THE CONCISE OXFORD DICTIONARY

OF CURRENT ENGLISH

Based on
The Oxford English Dictionary
and its Supplements

First edited by H. W. Fowler and F. G. Fowler

SIXTH EDITION
edited by J. B. SYKES

OXFORD
AT THE CLARENDON PRESS

Oxford University Press, Walton Street, Oxford OX2 6DP

OXFORD LONDON GLASGOW
NEW YORK TORONTO MELBOURNE WELLINGTON
KUALA LUMPUR SINGAPORE JAKARTA HONG KONG TOKYO
DELHI BOMBAY CALCUTTA MADRAS KARACHI
IBADAN NAIROBI DAR ES SALAAM CAPE TOWN

First edition 1911
New edition (*revised*) 1929
Third edition (*with Addenda*) 1934,
reprinted six times with corrections 1938–1949
Fourth edition 1951,
reprinted nine times with corrections 1952–1962
Fifth edition 1964,
reprinted 21 times with corrections 1964–1975
Sixth edition 1976
Thirteenth impression 1982

British Library Cataloguing in Publication Data

The Concise Oxford dictionary of current
English. – 6th ed
ISBN 0–19–861121–8
ISBN 0–19–861122–6 Thumb indexed ed.
1. Sykes, J B
423
PE 1625
English language – Dictionaries

Printed in the United States of America

CONTENTS

PREFACE TO THE SIXTH EDITION

In this sixth edition of the *Concise Oxford Dictionary* the changes made include revisions and additions resulting from a detailed scrutiny of the whole work, as well as modifications of typography and format to allow greater ease of use. Such a thorough recension has been possible because I have had access to the reference library and the very large collection of examples built up for the *Supplement to the Oxford English Dictionary* now in course of publication, and to the advice of members of the O.E.D. department and other officers of the Oxford University Press.

The opportunity has been taken to eliminate some matter that can no longer be regarded as pertaining to current English, to add many new words, phrases, and meanings that have entered the language in recent years (including technical expressions found in general literature), to increase the contribution from the English-speaking world outside the British Isles, to incorporate the appendix of abbreviations into the main list, to systematize the definitions of interrelated terms, to eliminate some duplication of definitions, to expand some unduly concise wordings, and to add an enlarged Introduction (which the reader is strongly recommended to study) explaining the use of the dictionary.

In these tasks I have been ever conscious of the extent to which I depended on the labours of others: my predecessors H. W. and F. G. Fowler, the first editors (1911), H. W. Fowler in the second edition (1929) and (with H. G. Le Mesurier) the third edition (1934), and E. McIntosh in the fourth (1951) and fifth (1964) editions; and my contemporaries on the staff of the Oxford dictionaries, especially the Chief Editor, Mr. Robert W. Burchfield, C.B.E., for much valuable guidance, Miss Joyce Hawkins for several years' devoted assistance and counsel, Mrs. Joan Pusey (Editor of the *Oxford School Dictionary*) and Dr. Rashid Ball for detailed comments and practical help, Miss Sandra Raphael for advice on some botanical points, and Mrs. Anne Whear for many hours' typing and other help. I have also had great benefit from the work of Dr. G. W. S. Friedrichsen mentioned under 'Etymology' in the Introduction, from Mrs. Dorothy Eagle's revision of the *Oxford Illustrated Dictionary* (1975), and (like all lexicographers of the present day) from the third edition of *Webster's New International Dictionary*. Thanks are due to Mrs. W. K. Davin, Mr. M. W. Grose, and Mr. T. F. Hoad, who each read a substantial section of the galley proofs and made many valuable comments, and to a very large number of correspondents who have written to comment on individual entries or general topics; of them I would specially mention Mr. A. R. Babcock of Summit, New Jersey, the sender of frequent and interesting lists of suggestions since 1972.

I must confess, with Henry Fowler in his acknowledgements preceding the 1929 edition, that 'a dictionary-maker, unless he is a monster of omniscience, must deal with a great many matters of which he has no firsthand knowledge', and consequently expect to be found 'guilty of errors and omissions in some of these'. To those who will take the trouble to inform me of such shortcomings, and so help the further improvement of this attempt to summarize and present in a small dictionary one of the great languages of the world, I here express my thanks in advance.

J. B. S.

July, 1975

From the
PREFACE TO THE FIRST EDITION

THE book is designed as a dictionary, and not as an encyclopaedia; that is, the uses of words and phrases as such are its subject matter, and it is concerned with giving information about the things for which those words and phrases stand only so far as correct use of the words depends upon knowledge of the things. The degree of this dependence varies greatly with the kind of word treated, the difference between cyclopaedic and dictionary treatment varies with it, and the line of distinction is accordingly a fluctuating and dubious one. It is to the endeavour to discern and keep to this line that we attribute whatever peculiarities we are conscious of in this dictionary as compared with others of the same size. One of these peculiarities is the large amount of space given to the common words that no one goes through the day without using scores or hundreds of times, often disposed of in a line or two on the ground that they are plain and simple and that every one knows all about them by the light of nature, but in fact entangled with other words in so many alliances and antipathies during their perpetual knocking about the world that the idiomatic use of them is far from easy; chief among such words are the prepositions, the conjunctions, the pronouns, and such 'simple' nouns and verbs as *hand* and *way*, *go* and *put*. Another peculiarity is the use, copious for so small a dictionary, of illustrative sentences as a necessary supplement to definition when a word has different senses between which the distinction is fine, or when a definition is obscure and unconvincing until exemplified; these sentences often are, but still more often are not, quotations from standard authors; they are meant to establish the sense of the definition by appeal not to external authority, but to the reader's own consciousness, and therefore their source, even when authoritative, is not named. A third and a fourth peculiarity are the direct results of the preceding ones; if common words are to be treated at length, and their uses to be copiously illustrated, space must be saved both by the curtest possible treatment of all that are either uncommon or fitter for the encyclopaedia than the dictionary, and by the severest economy of expression—amounting to the adoption of telegraphese—that readers can be expected to put up with.

H. W. F.
F. G. F.

June, 1911

From the
PREFACE TO THE SECOND EDITION

WHEN we began, more than twenty years ago, the work that took shape as *The Concise Oxford Dictionary*, we were plunging into the sea of lexicography without having been first taught to swim. But lexicography for us was fortunately of the minor or dependent kind; and, fortunately also, the time was one at which the major or firsthand kind was reaching greater excellence than ever before, and the *Oxford English Dictionary*, four-fifths completed, already provided popularizers with unlimited material.

The object we set before us, hinted at by the word *current* on our title-page, was to present as vivid a picture as the small dictionary could be made to give of the English that was being spoken and written at the time. The vividness was to be secured by allotting space to words more nearly in proportion to the frequency and variety of their use, and consequently to their practical value, than had been the custom; and further by an unprecedented abundance of illustrative quotation; define, and your reader gets a silhouette; illustrate, and he has it 'in the round'. That at least was our belief; and we hailed as confirmation of it one or two letters from persons unknown congratulating us on having 'produced a live dictionary', or 'treating English at last as a living language'.

H. W. F.

1929

INTRODUCTION

THIS introduction is designed to help the reader understand the way in which information is presented in the *Concise Oxford Dictionary*, where, as the name suggests, compactness has been a primary aim. Although many changes have been made in the sixth edition, users acquainted with previous editions will not find much that is unfamiliar as regards the style.

I. *Vocabulary*

The general aims of the dictionary have remained as they were specified by the original editors. The words, phrases, and meanings given are those current in the English of the present day—either in living use, or familiar through their occurrence in frequently quoted literature of the past. The attitude taken, however, is now essentially descriptive rather than prescriptive: that is, the dictionary seeks to record what is found to exist in the educated use of modern English. Restricted usage is regularly shown by usage labels such as (literary) and (colloq.) or subject labels such as (Law) and (Cricket); see paragraph IV. Admission has also been granted to many vulgar or slang expressions that are often met in print, or heard, at the present time. Limitations of space make it impossible to include every possible and legitimate derivative (e.g. compounds of obvious meaning such as *boiler-room*, the obvious literal senses where the figurative meaning is more important, the less common adverbs in *-ly*, or phrase-based compounds such as *arm-twisting* from *twist a person's arm*). Likewise, standard grammatical procedures such as the attributive use of nouns, or the intransitive use of transitive verbs as notional passives (*the car handles well*) are not often mentioned. The reader in search of a broader canvas of English words and their history is recommended to consult the twelve-volume *Oxford English Dictionary* and its Supplements on which this work is based, the intermediate abridgement in the *Shorter Oxford English Dictionary*, the encyclopaedic matter in the *Oxford Illustrated Dictionary*, and such specialized works as the Oxford Companions to art, English literature, music, and the theatre.

II. *Arrangement of dictionary entries*

For conciseness, derivatives and compounds are often put in the entry headed by their first element, even if this brings them out of their alphabetical position. It is therefore advisable to seek any word in its alphabetical place and then (if necessary) in the entry for its first part, for example *ant-eater* under *ant*, *playboy* under *play*². Cross-references are provided where the placing of a word may not be obvious; here, as in all other cross-references, the word to which reference is necessary is printed in SMALL CAPITALS. Raised figures (as in PLAY²) are used to distinguish two or more entry words having the same spelling; plain figures (as in FLOW 3) refer to bold-type arabic sense-numbers (see paragraph III). There are separate entries for the principal prefixes and suffixes, and cross-reference to these is often made for the explanation of derivative forms; for instance, most adverbs in *-ly* are entered with -LY², and similarly for nouns in -NESS, and verbs in -IZE (1) etc. (where the figure indicates the specific meaning among those listed in the entry for -IZE). Cross-references are also used to clarify the sense of an ambiguous word in a definition (as PIKE³, the fish, at *jack*¹ 6), to indicate an entry where further relevant information may be found (as LIBEL at *slander*), and to lead to definitions of phrases such as *let* SLEEP²*ing dogs lie*, which are usually defined under only one of their constituent words; such a phrase or compound is not itself a sense of the entry word unless preceded by an equals sign (for example *paper*¹. . . = NEWS-*paper* implies that 'paper' can mean 'newspaper'; *hare* . . . BELGIAN *hare*; = ELECTRIC *hare* implies that 'hare' alone can mean 'electric hare' but not 'Belgian hare').

III. *Structure of entries*

The entry word (headword) is printed in **bold** type, or in ***bold italic*** if it is not yet naturalized in English and is usually found in italics in printed matter. Alternative forms are shown either by the use of parentheses as at **rac(c)oon** (where the position of the entry implies that the spelling *racoon* is given preference over *raccoon*) or by placing them, either in full or abbreviated, after a comma (**carcass, carcase**; **pygmy, pigmy**; **organize, -ise**). These are followed by any necessary indication of the pronunciation where it cannot be shown in the headword itself (see 'Pronunciation' below), by the italic abbreviation for the part or parts of speech (*n.* for noun, etc.), and by an indication of any irregular inflexions (see 'Inflexion' below). The order of senses is normally based on frequency and convenience rather than historical evolution. The definitions of the senses of a word are separated by commas if very close in meaning, by semicolons if somewhat more distinct, and by bold-type arabic numbers (**1.**) if quite distinct. When an entry deals with more than one part of speech, the relevant part-of-speech abbreviation follows **1.**, and any subsequent number where it changes. Derivatives are in **bold** type (often partly replaced by the swung dash—see paragraph V—and by small capitals—see paragraph II); defined compounds and phrases in **semi-bold** (or in ***bold italic*** where not yet naturalized); examples and expressions defined by cross-reference, in *italic*. Definitions may include words in *italic* that are normally used with the headword in the sense concerned: '**contingent** . . . incidental *to*' implies that the idiomatic construction for this sense is *contingent to*; '**soak** . . . place or leave or lie in or *in* liquid' implies that either *soak* or *soak in water* etc. can be used for this sense; '**gather** . . . infer, deduce, (*that*)' implies that the word *gather* may, but need not, be used with a clause beginning with the conjunction *that*. Italicized examples may include words in ordinary (roman) type that are replaceable by others: *pull* one's *weight* covers *pull my weight*, *pull his weight*, and so on; *pull* person's *leg* is used similarly, where the person is not the subject of the verb. The etymology is at the end of the entry, in square brackets [ ] (see 'Etymology' below). Round brackets ( ) may be used anywhere in the entry to enclose letters or words that are optional or explanatory, for example definitions that are explanatory rather than formal; '(of . . .)' often precedes the definition of a verb or adjective to indicate the type of noun to which it can be applied, and a definition of a transitive verb may be followed by words in round brackets indicating the type of noun that occurs as its object. The expression 'in vbl senses' denotes 'in senses that may be deduced from the meanings of the corresponding verb'; 'abs.' refers to the use of a transitive verb without object, an adjective without noun, etc. (see ABSOLUTELY). Systematic names of animals and plants are given where they are appropriate as a guide to further information in specialized books on mammals, ferns, etc. (Here, as in definitions, 'etc.' is used to denote other items of the same general kind.)

IV. *Usage and subject labels*

Words (usually abbreviated) in round brackets ( ) preceding a definition are used to show that all or some of the senses are restricted to a particular type of discourse or subject field in current English. The principal usage labels are (colloq.): colloquial, not used in formal discourse, but widely used and entirely acceptable in informal circumstances; (sl.): slang, used only in certain circumstances (see SLANG); (joc.): jocular, used only in humorous or playful style; (derog.): derogatory, used only contemptuously; (vulg.): vulgar, used only by those who have no wish to be thought either polite or educated; (arch.): archaic, used only in old-fashioned (or religious or legal) speech or writing; (literary): in sense 2 as given at LITERARY. See p. xxiii for the geographical restrictions denoted by the symbols * and ||. The many subject labels, such as (Law), (Math.), (Naut.) (see the list of 'Abbreviations used in the Dictionary', p. xx), show that a word or sense is current only in a particular field of activity. When preceding all numbered senses, labels apply to the whole entry; when followed by a definition beginning with a capital letter, they apply as far as the next full stop; otherwise, as far as the next semicolon or full stop. Proprietary terms are treated as described in the note on p. xxiii.

V. *The swung dash*

A considerable amount of space is saved by the swung dash ~, which stands for the headword of the entry (or any of the alternative spellings of the headword) or for that part of it which precedes the vertical rule: for example, in the entry at **hair**, ~ stands for *hair*, *~'brush* for *hair'brush*, (-)*~ed* for *haired* or *-haired*; at **hungr|y**, *~y* stands for *hungry*, *~ily* for *hungrily*. Where the headword begins or ends with a hyphen, the swung dash does not include that hyphen (at **inter-**, *~stellar* = *interstellar*, but *~-city* = *inter-city*); a capital or small letter preceding the swung dash replaces an initial small or capital letter in the headword (at **genesis**, *G~* = *Genesis*; at **Renaissance**, *r~* = *renaissance*). Any indication of pronunciation or stress corresponding to the relevant part of the headword is transmitted by the swung dash unless cancelled by a respelling in round brackets or by a new stress (thus ~A'TION cancels the main stress on the first syllable of **co'git|ate**, **to'ler|ate**, etc.); otherwise, the normal pronunciation rules are implied (at **impact**, **~ion** is pronounced -sh*o*n; the second *c* in *caecitis* is pronounced s as usual before *i*, although in **caec|um** it is pronounced k; the plural *~e* (=*nebulae*) at **nebula** is pronounced nĕ'būlē (see 'Pronunciation')).

VI. *Hyphenation*
There is great variety in the use of the hyphen in English, especially between British and American styles, and there are few clearly defined rules on the subject. To clarify the intention in this dictionary (which conforms essentially to the British style), a hyphen that falls at the end of a line is repeated at the start of the next line to make clear that it is not simply the result of the printing convention whereby any word so divided is hyphenated.

VII. *Entries for abbreviations in general use*
These are to be found in their alphabetical places among ordinary words, the ampersand (&) being treated as if written 'and'. There are frequent variations in the presence or absence of capitals and full stops in abbreviations, and no attempt is made to show all possible forms. Abbreviations not in general use but employed in this dictionary are listed at p. xx below.

PRONUNCIATION

The pronunciation given in this dictionary is the standard one 'without any accent', associated especially with Southern England (sometimes called 'Received Pronunciation'). No attempt is made here to show the many variations heard in educated speech in Northern England, the rest of the British Isles, the United States, and the rest of the English-speaking world. Further information may be sought in dictionaries concerned primarily with pronunciation.

Where possible, the pronunciation is shown in the bold type of the headword that begins each entry, or of a derivative within an entry. If not, part or all of the word is respelt in round brackets ( ) immediately following it. Occasionally a group of forms is followed by a comma and then by a respelling that relates to the whole group. The pronunciation of a derivative formed by a suffix printed in small capitals is often to be found by means of the marking or respelling at the suffix entry. No attempt is made to show syllables or to indicate suitable points of division of words at the end of printed lines.

I. *With respelling*

Respelling in round brackets is according to the following scheme, which also shows the corresponding symbols in the International Phonetic Alphabet. See section IV below for the use of the stress-mark ʹ.

Consonants		IPA			IPA
b	as in (băt)	b	ng	as in (sĭng)	ŋ
ch	as in (chĭn)	tʃ	ngg	as in (fĭʹngg*er*) = finger	ŋg
d	as in (dŏg)	d	p	as in (pĕt)	p
dh	as in (dhĕn) = then	ð	r	as in (răt)	r
f	as in (făt)	f	s	as in (sĭp)	s
g	(except after n) as in (gō)	g	sh	as in (shĭp)	ʃ
h	(except after c, d, s, t, z) as in (hăt)	h	t	as in (tĭp)	t
			th	as in (thĭn)	θ
j	as in (jăm)	dʒ	v	as in (văn)	v
k	as in (kĭt)	k	w	as in (wĭn)	w
l	as in (lŏt)	l	y	as in (yĕt)	j
m	as in (măt)	m	z	as in (zĭp)	z
n	as in (nĕt)	n	zh	as in (vĭʹzh*o*n) = vision	ʒ
ṅ	(French nasalization) as in (ga͡rʹsawṅ) = *garçon* etc.	(æ̃, ɔ̃, etc.)	χ	(Scots etc.) as in (lŏχ) = loch	x

Vowels					
ā	as in (fāt) = fate	eɪ	ō	as in (gōt) = goat	əʊ
ă	as in (făt)	æ	ŏ	as in (gŏt)	ɒ
a	as in (*a*gōʹ)	ə	*o*	as in (flăʹg*o*n)	ə
ah	as in (bah)	ɑ	oi	as in (boil)	ɔɪ
a̅r̅	as in (fa̅r̅) = fare	eə(r)	o͞o	as in (bo͞ot)	u
a͡r	as in (fa͡r)	ɑ(r)	o͝o	as in (bo͝ok)	ʊ
aw	as in (paw)	ɔ	oor	as in (poor)	ʊə(r)
ē	as in (mēt) = meet	i	o͡r	as in (po͡rt)	ɔ(r)
ĕ	as in (mĕt)	e	ow	as in (brow)	ɑʊ
e	as in (tōʹk*e*n)	ə	owr	as in (sowr) = sour	ɑʊə(r)
e̅r̅	as in (fe̅r̅) = fear	ɪə(r)	ū	as in (dū) = due	ju
e͡r	as in (fe͡r) = fur	ɜ(r)	ŭ	as in (dŭg)	ʌ
er	as in (tāʹk*er*)	ə(r)	*u*	as in (bōʹn*u*s)	ə
ī	as in (bīt) = bite	ɑɪ	u̅r̅	as in (pu̅r̅) = pure	jʊə(r)
ĭ	as in (bĭt)	ɪ		See ṅ (under 'Consonants' above) for French nasalized vowels.	
i	as in (bāʹs*i*n)	ə			
i̅r̅	as in (fi̅r̅) = fire	ɑɪə(r)			

Vowels such as ā̆ may be pronounced in two ways, e.g. either as ā or as ă (pā̆'trĭot); similarly (zē̆'bra). Vowel combinations in -r include the consonantal value of r when followed by another vowel in the next syllable or word (*fearing*, *fear it*). Apart from this, the vowels *a*, *e*, *i*, *o*, *u*, and *er* are usually indistinguishable except in very precise speech.

II. *Without respelling*

Words or parts of words that are not respelt are pronounced in accordance with the foregoing scheme—for example: **bă'nĭsh, stū'dĭō, rĭ'nger**, but **fĭ'nger** (-ngg-), **dā'nger** (-nj-)—together with the symbols and values stated in the following seven rules.

1. **ė** = ĭ (**nā'kėd**)
   ir͡ = er͡ (**bir͡th**)
   ur͡ = er͡ (**bur͡n**)
   ȳ = ī (**rėlȳ'**)
   y̆ = ĭ (**dū'ty̆**)
   ȳr = īr (**tȳre**)

2. **e** final is silent (**ă'ctĭve, āpe, galōr͡'e**; cf. **rĕ'cĭpė**); **-le** final after a consonant = -*el* (**cā'ble, stā'ple, mă'ntle**).

3. Unmarked vowels (other than final **e**), if not respelt and not part of a compound vowel (**ah** etc.), correspond to *a* etc. above (**agō', tō'ken, bā'sin, flă'gon, bō'nus**); **y** (except in **yr**) = y (consonant); **ar** etc. = *er* (**partĭ'cūlar, mā'ker, tā'pir, sai'lor, lē'mur, zĕ'phyr**).

4. A doubled consonant is pronounced as single (**sĭ'lly̆, hă'ppen, bŭ'tter, bŭtt**). This applies also to the combinations **ck** (= k), **cq, dg(e, i, y), dj, sc(e, i, y), tch, xc(e, i, y), xs, ar͡r, arr**, etc.

5. The following letters and combinations have the values shown:
   ae = ē (**ae'gĭs**)
   ai = ā (**pain**)
   air = ār (**fair**)
   au = aw (**maul**)
   aur = or͡ (**dī'nosaur**)
   ay = ā (**say**)
   c before **e, i, y̆, ȳ** is 'soft' and = s (**īce, cĭ'ty̆, ī'cy̆, cȳ'der**), elsewhere is 'hard' and = k (**cŏb, crȳ, ar͡c**)
   ea = ē (**mean**)
   ear = ēr (**fear**)
   ee = ē (**meet**)
   eer = ēr (**beer**)
   eu = ū (**feud**)
   ew = ū (**few**)

g before **e, i, y̆, ȳ** is 'soft' and = j (**āge, gĭn, o͡r'gy̆, gȳbe**), elsewhere is 'hard' and = g (**gāme, băg, o͡r'gan**)
ie = ē (**thief**)
ier = ēr (**pier**)
n before 'hard' **c, k, q, x** = ng (**zĭnc, ŭ'ncle, tănk, bă'nquėt, mĭnx**)
oa = ō (**boat**)
oar = o͡r (**boar**)
ou = ow (**bound**)
our = owr (**sour**)
oy = oi (**boy**)
ph = f (**phō'tō**)
qu = kw (**quĭt**)
tion = sh*o*n (**nā'tion, nă'tional**)
wh = w (**whĭch**) or (by some speakers) hw (not shown in respelling)
x = ks (**fŏx**)

6. The following combinations, beginning a word, have the values shown:
kn- = n (**knŏt**)
rh- = r (**rhȳme**)
wr- = r (**wrĭst**)

7. The following, ending a word, have the values shown:
-age = ĭj (**vĭ'llage**)
-ate = *a*t (**dĕ'lĭcate**) or (by some speakers) ĭt
-e (see 2 above)
-ey = ĭ (**dŏ'nkey**)
-le (see 2 above)
-nch = nch or nsh (**trĕnch**)
-ous = *u*s (**fūr'ĭous**), and similarly for **-ouslȳ, -ousnėss**
-sm = z*e*m (**spă'sm**)
-ture = ch*er* or (sometimes, esp. in less common words) tūr

Note that all the above rules may be overridden by respelling, for example **shrĭ'llȳ** (-l-lĭ), **break** (-āk), **gĕt** (g-), **quay** (kē), **fā'vour** (-v*er*), **grā'teful** (-tf-), **ahea'd** (*a*-hĕ'd), **lōō'phōle** (-p-h-), the hyphen being used to make it clear that letters are to be taken separately and not as parts of combined symbols.

Where a word has no marking at all, its pronunciation will be found within the entry (**housewife**), or (in the case of a cross-reference) at the principal word. Acronyms are usually pronounced either as words (if thus shown by respelling) or as sequences of letters; other abbreviations are usually pronounced as their full forms. See 'Inflexion' below for a description of the pronunciations of inflected forms of words.

The occasional accents on letters as in **attaché**, **fête**, should not be confused with pronunciation markings.

III. *Alternative pronunciations*

Semicolons in the respelling separate different parts of the word, as in **brea'thalȳser** (brĕ'-; -*zer*). Alternative accepted pronunciations are introduced by the word *or*, and their order is not necessarily that of decreasing frequency of occurrence.

Unstressed vowels often have a reduced value, for example (ū) becoming (yo͝o) in **cĭr'cūlar**. The combinations of (ĭ) with preceding c, s, t; d, g, j; z, when followed by a vowel, are often palatalized into (sh, j, zh) respectively (as is normal in *acacia, Alsatian,* etc.); similarly, (ĭ) followed by a vowel tends to become consonantal (y), and (tū), (dū) tend to become (cho͞o) or (cho͝o), (jo͞o) or (jo͝o), when not beginning a word or stressed syllable.

In speech at normal speed the indeterminate vowel in words ending in **-ble, -den, -gon, -sm, -thm**, and the like, is often barely discernible.

IV. *Stress*

The usual main stress is shown by a stress-mark ' after the stressed vowel. No attempt is made to show secondary stress, and even the main stress may change when the word is used in different positions, e.g. *Chi'nese, i'deal* attributively, *Chine'se, ide'al* predicatively, or when a compound is used in different positions.

Unless otherwise shown, the stress falls on the first part of a hyphenated compound; it is usually on the second part of a compound written as two words. Where the swung dash ~ (see Introduction, paragraph v) is used, it may be followed immediately by a stress-mark to indicate a stress on the syllable it represents, or a suffix may have the stress-mark; otherwise, the stress is the same as in the word or part-word represented by the swung dash.

INFLEXION

The following are the rules for the formation of normal inflected forms of nouns, adjectives, adverbs, and verbs, and are applicable except where a different form is shown in round brackets ( ) in the dictionary entry immediately after the part-of-speech abbreviation *n., a., v., v.t.,* etc. The absence of any such different form is to be taken (for example at **virus** *n.*, **jacket** *v.t.*, and **parallel**[2] *v.t.*) as implying that the inflected forms are in accordance with the rules given below; the word *or* indicates the existence of more than one accepted form, not necessarily arranged in order of decreasing frequency of occurrence.

In these rules, 'sibilant wds' denotes all words ending in the sound of s (or x), z, sh (or ch), or zh (or j); '-*o* wds' denotes all words ending in the letter *o* except those in -*oo*; '-*e* wds' denotes all words ending in a silent *e*; and '-*y* wds' denotes all words ending in the letter *y* preceded by a consonant, together with those in -*quy*.

I. *Plural of nouns*

Sibilant wds add *-es*, pronounced (ĭz), *-e* wds dropping the *e*: *boxes, cases, mazes, porches*; *-y* wds change *-y* into *-ies*, pronounced (ĭz): *puppies*, or (īz): *skies*; *-o* wds add *-s* or *-es*, pronounced (-z), as shown in round brackets in the dictionary for all such words except those where no plural is in use (e.g. *blanco, quattrocento*); other nouns add *-s*, pronounced (s) after voiceless consonants (*books, cats, cliffs, faiths, hopes*) and (z) after voiced consonants and vowel sounds (*bags, hoods, knaves, scythes, tubs, views, ways*). A compound consisting of a noun followed by a word other than a noun usually adds the plural ending to the noun (*courts martial, passers-by*). Abbreviations etc. add *-s* (*M.P.s, 1960s*) or sometimes *'s*; some abbreviations of units remain unchanged (*m.* = *mile* or *miles*).

II. *Possessive of nouns*

Singular nouns add *'s*, pronounced (-ĭz) for sibilant wds (*fox's, goose's, witch's*), (s) after other voiceless consonants (*book's, cat's*), and (z) after other voiced consonants and vowel sounds (*boy's, dog's, man's*). Plural nouns not ending in the sound of s or z are treated like singular nouns (*men's, women's, sheep's*). Plural nouns ending in the sound of s or z add an apostrophe without change of pronunciation (*books', cats', boys', beaux'*); the same is sometimes done with singular nouns of this type (*for goodness' sake*). Abbreviations etc. add *'s* (*M.P.'s*, in plural *M.P.s'*; *1960's*).

III. *Comparative and superlative of adjectives and adverbs*

The syllables -ER[3] and -EST[1] are added to adjectives and adverbs of one syllable (*bolder, boldest; faster, fastest*), *-e* wds dropping the *e* (*braver, bravest; later, latest*), and a final single consonant (except *h, w*, or *x*) being doubled, without change of pronunciation, if preceded by a single-letter vowel (*grimmer, fattest; bigger* pr. bĭ'ger). The same applies to adjectives of two syllables that are *-y* wds, the *y* becoming *i* (*happier, luckiest*; similarly for some *-ey* wds such as *gooey*: *gooier*), to some adverbs of this type, especially *early*; to adjectives of two syllables ending in *-er, -le* after a consonant, or *-ow* (*cleverer, tenderest, nobler, simplest, narrower, mellowest*); and to negative forms of adjectives of all the types mentioned so far (*unfairest, ignobler, unluckiest*). The comparative and superlative of all other adjectives and adverbs must (except where otherwise shown), and those of any adjective or adverb may, be formed by prefixing *more* and *most* (*more beautiful, most splendid, most unfair, more brave, most nobly*). Similar rules apply to the formation of derived adjectives in -ISH[1] (*fattish, biggish, yellowish*; but *prettyish*).

IV. *Third person singular present indicative of verbs*

Sibilant wds (*-e* wds dropping the *e*) and *-o* wds add *-es*, pronounced (ĭz) and (z) respectively: *pushes, places, goes*; *-y* wds change *-y* into *-ies*, pronounced (ĭz): *carries*, or (īz): *cries*; other verbs add *-s*, pronounced (s) after voiceless consonants (*bakes, cuts, peeps*) and (z) after voiced consonants and vowel sounds (*begs, boos, fades, rubs, stays, ties, wallows*).

V. *Past tense and past participle of verbs*

-e wds add *-d* (*moved*); *-y* wds change *-y* into *-ied*, pronounced (ĭd): *carried*, or (īd): *cried*; other verbs add *-ed*; the final *-ed* is pronounced (ĭd) after the sound of t or d (*trusted, hated, ended, faded*), (t) after other voiceless consonants (*baked, peeped, pushed*), and (d) after other voiced consonants and vowel sounds (*absorbed, booed, seemed, stayed, vetoed, wallowed*). A final single consonant is often doubled (cf. paragraph III above), but this is always indicated in the dictionary by (**-bb-**) etc. (*rubbed, tinned, mimicked, preferred*; *sagged, tugged*, pr. -gd). There are many irregular forms; if the past tense and past participle are different, they are separated by a semicolon (**ran**; **run**); a single form stands for both (**brought**, **cut**, **found**). In archaic and poetical use, *-ed* after a voiceless consonant may be written *-t*, the consonant never being doubled (*blest, kist, wrapt*). Some past participles when used as adjectives have different forms (*drunken*) or pronunciations in (-ĭd) (*blessed, learned*); this pronunciation also occurs in archaic and poetical use (*the hornèd Moon*) and for some derived adverbs in *-edly* (*advisedly*). Similar rules apply to the formation of derived nouns in -ER[1] (*carrier, winner*) and adjectives in -ABLE (*carriable, winnable*).

VI. *Present participle and gerund of verbs*

All verbs add *-ing* (*fishing, playing, studying*), *-e* wds (except those in *-ee, -ie, -oe*) dropping the *e* (*dancing, moving*; *seeing*). A final single consonant is often doubled (cf. paragraph III above), but this is always indicated in the dictionary by (**-bb-**) etc. (*rubbing, tinning, mimicking, sitting, preferring*; *sagging, tugging*, pr. -gĭng).

VII. *Archaic second and third person singular of verbs*

These are formed in -(*e*)*st* for the second person singular present and past (*playest, canst, hearest, hear'st*; *madest, knewest, haddest, hadst, wouldst*), and -(*e*)*th* for the third person singular present indicative (*goeth, saith*). They are retained in some religious, legal, poetical, and dialectal usage.

ETYMOLOGY

The word-derivations given in this dictionary are based almost entirely on those by Dr. G. W. S. Friedrichsen in the previous edition of the *Concise Oxford Dictionary* and in the 1973 printing of the *Shorter Oxford English Dictionary*, but he does not bear any responsibility for the exact formulations used here. More detailed information may be sought in the latter of those works and in the *Oxford Dictionary of English Etymology* by Onions, Friedrichsen, and Burchfield (1966).

The etymology is given in square brackets [ ] at the end of nearly every entry. It begins with 'f.' (= from) or 'f. as' (= formed from the same source as) except where the word in the immediate source (foreign) language has exactly the same form as in English (in which case that form is not repeated in the etymology: at **formula**, [L . . .] means [f. Latin *formula* . . .]; at **basis**, [L f. Gk . . .] means [f. L *basis* f. Gk *basis* . . .]). Thereafter, the word may be traced back to earlier forms in other languages (preceded by 'f.') or in the same language (usually placed in round brackets). Where no form is given after the name of a language, it is understood to be the same as in the next language mentioned: at **high**, 'OS, OHG *hōh*' implies that the Old Saxon form is also *hōh*; at **Moor**[2], 'ME f. OF *More*' implies that the Middle English form is also *More*. Where no meaning is given for a form, it is understood to be the same as for the last one previously given in the etymology: at **knave**, 'OE *cnafa* boy, servant, = OHG *knabo*' implies that the Old High German form also had those meanings. Where no meaning is given for the first form in an etymology, it is understood to be the same as the first listed meaning of the English word.

There are frequent cross-references to other entries which represent component parts of a word, or which share some aspect of the derivation; these are printed in SMALL CAPITALS. An asterisk (*) precedes any form that is not recorded in known documents, but merely inferred to have existed.

Where the exact path of derivation is uncertain, the word 'or' is used: for instance, many English words have corresponding forms in both French and Latin and present a special problem in that we cannot be certain whether the word was adopted from one or the other, or from both at different times or by different persons. At **inclement**, 'f. F *inclément* or f. L *inclemens*', and at **hostility**, 'f. F *hostilité* or f. LL *hostilitas*', indicate situations of this kind.

Where the origin of a word cannot be reliably established at all, it is described as 'uncertain' or 'unknown', even if there are frequently-repeated speculative derivations (as with *pommy*). In such cases the century in which the word was first used in English is stated.

'After' introduces a word or form or language that has served as a basis for analogical formation.

The source of derivatives within an entry is usually indicated by printing in small capitals the suffixes such as -NESS, -LY[1], -LY[2], -ATION, -IZE (3), which are explained in their alphabetical places; the raised figures refer to different entries for suffixes spelt alike, and the figures in round brackets to particular senses of the suffix concerned. 'Hence' is used to introduce a derivative of the entry word itself (*brewer* from *brew*[1]) or of one or all of its numbered senses (*briefly* from *brief*[3] 1; *bringer* from *bring* 1–3); 'whence' introduces a derivative of one particular sense, separated only by semicolons, of that word (*careenage* from the first sense of *careen*); 'so' introduces a derivative formed from a predecessor given in the etymology of the entry word (*Carnivora* from Latin *carnivorus*, like *carnivorous*); 'hence or cogn.' introduces two or more derivatives describable partly by 'hence' and partly by 'so' (*censorial* from Latin, *censorship* from English *censor*).

An equals sign (=) precedes forms in other languages that are cognates rather than sources. The description of a form as F (French), G (German), and so on, does not necessarily imply that it is still current, or so spelt, in that language, nor does OF (Old French) or the like imply that it is now obsolete.

Words are usually given their customary dictionary forms for each language, e.g. verbs in the infinitive (French, German, Latin, etc.), first person singular present indicative (Greek), third person singular perfect (Semitic languages), but the English translation is not made to correspond grammatically to each of these.

'ME' (Middle English) refers to the period 1150–1500, no distinction being made between early and late ME; 'OE' (Old English) to the period before 1150. Words of Gmc (Germanic) or WG (West Germanic) origin that have come down from OE or ME are illustrated, so far as possible, by some or all of the forms known or inferred for the older stages of the cognate dialects, usually in the order OS (Old Saxon), OHG (Old High German), ON (Old Norse), and Goth. (Gothic), followed by reconstructed Germanic and IE (Indo-European) forms where appropriate: **hard** . . . [OE *h(e)ard*, = OS *hard*, OHG *hart*, ON *harthr*, Goth. *hardus* f. Gmc **hardhuz* f. IE **kratus*]. In OE, OS, ON, and Goth., the letters thorn and edh (or letters corresponding to them) are both represented by *th*; in OS the plain *b* and *d* are used irrespective of their phonetic value in that dialect; but in Gmc forms, *bh*, *dh*, and *th* are written where appropriate. Long vowels are denoted in ON (as also in Icelandic, Irish, and Magyar) by an acute accent (*á*), but in other languages by a macron (*ā*). LDu. (Low Dutch) stands for Low German and Dutch regarded as a linguistic unit.

Words of Romance origin are referred to their immediate source, usually F (French) or OF (Old French before 1400), and thence briefly to earlier sources where known; Rom. (Romanic) denotes the vernacular descendants of Latin that gave rise to French, Spanish, Italian, etc. L (Latin) without prefix denotes classical Latin before about A.D. 200; OL (Old Latin) Latin before about 75 B.C.; LL (Late

Latin) about A.D. 200–600; med. L (medieval Latin) about 600–1500; mod. L (modern Latin) since about 1500.† French nouns of Latin origin normally represent the Latin accusative case, but in this dictionary the Latin nominative is cited, followed by the genitive where necessary to show the relevant stem. Here, as elsewhere, a sequence of two forms in one language without punctuation indicates one word in different cases, tenses, or the like. For example, **hearse** . . . [ME, f. OF *herse* harrow f. med. L *erpica* f. Rom. **herpica* f. L. *(h)irpex -picis* large rake f. Samnite *(h)irpus* wolf . . .] traces the chain of derivation through Middle English to the Old French *herse* 'harrow', the medieval Latin *erpica* and the inferred Romanic form *herpica* 'harrow', the Latin *hirpex* or *irpex*, genitive *hirpicis* or *irpicis*, 'large rake', and the Samnite word *hirpus* or *irpus* 'wolf'. Latin vowels are left unmarked as to quantity, except for the *-ēre* of the second conjugation.

Greek and Russian words are transliterated in accordance with Appendix II. The Latin form of a word derived through Latin from Greek is usually omitted, being either identical with the transliterated Greek or obtainable from it according to the following scheme:

Greek	*Latin*	*Greek*	*Latin*
-a (m. & f. acc. sing.)	-em	ō	o
ai	ae	-oi (nom. pl.)	-i
ē	e	oi (elsewhere)	oe
-ē, -ēs (1st decl. nom.)	-a	-on	-um
ei	i *or* e	-ōn (nom.)	-o
gg	ng	-os (masc. nom.)	-us
gk	nc	-os (gen.)	-is
gx	nx	ou	u
k	c	u (exc. in diphthong)	y

The first element of a compound word is often referred to a prefix entry, and the remainder treated separately within round brackets; meanings given within the bracket belong to the simple word, those of the compound being added if necessary outside it. Thus at **convene** '[. . . f. L CON(*venire vent-* come) assemble, agree, fit]' indicates that *convene* is derived from the Latin *convenire* to assemble, which is from the Latin prefix *con-* (explained in a separate entry) and *venire* to come; the supine stem *vent-* and the senses 'agree, fit' are added for the elucidation of **convention** and **convenience**, which are referred to CONVENE.

The first element of a Greek compound thus treated is sometimes written in the Latin transliteration to assist reference to the prefix entry; for example, at **synagogue**, *sunagō* appears as 'SYN(*agō* bring)' in order to refer to the prefix entry SYN-.

† Gk (Greek) is similarly classified.

ABBREVIATIONS USED IN THE DICTIONARY

Abbreviations in general use (for example, those for the books of the Bible) appear in the dictionary itself. Some of those shown below may be printed in *italic* type where this helps to make the meaning clear. Similarly, the subject labels such as Aeron. may sometimes be used without the capital initial. The addition of 'etc.' to the full form in this list means that the abbreviation may also stand for a related word, e.g. sometimes adj. = adjectival, transl. = translated, Zool. = zoological.

a. adjective
abbr./eviation etc.
abbrs. abbreviations
abl./ative
abs./olute(ly) (see p. ix)
acc. according; accusative
act./ive(ly)
adj./ective etc.
adjs. adjectives
adv./erb etc.
advs. adverbs
Aeron./autics etc.
AF Anglo-French
Afr./ica(n)
Afrik./aans
Akkad./ian
AL Anglo-Latin
Alch./emy etc.
Alg./ebra etc.
allus./ive etc.
alt./eration etc.
alw./ays
Amer./ica(n)
Amh./aric
anal./ogy etc.
Anat./omy etc.
Anglo-Ind./ian
Ant./iquities
Anthrop./ology etc.
app./arently
Arab./ic
Aram./aic
arbitr./ary
arch./aic (see p. ix)
Archaeol./ogy etc.
Archit./ecture etc.
Arith./metic etc.
assim./ilated etc.
assoc./iated etc.
Assyr./ian
Astrol./ogy etc.
Astron./omy etc.
Astronaut./ics etc.
Athl./etics etc.
attrib./utive(ly)
augment./ative etc.
Austral./ia(n)
aux./iliary

back form./ation
bef./ore
Bibl./ical etc.
Bibliog./raphy etc.
Bill./iards
Biol./ogy etc.
Bookk./eeping
Bot./any etc.
Braz./il(ian)
Bret./on
Brit./ish
Bulg./arian
Burm./ese
Byz./antine

c. century
c. circa
Can./ada etc.
Carpent./ry
Cat./alan
Celt./ic
Ch./urch
Chald./ee
Chem./istry etc.
Chin./ese
Cinemat./ography etc.
cl./assical
cogn./ate (see p. xviii)
collat./eral
collect./ive(ly)
colloq./uial(ly) (see p. ix)
com./mon
comb. combination; combining
Commerc./ial etc.
compar./ative
compd. compound
compl./ement
comps. compounds
Conch./ology
condit./ional(ly)
confus./ion etc.
conj./unction
conjug./ation
conn./ected etc.
constr./uction etc.
contr./action etc.
cop./ulative
Copt./ic
Corn./ish
corresp./onding etc.
corrupt./ion
Cryst./allography etc.

Da./nish
dat./ive
decl./ension
def./inite
dem./onstrative
Dent./istry
deriv./ative etc.
derog./atory etc. (see p. ix)
dial./ect etc.
diff./erent
different./iated etc.
dim./inutive etc.
dims. diminutives
Diplom./acy
dir./ect etc.
dissim./ilated etc.
dist. distinct; distinguished

distrib./utive etc.
Du./tch

E English
Eccl./esiastical etc.
Ecol./ogy etc.
Econ./omics etc.
EFris. East Frisian
Egypt./ian
E. Ind. East Indian, of the East Indies
Electr./icity etc.
elem./entary etc.
ellipt./ical(ly)
emphat./ic(ally)
Engin./eering etc.
Engl. England; English
Entom./ology etc.
equiv./alent
erron./eous(ly)
esp./ecial(ly)
Eth./ics etc.
etym./ology etc.
euphem./ism etc.
Eur./ope(an)
ex./ample
exagg./eration etc.
exc./ept
excl. exclamation etc.; exclusive etc.
expr./essing etc.

F French
f. from
fam./iliar etc.
fem./inine
Fenc./ing
fig./urative(ly)
Finn./ish
Flem./ish
foll./owing entry
Footb./all
form./ation
Fortif./ication
Fr./ench
Frank./ish
freq./uent(ly)
frequent./ative(ly)
fut./ure (tense)

G German
Gael. GAELIC 1
Gallo-Rom./an
gen. general etc.; genitive
Geog./raphy etc.
Geol./ogy etc.
Geom./etry etc.
Ger./man
Gk Greek (classical if not otherwise described)
Gmc Germanic
Goth./ic
Gram./mar etc.

Hawk./ing
Heb./rew
Her./aldry etc.
Hind./ustani
Hist. historical; history
Horol./ogy etc.
Hort./iculture etc.
Hung./arian
Hunt./ing

i. intransitive
Icel./andic
IE Indo-European
illit./erate etc.
imit./ative etc.
immed./iate(ly)
imper./ative
impers./onal
improp./er(ly)
incept./ive
incl. including; inclusive
Ind. of the subcontinent comprising India, Pakistan, and Bangladesh
ind. indicative; indirect
indecl./inable
indef./inite
inf./initive
infl./uence etc.
instr./umental (case)
int./erjection
interrog./ative(ly)
intr./ansitive
ints. interjections
Ir./ish (language or usage)
iron./ical(ly)
irreg./ular(ly)
It./alian

Jap./an(ese)
Jav./anese
joc./ular(ly) (see p. ix)
Journ./alism etc.

L Latin (classical if not otherwise described)
lang./uage
LDu. Low Dutch
LG Low German
LHeb. Late Hebrew
Ling./uistics etc.
lit./eral(ly)
LL Late Latin

M Middle (with languages)
Magn./etism etc.
masc./uline
Math./ematics etc.
MDa. Middle Danish
MDu. Middle Dutch
ME Middle English
Mech./anics etc.
Med./icine etc.
med./ieval
metaph./or etc.
Metaphys./ics etc.
metath./esis etc.
Meteorol./ogy etc.
Mex./ican
MFlem. Middle Flemish
MHG Middle High German
Mil./itary etc.
Min./eralogy etc.
mistransl./ation
MLG Middle Low German
mod./ern
Mount./aineering
MSw. Middle Swedish
Mus./ic etc.
Myth./ology etc.

n. noun
N. Amer. North America(n)
Nat. National
Naut./ical etc.
neg./ative(ly)
N. Engl. north of England
neut./er
nom./inative
Norm./an
north./ern

Norw./egian
ns. nouns
num./eral

O Old (with languages)
obj. object; objective
obl./ique
OBret. Old Breton
OBrit. Old British
obs./olete
Obstet./rics etc.
OBulg. Old Bulgarian
occas./ional(ly)
OCelt. Old Celtic
ODa. Old Danish
ODu. Old Dutch
OE Old English
OF Old French
OFrank. Old Frankish
OFris. Old Frisian
OGael. Old Gaelic
OHG Old High German
OIcel. Old Icelandic
OIr. Old Irish
OIt. Old Italian
OL Old Latin
OLG Old Low German
ON Old Norse
ONF Old Northern French
ONorw. Old Norwegian
OPers. Old Persian
OPort. Old Portuguese
opp. (as) opposed (to); opposite
OProv. Old Provençal
Opt./ics etc.
ord./inary etc.
orig. origin; original(ly)
Ornith./ology etc.
OS Old Saxon
OScand. Old Scandinavian
OSlav. Old Slavonic
OSp. Old Spanish
OSw. Old Swedish

P: see note below
Paint./ing
Palaeog./raphy etc.
parenth./etic etc.
Parl./iament(ary)
part. (present) participle
pass./ive(ly)
Path./ology etc.
pej./orative
perf./ect (tense)
perh./aps
Pers./ian
pers./on(al)
Peruv./ian
Pharm./acy etc.
Philol./ogy etc.
Philos./ophy etc.
Phoen./ician
Phonet./ics etc.
Photog./raphy etc.
phr./ase
Phren./ology etc.
phrs. phrases
Phys./ics
Physiol./ogy
pl./ural
poet./ical etc.
Pol./ish
Polit./ics etc.
pop. popular etc., not technical
pop. L popular Latin, informal spoken Latin
Port./uguese
poss. possessive; possible etc.
p.p. past participle
pr./onounced etc.
prec./eding entry
pred. predicate; predicative(ly)
pref./ix
prep./osition
pres./ent (tense)
pret./erite
Print./ing
prob./able etc.
pron./oun etc.
pronunc./iation
prop./er(ly)
Pros./ody etc.
Prov./ençal (medieval if not otherwise described)
prov. proverb etc.; provincial etc.
Psych./ology etc.

redupl./icated etc.
ref./erence
refash./ioned
refl./exive(ly)
rel. related; relative
repl./acing etc.
repr./esenting etc.
Rhet./oric etc.
rhet./orical(ly)
Rom. Roman; (in etymologies) Romanic
Russ./ian

S. Afr. South Africa(n)
S. Amer. South America(n)
Sc./ottish etc.
Scand./inavia(n)
sent./ence
Shak./espeare
sim./ilar(ly)
sing./ular
Sinh./alese
Skr. Sanskrit
sl./ang
Slav./onic
Sociol./ogy etc.
Sp./anish
sp./elling etc.
spec./ial(ly)
st./em
St. Exch. Stock Exchange
subj. subject etc.; subjunctive
subord./inate
subst./antive
suf./fix
superl./ative
Surg./ery etc.
Surv./eying etc.
Sw./edish
syl./lable etc.
symb./ol
syn./onym etc.

t. transitive
tech./nical(ly)
Teleph./ony etc.
Telev./ision etc.
Teut./onic
Theatr./ical etc.
Theol./ogy etc.
thr./ough
transf. in transferred sense
transl./ation etc.
Turk./ish
Typogr./aphy etc.

ult./imate(ly)
uncert./ain
unexpl./ained
univ./ersity
unkn./own
usu./al(ly)

v. verb
var. variant; various
vars. variants
v. aux. auxiliary verb

vb. verb
vbl verbal
vbs. verbs
v.i. intransitive verb
voc. vocative
v. refl. reflexive verb
v.t. transitive verb
vulg./ar (see p. ix)

W Welsh
w. with

wd word
wds words
WFris. West Frisian
WG West Germanic
wh./ich
W. Ind. West Indian, of the West Indies
WS West Saxon
WSlav. West Slavonic

Zool./ogy etc.

P Proprietary name. See below.

***P** Proprietary name in U.S.

* (except in etymologies): chiefly U.S. (often also Canadian, Australian, etc.).

* in etymologies: form not recorded but merely inferred.

|| chiefly not U.S. (where this is not indicated by 'Sc.' or other label, or implied by the definition; usu. = U.K. and Commonwealth).

~ (swung dash; see page ix).

^{1} ^{2} ^{3} etc. used to distinguish several entries for words, prefixes, or suffixes spelt identically.

1 2 3 etc. or (1) (2) (3) etc. } used to distinguish senses within an entry.

1 2 3 1st, 2nd, 3rd person of verb.

NOTE ON PROPRIETARY TERMS

THIS dictionary includes some words which are or are asserted to be proprietary names or trade marks. Their inclusion does not imply that they have acquired for legal purposes a non-proprietary or general significance, nor is any other judgement implied concerning their legal status. In cases where the editor has some evidence that a word is used as a proprietary name or trade mark this is indicated by the letter **P**, but no judgement concerning the legal status of such words is made or implied thereby.

A

A, a¹, (ā) *n.* (*pl.* **As** *or* **A's**). First letter of alphabet; (Mus.) sixth note in diatonic scale of C major; first hypothetical person or example; highest class (of road, academic marks, population as regards affluence, etc.); **from A to Z,** over the entire range, completely; **from A to B,** from any place to some other place (*use* one's *car simply as a means of getting from A to B*); (Alg., usu. *a*) first known quantity; **A1** (ā wŭ'n), (Naut.) first-class (vessel in Lloyd's Register of Shipping), (colloq.) excellent, first-rate; **A1, A2,** etc., standard paper-sizes each half the previous one, e.g. A4=297×210 mm, A5=210×148 mm.

a², an, (a, an; *or, when stressed,* ā, ăn) *a.* (Called the *indefinite article*; unemphatic substitute for) one, some, any; one like (*a Daniel*); one single (*could not see a thing*; *reduce unemployment at a stroke*); (after *all of,* etc.) the same (*all of a size*); (distrib.) in, to, or for, each (*£40 a year, twice a day, seven a side,* where *a* is orig. = foll.). For usage see AN¹. [weakening of OE *ān* one]

a³ *prep.* (usu. as *pref.*) On (*afire, afoot*); to (*ashore*); towards (*aback, aside*); in (*nowadays*); in the process of (w. vbl ns. passively (*a-building*) or actively esp. w. *go, set* (*he went a-begging, they set the bells a-ringing*) and w. vbs. in same sense (*abuzz, aflutter*)). [weakening of OE prep. *an, on* (see ON¹)]

a- *pref.* **1.** f. OE *a-*, orig. *ar-*, away, on, up, out, (*arise*). **2.** f. ME *a-* f. OE *an, on,* prep. (see prec.). **3.** f. ME *a-* f. OE *of* prep. (*akin*). **4.** f. ME *a-* (= OF pref. *a-*), either directly f. L *ad* to, at (*ascend*) or thr. F. *a-* (*agree*); many wds derived in the latter way have been later assim. to L spelling, as *a(d)dress, a(g)grieve.* **5.** f. ME *a-*, = OF *a-*, f. L *ab* from, away, (*abridge*). **6.** f. ME, AF *a-* = OF *e-, es-* f. L *ex* out, utterly, (*affray*). **7.** f. Gk *a-*, not, without—derived directly (*agnostic, amoral*), thr. L (*apetalous*), or thr. L and F (*adamant, amethyst*).

-a *suf.* forming: **1.** *ns.* f. Gk, L, and Rom. fem. sing., as *idea* (Gk), *arena* (L), *piazza* (It.), *duenna* (Sp.), esp. names of animals and plants, ancient or Latinized mod. (*hyena, dahlia*), oxides (*alumina*), geog. names (*Africa*), and names of women, ancient or Latinized mod. (*Lydia, Hilda*). **2.** *pl. ns.* [f. Gk and L neut. pl.] (*phenomena, genera*), esp. names, often f. mod. L, of Zool. groups (*Carnivora*). **3.** Colloq. or sl. for *of* (*coupla, kinda, pinta*) or *have* (*mighta*).

A. *abbr.* ‖(Of films) certified as suitable for adult audiences but possibly not for children; ampere(s); ångström(s); answer; Associate of; atomic (energy etc.).

a *abbr.* atto-.

A *symb.* argon.

A.A. *abbr.* *Alcoholics Anonymous; anti-aircraft; ‖Automobile Association; ‖(of films) to be seen only by persons over 14.

A.A.A. *abbr.* ‖Amateur Athletic Association; *Automobile Association of America.

A. & M. *abbr.* (Hymns) Ancient and Modern.

A. & R. *abbr.* Artists and recording (*or* repertoire).

aar'dvârk (ar'd-) *n.* Termite-eating nocturnal African mammal. [Afrik. (*aarde* earth, *vark* pig)]

aar'dwol|f (ar'dwŏŏlf) *n.* (*pl.* **~ves**). Insectivorous African mammal of hyena family. [Afrik. (*aarde* earth, *wolf* wolf)]

Aaron's beard (āronz-) *n.* Popular name for several plants, esp. a St. John's wort (*Hypericum calycinum*). [ref. to Ps. 133: 2]

Aaron's rŏd (āronz-) *n.* Popular name for several tall plants, esp. a mullein (*Verbascum thapsus*). [ref. to Num. 17: 8]

A'asia *abbr.* Australasia.

aa'svogel (ah'sfōgel) *n.* S. Afr. vulture. [Afrik. (*aas* carrion, *vogel* bird)]

***A.A.U.** *abbr.* Amateur Athletic Union.

ab- *pref.* Off, away, from (*abduct, abnormal, abuse*). [F or f. L]

A.B. *abbr.* Able rating or seaman [f. *able-bodied*]; *Bachelor of Arts [f. L *Artium Baccalaureus*].

ă'ba, abaya (abā'ya), **ă'bba,** *n.* Sleeveless outer garment as worn by Arabs. [f. Arab. '*abā'*]

‖**ā'băc** *n.* Nomogram. [f. F *abaque* f. L ABACUS]

ă'baca *n.* (Plant yielding) Manila hemp. [f. Sp. *abacá*]

abă'ck *adv.* Backwards, behind; (Naut., of square sails) pressed against mast by head wind; **taken ~,** (of ship) with sails in that state; **take ~,** (fig.) surprise, disconcert. [OE *on bæc* (as A³, BACK¹)]

ă'bac|us *n.* (*pl.* **~uses,** *or* **~i** *pr.* -sī). **1.** Calculating frame with balls sliding on wires, used before adoption of the nine figures and zero, and still in elementary teaching. **2.** (Archit.) Upper member of capital, supporting architrave. [L, f. Gk *abax abakos* slab, drawing-board, f. Heb. *'ābāk* dust]

Abă'ddon (a-) *n.* Hell; the Devil (Rev. 9:11). [Heb., = destruction]

aba'ft (-ah'-) *adv.* & *prep.* (Naut.) **1.** *adv.* In stern half of ship. **2.** *prep.* Nearer stern than, aft of. [f. A³ + *baft* f. OE *beæftan* (*be* BY¹, *æftan* behind)]

***ăbalō'nė** *n.* Edible mollusc of genus *Haliotis,* with ear-shaped shell lined with mother-of-pearl; ormer, sea-ear. [f. Amer. Sp. *abulón*]

abă'ndon¹ *v.t.* Give up to another's control or mercy; yield one*self* completely to a passion or impulse; give up (possession, habit, game); forsake (person, post, ship). [ME, f. OF *abandoner* (*à bandon* under control f. Rom. **bando -onis* f. med. L *bandum,* var. of LL *bannus, -um* BAN²]

abă'ndon² (*or* ăbah'ndawn) *n.* Careless freedom of manner, letting oneself go. [F; see prec.]

abă'ndoned (-ond) *a.* Forsaken; profligate. [p.p. of ABANDON¹]

abăndonee' *n.* (Law). One to whom anything is relinquished, esp. underwriter entitled to salvage a wreck. [f. ABANDON¹ + -EE]

abă'ndonment *n.* Giving up or forsaking; being forsaken; self-surrender; careless freedom of manner, impulsiveness. [f. F *abandonnement* (as ABANDON¹; see -MENT)]

abā'se *v.t.* Lower, humiliate, debase; hence **~MENT** (-sm-) *n.* [ME, f. OF *abaissier* (*a* = A- 4, *baissier* to lower f. Rom. **bassiare* f. LL *bassus* short of stature); infl. by BASE³]

abă'sh *v.t.* (usu. in *pass.*) Embarrass, disconcert; hence **~MENT** *n.* [ME, f. OF *esbaïr* (*es-* = A- 6, *baïr* astound or *baer* yawn)]

aba'sk (-ah'-) *adv.* Basking. [f. A³ + BASK]

abā'te *v.* **1.** *v.t.* & *i.* Diminish; make or grow less. **2.** *v.t.* Do away with (nuisance); lower (price);

deduct (specified or unspecified part of price); mitigate (violence, pain); weaken (energy). **3.** (Law). Quash (writ or action). **4.** So ~MENT (-tm-) *n.* [ME, f. OF *abatre* f. Rom. **abbatt(u)ere* (A- 4, L *batt(u)ere* beat)]

ă'batĭs, abă'ttĭs, *n.* (*pl.* same *or* **~es**). Defence made of felled trees with boughs pointing outwards; hence ~ED² (-st) *a.* [F (*abatre* fell; see prec.)]

ă'battoir (-twâr) *n.* Slaughterhouse. [F (as prec.)]

abaya, abba. See ABA.

ă'bbacy̆ *n.* Office, jurisdiction, or tenure, of an abbot or abbess. [ME, f. eccl. L *abbacia* (*abbat-* ABBOT; see -ACY)]

abbā'tial (-shal) *a.* Of an abbey, abbot, or abbess. [F, or f. med. L *abbatialis* (as ABBOT; see -IAL)]

abbé (ă'bā) *n.* Frenchman (orig. abbot) entitled to wear ecclesiastical dress, with or without official duties. [F, f. eccl. L *abbas abbatis* ABBOT]

ă'bbėss *n.* Head of abbey of nuns. [ME, f. OF *abbesse* f. eccl. L *abbatissa* (as ABBOT; see -ESS¹)]

Abbevĭ'llian (ăbv-) *a.* & *n.* (Culture) of earliest palaeolithic period in Europe. [F (*-ien*), f. *Abbeville* in N. France; see -IAN]

ă'bbey *n.* Building(s) occupied by monks or nuns under an abbot or abbess; the monks or nuns as a body; church or house that was once an abbey or part of it; **the A~,** ‖(esp.) Westminster Abbey. [ME, f. OF *abbeie* etc. f. med. L *abbatia* ABBACY]

ă'bbot *n.* Head of abbey of monks. [OE *abbod* etc., f. eccl. L *abbas -atis* f. Gk *abbas* father f. Aram. *'abbā*]

abbrē'vĭate¹ *a.* Relatively short. [ME, f. LL *abbreviatus* (as foll.; see -ATE²)]

abbrē'vĭ|āte² *v.t.* Make short (usu. of writing part of word for whole; occas. of story etc.); so ~A'TION *n.* [ME, f. LL *abbreviare* shorten (*ab* or *ad, brevis* short) + -ATE³; cf. ABRIDGE]

ABC (ābēsē') *n.* The alphabet (*as easy as ABC*); rudiments of any subject; alphabetical guide. [f. A + B + C]

A.B.C. *abbr.* Australian Broadcasting Commission; *American Broadcasting Company.

ă'bdĭc|āte *v.t.* Renounce formally or by default (a power, office, duty, right, or abs., esp. of the crown); so ~A'TION *n.* [f. L AB(*dicare* declare) + -ATE³]

ă'bdomĕn (*or* ăbdō'-) *n.* **1.** (Anat.) Belly, part of body containing stomach, bowels, and other digestive organs. **2.** (Zool.) Hinder part of insect, crustacean, spider, etc. [L]

ăbdŏ'mĭnal *a.* Of the abdomen (in either sense). [f. mod. L *abdominalis* f. L. *abdomin-* stem of prec. + -AL]

ăbdŏ'mĭnous *a.* Corpulent. [f. L *abdomin-* stem of ABDOMEN + -OUS]

abdŭ'ct *v.t.* Kidnap (child); take away (esp. a woman) by illegal force or fraud; (of muscle etc.) draw (limb etc.) away from middle line of body etc.; so ~ION, ~OR, *ns.* [f. L AB(*ducere duct-* draw)]

abea'm *adv.* On a line at right angles to ship's or aircraft's length; opposite middle *of* (ship etc.). [f. A³ + BEAM¹]

ābėcėdār'ian *a.* & *n.* **1.** *a.* Arranged alphabetically. **2.** *n.* Person learning the alphabet or rudiments of a subject. [f. LL *abecedarius* (*a, b, c, d*; see -ARY¹) + -AN]

abĕ'd *adv.* (arch.) In bed. [OE (as A³, BED¹)]

abele (abē'l *or* ā'bel) *n.* The white poplar, *Populus alba.* [f. Du. *abeel* f. OF *abel*, earlier *aubel* f. med. L *albellus* dim. of *albus* white]

A'berdeen (ă'-) *n.* ~ **(Angus),** (animal of) Scottish breed of polled black beef cattle; ~ **(terrier),** Scotch terrier. [~ in Scotland]

Aberdō'nĭan (ă-) *a.* & *n.* (Native or inhabitant) of Aberdeen. [f. med. L *Aberdonia* + -IAN]

Abernĕ'thy̆ (ă-) *n.* Hard biscuit flavoured with caraway seeds. [prob. f. John ~, Engl. surgeon d. 1831]

abĕ'rr|ant *a.* Straying from moral standard; (esp. Biol.) diverging from normal type; so ~ANCE, ~ANCY, *ns.* [f. L AB(*errare* stray); see -ANT]

ăberrā'tion *n.* **1.** A straying from the path (lit. or fig.); breaking of rules; moral slip; temporary lapse of memory; deviation from type. **2.** (Opt.) Non-convergence of rays from a point to one focus. **3.** (Astron.) Apparent displacement of celestial body from its true position, caused by observer's motion. [f. L. *aberratio* (as prec.; see -ATION)]

abĕ't *v.t.* (**-tt-**). Encourage or assist (offence or offender; esp. *aid and abet*); so ~MENT, ~TER¹, (esp. Law) ~TOR, *ns.* [ME, f. OF *abeter* (*à* to, *beter* BAIT¹)]

ab extra (ăbĕ'kstra) *adv.* From outside. [LL]

abey'ance (-bā-) *n.* State of suspension or temporary disuse; (of rights etc.) dormant condition liable to revival (usu. *be in* or *fall into abeyance*). [f. AF *abeiance* f. OF *abeer* (*à* to, *beer* f. med. L *batare* gape)]

abhôr' *v.t.* (**-rr-**). Regard with disgust and hatred. [ME, f. L AB(*horrēre* shudder)]

abhŏ'rrence *n.* Detestation; detested thing. [f. foll. + -ENCE]

abhŏ'rrent *a.* (Of conduct etc.) inspiring disgust, hateful, *to* (person etc.); not according *to* (*abhorrent to the spirit of the law*); (arch.) feeling disgust; ~ **from,** inconsistent with. [f. as ABHOR; see -ENT]

abī'dance *n.* Continuance, dwelling (*in*); abiding (*by* rules etc.). [f. foll. + -ANCE]

abī'de *v.* (**abō'de** *pr.* -ō'd, *or* **~d**). **1.** *v.i.* Remain, continue; (arch.) dwell; ~ **by** (*past* and *p.p.* usu. **-d**), remain faithful to, act upon (terms, promise). **2.** *v.t.* Encounter, sustain; submit to, suffer; (neg. or interrog., with n. or inf.) put up with, tolerate; (arch.) wait for. [OE *ābīdan* (A- 1, *bīdan* BIDE)]

abī'dĭng *a.* Enduring, permanent; hence ~LY² *adv.* [f. prec. + -ING²]

ă'bĭgail *n.* Lady's-maid. [character in Beaumont & Fletcher's *Scornful Lady*; cf. 1 Sam. 25]

abĭ'lĭty̆ *n.* Sufficient power, capacity (*to* do something); legal competency (to act); cleverness, talent, mental power, (*his undoubted ability; his manifold abilities*). [ME f. OF *ablete* f. L *habilitas -tatis* (*habilis* deft; see -TY¹)]

-abĭ'lĭty̆ *suf.* forming *ns.* f. *adjs.* in -ABLE (*communicability*). [f. F *-abilité* or f. L *-abilitas*; see -ITY]

ab initio (ăbĭnĭ'shĭō) *adv.* From the beginning. [L]

ābio|gĕ'nėsĭs *n.* Spontaneous generation; supposed origin of life by formation of organic from inorganic substances; hence ~GE'NIC *a.* [f. A- 7 + Gk *bios* life + GENESIS]

ābiŏ'tĭc *a.* Devoid of life. [f. A- 7 + BIOTIC]

ă'bjėct *a.* Brought low, miserable; craven, degraded, despicable, self-abasing; hence ~LY² *adv.*, ~NESS *n.* [ME, f. L *abjectus* p.p. of AB(*icĕre* = *jacĕre* throw)]

abjĕ'ction *n.* State of misery or degradation. [ME f. OF, or f. L *abjectio* (as prec.; see -ION)]

abjur'e (-joor') *v.t.* Renounce on oath (an opinion, heresy, cause, claim, claimant); swear perpetual absence from (one's country etc.); so **ăbjur**A'TION *n.* [f. L AB(*jurare* swear)]

ăblā'te *v.t.* Remove by ablation. [back form. f. foll.]

ăblā'tion *n.* (Surg.) removal of any part of body; (Geol.) wasting or erosion of a glacier, iceberg, or rock by melting or water action; (Astronaut.)

evaporation or melting of part of outer surface of spacecraft through heating by friction with atmosphere. [F, or f. LL *ablatio* f. L AB(*lat-* p.p. st. of *ferre* carry)]

ă'blative *a.* & *n.* (Gram.) ~ (**case**), case of (esp. Latin) nouns etc., expressing source, agent, cause, or instrument, of action, =*from* or *by* w. the noun etc.; *ablative* ABSOLUTE. [ME, f. OF *ablatif -ive* or f. L *ablativus* (as prec.; see -IVE)]

ă'blaut (-owt) *n.* Vowel change in related words in (esp. the parent Indo-European) language, arising out of differences of accent and stress, and surviving e.g. in *sing, sang, sung*. [G]

ablā'ze *adv.* & *pred. a.* On fire; glittering; excited. [f. A³ + BLAZE¹]

ā'ble *a.* **1.** Talented, clever; competent, having the means or power (*to*) (esp. used w. parts of *be* to supply the deficiencies of *can*, e.g. *shall be able to* as fut. of *can*); legally qualified. **2.** **~-bodied,** fit, skilled; **~(-bodied) rating, seaman,** one able to perform all duties. **3.** Hence **ā'b**LY² *adv.*, capably, cleverly. [ME, f. OF *hable, able* f. L *habilis* handy (*habēre* to hold)]

-able *suf.* forming *adjs.*, in wds formed at early date freq. w. act. sense (*comfortable, suitable*), now always w. pass. sense: 'that can, may, must, be —d' (*eatable, execrable, forgivable, payable*), 'that can be made the subject of' (*dutiable, objectionable*), 'that is relevant to or in accordance with' (*fashionable, seasonable, serviceable*). [F, or f. L *-a-* of first conjug. + *-bilis* (see -BLE), in F extended to vbs. of all conjugs.; in E now appended even to native vbs. as *bearable*, nouns as *clubbable*, and phrasal vbs. as *get-at-able*, prob. f. confusion w. prec.]

ablōō'm *adv.* & *pred. a.* In or into bloom. [f. A³ + BLOOM¹]

ablŭ'sh *adv.* & *pred. a.* Blushing. [f. A³ + BLUSH¹]

ablu'tion (-lōō'-) *n.* (usu. in *pl.*) Ceremonial washing of person, hands, or sacred vessels; water that has been used for this; (joc.) ordinary personal washing; ||building containing washing-places etc. in camp, ship, etc.; hence ~ARY¹ *a.* [ME f. OF, or f. LL AB(*lutio* f. *luere lut-* wash; see -ION)]

ā'bly̆ *adv.* See ABLE.

-ably̆ *suf.* forming *advs.* corresp. to *adjs.* in *-able*. [f. -ABLE + -LY²]

A.B.M. *abbr.* anti-ballistic-missile missile.

ă'bnėgāte *v.t.* Deny oneself (something); renounce (a right or belief). [f. L AB(*negare* deny) + -ATE³]

ăbnėgā'tion *n.* Denial; renunciation (of doctrine); (**self-**)~, self-sacrifice. [f. OF, or f. LL *abnegatio* (as prec.; see -ATION)]

ăbnôr'mal *a.* Exceptional, irregular; deviating from type; relating to what is abnormal (*abnormal psychology*); hence **ăbnôrmă'l**ITY *n.*, the quality or an instance of it, ~LY² *adv.* [earlier and F *anormal, anomal* f. Gk *anōmalos* ANOMALOUS, assoc. w. L *abnormis*; see foll.]

ăbnôr'mity̆ *n.* Irregularity; a monstrosity. [f. L AB(*normis* f. *norma* rule) + -ITY]

A'bō (ă'-), **ă'bō,** *n.* (*pl.* **~s**) & *a.* (Austral. sl.) Aboriginal. [abbr.]

aboar'd *adv.* & *prep.* On or into ship, aircraft, train, *bus, etc. (*ship* etc. either expressed or omitted); alongside; near; **all ~!** (call that warns of imminent departure). [ME, f. A³ + BOARD¹ & F *à bord*]

abō'de¹ *n.* Dwelling-place, house; stay, habit of dwelling (*make* one's *abode*). [vbl n. of ABIDE; cf. *ride, rode, road*]

abō'de². See ABIDE.

abŏ'lish *v.t.* End existence of (custom, institution); hence ~ABLE *a.*, ~ER¹, ~MENT, *ns.* [ME, f. F *abolir* (-ISH²) f. L *abolēre* destroy]

ăboli'tion *n.* Abolishing, being abolished (esp. w. ref. to capital punishment, or (Hist.) Negro slavery, and the movement against it, whence ~ISM(3), ~IST(2), *ns.*). [F, or f. L *abolitio* (as prec.; see -ION)]

ăbomā's|um *n.* (*pl.* **~a**). Fourth STOMACH of ruminant. [mod. L, f. AB- + OMASUM]

A-bomb (ā'bŏm) *n.* Atomic bomb. [f. *A* (for ATOMIC) + BOMB]

abŏ'mĭnab|le *a.* Detestable, odious; morally or physically loathsome; (by exagg.) unpleasant (*abominable weather*); **A~le Snowman,** yeti, unidentified anthropoid or ursine animal alleged to exist in Himalayas; hence ~LY² *adv.* [ME f. OF, f. L *abominabilis* f. AB(*ominari* f. OMEN) deprecate; see -ABLE]

abŏ'mĭnāte *v.t.* Loathe; (by exagg.) dislike. [f. L *abominari* (as prec.) + -ATE³]

abŏmĭnā'tion *n.* Loathing; odious or degrading habit or act; an object of disgust (*to*). [ME f. OF (as ABOMINATE; see -ATION)]

ăbori'gĭnal *a.* & *n.* **1.** *a.* (Of races and natural objects) indigenous, existing in a land at the dawn of history, or before arrival of colonists; of the Australian Aboriginals; hence ~ITY (-ă'l-) *n.*, ~LY² *adv.* **2.** *n.* Aboriginal inhabitant, esp. (usu. *A~*) of Australia. [f. as foll. + -AL]

ăbori'gĭnė *n.* Aboriginal inhabitant, esp. (usu. *A~*) of Australia; (usu. in *pl.*) aboriginal plant or animal. [L, prob. f. phr. *ab origine* from the beginning]

***abôr'ning** *adv.* & *pred. a.* (While) being born or produced. [f. A³ + BORN + -ING²]

abôr't *v.* & *n.* **1.** *v.i.* Suffer abortion; (Biol.) remain undeveloped, shrink away. **2.** *v.t.* Cause abortion of; (fig.) cause to end fruitlessly; stop (growth, disease) in early stages. **3.** *v.t.* & *i.* (Aeron. & Astronaut.) Terminate (flight), stop, abandon, or destroy (rocket etc.), fail to complete flight. **4.** Hence ~ĬFA'CIENT *a.* & *n.*, (drug or other agent) causing abortion. **5.** *n.* (Aeron. & Astronaut.) Unsuccessful (flight by) rocket etc.; termination of such flight. [f. L AB(*oriri ort-* be born) miscarry]

abôr'tėd *a.* Untimely born; undeveloped; (Biol.) rudimentary (*thorns are aborted branches*). [f. prec. + -ED¹ (2)]

abôr'tion *n.* Miscarriage of birth, esp. if deliberately induced; procuring of this, esp. illegally, whence ~IST (1) *n.*; (Med.) delivery of (prob. non-viable) foetus in first 28 weeks of pregnancy; arrested development of any organ; dwarfed or misshapen creature; failure of a project or action. [f. L *abortio* (as ABORT; see -ION)]

abôr'tĭve *a.* Resulting in abortion; (Biol., of organ etc.) rudimentary, arrested in development; fruitless, unsuccessful; hence ~LY² (-vlĭ) *adv.*, ~NESS (-vn-) *n.* [ME, f. OF *abortif -ive* f. L *abortivus* (as ABORT, -IVE)]

abou'lĭa, abū'lĭa, *n.* Loss of will-power (as mental disorder). [f. Gk *a-* not + *boulē* will]

abou'nd *v.i.* Be plentiful; be rich (*in*); teem or be infested (*with*). [ME, f. OF *abunder* etc. f. L AB(*undare* f. *unda* wave) overflow]

abou't *adv.* & *prep.* **1.** All round from outside (*compass it about*; *go a long way about*; *He is about my path*; BEAT¹ *about the bush*); all round from a centre (*look,* LAY³, *about you*). **2.** Somewhere near (HANG¹ *about*; *people* or *objects about us*; *have* or *keep* one's WIT²*s about* one); carried with (*have no money about me*); here and there (*in* a place, or abs.) (*measles is about*; *move,* ORDER², *about*; PUT¹ *about*; *dotted about the fields*; *man about* TOWN); **out and ~,** (of person, esp. after illness) engaging in normal outdoor activity; **up and ~,** arisen after sleep or illness. **3.** Near in number, scale, degree, etc., (*about half, fifty, right, midnight, my size, the best*); (colloq., in iron. understatement or comparison; ***I'm** about tired of this*; *about as* *exciting as cold semolina*). **4.** Facing in opposite direction (RIGHT[1] *about turn* or *face*; *the wrong way about*); ~ **turn** or ***face** (as Mil. command). **5.** In rotation (*take turns about*; *on duty* (*week and*) *week about*). **6.** Occupied with (*about my father's business*; *send him about his* BUSINESS; *what are you about?*); **am ~ to do,** am on the point of doing (so all vbs. forming fut. participles). **7.** In connection with, on the subject of, (*quarrels, a book, about money*; *something wrong about it*; *have read, do not know, about it*; SET[1], SEE[1], GO[1], *about*); in relation to (*symmetry about a line or plane*); **how about,** = WHAT *about*. **8.** In the course of events (*I brought it about*; *it came about*). **9.** (Naut.) On or to the opposite tack (*go about*; *put about*). [OE *onbūtan* (*on* A[3], *būtan* BUT[1])]

about-fā'ce, about-tŭr'n, *n.*, & *v.i.* (Make) reversal of direction, opinion, policy, or behaviour. [f. Mil. commands (ABOUT 4)]

abo've (-ŭ'v) *adv.*, *prep.*, *a.*, & *n.* **1.** *adv.* At or to a higher point; overhead, on high; upstream; upstairs; in heaven. **2.** On the upper side; earlier in a book or article (*as was remarked above*; *the above-cited passages*; *the above-mentioned facts*); in addition (*over and above*). **3.** *prep.* Over, on the top of, higher than (*above average*, PAR[1]; *heard above the din*; *head above water*); ~ **ground,** alive; *above* one's HEAD[1]; ~ **oneself,** carried away by high spirits, conceit, etc.; **~-boar'd** *adv.* & *pred. a.*, undisguised(ly), fair(ly), open(ly) [metaph. f. card-playing]. **4.** More than (*above a hundred*); upstream from; further north than; (arch.) to an earlier time than (*not traced above the third century*); out of reach of (*above criticism, suspicion, my understanding*); too great or good for (*above meanness, ideas above* one's *station*); more important than (*above all*); of higher rank than. **5.** *a.* Preceding, previous (*the above statements*). **6.** *n.* That which is above. [f. A[3] + OE *bufan* (*be* BY[1], *ufan* above)]

ab ovo (ăb ō'vō) *adv.* (Relating tediously) from the very beginning. [L, = from the egg]

Abp. *abbr.* Archbishop.

ăbracadă'bra *n.* Spell, magic formula; gibberish. [cabbalistic word supposed when written triangularly, and worn, to cure fevers etc.; L f. Gk]

abrā'de *v.t.* Scrape off, wear away, injure, (skin, rock, fabric, etc.) by rubbing. [f. L AB(*radere ras-* scrape)]

A'brahăm-măn (ā'-; -*a*-h-) *n.* (*pl.* **-men**). (Hist.) Wandering beggar of 16th c., usu. feigning insanity; **sham Abraham,** feign illness or insanity. [perh. after Luke 16]

abrā'sion (-zh*o*n) *n.* Scraping off, wearing away, (of skin, rock, etc.); damaged area resulting from this. [f. L *abrasio* (as ABRADE; see -ION)]

abrā'sĭve *a.* & *n.* **1.** (Substance) capable of rubbing or grinding down. **2.** *a.* Tending to graze the skin; (fig.) tending to hurt person's feelings. [f. as prec. + -IVE]

ăbrėă'ct|ion *n.* (Psych.) Free expression and release of a previously repressed emotion; hence ~IVE *a.*, **ăbrėă'ct** *v.t.* release by abreaction. [f. AB- + REACTION, after G *abreagierung*]

abrea'st (-rĕ'st) *adv.* Side by side and facing the same way; keeping up, not behind, (*of* or *with* progress, thought, etc.). [ME, f. A[3] + BREAST[1]]

abrĭ'dge *v.t.* Condense (book etc.); curtail (liberty); (arch.) deprive (person *of*). [ME, f. OF *abreg*(*i*)*er* f. LL *abbreviare* ABBREVIATE[2]]

abrĭ'dgement, -dgm-, (-jm-) *n.* Shortening (of book etc.); curtailment (of rights); epitome, abstract. [f. F *abrégement* (as prec.; see -MENT)]

abroa'ch *adv.* & *pred. a.* (Of cask) pierced, so as to let the liquor run. [ME, f. AF *abroche* f. OF *abrochier* (as A- 4, BROACH[1])]

abroa'd (-raw'd) *adv.* **1.** In or to foreign lands; **from ~,** from another country. **2.** (arch.) Out of doors; in error. **3.** Broadly, in different directions (*scattered abroad*); in motion, current, (*there is a rumour abroad*). [ME, f. A[3] + BROAD]

ă'brogāte *v.t.* Repeal, cancel, (law, custom); so **ăbrog**A'TION *n.* [f. L AB(*rogare* propose law) + -ATE[3]]

abrŭ'pt *a.* Sudden, hasty; disconnected, not smooth (*abrupt manner of speaking*); steep, precipitous; (Bot.) truncated; (Geol., of strata) suddenly cropping out; hence ~LY[2] *adv.*, ~NESS *n.* [f. L *abruptus* p.p. of AB(*rumpere* break)]

abrŭ'ption *n.* Breaking away of part from a mass. [f. L *abruptio* (as prec.; see -ION)]

abs- *pref.* = AB-. [var. of L *ab-* used before *c, q, t*]

ă'bscėss *n.* Localized collection of pus formed in the body by disintegration of tissue. [f. L *abscessus* a going away f. ABS(*cedere cess-* go)]

absci'ssa *n.* (*pl.* **~s** *or* **~e**). (Math.) Part of line between fixed point on it and ordinate drawn to it from any other point; co-ordinate parallel to *x*-axis. [mod. L *abscissa* (*linea*) fem. p.p. of AB(*scindere sciss-* cut)]

absci'ssion (-sh*o*n) *n.* Cutting off; (Bot.) natural separation. [f. L *abscissio* (as prec.; see -ION)]

abscŏ'nd *v.i.* Depart secretly; flee from the law; hence ~ER[1] *n.* [f. L ABS(*condere* stow)]

ă'bseil (-sāl *or* -zīl) *n.*, & *v.i.* (Make) descent of steep rock-face by using doubled rope fixed at higher point. [f. G *abseilen* (*ab* down, *seil* rope)]

ă'bsence *n.* Being away from a place or person; time of being away; non-existence or lack *of*; inattention due to thought of other things (esp. *absence of mind*). [ME f. OF, f. L *absentia* (*absent-* ABSENT[1])]

ă'bsent[1] *a.* **1.** Not present (~ **from,** at another place than; ~ **voter,** one who votes by post because absent from usu. voting-place); not existing. **2.** Inattentive, abstracted in mind; hence ~LY[2] *adv.*, **~-mī'nd**ED[2] *a.*, **~-mī'ndėd**LY[2] *adv.*, **~-mī'ndėd**NESS, ~NESS, *ns.* [ME f. OF, f. L *absens absentis* part. of AB(*esse* be)]

absĕ'nt[2] *v.refl.* Keep one*self* away; withdraw one*self*. [ME, f. OF *absenter* or f. LL *absentare* (*absent-* ABSENT[1])]

ăbsentee' *n.* Person not present; ABSENT[1] voter; person, esp. landlord, habitually living elsewhere; hence ~ISM(2) *n.*, practice of being an absentee, practice of workers, pupils, etc., of absenting themselves from work, esp. frequently or without good reason. [f. ABSENT[2] + -EE]

ă'bsĭnth *n.* Wormwood, the plant or its essence; ~(e), a green liqueur made (at least orig.) from wine and wormwood. [f. F *absinthe* f. L f. Gk *apsinthion*]

absit omen (ăbsĭt ō'mĕn) *int.* May suggested foreboding not become fact. [L, = may this (evil) omen be absent]

ă'bsolūte (*or* -ōōt) *a.* **1.** Complete, perfect. **2.** Pure; ~ **alcohol** (free from water). **3.** Unrestricted, independent (~ **majority,** more than half, majority over all rivals combined); ruling arbitrarily, despotic. **4.** Not in usu. grammatical relation; **ablative** ~ in L, **accusative** ~ in G, **genitive** ~ in Gk, **nominative** ~ or ~ **construction** in E, noun and participle (or E infinitive) used as adverbial clause (*dinner being over, we left the table*; *let us toss for it, loser to pay*). **5.** Not relative or comparative; unqualified, unconditional; (Philos.) self-existent and conceivable without relation to other things (**the ~,** that which is absolute); *absolute* MAGNITUDE; ~ **music,** self-dependent instrumental music devoid of literary etc. suggestions; ~ **pitch,** (Mus.) (1) ability to recognize or reproduce the pitch of a note, (2) fixed standard of pitch defined by rate of vibration; ~ **temperature** (measured from *absolute* ZERO). **6.** Hence ~NESS

(-tn-) *n.* [ME, f. L *absolutus* p.p. (see ABSOLVE); infl. by OF *absolut*]

ă'bsolūtelÿ (-tlĭ; *or* -ōōtlĭ) *adv.* **1.** Independently, in and by itself; arbitrarily, without external control. **2.** Without qualification; (esp. Gram.) without the usual accompaniments (*transitive verb used* ~, without its object). **3.** Unconditionally; positively, actually, (*it absolutely exploded*); conclusively, completely, quite; (w. neg.) at all; (colloq., *pr.* -ōō'-) quite so, yes. [f. prec. + -LY²]

ăbsolū'tion (*or* -lōō'-) *n.* Formal setting-free from guilt, sentence, or obligation; ecclesiastical declaration of forgiveness of sins; remission of penance; forgiveness. [ME f. OF, f. L *absolutio -onis* (as ABSOLVE; see -ION)]

ă'bsolūt|ĭsm (*or* -lōō-) *n.* (Theol.) doctrine that God acts absolutely in the matter of salvation; (Polit.) principle of absolute government; philosophy of the absolute; hence ~IST(2) *n.* [f. ABSOLUTE + -ISM]

absŏ'lve (*or* -z-) *v.t.* Set or pronounce free (*from* blame, *of* sin, *from* obligation, or abs.); acquit, pronounce not guilty. [f. L AB(*solvere solut-* loosen)]

absôr'b (*or* -z-) *v.t.* Swallow up, incorporate (**be ~ed by,** lose one's identity in); engross the attention of; take in (fluid, food, knowledge); reduce intensity of (heat, light, sound, particles, impact, etc.) by physical or chemical action; consume (income, labour, strength, etc.); hence ~ABLE *a.*, ~ABI'LITY, ~ER¹(2), *ns.* [ME, f. F *absorber* or f. L AB(*sorbēre sorpt-* suck in)]

absôr'bed (-bd; *or* -z-) *a.* Intensely engaged or interested; hence ~LY² (-bĭdlĭ) *adv.* [p.p. of ABSORB]

absôr'bent (*or* -z-) *a.* & *n.* **1.** *a.* Having tendency to absorb; ***~ cotton,** cotton wool. **2.** *n.* Substance of this kind; one of the vessels in plants and animals (e.g. root tips) that absorb nutriment. [f. L (as ABSORB); see -ENT]

absôr'bĭng (*or* -z-) *a.* Engrossing, intensely interesting; hence ~LY² *adv.* [f. ABSORB + -ING²]

absôr'pt|ion (*or* -z-) *n.* Disappearance through incorporation in something else; mental engrossment; process of absorbing fluid, light, etc.; hence ~IVE *a.*, **~ĭve**NESS (-vn-) *n.* [f. L *absorptio* (as ABSORB; see -ION)]

ăbsqua'tūlāte (-ŏ'-) *v.i.* (joc.) Depart; decamp. [joc. after *abscond, squattle* decamp, *perambulate*]

abstai'n *v.i.* **1.** Restrain oneself (*from*); (esp.) refrain from alcohol. **2.** Decline to use one's vote. **3.** Hence ~ER¹ *n.*, ~ING² *a.* [ME, f. AF *astener* f. OF *abstenir* f. L ABS(*tinēre tent-* = *tenēre* hold)]

ăbstē'mĭous *a.* (Of persons, habits, etc.) sparing, moderate, not self-indulgent, esp. in food and drink; hence ~LY² *adv.*, ~NESS *n.* [f. L *abstemius* (ABS-, *temetum* strong drink) + -OUS]

abstĕ'ntion *n.* Abstaining (*from*, or abs.), (esp.) not using one's vote. [F, or f. LL *abstentio -onis* (as ABSTAIN; see -ION)]

abstêr'|gent *a.* & *n.* Cleansing (substance); so ~SION (-shon) *n.*, ~SIVE *a.* [f. L ABS(*tergēre ters-* wipe); see -ENT]

ă'bstĭnence *n.* Abstaining (*from* any pleasure etc.); continence; partial fasting; (**total**) ~, going without alcohol; = foll. [ME f. OF, f. L *abstinentia* (as ABSTINENT; see -ENCE)]

ă'bstĭnencÿ *n.* Habit of abstaining from pleasure, food, etc. [f. as prec.; see -ENCY]

ă'bstĭnent *a.* Practising abstinence; hence ~LY² *adv.* [ME f. OF, f. L (as ABSTAIN; see -ENT)]

ă'bstrăct¹ *a.* **1.** Separated from matter, practice, or particular examples; not concrete; **~ noun** (denoting quality or state); **the ~**, ideal or theoretical way of regarding things. **2.** Idealistic, not practical; abstruse; (Art etc.) free from representational qualities (**~ expressionism,** ACTION painting). **3.** Hence ~LY² *adv.*, ~NESS *n.* [ME f. OF, or f. L *abstractus* p.p. of ABS(*trahere* draw)]

ă'bstrăct² *n.* Brief statement of content of book etc., summary; abstraction or abstract term; abstract painting etc. [as prec.]

ăbstră'ct³ *v.t.* Deduct, remove; (euphem.) steal; disengage (attention etc.) *from*; consider abstractly; summarize; hence ~OR *n.* [f. ABSTRACT¹]

ăbstră'ctėd *a.* Withdrawn in thought; not attending; hence ~LY² *adv.*, ~NESS *n.* [p.p. of prec.]

ăbstră'ction *n.* Taking away, withdrawal; (euphem.) stealing; process of stripping an idea of its concrete accompaniments; an idea so stripped, something visionary; piece of abstract art, whence ~ISM(3), ~IST(2), *ns.*; absence of mind. [F, or f. L *abstractio* (as ABSTRACT¹; see -ION)]

ăbstru'se (-ōō's) *a.* Hard to understand, profound; hence ~LY² (-slĭ) *adv.*, ~NESS (-sn-) *n.* [F, or f. L ABS(*trusus* p.p. of *trudere* push)]

absûr'd *a.* Incongruous, inappropriate; unreasonable; ridiculous, silly; hence ~LY² *adv.* [f. F *absurde* or f. L *absurdus* (AB-, *surdus* deaf, dull)]

absûr'dĭtÿ *n.* Folly, unreasonableness; absurd statement or act. [f. F *absurdité* or f. L *absurditas* (as ABSURD; see -ITY)]

abū'lĭa. See ABOULIA.

abŭ'ndance *n.* Quantity more than enough, plenty; overflowing emotion (*abundance of the heart*); relative quantity or number (of plants, substances, etc.) present; affluence, wealth; call undertaking to make nine tricks in solo whist. [ME, f. OF (*h*)*abundance* f. L *abundantia* (as foll.; see -ANCE)]

abŭ'ndant *a.* More than enough, plentiful; rich (*in*); hence ~LY² *adv.* [ME, f. L (as ABOUND; see -ANT)]

ab urbe condita (ăb êrbĭ kŏ'ndĭta) *adv.* (Of date) reckoning from the foundation of Rome in 753 B.C. [L, = from the founding of the city]

abū'se¹ (-z) *v.t.* Misuse, make bad use of; maltreat; speak insultingly or unkindly to or of. [ME, f. OF *abuser* f. Rom. **abusare* f. L AB(*uti us-* USE²)]

abū's|e² *n.* **1.** Misuse, perversion, (*of*); unjust or corrupt practice. **2.** Reviling; insulting or unkind speech. **3.** Hence ~IVE *a.* [ME, f. OF *abus* or f. L *abusus* (as prec.)]

abŭ't *v.* (-tt-). **1.** *v.i.* (Of estates or countries) have common boundary, border *on*; (of part of building) end *on* or *against*, lean *on*. **2.** *v.t.* Abut on. [sense 'border upon' f. OF *abouter* (BUTT⁴); sense 'end on' f. AL *abuttare* (OF *but* end)]

abŭ'tment *n.* Lateral support (esp. of arch or bridge); point of junction between such support and thing supported. [f. prec. + -MENT]

abŭ'tter *n.* (Law). Owner of adjoining property. [f. ABUT + -ER¹]

abӯ(e)' *v.t.* (**abou'ght** *pr.* -aw't). (arch.) Redeem, pay the penalty of, (offence). [OE *ābycgan* redeem (as A- 1, BUY)]

abӯ'sm *n.* (arch. or poet.) = ABYSS. [ME, f. OF *abi(s)me* f. LL *abysmus* assim. (to -ISM) of *abyssus* ABYSS]

abӯ'smal (-z-) *a.* Bottomless (esp. fig.; *abysmal ignorance*); (colloq.) extremely bad (*his taste is abysmal*); hence ~LY² *adv.* [f. prec. + -AL]

abӯ'ss *n.* Bottomless chasm, deep gorge; immeasurable depth, esp. fig. (*abyss of despair*); primal chaos. [ME, f. L f. Gk *abussos* bottomless (*a-* not, *bussos* depth)]

abӯ'ssal *a.* At or of ocean depths or floor; (Geol.) plutonic. [f. prec. + -AL]

ac- *pref.* **1.** Assim. form of AD- before *c, k, q.* **2.** Erron. for *a-* [of various orig.; see A-], as in *acknowledge*. **3.** See AD- 2.

-ăc *suf.* forming *adjs.* (*cardiac, iliac, maniac*), which are often also (or only) used as *ns.* (cf. -ACAL). [f. F *-aque* or L *-acus* or Gk *-akos* adj. suf.]

A.C. *abbr.* ‖Aircraftman; alternating current; before Christ [f. L *ante Christum*].

a/c *abbr.* account. [f. *account current* (ACCOUNT[2] 3)]

Ac *symb.* actinium.

acā'cia (-sha) *n.* Tree or shrub of genus *Acacia*, some members of which yield gum ARABIC; (**false**) ~, the locust-tree (*Robinia pseudoacacia*), grown for ornament. [L, f. Gk *akakia*]

ă'cadēme *n.* (literary). College, university; **grove(s) of A~**, (fig.) university environment. [f. Gk *Akadēmos* (see ACADEMY); improp. transf., perh. from Milton's 'grove of Academe', *Paradise Regained* iv. 244]

ăcadĕ'm|ĭc *a.* & *n.* **1.** *a.* Scholarly; of a university etc. (*academic dress*; *academic* YEAR). **2.** Abstract, unpractical, theoretical, cold, merely logical, (Art) conventional, over-formal, whence **~ĭcISM** (3), **acă'demISM** (3), *ns.* **3.** Of the philosophy of Plato; sceptical. **4.** Hence ~ICALLY *adv.* **5.** *n.* Member of a university. [f. F *académique* or f. L *academicus* (as ACADEMY; see -IC)]

ăcadĕ'mĭcal *a.* & *n.* **1.** *a.* Belonging to a college or university. **2.** *n.* (in *pl.*) University costume. [f. prec. + -AL]

acădemĭ'cian (-shan) *n.* Member of an Academy, esp. of the Royal Academy of Arts or the Académie française or the U.S.S.R. Academy of Sciences. [f. F *académicien* (as ACADEMIC; see -ICIAN)]

Acă'demў (*a*-) *n.* **1.** Garden near Athens where Plato taught; Plato's followers or philosophical system (cf. GARDEN, LYCEUM, PORCH). **2.** (*a*~). Place of study; secondary school, esp. (Sc.) grammar school. **3.** Place for special training (*Royal Military Academy*). **4.** Society for cultivating literature, art, science, etc., of which membership is an honour, esp. the Royal Academy (of Arts). [f. F *académie* or f. L f. Gk *akadēmeia* (*Akadēmos* the man or demigod f. whom Plato's garden was named)]

Acā'dĭan (*a*-) *a.* & *n.* (Native or inhabitant) of Nova Scotia. [f. F *Acadie* Nova Scotia + -AN]

-acal *suf.* forming *adjs.* (*heliacal*); often used to distinguish them from *ns.* in -AC (*maniac, maniacal*). [f. -AC + -AL]

acă'nthus *n.* Herbaceous plant of genus *Acanthus*, with prickly leaves; (Gk Archit.) conventional representation of its leaf. [L, f. Gk *akanthos* (*akantha* thorn perh. f. *akē* sharp point)]

ă cappĕ'lla (*or* ah-) *a.* & *adv.* (Of choral music) unaccompanied. [It., =in church style]

ă'carĭd *n.* & *a.* (Mite or tick) of order Acarida, esp. of family Acaridae. [f. mod. L *acarida* (*acarus* f. Gk *akari* mite; see -ID[3])]

acâr'pous *a.* (Bot.) Not producing fruit. [f. A- 7 + Gk *karpos* fruit + -OUS]

acătalĕ'ctĭc *a.* & *n.* (Pros.) (Line) that is complete, not catalectic. [f. LL *acatalecticus* f. Gk *akatalēktos* (as A- 7, CATALECTIC)]

Accadian. See AKKADIAN.

ăccē'de (ăks-) *v.i.* (abs. or w. *to*). **1.** Enter upon an office; become monarch. **2.** Join a party; become part of a country; assent to an opinion or policy; formally accept a treaty etc. [ME, f. L AC(*cedere cess-* go)]

accĕlerā'nd|ō (aks- *or* ăch-) *adv., a.,* & *n.* (*pl.* **~os** *or* **~i**). (Mus.) (Passage performed) with gradual increase of speed. [It.]

accĕ'lerāte (aks-) *v.* **1.** *v.t.* Make quicker (*accelerated motion*); cause to move faster or happen earlier. **2.** *v.i.* (Of motion or process) become swifter; begin to move more quickly. [f. L AC(*celerare* f. *celer* swift) + -ATE[3]]

accĕlerā'tion (aks-) *n.* **1.** Making quicker; being made quicker; (of vehicle) ability to gain speed. **2.** (Phys.) Rate of change of velocity per unit time. [f. F *accélération* or f. L *acceleratio* (as ACCELERATE; see -ION)]

accĕ'lerātĭve (aks-) *a.* Tending to increase speed, quickening. [f. ACCELERATE + -IVE]

accĕ'lerātor (aks-) *n.* Thing that increases anything's speed, esp. pedal in motor vehicle for this purpose; substance that speeds up a chemical reaction; (Phys.) apparatus for imparting high speeds to charged particles. [f. ACCELERATE + -OR]

accĕlerŏ'mèter (aks-) *n.* Instrument for measuring acceleration or vibrations. [f. ACCELERATE + -O- + -METER]

ă'ccent[1] (ă'ks-) *n.* **1.** Prominence given to syllable by stress or (in some languages) by pitch; mark used with letter to show quality of vowel, metrical stress, speech stress, distinction of homonyms, etc. **2.** Individual, local, or national mode of pronunciation; modulation to express feeling; (in *pl.*) person's (mode of) speech. **3.** Rhythmical stress in verse or prose, whence **accĕ'ntūAL** (aks-) *a.* **4.** Recurrent or other stress in music. **5.** Intensity, sharp emphasis; distinctive character; a contrasting detail. [F, or f. L *accentus* (AC-, *cantus* song) repr. Gk *prosōidia* (PROSODY)]

accĕ'nt[2] (aks-) *v.t.* Pronounce with accent, emphasize (word or syllable); put written accents on; (fig.) accentuate. [f. obs. F *accenter* (as prec.)]

accĕ'ntor (aks-) *n.* Bird of genus *Prunella*, e.g. HEDGE[1]-sparrow. [cf. med. L *accentor*, f. L *ad* to + *cantor* singer]

ăccĕ'ntū|āte (ăks-) *v.t.* Emphasize, heighten; make conspicuous; hence **~A'TION** *n.* [f. med. L *accentuare* (as ACCENT[1]) + -ATE[3]]

accĕ'pt (aks-) *v.t.* & (arch., w. *of*) *v.i.* **1.** Consent to receive (person, something offered, or abs.); answer affirmatively (invitation, suitor). **2.** Regard with favour. **3.** Tolerate; submit to (*accept the umpire's decision*); receive as adequate or valid (*will accept your explanation*; *slot machine accepts only pennies*; *accept service of writ*); allow the truth of, believe; **~ed opinion** (generally held to be correct). **4.** Undertake (office); take responsibility for, agree to meet, (draft or bill of exchange). **5.** Hence **~ER**[1] *n.* [ME, f. OF *accepter* or f. L *acceptare* f. AC(*cipere cept-* =*capere* take)]

accĕ'pt|able (aks-) *a.* Worth accepting; pleasing, welcome; tolerable (*acceptable risk*); hence or cogn. **~ablY**[2] *adv.*, **~ABI'LITY**, **~ableNESS** (-beln-), *ns.* [ME f. OF, f. LL *acceptabilis* (as ACCEPT; see -ABLE)]

accĕ'ptance (aks-) *n.* **1.** Consent to receive (gift, thing delivered, payment, pleasure, duty); favourable reception (*of* person or thing, *by* or *with* person); affirmative answer to invitation. **2.** Approval, belief; toleration. **3.** Engagement to meet a bill; a bill so accepted. [F (*accepter* f. as ACCEPT; see -ANCE)]

accĕ'ptant (aks-) *a.* ~ **of,** willingly accepting. [F (as prec.; see -ANT)]

ăccĕptā'tion (ăks-) *n.* A particular sense, or the generally recognized meaning, of a word or phrase. [ME f. OF, f. LL *acceptatio* (as ACCEPT; see -ATION)]

accĕ'ptor (aks-) *n.* One who accepts a bill; (Phys.) atom or molecule able to receive an extra electron, esp. impurity in a semiconductor; (Chem.) substance able to combine with another; (Electr.) circuit able to accept a given frequency. [f. ACCEPT + -OR]

ă'ccĕss (ă'ks-) *n.* **1.** Approach; ~ **(to),** right or means of approaching or reaching. **2.** Being approached (*easy of access*); ~ **time,** (Computers) time needed to retrieve stored information.

3. Passage, channel, doorway. **4.** Attack or outburst (*of* illness, anger, emotion). [ME, f. OF *acces* or f. L *accessus* f. AC(*cedere cess-* go)]

accĕ'ssarȳ (*a*ks-) *n.* & *a.* (One) that helps in or is privy *to* any act, esp. a crime; ~ **before, after, the fact,** helping to plan, conceal, it. [f. med. L *accessarius* (as ACCEDE; see -ARY[1])]

accĕ'ss|ĭble (*a*ks-) *a.* Able to be reached, entered, influenced, or understood; **~ible to,** able to be reached etc. by; hence ~IBI'LITY *n.*, **~ĭb**LY[2] *adv.* [F, or f. LL *accessibilis* (as ACCEDE; see -IBLE)]

accĕ'ssion (*a*ksĕ'sh*o*n) *n.*, & *v.t.* **1.** *n.* Entering upon an office (esp. the throne) or condition (as manhood). **2.** Being added; thing added (e.g. book *to* library), increase, addition; (Law) improvement or natural growth of property. **3.** Assent; formal acceptance of treaty etc. **4.** *v.t.* Record addition of (book etc.) to library. [F, or f. L *accessio -onis* (as ACCEDE; see -ION)]

accĕ'ssor|ȳ (*a*ks-) *a.* & *n.* **1.** *a.* Additional; (of things) subordinately contributing, dispensable; adventitious. **2.** *n.* (esp. in *pl.*) Accessory thing, accompaniment; minor fitting or attachment; small article of (esp. woman's) dress, whence ~IZE (5) *v.t.*; accessary. [f. med. L *accessorius* (as ACCEDE; see -ORY)]

acciaccatu'ra (*a*chahk*a*toō'r*a*) *n.* (Mus.) Grace-note performed quickly before an essential note of a melody. [It.]

ă'ccĭdence (ă'ks-) *n.* Part of grammar dealing with the variable forms of words. [f. L *accidentia* (tr. Gk *parepomena*) neut. pl. of *accidens* (as foll.); see -ENCE]

ă'ccĭdent (ă'ks-) *n.* **1.** Event that is without apparent cause or unexpected; **chapter of ~s,** unforeseen course of events. **2.** Unintentional act, chance, misfortune, (*by accident*); unlucky event, esp. one causing injury or damage, (*accident*-PRONE). **3.** Irregularity in structure; property or quality not essential to our conception of a substance (so of material qualities of bread and wine after transubstantiation); mere accessory. [ME f. OF, f. L AC(*cidere* = *cadere* fall); see -ENT]

ăccĭdĕ'ntal (ăks-) *a.* & *n.* **1.** *a.* Happening by chance, undesignedly, or unexpectedly, whence ~LY[2] *adv.*; occasional. **2.** *a.* & *n.* (Thing) not essential to a conception; subsidiary; (Mus.) ~ (**sharp, flat, natural**), sign attached to single note, not in key signature. [ME, f. LL *accidentalis* (as prec.; see -AL)]

ă'ccĭdĭe (ă'ks-), **acē'dĭa,** *ns.* Laziness, torpor; apathy. [ME f. AF *accidie* f. OF *accide* f. med. L *accidia* alt. f. LL *acedia* f. Gk *akēdia* listlessness]

acclai'm *v.t.*, & *n.* **1.** *v.t.* Welcome or applaud enthusiastically; (w. obj. & compl.) hail as (king, winner, saviour; *acclaimed him king*). **2.** *n.* (Shout of) applause or welcome. [ME, f. L AC(*clamare* shout), sp. assim. to *claim*]

ăcclamā'tion *n.* Loud and eager assent to a proposal (*voted, carried, by acclamation*); (usu. in *pl.*) shouting in a person's honour. [f. L *acclamatio* (as prec.; see -ATION)]

***ă'cclĭmāte** (*or* -ī'-) *v.t.* Acclimatize; hence ***acclimat**A'TION *n.* [f. F *acclimater* (*à* to, *climat* CLIMATE)]

ăcclĭmā'tion *n.* Acclimatization. [irreg. f. prec.]

acclī'matiz|e, -is|e (-īz), *v.t.* & *i.* Habituate (animals, plants, one*self*), become habituated, to new climate or surroundings; hence ~A'TION *n.* [f. F *acclimater* (see ACCLIMATE) + -IZE]

acclĭ'vĭt|ȳ *n.* Upward slope; hence ~OUS *a.* [f. L *acclivitas* f. AC(*clivis* f. *clivus* slope); see -ITY]

ă'ccolāde (*or* -ā'd) *n.* **1.** Sign at bestowal of knighthood, now usu. stroke on shoulder with flat of sword; (fig.) bestowal of praise, acknowledgement of merit. **2.** (Mus.) Vertical line or brace coupling staves. [F, f. Prov. *acolada* f. Rom. **accollare* embrace (as AC-, L *collum* neck); see -ADE]

accŏ'mmodāte *v.t.* **1.** Adapt (thing or person *to* another); harmonize; reconcile, settle differences between. **2.** Equip, supply, (person *with*); oblige, confer favour on; provide lodging or room for. [f. L AC(*commodare* f. *commodus* fitting) + -ATE[3]]

accŏ'mmodātĭng *a.* Obliging, easy to deal with; compliant; hence ~LY[2] *adv.* [f. prec. + -ING[2]]

accŏmmodā'tion *n.* **1.** Adjustment (e.g. of lens of eye to focus for various distances); adaptation of anything or oneself to a purpose or meaning different from the original. **2.** Settlement, compromise. **3.** Serviceable thing, convenience; loan of money; (in *sing.* or **pl.*) lodgings, living premises; (in *pl.*) *seat in vehicle etc. **4.** ~ **address** (used on letters to person unable or unwilling to give permanent address); *accommodation* BILL[4]; ~ **ladder** (up side of ship from small boat); ~ **road** (for access to place not on public road). [F, or f. L *accommodatio -onis* (as ACCOMMODATE; see -ATION)]

acco'mpanĭment (-ŭ'm-) *n.* **1.** Appendage, accompanying thing. **2.** (Mus.) Subsidiary part, usu. instrumental, supporting solo instrument or voice, choir, etc. [f. *accompagnement* (as ACCOMPANY; see -MENT)]

acco'mpan|ȳ (-ŭ'm-) *v.t.* **1.** Supplement (a thing *with*, as word with blow); go or be put or be found with; escort, attend; (of things) coexist with, characterize. **2.** (Mus.) Support (singer, player, chorus) by performing subsidiary (usu. instrumental) part, whence ~(ȳ)IST (1) *n.* [ME, f. F *accompagner* (*à* to, OF *compaing* COMPANION[1]), assim. to COMPANY]

accŏ'mplĭce (*or* -ŭ'm-) *n.* Partner in crime. [ME, f. earlier and F *complice* (prob. by assoc. w. prec.), f. LL *complex complicis* confederate (cf. COMPLICATE)]

accŏ'mplĭsh (*or* -ŭ'm-) *v.t.* Perform, complete; succeed in doing; hence ~ED[1] (-sht) *a.*, clever, skilled, well trained or educated. [ME, f. OF *acomplir* f. Rom. *ACcomplēre f. L *complēre* COMPLETE[2]; see -ISH[2]]

accŏ'mplĭshment (*or* -ŭ'm-) *n.* Fulfilment, completion; thing done or attained, achievement; acquired skill, esp. social. [ME, f. prec. + -MENT]

accompt. Var. (arch.) of ACCOUNT[1,2].

accor'd[1] *v.* **1.** *v.i.* (Esp. of things) be in harmony or consistent (*with*, or abs.). **2.** *v.t.* Grant (permission, request, etc.); give (welcome etc.). [ME, f. OF *acorder* f. Rom. *AC(*cordare* f. L *cor cordis* heart)]

accor'd[2] *n.* **1.** Consent, mutual agreement; **with one ~**, all agreeing. **2.** Treaty of peace; harmonious correspondence in colour, pitch, tone, etc. **3.** Volition (*of* one's *own accord*). [ME, f. OF *acord* (*acorder*; see prec.)]

accor'dance *n.* Conformity, agreement, (*in accordance with*). [ME, f. OF *acordance* (as ACCORD[1]; see -ANCE)]

accor'dant *a.* In tune, agreeing, (*with*, or abs.); hence ~LY[2] *adv.* [ME, f. OF *acordant* (as ACCORD[1]; see -ANT)]

accor'dĭng *adv.* **1.** ~ **as,** in proportion as (of a process varying with another); in a manner depending on which of certain alternatives is true. **2.** ~ **to,** in a manner consistent with or degree proportioned to (*value them according to their merits*); as stated by. [f. ACCORD[1] + -ING[2]]

accor'dĭnglȳ *adv.* As the (stated) circumstances suggest; therefore; ~ **as,** according as. [f. prec. + -LY[2]]

accor'dĭon *n.* Portable musical instrument having bellows, metal reeds, and keyboard and/or buttons; ~ **pleat,** ~ **wall,** (folded like bellows of accordion); hence ~IST (3) *n.* [f. G *akkordion* f. It. *accordare* to tune]

accŏ'st *v.t.* Approach and address, esp. boldly; open conversation with; (of prostitute) solicit. [f. F *accoster* f. It. *accostare* f. Rom. *AC(*costare* f. L *costa* rib; see COAST^1)]

accouchement (ăkōō'shmahṅ) *n.* Childbirth; lying in. [F (*accoucher* act as midwife; see -MENT)]

accouch|eur (ăkōōshẽr') *n.* (*fem.* ***~euse*** *pr.* -ẽr'z). Man who acts as midwife. [F (as prec.)]

accou'nt^1 *v.* **1.** *v.t.* Consider, regard as, (w. obj. & compl. or inf.; *account him a hero, wise, to be guilty*). **2.** *v.i.* ~ **for,** give reckoning of (money held in trust), answer for (conduct, performance of duty), explain the cause of, serve as explanation of (*that accounts for it*), (Sport) be responsible for the death, defeat, dismissal, etc., of. [ME, f. OF *aconter* (*a-* AC-, *conter* COUNT^2)]

accou'nt^2 *n.* **1.** Reckoning of debit and credit, in money or service (**money of** ~, name of sum of money not repr. by actual coin etc.); statement of moneys or goods or services received and expended, with balance (*render* or *send in, pay* or *settle, an account*); *account* RENDERE*d*; **keep ~s,** enter all expenditure for comparison with income; **settle** or **square ~s with,** receive or pay the balance due from or to, (fig.) have revenge on; **on** ~, as interim payment; **on** one's **own** ~, for and at one's own purposes and risk; **on** ~ **of,** because of; **on no** ~, under no circumstances, certainly not. **2.** Favourable result of the reckoning, profit; **turn to (good)** ~, make useful. **3.** Business relationship involving reckoning of debit and credit, esp. with bank or with firm granting credit; **current** ~ (formerly ~ **current**) (at bank in order to withdraw money on demand); DEPOSIT^1 *account*; **joint** ~ (held by two or more persons in conjunction); **on** ~, debited by firm instead of being paid for immediately. **4.** Periodic settlement of accounts on Stock Exchange; ~ **day** (when this takes place). **5.** Statement of administration as required by creditor, or of discharge of any responsibility; answering for conduct (*demand, render, an account; call to account*); **gone to his** ~, dead; **give a good** ~ **of oneself,** be successful, make favourable impression. **6.** Consideration (*take into account* or *take account of; leave out of account* or *take no account of*); importance (*of some* or *no account*). **7.** Narration, report, description, (*of* event, person, etc.); performance (*of* piece of music etc.); **by all ~s,** in everyone's opinion. [ME, f. OF *acont* (*aconter*; see prec.)]

accou'nt|able *a.* Bound to give account, responsible, (*for* things, *to* persons, or abs.); explicable; hence ~ABI'LITY, **~able**NESS (-bełn-), *ns.*, **~ab**LY^2 *adv.* [f. ACCOUNT^1 + -ABLE]

accou'nt|ant *n.* Professional keeper and inspector of accounts; ||CHARTER^2*ed accountant*; TURF *accountant*; hence ~ANCY *n.*, profession or duties of an accountant. [law F, f. part. of OF *aconter* ACCOUNT^1; see -ANT]

accou'nting *n.* Process or art of keeping and verifying accounts. [f. ACCOUNT^1 + -ING^1]

accou'tre, *accou'ter, (-ōō'ter) *v.t.* (usu. in *p.p.*) Attire, equip, esp. with special costume. [f. F *accoutrer* f. OF *acoustrer* (A- 4, *cousture* sewing; cf. CON-, SUTURE)]

accou'trement, *accou'terment, (-ōō't-) *n.* (usu. in *pl.*) Equipment, trappings; (Mil.) soldier's outfit other than arms and garments. [F (as prec.; see -MENT)]

accrĕ'dit *v.t.* Gain belief or influence for (adviser, statement, etc.); send out (ambassador etc.) with credentials *to* person, *to* or *at* a court or government; attribute (thing *to* person), credit (person *with* thing); hence ~A'TION *n.* [f. F AC(*créditer* f. *crédit* CREDIT^1)]

accrĕ'dĭtĕd *a.* (Of person or organization) officially recognized; (of belief) generally accepted, orthodox; (of cattle, milk, etc.) having guaranteed quality. [p.p. of prec.]

accrē'te *v.* **1.** *v.i.* Grow together or into one; form round or on *to,* as round a nucleus. **2.** *v.t.* Attract (such additions). [f. L AC(*crescere cret-* grow)]

accrē'tion *n.* Growth by organic enlargement; growing of separate things into one; product of such growing; (adhesion of) extraneous matter added to anything; (Law) (1) = ACCESSION, (2) increase of legacy etc. by share of failing co-legatee. [f. L *accretio* (as prec.; see -ION)]

accru|e' (-ōō') *v.i.* Come (*to* one, *from* a thing) as natural increase, advantage, result (esp. of interest on invested money); hence ~AL 2 *n.*, ~ED^1 (2) (-ōō'd) *a.* [ME, f. AF *acru,* p.p. of *acreistre* increase f. L *accrescere* ACCRETE]

accŭ'ltūr|āte *v.t.* & *i.* Adapt to, adopt, a different culture; hence ~A'TION *n.* [f. AC- + CULTURE + -ATE^3]

accū'mūlāte *v.* **1.** *v.t.* Heap up, gradually get increasing number or quantity of (lit., or fig. of a fortune, ill will, etc.); produce or acquire thus. **2.** *v.i.* Grow numerous, form an increasing mass or quantity (lit. or fig.; *dirt, disasters, had accumulated*). [f. L AC(*cumulare* f. *cumulus* heap) + -ATE^3]

accūmūlā'tion *n.* Accumulating or being accumulated; growth of capital by continued interest; taking of higher and lower university degrees simultaneously; accumulated mass (*of* snow, papers, property, etc.). [f. L *accumulatio* (as prec.; see -ION)]

accū'mūlatĭve *a.* Arising from accumulation (*accumulative proof, evidence*); arranged so as to accumulate; acquisitive, given to hoarding; hence ~LY^2 (-vlĭ) *adv.* [f. ACCUMULATE + -IVE]

accū'mūlātor *n.* One who accumulates things; ||rechargeable electric cell; bet placed on a sequence of events, winnings from each being staked on next; storage register in computer. [f. ACCUMULATE + -OR]

ă'ccūr|ate *a.* Careful, precise; in exact conformity with a standard or with truth; hence ~ACY *n.*, **~ate**LY^2 (-tlĭ) *adv.* [f. L *accuratus* done carefully, p.p. of AC(*curare* f. *cura* care); see -ATE^2]

accûr'sĕd, (arch.) **accûr'st,** *a.* Lying under a curse, ill-fated; involving misery; (colloq.) execrable, detestable. [p.p. of *accurse,* f. A- 1 + CURSE^2; cf. AD- 2]

accū'sal (-z-) *n.* Accusation. [f. ACCUSE + -AL 2]

ăccūsā'tion (-z-) *n.* Accusing; being accused; a charge of offence or crime; indictment. [ME f. OF, f. L *accusatio -onis* (as ACCUSE; see -ATION)]

accū'satĭve (-z-) *a.* & *n.* (Gram.) ~**(case),** case of nouns etc., expressing goal of motion or obj. of action (in uninflected languages, applied to the wd that stands as obj., though with no mark of case); *accusative* ABSOLUTE; hence **accūsatī'v**AL (-z-) *a.*, ~LY^2 (-vlĭ) *adv.* [ME, f. OF *accusatif -ive* or f. L (*casus*) *accusativus,* transl. Gk (*ptōsis*) *aitiatikē*]

accūsatôr'ial (-z-) *a.* ~ **procedure** etc. (in which prosecutor and judge are not the same, opp. *inquisitorial*). [f. as foll. + -AL]

accū'satorў (-z-) *a.* (Of language, manner, etc.) conveying or implying accusation. [f. L *accusatorius* (as foll.; see -ORY)]

accū's|e (-z) *v.t.* **1.** Charge with a fault, indict, (person *as* offender or *of* offence); **the ~ed** (person, esp. on criminal charge). **2.** Lay the blame on. **3.** (arch.) Betray, disclose. **4.** Hence

~ER¹ *n.*, ~**ing**LY² *adv.* [ME *acuse* f. OF *ac(c)user* f. L AC(*cusare* f. *causa* CAUSE¹)]

accŭ'stom *v.t.* Make (one*self*, person or thing) used *to*; hence ~ED² (-md) *a.*, (esp.) customary, usual. [ME, f. OF *acostumer* (A- 4, *costume* CUSTOM); *accustomed* also f. obs. sense 'make usual']

āce *n.* **1.** The 'one' on cards, dice, or dominoes; card etc. so marked (||~ **up one's sleeve,** *~ **in the hole,** something effective kept in reserve); **play** one's ~, use one's best resource. **2.** (Lawn Tennis etc.) Stroke (esp. service) that opponent cannot return; point thus scored. **3.** Smallest possible amount, hair's breadth, (*within an ace of collapse*). **4.** Pilot who has brought down many enemy aircraft; one who excels at something, champion. [ME, f. OF f. L *as* unity]

-ā'cea (-sh*a*) *suf.* forming pl. names of orders and classes of animals (*Crustacea*); cf. -ACEAN. [neut. pl. of L adj. suf. *-aceus* of the nature of]

-ā'ceae (-siē) *suf.* forming pl. names of families of plants (*Rosaceae*). [fem. pl. of L adj. suf. *-aceus* (see prec.)]

-ā'cean (-sh*a*n) *suf.* forming *adjs.*, = -ACEOUS, and *ns.* as sing. of names in -ACEA (*crustacean*). [f. L *-aceus* (see -ACEA) + -AN]

acē'dia. See ACCIDIE.

Acĕ'ldama (*a*k- *or* *a*s-) *n.* Field of bloodshed; scene of slaughter. [Acts 1:19; ME, f. Gk *Akeldama* f. Aram. *ḥᵃkēl dᵉmâ* field of blood]

-ā'ceous (-sh*u*s) *suf.* forming *adjs.* (*carbonaceous, herbaceous*), esp. from *ns.* in -ACEA, -ACEAE (*crustaceous, rosaceous*). [f. L *-aceus* (see -ACEA) + -OUS]

acĕ'phalous *a.* Headless; (Zool.) having no part of body specially organized as head; (Bot.) with head aborted or cut off. [f. med. L f. Gk *akephalos* headless (*a-* not, *kephalē* head) + -OUS]

acer'b|(ic) *a.* Astringently sour, harsh-tasting; bitter or sharp in speech, manner, or temper; so ~ITY *n.* [f. L *acerbus* sour-tasting, -IC]

acĕ'sc|ent *a.* Turning sour; somewhat sour (lit. or fig.); so ~ENCE *n.* [F, or f. L *acescere* become sour; see -ENT]

ăcėtă'būl|um *n.* (*pl.* ~a). **1.** (Rom. Ant.) Cup to hold vinegar. **2.** (Zool.) Cup-shaped sucker of cuttlefish etc.; socket for head of thigh-bone, or of leg in insects. [ME f. L (*acetum* vinegar, *-abulum* dim. of *-abrum* holder)]

ăcėtă'ldėhȳde *n.* = ALDEHYDE 1. [f. ACETIC + ALDEHYDE]

ă'cėtāte *n.* Salt or ester of acetic acid, esp. its cellulose ester used to make textiles, gramophone records, etc.; ~ **fibre,** ~ **silk,** (made artificially from cellulose acetate). [f. foll. + -ATE¹ (3)]

acē'tic *a.* Pertaining to vinegar; ~ **acid,** the acid (CH_3COOH) that gives vinegar its characteristic taste. [f. F *acétique* f. L *acetum* vinegar; see -IC]

ă'cėto- *comb. form.* (Chem.) Acetic, acetyl, (*acetonitrile*). [f. as prec. + -O-]

ă'cėtōne *n.* Colourless volatile liquid ketone valuable as solvent of organic compounds. [f. prec. + -ONE]

ă'cėtous *a.* Having the qualities of vinegar; producing vinegar; sour. [f. LL *acetosus* sour (as ACETIC; see -OUS)]

ă'cėtўl *n.* (Chem.) The radical of acetic acid; ~**choline,** compound serving to transmit impulses from nerve fibres; ~ **silk,** = ACETATE *silk*. [f. ACETIC + -YL]

acĕ'tўlēne *n.* Colourless hydrocarbon gas, C_2H_2, burning with a bright flame, used esp. in lighting and welding. [f. ACETIC + -YL + -ENE]

Achae'an (*a*kē'-) *a.* & *n.* (Inhabitant) of Achaea in ancient Greece; (in Homer) Greek. [f. L f. Gk *Akhaios* + -AN]

acharnement (ăshar'nmahṅ) *n.* Ferocity; gusto. [F]

āche¹ (āk) *v.i.* Suffer or be source of continuous or prolonged dull pain or mental distress. [ME, f. OE *acan*; sp. after foll.]

āche² (āk) *n.* Continuous or prolonged dull pain; hence **ā'ch**Y² (ā'kĭ) *a.* [ME, f. OE *æce*; pr. after prec.]

achē'ne (*a*kē'n) *n.* (Bot.) Small dry one-seeded fruit that does not open, e.g. strawberry pip. [f. mod. L *achaenium* (A- 7, Gk *khainō* gape)]

Acheu'lĭan, -lėan, (*a*shōō'-) *a.* & *n.* (Culture) of the palaeolithic period in Europe etc. following the Abbevillian and preceding the Mousterian. [F (*-éen*), f. St-*Acheul* in N. France]

à cheval (ahsh*e*vah'l) *adv.* With one foot on each side; (of gambling stake) risked equally on two chances. [F, = on horseback]

achie'v|e *v.* **1.** *v.t.* Accomplish, carry out; acquire; reach (success, glory, one's objective); hence ~ABLE *a.* **2.** *v.i.* Attain desired level of performance. **3.** Hence ~ER¹ *n.* [ME, f. OF *achever* f. phr. *a chief* to a head; see A- 4, CHIEF¹]

achie'vement (-vm-) *n.* Completion, accomplishment; thing accomplished; (Psych.) performance in test; (Her.) escutcheon with adjuncts, or bearing, in memory of a distinguished feat, = HATCHMENT. [f. prec. + -MENT, or f. F *achèvement*]

Achĭ'llēs (*a*kĭ'lēz) *n.* *Achilles'* HEEL¹; *Achilles* TENDON. [L, name of Gk hero in Homer's *Iliad*, invulnerable except in heel]

ăchromă't|ĭc (ăk-) *a.* (Opt.) Free from colour; transmitting light without decomposing it into constituent colours; hence ~ICALLY *adv.*; ~**ĭ'**CITY, ~ISM (2) (*a*krō'm*a*-), *ns.* [f. F *achromatique* f. Gk *akhrōmatos* (as A- 7, CHROMATIC); see -IC]

achy. See ACHE².

ă'cĭd¹ *a.* Sharp-tasting, sour (||~ **drop,** kind of sweet with acid taste); (fig.) biting, severe, unpleasant, whence ~LY² *adv.*; (Chem.) having the essential properties of an ACID²; (Geol.) containing much silica; so **acĭ'd**ITY *n.*, (esp.) excessively acid condition of stomach. [f. F *acide* or f. L *acidus* (*acēre* be sour)]

ă'cĭd² *n.* **1.** Sour substance; (Chem.) one of a class of substances that neutralize and are neutralized by alkalis, and contain hydrogen that can be replaced by metals, and of which the principal types are sour and able to corrode or dissolve metals; ~ **radical** (formed by removal of hydrogen or hydroxyl groups from acid); ~ **test** (in which acid is applied to test for gold etc., often fig. of severe or conclusive test); **put the ~ on,** (Austral. sl.) seek to extract loan, favour, etc., from. **2.** (sl.) The drug LSD; ~**-head,** user of this. **3.** Hence **acĭ'd**IC *a.* (Chem. & Geol.), **acĭ'dĭ**FY *v.t.*, **ăcĭdĭ'**METER, **ăcĭdĭ'**METRY, *ns.* [f. prec.]

ăcĭdō's|ĭs *n.* (*pl.* ~**es** *pr.* -ēz). (Path.) Over-acid condition of blood or body tissues. [f. prec. + -OSIS]

acĭ'dūlāte *v.t.* Make somewhat acid. [f. L *acidulus* (dim. of *acidus* sour) + -ATE³]

acĭ'dūlous *a.* Somewhat acid. [f. as prec. + -OUS]

ă'cĭn|us *n.* (*pl.* ~**i** *pr.* -ī). (One of the small berries that make up) compound fruit such as blackberry; seed of grape or berry; (Anat.) racemose gland, or terminus of duct in it. [L, = berry, kernel]

-ā'cious (-sh*u*s) *suf.* forming *adjs.* w. sense 'inclined to' (*pugnacious*), 'abounding in' (*capacious*). [f. L *-ax -acis*, added to vbl stems to form *adjs.*, + -OUS]

-ă'cĭtў *suf.* forming *ns.* of quality corresponding to *adjs.* in -ACIOUS. [f. F *-acité* or f. L *-acitas -tatis*]

ăck-ă'ck *a.* & *n.* (colloq.) Anti-aircraft (gun etc.). [formerly signallers' name for letters *A.A.*]

ă'ckee, ă'kee, *n.* Tropical tree (*Blighia sapida*); its fruit, edible when cooked. [f. Kru *ākee*]

‖**ăck ĕ'mma** *adv.* & *n.* (colloq.) = A.M. [formerly signallers' name for letters *A.M.*]

acknow'ledge (aknŏ'lĭj) *v.t.* Agree to the truth of; own (person etc. *to be* something); own to knowing, take notice of; recognize the authority or claims of; express appreciation of, reward (a service); announce receipt of; recognize in legal form. [f. A- 2 + KNOWLEDGE, or from obs. n. *acknowledge*]

acknow'ledgement, -dgm-, (aknŏ'lĭjm-) *n.* Act of acknowledging; thing given or done in return for a service, message, etc.; (esp., in *pl.*) author's statement of indebtedness to others. [f. prec. + -MENT]

aclĭ'nĭc *a.* ~ **line,** magnetic equator, on which magnetic needle has no dip. [f. Gk *aklinēs* (*a*- not, *klinō* bend) + -IC]

ă'cmė *n.* Highest point; point or period of perfection. [Gk, = highest point]

ă'cnė *n.* Skin eruption characterized by red pimples. [mod. L, f. erron. Gk *aknas* for *akmas* acc. pl. of *akmē* facial eruption; cf. prec.]

ă'colȳte *n.* Church officer attending priest; attendant, assistant; beginner. [ME, f. OF *acolyt* or f. eccl. L *acolytus* f. Gk *akolouthos* follower]

ă'conīte *n.* Poisonous plant of genus *Aconitum,* esp. monkshood or wolfsbane; drug obtained from this; **winter** ~, yellow-flowered winter plant of genus *Eranthis*; hence **ăconĭ'tic** *a.* (Chem.), **acŏ'nĭtine**[5] *n.*, a poisonous alkaloid got from aconite. [f. F *aconit* or f. L *aconitum* f. Gk *akoniton*]

ā'cŏrn *n.* Fruit of the oak; ~ **barnacle,** ~ **shell,** multi-valve cirriped living on rocks; ~ **worm,** a primitive chordate. [OE *æcern,* cogn. w. *æcer* ACRE, later assoc. w. OAK and CORN[1]]

acŏtȳlē'don *n.* Plant with no distinct seed-leaves; hence ~OUS *a.* [f. mod. L *acotyledones* pl.; see A- 7, COTYLEDON]

acou'st|ĭc (-ōō'-) *a.* Relating to sound or sense of hearing; (of building materials) used for soundproofing; (of a mine) that can be exploded by sound waves transmitted under water; (Mus. etc., of instrument or recording) not electric; hence **~ĭcal** *a.*, **~ĭcally**[2] *adv.*, ~I'CIAN *n.*, ~ICS *n. pl.*, acoustical properties (of room etc.), (usu. treated as *sing.*) science of sound. [f. Gk *akoustikos* (*akouō* hear; see -IC)]

acquai'nt *v.t.* Make (person, one*self*) familiar (*with* circumstances, *that*); ~ **with,** make (person) aware of (facts etc.); **be ~ed (with),** have personal knowledge of (person or thing). [ME, f. OF *acointier* f. med. L *accognitare* (AC-, *cognoscere cognit-* come to know)]

acquai'ntance *n.* **1.** Knowledge more than mere recognition and usu. less than intimacy (*with* person or thing; **make the ~ of,** come to know). **2.** Person with whom one is acquainted. **3.** Hence ~SHIP (-s-sh-) *n.*, = sense 1. [ME, f. OF *acointance* (as prec.; see -ANCE)]

acquĕ'st *n.* Thing acquired; (Law) property gained otherwise than by inheritance. [obs. F, f. Rom. **acquaesitum* neut. p.p. (as n.) of **acquaerere* ACQUIRE]

ăcquiĕ'sc|e *v.i.* Agree, esp. tacitly; raise no objection; **~e in,** accept (arrangements, conclusions); hence ~ENCE *n.*, ~ENT *a.* [f. L AC(*quiescere* rest)]

acquīr'e *v.t.* Gain by and for oneself; come into possession (lit. or fig.) of; **~d characteristic,** (Biol.) one caused by environment, not inherited; **~d taste,** (object of) liking gained by experience; hence ~MENT (-īr'm-) *n.*, (esp.) mental attainment. [ME, f. OF *aquerre* f. Rom. **acquaerere* f. L AC(*quirere quisit-* = *quaerere* seek)]

ăcquisĭ'tion (-z-) *n.* Act of acquiring; thing acquired, useful or welcome addition; so **acquĭ'sĭtive** (-z-) *a.*, keen to acquire things, **acquĭ'sĭtiveness** (-z-; -vn-) *n.* [f. L *acquisitio* (as prec.; see -ION)]

acquĭ't *v.t.* (-tt-). Declare (person) not guilty (*of* offence); discharge one*self of* (duty, responsibility); ~ **oneself,** perform one's part *well, ill,* etc.; (arch.) pay (a debt). [ME, f. OF *aquiter* f. med. L *acquitare* pay debt (as AC-, QUIT[2])]

acquĭ'ttal *n.* Deliverance from a charge by verdict etc.; performance (of duty). [f. prec. + -AL]

acquĭ'ttance *n.* Payment of debt; release from debt; receipt in full. [ME, f. OF *aquitance* (as ACQUIT; see -ANCE)]

ā'cre (-*ker*) *n.* Measure of land, 4840 sq. yds. or about 4050 sq. metres; piece of tilled or enclosed land, field, (**land of broad ~s,** Yorkshire; GOD'*s Acre*); hence **(-)ā'cred** (-*erd*) *a.*, ~AGE (1) *n.* [OE *æcer,* = OHG *ackar,* ON *akr,* Goth. *akrs,* f. Gmc **akraz* f. IE **agros*]

ă'crĭd *a.* (~er, ~est). Bitterly pungent, irritating, corrosive; bitter in temper or manner; hence **ăcrĭ'dity** *n.* [irreg. f. L *acer acris* keen + -ID[1], prob. after *acid*]

ă'crĭdine (-ēn) *n.* Colourless crystalline compound got from coal tar, source of dyes and drugs. [f. prec. + -INE]

ăcrĭflā'vine (*or* -ēn) *n.* Reddish powder used as antiseptic. [irreg. f. prec. + FLAVINE]

ă'crĭmonȳ *n.* Bitterness of temper or manner; hence **ăcrĭmō'nĭous** *a.*, **ăcrĭmō'nĭously**[2] *adv.* [f. F *acrimonie* or f. L *acrimonia* pungency (as ACRID; see -MONY)]

ă'crobăt *n.* Performer of spectacular gymnastic feats, e.g. rope-walking; (fig.) one who changes position nimbly in argument; hence **ăcrobă'tic** *a.*, **ăcrobă'tics** *n.*, (doing of) acrobatic feats (also = AEROBATICS). [f. F *acrobate* f. Gk *akrobatēs* (*akron* summit, *bainō* walk)]

ă'crogėn *n.* (Bot.) Cryptogamous plant having perennial stem with growing point at extremity, e.g. fern or moss; hence **acrŏ'gėnous** *a.* [f. Gk *akron* tip + -GEN]

ăcromĕ'galȳ *n.* (Med.) Excessive growth of hands, feet, and face, caused by excessive activity of pituitary gland. [f. F *acromégalie* f. Gk *akron* extremity + *megas megal-* great; see -Y[1]]

acrŏ'nȳc(h)al (-ĭk-) *a.* Happening at nightfall (esp. of rising or setting of stars); hence ~LY[2] *adv.* [f. Gk *akronukhos* (*akron* peak, *nux nuktos* night) + -AL]

ă'cronȳm *n.* Word formed from initial letters of other words (*Ernie, laser, Nato, radar, Unesco*). [f. Gk *akron* end + *-onum-* = *onoma* name]

acrŏ'pėtal *a.* (Bot.) Developing from below upwards; hence ~LY[2] *adv.* [f. Gk *akron* tip + L *petere* seek + -AL]

ăcrophō'bĭa *n.* (Psych.) Morbid dread of heights. [f. Gk *akron* peak + -PHOBIA]

acrŏ'polĭs *n.* Citadel or upper fortified part of Greek city, esp. of Athens. [f. Gk *akropolis* (*akron* summit, *polis* city)]

acrŏ'ss (*or* -aw's) *adv.* & *prep.* **1.** Forming a cross with, making angles with, (obj. expressed or understood: *a line drawn across* or *across the road*); GET[1] *across.* **2.** Into contact with; COME, RUN[1], *across.* **3.** From side to side (of) (*run across, across the road*; *stretched across, across the road*; *half a mile across*); COME *across with*; ~ **the board** *a.* & *adv.*, general(ly), all-embracing(ly). **4.** On the other side (of) (*by this time he is across* (*the Channel*)); PUT[1] (*it*) *across.* [ME f. OF *a croix, en croix,* later regarded as f. A[3] + CROSS[1]]

acrŏ'stĭc *n.* Poem or other composition in which the initial (**single** ~), the initial and final (**double ~**), or the initial, middle, and final (**triple ~**) letters of the lines make words; word-puzzle so made. [f. F *acrostiche* or f. Gk *akrostikhis* (*akron* end, *stikhos* row, line of verse)]

acrȳ'lĭc *a.* & *n.* **~ acid,** unsaturated organic acid from which synthetic substances are derived by polymerization; **~ (fibre, plastic, resin),** synthetic substance of this kind. [f. *acrolein* (f. L *acer acris* pungent + *olēre* smell + -IN) + -YL + -IC]

ăct[1] *n.* **1.** Thing done, deed (*act of* GOD; *act of* GRACE); this as outward sign of a condition etc. (*act of faith*); **~** (short prayer) **of contrition; Acts (of the Apostles),** N.T. book following Gospels. **2.** Process of doing, operation (*in the very act of*; *caught in the act*). **3.** Decree passed by a legislative body etc., statute; verificatory legal document (esp. *act and deed*). **4.** Main division of a play; one of a series of short performances in circus or variety programme; performer(s) of this; **get into the ~,** (sl.) become participant (esp. for profit); **put on an ~,** (colloq.) show off, talk for display, pretend. **5.** (Hist.) Thesis publicly defended by candidate for university degree. [ME, f. OF *acte* and L *actus, -um* (see foll.)]

ăct[2] *v.* **1.** *v.t.* Portray (incident or story) by actions; **~ out,** translate (ideas etc.) into action. **2.** Personate (character in a play or in life) (*act Othello*; *act the* FOOL[1]). **3.** *v.i.* Perform actions, behave (*generously*, etc.); **~** (serve) **as** *interpreter*; **~ for** *me* (be my representative) *in the matter*; **~ (up)on** (execute) *a suggestion*; **~ up,** (colloq.) misbehave, give trouble; **~ up to** (put into practice) *a principle*. **4.** Perform special functions (*the policeman declined to act*; *the brake refused to act*); perform a play or part, be actor or actress; exert energy or influence (*on*; *alcohol acts on the brain*; *acid acts on metal*). [partly f. L *agere act-* do; partly f. prec.]

A.C.T. *abbr.* Australian Capital Territory.

ACTH *abbr.* adrenocorticotrophic hormone.

ă'ctĭng *a.* & *n.* **1.** In vbl senses. **2.** *a.* (Before title etc.) doing duty temporarily (*Acting Captain*); doing alone duties nominally shared with others (*Acting Manager*). **3.** *n.* Art or occupation of performing parts in plays, films, etc.; **~ copy** (for actors' use, with stage-directions and cuts). [f. ACT[2] + -ING[2,1]]

ăctĭ'nĭa *n.* (*pl.* **~e**). Sea ANEMONE, esp. of genus *Actinia*. [mod. L, f. Gk *aktis -inos* ray; see -IA[2]]

ă'ctĭnīde *n.* (Chem.) Any element in the series of fifteen starting with actinium. [f. ACTINIUM + -IDE as in *lanthanide*]

ă'ctĭnĭsm *n.* Property of short-wave radiant energy by which chemical changes are produced as in photography; hence **ăctĭ'nĭc** *a.* [f. Gk *aktis -inos* ray + -ISM]

ăctĭ'nĭum *n.* (Chem.) Radioactive metallic element found in pitchblende. [f. as prec. + -IUM]

ăctĭnŏ'mèter *n.* Instrument for measuring intensity of radiation. [f. Gk *aktis -inos* ray + -O- + -METER]

ăctĭnomŏr'phĭc *a.* (Biol.) Radially symmetrical. [f. as prec. + Gk *morphē* form + -IC]

ăctĭnomȳcē'tēs (-ēz) *n.* Group of minute organisms of order Actinomycetales, thought to be filamentous bacteria. [f. as prec. + *mycetes* (Gk *mukēs -ētos* mushroom)]

ă'ction *n.*, & *v.t.* **1.** *n.* Process of acting, exertion of energy or influence, (*men of action*; *put into action*; *action of an acid on metal*); **take ~,** begin to act; **out of ~,** not working. **2.** Thing done, act. **3.** (Theatr.) series of events represented; (sl.) principal activity or operations. **4.** Mode or style of movement (*action of a player*, *of a horse*); mechanism of piano or other instrument. **5.** Legal process; engagement between opposing forces (*killed in action*); **go into ~,** (fig.) start work. **6. ~ committee, group,** one formed to take active steps, esp. in politics; **~ painting** (with paint applied by artist's random or spontaneous actions); **~ stations,** positions taken up by troops, sailors, etc., before going into action. **7.** *v.t.* Bring a legal action against. [ME f. OF, f. L *actio -onis* (as ACT[2]; see -ION)]

ă'ctionab|le *a.* Affording ground for an action at law; hence **~LY**[2] *adv.* [f. prec. + -ABLE]

ă'ctĭv|āte *v.t.* Make active; (Phys.) make radioactive; **~ated carbon,** carbon, esp. charcoal, treated to increase its adsorptive power; **~ated sludge,** aerated sewage containing aerobic bacteria; hence **~A'TION, ~ātor,** *ns.* [f. ACTIVE + -ATE[3]]

ă'ctĭve *a.* & *n.* **1.** *a.* Given to action; working, effective; practical; diligent; radioactive; able to rotate plane of vibration of polarized light; **~ carbon** = ACTIVATE*d carbon*; *active* LIST[1]; **~ service,** full-time service in armed forces; **~ volcano** (likely to erupt, not extinct). **2.** (Gram.) **~ voice,** that comprising all forms of intransitive verbs, and those forms of transitive verbs that attribute the verbal action to the person or thing whence it proceeds (the logical subject), as *We saw him*; (of verb etc.) in active voice; cf. MIDDLE[1], PASSIVE. **3.** Hence **~LY**[2] (-vlĭ) *adv.*, **~NESS** (-vn-) *n.* **4.** *n.* (Gram.) Active voice or form of verb. [ME, f. OF *actif -ive* or f. L *activus* (as ACT[2]; see -IVE)]

ă'ctĭv|ĭsm *n.* Policy of vigorous action in politics etc.; hence **~IST** (2) *n.* [f. ACTIVE + -ISM]

ăctĭ'vĭtȳ *n.* Exertion of energy; state or quality of being active; diligence, nimbleness; = RADIOACTIVITY; (in *pl.*) actions, occupations. [f. F *activité* or f. LL *activitas* (as ACTIVE; see -ITY)]

ă'cton *n.* (Hist.) Jacket of quilted cotton worn under mail; mail-plated jacket of leather etc. [ME, f. OF *auqueton* padding, padded jacket, prob. f. Prov. *alcoton* cotton f. Arab. *alḳuṭun* the cotton]

ă'ctor *n.* Performer of part in play, film, etc.; hence **ă'ctrESS**[1] *n.* [L, = doer, actor (as ACT[2]; see -OR)]

A.C.T.U. *abbr.* Australian Council of Trade Unions.

ă'ctūal *a.* Existing in fact, real; present, current. [ME f. OF *actuel* f. LL *actualis* (*actus* vbl n. f. *agere* ACT[2]; see -AL)]

ăctūă'lĭtȳ *n.* Reality; realism; (in *pl.*) existing conditions. [ME, f. OF *actualité* entity or f. med. L *actualitas* (as prec.; see -ITY)]

ă'ctūallȳ *adv.* In actual fact, really; at present, for the time being; as a matter of fact, even (strange as it may seem). [f. ACTUAL + -LY[2]]

ă'ctūarȳ *n.* Expert in statistics, esp. one who calculates insurance risks and premiums; hence **ăctūār'ĭAL** *a.* [f. L *actuarius* bookkeeper (*actus*; see ACTUAL, -ARY[1])]

ă'ctū|āte *v.t.* Communicate motion to (machine etc.); cause operation of (electrical device etc.); be motive for action of (person); hence **~A'TION, ~ātor,** *ns.* [f. med. L *actuare* (*actus*; see ACTUAL, -ATE[3])]

acū'ĭtȳ *n.* Sharpness, acuteness (lit. or fig., of needle, senses, understanding). [f. F *acuité* or f. med. L *acuitas* (*acuere* sharpen; see ACUTE, -ITY)]

acū'lèate *a.* Pointed, incisive; (Zool.) having a sting; (Bot.) prickly. [f. L *aculeatus* (*aculeus* sting, dim. of *acus* needle; see -ATE[2])]

acū'mĕn *n.* Keen insight or discernment, penetration. [L *acumen -minis* anything sharp (*acuere* sharpen; see ACUTE)]

acū'mĭnate *a.* (Biol.) Tapering to a point. [f. L *acuminatus* pointed (as prec.; see -ATE[2])]

ă'cūpŭncture *n.* (Med.) (Orig. Chinese) method of pricking skin or tissues with needles as treatment for various conditions. [f. L *acu* with a needle + PUNCTURE]

acu'shla (-ōō'-) *n.* (Ir.) Darling. [f. Ir. *a cuisle* O pulse (of my heart)!]

acū'te *a.* (~**r**, ~**st**). **1.** Sharp, pointed; penetrating (*an acute critic*); (of angle) less than a right angle. **2.** (Of disease) coming sharply to a crisis, opp. CHRONIC; (of controversy, difficulty, shortage) critical, serious; (of sensation, senses) keen; (of sound) high, shrill. **3.** ~ **accent,** mark (′) placed over letters in some languages to show quality, vowel length, pronunciation (e.g. *maté*), etc. **4.** Hence ~LY² (-tlĭ) *adv.*, ~NESS (-tn-) *n.* [f. L *acutus* p.p. of *acuere* sharpen (*acus* needle)]

||**A.C.W.** *abbr.* Aircraftwoman.

-acy̆ *suf.*, branch of suf. -CY forming *ns.* of state or quality (*accuracy, advocacy, conspiracy, diplomacy, episcopacy, fallacy, lunacy, obstinacy, piracy, primacy, supremacy*); see also -CRACY. [f. or after F *-acie* or L *-acia* or *-atia* or Gk *-ateia*]

ă'cy̆l *n.* (Chem.) Acid RADICAL. [G (as ACID², -YL)]

ăd *n.* (colloq.) Advertisement; advertising. [abbr.]

ad- *pref.* **1.** [(thr. OF *a-* or) f. L *ad* to] w. sense of motion or direction to, reduction or change into, addition, adherence, increase, or intensification; usu. assim. to *ac-* bef. *c, k, q,* and similarly to *af-* etc. bef. *f, g, l, n, p, r, s, t*; reduced to *a-* bef. *sc, sp, st.* **2.** [f. *a-* repr. *prefs.* other than *ad-*] (*accurse, admiral, advance, affray*).

-ad *suf.* **1.** forming *ns.* (*a*) [f. Gk *-as -ada*]: in collective numerals (*myriad, triad*); in fem. patronymics (*Dryad, Naiad*); in names of poems (*Iliad*, and by anal. *Dunciad*; so *jeremiad*). (*b*) [f. F *-ade*] (*ballad, salad*); see the more usual -ADE 1. **2.** (Biol.) Invented to form *adjs.* and *advs.* w. sense 'towards' (part indicated by main element of wd): *caudad* towards the tail [L *cauda* tail].

A.D. *abbr.* Of the Christian era. [f. ANNO DOMINI]

ă'dage *n.* Traditional maxim, proverb of common experience. [F, f. L *adagium* (*ad* to, root of *aio* say)]

ada'giō (adah'jyō) *adv.*, *a.*, & *n.* (*pl.* ~**s**). (Mus.) (movement) in slow time; ~ **dancing,** kind involving feats of balance etc. [It.]

A'dam¹ (ă'-) *n.* First man, in Hebrew tradition; **not know** person **from** ~, have no knowledge of his appearance; **old** ~, sinful nature innate in a person; ~**'s ale** or **wine,** water; ~**'s apple,** projection of thyroid cartilage of larynx, esp. as prominent in men. [f. Heb. *'ādām* man]

A'dam² (ă'-) *a.* Of the decorative style of architecture and furniture created by the Scottish brothers Robert and James *Adam* (18th c.).

ă'damant *n.* & *a.* **1.** *n.* (arch.) Diamond or other hard substance; hence **ădamă'nt**INE² *a.* **2.** *a.* Unyielding to requests. [f. OF *adamaunt* f. L f. Gk *adamas -mant-* untameable (*a-* not, *damaō* to tame)]

A'damīte (ă'd-) *n.* Human being as descendant of Adam; member of sect living naked like Adam. [f. ADAM¹ + -ITE¹]

adă'pt *v.* **1.** *v.t.* Fit, adjust, (a thing *to* another); make suitable (*to* or *for* a purpose); modify, alter, (*adapted from the Bible story*); hence or cogn. ~ABI'LITY *n.*, ~ABLE *a.*, (esp.) able to adapt oneself to new surroundings, **ădapt**A'TION *n.*, (esp., Biol.) process by which organism or species becomes adjusted to its environment, ~ER¹, ~OR, *ns.*, (esp.) device allowing connection of pieces of equipment not orig. designed to be connected, ~IVE *a.* **2.** *v.i.* Adapt oneself (*to* conditions). [f. F *adapter* f. L AD(*aptare* f. *aptus* fit)]

A.D.C. *abbr.* aide-de-camp.

***ad captandum* (*vulgus*)** (ăd kăptă'ndum vŭlgus) *adv.* & *a.* (Designed) to appeal to the emotions (of the rabble). [L, = for alluring (the crowd)]

ădd *v.t.* & *i.* **1.** Join (one thing *to* another) as increase or supplement (*add your efforts to mine*; *add insult to injury*; ~ **in,** include; *this* ~**s to** (increases) *our difficulties*); say further (*he added a remark*). **2.** Unite two or more numbers to get number equal to their total amount; ~ **up,** find the sum of, amount *to*, (colloq.) make sense. **3.** Hence ~'ED¹ *a.* (~**ed value tax** = VALUE-*added tax*). [ME, f. L AD(*dere dit-* = *dare* put)]

ă'ddăx *n.* Large antelope of N. Africa and Arabia, with twisted horns. [L, f. African wd]

addĕ'nd|um *n.* (*pl.* ~**a**). Thing (esp. omitted thing) to be added; appendix, addition; (esp., in *pl.*) additional matter at end of book. [L, gerundive of *addere* ADD]

ă'dder *n.* Small venomous snake, esp. common viper; DEATH *adder*, **horned** ~, PUFF¹-*adder*, species of Viperidae; **deaf as an** ~, completely deaf; ~**'s tongue,** kind of fern (*Ophioglossum*). [OE *nædre*, = OS *nādra*, OHG *nātara*, ON *nathra*, Goth. *nadrs*; *n-* lost in ME by wrong division of *a naddre*, cf. APRON, AUGER, UMPIRE]

addĭ'ct¹ *v.t.* (esp. in *pass.*) Devote, apply habitually or compulsively, (*to* a practice); hence ~ION *n.*, (esp.) condition of taking drug excessively and being unable to cease doing so without adverse effects, ~IVE *a.*, causing addiction and dependence. [f. L AD(*dicere dict-* say) assign]

ă'ddĭct² *n.* Person addicted to a habit, esp. one dependent on a (specified) drug (*drug addict, heroin addict*); (colloq.) enthusiastic devotee of sport or pastime (*film addict*). [f. prec.]

A'ddĭson (ă'd-) *n.* ~**'s disease** (characterized by progressive anaemia and debility and brown discoloration of the skin). [first recognized by T. *Addison*, Engl. physician d. 1860]

addĭ'tion *n.* **1.** Process of adding; **in** ~, as an added thing etc. (*to*). **2.** Thing added (*a useful addition*). [ME f. OF, or f. L *additio* (as ADD; see -ITION)]

addĭ'tional *a.* Added, supplementary; hence ~LY² *adv.* [f. prec. + -AL]

ă'ddĭtive *a.* & *n.* **1.** *a.* To be added; characterized by addition (*additive process*). **2.** *n.* Thing to be added, esp. substance added to another so as to give it specific qualities. [f. LL *additivus* (as ADD; see -IVE)]

ă'ddle *a.* & *v.* **1.** *a.* Empty, vain; muddled, unsound, (*addle-brained, addle-head*); (of egg) addled. **2.** *v.t.* Muddle, confuse. **3.** *v.i.* (Of egg) become addled. [OE *adela* filth (MLG *adele*) used as a., then as v.]

ă'ddled (ă'deld) *a.* Made addle; (of egg) rotten, producing no chick. [f. ADDLE *a.*, assim. to p.p. form, app. bef. *addle* v. existed]

addrĕ'ss¹ *v.t.* **1.** Direct in speech or writing (*address remarks, a protest, petition*, etc. *to* person); ~ one**self to,** speak or write to. **2.** Write directions for delivery (esp. name and place of residence etc. of intended recipient) on (envelope etc.). **3.** Speak or write to, esp. deliver a speech to, (person, audience). **4.** Apply (one*self to* a task); (Golf) take aim at, prepare to hit, (ball). [ME, f. OF *adresser* f. Rom. *AD(*drictiare* f. **drictus* = L *directus* DIRECT²)]

addrĕ'ss² *n.* **1.** Superscription of letter; name of place to which letters etc. for a person or firm are directed; number etc. giving position of information in computer; place of residence. **2.** Discourse delivered to audience. **3.** Readiness, skill, dexterity. **4.** (arch.) Manner in conversation. **5.** (in *pl.*) Courteous approach, courtship (*pay* one's *addresses to*). [f. prec. & F *adresse*]

ăddrĕssee′ *n.* Person to whom something (esp. a letter) is addressed. [f. ADDRESS[1] + -EE]
addrĕ′ssograph (-ahf) *n.* Machine for printing addresses on envelopes. [f. ADDRESS[2] + -O- + -GRAPH; **P**]
addū′c|e *v.t.* Cite as proof or instance; hence ~IBLE *a.* [f. L AD(*ducere duct-* lead)]
addŭ′ct *v.t.* Draw (limb etc.) towards middle line of body etc.; so ~ION *n.* [f. as prec.]
-āde *suf.* forming *ns.* **1.** [f. or after F *-ade* f. Prov., Sp., or Port. *-ada* or It. *-ata* f. L *-ata* fem. sing. p.p. of vbs in *-are*] w. senses (1) action done (*blockade, tirade*); (2) body concerned in action or process (*cavalcade*); (3) product of material or action (*arcade, lemonade, masquerade*). **2.** [f. F *-ade* f. Gk *-as -ada*] (*decade*); cf. -AD 1. **3.** [f. Sp. or Port. *-ado*, masc. form of 1 above] w. senses (1)–(3) (*brocade*) or 'person concerned' (*renegade*).
ă′denine (-ēn) *n.* Crystalline base found in some glands and as constituent of DNA. [f. G *adenin* f. as foll.; see -INE[5]]
ă′dėnoids (-z) *n. pl.* (Path.) Mass of enlarged lymphatic tissue between back of nose and throat, often hindering speaking and breathing; hence **ădėnoi′d**AL *a.* [f. Gk *adēn -enos* gland + -OID]
ădėnō′ma *n.* (*pl.* **~s** *or* **~ta**). Glandlike benign tumour. [mod. L, f. Gk *adēn* gland + -OMA]
adĕ′nosĭne *n.* Nucleoside found in muscle, from which compounds providing muscular energy are derived. [f. ADENINE + RIBOSE]
ă′dĕpt[1] (*or* adĕ′-) *a.* Thoroughly proficient (*at* or *in*). [f. L *adeptus* p.p. of AD(*ipisci* attain)]
ă′dĕpt[2] *n.* Skilled performer, expert. [f. prec.]
ă′dėqu|ate *a.* Proportionate (*to* the requirements); sufficient, satisfactory; barely sufficient; hence ~ACY *n.*, **~ate**LY[2] (-tlĭ) *adv.* [f. L *adaequatus* p.p. of AD*aequare* make equal (*aequus*); see -ATE[2]]
ad eundem (***gradum***) (ăd ēŭ′ndem grā′dum) *adv.* (Admitted) to the same degree at another university. [L, = to the same (degree)]
à deux (ahdėr′) *adv.* & *a.* For two; between two. [F]
ad fin. *abbr.* at or near the end. [f. L *ad finem*]
adhēr′e (-h-) *v.i.* Stick fast *to* (substance); give support *to* (agreement, opinion, party); behave according *to* (rule). [f. F *adhérer* or f. L AD(*haerēre haes-* stick)]
adhēr′|ent (-h-) *a.* & *n.* **1.** *a.* Sticking (*to* substance); adhering *to* (rule etc.); so ~ENCE *n.* **2.** *n.* Supporter (*of* party etc.). [f. F *adhérent* (as prec.; see -ENT)]
adhē′sion (-hē′zhon) *n.* Adhering (lit. or fig.; **give** one's **~ to,** declare acceptance of); maintenance of contact between wheels and road or rail; (Path.) unnatural union of surfaces due to inflammation. [f. F *adhésion* or f. L *adhaesio* (as ADHERE; see -ION)]
adhē′sĭve (-h-) *a.* & *n.* Having the property of adhering, sticky, (substance); *adhesive* TAPE; hence ~LY[2] (-vlĭ) *adv.*, ~NESS (-vn-) *n.* [f. F *adhésif -ive* (as ADHERE; see -IVE)]
adhĭ′bĭt (-h-) *v.t.* Affix; apply, administer, (remedy); hence **ădhĭbĭ′t**ION (-h-) *n.* [f. L AD(*hibēre hibit-* = *habēre* have)]
ad hoc (ăd hŏ′k) *adv.* & *a.* For this particular purpose; special(ly). [L]
ad hominem (ăd hŏ′mĭnĕm) *adv.* & *a.* To the man; personal. [L]
ādĭabă′t|ĭc *a.* & *n.* (Phys.) **1.** *a.* Impassable to heat; occurring without heat entering or leaving system; hence ~ICALLY *adv.* **2.** *n.* Curve or formula for adiabatic phenomena. [f. Gk *adiabatos* impassable (*a-* not, *diabainō* pass)]
ădĭă′ntum *n.* Fern of genus *Adiantum*, e.g. true maidenhair; (pop.) black maidenhair, a spleenwort. [L, f. Gk *adianton* maidenhair (*a-* not, *diantos* wettable)]
adieu′ (adū′) *int.* & *n.* (*pl.* **~s, ~x,** *pr.* adū′z). Goodbye. [ME f. OF (*à* to, *Dieu* God)]
ad infinitum (ăd ĭnfĭnī′tum) *adv.* Without limit, for ever. [L]
ad interim (ăd ĭ′nterĭm) *adv.* & *a.* For the meantime. [L]
ă′dĭpocēre *n.* Greyish fatty or soapy substance generated in dead bodies subjected to moisture. [f. F *adipocire* f. L *adeps adipis* fat + -O- + F *cire* wax f. L *cera*)]
ă′dĭpōse *a.* Pertaining to fat, fatty; **~ tissue,** fat-containing connective tissue in animals; hence **ădĭpŏ′s**ITY *n.* [f. mod. L *adiposus* (*adeps -ipis* fat; see -OSE[1])]
ă′dĭt *n.* (In mines) horizontal entrance or passage. [f. L AD(*itus* f. *ire it-* go)]
Adj. *abbr.* Adjutant.
adjā′c|ent *a.* Lying near, contiguous (*to*); so ~ENCY *n.* [ME, f. L AD(*jacēre* lie); see -ENT]
ă′djėctĭve *a.* & *n.* **1.** *a.* Additional, not standing by itself, dependent; **~ dye** (which needs mordant to fix it); **~ law,** subsidiary part of law, enforcement procedure. **2.** *n.* Word naming an attribute, added to a noun to describe the thing etc. more fully; hence **ădjėctī′v**AL *a.* (also euphem. for expletive adj.). [ME, f. OF *adjectif -ive* f. LL *adjectivus* f. L AD(*jicere ject-* = *jacere* throw); see -IVE]
adjoi′n *v.t.* Be contiguous with; (arch.) = ADD 1. [ME, f. OF *ajoindre, ajoign-* f. L AD(*jungere junct-* join)]
adjour′n (ajėr′n) *v.* **1.** *v.t.* Put off, postpone; break off for later resumption. **2.** *v.i.* (Of persons met together) suspend joint proceedings and separate; transfer meeting *to* another place. **3.** Hence ~MENT *n.* [ME, f. OF *ajorner* (*a-* AD-, *jorn* day f. LL *diurnum* day f. L *diurnus* DIURNAL); cf. JOURNAL, JOURNEY]
adjŭ′dg|e *v.t.* Adjudicate (a matter); pronounce judicially (*that* a thing is; a thing *to be*); award judicially (thing *to* person); (arch.) condemn (person *to* penalty or *to* do); hence ~(**e**)MENT (-jm-) *n.* [ME, f. OF *ajuger* f. L *adjudicare* (see foll.)]
adju′dĭc|āte (ajōō′-) *v.* **1.** *v.t.* Decide judicially regarding (claim etc.); pronounce (person *to be* bankrupt etc.). **2.** *v.i.* Act as judge in court, tribunal, competition, etc. **3.** Hence ~A′TION, **~āt**OR, *ns.*, **~āt**IVE *a.* [f. L AD(*judicare* f. *judex -icis* judge) + -ATE[3]]
ă′djŭnct *n.* Thing subordinate or incidental (*to* or *of*); assistant, subordinate person, esp. with temporary appointment only; (Gram.) amplification of the predicate, subject, etc.; (Logic) non-essential attribute; hence **adjŭ′nct**IVE *a.* [f. L (as ADJOIN)]
adjur′e (ajoor′) *v.t.* Charge (person) under oath (*to* do); request earnestly; hence **ădjur**A′TION (ăjoor-) *n.* [ME, f. L AD(*jurare* swear) in LL sense 'put person to an oath']
adjŭ′st *v.* **1.** *v.t.* Arrange, put in order; regulate, esp. by small amount; assess (loss or damages); harmonize (discrepancies); adapt (*to* standard or purpose). **2.** *v.i.* Adapt oneself (*to* one's environment etc.). **3.** Hence ~ABLE *a.*, ~ER[1], ~MENT, *ns.* [f. F *adjuster* refash. (after *juste* JUST[1]) of OF *ajoster* f. Rom. **adjuxtare* f. L *juxta* near]
ă′djutage, ă′j-, (ă′jōō-) *n.* Mouthpiece of artificial fountain. [f. F. *aj(o)utage* (*ajouter* add, join, f. OF *ajoster*; see prec., -AGE)]
ă′djut|ant (ă′jōō-) *n.* **1.** Assistant; (Mil.) officer who assists superior officers by communicating orders, conducting correspondence, etc., whence ~ANCY *n.*; **A~ant-General,** high-ranking Army administrative officer. **2.** **~ant** (**bird**), giant Indian stork. [f. L *adjutare* frequent. of *adjuvare* (see foll.) + -ANT]
ă′djuvant (ă′jōō-) *a.* & *n.* Helpful, auxiliary,

(person or thing). [F, or f. L AD(*juvare jut-* help); see -ANT]

Adler̄'ian (ăd-) *a.* & *n.* (Disciple) of Adler or his system of psychology. [f. A. *Adler*, Austrian psychologist d. 1937 + -IAN]

ăd lĭ'b *adv.*, *a.*, & *v.i.* (**-bb-**). **1.** *adv.* To any desired extent. **2.** (*ad-lib*). *a.*, & *v.i.* (colloq.) (Speak) without preparation; improvise(d). [abbr. of foll.]

ad libitum (ăd lĭ'bĭtum) *adv.* = prec. [L, = according to pleasure]

ad litem (ăd lī'tĕm) *a.* (Of guardian etc.) appointed for a lawsuit. [L]

Adm. *abbr.* Admiral.

ă'd|măn *n.* (*pl.* **~men**). One who produces advertisements commercially. [f. AD + MAN[1]]

||**ă'dmăss** *n.* Section of the community that is readily influenced by advertising etc. [f. AD + MASS[2]]

admea'sure (-mĕ'zh*er*) *v.t.* Apportion, assign in due shares; so **~**MENT *n.* [ME, f. OF *amesurer* f. med. L AD(*mensurare* MEASURE[1])]

ă'dmĭn *n.* (colloq.) Administration. [abbr.]

admĭ'nĭcle *n.* Thing that helps; (Law) corroboratory evidence; hence **ădmĭnĭ'cŭl**AR[1] *a.* [f. L *adminiculum* prop]

admĭ'nĭster *v.* **1.** *v.t.* Manage (affairs); formally give out (sacrament, justice) or present (oath) *to*; furnish, give, (thing *to*); apply (remedies *to*); hence **admĭ'nĭstr**ABLE *a.* **2.** *v.i.* Act as administrator; (arch.) contribute *to* (one's comfort etc.). [ME, f. OF *aministrer* f. L AD(*ministrare* MINISTER[2])]

admĭ'nĭstrāte *v.t.* & *i.* Administer. [f. L *administrare* (see prec.) + -ATE[3]]

admĭnĭstrā'tion *n.* Management (*of* business); management of public affairs, government; the ministry, the Government; *President's period of office; (Law) management of deceased person's estate (**letters of ~**, authority to administer estate of an intestate; cf. *probate*); administering (*of* justice, oath, etc.); application (*of* remedies). [ME f. OF, or f. L *administratio* (as prec.; see -ATION)]

admĭ'nĭstratĭve *a.* Pertaining to management of affairs; hence **~**LY[2] (-vlĭ) *adv.* [f. F *administratif -ive* or f. L *administrativus* (as prec.; see -IVE)]

admĭ'nĭstrā|tor *n.* Manager; one capable of organizing; one who performs official duties (of religion, justice, etc.); applier or giver (*of*); (Law) one authorized to manage estate for legal owner during minority, absence, etc., or estate of one who dies without appointing competent executors; hence **~tor**SHIP, **~**TRIX, *ns.* [L (as ADMINISTER; see -OR)]

ă'dmirab|le *a.* Worthy of admiration; excellent; **A~le Crichton** (krī'ton), one who excels in many things [from J. Crichton, Scottish scholar, poet, athlete d. 1585]; hence **~**LY[2] *adv.* [F, f. L *admirabilis* (as ADMIRE; see -ABLE)]

ă'dmiral *n.* **1.** Commander-in-chief of a country's navy (||**Lord High A~**, title of sovereign); naval officer of high rank, commander of fleet or squadron; **A~ of the Fleet** (***Fleet A~**), **A~**, **Vice-A~**, **Rear-A~**, the four grades of such officers. **2. Red ~**, **white ~**, European species of butterfly. **3.** Hence **~**SHIP *n.* [ME, f. OF *a(d)mira(i)l* etc. f. med. L *a(d)miralis* etc., f. Arab. *'amīr* commander (cf. AMIR), assoc. w. prec.]

ă'dmiraltȳ *n.* **1.** ||**A~ (Board)**, Department administering the Navy. **2.** (Law). Trial and decision of maritime questions and offences. [ME, f. OF *admiral(i)té* (as prec.; see -TY[1])]

ădmirā'tion *n.* Pleased contemplation; (arch.) wonder; respect, warm approval; object of this (*was the admiration of the whole town*); **to ~**, marvellously. [F, or f. L *admiratio* (as foll.; see -ATION)]

admīr'|e *v.t.* Regard with pleased surprise, respect, or approval; (arch.) wonder at; (colloq.) express admiration of (*forgot to admire her cat*); hence **~**ER[1] *n.*, (esp., woman's) suitor, **~**ING[2] *a.*, showing or feeling admiration. [f. F *admirer* or f. L AD(*mirari* wonder at)]

admĭ'ss|ĭble *a.* (Of idea or plan) worthy of being accepted or considered; (Law) allowable as judicial evidence; capable of being admitted (*to* office or position); hence **~**IBI'LITY *n.* [F, or f. med. L *admissibilis* (as ADMIT; see -IBLE)]

admĭ'ss|ion (-shon) *n.* Admitting, being admitted, (*to*); charge for this; acknowledgement (*of* error etc.); so **~**IVE *a.* [ME, f. L *admissio* (as foll.; see -ION)]

admĭ't *v.* (**-tt-**). **1.** *v.t.* Let in, permit (person etc.) entrance or access (*to* place, class, privilege, etc.), whence **~t**ABLE *a.*; accept as valid or true, whence **~tėd**LY[2] *adv.*; acknowledge, confess, (thing *to be*, *that* it is, *to* being, or abs.); (of enclosed space) have room for. **2.** *v.i.* **~ of**, leave room for, be open to, (doubt, improvement). [ME, f. L AD(*mittere miss-* send)]

admĭ'ttance *n.* Admitting, being admitted (usu. to a place; *no admittance except on business*); (Electr.) reciprocal of IMPEDANCE. [f. ADMIT + -ANCE]

admĭ'x *v.* **1.** *v.t.* Add as an ingredient. **2.** *v.t.* & *i.* Mingle (*with* something). **3.** So **~t**URE *n.*, admixing, thing added (esp. minor ingredient). [f. AD- + MIX]

admŏ'nĭsh *v.t.* Urge (person *to* do, *that* he should do); give advice to; reprove; warn (*of* a thing); so **~**MENT *n.* [ME, f. OF *amonester* f. Rom. **admonestare* unexpl. alt. of L AD(*monēre monit-* warn); assim. to L wd and -ISH[2]]

ădmonĭ'tion *n.* Admonishing; warning; reproof; so **admŏ'nĭt**ORY *a.* [ME, f. OF *amonition* f. L *admonitio -onis* (as prec.; see -ITION)]

ad nauseam (ăd naw'sĭăm; *or* -z-) *adv.* To a disgusting extent. [L, = to sickness]

ădnŏ'mĭnal *a.* (Gram.) Attached to a noun. [f. L *adnomen -minis* (=AGNOMEN) + -AL]

ado' (adōō') *n.* (*pl.* **~s**). Action, business, fuss, (**without more ~**, forthwith); difficulty. [orig. in *much ado* = much to do, f. north. ME *at do* (= *to do*) f. ON *at* AT as sign of inf. + DO[1]]

-ado *suf.* forming *ns.* (*desperado*); cf. -ADE 3. [f. Sp. or Port. *-ado* f. L *-atus* p.p. of vbs. in *-are*]

adō'bė (*or* -ō'b) *n.* Unburnt sun-dried brick; clay from which such bricks can be made. [Sp.]

ădolĕ'sc|ent *n.* & *a.* (Person) growing up, between childhood and manhood or womanhood; so **~**ENCE *n.* [ME f. OF, f. L *adolescere* grow up + -ENT]

Adō'nĭs (*ad-*) *n.* Handsome young man; **~ blue**, species of butterfly (*Lysandra bellargus*). [name of youth loved by Venus; L f. Gk, f. Phoen. *adōn* lord]

adŏ'pt *v.t.* Take (person) into a relationship he did not previously occupy, esp. *as* one's child; take (idea etc.) from someone else; choose, take up; ||(of local authority) accept responsibility for maintenance of (road etc.); approve, accept, (report etc.); hence **~**ABLE *a.*, **~**ION *n.* [f. F *adopter* or f. L AD(*optare* choose)]

adŏ'ptĭve *a.* Due to adoption (*adoptive son, father*); hence **~**LY[2] (-vlĭ) *adv.* [ME, f. OF *adoptif -ive* f. L *adoptivus* (as prec.; see -IVE)]

adôr'|e *v.t.* Regard with deep respect and affection; worship as divine; (R.C. Ch.) offer reverence to (Host etc.); (colloq.) like greatly; so **~**ABLE *a.*, **~ab**LY[2] *adv.*, **ădor**A'TION *n.* [ME, f. OF *aourer* f. L AD(*orare* speak, pray) worship]

adôr'er *n.* Worshipper; ardent admirer. [f. prec. + -ER[1]]

adō̂r′n *v.t.* Add beauty or lustre to; furnish with ornament(s); so ~MENT *n.* [ME, f. OF *ao(u)rner* f. L AD(*ornare* furnish, deck)]

adow′n *adv.* & *prep.* (arch. or poet.) = DOWN[3,4]. [OE *adūn(e)*, earlier *ofdūne* (as OF, cf. A- 3; *dūne* dat. of *dūn* hill, DOWN[1])]

ADP *abbr.* adenosine diphosphate; automatic data processing.

ad personam (ăd persō′năm) *adv.* & *a.* To the person; personal. [L]

ad rem (ăd rĕ′m) *adv.* & *a.* To the point; to the purpose. [L, = to the matter]

adrē′nal *a.* & *n.* **1.** *a.* At or near the kidneys; ~ **glands,** ductless glands on top of kidneys, secreting ADRENALIN. **2.** *n.* Adrenal gland. [f. AD- + RENAL]

adrĕ′nalĭn, -ĭne, *n.* Hormone secreted by adrenal glands, affecting circulation and muscular action, and causing excitement and stimulation; same substance got from animals or by synthesis, used as stimulant. [f. ADRENAL + -IN, -INE[5]; *-in* *P]

adrēnocō̂rtĭcotrŏ′p(h)|ĭc *a.* ~**ic hormone,** ~IN, hormone secreted by pituitary gland and stimulating adrenal cortex. [f. ADRENAL + CORTEX + TROPHIC, TROPIC]

adrĭ′ft *adv.* & *pred. a.* Drifting; exposed to the elements or (fig.) the circumstances; (colloq.) unfastened, out of touch, out of order, ill--informed. [f. A[3] + DRIFT[1]]

adroi′t *a.* Dextrous; skilful; hence ~LY[2] *adv.*, ~NESS *n.* [F (*à droit* according to right)]

ădscītĭ′tious (-ĭ′sh*us*) *a.* Adopted from without; supplemental. [f. L AD(*sciscere scit-* incept. of *scire* know) + -ITIOUS[2]]

ădsō̂′b *v.t.* (Usu. of solid) hold (molecules of a gas or liquid or solute) to its surface; so ~ATE[1] (5) *n.*, ~ENT *a.* & *n.*, **ădsō̂r′pt**ION *n.* [f. AD-, after *absorb*]

ă′dsŭm *v.i.* (As answer in roll-call etc.) I am present. [L]

ă′dūl|āte *v.t.* Flatter obsequiously; so ~A′TION, ~**āt**OR, *ns.*, ~**āt**ORY *a.* [f. L *adulari* fawn on + -ATE[3]]

Adŭ′llamīte (ad-) *n.* Member of a dissident political group. [orig. of Liberal rebels 1866; f. cave of *Adullam* (1 Sam. 22:1, 2) + -ITE[1]]

ă′dŭlt (*or* adŭ′lt) *a.* & *n.* **1.** (One who is) grown up; ~ **education** (for those over usual school age). **2.** *a.* Mature, fully developed. **3.** Hence ~HOOD (-t-h-) *n.*, ~LY[2] *adv.* [f. L *adultus* p.p. of *adolescere* grow up; cf. ADOLESCENT]

adŭ′lterant *a.* & *n.* (Substance) used in adulterating. [f. as foll. + -ANT]

adŭ′lterate[1] *a.* Tainted by adultery; spurious, base. [f. L *adulteratus* p.p. of *adulterare*; see foll., -ATE[2]]

adŭ′lter|āte[2] *v.t.* Debase (esp. foods) by admixture of other substances; so ~A′TION, ~**āt**OR, *ns.* [f. L *adulterare* corrupt (*adulter* adulterer) + -ATE[3]]

adŭ′lter|er *n.* One guilty of adultery; so ~ESS[1] *n.* [f. obs. v. *adulter* f. OF *avoutrer* f. L *adulterare* (see prec.), + -ER[1]]

adŭ′lterine *a.* (Born) of adultery; spurious; illegal. [f. L *adulterinus* (*adulter*; see foll., -INE[1])]

adŭ′lter|ȳ *n.* Voluntary sexual intercourse of married person other than with spouse; so ~OUS *a.*, ~**ous**LY[2] *adv.* [ME, f. OF *avoutrie* etc. (*avoutre* adulterer f. L *adulter*); assim. to L *adulterium*]

ă′dumbrāte *v.t.* Represent in outline; faintly indicate; typify, foreshadow; overshadow; hence or cogn. **ădumbr**A′TION *n.*, **adŭ′mbrat**IVE *a.* [f. L AD(*umbrare* f. *umbra* shade) + -ATE[3]]

adŭ′st *a.* (arch.) Scorched, parched; sunburnt; gloomy, melancholy. [ME, f. F *aduste* or f. L *adustus* p.p. of AD(*urere* burn)]

ad valorem (ăd valō̂r′ĕm) *adv.* & *a.* (Of taxes) in proportion to estimated value of goods. [L, = according to the value]

adva′nce[1] (-vah′-) *v.* **1.** *v.t.* Move or put forward; promote, help on, (plan, person); bring forward (claim, suggestion); bring (event) to earlier date; pay (money) before it is due; lend (money); raise (price); so ~MENT (-sm-) *n.* (esp. of promotion of plan or person). **2.** *v.i.* Move forward; make progress; rise (in price); (in *p.p.*) far on in progress (*the work is well advanced*), ahead of the times (*advanced ideas*); ||~**d level,** G.C.E. examination for university entrance qualification; ~**d studies** (in higher branches of a subject). [ME, f. OF *avancer* f. Rom. **abantiare* f. LL *abante* in front f. L *ab* away + *ante* before]

adva′nce[2] (-vah′-) *n.* Going forward; progress; (esp. in *pl.*) friendly or amorous approach; rise in price; payment beforehand; loan; **in ~,** ahead in place or time; ~ **booking** (made before day of journey, performance, etc.); ~ **copy** (of book etc., supplied before publication); ~ **guard** (preceding main body of army). [f. prec. & F *avance* n. (as prec.)]

adva′ntage[1] (-vah′-) *n.* **1.** Better position, precedence, superiority (*gain an advantage over*); **have the ~ of,** have better position than; **you have the ~ of me,** (esp.) you know me but I do not know you; **take ~ of,** avail oneself of (circumstance), outwit (person) esp. unfairly, (euphem.) seduce; **take at ~,** (arch.) take (person) by surprise; **to ~,** in a way to exhibit the merits (*was seen, heard, to advantage*). **2.** Benefit, profit, (*it could be shortened with advantage*); **turn to ~,** benefit from. **3.** (Tennis). Next point won after deuce; ~ **in, out,** (to server, receiver of service). **4.** Hence **ădvantā′ge**OUS (-j*us*) *a.*, **ădvantā′geous**LY[2] (-jus-) *adv.* [ME, f. OF *avantage* (*avant* in front f. LL *abante*; see ADVANCE[1])]

adva′ntage[2] (-vah′-) *v.t.* Be beneficial or favourable to; further, promote. [ME, f. prec. or F *avantager*]

advĕ′ct|ion *n.* (Meteorol.) Heat transfer by horizontal flow of air; hence ~IVE *a.* [f. L *advectio* f. AD(*vehere vect-* carry); see -ION]

ă′dvent *n.* Arrival of important person or thing; (*A*~) season before Christmas; coming or second coming of Christ, whence ~ISM (3), ~IST (2), *ns.*, (tenets of) member of a sect believing in the imminent millennium of Christ. [OE, f. OF *advent, auvent* f. L *adventus* arrival f. AD(*venire vent-* come)]

ădventĭ′tious (-sh*us*) *a.* Coming from outside; accidental, casual; ||(Law, of property) coming from a stranger or by collateral, not direct, succession; (Biol.) occurring in an unusual place; hence ~LY[2] *adv.* [f. L *adventicius* (as prec.; see -ITIOUS[1])]

advĕ′nture[1] *n.* Daring enterprise; unexpected or exciting incident; commercial speculation; hazardous activity; ~ **playground** (where children are provided with waste materials etc. as basis for play); hence ~SOME[1] (-ch*ers*-) *a.* [ME, f. OF *aventure* f. Rom. **adventura* (*res* thing) about to happen (as ADVENT)]

advĕ′nture[2] *v.* **1.** *v.i.* Incur risk; dare to go or come (*into, upon,* a place); dare to enter (*up*)*on* (undertaking). **2.** *v.t.* (arch.) Hazard, imperil, (one*self*, thing). [ME, f. OF *aventurer* (as prec.)]

advĕ′ntur|er (-cher-) *n.* One who seeks adventures; mercenary soldier; speculator; one who lives by his wits; hence ~ESS[1] *n.* [f. F *aventurier* (as ADVENTURE[1]; see -ER[1])]

advĕ′ntur|ism (-cher-) *n.* Tendency to take risks in foreign policy etc.; hence ~IST (2) *n.* [f. ADVENTURE[1] + -ISM]

advĕ′nturous (-ch*er*-) *a.* Rash, venturesome;

filled with adventures; enterprising; hence ~LY[2] *adv.* [ME, f. OF *aventuros* (as ADVENTURE[1]; see -OUS)]

ă'dverb *n.* Word that modifies or qualifies another word (esp. adjective, verb, or other adverb) or a word-group, expressing a relation of place, time, circumstance, manner, cause, degree, etc. (*gently, so, now, accordingly, here, why*); hence **adver'b**IAL *a.* [f. F *adverbe* or f. L *adverbium* (*ad* to, *verbum* word, VERB) transl. of Gk *epirrhēma*]

ad verbum (ăd vėr'bum) *adv.* & *a.* Verbatim. [L, = to the word]

ă'dversarў *n.* Opponent, antagonist; enemy; **the A~**, the Devil. [ME, f. OF *adversarie* f. L *adversarius* (*adversus*; see ADVERSE, -ARY[1])]

adver'sative *a.* (Of words etc.) expressing opposition or antithesis; hence ~LY[2] (-vlĭ) *adv.* [f. F *adversatif -ive* or f. LL *adversativus* (*adversari* oppose f. *adversus*; see foll., -IVE)]

ă'dverse *a.* Contrary, hostile, (*to*); hurtful, injurious, (*to*); (arch.) placed opposite; hence ~LY[2] (-slĭ) *adv.* [ME, f. OF *advers* f. L *adversus* p.p. of AD(*vertere vers-* turn)]

adver'sitў *n.* Condition of adverse fortune; misfortune. [ME, f. OF *adversité* f. L *adversitas -tatis* (as prec.; see -ITY)]

||**ă'dvert**[1] *n.* (colloq.) Advertisement. [abbr.]

adver't[2] *v.i.* Refer *to* (in speaking or writing). [ME, f. OF *avertir* f. Rom. **advertire* f. L *advertere* (see ADVERSE)]

ă'dvertis|e (-z) *v.* **1.** *v.t.* Make (thing, one*self*, or abs.) generally or publicly known; (esp.) describe (goods) publicly with view to increasing sales; notify (person *of* thing, *that*). **2.** *v.i.* ~**e for,** ask for by public notice. **3.** Hence ~ER[1] *n.* [ME, f. OF *avertir* (st. *-iss-*); see ADVERT[2], -ISH[2]]

adver'tisement (-sm-) *n.* Public announcement (esp. in newspapers, on posters, by television, etc.); advertising; (arch.) notice to readers in book etc. [earlier *avert-* f. F *avertissement* (as prec.; see -MENT)]

advī'ce *n.* Opinion given or offered as to action, counsel, (**take ~**, seek it esp. from legal etc. expert, or act according to it when given); information given, news; formal notice of transaction; (in *pl.*) communications from a distance. [ME f. OF *avis* f. Rom. **advisum* f. L *ad* to + *visum* p.p. of *vidēre* see]

advī's|able (-z-) *a.* To be recommended; expedient; hence ~ABI'LITY, ~**able**NESS (-beln-), *ns.*, ~**ab**LY[2] *adv.* [f. foll. + -ABLE]

advī's|e (-z) *v.t.* & *i.* Offer advice (to); recommend (*they advise caution*; *advised me to rest*); inform, notify; *consult *with*; hence ~ER[1], ~OR, *ns.*, (esp.) person habitually consulted, *person advising students. [ME, f. OF *aviser* f. Rom. **advisare* (*ad* to, *visare* frequent. of *vidēre* see)]

advī'sed (-zd) *a.* Deliberate, considered, whence ~LY[2] (-ī'zĭdlĭ) *adv.*; judicious (**ill-~**, imprudent). [p.p. of prec.]

advī'sorў (-z-) *a.* Giving advice; consisting in giving advice. [f. ADVISE + -ORY]

ădvocaa't (-ah't) *n.* Liqueur of eggs, sugar, and brandy. [Du.]

ă'dvocacў *n.* Function of an advocate; pleading in support *of*. [ME, f. OF *a(d)vocacie* f. med. L *advocatia* (as foll.; see -ACY)]

ă'dvocate[1] *n.* One who pleads for another; one who speaks in favour *of* (proposal etc.) (DEVIL'*s advocate*); professional pleader in courts of justice (**Faculty of A~s,** Scottish bar; **Lord A~**, principal law-officer of Crown in Scotland); hence ~SHIP (-tsh-) *n.*, **ă'dvocāt**ORY *a.* [ME f. OF *avocat* f. L *advocatus* p.p. (as n.) of AD(*vocare* call)]

ă'dvocāte[2] *v.t.* Plead for, defend; recommend, support (policy etc.). [f. prec.]

||**advow'son** (-z-) *n.* Right of presentation to a benefice. [ME, f. AF *a(d)voweson* f. OF *avoeson* f. L *advocatio -onis* (as ADVOCATE[1]; see -ION)]

advt. *abbr.* advertisement.

ă'dўt|um *n.* (*pl.* ~**a**). Innermost part of a temple; private chamber, sanctum. [L, f. Gk *aduton* neut. (as n.) of *adutos* impenetrable (*a-* not, *duō* enter)]

ădze, *ădz, *n.*, & *v.t.* (Dress or cut with) tool for cutting away surface of wood, like axe with arched blade at right angles to handle. [OE *adesa*, of unkn. orig.]

-ae, *pl. suf.* used in names of animal and plant families (*Felidae, Rosaceae*) and (esp. ||) instead of *-as* in pl. of many non-naturalized or unfamiliar ns. in *-a* derived f. L or Gk (*larvae*, mathematical *formulae, actiniae*). [f. pl. *-ae* of L ns. in *-a* or pl. *-ai* of some Gk ns.]

ae'dīle *n.* Roman magistrate who superintended public buildings and other matters; hence ~SHIP (-lsh-) *n.* [f. L *aedilis* (*aedes* building; see -IL)]

ae'gĭs *n.* Protection, impregnable defence; **under the ~** (auspices) **of.** [L, f. Gk *aigis* mythical shield of Zeus or Athene]

||**ae'grōtăt** *n.* Certificate that university student is too ill to attend examination etc.; examination pass awarded for this reason. [L, = he is sick (*aeger*)]

-ae'mĭa, *-ē'mĭa, *suf.* forming *ns.* denoting that a substance is (excessively) present in the blood (*bacteriaemia, pyaemia*). [mod. L, f. Gk *-aimia* (*haima* blood; see -IA[1])]

aeō'lĭan, *ēō'lĭan, *a.* **1.** Wind-borne; ~ **harp,** stringed instrument producing musical sounds on exposure to wind. **2. Aeolian mode,** (Mus.) (1) ancient Greek MODE, (2) ninth of church modes (with A as final and E as dominant). [f. L *Aeolius*: sense 1 f. *Aeolus* god of winds f. Gk *Aiolos*; sense 2 f. *Aeolis* Gk colony district in Asia Minor f. Gk *Aiolis*; see -AN]

Aeŏ'lĭc *a.* & *n.* (Dialect) of Aeolia. [f. as prec. 2 + -IC]

aeolŏ'tropў *n.* Change of physical properties consequent on change of orientation; anisotropy. [f. Gk *aiolos* changeful + *-tropia* turning; see -Y[1]]

ae'on, ē'on, *n.* An age of the universe, immeasurable period; eternity; (Platonic & Gnostic Philos.) a power existing from eternity, emanation or phase of the supreme deity. [f. eccl. L f. Gk *aiōn* age]

aepўor'nĭs *n.* Extinct giant flightless bird of genus *Aepyornis*, like moa. [mod. L, f. Gk *aipus* high + *ornis* bird]

ā'er|āte (*or* ār'-) *v.t.* Expose to mechanical or chemical action of air; charge with carbon dioxide (||*aerated water*); hence ~A'TION, ~**ātor**, *ns.* [f. L *aer* AIR[1] + -ATE[3], after F *aérer*]

aer'ial (ār'-) *a.* & *n.* **1.** *a.* (*or* āēr'ĭal). Of air, gaseous; thin as air, ethereal; immaterial, imaginary; hence ~ITY (-ă'l-) *n.* **2.** Of or in the atmosphere, atmospheric; existing, moving, happening, in the air; ~ **cableway, railway, ropeway,** system of overhead cables from which cars or containers are suspended, usu. driven electrically; hence ~IST *n.*, high-wire or trapeze artist. **3.** By or from aircraft (*aerial bombardment, photography*, TORPEDO). **4.** Hence ~LY[2] *adv.* **5.** *n.* Wire or rod used to transmit or receive radio waves. [f. L f. Gk *aerios* (*aēr* air) + -AL]

aerie. See EYRIE.

aer'ĭform (ār'-) *a.* Of the form of air, gaseous; unsubstantial, unreal. [f. L *aer* AIR[1] + -I- + -FORM]

aero- (āro) *comb. form.* **1.** Air, as: ~**bio'logy,** study of airborne micro-organisms, pollen, spores, etc., esp. as agents of infection; **~dyna'mics,** study of interaction between air and solid bodies moving through it (so **~dyna'mic** *a.*, **~dyna'micist** *n.*); **aero'logy** (-ŏ'l-), study of atmosphere away from ground (hence **~lo'gical** *a.*); **~nau'tics,** science, art, or practice of aerial navigation (hence **~nau'tic(al)** *adjs.*); **aero'nomy** (-ŏ'n-), science of upper atmosphere. **2.** Aircraft, as: **~-engine** (for propelling aircraft); ||**aer'ofoil** [FOIL¹], aircraft wing, fin, or tailplane. [f. Gk *aero-* (*aēr* air)]

aerobă'tics (ār-) *n. pl.* (usu. treated as *sing.*) Feats of expert and usu. spectacular flying of aircraft. [f. prec. + ACROBATICS]

aer'ōbe (ār'-) *n.* Micro-organism that lives only in presence of free oxygen from the air; hence **aerŏ'bIC** (ār-) *a.* [f. AERO- + Gk *bios* life]

||**aer'odrōme** (ār'-) *n.* = AIR¹field. [f. AERO- + -DROME]

aer'olīte (ār'-) *n.* Stony meteorite. [f. AERO- + -LITE]

||**aer'oplāne** (ār'-) *n.* Mechanically driven winged heavier-than-air flying machine. [f. F *aéroplane* (as AERO-, PLANE³)]

aer'osŏl (ār'-) *n.* System of colloidal particles dispersed in gas (e.g. fog or smoke); (container of) substance packed under pressure with device for releasing it as fine spray. [f. AERO- + SOL³]

aer'ospāce (ār'-) *n.* Earth's atmosphere and outer space; technology of aviation in this region. [f. AERO- + SPACE¹]

aeru'gĭnous (ērōō'-) *a.* Of the nature or colour of verdigris. [f. L *aeruginosus* (*aerugo -inis* verdigris f. *aes aeris* bronze; see -OUS)]

Aesculā'pĭan *a.* Of medicine or physicians. [f. L *Aesculapius* f. Gk *Asklēpios* god of medicine + -IAN]

ae'sthēte *n.* Professed admirer of the beautiful; ||(at university) studious person (opp. HEARTY). [f. Gk *aisthētēs* one who perceives (as foll.), or f. foll. after *athlete* f. *athletic*]

aesthĕ't|ĭc *a.* & *n.* **1.** *a.* Belonging to the appreciation of the beautiful; having such appreciation; in accordance with principles of good taste; hence ~ICALLY *adv.*, **~ĭcISM** (3) *n.*, ~ICS *n.*, philosophy of the beautiful or of art. **2.** *n.* Set of principles of good taste and appreciation of beauty. [f. Gk *aisthētikos* (*aisthanomai* perceive; see -ETIC)]

aestival, *estival, (ĕ'stĭval; *or* ēstī'val) *a.* Belonging to or appearing in summer. [ME f. OF *estival*, f. L *aestivalis* f. *aestivus* (*aestus* heat); see -IVE, -AL]

ae'stĭv|āte (*or* ē'st-) *v.i.* Spend the summer, esp. (Zool.) in state of torpor; hence ~A'TION *n.*, (esp., Bot.) arrangement of petals in flower-bud before expansion (cf. VERNATION). [f. L *aestivare* + -ATE³]

aetatis (ētā'tĭs; *or* ītah'-) *a.* (*abbr.* ***aet., aetat.***) Of or at the age of (*aet. 17*). [L]

ae'ther. Var. of ETHER 1, 2.

aetĭŏ'logy̆, *ētĭŏ'logy̆, *n.* Assignment of a cause; philosophy of causation; (Med.) science of the causes of disease; hence **aetĭolŏ'gIC(AL)** *adjs.*, **aetĭolŏ'gicalLY²** *adv.* [f. LL f. Gk *aitiologia* (*aitia* cause; see -LOGY)]

af- *pref.*, assim. form of AD- before *f.*

A.F. *abbr.* audio frequency.

afar' *adv.* At, to, a distance (esp. *afar off*); **from ~,** from a distance. [ME, f. A- 2, 3 + FAR¹]

||**A.F.C.** *abbr.* Air Force Cross; Association Football Club.

ă'ffable *a.* (Of person) easy to approach and converse with; courteous, esp. to inferiors; hence or cogn. **ăffABI'LITY** *n.*, **ă'ffabLY²** *adv.* [F, f. L *affabilis* f. AF(*fari* speak); see -ABLE]

affair' *n.* **1.** Thing to be done; concern, business, matter, (*that is my affair*; *the Dreyfus affair*); love affair; (colloq.) thing, happening; **~ of honour,** duel to settle question of honour. **2.** (in *pl.*) Ordinary pursuits of life; business dealings; public matters (*current affairs, world affairs*). [ME, f. AF *afere* f. OF *afaire* (*à faire* to do); cf. ADO]

affaire (de cœur) (ăfārdekẽr') *n.* Love affair. [F]

affairé (ăfār'ā) *a.* Busy; involved. [F]

affĕ'ct¹ *v.t.* Assume (character) (*affect the free thinker*); use by preference; pretend to have or feel (indifference etc.); pretend (*to* do). [f. F *affecter* or f. L *affectare* aim at, frequent. of AF(*ficere fect-* = *facere* do) influence]

affĕ'ct² *v.t.* **1.** Move, touch, (in mind); hence ~ING² *a.*, **~ĭng**LY² *adv.* **2.** Produce (material) effect on; (of disease etc.) attack; (in *pass.*, arch.) be assigned *to.* [f. F *affecter* or f. L *affect-* (see prec.)]

ă'ffĕct³ *n.* (Psych.) Feeling, emotion, desire, esp. as leading to action. [f. G *affekt* f. L *affectus* disposition (*afficere*; see AFFECT¹)]

ăffĕctā'tion *n.* Studied display *of*; artificiality of manner; pretence. [F, or f. L *affectatio* (as AFFECT¹; see -ATION)]

affĕ'ctėd *a.* In vbl senses; artificially assumed or displayed, pretended; (of person) full of affectation, artificial, whence ~LY² *adv.*, ~NESS *n.*; (w. *adv.*) disposed, inclined, (*towards*, or abs.). [p.p. of AFFECT¹,²]

affĕ'ction *n.* Affecting; being affected; mental state, emotion, whence ~AL *a.*; mental disposition; goodwill, kindly feeling, love, (*for, towards*); bodily state due to any influence; (esp.) malady, disease. [ME f. OF, f. L *affectio -onis* (as AFFECT²; see -ION)]

affĕ'ctionate *a.* Loving, fond; (of things) showing love or tenderness; hence ~LY² (-tlĭ) *adv.*, ~NESS (-tn-) *n.* [f. F *affectionné* or f. med. L *affectionatus* (as AFFECTION; see -ATE²)]

affĕ'ctĭve *a.* Pertaining to the affections, emotional; (Psych.) pertaining to affects; hence **ăffĕctĭ'VITY** *n.* [f. F *affectif -ive* f. LL *affectivus* (as AFFECT²; see -IVE)]

ă'ffenpĭnscher (-nsher) *n.* (Animal of) small breed of dog like griffon. [G (*affe* monkey, *pinscher* terrier)]

ă'fferent *a.* (Physiol.) Conducting inwards or towards (*afferent nerves, vessels*) (opp. *efferent*). [f. L AF(*ferre* bring); see -ENT]

affī'ance¹ *n.* (arch.) Faith, trust, (*in*); pledging of faith, esp. in marriage. [ME, f. OF *afiance* (see foll.)]

affī'ance² *v.t.* (usu. in *pass.*) Promise solemnly in marriage. [f. OF *afiancer* (*afiance* f. *afier* f. med. L AF*fidare* f. *fidus* trusty); see -ANCE]

***affī'ant** *n.* Maker of affidavit. [F, part. of *afier* (see prec.)]

affiche (ăfē'sh) *n.* Notice affixed to wall etc. [F (*afficher* post up)]

ăffĭdā'vĭt *n.* Written statement, confirmed by oath, to be used as judicial evidence (*deponent made* or *swore* or *took an affidavit*). [med. L, = has stated on oath, f. *affidare* (see AFFIANCE²)]

affĭ'lĭāte *v.t.*, & *n.* **1.** *v.t.* (Of institution) adopt (persons as members, societies as branches); attach (persons, societies) *to*, connect (them) *with*, (a society); so **affĭlĭA'TION** *n.* (||**affiliation order,** legal order that putative father of illegitimate child must help to support it). **2.** *n.* Affiliated person or organization. [f. med. L AF*filiare* adopt (*filius* son) + -ATE³]

aff'ined (-nd) *a.* Related, connected. [f. *affine* a. f. L *affinis* related (see foll.) + -ED¹]

affĭ'nĭty̆ *n.* Relationship, relations, esp. by marriage; structural resemblance (between animals, plants, languages); (fig.) similarity of character suggesting relationship, family likeness; liking, attraction; person having attraction for another; (Chem.) tendency of certain

substances to combine with others. [ME, f. OF *afinité* f. L *affinitas -tatis* (AF*finis* related, lit. bordering on, f. *finis* border; see -ITY)]
affir'm *v.* **1.** *v.t.* Assert strongly, state as a fact; (Law) confirm, ratify, (judgement). **2.** *v.i.* Make formal declaration; esp. (Law) make affirmation. **3.** Hence ~ABLE, **~at**ORY, *adjs.* [ME, f. OF *afermer* f. L AF*firmare* (*firmus* strong)]
ăffirmā'tion *n.* Affirming; (Law) solemn declaration by person who conscientiously declines taking an oath. [F, or f. L *affirmatio* (as prec.; see -ATION)]
affir'mative *a.* & *n.* **1.** *a.* Affirming, answering that a thing is so; (Logic) asserting that a proposition is valid; hence ~LY[2] (-vlĭ) *adv.* **2.** *n.* That which affirms; **answer in the ~**, say that thing is so. [ME f. OF *affirmatif -ive* f. LL *affirmativus* (as prec.; see -IVE)]
affi'x[1] *v.t.* Fix, fasten, (thing *to*, *on*; lit. or fig.); impress (seal, stamp); add in writing (signature, postscript). [f. F *affixer* or f. med. L *affixare* frequent. of L AF(*figere fix-* fix)]
ă'ffix[2] *n.* Appendage, addition; (Gram.) addition placed at the beginning (*prefix*) or end (*suffix*) of root, stem, or word, or in body of word (*infix*), to modify its meaning. [f. F *affixe* f. L *affigere* (see prec.)]
affi'xture *n.* Affixing. [f. AFFIX[1], after *fixture*]
afflā'tus *n.* Divine impulse (esp. poetic); inspiration. [L, f. AF(*flare flat-* blow)]
affli'ct *v.t.* Distress with bodily or mental suffering; **~ed with,** suffering from. [ME, f. L *afflictare*, or *afflict-* p.p. st. of AF(*fligere flict-* dash)]
affli'ct|ion *n.* Misery, distress; (cause of) pain or calamity; so ~IVE *a.* [ME f. OF, f. L *afflictio -onis* (as prec.; see -ION)]
ă'fflu|ent (-lōō-) *a.* & *n.* **1.** *a.* Flowing freely, copious; abounding (esp. in riches); wealthy; **~ society,** one in which material wealth is widely distributed; hence or cogn. ~ENCE *n.*, **~ent**LY[2] *adv.* **2.** *n.* Tributary stream. **3.** So **ă'fflŭx** *n.*, flow towards a point, influx. [ME f. OF, f. L AF(*fluere flux-* flow); see -ENT]
affor'ce *v.t.* Reinforce (group of persons, e.g. jury) by adding experts. [ME, f. OF *aforcier* (*a* to, FORCE[1])]
affor'd *v.t.* Provide; (of thing) yield supply of; **can ~**, have means for or be rich enough *to* do, be in a position *to* do (*can't afford to let him think so*), be able to spare. [ME, f. OE *geforthian* promote (as Y-, FORTH), assim. to wds in AF-]
affŏ'rėst *v.t.* Convert into forest; plant with trees; so ~A'TION *n.* [f. med. L AF*forestare* (*foresta* FOREST)]
affră'nchise (-z) *v.t.* Release from servitude or obligation. [f. OF *afranchir* (as ENFRANCHISE, w. pref. A- 4)]
affray' *n.* Breach of the peace by fighting or rioting in public. [ME, f. AF *afrayer* v. f. OF *esfreer*, f. Rom. *EX[1]*fridare* (Gmc **frithuz* peace)]
affrei'ghtment (-rā't-) *n.* Hiring of ship to carry cargo. [f. *affreight* v. hire ship to carry cargo f. F AF(*fréter* f. *fret* FREIGHT); see -MENT]
ă'ffricate *n.* (Phonet.) Combination of plosive with immediately following fricative or spirant, e.g. *ch*. [f. L AF(*fricare* rub); see -ATE[1]]
affrī'ght (-ī't) *v.t.*, & *n.* (arch.) Fright(en). [f. A- 1 + FRIGHT 2]
affro'nt (-ŭ'nt) *v.t.*, & *n.* **1.** *v.t.* Insult openly; offend modesty or self-respect of; face, confront. **2.** *n.* Open insult (*feel it an affront*; *offer an affront to*). [ME, f. OF *afronter* slap in the face, insult, f. Rom. *AF*frontare* f. L *frons frontis* face]
affū'sion (-zhon) *n.* Pouring on (esp. of water on body in baptism). [F, or f. LL *affusio* f. L AF(*fundere fus-* pour); see -ION]
A'fghăn (ă'fgăn) *n.* Native, inhabitant, or language (Pushtu), of Afghanistan; (*a~*) knitted and sewn woollen blanket or shawl; **~ hound**, hunting dog with long silky hair. [f. Pushtu *afghānī*]
aficionado (afĭsyonah'dō) *n.* (*pl.* *~s*). Devotee of bullfighting; devotee of any sport or pastime. [Sp.]
afie'ld *adv.* In the field; away from home, to or at a distance. [OE (as A[3], FIELD)]
afir'e *adv.* & *pred. a.* On fire (lit. or fig.). [ME, f. A[3] + FIRE[1]]
aflā'me *adv.* & *pred. a.* In flames (lit. or fig.). [f. A[3] + FLAME[1]]
ă'flatŏxin *n.* Carcinogen produced by the mould *Aspergillus flavus*. [f. *Aspergillus* + *flavus* + TOXIN]
***A.F.L.-C.I.O.** *abbr.* American Federation of Labor and Congress of Industrial Organizations.
afloa't *adv.* & *pred. a.* Floating in water or air; at sea, on board ship; full of or covered with water; out of debt; in full swing; in general circulation, current. [OE (as A[3], FLOAT[1])]
||**A.F.M.** *abbr.* Air Force Medal.
à fond (ahfaw'ṅ) *adv.* Thoroughly, fully. [F, = to bottom]
afōō't *adv.* & *pred. a.* Astir, on the move; in operation or employment; (arch.) on one's own feet. [ME, f. A[3] + FOOT[1]]
afor'e *adv.* & *prep.* (Naut.) in front (of) (*afore the mast*); (arch.) previously. [OE *onforan* (as A[3], FORE[2])]
afor'e- *comb. form.* Before, previously, (*aforementioned*, *aforesaid*); **~thought,** premeditated (*malice aforethought*). [f. prec.]
a fortiori (ā fortĭor'ī) *adv.* & *a.* With yet stronger reason; more conclusively. [L]
***afou'l** *adv.* Foul (*fall*, *run*, *afoul of*). [f. A[3] + FOUL]
afrai'd *pred. a.* Alarmed, frightened, (*of*, *lest*, *that*, or abs.); ~ (of the consequences, and therefore unwilling) **to** do a thing; **I'm ~**, (colloq.) I admit with (real or politely simulated) regret (*I'm afraid I'm late*; *I'm afraid there's none left*). [ME, p.p. of obs. *affray* v. f. AF *afrayer* f. OF *esfreer* (see AFFRAY)]
ă'freet, ă'frit, (-rēt) *n.* Evil demon in Muslim mythology. [f. Arab. '*ifrīt*]
afrĕ'sh *adv.* Anew, with fresh beginning. [f. A- 3 + FRESH]
A'frĭc (ă'f-) *a.* & *n.* (arch. or poet.) (Of) Africa. [f. L *Africus* African]
A'frĭcan (ă'f-) *a.* & *n.* (Native, esp. dark-skinned, or inhabitant) of Africa; *Negro; **~ violet,** saintpaulia; hence ~ISM (3, 4), ~IST (2), *ns.*, ~IZE (3) *v.t.*, make African, place under control of African Negroes. [f. L *Africanus* (*Africa*; see -AN)]
Afrĭkaa'ns (ăfrĭkah'ns) *n.* Modified form of Dutch language used in S. Africa. [Du., = African]
ăfrĭkă'nder *n.* S. Afr. breed of cattle or sheep; (S. Afr.) kind of gladiolus. [f. Afrik. *Afrikaander* alt. of Du. *Afrikaner* after *Hollander* etc.]
Afrĭka'ner (ăfrĭkah'ner) *n.* Afrikaans-speaking white person in S. Africa, esp. of Dutch descent; afrikander. [Afrik., f. as prec.]
A'frō (ă'f-) *a.* (Of hair style) long and bushy, as naturally grown by some Negroes. [f. foll., or abbr. of AFRICAN; see -O]
A'fr(ō)- (ă'f-) *comb. form.* African, as: *Aframerican*, *Afro-American*, (esp. of Amer. Negroes); *Afro-Asian*, *Afro-Asiatic*. [f. L *Afer Afr-* African]
ăfrormō'sĭa (-z-) *n.* (Afr. tree of genus *Afrormosia* yielding) wood like teak in appearance, used for furniture. [mod. L, f. AFRO- + *Ormosia* genus of trees]
aft (ahft) *adv.* (Naut. & Aeron.) In or near or to or towards stern or tail. [prob. alt. f. ME *baft* (see ABAFT) on anal. of AFTER]
a'fter[1] (ah'-) *adv.*, *prep.*, & *conj.* **1.** *adv.* Behind

in place (*Jill came tumbling after*; *look before and after*); later in time (*soon after*; *a week after*). **2.** *prep.* In pursuit or quest of (*run, inquire, after him*; *hanker after*); behind (*shut the door after you*); about, concerning (*ask after her, her health* etc.; LOOK *after*). **3.** Following in time, later than, (**a quarter after ten o'clock*); **~ you** (formula in yielding precedence); **~ you with,** (colloq.) may I have next turn at; **~ six months,** when six months have or had elapsed; **time ~ time** (& sim. phrs.), many times (etc.) in succession. **4.** In view of (*after such behaviour*); next in importance to; according to (*after a* FASHION; *after* one's *own* HEART); in imitation of (person, word, etc.) (*a picture after Rubens*; '*aesthete*' *is formed after* '*athlete*'); in allusion to (*named after*). **5. ~ all,** in spite of all that has happened or has been said etc. (*after all, what does it matter?*) or of one's exertions, expectations, etc., (*he tried for an hour and failed after all*; *so you have come after all!*). **6.** *conj.* In or at the time subsequent to that when (*after he went, goes, has gone, had gone*). [OE *æfter*, = OS, OHG *aftar*, ON *aptr*, Goth. *aftra*, Gmc f. **af-* (cogn. w. Gk *apo* or *opisō*) + compar. suf. **-ter*]

a'fter² (ah'-) *a.* **1.** Later, following, (*in after years*); (Naut.) nearer stern (*after cabins*; *after*-PEAK¹), whence **~**MOST *a.* **2. ~birth,** placenta and foetal membrane discharged after birth; **~-care,** attention given after a stay in hospital, prison, etc.; **~-effect,** effect that follows after an interval or after the primary action of something; **~glow,** radiance (lit. or fig.) remaining after removal of source; **~grass,** = AFTERMATH (lit.); **~-image** (retained by sense-organ, esp. eye, and producing sensation after cessation of stimulus); **~life,** life at a later time or after death; **~light,** hindsight; **~pains** (caused by contraction of womb after childbirth); **~shave** *a.* & *n.*, (lotion) for use after shaving; **~-taste** (remaining or recurring after eating or drinking); **~thought,** something that is thought of or added later; **~word,** concluding remarks in book, esp. by person other than its author. [f. prec.]

a'ftermăth (ah'-; *or* -ahth) *n.* Grass growing after mowing or harvest; (fig.) consequences (*the aftermath of war*). [f. prec. + *math* mowing f. OE *mǣth* f. Gmc **mǣ-* MOW³]

afternōō'n (ah-) *n.* Time from noon to evening (lit. or fig.; *in* or *during the afternoon*; *on Wednesday afternoon*; *the afternoon of life*); this time spent in a particular way; *afternoon* TEA. [f. AFTER¹ 3 + NOON]

‖**a'fters** (ah'-; -z) *n.pl.* (colloq.) Course following main course at meal. [f. AFTER¹ 1 or AFTER²]

a'fterwards (-z), ***a'fterward,** (ah'-) *adv.* Later, subsequently. [OE *æftanwearde* a. (*æftan* AFT, -WARD) + -S³]

ag- *pref.*, assim. form of AD- before *g.*

Ag *symb.* silver. [f. L *argentum*]

a'ga (ah'ga) *n.* (In Muslim countries, esp. under Ottoman Empire) commander, chief; **Aga Khan,** spiritual leader of Ismaili Muslims. [f. Turk. *ağa* master]

agai'n (*or* agĕ'n) *adv.* **1.** Another time, once more; **~ and ~, time and (time) ~,** repeatedly; **back ~, home ~,** to or in original position or condition; **come ~,** (esp.) make second effort, (as *imper.*, colloq.) what did you say?; NOW *and again*; **as much ~,** twice as much; **half as much** or **many ~,** one-and-a-half times as much or many. **2.** Further, besides (*again, what about the children?*); on the other hand (*I might, and again I might not*); in accordance or response (*glasses rang again*; *the loaded table groaned again.* [orig. north. form of ME *ayen* etc., f. OE *ongēan*, *ongægn*, etc., OS *angegin*, OHG *ingagan*, f. Gmc (as ON¹, **gagan-*, **gagin-* straight)]

agai'nst (*or* agĕ'nst) *prep.* **1.** In opposition to (*fight against*; *I am against reform*; *arson is against the law*; *against the* GRAIN 5; OVER *against*); to the disadvantage of (*his age is against him*); in contrast to (*against a dark background*; *99 as against 102 yesterday*). **2.** In anticipation of or preparation for (*against his coming*; *against a rainy day*; *protected against the cold*; *warned against pickpockets*); in return for (*issued against payment of the fee*); into collision or in contact with (*ran against a rock*; *lean, stand, against the wall*; UP *against*). [f. ME *ayenes* etc. (*ayen* AGAIN; see -S³), + *-t* as in *amidst, amongst, betwixt, whilst*]

ă'gama *n.* Old World lizard like iguana. [Carib]

ă'gamĭ *n.* Tropical Amer. heron-like bird. [F, f. Carib]

agă'mĭc *a.* (Zool.) Characterized by absence of sexual action. [f. as AGAMOUS + -IC]

ăgamo|gĕ'nėsĭs *n.* (Biol.) Asexual reproduction; so **~gėnĕ'tĭc** *a.* [f. as foll. + Gk *genesis* birth]

ă'gamous *a.* (Biol.) Without (distinguishable) sexual organs. [f. Gk *agamos* (*a-* not, *gamos* marriage) + -OUS]

ăgapă'nthus *n.* S. Afr. ornamental lily of genus *Agapanthus*, with blue or white flowers. [mod. L, f. Gk *agapē* love + *anthos* flower]

agā'pe¹ *adv.* & *pred. a.* Gaping; open-mouthed with wonder or expectation. [f. A³ + GAPE]

agape² (ă'gapē) *n.* Love-feast held by early Christians in connection with Lord's Supper; (Theol.) Christian love, charity. [Gk, = brotherly love]

ăgapĕ'monė *n.* Abode of free love. [f. *A~*, name of a community founded in Somerset *c.* 1850, believed to practise free love; irreg. f. Gk *agapē* love + *monē* abode]

ā'gar(-ā'gar) *n.* Seaweed of various kinds, esp. Ceylon moss; gelatinous substance made from this and used in food, bacterial cultures, etc. [Malay]

ă'garĭc *n.* Fungus of family Agaricaceae, with cap and stalk, incl. common mushroom; FLY¹ *agaric*. [f. L f. Gk *agarikon*]

ă'gate *n.* One of several varieties of hard usu. banded chalcedony; coloured toy marble resembling this. [f. F *agate, -the*, f. L f. Gk *akhatēs*]

agā'vė *n.* (Bot.) Plant of genus *Agave*, with spiny leaves, flowering only once, e.g. American aloe. [L, f. Gk *Agauē*, proper name in myth (*agauos* illustrious)]

agā'ze *adv.* Gazing. [ME, f. A³ + GAZE]

āge¹ *n.* **1.** Length of past life or of existence; **be your ~,** (colloq.) act sensibly; **look** one's **~,** look as old as one really is; MENTAL¹, READING, *age*; **moon's ~,** time elapsed since new moon; **of an ~ with,** of same age as. **2.** Duration or period of life required for a purpose; **come of ~,** reach adult status (esp. in Law at 18, formerly 21); *age of* CONSENT², *of* DISCRETION; **over ~,** (1) old enough, (2) too old; **under ~,** not old enough, esp. not yet of adult status. **3.** Latter part of life (*peevishness of age*); **~ before beauty,** children must give precedence to their elders. **4.** A generation; (Hist.) great period (*Age of* REASON¹; *brazen*, BRONZE, GOLDEN, IRON¹, SILVER¹, STONE, *age*; MIDDLE¹ *Ages*); (colloq., esp. in *pl.*) long time (*waiting for ages*); **~-long, ~-old,** having existed for a very long time. **5.** (Geol.) Period of time, esp. one shorter than an EPOCH, corresp. to STAGE¹ in rocks; ICE¹-*age*. [ME f. OF, f. Rom. **aetaticum* f. L *aetas -atis* age; see -AGE]

āge² *v.t.* & *i.* (part. **~ing** *or* **aging,** *pr.* ā'jĭng). (Cause or allow to) grow old or mature or show effects of passage of time; begin to appear older

(*he's aged a lot recently*); hence **ā'g(e)**ING¹ (ā'jĭng) *n.*, change of properties occurring in some metals after heat treatment or cold working. [f. prec.]
-age (-ĭj) *suf.* forming *ns.* w. sense: (1) aggregate or number of (*coverage*, the *peerage*, *acreage*); (2) function or condition (*bondage*, a *peerage*); (3) action (*breakage*, *spillage*); (4) fees payable for, cost of using, (*porterage*, *postage*); (5) place, abode, (*anchorage*, *orphanage*, *parsonage*); (6) product of action (*dosage*, *wreckage*). [OF, f. Rom. **-aticum* (**aetaticum* AGE¹, **coraticum* COURAGE), f. L *-aticum* neut. of adj. suf. *-aticus* -ATIC]
aged *a.* **1.** (ā'jĭd). Having lived long, old; hence **ā'gėd**NESS *n.* **2.** (ājd). Of the age of (*aged ten*); that has been subjected to ageing; (of horse) over six years old. [p.p. of AGE²]
ā'gelėss (-jl-) *a.* Never growing or appearing old or outmoded. [f. AGE¹ + -LESS]
ā'gencȳ *n.* **1.** Active operation, action (*moral*, *free*, *agency*); intervening action (*fertilized by the agency of insects*); action personified (*an invisible agency*). **2.** Function of an agent or representative; business establishment of an agent (*employment*, *news*, *agency*); specialized department of United Nations. [f. med. L *agentia* f. L *agere* do; see -ENCY]
agĕ'nda *n.* Things to be done; (list of) items of business to be considered at a meeting. [L, neut. pl. of gerundive of *agere* do; now usu. treated as sing.]
ā'gēne *n.* Nitrogen trichloride formerly used to whiten flour. [***P**, f. AGE¹˒² + -ENE]
ā'gent *n.* **1.** One who or that which exerts power or produces an effect (**free ~**, one whose actions are not subject to another's control); (cause of) natural force or effect on matter (*oxidizing agent*). **2.** One who acts for another in business, politics, etc., (*estate*, *insurance*, *secret*, *agent*); **law ~**, (Sc.) solicitor; **~-general**, London representative of Australian state or Canadian province. **3.** So **agĕ'nt**IAL (-shal) *a.* [f. L *agere* do; see -ENT]
agent provocateur (ahzhahṅ prŏvŏkatėr') *n.* (*pl.* ***-ts -rs*** *pr.* same). Person employed to detect suspected offenders by tempting them to overt action. [F, = provocative agent]
aggiornament|o (ajôrnamĕ'ntō) *n.* (*pl.* ***~i*** *pr.* -ē). Bringing up to date, esp. of R.C. Church policy. [It.]
agglŏ'mer|āte¹ *v.t.* & *i.* Collect into a mass; accumulate in a disorderly way; hence **~**A'TION *n.*, **~at**IVE *a.* [f. L AG*glomerare* (*glomus -meris* ball) + -ATE³]
agglŏ'merate² *a.* & *n.* (Collected into) a mass; (Geol.) mass of volcanic fragments united under heat (cf. CONGLOMERATE). [f. as prec.; see -ATE¹˒²]
agglu'tĭn|āte (-lōō'-) *v.t.* & *i.* Unite as with glue; (of language) combine simple words without change of form to express compound ideas; (Biol.) cause or undergo coalescence (of bacteria, erythrocytes, etc.); hence **~**A'TION *n.*, **~at**IVE *a.* [f. L AG*glutinare* (*gluten -tinis* glue) + -ATE³]
aggră'ndīze, -ise (-īz), *v.t.* Increase power, rank, wealth, of (person, State); make appear greater than the reality; hence **aggră'ndize**MENT, **-ise-**, (-zm-) *n.* [f. F *agrandir* (st. *-iss-*), prob. f. It. AG(*grandire* f. L *grandis* large); assim. to vbs in -IZE]
ă'ggrav|āte *v.t.* Increase gravity of (illness, offence, etc.); (colloq.) exasperate (person); so **~**A'TION *n.* [f. L AG*gravare* make heavy (*gravis*) + -ATE³]
ă'ggrėgate¹ *a.* & *n.* **1.** *a.* Collected into one body; collective, total; CORPORATION *aggregate*; (Bot., of fruit) formed from carpels of one flower (e.g. raspberry). **2.** *n.* Sum total; assemblage (**in the ~**, as a whole); broken stone etc. used in making concrete; mass of particles in soil etc.; (Geol.) mass of minerals formed into one rock. [f. L AG*gregare* herd together (*grex gregis* flock); see -ATE¹˒²]
ă'ggrėg|āte² *v.t.* & *i.* Collect together; unite (individual to company); (colloq.) amount to (specified total); hence **~**A'TION *n.*, **~at**IVE *a.* [f. as prec. + -ATE³]
aggrĕ'ss|ion (-shon) *n.* Act of beginning quarrel or war; unprovoked attack; (Psych.) hostile or destructive tendency or behaviour; so **~**OR *n.* [f. F *agression* or f. L *aggressio* attack f. AG(*gredi* = *gradi* walk); see -ION]
aggrĕ'ssĭve *a.* **1.** Of aggression; offensive. **2.** Disposed to attack; forceful, self-assertive. **3.** Hence **~**LY² (-vlĭ) *adv.*, **~**NESS (-vn-) *n.* [f. as prec.; see -IVE]
aggrie've *v.t.* (usu. in *pass.*) Grieve, distress; oppress, treat unfairly. [ME, f. OF *agrever* f. Rom. *AG(*grevare*) GRIEVE¹]
ă'ggrō *n.* (sl.) Deliberate trouble-making. [abbr. of AGGRAVATION or AGGRESSION; see -O]
agha'st (agah'st) *a.* Terrified; struck with amazement. [ME, p.p. of obs. v. *agast*, *gast* frighten; see GHASTLY]
ă'gīle *a.* Quick-moving, nimble, active; hence or cogn. **agĭ'l**ITY *n.*, **~**LY² (-l-lĭ) *adv.* [F, f. L *agilis* (*agere* do; see -IL)]
agĭ'n (ag-) *prep.* (joc. or dial.) Against; **~ the government**, uncooperative. [corrupt. of (AGAIN obs. prep. =) AGAINST]
ă'gĭō *n.* (*pl.* **~s**). Percentage charged on exchange of paper money into cash, or of one currency into another more valuable; excess value of one currency over another; money-exchange business. [It., = ease]
ă'gĭotage *n.* Money-exchange business; speculation in stocks; stock-jobbing. [F (*agioter* f. as prec. + connecting *-t-*; see -AGE)]
agĭ'st *v.t.* Take in livestock to feed; charge (land or its owner) with a public burden; so **~**MENT *n.* [f. OF *agister* (*à* to, *gister* lodge f. Rom. **jacitare* frequent. of L *jacēre* lie)]
ă'gĭtāte *v.* **1.** *v.t.* Shake, move; disturb, excite, (feelings, person); revolve mentally, discuss, debate, (plan etc.). **2.** *v.i.* Keep up an agitation (*for* or *against*). [f. L *agitare* + -ATE³]
ăgĭtā'tion *n.* Shaking, moving; (mental or physical) commotion, disturbance; debate, discussion; keeping of a matter constantly before the public. [F, or f. L *agitatio* (as prec.; see -ATION)]
ăgĭta'tō (-ah'-) *adv.* (Mus.) In an agitated manner. [It.]
ă'gĭtātor *n.* One who agitates, esp. politically; apparatus for shaking or mixing liquid etc. [L (as AGITATE; see -OR)]
ă'gĭtprŏp (*or* ă'g-) *n.* (System of) Russian Communist propaganda. [Russ. (as AGITATION, PROPAGANDA)]
ă'glėt *n.* **1.** Metal tag of a lace; metallic ornament of dress. **2.** = AIGUILLETTE. [ME, f. F *aiguillette* dim. of *aiguille* needle f. LL *acucula* dim. of *acus* needle]
agley' (-ā' *or* -ē') *adv.* (Sc.) Askew, awry. [f. A³ + Sc. *gley* squint]
aglow' (-ō') *adv.* & *pred. a.* Glowing(ly). [f. A³ + GLOW]
A.G.M. *abbr.* annual general meeting.
ă'gnail *n.* Torn skin at root of finger-nail; soreness resulting from this. [OE *angnægl* f. Gmc (**ang-* tight, painful, *nægl* NAIL¹ 3, hard excrescence fixed in the flesh); mod. sense, and form *hangnail*, result from pop. etym., *nail* being taken as NAIL¹ 1]
ă'gnāte *n.* & *a.* (One who is) descended esp. by male line from same male ancestor (cf. COGNATE); descended from same forefather, of same

clan or nation; (fig.) akin, of same nature; hence **ăgnă′**TIC *a.*, **ăgnā′**TION *n.* [f. L *agnatus* (*ad* to, **gnatus* born p.p. of (*g*)*nasci* f. stem *gen*- beget)]

ăgnō′mĕn *n.* (Rom. Ant.) fourth name occas. given as honour (see COGNOMEN); nickname. [L (as AG-, (**g*)*nomen* name)]

ăgnŏ′stĭc *n.* & *a.* (Adherent) of the view that nothing is known, or likely to be known, of the existence of God or of anything beyond material phenomena; hence ~ISM (3) *n.* [f. A- 7 + GNOSTIC]

Agnus Dē′ī (ă-; *or* -ōōs dā′ē) *n.* Part of R.C. Mass beginning *Agnus Dei*; figure of lamb bearing cross or flag, as emblem of Christ; cake of wax stamped with such figure and blessed by pope. [L, = lamb of God]

agō′ *adv.* Past, gone by, (*ten years ago*); **long ~**, long since. [ME (*ago, agone*), p.p. of obs. v. *ago* (A- 1, GO¹)]

agŏ′g *adv.* & *pred. a.* Eager, expectant. [f. F *en gogues* (*en* in, pl. of *gogue* fun; orig. unkn.)]

agŏ′nĭc *a.* ~ **line,** line of zero magnetic declination. [f. Gk *agōnios* without angle (*a*- not, *gōnia* angle) + -IC]

ăgonĭ′st|ĭc *a.* Polemical, combative; hence ~ICALLY *adv.* [f. LL f. Gk *agōnistikos* (*agōnistēs* contestant f. *agōn* contest); see -IST, -IC]

ă′goniz|e, -ĭs|e (-īz), *v.* **1.** *v.i.* Suffer agony, writhe in anguish; contend, wrestle (lit. or fig.). **2.** *v.t.* Cause agony to; hence **~ĭng**LY² *adv.* [f. F *agoniser* or f. LL *agonizare* f. Gk *agōnizomai* contend (*agōn* contest)]

ă′gonȳ *n.* Extreme mental or physical suffering (‖**~ column,** (colloq.) = PERSONAL *column*; **death ~, last ~,** pangs of death); severe struggle. [ME, f. OF *agonie* or f. LL f. Gk *agōnia* (*agōn* contest; see -Y¹)]

ăgoraphō′b|ĭa *n.* (Psych.) Morbid dread of public places or open spaces (opp. *claustrophobia*); hence ~IC *a.* & *n.* [f. Gk *agora* place of assembly, market-place + -PHOBIA]

agou′tĭ, -tȳ, agu′tĭ, (-gōō′-) *n.* Rodent of genus *Dasyprocta* or *Myoprocta* of Central and S. America, related to guinea-pig. [f. F *agouti* or Sp. *aguti* f. Tupi *aguti*]

A.G.R. *abbr.* advanced gas-cooled (nuclear) reactor.

ă′grapha *n. pl.* Sayings of Christ not recorded in canonical Gospels. [Gk, = unwritten things]

agrār′ĭan *a.* & *n.* **1.** *a.* Relating to landed property; relating to cultivated land. **2.** *n.* Advocate of redistribution of landed property. [f. L *agrarius* (*ager agri* land; see -ARY¹) + -AN]

agree′ *v.* **1.** *v.i.* Consent (*to* proposal, statement, *to* do); **~ to differ** or **disagree,** no longer try to convince each other. **2.** Hold similar opinion (*with* person *that* or *about*); **be ~d,** have reached similar opinion. **3.** Become or be in harmony (*with* person); **~ on,** decide by mutual consent. **4. ~ with,** suit constitution of (*this work, lobster, the climate, does not agree with him*). **5.** (Gram.) Have same number, gender, case, or person. **6.** *v.t.* Bring into harmony; ‖reach agreement concerning (*agree a price*); consent to or approve of (proposal, terms, etc.). [ME, f. OF *agreer* f. Rom. *AG*gratare* make agreeable (*gratus*)]

agree′ab|le (-rĭ′*abel*) *a.* Pleasing (*to*, or abs.); (colloq., of person) willing to agree (*to* a thing, *to* do, or abs.); conformable *to*; hence **~le**NESS *n.*, ~LY² *adv.* (**~ly surprised,** surprised and pleased). [ME, f. OF *agreable* (*agreer* AGREE; see -ABLE)]

agree′ment *n.* Mutual understanding; covenant, treaty; (Law) contract legally binding on parties; holding of similar opinion; state of being harmonious; (Gram.) having the same number, gender, case, or person. [ME, f. OF (as AGREE; see -MENT)]

agrĕ′stĭc *a.* Rural, rustic; uncouth. [f. L *agrestis* (*ager* field) + -IC]

ă′grĭbusinĕss (-bĭzn-) *n.* Group of industries dealing with farming produce and services. [f. AGRICULTURE + BUSINESS]

ă′grĭcŭlture *n.* Science or practice of cultivating the soil and rearing animals; hence **ăgrĭcŭ′ltur**AL *a.*, **ăgrĭcŭ′ltur(al)**IST (3) *ns.*, (-cher-). [F, or f. L *agricultura* (*ager agri* field, *cultura* CULTURE)]

ă′grĭmonȳ *n.* Perennial plant of genus *Agrimonia*, esp. *A. eupatoria* with small yellow flowers; HEMP *agrimony*. [ME, f. OF *aigremoine* f. L *agrimonia* alt. of *argemonia* f. Gk *argemōnē*]

agrŏ′nom|ȳ *n.* Science of soil management and crop production; so **ăgronŏ′m**IC(AL) *adjs.*, **ăgronŏ′m**ICS, ~IST (3), *ns.* [f. F *agronomie* (*agronome* agriculturist f. Gk *agros* land + -*nomos* f. *nemō* arrange); see -Y¹]

agrou′nd *adv.* & *pred. a.* (Of ship) on the bottom of shallow water (*be, run, aground*). [ME, f. A³ + GROUND¹]

ā′gū|e *n.* Malarial fever, with cold, hot, and sweating stages; shivering fit (lit. or fig.); hence **ā′gūe**D² (-ūd), ~ISH¹, *adjs.* [ME f. OF, f. med. L *acuta* (*febris* fever) ACUTE]

aguti. See AGOUTI.

ah *int.* expr. sorrow or regret (*ah me!*), surprise, pleasure, admiration, entreaty, remonstrance, dislike, boredom, contempt, mockery. [ME f. OF *a*]

A.H. *abbr.* in the year of the Hegira; of the Muslim era. [f. L *anno Hegirae*]

aha′ (ahhah′ *or* a-hah′) *int.* expr. surprise, triumph, mockery, irony. [ME, f. AH + HA¹]

ahea′d (*a*-hĕ′d) *adv.* **1.** Farther forward in space or time; **~ of,** farther advanced than (lit. or fig.). **2.** In the line of one's forward motion (*breakers ahead*); straight forwards; GO¹ *ahead.* [f. A³ + HEAD¹]

ahĕ′m (*a*-h-) *int.* (used to attract attention, express disapproval, or gain time). [lengthened form of HEM³]

ahĭ′msa (*a*-hĭ′msah) *n.* (Hindu, Buddhist, & Jainist Philos.) Doctrine of non-violence or non-killing. [Skr. (*a* without, *himsa* injury)]

āhĭstŏ′rĭc(al) *adjs.* Not historic(al); unrelated to history. [f. A- 7 + HISTORIC(AL)]

ahoy′ (*a*-h-) *int.* (Naut.) used in hailing. [f. AH + HOY²]

à huis clos (ah wē klō′) *adv.* In private. [F, = with closed doors]

ahŭ′ll (*a*-h-) *adv.* (Naut.) With sails taken in and helm lashed on lee side. [f. A³ + HULL²]

a′ĭ (ah′ĭ) *n.* Three-toed sloth of S. America, of genus *Bradypus*. [f. Tupi *ai*, repr. its cry]

A.I. *abbr.* artificial insemination.

aid¹ *v.t.* Help (person *to* do, or abs.); promote (recovery etc.). [ME, f. OF *aïdier* f. L *adjutare* frequent. of AD(*juvare jut*- help)]

aid² *n.* Help; helper; material source of help (*teaching aid; aids and appliances*); (Hist.) grant of subsidy or tax to king; **in ~ of,** in support of; **what's (all) this in ~ of?**, (colloq.) what is the purpose of this?; PRAY *in aid.* [ME, f. OF *aïde* f. Rom. **adjuta* fem. p.p. (as n.) of *adjuvare* AID¹]

A.I.D. *abbr.* *Agency for International Development; artificial insemination by donor.

aide *n.* = foll.; *assistant. [abbr.]

aide-de-camp (ād-dekah′ṅ) *n.* (*pl.* **aides-de-camp** *pr.* same). Officer acting as confidential assistant to senior officer. [F]

aide-mémoire (ā′dmĕmwār) *n.* (Book or document serving as) an aid to the memory; (Diplom.) memorandum. [F (*aider* to help, *mémoire* memory)]

ai′grĕtte (*or* -ĕ′t) *n.* Egret; its white plume; tuft of feathers or hair; spray of gems etc. [F]

ai'guille (-gwēl) *n.* Sharp peak of rock, esp. in Alps. [F (see AGLET)]
aiguillě'tte (āgwĭlě't) *n.* Tagged point hanging from shoulder upon breast of some uniforms. [F (see AGLET)]
A.I.H. *abbr.* artificial insemination by husband.
ail *v.* **1.** *v.t.* (in 3rd person *act.* w. pron. subj.) Trouble, afflict, (*what ails him?*). **2.** *v.i.* Be ill; hence ~'MENT *n.*, (esp. slight) illness. [OE *egl(i)an* (*egle* troublesome, Goth. *agls* disgraceful)]
ai'lerŏn *n.* Hinged flap on rear edge of aeroplane wing, used to control sideways balance. [F, dim. of *aile* wing f. L *ala*]
ai'lĭng *a.* Ill, esp. often ill; (fig.) in poor condition. [f. AIL + -ING²]
ailuro- (īlūr'o) *comb. form.* Cat, as ~PHIL(E), ~PHOBE, *ns.* & *adjs.*, ~PHO'BIA *n.* [f. Gk *ailouros* cat + -O-]
aim¹ *v.* **1.** *v.t.* Direct (blow, missile, act, remark, *at*); ~ **at,** point (gun etc.) towards. **2.** *v.i.* Take aim (~ **high,** show ambition); intend or try (*to* do, *at* do*ing*); ~ **at,** (fig.) seek to attain (*aim at a bishopric*). [ME, partly f. OF *amer* f. L *aestimare* reckon, partly f. OF *ae(s)mer* f. Rom. *AD*aestimare*]
aim² *n.* Directing of weapon, missile, etc. at object (**take** ~, direct weapon etc. thus); design, purpose, object aimed at; hence ~'LESS *a.*, ~'**lĕss**LY² *adv.*, ~'**lĕss**NESS *n.* [ME, f. prec.]
ain't. See BE, HAVE¹.
air¹ *n.* **1.** Invisible gaseous substance enveloping earth, mixture mainly of oxygen and nitrogen, breathed by all land animals and plants; the earth's atmosphere; free or unconfined space in atmosphere (*birds of the air*; *in the open air*); CLEAR² *the air*; ***give** person **the air,** (sl.) dismiss him; **in the** ~, (of opinions, feelings) spreading about, (of projects etc.) uncertain; **on the** ~, broadcast(ing) by radio; **take the** ~, go out of doors; THIN¹ *air.* **2.** The atmosphere as place of (esp. warlike) operations with aeroplanes etc.; **by** ~, in or by aircraft. **3.** Breeze, light wind. **4.** Appearance (*an air of absurdity*); bearing, gesture, (*with a triumphant air*); confident bearing (*does things with an air*); (esp. in *pl.*) affected manner, pretentiousness, (*gave himself airs*; *airs and* GRACE*s*). **5.** (Mus.) Melody, tune, esp., in harmonized composition, predominant (usu. soprano) part. **6.** ~ **bag,** safety device filling with air to protect occupants of motor car in collision; ~**-bed,** inflated mattress; ~**-bladder,** one filled with air in animals or plants; ~'**borne,** transported by air, (of aircraft) in the air after taking off (*the squadron was soon airborne*); ~ **brake,** (1) brake worked by air pressure, (2) movable flap to retard aircraft; ~**-brick** (perforated for ventilation); ~'**brush,** device for spraying paint by means of compressed air; ~ **bus,** aircraft providing passenger service like bus; ||*air* COMMODORE; ~**-conditioned,** (of room, building, etc.) having the air in it cleaned and brought to required humidity (and temperature); ~**-conditioner,** ~**-conditioning,** (apparatus for) this process; ~**-cooled** (by a current of cool air); *air* CORRIDOR; ~'**craft,** aeroplane(s), helicopter(s), (occas. also) airship(s) and balloon(s); ~'**craft-carrier,** ship that carries and serves as a base for aeroplanes; ~'**craftman,** ~'**craftwoman,** lowest rank in (Women's) Royal Air Force; ~**-cushion,** (1) cushion inflated with air, (2) layer of air supporting vehicle of hovercraft type; ~ **ferry,** transport of cars etc. over water by aircraft; ~'**field,** area of land where aircraft are kept and may take off and land; *~'**foil,** = AERO*foil*; ~ **force** (||ROYAL *Air Force*), branch of armed forces fighting in the air; ~'**frame,** body of aircraft as dist. from engine(s); ~'**glow,** radiation from upper atmosphere, detectable at night; ~'**gun** (using compressed air to propel missile); ~ **hostess,** stewardess in passenger aircraft; ~**-jacket** (inflated, to support wearer in water); ||~ **letter,** sheet of light paper that may be sent cheaply by air mail; ~'**lift,** (*n.*) transport of troops, supplies, etc. by air, esp. in emergency, (*v.t.*) transport thus; ~'**line,** line of aircraft for public service; ~ **liner,** large passenger aircraft; ~'**lock,** (1) stoppage of flow in pump or pipe caused by air, (2) compartment with double doors for entering or leaving vessel under pressure; ~ **mail** (carried by air); ~'**-man,** man who flies in an aircraft, esp. as pilot or member of crew; **Air Marshal,** ~ **mechanic,** ranks in Royal Air Force; ~**-minded,** interested in aviation; ~'**miss,** narrow escape from collision between aircraft; **Air Officer,** R.A.F. officer above rank of Group Captain; *~'**plane,** aeroplane; ~ **pocket,** apparent vacuum in air causing aircraft to drop some distance; ~'**port,** airfield, esp. one fully equipped, usu. with customs-house, at which passengers by air embark or disembark; ~'**post,** = *air mail*; ~ **power,** ability to defend and attack by means of aircraft, missiles, etc.; ~ **pump** (for pumping air into or out of a vessel); ~ **raid,** attack by aircraft; ~ **rifle** (as *airgun*); ~'**screw,** propeller of aircraft; ~**-sea rescue** (from the sea by aircraft); ~'**ship,** flying machine lighter than air; ~'**sick,** affected with nausea due to motion of aircraft; ~'**space,** air above country etc., esp. considered as subject to its jurisdiction; ~ **speed,** speed of aircraft etc. relative to the air through which it is moving; ~'**strip,** strip of ground used or usable for landing and take-off of aircraft; ~ **terminal,** place in a town where transport is provided to and from airport; ~'**tight,** impermeable to air; ~**-to-**~, from one aircraft to another in flight; ~'**way,** (1) ventilating passage in mine, (2) route regularly followed by aircraft; ~'**woman,** woman who flies in an aircraft, esp. as pilot or member of crew; ~'**worthy,** (of aircraft) fit to fly. [senses 1–3 ME f. OF, f. L f. Gk *aēr*; sense 4 F, prob. f. OF *aire* place, disposition f. L *area*; sense 5 f. It. *aria* air]
air² *v.t.* **1.** Expose to open air, ventilate; finish drying at fire or in heated ~'**ing cupboard,** whence ~'ER¹ *n.*, frame for drying clothes etc. **2.** Parade (qualities, fine clothes); make public (grievances, theories). **3.** ~ **oneself,** go out in fresh air. [f. prec.]
Air'edāle (ār'd-) *n.* Large rough-coated terrier. [~ in W. Yorkshire]
air'lĕss *a.* Stuffy; breezeless, still. [f. AIR¹ + -LESS]
air'ỹ *a.* **1.** Aerial, lofty; breezy. **2.** Superficial, flippant; immaterial, unsubstantial; of thin texture. **3.** Light in movement; sprightly; graceful, delicate. **4.** Hence **air'ĭ**LY² *adv.*, **air'ĭ**NESS *n.* **5.** ~**-fairy,** (colloq.) delicate or light as a fairy, nonchalant, (derog.) fanciful, unsubstantial. [f. AIR¹ + -Y²]
aisle (īl) *n.* Part of church, esp. one parallel to and divided by pillars from the main nave, choir, or transept; passage between rows of pews or seats; hence **aisl**ED² (īld), ~LESS (ī'l-l-), *adjs.* [ME f. OF *ele*, f. L *ala* wing; confus. w. *island* and F *aile* wing]
||**ait,** ||**eyot,** (āt) *n.* Small isle, esp. in a river. [f. OE *iggath* etc. f. *īeg* ISLAND + dim. suf.]
aitch *n.* Name of letter H; **drop** one's ~**es,** fail to pronounce initial *h* in words. [phonet. sp.]
||**ai'tchbōne** *n.* (Cut of beef lying over) buttock or rump bone. [ME *nage-*, *nache-bone* buttock f. OF *nage*, *nache* f. LL (pl.) *naticas* f. L *natis*, *-es* buttock(s); for loss of *n-* cf. ADDER, APRON]

ajar′[1] *adv.* & *pred. a.* (Of door) slightly open. [f. A[3] + obs. *char* f. OE *cerr* a turn]
ajar′[2] *adv.* Out of harmony. [f. A[3] + JAR[1]]
A.J.C. *abbr.* Australian Jockey Club.
ajutage. See ADJUTAGE.
***a.k.a.** *abbr.* also known as.
A.K.C. *abbr.* Associate of King's College, London.
ă′kee. See ACKEE.
akĭ′mbō *adv.* (Of the arms) with hands on hips and elbows turned outwards. [ME *in kenebowe*, prob. f. ON **i keng boginn* bent in a curve; assim. to A[3]]
akĭ′n *pred. a.* Related by blood; (fig.) of similar or kindred character. [f. A- 3 + KIN]
Akkā′dĭan, Accā′dĭan, (ăk-) *n.* & *a.* (Semitic language) of Akkad in ancient Babylonia. [f. *Akkad* + -IAN]
akvavit. See AQUAVIT.
al- *pref.*, assim. form of AD- before *l.*
-al *suf.* **1.** forming *adjs.* f. (or f. *ns.* f.) L (*central, general, postal, regimental, sensational*) or Gk (*colossal, rhomboidal, tropical*; cf. also -IAL, -ICAL) or f. E *ns.* (*tidal*) [f. F *-el* or f. L *-alis* adj. suf. cogn. w. *-aris* (-AR[1])]. **2.** forming *ns.* [f. F *-aille* or f. (or after) L *-alis* etc. used as *n.*] (*animal, cardinal, rival*), esp. of vbl action (*arrival, proposal, recital, trial, withdrawal*).
Al *symb.* aluminium.
à la (ah lah) *prep.* After the manner of; **~ *russe*,** in the Russian manner. [F, f. À LA MODE]
Ala. *abbr.* Alabama.
ă′labast|er (-bah-) *n.* & *a.* **1.** *n.* Translucent usu. white form of gypsum, often carved into ornaments; hence **~RINE**[1] (-ah′s-) *a.* **2.** *a.* Of alabaster; like alabaster in whiteness or smoothness. [ME, f. OF *alabastre* f. L *alabaster, -trum,* f. Gk *alabast(r)os*]
à la carte (ah lah kar̂′t) *adv.* & *a.* By the bill of fare; ordered as separately priced item(s) from menu, not as part of table d'hôte meal. [F]
ală′ck *int.* (arch.) expr. regret or surprise, esp. in phr. **~-a-day.** [prob. f. AH + LACK]
ală′crĭtȳ *n.* Briskness, cheerful readiness. [f. L *alacritas* (*alacer* brisk; see -ITY)]
Ală′ddĭn (*a-*) *n.* **~'s cave,** place of great riches; **~'s lamp,** talisman enabling holder to gratify any wish. [character in *Arabian Nights*]
à la mode (ah lah mō′d) *adv.* & *a.* In the fashion, fashionable; (of beef) braised in wine; *(of food) served with ice cream. [F, = in the fashion]
ală′nna(h) *int.* (Ir.) of address or endearment. [f. Ir. *a leanbh* my child!]
à la page (ah lah pah′zh) *adv.* Up to date; in the latest fashion. [F]
ā′lar *a.* Pertaining to wings; winglike, wing-shaped; axillary. [f. L *alaris* (*ala* wing; see -AR[1])]
alar̂′m[1] *n.* **1.** Warning sound giving notice of danger; warning (*give, raise, the alarm*). **2.** Frightened anticipation of danger; uneasiness. **3.** Mechanism that sounds the alarm (*burglar alarm*); apparatus that rings at set time; **~ (clock)**, clock with this; cf. ALARUM. [ME, f. OF *alarme* f. It. *allarme* (*all' arme!* to arms)]
alar̂′m[2] *v.t.* Arouse to sense of danger; disturb; agitate with fear; hence **~ING**[2] *a.*, **~ingLY**[2] *adv.* [f. prec.]
alar̂′m|ĭst *n.* One who raises alarms on slight grounds; panic-monger; so **~ISM** (1) *n.* [f. ALARM[1] + -IST]
alar̂′um *n.* Var. of ALARM[1]; **~s and excursions,** (joc., f. old stage-direction) confused noise and bustle.
ală′s (*or* -ah′s) *int.* expr. grief, pity, concern. [ME, f. OF *a las(se)* (*a* ah, *las(se)* f. L *lassus* weary)]
Alas. *abbr.* Alaska.
Ală′ska (*a-*) *n.* **Baked ~,** sponge-cake and ice cream in meringue covering. [name of northernmost state of U.S.]
Ala′stor (alah′s-) *n.* Avenging deity, nemesis. [f. Gk *alastōr* (*a-* not, *last-* f. *lath-* forget)]
ā′lāte *a.* Having wings or winglike appendages. [f. L *alatus* (*ala* wing; see-ATE[2])]
ălb *n.* White vestment reaching to feet, worn by Christian priests etc. [OE *albe* f. eccl. L *alba* fem. (as n.) of L *albus* white]
ă′lbacor̂e *n.* **1.** Large W. Ind. species of tunny. **2.** One of various other related fish. [f. Port. *albacor, -cora,* f. Arab. *al* the + *bakr* young camel or *bakūr* premature, precocious]
Albā′nĭan (ăl-) *a.* & *n.* (Native, inhabitant, or language) of Albania. [f. *Albania* in S.E. Europe + -AN]
albā′ta *n.* White metal, German silver. [f. L *albata* whitened (*albus* white)]
ă′lbatrŏss *n.* One of a family of long-winged birds allied to petrels, inhabiting Pacific and Southern Oceans; ‖(Golf) hole played in three strokes under par or bogey. [alt. (after L *albus* white) of 17th-c. *alcatras*, applied to various sea-birds, f. Sp. and Port. *alcatraz*, var. of Port. *alcatruz* f. Arab. *alḳādūs* the pitcher (*al* the, *ḳādūs* f. Gk *kados* jar)]
ălbē′dō *n.* (*pl.* **~s**). Fraction of incident radiation reflected by a surface. [eccl. L, = whiteness, f. L *albus* white]
albē′ĭt (awl-) *conj.* (literary). Though (*he tried, albeit without success*). [f. ALL + BE + IT[1], = all though it be that]
ă′lbert *n.* Watch-chain with crossbar. [f. Prince *Albert*, consort of Queen Victoria, d. 1861]
ălbĕ′scent *a.* Growing white; shading into white. [f. L *albescere* (*albus* white); see -ESCENT]
Albĭgĕ′ns|ēs (ăl-; -z) *n. pl.* Members of Manichaean sect in S. France in 11th–13th c.; hence **~IAN** *a.* [L, f. *Albi* in S. France]
ălbī′nō (-bē′-) *n.* (*pl.* **~s**). Person or animal having congenital absence of colouring pigment in skin and hair, which are white, and eyes, which are usu. pink and unduly sensitive to light; plant lacking normal colouring; hence **ă′lbĭnISM** (5) *n.*, **ălbĭnŏ′tIC** *a.* [Sp. & Port., orig. of white Negroes, f. *albo* (L *albus*) white + *-ino* (-INE[1])]
A′lbĭon (ă′l-) *n.* (poet. or rhet.) (Orig. Greek and Roman name for) Britain; **perfidious ~**, England (f. F *la perfide Albion* w. ref. to her alleged treachery to other nations). [OE f. L, f. Celt. **Albio*]
ă′lbīte *n.* White or soda felspar. [f. L *albus* white + -ITE[1]]
ă′lbum *n.* **1.** Blank book for insertion of autographs, stamps, photographs, etc. **2.** Holder for set of gramophone records; set of records; one record comprising several pieces of music etc. [L, = blank tablet, neut. of *albus* white]
ă′lbūmėn *n.* White of egg; (Bot.) endosperm, substance found between skin and germ of many seeds, usu. the eatable part. [L *albumen -minis* white of egg (*albus* white)]
ă′lbūmĭn *n.* Any of a class of water-soluble proteins found in egg-white, milk, blood, etc.; hence **ălbū′mĭnOUS** *a.* [f. F *albumine* f. L *albumin-* (see prec.)]
ălbū′mĭnoid *n.* Complex protein forming framework of organs and tissues of animals and plants. [f. ALBUMIN + -OID]
ălbūmĭnūr̂′ĭa *n.* Presence of proteins in the urine, usu. as symptom of kidney disease. [f. ALBUMEN + -URIA]
ălbur̂′num *n.* = SAP[1]*wood.* [L (*albus* white)]
alcahest. Var. of ALKAHEST.
ălcā′ĭc *a.* & *n.* **1.** *a.* Of verse metre in four-line stanza invented by Alcaeus. **2.** *n.* (in *pl.*) Alcaic

verses. [f. LL f. Gk *alkaikos* (*Alkaios* Alcaeus, lyric poet of Mitylene *c.* 600 B.C.; see -IC)]

alca'lde (ahlkah'ldā) *n.* Magistrate or mayor in Spanish, Portuguese, or Latin-Amer. town. [Sp., f. Arab. *al-ḳādī* the judge (see CADI)]

ă'lchem|ў (-k-) *n.* Medieval forerunner of chemistry, esp. pursuit of transmutation of baser metals into gold or silver; (fig.) transformation like those sought in alchemy; hence or cogn. **ălchĕ'mIC(AL)** (-k-) *adjs.*, ~IST (3) *n.*, ~IZE (1) *v.t.* [ME, f. OF *alkemie*, *alkamie* f. med. L *alchimia*, *-emia*, f. Arab. *alkīmiā* (*al* the, *kīmiā* f. Gk *khēmia*, *-meia* art of transmuting metals)]

ălcherĭ'nga (-ngg*a*) *n.* 'Golden age' in mythology of some Australian Aboriginals. [Aboriginal, = dream-time]

ă'lcohŏl *n.* **1.** (**Ethyl**) ~, colourless volatile inflammable liquid, intoxicant present in wine, beer, whisky, etc., also used as solvent, fuel, etc. **2.** Any liquor containing this. **3.** (Chem.) One of large class of compounds of same type as ethyl alcohol. [F or med. L, f. Arab. *alkuḥl* (*al* the, *kuḥl* KOHL)]

ălcohŏ'lĭc *a.* & *n.* **1.** *a.* Of, relating to, containing, caused by, alcohol. **2.** *n.* Person addicted to excessive consumption of alcohol. [f. prec. + -IC]

ă'lcohŏlĭsm *n.* Continual heavy drinking of alcoholic liquor; diseased condition resulting from this. [f. mod. L *alcoholismus* (as ALCOHOL; see -ISM)]

ălcohŏlŏ'|mėter *n.* Instrument for measuring alcoholic strength of spirits; hence ~METRY *n.* [f. ALCOHOL + -O- + -METER]

Alcoran, Alkoran, (ălk*o*rah'n, ă'l-) *n.* (arch.) Koran. [ME f. OF, f. Arab. *al-ḳur'ān* the reading, the recitation (see KORAN)]

ă'lcōve *n.* Vaulted recess in room-wall; recess in garden wall or hedge; (arch.) summer-house. [F, f. Sp. *alcoba* f. Arab. *al-ḳubba* (*al* the, *ḳubba* vault)]

ă'ldėhўde *n.* **1.** Colourless volatile fluid with suffocating smell, obtained by oxidation of alcohol, acetaldehyde. **2.** One of a class of compounds of this type. **3.** Hence **ăldėhў'dIC** *a.* [abbr. of mod. L *alcohol dehydrogenatum* alcohol deprived of hydrogen]

al dente (ăl dĕ'ntĭ) *a.* (Of pasta etc.) cooked so as to be still firm when bitten. [It., lit. 'to the tooth']

a'lder (aw'l-) *n.* Tree of genus *Alnus*, related to birch; one of various other similar trees not related; ~ **buckthorn,** shrub of buckthorn genus. [OE *alor*, *aler*, = MLG *aller*, OHG *elira*, *erila*, ON *ölr*, cogn. w. L *alnus*, w. euphonic *d*]

a'lder|man (aw'l-) *n.* (*pl.* ~**men**). (chiefly Hist.) co-opted member of English county or borough council, next in dignity to Mayor; (U.S. & Austral.) elected governor of city; hence ~**mă'nIC** *a.*, ~**manSHIP** *n.* [f. OE *aldor* patriarch (*ald* old, *-or*, n. suf.) + MAN[1]]

a'ldermanrў (aw'l-) *n.* (Hist.) District having its own alderman; rank of alderman. [ME, f. prec. + -RY]

A'lderney (aw'l-) *a.* & *n.* (Animal) of breed of dairy cattle from *Alderney* or elsewhere in the Channel Islands.

A'ldīne (aw'l-) *a.* Of or by Aldus Manutius, Venetian printer of 16th c., who introduced italic type; name of a type-face. [f. mod. L *Aldinus* (*Aldus*; see -INE[1])]

A'ldĭs (aw'l-) *n.* ~ **lamp,** hand lamp for signalling in Morse code. [f. A.C.W. ~, inventor]

ă'ldrĭn *n.* White crystalline chlorinated hydrocarbon used as insecticide. [f. K. *Alder*, Ger. chemist d. 1958 + -IN]

āle *n.* (arch. exc. as trade wd). Beer; ~'**cost,** costmary; ~'**house,** (Hist.) one at which ale was retailed; *~'**wife,** one of several species of fish allied to herring. [OE *alu*, = ON *öl*]

ālėatŏr'ĭc, ā'lėatorў, *adjs.* Depending on the throw of a die or on chance; (Mus. & Art) involving random choice by performer. [f. L *aleatorius* (*aleator* dice-player f. *alea* die); see -IC, -Y[2]]

alee' *adv.* & *pred. a.* On the lee or sheltered side of ship; to leeward. [ME, f. A[3] + LEE]

ā'lėgar *n.* Sour ale; malt vinegar. [f. ALE, after VINEGAR]

alĕ'mbĭc *n.* Apparatus formerly used in distilling; (fig.) means of transmutation. [ME f. OF, f. med. L *alembicus* f. Arab. *al-'inbīḳ* (*al* the, *'inbīḳ* still f. Gk *ambix -ikos* cup, cap of a still)]

alĕ'mbĭcātėd *a.* (Of literary style) over-refined, as if by distillation; so **alĕmbĭcA'TION** *n.* [f. prec. + -ATE[3] + -ED[1]]

a'lĕph (ah'-) *n.* First letter of Hebrew alphabet. [f. Heb. *'ālep*, prob. f. ALPHA]

alĕr't *a.*, *n.*, & *v.t.* **1.** *a.* Watchful, vigilant; lively, nimble; hence ~LY[2] *adv.*, ~NESS *n.* **2.** *n.* Warning call, alarm; (period of) warning of air raid etc.; **on the** ~, on the look-out against danger or attack. **3.** *v.t.* Make alert, warn. [f. F *alerte* f. It. *all' erta* (*alla* to the, *erta* watch-tower)]

-ā'lēs (-z) *suf.* forming pl. names of orders of plants (*Rosales*). [pl. of L adj. suf. *-alis* (see -AL)]

aleur'on, aleur'ōne, (-lūr'-) *n.* Protein found in seeds of plants etc. [f. Gk *aleuron* flour]

‖A lĕvel (ā'-) *n.* = ADVANCE*d level* (in G.C.E.). [abbr.]

ălėxa'nders (-ĭgzah'nd*e*rz) *n.* Umbelliferous plant, formerly used in salads. [OE, f. med. L *alexandrum*]

Alėxa'ndrĭan (ălĭgzah'-) *a.* Of Alexandria, esp. as chief centre of Hellenistic literature in 3rd and 2nd C. B.C.; (of writer) imitative, or fond of recondite learning. [f. *Alexandria* in Egypt, founded by *Alexander* the Great]

ălėxă'ndrīne (-ĭgz-) *a.* & *n.* ~ (**verse**), iambic line of six feet or twelve syllables. [f. F *alexandrin* f. *Alexandre* Alexander (the Great), subj. of an OF poem in this metre]

alėxă'ndrīte (-ĭgz-) *n.* Green variety of chrysoberyl. [f. Tsar *Alexander* I of Russia + -ITE[1] (2)]

alĕ'xĭn, -īne, *n.* One of a class of proteins found in blood serum and capable of destroying bacteria etc. (also called *complement*). [G, f. Gk *alexō* ward off; see -IN, -INE[5]]

alĕ'xĭphar'mĭc *a.* & *n.* (Having the quality of) an antidote. [earlier *-ac* f. F *alexipharmaque* f. Gk *alexipharmakon* remedy for poison (*alexō* ward off, *pharmakon* poison)]

ă'lfa *n.* N. Afr. esparto grass. [f. Arab. *ḥalfā'*]

ălfă'lfa *n.* Lucerne. [Sp., f. Arab. *al-faṣfaṣa*, a green fodder]

ălfrĕ'scō *adv.* & *a.* In the open air (*lunched alfresco*; *an alfresco lunch*). [f. It. *al fresco* in the fresh (air)]

ă'lg|a *n.* (usu. in *pl.* ~**ae** *pr.* -jē *or* -gē). (Bot.) Primitive cryptogam, e.g. some seaweeds, some plankton, water bloom; hence ~AL, ~OID, ~**olŏ'gĭcAL**, *adjs.*, ~**ĭCIDE** (1), ~**ŏ'LOGIST**, ~**ŏ'LOGY**, *ns.* [L]

ă'lgėbr|a *n.* Branch of mathematics dealing with properties of numbers and quantities by means of letters and other general symbols; system of this based on given axioms; hence ~**ā'IC(AL)** *adjs.*, ~**ā'ĭcalLY**[2] *adv.*, ~(**ā**)IST (3) *ns.* [It., Sp., med. L, f. Arab. *al-jabr* (*al* the, *jabr* reunion of broken parts f. *jabara* reunite)]

-ă'lgia (-j*a*) *suf.* (Med.) denoting pain in a specified part (*neuralgia*); hence **-ă'lgIC** *a.* [Gk (*algos* pain; see -IA[1])]

ă'lgĭcīde. See ALGA.

ă'lgĭd *a.* (esp. Med.) Cold, chilly; hence

ălgĭ'dɪᴛʏ *n.* [f. L *algidus* (*algēre* be cold; see -ɪᴅ¹)]
ălgĭ'nĭc *a.* ~ **acid,** insoluble colloidal acid found as salts in some algae; hence **ă'lgĭnᴀᴛᴇ¹** (3) *n.* [f. ᴀʟɢᴀ + -ɪɴ + -ɪᴄ]
A'lgŏl (ă'-) *n.* Algebraic computer language. [f. ᴀʟɢᴏʀɪᴛʜᴍɪᴄ + ʟ(ᴀɴɢᴜᴀɢᴇ)]
ălgolă'gn|ĭa *n.* Sexual perversion in which pleasure is got from inflicting pain on oneself or others; hence ~ɪᴄ *a.* & *n.* [mod. L, f. G *algolagnie* f. Gk *algos* pain + *lagneia* lust]
ălgŏ'logy̆, etc. See ᴀʟɢᴀ.
Algŏ'nquĭan (*or* -kĭ-), **-nkĭan,** (ăl-) *a.* & *n.* (Member or language) of a large group of N. Amer. Indian tribes. [f. *Algonquin* people + -ɪᴀɴ]
ă'lgorĭsm, ă'lgorĭthm (-dhem), *ns.* **1.** Arabic (decimal) notation of numbers. **2.** Process or rules for (esp. machine) calculation etc.; hence **ălgorĭ'thmɪᴄ** (-dh-) *a.* [ME, f. OF *augori(s)me* f. med. L *algorismus* f. Arabicized Pers. *al-Kuwārizmi* man of Kuwārizm, surname of a 9th-c. mathematician; assim. to -ɪsᴍ and F *algorithme*, Gk *arithmos* number]
ălguazĭ'l (-gw-) *n.* Spanish warrant-officer or sergeant. [Sp., f. Arab. *al-wazīr* (*al-* the; see ᴠɪᴢɪᴇʀ)]
Alhă'mbr|a (ăl-) *n.* Palace of Moorish kings at Granada; hence ~ᴇ'sǫᴜᴇ *a.* [Sp., f. Arab. *al-ḥamrā'* the red (f. name of founder, 1273)]
ā'lĭas *adv.* & *n.* (Name by which one is or has been) called on other occasions. [L, = at another time, otherwise]
ă'lĭbi *n.* & *v.* **1.** *n.* Plea that when an alleged act took place one was elsewhere; (colloq.) excuse of any kind. **2.** *v.i.* & *t.* (colloq.) Offer excuse (for). [L, = elsewhere]
A'lĭce (ă'-) *n.* ~**-in-Wo'nderland,** (attrib.) fantastic, absurd. [heroine of two books by L. Carroll]
ălĭcy̆'clĭc *a.* (Chem.) Combining the structural properties of aliphatic and cyclic compounds. [f. G *alicyclisch* (as ᴀʟɪᴘʜᴀᴛɪᴄ, ᴄʏᴄʟɪᴄ)]
ă'lĭdāde *n.* (Surv. & Astron.) Instrument for determining directions. [F, & ME f. med. L, f. Arab. *al-'iḍāda* the revolving radius (*'aḍud* upper arm)]
ā'lĭen *a.* & *n.* **1.** *a.* Not one's own; foreign, under foreign allegiance (*alien* ᴘʀɪᴏʀʏ); differing in nature (*from, to*); out of harmony; repugnant (*to*). **2.** *n.* Non-naturalized foreigner; a being from another world; (arch.) person excluded (*from*); hence ~ᴀɢᴇ (2) *n.* [ME f. OF, f. L *alienus* belonging to another (*alius*)]
ā'lĭen|āte *v.t.* Estrange; transfer ownership of; turn away, divert, (*from*); hence or cogn. ~ᴀʙʟᴇ *a.*, ~ᴀ'ᴛɪᴏɴ *n.*, (esp., Theatr.) objectivity of spectator's reaction, sought by some dramatists, ~**āt**ᴏʀ *n.* [ME, f. L *alienare* (as prec.) + -ᴀᴛᴇ³]
ā'lĭen|ĭsm *n.* (arch.) Study and treatment of mental diseases, psychiatry; hence ~ɪsᴛ (3) *n.* (esp. *legal adviser on psychiatric problems). [f. ᴀʟɪᴇɴ + -ɪsᴍ]
ā'lĭfŏrm *a.* Wing-shaped. [f. mod. L *aliformis* f. L *ala* wing (see -ꜰᴏʀᴍ)]
alĭ'ght¹ (-ī't) *v.i.* Dismount (*from* horse); descend (*from* vehicle); settle, come to earth, from the air. [OE *ālīhtan* (ᴀ- 1, *līhtan* ʟɪɢʜᴛ⁵)]
alĭ'ght² (-ī't) *pred. a.* On fire; lighted up. [ME, prob. f. phr. *on a light* (= lighted) *fire*]
alĭ'gn (-ī'n), **alĭ'ne,** *v.t.* Place or lay in a line; bring into line, (esp.) bring three or more points into a straight line; (Polit. etc.) place in relation of agreement or alliance with others; hence ~ᴍᴇɴᴛ (-ī'nm-) *n.* [f. F *aligner* f. phr. *à ligne* into ʟɪɴᴇ²]
alĭ'ke *adv.* & *pred. a.* **1.** *adv.* In like manner. **2.** *a.* Similar, like; indistinguishable. [ME, f. OE *gelīc* and ON *glíkr* (ʟɪᴋᴇ¹)]
ă'lĭment *n.* Food; (fig.) support, mental sustenance; hence **ălĭmĕ'ntᴀʟ** *a.* [ME f. F, or f. L *alimentum* (*alere* nourish; see -ᴍᴇɴᴛ)]
ălĭmĕ'ntary̆ *a.* Nourishing; performing functions of nutrition; providing maintenance; ~ **canal** (transmitting food through animal body from mouth to anus). [f. L *alimentarius* (as prec.; see -ᴀʀʏ¹)]
ălĭmentā'tion *n.* Nourishment; maintenance. [F, or f. med. L *alimentatio* (*alimentare*, as ᴀʟɪᴍᴇɴᴛ; see -ᴀᴛɪᴏɴ)]
ă'lĭmony̆ *n.* **1.** (arch.) Maintenance. **2.** Allowance due to woman from (ex-)husband after divorce or legal separation, or during proceedings for these. [f. L *alimonia* nutriment (*alere* nourish])
alĭ'ne etc. See ᴀʟɪɢɴ.
A'-līne (ā'-) *a.* (Of garment) having narrow waist or shoulders and somewhat flared skirt. [f. A + ʟɪɴᴇ² 14]
ălĭphă'tĭc *a.* (Chem.) Related to fats; of organic compounds in which carbon atoms form open chains, not rings. [f. Gk *aleiphar -atos* fat + -ɪᴄ]
ă'lĭquŏt *a.* & *n.* ~ **(part),** part contained by the whole an integral number of times, integral factor; (loosely) any known fraction of a whole. [f. F *aliquote* f. L *aliquot* some, so many]
-ă'lĭty̆ *suf.* forming *ns.*, w. senses as -ɪᴛʏ (*banality, generality*). [f. -ᴀʟ + -ɪᴛʏ]
alĭ've *adv.* & (usu. *pred.*) *a.* **1.** Living; **any man** ~ (whatever); **man** ~**!** (colloq. expletive); **keep the matter** ~ (still under discussion); **microphone is** ~ (switched on and working); **wire is** ~ (electrically charged). **2.** Fully responsive *to* (an idea etc.). **3.** ~ **(and kicking),** active, brisk; **look** ~, (colloq.) be brisk. **4.** Swarming *with* (*river alive with boats*). **5.** Hence ~ɴᴇss (-vn-) *n.* [OE *on life* (as ᴀ³, ʟɪꜰᴇ)]
alĭ'zarĭn *n.* Red colouring matter of madder; (*attrib.*, of a dye) derived from or similar in action to this pigment. [f. F *alizarine* (*alizari* madder f. Arab. *al-'iṣara* pressed juice f. *'aṣara* to press fruit); see -ɪɴ]
ă'lkahĕst (-a-h-) *n.* Universal solvent sought by alchemists (lit. or fig.). [sham Arab., prob. invented by Paracelsus]
ă'lkal|ī *n.* (*pl.* ~**is** *or* ~**ies**). One of a class of substances that neutralize and are neutralized by acids, and form caustic or corrosive solutions in water, including caustic soda, caustic potash, and ammonia; other substance with similar but weaker properties, e.g. sodium carbonate; ~**i metals,** those whose hydroxides are alkalis, members of the sodium group; hence ~ɪꜰʏ *v.t.*, **ălkalĭ'ᴍᴇᴛᴇʀ, ălkalĭ'ᴍᴇᴛʀʏ,** *ns.*, ~ɪɴᴇ¹ *a.* (~**ine earth,** oxide of the lime group). [ME f. med. L, f. Arab. *al-ḳali* calcined ashes (*ḳala* fry)]
ă'lkaloid *n.* One of a large group of nitrogenous bases of vegetable origin, many used as drugs, e.g. morphine, quinine, strychnine. [f. G (as prec.; see -ᴏɪᴅ)]
ălkalō's|ĭs *n.* (*pl.* ~**es** *pr.* -ēz). (Path.) Over-alkaline condition of blood or body tissues. [f. ᴀʟᴋᴀʟɪ + -ᴏsɪs]
ă'lkanĕt *n.* (Plant, *Alkanna tinctoria*, whose root yields) a red dye. [ME, f. Sp. *alcaneta* dim. of *alcana* f. Arab. *al-ḥinnā'* the henna shrub]
Alkoran. See Aʟᴄᴏʀᴀɴ.
ă'lky̆d *n.* Any of a group of synthetic resins derived from various alcohols and acids. [f. ᴀʟᴋʏʟ + ᴀᴄɪᴅ²]
ă'lky̆l *a.* Derived from or related to a paraffin hydrocarbon. [f. G *alkohol* ᴀʟᴄᴏʜᴏʟ + -ʏʟ]
all (awl) *a., n.,* & *adv.* **1.** *a.* Whole amount, quantity, or extent of (*all day; all England; all his life; and all* ᴛʜᴀᴛ¹; *take it all*); ~ **hail,** *int.* of greeting (*to*) [*hail* = health]; **get away from it** ~ (from everyday tasks and worries); *stop* ~ **this** (this excessive) *grumbling*; *all the* ᴛɪᴍᴇ¹ 9;

all the WAY 3. **2.** Greatest possible (*with all speed*). **3.** (w. *pl.*) Entire number of (*all men*; *all ten men*; *his children are all boys*; *admirals all*; *all the others*); **All Fools' Day,** 1 Apr.; *all* FOURS; *All* HALLOW[1]*s*; *all* HAND[1]*s*; ~ **kind**(s) **of,** ~ **manner of,** many different kinds of; **All Saints' Day,** 1 Nov.; **All Souls' Day,** 2 Nov. **4.** Any whatever (*beyond all doubt*; *disclaim all knowledge of*). **5.** *n.* All persons concerned (*all were agreed*); *all* SUCH 11; **one and** ~, ~ **and sundry,** all individually and collectively. **6.** (In games) for both sides (*score was two goals all*); LOVE[1] *all.* **7.** ~ **of,** the whole of (*take all of it*), every one of (*all of us*), (colloq.) as much as (*all of seven feet tall*; *walked all of two miles*), (colloq.) affected by (*was all of a dither*). **8.** Everything (*that is all*; *all is lost*); one's whole property (*he lost his all*); ~ **but** *adv.*, everything short of (*all but impossible*; *he was all but drowned*); ~ **in** ~, (1) taken as a whole, (2) of supreme importance; ~ **one,** a matter of indifference (*it is all one to me*); *all* UP; ~ **very fine** or **very well,** (colloq. phr. expr. dissatisfaction, or rejection of consolation etc.); **and** ~ (the rest); **at** ~, (usu. w. neg. or interrog.) in any way or to any extent (*not at all*; *did you see him at all?*; *occurs very rarely if at all*); **in** ~, in total number. **9.** *adv.* Entirely, quite, (*dressed all in white*; *all covered with mud*; *all round the room*; *all the better*; *was all smiles*; *all at once*; *all too soon*; *an all--powerful dictator*; *the all-important thing*); (colloq.) very (*went all high-falutin*); ~ **for,** (colloq.) strongly in favour of (*am all for fair play*); **what** thing **is** ~ **about,** its essential nature; *all* ALONG; **All Blacks,** (colloq.) New Zealand international Rugby Union football team; ~ **in,** exhausted; ~ **out,** involving all one's strength or resources; *going* ~ **out** (at full speed); *all* OVER 8, 10, 13; ~ **right,** (*adv.*) as desired, satisfactorily, certainly (*that's the man all right*), (*int.*) I assent to your order or proposal, (*pred. a.*) safe and sound, in good condition, satisfactory, acceptable (*a* BIT[2] *of all right*); ~ **round,** (1) in all respects, (2) for each person present etc.; *all* SET[3]; *all* SQUARE[2]; (*not*) *all* THAT[1] 3; ~ **there,** (colloq.) not deficient in intellect etc.; ~ **the same,** (*adv.*) in spite of this, notwithstanding (*he was punished all the same,* in spite of extenuating circumstances etc.), (*pred. a.*) just the same, making no difference (*if it's all the same to you,* if you don't mind). **10.** **~-American,** representing whole of, or only, America or U.S.; ***~-around,** = *all-round*; **~-clear',** signal that danger or difficulty is over; **~-ele'ctric,** using only electricity for heating and lighting; ***~-fired,** (sl.) extreme(ly), excessive(ly); **~-in,** inclusive of all; **~-in wrestling** (with few or no restrictions); **~-o'verish,** (colloq.) indisposed all over the body; **~-purpose,** suitable for several uses; **~-red,** (Hist.) entirely on British territory (usu. coloured red in maps); **~-round,** having ability in many departments; **~-rou'nder,** one able to perform several tasks (esp. ||in sports); **~-sorts,** miscellany, esp. of liquorice sweets; **~-time,** (of record) hitherto unsurpassed; **~-up,** total (weight of aircraft) incl. crew, passengers, cargo, etc., when in air. [OE *all, eall,* = OS, OHG *al,* ON *allr,* Goth. *alls,* prob. f. Gmc **alnaz*]

ălla bre've (brā'vā). See BREVE.

ălla cappĕ'lla. Var. of A CAPPELLA.

A'llah (ă'la) *n.* Muslim name of God. [f. Arab. '*allāh* contr. of *al-'ilāh* (*al* the, *ilāh* god)]

allă'ntō|ĭs *n.* (*pl.* **~ides** *pr.* -ĭdēz). (Zool.) Foetal membrane in mammal, bird, or reptile. [mod. L, f. Gk *allantoeidēs* sausage-shaped]

allay' *v.t.* Alleviate (pain, hunger, etc.); diminish (fears, pleasure, etc.). [OE *ālecgan* (as A- 1, LAY[3])]

ăllėgā'tion *n.* Alleging; (esp. unproved) assertion. [ME f. F, or f. L *allegatio* (*allegare* allege; see -ATION)]

allĕ'g|e *v.t.* Affirm, esp. without proof, (thing, *that*); advance as argument or excuse; hence ~ED[1] (-ĕ'jd) *a.*, **~ėd**LY[2] *adv.*, (used in statements for which author disclaims responsibility). [ME, f. AF *alegier,* OF *esligier* f. Rom. *EX[1]*litigare* clear at law; confused in sense w. L *allegare* (see prec.)]

allē'giance (-jans) *n.* Duty of subject to sovereign or government; loyalty (lit. or fig.). [ME, f. AF **alligeance* f. OF *ligeance* (as LIEGE; see -ANCE); perh. assoc. w. ALLIANCE]

ă'llėgor|ў *n.* Narrative description of a subject under guise of another having similarities to it, e.g. Bunyan's *Pilgrim's Progress* describing life as journey; picture in which meaning is symbolically represented; emblem; hence or cogn. **ăllėgŏ'**RIC(AL) *adjs.*, ~IST (1) *n.*, ~IZE (1) *v.t.* [ME f. OF *allegorie* f. L f. Gk *allēgoria* (*allos* other, *-agoria* speaking)]

ăllėgrĕ'ttō *adv.*, *a.*, & *n.* (*pl.* **~s**). (Mus.) (Movement) in fairly brisk time. [It., dim. of ALLEGRO]

ălle'grō (-lā'-) *adv.*, *a.*, & *n.* (*pl.* **~s**). (Mus.) (Movement) in brisk time. [It., = lively, gay]

ă'llēle, ă'llĕl, allē'lomōrph, *ns.* (Gene determining) one of two alternative Mendelian characters. [(*allele* f. G *allel* abbr. of) *allelomorph* f. Gk *allēl-* one another + -o- + *morphē* form]

ăllėlu'ia, -u'ya, hăllėlu'jah, (-lōō'ya) *n.* (Song of) praise to God; (R.C. Ch.) part of mass including this. [ME f. eccl. L f. (Septuagint) Gk *allēlouia* f. Heb. *hallᵉlûyāh* praise ye the Lord]

ă'llemande (ă'lmahnd) *n.* Name of several German dances; music for one of these, e.g. as suite movement; country-dance figure. [F, = German (dance)]

ă'llergėn *n.* Substance that causes allergic reaction; hence **ăllergĕ'n**IC *a.* [f. ALLERGY + -GEN (1)]

ă'llergў *n.* (Med.) Unusual sensitiveness to the action of particular foods, pollens, insect-bites, etc.; (colloq.) antipathy; hence **allêr'g**IC *a.*, relating to or characterized by allergy, (colloq.) sensitive (esp. antipathetic) *to.* [f. G *allergie,* after *energie* ENERGY, f. Gk *allos* other]

allē'vĭ|āte *v.t.* Lessen; make less burdensome or severe; hence ~A'TION, **~ā**TOR, *ns.*, **~ā**TIVE, **~ā**TORY, *adjs.* [f. LL *alleviare* lighten f. L AL(*levare* raise) + -ATE[3]]

ă'lley[1] *n.* Walk or passage, esp. in park or garden; ~(**-way**), narrow street or passage (**up** one's ~, = *up* one's STREET); enclosure for skittles, bowling, etc.; side strip added to tennis singles court when doubles are played. [ME, f. OF *alee* walking, passage (*aler* go f. L *ambulare* walk)]

ă'lley[2]. See ALLY[3].

||**Alley'nĭan** (alā'n-) *a.* & *n.* (Past or present member) of Dulwich College. [f. E. *Alleyn,* founder of the college d. 1626 + -IAN]

ăllĭā'ceous (-shus) *a.* Of the genus ALLIUM; smelling or tasting of garlic etc. [f. mod. L *alliaceus* f. L *allium* garlic; see -ACEOUS]

allī'ance *n.* Union by marriage; kinship; (esp. of countries) joining in pursuit of common interests; league, association; community in nature or qualities; (Biol.) group of allied families. [ME, f. OF *aliance* (as ALLY[1]; see -ANCE)]

ă'llīed (-īd) *a.* See ALLY[1].

ă'llĭgātor *n.* Amer. saurian reptile of genus *Alligator*; other large American or Chinese saurian; skin of such an animal; ~ **clip** (with teeth for gripping); ~ **pear,** avocado; ~ **tortoise,** snapping turtle. [f. Sp. *el lagarto* the lizard f. L *lacerta*]

allĭ'terāt|e *v.i.* (Use words that) begin with same letter or sound; hence ~IVE *a.* [back form. f. foll.; see -ATE[3]]

allĭterā'tion *n.* Commencement of adjacent or closely connected words with same letter or sound (*cool, calm, and collected*; *sing a song of sixpence*). [f. mod. L AL(*literatio* f. *littera* letter; see -ATION)]

ă'llĭum *n.* Plant of genus *Allium*, incl. garlic, onions, leeks, and various garden flowers. [L, = garlic]

ăllo- *comb. form.* Other (*allogamy, allopathy*). [f. Gk *allos* other]

ă'lloc|āte *v.t.* Assign, devote, (*to* person or purpose); assign to a place; hence or cogn. ~ABLE *a.*, ~A'TION *n.* [f. med. L *allocare* (*locus* place) + -ATE[3]]

ăllocū'tion *n.* Formal or hortatory address. [f. L *allocutio* f. AL(*loqui locut-* speak; see -ION)]

al(l)ō'dĭ|um *n.* (Hist.) Estate held in absolute ownership, without acknowledgement to a superior; so ~AL *a.* [f. med. L f. Frank. **allōd-* entire property (as ALL, *ōd* estate)]

ăllŏ'gamȳ *n.* (Bot.) Cross-fertilization. [f. ALLO- + Gk *-gamia* f. *gamos* marriage]

ă'llomôrph *n.* One of two or more alternative forms of a morpheme; hence **ăllomôr'ph**IC *a.* [f. ALLO- + MORPHEME]

ă'llopăth *n.* One who practises allopathy. [f. F *allopathe* back form. f. *allopathie* = foll.]

ăllŏ'path|ȳ *n.* Treatment of disease by usual means, i.e. by inducing an opposite condition (opp. *homoeopathy*); hence **ăllopă'th**IC *a.*, ~IST (3) *n.* [f. G *allopathie* (as ALLO-, -PATHY)]

ă'llophōne *n.* One of the variant sounds forming a phoneme; hence **ăllophŏ'n**IC *a.* [f. ALLO- + PHONEME]

allŏ't *v.t.* (-tt-). Distribute by lot or with authority; apportion (*to*). [f. OF *aloter* f. (*a* to, LOT)]

allŏ'tment *n.* Apportioning; share allotted to one; one's lot in life; ||small portion of usu. public land let out for cultivation. [f. prec. + -MENT]

ă'llotrōpe *n.* One form of a substance which exhibits allotropy. [back form. f. foll.]

ăllŏ'tropȳ *n.* Existence of several forms of a chemical element in same state (gas, liquid, solid) but with different physical or chemical properties; hence **ăllotrŏ'p**IC(AL) *adjs.* [f. Gk *allotropos* of another form (*allos* different, *tropos* manner f. *trepō* turn)]

ăllŏttee' *n.* One to whom allotment is made. [f. ALLOT + -EE]

allow' *v.* **1.** *v.t.* Admit (thing *to be, that*); permit (practice, person *to* do); indulge one*self* in (conduct); *consider, assert, (*that*); give (limited quantity or sum; *allow him £200 a year*); add or deduct in consideration of something; hence ~ABLE *a.* **2.** *v.i.* Admit *of*; ~ **for,** take into consideration, make addition or deduction corresponding to. [ME, orig. = 'praise', f. OF *alouer* f. L AL*laudare* praise & med. L AL*locare* place]

allow'ance[1] *n.* Tolerance (*of*); limited quantity or sum esp. of money or food; money paid to cover special expenses (*entertainment, family, allowance*); deduction, discount; **make** ~(s) **for,** allow for (esp. mitigating circumstances). [ME, f. OF *alouance* (as prec.; see -ANCE)]

allow'ance[2] *v.t.* Make allowance to (person); supply in limited quantities. [f. prec.]

ă'lloy[1] (*or* aloi') *n.* Mixture composed wholly or mainly of metals; inferior metal mixed esp. with gold or silver (lit. or fig.). [f. F *aloi* f. OF *aloier, aleier* combine f. L AL*ligare* bind]

ă'lloy[2] (*or* aloi') *v.t.* Mix (metals); debase by admixture; moderate. [f. F *aloyer* (*aloi*; see prec.)]

a'llseed (aw'l-) *n.* Any of various plants producing much seed. [f. ALL + SEED]

a'llspīce (aw'l-) *n.* Pimento, dried ground berry of *Pimenta officinalis*, supposed to combine flavour of cinnamon, nutmeg, and cloves; plant yielding this; one of various other aromatic shrubs. [f. ALL + SPICE]

allū'de (*or* -ōō'd) *v.i.* Refer covertly, transiently, or indirectly, *to* (something assumed known); refer in any manner *to*. [f. L AL(*ludere lus-* play)]

allūr'e *v.t.*, & *n.* **1.** *v.t.* Tempt, entice, win over, (*to, from*, person, place, conduct); fascinate, charm; hence ~MENT (-ūr'm-) *n.* **2.** *n.* Personal charm, attractiveness. [ME, f. OF *alurer* attract (*a* AD-, *luere* LURE[1] 1)]

allū'sion (-zhon; *or* -lōō'-) *n.* Covert, passing, or indirect reference (*to*); any reference *to*. [F, or f. LL *allusio* (as ALLUDE; see -ION)]

allū'sĭve (*or* -lōō'-) *a.* Containing an allusion (*to*); abounding in allusions; hence ~LY[2] (-vlĭ) *adv.*, ~NESS (-vn-) *n.* [as prec.; see -IVE]

allū'vĭal (*or* -ōō'-) *a.* & *n.* **1.** *a.* Pertaining to alluvium. **2.** *n.* Alluvial (esp. gold-bearing) deposit. [f. ALLUVIUM + -AL]

allū'vĭon (*or* -ōō'-) *n.* Wash of sea or river against shore or banks; flood; matter deposited by flood, esp. alluvium; (Law) formation of new land by water's action. [F, f. L AL*luvio -onis* (*luere* wash)]

allū'vĭ|um (*or* -ōō'-) *n.* (*pl.* **~a** *or* **~ums**). Deposit of earth, sand, etc., left by flood, esp. in river valley or delta. [L, neut. of AL*luvius* a. (*luere* wash)]

allȳ'[1] (*or* ă'lī) *v.t.* (*attrib. p.p.* usu. *pr.* ă'līd). Combine or unite for special purpose *to* or *with* (esp. of marriage and alliance with foreign States); (in *p.p.*) pertaining to allied forces or States, esp. to Britain and her allies in wars of 1914–18 and 1939–45; **allied to,** (of thing) related to, connected with. [ME, f. OF *al(e)ier* f. L AL*ligare* bind; cf. ALLOY[1]]

ă'llȳ[2] *n.* Person, State, etc., allied with another. [f. prec.]

ă'llȳ[3], **ă'lley**[2], *n.* Choice playing-marble of marble, alabaster, or glass. [perh. dim. of ALABASTER]

-allȳ *suf.* forming *advs.* f. *adjs.* in -AL; cf. -LY[2].

ă'llȳl *n.* (Chem.) Unsaturated univalent radical, C_3H_5. [f. L *allium* garlic + -YL]

ălmacă'ntar. See ALMUCANTAR.

Alma Mā'ter (ă-; *or* -mah'-) *n.* Title used of universities and schools by their past and present pupils. [L, = bounteous mother]

a'lmanăc, (rare) **-ăck,** (aw'l- *or* ŏ'l-) *n.* Annual calendar of months and days, usu. with astronomical data and other information. [ME, f. med. L *almanac(h)* f. Gk *almenikhiaka*]

ă'lmandīne *n.* Violet-tinted garnet. [F, alt. of obs. *alabandine* f. med. L *alabandina* (*Alabanda*, ancient city in Asia Minor)]

almī'ghtȳ (awlmī'tĭ) *a.* & *adv.* **1.** *a.* All-powerful (esp. *Almighty God*; **the A~,** God); (sl.) very great. **2.** *adv.* (sl.) Exceedingly. [OE *ælmihtig* (as ALL 9, MIGHTY)]

almīr'ah (-*a*) *n.* (Ind.) Wardrobe, movable cupboard. [f. Urdu *almari* f. Port. *almario* f. L *armarium* closet, chest]

a'lmond (ah'm-) *n.* Kernel of stone-fruit borne by two trees (**sweet, bitter,** ~), varieties of *Amygdalus communis*, allied to plum and peach; either tree; ~ **eyes** (apparently almond-shaped). [ME, f. OF *alemande* etc. f. med. L *amandula* f. L *amygdala* f. Gk *amugdalē*; assoc. w. wds in AL-]

ă'lmon|er (*or* ah'm-) *n.* Official distributor of alms, whence ~RY (3) *n.*; ||social worker attached to hospital, seeing to after-care of patients. [ME f. AF *aumoner*, OF *aumonier* f. Rom. **almosinarius* f. med. L *eleēmosynarius* (as ALMS; see -ARY[1])]

a'lmōst (aw'l-) *adv.* All but; as the nearest thing to. [f. ALL + MOST 2]

alms (ahmz) *n.* (usu. as *sing.*) Charitable relief

of the poor; charitable donation; **~'folk, ~'man,** person(s) supported by alms; **~'house,** one founded by charity for reception of poor. [OE *ælmysse, -messe,* f. Gmc **alemos(i)na* f. Rom. **alimosina,* alt. after *alimonia* (see ALIMONY) f. LL f. Gk *eleēmosunē* compassionateness (*eleēmōn* a. f. *eleos* compassion)]

ălmucă'ntar, -mac-, *n.* Line of constant altitude above the horizon. [ME, f. med. L *almucantarath* or F *almucantara* etc., f. Arab. *almuḳanṭarāt* sundial (*ḳanṭara* bridge)]

alō'dĭum. See ALLODIUM.

ă'lōe *n.* Plant of genus *Aloe,* with erect spikes of flowers, and leaves yielding bitter juice; (in *pl.*) purgative drug procured from juice of aloes; one of various other plants, e.g. agave. [OE *al(e)we* f. L f. Gk *aloē*]

ălōĕ'tĭc *a.* & *n.* (Medicine) containing aloes. [f. Gk *aloē* aloe, on false anal. of *diuretic* etc.]

alŏ'ft (*or* -aw'-) *adv.* & *pred. a.* High up (lit., esp. Naut., or fig.); upward. [ME, f. ON *á lopt(i)* (*á* in, on, to, *lopt* air); cf. LIFT, LOFT]

ālŏ'gĭcal *a.* Non-logical; opposed to logic. [f. A- 7 + LOGICAL]

alō'ha *int.* (used in Hawaii at greeting or parting); ***A~ State,** Hawaii. [Hawaiian, = love]

alō'ne *pred. a.,* & *adv.* **1.** *a.* Not with others (*this fact alone would discredit him*); **go it ~,** act by oneself without assistance; LEAVE[2] *alone*; LET[2] *alone.* **2.** Standing by oneself (*in* opinion etc.). **3.** *adv.* Only, exclusively, (*you alone can help me*). [ME, f. ALL + ONE]

alŏ'ng *adv.* & *prep.* **1.** From end to end (of); through any part of the length (of). **2.** *adv.* Onward (GET[1] *along*); in(to) more advanced state (*coming along nicely*); in company or conjunction (*with*) (GO[1] *along with*); with a person (*take a torch along*; *I'll be along in ten minutes*); **all ~,** all the time; **~shore,** by the shore, along and on the shore; **~side,** close to side of ship, pier, etc.; **~si'de of,** side by side with (lit. or fig.). [OE *andlang* f. WG **and-* opposite + **lang-* extended, LONG[1]]

alōō'f *adv.* & *a.* **1.** *adv.* Away, apart, (lit. or fig.; *stand, keep, hold, aloof*). **2.** *a.* Distant, unsympathetic; hence **~**LY[2] *adv.,* **~**NESS *n.* [f. A[3] + LUFF]

ălōpē'cĭa *n.* (Med.) Baldness, complete or partial. [L, f. Gk *alōpekia* fox-mange (*alōpēx* fox; see -IA[1])]

alou'd *adv.* Audibly, not silently or in a whisper (THINK *aloud*); (arch.) loudly. [f. A[3] + LOUD]

alow' (-ō') *adv.* (Naut.) In or into lower part of vessel. [f. A[3] + LOW[1] 2]

ălp *n.* Mountain-peak, esp. (in *pl., Alps*) those in Switzerland and adjacent countries; (in Switzerland) green pasture-land on mountain-side. [orig. pl., f. F f. L *Alpes* f. Gk *Alpeis*]

ălpă'ca *n.* Kind of llama with long woolly hair; its wool; fabric made from the wool, with or without other fibres. [Sp., f. Quechua *alpako* (*pako* reddish-brown)]

ălpar̂ga'ta (-gah'-) *n.* Light canvas shoe with plaited fibre sole, espadrille. [Sp.]

ă'lpenhor̂n *n.* Long wooden horn used by Alpine herdsmen. [G, = Alp-horn]

ă'lpenstŏck *n.* Long iron-tipped staff used in mountain-climbing. [G, = Alp-stick]

ă'lpha *n.* First Greek letter (A, α) = a (**A~ and Omega,** beginning and end); first-class mark in examination (**~ plus,** superlatively good); (Astron.) chief star in a constellation; **~ particles, ~ rays,** helium nuclei emitted by radioactive substances (orig. regarded as rays). [ME f. L f. Gk]

ă'lphabĕt *n.* Set of letters used in a language (*Russian alphabet*) or symbols or signs for them (*Morse, deaf-and-dumb, alphabet*); **phonetic ~** (used to represent sounds of speech); hence **ălphabĕ'tɪc**(AL) *adjs.* (esp. of order of letters or words), **~**IZE (3) *v.t.* [f. LL *alphabetum* f. Gk *alpha, bēta,* first two letters of alphabet]

ălphamĕ'rĭc, ălphanūmĕ'rĭc(al), *adjs.* Containing both alphabetic and numerical symbols. [f. ALPHABETIC + NUMERICAL]

A'lpīne (ă'-) *a.* & *n.* **1.** *a.* Of the Alps or any lofty mountains. **2.** *n.* Plant native or suited to mountain districts. [f. L *Alpinus* (*Alpes*; see ALP, -INE[1])]

A'lpĭn|ĭst (ă'-) *n.* Alpine climber; so **~**ISM (2) *n.* [f. F *alpiniste* (as prec.; see -IST)]

alrea'dy̆ (awlrĕ'dĭ) *adv.* Before this or that time; as early as this. [f. ALL 9 + READY]

A.L.S. *abbr.* autograph letter signed.

Alsă'ce (ă-) *n.* Dry white wine. [~ in E. France]

Alsā'tia (ălsā'sha) *n.* (Hist.) Precinct of White Friars in London as sanctuary for debtors and criminals. [med. L, = prec., as being a much disputed territory]

‖**Alsā'tian** (ălsā'shan) *n.* Breed of wolfhound, German shepherd dog. [f. *Alsatia* (= ALSACE) + -AN]

ă'lsīke *n.* Species of clover (*Trifolium hybridum*). [f. *A~* in Sweden]

a'lsō (aw'l-) *adv.* In addition, besides; **~-ran** *n.,* horse or dog not placed in first three in race, (fig.) person(s) who failed to win distinction. [OE *alswā* (as ALL 9, SO[1])]

ălt *n.* (Mus.) High note; **in ~,** in octave beginning with G above treble staff, (fig.) in exalted mood. [f. It. *alto* ALTO f. L *altus* high]

Alta. *abbr.* Alberta.

a'ltar (aw'l- *or* ŏ'l-) *n.* Flat-topped block for offerings to deity; Communion table; **lead to the ~,** marry (woman); **~-piece,** reredos, esp. a painting. [OE *altar, -er,* Gmc f. LL *altar(e), -ium* f. L *altus* high]

ăltă'zĭmuth *n.* Instrument for determining altitude and azimuth of heavenly bodies. [f. ALTITUDE + AZIMUTH]

a'lter (aw'l- *or* ŏ'l-) *v.t.* & *i.* Change in characteristics, position, etc.; *castrate or spay; so **~**ABLE *a.,* **~**A'TION *n.* [ME, f. OF *alterer* f. LL *alterare* f. L *alter* other]

a'lteratĭve (aw'l- *or* ŏ'l-) *a.* & *n.* **1.** *a.* Tending to alter. **2.** *a.* & *n.* (Medicine, treatment) that alters bodily processes. [ME, f. med. L *alterativus* (as prec.; see -ATIVE)]

a'lterc|āte (aw'l- *or* ŏ'l-) *v.i.* Dispute hotly, wrangle, (*with*); so **~**A'TION *n.* [f. L *altercari* + -ATE[3]]

alter ego (ălter ĕ'gō) *n.* (*pl.* **~s**). Intimate friend. [L, = other self]

alter̂'n|ant (awl- *or* ŏl-) *a.* Alternating; hence **~**ANCE *n.* [f. L *alternare*; see foll., -ANT]

alter̂'nate[1] (awl- *or* ŏl-) *a.* & *n.* **1.** *a.* (Of things of two kinds) coming each after one of the other kind (**~ leaves, angles,** those placed alternately on the two sides of stem, line); alternative; hence **~**LY[2] (-tlĭ) *adv.* **2.** *n.* Deputy; substitute. [f. L *alternatus* p.p. of *alternare* do things by turns (*alternus* every other f. *alter* other); see -ATE[2]]

a'ltern|āte[2] (aw'l- *or* ŏ'l-) *v.* **1.** *v.t.* Arrange, perform, (two sets of things) alternately; interchange (one thing) alternately *with* or *by* another. **2.** *v.i.* (Of two things) succeed each other by turns; (of a whole) consist of alternate things (**~ating current,** electric current reversing its direction at regular intervals); (of one class of things) appear alternately with another. **3.** So **~**A'TION *n.* (**~ation of generations,** reproduction by alternate processes, e.g. sexual and asexual), **~āt**OR *n.,* dynamo giving alternating current. [f. as prec. + -ATE[3]]

alter̂'natĭve (awl- *or* ŏl-) *a.* & *n.* **1.** *a.* (Of two things) mutually exclusive; (of one or more things) available in place of another (**the ~**

society, group of persons dissociating themselves from conventional social practices); hence ~LY[2] (-vlĭ) *adv.* **2.** *n.* Liberty to choose between two or more things; either of two or more possibilities. [f. F *alternatif -ive* or f. med. L *alternativus* (as prec.; see -ATIVE)]

ă'lthōrn (-t-h-) *n.* (Usu. high-pitched) wind instrument of saxhorn family. [G (as ALT, HORN[1])]

althou'gh (awldhō') *conj.* = THOUGH 1, 3. [ME, f. ALL 9 + THOUGH]

ă'ltĭmēter *n.* Instrument for showing height above sea level, esp. aneroid barometer in aircraft. [f. L *altus* high + -I- + -METER]

ă'ltĭtūde *n.* Height (of object, esp. above sea level or horizon); depth; (Geom.) length of perpendicular from vertex to base; (fig.) eminence. [ME, f. L *altitudo* (*altus* high; see -TUDE)]

ă'ltō *n.* (*pl.* ~s). (Mus.) Highest adult male voice, above tenor; female voice of similar range, contralto; singer with alto voice; part written for alto voice; second-highest-pitched member of a group of similar instruments; ~ **clef** (placing middle C on middle line of staff). [It. *alto* (*canto*) high (singing)]

ăltocū'mūl|us (*pl.* ~i *pr.* -ī). (Meteorol.) Clouds like cumulus but at higher level. [mod. L, f. L *altus* high + -o- + CUMULUS]

altogĕ'ther (awl- *or* ŏltogĕ'dh-) *adv.* & *n.* **1.** *adv.* Totally; on the whole. **2.** *n.* (colloq.) **In the** ~, nude. [ME, f. ALL + TOGETHER]

ăltō-rėlie'vō *n.* (*pl.* ~s). (Sculpture in) high RELIEF[2]. [It.]

ăltostrā't|us (*or* -ah'-) *n.* (*pl.* ~i *pr.* -ī). (Meteorol.) Clouds forming continuous layer at medium altitude. [mod. L, f. L *altus* high + -o- + STRATUS]

ăltrĭ'cial (-shal) *a.* (Of bird) whose young have to be fed by parents after hatching. [f. L *altrix altricis* fem. nourisher (*altor* f. *alere altus* nourish; see -TRIX) + -IAL]

ă'ltru|ĭsm (-rōō-) *n.* Regard for others as a principle of action; unselfishness; hence ~IST (2) *n.*, ~**ĭ'stic** *a.*, ~**ĭ'stically** *adv.* [f. F *altruisme* f. It. *altrui* somebody else f. Rom. **alteri huic* to this other; see -ISM]

ă'lum *n.* Double sulphate of aluminium and potassium; one of a series of similar compounds. [ME f. OF, f. L *alumen aluminis*]

alu'mĭna (-lōō'-) *n.* Aluminium oxide. [f. L *alumen* alum, after *soda* etc.]

ălūmĭ'nĭum, *alū'mĭnum, *n.* Silvery light ductile and malleable metallic element, not tarnished by air; ~ **bronze,** alloy of this with copper. [*aluminium* alt. (after *sodium* etc.) f. *aluminum*, earlier *alumium* f. ALUM + -IUM]

alū'mĭnīz|e, -īs|e (-īz), *v.t.* Coat with aluminium; hence ~A'TION *n.* [f. prec. + -IZE]

***alŭ'mn|us** *n.* (*pl.* ~i *pr.* -ī; *fem.* ~a, *pl.* ~ae). (Former) pupil or student (lit. or fig.). [L, = nursling, pupil (*alere* nourish)]

ălvē'olar *a.* Of tooth-socket; (Phonet., of consonant) pronounced with tongue-tip at or near ridge of teeth, e.g. *n, s, t.* [f. foll. + -AR[1]]

ălvē'ol|us *n.* (*pl.* ~i *pr.* -ī). Small cavity; socket of tooth; cell of honeycomb; terminal air-sac of lung; conical chamber of belemnite; so ~ATE[2] *a.* [L, dim. of *alveus* cavity]

a'lways (aw'lwāz *or* -ĭz), (arch.) **a'lway** (aw'-), *adv.* At all times; on all occasions; whatever the circumstances (*I can always sleep on the floor*); repeatedly (*they are always complaining*). [ME, prob. distrib. gen. f. ALL + WAY + 's 1]

ă'lÿssum *n.* One of various cruciferous plants of genus *Alyssum* etc. with usu. yellow or white flowers. [f. L f. Gk *alusson*]

am. See BE.

A.M. *abbr.* ||Albert Medal; amplitude modulation; *Master of Arts [f. L *Artium Magister*]; in the year of the world [f. L *anno mundi*].

a.m. *abbr.* before noon. [f. L *ante meridiem*]

Am *symb.* americium.

A.M.A. *abbr.* American Medical Association; Australian Medical Association.

ămadavă't, ăvadavă't, *n.* Small Indian song-bird. [f. *Ahmadabad* in India]

ă'madou (-ōō) *n.* Tinder from fungi. [F f. mod. Prov., lit. = lover (because quickly afire)]

a'mah (ah'ma) *n.* (China etc.) Nursemaid. [f. Port. *ama* nurse]

amai'n *adv.* (arch. or poet.) Vehemently; in all haste. [f. A[3] + MAIN[2]]

amă'lgam *n.* Mixture of a metal with mercury (*gold amalgam*); plastic mixture of any substances (lit. or fig.). [ME, f. F *amalgame* or f. med. L *amalgama*, prob. f. Gk *malagma* an emollient]

amă'lgam|āte *v.t.* & *i.* Mix; unite (classes, societies, companies, ideas, etc.); (of metals) alloy with mercury; hence ~A'TION *n.*, amalgamating or being amalgamated, merging of two or more business concerns into one. [f. med. L *amalgamare* (as prec.) + -ATE[3]]

amănūĕ'ns|ĭs *n.* (*pl.* ~es *pr.* -sēz). One who writes from dictation or copies manuscript; literary assistant. [L, a. (as n.) f. (*servus*) *a manu* secretary + *-ensis* belonging to]

ă'marănth *n.* Imaginary unfading flower, whence **ămară'nth**INE[1] *a.*; flower of genus *Amaranthus*, e.g. prince's feather and love-lies-bleeding; purple colour. [f. F *amarante* or mod. L *amaranthus* f. L f. Gk *amarantos* everlasting (*a-* not, *marainō* wither), alt. after *polyanthus* etc.]

ămarÿ'llĭs *n.* Bulbous S. Afr. plant of genus *Amaryllis*; one of various related plants. [L f. Gk *Amarullis*, name of a country girl]

amă'ss *v.t.* Heap together; accumulate (esp. riches). [f. F *amasser* or f. med. L *amassare* f. Rom. *AD(*massare* f. L *massa* MASS[2])]

ă'mateur (-tūr *or* -ter) *n.* One who is fond *of* (thing); one who practises a thing (esp. an art or game) only as a pastime, esp. unpaid player etc. (opp. *professional*); hence ~ISH[1] *a.*, having the faults of amateurs' work, unskilful in execution, ~ISM (2) *n.* [F, f. It. *amatore* f. L *amator -oris* lover (*amare* love)]

Ama'ti (ahmah'tē) *n.* Violin or violoncello made by *Amati* family in Cremona *c.* 1550–1700.

ă'matĭve *a.* Disposed to loving. [f. med. L *amativus* f. L *amare* love; see -ATIVE]

ă'matorÿ *a.* Pertaining to a lover or to sexual love. [f. L *amatorius* (*amare* love; see -ORY)]

ămaur|ō'sĭs *n.* (*pl.* ~oses *pr.* -ēz). Partial or total loss of sight from disease of optic nerve; hence ~O'TIC *a.* [mod. L, f. Gk (*amauroō* darken f. *amauros* dim; see -OSIS)]

amā'ze *v.t.*, & *n.* **1.** *v.t.* Overwhelm with wonder; hence ~MENT (-zm-) *n.* **2.** *n.* (arch. or poet.) Amazement. [ME, f. OE *āmasod* p.p. of *āmasian*, of uncert. orig.]

A'mazon (ă'-) *n.* One of a fabulous race of female warriors in Scythia; female warrior (lit. or fig.); tall, strong, or athletic woman; hence **Amazō'n**IAN (ă-) *a.* [ME f. L f. Gk (prob. foreign word, but explained by Greeks as *a-* not + *mazos* breast, from removal of right breast to facilitate use of bow)]

ămbā'gēs (-z) *n. pl.* Indirect or roundabout paths (lit. or fig.). [ME f. OF f. L (*amb-* both ways, *agere* drive)]

ămbă'ssador *n.* Diplomat sent by one sovereign or State on mission to another; diplomat of highest rank permanently representing sovereign or State at foreign court or government (*ambassador-at-*LARGE); official messenger; hence **ămbăssadōr'**IAL *a.* [ME, f. F *ambassadeur* f. It.

ambasciator f. Rom. **ambactiator* (**ambactiare* f. med. L *ambactia* charge, office, f. Gmc **ambahtaz* f. L *ambactus* servant, of Gaulish orig.)]

ămbă'ssadrėss *n.* Female ambassador; ambassador's wife. [f. prec. + -ESS¹]

ă'mbătch *n.* Tropical Afr. tree with very light spongy wood. [Ethiopic]

ă'mber *n.* & *a.* **1.** *n.* Yellow translucent fossil resin; yellow traffic light shown as caution between red (= *stop*) and green (=*go*). **2.** *a.* Made of or coloured like amber; ***~jack,** large game-fish of W. Atlantic. [ME, f. OF *ambre* f. Arab. *ʿanbar* ambergris, amber]

ă'mbergrĭs (*or* -ēs) *n.* Waxlike odoriferous substance found floating in tropical seas, and in intestines of sperm whale. [ME, f. OF *ambre gris* grey AMBER]

ambiance (ahǹbĭah'ǹs) *n.* Surroundings, milieu. [F (as AMBIENT; see -ANCE)]

ămbĭdĕ'xtrous, -terous, *a.* Able to use left and right hands equally well; (fig.) working in either of two media (e.g. verse and prose); deceitful; hence **ămbĭdĕxtĕ'**RITY *n.*, ~LY² *adv.*, ~NESS *n.* [f. LL *ambidexter* (*ambi-* on both sides, *dexter* right-handed) + -OUS]

ă'mbĭ|ent *a.* Surrounding; hence ~ENCE *n.*, (esp.) surroundings. [f. F *ambiant* or f. L *ambiens -entis* part. of *ambire* go round (*ambi-* on both sides, *ire* go)]

ămbĭgū'ĭtў *n.* Double meaning; instance of this; expression capable of more than one meaning. [ME, f. OF *ambiguité* or f. L *ambiguitas* (as foll.; see -ITY)]

ămbĭ'gūous *a.* Obscure; having double meaning; of doubtful classification; of uncertain issue; hence ~LY² *adv.*, ~NESS *n.* [f. L *ambiguus* doubtful f. *ambigere* (*ambi-* both ways, *agere* drive) + -OUS]

ă'mbĭt *n.* Precincts; bounds; scope, extent. [ME, f. L *ambitus* circuit (*ambire*; see AMBIENT)]

ămbĭ'tion *n.* Ardent desire for distinction; aspiration (*to* be, *to* do); object of such desire. [ME f. OF, f. L *ambitio -onis* (*ambire ambit-* canvass for votes; see AMBIENT, -ION)]

ămbĭ'tious (-sh*u*s) *a.* Full of ambition; strongly desirous (*of* a thing, *to* do); showing ambition (*an ambitious attempt*); hence ~LY² *adv.*, ~NESS *n.* [ME, f. OF *ambitieux* f. L *ambitiosus* (as prec.; see -ITIOUS²)]

ămbĭ'val|ence, ~|encў, *n.* (Psych.) Coexistence in one person of the emotional attitudes of love and hate, or other opposite feelings, towards the same object or situation; so ~ENT *a.* [f. G *ambivalenz* f. L *ambo* both, after EQUIVALENCE, -CY]

ămbĭvêr'sion (-sh*o*n) *n.* (Psych.) Balance between introversion and extroversion; hence **ă'mbĭvêrt** *n.*, person having such balance. [f. L *ambi-* on both sides + *-version* after EXTROVERSION, INTROVERSION]

ă'mble *v.i.*, & *n.* **1.** *v.i.* (Of horse etc.) move by lifting two feet on one side together; ride an ambling horse; ride at an easy pace; move in a way suggesting an ambling horse. **2.** *n.* Gait of ambling horse; easy pace. [ME, f. OF *ambler* f. L *ambulare* walk]

ămblў|ō'pĭa *n.* Impaired vision without apparent change in eye; hence **~ŏ'p**IC *a.* [Gk (*ambluōpos* a., f. *amblus* dull + *ōps ōpos* eye; see -IA¹)]

ă'mbō *n.* (*pl.* **~s,** *or* **~nes** *pr.* -ō'nēz). Pulpit in early Christian church etc. [med. L, f. Gk *ambōn* rim (in med. Gk = pulpit)]

ămboy'na *n.* Ornamental wood of an Asian tree. [f. *A~* Island in Indonesia]

ămbrō'sĭ|a (-zĭa *or* -zhy*a*) *n.* **1.** (Gk & Rom. Myth.) food of the gods; anything delightful to taste or smell; so ~AL *a.* **2.** Food of certain bees and beetles. [L, f. Gk, = elixir of life (*ambrotos* immortal)]

ă'mbrў, au'mbrў, *n.* Closed recess in wall of church; (Hist.) small cupboard. [ME, f. OF *almarie, armarie,* f. L *armarium* closet, chest (*arma* utensils)]

ămbs-ā'ce (-mz-) *n.* (arch.) Lowest throw at dice, pair of aces; bad luck; worthlessness. [ME, f. OF *ambes as* f. L *ambo* both + *as* ACE]

ă'mbūlance *n.* Conveyance for sick or injured persons (***~-chaser,** (sl.) one who seeks profit through lawsuits for others' personal injuries); mobile hospital following army. [F (as foll.; see -ANCE)]

ă'mbūlant *a.* (Med.) (Of treatment) not confining patients to bed; (of patient) able to walk about, not confined to bed. [f. L *ambulare* walk; see -ANT]

ă'mbūlatorў *a.* & *n.* **1.** *a.* Pertaining to walking; adapted for walking; movable; not permanent; = prec. **2.** *n.* Place for walking; arcade, esp. in apse; cloister. [f. L *ambulatorius* (*ambulare* walk; see -ORY)]

ămbuscā'de *n.*, & *v.t.* & *i.* (Lie or conceal in) ambush. [f. F *embuscade* f. It. *imboscata* or Sp. *emboscada* (*imboscare*; see AMBUSH², -ADE)]

ă'mbush¹ (-ŏŏsh) *n.* Concealment of troops, troops concealed, in a wood etc. (*lie in ambush*); (generally) lying in wait. [ME, f. OF *embusche* (*embuschier*; see foll.)]

ă'mbush² (-ŏŏsh) *v.t.* & *i.* Lie in wait (for); attack from ambush. [ME, f. OF *embuschier* f. Rom. *IM¹(*boscare* f. **boscus* BUSH¹)]

A.M.D.G. *abbr.* to the greater glory of God. [f. L *ad majorem Dei gloriam*]

***amē'ba.** See AMOEBA.

âme damnée (ahm dah'nā) *n.* (*pl.* **-es -es** *pr.* same). Devoted adherent. [F, = damned soul]

ameer'. See AMIR.

amē'lĭor|āte *v.t.* & *i.* (Cause to) become better; hence ~A'TION, **~āt**OR, *ns.*, **~at**IVE *a.* [f. MELIORATE after F *améliorer* alt. f. OF *ameillorer* (*meilleur* f. L *melior -oris* better)]

āmĕ'n (*or* ah-) *int.* & *n.* (Saying of) 'so be it' esp. at end of prayer etc.; **say ~** (assent) **to.** [ME f. eccl. L f. Gk f. Heb. *'āmēn* certainly]

amē'n|able *a.* (Of persons) responsible (*to* law etc., or abs.); (of things) subject or liable *to*; responsive, tractable; hence ~ABI'LITY, **~able**NESS (-beln-), *ns.*, **~ab**LY² *adv.* [AF (Law Fr.), f. F *amener* bring to (*a-* AD-, *mener* bring f. LL *minare* drive animals f. L *minari* threaten); see -ABLE]

amĕ'nd *v.t.* Correct error in (document); make proposed minor improvements in (motion etc. under discussion); make better; so ~MENT *n.*, minor improvement in document, e.g. added article in U.S. Constitution. [ME, f. OF *amender* f. Rom. **admendare* f. L *emendare* EMEND]

amende honorable (amahǹd ŏnŏrah'bl) *n.* (*pl.* **-es -es** *pr.* same). Public or open apology and reparation. [F, = honourable reparation]

amĕ'nds (-z) *n.* Reparation, restitution, compensation, (*make amends*). [ME, f. OF *amendes* penalties, fine, pl. of *amende* reparation (*amender* AMEND)]

amĕ'nĭtў *n.* Pleasantness (of place, person, etc.; ‖**~ bed,** bed available in hospital to give more privacy for small payment); (in *pl.*) pleasant manners or features. [ME, f. OF *amenité* or f. L *amoenitas* (*amoenus* pleasant; see -ITY)]

āmĕnorrhoe'a (-rē'*a*) *n.* (Physiol.) Abnormal absence of menstruation. [f. A- 7 + MENO- + Gk *-rrhoia* (*rheō* flow)]

ā'mĕnt¹ (*or* amĕ'-) *n.* Person with congenital mental deficiency; so **āmĕ'nt**IA¹ (-sh*a*) *n.* [f. L *amens -ent-* mad (*a* away from, *mens mentis* mind)]

amĕ'nt², amĕ'nt|um (*pl.* **~a**), *ns.* Catkin. [L, = thong]

amĕr'ce *v.t.* Fine; (loosely) punish; hence or cogn. **amĕr'ci**ABLE *a.*, ~MENT (-sm-) *n.* [ME *amercy*, f. AF *amercier* (*a* at, *merci* MERCY)]
Amĕ'rican (*a*-) *a.* & *n.* **1.** *a.* Belonging to continent of America (usu. in comb., as *Latin-American*); belonging to the United States; ||~ **cloth,** cotton cloth enamelled or waterproofed with shiny surface; *American* INDIAN; ~ **organ,** harmonium with suction-operated instead of blown reeds; *~ **plan** (charging for hotel-room with inclusion of meals); ~ **tiger,** jaguar. **2.** *n.* Native of America of Old-World descent; citizen of United States; English language as spoken in United States. [f. mod. L *Americanus* (*America* f. Latinized name of *Amerigo* Vespucci, It. navigator d. 1512; see -AN)]
Amĕ'ricanism (*a*-) *n.* Word or sense or phrase peculiar to or originating from United States; attachment to or sympathy with the United States. [f. prec. + -ISM]
Amĕ'ricanize (*a*-), **-ise** (-īz), *v.t.* & *i.* Naturalize as an American; make or become American in character. [f. as prec. + -IZE]
ămerĭ'cium (-ĭ'sĭ- *or* -ĭ'shĭ-) *n.* (Chem.) Artificially made transuranic radioactive metallic element. [f. *America* (where first made) + -IUM]
A'merind, Amerĭ'ndian, (ă-) *adjs.* & *ns.* American Indian or Eskimo; so **Amerĭ'nd**IC (ă-) *a.* [portmanteau wds]
à merveille (ahmārvā'y) *adv.* Admirably, wonderfully. [F, lit. 'to a marvel']
ă'mėthўst *n.* Precious stone, purple or violet quartz; hence ~INE[1] (-ĭ's-) *a.* [ME, f. OF *ametiste* f. L f. Gk *amethustos* not drunken, the stone being supposed to prevent intoxication]
Amhă'ric (ă-) *n.* & *a.* (Of the) official and trade language of Ethiopia. [f. *Amhara*, Ethiopian province + -IC]
ā'miable *a.* Feeling and inspiring friendliness; lovable; hence **āmi**ABI'LITY, ~NESS (-beln-), *ns.*, **ā'miab**LY[2] *adv.* [ME f. OF, f. LL *amicabilis* amicable; confused w. F *aimable* lovable]
ămiă'nt(h)us *n.* Mineral variety of asbestos, splitting into flexible fibres. [L, f. Gk *amiantos* undefiled (*a*- not, *miainō* defile) i.e. purified by fire, being incombustible; for *-h-* cf. AMARANTH]
ă'mic|able *a.* Friendly; done in a friendly spirit; hence ~ABI'LITY, ~**able**NESS (-beln-), *ns.*, ~**ab**LY[2] *adv.* [f. LL *amicabilis* (*amicus* friend; see -ABLE)]
ă'mice[1] *n.* Square of white linen worn by celebrant priests, formerly on head, now on neck and shoulders. [ME, f. med. L *amicia, -sia*; earlier *amit* f. OF, f. L *amictus* garment]
ă'mice[2] *n.* Cap, hood, or cape, of religious orders. [ME, f. OF *aumusse* f. med. L *almucia* etc., of unkn. orig.]
amicus curiae (amīkus kūr'ĭē) *n.* (*pl.* *-ci pr.* -sī). Friend of the (law)court, disinterested adviser. [mod. L]
amĭ'd(st) *prep.* In the middle of (lit. or fig.); in the course of. [ME *amidde(s)* f. OE *on* ON + oblique case of MID[1]; *-st* w. adv. gen. *-s* + *-t* as in AGAINST]
ă'mide *n.* (Chem.) Compound formed from ammonia by replacing one (or occas. more than one) hydrogen atom by metal or acid radical. [f. AMMONIA + -IDE]
ă'midōne *n.* Synthetic analgesic drug, methadone. [f. AMINE + *d*(iphenyl) + -ONE]
amĭ'dships, *-ĭp, *adv.* In middle of ship (lit. or fig.). [f. MIDSHIP(s) after AMID]
amĭ'dst. See AMID.
ā'mine (-ēn) *n.* (Chem.) Compound formed from ammonia by replacing one or more hydrogen atoms by alkyl or other non-acidic radical. [f. AMMONIA + -INE[5]]
aminō-ă'cid (-ēn-) *n.* (Chem.) Organic acid containing the group NH_2 derived from ammonia, esp. as constituent of proteins. [f. AMINE + ACID[2]]
amir' (-ēr'), **ameer',** *n.* Title of various Muslim rulers; hence ~ATE[1] (1) *n.* [f. Arab. *'amīr* commander (*amara* command); cf. EMIR]
A'mish (ă'-) *a.* Belonging to a strict U.S. Mennonite sect. [prob. f. G *amisch* f. J. *Amen* 17th c. Swiss preacher; see -ISH[1]]
amĭ'ss *adv.* & *pred. a.* Out of order; wrong(ly); inappropriate(ly) (*come, go, amiss*); **take ~,** take offence at (thing). [ME, prob. f. ON *á mis* so as to miss (*á* on, *mis* cogn. w. MIS-[1], MISS[2])]
ă'mitў *n.* Friendship, friendly relationship. [ME, f. OF *amitié* f. Rom. **amicitas -tatis* f. L *amicus* friend; see -ITY]
ă'mmėter *n.* Instrument for measuring electric current, esp. in amperes. [f. AMPERE + -METER]
ă'mmō *n.* (colloq.) Ammunition. [abbr.]
ammō'nia *n.* Colourless gas with pungent smell and strong alkaline reaction, nitrogen trihydride, NH_3; (**liquid**)~, ~ **water,** solution of ammonia in water. [mod. L, f. SAL AMMONIAC]
ămmonī'acal *a.* Pertaining to ammonia or sal ammoniac. [f. ME *ammoniac*, f. OF (*arm-, amm-*) f. L f. Gk *ammōniakos* of Ammon (cf. SAL AMMONIAC), + -AL]
ammō'niātėd *a.* Combined or treated with ammonia. [f. AMMONIA + -ATE[1] (3) + -ED[1]]
ă'mmonite *n.* Fossil cephalopod of order Ammonoidea, with flat spiral shell. [f. mod. L *ammonites,* after med. L *cornu Ammonis,* = L *Ammonis cornu* (Pliny), horn of (Jupiter) Ammon; see -ITE[1] (2)]
ammō'nium *n.* Univalent radical of ammonia salts. [mod. L (as AMMONIA; see -IUM)]
ămmūnĭ'tion *n.* Military projectiles (bullets, shells, grenades, etc.) and propellants; (fig.) facts, arguments, etc., used in attack or defence. [f. obs. F *amunition*, corrupt. of (*la*) *munition* (the) MUNITION]
ămnē's|ia (-zĭa) *n.* Loss of memory; hence ~ĭAC *n.*, ~IC *a.* & *n.* [mod. L, f. Gk, = forgetfulness]
ă'mnėstў *n.*, & *v.t.* **1.** *n.* General pardon, esp. for political offence. **2.** *v.t.* Give amnesty to. [f. F *amnestie* or f. L f. Gk *amnēstia* oblivion]
ămniocĕntē's|is *n.* (*pl.* ~**es** *pr.* -ēz). (Med.) Sampling of amniotic fluid by insertion of hollow needle. [f. foll. + -o- + Gk *kentēsis* pricking (*kentō* to prick)]
ă'mnĭ|ŏn *n.* (*pl.* ~**a**). (Zool. & Physiol.) Innermost membrane enclosing foetus before birth; hence ~O'TIC *a.* [Gk, = caul (dim. of *amnos* lamb)]
amoe'b|a (-mē'-), ***amē'b|a,** *n.* (*pl.* ~**as** *or* ~**ae**). Single-celled aquatic protozoan, perpetually changing shape; hence ~IC, ~OID, *adjs.* [mod. L, f. Gk *amoibē* change]
ămoebē'an (-mēb-) *a.* (Esp. of verse dialogue) alternately answering. [f. L f. Gk *amoibaios* interchanging (as prec.) + -AN]
amŏ'k, amŭ'ck, *adv.* **Run ~,** run about in frenzied thirst for blood (lit. or fig.). [f. Malay *amok* rushing in frenzy]
amo'ng(st) (-mŭ'-) *prep.* In the assemblage of, surrounded by; in the general practice or views of (*there is honour among thieves*); in the number of (*reckoned among his best works*); within the limits of (collectively or distributively: *five pounds among us*; *divided among us*); in comparison with (*one among many*); by joint action of (*kill him among you*); by reciprocal action of; *quarrelled* ~ **themselves,** with one another. [OE *ongemang* (*on* ON, *gemang* assemblage, cf. MINGLE); *-st* w. adv. gen. *-s* + *-t* as in AGAINST]
Amŏntĭlla'dō (*a*-; -lah'-) *n.* (*pl.* ~**s**). Medium dry sherry of a matured type. [Sp. (*Montilla* in Spain, *-ado* = -ATE[2])]

āmŏ'ral *a.* Unconcerned with or outside morals; non-moral. [f. A- 7 + MORAL]
ă'morĭst *n.* One who professes (esp. sexual) love; one who writes of love. [f. L *amor* or F *amour* love + -IST]
ămorō'sō *n.* (*pl.* ~**s**). Full rich type of sherry. [Sp., = amorous]
ă'morous *a.* Inclined to (esp. sexual) love; in love; of or pertaining to love; hence ~LY[2] *adv.*, ~NESS *n.* [ME f. OF, f. med L *amorosus* f. L *amor* love; see -OUS]
amŏr'ph|ous *a.* Shapeless; (Min. & Chem.) uncrystallized; unorganized: hence ~**ous**LY[2] *adv.*, ~**ous**NESS *n.* [f. mod. L *amorphus* f. Gk *amorphos* shapeless (*a*- not, *morphē* form) + -OUS]
amŏr'tīz|e, -īs|e (-īz), *v.t.* Transfer (land) to corporation in mortmain; extinguish (debt, usu. by means of sinking fund); gradually write off initial cost of (assets); hence ~A'TION *n.* [ME, f. OF *amortir* (st. *-iss-*) f. Rom. **admortire* (*ad* to, *mort-* death)]
amou'nt[1] *v.i.* Be equivalent (in total value, quantity, significance, etc.) *to.* [ME, f. OF *amunter* (*amont* upward, lit. uphill, f. L *ad montem*)]
amou'nt[2] *n.* Total to which a thing amounts; full value, significance, etc.; quantity; **any** ~, a great deal (*of*); **no** ~ **of,** not even the greatest possible amount of. [f. prec.]
amour' (-oor') *n.* Love affair, esp. secret one. [F, = love, f. L *amor amoris*]
amourĕ'tte (-oor-) *n.* Petty love affair. [F, dim. of prec.]
amour propre (ămoor prŏ'pr) *n.* Self-esteem; vanity. [F]
ămp *n.* (colloq.) Ampere; amplifier. [abbr.]
AMP *abbr.* adenosine monophosphate.
ămpėlŏ'psĭs *n.* Climbing plant allied to vine, esp. Virginia creeper. [mod. L, f. Gk *ampelos* vine + *opsis* appearance]
ă'mpērage (*or* -ār-) *n.* (Electr.) Strength of current in amperes. [f. AMPERE + -AGE]
ă'mpēre (*or* -ār) *n.* (Electr.) Fundamental unit of current. [f. A. M. *Ampère*, Fr. physicist d. 1836]
ă'mpersănd *n.* The sign & (= *and*, L *et*). [corrupt. of '& per se (i.e. by itself) *and*', the old way of naming and explaining the character &]
ămphĕ'tamĭne (*or* -ēn) *n.* Synthetic stimulant and decongestant drug. [f. *a*lpha-*m*ethyl-*-phe*nethyl*amine*]
ămphĭ- *comb. form.* Both; of both kinds; on both sides; around. [Gk]
Amphĭ'bĭa (ă-) *n. pl.* Class of Vertebrata, intermediate between reptiles and fishes, incl. frogs, newts, etc., able to live on land or in water. [mod. L f. Gk, neut. pl. of *amphibios* (AMPHI-, *bios* life)]
ămphĭ'bĭan *a.* & *n.* (Animal) living both on land and in water; (Zool.) (member) of the Amphibia; (tank, aircraft, etc.) adapted to operate on both land and water. [f. as prec. + -AN]
ămphĭbĭŏ'logy̆ *n.* Branch of zoology treating of Amphibia. [f. as prec. + -O- + -LOGY]
ămphĭ'bĭous *a.* Living both on land and in water; connected with or operating on both land and water; (Mil.) involving co-operation of sea and land (and occas. air) forces organized for invasion, (of forces) trained for such action; having a twofold life, connected with two classes, etc.; hence ~LY[2] *adv.* [f. AMPHIBIA + -OUS]
ămphĭbŏ'logy̆ *n.* Quibble; ambiguous wording. [ME, f. OF *amphibologie* f. LL *amphibologia* for L f. Gk *amphibolia* ambiguity]
ă'mphĭbrăch (-k) *n.* (Pros.) Foot consisting of one long syllable between two short; hence **ămphĭbră'ch**IC (-k-) *a.* [f. L *amphibrachys, -us* f. Gk *amphibrakhus* short at both ends (as AMPHI-, *brakhus* short)]
ămphĭ'ctȳon *n.* Delegate to amphictyonic council; **the A~s,** the Greek amphictyonic council. [f. Gk AMPHI*ktuones* pl. dwellers around]
ămphĭ'ctȳ|onȳ *n.* Association of tribes etc. for common welfare esp. in ancient Greece; so ~**ŏ'n**IC *a.* [f. Gk *amphiktuonia* (as prec.; see -Y[1])]
ămphĭ'gamous *a.* (Bot.) Without distinct sexual organs. [f. F *amphigame* (as AMPHI-, Gk *gamos* marriage) + -OUS]
ămphĭgour'ĭ (-oor'ĭ), **ămphĭ'gorȳ,** *n.* Nonsensical verse etc. composition. [F *amphigouri*, of uncert. orig.]
ămphĭmĭ'x|ĭs *n.* (*pl.* ~**es** *pr.* -ēz). (Biol.) Fusion of gametes from two individuals in sexual reproduction; so **ămphĭmĭ'ct**IC *a.* [mod. L, f. as AMPHI- + Gk *mixis* mingling]
ămphĭŏ'xus *n.* Lancelet of genus *Branchiostoma*. [mod. L, f. as AMPHI- + Gk *oxus* sharp]
ă'mphĭpŏd *n.* Small usu. marine crustacean of order Amphipoda, with feet of two kinds, e.g. sandhopper. [f. AMPHI- + Gk *pous podos* foot]
ămphĭ'prostȳle *a.* & *n.* (Building) with portico at each end. [f. L f. Gk AMPHI(*prostulos* PROSTYLE)]
ămphĭsbae'na *n.* Fabulous serpent with head at each end; (Zool.) wormlike lizard of genus *Amphisbaena*. [ME f. L, f. Gk *amphisbaina* (*amphis* both ways, *bainō* go)]
ă'mphĭtheatre, *-ter, (-ĭater) *n.* Oval or circular building, with seats rising in tiers round central open space; large circular hollow; semicircular gallery in a theatre; (fig.) scene of a contest. [f. L f. Gk *amphitheatron* (as AMPHI-, THEATRE)]
ă'mphora *n.* (*pl.* ~**e** *or* ~**s**). Greek or Roman two-handled vessel. [L, f. Gk *amphoreus*]
ămphotĕ'rĭc *a.* Acting both ways; (Chem.) capable of reacting as acid and base. [f. Gk *amphoteros* compar. of *amphō* both + -IC]
ă'mple *a.* (~**r,** ~**st**). Spacious; extensive; abundant, copious; (euphem.) stout; quite enough; hence ~NESS (-peln-) *n.*, **ă'mp**LY[2] *adv.* [ME f. F, f. L *amplus*]
ă'mplĭ|fȳ *v.* **1.** *v.t.* Enhance; increase loudness of (sounds), strength of (electrical signals), etc., whence ~**fīe**R[1] *n.*; enlarge (story, statement). **2.** *v.i.* Expatiate. **3.** Hence ~FICA'TION *n.* [ME, f. OF *amplifier* f. L *amplificare* (as AMPLE; see -FY)]
ă'mplĭtūde *n.* **1.** Breadth; abundance; wide range. **2.** (Phys.) maximum extent of vibration or oscillation from position of equilibrium; (Electr.) maximum departure from average of alternating current or wave; ~ **modulation** (in which amplitude of carrier wave is varied). [F, or f. L *amplitudo* (as AMPLE; see -TUDE)]
ă'mpoule (-o͞ol) *n.* (Med.) Small sealed glass vessel for containing materials before injection. [F, f. as foll.]
ămpŭ'lla *n.* (*pl.* ~**e**). Roman two-handled globular flask; vessel for sacred uses; (Zool. & Physiol.) dilated end of vessel, canal, or duct. [L]
ă'mpūt|āte *v.t.* Cut off (part of animal body etc., esp. limb because of injury or disease); hence ~A'TION, ~**āt**OR, *ns.*, ~EE' *n.*, one who has lost limb etc. by amputation. [f. L *amputare* (*amb*- about, *putare* prune) + -ATE[3]]
amŭ'ck. See AMOK.
ă'mūlėt *n.* Thing worn as charm against evil (lit. or fig.). [f. L *amuletum*; orig. unkn.]
amū's|e (-z) *v.t.* **1.** Interest *with* pleasant trifling matters; ~**e** one**self,** pass time in small diversions. **2.** Make (person) laugh or smile (*be amused with, by, at*). **3.** Hence ~IVE *a.* [ME, f. OF *amuser* cause to MUSE[2] (causal *a* to, *muser* stare)]
amū'sement (-zm-) *n.* Pleasant diversion;

causing of laughter or smiles; pastime; ||~ **arcade,** place for recreation with automatic game-machines etc. [F (*amuser*; see prec., -MENT)]

ă'mȳl *n.* (Chem.) Radical, C_5H_{11}, derived from pentane. [f. L *amylum* starch, from which oil containing it was distilled]

ă'mȳlāse (*or* -z) *n.* Diastase. [f. prec. + -ASE]

ămȳlŏ'psĭn *n.* Pancreatic enzyme that converts starch into sugar. [f. AMYL after *pepsin*]

ă'mȳtăl *n.* White crystalline powder used as sedative and hypnotic, esp. as sodium salt. [P]

an[1] (*an or, when stressed,* ăn) *a.* See A[2]; *an* is the form generally used before words beginning with vowel sounds (*an egg, an hour, an M.P.*), and sometimes used before words beginning with *h* in unstressed syllable (*an historical novel, an hypothesis*).

ăn[2] *conj.* (arch. or dial.) If. [ME weakening of AND]

an- *pref.* **1.** f. OE, ME *an* = on (*anon, anent*). **2.** assim. form of AD- before *n.* **3.** f. Gk ANA- (*anode*). **4.** f. Gk *an-* = *a-* not (A- 7) (*anarchy*).

-an *suf.* forming *adjs.* (often used as *ns.*) esp. f. names of places, systems, Zool. classes or orders, and founders (*Australasian, Chilean, Anglican, crustacean, crocodilian, Lutheran*); cf. also -ANE, -EAN, -IAN, -ICIAN. [f. or after F *-ain, -(i)en* or f. L *-anus*]

ā'na (*or* ah'-) *n.* **1.** (as *pl.*) Anecdotes, literary gossip, about a person. **2.** (as *sing.*) Collection of person's memorable sayings. [= -ANA]

ăna- *pref.* (usu. **an-** bef. vowel) w. sense 'up' (*anadromous*), 'back' (*anamnesis*), 'again' (*anabaptism*). [f. Gk *ana* up]

-a'na (ah'-) *suf.* forming *pl. ns.*, w. sense 'anecdotes or publications or other items concerning persons, places, or topics' (*Shakespeareana, Victoriana, Americana, cricketana*). [neut. pl. of L *-anus*; cf. -AN]

ănabă'pt|ĭsm *n.* (Hist.) Doctrine that persons baptized as infants should be rebaptized as adults; so ~IST (2) *n.* [f. eccl. L f. Gk ANA(*baptismos* BAPTISM)]

ă'nabăs *n.* Perchlike freshwater fish of genus *Anabas*, able to leave water and ascend trees. [mod. L, f. Gk, part. of *anabainō* walk up]

ană'bas|ĭs *n.* (*pl.* **~es** *pr.* -ēz). Up-country march, esp. that of Cyrus the younger into Asia, narrated by Xenophon. [Gk, = ascent, f. ANA(*bainō* go)]

ănabă'tĭc *a.* (Meteorol.) (Of wind) caused by air flowing upwards; cf. KATABATIC. [f. Gk *anabatikos* ascending (as prec.; see -IC)]

ănabĭ|ō'sĭs *n.* (*pl.* **-oses** *pr.* -ō'sēz). (Biol.) Ability to regain life after apparent death by drying etc.; state of reduced animation; so ~O'TIC *a.* [mod. L, f. Gk *anabiōsis* (ANA*bioō* return to life; see -OSIS)]

ană'bolĭsm *n.* (Biol.) Constructive metabolism, synthesis of complex substances for body tissues etc., (opp. CATABOLISM); so **ănabŏ'lĭc** *a.* [f. Gk ANA(*bolē* f. *ballō* throw) ascent + -ISM]

ă'nabranch (-ahn-) *n.* (esp. Austral.) Stream that leaves river and re-enters it lower down. [f. ANASTOMOSE + BRANCH[1]]

ănachrŏ'nĭc (-k-) *a.* Involving anachronism; out of date. [f. foll. after *synchronic* etc.]

ană'chron|ĭsm (-k-) *n.* Error in computing of time; person or thing out of harmony with the time; relating of an event, custom, or circumstance to a wrong period of time; hence **~ĭ'stĭc** *a.* [f. F *anachronisme* or f. Gk ANA(*khronismos* f. *khronos* time); see -ISM]

ănacolū'th|on *n.* (*pl.* **~a**). Sentence or construction lacking grammatical sequence; hence ~IC *a.* [LL, f. Gk *anakolouthon* (as AN- 4, *akolouthos* following)]

ănacŏ'nda *n.* Large tropical S. Amer. aquatic and arboreal boa. [alt. of *anacondaia* f. Sinh. *henakandayā* whip-snake (*hena* lightning, *kanda* stem); orig. of a snake in Sri Lanka (Ceylon)]

anăcrēŏ'ntĭc *a.* & *n.* **1.** (Poem) after the manner of Anacreon. **2.** *a.* Convivial and amatory in tone. [f. LL *anacreonticus* f. Gk *Anakreōn -ont-* Anacreon, Gk lyric poet d. 478 B.C.]

ănacru's|ĭs (-ōō'-) *n.* (*pl.* **~es** *pr.* -ēz). (Pros.) unstressed syllable at beginning of verse; (Mus.) unstressed note(s) before first bar-line. [f. Gk ANA(*krousis* f. *krouō* strike)]

ană'dromous *a.* (Of fish) ascending rivers to spawn. [f. Gk ANA(*dromos* -running) + -OUS]

anae'm|ĭa, *anē'm|ĭa, *n.* (Med.) Deficiency of red blood-corpuscles or their haemoglobin, often causing pallor; PERNICIOUS *anaemia*; hence ~IC *a.* (lit., or fig., lacking vigour etc.). [mod. L, f. Gk *anaimia* (as AN- 4, -AEMIA)]

anaer'ōbe (-ār'-; *or* ă'-) *n.* Micro-organism that can or must live without free oxygen from the air; hence **ănaerō'bĭc** (-ār-) *a.* [f. F *anaérobie* f. as AN- 4 + AEROBE]

ănaesthē'sĭ|a (ănĭs-), ***ănės-,** (-zĭa) *n.* Absence of sensation, esp. artificially induced insensibility to pain; hence **~ŏ'LOGY** *n.* [mod. L, f. Gk *anaisthēsia* (as AN- 4, *aisthēsis* sensation; see -IA[1])]

ănaesthĕ'tĭc (ănĭs-), ***ănės-,** *a.* & *n.* (Agent) that produces partial or complete insensibility to pain etc.; **general ~** (affecting whole body, usu. with loss of consciousness); **local ~** (affecting limited part of body). [f. Gk *anaisthētos* insensible (as prec.) + -IC]

anae'sthet|īze, -īse (-īz), ***anē's-,** *v.t.* Deprive of sensation (lit. or fig.); administer anaesthetic to; hence ~IST (1), **~īzA'TION,** *ns.* [f. as prec. + -IZE]

ă'naglȳph *n.* Embossed ornament in low relief; (Photog.) composite stereoscopic picture printed in superimposed complementary colours; hence **ănaglȳ'phĭc** *a.* [f. Gk ANA(*gluphē* f. *gluphō* carve)]

ănagnŏ'rĭs|ĭs *n.* (*pl.* **~es** *pr.* -ēz). Recognition, dénouement in drama. [Gk *anagnōrisis*]

ănagō'gē *n.* Spiritual, allegorical, or mystical interpretation; hence **ănagŏ'gĭc(AL)** *adjs.* [eccl. L f. Gk, f. *anagō* lead up (AN- 3)]

ă'nagrăm *n.* Transposition of letters of word or phrase, to form new word or phrase; hence or cogn. **ănagrammă'tĭc(AL)** *adjs.*, **ănagră'mmatIZE** (1) *v.t.* [f. F *anagramme* or mod. L *anagramma*, f. Gk ANA- + *gramma -atos* letter; cf. -GRAM]

ā'nal *a.* Pertaining to or situated near the anus. [f. mod. L *analis* (as ANUS; see -AL)]

ă'nalĕcts, ănalĕ'cta, *n. pl.* Literary gleanings. [L f. Gk *analekta* things gathered (ANA*legō* pick up)]

ănalĕ'ptĭc *a.* & *n.* Restorative (medicine). [f. Gk *analēptikos* (ANA*lambanō* take back; see -IC)]

ănălgē'sĭa (*or* -zĭa) *n.* Absence or relief of pain; so **ănălgē'sĭc** *a.* & *n.*, (drug) producing analgesia. [mod. L, f. Gk, = painlessness]

***ă'nalŏg.** See ANALOGUE.

ănalŏ'gĭc *a.* Of analogy. [f. F *analogique* or f. L f. Gk *analogikos* (as ANALOGUE; see -IC)]

ănalŏ'gĭcal *a.* According to analogy; expressing an analogy; hence ~LY[2] *adv.* [f. as prec.; see -ICAL]

ană'logist *n.* One who argues from or seeks analogies. [f. foll. + -IST]

ană'logize, -īse (-īz), *v.* **1.** *v.t.* Represent by analogy; show to be analogous. **2.** *v.i.* Use analogy; be in harmony (*with*). [f. ANALOGY + -IZE]

ană'logous *a.* Similar, parallel, (*to*); showing analogy; hence ~LY[2] *adv.*, ~NESS *n.* [f. L f. Gk *analogos* proportionate + -OUS]

ă'nalŏgue (-ŏg), ***ă'nalŏg,** *n.* Analogous or parallel word or thing (e.g. narrative); ~ **computer,** one using physical quantities (voltage, weight, length, etc.) to represent numbers. [F, f. Gk *analogon* neut. adj. (see prec.)]

ană'logy̆ *n.* Agreement, similarity, (*to, with, between*); analogue; (Logic) process of reasoning from parallel cases; (Philol.) imitation of existing words in forming inflexions or constructions of others, without the existence of corresponding intermediate stages; (Biol.) resemblance of function between organs essentially different. [f. F *analogie* or f. L f. Gk *analogia* proportion (as ANALOGOUS; see -Y[1])]

ă'nalȳs|e (-z), ***ă'nalȳz|e,** *v.t.* Examine the detailed constitution of; =PSYCHO-ANALYSE; (Chem.) ascertain constituents of (sample of mixture or compound); find or show the essence or structure of (book, music, etc.); (Gram.) resolve (sentence) into its grammatical elements; hence ~ABLE *a.*, ~ĂND[1] *n.*, person undergoing psycho-analysis, ~ER[1] *n.* [f. obs. *analyse* n. or f. F *analyser* (*analyse* n. f. med. L ANALYSIS)]

ană'ly̆sĭs *n.* (*pl.* **ana'lyses** *pr.* -sēz). **1.** Resolution into simpler elements by analysing (opp. *synthesis*); statement of result of this; **in the final, last, ultimate,** ~, after all due consideration, in the end; **bowling** ~, (Cricket) statement usu. of overs and maiden overs bowled, runs conceded, and wickets taken, by bowler. **2.** (Math.) Use of algebra and calculus in problem-solving. **3.** =PSYCHO-ANALYSIS. [med. L, f. Gk ANA(*lusis* f. *luō* set free)]

ă'nalȳst *n.* One skilled in (esp. chemical) analysis; =PSYCHO-ANALYST. [f. F *analyste* (*analyser* ANALYSE, after ns. in *-iste* -IST f. vbs in *-iser* -IZE)]

ănalȳ'tĭc *a.* Pertaining to analysis; (Philol.) analytical. [f. LL f. Gk *analutikos* (as ANALYSIS; see -IC)]

ănalȳ'tĭcal *a.* Employing analytic methods; (Philol.) using separate words instead of inflexions; ~ **geometry** (using co-ordinates); hence ~LY[2] *adv.* [f. as prec.; see -ICAL]

***ă'nalȳze.** See ANALYSE.

ănamnē's|ĭs *n.* (*pl.* ~**es** *pr.* -ēz). Recollection (esp. of a previous existence); patient's account of his medical history. [Gk, =remembrance]

ănamôr'phos|ĭs *n.* (*pl.* ~**es** *pr.* -ēz). Distorted drawing or picture appearing regular from one point; (Bot.) abnormal transformation. [Gk (ANA*morphoō* transform f. *morphē* form; see -OSIS)]

anā'nas (*or* -ah'n-) *n.* Pineapple; pinguin. [F or Sp., f. Guarani *anānā*]

ană'ndrous *a.* (Bot.) Having no stamens. [f. Gk *anandros* without males (*an-* not, *anēr andros* male) + -OUS]

ă'napaest, *-pēst, *n.* (Pros.) Foot consisting of two short syllables followed by one long; so **ănapae'st**IC *a.* [f. L f. Gk ANA(*paistos* f. *paiō* strike) reversed (because reverse of dactyl)]

ană'phora *n.* **1.** Repetition of word or phrase at beginning of successive clauses; use of word referring to or replacing earlier word(s) (e.g. DO[1] 9), whence **ănaphŏ'r**IC *a.* **2.** (Eccl.) Part of Eucharistic service where oblation is made. [L f. Gk, =repetition (as ANA-, *pherō* carry)]

ănăphrodī'sĭăc (-z-) *a.* & *n.* (Drug) reducing sexual desire. [f. AN- 4 + as APHRODISIAC]

ănaphȳlă'|xĭs *n.* (*pl.* ~**xes** *pr.* -ksēz). (Med.) Hypersensitivity of tissues to second dose of antigen; hence ~**ct**IC *a.* [mod. L, f. F *anaphylaxie* f. as ANA- + Gk *phulaxis* guarding]

ănaptȳ'|xĭs *n.* (*pl.* ~**xes** *pr.* -ksēz). (Phonet.) Development of vowel between two consonants (*she went thataway*); hence ~**ct**IC *a.* [mod. L, f. Gk ANA(*ptuxis* f. *ptussō* fold)]

ă'nârch (-k) *n.* **1.** Anarchist. **2.** (poet.) Leader of revolt. [f. Gk *anarkhos* leaderless (as AN- 4, *-arkhos* ruling f. *arkhō* rule)]

ă'narch|ȳ (-kĭ) *n.* Absence of government in a society; disorder; political or social confusion; hence **anâr'ch**IC(AL) (-k-) *adjs.*, ~ISM (3), ~IST (2), *ns.*, (adherent of) doctrine that all government should be abolished, ~**ĭ'st**IC *a.* [f. med. L f. Gk *anarkhia* (*anarkhos*; see prec.)]

ănastĭgmă'tĭc *a.* Free from astigmatism; so [by back form. thr. G] **ănă'stĭgmăt** *n.*, lens, or lens-system, made anastigmatic by correction. [f. AN- 4 + ASTIGMATIC]

ănastomō's|ĭs *n.* (*pl.* ~**es** *pr.* -ēz). Cross-connection of arteries, branches, rivers, etc.; so **ană'stomōse** (-z) *v.i.*, communicate by anastomosis. [mod. L f. Gk, f. ANA*stomoō* furnish with mouth (*stoma*); see -OSIS]

ană'strophė *n.* (Rhet.) Inversion of usual order of words or clauses. [Gk ANA(*strophē* f. *strephō* to turn) turning back]

ană'thėma *n.* Accursed thing; curse of God; curse of Church, excommunicating a person or denouncing a doctrine; imprecation; detested thing or person (*he, it, is anathema to me*); so ~TIZE *v.t.* & *i.*, curse. [eccl. L, =excommunicated person, excommunication, f. Gk *anathema* thing devoted, (later) accursed thing (ANA*tithēmi* set up)]

ănatŏ'mĭcal *a.* Belonging to anatomy; structural; hence ~LY[2] *adv.* [f. F *anatomique* or f. LL *anatomicus* (as ANATOMY, -IC); see -ICAL]

ană'tomĭst *n.* Dissecter of dead bodies; person skilled in anatomy; (fig.) analyser. [f. F *anatomiste* or med. L **anatomista* f. as foll.; see -IST]

ană'tomīze, -īse (-īz), *v.t.* Dissect; (fig.) analyse. [f. F *anatomiser* or med. L *anatomizare* f. *anatomia* (see foll., -IZE)]

ană'tomy̆ *n.* Dissection of human body, animals, or plants; (science of) bodily structure of human beings, animals, or plants; (joc.) human body; (fig.) analysis. [f. F *anatomie* or f. LL f. Gk *anatomia* (as ANA-, -TOMY)]

ană'tta, ană'ttō. See ANNATTO.

ă'nbury̆ *n.* Soft tumour of horse or ox; disease of root-plants. [perh. f. *ang-* (cf. AGNAIL) + BERRY[1]]

-ance *suf.* forming *ns.* of quality (or instance of it) (*arrogance, protuberance, relevance, resemblance*) or action (*assistance, furtherance, penance*). [f. or after F *-ance* f. L *-antia, -entia* (cf. -ENCE) f. part. st. *-ant-, -ent-*]

ă'ncėst|or *n.* Any person from whom one's father or mother is descended, forefather; hence ~RESS[1] *n.* [ME, f. OF *ancestre* f. L *antecessor -oris* f. ANTE(*cedere cess-* go); see -OR]

ăncĕ'stral *a.* Belonging to or inherited from ancestors. [f. F *ancestrel*; see prec., -AL]

ă'ncėstry̆ *n.* (Lineage of) ancestors, esp. noble or aristocratic; ancient descent. [ME, alt. f. OF *ancesserie* (as ANCESTOR; see -Y[1])]

ă'nchĭthēre (ă'ngkĭ-) *n.* Fossil animal of genus *Anchitherium*, of size of small pony, regarded as ancestor of horse. [f. mod. L *anchitherium* f. Gk *agkhi* near + *thērion* beast]

ă'nchor[1] (-k-) *n.* **1.** Heavy metal structure used to moor ship to sea-bottom etc. or balloon etc. to ground (**at** ~, thus moored; **cast, come to,** (let down), **weigh** (take up), ~; SHEET[3]-*anchor*); (fig.) source of confidence. **2.** ~**man,** one playing vital part (at back of tug-of-war team, as last runner in relay race, as compère in broadcast programme, etc.); ~**-plate,** heavy piece of timber or metal, e.g. as support for suspension-bridge cables; ~**-ring,** TORUS (sense 4) of circular cross-section. [f. OE *ancor* etc. & OF *ancre* f. L *ancora* f. Gk *agkura*]

ă'nchor² (-k-) *v.* **1.** *v.t.* Secure (ship) with anchor; fix firmly (lit. or fig.). **2.** *v.i.* Cast anchor; be moored by anchor. [ME, f. OF *ancrer* f. med. L *anc(h)orare*]

ă'nchorage (-k-) *n.* (Place for) anchoring; lying at anchor; (fig.) thing to depend upon. [f. ANCHOR¹ + -AGE]

ă'nchor|īte, ă'nchor|ėt, (-k-) *n.* Hermit, recluse; person of secluded habits; hence or cogn. ~ESS¹ *n.*, ~**ĕ'tic**, ~**ĭ'tic**, *adjs.* [ME, f. med. L *anc(h)orita*, eccl. L *anchoreta* f. eccl. Gk *anakhōrētēs* (ANA*khōreō* retire); see -ET²]

ănchovē'ta *n.* Small Pacific anchovy caught for use as bait or to make fish-meal. [Sp., dim. of *anchova* (cf. foll.)]

ă'nchovy̆ (*or* ănchō'-) *n.* Small fish of herring family with rich flavour; ~ **pear,** W. Ind. fruit like mango; ~ **toast** (spread with paste made from anchovies). [f. Sp. & Port. *ancho(v)a*, of uncert. orig.]

ănchū'sa (-k-; *or* -chōō'-) *n.* Plant of genus *Anchusa*, akin to borage; related plant, e.g. bugloss. [L, f. Gk *agkhousa*]

anchylose etc. Var. of ANKYLOSE etc.

ancien régime (ahṅsyăṅ rāzhē'm) *n.* (*pl.* ***-ns -es*** *pr.* same). System of government in France before the Revolution; (transf.) a superseded regime. [F, = old rule]

ā'ncient¹ (-shent) *a.* & *n.* **1.** *a.* Belonging to times long past; ~ **history** (esp. before fall of Western Roman Empire in 476, (fig.) something already long familiar); hence ~LY² *adv.*, long ago. **2.** Having existed, or lived, long; ~ **lights,** window that neighbour may not deprive of light by building; ‖~ **monument,** old building etc. preserved usu. under Government control. **3.** *n.* (arch.) Old man. **4. A~ of Days,** God; **the ~s,** civilized nations of antiquity, esp. Greeks and Romans. **5.** Hence ~NESS *n.* [ME f. AF *auncien*, f. OF *ancien*, f. Rom. **anti-*, *anteanus* (*ante* before; see -AN)]

ā'ncient² (-shent) *n.* (arch.) = ENSIGN. [corrupt. of form *ensyne* etc. by assoc. w. *ancien* = prec.]

ăncĭ'llary̆ (*or* ă'n-) *a.* Subservient, subordinate, (*to*). [f. L *ancillaris* (*ancilla* handmaid; see -ARY²)]

ă'ncon *n.* (Archit.) Console, usu. of two volutes, (apparently) supporting cornice. [L, f. Gk *agkōn* elbow]

-ancy̆ *suf.* forming *ns.* denoting quality (*constancy, relevancy*) or state (*expectancy, infancy*), but not action (cf. -ANCE). [f. or after L *-antia* (cf. -ENCY)]

and (and, an, *or, when stressed,* ănd) *conj.* (connecting words, clauses, or sentences, that are to be taken jointly; *cakes and buns*; *white and brown bread*; *buy and sell*; *two hundred and forty*); *better* ~ (steadily) *better*; *she cried* ~ *cried* (cried for a long time); *and* ALL; GOOD *and*; *miles* ~ (very many) *miles*; NICE *and*; TRY *and*; *there are books* ~ (different kinds of, good and bad) *books*; *two* ~ *two*, (1) two added to two, (2) by twos; *move* ~ (= if you move) *I shoot*; *A* **and/or** *B*, A or B or both. [OE *and*, = OS *anda, endi*, OHG *anti, enti*, f. IE **n̥tha*]

-ănd *suf.* See -ND¹.

ăndă'ntė (*or* -ā) *adv.*, *a.*, & *n.* (Mus.) (Movement) in moderately slow time. [It., part. of *andare* go]

ăndantī'nō (-tē'-) *adv.*, *a.*, & *n.* (*pl.* ~**s**). (Movement) rather quicker (orig. slower) than andante. [It., dim. of prec.]

ă'ndiron (-iern) *n.* Metal stand for supporting burning wood on hearth etc., FIRE¹dog. [ME, f. OF *andier*, of unkn. orig.; assim. to IRON¹]

ăndroe'cĭ|um (-rē'-) *n.* (*pl.* ~**a**). (Bot.) Stamens taken collectively. [mod. L, f. Gk *andro-* male + *oikion* house]

ă'ndrogėn *n.* Male sex hormone or other substance capable of developing and maintaining certain male sexual characteristics; hence **ăndrogĕ'nic** *a.* [f. Gk *andro-* male + -GEN]

ă'ndrogy̆ne *a.* & *n.* Hermaphrodite (person). [OF, or f. L f. Gk *androgunos* (*anēr andros* male, *gunē* woman)]

ăndrŏ'gy̆n|ous *a.* Hermaphrodite, whence ~Y¹ *n.*; (Bot.) with stamens and pistils in same flower or inflorescence. [f. prec. + -OUS]

ă'ndroid *n.* Robot with human form. [f. Gk *andro-* male, man + -OID]

-ă'ndrous *suf.* (Bot.) forming *adjs.* w. sense 'having specified male organs or stamens' (*monandrous*). [f. mod. L f. Gk *-andros* (*anēr andros* male) + -OUS]

-āne *suf.* **1.** Var. of -AN, usu. w. differentiation (*germane, humane, urbane*) but occas. alone (*mundane*). **2.** (Chem.) forming names of paraffins and other saturated hydrocarbons (*methane, propane*) [after *-ene*, *-ine*, etc.].

anear' *adv.* & *prep.* (arch.) = NEAR¹. [f. A- + NEAR¹]

ă'nėcdōtage *n.* Anecdotes; (joc., after *dotage*) garrulous old age. [f. foll. + -AGE]

ă'nėcdōt|e *n.* Narrative (or painting etc.) of amusing or interesting incident; hence ~(**al**)IST (3) *n.*, ~AL, ~IC, (*or* -dō'-) *adjs.* [F, or f. mod. L f. Gk *anekdota* things unpublished (as AN- 4, *ekdotos* f. *ekdidōmi* publish)]

ănėchō'ic (-kō'-) *a.* Free from echo. [f. AN- 4 + ECHO¹ + -IC]

anē'le *v.t.* (arch.) Anoint; give extreme unction to. [ME, f. AN- 1 + *elien* f. OE *ele* f. L *oleum* oil]

***anē'mĭa.** See ANAEMIA.

anĕ'mo|graph (-ahf) *n.* Instrument for recording on paper the direction and force of wind; hence ~**gră'phic** *a.* [f. Gk *anemos* wind + -GRAPH]

ănėmŏ'mėter *n.* Instrument for measuring force of wind; hence **ănėmomĕ'tric** *a.*, **ănėmŏ'metry** *n.* [f. as prec. + -METER]

anĕ'monė *n.* Plant of genus *Anemone*, akin to buttercup; **sea** ~, large polyp with petal-like tentacles round mouth; **wood** ~, wild kind of anemone, wind-flower. [f. L f. Gk *anemōnē* wind-flower (*anemos* wind)]

ănėmŏ'phĭlous *a.* Wind-pollinated. [f. Gk *anemos* wind + -PHILOUS]

anĕ'nt *prep.* (arch., joc., or Sc.) Concerning. [OE *on efen* on a level with]

-ā'nėous *suf.* forming *adjs.* (*cutaneous, miscellaneous*). [f. L *-aneus* + -OUS]

ă'neroid *a.* & *n.* (Barometer) that measures air-pressure by its action on elastic lid of evacuated box, not by height of fluid column. [f. F *anéroïde* f. Gk *a-* not + *nēros* wet; see -OID]

***anesthesia,** etc. See ANAESTHESIA, etc.

aneur'ĭn (-nūr'-) *n.* Vitamin B_1. [f. *a*nti- + poly*neur*itis + vitam*in*]

ă'neury̆sm, -ĭsm, (-nūr-) *n.* Morbid dilatation of an artery; hence **ăneury̆'smal, -ĭ'smal,** (-nūrĭ'z-) *a.* [f. Gk *aneurusma* (*aneurunō* widen out f. *eurus* wide)]

anew' *adv.* Again; in a different way. [ME, f. A- (3) + NEW¹]

ănfrăctūŏ'sĭty̆ *n.* Circuitousness, intricacy, (lit. or fig.). [f. F *anfractuosité* f. LL *anfractuosus* f. L *anfractus* a bending; see -OSITY]

ă'ngary̆ (ă'ngg-) *n.* (Law). Belligerent's right (subject to compensation of loss) of seizing or destroying neutral property under military necessity. [f. F *angarie* f. It. or LL *angaria* forced service f. Gk *aggareia* (*aggaros* courier f. Pers. *angaros*)]

ā'ngel (-nj-) *n.* **1.** Divine attendant or messenger (**good, evil,** ~, attendant spirits; GUARDIAN *angel*); one of the lowest ORDER¹ of ninefold celestial hierarchy; **on the side of the ~s,** favouring the pleasanter or more spiritual view of a question, believing that good will prevail. **2.** Lovely or innocent being; obliging or loving person; (sl.) financial backer of (esp. theatrical) enterprise; unexplained radar echo; ~(**-noble**), old English gold coin bearing figure of archangel Michael piercing dragon. **3.** ~ **cake,** ~ **food,** very light sponge cake; **~-fish,** one of various fish with winglike fins; **~s, devils, -on-horse-back,** savoury of oysters wrapped in slices of bacon. [ME, f. OF *angele* f. eccl. L *angelus* f. Gk *aggelos* messenger]

ăngĕ'lĭc (-nj-) *a.* Pertaining to angels; like an angel in beauty or sublimity or power; **A~ Doctor,** St. Thomas Aquinas; hence ~AL *a.*, ~alLY² *adv.* [ME, f. F *angélique* or f. LL f. Gk *aggelikos* (as prec.; see -IC)]

ăngĕ'lĭca (-nj-) *n.* Aromatic umbelliferous plant, used in cooking and medicine; its candied stalks. [f. med. L (*herba*) *angelica* angelic herb]

ă'ngėlus (-nj-) *n.* Devotional exercise commemorating Incarnation, said by Roman Catholics at morning, noon, and sunset, at sound of ~ **bell.** [f. opening words *Angelus domini* (L, = the angel of the Lord)]

ă'nger¹ (ă'ngg-) *n.* Extreme displeasure. [ME, f. ON *angr* grief (**ang* narrow)]

ă'nger² (ă'ngg-) *v.t.* Make angry, enrage. [ME, f. ON *angra* vex (as prec.)]

A'ngėvĭn (ă'nj-) *a.* & *n.* (Native or inhabitant) of Anjou; (one) of the Plantagenets, including English kings from Henry II to Richard II. [F]

ăngī'na (pĕ'ctorĭs) (-nj-) *n.* Pain in chest resulting from over-exertion when heart is diseased. [L, = spasm of the chest (*angina* quinsy f. Gk *agkhonē* strangling)]

ă'ngĭospẽrm (-nj-) *n.* Flowering plant, opp. *gymnosperm*; hence ~OUS (-ẽr'-) *a.* [f. Gk *aggeion* vessel + *sperma* seed]

ă'ngle¹ (ă'nggel) *n.* Space between two meeting lines or planes; inclination of two lines to each other (ACUTE, OBTUSE, RIGHT¹, *angle*); corner; sharp projection; direction from which photograph etc. is taken; (fig.) aspect from which a matter is considered; ~ **brackets,** brackets ⟨ ⟩ (see BRACKET¹ 2); **~dozer,** bulldozer with blade set obliquely; **~-iron,** piece of iron with L-shaped cross-section to strengthen framework; **~-parking** (of cars obliquely to roadside). [ME f. OF, or f. L *angulus* dim. of **angus*]

ă'ngle² (ă'nggel) *v.t.* & *i.* Move or place obliquely; (colloq.) present (news etc.) from particular viewpoint; hence **ă'nglED²** (ă'nggeld) *a.*, placed obliquely, having an angle (also in *comb.*). [f. prec.]

ă'ngle³ (ă'nggel) *n.*, & *v.i.* **1.** *n.* (arch.) Fish-hook; **brother of the** ~, angler. **2.** *v.i.* Fish with hook and bait (*for*, or abs.; lit., or fig.: *angle for compliments, votes*, etc.). [OE *angul*, = OS, OHG *angul*, ON *öngull*]

A'ngl|e⁴ (ă'nggel) *n.* Member of tribe from Schleswig that settled in Eastern Britain in 5th c.; hence ~IAN *a.* [f. L *Anglus* f. Gmc **angli-* (OE *Engle*; cf. ENGLISH¹) f. *Angul* a district of Schleswig (now in N. Germany) (as prec.)]

ă'ngler (ă'ngg-) *n.* One who fishes with hook and line; ~(**-fish**), one of various fishes that prey upon small fish, attracting them by filaments attached to head and mouth. [f. ANGLE³ + -ER¹]

A'nglĭcan (ă'ngg-) *a.* & *n.* (Adherent) of the reformed Church of England or of any church in communion with it; hence ~ISM (3) *n.* [f. med. L *Anglicanus* (Magna Carta) f. *Anglicus* (Bede) f. *Anglus* ANGLE⁴]

ă'nglĭcė (ă'ngg-) *adv.* In English. [med. L]

A'nglĭcĭsm (ă'ngg-) *n.* English idiom; Englishness; preference for what is English. [f. L *Anglicus* (see ANGLICAN) + -ISM]

A'nglĭcīze, -īse, (ă'ngglĭsīz) *v.t.* Make English in form or character. [f. as prec. + -IZE]

A'nglĭst (ă'ngg-) *n.* Student of or scholar in English language or literature; hence **Anglĭ'stics** (ăngg-) *n.* [G, f. L *Anglus* English; see -IST]

Anglō- (ăngg-) *comb. form.* English (*Anglo-Catholic*); of English origin (*an Anglo-American*); English or British and (*an Anglo-American agreement*). [mod. L, f. L *Anglus* English; see -O-]

Anglō-Că'tholĭc (ăngg-) *a.* & *n.* (Member) of party holding that the Church of England is a branch of the Catholic Church and rejecting its Protestant element. [f. prec. + CATHOLIC]

Anglōcĕ'ntrĭc (ăngg-) *a.* Centred on England. [f. ANGLO- + -CENTRIC]

Anglō-Frĕ'nch (ăngg-) *a.* & *n.* **1.** (Of) French language as retained and separately developed in England after Norman Conquest. **2.** *a.* English (or British) and French. [f. ANGLO- + FRENCH]

Anglō-I'ndĭan (ăngglōĭ'-) *a.* & *n.* (Person) of British birth but living or having lived long in India; Eurasian; (of word) adopted into English from an Indian language. [f. ANGLO- + INDIAN]

Anglomā'nĭa (ăngg-) *n.* Excessive admiration of English customs; so **AngloMA'NIAC, A'ngloPHIL(E), A'ngloPHOBE,** *ns.* & *adjs.*, **AngloPHO'BIA** *n.*, (ăngg-). [f. ANGLO- + -MANIA]

Anglō-Nŏr'man (ăngg-) *a.* & *n.* (Of the) dialect of Normans as used in England after Norman Conquest. [f. ANGLO- + NORMAN]

ă'nglophōne (ăngg-) *a.* & *n.* English-speaking (person). [f. ANGLO-, after FRANCOPHONE]

Anglō-Să'xon (ăngg-) *n.* & *a.* English Saxon (as distinct from Old Saxons of the continent); Old English (person, language) before Norman Conquest; *modern English, (colloq.) plain English; (person) of English descent (wherever found); hence ~ISM (2, 3, 4) *n.* [f. mod. L *Anglo-Saxones*, med. L *Angli Saxones* after OE *Angulseaxe, -an*]

ăngōr'a, (arch.) **ăngō'la,** (ăngg-) *n.* Fabric made from hair of angora goat; ~ **cat, goat, rabbit,** (long-haired varieties); ~ (**wool**), mixture of sheep's wool and angora rabbit hair. [f. *Angora* (Ankara) in Turkey; *angola* is a corruption]

ăngostūr'a (ăngg-) *n.* ~ **bark,** aromatic bark formerly used as febrifuge and tonic; ~ **bitters,** kind of tonic first made in Angostura (**P**). [f. *Angostura*, town in Venezuela on the Orinoco, now Ciudad Bolivar]

ă'ngr|ȳ (ăngg-) *a.* Showing anger, extremely displeased, resentful, (*at, about,* thing; *at, with,* person); (fig.) seeming to show anger (*an angry sky*); irritable; (of wound, sore, etc.) inflamed, painful; hence ~ĬLY² *adv.* [ME, f. ANGER¹ + -Y²]

Angst (ă-) *n.* Anxiety; feeling of guilt or remorse. [G]

å'ngström (ă'ngstrẽm; *or* ŏ'ng-) *n.* Unit of wavelength measurement, 10^{-10} metre. [f. A. J. *Ångström*, Swedish physicist d. 1874]

ă'nguīne (ă'nggw-) *a.* Snakelike. [f. L *anguinus* (*anguis* snake); see -INE¹]

ă'nguĭsh (ă'nggw-) *n.* Severe bodily or mental pain. [ME, f. OF *anguisse* choking f. L *angustia* tightness (*angustus* narrow); cf. -ISH²]

ă'nguĭshed (ă'nggwĭsht) *a.* Suffering or expressing anguish. [p.p. of *anguish* v. f. OF *anguissier* f. eccl. L *angustiare* to distress f. as prec.]

ă'ngūlar (ă'ngg-) *a.* **1.** Having angles; sharp-cornered; lacking plumpness, smoothness, or suavity. **2.** Placed in or at an angle; measured by angle (*angular distance*; ~ **momentum,** quantity of rotation of a body, product of its moment of inertia and angular velocity; ~ **velocity,** rate of change of angular position of rotating body). **3.** Hence ~ITY (-ă'r-) *n.*, ~LY² *adv.* [f. L *angularis* (*angulus* ANGLE¹; see -AR¹)]

ănhē'dral *a.* & *n.* **1.** (Aeron.) (Having) negative dihedral angle. **2.** *a.* (Of crystals etc.) not having normal external form. [f. AN- 4 + -HEDRAL]
ănhȳ'drīde *n.* (Chem.) Substance obtained by removing the elements of water from a compound, esp. from an acid. [f. as foll. + -IDE]
ănhȳ'drous *a.* (Chem.) Without water, esp. water of crystallization. [f. Gk *anudros* (as AN- 4, *hudōr* water) + -OUS]
ănīcŏ'nĭc *a.* (Of idols, symbols, etc.) not shaped in human or animal form. [f. AN- 4 + ICONIC]
ă'nĭcŭt, ă'nn-, *n.* River-dam in S. India built for irrigation purposes. [f. Tamil *aṉai-kaṭṭu* dam-building]
anī'gh (-ī') *adv.* & *prep.* (arch.) = NEAR¹. [f. NIGH after *anear*]
ă'nīle *a.* Old-womanish; imbecile; so **anĭ'lITY** *n.* [f. L *anilis* (*anus* old woman; see -IL)]
ă'nĭlĭne (*or* -ēn *or* -īn) *n.* Oily liquid got from coal tar, an organic base; ~ **dye,** (1) one of numerous dyes made from aniline, (2) any synthetic dye. [f. G *anilin* f. *anil* indigo (whence orig. obtained) f. F or Port. f. Arab. *an-nīl* (*al* the, *nīl* f. Skr. *nīlī* indigo f. *nīla* dark blue); see -INE⁵]
ă'nĭma *n.* (Psych.) Inner personality (opp. *persona*); feminine part of a man's personality. [L, = mind, soul]
ănĭmadvēr'|t *v.i.* Pass criticism or censure *on* (conduct, fault, etc.); so ~**SION** (-shon) *n.* [f. L *animadvertere* f. *animus* mind + AD(*vertere vers-* turn)]
ă'nĭmal *n.* & *a.* **1.** *n.* Organized being endowed (more or less perceptibly) with life, sensation, and voluntary motion; (esp.) such being other than man; (colloq.) **there is no such** ~ (person or thing). **2.** Quadruped; a brutish man. **3.** *a.* Characteristic of animals; ~ **magnetism,** (Hist.) mesmerism; ~ **spirits,** natural exuberance. **4.** Of animals as opp. to vegetables (*animal charcoal*); carnal, sensual. [L, f. *animale* neut. of *animalis* having breath (*anima* breath; see -AL)]
ănĭmă'lcūle *n.* Microscopic animal. [f. mod. L *animalculum* (*animal*; see prec., -CULE)]
ă'nĭmalĭsm *n.* Animal activity; sensuality; doctrine that men are mere animals. [f. ANIMAL + -ISM]
ănĭmă'lĭtȳ *n.* Animal nature or system; merely animal nature; the animal world. [f. F *animalité* (*animal* a.; see -ITY)]
ă'nĭmalīz|e, -īs|e (-īz), *v.t.* Convert to animal substance; sensualize; hence ~**A'TION** *n.* [f. ANIMAL + -IZE]
anima mundi (ănĭma mŭ'ndī) *n.* Power supposed to organize and regulate the material universe. [med. L, = soul of the world]
ă'nĭmate¹ *a.* Living; lively. [f. L *animatus* p.p. of *animare* give life to (*anima* life, soul); see -ATE²]
ă'nĭmāt|e² *v.t.* Breathe life into; enliven, make lively (*an animated discussion*); give (film etc.) appearance of movement by using quick succession of gradually varying drawings; encourage; inspire, actuate; hence ~**ėdLY²** *adv.*, **ănĭmA'TION** *n.*, (esp.) state of being alive, ardour, vivacity, ~**OR** *n.*, (Cinemat.) artist who prepares animated cartoons. [f. as prec. + -ATE³]
ă'nĭmé (-mā) *n.* One of various resins, esp. W. Ind. resin used in making varnish. [F, of uncert. orig.]
ă'nĭm|ĭsm *n.* Doctrine of *anima mundi*; attribution of living soul to plants, inanimate objects, and natural phenomena; hence ~**IST** (2) *n.*, ~**ĭ'stIC** *a.* [f. L *anima* life, soul + -ISM]
ănĭmŏ'sĭtȳ *n.* Spirit of enmity (*against, between, towards*). [ME, f. OF *animosité* or f. LL *animositas* (*animosus* spirited f. as foll.; see -OSITY)]
ă'nĭmus *n.* Animating spirit; animosity shown in speech or action; (Psych.) masculine part of a woman's personality. [L, = spirit, mind]
ă'nīon *n.* Ion with negative charge that moves towards anode in presence of electric field (opp. CATION). [f. ANA- + ION]
ănīŏ'nĭc *a.* Of anion(s); having an active anion. [f. prec. + -IC]
ă'nĭse *n.* Umbelliferous plant (*Pimpinella anisum*) with aromatic seeds (see foll.). [ME, f. OF *anis* f. L f. Gk *anison* anise, dill]
ă'nĭseed *n.* Seed of anise, used to flavour liqueurs and sweets. [ME, f. prec. + SEED]
ănĭsĕ'tte (-z-) *n.* Liqueur flavoured with aniseed. [F, dim. of *anis* ANISE; see -ETTE]
ănīsotrŏ'p|ĭc *a.* Having physical properties (e.g. elasticity) that depend on direction; hence ~**ICALLY** *adv.*, **ănīsŏ'tropY¹** *n.* [f. AN- 4 + ISOTROPIC]
ă'nker *n.* (Hist.) (Cask containing) quantity of about 8 gal. of wine. [LG & Du., f. med. L *anc(h)eria*]
ănkh (ăngk) *n.* Keylike cross used in ancient Egypt as symbol of life. [Egypt., = life, soul]
ă'nkle *n.*, & *v.i.* **1.** *n.* Joint connecting foot with leg; slender part between this and calf; ~ **sock,** short sock just covering ankle. **2.** *v.i.* (sl.) Walk. [ME, f. ON **ankul-* f. Gmc **ank-* f. IE **ang-* (as in ANGLE¹)]
ă'nklėt *n.* Ornament or fetter for ankle; *ankle sock. [f. prec. + -LET, after *bracelet*]
ă'nkȳlōse (-ōz) *v.t.* & *i.* Stiffen or unite by ankylosis. [back form. f. foll. after *anastomose* etc.]
ănkȳl|ō'sĭs *n.* (*pl.* ~**oses** *pr.* -ō'sēz). Formation of stiff joint by consolidation of articulating surfaces; growing together of separate bones; hence ~**O'TIC** *a.* [mod. L, f. Gk *agkulosis* (*agkuloō* crook; see -OSIS)]
ă'nlāce *n.* (arch.) Short tapering two-edged dagger. [ME, of unkn. orig.]
ă'nna *n.* Former coin of India and Pakistan, one-sixteenth of rupee. [f. Hind. *ānā*]
ă'nnal *n.* Annals of one year; record of one item in chronicle. [back form. f. ANNALS]
ă'nnal|ĭst *n.* Writer of annals; hence ~**ĭ'stIC** *a.* [f. foll. + -IST]
ă'nnals (-z) *n. pl.* Narrative of events year by year; historical records. [f. F *annales* or f. L *annales* (*libri*) yearly (books) (*annus* year; see -AL)]
ă'nnātes (-ts) *n. pl.* (R.C. Ch.) First year's revenue of see or benefice, paid to pope. [f. F *annate* f. med. L *annata* year's proceeds (*annus* year; see -ADE)]
an(n)ă'ttō, ană'tta, *n.* Orange-red dye from pulp of Central Amer. fruit, used for colouring cheese etc. [f. Carib name of the fruit-tree]
annea'l *v.t.*, & *n.* **1.** *v.t.* Toughen (glass or metals) by heating and usu. slow cooling; (fig.) toughen. **2.** *n.* Treatment by annealing. [OE *onǣlan* (*on* AN- 1, *ǣlan* burn, bake f. *āl* fire]
annĕ'ctent *a.* (Biol.) Connecting (*annectent link*). [f. L *annectere* (see ANNEX¹, -ENT)]
ă'nnelĭd *n.* Segmented worm of phylum Annelida, e.g. earthworm; hence **annĕ'lĭdAN** *a.* & *n.* [f. F *annélide* or mod. L *annelida* pl. f. F *annelés* ringed animals (OF *anel* ring f. L *anellus* dim. of *anulus* ring)]
annĕ'x¹ *v.t.* Add as subordinate part; append (*to* book etc.); take possession of (territory etc.), esp. (colloq.) take without right; attach as an attribute, addition, or consequence; so **ănnėxA'TION** *n.* [ME, f. OF *annexer* f. L AN(*nectere nex-* bind)]
ă'nnĕx², -ĕxe, *n.* Addition to a document; (‖usu. *-exe*) supplementary building, esp. for extra accommodation. [f. F *annexe* f. L *annexum* p.p. (as n.) of *annectere* bind; cf. prec.]

ă'nnĭcŭt. See ANICUT.

annī'hĭlāt|e (-nī'ĭ-) *v.t.* Destroy largely or completely; (fig.) make insignificant; hence ~OR *n.* [f. LL ANnihilare (*nihil* nothing) + -ATE³]

annĭhĭlā'tion (-nīĭ-) *n.* Destruction etc. (cf. prec.); (Phys.) conversion of particle and antiparticle into radiation; (Theol.) destruction of soul as well as body, whence ~ISM (3), ~IST (2), *ns.* [F, or f. LL *annihilatio* (see prec., -ATION)]

ănnĭvĕr'sarȳ *n.* Yearly return of a date; celebration of this; **A~ Day,** (Austral.) 26 Jan. (commemorating British landing 1788). [ME, f. L *anniversarius* (*annus* year, *versus* turned; see -ARY¹)]

Annō Dŏ'mĭnī (ă-) *adv.* & *n.* **1.** *adv.* In the year of our Lord, of the Christian era. **2.** *n.* (colloq.) Advancing age (*suffering from Anno Domini*). [L, = in the year of the Lord]

ă'nnot|āte *v.t.* Furnish (book etc.) with notes; hence or cogn. **~āt**ABLE *a.*, ~A'TION, **~āt**OR, *ns.* [f. L ANnotare (*nota* mark) + -ATE³]

annou'nce *v.t.* Make publicly known (*that*); make known the approach of; make known (without words) to senses or mind, be sign of; hence ~MENT (-sm-), **annou'nc**ER¹ (esp. in broadcasting), *ns.* [ME, f. OF *annoncer* f. L ANnuntiare (*nuntius* messenger)]

annoy'¹ *n.* (arch. or poet.) Annoyance. [ME, f. OF *anui, anoi* f. Rom. **inodio* (see foll.)]

annoy'² *v.t.* **1.** Irritate; **be ~ed** (somewhat angry) *with* person, *at* thing, *to discover* etc. **2.** Molest, harass. **3.** So ~ANCE *n.* [ME, f. OF *anuier* etc., LL *inodiare*, f. Rom. **inodio* f. L *in odio* hateful]

ă'nnūal *a.* & *n.* **1.** *a.* Reckoned by the year; recurring yearly (~ **ring,** ring in cross-section of tree, fish, etc., from one year's growth); lasting for one year; hence ~LY² *adv.* **2.** *n.* Plant that lives only for a year; book etc. published in yearly numbers. [ME f. OF *annuel* f. LL *annualis* f. L *annalis* (*annus* year; see -AL)]

annū'ĭtant *n.* One who holds or receives an annuity. [f. foll. + -ANT, by assim. to *accountant* etc.]

annū'ĭtȳ *n.* Sum payable in respect of a particular year; yearly grant; investment of money entitling investor to series of equal annual sums. [ME, f. F *annuité* f. med. L *annuitas -tatis* f. L *annuus* yearly (as ANNUAL; see -ITY)]

annŭ'l *v.t.* (-ll-). Abolish, cancel; declare invalid; hence ~MENT *n.* [ME, f. OF *anuller* f. LL AN(*nullare* f. *nullus* none)]

ă'nnūlar *a.* Ringlike; ~ **eclipse** of sun (when moon, projected on sun's disc, leaves ring of light visible); hence ~LY² *adv.* [f. F *annulaire* or f. L *annularis* (*an(n)ulus* ring; see -AR¹)]

ă'nnūlate *a.* Having, or marked with, or formed of, rings. [f. L *annulatus* (as ANNULUS; see -ATE²)]

ă'nnūlėt *n.* Small ring; (Archit.) small fillet or band encircling column. [f. L (as foll.) + -ET¹]

ă'nnūl|us *n.* (*pl.* ~i *pr.* -ī). (esp. Math. & Biol.) Ring. [L *an(n)ulus*]

annŭ'ncĭāte (-shĭ-) *v.t.* Proclaim; indicate as coming or ready. [f. LL *annunciare* f. L *annuntiare* announce + -ATE³]

annŭncĭā'tion *n.* Announcement; (*A~*) that of the Incarnation, made by Gabriel to Mary; festival commemorating this, Lady Day, 25 March. [ME, f. OF *annonciation* f. LL *annuntiatio -onis* (as prec.; see -ATION)]

annŭ'ncĭātor (-shĭ-) *n.* Announcer; audible or visible indicator of where bell has been rung, position of train, etc. [f. LL *annuntiator* (as prec.; see -OR)]

annus mirabilis (ănus mĭrah'bĭlĭs) *n.* Remarkable or auspicious year. [mod. L, = wonderful year]

anō'a *n.* Small wild ox of Celebes. [name in Celebes]

ă'nōde *n.* (Electr.) Positive electrode or terminal (opp. CATHODE); ~ **ray,** beam of particles from anode of high-vacuum tube; hence **ă'nod**AL, **anŏ'd**IC, *adjs.* [f. Gk *anodos* way up (*ana* up, *hodos* way)]

ă'nodīze, -īse (-īz), *v.t.* Coat (metal) with protective layer (e.g. of alumina) by making it anode in electrolysis. [f. ANODE + -IZE]

ă'nodȳne *a.* & *n.* (Medicine etc.) able to assuage pain; (anything) mentally soothing and harmless. [f. L f. Gk *anōdunos* painless (as AN- 4, *odunē* pain)]

ănoē's|ĭs *n.* (*pl.* ~**es** *pr.* -ēz). (Psych.) Consciousness with sensation but without thought; so **ănoē'**TIC *a.* [f. A- 7 + Gk *noēsis* understanding]

anoi'nt *v.t.* Apply ointment or oil to (esp. as religious ceremony at baptism or on consecration as priest or king); smear, rub; **the Lord's Anointed,** (1) Christ, (2) king by divine right. [ME, f. AF *anoint* a. f. OF *enoint* p.p. of *enoindre* f. L IN¹(*ungere unct-*)]

anŏmalĭ'stĭc *a.* (Astron.) Of anomaly; ~ **month** (between successive perigees of moon); ~ **year** (between successive perihelia of earth). [f. Gk *anōmalos* (see foll.) + -IST + -IC]

anŏ'malous *a.* Irregular; abnormal; hence ~LY² *adv.*, ~NESS *n.* [f. LL f. Gk *anōmalos* (as AN- 4, *homalos* even) + -OUS]

anŏ'malūre *n.* African rodent of genus *Anomalurus*, with projecting scales on tail. [f. mod. L *anomalurus* f. Gk *anōmalos* ANOMALOUS + *oura* tail]

anŏ'malȳ *n.* Irregularity of motion, behaviour, etc.; (Astron.) angular distance of planet or satellite from its last perihelion or perigee. [f. L f. Gk *anōmalia* (*anōmalos* ANOMALOUS; see -Y¹)]

ă'nomȳ, ă'nomĭe, *n.* Lack of the usual social standards in group or person; hence **anŏ'm**IC *a.* [f. Gk *anomia* (*anomos* lawless); *-ie* f. F]

anŏ'n *adv.* (arch. or literary). Soon, presently, (*will say more of this anon*); EVER *and anon.* [OE *on ān* into one, *on āne* in one]

anŏ'n. *abbr.* anonymous (author).

ănonā'ceous (-ā'shus) *a.* Of the custard-apple family Annonaceae. [f. mod. L *An(n)ona* genus of edible fruits typical of family + -ACEOUS]

ă'nonȳm *n.* Person who remains nameless; anonymous publication; pseudonym. [f. F *anonyme* f. Gk *anōnumos* (see foll.)]

anŏ'nȳmous *a.* Of unknown name; of unknown or undeclared source or authorship; hence ~LY² *adv.*, **ănonȳ'm**ITY, ~NESS, *ns.* [f. L f. Gk *anōnumos* nameless (as AN- 4, *onoma* name); see -OUS]

anŏ'phelēs (-z) *n.* Mosquito of genus *Anopheles*, esp. one carrying malaria. [mod. L, f. Gk *anōphelēs* unprofitable]

ă'norăk *n.* Skin or cloth hooded jacket for wear in polar regions; similar weatherproof garment for ordinary wear. [f. Greenland Eskimo *anoraq*]

ănorĕ'xia *n.* (Path.) Absence of appetite or desire; ~ **nervo'sa** (-ō-), condition of which chronic anorexia induced by emotional disturbance is a symptom. [LL f. Gk (*an-* not, *orexis* appetite; see -IA¹)]

ănŏ'sm|ĭa (-z-) *n.* Loss of sense of smell; hence ~IC *a.* [mod. L f. as AN- 4 + Gk *osmē* smell + -IA¹]

ano'ther (-ŭ'dh-) *pron.* (*pl.* **others**) & *a.* (*pl.* **other**). An additional (one) (*have another pear*; *have another*; YOU'*re another*; *after another month*; *after another six months*); a different (one) (*take this towel away and bring me another*; *another person than yourself*; *one man's* MEAT *is another man's poison*; ONE *another*); ‖~ **place,** the other House of Parliament (used in Commons to refer to Lords, and vice versa); ‖unnamed additional party to legal action (*X versus Y and another*);

||(also **A. N. Other**) player unnamed or not yet selected; someone like (*another Solomon*); **such ~**, another of the same sort. [ME, f. AN[1] + OTHER]

ănŏ'vūlant *a.* & *n.* (Drug) preventing ovulation. [f. AN- 4 + OVULATION + -ANT]

ănŏxae'mĭa *n.* (Med.) Defective oxygenation of the blood. [mod. L, f. as AN- 4 + OXYGEN + -AEMIA]

anŏ'x|ĭa *n.* (Med.) Deficiency of oxygen in tissues; hence **~IC** *a.* [mod. L, f. as AN- 4 + OXYGEN + -IA[1]]

anschluss (ă'nshlōōs) *n.* Union, esp. annexation of Austria by Germany in 1938. [G (*anschliessen* join)]

ă'nserīne *a.* Of or like a goose; silly. [f. L *anserinus* (*anser* goose; see -INE[1])]

a'nswer[1] (ah'nser) *n.* Something said or done to deal with a question, accusation, etc.; solution to a problem; **know all the ~s**, (colloq.) be very experienced. [OE *andswaru* f. Gmc **andswarō* (**and-* against, **swar*; cf. OE *swerian* swear)]

a'nswer[2] (ah'nser) *v.* **1.** *v.t.* Make answer to (*answer me, my question*); ~ (summons to) *the door, the telephone*, etc.; be satisfactory for (purpose etc.). **2.** *v.i.* Make answer (*to*); be responsible (*for* person or thing); correspond *to* (description etc.); be satisfactory or successful; **~ to the name of**, be called; **~ back**, (colloq.) make impudent answer to rebuke etc. [OE *andswarian* (as prec.)]

a'nswerable (ah'nser-) *a.* Responsible (*to* person, *for* person or thing); that can be answered. [f. prec. + -ABLE]

ănt *n.* Small social hymenopterous insect proverbial for industry; **white ~**, termite; **~-bear**, (1) tamanoir, (2) aardvark; **~-eater**, name of various mammals that live on ants, e.g. aardvark, echidna, pangolin; **~(s')-eggs**, pupae or larvae of ants, used as animal food; **~'heap, ~'hill**, (-t-h-) mound over ants' nest, conical nest of termites, (fig.) crowded dwelling; **~-lion**, (larva of) nocturnal neuropterous insect that traps ants. [OE *ǣmet(t)e, ēmete* (see EMMET) f. WG **āmaitja* (*ā* off, *mait-* cut)]

an't (ahnt) *v.i.* (arch.) = *are not*; (arch. colloq.) = *am not*; (arch. vulg.) = *is not, has not, have not*. [contr.]

ant-. See ANTI-.

-ant *suf.* forming *adjs.* denoting existence of action (*pendant, repentant*), and *ns.* denoting agent (*assistant, celebrant, deodorant*), usu. f. *vbs.* [f. or after F *-ant* or f. L *-ant-, -ent-*, part. st. of vbs (cf. -ENT)]

ăntă'cĭd *a.* & *n.* Preventive or corrective of acidity (esp. in stomach). [f. ANT- + ACID[2]]

ăntă'gonĭsm *n.* Active opposition (*to, against*, person or thing; *between* two). [f. F *antagonisme* (as foll.; see -ISM)]

ăntă'gon|ĭst *n.* Opponent; (Biol.) substance or organ that interferes with the action of another; hence **~ĭ'stIC** *a.* [f. F *antagoniste* or f. LL *antagonista* f. Gk *antagōnistēs* (as foll.; see -IST)]

ăntă'gonīze, -īse (-īz), *v.t.* (Of force etc.) counteract, tend to neutralize, (another); evoke hostility or opposition or enmity in. [f. Gk ANT(*agōnizomai* f. *agōn* contest; see -IZE)]

ăntar̄'ctĭc *a.* & *n.* (Of) the south polar regions; **A~ Circle**, parallel of latitude 66° 33′ S. [ME, f. OF *antartique* or f. L f. Gk ANT(*arktikos* ARCTIC)]

ă'ntė *n.*, & *v.t.* **1.** *n.* (In poker etc.) stake put up by player before drawing cards; (transf.) advance payment. **2.** *v.t.* Put up as ante; *(transf.) bet, stake, pay *up*. [L, = before]

ăntė- *pref.* forming *ns.* (*ante-room*), and *adjs.* with (*antenatal*) or without (*ante-post*) adj. ending, w. sense 'before, preceding'. [L *ante* prep. & adv., = before]

ăntė-bĕ'llum *a.* Occurring or existing before a (specified) war, esp. *the Civil War. [L (*ante* before, *bellum* war)]

ăntėcē'd|ent *a.* & *n.* **1.** *a.* Previous (*to*); presumptive, a priori; hence or cogn. **~ENCE** *n.*, **~entLY[2]** *adv.* **2.** *n.* Preceding thing or circumstance; (Logic) the part of a conditional proposition on which the other part depends; (Gram.) noun, clause, sentence, to which a (usu. following and esp. relative) pronoun or adverb refers; (in *pl.*) past history (esp. of person). [ME f. F, or f. L ANTE(*cedere* go); see -ENT]

ă'ntėchāmber *n.* Room leading to a more important one. [earlier *anti-*, f. F *antichambre*, f. It. *anticamera* (as ANTE-, CHAMBER)]

ă'ntėchăpel *n.* Outer part at west end of chapel. [f. ANTE- + CHAPEL]

ă'ntėdāte[1] *n.* Date before the true time (esp. of writing). [f. ANTE- + DATE[2]]

ăntėdā'te[2] *v.t.* Affix, assign, an earlier (esp. than the true) date to (document, event); precede. [f. prec.]

ăntėdĭlū'vĭan (*or* -lōō'-) *a.* & *n.* **1.** *a.* Belonging, referring, appropriate, to the time before the Flood; (colloq.) utterly out of date. **2.** *n.* Old--fashioned or aged person. [f. ANTE- + L *diluvium* DELUGE + -AN]

ă'ntėlōpe *n.* (*pl.* same *or* **~s**). Deerlike ruminant animal, e.g. chamois, gazelle, gnu; leather made from its skin. [ME, f. OF *antelop* or f. med. L *ant(h)alopus* f. late Gk *antholops*, of unkn. orig.]

ăntė-mor̄'tem *a.* Made before death. [L, = before death]

ăntėmŭ'ndāne *a.* Existing or occurring before creation of world. [f. ANTE- + L *mundus* world + -ANE]

ăntėnā'tal *a.* Existing or occurring previous to birth; pertaining to the period of pregnancy. [f. ANTE- + NATAL]

ăntĕ'nn|a *n.* **1.** (*pl.* **~ae**). Sensory organ found in pairs on heads of insects, crustaceans, etc., feeler; (Bot.) irritable process in male flower of some orchids; hence **~AL**, **~ARY[1]**, *adjs.* **2.** (*pl.* **~as**). * = AERIAL 5. [L, = sail-yard]

ăntėnŭ'ptial (-shal) *a.* Born, occurring, etc., before marriage. [f. LL ANTE(*nuptialis* NUPTIAL)]

ăntėpĕ'ndĭ|um *n.* (*pl.* **~a**). Veil or hanging for front of altar. [med. L (ANTE-, *pendēre* hang)]

ăntėpėnŭ'lt (*or* -pē'n-) *a.* & *n.* = foll. [abbr. of LL ANTE(*paenultimus* PENULT)]

ăntėpėnŭ'ltĭmate *a.* & *n.* Last but two (esp. syllable). [f. ANTE- + PENULTIMATE]

||**ăntė-pō'st** *a.* (Of racing bets) made before the runners' numbers are displayed on the board. [f. ANTE- + POST[1]]

ăntėpră'ndĭal *a.* Before-dinner. [f. ANTE- + L *prandium* dinner + -AL]

ăntēr̄'ĭor *a.* More to the front; prior (*to*); hence **ăntēr̄ĭŏ'rITY** *n.*, **~LY[2]** *adv.* [f. F *antérieur* or f. L *anterior*, compar. f. *ante* before]

ă'ntė-rōōm (*or* -ŏŏm) *n.* Room leading to a more important one; ||(Mil.) sitting-room in officers' mess. [f. ANTE- + ROOM, after earlier ANTECHAMBER]

ănthē'lĭ|on *n.* (*pl.* **~a**). Luminous halo projected on cloud or fog-bank opposite to sun. [Gk, neut. of *anthēlios* opposite to sun (as ANTI-, *hēlios* sun)]

ănthĕlmĭ'ntĭc, -nthĭc, *a.* & *n.* (Medicine) acting against parasitic (esp. intestinal) worms. [f. ANTI- + Gk *helmins helminthos* worm + -IC]

ă'nthem *n.* Composition for church use sung antiphonally; non-metrical musical setting of sacred words; song of praise or gladness; NATIONAL *anthem*. [OE *antefn, antifne* f. LL *antiphona* ANTIPHON]

ănthē'mĭ|on *n.* (*pl.* ~**a**). Flower-like ornament used in art. [Gk, = flower]

ă'nther *n.* (Bot.) Part of stamen containing pollen; hence ~AL *a.* [f. F *anthère* or mod. L *anthera*, in L 'medicine extracted from flowers' f. Gk *anthēra* flowery, fem. a. f. *anthos* flower]

ăntherĭ'dĭ|um *n.* (*pl.* ~**a**). (Bot.) Male sex organ in cryptogams. [mod. L, f. *anthera* (as prec.) + Gk *-idion* dim. suf.]

ănthŏ'log|ȳ *n.* Choice collection of passages from literature (esp. poems), songs, paintings, etc.; hence ~IST (1) *n.*, ~IZE *v.i.*, compile anthology. [f. F *anthologie* or med. L f. Gk *anthologia* (*anthos* flower, *-logia* collection f. *legō* gather)]

ănthozō'an *a.* & *n.* (Marine animal) of the class Anthozoa, including corals, sea anemones, etc. [f. mod. L *Anthozoa* f. Gk *anthos* flower + *zōa* animals; see -AN]

ă'nthracēne *n.* Aromatic hydrocarbon obtained in the distillation of coal tar. [f. Gk *anthrax -akos* coal + -ENE]

ă'nthrac|ite *n.* Non-bituminous hard variety of coal; hence ~**ĭ'**TIC *a.* [f. Gk *anthrakitis* a kind of coal (as prec.; see -ITE[1])]

ă'nthrăx *n.* Disease of sheep and cattle, transmissible to man by infection from animals so affected. [LL f. Gk, = carbuncle]

ănthropo- *comb. form.* Human, mankind, as: ~**ce'ntric** *a.*, ~**ce'ntrism** *n.*, regarding man as central fact of universe; ~**geny** (-ŏ'j-), study of origin of man; ~**ge'nic,** (1) of anthropogeny, (2) originated by man; ~**graphy** (-ŏ'g-), science of geographical distribution of man. [f. Gk *anthrōpos* human being]

ă'nthropoid *a.* & *n.* **1.** *a.* Manlike in form; (colloq., of person) apelike. **2.** *n.* Being that is human in form only, esp. anthropoid ape. [f. Gk *anthrōpoeidēs* (as ANTHROPO-; see -OID)]

ănthropŏ'log|ȳ *n.* Study of mankind, esp. of its societies and customs; study of structure and evolution of man as an animal; hence **ănthropolŏ'g**ICAL *a.*, ~IST (3) *n.* [f. ANTHROPO- + -LOGY]

ănthropŏ'mĕtrȳ *n.* Measurement of the human body; hence **ănthropomĕ'tr**IC *a.* [f. ANTHROPO- + -METRY]

ănthropomôr'phĭc *a.* Of the nature of anthropomorphism. [f. as foll. + -IC]

ănthropomôr'ph|ĭsm *n.* Attribution of human form or personality to (god, animal, etc.); hence ~IZE (4) *v.t.* [f. as foll. + -ISM]

ănthropomôr'phous *a.* Of human form. [f. Gk ANTHROPO*morphos* (*morphē* form) + -OUS]

ănthropŏ'phag|ȳ *n.* Cannibalism; hence ~OUS *a.* [f. Gk ANTHROPO*phagia* (*phagō* eat)]

ă'ntĭ[1] *n.* Opponent. [f. ANTI-]

ă'ntĭ[2] *prep.* Against, opposing. [f. foll.]

ăntĭ- *pref.* (sometimes **ant-** before vowel or *h*) freely used to form *ns.* from *ns.* (*antibody, anticlimax, antipope*) and *adjs.* from *ns.* (*anti-aircraft, antitrust*) or from *adjs.* (*antarctic, anticlerical, anticoagulant, anti-Semitic*), w. senses: 'opposite, against, preventing'; (Phys.) antiparticle of specified particle (*antineutrino, antiproton*); unlike the conventional form (*anti-hero, anti-novel*); (w. suf. *-ism, -ist*) (doctrine of) person opposed to (*antivivisectionism, -ist*). [f. or after Gk *anti-* against]

ăntĭ-air'craft (-ahft) *a.* (Of gun etc.) for defence against hostile aircraft. [f. prec. + AIR[1]*craft*]

ă'ntĭar *n.* Upas tree of Java; poison obtained from it. [f. Jav. *antjar*]

ăntĭbiō's|ĭs *n.* (*pl.* ~**es** *pr.* -ēz). Condition of antagonism between (esp. micro-)organisms. [mod. L, f. F *antibiose* (as ANTI-, SYMBIOSIS)]

ăntĭbiŏ'tĭc *a.* & *n.* (Substance) capable of destroying or injuring living organisms, esp. bacteria. [f. F *antibiotique* f. as ANTI- + Gk *biōtikos* fit for life (*bios* life; see -OTIC)]

ă'ntĭbŏdȳ *n.* (Physiol.) Any of various proteins in the human body, produced by and counteracting antigens. [transl. of G *antikörper* (as ANTI-, *körper* body)]

ă'ntĭc *n.* & *a.* **1.** *n.* (usu. in *pl.*) Grotesque or absurd posture or action. **2.** *a.* (arch.) Grotesque, bizarre. [f. It. *antico* ANTIQUE, used as = grotesque]

ăntĭcă'thōde *n.* Target in X-ray tube on which electrons from cathode impinge. [f. ANTI- + CATHODE]

A'ntĭchrīst (ă'-; -k-) *n.* Enemy of Christ; great personal opponent of Christ expected by early Church to appear before end of world. [ME, f. OF *antecrist* f. eccl. L. f. Gk ANTI*khristos* (*Khristos* CHRIST)]

ăntĭchrĭ'stian (-krĭ'styan) *a.* Pertaining to Antichrist; opposed to Christianity. [f. prec., w. extended meaning]

antĭ'cĭpāt|e *v.t.* Look forward to; expect; discuss, consider, use, spend, etc., before the due or natural time; forestall (person or thing); hence ~IVE, ~ORY, *adjs.*, ~OR *n.* [f. L *anticipare* (*anti-* for ANTE-, *-cipare* f. *capere* take) + -ATE[3]]

ăntĭcĭpā'tion *n.* **1.** Action of anticipating; **thanking you in** ~ (closing formula in letter of inquiry or request). **2.** (Mus.) Introduction beforehand of part of chord about to follow. [F, or f. L *anticipatio* (as prec.; see -ATION)]

ăntĭclĕ'rĭcal *a.* & *n.* (Person) opposed to strong influence of clergy, esp. in politics; hence ~ISM (3) *n.* [f. ANTI- + CLERICAL]

ăntĭclī'măx *n.* Opposite of climax; ineffective end to anything that has suggested a climax; descent contrasting with previous rise; hence **ăntĭclīmă'ct**IC *a.* [f. ANTI- + CLIMAX]

ă'ntĭclin|e *n.* (Geol.) Ridge or fold from which strata slope down in opposite directions; so ~AL (-ī'n-) *a.* [f. ANTI- + Gk *klinō* lean, after INCLINE[2]]

ăntĭclŏ'ckwīse (-z) *adv.* & *a.* See CLOCK[1] 3.

ăntĭcōă'gūlant *a.* & *n.* (Drug) retarding or preventing clotting of blood. [f. ANTI- + COAGULANT]

ăntĭconvŭ'lsant *a.* & *n.* (Drug) retarding or preventing convulsions. [f. ANTI- + CONVULSANT]

ăntĭcȳ'cl|ōne *n.* System of winds rotating outwards from area of high barometric pressure; so ~**ŏ'n**IC *a.* [f. ANTI- + CYCLONE]

ă'ntĭdōt|e *n.* Medicine etc. taken or given to counteract poison; (fig.) thing that counteracts an evil; hence ~AL *a.* [F, or f. L f. Gk *antidoton* neut. of ANTI*dotos* given against]

ă'ntĭfreeze *n.* Substance (usu. ethylene glycol) added to water to lower its freezing-point, esp. for use in radiator of engine. [f. ANTI- + FREEZE]

ăntĭ-g (-jē') *a.* (Of clothing for astronaut etc.) designed to counteract effects of high acceleration. [f. ANTI- + *g* symb. for acceleration due to gravity]

ă'ntĭgĕn *n.* Substance (e.g. toxin) that stimulates production of antibodies when introduced into the body; hence **ăntĭgĕ'n**IC *a.* [G (as ANTIBODY, -GEN)]

ăntĭ-gră'vĭtȳ *n.* Hypothetical force opposing gravity. [f. ANTI- + GRAVITY]

ăntĭgrŏ'pĕlōs (-z) *n. pl.* (Hist.) Waterproof leggings. [perh. f. ANTI- + Gk *hugros* wet + *pēlos* mud]

ă'ntĭ-hērō *n.* (*pl.* ~**es**). (In novel etc.) hero of unconventional or non-traditional type. [f. ANTI- + HERO]

ăntĭhĭ'stamĭne (*or* -ēn) *n.* & *a.* (Substance) that

For other words in *anti-* see ANTI-.

counteracts effects of histamine, used esp. in cases of allergy. [f. ANTI- + HISTAMINE]

ăntĭ-Jă′cobĭn *a.* & *n.* (Person) opposed to Jacobins (1789) or to the French Revolution. [f. ANTI- + JACOBIN^1]

ă′ntĭknŏck (-ĭn-) *n.* Substance added to motor fuel to prevent detonation. [f. ANTI- + KNOCK^2]

ăntĭlŏ′garĭthm (-dhem), (colloq.) **ă′ntĭlŏg,** *ns.* Number to which a logarithm belongs (*100 is the common antilogarithm of 2*). [f. ANTI- + LOGARITHM]

ăntĭ′logy̆ *n.* Contradiction in terms. [f. F *antilogie* f. Gk *antilogia* (as ANTI-, -LOGY)]

ăntĭmacă′ssar *n.* (esp. Hist.) Covering put over backs (and arms) of chairs etc., as protection from grease or as ornament. [f. ANTI- + MACASSAR (*oil*)]

ă′ntĭmasque (-mahsk) *n.* Grotesque interlude between acts of masque. [f. ANTI- + MASQUE]

ă′ntĭmătter *n.* (Hypothetical) matter composed solely of antiparticles. [f. ANTI- + MATTER^1]

ăntĭmonar′chĭcal (-k-) *a.* Opposed to monarchy. [f. ANTI- + MONARCHICAL]

ă′ntĭmony̆ *n.* Brittle silvery-white metallic element, used esp. in alloys; hence **ăntĭmō′nI**AL, **ăntĭmŏ′nI**C, **ăntĭmō′nI**OUS, *adjs.* [ME, f. med. L *antimonium* (11th c.), of unkn. orig.]

ă′ntĭng *n.* Rubbing or placing of ants etc. in plumage by birds, perh. to kill parasites. [f. ANT + -ING^1]

ăntĭnō′mĭan *a.* & *n.* **1.** *a.* Opposed to the obligatoriness of moral law. **2.** *n.* One who maintains that moral law is not binding on Christians; hence ~ISM (3) *n.* [f. med. L *Antinomi*, name of sect in Germany (1535) alleged to hold this opinion (as ANTI-, Gk *nomos* law) + -AN]

ăntĭ′nomy̆ *n.* Contradiction in a law, or between two laws; conflict of authority; paradox. [f. L f. Gk ANTI(*nomia* f. *nomos* law)]

ă′ntĭ-nŏvel *n.* Novel of unconventional or non-traditional type. [f. ANTI- + NOVEL^1]

ă′ntĭparticle *n.* (Phys.) Elementary particle having same mass as given particle but opposite electric charge or magnetic moment. [f. ANTI- + PARTICLE]

ăntĭpa′st|ō (-pah′-) *n.* (*pl.* ~*i or* ~*os*). Hors d'œuvre. [It.]

ăntĭpathĕ′tĭc *a.* Opposed in nature or disposition (*to*); hence ~AL *a.*, ~**al**LY^2 *adv.* [f. as ANTIPATHY after *pathetic*]

ăntĭpă′thĭc *a.* Of contrary character (*to*); (Med.) having or producing contrary symptoms. [f. foll. + -IC]

ăntĭ′pathy̆ *n.* Constitutional or settled aversion (*to*; *for*; *between* persons etc.). [f. F *antipathie* or L *antipathia* f. Gk *antipatheia* f. ANTI*pathēs* opposed in feeling (*pathos -eos*)]

ăntĭ-personnĕ′l *a.* (Of bombs etc.) designed to kill or injure human beings. [f. ANTI- + PERSONNEL]

ăntĭper′spirant *a.* & *n.* (Substance) tending to inhibit perspiration. [f. ANTI- + PERSPIRE + -ANT]

ăntĭphlogĭ′stĭc *a.* & *n.* (Medicine etc.) reducing inflammation. [f. ANTI- + PHLOGISTIC]

ă′ntĭphon *n.* Verse of psalm etc. sung usu. responsively by choir; (fig.) response. [f. eccl. L *antiphona*, fem. sing., f. Gk ANTI*phōna* (neut. pl. of *antiphōnos* responsive) f. *phōnē* sound]

ăntĭ′phonal *a.* & *n.* **1.** *a.* Sung alternately; responsive; hence ~LY^2 *adv.* **2.** *n.* Collection of antiphons. [f. prec. + -AL]

ăntĭ′phonary̆ *n.* Book of antiphons. [f. eccl. L *antiphonarium* (as ANTIPHON; see -ARY^1)]

ăntĭ′phony̆ *n.* Antiphonal singing; response, echo. [f. ANTIPHON + -Y^1]

ăntĭ′pod|ēs (-z) *n. pl.* Place(s) diametrically opposite (to each other), esp. Australasia as region on opposite side of earth to Europe; (w. back-form. *sing.* **ă′ntĭpōde**) exact opposite (*of*, *to*); hence ~AL, ~E′AN, *adjs.* [F, or LL f. Gk *antipodes* having the feet opposite, pl. of ANTI*pous* a. (*pous podos* foot)]

ă′ntĭpōle *n.* Opposite pole; direct opposite. [f. ANTI- + POLE^2]

ă′ntĭpōpe *n.* Pope elected in opposition to one (held to be) canonically chosen. [f. F *antipape* f. med. L *antipapa*, assim. to *pope*]

ăntĭprō′tŏn *n.* (Phys.) Antiparticle of proton. [f. ANTI- + PROTON]

ăntĭpy̆rĕ′tĭc *a.* & *n.* (Drug) allaying or preventing fever. [f. ANTI- + PYRETIC]

ăntĭquar′ĭan *a.* & *n.* **1.** *a.* Connected with study of antiques or antiquities. **2.** *n.* Antiquary. **3.** Hence ~ISM (2) *n.* [f. as foll. + -AN]

ă′ntĭquary̆ *n.* Student or collector of antiques or antiquities. [f. L *antiquarius* (*antiquus* ancient; see -ARY^1)]

ă′ntĭquātėd *a.* Old-fashioned; out of date. [p.p. of *antiquate* v. f. *antiquate* a., f. eccl. L *antiquare* make old; see -ATE^{2,3}]

ăntĭ′que (-ē′k) *a.*, *n.*, & *v.t.* **1.** *a.* Of old times; existing since old times; old-fashioned; archaic. **2.** *n.* Relic of old times, esp. furniture etc. sought by collectors. **3.** *v.t.* Make (furniture etc.) appear antique by artificial means. [F, or f. L *antiquus*, *anticus*, former, ancient (*ante* before)]

ăntĭ′quĭty̆ *n.* Ancientness (*a city of great antiquity*); old times, esp. time before Middle Ages; the ancients; (in *pl.*) customs, events, etc., of ancient times; (usu. in *pl.*) ancient relics. [ME, f. OF *antiquité* f. L *antiquitas -tatis* (*antiquus*; see prec., -ITY)]

ăntĭrrhī′num (-rī′-) *n.* (Bot.) Snapdragon, plant of genus *Antirrhinum*. [L, f. Gk *antirrhinon* (*anti* counterfeiting, *rhis rhinos* nose, from resemblance of flower to animal's mouth)]

ăntĭsăbbatar′ĭan *a.* & *n.* (Person) opposed to observance of the Sabbath. [f. ANTI- + SABBATARIAN]

ăntĭscorbū′tĭc *a.* & *n.* (Medicine) preventing or curing scurvy. [f. ANTI- + SCORBUTIC]

ăntĭscrĭ′ptural (-choor-) *a.* Opposed to Scripture. [f. ANTI- + SCRIPTURAL]

ăntĭ-Sĕ′m|īte *a.* & *n.* (Person) hostile to Jews; so **ăntĭ-Sėmĭ′t**IC *a.*, ~**ĭt**ISM (3) *n.* [f. ANTI- + SEMITE]

ăntĭsĕ′psĭs *n.* Process or principles of using antiseptics. [mod. L (as ANTI-, SEPSIS)]

ăntĭsĕ′ptĭc *a.* & *n.* **1.** *a.* Counteracting sepsis, esp. by preventing growth of bacteria; scrupulously clean; sterile (lit. or fig.). **2.** *n.* Antiseptic agent. [f. ANTI- + SEPTIC]

ă′ntĭser|um *n.* (*pl.* ~**a**). Serum with high antibody content. [f. ANTI- + SERUM]

ăntĭsō′cial (-shal) *a.* Opposed to principles or instincts on which society is based, or to normal social practices; not sociable. [f. ANTI- + SOCIAL]

ăntĭstă′tĭc *a.* Counteracting the effects of static electricity. [f. ANTI- + STATIC]

ăntĭ′strophė *n.* See STROPHE. [LL, f. Gk *antistrophē* (ANTI*strephō* turn against)]

ăntĭthē′|ĭsm *n.* Opposition to belief in existence of a God; hence ~IST (2) *n.* [f. ANTI- + THEISM]

ăntĭ′thės|ĭs *n.* (*pl.* ~**es** *pr.* -ēz). Contrast of ideas expressed by parallelism of strongly contrasted words; opposition, contrast, (*of*, *between*, two things); direct opposite (*of*, *to*). [LL f. Gk (ANTI*tithēmi* set against)]

ăntĭthĕ′tĭc *a.* Of the nature of antithesis; contrasted; consisting of two opposites; so ~AL *a.*, ~**al**LY^2 *adv.* [f. Gk *antithetikos* (as prec.; see -IC)]

ăntĭtŏ′x|ĭn *n.* Substance that neutralizes a toxin; so ~IC *a.* [f. ANTI- + TOXIN]

ă′ntĭtrāde *a.* & *n.* (Wind) that blows in opposite

direction to trade wind, at different altitude or place. [f. ANTI- + TRADE]

ăntĭtrĭnĭtār'ian *a.* & *n.* (Person) opposed to doctrine of the Trinity. [f. ANTI- + TRINITARIAN]

***ăntĭtrŭ'st** *a.* (Of law etc.) opposed to trusts or other monopolies. [f. ANTI- + TRUST 8]

ă'ntĭtȳpe *n.* That which a type or symbol represents; one of the opposite type; hence **ăntĭtȳ'pICAL** *a.* [f. Gk ANTI*tupos* corresponding as an impression to the die (*tupos* stamp)]

ăntĭvĕnē'ne, ăntĭvĕ'nĭn, *ns.* Antitoxin, esp. against snake poison. [f. ANTI- + L *venenum* poison + -IN]

ăntĭvĭvĭsĕ'ction|ĭsm *n.* Opposition to vivisection or to experiments with animals; so ~IST (2) *n.* [f. ANTI- + VIVISECTION]

ă'ntler *n.* (Branch of) horn of stag or other (usu. male) deer; hence (-)~ED[2] (-*lerd*) *a.* [ME f. AF, var. of OF *antoillier*, of unkn. orig.]

ăntonomā'sĭa (-z-) *n.* Substitution of epithet etc. for proper name (e.g. *the Iron Duke* for 'the Duke of Wellington'); use of a proper name to express a general idea (e.g. *a Solomon* for 'a wise man'). [L f. Gk (*antonomazō* name instead f. as ANTI- + *onoma* name)]

ă'ntonȳm *n.* Word of contrary meaning to another, as *bad* to *good* (opp. *synonym*); hence **ăntŏ'nȳmOUS** *a.* [f. F *antonyme* (as ANTI-, SYNONYM)]

ă'ntr|um *n.* (*pl.* ~**a**). Cavity in the body (esp. one in the upper jaw-bone); hence ~AL *a.* [L, f. Gk *antron* cave]

ā'nus *n.* Terminal excretory opening of alimentary canal. [L]

ă'nvĭl *n.* Block (usu. iron) on which smith works metal; (Anat.) a bone of the ear, the incus. [OE *anfilte* etc., = OHG *anafalz*, f. Gmc **ana* on + vbl stem w. sense 'beat']

ănxī'etȳ (ăngz-) *n.* State of being anxious; concern about the future; earnest desire (*for* a thing, *to* do); (Psych.) morbid state of excessive uneasiness. [f. F *anxieté* or f. L *anxietas -tatis* (as foll.; see -TY[1])]

ă'nxious (ă'ngkshus) *a.* Troubled, uneasy in mind, (*about*); earnestly desirous (*for* a thing, *to* do); causing anxiety; hence ~LY[2] *adv.* [f. L *anxius* (*angere* choke) + -OUS]

a'nȳ (ĕ'-) *a., pron.,* & *adv.* **1.** *a.* & *pron.* (With interrog. or neg. expressed or implied) one or some but no matter which (*have you any wool?*; *have you any of them?*; *cannot find any of them*; *hardly any difference*; *to avoid any delay*; **not having ~,** (colloq.) unwilling to participate); whichever (of all) is chosen (*any fool knows that*; *in any* CASE[1] 4; *any* MORE; *at any* RATE[1]; ~ **time,** (colloq.) at any time; *has* ~ **amount** (a great deal) *of money*); an appreciable or significant (*did not stay for any length of time*). **2.** *adv.* (Usu. w. compar. in neg. or interrog. context) at all, in some degree (*is that any better?*; *without being any the wiser*). [OE *ǣnig*, = OHG *einag*, f. Gmc **ain-*one + **-ig* -Y[2]]

a'nȳbŏdȳ (ĕ'-) *n.* & *pron.* Whatever person; a person, no matter who, (~**'s** *game* etc., evenly balanced contest; **~'s guess,** an unpredictable matter); a person of any kind; a person of importance. [f. ANY + BODY[1] (=person)]

a'nȳhow (ĕ'-) *adv.* Anyway; haphazardly (*does his work anyhow*; *things are all anyhow*). [f. ANY + HOW]

a'nȳone (ĕ'nĭwŭn; *or* -wun) *n.* & *pron.* Anybody. [f. ANY + ONE]

***a'nȳplāce** (ĕ'-) *adv.* Anywhere. [f. ANY + PLACE[1]]

a'nȳthĭng (ĕ'-) *n.* & *pron.* Whatever thing; a thing, no matter which (~ **but,** far from; **like** ~, with great intensity etc.); a thing of any kind. [f. ANY + THING]

a'nȳway (ĕ'-) *adv.* In any way; in any case; at any rate. [f. ANY + WAY]

a'nȳwhere (ĕ'nĭwār) *adv.* & *pron.* (In or to) any place. [f. ANY + WHERE]

a'nȳwīse (ĕ'-; -z) *adv.* In any manner. [OE *on ǣnige wīsan* in any wise]

A'nzăc (ă'-) *n.* & *a.* **1.** (Member) of the Australian and New Zealand Army Corps (1914–18); ~ **Day,** 25 Apr. **2.** Australian or New Zealand (person, esp. serviceman). [f. initials]

***AOK** (āōkā') *a.* (colloq.) In perfect order. [f. *all systems O.K.*]

ā'orĭst *a.* & *n.* (Gram.) indefinite, not implying limitation; ~ (**tense**), past tense merely denoting occurrence without limitation as to duration etc.; so **āorĭ'stIC** *a.* [f. Gk *aoristos* indefinite (*a-* not, *horizō* define)]

āor̂'t|a *n.* Great artery or trunk of the arterial system, issuing from heart; hence ~IC *a.* [f. Gk *aortē* (*a*(*e*)*irō* raise)]

a'oudăd (ah'oo-) *n.* N. Afr. wild or domesticated sheep (*Ammotragus tragelaphus*). [F, f. native name]

à outrance (ahōō'trahṅs) *adv.* To the death; to the bitter end. [F, = to the utmost]

ap- *pref.* **1.** Assim. form of AD- before *p*. **2.** See APO-.

***ap.** *abbr.* apothecaries'.

apā'ce *adv.* Swiftly, quickly. [f. OF *a pas* at (a considerable) PACE[1]]

apa'che *n.* **1.** (*A*~) (apă'chĭ). Member of N. Amer. Indian tribe. **2.** (apă'sh). Violent street ruffian, orig. in Paris; ~ **dance,** a vigorous dance for two. [Mex. Sp.]

ă'panage, ă'pp-, *n.* Provision for maintenance of younger children of kings etc.; perquisite, subsidiary title; natural accompaniment or attribute. [F, f. OF *apaner* dower f. med. L AP*panare* (*panis* bread) endow with means of subsistence; see -AGE]

apar̂'t *adv.* **1.** Aside, separately, independently; ~ **from,** not considering; **joking** ~, seriously; **set** ~, devote, reserve (*for*); **tell** ~, distinguish between. **2.** To or at a distance. **3.** Into pieces (*come apart*); **take** ~, (fig.) deal with severely or thoroughly. [ME f. OF (*à* to, *part* side)]

apar̂'theid (-t-hāt) *n.* (S. Afr.) (policy of) racial segregation; (fig.) similar segregation elsewhere. [Afrik. (as prec., -HOOD)]

apar̂'tment *n.* Single room in a house; *flat (~ **house,** block of flats); (in *pl.*) set of (usu. rented furnished) rooms. [f. F *appartement* f. It. *appartamento* (*appartare* separate f. *a parte* apart; see -MENT)]

ăpathĕ't|ic *a.* Not feeling emotion; uninterested; hence ~ICALLY *adv.* [f. foll., after *pathetic*]

ă'pathȳ *n.* Insensibility to suffering; passionless existence; lack of interest or desire. [f. F *apathie* f. L f. Gk *apatheia* (*apathēs* without feeling f. *a-* not + *pathos* suffering)]

ă'patīte *n.* Crystalline mineral of calcium phosphate and fluoride. [f. G *apatit* f. Gk *apatē* deceit (from its deceptive forms); see -ITE[1]]

āpe[1] *n.* **1.** Tailless monkey, esp. anthropoid; any monkey. **2.** Imitator, mimic; apelike person; **go** ~, (sl.) become crazy. [OE *apa*, = OHG *affo*, ON *api* f. Gmc **apan-*]

āpe[2] *v.t.* Imitate, mimic. [f. prec.]

apea'k *adv.* & *pred. a.* (Naut.) Vertical(ly) (*oars apeak*). [f. F *à pic* (*à* at, *pic* PEAK[1])]

aperçu (ăpĕrsū') *n.* Summary, conspectus; an insight. [F, p.p. of *apercevoir* perceive]

apēr̂'ient *a.* & *n.* Laxative (medicine). [f. L *aperire* to open; see -ENT]

For other words in *anti-* see ANTI-.

āpĕrĭŏ'dĭc *a.* (Phys.) Without a natural period. [f. A- 7 + PERIODIC[1]]
apĕ'rĭtif (-ēf) *n.* Alcoholic drink as appetizer. [f. F *apéritif* f. med. L *aperitivus* var. of LL *apertivus* f. L *aperire* to open; see -IVE]
ă'perture *n.* Opening, gap; space through which light passes in optical or photographic instrument. [f. L *apertura* (as prec.; see -URE)]
ā'perȳ *n.* Mimicry; ape-house. [f. APE[1] + -ERY]
apĕ'talous *a.* Without petals. [f. mod. L f. Gk *apetalos* leafless (*a-* not, *petalon* leaf) + -OUS]
ā'pĕx *n.* (*pl.* **~es,** *or* **apices** *pr.* ā'pĭsēz). Tip; top, climax; vertex (of triangle, cone); pointed end (of heart, lung, etc.). [L, = peak, tip]
ă'pfelstrudel (-rōō-) *n.* Baked spiced apples in flaky pastry. [G (*apfel* apple, STRUDEL)]
aphaer'ĕs|ĭs (afēr'-) *n.* (*pl.* **~es** *pr.* -ēz). Removal of letter or syllable at beginning of word (e.g. in derivation of ADDER). [LL, f. Gk *aphairesis* (as APO-, *haireō* take)]
aphā'sĭa (-zĭa) *n.* Loss of speech, or of understanding of language, owing to brain damage; hence **~IC** *a.* & *n.* [mod. L f. Gk, f. *aphatos* speechless (*a-* not, *pha-* speak; see -IA[1])]
aphē'lĭ|on (*or* -lyon) *n.* (*pl.* **~a**). Point (of planet's or comet's orbit) farthest from sun. [Graecized f. mod. L *aphelium* f. Gk *aph' hēliou* from the sun]
ă'phĕs|ĭs *n.* (*pl.* **~es** *pr.* -ēz). Gradual loss of unaccented vowel at beginning of word (e.g. of *e* from *esquire* to form *squire*); hence **aphĕ'tic** *a.* [Gk, = letting go (as APO-, *hiēmi* send)]
ā'phĭd *n.* Plant-louse, small insect infesting and damaging plants, e.g. greenfly. [back form. f. *aphides* (see foll.)]
ā'phĭs *n.* (*pl.* **aphides** *pr.* ā'fĭdēz). Aphid, esp. of genus *Aphis*. [mod. L (Linnaeus) f. Gk (1523), perh. misreading of *koris* bug]
aphō'nĭa, ă'phonȳ, *n.* Loss or absence of voice. [mod. L *aphonia* f. Gk (*aphōnos* voiceless f. *a-* not + *phōnē* voice; see -IA[1], -Y[1])]
ă'phor|ĭsm *n.* Short pithy statement or maxim; hence **~IST** (1) *n.*, **ăphorĭ'stic** *a.*, **~IZE** (2) *v.i.* [f. F *aphorisme* or f. LL f. Gk *aphorismos* definition (APhorizō f. *horos* boundary; see -ISM)]
ăphrodĭ'sĭăc (-z-) *a.* & *n.* (Drug etc.) arousing sexual desire. [f. Gk *aphrodisiakos* (*aphrodisios* f. *Aphroditē* Gk goddess of love; see -AC)]
aphȳ'llous *a.* (Bot.) Naturally without leaves. [f. mod. L f. Gk *aphullos* (*a-* not, *phullon* leaf) + -OUS]
ā'pĭan *a.* Pertaining to bees. [f. L *apianus* (*apis* bee; see -AN)]
āpĭār'ĭan *a.* Pertaining to bee-keeping. [f. as foll. + -AN]
ā'pĭar|ȳ *n.* Place where bees are kept; hence **~IST** (1) *n.* [f. L *apiarium* (*apis* bee; see -ARY[1])]
ā'pĭcal *a.* Belonging to an apex; situated at the tip; hence **~LY**[2] *adv.* [f. L APEX -*icis* + -AL]
apices. See APEX.
ā'pĭcŭlture *n.* Bee-keeping; hence **āpĭcŭ'ltur**AL *a.*, **āpĭcŭ'lturist** (3) *n.*, (-cher-). [f. L *apis* bee, after *agriculture*]
apie'ce *adv.* Severally, each (*had five pounds apiece*). [f. A[2] + PIECE[1]]
ā'pĭsh *a.* Of the nature or appearance of an ape; apelike in manner, silly; hence **~LY**[2] *adv.*, **~NESS** *n.* [f. APE[1] + -ISH[1]]
ăplană'tĭc *a.* Free from spherical aberration; so [by back form. thr. G] **ă'planăt** *n.*, lens, or lens-system, made aplanatic by correction. [f. Gk *aplanētos* free from error (*a-* not, *planaō* wander) + -IC]
aplā'sĭa (-z-) *n.* (Med.) Congenital irregularity or absence of organ or structure; hence **aplă'stic** *a.* [mod. L, f. Gk (*a-* not, *plasis* formation); see -IA[1]]
aplĕ'ntȳ *adv.* In plenty. [f. A[3] + PLENTY]
aplŏ'mb (-m) *n.* Self-possession. [F, = perpendicularity, f. *à plomb* according to plummet]
ăpnoe'a (-nē'*a*), ***ăpnē'a,** *n.* (Med.) Cessation of breathing. [mod. L, f. Gk *apnoia* (*apnous* breathless)]
ăpo- *pref.* (usu. **ap-** bef. vowel or *h*) w. sense 'away from' (*apogee*), 'separate' (*apocarpous*). [f. Gk *apo* from, away, un-, quite]
apŏ'calȳpse *n.* Revelation, esp. that made to St. John in island of Patmos; book recording this; grand or violent event resembling those described in St. John's book; so **apŏcalȳ'ptic**(AL) *adjs.* [ME f. OF, f. eccl. L f. Gk *apokalupsis* (APOkaluptō uncover)]
ăpocar'pous *a.* (Bot.) Having carpels distinct. [f. APO- + Gk *karpos* fruit + -OUS]
ăpochromă'tĭc (-k-) *a.* Free from spherical and chromatic aberrations; so [by back form. thr. G] **ă'pochromăt** (-k-) *n.*, lens, or lens-system, made apochromatic by correction. [f. APO- + CHROMATIC]
apŏ'copė *n.* Removal of letter or syllable at end of word (e.g. in derivation of CURIO). [LL, f. Gk APO(*kopē* f. *koptō* cut)]
Apocr. *abbr.* Apocrypha.
ă'pocrĭne *a.* (Of gland) losing parts of cells when secreting. [f. APO- + Gk *krinō* separate]
Apŏ'crȳpha (*a*-) *n.* Books of Old Testament included in Septuagint and Vulgate, but not in Hebrew Bible and not in all modern Bibles. [ME, f. eccl. L *apocrypha* (*scripta*) pl., hidden writings f. Gk *apokruphos* (APOkruptō hide away)]
apŏ'crȳphal *a.* Of the Apocrypha; of doubtful authenticity (esp. of some early Christian texts resembling those of N.T.); invented. [f. prec. + -AL]
ă'podal *a.* Without (or with undeveloped) feet or ventral fins. [f. *apod* apodal creature f. Gk *apous* footless (*a-* not, *pous podos* foot) + -AL]
ăpodĭ'ctĭc, -dei'ctĭc (-dī'-), *a.* Of clear demonstration; clearly established. [f. L f. Gk *apodeiktikos* (APOdeiknumi show; see -IC)]
apŏ'dos|ĭs *n.* (*pl.* **~es** *pr.* -ēz). Consequent clause of conditional sentence. [LL, f. Gk (APOdidōmi give back)]
ă'pogee *n.* Point (in orbit of moon, planet, or artificial satellite) farthest from earth; (fig.) most distant or highest point; hence **ăpogē'**AN *a.* [f. F *apogée* or f. mod. L f. Gk APOgeion away from earth (*gē* earth)]
ăpolau'stĭc *a.* Seeking enjoyment. [f. Gk *apolaustikos* (APOlauō enjoy; see -IC)]
āpolĭ'tĭcal *a.* Unconcerned with or detached from politics. [f. A- 7 + POLITICAL]
Apŏllĭnār'ĭs (*a*-) *n.* Effervescent mineral water from *Apollinaris*burg in the Rhineland.
Apŏ'llō (*a*-) *n.* (*pl.* **~s**). Young man of great beauty. [L, f. Gk *Apollōn* name of sun-god]
Apŏ'llyon (*a*-) *n.* The Devil (Rev. 9:11). [L (Vulgate), f. Gk *apolluōn* part. of *apollumi* (APO-, *ollumi* destroy)]
apŏlogĕ't|ĭc *a.* & *n.* **1.** *a.* Regretfully acknowledging or excusing fault or failure; diffident; vindicatory; hence **~ICALLY** *adv.* **2.** *n.* (usu. in *pl.*) Reasoned defence, esp. of Christianity. [f. F *apologétique* f. LL f. Gk *apologētikos* (APOlogeomai speak in defence; see -IC)]
ăpolō'gĭa *n.* Written defence of one's conduct or opinions. [L; see APOLOGY]
apŏ'logĭst *n.* One who defends (e.g. Christianity) by argument. [f. F *apologiste* f. Gk *apologizomai* render account (*apologos* account); see -IST]
apŏ'logīze, -īse (-īz), *v.i.* Make an apology (*to* person, *for* person or thing). [f. Gk (see prec.)]
ă'polŏgue (-ŏg) *n.* Moral fable. [F, or f. L f. Gk APO(*logos* discourse) story]
apŏ'logȳ *n.* Regretful acknowledgement of fault

or failure; assurance that no offence was intended; explanation, vindication; ~ **for,** poor or scanty specimen of (*this apology for a letter*). [f. F *apologie* or f. LL f. Gk *apologia* (as APOLOGETIC)]

ă'polūne *n.* Point in body's orbit about moon where it is farthest from moon's centre. [f. APO- + L *luna* moon, after *apogee*]

ăpomĭ'x|ĭs *n.* (*pl.* ~**es** *pr.* -ēz). (Biol.) Reproduction without fertilization; so **ăpomĭ'ct**IC *a.* [mod. L, f. as APO- + Gk *mixis* mingling]

ăpophă'tĭc *a.* (Theol.) (Of knowledge of God) obtained by negation. [f. Gk APO*phatikos* negative]

ă'pophthĕgm (-ofthĕm *or* -othĕm), ***ă'pothĕgm** (-ĕm), *n.* Terse saying; pithy maxim; hence ~**ă'**TIC (-ofthĕg- *or* -othĕg-) *a.* [f. F *apophthegme* or mod. L f. Gk *apophthegma -matos* (APO*phtheggomai* speak out)]

ăpoplĕ'ct|ĭc *a.* Pertaining to, causing, suffering from, tending to, apoplexy; hence ~ICALLY *adv.* [f. F *apoplectique* or f. LL f. Gk *apoplēktikos* (APO*plēssō* strike completely; see -IC)]

ă'poplĕxȳ *n.* Inability to feel and move, caused by blockage or rupture of brain artery. [ME, f. OF *apoplexie* f. LL f. Gk *apoplēxia* (as prec.)]

ăposėmă'tĭc *a.* (Zool.) (Of coloration, markings, etc.) serving to warn or repel. [f. APO- + Gk *sēma sēmatos* sign + -IC]

ăposĭopē's|ĭs *n.* (*pl.* ~**es** *pr.* -ēz). (Rhet.) Sudden breaking-off in speech. [L f. Gk, f. APO(*siōpaō* keep silent)]

apŏ'stasȳ *n.* Abandonment of religious faith, vows, principles, or party. [ME, f. eccl. L f. N.T. Gk *apostasia* (APO*stasis* defection f. *stat-* stand)]

apŏ'state *n.* & *a.* (One) guilty of apostasy; so **ăpostă'**TICAL *a.* [ME f. OF, or f. eccl. L *apostata* f. Gk *apostatēs* deserter (as prec.)]

apŏ'statīze, -īse (-īz), *v.i.* Become an apostate. [f. med. L *apostatizare* (*apostata*; see prec.)]

ā pŏstērĭōr'ī (*or* -ĕr-) *adv.* & *a.* (Reasoning) from effects to causes; inductive(ly). [L, = from what comes after]

apŏ'stĭl *n.* (arch.) Marginal note. [f. F *apostille* (*apostiller* v. f. *postille* POSTIL)]

apŏ'stle (-sel) *n.* **1.** Messenger, esp. (*A*~) any of the twelve whom Christ sent forth to preach Gospel; ~**-bird,** one of various Austral. birds forming flocks of about a dozen; **A~s' Creed,** simplest and prob. earliest form of Christian creed, anciently ascribed to the Apostles; ~ **spoon** (with figure of Apostle on handle). **2.** First successful Christian missionary in a country (*St. Boniface, the Apostle of Germany*); leader of reform (*apostle of temperance*). **3.** Hence ~SHIP *n.* [OE *apostol* f. eccl. L f. Gk *apostolos* (APO*stellō* send forth)]

apŏ'stolate *n.* Apostleship; leadership in reform. [f. eccl. L *apostolatus* (as prec.; see -ATE^{1})]

ăpostŏ'lĭc *a.* Pertaining to the Apostles (**A~ Fathers,** Christian leaders immediately after the Apostles; *apostolic* SUCCESSION); of the character of an apostle (VICAR *apostolic*); of the pope as successor of St. Peter; hence ~AL *a.*, ~**al**LY^{2} *adv.* [f. F *apostolique* or eccl. L f. Gk *apostolikos* (as APOSTLE; see -IC)]

apŏ'stroph|ė^{1} *n.* Exclamatory passage by orator or poet, addressed to particular person (often dead or absent) or thing; hence ~IZE (1, 2) *v.t.* & *i.* [L f. Gk, lit. 'turning away' (as foll.)]

apŏ'strophė^{2} *n.* Sign of omission of letters (*can't*) or numbers (*the spirit of '76*, i.e. 1776), or of possessive case (*a man's coat*) (see also 'D^{1,2}, 's). [F, or LL f. Gk *apostrophos* adj. as n., accent of elision (APO*strephō* turn away)]

ăpostrŏ'phĭc *a.* In senses of the above *ns.* [f. APOSTROPHE^{1,2} + -IC]

apŏ'thėcar|ȳ *n.* **1.** (arch.) Druggist, pharmaceutical chemist. **2.** ~**ies' measure, weight,** sets of units used in pharmacy for liquid volume (with fluid OUNCE^{1} of 8 drachms = 480 minims) and for weight (with OUNCE^{1} of 8 drachms = 24 scruples = 480 grains) respectively. [ME, f. OF *apotecaire* f. LL *apothecarius* f. L *apotheca* f. Gk *apothēkē* storehouse; see -ARY^{1}]

***apothegm.** See APOPHTHEGM.

ă'pothĕm *n.* (Geom.) Line from centre of regular polygon perpendicular to a side. [f. Gk APO(*tithēmi* to place); cf. THEME]

apŏthėō's|ĭs *n.* (*pl.* ~**es** *pr.* -ēz). Deification (lit. or fig.); canonization; deified ideal or highest development; hence **apŏ'thėos**IZE (1) *v.t.* [eccl. L, f. Gk (APO*theoō* make a god of, f. *theos* god; see -OSIS)]

ăpotropā'ĭc *a.* Having power to avert evil influence or bad luck. [f. Gk APO(*tropaios* f. *trepō* turn) averting evil + -IC]

appa'l (-aw'l) *v.t.* (**-ll-**). Dismay, terrify; hence ~**l**ING^{2} *a.*, (esp., colloq.) shocking, unpleasant. [ME, f. OF *apalir* grow pale; cf. PALE^{2}]

***appa'll** (-aw'l). Var. of prec.

Appalōō'sa (ă-) *n.* Horse of N. Amer. breed with dark spots on light background. [f. *Opelousa* in Louisiana, or *Palouse*, river in Idaho]

ă'ppanage. See APANAGE.

apparat (ăparah't) *n.* Communist party machine in U.S.S.R. and other countries. [Russ. f. G, = apparatus]

apparatchik (ăparah'chĭk) *n.* (*pl.* ~**s** *or* ~**i**). Member of *apparat*; Communist agent or spy. [Russ.]

ăpparā'tus *n.* Equipment for doing something, esp. scientific experiments; organs effecting a natural process; *apparat* or other political organization; ~ (**criticus**), list of variant readings, materials for textual study of document. [L (AP*parare* make ready for; see -ATE^{1})]

appă'rel^{1} *v.t.* (‖**-ll-**). (arch.) Attire, dress. [ME, f. OF *apareiller* f. Rom. *AD*pariculare* make fit (*pariculum* dim. of *par* equal)]

appă'rel^{2} *n.* Clothing, dress; ornamental embroidery on some ecclesiastical vestments. [ME, f. OF *apareil* (*apareiller*; see prec.)]

appă'rent *a.* Manifest, palpable, (**heir** ~, one whose right of inheritance cannot be superseded by birth of another heir; cf. PRESUMPTIVE); seeming; *apparent* MAGNITUDE; ~ **time,** solar time; hence ~LY^{2} *adv.* [ME, f. OF *aparant* f. L (as APPEAR; see -ENT)]

ăppari'tion *n.* Appearance, esp. (as) of a supernatural being; ghost. [ME f. F, or f. L *apparitio* attendance (as APPEAR; see -ION)]

appă'rĭtor *n.* Officer of ecclesiastical synod or court. [L, = public servant (as APPEAR; see -OR)]

appea'l^{1} *v.* **1.** *v.i.* Call (*to* higher tribunal, or abs.) for alteration of decision of lower one; call attention *to* (evidence); make earnest request (*to* person, *for* thing or *to* do); address oneself *to* (person, etc.) for help or corroboration or decision (‖*appeal to the* COUNTRY); (Cricket) ask umpire whether batsman is out; (seek to) be attractive (*she does not appeal to me*; *films that appeal to depraved tastes*). **2.** *v.t.* Remove (case) to higher court; hence ~ABLE *a.* [ME, f. OF *apeler* f. L AP(*pellare* f. *pellere* drive) address]

appea'l^{2} *n.* Act of appealing; feature or quality that appeals (*has sex, snob, appeal*); right of appealing; **Court of A~(s)** (hearing cases previously tried in inferior courts); LORD (*Justice*) *of Appeal*. [ME, f. OF *apel* (as prec.)]

appear' *v.i.* Become or be visible; present oneself formally or publicly; (Law) act as counsel; be published; be manifest; have the appearance of being, seem (*to* be, do, etc.). [ME, f. *aper-*

stressed st. of OF *apareir* f. L APp*arēre -rit-* come in sight]

appear'ance *n.* **1.** Act of appearing; **put in an ~,** be present, esp. briefly. **2.** Look, aspect; **to all ~(s),** so far as can be seen; **keep up** or **save ~s** (outward show of prosperity etc.). **3.** Semblance. [ME, f. OF *aparance, -ence,* f. LL *apparentia* (as prec.; see -ENCE)]

appea'se (-z) *v.t.* Make calm or quiet (strife, anger, person); (Polit.) try to conciliate or bribe (potential aggressor) by making concessions, freq. with implication of sacrifice of principles; soothe; satisfy (appetite, prejudice); hence ~MENT (-zm-) *n.* [ME, f. AF *apeser,* OF *apaisier* (*à* to, *pais* PEACE)]

appĕ'llant *n.* & *a.* (One) who appeals to higher court; =foll. [ME, f. F (as APPEAL¹; see -ANT)]

appĕ'llate *a.* (Law). Taking cognizance of appeals. [f. L *appellatus* (as APPEAL¹; see -ATE²)]

ăppellā'tion *n.* Name, title; nomenclature. [ME f. OF, f. L *appellatio -onis* (as APPEAL¹; see -ATION)]

appĕ'llatĭve *a.* (Of words) designating a class, common (as opp. to *proper*). [f. LL *appellativus* (as APPEAL¹; see -ATIVE)]

appĕ'nd *v.t.* Hang on, annex; add, esp. in writing. [f. L AP(*pendere* hang)]

appĕ'ndage *n.* Thing attached, esp. (Zool.) leg etc. of arthropod; addition; accompaniment. [f. prec. + -AGE]

appĕ'ndant *a.* & *n.* (Person or thing) attached in subordinate capacity (*to* another). [f. OF *apendant* (*apendre* f. as APPEND; see -ANT)]

appĕ'nd|ĭx *n.* (*pl.* **~ices** *pr.* -sēz, *or* **~ixes**). Subsidiary addition (*to* book or document); (Anat.) small process developed from surface of any organ, esp. the vermiform process of the caecum; hence ~(**ĭc**)E'CTOMY, **~ĭcĭ'**TIS, *ns.* [L *appendix -icis* (AP*pendere* APPEND)]

ăppercei've (-sē'v) *v.t.* Be conscious of perceiving; (Psych.) unite and assimilate (a perception) to ideas already possessed, and so comprehend and interpret. [ME (in obs. sense 'observe'), f. OF *aperceveir* f. Rom. *AP(*percipere* f. L *percipere* PERCEIVE)]

ăppercĕ'pt|ion *n.* Mind's perception of itself; (Psych.) perception with recognition or identification by association with previous ideas; hence ~IVE *a.* [f. F *aperception* f. mod. L *apperceptio -onis* (as prec.; see -ION)]

ăppertai'n *v.i.* Belong as possession or right *to*; be appropriate *to*; relate *to*. [ME, f. OF *apertenir* f. LL AP(*pertinēre* PERTAIN)]

ă'ppėtence, -cy̆, *ns.* Longing or desire *for*. [f. F *appétence* or f. L *appetentia* (AP*petere* seek after; see -ENCE, -ENCY)]

ă'ppėtent *a.* Eagerly desirous. [ME, f. L *appetere* (see prec., -ENT)]

ă'ppėtīte *n.* Desire, inclination, (*for*); desire to satisfy natural needs, esp. for food or sexual pleasure; so **appĕ'tĭtIVE** *a.* [ME, f. OF *apetit* f. L *appetitus* (AP*petere* seek after; see -ITE²)]

ă'ppėtīzer, -īser (-z-), *n.* Thing eaten or drunk to stimulate appetite. [f. *appetize* (back form. f. foll.) + -ER¹ (2)]

ă'ppėtīzĭng, -īsĭng (-z-), *a.* Giving appetite. [f. F. *appétissant* irreg. f. *appetit* f. as APPETITE]

applau'd *v.* **1.** *v.i.* Express approval loudly, as by clapping hands. **2.** *v.t.* Express approval of, praise. [f. L AP*plaudere -plaus-* clap hands]

applau'se (-z) *n.* Approbation loudly expressed; marked approval. [f. med. L *applausus* (as prec.)]

ă'pple *n.* **1.** Rounded firm edible juicy fruit of a tree of the genus *Malus*; any of various similar fleshy many-celled fruits; **~ of the** or one's **eye,** the pupil, eyeball, any cherished object. **2.** **~ brandy,** spirit distilled from cider; **upset** person's **~cart,** spoil his plans; **~-green,** yellowish green; **~head,** rounded head of toy dog; ***~jack,** apple brandy; **~-pie bed** (with sheets so folded that one's legs cannot get down); **~-pie order,** perfect order; ***~-polisher,** (sl.) toady; **~s (and pears),** ||(rhyming sl.) stairs; **~ sauce,** apples stewed to a pulp, *(sl.) insincere flattery, nonsense. [OE *æppel,* = OHG *apful,* ON *epli* f. Gmc **aplu-*]

applī'ance *n.* Thing applied as means to an end; utensil, device, equipment; fire-engine. [f. APPLY + -ANCE]

ă'pplĭc|able *a.* Capable of being applied; having reference, appropriate, (*to*); hence ~ABI'LITY *n.,* **~abLY**² *adv.* [OF, or f. med. L *applicabilis* (as APPLY; see -ABLE)]

ă'pplĭcant *n.* One who applies (*for*). [f. foll. + -ANT]

ăpplĭcā'tion *n.* **1.** Putting of one thing *to* another; thing (e.g. medicament) so put. **2.** Employment of means; bringing (*of* general rule etc.) to bear upon particular case. **3.** Relevance, applicability; diligence; (making of) a request. [ME f. F, f. L *applicatio -onis* (as APPLY; see -ATION)]

ă'pplĭcātor *n.* Device for applying something, esp. to the body. [f. prec. + -OR]

ăppli'qué (-lē'kā) *n.* & *a.,* & *v.t.* **1.** *n.* & *a.* (Ornamental work) cut out from one material and affixed to surface of another (esp. in needlework). **2.** *v.t.* Ornament thus. [F, p.p. of *appliquer* apply f. L *applicare*; see foll.]

applȳ' *v.* **1.** *v.t.* Put close (*to*) or in contact; administer (remedy etc. *to*; lit. or fig.); devote (*to*); make use of (**applied,** put to practical use, opp. *theoretical* or *pure*; *applied* MATHEMATICS); use as relevant or suitable (*to*). **2.** *v.i.* Have relevance (*to*); address oneself (*for* help etc. *to*); make application (*for* employment etc.). [ME, f. OF *aplier* f. L AP*plicare* fold, fasten to]

appŏggiatu'ra (-ŏj*a*tōō'r*a*) *n.* (Mus.) Grace-note just above or below primary note, performed before it and delaying it. [It.]

appoi'nt *v.t.* Fix (time, place, *for* purpose); prescribe, ordain; (Law) declare destination of (property, or abs.); assign to office (*appoint him governor, to govern, to be governor, appoint him*); *well, badly,* **~ed,** furnished or equipped; hence ~EE' *n.,* ~IVE *a.* [ME, f. OF *apointer* (*à point* to a point)]

appoi'ntment *n.* Appointing, esp. of time and place for meeting; office assigned; (usu. in *pl.*) equipment, furnishing, fittings. [ME, f. OF *apointement* (as prec.; see -MENT)]

appôr't *n.* Production of material objects by allegedly occult means at spiritualist seance; object thus produced. [ME (in obs. senses), f. OF *aport* (*aporter* f. *à* to, *porter* bring)]

appôr'tion *v.t.* Give as due share (*to*); portion out; hence ~MENT *n.* [f. F *apportionner* or f. med. L *apportionare* (as AP-, PORTION)]

ă'ppŏsĭte (-z-) *a.* Well expressed; appropriate (*to*); hence ~LY² (-tlĭ) *adv.,* ~NESS (-tn-) *n.* [f. L *appositus* p.p. of AP(*ponere* put); see -ITE²]

ăpposĭ'tion (-z-) *n.* Placing side by side; (Gram.) placing of word syntactically parallel with another, esp. addition of one noun to another; hence ~AL *a.* [ME f. F, or f. LL *appositio* (as prec.; see -ITION)]

apprai's|e (-z) *v.t.* (Esp. of official valuer) value or fix price for; estimate; hence ~AL, **~e**MENT (-zm-), ~ER¹, *ns.,* ~ABLE, ~IVE, *adjs.* [f. APPRIZE by assim. to PRAISE]

apprē'ciab|le (-sh*a*-) *a.* Capable of being estimated; perceptible; considerable; hence ~LY² *adv.* [F (*apprécier*; see foll., -ABLE)]

apprē'cĭ|āte (-shĭ-) *v.* **1.** *v.t.* Estimate worth, quality, amount, of; estimate rightly; understand, recognize, *that*; be sensitive to; esteem highly, be grateful for; raise in value; hence ~atIVE, ~atORY, *adjs.* **2.** *v.i.* Rise in value. [f. LL AP*pretiare* appraise (*pretium* price) + -ATE³]

apprēcĭā'tion (-shĭ-) *n.* Estimation, judgement; adequate recognition; rise in value; (usu. favourable) review of book etc. [F, f. LL *appretiatio -onis* (as prec.; see -ATION)]

ăpprėhĕ'nd *v.t.* Seize, arrest; perceive (by senses or intellect); understand; anticipate with fear. [f. F *appréhender* or L AP(*prehendere -hens-* lay hold of)]

ăpprėhĕ'ns|ĭble *a.* Capable of being grasped (by senses or intellect); hence ~IBI'LITY *n.* [f. LL *apprehensibilis* (as prec.; see -IBLE)]

ăpprėhĕ'nsion (-shon) *n.* Seizure, arrest; grasping (of ideas), conception; understanding; uneasiness. [F, or f. LL *apprehensio* (as prec.; see -ION)]

ăpprėhĕ'nsĭve *a.* Pertaining to perception by senses or intellect; uneasy in mind, fearful, (*of* thing, *that* it may happen, *for* person, *for* his safety); (arch.) perceptive, intelligent; hence ~LY² (-vlĭ) *adv.*, ~NESS (-vn-) *n.* [f. F *appréhensif* or med. L *apprehensivus* (as prec.; see -IVE)]

apprĕ'ntĭce *n.*, & *v.t.* **1.** *n.* Learner of a craft, bound to serve, and entitled to instruction from, his employer for specified term; (esp. of jockey) beginner, novice; hence ~SHIP (-s-sh-) *n.* **2.** *v.t.* Bind as apprentice. [ME, f. OF *aprentis* (*apprendre* learn, as APPREHEND), after wds in *-tis*, *-tif*, f. L *-tivus* (see -IVE)]

apprī'se (-z) *v.t.* Inform; **be ~d** (aware) **of.** [f. F *appris -ise* p.p. of *apprendre* learn, teach, (as APPREHEND)]

apprī'ze *v.t.* (arch.) Appraise; esteem highly. [ME, f. OF *aprisier* (*à* to, *pris* PRICE)]

||**ă'pprō** *n.* (colloq.) **On** ~, on APPROVAL. [abbr. of *approval* or *approbation*]

approa'ch¹ *v.* **1.** *v.i.* Come near(er) in space or time; (Golf) play approach shot; (Aeron.) make approach. **2.** *v.t.* Be similar in character etc. to; come near to; set about (task); approximate to; make tentative proposal to; attempt to influence or bribe; (arch.) bring near; hence ~ABI'LITY *n.*, ~ABLE *a.*, (esp.) friendly. [ME, f. OF *aproch(i)er* f. eccl. L AP*propiare* draw near (*propius* compar. of *prope* near)]

approa'ch² *n.* Act or means of approaching; approximation; (Bridge) bidding method with gradual advance to final contract; (Golf) stroke, not from tee, played to reach the green; (Aeron.) final part of flight before landing. [f. prec.]

***ă'pprobāte** *v.t.* Approve formally, sanction. [ME, f. L AP(*probare* test f. *probus* good) + -ATE³]

ăpprobā'tion *n.* Sanction; approval; so **ă'pprobāt**ORY *a.* [ME f. OF, f. L *approbatio -onis* (as prec.; see -ATION)]

apprō'prĭate¹ *a.* Belonging or peculiar (*to*); suitable or proper (*to*, *for*); hence ~LY² (-tlĭ) *adv.*, ~NESS (-tn-) *n.* [f. LL *appropriatus* p.p. of AP*propriare* (*proprius* own); see -ATE²]

apprō'prĭ|āte² *v.t.* Take possession of; take to oneself; devote (money etc.) to special purposes; hence or cogn. ~A'TION, **~ātor**, *ns.*, **~at**IVE *a.* [f. prec.; see -ATE³]

appro'val (-ōō'-) *n.* Act of approving; sanction; **on** ~, (of goods supplied) to be returned if not satisfactory. [f. foll. + -AL 2]

appro've (-ōō'v) *v.* **1.** *v.t.* Confirm, sanction; commend; (arch.) show one*self* to be. **2.** *v.t.* & *i.* ~ **(of)**, pronounce or consider good or satisfactory, agree to; **~d school,** (Hist.) community home for training of young offenders. [ME, f. OF *aprover*, f. L (as APPROBATE)]

approx. *abbr.* approximate(ly).

apprŏ'xĭmate¹ *a.* Very near; fairly correct, near to the actual; hence ~LY² (-tlĭ) *adv.* (**very ~ly,** as only a rough approximation). [f. LL *approximatus* p.p. of AP*proximare* (*proximus* very near); see -ATE²]

apprŏ'xĭm|āte² *v.t.* & *i.* Bring or come near but not exactly (*to* thing, esp. in quality, number, etc.); hence ~A'TION *n.*, **~at**IVE *a.* [f. prec.; see -ATE³]

appūr'tėnance *n.* (usu. in *pl.*) Belonging; appendage; accessory. [ME, f. AF *apurtenaunce*, OF *apertenance*, f. Rom. **appertinentia* (as APPERTAIN; see -ANCE)]

appūr'tėnant *a.* Belonging, appertaining, pertinent, (*to*). [ME, f. OF *apartenant* part. (as APPERTAIN)]

Apr. *abbr.* April.

après-ski (ăprăskē') *a.* & *n.* (Worn or done at) time after day's skiing at resort. [F]

ā'prĭcŏt *n.* Juicy stone-fruit allied to plum and peach; its colour when ripe, orange-pink. [f. Port. *albricoque* or Sp. *albaricoque* f. Arab. *al* the + *barḳuḳ* f. late Gk *praikokion* f. L *praecoquum* variant of *praecox* early-ripe; *apri-* after L *apricus* ripe, *-cot* by assim. to F *abricot*]

A'prĭl (ā'-; *or -il*) *n.* Fourth month of year; **~ fool,** person jokingly fooled on 1 Apr. (~ *Fool's Day*); **~ weather,** alternating sunshine and showers. [ME, f. L *Aprilis*]

ā priōr'ī *adv.* & *a.* (Reasoning) from causes to effects; deductive(ly); presumptive(ly), without investigation, as far as one knows; (of knowledge) obtained by deduction without sensory experience; hence **āpriōr'**ISM *n.*, doctrine of a priori ideas. [L, = from what is before]

ā'pron *n.* **1.** Garment worn in front of body to protect clothes; **tied to ~-strings of** (*wife*, *mother*, etc.), unduly controlled by. **2.** Official dress of this kind (*bishop's*, *freemason's*, *apron*); leather covering for use in open carriage; endless conveyor-belt; hard-surfaced area on airfield, used for manœuvring and (un)loading aircraft; (Theatr.) advanced strip of stage for playing scenes in front of curtain. **3.** Hence ~ED² (-nd) *a.*, ~FUL 2 *n.* [ME *naperon* etc., f. OF dim. of *nape* table-cloth f. L *mappa*; for loss of *n-* cf. ADDER]

ăpropō's (-pō'; *or* ă'-) *adv.* & *a.* To the purpose; appropriate(ly); (abs.) incidentally, by the way; in respect *of*; (colloq.) concerning. [f. F *à propos* (*à* to, *propos* PURPOSE¹)]

ăpse *n.* Large semicircular or polygonal recess, arched or dome-roofed, esp. at end of church; apsis. [f. L APSIS]

ă'psĭdal *a.* Of the form of an apse; of apsides. [f. foll. + -AL]

ă'psĭ|s *n.* (*pl.* **~des** *pr.* -dēz). Point on orbit of planet, satellite, etc. nearest to or farthest from body round which it moves. [L, f. Gk (*h*)*apsis -idos* arch, vault]

ăpt *a.* Suitable, appropriate; having a tendency (*to* do etc.); quick-witted (*at*); hence ~'LY² *adv.*, ~'NESS *n.* [ME, f. L *aptus* fitted p.p. of *apere* fasten]

ă'pterous *a.* (Zool.) wingless; (Bot.) having no winglike expansions. [f. Gk *apteros* (*a-* not, *pteron* wing) + -OUS]

ă'ptery̆x *n.* Flightless New Zealand bird of genus *Apteryx*, with rudimentary wings and no tail, kiwi. [mod. L, f. Gk *a-* not + *pterux* wing]

ă'ptĭtūde *n.* Fitness; natural propensity or talent (*for*); ability, esp. (Psych.) to acquire a particular skill. [F, f. LL *aptitudo -inis* (as APT; see -TUDE)]

ă'qua *n.* The colour aquamarine. [abbr.]

ăqua- *pref.* denoting water, esp. w. ref. to aquatic entertainments or sports. [f. L *aqua* water]

ă'quacŭlture *n.* Cultivation of plants or breeding of animals in water. [f. AQUA-, after *agriculture*]

ăqua fŏr′tĭs *n.* (Chem.) Nitric acid. [L, = strong water]

ă′qualŭng *n.*, & *v.i.* **1.** *n.* Diver's portable breathing apparatus with cylinders of compressed air strapped on back, feeding air automatically through mask. **2.** *v.i.* Use this. [f. L *aqua* water + LUNG]

ăquamari′ne (-ē′n) *n.* Bluish-green beryl; its colour. [f. L *aqua marina* sea water]

ă′quanaut *n.* Underwater explorer or swimmer. [f. AQUA- + Gk *nautēs* sailor]

ă′quaplāne *n.*, & *v.i.* **1.** *n.* Board on which person rides, towed behind speedboat. **2.** *v.i.* Ride standing on aquaplane; (of vehicle) glide uncontrollably on water covering road surface. [f. L *aqua* water + PLANE[3]]

ăqua rē′gĭa *n.* (Chem.) Mixture of nitric and hydrochloric acids, able to dissolve gold and platinum. [L, = royal water]

ăquarĕ′lle *n.* Painting in thin usu. transparent water-colours. [F, f. It. *acquerella* water-colour dim. of *acqua* f. L *aqua* water]

aquār′ĭ|um *n.* (*pl.* **~ums** *or* **~a**). Artificial pond or tank usu. with transparent sides, for keeping live aquatic plants and animals; place containing such tanks; hence **ă′quarIST** *n.*, keeper of an aquarium. [f. neut. of L *aquarius* of water (*aqua*), after *vivarium*]

Aquār′ĭus (*a*-) *n.* Sign of the ZODIAC, the Water-carrier. [L (as prec.; see -ARY[1])]

aquă′tĭc *a.* & *n.* **1.** *a.* Growing or living in or near water; (of sports) conducted in or on water. **2.** *n.* Aquatic plant or animal; (in *pl.*) aquatic sports. [ME, f. F *aquatique* or f. L *aquaticus* (*aqua* water; see -ATIC)]

ă′quatĭnt *n.* Method of etching on copper with nitric acid; engraving so made. [f. F *aquatinte* f. It. *acqua tinta* coloured water]

ăquavi′t, ăkvavi′t, (-ē′t) *n.* Alcoholic spirit from potatoes etc. [Scand.]

ăqua vī′tae *n.* Alcoholic spirits, esp. of the first distillation. [L, = water of life, orig. alchemists' term]

ă′quėdŭct *n.* Artificial channel, esp. elevated structure of masonry, for conveyance of water; (Physiol.) small canal, esp. in head of mammals. [f. L *aquae ductus* conduit (*aqua* water, *ducere duct-* lead)]

ā′quėous *a.* Of water; containing water; (Geol.) produced by water (*aqueous rocks*); **~ humour,** (Anat.) transparent fluid between lens of eye and cornea. [f. med. L *aqueus* f. L *aqua* water, + -OUS]

ă′quĭfer *n.* (Geol.) Layer of rock or soil able to hold or transmit much water. [f. L *aqui-* (*aqua* water) + *-fer* bearing (*ferre* bear)]

ăquĭlē′gĭa *n.* (Usu. blue-flowered) plant of genus *Aquilegia*, columbine. [mod. use of med. L wd, of unkn. orig.]

ă′quĭlīne *a.* Of or like an eagle; (of nose) curved like eagle's beak. [f. L *aquilinus* (*aquila* eagle; see -INE[1])]

ar- *pref.*, assim. form of AD- before *r*.

-ar[1] *suf.* forming (1) adjs. (*angular, annular, linear, molecular, nuclear, titular*) and ns. (*scholar*) [f. or after OF *-aire* or *-ier* or f. L *-aris*], (2) ns. (*pillar*) [f. F *-er* or f. L *-ar, -are*, neut. of *-aris*].

-ar[2] *suf.* forming ns. (*bursar, exemplar, mortar, vicar*). [f. OF *-aire* or *-ier* or f. L *-arius, -arium*]

-ar[3] *suf.* var. of -ER[1], -OR, (*liar, pedlar*).

Ar *symb.* argon.

A.R.A. *abbr.* Associate of the Royal Academy.

A′rab (ă′-) *n.* & *a.* **1.** (One) of the Semitic people originally inhabiting Saudi Arabia and neighbouring countries, now the Middle East generally. **2.** *n.* Arabian horse; **street arab,** homeless child. [f. F *Arabe* f. L *Arabs Arabis* f. Gk *Araps -abos* f. Arab. *'arab*]

ărabĕ′sque (-k) *n.* Decoration with fanciful intertwining of leaves, scrollwork, etc.; (Mus.) passage or composition suggesting this decoration; (Ballet) posture in which body is supported on one leg with the other leg extended horizontally backwards, and arms are extended one forwards and one backwards. [F, f. It. *arabesco* (*arabo* Arab; see -ESQUE)]

Arā′bĭan (*a*-) *a.* & *n.* (Native or inhabitant) of Arabia. [ME, f. OF *arabi* prob. f. Arab. *'arabī*, or f. L *Arab*(*i*)*us* f. Gk *Arabios*, + -AN]

A′rabĭc (ă′-) *a.* & *n.* **1.** *a.* Of Arabia; **gum a~** (exuded by some kinds of acacia); **a~ numerals,** 1, 2, 3, etc. (opp. *Roman numerals*). **2.** Of the Arabs' language or literature. **3.** *n.* Language orig. of the Arabs, now spoken in much of N. Africa and Middle East. [ME, f. OF *arabic* f. L f. Gk *Arabikos*]

ă′rabĭs *n.* Cruciferous plant of genus *Arabis*, with white or purple flowers. [med. L f. Gk, = Arabian]

A′rabĭsm (ă′-) *n.* Arabic usage; Arab nationalism etc. [f. ARAB + -ISM]

A′rabĭst (ă′-) *n.* Student of Arabic language or Arab civilization. [f. ARAB + -IST]

ă′rable *a.* & *n.* (Land) ploughed or fit for ploughing; ‖(of crops) that can be grown on arable. [F, or f. L *arabilis* (*arare* plough; see -ABLE)]

A′rabȳ (ă′-) *n.* (poet.) Arabia. [f. OF *Arabie* f. L f. Gk *Arabia*]

ară′chnĭd (-k-) *n.* (Zool.) Member of the class Arachnida, comprising spiders, scorpions, ticks and mites. [f. F *arachnide* or mod. L *arachnida* f. Gk *arakhnē* spider; see -ID[3]]

ară′chnoid (-k-) *a.* & *n.* **1.** *a.* (Bot.) Covered with long cobweb-like hairs. **2.** *n.* (Anat.) Middle MENINX, between dura mater and pia mater. [f. mod. L *arachnoides* f. Gk *arakhnoeidēs* (*arakhnē* cobweb; see -OID)]

ară′k. See ARRACK.

A′raldīte (ă′-) *n.* One of various epoxy resins used as strong cements, insulators, etc. [P]

Aramā′ĭc (ă-) *a.* & *n.* (Of) language of Syria, widely used as lingua franca by Jews and others in time of Christ; (of) northern branch of Semitic family of languages, including Syriac and Mandaean. [f. L f. Gk *Aramaios* of Aram (bibl. name of Syria); see -IC]

ărapai′ma (-pī′-) *n.* Large S. Amer. food-fish of genus *Arapaima*, pirarucú. [Tupi]

ărapŏ′nga, -pŭ′nga, (-ngg*a*) *n.* S. Amer. bell-bird. [F f. Port.]

ăraucār′ĭa *n.* Evergreen tree of genus *Araucaria*, e.g. monkey-puzzle. [mod. L, f. *Arauco*, name of province in Chile; see -ARY[1]]

ar′balĕst *n.* (Hist.) Crossbow with special mechanism for drawing. [OE *arblast* f. OF *arbaleste* f. LL *arcubalista* (*arcus* bow, BALLISTA)]

ar′bĭter *n.* Judge; arbitrator; one who has entire control (*of*); **~ elegantiar′um** (or **elega′ntiae**) (-shĭ-), judge of taste and etiquette (lit. of elegance). [L]

ar′bĭtrag|e (-ahzh) *n.* Traffic in bills of exchange or stocks to take advantage of different prices in other markets; so **~eur′** (-ahzhêr′) *n.*, one who engages in arbitrage. [F, f. *arbitrer* (as ARBITRATE); see -AGE]

ar′bĭtral *a.* Pertaining to arbitration. [F, or f. LL *arbitralis* (ARBITER); see -AL]

arbĭ′trament *n.* Deciding of dispute by arbiter; authoritative decision. [ME, f. OF *arbitrement* f. med. L *arbitramentum* (as ARBITRATE; see -MENT)]

ar′bĭtrar|ȳ *a.* & *n.* **1.** *a.* Derived from mere opinion or random choice; capricious; unrestrained; despotic; hence **~ĬLY[2]** *adv.*, **~ĬNESS** *n.* **2.** *n.* (Print.) Character additional to usual fount. [f. L *arbitrarius* or F *arbitraire*; see ARBITER, -ARY[1]]

a͡r'bĭtrāte *v.t.* & *i.* Decide by arbitration. [f. L *arbitrari* judge (ARBITER) + -ATE[3]]

a͡rbĭtrā'tion *n.* Settlement of a dispute by an arbitrator. [ME f. OF, f. L *arbitratio -onis* (as prec.; see -ATION)]

a͡r'bĭtrātor *n.* One appointed by two parties to settle dispute; arbiter; hence ~SHIP *n.* [ME f. LL, f. as prec. + -OR]

a͡r'bĭtrėss *n.* Female arbiter. [ME, f. OF *arbitresse* fem. of *arbitre* f. L (as ARBITER; see -ESS[1])]

a͡r'blast (-ahst) *n.* = ARBALEST.

a͡r'bor[1] *n.* Axle or spindle on which something revolves; *tool-holder in lathe etc. [f. F *arbre* tree, axis, f. L *arbor*; refash. on L]

***a͡r'bor**[2]**.** See ARBOUR.

a͡rborā'ceous (-shus) *a.* Treelike; wooded. [f. L *arbor* tree + -ACEOUS]

Ar'bor Day (a͡r'-) *n.* Day set apart annually in U.S., Australia, and elsewhere for public tree-planting. [f. L *arbor* tree + DAY]

a͡rbŏr'ėal *a.* Of, living in, connected with, trees. [f. L *arboreus* (*arbor* tree) + -AL]

a͡rbŏr'ėous *a.* Wooded; arboreal. [f. as prec. + -OUS]

a͡rborĕ'sc|ent *a.* Treelike in growth or general appearance; hence ~ENCE *n.* [f. L *arborescere* grow into a tree (*arbor*); see -ESCENT]

a͡rborē't|um *n.* (*pl.* **~a** *or* ***~ums**). Botanical tree-garden. [L (*arbor* tree)]

a͡r'borĭ|cŭlture *n.* Cultivation of trees and shrubs; hence **~cŭ'ltur**AL *a.*, **~cŭ'ltur**IST (3) *n.*, (-cher-). [f. L *arbor -oris* tree, after *agriculture*]

a͡rborizā'tion, -īsā'tion (-z-), *n.* Treelike appearance of crystal etc. [f. as prec. + -IZE + -ATION]

a͡rbor vī'tae *n.* Evergreen conifer of genus *Thuja*. [L, = tree of life]

a͡r'bour, *a͡r'bor[2]**,** (-*er*) *n.* Bower, shady retreat with sides and roof formed mainly by trees or climbing plants; hence ~ED[2] (-*erd*) *a.* [ME f. AF *erber*, f. OF *erbier* (*erbe* herb f. L *herba*; see -ARIUM); phonetic change to *ar-* assisted by assoc. with L *arbor* tree]

a͡rbū'tus *n.* Evergreen of genus *Arbutus*, e.g. strawberry-tree; ***trailing ~**, mayflower. [L]

a͡rc *n.*, & *v.i.* (**~ing** *pr.* a͡r'k-, **~ed** *pr.* a͡rkt). **1.** *n.* Part of circumference of circle or other curve; (Electr.) luminous bridge formed by discharge between electrodes in gas; **~ lamp, ~ light,** light sources using electric arc; **~ welding** (using electric arc to melt metals to be welded). **2.** *v.i.* Form arc. [ME f. OF, f. L *arcus* bow, curve]

a͡rcā'de *n.* Passage arched over; any covered walk, esp. with shops etc. along one or both sides; ||AMUSEMENT *arcade*; (Archit.) series of arches supporting or along wall; hence **a͡rcā'd**ED[2] *a.* [F, f. Prov. *arcada* or It. *arcata* f. Rom. **arca* ARCH[1]; see -ADE]

Arcā'dĭan (a͡r-) *a.* & *n.* Ideal(ly) rustic; hence ~ISM *n.*, pastoral simplicity. [f. L *Arcadius* f. Gk *Arkadia* mountain district in Peloponnese, taken as ideal rustic paradise, + -AN]

Ar'cadȳ (a͡r'-) *n.* (poet.) Ideal rustic paradise. [f. Gk *Arkadia* (see prec.)]

a͡rcā'ne *a.* Mysterious, secret; hence ~LY[2] (-nlĭ) *adv.*, ~NESS (-n-n-) *n.* [F, or f. L *arcanus* (*arcēre* shut up f. *arca* chest; see -ANE)]

a͡rcā'n|um *n.* (usu. in *pl.* **~a**). Mystery, secret. [L, neut. of *arcanus* (see prec.)]

a͡rch[1] *n.* Curved structure as support for bridge, roof, floor, etc., or as ornament; curvature in shape of arch, e.g. on inner side of foot; vault; **Court of Arches,** (Eccl.) court of appeal for the province of Canterbury, orig. held in the church of St. Mary-le-Bow (or 'of the Arches'); **~'way,** vaulted passage, arched entrance. [ME, f. OF *arche* f. Rom. **arca,* n. pl. by-form of L *arcus* arc]

a͡rch[2] *v.* **1.** *v.t.* Furnish with or form into arch; span like arch; *arched* SQUALL. **2.** *v.i.* Form arch. [ME, f. prec.]

a͡rch[3] *a.* Consciously or affectedly playful or teasing; hence ~'LY[2] *adv.*, ~'NESS *n.* [f. foll. (2), orig. in ~ *rogue* etc.]

arch- *pref.* w. sense (1) chief, superior, (*archbishop, archdiocese, archduke*), (2) pre-eminent, esp. extremely bad, (*arch-fiend*). [f. OE *arce-* or OF *arche-*, f. L f. Gk *arkhi-* etc. (*arkhos* chief)]

Archae'an, *Archē'an, (a͡rk-) *a.* & *n.* (Of) the earliest geological period. [f. Gk *arkhaios* ancient (*arkhē* beginning) + -AN]

a͡rchae|ŏ'logȳ, *a͡rchė|ŏ'logȳ, (-kĭ-) *n.* Study of human antiquities, esp. of the prehistoric period and usu. by excavation; **industrial ~ology,** study of machines etc. formerly used in industry; hence or cogn. **~olŏ'g**IC(AL) *adjs.*, **~ŏ'log**IST (3) *n.*, **~ŏ'log**IZE (2) *v.i.* [f. mod. L f. Gk *arkhaiologia* ancient history (as prec.; see -LOGY)]

a͡rchaeŏ'pterȳx (-kĭŏ'-) *n.* Oldest known fossil bird, with tail like reptile's. [f. Gk *arkhaios* ancient + *pterux* wing]

a͡rchā'|ic (-k-) *a.* Primitive; antiquated; (of word etc.) no longer in ordinary use, though retained for special purposes; hence ~ICALLY *adv.* [f. F *archaïque* f. Gk *arkhaïkos* (as prec.; see -IC)]

a͡r'chā|ism (-k-) *n.* Retention or imitation of the old or obsolete (esp. in language and art); archaic word or expression; hence ~IST (1) *n.*, **~ĭ'st**IC *a.* [f. mod. L f. Gk *arkhaïsmos* (*arkhaïzō*; see foll., -ISM)]

a͡r'chāïze (-k-), **-ise** (-īz), *v.* **1.** *v.i.* Imitate the archaic. **2.** *v.t.* Render archaistic. [f. Gk *arkhaïzō* be old-fashioned (*arkhaios* ancient; see -IZE)]

a͡r'chāngel (-kānj-) *n.* Angel of highest rank; one of the eighth ORDER[1] of ninefold celestial hierarchy; hence **a͡rchăngĕ'l**IC (-kănj-) *a.* [OE, f. AF *archangele* f. eccl. L f. eccl. Gk *arkhaggelos* (as ARCH-, ANGEL)]

a͡rchbĭ'shop *n.* Chief bishop; hence **a͡rch-**BI'SHOPRIC *n.* [OE (as ARCH-, BISHOP)]

a͡rchdea'con *n.* Anglican clergyman next below bishop; dignitary of similar rank in other Churches; hence ~RY (2, 3), ~SHIP, *ns.* [OE *arce-, ercediacon*, f. eccl. L f. eccl. Gk *arkhidiakonos* (as ARCH-, DEACON[2])]

a͡rchdī'ocėse *n.* See of an archbishop. [f. ARCH- + DIOCESE]

a͡r'ch|dūke *n.* (*fem.* **~duchess**). (Hist.) Chief duke (esp. as title of son of Emperor of Austria); hence or cogn. ~DU'CAL *a.*, ~DUCHY *n.* [f. OF *archeduc* f. med. L *archidux -ducis* (as ARCH-, DUKE)]

***Archean.** See ARCHAEAN.

a͡rchėgō'nĭ|um (-kĭ-) *n.* (*pl.* **~a**). (Bot.) Female sex organ in mosses, ferns, etc. [mod. L, dim. of Gk *arkhegonos* (*arkhe-* chief, *gonos* race)]

a͡rch-ĕ'nemȳ *n.* Chief enemy; the Devil. [f. ARCH- (2) + ENEMY]

***archeology.** See ARCHAEOLOGY.

a͡r'cher *n.* One who shoots with bow and arrows; (*A~*) *the* zodiacal sign Sagittarius; **~-fish,** E. Ind. fish shooting water from mouth to dislodge and catch insects; so **a͡r'ch**ERY (2) *n.* [AF, f. OF *archier* f. Rom. **arcarius* (*arcus* bow; see -ARY[1])]

a͡r'chėtȳp|e (-k-) *n.* Original model, prototype; typical specimen; (Psych.) primordial mental image inherited by all; recurrent symbol or motif; so ~AL, **a͡rchėtȳ'p**ICAL (-k-), *adjs.* [f. L f. Gk *arkhetupon* (*arkhe-* ARCH-, *tupos* stamp)]

a͡rch-fie'nd *n.* The Devil. [f. ARCH- (2) + FIEND]

ar̂chĭdiă'con|al (-kĭ-) *a.* Pertaining to an archdeacon; so ~ATE^1 (1) *n.* [f. med. L *archidiaconalis* (as ARCH-, DIACONAL)]

ar̂chĭėpĭ'scop|al (-kĭĭ-) *a.* Pertaining to an archbishop; so ~ATE^1 (1) *n.* [f. eccl. L f. Gk *arkhiepiskopos* archbishop + -AL]

ar̂'chĭl (*or* -k-) *n.* (Violet dye from) one of various kinds of lichen. [var. of ORCHIL]

ar̂chĭmă'ndrīte (-k-) *n.* Superior of large monastery in Orthodox Church. [F, or f. eccl. L *archimandrita* f. eccl. Gk *arkhimandritēs* (*arkhi-* ARCH-, *mandra* monastery)]

Archĭmē'dėan (ar̂k-) *a.* Of Archimedes (Greek mathematician d. 212 B.C.); ~ **screw,** instrument raising water by turning of inclined screw. [f. LL *Archimedeus* + -AN]

Archĭmē'dēs (ar̂k-; -z) *n.* ~**' principle** (that a body immersed in a fluid is subject to an upward force equal in magnitude to the weight of fluid it displaces). [see prec.]

ar̂chĭpĕ'lagō (-k-) *n.* (*pl.* ~**s** *or* ~**es**). Sea with many islands; group of islands. [f. It. *arcipelago* f. Gk *arkhi-* chief + *pelagos* sea (orig. = the Aegean Sea)]

ar̂'chĭtĕct (-kĭ-) *n.* Designer of buildings, who prepares plans and superintends construction; designer of complex structure; the Creator; designer of ships etc.; (fig.) achiever (*architect of his own fortunes*). [f. F *architecte* f. It. *architetto*, or f. L *architectus* f. Gk *arkhitektōn* (*arkhi-* ARCH-, *tektōn* builder)]

ar̂chĭtĕctŏ'n|ĭc (-kĭ-) *a.* Of architecture or architects; constructive; pertaining to systematization of knowledge; hence ~ICS *n.* [f. L f. Gk *arkhitektonikos* (as prec.; see -IC)]

ar̂'chĭtĕcture (-kĭ-) *n.* Art or science of building; thing built, structure; style of building; construction; hence **ar̂chĭtĕ'ctur**AL (-kĭtĕ'kcher-) *a.* [F, or f. L *architectura* (*architectus* ARCHITECT; see -URE)]

ar̂'chĭtrāve (-k-) *n.* Main beam resting immediately on abacus of column; the various parts surrounding doorway or window; moulding round exterior of arch. [F f. It. (*archi-* ARCH-, *trave* f. L *trabs trabis* beam)]

ar̂'chīve (-k-) *n.* (usu. in *pl.*) Place in which collected public or corporate records are stored; records so kept. [f. F *archives* pl. f. L *archi*(*v*)*a* f. Gk *arkheia* public office (*arkhē* government)]

ar̂'chĭvĭst (-k-) *n.* Keeper of archives. [f. prec. + -IST]

ar̂'chĭvōlt (-k-) *n.* Lower curve of arch from impost to impost; band of mouldings on this. [f. F *archivolte* or It. *archivolto* (as ARC, VAULT^1)]

ar̂'chon (-k-) *n.* One of nine chief magistrates in ancient Athens; hence ~SHIP *n.* [f. Gk *arkhōn* ruler (part., as n., of *arkhō* rule)]

ar̂'ctĭc *a.* & *n.* **1.** *a.* Of the north polar regions (**A~ Circle**, parallel of latitude 66° 33′ N.); (colloq., of weather) very cold. **2.** *n.* Arctic regions; *thick waterproof overshoe. [ME, f. OF *artique* f. L *ar*(*c*)*ticus* f. Gk *arktikos* (*arktos* bear, Ursa Major; see -IC)]

ar̂'cūate *a.* Bent like a bow; arched. [f. L *arcuatus* p.p. of *arcuare* curve (*arcus* bow, curve); see -ATE^2]

arcus senilis (ar̂kus sĕnī'lĭs) *n.* Narrow opaque band often encircling cornea in old age. [L, lit. 'senile bow']

-ard, -art, *suf.* forming *ns.* (*placard, pollard, Spaniard, standard, wizard*), usu. depreciatory (*braggart, drunkard, dullard, sluggard*). [ME & OF, f. G *-hard, -hart* hardy (in proper names)]

ar̂'dent *a.* **1.** Burning; ~ (alcoholic) **spirits. 2.** Eager, zealous; (of person or feelings) fervent. **3.** Hence **ar̂'d**ENCY *n.*, ~LY^2 *adv.* [ME, f. OF *ardant* f. L *ardens -entis* (*ardēre* burn); see -ANT]

ar̂'dour, *ar̂'dor, (*-er*) *n.* Fierce heat; warm emotion; fervour, zeal, (*for*). [ME f. OF, f. L *ardor -oris* (*ardēre* burn; see -OR)]

ar̂'dūous *a.* Hard to achieve or overcome; laborious; strenuous, energetic; (arch.) steep; hence ~LY^2 *adv.*, ~NESS *n.* [f. L *arduus* steep, difficult + -OUS]

âre^1 *n.* Metric unit of square measure, 100 square metres. [F, f. L AREA]

âre^2. See BE.

âr'ėa *n.* **1.** Superficial extent; region, tract; hence **âr'ė**AL *a.* **2.** Defined space for particular use (*parking area, picnic area*); subject field (*areas of discussion*), branch of study; scope, range; (*or* *~**way**) sunk court in front of house basement. [L, = vacant piece of level ground]

ă'rėca (*or* arē'ka) *n.* Tropical Asiatic palm-tree of genus *Areca*; ~ **nut,** astringent seed of a species of areca. [Port., f. Malayalam *áḍekka*]

ar̂'ĕg. See ERG^2.

arē'na *n.* Central part of amphitheatre etc., in which contests take place; (fig.) scene of conflict, sphere of action; ~ **stage** (Theatr., placed amid audience); ~ **theatre,** theatre-in-the-round. [L (*h*)*arena* sand, sand-strewn place of combat]

ărėnā'ceous (-shus) *a.* Sandlike; sandy; growing in sand. [f. L *arenaceus* (as prec.; see -ACEOUS)]

aren't (ar̂nt). See BE.

arē'ol|a *n.* (*pl.* ~**ae**). Interstice; (Anat.) circular pigmented area, e.g. that surrounding nipple or pupil; hence ~AR^1 *a.* [L, dim. of AREA]

ărē'te (-ā't) *n.* Sharp ridge of mountain, esp. in Switzerland. [F, f. L *arista* ear of corn, fishbone, spine]

ar̂'gala *n.* Adjutant bird. [f. Hindi *haṛgīlā*]

ar̂'galĭ *n.* Large Asiatic wild sheep; bighorn. [Mongol]

ar̂'gent *n.* & *a.* (esp. Her.) Silver (colour). [F, f. L *argentum*]

ar̂gentĭ'ferous *a.* Yielding silver. [f. L *argentum* + -I- + -FEROUS]

ar̂'gentīne *a.* Of silver; silvery; **the A~**, Argentina, whence **Argentĭ'n**IAN (ar̂-) *a.* & *n.* [f. F *argentin* (*argent* silver; see -INE^1); *the A~* f. Sp.]

ar̂'gĭl *n.* Clay (esp. potter's); so ~**IA'**CEOUS *a.*, of or like clay. [f. F *argille* f. L *argilla* f. Gk *argillos* (*argos* white)]

Ar'gīve (ar̂'g-; *or* -j-) *a.* & *n.* (Inhabitant) of Argos in ancient Greece; Greek. [f. L *Argivus* f. Gk *Argeios*]

ar̂'gle-bar̂'gle *v.i.*, & *n.* (joc.) Dispute, wrangle. [corrupt. and redupl. of *argue*, as in *haggle*]

ar̂'gol *n.* Crude TARTAR^1 1. [ME f. AF *argoile*, of unkn. orig.]

ar̂'gŏn *n.* (Chem.) Gaseous element, an almost inert constituent of the atmosphere. [Gk, neut. of *argos* idle (*a-* not, *ergon* work)]

ar̂'gonaut *n.* **1.** (in *pl.*, *A~s*). Legendary heroes who sailed with Jason in the ship 'Argo' for the golden fleece. **2.** Cephalopod of genus *Argonauta*, paper NAUTILUS. [f. L *argonauta* f. Gk *Argonautēs* sailor in the Argo]

ar̂'gosy̆ *n.* (Hist. or poet.) Large merchant-vessel, esp. of Ragusa or Venice; (poet.) ship, venture. [prob. f. It. *Ragusea* (*nave*) Ragusan (vessel)]

ar̂'gōt (-gō) *n.* Jargon or slang of a class or group, formerly esp. of thieves. [F, of unkn. orig.]

ar̂'gūe *v.* **1.** *v.t.* Maintain by reasoning (*that*); hence **ar̂'gū**ABLE *a.* **2.** Treat (matter) by reasoning; persuade (person) *into, out of*; ~ **away,** get rid of by argument; *argue the* TOSS 8. **3.** Prove; indicate. **4.** *v.i.* Reason, esp. contentiously, (*with, against,* person; *for, against, about,* thing). [ME, f. OF *arguer* f. L *argutari* prattle, frequent. of *arguere* make clear, prove, accuse]

ar̂'gūfy̆ *v.i.* (colloq.) Dispute excessively. [illit. f. ARGUE; cf. *speechify*]

ar'gument *n.* **1.** Reason advanced (*for, against,* proposition or course of action); reasoning process; ~ **from silence** (based on opponent's silence or on absence of evidence). **2.** Debate, esp. heated one. **3.** Summary of subject-matter of book etc. **4.** (Math.) Independent variable determining value of function. [ME f. OF, f. L *argumentum* (*arguere*; see ARGUE, -MENT)]

argŭmĕntā'tion *n.* Methodical reasoning; debate. [F, f. L *argumentatio* (*argumentari* as prec.; see -ATION)]

argŭmĕ'ntative *a.* Logical; fond of arguing; hence ~LY[2] (-vlĭ) *adv.*, ~NESS (-vn-) *n.* [f. F *argumentatif -ive* or f. LL *argumentativus* (as prec.; see -ATIVE)]

argumentum e silentio (argŭmĕntum ē silĕ'n-shĭō) *n.* = ARGUMENT *from silence.* [L]

Ar'gus (ar'-) *n.* Watchful guardian; Asiatic pheasant; butterfly with ocellated wings; **~-eyed,** vigilant. [ME f. L, f. Gk *Argos* mythical person with a hundred eyes]

argū'te *a.* Sharp, shrewd; (of sounds) shrill; hence ~LY[2] (-tlĭ) *adv.*, ~NESS (-tn-) *n.* [ME, f. L *argutus* p.p. of *arguere* (see ARGUE)]

ar'gy̆-bargy̆. Var. of ARGLE-BARGLE.

ar'ia *n.* (Mus.) Long accompanied song for one voice in opera, oratorio, etc. [It.]

Ar'ian (ar'-) *a.* & *n.* (Holder) of the doctrine of Arius of Alexandria (4th c.), who denied full divinity of Christ; hence ~ISM (3) *n.* [f. eccl. L *Arianus* (*Arius* f. Gk *Arios, Areios*; see -AN)]

-ar'ian *suf.* forming *adjs.* and *ns.* (*agrarian, antiquarian, disciplinarian*), esp. w. sense '(member) of a sect etc., believer in' (*humanitarian, Unitarian, vegetarian*). [f. L *-arius* (see -ARY[1]) + -AN]

ă'rĭd *a.* Dry, parched; (fig.) uninteresting; (Geog.) too dry to support vegetation; (of ground) barren, bare; hence **arĭ'd**ITY, ~NESS, *ns.*, ~LY[2] *adv.* [f. F *aride* or f. L *aridus* (*arēre* be dry; see -ID[1])]

ar'iel *n.* Species of gazelle in W. Asia and Africa. [f. Arab. *'aryal* stag]

Ar'ies (ar'ēz) *n.* Sign of the ZODIAC, the Ram; **first point of** ~, vernal EQUINOCTIAL point. [ME f. L, = ram]

ari'ght (-i't) *adv.* Rightly. [OE (as A[3], RIGHT[3])]

ă'rĭl *n.* (Bot.) Extra seed-covering in certain plants, e.g. yew. [f. mod. L *arillus*; cf. med. L *arilli* dried grape-stones]

-ar'ious *suf.* forming *adjs.* (*gregarious, vicarious*). [f. L *-arius* (see -ARY[1]) + -OUS]

ari'se (-z) *v.i.* (**aro'se** *pr.* -ō'z; **ari'sen** *pr.* -ĭ'zen). Originate; be born; come into notice; result (*from, out of*); present itself; rise, esp. from the dead. [OE *ārīsan* (as A- 1, RISE[1])]

ari'sings (-z-; -z) *n. pl.* Materials forming secondary or waste products of operations. [f. prec. + -ING[1] (2)]

ărĭstŏ'cracy̆ *n.* Government by the best or most outstanding citizens; State so governed; ruling body of nobles; class of nobles; the best representatives *of* (intellect etc.). [f. F *aristocratie* f. Gk *aristokratia* (*aristos* best; see -CRACY)]

ă'rĭstocrăt *n.* One of the class of nobles. [f. F *aristocrate* (as foll.)]

ărĭstocră't|ic *a.* Pertaining to or attached to aristocracy; grand; stylish; with distinguished bearing and manners; hence ~ICALLY *adv.* [f. F *aristocratique* f. Gk *aristokratikos* (as ARISTOCRACY; see -IC)]

Arĭstotē'lian (ă-) *a.* & *n.* (Disciple or student) of the Greek philosopher Aristotle (d. 322 B.C.); logical, deductive. [f. L *Aristotelius, -eus,* f. Gk *Aristoteleios* (*Aristotelēs* Aristotle) + -AN]

ari'thmetic[1] *n.* Science of numbers; knowledge of this; computation, use of numbers; hence **arĭthmeti'**CIAN *n.* [ME, f. OF *arismetique* f. Rom. **arismetica* f. L *arithmetica* f. Gk *arithmētikē* (*tekhnē*) (art) of counting (*arithmeō* count f. *arithmos* number; see -IC)]

ărĭthmĕ'tĭc[2], **-ĭc|al,** *adjs.* Of arithmetic; *arithmetic* MEAN[1]; **~al progression,** (series of numbers showing) increase or decrease by a constant quantity (e.g. 1, 2, 3, 4, etc., 9, 7, 5, 3, etc.). [f. L f. Gk *arithmētikos* (see prec.) + -AL]

-ar'ium *suf.* forming *ns.* usu. denoting place (*aquarium, planetarium*). [L, neut. of adjs. in *-arius* (see -ARY[1])]

Ariz. *abbr.* Arizona.

ark *n.* Chest, box; **Ark (of the Covenant** or **of Testimony),** chest or cupboard containing scrolls or tables of Jewish Law; NOAH'*s ark.* [OE *ærc,* = OHG *archa,* ON *örk,* Goth. *arka,* f. L *arca* chest]

Ark. *abbr.* Arkansas.

arm[1] *n.* **1.** Upper limb of human body from shoulder to hand; ~ **in** ~, with arms interlinked; **at ~'s length,** as far as arm can reach, far enough to avoid undue familiarity, (of dealings) with neither party controlled by the other; **on** one's ~, supported by it; **under** one's ~, between it and body; **in ~s,** (of child) too young to walk; **in** person's **~s,** embraced by him; **with open ~s,** cordially; **within ~'s reach,** reachable by extending arm without moving from chair etc. **2.** Forelimb of animal; flexible limb of invertebrate; sleeve of garment; side part of chair to support sitter's arm; large branch of tree; thing resembling arm (*arm of the sea*). **3. ~chair'** (with side supports); **~'chair** *a.*, (fig.) theorizing, not practical or participating (*armchair critic, traveller*); **~'hole** (through which arm is put into garment sleeve or out of sleeveless garment); **~'pit,** hollow under arm at shoulder. **4.** Hence (-)**arm**ED[2] (-md) *a.*, ~'FUL 2 *n.*, quantity that can be held by one or both arms, ~'LESS *a.* [OE, = OHG *arm,* ON *armr,* Goth. *arms* f. Gmc **armaz*]

arm[2] *n.* **1.** (usu. in *pl.*) Weapon; =*firearm* (see FIRE[1] 8); **small ~s,** portable firearms, esp. rifles, pistols, light machine-guns, sub-machine-guns, etc.; **~s race,** contest between nations in accumulating weapons; **bear ~s,** be armed, serve as soldier, have coat of arms; **in ~s,** armed; **lay down, take up, ~s,** cease, begin, fighting; **under ~s,** ready for war or battle; **up in ~s,** actively rebelling (*against,* lit. or fig.; *about,* fig.). **2.** (in *pl.*) Military profession. **3.** Each kind of troops or branch of military forces, infantry, cavalry, etc. **4.** (in *pl.*) Heraldic devices; COAT *of arms*; ||KING[1] *of Arms.* [ME, f. OF *armes* pl. f. L *arma* arms, fittings]

arm[3] *v.t.* **1.** Furnish (person, one*self*, or abs.) with weapons; **~ed neutrality** (of nations prepared for war). **2.** Furnish with tools or other requisites or (fig.) advantages. **3.** Make (bomb etc.) able to explode. [ME, f. OF *armer* f. L *armare* (*arma* arms)]

arma'da (-ah'-) *n.* Fleet of warships, esp. that sent by Spain against England in 1588. [Sp., f. Rom. *armata* army; see -ADE]

armadĭ'llō *n.* (*pl.* ~s). Burrowing mammal of S. America, with body encased in bony plates, and often with habit of rolling itself into ball when captured. [Sp., dim. of *armado* armed man f. L *armatus* p.p. of *armare* ARM[3]]

Armagĕ'ddon (armag-) *n.* (Scene of) supreme or large-scale conflict between the nations. [Rev. 16:16 (A.V.)]

ar'mament *n.* Force equipped for war; military weapons and equipment, esp. guns on warship; process of equipping for war. [f. L *armamentum* (as ARM[2]; see -MENT)]

armamĕntar'i|um *n.* (*pl.* ~a). Set of equipment available to physician etc. (also fig.). [L, = arsenal]

ar'mature *n.* Defensive covering of animals or plants; framework to support sculpture etc. during construction; piece of soft iron placed in contact with poles of magnet, to preserve its power or transmit force to support load; wire-wound core of dynamo or electric motor; moving part of electric bell etc.; (arch.) arms, armour. [F, f. L *armatura* armour (as ARM²; see -URE)]

arme blanche (arm blah'ńsh) *n.* (*pl.* ***-es -es*** *pr.* same). Cavalry sword or lance; cavalry. [F, = white ARM²]

Armē'nian (ar-) *a.* & *n.* (Native, inhabitant, or language) of Armenia; (member) of Monophysite church established in Armenia *c.* 300. [f. *Armenia* in U.S.S.R. + -AN]

ar'mĭger *n.* Person entitled to heraldic arms; hence ~OUS (-ĭ'j-) *a.* [L, = bearing arms (*arma* ARM²s, *gerere* bear)]

armĭ'llarў *a.* Pertaining to bracelets; ~ **sphere,** (Hist.) skeleton celestial globe of metal rings representing equator, tropics, etc. [f. mod. L *armillaris* f. L *armilla* bracelet; see -ARY²]

Armĭ'nian (ar-) *a.* & *n.* (Holder) of the doctrine of Arminius, Dutch Protestant theologian d. 1609, who opposed the views of Calvin, esp. on predestination; hence ~ISM (3) *n.* [f. *Arminius,* Latinized f. *Harmensen,* + -AN]

ar'mĭstice *n.* Cessation from hostilities (lit. or fig.); short truce; **A~ Day,** 11 Nov., anniversary of the armistice of 1918 (now replaced by Remembrance Sunday and *Veterans' Day). [F, or f. mod. L *armistitium* (*arma* arms, *-stitium* stoppage; cf. SOLSTICE)]

ar'mlėt *n.* Band worn round arm; small inlet of sea or branch of river. [f. ARM¹ + -LET]

***ar'mor** etc. See ARMOUR¹,² etc.

armor'ial *a.* Pertaining to heraldic arms. [f. foll. + -AL]

ar'mor|ў¹ *n.* Heraldry; hence ~IST (3) *n.* [f. OF *armoierie*; see ARMOURY]

***ar'morў²**. See ARMOURY.

ar'mour¹, *ar'mor¹, (-mer) *n.* **1.** (Hist.) Defensive covering for the body worn in fighting. **2.** ~**(-plate)**, metal sheathing of warship, composed of plates (**~-clad,** furnished with this); steel plates etc. protecting cars, tanks, etc., from projectiles; armoured vehicles collectively, e.g. tanks, armoured cars. **3.** Diver's suit. **4.** Protective covering of animals or plants. **5.** Heraldic devices. [ME, f. OF *armure* f. L *armatura* (see ARMATURE)]

ar'mour², *ar'mor², (-mer) *v.t.* Furnish with protective covering; toughen (glass); **~ed car, train,** etc., one with protective plates of steel etc., and (usu.) guns; **~ed division** etc., one equipped with armoured cars, tanks, etc. [f. prec.]

ar'mourer, *ar'morer, (-mer-) *n.* Maker or repairer of arms or armour; official in charge of ship's or regiment's arms. [f. AF *armurer,* OF *-urier,* (as ARMOUR¹; see -ER²)]

ar'mourў, *ar'morў², (-erĭ) *n.* Place where arms are kept, arsenal; array of weapons, resources, etc.; *drill hall; *armourer's workshop. [ME, f. OF *armoi(e)rie* (*armoier* to blazon f. *arme* ARM²); assim. to ARMOUR¹]

ar'mў *n.* Organized force armed for fighting on land; *the* military profession; large number (*an army of locusts, of helpers*); organized body for a cause (*Salvation Army; Church Army*); ~ **corps,** main subdivision of army in the field; ||**A~ List,** official list of commissioned officers; **~-worm,** larva of various moths and flies, gathering in large numbers. [ME, f. OF *armee* f. Rom. *armata* fem. p.p. of *armare* arm; see -Y⁴]

ar'nĭca *n.* Composite plant of genus *Arnica,* e.g. mountain tobacco; medicine prepared from this, used for bruises etc. [mod. L, of unkn. orig.]

aroi'nt *v.* or *int.* (arch.) ~ **thee,** begone. [17th c.; orig. unkn.]

arō'ma *n.* Fragrance, sweet smell; subtle pervasive quality. [f. L f. Gk *arōma -atos* spice]

ăromă't|ĭc *a.* & *n.* **1.** *a.* Fragrant, spicy; (of smell) pleasantly pungent; (Chem.) of organic compounds containing rings of (usu. six) carbon atoms; *aromatic* VINEGAR; hence ~ICALLY *adv.* **2.** *n.* Aromatic substance. [ME, f. OF *aromatique* f. LL f. Gk *arōmatikos* (as AROMA; see -IC)]

arose. See ARISE.

arou'nd *adv.* & *prep.* **1.** *adv.* On every side, in every direction; round, round about; (colloq.) near at hand, in existence; in various places, here and there, at random, (*fool around; shop around*); **have been ~**, have gained worldly experience. **2.** *prep.* On or along the circuit of; on every side of, enveloping; here and there in or near; *round (*the church around the corner*); *approximately at, approximately equal to. [f. A- 2 + ROUND²]

arou's|e (-z) *v.t.* Awake from sleep; stir into activity; call into existence (*his behaviour aroused suspicion*); so ~AL *n.* [f. A- 1 + ROUSE², after *arise*]

arow' (-ō') *adv.* In a row or line. [ME, f. A³ + ROW¹]

A.R.P. *abbr.* air-raid precautions.

arpĕ'ggĭō (*or* -ĕ'jō) *n.* (*pl.* ~**s**). (Mus.) Sounding of notes of chord in (usu. rapid upward) succession, not simultaneously; chord so played. [It. (*arpeggiare* play harp, f. *arpa* harp)]

ar'quėbus. See HARQUEBUS.

arr. *abbr.* arranged by; arrives.

ă'rrack, ară'k, *n.* Alcoholic spirit, esp. distilled from coco sap or rice. [f. Arab. *'araḳ* sweat, alcoholic spirit from grapes or dates]

arrai'gn (-ā'n) *v.t.* Indict before tribunal; accuse; find fault with, call in question, (action, statement); so ~MENT *n.* [ME, f. AF *arainer* f. OF *araisnier* f. Rom. *ADrationare reason, talk reasonably f. L *ratio -onis* reason, discourse]

arrā'nge (-nj) *v.* **1.** *v.t.* Put into order, adjust; (Mus.) adapt (composition) for different medium, instrumental or vocal; adapt (play etc.) for broadcasting; settle (dispute etc.); settle beforehand the order or manner of; plan, cause to occur. **2.** *v.i.* Take steps, form plans, give instructions, (*arrange to be there, for the car to be there; arrange about it*); come to agreement (*with* person, *about* thing). [ME, f. OF *arangier* (*à* to, *rangier* RANGE¹)]

arrā'ngement (-njm-) *n.* Arranging or being arranged; condition or manner of being arranged; thing arranged; settlement of dispute etc.; (in *pl.*) plans, measures, (*make your own arrangements*). [F (as prec.; see -MENT)]

ă'rrant *a.* Downright, complete, (*arrant liar, nonsense*); hence ~LY² *adv.* [ME, var. of ERRANT, orig. in phrs. like *arrant* (=outlawed roving) *thief*]

ă'rras *n.* Rich tapestry; (Hist.) hanging screen of this on wall(s) of room. [f. *A~*, town in N.E. France famous for the fabric]

array'¹ *v.t.* Marshal, dispose, (forces); (Law) empanel (jury); dress, esp. with display; adorn. [ME, f. AF *araier,* OF *areer,* f. Rom. *ARredare f. Gmc *rǣdh- prepare]

array'² *n.* Imposing or well-ordered series of persons or things; (Law) order of empanelling jury; (Math.) matrix; (Hist.) arming of militia; (poet.) outfit, dress. [ME, f. AF *arai,* OF *arei* (*areer*; see prec.)]

arrear' *n.* (in *pl.*) Outstanding debts; what remains undone (*arrears of work*); **in ~(s)**, behindhand, esp. in payment; so ~AGE (1, 2) *n.* [ME, orig. adv. f. OF *arere* f. med. L *adretro* (AD-, *retro* backwards); first used in phr. *in arrear*]

arrĕ'st[1] *v.t.* **1.** Stop (growth, motion, progress of disease, decay); ~ **judgement,** (Law) stay proceedings after verdict, on ground of error. **2.** Seize (person or ship), esp. by legal authority; catch (attention); catch attention of. **3.** Hence ~ABLE *a.*, (esp., of offence) such that offender may be arrested without warrant; ~A'TION *n.*; ~ER[1], ~OR, *ns.*, (esp.) device for retarding aircraft by hook and cable on landing; ~MENT *n.*, (esp., Sc.) attachment of earnings. [ME, f. OF *arester* f. Rom. *ARrestare remain, stop (REST[3])]

arrĕ'st[2] *n.* **1.** Stoppage, check; **cardiac ~,** heart failure; ~ **of judgement** (Law) (see prec.). **2.** Seizure; legal apprehension; **under** ~ (legal restraint). [ME, f. OF *arest(e)* (*arester*; see prec.)]

arrière-ban (ă'rïerbăn) *n.* (Hist.) (Calling together of) vassals summoned for military service. [F, f. Frank. **hariban* (*hari* army, *ban* proclamation)]

arrière-pensée (ărïarpah'ṅsā) *n.* Ulterior motive; mental reservation. [F]

ă'rrĭs *n.* (Archit.) Sharp edge formed by angular contact of two plane or curved surfaces. [corrupt. f. F *areste*, mod. ARÊTE]

arrī'val *n.* Act of arriving; appearance upon scene; person or thing that has arrived; (**new**) ~, (colloq.) new-born child. [ME, f. AF *arrivaille* (*arriver* as foll.; see -AL 2)]

arrī've *v.i.* ~ **(at, in,** etc.), come to destination (lit., or fig.: *arrive at conclusions*) or end of journey or specified point on journey; establish one's reputation or position; (colloq., of child) be born; (of thing) be brought; (of time) come. [ME, f. OF *ariver* f. Rom. *AR*ripare* come to shore (L *ripa*)]

arriviste (ărēvē'st) *n.* Ambitious or self-seeking person; so ***arrivisme*** (ărēvē'zem) *n.*, behaviour of an *arriviste*. [F (*arriver* f. as prec.; see -IST)]

ă'rrog|ant *a.* Overbearing; presumptuous; haughty; hence or cogn. ~ANCE, ~ANCY, *ns.*, ~**ant**LY[2] *adv.* [ME f. OF (as foll.; see -ANT)]

ă'rrog|āte *v.t.* Claim unduly (thing *to oneself*); attribute unjustly (*to* person); so ~A'TION *n.* [f. L AR(*rogare* ask) + -ATE[3]]

arrondissement (ărŏndē'smahṅ) *n.* Administrative subdivision of French department. [F]

ă'rrow (-ō) *n.* Pointed straight slender missile shot from bow; pointer etc. of similar shape; ||**broad** ~, mark distinguishing British Government stores, e.g. (formerly) prison clothing; ~**head,** pointed end of arrow, water-plant with sagittate leaves; ~**root,** plant from which a nutritious starch is prepared; hence ~Y[2] *a.* [OE *ar(e)we* f. ON *ör*, st. **arw-*, f. Gmc **arhw-* f. IE **arkw-*]

***arroy'ō** *n.* (*pl.* ~**s**). Brook, stream. [Sp.]

||**ar͡se**[1], ***ăss**[2], *n.* (vulg.) Buttocks, rump; ~-**licking** *n.* & *a.*, toadying. [OE *ærs*, = OHG, ON *ars*, Gmc **arsaz*, IE **órsos*]

||**ar͡se**[2]. Var. of ASS[3].

ar͡'senal *n.* Government establishment for storage or manufacture of weapons and ammunition; store of weapons (lit. or fig.). [F, or f. It. *arzanale* f. Arab. *dār-ṣinā'a* (*dār* house, *ṣinā'a* art f. *ṣana'a* fabricate)]

ar͡'senĭc[1] *n.* (Chem.) Brittle steel-grey semi-metallic element; (pop.) arsenic trioxide, white mineral substance, a violent poison; **red** ~, realgar; hence **ar͡sē'nĭ**OUS *a.* [ME f. OF, f. L f. Gk *arsenikon* yellow orpiment (identified with *arsenikos* male, but in fact) f. Arab. *al-zarnīḵ* (*al* the, *zarnīḵ* orpiment f. Pers. f. *zar* gold)]

ar͡sĕ'nĭc[2] *a.* Pertaining to arsenic; (Chem.) containing arsenic with valence five. [f. prec. + -IC]

ar͡sĕ'nĭcal *a.* & *n.* (Drug) containing arsenic. [f. ARSENIC[1] + -AL]

ar͡'sine (-ēn) *n.* (Chem.) Compound AsH_3, like phosphine but with arsenic in place of phosphorus. [f. ARSENIC[1] after *amine*]

ar͡'s|ĭs *n.* (*pl.* ~**es** *pr.* -ēz). Stressed syllable or part of metrical foot (opp. THESIS). [ME f. LL f. Gk, = lifting (*airō* raise)]

ar͡'son *n.* Malicious setting on fire of house etc.; hence ~IST *n.*, person guilty of arson. [legal AF, OF, f. med. L *arsio -onis* f. L *ardēre ars-* burn]

ar͡sphĕ'namīne (*or* -ēn) *n.* Drug formerly used in treating yaws and syphilis. [f. ARSENIC + PHENYL + AMINE]

ar͡sy̆-ver͡'sy̆ *adv.* (vulg.) Back to front; upside down. [f. ARSE[1] + L *versus* p.p. of *vertere* turn, after *hurly-burly* etc.]

art[1]. See BE.

ar͡t[2] *n.* **1.** Skill, esp. human skill as opposed to nature; (ability in) skilful execution as an object in itself; cunning; imitative or imaginative skill applied to design, as in paintings, architecture, etc. (WORK[1]*s of art*); (*attrib.*) pertaining to use of such skill (*art music; art needlework*); (in *pl.*) = FINE[2] *arts*. **2.** Thing in which skill may be exercised; (in *pl.*) certain branches of university or school study serving as preparation for life or for more advanced studies, esp. languages, literature, philosophy, history, etc., as dist. from sciences; **Bachelor, Master, of Arts,** one who has attained standard of proficiency in these at university. **3.** Practical application of any science; industrial pursuit, craft. **4.** Knack; stratagem. **5.** ~**s and crafts,** decorative design and handicraft; ~ **and part,** accessory, participant; ~ **deco** (dĕ'kō), decorative art style of 1920s and 1930s; ~**-form,** established form of composition (e.g. novel, sonata, sonnet), medium of artistic expression; ~ **nouveau** (ar͡nōōvō') [F, = new art], art style of late 19th c. with ornamented and flowing designs; ~ **paper** (coated with smooth-surfaced clay etc.); ~ **union,** (Austral. & N.Z.) lottery (orig. with work of art as prize); ~**'work,** illustrative matter in printed text. [ME f. OF, f. L *ars artis*]

-art. See -ARD.

art. *abbr.* article.

ar͡'tėfăct, ar͡'tĭ-, *n.* Product of human art and workmanship; (Archaeol.) product of prehistoric or aboriginal art as dist. from similar object naturally produced; (Biol. etc.) thing not naturally present, introduced during preparation or investigation. [f. L *arte* (abl. of *ars* art) + *factum* (neut. p.p. of *facere* make)]

ar͡tĕ'l *n.* Collective enterprise of craftsmen etc. in Russia. [Russ.]

ar͡ter͡'ĭal *a.* Belonging to an artery; of the nature of or resembling an artery (esp. of important main roads etc.). [F (*artère* artery; see -AL)]

ar͡ter͡'ĭalīz|e, -īs|e (-īz), *v.t.* Convert venous into arterial (blood) by exposure to oxygen in lungs; furnish with arterial system; hence ~A'TION *n.* [f. prec. + -IZE]

ar͡ter͡'ĭōle *n.* Small artery adjoining capillaries. [F, dim. of *artère* ARTERY]

ar͡tēr͡ĭōscler͡|ō'sĭs *n.* (*pl.* ~**o'ses** *pr.* -ēz). Hardening and thickening of walls of arteries, esp. in old age; hence ~O'TIC *a.* [f. ARTERY + -O- + SCLEROSIS]

ar͡'ter|y̆ *n.* **1.** Muscular-walled tube forming part of system by which blood is conveyed from heart (cf. VEIN) to all parts of body; hence ~I'TIS *n.* **2.** (fig.) Important channel of transport. [ME, f. L f. Gk *artēria* prob. f. *airō* raise]

ar͡tē'sian (-zhan) *a.* ~ **well,** perpendicular boring into oblique strata, producing constant supply of water at surface with little or no pumping. [f. F *artésien* (*Artois*, old French province)]

ar'tful *a.* (Of person or action) crafty, deceitful; hence ~LY² *adv.*, ~NESS *n.* [f. ART² + -FUL]
arthr|ī'tis *n.* Inflammation of joint(s); so ~**ĭ'tic** *a.* & *n.* [L f. Gk (*arthron* joint; see -ITIS)]
ar'thrōpŏd *n.* (Zool.) Animal of phylum Arthropoda, with segmented body and jointed limbs, e.g. insect, spider, crustacean. [f. Gk *arthron* joint + *pous podos* foot]
Arthur'ian (ar-) *a.* Relating to King Arthur or his knights. [f. *Arthur*, legendary British king + -IAN]
ar'tic *n.* (colloq.) Articulated lorry. [abbr.]
ar'tichōke *n.* Plant allied to thistle; (**globe**) ~, its partly edible flower-head; **Jerusalem** [corrupt. of It. *girasole* sunflower] ~, species of sunflower with edible tuberous roots. [f. It. *articiocco* alt. of **alcarcioffo* f. Arab. *alkaršūfa*]
ar'ticle¹ *n.* **1.** Separate portion of anything written; separate clause (of agreement etc.; *the* THIRTY-*nine Articles*; *articles of apprenticeship*); literary composition (other than fiction) forming part of magazine etc. but independent of others. **2.** Particular part or thing; ~ **of faith,** basic point of belief. **3.** (Gram.) **Definite** ~, 'the'; **indefinite** ~, 'a, an'; corresponding adj. in other languages. **4.** (arch.) **In the** ~ (moment) **of death.** [ME f. OF, f. L *articulus* dim. of *artus* joint]
ar'ticle² *v.t.* Bind by articles of apprenticeship. [f. prec.]
arti'cūlar *a.* Pertaining to the joints. [ME, f. L *articularis* (as ARTICLE¹; see -AR¹)]
arti'cūl|ate¹ *a.* Jointed; distinctly jointed; with clearly distinguishable parts (*articulate speech*); able to express oneself coherently; hence ~ACY, ~**ate**NESS (-tn-), *ns.*, ~**ate**LY² (-tlĭ) *adv.* [f. L *articulatus* (as prec.; see -ATE²)]
arti'cūlāt|e² *v.* **1.** *v.t.* (usu. in *pass.*) Connect by joints; ~**ed lorry** etc. (with flexibly connected sections). **2.** (usu. in *pass.*) Mark with apparent joints. **3.** Divide into words, pronounce, distinctly; utter. **4.** Hence ~ORY *a.* (esp. of speech). **5.** *v.i.* Speak distinctly; speak. **6.** Form joint *with*. [f. as prec.; see -ATE³]
articulā'tion *n.* Act or mode of jointing; joint; act of speaking; articulate utterance, speech. [F, or f. L *articulatio* (*articulare* joint, as ARTICLE¹; see -ATION)]
ar'tifăct. See ARTEFACT.
ar'tifice *n.* Device, contrivance; (piece of) cunning; address, skill. [F, f. L *artificium* (*ars artis* art, *-ficium* making f. *facere* make)]
arti'ficer *n.* Craftsman; (Mil., Navy) skilled mechanic; inventor (*of*). [ME, f. AF, prob. alt. of OF *artificien*, f. as prec.]
artifi'cial (-shal) *a.* **1.** Made by art; not natural (*artificial limb, satellite*); ~ **insemination,** injection of semen into uterus by artificial means; *artificial* KIDNEY; ~ **language** (made from words etc. in several languages, esp. one meant for international use); ~ **respiration,** restoration or initiation of breathing by manual or mechanical means; *artificial* TOOTH. **2.** Not real (*artificial flowers*); ~ **horizon,** dish of mercury etc. for use with sextant on land, gyroscopic device showing position of aircraft rel. to horizon plane; *artificial* MOTHER¹; ~ **silk,** (arch.) rayon. **3.** Affected, insincere; factitious, not arising naturally. **4.** Hence **artificiă'l**ITY (-shĭ-), ~NESS, *ns.*, ~IZE (3) *v.t.*, ~LY² *adv.* [ME, f. OF *artificiel* or f. L *artificialis* (as ARTIFICE; see -AL)]
arti'llerў *n.* Large guns used in fighting on land; branch or arm of the service that uses these; hence **arti'ller**IST (3), ~**man,** *ns.* [ME, f. OF *artillerie* (*artiller* alt. of *atillier*, *atirier* equip, arm, f. *à* to, *tire* order; see -ERY)]
artisă'n (-z-) *n.* Mechanic, skilled (esp. manual) worker; hence ~ATE¹ (4) *n.* [F, f. It. *artigiano* f. Rom. **artitianus* f. L *artitus* p.p. of *artire* instruct in arts; see -AN]
ar'tist *n.* One who practises one of the fine arts, esp. painting; one who makes his craft a fine art (*artist in words* etc.); artiste; (Austral., N.Z.) devotee (usu. w. defining wd; *booze artist*); ~**'s proof,** copy of engraving taken for the artist and valued as fresher than ordinary copies; hence ~RY (5) *n.* [f. F *artiste* f. It. *artista* (*arte* ART²; see -IST)]
arti'ste (-tē'-) *n.* Professional singer, dancer, etc. [F; see prec.]
arti'st|ic *a.* Of art or artists; made or done with art; appreciative of art; having natural skill in art; hence ~ICALLY *adv.* [f. prec. + -IC]
ar'tlėss *a.* Not resulting from or displaying art; clumsy; guileless, ingenuous; hence ~LY² *adv.*, ~NESS *n.* [f. ART² + -LESS]
ar'tў *a.* (colloq.) (Of person, furniture, etc.) pretentiously or quaintly artistic; ~**-(and-) crafty,** (joc.) (of furniture) remarkable rather for specially artistic style than for usefulness or comfort (after the *Arts and Crafts* Exhibition Society founded 1888), (of person) arty. [f. ART² + -Y²]
ar'um *n.* Plant of genus *Arum*, e.g. lords-and--ladies; ~ **lily** (tall and white-spathed). [L, f. Gk *aron*]
-arў¹ *suf.* forming adjs. (*budgetary*, *contrary*, *primary*, *unitary*) or ns. (*dictionary*, *fritillary*, *granary*, *January*). [f. or after F *-aire* or f. L *-arius -aria -arium* 'connected with']
-arў² *suf.* forming adjs. (*military*). [f. F *-aire* or f. L *-aris* 'belonging to']
Ar'ўan (ar'-) *a.* & *n.* **1.** (arch.) Indo-European; Indo-Iranian. **2.** (Of) the parent language of the Indo-European (esp. Indo-Iranian) family; (member) of the peoples speaking any of these languages; (improp., esp. in Nazi Germany) non-Jewish German. [f. Skr. *āryas* noble, earlier used as a national name]
ă'rўl *a.* Derived from or related to an aromatic hydrocarbon. [f. G (as AROMATIC, -YL)]
as¹ (az *or, when stressed,* ăz) *adv., conj.,* & *rel. pron.* **1.** *adv.* (in main sentence, foll. by *as* in expressed or understood subord. clause). In the same degree (*I came as quickly as I could*; *is twice as big*; *I know that as well as you*; *you might as well help me*). **2.** *rel. adv.* or *conj.* (in subord. clause, with or without antecedent *as*, *so*, expressing degree, manner, etc., of the principal sentence): (degree) *you are as good as he* (see also GOOD 12); *it is not so* (or *as*) *easy as you think*; *as recently as* (no longer ago than) *last week*; *quick as a flash he jumped out*; *fair as* (= though) *she is*; *try as he might*, however hard he tried; (*as*) *sure as fate* (and in many other proverbial expressions); (manner) *do as you like*; *as you well know*; *according as we decide*; *Olivier as Hamlet*; *did this as* (in the function of) *their legal representative*; *treat him as a stranger*; *you are*, **as it were** (= to a certain extent, or as if it were actually so), *compromised*; *friends as distinct from mere acquaintances*; *they rose as one man*; *late as usual*; *he smiled, as who should say* (arch., = as a man would smile who said); **as you were!** (order, esp. Mil., to return to previous position); (time) *it struck me as I was speaking*; *I knew him as a boy*; (reason) *as you are ready, we can go at once*; (result) *he so arranged matters as to suit everyone*; *be so good as to come*; (purpose) *turned aside so as to avoid meeting her*; (illustration) *cathedral cities, as Norwich*. **3.** *rel. pron.* That, who, which, (*I had the same trouble as you*; *such countries as Spain*; (vulg.) *it was him as did it*); (with antecedent inferred from main sentence) *he was a foreigner, as* (which fact) *they perceived from his accent*; *he was a playwright, as was his wife*. **4.** *As* FAR¹ *as*; **as for,** with regard to (*as for you, I despise you*);

as from, (in formal dating; *prices will be raised as from 31 March*); *as* IF; **as (it) is,** in the existing state; *as* LONG[2] *as*; *as* MUCH; **as of,** *as from, as at (date); *as* PER; *as* REGARD[1]*s*; *as* SOON *as*; *as* SUCH 11; **as though,** = *as* IF; **as to,** with respect to (*said nothing as to hours, as to when he would come; as to you, I despise you*); **as was,** in the previously existing state; *as* WELL[3] (*as*); **as yet,** up to this or that time (though not at some later time) (*has worked well as yet*). [reduced form of OE *alswā* ALSO]

ăs[2] *n.* (*pl.* **a'sses**). Roman copper coin. [L]

as- *pref.*, assim. form of AD- before *s*.

A.S. *abbr.* Anglo-Saxon.

As *symb.* arsenic.

A.S.A. *abbr.* ||Amateur Swimming Association; *American Standards Association.

ăsafoe'tĭda (-fē't-), ***-fē't-,** *n.* Resinous plant gum with strong smell, used in medicine. [ME f. med. L (*asa* f. Pers. *azā* mastic; *fetida* as FETID)]

ăsbĕ'st|ŏs (*or* ăz-) *n.* Fibrous silicate mineral that can be woven into an incombustible fabric; this fabric; hence ~INE[2] *a.* (lit. or fig.), ~O'SIS *n.*, lung disease from inhaling asbestos particles. [ME, f. OF *a(l)beston* f. L f. Gk *asbeston* (acc.) unquenchable (*a-* not, *sbestos* f. *sbennumi* quench)]

ă'scarĭd *n.* Intestinal roundworm of family Ascaridae. [f. mod. L f. Gk *askaris*]

ascĕ'nd *v.* **1.** *v.i.* Go or come up; (of thing) rise, be raised; (Print., of letter) have part projecting upwards, whence ~ER[1] (2) *n.*; slope upwards, lie along ascending slope; rise in thought, rank, or degree of quality; (of sound) rise in pitch; go back in point of time. **2.** *v.t.* Go up, climb, (hill, stairs); go along (river) towards its source; mount upon (~ **the throne,** become king or queen). [ME, f. L *ascendere*, AD(*scendere scens-* = *scandere* climb)]

ascĕ'ndancy̆, -ency̆, *n.* Dominant control (*over*). [f. foll. + -ANCY, -ENCY]

ascĕ'ndant *a.* & *n.* **1.** *a.* Rising; (Astron.) rising towards zenith; (Astrol.) just above eastern horizon; predominant. **2.** *n.* (Astrol.) point o ecliptic that is ascendant at a given time; **in the ~,** supreme, dominating, (pop.) rising. **3.** Ancestor. [ME f. OF, f. L (as ASCEND; see -ANT)]

ascĕ'nsion (-shon) *n.* Act of ascending; (*A~*) ascent of Christ into Heaven on fortieth day after Resurrection (**A~ Day,** Thursday on which this is commemorated; **A~tide,** period of ten days from Ascension Day to Whitsun Eve); **right ~,** (Astron.) longitude measured along celestial equator; hence ~AL *a.* [ME f. OF, f. L *ascensio -onis* (as ASCEND; see -ION)]

ascĕ'nt *n.* Act of ascending; upward movement, rise, (lit. or fig.); way by which one may ascend; upward slope; flight of steps; SONG *of Ascents*. [f. ASCEND, after *descent*]

ăscertai'n *v.t.* Find out (for certain), get to know; hence ~ABLE *a.*, ~MENT *n.* [ME, f. OF *acertener*, st. *acertain-* (*à* to, CERTAIN)]

ascē's|ĭs *n.* (*pl.* ~**es** *pr.* -ēz). Practice of self-discipline. [f. Gk *askēsis* training (*askeō* exercise)]

ascĕ'tĭc *a.* & *n.* **1.** *a.* Severely abstinent, austere; having the appearance of an ascetic; hence **ascĕ'tĭ**CALLY *adv.*, ~ISM (2) *n.* **2.** *n.* One who practises severe self-discipline; (Eccl. Hist.) one who retired into solitude for this purpose. [f. med. L or f. Gk *askētikos* (*askētēs* monk f. *askeō* exercise; see -ET[2], -IC)]

ascĭ'dĭan *n.* (Zool.) Tunicate of order Ascidiacea, esp. sea-squirt. [f. mod. L *Ascidia* f. Gk *askidion* dim. of *askos* wineskin + -AN]

ascī'tēs (-z) *n.* (*pl.* same). Abdominal dropsy. [ME f. LL f. Gk (*askos* wineskin)]

Asclē'pĭad (*a-*) *n.* (Gk & L Pros.) Verse of spondee, two (or three) choriambi, and iambus. [f. LL f. Gk *asklēpiadeios* (*Asklēpiadēs* Gk poet of 3rd C. B.C., its inventor)]

ascŏr'bĭc *a.* ~ **acid,** vitamin C. [f. A- 7 + SCORBUTIC]

***ă'scŏt** *n.* Man's broad tie; broad scarf looped under chin. [*A~* in Berkshire, England, where race-meetings are held]

ascrī'b|e *v.t.* Regard as belonging (*to* person or cause); attribute, impute, (*to*); so ~ABLE *a.*, **ascrĭ'pt**ION *n.*, (esp.) preacher's words ascribing praise to God at end of sermon. [ME, f. L *ascribere*, AD(*scribere script-* write)]

ă'sdĭc (-z-) *n.* Earlier form of sonar. [f. initials of *A*nti-*S*ubmarine *D*etection *I*nvestigation *C*ommittee]

-āse *suf.* (Chem.) forming names of enzymes (*amylase*). [f. DIASTASE]

āsē'ĭty̆ *n.* (Metaphys.) Independent or underived existence. [f. med. L *aseitas* f. L *a* from + *se* oneself; see -ITY]

āsē'psĭs *n.* Absence of sepsis or of harmful bacteria; aseptic method in surgery. [f. A- 7 + SEPSIS]

āsĕ'ptĭc *a.* Free from sepsis, esp. that caused by micro-organisms; (of wound, instrument, dressing) surgically sterile, sterilized; (of method etc.) aiming at the absence (rather than counteraction, cf. ANTISEPTIC) of septic matter. [f. A- 7 + SEPTIC]

āsĕ'xūal *a.* **1.** (Biol.) Without sex; (of reproduction) not involving fusion of gametes. **2.** Without sexuality. **3.** Hence ~ITY (-ă'l-) *n.* [f. A- 7 + SEXUAL]

ăsh[1] *n.* **1.** Forest-tree of genus *Fraxinus*, with silver-grey bark, pinnate foliage, and hard, tough, pale wood; its wood; MOUNTAIN *ash*. **2.** **~-key,** winged seed of the ash; **~-plant,** sapling of ash, used as stick etc. [OE *æsc*, = OHG *ask*, ON *askr*, f. Gmc **askiz*]

ăsh[2] *n.* (freq. in *pl.*) Powdery residue left after combustion of any substance (**lay in ~es,** burn to the ground; SACK[1]*cloth and ashes*); (in *pl.*) remains of human body after cremation or disintegration, ||(Cricket) imaginary trophy for winner of series of test matches between England and Australia; ashlike material ejected by volcano; **~-bin, *~'can,** dustbin; ~ **blonde,** (woman with) very fair (hair); **~'pan,** tray under grate; **~'tray,** receptacle for tobacco ash etc.; **Ash Wednesday,** first day of Lent (from former custom of sprinkling ashes on penitents' heads). [OE *æsce*, = OHG *asca*, ON *aska*, Goth. *azgo*]

ashā'med (-md) *a.* (usu. *pred.*) Embarrassed, disconcerted, by shame (*ashamed of having lied, that one lied*); ~ **for** *you* (on account of); ~ **to** *say* (reluctant, but not necessarily refusing). [OE *āscamod* p.p. of *āscamian* feel shame (as A- 1, SHAME[2])]

ă'shen[1] *a.* Pertaining to an ash-tree; (arch.) made of ash wood. [f. ASH[1] + -EN[5]]

ă'shen[2] *a.* Of ashes; ash-coloured, grey, pale. [f. ASH[2] + -EN[5]]

ă'shĕt *n.* (Sc. & N.Z.) Large plate or dish. [f. F *assiette*]

Ashkĕna'z|ĭ (ă-; -ah'-) *n.* (*pl.* ~**im**). E. European Jew (cf. SEPHARDI); hence ~IC *a.* [mod. Heb., f. *Ashkenaz* (Gen. 10: 3)]

ă'shlar *n.* Square-hewn stone(s); masonry constructed of this; similar masonry as facing to rubble or brick wall. [ME, f. OF *aisselier* f. L *axilla* dim. of *axis* board; see -AR[2]]

ă'shlarĭng *n.* Short upright boarding in garret, cutting off acute angle of roof with floor. [f. prec. + -ING[1]]

ashŏr'e *adv.* To or on shore or land. [f. A[3] + SHORE[1]]

ă'shram *n.* (In India) place of religious retreat, hermitage. [f. Skr. *asrama* hermitage]

ă'shȳ *a.* = ASHEN[2]; covered with ashes. [f. ASH[2] + -Y[2]]

A'sian (ā'shan) *a.* & *n.* (Native or inhabitant) of Asia (freq. preferred to foll.). [f. L f. Gk *Asianos* (*Asia*; see -AN)]

Asiă'tic (āshĭ-) *a.* & *n.* Asian. [f. L f. Gk *Asiatikos*; see -IC]

asī'de *adv.* & *n.* **1.** *adv.* To or on one side, away; *~ (apart) **from**; **set** ~, quash (verdict), assign for future use; **take** ~ (esp. for private conversation). **2.** *n.* Words spoken aside, esp. spoken by actor and heard by audience but supposed not to be heard by other actors; incidental remark of author etc. [orig. *on side*; see A[3]]

ă'sĭnīne *a.* Pertaining to asses; stupid; hence **ăsinĭ'nITY** *n.* [f. L *asininus* (*asinus* ass; see -INE[1])]

-asĭs *suf.* forming names of diseases (*psoriasis, satyriasis*). [L, f. Gk *-asis* in ns. of state f. vbs in *-aō*]

ask (ah-) *v.* **1.** *v.t.* Call for an answer to or about (*ask* (*him*) *a question*; *ask* (*him*) *this*, (*him*) *who it is*; *ask him the time* ; *ask* (*him*) *his name*; *ask a question of a person*; *ask him about a thing*); **I ~ you** (excl. of disgust etc.); **if you ~ me,** (colloq.) in my opinion; **~ me another,** (colloq.) I do not know. **2.** Seek to obtain from another person (*ask a favour of him*; *ask* (*him*) *a favour*; *asked £5 for the book*; *ask him to do it*; *ask that it may be done*; *ask to be allowed out*; *you have only to ask*); **~'ing price** (set by seller); **for the** (mere) **~ing. 3.** Invite (person *to* dinner etc., or *out* or OVER); (arch., of thing) require. **4.** *v.i.* **~ for,** seek to obtain or meet (*ask* (*him*) *for it*; *someone is asking for you*); **~ for it,** (sl.) = *ask for* TROUBLE. [OE *āscian* etc., = OHG *eiscōn*, f. WG **aiskōjan*]

askă'nce, askă'nt, (*or* -ah'n-) *adv.* Sideways, squinting (**look ~ at,** view suspiciously); with oblique meaning. [16th c., of unkn. orig.]

ăskar'ĭ *n.* E. African native soldier or policeman. [f. Arab. ʻ*askarī* soldier]

askē'sĭs. Var. of ASCESIS.

askew' *adv.* & *pred. a.* Oblique(ly); awry. [f. A[3] + SKEW]

asla'nt (-ah'nt) *adv.* & *prep.* Obliquely (across). [f. A[3] + SLANT]

aslee'p *adv.* & *pred. a.* In or into a state of sleep (lit. or fig.); (euphem.) dead; (of limb) benumbed; (of top) spinning without apparent motion. [f. A[3] + SLEEP[1]]

||**A.S.L.E.F.** (ă'zlĕf) *abbr.* Associated Society of Locomotive Engineers and Firemen.

aslō'pe *adv.* & *pred. a.* Sloping, crosswise. [ME, of uncert. orig.]

A.S.M. *abbr.* air-to-surface missile.

āsō'cial (-shal) *a.* Not social; antisocial; (colloq.) inconsiderate of or hostile to others. [f. A- 7 + SOCIAL]

ăsp *n.* Small viper of S. Europe; viper of N. Africa and Arabia. [ME, f. OF *aspe* or f. L f. Gk *aspis*]

aspă'ragus *n.* Plant of genus *Asparagus*; one species of this (*A. officinalis*) whose young shoots are eaten; this food; **~ fern,** decorative plant of genus *Asparagus*. [L, f. Gk *asparagos*]

ă'spĕct *n.* Way of looking; looking or fronting in a given direction; side so fronting; phase; particular component of complicated matter; look, expression; appearance (esp. to the mind); (Gram.) verbal category or form expressing inception, duration, or completion, whence **ăspĕ'ctūAL** *a.*; (Astrol.) relative position of planets etc.; **~ ratio** (Aeron., of aerofoil span to mean chord; Telev., of picture width to height). [ME, f. L *aspectus* (ADspicere *-spect-* look at)]

ă'spen *n.* Kind of poplar with especially tremulous leaves. [f. earlier name *asp* f. OE *æspe*, = OHG *aspa*, Gmc **aspōn*, + -EN[5] forming adj. taken as n.]

ăspergĭ'll|um *n.* (*pl.* **~ums** *or* **~a**). Brush etc. for sprinkling holy water. [mod. L, f. L *aspergere* (*ad* to, *spargere* sprinkle) + *-illum* dim. suf.]

ăspĕ'rĭtȳ *n.* Roughness; rough excrescence; harshness, sharpness, (of temper or tone). [ME, f. OF *asperité* or f. L *asperitas* (*asper* rough; see -ITY)]

aspĕr'se *v.t.* Attack reputation of (person *with* allegations etc.); calumniate; so **aspĕr'sION** (-shon) *n.* (*cast aspersions on*). [ME, = besprinkle, f. L *aspergere -ers-*; see ASPERGILLUM]

ăspersŏr'ĭ|um *n.* (*pl.* **~a**). Vessel for holy water. [med. L (as prec.; see -ORY)]

ă'sphălt *n.*, & *v.t.* **1.** *n.* Dark bituminous pitch from petroleum; mixture of this with sand etc. for surfacing roads etc.; hence **ăsphă'ltIC** *a.* **2.** *v.t.* Surface (road etc.) with asphalt. [ME; ult. f. LL *asphalton, -um*, f. Gk *asphalton*, of foreign orig.]

ă'sphodĕl *n.* Plant of genus *Asphodeline* or *Asphodelus*, of lily family; (poet.) immortal flower in Elysium. [f. L f. Gk *asphodelos*; cf. DAFFODIL]

ăsphȳ'xĭ|a *n.* Defective aeration of blood through impaired respiration; suffocation; hence **~ANT** *a.* & *n.*, **~ATE**[3] *v.t.* & *i.*, **~A'TION** *n.* [mod. L f. Gk *asphuxia* (*a-* not, *sphuxis* pulse); see -IA[1]]

ă'spĭc[1] *n.* (poet.) Asp. [F, f. OF *aspide* f. L (as ASP); prob. infl. by F *piquer* to sting]

ă'spĭc[2] *n.* Savoury meat jelly used as garnish or to contain game, eggs, etc. [F, = ASP, f. the colours of the jelly (compared to those of the asp)]

ăspidĭ'stra *n.* Foliage plant of genus *Aspidistra*, with broad tapering leaves, freq. grown as house plant. [mod. L f. Gk *aspis aspidos* shield, after *Tupistra*]

ă'spirant (*or* aspīr'-) *a.* & *n.* (One) who aspires (*to, after, for*). [F, or f. L, as ASPIRE; see -ANT]

ă'spirate[1] *a.* & *n.* (Consonant) pronounced with a breathing, blended with sound of *h*; sound of *h*. [f. L *aspiratus* p.p. of *aspirare*; see ASPIRE, -ATE[2]]

ă'spirāte[2] *v.t.* Pronounce with a breathing; draw (fluid) by suction from vessel or cavity. [f. as prec. + -ATE[3]]

ăspirā'tion *n.* Drawing of breath; desire (*for, to, after*); action of aspirating. [ME f. OF, or f. L *aspiratio* (as prec.; see -ATION)]

ă'spirātor *n.* Apparatus for aspirating fluid. [f. L *aspirare*; see foll., -OR]

aspīr'e *v.i.* Desire earnestly (*to, after*); rise high (usu. fig.). [ME, f. F *aspirer* or f. L *aspirare*, AD(*spirare* breathe)]

ă'spirĭn *n.* Acetylsalicylic acid, an analgesic and febrifuge; tablet of this. [G, f. as ACETYL + *spiraeic* (= salicylic) *acid* + -IN]

asquĭ'nt *adv.* & *pred. a.* (*Look* etc.) to one side or from corner of eye or with squint. [ME, perh. f. A- + LDu. wd; cf. Du. *schuinte* slant]

ăss[1] (*or* ahs) *n.* Quadruped of horse genus with long ears, donkey, (esp. fig., as type of ignorance, stupidity, etc.); stupid person (**make an ~ of,** make (person) look absurd or foolish); **asses' bridge,** PONS *asinorum*. [OE *assa*, f. OCelt. **as(s)in* f. L *asinus*]

***ăss**[2] (*or* ahs) *n.* (vulg.) = ARSE[1].

ăss[3] (*or* ahs) *v.i.* (sl.) Fool *about, around*. [f. ASS[1]]

assagai. See ASSEGAI.

assai (asah'ē) *adv.* (Mus.) Very (*adagio assai*). [It.]

assai'l *v.t.* Make hostile attack upon (lit. or fig.); make resolute start on (task); overwhelm (*with* questions etc.); hence **~ABLE** *a.*, **~ANT** *n.* [ME, f. OF *asaill-* stressed st. of *asalir* f. med. L *assalire* f. L ASsilire (*salire salt-* leap)]

assă'ssin *n.* One who undertakes to kill treacherously; (Hist.) Muslim fanatic in time of Crusades, sent on murder errands by the Old Man of the Mountains or later leaders. [F, or f. med. L *assassinus* f. Arab. *ḥaššāšin* obl. pl. of *ḥaššāš* hashish-eater]

assă'ssin|āte *v.t.* Kill (esp. political or religious leader) by violence; hence ~A'TION *n.* (CHARACTER *assassination*), **~ātor** *n.* [f. med. L *assassinare* (*assassinus*; see prec.) + -ATE[3]]

assau'lt[1] (*or* -ŏ'lt) *n.* Hostile attack (lit. or fig.); rush against walls of fortress etc. (*carry by assault*); (Law) unlawful personal attack (even if only with menacing words), cf. BATTERY; (euphem.) rape (of woman); hence ~IVE *a.* [ME, f. OF *asaut* f. Rom. **assaltus* (as ASSAIL)]

assau'lt[2] (*or* -ŏ'lt) *v.t.* Make violent or hostile attack upon (lit. or fig.); attack (fortress) by sudden rush; (euphem.) rape (woman). [ME, f. OF *assauter* f. Rom. **assaltare* spring at f. L *AS(*sultare* frequent. of *salire salt-* leap)]

assay'[1] *n.* **1.** Trial of metals or ore for quality; **A~ Office** (awarding hallmarks). **2.** (Chem. etc.) Determination of content of a substance. [ME, f. OF *assai*, var. of *essai* (see ESSAY[1])]

assay'[2] *v.t.* & *i.* Test quality of (metals, ore); (Chem. etc.) perform assay; show (content) on assay; (arch.) attempt (task, *to* do); hence ~ABLE *a.* [ME, f. OF *assaier*, *essayer* (see ESSAY[2])]

ă'ssėgai, ă'ssagai, (-gī) *n.* Slender iron-tipped spear of hard wood, esp. missile of S. Afr. tribes. [f. obs. F *azagaie* or Port. *azagaia* f. Arab. *az-zaġāyah* (*al* the, *zaġāyah* spear)]

assĕ'mblage *n.* Bringing or coming together; concourse of persons; collection of things; fitting together; object made of pieces fitted together; (Art) object made of unrelated things joined together. [f. foll. + -AGE]

assĕ'mble *v.t.* & *i.* Gather together, collect; arrange in order; (Mech.) fit together the parts of (machine, structure). [ME, f. OF *asembler* f. Rom. **assimulare* bring together (L *ad* to, *simul* together)]

assĕ'mblȳ *n.* Gathering together, concourse; meeting for discussion, recreation, etc.; deliberative body, legislative council; military call by drum or bugle; assembling of a machine or structure or its parts; ~ **line,** group of machines and workers progressively assembling some product; **~man,** member of legislative assembly; ~ **room, shop,** place where a machine or its parts are assembled; ~ **rooms** (in which dances etc. are held). [ME, f. OF *asemblee* fem. p.p. of *asembler* (see prec.)]

assĕ'nt[1] *v.i.* Consent (*to* proposal, request); express agreement (*to* statement or opinion, or abs.); hence ~OR *n.* (||esp. election-candidate's supporter other than proposer and seconder). [ME, f. OF *asenter* f. Rom. **assentare* f. L *assentari* (*ad* to, *sentire* think)]

assĕ'nt[2] *n.* (Official) consent or sanction (**royal** ~ of sovereign to bill passed by Parliament); (mental) acceptance. [ME, f. OF *as(s)ente* (as prec.)]

assĕ'ntient (-shĭ- *or* -shent) *a.* & *n.* (Person) that assents. [f. L *assentire* (as ASSENT[1]; see -ENT)]

assêr't *v.t.* Vindicate claim to (rights); give effect to (~ one**self,** insist on one's rights or opinions); declare; so ~IVE *a.*, tending to assert (oneself), dogmatic, ~OR *n.* [f. L AS(*serere sert-* join)]

assêr'tion *n.* Insistence on a right or opinion; (**self-**)~, insistence on recognition of one's claims; declaration, positive statement. [ME f. F, or f. L *assertio* (as prec.; see -ION)]

asses. *Pl.* of AS[2] or ASS[1,2].

assĕ'ss *v.t.* Fix amount of (taxes, fine); fix amount of and impose (*on* person or community); fine or tax (person, community, property, *in*, *at*, so much); estimate value of (esp. property for taxation); estimate magnitude or quality of; hence ~ABLE *a.*, ~MENT *n.* [ME, f. F *assesser* f. L AS(*sidēre sess-* = *sedēre* sit)]

assĕ'ssor *n.* One who sits as adviser to judge etc.; one who assesses taxes or estimates value of property for taxation or insurance purposes; hence ~IAL (ăsĕsôr'-) *a.* [ME, f. OF *assessour* f. L *assessor -oris* assistant-judge (as prec.; see -OR); 2nd sense f. med. L]

ă'ssĕt *n.* Property available to meet debts; any possession; (person or thing having) any useful quality. [f. *assets* (taken as pl.), f. AF *asetz* f. OF *asez* enough f. Rom. **assatis* f. L *ad* to + *satis* enough]

assĕ'ver|āte *v.t.* Solemnly declare; so ~A'TION *n.* [f. L ASSEVERARE (*severus* serious) + -ATE[3]]

assĭ'bĭl|āte *v.t.* (Phonet. & Philol.) Pronounce as or change to sibilant or fricative; hence ~A'TION *n.* [f. L AS(*sibilare* hiss) + -ATE[3]]

assĭ'dūous *a.* Persevering, diligent; attending closely; hence or cogn. **ăssĭdū'**ITY, ~NESS, *ns.*, ~LY[2] *adv.* [f. L *assiduus* (as ASSESS) + -OUS]

assī'gn[1] (-ī'n) *v.t.* **1.** Allot as share (*to*); transfer formally (esp. personal property, *to*); hence ~OR (*or* asĭnôr') *n.* **2.** Appoint (place etc. *to*); fix, specify; ascribe, refer, (event *to* date); ascribe (reason *to*, *for*, thing). **3.** Hence ~ABLE *a.* [ME, f. OF *asi(g)ner* f. L ASSIGNARE mark out to (*signum* sign)]

assī'gn[2] (-ī'n) *n.* One to whom property or right is legally transferred. [ME, f. F *assigné* (see ASSIGNEE)]

ăssĭgnā'tion *n.* Apportionment; attribution *to*; formal transference; appointment (of time and place); illicit love meeting; *~ **house,** brothel. [ME f. OF, f. L *assignatio -onis* (as ASSIGN[1]; see -ATION)]

assignee' (-ĭn-) *n.* One appointed to act for another; assign. [ME, f. OF *assigné*, p.p. of *assigner* ASSIGN[1]]

assī'gnment (-ī'n-) *n.* Allocation; legal transference, document effecting this; attribution; statement (of reasons); task allotted to person (*esp. to student). [ME, f. OF *assignement* f. med. L *assignamentum* (as ASSIGN[1]; see -MENT)]

assĭ'mĭl|āte *v.* **1.** *v.t.* Make like (*to*, *with*); (Philol.) make (sound) more like another in same or contiguous word; absorb into the system (lit. or fig.). **2.** *v.i.* Be so absorbed. **3.** Hence or cogn. ~A'TION, **~ātor,** *ns.*, ~ABLE, **~at**IVE, **~at**ORY, *adjs.* [ME, f. L ASSIMILARE (*similis* like) + -ATE[3]]

assĭ'st *v.* & *n.* **1.** *v.t.* Help (person, process, person *in* doing); hence ~ANCE *n.* (||NATIONAL *Assistance*). **2.** *v.i.* Take part (*in*); be present (*at*). **3.** *n.* *Help; *act of helping; *(Baseball etc.) player's action in helping to put out opponent, score goal, etc. [ME, f. F *assister* f. L ASSISTERE take one's stand by]

assĭ'stant *a.* & *n.* **1.** *a.* Helping; subordinate. **2.** *n.* Helper; subordinate worker, esp. in shop to serve customers. [ME *assistent*, f. med. L *assistens -ent-* present (as ASSIST; see -ANT, -ENT)]

assī'ze *n.* (Hist.) **1.** (usu. in *pl.*) Periodical session in each county of England and Wales for administration of civil and criminal justice. **2.** Statutory price of bread and ale. [ME, f. OF *as(s)ise*, fem. p.p. (as n.) of *aseeir* sit at, f. L *assidēre*; cf. ASSESS]

Assoc. *abbr.* Association.

assō'ciable (-sha-) *a.* That can be connected in thought (*with*); hence ~ABI'LITY *n.* [F, f. *associer* (as foll.; see -ABLE)]

assō'ciate[1] (*or* -shĭ-) *a.* & *n.* **1.** *a.* Joined in companionship, function, or dignity; allied. **2.** *n.* Partner; companion; colleague; subordinate member of a body, institute, etc.; thing connected with another; hence ~SHIP (-tsh-) *n.* [ME, f. L *associatus* p.p. of ASSOCIARE (*socius* sharing, allied); see -ATE[2]]

assō'ciăt|e[2] (*or* -shĭ-) *v.* **1.** *v.t.* Join (persons, things, or one *with* another); connect as an idea; make one*self* a partner *in* (a matter); declare one*self* in agreement *with.* **2.** *v.i.* Combine for common purpose; have frequent dealings (*with*). **3.** Hence ~IVE, ~ORY, *adjs.*, ~OR *n.* [f. L *associare* (as prec.) + -ATE[3]]

assōciā'tion *n.* Act of associating; organized body of persons for a joint purpose (**articles** or **deed of** ~, document giving particulars of limited liability company); fellowship, companionship; mental connection between related ideas; (Chem.) loose aggregation of molecules; (Ecol.) group of associated plants; ||**A~ football,** kind played with round ball which may not be handled during play exc. by goalkeeper (cf. RUGBY); hence ~ISM *n.*, theory accounting for mental phenomena by association of ideas. [F, or f. med. L *associatio* (as prec.; see -ATION)]

assoi'l *v.t.* (arch.) Absolve from sin; acquit; release; atone for. [ME, f. AF *as(s)oili(e)r*, OF *assoil-* stressed stem of *asoldre* f. L (as ABSOLVE)]

ă'sson|ance *n.* Resemblance of sound between two syllables; rhyming of one word with another in accented vowel and those that follow, but not in consonants (*sonnet, porridge*), or in consonants but not in vowels (*killed, cold*); so ~ANT *a.*, ~ATE[3] *v.i.* [F, f. L ASSONARE respond to (*sonus* sound); see -ANCE]

assor't *v.* **1.** *v.t.* Classify, arrange in sorts; group *with* others. **2.** *v.i.* Suit *well* or *ill with.* [f. OF *assorter* (*à* to, *sorte* SORT[1])]

assor'tative *a.* Assorting (esp. ~ **mating,** not random but based on similarity of partners' characteristics etc.). [f. prec. + -ATIVE]

assor'tėd *a.* Of various sorts put together; **ill-~**, not well matched. [p.p. of ASSORT]

assor'tment *n.* Set of various sorts put together. [f. ASSORT + -MENT]

A.S.S.R. *abbr.* Autonomous Soviet Socialist Republic.

Asst. *abbr.* Assistant.

assuā'ge (*a*sw-) *v.t.* Calm, soothe, (person, feelings, pain); appease (appetite, desire); hence ~MENT (-jm-) *n.* [ME, f. OF *as(s)ouagier* f. Rom. *ASSUAVIARE f. L *suavis* sweet]

assū'm|e *v.t.* **1.** Take or put on oneself (aspect, garment); **~ing,** taking much upon oneself, arrogant. **2.** Undertake (office, duty). **3.** Simulate (ignorance etc.); arrogate (credit etc.) *to* one*self.* **4.** Take as being true, for purpose of argument or action. [ME, f. L AS(*sumere sumpt-* take)]

assŭ'mption *n.* **1.** Act of assuming; thing assumed; arrogance. **2.** (*A~*). Reception of Virgin Mary bodily into Heaven; feast in honour of this (15 Aug.). [ME, f. OF *asompsion* or f. L *assumptio* (as ASSUME; see -ION)]

assŭ'mptive *a.* Taken for granted; arrogant. [f. L *assumptivus* (as ASSUME; see -IVE)]

assur'ance (*a*shoor'-) *n.* Formal guarantee; positive declaration that thing is true; ||insurance, esp. of life; certainty; self-confidence; impudence. [ME, f. OF *aseürance* (*aseürer*; see foll., -ANCE)]

assur'e (*a*shoor') *v.t.* Make safe; ||insure (esp. life); make certain, ensure the happening etc. of; make (person) sure (*of* fact; REST[3] *assured*); tell (person) confidently (*of* a thing, *of* its being so, *that* it is so); hence **assur'ėd**LY[2] (*a*shoor'-) *adv.*, certainly. [ME, f. OF *aseürer* f. Rom. *ASSECURARE f. L *securus* safe, SECURE]

Assȳ'rian (*a*-) *a.* & *n.* (Inhabitant or language) of Assyria. [f. L f. Gk *Assurios* of Assyria, ancient empire in Mesopotamia, + -IAN]

Assȳriŏ'|logȳ (*a*-) *n.* Study of language, history, antiquities, of Assyria; hence ~LOGIST *n.* [f. L f. Gk *Assuria* + -O- + -LOGY]

AST *abbr.* Atlantic Standard Time.

āstā'ble *a.* Not stable; (Electr.) not having a stable state. [f. A- 7 + STABLE[1]]

astă'tĭc *a.* (Electr.) Not tending to keep one position; ~ **galvanometer,** one in which the effect of the earth's magnetic field on the needle is greatly reduced. [f. Gk *astatos* unstable (*a-* not, *sta-* stand) + -IC]

ă'statine (-ēn) *n.* (Chem.) Artificial radioactive element, heaviest of halogen group. [f. as prec. + -INE[5]]

ă'ster *n.* Composite plant of genus *Aster*, with showy radiated flowers, e.g. Michaelmas daisy; **China** ~, flower of allied species, *Callistephus chinensis.* [L, f. Gk *astēr* star]

-ă'ster *suf.* forming *ns.* denoting poor quality (*criticaster, poetaster*) or (Bot.) incomplete resemblance (*oleaster, pinaster*). [L]

ă'sterĭsk *n.*, & *v.t.* **1.** *n.* Star-shaped symbol (*) used to mark words etc. for reference or distinction, or to replace omitted matter. **2.** *v.t.* Mark with asterisk. [ME, f. LL f. Gk *asteriskos* dim., as ASTER]

ă'sterĭsm *n.* Cluster of stars; group of three asterisks (⁂), calling attention. [f. Gk *asterismos* (as ASTER; see -ISM)]

astēr'n *adv.* (Naut. & Aeron.) Aft; away to the rear (*of*); backwards. [f. A[3] + STERN[2]]

ă'steroid *n.* One of the small planets revolving round sun mainly between orbits of Mars and Jupiter; (Zool.) starfish; hence ~AL (-oi'd-) *a.* [f. Gk *asteroeidēs* (as ASTER; see -OID)]

ăsthē'nĭa *n.* (Med.) Loss of strength, debility. [mod. L, f. Gk *astheneia* (*asthenēs* weak; see -IA[1])]

ăsthĕ'nĭc *a.* & *n.* **1.** (Person) of lean and long-limbed build. **2.** *a.* Of or characterized by asthenia. [f. prec. + -IC]

ă'sthma (-sm-) *n.* Disease (esp. allergic) of respiration, esp. with paroxysms of difficult breathing. [ME f. med. L *asma*, f. Gk *asthma -matos* (*azō* breathe hard)]

ăsthmă't|ic (-sm-) *a.* & *n.* Pertaining to or effective against asthma; (person) suffering from asthma; hence ~ICALLY *adv.* [f. L f. Gk *asthmatikos* (as prec.; see -IC)]

A'sti (ă'-) *n.* Still or (~ **spūmă'ntė**) sparkling Italian white wine. [~ in Piedmont]

astĭ'gmatĭsm *n.* Structural defect in eye or lens, preventing rays of light from being brought to common focus; so **ăstĭgmă'**TIC *a.* [f. A- 7 + Gk *stigma -matos* point + -IC]

astĭ'lbė *n.* White- or red-flowered perennial plant of genus *Astilbe.* [mod. L, f. Gk *a-* not + *stilbē* fem. of *stilbos* glittering; f. the inconspicuous (individual) flowers]

astīr' *adv.* & *pred. a.* In motion; out of bed; excited(ly). [f. A[3] + STIR[1] 5]

||**A.S.T.M.S.** *abbr.* Association of Scientific, Technical, and Managerial Staffs.

astŏ'nĭsh *v.t.* Amaze; surprise greatly; hence ~MENT *n.* [f. obs. *astone* f. OF *estoner* f. Gallo-Rom. *EX(*tonare* thunder); see -ISH[2]]

astou'nd *v.t.* Shock with alarm or surprise; amaze. [f. obs. *astound* a. = *astoned* p.p. of obs. *astone*; see prec.]

astră'ddle *adv.* & *pred. a.* In a straddling position. [f. A[3] + STRADDLE]

ă'stragal *n.* (Archit.) Small moulding round top or bottom of column. [f. foll.]

astră'galus *n.* (Anat. & Zool.) ankle-bone supporting tibia, talus; (Bot.) leguminous plant of genus *Astragalus.* [L, f. Gk *astragalos* ankle-bone, moulding, a plant]

ăstrakhă'n (-kă'n) *n.* Dark curly fleece of young lambs from *Astrakhan* in Russia; cloth imitating this.

ă'stral *a.* Connected with or consisting of stars; **~ body,** spiritual counterpart of body, thought to survive death; **~ spirits** (formerly thought to inhabit heavenly bodies). [f. LL *astralis* (*astrum* star; see -AL)]

astray' *adv.* & *pred. a.* Out of the right way; (esp., fig.) in or into error or sin; **go ~**, (fig.) be lost or mislaid. [ME, f. OF *estraié* p.p. of *estraier* f. Rom. **extravagare* f. L *extra* out of bounds + *vagari* wander]

astrī'de *adv.* & *prep.* **1.** *adv.* With legs apart; with legs on either side (*of*). **2.** *prep.* Astride of; extending across. [f. A[3] + STRIDE 3.]

astrĭ'ng|ent (-nj-) *a.* & *n.* **1.** *a.* Causing contraction of body tissues, styptic; severe; austere; hence **~ENCY** *n.*, **~entLY**[2] *adv.* **2.** *n.* Astringent medicine. [F, f. L *astringere* (*ad* to, *stringere* bind); see -ENT]

ă'strō- *comb. form.* Star, heavenly body, as: **~bo'tany,** study of plants on celestial bodies; **~dome, ~hatch,** domed window in aircraft for astronomical observations. [Gk (*astron* star)]

ă'strolābe *n.* Instrument for measuring altitudes of stars etc. [ME, f. OF *astrelabe* f. med. L *astrolabium* f. Gk *astrolabon,* neut. (as n.) of ASTRO*labos* star-taking]

astrŏ'logȳ *n.* Art of judging reputed occult influence of stars, planets, etc. on human affairs; so **astrŏ'LOGER** *n.*, **ăstrolŏ'GIC(AL)** *adjs.* [ME, f. OF *astrologie* f. L f. Gk ASTRO(*logia* -LOGY)]

ă'stronaut *n.* Space traveller; hence or cogn. **~ICAL** *a.*, **~ICS** *n.*, science of space travel, (-aw'-). [f. ASTRO-, after *aeronaut*]

astrŏ'nom|ȳ *n.* Science of the heavenly bodies; hence or cogn. **~ER**[1] (3) *n.*, person who studies or practises astronomy, **ăstronŏ'mIC(AL)** *adjs.* (**~ical figures, distances,** as enormous as those familiar to astronomers; **~ical unit,** earth's mean distance from sun, about 150 million kilometres; *astronomical* YEAR); **ăstronŏ'mĭcalLY**[2] *adv.* [ME, f. OF *astronomie* f. L f. Gk *astronomia* f. ASTRO*nomos* a. star-arranging (*nemō* arrange)]

ăstrophȳ'sĭc|s (-ĭ'z-) *n.* Branch of astronomy concerned with physics and chemistry of the heavenly bodies; hence **~AL** *a.*, **~IST** (3) *n.* [f. ASTRO- + PHYSICS]

astū'te *a.* Shrewd, sagacious; crafty; hence **~LY**[2] (-tlĭ) *adv.*, **~NESS** (-tn-) *n.* [f. obs. F *astut* or L *astutus* (*astus* craft)]

asŭ'nder *adv.* (rhet.) Apart. [OE *on sundran* into pieces; cf. SUNDER]

asȳ'lum *n.* Sanctuary, place of refuge and safety, esp. for criminals, (**political ~**, protection from arrest by another country); (Hist.) institution for shelter and support of afflicted (e.g. blind, deaf, and esp. insane) or destitute persons. [ME f. L f. Gk *asulon* refuge (*a-* not, *sulon* right of seizure)]

asȳ'mmėtrȳ (*or* ā-) *n.* Lack of symmetry; hence **ăsȳmmĕ'trIC(AL)** *adjs.* [f. Gk *asummetria* (*a-* not; see SYMMETRY)]

ă'sȳmpt|ōte (*or* -mt-) *n.* Line that continually approaches given curve but does not meet it at a finite distance; hence **~o'TIC** *a.*, **~ŏ'tICALLY** *adv.* [mod. L *asymptota* (*linea* line) f. Gk *asumptōtos* not falling together (*a-* not, *sum-* together, *ptōtos* falling f. *piptō* fall)]

ăsȳ'nchronous (-ngk-) *a.* Not synchronous; hence **~LY**[2] *adv.* [f. A- 7 + SYNCHRONOUS]

asȳ'ndėt|on *n.* (*pl.* **~a**). (Rhet.) Omission of conjunction; hence **~IC** (ăsĭndĕ't-) *a.* [mod. L, f. Gk *asundeton* neut. a. (*a-* not, *sundetos* bound together)]

at (*or, when stressed,* ăt) *prep.* **1.** Expr. exact, approximate, or vague position, lit. or fig. of condition, occasion, price, time, etc., (*meet at a point*; *wait at the corner*; *at the top*; *at Bath* (or any town etc. except those of public or private importance; cf. IN[1]); *at school*; *at* HOME[1] 7; *at* SEA; *at a distance*; *at* ARM[1]*'s length*; *sick at heart*; *at* HAND[1]; *out at elbows*; *at work*; *at* ONE 3; *at* EASE[1]; *at dinner*; *at* WAR[1]; *at a standstill*; *play at fighting*; *good at repartee*; *at daggers drawn*; *at a disadvantage*; *at his* MERCY; *came at a run*; *sold at £1 each*; *at a low price*; *at* ONCE 4; *at short notice*; *at midday*; *at Easter*; *at* (*the age of*) *70*; *at all events*; *at* ALL 8; *at* BEST[1]; *at* FIRST 6; *at* LAST[3] 8; *at* LEAST 2; *at* MOST 6; *at* WORST 2; *annoyed at finding*; *impatient at delay*); **at it,** at work or other activity; **where it's at,** (sl.) the (true) scene of action; **at that,** at that point, estimate, etc., (*leave it at that,* not do more), moreover (*lost in twenty moves, and to an amateur at that*), nevertheless (*delayed ten minutes, but caught the train at that*). **2.** Expr. motion towards, lit. or fig., (*arrive at a place*; *get, rush, shoot, laugh, look, grumble, guess, hint, snatch, aim, at*). [OE *æt,* = OHG *az,* OS, ON, Goth. *at,* Gmc cogn. w. L *ad* to]

at- *pref.*, assim. form of AD- before *t.*

At *symb.* astatine.

ă'tabrĭne. See ATEBRIN.

ă'tarăxȳ, -ă'xĭa, *n.* Stoical indifference; imperturbability; so **ătară'ctIC, ătară'xIC,** *adjs.* & *ns.*, tranquillizing (drug). [f. F *ataraxie* f. Gk *ataraxia* impassiveness]

ă'tavĭsm *n.* Resemblance to remote ancestors rather than parents; reversion to earlier type; hence **ătavĭ'stIC** *a.* [f. F *atavisme* f. L *atavus* great-grandfather's grandfather; see -ISM]

ată'xȳ, -xĭa, *n.* Imperfect control of bodily functions; **locomotor ~**, disease affecting co-ordination of movements; hence **ată'xIC** *a.* [f. mod. L f. Gk *ataxia* (*a-* not, *taxis* order)]

||**A.T.C.** *abbr.* air traffic control; Air Training Corps.

ate. See EAT.

-ate[1] (*or* āt) *suf.* forming *ns.*, denoting (1) office (*episcopate, marquisate*), (2) state or function (*curate, legate, magistrate, mandate*), (3) (Chem.) salt of acid w. corresp. name in *-ic* (*chlorate, nitrate*), (4) group (*electorate*), (5) product (*condensate, filtrate*). [f. or after OF *-at* or *-é(e)* or f. L *-atus* n. or p.p. (cf. foll.)]

-ate[2] (*or* āt) *suf.* forming *adjs.* & *ns.* (*associate*[1], *delegate, desolate, duplicate*[1], *separate*[1]) or *adjs.* f. L or E *n.* or *adj.* (*cordate, insensate, Italianate*). [f. or after (F *-é* f.) L *-atus* p.p. of vbs. in *-are*]

-āte[3] *suf.* forming *vbs.* (*associate*[2], *camphorate, duplicate*[2], *fascinate, felicitate, hyphenate, separate*[2]). [f. or after (F *-er* f.) L *-are* (p.p. *-atus*); cf. prec.]

ă'tĕbrĭn, ă'tabrĭne, *n.* Antimalarial drug, mepacrine. **[P]**

atĕ'lier (-lyā) *n.* Workshop, studio, esp. of artist or *couturier.* [F]

a tempo (ahtĕ'mpō) *adv.* (Mus.) In the previous tempo. [It., lit. 'in time']

Athanā'sian (ă-; -shan) *a.* Of Athanasius, bishop of Alexandria d. 373; **~ Creed,** that beginning *Quicunque vult,* = *Whosoever will,* formerly ascribed to Athanasius. [f. LL *Athanasius* + -AN]

ā'thė|ĭsm *n.* Disbelief in the existence of God or gods; godlessness; so **~IST** (2) *n.*, **~ĭ'stIC** *a.* [f. F *athéisme* f. Gk *atheos* without God (*a-* not, *theos* god); see -ISM]

ă'thelĭng *n.* (Hist.) Prince or lord. [OE *ætheling,* = OHG *ediling* f. WG **athelinga* (**athal* family; see -ING[3])]

ăthėmă'tĭc *a.* **1.** (Mus.) Not based on the use of themes. **2.** (Gram., of form of verb) having suffix attached to stem without thematic vowel. [f. A- 7 + THEMATIC]

Athē'nĭan (*a-*) *a.* & *n.* (Native or inhabitant) of Athens. [f. L *Atheniensis* (*Athenae* f. Gk *Athēnai* Athens, principal city of Greece) + -IAN]

ătherōsclēr|ō'sĭs *n.* (*pl.* **~o'ses** *pr.* -ēz). Form of arteriosclerosis with fatty degeneration; hence ~O'TIC *a.* [f. G (*-sklerose*) f. Gk *athērē* groats + -O- + SCLEROSIS]

athīr'st *pred. a.* Thirsty; eager (*for*). [OE *ofthyrst* for *ofthyrsted* p.p. of *ofthyrstan* be thirsty]

ă'thlēte *n.* Competitor or skilled performer in physical exercises; robust or vigorous person; **~'s foot,** contagious ringworm of the feet. [f. L *athleta* f. Gk *athlētēs* f. *athleō* contend for prize (*athlon*); see -ET²]

ăthlĕ'tĭc *a.* & *n.* **1.** *a.* Pertaining to athletes (*athletic* SPORTS); physically powerful; large and muscular in build; hence **ăthlĕ'tICALLY** *adv.*, ~ISM (2) *n.* **2.** *n.* (in *pl.*, occas. treated as *sing.*). Practice of or competition in physical exercises (running, jumping, throwing, etc.); *physical sports and games of any kind. [f. F *athlétique* or f. L f. Gk *athlētikos* (as prec.; see -IC)]

athwar't (-ŏr't) *adv.* & *prep.* Across from side to side (usu. obliquely); crosswise, perversely; in opposition (to); **~-hawse,** (Naut.) lying transversely in front of anchored ship. [f. A³ + THWART]

-atĭc (*or* ă'tĭk) *suf.* forming *adjs.* & *ns.* (1) [f. F *-atique* or f. L *-aticus* f. p.p. st. *-at-* of vbs in *-are* + *-icus* (see -IC; cf. -AGE)] (*aquatic, erratic, fanatic, lunatic*), (2) [f. F *-atique* or f. LL f. Gk *-atikos*] (*aromatic, idiomatic, problematic*).

atĭ'lt *adv.* Tilted and nearly falling; **run** or **ride ~** (arch., on horseback with thrust of lance; usu. fig.). [f. A- + TILT¹]

-ā'tion *suf.* forming *ns.* denoting (1) vbl action, (2) instance of this, (3) resulting state, (4) resulting thing, (*alteration, civilization, constellation, creation, filtration, flirtation, hesitation, plantation, preservation, starvation, vexation, visitation*); cf. also -FICATION. [f. or after F, or f. L *-atio -ationis* f. vbs in *-are* (see -ION)]

-atĭve (*or* ā-) *suf.* forming *adjs.* (*authoritative, imitative, pejorative, qualitative, talkative*). [f. or after F *-atif -ative* or f. L *-ativus* f. p.p. st. *-at-* of vbs in *-are* + *-ivus* (see -IVE; cf. -ATIC)]

Atlă'ntėan (*a-*) *a.* Of or like the giant Atlas, esp. w. ref. to strength. [f. L *Atlanteus* (as ATLAS) + -AN]

atlă'ntēs (-z) *n. pl.* (Archit.) Male figures used as pillars to support entablature. [Gk, pl. of ATLAS]

Atlă'ntĭc (*a-*) *a.* & *n.* (Of or adjoining) the ocean between Europe and Africa on the east and America on the west; **~ Time,** standard time used in eastern Canada. [ME, f. L f. Gk *Atlantikos* (as ATLAS; see -IC); orig. of Atlas mountains, then of sea near W. Afr. coast]

atlăntosaur'us *n.* Extinct gigantic reptile of genus *Atlantosaurus*. [mod. L, f. Gk (as ATLAS, *sauros* lizard)]

ă'tlas *n.* Book of maps or charts, orig. with figure of Atlas at front; (Anat.) uppermost cervical vertebra, supporting skull. [L, f. Gk *Atlas -antos* giant who held up pillars of universe, hence the mountains in N. Africa, regarded as supporting the heavens]

atm. *abbr.* (Phys.) atmosphere(s).

ă'tmosphēre *n.* Gaseous envelope surrounding heavenly body; that surrounding the earth; one surrounding any substance; mental or moral environment esp. artistic or emotional; pervading tone or mood, esp. attractive one; air (in any place), esp. w. ref. to effects on those present; (Phys.) pressure exerted by atmosphere on earth's surface, taken as unit of pressure, about 1 kg per sq. cm; hence **ătmosphĕ'rIC(AL)** *adjs.*, **ătmosphĕ'rICS** *n. pl.*, (interference with telecommunications, due to) electric disturbances in atmosphere. [f. mod. L *atmosphaera* f. Gk *atmos* vapour; see SPHERE]

ă'toll (*or* atŏ'l) *n.* Ring-shaped coral reef enclosing lagoon. [f. Maldive *atolu*]

ă'tom *n.* Smallest particle of a chemical element; this as source of atomic energy; very small portion or thing or quantity; (*attrib.*) = foll. (*atom bomb*). [ME, f. OF *atome*, f. L f. Gk *atomos* indivisible]

atŏ'mĭc *a.* Of or relating to atom(s); concerned with or using atomic energy or atomic bombs; **~ bomb** (deriving its destructiveness from atomic energy); **~ clock** (using atomic vibrations as standard of time); **~ energy,** nuclear energy; **~ mass,** = *atomic weight*; **~ number,** (of a chemical element) number of unit positive charges carried by the nucleus of its atom; **~ philosophy,** atomism; **~ pile,** nuclear REACTOR; **~ power,** nuclear power; **~ theory,** (1) (Philos.) = foll., (2) theory that chemical elements consist of atoms of definite relative weight uniting with those of other elements in fixed proportions; **~ warfare** (in which atomic bombs are used); **~ weight,** ratio between the mass of one atom of an element or isotope and one-twelfth of the weight of an atom of the isotope carbon 12; hence **atŏ'mICALLY** *adv.* [f. mod. L *atomicus* (as prec.; see IC)]

ă'tom|ĭsm *n.* (Philos.) theory that all matter consists of minute individual particles; (Psych.) theory that mental states are made up of elementary units; hence ~IST (2) *n.*, **~ĭ'stIC** *a.* [f. ATOM + -ISM]

ă'tomīz|e, -īs|e (-īz), *v.t.* Reduce to atoms or fine particles; hence ~A'TION *n.*, ~ER¹ *n.*, instrument for reducing liquids to fine spray. [f. ATOM + -IZE]

ă'tomȳ¹ *n.* (arch.) Skeleton; emaciated body. [f. ANATOMY, taken as *an atomy*]

ă'tomȳ² *n.* (arch.) Atom; tiny being. [prob. f. *atomi* pl. of L *atomus* ATOM, assoc. w. prec.]

ātō'nal (or *a-*) *a.* (Mus.) Not written in any particular key or mode. [f. A- 7 + TONAL]

atō'ne *v.i.* Make amends; **~ for,** expiate. [back form. f. foll.]

atō'nement (-nm-) *n.* Atoning; expiation, reparation for wrong or injury; reconciliation of God and man; **the A~,** expiation of man's sin by Christ; **Day of A~,** most solemn religious fast of Jewish year, eight days after Jewish New Year. [f. *at* ONE 3 + -MENT, after med. L *adunamentum* and earlier *onement* f. obs. v. *one* unite]

atŏ'nĭc *a.* Without accent or stress; (Path.) lacking tone; so **ă'tonY¹** *n.* [f. A- 7 + TONIC]

atŏ'p *adv.* & *prep.* On the top (*of* or of). [f. A³ + TOP¹]

-ator *suf.* See -OR.

-atorȳ *suf.* See -ORY.

ATP *abbr.* adenosine triphosphate.

ătrabĭ'lious (-lyus) *a.* Melancholy; ill-tempered; hence ~NESS *n.* [f. L *atra bilis* (black bile, transl. Gk *melagkholia* MELANCHOLY) + -OUS; cf. TEMPERAMENT]

ā'trĭ|um *n.* (*pl.* **~a** *or* **~ums**). Central court of Roman house; cavity in body, esp. (Anat.) one of two upper cavities of heart that receive blood from veins; hence ~AL *a.* [L]

atrō'cious (-shus) *a.* Extremely wicked; very bad (*atrocious weather*); hence ~LY² *adv.*, ~NESS *n.* [f. L *atrox -ocis* cruel + -OUS]

atrŏ'cĭtȳ *n.* Extreme wickedness; atrocious deed; (colloq.) repellent act or thing. [f. F *atrocité* or f. L *atrocitas* (as prec.; see -ITY)]

ă'trophȳ *n.* & *v.* **1.** *n.* Wasting away through under-nourishment or lack of use; emaciation (lit. or fig.). **2.** *v.t.* & *i.* (Cause to) undergo atrophy. [f. F *atrophie* or f. LL f. Gk *atrophia* (*a-* not, *trophē* food); see -Y[1]]

ă'tropĭne (*or* -ēn) *n.* Poisonous alkaloid found in deadly nightshade, used in medicine. [f. mod. L *Atropa belladonna* deadly nightshade f. Gk *Atropos* inflexible, name of one of the Fates; see -INE[5]]

***ă'ttaboy** *int.* (sl.) expr. encouragement or admiration. [prob. corrupt. of *that's the boy!*]

attă'ch *v.* **1.** *v.t.* Fasten (thing *to* another); join one*self* (*to* person, company, expedition); (usu. in *pass.*) bind in friendship, make devoted (*is deeply attached to her*); appoint for special or temporary duties; affix (immaterial things, name, liability, etc., *to*); attribute (importance, meaning, etc. *to*); (Law) seize (person, property) by legal authority; hence ~ABLE *a.* **2.** *v.i.* Be attributable (*no blame attaches to the bystanders*). [ME, f. OF *estachier* fasten f. Gmc **stakōn* f. **stak*- STAKE; in Law sense thr. OF *atachier*]

attă'ché (-shā) *n.* One attached to ambassador's staff (*military, press, attaché*); ~ **case,** small rectangular case for carrying documents etc. [F, p.p. of *attacher* (as prec.)]

attă'chment *n.* Act of attaching; thing (to be) attached; means of attaching; affection, devotion; legal seizure. [ME, f. F *attachement* (*attacher* attach; see -MENT)]

attă'ck[1] *v.* **1.** *v.t.* Act against with (esp. armed) force; seek to hurt or defeat; criticize adversely; act harmfully on; begin vigorous work on; hence ~ABLE *a.* **2.** *v.i.* Make attack. [f. F *attaquer* f. It. *attaccare* ATTACH, join (battle)]

attă'ck[2] *n.* Act of attacking; offensive operation or behaviour; (Mus.) action or manner of beginning piece, passage, etc.; sudden start of illness etc. (*bilious, heart, attack*; *an attack of the blues*); (Lacrosse, Netball) player in forward position. [f. prec., or f. F *attaque* f. It. *attacco*]

attai'n *v.* **1.** *v.t.* Arrive at, reach; gain, accomplish; hence ~ABI'LITY *n.*, ~ABLE *a.*, **~able**NESS (-beln-) *n.* **2.** *v.i.* ~ **to,** arrive at. [ME, f. AF *atain-*, *atein-*, OF *ataign-* st. of *ataindre* f. L AT*tingere* (*tangere* touch)]

attai'nder *n.* (Hist.) Consequences of sentence of death or outlawry (forfeiture of estate, loss of civil rights); **bill of** ~, legislation inflicting attainder without trial. [ME f. AF, = OF *ateindre* ATTAIN used as n. (see -ER[4])]

attai'nment *n.* Act of attaining; thing attained, esp. (in *pl.*) personal accomplishments. [f. ATTAIN + -MENT]

attai'nt *v.t.* (Hist.) subject to attainder; (of disease etc.) strike, affect; taint. [ME, f. obs. *attaint* a. f. OF *ataint*, *ateint* p.p. f. as ATTAIN; confused in meaning with TAINT]

ă'ttar, ŏ'ttō[1], *n.* Fragrant essential oil, esp. from rose-petals. [f. Pers. (Arab.) '*aṭṭār* ('*iṭr* perfume)]

attĕ'mper *v.t.* (arch.) Modify by admixture; soothe, mollify; accommodate or attune *to*; hence ~MENT *n.* [ME, f. OF *atemprer* f. L AT(*temperare* TEMPER[1])]

attĕ'mpt[1] *v.t.* Try (thing, action, *to* do); try to conquer (mountain, fortress) or accomplish; ~ **the life of,** (arch.) try to kill; hence ~ABLE *a.* [f. OF *attempter*, f. L AT(*temptare* TEMPT)]

attĕ'mpt[2] *n.* Act of attempting (*to* do, *at* thing or doing, *on the life of*); endeavour; result of attempting, esp. unsuccessfully. [f. prec.]

attĕ'nd *v.* **1.** *v.i.* Turn the mind *to*; apply oneself (*to*, or abs.). **2.** Be present (*at*); wait *on*. **3.** *v.t.* Wait on; escort, accompany; follow as result from; be present at (lecture etc.); go regularly to (school, church, etc.). **4.** Hence ~ER[1] *n.* [ME, f. OF *atendre* f. L AT*tendere -tent-* stretch]

attĕ'ndance *n.* Act of ATTENDing (senses 2 and 3; ||**~ centre,** place where young delinquents must attend regularly instead of being sent to prison; DANCE[1] *attendance*); number of persons present. [ME f. OF *atendance* (as prec.; see -ANCE)]

attĕ'ndant *a.* & *n.* **1.** *a.* Waiting (*on*); accompanying (*attendant circumstances*). **2.** *n.* One who attends; person providing service (*cloakroom attendant*; **medical ~**, one's physician; **museum** etc. ~, custodian or guide). [ME f. OF (as ATTEND; see -ANT)]

attĕ'ntion *n.* & *int.* **1.** *n.* Act of ATTENDing (sense 1; *give, pay, attention*); faculty of attending (sense 1; *attract attention*; *call, draw, attention to*); consideration, care; (in *pl.*) ceremonious politeness (**pay** one's **~s to,** woo); (Mil.) erect attitude of readiness. **2.** *int.* **A~!,** order to take notice or to assume attitude of attention. [ME, f. L *attentio* (as ATTEND; see -ION)]

attĕ'ntĭve *a.* Heedful; ATTENDing (sense 1) *to*; polite, assiduous; hence ~LY[2] (-vlĭ) *adv.*, ~NESS (-vn-) *n.* [ME, f. F *attentif -ive* f. *attente*, OF *atente*, fem. p.p. (as n.) of *atendre* ATTEND; see -IVE]

attĕ'nū|āte[1] *v.t.* Make thin; reduce in force, value, or virulence; reduce amplitude of (signal or current); so ~A'TION, **~āt**OR, *ns.* [f. L AT*tenuare* (*tenuis* thin) + -ATE[3]]

attĕ'nuate[2] *a.* Slender; rarefied; tapering gradually. [f. L *attenuatus* p.p. of *attenuare* (see prec., -ATE[2])]

attĕ'st *v.* **1.** *v.t.* Certify validity of; enrol (recruit) for military service; ||**~ed cattle, milk,** (certified free from disease). **2.** *v.i.* Bear witness *to*; (of recruit) enrol for military service. **3.** Hence ~OR *n.* [f. F *attester* f. L AT*testari* (*testis* witness)]

ăttĕ**stā'tion** *n.* Act of attesting; testimony. [F, or f. LL *attestatio* (as prec.; see -ATION)]

A'ttĭc[1] (ă'-) *a.* & *n.* Of Athens or Attica; ~ (**dialect**), Greek as used by the ancient Athenians; ~ **order,** (Archit.) square column of any of the five ORDER[1]S; ~ **salt, wit,** refined wit. [f. L f. Gk *Attikos*]

ă'ttĭc[2] *n.* Highest storey of house, usu. immediately under roof; room in this. [f. F *attique*, as prec.; orig. (Archit.) small order above a taller one]

ă'ttĭcĭsm *n.* Extreme elegance of speech. [f. Gk *Attikismos* (as ATTIC[1]; see -ISM)]

attīr'e *v.t.*, & *n.* Dress (esp. w. ref. to fine or formal or special clothing). [ME, f. OF *atir(i)er* equip f. *à tire* in order, of unkn. orig.]

ă'ttĭtūde *n.* Disposition of figure (in painting etc.); posture of body (**strike an** ~, assume it theatrically); position of aircraft etc. relative to specified directions; settled behaviour, as indicating opinion; ~ (**of mind**), settled mode of thinking; hence **ăttĭtū'dĭn**AL *a.* [F, f. It. *attitudine* fitness, posture, f. LL *aptitudo -dinis* (*aptus* fit; see -TUDE)]

ăttĭtū'dĭnīze, -īse (-īz), *v.i.* Practise or adopt attitudes; speak, write, behave, affectedly. [f. It. *attitudine* f. LL (as prec.) + -IZE]

attn. *abbr.* (for the) attention (of).

ă'ttō- *pref.* denoting factor of 10^{-18}, as *atto*METRE[2]. [f. Da. or Norw. *atten* eighteen + -O-]

attor'ney (-tẽr'-) *n.* **1.** One appointed to act for another in business or legal matters (**power of** ~, authority to act thus); *qualified lawyer, esp. representing client in proceedings; *DISTRICT *attorney*; hence ~SHIP (-nĭsh-) *n.* **2. A~-General,** chief legal officer of some countries and states. [ME, f. OF *atorné* p.p. (as n.) of *atorner* assign (*à* to, *torner* turn); see -Y[4]]

attră'ct *v.t.* Draw or bring to oneself or itself (*he attracted a crowd with his tricks*; *magnet attracts iron*; *publicity attracts new members*); give or promise pleasure to (person); draw forth and fix on oneself (attention etc.); hence ~ABLE *a.* [f. L AT(*trahere tract-* draw)]

attră'ctant *a.* & *n.* (Substance) which attracts (esp. insects). [f. prec. + -ANT]

attră'ction *n.* Act or faculty of drawing to oneself or itself (lit. or fig.); (Phys.) tendency of bodies to attract or approach each other (opp. *repulsion*); thing that attracts (fig.); (Gram.) influence of word in context to cause incorrect form of adjacent word. [F, or f. L *attractio* (as ATTRACT; see -ION)]
attră'ctĭve *a.* Attracting or capable of attracting (esp. fig.); hence ~LY² (-vlĭ) *adv.*, ~NESS (-vn-) *n.* [f. F *attractif -ive* f. LL *attractivus* (as ATTRACT; see -IVE)]
ă'ttrĭbūte¹ *n.* Quality ascribed to anything; material object recognized as appropriate to person or office; characteristic quality; (Gram.) attributive word. [ME, f. OF *attribut* or f. L *attributum* (ATtribuere *-ut-* assign)]
attrĭ'būt|e² *v.t.* Regard as belonging or appropriate *to* (author etc.); refer (effect *to* its cause); assign (*to* time or place); hence ~ABLE *a.* [f. L as prec.]
ăttrĭbū'tion *n.* Act of attributing. [ME, f. OF, f. L *attributio -onis* (as ATTRIBUTE¹; see -ION)]
attrĭ'būtĭve *a.* (Gram., of *a.* or *n.*, opp. *predicative*) expressing an attribute (e.g. *old* in *the old dog* but not in *the dog is old*); hence ~LY² (-vlĭ) *adv.* [f. F *attributif -ive* (as ATTRIBUTE¹; see -IVE)]
attrĭ'tion *n.* Friction; gradual wearing out (esp. Mil.; **war of** ~, one whose outcome depends on which side can last longer); abrasion; (Theol.) sorrow for sin (short of *contrition*); hence ~AL *a.* [ME, f. LL *attritio* (ATterere *-trit-* rub)]
attū'ne *v.t.* Bring into musical accord (*to*, lit. or fig.); tune (instrument). [f. AT- + TUNE 4]
Atty. *abbr.* Attorney.
A.T.V. *abbr.* ||Associated Television.
ătȳ'pĭcal *a.* Not conforming to type; hence ~LY² *adv.* [f. A- 7 + TYPICAL]
A.U. *abbr.* ångström unit; astronomical unit.
Au *symb.* gold. [f. L *aurum*]
auba'de (ōbah'd) *n.* Poem or piece of music appropriate to dawn. [F, f. Sp. *albada* (*alba* dawn)]
auberge (ōbār'zh) *n.* Inn. [F]
au'bergine (ō'berzhēn) *n.* Fruit of egg-plant, used as vegetable. [F, f. Cat. *alberginia* f. Arab. *al-bādinjān* f. Pers. *bādingān* f. Skr. *vātimgaṇa*]
aubrie'tia, (erron.) **-rē'tia,** (-sha) *n.* Spring-flowering dwarf perennial rock-plant of genus *Aubrieta.* [mod. L, f. Claude *Aubriet*, Fr. botanist d. 1743; see -IA¹]
au'burn *a.* Reddish brown (usu. of person's hair). [ME, orig. yellowish white, f. OF *auborne, alborne*, f. L *alburnus* whitish (*albus* white)]
A.U.C. *abbr. ab urbe condita.*
au courant (ōkoo'rahṅ) *pred. a.* Acquainted *with* or *of* what is going on; well-informed. [F, = in the (regular) course]
au'ction *n.*, & *v.t.* **1.** *n.* Public sale in which articles are sold to maker of highest bid; **all over the** ~, (Austral. sl.) everywhere; **Dutch** ~, sale in which price is reduced by auctioneer till a buyer is found. **2.** ~ (**bridge**), form of bridge in which players bid for right to name trumps; sequence of bids made at bridge. **3.** *v.t.* Sell by auction. [f. L *auctio* increase, auction (*augēre auct-* increase; see -ION)]
auctioneer' *n.* One whose business is to conduct auctions; hence ~ING¹ (1) *n.* [f. prec. + -EER]
audā'cious (-shus) *a.* Daring, bold; impudent; hence or cogn. ~LY² *adv.*, ~NESS, **aud**A'CITY, *ns.* [f. L *audax -acis* bold (*audēre* dare; see -ACIOUS)]
au'dĭble *a.* That can be heard; hence **audi**BI'LITY, ~NESS (-beln-), *ns.*, **au'dĭ**BLY² *adv.* [f. LL *audibilis* (*audire* hear; see -IBLE)]
au'dĭence *n.* Hearing (**give** ~, listen); formal interview (*had audience of*; *had an audience with*); persons within hearing; whole group of listeners or spectators; readers (of book, writer, etc.). [ME f. OF, f. L *audientia* (*audire* hear; see -ENCE)]
au'dīle *a.* Pertaining to sense of hearing. [irreg. f. L *audire* hear, after *tactile*]
au'dĭō *n.* (Reproduction of) sound; ~ **frequency** (comparable to that of normally audible sound); ~ **typist** (who types direct from tape or other recording). [f. foll.]
au'dĭō- *comb. form.* Hearing, as: ~LOGY (-ŏ'l-) *n.*, science of hearing, whence ~LOGIST (-ŏ'l-) *n.*; ~METER (-ŏ'm-) *n.*, instrument for testing hearing; ~PHILE *n.*, devotee of high-fidelity sound reproduction; **~-vi'sual,** using both sight and sound. [f. L *audire* hear + -o-]
au'dĭt *n.*, & *v.t.* **1.** *n.* Official examination of accounts; ~ **ale** (of special quality, formerly brewed in English colleges, orig. for use on day of audit). **2.** *v.t.* Conduct audit of; *attend (class) without intending to obtain credits. [ME, f. L *auditus* hearing (*audire -it-* hear)]
audĭ'tion *n.* & *v.* **1.** *n.* Power of hearing; listening; trial hearing or seeing of applicant for employment as singer, dancer, etc. **2.** *v.t.* & *i.* Hear etc., be heard etc., as such applicant. [F, or f. L *auditio* (*audire -it-* hear; see -ION)]
au'dĭtĭve *a.* Concerned with hearing. [f. F *auditif -ive* (as prec.; see -IVE)]
au'dĭtor *n.* Listener; one who audits accounts; hence **audĭtōr'**IAL *a.* [ME, f. AF *auditour* f. L *auditor -oris* (as prec.; see -OR)]
audĭtōr'ĭ|um *n.* (*pl.* **~ums** *or* **~a**). Building or part of building occupied by audience. [L, neut. (as n.) of *auditorius* a. (see foll., -ORIUM)]
au'dĭtorȳ *a.* & *n.* **1.** *a.* Concerned with hearing; received by the ear. **2.** *n.* (arch.) Assembly of hearers, audience; auditorium. [f. L *auditorius* (as AUDITOR; see -ORY)]
||**A.U.E.W.** *abbr.* Amalgamated Union of Engineering Workers.
au fait (ōfā') *pred. a.* Conversant, instructed; **put** or **make** ~ **with,** instruct in. [F]
au fond (ōfaw'ṅ) *adv.* At bottom, basically. [F]
Aug. *abbr.* August.
Augē'an *a.* Filthy, like the stables of Augeas, which Hercules cleansed by diverting river Alpheus to flow through them. [f. L *Augeas* f. Gk *Augeias* + -AN]
au'ger (-g-) *n.* Tool for boring holes in wood, having long shank with helical groove, cutting edge, and transverse handle; similar instrument for boring in soil. [OE *nafogār* (*nafu* NAVE¹, *gār* piercer); cf. OS, OHG *nabugēr*, ON *nafarr*; for loss of *n-* cf. ADDER]
aught¹ (awt) *n.* (arch. or poet.) Anything. [OE *āwiht* etc., = OS *ēowiht*, f. WG (as AYE², WIGHT)]
aught². See OUGHT¹.
au'gment¹ *n.* (Gram.) Vowel prefixed to past tenses in the older IE languages. [ME f. OF, or f. LL *augmentum* (as foll.)]
augmĕ'nt² *v.t.* & *i.* Make or become greater; increase; **~ed interval** (Mus., greater by a semitone than corresp. major or perfect interval). [ME, f. F *augmenter* or f. LL *augmentare* increase f. L *augmentum* (*augēre* increase)]
augmentā'tion *n.* Enlargement; growth, increase; (Mus.) repetition of passage in notes longer than those previously used. [ME f. F, f. LL *augmentatio -onis* (*augmentare*; see prec., -ATION)]
augmĕ'ntatĭve *a.* Having the property of increasing; (Gram., of affix or derived word) increasing in force the idea of the original word. [f. F *augmentatif -ive* or f. med. L *augmentativus* (as AUGMENT²; see -ATIVE)]
au grand sérieux (ōgrahṅsĕrēer') *adv.* Quite seriously (*take it, him*, etc., *au grand sérieux*). [F]
au gratin. See GRATIN.
au'gur¹ *n.* Roman religious official who foretold future events by observing behaviour of birds etc.; soothsayer; hence ~SHIP *n.* [L]
au'gur² *v.* **1.** *v.t.* Foresee, predict; portend. **2.** *v.i.*

~ **well, ill,** have good, bad, implications *for*. [f. prec.]

au'gūral *a.* Of augurs; significant as regards the future. [f. L *auguralis* (AUGUR¹; see -AL)]

au'gūrў *n.* Divination by omens; omen. [ME, f. OF *augurie* or f. L *augurium* (AUGUR¹)]

augŭ'st¹ *a.* Majestic; venerable; noble; impressive; hence ~LY² *adv.*, ~NESS *n.* [f. F *auguste* or L *augustus* consecrated, venerable]

Au'gust² *n.* Eighth month of year. [OE, f. L *augustus* (see prec.), name of Augustus Caesar, first Roman emperor]

Augŭ'stan *a.* & *n.* **1.** *a.* Connected with reign of Augustus Caesar, outstanding period of Latin literature; (of any national literature) classical (in Engl. literature 17th–18th c.). **2.** *n.* Writer of the Augustan age of any literature. [f. L *Augustanus* (*Augustus*; see -AN)]

Augŭ'stĭne *n.* Augustinian monk. [ME, f. OF *augustin* f. L *Augustinus* (see foll.)]

Augŭstĭ'nĭan *a.* & *n.* **1.** *a.* Of or relating to St. Augustine, a Doctor of the Church (d. 430), or his doctrines; belonging to a religious order observing rule derived from St. Augustine's writings. **2.** *n.* Adherent of the doctrines of St. Augustine; one of the order of Augustinian monks. [f. L *Augustinus* Augustine + -IAN]

auk *n.* Sea-bird of family Alcidae, e.g. great auk (flightless and extinct), little auk, guillemot, puffin, razorbill. [f. ON *álka*]

auld *a.* (Sc.) Old; ~ **lang syne** (-sīn), 'old long since', the days of long ago (esp. as title and refrain of song sung at parting etc.). [OE *ald*, Anglian form of OLD]

au'lĭc *a.* Pertaining to a court. [f. F *aulique* or f. L f. Gk *aulikos* (*aulē* court; see -IC)]

au'mbrў. See AMBRY.

au naturel (ōnătūrĕ'l) *adv.* & *pred. a.* Uncooked; (cooked) in the most natural or simplest way. [F, = in the natural state]

aunt (ahnt) *n.* Father's or mother's sister; uncle's wife; (colloq.) unrelated woman friend of children; **A~ Sally,** game in which players throw sticks or balls at wooden dummy, (fig.) object of unreasonable attack; **my** (**sainted** etc.) ~ (excl. of surprise etc.); hence (colloq.) ~'IE, ~'Y³, *ns.* [ME, f. AF *aunte*, OF *ante* f. L *amita*]

au pair' (ōp-) *a.* & *n.* (Of arrangements between two parties) paid for by mutual services (no money passing); ‖~ (**girl**), young (usu. foreign) woman helping with housework etc. in return for room and board. [F]

aur'a *n.* (*pl.* ~**e** *or* ~**s**). Subtle emanation (from flowers etc.); atmosphere diffused by or attending person, place, etc. (esp. in mystical or spiritualistic use); (Path.) premonitory symptom in epilepsy etc.; hence **aur'al¹** [-AL] *a.* [ME f. L f. Gk, = breeze, breath]

aur'al² *a.* Pertaining to or received by the ear; hence ~LY² *adv.* [f. L *auris* ear + -AL]

aur'ėate *a.* Golden, gold-coloured; resplendent; (of language) highly ornamented. [ME, f. LL *aureatus* f. L *aureus* golden (*aurum* gold); see -ATE²]

aurē'ola, aur'ėōle, *n.* Celestial crown of martyr etc.; glory round head or body of pictured divine figure; halo or ring round sun or moon. [ME; *aureola* (*corona*) L, = golden (crown), fem. of *aureolus* f. *aureus* (*aurum* gold); *aureole* f. OF f. L *aureola*]

aurėomȳ'cĭn *n.* Antibiotic used esp. in lung diseases. [f. L *aureus* golden + Gk *mukēs* fungus + -IN]

au revoir (ōrevwar̂') *int.* & *n.* (Goodbye) till we meet again. [F]

aur'ĭc *a.* Pertaining to gold. [f. L *aurum* gold + -IC]

aur'ĭcle *n.* External ear of animals; process shaped like lower lobe of ear; (Anat.) (small appendage to) atrium of heart. [f. foll.]

aurĭ'cūla *n.* Species of primula, with ear-shaped leaves; mollusc of genus *Auricula*. [L, dim. of *auris* ear]

aurĭ'cūlar *a.* **1.** Pertaining to the ear; ~ **confession** (made privately in priest's ear). **2.** Pertaining to auricle of heart; shaped like an auricle. **3.** Hence ~LY² *adv.* [f. LL *auricularis* (AURICULA; see -AR¹)]

aurĭ'cūlate *a.* Having ear-shaped appendages. [f. L AURICULA + -ATE²]

aurĭ'ferous *a.* Yielding gold. [f. L *aurifer* (*aurum* gold); see -FEROUS]

Aurĭgnā'cian (-shan) *a.* & *n.* (Culture) of the palaeolithic period in Europe following the Mousterian and preceding the Solutrean. [F (*-ien*), f. *Aurignac* in S.W. France]

aur'ĭst *n.* Ear specialist. [f. L *auris* ear + -IST]

aur'ŏchs (owr'ŏks; *or* ŏr̂'-) *n.* **1.** Extinct European wild ox, urus. **2.** European bison, wisent. [G, f. OHG *ūrohso* (*ūr-* urus, *ohso* ox)]

auror̂'a *n.* (*pl.* ~**s** *or* ~**e**). Luminous atmospheric (prob. electrical) phenomenon, usu. of streamers radiating from above northern (~ **bor̂ėā'lĭs**) or southern (~ **austrā'lĭs**) magnetic pole; dawn; (*A*~) Roman goddess of dawn; hence **auror̂'**AL *a.* [L, = dawn, goddess of dawn]

auscultā'tion *n.* Act of listening, esp. (Med.) to sounds of heart, lungs, etc.; so **auscŭ'ltat**ORY *a.* [f. L *auscultatio* (*auscultare* listen to; see -ATION)]

au sérieux (ōsĕrēer̂') *adv.* Seriously (*take it, him*, etc., *au sérieux*). [F]

au'spĭcāte *v.t.* (arch.) Inaugurate, initiate. [f. L *auspicari* prognosticate (*auspex*; see foll.) + -ATE³]

au'spĭce *n.* Forecast; (in *pl.*) patronage (*under the auspices of*). [orig. 'observation of bird-flight in divination'; F, or f. L *auspicium* (*auspex* observer of birds f. *avis* bird)]

auspĭ'cious (-sh*u*s) *a.* Of good omen, favourable; prosperous; hence ~LY² *adv.*, ~NESS *n.* [f. prec. + -OUS]

Au'ssĭe (ŏ'zĭ *or* ŏ'sĭ) *n.* & *a.* (colloq.) Australia(n). [abbr.; see -IE]

austēr̂'e (*or* ŏ-) *a.* (~**r**, ~**st**). Harsh, stern; morally strict; severely simple; hence or cogn. ~LY² (-ēr̂'lĭ) *adv.*, ~NESS (-ēr̂'n-) *n.*, **austĕ'r**ITY (*or* ŏ-) *n.* (esp. of nation-wide economies). [ME f. OF, f. L f. Gk *austēros* severe]

Au'stĭn (*or* ŏ'-) *a.* & *n.* = AUGUSTINIAN. [contr. of AUGUSTINE]

au'stral (*or* ŏ'-) *a.* Southern; of Australia. [ME, f. L *australis* (*Auster* south wind; see -AL)]

Australā'sian (-shan; *or* ŏ-) *a.* & *n.* (Native or inhabitant) of Australasia. [f. *Australasia* Australia and islands of S.W. Pacific (f. F *Australasie* f. as *Australia* + *Asia*) + -AN]

Austrā'lĭan (*or* ŏ-) *n.* & *a.* (Native or inhabitant) of Australia; ~ **bear,** koala; ~ (**National**) **Rules,** form of football played with Rugby ball by teams of 18; ~ **terrier** (wire-haired Australian breed); hence ~ISM (2, 4) *n.* [f. F *australien* f. L (as AUSTRAL)]

Austrālopĭ'thėc|us *n.* Small-brained fossil hominid of genus *Australopithecus*; hence ~INE¹ *n.* & *a.* [mod. L, f. L *australis* southern + -o- + Gk *pithēkos* ape]

au'tarchў (-kĭ) *n.* Absolute sovereignty; despotism; hence **autar̂'ch**IC(AL) (-k-) *adjs.* [f. mod. L *autarchia* (as AUTO-, Gk *-arkhia* f. *arkhō* rule)]

au'tarkў *n.* Self-sufficiency, esp. economic; hence **autar̂'k**IC(AL) *adjs.*, **au'tark**IST *n.* [f. Gk *autarkeia* (as AUTO-, *arkeō* suffice)]

authĕ'nt|ĭc *a.* Reliable, trustworthy; of undisputed origin, genuine; (of church mode) having sounds within an octave of the final (cf. PLAGAL);

hence ~ICALLY *adv.*, ~ĭ'CITY *n.* [ME, f. OF *autentique* f. LL f. Gk *authentikos* principal, genuine; see -IC]

authĕ'ntĭc|āte *v.t.* Establish truth or authorship or validity or genuineness of; hence ~A'TION, ~**ātor**, *ns.* [f. med. L *authenticare* (LL *authenticus*; see prec.) + -ATE³]

au'thor *n.*, & *v.t.* **1.** *n.* Originator (*of* a condition of things, event, etc.); writer of book, essay, etc.; author's writings; hence ~ESS¹ *n.*, **authôr'-IAL** *a.* **2.** *v.t.* Be author of. [ME f. AF *autour*, OF *autor* f. L *auctor* (*augēre auct-* increase, originate, promote; see -OR)]

authŏrĭtār'ĭan *a.* & *n.* (esp. Polit.) (Person) favouring obedience to authority as opp. to individual liberty; tyrannical (person); (of State etc.) that is a dictatorship. [f. AUTHORITY + -ARIAN]

authŏ'rĭtatĭve *a.* Possessing or claiming authority; proceeding from competent authority; commanding, imperative; hence ~LY² (-vlĭ) *adv.*, ~NESS (-vn-) *n.* [f. foll. + -ATIVE]

authŏ'rĭtȳ *n.* Power or right to enforce obedience; delegated power (*to* do, *for* an act, or abs.); person or (esp. in *pl.*) body having authority; personal influence, esp. over opinion; weight of testimony; book, quotation, considered to settle a question; evidence or declaration that may be cited in support of a statement (*on the authority of Plato*); person whose opinion is accepted, esp. expert in a subject (*an authority on bees*). [ME, f. OF *autorité* f. L *auctoritas* (*auctor*; see AUTHOR, -ITY)]

au'thorīz|e, -īs|e (-iz), *v.t.* **1.** Sanction; **A~ed Version,** English transl. of Bible (1611). **2.** Give authority to, commission, (person *to* do). **3.** Hence ~A'TION *n.* [ME, f. OF *autoriser* f. med. L *auctorizare* (*auctor*; see AUTHOR, -IZE)]

au'thorshĭp *n.* Occupation or career as a writer; origin (*of* book). [f. AUTHOR + -SHIP]

au'tĭsm *n.* Morbid absorption in fantasy; mental condition esp. in children, preventing proper response to environment; hence **autĭ'stIC** *a.* [f. mod. L *autismus* (as AUTO-, -ISM)]

***au'tō** *n.* (*pl.* ~**s**). (colloq.) Motor car. [abbr. of AUTOMOBILE]

au'to- *comb. form.* Self (*autism*); one's own (*autobiography*); by oneself, spontaneous, (*autarky, auto-suggestion*); by itself, automatic, (*autocycle, automobile*). [f. or after Gk *auto-* f. *autos* self]

autobahn (aw'tobahn) *n.* (*pl.* ~*s or* ~*en*). German motorway. [G (*auto* motor car, *bahn* path, road)]

autobīŏ'graph|ȳ *n.* Writing the story of one's own life; story so written; hence ~ER¹ *n.*, **autobīogră'phIC(AL)** *adjs.* [f. AUTO- + BIOGRAPHY]

***au'tocāde** *n.* Motorcade. [f. AUTOMOBILE + CAVALCADE]

au'tocâr *n.* (arch.) Motor vehicle. [f. AUTO- + CAR]

autocĕ'phalous *a.* Having its own head; (of bishop, church, etc.) independent. [f. Gk *autokephalos* (as AUTO-, *kephalē* head) + -OUS]

autŏ'chthon (-k-) *n.* (in *pl.* ~**s**, *or* ~**es** *pr.* -ēz) Original or earliest known inhabitants; aborigines; hence ~AL, **autochthŏ'nIC**, ~OUS, (-k-) *adjs.* [Gk, = sprung from that land itself (as AUTO-, *khthōn -onos* land)]

au'toclāve *n.* Strong vessel used for chemical reactions at high pressures and temperatures; sterilizer using high-pressure steam. [f. AUTO- + L *clavus* nail or *clavis* key]

autŏ'cracȳ *n.* Absolute government by one person; controlling influence. [f. Gk *autokrateia* (as foll.)]

au'tocrăt *n.* Absolute ruler; dictatorial person; so **autocră'tIC** *a.* [f. F *autocrate* f. Gk *autokratēs* (as AUTO-, *kratos* power)]

au'tocrŏss *n.* Motor-racing across country or on unmade roads. [f. AUTOMOBILE + CROSS-COUNTRY]

au'tocȳcle *n.* (arch.) Bicycle with auxiliary engine. [f. AUTO- + CYCLE]

auto-da-fé (awtodahfā') *n.* (*pl.* ***autos-da-fé***). Sentence of the Inquisition; execution of this, esp. burning of heretic. [Port., = act of the faith]

au'todĭdăct *n.* Self-taught person; so **autodĭdă'ctIC** *a.* [f. AUTO- + as DIDACTIC]

autō-ĕ'rotĭsm *n.* Sexual excitement generated without external stimulus; so **autō-ėrŏ'tIC** *a.*, **autō-ėrŏ'tiCISM** *n.* [f. AUTO- + EROTISM]

autŏ'gamȳ *n.* (Bot.) Self-fertilization. [f. AUTO- + Gk *-gamia* f. *gamos* marriage]

autŏ'gėnous *a.* Self-produced; ~ **welding** (by melting edges together without adding different material). [f. AUTO- + -GENOUS]

autogīr'ō *n.* (*pl.* ~**s**). Early form of helicopter with propeller and freely rotating horizontal vanes. [Sp. (as AUTO-, *giro* gyration)]

au'tograft (-ahft) *n.* (Surg.) Graft from another part of same individual. [f. AUTO- + GRAFT¹]

au'tograph (-ahf) *n.*, & *v.t.* **1.** *n.* Author's own manuscript; person's own handwriting, esp. signature; document signed by its author. **2.** *v.t.* Write with one's own hand; sign. [F, or f. LL f. Gk *autographon* neut. (as n.) of *autographos* (as AUTO-, *-graphos* written); cf. -GRAPH]

autŏ'graphȳ *n.* Writing with one's own hand; reproduction of writing or drawing by direct facsimile; so **autogră'phIC** *a.* [f. prec. + -Y¹]

autogȳr'ō. Var. of AUTOGIRO.

au'tohârp *n.* Kind of zither with mechanical device to allow playing of chords. [f. AUTO- + HARP¹]

autō-ĭmmū'n|e *a.* (Med.) Caused by the production of antibodies to substances naturally present; so ~ITY *n.* [f. AUTO- + IMMUNE]

autō-ĭntŏxĭcā'tion *n.* (Med.) Poisoning by toxin produced within the body. [f. AUTO- + INTOXICATION]

autŏ'lȳsĭs *n.* Destruction of body cells by their own enzymes; hence **autolȳ'tIC** *a.* [f. G *autolyse* f. as AUTO- + -LYSIS]

***au'tomăt** *n.* Cafeteria in which meals etc. are provided from slot-machines; slot-machine. [G, f. F *automate*, f. as AUTOMATON]

au'tomāte *v.t.* Subject to or operate by automation. [back form. f. AUTOMATION]

automă'tĭc *a.* & *n.* **1.** *a.* Working of itself, without direct human actuation; (of firearm) having mechanism for loading, firing, and ejecting until ammunition is exhausted or pressure on trigger etc. is released; (of telephone system) operated by automatic switches; (of gear system in motor car) not operated directly by driver; ~ **pilot,** device for keeping aircraft or ship on set course. **2.** Mechanical, unconscious; unintelligent, merely mechanical; necessary (*an automatic consequence*; *incurs automatic disqualification*). **3.** (Psych.) performed unconsciously or subconsciously; ~ **writing** (with planchette etc.). **4.** Hence **automă'tICALLY** *adv.*, **automatĭ'CITY** *n.* **5.** *n.* Automatic firearm, tool, etc. [f. as AUTOMATON + -IC]

automā'tion *n.* Automatic control of manufacture of product through successive stages; use of automatic equipment to save mental and manual labour. [irreg. f. prec. + -ATION]

autŏ'matĭsm *n.* Involuntary action; unthinking routine; (Psych.) action performed unconsciously or subconsciously, mental state

For other words in *auto-* see AUTO-.

accompanying such actions. [f. F *automatisme* (*automate* AUTOMATON; see -ISM)]
autŏ'matize, -ise (-iz), *v.t.* Make automatic; subject to automation. [f. AUTOMATIC + -IZE]
autŏ'mat|on *n.* (*pl.* **~a** *or* **~ons**). Piece of mechanism with concealed motive power; organism, esp. person, whose actions are involuntary or without active intelligence. [L f. Gk, neut. (as n.) of AUTO*matos* acting of itself]
***au'tomobile** (-ēl) *n.* Motor car. [F (as AUTO-, MOBILE)]
automō'tive *a.* Concerned with motor vehicles. [f. AUTO- + MOTIVE[1]]
autŏ'nom|y̆ *n.* Right of self-government; personal freedom; freedom of the will; hence or cogn. **autonŏ'mIC** *a.*, (esp. Physiol., functioning involuntarily), ~OUS *a.* [f. Gk *autonomia* f. AUTO(*nomos* law); see -Y[1]]
au'tōpilot *n.* Automatic pilot. [abbr.]
autopista (aw'topĭsta) *n.* Spanish motorway. [Sp. (as AUTOMOBILE, *pista* track)]
au'tŏpsy̆ (*or* -ŏ'-) *n.* Personal inspection; post--mortem examination; (fig.) critical dissection. [f. F *autopsie* or f. mod. L f. Gk *autopsia* (*autoptēs* eye-witness)]
autorā'dĭograph (-ahf) *n.* Photograph of object, produced by radiation from radioactive material in the object; so **autorādĭogră'phIC** *a.*, **autorādĭŏ'GRAPHY** *n.* [f. AUTO- + RADIOGRAPH]
autoroute (aw'torōōt) *n.* French motorway. [F (as AUTOMOBILE, ROUTE)]
autostrad|a (owtostrah'da) *n.* (*pl.* **~e** *pr.* -dā). Italian motorway. [It. (as AUTOMOBILE, *strada* road)]
auto-suggĕ'stion (-schon) *n.* Hypnotic or subconscious suggestion from subject himself. [f. AUTO- + SUGGESTION]
autotĕ'lĭc *a.* Having or being a purpose in itself. [f. AUTO- + Gk *telos* end + -IC]
autŏ'tomy̆ *n.* (Zool.) Casting off of part(s) of body. [f. AUTO- + -TOMY]
autotŏ'x|ĭn *n.* Poisonous substance produced by changes within the organism; so ~IC *a.* [f. AUTO- + TOXIN]
autotrŏ'phĭc *a.* Self-nourishing; able to feed on simple substances. [f. AUTO- + Gk *trophos* feeder + -IC]
au'toty̆pe *n.* Facsimile; photographic printing process for monochrome reproduction. [f. AUTO- + TYPE[1]]
au'tumn (-m) *n.* Third season of the year, in N. hemisphere September–November (Astron., from autumnal equinox to winter solstice); (fig.) season of maturity or incipient decay; ~ **crocus,** plant of genus *Colchicum*, esp. meadow saffron; ~ **tints,** brown and gold colours of dying leaves. [ME f. OF *autompne* f. L *autumnus*]
autŭ'mnal *a.* Of or like, appearing or occurring or done in, appropriate to, autumn (*autumnal tints* (cf. prec.); *autumnal* EQUINOX); maturing or blooming in autumn; past prime of life. [f. L *autumnalis* (as prec.; see -AL)]
auxanŏ'mėter *n.* Instrument for measuring growth of plants. [f. Gk *auxanō* increase + -o- + -METER]
auxĭ'liar|y̆ (-gzĭ'lyerĭ) *a.* & *n.* (One who is) helpful *to* (**~y troops, ~ies,** (Mil.) foreign or allied troops in a nation's service); (of services or equipment) subsidiary; (Gram.) **~y (verb)**, one used in forming tenses, moods, voices, of other verbs. [f. L *auxiliarius* (*auxilium* help; see -ARY[2])]
au'xĭn *n.* Substance which stimulates growth of plants, growth hormone. [G, f. Gk *auxō* increase + -IN]
A.V. *abbr.* Authorized Version.
ăvadavă't. See AMADAVAT.
avai'l[1] *v.* **1.** *v.i.* Afford help; be of value or profit. **2.** *v.t.* Help, benefit; ~ **oneself of,** profit by, take advantage of. [ME, f. obs. *vail* v. f. stressed st. of OF *valoir* be worth f. L *valēre*]
avai'l[2] *n.* Use, profit (usu. in neg. or interrog. phrs.: *of no avail, without avail, of what avail?*). [f. prec.]
avai'l|able *a.* Capable of being used; at one's disposal; within one's reach; hence ~ABI'LITY, **~able**NESS (-beln-), *ns.*, **~ab**LY[2] *adv.* [ME, f. AVAIL[1] + -ABLE]
ă'valanche (-ahnsh) *n.* & *v.* **1.** *n.* Mass of snow, rock, and ice, descending mountain rapidly; (fig.) sudden onrush of anything. **2.** *v.t.* & *i.* Carry or descend like avalanche. [F, alt. of dial. *lavanche* after *avaler* descend]
avant-gar̂'d|e (ăvahṅ-) *n.* & *a.* (Of) pioneers or innovators in any art in a particular period; hence ~ISM (3), ~IST (2), *ns.* [F, = vanguard]
ă'varĭce *n.* Greed for gain, cupidity; (fig.) eager desire to get or keep; hence **ăvarĭ'ci**OUS (-shus) *a.* [ME f. OF, f. L *avaritia* (*avarus* greedy; see -ICE)]
ava'st (-ah'st) *int.* (Naut.) Stop, cease. [f. Du. *houd vast* hold fast]
ă'vatar̂ *n.* (Hindu Myth.) descent of deity to earth in incarnate form; incarnation; manifestation; phase. [f. Skr. *avatāra* descent (*áva* down, *tar-* pass over)]
avau'nt *int.* (arch.) Begone. [ME f. AF, f. OF *avant* f. Rom. **abante* before f. L *ab* from + *ante* before]
a've (ah'vĭ; *or* -vā) *int.* & *n.* **1.** *int.* Welcome; farewell; **Ave (Maria)** (Hail, Mary), devotional recitation (cf. Luke 1:28 & 42) and prayer to the Virgin Mary. **2.** *n.* Shout of welcome or farewell. [ME f. L, 2nd sing. imper. of *avēre* fare well]
Ave. *abbr.* Avenue.
avĕ'nge (-nj) *v.t.* Inflict retribution, exact satisfaction, on behalf of (person, violated right, etc.); (in *pass.*) avenge oneself; take vengeance for (injury). [ME, f. OF *avengier* (*à* to, *vengier* f. L *vindicare* vindicate)]
ă'vens (-z) *n.* One of various plants of genus *Geum*; **mountain** ~, a related plant (*Dryas octopetala*). [ME f. OF *avence* (med. L *avencia*), of unkn. orig.]
avĕ'ntūrĭne *n.* Brownish glass with copper crystals; variety of spangled quartz resembling this. [F, f. It. *avventurino* (*avventura* chance, from its accidental discovery)]
ă'vėnūe *n.* Way of approach (usu. fig.; *explore every avenue*); ||tree-lined approach to country house; roadway with trees or other objects at regular intervals; broad street. [F, fem. p.p. (as n.) of *avenir* f. L AD*venire* come to]
aver̂' *v.t.* (-rr-). Assert, affirm. [ME, f. OF *averer* (*a-* AD-, L *verus* true)]
ă'verage[1] *n.* **1.** Generally prevailing rate, degree, or amount; ordinary standard; middle estimate (*on the* or *an average*); **law of ~s,** proposition that occurrence of one extreme will be matched by that of the other extreme so as to maintain the normal average. **2.** Arithmetic mean; **batting** ~, (Baseball) batter's safe hits per time at bat, (Cricket) batsman's runs scored per completed innings; **bowling** ~, (Cricket) bowler's conceded runs per wicket taken. **3.** Damage to or loss of insured ship or cargo; **general** ~, deliberate partial sacrifice of insured ship or cargo to avoid total loss; **particular** ~, partial damage to or loss of insured ship or cargo; ~ **adjustment,** apportionment of liability resulting from average. [f. F *avarie* damage to ship or cargo, f. It. *avaria* f. Arab. *'awārīya* damaged goods (*'awār* damage at sea, loss); *-age* after *damage*]

ă'verage[2] *a.* Estimated by average; of the ordinary standard or kind; hence ~LY[2] (-jlĭ) *adv.* [f. prec.]

ă'verage[3] *v.t.* Estimate average of, esp. as arithmetic mean; estimate general standard of; amount on an average to; do etc. on an average (*average six hours' work a day*). [f. as prec.]

avēr'ment *n.* Positive statement, affirmation, esp. (Law) with offer of proof. [ME, f. AF, OF *aver(r)ement* (as AVER; see -MENT)]

avēr'se *pred. a.* Opposed, disinclined, (*to, from*); hence ~NESS (-sn-) *n.* [f. L *aversus* (as AVERT)]

avēr'sion (-shon) *n.* **1.** Dislike, antipathy, (*to, from, for*); ~ **therapy** (designed to make patient averse to an existing habit). **2.** Object of dislike (*my pet aversion*). [F, or f. L *aversio* (as AVERT; see -ION)]

avēr't *v.t.* Turn away (eyes, thoughts, *from*); prevent, ward off; hence ~ABLE, ~IBLE, *adjs.* [ME, f. L *avertere* (*a* AB- away, *vertere vers-* turn); partly f. OF *avertir* f. Rom. **avertire*]

Avĕ'st|a (*a*-) *n.* See ZEND; hence ~AN, ~IC, *adjs.* & *ns.*, (ancient Iranian language) of the Avesta. [Pers.]

ā'vĭan *a.* Pertaining to birds. [f. L *avis* bird + -AN]

ā'vĭarў *n.* Large cage or building for keeping birds. [f. L *aviarium* (as prec.; see -ARY[1])]

ā'vĭāte *v.i.* & *t.* Fly in aeroplane; pilot (aeroplane). [back form. f. foll.]

āvĭā'tion *n.* Art or practice of operating aeroplanes, helicopters, etc.; aircraft manufacture. [F, irreg. f. L *avis* bird; see -ATION]

ā'vĭā|tor *n.* Airman; pilot of an aeroplane; so ~TRIX *n.* [f. F *aviateur* f. L *avis* bird; see -OR]

ă'vĭd *a.* Eager, greedy (*of, for*); hence or cogn. **avĭ'd**ITY *n.*, ~LY[2] *adv.* [f. F *avide* or f. L *avidus* (*avēre* crave; see -ID[1])]

ā'vĭfauna *n.* Birds (of district, country) collectively. [f. L *avis* bird + FAUNA]

āvĭŏ'nĭcs *n.* Application of electronics in aviation. [f. AVIATION + ELECTRONICS]

āvĭtamĭnō's|ĭs *n.* (*pl.* ~**es** *pr.* -ēz). (Path.) Condition resulting from deficiency of one or more vitamins. [mod. L, f. as A- 7 + VITAMIN + -OSIS]

ăvĭză'ndum *n.* (Sc. Law). Private consideration by judge etc. [med. L, gerund of *avizare* consider (as ADVISE)]

ăvoca'dō (-ah'-) *n.* (*pl.* ~**s**). ~ (**pear**), succulent rough-skinned pear-shaped tropical Amer. and W. Ind. fruit, alligator pear. [Sp., = advocate (pop. rendering of Aztec *ahuacatl*)]

ăvocā'tion *n.* Minor occupation; (colloq.) vocation, calling. [f. L *avocatio* (*avocare* call away; see -ATION)]

ă'vocĕt *n.* Wading bird with upturned bill. [f. F *avocette* f. It. *avosetta*]

Avoga'drō (ă-; -gah-) *n.* ~**'s constant** or **number,** number of atoms in one gram-atom; ~**'s law** (that gases at same temperature and pressure have same number of molecules per unit volume). [f. A. ~, It. physicist d. 1856]

avoi'd *v.t.* Keep away or refrain from (thing, doing); escape, evade; (Law) defeat (pleading), quash (sentence); hence ~ABLE *a.*, ~ANCE *n.* [f. AF *avoider*, OF *evuider* clear out, get quit of (*es* out, *vuidier* f. *vuide* empty, VOID)]

ăvoirdūpoi's (ăver-; -z) *a.* & *n.* ~ (**weight**), system of weights based on ~ **pound** of 16 ounces or 7,000 grains; bodily weight, heaviness. [ME, f. OF *aveir de peis* goods of weight (*aveir* f. L *habēre* have, *peis* see POISE)]

avou'ch *v.t.* & *i.* (arch. or rhet.) Guarantee; affirm; confess; hence ~MENT *n.* [ME, f. OF *avochier* f. L AD(*vocare* call)]

avow' *v.t.* Admit, confess; (in *refl.* and *pass.*) admit oneself to be (*avowed himself the author*; *the avowed author*); hence ~ABLE *a.*, ~AL *n.*, ~**ĕd**LY[2] *adv.* [ME, f. OF *avouer* acknowledge f. L AD(*vocare* call)]

avŭ'lsion (-shon) *n.* Tearing away; (Law) sudden removal of land by flood etc. to another person's estate. [F, or f. L *avulsio* (*avellere avuls-* pluck away; see -ION)]

avŭ'ncŭlar *a.* Of or resembling an uncle. [f. L *avunculus* maternal uncle (dim. of *avus* grandfather) + -AR[1]]

aw *int.* expr. mild remonstrance, commiseration, disgust, etc. [imit.]

awai't (*a*-) *v.t.* Wait for; (of thing) be in store for (*a surprise awaits you*). [ME, f. AF *awaitier*, OF *aguaitier* (*a* AD-, *waitier* WAIT[1])]

awā'ke[1] (*a*-) *v.* (*past* **awo'ke** *pr.* -ō'k; *p.p.* **awo'ken** *or* ~**d**). **1.** *v.i.* Cease to sleep; (fig.) become active; ~ **to,** become conscious of. **2.** *v.t.* Cause to cease sleeping (lit. or fig.). [OE *āwæcnan* and *āwacian* (as A- 2, WAKE[1])]

awā'ke[2] (*a*-) *pred. a.* No longer or not yet asleep; vigilant; WIDE *awake*; ~ **to,** aware of. [short for *awaken*, orig. p.p. of prec.]

awā'ken (*a*-) *v.t.* & *i.* = AWAKE[1] (lit. or fig.), esp. (fig.) arouse (*to* a sense of), make aware. [OE *onwæcnan*, *āwæcnan*, *āwæcnian* (as A- 2, WAKE[1], WAKEN)]

awar'd[1] (awôr'd) *v.t.* Order to be given as payment, penalty, or prize; grant; assign. [ME, f. AF *awarder* f. ONF *eswarder* = OF *esguarder* consider, ordain, f. Rom. *EX*wardare* f. WG **ward-*; see WARD[1]]

awar'd[2] (awôr'd) *n.* Judicial decision; payment, penalty, or prize awarded. [ME f. AF (*awarder*; see prec.)]

awār'e (*a*-) *pred. a.* Conscious, not ignorant, having knowledge, (*of, that*); well-informed; hence ~NESS (-ār'n-) *n.* [OE *gewær*, = OS *giwar*, OHG *giwar, gawar*, WG f. as Y-, WARE[2]]

awa'sh (awŏ'-) *pred. a.* Level with surface of water; carried or washed by the waves; flooded. [f. A[3] + WASH[1]]

away (*a*-) *adv., a.,* & *n.* **1.** *adv.* To or at a distance (lit. or fig.) from the place, person, thing, in question (*go away*; *throw it away*; *give it away*; *he is away*); FAR[1] *and away*; **out and** ~, by far; PUT[1] *away*; **turn** ~ (in another direction). **2.** Towards or into non-existence (*sound dies away*; *explain it away*; *idle* one's *time away*). **3.** Constantly, persistently, continuously (*laughing away*; *peg away*; *working away*). **4.** Without delay; **fire** ~, begin, go ahead; RIGHT[4] *away*; STRAIGHT *away*. **5.** ~ **with,** (*imper.*) go away with, take away; **do** ~ **with,** abolish; **get** ~ **with it,** (colloq.) do something with impunity; **make** ~ **with,** destroy. **6.** *a.* Played on opponents' ground etc. (*away match, win*). **7.** *n.* Away match or win. [OE *onweg, aweg* on (the, his, one's) way; f. A[3] + WAY]

awe *n.*, & *v.t.* **1.** *n.* Reverential fear or wonder (*stand in awe of*; *hold in awe*); ~**'stricken,** ~**'struck,** struck with awe; hence ~'SOME[1] (aw's-) *a.* **2.** *v.t.* Inspire with awe. [ME *age* f. ON *agi* f. Gmc **ag-*]

awear'ў (*a*-) *pred. a.* (poet.) Tired, weary, (*of*). [f. A- + WEARY]

awei'gh (awā') *pred. a.* (Of anchor) just lifted from ground in weighing. [f. A[3] + WEIGH]

aw'ful *a.* Inspiring awe; solemnly impressive; (colloq.) notable (esp. for badness) in its kind (*awful writing*; *has an awful lot of money*); hence ~NESS *n.* [f. AWE + -FUL]

aw'fullў *adv.* **1.** In adj. senses. **2.** (colloq., *pr.* aw'flĭ). Extremely (*an awfully nice fellow*; *thanks awfully*). [f. prec. + -LY[2]]

awhee'l (awē'l) *adv.* & *pred. a.* On wheels, esp. cycling. [f. A[3] + WHEEL[1]]

awhī'le (awī'l) *adv.* For a short time. [OE *āne hwīle* a while]

aw'kward *a.* Ill-adapted for use; clumsy

(person, thing); bungling (~ **age,** callow adolescence; *awkward* SQUAD); embarrassing; embarrassed (*felt awkward about it*); difficult or dangerous to deal with (*awkward customer, situation*); hence ~LY² *adv.*, ~NESS *n.* [f. obs. *awk* backhanded, untoward (ME, f. ON *afugr* turned the wrong way) + -WARD]

awl *n.* Small pointed tool for pricking, esp. that used by shoemakers. [OE *æl*, = OHG *ala*, ON *alr*]

awn *n.* Stiff bristle at top of grain-sheath of barley, oats, grasses, etc. [ME, f. ON *ögn* pl. *agnar*, = OHG *agana*, Goth. *ahana* chaff]

aw'nĭng *n.* Sheet of canvas etc. as shelter against sun or rain, esp. on ship's deck. [17th c. (Naut.), of uncert. orig.]

awō'ke, -en, (*a*-). See AWAKE¹.

AWOL (ā'wŏl) *abbr.* absent without leave.

awrȳ' (*a*rī') *adv.* & *a.* **1.** *adv.* Crookedly, askew; amiss, improperly; **go** ~, go or do wrong. **2.** *a.* (usu. *pred.*) Crooked (lit. or fig.). [ME, f. A³ + WRY]

ăxe, *ăx, *n.*, & *v.t.* **1.** *n.* Chopping-tool, usu. of iron with steel edge and wooden handle (~ **to grind,** private ends to serve); drastic reduction or elimination of expenditure, staff, etc.; ~**-breaker,** hard-wooded Austral. tree. **2.** *v.t.* Cut down drastically (costs, services); remove, eliminate, dismiss. [OE *æx*, = OS *akus*, OHG *ackus*, ON *öx*, Goth. *aqizi* f. Gmc **akuwizjō*, **akuzjō*]

ă'xel *n.* Jumping movement in skating. [f. *Axel* R. Paulsen, Norw. skater d. 1938]

axes. *Pl.* of AXE or AXIS¹.

ă'xĭal *a.* Forming or belonging to an axis; round an axis (*axial rotation, symmetry*); hence ~ITY (-ă'l-) *n.*, ~LY² *adv.* [f. AXIS¹ + -AL]

ă'xĭl *n.* Upper angle between leaf and stem it springs from, or between branch and trunk. [f. L AXILLA]

ăxĭ'lla *n.* (*pl.* ~*e*). Armpit; axil. [L, = armpit, dim. of *ala*, **acsla*, wing]

ă'xĭllarȳ *a.* Pertaining to the armpit; (Bot.) in or growing from the axil. [f. AXILLA + -ARY¹]

ăxĭo'log|ȳ *n.* (Philos.) Theory of value; hence **ăxĭo**LO'GICAL *a.*, ~IST (3) *n.* [f. F *axiologie* f. Gk *axia* value; see -LOGY]

ă'xĭom *n.* Established principle; (esp. Geom.) self-evident truth. [f. F *axiome* or f. L f. Gk *axiōma* (*axios* worthy)]

ăxĭomă't|ĭc *a.* Self-evident; characterized by axioms; hence ~ICALLY *adv.* [f. Gk *axiomatikos* (*axiōma -matos*; see prec., -IC)]

ă'xĭs¹ *n.* (*pl.* **a'xes** *pr.* -ēz). **1.** Imaginary line about which a body rotates; imaginary line by revolution about which a plane figure is conceived as generating a solid; line dividing regular figure symmetrically. **2.** Fixed reference line for measurement of co-ordinates etc. **3.** (Bot.) Central column of inflorescence or other growth. **4.** (Anat.) Second cervical vertebra. **5.** Central part of organ or organism. **6.** (Polit. etc.) Agreement or alliance between two or more countries intended to form a centre round which like-minded nations may rally; **the A~,** (Hist.) (alliance of 1939 between) Germany and Italy, later extended to include Japan and other countries. [L, = axle, pivot]

ă'xĭs² *n.* White-spotted deer (*Axis axis*) of S. Asia. [L]

ă'xle *n.* Spindle upon or with which wheel revolves; rod connecting pair of wheels of vehicle (orig. ~**-tree**). [earliest in ME *axel-tre* f. ON *öxull-tré*]

A'xmĭnster (ă'-) *n.* ~ **carpet,** machine-woven tufted kind with cut pile. [~ in Devon]

ă'xolŏtl *n.* Newtlike amphibian found in Mexican lakes. [Nahuatl (*atl* water, *xolotl* servant)]

ă'xŏn *n.* (Anat. & Zool.) Long appendage of nerve cell, usu. carrying signals from it. [mod. L, f. Gk *axōn* axis]

ay¹, aye¹, (ī) *adv.* & *n.* (*pl.* **ayes** *pr.* īz). **1.** *adv.* (esp. arch., dial., Naut., or in formal voting). Yes. **2.** *n.* Affirmative answer or vote; **the ayes have it,** affirmative voters are in majority. [16th c.; prob. f. pron. *I* expr. assent]

ay² *int.* ~ **me!** (expr. regret, sorrow, or pity). [ME; *ay me!* prob. after OF *aimi* etc.]

ay'ah (ī'*a*) *n.* Native nurse or maidservant esp. of Europeans in India etc. [Anglo-Ind., f. Port. *aia* nurse, fem. of *aio* tutor]

aye¹ (ī). See AY¹.

aye² (ā) *adv.* (arch.) Ever, always; at all times; **for** ~, for ever. [ME, f. ON *ei*, *ey*, cogn. w. Goth. *aiws* age, eternity, f. Gmc **aiwaz*]

ay'e-aye (ī'ī) *n.* Squirrel-like cat-sized nocturnal tree-climbing lemur of Madagascar. [F, f. Malagasy *aiay*]

Ay'lesburȳ (ā'lzb-) *n.* (Bird of) breed of white domestic ducks. [~ in Buckinghamshire]

Ayr'shire (ār'-) *n.* (Animal of) breed of mainly white dairy cattle. [former Scottish county]

azā'lėa *n.* Flowering shrubby plant of genus or subgenus *Azalea*. [mod. L f. Gk, fem. of *azaleos* dry (from the dry soil in which Linnaeus believed that it flourished)]

azē'otrōpe *n.* (Chem.) Mixture of liquids with boiling-point remaining constant during distillation; hence **azēotrŏ'p**IC *a.* [f. A- 7 + Gk *zeō* boil + *tropos* turning]

Azĭ'lĭan (*a*-) *a.* & *n.* (Of) the transitional period between the palaeolithic and neolithic ages in Europe. [f. Mas d'*Azil* in French Pyrenees]

ă'zĭmuth *n.* Arc of celestial great circle from zenith to horizon; arc of horizon between north or south point and point where the great circle passing through a heavenly body and the zenith cuts the horizon; hence **ăzĭmū'th**AL *a.* [ME, f. OF *azimut* f. Arab. *as-sumūt* (*al* the, *sumūt* pl. of *samt* way, direction)]

ă'zō- *pref.* (Chem.) Containing two adjacent nitrogen atoms between carbon atoms. [f. F *azote* nitrogen f. Gk *a-* not + *zōō* live]

azō'ĭc *a.* Having no trace of life; (Geol.) containing no organic remains. [irreg. f. Gk *azōos* (*a-* not, *zōē* life) + -IC]

A'ztĕc (ă'-) *a.* & *n.* (One) of the native people dominant in Mexico till the conquest by Cortes (1519); (of) their language. [f. F *Aztèque* or Sp. *Azteca* f. Nahuatl *aztecatl* men of the north]

ă'zūre (*or* -zh*er or* -zhyer) *n.* & *a.* **1.** *n.* Sky blue; (Her.) blue; unclouded vault of heaven. **2.** *a.* Sky-blue; (Her., usu. after *n.*) blue; (fig.) cloudless, serene. [ME, f. OF *asur*, *azur* f. med. L *azzurum*, *azolum* f. Arab. *al* the + *lāzaward* f. Pers. *lāžward* lapis lazuli]

ă'zȳgous *a.* & *n.* (Anat.) (Organic part) not existing in pairs. [f. Gk *azugos* unyoked (*a-* not, *zugon* yoke) + -OUS]

B

B, b, (bē) *n.* (*pl.* **Bs** *or* **B's**). Second letter of alphabet; (Mus.) seventh note in diatonic scale of C major; second hypothetical person or example; second highest class (of road, academic marks, population as regards affluence, etc.); (Alg., usu. *b*) second known quantity; **B film** (made for use as supporting feature in cinema programme).

B. *abbr.* Bachelor; bel(s); bishop; black (pencil-lead); Blessed.

b. *abbr.* bay horse; born; bowled by; bye.

B *symb.* boron.

B.A. *abbr.* Bachelor of Arts; British Academy; British Association.

Ba *symb.* barium.

baa (bah) *n.*, & *v.i.* (**~ed** *or* **~'d** *pr.* bahd). (Esp. of sheep) bleat; **~-lamb,** childish name for lamb. [imit.]

B.A.A. *abbr.* British Airports Authority.

Bā'al *n.* (*pl.* **~im**). Phoenician and Canaanite god; false god; hence ~ISM (3) *n.* [ME, f. Heb. *ba'al* lord]

baas (bahs) *n.* (S. Afr.) Master (freq. as *voc.*). [Du.; cf. BOSS[2]]

baa'sskap (bah'skahp) *n.* (S. Afr.) Domination, esp. of non-whites by whites. [Afrik.]

ba'ba (bah'bah) *n.* (**Rum**) **~**, rich sponge-cake soaked in rum syrup. [F]

ba'bacōōte (bah'-) *n.* Woolly lemur of Madagascar, indri. [f. Malagasy *babakoto*]

bă'bbĭtt[1] *n.* Soft alloy of tin, antimony, copper, and usu. lead; bearing-lining made of this. [f. I. *Babbitt*, Amer. inventor d. 1862]

Bă'bbĭtt[2] *n.* Materialistic complacent businessman; hence ~RY (4) *n.* [character in & title of novel (1922) by S. Lewis]

bă'bble[1] *v.* **1.** *v.i.* Talk half-articulately, foolishly, incoherently, or excessively; (of stream etc.) murmur. **2.** *v.t.* Divulge or repeat foolishly; reveal (secret). **3.** Hence ~MENT (-belm-) *n.* [ME, f. MLG *babbelen*, or imit.]

bă'bble[2] *n.* Imperfect, foolish, or childish speech; idle talk; murmur of water etc.; (Teleph.) unwanted interference from several other conversations. [f. prec.]

bă'bbler *n.* Chatterer; teller of secrets; one of a large group of passerine birds with loud chattering voices. [f. BABBLE[1] + -ER[1]]

bābe *n.* **1.** (poet.) Young child, baby. **2.** Inexperienced or guileless person (in *pl.* often *babes and sucklings, babes in the wood*); MILK[1] *for babes.* **3.** *(sl.) Young woman. [ME, imit. of child's *ba, ba*]

bā'bel *n.* Scene of confusion; confusion of tongues; noisy assembly; meaningless noise; **tower of B~,** visionary plan. [ME, f. Heb. *bābel* Babylon f. Akkad. *bāb ili* gate of god; ref. to Gen. 11]

Ba'b|ĭ (bah'-) *n.* (Member of) Persian eclectic sect founded in 1844; = BAHA'I; hence ~ISM (3), ~IST (2), *ns.* [f. Pers. *Bab*-ed-Din, gate (= intermediary) of the Faith, whence the founder's usual title of (the) *Bab*]

băbĭrou'ssa, -ru'sa, -ru'ssa, (-rōō'-) *n.* E. Ind. wild hog with upturned hornlike tusks. [f. Malay *bābi* hog + *rūsa* deer]

baboo. See BABU.

babōō'n *n.* Large African and Arabian monkey with doglike snout; ugly or uncouth person. [ME, f. OF *babuin* or med. L *babewynus*, of unkn. orig.]

babou'che (-ōō'sh) *n.* Oriental heelless slipper. [F, f. Arab. *bābūj* f. Pers. *pāpūš* (*pā* foot, *pūš* covering)]

ba'bu, ba'boo, (bah'bōō) *n.* (Ind.) title of respect, esp. to Hindus; (Hist., derog.) English-writing Indian clerk; **~ English** (ornate and somewhat unidiomatic). [f. Hindi *bābū*]

babu'l (-ōō'l) *n.* Thorny mimosa of India. [Urdu & Pers.]

babu'shka (-ōō'-) *n.* Head-scarf tied under chin. [Russ., = grandmother]

bā'bȳ *n.*, & *v.t.* **1.** *n.* Very young child, esp. one unable to walk; **carry** or **hold the ~,** bear unwelcome responsibility; **it's your ~,** you must deal with it; **throw away the ~ with the bathwater,** reject essential with inessential; hence ~HOOD *n.* **2.** Youngest member (*of* family, team, etc.); unduly childish person, whence ~ISH[1] *a.*; animal or thing small of its kind; (sl.) young woman, sweetheart; (sl.) person or thing. **3. ~-bouncer,** = *baby-jumper*; ***~ buggy,** pram; **~ car,** motor car of small size and power; **~ carriage,** pram; **~-face,** (person having) smooth rounded face like baby's; **~-farmer,** (usu. derog.) person who looks after babies for payment; **~ grand,** small grand piano; ||**~-jumper,** hanging frame on springs, in which child is fastened to exercise limbs; **~-sit** *v.i.*, act as **~-sitter,** person looking after child while its parents are out; **~-talk,** imperfect speech as used by or to young children; **~-walker,** device for helping baby learning to walk. **4.** *v.t.* Treat like baby. [ME, f. as BABE, -Y[3]]

Bă'bȳlon *n.* (rhet.) Great and luxurious city; so **Băbȳlō'n**IAN *a.* [L, f. Gk *Babulōn* capital of Chaldea, f. Heb. *bābel*]

B.A.C. *abbr.* British Aircraft Corporation.

băccalaur'eate *n.* University degree of bachelor. [f. F. *baccalauréat* or f. med. L *baccalaureatus* (*baccalaureus* bachelor; see -ATE[1])]

bă'ccarat (-rah) *n.* Gambling card game, played by punters in turn against banker. [F]

bă'ccāte *a.* (Bot.) Bearing berries; berry-shaped. [f. L *baccatus* berried (*bacca* berry; see -ATE[2])]

Bă'cchanal (-ka-) *a.* & *n.* **1.** *a.* Of or like Bacchus (Greek and Roman god of wine) or his rites; riotous, roistering. **2.** *n.* Priest, priestess, votary, of Bacchus; noisy or drunken reveller or revelry. [f. L *bacchanalis* (*Bacchus* f. Gk *Bakkhos* god of wine; see -AL)]

Băcchanā'lĭ|a (-ka-) *n. pl.* Festival of Bacchus; drunken revelry; so ~AN *a.* & *n.*, riotous or drunken (person). [L, neut. pl. of *bacchanalis* (see prec.)]

Bă'cchant (-ka-) *n.* (*pl.* **~s,** *or* **~es** *pr.* bakă'ntēz) & *a.*, **Bacchante** (bă'kant, bakă'nt, bakă'ntĭ) *n. fem.* Bacchanal; hence **Bacchă'nt**IC (-kă'-) *a.* [f. F *bacchante* f. L *bacchari* celebrate Bacchanal rites]

Bă'cchĭc (-kĭk) *a.* Bacchanal. [f. L f. Gk *bakkhikos* of Bacchus; see -IC]

||**bă'ccȳ** (-kĭ) *n.* (colloq.) Tobacco. [abbr.]

băch *n.*, & *v.i.* (colloq.) **1.** *n.* (N.Z.) Small hut or seaside house. **2.** *v.i.* Live as bachelor. [abbr.]

bă'chelor *n.* Unmarried man; (Hist.) young knight serving under another's banner (**knight**

~, knight not belonging to a special order); man or woman who has taken university etc. degree below that of Master (usu. the first degree in a faculty); **~'s button(s)**, one of various button-shaped flowers, esp. double buttercup; **~ flat** (suitable for unmarried person); **~ girl** (unmarried and living independently); **~ (seal)**, young male fur-seal with no mate; hence ~HOOD, ~SHIP, *ns.* [ME & OF *bacheler* aspirant to knighthood, f. Rom. **baccalaris*, in med. L altered to *baccalaureus*, w. pun on *bacca lauri* laurel berry]

baci'llary̆ *a.* Relating to or caused by bacilli. [f. BACILLUS + -ARY[1]]

baci'llifôrm *a.* Rod-shaped. [f. as foll. + -I- + -FORM]

baci'll|us *n.* (*pl.* **~i** *pr.* -ī). Rod-shaped bacterium, esp. one that causes disease by entering and multiplying in animal and other tissues; (loosely, usu. in *pl.*) any pathogenic bacterium. [LL, dim. of L *baculus* stick]

băck[1] *n.* & *a.* **1.** *n.* Hinder surface of human body from shoulders to hips; **at the ~ of,** behind in support, pursuit, or concealment; **~ to ~**, with backs adjoining and opposite each other (e.g. of houses), (fig.) in succession; BEHIND person's *back*; **get** or **put** person's **~ up,** make him angry or stubborn; **give** or **make a ~**, bend down for leapfrog or wall-climbing; **on** one's **~**, ill in bed; SEE[1] *the back of*; **turn** one's **~ on,** run away from, abandon, ignore; **with** one's **~ to the wall,** at bay, hard pressed. **2.** Body as needing clothes or as weight-carrier; BREAK[1] one's *back*; **have on** one's **~**, be burdened with or harassed by; **put** one's **~ into,** use all one's efforts on. **3.** Surface of things corresponding to human back; **~** (outer surface) **of hand** (*know like the ~ of* one's *hand,* be entirely familiar with); **~** (rear surface) **of head, leg;** less active or important part; **~ of book,** spine or final pages; **~ of knife,** non-cutting edge. **4.** Upper surface of animal's body; similar ridge-shaped surface (*back of hill*); **~ of ship,** keel (*broke her back*). **5.** Side or part normally more remote or away from spectator or direction of motion (*back of car, chair, door, house, mouth*); **at the ~ of** one's **mind,** in memory but not consciously thought of; *talk through the back of* one's NECK[1]; *back of* BEYOND; ***in ~ (of),** behind. **6.** Part of dress covering back from shoulders to waist; hence ~'LESS *a.*, (of dress) low-cut at back. **7. The B~s,** grounds on the Cam at back of some Cambridge colleges. **8.** (Position of) defensive player in football etc. **9. ~'ache,** pain in the back; **~'board** (esp. worn to support or straighten the back); **~'bone,** spine (*of book), (fig.) main support, firmness of character; *to the ~bone,* thoroughly; **~-breaking,** extremely laborious; **~'rest,** support for the back; **~'scratcher,** implement for scratching one's own back, (fig.) one who performs mutual services for gain; **~'slapping,** (fig.) vigorously hearty; **~'stroke** (made by swimmer lying on back). **10.** *a.* (no compar.; superl. **~'most**). Situated behind (*back street, teeth*); (Cricket) of playing BACK[3]; of the past; remote; inferior; overdue (*back pay*); reversed (*back flow*); (Phonet.) formed at back of mouth. **11.** ‖**~-be'nch(er)**, (occupant of) seat in House of Commons etc. used by member not entitled to sit on front bench; **~'blocks,** (Austral., N.Z., etc.) land in remote and sparsely-inhabited interior; ‖**~-boiler** (behind domestic fire or cooking range); **~'chat,** (colloq.) impudent repartee; ‖**~'cloth,** (Theatr.) painted cloth at back of stage as main part of scenery; **~ country,** (Austral., N.Z., etc.) area away from settled districts; **~ door,** (fig.) secret means of approach; **~-door** *a.*, (fig.) clandestine, underhand; **~'drop,** backcloth; **~'ground,** part of scene, picture, or description, that serves as setting to chief figures or objects and foreground, (fig.) obscurity or retirement, (fig.) person's cultural knowledge, education, experience, etc., information needed to understand problem etc., (Phys.) radiation from natural sources, (Radio) adventitiously received signals; *~ground heating* (for general warmth); *~ground music* (used as accompaniment to film etc.); **~'hand,** (Tennis etc.) (stroke) played with back of hand in direction of opponent; **~-ha'nded,** delivered with back of hand or in opposite of usual direction, indirect, ambiguous (*backhanded compliment*); **~'hander,** backhand stroke, backhanded blow, indirect attack, (sl.) bribe; **~'list,** publisher's list of books still in print; **~'log,** reserves, arrears of unfulfilled orders, uncompleted work, etc.; **~'marker,** scratch man in race etc.; **~ number,** old issue of magazine etc., (sl.) out-of-date method or person; ***~'pack** *n.*, & *v.i.*, (travel with) rucksack etc.; *back* PASSAGE[1]; **~ room,** (fig.) place where (secret) research is done; **~ seat,** (fig., colloq.) inferior or unimportant position; *~-seat driver*, one who rides in back seat of motor car and gives unwanted advice to its driver, (fig.) one who attempts to control without responsibility; **~'side,** buttocks; **~'sight,** that nearer stock of rifle etc., (Surv.) sight taken backwards; **~ slang,** form of slang in which words are spelt and pronounced backwards; **~'stage** *a.* & *adv.*, (Theatr.) behind the curtain, esp. in wings or dressing-rooms, (fig.) behind the scenes; **~ stairs, ~-stair(s)** *a.*, (fig.) = *back-door*; **~'stay,** rope etc. downwards and aft from top of mast; ***~ talk,** backchat; **~'veld,** (S. Afr.) back country; **~'water,** still water beside stream and fed by its back flow, (fig.) (condition or place of) intellectual stagnation; **~'woods,** wholly or partly uncleared forest, remote or sparsely inhabited region; **~'woodsman,** inhabitant of backwoods, uncouth person, ‖(fig.) peer who rarely or never attends the House of Lords; **~'yard,** yard at back of house, (fig.) somewhere easily accessible (esp. one's *own backyard*). [OE *bæc*, = OS, ON *bak*, f. Gmc **bakam*]

băck[2] *v.* **1.** *v.t.* Act as or put a back, lining, support, or background, to; assist with money or argument, bet on success of, whence ~'ER[1] *n.*; lie at back of; countersign, endorse. **2.** Cause (horse, boat, car, etc.) to move back; **~ water,** reverse boat's forward motion with oars. **3.** *v.i.* Go backwards; ***~ and fill,** move to and fro, vacillate. **4.** (Of wind) change direction counter-clockwise (cf. VEER[2]). **5. ~ down,** abandon claim; so *~-down* n.; **~ out,** (fig.) withdraw; **~ up,** help by subordinate action, (of running water) accumulate behind obstruction, *form queue of vehicles etc., *reverse (vehicle); *~-up* n., support, spare or reserve, *queue of vehicles etc. (**~-up light*, reversing light). [f. prec.]

băck[3] *adv.* **1.** To the rear; away from what is considered the front; **~ and forth,** to and fro; ***~ of,** behind; **play ~**, (Cricket) step back to play defensive stroke. **2.** Away from a promise (*go back on* one's *word*); in or into the past or an earlier or normal position or condition; home (*will be back at six*). **3.** In return (*pay back*); ANSWER[2] *back*; GET[1] *back*. **4.** At a distance (*back from the road*); in check (*keep back from*). **5. ~'bite** *v.t.*, slander, speak ill of; hence **~'biter; ~'comb** *v.t.*, comb (under-hair) back towards scalp; **~'date** *v.t.*, put earlier date to, make retrospectively valid; **~-fill,** replace excavated earth etc. round foundations etc. placed in hole made; **~'fire,** premature explosion in cylinder or explosion in exhaust-pipe of vehicle engine; **~fir'e** *v.i.*, undergo backfire, (of plan etc.) recoil on originator, have opposite effect to what was intended; **~ formation,** (word got by) making from an existing supposed derivative (as *automation, lazy, pedlar*) a previously non-existent word (*automate, laze, peddle*) from which it might have come; **~'lash,** irregular recoil in machinery, excessive play between parts of machine, (fig.) excessive or violent reaction; **~-pe'dal** *v.i.*, work pedal backwards, (fig.) reverse one's previous action; **~-projection** (of picture from behind transparent screen for viewing or filming); **~-scattering** (of radiation in reverse direction); **~'slide** *v.i.*, relapse into sin or error; **~'space** *v.i.*, cause typewriter carriage to move backwards one space; **~'-stitch** *n.*, & *v.t.* & *i.*, sew(ing) with overlapping stitches; **~'track** *v.i.*, (fig.) = *back-pedal*; **~'-wash,** motion of receding wave, repercussions. [f. ABACK]

băckgă'mmon *n.* Game for two, played on special double board with dice and pieces like draughtsmen; most complete form of win in this. [f. BACK³ (because pieces go back or re-enter) + GAMMON²]

bă'cking *n.* In vbl senses; body of supporters; material used to form thing's back or support; accompaniment to a singer. [f. BACK² + -ING¹]

bă'cksheesh. Var. of BAKSHEESH.

bă'ckward(s) (-dz) *adv.*, **bă'ckward** *a.* **1.** *adv.* Away from one's front (*look, lean*, etc. *backwards*; **bend, fall, lean, over ~**, go to opposite extreme, do one's utmost (*to agree* etc.)); back foremost (*walk* etc. *backwards*); (of thing's motion) back to starting-point (*flow, roll*, etc. *backward*); **~ and forwards,** in both directions alternately, to and fro. **2.** Into a worse state (*go* etc. *backward*); into the past (*reckon* etc. *backwards*); reverse way (*spell* etc. *backwards*); **know ~**, be entirely familiar with; **ring the bells ~** (from bass upwards). **3.** *a.* Directed to rear or starting-point; reversed; reluctant, shy; behindhand, dull; hence **bă'ckward**NESS *n.* [f. *abackward*, later assoc. w. BACK¹; see -WARD(s)]

‖**băckwardā'tion** *n.* Percentage paid by seller of stock for right of delaying delivery (cf. CONTANGO). [f. prec. used as v. + -ATION]

bā'con *n.* (Piece of) cured back or side of pig; **bring home the ~**, (colloq.) succeed in one's undertaking; **save** one's **~**, escape death or injury. [ME f. OF, f. Frank. *bako* = OHG *bahho* ham, flitch, f. Gmc **bakkon-*]

Bācō'nĭan *a.* & *n.* **1.** *a.* Of Bacon or his philosophy; experimental, inductive. **2.** *n.* Follower of Bacon; believer that Bacon was author of Shakespeare's plays. [f. Francis *Bacon*, Engl. philosopher d. 1626 + -IAN]

băctērĭŏ'log|ȳ *n.* Science of bacteria; hence **băctērĭo**LO'GICAL *a.* (**~ical warfare,** deliberate use of bacteria to spread disease among enemy), ~IST (3) *n.* [f. BACTERIUM + -O- + -LOGY]

băctērĭ|ŏ'lȳsĭs *n.* (*pl.* **~o'lyses** *pr.* -ēz). Destruction of bacteria by antibodies; so **~olȳ'tic** *a.*, capable of destroying bacteria. [f. BACTERIUM + -O- + -LYSIS]

băctēr'iophāge (*or* -fahzh) *n.* Virus which destroys bacteria. [F, f. as foll. + Gk *phagein* eat]

băctērĭo|stă'sĭs *n.* (*pl.* **~sta'ses** *pr.* -ēz). Inhibition of growth of bacteria without destroying them; hence ~STA'TIC *a.* [f. foll. + -O- + -STASIS]

băctēr'|ĭum *n.* (*pl.* **~ia**). Microscopic unicellular plant of widely distributed class, esp. of kind which causes disease; hence ~IAL *a.*, ~ĬCIDE (1) *n.* [mod. L, f. Gk *baktērion* dim. of *baktron* stick]

Bă'ctrĭan *a.* Of Bactria in central Asia; **~ camel** (with two humps). [f. L f. Gk *Baktrianos*; see -AN]

băd *a.* & *adv.* (WORSE, WORST) & *n.* **1.** *a.* Worthless (*bad cheque*); inferior; deficient (*bad light*); of poor quality (*bad driver, English, liar*); incorrect, not valid; counterfeit or debased (*bad* PENNY); unpleasant (*bad breath, weather*). **2.** *Bad* BOOK¹*s*, BREAK²; **~ debt** (not recoverable); *bad* EGG¹, FAITH, FORM¹; *with a bad* GRACE; ‖*bad* HAT; *bad* JOB¹; ***~ lands,** extensive uncultivable eroded tracts; **~ law** (not sustainable); *bad* LOT; **in a ~ sense** (unfavourable); *bad* TEMPER²; **go ~**, decay; **not ~, not half ~, not so ~**, (colloq.) fairly or very good; **too ~**, (colloq.) regrettable. **3.** Noxious (*sweets are bad for your teeth*); wicked (***~ man,** desperado; ***~ mouth,** malicious gossip or criticism); offensive (*bad* LANGUAGE); painful (**~ blood,** ill feeling; **a ~ business,** an unfortunate matter; **~ news,** unwelcome news); in ill health, injured, in pain, (*she is bad, worse, today*; *a bad leg*); **in a ~ way,** ill or in trouble. **4.** (colloq., of things in no case good). Notable, decided, pronounced, (*bad accident, blunder, headache*). **5.** (colloq.) Regretful (*feel bad about it*). **6.** Hence **~'dish**¹ 2 *a.*, **~'dy**³ *n.*, (colloq.) criminal, villain, ~'LY² *adv.* (WORSE, WORST), (esp.) by much (*badly beaten*), very much (*want a thing badly*; *hair badly needs cutting*), (colloq.) regretfully (*feel badly about it*), ~'NESS *n.* **7.** *adv.* *(colloq.) Badly. **8.** *n.* Ill fortune (*take the bad with the good*); debit side of account (*£500 to the bad*); ruin (*go to the bad*); **in ~**, (colloq.) in disfavour *with*; *from bad to* WORSE. [ME, perh. f. OE *bæddel* hermaphrodite, womanish man; for loss of *l* cf. MUCH, WENCH]

băde. See BID¹.

bădge *n.* Distinctive mark worn as sign of office or achievement or licensed employment or membership of a society; symbol; thing that reveals a quality or condition. [ME, of unkn. orig.]

bă'dger *n.*, & *v.t.* **1.** *n.* Grey-coated strong-jawed fiercely defensive nocturnal burrowing hibernating plantigrade mammal of weasel family; fishing-fly, or painting or other brush, made of its hair; **~-baiting,** setting dogs to draw badger from its burrow or from a cask; ***B~ State,** Wisconsin. **2.** *v.t.* Pester as dogs worry a badger; torment, tease. [16th c., perh. f. BADGE + -ARD, w. ref. to its white forehead mark]

badinage (bă'dĭnahzh) *n.* Humorous ridicule. [F (*badiner* to joke)]

ba'dmash (bŭ'dmahsh) *n.* (Ind.) Rascal, hooligan. [Pers. & Urdu]

bă'dmĭnton *n.* **1.** Summer drink of claret, soda, and sugar. **2.** Game with net, rackets, and shuttlecock. [*B~* in Avon]

Bae'dėker (bā'd-) *n.* Guidebook published by firm founded by Karl *Baedeker* (d. 1859); **~ raids,** German reprisal air raids in 1942 on places in England of cultural and historical importance.

bā'el *n.* Thorny Indian tree with aromatic orange-like fruit. [f. Hindi *bel*, Marathi *bail*]

bă'ffle *v.t.*, & *n.* **1.** *v.t.* Frustrate, reduce to perplexity, (person, curiosity, faculties); stop progress of (efforts, ship); hence ~MENT (-felm-) *n.* **2.** *n.* State of being baffled; **~(-plate), bă'ffl**ER¹, plate hindering or regulating passage of fluid or gas or radiation through outlet or inlet (e.g. a damper); **~-board,** device to prevent spread of sound, esp. round loudspeaker cone to improve tone. [perh. conn. w. F *bafouer* ridicule, OF *beffer* mock]

băg¹ *n.* **1.** Receptacle of flexible material with closable opening at top (esp. w. prefixed word showing contents or purpose; DIPLOMATIC *bag*,

GAME[1]*bag*, HAND[1]*bag*, KIT[1]*bag*, *mailbag*, *travelling-bag*, VANITY *bag*); (w. such prefix understood) particular kind of this; hence ~'FUL 2 *n.* **2.** Contents of bag; MIXED *bag*; amount of game a sportsman has shot or caught (also fig.). **3.** **~ and baggage,** with all belongings; **~ of bones,** lean creature; **(whole) ~ of tricks,** every device, everything, the whole lot; ***hold the ~,** = *hold the* BABY; **in the ~,** (colloq.) in one's possession or power, (as good as) secured; *let the* CAT[1] *out of the bag.* **4.** (in *pl.*, sl.) Wealth, large amount, plenty; ||trousers. **5.** Sac in animal body containing honey, poison, etc.; baggy place under eye etc.; (sl., derog.) woman (*old bag*); (sl.) distinctive mode of behaviour, esp. in playing jazz; (sl.) one's current interest. **6.** **~'man,** commercial traveller, (Austral.) tramp, *(sl.) agent who collects or distributes money for illicit purposes; **~'pipe(s),** reed-pipe wind instrument with bag as receptacle for air, melody pipe (chanter), and fixed-note pipes (drones), used in Scotland and elsewhere; ||**~'wash,** (laundry that undertakes) rough unfinished washing of clothes; **~-wig,** 18th-c. wig with back hair enclosed in bag. [ME, perh. f. ON *baggi*, of unkn. orig.]

băg[2] *v.* (-gg-). **1.** *v.t.* & *i.* (Cause to) swell, bulge, or hang loosely. **2.** *v.t.* Put in a bag, secure (game, whether lit. bagged or not), take possession of (*bag the best chair*), (euphem.) steal; ||(school sl.) claim on the ground of being first to do so (usu. *bags I, bags first innings!*, etc.). [f. prec.]

băg[3] *v.t.* (-gg-). Cut (wheat etc.) with reaping-hook. [17th c., also *badge*; orig. unkn.]

bagarre (bahgar̄') *n.* Scuffle, brawl. [F]

bagă'sse *n.* Residue after extraction of juice from sugar-cane or sugar-beet. [F, f. mod. Prov. *bagasso*]

băgatĕ'lle *n.* Trifle, negligible amount; (Mus.) short unpretentious piece; game in which small balls are struck into numbered holes on board with semicircular end. [F, f. It. *bagatella* dim., perh. f. *baga* BAGGAGE]

***bā'gel** (-g-) *n.* Hard ring-shaped bread roll. [f. Yiddish *beygel*]

bă'ggage *n.* **1.** Belongings with which one travels by sea or air (*or land); BAG[1] *and baggage*; ***~ car,** luggage van; ***~ check,** luggage ticket; ***~ room,** cloakroom; ***~ tag,** luggage label. **2.** Portable equipment of army; (fig.) mental equipment etc. **3.** (joc.) Good-for-nothing woman, saucy girl. [ME, f. OF *bagage* (*baguer* tie up or *bagues* bundles, perh. rel. to BAG[1]; see -AGE)]

bă'gg|y̆ (-gĭ) *a.* Puffed out, hanging in loose folds; hence **~ĭNESS** *n.* [f. BAG[1] + -Y[2]]

ba'gnio (bah'nyō) *n.* (*pl.* **~s**). Oriental prison; brothel. [f. It. *bagno* f. L *balneum* bath]

băguĕ'tte (-gĕ't) *n.* (Archit.) small moulding of semicircular section, like astragal; gem cut in long rectangular shape; long narrow French loaf. [F, f. It. *bacchetto* dim. of *bacchio* f. L *baculum* staff]

bah *int.* expr. contempt. [prob. f. F]

Baha'dur (bahah'-) *n.* Title of respect appended in India to a person's name (and to other titles). [Hindi, = hero]

Baha'|ī (bah-hah'ĭ) *n.* Religious faith developed from BABI by Bahá'u'lláh (d. 1892), emphasizing unity of mankind and its religions, and seeking world peace; hence ~ISM (3), ~IST (2), ~ITE[1] (1), *ns.* [f. Pers. *bahā* splendour]

baignoire (bā'nwar̄) *n.* Box at theatre on level of stalls. [F, = bath-tub]

bail[1] *n.* **1.** Security for prisoner's appearance for trial; **forfeit** or ***jump** one's **~,** fail to appear for trial after being bailed; **give leg ~,** (joc.) run away; **~'sman** (-z-), one who gives bail for another. **2.** Person(s) acting as surety for prisoner's appearance for trial; **go ~ for,** (fig.) guarantee truth of. [ME f. OF *bail* custody (*bailler* take charge of f. L *bajulare* bear a burden f. *bajulus* carrier)]

bail[2] *v.t.* **1.** Deliver (goods) in trust for a purpose; hence ~EE', ~'OR, *ns.* **2.** (Of magistrate etc.) release on security given for appearance; secure liberation of, by becoming bail or security for; **~ out,** thus liberate prisoner, (fig.) release from difficulty. **3.** So ~'ABLE *a.*, ~'MENT *n.* [f. OF *bailler*; see prec.]

bail[3] *n.* **1.** (Hist.) Outer line of fortification; wall of castle or court within it. **2.** Bar separating horses in open stable; (Cricket) one of two cross pieces over stumps; bar on typewriter holding paper against platen. [ME, f. OF *bail(e)*, perh. f. *bailler* enclose, of unkn. orig.]

bail[4] *n.* Hoop-handle of kettle, pail, etc.; (esp. Austral.) frame holding cow's head at milking. [ME, prob. f. ON *beygla* (*beygja* to bend, bow)]

bail[5] *v.* (Austral.) **1.** *v.t.* **~ up,** secure (cow; see prec.); (of bushranger) make (person) hold up the arms to be robbed; buttonhole (person). **2.** *v.i.* (Of victim) throw up the arms. [perh. f. OF *bailler* enclose; cf. BAIL[3]]

bail[6], **bāle**[3], *v.* **1.** *v.t.* Scoop water out of (boat etc.); hence **bai'lER**[1] *n.*, utensil for doing this. **2.** *v.i.* **~ out,** (of airman) make emergency parachute descent from aircraft, (of surfer) leave surfboard, (fig.) = BAIL[2] *out.* [f. obs. n. *bail* bucket f. F *baille* f. Rom. **bajula* fem. of L *bajulus* carrier]

bai'ley[1] *n.* Outer wall of castle; any of its inner defensive circuits; any of the courts enclosed between these; **Old B~,** London Central Criminal Court, formerly standing in ancient bailey of city wall. [ME, var. of BAIL[3]]

Bai'ley[2] *n.* **~ bridge,** prefabricated kind made of lattice steel and designed for rapid construction. [f. Sir D. ~, Engl. engineer b. 1901, its designer]

bai'lĭe *n.* Scottish municipal councillor serving as magistrate. [ME, f. OF *bailli(s)* BAILIFF]

bai'lĭff *n.* Officer under sheriff executing writs and processes, and performing distraints and arrests; agent or steward of landlord; *official in court of law; (Hist. exc. in formal titles) sovereign's representative in a district, esp. chief officer of a hundred; first civil officer in Channel Islands. [ME, f. OF *baillif* obl. case of *baillis* f. med. L *bajulivus* f. L *bajulus* carrier, manager]

bai'lĭwĭck *n.* District or jurisdiction of bailie or bailiff; (joc.) person's sphere of operations. [f. BAILIE + WICK[2]]

bain-marie' (băn-) *n.* (*pl.* **-ns-** *pr.* same). Vessel of hot water in which cooking-pans are slowly heated; DOUBLE[1] *boiler.* [F, transl. med. L *balneum Mariae* transl. Gk *kaminos Marias* furnace of Mary (supposed Jewish alchemist)]

Baira'm (bīrah'm) *n.* One of two annual Muslim festivals (**Lesser** and **Greater ~**). [Turk. & Pers.]

bairn *n.* (Sc., N. Engl., or literary). Child. [OE *bearn*, = OS, OHG, ON *barn*, f. Gmc **barnam*, conn. w. **beran* BEAR[3]]

bait[1] *v.* **1.** *v.t.* Torment (chained animal) by setting dogs at it; torment (helpless person) with jeers etc. **2.** (arch.) Give food to (horses on journey). **3.** Put (real or sham) food on or in (hook, trap, fishing-place). **4.** *v.i.* (arch.) Stop on journey to take food or rest. [ME, f. ON *beita* causal of *bíta* BITE[1]; sense 3 prob. f. foll.]

bait[2] *n.* Food to entice prey (**live ~,** small fish or worms so used); (fig.) an allurement, temp-

tation; (arch.) halt in journey for refreshment or rest. [partly f. ON *beita* food, partly f. prec.]
||**bait**³. See BATE².
baize *n.* Coarse usu. green woollen stuff with long nap used for coverings and linings. [f. F *baies* pl. fem. of *bai* chestnut-coloured, BAY⁶, treated as sing.; cf. BODICE]
ba'jra (bah'-) *n.* (Ind.) Pearl millet or similar grain. [Hindi]
bāke *v.* & *n.* **1.** *v.t.* Cook by dry heat in closed place or on hot surface (not by direct exposure to fire); harden by heat; (of sun) ripen (fruit), tan (skin). **2.** *v.i.* Undergo the process of being baked; be cooked, hardened, tanned, by heat. **3.** **~'apple,** (Can.) (dried) cloudberry; **~'house,** house or room for baking bread; **~d beans,** haricot beans baked and usu. tinned with tomato sauce; **~d potato** (usu. cooked in its skin); **baking-powder,** mixture of sodium bicarbonate, cream of tartar, etc., used instead of yeast to make cakes etc. rise; **baking-soda,** sodium bicarbonate. **4.** *n.* *Party, esp. for eating baked food. [OE *bacan,* = OHG *bachan,* ON *baka,* f. Gmc **bak-,* IE **bhog-*]
Bā'kelīte *n.* Plastic made from formaldehyde and phenol etc. [**P**; G *Bakelit* f. name of L. H. *Baekeland,* Belgian-Amer. inventor d. 1944; see -ITE¹ (2)]
bā'ker *n.* One who bakes and sells bread; **~'s dozen,** thirteen [13th loaf being retailer's profit]; hence **bā'kERY** (3) *n.* [OE *bæcere* (as BAKE, -ER¹)]
ba'klava (bah'-) *n.* Dessert of flaky pastry, honey, and nuts. [Turk.]
bă'ksheesh *n.* Gratuity, tip, (*give baksheesh to*); alms. [ult. f. Pers. *bakšīš* (*bakšīdan* give)]
Bălacla'va (-ah'-) *n.* **~ (helmet),** woollen covering for head and neck, worn orig. by soldiers on active service. [~ in the Crimea, site of battle (1854)]
bălalai'ka (-lī'-) *n.* Triangular-bodied guitar-like musical instrument with 2–4 strings, popular in Slav countries. [Russ.]
bă'lance¹ *n.* **1.** Weighing-apparatus with central pivot, beam, and two scales (TIP² *the balance*); spring or lever substitute for this; **~(-wheel),** speed-regulating gear of clock or watch; (*B~*) *the* zodiacal sign Libra. **2.** Weighing of actions or opinions; wavering of fortune or chance; **in the ~,** remaining uncertain. **3.** Power to decide (*hold the balance*); counterpoise, set-off; even distribution of weight or amount; **~ of mind,** sanity; **~ of nature,** constancy of conditions resulting from interaction of living things; **~ of power** (with no nation greatly preponderant). **4.** (Art etc.) Harmony of design and proportion. **5.** Steady position; **keep** one's ~, not fall; **lose** one's ~, fall physically or be upset mentally; **off** one's ~, in danger of falling. **6.** Preponderating weight or amount (*the balance of advantage lies with him*). **7.** (Accountancy). Difference between credits and debits; statement of this (STRIKE *a balance*); **~ sheet,** written statement of it with details, esp. for public company; **~ of payments,** difference of value between payments into and out of a country, including INVISIBLE items; **~ of trade,** difference between exports and imports; **on ~,** taking everything into consideration. **8.** Difference between amount due and greater amount offered (*you may keep the balance*); (colloq.) rest, remainder. [ME f. OF, f. Rom. **bilancia* f. LL (*libra*) *bilanx bilancis* two-scaled (balance) (as BI-, *lanx* scale)]
bă'lance² *v.* **1.** *v.t.* Weigh (a question, two arguments etc. against each other); match (thing) *with, by, against,* another; bring (thing, one*self,* or abs.) into, or keep in, equilibrium; equal or neutralize weight of; make up for; exclude undue preponderance of any constituent in (*balanced diet*). **2.** (Accountancy). Compare debits and credits of (account); make entry necessary to equalize them; settle (account) by paying deficit. **3.** *v.i.* Oscillate, waver; (of account) have two sides equal. [f. F *balancer* (*balance*; see prec.)]
bă'las *n.* Rose-coloured spinel ruby. [ME, f. OF *balais* f. med. L *balascus* f. Arab. *balakš* f. Pers. *Badakšān,* district of origin]
bă'lata (*or* -lah'-) *n.* Central Amer. tree of family Sapotaceae; its dried juice, used as substitute for gutta-percha. [S. Amer. Sp.]
Bălbrĭ'ggan *n.* Knitted cotton fabric used for underwear etc. [~ in Ireland, where orig. made]
bă'lconȳ *n.* External balustraded platform with access from upper-floor window; (in theatre) tier of seats above dress-circle, usu. = gallery; *dress-circle; (in cinema etc.) upstairs seats. [f. It. *balcone* prob. f. Gmc **balkon* (as BALK¹, -OON)]
bald (bawld) *a.* With scalp wholly or partly hairless (*bald as a* COOT; **go ~-headed,** (sl.) proceed (*at, for, into*) regardless of consequences); (of animal etc.) hairless, featherless, treeless, leafless, napless; (of horse etc.) marked with white, esp. on face (**~-faced**); (of tyre, colloq.) having lost its tread by wear; (of style etc.) meagre, dull, (of bad qualities) undisguised, whence ~'LY² *adv.*; **~'head, ~'pate,** (person) with bald head, white-crowned Amer. widgeon; **~'ing** *a.*, becoming bald; hence ~'NESS *n.* [ME, perh. f. **ball-* white patch + -ED²]
bă'ldachĭn, -quĭn, (-kĭn; *or* baw'-) *n.* Canopy projecting, suspended, or carried, over altar, throne, priest, etc. [orig. 'rich brocade', f. It. *baldacchino* (*Baldacco* Baghdad, its place of origin; see -INE¹)]
ba'lderdăsh (baw'l-) *n.* Jumble of words; nonsense. [earlier sense (16th c.) 'frothy liquid'; orig. unkn.]
ba'ldmoney (baw'ldmŭnĭ) *n.* Aromatic white-flowered umbelliferous mountain plant (*Meum athamanticum*). [ME in sense 'gentian'; orig. unkn.]
ba'ldrĭc (baw'l-) *n.* (Hist.) Belt for sword, bugle, etc., hung from shoulder across body to opposite hip. [ME *baudry* f. OF *baudrei*; cf. MHG *balderich*]
bāle¹ *n.* (arch. & poet.) Evil; destruction; woe, pain, misery. [OE *b(e)alu,* = OS *balu,* OHG *balo,* ON *böl* f. Gmc **balw-*]
bāle² *n.*, & *v.t.* (Make up into) package of merchandise usu. wrapped in canvas etc. and corded or hooped; quantity in bale as measure (e.g. *500 lb. of cotton). [ME, prob. f. MDu. *bale,* ult. identical w. BALL¹]
bāle³. See BAIL⁶.
balee'n *n.* & *a.* Whalebone; **~ whale,** kind that yields baleen. [ME, f. OF *baleine* f. L *balaena* whale]
bā'lefīre (-lf-) *n.* (literary). Funeral pyre; beacon-fire; bonfire. [f. OE *bǣl* & ON *bál* great fire + FIRE¹]
bā'leful (-lf-) *a.* Pernicious, destructive; malignant; hence ~LY² *adv.* [f. BALE¹ + -FUL]
bălĭbŭ'ntal *n.* (Hat of) fine close-woven straw. [f. *Baliuag buntal* (*Baliuag* in Philippines + BUNTAL)]
Balinē'se (bah-; -z) *a.* & *n.* (*pl.* same). (Native or language) of Bali. [f. *Bali* island in Indonesia + -ESE]
balk¹, **baulk**¹, (bawk *or* bawlk) *n.* Ridge left unploughed between furrows; stumbling-block, hindrance; (usu. *baulk*) area marked on billiard table where ball may be exempt from direct stroke; roughly squared timber beam;

tie-beam of house; (Baseball) illegal action of pitcher. [OE *balc* f. ON *bálkr* f. Gmc **balkuz*]

balk[2], **baulk**[2], (bawk *or* bawlk) *v.* **1.** *v.t.* Shirk, ignore, miss, (topic, turn, duty, chance); hinder, thwart, disappoint, (*balked their plans*; *baulked of his prey*). **2.** *v.i.* Jib, shy; hence ~'Y[2] *a.*, reluctant, perverse. [f. prec.]

Ba'lkan (baw'l-) *a.* & *n.* **1.** *a.* Of the peninsula in Europe bounded by the Adriatic, Aegean, and Black Seas; of its peoples and countries; hence ~IZE (3) *v.t.*, divide (an area) into small antagonistic States. **2.** *n.* (in *pl.*) *The* Balkan countries.

ball[1] (bawl) *n.* **1.** Solid or hollow sphere (**terrestrial ~**, the earth; **three ~s**, pawnbroker's sign). **2.** Hard or soft, inflated or solid, large or small, sphere used in games (*ball is in your* COURT[1]; **have the ~ at** one's **feet,** have one's opportunity; **keep** one's **eye on the ~**, remain alert; **keep the ~ rolling,** do one's part in talk etc.; **start the ~ rolling,** make a beginning; **on the ~**, (colloq.) alert; **play ~**, (colloq.) co-operate (*with*)); (Cricket) single delivery of it by bowler (NO[1]-*ball*); (Baseball) single delivery of it by pitcher, esp. if outside specified limits and not struck at by batter, four such deliveries entitling batter to go to first base (*base on balls*). **3.** Solid non-explosive missile (not always spherical) for cannon, rifle, pistol, etc.; hence ~-PROOF[2] *a.* **4.** (in *pl.*, vulg.) Testicles, (fig.) nonsense, muddle (*make a balls of*), unsuccessful attempt; **~s-up,** confusion, muddle. **5.** Material gathered or wound in round mass, e.g. of snow, soil, wool, string, minced meat, animal medicine, (**~ of fire,** very energetic etc. person); EYE[1]*ball*; rounded part of hand or foot at base of thumb or big toe. **6. ~ (and socket) joint,** form of joint with rounded end in concave cup or socket, having great freedom of movement; **~-bear'ing,** (Mech.) bearing avoiding friction by use of small balls, ball for this purpose; **~'boy** (retrieving balls in lawn tennis etc.); ***~ clay,** pipeclay; **~'cock,** automatic device to control water level in cistern, with floating ball; **~-flower,** (Archit.) ornament resembling ball within hollow flower; ***~ game,** baseball game; **~ lightning** (rare globular form); ***~'park,** baseball ground (**not in the right ~park*, nowhere near one's objective); **~-pen, ~-point,** (pen) having tiny ball as its writing point. [ME, f. ON *böllr* f. Gmc **balluz*]

ball[2] (bawl) *n.* Social assembly for dancing (so **~'room;** *~room dancing*, social dancing as recreation); **give a ~**, be host at ball; **have** (one**self**) **a ~**, (sl.) enjoy oneself; **open the ~**, (fig.) commence operations. [f. F *bal* (obs. *baler*, *baller*, f. LL *ballare* to dance f. Gk *ballō*)]

ball[3] (bawl) *v.* **1.** *v.t.* Squeeze or wind into a ball; **~ up,** (sl.) muddle, entangle. **2.** *v.i.* Grow into a lump or lumps. [f. BALL[1]]

bă'llad *n.* Simple song, esp. sentimental or romantic or narrative composition of several verses, each sung to same melody, with accompaniment merely subordinate (**~ metre,** COMMON[1] *metre*); poem in short stanzas narrating popular story; hence ~EER', ~-MONGER (usu. derog.), ~RY (5), *ns.* [ME f. OF *balade* f. Prov. *balada* dancing-song (*balar* dance; see BALL[2], -ADE 1)]

balla'de (-ah'd) *n.* Poem of one or more triplets of stanzas with 7, 8, or 10 lines, each ending with same refrain line, and envoy. [earlier spelling and pronunc. of prec.]

bă'llast *n.*, & *v.t.* **1.** *n.* Heavy material placed in ship or balloon-car to secure stability; **in ~**, (of ship) laden with ballast only or unladen. **2.** Experience, principles, etc., that give stability to character. **3.** Coarse stone etc. used to form bed of railway or substratum of road. **4.** (Electr.) Device to stabilize current in circuit. **5.** *v.t.* Furnish with ballast; make steady, or fill, with ballast. [16th c., f. LG or Scand.]

băllerī'na (-ē'na) *n.* Female ballet-dancer, esp. (**prima ~**) dancer taking one of the leading classical female roles in ballet. [It., fem. of *ballerino* dancing-master (*ballare* dance f. LL; see BALL[2])]

bă'llet (-lā) *n.* Theatrical performance of dancing and mime to music; company performing this; hence **băllĕ'**TIC *a.*, **bă'llėtomāne** *n.*, enthusiast of ballet, **băllėto**MA'NIA *n.* [F, f. It. *balletto* dim. of *ballo* BALL[2]]

ballī'sta *n.* (*pl.* ~*e*). Ancient military engine for hurling great stones etc. [L, f. Gk *ballō* throw]

ballī'st|ic *a.* Of projectiles; moving under force of gravity only (**~ic missile,** one which moves under gravity after initial powered and guided stage); hence ~ICS *n.*, science of projectiles or of firearms. [f. prec. + -IC]

bă'llocks *n. pl.* = BALL[1] 4. [OE *bealluc* dim. f. Gmc **ball-* BALL[1]]

ballon d'essai (bălawn̈dĕsā') *n.* (*pl.* *-ns pr.* same). Experiment to see how new policy etc. will be received. [F, = trial balloon]

bă'llonėt *n.* Air-compartment in balloon etc. to maintain pressure as buoyant gas is released. [f. F *ballonnet*, dim. of *ballon* (see foll., -ET[1])]

ballōō'n[1] *n.* **1.** Round or pear-shaped airtight envelope inflated with hot air or other gas lighter than ordinary air and so able to rise skywards, esp. one with car attached for passengers; BARRAGE *balloon*; **when the ~ goes up,** when action or trouble begins. **2.** Small air-inflated rubber bag as child's toy etc. **3.** Anything hollow and inflated; (colloq.) balloon-shaped line enclosing words or thoughts of characters in strip cartoons etc.; large globular drinking-glass. **4. ~ tyre,** low-pressure pneumatic tyre with large cross-section; **~ vine,** tropical Amer. vine with balloon-like pods. [f. F *ballon* or It. *ballone* large ball (*balla* ball; see -OON)]

ballōō'n[2] *v.* **1.** *v.i.* Travel by balloon; (of gown, sail, etc.) swell out like balloon. **2.** *v.t.* Hit or kick (ball etc.) high in the air. [f. prec.]

bă'llot[1] *n.* (Usu. secret) voting; small ball, ticket, or paper (**~-paper**) used in voting; votes so recorded; lot-drawing; **~-box** (used in voting esp. to contain ballot-papers marked by voters and to preserve secrecy). [f. It. *ballotta* dim. of *balla* BALL[1]]

bă'llot[2] *v.i.* Give (usu. secret) vote (**~ for,** select (officials etc.) by ballot); draw lots (*for* precedence etc.). [f. It. *ballottare* (*ballotta*; see prec.)]

||**bă'llȳ** *a.* & *adv.* (sl.) euphem. form of BLOODY[1] as vague intensive (*took the whole bally lot*). [pronunciation of *bl—y* = *bloody*]

băllȳhōō' *n.*, & *v.t.* **1.** *n.* Factitious vulgar or misleading or noisy publicity; showman's touting speech; bombastic nonsense. **2.** *v.t.* Advertise, cajole, by ballyhoo. [20th c., orig. U.S.; etym. unkn.]

bă'llȳrăg *v.* (-gg-). (sl.) **1.** *v.t.* Maltreat by jeering at or playing practical jokes on. **2.** *v.i.* Indulge in horseplay. [18th c.; orig. unkn.]

balm (bahm) *n.* **1.** Fragrant and medicinal exudation from certain trees; aromatic ointment for anointing, soothing pain, or healing; perfume, fragrance; healing or soothing influence, consolation. **2.** Asian and N. Afr. tree yielding balm; aromatic herb of genus *Melissa*; **~ of Gilead,** (1) (plant of genus *Commiphora* yielding) fragrant resin formerly much used as unguent, (2) balsam fir or poplar. [ME, f. OF *ba(s)me* f. L *balsamum* BALSAM]

ba'lm-crĭckėt (bah'm-) *n.* Cicada. [earlier

baum-, partial transl. of G *baumgrille* tree--cricket]

bălmŏ'ral *n.* Round flat cap worn by some Scottish regiments. [f. *B*~ Castle, royal residence in Grampian, Scotland]

ba'lm|y (bah'mĭ) *a.* Yielding balm; fragrant; soft, mild; soothing, healing; (sl.) crazy; hence ~ĭLY[2] *adv.*, ~ĭNESS *n.* [f. BALM + -Y[2]]

bă'lnėarў *a.* Pertaining to baths or bathing. [f. L *balneum* bath + -ARY[1]]

bălnėŏ'logў *n.* Scientific study of bathing and medicinal springs. [f. as prec. + -O- + -LOGY]

balō'ney. See BOLONEY.

B.A.L.P.A. *abbr.* British Airline Pilots' Association.

ba'lsa (baw'l- *or* bŏ'l-) *n.* Amer. tropical tree (*Ochroma lagopus*); ~(**-wood**), its light strong wood, used for lifebelts etc.; raft or float. [Sp., = raft]

ba'lsam (baw'l- *or* bŏ'l-) *n.* **1.** Resinous product = BALM (exudation or ointment); any of various other medicinal oleo-resins; **Canada** ~, (from balsam fir, used in mounting for microscope). **2.** Artificial ointment, esp. one of various substances dissolved in oil or turpentine. **3.** (fig.) Healing or soothing agency. **4.** Tree yielding balsam; flowering plant of genus *Impatiens*; ~ **apple,** gourdlike plant with highly coloured fruit; ~ **fir,** ~ **poplar,** Amer. trees (*Abies balsamea, Populus balsamifera*) yielding balsam. **5.** Hence **bălsă'mic**, **bălsamĭ'ferous**, (*or* bawl- *or* bŏl-), *adjs.* [OE, f. L *balsamum*]

Ba'ltĭc (baw'l- *or* bŏ'l-) *a.* & *n.* **1.** ~ (**Sea**), almost land-locked sea of N.E. Europe. **2.** *a.* Of the branch of Indo-European languages that includes Lithuanian and Lettish. [f. med. L *Balticus* f. LL *Balthae* dwellers near the Baltic Sea; see -IC]

ba'ltĭmōre (baw'l- *or* bŏ'l-) *n.* N. Amer. orange and black starling (*Icterus galbula*). [f. its colours' being those of coat of arms of Lord *B*~, governor of Maryland d. 1632]

bă'luster *n.* Short pillar with curving outline, esp. in balustrade; post helping to support rail; (in *pl.*, arch.) banisters. [f. F *balustre* f. It. *balaustro* f. L f. Gk *balaustion* wild-pomegranate flower (from resemblance of shape)]

bălustrā'de *n.* Row of balusters with rail or coping as ornamental parapet to terrace, balcony, etc. [F (as prec.; see -ADE)]

bambin|o (bămbē'nō) *n.* (*pl.* ~*i pr.* -ē). Image of infant Jesus in swaddling-clothes; (colloq.) young child in Italy. [It., dim. of *bambo* silly]

bămboō' *n.* Mainly tropical giant grass of genus *Bambusa*; its hollow jointed stem, used as stick or material or food; ~ **curtain,** (Polit.) 'IRON[1] curtain' in respect of Communist China. [f. earlier *bambous* etc. taken as pl., f. Du. *bamboes*, unexpl. alt. of Port. *mambu* f. Malay]

bămboō'zle *v.t.* (sl.) Hoax, mystify; cheat *into* doing something or *out of* property etc.; hence ~MENT (-zelm-) *n.* [*c.* 1700, prob. of cant orig.]

băn[1] *v.t.* (**-nn-**). Formally prohibit, interdict. [OE *bannan* summon, = OHG *bannan*, ON *banna* f. Gmc **bannan* proclaim to be under penalty]

băn[2] *n.* Formal or authoritative prohibition; tacit prohibition by public opinion; ecclesiastical anathema, interdict; curse supposed to have supernatural power; sentence of outlawry; (arch.) angry execration. [f. prec.]

bănă'l (*or* banah'l *or* bā'nal) *a.* Commonplace, trite; hence or cogn. **bană'lITY** *n.*, ~LY[2] *adv.* [orig. in sense 'compulsory', hence 'common to all'; F (f. Gmc as BAN[1], -AL)]

bana'na (-nah'-) *n.* Tropical and subtropical fruit-tree (*Musa sapientum*); its pulpy fruit, finger-shaped with yellow skin when ripe, growing in clusters; **hand of** ~**s** (bunch, esp. 10–20, like fingers of hand); ~**lander,** (Austral.) Queenslander; ~ **republic,** (usu. derog.) small tropical country economically dependent on its fruit export; *banana* SPLIT[2]. [Port. or Sp., f. name in Guinea]

banau'sĭc *a.* (derog.) Suitable (only) for artisans; uncultivated; materialistic. [f. Gk *banausikos* for artisans]

Bă'nburў *n.* ~ **cake,** pastry filled with currant mixture. [~ in Oxfordshire, where orig. made]

bănc *n.* **In** ~, (Law) sitting as full court. [AF, = bench, f. med. L (as BANK[3])]

bănd[1] *n.* **1.** (arch.) Thing that restrains, binds together, connects, or unites; BOND[1]. **2.** Flat strip of thin material; hoop or loop (of iron, RUBBER[2], etc.) put round a thing to keep it together; metal etc. ring round bird's leg to identify it; strip forming part of garment (shirt, hat, skirt, etc.); (in *pl.*) development of neckband or collar into two pendent strips in clerical, legal, or academic dress; (Mech.) belt connecting wheels or pulleys; stripe of colour or distinguishable material on object; range of values in a series; range of frequency or wavelength in spectrum. **3.** ~**'box,** box of paper-covered cardboard or thin wood for millinery, orig. for neckbands, (*look as if* one *came out of a* ~*box*, look extremely neat); ~**-saw,** endless saw running over wheels; ~**'width,** range of frequencies used in telecommunications. **4.** Organized company of persons with common object, esp. robbers etc. (**B**~ **of Hope,** total-abstinence association); *herd or flock. **5.** Body of musicians, esp. wind--instrument performers (*brass band*; *dance band*); **the** ~ **begins to play,** (fig.) matters become serious or exciting; BEAT[1] *the band*; ~**'master,** conductor of band; ~**'stand,** covered outdoor platform for band etc.; ~**'sman** (-z-), member of band; ~**'wagon,** wagon for band of musicians esp. in circus parade, (fig.) imaginary vehicle regarded as carrying a band of political leaders likely to be successful (*climb on the* ~*wagon*, seek to join the party etc. that seems likely to win). [senses 1–3 ult. f. Gmc **bindan* BIND[1]. (1) (tie), ME f. ON, f. Gmc **bandam*; (2, 3) (strip), ME f. OF *bande, bende*, med. L *benda* f. Gmc **bendōn*; (4, 5) (company), ME f. OF *bande*, med. L *banda*, prob. of Gmc orig.]

bănd[2] *v.t.* Put a band on; mark with stripes, (in *p.p.*, Bot. & Zool.) marked with coloured bands or bars; form into a league (usu. refl., or abs. w. *together*). [f. F *bander* (*bande*; see prec.)]

bă'ndage *n.*, & *v.t.* **1.** *n.* Strip of material for binding up wound etc., or for blindfolding. **2.** *v.t.* Tie up with bandage. [F (*bande*; see BAND[1], -AGE)]

băndă'nna *n.* Coloured handkerchief or neckerchief with yellow or white spots. [prob. Port., f. Hindi]

b. & b. *abbr.* bed and breakfast.

bă'ndeau (-dō; *or* -ō') *n.* (*pl.* ~**x** *pr.* -z). Strip of material for binding woman's hair; band inside woman's hat. [F]

banderilla (bănderĭ'lya) *n.* Decorated dart thrust into bull's neck or shoulders during bullfight; so ***banderillero*** (bănderĭlyār'ō) *n.* (*pl.* ~*s*), bullfighter using banderillas. [Sp.]

bănderō'l(e) *n.* Long narrow flag with cleft end, flown at mast-head; ornamental streamer on knight's lance; ribbon-like scroll or stone band with inscription. [f. F *banderole* f. It. *banderuola* dim. of *bandiera* BANNER]

bă'ndĭcoōt *n.* (Ind.) large destructive rat (*Nesocia bandicota*); (Austral.) insectivorous and herbivorous marsupial of genus *Perameles*. [f. Telugu *pandikokku* pig-rat]

bă'ndĭt *n.* (*pl.* ~**s** *or* **bandi'tti**). Outlaw;

lawless robber or murderer; gangster; hence ~RY (4) *n.* [f. It. *bandito* (pl. *-iti*), p.p. (as n.) of *bandire* ban, = med. L *bannire* proclaim; see BANISH]

bă'ndŏg *n.* (Hist.) Dog kept on chain. [ME, f. BAND[1] + DOG[1]]

băndoleer', -ier', *n.* Shoulder-belt with loops or pockets for cartridges. [f. Du. *bandelier* or f. F *bandoulière*, prob. f. as BANDEROLE]

bă'ndy̆[1] *v.t.* ~ (**about**), throw, strike, pass, to and fro (ball, or fig. stories, insults, etc.); discuss (names etc.), esp. disparagingly; give and take (blows etc.), exchange (compliments etc.) *with* person. [perh. f. F *bander* take sides (*bande* BAND[1] 4)]

bă'ndy̆[2] *a.* (Of legs) curved so as to be wide apart at the knees; **~-legged,** having bandy legs. [perh. f. obs. *bandy* curved stick]

bāne *n.* Cause of ruin or trouble (*he is the bane of my life*); (poet.) ruin, woe; (arch., fig., or in comb., e.g. *henbane*, RAT[1]*sbane*) poison; **~'berry,** (bitter poisonous berry of) plant of genus *Actaea*; hence ~'FUL (-nf-) *a.* [OE *bana*, = OHG *bano*, ON *bani* f. Gmc **banon*]

băng[1] *v.t.* & *i.* Strike or shut noisily; (cause to) make sound of blow or explosion; hence ~'ER[1] *n.*, (esp., sl.) sausage, firework, noisy old car. [16th c., perh. f. Scand.]

băng[2] *n.* Sharp blow; sound of a blow; report of gun; sound of explosion (BIG *bang*; **with a ~,** successfully or impressively); (sl.) drug injection [cf. BHANG]; (sl.) copulation. [f. prec.]

băng[3] *adv.* With sudden impact; abruptly; (colloq.) completely (*bang in the middle*); explosively (as conventional imitation of shot or explosion, lit. or fig., *bang went my hopes of success*); **go ~,** shut etc. noisily, explode; **~ off,** (sl.) immediately; **~ on,** (sl.) exactly right; ***~-up,** (sl.) first-class. [f. BANG[1]]

băng[4] *v.t.*, & *n.* **1.** *v.t.* Cut (front hair) straight across forehead. **2.** *n.* Fringe thus formed; **~'tail,** horse esp. with tail cut straight across; *~tail muster*, (Austral.) counting of cattle by cutting across tufts at tail-ends. [f. prec.]

bă'ngle (-nggel) *n.* Rigid ring as bracelet or anklet. [f. Hindi *bangri* glass bracelet]

bă'nĭan, bă'nyan, *n.* Hindu trader; loose flannel jacket etc.; ~(**-tree**), Indian fig, branches of which root themselves over wide area. [Port. *banian* f. Gujarati *vāṇiyo* man of trading caste, f. Skr.; applied orig. to one such tree under which banians had built pagoda]

bă'nĭsh *v.t.* Condemn (person) to exile (*from* place); dismiss from one's presence or mind; hence ~MENT *n.* [ME, f. OF *banir* (-ISH[2]) f. Rom. **bannire* f. Gmc **bannjan* (**bann-* BAN[1])]

bă'nĭster, bă'nnĭster, *n.* (usu. in *pl.*) Upright(s) supporting stair handrail; (in *pl.*) these uprights and rail together. [f. earlier *barrister*, corrupt. of BALUSTER]

bă'njō *n.* (*pl.* ~s *or* ~es). Stringed musical instrument with neck and head like guitar and body shaped like tambourine, played with fingers or plectrum; hence ~IST (3) *n.* [Negro corrupt. of earlier *bandore* ult. f. Gk *pandoura* three-stringed lute]

bănk[1] *n.* **1.** Raised shelf of ground, slope; elevation in sea or river bed; artificial slope of road etc. enabling car etc. to maintain speed round a curve; (flat-topped) mass of cloud, fog, snow, etc. **2.** Sloping margin of river, ground near river (**right, left,** ~, to one looking down stream); edge of hollow place (e.g. top of mine-shaft). [ME, f. ON **banki* f. Gmc **bankon*; cf. BANK[5], BENCH]

bănk[2] *v.t.* & *i.* Contain or confine with bank(s); (of car or aeroplane or its occupant) travel with one side higher; cause (car etc.) to do this; build (road etc.) higher at outer edge of bend to help fast cornering; ~ (**up**), heap or rise into banks, pack tightly (fire, for slow burning). [f. prec.]

bănk[3] *n.* **1.** Establishment for custody of money, which it pays out on customer's order; **central ~,** national (not commercial) bank; ‖**the B~,** Bank of England, issuing legal-tender notes, and having the Government as chief customer. **2.** Small domestic receptacle for money; (Gaming) amount of money held by keeper of table; place for storing anything for future use (*blood bank*; *data bank*). **3. ~-bill,** ‖bill drawn by one bank on another, *banknote; **~-book** (containing customer's private copy of his account with bank); **~ card** (issued by bank to customer and guaranteeing payment on his cheques up to stated amount); **~ holiday,** day on which banks are legally closed, ‖usu. kept as general holiday also; **~ manager,** person in charge of local branch of bank; **~'note,** banker's promissory note (esp. from central bank) payable to bearer on demand and serving as money; ‖**B~ Rate,** announced minimum percentage at which central bank will discount bills; ***~'roll,** (*n.*) roll of banknotes, funds, (*v.t.*, colloq.) support financially. [f. F *banque* or f. It. *banca* f. med. L *banca, bancus*, f. Gmc **bank-* bench; cf. BANK[1, 5]]

bănk[4] *v.* **1.** *v.i.* Keep BANK[3], trade in money; keep money *at* (or *with*) bank; (Gaming) be keeper of the bank; **~ on,** base one's hopes on, count upon, reckon reliable. **2.** *v.t.* Deposit (money etc.) in bank. [f. prec.]

bănk[5] *n.* Row of keys, lights, switches, etc.; group of similar objects connected in line; tier *of oars*. [ME, f. OF *banc* f. Gmc **bank-*; cf. BANK[1], BENCH]

bă'nkable *a.* That will be accepted at a BANK[3]; (fig.) reliable. [f. BANK[4] + -ABLE]

bă'nker[1] *n.* **1.** One who manages a BANK[3]; **let me be your ~** (lend the money you need); **~'s card,** = BANK[3] *card*; *banker's* ORDER[1]. **2.** (Gaming) keeper of the bank; dealer in some games of chance; a gambling game of cards. **3.** Result forecast identically (while other forecasts differ) in several football-pool entries on one coupon. [f. F *banquier* (*banque* BANK[3]; see -ER[2])]

bă'nker[2] *n.* Fishing boat or fisherman off Newfoundland; (Austral.) river flooded to top of banks. [f. BANK[1] + -ER[1]]

bă'nkėt *n.* Auriferous conglomerate like pudding-stone, found in S. Africa. [Du., = kind of hard-bake (BANQUET[1])]

bă'nkĭng *n.* In vbl senses of BANK[2,4]; fishing on a sea bank (esp. off Newfoundland). [f. BANK[1,2,4] + -ING[1]]

bă'nkrŭpt *n.*, *a.*, & *v.t.* **1.** *n.* (Law) insolvent person whose estate is administered and distributed for benefit of all his creditors; insolvent debtor. **2.** *a.* Insolvent; undergoing legal process because of insolvency; (fig.) bereft *of* (some quality etc.); hence ~CY *n.* **3.** *v.t.* Reduce to bankruptcy. [16th c., f. It. *banca rotta* (BANK[3], L *rumpere rupt-* break) broken bench, assim. to L]

bă'nksĭa *n.* Flowering shrub of genus *Banksia*, orig. Australian. [f. Sir J. *Banks*, Engl. naturalist d. 1820 + -IA[1]]

bă'nner *n.* & *a.* **1.** *n.* Cloth flag on pole used as standard of king, knight, etc.; **join, follow, the ~ of,** (fig.) adhere to the cause of. **2.** Ensign (esp. on two poles or crossbar) borne in religious or political demonstrations; anything used as symbol of principles. **3.** Hence ~ED[2] (-erd) *a.* **4.** *a.* Conspicuous (*banner headline* in newspaper); *pre-eminent. [ME, f. AF *banere*, OF *baniere*, f. Rom. **bandaria* f. med. L *bandum* standard (BAND[1] 4), f. Gmc]

bă'nnerėt *n.* (Hist.) Knight having vassals in the field under his own banner; knighthood conferred on the field for valour. [ME & OF *baneret* (*baniere* BANNER; *-et* as -ATE[1])]

bă'nnĭster. See BANISTER.

bă'nnock *n.* (Sc. & N. Engl.) Round flat loaf, usu. unleavened. [OE *bannuc*, perh. f. Celt.]

bănns (-z) *n. pl.* Notice in church etc. of intended marriage, read on three Sundays to give opportunity of objection; **forbid the ~**, raise such objection. [pl. of BAN[2]]

bă'nquėt[1] *n.* Sumptuous feast; dinner with speeches in celebration of something or to further a cause. [F, dim. of *banc* bench, BANK[3]]

bă'nquėt[2] *v.* **1.** *v.t.* Regale (person). **2.** *v.i.* Feast; carouse; hence **~ER**[1] *n.* [f. F *banqueter* (*banquet*; see prec.)]

bănquĕ'tte (-ngk-) *n.* Raised step behind rampart etc.; upholstered seat along wall. [F, f. It. *banchetta* dim. of *banca* bench, BANK[3]]

bă'nshee *n.* (Ir. & Sc.) Female spirit whose wail portends death in a house. [f. Ir. *bean sídhe* f. OIr. *ben síde* woman of the fairies]

bănt *v.i.* Undergo banting treatment. [back form. f. BANTING; cf. -ING[1]]

bă'ntam *n.* Small kind of domestic fowl, of which the cock is very pugnacious; small but spirited person; **~weight** (Boxing; see BOX[5]*ing-weights*). [app. f. *Bāntān* in Java (not their orig. home)]

bă'nter *n.* & *v.* **1.** *n.* Humorous ridicule; good-humoured personal remarks. **2.** *v.t.* Make fun of, rally. **3.** *v.i.* Talk jestingly. [17th c., of unkn. orig.]

bă'ntĭng *n.* (arch.) Treatment of obesity by abstinence from sugar, starch, and fat. [f. W. *Banting*, Engl. undertaker and dietitian d. 1878]

bă'ntlĭng *n.* Young child, brat. [16th c., perh. f. G *bänkling* (*bank* bench; cf. BASTARD)]

Bă'ntu (-ōō; *or* -ōō') *n.* (*pl.* ~ *or* ~s) & *a.* (Member) of a group of Negroid peoples in equatorial and southern Africa; (group) of languages spoken by them. [Bantu, = people]

Băntustă'n (-ōōstah'n) *n.* (S. Afr.) Area reserved for Bantu members of population. [f. BANTU + *-stan* as in *Hindustan*]

bă'nxrĭng *n.* Javanese squirrel-like insectivorous animal, tree-shrew. [f. Jav. *bangsring*]

bă'nyan. See BANIAN.

bănzai' (-zī') *int.* Form of greeting by Japanese to their Emperor, cheer used in battle, etc. [Jap., = ten thousand years (of life to you)]

bā'obăb *n.* African tree (*Adansonia digitata*) with enormously thick trunk and large fruit with edible pulp. [L (1592), prob. f. an Afr. lang.]

B.A.O.R. *abbr.* British Army of the Rhine.

băp *n.* (esp. Sc.) Large soft bread roll. [16th c.; orig. unkn.]

bă'ptĭsm *n.* **1.** Religious rite of immersing person in, or sprinkling him with, water in sign of purification and (with Christians) of admission to the Church, generally accompanied by name-giving. **2.** (fig.) **~ of blood,** martyrdom of the unbaptized; **~ of fire,** soldier's first battle. **3.** Naming of church bells and of ships. **4.** So **băptĭ'smAL** (-z-) *a.* [ME, f. OF *ba(p)te(s)me* f. eccl. L f. Gk *baptismos* (*baptizō* BAPTIZE; see -ISM)]

bă'ptĭst *n.* One who baptizes, esp. John the Baptist; (*B~*) one of a Christian religious body objecting to infant baptism, and practising immersion. [ME, f. OF *baptiste*, f. eccl. L f. eccl. Gk *baptistēs* (*baptizō*; see BAPTIZE)]

bă'ptĭst(e)rў *n.* Part of church (or, formerly, separate building) used for baptism; (in Baptist chapel) immersion receptacle for baptism. [ME, f. OF *baptisterie* f. eccl. L f. Gk *baptistērion* bathing-place (*baptizō*; see BAPTIZE)]

băptī'ze, -ī'se (-ī'z), *v.t.* Administer baptism to (person, or abs.); christen; name or nickname. [ME, f. OF *baptiser* f. eccl. L *baptizare* f. Gk *baptizō* immerse, baptize]

bar̂[1] *n.* **1.** Long piece of rigid material (metal, wood, etc.); oblong piece (of chocolate, soap, etc.); CROSS*bar*; heating element of electric fire; **~'bell,** iron bar with heavy ball at each end used in exercising; *bar* TRACERY. **2.** Strip of silver below clasp of medal as additional distinction; band of colour etc. on surface (~ **chart** etc., using bars to represent quantities); (Her.) narrow horizontal stripe across field (~ **sinister,** erron. for BEND[1] or BATON, supposed sign of bastardy). **3.** Rod or pole used to fasten or confine or obstruct (window, door, grate, gate, etc.; **behind ~s,** in prison); barrier of any shape; sandbank or shoal at mouth of harbour or estuary. **4.** (Mus.) vertical line (also **~-line**) across staff dividing piece into sections of equal time-value, such section; immaterial barrier or obstacle; restriction; (Law) plea arresting action or claim. **5.** (In lawcourt) place at which prisoner stands, (fig.) *bar of conscience, opinion*, etc.; a particular court; **be called to the ~** (i.e. that in Inns of Court separating benchers), be admitted a barrister; **be called within the ~** (i.e. that in courts within which Q.C.s plead), be appointed Queen's Counsel; **the ~,** barristers, profession of barrister; **the outer ~,** those not Q.C.s. **6.** ||(Parl.) Rail dividing off space to which non-members may be admitted on business. **7.** (In inn etc.) counter across which alcoholic refreshments are served, space behind or room or premises containing it; **~'fly,** person frequenting such places; ***~'keep,** ||**~'maid, ~'man, ~'tender,** attendant at such counter. **8.** Place where anything is served across counter etc., esp. refreshments (COFFEE *bar*; SNACK-*bar*); specialized department in large shop (*heel bar*; *slipper bar*). [ME, f. OF *barre*, f. Rom. **barra* of unkn. orig.]

bar̂[2] *v.t.* (**-rr-**). Fasten (door etc.) with bar(s); keep (person) *in* or *out*; obstruct (path etc.); (Law) stay (process or party) by objection; exclude from consideration (cf. BAR[5], BARRING); prohibit; ||(sl.) object to, dislike, (person, habit, etc.); mark with stripe(s). [ME, f. OF *barrer* (*barre*; see prec.)]

bar̂[3] *n.* Large Mediterranean food-fish (*Sciaena aquila*). [F]

bar̂[4] *n.* (esp. Meteorol.) Unit of pressure, 10^5 newton per square metre, approx. one atmosphere. [f. Gk *baros* weight]

bar̂[5] *prep.* Except (*all over bar the shouting*); **~ three** etc., (in stating odds in Racing) except the three etc. horses already named (also ellipt. w. omission of *three* etc.). [imper. of BAR[2], prob. by anal. w. *except* etc.]

bărathē'a *n.* Fine cloth made from wool (with or without silk or cotton). [19th c.; orig. unkn.]

bar̂b[1] *n.*, & *v.t.* **1.** *n.* Secondary backward-projecting point of arrow, fish-hook, etc.; (fig.) sting, wounding remark; beardlike filament at mouth of barbel or other fish; lateral filament branching from shaft of feather. **2.** *v.t.* Furnish (arrow etc.) with barb; **~ed wire** (for fences and esp. as obstruction in war, with short pointed pieces of wire inserted at intervals). [ME, f. OF *barbe* f. L *barba* beard]

bar̂b[2] *n.* Breed of horse or pigeon imported from Barbary; (Austral.) black kelpie. [f. F *barbe* f. It. *barbero* of BARBARY]

Bar̂bā'dĭan *a.* & *n.* (Native or inhabitant) of Barbados. [f. *Barbados* in W. Indies + -IAN]

bar̂bar̂'ĭan *n.* & *a.* Rough, wild, or uncultured (person). [orig. of any foreigner w. different language or customs; f. F *barbarien* f. *barbare* (as BARBAROUS; see -IAN)]

barbă'r|ic *a.* Rough, uncultured; like or of barbarians and their art or taste, unrestrained; hence ~ICALLY *adv.* [ME, f. OF *barbarique* or f. L f. Gk *barbarikos* (*barbaros* foreign; see -IC)]

bar'barism *n.* (Use of) word or action not in accordance with normal standards; absence of culture; ignorance and rudeness; instance of this. [f. F *barbarisme* f. L f. Gk *barbarismos* (*barbarizō* speak like a foreigner f. *barbaros* foreign; see -ISM)]

barbă'rity *n.* Savage cruelty; instance of it. [f. as BARBAROUS + -ITY]

bar'bariz|e, -is|e (-īz), *v.t.* & *i.* Make or become barbarous; hence ~A'TION *n.* [f. as foll. + -IZE]

bar'barous *a.* Uncivilized; cruel; coarse; hence ~LY[2] *adv.*, ~NESS *n.* [orig. of any foreign language or people; f. L f. Gk *barbaros* foreign + -OUS]

Bar'bary *n.* Old name of western part of N. Africa; ~ **ape,** macaque of N. Africa and Gibraltar. [ult. f. Arab. *barbar* BERBER]

bar'bėcūe *n.*, & *v.t.* **1.** *n.* Metal frame for cooking meat above open fire; fireplace containing this; meat etc. thus cooked; open-air party at which such food is served. **2.** *v.t.* Cook on barbecue. [f. Sp. *barbacoa* f. Haitian *barbacòa* wooden frame on posts]

bar'bel *n.* Large European freshwater fish of genus *Barbus* with fleshy filaments hanging from mouth; such filament in any fish. [ME f. OF, f. LL *barbellus* dim. of *barbus* barbel (*barba* beard)]

bar'ber *n.*, & *v.t.* **1.** *n.* One who cuts men's hair and shaves beards, men's hairdresser; ~**-shop** *a.* *(fig., colloq.) of close-harmony male quartet singing; ~**'s itch, rash,** ringworm of face communicated by (unsterilized) shaving apparatus; ~**'s pole** (spirally painted red and white and used as barber's sign). **2.** *v.t.* Cut hair of; (fig.) cut (grass etc.) short. [ME & AF, f. OF *barbeor* f. med. L *barbator -oris* (*barba* beard); see -OR, -ER[2]]

bar'berry *n.* Shrub of genus *Berberis,* with spiny shoots, yellow flowers, and oblong red berries; its berry. [ME, f. OF *berberis,* of unkn. orig.; assim. to BERRY[1]]

bar'bet *n.* Tropical bird with bristle-tufts at base of bill. [F (*barbe* beard; see -ET[1])]

barbĕ'tte *n.* Platform in fort or ship from which guns fire over parapet etc. without embrasure. [F, dim. of *barbe* beard; see -ETTE]

bar'bĭcan *n.* Outer defence of city or castle, esp. double tower over gate or bridge. [ME, f. OF *barbacane,* of unkn. orig.]

***bar'bĭtal,** ||**bar'bĭtōne,** *ns.* Soporific drug, veronal. [f. BARBITURIC + *-al* as in *veronal,* -ONE]

barbĭtur'ic *a.* (Chem.) ~ **acid,** an acid, malonyl urea, from which various soporific and sedative drugs are derived; hence **barbĭ'turATE**[1] (3) *n.* [f. F *barbiturique* f. G *barbitur*(*säure* acid) f. woman's name *Barbara*]

Bar'bĭzŏn *n.* ~ **School,** coterie of mid-19th-c. French naturalistic painters. [~ near Paris]

barbō'la *n.* ~ (**work**), embellishment of small articles by attachment of coloured models of flowers, fruit, etc. made from a plastic paste. [P, arbitrarily from *barbotine* clay slip for ornamenting pottery]

bar'būle *n.* Filament branching from barb (of feather) as barb from shaft. [f. L *barbula* dim. of *barba* beard; see -ULE]

bar'carōle, -ŏlle, *n.* Song of gondolier; music in imitation of it. [f. F *barcarolle* f. Venetian It. *barcarola* boatman's song (*barca* boat)]

Barcėlōna *n.* ~ (**nut**), hazel-nut imported from Spain etc. [~ in Spain]

bard[1] *n.* **1.** Celtic minstrel; poet honoured at Eisteddfod; hence ~'IC *a.* **2.** Poet; **the B~ (of Avon),** Shakespeare; ~**ŏ'**LATRY *n.*, excessive admiration of Shakespeare. [f. Gael. & Ir. *bárd,* W *bardd,* f. OCelt. **bardos*]

bard[2] *n.*, & *v.t.* **1.** *n.* Slice of bacon placed on meat or game before roasting. **2.** *v.t.* Cover with bards. [f. F *barde,* orig. = horse's breastplate, ult. f. Arab.]

bar'dy *n.* (Austral.) Edible wood-boring grub or its larva. [Aboriginal]

bare[1] *a.* **1.** Unclothed, uncovered; (of head) hatless; (of tree) leafless; unfurnished, unprotected, (of floor) without carpet; undisguised (*lay bare the truth*); unadorned (*bare facts, walls*); empty (*cupboard was bare*); scanty (*a bare majority*); mere (*bare necessities of life*). **2.** ~ **of,** unprovided with; **with** one's ~ **hands,** not using tool or weapon. **3.** ~**'back** *a.* & *adv.*, (esp.) on unsaddled horse; ~**'faced,** (fig.) undisguised, impudent; ~**'foot** *a.* & *adv.*, ~**'footed** *a.*, without shoes or stockings; ~**hea'ded,** without hat or cap. **4.** Hence ~'NESS (bar'n-) *n.* [OE *bær,* = OS, OHG *bar,* ON *berr,* f. Gmc **bazaz* f. IE **bhosós*]

bare[2] *v.t.* Uncover, unsheathe; reveal (*bared its teeth in a snarl*). [OE *barian* (*bær*; see prec.)]

bare[3]. See BEAR[3].

barège (barā'zh) *n.* & *a.* (Of) silky gauze made from wool etc. [F, f. *Barèges* in S.W. France, where orig. made]

bar'ely (bar'lĭ) *adv.* Merely; only just; scarcely (*barely escaped disaster*); scantily (*barely furnished rooms*); (arch.) openly, explicitly. [f. BARE[1] + -LY[2]]

bar'gain[1] (-gĭn) *n.* **1.** Agreement on terms of a transaction; **into** or ***in the** ~, beyond the strict terms, moreover; **make** or **strike a** ~, come to terms; HARD *bargain.* **2.** Thing acquired by such agreement; **good, bad,** ~, thing or result cheaply or dearly bought; *make the* BEST[1] *of a bad bargain.* **3.** Thing acquired or offered cheap, esp. in special shop-sale; ~ **basement** (in shop, where bargains are offered). [ME, f. OF *bargaine* (*bargaignier*; see foll.)]

bar'gain[2] (-gĭn) *v.* **1.** *v.i.* Discuss terms of a transaction (*with* person, or abs.); ~ **for,** be prepared for, expect, (usu. w. neg. or *more than*: *did not bargain for her coming too*). **2.** *v.t.* ~ **away,** part with for a consideration. **3.** Hence ~ER[1] *n.* [ME, f. OF *bargaignier,* prob. f. Gmc **borganjan* (**borgan* look after)]

barge *n.*, & *v.i.* **1.** *n.* Flat-bottomed freight-boat for canals, rivers, and harbours, with or without sails; large ornamental oared vessel for state occasions; ornamental house-boat (e.g. *College barge*); second boat of man-of-war; *~**'man,** bargee; ~**-pole** (for fending; *would not touch with a* ~*-pole,* refuse to associate or be concerned with). **2.** *v.i.* Lurch or rush heavily *into, against, about*; ~ **in,** intrude. [ME f. OF, perh. f. med. L *barica* f. Gk *baris* Egyptian boat]

bar'ge-board *n.* (Archit.) Board or ornamental screen along edge of gable. [cf. med. L *bargus* gallows; BOARD[1]]

||**bargee'** *n.* Man in charge of or working on barge. [f. BARGE + -EE]

barĭ'lla *n.* Plant of genus *Salsola* in Spain, Sicily, etc.; impure alkali made by burning either this or kelp. [Sp.]

bă'rĭtōne *n.* (Mus.) Male voice between tenor and bass; singer with this voice; part written for baritone voice; member of a group of similar instruments, between tenor and bass. [f. It. *baritono* f. Gk *barutonos* (*barus* heavy, *tonos* TONE[1])]

bar'ĭum *n.* (Chem.) White metallic element, of which baryta is the oxide; ~ **meal,** mixture containing barium sulphate, used in radiography of alimentary canal. [f. BARYTA + -IUM]

bark[1] *n.* Outer sheath of tree trunks and branches; this material used as TAN[1]; ~**'cloth** (made from inner bark of paper mulberry etc.). [ME, f. OIcel. *börkr bark-,* perh. rel. to BIRCH]

bar̂k[2] *v.t.* Strip bark from (tree); abrade (knuckles etc.). [f. prec.]

bar̂k[3] *n.* (poet.) Ship, boat. [= BARQUE]

bar̂k[4] *n.* Sharp explosive cry of dogs, foxes, squirrels; **his ~ is worse than his bite,** he is irritable but harmless; hence ~'LESS *a.* [f. foll.]

bar̂k[5] *v.i.* (Of dog etc.) utter bark; speak petulantly or imperiously; *act as tout; **~ at,** abuse; **~ up the wrong tree,** (fig.) be on wrong track, make effort in wrong direction; **~'ing deer,** muntjak; *barking* SQUIRREL. [OE *beorcan*, repr. earlier **berkan*, perh. var. of BREAK[1]]

barkentine. See BARQUENTINE.

bar̂'ker *n.* Tout at auction, side-show, etc. [f. BARK[5] + -ER[1]]

bar̂'ley *n.* Hardy awned cereal of genus *Hordeum* used as food and in making malt liquors and spirits; **~(corn)**, its grain (**John B~corn,** malt liquor personified), (Hist.) length of its grain as measure ($\frac{1}{3}$ inch); PEARL[1] *barley*; **~-mow,** stack of barley; **~ sugar,** usu. twisted sweetmeat of boiled sugar; **~-water,** decoction of pearl barley for invalids etc. [OE *bærlic* a. f. *bære, bere* barley + *-lic* -LY[1]]

bar̂m *n.* Froth on fermenting malt liquor; yeast, leaven. [f. OE *beorma* f. OLG **bermon*]

Bar̂'mėcide *n.* & *a.* (Giver of benefits that are) illusory, imaginary, disappointing. [name of Arabian-Nights prince whose feast to beggar was rich dish-covers with nothing below]

bar̂ mi'tzvah *n.* (Religious initiation ceremony for) Jewish boy aged 13. [Heb., = 'son of commandment']

bar̂'mȳ *a.* Full of barm; (sl.) crazy. [f. BARM + -Y[2]]

bar̂n[1] *n.* Roofed building for storing grain, hay, *livestock, *vehicles, etc.; (derog.) large unadorned building; **~ dance,** kind of schottische; **~-door,** lit., or fig. target too large to be missed; **~-owl,** kind of owl frequenting barns; **~'storm,** act as **~'stormer,** itinerant actor (esp. given to ranting), *politician, or *aviator; **~'yard,** farmyard. [OE *bern, beren* (*bere* barley, *ern, ærn* house)]

bar̂n[2] *n.* (Phys.) Unit of nuclear cross-section, 10^{-28} square metre. [perh. f. phr. 'as big as a barn']

bar̂'nacle *n.* **1. ~ (goose),** Arctic goose (*Anas leucopsis*) visiting Britain in winter. **2.** Cirriped clinging to rock or by fleshy foot-stalk to ship's bottom; follower who cannot be shaken off. [ME, earlier *bernak*, med. L *bernaca*, of unkn. orig.]

bar̂'ney *n.* (colloq.) Noisy quarrel. [perh. f. dial.]

bă'rograph (-ahf) *n.* Self-recording barometer. [f. Gk *baros* weight + -O- + -GRAPH]

barŏ'mėter *n.* Instrument measuring atmospheric pressure used for forecasting weather and ascertaining height above sea-level; (fig.) *barometer of opinion* etc.; hence **băromĕ'tric(al)** *adjs.*, **băromĕ'tricalLY**[2] *adv.*, **barŏ'METRY** *n.* [f. as prec. + -METER]

bă'ron *n.* Member of the lowest order of British nobility; holder of similar foreign title; great merchant in a specified commodity (*beer baron*); powerful or influential person; (Hist.) one who held lands etc. from king; **~ of beef,** double sirloin undivided. [ME, f. AF *barun*, OF *baron* f. med. L *baro -onis* man, of unkn. orig.]

bă'ronage *n.* Barons or nobles collectively; annotated list of barons or peers. [ME f. OF *barnage* (as prec.; see -AGE)]

bă'ronėss *n.* Baron's wife or widow; woman holding rank of baron in her own right. [ME, f. OF *baronesse*; see BARON, -ESS[1]]

bă'ronėt *n.*, & *v.t.* **1.** *n.* Member of lowest hereditary titled British order; hence ~CY *n.* **2.** *v.t.* Raise to rank of baronet. [ME, f. AL *baronettus* (as BARON; see -ET[1])]

bă'ronėtage *n.* Baronets collectively; annotated list of baronets. [f. prec. + -AGE; cf. BARONAGE]

barō'nial *a.* Of, belonging to, befitting, baron(s); (Archit.) in turreted style used by Sc. land-owners. [f. foll. + -AL]

bă'ronȳ *n.* Domain, rank, tenure, of baron; (Ir.) division of county; (Sc.) large manor. [ME, f. OF *baronie* (as BARON; see -Y[1])]

barŏ'que (-k) *a.* & *n.* **1.** (Of) certain stylistic tendencies in 17th–18th c. arts, characterized by exuberance and extravagance. **2.** *a.* Grotesque, whimsical. [F, orig. 'misshapen pearl']

barou'che (-ōō'sh) *n.* (Hist.) Four-wheeled horse-drawn carriage with collapsible half-hood. [f. G (dial.) *barutsche* f. It. *baroccio* f. **biroccio* f. LL *birotium* f. L *birotus* (BI- 1(a), *rota* wheel)]

bar̂que (-k) *n.* Vessel with aftermost mast fore-and-aft rigged and remaining (usu. two) masts square-rigged. [ME f. F, prob. f. Prov. f. L *barca* ship's boat]

bar̂'quentine, bar̂'k-, (bar̂'kentēn) *n.* Three-masted vessel with foremast square-rigged, main and mizen fore-and-aft rigged. [f. prec., after *brigantine*]

bă'rrack[1] *n.*, & *v.t.* **1.** *n.* (usu. in *pl.*, often treated as *sing.*) Building(s) in which soldiers are lodged (**~-square,** drill-ground near barracks); building in which many persons are similarly herded together; large building of severely dull or plain appearance. **2.** *v.t.* Place in barracks. [f. F *baraque* f. It. *baracca* or Sp. *barraca* soldier's tent, of unkn. orig.]

bă'rrack[2] *v.i.* & *t.* (Of spectators at games etc.) shout or jeer (at). [app. f. BORAK]

bărracōō'n *n.* (Hist.) Enclosure for slaves, convicts, etc. [f. Sp. *barracón* (as BARRACK[1]; see -OON)]

bărracu'da (-ōō'da), **-couta** (-ōō'ta), *n.* **1.** (usu. *-uda*). Large voracious W. Ind. sea-fish of family Sphyraenidae. **2.** (usu. *-outa*). Long slender food-fish of Pacific etc. (*Thyrsites atun*). [Amer. Sp. *barracuda*]

bă'rrage (-rahzh) *n.* **1.** Artificial barrier in river etc. (esp. in Nile). **2.** (Mil.) barrier to enemy's offensive or defensive action, usu. an area which is intensively bombarded; (fig.) rapid succession (*of* questions etc.); **~ balloon,** large captive balloon supporting steel cable as part of barrier against aircraft. **3.** Heat or deciding event in fencing, show-jumping, etc. [F (*barrer*; see BAR[2], -AGE)]

bărramŭ'ndĭ *n.* One of various Austral. freshwater food-fishes. [Aboriginal]

bă'rrator *n.* (Law) vexatious litigant; malicious raiser of discord. [ME, f. AF *baratour*, OF *barateor* trickster (*barater* f. Rom. **prattare* exchange, cheat f. Gk *prattō* manage)]

bă'rratr|ȳ *n.* (Marine law) fraud or gross and criminal negligence of master or crew to prejudice of ship's owners; (Law) vexatious litigation or incitement to it; trade in Church or State appointments; hence ~OUS *a.* [ME, f. OF *bar(a)terie* (*barat* deceit f. as BARRATOR)]

bar̂re *n.* Waist-level horizontal bar to help dancers keep their balance when exercising. [F, = BAR[1]]

bă'rrel[1] *n.* **1.** Wooden vessel of hooped staves with flat ends and usu. outward-bulging sides, cask, (**over a ~,** helpless; **scrape the ~,** use one's last resources); contents of this; measure of capacity (variable, *c.* 30–40 gallons); revolving cylinder in capstan, watch, and other machines; cylindrical body or trunk of an object (e.g. fountain-pen); belly and loins of horse, etc.; metal tube of gun. **2. ~-chested,** having a large rounded chest; ***~house,** low-

-class saloon, unrestrained forceful jazz-playing; **~-organ,** musical instrument with pin-studded cylinder turned by handle and mechanism opening pipes or striking metal tongues; **~ vault** (with uniform concave roof). [ME, f. OF *baril*, perh. f. Rom. **barra* (BAR[1])]

bă'rrel[2] *v.* (‖-ll-). **1.** *v.t.* Put in barrel(s). **2.** *v.i.* *(sl.) Drive fast. [f. prec.]

bă'rren *a.* (**-er, -est**) & *n.* **1.** *a.* Not bearing, or incapable of bearing, children, young, fruit, vegetation, or produce, (**~wort,** herb of genus *Epimedium*, thought to cause sterility); meagre, unprofitable, dull; hence ~LY[2] *adv.*, ~NESS (-n-n-) *n.* **2.** *n.* Barren tract of land, esp. (in *pl.*) in N. Amer. [ME, f. AF *barai(g)ne*, OF *barhaine* etc., of unkn. orig.]

bă'rrėt *n.* Small flat cap, esp. biretta. [f. F *barrette* f. It. *baretta* (as BIRETTA)]

***barrĕ'tte** *n.* Woman's bar-shaped clip or ornament for hair. [F, dim. of *barre* BAR[1]]

bărrĭcā'de[1] *n.* Hastily erected rampart across street etc. of barrels, carts, stones, furniture, esp. during revolution; barrier (lit. or fig.). [F (*barrique* f. Sp. *barrica* cask f. as *barril* BARREL[1]; see -ADE)]

bărrĭcā'de[2] *v.t.* Block (street etc.) with barricade; defend (place or person) with barricade. [f. prec.]

bă'rrĭer *n.* Fence barring advance or preventing access; gate at railway station where tickets must be shown; obstacle, boundary, or agency that prevents communication, success, etc.; **~ cream** (to protect skin against damage, infection, etc.); **~ reef,** coral reef separated from adjacent land by broad deep channel; SOUND[2] *barrier*. [ME f. AF *barrere*, OF *barriere* f. Rom. **barraria* (**barra* BAR[1])]

bar'rĭng *prep.* Except, not including. [f. BAR[2] + -ING[2]]

bar'rĭō *n.* (*pl.* **~s**). Spanish-speaking quarter of U.S. town or city. [Sp., = district of town]

bă'rrĭster *n.* ‖**~(-at-law)**, person called to bar and having right of practising as advocate in the higher courts; *lawyer. [16th c., f. BAR[1], perh. after *minister*]

bă'rrow[1] (-ō) *n.* (Archaeol.) Grave-mound, tumulus. [OE *beorg*, = OS, OHG *berg*, f. Gmc **bergaz*]

bă'rrow[2] (-ō) *n.* (**Whee'l**)**~**, shallow open box with shafts and one wheel for carrying loads etc.; = HAND[1]-*barrow*; ‖two-wheeled handcart (**~ boy,** coster); metal frame with two wheels for transporting luggage etc.; quantity carried in barrow. [OE *bearwe* f. Gmc **barwōn*, conn. w. BEAR[3]]

Bar'săc *n.* Somewhat sweet white Bordeaux wine. [~ in S.W. France]

Bart. *abbr.* Baronet.

bar'ter[1] *v.* **1.** *v.t.* Exchange (goods or intangible things) *for* other goods or *away*; **~ away,** part with for a (usu. unworthy) consideration. **2.** *v.i.* Trade by exchange. [prob. f. OF *barater*; see BARRATOR]

bar'ter[2] *n.* Traffic by exchange of goods (also fig., e.g. of talk). [f. prec.]

bartĭză'n *n.* Battlemented parapet, or overhanging battlemented corner turret, at top of church tower or castle. [spurious form (Scott) f. *bertisene* illit. spelling of *bratticing*; see BRATTICE]

bar'ton *n.* (arch.) Farmyard. [OE *bere-tūn* (*bere* barley, *tūn* enclosure; see TOWN)]

‖**Bart's** *n.* (colloq.) St. Bartholomew's Hospital in London. [abbr.]

bă'ryŏn *n.* (Phys.) Heavy elementary particle (nucleon or hyperon); hence **băryŏ'n**IC *a.* [f. Gk *barus* heavy + -ON]

bă'rysphēre *n.* Dense core of the earth, within the lithosphere. [f. Gk *barus* heavy + *sphaira* sphere]

barȳ'ta *n.* Barium oxide or hydroxide; hence **barȳ't**IC *a.* [f. foll., after *soda* etc.]

barȳ'tēs (-z) *n.* Native barium sulphate, heavy spar, used in some white paints. [f. Gk *barus* heavy, partly assim. to mineral names in *-ites*]

bă'rytōne *a.* & *n.* (Gk Gram.) (Word) with no or grave accent on last syllable. [f. Gk *barutonos* (see BARITONE)]

bā'sal *a.* Of, at, or forming, the base; fundamental; *basal* METABOLISM. [f. BASE[1] + -AL]

basalt (bă'sawlt *or* basaw'lt) *n.* **1.** Dark igneous rock often in columnar strata; hence **basa'lt**IC (-saw'l-) *a.* **2.** Black porcelain invented by Wedgwood. [f. L *basaltes* var. of *basanites* f. Gk (*basanos* touchstone)]

bas bleu (bah blėr') *n.* Bluestocking. [F]

bă'scūle *n.* Lever apparatus used in **~-bridge,** kind of drawbridge raised and lowered with counterpoise. [F, earlier *bacule* see-saw (*battre* bump, *cul* buttocks)]

bāse[1] *n.* **1.** That on which anything stands or depends; support, foundation, (lit. or fig.); principle, starting-point; main or important ingredient of mixture; material supporting film etc.; root or stem as origin of word or derivative; middle part of transistor. **2.** (Archit.) Part of column between shaft and pedestal or pavement; (Her.) lowest part of shield. **3.** (Bot. & Zool.) End at which an organ is attached to trunk. **4.** (Geom.) Line or surface on which plane or solid figure is regarded as standing. **5.** (Chem.) Substance capable of combining with an acid to form a salt (including, but wider than, ALKALI). **6.** (Mil.) Town or other area in rear of an army where drafts, stores, hospitals, etc., are concentrated; operational headquarters. **7.** (Surv.) Known line used as geometrical base for trigonometry. **8.** (Math.) Starting-number for system of numeration or logarithms (as 10 in decimal counting). **9.** (Baseball). One of the four stations that must be reached in turn when scoring a run; **get to first ~**, (fig.) achieve first step towards objective; **off ~**, (fig.) mistaken. **10.** ***~'board,** skirting-board; **~ hit** (enabling batter to reach first base safely); **~'line,** starting-point, (Tennis) line at each end of court; **~'load,** permanent load on power supplies etc.; **~'man,** fielder near a base in baseball. [F, or f. L f. Gk *basis* stepping]

bāse[2] *v.t.* Found (something) *on*; establish (*firmly* etc.); **~ oneself on,** rely upon (in argument etc.); **~d on, -~d,** using as fundamental station or means (*submarine based on Malta*; *land-based forces*; *computer-based accountancy*). [f. prec.]

bāse[3] *a.* **1.** Morally low; cowardly, selfish, mean, or despicable; menial; hence ~'LY[2] (-slĭ) *adv.*, ~'NESS (-sn-) *n.* **2. ~'born,** of low birth, illegitimate; **~ coin** (spurious, alloyed); **~ metals** (opposed to noble or precious). [ME in sense 'of small height', f. F *bas* f. med. L *bassus* short (in L as cognomen)]

bā'seball (-sbawl) *n.* (Ball used in) U.S. national game, with teams of nine who in turn seek to strike ball thrown by opponent and traverse circuit of four points called bases. [f. BASE[1] + BALL[1]]

bā'selėss (-sl-) *a.* Groundless, unfounded; hence ~LY[2] *adv.*, ~NESS *n.* [f. BASE[1] + -LESS]

bā'sement (-sm-) *n.* Lowest or fundamental part of structure; inhabited storey below ground level. [prob. Du., perh. f. It. *basamento* base of column (*basare* BASE[2])]

basĕ'nji *n.* Smallish rarely-barking African hunting-dog. [Bantu]

bases. *Pl.* of BASE[1] or BASIS.

băsh *v.t.*, & *n.* **1.** *v.t.* Strike heavily so as to smash in or *in*; make violent attack on. **2.** *n.* Heavy blow; (sl.) attempt (*have a bash*); (sl.) party, entertainment. [ult. imit., perh. f. *bang, smash, dash*, etc.]

bashaw'. Var. (arch.) of PASHA.

bă'shful *a.* Shy, diffident; shamefaced, sheepish; hence ~LY² *adv.*, ~NESS *n.* [f. obs. *bash* v. (ABASH) + -FUL]

băshĭ-bazou'k (-ōō'k) *n.* (Hist.) Mercenary of Turkish irregulars, notorious for pillage and brutality. [f. Turk. *başıbozuk* irregular soldier]

bā'sĭc *a.* Of, at, or forming, base; fundamental; (Chem.) having the properties of or containing a base; (Geol.) with low silica content; standard minimum (allowance, pay, etc.); ~ **dye** (consisting of salts of organic bases); **B~ English** (simplified form with select vocabulary of 850 words for international use); ~ **industry,** one of great economic importance; ~ **slag,** fertilizer containing phosphates formed as by-product in steel manufacture; hence **bā'**SICALLY *adv.* [f. BASE¹ + -IC]

bāsĭ'cĭty̆ *n.* (Chem.) Number of equivalents of base reacting with one molecule of a particular acid. [f. prec. + -ITY]

basĭ'dĭ|um *n.* (*pl.* ~**a**). Spore-bearing structure in some fungi. [mod. L, f. Gk *basidion* dim. of BASIS]

bă'sĭl (-z-) *n.* Aromatic herb of genus *Ocimum*, esp. **sweet** ~ and **bush** ~, both culinary. [ME, f. OF *basile* f. med. L f. Gk *basilikos* royal]

basĭ'lĭc|a *n.* Oblong hall with double colonnade and apse used for lawcourts and assemblies; such building used as Christian church; church with special privileges from Pope; hence ~AN *a.* [L, f. Gk *basilikē* (*oikia, stoa*) royal (house, portico) f. *basileus* king; see -IC]

bă'sĭlĭsk (bă'z-) *n.* **1.** Fabulous reptile hatched by serpent from cock's egg, with lethal breath and look; ~**-glance** etc., (fig.) evil eye, person or thing that blasts (reputation etc.). **2.** (Her.) cockatrice; (Zool.) small American lizard of genus *Basiliscus*, with hollow crest inflated at will. [ME, f. L f. Gk *basiliskos* (dim. of *basileus* king) kinglet, serpent, golden-crested wren]

bā'sin *n.* Hollow round metal or pottery vessel, less deep than wide, and narrowing downwards, for holding water etc., bowl; hollow depression; dock with floodgates; land-locked harbour; area drained by river and tributaries; circular or oval valley; (Geol.) formation with strata dipping towards centre, deposit (e.g. of coal) contained in this; hence ~FUL 2 *n.* [ME, f. OF *bacin* f. med. L *ba(s)cinus*, perh. f. Gaulish]

bāsĭ'pėtal *a.* Developing from above downwards; hence ~LY² *adv.* [f. BASIS + L *petere* seek + -AL]

bā'sĭs *n.* (*pl.* **ba'ses** *pr.* -sēz). Main ingredient; foundation; beginning; determining principle (*on a purely friendly basis*); common ground for negotiation etc. [L f. Gk, = BASE¹]

bask (bah-) *v.i.* Revel in warmth and light (usu. *in* the sun, firelight, etc., fig. *in* popularity etc.); ~**'ing shark,** very large species of shark (*Cetorhinus maximus*), accustomed to lie near water surface. [ME, app. f. ON **bathask* refl. of *batha* BATHE¹]

Bă'skervĭlle *n.* Style of type (as used in this dictionary). [orig. designed by J. ~, Engl. printer d. 1775]

ba'skėt (bah'-) *n.* Container made of plaited or interwoven osiers, cane, rushes, wire, etc.; ~**(ful)**, quantity contained in it; structure resembling basket; **(type)** ~, keybars of typewriter; net used, goal scored, in basketball; (euphem., colloq.) bastard; ~**ball,** (large inflated ball used in) game played by teams of five or six in which goal is scored when ball is thrown into net fixed on ring 10 ft. above ground; ~ **chair** (made of wickerwork); ~ (comprehensive) **clause;** ~ **weave** (resembling basket material in design); ~**work,** ~RY (5), (art of making) structure of interlaced osiers etc. [AF & OF, AL *baskettum*, of unkn. orig.]

bā'son. Var. (arch.) of BASIN.

Băsque (-sk; *or* bah-) *n.* & *a.* **1.** (Native or language) of Western Pyrenees. **2.** *n.* (*b*~). Short continuation of bodice below waist; bodice having this. [F, f. L *Vasco -onis*]

bă's-rėlief *n.* (Sculpture in) low RELIEF². [earlier *basse relieve*, f. It. *basso rilievo* low relief; later alt. to F form]

băss¹ *n.* (*pl.* ~ *or* ~**'es**). Common perch; one of many similar sea or freshwater fish with spiny fins. [earlier *barse* f. OE *bærs*, OS, MHG *bars*]

băss² *n.* Inner bark of lime or palm tree used as fibre; ~**'wood,** Amer. lime tree or its wood. [alt. f. BAST]

bāss³ *a.* & *n.* **1.** *a.* Deep-sounding; of or suited to bass part; ~ **clef** (placing F below middle C on second highest line of staff); ~ **viol,** viola da gamba, *double-bass. **2.** *n.* Lowest part in harmonized music; male voice of lowest range; singer with this voice; part written for bass voice; lowest-pitched member of a group of similar instruments; (colloq.) double-bass, whence ~'IST (3) *n.*; **figured** or **thorough** ~, (1) bass part with numerals etc. below to indicate the proper harmony, (2) theory of harmony; GROUND¹ *bass.* [=BASE³, alt. after It. *basso*]

bă'ssėt *n.* ~**(-hound)**, short-legged hound for hunting hares etc. [F, dim. of *bas basse* low; see BASE³]

bă'ssėt-hôrn *n.* Tenor clarinet with extended compass. [G, transl. of F *cor de bassette* f. It. *corno di bassetto* (*corno* horn, *di* of, *bassetto* dim. of *basso* BASE³)]

băssinĕ't *n.* Hooded wicker cradle or pram. [F, dim. of *bassin* BASIN]

bă'ss|ō *n.* (*pl.* ~**os** *or* ~**i**). Man with bass voice; ~**o ostina'to** (-ah'-), = GROUND¹ *bass*; ~**o profu'ndo,** man with unusually deep bass voice. [It., = BASS³; *ostinato* persistent, *profondo* deep]

bassōō'n *n.* Bass instrument of oboe family, whence ~IST (3) *n.*; its player; organ and harmonium stop of similar quality. [f. F *basson* f. It. *bassone* (*basso* BASE³; see -OON)]

basso-relievo (băsōrĕlyā'vō) *n.* (*pl.* ~*s*). = BAS-RELIEF. [It.]

băst *n.* Inner bark of lime (see BASS²); other flexible fibrous bark. [OE *bæst* f. Gmc **bastaz*]

bă'stard (*or* bah'-) *a.* & *n.* **1.** *a.* Born out of wedlock, illegitimate; (of things) unauthorized, hybrid, counterfeit; (Bot. & Zool.) closely resembling another species; ~ **title,** half-title; ~ **wing,** (Zool.) rudimentary extra digit with quill-feathers. **2.** *n.* Bastard person; (S. Afr., also **bastaard**) person of mixed race, Griqua; (colloq.) disliked or unfortunate person or thing. [ME f. OF, f. med. L *bastardus*, perh. f. *bastum* pack-saddle; see -ARD]

bă'stardĭz|e, -ĭs|e (-īz), *v.t.* Declare illegitimate; hence ~A'TION *n.* [f. prec. + -IZE]

bă'stardy̆ *n.* State of being bastard, illegitimacy. [f. AF & OF *bastardie* (as BASTARD; see -Y¹)]

bāste¹ *v.t.* Stitch loosely together, tack, (as preparation for regular sewing). [ME, f. OF *bastir* sew lightly f. Frank. **bastjan* f. Gmc **bastaz* (BAST)]

bāste² *v.t.* Moisten (roasting meat) with gravy or melted fat to prevent drying. [16th c., of unkn. orig.]

bāste³ *v.t.* Thrash, cudgel. [perh. fig. use of prec.]

băstĭ'lle (-ē'l) *n.* (Hist.) Fortress; prison. [ME f. OF *bastille, bastide* f. Prov. *bastida* (*bastir* build);

applied to a 14th-c. prison-fortress in Paris, destroyed 1789]

băstĭnā'dō *n.* (*pl.* **~s** *or* **~es**), & *v.t.* (Punish or torture by) caning on soles of feet. [f. Sp. *bastonada* (*baston* BATON); see -ADO]

bă'stĭon *n.* Projecting part of fortification, irregular pentagon with its base in the line (or at an angle) of the main works; similar natural rock formation; (fig.) institution serving as defence. [F, f. It. *bastione* (*bastire* build)]

băt[1] *n.* Furry mammal of order Chiroptera flying esp. at nightfall, with forelimbs modified to carry membranous wings; **blind as a ~**, completely blind; **have ~s in the belfry,** (colloq.) be crazy or eccentric, whence BATS *a.*; **like a ~ out of hell,** (sl.) very quickly; **~'wing sleeve** (with deep armhole and tight cuff). [16th c., alt. of ME *bakke* f. Scand.]

băt[2] *n.* & *v.* (**-tt-**). **1.** *n.* Implement with handle, for striking ball in cricket, baseball, table tennis, etc.; **carry** one's **~**, (Cricket) be not out at end of side's completed innings; ||**off** one's **own ~**, (fig.) unaided; ***right off the ~**, immediately. **2.** Act of using this; (usu. in *pl.*) object like table-tennis bat used to guide aircraft when landing; batsman (*a good* etc. *bat*). **3. ~'sman,** performer with cricket etc. bat, signaller using bats to guide aircraft; *~sman's wicket*, cricket pitch favouring batsmen; hence *~'sman*SHIP *n.* **4.** *v.i.* Use bat, have innings; (sl.) move (*along*, *around*, etc.). **5.** *v.t.* Strike (as) with bat; **~ in,** (Baseball) effect scoring of (run) by batting. [ME, f. OE *batt* club, perh. partly f. OF *batte* club (*battre* strike)]

||**băt**[3] *n.* (sl.) Pace of stroke or step (*went off at a rare bat*). [19th c., perh. f. BAT[1]]

băt[4] *n.* (sl.) Spree, binge. [orig. uncert.; cf. BATTER[4]]

băt[5] *v.t.* (**-tt-**). Wink; **never ~ted an eyelid,** (1) did not sleep a wink, (2) betrayed no emotion. [var. of obs. *bate* flutter]

bata'ta (-ah'ta) *n.* Sweet POTATO. [Sp., f. Taino]

Batā'vĭan *a.* & *n.* (Inhabitant) of ancient Batavia (between Rhine and Waal) or of modern Holland, Dutch(man). [f. L *Batavia* (*Batavi* the Batavians) + -AN]

bătch *n.*, & *v.t.* **1.** *n.* Loaves produced at one baking; quantity or number of things or persons coming at once and treated as a set; **~ production,** treating materials in batches, not continuously. **2.** *v.t.* Arrange in batches. [ME, f. OE *bæcce* (*bacan* BAKE)]

bă'tchy̆. Var. of BATTY.

bāte[1] *v.t.* Restrain; **with ~d breath,** anxiously. [f. ABATE]

||**bāte**[2], ||**bait**[3], *n.* (sl.) Rage (*was in an awful bate*). [f. BAIT[1] = state of baited person]

bă'teau (-tō) *n.* (*pl.* **~x** *pr.* -ōz). Light river-boat, esp. flat-bottomed kind used in Canada. [F, = boat]

bă'teleur (-lẽr) *n.* Short-tailed Afr. and Arabian eagle (*Terathopius ecaudatus*). [F, = juggler]

Bā'tesĭan (-ts-) *a.* **~ mimicry** (in which edible species is protected by resemblance to harmful one). [f. H. W. *Bates*, Engl. naturalist d. 1892 + -IAN]

bath[1] (bahth; *pl. pr.* -dhz) *n.* **1.** Immersion in liquid etc. for cleansing or therapy (*have, take, a bath*); BLOOD[1]-*bath*; MUD-*bath*; SHOWER-*bath*; SUN-*bath*; TURKISH *bath*. **2.** Water etc. for bathing in; surrounding medium for developing films, controlling temperature, etc. **3. ~(-tub)**, vessel for bathing in; BIRD-*bath*; EYE[1]-*bath*. **4.** (usu. in *pl.*) Building for bathing or swimming in. **5. ~ cube, salts,** etc., (for softening or scenting bath-water); ***~'robe,** dressing-gown; **~'room,** room containing bath, (euphem.) lavatory. **6.** ||**Order of the B~,** order of knighthood, named from bath preceding installation. **7.** (*B~*). Town in Avon named from hot springs; **B~ brick,** preparation for cleaning metal; **B~ bun,** round spiced kind with currants and icing; **B~ chair** (wheeled, for invalid); *Bath* CHAP[2]; **B~ Oliver,** unsweetened biscuit invented by Dr. W. Oliver of Bath, d. 1764; **B~ stone,** oolite building-stone. [OE *bæth*, = OHG *bad*, OS, ON *bath* f. Gmc **batham*]

||**bath**[2] (bahth) *v.* **1.** *v.t.* Wash (child, invalid, animal, etc.) in bath. **2.** *v.i.* Take a bath, bath oneself. [f. prec.]

bāth|e[1] (-dh) *v.* **1.** *v.t.* Immerse in liquid etc.; moisten all over (*bathe* one's *eyes*); (of sunlight etc.) envelop. **2.** *v.i.* Immerse oneself in water etc., ||usu. as recreation; **~'ing beauty, belle,** attractive woman in bathing-suit; **~'ing-machine,** (Hist.) wheeled dressing-box drawn into sea for bathing from; **~'ing-suit,** garment worn when bathing. [OE *bathian*, = OHG *badon*, ON *batha* f. Gmc **bathōn* (**batham* BATH[1])]

||**bāthe**[2] (-dh) *n.* Immersion in liquid, esp. in sea, river, or swimming-bath. [f. prec. 2]

bā'ther (-dh-) *n.* One who bathes; (in *pl.*, Austral.) bathing-suit. [f. BATHE[1] + -ER[1]]

bathĕ'tĭc *a.* Marked by bathos. [irreg. f. Gk BATHOS after *pathos*, *pathetic*]

bă'tholĭth *n.* Dome of intrusive igneous rock extending to unknown depth. [G, f. as foll. + -LITH]

bathŏ'mèter *n.* Instrument used to ascertain depth of water. [f. Gk *bathos* depth + -o- + -METER]

Bathō'nĭan *a.* & *n.* **1.** (Native or inhabitant) of BATH[1] 7. **2.** (Geol.) (Of) subdivision of Jurassic typified by formations at Bath. [f. mod. L *Bathonia* Bath + -AN]

bā'thŏs *n.* Fall from sublime to commonplace; anticlimax; performance absurdly unequal to occasion. [Gk, = depth]

bathŏ'tĭc *a.* Marked by bathos. [irreg. f. prec. after *chaos*, *chaotic*]

bă'thy̆scăphe *n.* Manned vessel for deep-sea diving, with special buoyancy gear. [F, f. Gk *bathus* deep + *skaphos* ship]

bă'thy̆sphēre *n.* Large strong submersible sphere for deep-sea observation. [f. Gk *bathus* deep + SPHERE]

bă'tĭk (*or* batē'k) *n.* Method (orig. in Java) of printing coloured design on textiles by waxing parts not to be dyed; material so treated. [Jav., lit. 'painted']

bati'ste (-ē'st) *n.* & *a.* (Of) fine light cotton or linen fabric like cambric. [F, f. *Baptiste* of Cambrai, first maker]

bă't|man *n.* (*pl.* **~men;** *fem.* **~woman** *pl.* **~women**). (Mil.) Officer's servant. [f. *bat* (OF *ba(s)t* f. Prov., f. med. L *bastum* pack-saddle) + MAN[1]]

bă'ton *n.* Staff of office, esp. field marshal's; constable's truncheon; short tube or stick carried in relay race; (Her.) narrow truncated bend (**~ sinister,** sign of bastardy); (Mus.) conductor's wand for beating time, drum major's stick; (Horol.) short bar replacing some figures on dials. [f. F *bâton*, *baston* f. Rom. **baston*- (**bastare* drive with stick f. LL *bastum* stick)]

batrā'chĭan (-k-) *a.* & *n.* **1.** *a.* Of frogs and toads. **2.** *a.* & *n.* (One) of the Batrachia or Salientia, animals that discard gills and tail. [f. Gk *batrakheios* (*batrakhos* frog) + -AN]

băts *a.* (usu. *pred.*) (sl.) Crazy. [f. BAT[1]*s in the belfry*]

bă'tsman. See BAT[2].

battă'lion (-yon) *n.* Large body of men in battle array (**God is for the big ~s,** force prevails); unit of infantry composed of several companies and forming part of brigade; large group of persons with similar tasks etc. [f. F *battaillon* f. It. *battaglione* (*battaglia* BATTLE¹; cf. -OON)]

||**bă'ttels** (-z) *n. pl.* College account at Oxford for board and provisions supplied, or for all college expenses. [perh. f. obs. v. *battle* fatten f. obs. a. *battle* nutritious; cf. BATTEN³]

bă'tten¹ *n.* Long narrow piece of squared timber; bar of wood used for clamping boards of door etc.; strip of wood carrying electric lamps; (Naut.) strip of wood or metal securing hatchway tarpaulin; hence ~ING¹ (6) *n.* [f. OF *batant* part. of *batre* beat (see BATTERY)]

bă'tten² *v.t.* Strengthen with battens; ~ **down,** (Naut.) close (*the hatches*; see prec.). [f. prec.]

bă'tten³ *v.i.* Feed gluttonously *on*; grow fat; thrive, esp. at expense of another. [f. ON *batna* get better (*bati* advantage)]

bă'tter¹ *v.* **1.** *v.t.* & *i.* Strike repeatedly so as to bruise or break (person, thing, or abs.; *against, at,* door etc.; *about, down, in*); **~ed baby** (with symptoms of repeated violence by adults). **2.** *v.t.* Operate against (walls etc.) with artillery; (fig.) handle severely (theory, person); beat out of shape, indent; **~ing-ram,** swinging beam anciently used for breaching walls, sometimes with ram's-head end. [ME, f. AF *baterer* f. OF *batre* beat (see BATTERY)]

bă'tter² *n.* Runny mixture of flour and egg beaten up with milk or water for cooking. [ME, f. AF *batour* f. OF *bateüre* (*batre*; see prec.)]

bă'tter³ *n.* (Baseball) player using bat. [f. BAT² 4 + -ER¹]

bă'tter⁴ *n.* (sl.) Spree, binge. [19th c., orig. unkn.]

bă'tter⁵ *v.i.,* & *n.* (Have) receding slope from ground upwards. [ME, of unkn. orig.]

bă'ttery̆ *n.* **1.** (Law). Infliction of blows, or of any menacing touch to clothes or person (esp. in phr. *assault and battery*). **2.** (Mil.) Emplacement for one or more guns on land or ship; artillery unit of guns and men and vehicles. **3.** Set of connected similar units of equipment; portable cell(s) supplying electricity; (Psych.) series of tests; series of cages, etc., in which hens are confined for intensive laying, or poultry or cattle reared and fattened; (Baseball) pitcher and catcher. [f. F *batterie* (*bat(t)re* strike f. L *battuere*; see -ERY)]

bă'ttĭng *n.* In vbl senses; cotton fibre prepared in sheets for quilts etc. [f. BAT² + -ING¹]

bă'ttle¹ *n.* **1.** Fight, esp. between large organized forces (**do ~, join ~,** enter into combat; PITCH²*ed battle*; **~ royal,** battle in which several combatants or all available forces engage, free fight, (fig.) heated argument); victory in fighting (*the battle is to the strong*; *youth is* **half the ~,** a great help); (fig.) contest (*battle of wits*). **2.** **~axe,** medieval or prehistoric weapon, (colloq.) domineering or formidable (usu. middle-aged) woman; **~-cruiser,** heavy-gunned ship of higher speed and lighter armour than battleship; **~-cry,** war-cry, slogan; **~dress,** soldier's etc. everyday uniform of blouse and trousers; **~ fatigue,** = COMBAT *fatigue*; **~field, ~ground,** scene of battle; **~ship,** most heavily armed and armoured warship, designed to meet the most powerful ships in battle. [ME, f. OF *bataille* f. Rom. **battalia* f. LL *battualia* pl. gladiatorial exercises f. L *battuere* beat; see -LE 2]

bă'ttle² *v.* **1.** *v.i.* Struggle (*with* or *against* difficulties, waves, etc., *for* one's rights etc.). **2.** *v.t.* Fight (one's way etc.); *battle with. [f. F *batailler* (*bataille*; see prec.)]

băttledōre (-teld-) *n.* **1.** (Hist.) Wooden instrument like canoe paddle used in washing, baking, etc. **2.** Small racket used with shuttlecock in the game of **~ and shuttlecock.** [15th c., perh. f. Prov. *batedor* beater (*batre* beat)]

bă'ttlement (-telm-) *n.* (usu. in *pl.*) Indented parapet at top of wall, for defence of building; roof enclosed by this (*walking on the battlements*); hence ~ED² *a.* [f. OF *bataillier* furnish with ramparts + -MENT]

battue (bătū' *or* -ōō') *n.* Driving of game by beaters towards sportsmen; shooting-party on this plan; wholesale slaughter. [F, fem. p.p. (as n.) of *battre* beat f. L *battuere*]

bă'ttȳ *a.* (sl.) Crazy. [f. BAT¹ + -Y²]

batwoman. See BATMAN.

bau'ble *n.* Showy trinket; (Hist.) jester's emblem; trifle, toy; thing of no worth. [ME f. OF *ba(u)bel* child's toy, of unkn. orig.]

baud (bōd) *n.* Unit of telegraphic signalling speed, corresp. to one dot etc. per second. [f. J. M. E. *Baudot*, Fr. engineer d. 1903]

Bauhaus (bow'hows) *n.* (Principles of) a German school of architectural design (1919–33). [G (*bau* building, *haus* house)]

baulk¹,². See BALK¹,².

bau'xīte *n.* Earthy mineral containing varying proportions of alumina, the chief commercial source of aluminium; hence **bauxĭ'tIC** *a.* [F, f. *Les Baux* near Arles in S. France + -ITE¹ (2)]

bawbee' (*or* baw'-) *n.* (Sc.) Halfpenny. [f. name of the laird of *Sillebawby*, 16th-c. Scots mint-master]

bawd *n.* Procuress. [f. ME *bawdstrot* f. OF *baude(s)tro(y)t* procuress]

baw'd|ȳ *a.* & *n.* Humorously indecent (talk); **~y-house,** brothel; hence ~ĭLY² *adv.,* ~ĭNESS *n.* [f. prec. + -Y²]

bawl *v.t.* & *i.* Speak or weep at top of voice; **~ out,** (colloq.) reprimand severely. [imit.; cf. med. L *baulare* bark, Icel. *baula* (Sw. *böla*) to low]

bay¹ *n.* **1.** Kind of laurel, esp. *Laurus nobilis*; (in *pl.*) wreath of its leaves worn by conquerors or poets; fame as hero or poet. **2.** **~'berry,** fragrant W. Indian tree (*Pimenta acris*); **~-leaf,** (usu. dried) leaf of *L. nobilis* used as flavouring; **~ rum,** perfume (esp. for the hair) distilled from rum and bayberry leaves. [f. OF *baie* f. L *baca* berry]

bay² *n.* Part of sea filling wide-mouthed opening of land; recess in mountain range; **~ salt,** salt crystals from evaporation of sea-water; ***Bay State,** Massachusetts. [ME, f. OF *baie* f. OSp. *bahia*]

bay³ *n.* Division of wall between columns or buttresses; recess or compartment (**sick-~,** part of ship's deck used as hospital, any quarters for sick persons); space added to room by advancing window from wall line (**~ window,** window filling such space, (sl.) protuberant abdomen); ||railway line at station, ending in cul-de-sac and acting as starting-point or terminus for side-line; platform adjoining this. [ME, f. OF *baie* (*ba(y)er* gape f. med. L *batare*)]

bay⁴ *n.* Deep bark of large dog or of hounds in pursuit, esp. chorus raised as they draw close to quarry; **at ~,** in desperate situation; **bring to ~,** come close to (quarry); **hold, keep, at ~,** keep at a distance; **stand at ~,** turn against pursuers. [ME f. OF *(a)bai* f. *bayer, baiier* (see foll.)]

bay⁵ *v.i.* & *t.* (Of large dog) bark or howl (at). [ME f. OF *(a)baiier* bark f. It. *(ab)baiare*, of imit. orig.]

bay⁶ *a.* & *n.* Reddish-brown (horse) with black mane and tail. [f. OF *bai* f. L *badius*]

bayadère (-dār') *n.* Hindu dancing-girl (esp. at S.-Indian temple); striped textile fabric. [F, f. Port. *bailadeira* dancer]

Bay'ard *n.* Chivalrous person. [f. Seigneur de ~, Fr. soldier d. 1524]

bay'onĕt *n.,* & *v.t.* **1.** *n.* Stabbing blade attachable to rifle-muzzle; ~ **plug** etc., electric etc. plug with push-and-twist engagement of parts to prevent detachment by simple pull. **2.** *v.t.* Stab with bayonet. [f. F *baïonnette*, perh. f. *Bayonne* in S.W. France, as first made there; cf. -ET[1]]

bay′ou (bī′o͞o) *n.* Marshy offshoot of river etc. in southern U.S. [Amer. F; cf. Choctaw *bayuk*]

bazaar′ (-zar̂′) *n.* Oriental market; large shop selling fancy goods; sale of goods for charity. [f. Pers. *bāzār*, prob. through Turk. and It.]

***bazo͞o′** *n.* (sl.) Mouth. [19th c.; orig. unkn.]

***bazo͞o′ka** *n.* Crude trombone-like musical instrument; anti-tank rocket-gun of similar form. [arbitr. name; cf. prec.]

BB *abbr.* double-black (pencil-lead).

***BBB** *abbr.* Better Business Bureau.

B.B.C. *abbr.* British Broadcasting Corporation.

bbl. *abbr.* barrels (esp. of oil).

B.C. *abbr.* BEFORE Christ; British Columbia; British Council.

B.C.E. *abbr.* Before the COMMON[1] Era.

B.D. *abbr.* Bachelor of Divinity.

Bde. *abbr.* (esp. Mil.) Brigade.

bdĕ′llium (d-) *n.* (Tree esp. of genus *Commiphora* yielding) resin used as perfume etc. [L, f. Gk *bdellion* rendering Heb. *b^{e}dhōlah*]

B.D.S. *abbr.* Bachelor of Dental Surgery.

bē (bē *or* bĭ) *v.* (*pres. ind.*: **am** *pr.* ăm *or* am; **art** (arch.) *pr.* ar̂t *or* ert; **is** *pr.* ĭz; *pl.* **are** *pr.* ar̂ *or* er, or **be** (arch.; *powers that be*); *past ind.*: 1 and 3 **was** *pr.* wŏz *or* woz; 2 **wast** (arch.) *pr.* wŏst *or* wost; *pl.* & 2 *sing.* **were** *pr.* wer̂ *or* war̂ *or* wer; *pres. subj.* **be;** *past subj.* **were,** exc. 2 *sing.* **wert** (arch.) *pr.* wer̂t *or* wert; *imper.* **be;** *part.* **being** *pr.* bē′ĭng; *p.p.* **been** *pr.* bēn *or* bĭn; colloq. abbr. forms: **'m** = *am*, **'s** = *is*, **'re** = *are*; **aren't** (ar̂nt) = *am not* (interrog.), *are not*; **isn't** (ĭ′zent) = *is not*; **wasn't** (wŏ′zent) = *was not*; **weren't** (wer̂nt *or* war̂nt) = *were not*; **ain't** (colloq.) = *am not*, (vulg.) = *is not, are not*. **1.** (As full verb) Exist, occur, live, (often with *there*; *God is*, *there is a God*; *there is a green hill far away*; *I think, therefore I am*; *can such things be?*; **to be or not to be,** should existence be terminated? (f. Shak. *Hamlet* III. i. 56); **Miss X that was,** her maiden name being X; **for the time being,** = *for the* PRESENT[2]; **be that as it may,** no matter what is the fact concerning that); remain, continue, (**let it be,** do not disturb it); (w. *adv.* or *adv. phr.*) occupy position in space or time (*is in the garden*; *her birthday is on Tuesday*), take or direct oneself (*be off!*; *are you for London?*; *is from Canada*), experience condition (*he is better today*), occupy oneself (*what are you about?*; *mice have been at the food*), hold view (*I am for, against, capital punishment*), (in perf. tenses) go (to place etc.) (*has been to Rome, into the matter*); (w. ind. obj.) befall (*woe is me*); (in *p.p.*, colloq.) called, visited, (*has anyone been?*); **been (and gone) and,** (colloq. phr. expr. protest or surprise; *you have been and moved my papers!*). **2.** (As cop. v., with *n.*, *a.*, or *adj. phr.*) Have state or quality (*I am a man*; *he is ill*; *be of good courage*; *be quick about it*); coincide in identity with (*you are the man I want*; *today is Thursday*; *it is I*, colloq. *it is me*); (emphat.) form main constituent of (*Kingsley Martin* was *the 'New Statesman'*); amount to (*twice two is four*); cost (*how much are these pears?*); signify (*it is nothing to me*); act the part of (*Miss X is Desdemona*). **3.** (As aux. v.) (with *p.p.* of *v.t.* forming passives) (*this was done*); (arch., with *p.p.* of *v.i.* such as *fall, come, flee, grow*, forming past tenses) (*the sun is set*; *Babylon is fallen*); (with *pres. part. act.* forming continuous tenses act. and pass.) (*he is building a house*; *am leaving tomorrow*; *the house was building*); (with *pres. part. pass.* forming continuous tenses pass.) (*the house was being built*); (w. inf. expr. duty (*I am to inform you*), intention (*he is to be there*), possibility (*the house is to let*; *it was not to be found*), destiny (*they were never to meet again*)); *were* (w. inf. in hypotheses) (*if I were*, or *were I, to tell you*). **4. be-all (and end-all)** *n.*, whole being or essence (*of*); **be-in** *n.*, (sl.) usu. spontaneous meeting of hippies etc. in public place; **-to-be** *a.*, future (*his bride-to-be*). [*am, is* f. Gmc **es-*; past forms f. Gmc **wes-*; *be, been, being* f. OE *bēon* f. IE **beu-*; *are, art* f. Gmc **ar-*]

bė- *pref.* forming *vbs.* **1.** (to *v.t.*) All over, all round, (*beset, besmear*). **2.** (to *v.t.*) Thoroughly, excessively, (*begrudge, belabour*). **3.** (to *v.i.*, expr. transitive action) (*bemoan, bestride*). **4.** (to *a.* or *n.*, expr. transitive action) (*befool, befoul*). **5.** (to *n.*) = to call (so and so). **6.** (to *n.*) = to surround with, to affect with, to treat in the manner of, (*becloud, befriend*). **7.** (to *n.*, w. *suf.* -ED[2]) = having (*bejewelled, beribboned, bespectacled, bewigged*). [OE *be-*, weak form of *bī* BY[1] prep. & adv., as used in *bygone, by-law, byword*, etc.]

B.E. *abbr.* Bachelor of Education; Bachelor of Engineering; bill of exchange.

Be *symb.* beryllium.

B.E.A. *abbr.* British Epilepsy Association; (formerly) British European Airways.

beach *n.*, & *v.t.* **1.** *n.* (arch.) Water-worn pebbles or sand. **2.** Sea-shore or lake-shore covered with these; shore between high and low water mark. **3. ~-ball,** large inflated ball for games on beach; **~′comber,** (1) white man in Pacific Islands etc. who lives by collecting jetsam, longshore vagrant, (2) long wave rolling in from sea; **~-head,** fortified position established on beach by landing forces [after *bridgehead*]; **~ plum,** (edible fruit of) maritime N. Amer. shrub (*Prunus maritima*). **4.** *v.t.* Run or haul up (ship, whale, etc.) on shore. [16th c., of unkn. orig.]

‖**beach-la-mar̂′** *n.* Commercial jargon English used in W. Pacific. [corrupt. f. Port. *bicho do mar* BÊCHE-DE-MER]

bea′con *n.* **1.** Signal or signal-fire on pole or hill; ‖conspicuous hill suitable for this. **2.** Signal station; radio station whose signal helps to fix position of ship or aircraft or spacecraft. **3.** Signal light; guide or warning; ‖amber globe on pole marking some pedestrian crossings. [OE *bēacn*, = OS *bōkan*, OHG *bouhhan* f. WG **baukna*]

bead[1] *n.* Small rounded usu. perforated object for threading with others on string or wire, sewing on fabric, etc. (**tell** one's **~s,** use beads of rosary etc. in counting prayers); drop of liquid, bubble; small knob in foresight of gun (**draw a ~ on,** take aim at); **~('ing),** inner edge of pneumatic tyre gripping rim of wheel; (Archit.) moulding like a series of beads, or narrow moulding of semicircular section; **~-roll,** list of names, long series, (orig. of persons to be prayed for); **~′sman** (-z-), (Hist.) pensioner bound to pray for benefactor, almsman. [orig. 'prayer', f. OE *gebed*, = OS *beda*, OHG *beta*, Goth. *bida*, f. Gmc **bedh-*; see BID[1]]

bead[2] *v.* **1.** *v.t.* Furnish with beads; string together. **2.** *v.i.* Form or grow into beads. [f. prec.]

bea′dĭng *n.* In vbl senses; (Archit.) = BEAD[1]. [f. BEAD[1,2] + -ING[1]]

‖**bea′dle** *n.* Ceremonial officer of church, college, city company, etc.; (Hist.) parish officer appointed by vestry to keep order in church, etc.; (Sc.) church officer attending on the minister; hence **~DOM** (-deld-) *n.*, stupid officiousness, **~SHIP** (-delsh-) *n.* [ME f. OF *bedel* f. Rom. **bidellus*, of Gmc orig.; see -LE 1]

For other words in *be-* see BE-.

bea'dy̆ *a.* (Of eyes) small and bright; covered with beads or drops. [f. BEAD[1] + -Y[2]]

bea'gle *n.* Small hound, used for hare-hunting when field follows on foot; spy, informer, constable; **bea'gling,** hunting with beagles. [ME, f. OF *beegueule* noisy person, prob. f. *beer* open wide + *gueule* throat]

beak[1] *n.* Bird's horny projecting jaws (esp. in bird of prey, and when strong and hooked); similar mandible-end of other animals, e.g. turtle; hooked nose; projection at prow of ancient warship; spout; hence (-)~ED[2] (-kt) *a.* [ME f. OF *bec* f. L *beccus*, of Celt. origin]

||**beak**[2] *n.* (sl.) Magistrate; schoolmaster. [19th c., prob. f. thieves' cant]

bea'ker *n.* Lipped cylindrical glass vessel for scientific experiments; tall wide-mouthed pottery drinking-vessel found in graves of European Bronze Age **B~ Folk**; (arch. or literary) large drinking-cup. [ME, f. ON *bikarr* = OS *bikeri*, OHG *behhari* f. pop. L **bicarium* perh. f. Gk *bikos* drinking-bowl]

beam[1] *n.* **1.** Long piece of squared timber supported at both ends, used in houses, ships, etc., (**~ in** one's **eye,** fault great compared to another's; see Matt. 7:3); cylinder in loom on which warp or cloth is wound; chief timber of plough; bar of balance; shank of anchor; lever in engine connecting piston-rod and crank; main stem of stag's antlers; (in *pl.*) horizontal cross-timbers of ship supporting deck and joining sides (**on her ~-ends,** on her side, almost capsizing; **on** one's **~-ends,** (fig.) near end of resources); side of ship (*land on the port beam*); ship's breadth (**broad in the ~**, (colloq.) having wide hips); *beam*-COMPASS[1](*es*). **2.** Ray or pencil of radiation; this as guide to aircraft or missile; course so indicated (**off ~**, (colloq.) mistaken; **on the ~**, (colloq.) on the right track); directional flow of particles; radiance; bright look, smile. [OE *bēam* tree, = OS *bām*, OHG *boum* f. WG **bauma*; cf. ON *bathmr*, Goth. *bagms*]

beam[2] *v.* **1.** *v.t.* Emit (light, affection, etc.); direct (radio signals etc., and fig.) *at.* **2.** *v.i.* Shine; smile radiantly; hence ~'ING[2] *a.* [f. prec.]

bea'my̆ *a.* (Of ship) broad-beamed. [f. BEAM[1] + -Y[2]]

bean *n.*, & *v.t.* **1.** *n.* (Seed, used as food, of) leguminous plant bearing smooth usu. kidney-shaped seeds in long pods; **full of ~s,** (colloq.) in high spirits; **give** person **~s,** (sl.) punish or scold him; **not a ~**, (sl.) no money; ||OLD *bean*; SPILL[1] *the beans.* **2.** Similar seed of other plants (e.g. cocoa, coffee); *(sl.) head. **3. ~'pole,** (fig.) tall thin person; **~'stalk,** stem of bean plant. **4.** Hence *~'ERY *n.*, cheap restaurant. **5.** *v.t.* *(sl.) Hit on head. [OE *bēan*, = OHG *bōna*, ON *baun* f. Gmc **baunō*]

||**bea'nfeast** *n.* Employer's annual dinner given to employees; (colloq.) festival, celebration, merry time. [f. prec. + FEAST, beans and bacon being regarded as indispensable dish]

bea'nĭe *n.* Small close-fitting hat worn on back of head. [perh. f. BEAN 'head' + -IE]

||**bea'nō** *n.* (*pl.* ~s). (sl.) Beanfeast. [abbr. + -o]

bear[1] (bār) *n.* **1.** Thick-furred plantigrade mammal of family Ursidae (**Great B~, Little B~**, constellations near north pole; **the B~**, Russia; **like a ~ with a sore head,** (colloq.) ill-tempered); child's toy like this animal (cf. TEDDY 2); rough, unmannerly, or uncouth person; (St. Exch.) one who sells for future delivery hoping to buy cheaper meanwhile (cf. BULL[1]) [perh. w. ref. to selling bear's skin before killing bear]. **2. ~-baiting,** (Hist.) setting dogs to attack captive bear; **~'garden,** (fig.) scene of tumult; **~-hug,** powerful embrace; **~'leader,** (fig.) rich young man's travelling tutor; **~ market** (with falling prices); **~'s-breech,** (Bot.) kind of acanthus; **~'s-ear,** auricula; **~'s-foot,** a hellebore (*Helleborus fetidus*); **~'s-grease,** (arch.) pomade; **~'skin,** (wrap etc.) of bear's skin, Guards' tall furry cap; ***B~ State,** Arkansas; hence ~'ISH[1] *a.* [OE *bera*, = OHG *bero*, f. WG **bero*]

bear[2] (bār) *v.* (St. Exch.) **1.** *v.i.* Speculate for a fall. **2.** *v.t.* Produce fall in price of (stocks etc.). [f. prec.]

bear[3] (bār) *v.* (**bore,** arch. **bare; borne** or BORN; in pass. *born* is used w. ref. to birth, but *borne by* w. name of mother). **1.** *v.t.* (poet. or formal). Carry. **2.** Carry visibly, show, be known by, (banner, device, arms, the marks *of*, name, relation or ratio *to*); **~ (away** or **off)**, win (prize etc.); **~ oneself** (behave) *well* etc. **3.** Bring something needed (*bear witness*; *bear* person *company*); **~ a hand,** help. **4.** Exercise (office, rule); carry in the mind (*bear a grudge*); **~ in mind,** not forget. **5.** Wear; **~ arms** (as soldier, or of heraldic arms). **6.** (in *p.p.*) Carried or transported by (AIR[1]*borne*); **be borne away** (by external force or influence, or internal impulse); **is borne in upon** one, becomes one's conviction. **7. ~ out,** confirm (story etc.), confirm account etc. given by (person). **8.** Sustain (weight, responsibility, cost); **~ a part in,** share. **9.** Stand (test etc.), endure (GRIN *and bear it*); (usu. w. neg. or interrog.) tolerate, put up with, (*cannot bear him*), admit of; hence ~'ABLE *a.* **10.** Be fit for (*his language won't bear repeating*). **11. ~ up,** uphold, (abs.) not despair, (Naut.) sail to leeward; **~ with,** treat forbearingly, tolerate patiently. **12.** Give birth to; produce, yield (*land bears crops*, and abs.); **~ fruit,** (fig.) have results. **13.** *v.i.* Thrust, strive, apply weight, tend; **~ down,** exert downward pressure; **~ down on,** move rapidly or purposefully towards; **~ hard on,** oppress; **~ (up)on,** be relevant to; ~ (diverge) **to** *the right, left*, etc.; **bring to ~**, apply, aim (gun etc.). [OE *beran*, = OS, OHG *beran*, ON *bera*, Goth. *bairan* f. Gmc **ber-* f. IE **bher-*]

beard[1] *n.* **1.** Hair of man's lower face (excluding WHISKERS and MOUSTACHE); OLD *man's beard.* **2.** Chin tuft of animal; gills of oyster; byssus of mollusc; beak-bristles of birds (*bearded* TIT[1]); awn of grass. **3.** Hence ~'ED[2], ~'LESS, *adjs.* [OE, = OHG *bart* f. WG **bardha*]

beard[2] *v.t.* Oppose openly, defy; **~ the lion in his den,** (fig.) openly attack person on his own subject etc. [f. prec.]

bear'dĭe *n.* (colloq.) Bearded man. [f. BEARD[1] + -IE]

bear'er (bār'-) *n.* Person or thing that carries or helps to carry; Indian palanquin-carrier (Hist.) or personal servant; carrier of equipment on safari etc.; bringer of letters or message; presenter of cheque; possessor of shares; (**good** etc.) ~, plant etc. that produces (well etc.). [f. BEAR[3] + -ER[1]]

bear'ing (bār'-) *n.* **1.** In vbl senses. **2.** Outward behaviour; bodily attitude; endurability (*past bearing*). **3.** Heraldic charge or device. **4.** Relation, reference, aspect, (*consider it in all its bearings*; *what is the bearing of this on the argument?*). **5.** (usu. in *pl.*) Part of machine that bears the friction, esp. between rotating shaft and its housing; BALL[1]-*bearings.* **6.** Compass direction in which a place etc. lies; (in *pl.*) relative position; **have lost my ~s,** do not know where I am. **7. ~-rein,** fixed rein from bit to saddle forcing horse to arch its neck. [f. BEAR[3] + -ING[1]]

Béar̂nai'se (bā-; -z) *a.* **~ sauce,** rich usu. tarragon-flavoured white sauce. [F, fem. of *béarnais* of *Béarn* in S.W. France]

beast *n.* (Esp. wild) animal (*beast of* BURDEN[1], *of*

PREY[1]); quadruped (*man and beast*); domesticated bovine animal; brutal man; disliked person or thing; **The B~**, Antichrist; **the ~**, animal nature in man. [ME, f. OF *beste* f. Rom. *besta* f. L *bestia*]

***beastings.** See BEESTINGS.

bea'stl|y̆[1] *a.* **1.** Like a beast or its ways; foul; sensual. **2.** Unfit for human use, dirty; (colloq.) unpleasant, undesirable. **3.** Hence **~ĭness** *n.* [f. BEAST + -LY[1]]

bea'stly̆[2] *adv.* (sl.) Very (esp. of bad things), regrettably, (*beastly drunk, wet; raining beastly hard*). [f. BEAST + -LY[2]]

beat[1] *v.* (**beat;** BEATEN, *or* **beat** esp. in senses 3 and 4). **1.** *v.t.* & *i.* Strike repeatedly (**~ the air,** strive in vain; **~** one's **breast,** in mourning or woe); remove dust from (carpet) by beating; knock loudly *at door* etc.; make (path) by trampling. **2.** Inflict blows on; (of sun, rain, etc.) strike persistently (*on*, or abs.). **3.** *v.t.* Overcome, surpass; **~ the band,** (sl.) surpass everything; **~** person **to it, to the punch,** etc., get there first (lit. or fig.); **can you beat it?** (sl., expr. surprise or amazement). **4.** Exhaust (DEAD *beat*); be too hard for, perplex. **5.** *v.t.* & *i.* (Of wings) move up and down; move rhythmically (*heart* etc. *beats* or *is beating*); **~ time,** mark or follow time of music with baton, foot, etc. **6.** *v.i.* (Phys.) create BEAT[2] 4; (Naut.) sail to windward. **7.** *v.t.* Shift, drive, alter, shape, deform, by blows; strike (bushes, water) to rouse game; **~ (up)**, make (eggs etc.) into frothy smooth mixture by vigorous stirring etc.; ||**~ the bounds,** mark parish boundaries by striking certain points with rods; **~** one's **brains,** search for ideas. **8.** *v.i.* & *t.* Play on drum; *beat to* QUARTER[1]*s*; *beat a* RETREAT; **~ it,** (sl.) go away. **9.** **~ about,** search (*for* excuse etc.); **~ about the bush,** approach subject indirectly; **~ down,** bargain with (seller), cause seller to lower (price); **~ in,** crush; **~ off,** drive back (attack etc.); **~ out,** forge (metal), *defeat (one's competitors); **~ up,** beat (person) severely, collect (recruits etc.). [OE *bēatan*, = OHG *bōzan*, ON *bauta* f. Gmc **bautan*]

beat[2] *n.* **1.** Stroke on drum, signal so given. **2.** (Mus.) Movement of conductor's baton; principal recurring accent; interval between two such accents. **3.** Measured sequence of strokes or sounds; throbbing; strongly marked rhythm of popular music. **4.** (Phys.) Pulsation due to combination of two sounds or electric currents of (slightly) different frequencies. **5.** Sentinel's or policeman's appointed course; area covered by this; one's habitual round. **6.** Sportsman's range in search of game. **7.** *(sl.) **The ~ of,** something surpassing (*did you ever see the beat of that?*). **8.** *(Journ.) Scoop. [f. prec.]

beat[3] *n.* & *a.* (One) of the **~ generation** (young people with unconventional dress and behaviour as expression of social philosophy). [prob. f. p.p. of BEAT[1]]

bea'ten *a.* In vbl senses; worn; (**~ track,** well-trodden way, lit. or fig.); shaped by the hammer; exhausted, dejected. [p.p. of BEAT[1]]

bea'ter *n.* In vbl senses; man employed to rouse game; implement for beating carpets, eggs, etc. [f. BEAT[1] + -ER[1]]

bēatĭ'f|ĭc *a.* Making blessed; (colloq.) blissful (*beatific smile*); hence **~ICALLY** *adv.* [f. F *béatifique* or L *beatificus* (*beatus* blessed; see -FIC)]

bėătĭfĭcā'tion *n.* Making or being blessed; (R.C. Ch.) first step to canonization, announcement that dead person is in bliss. [F, or f. eccl. L *beatificatio* (as foll.; see -ATION)]

bėă'tĭfy̆ *v.t.* Make happy; (R.C. Ch.) announce beatification of. [f. F *béatifier* or f. eccl. L *beatificare* f. L *beatus* blessed; see -FY]

bea'tĭng *n.* In vbl senses; chastisement (*take a beating*); defeat (**take some, a lot of, ~,** be difficult to surpass). [f. BEAT[1] + -ING[1]]

bėă'tĭtūde *n.* Blessedness; (in *pl.*) the declarations of blessedness in Matt. 5: 3–11; patriarchal title in Orthodox Church. [F, or f. L *beatitudo* (*beatus* blessed; see -TUDE)]

bea'tnĭk *n.* Member of the BEAT[3] generation. [f. BEAT[3] + *-nik* after *sputnik*, perh. infl. by U.S. use of Yiddish *-nik* agent-suf.]

beau (bō) *n.* (*pl.* **~x** *or* **~s,** *pr.* bōz). Fop, dandy; ladies' man, admirer; *boy-friend, lover. [F]

Beau'fort (bō'f-) *n.* **~ scale,** scale of wind speed ranging from 0 (calm) to 12 (hurricane over 73 m.p.h.). [f. Sir F. ~, Engl. admiral d. 1857]

beau geste (bōzhĕ'st) *n.* Display of magnanimity. [F, = splendid gesture]

beau idė'al (bō) *n.* One's highest or ideal type of excellence or beauty. [F *beau idéal* = ideal beauty, often misunderstood in E as a beautiful ideal; see BEAU, IDEAL]

Beau'jolais (bō'zholā) *n.* Red or white burgundy wine from *Beaujolais* district of France.

beau mo'nde (bōmaw'nd) *n.* Fashionable society. [F]

Beaune (bōn) *n.* Red burgundy wine from *Beaune* district of France.

beaut (būt) *n.* & *a.* (Austral., N.Z., & U.S.; sl.) Beautiful (person or thing). [abbr. of BEAUTY]

beau'tėous (bū'-) *a.* (rhet.) Beautiful. [ME, f. BEAUTY + -OUS, after *bounteous, plenteous*]

beautĭ'cian (būtĭ'shan) *n.* One who runs a beauty parlour; specialist in beauty treatment. [f. BEAUTY + -ICIAN]

beau'tĭful (bū'-) *a.* Delighting the eye or ear (*beautiful face, voice*); gratifying any taste (*beautiful poem, picture, roast beef, batting, batsman*); morally or intellectually impressive, charming, or satisfactory, (*beautiful patience, organization, specimen*; ***~ letters,** *belles-lettres*); hence **~LY**[2] *adv.*, (esp., colloq.) excellently (*beautifully warm; that will do beautifully*). [f. BEAUTY + -FUL]

beau'tĭ|fy̆ (bū'-) *v.t.* Make beautiful; adorn; hence **~FICA'TION, ~fīer**[1] (1, 2), *ns.* [f. foll. + -FY]

beau'ty̆ (bū'-) *n.* **1.** Combination of qualities, as shape, proportion, colour, in human face or form, or in other objects, that delights the sight (**~ is only skin deep,** one cannot judge by appearances); combined qualities delighting the other senses, the moral sense, or the intellect. **2.** Beautiful person or thing; exceptionally good specimen (*here is a beauty*); beautiful women; beautiful feature, ornament, (**the ~ of it,** the particular point that gives satisfaction). **3.** **~ parlour,** establishment in which the art or trade of face-massage, hairdressing, manicuring, applying cosmetics, etc. is carried on; **~ queen,** woman judged most beautiful in a competition; **~ sleep** (before midnight); **~ spot,** (1) small patch placed on lady's face as foil to complexion, (2) beautiful locality; **~ treatment,** use of cosmetics etc. to enhance person's beauty. [ME, f. AF *beuté*, OF *bealté, beauté*, f. Rom. **bellitas* f. L *bellus* pretty; see -TY[1]]

beaux. See BEAU.

beaux arts (bōzar̄') *n.* & *a.* **1.** *n. pl.* Fine arts. **2.** *a.* Of classical decorative style maintained esp. in 19th c. by École des Beaux-Arts in Paris. [F *beaux-arts*]

beaux yeux (bōzyer̄') *n.* Person's favour; **for the ~ of,** just to gratify (person). [F, = fine eyes]

bea'ver[1] *n.* (*pl.* same *or* **~s**). Amphibious broad-

-tailed soft-furred rodent of genus *Castor*, able to cut down trees and build dams, (**eager ~**, (colloq.) (over-)zealous person); its light-brown fur; hat of this; ~ (**cloth**), heavy woollen cloth like beaver fur; **~board,** kind of fibreboard [*P]; ~ **lamb,** lamb's wool made to look like beaver fur. [OE *be(o)for*, = OHG *bibar*, ON *bjórr* f. Gmc **bebruz* f. IE **bhebhrús* (**bhru* brown)]

bea'ver² *n.* (Hist.) Lower face-guard of helmet. [f. OF *baviere* bib (*baver* slaver f. *beve* saliva f. Rom. **baba*)]

bea'ver³ *n.* (sl.) Bearded man. [20th c.; orig. uncert.]

bea'ver⁴ *v.i.* ~ **away,** work hard *at*. [f. BEAVER¹]

bē'bŏp *n.* Kind of jazz music, with complex harmony and highly syncopated rhythm; hence **~PER**¹ (3) *n.* [imit. of typical phr.]

bėca'lm (-ah'm) *v.t.* (usu. in *pass.*) Deprive (ship) of wind. [f. BE- 6 + CALM¹]

bėcā'me. See BECOME.

bėcau'se (-ŏ'z) *adv.* & *conj.* **1.** *adv.* By reason, on account, (*of*). **2.** *conj.* For the reason that, inasmuch as, since. [ME, f. BY¹ prep. + CAUSE¹, after OF *par cause de* by reason of]

bĕccafi'cō (-fē'-) *n.* (*pl.* **~s**). Small migrant bird eaten in Italy. [It. (*beccare* peck, *fico* fig)]

béchamĕl (bĕ'sh-) *n.* Kind of fine white sauce. [invented by Marquis de *B~*, Fr. courtier d. 1703]

bêche-de-mer (bāshdemār') *n.* (*pl.* same *or* ***bêches-***, *pr.* same). **1.** Holothurian animal eaten as a delicacy in China. **2.** Beach-la-mar. [F, alt. of *biche de mer* f. Port. *bicho do mar* sea-worm]

Bĕchua'na (-chŏŏah'- *or* -kūah'-) *n.* (*pl.* **~s** *or* same). Member of Negroid people between Orange and Zambezi rivers. [Tswana]

bĕck¹ *n.* (N. Engl.) Brook, mountain stream. [ME, f. ON *bekkr* f. Gmc **bakkiz*]

bĕck² *n.* (literary). Significant gesture, nod, etc.; the order implied by such gesture etc.; **at** person's ~ **and call,** entirely obedient to him. [f. *beck* v. f. BECKON]

bĕ'ckėt *n.* (Naut.) Contrivance of rope-loop, hook, bracket, etc., for securing loose ropes, tackle, or spars. [18th c.; orig. unkn.]

bĕ'ckon *v.* **1.** *v.t.* Summon, call attention of, by gesture. **2.** *v.i.* Make mute signal (*to* person). [OE *biecnan*, *bēcnan*, = OS *bōknian*, OHG *bouhnen* f. WG **bauknian* (*baukna* BEACON)]

bėclou'd *v.t.* Cover with clouds; obscure. [f. BE- 6 + CLOUD 1]

bėco'm|e (-ŭ'm) *v.* (**beca'me; beco'me**). **1.** *v.i.* Come into being; **what has ~e of** (happened to) **him? 2.** (As cop. v., with *n.*, *a.*, or *adj. phr.*) Begin to be (*became known*; *became Prime Minister*). **3.** *v.t.* Suit, befit (*it ill becomes you to complain*); adorn, look well on; hence **~ING**² *a.* [OE *becuman*, = OHG *biqueman*, Goth. *biquiman* f. Gmc **bi-* BE- + **kweman* COME]

bĕd¹ *n.* **1.** Thing to sleep or rest on; mattress (*feather bed* etc.); framework with mattress and coverings; animal's resting place, litter; use of bed; being in bed. **2.** ~ **and board,** (1) lodging and food, (2) connubial relations; ~ **and breakfast,** sleeping accommodation and food next morning, as offered by hotels etc.; ~ **of roses,** easy position; ~ **of sickness,** invalid state; **brought to** ~ (in childbirth, *of* child, or abs.); DIE² *in* one's *bed*; **go to ~,** retire for the night, (fig.) have sexual intercourse *with*, (of newspaper) go to press; **has got out of ~ on the wrong side,** is bad-tempered for the day; KEEP¹ one's *bed*; **lie in the ~ one has made,** accept consequences of one's acts; **make the ~,** arrange its coverings; NARROW *bed*; **put to ~,** cause (child, newspaper, etc.) to go to bed; **take to** one's **~,** become ill and have to remain in bed. **3.** *Bed*BUG; **~'chamber,** (arch. exc. in titles of sovereign's attendants) bedroom; **~'clothes,** sheets, pillows, blankets, etc.; **~'fast,** bedridden; **~'fellow,** sharer of bed, (fig.) associate; **~'jacket** (worn when sitting up in bed); **~-linen,** sheets and pillow-cases; ||**~'maker,** person tending rooms in college, hotel, etc.; **~'pan,** invalid's utensil for urination or defecation when in bed; **~'post,** upright support of bed (*between you and me and the ~post*, in strict confidence); **~-rest,** confinement of patient to bed; **~'ridden,** confined to bed by infirmity, (fig.) decrepit, [OE *bedreda* (*ridan* ride)]; **~'roll,** (U.S. & N.Z.) bedding rolled into a bundle; **~'room,** room for sleeping in (sometimes w. ref. to sexual intimacy: *~room comedy* etc.); **~'side,** side of esp. invalid's bed; *~side book* (for reading in bed); *good ~side manner* (of tactful doctor); ||**~-si'tting-room,** (colloq.) **~-si'tter,** (sl.) **~-si't,** combined bedroom and sitting-room; **~'sock,** warm sock worn in bed; **~'sore** (developed in invalid by lying in bed); **~'spread,** cloth or sheet put over bed during day etc. when not in use; **~'stead,** framework of bed; **~'straw,** herbaceous plant of genus *Galium* once used as straw for beds, esp. (*Our*) *Lady's ~straw* (yellow-flowered species); **~'table** (for use by person sitting up in bed); **~'time,** hour for going to bed; **~-wetting,** nocturnal enuresis. **4.** Flat base on which anything rests; **~'plate,** metal plate forming base of machine. **5.** Garden plot (to be) filled with plants; place where osiers etc. are grown. **6.** Bottom of sea, river, etc.; **~'rock,** solid rock underlying alluvial deposits etc., (fig.) ultimate facts or principles of a theory, character, etc. **7.** Foundation of road or railway; slates etc. of billiard-table. **8.** Stratum; layer of oysters etc. [OE *bed(d)*, = OS *bed*, *beddi*, OHG *betti*, Goth. *badi* f. Gmc **badhjam*]

bĕd² *v.t.* & *i.* (**-dd-**). **1.** ~ (**down**), put or go to bed; (fig.) have sexual intercourse with. **2.** *v.t.* ~ (**out**), plant in a garden bed. **3.** *v.t.* Cover up or fix firmly in something. **4.** *v.t.* & *i.* Arrange as, be or form, a layer. [OE *beddian* (*bedd*; see prec.)]

B.Ed. *abbr.* Bachelor of Education.

bėdă'bble *v.t.* Stain or splash with dirty liquid, blood, etc. [f. BE- 1 + DABBLE]

bėdă'd *int.* (Ir.) By GAD¹. [corrupt.]

bėdau'b *v.t.* Smear with paint etc.; bedizen. [f. BE- 1 + DAUB 1]

bėdă'zzle *v.t.* Completely dazzle; confuse (person). [f. BE- 2 + DAZZLE 1]

bĕ'ddable *a.* Sexually attractive. [f. BED² + -ABLE]

bĕ'dder *n.* In vbl senses; plant suited for garden bed; ||(colloq.) college bedmaker. [f. BED² + -ER¹]

bĕ'ddĭng *n.* In vbl senses; mattress, bedclothes, etc.; litter for cattle, horses, etc.; bottom layer; (Geol.) (esp. visible) stratification; ~ **plant** (suitable for garden bed). [f. BED² + -ING¹]

bėdĕ'ck *v.t.* Adorn. [f. BE- 1 + DECK²]

bĕ'dėguar (-gār) *n.* Mosslike excrescence on rose-bush produced by insect's puncture. [f. F *bédégar* f. Pers. *bād-āwar* wind-brought]

||**bē'del(l)** (*or* bedĕ'l) *n.* University official with chiefly processional duties. [= BEADLE]

bėdĕ'vĭl *v.t.* (||**-ll-**). Treat with diabolical violence or abuse; possess, bewitch; spoil, confound; plague, afflict; hence **~MENT** *n.* [f. BE- 6 + DEVIL¹]

bėdew' *v.t.* Cover or sprinkle with dew or dew-like water. [f. BE- 6 + DEW¹]

Bĕ'dford *n.* ~ **cord,** woven fabric with prominent ridges in direction of warp. [~ in England]

bėdī'ght (-ī't) *a.* (arch.) Arrayed, adorned. [ME, p.p. of *bedight* v. (BE- 1; see DIGHT)]

bėdĭ'm *v.t.* (**-mm-**). Make (eyes, mind) dim. [f. BE- 4 + DIM 1]

bėdī'zen *v.t.* Deck out gaudily. [f. BE- 2 + obs. *dizen* deck out]

bĕ'dlam *n.* Madhouse; scene of uproar; hence ~ITE[1] (1) *n.*, (arch.) insane person. [f. hospital of St. Mary of *Bethlehem* in London]

Bĕ'dlĭngton *n.* ~ **(terrier)**, narrow-headed sporting terrier with fairly long legs and curly grey hair. [~ in Northumberland]

bĕ'd(o)uĭn (-ōō-) *n.* (*pl.* same) & *a.* (Arab) of the desert; wandering (person). [ME, f. OF *beduin* ult. f. Arab. *badawiyyūn* (obl. case) dwellers in the desert]

bėdră'ggle *v.t.* Wet (dress etc.) by trailing it, or so that it trails or hangs limp; (esp. in *p.p.*) make (person) untidy or dishevelled. [f. BE- 2 + DRAGGLE]

Beds. *abbr.* Bedfordshire.

bee *n.* **1.** Four-winged stinging social insect collecting nectar and pollen and producing wax and honey; insect of similar type; busy worker; *meeting for combined work or amusement; SPELLING-*bee*. **2. Have a ~ in** one's **bonnet,** be obsessed on some point; **~-bread,** (honey and) pollen used as food by bees; **~-eater,** bright-plumaged bird of family Meropidae; ~'HIVE, (fig.) domed structure resembling hive for bees, busy place; **~-line,** straight line between two places, esp. if quickly traversed; **~-master,** keeper of bees; ~ **orchis** (with bee-shaped flowers); **~'s knees,** (sl.) something outstandingly good; **bee'swax** (-z-), WAX[1] secreted by bees as comb material, and used to polish wood; **bee'swing** (-z-), filmy second crust on old port wine. [OE *bēo*, = OHG *bia*, ON *bý* f. Gmc **bīōn*]

||**Beeb** *n.* (colloq.) *The* B.B.C. [abbr.]

beech *n.* Smooth-barked glossy-leaved mast-bearing forest tree of genus *Fagus*; ~(**'wood**), its wood; (Austral.) one of various similar trees; **~-fern,** kind of polypody; **~-marten,** white-breasted marten found in S. Europe and Asia; **~'mast,** fruit of beech; hence ~'EN[5], ~'Y[2], *adjs.* [OE *bēce* f. Gmc **bōkjōn*]

beef *n.* & *v.* **1.** *n.* (*pl.* ~s). Flesh of ox, bull, or cow; (in men) size, muscle. **2.** (usu. in *pl.* **beeves** *pr.* -vz, *or* *~s). Ox(en), esp. fattened, or their carcasses. **3.** (sl., *pl.* ~s). Complaint, protest. **4. ~'burger,** hamburger; ***~'cake,** (sl.) display of sturdy masculine physique; ||**~'eater,** (colloq.) warder in Tower of London [f. obs. sense 'well-fed menial']; *bee'f*STEAK (*~steak fungus*, red edible fungus resembling beef); ~ **tea,** stewed beef juice for invalids; **~-wood,** red timber of various Austral. and W. Ind. trees. **5.** *v.i.* (sl.) Complain. **6.** *v.t.* ~ **up,** (sl.) reinforce, strengthen. [ME, f. AF, OF *boef* f. L *bos bovis* ox]

bee'f|ȳ *a.* Like beef; solid, muscular; hence ~INESS *n.* [f. prec. + -Y[2]]

Bēē'lzėbŭb *n.* The Devil. [OE f. L, f. Gk *beelzeboub* & Heb. *ba'al zᵉbûb* lord of flies]

been. See BE.

beep *n.*, & *v.i.* **1.** *n.* Sound of motor-car horn; short high-pitched sound of various devices. **2.** *v.i.* Emit beep; hence ~'ER[1] *n.*, device emitting beep. [imit.]

beer *n.* Alcoholic liquor (esp. of lighter kinds) from fermented malt etc. flavoured with hops etc.; glass of this (*two beers, please*); other fermented drink (GINGER *beer*, ROOT[1] *beer*); *beer and* SKITTLES; **small** ~, (lit.) weak beer, (fig.) trifling matters; *think no small ~ of*, have high opinion of; **~-engine** (for drawing beer up from barrel in cellar); ~ **garden,** ~ **hall,** etc., (where beer is served); ||**~'house** (licensed for beer, not spirits); hence ~'Y[2] *a.*, (esp.) betraying influence of beer. [OE *bēor*, = MDu. *bēr*, OHG *bior*, WG, f. LL *biber* drink f. L *bibere*]

bee'stĭngs, *bea'-, (-z) *n. pl.* First milk (esp. of cow after calving). [OE **bēsting* (*bēost*, OHG *biost*, of unkn. orig.)]

beeswax, beeswing. See BEE.

beet *n.* Plant of genus *Beta* with succulent root (SUGAR-*beet*); *beetroot; ||**~'root,** root of beet, esp. crimson root of garden beet as vegetable. [OE *bēte*, = LG *beete*, OHG *bieza*, WG, f. L *beta*, perh. of Celt. orig.]

bee'tle[1] *n.* Tool with heavy head and handle for ramming, crushing, driving wedges, etc.; machine for finishing cloth e.g. by beating; **~-brain** etc., blockhead. [OE *bētel* f. Gmc **bautilaz* (**bautan* BEAT[1]; see -LE 1)]

bee'tle[2] *n.*, & *v.i.* **1.** *n.* Insect of order Coleoptera, having front wings converted to hard wing-cases closing over back wings; (pop.) large black insect of this kind; (pop.) similar insect; **black-~,** common cockroach. **2.** Short-sighted person; dice game in which beetle-figure is drawn or assembled; **~-crusher,** large boot or foot. **3.** *v.i.* ~ **off,** (sl.) depart. [OE *bitula* biter (*bītan* BITE[1])]

bee'tle[3] *a.* Projecting, shaggy, scowling, (*beetle brows, beetle-browed*). [ME, of unkn. orig.]

bee'tle[4] *v.i.* (Of brows or cliffs) overhang. [f. prec.]

bee'trōōt. See BEET.

beeves. See BEEF.

bee'zer *n.* (sl.) Nose; person. [20th c.; orig. uncert.]

||**B.E.F.** *abbr.* (Hist.) British Expeditionary Force.

bėfa'll (-aw'l) *v.* (**befe'll; ~en**). **1.** *v.i.* Happen. **2.** *v.t.* Happen to (person etc.). [OE *befeallan* (as BE- 2, *feallan* FALL[1])]

bėfĭ't *v.t.* (**-tt-**). Suit, be fitted or appropriate for; be incumbent on; hence ~TING[2] *a.* [f. BE- 2 + FIT[4]]

bėfŏ'g *v.t.* (**-gg-**). Envelop in fog; confuse; obscure. [f. BE- 6 + FOG[2] 1]

bėfōō'l *v.t.* Delude, make fool of. [f. BE- 4 + FOOL[1] 1]

bėfôr'e *adv.*, *prep.*, & *conj.* **1.** *adv.* Ahead (*go before*); on the front (*before and behind*); earlier than the time in question, already; in the past (*long before*). **2.** *prep.* In front of; ahead of; under the impulse of (*before the wind*; *recoil before the attack*; *carry all before you*); in presence of (*appear before judge*; *bow before authority*; ~ **God,** as God sees me); awaiting (*the future before them*); earlier than (~ **Christ,** (of date) reckoned backwards from birth of Jesus Christ); earlier than the coming of (future event); farther on than; rather than (*would starve before stealing*). **3.** *conj.* Earlier than the time when; rather than (*would starve before he stole*). [OE *beforan*, = OS *biforan*, OHG *bifora* f. Gmc *bi-* BY[1] + **forana* from the front (**fora* FOR)]

bėfôr'ehănd (-ôr'h-) *adv.* In anticipation; in advance; in readiness; **be ~ with,** anticipate, forestall. [ME, f. prec. + HAND[1]; cf. AF *avant main*]

bėfou'l *v.t.* Make foul (lit. or fig.). [f. BE- 4 + FOUL[1]]

bėfrie'nd (-rĕ'nd) *v.t.* Act as friend to; help, favour. [f. BE- 6 + FRIEND]

bėfŭ'ddle *v.t.* Make drunk; confuse. [f. BE- 3 + FUDDLE 1]

bĕg *v.* (**-gg-**). **1.** *v.t.* Ask for (food, money, etc., or abs.) as gift; ~ one's **bread,** live by begging. **2.** *v.i.* Ask (*for* alms etc.); live by alms; (of dog) sit up with forepaws raised expectantly. **3.** *v.t.*

& *i.* Ask earnestly or humbly (thing, *for* thing, *of* person, person *to* do, *of* person *to* do, *that* something may be done); ask formally (*beg leave*; *beg* PARDON[1]); take leave *to* do (*I beg to differ, enclose, announce,* etc.). **4.** ~ **off,** get (person) excused penalty etc., decline to take part etc.; ~ **the question,** assume truth of thing to be proved or thing equivalent to it, (pop.) evade difficulty; **go (a-)begging,** (fig., of opportunity etc.) find no accepter, (of thing) be unwanted. [ME, prob. f. OE *bedecian* f. Gmc **bedh-* base of BID[1]]

bėgă'd *int.* (colloq.) By God! [corrupt.]

bėgă'n. See BEGIN.

bėgă't. See foll.

bėgĕ't (-g-) *v.t.* (**-tt-; bego't,** (arch.) **bega't; bego'tten**). Procreate (usu. of father, sometimes of father and mother); give rise to, occasion; hence **~TER**[1] *n.* [OE *begietan,* = OS *bigetan* seize, OHG *bigezzan* receive; f. as BE- 1 + GET[1] procreate]

bĕ'ggar[1] *n.* One who begs; one who lives by begging; poor person (**~s must not** or **cannot be choosers,** must take what is offered); (colloq.) person, fellow. [ME, f. BEG + -AR[3]]

bĕ'ggar[2] *v.t.* Reduce to poverty; outshine; exhaust resources of (*beggar description*); **~-my--neighbour,** card-game in which player seeks to capture opponent's cards (also fig. of national policy etc.). [f. prec.]

bĕ'ggarl|ў *a.* Needy, poverty-stricken; intellectually poor; mean, sordid; ungenerous; hence **~ĭNESS** *n.* [f. BEGGAR[1] + -LY[1]]

bĕ'ggarў *n.* Extreme poverty. [f. BEGGAR[1] + -Y[1]]

bėgĭ'n (-g-) *v.* (**-nn-; bega'n; begu'n**). **1.** *v.t.* Perform first part of (*begin work*; *begin crying*; *begin to cry*; *it has begun to be done, it has been begun*); ~ **school,** attend it for first time. **2.** Come *to* do at a certain time (*begin to feel ill*; *food was beginning to decay*; *this is beginning to get wearisome*). **3.** (colloq.) Show any attempt or likelihood *to* (*can't, does not, begin to compete with him*). **4.** *v.i.* Be the first to do something; take the first step (**beginning student*); start speaking; be begun (*meeting will begin at 7*); come into being, arise; have its commencement, nearest boundary, etc., (at some point in space or time); ~ **at,** start from; ~ **(up)on,** set to work at; ~ **with,** take first or as starting-point; **to ~ with,** as the first thing, in the first place. [OE *beginnan,* = OS, OHG *biginnan,* WG f. *bi-* BE- + Gmc **-ginnan,* of unkn. orig.]

bėgĭ'nner (-g-) *n.* In vbl senses; one just beginning to learn a skill etc.; **~'s luck,** good luck supposed to attend beginner at games etc. [f. prec. + -ER[1]]

bėgĭ'nnĭng (-g-) *n.* In vbl senses; time at which anything begins; source, origin; first part; **the ~ of the end,** first clear sign of final result. [f. BEGIN + -ING[1]]

bėgĭr'd (-g-) *v.t.* (**begir't**). (literary; esp. in *p.p.*) Gird round, encircle. [OE *begyrdan* (as BE- 1, GIRD[1])]

bėgŏ'ne (*or* -aw'n) *v.* (in *imper.* & *inf.* only). Go away immediately. [f. BE + GONE]

bėgō'nĭa *n.* Plant of genus *Begonia,* with coloured perianth but no petals, and often with brilliant foliage also. [f. M. *Bégon,* Fr. patron of science d. 1710 + -IA[1]]

bėgŏ'rra *int.* (Ir.) By God! [corrupt.]

bėgŏ't(ten). See BEGET.

bėgrī'me *v.t.* Make grimy. [f. BE- 1 + GRIME 2]

bėgrŭ'dge *v.t.* Feel or show dissatisfaction at (thing); envy (person) the possession of. [f. BE- 2 + GRUDGE 1]

bėguī'le (-gī'l) *v.t.* Delude; cheat (person *of, out of,* or *into* doing); charm, amuse; divert attention from (toil, passage of time); hence **~MENT** (-gī'lm-) *n.* [f. BE- 2 + obs. *guile* to deceive]

béguine[1] (bāgē'n) *n.* Member of Netherlands religious lay sisterhood not bound by vows. [ME f. OF, f. (le) *Bègue* 12th-c. priest who founded the order; cf. -INE[3]]

bėguī'ne[2] (-gē'n) *n.* Dance of W. Ind. orig.; its rhythm. [Amer. F, f. F *béguin* infatuation]

bē'gum (*or* bā'-) *n.* Indian Muslim lady of high rank. [f. Urdu *begam* f. E. Turk. *bīgam* princess fem. of *big* prince; cf. BEY]

bėgŭ'n. See BEGIN.

bėha'lf (-ah'f) *n.* **On** or ***in ~ of,** in the interest of (person, principle, etc.), as representative of. [mixture of earlier phrs. *on his halve* and *bihalve him,* both = on his side; see BY[1], HALF]

bėhā've *v.i.* & *refl.* **1.** *v.i.* Act or react (in specified way); ~ **towards,** treat (*well* etc.); **ill-~d, well-~d,** having bad, good, manners or conduct. **2.** (Of machine etc.) work (well etc.); (esp. to or of child) conduct oneself with propriety. **3.** *v. refl.* (esp. of or to child) Show good manners. [f. BE- 2 + HAVE[1]]

bėhā'viour, *-ior, (-vyer) *n.* Deportment, manners; way of conducting oneself (**be on** one's **good** or **best ~,** take care to behave well when being observed or tested); moral conduct, treatment shown to or towards others; way in which ship, machine, substance, etc., acts or works; (Psych.) response to stimulus (~ **therapy,** treatment of neurotic condition by gradual training to react normally); hence **~AL** *a.* [f. prec. after *demeanour* and obs. *haviour* f. *have*]

bėhā'viour|ĭsm, *-ior|-, (-vyer-) *n.* (Psych.) Study of human actions by analysis into stimulus and response; doctrine that such study is the only valid method in psychology; hence **~IST** (2) *n.,* **~ĭ'stIC** *a.* [f. prec. + -ISM]

bėhea'd (-hĕ'd) *v.t.* Cut off the head of; kill thus. [OE *behēafdian* (*be-* (from) about, *hēafod* HEAD[1])]

bėhĕ'ld. See BEHOLD.

bėhē'moth (*or* bē'ĭ-) *n.* Enormous creature. [ME, f. Heb. *b^ehēmôṯ* intensive pl. of *b^ehēmāh* beast, perh. f. Egyptian *p-ehe-mau* water-ox]

bėhĕ'st *n.* (literary). Command. [OE *behǣs* f. Gmc **bihaissi-* (**bi-* BE-, **haitan* bid, call)]

bėhī'nd *adv., prep.,* & *n.* **1.** *adv.* & *prep.* In or to the rear (of); ~ person's **back,** without his knowledge; **put ~** one, refuse to consider. **2.** On farther side (of); hidden (by) (*what is behind all this?*); *behind the* SCENES. **3.** Towards one's rear (*glance behind before moving off*); farther back in space or time (than; ~ **the times,** antiquated; **come from ~,** win after lagging; **fall** or **lag ~,** not keep up); past in relation to (*all that trouble is behind me*). **4.** In support of (*the man behind the project*); in an inferior position (to); remaining after departure of oneself (*leave behind*) or of others (*remain* or *stay behind*); later than; (~ **schedule** or **time,** unpunctual); in the tracks of; in arrear (*with* payments etc.). **5.** *n.* Buttocks; (Austral. Nat. Football) kick etc. scoring one point. [OE *behindan, bihindan* (*bi* BY[1], *hindan* from behind, *hinder* below = OHG *hintana* behind, Goth. *hintana* beyond)]

bėhī'ndhănd (-d-h-) *adv.* & *pred. a.* In arrear (*with* or *in* payments etc.); out of date, behind time. [f. prec. + HAND[1]; cf. BEFOREHAND]

bėhō'ld *v.t.* (**behe'ld**). (arch. or literary). See, become aware of by sight; (in *imper.,* calling attention) *behold, a pale horse*; hence **~ER**[1] *n.* [OE *bihaldan* (as BE- 2, *haldan* hold)]

bėhō'lden *pred. a.* Under obligation (*to*). [p.p. (obs. exc. in this use) of prec., = bound]

bėhōō'f *n.* (arch.) Benefit, advantage (*to, for, on,* (*the*) *behoof of*). [OE *behōf,* = MDu. *behoef,* MHG *behuof,* WG (**bi-* BE-, **hōf-* cogn. w. HEAVE[1])]

bėhō've, *bėhōō've, *v.t. impers.* Be incumbent on (person) *to* (do something); (w. neg. etc.)

befit (*it ill behoves me to complain*). [OE *behōfian* (*behōf*; see prec.)]

beige (bāzh) *n.* & *a.* (Of) yellowish-grey colour of undyed and unbleached wool. [F, of unkn. orig.]

beigel. Var. of BAGEL.

bē'ing *n.* In vbl senses; existence (**in ~**, existing); constitution, nature, essence; anything (esp. person), that exists (**the Supreme B~**, God). [f. BE + -ING[1]]

bėjā'bers, bėjă'bbers, (-z) *int.* (Ir.) By Jesus! [corrupt.]

|**bėjew'elled, *-eled,** (-ōō'eld) *a.* Adorned with jewels. [f. BE- 7 + JEWEL + -ED[2]]

bĕl *n.* Unit used in comparison of power levels in electrical communication or intensities of sound, corresponding to an intensity ratio of 10 to 1; cf. DECIBEL. [f. A. G. *Bell*, Amer. inventor of telephone d. 1922]

bėlā'bour (-b*er*), ***bėlā'bor,** *v.t.* Thrash (lit. or fig.); labour (a subject). [f. BE- 2 + LABOUR[2] (exert one's strength)]

bėlā'tėd *a.* Coming (too) late; overtaken by darkness. [p.p. of obs. *belate* delay (BE- 4, LATE[1])]

bėlay' *v.t.*, & *n.* **1.** *v.t.* Fix (running rope) round cleat, pin, rock, etc., to secure it; **~ (there)!,** (Naut. sl.) stop!, enough!; **~ing-pin,** fixed wooden or iron pin for belaying on. **2.** *n.* (Spike of rock used for) act of belaying. [f. Du. *beleggen*]

bĕl că'ntō (*or* -ah'-) *n.* Singing with full rich broad tone and accomplished vocal technique. [It., = fine song]

bĕlch *v.* & *n.* **1.** *v.i.* Emit wind noisily from stomach through mouth. **2.** *v.t.* (Of gun, chimney, volcano, etc.) send out or up; utter forcibly. **3.** *n.* Act of belching. [OE *belcettan* or **belcan*]

bĕ'lcher *n.* (arch.) Neckerchief with white spots on blue ground. [f. J. *Belcher*, Engl. pugilist d. 1811]

bĕ'ldam(e) *n.* (arch.) Old woman, hag; virago. [f. ME & OF *bel* beautiful + DAM[2], DAME]

bėlea'guer (-g*er*) *v.t.* Besiege (lit. or fig.). [f. Du. *belegeren* camp round (as BE- 6, *leger* a camp)]

bĕ'lemnīte *n.* Tapering sharp-pointed fossil bone of extinct cuttlefish. [f. mod. L *belemnites* f. Gk *belemnon* dart + -ITE[1] (2)]

bel esprit (bĕl ĕsprē') *n.* (*pl.* ***beaux esprits*** *pr.* bōz ĕsprē'). Witty person. [F, lit. fine mind]

bĕ'lfrȳ *n.* Bell tower, attached to church etc. or separate; bell space in church tower; BAT[1]*s in the belfry*. [ME, f. OF *berfrei* f. Frank. **bergfridh*-, prob. f. **bergan* protect + **frithuz* peace; alt. by assoc. w. *bell*]

Bĕ'lgian (-j*a*n) *a.* & *n.* (Native or inhabitant) of Belgium; **~ hare,** dark-red long-eared breed of domestic rabbit. [f. *Belgium* + -AN]

Bĕ'lgĭc *a.* Of the ancient Belgae of N. Gaul; of the Low Countries. [f. L *Belgicus* (*Belgae*; see -IC)]

Bĕlgrā'vĭ|a *n.* Fashionable residential part of London S. of Knightsbridge; hence **~AN** *a.* & *n.* [f. *Belgrave* Square in this district (*Belgrave* in Leicestershire) + -IA[1]]

Bē'lĭal *n.* The Devil. [f. Heb. *b[e]liyya'al* worthless]

bėlī'e *v.t.* (**bely'ing**). Give false notion of; fail to fulfil (promise etc.); fail to justify (hope etc.); fail to corroborate. [OE *belēogan* (as BE- 3, *lēogan* LIE[2])]

bėlie'f *n.* Trust or confidence (*in*); acceptance of any received theology; acceptance (of thing, fact, statement, etc.) as true or existing (*belief in his honesty, that he is honest*; **beyond ~**, incredible; **to the best of my ~**, in my genuine opinion); thing believed; religion; firm opinion (*it is my belief that he did it*). [ME, f. OE *gelēafa* (as foll.)]

bėlie'v|e *v.* **1.** *v.i.* Have faith *in* (arch. *on*). **2.** Put trust *in* truth of (statement), efficacy of (principle or system), advisability of (practice), existence of (thing). **3.** Suppose, think, (*Mr. Smith, I believe?*). **4.** Hence **~ER**[1] *n.*, (esp.) adherent of a specified religion (OLD *Believer*); so **~ING**[2] *a.* **5.** *v.t.* Accept truth of (statement etc.); **~e it or not, would you ~e it?,** (colloq.) it is surprising though true. **6.** Accept veracity of (person); **~e** one's **ears, eyes,** etc., accept that what one apparently hears, sees, etc., is true. **7.** Be of opinion *that*; suppose, think, (*is believed to be in Rome*); **make ~e,** pretend (*to* do or *that*). **8.** Hence **~ABLE** *a.* [OE *belȳfan, belēfan*, w. change of pref. f. *gelēfan*, = OS *gilōbian*, OHG *gilouben*, Goth. *galaubjan* f. Gmc **glaubjan* hold dear, f. same root as LIEF]

bėlī'ke *adv.* (arch., often iron.) Probably; perhaps. [f. BY[1] + LIKE[1] as *n.* = likelihood]

||**Belī'sha** (-ē'sh*a*) *n.* **~ beacon,** = BEACON 3 (marking pedestrian crossing). [f. L. Hore-*Belisha* d. 1957, Minister of Transport 1934]

bėlĭ'ttle *v.t.* Make small, dwarf; depreciate. [f. BE- 4 + LITTLE]

bĕll[1] *n.* **1.** Hollow object of cast metal in deep cup shape widening at lip made to emit clear musical sound when struck. **2.** Stroke of bell; (Naut.) **one** to **eight ~s,** half-hours of watch; (Boxing) signal for start or end of round. **3.** Bell-shaped object or part; flower corolla (BLUE[1]*bell*; CANTERBURY *bell*); any object designed to emit bell-like sound for calling attention etc. **4. Bear away the ~**, be first, win; **~, book, and candle** (in allusion to eccl. cursing formula); **sound** or **clear as a ~**, quite sound or clear (in other senses besides the acoustic). **5. ~-bird,** one of various S. Amer. and Austral. birds with bell-like note; **~-bottomed,** (of trousers) bell-shaped below knee; ***~'boy,** page in hotel or club; **~-buoy** (with warning bell rung by waves' motion); *bell*-COT[1]; **~-flower,** herbaceous plant of genus *Campanula*; **~-founder, -founding, -foundry,** caster, casting, and manufactory, of large bells; **~-glass** (bell-shaped as cover for plants); **~-heather,** plant *Erica cinerea* or *E. tetralix*; ***~'hop,** (sl.) bellboy; **~s of Ireland,** plant (*Molluccella laevis*) with green bell-shaped calyx; **~-jar,** bell-shaped glass to cover instruments or contain gas in laboratory; **~'man,** (Hist.) town crier; **~-metal,** alloy of copper and tin (with more tin than in bronze) for bells; **~-pull,** cord or handle attached to bell-wire; **~-punch** (for punching ticket and making ringing sound at same time); **~-push,** button to operate electric bell; **~-ringer, -ringing,** (of church bells or handbells with changes etc.); **~-tent,** conical tent with central pole; **~-wether,** leading sheep of flock with bell on neck, ringleader; **~-wire,** wire pulled at door etc. to sound bell. [OE *belle*, = MDu., MLG *belle*; a LG wd perh. related to BELL[3]]

bĕll[2] *v.* **1.** *v.t.* Furnish with bell(s); **~ the cat,** take the danger of a common enterprise on oneself [f. fable of cat and mice]. **2.** *v.i.* Widen *out* like bell lip. [f. prec.]

bĕll[3] *n.*, & *v.i.* (Make the) cry of stag or buck at rutting-time. [OE *bellan* bark, bellow, = OHG *bellan*; cf. ON *belja* and BELLOW]

bĕlladŏ'nna *n.* **1.** (Bot.) Deadly nightshade, a poisonous plant (*Atropa belladonna*) with purple flowers and purple-black berries. **2.** (Med.) Drug prepared from this. **3. ~ lily,** S. Afr. amaryllis with white or pink flowers. [mod. L f. It., = fair lady, perh. because a cosmetic is made from it]

bĕlle *n.* Handsome woman; reigning beauty (*the*

belle of the ball, of New York). [F, f. L *bella* fem. of *bellus* pretty]

belle époque (bĕl ĕpŏ'k) *n.* Period of settled and comfortable life preceding war of 1914–18. [F, = fine period]

belle laide (bĕl lā'd) *n.* (*pl.* ***belles laides*** *pr.* same). Woman who is ugly but fascinatingly so. [F (*belle* beautiful, *laide* ugly, fem. adjs.)]

belles-lettres (bĕl-lĕ'tr) *n. pl.* (occas. treated as *sing.*) Studies or writings of the purely literary kind, (esp.) essays, criticisms, etc.; hence **bĕllĕ'trɪsm** (2), **bĕllĕ'trɪst** (3), (-l-l-) *ns.*, **bĕllĕtrĭ'stɪc** (-l-l-) *a.* [F, = fine letters]

bĕ'llĭc|ōse *a.* Inclined to fighting; hence ~o'sity *n.* [ME, f. L *bellicosus* (*bellum* war; see -IC, -OSE[1])]

bĕllĭ'gerencў *n.* Status of a belligerent. [f. foll.; see -ENCY]

bĕllĭ'gerent *a.* & *n.* (Nation, party, or person) waging regular war as recognized by the law of nations; of such nation etc.; any opponent engaged in conflict; pugnacious. [f. L *belligerare* wage war (*bellum* war, *gerere* wage); see -ENT]

bĕ'llow (-ō) *v.* & *n.* **1.** *v.i.* Roar like a bull; shout or roar with pain. **2.** *v.t.* Utter loudly and usu. angrily. **3.** *n.* Bellowing sound. [ME, of uncert. orig.; perh. related to BELL[3]]

bĕ'llows (-ōz) *n. pl.* (occas. treated as *sing.*) **1.** Portable or fixed contrivance for driving blast of air into a fire or through pipes of organ, reeds of harmonium, etc.; **pair of** ~ (two-handled for fire). **2.** Expansible part of camera etc. [ME, prob. f. OE *belga* pl. of *bel(i)g*, *bæl(i)g* BELLY[1], abbr. of *blǣstbel(i)g* blowing-bag]

bĕ'llў[1] *n.* **1.** Cavity of human body below diaphragm with stomach and bowels and other contents, abdomen; front surface of body from waist to groin; womb; corresponding parts of animals. **2.** Stomach; body as needing food; appetite, gluttony. **3.** Cavity of anything, bulging part (concave or convex); front, inner, or lower surface; surface of violin etc. across which strings pass. **4.** **~ache,** (*n.*) colic, (*v.i.*, sl.) complain whiningly; **~-band** (below horse's belly, holding shafts etc. in place); **~-button,** (colloq.) navel; **~-dance,** oriental solo dance by woman, with much abdominal movement; **~-flop,** (*n.*, & *v.i.*, colloq.) dive landing flat on belly; **~-landing,** crash-landing of aircraft on belly without use of undercarriage; **~-laugh,** deep unrestrained laugh. [OE *belig*, *bæl(i)g*, = OHG *balg*, ON *belgr*, Goth. *balgs* f. Gmc **balgiz* bag (**balg-*, **belg-* swell)]

bĕ'llў[2] *v.t.* & *i.* ~ (**out**), (usu. of sails) swell out. [f. prec.]

bĕ'llўful (-ŏŏl) *n.* As much as or more than one wants of anything. [f. BELLY[1] + -FUL 2]

bėlŏ'ng *v.i.* **1.** Be rightly assigned *to* (as duty, right, possession, natural or usual accompaniment, example in classification, characteristic, part, member, inhabitant, appendage); ~ **to,** be member of (club, household, grade of society, etc.). **2.** *Be resident *in* or connected *with*. **3.** Be rightly placed or classified (*in*, *under*, etc.); fit a specified environment etc. [ME, app. an intensive, f. BE- 2, of ME *longen* belong f. OE *langian* (*gelang* at hand)]

bėlŏ'ngings (-z) *n. pl.* Person's movable property or luggage; (colloq.) person's relatives etc. [f. prec. + -ING[1]]

Bĕlōrŭ'ssian, Byĕlō-, (-shan) *a.* & *n.* (Native or language) of Belorussia in western U.S.S.R. [f. *Belorussia* f. Russ. *Belorussiya* (*belyi* white, *Russiya* Russia) + -AN]

bėlo'ved (as *a.* or *n.* usu. -ŭ'vĭd, as *p.p.* -ŭ'vd) *p.p.*, *a.*, & *n.* **1.** *p.p.*, & *a.* Dearly loved (*of* or *by*, or abs.). **2.** *n.* Beloved person. [f. obs. vb *belove* f. BE- 2 + LOVE[2]]

bėlow' (-ō') *adv.* & *prep.* **1.** *adv.* At or to a lower point; downstream; downstairs (esp. Naut., **go** ~, from deck); (rhet.) on earth; (rhet.) in hell. **2.** In lower rank (*the judge in the court below*); at foot of page, or later in a book or article. **3.** *prep.* Lower than; *below* PAR[1]; *below* STAIRS; *temperature is 20 below* (*freezing-point*). **4.** Downstream from; at or to greater depth than; covered by, lower in amount, degree, etc., than (*below* one's BREATH); of lower rank than; unworthy of. [f. *be* BY[1] + LOW[1] *a.*]

bĕl pae'se (-ahā'zā) *n.* Rich white mild creamy cheese orig. from Italy. [It., = fair country]

bĕlt[1] *n.* **1.** Encircling strip of cloth, leather, etc., worn round waist or baldric-wise to confine or support clothes or weapons etc.; ~ **and braces** (w. ref. to policy of twofold security); **hit below the** ~, fight unfairly; TIGHTEN one's *belt*; **under** one's ~, eaten, or otherwise secured; SEAT-*belt*. **2.** Belt worn as mark of rank by earl or knight, or by champion at boxing, expert in judo, etc. **3.** Strip of colour, special surface, trees, etc., round or on anything; region (*cotton*, *wheat*, *fever*, *commuter*, *belt*; GREEN[1] *belt*); flexible strip carrying machine-gun cartridges; endless strap connecting pulleys, whence ~'ING[1] (3) *n.*; (sl.) heavy blow; *~ **line,** *~**'way,** etc., railway or road around city. [OE, = OHG *balz*, ON *belti* f. Gmc **baltjaz*, **baltjōn-*, f. L *balteus*]

bĕlt[2] *v.* **1.** *v.t.* Put belt round; fasten *on* with belt; mark with belt of colour etc.; thrash with belt; ~ **out,** (sl.) utter forcibly. **2.** *v.i.* (sl.) Rush; ~ **up,** (colloq.) wear seat-belt, (sl.) be quiet. [f. prec.]

bĕ'ltāne *n.* (Ancient Celtic festival on) May Day. [f. Gael. *bealltainn*]

bėlu'ga (-lōō'-) *n.* Large kind of sturgeon; caviare from it; white whale. [f. Russ. *beluga*, *belukha* (*belo-* white)]

bĕ'lvėdēre *n.* Raised turret or summer-house to view scenery from. [It. (*bel* beautiful, *vedere* see)]

bėlў'ing. See BELIE.

B.E.M. *abbr.* British Empire Medal; bug-eyed monster.

bē'ma *n.* Platform in ancient Athenian public assembly; reading platform in synagogue; sanctuary in Orthodox Church. [Gk]

bėmīr'e *v.t.* Cover or stain with mud; (in *pass.*) be stuck in mud. [f. BE- 6 + MIRE[1]]

bėmoa'n *v.t.* Weep or express sorrow for or over. [f. BE- 3 + MOAN[2]]

bėmū'se (-z) *v.t.* Stupefy; make (person) confused. [f. BE- 2 + MUSE[2]]

bĕn[1] *n.* (Sc.) Inner room (usu. of two-roomed cottage); **but and** ~, outer and inner rooms, cottage having only these. [ellipt. use of *ben* adv., within (OE *binnan*), BUT[1] outside]

bĕn[2] *n.* (Sc.) Mountain peak; high mountain. [f. Gael. *beann*]

bĕnch *n.*, & *v.t.* **1.** *n.* Long seat of wood or stone; seat across boat. **2.** Judge's seat; office of judge; lawcourt (‖**Queen's, King's, B~,** division of High Court); (collect.) judges, magistrates; **on the** ~, serving as judge or magistrate. **3.** ‖(Parl.) Seat appropriated to certain group etc. (FRONT, BACK[1]-, CROSS-, *bench*). **4.** *Seat used by players not participating in a game for the time being. **5.** Working-table in carpenter's shop, laboratory, etc. **6.** Level ledge in masonry or earthwork, on hill-slope, etc. **7.** **~-mark,** mark cut in rock etc. by surveyors to mark point in line of levels, (fig.) criterion or point of reference; ~ **seat** (across whole width of car); **~-warrant,** one issued by a judge. **8.** *v.t.* Exhibit (dog) at show; *retire (player) to bench. [OE *benc*, = OS *banc*, OHG *bank*, ON **benkr* f. Gmc **bankiz*; cf. BANK[1]]

‖**bĕ'ncher** *n.* Senior member, sharing management, of Inns of Court; (Parl.) occupant of (specified) bench (CROSS-, *front-*, BACK[1]-, *bencher*). [f. prec. + -ER[1]]

bĕnd[1] *n.* **1.** (Naut.) Knot of various kinds (*fisherman's, weaver's*, etc., *bend*). **2.** (Her.) Stripe from dexter chief to sinister base; ~ **sinister** (from sinister chief to dexter base, sign of bastardy). [OE *bend* band, bond, = Goth. *bandi* f. Gmc **bandjō* (**band-*, **bend-* BIND[1]); cf. BAND[1], BOND[1]]

bĕnd[2] *n.* Bending; curve in road, racecourse, etc., (**round the** ~, (colloq.) crazy); bent part of a thing; (in *pl.*, colloq.) caisson disease, its painful symptoms; (sl.) spree. [f. foll.]

bĕnd[3] *v.* (*past* **bent**; *p.p.* **bent** exc. in *bended* KNEE[1]*s*). **1.** *v.t.* & *i.* Force out of straightness; modify (rules etc.) to suit oneself; impart to (rigid object) or receive a curved or angular shape; **be'ntwood** (artificially curved for chairs etc.). **2.** *v.t.* Bring to bear (energies, ears, eyes, one*self*, etc. *on, to*); (in *pass.*) be determined (*on* thing or do*ing*; *on pleasure bent*). **3.** (sl.) Make illicit or dishonest, pervert. **4.** Attach (cable, sail) with knot. **5.** *v.t.* & *i.* Turn (steps, eyes) in new direction; incline from the perpendicular. **6.** *v.i.* Bow, stoop, submit, (*to* or *before*); **catch** person **~'ing,** (colloq.) take him at disadvantage. **7.** *v.t.* Force to submit. **8.** Hence ~'ER[1] *n.* (esp., sl.) drinking-spree, ~'Y[2] *a.* (colloq.) flexible. [OE *bendan*, = ON *benda*, f. Gmc **bandjan* (**band-*; cf. BEND[1])]

bēnea'th *adv.* & *prep.* **1.** (arch. & literary). Below, under, underneath. **2.** *prep.* In manner unworthy of (person, one's status, etc.); ~ **contempt** etc., not worth despising etc. [OE *binithan, bineothan* (*bi* BY[1], *nithan, neothan* below f. Gmc **nith-*; cf. NETHER)]

bĕnēdī'cĭtē *n.* **1.** Blessing invoked; grace at table. **2.** (*B*~). Canticle beginning *Benedicite, omnia opera*, from Song of 3 Children in Apocrypha. [ME f. L, = bless ye (*benedicere*; see BENEDICTION); *omnia opera* = all the works (of the Lord)]

bĕ'nēdĭck *n.* Newly married man, esp. confirmed bachelor who marries. [f. *Benedick*, character in Shak. *Much Ado*]

Bĕnēdĭ'ctĭne *a.* & *n.* (Monk) of order founded 529 by St. Benedict; (*b*~; pr. -ēn), liqueur of brandy flavoured with herbs, made orig. by Benedictine monks. [f. F *bénédictine* or mod. L *benedictinus* (*Benedictus* Benedict; see -INE[1])]

bĕnēdĭ'ction *n.* Utterance of a blessing, generally at table, at end of church service, or as special R.C. service; a blessing, blessedness. [ME f. OF, f. L *benedictio -onis* (*benedicere -dict-* bless; see -ION)]

bĕnēdĭ'ctorў *a.* Of or expressing benediction. [f. L *benedictus* (see prec.) + -ORY after *valedictory*]

Bĕnēdĭ'ctus *n.* **1.** Part of R.C. Mass beginning *Benedictus qui venit* (Blessed is he who cometh). **2.** Canticle beginning *Benedictus Dominus Deus* (Blessed be the Lord God) from Luke 1:68–79. [L, = blessed, p.p. of *benedicere* (see BENEDICTION)]

bĕnēfă'ction *n.* Doing good; gift for charitable purpose. [f. LL *benefactio* (as BENEFIT[1]; see -ION)]

bĕ'nēfăct|or *n.* Person who has given friendly aid; patron of or donor to a cause or charitable institution; hence ~**r**ESS[1] *n.* [ME f. LL (as BENEFIT[1]; see -OR)]

bēnĕ'fĭc *a.* Having a favourable influence. [f. L *beneficus* (as BENEFIT[1]; see -FIC)]

bĕ'nēfĭc|e *n.* Church living; property held by an ecclesiastical officer, esp. by rector or vicar; hence ~ED[2] (-st) *a.* [ME f. OF, f. L *beneficium* favour (*bene* well + *-fic-* f. *facere* do)]

bēnĕ'fĭc|ent *a.* Doing good; (showing) active kindness; hence or cogn. ~ENCE *n.*, **~ent**LY[2] *adv.* [f. L *beneficent-* (*beneficus* BENEFIC; see -ENT)]

bĕnēfĭ'cial (-shal) *a.* Advantageous; (Law) of, or having, the use or benefit of property etc.; hence ~LY[2] *adv.* [ME, f. F *bénéficial* or f. LL *beneficialis* (as BENEFICE; see -AL)]

bĕnēfĭ'ciarў (-sherĭ) *n.* Holder of church living; receiver of benefits, esp. under person's will. [f. L *beneficiarius* (as BENEFICE; see -ARY[1])]

bĕnēfĭcĭā'tion *n.* Treatment of raw materials, ores, etc., to improve their properties. [f. Sp. *beneficiar* to benefit (*beneficio* f. L *beneficium*; see BENEFICE, -ATION)]

bĕ'nēfĭt[1] *n.* **1.** Advantage; **for the ~ of,** on behalf of, (iron.) for the instruction or disadvantage of; **the ~ of the doubt,** assumption of innocence rather than guilt. **2.** Allowance etc. to which person is entitled under insurance or social security (*sickness, unemployment, supplementary, benefit*) or as member of benefit-club or society; (Hist.) exemption from ordinary courts by the privilege of one's order (*benefit of clergy*); **without ~ of clergy,** (joc.) without formal marriage etc. **3.** Performance at theatre, game, etc., of which proceeds go to particular player etc. **4. ~-club, ~ society,** (for mutual insurance against illness or effects of old age). [ME f. AF *benfet*, OF *bienfet*, f. L *benefactum* neut. p.p. of *bene facere* do well]

bĕ'nēfĭt[2] *v.* (**or* **-tt-**). **1.** *v.t.* Do good to. **2.** *v.i.* Receive benefit (*by, from*). [f. prec.]

Bĕ'nēlŭx *n.* Belgium, the Netherlands, and Luxemburg in association as a regional economic group. [f. *Be*lgium + *Ne*therlands + *Lux*emburg]

bēnĕ'vol|ent *a.* Desirous of doing good; charitable (*benevolent fund, society*); kind and helpful; hence or cogn. ~ENCE *n.*, **~ent**LY[2] *adv.* [ME, f. OF *benivolent* f. L *bene volens -entis* well wishing (*velle* wish)]

B. Eng. *abbr.* Bachelor of Engineering.

Bĕnga'l (-nggaw'l) *a.* ~ **light,** kind of firework used for signals; ~ **quince,** bael; ~ **tiger,** the true tiger; so ~I *a.* & *n.*, (native or language) of Bengal. [former Indian province, now consisting of Bangladesh and Indian state of W. Bengal]

bēnī'ghtēd (-nī't-) *a.* Overtaken by night; in intellectual or moral darkness; ignorant. [p.p. of obs. *benight* v. f. BE- 6 + NIGHT]

bēnī'gn (-ī'n) *a.* Gracious, gentle; (of climate etc.) mild; fortunate, salutary; (Med.) mild, not malignant; hence **bēnĭ'gn**ITY *n.*, ~LY[2] *adv.* [ME, f. OF *benigne* fem., f. L *benignus* prob. f. **benigenus* (*bene* well, *-genus* born); cf. MALIGN]

bēnĭ'gn|ant *a.* Kind or gracious to inferiors; salutary; (Med.) = prec.; hence ~ANCY *n.*, **~ant**LY[2] *adv.* [18th c., f. prec. or L *benignus*, after *malignant*]

bĕ'nison (-z-) *n.* (arch.) A blessing. [ME, f. OF *beneiçun* etc. f. L *benedictio -onis* BENEDICTION]

Bĕ'njamĭn[1] *n.* Youngest (and favourite) child. [name of youngest son of Jacob (Gen. 43 etc.)]

bĕ'njamĭn[2] *n.* = BENZOIN; ~ **tree,** (1) tree yielding benzoin, (2) spicebush. [corrupt. of BENZOIN]

bĕ'nnēt *n.* **1.** See HERB *bennet*. **2.** = BENT[1] 2.

bĕ'nnĭ *n.* Sesame plant; **~seed,** sesame seed. [f. Mende *bene*]

***bĕ'nnў**[1] *n.* (sl.) Overcoat. [abbr. of *benjamin*, perh. f. a tailor's name]

***bĕ'nnў**[2] *n.* (sl.) Benzedrine. [abbr.]

bĕnt[1] *n.* **1.** Stiff-stemmed reedy or rushlike grass. **2.** Stiff flower-stalk or old stalk of grasses. **3.** Grass of genus *Agrostis*. **4.** Heath, unenclosed pasture. [ME, repr. OE *beonet-* (in place-names), OS *binet*, OHG *binuz* f. WG **binut-*]

For other words in *be-* see BE-.

bĕnt[2] *n.* Inclination, bias, tendency; **to the top of** one's ~, to heart's content. [prob. f. BEND[3] after *descend, descent,* etc.]
bĕnt[3]. See BEND[3].
Bĕ'ntham|ism (*or* -*ta*-) *n.* Utilitarian philosophy based on measurability of pleasure and aim of greatest happiness of the greatest number; so ~ITE[1] (1) *n.* [f. J. *Bentham,* Engl. philosopher d. 1832 + -ISM]
bĕ'nth|ŏs *n.* Flora and fauna found at bottom of ocean or lake; hence ~IC *a.* [Gk, = depth of the sea]
bĕ'ntonite *n.* Kind of clay used as absorbent, filler, etc. [f. Fort *Benton* in Montana + -ITE[1] (2)]
ben trovato (bĕn trovah'tō) *a.* Well invented, characteristic if not true. [It., = well found]
bĕ'ntwŏŏd. See BEND[3].
bėnŭ'mb (-m) *v.t.* (Usu. of cold) make torpid, insensible, powerless; paralyse (mind, action). [earlier p.p. of ME *benimen* deprive f. OE *beniman* (*bi*- BE-, *niman* take)]
Bĕ'nzėdrīne (*or* -ēn) *n.* Amphetamine. **[P]**
bĕ'nzēn|e *n.* Aromatic liquid hydrocarbon got from coal and petroleum, used as solvent, fuel, and in manufacture of plastics etc.; **~e ring,** arrangement of 6 carbon atoms in benzene molecule; hence ~OID *a.* [f. BENZOIC + -ENE]
bĕ'nzine (-ēn) *n.* Mixture of liquid hydrocarbons got from petroleum and used as solvent, esp. in dry-cleaning. [f. foll. + -INE[5]]
bĕ'nzōĭn *n.* **(Gum)** ~, fragrant aromatic resin of E. Asian tree of genus *Styrax*; (Chem.) white crystalline constituent of this; hence **bĕnzō'**IC *a.* [earlier *benjoin* thr. F etc. f. Rom. *lobenjoi* f. Arab. *lubān jāwī* incense of Java (*lo*- being dropped in Rom. as if the def. article)]
bĕ'nzŏl, -ōle, *n.* Benzene, esp. unrefined. [f. BENZOIC + -OL]
bėquea'th (-dh) *v.t.* Leave (personal estate *to* person) by will; transmit (example etc.) to posterity. [OE *becwethan* (as BE- 3, *cwethan* say; cf. QUOTH)]
bėquĕ'st *n.* Bequeathing; thing bequeathed. [ME, f. BE- + obs. *quiste* f. OE -*cwiss, cwide* saying]
bėrā'te *v.t.* Scold. [f. BE- 1 + RATE[3]]
Ber'ber *n.* & *a.* (Member) of the N. Afr. stock including the aboriginal races, speaking allied languages; language of Berber people. [f. Arab. *barbar*]
ber'berĭs *n.* Plant of genus *Berberis,* barberry. [med. L & OF, of unkn. orig.]
berceuse (bārser'z) *n.* Cradle-song; (Mus.) piece in this style. [F]
bėrea've *v.t.* **1.** (**bere'ft**). Rob, dispossess, *of* (usu. immaterial things, e.g. life, hope). **2.** (**~d**). Leave desolate (esp. in *p.p.*); (of death etc.) deprive *of* a relation, wife, etc.; hence ~MENT (-vm-) *n.* [OE *berēafian* (as BE- 2, REAVE)]
bėrĕ'ft. See prec.
be'ret (bĕ'rā *or* -rĭ) *n.* Round flat felt or cloth cap. [F, f. dial. & Prov. *berret*; cf. BIRETTA]
berg[1] *n.* = ICEBERG. [abbr.]
berg[2] *n.* (S. Afr.) Mountain or hill (esp. in comb.); **~ wind,** hot dry northerly wind blowing in coastal regions. [Afrik. f. Du.]
ber'gamăsque (-sk) *n.* Dance like tarantella. [f. *Bergamo* in Italy]
ber'gamŏt[1] *n.* Citrus tree (*Citrus bergamia*); perfume extracted from rind of its fruit; aromatic herb, esp. *Mentha citrata.* [as prec.]
ber'gamŏt[2] *n.* Kind of fine pear. [f. F *bergamotte* f. It. *bergamotta* f. Turk. *begarmūdī* prince's pear]
ber'gschrund (bār'kshrŏŏnt) *n.* (Mountaineering). Crevasse or gap at junction of steep upper slope with glacier or névé. [G]
ber'gy̆lt (-g-) *n.* Red sea-fish, the Norway haddock. [perh. f. ON *berg* rock]
bėrhȳ'me (-rī'm) *v.t.* (arch.) Write verses about, lampoon. [f. BE- 3 + RHYME[2]]
bĕ'rĭbĕrĭ *n.* Mainly tropical polyneuritic disease caused by deficiency of vitamin B_1, esp. in rice-based diet. [Sinh., f. *beri* weakness]
berk, birk, burk(e), *n.* (sl.) Fool. [abbr. of *Berkeley* or *Berkshire Hunt,* rhyming sl. for *cunt*]
Berkelei'an (barklē'an) *n.* & *a.* (Follower) of Berkeley or his philosophy, which denied the objective existence of the material world. [f. G. *Berkeley,* Ir. philosopher d. 1753; see -IAN]
berkē'lium (*or* ber'klĭum) *n.* (Chem.) Artificially made transuranic radioactive metallic element. [mod. L, f. *Berkeley* in California (where first made) + -IUM]
Berks. *abbr.* Berkshire.
berli'n, berli'ne (-ē'n), *n.* Four-wheeled covered carriage with hooded seat behind; so **Berlĭ'n**ER[1] (4) *n.* [f. *Berlin* in Germany (-*ine* thr. F)]
berm *n.* Narrow ledge, esp. in fortification between ditch and base of parapet; narrow path or grass strip beside road. [f. F *berme* f. Du. *berm,* prob. cogn. w. ON *barmr* brim]
Bermū'd|a *n.* **~a rig,** (Naut., with high tapering sail called **~ian mainsail**); **~as, ~a shorts,** knee-length shorts; hence ~IAN *a.* & *n.* [~ (Islands) in W. Atlantic]
Ber'nardīne *a.* & *n.* = CISTERCIAN. [f. St. *Bernard* of Clairvaux, Fr. churchman d. 1153, who founded a branch of the order, + -INE[1]]
bĕ'rrȳ[1] *n.* Small roundish juicy fruit without stone; (Bot.) fruit with seeds enclosed in pulp (e.g. gooseberry, tomato, banana); egg in fish or lobster roe; (sl.) ‖pound, *dollar; hence **(-)bĕ'rri**ED[2] (-ĭd) *a.* [OE *beri(g)e,* = OS, OHG *beri,* ON *ber,* Goth. *basi* f. Gmc **basj*-, **bazj*-]
bĕ'rrȳ[2] *v.i.* Form berry; go gathering berries. [f. prec.]
bersaglieri (barsahlyar'ē) *n. pl.* Highly trained Italian infantry, orig. riflemen. [It.]
ber'serk *n.* & *a.* **1.** *n.* ~**(er)**, wild Norse warrior fighting with mad frenzy. **2.** *a.* (*or* berser'k, -z-). Wild, frenzied, (esp. *go berserk*). [f. Icel. *berserkr* prob. f. *bern*- BEAR[1] + *serkr* coat]
berth[1] *n.* Adequate sea-room (*give* WIDE *berth to*); room for ship to swing at anchor; ship's place at wharf; proper place for anything; sleeping-place in ship, train, etc.; situation, appointment. [prob. f. naut. use of BEAR[3] + -TH[1]]
berth[2] *v.* **1.** *v.t.* Moor (ship) in suitable place; provide sleeping-place for. **2.** *v.i.* (Of ship) come to mooring. [f. prec.]
ber'tha *n.* Deep falling collar or small cape on dress. [f. F *berthe* (*Berthe* Bertha, woman's Christian name)]
bĕ'rȳl *n.* Transparent precious stone, pale-green, light blue, yellow, or white; mineral species including this, emerald, and aquamarine. [ME f. OF, f. L f. Gk *bērullos*]
bėrȳ'llĭum *n.* Very light hard white metallic element. [f. prec. + -IUM]
bėsee'ch *v.t.* (**besought** *pr.* -saw't, *or* **~ed**). Ask earnestly for; entreat (person, person *that* or *to* do or *for* thing); hence ~ING[2] *a.*, suppliant. [ME, f. *bi*- BE- 2 + *secen* etc. SEEK]
bėsee'm *v.t.* (arch.; impers.) Suit; be fitting or creditable to. [f. BE- 2 + SEEM]
bėsĕ't *v.t.* (-tt-; **beset**). Hem in; occupy and make impassable (road etc.); (of difficulties, doubts, temptations, etc.) assail, encompass; **~ting sin** (that especially or most frequently tempts one); hence ~MENT *n.* [OE *besettan,* = OS *bisettian,* OHG *bisezzan,* Goth. *bisatjan* f. Gmc **bi*- BE- 1 + **satjan* SET[1]]
bėshrew' (-rōō') *v.t.* (arch., as mock-heroic imprecation). The Devil etc. take (*me,* person, or thing). [f. BE- 2 + obs. *shrew* to curse f. SHREW]

bėsī′de *prep.* Close to, by, near; on a level with; compared with; wide of (*beside the mark, point, question,* etc.); ~ one**self,** distraught. [OE *be sīdan* (as BY[1], SIDE[1])]
bėsī′des (-dz) *adv.* & *prep.* In addition (to); moreover; otherwise, else, (than). [f. prec. + -S[3]]
bėsie′g|e *v.t.* Invest, lay siege to; crowd round; assail with requests; hence ~ER[1] *n.* [ME, f. *assiege* (by substitution of pref. BE-), f. OF *asegier* f. Rom. *AS(*sedicare* f. **sedicum* siege)]
bėslă′ver, bėslŏ′bber, *vbs. t.* Slaver on or over; flatter fulsomely. [f. BE- 1 + SLAVER[2], SLOBBER]
bėsmear′ *v.t.* Smear with greasy or sticky stuff; (fig.) sully (reputation etc.). [f. OE *bismierwan* (*bi-* BE- 1, *smierwan* SMEAR V.]
bėsmĭr′ch *v.t.* Soil, discolour; dim brightness of; (fig.) sully (reputation etc.). [f. BE- 1 + SMIRCH]
bē′som (-z-; *or* bĭ′-) *n.*, & *v.t.* (Sweep with) broom made of twigs tied round stick; (prov., derog.) woman. [OE *besema,* = OS *besmo,* OHG *besamo,* f. WG **besmo*]
bėsŏ′t *v.t.* (-tt-). (usu. in *p.p.*) Stupefy mentally or morally; infatuate. [f. BE- 4 + SOT]
besought. See BESEECH.
bėspă′ngle (-ă′ngg*e*l) *v.t.* Cover with spangles. [f. BE- 6 + SPANGLE]
bėspă′tter *v.t.* Spatter (object) all over; spatter (liquid etc.) about; cover with abuse or flattery. [f. BE- 1 + SPATTER]
bėspea′k *v.t.* (*past* **bespo′ke** *pr.* -ō′k, *p.p.* **bespo′ke** as *adj.*, otherwise **bespo′ken**). Engage beforehand; order (goods); suggest, be evidence of; **bespoke** *tailor, overcoat,* etc., (seller of) clothes made to order, opp. ready-made clothes etc. [OE *bisprecan,* = OS *besprekan,* OHG *bisprehhan*; see BE- 3, SPEAK]
bėspĕ′ctacled (-k*e*ld) *a.* Wearing spectacles. [f. BE- 7 + SPECTACLE + -ED[2]]
bėspō′ke(n). See BESPEAK.
bėsprĕ′nt *a.* (arch.) Sprinkled (*with*). [ME, p.p. of obs. *besprenge* f. OE *besprengan* (as BE- 1, *sprengan* sprinkle; see SPRENT)]
bėsprĭ′nkle *v.t.* Sprinkle or strew over (*with*; lit. or fig.); sprinkle (liquid etc.) *over.* [ME, f. BE- 3 + *sprenkel* freq. of *sprengen* besprinkle (as prec.)]
Bĕ′ssėmer *a.* ~ **process** (formerly much used for removing carbon, silicon, etc., from molten pig-iron by passage of air, thus converting it to a material suitable for steel-making). [f. Sir H. ~, Engl. engineer d. 1898]
bĕst[1] *a., adv.,* & *n.* **1.** *a.* (*superl.* of GOOD). Of the most excellent or outstanding or desirable kind (*the best friend I have*; *the best thrashing he ever had*; *the best bedroom*; *the best thing to do would be to leave*); *best* BUY; ~ **end,** rib end of neck of lamb etc. for cooking; **put** one's ~ **foot forward,** go at full pace, exert all one's efforts; ~ **girl,** (colloq.) sweetheart; ~ **man,** bridegroom's chief attendant; ~ **part,** most *of*; ~ **seller,** (author of) book with large sale; ~ **way** (shortest, surest, easiest, etc.). **2.** *adv.* (*superl.* of WELL[3]). In the best manner; to the greatest degree; most usefully (*is best ignored*); **as** ~ one **can** or **may,** as well as one is able to do under the circumstances; **had** ~, would find it wisest to. **3.** *n.* That which is best; victory; ~ **of three games,** winning 2; **get** or **have the** ~ **of it,** win fight or argument; **give** person ~, admit his superiority. **4.** Chief advantage or merit (*that is the best of knowing French*; *bring out the best in* person). **5.** *The* best persons or things. **6. All the** ~ (expr. good will); **at** ~, on the most hopeful view; **at its,** one's, ~, in the best state; **at the** ~ **of times,** even in the most favourable circumstances; **do** one's ~ (*to* win etc.), do all one can; *did it* (**all**) **for the** ~, with good intentions; *it was* (**all**) **for the** ~, desirable in the end; **look** one's ~ (most attractive); **make the** ~ **of it, things, a bad bargain,** etc., be as contented as possible; **make the** ~ **of** one's **opportunities, way,** one**self,** etc., do as well as possible, progress as fast as possible, etc.; one's (**Sunday**) ~, best clothes; **six of the** ~, vigorous caning; **to the** ~ **of** one's **ability, belief, power,** etc., so far as one can do, judge, etc.; **with the** ~ (**of them**), as well as anyone. [OE *betest* a., *bet(o)st* adv., = OS *best,* OHG *bezzisto,* ON *beztr,* Goth. *batists* f. Gmc **batistaz* superl. of **bat-*; cf. BETTER[1]]
bĕst[2] *v.t.* (colloq.) Defeat, outwit. [f. prec.]
bėstea′d (-ĕ′d) *v.t.* & *i.* (arch.) Avail, help. [f. BE- 2 + *stead* v. f. STEAD]
bėstĕ′d *a.* (arch.) (*Ill, hard, sore,* etc.) situated, circumstanced. [ME, f. BE- 2 + *stad* f. ON *staddr* p.p. of *stethja* place]
bĕ′stĭal *a.* Of or like a beast or beasts; brutish; barbarous; savage; depraved, lustful; hence or cogn. ~ITY (-ă′l-) *n.*, (esp.) unnatural form of copulation between person and animal, ~IZE (3) *v.t.*, ~LY[2] *adv.* [ME f. OF, f. LL *bestialis* (*bestia* beast; see -AL)]
bĕ′stĭarӯ *n.* Medieval moralizing treatise on beasts. [f. med. L *bestiarium* f. L *bestia* beast; see -ARY[1]]
bėstĭr′ *v.t.* (-rr-). Exert, rouse, (one*self*). [f. BE- 2 + STIR[1] V.]
bėstow′ (-ō′) *v.t.* Deposit; lodge; confer (thing) (*up*)*on* (person) as gift; hence ~AL, ~MENT, *ns.* [ME, f. BE- 2 + OE *stow* a place]
bėstrew′ (-rōō′) *v.t.* (*p.p.* ~**ed** *or* ~**n**). Strew (surface) *with*; scatter (things) about; lie scattered over. [OE *bestrēowian* (as BE- 1, STREW)]
bėstrĭ′dden. See foll.
bėstrī′de *v.t.* (**bestro′de; bestri′dden**). Get or sit on (horse, chair, etc.) with legs astride; stand astride over. [OE *bestrīdan* (as BE- 3, STRIDE V.)]
bėstrō′de. See prec.
bĕt *v.* (-tt-; ~ *or* ~′**ted**) & *n.* **1.** *v.i.* & *t.* Risk one's money etc., risk (an amount etc.) against another's, on the result of a doubtful event (*on* or *against* result or competitor, *that* a thing will happen; **you** ~, (colloq.) you may take it as certain); (colloq.) be certain (*I bet he's forgotten it*); ~′**ting-shop,** bookmaker's shop or office. **2.** *n.* Act of betting; sum of money bet; (colloq.) course of action (*your best bet is to call tomorrow*); (colloq.) opinion (*my bet is that he won't come*). [16th c., of uncert. orig.; perh. v. f. n., f. *abet* n., in sense 'instigation, support of a cause']
bē′ta *n.* Second Greek letter (Β, β) = b; (Astron.) second brightest star in a constellation; second-class mark in examination (~ **plus,** ~ **minus,** rather better, worse, than average second-class) ~ **particles,** ~ **rays,** fast-moving electrons emitted by radioactive substances (orig. regarded as rays). [ME f. L f. Gk]
bėtā′ke *v. refl.* (**betoo′k;** ~**n**). ~ **oneself to,** go to (place or person). [ME, f. BE- 2 + TAKE[1]]
bē′tatrŏn *n.* (Phys.) Apparatus for accelerating electrons in circular path. [f. BETA + -TRON]
bē′tel *n.* Leaf of evergreen plant *Piper betle,* chewed in the East with areca-nut parings; ~**-nut,** the areca nut. [Port., f. Malayalam *veṭṭila*]
bête noire (bāt nwar̃) *n.* (*pl.* ***bêtes noires*** *pr.* same). Particularly disliked person or thing. [F, = black beast]
bĕ′thel *n.* Nonconformist chapel; seamen's church. [f. Heb. *bêt-'ēl* house of God (Gen. 28: 17–19)]

For other words in *be-* see BE-.

bėthĕ'sda (-z-) *n.* Nonconformist chapel. [John 5:2]
bėthĭ'nk *v. refl.* (**bethou'ght** *pr.* -thaw't). ~ **oneself** or (arch.) one, reflect, stop to think, remind oneself *of, how,* or *that.* [OE *bithencan,* = OS *bithenkian,* OHG *bidenken,* Goth. *bithagkjan,* Gmc (**bi-* BE-, **thankjan* THINK)]
bėtī'de *v.i.* & *t.* (only in *inf.* & 3 *sing. pres. subj.*) Happen (*whate'er may betide*); happen to (*woe betide him* etc.). [ME, f. BE- 2 + obs. *tide* befall f. OE *tīdan*]
bėtī'mes (-mz) *adv.* Early in day, year, life, etc.; in good time. [ME, f. obs. *betime* (BY[1], TIME[1]) + -S[3]]
bêtise (bātē'z) *n.* Foolish or ill-timed remark or action; piece of folly. [F]
bėtō'ken *v.t.* Augur, indicate; suggest, be token of. [OE **bitācnian* (as BE- 2, *tācnian* signify f. as TOKEN)]
bĕ'tonȳ *n.* Purple-flowered plant (*Stachys officinalis*); one of various similar plants (**water** ~; **wood** ~). [ME, f. OF *betoine* f. pop. L **betonia* for L *betonica* f. *vettonica* perh. f. name of Iberian tribe]
bėtŏŏ'k. See BETAKE.
bėtray' *v.t.* Give up treacherously (person or thing *to* enemy); be disloyal to; lead astray; reveal treacherously or involuntarily; be evidence or symptom of; hence ~AL *n.* [ME f. BE- 2 + obs. *tray* f. OF *trair* f. Rom. **tradire* f. L *tradere* hand over]
bėtrō'th (-ō'dh) *v.t.* (usu. in *p.p.*). Bind with promise to marry; hence ~AL *n.*, ~ED[1] (-dhd) *a.* & *n.* [ME, f. BE- 6 + *trouthe, treuthe* TRUTH, later assim. to TROTH]
bĕ'tter[1] *a., adv.,* & *n.* **1.** *a.* (*compar.* of GOOD). Of a more excellent or outstanding or desirable kind; partly or fully recovered from illness; ~ **feelings,** conscience; ~ **half,** (joc.) wife; ~ **part,** most *of*; **for** ~ (or) **for worse,** on terms of accepting all results, whatever the (unpredictable) outcome; **no** ~ **than,** practically (*no ~ than she should be,* of doubtful virtue). **2.** *adv.* (*compar.* of WELL[3]). In a better manner; to a greater degree; more usefully (*is better ignored*); ~ **than** (number etc.), above; **go one** ~, outbid etc. by one, (fig.) outdo person, *outdo (person); **had** ~, (colloq.) ~, would find it wiser to; *better* OFF; **know** ~ **than,** not be so foolish as; THINK *better of.* **3.** *n.* That which is better (*change for the better*; **get the** ~ **of,** defeat, outwit; **think (all) the** ~ **of,** have higher opinion of); person who is more skilful etc. than oneself; (in *pl.*) persons of higher rank than oneself. [f. OE *betera,* OS *betiro,* OHG *bezziro,* ON *betri,* Goth. *batiza* f. Gmc **batizon* (**bat-* cogn. w. BOOT[2]; see -ER[3])]
bĕ'tter[2] *v.t.* Amend, improve; surpass (a feat etc.); ~ **oneself,** get better situation, wages, etc., hence ~MENT *n.*, improvement, enhanced value (of real property) arising from local improvements. [ME f. prec.]
bĕ'tter[3], **bĕ'ttor,** *n.* One who bets. [f. BET + -ER[1], -OR]
bėtwee'n *prep.* & *adv.* In, into, along, or across, a space, line, interval, or route, bounded by (any number of, esp. two, points, lines, dates, etc.; *between* TIME[1]*s,* WHILE[1]*s*); separating (*difference between right and wrong*; **stand** ~, act as mediator or protector); connecting; (**in**) ~, intermediately in place, time, amount, or order (to); owing partly to, partaking of the nature of, shared by, (each); to and from (*runs between London and Brighton*); reciprocally on the part of (*agreement between us*); confined to (*between ourselves*; *between you and me*); by combination of; taking one and rejecting the other of (*choose between*); separated (**far** ~, at wide intervals); ||~**-maid,** servant assisting two others, e.g. cook and housemaid. [OE *betwēonum* f. Gmc **bi* BY[1] + **twēon* (**twihnai,* ult. rel. to TWO)]
bėtwĭ'xt *prep.* & *adv.* (poet., arch., or dial.) Between; ~ **and between,** (colloq.) intermediate(ly). [ME, f. OE *betwēohs, betwēox,* etc. f. Gmc **bi* BY[1] + **twisk-* twofold (**twa* TWO, **-isk* -ISH[1]); cf. AGAINST]
BeV *abbr.* billion (= 10^9) electron-volts.
bĕ'vel[1] *n.* Joiner's and mason's tool for adjusting angles; slope from horizontal or vertical; sloping surface; ~ **gear** (working one shaft from another at angle to it by ~ **wheels,** toothed wheels with working face oblique to axis). [f. OF **bevel* (*baïf* open-mouthed f. *baer* gape; cf. BAY[3])]
bĕ'vel[2] *v.t.* & *i.* (||**-ll-**). Impart bevel to, slant. [f. prec.]
bĕ'verage *n.* (formal or joc.) Liquid for drinking. [ME, f. OF *be(u)vrage* f. Rom. **biberaticum* f. L *bibere* drink; see -AGE]
bĕ'vȳ *n.* Company (orig. of ladies, roes, quails, larks). [15th c.; orig. unkn.]
bėwai'l *v.t.* Wail over; mourn for. [f. BE- 3 + WAIL V.]
bėwār'e *v.i.* & *t.* (only in *imper.* and *inf.*) Be cautious, take heed, (of); take heed *of, lest, how, that . . . not.* [f. BE + WARE[2]]
bėwĭ'lder *v.t.* Lead astray; perplex, confuse; hence ~MENT *n.* [f. BE- 2 + obs. *wilder* lose one's way]
bėwĭ'tch *v.t.* Affect by magic, put a spell on; delight exceedingly. [ME, f. BE- 2 + OE *wiccian* enchant (*wicca* WITCH)]
bėwray' (bĭrā') *v.t.* (arch.) Reveal, esp. involuntarily. [ME, f. BE- 2 + obs. *wray* accuse f. OE *wrēgan,* = OS *wrōgian,* OHG *ruogen,* ON *rœgja* f. Gmc **wrōgjan*]
bey (bā) *n.* (Hist.) Turkish governor; **Bey of Tunis,** ruler of Tunisia; ~**'lĭc** *n.*, bey's province or jurisdiction. [Turk.]
bėyŏ'nd *adv., prep.,* & *n.* **1.** *adv.* & *prep.* At or to the farther side (of); past, outside; later than; out of reach, comprehension, or range, of (*it is beyond me*; *living beyond* one's *means*; *beyond repair*; ~ **measure,** exceedingly); surpassing; not subject to (*beyond argument*; *beyond question*); more (than) (*this is beyond a joke*). **2.** *n.* **The** ~, the future life, the unknown; **the back of** ~, very remote or out-of-the-way place. [OE *beg(e)ondan* (*be* BY[1], *g(e)ondan* f. Gmc **jandana* f. **jand-,* see YON, YONDER)]
bĕ'zant (*or* bĭză'-) *n.* **1.** (Hist.) Gold or silver coin, orig. minted at Byzantium. **2.** (Her.) Gold roundel. [ME, f. OF *besanz -ant* f. L *Byzantius* adj. of *Byzantium*]
bĕ'zel *n.* Sloped edge of chisel etc.; oblique faces of cut gem; groove holding watch-glass or gem; rim holding glass etc. cover. [f. OF **besel,* of unkn. orig.]
bėzi'que (-ē'k) *n.* Card-game for two, with double pack of 64 cards (ace to seven only); combination of queen of spades and jack of diamonds in this game. [f. F *bésigue,* perh. f. Pers. *bāzīgar* juggler]
bē'zoar *n.* Concretion with hard nucleus found in stomach or intestines of certain animals (chiefly ruminants), formerly believed antidotal. [ult. f. Pers. *pādzahr* antidote, Arab. *bāzahr*]
bėzō'nian *n.* (arch.) Rascal, beggarly fellow. [f. It. *bisogno* & Sp. *bisoño* need + -IAN]
||**b.f.** (bēē'f) *n.* (euphem.) Bloody fool. [abbr.]
b.f. *abbr.* bold face; brought forward.
||**B'ham** *abbr.* Birmingham.
bhăng (bă-) *n.* Indian hemp; its leaves etc. used as narcotic and intoxicant. [f. Port. *bangue,* Pers. *bang,* & Urdu etc. *bhāng*]

bha'ral (bŭ'-) *n.* Himalayan wild sheep. [Hindi]
b.h.p. *abbr.* brake horsepower.
bī- *pref.* (often **bin-** before vowel) to *adjs.* & *ns.*, forming other *adjs.* & *ns.* **1.** *adjs.*, w. sense (a) having two (*bilateral*, *bilingual*, *binaural*), (b) doubly, in two ways, (*biconcave*), (c) (Bot. & Zool.) twice over, i.e. divided into similarly divided parts, (*bipinnate*), (d) lasting for two, appearing etc. every two, (*biennial*), (e) appearing etc. twice in, (*biannual*, *bimonthly*), (f) joining two (*bi-parietal*). **2.** *ns.*, w. sense (a) thing having two (*biplane*), (b) (Chem.) salt having twice the proportion of acid to base molecules indicated by the simple word (*bicarbonate*, *bisulphate*). [L]
Bi *symb.* bismuth.
biă'nnūal *a.* Appearing etc. twice a year; hence ~LY[2] *adv.* [f. BI- 1(e) + ANNUAL]
bī'as[1] *n.* **1.** (Bowls). Lopsided form of a bowl, its oblique course. **2.** Inclination, predisposition (towards); prejudice; influence. **3.** (Statistics). Distortion of result by neglected factor. **4.** (Dressmaking etc.) **Cut on the ~**, cut obliquely across the warp; **~ binding,** strip so cut, used to finish edges etc. [f. F *biais* f. LL *bifax* looking two ways f. as BI- + L *facies* face]
bī'as[2] *v.t.* (**-s-** *or* **-ss-**). Give a bias to; influence (usu. unfairly); inspire with prejudice. [f. prec.]
biă'thlon *n.* Athletic contest in which competitors engage in skiing and shooting. [f. BI- 1(a), after PENTATHLON]
biă'xial *a.* Having two (optic) axes. [f. BI- 1(a) + AXIAL]
bĭb[1] *n.* Edible sea-fish (*Trisopterus luscus*) akin to cod, with inflatable head-membrane. [f. foll.]
bĭb[2] *n.* Piece of cloth etc. put under child's chin to keep dress-front clean; top front part of apron or overall (**best ~ and tucker,** best clothes). [perh. f. foll.]
bĭb[3] *v.i.* (**-bb-**). (arch.) Drink much or often; hence **~'b**ER[1] *n.* [ME, perh. f. L *bibere* drink]
bĭ'b-cŏck *n.* Tap with bent nozzle fixed at end of pipe. [perh. f. BIB[2] + COCK[1]]
bi'belot (bē'blō) *n.* Small curio or artistic trinket. [F]
Bī'ble *n.* **1.** Christian scriptures of the Old and New Testament; copy of them; particular edition of them (BISHOPS', BREECHES, PRINTERS', VINEGAR, WICKED, *Bible*). **2.** Scriptures of other religion; authoritative book. **3.** ***~ Belt,** reputedly puritanical area of S. and central U.S.; **~ oath** (taken on the Bible); **~-pounding, -punching, -thumping,** etc., (sl.) aggressively expounding or following the Bible. [ME f. OF, f. eccl. L f. Gk *biblia* books pl. of *biblion*, orig. dim. of *biblos*, *bublos* papyrus]
bĭ'blĭcal *a.* Of, concerning, contained in, the Bible; resembling the language of the Bible; hence ~LY[2] *adv.* [f. prec. + -ICAL]
bĭblĭŏ'graph|ȳ *n.* History or description of books, their authorship, editions, etc.; book containing such details; list of books etc. of any author, printer, country, subject; hence or cogn. ~ER[1] *n.*, **bĭblĭogră'phic**(AL) *adjs.*, ~IZE (1) *v.t.* [f. F (*-phie*) or f. mod. L f. Gk *bibliographia* (*biblion* book; see BIBLE, -GRAPHY)]
bĭ'blĭomăncȳ *n.* Divination by books, esp. by the Bible. [f. Gk *biblion* book (see BIBLE) + -O- + -MANCY]
bĭblĭomā'nĭ|a *n.* Craze for collecting books; hence ~AC *n.* [f. as prec. + -MANIA]
bĭblĭophĭl, -phīle, *n.* Lover of books; collector of books; hence **bĭblĭophĭ'lı**c *a.*, **bĭblĭŏ'phĭly**[1] *n.* [f. F *bibliophile* (as prec.; see -PHIL, -PHILE)]
bĭ'blĭopōle *n.* Seller of (esp. rare) books; so **bĭblĭŏ'pol**Y[1] *n.* [f. L f. Gk *bibliopōlēs* (*biblion* book, *pōlēs* seller)]
bĭ'būlous *a.* Addicted to drinking alcoholic liquor; hence ~LY[2] *adv.* [f. L *bibulus* freely drinking (*bibere* drink) + -OUS]
bīcă'meral *a.* Having two (legislative) chambers. [f. BI- 1(a) + L *camera* chamber + -AL]
bīcar̂'b *n.* (colloq.) = foll. 2. [abbr.]
bīcar̂'bonāte *n.* **1.** (Chem.) Salt containing double proportion of carbon dioxide. **2.** (pop.) Sodium bicarbonate, used as antacid, in baking-powder, etc. [f. BI- 2(b) + CARBONATE[1]]
bīce *n.* ~ or **blue ~, green ~,** pigments made from blue, green, basic copper carbonate; similar pigment made from smalt etc.; dull shade of blue or green given by these. [orig. = brownish grey, f. OF *bis* dark grey, of unkn. orig.]
bīcĕntē'narȳ (*or* -sĕ'ntĭ-) *a.* & *n.* (Festival) of the two-hundredth anniversary. [f. BI- 1(d) + CENTENARY]
bīcĕntĕ'nnĭal *a.* & *n.* **1.** *a.* Lasting, occurring every, two hundred years. **2.** *n.* = prec. [f. BI- 1(d) + CENTENNIAL]
bīcĕ'phalous *a.* Two-headed. [f. BI- 1(a) + -CEPHALOUS]
bī'cĕps *n.* Muscle with double head or attachment, esp. that which bends elbow; muscularity. [L, = two-headed, f. as BI- 1(a) + *-ceps* (*caput* head)]
bĭ'cker *v.i.* Quarrel, wrangle; (of stream, rain, etc.) brawl, patter; (of flame, light, etc.) flash, flicker. [ME *biker*, *beker*, of unkn. orig.]
bīcŏ'ncāve (-n-k-), **bīcŏ'nvĕx,** *adjs.* (Of lens etc.) concave, convex, on both sides. [f. BI- 1(b) + CONCAVE, CONVEX]
bīcŭ'ltural (-cher-) *a.* Having or combining two cultures. [f. BI- 1(a) + CULTURAL]
bīcŭ'spĭd *a.* & *n.* (Tooth) with two cusps, human premolar. [f. BI- 1(a) + L *cuspis -idis* sharp point]
bī'cȳcle *n.*, & *v.i.* (Ride on) two-wheeled pedal-driven road vehicle; **~-chain,** chain transmitting power from bicycle pedals to wheel; **~-clip** (used to confine cyclist's trouser-leg at ankle); **~-pump,** portable pump for inflating tyres of bicycle; hence **bī'cȳcl**IST (1) *n.* [F, f. BI- 2(a) + Gk *kuklos* wheel]
bĭd[1] *v.* (**-dd-**). **1.** *v.t.* (arch. or poet.; *past* **bade** *pr.* băd, *or* ~; *p.p.* ~ *or* **~'den**). Command to, tell to, (*bid the soldiers shoot*; *do as you are bid*); proclaim (defiance etc.); invite (*bidden guest*; **~'ding-prayer,** one inviting congregation to join in, now usu. a group of intercessory prayers); salute (person) with *welcome*, *farewell*, etc. **2.** *v.i.* & *t.* (*past* & *p.p.* ~). (Esp. at auction) offer price, offer (a certain price) *for*; offer to do work etc. for stated price; (Cards) make a BID[2] of or in, make a bid on the basis of (one's hand), make a bid; **~ fair to do,** show promise of doing; hence **~'d**ER[1] *n.* [OE *biddan* ask, = OS *biddian*, OHG *bitten*, ON *bithja*, Goth. *bidjan* f. Gmc **bidhjan* pray, & OE *bēodan* offer, command, OS *biodan*, OHG *biotan*, ON *bjótha*, Goth. *biudan*, IE **bh(e)udh-*]
bĭd[2] *n.* Offer of price, esp. at auction; offer made for stated price, TENDER[2] 3, (**make a ~ for,** (fig.) make an attempt to secure); (Cards) statement of number of tricks player proposes to win in specified suit or no-trumps; attempt, effort. [f. prec.]
bĭ'dd|able *a.* Obedient; (of hand or suit at cards) suitable for being bid; hence ~ABI'LITY *n.* [f. BID[1] + -ABLE]
bĭ'dden. See BID[1].
bĭ'ddĭng *n.* In vbl senses; the offers at auction; (Cards) the bids made; a command. [f. BID[1] + -ING[1]]
bĭ'ddȳ *n.* (sl., derog.) Woman. [f. *Bridget*]
bĭ'ddȳ-bĭddȳ *n.* (N.Z.) (Bur of) the piripiri. [corrupt. of Maori PIRIPIRI]

bīde *v.* **1.** *v.t.* ~ one's **time,** await best opportunity. **2.** *v.i.* (arch. or dial.) Remain. [OE *bidan,* = OS *bīdan,* OHG *bītan,* ON *bítha,* Goth. *beidan* f. Gmc **bidhan*]
bi'det (bē'dā) *n.* Low basin for washing, esp. of the genital region. [F, = pony]
bĭ'donvĭlle *n.* Shanty-town built of oil drums etc. [F (*bidon* oil drum, petrol tin, *ville* town)]
Bie'dermeier (-mī-) *a.* (derog.) Conventional; bourgeois. [f. *Biedermaier* fictitious Ger. poet (1854), applied to a style of furniture etc. in Germany 1815–1848]
bīĕ'nnĭal *a.* & *n.* **1.** *a.* Lasting, recurring every, two years; hence ~LY² *adv.* **2.** *n.* (Bot.) Plant that springs one year, and flowers, fructifies, and perishes, the next. [f. L *biennis* (as BI- 1(d), *annus* year) + -AL]
bīĕ'nnĭ|um *n.* (*pl.* **~ums** *or* **~a**). Period of two years. [L (as prec.)]
bier *n.* Movable frame on which coffin or corpse is placed, or taken to grave. [OE *bēr,* = OS, OHG *bāra* f. WG **bērō* f. Gmc **beran* BEAR³]
bĭff *n.,* & *v.t.* (sl.) **1.** *n.* Smart blow. **2.** *v.t.* Strike (person). [imit.]
||**bĭ'ffĭn** *n.* Deep-red cooking-apple. [= *beefing* f. BEEF + -ING¹ (3), w. ref. to the colour]
bī'fĭd *a.* Divided by deep cleft into two parts. [f. L BI(*fidus* f. st. of *findere* cleave)]
bīfō'cal *a.* & *n.* **1.** *a.* Having two foci (esp. of combined distant and near vision spectacles). **2.** *n.* (in *pl.*) Bifocal spectacles. [f. BI- 1(a) + FOCAL]
bī'furcāte *v.t.* & *i.* Divide into two branches, fork. [f. med. L *bifurcare* f. L *bifurcus* two-forked (as BI-, *furca* fork), + -ATE³]
bīfurcā'tion *n.* Division into two branches; point of such division; such branches or one of them. [f. prec. + -ATION]
bĭg *a.* & *adv.* **1.** *a.* Of considerable size, amount, intensity, etc. (usu. without emotional implications of *great*; *elected by a big majority*; **in a ~ way,** (colloq.) with great enthusiasm, display, etc.); of largest, larger than usual, size (*big drum, game, toe*); (more) grown up (*you're a big boy now*); elder (*big brother, sister*); **too ~ for** one's **boots** or **breeches,** (sl.) conceited. **2.** Advanced in pregnancy (esp. of animals or fig., *big with consequences*); important (*the big fight, league, race,* etc.); **a ~ man** (in eminence or range of operation); **~ money,** large amounts, high profit or pay; **the Big Three, Four,** etc., the predominant few. **3.** Boastful (*big words*); (colloq.) generous; (colloq.) ambitious (*have big ideas*; *the big* IDEA); (colloq.) outstanding (*his big opportunity, my big moment*). **4.** **~ bang,** assumed violent event creating the universe; ||**Big Ben,** great bell, clock, and tower, of Houses of Parliament; ***Big Board,** (colloq.) New York Stock Exchange; **Big Brother,** all-powerful dictator simulating benevolence [Orwell's *1984*]; **~ bud,** plant disease caused by gall-mite; **~ bug,** (sl.) bigwig; **~ business,** (persons concerned in) commerce on the grand scale (freq. with sinister implications); **~ Chief, ~ Daddy,** (sl.) bigwig; ***~ deal!,** (sl., iron.) I am not impressed; **~ dipper,** ||fairground switchback, *Great BEAR¹; **~ end,** end of connecting-rod that encircles crankpin; **~ gun,** (sl.) bigwig; **~ head,** (colloq.) conceit(ed person); **~-hearted,** generous; **~'horn,** Rocky Mountains sheep; **~ house,** principal house in a village etc., (sl.) prison; **~-mouthed,** boastful; **~ name,** famous person; **~ noise, ~ pot, ~ shot,** (sl.) bigwig; **the ~ smoke,** ||(sl.) London, (orig. Austral. Aboriginal) a large town; **~ stick,** display of force; *big* STIFF; **~ time,** (sl.) highest rank among entertainers etc.; **~ top,** main tent at circus; ***~ tree,** giant sequoia; **~ wheel,** Ferris wheel, *(sl.) bigwig; **~'wig,** important person. **5.** Hence ~'NESS *n.* **6.** *adv.* In a big manner; **come, go, over ~** (with great effect); **look, talk, ~** (boastfully); **think ~** (ambitiously). [ME, of unkn. orig.]
bĭ'gamĭst *n.* Person guilty of bigamy. [f. foll. + -IST]
bĭ'gam|ȳ *n.* Crime of going through form of marriage while previous marriage is still in existence; hence ~OUS *a.* [ME, f. OF *bigamie* (-Y¹) (*bigame* bigamous f. LL *bigamus* f. as BI- + Gk *gamos* marriage)]
bīght (bīt) *n.* Loop of rope; curve or recess of coast, river, etc. [OE *byht,* MLG *bucht* f. Gmc **b(e)ug-*; see BOW³]
bĭ'got *n.* Obstinate and intolerant adherent of a creed or view; hence ~ED² *a.,* ~RY (4, 5) *n.* [16th c. f. F; orig. unkn.]
Bĭhar'ĭ *a.* & *n.* (Native or language) of Bihar. [Hindi, f. *Bihar* in India + -I]
bijou (bē'zhōō) *n.* (*pl.* **~x** *pr.* same) & *a.* **1.** *n.* Jewel, trinket. **2.** *a.* Small and elegant. [F]
bijouterie (bēzhōō'terē) *n.* Jewellery, trinkets, etc. [F; see prec. and -ERY]
bīk|e *n.,* & *v.i.* (colloq.) (Ride on) bicycle or motor cycle; hence *~'ER¹ (1) *n.* [abbr.]
bĭki'nĭ (-ē'-) *n.* Scanty two-piece beach garment worn by women; **~ briefs** etc., women's briefs of similar design. [f. *B~,* atoll in Marshall Islands in Pacific where atomic bomb was exploded 1946]
bīlă'teral *a.* **1.** Of, on, with, two sides; **~ symmetry** (about a plane). **2.** Affecting or between two parties, countries, etc. **3.** Hence ~LY² *adv.* [f. BI- 1(a) + L *latus lateris* side + -AL]
bĭ'lberrȳ *n.* (Small blue fruit of) dwarf hardy N. European shrub (*Vaccinium myrtillus*) growing on heaths and stony moors and in mountain woods. [cf. Da. *böllebær*]
bĭ'lbō *n.* (*pl.* **~s** *or* **~es**). (Hist.) Sword of notable temper. [f. *Bilboa* = Bilbao in Spain]
bĭ'lbōes (-ōz) *n. pl.* (Hist.) Iron bar with sliding shackles for prisoner's ankles. [16th c.; orig. unkn.]
Bildungsroman (bĭ'ldōōngzrəmahn) *n.* Novel dealing with one person's early life and development. [G]
bīle *n.* Brownish-yellow bitter fluid secreted by liver to aid digestion; derangement of the bile; (fig.) peevishness. [F, f. L *bilis*]
bĭlge¹ *n.* Nearly horizontal part of ship's bottom, inside or out; filth that collects inside the bilge; (sl.) nonsense, rot; **~-keel,** timber or plate fastened under bilge to prevent rolling; **~-water,** stinking water collected in bilge. [prob. var. of BULGE¹]
bĭlge² *v.* **1.** *v.t.* Stave in the bilge of. **2.** *v.i.* Spring a leak in the bilge; bulge, swell out. [f. prec.]
bĭlhar'zĭa *n.* Tropical flatworm of genus *Bilharzia* parasitic in human pelvic region; bilharziasis; hence **bĭlharzī'**ASIS *n.,* chronic disease produced by its presence, schistosomiasis. [mod. L, f. T. *Bilharz,* Ger. physician d. 1862 + -IA²]
bĭ'liarȳ (-lyerĭ) *a.* Of the bile. [f. F *biliaire*; see BILE, -ARY²]
bīlĭ'ngual (-ĭ'nggwal) *a.* & *n.* **1.** *a.* Having, speaking (fluently), spoken or written in, two languages; hence ~ISM (1) *n.* **2.** *n.* Person able to speak two languages, esp. fluently. [f. L *bilinguis* (as BI- 1(a), *lingua* tongue, -AL)]
bĭ'lious (-lyus) *a.* Liable to, affected by, causing, or arising from, derangement of the bile; (fig.) peevish, having bilious TEMPERAMENT; hence ~LY² *adv.,* ~NESS *n.* [f. L *biliosus* (*bilis* bile; see -OUS)]
-bĭ'lĭtȳ. See -ABILITY, -IBILITY, -UBILITY. [f. as -BLE, -ITY]
bĭlk *v.t.* Evade payment of (creditor, bill); cheat;

give the slip to. [orig. uncert., perh. = BALK[2]; earliest use (17th c.) in cribbage, = spoil opponent's score]

bĭll[1] *n.* **1.** (Hist.) Weapon like halberd with hook instead of blade. **2.** ~(**'hook**), concave-edged lopping implement for pruning etc. [OE *bil*, = OS *bil*, OHG *bill* f. WG **bilja*]

bĭll[2] *n.* Bird's beak (esp. when slender, flattened, or weak, and in pigeons and web-footed birds); muzzle of platypus; narrow promontory; point of anchor-fluke; hence (-)~ED[2] (-ld) *a.* [OE *bile*, of unkn. orig.]

bĭll[3] *v.i.* (Of doves) stroke bill with bill; exchange caresses (esp. *bill and coo*). [f. prec.]

bĭll[4] *n.* **1.** Draft of proposed law; (Law) written statement of (esp. plaintiff's) case; TRUE *bill*. **2.** Note of charges for goods supplied or services rendered; amount thus owed; *banknote; poster, placard; (programme of) entertainment. **3.** ~ (**of exchange**), written order to pay sum on given date to drawer or to named payee; **accommodation** ~ (to raise money on credit). **4.** ~ **of fare,** menu, (fig.) programme; ~ **of health,** certificate regarding infectious disease on ship or in port at time of sailing (*clean ~ of health*, certificate that there is no disease, also fig. of person or thing examined and found in good condition); *bill of* INDICTMENT; ~ **of lading,** shipmaster's detailed receipt to consignor, *waybill; ~ **of mortality,** (Hist.) weekly statement of deaths in and near London; ||~ **of quantities,** detailed statement of work, prices, dimensions, etc., for the erection of a building; *Bill of* RIGHT[3]*s*; ~ **of sale,** certificate of transfer of personal property, esp. borrower's certificate that chattel is pledged as security. **5.** ~**'board,** large outdoor board for advertisements; *~**'fold,** wallet for banknotes; ~**'head,** printed account form; ~**'poster,** ~**'sticker,** man who pastes up placards. [ME f. AF *bille*, AL *billa*, prob. alt. of med. L *bulla* seal, sealed document, BULL[3]]

bĭll[5] *v.t.* Announce, put in the programme (~**ed to appear** etc., announced as going to); advertise *as*; send note of charges to. [f. prec.]

bĭ'llabŏng *n.* (Austral.) River branch that forms backwater or stagnant pool. [f. Aboriginal *Billibang* Bell River (*billa* water)]

bĭ'llĕt[1] *n.* Order requiring person to board and lodge the soldier etc. bearing it; place where troops etc. are lodged; destination (**every bullet has its** ~, hits only by providential order); appointment, situation. [ME f. AF *billette*, AL *billetta*, dim. of *billa* BILL[4]; see -ET[1]]

bĭ'llĕt[2] *v.t.* Quarter (soldiers etc.) *on* (town, householder, etc.), *in*, *at*; (of householder) provide (soldier etc.) with board and lodging; hence ~EE', ~ER[1], *ns.* [f. prec.]

bĭ'llĕt[3] *n.* Thick piece of firewood; small bar of metal; (Archit.) short roll inserted at intervals in hollow moulding. [ME, f. F *billette* and *billot* dims. of *bille* tree-trunk f. med. L *billa*, *billus*, prob. of Celt. orig.]

bĭllet-doux (bĭlĭdōō') *n.* (*pl.* **billets-** *pr.* -ōō'z). (joc.) Love-letter. [F]

bĭ'lliard|s (-lyerdz) *n. pl.* (usu. treated as *sing.*) Game played with cues and three balls on oblong smooth cloth-covered table; ||**bar ~s,** variant in which balls are to be struck into holes on table; **~-ball, ~-table,** kinds used in billiards; **~-marker,** attendant, or apparatus for, keeping the score. [f. F *billard* billiards, cue, dim. of *bille*; see BILLET[3]]

bĭ'llĭngsgāte (-z-) *n.* Abuse, violent invective. [17th c., from the scolding of fish-sellers in *B~* market, London]

bĭ'llion (-yon) *n.* (for *pl.* usage see HUNDRED). ||A million millions; *a thousand millions; *~**air'e,** person possessing a thousand million dollars [after MILLIONAIRE]; hence ~TH[2] *a.* & *n.* [F (as BI-, MILLION)]

bĭ'llon *n.* Alloy of gold or silver with predominating amount of base metal. [F (*bille* BILLET[3])]

bĭ'llow (-ō) *n.*, & *v.i.* **1.** *n.* Great wave; (poet., in *sing.* or *pl.*) *the* sea; (fig.) anything that sweeps along as if in waves; hence ~Y[2] *a.* **2.** *v.i.* Rise or move or swell in billows. [f. ON *bylgja* f. Gmc **bulg-*, **belg-* swell]

bĭllȳ[1] *n.* (orig. Austral. & N.Z.) Cylindrical tin etc. or enamelled container used as kettle, cooking-pot, food-carrier, etc. [perh. f. Aboriginal *billa* water]

bĭ'llȳ[2] *n.* **1.** = BILLY-GOAT. **2.** *~ (**club**), policeman's truncheon. [f. *B~*, pet-form of name *William*]

bĭ'llȳcăn *n.* = BILLY[1]. [f. BILLY[1] + CAN[1]]

||**bĭ'llȳcŏck** *n.* (arch.) Bowler hat. [said to have been orig. designed for *William Coke* 1850]

bĭ'llȳ-goat *n.* Male goat. [f. as BILLY[2] + GOAT]

bĭ'llȳ-ō(h) (-ō) *n.* (colloq.) **Like** ~ (intensive phr.): *raining like* ~ (very hard), *fighting like* ~ (fiercely). [19th c.; orig. unkn.]

bīlō'bate, bī'lōbed (-ōbd), *adjs.* Having two lobes. [f. BI- 1(a) + LOBE + -ATE[2], -ED[2]]

bĭ'ltŏng *n.* (S. Afr.) Strips of sun-dried lean meat. [Afrik. (*bil* buttock, whence it is cut, *tong* tongue, which it looks like)]

Bĭm *n.* (colloq.) Inhabitant of Barbados. [19th c.; orig. unkn.]

B.I.M. *abbr.* British Institute of Management.

bī'manal, bī'manous, *adjs.* Having two hands. [f. BI- 1(a) + L *manus* hand + -AL, -OUS]

bĭmba'shi (-ah'-) *n.* Turkish major or naval commander. [Turk., = head of a thousand (*bin* thousand, *baş* head)]

bĭ'mbō *n.* (*pl.* ~**s** *or* ~**es**). (sl., usu. derog.) Person; woman. [It., = little child]

bīmĕtă'llĭc *a.* **1.** Of two metals; ~ **strip** (in thermostat etc., made of two bands of metals with different thermal expansion, thus bending when heated, in a way that can be used to control temperature). **2.** Using gold and silver as legal tender to any amount at fixed ratio to each other; hence **bīmĕtall**ISM (3), **bīmĕtall**IST (2), *ns.* [f. F *bimétallique* (as BI- 1(a), METALLIC)]

bīmĭllē'narȳ (*or* -mĭ'lĭ-) *a.* & *n.* (Festival) of the two-thousandth anniversary. [f. BI- 1(d) + MILLENARY]

bīmo'nthlȳ (-mŭ'-) *a.* & *n.* (Periodical) produced or occurring every two months or twice a month. [f. BI- 1(d, e) + MONTHLY]

bĭn *n.* Receptacle for corn, coal, bottled wine, etc.; receptacle for household rubbish, litter, etc.; ||canvas receptacle used in hop-picking. [OE *bin(n)*, *binne* f. OBrit. **benna*, or f. med. L *benna* f. Gaulish]

bín-. See BI-.

bī'narȳ *a.* & *n.* Dual, of or involving pairs; ~ **fission,** (Biol.) division of cell or organism into two parts; (Mus.) ~ **form** (of movement in two sections), ~ **measure** (of two beats to bar); ~ (**star**), system of two stars revolving round each other; ~ **compound** (Chem., of two elements or radicals); *binary* SCALE[3]; ~ **digit,** one of two (usu. 0 and 1) used in binary scale. [f. LL *binarius* (*bini* two together; see -ARY[1])]

bī'nate *a.* (Bot.) Composed of two equal parts; growing in pairs. [f. mod. L *binatus* f. L *bini* (as prec.; see -ATE[2])]

bīnaur'al *a.* Of, used with, both ears (*binaural stethoscope*); (of sound) recorded by two microphones and usu. transmitted separately to the two ears. [f. BI- + AURAL[2]]

bīnd[1] *v.* (**bound;** see also BOUNDEN). **1.** *v.t.* Tie; fasten, attach, *to* or *on*. **2.** Put in bonds, restrain;

obstruct (*fog-*, *snow-bound*); fasten or hold together; constipate; (esp. Cookery) cause to cohere; **bound up,** closely associated *with*. **3.** Be obligatory, exercise authority, impose constraint or duty, on; indenture as apprentice; ratify (bargain etc.); (in *pass.*) be required by duty, be certain, *to* (do something); ~ (**over**), subject to legal obligation, promise, etc.; **I'll be bound,** (fig.) I guarantee truth of (statement), I feel certain. **4.** (sl.) Bore, weary. **5.** ~ (**up**), bandage; encircle (head etc.) *with*, wreathe (material) *round*, *on*; edge with braid, iron, etc.; fasten (sheets of book) into (usu. stiff) cover. **6.** *v.i.* (Of snow etc.) cohere, stick; be prevented from moving freely; (sl.) complain. [OE *bindan*, = OS *bindan*, OHG *bintan*, ON *binda*, Goth. *bindan* f. IE **bhendh-*]

bīnd[2] *n.* = BINE; (Mus.) = TIE[2] 5; (sl.) nuisance, bore; ***in a** ~, (sl.) in difficulty. [f. prec.]

bī'nder *n.* In vbl senses; bookbinder; cementing substance; tie-beam; bondstone in wall; machine for reaping and binding grain into sheaves; loose cover for unbound newspapers etc. [f. BIND[1] + -ER[1]]

bī'nderў *n.* Bookbinder's workshop. [f. prec. + -ERY (3)]

bī'ndĭng[1] *a.* Obligatory (*on*). [f. BIND[1] + -ING[2]]

bī'ndĭng[2] *n.* In vbl senses; book-cover; tape, braid, etc., for protecting raw edges. [f. BIND[1] + -ING[1]]

bī'ndweed *n.* Convolvulus; other climbing plant, e.g. honeysuckle. [f. BIND[1] + WEED]

bīne *n.* Flexible shoot; stem of climbing plant, esp. the hop. [orig. dial. form of BIND[2]]

Binet(-Simo'n) (bē'nā sēmaw'ṅ) *a.* ~ **scale, test,** (for measuring intelligence). [f. A. *Binet* d. 1911 and T. *Simon* d. 1961, Fr. psychologists]

bĭnge (-nj) *n.* (sl.) Drinking-bout, spree. [prob. orig. dial., = soak]

bĭ'ngō[1] (-nggō) *n.* (*pl.* ~**s**). Popular gambling game like lotto, played esp. in public halls, with cards divided into numbered squares, in which player first covering all or specified set of numbers on card wins prize. [perh. f. winner's excl.; cf. dial. *bing*, imit.]

bĭ'ngō[2] (-nggō) *int.* expr. sudden action or event, e.g. winning of game of bingo (see prec.). [imit. of sudden sound]

bĭ'nnacle *n.* Receptacle for ship's compass. [earlier *bittacle* etc., ME, f. Sp. *bitácula* or Port. *bitacola* f. L *habitaculum* habitation (*habitare* inhabit)]

bīnŏ'cūlar *a.* & *n.* **1.** *a.* Adapted for or using two eyes. **2.** *n.* (usu. in *pl.*) Field or opera glasses for use with both eyes. [f. L *bini* two together + *oculus* eye + -AR[1]]

bīnō'mĭal *a.* & *n.* (Algebraic sum or difference) consisting of two terms (~ **theorem,** formula for finding any power of a binomial without multiplying at length); = BINOMINAL (name). [f. F *binôme* or mod. L *binomium* (as BI-, Gk *nomos* part, portion) + -AL]

bīnŏ'mĭnal *a.* Composed of or using two names; ~ **system** (of scientific nomenclature by genus and species). [f. L *binominis* (BI- 1(a), *nomen -inis* name) + -AL]

bĭnt *n.* (colloq., usu. derog.) Girl; woman. [Arab., = daughter, girl]

bĭ'ntūrŏng *n.* S. Asian prehensile-tailed civet (*Arctictis binturong*). [Malay]

bīo- *comb. form.* (1) Life (*biography*); (2) biological (*biomathematics*); (3) of living beings (*bioscience*). [f. Gk *bios* (course of) human life]

bīochĕ'm|ĭstrў (-kĕ'-) *n.* Study of chemical or physico-chemical processes and products involved in life phenomena of plants and animals; hence ~ICAL *a.*, ~IST (3) *n.* [f. prec. + CHEMISTRY]

bīocoen|ō'sĭs (-sēn-), ***-cēn|-,** *n.* (*pl.* ~**oses** *pr.* -ō'sēz). Association of organisms forming a community; relationship existing between such organisms; hence ~**ŏ'**LOGY *n.*, ~O'TIC *a.* [mod. L, f. BIO- + Gk *koinōsis* sharing (*koinos* common)]

bīōdėgrā'dable *a.* Capable of being decomposed by living matter, esp. by bacteria; so **bīōdėgrād**ABI'LITY, **bīōdĕgrad**A'TION, *ns.* [f. BIO- + DEGRADE + -ABLE]

bīōfee'dbăck *n.* Technique of using feedback of a normally automatic bodily response to a stimulus, in order to acquire voluntary control of the response. [f. BIO- + FEEDBACK]

bīogĕ'nėsĭs *n.* Hypothesis that living matter arises only from living matter; synthesis of chemical substances by living matter; hypothetical development of living matter from complex inanimate substances; hence **bīogėnĕ'**TIC *a.* [f. BIO- + Gk *genesis* birth]

bīogĕ'nĭc *a.* Produced by living matter. [f. BIO- + -GENIC]

bīŏ'graphў *n.* Written life of a person; branch of literature dealing with persons' lives; life-course of a living (usu. human) being; so **bīŏ'**GRAPHER *n.*, **bīo**GRA'PHIC(AL) *adjs.* [f. F *biographie* or mod. L f. med. Gk *biographia* (as BIO-, -GRAPHY)]

bīolŏ'gĭcal *a.* Of or relating to biology or life phenomena; ~ **clock,** innate mechanism controlling rhythmic activities of an organism; ~ **control** (of pest by introducing a natural enemy of it); ~ **warfare,** use of organisms against an enemy, esp. of bacteria to spread disease; hence ~LY[2] *adv.* [f. BIOLOGY + -ICAL]

bīŏ'log|ў *n.* Science of life, dealing with morphology, physiology, anatomy, behaviour, origin, and distribution, of animals and plants; hence ~IST (3) *n.* [f. F f. G *biologie* (as BIO-, -LOGY)]

bīolūmĭnĕ'sc|ence (*or* -lōō-) *n.* Emission of light by living organisms; hence ~ENT *a.* [f. BIO- + LUMINESCENCE]

bī'ōmăss *n.* Total quantity or weight of organisms in a given area. [f. BIO- + MASS[2]]

bīōmăthėmă'tĭcs *n.* Science of the application of mathematics to biology. [f. BIO- + MATHEMATICS]

bīŏ'mėtrў *n.*, **bīomĕ'trĭcs** *n. pl.* (usu. treated as *sing.*) Science of the application of statistical methods to biological facts; so **bīomĕ'tr**IC(AL) *adjs.*, **bīomėtri**'CIAN *n.* [f. BIO- + -METRY]

bī'omōrph *n.* Decorative form representing living object. [f. BIO- + Gk *morphē* form]

bīŏ'nĭcs *n. pl.* (usu. treated as *sing.*) Study of mechanical systems that behave like living beings. [f. BIO- after *electronics*]

bīonŏ'mĭcs *n. pl.* (usu. treated as *sing.*) Branch of biology dealing with organisms' habits and modes of life in their natural environment. [f. BIO-, after ECONOMICS]

bīophў'sĭc|s (-z-) *n. pl.* (usu. treated as *sing.*) Science of the application of the laws of physics to biological phenomena; hence ~AL *a.*, ~IST (3) *n.* [f. BIO- + PHYSICS]

bī'ŏpsў *n.* Examination of tissue cut from the living body; removal of such tissue. [f. F *biopsie* f. Gk *bios* life + *opsis* sight, after *necropsy*]

bī'oscōpe *n.* (S. Afr.) Cinema. [f. BIO- + -SCOPE]

bī'ōsphēre *n.* Regions of earth's crust and atmosphere occupied by living matter. [f. G *biosphäre* (as BIO-, SPHERE)]

biosў'nthės|ĭs *n.* (*pl.* ~**es** *pr.* -ēz). Production of chemical substance by living organism. [f. BIO- + SYNTHESIS]

bīō'ta *n.* Animal and plant life of a region. [mod. L; cf. Gk *biotē* life]

bīŏ'tĭc *n.* Relating to life or to living things. [f. F *biotique* or f. LL f. Gk *biōtikos* (*bios* life; see -IC)]

bī'otĭn *n.* Crystalline vitamin in yeast etc., controlling growth. [G, f. Gk *bios* life + -IN]

bīpar̂tisă'n (-z-; *or* -par̂'t-) *a.* Of or involving two (political) parties. [f. BI- 1(a) + PARTISAN[1]]

bīpar̂'tīte *a.* Having two parts; (of treaty, contract, etc.) drawn up in two corresponding parts; shared by or involving two parties. [f. L *bipartitus* f. BI(*partire* PART[2])]

bī'pĕd *a.* & *n.* Two-footed (animal); so **bī'pĕdAL** *a.* [f. L *bipes -edis* (as BI- 1(a), *pes pedis* foot)]

bīpĭ'nnate *a.* Having lobes that themselves have lobes. [f. BI- 1(c) + PINNATE]

bī'plāne *n.* Aeroplane having two sets of wings, one above the other. [f. BI- 1(a) + PLANE[3]]

bīpō'lar *a.* Having two poles or extremities. [f. BI- 1(a) + POLAR]

bīquadră'tĭc *a.* & *n.* (Math.) (Number) that is a fourth power, square of a square; ~ **(equation)**, equation in which there is the fourth power of a variable. [f. BI- 1(b) + QUADRATIC]

bir̂ch *n.*, & *v.t.* **1.** *n.* Smooth-barked slender-branched northern forest tree of genus *Betula*; **~('wood)**, its wood; (N.Z.) one of various similar trees; **~-bark,** bark of *B. papyrifera* for canoes etc., *such canoe; **~(-rod)**, bundle of birch twigs used for flogging delinquents; hence ~'EN[5] *a.* **2.** *v.t.* Flog with birch. [OE *bi(e)rce*, = OHG *birka* f. Gmc **berkjōn*]

bir̂d *n.*, & *v.i.* **1.** *n.* Feathered vertebrate with two wings and two feet; game-bird; (sl.) young woman; (colloq.) person; (sl.) prison (sentence). **2.** (fig.) **A ~ in the hand,** something certain; **~ is** or **has flown,** prisoner etc. has escaped; **~s of a feather,** people of like character; **(strictly) for the ~s,** (sl.) trivial, uninteresting; **get the ~**, (sl.) be dismissed, be hissed and booed; **kill two ~s with one stone,** achieve two aims at once; **like a bird,** without difficulty or hesitation; **little ~**, unnamed informant (*told me* etc.); OLD *bird.* **3. ~ of paradise,** New Guinea bird with beautiful brilliantly coloured plumage; **~ of passage,** migrant, (fig.) transient visitor; *bird of* PREY[1]. **4. ~-bath,** basin in garden etc. with water for birds to bathe in; **~'brain(ed)**, stupid or flighty (person); **~'cage,** wire cage for bird(s), object of similar design; **~-call,** bird's natural call, instrument imitating it; **~ cherry,** wild cherry (*Prunus padus*); ***~ dog,** retriever (lit., or fig. of person); **~-fancier,** one who knows about, collects, breeds, or deals in, birds; *bird*LIME[1]; **~ sanctuary,** area where birds are protected and helped to breed; **~'seed,** special seeds given to caged birds; **~'s-eye,** plant (esp. ‖germander speedwell) with small bright round flowers, pattern with many small spots; **~'s-eye view,** general overhead view *of* town etc. or (fig.) *of* subject; **~'s-foot,** plant like foot of bird, esp. of genus *Lotus* with claw-shaped pods; **~'s nest,** nest of bird (*~'s nest soup*, made from edible kind of S. Asian swift's nest); **~'s-nesting** (-zn-), hunting for birds' nests, usu. to get eggs; **~-strike,** collision between bird and aircraft; **~-table,** raised platform on which food for birds is placed; **~-watcher,** one who observes birds in their natural surroundings; **~-watching,** this occupation; hence **~(-watch)** *v.i.* [OE *brid*, of unkn. orig.]

bir̂'dĭe *n.* Little bird; (Golf) hole played in one stroke under par or bogey. [f. prec. + -IE]

bīrĕfrĭ'ng|ent (-nj-) *a.* (Phys.) Having double REFRACTION; so **~ENCE** *n.* [f. BI- 1(b) + REFRINGENT]

bir̂'ēme *n.* Ancient galley with two banks of oars. [f. L *biremis* (as BI- 1(a), *remus* oar)]

bĭrĕ'tta *n.* Square cap of various colours (cf. ZUCCHETTO) worn by R.C. and other clergymen. [f. It. *berretta* or Sp. *birreta* fem. dims. corresp. to Prov. BERET f. LL *birrus* cape]

bir̂k. See BERK.

Bīr'ō *n.* (*pl.* ~s). (Make of) ball-point pen. [**P,** f. L. *Biró*, Hung. inventor]

bir̂th *n.* **1.** Emergence of young from body of mother; **give ~ to,** produce (young) thus, also fig.; **new ~**, (Theol.) spiritual regeneration. **2.** Coming into existence; origin, beginning; parentage, descent, inherited position; noble lineage. **3. ~ certificate,** official document giving date and place of person's birth; **~ control,** (practice of) methods of preventing undesired pregnancy; **~'day,** (anniversary of) day of one's birth; *~day card, party, present*, (given on this); ‖*~day honours*, titles etc. given on sovereign's (official) birthday; *~day suit*, (joc.) state of nakedness; **~'mark,** unusual mark on one's body at or from birth, usu. an irregularly-shaped blotch of brown or dark red skin; **~ pill,** contraceptive pill; **~'place** (at which one was born); **~ rate,** number of births per thousand of population per year etc.; **~'right,** rights or possessions belonging to one as eldest son, as born in a certain status or country, or as a human being. [ME, f. ON *byrth*, Goth. *gabaurths* f. Gmc **gaburthiz* f. stem **ber-* BEAR[3] + -TH[1]]

B.I.S. *abbr.* Bank for International Settlements.

bĭ'scuĭt (-kĭt) *n.* & *a.* **1.** *n.* ‖Piece of usu. unleavened cake or bread of various materials, usu. crisp, dry, hard, and in small flat thin shape; TAKE[1] *the biscuit.* **2.** *Soft round cake like scone. **3.** Porcelain etc. after firing but before glazing and painting. **4.** One of three square sections of soldier's mattress. **5.** *n.* & *a.* (Of) light-brown colour. [ME, f. OF *bescoit* etc. f. med. L **biscoctus* twice baked f. L *bis* + *coctus* p.p. of *coquere* cook]

bise (bēz) *n.* Keen dry N. wind in Switzerland, S. France, etc. [ME f. OF]

bīsĕ'ct *v.t.* Cut or divide into two (prop. equal) parts; hence **bīsĕ'ctION** *n.* [f. BI- + L *secare sect-* cut]

bīsĕ'ctor *n.* Bisecting line. [f. as prec. + -OR]

bīsĕ'xūal *a.* Of two sexes; having both sexes in one individual; (of person) sexually attracted by members of both sexes; hence ~ITY (-ă'l-) *n.* [f. BI- 1(a) + SEXUAL]

bĭsh *n.* (sl.) Mistake. [20th c.; orig. unkn.]

bĭ'shop *n.* Clergyman consecrated as governor of diocese and possessing powers of confirming, instituting, and ordaining; bishop SUFFRAGAN; chess piece with mitre-shaped top; mulled and spiced wine; **Bishops' Bible** (version of 1568); **~ sleeve,** full sleeve gathered at wrist. [OE *bisc(e)op*, = OS *biskop*, OHG *biscof*, ON *biskup* f. pop. L **biscopus* f. eccl. L f. Gk *episkopos* overseer (as EPI-, *-skopos* -looking)]

bĭ'shoprĭc *n.* Office or diocese of bishop. [OE *bisceoprīce* (as prec., *rīce* realm)]

bĭsk. See BISQUE[3].

Bĭ'smar̂ck (-z-) *n.* **~ herring** (marinaded fillet served cold). [f. Prince O. von ~, Ger. statesman d. 1898]

bĭsmĭ'llah (-*a*) *int.* (used by Muslims before action). [Arab., = in the name of Allah]

bĭ'smuth (-z-) *n.* Reddish-white easily fusible metallic element; compound of it used medicinally. [f. mod. L *bisemutum*, latinization of G *wismut*, of unkn. orig.]

bī'son *n.* (*pl.* same). Wild ox of two species of genus *Bison*, European (also called *wisent*) and American (also called *buffalo*). [ME f. L, f. Gmc **wisand-*]

bĭsque[1] (-k) *n.* (Tennis) right of scoring one point without winning it, at any time in the set; (Croquet) right of playing extra turn; (Golf) handicap stroke to be taken when desired. [F; etym. unkn.]

bĭsque[2] (-k) *n.* Unglazed white porcelain used in statuettes. [f. BISCUIT]

bĭsque[3] (-k), **bĭsk,** *n.* Rich soup made from shellfish etc. [F; etym. unkn.]

bĭssĕ'xtile *a.* & *n.* Leap(-year). [f. LL *bi(s)sextilis (annus)*, (year) containing the *bis sextus dies* or doubled 24 Feb. (sixth day before calends of March)]

bĭstā'ble *a.* Having two stable states. [f. BI- 1(a) + STABLE[1]]

bĭ'stôrt *n.* Herb with twisted root and cylindrical spike of flesh-coloured flowers. [f. F *bistorte* or f. med. L *bistorta* (*bis* twice + *torta* fem. p.p. of *torquēre* twist)]

bĭ'stourў (-terĭ) *n.* Surgeon's scalpel. [f. F *bistouri, bistorie*, orig. = dagger; orig. unkn.]

bĭ'stre (-*ter*), ***bĭ'ster,** *n.* & *a.* Brown pigment prepared from soot; (of) its colour. [F; orig. unkn.]

bĭ'strō (*or* bē'-) *n.* (*pl.* **~s**). Small bar or restaurant. [F]

bĭsŭ'lphāte *n.* (Chem.) Salt containing double proportion of sulphate radical. [f. BI- 2(b) + SULPHATE]

bĭt[1] *n.* Boring-piece of drill, cutting-iron of plane, nipping-part of pincers etc.; part of key that engages with lock-lever; copper head of soldering-iron; mouthpiece of bridle; **take the ~ between** one's **teeth,** (fig.) escape from control. [OE *bite*, = OS *biti*, OHG *biz*, ON *bit* f. Gmc **bitiz* (**bitan* BITE[1])]

bĭt[2] *n.* **1.** Morsel of food; (small) piece or quantity or portion of anything; **~ by ~,** gradually. **2.** (colloq.) **A ~,** somewhat (*feeling a bit tired*); **a ~ of,** rather (*a bit of a coward*), a small or unimportant (*only a bit of a book*), a fair quantity of (*takes a bit of remembering*); **a ~ of all right,** very pleasing person or thing; **~s and pieces, ~s and bobs,** odds and ends; **~s of,** poor little (*children, furniture*); **do** one's **~,** contribute service or money to a cause; **every ~ as,** quite as; **not a ~ (of it),** not at all. **3.** A short time (*wait a bit*) or distance (*move up a bit*); small coin; *amount of 12½ cents (*two, four, six, bits*). **4. ~ (part),** small part in a play or film. **5.** (sl.) **~ (of stuff),** young woman. [OE *bita*, = OHG *bizzo*, ON *biti* f. Gmc **biton* (**bītan* BITE[1])]

bĭt[3] *v.t.* (**-tt-**). Put bit into mouth of (horse); restrain. [f. BIT[1]]

bĭt[4] *n.* (Computers etc.). Unit of information expressed as choice between two possibilities. [f. BINARY + DIGIT]

bĭt[5]. See BITE[1].

bĭtch *n.* & *v.* **1.** *n.* Female of dog; **~ (fox, otter, wolf),** female of fox etc.; (derog.) woman, esp. lewd or malicious or treacherous one (SON *of a bitch*); unpleasant or difficult thing; hence **~'Y**[2] *a.*, immoral, spiteful, ill-tempered. **2.** *v.i.* Be spiteful or unfair; (colloq.) grumble. **3.** *v.t.* Be spiteful or unfair to; **~ (up),** (colloq.) muddle. [OE *bicce*, rel. to ON *bikkja*]

bīte[1] *v.* (*past* **bit;** *p.p.* **bi'tten,** occas. **bit**). **1.** *v.t.* Cut into or nip with the teeth; **~ off** etc., detach with the teeth. **2.** (Of snake, mosquito, etc.) sting, suck; **bitten with,** infected by (enthusiasm etc.); **what's biting you?,** (colloq.) what is worrying you? **3.** Cause glowing, smarting, etc., pain to (*frost-bitten*). **4.** (Of wheel, screw, anchor, etc.) grip; (of sword) penetrate. **5.** (usu. in *pass.*) Take in, swindle; **once bitten twice shy,** being cheated or deluded promotes later caution. **6.** *v.i.* Snap *at*; accept bait (lit. or fig.); have (desired) adverse effect. **7. ~ back,** restrain (speech etc.) by biting the lips; **~ on the bullet,** be stoical; **~ the dust,** (rhet.) fall and die; **~ the hand that feeds** one, injure a benefactor; **~** person's **head off,** respond curtly or angrily; *bite* one's LIP[1]; **~ off more than** one **can chew,** attempt too ambitious a task; **something to ~ on,** (esp. fig.) enough to get a grip or understanding. [OE *bītan*, = OS *bītan*, OHG *bīzan*, ON *bíta*, Goth. *beitan* f. Gmc **bītan*]

bīte[2] *n.* **1.** Act of, wound made by, piece detached by, biting; ***put the ~ on,** (sl.) borrow or extort money from. **2.** Food to eat; small meal. **3.** Taking of bait by fish; grip, hold, (lit. or fig.); bringing together of teeth in occlusion; (fig.) incisiveness, pungency. [f. prec.]

bī'ter *n.* In vbl senses; **the ~ bit,** swindler himself duped. [f. BITE[1] + -ER[1]]

bī'tĭng *a.* In vbl senses; pungent, stinging (*biting wind*); sarcastic; hence **~LY**[2] *adv.* [f. BITE[1] + -ING[2]]

bĭ'tten. See BITE[1].

bĭ'tter *a.* & *n.* **1.** *a.* Tasting like wormwood or quinine, opp. *sweet*, (**~-apple,** colocynth; **~ orange,** SEVILLE orange); (of beer) much flavoured with hops, opp. *mild*; unwelcome to the mind (*know from bitter experience*; **the ~ end,** last extremity; *bitter* PILL[1]). **2.** Caused by or showing mental pain (*a bitter rejoinder*); full of affliction or resentment; virulent, relentless; biting, harsh; piercingly cold. **3.** Hence **~LY**[2] *adv.*, **~NESS** *n.* **4.** *n.* Bitterness; (in *pl.*) liquors impregnated with wormwood etc. used to promote appetite or digestion or as flavourings; ||bitter beer; **~-sweet,** sweet(ness) with bitter after-taste or element (lit. or fig.), woody NIGHTSHADE. [OE *biter*, = OS, OHG *bittar*, ON *bitr*, Goth. *baitrs*, prob. f. Gmc **bitan* BITE[1]; *the bitter end* may be f. Naut., where the wds mean the last part of a cable left round the bitts when the rest is overboard]

bĭ'tterlĭng *n.* Small carplike freshwater fish from Central Europe. [G (*bitter* BITTER, *-ling* -LING[1])]

bĭ'ttern *n.* Marsh bird of genus *Botaurus* allied to herons, esp. one known for male's booming note in breeding-season. [ME, f. OF *butor* f. Rom. **butitaurus* f. L *butio* bittern + *taurus* bull; *-n* perh. f. assoc. w. HERN]

bĭtts *n. pl.* (Naut.) Pair of posts on deck for fastening cables etc. [ME, prob. f. LG; cf. LG, Du. *beting*]

bĭ'ttў *a.* Made up of unrelated bits, scrappy. [f. BIT[2] + -Y[2]]

bĭ'tūmen *n.* **1.** Any of various brown or black mixtures of tarlike hydrocarbons derived from petroleum naturally or by distillation; (Austral. colloq.) tarred road. **2.** So **bĭtū'mĭnous** *a.*; **bituminous coal,** kind burning with smoky flame. [L *bitumen -minis*]

bĭtū'mĭnĭz|e, -is|e (-īz), *v.t.* Convert into, impregnate or cover with, bitumen; hence **~A'TION** *n.* [f. prec. + -IZE (3, 5)]

bīvā'lent *a.* (Chem.) Having a valence of two. [f. BI- 1(a) + *valent-* part. st. f. as VALENCE[2]]

bī'vălve *a.* & *n.* **1.** *a.* (Biol.) Having two valves. **2.** *a.* & *n.* (Mollusc) with hinged double shell, e.g. oyster. [f. BI- 1(a) + VALVE]

bĭ'vouăc (-ōō-) *v.i.* (**-ck-**), & *n.* (Remain, esp. for the night, in) temporary encampment without tents. [F, prob. f. Swiss G *beiwacht* additional guard at night (formed by citizens' patrol in Aargau and Zürich)]

bĭ'vvў *n.* (sl.) Shelter; small tent. [abbr. of prec.]

bī-wee'klў *a.* & *n.* (Periodical) produced or occurring every two weeks or twice a week. [f. BI- 1(d, e) + WEEKLY]

bī-year'lў *a.* & *adv.* (Produced or occurring) every two years or twice a year. [f. BI- 1(d, e) + YEARLY]

bĭz *n.* (colloq.) Business. [abbr.]

bĭzar̄′re (-zar̄′) *a.* Eccentric, fantastic, grotesque; so **~rie** (-rerē) *n.*, bizarre quality [-ERY]. [F, = handsome, brave, f. Sp. & Port. *bizarro*, f. Basque *bizarra* beard]

bk. *abbr.* book.

Bk *symb.* berkelium.

B.L. *abbr.* Bachelor of Law; bill of lading; British Library.

bl. *abbr.* barrel; black.

blăb *v.* (-bb-) & *n.* **1.** *v.t.* & *i.* Talk or tell foolishly or indiscreetly, reveal, let out, (secrets etc., or abs.); hence **~′BER**[1] *n.* **2.** *n.* Person who blabs. [v. f. n., ME; cf. OHG *blabbizōn*, prob. f. Gmc **blab-* imit.]

blăck[1] *a.* **1.** Opposite to white, colourless from the absence or complete absorption of all light (like coal or soot); so near this as to have no distinguishable colour; very dark-coloured (**~ in the face,** purple with strangulation, exertion, or passion). **2.** Dark-skinned; (usu. *B~*) pertaining to Negroes; dark-clothed; (of sky, cloud, deep water, etc.) dusky, gloomy; (of hands, clothes) dirty; (as distinguishing epithet) *black bear, pine, snake, vulture, black-backed gull*, etc. **3.** Deadly, sinister, wicked, hateful, (*black-hearted*; *black ingratitude*; **not so ~ as** one **is painted,** better than one's reputation); dismal (*black despair*); angry, sulky, threatening, (*black looks*); implying disgrace or condemnation; presenting tragedy or bitter reality in comic terms (*black comedy, humour, joke*); performed by blackleg labour; (of goods etc.) not to be handled by workers on strike; contravening economic regulations (*black market*). **4. ~ and blue,** discoloured by bruises; **B~ and Tans,** armed force recruited to fight Sinn Fein 1921, wearing mixture of military and constabulary uniforms; **~ and white,** written etc. in black ink on white paper, (of film etc.) not in colour, (fig.) comprising only opposite extremes; (*down*) *in ~ and white*, recorded in writing or print; **~ art,** magic [partly f. *black* in sense 'wicked', partly by assoc. w. med. L *nigromantia* corrupt. of *necromantia* NECROMANCY]; **~ ball** (placed in ballot-box etc. to reject candidate), whence **~′ball** *v.t.*, reject by this or other means of voting; **~-beetle,** common cockroach; **~ belt,** region in U.S. where Negroes predominate, (holder of) mark of proficiency in judo; **~′berry,** dark-fruited bramble or its fruit (*plentiful as ~berries*, as plentiful as can be; *~′berrying*, gathering them); **~′bird,** European song-bird of thrush family, *grackle or similar bird, (Hist.) kidnapped Negro or Polynesian on slave-ship (*~′birding*, trade in these); **~′board** (with black or dark surface, used in schools etc. for writing or drawing on in chalk); **~ body,** (Phys.) hypothetical perfect absorber and radiator; **in** person's **~ books,** out of favour with him; **~ box,** (1) flight-recorder in aircraft, (2) apparatus of unknown internal design; **~′boy,** Austral. tree with thick dark trunk and head of spearlike leaves; **~ bread,** coarse rye bread; *black* BRYONY; **~′buck,** Ind. or S. Afr. antelope; ||**~ cap,** (Hist.) cap put on by judge in sentencing to death; **~′cap,** bird with black-topped head, esp. a warbler (*Sylvia atricapilla*); *black* CATTLE; ||**~-coat worker,** clerk etc. (opp. industrial employee); **~′cock,** male of black grouse (cf. GREY-*hen*); **~ coffee** (without milk or cream); ||**B~ Country,** smoky grimy district in Staffs. and War.; *black* CURRANT; **~ damp,** = CHOKE[1]-*damp*; *Black* DEATH; *black* DIAMOND; **~ dog,** sulks, melancholy mood; **~ earth,** chernozem; **~ eye** (with surrounding skin discoloured by bruise, or with dark iris), whence *~-eyed*; **~-eyed Susan,** flower with light petals and dark centre, esp. of genus *Rudbeckia*; **~-face,** (1) dark-faced sheep, (2) make-up for Negro role; **~′fellow,** Australian aboriginal; **~′fish,** (1) one of several dark-coloured species of fish (e.g. tautog), (2) salmon just after spawning; *black* FLAG[4]; **~′fly,** thrips or aphid infesting plants; **B~ Friar,** Dominican; *black* FROST; **~ game, ~ grouse,** a European GROUSE[1] (*Lyrurus tetrix*); **~′head,** (1) bird with black head, esp. scaup, (2) black-topped pimple in hair follicle on face etc.; **~ hole,** (Astron.) region from which no matter or radiation can escape, (esp. Mil.) place of confinement for punishment; **~ ice,** thin hard transparent ice; *black* IVORY; **~′jack,** (1) tarred-leather vessel for alcoholic liquor, (2) pirates' black flag, (3) *flexible loaded bludgeon, (4) vingt-et-un; **~′lead,** (polish with) graphite [named from its making marks like lead]; **~′leg,** (1) swindler esp. on turf, (2) || = SCAB 3, (*v.i.* & *t.*) act as blackleg, betray or injure thus [origin of senses unknown]; *black* LEOPARD; **~ letter,** old heavy style of type; **~ light,** invisible ultraviolet or infra-red radiation; **~ list** (of persons under suspicion, liable to punishment or unfavourable treatment, etc.); **~′list** *v.t.*, enter name of (person) on black list; *black* MAGIC; **~′mail** *v.t.*, & *n.*, compel, compulsion, to make payment or action in return for concealment of discreditable secrets etc., (fig.) use (of) threats or moral pressure [f. obs. *mail* rent, OE *māl* f. ON *mál* agreement, perh. = OHG *mahal* assembly]; **B~ Maria,** vehicle for taking prisoners from and to gaol; **~ mark** (of discredit against one's name); **~ market,** (place of) illegitimate traffic in officially controlled goods or currencies or in commodities in short supply (*~ marketeer*, one who engages in this); **~ mass,** (1) travesty of the Mass said to be used in the cult of Satanism, (2) Requiem Mass; **B~ Monk,** Benedictine; ***B~ Muslim,** member of Negro sect proposing separation of Negroes and Whites; *black* MUSTARD; *black* NIGHTSHADE; ***B~ Panther,** one of a group of extremist fighters for Negroes' rights; *black* PEPPER[1]; **B~ Power,** movement in support of civil rights etc. of Negroes; **~ pudding** (sausage-shaped, of blood, suet, etc.); ||**B~ Rod,** gentleman usher of Lord Chamberlain's department, House of Lords, etc.; **B~ Sash,** (S. Afr.) women's anti-apartheid organization; **~ sheep,** scoundrel, unsatisfactory member (*of* family etc.); **~′shirt,** Fascist [f. It. Fascist uniform]; **~′smith,** smith working in iron; **~ spot,** place of danger or difficulty, esp. area with high accident rate etc.; *black* SQUALL; *black* SWAN; **~ tea** (fully fermented before drying); **~′thorn,** (1) thorny shrub bearing white flowers before leaves and small plums or sloes (*~thorn winter*, time of its flowering, cold with N.E. winds), (2) cudgel or walking-stick of its wood; **~ tie,** man's black bow-tie worn with dinner-jacket; ***~′top,** type of road surfacing; **~ tracker,** (Austral.) Aboriginal employed to help find persons lost or hiding in the bush; **~ velvet,** mixture of stout and champagne, (Austral. & N.Z. sl.) dark-skinned woman; *black* VOMIT; ||**B~ Watch,** Royal Highland Regiment [f. their dark-coloured tartan]; **~-water fever,** tropical disease caused by malarial infection, with dark urine; **~ widow,** common Amer. spider, the female of which devours its mate. **5.** Hence **~′ISH**[1] 2 *a.*, **~′LY**[2] *adv.*, **~′NESS** *n.* [OE *blæc*, = OHG *blah-*, of unkn. orig.]

blăck[2] *n.* Black colour; black pigment; black clothes or material (*dressed in black*); fungus or smut in wheat etc.; the black colour in roulette and rouge-et-noir; black ball in snooker etc.; (player of) black men in chess etc.; credit side of account (**in the ~**, solvent); (usu. *B~*) Negro, whence ~'Y[3] *n.* (sl.). [f. prec.]

blăck[3] *v.t.* **1.** Make black; polish with blacking; declare (goods etc.) 'black'. **2. ~ out,** (*v.t.*) obliterate or obscure, obscure (windows etc.) to prevent any light being seen from outside, esp. from the air, (*v.i.*) undergo black-out. **3. ~-out** *n.*, blacking out or being blacked out, period when obscuring of lights is compulsory, sudden darkening of theatre stage, loss of radio reception through fading or jamming, temporary complete loss of consciousness or failure of memory, aviator's temporary blindness etc. esp. resulting from centrifugal force when a sudden turn is made. [f. BLACK[1]]

blă'ckamoor (*or* -oo͝r) *n.* Negro; dark-skinned person. [f. BLACK[1] + MOOR[2]]

blă'ckavīsed (-zd) *a.* (arch.) Dark-complexioned. [f. BLACK[1] + F *vis* face]

blă'cken *v.t.* & *i.* Make or become black(er) or dark(er); speak evil of, defame, (person's character). [ME, f. BLACK[1] + -EN[6]]

blă'ckguard (blă'gard) *n.*, *a.*, & *v.t.* **1.** *n.* & *a.* Scoundrel(ly); foul-mouthed (person); hence ~LY[1] *a.* **2.** *v.t.* Call blackguard; abuse scurrilously. [f. BLACK[1] + GUARD[1]; orig. collect. n. and applied to menials of royal household, camp-followers, bodyguard, criminals, vagrants]

blă'cking *n.* In vbl senses; paste or liquid for blacking or polishing boots etc. [f. BLACK[1] + -ING[1]]

Blă'ckwood *n.* (Bridge). Convention of bidding four and five no-trumps to find number of aces and kings held by partner. [f. E.F. ~, 20th-c. Amer. bridge-player]

blă'dder *n.* **1.** Membranous bag in human and other animal bodies, containing urine, bile (*gall-bladder*), air, etc., (esp. the urinary bladder); this or part of it or similar object prepared for various uses, inflated, etc. **2.** (fig.) Anything inflated and hollow; wordy man, windbag; inflated pericarp or vesicle in plants and seaweeds (**~-wrack,** common seaweed with these in its fronds). [OE *blǣdre*, = OS *blādara*, OHG *blātara*, ON *bláthra* f. Gmc **blǣdrōn* (**blǣ-* BLOW[1])]

blāde *n.* **1.** Flat spear-shaped leaf esp. of grass and cereals; whole of such plants before ear comes (*in the blade*); (Bot.) broad thin part of leaf apart from petiole. **2.** Flattened part of oar, bat, spade, paddle-wheel, turbine, propeller, etc.; cutting-piece of sword, chisel, knife, etc.; sword; (**razor-**)~, flat piece of metal with usu. two sharp edges, used in safety razor; ~(**-bone**), flat bone, esp. shoulder-blade as joint of meat or otherwise. **3.** Jovial, dashing, gay, etc., fellow. **4.** Hence (-)**blā'd**ED[2] *a.* [OE *blæd*, = OHG *blat*, ON *blath* f. Gmc **bladham* perh. f. **blō-* BLOW[3]]

||**blae'berry̆** (blā'-) *n.* = BILBERRY. [ME, f. *blae* (Sc. and N. Engl. dial. f. ME *blo* f. ON *blár* f. Gmc; see BLUE[1]) + BERRY[1]]

blague (blahg) *n.* Humbug, claptrap; hence ***blagueur*** (blahger'), pretentious talker. [F]

blah(-blah) *n.* (colloq.) Pretentious nonsense. [imit.]

blain *n.* Inflamed swelling or sore on skin. [OE *blegen*, = LG *bleien* f. WG **blegen*]

blāme[1] *v.t.* Find fault with (*for* offence etc.) (**be to ~**, deserve censure); fix the responsibility on; (colloq.) ~ thing **on** person, hold him responsible for it; hence ~'ABLE (-ma-) *a.* [ME, f. OF *bla(s)mer* f. pop. L *blastemare* f. eccl. L *blasphemare* reproach f. Gk *blasphēmeō* blaspheme]

blāme[2] *n.* Censure; responsibility for bad result (*lay the blame on*; *bear the blame*). [ME, f. OF *blame* (*blamer*; see prec.)]

blā'meful (-mf-) *a.* Deserving blame. [ME, f. BLAME[2] + -FUL]

blā'melėss (-ml-) *a.* Innocent; hence ~LY[2] *adv.*, ~NESS *n.* [ME, f. BLAME[2] + -LESS]

blā'meworth|y̆ (-mwerdhĭ) *a.* Deserving blame; hence ~ĭNESS *n.* [f. BLAME[2] + -WORTHY]

blanch (-ah-) *v.* **1.** *v.t.* Make white by withdrawing colour, peeling (almonds esp. by scalding), or depriving (plants) of light; immerse (food) in boiling water. **2.** *v.t.* & *i.* Make or grow pale with fear, cold, etc. **3.** *v.t.* **~ over,** palliate by misrepresentation. [ME, f. OF *blanchir* (*blanc* BLANK[1])]

blancma'nge (blamŏ'nzh) *n.* Opaque jelly of (usu. flavoured and sweetened) cornflour and milk. [ME, f. OF *blancmanger* (*blanc* white, BLANK[1], *manger* eat f. L *manducare* MANDUCATE)]

blă'ncō *n.* & *v.t.* (Mil.) (Treat with) white substance for whitening belts etc. [**P** as noun f. F *blanc* white, BLANK[1]]

blănd *a.* Gentle or suave in manner; mild; not irritating or stimulating; hence ~'LY[2] *adv.*, ~'NESS *n.* [f. L *blandus* soft, smooth]

blă'ndĭsh *v.t.* Flatter, coax; hence ~MENT *n.* (usu. in *pl.*), flattery, cajolery. [ME, f. OF *blandir* (-ISH[2]) f. L *blandiri* (*blandus* soft, smooth)]

blănk[1] *a.* **1.** (Of paper) not written or printed on; (of document) with spaces left for signature or details (**~ cheque,** with amount left for payee to fill in, hence = CARTE BLANCHE). **2.** Empty, not filled, (*blank space* etc.); **~ cartridge** (without bullet, to make sound only); **~ test** (done without specimen, to verify absence of effects of reagents etc.); *blank* WINDOW. **3.** Having no interest, incident, result, or expression (**look ~**, appear puzzled); unrelieved, sheer, (*blank* WALL); unrhymed (**~ verse,** esp. iambic pentameters). **4.** Hence ~'LY[2] *adv.*, ~'NESS *n.* [ME, f. OF *blanc* white f. Rom. **blancus* f. Gmc **blankaz*]

blănk[2] *n.* Lottery ticket that gains no prize (**draw (a) ~**, elicit no response, fail); space left to be filled up in document; empty surface or interval (one's *mind*, *memory*, etc., **is a ~**, has no impressions etc.); document having blank space(s) to be filled up; domino with one or both halves blank; coin-disc before stamping, metal or wooden block before final shaping; = BLANK[1] *cartridge*; dash written instead of word or letter, whence **~**, **~ed** (-kt), **~'ety,** ||**~'y,** as euphem. substitutes for profane or abusive *ns.* and *adjs.* [f. prec.]

blănk[3] *v.t.* Screen *off* or *out*; *defeat without allowing to score. [f. prec.]

blă'nkėt[1] *n.* & *a.* **1.** *n.* Large piece of woollen etc. material used for warmth, esp. as bed-covering, horse-cloth, etc.; **~ stitch** (for finishing edges of blankets etc.); **electric ~** (that can be connected to mains and heated by internal wiring); **wet ~**, gloomy person preventing others' enjoyment etc.; **born on the wrong side of the ~**, illegitimate; hence ~ING[1] (3) *n.* **2.** Thick mass or layer (*of* fog, snow, etc.) that covers something; rubber sheet transferring impression from plate to paper etc. in offset printing. **3.** *a.* General rather than individual, covering all cases or classes, inclusive, (*blanket term*, *agreement*). [ME, f. OF *blancquet*, *blanchet* (*blanc* white, BLANK[1]; see -ET[1])]

blă'nkėt[2] *v.t.* Cover with blanket (lit. or fig.); stifle, keep quiet, (scandal, question, etc.); take wind from sails of (another craft) by passing to windward. [f. prec.]

blanquette (blahṅkĕ't) *n.* (Cookery). Dish of white meat, e.g. veal, in white sauce. [F (as BLANKET[1])]

blâre *v.i.* & *t.*, & *n.* (Make) sound of trumpet; utter loudly. [ME, f. MDu. *blaren*, *bleren*, imit.]

blâr'ney *n.*, & *v.t.* & *i.* (Use, subject to) cajoling talk; nonsense. [f. *B~*, Irish castle near Cork with stone said to confer cajoling tongue on whoever kisses it]

blasé (-ah'zā) *a.* Cloyed with or tired of pleasure. [F]

blăsphē'me *v.* **1.** *v.i.* Talk impiously. **2.** *v.t.* Utter profanity about, revile. [ME, f. OF *blasfemer* f. eccl. L *blasphemare* f. Gk *blasphēmeō*; cf. BLAME^1]

blă'sphem|y̆ *n.* Impious or profane talk; hence ~OUS *a.* [ME, f. OF *blasfemie* f. eccl. L f. Gk *blasphēmia* slander, blasphemy]

blast^1 (-ah-) *n.* **1.** Strong gust of wind; sound of wind-instrument, car horn, whistle, etc.; current of air in smelting etc.; **at full ~**, (colloq.) working at maximum speed etc. **2.** Destructive wave of highly compressed air spreading outwards from an explosion; (colloq.) severe reprimand. **3. ~-furnace,** smelting furnace into which compressed hot air is driven; **~-hole** (containing explosive charge for blasting). [OE *blǣst*, = OHG *blāst*, ON *blástr* f. Gmc **blǣstaz* (**blǣs-* blow)]

blast^2 (-ah-) *v.* **1.** *v.t.* Blow up (rocks etc.) with explosives; hence ~'ER^1 *n.*, (esp., fig.) heavy lofted golf-club for playing from bunker. **2.** *v.i.* **~ off,** (of rocket etc.) take off from launching site; **~-off** *n.*, (initial thrust for) launching of rocket etc. **3.** *v.t.* Wither, shrivel, blight, (plant, animal, limb, prosperity, character; esp., w. subj. *God* expr. or understood in curses, also abs. as *int.*; hence ~'ED^1 *a.*, damnable). [f. prec.]

-blăst *suf.* (Biol.) Embryonic cell (*erythroblast*; cf. -CYTE); germ layer of embryo (*epiblast*). [f. Gk *blastos* sprout]

blă'stūla *n.* (*pl.* **~e** *or* ***~s**). (Biol.) Hollow ball of cells formed by cleavage of ovum. [mod. L, f. Gk *blastos* sprout + dim. suf.; cf. -ULE]

blā't|ant *a.* Noisy, vulgarly clamorous; flagrant, palpable; obtrusive, conspicuous; unashamed; hence ~ANCY *n.*, **~ant**LY^2 *adv.* [wd used by Spenser (1596), perh. after Sc. *blatand* = bleating]

blather(skite). See BLETHER.

blāze^1 *n.* **1.** Bright flame or fire; state of being on fire; (in *pl.*, sl.) hell (*go to blazes*; *what the blazes!*; *like blazes*). **2.** Violent outburst (*of* passion etc.); glow of colour, bright display; full light (*blaze of publicity*). [OE *blæse* torch, f. Gmc **blasōn*; ult. cogn. w. BLAZE^3]

blāze^2 *v.i.* **1.** Burn with flame (**~ up,** burst into blaze); be brilliantly lighted; burn with anger, excitement, etc., (**~ up,** burst out in anger). **2.** Show bright colours; emit light; **~ away,** fire continuously with rifles etc., work enthusiastically at anything; ***blazing star,** plant with brilliant star-shaped flowers esp. of genus *Aletris*. [f. prec.]

blāze^3 *n.* White mark on animal's face; mark made on tree by chipping bark to mark route. [17th c.; = ON *blesi*, OHG *blassa* in same sense]

blāze^4 *v.t.* Mark (tree, path) by chipping bark; esp. *blaze a trail* (lit., show the way for others to follow, or fig.). [f. prec.]

blāze^5 *v.t.* Proclaim as with trumpet; **~ abroad,** spread (news) about. [ME, f. MLG, MDu. *blāzen* blow, = ON *blása*, OHG *blāsan*, Goth. *-blesan* f. Gmc **blǣsan* (cf. BLAST^1) f. **blǣ-* (BLOW^1)]

blā'zer *n.* Coloured light unlined jacket worn by schoolchildren, sportsmen, etc.; man's plain jacket not matching trousers. [f. BLAZE^2 + -ER^1]

blā'zon^1 *n.* Heraldic shield, coat of arms, bearings, or banner; correct description of these; record, description, esp. of virtues etc. [ME, f. OF *blason* shield, of unkn. orig.]

blā'zon^2 *v.t.* Describe or paint (arms) heraldically; inscribe (object) with arms, names, etc., in colours or ornamentally; proclaim; hence ~MENT *n.* [ME, f. prec. and BLAZE^5]

blā'zonry̆ *n.* (Art of describing or painting) heraldic devices or armorial bearings; brightly coloured display. [f. prec. + -RY]

-ble *suf.* See -ABLE, -IBLE, -UBLE. [OF, f. L *-bilis* forming vbl adjs. act. or pass. f. vbs. or p.p. stems]

bleach *v.* & *n.* **1.** *v.t.* & *i.* Whiten by exposure to sunlight or by chemical process; **~'ing-powder,** chloride of lime, used esp. to remove colour from materials; hence ~'ER^1 *n.*, one who bleaches (esp. textiles), vessel or chemical used in bleaching, (usu. in *pl.*) outdoor uncovered plank-seat for spectators at sports ground. **2.** *n.* Bleaching substance or process. [OE *blǣcan*, = ON *bleikja* f. Gmc **blaikjan* (**blaik-* white)]

bleak^1 *n.* Small river-fish of various species, esp. *Alburnus lucidus*. [ME, prob. f. ON *bleikja*, OHG *bleicha* f. Gmc **blaikjōn* (**blaik-* white)]

bleak^2 *a.* Bare, exposed, wind-swept; chilly; dreary, unpromising (*bleak prospects*). [16th c.; rel. to obs. adjs. *bleach*, *blake* (f. ON *bleikr*) pale, ult. f. Gmc **blaikaz*; cf. BLEACH]

blear *a.*, & *v.t.* (Make) (eyes or mind) dim-sighted, dull, filmy; (make) indistinct in outline; hence ~'Y^2 *a.*; **~(y)-eyed,** having blear eyes or wits. [ME, cogn. w. MHG *blerre* blurred vision, LG *blarr-*, *blerr-oged* blear-eyed]

bleat *v.i.* & *t.*, & *n.* (Make) sheep's, goat's, or calf's, tremulous cry; speak (*out*) feebly or foolishly or plaintively. [OE *blǣtan*, = OHG *blāzen*, Du. *blaten*; imit.]

blĕb *n.* Small blister or bubble on skin or in water or glass. [var. of BLOB]

blĕd. See foll.

bleed *v.* (**bled**) & *n.* **1.** *v.i.* Emit blood (one's **heart ~s,** one is very sorrowful); suffer wounds or violent death (*for* cause etc.). **2.** (Of plant) emit sap; (of dye) come out in water; (Print.) be cut into when pages are trimmed. **3.** Part with money, pay lavishly, suffer extortion. **4.** *v.t.* Draw blood surgically from; (fig.) extort money from; (Print.) extend (illustration) to cut edge of page, cut into printed area of when trimming; allow (fluid) to escape from closed system through valve etc., treat (system) thus. **5.** *n.* Act of bleeding. [OE *blēdan*, = ON *blœtha* f. Gmc **blōdhjan* (**blōdham* BLOOD^1)]

blee'der *n.* In vbl senses; person inclined to bleed excessively from slight wound, haemophiliac; (vulg.) person (esp. unpleasant). [f. prec. + -ER^1]

blee'ding *a.* & *adv.* In vbl senses; (vulg. euphem.) = BLOODY 2, 4; **~ heart,** pop. name of various plants, esp. of genus *Dicentra*, (colloq.) too soft-hearted person. [f. BLEED + -ING^2]

bleep *n.*, & *v.i.* (Emit) intermittent high-pitched sound, esp. as signal. [imit.]

blĕ'mĭsh^1 *v.t.* Mar; spoil the beauty or brightness (lit. or fig.) or perfection of. [ME, f. OF *ble(s)mir* (-ISH^2) make pale, prob. of Gmc orig.]

blĕ'mĭsh^2 *n.* Physical or moral defect; stain, flaw. [f. prec.]

blĕnch *v.i.* Flinch, quail. [ME, f. OE *blencan*, ON *blekkja* deceive f. Gmc **blankjan*; for later senses cf. BLINK^1]

blĕnd^1 *v.t.* & *i.* (**~'ed,** poet. or rhet. **blent**). **1.** *v.t.* Mix (things) together (esp. sorts of tea, spirit, tobacco, to get certain quality); mingle intimately *with*; mix (components) so as to be inseparable and indistinguishable. **2.** *v.i.* Be blended *with*; become one, form harmonious compound; (esp. of colours) pass imperceptibly into each other. **3.** Hence ~'ER^1 (1, 2) *n.* [ME, prob. f. ON *blanda* mix]

blĕnd^2 *n.* Mixture made of various sorts of tea, spirits, wool, tobacco, etc.; portmanteau word. [f. prec.]

blĕnde *n.* Native zinc sulphide. [G (*blenden*

deceive, 'because while often resembling galena it yielded no lead')]

Blĕ'nheim (-nĭm) *n.* Kind of small red and white spaniel; ~ **Orange,** golden-coloured late-ripening apple. [f. Duke of Marlborough's seat at Woodstock, Oxfordshire, named after his victory at ~ in Bavaria (1704)]

blĕ'nnў *n.* Spiny-finned sea-fish esp. of genus *Blennius.* [f. L *blennius* f. Gk *blennos* mucus, from mucous coating of its scales]

blĕnt. See BLEND¹.

blĕpharī'tĭs *n.* Inflammation of eyelids. [f. Gk *blepharon* eyelid + -ITIS]

blĕ'sbŏk, -bŭck, *n.* Large S. Afr. antelope (*Damaliscus albifrons*). [Afrik. (*bles* BLAZE³, from white mark on forehead, *bok* goat)]

blĕss *v.t.* (BLESSED *or* **blest**). Consecrate (esp. food); sanctify by sign of cross (**not have a penny to ~ oneself with,** be impoverished, w. ref. to cross on silver penny); call holy, adore, (God); attribute one's good fortune to (esp. one's stars); (of father, priest, etc.) pronounce words held to bring divine or supernatural favour upon; invoke God's favour on; make happy or successful (abs. or *with* something); (**God**) **~ me, ~ you, ~ my soul, I'm blest,** (excl. of surprise or pleasure or indignation, (**God**) **~ you** also as well-wishing or to one who sneezes); *bless my* etc. HEART; (euphem.) = damn, curse, etc. [OE *blǣdsian, blēdsian, blētsian,* (*blōd* blood; hence mark with blood, consecrate); meaning infl. by wd's being used at the conversion of the English to translate L *benedicere* praise]

blĕ'ssėd (usu. *pr.* blĕst as *pred. a.*), **blĕst** (usu. poet.), *a.* Consecrated (*Blessed* SACRAMENT, VIRGIN); revered; fortunate (~ **with,** (esp. iron.) fortunate in the possession of); in paradise; (R.C. Ch.) beatified; blissful, bringing happiness (*blessed ignorance* etc.); (euphem.) cursed. [p.p. of prec.]

blĕ'ssėdnėss *n.* Happiness; enjoyment of divine favour; **single ~,** (joc.) state of being unmarried (perversion of Shak. *Midsummer Night's Dream* I. i. 78). [f. prec. + -NESS]

blĕ'ssĭng *n.* Declaration, invocation, or bestowal, of (esp. divine) favour; grace before or after food (*ask a blessing*); gift of God, nature, etc., thing one is glad of; **~ in disguise,** unwelcome but salutary experience, apparent misfortune that eventually does good. [f. BLESS + -ING¹]

blĕ'ther, blă'ther, (-dh-) *v.i.,* & *n.* (Talk) loquacious nonsense; hence **blă'therskīte, blĕ'therskāte,** (-dh-) *ns.,* blether(ing person). [ME *blather,* Sc. *blether,* f. ON *blathra* talk nonsense (*blathr* nonsense); derog. use of SKATE¹]

blew. See BLOW¹,³.

blew'ĭts (-ōō'-) *n.* Late edible mushroom with lilac stem. [prob. f. BLUE¹]

blight¹ (-īt) *n.* Plant disease caused by fungoid parasite, mildew, rust, smut; ‖species of aphid; any obscure malignant influence; unsightly urban area. [17th c., of unkn. orig.]

blight² (-īt) *v.t.* Affect with blight; exert baleful influence on, frustrate, wither, mar; hence **~'ER¹** *n.,* (esp., sl.) (usu. contemptible or annoying) person or thing. [f. prec.]

‖**Blī'ghtў** (-ī'tĭ) *n.* (Army sl.) England, home, after foreign service (**a ~ one** etc., wound ensuring return to England). [Anglo-Ind. corrupt. of Hindi *bilāyatī, wilāyatī* foreign, European]

‖**blī'mey** *int.* (vulg.) expr. surprise, contempt, etc. [corrupt. of (*God*) *blind me!*]

blĭmp *n.* **1.** Small non-rigid airship; barrage balloon; soundproof cover for cine-camera. **2.** ‖(**Colonel**) **Blimp,** character invented by the cartoonist David Low (d. 1963), representing a pompous, obese, elderly figure, pop. interpreted as type of diehard or reactionary; hence **~'ERY** (4) *n.,* **~'ISH¹** *a.* [20th c., of uncert. orig.]

blīnd¹ *a.* & *adv.* **1.** *a.* Without sight (**~ corner,** one round which motorist etc. cannot see; **turn a** or one's **~ eye to,** pretend not to notice); (Aeron.) without direct observation, using instruments only. **2.** Without foresight, discernment, intellectual perception, or adequate information, (**~ to,** incapable of appreciating; one's **~ side,** direction in which one cannot see approach of danger etc.); reckless; not ruled by purpose (*blind forces*). **3.** Concealed (*blind ditch*; **~-stitch,** (*n.*) sewing visible on one side only, (*v.t.* & *i.*) sew thus); (of door, window, etc.) walled up; closed at one end (**~ alley,** cul-de-sac, unprofitable course of action; *~-alley job* etc., one with no prospect of advancement); (Cookery) baked without filling; (sl.) drunk(en); **not a ~ (bit of),** (sl.) not the slightest. **4. ~ coal** (burning without flame); **~ date,** social engagement between two persons of opposite sex who have not met; **~ god,** Eros or Cupid; **~ gut,** caecum; *blind* HOOKEY; **~-man's buff,** game in which blindfold player tries to catch others, who push him about [f. obs. *buff* = buffet]; **~ man's holiday,** time before lamps are lit; **~ spot,** (Anat.) point of entry of optic nerve on retina, insensitive to light, (Radio) point of unusually weak reception, (fig.) area where vision or understanding is lacking; **~ stamping, tooling,** (in bookbinding without use of colour or gold-leaf); **~'worm,** slow-worm [f. small size of eyes]. **5.** Hence **~'LY²** *adv.,* **~'NESS** *n.* **6.** *adv.* Blindly (*flying blind*; *bake it blind*); **~ drunk,** insensible through drink; **go it ~,** act recklessly or without proper consideration. [OE, = OS *blind,* OHG *blint,* ON *blindr,* Goth. *blinds* f. Gmc **blindaz*]

blīnd² *v.* **1.** *v.t.* Make unable to see, permanently or temporarily; rob of judgement, deceive, (**~ with science,** overawe by display of knowledge). **2.** *v.i.* ‖(sl.) Go blindly or heedlessly (esp. in motor vehicle). **3.** Hence **~'ER¹** *n.,* (esp., in *pl.*) *blinkers; **~'ING¹** *n.,* (process of covering newly made road with) fine material to fill interstices. [ME, f. prec.]

blīnd³ *n.* Obstruction to sight or light; screen for window, esp. on roller, (VENETIAN *blind*); ‖awning of shop-window; *screen for hunters; screen to keep cold air from radiator of vehicle; pretext; legitimate business concealing illegitimate one; ‖(sl.) heavy drinking-bout; (Poker) stake put up before seeing one's cards. [f. prec.]

blī'ndfōld¹ *v.t.* Deprive (eyes, person) of sight with bandage (lit. or fig.). [replacing (by assoc. w. FOLD²) ME *blindfellen* (FELL⁴) strike blind]

blī'ndfōld² *a.* & *adv.* With eyes bandaged; (Chess) without sight of board and men; without circumspection. [earlier p.p. *blindfelled*; see prec.]

blī'ndfōld³ *n.* Bandage to prevent person from seeing; (fig.) obstruction to perception. [f. prec.]

blĭnk¹ *v.* **1.** *v.i.* Move the eyelids; look with eyes opening and shutting; shut the eyes for a moment, esp. involuntarily; shine with unsteady or intermittent light, cast momentary gleam; hence **~'ING²** *a.* & *adv.,* (vulg. euphem.) = BLOODY¹ 2, 4. **2.** *v.t.* Prevent (tears) by blinking; blink with (eyes); (fig.) ignore, shirk consideration of, (esp. *the fact*). [partly var. of *blenk* = BLENCH, partly f. MDu. *blinken* shine]

blĭnk² *n.* Blinking; momentary gleam or glimpse; = ICE¹*blink*; **on the ~,** (sl.) out of order. [f. prec.]

blĭ'nker *n.,* & *v.t.* **1.** *n.* In vbl senses; (usu. in *pl.*) leather screen(s) on bridle preventing horse from seeing sideways. **2.** *v.t.* (esp. fig.) Obscure with blinkers. [f. BLINK[1] + -ER[1]]

blĭp *v.t.* (**-pp-**), & *n.* **1.** *v.t.* Strike briskly. **2.** *n.* Act or sound of blipping; small image of object on radar screen. [imit.]

blĭss *n.* Gladness, enjoyment; perfect joy or happiness; blessedness; being in heaven; hence ~'FUL *a.*, (esp.) happily oblivious (*blissful ignorance*). [OE *blīths*, *bliss*, = OS *blīdsea* f. Gmc *blīthsjō* (*blīthiz* BLITHE); sense infl. by BLESS]

blĭ'ster *n.* & *v.* **1.** *n.* Thin vesicle on skin filled with serum, caused by friction, burning, etc.; similar swelling on surface of plant, metal, painted wood, (~ **pack,** bubble pack); (Med.) anything applied to raise a blister; (sl.) annoying person; ~ **copper** (almost pure); ~ **gas,** poison gas causing blisters on skin. **2.** *v.t.* Raise blister on; (fig.) attack sharply (*blistering criticism*). **3.** *v.i.* Become covered with blisters. [ME, perh. f. OF *blestre*, *blo(u)stre* swelling, pimple]

blīthe (-dh) *a.* **1.** (chiefly poet.) Gay, joyous; hence ~'SOME[1] (-dhs-) *a.* **2.** Careless, casual. **3.** Hence ~'LY[2] (-dhlĭ) *adv.*, ~'NESS (-dhn-) *n.* [OE *blīthe*, = OS *blīthi*, OHG *blīdi*, ON *blíthr*, Goth. *bleiths* f. Gmc **blīthiz*]

blĭ'therĭng (-dh-) *a.* (colloq.) Senselessly talkative; utter, hopeless, (*blithering idiot*); contemptible. [f. *blither*, var. of BLETHER + -ING[2]]

B. Litt. *abbr.* Bachelor of Letters. [f. L *Baccalaureus Litterarum*]

blĭtz (-ts) *n.*, & *v.t.* (colloq.) **1.** *n.* Intensive or sudden (esp. aerial) attack (lit. or fig.); *the* air raids on London in 1940. **2.** *v.t.* Attack or damage or destroy by blitz. [abbr. of foll.]

blĭ'tzkrieg (-tsk-) *n.* Violent campaign intended to bring about speedy victory. [G, = lightning war]

|**blĭ'zzard** *n.* Severe snowstorm. [U.S. 'violent blow' (1829), 'snowstorm' (1859), perh. imit.]

bloat[1] *v.t.* Cure (herring) by salting and smoking slightly. [f. obs. *bloat* soft and wet, perh. f. ON *blautr* soaked]

bloat[2] *v.t.* & *i.* Inflate, swell; hence ~'ED[1] *a.*, puffed up, esp. with gluttony, pride, excessive wealth, etc. [f. obs. *bloat* swollen, perh. f. ON *blautr* soft, flabby; cf. prec.]

bloa'ter *n.* Herring cured by bloating. [f. BLOAT[1] + -ER[1]]

blŏb *n.* Drop of liquid; small roundish mass; spot of colour; (Cricket sl.) score of 0. [imit.; cf. BLEB]

blŏc *n.* Combination of parties, governments, groups, etc., to foster a particular interest; ~ **vote** = BLOCK[1] vote. [F, = BLOCK[1]]

blŏck[1] *n.* **1.** Log of wood, tree-stump, (**chip off the old** ~, child like his father esp. in character); large piece of wood for chopping, beheading, or hammering on, or mounting horse from (***on the** ~, being auctioned); mould for shaping hats on. **2.** Pulley or system of pulleys mounted in case; *block and* TACKLE. **3.** Piece of wood or metal engraved for printing on paper or fabric; (in *pl.*) set of wooden cubes etc. as child's toy. **4.** Bulky or massive piece of anything; unhewn lump of rock; prepared piece of building-stone; (sl.) head (*knock* person's *block off*). **5.** Compact mass of buildings bounded by (usu. four) streets (**~-buster,** (sl.) huge bomb capable of destroying this, (fig.) thing of great power); *area between streets in town or suburb; *length of such area (*lives three blocks away*); large building (*block of flats*). **6.** Stolid or hard-hearted person. **7.** Obstruction; (Amer. Footb. etc.) blocking action; group of jammed vehicles unable to proceed; ~ **system,** (Railways) system by which no train may enter a section that is not clear; **mental** or **psychological** ~, particular mental inability due to subconscious emotional factors. **8.** (Cricket) spot on which batsman blocks ball, and rests bat before playing; (Athletics) = STARTING-*block*. **9.** (Austral. etc.) Tract of land offered to individual settler by government; large area of land. **10.** Large quantity of shares, seats, etc., esp. if treated as unit; set of sheets of paper for writing or drawing on, fastened together at edge; (*attrib.*) made or treated as a large unit (*block booking*, *grant*). **11.** **~'board,** plywood board with core of thin wooden strips; ~ **diagram** (showing general arrangement of parts of apparatus); **~'head,** stupid person; ~ **heater,** storage heater; **~'house,** (1) one-storeyed timber building with loopholes used as fort, (2) house of squared logs, (3) reinforced concrete shelter; ~ **letters** (with each letter separate as in print, and usu. in capitals); **~-ship** (used to block a channel etc.); ~ **tin,** refined tin cast in ingots; ~ **vote** (in which voter has influence according to number of persons he represents). [ME, f. OF *bloc* f. MDu. *blok*, of unkn. orig.]

blŏck[2] *v.t.* **1.** Obstruct (passage etc.); put obstacles in way of (progress etc.; ~ **up, in,** confine); (Amer. Footb. etc.) intercept (opponent) with one's body; (esp. in *p.p.*) restrict use or conversion of (currency or other asset); (Cricket) stop (ball) with bat. **2.** Emboss or impress design on (book cover); ~ **out, in,** sketch roughly, plan. **3.** Hence ~'AGE (3) *n.*, blocked(-up) state. [f. prec. or f. F *bloquer* (*bloc*; see prec.)]

blŏckā'de[1] *n.* Surrounding of place, blocking of harbour etc., by hostile forces to prevent goods etc. from reaching or leaving it (**run** ~, evade blockading force); *obstruction by snow etc. [f. prec. + -ADE, prob. after *ambuscade*]

blŏckā'de[2] *v.t.* Subject to blockade; obstruct (passage, view, etc.). [f. prec.]

||**blōke** *n.* (colloq.) Man, fellow, chap. [Shelta]

blŏnd *a.* & *n.* **1.** *a.* (Of hair) light-coloured, flaxen; (of complexion) fair. **2.** *n.* Person having such hair and skin. [ME f. F, f. med. L *blondus*, *blundus* yellow, perh. of Gmc orig.]

blŏnde *a.* & *n.* (Of woman or woman's hair) blond. [F, fem. of *blond* (see prec.)]

blood[1] (blŭd) *n.* **1.** Liquid (usu. red) circulating in arteries and veins of higher animals; corresponding liquid in lower animals; one's *blood* BOIL[2]*s*; one's ~ **runs cold,** one is horrified; **first** ~, first shedding of blood (in Boxing, or fig.); **out for** person's ~, determined to defeat him; **taste** ~, (fig.) be stimulated by early success. **2.** Taking of life; guilt of bloodshed. **3.** Passion, temperament, mettle, (**bad** ~, ill feeling; ~ **out of** (or **from**) **a stone,** pity from the pitiless or money from the avaricious; **in cold** ~, without passion, deliberately; **his** ~ **is up,** he is in a fighting mood). **4.** Race, descent, parentage; BLUE[1] *blood*; **fresh** or **new** ~, new members admitted to family, society, etc.; **young** ~, younger member(s) of party etc.; **in** one's ~, fundamental in one's character (*the sea is in his blood*); *prince* etc. **of the** ~, royal. **5.** Relationship, relations, (*own flesh and blood*; ~ **is thicker than water,** the tie of kinship is strong). **6.** Dandy, man of fashion, (*young blood*). **7.** ||(esp. in *pl.*) Blood-and-thunder story. **8.** ~ **and iron,** relentless use of military force (esp. as motto of Bismarckian policy); **~-and-thunder,** sensational, melodramatic; ~ **bank,** place where supply of blood for transfusion is stored; **~-bath,** massacre; **~-brother** (by birth or ceremonial mingling of blood); ~ **count,** (counting of) number of corpuscles in a definite volume of blood;

~-curdling, so horrific as to seem to curdle the blood; *blood*-DONOR; **~ feud** (between families of which one has killed or injured member(s) of the other); **~ group,** any one of the (usu. four) types into which human blood may be divided according to its compatibility in transfusion; **~-guilt,** responsibility for murder or death; **~-heat,** ordinary heat of human blood in health, about 98°F. or 37°C.; **~ horse,** thoroughbred; **~'hound,** large keen-scented dog formerly used to track cattle, criminals, etc., (fig.) detective; **~-letting,** surgical removal of some of patient's blood, (joc.) bloodshed; **~-lust** (for shedding of blood); **~-money,** (1) reward to witness for securing capital sentence, (2) fine paid to next of kin for slaughter of relative; **~ orange** (with red-streaked pulp); **~-poisoning,** state resulting from presence of pathogenic bacteria in blood; *blood* PRESSURE; **~ pudding,** black pudding; **~-red,** red as blood; **~-relation,** one related by blood, not by marriage; **~ royal,** *the* royal family; **~'shed,** spilling of blood, slaughter [f. phr. *to shed blood*]; **~'shot,** (of eyeball) tinged with blood; *blood* SPAVIN; **~ sports,** those involving bloodshed or killing of animals, esp. hunting; **~-stained,** (1) stained with blood, (2) disgraced by bloodshed; **~'stock,** thoroughbred horses; **~'stone,** green chalcedony spotted or streaked with red; **~'stream,** circulating blood; **~'sucker,** leech, extortioner; **~ test,** examination of blood for diagnosis etc.; **~'thirsty,** eager for bloodshed; *blood* TRANSFUSION; **~-vessel,** vein, artery, or capillary, conveying blood; **~'worm,** bright-red midge-larva used as fishing bait; **~-wort,** plant with red roots or leaves, esp. red-veined dock. **9.** Hence -~'ED² *a.* [OE *blōd*, = OS *blōd*, OHG *bluot*, ON, Goth. *blōth* f. Gmc **blōdham*]

blood² (blŭd) *v.t.* Allow first taste of blood to (hound, or fig. of initiating persons). [f. prec.]

bloo'dlėss (-ŭ'-) *a.* Without blood; unemotional; pale; without bloodshed; hence ~LY² *adv.* [f. BLOOD¹ + -LESS]

bloo'dў¹ (-ŭ'-) *a.* & *adv.* **1.** *a.* Of, like, running or smeared with, blood (*bloody* FLUX; *bloody* SWEAT); red (**~ hand,** armorial device of baronet; **B~ Mary,** mixed drink of vodka and tomato juice); involving, loving, resulting from, bloodshed (**~-minded,** (colloq.) deliberately uncooperative); sanguinary, cruel. **2.** ‖(in strong language) = DAMNED 2 etc. (*a bloody shame*), or as mere intensive (*not a bloody one*); unpleasant. **3.** Hence **bloo'dĭLY²** *adv.*, **bloo'dĭNESS** *n.* (-ŭ'-). **4.** *adv.* ‖(as in 2) = DAMNED 3, confoundedly, very, or as intensive. [OE *blōdig* (as BLOOD¹, -Y²)]

bloo'dў² (-ŭ'-) *v.t.* Make bloody; stain with blood. [f. prec.]

blōōm¹ *n.* **1.** Flower, esp. of plant grown or admired chiefly for the flower, florescence (*in bloom*); prime, perfection. **2.** Flush, glow; delicate powdery deposit on grapes, plums, etc., freshness, (**take the ~ off,** make stale); cloudiness on shiny surface; (**water-**)**~,** scum formed by algae on water surface. [ME, f. ON *blóm*, *blómi*, OS *blōmo*, OHG *bluomo*, *-ma*, Goth. *blōma* f. Gmc **blōmon*, *-ōn* (**blō-* BLOW³; cf. BLOSSOM¹)]

blōōm² *v.* **1.** *v.i.* Bear flowers, be in flower; come into, be in, full beauty; culminate, flourish. **2.** *v.t.* ‖(Photog.) Coat (lens) so as to reduce reflection from surface. [ME, f. prec.]

blōōm³ *n.*, & *v.t.* **1.** *n.* Mass of puddled iron hammered or squeezed into thick bar. **2.** *v.t.* Make into bloom. **3.** Hence ~'ERY (3) *n.* [OE *blōma*]

‖**blōō'mer** *n.* (sl.) Blunder. [= BLOOMING *error*; see -ER¹]

blōō'mers (-z) *n. pl.* **1.** (Hist.) Woman's costume with loose knee-length trousers. **2.** Woman's undergarment of this shape; (colloq.) knickers. [f. Mrs. A. *Bloomer*, Amer. social reformer d. 1894, who advocated similar costume]

blōō'mĭng *a.* & *adv.* In vbl senses; (sl. euphem.) = BLOODY¹ 2, 4. [f. BLOOM² + -ING²]

Blōō'msburў (-z-) *n.* & *a.* (Associated with or similar to) early 20th-c. school of writers and aesthetes living in Bloomsbury; intellectual, highbrow. [f. ~ in west-central London]

***blōō'per** *n.* (colloq.) Embarrassing error. [f. imit. *bloop* + -ER¹]

blŏ'ssom¹ *n.* Flower, esp. as promising fruit; mass of flowers on fruit-tree etc. (*in blossom*); early stage of growth, promise; hence ~Y² *a.* [OE *blōstm(a)*, cogn. w. MDu. *bloesem*, MLG *blōs(s)em* (cf. also ON *blómstr*), prob. f. as BLOOM¹]

blŏ'ssom² *v.i.* Open into flower (lit., or fig.; *blossom out into a statesman*). [OE *blōstmian* (as prec.)]

blŏt¹ *n.* Spot or stain of ink etc., dark patch; disfigurement, blemish; defect; disgraceful act or quality in good character. [ME, prob. f. Scand.; cf. Icel. *blettr* spot, stain]

blŏt² *v.t.* & *i.* (-tt-). Spot or stain with ink (**~ one's copy-book,** (colloq.) spoil one's character or record, commit an indiscretion); smudge; (of pen, ink) make blots; disgrace; **~ out,** obliterate (writing), obscure (view), exterminate, destroy; dry with **~'ting-paper,** absorbent paper for drying wet ink, whence ~'TER¹ (2) *n.*, (esp. pad of this, *temporary recording-book, e.g. police charge-sheet). [f. prec.]

blŏtch *n.* Discoloured or inflamed patch on skin; irregular patch of ink or colour; hence ~'Y² *a.* [17th c., f. obs. *plotch* and BLOT¹]

blŏ'ttō *a.* (sl.) Very drunk. [20th c.; perh. f. BLOT¹]

blouse (-z) *n.*, & *v.t.* **1.** *n.* (Esp. French) workman's or peasant's loose linen or cotton garment, usu. belted at waist. **2.** Woman's loose upper garment, usu. tucked into skirt or trousers at waist; upper part of soldier's or airman's battledress. **3.** *v.t.* Make (bodice etc.) loose like blouse. [19th c.; F, of unkn. orig.]

blou'son (blōō'zawṅ) *n.* Short blouse-shaped jacket. [F]

blow¹ (-ō) *v.* (**blew** *pr.* blōō; **~n** exc. in sense 'cursed'). **1.** *v.i.* (Of wind, air, or impers.) move along, act as air-current, (*blow great* GUNS); send directed air-current from mouth (**~ hot and cold,** vacillate); puff, pant; (U.S. & Austral. colloq.) boast; be driven or sounded by blowing; (sl.) depart suddenly; (of whale) eject air and water; (of electric filament or fuse) melt when overloaded; (of food-tin etc.) swell from internal gas pressure. **2.** *v.t.* Work bellows of (organ); (esp. in *pass.*) exhaust of breath; send out by breathing (*blow air into*; **~ a kiss,** kiss one's hand and wave it to distant person); drive by blowing; make or shape (bubble, glass) by blowing air in; sound (wind instrument, note or signal *on* or *with* it; **~ one's own trumpet,** praise oneself); direct air-current at (*blow fingers, fire*); clear (nose, egg) by air-current. **3.** Send flying (*off* etc.) by explosion; cause (electric fuse etc.) to melt under overload; break into (safe etc.) with explosives; (sl.) reveal (*blow the* GAFF²); **~ one's mind,** (sl.) indulge in hallucinations; **~ one's top** or ***stack,** (colloq.) become very angry. **4.** (of flies) deposit eggs in; (sl.) curse, confound, (*I'll be blowed if* etc.; esp. in *imper.* (*blow you, Jack*) and abs. (*oh blow!*)); (sl.) squander, spend (money) recklessly (cf. BLUE⁴). **5.** **~-ball,** globular seed-head of dandelion etc.; **~-fish,** kind able to inflate its body when frightened etc.; **~'fly,** meat-fly, bluebottle; **~-hard,** boastful (person); **~-hole,** hole for blowing or breathing through, nostril of whale etc., vent for air, smoke, etc., in tunnel etc.; **~'lamp** (for directing very hot flame on a selected spot); **~'pipe,** tube for heating flame by blowing air or other gas into it, tube used in glass-blowing, tube for propelling arrows or darts by blowing; **~'torch,** = *blowlamp*. **6.** ~ **in,** break inwards by explosion, (colloq.) come in unexpectedly; ~ **on, upon,** make stale, discredit; ~ **out,** (*v.t.*) extinguish, send outwards by explosion (~ *out* one's *brains*, shoot oneself in the head), (*v.i.*) (of tyre) burst, (of fuse etc.) melt; so *~-out n.*, (also, colloq.) large meal; ~ **over,** pass off; ~ **up,** (*v.t.*) send upwards or shatter by explosion, reprove, (colloq.) enlarge (photograph etc.), exaggerate, (*v.i.*) arise, come to notice, be shattered by explosion, lose one's temper; *~-up* n., explosion, (colloq.) enlargement (of photograph etc.). [OE *blāwan*, = OHG *blā(h)an* f. IE **bhlá-*]

blow² (-ō) *n.* Blowing; inhaling of fresh air; blowing of flute, one's nose, etc.; = FLY¹-*blow*; *boast(er). [f. prec.]

blow³ (-ō) *v.i.* (**blew** *pr.* bloo͞; **~n**). (arch.) Burst into or be in flower. [OE *blōwan*, = OS *blōjan*, OHG *bluojan* f. Gmc **blō-*; cf. *blade*, BLOOM¹]

blow⁴ (-ō) *n.* (arch.) Blossoming (*in full blow* etc.). [f. prec.]

blow⁵ (-ō) *n.* **1.** Hard stroke with fist, instrument, etc.; **at one ~,** by a single stroke, in one operation; **~-by-~,** (of description etc.) giving all details in sequence; **come to ~s,** fight; **strike a ~ for, against,** help, oppose. **2.** Disaster, shock, (*to* person). [15th c., of unkn. orig.]

blow'er (-ō'*er*) *n.* In vbl senses; apparatus for increasing a fire's draught, e.g. sheet of iron across fireplace; (colloq.) telephone. [f. BLOW¹ + -ER¹]

blown. See BLOW¹,³.

blow'ȳ (-ō'ĭ) *a.* Windy, wind-swept. [f. BLOW¹ + -Y²]

blow'zȳ *a.* Red-faced, coarse-looking; slatternly. [f. obs. *blowze* beggar's wench; orig. unkn.]

blŭb *v.i.* (**-bb-**). (sl.) Shed tears. [abbr. of BLUBBER³]

blŭ'bber¹ *n.* Whale fat; SEA *blubber*; weeping. [ME, perh. imit. (obs. meanings 'foaming, bubble')]

blŭ'bber² *a.* (Of lips) swollen, protruding. [earlier *blabber*, *blobber*, imit.]

blŭ'bber³ *v.t.* & *i.* Utter with sobs; weep noisily; wet, disfigure, swell, (face) with weeping. [f. BLUBBER¹]

blu'chers (-oo͞'kerz) *n. pl.* (Hist.) Strong leather half-boots or high shoes. [f. G. L. von *Blücher*, Prussian general d. 1819]

blŭ'dgeon (-ŭ'jon) *n.*, & *v.t.* **1.** *n.* Heavy-headed stick. **2.** *v.t.* Strike repeatedly with bludgeon; coerce. [18th c., of unkn. orig.]

blue¹ (bloo͞) *a.* **1.** Of the colour between green and violet in the spectrum, coloured like the clear sky or deep sea (also of things much paler, darker, etc., e.g. smoke, distant hills, bruises); with blue-coloured skin through cold, fear, anger, etc.; wearing blue clothes; (as distinguishing epithet) *blue fox, vitriol*, etc. **2.** Nervous, depressed; (of state of affairs etc.) dismal; (of music) characteristic of the blues; belonging to a particular political party, in U.K. usu. Conservative; (of woman, arch.) that is a bluestocking; (of talk, film, etc.) indecent or profane. **3.** ~ **baby** (with congenital cyanosis from heart defect); ~ **bag** (for lawyer's brief); **~'bell,** any of several plants with blue bell-shaped flowers, esp. (Sc.) light-blue-flowered *Campanula*, harebell, (Engl.) wild hyacinth; **~'berry,** (blue fruit of) one of several plants of genus *Vaccinium*; **~-bird,** N. Amer. song-bird of genus *Sialis*, with blue back; ~ **blood,** noble birth; ~ **book,** Parliamentary or Privy-Council report, *book giving personal details of U.S. government officials; **~'bottle,** dark blue cornflower, large buzzing fly with blue body, (Austral.) Portuguese man-of-war; ~ **cheese** (with veins of blue mould); **~-chip,** [f. high-valued blue chips in Poker] of highest quality, (St. Exch., of shares) constituting a fairly reliable investment, though less secure than gilt-edged; ||**~-coat boy, girl, school,** (scholar in) charity school, esp. Christ's Hospital; **~-collar worker,** manual or industrial (opp. office) worker; *blue* DAHLIA; ~ **devils,** mood of depression; *blue* ENSIGN; ~ **eye** (with blue iris); **~-eyed boy,** (colloq.) pet, favourite; **~'fish,** a voracious game-fish (*Pomatomus saltatrix*); *blue* FUNK 1; ***~'gill,** a freshwater sunfish; *~ **grass,** a bluish-coloured grass, esp. of Kentucky; ~ **ground,** dark usu. blue soil in which diamonds are found in S. Africa etc.; ~ **gum,** kind of eucalyptus tree, esp. *Eucalyptus globulus*; **~'jacket,** seaman in Navy; *~ **laws,** severe puritanical laws alleged to have been in force among early colonists of New England; ||**B~ Mantle,** one of four pursuivants of College of Arms; ~ **metal,** broken blue stone for road-making; **once in a ~ moon,** very rarely; ~ **mould,** a fungus in food, esp. in certain cheeses when mature; *blue* MURDER¹; ***B~-nose,** (colloq.) Nova-Scotian; ~ **pencil** (used in marking corrections, obliterations, etc.); **~-pencil** *v.t.* (||*-ll-*), mark etc. with blue pencil, make cuts in, censor; **B~ Peter,** blue flag with white square, hoisted by ship before sailing; ~ **pill,** mercurial aperient; **~'print,** (*n.*) blue photographic print representing final stage of engineering or other plans, (fig.) detailed plan of work to be done, *(*v.t.*) work out (programme etc.); ~ **ribbon,** ribbon of the Garter, greatest honour in any sphere, sign of teetotalism; *blue* ROAN¹, ROCK¹; ||~ **rod,** official of order of St. Michael & St. George; ***~-sky laws** (preventing sales to gullible investors); **~'stocking,** woman having or affecting literary tastes and learning [Blue Stocking Society, met about 1750 to talk on literature etc., some of the men wearing ordinary blue (not dress) stockings]; ~ **streak,** (colloq.) fast-moving thing or person; **~'-stone,** copper sulphate; **~'throat,** thrush of genus *Erithacus*; *blue* TIT¹; *blue* VITRIOL; ~ **water,** open sea; ~ **whale,** a rorqual, largest known living animal. **4.** Hence **blu'**ISH¹ 2 (bloo͞'-) *a.*, ~'NESS (-oo͞'n-) *n.* [ME, f. OF *bleu* f. Rom. **blavus* f. Gmc **blæwaz*]

blue² (bloo͞) *n.* Blue colour; blue pigment; blue powder used as whitener in laundering; blue clothes or material (*dressed in blue*); blue butterfly; blue ball in snooker etc.; **the ~,** the clear sky (BOLT¹ *from the blue*; *out of the blue*), the sea; ||**the B~s,** the Royal Horse Guards; colour or member of a political party, in U.K. usu. Conservative; ||one who has represented his university etc., esp. Oxford (**dark** ~) or Cambridge (**light** ~), in athletics etc. (**get** one's ~, be chosen as representative); (Austral. sl.) argument, row; (in *pl.*) melancholy; in *pl.*, sometimes treated as *sing.*) (type of) melancholy song of Amer. Negro origin. [f. prec.]

blu|e³ (bloo͞) *v.t.* (*part.* **~eing** *or* **~ing,** *pr.* -oo͞'ĭ-). Make blue; treat with laundering blue. [f. BLUE¹]

blu|e⁴ (bloo͞) *v.t.* (*part.* **~eing** *or* **~ing,** *pr.* -oo͞'ĭ-). (sl.) Squander (money). [perh. var. of BLOW¹]

Blue'beard (bloo'-) *n.* Person who murders several wives in succession, or has mysterious or horrible things to conceal. [f. character in fairy-tale told in F (*Barbe-bleue*) by Perrault]

***blu'ėt** (bloo'-) *n.* Blue-flowered plant of genus *Houstonia.* [f. BLUE[1] + -ET[1]]

blu'ey (bloo'ĭ) *n.* (Austral.) Bushman's bundle (HUMP *bluey*); (colloq.) blue summons-paper or cattle-dog. [f. BLUE[1] + -Y[2]]

blŭff[1] *a.* (Of ship's bows, cliffs) having perpendicular broad front; (of person or his manner) abrupt, blunt, frank, hearty; hence ~'LY[2] *adv.*, ~'NESS *n.* [17th c. Naut. wd, of unkn. orig.]

blŭff[2] *n.* Headland or cliff with perpendicular broad face. [f. prec.]

blŭff[3] *v.* **1.** *v.i.* Make pretence of strength to gain advantage etc. **2.** *v.t.* Deceive (opponent, rival) thus. [19th c., orig. in Poker; earlier sense *blindfold*, f. Du. *bluffen* brag]

blŭff[4] *n.* Act of bluffing (**call** person's ~, challenge his attempt to deceive by bluffing); threats designed to operate without action. [19th c., orig. in Poker; earlier sense 'horse's blinker', prob. f. prec.]

bluish. See BLUE[1] 4.

blŭ'nder[1] *v.* **1.** *v.i.* Move blindly, stumble, (*along*; ~ **upon,** find by chance); make gross mistake. **2.** *v.t.* Mismanage; ~ **away,** waste or lose by mismanagement. [ME, prob. f. Scand.; cf. MSw. *blundra* shut the eyes]

blŭ'nder[2] *n.* Stupid or careless mistake. [prob. f. prec., but found earlier]

blŭ'nderbŭss *n.* (Hist.) Short gun with large bore firing many balls or slugs. [alt. of Du. *donderbus* thunder gun, assoc. w. BLUNDER[1]]

blŭng|e (-nj) *v.t.* (Pottery). Mix (clay, bone, flint-powder, etc.) with water by revolving machinery; hence ~'ER[1] (2) *n.* [after *plunge, blend*]

blŭnt *a.*, *n.*, & *v.t.* **1.** *a.* Dull, not sensitive; without sharp edge or point; outspoken; uncompromising (*a blunt refusal to go*); hence ~'LY[2] *adv.*, ~'NESS *n.* **2.** *n.* (arch. sl.) Ready money. **3.** *v.t.* Make blunt(er). [ME, perh. f. Scand. (ON *blunda* shut the eyes; cf. BLUNDER[1])]

blûr[1] *n.* Smear of ink etc.; dimness, confused effect. [16th c.; perh. rel. to BLEAR]

blûr[2] *v.t.* & *i.* (**-rr-**). Smear (clear writing etc.) with ink etc.; sully, disfigure; make or become indistinct, efface; dim (perception etc.). [as prec.]

blûrb *n.* Publisher's (usu. eulogistic) brief description of book printed on its jacket or in advertisements elsewhere; descriptive or commendatory matter. [coined by G. Burgess, Amer. humorist d. 1951]

blûrt *v.t.* Burst *out* with, utter abruptly. [prob. imit.]

blŭsh[1] *v.i.* Become red in the face with shame or other emotion (*at* sight or word, *with* or *for* joy or usu. shame); be ashamed (*blush to own* etc.); be red or pink. [ME, f. OE *blyscan*]

blŭsh[2] *n.* **1.** Glance, glimpse; **at** (**the**) **first** ~, on first glimpse or impression. **2.** Reddening of face in shame etc. (*put to the blush*); **spare** person's ~**es,** not embarrass him by praise. **3.** Rosy glow, flush of light. [f. prec.]

blŭ'sher *n.* Cosmetic used to give colour to the face. [f. BLUSH[1] + -ER[1]]

blŭ'ster[1] *v.i.* (Of wind, waves, person) storm boisterously. [16th c.; ult. imit.]

blŭ'ster[2] *n.* Boisterous blowing; noisy self-asserting talk, threats; hence ~Y[2] *a.* [f. prec.]

B.M. *abbr.* Bachelor of Medicine; British Museum.

B.M.A. *abbr.* British Medical Association.

B. Mus. *abbr.* Bachelor of Music.

Bn. *abbr.* (esp. Mil.) Battalion.

B.N.C. *abbr.* Brasenose College, Oxford.

bō[1] *int.* = BOO. [imit.]

***bō**[2] *n.* (Form of address, =) mate, old chap. [19th c.; perh. f. BOY]

B.O. *abbr.* (colloq.) body odour.

bō'a *n.* **1.** Large S. Amer. non-poisonous snake of genus *Boa* etc. killing by compression; Old-World python; woman's long fur or feather throat-wrap. **2.** ~ **constrictor,** Brazilian species of boa; python. [L]

B.O.A.C. (formerly) British Overseas Airways Corporation.

boar *n.* Uncastrated male pig; its flesh; WILD *boar*; male guinea-pig etc. [OE *bār*, = OS *bērswīn*, OHG *bēr* f. WG **baira*]

board[1] *n.* **1.** Long thin usu. fairly narrow piece of sawn timber; slab made of one or more such pieces of wood etc., bare or covered with cloth, leather, etc., used for various purposes, as in games, for posting notices, etc., (BLACK[1]*board*, *chessboard*, *notice-board*, SPRING[2]*board*; ACROSS *the board*); (in *pl.*) theatre stage, actor's profession; material compressed from wood fibres etc. into stiff sheets; = STRAW[1]*-board*; *~ **foot,** 144 cu. in. (of timber); *~'**walk,** footway (orig.) made of boards. **2.** Table (ABOVE-*board*; SWEEP[1] *the board*); table spread for meals; food served, daily meals provided at contract price or in return for services (esp. *board and lodging*); council-table, councillors, committee (‖**B~ of Trade,** ‖**B~ of Inland Revenue,** government departments; *~ **of trade,** chamber of commerce); body of examiners or interviewers; directors of company (~'**room,** their meeting-place). **3.** Ship's side: **go by the** ~, (of mast etc.) fall overboard, (fig.) be entirely neglected; **on** ~ = ABOARD, esp. on or into ship, aircraft, train, bus, etc. **4.** (Naut.) Distance covered in one tack. [OE *bord*, f. two distinct Gmc wds meaning (1) board (2) border, respectively f. Gmc **bordham* and **bordhaz*; reinforced in ME by F *bord*, ON *borth*]

board[2] *v.* **1.** *v.t.* Cover or close (*up*) with boards. **2.** *v.t.* & *i.* Provide (lodger or daily guest) with, (of lodger etc.) receive, stated meals at fixed rate (~ **out,** eat away from home, place (destitute etc. child) in family; ~ **with,** be lodger boarding in house of); bring (candidate etc.) before board of interviewers. **3.** *v.t.* Come alongside (ship, usu. to attack); force one's way on board (ship, or abs.); go on board (ship, aircraft, train, bus, etc.). **4.** (Of ship) tack. [f. prec.]

boar'der *n.* One who boards (sense 2) with someone, esp. pupil at boarding-school; one who boards an enemy ship. [f. prec. + -ER[1]]

boar'dĭng *n.* In vbl senses; ~**-house, -school,** (in which persons, schoolchildren, board (sense 2)). [f. BOARD[2] + -ING[1]]

boart. See BORT.

boast[1] *n.* Excessively proud statement; cause of pride; hence ~'FUL *a.*, ~**ful**LY[2] *adv.*, ~**ful**NESS *n.* [ME f. AF *bost*; orig. unkn.]

boast[2] *v.* **1.** *v.i.* Praise oneself; make boasts *of* or *about.* **2.** *v.t.* Make boasts of; possess as thing to be proud of. **3.** Hence ~'ER[1] *n.* [ME f. AF **boster* (as prec.)]

boat[1] *n.* **1.** Small open oared or sailing vessel, fishing-vessel, mail packet, or small steamer, (BURN[2] one's *boats*; MISS[2] *the boat*; **push the** ~ **out,** (colloq.) celebrate; ROCK[3] *the boat*; **in the same** ~, in same predicament, with like risks etc.; **ship's** ~ (carried on board ship); **take to the** ~**s,** use ship's boats to escape from sinking ship etc., (fig.) precipitously abandon one's undertaking); *large sea-going vessel; boat-shaped utensil for sauce etc. **2.** ~**-bill,** S. Amer. heron with bill like overturned boat;

~-deck (from which ship's boats are launched); **~ drill,** exercise of launching ship's boats; **~-hook,** long pole with hook and spike; **~-house,** shed at water's edge for housing boats; **~'load,** as many or as much as a boat can hold; **~'man,** one who hires out his boat(s), one who provides transport by boat; **~ race** (between rowing crews, esp. between Oxford and Cambridge Universities); **~'swain, bo's'n, bo'sun, bosun,** (bō'*sun*), ship's officer in charge of sails, rigging, etc., and summoning men to duty (*~swain's chair,* wooden seat suspended from ropes for work on side of ship or building); **~-train** (timed to catch or meet boat). **3.** Hence ~'FUL 2 *n.* [OE *bāt,* = ON *beit* f. Gmc **bait-*]

boat^2 *v.i.* Go in a boat; amuse oneself thus (*boating man*); hence ~'ER^1 *n.,* hard flat straw hat (as formerly worn in boating). [f. prec.]

boatĕ'l. See BOTEL.

bŏb^1 *n.* & *v.* (**-bb-**). **1.** *n.* Weight on pendulum, plumb-line, or kite-tail; knot of hair, tassel-shaped curl (**~-wig,** wig with short curls, opp. to *full-bottomed wig*); CHERRY-*bob*; = BOB-SLEIGH; short line at end of stanza; horse's docked tail; bobbed hair; ***~'cat,** Amer. short-tailed lynx; **~'tail,** (horse or dog with) docked tail; RAG^1*tag and bobtail.* **2.** *v.t.* Cut (woman's or child's hair) to hang short of shoulders. **3.** *v.i.* Ride on bob-sleigh. [14th c.; orig. unkn.]

||**bŏb^2** *n.* (*pl.* same). (sl.) Shilling; five decimal pence, 5p. [19th c.; orig. unkn.]

bŏb^3 *v.i.* (**-bb-**). **1.** Move up and down, dance, rebound; curtsy; **~ up (like a cork),** (fig.) emerge suddenly, become active or conspicuous again after defeat. **2. ~ for,** try to catch with the mouth (fruit floating or hanging). [14th c.; app. imit.]

bŏb^4 *n.* Jerk, bouncing movement; curtsy; (Bell-ringing) one of several kinds of change in long peals. [f. prec.]

||**bŏb^5** *n.* **Dry, wet, -~,** cricketing, boating, Etonian; **~'s your uncle,** (sl.) all is well. [prob. = *Robert*]

bŏ'bbĭn *n.* Cylinder from which thread, yarn, wire, etc., is unwound as wanted; reel, spool; small bar and string for raising door-latch; **~-lace** (made by hand with thread wound on bobbins). [f. F *bobine*]

bŏ'bbĭnĕt *n.* Machine-made cotton net (imitating lace made with bobbins on pillow). [f. prec. + NET^1]

||**bŏ'bbĭsh** *a.* (sl.) Brisk, well. [f. BOB^3 + -ISH^1]

bŏ'bble *n.* Small woolly ball as ornament or trimming. [dim. of BOB^1]

||**bŏ'bbȳ^1** *n.* **1.** (colloq.) Policeman [f. Sir *Robert* Peel, Engl. statesman d. 1850]. **2. ~ (calf),** unweaned calf slaughtered soon after birth. [f. as BOB^5 + -Y^3]

bŏ'bbȳ^2 *n.* ***~ pin,** flat hairpin; **~ socks,** short socks covering ankle; **~-soxer,** (usu. derog.) adolescent girl wearing bobby socks. [f. BOB^1 + -Y^3]

bŏ'bbȳ-dăzzler *n.* Remarkable or excellent thing or person. [dial., rel. to DAZZLE]

bŏ'blĕt *n.* Bob-sleigh for two persons. [f. BOB^1 + -LET]

bŏ'bolĭnk *n.* N. Amer. song-bird (*Dolichonyx oryzivorus*). [orig. *Bob (o') Lincoln*; imit. of its call]

bŏ'b-sleigh (-lā), **-slĕd,** *n.* (One of) two short sledges coupled, used in tobogganing and for drawing logs. [f. BOB(^{1}?) + SLEIGH, SLED]

bŏ'bstay *n.* Rope holding bowsprit down. [f. BOB(^{3}?) + STAY^2]

bŏ'b-white *n.* N. Amer. quail of genus *Colinis.* [imit. of its call]

boca'ge (-ah'zh) *n.* Representation of silvan scenery in ceramics. [F, f. OF *boscage* (see BOSCAGE)]

Bŏche (-sh) *n.* & *a.* (sl., derog.) German. [F sl., orig. = rascal; applied to Germans in 1914–18 war]

bŏck *n.* Strong dark-coloured German beer; glass of (any) beer. [F f. G abbr. of *Eimbockbier* (*Einbeck* in Hanover, *bier* BEER)]

||**bŏd** *n.* (sl.) Person. [f. BODY^1]

B.O.D. *abbr.* biochemical oxygen demand.

bōde *v.* **1.** *v.t.* Foresee, foretell, (evil); portend, foreshow. **2.** *v.i.* Promise *well* or *ill.* **3.** Hence **bō'd**ING^1, ~'MENT (-dm-), *ns.* [OE *bodian* (*boda* messenger, = OS *bodo,* OHG *boto,* ON *bothi* f. Gmc **budhon*)]

bō'deful (-df-) *a.* Ominous, presageful. [19th c., f. *bode* omen + -FUL]

bodē'ga *n.* Cellar or shop selling wine. [Sp., f. L f. Gk *apothēkē* storehouse]

bŏdge. Var. of BOTCH.

Bŏdhĭsa'ttva (-dĭsah'-) *n.* (Buddhism). One who is able to reach nirvana but delays doing so through compassion for human suffering. [Skr., = one whose essence is perfect knowledge]

bŏ'dĭce *n.* Upper part of woman's dress, down to waist; woman's undergarment for same part of body. [orig. *pair of bodies* = whalebone corset]

bŏ'dĭlĕss *a.* Incorporeal; separated from the body. [f. BODY^1 + -LESS]

bŏ'dĭlȳ^1 *a.* Of or affecting the human body or physical nature. [f. BODY^1 + -LY^1]

bŏ'dĭlȳ^2 *adv.* With the whole bulk, as a whole; in the body, in person. [f. BODY^1 + -LY^2]

bŏ'dkĭn *n.* Blunt thick needle with large eye for drawing tape etc. through hem; long pin for fastening hair; small pointed instrument for piercing cloth, removing piece of type for correction, etc.; ||(arch.) person squeezed between two others (*ride bodkin*). [ME, perh. f. Celt.]

Bŏ'dleian^1 (-lĭan) *a.,* **Bŏdlei'an^2** (-lē'an) *n.,* (colloq.) **Bŏ'dley** *n.* (Of) the Library of Oxford University. [f. Sir T. *Bodley,* Engl. diplomat d. 1613, who re-founded it 1603, + -AN]

Bodō'nĭ *n.* Style of type for printing and typewriting. [f. G. ~, It. printer d. 1813]

bŏ'dȳ^1 *n.* **1.** Man or animal as material organism (**keep ~ and soul together,** remain alive); (**dead**) **~,** corpse. **2.** Trunk apart from head and limbs; main portion (stem, hull, nave, etc.; *of* motor car, document, etc.); majority. **3.** Human being, person, (HEIR *of the* or one's *body*; *good sort of body, anybody,* etc.). **4.** Aggregate of persons (*governing body*), things, or substance (*body of ore, of water*; **in a ~,** all together; *body* CORPORATE, *body* POLITIC); society, league, military force; collection *of* facts etc. **5.** Piece of matter (**heavenly ~,** sun, star, etc.); bulk, quantity; comparative solidity or substantial character or flavour (*wine of good body*); thing perceptible to senses. **6. ~-blow,** (fig.) severe set-back; **~-building,** strengthening the body esp. by exercise; **~-colour,** opaque pigment; **~guard,** escort or personal guard of dignitary etc.; **~line bowling,** (Cricket) persistent fast bowling on leg side threatening batsman's body; **~ odour,** (esp. unpleasant) smell of the body; **~-servant,** valet; **~-snatcher,** (Hist.) illicit exhumer of corpses for dissection; **~ stocking,** woman's undergarment covering trunk and legs; **~'work,** structure of vehicle body. **7.** Hence (-)**bŏ'dĭ**ED^2 (-ĭd) *a.* [OE *bodig,* corresp. to OHG *botah*; orig. unkn.]

bŏ'dȳ^2 *v.t.* **~ forth,** give mental shape to, exhibit in outward shape, typify. [f. prec.]

Boeō'tian (bēō'shan) *a.* & *n.* Crass or dull (person). [f. *Boeotia* in ancient Greece, proverbial for stupidity of inhabitants, + -AN]

Bō'er (*or* boor) *n.* & *a.* (Of) Dutch or Dutch--descended S. African(s). [Du.; see BOOR]
bŏ'ffin *n.* (sl.) Person engaged in (esp. technical) research. [20th c.; orig. unkn.]
Bō'fors (-z) *n.* ~ (**gun**), type of light anti--aircraft gun. [~ in Sweden]
bŏg[1] *n.* **1.** (Piece of) wet spongy ground (~ **violet** etc., plant growing in bogs); ||(sl.) lavatory. **2.** ~**-bean,** = BUCK[1]*bean*; ~ **myrtle,** shrub with fragrant leaves found in bogs; ~ **oak,** ancient oak preserved in black state in peat; *bog* SPAVIN; ~**-trotter,** (derog.) Irishman. **3.** Hence ~**'gy**[2] (-gĭ) *a.* [f. Ir. or Gael. *bogach* (*bog* soft)]
bŏg[2] *v.t.* (**-gg-**). (Usu. in *pass.*) Submerge in bog (lit., or fig.: *bogged down in* or *by difficulties*). [f. prec.]
bō'gey[1] (-gĭ) *n.* Score that good golf-player should do hole or course in. [perh. f. BOGY as imaginary person]
bogey[2]. See BOGY.
bŏ'ggle *v.i.* Hesitate, demur, *at* or *about*; equivocate; be startled or baffled. [prob. f. dial. *boggle* BOGY]
||**bō'gie** (-gĭ) *n.* Undercarriage with two or more wheel-pairs, pivoted below end of rail vehicle. [19th c.; north. dial. wd, of unkn. orig.]
bō'gle *n.* Bugbear; scarecrow; phantom; goblin. [orig. Sc. (16th c.), prob. rel. to BOGY]
bō'gus *a.* Sham, fictitious, spurious. [19th c. U.S. wd; orig. unkn.]
bō'gy̆, bō'gey[2], (-gĭ) *n.* The Devil; ~(**man**), evil spirit, goblin; bugbear. [19th c., orig. as proper name; cf. BOGLE]
bōh (bō) *int.* = BOO. [imit.]
bōhea' *n.* Black tea of lowest quality (last crop of season). [f. *Bu-i* or *Wu-i* in China]
Bōhē'mĭan *a.* & *n.* **1.** (Native or inhabitant) of Bohemia; Czech. **2.** Socially unconventional (person); person, esp. artist or writer, of free--and-easy habits, manners, and sometimes morals; hence **bōhē'mĭan**ISM (2) *n.* [f. *Bohemia* + -AN; sense 2 f. F *bohémien* gipsy]
***bō'hŭnk** *n.* (sl.) Immigrant from central or S.E. Europe; rough fellow. [app. f. prec. + HUNGARIAN]
boil[1] *n.* Inflamed suppurating swelling caused by infection of hair follicle etc. [OE *bȳl(e)*, = OS *būla*, OHG *būlla* bladder f. WG **būlja*]
boil[2] *v.* **1.** *v.i.* Bubble up, undulate, (of liquid at the temperature at which it changes into vapour, or of containing vessel: *kettle is boiling*); (of sea etc., feelings, person) seethe, be agitated, like boiling water or its vessel; be cooked by boiling; **blood** ~**s** (with indignation; *it makes my blood boil*); ~ **down to,** amount to, signify basically; ~ **over,** overflow by boiling; ~**'ing** (**hot**), (colloq.) very hot; **keep the pot** ~**ing,** get a living. **2.** *v.t.* Bring (liquid, vessel) to temperature at which it boils; manufacture (soap etc.) thus; subject to heat of boiling water, cook thus; ~ **down,** reduce by boiling (lit. or fig.); ~**ed shirt,** dress shirt with starched front; ||~**ed sweet,** sweetmeat made of boiled sugar. [ME, f. AF *boiller*, OF *boillir*, f. L *bullire* to bubble (*bulla* bubble)]
boil[3] *n.* Boiling, boiling-point, (*on, at, to, the boil*). [f. prec.]
boi'ler *n.* In vbl senses (*soap-boiler*); vessel for boiling, esp. for making steam under pressure; water-tank attached to fire etc. in house; metal tub for boiling laundry; vegetable, fowl, etc., suited to boiling; ~**-plate,** rolled steel for making boilers, *(fig.) stereotyped writings esp. as syndicated for newspapers; ~ **suit,** one-piece garment combining overalls and shirt. [f. BOIL[2] + -ER[1]]
boi'lĭng *n.* In vbl senses; **the whole** ~, (sl.) the whole lot; ~**-point,** temperature at which liquid (esp. water) boils, (fig.) high excitement. [f. BOIL[2] + -ING[1]]
boi'sterous *a.* Violent, rough, (wind, sea, behaviour, speech, persons); noisily cheerful; hence ~LY[2] *adv.*, ~NESS *n.* [var. of ME *boistous*, of unkn. orig.]
bō'las *n.* (as *sing.* or *pl.*) S. Amer. etc. missile consisting of balls connected by a strong cord (when thrown bringing down quarry by entangling limbs). [Sp. & Port., pl. of *bola* ball]
bōld *a.* **1.** Courageous, enterprising, confident; forward, immodest; **make** (**so**) ~ (**as**), presume, venture, (*to* do). **2.** Vigorous, free, well--marked, clear, (*bold imagination, drawing, description, features, headland*, etc.). **3.** ~(**-face, -faced**), (of type) having a heavy or conspicuous face, as **bōld** in this entry. **4.** Hence ~'LY[2] *adv.*, ~'NESS *n.* [OE *bald*, = OS, OHG *bald*, ON *ballr* dangerous f. Gmc **balthaz*]
bōle[1] *n.* Stem or trunk of tree. [ME, f. ON *bolr*, perh. rel. to BALK[1]]
bōle[2] *n.* Fine compact earthy clay. [f. LL BOLUS]
bolĕ'ction *a.* & *n.* (Moulding) placed above or round panel etc. [18th c.; orig. unkn.]
boler'ō (-ār'ō) *n.* (*pl.* ~**s**). Spanish dance; music for it; (*or* bŏ'lerō) woman's short open jacket with or without sleeves. [Sp.]
bō'līde *n.* Large meteor, fire-ball. [F, f. L f. Gk *bolis -idos* missile]
bōll *n.* Rounded seed-vessel, as in flax or cotton; ~**-weevil,** small destructive insect infesting cotton-plant. [ME, f. MDu. *bolle*; see BOWL[1]]
bŏ'llard *n.* Post on ship or quay for securing ropes to; short post on traffic island. [ME, perh. f. ON *bolr* BOLE[1] + -ARD]
bŏ'llĭx[1] *v.t.* (vulg.) Bungle, confuse. [f. foll.]
bŏ'llĭx[2], **bŏ'llocks.** Vars. of BALLOCKS.
***bolō'gna** (-nya) *n.* = *Bologna* SAUSAGE. [f. *B*~ in Italy]
bolŏ'mèter *n.* Electrical instrument for measuring heat radiation; hence **bolŏ'**METRY *n.*, **bŏlomĕ'tr**IC *a.* [f. Gk *bolē* ray + -O- + -METER]
bolō'ney, balō'ney, *n.* **1.** (sl.) Humbug, nonsense. **2.** *Bologna SAUSAGE. [20th c.; orig. uncert.]
Bŏ'lshèv|ĭk *n.* (Hist.) advocate of proletarian dictatorship in Russia by soviets, Russian communist; (pop.) socialist revolutionary; hence ~ISM (3) *n.*, ~IST (2) *n.*, ~IZE (3) *v.t.* [Russ., = member of majority, one who (in 1903) favoured extreme measures, f. *bol'she* greater]
Bŏ'lshĭe, -shy̆, *n.* & *a.* (sl.) **1.** *n.* Bolshevik. **2.** *a.* Of Bolsheviks; left-wing; uncooperative. [abbr.]
bō'lster[1] *n.* Long (esp. under-)pillow across bed or couch; pad or support in machine or instrument. [OE, = OHG *bolstar*, ON *bolstr* f. Gmc **bolstraz* (**bolg-* swell)]
bō'lster[2] *v.t.* ~ (**up**), support with bolster, (fig.) prop, aid. [f. prec.]
bō'lster[3] *n.* Chisel for cutting bricks. [20th c.; orig. uncert.]
bōlt[1] *n.* Short heavy arrow of crossbow (**my** ~ **is shot,** I have done all I can); discharge of lightning (~ **from the blue,** complete surprise); door-fastening of sliding bar and staple, sliding piece of lock or rifle-breech; metal pin with head for holding things together, usu. riveted or with nut; (as measure) roll of fabric, bundle of osiers; ~**-rope** (round sail-edge to prevent tearing). [OE, = MLG *bolte*, OHG *bolz*; ult. orig. unkn.]
bōlt[2] *v.* **1.** *v.i.* & *t.* Dart off or away, (of horse) escape from control; run to seed; (cause fox, rabbit, etc. to) escape from hole or burrow; gulp down hastily without chewing; *(Polit.)

break away, refuse to support party or policy; ~-**hole,** (fig.) means of escape. **2.** *v.t.* Fasten (door etc.) with bolt, keep *in* or *out* by bolting door; fasten together with bolts; ~-**on** *a.*, (of car parts etc.) able to be fixed thus. [f. prec.]

bōlt[3] *n.* Act of bolting (see prec.); sudden start; running away. [f. prec.]

bōlt[4] *adv.* ~ **upright,** rigidly erect (like a bolt). [f. BOLT[1]]

bōlt[5], **boult,** (bōlt) *v.t.* Sift; investigate. [ME f. OF *bul(e)ter*, prob. f. **bureter* = It. *burattare*, of unkn. orig.]

bō'lter *n.* In vbl senses; horse apt to bolt; (or **bou'lter** *pr.* same) sieve, sifting machine. [f. BOLT[2,5] + -ER[1]]

bō'lus *n.* Large pill; quantity of food at moment of swallowing. [LL, f. Gk *bōlos* clod]

bō'ma *n.* (E. Afr.) Defensible enclosure; police or military post; magistrate's office. [Swahili]

bŏmb (-m) *n.* & *v.* **1.** *n.* High-explosive or incendiary material or smoke or gas etc. in container fired from gun, or thrown or deposited by hand, or dropped from aircraft, and exploded by impact or by time mechanism; ATOMIC *bomb*, HYDROGEN *bomb*; **the** ~, atomic or hydrogen bomb as supreme weapon; **like a** ~, (colloq.) very successfully. **2.** Mass of lava discharged from volcano; (sl.) large sum of money; (sl.) drugged cigarette; *(colloq.) a failure. **3.** ~-**bay,** compartment in aircraft to hold bombs; ~-**disposal,** removal and detonation of unexploded and delayed-action bombs; ~-**happy,** (colloq.) suffering from shell-shock; *bomb*-PROOF[2]; ~'**shell,** artillery bomb (esp. fig., cause of great surprise; *news came as a bombshell* etc.); ~-**sight,** device in aircraft for aiming bombs; ~-**site,** area where buildings have been destroyed by bombs. **4.** *v.t.* Attack with bombs; ~ **out,** (esp. in *p.p.*) drive by bombs out of a building etc. **5.** *v.i.* Throw or drop bombs; (sl.) fail; hence ~'ER[1] (-m*er*) *n.*, (esp.) aircraft used for bombing. [f. F *bombe* f. It. *bomba* f. L f. Gk *bombos* hum]

bŏmbar'd *v.t.* Attack with heavy guns; (Phys.) subject (substance) to stream of high-speed particles; (fig.) assail persistently with abuse, argument, etc.; hence ~MENT *n.* [f. F *bombarder* (*bombarde* f. med. L *bombarda* stone-throwing engine prob. f. L *bombus*; see prec.)]

bŏmbardier' *n.* **1.** ||Artillery non-commissioned officer. **2.** *Aimer and releaser of bombs from aircraft. **3.** ~ **beetle** (audibly releasing unpleasant vapour when alarmed). [F, f. as prec.; see -IER]

bŏ'mbardon *n.* (Mus.) Low-pitched brass wind instrument; organ stop imitating this. [f. It. *bombardone* (*bombardo* bassoon, *-one*; see -OON)]

bombasine. See BOMBAZINE.

bŏ'mbast *n.* Pompous or extravagant language; hence **bŏmbă'st**IC *a.*, **bŏmbă'st**ICALLY *adv.* [f. earlier *bombace* f. F f. med. L *bombax -acis* alt. f. *bombyx*; see BOMBAZINE]

Bŏmbay dŭ'ck *n.* Bummalo, esp. as relish. [corrupt. of *bombil*; see BUMMALO]

bŏ'mbazine, -sine, (-zēn) *n.* Twilled dress-material of worsted with or without silk or cotton, esp. black kind formerly much used for mourning. [f. F *bombasin* f. med. L *bombacinum* f. LL *bombycinus* silken (*bombyx -ycis* silk or silk-worm f. Gk *bombux*)]

bombe (bawṅb) *n.* (Cookery). Cone-shaped or cup-shaped dish or confection, freq. frozen. [F, = BOMB]

bomber. See BOMB 5.

bŏ'mbĭlāte, bŏ'mbĭnāte, *vbs. i.* (literary). Hum, buzz. [f. med. L *bombilare, bombinare* buzz f. L *bombus* (see BOMB) + -ATE[3]]

bŏmbōr'a *n.* (Austral.) Dangerous sea area with waves breaking over submerged reef. [Aboriginal]

bōna fī'dė *a.* & *adv.* Genuine(ly), sincere(ly). [L, abl. sing. of foll.]

bōna fī'dēs (-z) *n.* (Law). Honest intention, sincerity. [L, = good faith]

bonă'nza *n.* & *a.* **1.** *n.* Prosperity, good luck; large output (esp. of mines); unexpected success (orig. in mining), run of luck. **2.** *a.* Greatly prospering or productive. [orig. U.S. f. Sp., = fair weather f. L *bonus* good]

bona vacantia (bōn*a* vakă'ntĭ*a*) *n.* (Law). Goods without apparent owner. [L, = ownerless goods]

bŏ'n-bŏn *n.* Piece of confectionery, sweet. [F (*bon* good f. L *bonus*)]

||**bŏnce** *n.* Large playing-marble; (sl.) head. [19th c.; orig. unkn.]

bŏnd[1] *n.* **1.** Thing that ties another down or together; (in *pl.*) thing restraining bodily freedom, imprisonment, (*burst* one's *bonds*). **2.** Restraining or uniting force; adhesion; (Chem.) linkage between atoms in a molecule. **3.** Binding engagement, agreement, (*his word is as good as his bond*); deed by which person binds himself to pay another; government's or public company's documentary promise to repay borrowed money, usu. with interest, debenture; insurance policy; ~ (**paper**), high-quality writing-paper suitable for bonds; ~-**washing,** dividend-stripping. **4. In** ~, (of goods) stored under charge of Customs in 'bonded warehouse' till importer pays duty. **5.** (Bricklaying). One of various methods (*English bond, Flemish bond*, etc.) of holding wall together by making bricks overlap; ~'**stone,** stone or brick running through wall. [ME var. of BAND[1]]

bŏnd[2] *v.t.* Bind together (bricks etc., see prec.; resin etc. with fibres); connect with bond; put goods into bond. [f. prec.]

bŏnd[3] *a.* (arch.) In serfdom or slavery; hence ~'**maid,** ~'**man,** ~'**servant,** ~'**service,** ~'**slave,** ~'**woman.** [adj. use of ME *bonde* f. OE *bonda* husbandman f. ON *bóndi* = *bóandi*, part. of *búa, bóa* dwell]

bŏ'ndage *n.* Serfdom, slavery; subjection to constraint, influence, obligation, etc. [ME, f. AL *bondagium*; see prec. and -AGE; infl. by BOND[1]]

bŏ'ndėd *a.* (Of goods) placed in bond; (of warehouse) for such goods; (of debt) secured by bonds; (of material) reinforced by or cemented to another. [f. BOND[1] + -ED[2]]

bŏ'nds|man (-z-) *n.* (*pl.* ~**men**). Slave (lit. or fig.). [var. of *bondman* (BOND[3]) as though f. *bond's* gen. of BOND[1]]

bōne[1] *n.* **1.** One of the pieces of hard tissue making up vertebrate animal's skeleton; (in *pl.*) the body (**feel in** one's ~**s,** feel sure; **make old** ~**s,** live to old age), its remains (*his bones were laid*); body's hard, solid, or essential part (*flesh and bone*; **bare** ~**s,** mere essentials; **close to** or **near the** ~, (1) destitute, (2) indecent; **to the** ~, penetratingly, to the bare minimum; **work** one's **fingers to the** ~, work very hard); (Austral.) bone used by Aboriginals in spells to cause sickness or death (*point the bone*). **2.** Material of which bones consist; similar substance, e.g. ivory, dentine, whalebone; thing made of bone, e.g. domino; (in *pl.*) dice, castanets; strip of stiff substance in corset etc. **3.** Subject of dispute (*bone of contention*; *bone to pick with someone*); **make no** ~**s,** not hesitate or scruple. **4.** ~ **china,** (made of clay mixed with bone ash); ~-**dry,** quite dry; *~'**fish,** large game-fish with many small bones; ~'**head**(**ed**), (sl.) stupid (person); ~ **idle, lazy,** utterly idle or lazy; ~-**meal,** crushed or ground bones used esp. as fertilizer; ~-**oil,** dark oil got by carbonizing bones; **~-seeking,** (Med.) tending to be deposited in the bones; **~-setter,** one who sets broken or dislocated bones, esp. without being qualified surgeon; **~-shaker,** old shaky vehicle, (Hist.) bicycle without rubber tyres; *bone* SPAVIN; **~ weary,** utterly weary; **~-yard,** (sl.) cemetery. [OE *bān*, = OS *bēn*, OHG, ON *bein* f. Gmc **bainam*]

bōne[2] *v.t.* **1.** Take out the bones from (meat, fish). **2.** Stiffen with bone. **3.** (sl.) Steal; ***~ up on,** study intensively. [f. prec.; sense 3 perh. diff. wd]

bō'ner *n.* (sl.) Stupid mistake. [f. BONE[1] + -ER[1]]

bŏ'nfīre *n.* Large open-air fire to celebrate event (‖**B~ Night,** 5 Nov.; cf. GUY[2]) or as signal; fire for consuming rubbish (**make a ~ of,** destroy). [earlier *bonefire* f. BONE[1] (bones being the chief material formerly used) + FIRE[1]]

bŏ'ngō[1] (-nggō) *n.* (*pl.* same *or* **~s**). Large striped African antelope. [cf. Bangi *mbangani*, Lingala *mongu*]

bŏ'ngō[2] (-nggō) *n.* (*pl.* **~s** *or* **~es**). One of pair of small drums usu. held between knees and played with fingers. [Amer. Sp. *bongó*]

bonhomie (bŏ'nomē) *n.* Geniality; good-natured friendliness. [F (*bonhomme* good fellow, *-ie* = -Y[1])]

bŏ'nhomous (-nom-) *a.* Showing *bonhomie*. [f. prec. + -OUS]

Bŏ'nĭfāce *n.* Keeper of inn etc. [character in Farquhar's *Beaux' Stratagem* (1707)]

bŏ'n|ĭsm *n.* Doctrine that the world is good, but not the best possible; so **~IST** (2) *n.* [f. L *bonus* good + -ISM]

bŏni'tō (-ē'-) *n.* (*pl.* **~s**). Large mackerel-like fish. [Sp.]

‖**bŏ'nkers** (-z) *a.* (sl.) Crazy. [20th c.; orig. unkn.]

bon mot (bawṅ mō'; *or* bŏn-) *n.* (*pl.* ***bons mots*** *pr.* same *or* -mō'z). Witty saying. [F]

bonne bouche (bŏn bōō'sh) *n.* (*pl.* **~s** *or* ***bonnes bouches,*** *pr.* same). Titbit, esp. to end up with. [F (*bonne* fem. good, *bouche* mouth)]

bŏ'nnėt *n.* **1.** (Man's) round brimless Scotch cap (BEE *in* one's *bonnet*); woman's or child's outdoor head-dress with strings; Amer. Indian's ceremonial head-dress; **~ *rouge*** (F, *pr.* bŏnā rōō'zh), red cap as revolutionary symbol. **2.** (Naut.) additional canvas laced to sail-foot; cowl of chimney etc.; protective cap in various machines, ‖hinged cover over engine of motor vehicle; **~-head,** = SHOVEL-*head* (1); **~-monkey,** Ind. macaque with bonnet-like tuft of hair; hence **~ED**[2] *a.* [ME, f. OF *bonet* short for *chapel de bonet* cap of some kind of material (med. L *bonetus*)]

bŏ'nn|ȳ *a.* **1.** (chiefly Sc. & N. Engl.) Comely. **2.** Healthy-looking; pleasing. **3.** Hence **~ĭLY**[2] *adv.* [16th c.; perh. f. F *bon* good]

bŏ'nsai (-sī) *n.* (Method of cultivating) artificially dwarfed potted plant or small tree. [Jap.]

bŏ'nspiel *n.* (esp. Sc.) Curling-match (usu. between two clubs). [16th c., perh. f. LG]

bŏ'nt(e)bŏk *n.* (S. Afr.) Reddish white-faced antelope. [Afrik. (*bont* spotted, *bok* BUCK[1])]

bon ton (bawṅ taw'ṅ) *n.* (arch.) Good breeding; the fashionable world. [F, lit. good tone]

bō'nus *n.* Something to the good, into the bargain; extra dividend or issue to shareholders of company, distribution of profits to insurance-policy-holders, gratuity to employees beyond their normal pay. [joc. or ignorant use of L *bonus*, *bonum* good (thing)]

bon vivant (bawṅ vē'vahṅ) *n.* Gourmand. [F, lit. good liver (*vivre* to live)]

bon viveur (bawṅ vēver') *n.* One who lives luxuriously. [pseudo-F]

bō'nȳ *a.* Of or like bone(s); big-boned with little flesh; (of fish) having bones rather than cartilage. [f. BONE[1] + -Y[2]]

bŏnze *n.* Japanese or Chinese Buddhist priest. [F, or f. Port. *bonzo* perh. f. Jap. *bonzō* f. Chin. *fan seng* religious person, or f. Jap. *bō-zi* f. Chin. *fa-sze* teacher of the law]

bŏ'nzer *a.* (Austral. sl.) Excellent, first-rate. [perh. f. BONANZA]

bōō *int.*, *n.*, & *v.t.* & *i.* expr., (make) sound of, disapproval or contempt (**can't say ~ to a goose,** is very shy or timid); jeer at (speaker, performer, announcement, etc.). [imit.]

bōōb *n.*, & *v.i.* (sl.) **1.** Simpleton; (make) mistake. **2.** *n.* (in *pl.*; prob. f. BUB[1]). Woman's breasts. [abbr. of BOOBY]

bōō'bōō *n.* (sl.) Mistake. [f. prec.]

bōō'bŏŏk *n.* (Austral.) Medium-sized brown spotted owl. [imit.]

bōō'bȳ *n.* **1.** Silly or stupid or childish person; small gannet. **2.** ***~ hatch,** (sl.) mental hospital; **~ prize,** awarded to last competitor or lowest scorer in contest of any kind; **~ trap,** thing placed on top of door ajar to fall on first opener, (Mil.) apparently harmless device concealing explosive charge designed to go off when tampered with; **~-trap** *v.t.*, place booby trap(s) in or on. [prob. f. Sp. *bobo* (in both senses 1) f. L *balbus* stammering]

bōō'dle *n.* (sl.) Money, esp. for political bribery. [f. Du. *boedel* possessions]

bōōgĭe-wōō'gĭe (-gĭ-; -gĭ) *n.* Style of playing blues on piano, marked by persistent bass rhythm. [20th c.; orig. unkn.]

bŏŏk[1] *n.* **1.** Portable written or printed work filling a number of sheets fastened together, usu. with sheets sewn or pasted hingewise and enclosed in cover (**closed ~,** thing of which one has no understanding); literary composition that would fill such a set of sheets (or several) if printed; telephone directory; (colloq.) magazine. **2.** Anything from which one may learn (**throw the ~ at,** make all possible charges against); imaginary record, list, etc., (**~ of fate,** future as being predetermined; **~ of life,** list of those who shall be saved); **the (good) ~,** the Bible (*swear on the book*; *people of the B~*, Jews); main division of literary work or of Bible; **~ (of words)** = LIBRETTO; script of play. **3.** Back-hinged set of blank sheets for writing accounts, notes, exercises, etc., in; (in *pl.*) society's records, trader's accounts; bets on a horse-race etc. or at a race-meeting (*make a book*; **in my ~,** as I see the matter; **won't suit my ~,** is inconvenient to me); set of tickets, stamps, matches, cheques, pieces of cloth, six tricks at cards, etc., bound up or collected. **4. Bring to ~,** call to account; **in** person's **bad** or **black, good, ~s,** in disfavour, favour, with him; **not in the ~,** disallowed; **on the ~s,** in list of members etc.; **read** person **like a ~,** understand his motives etc. fully; **speak by the ~** (with correct information); **speak** or **talk like a ~** (in formal phrases); **speak without ~,** give facts from memory; **take a leaf out of** person's **~,** imitate him. **5. ~'binder, -ding,** binder, binding, of books; **~'case** (-k-k-), case containing shelves for books; **~ club,** society whose members can buy selected books on special terms; **~-ends,** pair of usu. ornamental props to keep row of books upright; **~'keeper, -ping,** (-k-k-) one who keeps, (art or business of) keeping, accounts of trader, public office, etc.; **~'land,** (Hist.) area of common land granted by charter to private owner; **~-learned,** knowing books (but lacking practical experience); **~-learning** or **-lore,** mere theory; **~'maker, ~'making,** (1) compiler, compiling, of books (esp. for mercenary motives), (2) professional betting (man); **~'man,** literary man; **~'mark(er)**, strip of leather, paper, etc., to mark place in book; ***~'mobile** (-ēl), mobile library; **~ page,** (1) page of book, (2) page of newspaper etc. on which reviews of books appear; **~-plate,** ex-libris; ||**~-post,** transmission of books by post at especially low rates; **~-rest,** adjustable support for open book on table; **~'seller,** dealer in books; **~'shop** (where books are sold); ||**~'stall** (for sale of books out of doors or in station etc.); ***~'store,** bookshop; ||**~ token,** voucher for sum of money to buy book(s); **~-trough,** V-shaped rack for display of titles of books on table etc.; **~ value,** value of a commodity as entered in firm's books (opp. *market value*); **~'work,** study of books (opp. *practical work*); **~'worm,** larva of moth or beetle eating its way through books, (fig.) person devoted to reading. **6.** Hence ~'IE *n.*, (colloq.) bookmaker (2); ~'ISH[1] *a.*, addicted to reading books, studious, getting knowledge from books only, literary rather than colloquial; ~'LET *n.*, small book (usu. paper-covered). [OE *bōc*, = OHG *buoh*, ON *bók* f. Gmc **bōks*, usu. taken to be cogn. w. BEECH]

boo͝k[2] *v.* **1.** *v.t.* Enter in book or list; engage (seat etc.) in advance, (guest, supporter, etc.) for some occasion; enter name of (person engaging seat, suspect, etc.); issue railway etc. ticket to (whence **~'ing-clerk, -hall, -office**); (in *p.p.*, sl.) caught, unable to escape. **2.** *v.i.* Obtain ticket for journey etc.; **~ in,** register at hotel etc. [OE *bōcian* (as prec.)]

boo͝'ksy̆ *a.* (colloq.) Having literary or bookish pretensions. [f. pl. of BOOK[1] + -Y[2]]

Boo͞'lėan *a.* **~ algebra** etc., abstract system of postulates and symbols applicable to logical problems. [f. G. *Boole*, Engl. mathematician d. 1864 + -AN]

boo͞m[1] *n.* Long pole with one end fixed, to support sail-foot, camera, microphone, etc.; floating barrier of timber across river or harbour mouth. [Du., = BEAM[1]]

boo͞m[2] *v.i.*, & *n.* (Make, speak etc. with) deep resonant sound; hum, buzz; SONIC *boom*. [imit.]

boo͞m[3] *v.i.*, & *n.* (Esp. of commercial ventures, prices, etc.) (show) sudden activity or development; **~ town,** town undergoing sudden growth due to boom; hence ~'LET *n.* [19th c.; U.S. wd, perh. f. prec. (cf. *make things hum*)]

boo͞'mer *n.* Large male kangaroo; N. Amer. mountain beaver; large wave. [f. BOOM[2] + -ER[1]]

boo͞'merăng *n.*, & *v.i.* **1.** *n.* Australian thin curved hardwood missile that can be thrown so as to return to its thrower; (fig.) scheme etc. that recoils on its author. **2.** *v.i.* Act as a boomerang; (fig.) recoil on originator. [Aboriginal name, perh. modified]

boo͞'mslăng *n.* (S. Afr.) Large tree-snake. [Afrik. (*boom* tree, *slang* snake)]

boo͞n[1] *n.* Request, thing asked for; favour, gift; blessing, advantage. [ME, orig. = prayer f. ON *bón* f. Gmc **bōniz*, of unkn. orig.]

boo͞n[2] *a.* Congenial, jolly, (*boon companion*). [ME, f. OF *bon* f. L *bonus* good]

***boo͞'ndŏck** *n.* (sl., usu. in *pl.*) Rough or isolated country. [f. Tagalog *bundok* mountain]

***boo͞'ndŏggle** *n.*, & *v.i.* (Engage in) trivial or unnecessary work. [20th c.; orig. unkn.]

boor *n.* Clumsy or ill-bred person; hence ~'ISH[1] *a.* [f. LG *būr* or Du. *boer* farmer; cf. BOWER[3]]

boo͞st *v.t.*, & *n.* **1.** *v.t.* (colloq.) Push from below; assist. **2.** Increase reputation, value, etc., of (person, scheme, commodity, etc.) by praise, advertising, etc. **3.** Raise (voltage in electric circuit etc.); amplify (radio signal). **4.** *n.* Act or process of boosting; scheme of advertisement; resulting advance in value etc. [19th c. U.S. wd; orig. unkn.]

boo͞'ster *n.* Device for boosting voltage or signal strength; auxiliary engine or rocket to give initial acceleration; (Med.) dose increasing or renewing effect of earlier one. [f. prec. + -ER[1]]

boo͞t[1] *n.*, & *v.t.* **1.** *n.* Outer foot-covering, esp. of leather, coming (*well) above ankle; covering to protect lower part of horse's leg; **~ and saddle** [corrupt. of F *boute-selle* place saddle], cavalry signal to mount; DIE[2] *in* one's *boots*; **get** or **give the ~**, (sl.) be dismissed, dismiss, from employment; HEART *in* one's *boots*; **like old ~s,** (sl.) tremendously; **put the ~ in,** kick brutally, take decisive action; *too* BIG *for* one's *boots*; **the ~ is on the other leg** or **foot,** truth or responsibility is just the other way round; **you bet your ~s,** (sl.) it is quite certain; hence ~'ED[2] *a.* **2.** (Hist.) Instrument of torture encasing the foot. **3.** (Hist.) luggage-receptacle in coach under guard's and coachman's seats; ||luggage-receptacle at back (or occas. front) of motor car. **4.** ***~'black,** shoeblack; **~-faced,** grim or expressionless; **~'jack,** contrivance for pulling boots off; **~'lace,** cord or leather strip for lacing boots; **~'leg,** smuggle(d) (esp. of liquor); **~'licker,** toady; **~'straps,** (fig.) unaided effort (*raise oneself by one's own bootstraps*); **~-tree,** mould for keeping boot in shape. **5.** *v.t.* Kick; (sl.) kick or drive (person) *out* (of house, of employment, etc.). [ME, f. ON *bóti* or f. OF *bote*, of unkn. orig.]

boo͞t[2] *n.* **To ~**, as well, to the good, additionally. [OE *bōt*, = OS *bōta*, OHG *buoza*, ON *bót*, Goth. *bōta* f. Gmc **bōtō* remedy (**bōt-*, **bāt-*; cf. BETTER[1], BEST)]

boo͞t[3] *v.t.* (arch.; usu. *impers.* and abs.). Do good, avail (*what boots it to repeat how time is slipping underneath our feet?*). [ME, f. prec.]

boo͞tee' *n.* Woman's short lined boot; infant's woollen etc. boot. [f. BOOT[1] + -EE; cf. *coatee*]

boo͞th (-dh) *n.* Temporary shelter of canvas etc.; covered stall in market, tent at fair, etc.; (partly) enclosed area for telephoning, voting, sitting in restaurant, etc. [ME, f. Old East Norse **bóth* (*bóa* dwell; cf. BOND[3], BOWER[1])]

boo͞'tlėss *a.* Unavailing. [OE *bōtlēas*; see BOOT[2], -LESS]

||**boo͞ts** *n.* Hotel servant who cleans boots and shoes, carries luggage, etc. [pl. of BOOT[1]]

boo͞'ty̆ *n.* Plunder or profit acquired in common and to be divided; gain, prize. [ME, f. MLG *būte*, *buite* exchange, of uncert. orig.]

boo͞z|e *v.i.*, & *n.* **1.** *v.i.* Drink (alcoholic liquor) habitually or excessively. **2.** *n.* (Esp. alcoholic) drink; drinking-bout. **3.** Hence ~'ER[1] *n.*, one who boozes, ||(sl.) public house; ~'Y[2] *a.*, addicted to drink, intoxicated. [earlier *bouse*, *bowse*, f. MDu. *būsen* drink to excess]

bŏp *n.* = BEBOP; hence **~'per**[1] (3), ~'STER, *ns.* [abbr.]

bō-pee'p *n.* Game of hiding and suddenly reappearing, played with young child. [f. BO[1] + PEEP[2]]

bor'a[1] *n.* Cold dry N.E. wind blowing in the upper Adriatic. [It. dial., f. L *boreas* north wind; see BOREAL]

bor'a[2] *n.* (Austral.) Rite of admission to manhood among Aborigines. [Aboriginal]

borā'cic *a.* Of borax (**~ acid,** boric acid). [f. med. L BORAX *boracis* + -IC]

bŏ'rage (*or* bŭ'-) *n.* Blue-flowered hairy-leaved plant used in salads etc. [f. OF *bourrache* f. med. L *borrago* f. Arab. *'abu 'āraḳ* father of sweat (from its use as a diaphoretic)]

bor'ăk *n.* (Austral. & N.Z. sl.) Nonsense; banter. [Aboriginal Austral.]

bor'āte *n.* Salt of boric acid. [f. BORIC + -ATE[1]]

bŏr'ăx *n.* Sodium borate as native deposit or purified white powder or crystals. [ME f. OF *boras* f. med. L *borax* f. Arab. *būrak* f. Pers. *būrah*]
bŏr'azŏn *n.* Hard oxidation-resistant form of boron nitride. [f. BORON + AZO- nitrogen + *-on*]
bŏrborў'gm|us *n.* (*pl.* ~i *pr.* -ī). Rumbling of gas in intestines; hence ~IC *a.* [mod. L f. Gk]
Bŏrdeau'x (-dō') *n.* (*pl.* same *pr.* -ōz). Red (claret) or white wine esp. from district of Bordeaux; ~ **mixture,** fungicide for fruit-trees etc. [~ in S.W. France]
***bŏrdĕ'l, *bŏrdĕ'llō** (*pl.* **-os**), *ns.* Brothel. [ME, f. OF *bordel* small farm, dim. of *borde* f. Gallo-Rom. **borda* f. Frank. **bord* BOARD¹]
bŏr'der¹ *n.* **1.** Side, edge, boundary or part near it; frontier of country; **the B~,** boundary and adjoining districts between England and Scotland, N. Ireland and Irish Republic, U.S. and Mexico, etc.; **B~ terrier,** small rough-haired kind. **2.** Continuous bed round garden or part of it; distinct edging for strength or ornament or definition round anything. **3. ~land,** district on either side of border, (fig.) intermediate condition (e.g. between sleeping and waking), debatable ground; **~line,** (*n.*) line of demarcation, (*a.*) on the borderline (*~line case,* e.g. one verging on obscenity or insanity). [ME f. OF *bordure,* f. Rom. **bordare* (**bordus* f. Gmc **bordhaz*; cf. BOARD¹, -URE)]
bŏr'der² *v.t.* & *i.* Put or be a border to; ~ (**on**), adjoin, resemble, come close to being. [ME, f. prec.]
bŏrdereau' (-ō') *n.* (*pl.* **~x** *pr.* -z). Memorandum of contents, docket. [F]
bŏr'derer *n.* Dweller on or near frontier, esp. that between England and Scotland. [f. BORDER¹ + -ER¹ (4)]
bŏr'dūre *n.* (Her.) Border round edge of shield. [ME form of BORDER¹]
bŏre¹ *v.* **1.** *v.t.* Make hole in, usu. with revolving tool; hollow out (tube etc.) evenly; make (hole, one's way), by boring, persistent pushing, or excavation. **2.** *v.i.* (Of racehorse) push another horse out of the way; drill a well (for oil etc.). [OE *borian,* = OHG *borōn,* ON *bora* f. Gmc **borōn*]
bŏre² *n.* Hollow of firearm barrel or of cylinder in internal combustion engine; diameter of this, calibre; ~(**'hole**), deep narrow hole made in earth to find water etc. [partly f. prec., partly f. ON *bora* borehole f. Gmc **borōn*]
bŏre³ *n.* Nuisance (usu. as *pred.*); tiresome or dull person. [18th c.; orig. unkn.; early contexts suggest F deriv.]
bŏre⁴ *v.t.* Weary by tedious talk or dullness. [app. f. contemporary BORE³]
bŏre⁵ *n.* Tide-wave with steep front moving up some estuaries and bays; eagre. [ME, perh. f. ON *bára* wave]
bŏre⁶. See BEAR³.
bŏr'ėal *a.* Of the North or the Arctic or the north wind. [ME, f. F *boréal* or f. LL *borealis* f. L f. Gk *Boreas* god of north wind; see -AL]
bŏr'ecōle (bŏr'k-) *n.* = KALE. [f. Du. *boerenkool* peasant's cabbage]
bŏr'edom (bŏr'd-) *n.* Being bored, ennui. [f. BORE³ + -DOM]
bŏr'er *n.* In vbl senses; boring worm, mollusc, or insect. [f. BORE¹ + -ER¹]
bŏr'ĭc *a.* Of boron; ~ **acid** (derived from borax and used as mild antiseptic). [f. BORON + -IC]
bŏrn *a.* Having come into existence by birth; destined to be (*born rich, tired, to be hanged, a poet*; *a ~ orator, an orator ~,* by natural ability); utter, hopeless, (*born fool, idiot*); (in comb.) born as (*English-born, first-born*); **~ again,** regenerate; *born and bred* (see BREED¹); **~ of,** owing origin to; **not ~ yesterday,** (fig.) far from foolish; **in all my ~ days,** (colloq.) in my life hitherto. [p.p. of BEAR³]
bŏrne. See BEAR³.
borné (bŏr'nā) *a.* Having limitations, of limited ideas, narrow-minded. [F]
Bŏr'nhōlm (-ōm) *n.* ~ **disease,** epidemic virus disease with intercostal pain. [~ in Denmark]
bŏro- *comb. form.* Boron, as: **boroflu'oride, borosi'licate,** etc., salts containing boron. [f. foll.]
bŏr'ŏn *n.* Non-metallic solid element (brown amorphous powder or black crystals). [f. BORAX w. ending of *carbon,* which it resembles in some respects]
bŏrō'nĭa *n.* (Austral.) Sweet-scented shrub of genus *Boronia.* [f. F. *Borone,* It. botanist d. 1794 + -IA¹]
bo'rough (bŭ'ro) *n.* **1.** (Hist.) ||Town with corporation and privileges conferred by royal charter; town sending member(s) to parliament; ||**pocket ~,** (Hist.) borough where election was controlled by private person or family; ||**rotten ~,** (Hist.) borough no longer having real constituency. **2.** *Town or village; *one of five parts of New York City; *(in Alaska) county. [OE *burg, burh,* = OS *burg,* OHG *burug,* ON *borg,* Goth. *baurgs* f. Gmc **burgs* cogn. w. **bergan* shelter; cf. BURGH]
borough-E'nglĭsh (bŭroĭ'nggl-) *n.* (Hist.) Tenure in some parts of England whereby youngest son inherited all lands and tenements. [ME, f. AF (*tenure en*) *Burgh Engloys* English borough (tenure); so called as not existing in France]
bŏ'rrow (-ō) *v.t.* & *i.* Get temporary use of (money or property to be returned; *from* or *of* person); adopt, use without being the true or original owner or inventor, derive from another, import from an alien source; (Golf) (1) play ball uphill to roll back, (2) allow for wind or slope; **~ed light,** (1) reflected light, (2) internal window; *borrowed* PLUME¹*s* or *plumage*; **~ed time,** unexpected extension esp. of life; hence ~ER¹, ~ING¹ (2), *ns.* [OE *borgian* give a pledge (= OHG *borgēn* take heed) f. *borg* (= OS *borg*) pledge, f. root of Gmc **bergan* protect (cf. prec.)]
bŏrsch (-sh), **bŏrtsch** (-ch), *n.* Highly seasoned Russian or Polish soup of various ingredients including beetroot and cabbage. [f. Russ. *borshch*]
||**Bŏr'stal** *n.* Institution to which young offenders may be sent for reformative training. [~ in Kent]
bŏrt, boart, *n.* Diamond fragments made in cutting; diamond malformed in the making. [f. Du. *boort*]
bŏr'zoi *n.* Large Russian wolfhound with usu. white silky coat. [Russ. (*borzyi* swift)]
bŏ'scage, -kage, *n.* Masses of trees or shrubs; wooded scenery. [ME, f. OF *boscage* f. Gallo-Rom. **boscaticus* (**boscos*; cf. BUSH¹, -AGE)]
bŏsh¹ *n.* & *int.* (sl.) Nonsense, foolish talk. [f. Turk. *boş* empty]
bŏsh² *n.* Lower sloping part of blast-furnace shaft, from belly to hearth. [17th c.; orig. unkn.]
bō'sĭe (-zĭ) *n.* (Austral.) = GOOGLY. [f. B. J. T. *Bosanquet,* Engl. cricketer d. 1936 + -IE]
bŏ'skage. See BOSCAGE.
bŏ'skў *a.* Wooded, bushy. [f. ME *bosk* thicket + -Y²]
bō's'n. See BOAT¹*swain.*
bo'som (bŏŏ'z-) *n.* **1.** Person's breast; *(in *pl.*) woman's breasts; enclosure formed by breast and arms. **2.** Breast of dress, space between dress and breast; *shirt-front; surface of lake, sea, ground, etc.; enfolding relationship (*bosom of* one's *family, of the church*); the heart, thoughts, desires, etc. (~ **friend,** intimate); hence **~Y²** *a.,*

(of woman) having prominent bosom. [OE *bōsm*, = OS *bōsom*, OHG *buosam* f. WG **bōsm-*, perh. f. **bōhsm-* f. **bōg-* (cf. BOUGH)]

bō'sŏn (-z-) *n.* (Phys.) Particle obeying relations stated by Bose and Einstein, with integral spin. [f. S. N. *Bose*, Ind. physicist d. 1974 + -ON]

bŏss¹ *n.* Protuberance; round metal knob or stud on centre of shield or ornamental work; (Archit.) carved or sculptured projection at intersecting-point of ribs; (Geol.) large mass of igneous rock; (Mech.) enlarged part of shaft. [ME, f. OF *boce* f. Rom. **bokja*, **botja*, of unkn. orig.]

bŏss² *n.* (colloq.) ~**(-man)**, master, person in authority, overseer; *manager of political organization, whence ~'ISM (3) *n.*; hence ~'Y² *a.*, domineering. [19th c.; U.S. wd f. Du. *baas* master]

bŏss³ *v.t.* (sl.) Be master or manager of; give orders to (~ person **about**, continually give peremptory orders to him). [f. prec.]

||**bŏss⁴** *n.*, & *v.t.* **1.** *n.* (sl.) ~**(-shot)**, bad shot or guess, miss; bungle, mess; ~**-eyed**, (sl.) blind in one eye, cross-eyed, crooked, one-sided. **2.** *v.t.* (sl.) Miss, bungle. [19th c.; orig. unkn.]

bŏssa nō'va *n.* Brazilian dance like samba; music for it. [f. Port. *bossa* tendency + *nova* fem. of *novo* new]

Bŏ'ston *n.* ~ **terrier**, small smooth-haired terrier. [~ in Massachusetts]

bō'sun, bo'sun. See BOAT¹*swain*.

Bŏ'swĕll (-z-) *n.* Biographer like James ~ d. 1795, writer of Samuel Johnson's life; hence **Bŏswĕ'lli**AN (-z-) *a.*, ~ISM (3) *n.*, ~IZE (4) *v.i.*

bŏt(**t**) *n.* Parasitic worm infesting horses etc., larva of ~**-fly.** [prob. of LG orig.]

bot. *abbr.* bottle; bought.

bŏ'tan|y̆¹ *n.* Science of structure, physiology, classification, and distribution of plants; so **botă'ni**CAL, (arch.) **botă'ni**C, *adjs.*, ~IST (3) *n.*, ~IZE (2) *v.i.*, (esp.) study plants where they grow. [f. *botanic* f. F *botanique* or LL f. Gk *botanikos* (*botanē* plant); see -IC, -Y¹]

Bŏ'tany̆² *a.* & *n.* ~ **(wool)**, merino wool, esp. from Australia. [f. ~ *Bay*, New S. Wales, named from the variety of its flora]

botar̂'gō *n.* (*pl.* ~**es** *or* ~**s**). Relish of mullet or tunny roe. [f. It. *bottarga* f. Egypt. Arab. *baṭārikh* fish-roe, of Coptic orig.]

bŏtch *n.*, & *v.t.* & *i.* (Make a) clumsy patch; spoil(t) or bungle(d) work; repair badly. [ME, of unkn. orig.]

bōtĕ'l, boatĕ'l, *n.* Hotel for boat-owners; ship serving as hotel. [f. BOAT¹ + HOTEL]

bōth *a.*, *pron.*, & *adv.* **1.** *a.* & *pron.* The two (and not only one) (*both* (*the*) *brothers are dead*; *both* (*of the brothers*) *are dead*; *the brothers are both dead*); ||~ **ways,** (Racing) = EACH *way*; **have it** ~ **ways,** choose now one now the other of alternatives or contradictories to suit one's argument etc. **2.** *adv.* With equal truth in two (or arch. more) cases (*both brother and sister are dead*; *she is both dead and buried*; *both God and man and beast*). [ME, f. ON *báthir* etc. (= OS *bethia*, OHG *bēde*), extended form of base repr. by OE *bēgen* etc.]

bŏ'ther¹ (-dh-) *v.* & *int.* **1.** *v.t.* Give trouble to; worry; ~ one**self,** one's **head,** be anxious (*about*); **can't be** ~**ed,** will not make the effort needed. **2.** *v.i.* Worry or trouble oneself (*to* do, *about*); be concerned *with*. **3.** *v.t.* (subj.) & *int.* (colloq., expr. impatience). Confound, damn. [18th c., Anglo-Ir., perh. f. POTHER]

bŏ'ther² (-dh-) *n.* (Cause of) worry, fuss, minor trouble; worried state. [f. prec.]

bŏtherā'tion (-dh-) *n.* & *int.* **1.** *n.* = prec. **2.** *int.* = BOTHER¹. [f. BOTHER¹ + -ATION]

bŏ'thersome (-dh-) *a.* Annoying, troublesome. [f. BOTHER¹ + -SOME¹]

bŏ'thy̆, -ie, *n.* (Sc.) Hut, cottage; one-roomed building in which labourers are lodged. [18th c., orig. unkn.; perh. rel. to BOOTH]

bō'-tree *n.* Sacred pipal tree of India. [repr. Sinh. *bogaha* f. *bo* = Pali and Skr. *bodhi* perfect knowledge + *gaha* tree (Buddha's enlightenment having occurred beneath such a tree)]

bŏtt. See BOT.

bŏ'ttle¹ *n.* **1.** Narrow-necked vessel, usu. of glass or plastic for storing liquid; amount of liquid in it; act or habit of drinking alcoholic liquor (**on the** ~, addicted to drink; **over a** ~, while drinking); FEED¹*ing-bottle*; HOT¹*-water bottle*; metal cylinder for liquefied gas. **2.** ~**-brush,** cylindrical brush for cleaning bottles, plant with flower of this shape; ~**-fed,** fed with milk from feeding-bottle, not with mother's milk; ~**-glass,** coarse dark-green glass; ~**-green,** dark green; ~**-neck,** (fig.) narrow stretch or restricted outlet of road, anything obstructing an even flow of production etc.; ~**-nose,** swollen nose; ~**-nosed,** (of dolphin, whale) with bottle-shaped snout; ~**-opener,** device for opening bottles of beer etc.; ~**-party** (to which each guest brings bottle of wine etc.), drinking-party; ~**-tree,** Austral. tree with swollen bottle-shaped trunk; ~**-washer,** (colloq.) factotum, underling. [ME, f. OF *botele*, *botaille* f. med. L *butticula* dim. of LL *buttis* BUTT¹]

bŏ'ttle² *v.t.* Store in bottle(s); preserve (fruit etc.) in jars; (in *p.p.*, sl.) drunk; ~ **up,** conceal, restrain for a time, (resentment etc.), entrap or keep entrapped (enemy forces etc.). [f. prec.]

bŏ'ttom¹ *n.* & *a.* **1.** *n.* Lowest point or part, part on which thing rests (~ **up,** upside-down; ~**s up!,** call to drain one's glass); buttocks; seat (of chair); ~ **falls out,** collapse occurs; **knock** ~ **out of,** prove (thing) worthless. **2.** Ground under water of sea, lake, etc., (**go, send, to the** ~, sink; **touch** ~, reach bottom of water with feet, (fig.) be at the lowest or worst point or on firm facts), whence ~LESS *a.*, without bottom, baseless, inexhaustible, (*the* ~*less pit*, hell); low-lying land. **3.** Less honourable end of table, class, etc.; farthest or inmost point (*bottom of garden*, HEART, *bay*). **4.** Keel, horizontal part near keel, hull, ship esp. as cargo-carrier (*in British bottoms*). **5.** Basis, origin, (**be at the** ~ **of,** cause); essential character, reality, (**at** ~, basically, essentially; **get to the** ~ **of,** fully investigate and explain). **6.** *a.* Lowest, last (**bet** one's ~ **dollar,** stake all); ~ **dog,** = UNDERDOG; ~ **drawer,** ||(fig.) woman's store of clothes etc. in preparation for marriage; ||*bottom* GEAR; hence ~MOST (-m-m-) *a.* [OE *botm*, = OS *bodom* f. Gmc **buthm-*, **buthn-*]

bŏ'ttom² *v.* **1.** *v.t.* Put bottom to (saucepan, chair); touch bottom of, find the extent or real nature of; base (argument etc.) *on*. **2.** *v.i.* Reach or touch bottom; ~ **(out),** reach lowest level. [f. prec.]

bŏ'ttomry̆ *n.*, & *v.t.* **1.** *n.* System of lending money to shipowner for purposes of voyage on security of ship, lender losing the money if ship is lost. **2.** *v.t.* Pledge (ship) thus. [f. BOTTOM¹ = ship + -RY, after Du. *bodemerij*]

bŏ'tūlĭsm *n.* (Med.) Poisoning by a bacillus found esp. in infected sausages or tinned food etc. [f. G *botulismus* f. L *botulus* sausage; see -ISM (5)]

bou'clé (bo͞o'klā) *n.* Yarn of looped or curled ply; fabric of this. [F, = buckled, curled]

bou'doir (bo͞o'dwar̂) *n.* (Woman's) small private room. [F, lit. sulking-place (*bouder* sulk)]

bou'ffant (bo͞o'fahṅ) *a.* (Of dress, hair, etc.) puffed out. [F]

bougainvĭ'llaea (bo͞ogan-) *n.* Tropical plant of

genus *Bougainvillaea*, with large bright-coloured bracts almost concealing flowers. [f. L. A. de *Bougainville*, Fr. navigator d. 1811 + -A 1]

bough (bow) *n.* Tree-branch (esp. one of the chief branches). [OE *bōg*, *bōh*, = OHG *buog*, ON *bógr* shoulder of an animal f. Gmc **bōguz*]

bought. See BUY.

bou'ghten (baw'ten) *a.* (dial. & U.S.) Purchased at shop, opp. home-made. [var. p.p. of BUY]

bougie (bōō'zhē) *n.* Wax candle; thin flexible surgical instrument for exploring, dilating, etc., the passages of the body. [F, f. Arab. *Bujiya* Algerian town with wax trade]

bouillabai'sse (bōōyabā's) *n.* Rich fish-stew, orig. from Provence. [F]

bouilli (bōōyē') *n.* Stewed or boiled meat. [F, = boiled]

bouillon (bōō'yawn) *n.* Broth, thin soup. [F (*bouillir* to boil)]

bou'lder (bō'l-) *n.* Large water-worn or weather-worn stone; ~ **clay,** (Geol.) mixture of boulders etc. in clay as glacial formation. [short for *boulderstone*, ME f. Scand.]

bou'lė[1] *n.* Legislative body of ancient or modern Greece. [Gk *boulē* senate]

boule[2] (bōōl) *n.* French form of bowls, played on rough ground with usu. metal balls. [F, = BOWL[2]]

boule[3]**.** See BUHL.

bou'levard (bōō'-) *n.* Broad street with rows of trees along it; *broad main road. [F, f. G *bollwerk* BULWARK, orig. of promenade on demolished fortification]

boulle. See BUHL.

boult. See BOLT[5].

boulter. See BOLTER.

bounc|e[1] *v.i.* & *t.* **1.** (Cause to) rebound; (sl., of cheque) be returned by bank when there are no funds to meet it; *(sl.) dismiss. **2.** Throw oneself *about*; rush (noisily, angrily, etc.) *into* or *out of* (room), *in* or *out*; talk big; hustle (person) by bluff or assumptions *into* doing or *out of* (something). **3.** Hence ~'ING[2] *a.*, big and healthy, boisterous, ~'Y[2] *a.* [ME *bunsen* beat, thump, perh. imit., or f. LG *bunsen*, Du. *bons* thump]

bounce[2] *n.* Rebound(ing power); ejection; boast, exaggeration, swagger. [f. prec.]

bou'ncer *n.* In vbl senses; (sl.) chucker-out. [f. BOUNCE[1] + -ER[1]]

bound[1] *n.* Limit of territory (BEAT[1] *the bounds*); (usu. in *pl.*) limitation, restriction, (‖**out of ~s,** beyond limits set by rules of school etc.); hence ~'LESS *a.* [ME, f. AF *bounde*, OF *bonde* etc., f. med. L *bodina*, earlier *butina*, of unkn. orig.]

bound[2] *v.t.* Set bounds to, limit, (esp. in *pass.* w. *by*); be the boundary of. [f. prec.]

bound[3] *v.i.* (Of ball etc.) recoil from wall or ground, bounce; (of living thing, wave, etc.) spring, leap, advance lightly. [f. F *bondir* (orig. of sound) f. Rom. **bombitire* var. of LL *bombitare* f. L *bombus* hum]

bound[4] *n.* Springy movement upward or forward (*by* LEAP[2]*s and bounds*); (of ball etc.) recoil, bounce. [f. F *bond* (*bondir*; see prec.)]

bound[5] *a.* Ready to start or having started (*for*); moving in specified direction (*northbound*). [ME f. ON *búinn* p.p. of *búa* get ready; -*d* euphonic, or partly after foll.]

bound[6]**.** See BIND[1].

bou'ndarў *n.* Limit-line; (Cricket) hit to limit of field, scoring 4 or 6 runs; ~ **layer** (of fluid adjacent to body moving through it); ~ **rider,** (Austral. & N.Z.) rider round sheep or cattle station mending fences etc. [f. dial. *bounder* f. BOUND[2] + -ER[1], perh. after *limitary*]

bou'nden *a.* (Of duty etc.) obligatory. [arch. p.p. of BIND[1]]

bou'nder *n.* In vbl senses; (sl.) (ill-bred) person, cad. [f. BOUND[2,3] + -ER[1]]

bou'ntėous *a.* (rhet.) Beneficent, liberal; freely bestowed; hence ~LY[2] *adv.*, ~NESS *n.* [ME, f. OF *bontif* (*bonté* BOUNTY) + -OUS, after *plenteous*]

bou'ntĭful *a.* = prec. (**Lady B~,** beneficent lady of a neighbourhood [character in Farquhar's *Beaux' Stratagem* (1707)]); ample; hence ~LY[2] *adv.* [f. foll. + -FUL]

bou'ntў *n.* Munificence, liberality in giving; gift (**king's, queen's, ~,** (Hist.) grant made to mother of triplets; **Queen Anne's ~,** (Hist.) fund for augmenting poor benefices); sum paid to encourage trade enterprise, or for killing dangerous animals etc.; gratuity to recruits on enlistment. [ME, f. OF *bonté* f. L *bonitas -tatis* (*bonus* good; see -TY[1])]

bouque't (bōōkā', bō-, *or* bōō'kā) *n.* Bunch of flowers; (fig.) praise; perfume of wine; ~ **garni,** bunch of herbs for flavouring. [F, f. dial. var. of OF *bos*, *bois* wood; see -ET[1]]

bou'quetĭn (bōō'k-) *n.* Alpine ibex. [F, f. OF *boc estaign* f. MHG *steinbock* (as STONE, BUCK[1])]

***bour'bon**[1] (boor'-) *n.* Whisky distilled from maize and rye. [f. *B~* County, Kentucky, where first made]

Bour'bon[2] (boor'-) *n.* *Reactionary; ~ **biscuit** (chocolate-flavoured with chocolate-cream filling). [f. the ~ family, whose descendants founded dynasties in France and Spain]

bour'don (boor'-) *n.* Low-pitched stop in organ or harmonium; lowest bell in peal of bells; drone pipe of bagpipe. [F, = bagpipe-drone, f. Rom. **burdo -onis*, imit.]

bourgeois (boor'zhwah) *n.* & *a.* (Member) of middle class; (person) of humdrum or conventional middle-class ideas; selfish(ly) materialist; capitalist(ic). [F; see BURGESS]

bourgeoisie (boorzhwahzē') *n.* The middle or bourgeois class. [F]

bourn[1] (boorn *or* bōrn) *n.* Small stream. [ME, S. Engl. var. of BURN[1]]

bourn[2]**, bourne,** (boorn *or* bōrn) *n.* (arch.) Limit; goal. [f. F *borne* f. OF *bodne* BOUND[1]]

bourrée (boor'ā) *n.* (Music for) old lively dance like gavotte. [F]

bourse (boors) *n.* Money-market, esp. (*B~*) Paris equivalent of Stock Exchange. [F, = purse, f. med. L *bursa*; cf. PURSE[1]]

boustrophē'don (*or* bōō-) *a.* & *adv.* (Written) from right to left and from left to right in alternate lines. [Gk, adv. = as ox turns in ploughing (*bous* ox, *-strophos*, STROPHE turning, *-don* adv. suf.)]

bout *n.* Spell of or turn at work or exercise; fit of drinking or illness; trial of strength, wrestling- or boxing-match. [16th c., app. same as obs. *bought* bending]

bouti'que (bōōtē'k) *n.* Small shop or department selling (esp. fashionable) clothes or accessories. [F, = small shop, f. L (as BODEGA)]

boutonnière (bōōtŏnyār') *n.* Spray of flowers worn in buttonhole. [F]

bouzou'kĭ (bōōzōō'-) *n.* Greek form of mandoline. [f. mod. Gk *mpouzouki* pr. b-]

bō'vīne *a.* Of or like an ox, esp. in stupidity or slowness; of the genus *Bos* of ruminants. [f. LL *bovinus* f. L *bos bovis* ox; see -INE[1]]

‖**Bŏ'vrĭl** *n.* Concentrated essence of beef. [P]

bow[1] (bō) *n.* **1.** Curve; rainbow. **2.** Weapon for shooting arrows (**two strings to** one's ~, a twofold resource; *draw the* LONG[1]*bow*); = SADDLE-*-bow*; rod with stretched horsehair for playing violin etc., single passage of this across strings; = BAIL[4]; metal ring forming handle of scissors, key, etc.; *side-piece of spectacle-frame. **3.** Slip-knot with single or double loop; ribbon etc. so tied. **4.** ~**-compass**(**es**), compass with jointed legs; **~'fin,** voracious Amer. freshwater fish; **~-head,** Greenland whale; **~-legged, ~-legs,** (having) bandy legs; **~'man,** archer; **~-saw,** narrow saw stretched like bowstring on light frame; **~'shot,** distance to which bow can send arrow; **~'string** *n.*, & *v.t.*, (strangle with) string of bow (former Turkish method of execution); **~-tie,** necktie (to be) tied in shape of bow (sense 3); **~-wi'ndow,** curved bay window. [OE *boga,* = OS, OHG *bogo*, ON *bogi* f. Gmc **bugon* (**bug-* BOW[3])]

bow[2] (bō) *v.t.* Use the bow on (violin etc., or abs.). [f. prec.]

bow[3] *v.* **1.** *v.i.* Submit (*to the inevitable* etc.); ~ (**down**), bend or kneel in sign of submission or reverence *to* or *before*; incline head in salutation, assent, etc., (**~ing acquaintance,** slight degree of acquaintance that stops at this); **~ out,** make one's exit (esp. formally); *bow and* SCRAPE. **2.** *v.t.* Express (thanks etc.), usher *in* or *out*, by bowing; cause to bend (lit. or fig., *knee, back* etc. for burden, *will*); **~ down,** crush, make stoop, (esp. *bowed down by* or *with* care etc.). [OE *būgan*; cf. OHG *biogan*, ON **bjuga*, Goth. *biugan* f. Gmc **beugan*, cf. BOW[1]]

bow[4] *n.* Bending of head or body in salutation, respect, consent, etc.; **make** one's ~, make formal entrance or exit; **take a** ~, acknowledge applause. [f. prec.]

bow[5] *n.* (often in *pl.*) Fore-end of boat or ship from where it begins to curve inwards (**on the** ~, within 45° of the point right ahead; **shot across the ~s,** (fig.) warning); rower nearest the bow; **~'man** (stationed in bow); **~ wave** (set up at bows of ship or in front of body moving in air). [f. LG *boog*, Du. *boeg*, ship's bow, orig. shoulder; see BOUGH]

bow'dler|ize, -|ise (-īz), *v.t.* Expurgate (book, author); hence **~ISM** (3), **~IZA'TION,** *ns.* [f. T. *Bowdler* (d. 1825), expurgator of Shakespeare, + -IZE (4)]

bow'el *n.* Division of alimentary canal below stomach, intestine, gut, (*bowel* MOTION[1]); (in *pl.*, arch.) pity, tender feelings, (*bowels of mercy* etc.); (in *pl.*) innermost parts (*bowels of the earth*). [ME, f. OF *buel* etc. f. L *botellus* dim. of *botulus* sausage]

bow'er[1] *n.* Place closed in with foliage, arbour, summer-house, whence **~Y**[2] *a.*; (poet.) inner room; **~-bird,** Austral. bird of the bird-of--paradise family constructing elaborate runs adorned with feathers, shells, etc. during courtship. [OE *būr,* = OS, OHG, ON *būr* f. Gmc **būraz* (**bū-* dwell)]

bow'er[2] *n.* ~(**-anchor**), either of two anchors (**best** ~ and **small** ~) carried at ship's bow; ~(**-cable**), cable of bower-anchor. [f. BOW[5] + -ER[1]]

bow'er[3] *n.* One of two cards (**right** ~, jack of trumps, **left** ~, jack of same colour) at euchre and similar games. [f. G *bauer* peasant, jack at cards, cogn. w. Du. *boer*; see BOOR]

***bow'erў** *n.* District (orig. **the B~,** street in New York City) known as resort of drunks and down-and-outs. [f. Du. *bouwerij* farm]

bow'ĭe (bō'ĭ) *n.* ~ (**knife**), long knife with blade double-edged at point used as weapon by Amer. pioneers. [f. J. *Bowie*, Amer. soldier d. 1836]

bowl[1] (bōl) *n.* Basin, esp. deep-shaped or for food or liquid; (arch.) drinking-vessel; contents of a bowl; *bowl-shaped region; bowl-shaped part of tobacco-pipe, spoon, balance, etc.; amphitheatre; hence **~'FUL** 2 *n.* [OE *bolle, bolla,* = OS *bollo*, OHG *bolla* f. Gmc **bul-* swell]

bowl[2] (bōl) *n.* **1.** Wooden ball made slightly out of spherical shape to make it run on curved course. **2.** Flattened or spherical wooden ball at skittles. **3.** (in *pl.*, usu. treated as *sing.*) Game played with bowls (sense 1) on grass, or with round balls in room. [ME & F *boule* f. L *bulla* bubble]

bowl[3] (bōl) *v.t.* & *i.* **1.** Play bowls or skittles; roll (ball, hoop, etc.) along ground; go along by revolving or by means of wheels; **~ along,** go fast and smoothly; **~ over,** knock down, (fig.) disconcert, render helpless, impress greatly. **2.** (Cricket). Deliver (*ball, over*, or abs.); knock *down* (wicket); ~ (**out**), dismiss (batsman) by knocking down wicket with delivered ball; **~ out,** dismiss (side). [f. prec.]

bow'ler[1] (bō'-) *n.* Player at bowls; (Cricket) fieldsman who bowls. [f. prec. + -ER[1]]

‖**bow'ler**[2] (bō'-) *n.* ~ (**hat**), round-crowned hard felt hat; **~-hat** *v.t.* (*-tt-*), (sl.) retire from the army etc. [f. *B~*, hatter, who designed it 1850]

bow'lĭne (bō'-) *n.* Rope from weather side of square sail to bow; ~ (**knot**), simple knot for forming non-slipping loop at end of rope. [ME, f. MLG *bōlīne* = MDu. *boechlijne* (as BOW[5], LINE[2])]

bow'lĭng (bō'-) *n.* In vbl senses; **~-alley,** long enclosure for playing skittles, building containing such; **~-crease,** (Cricket) line from behind which bowler delivers ball; **~-green,** lawn for playing bowls. [f. BOWL[3] + -ING[1]]

bowman. See BOW[1,5].

bow'ser (-z-) *n.* Tanker for fuelling aircraft etc.; (Austral. & N.Z.) petrol pump. [P]

bowsprĭt (bō'-) *n.* Spar running out from ship's stem to which forestays are fastened. [ME, f. MLG *bōgsprēt* = MDu. *boechspriet* (as BOW[5], SPRIT)]

Bow Street (bō'-) *n.* (Hist.) London street containing chief metropolitan police-court; **~ officer, runner,** London policeman.

bow'-wow *int.* & *n.* Dog's bark or imitation of it; (childish colloq.) dog. [imit.]

bow'yăng (bō'-) *n.* (Austral. & N.Z.) Band or strap round trouser-leg below knee. [f. dial. *bowy-yangs* etc.]

bow'yer (bō'-) *n.* Maker or seller of archers' bows. [f. BOW[1] + -YER]

bŏx[1] *n.* Evergreen shrub or small tree of genus *Buxus*, esp. one of a species with small dark leathery leaves, much used in garden borders; ~(**'wood**), its wood, used by turners and engravers; (Austral.) tree with similar wood; **~ elder,** Amer. maple (*Acer negundo*). [OE, f. L *buxus*, Gk *puxos*]

bŏx[2] *n.* **1.** Container (usu. with lid, rectangular or cylindrical, for solids) of wood, metal, cardboard, etc.; boxful, quantity contained in box; coachman's seat; = LETTER-*box*, *MAIL[3]*box*, MONEY-*box*, POST[2]-*office box*, etc.; receptacle at newspaper office for replies to advertisement; **the** ~, (colloq.) television (set); *in the* WRONG *box.* **2.** Separate compartment in theatre, restaurant, etc.; compartment for horse in stable or vehicle (HORSE[1]-*box*; **loose** ~, one in which it can move about); = CALL[2]-*box*, JURY-*box*, SENTRY-*box*, SIGNAL[2]-*box*, ‖TELEPHONE--*box*, WITNESS-*box*, etc.; small country house for use when fishing, shooting, etc.; protective case for piece of mechanism; cricketer's light shield to protect genitals. **3.** Confined area; space enclosed by printed lines; (Football, colloq.) penalty area; (Baseball) area occupied by batter or pitcher. **4.** **~ barrage** (on all sides of an area, to prevent escape from it); **~ camera,** simple box-shaped hand camera; ***~'car,** closed railway goods wagon; **~ coat,** heavy overcoat (for coachman etc.); **~ girder** (made of plates fastened in box shape); ‖**~ junction,** yellow-striped road area which vehicle must not enter if it cannot leave immediately; **~-kite,**

tailless kite with light rectangular frame at each and; ~ **number** (to identify box in newspaper office or post office); **~-office** (for booking seats etc. in theatre, (fig.) entertainment etc. likely to attract audiences); ~ **pew** (enclosed like box); **~-pleat** (of two parallel contrary pleats forming raised band); ||**~-room** (in which boxes, trunks, etc. are stored); ~ **score,** tabulated results of baseball etc. game; **~-spanner** (with head fitting over nut etc.); **~-spring,** one of set of vertical springs in mattress; ~ **tortoise** (that can enclose itself entirely within shell); **~-wallah,** (India) dealer or pedlar. **5.** Hence ~′FUL 2 *n.*, ~′Y[2] *a.* [OE, prob. f. **bux* f. LL *buxis -id-* var. of L PYXIS box of boxwood]

bŏx[3] *v.t.* Provide with or put into a box; ~ **the compass,** (Naut.) rehearse the points in correct order, (fig.) make complete revolution and end where one began (in politics, argument, etc.); **~-haul,** veer ship round on keel for lack of room; ~ **in,** confine and restrict movement of; ~ **up,** confine uncomfortably, muddle. [f. prec.]

bŏx[4] *n.* Slap with hand on ear(s). [ME, of unkn. orig.]

bŏx[5] *v.t.* & *i.* Slap (person's ears); fight (person, or abs.) with fists (usu. in padded gloves, as sport); ~ **clever,** (sl.) behave cleverly; **~′ing-glove,** padded glove worn in boxing; **~′ing-weight,** weight at which boxers are matched (British amateur scale, somewhat modified for professionals, wrestlers, weight-lifters, and in U.S.: *heavyweight* no limit, *light heavyweight* or *cruiserweight* 81 kg, *middleweight* 75 kg, *light middleweight* 71 kg, *welterweight* 67 kg, *light welterweight* 63½ kg, *lightweight* 60 kg, *featherweight* 57 kg, *bantamweight* 54 kg, *flyweight* 51 kg, *light flyweight* 48 kg). [f. prec.]

Bŏx and Cŏx *n.* Two persons who are never together, never at home at the same time; two persons who take turns in a part, position, etc. (also as *a.*, *adv.*, & *v.i.*). [name of play (1847) by J. M. Morton, in which two persons unknowingly become tenants of same room]

bŏ′xcalf (-kahf) *n.* Chrome-tanned calfskin with hatched grain. [after Joseph *Box*, London bootmaker *c.* 1890]

bŏ′xer *n.* One who boxes (BOX[5]); (*B~*, Hist.) member of Chinese anti-foreign secret society; medium-sized smooth-haired kind of dog derived from German bulldog; ~ **shorts,** men's loose underpants. [f. BOX[5] + -ER[1]]

||**Bŏ′xĭng Day** *n.* First weekday after Christmas. [on which Christmas-boxes were traditionally given, f. obs. sense of BOX[3] f. (money-)BOX[2]]

boy *n.* & *int.* **1.** *n.* Male child; young man; (as familiar *voc.*, **my** ~; also to dog); **old** ~ (see OLD 7); male native servant, labourer. **2.** **~-and-girl,** juvenile (romance etc.); **~-friend,** girl's or woman's usual or preferred male companion; **~-meets-girl,** conventional (romance etc.); **~ scout,** = SCOUT[1] 2; ||**~'s-love,** southernwood; **the ~,** (arch. sl.) champagne; **the ~s,** group of men esp. with similar interests, grown-up sons of family; **~s will be ~s,** juvenile behaviour must be tolerated; **jobs for the ~s,** assurance of gain for one's friends. **3.** Hence ~′HOOD *n.*, ~′ISH[1] *a.*, (esp.) high-spirited. **4.** *int.* (**oh**) ~ (expr. surprise, excitement, etc.). [ME, = servant, perh. f. AF **abuié*, **embuié* fettered f. LL IM[1]*boiare* (L *boia* fetter; see BUOY[1])]

bōyâr′ *n.* (Hist.) Member of aristocratic order in Russia. [f. Russ. *boyarin* grandee]

boy′cott *v.t.*, & *n.* **1.** *v.t.* Combine to punish or coerce (person, class, nation) by systematic refusal of social or commercial relations; refuse to handle (goods etc.) with this aim. **2.** *n.* Such treatment. [f. Capt. C. C. *Boycott*, Irish land-agent d. 1897, so treated f. 1880]

Boyle *n.* **~'s law** (that gas pressure and volume are inversely proportional at constant temperature). [f. Robert ~, Brit. scientist d. 1691]

boy′ō *n.* (*pl.* **~s**). (colloq., Ir.) Boy (esp. as *voc.*). [f. BOY]

boy′senbĕrry̆ (*or* -z-) *n.* (Fruit of) a hybrid of several species of bramble. [f. R. *Boysen*, 20th-c. Amer. horticulturist + BERRY[1]]

***bō′zō** *n.* (*pl.* **~s**). (sl.) Person, fellow. [20th c.; orig. unkn.]

B.P. *abbr.* boiling-point; British Petroleum; British Pharmacopoeia.

Bp. *abbr.* Bishop.

B.P.C. *abbr.* British Pharmaceutical Codex.

B.R. *abbr.* British Rail(ways).

Br. *abbr.* British; Brother.

br. *abbr.* brown.

Br *symb.* bromine.

bra (-ah) *n.* Brassière. [abbr.]

brāce[1] *n.* **1.** Thing that clasps, tightens, supports, unites, or secures; ||(in *pl.*) straps to support trousers from shoulders; wire device for straightening teeth. **2.** Connecting mark in printing ({ or }); (Mus.) similar mark connecting staves to be performed at same time; (*pl.* same) pair, couple, (of dogs, game, pistols, derog. of persons). **3.** Strengthening-piece of iron or timber in building; (Naut.) rope attached to yard for trimming sail (*splice the* MAIN[3] *brace*); ~ **and bit,** revolving tool for boring. [ME, f. OF *brace* two arms, f. L *bracchia* (pl.) arms; some senses f. foll.]

brāce[2] *v.t.* Fasten tightly, stretch, string up, give firmness to, invigorate, (~ **oneself,** ~ **up,** prepare for effort); support; (Naut.) move (sail) by braces. [ME, partly f. OF *bracier* embrace, partly f. prec.]

brā′celėt (-sl-) *n.* Ornamental band, chain, etc., for wrist or arm; (sl.) handcuff. [ME f. OF, dim. of *bracel* f. L *bracchiale* (*bracchium* arm)]

brā′cer[1] *n.* In vbl senses; (colloq.) pick-me-up. [f. BRACE[2] + -ER[1]]

brā′cer[2] *n.* Wrist-guard of archer, fencer, etc. [ME, f. OF *brasseüre* (*bras* arm, *-eüre* -URE)]

brā′chĭal (-kĭ-) *a.* Of the arm (*brachial artery*); like an arm. [f. L *brachialis* (*brachium* arm); see -AL]

brā′chĭ|āte (-kĭ-) *v.i.* (Of ape) move by using the arms to swing from branch to branch; hence ~A′TION, **~ātor**, *ns.* [f. L *brachium* arm + -ATE[3]]

brăchĭosaur′us (-kĭ-) *n.* Huge dinosaur of genus *Brachiosaurus*, with forelegs longer than hind legs. [mod. L, f. Gk *brakhiōn* arm + *sauros* lizard]

brachĭ′stochrōne (-kĭ′stokr-) *n.* Curve between two points along which body moves in shorter time than for any other curve. [f. Gk *brakhistos* shortest + *khronos* time]

brăchy̆- (-k-) *comb. form.* Short, as: **~cepha′lic, ~ce′phalous,** having a short or broad head; **~logy** (brakĭ′lojĭ), (over-)conciseness of expression. [f. Gk *brakhus* short]

bră′cken *n.* Kind of large fern abundant on heaths, hillsides, etc.; mass of such ferns. [north. ME, f. ON **brakni*]

bră′ckėt[1] *n.* **1.** Flat-topped projection from wall serving as support to statue, arch, etc.; shelf with slanting under-prop for hanging against wall; wooden or metal angular support; support of lamp, projecting from wall. **2.** Mark used in pairs ( ), [ ], { } (cf. BRACE[1]), ⟨ ⟩, for enclosing words, figures, etc.; skating-figure resembling {; (Mil. etc.) distance between two shots either side of target in range-finding; group bracketed together as similar (*social bracket*) or falling between certain limits (*income* *bracket*). [f. F *braguette* or Sp. *bragueta* codpiece dim. of F *brague* f. Prov. *braga* f. L *braca*, pl. *bracae* breeches]

brăʹckĕt[2] *v.t.* Enclose in brackets as parenthetic, spurious, or (Math.) having spec. relations to what precedes or follows, etc.; couple (names etc.) with brace, imply connection or equality between; (Mil. etc.) place two shots one short of and one beyond (target) in range-finding. [f. prec.]

brăʹckĭsh *a.* (Of water) slightly salt. [f. obs. *brack* a. f. MLG, MDu. *brac* + -ISH[1]]

brăct *n.* (Usu. small) leaf or scale below calyx. [f. L *bractea* thin plate, gold-leaf]

brăd *n.* Thin flat small-headed nail. [var. of ME *brod* goad, pointed instrument, f. ON *broddr* spike]

brăʹdawl *n.* Small non-spiral boring-tool. [f. prec. + AWL]

‖**Brăʹdshaw** *n.* (Hist.) Time table of (esp. British) passenger trains. [f. G. ~, Brit. printer d. 1853, first publisher of *Bradshaw's Railway Guide*]

brăʹdȳ- *comb. form.* Slow, as: **~carʹdia,** abnormally slow heart-action; **~seism** (-sīzem), slow rise and fall of earth's crust. [f. Gk *bradus* slow]

brae (-ā) *n.* (Sc.) Steep bank, hillside. [ME, f. ON *brá* eyelash, = OS, OHG *brāwa* eyebrow; for sense cf. BROW]

brăg *n.*, & *v.i.* & *t.* (**-gg-**). Boast, boasting; card-game like poker. [ME, orig. a. = spirited, boastful, of unkn. orig.]

brăggadōʹcĭō (-shĭō) *n.* (*pl.* **~s**). Empty boasting. [formed by Spenser 1590 as name (meaning boaster) on prec. or foll. and It. augment. suf. *-occio*]

brăʹggart *n.* & *a.* (Person) given to bragging. [f. F *bragard* (*braguer* BRAG; see -ARD)]

Brahʹma[1] *n.* Supreme Hindu deity; divine reality of which world is manifestation. [Skr., = creator]

brahmapuʹtra (-ōō't-), **brahʹma**[2], *n.* (Bird of) large Asian breed of domestic fowl. [f. river *Brahmaputra* in India, whence brought]

brahʹmĭn, -man, *n.* Member of Hindu priestly caste; ***B~**, (colloq.) highly cultured or intellectual aloof person; hence **brahmiʹnic(al)**, **-măʹnic(al)**, *adjs.*, ~ISM (3) *n.* [f. Skr. *brāhmaṇas* (*brahmaṇ* priest)]

braid[1] *n.* Entwined hair, plait; band etc. entwined with the hair; silk, thread, etc., woven into a band; hence ~ʹING[1] (3, 6) *n.* [f. foll.]

braid[2] *v.t.* Plait, interweave, (hair, flowers, thread); arrange (hair) in braids; confine (hair etc.) with ribbon etc.; trim, edge, with braid. [OE *bregdan*, = OS *bregdan*, OHG *brettan*, ON *bregtha* f. Gmc **bregdhan*]

brail *n.*, & *v.t.* (Haul up with) small rope(s) on sail-edges for trussing sails before furling. [ME, f. OF *brai(e)l* f. med. L *bracale* girdle (*bracae* breeches; see -AL 2)]

Braille (-āl) *n.*, & *v.t.* **1.** *n.* System of writing and printing for the blind, in which the characters are represented by raised dots. **2.** *v.t.* Print or transcribe in Braille characters. [f. L. ~, Fr. teacher d. 1852, its inventor]

brain *n.*, & *v.t.* **1.** *n.* Convoluted nervous tissue in skull of vertebrates (in *sing.* of the whole as an organ, in *pl.* of the substance esp. as food; BLOW[1] *out* one's *brains*); centre of sensation, thought, etc., (BEAT[1], CUDGEL, RACK[3], one's *brains*; **get** or **have on the** ~, be constantly thinking of (person or thing); **turn** person's ~, make him vain and silly); (source of) intellectual power, whence ~ʹLESS *a.* (PICK[2] person's *brains*); (colloq.) clever person; electronic device comparable to brain. **2. ~-child,** (colloq.) product of thought; ~ **drain,** (colloq.) loss of intellectual or highly trained workers by emigration; **~-fag,** mental exhaustion; ~ **fever,** inflammation of the brain; **~-fever bird,** Ind. cuckoo with maddeningly persistent cry; **~-pan,** (colloq.) skull; **~ʹpower,** mental ability or intelligence; **~-stem,** medulla oblongata; **~ʹstorm,** violent symptoms of mental disturbance, *(colloq.) brainwave; ***~ʹstorming,** spontaneous discussion in search for new ideas; **~s trust,** group of experts giving impromptu answers to questions; ***~ trust,** group of experts guiding or advising the government; **~-teaser, ~-twister,** difficult puzzle esp. for amusement; **~ʹwashing,** systematic replacement of established ideas in person's mind by new ones (so **~ʹwash** *v.t.*); **~ʹwave,** electrical impulse in brain, (colloq.) sudden bright idea; **~ʹwork,** mental activity. **3.** *v.t.* Dash out brains of. [OE *brægen*, = MLG *bregen*, f. WG **bragna*]

braiʹnȳ *a.* Intellectually clever or active. [f. prec. + -Y[2]]

braise (-z) *v.t.* Steam (meat) slowly in closed container. [f. F *braiser* (*braise* live coals)]

brāke[1] *n.* Bracken. [ME, perh. shortened f. BRACKEN, *-en* being taken to be the pl. ending]

brāke[2] *n.* Thicket, brushwood. [ME, f. OE *bracu*, MLG *brake* branch, stump]

brāke[3] *n.* Toothed instrument for braking flax and hemp; ~(**-harrow**), heavy harrow; instrument for peeling off willow-bark; baker's kneading-machine. [ME, MLG, MDu., = flax-brake, cogn. w. BREAK[1]]

brāke[4] *v.t.* Crush (flax, hemp) by beating. [f. prec.]

brāke[5] *n.* Apparatus for checking (usu. rotary) motion (**apply** or **put on the ~s,** lit., or fig. moderate one's enthusiasm); **~-block,** block holding brake-shoe; **~-drum,** cylinder attached to wheel receiving pressure of brake-shoe; ~ **fluid,** liquid used in hydraulic brake; ~ **horsepower,** engine horsepower measured in terms of force needed to brake it; ~ **lining,** piece of fabric to increase friction of brake-shoe; **~ʹman,** man in charge of brake(s); **~-shoe,** part of brake coming in contact with wheel etc.; ‖**~ʹsman,** = *brakeman*; **~-van,** railway carriage from which train's brakes can be controlled; hence ~ʹLESS (-kl-) *a.* [prob. f. obs. *brake* in sense machine-handle or bridle]

brāke[6] *v.t.* & *i.* Retard (wheel, car, train, etc., with brake; apply brake. [f. prec.]

brāke[7] *n.* Large wagonette; estate car. [var. of BREAK[3]]

brāke[8]**.** See BREAK[1].

brăʹmble *n.* Rough prickly shrub of genus *Rubus* with long trailing shoots, esp. blackberry-bush; blackberry; hence **brăʹmbly**[2] *a.* [OE *bræmbel* (earlier *brǣmel*); see BROOM]

brăʹmblĭng *n.* Brightly coloured finch (*Fringilla montifringilla*). [f. G *brämling* prob. f. WG **brām-* (cf. prec.)]

Brăʹmley *n.* ~(**'s seedling**), large green variety of cooking apple. [f. M. ~, Engl. butcher in whose garden it may have first grown *c.* 1850]

brăn *n.* Husks of grain separated from flour after grinding; ‖**~-tub** (filled with bran into which children dip for toys etc.). [ME f. OF, of unkn. orig.]

branch[1] (-ah-) *n.* Limb springing from tree or bough; lateral extension or subdivision of mountain-range, river, road, railway, family, genus, subject of knowledge, or argument; local establishment of library, bank or other business, etc.; nozzle of fireman's hose; hence (-)~ED[2] (-cht) *a.*, ~ʹLET *n.*, ~ʹY[2] *a.* [ME, f. OF *branche*, f. LL *branca* paw]

branch[2] (-ah-) *v.i.* Put branches *out, forth*; spread or spring *out*, tend *away* or *off*, diverge *into*. [f. prec.]

bră'nchĭ|ae, bră'nchĭ|a, (-ngk-) *n. pl.* Gills; hence ~AL, ~ATE², *adjs.* [L *branchia*, pl. *-ae*, f. Gk *bragkhia* pl.]

brănd¹ *n.* Burning or charred log or stick, (poet.) torch, (~ **from the burning,** rescued person, convert); permanent mark deliberately made by hot iron; stigma (~ **of Cain,** blood-guilt); trade mark, goods of particular make or trade mark (lit. or fig.); iron stamp for burning-in a mark; (poet.) sword; kind of blight in which leaves look burnt; ~**-new',** conspicuously or completely new. [OE, = OHG *brant*, ON *brandr* f. Gmc **brandaz* (**bran-* BURN²)]

brănd² *v.t.* Burn with hot iron (penally, or to show ownership or quality); label with trade mark; impress on memory; stigmatize. [f. prec.]

bră'ndĭsh *v.t.* Wave about, flourish, (weapon, etc.) in display or threat. [f. OF *brandir* (-ISH²) f. Rom. **brandire* f. Gmc **brand-* sword-blade]

bră'ndlĭng *n.* Red earthworm with rings of brighter colour, used as bait. [f. BRAND¹ + -LING¹ 1]

bră'ndў *n.* Strong spirit distilled from wine, or from fermented fruit-juice (*apple* etc. *brandy*); ||~**-ball,** kind of brandy-flavoured sweet; ~**-snap,** rolled gingerbread wafer. [earlier *brand(e)wine* f. Du. *brandewijn* burnt (distilled) wine]

brănk-ūr'sīne *n.* Bear's-breech, kind of acanthus. [f. F *branche ursine*, med. L *branca ursina* bear's claw; see BRANCH¹, URSINE]

brăn-new'. Var. of BRAND¹*-new*.

***brănt.** See BRENT.

brăsh¹ *n.* Loose broken rock or ice; hedge refuse, clippings, etc. [18th c., of unkn. orig.]

brăsh² *a.* (colloq.) Rash; cheeky, saucy; vulgarly self-assertive; hence ~'LY² *adv.*, ~'NESS *n.* [orig. dial., perh. f. RASH²]

brăsh³ *n.* Eruption of fluid from stomach. [16th c., perh. imit.]

brass (-ahs) *n.*, *a.*, & *v.* **1.** *n.* Yellow alloy of copper and zinc (**as bold as** ~, excessively bold or self-assured); inscribed monumental or sepulchral tablet of brass (~**-rubbing,** cf. RUB¹ 3); (**horse-**)~, brass ornament worn by horse; brass block used for design etc. on book-cover; (Mus.) brass instruments; brassware; ||(sl.) money; (sl.) prostitute; effrontery; (**top**) ~, (colloq.) = (highest-ranking) officers or *brass hats* (also of leaders in industry, politics, etc.). **2.** *a.* Made of brass; ~ **band,** set of musicians with brass (and percussion) instruments; ~ **farthing,** least possible amount; ||~ **hat,** (sl.) officer of high rank with gold braid on cap; ~ **plate** (on door, gate, or window-ledge, with name, trade, etc.); ~ **rags,** sailors' cleaning cloths (*part* ~ *rags*, (sl.) cease friendship *with*); ~ **tacks,** (sl.) actual details, real business, (*get down to brass tacks*); ~**'ware,** utensils etc. made of brass. **3.** *v.i.* (sl.) Pay *up*. **4.** *v.t.* ~ **off,** (in *p.p.*, sl.) fed up. [OE *bræs*, = MLG *bras*, of unkn. orig.]

bră'ssage *n.* Mint-charge for coining money. [F, f. *brasser* stir melted metals together, brew, f. pop. L **braciare* f. L *brace* kind of grain]

bră'ssârd *n.* Badge worn on arm; band worn on sleeve, esp. with uniform. [F (*bras* arm; see -ARD)]

bră'sserĭe *n.* Beer saloon; restaurant serving beer with food. [F, = brewery (*brasser* brew)]

bră'ssĭca *n.* Plant of genus *Brassica* (cabbage, turnip, etc.). [L, = cabbage]

bră'ssĭe, -ў², *n.* Wooden-headed golf-club with brass sole. [f. BRASS + -IE]

bră'ssière (-syār) *n.* Woman's undergarment worn to support breasts. [F]

bra'ss|ў¹ (-ah-) *a.* Like brass in colour, sound, or taste; impudent; pretentious; hence ~ĬLY² *adv.*, ~ĬNESS *n.* [f. BRASS + -Y²]

bră'ssў². See BRASSIE.

brăt *n.* (usu. derog.) Child. [perh. abbr. f. Sc. *bratchart* hound, or f. *brat* rough garment]

bră'ttĭce *n.* Wooden partition or shaft-lining in coal-mine. [ME, = temporary breastwork on parapet f. AF *breteske*, OF *bretesche* f. med. L *brittisca* f. OE *brittisc* BRITISH]

brava'dō (-vah'-) *n.* (occas. *pl.* ~**es** *or* ~**s**). Show of boldness. [f. Sp. *bravata* (*bravo*; cf. foll., -ADO)]

brāve¹ *a.* & *n.* **1.** *a.* Able to face and endure danger or pain; (literary) splendid, spectacular, admirable, (*make a brave show*); hence ~'LY² (-vlĭ) *adv.* **2.** *n.* Amer. Indian warrior. [ME f. F, f. It. or Sp. *bravo*, f. Rom. **brabus* (**brabarus* f. L *barbarus* BARBAROUS)]

brāve² *v.t.* Defy, encounter with bravery; ~ **it out,** behave defiantly under suspicion or blame. [f. F *braver* (as prec.)]

brā'verў *n.* Brave conduct; (literary) splendour. [f. F *braverie* or It. *braveria* (as prec.; see -ERY)]

bra'vō¹ (-ah'-) *n.* (*pl.* ~**es** *or* ~**s**). Hired ruffian; desperado. [It.; see BRAVE¹]

bra'vō² (-ah'-) *n.* (*pl.* ~**s**) & *int.* Cry of approval, esp. to actor etc. [F f. It.]

bravūr'a (*or* -oor'*a*) *n.* Brilliant or ambitious performance; passage or style of (esp. vocal) music requiring exceptional powers. [It.]

braw *a.* (Sc.) Fine, good. [var. of *brawf* BRAVE¹]

brawl *v.i.*, & *n.* (Engage in) noisy quarrel; (of stream) run noisily; hence ~'ER¹ *n.* [ME, f. OProv. *braular*, rel. to BRAY¹]

brawn *n.* Muscle; muscularity; pig's head etc. boiled, chopped, and moulded. [ME, f. AF *braun*, OF *braon* f. Gmc **brādon* roast flesh]

braw'n|ў *a.* Strong, muscular; hence ~ĬNESS *n.* [f. prec. + -Y²]

bray¹ *n.*, & *v.i.* (Make) the cry, or a sound like the cry, of an ass; (make) sound of harshly played trumpet. [ME, f. OF *braire* f. Rom. **bragere*, perh. f. Celt.]

bray² *v.t.* Pound, beat small, esp. with pestle and mortar. [ME, f. AF *braier*, OF *breier* f. Gmc **brekan* BREAK¹]

brāze *v.t.*, & *n.* **1.** *v.t.* Solder with alloy of brass and zinc. **2.** *n.* Brazed joint. [f. F *braser* solder (*braise* live coals)]

brā'zen¹ *a.* Made of brass; strong, yellow, or harsh-sounding, as brass; ~(**-faced**), shameless; hence ~LY² *adv.*, ~NESS (-n-n-) *n.* [OE *bræsen* (*bræs* brass; see -EN⁵)]

brā'zen² *v.t.* ~ **out,** face or undergo impudently (esp. ~ *it out*, be unashamed of one's misbehaviour). [f. prec.]

brā'zĭ|er¹ (*or* -zh*er*) *n.* Worker in brass; hence ~ERY (1) *n.* [ME, prob. f. BRASS + -IER, after *glass*, *glazier*]

brā'zĭer² (*or* -zh*er*) *n.* Pan or stand for holding lighted coals. [f. F *brasier* (*braise* hot coals)]

Brazĭ'l *n.* ~(**-nut**), large three-sided nut from S. Amer. tree; ~(**-wood**), hard red wood from tropical tree of genus *Caesalpinia*, yielding dyes; hence ~IAN *a.* & *n.* [~ in S. America, named from ~*-wood* f. ME *brasile* f. med. L *brasilium*]

B.R.C.S. *abbr.* British Red Cross Society.

breach¹ *n.* **1.** Breaking or neglect (*of* rule, duty, contract, someone's privileged rights; ~ **of the peace,** riot or affray; ~ **of promise,** (esp.) breaking of promise to marry); breaking of relations, separation, estrangement, quarrel. **2.** Broken state; gap, esp. in fortifications made by artillery; **stand in the** ~, bear brunt of attack, lit. or fig.; **step into the** ~, give help in crisis. [ME f. OF *breche* f. Gallo-Rom. **brecca* f. Frank. **breka*, Gmc **brekan* BREAK¹]

breach² *v.t.* Break through, make gap in. [f. prec.]

bread (-ĕd) *n.*, & *v.t.* **1.** *n.* Flour moistened, kneaded, and baked, usu. with leaven (BLACK¹,

BROWN[1], WHITE[1], *bread*); ~ **and butter,** bread slices spread with butter, necessary food, a livelihood, routine work to ensure an income; **~-and-butter letter** (of thanks for hospitality, sent by departed guest); ~ **and circuses,** public provision of food and entertainment; ~ **and milk,** broken bread in hot boiled milk; ~ **and scrape,** stingily buttered bread; ~ **and water,** plainest possible diet; *cast bread upon* WATER[1]*s*; ~ **and wine,** Eucharist; ~ **buttered on both sides,** easy prosperity; **know which side** one's ~ **is buttered** (where one's advantage lies). **2.** Necessary food (**break** ~, (arch.) take food; **breaking of** ~, Eucharist; (**daily**) ~, livelihood; **eat the** ~ **of,** be subjected to (*affliction* etc.); **take the** ~ **out of** person's **mouth,** take away his living by competition etc.); (sl.) money. **3.** **~-basket,** (sl.) stomach; **~-bin,** container for loaves; **~'board** (for cutting bread on or (sl.) making flat model of electric circuit etc.); **~'crumb,** crumb of loaf, (esp. in *pl.*) bread crumbled for use in cooking; **~-fruit** (of tropical tree *Artocarpus incisa*, with white pulp like new bread); ***~'line,** queue of poor people waiting to receive food, (fig.) subsistence level; *bread* ROLL[1]; ~ **sauce,** milk sauce thickened with breadcrumbs; **~-stick,** long thin roll of crisp bread; **~'stuffs,** (1) grain flour, (2) articles of bread; **~-winner,** person whose work supports a family. **4.** *v.t.* Coat with breadcrumbs for cooking. [OE *brēad*, = OS *brōd*, OHG *brōt*, ON *brauth* f. Gmc **braudham*, of unkn. orig.]

breadth (-ĕd-) *n.* Broadness, measurement from side to side; piece (of cloth etc.) of full breadth; extent, distance, room; (fig.) largeness, freedom from limitations (*of* mind, view, etc.); liberality, catholicity, toleration; (Art) unity of whole, achieved by disregard of unnecessary detail; hence ~'WAYS, ~'WISE, *advs.* [f. obs. *brede*, OE *brǣdu*, OHG *breitī*, ON *breidd*, Goth. *braidei* f. Gmc **braidjōn* abstr. n. f. **braidh-* BROAD, + -TH[1] after *length* etc.]

break[1] (-āk) *v.t.* & *i.* (**broke** *pr.* -ōk, (arch.) **brake;** BROKEN, see also BROKE). **1.** (Of a whole) make or become discontinuous otherwise than by cutting, divide or disperse into two or more parts, (*break* BULK[1], *the* ICE[1]; ~ **a set,** sell its parts separately); (of waves) curl over and disintegrate in foam; (of prices) fall suddenly; (of weather) change suddenly esp. after settled period; (of troops) disperse in confusion; (of clouds) show gap; disconnect (electric circuit); subject (vowel) to fracture. **2.** Crack, graze, (*broken heads*); shatter (*break a window*); break bone in (arm, back, leg, etc.), fracture or dislocate (neck; ~ **the back of,** do hardest or greatest part of, overburden (person)); make by separating obstacles (*trail, a way*, etc.); penetrate by breaking (*break open*; **~ing and entering,** housebreaking); surpass (record); cause to cease or be discontinuous (*break gloom, spell, journey, silence*, STEP[2], one's *fast*); (of voice) change tone with emotion or at manhood; change (banknote etc.) for coins; unfurl (flag etc.); defeat object of (strike); solve (cipher etc.); disprove (alibi); (Tennis) win a game against (opponent's service); (Boxing, usu. as command from referee) come out of clinch; have interval between spells of work (*we broke for coffee*). **3.** (Of a part) disconnect or become separate from something otherwise than by cutting (~ **with,** quarrel or cease relations with); dismiss (officer); (of bowled ball in Cricket) deviate from original direction on pitching. **4.** Make a way, come, produce, with effort, suddenness, violence, etc., (*break into* house, *out of* prison, *through* obstacles); (of day) dawn; (of storm) begin violently; reveal, (of news) be revealed; escape, emerge from, (prison, bounds, cover(t); *break free* or *loose*); fail to rejoin (ship) after absence on leave; ~ **into,** suddenly begin to utter, perform, etc., (*laughter, a run, tears*), establish oneself in (profession); *break* WIND[1] 6. **5.** Make or become weak, disable, discourage, destroy, cease, exhaust, (~ **bank,** exhaust its resources or its limit of payment; ~ **blow, fall,** weaken its effect); make or become bankrupt; tame, subdue, (*break* person's HEART, *will, spirit*; *break resistance, a rebellion*; ~ **a habit,** be no longer subject to it; ~ person etc. **of a habit,** make him no longer subject to it; ~ **horse** (**to the rein**), make him accustomed to it); make of no effect, act contrary to (*law, contract*, one's *promise*, one's WORD[1]). **6.** ~ **away,** make or become free or separate; **~'away,** (*n.*) breaking away, secession, false start in race, (Rugby Footb.) outside second-row forward, (Austral.) stampede, (*a.*) that breaks away or has broken away; ~ **down,** collapse, fail, cease to function, demolish, suppress (resistance), analyse (total) into components, lose self-control; **~'down** *n.*, collapse, failure of mechanical action or health or (esp. mental) power, analysis, disintegration; ~ **even,** emerge from transaction etc. with neither gain nor loss; ~ **in,** intrude forcibly esp. as thief (whence *~-in* n.), interrupt, accustom to habit, tame, discipline, wear etc. until comfortable; ~ **in on,** disturb, interrupt; ~ **off,** detach by breaking, bring to an end, cease; ~ **out,** open up and remove contents (esp. of cargo), burst from restraint or concealment (whence *~-out* n.), release (run-up flag), become covered *in* (*a rash* etc.), exclaim; **~'through** *n.*, act of breaking through obstacle etc., major advance in knowledge etc.; ~ **up,** disband, depart, disconcert, break into small pieces, become feeble, be convulsed (*with laughter* etc.), cease (conversation etc.), (of weather) = sense 1; **~'up** *n.*, disintegration, decay, collapse, dispersal. **7.** ~ **crop** (grown to avoid continual growing of cereals); **~-line,** (Print.) last line of paragraph (usu. not of full length); **~'neck** *a.*, dangerous (pace); **~'water,** object (esp. groyne or pier) breaking force of waves; **~'wind,** (Austral.) wind-break. **8.** Hence ~'ABLE *a.*, & *n.* in *pl.*, (things) easily broken, ~'AGE (3) *n.* [OE *brecan*, = OS *brekan*, OHG *brehhan*, Goth. *brikan* f. Gmc **brekan*]

break[2] (-āk) *n.* Breaking (~ **of day,** dawn); escape from prison; sudden dash; (Cricket) deviation of ball on pitching; (Bill.) points scored continuously; gap, broken place, interruption of continuity; (Electr.) breaking of circuit; (Jazz) short unaccompanied passage; short spell of recreation between periods of work etc. (esp. *coffee-break, tea-break*); (colloq.) a fair chance, piece of good luck; (**bad**) ~, (colloq.) unfortunate remark or ill-judged action, piece of ill luck. [f. prec.]

break[3] (-āk) *n.* Carriage-frame without body, for breaking-in young horses; = BRAKE[7]. [perh. = *brake* framework, 17th c., of unkn. orig.]

brea'ker[1] (-ā'k-) *n.* In vbl senses (esp. in comb., as *horse-breaker*); heavy ocean-wave breaking on coast or over reefs. [f. BREAK[1] + -ER[1]]

brea'ker[2] (-ā'k-) *n.* (Naut.) Small keg. [f. Sp. *bareca, barrica* cask, cogn. w. BARREL[1]]

brea'kfast (brĕ'k-) *n.*, & *v.i.* (Take) first meal of day; WEDDING *breakfast.* [f. BREAK[1] interrupt + FAST[2]]

brea'king (-ā'k-) *n.* In vbl senses; (of vowel) = FRACTURE 2; **~-point** (at which thing or person gives way under stress); **~-strength,** maximum stress that a body can withstand without breaking. [f. BREAK[1] + -ING[1]]

bream[1] *n.* (*pl.* same). Yellowish arch-backed freshwater fish of genus *Abramis*; (**sea-**)~, similarly shaped sea-fish of family Sparidae, esp. porgy or POMFRET 2; *sunfish of genus *Lepomis* etc. [ME, f. OF *bre(s)me* f. Frank. **brachsima*, OS *bressemo*, OHG *brahsema*]

bream[2] *v.t.* Clear (ship's bottom) by burning and scraping. [prob. f. LG, cogn. w. BROOM]

breast[1] (-ĕst) *n.* **1.** Either of two milk-secreting organs on upper front of woman's body; corresponding usu. rudimentary part of man's body; (fig.) source of nourishment. **2.** Upper front of human body or of coat, dress, etc.; corresponding part of animals; CHIMNEY-*breast*; heart, emotions, thoughts, (**make clean ~ of,** confess fully); BEAT[1] one's *breast*. **3.** **~'bone,** thin flat vertical bone or cartilage in chest connecting ribs; **~-drill** (pushed with breast to press against workpiece); **~-fed, -feeding,** (at mother's breast, opp. from bottle); **~-high,** high as the breast, (submerged) to the breast, (of scent) so strong that hounds race with heads up; **~-pin** (jewelled etc., worn in tie); **~'plate,** vestment or piece of armour covering breast, lower shell of turtle, tortoise, etc., inscription-plate on coffin; **~-stroke,** stroke made while swimming on the breast by extending the arms in front and sweeping them back; **~-wall** (confining a bank of earth); **~-wheel,** water-wheel with water admitted near axle; **~'work,** temporary defence or parapet a few feet high. **4.** Hence (-)~'ED[2] *a.* [OE *brēost*, = OS *briost*, ON *brjóst* f. Gmc **breustam*]

breast[2] (-ĕst) *v.t.* Oppose the breast to; face, contend with, (waves, hill); climb (hill); *breast the* TAPE. [f. prec.]

brea'stsŭmmer (-ĕ'st-) *n.* Beam across broad opening, sustaining superstructure. [f. BREAST[1] + SUMMER[2]]

breath (-ĕth) *n.* Exhalation as perceptible to sight or smell or hearing (**below** or **under** one's ~, in a whisper); slight movement of air; whiff of perfume etc.; air taken into and expelled from lungs (**draw ~,** breathe, live; **a ~ of** (brief time in or small amount of) **fresh air; waste ~,** talk in vain; **keep ~ to cool porridge, save** one's ~, abstain from useless talk; **~ of life,** a necessity); process of respiration (**catch, hold,** one's ~, in fear or absorbing emotion); one respiration (*say* inconsistent things *in the same breath*); power of breathing (**out of ~,** not able to breathe quick enough; **take ~,** pause to rest; **take** person's **~ away,** make him breathless with delight, surprise, etc.; so **~-taking** *a.*); whisper, murmur, (*not a breath of suspicion*); **~ test** (given with breathalyser). [OE *brǣth* f. Gmc **brǣthaz* f. IE **bhrētos* (**bhrē-* burn)]

brea'thalȳser, *-ȳzer, (brĕ'-; *-zer*) *n.* Instrument measuring amount of alcohol in breath; so **brea'thalȳse** (brĕ'-; -z) *v.t.*, carry out such measurement on. [f. BREATH + ANALYSE + -ER[1]]

breathe (-ēdh) *v.* **1.** *v.i.* Take air into and expel it from the lungs (**~ down** person's **neck,** be close behind him esp. in pursuit or mistrust); be or seem alive; take breath, pause, (**~ again, freely,** recover from fear etc., be at ease); (of wine, fabric) be exposed to fresh air; sound, speak, (of wind) blow, softly (**~ upon,** tarnish, taint). **2.** *v.t.* Send out or take in (as if) with breathed air (**~** one's **last,** die); utter (**not ~ a word of,** keep quite secret); exhibit (*breathe defiance, simplicity*); allow (horse etc.) to breathe, give rest after exertion. [ME, f. BREATH]

brea'ther (-ē'dh-) *n.* In vbl senses; short spell of exercise; brief pause for rest; safety-vent in crankcase etc. [f. prec. + -ER[1]]

brea'thĭng (-ē'dh-) *n.* In vbl senses; (Gk Gram.) **rough, smooth, ~,** signs (cf. Appendix II) indicating that initial vowel or rho is or is not aspirated; **~-space,** time to breathe, pause. [f. BREATHE + -ING[1]]

brea'thlėss (-ĕ'th-) *a.* Panting; holding the breath through excitement etc.; unstirred by wind; hence ~LY[2] *adv.*, ~NESS *n.* [f. BREATH + -LESS]

brea'th|ȳ (-ĕ'thĭ) *a.* (Of singing-voice) with sound of emission of breath; hence ~ĭNESS *n.* [f. BREATH + -Y[2]]

brĕ'ccia (-cha) *n.* Rock of angular stones etc. cemented by lime etc.; hence **brĕ'cciATE**[3] (-chĭ-) *v.t.*, form into breccia. [It., = gravel, f. Gmc **brekan* BREAK[1]]

brĕd. See BREED[1].

breech *n.*, & *v.t.* **1.** *n.* (**Pair of**) **~es** (brĭ'chĭz), short trousers esp. fastened below knee, now used esp. for riding or in court costume etc. (**B~es Bible,** Geneva Bible of 1560 with *breeches* for *aprons* in Gen. 3:7; **~'es-buoy,** lifebuoy on rope with canvas breeches for user's legs); trousers or knickerbockers; *too* BIG *for* one's *breeches*; WEAR[1] *the breeches*. **2.** Buttocks (arch. exc. w. ref. to baby's position at or before birth); **~ birth** (with buttocks foremost). **3.** Part of cannon behind bore, back part of rifle or gun barrel; **~-block** (closing breech aperture in gun); **~-loader, -loading,** (gun) loaded at breech, not through muzzle. **4.** *v.t.* (arch.) Put (boy) into breeches instead of petticoats. [OE *brōc*, pl. *brēc* (treated as sing. in ME), = OS *brōk*, OHG *bruoh*, ON *brók* f. Gmc **brōks*]

breed[1] *v.t.* & *i.* (**bred**). **1.** Bear, generate, (offspring); propagate (**~ in,** always mate with or marry near relations); yield, produce, result in; cause to propagate, raise, (cattle, domestic animals); **bred in the bone,** hereditary. **2.** Train up (*bred to the law*); bring up; arise, spread; **bred and born** or **born and bred,** by birth and upbringing. **3.** (Phys.) Create (fissile material) by nuclear reaction. **4.** Hence ~'ER[1] *n.*; **~er reactor,** nuclear reactor that can create more fissile material than it consumes in the chain reaction. [OE *brēdan*, = OHG *bruotan* f. WG **brōdjan* (**brōd-* BROOD[1])]

breed[2] *n.* **1.** Stock of animals etc. within a species, having similar appearance and usu. developed by deliberate selection. **2.** Race, lineage. **3.** Sort, kind. [f. prec.]

bree'dĭng *n.* In vbl senses; result of training, behaviour; good manners. [f. BREED[1] + -ING[1]]

breeze[1] *n.* Gadfly. [OE *briosa*, of unkn. orig.]

breeze[2] *n.*, & *v.i.* **1.** *n.* Gentle wind; (on Beaufort scale) wind of 4–31 m.p.h.; wind blowing from land at night or sea during day; (sl.) easy task; (sl.) quarrel, display of temper; **~'way,** roofed outdoor passage; hence ~'LESS (-zl-) *a.* **2.** *v.i.* (colloq.) Go like a breeze, move *along* or come *in* in lively or offhand manner. [prob. f. OSp. & Port. *briza* N.E. wind]

breeze[3] *n.* Small cinders etc. used with sand and cement in making **~-blocks** (lightweight building blocks). [f. F *braise* live coals]

bree'z|ȳ *a.* Wind-swept; pleasantly windy; fresh, lively, jovial; careless; hence ~ĭLY[2] *adv.*, ~ĭNESS *n.* [f. BREEZE[2] + -Y[2]]

brĕ'msstrahlung (-mzshtrahlo͝ong) *n.* (Phys.) Radiation due to retardation of charged particle by electric field, esp. of nucleus. [G, = braking radiation]

Brĕn *n.* **~ (gun),** light-weight quick-firing machine-gun. [f. *Br*no in Czechoslovakia (where orig. made) + *En*field in England (where later made)]

brĕnt, *brănt, *n.* **~(-goose),** smallest species of wild goose (*Bernicla brenta*), visiting Britain in winter. [16th c., of unkn. orig.]

brethren. See BROTHER.
Brĕ'ton *a.* & *n.* (Native, or Celtic language) of Brittany. [OF, = BRITON]
brĕ'tzel. Var. of PRETZEL.
brēve *n.* **1.** (Hist.) Authoritative letter from sovereign or pope. **2.** (Mus.) Note = two semibreves, now rarely used (**alla** ~ *pr.* ălabrā'vā, time signature indicating 2 or 4 minim beats in bar). **3.** Written or printed mark (˘) of short or unstressed vowel. [ME, var. of BRIEF[1]]
brĕ'vėt *n.*, & *v.t.* **1.** *n.* Document conferring a privilege from sovereign or government, esp. rank without corresponding pay in army (*brevet rank, major*). **2.** *v.t.* Confer brevet rank on. [ME f. OF, dim. of *bref* BRIEF[1]]
brē'vĭarў *n.* (R.C. Ch.) Book containing the Divine Office for each day, to be recited by those in orders. [f. L *breviarium* summary (*breviare* abridge); see ABBREVIATE[2], -ARY[1]]
brĕ'vĭtў *n.* Compact written or spoken expression, conciseness; short span (*of* life etc.). [f. AF *breveté*, OF *brieveté* (*bref* BRIEF[1]; see -ITY)]
brew[1] (-ōō) *v.t.* & *i.* Make (beer etc.) by infusion, boiling, and fermentation; make (tea etc.) by infusion or mixture (~ **up,** make tea); undergo these processes; concoct, bring about, set in train; grow to ripeness, fester, gather force, (usu. of evil results; *mischief is brewing*); hence ~'ER[1], ~'ERY (3), *ns.* (esp. w. ref. to beer etc.). [OE *brēowan*, = OS *breuwan*, OHG *briuwan*, ON *brugga* f. Gmc **breu(w)an*]
brew[2] (-ōō) *n.* Process of brewing; amount brewed at once; (quality of) what is brewed (*a good strong brew*). [f. prec.]
||**brew'ster** (-ōō'-) *n.* **B~ Sessions,** magistrates' sessions for issue of licences to permit trade in alcoholic liquors. [f. obs. *brewster* (orig. female) brewer; see -STER]
brī'ar[1,2]. See BRIER[1,2].
brībe[1] *n.* Money etc. offered to procure (often illegal or dishonest) action or decision in favour of giver. [f. foll.]
brīb|e[2] *v.t.* Persuade by bribe; (abs.) practise bribery; hence ~'ABLE *a.*, ~'ERY (4) *n.* [ME f. OF *briber*, *brimber* beg, of unkn. orig.]
brĭ'c-à-brăc *n.* Miscellaneous old ornaments, furniture, trinkets, etc. [F, f. obs. *à bric et à brac* at random]
brĭck[1] *n.* & *a.* **1.** *n.* Clay kneaded, moulded, and baked or sun-dried; small usu. rectangular block of this (**drop a** ~, (sl.) say indiscreet thing; *bricks without* STRAW[1]; **like a load** or **ton of ~s,** (colloq.) with crushing weight or force); similar block of concrete etc.; brick-shaped loaf, block of tea, ice cream, etc.; child's toy building-block; (sl.) generous or loyal person. **2.** **~'bat,** piece of brick, esp. as missile [BAT[2]], (fig.) uncomplimentary remark; **~-field** (in which bricks are made); **~'fielder,** (Austral.) hot dry N. wind; **~'layer,** workman building with bricks; *brick*-NOG[1]; **~-red,** of the red colour of bricks; **~'work,** building in brick; **~'yard,** place where bricks are made. **3.** Hence ~'IE *n.*, (sl.) bricklayer. **4.** *a.* Built of brick (*brick* WALL); of the red colour of bricks. [ME, f. MLG, MDu. *bri(c)ke*, of unkn. orig.]
brĭck[2] *v.t.* Block *up* (window etc.), close *in,* with brickwork. [f. prec.]
brī'dal *a.* Of bride or wedding; hence ~LY[2] *adv.* [orig. n., = wedding-feast, f. OE *brȳd-ealu* (*brȳd* BRIDE, *ealu* ALE-drinking)]
brīde *n.* Woman on her wedding-day and for some time before and after it; **~-cake,** wedding-cake; **~-price,** money etc. paid to bride's family esp. in primitive societies. [OE *brȳd*, = OS *brūd*, OHG *brūt*, ON *brúthr*, Goth. *brūths* f. Gmc **brūdhiz*]
brī'degrōōm (-dg-) *n.* Man on his wedding-day and for some time before and after it. [OE *brȳdguma* (as BRIDE, *guma* man, assim. to GROOM)]
brī'desmaid (-dz-) *n.* Unmarried woman (usu. one of several) attending bride at wedding. [earlier *bridemaid*, f. BRIDE + MAID]
brī'dewĕll (-dw-) *n.* (arch.) Prison, reformatory. [f. St. Bride's Well in London, near which such a building stood]
brĭdge[1] *n.* **1.** Structure carrying road, path, railway, etc., across stream, ravine, road, railway, etc.; ~ **of asses,** = PONS *asinorum*; ~ **of boats** (over boats moored abreast); BURN[2] one's *bridges*; **cross a ~ when** one **comes to it,** deal with a problem when and if it arises. **2.** (Naut.) raised platform from which ship is directed; upper bony part of nose; movable piece over which strings of violin etc. are stretched; (Bill.) long stick with device at end to support cue, support for cue formed with hand; bridgework; LAND[1]-*bridge*. **3.** **~'head,** post held on far side of river or other obstacle, facing enemy's position; ~ **passage,** (Mus. etc.) transition between main subjects; **~'work,** partial denture supported by teeth on each side. [OE *brycg*, = OS *bruggia*, OHG *brucca*, ON *bryggja* f. Gmc **brugjō*]
brĭdge[2] *v.t.* Be or make bridge over; span as if with bridge. [OE *brycgian* (as prec.)]
brĭdge[3] *n.* Card-game derived from whist, in which one player's cards are exposed and are played by his partner; (esp.) AUCTION *bridge* or CONTRACT[1] *bridge*; ~ **roll,** small soft bread roll. [19th c.; orig. unkn.]
brī'dle[1] *n.* Headgear to control horse, including headstall, bit, and rein; restraint, curb; (Naut.) mooring-cable; (Physiol.) ligament checking motion of a part; **~-path, -road,** etc., (fit for riders but not for vehicles). [OE *bridel*, = OHG *brittil*, WG f. as BRAID[2], + -LE 1]
brī'dle[2] *v.* **1.** *v.t.* Put bridle on (horse etc.); curb, hold in, bring under control. **2.** *v.i.* ~ (**up**), express offence, resentment, etc., (as if) by throwing up head and drawing in chin. [OE *brīdlian* (as prec.)]
brĭdōō'n *n.* Snaffle and rein of military bridle. [f. F *bridon* (*bride* bridle; see -OON)]
Brie *n.* Kind of soft cheese. [~ in N. France]
brief[1] *n.* Pope's letter on matter of discipline to person or community (less formal than bull); (Law) summary of facts and law-points of a case drawn up for counsel (**hold ~ for,** be retained as counsel for, be obliged to argue in favour of); ||piece of employment for barrister (DOCK[5] *brief*, WATCH[2]*ing brief*), whence ~'LESS *a.*; *(Law) statement of arguments to support case; instructions given to aircraft crews etc.; ||**~-bag** (in which barrister carries briefs); **~-case,** rectangular case for documents etc. [ME f. AF *bref*, OF *brief*, f. LL *breve* dispatch, note, neut. of L *brevis* short]
brief[2] *v.t.* ||Instruct (barrister) by brief; instruct (aircraft crews etc.) with regard to raid etc.; instruct or inform thoroughly in advance. [f. prec.]
brief[3] *a.* & *n.* **1.** *a.* Of short duration; concise in expression (**be** ~, speak in few words; **in** ~, in short); hence ~'LY[2] *adv.*, ~'NESS *n.* **2.** *n.* (in *pl.*) Men's very short underpants, women's very short knickers. [ME f. AF *bref*, OF *brief*, f. L *brevis* short]
brī'er[1], **brī'ar**[1], *n.* Prickly bush, esp. of wild rose; **~-rose,** dog-rose; **sweet-~,** wild rose with small fragrant leaves and flowers; hence ~Y[2] *a.* [OE *brǣr*, *brēr*, of unkn. orig.]
brī'er[2], **brī'ar**[2], *n.* White heath (*Erica arborea*) of S. Europe; tobacco pipe made from its root. [19th c. *bruyer* f. F *bruyère* heath f. Gallo-Rom. **brūcaria* (**brūcus* f. Gaulish **brūko*); assim. to prec.]

brĭg[1] *n.* Two-masted square-rigged vessel, with additional lower fore-and-aft sail on gaff and boom to mainmast; *prison, esp. in warship. [abbr. of BRIGANTINE]

brĭg[2]. Sc. & N. Engl. var. of BRIDGE[1].

Brig. *abbr.* Brigadier.

brigā'de *n.*, & *v.t.* **1.** *n.* Subdivision of army; ||infantry unit consisting usu. of 3 battalions and forming part of a division; corresponding armoured unit. **2.** Organized or uniformed band of workers (*fire brigade*). **3.** *v.t.* Form into brigade. [F, f. It. *brigata* company (*brigare* be busy with, f. *briga* strife); see -ADE]

brĭgadier' *n.* ~(**-general**), officer commanding a brigade, (titular rank granted to) staff officer of similar standing, above colonel and below major-general. [F; see prec., -IER]

brĭ'galow (-ō) *n.* (Austral.) One of various acacia trees. [Aboriginal]

brĭ'gand *n.* Member of robber band living by pillage and ransom; hence or cogn. ~AGE (3), ~ISM (2), ~RY (5), *ns.*, ~ISH[1] *a.* [ME f. OF, f. It. *brigante* (*brigare*; see BRIGADE)]

brĭ'gandīne *n.* Coat of mail, esp. made of iron rings or plates within canvas etc. [ME f. OF, or f. It. *brigantina* (as prec.; see -INE[4])]

brĭ'gantine (-ēn) *n.* Two-masted vessel with square-rigged foremast and fore-and-aft-rigged mainmast. [f. OF *brigandine* or f. It. *brigantino* (*brigante*; see BRIGAND)]

brīght[1] (-īt) *a.* & *adv.* **1.** *a.* Emitting or reflecting much light, shining, (~ **lights,** urban places of entertainment; ~**'work,** polished metal on ships etc.); lit up with joy, hope, etc.; (of colour) intense, shining; illustrious; vivacious; quick-witted; clever, talented, (*bright boy, idea*); hence ~'EN[6] (*up*) *v.t.* & *i.*, ~'ISH[1] 2 *a.*, ~'LY[2] *adv.*, ~'NESS *n.* **2.** *adv.* Brightly (*moon shines bright*); ~ **and early,** very early in the morning. [OE *beorht*, adv. *beorhte*, = OS, OHG *beraht*, ON *bjartr*, Goth. *bairhts* f. Gmc **berhtaz*]

Brīght[2] (-īt) *n.* ~**'s disease,** one of various forms of degeneration of the kidneys. [f. R. ~, Engl. physician d. 1858]

brĭll *n.* European flat-fish (*Scophthalmus rhombus*) resembling turbot. [15th c.; orig. unkn.]

brĭ'lli|ant[1] (-ly*a*-) *a.* Bright, sparkling; illustrious, striking; highly talented; showy; hence ~ANCE, ~ANCY, *ns.*, ~**ant**LY[2] *adv.* [f. F *brillant* part. of *briller* shine, f. It. *brillare*, of unkn. orig.]

brĭ'lliant[2] (-lya-) *n.* Diamond of finest cut and brilliance; ~ **shape** (with two horizontal surfaces joined by facets). [f. F as prec. used as n.]

brĭ'lliantine (-ly*a*ntēn) *n.* Cosmetic for making hair smooth and glossy; *shiny dress fabric. [f. F *brillantine* (as BRILLIANT[1]; see -INE[4])]

brĭm[1] *n.* Edge or lip of cup, bowl, or hollow; projecting edge of hat; ~**-full,** full to the brim; hence ~'LESS, ~**m**ED[2] (-md), *adjs.* [ME *brimme*, of unkn. orig.; cf. ON *barmr* brim, MHG *brem* border]

brĭm[2] *v.t.* & *i.* (**-mm-**). Fill or be full to the brim (lit. or fig.); ~ **over,** overflow (lit. or fig.). [f. prec.]

brĭm[3] *n.* (U.S. & Austral.) Var. of BREAM[1].

brĭ'mstone *n.* **1.** (arch.) Sulphur. **2.** Fuel of hell-fire; ~ (**butterfly, moth**), kind that is yellow like sulphur; hence **brĭ'mston**Y[2] *a.* [ME, prob. f. OE *bryne* burning + STONE]

brĭ'ndled (-deld), **brĭ'ndle,** *a.* Brownish or tawny with streaks of other colour. [*brindled* (whence back form. *brindle*) alt. of *brinded* f. earlier *brended* f. *brend*, perh. of Scand. orig.]

brīne *n.*, & *v.t.* **1.** *n.* Water saturated or nearly so with salt; the sea; ~**-pan,** salt-pan; hence **brī'n**Y[2] *a.* (**the briny,** ||(sl.) the sea). **2.** *v.t.* Steep in or saturate with brine. [OE *brīne*, = MDu. *brine*, of unkn. orig.]

brĭng *v.t.* (**brought** *pr.* -awt). **1.** Cause to come, come with or convey by carrying, leading, impelling, or attracting, (~**-and-buy** *sale* etc., at which customers bring things for sale and buy what is brought by others); be sold for (price); cause, result in; prefer (charge), initiate (legal action), adduce (argument); cause to become (*bring low*); cause despite reluctance (*cannot bring myself to believe, to do it*). **2.** ~ **home to,** convict or convince of; ~ **into being,** cause to exist; ~ **into play,** cause to operate; ~ **into the world,** give birth to; *bring to* BEAR[3]; *bring to* BOOK[1]; ~ **to mind,** (cause oneself to) remember; ~ **to pass,** cause to happen. **3.** ~ **about,** cause to happen, reverse (ship); ~ **back,** call to mind; ~ **down,** kill or wound, cause (penalty) to fall *on*, abase, make (flying bird, aircraft, etc.) fall, lower (price etc.), continue (record) *to* a point; ~ **the house down,** ~ **down the house,** (Theatr.) get loud applause; ~ **forth,** give birth to, produce, cause; ~ **forward,** draw attention to, move to earlier time, transfer from previous page or account; ~ **in,** introduce (custom, fashion, topic, legislation), produce as profit or increase, adduce, pronounce (verdict; person *guilty, not guilty*); ~ **off,** rescue from wreck etc., conduct (attempt) successfully; ~ **on,** cause, cause discussion of, advance progress of; ~ **out,** express, exhibit clearly, introduce (girl) to society, publish, make known; ~ **over,** convert; ~ **round,** restore to consciousness, bring incidentally or informally, win over (*to* other person's opinion); ~ **through,** save (sick person); ~ **to,** check motion of, (abs.) come to a stop, restore to consciousness; ~ **under,** subdue; ~ **up,** educate, rear, cause to appear in court, anchor (ship), (abs.) come to a stop, call attention to, vomit; ~ **up to date,** provide with what is needed to deal with latest developments; *bring up the* REAR[1]. **4.** Hence ~'ER[1] *n.* [OE *bringan*, = OS, OHG *bringan*, Goth. *briggan* f. Gmc **brengen*]

brĭ'njal (-awl) *n.* (Ind. & Afr.) Aubergine. [ult. f. Port. *berinjela* f. as AUBERGINE]

brĭnk *n.* Edge of steep place; border of water, esp. when steep (**shiver on the** ~, hesitate to plunge, usu. fig.); verge (*of* discovery, ruin, eternity, etc.); *the* verge of war; ~**'manship,** art of advancing to the very brink of war etc. but not engaging in it. [ME, f. ON **brenkōn* (OIcel. *brekka* slope), of unkn. orig.]

brī'nў. See BRINE.

brio (brē'ō) *n.* Vivacity. [It.]

bri'ŏche (brē'ŏsh) *n.* Small sweet cake made with light yeast dough. [F]

brĭquĕ'tte, brĭquĕ't, (-kĕ't) *n.* Block of compressed coal-dust. [F *briquette*, dim. of *brique* brick]

brĭsk *a.* & *v.* **1.** *a.* (Esp. of movement) active, lively, (*brisk pace, trade, wind*, etc.); enlivening, keen, (*air* etc.); hence ~'EN[6] *v.t.* & *i.*, ~'LY[2] *adv.*, ~'NESS *n.* **2.** *v.t.* & *i.* ~ (**up**), make or become brisk. [prob. f. F BRUSQUE]

brĭ'skėt *n.* Breast of animals (esp. as joint of meat). [f. AF **brusket, brisket*, OF *bruschet* etc., perh. f. ON *brjósk*; see -ET[1]]

brĭ'slĭng (*or* -z-) *n.* Small herring or sprat. [Norw. & Da., = sprat]

brĭ'stle[1] (-ĭ'sel) *n.* One of stiff hairs on pig's back and sides; short stiff hair of other animals, man's short-cropped beard, or plants; short stiff piece of wire etc.; ~**tail,** wingless insect of order Thysanura; ~**worm,** polychaete; hence **brĭ'stl**Y[2] (-ĭ'slĭ) *a.* [ME, prob. f. OE **brystel*, **byrstel* f. *byrst* (= OHG, ON *burst*) + -LE 1]

brĭ'stle[2] (-ĭ'sel) *v.i.* & *t.* (Cause to) stand upright (hair etc.); ~ (**up**), raise or rise like bristles or into roughness; show temper, prepare for fight; be thickly set *with* hair, difficulties, etc. [f. prec.]

brĭ'stlĭng (-sl-). Var. of BRISLING.

Brĭ'stol *n.* **1.** ~ **board,** kind of fine pasteboard for drawing on; (**shipshape and**) ~ **fashion,** (Naut. or transf.) with all in good order. **2.** (*b*~; in *pl.*, sl.) Woman's breasts. [~ in England]

Brit *n.* (colloq.) British person. [abbr.]

Brit. *abbr.* Britain; British.

Brĭtă'nnia (-ny*a*) *n.* Personification of Britain, usu. as woman with shield, helmet, and trident; ~ **metal,** alloy of tin, antimony, and copper, resembling silver; ~ **silver** (about 96% pure). [L, also *Brittan(n)ia* = Gk *Brettania* (*Brettanoi* Britons; see BRITISH)]

Brĭtă'nnĭc *a.* Of Britain (chiefly in phr. *Her* or *His Britannic Majesty*). [f. L *Britannicus* (as prec.; see -IC)]

Brĭ'tĭcism, Brĭ'tĭshĭsm, *n.* Idiom used in Gt. Britain and not in U.S. etc. [f. foll. + -ISM (4); *-icism* after *gallicism*]

Brĭ'tĭsh *a.* Of (Great) Britain or its inhabitants or language; *English; **the** ~, (*pl.*) British people; ~ **English** (esp. as contrasted with language of U.S. etc.); *British* LEGION; *British* THERMAL *unit*; ~ **warm,** kind of short military overcoat. [OE *Brettisc* etc. f. *Bret* (L *Britto* or OCelt. **Britto(s)*); see -ISH[1]]

Brĭ'tĭsher *n.* (U.S. etc. term for) British subject esp. of British descent. [f. prec. + -ER[1]; cf. *foreigner*]

Brĭ'tĭshĭsm. See BRITICISM.

Brĭ'ton *n.* One of the people living in S. Britain before the Roman conquest; native or inhabitant of Great Britain, or (Hist.) the British Empire. [ME & OF *Breton* f. L *Britto -onis* f. OCelt. **Britto(s)*]

brĭ'ttle *a.* & *n.* **1.** *a.* Apt to break, fragile; insecure; hard-natured; ~**-star,** kind of starfish; hence ~LY[2] (-tel-lĭ), **brĭ'ttLY**[2], *advs.*, ~NESS (-teln-) *n.* **2.** *n.* Brittle sweet made from nuts and melted sugar. [ME, f. *bryt-* f. Gmc **brut-* break up]

brĭ'tzka, -tzska, (-ĭ'tsk*a*) *n.* Open carriage with calash top and space for reclining. [f. Pol. *bryczka* dim. of *bryka* goods wagon]

brize (-ēz). Var. of BREEZE[1].

bro. *abbr.* brother.

broach[1] *n.* Roasting-spit; octagonal church-spire rising from tower without parapet; boring-bit. [ME f. OF *broche* f. Rom. **brocca* spike f. L *brocc(h)us* in *brocci dentes* projecting teeth; cf. BROOCH]

broach[2] *v.t.* Pierce (cask) to draw liquor, begin drawing (liquor); open and start using contents of (bale, box, cargo, etc.); begin discussion of (subject). [ME, f. OF *brocher* f. Rom. deriv. of prec.]

broach[3] *v.t.* & *i.* ~ (**to**), veer or cause (ship) to veer and present side to wind and waves. [18th c.; orig. unkn.]

broad (-awd) *a.*, *n.*, & *adv.* **1.** *a.* Large across, wide, not narrow; (appended to measurement) = in breadth (*6 ft. broad*); extensive (*broad* ACRES). **2.** Full, clear, main, explicit, (*broad daylight, facts, distinction, hint*); somewhat coarse (*broad story*), strongly dialectal etc. (*broad Yorkshire, Scots*), whence ~'NESS *n.*; generalized (*broad rule*; *in the broadest sense of the word*); tolerant (**B~ Church,** Anglican churchmen favouring comprehensiveness and not pressing doctrines); bold in effect or style; **as ~ as it is long,** without preference for either aspect. **3.** *Broad* ARROW; ~ **bean,** (large flat seed of) an edible bean; ~**-brow,** (colloq.) person with broad interests; ~**'cloth,** fine twilled woollen or worsted cloth, plain-woven cotton etc. cloth, [phr. in Act of Parl. 1482 kept as name for quality rather than width]; *~ **jump,** long jump; ~**-leaved,** (of tree) deciduous but hard-timbered; ~**'loom,** (carpet) woven in broad width; ~**mi'nded(ness),** (condition of) being tolerant or liberal in thought or opinion; *broad* PENNANT; ~**'sheet,** large sheet of paper printed on one side only; ~**'side,** (1) = *broadsheet*, (2) ship's side above water between bow and quarter (~*side on, to*, with this presented), (3) (discharge of) all guns on one side of ship, (fig.) powerful verbal attack; ~**'sword,** broad-bladed cutting-sword; ~**'tail,** caracul sheep, its lamb's fur; ~**'way,** a broad road; ***B~'way,** New York theatre life. **4.** *n.* The broad part (*broad of the back*); ||(in E. Anglia) large piece of fresh water formed by widening of river; *(sl.) woman, prostitute. **5.** *adv.* Broadly, fully (*broad awake*). **6.** Hence ~'EN[6] *v.t.* & *i.*, ~'LY[2], ~'WAYS, ~'WISE, *advs.* [OE *brād*, = OS *brēd*, OHG *breit*, ON *breithr*, Goth. *braiths* f. Gmc **braidhaz*]

broa'dcast (-aw'dkah-) *a.*, *adv.*, *v.* (*past* **-cast** *or* **-casted,** *p.p.* **-cast**), & *n.* **1.** *a.* (Of seed) scattered freely, not in drills or rows, (fig.) widely disseminated. **2.** *adv.* In broadcast manner. **3.** *v.t.* Sow or disseminate thus; disseminate (news, music, etc.) by radio or television. **4.** *v.i.* Speak, sing, play, etc., for radio or television transmission. **5.** *n.* Transmission by radio or television. [f. prec. + CAST[1] p.p.]

||**Broa'dmoor** (-aw'-; *or* -ŏŏr) *n.* Institution at Broadmoor for treatment of mental patients under special conditions (formerly housing insane criminals). [~ in Berkshire]

Brŏ'bdĭngnăg *n.* Land of giants; hence ~IAN (-ă'g-) *a.* [place in Swift's *Gulliver's Travels*]

brocā'de *n.*, & *v.t.* **1.** *n.* Fabric woven with raised patterns, orig. of added metal threads. **2.** *v.t.* Work with raised pattern. [f. Sp. & Port. *brocado* f. It. *broccato* & F *brocart* (It. *brocco* twisted thread; see -ADE)]

brŏ'ccolĭ *n.* Hardy variety of cauliflower; (**sprouting**) ~, form of this which produces many small heads. [It., pl. of *broccolo* cabbage-top dim. of *brocco*; see BROACH[1]]

brŏch (-ŏk *or* -ŏχ) *n.* Prehistoric circular stone tower in N. Scotland and adjacent islands. [f. ON *borg* castle]

brochĕ'tte (-shĕ't) *n.* Skewer on which chunks of meat are cooked. [F, dim. of *broche* BROACH[1]]

brō'chūre (-sh-) *n.* Booklet, pamphlet, esp. giving information about place etc. [F, lit. 'stitching' (*brocher* stitch; see -URE)]

brŏck *n.* Badger. [OE *broc(c)* f. OBrit. **brokkos*]

brŏ'ckĕt *n.* Second-year male red deer with straight horns. [ME, f. AF **broquet* dim. of *broque* (= *broche* BROACH[1]); see -ET[1]]

brō'derer *n.* (arch.) Embroiderer (now only as guild-name). [f. obs. *brouder* etc. f. OF (see EMBROIDER) + -ER[1]]

broderie anglaise (brōdrĭ ahṅglā'z) *n.* Open embroidery on white linen, cambric, etc.; fabric so embroidered. [F, = English embroidery]

brōgue[1] (-ōg) *n.* Rough shoe of untanned leather; strong outdoor shoe with ornamental perforated bands. [f. Gael. & Ir. *brōg* f. ON *brók*]

brōgue[2] (-ōg) *n.* Dialectal, esp. Irish, accent. [18th c., orig. unkn.; perh. allusively f. prec.]

broil[1] *v.t.* & *i.* Cook (meat) or be cooked on fire or gridiron; make or be very hot (of person in sun etc.); hence ~'ER[1] *n.*, young chicken reared for broiling, apparatus or compartment for broiling, very hot day; ~**'er house,** building for rearing broiler chickens in close confinement. [ME, f. OF *bruler* burn f. Rom. **brustulare*]

broil[2] *n.* (arch.) Quarrel; tumult. [f. obs. *broil* to muddle; cf. EMBROIL]

brōke *past* & *p.p.* of BREAK[1]; as *p.p.* arch. exc.: (colloq.) ruined, without money; ***go for** ~, (sl.) exert strenuous efforts.

brō'ken *a.* In vbl senses; ~ **chord,** (Mus.) chord in which notes are performed successively not simultaneously; ~ **cloud** (covering large part of sky); ~ **colour** (mixed or juxtaposed closely with another); ~**-down,** used or worn and hence broken or about to break; ~ **English** etc. (imperfect); ~ **ground** (uneven); ~**-hearted,** crushed by grief; ~ **home** (of family lacking one parent esp. through divorce or separation); ~ **line** (made up of dashes); ~ **man** (reduced to despair); *broken* REED[1]; ~ **sleep** (disturbed and intermittent); ~ **tea,** tea-siftings; ~ **time,** (esp. working) time reduced by interruptions; ~ **water** (choppy); ~**-winded,** (of horse) disabled by ruptured air-cells in lungs; hence ~LY[2] *adv.* [p.p. of BREAK[1]]

brō'ker *n.* Middleman in business; agent, commissioner; pawnbroker; stockbroker; ‖person licensed to sell or appraise distrained goods; hence ~AGE *n.*, (esp.) broker's fee or commission. [ME f. AF *brocour* = Prov. *abrocador,* of unkn. orig.]

brō'kĭng *n.* Broker's trade, acting as broker. [f. obs. *broke* v. (cf. prec.) + -ING[1]]

brŏ'lga *n.* (Austral.) Species of crane (*Grus rubicunda*) often seen in pairs. [Aboriginal]

‖**brŏ'llȳ** *n.* **1.** (colloq.) Umbrella. **2.** (sl.) Parachute. [abbr.]

brōm-. See BROMO-.

bromē'lĭa, -ĭad, *ns.* Amer. plant of family Bromeliaceae (esp. of genus *Bromelia*) usu. with spiny leaves, e.g. pineapple. [f. O. *Bromel,* Sw. botanist d. 1705 + -IA[1]]

brō'mĭc *a.* Containing bromine in chem. combination, esp. ~ **acid** ($HBrO_3$); hence **brō'm**ATE[1] (3) *n.* [f. BROMINE + -IC]

brō'mīde *n.* Binary compound of bromine, used in various preparations as sedative; commonplace bore, trite remark; ~ **paper,** photographic printing paper coated with silver bromide emulsion. [f. foll. + -IDE]

brō'mine (-ēn) *n.* Non-metallic element, a poisonous dark liquid with rank smell; hence **brō'm**ISM (5) *n.* [f. F *brome* f. Gk *brōmos* stink + -INE[5]]

brōmo-, (esp. bef. vowel) **brōm-,** *comb. form.* (Chem.) Bromine. [f. prec. + -O-]

***brŏnc** *n.* (colloq.) = BRONCO. [abbr.]

brŏ'nchĭa (-k-) *n. pl.* Ramifications of bronchi in lungs. [LL f. Gk (*brogkhos* windpipe)]

brŏ'nchĭal (-k-) *a.* Of bronchi or bronchia. [f. prec. + -AL]

brŏ'nchĭōle (-k-) *n.* Minute branch of bronchus. [f. mod. L **bronchiola* dim. of BRONCHIA]

brŏnch|ī'tĭs (-k-) *n.* Inflammation of bronchial mucous membrane; hence ~**ĭ't**IC *a.* & *n.* [mod. L, f. BRONCHUS + -ITIS]

brŏ'ncho- (-k-) *comb. form.* Bronchi, bronchia, throat, as: ~**cele** (-sēl), goitre; ~**scope,** instrument for inspecting interior of bronchi. [f. foll.]

brŏ'nch|us (-k-) *n.* (*pl.* ~**i** *pr.* -kī). Either of two main divisions of windpipe. [LL, as BRONCHIA]

brŏ'ncō *n.* (*pl.* ~**s**). Wild or half-tamed horse of California etc.; *~**-buster,** (sl.) breaker-in of broncos. [Sp., = rough]

brŏntosaur'us *n.* Herbivorous large dinosaur of genus *Brontosaurus* of the Jurassic and Cretaceous periods. [f. Gk *brontē* thunder + -O- + *sauros* lizard]

***Brŏnx** *n.* Cocktail of gin, vermouth, and orange-juice; ~ **cheer,** (sl.) sound of contempt or derision made with tongue between lips. [~ in New York]

brŏnze *n., a.,* & *v.* **1.** *n.* Brown alloy chiefly of copper and tin (**B~ Age,** time when weapons and tools were usu. made of bronze); work of art made of bronze; bronze medal; colour of bronze; hence **brŏ'nz**Y[2] *a.* **2.** *a.* Made of or coloured like bronze; ~ **medal,** medal of bronze usu. awarded as third prize. **3.** *v.t.* & *i.* Give bronzelike surface to; make or become brown, tan. [F, f. It. *bronzo,* prob. f. Pers. *birinj* copper]

brooch (-ō-) *n.* Ornament with hinged pin and catch, usu. worn fastened to woman's dress etc. or as badge etc. [ME *broche* = BROACH[1]]

brōōd[1] *n.* Young birds etc. from one hatching; (usu. derog. or joc.) human family, children; bee or wasp larvae; group of related things; ~**-mare** etc. (kept for breeding). [OE *brōd,* cogn. w. MDu. *broet,* OHG *bruot* f. Gmc **brōd-* (**brō-* warm, heat)]

brōōd[2] *v.i.* Sit as hen on eggs; (of night etc.) hang close *over* or *on*; meditate (esp. resentfully) (*on* or *over,* or abs.). [f. prec.]

brōō'der *n.* Heated house for chicks, piglets, etc. [f. prec. + -ER[1]]

brōō'd|ȳ *a.* (Of hen) wishing to incubate eggs; (fig.) feeling depressed; hence ~**ĭ**NESS *n.* [f. BROOD[1] + -Y[2]]

brŏŏk[1] *n.* Small stream; ~**'lime,** kind of speedwell common in ditches; hence ~'LET *n.* [OE *brōc,* = MLG *brōk,* OHG *bruoh* marsh, WG, of unkn. orig.; ~*lime* f. OE *hleomoce* name of the plant]

brŏŏk[2] *v.t.* (literary; usu. w. neg.) Put up with, tolerate. [OE *brūcan,* = OS *brūkan,* OHG *brūhhan,* Goth. *brūkjan* f. Gmc **brūk-* use f. IE **bhrug-*]

brōōm *n.* Yellow-flowered shrub of genus *Cytisus* or *Genista*; sweeping-implement usu. on long handle (**new** ~, newly appointed person eager to sweep away abuses); ~**'rape,** brown leafless parasitic plant growing on roots of broom etc. [L *rapum* tuber]; ~**'stick,** handle of broom (allegedly ridden on through the air by witches, and jumped over by parties to sham marriage). [OE *brōm,* = MLG *brām,* OHG *brāmo*; cf. BRAMBLE]

Bros. *abbr.* Brothers (esp. in title of firm).

‖**brōse** (-z) *n.* Dish of oatmeal with boiling water or milk poured on it; **Athole** ~, mixture of whisky, oatmeal, and honey. [Sc. form of *brewis* broth. ME f. OF *bro(u)ez* (*breu* f. Rom. **brodo* f. Gmc **brotham* BROTH)]

brŏth (*or* -aw-) *n.* Unclarified meat or fish stock; thin soup made from it; meat stock as nutrient medium for bacteria; ~ **of a boy,** (Ir.) good fellow. [OE, = ON *broth,* OHG *brod* f. Gmc **brotham* (**bru-* BREW; see -TH[1])]

brŏ'thel *n.* House etc. where prostitutes may be visited. [orig. ~*-house* f. ME *brothel* worthless man, prostitute, f. OE *brēothan* go to ruin]

bro'ther (-ŭ'dh-) *n.* **1.** Son of same parents or (also **half-**~) same parent as another person. **2.** Man who is a close friend, fellow citizen, countryman, associate, or equal. **3.** (*pl.* **brethren** *pr.* brĕ'dhrĭn). Man who is a fellow member of religious society (LAY[2] *brother*), trade union, regiment, guild, order, profession, etc.; official of certain companies etc.; ELDER[1] *brother.* **4.** (*pl.* also **brethren**). (As title) Member of religious order. **5.** ~ **german** (having same parents); ~ **uterine** (having same mother only); ~**-in-law,** brother of one's husband or wife, husband of one's sister; ‖*Brother* JONATHAN. **6.** Hence ~LY[1,2] *a.* & *adv.* [OE *brōthor,* = OS *brōthar,* OHG *bruodar,* ON *bróthir,* Goth. *brōthar* f. Gmc **brōthar* f. IE **bhrāter*]

bro'therhŏŏd (-ŭ'dh-) *n.* Relationship (as) between brothers; companionship; (members of) association for mutual help etc.; community of feeling; *trade union esp. of railwaymen; *(members of) a profession. [ME, alt. f.

brotherrede (f. OE *brōthor-rǣden*, cf. (KIND)RED) after wds in -HOOD, -HEAD]

brougham (-ōōm *or* -ōō'am) *n.* (Hist.) one-horse (or electric) closed carriage; motor car with driver's seat open. [f. Lord *B*~ d. 1868]

brought. See BRING.

brou'haha (brōō'hah-hah) *n.* Commotion, sensation; hubbub, uproar. [F]

brow *n.* **1.** Eyebrow (KNIT one's *brows*); forehead; (colloq.) level of intellect [after *highbrow* etc.]; hence (-)~ED² (-owd) *a.* **2.** Edge, projection, of cliff etc., top of hill in road. [OE *brū* f. Gmc **brūs* f. IE **bhrūs*]

brow'beat *v.t.* (**-beat; -beaten**). Bully or intimidate with looks and words. [f. BROW + BEAT¹]

brown¹ *a.* **1.** Of the colour given by mixing red, yellow, and black, or by toasting bread; (as distinguishing epithet) *brown bear, willow*; dark-skinned, sun-tanned. **2.** ~ **bread** (of unbolted flour); ~ **coal,** lignite; *brown* HOLLAND; ~ **paper,** unbleached kind used for packing etc.; *brown* STUDY¹ 2; ~ **sugar** (partly refined); **do** ~, (sl.) cheat. **3.** Hence ~'ISH¹ 2 *a.*, ~'NESS (-n-n-) *n.* [OE *brūn*, = OS, OHG *brūn*, ON *brúnn* f. Gmc **brūnaz*]

brown² *n.* Brown colour; brown pigment; brown clothes or material (*dressed in brown*); brown butterfly; brown ball in snooker etc.; ||**the** ~, brown mass of flying game-birds; *fire into the* ~, let fly into a covey without singling out a bird, (transf.) shoot at random into a mass. [f. prec.]

brown³ *v.t.* & *i.* Make or become brown by roasting, sunburn, etc.; ||**~ed off,** (sl.) bored, fed up; **~-out** *n.*, partial black-out or power cut. [f. BROWN¹]

Brow'nĭan *a.* ~ **movement** etc., irregular oscillations of microscopic particles suspended in a fluid. [f. R. *Brown*, Sc. botanist d. 1858, + -IAN]

brow'nĭe *n.* Benevolent shaggy goblin said to haunt house and do household work secretly; (*B*~) member of junior branch of Guides; (Austral. & N.Z.) sweet currant-bread; *square of rich cake with nuts. [f. BROWN¹ + -IE]

brow'nĭng *n.* Browned sugar or flour used to colour gravy etc. [f. BROWN³ + -ING¹]

***brow'nstōne** *n.* Kind of reddish-brown sandstone used for building (esp. in front elevation); house faced with this. [f. BROWN¹ + STONE]

browse¹ (-z) *n.* Twigs, young shoots, etc., as fodder for cattle; act of browsing. [earlier *brouse* f. OF *brost* young shoot, prob. f. Gmc]

browse² (-z) *v.t.* & *i.* **1.** Feed *on*, crop, (leaves, twigs, scanty vegetation). **2.** *v.i.* Feed thus; (fig.) read desultorily. [f. F *broster* (*brost*; see prec.)]

B.R.S. *abbr.* British Road Services.

brucĕllō'sĭs (brōō-) *n.* Disease caused by bacteria of genus *Brucella* (undulant fever in man, contagious abortion in cattle). [f. *Brucella* (f. Sir D. *Bruce*, Sc. physician d. 1931) + -OSIS]

Bru'ĭn (-ōō'-) *n.* (Personal name for) bear. [ME f. Du., = BROWN¹, name in *Reynard the Fox*]

bruise¹ (-ōōz) *n.* Injury by blow to body (also to fruit etc.) discolouring skin. [f. foll.]

bruise² (-ōōz) *v.t.* Injure by blow that discolours skin without breaking it or a bone (of human or animal body, also fruit, plant, etc.); crush, grind small; (fig.) hurt mentally; *bruised* REED¹. [ME, f. OE *brȳsan* crush, reinforced by AF *bruser*, OF *bruisier* break]

brui'ser (-ōō'z-) *n.* In vbl senses; prize-fighter. [f. prec. + -ER¹]

bruit¹ (-ōōt) *n.* (arch.) Report, rumour. [F, = noise (*bruire* roar)]

bruit² (-ōōt) *v.t.* (arch. or U.S.) Spread (report) *abroad* or *about*. [f. prec.]

||**Brŭm** *n.* (colloq.) Birmingham (England); hence ~'MIE *n.*, person from Birmingham. [abbr. of BRUMMAGEM]

brŭ'mbȳ *n.* (Austral.) Wild or unbroken horse. [19th c.; orig. unkn.]

brume (-ōōm) *n.* (poet.) Mist, fog. [F, f. L *bruma* winter]

Brŭ'mmagem *a.* Counterfeit; cheap and showy. [dial. form of *Birmingham*, England, w. ref. to counterfeit coins and plated goods once made there]

bru'mous (-ōō'-) *a.* Wintry; foggy. [f. F *brumeux* f. LL *brumosus* rainy (*bruma* winter; see -OUS)]

brŭnch *n.* (colloq.) Single meal instead of breakfast and lunch. [portmanteau wd]

brunĕ't (-ōō-) *n.* & *a.* Dark-skinned (person). [F, dim. of *brun* BROWN¹; see -ET¹]

brunĕ'tte (-ōō-) *n.* & *a.* Dark-skinned and/or brown-haired (woman). [F, fem. of prec.; see -ETTE]

brŭnt *n.* Chief stress *of* shock, attack, etc. (usu. in phr. *bear the brunt of*). [ME; orig. unkn.]

brŭsh¹ *n.* **1.** (arch. exc. U.S., Austral., etc.) Undergrowth, thicket, small trees and shrubs growing or (in U.S.) cut in faggots; land covered with such growth; (Austral.) dense forest. **2.** Implement of bristles, hair, wire, etc., set in wood etc. for scrubbing or sweeping; bunch of hairs etc. in straight handle, quill, etc., for painting, drawing, writing, etc.; one of pair of thin sticks with long wire bristles for striking drum, cymbal, etc. **3.** Bushy tail, esp. of fox; brushlike tuft. **4.** (Electr.) Brushlike discharge of sparks; piece of carbon or metal ending in wires or strips securing good metallic connection; movable strip of conducting material for making and breaking connection. **5.** (Austral. & N.Z. sl.) Girl, young woman. **6.** Application of brush, brushing; short smart encounter, skirmish, graze. **7.** **~'fire** (small-scale) *war*; ~ **turkey,** (Austral.) large mound-building bird; **~'wood,** undergrowth, thicket, cut or broken twigs etc.; **~'work,** painter's (style of) manipulation of brush. **8.** Hence ~'LESS *a.*, not requiring use of brush; ~'Y² *a.* [sense 1 ME, f. AF *brousse*, OF *brosse*, *broce*, sense 6 f. foll., other senses ME f. OF *brosse*, *broisse*, perh. both f. Rom. **bruscia*]

brŭsh² *v.t.* & *i.* **1.** Move briskly (esp. *by, through, against*); sweep or scrub clean, put in order, with brush; graze or touch in passing; remove (dust etc.) with brush; treat (surface) with brush to change its nature or appearance; **~ed aluminium** (lustreless); **~ed fabric** (with nap raised). **2.** ~ **aside,** dismiss or dispose of curtly or lightly; ~ **off,** dismiss, rebuff; *~-off* n., dismissal; ~ **over,** paint lightly; ~ **up,** furbish, renew one's acquaintance with (subject); so *~-up* n. [f. prec.]

brŭsque (-k; *or* -ŏŏsk) *a.* Blunt, offhand, abrupt, (of or in manner, speech); hence ~'LY² (-klĭ) *adv.*, ~'NESS (-kn-), **~'rie** (-skerē) [-ERY], *ns.* [F, f. It. *brusco* sour, as n. butcher's broom, f. Rom. **bruscum*]

Brŭ'ssels (-z) *n.* ~ **carpet** (with wool pile and stout linen back); ~ **lace,** rich pillow-lace or needle-point; ~ **sprouts,** edible buds of the cabbage *Brassica oleracea gemmifera*. [~ in Belgium]

brut (brōōt) *a.* (Of wine) unsweetened. [F]

bru'tal (-ōō'-) *a.* Coarse; savagely cruel; merciless (*brutal frankness*); hence ~ISM (2), **brută'l**ITY (-ōō-), *ns.*, ~IZE (1, 3) *v.t.* & *i.*, ~LY² *adv.* [F, or f. med. L *brutalis* (*brutus* BRUTE; see -AL)]

brute (-ōōt) *a.* & *n.* **1.** *a.* Not possessing capacity to reason; stupid, sensual, beastlike, cruel, or passionate (person, act, motive, etc.); unconscious, merely material, (*brute force, matter*). **2.** Brute person or beast; (colloq.) disliked person. **3.** Hence ~'HOOD (-t-h-) *n.*, **bru'tish**[1] 1 (-ōō'-) *a.* [f. F *brut(e)* f. L *brutus* stupid]

brȳŏ'log|ȳ *n.* Science of mosses; hence ~IST (3) *n.* [f. Gk *bruon* moss + -O- + -LOGY]

brȳ'onȳ *n.* Climbing plant of genus *Bryonia*; **black ~,** similar plant (*Tamus communis*). [f. L f. Gk *bruōnia*]

brȳ'ophȳte *n.* Moss or liverwort. [f. mod. L *Bryophyta* f. Gk *bruon* moss + *phuton* plant]

brȳozō'|an *a.* & *n.* (Member) of phylum Bryozoa of aquatic animals forming colonies; hence **~ŏ'**LOGY *n.* [f. Gk *bruon* moss + *zōia* animals + -AN]

Brȳthŏ'nĭc *a.* & *n.* (Language) of the Celts of S. Britain. [f. W *Brython* Britons f. OCelt. **Brittones*, + -IC]

B.S. *abbr.* *Bachelor of Science; Bachelor of Surgery; British Standard.

||**B.S.A.** *abbr.* Birmingham Small Arms (Company).

B.Sc. *abbr.* Bachelor of Science.

B.S.I. *abbr.* British Standards Institution.

B.S.T. *abbr.* British Standard Time; British Summer Time.

Bt. *abbr.* Baronet.

B.th.u., B.t.u., *abbr.* British thermal unit(s).

bu. *abbr.* bushel(s).

bŭb[1] *n.* (usu. in *pl.*) Woman's breast. [f. earlier *bubby*; cf. dial. G *bübbi* teat]

***bŭb**[2] *n.* (colloq.) (Word of address to) boy, man. [f. earlier *bubby*, perh. childish form of BROTHER or f. G *bube* boy]

bū'bal *n.* N. Afr. and Arabian antelope (*Alcelaphus buselaphus*). [f. L f. Gk *boubalos* oxlike antelope]

bŭ'bble[1] *n.* **1.** Spherical or hemispherical envelope of liquid enclosing air etc.; air-filled cavity in solidified liquid, as glass or amber; transparent domed canopy; unsubstantial or visionary project, enterprise, etc. (SOUTH *Sea Bubble*). **2.** Sound or appearance of boiling. **3.** **~ and squeak,** cold meat or potatoes fried with chopped vegetables; **~ bath** (in which water is made to foam by perfumed toilet preparation); **~ car,** small motor car with transparent dome; *bubble* CHAMBER; **~ gum,** chewing-gum that can be blown into large bubbles; **~ pack,** small package enclosing goods in transparent material on backing. **4.** Hence **bŭ'bbly**[2] *a.*, & *n.*. ||(sl.) champagne. [ME, prob. imit.]

bŭ'bble[2] *v.i.* Send up, rise in, make the sound of, bubbles (lit. or fig.; **~ (over)**, be exuberant *with* laughter, anger, excitement). [ME, prob. imit.]

bŭ'bblȳ-jŏck *n.* (Sc.) Turkey-cock. [f. *bubbly* (imit., BUBBLE[1]) + *Jock* = *Jack*]

bū'b|ō *n.* (*pl.* **~oes**). Inflamed swelling in glandular part, esp. groin or armpit; hence **~ŏ'nic** *a.* (esp. **~onic plague,** contagious bacterial disease characterized by presence of buboes), **~ŏ'no**CELE *n.*, hernia of groin. [L, f. Gk *boubōn* groin]

bū'ccal *a.* Of the cheek; of or in the mouth. [f. L *bucca* cheek + -AL]

bŭccaneer' *n.*, & *v.i.* (Be) pirate, orig. of the Spanish-American coasts; (be) unscrupulous adventurer; hence ~ISH[1] *a.* [f. F *boucanier* f. *boucaner* cure meat on a *boucan* (i.e. barbecue), f. Tupi *mukem*]

bŭ'ccinātor (-ksĭ-) *n.* Flat thin cheek-muscle. [L, f. *buccinare* blow trumpet (*buccina*); see -OR]

Bu'chman|ĭsm (bōō'k- *or* bŭ'k-) *n.* (usu. derog.) Theories or practice of the Oxford Group Movement; so ~ITE[1] *a.* & *n.* [f. F. *Buchman*, Amer. evangelist d. 1961 + -ISM]

bŭck[1] *n.* **1.** Male of fallow-deer, roe-deer, reindeer, chamois, antelope, hare, rabbit, ferret, or rat; (arch.) dandy; (*attrib.*, sl.) male (*buck nigger*, derog.), *(Mil.) of lowest rank (*buck private* etc.). **2.** **~'bean,** bog-plant with white or pinkish flowers; **~'eye,** (*n.*) shrub or tree of genus *Aesculus*, its nut or fruit, (*a.*) *showy but not impressive; ***B~eye State,** Ohio; ***~ fever,** nervousness when called on to act; **~-horn,** horn of buck as material for knife-handles etc.; **~-hound,** small variety of staghound; **~ rarebit,** Welsh rarebit with poached egg; **~'shot,** coarse shot; **~'skin,** (leather made of) buck's or similar skin, thick smooth cotton or woollen cloth; **~'thorn,** thorny shrub with cathartic berries, esp. of genus *Rhamnus*; **~-tooth,** one that projects. [OE *buc* male deer, = OHG *boc*, ON *bukkr* f. Gmc **bukkaz*, and OE *bucca* male goat, f. ON **bukkon*]

bŭck[2] *v.* **1.** *v.i.* (Of horse) jump vertically with back arched and feet drawn together. **2.** *v.t.* **~ (off)**, throw (rider or burden) thus; *oppose, resist. [f. prec.]

bŭck[3] *v.i.* & *t.* (sl.) **~ (up)**, make haste, become or make vigorous or cheerful (esp. in *imper.*); (in *p.p.*) encouraged, elated. [f. BUCK[1] in sense *dandy*]

bŭck[4] *n.* Basket for trapping eels. [19th c.; orig. unkn.]

bŭck[5] *n.* Body of cart; ***~'board,** (vehicle with) body formed by plank on wheels. [perh. f. obs. *bouk* belly, f. OE *būc* f. Gmc **būkaz*]

bŭck[6] *n.* Conversation; boastful talk. [f. Hindi *buk buk*]

bŭck[7] *n.* (sl.) Article placed as reminder before player whose turn it is to deal at poker; **pass the ~,** (colloq.) shift responsibility (*to* another). [19th c.; orig. unkn.]

bŭck[8] *n.* (U.S. & Austral. sl.) Dollar; **a fast ~,** easy money. [19th c.; orig. unkn.]

bŭck[9] *n.* *Saw-horse; vaulting-horse. [f. Du. (*zaag*)*boc*]

bŭ'ckėt[1] *n.* **1.** Vessel for drawing, holding, or carrying water etc.; **~(ful)**, amount contained in this; (in *pl.*) large quantities (of rain, tears, etc.). **2.** Compartment of water-wheel, scoop of dredger or grain-elevator. **3.** **Kick the ~,** (sl.) die [perh. f. obs. *bucket* beam, yoke]; **~ seat** (with rounded back to fit one person); **~-shop,** office for gambling in stocks, speculating on markets, etc. [ME & AF *buket*, *buquet*, perh. f. OE *būc* pitcher; see -ET[1]]

bŭ'ckėt[2] *v.i.* & *t.* Move or drive jerkily or bumpily; (of rain etc.) pour down heavily. [f. prec.]

bŭ'ckle[1] *n.* Metal rim with hinged spiked tongue for securing strap, belt, etc. [ME, f. OF *boucle* f. L *buccula* cheek-strap of helmet (*bucca* cheek; see -ULE)]

bŭ'ckle[2] *v.t.* & *i.* **1.** Fasten (*up*, *on*, etc.) with buckle; **~ (down) to,** prepare for, set about, (work etc.); **~ to,** get to work, make vigorous start. **2.** **~ (up)**, (cause to) give way, crumple up, under longitudinal pressure. [f. prec.; in sense 2 f. F *boucler* bulge]

bŭ'ckler *n.* (Hist.) small round shield usu. held by a handle; (Bot.) shield-fern. [ME, f. OF *bocler* lit. 'having a boss' (*boucle* BOSS[1]; see -ER[2])]

bŭ'cklĭng *n.* Smoked herring. [f. G *bückling* bloater]

bŭ'ckō *n.* (*pl.* **~es**) & *a.* (Naut. sl.) Swaggering or domineering (fellow). [f. BUCK[1] + -O]

bŭ'ckram *n.* & *a.* Coarse linen or cloth stiffened with gum or paste; stiff(ness) in manner; **men in ~,** figment (Shak. *1 Henry IV* II. iv. 210–50). [ME, f. AF *bukeram*, OF *boquerant*, perh. f. *Bokhara* in central Asia]

Bŭcks. *abbr.* Buckinghamshire.

||**bŭ'ckshee** *n.*, *a.*, & *adv.* (sl.) **1.** *n.* Something in addition to the usual allowance; something extra or free. **2.** *a.* & *adv.* Gratuitous(ly), free of charge. [corrupt. of BAKSHEESH]

bŭ'ckwheat (-wēt) *n.* Cereal plant of genus *Fagopyrum*, whose seed is used esp. for horse and poultry food, and in U.S. for breakfast pancakes. [f. MDu. *boecweite* beech wheat, its grains being shaped like beechmast]

būcŏ'l|ĭc *a.* & *n.* **1.** *a.* Of shepherds, pastoral, rustic; hence ~ICALLY *adv.* **2.** *n.* (usu. in *pl.*) Pastoral poem, e.g. Virgil's eclogues. [f. L f. Gk *boukolikos* (*boukolos* herdsman f. *bous* ox)]

bŭd[1] *n.* Rudiment of shoot, foliage, or flower; leaf or flower not fully open; (Zool.) asexual growth later separating to form new animal; anything still undeveloped; **in** ~, putting forth buds; **nip in the** ~, (fig.) destroy at early stage of development. [ME, of unkn. orig.]

bŭd[2] *v.i.* & *t.* (**-dd-**). Put forth buds; begin to grow or develop (*budding lawyer, cricketer*); (Zool.) form (as) bud; (Hort.) graft bud of (plant) on to another plant. [f. prec.]

***bŭd**[3] *n.* (colloq.) = BUDDY (esp. as *voc.*). [abbr.]

Bu'ddh|a (bŏŏ'd*a*) *n.* Title of successive teachers past and future of the Asian religion ~ISM (3) *n.*, esp. of its founder, the Ind. philosopher Gautama (5th c. B.C.); hence ~IST (2) *n.* & *a.*, ~**ĭ'st**IC(AL) *adjs.* [Skr., = enlightened, p.p. of *budh* know]

bŭ'ddleia (-lĭ*a*) *n.* Shrub or tree of genus *Buddleia*, with fragrant lilac or yellow flowers. [f. A. *Buddle*, Engl. botanist d. 1715 + -IA[1]]

bŭ'ddy̆ *n.*, & *v.i.* (colloq.) **1.** *n.* (often as *voc.*) Brother, companion, friend. **2.** *v.i.* ~ (**up**), become friendly. [perh. corrupt. of *brother*, or var. of BUTTY[1]]

bŭdge *v.* (In neg. sentences). **1.** *v.i.* Make slightest movement; change opinion. **2.** *v.t.* Compel to budge. [f. F *bouger* stir f. Rom. **bullicare* frequent. of L *bullire* boil]

bŭ'dgerĭgar̂ *n.* Austral. grass parakeet, often kept as cage-bird. [Aboriginal, = good cockatoo]

bŭ'dgėt *n.* & *v.* **1.** *n.* Annual estimate of revenue and expenditure of a country or organization; private person's or family's similar estimate; amount of money needed or available; (*attrib.*) inexpensive; **on a** ~, avoiding undue expense; hence ~ARY[1] *a.* **2.** (arch.) Quantity of material etc., esp. written or printed matter. **3.** *v.i.* & *t.* ~ (**for**), allow or arrange for in budget. [ME = pouch, f. OF *bougette* dim. of *bouge* leather bag f. L *bulga* (f. Gaulish) knapsack; cf. BULGE[1]]

bŭ'dgĭe *n.* (colloq.) = BUDGERIGAR. [abbr.; see -IE]

bŭff[1] *n.* & *a.* (Of) velvety dull-yellow ox-leather; human skin (**in the** ~, naked); (of) dull-yellow colour (**the B**~**s**, former East Kent Regiment, from colour of facings); *(colloq.) enthusiast [orig. for watching fires, f. buff uniforms formerly worn by New York volunteer firemen]; ~**-stick,** stick covered with buff for polishing. [orig. sense 'buffalo', prob. f. F *buffle*]

bŭff[2] *v.t.* Polish (metal, finger-nails, etc.); make (leather) velvety like buff. [f. prec.]

bŭ'ffalō *n.* (*pl.* ~**es,** *or* same). **1.** Ox esp. of one of three species: *Bubalus bubalis* of Asia, *Syncerus caffer* of S. Africa, and *Bison bison* of N. America; ||member of a sociable and benevolent organization (*Royal Antediluvian Order of Buffaloes*); amphibious tank. **2.** ~ **chips,** dried dung of buffalo etc. as fuel; *~ **grass,** prairie grass formerly common on buffalo pastures; *~ **robe,** lined trimmed hide of buffalo as rug etc. [prob. f. Port. *bufalo* f. LL *bufalus* f. L f. Gk *boubalos* antelope, wild ox]

bŭ'ffer[1] *n.*, & *v.t.* **1.** *n.* Apparatus for deadening impact, esp. ||of railway vehicles; (Chem.) substance tending to maintain constant acidity of solution; intermediate store in computer; ~ **solution** (Chem., containing buffer); ~ **state,** small State between two possible belligerents, diminishing chance of hostilities; ~ **stock,** reserve of commodity to offset price fluctuations. **2.** *v.t.* Act as buffer to; (Chem.) treat with buffer. [prob. f. obs. *buff* v., imit. of sound of soft body struck, + -ER[1]]

bŭ'ffer[2] *n.* (sl.) (**Old**) ~, (old-fashioned or incompetent) fellow. [18th c., prob. f. as prec. or w. sense 'stutterer']

bŭ'ffėt[1] *n.*, & *v.t.* (Strike with) blow of or as of hand; (of fate etc.) knock, hurt, plague; contend with (waves etc.); hence ~ING[1] (1, 2) *n.*, beating, repeated blows, (Aeron.) irregular oscillation, caused by air eddies, of any part of an aircraft. [ME f. OF, dim. of *bufe* blow]

bu'ffet[2] (bŏŏ'fā) *n.* **1.** (*or* bŭ'fĭt). Sideboard or recessed cupboard for china, plate, etc. **2.** (Place offering) service of food from sideboard or counter where guests or customers serve themselves; ~ **car,** railway coach serving light meals; ~ **meal** (served from sideboard etc.). [F, f. OF *bufet* stool, of unkn. orig.]

bŭ'fflehead (-felhĕd) *n.* N. Amer. duck with seemingly over-large head. [f. obs. *buffle* BUFFALO + HEAD[1]]

buffo (bŏŏ'fō) *n.* (*pl.* ~**s**) & *a.* Burlesque, comic, (actor). [It.]

buffōō'n *n.*, & *v.i.* (Play the) wag, jester, or mocker; hence ~ERY (4) *n.* [f. F *bouffon* f. It. *buffone* f. med. L *buffo* clown f. Rom. **buffare* puff; see -OON]

bŭg *n.*, & *v.t.* (**-gg-**). **1.** *n.* Hemipterous insect, esp. (**be'd**)~, flat evil-smelling blood-sucking one (*Cimex lectularius*) infesting beds; *any small insect. **2.** (sl.) Micro-organism, esp. virus, or disease caused by it; (person having) obsession; enthusiast; concealed microphone; defect. **3.** BIG *bug*; ~**-eyed,** with bulging eyes; ~**'house,** (sl.) (*n.*) mental hospital, (*a.*) *crazy; ~**-hunter,** (colloq.) entomologist. **4.** *v.t.* (sl.) Install concealed microphone in, listen to by this means; *annoy, bother. **5.** *v.i.* (sl.) *~ **out,** leave quickly. [17th c.; orig. unkn.]

bŭ'gabōō, bŭ'gbear (-bār̆), *ns.* Object of baseless fear; false belief used to intimidate or dissuade; *bête noire*, cause of annoyance. [*bugbear* f. obs. *bug* + BEAR[1]; *bugaboo* prob. dial.]

bŭ'gger (-g-) *n.* & *v.* **1.** *n.* Sodomite; (Law) person who commits bestiality; hence **bŭ'gg**ERY (4) *n.* **2.** (vulg.) (Esp. unpleasant) fellow or thing; = DAMN 3; ~**-all,** nothing. **3.** *v.t.* Commit buggery with. **4.** *v.t.* & *i.* (vulg.) = DAMN 2; ~ **about, around,** persecute, mess about (*with*); ~ **off,** go away; ~ (**up**), ruin, spoil. [ME f. MDu., f. OF *bougre*, orig. 'heretic' f. med. L *Bulgarus* Bulgarian (member of Greek Church)]

||**Bŭ'ggĭns** (-gĭnz) *n.* ~**'s turn,** appointment by rotation rather than by merit. ['typical' name used generically]

bŭ'ggy̆[1] (-gĭ) *a.* Infested with bugs. [f. BUG + -Y[2]]

bŭ'ggy[2] (-gĭ) *n.* Light horse-drawn vehicle for one or two persons; small sturdy motor vehicle (*beach, dune*, etc. *buggy*); *BABY *buggy*. [18th c.; orig. unkn.]

bū'gle[1] *n.* & *v.* **1.** *n.* ~(**-horn**), brass instrument like small trumpet used by huntsmen and for military signals. **2.** *v.i.* Sound bugle. **3.** *v.t.* Sound (call) on bugle. **4.** Hence **bū'gl**ER[1], **bū'gl**ET[1], *ns.* [ME, orig. = 'buffalo', f. OF f. L *buculus* dim. of *bos* ox]

bū'gle[2] *n.* Creeping plant of genus *Ajuga* with usu. blue flowers. [ME, f. LL *bugula*]

bū'gle[3] *n.* Tube-shaped glass bead sewn on dress etc. for ornament. [16th c.; orig. unkn.]

bū'glŏss *n.* Plant allied to borage, of various genera; VIPER's *bugloss*. [f. F *buglosse* or L f. Gk *bouglōssos* ox-tongued]

buhl, boule[3]**, boulle,** (bōōl) *n.* & *a.* (Inlaid with) brass, tortoise-shell, etc., cut in ornamental patterns for inlaying. [(*buhl* Germanized) f. A. C. *Boule*, Fr. wood-carver d. 1732]

buĭld[1] (bĭ-) *v.* (**built** *pr.* bĭ-, arch. **~'ed**). **1.** *v.t.* Construct by putting parts or material together (house, ship, nest, vehicle, fire, road, or other structure large or intricate relative to the user); (in *p.p.*) having specified build (*sturdily built, clinker-built*, etc.); **~ in, round, up,** surround with houses etc., block up; lay (material) *in(to* wall etc.) as part of structure; **built-in,** forming integral part of structure, (fig.) personality, etc.; **built-up,** (1) increased in height etc. by addition of parts, (2) composed of separately prepared parts, (3, of locality) fully occupied by houses etc. **2.** Establish, make (*up*) or accumulate gradually; base (hopes etc.); **~ up,** praise, boost; **~'up** *n.*, favourable description in advance, gradual approach to a climax or maximum. **3.** *v.i.* **~ on,** rely on; **~ up,** gradually establish itself. [OE *byldan* (*bold* dwelling f. Gmc **bu-* dwell; cf. BOWER[1], BOOTH)]

buĭld[2] (bĭ-) *n.* Style of construction, make; proportions of human body (*sturdy build* etc.). [f. prec.]

buĭ'lder (bĭ'-) *n.* In vbl senses; master builder, contractor for building houses. [f. BUILD[1] + -ER[1]]

buĭ'ldĭng (bĭ'-) *n.* In vbl senses; house, school, factory, stable, etc.; **~ line,** limit relative to frontage beyond which owners may not build; ||**~ society** (of investors in fund for loan to persons buying houses etc.). [f. BUILD[1] + -ING[1]]

built. See BUILD[1].

bŭlb *n.* Globular base of stem of lily, onion, etc., sending roots downwards and leaves etc. upwards; compressible globular rubber attachment for pneumatic operation of syringe etc.; (Anat.) roundish swelling of any cylindrical organ, as of hair-root or spinal cord; dilated part of glass tube, e.g. reservoir of thermometer; (glass container of) electric lamp; so **~'**OUS *a.*, of, having, like, bulb(s), (esp. of plant) growing from a bulb. [f. L *bulbus* f. Gk *bolbos* onion]

bu'lbul (bōō'lbōōl) *n.* Asian song-thrush; singer, poet. [Pers. f. Arab., of imit. orig.]

Bŭ'lgar *n.* Native or inhabitant of Bulgaria; so **Bŭlgar'**IAN *a.* & *n.*, (native, inhabitant, or language) of Bulgaria. [f. med. L *Bulgarus* f. OBulg. *Blugarinu*]

bŭlge[1] *n.* Convex part, irregular swelling, tendency to swell out, on flat or flatter surface; bilge of ship; (colloq.) temporary increase in volume or numbers; (Mil.) salient; (sl.) advantage (esp. in phr. **have,** or **get, the ~ on,** have, get, the advantage over); hence **bŭ'lg**Y[2] *a.* [ME, f. OF *boulge, bouge* f. L *bulga*; see BUDGET]

bŭ'lge[2] *v.i.* & *t.* Swell outwards; be replete; extend (bag etc.) by stuffing it. [f. prec.]

bŭlĭ'mĭa *n.* (Med.) Morbid hunger. [mod. L f. Gk *boulimia* (*bous* ox, *limos* hunger)]

bŭlk[1] *n.* Cargo (**break ~,** begin unloading; **in ~,** loose, not in package); large quantity (*save money by posting in bulk*); large shape, person, or body; size, magnitude; great size; mass, large mass; roughage; *the* greater part or number *of*; **~ buying,** buying in large amounts, purchase by one buyer of all or most of a producer's output. [sense 'cargo' f. OIcel. *búlki*; sense 'mass' etc. perh. alt. f. obs. *bouk* (cf. BUCK[5])]

bŭlk[2] *v.* **1.** *v.i.* Seem in respect of size or importance (*bulk large, larger*). **2.** *v.t.* Combine (consignments etc.); make (book, textile yarn, etc.) seem thicker by suitable treatment. [f. prec.]

bŭ'lkhead (-hĕd) *n.* Upright partition separating compartments in ship, aircraft, vehicle, etc. [f. *bulk* stall f. ON *bálkr* + HEAD[1]]

bŭ'lk|y̆ *a.* Of great or too great size; unwieldy; hence **~ĭLY**[2] *adv.*, **~ĭNESS** *n.* [f. BULK[1] + -Y[2]]

bull[1] (bōōl) *n.* & *a.* **1.** *n.* Uncastrated male of ox 2, or of any bovine animal (**~ in a china shop,** reckless or clumsy destroyer; **take the ~ by the horns,** meet difficulty boldly); male of whale, elephant, and other large animals; (*B~*) *the* zodiacal sign Taurus; *(sl.) policeman. **2.** (St. Exch.). One who buys, hoping to sell at higher price later (cf. BEAR[1]); hence **~'**ISH[1] *a.* **3.** = *bull's-eye* (of target). **4.** *a.* Like that of a bull (*bull head, neck*). **5. ~ ant,** (Austral.) = *bull-dog ant*; **~-at-a-gate,** directly attacking; **~'dog,** dog of powerful and courageous large-headed smooth-haired breed, tenacious and courageous (person), (Oxf. & Camb.) University proctor's attendant; **~dog ant,** (Austral.) large ant with vicious sting; **~dog clip,** fastener with strong closure; **~'doze** *v.t.*, (colloq.) clear with bulldozer, make one's *way* forcibly, intimidate, coerce; **~'dozer,** powerful tractor with broad vertical blade in front, used for clearing ground etc.; ***~-fiddle,** (colloq.) double-bass; **~'fight(ing),** Spanish etc. sport of baiting and usu. killing bull with horsemen etc.; **~'finch,** (1) strong-beaked handsome-plumaged song-bird, (2) quickset hedge with ditch [perh. f. 'bull fence']; **~'frog,** large Amer. frog with loud bellow; **~'head,** small big-headed fish, esp. MILLER's thumb; **~-headed,** obstinate, impetuous, blundering; **~-horn,** megaphone; **~ market** (with rising prices); **~-nose(d),** with rounded end; **~-of-the-bog,** bittern; ***~'pen,** exercise area for baseball pitchers; ***~-pine,** ponderosa; **~ point,** (colloq.) point of superiority; **~-puncher,** (Austral.) bullock-driver; **~'ring,** arena for bullfight; **~'roarer,** flat strip of wood tied to a string, making a roaring sound when whirled round, used esp. in religious rites of Australian Aboriginals; ***~ session,** informal group discussion; **~'s-eye,** boss of glass formed at centre of blown glass sheet, hemispherical piece or thick disc of glass as light in ship's deck or side, hemispherical lens, (lantern) with such lens, small circular window, centre of target, large round peppermint sweetmeat; **~'shit,** (vulg.) nonsense, BULL[6]; **~-terrier,** dog of short-haired breed that is cross between bulldog and terrier; ||**~'trout,** salmon trout. [ME, f. ON *boli* = MLG, MDu. *bulle*]

bull[2] (bōōl) *v.i.* & *t.* Act or treat violently etc.; (St. Exch.) speculate for a rise; raise price of (stocks etc.). [f. prec.]

bull[3] (bōōl) *n.* Papal edict. [ME, f. OF *bulle* f. L *bulla* rounded object, in med. L 'seal']

bull[4] (bōōl) *n.* (**Irish**) **~,** expression containing contradiction in terms or implying ludicrous inconsistency. [17th c.; orig. unkn.]

bull[5] (bōōl) *n.* Drink made of water flavoured by being put in empty spirit cask. [19th c.; orig. unkn.]

bull[6] (bōōl) *n.* (sl.) Unnecessary routine tasks or discipline; nonsense; trivial or insincere talk or writing; *bad blunder. [f. BULL[4]]

bull[7] (bōōl) *n.* Deck-game in which small flat sandbags are thrown on an inclined board marked with numbered squares. [19th c.; orig. unkn.]

bu'llace (bōō'lĭs) *n.* Species of wild (or semi-cultivated) plum-tree (*Prunus insititia*) or its fruit. [ME, f. OF *buloce, beloce* f. Rom. **bulluca* sloe]

bu'llāte (bŏŏ'-) *a.* (Bot. etc.) Having blisters. [f. med. L *bullatus* f. L *bulla* bubble; see -ATE[2]]

bu'ller (bŏŏ'-) *n.* (sl.) = BULL[1]*dog* (proctor's attendant). [f. *bulldog* + -ER[1] (5)]

bu'llėt (bŏŏ'-) *n.* Missile of lead etc. (usu. round, or cylindrical and pointed) used in rifles, revolvers, etc.; **~-head(ed)**, (with) round head; *bullet*-PROOF[2]. [f. F *boulet, boulette* dim. of *boule* ball f. L *bulla* bubble; cf. -ET[1]]

bu'llėtĭn (bŏŏ'-) *n.* Short official statement or broadcast report of public event or news or of invalid's condition; ***~-board,** notice-board. [F, f. It. *bullettino* dim. of *bulletta* passport dim. of *bulla* seal, BULL[3]]

Bu'llī (bŏŏ'-) *n.* (Austral.) Type of soil used for cricket pitches etc. [~ in New South Wales]

bu'llion (bŏŏ'lyon) *n.* Metal, esp. gold or silver, before (or as valued apart from) coining or manufacture. [AF, = mint, var. of OF *bouillon* f. Rom. **bullio -onis* (*bullire* BOIL[2]; see -ION)]

bu'llock[1] (bŏŏ'-) *n.* Bull after castration; **~-cart,** cart drawn by bullock(s). [OE *bulluc*, dim. of BULL[1]; see -OCK]

bu'llock[2] (bŏŏ'-) *v.t.* Make one's *way* with heavy violence. [f. prec.]

bu'llockỹ (bŏŏ'-) *n.* (Austral. & N.Z. colloq.) Bullock-driver. [f. BULLOCK[1] + -Y[3]]

bu'llỹ[1] (bŏŏ'-) *n.* Person who uses strength or power to coerce others by fear; (arch.) pimp; **~(-boy)**, hired ruffian. [orig. as term of endearment, prob. f. MDu. *boele* lover]

bu'llỹ[2] (bŏŏ'-) *v.t.* Persecute, oppress, physically or morally, by (threat of) superior force; frighten *into* or *out of*. [f. prec.]

bu'llỹ[3] (bŏŏ'-) *a.* & *int.* Very good, first-rate; **~ for you, him,** etc., bravo. [perh. f. BULLY[1]]

bu'llỹ[4] (bŏŏ'-) *n.*, & *v.i.* (Hockey). **1.** *n.* Procedure for putting ball in play, beginning with threefold striking of two opposing players' sticks. **2.** *v.i.* **~ off,** start play in this way. [19th c., perh. f. *bully* scrum in Eton football; orig. unkn.]

bu'llỹ[5] (bŏŏ'-) *n.* **~ (beef)**, corned beef. [f. F *bouilli* boiled beef (*bouillir* BOIL[2])]

bu'llỹrăg (bŏŏ'-). Var. of BALLYRAG.

bu'llỹ tree (bŏŏ'-) *n.* = BALATA. [corrupt.]

bu'ln-buln (bŏŏ'-; -bŏŏ-) *n.* (Austral.) Lyre-bird. [Aboriginal, imit.]

bu'lrŭsh (bŏŏ'-) *n.* Kind of tall rush (*Scirpus lacustris*); cat's tail of genus *Typha*; (O.T.) papyrus plant. [perh. f. BULL[1] = large, coarse, as in *bullfrog, bulltrout*, etc.]

bu'lwark (bŏŏ'-) *n.* Rampart, earthwork, etc.; mole, breakwater; person, principle, etc., that acts as a defence; ship's side above deck. [ME, f. MLG, MDu. *bolwerk*; see BOLE[1], WORK[1]]

bŭm[1] *n.* **1.** ||(sl.) Buttocks. **2.** ||**~(-bailiff)**, (Hist.) bailiff employed for arrests [from touching debtor on the back]; **~-boat** (plying with fresh provisions etc. for ships); **~-sucker, -sucking,** ||(sl.) toady(ing). [ME *bom*, of unkn. orig.]

***bŭm[2]** *n.*, *a.*, & *v.* **(-mm-)**. (sl.) **1.** *n.* Habitual loafer or tramp; lazy dissolute person; **on the ~,** vagrant, begging; **~ rap,** imprisonment on false charge; **~'s rush,** forcible ejection. **2.** *a.* Of poor quality; **~ steer,** false information. **3.** *v.i.* Loaf, wander *around*, be a bum. **4.** *v.t.* Get by begging, cadge. [prob. abbr. or back form. f. BUMMER]

||**bŭ'mble[1]** *n.* Self-important official; hence **~DOM** (-beld-) *n.* [f. *Bumble*, name of beadle in Dickens's *Oliver Twist*; earlier = jumble, blunderer]

bŭ'mble[2] *v.i.* Make buzz or hum; ramble *on* in speaking; move or act ineptly or flounderingly. [f. BOOM[2] + -LE, and partly f. prec. in earlier sense 'blunderer']

bŭ'mble-bee *n.* Large loud-humming bee of genus *Bombus*. [f. prec. + BEE]

bŭ'mble-pŭppỹ *n.* Unskilful bridge, whist, etc.; game with tennis-ball attached by string to post. [19th c.; orig. unkn., but cf. BUMBLE[2]]

||**bŭmf** *n.* (sl.) Toilet-paper; (usu. derog.) papers, documents. [abbr. of *bum-fodder* (BUM[1], FODDER)]

bŭ'mmalō *n.* (*pl.* same). Small fish (*Harpodon nehereus*) of S. Asian coasts. [perh. f. Marathi *bombīl(a)*]

bŭmmaree' *n.* (Hist.) middleman at Billingsgate fish-market, London; self-employed licensed porter at Smithfield meat-market, London. [18th c.; orig. unkn.]

***bŭ'mmer** *n.* Idler, loafer; unpleasant occurrence. [19th c.; perh. f. G *bummler*]

bŭmp[1] *v.* & *adv.* **1.** *v.t.* Push, throw down, (box etc.) *against* or *on* (wall, person, floor, etc.); hurt (one's head etc.) by striking it (*against, on,* or abs.); overtake and touch in boat-race (**~'ing-race;** see foll.); *displace; **~ (off)**, (sl.) murder; **~ up,** (colloq.) increase (prices etc.). **2.** *v.i.* Come with a bump *against*; go *along* with repeated bumps; (of liquid) boil explosively; **~ into,** (colloq.) meet by chance. **3.** *adv.* With a bump, suddenly, violently, (*come, go*, etc., *bump*; cf. BANG[3]). [16th c., imit., perh. f. Scand.]

bŭmp[2] *n.* **1.** Dull-sounding blow, knock, collision; (in races where boats start at fixed intervals) overtaking and touching of boat by next in line, giving victory to latter (**~-supper,** celebration of success in bumping-races); **~-ball,** (Cricket) ball hit hard on ground close to bat and coming to fieldsman like possible catch. **2.** Swelling caused by bump; uneven patch on road, cricket-pitch, etc.; (Phren.) prominence on skull, faculty indicated by it, esp. **~ of locality,** supposed faculty of recognizing places and finding one's way; (rising air current causing) irregularity in aircraft's motion; (sl.) dancer's forward thrust of abdomen; hence **~'Y[2]** *a.* [f. prec.]

bŭmp[3] *n.*, & *v.i.* (Make) bittern's cry. [imit.]

bŭ'mper *n.* In vbl senses; brim-full glass of wine; anything unusually large or abundant or excellent (harvest, theatre audience); metal bar attached to (usu. front or back of) motor vehicle to reduce damage in collisions (**~-to-~**, travelling very close together); *railway buffer; (Cricket) ball that rises high after pitching. [f. BUMP[1] + -ER[1]]

||**bŭmph.** Var. of BUMF.

bŭ'mpkĭn *n.* Rustic or awkward fellow. [perh. f. Du. *boomken* little tree or MDu. *bommekijn* little barrel]

bŭ'mptious (-pshus) *a.* Self-assertive, offensively conceited; hence **~LY[2]** *adv.*, **~NESS** *n.* [joc., f. BUMP[1] after *fractious*]

bŭn *n.* **1.** Small soft round sweet bread or cake with currants etc.; ||**~-fight,** (sl.) tea-party; **hot cross ~** (marked with cross and eaten, usu. hot, on Good Friday); TAKE[1] *the bun*. **2.** (Sc.) Rich fruit cake or currant bread. **3.** Hair dressed in bun shape. [ME, of unkn. orig.]

bū'na (*or* bŏŏ'-) *n.* Synthetic rubber made by polymerization of butadiene. [G (as BUTADIENE, *natrium* sodium)]

Bŭ'nburỹ *n.* Fictitious excuse for making visit or avoiding obligation. [f. use in Wilde's *Importance of Being Earnest*]

bŭnch[1] *n.* Cluster of things growing or fastened together (*bunch of flowers, grapes, keys*); lot, collection, (*best of the bunch*); (sl.) gang, group; **~ grass,** N. Amer. grass growing in clumps; hence **~'Y[2]** *a.* [ME; orig. unkn.]

bŭnch[2] *v.* **1.** *v.t.* Make into bunch(es); gather (material) into close folds. **2.** *v.i.* Form group or crowd. [f. prec.]

***bŭ'ncō** *n.* (*pl.* **~s**), & *v.t.* (sl.) Swindle (esp. by card-sharping or confidence trick); **~-steerer,** swindler. [perh. f. Sp. *banca* a card-game]

buncombe. Var. of BUNKUM.
bŭnd *n.* (In Far East) embankment, causeway, quay. [f. Hindi *band*, f. Pers.]
bŭ'nder *n.* (Ind.) Landing-place, quay, harbour; **~-boat** (used for coastal and harbour work). [f. Hindi *bandar*, f. Pers.]
bŭ'ndle[1] *n.* **1.** Collection of things loosely fastened together (esp. clothes, or odds and ends in handkerchief or paper); set of sticks, rods, etc., bound up; set of parallel fibres, nerves, etc. **2.** (sl.) Large amount of money; **do** or **go a ~ on,** be very fond of (thing). [ME, perh. f. OE *byndelle* a binding, but also f. LG & Du. *bundel*]
bŭ'ndle[2] *v.* **1.** *v.t.* Tie in or make *up* into a bundle; throw confusedly *into* any receptacle; put or send (esp. person) in a hurry or unceremoniously *out, off, away*, etc. **2.** *v.t.* & *i.* **~ up,** dress warmly or cumbersomely. **3.** *v.i.* Sleep clothed *with* another person (esp. as local custom during courtship). [f. prec.]
bŭ'ndobŭst *n.* (Ind.) Arrangements, organization. [f. Hindi *band-o-bast* tying and binding]
bŭng[1] *n.* Stopper, esp. large cork stopping hole in cask; brewer or publican; **~-ho'** (excl. at parting or as toast); **~-hole** (for filling or emptying cask). [f. MDu. *bonghe*]
bŭng[2] *v.t.* Stop (cask) with bung (**~ed up,** closed, blocked); (sl.) throw, toss. [f. prec.]
bŭng[3] *a.* (Austral. & N.Z. sl.) Dead; ruined, useless. [Aboriginal]
bŭ'ngal|ow (-ngg*a*lō) *n.* One-storeyed house; hence **~**OID *a.*, (usu. derog.) resembling a bungalow, consisting of bungalows. [orig. in India, f. Gujarati *bangalo* f. Hindi *baṅglā* belonging to Bengal]
bŭ'ngl|e (-ngg*e*l) *v.i.* & *t.*, & *n.* (Make) clumsy work, confusion; blunder over, fail to accomplish, (task); hence **~**ER[1] *n.* [imit.; cf. BUMBLE[2]]
bŭ'nion (-y*o*n) *n.* Inflamed swelling on foot, esp. at first joint of big toe. [f. OF *buignon* (*buigne* bump on head)]
bŭnk[1] *n.* Sleeping-berth, esp. one of two or more arranged vertically; **~-bed,** piece of furniture comprising two bunks. [19th c.; orig. unkn.]
bŭnk[2] *v.i.*, & *n.* (sl.) (**Do a**) **~**, make off, vanish. [19th c.; orig. unkn.]
bŭnk[3] *n.* (sl.) Nonsense, humbug. [abbr. of BUNKUM]
bŭ'nker *n.*, & *v.t.* **1.** *n.* Container for fuel; (Golf) pit containing sand etc. and constituting a hazard; (Mil.) reinforced underground shelter. **2.** *v.t.* Fill bunkers of (ship etc.); (usu. in *p.p.*) trap in bunker, (fig.) bring into difficulties. [19th c.; orig. unkn.]
bŭ'nkum *n.* Nonsense; ostentatious talking. [orig. *buncombe*, f. *Buncombe* County in N. Carolina, whose member spoke needlessly in Congress *c.* 1820 to impress his constituents]
bŭ'nnȳ *n.* (Child's name for) rabbit; **~ (girl)**, club hostess wearing costume suggestive of rabbit. [f. *bun* rabbit + -Y[3]]
Bŭ'nsen *n.* **~ burner** (burning air with gas for heating substances in chemical laboratories etc.). [f. R. W. ~, Ger. chemist d. 1899]
bŭnt[1] *n.* Cavity or baggy part of fishing-net, sail, etc.; **~-line** (confining bunt when furling sail). [16th c.; orig. unkn.]
bŭnt[2] *n.* Disease of wheat caused by smut-ball fungus of genus *Tilletia*. [18th c.; orig. unkn.]
bŭnt[3] *v.* & *n.* **1.** *v.t.* & *i.* Push with head or horns, butt. **2.** *v.t.* *(Baseball). Stop (ball) with bat without swinging. **3.** *n.* Act of bunting. [19th c.; cf. BUTT[4]]
bŭ'ntal *n.* Straw from talipot palm. [Tagalog]
bŭ'ntĭng[1] *n.* Bird of sub-family Emberizinae, allied to finches. [ME; orig. unkn.]
bŭ'ntĭng[2] *n.* (Loosely-woven fabric used for) flags and festive decorations. [18th c.; orig. unkn.]
bŭ'nya *n.* (Austral.) Tall tree (*Araucaria bidwillii*) bearing large nutritious cones. [Aboriginal]
bŭ'nyĭp *n.* (Austral.) Fabulous monster of swamps and lagoons. [Aboriginal]
buoy[1] (boi) *n.* Anchored float showing navigable course or reefs etc.; (**li'fe**)**~**, device to keep person afloat; hence **~'**AGE (1, 3, 4) *n.* [ME, prob. f. MDu. *bo(e)ye*, perh. f. OF *boie* chain f. L *boia*, pl. *boiae* f. Gk *boeiai* (*dorai*) ox-hides, ox-leather straps]
buoy[2] (boi) *v.t.* **1. ~ (up)**, keep afloat; sustain (person, courage, etc.), uplift, encourage. **2.** Mark (*out*) with buoy(s). [sense 1 f. Sp. *boyar* (see BUOYANT); sense 2 f. prec.]
buoy'ancȳ (boi'-) *n.* Floating power on liquid or in air; resilience, recuperative power, (of spirits, also of stock-market prices, etc.); cheerfulness. [f. foll.; see -ANCY]
buoy'ant (boi'-) *a.* Apt to float, rise, keep up, or recover; able to keep things up; light-hearted; hence **~**LY[2] *adv.* [f. F *bouyant* or Sp. *boyante* part. of *boyar* float (*boya* BUOY[1]; see -ANT)]
bûr, bûrr[3], *n.* (Any plant with) clinging seed-vessel or flower; person hard to shake off; = BURR[1] 1; **~ oak,** N. Amer. oak with large fringed acorn-cups. [ME; cf. Da. *burre* bur, burdock, Sw. *kard-borre* burdock]
bûr'ble *v.i.* Speak lengthily; make murmuring noise; (Aeron., of air-flow) break up into turbulence. [19th c., imit.]
bûr'bot *n.* Eel-like flat-headed bearded freshwater fish (*Lota lota*). [ME; cf. OF *barbote*]
bûr'den[1] *n.* Load (lit., or of labour, duty, sorrow, etc.; **~ of proof,** obligation to prove one's assertion); obligatory expense; (also arch. **bur'then** *pr.* -dh-) ship's carrying-capacity, tonnage; bearing of loads (*ship, beast, of burden*); refrain, chorus, of song [partly f. BOURDON]; chief theme or gist of poem, book, speech, etc.; hence **~**SOME[1] *a.* [OE *byrthen*, = OS *burthinnia* f. WG **burthinnja* (**burthi-* BIRTH, *-*innja* -EN[3]); for *-d-* cf. *murder*]
bûr'den[2], (arch.) **bûr'then** (-dh-), *v.t.* Load (lit. or fig.), encumber; oppress. [f. prec.]
bûr'dock *n.* Coarse weed of genus *Arctium*, with prickly flower-heads and docklike leaves. [f. BUR + DOCK[1]]
bur'eau (būr'ō; *or* -ō') *n.* (*pl.* **~x** *or* **~s**, *pr.* -ōz). **1.** ‖Writing-desk with drawers; *chest of drawers. **2.** Office or department for transacting specific business; government department. [F, = desk, orig. its baize covering, f. OF *burel* (*bure, buire* dark brown f. Rom. **burius* dark red f. L *burrus* bright red f. Gk *purros* red)]
bûreau'|cracȳ (būrŏ'-) *n.* Government by central administration; officialism or officials of such government; so **~**CRAT (būr'*o*-) *n.*, (esp. unimaginative) official in bureaucracy, **~cră'**TIC (būr'*o*-) *a.*, **~cratIZE** (3) *v.t.* [f. F *bureaucratie* (as prec.; see -CRACY)]
bûrĕ'tte, *bûrĕ't, *n.* Graduated glass tube with end-tap for measuring small quantities of liquid in chemical analysis. [F]
***bûrg** *n.* (colloq.) Town or city. [see BOROUGH]
bûr'gage *n.* (Hist.) Tenure of land in town on yearly rent. [ME, f. med. L *burgagium* (*burgus* BOROUGH; see -AGE)]
bûrgee' *n.* Triangular or swallow-tailed flag bearing colours or emblem of yacht club or sailing club. [19th c.; perh. for *~'*s flag*, with ~ = 'owner' f. F *bourgeois* f. OF *burgeis* (see BURGESS)]
bûr'geon (-j*o*n) *n.*, & *v.i.* (Put forth, spring forth as) young shoot(s); bud; (fig.) begin to grow rapidly. [ME, f. OF *bor-, burjon* f. Rom. **burrio -onis* f. LL *burra* wool]

***bur'ger** (-g-) *n.* (colloq.) Hamburger; (in comb.) food resembling hamburger (*beefburger, nutburger*). [abbr.]
bur'gess *n.* ||Inhabitant of borough with full municipal rights, citizen; ||(Hist.) member of parliament for borough, corporate town, or university; *borough magistrate or governor. [ME f. OF *burgeis* f. Rom. **burgensis* f. LL *burgus* BOROUGH]
burgh (bŭ'r*o*) *n.* (Sc.) Borough, chartered town; hence ~'AL (bĕr'g*a*l) *a.* [Sc. form of BOROUGH]
bur'gher (-*ger*) *n.* Freeman or citizen of a foreign town; (S. Afr., Hist.) citizen of a Boer republic; descendant of Dutch or Portuguese colonist in Sri Lanka. [f. G or Du. *burger* (*burg* BOROUGH; see -ER[1])]
bur'glar *n.* One who enters building illegally (in Engl. law formerly by night only) with intent to commit felony; hence ~Y[1] *n.*, **burglar'**IOUS *a.*, *~IZE (1) *v.t.* [f. legal AF *burgler* = AL *burg(u)lator*, f. **burg-* pillage]
bur'gle *v.* **1.** *v.i.* Commit burglary. **2.** *v.t.* Rob by burglary. [19th c.; back form. f. prec.]
bur'gomaster (-ah-) *n.* Mayor of Dutch or Flemish town. [f. Du. *burgemeester* (*burg* BOROUGH), assim. to MASTER[1]]
bur'gonĕt *n.* (Hist.) Visored helmet. [f. F *bourguignotte* perh. fem. of *bourguignot* Burgundian (*Bourgogne* Burgundy); assim. to -ET[1]]
burgoo' *n.* (Naut. sl.) porridge; *soup or stew for outdoor meal. [f. Arab. *burġul* f. Turk. *bulgur* bruised grain]
bur'gundy̆ *n.* (Usu. red) wine of *Burgundy* in E. France; similar wine from other countries; red colour of such wine.
bŭ'rhel (-r*e*l). Var. of BHARAL.
bu'rial (bĕ'-) *n.* Burying, esp. of dead body; funeral; **~-ground,** cemetery; **~-service,** religious ceremony at funeral. [ME, erron. formed as sing. of OE *byrgels,* f. Gmc **burgisli* (**burg-* BURY, *-*isli*; cf. RIDDLE[1])]
bur'in *n.* Tool for engraving on copper; (Archaeol.) chisel-pointed flint tool. [F]
burk. See BERK.
bur'ka *n.* Muslim woman's long enveloping garment worn in public. [Hindi, f. Arab. *burḳa'*]
burke[1] *v.t.* Avoid, smother, (publicity, inquiry); hush up, suppress, (rumour). [f. W. *Burke,* executed in 1829 for smothering people to sell bodies for dissection]
||**Burke**[2] *n.* (colloq.) (Used for) '~'s Peerage etc.' [f. John ~, compiler d. 1848]
burl *n.* Knot in wool or cloth. [ME, f. OF *bourle* tuft of wool, dim. of *bourre* coarse wool f. LL *burra* wool]
bur'lăp *n.* Coarse canvas esp. of jute for sacking etc.; similar material for dress or furnishing. [17th c.; orig. unkn.]
burlĕ'sque (-k) *a.* & *n.*, & *v.t.* **1.** Imitative, imitation, imitate, for purpose of deriding or amusing; bombast(ic), mock-serious(ness); caricature, parody, esp. (of) literary or dramatic work. **2.** *n.* *Variety show freq. featuring strip-tease. [F, f. It. *burlesco* (*burla* mockery; see -ESQUE)]
bur'l|y̆ *a.* Sturdy; big and strong; hence ~INESS *n.* [ME *borli(ch)* prob. f. OE **būrlic* fit for the BOWER[1]; see -LY[1]]
Bur'man *a.* & *n.* = foll. [f. *Burma* + -AN]
Burmē'se (-z) *a.* & *n.* (*pl.* same). (Native or language) of Burma. [f. *Burma* + -ESE]
burn[1] *n.* (Sc.) Small stream. [OE *burna* etc., = MDu. *borne,* f. Gmc **brunnon, -az*; cf. BOURN[1]]
burn[2] *v.t.* & *i.* (**~t** *or* **~ed**). **1.** Consume, be consumed, waste, by fire, (of heat, person heating, or heated thing; ~ one's **boats** or **bridges,** commit oneself irrevocably to a course); blaze or glow with fire; use energy of (propellant, nuclear fuel); **money to ~** (in great abundance). **2.** Give or cause to give light (of lamp, candles, gas, oil, electricity, etc.); *burn* CANDLE *at both ends*; *burn* DAYLIGHT; *burn the midnight* OIL[1]. **3.** Put or be put to death by fire. **4.** Subject (clay, chalk, etc.) to heat for a purpose; harden (bricks), make (lime, charcoal) by heat. **5.** Make (hole etc.) by heat (**money ~s hole in pocket,** one is eager to spend it). **6.** Injure or be injured by fire, sun's rays, or great heat (~ one's **fingers,** suffer for meddling or rashness); char or scorch in cooking, (cause to) adhere to pan etc. and char; cauterize, brand; eat, make acid etc. eat, its way (*into* material). **7.** Parch, colour, (*brown, dry,* etc., or abs.). **8.** Give or feel sensation or pain (as) of heat; **ears ~** (esp., allegedly, when one is talked of). **9.** Make or be hot or passionate; glow, rage, yearn. **10. ~ away,** diminish to nothing by burning; **~ down,** burn less vigorously as fuel fails, destroy (building) by burning; **~ in,** imprint by burning (lit. or fig.); **~ out,** burn away, (make) fail by burning, consume contents of by burning (also fig.), make homeless by burning of house; **~ up,** get rid of by fire, flash into blaze, *(sl.) be or make furious. **11. ~'ing-glass,** lens to concentrate sun's rays on object and burn it; **~t almond** (enclosed in burnt sugar); **~t cork** (used to blacken face etc.); **~t ochre,** SIENNA, UMBER, (calcined to deeper colour); **~t offering,** sacrifice offered by burning. [OE *birnan* v.i., *bærnan* v.t., f. Gmc **bren-* etc.]
burn[3] *n.* Sore or mark made by burning; provision of thrust by engine of spacecraft; (U.S. etc.) forest area cleared by burning; (sl.) cigarette; (sl.) car race. [f. prec.]
bur'ner *n.* In vbl senses; part of lamp, gas cooker, etc., that shapes the flame. [f. BURN[2] + -ER[1]]
bur'nėt *n.* Brown-flowered plant of genus *Sanguisorba* or *Poterium*; diurnal moth, greenish-black with crimson spots on wings. [f. obs. *burnet* a. dark brown f. OF *burnete*; see BRUNET]
||**Bur'nham** (-n*a*m) *n.* ~ **scale,** national salary scale (since 1924) for teachers in State-aided schools. [f. Lord ~, chairman of committee which recommended this scale]
bur'nĭng *a.* In vbl senses; ardent (*burning desire*); flagrant (*burning shame*); hotly discussed, exciting, (*burning question*); ~ **bush,** (1) one of various shrubs with red fruits or red autumn leaves (w. ref. to Exod. 3:2), (2) fraxinella. [f. BURN[2] + -ING[2]]
bur'nĭsh *v.t.* Polish by rubbing. [ME, f. OF *burnir* = *brunir* (*brun* BROWN[1]); see -ISH[2]]
burnou's (-ōō's) *n.* Arab or Moorish hooded cloak. [F, f. Arab. *burnus* f. Gk *birros* cloak]
burnt. See BURN[2].
burp *n.*, & *v.i.* & *t.* (sl.) (Cause to) belch; *~ **gun,** automatic pistol. [imit.]
burr[1] *n.* **1.** Rough edge left on cut or punched metal or paper; surgeon's or dentist's small drill. **2.** Siliceous rock used for millstones; whetstone; kind of limestone. **3.** Rough sounding of letter *r*; whirring sound. **4.** Coronet of deer's antler. [var. of BUR]
burr[2] *v.t.* & *i.* Pronounce with burr; speak indistinctly; make whirring sound. [f. prec.]
burr[3]. See BUR.
bŭ'rrawăng (-*a*-w-) *n.* (Austral.) (Nut of) a palmlike tree of genus *Macrozamia.* [f. Mount *Budawang* in New South Wales]
***bŭ'rrō** (*or* bŏŏ'-) *n.* (*pl.* **~s**). (colloq.) Small donkey used as pack-animal. [Sp.]
bŭ'rrow (-ō) *n.*, & *v.i.* & *t.* (Make or live in) hole excavated in earth, as of foxes, rabbits, etc.; make by excavating (hole, one's way); hide oneself; ~ **into,** (fig.) investigate mysteries etc. of; hence ~ER[1] *n.* [ME, app. var. of BOROUGH]

bûr′s|a *n.* (*pl.* **~ae** *or* **~as**). (Anat. & Zool.) Sac or saclike cavity to lessen friction; hence ~AL *a.*, ~I′TIS *n.* [med. L, = bag; cf. PURSE[1]]

bûr′sar *n.* Treasurer, esp. of college; holder of bursary; hence ~SHIP *n.*, (esp.) endowment given to student. [f. F *boursier* or (in first sense) med. L *bursarius* (BURSA; see -AR[2])]

bûrsăr′ĭal *a.* Of bursar(y). [f. prec. + -AL]

bûr′sarў *n.* Bursarship; bursar's room in college etc. [f. med. L *bursaria* (as BURSAR; see -ARY[1])]

bûrsī′tĭs. See BURSA.

bûrst[1] *v.t.* & *i.* (**burst**). **1.** Fly by expansion of contents or internal pressure, or send (containing case), violently asunder; split; be as if about to burst because of excitement etc. **2.** Get away from or through, make way *out* or *in*, or express one's feelings, by force or suddenly (*river bursts banks*). **3.** Open, come open, or be opened, forcibly (*abscess, bud, cloud, bursts; burst door, door bursts, open*). **4.** Fill or be full to overflowing. **5.** Appear or come suddenly (*burst into flame, upon the view; sun burst out*). **6.** Suffer bursting of (some part; *burst a blood-vessel*, (fig.) one's *sides with laughing*). **7.** ~ **in,** come in abruptly, break in by violence; ~ **into,** suddenly begin to utter etc. (song, laughter, tears); ~ **out,** go out abruptly, exclaim, suddenly begin (laughing etc.). [OE *berstan*, = OS, OHG *brestan*, ON *bresta* f. Gmc **brestan*]

bûrst[2] *n.* Bursting, split; sudden issuing forth (*burst of flame*), explosion, outbreak, (lit. or fig., *burst of applause, firing*); = SPURT[1]; **~′proof,** (of door lock) able to withstand violent impact. [f. prec.]

burthen. See BURDEN[1,2].

bûr′ton[1] *n.* Light handy two-block tackle. [f. ME BRETON *tackles*]

||**bûr′ton**[2] *n.* (sl.) **Go for a ~,** be lost, destroyed, or killed. [20th c.; perh. f. *Burton* ale f. *B~-on--Trent* in Staffordshire]

bu′rў (bĕ′rĭ) *v.t.* **1.** Deposit (corpse etc.) in earth, tomb, or sea; lose by death (*has buried three husbands*); put under ground (*bury alive*; ~ **the hatchet** or ***tomahawk,** cease to quarrel); hide (treasure etc.) in earth, cover up, submerge; **~ing-beetle,** sexton beetle; **~ing-ground, ~ing-place,** cemetery. **2.** Put away, forget; consign to obscurity; put out of sight (face *in* hands, hands *in* pockets); involve deeply (*bury oneself in* one's *work*). [OE *byrgan* f. WG **burgjan* (*burg-* st. of Gmc **bergan* shelter, protect; cf. BURIAL)]

bŭs *n.* (*pl.* ***~′ses**) & *v.* (***-ss-**). **1.** Large passenger vehicle running on fixed route; (colloq.) aeroplane, motor car, etc.; MISS[2] *the bus*; **~′bar,** (Electr.) system of conductors carrying all power to or from a station; ***~′boy,** waiter's assistant; **~-conductor,** (1) conductor of bus, (2) busbar; ||~ **lane,** strip of road for use by buses only; **~′man,** driver of a bus (*~man's holiday*, leisure time spent in same kind of occupation as one's regular work); **~-shelter,** roadside structure for protection against rain etc. for persons waiting for bus; **~-stop,** regular stopping-place of bus. **2.** *v.i.* Go by bus. **3.** *v.t.* *Transport by bus (esp. schoolchildren to counteract racial segregation). [abbr. of OMNIBUS]

||**bŭ′sbў** (-z-) *n.* Tall fur cap of hussars and guardsmen. [18th c.; orig. unkn.]

bush[1] (bŏŏ-) *n.* **1.** Shrub or clump of shrubs with stems of moderate length (BEAT[1] *about the bush*); bunch of ivy as ancient vintner's sign (**good wine needs no ~,** merit needs no special advertisement); luxuriant growth of hair etc. **2.** Woodland, forest, untilled district, (esp. in Australia, N.Z., S. Afr.); **go ~,** (Austral.) leave one's usual surroundings, run wild. **3. ~-baby,** galago; *bush* BASIL; **~′buck,** small S. Afr. antelope; **~′craft,** skill in living in the bush; **~--fighting,** fighting in the bush, guerrilla warfare; ~ **jacket,** belted cotton jacket; ~ **lawyer,** (N.Z.) a bramble, (Austral. & N.Z.) layman pretending to legal knowledge; ***~ league,** minor baseball league; **B~′man,** aboriginal or language of a S. Afr. people [after Du. *boschjesman* (*bosch* bush)]; **~′man,** dweller, farmer, or traveller in the Australian bush; **~′manship,** bushcraft; **~′master,** venomous S. Amer. snake; **~-ranger,** (Hist.) Australian brigand living in the bush; ~ **shirt,** = *bush jacket*; ~ **sickness,** disease of animals due to lack of cobalt in soil; ~ **telegraph,** rapid spreading of information, rumour, etc.; **~′veld** (-fĕlt), veld composed largely of bush, wooded region in Transvaal; **~-whacker,** one who clears land of bush, backwoodsman, *(Hist.) deserter or guerrilla. [ME, partly f. OE **bysc*, partly f. ON *buski*, partly (cf. BOSKY) f. OF *bos(c)*, all ult. f. Gmc **busk-*]

bush[2] (bŏŏ-) *n.*, & *v.t.* **1.** *n.* Metal lining of axle--hole or other circular orifice; perforated plug; box or bearing in which shaft revolves; (Electr.) insulating sleeve. **2.** *v.t.* Furnish with bush. [f. MDu. *busse* BOX[2]]

bushed (bŏŏsht) *a.* (Austral. & N.Z. colloq.) lost in the bush, bewildered; *(colloq.) tired out. [f. BUSH[1] + -ED[2]]

bu′shel[1] (bŏŏ′-) *n.* Measure of capacity (|| 8 gallons, *32 quarts) for corn, fruit, ||liquids, etc., (**hide** one's **light under a ~,** conceal one's merits); hence ~FUL 2 *n.* [ME, f. OF *buissiel* etc., perh. of Gaulish orig.]

***bu′shel**[2] (bŏŏ′-) *v.t.* & *i.* Mend or alter (clothes). [perh. f. G *bosseln* do odd jobs]

bu′shidō (bŏŏ′shē- *or* bŏŏ′-) *n.* Code of honour and morals evolved by the samurai. [Jap., = military knight's way]

bu′shĭng (bŏŏ′-) *n.* = BUSH[2]. [f. BUSH[2] + -ING[1] (3)]

bu′shў[1] (bŏŏ′-) *n.* (Austral. & N.Z.) Dweller in the bush. [f. BUSH[1] + -Y[3]]

bu′sh|ў[2] (bŏŏ′-) *a.* Abounding in bushes; growing thickly; covered with bush; hence ~ĬNESS *n.* [f. BUSH[1] + -Y[2]]

busily. See BUSY[1].

bu′sinĕss (bĭ′zn-) *n.* **1.** Task, duty, province, (**make it** one's **~,** undertake *to*); cause of coming (*what is your business?*). **2.** Habitual occupation, profession, trade; ~ **as usual,** things will proceed normally despite disturbances; ***~ cycle,** trade cycle; ~ **hours** (of regular work, of shop or office opening); ~ **studies,** training in economics, management, etc.; ***~ suit,** lounge suit; BIG *business*; **in ~,** trading or dealing, (fig.) able to begin operations. **3.** Serious work; ~ **end,** (colloq.) working end of tool etc.; **get down to ~,** begin in earnest; **mean ~,** be in earnest; **on ~,** with definite purpose, esp. one relating to business (sense 2). **4.** Thing needing attention, agenda, (*the business of the day, meeting*, etc.); dealings with men and matters. **5.** Difficult matter (*what a business it is!; make a great business of it*). **6.** Thing that concerns one, that one may meddle with; **mind your own, go about your, send about his, ~** (expr. reproof of meddlesomeness, or dismissal); **has no ~ to** (no right); **like nobody's ~,** (colloq.) extraordinarily. **7.** (derog.) Process, concern, affair, structure, (*sick of the whole business; a lath-and-plaster business*). **8.** (Theatr.) Action on stage. **9.** Buying and selling, trade, (*doing a great business; good stroke of business*); ~ **man, woman,** (engaged in trade or commerce); ~ **is ~,** commercial considerations have priority. **10.** Commercial house, firm. **11.** Hence ~-LIKE *a.*, practical, systematic. [OE *bisignis* (as BUSY[1], -NESS)]

bŭ'sker *n.* Itinerant musician or actor, esp. performing in street; so **bŭ'sk**ING[1,2] *a.* & *n.* [f. *busk* peddle etc. (perh. f. obs. F *busquer* seek)]

bŭ'skĭn *n.* Thick-soled boot lending height to ancient Athenian tragic actor; (fig.) tragic drama; (Hist.) half-boot; hence ~ED[2] (-nd) *a.* [prob. f. OF *bouzequin*, var. of *bro(u)sequin*, or unkn. orig.]

bŭss *n.*, & *v.t.* (arch.) Kiss. [earlier *bass* n. & v.; cf. F *baiser*, f. L *basiare*]

bŭst[1] *n.* **1.** Sculpture of person's head, shoulders, and chest. **2.** Upper front of body, bosom, esp. of woman; circumference of this; hence ~'Y[2] *a.*, (of woman) having prominent bust. [f. F *buste* f. It. *busto*, of unkn. orig.]

bŭst[2] *n.* & *v.* (colloq.) **1.** *n.* Sudden failure; worthless thing; bad hand at cards; drinking--bout. **2.** *v.t.* & *i.* Burst, break; dismiss, reduce to lower rank; ~ **up,** explode, bring or come to collapse; ~**-up** *n.*, explosion, quarrel, collapse; hence ~'ER *n.*, (esp.) violent gale, (sl., as form of usu. disrespectful address) mate, fellow. [f. BURST[1,2]]

bŭst[3], **bŭ'stĕd,** *adjs.* (colloq.) Broken, burst, collapsed; bankrupt. [f. prec.]

bŭ'stard *n.* Large swift-running bird of genus *Otis*. [ME, perh. f. AF **bustarde*, mixture of OF *bistarde*, *oustarde*, both f. L *avis tarda* slow bird (the inappropriate adj. unexplained)]

bŭ'stee *n.* (Ind.) Shanty town, slum. [f. Hindi *bastī* dwelling]

bŭ'stle[1] (-*sel*) *v.* **1.** *v.i.* Bestir oneself; make show of activity, hurry *about*; hence **bŭ'stl**ING[2] (-sl-) *a.*, full of activity. **2.** *v.t.* Make (person) hurry or work hard. [perh. var. of obs. *buskle* frequent. of obs. *busk* prepare (ON *búask* refl. of *búa* prepare; cf. BOUND[5]); see -LE 3]

bŭ'stle[2] (-*sel*) *n.* Excited activity, fuss. [f. prec.]

bŭ'stle[3] (-*sel*) *n.* (Hist.) Pad or frame puffing out top of woman's skirt at back. [18th c.; orig. unkn.]

bu'sў[1] (bĭ'zĭ) *a.* & *n.* **1.** *a.* Occupied, working, engaged, with attention concentrated, (*in*, *with*, *at*; also, prep. being dropped, with vbl n. now looking like part.: *he was busy packing*); full of activity or detail; (of telephone line) engaged; unresting, ever employed, (*busy as a bee*); fussy, meddlesome, prying; ~**body,** meddlesome person, mischief-maker; ~ **Lizzie,** house-plant of genus *Impatiens*; hence **bu'sĭ**LY[2] (bĭ'z-) *adv.*, ~NESS *n.* **2.** *n.* (sl:) Detective. [OE *bisig*, = MLG, MDu. *besich*, of unkn. orig.]

bu'sў[2] (bĭ'zĭ) *v.t.* Occupy (esp. one*self*, one's *hands*, etc.), keep busy, (*with*, *in*, *at*, *about*, doing, or abs.). [OE *bisgian* (as prec.)]

but[1] (*or, when stressed,* bŭt) (orig. *adv.* & *prep.* = outside, without; developed into *conj.*, under which most mod. uses belong; is now *adv.*, *prep.*, negative *rel. pron.*, & *conj.*; clear distinction of these is not possible here). **1.** Only, no more than, (*she is but a child*; *it was used but once*; *I can but do it*). **2.** Except, if not, short of, except that, if it were not that, short of the condition that, (*they are all wrong but he* or *him*; *no one but me* or *I*; *but for you I should have drowned*; *never saw her but once*; *he all but did it*; *what can he do but die?*; *nothing would content him but I must come*); *last*, *next*, etc. ~ **one, two,** etc., if one, two, etc., were excluded from the count. **3.** Other(wise) than (*cannot choose but*, *cannot but*, *do it*); ANYTHING *but*. **4.** Who or that not (*no one but knows that*). **5.** Without the result etc. that (*never rains but it pours*; *justice was never done but someone complained*). **6.** Rather than so-and-so shall prove untrue (*it shall go* HARD *but I will get there*); that not (*not such a fool but*—also *but that*, *but what*—*he can see the reason*). **7.** To say (that) not (*who knows but that*—also (colloq.) *but what*—*it is true?*; NOT *but that* or *what*). **8.** ~ **that,** (after neg.) that (*I don't deny*, *doubt*, *but that*). **9.** ~ (**then, yet**), on the contrary, nevertheless, however, on the other hand, moreover, yet. **10.** (Introducing emphasized word) *it must be used always, but always.* [OE *be-ūtan*, *būtan*, *būta* outside, without, = OS *biūtan*, OHG *biūzan* f. WG **be*, **bi* BY[1] + **ūtana* from outside]

bŭt[2] *n.*, & *v.t.* (-tt-). **1.** *n.* An objection (*ifs and buts*). **2.** *v.t.* Utter or use ('but'); ~ **me no** ~**s,** do not raise objections. [f. prec.]

bŭt[3]. See BEN[1].

būtadī'ēne *n.* (Chem.) Gas used in making synthetic rubber. [f. BUTANE + DI-[2] + -ENE; cf. BUNA]

bū'tāne *n.* (Chem.) Hydrocarbon of the paraffin series, C_4H_{10}, used in liquefied form as fuel. [f. BUTYL + -ANE]

butch (bŏŏ-) *n.* (sl.) Tough youth or man; mannish woman; *~ **haircut,** crew cut. [perh. abbr. of foll.]

bu'tcher[1] (bŏŏ'-) *n.* **1.** One who slaughters animals for food; dealer in meat (**the** ~, **the baker, the candlestick-maker,** people of all trades); *(colloq.) seller of sweets etc. on train; judge, general, etc., who has men killed needlessly or brutally. **2.** ~**-bird,** shrike esp. of genus *Lanius*; ~**-boots,** high boots without tops; ~**'s-broom,** low spiny-leaved evergreen shrub; ~**'s (hook)**, (rhyming sl.) a look; ~**'s meat** (excluding poultry, game, and bacon etc.). **3.** Hence ~LY[1] *a.* [ME, f. OF *bo(u)chier* (*boc* BUCK[1])]

bu'tcher[2] (bŏŏ'-) *v.t.* Slaughter or cut up (animal); kill (people) wantonly or cruelly; ruin by bad performance etc. [f. prec.]

bu'tcherў (bŏŏ'-) *n.* Slaughterhouse; butcher's trade; needless or cruel slaughter of people. [ME, f. OF *boucherie* (as BUTCHER[1]; see -Y[1])]

bŭ'tler *n.* Servant in charge of wine-cellar and plate etc.; principal manservant. [ME, f. AF *buteler*, OF *bouteillier*; see BOTTLE[1], -ER[2] (2)]

bŭtt[1] *n.* Cask, esp. as measure of wine or ale. [f. AL *butta*, *bota*, AF *but*, f. OF *bo(u)t* f. LL *buttis*]

bŭtt[2] *n.* ~(**-end**), thicker end, esp. of tool or weapon; trunk of tree, esp. part just above ground; ~(**-end**), remnant; stub of cigar or cigarette; flat-fish (sole, plaice, turbot); ~(**-end**), square end of plank meeting a similar end; ~ **weld** (in which pieces are joined end to end). [ME, (a) f. MLG, MDu. *but* flat-fish (see HALIBUT, TURBOT), (b) = Du. *bot* stumpy (see BUTTOCK)]

bŭtt[3] *n.* **1.** Mound behind target; grouse--shooter's stand screened by low turf or stone wall; (in *pl.*) shooting-range; target. **2.** Aim, object; object *of* (ridicule etc.), object of teasing and ridicule (*make a butt of* person). [ME, f. OF *but* goal, of unkn. orig.]

bŭtt[4] *v.i.* & *t.*, & *n.* **1.** Push with head; ~ **in,** (fig.) intervene, meddle; *~**i'nsky,** (sl.) meddler. **2.** *v.i.* & *t.* Meet end to end (*butt against*, *upon*); come, place (timber etc.), with end flat *against* wall etc. [ME, f. AF *buter*, OF *boter* f. Gmc **buttan* sprout; infl. by prec. and ABUT]

***būtte** *n.* Conspicuous isolated hill, esp. one with steep or clifflike sides. [F, = mound]

bŭ'tter[1] *n.* **1.** Edible fatty substance made from cream by churning, used on bread and in cookery, (**look as if** ~ **would not melt in** one's **mouth,** seem demure; **melted** ~, (also) sauce of butter, flour, etc.); substance of similar consistency or look (COCOA[2] *butter*; PEA*nut butter*; **vegetable** ~, such substance got from plant); fulsome flattery. **2.** ~**-and-eggs,** plant with two yellows in flower, e.g. toadflax; ~**-ball,** (1) piece of butter moulded into a ball, (2) *buffle-head [because very fat in autumn]; **~-bean,** (1) yellow-podded bean, (2) dried white Lima bean; **~bur,** plant of genus *Petasites* with large soft leaves; **~cup,** yellow-flowered plant of genus *Ranunculus*; **~-fingers,** person likely to drop things or unable to catch ball etc.; **~-fish,** slippery kind, of various species; **~-knife,** blunt knife for cutting butter at table; **~milk,** somewhat acid liquid fat left after churning butter; **~ muslin,** thin loosely woven cloth with fine mesh, used orig. for wrapping butter; **~-nut,** N. Amer. (oily nut of) tree *Juglans cinerea*; **~scotch,** kind of toffee made chiefly with butter and sugar; **~wort,** fleshy-leaved violet-flowered bog-plant, *Pinguicula vulgaris*. [OE *butere*, = OHG *butera*, WG f. L *butyrum* f. Gk *bouturon*]

bŭ'tter[2] *v.t.* Spread, cook, serve, with butter (**fine words ~ no parsnips,** mere protestations do not alter facts; see BREAD 1); **~ up,** flatter. [f. prec.]

bŭ'tterfly̆ *n.* Diurnal insect of order Lepidoptera with large often showy wings erect when at rest and knobbed antennae (**break ~ on wheel,** use needless destructive force); (in *pl.*, colloq.) nervous tremors (esp. *in stomach* etc.); showy or frivolous person; **~-fish,** fish (esp. a blenny) with variegated colours or broad fins; **~-nut** (Mech., with wings to be turned by thumb and finger); **~ stroke** (Swimming, in which both arms are lifted at same time); **~ valve** (with hinged semicircular plates). [OE *buttor-flēoge* (as BUTTER[1], FLY[1])]

bŭ'ttery̆[1] *n.* Place in college etc. where provisions are kept and supplied. [ME, f. AF **buterie*, *boterie* butt-store (as BUTT[1]; see -ERY)]

bŭ'tter|y̆[2] *a.* Like or containing butter; hence **~ĭness** *n.* [f. BUTTER[1] + -Y[2]]

bŭ'ttock *n.* Either of two fleshy protuberances on lower rear part of human body; corresponding part of animal; ||manœuvre in wrestling using buttock or hip. [f. *butt* ridge + -OCK]

bŭ'tton[1] *n.* **1.** Knob or disc sewn to garment to fasten it by passing through buttonhole, or for ornament, or attached as badge, (**a ~ short,** (colloq.) mentally deficient; ***on the ~,** precisely); thing of little value. **2.** Bud; mushroom not yet open. **3.** Knob etc. pressed to operate electric bell etc.; small rounded object; terminal knob (on fencing foil, making it harmless; also as ornament). **4. ~ chrysanthemum** (with many small round flower-heads); **~ day,** (Austral.) FLAG[4]-*day* (but with buttons not flags); **~hole,** (*n.*) slit made to receive fastening button, ||flower(s) worn in coat-lapel buttonhole, (*v.t.*) make buttonholes in, hold by coat or waistcoat button, detain (reluctant listener); *~hole stitch*, looped stitch for edging buttonholes; **~hook** (for pulling button into place); **~-stick,** appliance to protect cloth in button-polishing; **~-through,** (of dress) fastening by buttons over its whole length; ***~-tree,** ***~-wood,** plane-tree. **5.** Hence (-)~ED[2] (-nd), ~LESS, ~Y[2], *adjs.* [ME, f. OF *bouton* f. Rom. **bottone* (**bottare* f. Gmc **button* sprout)]

bŭ'tton[2] *v.* **1.** *v.t.* Furnish with button(s). **2.** *v.t.* & *i.* **~ (up),** fasten with buttons, (fig.) complete satisfactorily, (in *p.p.*, of person) taciturn; ***~** one's **lip,** (sl.) remain silent. [f. prec.]

bŭ'ttons (-z) *n.* Liveried page-boy. [f. BUTTON[1] (from rows of buttons on his jacket)]

bŭ'ttrĕss *n.*, & *v.t.* **1.** *n.* Support built against wall etc. (FLYING[2] *buttress*); prop (lit. or fig.); buttress-like projection of hill. **2.** *v.t.* **~ (up),** support (lit. or fig.) with buttress, by argument, etc. [ME, f. OF (*ars*) *bouterez* thrusting (arch) f. *bouteret* f. *bouter* BUTT[4]]

bŭ'tty̆[1] *n.* **1.** (colloq.) Mate, chum, companion. **2.** Middleman between mine-proprietor and miners; **~-gang** (of men undertaking part of large job, sharing profits equally). [19th c., perh. f. BOOTY in phr. *play booty* join in sharing plunder]

||**bŭ'tty̆**[2] *n.* (dial.) Slice of bread and butter; sandwich. [f. BUTTER[1] + -Y[3]]

bū'ty̆l *n.* (Chem.) Radical, C_4H_9, derived from butane; **~ rubber,** kind of synthetic rubber. [f. foll. + -YL]

būty̆'rĭc *a.* (Chem.) **~ acid,** colourless syrupy liquid acid (C_3H_7COOH) found in rancid butter; hence **bū'ty̆r**ATE[1] (3) *n.* [f. L *butyrum* BUTTER[1] + -IC]

bŭ'xom *a.* Plump and comely; hence ~NESS *n.* [earlier sense *pliant*, ME f. st. of OE *būgan* BOW[3] + -SOME[1]]

buy (bī) *v.t.* (**bought** *pr.* bawt), & *n.* **1.** *v.t.* Obtain in exchange for money etc.; serve to procure (*money cannot buy happiness*); get by some sacrifice (*dearly bought*); win over (person) by bribery etc.; (sl.) accept, believe, be deceived by, suffer, receive as punishment etc. (**~ it,** be killed). **2. ~ in,** buy a stock of, withdraw at auction by naming higher price than highest offered; **~ into,** obtain share in by payment; **~ off,** pay to get rid of (claim, claimant, blackmailer); **~ out,** pay (person) to give up post, property, etc.; **~ over,** bribe; **~ up,** buy as much as possible of, absorb (other firm etc.) by purchase. **3.** Hence ~'ER[1] *n.*, (esp.) agent who selects and purchases stock for a large shop etc.; **~er's** or **~ers' market,** one in which goods are plentiful and cheap. **4.** *n.* Purchase (**best ~,** that giving best results in proportion to price; **good ~,** a favourable bargain, thing cheaply bought). [OE *bycgan*, = OS *buggian*, ON *byggja*, Goth. *bugjan* f. Gmc **bugjan*]

bŭzz[1] *n.* Hum of bee etc.; sound of buzzer; sound of people talking, stir, general movement; rumour; confused low sound; (sl.) telephone call; ***~-saw,** circular saw; **~-word,** catchword, slogan. [f. foll.]

bŭzz[2] *v.i.* & *t.* Make humming sound; signal with buzzer; move or hover *about* busily; (sl.) go *off* quickly; (of place) sound confusedly; (colloq.) throw hard; interfere with (aircraft) by flying very close to it. [imit.]

bŭ'zzard *n.* Raptorial bird of genus *Buteo*; *turkey buzzard. [ME, f. OF *busard*, *buson* f. L *buteo -onis* falcon; see -ARD]

bŭ'zzer *n.* In vbl senses; whistle or hooter; electric buzzing-machine for sending signals. [f. BUZZ[2] + -ER[1]]

B.V.M. *abbr.* Blessed Virgin Mary.

bwa'na (-ah'-) *n.* (Afr.) Master, sir. [Swahili]

B.W.I. *abbr.* (Hist.) British West Indies.

by[1] *prep.* & *adv.* **1.** *prep.* (bī *or, when unstressed,* bĭ). Near, at or to side of, about person or in possession of, in company of, in region of, slightly inclining to, (*come here by me*; STAND[1] *by*; ABIDE *by*; *have not got it by me*; COME *by*); **by oneself,** alone (& see 4); **North by East,** between N. and N.N.E.; **North-East by East,** between N.E. and E.N.E.; **by the head, stern,** (of ship) deeper in water there. **2.** Along, in passing along, through, via, avoiding, passing, outstripping, (*by nearest road*; *by the* WAY; *by the* BYE[1]; *travel by Paris, by sea*; *pass him by, go by him*). **3.** During, in the circumstances of, (*by day, night, daylight*). **4.** Through the agency, means, instrumentality, or causation, of, owing to, in such a manner, with, (*know, say, by* HEART; *multiply, divide, by*; *3 ft. by 2 ft.*; *lead by the hand*; *set by the ears* (EAR[1] 1); *go, be known, by the name of*; *what do you mean by that?*; *by all, no,* MEAN[1]*s*; *live by bread*; *do it by* one's *deputy*; *have children by* (man as father, woman as mother); *colt by* (sire); *approved, written, made, by*; *novel by Scott, play by Shaw*; *no light to read by*; *case goes by default*; *begin, end, by* doing; *by* WAY *of*; *cautious by nature*; **by** *cheque* etc., in credit entries; *by chance*; *by dint of*; *by reason of*; *by* VIRTUE *of*); **by** one**self,** without help or prompting (& see 1). **5.** As soon as, not later than, (*by now, next week, tomorrow, the time he gets here*); according to, after, from, (*by* ROTE; *by* RIGHT³; *by* RIGHT³*s*; *take warning, example, by*; *by your* LEAVE¹; *judge by appearances*; *ten minutes by the clock*; *sell, buy, by retail, the yard, the packet*; *paid by the hour*; **by the dozen** etc., in at least that quantity). **6.** With succession of, succeeding, (*by* DEGREE*s*, *by hundreds*, **getting worse by the minute*, *day by day*, *year by year*, *man by man*, LITTLE *by little*); **by and by,** (*adv.*) before long, (*n.*) *the* future. **7.** To the extent of (*missed by a foot*; *too clever by* HALF 2; *better by far*). **8.** Concerning, in respect of, (*do* one's *duty by*; *do as you would be done by*; *French by blood*, *Jones by name*; *pull up by the roots*; (colloq.) *all right by me*). **9.** As surely as one believes in (*by God*; SWEAR *by*). **10.** *adv.* (bī). Near (STAND¹ *by*; *lives close by*). **11.** Aside, in reserve, (PUT¹ *by*, LAY³ *by*). **12.** Past (*they marched by*; *all that is gone by*). **13.** **~ and large,** on the whole, everything considered, (orig. Naut., to the wind and off it); **by'gone,** (*a.*) past, antiquated, (*n.*, in *pl.*) past offences (**let bygones be bygones,** forgive and forget), domestic objects of the past; **by'line,** line in newspaper etc. naming writer of article, (Assoc. Footb.) goal-line; **by'stander,** spectator. [OE *bī, bi, be*, = OS, OHG *bī, bi*, Goth. *bi* f. Gmc **bi*]

bȳ², bȳe², *a.* Subordinate, incidental, secondary; side, out-of-the-way; **by-blow,** (1) side-blow not at main opponent, (2) bastard child; **by-effect,** side-effect; *by*-ELECTION; **by-form,** collateral form of word etc.; **by-lane,** side lane; **by'name,** sobriquet, nickname; **by'pass,** (*n.*) secondary channel for gas etc. to allow flow when main channel is blocked, road passing round town or its centre to provide alternative route for through traffic, (*v.t.*) provide with bypass, avoid; **by'path,** secluded path, minor branch of subject; **by-play,** subsidiary action in play (lit. or fig.); **by-product,** incidental or secondary product of manufacture etc.; **by-road,** minor road; **by-street,** side-street; **byway,** by-road or bypath; **by'word,** proverb, person etc. taken as typical (*a byword for laziness* etc.). [f. prec.]

bȳ³ *n.* Var. of foll.

bȳe¹ *n.* Something subordinate (**by the by** or **bye,** incidentally, parenthetically); (Cricket) run scored from ball that passes batsman without being hit, **leg-~,** from one that touches batsman; (Golf) hole(s) remaining after decision of match; (being) unpaired competitor in game etc. [f. BY¹, as *n.*]

bȳe². See BY².

bȳe³ *int.* (colloq.) = GOODBYE. [abbr.]

bȳe'-bȳe¹, bȳe'-bȳes (bī'bīz), *n.* (Child's wd for) sleep, bed. [ME, f. sound used in lullabies]

bȳe-bȳe'² *int.* (colloq.) = GOODBYE. [childish corrupt.]

Byelorussian. See BELORUSSIAN.

bȳ'-law, bȳe'-law, *n.* ||Regulation made by local authority or corporation; regulation of company etc. [ME, prob. f. obs. *byrlaw* local custom (ON *býjar* gen. sing. of *býr* town, but assoc. w. BY²; **lagu* LAW)]

bȳre *n.* Cow-shed. [OE *bȳre*, perh. cogn. w. BOWER¹]

Bȳrŏ'nĭc *a.* Characteristic of Byron or his romantic poetry. [f. Lord *Byron*, Engl. poet d. 1824 + -IC]

bȳssĭnō's|ĭs *n.* (*pl.* **-es** *pr.* -ēz). (Path.) Lung disease due to prolonged inhalation of textile fibre dust. [mod. L, f. Gk *bussinos* made of byssus + -OSIS]

bȳ'ssus *n.* (Hist.) fine textile fibre and fabric of flax; tuft of silky filaments by which some molluscs adhere to rock. [ME f. L, f. Gk *bussos*]

bȳte *n.* Group of binary digits in computer. [20th c., perh. based on BIT⁴ and BITE²]

bȳ'wōner (*or* bā'vō-) *n.* (S. Afr.) Holder of land under *métayage* system. [Afrik. (*by* with, *woon* live; see -ER¹)]

Bȳ̆ză'ntīne *a.* & *n.* (Inhabitant) of Byzantium or the E. Roman Empire; (Archit. etc.) of style developed in the Eastern Empire; complicated; inflexible; underhand. [f. F *byzantin* or f. L *Byzantinus* (*Byzantium*, later Constantinople and now Istanbul; see -INE¹)]

Bȳ̆ză'ntĭn|ĭsm *n.* Style and methods of architecture etc. developed in Byzantine Empire; so **~IST** (3) *n.* [f. prec. + -ISM]

C

C, c, (sē) *n.* (*pl.* **Cs** *or* **C's**). Third letter of alphabet; (Mus.) first note of natural major scale; third hypothetical person or example; third highest class (of academic marks, population as regards affluence, etc.); (Alg., usu. *c*) third known quantity; (as Roman numeral) 100 (**cc** 200, **cd** 400, **cm** 900); ||**C3** (sē thrē'), lowest medical grade in war of 1914–18, (colloq.) unfit, worthless.

C. *abbr.* Cape; Celsius, Centigrade; ||COMMAND² Paper (second series, 1870–1899); Conservative; coulomb(s).

c. *abbr.* about [L *circa*]; caught by; cent(s); centi-; century; chapter; cold; colt; cubic.

C *symb.* carbon; copyright (also ©).

c/- *abbr.* (Austral. & N.Z.) care of.

C.A. *abbr.* chartered accountant.

ca. *abbr. circa.*

Ca *symb.* calcium.

Caaba. Var. of KAABA.

căb *n.* Taxi or (Hist.) hackney carriage; shelter or compartment for driver of train, lorry, or crane; **~'man,** driver of cab; **~-rank,** place where cabs are authorized to wait. [abbr. of CABRIOLET]

C.A.B. *abbr.* Citizens' Advice Bureau; *Civil Aeronautics Board.

cabă'l *n.* Secret intrigue; political clique, faction; (Hist.) committee of five ministers under Charles II, whose surnames happened to begin with C, A, B, A, and L. [f. F *cabale* f. med. L *cabala*, CABBALA]

cabala. See CABBALA.

căballer'ō (-lyār'ō) *n.* (*pl.* **~s**). Spanish gentleman. [Sp.; see CAVALIER]

***caba'na** (-ah'-) *n.* Shelter at beach or swimming-pool. [f. Sp. *cabaña* f. LL (as CABIN)]

că'baret (-rā) *n.* Entertainment provided in restaurant etc. while customers are at table. [F, = wooden structure, tavern]

că'bbage *n.* Green culinary vegetable, variety of *Brassica oleracea*, with leaves forming a round heart or head; (colloq.) person without ambition or interests; **~-palm,** tree with edible cabbage-like terminal bud; **~-rose,** double rose with large round compact flower; **~-tree,** = *cabbage-palm*; **~ white,** butterfly of genus *Pieris* feeding on cabbage leaves; hence **că'bbag**Y² (-ĭjĭ) *a.* [earlier *cabache*, *-oche* f. OF (Picard) *caboche* head, OF *caboce*, of unkn. orig.]

că'b(b)al|a (*or* kabah'la) *n.* Jewish oral tradition; mystic interpretation, esoteric doctrine, occult lore; hence ~ISM (3), ~IST (2), *ns.*, **~ĭ'stɪc** *a.* [med. L, f. Rabbinical Heb. *ḳabbālâ* tradition]

că'bbў *n.* (colloq.) Cab-driver. [f. CAB + -Y³]

cā'ber *n.* Roughly trimmed tree-trunk used in Sc. Highland sport of **tossing the ~**. [f. Gael. *cabar* pole]

că'bĭn *n.*, & *v.t.* **1.** *n.* Small poor dwelling; room or compartment in ship or aircraft for passengers or crew, or in aircraft for cargo; driver's cab; **~-boy** (waiting on officers or passengers); **~ class,** intermediate class of accommodation in ship; **~ cruiser,** power-driven vessel with cabin and living accommodation. **2.** *v.t.* (esp. in *p.p.*) Confine in small space, cramp. [ME f. OF *cabane* f. Prov. *cabana* f. LL *capanna, cavanna*]

că'bĭnėt *n.* **1.** Case or cupboard with drawers, shelves, etc., for storing or displaying articles; piece of furniture containing radio or television set etc. **2.** (Polit.; *C~*). Inner circle of ministers controlling Government policy; ||**C~ Minister,** one of them; ||SHADOW¹ *Cabinet*. **3.** (arch.) Small private room. **4. ~-maker,** skilled joiner; ||**~ photograph** (about 6 by 4 inches); **~ pudding,** steamed pudding with dried fruit. [f. prec. + -ET¹, infl. by F *cabinet*]

cā'ble¹ *n.* **1.** Strong thick rope of hemp or wire; (Naut.) chain of anchor, (as measure) 200 yards; (esp. submarine or underground telegraph) line containing insulated wires; cablegram; (Archit.) rope-shaped ornament. **2. ~-car** (moved by endless cable); **~-laid,** (of rope) having three triple strands; **~ railway** (along which cars or carriages are drawn by endless cable moved by fixed engine); **~ (stitch),** knitted pattern looking like twisted rope; **~way,** transporting-system with usu. elevated cable. [ME f. AF, ONF **cable* f. OF *chable*, or f. Prov. *cable*, f. LL *cap(u)lum* halter f. Arab. *ḥabl*]

cā'ble² *v.t.* & *i.* Furnish or fasten with cable; (Archit.) fill with cables; transmit (message), communicate, inform (person), by cable. [f. prec.]

cā'blegrăm (-bėlg-) *n.* Message by submarine cable. [f. CABLE¹ + -GRAM]

că'bochŏn (-sh-) *n.* Gem polished but not faceted; ***en ~***, (of gem) so treated. [F, dim. of *caboche*; see CABBAGE]

caboo'dle *n.* (sl.) **The whole ~**, the lot, the whole number or quantity, (of persons or things). [19th c. U.S., perh. f. phr. *kit and boodle*]

caboo'se *n.* Cooking-room on ship's deck; *guard's van, car on goods train for workmen etc. [f. Du. *cabūse*, of unkn. orig.]

că'botage (*or* -ahzh) *n.* Coastal trade; reservation to a country of (esp. air) traffic operation within its territory. [F (*caboter* to coast, perh. f. Sp. *cabo* CAPE²; see -AGE)]

cabotin (kahbotă'ṅ) *n.* (*fem.* ~*e pr.* -ē'n). Second-rate actor. [F, = strolling player, perh. f. as prec., from resemblance to vessels travelling from port to port]

că'brĭōle *n.* Kind of curved leg characteristic of Queen Anne and Chippendale furniture. [F, f. *cabrioler, caprioler* f. It. *capriolare* to leap in the air; from resemblance to leaping animal's foreleg (see CAPRIOLE)]

căbrĭole't (-lā') *n.* (Hist.) Light two-wheeled hooded one-horse chaise; motor car with folding top. [F, f. *cabriole* goat's leap (cf. CAPRIOLE), applied to its motion; cf. -ET¹]

ca'că'nnў (kah-). See CANNY.

cacā'ō (*or* -kah'ō) *n.* (*pl.* ~s). Seed of orig. tropical Amer. tree, from which cocoa and chocolate are made; **~(-tree)**, this tree (*Theobroma cacao*). [Sp., f. Nahuatl *caca(uatl* tree)]

că'chalŏt (-sh-; *or* -lō) *n.* Sperm whale. [F, f. Sp. & Port. *cachalote*; orig. unkn.]

căche (kăsh) *n.*, & *v.t.* **1.** *n.* Hiding-place for treasure, provisions, ammunition, etc.; what is hidden in a cache. **2.** *v.t.* Place in cache. [F (*cacher* to hide)]

cachectic. See CACHEXIA.

că'chet (-shā) *n.* Distinguishing mark; internal evidence of authenticity; prestige; (Med.) small case of gelatine etc. enclosing dose of medicine, capsule. [F (*cacher* press f. Rom. **coacticare* f. L *coactare* constrain)]

cachĕ'xĭa, -xў, (-kĕ'-) *n.* Chronic debility of body or mind; so **cachĕ'ctɪc** (-kĕ'-) *a.* [f. F *cachexie* or f. LL f. Gk *kakhexia* (*kakos* bad, *hexis* habit; see -IA¹, -Y¹)]

că'chĭnn|āte (-k-) *v.i.* Laugh loudly; so ~A'TION *n.*, **~ātory** *a.* [f. L *cachinnare* + -ATE³]

că'cholŏng (-sh-) *n.* Kind of opal. [F, f. Mongolian *kashchilon* beautiful stone]

că'chou (-shōō) *n.* Catechu; lozenge to sweeten breath. [F, f. Port. *cachu* f. Malay *kāchu*; cf. CATECHU]

cachu'cha (-ōō'-) *n.* Spanish solo dance. [Sp.]

caci'que (-sē'k) *n.* W. Ind. or Amer. Ind. native chief; political boss in Spain or Latin America; hence **caci'quɪsm** (-sē'k-) *n.*, government by caciques. [Sp., f. Carib]

căck-hă'ndėd *a.* (colloq.) Left-handed; clumsy. [f. dial. *cack* excrement + HAND¹ + -ED²]

că'ckle *v.* & *n.* **1.** *v.i.*, & *n.* (Make) clucking of hen after laying; (indulge in) noisy inconsequent talk; (give) loud silly laugh; **cut the ~**, (colloq.) come to the point. **2.** *v.t.* Say cacklingly. [ME, prob. f. MLG, MDu. *kākelen*, imit.]

căcodē'mon, -ae'mon, *n.* Evil spirit; malignant person. [f. Gk *kakodaimōn* (*kakos* bad, *daimōn* spirit)]

că'codўl *n.* (Chem.) Radical formed from arsenic and methyl, occurring in malodorous compounds; hence **căcodў'lɪc** *a.* [f. Gk *kakōdēs* stinking (*kakos* bad) + -YL]

cacŏ'ĕpў (*or* kă'-) *n.* Bad pronunciation (opp. *orthoepy*). [f. Gk *kak(o)epeia* (*kakos* bad, *epos* word); see -Y¹]

cacoethes (kăkōē'thēz) *n.* Itch for doing something inadvisable; ***~ scribe'ndi,*** irresistible desire to write. [L, f. Gk *kakoēthes* neut. a. (*kakos* bad, *ēthos* disposition)]

cacŏ'graphў *n.* Bad handwriting or spelling; hence **cacŏ'**GRAPHER *n.*, **căco**GRA'PHIC(AL) *adjs.* [f. Gk *kakos* bad, after *orthography*]

cacŏ'logў *n.* Bad choice of words or pronunciation. [f. LL f. Gk *kakologia* vituperation (*kakos* bad; see -LOGY)]

că'comĭstle (-sėl) *n.* Racoon-like animal of southern N. America. [f. Amer. Sp. *cacomixtle* f. Nahuatl *tlacomiztli*]

cacŏ'phon|ў *n.* Discordant sound; so ~OUS *a.* [f. F *cacophonie* f. Gk *kakophōnia* f. *kakophōnos* (*kakos* bad, *phōnē* sound); see -Y¹]

că'ct|us *n.* (*pl.* ~i *pr.* -ī, *or* ~uses). Succulent plant of family Cactaceae, with thick fleshy stem, usu. spines but no leaves, and brilliantly coloured flowers; **~us dahlia,** kind of dahlia with rolled-back flower-rays resembling cactus flower; hence ~A'CEOUS, **~AL**, **~OID**, *adjs.* [L, f. Gk *kaktos* cardoon]

căcū'mĭnal *a.* (Phonet.) Pronounced with

tongue-tip curled up towards hard palate. [f. L *cacuminare* make pointed (*cacumen -minis* tree-top) + -AL]

căd *n.* Vulgar ill-bred person; person guilty or capable of ungentlemanly conduct, blackguard, whence **~'**DISH[1] *a.* [abbr. of CADDIE in sense 'odd-job man']

cadă'stral *a.* Of or showing extent, value, and ownership, of land for taxation. [F, f. *cadastre* register of property f. Prov. *cadastro* f. It. *catast(r)o*, earlier *catastico* f. late Gk *katastikhon* list, register (*kata stikhon* line by line)]

cadă'ver *n.* (esp. Med.) Corpse; so **cadă'ver**IC *a.* [ME f. L (*cadere* fall)]

cadă'verous *a.* Corpselike; deathly pale. [f. L *cadaverosus* (as prec.; see -OUS)]

că'ddie *n.*, & *v.i.* **1.** *n.* Golfer's attendant for carrying clubs etc.; ~ **car** or **cart,** light two-wheeled trolley for transporting golf-clubs during game. **2.** *v.i.* Act as caddie. [orig. Sc., f. F CADET]

că'ddis *n.* **~-fly,** feebly flying freq. nocturnal insect of order Trichoptera, living near water; ~(**-worm**), larva of caddis-fly etc., living in water and making cylindrical case of sticks etc., used as fishing-bait. [17th c., of unkn. orig.]

că'ddy[1] *n.* Small box for holding tea. [earlier *catty* weight of 1⅓ lb., f. Malay *kātī*]

că'ddy[2]. Var. of CADDIE.

cā'denc|e *n.* Rhythm; measured movement, esp. of sound; fall of voice, esp. at end of sentence etc.; intonation; close of musical phrase; hence ~ED[2] (-st) *a.* [ME f. OF **cadence* f. It. *cadenza* f. pop. L **cadentia* f. L *cadere* fall; see -ENCE]

cā'dency *n.* Status of younger branch of family. [f. as prec.; see -ENCY]

cadĕ'ntial (-shal) *a.* Of cadence or cadenza. [f. as CADENCE + -IAL]

cadĕ'nza *n.* (Mus.) Passage for solo instrument near close of movement, sometimes improvised. [It.; see CADENCE]

cadĕ't *n.* Younger son; student in naval or military or air force college; member of corps receiving elementary military or police training; (N.Z.) young man learning sheep-farming; hence ~SHIP *n.* [F, f. Gascon dial. *capdet* f. Rom. **capitellus* dim. of L *caput* head]

cădg|e *v.* **1.** *v.i.* Go about begging. **2.** *v.t.* Get by begging or sponging. **3.** Hence ~'ER[1] *n.* [19th c., earlier = ? bind, carry; orig. unkn.]

cā'di (*or* kah'-) *n.* Judge in Muslim country. [f. Arab. *ḳādī* (*ḳaḍā* to judge)]

Cădmē'an *a.* ~ **victory,** = PYRRHIC[2] *victory.* [f. L f. Gk *Kadmeios* (*Kadmos* Cadmus; see foll.)]

că'dmium *n.* Bluish-white metallic element, physically resembling tin; ~ **cell,** voltaic cell used as standard of e.m.f.; ~ **yellow,** intense yellow pigment containing cadmium sulphide. [f. obs. *cadmia* calamine f. L f. Gk *kadm(e)ia* (*gē*) Cadmean (earth), f. *Cadmus* legendary founder of Thebes; see -IUM]

cadre (kahdr, kah'der, *or* kă'drĭ) *n.* (Mil. etc.) permanent establishment of unit forming nucleus for expansion at need; (member of) group of workers promoting interests of Communist Party. [F, f. It. *quadro* f. L *quadrus* square]

cadū'c|ėus *n.* (*pl.* ~**ei** *pr.* -ĭī). Ancient Greek or Roman herald's wand, esp. as carried by messenger-god Hermes or Mercury. [L, f. Doric Gk *karuk(e)ion* (*kērux* herald)]

cadū'c|ous *a.* (Zool. & Bot., of organs and parts) falling off early; so ~ITY *n.* [f. L *caducus* falling (*cadere* fall) + -OUS]

caecĭ'lian (sĭs-) *a.* & *n.* (Zool.) (Member) of order Apoda of amphibians, mainly tropical and wormlike. [f. L *caecilia* kind of lizard + -AN]

cae'c|um (sē'-), ***cē'c|um,** *n.* (*pl.* ~**a**). Blind end of first part of large intestine; hence ~AL *a.*, ~I'TIS (sĭ-) *n.* [L, for *intestinum caecum* f. *caecus* blind, transl. of Gk *tuphlon enteron*]

caenozoic. See CAINOZOIC.

Caerns. *abbr.* Caernarvonshire (former county in Wales).

Caerphĭ'lly (kar̄-, kâr-, *or* ker-) *n.* Kind of mild white cheese. [~ in Wales]

Cae'sar (sē'z-) *n.* Any of the Roman emperors, esp. from Augustus to Hadrian; autocrat; (Med. sl.) (case of) Caesarean section; **~'s wife,** person required to be above suspicion. [L, family name of Gaius Julius ~, Roman statesman d. 44 B.C.]

Caesār'ėan, -ĭan, (sĭz-) *a.* & *n.* **1.** *a.* Of Caesar or the Caesars, imperial; ~ **birth, operation, section,** delivery of child by cutting walls of abdomen [from story that Julius Caesar was so delivered]. **2.** *n.* Adherent of Caesar or of an autocratic system; so **Cae'sar**ISM (3), **Cae'sar**IST (2), (sē'z-) *ns.* **3.** Caesarean operation. [f. L *Caesarianus*; see -EAN, -IAN]

cae'sĭous (sē'z-) *a.* (Bot.) Bluish or greyish green. [f. L *caesius* + -OUS]

cae'sĭum, *cē'sĭum, (sē'z-) *n.* Soft silver-white element of alkali-metal group. [as prec. f. its spectrum lines; see -IUM]

caesūr'|a (sĭz-) *n.* (Gk & L Pros.) break between words within a metrical foot; (mod. Pros.) pause near middle of line; hence ~AL *a.* [L (*caedere caes-* cut; see -URE)]

***C.A.F.** *abbr.* cost and freight.

cafâr'd (kahfâr') *n.* Melancholia. [F, = cockroach, hypocrite]

café[1]**, cafe,** (kă'fā *or* kă'fĭ, joc. or vulg. kăf) *n.* Coffee-house, tea-shop, restaurant, *bar; ~ **society,** regular patrons of fashionable restaurants and night-clubs. [F, = coffee(-house)]

café[2] (kă'fā) *n.* ~ ***au lait*** (ō lā), coffee with milk, colour of this; ~ ***noir*** (nwâr), coffee without milk. [F, as prec.; *noir* = black]

căfėtēr'ĭa *n.* Restaurant in which customers fetch food and drink from the counter. [f. Amer. Sp. *cafetería* coffee-shop]

||**căff** *n.* (sl.) Café. [abbr.]

că'ffėine (*or* -fēn) *n.* Vegetable alkaloid stimulant found in coffee and tea plants. [f. F *caféine* (*café* coffee; see -INE[5])]

Caffre. See KAFFIR.

că'ftăn, k-, (*or* kăftah'n) *n.* Eastern man's long tunic with waist girdle; woman's long loose dress; loose shirt. [f. Turk. *ḳaftān*, partly thr. F *cafetan*]

cāge *n.*, & *v.t.* **1.** *n.* Fixed or portable prison, of wire or barred, esp. for birds or animals or prisoners of war; prison (lit. or fig.); (Mining) frame for hoisting and lowering men, wagons, etc.; compartment for passengers etc. in lift; open framework of various kinds; **~-bird,** bird (of kind customarily) kept in cage. **2.** *v.t.* Place or keep in cage. [ME f. OF, f. L *cavea*]

cā'gey, cā'gy̆, *a.* (**ca'gier, ca'giest**). (colloq.) Shrewd; wary; secretive; uncommunicative; hence **cā'gĭ**LY[2] *adv.*, **cā'gey**NESS (-jĭn-), **cā'gĭ**NESS, *ns.* [20th c. U.S.; orig. unkn.]

***cahōō't** (ka-h-) *n.* (sl., usu. in *pl.*) Company, partnership; collusion; **in ~s,** in league *with.* [19th c.; orig. uncert.]

cai'man. See CAYMAN.

Cain *n.* **Raise ~,** (colloq.) make a disturbance. create trouble. [f. ~, eldest son of Adam (Gen. 4)]

cainozō'ic (kīn-), **caen-** (sēn-), ***cēn-,** *a.* & *n.* (Geol.) (Of) the third geological era; tertiary. [f. Gk *kainos* new + *zōion* animal + -IC]

cai'que (kaē'k *or* kīē'k) *n.* Light rowing-boat on Bosporus; Levantine sailing-ship. [F, f. It. *caicco* f. Turk. *kayik*]

cairn *n.* Pyramid of rough stones as memorial, to mark path, etc.; ~ (**terrier**), small short-

-legged longish-bodied shaggy-coated terrier (perh. f. its being used to hunt among cairns). [f. Gael. *carn*]

cair'ngôrm (-n-g-) *n.* Yellow or wine-coloured semi-precious stone. [found on *C*~, mountain in Scotland (Gael. *carn gorm* blue cairn)]

cai'sson (*or* kasōō'n) *n.* **1.** Ammunition chest or wagon. **2.** Large watertight chamber open at bottom, from which water is kept out by air pressure, used in laying foundations under water; floating vessel used as dock gate; ~ **disease,** sickness caused by too rapid decompression of workers in compressed air (as in caissons etc.). [F (f. It. *cassone*), assim. to *caisse* CASE²; see -OON]

cai'tiff *n.* & *a.* (poet. or arch.) Base or despicable (person); coward(ly). [ME, f. OF *caitif, chaitif,* f. Rom. **cactivus* f. L *captivus* CAPTIVE]

cajō'l|e *v.t.* Persuade by flattery, deceit, etc., (*into* do*ing, out of,* something); coax something *out of* person; hence ~EMENT (-lm-), ~ERY (4), *ns.* [f. F *cajoler*]

cāke *n.* & *v.* **1.** *n.* Sweet usu. unleavened bread with other ingredients besides flour, e.g. currants, spice, eggs, sugar; quantity of this baked in thick disc or ornamental shape (**slice of the** ~, (fig.) participation in benefits); (Sc. & N. Engl.) thin oaten bread (**land of ~s,** Scotland); flattish compact mass of other food (*fish cake,* PANCAKE) or of any compressed substance (‖CATTLE-*cake*; *cake of soap, wax, tobacco*). **2. ~s and ale,** merry-making; **~'walk,** (1) dance developed from Negro contest in graceful walking with cake for prize, (2) easy task; **go** or **sell like hot ~s** (very readily); **piece of ~,** (colloq.) something easy or pleasant; TAKE¹ *the cake*; **cannot have** one's **~ and eat it, cannot eat** one's **~ and have it,** cannot enjoy both alternatives. **3.** *v.t.* & *i.* Form into compact mass; cover *with* hardened mass (*caked with dirt*). [ME, f. ON *kaka*]

Cal. *abbr.* California.

cal. *abbr.* calorie(s).

Că'labâr *n.* ~ **bean,** poisonous seed of tropical Afr. climbing plant yielding medicinal extract. [~ in Nigeria]

că'labăsh *n.* Gourd whose shell serves for holding liquid; (fruit of) tropical Amer. tree of genus *Crescentia,* whose fruit is so used; pipe etc. made from these or of like shape. [f. F *calebasse* f. Sp. *calabaza,* perh. f. Pers. *karbuz* melon]

***călabōō'se** *n.* Prison, lock-up. [f. Negro F *calabouse* f. Sp. *calabozo* dungeon]

călabre'se (-ā'sā) *n.* Variety of sprouting broccoli. [It., = Calabrian]

călamă'ncō *n.* (*pl.* ~es). (Hist.) Glossy woollen material chequered on one side. [16th c., of unkn. orig.]

călamă'nder *n.* Hard wood of E. Ind. tree of genus *Diospyros,* used in furniture. [19th c.; orig. unkn., perh. conn. w. Sinh. *kalu-madiriya*]

că'lamarÿ *n.* Cuttlefish with pen-shaped internal shell, esp. squid of genus *Loligo.* [f. med. L *calamarium* pen-case f. L *calamarius* (*calamus* pen; see -ARY¹)]

că'lamīne *n.* Native zinc carbonate; pink powder of zinc carbonate or oxide etc. used in lotion or ointment. [ME f. F, f. med. L *calamina* alt. f. L *cadmia*; see CADMIUM]

că'lamĭnt *n.* Mintlike herb or shrub of genus *Calamintha.* [ME, f. OF *calament* f. med. L *calamentum* f. LL f. Gk *kalaminthē*]

cală'mĭt|ÿ *n.* Adversity; deep distress; grievous disaster; ***~y-howler, C~y Jane,** prophet of disaster; so ~OUS *a.* [ME, f. F *calamité* f. L *calamitas -tatis*; see -ITY]

calando (kală'ndō) *adv.* (Mus.) Gradually decreasing in speed and volume. [It., = slackening]

cală'ndrĭa *n.* Closed vessel carrying tubes and serving as heat-exchanger etc. [Sp., = lark]

cală'sh *n.* (Hist.) light low-wheeled carriage with removable folding hood; carriage hood; (Can.) two-wheeled horse-drawn vehicle; (Hist.) woman's hooped silk hood. [f. F *calèche* f. G *kalesche* f. Pol. *kolaska* or Czech *kolesa*]

călc- *comb. form.* Lime, as: **~-sinter,** crystalline deposit from calcareous springs, travertine; **~'spar,** calcite; **~-tuff,** porous calcareous deposit. [f. G *kalk* f. L CALX]

călcā'nė|um *n.* (*pl.* ~a). Heel-bone. [L]

călcār'ėous, -ĭous, *a.* Of or containing calcium carbonate. [f. L *calcarius* (CALX; see -ARY¹) + -OUS]

călcėolār'ĭa *n.* S. Amer. plant of genus *Calceolaria,* with slipper-shaped flower. [mod. L, f. L *calceolus* dim. of *calceus* shoe + *-aria* fem. (-ARY¹)]

că'lcėolāte *a.* (Bot.) Slipper-shaped. [f. as prec. + -ATE²]

calces. See CALX.

călcĭ'ferous *a.* Yielding calcium carbonate. [f. L CALX lime + -I- + -FEROUS]

că'lc|ifÿ *v.t.* & *i.* Convert or be converted into calcium carbonate; harden by deposit of calcium salts; petrify; hence ~Ĭ'FIC *a.,* ~ĬFICA'TION *n.* [f. as prec. + -FY]

că'lcĭn|e *v.* **1.** *v.t.* Reduce to quicklime or friable substance by roasting or burning; desiccate; refine by consuming baser part; burn to ashes. **2.** *v.i.* Undergo any of these processes. **3.** Hence **călcĭn**A'TION *n.* [ME, f. OF *calciner* or f. med. L *calcinare* f. LL *calcina* lime f. L CALX]

că'lcīte *n.* Crystalline calcium carbonate. [f. G *calcit* f. L CALX lime; see -ITE¹]

că'lcĭum *n.* Greyish-white metallic element whose oxide is quicklime and which occurs widely as calcium carbonate. [f. L CALX lime + -IUM]

că'lcūl|āte *v.* **1.** *v.t.* Ascertain by mathematics; ascertain esp. beforehand (nature of event, date, etc.) by exact reckoning. **2.** *v.t.* & *i.* Plan deliberately; rely *on*; (in *part.* and *p.p.*) shrewd, cold-blooded, selfish; (in *p.p.*) apt, fit, suitable, *to* do. **3.** *v.t.* *(colloq.) Suppose, believe. **4.** Hence ~ABLE, ~ATIVE, *adjs.* [f. LL *calculare* (as CALCULUS) + -ATE³]

călcūlā'tion *n.* (Result got by) calculating; forecast. [ME f. OF, f. LL *calculatio -onis* (as prec.; see -ATION)]

că'lcūlātor *n.* In vbl senses; set of tables for use in calculation; calculating-machine. [ME f. L (as CALCULATE; see -OR)]

că'lcūlous *a.* (Med.) Of or suffering from calculus. [f. L *calculosus* (as foll.; see -OUS)]

că'lcūl|us *n.* (*pl.* ~i *pr.* -ī, *or* ~uses). **1.** (Med.) Stone, concretion in some part of body (*renal* etc. *calculus*). **2.** (Math. etc.) Particular method of calculation or reasoning (*calculus of probabilities, variations*); (esp.) = INFINITESIMAL *calculus*; DIFFERENTIAL, INTEGRAL, *calculus.* [L, = small stone (-ULE) used in reckoning on abacus]

calder'a (kahldār'*a*) *n.* Deep cauldron-like cavity on summit of volcano. [Sp., f. LL *caldaria* boiling-pot]

caldron. See CAULDRON.

Călėdō'nĭan *a.* & *n.* (Native) of ancient Scotland; (usu. joc. exc. in titles of institutions) Scots(man); (Geol.) (of) episode of mountain-formation in Europe in the palaeozoic era. [f. L *Caledonia* northern Britain + -AN]

călėfā'cient (-shent) *a.* & *n.* (Med.) (Substance) producing warmth. [f. L *calefacere* (*calēre* be warm, *facere* make) + -ENT]

călėfă'ctorÿ *a.* & *n.* **1.** *a.* Producing warmth. **2.** *n.* Warm room in monastery. [f. LL *calefactorius* f. as prec.; see -ORY]

că'lėndar *n.,* & *v.t.* **1.** *n.* System by which

beginning, length, and subdivision of year are fixed (*calendar* MONTH, *calendar* YEAR); table(s) with months, weeks, and festivals etc., of a given year, or with dates important for certain classes (*gardener's calendar*); register or list, esp. of canonized saints, cases for trial, *matters for debate, or documents chronologically arranged with summaries; hence **calĕ'ndr**IC(AL) *adjs.* **2.** *v.t.* Register or enter in calendar; arrange, analyse, and index (documents). [ME, f. AF *calender*, OF *calendier*, f. L *calendarium* account-book (as CALENDS; see -AR[2])]

că'lėnder[1] *n.*, & *v.t.* **1.** *n.* Machine in which cloth, paper, etc., is pressed by rollers to glaze or smooth it. **2.** *v.t.* Press in calender. [f. F *calandre(r)*, of unkn. orig.]

că'lėnder[2] *n.* Mendicant dervish. [f. Pers. *ḳalandar*]

că'lėnds (-z) *n. pl.* First of month in Roman calendar; **on the Greek C~,** never. [ME, f. OF *calendes* f. L *kalendae* (**kal-* proclaim); from proclaiming of order of days]

calĕ'ndūla *n.* Marigold or other plant of genus *Calendula*, with large yellow or orange flowers. [mod. L, dim. of *calendae* (as prec.), perh. = little clock]

că'lĕnture *n.* Tropical delirium of sailors, who think the sea is green fields. [F, f. Sp. *calentura* fever (*calentar* be hot f. Rom. **calentare* f. L *calēre* be warm)]

calf[1] (kahf) *n.* (*pl.* **calves** *pr.* kahvz). **1.** Young of bovine animal, esp. domestic cow, for first year (*cow* **in** or **with ~**, pregnant; **golden ~**, wealth as object of worship (Exod. 32)); **~('skin)**, calf-leather, esp. in bookbinding and shoemaking. **2.** Young of elephant, whale, etc.; (Naut.) floating piece of ice detached from iceberg etc. **3. ~-love,** immature romantic affection; hence ~'HOOD *n.*, ~'ISH[1] 1 *a.* [OE *cælf*, = OS *calf*, OHG *kalb* f. WG **kalbha*]

calf[2] (kahf) *n.* (*pl.* **calves** *pr.* kahvz). Fleshy hinder part of leg below knee; hence **-calv**ED[2] (kahvd) *a.* [ME, f. ON *kálfi*, of unkn. orig.]

Că'lĭban *n.* Man of degraded bestial nature. [character in Shak. *The Tempest*]

că'lĭbr|āte *v.t.* Find calibre of; calculate irregularities of (tube, gauge) before graduating it; graduate (gauge) with allowance for irregularities; correlate readings of (instrument etc.) with a standard; hence ~A'TION, **~āt**OR, *ns.* [f. foll. + -ATE[3]]

că'lĭbre (*-er, or* kalē'ber), ***că'lĭber,** *n.* **1.** Internal diameter of gun or any tube; diameter of bullet or shell. **2.** Weight of character, standing, importance; ability (*we need a man of your calibre*). [f. F *calibre* f. Sp. or f. It. *calibro*, f. Arab. *ḳālib* mould]

calices. See CALIX.

cali'chė (-ē'-) *n.* Mineral deposit in dry areas of N. & S. America, esp. Chile saltpetre. [Amer. Sp.]

că'lĭcle *n.* (Biol.) Small cuplike body; so **calĭ'cūl**AR[1] *a.* [f. L *caliculus* dim. of *calix* cup]

că'lĭcō *n.* (*pl.* **~es** *or* *~s) & *a.* **1.** *n.* Cotton cloth, esp. plain white unprinted, bleached or unbleached (**~-printer, -printing,** producer, production, of coloured patterns on calico); *printed cotton fabric. **2.** *a.* Of calico; *multicoloured, piebald. [earlier *calicut*, f. name of town in India]

Calif. *abbr.* California.

călĭfor'nĭum *n.* (Chem.) Artificially made transuranic radioactive metallic element. [f. *California* (where first made) + -IUM]

că'lĭpăsh, că'lĭpee, *ns.* Gelatinous substances in turtle regarded as delicacies (*-ash*, dull green next to upper shell; *-ee*, light yellow next to lower shell). [17th c., perh. W. Ind. or alt. f. Sp. *carapacho* CARAPACE]

că'lĭper. See CALLIPER.

că'lĭph *n.* (esp. Hist.) Muslim chief civil and religious ruler; hence ~ATE[1] *n.* [ME, f. OF *caliphe* f. Arab. *ḳalīfa* successor (i.e. of Muhammad)]

călĭsthĕ'nĭc. Var. of CALLISTHENIC..

cā'lĭ|x *n.* (*pl.* **~ces** *pr.* -sēz). Cuplike cavity or organ. [L, = cup; cf. CALYX]

***calk.** See CAULK.

call[1] (kawl) *v.t.* & *i.* **1.** Cry, shout, speak loudly, (lit. or fig.); (of bird etc.) utter characteristic note; cry *out*; cry *to* (person); (Cards) name (suit, contract) in bidding; attempt to predict result of tossing coin etc.; pay brief visit (*at* house, port, station, etc., *on* person; *in*); read *over* (names to ascertain owners' presence); *call the* TUNE; **~ for,** order, demand, require, need, go and fetch; **~ off,** cancel (engagement etc.); **~ (up)on,** invoke, appeal to, request or require (*to* act, speak, etc.). **2.** Summon (lit. or fig.); demand presence of (taxi, witness, actor after curtain); invite to pastorate; communicate (with) by radio or telephone; *call to* ACCOUNT[2]; **~ into being,** create; *call* person's BLUFF[4]; **~ to mind** etc., recollect; **~ to order,** request to be orderly, declare (meeting) open; **~ into play,** give scope for; **~ in question,** dispute; **~ away,** divert, distract; **~ down,** invoke, reprimand; **~ forth,** elicit; **~ in,** withdraw from circulation, seek advice from; **~ out,** elicit, challenge to duel, order (workers) to strike, summon to action (esp. troops to aid the civil authorities); *call over the* COALS; **~ up,** imagine, recollect, summon (esp. to talk by telephone, to serve in army etc., whence **~-up** *n.*). **3.** Rouse from sleep; fix time for (*call a meeting*); announce as ensuing (*call a halt*, lit. or fig.); urge, invite, nominate, (*duty, pleasure, calls*; ||*call to the* BAR[1]; *call attention to*; *call to witness*). **4.** Name, describe as, (*call a* SPADE *a spade*; *call him John*; **~** person **names,** abuse him); consider, regard or estimate as, (*I call that mean*); *call it a* DAY; **~** (thing) one's **own,** possess. **5.** (Sc.) Drive (animal, vehicle, etc.). **6.** Hence ~'ABLE *a.* [OE *ceallian* f. ON *kalla*, = MLG, MDu. *kallen*, OHG *kallōn* talk (**kallōjan* f. Gmc **kal*)]

call[2] (kawl) *n.* **1.** Shout, cry; special cry of bird etc., imitation of this, instrument imitating it; signal on bugle etc., signalling-whistle; short esp. formal visit; **pay a ~**, make one (*pay a call on him*; *pay him a call*), (colloq.) go to lavatory. **2.** Invitation, summons, (to actor etc. to appear for rehearsal, performance, or applause; ||to the BAR[1]; from God, conscience, or congregation, to be pastor); duty, need, occasion, (*no call to blush*); demand *for* (money, esp. lent or unpaid capital; wares) or *on* (one's *purse, time*, etc.); (St. Exch.) option of buying stock at fixed price at given date; (Cards) player's right or turn to make a bid, bid etc. thus made; act of telephoning, conversation over telephone. **3. At ~, on ~,** ready or available when wanted; **within ~**, near enough to be summoned by calling. **4. ~-box,** structure containing public telephone; **~-boy,** prompter's attendant summoning actors; **~-day, -night,** (on which students are called to the bar); **~-girl,** prostitute accepting appointments by telephone; **~ of nature,** need to urinate or defecate; **~-over,** (1) = ROLL[1]-*call*, (2) reading aloud of a list of betting prices (in sporting club etc.); **~-sign(al)** (indicating identity of radio transmitter). [ME, f. prec.]

că'lla *n.* Aquatic plant of genus *Calla*; **~ (lily),** (pop.) arum lily. [mod. L]

ca'ller[1] (kaw'-) *n.* In vbl senses; person who pays call or visit, makes telephone call, announces numbers in bingo etc., or gives directions in square dance. [f. CALL[1] + -ER[1]]

că'ller[2] *a.* (Sc.) (Of fish) fresh, not decaying;

(of air) cool. [var. of ME *calver*, perh. f. OE *calwer* curds]
callĭ'graph|ў *n.* Beautiful handwriting; handwriting; so **callĭ'**GRAPHER, ~IST (1), *ns.*, **căllĭ**GRA'PHIC *a.* [f. Gk *kalligraphia* (*kallos* beauty; see -GRAPHY)]
ca'llĭng (kaw'-) *n.* In vbl senses; divine summons to salvation or self-devotion; occupation, profession, trade; ***~-card,** = *visiting*-CARD². [f. CALL¹ + -ING¹]
***callī'opė** *n.* Set of steam whistles producing musical notes, played by keyboard like that of organ. [f. name of Muse of epic poetry, Gk *Kalliopē*, lit. beautiful-voiced]
că'l(l)ĭper *n.*, & *v.t.* **1.** *n.* ~ **compasses** or **~s,** compasses with bowed legs for measuring diameter of convex bodies, or with out-turned points for measuring cavities; ~ **(splint)**, metal support for leg. **2.** *v.t.* Measure with callipers. [app. var. of CALIBRE]
căllĭpȳ'gous *a.* Having well-shaped buttocks. [f. Gk *kallipugos* (*kallos* beauty, *pugē* buttocks)]
căllĭsthĕ'n|ĭc *a.* Suitable for producing strength and grace; hence ~ICS *n.*, gymnastic exercises to achieve bodily health and grace of movement. [f. Gk *kallos* beauty + *sthenos* strength + -IC]
că'llop *n.* (Austral.) Golden perch. [Aboriginal]
callŏ'sĭtў *n.* Abnormal hardness and thickness of skin; hardened insensitive part, lump. [f. F *callosité* or f. L *callositas* (as foll.; see -ITY)]
că'llous *a.* & *n.* **1.** *a.* (Physiol. & Zool., of skin) hardened, hard; (of person, heart, etc.) unfeeling, insensitive, whence ~LY² *adv.*, ~NESS *n.* **2.** *n.* Callus. [ME, f. L *callosus* (as CALLUS; see -OUS) or F *calleux*]
că'llow (-ō) *a.* Unfledged; raw, inexperienced; hence ~LY² *adv.*, ~NESS *n.* [OE *calu* f. WG **kalwaz*, prob. f. L *calvus* bald]
callu'na (-ōō'-) *n.* Common heather, of genus *Calluna.* [mod. L, f. Gk *kallunō* beautify (*kallos* beauty)]
că'llus *n.* (Physiol.) thickened part of skin or soft tissue; (Path.) bony material formed while bone-fracture heals; (Bot.) new tissue over wound. [L]
calm¹ (kahm) *n.* Stillness, serenity, (of weather, air, sea, the mind, social or political conditions); windless period. [ME, perh. f. pop. L **calma* f. LL f. Gk *kauma* heat]
calm² (kahm) *a.* & *v.* **1.** *a.* Tranquil, quiet, windless, (lit. or fig.); (colloq.) self-confident, impudent, (*pretty calm of him*); hence ~'LY² *adv.*, ~'NESS *n.* **2.** *v.t.* Make calm, quiet, pacify. **3.** *v.i.* ~ **(down)**, become calm. [ME, f. med. L *calmus* f. as prec.]
că'lmatĭve (*or* kah'm-) *a.* & *n.* (Med.) Calming (agent), sedative. [f. prec. + -ATIVE]
că'lomĕl *n.* Mercurous chloride, esp. when used as purgative. [mod. L, perh. f. Gk *kalos* beautiful + *melas* black]
Că'lor *n.* ~ **gas,** liquefied butane etc. under pressure in containers for domestic use. [**P**; L *calor* heat]
că'lorĭc *n.* & *a.* **1.** *n.* Heat, esp. (Hist.) when regarded as a fluid. **2.** *a.* Pertaining to heat or calories. [f. F *calorique* (L *calor* heat; see -IC)]
că'lorĭe *n.* (Phys.) Unit of quantity of heat, the amount needed to raise temperature of one gram (**small** ~) or one kilogram (**large** or **great** ~) of water one degree C.; large calorie as unit of energy value of foods. [F, arbitr. f. L *calor* heat + *-ie* (-Y¹)]
călorĭ'fĭc *a.* Producing heat; ~ **value,** amount of heat given by specified quantity of fuel. [f. L *calorificus* (*calor* heat; see -I-, -FIC)]
călorĭ'mėter *n.* Apparatus for measuring heat; hence **călorĭmĕ'tr**IC *a.*, **călorĭ'**METRY *n.* [f. L *calor* heat + -I- + -METER]
că'lorў. Var. of CALORIE.
calŏ'tte *n.* Skull-cap of R.C. priests etc. [F, dim. of *cale* caul]
călque (-k) *n.* (Philol.) Loan-translation (*of* or *on*). [F, = copy, tracing (*calquer* trace f. It. f. L *calcare* tread)]
***Căltĕ'ch** (-k) *n.* California Institute of Technology. [abbr.]
că'ltrop, -ap, *n.* (Hist.) four-spiked iron ball thrown on ground to impede cavalry horses; (Her.) representation of this; (Bot.) plant with spined caltrop-like flower heads, which catch or entangle feet. [ME, f. OF *kauketrape, chauchetrape* (*chauchier* tread, *trappe* trap); (Bot.) f. OE *calcatrippe* f. med. L *calcatrippa*]
că'lūmėt *n.* Amer. Ind. clay-bowled reed-stemmed tobacco-pipe; symbol of peace. [F, dial. var. of *chalumeau* f. LL *calamellus* dim. of *calamus* reed]
calŭ'mnĭ|āte *v.t.* Slander; hence or cogn. ~A'TION, **~āt**OR, *ns.*, **~āt**ORY *a.* [f. L *calumniari* + -ATE³]
că'lumnў *n.*, & *v.t.* **1.** *n.* Malicious misrepresentation; false charge; slanderous report; so **calŭ'mnĭ**OUS *a.* **2.** *v.t.* Slander. [f. L *calumnia*]
că'lvadŏs *n.* Apple brandy. [f. *C*~, department of Normandy, France]
Că'lvarў *n.* Place or (R.C. Ch.) representation of Crucifixion. [ME, f. LL *calvaria* skull (*calvus* bald), transl. of Gk *golgotha*, Aram. *gûlgûltâ* (Matt. 27: 33)]
calve (kahv) *v.i.* & *t.* Give birth to calf; (esp. in *pass.*) give birth to (calf); (of iceberg etc.) break off mass of ice. [OE *c(e)alfian* (*cælf* CALF¹)]
-calved. See CALF².
calves. See CALF¹,².
Că'lvĭn|ĭsm *n.* Theology of Calvin or his followers; adherence to this; hence ~IST (2) *n.*, **~ĭ'st**IC(AL) *adjs.*, ~IZE (4) *v.i.* & *t.* [f. F *calvinisme* or mod. L *-ismus* f. J. *Calvin*, Fr. theologian d. 1564]
călx *n.* (*pl.* **ca'lces** *pr.* -sēz). Powder or friable substance left when a metal or mineral has been burnt. [L *calx calcis* lime, prob. f. Gk *khalix* pebble, limestone]
calў'psō *n.* (*pl.* ~**s**). Spontaneous topical W. Ind. song in Afr. rhythm. [20th c.; orig. unkn.]
că'l|ўx *n.* (*pl.* **~yces** *pr.* -ĭsēz, *or* **~yxes**). (Bot.) whorl of leaves forming outer case of bud or envelope of flower; (Biol.) = CALIX. [L, f. Gk *kalux* case of bud, husk (cf. *kaluptō* hide)]
căm *n.* Projecting part of wheel etc. in machinery, shaped to convert circular into reciprocal or variable motion; **~'shaft,** shaft carrying cam(s). [f. Du. *kam* comb; cf. Du. *kamrad* cog-wheel]
cămara'derĭe (-ah'd-) *n.* Mutual trust and sociability of comrades. [F]
cămarĭ'lla *n.* Cabal, clique. [Sp., dim. of *camara* chamber]
cămarō'n (*or* kă'maron) *n.* Freshwater shrimp or prawn like crayfish. [Sp., = shrimp]
Camb. *abbr.* Cambridge.
că'mber *n.* & *v.* **1.** *n.* Slight convexity above, arched form, (of beam, deck, road from side to side, aircraft wing, etc.); sideways inclination of motor vehicle's wheel. **2.** *v.i.* & *t.* Have, or impart to (beam etc.), such convexity. [f. F *cambre, chambre* arched, *cambrer* to arch, f. L *camurus* curved inwards]
Că'mberwĕll *n.* ~ **Beauty,** brown butterfly with yellow-bordered wings. [~ in London]
că'mbĭst *n.* Expert in, manual of, financial exchange; dealer in bills of exchange. [f. F *cambiste* f. It. *cambista* (*cambio* CHANGE¹)]
că'mbĭum *n.* (Bot.) Cellular tissue from which annual growth of wood and bark occurs. [med. L, = (ex)CHANGE¹]
Cămbō'dĭan *a.* & *n.* (Native or language) of

Cambodia (Khmer Republic). [f. *Cambodia* in S.E. Asia + -AN]

Că'mbrĭan *a.* & *n.* Welsh(man); (Geol.) (of) earliest palaeozoic period or system. [f. L *Cambria* var. of *Cumbria* f. W *Cymry* Welshmen or *Cymru* Wales (OCelt. **Kombroges* compatriots)]

că'mbrĭc *n.* Fine white linen; similar cotton fabric. [f. *Kamerijk*, Flem. form of *Cambrai* in N. France, where orig. made]

Cā'mbrĭdge *n.* **~ blue,** light blue. [~, university town in England]

Cambs. *abbr.* Cambridgeshire.

cāme[1] *n.* Grooved slip of lead as used in lattice windows. [app. = Sc. *calm* casting-mould]

cāme[2]. See COME.

că'mel *n.* Large hornless ruminant long-necked cushion-footed quadruped with (Arabian) one hump or (Bactrian) two humps (SWALLOW[1] *a camel*); shade of fawn colour; machine for floating a ship; **~-back,** inferior rubber for tyres; **~('s)-hair,** made of camel's hair or (paint--brushes) of squirrel's tail hairs. [OE, f. L f. Gk *kamēlos*, f. Semitic]

cămeleer' *n.* Camel-driver. [f. prec. + -EER]

camĕ'llĭa *n.* Shrub of genus *Camellia*, esp. flowering evergreen from China and Japan. [f. J. *Camellus* or *Kamel*, 17th-c. Jesuit and botanist + -IA[1]]

că'melopard (*or* -mĕ'-) *n.* (arch.) Giraffe. [f. L *camelopardus* f. Gk *camēlopardalis* (as CAMEL, PARD[1])]

că'melrў *n.* Troops mounted on camels. [f. CAMEL + -RY]

Că'membert (-mahṅbār) *n.* Small soft rich cheese. [~ in Normandy, France, where orig. made]

că'mėō *n.* (*pl.* **~s**). Small piece of relief-carving in stone (onyx, agate, etc.) usu. with colour--layers utilized to give background; relief design of similar form; short literary sketch or acted scene. [ME, f. OF *camahieu* etc. & med. L *cammaeus*]

că'mera *n.* **1.** Apparatus for taking photographs or television pictures; **on ~,** being filmed; **~man,** one who operates a camera professionally, esp. in cinema or television; **~ obscur'a,** darkened box with aperture for projecting image of distant object on screen; **~-shy,** not liking to be photographed. **2.** ***In*** **~,** (1, Law) in judge's private room, (2) privately, not in public. [L, = vault, f. Gk *kamara* thing with arched cover]

cămerlĭ'ngō, -lĕ'n-, (-nggō) *n.* (*pl.* **~s**). Pope's chamberlain and financial secretary; treasurer of the Sacred College. [It. *camerlingo* f. Frank., see CHAMBERLAIN]

||**că'mĭknĭckers** (-ĭnĭkerz) *n. pl.* Woman's one--piece close-fitting undergarment. [f. CAMISOLE + KNICKERS]

că'mĭon *n.* Dray; lorry; bus. [F]

că'mĭsōle *n.* (arch.) Under-bodice, usu. embroidered etc. [F, f. It. *camiciola* or Sp. *camisola* (*camicia*, *camisa* shirt; see CHEMISE)]

că'mlėt *n.* (arch.) Light cloth of various materials for cloaks etc. [orig. a costly Eastern material, ME, f. OF *cham-*, *camelot* perh. ult. f. Arab. *ḵamla*(*t*) nap; assoc. w. CAMEL]

că'momīle, ch- (k-), *n.* Aromatic composite plant of genus *Anthemis* or *Matricaria* with flowers used as tonic; **~ tea,** infusion of the flowers. [ME, f. OF *camomille* f. LL *c*(*h*)*amomilla* f. Gk *khamaimēlon* earth-apple (f. apple-smell of flowers)]

că'mouflage (-ŏŏflahzh; *or* -*o*f-) *n.*, & *v.t.* **1.** *n.* Disguise of guns, ships, etc., effected by obscuring with splashes of various colours, smoke-screens, foliage, etc.; means of disguise or evasion. **2.** *v.t.* Hide by camouflage. [F (*camoufler* (sl.) disguise f. It. *camuffare* disguise, deceive; see -AGE)]

cămp[1] *n.* **1.** Place where troops are lodged or trained; military life (*court and camp*); (arch.) army on campaign; (remains of) ancient fortified site; temporary quarters of nomads, gipsies, detainees, holiday-makers, Scouts, Guides, or travellers; (persons) camping out; (S. Afr.) portion of veld fenced off for pasture on farms; (Austral. & N.Z.) assembly place of sheep or cattle; adherents of a doctrine or party. **2. ~-bed, -chair,** etc., (folding and portable); **~'craft,** skill in living in camp; **~-fever,** typhus; **~-fire,** open-air fire in camp etc.; ***~ fire girl,** member of a recreational and training organization; **~-follower,** non-military worker or hanger-on in camp, disciple of group or theory; ***~-meeting,** religious open-air or tent meeting often lasting several days; **~'site,** place for camping; **~-stool,** light stool with folding legs. [F, f. It. *campo* f. L *campus* level ground]

cămp[2] *v.i.* Encamp, lodge in camp; **~ (out),** lodge in temporary quarters or in the open; (Austral. & N.Z., of sheep or cattle) flock together esp. for rest. [f. F *camper* (as prec.)]

cămp[3] *a.*, *n.*, & *v.* **1.** *a.* Affected, effeminate; homosexual; exaggerated, bizarre. **2.** *n.* Camp behaviour; hence **~'Y**[2] *a.* **3.** *v.i.* & *t.* Behave or do in a camp way; **~ it up,** overact. [20th c.; orig. uncert.]

cămpai'gn (-ā'n) *n.*, & *v.i.* **1.** *n.* Series of military operations in a definite area or with one objective or forming the whole or a distinct part of a war; military service in the field (*on campaign*); organized course of action, esp. (Polit. etc.) attempt to arouse public interest, esp. before an election. **2.** *v.i.* Serve on or conduct campaign; hence **~ER**[1] *n.* (**old ~er,** veteran, person skilled in adapting himself to circumstances). [f. F *campagne* open country, f. It. *campagna* f. LL *campania*; cf. CHAMPAIGN]

cămpani'lė (-nē'-) *n.* Bell-tower, usu. detached, esp. in Italy. [It. (*campana* bell)]

cămpanŏ'|logў *n.* Subject of bells (founding, ringing, etc.); hence **~LOGER, ~LOGIST,** *ns.*, **~LO'GICAL** *a.* [f. mod. L *campanologia* f. LL *campana* bell + -LOGY]

cămpă'nūla *n.* Plant of genus *Campanula*, with bell-shaped flowers, usu. blue, pink, or white. [mod. L, dim. of *campana* bell; see -ULE]

cămpă'nūlate *a.* (Bot. & Zool.) Bell-shaped. [f. as prec. + -ATE[2]]

Cămpea'chў *n.* **~ wood,** LOG[1]wood. [f. *Campeche* in Mexico, whence first exported]

că'mper *n.* In vbl senses; motor vehicle used as living-accommodation when camping. [f. CAMP[2] + -ER[1]]

că'mphor *n.* Whitish translucent crystalline volatile substance with aromatic smell and bitter taste, used in pharmacy and as insect--repellent; hence **cămphŏ'rIC** *a.* [ME, f. OF *camphore* or med. L *camphora*, f. Arab. *kāfūr* f. Skr. *karpūram*]

că'mphorāte *v.t.* Impregnate or treat with camphor. [f. prec. + -ATE[3]]

că'mpĭon *n.* Flowering plant of genus *Silene* or *Lychnis*. [transl. of Gk *lukhnis stephanōmatikē* a plant used for garlands, perh. f. obs. *campion* CHAMPION]

că'mpus *n.* Grounds of university or college; university as teaching etc. institution. [L, = field]

că'mwŏŏd *n.* Hard red W. Afr. wood yielding dye. [perh. f. Temne]

căn[1] *n.*, & *v.t.* (-nn-). **1.** *n.* Vessel for liquids, usu. of metal and with handle; **carry** or **take the ~ (back),** (sl.) bear the responsibility or blame. **2.** Jacket for nuclear fuel rod; *metal container (**~ of worms,** complex and largely uninvestigated topic); *(sl.) lavatory; (sl.) prison. **3.**

Tin-plate container for hermetic sealing (to preserve meat, fish, fruit, drink, etc.); whence (-)~'NER[1] *n.*, ~'NERY (3) *n.*, canning-factory; **~-opener,** tool for opening cans. **4.** *v.t.* Put into a can; preserve thus. [OE *canne,* = OHG *channa,* ON *kanna,* Gmc or f. LL *canna*]

can[2] (*or, when stressed,* kăn) *v. aux.* (*pres.* **can** exc. 2 *sing.* (arch.) **canst,** *neg.* **ca'nnot,** (colloq.) **can't** *pr.* kahnt; *past* **could** *pr.* kud *or* ko͝od exc. 2 *sing.* (arch.) **couldst** *pr.* ko͝odst or **couldest** *pr.* ko͝o'dĭst, *neg.* **could not,** (colloq.) **couldn't** *pr.* ko͝o'dent; no other parts used). Be able to; have right to; be permitted to (*all right, you can go*); know how to (*can you play bridge, speak French?*); **could,** feel inclined to (*could laugh for joy; could you please ring?; really couldn't think of it*); (ellipt.) *will do what I can, how could you?,* (I) ~ **do** (it), (that) **could be** (so). [OE *cunnan,* = OS *cunnan,* OHG *kunnan,* ON *kunna,* Goth. *kunnan* (preterite-present vbs.) know f. IE]

Can. *abbr.* Canada; Canadian.

Cā'naan (-nan) *n.* Land of promise; heaven. [ancient name of W. Palestine; eccl. L f. eccl. Gk *Khanaan* f. Heb. *kᵉna'an*]

Că'nada *n. Canada* BALSAM; ~ **goose,** N. Amer. wild goose (*Branta canadensis*); hence **Canā'd**IAN *a.* & *n.* [~ in N. America]

canaille (kanah'ē) *n.* The rabble, the populace. [F, f. It. *canaglia* pack of dogs]

că'nakĭn. Var. of CANNIKIN.

cană'l *n.* Duct in plant or animal body for food, liquid, air, etc.; artificial watercourse for inland navigation or irrigation; (on planet Mars) seasonal marking, like a narrow line when observed from the earth; (Zool.) groove in shell for protrusion of mollusc's breathing-tube; ~ **boat,** long narrow boat for use on canals; ~ **ray,** beam of particles moving to cathode of high-vacuum tube. [ME f. OF, earlier *chanel* f. L *canalis* or It. *canale*]

că'nalīz|e, -īs|e (-īz), *v.t.* Make canal through; convert (river) into canal; provide with canals; (fig.) give desired direction etc. to; hence ~A'TION *n.* [f. F *canaliser* (CANAL; see -IZE)]

că'napé (-pĭ) *n.* **1.** Piece of bread, toast, etc., with small savoury on top. **2.** Sofa. [F]

canar'd (*or* kă'nard) *n.* False report, hoax; extra surface attached to aircraft for stability or control. [F, = duck]

Canarese. Var. of KANARESE.

canar'y̆ *n.* Yellow-feathered song-bird, the finch *Serinus canarius*; (Hist.) sweet wine from Canary Islands; **~-coloured, ~-yellow,** bright yellow; ~ **creeper,** yellow-flowered climbing plant, *Tropaeolum peregrinum*; **~-seed** (used as food for canaries and other cage-birds). [f. *Canary* Islands f. F *Canarie* f. Sp. & L *Canaria* (*canis* dog), one of the islands being noted in Roman times for large dogs]

cană'sta *n.* Card-game of Uruguayan origin, resembling rummy; meld of seven cards in it. [Sp., = basket]

cană'ster *n.* Tobacco prepared by coarsely breaking the dried leaves. [orig. the rush basket container; f. Sp. *canastro,* f. med. L **canastrum,* f. Gk *kanastron*; see CANISTER]

că'ncăn (-n-k-) *n.* High-kicking dance by woman with display of legs and petticoats. [F]

că'ncel[1] *v.* (‖-**ll**-). **1.** *v.t.* Obliterate, cross out; annul, make void, abolish; countermand, revoke order for, neutralize; balance, make up for; deface (postage stamp) to prevent further use; (Math.) strike out (same factor) from numerator and denominator, from two sides of equation, etc.; *(Mus.) return to natural pitch after (sharp or flat). **2.** *v.i.* ~ (**out**), neutralize each other. **3.** Hence ~**l**A'TION *n.* [ME, f. F *canceller* f. L *cancellare* (*cancelli* cross-bars, lattice)]

că'ncel[2] *n.* Countermand; postal cancellation; (Print.) suppression and reprinting of leaf or leaves set up, the suppressed or the substituted leaf or leaves; *(Mus.) natural-sign. [f. prec.]

că'ncellate, că'ncellātėd, *adjs.* (Biol.) Marked with crossing lines; (of bone) porous. [f. as foll. + -ATE[2] (+ -ED[1])]

că'ncellous *a.* (Of bone) porous. [f. L *cancelli* lattice + -OUS]

că'ncer *n.* **1.** (*C*~). Sign of the ZODIAC, the Crab; TROPIC *of Cancer.* **2.** (Path.) (Condition in which there is) malignant tumour from uncontrolled growth of tissue, tending to spread and to recur when removed; (fig.) evil (corruption etc.) acting similarly; ~ **stick,** (sl.) cigarette; hence ~OUS *a.* [ME f. L, = crab, cancer, after Gk *karkinos*; cf. CARCINOMA]

că'ncroid *a.* & *n.* **1.** *a.* Crablike; like cancer. **2.** *n.* Crustacean of crab family; mild form of cancer. [f. as prec. + -OID]

c & b *abbr.* caught and bowled by.

că'ndėla (*or* -ē'la) *n.* Unit of luminous intensity in the international system. [L, = CANDLE]

căndėlă'br|um (*or* -ah'-) *n.* (*pl.* **~a** *or* ***~ums;** also *sing.* **~a,** *pl.* **~as**). Large, usu. branched, candlestick or lampstand; **~um tree,** tropical Afr. tree with foliage shaped like candelabrum. [L (*candela* CANDLE)]

căndĕ'sc|ent *a.* Glowing (as) with white heat; hence ~ENCE *n.* [f. L *candēre* be white; see -ESCENT]

că'ndĭd *a.* Frank, not hiding one's thoughts; (arch.) unbiased; ~ **camera,** small camera for taking informal pictures of persons freq. without their knowledge (so ~ **photograph** etc.); hence ~LY[2] *adv.*, ~NESS *n.* [f. F *candide* or L *candidus* white (*candēre*; see prec.)]

că'ndĭdacy̆ *n.* Candidature. [f. foll. + -ACY]

că'ndĭdāte *n.* One who seeks, or is nominated for, appointment to an office or honour or membership; one thought likely to gain any position; examinee. [f. F *candidat* or f. L *candidatus* white-robed (Roman candidates wearing white), f. *candidus* (*candēre* be white); see -ATE[2]]

‖**că'ndĭdature** *n.* Standing for election, being candidate. [F (as prec.; see -URE)]

că'ndle *n.*, & *v.t.* **1.** *n.* Cylinder of wax, tallow, etc., enclosing wick, for giving light by burning; ~(**-power**), unit of light-measurement; **Roman** ~, firework in form of tube discharging coloured balls. **2.** BELL[1], *book, and candle*; **burn ~ at both ends,** exhaust one's strength or resources through undertaking too much; **can't, is not fit to, hold a ~ to,** is not to be compared with, is much inferior to; *hold a candle to the* SUN; **game not worth the ~,** result not justifying the cost or trouble. **3.** **~berry-myrtle, ~berry-tree,** trees yielding wax and oil used for candles; **~-light,** (1) light of candles, (2) dusk; **~stick,** support for (usu. single) candle; **~-tree** (with long candle-like fruit); **~wick,** (material with raised usu. tufted pattern in) thick soft cotton yarn. **4.** *v.t.* Test (egg) for freshness etc. by holding between eye and light. [OE *candel* f. L *candela* (*candēre* shine)]

Că'ndlemas (-delm-) *n.* Feast of Purification of Virgin Mary and presentation of Christ in Temple, when candles are blessed (2 Feb.). [OE *Candelmæsse* (as CANDLE, MASS[1])]

că'ndour (-der), ***că'ndor,** *n.* Candid behaviour or action; frankness. [f. F *candeur* or f. L *candor* whiteness (*candēre* shine; see -OR)]

C. & W. *abbr.* country-and-western.

că'ndy̆ *n.*, & *v.t.* **1.** *n.* (**Sugar-**)~, crystallized sugar made by repeated boiling and slow evaporation; *sweetmeat; **~-floss,** mass of fluffy spun sugar; ***~-store,** sweet-shop; **~-stripe(d),** pattern(ed) in alternate stripes of white and colour. **2.** *v.t.* Preserve by coating and impregnating with candy (*candied* PEEL³). [earlier *sugar candy* f. F *sucre candi* f. Arab. *sūkkar ḳandī* (*ḳand* sugar f. Pers. *kand* f. Skr. *khaṇḍa* sugar in pieces)]

că'ndȳtŭft *n.* Plant of genus *Iberis* with white, pink, or purple flowers in flat tufts. [f. obs. *Candy* (*Candia* Crete) + TUFT]

cāne¹ *n.* **1.** Hollow jointed stem of giant reeds and grasses (*bamboo cane*) or solid stem of slender palms (rattan, Malacca, etc.); SUGAR-*-cane*; material of such stems for wickerwork etc.; this stem or a length of it used as walking-stick or instrument of punishment or to support plant; ‖any slender walking-stick. **2.** *~-**-brake,** tract of land overgrown with canes; ~ **chair** (with seat of woven cane strips); ~-**-sugar** (obtained from the sugar-cane); *cane-*-TRASH. [ME f. OF, f. L f. Gk *kanna* reed f. Semitic]

cāne² *v.t.* Beat with cane, whence **cā'ning**¹ (1) *n.*; weave cane into (chair etc.). [f. prec.]

căngue (kăng), **căng,** *n.* (Hist.) Heavy wooden board worn round neck as punishment in China. [F *cangue* f. Port. *canga* yoke, f. Vietnamese]

cā'nīne *a.* & *n.* Of or as of a dog or dogs; ~ (**tooth**), one of the four strong pointed teeth between incisors and molars. [ME, f. F *canin -ine* or f. L *caninus* (*canis* dog; see -INE¹)]

că'nĭster *n.* Small container usu. of metal for tea, shot, etc. [f. L *canistrum* f. Gk *kanastron* wicker basket (*kanna* CANE¹)]

că'nker *n.*, & *v.t.* **1.** *n.* Ulcerous disease of animals; necrotic disease of plants; (fig.) corrupting influence; ~(**-worm**), caterpillar destroying buds and leaves; hence ~OUS *a.* **2.** *v.t.* Consume with canker; infect, corrupt; (in *p.p.*) soured, malignant, crabbed. [OE *cancer* & ONF *cancre*, OF *chancre* f. L *cancer*; see CANCER, CHANCRE]

că'nna *n.* Plant of genus *Canna*, with bright yellow, red, or orange flowers and ornamental leaves. [L; see CANE¹]

că'nnabĭs *n.* Hemp plant of genus *Cannabis*; preparation of parts of it used as intoxicant or hallucinogen; ~ **resin,** sticky product esp. from flowering tops of female cannabis plant. [L f. Gk]

că'nned (-nd) *a.* In vbl senses; (sl.) drunk, (of music) recorded for reproduction. [p.p. of CAN¹]

că'nnel *n.* ~ (**coal**), bituminous coal burning with bright flame. [16th c.; orig. N. Engl.]

cănnellō'nĭ *n. pl.* Rolls of pasta containing meat and seasoning. [It., augment. pl. of *cannello* stalk; see -OON]

că'nnelūre *n.* Groove round bullet etc. [F (*canneler* f. *canne* reed, CANE¹; see -URE)]

că'nner(ȳ). See CAN¹.

că'nnĭbal *n.* & *a.* **1.** *n.* Person who eats human flesh; animal that eats its own species; hence ~ISM (2) *n.*, ~**ĭ'st**IC *a.* **2.** *a.* Of or having these habits. [orig. pl. *Canibales* f. Sp., var. of *Caribes* name of a W. Ind. nation]

că'nnĭbalīze, -īse (-īz), *v.t.* Use (machine etc.) as source of spare parts for others. [f. prec. + -IZE (4)]

că'nnĭkin *n.* Small can. [f. Du. *kanneken* (as CAN¹, -KIN)]

că'nnon¹ *n.* **1.** (Hist.; *pl.* usu. same) piece of ordnance, gun of kind that needs a mounting; aircraft's automatic shell-firing gun; **~-ball,** (Hist.) projectile fired by cannon; **~-bone,** tube-shaped bone between horse's hock and fetlock; **~-fodder,** men regarded merely as material to be consumed in war. **2.** (Mech.) Hollow cylinder moving independently on shaft. **3.** ~(**-bit**), smooth round bit for horse. **4.** ‖(Bill.) Hitting of two balls successively by player's ball. [f. F *canon* f. It. *cannone* great tube (*canna* CANE¹; see -OON); in sense 4 f. older CAROM]

‖**că'nnon**² *v.i.* Come into collision, strike obliquely, *against, into*; make cannon at billiards. [f. prec.]

cănnonā'de *n.*, & *v.t.* **1.** *n.* Continuous gunfire. **2.** *v.t.* Bombard with cannon. [f. F *canonnade*, f. It. *cannonata* (as prec.; see -ADE)]

că'nnot. See CAN².

că'nnūl|a *n.* (*pl.* **~ae** *or* **~as**). (Surg.) Small tube for inserting into a cavity or tumour to allow fluid to enter or escape; hence ~ATE³ *v.t.*, introduce cannula into. [L, dim. of *canna* CANE¹]

că'nn|ȳ *a.* Shrewd, worldly-wise, (esp. of Scots) thrifty; circumspect (**ca'~y,** [Sc., = proceed warily] go-slow, trade-union policy of limiting output); sly, pawky; hence ~**ĭ**LY² *adv.*, ~**ĭ**NESS *n.* [f. CAN² know + -Y²]

canoe' (-ōō') *n.*, & *v.i.* (**~ing**). (Go in, paddle) keelless boat propelled by paddle(s) (PADDLE² one's *own canoe*); hence ~IST (3) *n.* [f. Sp. and Haitian *canoa*]

că'non *n.* **1.** Church decree; ~ **law,** eccl. law esp. from papal and council pronouncements. **2.** General law, rule, or principle; criterion; list of sacred books etc. accepted as genuine; list of recognized genuine works of a particular author (*the Shakespeare canon*). **3.** Part of Mass containing words of consecration; (Mus.) piece with different parts taking up same subject successively in strict imitation. **4.** Member of cathedral chapter; MINOR *canon*; *canon* REGULAR; hence ~ESS¹, ~RY (2), *ns.* [OE f. L f. Gk *kanōn*, in ME also f. AF & OF *canun, -on*; in sense 4 ME, f. OF *canonie* f. eccl. L *canonicus*; cf. CANONICAL]

cañon. See CANYON.

canŏ'nĭc *a.* = foll.; so ~ATE¹ *n.*, canonry. [OE, f. OF *canonique* or f. L f. Gk *kanonikos* (as CANON; see -IC)]

canŏ'nĭcal *a.* & *n.* **1.** *a.* Appointed by canon law (~ **hours,** times for prayer, or for celebration of marriage); included in canon of Scripture; authoritative, standard, accepted; (Mus.) in canon form; of a cathedral chapter or a member of it; hence ~LY² *adv.* **2.** *n.* (in *pl.*) Canonical dress of clergy. [f. med. L *canonicalis*; see prec., -AL]

cănonĭ'cĭtȳ *n.* Status of canonical book. [f. L *canonicus* canonical + -ITY]

că'nonĭst *n.* Expert in canon law. [ME, f. F *canoniste* or f. med. L *canonista* (as CANON; see -IST)]

că'nonīz|e, -īs|e (-īz), *v.t.* Admit formally to list of saints; regard as a saint; sanction by church authority; so ~A'TION *n.* [ME, f. med. L *canonizare* (as CANON; see -IZE)]

că'nonrȳ. See CANON 4.

canōō'dle *v.i.* & *t.* (sl.) Cuddle amorously, fondle. [19th c.; U.S., of unkn. orig.]

Canō'pĭc *a.* ~ **jar, vase,** urn used for holding the entrails of an embalmed body in ancient Egyptian burial. [f. L *Canopicus*, f. *Canopus* in ancient Egypt; see -IC]

că'nopȳ *n.*, & *v.t.* **1.** *n.* Covering suspended or held over throne, bed, person, etc. (also fig. of any overhanging shelter, the sky, etc.); (Archit.) rooflike projection over niche etc.; expanding part of parachute; cover of cockpit in aircraft. **2.** *v.t.* Supply or be canopy to. [ME, f. med. L *canopeum* f. L f. Gk *kōnōpeion* mosquito-net (*kōnōps* gnat)]

canôr'ous *a.* Melodious, resonant. [f. L *canorus* (*canere* sing) + -OUS]

cănst. See CAN².

cănt¹ *n.* Bevel, oblique face, of crystal, bank, etc.; push, toss, movement, that partly or quite upsets; tilted or sloping position; ‖**~'rail,** timber etc. supporting railway-carriage roof. [ME, f.

MLG *kant, kante,* MDu. *cant,* point, side, edge, f. Rom. **canto* f. L *cant(h)us* iron tire]

cănt[2] *v.* **1.** *v.t.* Bevel off; tilt; turn over or upside down; push or pitch sideways. **2.** *v.i.* Take inclined position; lie aslant; (Naut.) swing round. **3. ~-dog, ~-hook,** iron hook at end of long handle, used for rolling logs. [f. prec.]

cănt[3] *n.,* & *v.i.* **1.** *n.* (usu. derog.) Language of class, profession, sect, etc., jargon. **2.** Ephemeral catchwords; words used for fashion without being meant, insincere use of words implying piety; hypocrisy. **3.** *v.i.* Use cant; **~'ing arms,** (Her.) arms containing allusion to name of bearer. [earlier of musical sound, of intonation, and of beggars' whining, perh. f. singing of religious mendicants; prob. f. L *cantare* frequent. of *canere* sing]

can't. See CAN[2].

Cant. *abbr.* Canticles (O.T.).

Că'ntăb. *abbr.* of Cambridge University. [f. L *Cantabrigiensis*]

cantabile (kăntah'bĭlĭ) *adv.* (Mus.) In smooth flowing style. [It., = singable]

Căntabrĭ'gĭan *n.* & *a.* (Member) of Cambridge (or *Harvard) University; (native or inhabitant) of Cambridge in England or *in Massachusetts. [f. L *Cantabrigia* Cambridge + -AN]

că'ntal *n.* Hard strong type of French cheese. [f. *C~*, department of Auvergne, France]

că'ntaloup, -oupe, (-ōōp) *n.* Small round ribbed melon with orange flesh. [F *cantaloup,* f. *Cantaluppi* near Rome, where first grown in Europe]

căntă'nkerous *a.* Bad-tempered, quarrelsome; hence **~**LY[2] *adv.,* **~**NESS *n.* [perh. f. Ir. *cant* outbidding + *rancorous*]

cănta'ta (-tah'-) *n.* (Mus.) Choral work, kind of short oratorio, or lyric drama set to music but not intended for acting. [It. *cantata* (*aria*) sung (air) f. *cantare* sing]

Cănta'tė (-ah'-) *n.* Canticle consisting of Ps. 98. [L, = sing ye, its first word]

cantatrice (kă'ntatrēs) *n.* Professional woman singer. [It. & F]

căntee'n *n.* Provision and liquor shop in camp or barracks (**dry, wet, ~**, without, chiefly for, liquor); ||bar, lunch-counter, etc. at outdoor entertainment or in large public or private institution; soldier's or camper's water-flask; case or chest of plate or cutlery for domestic use. [f. F *cantine* f. It. *cantina* cellar]

cante hondo (kahntĭ hŏ'ndō) *n.* Type of usu. mournful Spanish song. [Sp., = deep song]

că'nter *n.* & *v.* **1.** *n.* Easy gallop; *win* **in a ~**, easily. **2.** *v.i.* (Of horse or rider) go at this pace. **3.** *v.t.* Make (horse) go thus. [short for *Canterbury pace, gallop, trot,* etc., f. supposed easy pace of medieval pilgrims to Canterbury in Kent]

Că'nterburў *n.* **1. ~ bell,** kind of campanula [f. bells of Canterbury pilgrims' horses]. **2.** (*c~*). Stand with partitions for music etc. [~ in Kent]

căntha'rĭdēs (-z) *n. pl.* (Med.) Dried SPANISH fly. [pl. of L f. Gk *kantharis* Spanish fly]

că'nth|us *n.* (*pl.* **~i** *pr.* -ī). Outer or inner corner of eye, where lids meet. [L, f. Gk *kanthos*]

că'ntĭcle *n.* Hymn; one of the Anglican Prayer-Book hymns; (**C~ of**) **C~s,** SONG of Solomon. [ME f. OF, or f. L *canticulum* dim. of *canticum* (*cantus* song f. *canere* sing)]

căntĭlē'na *n.* (Mus.) Simple or sustained melody. [It.]

că'ntĭlēver *n.* Long bracket projecting from wall to support balcony etc.; beam or girder fixed at only one end; **~ bridge** (with piers each of which has two cantilevers, and long girders connecting cantilevers of adjacent piers). [17th c.; orig. unkn.]

că'ntĭll|āte *v.t.* & *i.* Chant, recite with musical tones; hence **~**A'TION *n.* [f. L *cantillare* sing low (as CHANT) + -ATE[3]]

căntĭ'na (-ē'-) *n.* Bar-room or wine-shop. [Sp. & It.]

că'ntle *n.* (arch.) Piece or slice cut off; hind-bow of saddle. [ME, f. AF *cantel,* OF *chantel* f. med. L *cantellus* dim. of L *cantus* CANT[1]]

că'ntō *n.* (*pl.* **~s**). Division of long poem. [It., = song, f. L *cantus*]

că'nton[1] (*or* kăntŏ'n) *n.* Subdivision of country; State of Swiss confederation; (Her.) square division, less than a QUARTER[1], in upper (usu. dexter) corner of shield; hence **~**AL *a.* [OF, = corner (as CANT[1]; see -OON)]

canto'n[2] *v.t.* **1.** (kăntŏ'n). Divide into cantons. **2.** (kantōō'n). Quarter (soldiers). [partly f. F *cantonner,* partly f. prec.]

Căntonē'se (-z) *a.* & *n.* (*pl.* same). (Native or inhabitant or Chinese dialect) of Canton. [f. *Canton* in China + -ESE]

cănto'nment (-ōō'n-) *n.* Lodging assigned to troops; (Ind.) permanent military station. [f. F *cantonnement* (as CANTON[2]; see -MENT)]

că'ntor *n.* Leader of singing in church, precentor; precentor in synagogue. [L, = singer (*canere cant-* sing; see -OR)]

căntôr'ial *a.* Of the precentor; of N. side of choir (cf. DECANAL). [f. prec. + -IAL]

căntôr'ĭs *a.* (Mus.) To be sung by cantorial side in antiphonal singing (cf. DECANI). [L, gen. of CANTOR precentor]

că'ntrĭp *n.* (Sc.) Witch's trick; piece of mischief, playful act. [18th c.; orig. unkn.]

***Canŭ'ck** *n.* & *a.* (derog.) (French) Canadian (person or horse or pony). [app. f. *Canada*]

că'nvas *n.,* & *v.t.* (||**-ss-**). **1.** *n.* (Piece of) strong unbleached cloth of hemp, flax, or other coarse yarn, for sails, tents, painting on; (esp. oil-) painting; open kind of canvas used as basis for tapestry and embroidery; racing-boat's covered end (*win* **by a ~**, by narrow margin in racing); **under ~**, (1) in tent(s), (2) with sails spread; **~-back,** N. Amer. wild duck *Aythya valisineria* (f. colour of back feathers). **2.** *v.t.* Cover with canvas. [ME & ONF *canevas,* OF *chanevaz* f. Rom. **cannapaceum* f. **cannapum* f. L CANNABIS]

că'nvass *v.* & *n.* **1.** *v.t.* & *i.* Discuss thoroughly; solicit votes, solicit votes from (electors in constituency), ascertain sentiments of, ask custom of; ||propose (plan etc.); *check validity of votes; hence **~**ER[1] *n.* **2.** *n.* Canvassing for or of votes. [f. prec., orig. = toss in a sheet, shake up, agitate, etc.]

că'nyon, cañon, (kă'nyon) *n.* Deep gorge, freq. with stream. [f. Sp. *cañón* tube (*caña* f. L *canna* CANE[1])]

cănzonĕ'tta, cănzonĕ't, *n.* Short light song; kind of madrigal. [It., dim. of *canzone* song f. L *cantio -onis* (*canere* sing)]

caou'tchouc (kow'chŏŏk) *n.* & *a.* (Of) unvulcanized rubber. [F, f. Carib *cahuchu*]

căp[1] *n.* **1.** Nurse's or woman servant's indoor head-dress; man's or boy's brimless soft outdoor head-dress; **~ fits,** (fig.) general remark is true of person in question; **~ in hand,** (fig.) humbly; **set** one's **~ at,** try to attract as suitor. **2.** Special head-dress (college mortar-board, as part of Highland costume, or ||awarded as sign of membership of sports team; **~ and bells** (worn by professional jester); **~ of liberty** (conical, given to Roman slave on emancipation, now (esp. French) Republican symbol); *cap of* MAINTENANCE); money collected in cap at fox-hunt etc. from those who are not subscribing members. **3.** Covering like cap in shape, position, etc., natural (mushroom top, kneecap, etc.), or designed for various purposes (windmill top, toe-cap; device to seal bottle, protect nib of fountain pen or lens of camera, etc.; = DUTCH[1] *cap*; = PERCUSSION *cap*); **~'stone,** top stone, coping. **4.** Hence ~'FUL 2 *n.*, (esp.) passing gust of wind. [f. OE *cæppe* f. LL *cappa*, perh. f. L *caput* head]

căp[2] *v.t.* (-pp-). **1.** Put cap on; (Sc. & N.Z.) confer university degree on; award cap to (player); protect (end of beam etc.) with metal etc., whence **~'p**ING[1] (3) *n.* **2.** Lie on top of, form cap of; follow with another (**~ anecdote, quotation,** etc., produce another esp. better or apposite one; **~ verses,** reply with verse beginning with the previous one's last letter). [f. prec.]

cap. *abbr.* capital (letter); chapter [f. L *capitulum* or *caput*].

cāpabĭ'lĭtȳ *n.* Power *of* (action etc., act*ing* etc.), *for* (be*ing* treated in some way), *to* (do something); undeveloped or unused faculty. [f. foll. + -ITY]

cā'pable *a.* Susceptible, admitting, (*of*); **~ of,** having the ability or fitness for, wicked enough for; gifted, able, competent; hence **cā'pab**LY[2] *adv.* [F, f. LL *capabilis* f. L *capere* hold; see -ABLE]

capā'cious (-sh*us*) *a.* Roomy, able to hold much; hence ~LY[2] *adv.*, ~NESS *n.* [f. L *capax -acis* (*capere* hold) + -IOUS]

capă'cĭtance *n.* (Electr.) **1.** Ratio of the change in the electric charge of a body to the corresponding change in its potential. **2.** Ability to store a charge of electricity, capacity. [f. CAPACITY + -ANCE]

capă'cĭtāte *v.t.* Render capable (*for*, *to* do); make legally competent. [f. CAPACITY + -ATE[3]]

capă'cĭtor *n.* (Electr.) Device having capacitance usu. consisting of conductors separated by insulator. [f. foll. + -OR]

capă'cĭtȳ *n.* **1.** Power of containing, receiving, experiencing, or producing, (*capacity for heat, moisture,* etc.); maximum amount that can be contained, produced, etc.; **to ~,** fully (*working to capacity*); (*attrib.*) fully occupying (*capacity audience* etc.). **2.** Cubic content (**measure of ~,** measure used for vessels and liquids, grain, etc.); mental power, faculty, talent; position, relative character, (*in a civil capacity*; *in my capacity as critic*); legal competency; (Electr.) capacitance, whence **capă'cĭt**IVE *a.* [ME, f. F *capacité* f. L *capacitas -tatis* (as CAPACIOUS; see -ITY)]

căp-à-pie' (-apē') *adv.* (arch.) From head to foot, (armed, ready, etc.). [f. OF *cap a pie*]

capă'rĭson *n.*, & *v.t.* **1.** *n.* (usu. in *pl.*) Horse's trappings; equipment, outfit. **2.** *v.t.* Put caparison on. [f. obs. F *caparasson* f. Sp. *caparazón* saddle-cloth (*capa* CAPE[1])]

cāpe[1] *n.* Short sleeveless cloak, either as separate garment or as fixed or detachable part of longer cloak or coat. [F, f. Prov. *capa* f. LL *cappa* CAP[1]]

cāpe[2] *n.* Headland, promontory. [ME, f. OF f. Prov. *cap* f. Rom. **capo* f. L *caput* head]

Cāpe[3] *n.* *The* CAPE[2] of Good Hope; *the* province containing it; **~ cart,** (S. Afr.) two-wheeled horse-drawn cart; **~ Coloured,** (member) of COLOURED population of Cape Province; **~ doctor,** (S. Afr.) strong S.E. wind; **~ Dutch,** (arch.) Afrikaans; **~ gooseberry,** kind of ground-cherry; **c~'skin,** soft leather from S. Afr. sheepskin; **~ smoke,** (Hist.) S. Afr. brandy. [f. prec.]

căp(e)lĭn *n.* Small smeltlike fish used as cod-bait. [f. F f. Prov. *capelan*; see CHAPLAIN]

cā'per[1] *n.* Bramble-like S. Eur. shrub (*Capparis spinosa*); (in *pl.*) its flower-buds pickled (esp. for *caper sauce*). [ME, f. L f. Gk *kapparis*; treated as pl., cf. CHERRY, PEA]

cā'per[2] *n.*, & *v.i.* **1.** *n.* Frisky movement, leap; fantastic proceeding; (sl.) any activity or occupation; **cut a ~** or **~s,** = sense 2. **2.** *v.i.* Move friskily, leap; hence ~ER[1] *n.* [abbr. of CAPRIOLE]

căpercai'llie, -lzie (-lyĭ *or* -lzĭ), *n.* Wood-grouse (*Tetrao urogallus*), largest European gallinaceous bird. [f. Gael. *capull coille* horse of the wood]

cā'pĭās *n.* (Law). Writ commanding arrest of person named. [L, = you are to seize, 2 sing. pres. subj. of *capere* take]

căpĭllă'rĭtȳ *n.* (Power of exerting) capillary attraction or repulsion. [f. F *capillarité*; see foll., -TY[1]]

capĭ'llarȳ *a.* & *n.* Of hair; hairlike, thin as hair; (tube) of minute or hairlike diameter (e.g. one of ramified blood-vessels intervening between arteries and veins); **~ attraction, repulsion,** (by which liquid is drawn up, down, in capillary tubes). [f. L *capillaris* (*capillus* hair; see -ARY[2])]

că'pĭtal[1] *n.* Head or cornice of pillar or column. [ME, f. OF *capitel* f. LL *capitellum* dim. of *caput* head]

că'pĭtal[2] *a.* & *n.* **1.** *a.* Involving loss of life (*capital punishment*); punishable by death (*capital offence*); vitally injurious, fatal, (*capital error*). **2.** Standing at the head; chief (**~ town** or **city,** head town of country, county, etc.); important, leading, first-class; (colloq.) excellent, first-rate, (also as *int.* of approval); original, principal. **3.** Hence ~LY[2] *adv.* **4.** (Of letter) having form and size used to begin sentence, name, etc. (*capital A* etc.); **with a ~ A** etc., emphatically such (*life with a capital L*). **5.** *n.* Capital letter; capital town or city. **6.** Stock with which company or person enters into business; accumulated wealth esp. as used in further production; holders of this as a class; **make ~ out of,** (fig.) turn to account. **7. ~ gain,** profit from sale of investments or property; **~ goods,** goods (to be) used in producing commodities, opp. *consumer goods*; *capital* LEVY; **~ ship,** battleship, or warship of similar class; **~ sum,** lump sum of money, esp. payable to insured person; **~ territory** (containing capital city of a country). [ME f. OF, f. L *capitalis* (*caput -itis* head; see -AL)]

că'pĭtal|ĭsm *n.* Possession of capital or wealth; system in which private capital or wealth is used in production and distribution of goods; (Polit.) dominance of private owners of capital and production for profit; hence or cogn. ~IST (2) *n.* (freq. derog.), **căpĭtalĭ'st**IC *a.* [f. prec. + -ISM]

că'pĭtalīz|e, -īs|e (-īz), *v.* **1.** *v.t.* Convert into or provide with capital; compute or realize present value of (income); reckon (value of asset) by setting future benefits against cost of maintenance; write (letter) as capital, begin (word) with capital letter. **2.** *v.t.* & *i.* **~e (on),** (fig.) turn to account, make use of to one's advantage. **3.** Hence ~A'TION *n.* [f. F *capitaliser* (as CAPITAL[2]; see -IZE)]

căpĭtā'tion *n.* (Levying of) tax or fee of so much a head; **~ grant** (of so much for every person fulfilling conditions). [F, or f. LL *capitatio* poll-tax (*caput -itis* head; see -ATION)]

Că'pĭtol *n.* Temple of Jupiter in ancient Rome; *Congress or State legislature building. [ME f. OF *capitolie*, f. L *capitolium* (*caput* head)]

capĭ'tūlar *a.* Of a cathedral chapter; (Anat.) of a terminal protuberance of bone. [f. LL *capitularis* f. L *capitulum* CHAPTER; see -AR[1]]

capĭ'tūlarȳ *n.* Collection of ordinances, esp. of Frankish kings. [f. LL *capitularius* f. L (as prec.); see -ARY[1]]

capĭ'tūl|āte *v.i.* Surrender esp. on stated conditions. [f. med. L *capitulare* draw up under headings (CAPITULUM) + -ATE[3]]

capĭtūlā'tion *n.* Capitulating; statement of

main divisions of subject; agreement, conditions. [f. LL *capitulatio* (as prec.; see -ATION)]

capĭ'tūl|um *n.* (*pl.* ~**a**). (Bot.) Rounded or flattened flower-head of composite plant etc. [L, dim. of *caput* head]

că'plĭn. See CAPELIN.

că'pō (tă'stō) *n.* (*pl.* ~**s**). Device on stringed instrument to adjust pitch of all strings simultaneously. [f. It. *capo tasto* head stop]

cā'pon *n.* Domestic cock castrated and fattened for eating; hence ~IZE (3) *v.t.* [OE f. AF *capun,* OF *capon,* f. Rom. **cappone* f. L *capo -onis*]

căponier' *n.* Covered passage across ditch of fort. [f. Sp. *caponera,* lit. pen for capons; see prec.]

capŏ't *n.,* & *v.t.* (**-tt-**). **1.** *n.* (In piquet) winning of all tricks by one player. **2.** *v.t.* Score capot against (opponent). [F]

capō'te *n.* Soldier's, traveller's, etc., long cloak with hood. [F, dim. of *cape* CAPE¹]

cappuccino (kahpŏŏchē'nō) *n.* (*pl.* ~**s**). Coffee with milk, esp. made with espresso coffee. [It., = CAPUCHIN]

Capri' (-ē') *n.* ~ **pants,** ~**s,** women's close-fitting tapered trousers. [~, island in Bay of Naples]

că'prĭc *a.* (Chem.) ~ **acid,** acid obtained from butter, coconut oil, etc. [f. L *caper -pri* goat + -IC (from its goatlike smell)]

caprĭ'ccĭō (-ĭ'chĭō) *n.* (*pl.* ~**s**). (Mus.) Lively (usu. short) musical composition. [It.; see CAPRICE]

capriccioso (kaprĭchĭō'sō) *adv.* (Mus.) In free and impulsive style. [It. (prec.; see -OUS)]

caprī'ce (-ē's) *n.* Unaccountable change of mind or conduct; inclination to these; work of lively fancy in art etc., esp. capriccio. [F, f. It. CAPRICCIO sudden start, orig. 'horror']

caprĭ'cious (-sh*u*s) *a.* Guided by whim, inconstant; irregular, unpredictable; hence ~LY² *adv.,* ~NESS *n.* [f. F *capricieux* f. It. CAPRICCIOSO]

Că'prĭcôrn *n.* Sign of the ZODIAC, the Goat; TROPIC *of Capricorn.* [ME, f. OF *capricorne* f. L *capricornus* (*caper -pri* goat, *cornu* horn)]

că'prīne *a.* Of or like a goat. [ME, f. L *caprinus* (*caper -pri* goat; see -INE¹)]

că'prĭōle *n.,* & *v.i.* (Give a) leap, caper; trained horse's high leap and kick without advancing. [F, f. It. *capriola, capriolare* leap (*capriolo* roebuck f. L *capreolus* dim. of *caper* goat)]

caprō'ic *a.* (Chem.) ~ **acid,** acid found with capric and butyric acids in butter etc. [f. as CAPRIC, w. *-oic* for differentiation]

căps. *abbr.* capital letters.

Că'psian *a.* & *n.* (Of) a palaeolithic culture of N. Africa and S. Europe. [f. L *Capsa* = Gafsa in Tunisia + -IAN]

că'psĭcum *n.* Tropical plant of genus *Capsicum,* with pungent capsules and seeds; its fruit. [mod. L, perh. f. L *capsa* CASE²]

că'psĭd¹ *n.* Bug of family Capsidae, esp. one carrying plant disease. [f. mod. L *Capsus* a genus of them + -ID³]

că'psĭd² *n.* Shell or coat of some viruses. [f. F *capside* f. L *capsa* box; see -ID²]

căpsī'z|e *v.* **1.** *v.t.* Upset, overturn, (ship etc.). **2.** *v.i.* Be capsized. **3.** Hence ~AL 2 *n.* [perh. ult. f. Sp. *capuzar* sink by the head (*cabo* head and *chapuzar* dive)]

că'pstan *n.* Revolving barrel with vertical axis, worked by men walking round and pushing horizontal levers, or by steam etc., for winding cable, halyard, etc.; revolving spindle on tape-recorder etc.; ~ **lathe** (with revolving tool-holder). [f. Prov. *cabestan,* earlier *cabestran* (*cabestre* halter f. L *capistrum* f. *capere* seize)]

că'psūl|e *n.* & *a.* **1.** *n.* (Physiol.) membranous envelope; (Bot.) dry seed-case opening when ripe by parting of valves; (Med.) small case of gelatine enclosing dose; metal bottle-top; detachable nose-cone of rocket etc. or cabin of spacecraft containing instruments or crew; hence ~AR¹ *a.* **2.** *a.* Highly condensed (description etc.). [F, f. L *capsula* (*capsa* CASE²; see -ULE)]

că'psūlize, -ise (-īz), *v.t.* Put (information etc.) in compact form. [f. prec. + -IZE]

Capt. *abbr.* Captain.

că'ptain¹ (-tĭn) *n.* **1.** Chief, leader (~ **of industry,** industrial magnate); great soldier, strategist, experienced commander (||~**-general,** honorary officer esp. of artillery); (Army) officer of rank below major and above lieutenant; (Navy) officer commanding warship, officer of rank below commodore and above commander (||**C**~ **of the Fleet,** staff officer in charge of maintenance); *policeman ranking below chief officer; master of merchant ship; pilot of civil aircraft; ~**'s biscuit,** hard fancy biscuit. **2.** Foreman; ||head boy or girl at school; leader of side in games; *supervisor of waiters or bellboys. **3.** Hence ~CY, ~SHIP, *ns.* [ME and OF *capitain* f. LL *capitaneus* chief (L *caput capitis* head)]

că'ptain² (-tĭn) *v.t.* Be captain of, lead. [f. prec.]

că'ption *n.,* & *v.t.* **1.** *n.* (Law) certificate attached to or written on document; heading of chapter, article, etc.; wording on cinema or television screen, appended to illustration or cartoon, etc. **2.** *v.t.* Provide with caption. [ME, f. L *captio* (*capere capt-* take; see -ION)]

că'ptious (-sh*u*s) *a.* Fond of taking exception or raising objections; hence ~LY² *adv.,* ~NESS *n.* [ME, f. OF *captieux* or f. L *captiosus* (as prec.; see -IOUS)]

că'ptĭv|āte *v.t.* Fascinate, charm; so ~A'TION *n.* [f. LL *captivare* take captive (as foll.) + -ATE³]

că'ptĭve *a.* & *n.* (Person or animal) taken prisoner, kept in confinement, under restraint, unable to escape; of or like prisoner (*captive state*); ~ **audience** (unable to avoid being addressed etc.); ~ **balloon** (held by rope from ground); so **căptĭ'**VITY *n.* (**the C**~, of Jews in Babylon, 6th c. B.C.). [ME, f. L *captivus* (*capere capt-* take; see -IVE)]

că'ptor *n.* One who takes a captive or prize. [L (as prec.; see -OR)]

că'pture *n.,* & *v.t.* **1.** *n.* Seizing, taking possession of; thing or person captured. **2.** *v.t.* Take prisoner, seize as prize; put in permanently accessible form (*could not capture the likeness*); (Chess etc.) remove (man) from board; (Phys.) absorb (atomic particle). [F, f. L *captura* (as prec.; see -URE)]

Că'pūchĭn *n.* & *a.* Franciscan (friar) of new rule of 1528; (Hist.) woman's cloak and hood; **c**~ **monkey, pigeon,** (with head hair, head and neck feathers, like cowl). [F, f. It. *cappuccino* (*cappuccio* cowl f. *cappa* CAPE¹)]

caput mortuum (kăp*u*t môr'tūum) *n.* Worthless residue. [L, = dead head; alch. term for residuum after distillation or sublimation]

căpÿbar'a *n.* Large S. Amer. rodent (*Hydrochoerus capybara*) allied to guinea-pig. [Tupi]

car *n.* **1.** Wheeled vehicle (of specified type; DINING-*car,* JAUNT*ing-car*); = MOTOR *car;* *railway carriage or van; *lift-cage; passenger compartment of airship or balloon or cableway; (poet.) wheeled vehicle, chariot. **2.** ~ **coat,** short coat designed esp. for car-drivers; *~**'fare,** passenger's fare to travel by bus etc.; *~**'hop,** (colloq.) waiter at drive-in restaurant etc.; ~**'load,** quantity that can be carried in a car, *minimum quantity of goods for which lower rate is charged for transport; ~**'man,** driver of van, carrier; ~**-park,** space for parking cars; ~**'port,** roofed open-sided shelter for car;

~'sick, affected with nausea caused by motion of car. [ME f. AF & ONF *carre*, f. Rom. **carra*, L *carrum, carrus*, f. OCelt. **karrom*, **karros*]
C.A.R. *abbr.* Central African Republic.
cărabĭneer', -ier', *n.* (Hist.) soldier with carbine; ||**The C~s,** Royal Scots Dragoon Guards. [f. F *carabinier* (*carabine* CARBINE; see -EER, -IER)]
carabini|ere (kărabĭnyār'ĭ) *n.* (*pl.* **~eri** *pr.* -ār'ē). Italian soldier in corps serving as policemen. [It.]
că'racăl *n.* Lynx of N. Africa and S.W. Asia (*Felis caracal*). [F or Sp., f. Turk. *karakulak* (*kara* black, *kulak* ear)]
că'racōle *n.*, & *v.i.* (Of horse or rider) (execute) half-turn(s) to right or left. [f. F *caracole(r)*]
că'racul, kă'rakul, (-ōōl) *n.* Asian sheep whose lambs have dark curled fleece; fur made from or resembling this. [Russ.]
carā'fe (*or* -ah'f) *n.* Glass bottle for water or wine at table, in bedroom, etc. [F, f. It. *caraffa* prob. f. Sp. *garrafa* f. Arab. *ġarrāfa* drinking vessel]
că'ramĕl *n.* Burnt sugar or syrup used for colouring spirits etc.; toffee made with sugar melted and further heated; light-brown colour of caramel; hence ~IZE (3) *v.t.* & *i.* [F, f. Sp. *caramelo*]
că'rapāce *n.* Upper shell of tortoise or crustacean. [F, f. Sp. *carapacho*]
că'rat *n.* **1.** Measure of weight for precious stones, 200 milligrams. **2.** Measure of purity of gold, pure gold being 24 carats. [F, f. It. *carato* f. Arab. *ķīrāţ* weight of four grains, f. Gk *keration* fruit of carob (dim. of *keras* horn)]
că'ravăn (*or* -vă'n) *n.*, & *v.i.* (||**-nn-**). **1.** *n.* Company of merchants, pilgrims, etc., travelling together, esp. across desert in Asia or N. Africa; covered cart or carriage; ||house on wheels, able to be towed by horse or car; ||**~ park** or **site,** place where caravans are parked as dwellings. **2.** *v.i.* Travel or live in caravan. [f. F *caravane* f. Pers. *kārwān*]
căravă'nserai (-rī) *n.* Eastern inn with inner court where caravans rest. [f. Pers. *kārwānsarāy* (as prec., SERAI)]
că'ravel, car'vel, *n.* (Hist.) Small light fast ship, chiefly Spanish and Portuguese of 15th–17th c. [f. F *car(a)velle* f. Port. *caravela*, f. Gk *karabos* horned beetle, crayfish, light ship]
că'raway (-*a*-wā) *n.* Umbelliferous plant, *Carum carvi*; **~ seed,** its fruit, used in cakes and as source of oil. [prob. f. OSp. *alcarahueya* f. Arab. *alkarāwiyā*, perh. f. Gk *karon, kareon* cumin]
car'bamāte *n.* Salt or ester of an amide of carbonic acid, $CONH_2OH$. [f. CARBONIC + AMIDE + -ATE[1] (3)]
car'bīde *n.* Binary compound of carbon; esp. (**calcium**) **~** (used in making acetylene gas). [f. CARBON + -IDE]
car'bīne *n.* Short firearm for cavalry use. [earlier & F *carabine*, weapon of the *carabin* mounted musketeer]
car'bo- *comb. form.* Carbon, as: CARBOHYDRATE, CARBOLIC, CARBOXYL. [f. CARBON + -O-]
carbohȳ'drāte *n.* (Chem.) Energy-producing organic compound of carbon with oxygen and hydrogen (e.g. starch, sugar, glucose). [f. CARBO- + HYDRATE[1]]
car'bŏ'lĭc *a.* **~ acid,** phenol; **~ soap** (containing this). [f. CARBO- + -OL + -IC]
car'bon *n.* **1.** Non-metallic chemical element occurring as diamond, graphite, and charcoal, in carbon dioxide and carbonates, and in all organic compounds; RADIO-*carbon*. **2.** Carbon copy; carbon paper; (Electr.) rod of carbon in arc lamp. **3. ~ copy,** copy made with carbon paper, (fig.) exact copy; **~ dating,** determination of age from decay of radio-carbon in timber etc.; **~ dioxide,** gas formed by combustion of carbon and by breathing; **~ monoxide,** very poisonous, colourless, almost odourless gas formed by incomplete combustion of carbon, occurring e.g. in exhaust of motor engines; **~ paper,** thin paper coated with carbon etc. for making copy of words written or typed; **~ steel** (with properties depending mainly on amount of carbon present); **~ tetrachloride,** colourless liquid used as solvent in dry cleaning etc. [f. F *carbone* f. L *carbo -onis* charcoal]
carbonā'ceous (-sh*u*s) *a.* Of or like coal or charcoal; consisting of or containing carbon. [f. prec. + -ACEOUS]
carbonā'de *n.* Rich beef stew made with onions and beer. [F]
carbonā'dō *n.* (*pl.* **~s**). Dark opaque kind of diamond used as abrasive etc. [Port.]
car'bonāte[1] *n.* Salt of carbonic acid. [f. F *carbonat* f. mod. L *carbonatum* (as CARBON, -ATE[1] (3))]
car'bonāte[2] *v.t.* Impregnate with carbon dioxide, aerate; convert into carbonate. [f. prec.]
carbŏ'nĭc *a.* (Chem.) Of carbon; **~ acid,** weak acid formed from carbon dioxide and water; **~ acid gas,** (arch.) carbon dioxide. [f. CARBON + -IC]
carbonĭ'ferous *a.* & *n.* Producing coal; (*C~*, Geol.) (of the) palaeozoic period or system, above Devonian and below Permian, often containing coal. [f. CARBON + -I- + -FEROUS]
car'bonīz|e, -īs|e (-īz), *v.t.* Convert into carbon; reduce to charcoal or coke; coat (paper) with carbon; hence **~A'TION** *n.* [f. CARBON + -IZE]
carborŭ'ndum *n.* Silicon carbide used as abrasive or refractory. [***P,** f. CARBON + CORUNDUM]
carbŏ'xȳl *n.* (Chem.) Univalent group (—COOH) present in many organic acids; hence **carbŏxȳ'lIC** *a.* [f. CARBO- + OXYGEN + -YL]
car'boy *n.* Large globular glass bottle to contain liquids safely, usu. protected by frame. [f. Pers. *ķarāba* large glass flagon]
car'bŭncle *n.* **1.** Red precious stone, esp. garnet cut in boss shape. **2.** Severe abscess, esp. on neck; face pimple; hence **carbŭ'ncūlAR**[1] *a.* [ME f. OF *charbucle* etc., f. L *carbunculus* small coal (*carbo* coal; see -UNCLE)]
carbūrā'tion *n.* Process of charging air with spray of liquid hydrocarbon fuel. [f. foll. + -ATION]
carbūrĕ't *v.t.* (||**-tt-**). Combine (any element) chemically with carbon. [f. CARBON + -URET]
carbūrĕ'ttor, -tter, *-ē'tor, *n.* Apparatus for carburation of air in petrol engines. [f. prec. + -OR, -ER[1]]
car'cajou (-jōō *or* -zhōō) *n.* (Zool.) American glutton, wolverine. [F, app. of Amer. Ind. orig.]
car'canėt *n.* (arch.) Jewelled necklace or collar. [f. obs. & F *carcan*, f. Gmc **querkbann* chin-strap + -ET[1]]
car'cass, ||**car'case,** *n.* Dead body of animal or bird; human body, (joc. or derog.) alive or (derog.) dead; animal's trunk without head or offal (**~ meat,** raw meat as dist. from corned or tinned meat); worthless remains (*of*); skeleton, framework, (of building, ship, etc.); foundation of motor-vehicle tyre; (Hist.) spherical projectile filled with combustible material to ignite buildings etc. [ME f. AF *carcois* (OF *charcois*), & f. F *carcasse*; ult. orig. unkn.]
carcĭ'no|gėn *n.* (Path.) Cancer-producing substance; so **~GE'NIC** (1) *a.* [f. foll. + -GEN]
carcĭnō'ma *n.* (*pl.* **~ta** *or* **~s**). (Path.) Cancer, esp. malignant epithelial tumour. [L, f. Gk *karkinōma* (*karkinos* crab; see -OMA)]

cārd[1] *n.*, & *v.t.* (Cleanse, comb, or scratch, with) toothed instrument or wire-brush etc. for raising nap on cloth or for disentangling fibres of wool, hemp, etc., before spinning; **~'ing-wool** (short--stapled). [ME, f. OF *carde* f. Prov. *carda* (*cardar* tease, comb f. pop. L **caritare* f. L *carere* card)]

cārd[2] *n.* **1.** = PLAYING-*card* (COURT[1]-*card*; HOUSE[1] *of cards*; **on the ~s,** likely, possible; **play** one's **~s well,** act cleverly; **put** (**all**) one's **~s on the table,** disclose all one's resources, plans, etc.; SHOW[1] one's *cards*; **~ up** one's **sleeve,** plan in reserve); **~s,** card-game, card-playing; (*sure, safe, doubtful,* etc.) plan, expedient; (*knowing, odd,* etc.) person; (colloq.) eccentric person. **2.** Flat piece of thick paper or pasteboard for various purposes; POST[2]*card*; ticket of admission or membership; invitation; (**visiting-**)**~** (with name etc., sent or left in lieu of formal visit); BIRTH*day*, WEDDING-, CHRISTMAS, etc., **~** (sent as notification or greeting to friends); programme of events at race--meeting etc., or for entering cricket scores; list of holes on golf course for entering player's scores; printed or written notice, rules, etc., for display; (in *pl.*, colloq.) employee's documents held by employer (**ask for, get,** one's **~s,** ask, be told, to leave one's employment). **3. ~'board,** pasteboard for cutting cards from or making boxes etc., (fig.) insubstantial thing; **~-carrying,** having valid membership (esp. of political party); **~-game,** game using playing-cards; **~ index** (in which each item is entered on separate card); **~-i'ndex** *v.t.*, make card index of; **~-playing,** use of playing-cards in game; **~-room** (in which games are played with cards); **~-sharp, ~-sharper,** swindler at card-games; **~-table,** (esp. folding) table for card-playing; **~ vote,** = BLOCK[1] *vote*, esp. in trade-union meetings. [ME, f. OE *carte* f. L *charta* f. Gk *khartēs* papyrus-leaf]

Card. *abbr.* Cardinal.

cār'damom, -mum, *n.* Spice from the seed--capsules of E. Ind. plants, esp. *Elettaria cardamomum.* [f. L *cardamomum* or F *cardamome* f. Gk *kardamōmon* (*kardamon* cress, *amōmon* a spice plant)]

cār'dan *a.* (Engin.) **~ joint,** universal joint; **~ shaft** (with universal joint at one or both ends). [f. G. *Cardano*, It. mathematician d. 1576]

cār'dĭăc *a.* & *n.* **1.** *a.* Of the heart (*cardiac* ARREST[2]); of upper orifice of stomach. **2.** *n.* Person with heart disease. [f. F *cardiaque* or f. L *cardiacus* f. Gk *kardiakos* (*kardia* heart; see -AC)]

cār'dĭgan *n.* Knitted woollen etc. jacket with or without sleeves. [named after 7th Earl of *C~* d. 1868]

cār'dĭnal *a.* & *n.* **1.** *a.* On which something hinges, fundamental, important, (*cardinal* HUMOUR[1]*s*; **~ numbers,** one, two, three, etc., as opp. to ordinal numbers; **~ points** (of compass), N., S., E., W.; *cardinal* VIRTUE*s*); of deep scarlet (like cardinal's cassock); (Zool.) of hinge of bivalve; **~-flower,** scarlet lobelia; hence **~**LY[2] *adv.* **2.** *n.* One of leading officials of R.C. Church, electing Pope; *cardinal* VICAR; hence **~**ATE[1], **~**SHIP, *ns.* **3.** Small scarlet Amer. song--bird of genus *Richmondena.* **4.** (Hist.) Woman's cloak, orig. of scarlet cloth with hood. [a. ME f. OF, f. L *cardinalis* (*cardo -inis* hinge; see -AL); n. OE f. OF, f. med. L *cardinalis*]

cār'dĭo- *comb. form.* Heart, as: **~**GRAM, record of heart movements, made by **~**GRAPH; so **~**GRAPHER, **~**GRAPHY, (-ŏ'g-); **~**LOGY (-ŏ'l-), study of the heart; **~-va'scular,** involving heart and blood-vessels. [f. Gk *kardia* heart + -O-]

cārdōō'n *n.* Thistle-like vegetable allied to globe artichoke. [f. F *cardon* (*carde* edible part of artichoke f. Prov. *cardo* f. Rom. **carda* f. L *cardu(u)s* thistle); see -OON]

Cards. *abbr.* Cardiganshire (former county in Wales).

cāre[1] *n.* **1.** Trouble, anxiety (*care killed the* CAT[1]); occasion for these; serious attention, heed, caution, pains, (**take, have a, ~,** be cautious, not neglect or fail); charge, protection, (*A* **~ of B,** at B's address; **take ~ of,** ensure safety of, deal with, dispose of); thing to be done or seen to; = CHILD *care.* **2. ~'free,** free from anxiety or responsibility; **~-laden, -worn,** (with anxieties); **~'taker,** person hired to take charge, esp. of house in owner's absence, ||person looking after public building, (*attrib.*) exercising temporary control (*caretaker government*). [OE *caru*, = OS *kara*, OHG *chara*, ON *kor*, Goth. *kara* f. Gmc **karō*]

cāre[2] *v.i.* Feel concern or interest (*for, about*); (usu. w. neg. expressed or implied) feel regard, deference, affection, liking, (*for, about*), be concerned *whether* etc., (often with expletive *a damn, a tinker's cuss,* etc.; **for all I ~, I couldn't ~ less,** (colloq.) I am utterly uninterested or indifferent); be willing or wishful *to* (*should not care to be seen with him*; *would you care to try them?*); **~ for,** provide for, look after. [OE *carian*, = OS *karon*, OHG *charōn*, Goth. *karōn* f. Gmc **karōjan*, or f. prec.]

caree'n *v.t.* & *i.* Turn (ship) on side for cleaning, caulking, etc., whence **~**AGE (4, 5) *n.*; (cause to) heel over; *(of vehicle etc.) career. [f. *careen* n. = careened position of ship f. F *carène* f. It. *carena* f. L *carina* keel]

career' *n.*, & *v.i.* **1.** *n.* Swift course, impetus, (*in full, mid,* etc., *career*); course or progress through life or history; way of making a livelihood and advancing oneself (**~ diplomat,** professional diplomat; **~ girl, woman,** woman who works permanently in a profession; **~s master, mistress,** teacher advising pupils on choice of career); hence **~**IST (3) *n.*, one intent mainly on personal advancement and success in life. **2.** *v.i.* Go swiftly or wildly (*about*). [f. F *carrière* f. It. *carriera* f. Prov. *-eira* f. Rom. **carraria* (*via*) carriage(-road) f. L *carrus* CAR]

cāre'ful (kār'f-) *a.* Concerned *for*, taking care *of*; painstaking, watchful, cautious, (*to* do, *that,* etc.); done with or showing care; hence **~**LY[2] *adv.*, **~**NESS *n.* [OE *carful* (as CARE[1], -FUL)]

cāre'lėss (kār'l-) *a.* Unconcerned, taking no heed *of*, light-hearted; inattentive, negligent (*of*), thoughtless; effortless; inaccurate; hence **~**LY[2] *adv.*, **~**NESS *n.* [OE *carlēas* (as CARE[1], -LESS)]

carĕ'ss *n.*, & *v.t.* **1.** *n.* Fondling touch, kiss. **2.** *v.t.* Bestow caress on; treat fondly or kindly. [f. F *caresse(r)* f. It. *carezza* f. Rom. **caritia* f. L *carus* dear]

că'rĕt *n.* Mark (‸) placed below line to show place of omission. [L, = is lacking]

||**cār'făx** *n.* Place where (usu. four) roads meet. [ME f. AF *carfuks*, OF *carrefurcs* f. pop. L *QUADRI(*furcus* f. *furca* fork)]

cār'gō *n.* (*pl.* **~es** *or* ***~s**). Goods carried by ship, aircraft, or *motor vehicle; **~ boat** (carrying only or chiefly cargo); **~ cult,** (orig. in Pacific Islands) belief in forthcoming arrival of supernatural benefactors. [Sp., f. as CHARGE[1]]

căria'ma (-ah'-) *n.* Var. of SERIEMA.

Că'rĭb *n.* & *a.* (One) of aboriginal inhabitants of southern W. Ind. islands and adjacent coasts; their language. [f. Sp. *Caribe* f. Haitian]

Cărĭbbē'an *n.* & *a.* Of the region occupied by the Caribs; **~ (Sea),** the part of the Atlantic between the southern W. Ind. islands and Central America. [f. prec. + -EAN]

că'rĭbou (-bōō) *n.* (*pl.* same). N. Amer. reindeer. [Can. F, prob. f. Amer. Ind.]

că'rĭcatūr|e *n.*, & *v.t.* **1.** *n.* Grotesque representation of person or thing by exaggeration of characteristic traits, in picture, writing, or mime; ridiculously poor imitation or version; hence ~AL *a.*, ~IST (1) *n.* **2.** *v.t.* Make or give a caricature of. [F, f. It. *caricatura* (*caricare* load, exaggerate; see CHARGE¹, -URE)]

cār'ĭēs (-z; *or* kār'ēz) *n.* (*pl.* same). Decay (of bones or teeth); hence **cārĭŏGE'NIC** (1) *a.* [L]

carĭ'llon (-lyon; *or* kă'rĭl(y)on) *n.* Set of bells sounded either from keyboard or mechanically; tune played on bells; instrument (or part of organ) imitating peal of bells. [F, f. Rom. **quatrinio* peal of four bells]

carī'n|a *n.* (Biol.) Ridge-shaped structure, esp. keel of bird's breastbone; hence ~AL *a.* [L, = keel]

că'rĭnate *a.* (Of bird) having keeled breastbone (opp. *ratite*). [f. L *carinatus* keeled (*carina* keel; see -ATE²)]

cărĭō'ca *n.* Native of Rio de Janeiro; (music for) Brazilian dance like samba. [Port.]

cārĭŏgĕ'nĭc. See CARIES.

cār'ĭous *a.* Decayed (esp. of bones or teeth). [f. L *cariosus* (CARIES; see -OUS)]

cār'kĭng *a.* (arch.) Burdensome (*care* etc.). [part. of obs. *cark* v. f. ONF *carkier* f. Rom. **carcare* (**carricare* CHARGE²)]

cārl *n.* (Sc.) Man, fellow. [OE, f. ON *karl*, cogn. w. CHURL]

Cār'ley *n.* ~ (**float**), large emergency raft on ship. [f. H. S. ~, Amer. inventor (1903)]

cār'līne *n.* Plant of genus *Carlina*, allied to thistle. [F, f. med. L *carlina* perh. for *cardina* (L *cardo* thistle), assoc. w. *Carolus Magnus* Charlemagne]

Carlovingian. See CAROLINGIAN.

Cār'mėlīte *n.* & *a.* (Member) of mendicant order of friars (also *White Friars* f. their white cloak) or of a similar order of nuns. [F, or f. med. L *carmelita* (Mt. *Carmel* in Palestine, place of foundation in 12th c.; see -ITE¹ (1))]

cār'mĭnatĭve *a.* & *n.* (Drug) curing flatulence. [f. F *carminatif -ive* or med. L *carminare* heal (by incantation); see CHARM¹, -ATIVE]

cār'mīne *n.* & *a.* (Coloured like, colour of) crimson pigment made from cochineal. [f. F *carmin* or f. med. L *carminium* perh. f. *carmesinum* CRIMSON + *minium* cinnabar]

Carms. *abbr.* Carmarthenshire (former county in Wales).

Cār'nabӯ Street *n.* (usu. *attrib.*) Fashionable clothing for young people. [name of street in central London]

cār'nage *n.* Great slaughter, esp. of human beings. [F, f. It. *carnaggio* f. med. L *carnaticum* f. L *caro carnis* flesh; see -AGE]

cār'nal *a.* Sensual, fleshly, (**have ~ knowledge of,** (Law) have sexual intercourse with); unsanctified, worldly; hence **cārnă'lITY** *n.*, ~IZE (3) *v.t.*, ~LY² *adv.* [ME, f. LL *carnalis* (*caro*; see prec., -AL)]

cārnā'tion¹ *n.* & *a.* (Of) rosy pink colour. [F, f. It. *carnagione* f. LL *carnatio -onis* (as prec.; see -ATION) fleshiness]

cārnā'tion² *n.* Cultivated clove pink. [in 16th c. also *coronation*, perh. the orig. form, later assim. to prec.]

cārnau'ba (*or* -naōō'- *or* -now'-) *n.* Brazilian palm (*Copernicia cerifera*); its yellowish leaf-wax, used as polish etc. [Port.]

cārnē'lĭan. See CORNELIAN¹.

cār'net (-nā) *n.* Permit to drive across frontier or use camping-site. [F, = notebook]

||**cār'ney.** See CARNY.

cār'nĭval *n.* Festivities usual during period before Lent in R.C. countries; riotous revelry; *travelling circus or fair; festivities esp. occurring at regular date. [f. It. *carne-*, *carnovale* f. med. L *carnelevarium* etc. Shrove-tide, f. L *caro carnis* flesh + *levare* put away]

cārnĭ'vorous *a.* Feeding on flesh or other animal matter; (esp.) belonging to the Carnivora, (of plant) digesting animal substance; so **Cārnĭ'**VORA *n. pl.*, large order of mainly carnivorous mammals (cats, dogs, foxes, bears, seals, etc.); **cār'nĭ**VORE *n.*, carnivorous animal or plant. [f. L *carnivorus* (*caro carnis* flesh; see -VOROUS)]

||**cār'nӯ, cār'ney,** *v.t.*, & *a.* (colloq.) **1.** *v.t.* Coax, wheedle. **2.** *a.* Artful, sly. [19th c.; orig. unkn.]

că'rob *n.* Horn-shaped edible pod of Mediterranean evergreen tree (**~-tree**), *Ceratonia siliqua*. [f. obs. F *car(r)obe* f. med. L *carrubia, -um* f. Arab. *karrūba*]

că'rol *n.* & *v.* (||-ll-). **1.** *n.* Joyous song, esp. Christmas hymn. **2.** *v.t.* & *i.* Sing (as) carol; sing joyfully. [ME, f. OF *carole(r)*, of unkn. orig.]

Cărolē'an, Că'rolīne, *adjs.* Of the time of Charles I or II of England. [f. L *Carolus* Charles + -EAN, -INE¹]

Cărolĭ'ngĭan, Cārlovĭ'ngĭan, (-nj-) *a.* & *n.* (Member) of second Frankish dynasty, founded by Charlemagne (d. 814); (style) of script developed in France at time of Charlemagne. [(*Caro-* after L *Carolus* Charles) f. F *carlovingien* f. *Karl* Charles after *mérovingien* MEROVINGIAN]

***că'rom** *n.*, & *v.i.* **1.** *n.* Cannon at billiards. **2.** *v.i.* Make carom; strike and rebound *off*. [abbr. of *carambole* f. Sp. *carambola*]

că'rotēne *n.* Orange or red substance formed in carrots etc. and acting as source of vitamin A; hence **carŏ'tėn**OID *n.*, pigment of class including carotene. [f. G *carotin* f. L *carota* CARROT; see -ENE]

carŏ'tĭd *a.* & *n.* (Of or near) one of the two great arteries carrying blood to head. [f. F *carotide* or mod. L *carotides* f. Gk *karōtides* pl. (*karoō* stupefy, compression of these arteries being thought to cause stupor)]

carou's|e (-z) *v.i.*, & *n.* (Have or engage in) drinking-bout; drink heavily; hence ~AL 2 *n.* [orig. as adv. = right out, in phr. *drink carouse* f. G *gar aus trinken*]

cărousĕ'l, *cărr-, (-ōō-; *or* -z-) *n.* (Hist.) kind of tournament; rotating delivery or conveyor system; *roundabout, merry-go-round. [f. F *carrousel* f. It. *carosello*]

cārp¹ *n.* (*pl.* same). Freshwater fish of genus *Cyprinus*, esp. a species usu. bred in ponds. [ME, f. OF *carpe* f. Prov. or f. LL *carpa*]

cārp² *v.i.* Talk querulously, find fault, (usu. *at*); (in *part.*, of tongue, criticism) captious. [obs. ME senses talk, say, sing, f. ON *karpa* to brag; mod. sense (16th c.) f. or infl. by L *carpere* pluck at, slander]

cār'pal. See CARPUS.

cār'pel *n.* (Bot.) One of the constituent units of a compound ovary; hence ~**l**ARY¹ *a.* [f. F *carpelle* or mod. L *carpellum* f. Gk *karpos* fruit; see -LE 2]

cār'pėnter *n.* & *v.* **1.** *n.* Craftsman in woodwork (esp. of rough solid kinds as in ship or house building; cf. JOINER, CABINET-*maker*); **~ ant, bee,** kinds boring into trees; so **cār'pėnt**RY (2, 5) *n.* **2.** *v.i.* & *t.* Do, or make by, carpenter's work, (fig.) construct, fit (things) *together*. [ME & AF; OF *carpentier*, f. LL *carpentarius* (*carpentum* wagon f. Gaulish; see -ER²)]

cār'pėt *n.*, & *v.t.* **1.** *n.* Thick fabric for covering floor and stairs (**figure in the ~**, pattern not immediately perceptible; **on the ~**, (1) being reprimanded, (2) under discussion [f. earlier use as table-cover]; RED *carpet*; **sweep under the ~**, conceal (thing) in the hope that others will overlook or forget it); area of intensive bombing etc.; smooth, soft, or bright expanse of grass, flowers, etc. **2. ~-bag,** travelling-bag, orig. made of carpet; ~-**bagger,** political candidate etc. without local connections; ~-**bed,** garden bed with dwarf plants arranged in pattern; ~-**knight,** (arch.) idler, ladies' man; ~-**shark** (with carpet-like pattern on back); ~ **slipper** (with upper made (orig.) of carpet-like material); ~-**snake,** large variegated Australian python; ~-**sweeper,** household implement with revolving brush(es) for sweeping carpets. **3.** *v.t.* Cover (as) with a carpet, whence ~ING[1] (3) *n.*; (colloq.) reprimand, reprove. [ME, f. OF *carpite* or med. L *carpita*, f. obs. It. *carpita* woollen counterpane f. Rom. **carpire* f. L *carpere* pluck, pull to pieces]

carphŏ'logy̆ *n.* Delirious fumbling with bedclothes etc. [f. Gk *karphologia* (*karphos* straw etc., *legō* pick; see -Y[1])]

carpo-[1] *comb. form.* Carpus. [f. CARPUS + -O-]

carpo-[2] *comb. form.* Fruit, as **carpŏ'**LOGY *n.* [f. Gk *karpos* fruit + -O-]

car'p|us *n.* (*pl.* ~**i** *pr.* -ī). Part of skeleton between forearm or foreleg and metacarpus, eight small bones in higher vertebrates (in man, wrist; in horse, knee); hence ~AL *a.* [mod. L, f. Gk *karpos* wrist]

că'rrack *n.* (Hist.) Large merchant-ship equipped for warfare. [ME, f. F *caraque* f. Sp. *carraca* f. Arab. *ḳarāḳir*]

că'rrageen, -gheen, (-gēn) *n.* Edible purple seaweed (*Chondrus crispus*) found in N. hemisphere. [f. *Carragheen* in Ireland]

că'rrel *n.* **1.** (Hist.) Small enclosure or study in cloister. **2.** Small cubicle for reader in (stack-room of) library. [var. of CAROL in obs. sense]

că'rriage (-rĭj) *n.* **1.** Conveying, transport; cost of conveying (~ **forward,** carriage to be paid by receiver; ~ **paid,** by sender); manner of carrying (head, body, etc.), bearing, deportment. **2.** Wheeled vehicle for persons (HACKNEY, INVALID[1], ‖*railway, carriage*); four-wheeled private vehicle for two (~ **and pair**) or more horses (**drive** ~ **and six** etc. **through,** cf. COACH 4); ‖railway passenger vehicle; (**gun-**)~, wheeled support of gun; (Mech.) sliding etc. part of machinery for shifting position of other parts, e.g. in typewriter. **3.** ~ **clock** (working in any position); ~-**dog,** Dalmatian; ~ **trade,** (trade with) those rich enough to own a private carriage; ~**way,** part of road intended for vehicular traffic. **4.** Hence ~ABLE (-ĭja-) *a.*, (of road) available to carriages. [ME, f. ONF *cariage* (*carier* CARRY[1]; see -AGE)]

că'rrĭck bĕnd *n.* (Naut.) Kind of knot or splice. [BEND[1]; *carrick* perh. f. CARRACK]

că'rrĭer *n.* **1.** In vbl senses; person or company undertaking for hire the conveyance of goods or passengers (COMMON[1] *carrier*); substance used to support or convey pigment, catalyst, radioactive material, etc.; part of bicycle etc. for carrying luggage or a passenger; person or animal that without suffering from a disease or showing a hereditary characteristic transmits it to others; (Phys.) mobile electron or hole in a semiconductor; = *aircraft carrier.* **2.** ~(**-bag**), paper or plastic bag for shopping etc.; *carrier* PIGEON[1]; ~ **wave,** continuous electromagnetic wave on which signal is superposed by modulation of amplitude or frequency. [f. CARRY[1] + -ER[1]]

că'rrĭōle *n.* Small open carriage for one; covered light cart; Canadian sledge. [F, f. It. *carriuola*, dim. of *carro* (CAR)]

că'rrĭon *n.* & *a.* **1.** *n.* Dead putrefying flesh; anything vile, garbage, filth; ~ **crow,** black crow (*Corvus corone*), feeding on carrion, small animals, etc. **2.** *a.* Rotten, loathsome. [ME, f. AF & ONF *caroine, -oigne*, OF *charoigne*, f. Rom. **caronia* f. L *caro* flesh]

cărronā'de *n.* (Hist.) Ship's short large-calibred gun. [f. *Carron* in Scotland, orig. place of making, + -ADE]

că'rrot *n.* Umbelliferous plant (*Daucus carota*) with tapering orange-coloured edible root; the root, used as vegetable; the vegetable used as incentive to donkey, (fig.) means of persuasion; (in *pl.*, sl.) red hair, red-haired person, whence ~Y[2] *a.* [f. F *carotte* f. L *carota* f. Gk *karōton*]

că'rry̆[1] *v.* **1.** *v.t.* Transport in vehicle, ship, aircraft, hand, or mind, or on person, or (of wind etc.) by its own motion; ~ **all before** one, succeed, overcome all opposition; *carry* COALS *to Newcastle*; *carrying-*TRADE; FETCH[1] *and carry*; *carry* WEIGHT[1]. **2.** Conduct (*pipes carry water*; *wires carry electric current*; *carry into effect*); ~ person **back** (in thought to past time). **3.** Transfer (figures to column of higher value); ~ **conviction,** persuade others; ~ **forward,** transfer to new page or account. **4.** (Of gun etc.) propel to specified distance. **5.** Be pregnant with (*she was carrying twins*). **6.** (Of motive, money, etc.) cause or enable to go *to*; (of day's journey etc.) bring *to.* **7.** Prolong or continue *to* (*carry tower to 500 ft., modesty to excess*). **8.** Win (prize; ~ **the day,** succeed; ~ **fortress** etc., capture it; ~ **hearers with** one, persuade them); win victory for (*carry* one's *point, a motion, bill*). **9.** Have with one, possess, (*arms, a watch,* etc.; *carry* one's BAT[2]; ~ **with** one, remember); involve, imply, (*loans carry interest, principles carry consequences*); stock (goods for sale); (of newspaper) publish, esp. regularly; (of radio station etc.) broadcast, esp. regularly. **10.** Hold in a certain way (*carry* one's *head* or *body*, one*self*, *erect* etc.). **11.** Endure weight of, support, (*ships carry sail, columns carry dome*); bear major responsibility for effectiveness of (*he carries that department*). **12.** ~-**all,** carriole, *car with sideways seats; ~-**cot,** portable cot for baby. **13.** ~ **away,** inspire, transport, deprive of self-control, (Naut.) lose (mast etc.) by breakage, break off or away; ~ **off,** remove from life, remove by force, win, render acceptable or passable; ~ **it off** (**well**), do well under difficulties; ~ **on,** advance (process) by a stage, continue, manage (business); ~ **out,** put (principles, instructions, etc.) into practice; ~ **over,** = *carry forward* (see sense 3), postpone (work etc.) to later time, (St. Exch.) keep over to next settling-day, whence ~-*over* n.; ~ **through,** bring safely out of difficulties, complete. **14.** *v.i.* (Of missile, sound, etc.) travel, penetrate; ~ **on,** go on with what one is doing, (colloq.) behave strangely or violently, flirt (*with*); ~-**on** *n.*, ~**ing(s)-on,** (sl.) excitement, questionable behaviour, flirtation. [ME, f. AF & ONF *carier* (as CAR)]

că'rry̆[2] *n.* Act of carrying; (Golf) ball's flight before pitching; portage between rivers etc.; range of gun etc. [f. prec.]

carse *n.* (Sc.) Lowland beside river. [ME, perh. f. *carrs* swamps]

cart *n.*, & *v.t.* **1.** *n.* Strong two-wheeled or four-wheeled usu. horse-drawn vehicle used in farming and for heavy goods; light two-wheeled one-horse vehicle for driving in; ‖**in the** ~, (sl.) in an awkward or losing position; **put the** ~ **before the horse,** reverse proper order, take effect for cause. **2.** ~-**horse** (thickset and fit for heavy work); ~-**load,** cartful, large quantity of anything; ~-**road** or **-track** (too rough for carriages); ~-**wheel,** wheel of cart, large coin or hat etc., lateral handspring with arms and legs extended; ~-**wright,** maker of carts. **3.** Hence ~'AGE (4), ~'ER[1], ~'FUL 2, *ns.* **4.** *v.t.* Carry (as) in a cart; (sl.) carry (esp. cumbersome thing) over unduly long distance; (Cricket) hit hard; ~ **off,** remove esp. by force.

[ME, f. ON *kartr* cart & OE *cræt*, prob. infl. by AF & ONF *carete* dim. of *carre* CAR]

că̄rte *n.* Var. of QUART[2].

carte blanche (kărt blah'ňsh) *n.* Full discretionary power given to person; hand of cards without court-card. [F, = blank paper (as CARD[2], BLANK[1])]

cărte-de-vĭsĭ'te (-zē't) *n.* (arch.) Small photograph for use as visiting-card. [F, = visiting-card]

cărtĕ'l *n.* Manufacturers' union to control production, marketing arrangements, prices, etc.; political combination between parties; hence ~IZE (3) *v.t.* & *i.*, combine to form a (business) cartel. [f. G *kartell* f. F *cartel* f. It. *cartello* dim. of *carta* CARD[2]]

Cărtē'sian (-zyan) *a.* & *n.* (Follower) of Descartes or his philosophy or mathematical methods; ~ **co-ordinates** (measured from intersecting straight axes); ~ **diver** etc., toy that rises and falls in liquid when cover of vessel is subjected to varying pressure; hence ~ISM (3) *n.* [f. mod. L *Cartesianus* (*Cartesius* name of René *Descartes*, Fr. philosopher d. 1650; see -IAN)]

Cărthagĭ'nĭan *a.* & *n.* (Native or inhabitant) of Carthage; ~ **peace,** treaty of peace that is very severe to the defeated contestant. [f. L *Carthago -ginis* Carthage, ancient city near Tunis + -IAN]

Cărthū'sian (-zyan) *a.* & *n.* (Member) of order of monks founded by St. Bruno 1086; ||(past or present member) of Charterhouse School (founded on site of Carthusian monastery). [f. med. L *Carthusianus* f. L *Cart(h)usia* (CHARTREUSE, near Grenoble); see -IAN]

căr'tĭlage *n.* (Structure in vertebrates made of) firm elastic tissue, gristle; **temporary** ~ (in the young, changing later to bone); hence **cărtĭlă'gĭn**OID, **cărtĭlă'gĭn**OUS, *adjs.* [F, f. L *cartilago -ginis*]

căr'togrăm *n.* Map with diagrammatic statistical information. [f. F *cartogramme* (*carte* map, CARD[2]; see -GRAM)]

cărtŏ'graphy̆ *n.* Map-drawing; hence **cărtŏ'**-GRAPHER *n.*, **cărto**GRA'PHIC(AL) *adjs.* [f. F *cartographie* (as prec.; see -GRAPHY)]

căr'tomăncy̆ *n.* Fortune-telling by playing-cards. [f. F *cartomancie* (*carte* CARD[2]; see -MANCY)]

căr'ton *n.* Light cardboard etc. box for holding goods. [F, f. as foll.]

cărtōō'n *n.* & *v.* **1.** *n.* Full-size drawing on stout paper as design for painting, tapestry, mosaic, etc.; full-page (or large) illustration, esp. satirical one on politics in newspaper or magazine; amusing drawing with or without caption; sequence of these in STRIP[2]; film made from a succession of drawings that simulate a cinema film; hence ~IST (3) *n.* **2.** *v.i.* Draw cartoon(s). **3.** *v.t.* Represent (person etc.) in cartoon. [f. It. *cartone* (*carta* CARD[2]; see -OON)]

cărtou'che (-ōō'sh) *n.* (Archit.) scroll ornament, e.g. volute of Ionic capital; tablet imitating, or drawing of, scroll with rolled-up ends, used ornamentally or bearing inscription; ornate frame; (Archaeol.) oval ring containing hieroglyphic names and titles of Egyptian kings etc. [F, = cartridge, f. It. *cartoccio* f. *carta* (CARD[2])]

căr'trĭdge *n.* **1.** Case containing charge of propellant explosive for firearms or blasting, with bullet or shot if for small arms (BLANK[1] *cartridge*); spool of film, magnetic tape, etc., in container; removable pick-up head of record-player; ink-container for insertion in pen. **2.** ~ **belt** (with sockets for cartridges); ~ **paper** (thick and rough, used for cartridges, for drawing, and for strong envelopes). [f. prec.]

c(h)ăr'tūlary̆ (k-) *n.* Collection of charters or records; place where these are kept. [f. med. L *c(h)artularium* (*c(h)artula* dim. of L *c(h)arta* CARD[2]; see -ARY[1])]

că'rŭncle (*or* karŭ'-) *n.* Fleshy excrescence, e.g. turkeycock's wattles. [obs. F, f. L *caruncula* (*caro carnis* flesh; see -UNCLE)]

cărve *v.* (*p.p.* ~**d** *or* arch. **car'ven**). **1.** *v.t.* Produce by cutting (statue, portrait, representation in relief or intaglio, inscription, design, or abs., *out of*, *in*, or *on*, material; *carve* one's *way* etc., lit. or fig.); change (material *into* something) by cutting; cover or adorn (material) *with* figures cut in it, cut designs etc., whence **căr'**VING[1] (2) *n.* **2.** *v.i.* & *t.* Cut up meat, cut up (meat etc.), at or for table (**carving knife,** long knife for this purpose); ~ **out,** take from larger whole; ~ **up,** divide into several pieces, whence ~**-up** *n.*, (sl.) sharing-out, esp. of booty. [OE *ceorfan* cut f. WG **kerfan*]

căr'vel *n.* See CARAVEL; ~**-built,** with planks flush (cf. CLINKER[3]-*built*). [f. as CARAVEL]

căr'ver[1] *n.* In vbl senses; carving knife, (in *pl.*) carving knife and fork; ||armchair in set of dining-room chairs. [f. CARVE + -ER[1]]

***Căr'ver[2]** *n.* ~ **chair** (with arms, rush seat, and back having horizontal and vertical spindles). [f. J. ~, first governor of Plymouth Colony, d. 1621]

căry̆ă'tĭd *n.* (*pl.* ~**es** *pr.* -ēz, *or* ~**s**). (Archit.) Female figure used as pillar to support entablature. [f. F *caryatide* f. It. *cariatide* or f. L f. Gk *karuatis -idos* priestess at Caryae (*Karuai*) in Laconia]

căry̆ŏ'ps|ĭs *n.* (*pl.* ~**es** *pr.* -ēz). (Bot.) One-seeded indehiscent fruit with pericarp fused to seed-coat, as in wheat and maize. [mod. L, f. Gk *karuon* nut + *opsis* appearance]

Căsanō'va (*or* -z-) *n.* Man engaging in promiscuous love-affairs. [f. G. J. ~ de Seingalt, It. adventurer d. 1798]

că'sbah, kă'sbah, (-z-) *n.* Arab quarter near citadel of N. Afr. city. [F *casbah* f. Arab. *kaṣ(a)ba* citadel]

căscā'de *n.*, & *v.i.* **1.** *n.* (Small) waterfall; section of large broken waterfall; succession of electrical devices or stages in a process; quantity of material etc. falling; wavy arrangement of hanging lace etc. **2.** *v.i.* Fall in or like cascade. [F, f. It. *cascata* f. *cascare* to fall f. Rom. **casicare* f. L *casus* (CASE[1]); see -ADE]

căscăr'a *n.* ~ (**sagrada** *pr.* -ah'da), bark of N. Amer. buckthorn, used as purgative. [Sp., = sacred bark]

cāse[1] *n.* **1.** Instance of thing's occurring; actual state of affairs (**is, is not, the** ~, is true, false; **as the** ~ **may be,** according to the situation); position, circumstances, in which one is (**in good, evil,** ~, well, badly, off); (Med.) diseased condition of a person, instance of any disease; *comical fellow. **2.** (Law) cause or suit for trial; statement of facts in cause *sub judice*, drawn up for higher court's consideration (*judge states a case*); cause that has been decided and may be cited (LEADING[2] *case*); sum of arguments on one side (*that is our case*; **make out a** ~, prove it); valid set of arguments (*have no case*; *there is a case for doing nothing at present*). **3.** (Gram.) Form of noun, adjective, or pronoun, in inflected languages expressing relation to some other word in sentence (in uninflected languages, this relation itself apart from form). **4. In** ~, if, in the event that, lest; (**just**) **in** ~, against some possible occurrence; **in** ~ **of,** in the event of; **in the** ~ **of,** as regards; **in any** ~, whatever the fact is, whatever may happen; **in no** ~, under no circumstances; **in that** ~, if that is true, should that happen. **5.** ~**-book** (with record of legal or medical cases; also fig.); ~ **history,** record of person's ancestry, personal history, information about patient, etc., for use in determining necessary treatment etc.; **~-law,** law as settled by decided cases; **~-load,** cases with which doctor etc. is concerned at one time; **~-study,** (record of) attempt to understand person etc. from collected information about his development; **~'work(er),** social work(er) concerned with individuals or groups. [ME f. OF *cas* f. L *casus* fall (*cadere cas-* to fall)]

cāse² *n.*, & *v.t.* **1.** *n.* What encloses something, box, bag, sheath, etc., (*bookcase, brief-case, spectacle-case, suitcase*); glass box for showing specimens, curiosities, etc.; outer protective covering part (of watch, sausage, seed-vessel, book, etc.); box with appropriate contents (*dressing-case*); (Print.) receptacle with compartments for type (**upper ~,** capitals; **lower ~,** small letters). **2. ~-bound,** (of book) in hard cover; **~-harden** *v.t.*, harden surface of, esp. give steel surface to (iron) by carbonizing, (fig.) render callous; **~-knife** (carried in sheath); **~-shot,** (1) bullets in iron case fired from cannon, (2) shrapnel. **3.** *v.t.* Enclose in case; surround *with*; (sl.) examine (house etc., esp. in preparation for robbery); hence **cā'sING**¹ (3) *n.* [ME, f. OF *casse, chasse*, f. L *capsa* (*capere* hold)]

cā'sèĭn (*or* -sēn) *n.* Protein of milk, the basis of cheese. [f. L *caseus* cheese + -IN]

cāsemāte (-sm-) *n.* Chamber in thickness of wall of fortress, with embrasures; armoured enclosure for guns in warship. [F, & f. It. *casamatta* or Sp. *-mata*, f. *camata*, perh. f. Gk *khasma -atos* gap]

cā'sement (-sm-) *n.* Metal or wooden vertically hinged frame with glass forming (part of) window; (poet. etc.) window; **~ cloth,** plain fabric used for curtains etc. [ME, f. AL *cassimentum* (*cassa* CASE²; see -MENT)]

cā'sèous *a.* Of or like cheese. [f. L *caseus* cheese + -OUS]

căsh¹ *n.*, & *v.t.* **1.** *n.* Ready money, actual coins, notes, etc., (opp. *credit*; **~ on delivery,** forwarding of goods against cash to be paid to postman or carrier; **~ down** (paid on the spot); HARD *cash*); (Banking etc.) coins, or coins and banknotes, opp. cheques and orders. **2. ~-account** (to which only cash is carried, and from which all payments are made); **~-book** (for record of cash received and paid); **~ and carry,** (of goods) paid for in cash and removed by buyer, not delivered; **~ crop** (to be sold, not used as food etc.); **~ desk** (where cash is taken in shop etc.); *cash* NEXUS; **~ payment** (in ready money); **~ price** (lowest, for ready money); **~ register,** mechanical till visibly recording amount of each purchase, totalling receipts, etc. **3.** *v.t.* Give or obtain cash for (note, cheque, etc.); (Bridge) lead (winning card); **~ in,** pay into bank etc.; **~ in** (one's **checks**), (colloq.) die. **4.** *v.i.* **~ in on,** realize profit on, (fig.) take advantage of. [f. obs. F *casse* box or f. It. *cassa* f. L *capsa* CASE²]

căsh² *n.* (*pl.* same). (Hist.) E. Ind. or Chinese small coin. [ult. f. Port. *ca*(*i*)*xa* f. Tamil *kāsu* f. Skr. *karsha*]

că'shew (-ōō) *n.* Large tropical tree (*Anacardium occidentale*) with edible kidney-shaped nut (**~-nut**). [f. Port. f. Tupi (*a*)*caju*]

căshier'¹ *n.* Person in charge of bank's or business's cash; person receiving payments in shop etc. [f. Du. *cassier* or f. F *caissier* (as CASH¹; see -IER)]

căshier'² *v.t.* Dismiss from service, esp. with disgrace; depose; (arch.) get rid of. [f. Flem. *kasseren* disband, revoke, f. F *casser* f. L *quassare* QUASH]

că'shmēre *n.* Fine soft wool of Kashmir goat; imitation of it. [f. *Kashmir* in Asia]

casi'nō (-sē'-) *n.* (*pl.* **~s**). Public room or building for amusements, esp. gambling. [It., dim. of *casa* house f. L *casa* cottage]

cask (kah-) *n.* Barrel, esp. for alcoholic drinks; its contents or capacity. [f. F *casque* or Sp. *casco* helmet]

ca'skėt (kah'-) *n.* Small box or chest, often ornamental, for jewels, letters, cremated ashes, etc.; *rectangular coffin. [perh. f. AF form of OF *cassette* f. It. *cassetta* dim. of *cassa* f. L *capsa* CASE²; see -ET¹]

Că'slon (-z-) *n.* Style of type cut by the Caslons or imitated from theirs. [f. W. ~, Engl. typographer d. 1766 and his son d. 1778]

casque (kăsk) *n.* (Hist. or poet.) Helmet. [F, f. Sp. *casco*]

Cassă'ndra *n.* Prophet of disaster, esp. if disregarded. [L f. Gk *Kas*(*s*)*andra*, daughter of Priam king of Troy; she was condemned by Apollo to prophesy correctly but not be believed]

căssa'ta (-ah'-) *n.* Neapolitan ice cream with fruit and nuts. [It.]

cassā'tion *n.* Annulment; **Court of C~,** court of appeal in France etc. [ME f. F (*casser*; see QUASH, -ATION)]

cassa'va (-ah'-) *n.* Tropical plant of genus *Manihot*, with tuberous roots; its starch or flour; bread made from these. [earlier *cas*(*s*)*avi* etc., f. Taino *casavi*, infl. by F *cassave*]

că'sserōle *n.*, & *v.t.* **1.** *n.* Covered heat-proof vessel in which food is cooked and served; food thus prepared. **2.** *v.t.* Cook in casserole. [F, f. *cassole* dim. of *casse* f. Prov. *casa* f. LL *cattia* ladle, pan f. Gk *kuathion* dim. of *kuathos* cup]

cassě'tte *n.* Container of film, magnetic tape, etc., for insertion into equipment. [F, dim. of *casse* CASE²]

că'ssĭa (*or* -sh*a*) *n.* Inferior kind of cinnamon; plant of genus *Cassia*, yielding senna-leaves. [f. L f. Gk *kasia* f. Heb. *ḳᵉṣīʿāh* bark like cinnamon]

că'ssĭs *n.* Syrupy black-currant flavouring for drinks etc. [F, = black currant]

cassĭ'terīte *n.* Native tin dioxide. [f. Gk *kassiteros* tin + -ITE¹ (2)]

că'ssock *n.* Long close garment worn esp. by clergy and choristers; hence **~ED**² (-kt) *a.* [f. F *casaque* long coat f. It. *casacca* horseman's coat, prob. f. Turkic *quzzāk* nomad; cf. COSSACK]

că'ssoulet (-ŏŏlā) *n.* Ragout of meat and beans. [F, dim. of dial. *cassolo* stew-pan]

că'ssowarȳ (-*o*-) *n.* Large flightless bird of genus *Casuarius*, related to emu. [f. Malay *kasuārī, kasavārī*]

cast¹ (kah-) *v.* (**cast**). **1.** *v.t.* Move by throwing; **~ adrift,** leave to drift; **~ ashore** (of waves etc.); **~ aspersions on,** utter them regarding (person etc.); **~ an eye,** glance; *cast the* LEAD¹; *cast* LOTS; **~ line, net,** throw it out into water etc. in fishing; **~ a shadow,** make it fall (*on*); **~ a spell on,** bewitch; **~ a vote,** give or deposit it; DIE¹ *is cast*. **2.** *v.i.* **~ing vote** (that decides between two equal parties) [f. obs. sense 'turn the scale']. **3.** *v.t.* Throw off, get rid of, shed esp. in process of growth; (of horse) lose (shoe); **~ aside,** give up using, abandon. **4.** *v.t.* & *i.* Reckon, calculate; calculate and record details of (horoscope). **5.** *v.t.* Arrange; assign (actors) *as* characters; allocate roles in (play, film, etc., or abs.). **6.** Shape, found, (molten metal), form (figure, type, etc.) of metal; **~ iron,** hard alloy of iron, carbon, and silicon cast in mould; **~-iron** *a.*, made of this, (fig.) hard, unchangeable, impregnable; hence **~'ING**¹ (2) *n.* **7. ~ about,** go this way and that in search, devise means, (*for, to* do, *how*); **~ away,** reject, (in *pass.*, of ship) be wrecked, see CASTAWAY; **~ down,** depress (cf. DOWNCAST²); **~ loose,** detach oneself; **~ in** one's **lot with,** decide to share fortunes of; **~ off,** abandon (so **~-*off*** a. & n.), (Knitting) take stitches off needle and loop each over next to finish edge, (Naut.) loosen and throw off (rope etc., or abs.), (Printing) estimate space taken in print by MS. copy; ~ **on,** (Knitting) make first row of loops on needle; ~ **up,** add (column of figures etc.). [ME, f. ON *kasta*]

cast[2] (kah-) *n.* **1.** Throwing of missile etc.; distance so attained; throw or number thrown at dice; throw of net, sounding-lead, or fishing-line (also, in fishing, the gut with hook and fly, and *good, bad,* etc., place for casting); **~-net** (thrown out and immediately drawn in, not set). **2.** Undigested food thrown up by hawk, owl, etc.; earth excreted by worm. **3.** Set of actors taking parts in play, film, etc. **4.** Form into which any work is thrown; model made by running molten metal or pressing soft material into mould; moulded mass of solidified material (*leg in a plaster cast*). **5.** Twist, inclination; ~ **in the eye,** slight squint. **6.** Tinge or shade of colour. **7.** Type, quality, (esp. *cast of features, cast of mind*). [ME, f. prec.]

Căstā'lian *a.* Of Castalia on Mt. Parnassus, fountain of the Muses; of the Muses. [f. L *Castalius* (*Castalia* f. Gk) + -AN]

căstanĕ't *n.* (usu. in *pl.*) Hardwood or ivory instrument(s) clicked or rattled in pairs as accompaniment to dance etc. [f. Sp. *castañeta* dim. of *castaña* f. L *castanea* chestnut]

ca'staway (kah'st*a*-) *n.* & *a.* Shipwrecked (person); (arch.) reprobate. [f. p.p. of CAST[1] + AWAY]

caste (kah-) *n.* Hindu hereditary class, with members socially equal, united in religion, and usu. following same trades, having no social intercourse with persons of other castes (~ **mark,** symbol on forehead denoting this); more or less exclusive social class; this system; the position it confers (**lose** ~, descend in social scale); (Zool.) form of a social insect having a particular function. [f. Sp. and Port. *casta* lineage, race, breed, fem. of *casto* pure, CHASTE]

că'stellan *n.* (Hist.) Governor of castle. [ME f. ONF *castelain* f. med. L *castellanus* (as CASTLE[1]; see -AN)]

că'stell|ātėd *a.* Castle-like; battlemented; so ~A'TION *n.* [f. med. L *castellatus* (as CASTLE[1]; see -ATE[2], -ED[1])]

ca'ster (kah'-) *n.* In vbl senses; machine for casting type; see also CASTOR[2]. [ME, f. CAST[1] + -ER[1]]

că'stig|āte *v.t.* Chastise, punish with blows or words; hence ~A'TION, ~ātor, *ns.*, ~ātory *a.* [f. L *castigare* reprove (*castus* pure) + -ATE[3]]

Căsti'le (-ē'l) *n.* ~ **soap,** fine hard white or mottled soap made with olive oil and soda. [f. as foll.]

Casti'lian *a.* & *n.* (Native or inhabitant) of Castile; language of Castile, standard literary Spanish. [f. *Castile* in Spain + -IAN]

ca'stle[1] (kah's*e*l) *n.* Large fortified building or set of buildings, stronghold, (**Englishman's house is his** ~, none may force entrance); mansion that was once such; (Chess) = ROOK[2]; **the C~,** (Ir. Hist.) viceroy's government and administration (with seat at Dublin Castle); ~ **in the air,** ~ **in Spain,** visionary project, day-dream; **~-nut,** (Mech.) one with notched extension for locking-pin; ~ **pudding** (steamed or baked in small mould); hence **ca'stl**ED[2] (kah'seld) *a.* [f. AF & ONF *castel, chastel* f. L *castellum* dim. of *castrum* fort; see -LE 2]

ca'stle[2] (kah's*e*l) *v.t.* & *i.* (Chess). Move rook next to king and king to other side of rook (~ **the king,** or abs.). [f. prec.]

ca'stor[1] (kah'-) *n.* Substance obtained from beaver and used in medicine and perfumery; (arch. sl.) hat. [F or L, f. Gk *kastōr* beaver]

ca'stor[2], **ca'ster,** (kah'-) *n.* **1.** Small bottle with holes in top for sprinkling contents; ~ **sugar,** white finely granulated kind. **2.** Small swivelled wheel on leg of chair, table, etc.; ~ **action,** swivelling of vehicle wheels to ensure stability. [f. CAST[1] + -OR, -ER[1]]

ca'stor[3] (kah'-) *n.* ~ **oil,** oil from seeds (~ **beans**) of the plant *Ricinus communis,* used as purgative and lubricant. [18th c., orig. uncert.; perh. so called as having succeeded CASTOR[1] in medical use]

căstr|ā'te *v.t.* Remove testicles of, geld; deprive of vigour; expurgate (book); hence ~A'TION *n.* (**~ation complex,** (Psych.) child's anxiety over imagined loss of genitals), **~ā'tive** *a.* [f. L *castrare* + -ATE[3]]

căstra't|ō (-rah'-) *n.* (*pl.* **~i** *pr.* -ē). (Hist.) Adult male singer castrated in boyhood so as to retain soprano or alto voice. [It., p.p. of *castrare* f. as prec.]

Că'strō|ism *n.* Political principles or actions of Fidel Castro or his followers; so ~IST (2) *n.* [f. Fidel *Castro* Ruz, Cuban statesman b. 1927 + -ISM]

că'sual (-zhōō- *or* -zyōō-) *a.* & *n.* Accidental; irregular; undesigned; unmethodical; careless; (colloq.) unconcerned, uninterested, unceremonious; ~ **clothes, ~s,** informal clothes; ~ (**labourer**), one without permanent employment, working when the chance comes; ~ (**shoe**), low-heeled slip-on shoe; ||~ **ward** (for temporary accommodation of vagrants); ~ **water,** (Golf) temporary accumulation of water (i.e. not one of the recognized hazards of the course); hence ~LY[2] *adv.*, ~NESS *n.* [ME, f. OF *casuel* & L *casualis* (*casus* CASE[1]; see -AL)]

că'sualtў (-zhōō- *or* -zyōō-) *n.* Accident, mishap, disaster; person killed or injured in war or accident; thing lost or destroyed. [ME, f. med. L *casualitas* (as prec.; see -ITY), after *royalty* etc.]

căsūari'na (-ē'n*a*) *n.* (Orig. Austral. and E. Ind.) tree of genus *Casuarina,* with jointed branches resembling gigantic horse-tails. [f. mod. L *casuarius* cassowary (from resemblance between branches and feathers)]

că'su|ĭst (-zhōō- *or* -zū-) *n.* Person, esp. theologian, who resolves cases of conscience, duty, etc.; sophist, quibbler; hence **~ĭ'stic(al)** *adjs.*, **~ĭstry** (4) *n.* [f. F *casuiste* f. Sp. *casuista* f. L *casus* CASE[1]; see -IST (3)]

casus belli (kās*u*s bĕ'lī *or* kahz*u*s bĕ'lĭ) *n.* Act or situation justifying or precipitating war. [L]

căt[1] *n.* **1.** Small furry domesticated carnivorous quadruped, *Felis catus*; WILD *cat*; (colloq., derog.) spiteful or malicious woman; (sl.) person, esp. jazz enthusiast; any member of genus *Felis,* e.g. lion, tiger, leopard (esp. *the Cats, the great Cats*); catlike animal of other species (*civet cat, polecat*). **2.** ~(**'head**), horizontal beam from each side of ship's bow for raising and carrying anchor. **3.** ~(**-o'-nine-tails**), (Hist.) rope whip with nine knotted lashes for flogging sailors, soldiers, or criminals. **4.** Tapered short stick in game of tipcat. **5. Let the ~ out of the bag,** reveal secret, esp. involuntarily; BELL[2] *the cat*; **like a ~ on hot bricks,** uneas(il)y; **like something the ~ brought in,** bedraggled; **care killed the ~,** (for all its nine lives; therefore,) be cheerful! (sim. *curiosity killed the cat,* do not be inquisitive); **~-and-dog** *life* etc., full of quarrels; **not a ~ in hell's chance,** no chance whatever; **see which way the ~ jumps,** wait for opinion or result to declare itself; **fight like** KILKENNY **~s** (to mutual destruction); **a ~ may look at a king,** even inferiors must be allowed some privileges; **enough to make a ~ laugh,** extremely amusing; **turn ~ in pan,** change sides, be turncoat; ~ **among the pigeons,** violent intruder; *rain* **~s and dogs,** very hard; **not**

room to swing a ~, very confined space; **has the ~ got your tongue?,** (colloq.) why are you silent? **6. ~'bird,** bird with mewing cry (N. Amer. mocking-bird, Austral. bower-bird, etc.); CATBOAT; ||~ **burglar** (who enters by climbing to upper storey); **~'call,** (*n.*) shrill whistle of disapproval at meetings etc., (*v.i.* & *t.*) make, reprove with, this; **~-door,** small door that cat can itself open; **~'fish,** (esp. freshwater) fish of sub-order Siluroides; CATGUT; **~'head** (see sense 2); **~-ice,** thin ice unsupported by water; **~-lap,** (sl.) slops, tea, etc.; **~'lick,** (colloq.) perfunctory wash; **~'mint,** blue-flowered aromatic plant (*Nepeta cataria*); **~'nap,** brief sleep in chair etc.; **~'nip,** catmint; **~'s-cradle,** child's game with string forming patterns between fingers; **~'s-eye,** precious stone of Sri Lanka and Malabar, one of line of reflector studs on road; **~'s-foot,** ground ivy; ||**~'s-meat,** horse's or other flesh prepared and sold as food for cats; **~'s-paw,** person used as tool by another, slight breeze rippling water in places; **~'s pyjamas,** (sl.) = *cat's whiskers*; **~'s-tail,** tall plant with long flat leaves; **~'suit,** single garment from neck to feet, with trouser legs; **~'s whiskers,** (sl.) something very fine; **~'walk,** narrow footway along a bridge, among large engines, etc. **7.** Hence ~'HOOD (-t-h-) *n.*, ~'LIKE *a.*, CATTERY, CATTISH, CATTY. [OE *catt(e)*, = OHG *kazza*, ON *köttr*, f. LL *cattus*, *catta*; ME *catt(e)* reinforced by AF & ONF *cat* f. same source]

căt² *v.t.* (**-tt-**). (Naut.) raise (anchor) from surface of water to cathead; ||(sl.) vomit. [f. prec.]

cat-. See CATA-.

||**C.A.T.** *abbr.* College of Advanced Technology.

căta- *pref.* (usu. **cat-** before vowel or *h*) meaning 'down' (*catadromous*), 'wrongly' (*catachresis*). [f. Gk *kata* down]

cată'bolism *n.* (Biol.) Destructive metabolism, breakdown of complex substances in the body, (opp. ANABOLISM); so **cătabŏ'lic** *a.* [f. Gk CATA(*bolē* a throwing) + -ISM]

cătachr|ē'sĭs (-k-) *n.* (*pl.* **~eses** *pr.* -ē'sēz). Incorrect use of words; hence **~ĕ'stic(al)** *adjs.* [L f. Gk CATA(*khrēsis* f. *khraomai* use)]

cătaclā's|ĭs *n.* (*pl.* **~es** *pr.* -ēz). (Geol.) Crushing of rocks; so **cătaclă'stic** *a.* [mod. L, f. Gk CATA(*klasis* breaking)]

că'taclăsm *n.* Violent break, disruption. [f. Gk CATA(*klasma* f. *klaō* to break)]

că'taclўsm *n.* Violent event; political or social upheaval; hence **~AL**, **~IC**, (-ĭ'zm-) *adjs.* [f. F *cataclysme* f. L f. Gk CATA(*klusmos* flood f. *kluzō* wash)]

că'tacomb (-kōōm *or* -kōm) *n.* Subterranean cemetery; (in *pl.*) the many Roman subterranean galleries with recesses excavated in sides for tombs; (in *pl.*) similar works elsewhere; cellar. [f. F *catacombes* f. LL *catacumbas* (name given in 5th c. to cemetery of St. Sebastian near Rome), of unkn. orig.]

cată'dromous *a.* (Of fish) descending to lower river or sea to spawn. [f. Gk CATA(*dromos* -running) + -OUS]

că'tafălque (-k) *n.* Decorated structure to carry coffin or effigy of distinguished person during funeral service, or for a lying in state; structure on which coffin is drawn in procession. [F, f. It. *catafalco*, of unkn. orig.; cf. SCAFFOLD]

Că'talan *a.* & *n.* (Native or language) of Catalonia in Spain. [F f. Sp.]

că'talāse (*or* -z) *n.* (Chem.) Enzyme that catalyses reduction of hydrogen peroxide. [f. CATALYSIS + -ASE]

cătalĕ'ctic *a.* & *n.* (Pros.) (Line) lacking one syllable in last foot. [f. LL f. Gk CATA(*lēktikos* ceasing f. *lēgō* cease; see -IC)]

că'talĕpsў *n.* Trance or seizure with loss of sensation and consciousness accompanied by rigidity of the body; so **cătalĕ'ptic** *a.* & *n.* [f. F *catalepsie* or f. LL *catalepsia* f. Gk CATA(*lēpsis* seizure); see -Y¹]

***că't(t)alō** *n.* (*pl.* **~es** *or* **~s**). Cross between male buffalo and domestic cow. [f. CATTLE + BUFFALO]

că'talŏgue (-g), ***-lŏg,** *n.*, & *v.t.* (Enumerate or enter in a) complete list, usu. alphabetical or under headings, and often with particulars added to items; *university course-list etc.; ~ ***raisonné*** (rāzonā'), descriptive catalogue with explanations or comments; hence **că'talŏg(u)ER¹** (-ger) *n.* [F, f. LL f. Gk *katalogos* f. CATA(*legō* choose) enrol]

cată'lpa *n.* Tree of genus *Catalpa*, with heart-shaped leaves, trumpet-shaped flowers, and long pods. [Amer. Ind. (Creek)]

că'talўse, *că'talўze, *v.t.* (Chem.) Accelerate (process) or produce by catalysis. [f. foll. after *analyse*]

cată'lўs|ĭs *n.* (*pl.* **~es** *pr.* -ēz). (Chem.) Effect produced by a substance that, without itself undergoing change, aids a chemical change in other substances; hence **cătalў'tic** *a.* [f. Gk CATA(*lusis* f. *luō* set free) dissolution]

că'talўst *n.* Substance causing catalysis; (fig.) something that facilitates a change. [f. prec. after *analyst*]

cătamară'n *n.* Raft or float of logs tied side by side, longest in middle; raft of two boats fastened side by side; sailing boat with two hulls side by side; (colloq.) quarrelsome woman. [f. Tamil *kaṭṭumaram* tied wood]

că'tamīte *n.* Boy kept for homosexual practices; passive partner in sodomy. [f. L *catamitus* thr. Etruscan f. Gk *Ganumēdēs* Ganymede, cupbearer of Zeus]

cătamou'ntain (-tĭn) *n.* Leopard, puma, or other tiger-cat; wild quarrelsome person. [ME, f. *cat of the mountain*]

cătană'nchė (-ngkĭ) *n.* Plant of genus *Catananche*, with blue or yellow flowers. [mod. L, f. L *catanancē* plant used in love-potions f. Gk *katanagkē* (*kata* down, *anagkē* compulsion)]

că'taplĕxў *n.* Sudden temporary paralysis due to fright etc.; hence **cătaplĕ'ctic** *a.* [f. Gk CATA*plēxis* stupefaction]

că'tapŭlt *n.* & *v.* **1.** *n.* (Hist.) Military machine worked by lever and ropes for discharging stones etc. **2.** ||Boy's contrivance of forked stick and elastic for shooting small stones etc.; mechanical contrivance for launching glider, aircraft from deck of ship, etc. **3.** *v.t.* Launch with catapult; fling forcibly (lit. or fig.). **4.** *v.i.* Move (as if) from catapult. [f. F *catapulte* or f. L *catapulta* f. Gk *katapeltēs* (*kata* CATA-, **pel-* cf. *pallō* hurl)]

că'tarăct *n.* Waterfall (prop. large and sheer; cf. CASCADE); downpour, rush of water; (Path.) progressive opacity of eye-lens. [f. L *cataracta* f. Gk *katarrhaktēs* down-rushing; in Path. sense prob. f. obs. sense *portcullis*]

catar̂'rh (-ar̂') *n.* Inflammation of mucous membrane; watery discharge in nose or throat due to this; hence **catar̂'rhAL** (-ral) *a.* [f. F *catarrhe* f. LL *catarrhus* f. Gk *katarrhous* f. *katarrheō* (CATA-, *rheō* flow)]

că'tarrhīne (-rīn) *a.* & *n.* (Zool.) (Monkey) having nostrils close together, and directed downwards. [f. Gk CATA- + *rhis rhinos* nose]

cată'strophė *n.* Sudden or widespread or noteworthy disaster; event subverting system of things; disastrous end, ruin; dénouement of drama; hence **cătastrŏ'phic** *a.*, **cătastrŏ'phically** *adv.* [f. L *catastropha* f. Gk CATA(*strophē* turning f. *strephō* turn)]

cată'stroph|ĭsm *n.* (Geol.) Theory that crustal

changes have occurred in sudden violent and unusual events; so ~IST (2) *n.* [f. prec. + -ISM]

cătatō'nĭa *n.* Schizophrenia with intervals of catalepsy and occas. violence; catalepsy; hence **cătatŏ'nIC** *a.* & *n.* [f. G *katatonie* (as CATA-, TONE[1], -IA[1])]

cataw'ba *n.* U.S. grape; white wine made from it. [f. River *C~* in Carolinas]

că'tboat *n.* Sailing-boat with single mast placed well forward and carrying only one sail. [perh. f. *cat* former type of coaler in N.E. England, + BOAT[1]]

cătch[1] *v.* (**caught** *pr.* kawt). **1.** *v.t.* Capture, ensnare; ~ (**up**), overtake, (abs.) make up arrears; lay hold of or *hold of* (*catch a* TARTAR[2]); be in time for (train etc., person about to depart); see (film), hear (broadcast), etc. **2.** Surprise, detect, (*at* or *in*, or do*ing*; ~ **me!, him!,** (iron.) you may be sure I etc. shall not); (in *pass.*, colloq.) become pregnant. **3.** Hit (usu. *on* part specified; *caught him on the nose*; *caught him a blow* or *one*). **4.** *v.i.* (Of fire or combustible) begin to burn. **5.** Become fixed or entangled, take hold; ~ **on,** (colloq.) (1) become popular, (2) understand what is meant. **6.** *v.t.* Snatch (esp. ~ **up, away**). **7.** Intercept motion of and hold (*nail catches dress*; *put something to catch the drips*); (Cricket etc.) prevent (ball) from touching ground after striking the bat, ~ (**out**), dismiss (batsman) by doing this; ~ **out,** (fig.) detect in a mistake etc., take unawares. **8.** Check suddenly (*catch* one's *breath*). **9.** Receive, incur, be infected with, (*cold, a* COLD[2], *a fever*; a scolding, thrashing, or 'it'; a habit; *catch* one's DEATH; *catch* FIRE[1]; *catch the* SUN). **10.** Grasp with senses or mind (meaning, sound, tune; ~ **a likeness,** see and reproduce it; ~ **a glimpse of,** see for a moment; *catch* SIGHT[1] *of*). **11.** Arrest, captivate, (attention, eye, fancy; ~ **Speaker's eye,** succeed in being called on to speak in House of Commons). **12.** **~-all,** (thing) designed to catch or include various items; **~-as-~-can,** wrestling style in which all holds are permissible; ~ **crop,** crop grown between two staple crops (in position or time); **~'fly,** plant (esp. of genus *Silene*) with sticky stem; **~'penny** *a.*, intended merely to sell readily, superficially attractive; **~-phrase,** one in frequent current use; ‖**~-points** (to derail train etc., e.g. when running away down slope); **~'weight** *a.* & *n.*, (Sports) unrestricted (as regards) weight; **~'word,** word so placed as to draw attention, e.g. first and last headwords repeated at top of dictionary etc. page, rhyming word in verse, last word (cue) of actor's speech, first word of page given at foot of previous one, word or phrase caught up and repeated esp. in connection with party politics, slogan. **13.** Hence ~'ABLE *a.* [ME, f. AF & ONF *cachier*, OF *chacier*, f. Rom. **captiare* for L *captare* try to catch; cf. CHASE[2]]

cătch[2] *n.* **1.** Act of catching; amount of fish etc. caught. **2.** (Cricket etc.) Chance of or success in catching ball (**a good** or **safe** ~, person skilful at catching). **3.** Cunning question, deception, surprise; unexpected difficulty; **~-22,** (sl.) dilemma where victim cannot win [f. novel by J. Heller 1961]. **4.** Contrivance for checking motion of door etc. **5.** Thing or person caught or worth catching, esp. in matrimony by virtue of wealth etc., (**no** ~, bad bargain, unwelcome acquisition). **6.** (Mus.) Round for three or more equal voices, occas. so devised as to produce punning or other humorous verbal combinations. [f. prec.]

că'tcher *n.* In vbl senses; (Baseball) fielder who stands behind batter. [f. CATCH[1] + -ER[1]]

că'tchĭng *a.* In vbl senses; infectious; attractive, captivating. [f. CATCH[1] + -ING[2]]

că'tchment *n.* ~ **area** (from which rainfall flows into river, reservoir, etc., (fig.) from which hospital patients, school pupils, etc. are drawn). [f. CATCH[1] + -MENT]

că'tchpōle, -pōll, *n.* (Hist.) Sheriff's officer. [OE *kæcepol* f. AF & ONF **cachepol*, OF *chacepol*, or f. AL *cacepollus* chase-fowl (as CATCH[1], L *pullus* fowl)]

că'tchup. Var. of KETCHUP.

că'tchȳ *a.* Attractive; (of tune etc.) easily remembered. [f. CATCH[1] + -Y[2]]

cāte *n.* (arch.; usu. in *pl.*) Choice food. [f. obs. *acate* purchase f. AF *acat*, OF *achat* f. *acater*, *achater* buy; see CATER[2]]

cătėchĕ't|ic(al) (-kĕ'-) *adjs.* Of or by oral teaching; according to a, or the Church, catechism; consisting of or proceeding by question and answer; hence ~ICALLY *adv.* [f. eccl. Gk *katēkhētikos* (*katēkhētēs* oral teacher; see CATECHIZE, -IC, -AL)]

că'tėchĭsm (-k-) *n.* Instruction by question and answer; published example of this, esp. on religious doctrine (**Church C~**, Anglican; **Longer** and **Shorter C~**, of Presbyterians); series of questions put to anyone; hence **cătėchĭ'smAL** (-kĭ'z-) *a.* [f. eccl. L *catechismus* (as foll.; see -ISM)]

că'tėch|ize (-k-), **-ise** (-īz), *v.t.* Instruct by question and answer, or by use of Church Catechism; put questions to, examine; so ~IST (1), **~izER**[1], *ns.* [f. LL *catechizare* f. eccl. Gk *katēkhizō* (*katēkheō* make hear f. as CATA-, *ēkheō* sound; see -IZE)]

că'tėchu (-ōō) *n.* Gambier or similar vegetable extract, containing much tannin. [mod. L, f. Malay *kachu*]

cătėchū'mĕn (-kū'-) *n.* Christian convert under instruction before baptism. [ME, f. OF *catechumene* or eccl. L *catechumenus* f. pass. part. of Gk *katēkheo* (see CATECHIZE)]

cătėgŏ'rĭcal *a.* Unconditional, absolute; explicit, direct, plain-speaking; ~ **imperative,** (Ethics) unconditional moral obligation derived from pure reason, bidding of conscience as ultimate moral law; hence ~LY[2] *adv.* [f. F *catégorique* or f. LL f. Gk *katēgorikos*; see foll., -IC, -AL]

că'tėgorȳ *n.* Class, division; (Philos.) one of a possibly exhaustive set of classes among which all things might be distributed; one of the a priori conceptions applied by the mind to sense-impressions; any relatively fundamental philosophical concept; hence **cătėgor'ĭAL** *a.* [f. F *catégorie* or f. LL f. Gk *katēgoria* statement (*katēgoros* accuser)]

catē'n|a *n.* (*pl.* **~ae** *or* **~as**). Connected series of patristic comments on Scripture, or of other things. [L, = chain; orig. *catena patrum* chain of the Fathers (of the Church)]

catē'narȳ *a.* & *n.* (Like) curve formed by uniform chain hanging freely from two points not in same vertical line; ~ **bridge,** suspension bridge hung from such chains. [f. L *catenarius* (*catena* chain; see -ARY[1])]

că'tėn|āte *v.t.* Connect like links of chain; hence ~A'TION *n.* [f. L *catenare* (as prec.) + -ATE[3]]

cā'ter[1] *n.* The four on dice. [f. F *quatre* four]

cā'ter[2] *v.i.* Purvey food; provide meals *for*; provide amusement, requisites, etc., *for*; pander *to* (evil inclinations); hence ~ER[1] *n.*, (esp.) one whose trade is to supply food for social events, ~ING[1] *n.*, such trade. [f. obs. n. *cater* (now *caterer*), f. *acater* f. AF *acatour* buyer f. *acater* buy f. Rom. *AC(*captare* catch)]

că'teran *n.* (Sc.) Highland irregular fighting-man, raider. [ME, f. med. L *cateranus* & f. Gael. *ceathairne* peasantry]

***că'tercorner, -cornered** (-erd), *adv.* & *a.*

(Placed or situated) diagonally. [f. dial. adv. *cater* diagonally (cf. CATER[1]) + CORNER + -ED[2]]

că'ter-cousin (-kŭz-) *n.* (arch.) Intimate friend. [perh. f. as CATER[2], w. ref. to boarding together]

că'terpillar *n.* Larva of butterfly or moth; similar larva of various insects; (Mech.; **P**) vehicle with endless articulated steel band (~ **track, tread**) passing round and worked by two wheels, to travel on rough ground. [perh. f. AF var. of OF *chatepelose* lit. hairy cat, infl. by obs. *piller* ravager]

că'terwaul *v.i.*, & *n.* (Make) cat's screaming. [ME, f. CAT[1] + *-waul* etc. imit.]

că'tgŭt *n.* Material used for strings of musical instruments and surgical sutures, made of twisted intestines of sheep, horse, or ass (not cat). [f. CAT[1] (reason unkn.) + GUT]

Cath. *abbr.* Cathedral; Catholic.

Că'thar *n.* (*pl.* **~s**, *or* **~i** *pr.* -ī). Member of medieval sect professing great purity; hence ~ISM (3), ~IST (2), *ns.* [f. med. L *Cathari* pl. f. Gk *katharoi* the pure]

cathar's|is *n.* (*pl.* **~es** *pr.* -ēz). **1.** (Med.) Purgation. **2.** Outlet to emotion afforded by drama etc. or (Psych.) by abreaction. [mod. L, f. Gk *katharsis* (*kathairō* cleanse); sense 2 f. Aristotle's *Poetics*]

cathar'tĭc *a.* & *n.* **1.** (Med.) Purgative (medicine). **2.** *a.* Effecting catharsis. [f. LL f. Gk *kathartikos* (as prec.; see -IC)]

Cathay' *n.* (arch. or poet.) The country China. [f. med. L *Cat(h)aya*]

cathĕ'ctĭc. See CATHEXIS.

cathē'dral *a.* & *n.* ~ **(church)**, principal church of diocese; ~ **city,** one in which there is a cathedral. [ME a. f. OF, or f. LL *cathedralis* f. L f. Gk *kathedra* chair (as CATA-, *hed-* sit); see -AL]

Că'therĭne *n.* ~ **wheel,** circular window with radial divisions, rotating firework, lateral handspring with arms and legs extended. [f. mod. L *Catharina* f. Gk *Aikaterina*, name of saint martyred on spiked wheel]

că'thèter *n.* (Med.) Tubular instrument for passing into body cavity to allow movement of fluid; hence ~IZE (1) *v.t.*, introduce catheter into. [LL, f. Gk *kathetēr* (*kathiēmi* send down)]

căthètŏ'mèter *n.* Instrument for measuring small vertical distances. [f. *cathetus* perpendicular line (L f. Gk as prec.) + -O- + -METER]

cathĕ'x|is *n.* (*pl.* **~es** *pr.* -ēz). (Psych.) Concentration of mental energy in one channel; so **cathĕ'ct**IC *a.* [f. Gk *kathexis* retention]

că'thōde *n.* (Electr.) Negative electrode or terminal (opp. ANODE); ~ **ray,** beam of electrons from cathode of high-vacuum tube caused by electric field, heat, radiation, etc.; **~-ray tube,** sealed evacuated vessel in which cathode rays produce luminous image on fluorescent screen; hence **că'thod**AL, **cathŏ'd**IC, *adjs.* [f. Gk *kathodos* descent (*kata* down, *hodos* way)]

că'tholĭc *a.* & *n.* **1.** *a.* Universal; of interest or use to all men; all-embracing, of wide sympathies, broad-minded, tolerant; **C~ Epistles** (of James etc., as not addressed to one person or church). **2. C~ Church,** (orig.) whole body of Christians; ~, belonging to or in accord with (a) this, (b) the church before separation into Greek or Eastern and Latin or Western, (c) the Latin Church after that separation (cf. ORTHODOX), (d) (often **Roman C~**) the part of the Latin Church that remained under the Roman obedience after the Reformation, (e) any church (as the Anglican) claiming continuity with (b). **3. C~ Apostolic Church,** IRVINGITES; **C~ King, his C~ Majesty,** (Hist.) King of Spain. **4.** Hence **cathŏ'l**ICALLY *adv.*, (Eccl.) **cathŏ'lĭc**ISM (2, 3) *n.*, (Eccl.) **cathŏ'lĭc**IZE (3) *v.t.*, **cătholĭ'**CITY *n.*, ~LY[2] *adv.* **5.** *n.* Member of catholic church, esp. (*C~*) Roman Catholic Church accepting jurisdiction of Pope as supreme head of that Church. [ME, f. OF *catholique* or f. LL f. Gk *katholikos* universal f. *kath' holou* in general (*kata* in respect of, *holos* whole)]

cathŏ'lĭcon *n.* Universal remedy, panacea. [ME f. F, f. mod. L *catholicum*, neut. (as n.) of LL *catholicus* (see prec.)]

Cătĭlĭnār'ĭan *a.* & *n.* (One who engages in) conspiracy, esp. against government. [f. *Catiline*, Rom. conspirator d. 63 B.C. + -ARIAN]

că'tion *n.* Ion with positive charge that moves towards cathode in presence of electric field (opp. ANION). [f. CATA- + ION]

cătiŏ'nĭc *a.* Of cation(s); having an active cation. [f. prec. + -IC]

că'tkĭn *n.* Cylindrical male or female inflorescence of willow, hazel, etc., usu. hanging and usu. downy or silky. [f. obs. Du. *katteken* kitten (as CAT[1], -KIN)]

catŏ'ptr|ĭc *a.* Of mirror, reflector, or reflection; hence ~ICS *n.* [f. Gk *katoptrikos* (*katoptron* mirror; see -IC)]

că'tsup. Var. of KETCHUP.

***că'ttalō.** See CATALO.

că'ttery̆ *n.* Place where cats are bred or looked after. [f. CAT[1] + -ERY]

că'ttĭsh, că'tty̆, *adjs.* Catlike; (esp., fig.) sly and spiteful; hence **că'ttĭsh**LY[2], **că'ttĭ**LY[2], *advs.*, **că'ttĭsh**NESS, **că'ttĭ**NESS, *ns.* [f. CAT[1] + -ISH[1], -Y[2]]

că'ttle *n. pl.* **1.** Oxen (*cattle and sheep*; **black ~,** oxen of Scottish and Welsh highland breeds, orig. black); (arch.) livestock. **2.** ||**~-cake,** concentrated food for cattle, in cake form; ||**~-grid,** ***~-guard,** ditch covered by spaced bars to allow passage of vehicles and pedestrians but not cattle etc.; **~-lifter,** cattle-thief; **~-plague,** rinderpest; ***~-rustler,** cattle-thief; **~-stop,** (N.Z.) = *cattle-grid*; **~-truck,** truck for transport of cattle, (fig.) crowded uncomfortable vehicle. [ME & AF, ONF *catel*, OF *chatel* (cf. CHATTEL) f. as CAPITAL[2]; see -LE 2]

că'ttleya (-lĭa) *n.* Amer. epiphytic orchid of genus *Cattleya*, with handsome violet, pink, or yellow flowers. [mod. L, f. W. *Cattley*, Engl. patron of botany d. 1832; see -A 1]

că'tty̆. See CATTISH.

***că'tty̆cōrner, -ered** (-*er*d). Var. of CATER-CORNER(ED).

Caucā'sĭan (-z-; *or* -zhan) *a.* & *n.* (Member) of the 'white' or light-skinned division of mankind; (native or inhabitant) of the Caucasus. [f. *Caucasus*, supposed place of origin + -IAN]

cau'cus *n.* (||usu. derog.) Local political usu. elective party committee for fighting elections, defining policy, etc.; this system as a political power; party meeting. [18th c. U.S., perh. f. Algonquin *cau'-cau-as'u* adviser]

cau'dal *a.* Of, at, like, tail; of posterior part of body; hence or cogn. ~LY[2] *adv.*, **cau'd**ATE[2] *a.* [f. mod. L *caudalis* f. L *cauda* tail; see -AL]

caudi'llō (kowdē'lyō) *n.* (*pl.* **~s**). (In Spanish-speaking countries) military or political leader. [Sp., f. LL *capitellum* dim. of *caput* head]

cau'dle *n.* (arch.) Warm gruel with spice, sugar, and wine, for invalids. [ME, f. ONF *caudel*, OF *chaudel* f. med. L **caldellum* dim. of L *caldum* hot drink (*calidus* warm)]

caught. See CATCH[1].

caul *n.* **1.** (Hist.) Woman's close-fitting indoor head-dress; plain back part of woman's indoor head-dress. **2.** Inner membrane enclosing foetus; portion of this occas. found on child's head at birth, thought to be of good omen; omentum. [ME, perh. f. OF *cale* small cap]

cau'ldron, ca'l- (kaw'-), (*or* kŏ'-) *n.* Large boiling-vessel (usu. of deep basin shape with hoop handle and removable lid). [ME, f. AF & ONF *caudron*, augment. (see -OON) f. Rom. **caldario*, L *caldarium* hot bath (*calidus* hot)]

cau'lĭflower (kŏ'l-) *n.* Variety of cabbage with large white flower-head; ~ **cheese,** savoury dish containing mainly cauliflower and cheese; ~ **ear,** ear (usu. boxer's) thickened by repeated blows. [earlier *cole-florie* etc., f. obs. F *chou-fleuri* flowered cabbage, assim. to COLE and FLOWER]

caulk, *calk, (kawk) *v.t.* Stop up seams of (ship), stop up (seams), with oakum etc. and waterproofing material or by driving plate-junctions together; hence ~'ER[1] *n.* [f. OF dial. *cauquer* tread, press with force, f. L *calcare* tread (*calx* heel)]

cau'sal (-z-) *a.* Of, acting as, expressing, due to, a cause or causes; of the nature of cause and effect; so **causă'lĭty** (-z-) *n.*, ~LY[2] *adv.* [f. LL *causalis* (as CAUSE[1]; see -AL)]

causā'tion (-z-) *n.* Causing or producing an effect; relation of cause and effect; doctrine that all things have causes. [F, or f. L *causatio* pretext etc., in med. L action of causing, f. *causare* (CAUSE[2]); see -ATION]

cau'satĭve (-z-) *a.* Acting as cause, productive *of*; (Gram.) expressing cause; hence ~LY[2] (-vlĭ) *adv.* [ME, f. OF *causatif* or f. LL *causativus* (as prec.; see -ATIVE)]

cause[1] (-z) *n.* **1.** What produces an effect; antecedent(s) invariably and unconditionally followed by a certain phenomenon; person who, agent that, occasions something; ground, reason, motive, for action etc. (*no cause for complaint*); adequate motive or justification (esp. *show cause*); **First C~,** the Creator of the universe; SECOND *cause*; hence ~'LESS (-zl-) *a.* **2.** (Law). Matter about which person goes to law; his case (*plead a cause*); lawsuit; ~ **list** (of cases awaiting trial). **3.** Side of any dispute espoused by person or party (**lost ~,** hopeless undertaking; **make common ~ with,** join side of); subject of interest (**good ~,** movement deserving support). [ME f. OF, f. L *causa*]

caus|e[2] (-z) *v.t.* Be the cause of, produce; induce, make, (person or thing *to* do, *to be* done); hence ~ER[1] *n.* [ME, f. OF *causer* or med. L *causare, causari* f. L *causa* CAUSE[1]]

'cause (kŏz *or* koz) *adv.* & *conj.* (colloq.) = BECAUSE. [abbr.]

cause célèbre (kōz sĕlĕ'br) *n.* (*pl.* ***causes célèbres*** *pr.* same). Lawsuit that attracts much attention. [F]

causerie (kōzerē') *n.* (*pl. pr.* same). Informal article or talk, esp. on literary subject. [F (*causer* talk)]

cau'seway (-zwā), (arch. or dial.) **cau'sey** (-zĭ), *n.* Raised road across low or wet place or piece of water; raised footway by road. [earlier *cauce(way)* f. AF **caucé(e)*, ONF *caucié(e)* f. Rom. **calciata* (*via*) f. L CALX lime(stone)]

cau'st|ĭc *a.* & *n.* (Substance) that burns or corrodes organic tissue (**~ic potash,** potassium hydroxide; **~ic soda,** sodium hydroxide); sarcastic, biting; (Phys.) (surface or curve) formed by intersection of rays reflected or refracted from curved surface; hence ~ICALLY *adv.*, **~ĭ'**CITY *n.*, **~ĭc**IZE (3) *v.t.* [f. L f. Gk *kaustikos* (*kaustos* burnt f. *kaiō* burn; see -IC)]

cau'terīz|e, -īs|e (-īz), *v.t.* Sear with hot iron or caustic, esp. in treatment of wound; (fig.) make callous; hence ~A'TION *n.* [f. F *cautériser* f. LL *cauterizare* f. Gk *kautēriazō* (*kautērion* branding-iron f. *kaiō* burn; see -IZE)]

cau'terў *n.* Metal instrument or caustic for searing tissue; cauterizing. [f. L f. Gk *kautērion*; see prec.]

cau'tion *n.*, & *v.t.* **1.** *n.* Prudence, taking care, avoidance of rashness, attention to safety; ||~ **money,** sum deposited as security for good conduct; hence **cau'tious** *a.*, **cau'tiousLY[2]** *adv.*, (-shus-). **2.** Warning; fact that acts as warning; warning and reprimand (*dismissed with a caution*); hence ~ARY[1] *a.* **3.** (colloq.) Surprising or amusing person or thing. **4.** *v.t.* Warn (person; *against, to* or *not to* do); warn and reprove. [ME f. OF, f. L *cautio -onis* (*cavēre caut-* take heed; see -ION)]

căvalcā'de *n.* Company or procession of riders, motor cars, etc.; any procession. [F, f. It. *cavalcata* (*cavalcare* ride f. Rom. **caballicare* f. L *caballus* pack-horse; see -ADE)]

căvalier' *n.* & *a.* **1.** *n.* Courtly gentleman, gallant, esp. as escorting a lady; (Hist.) supporter of Charles I in Civil War; (arch.) horseman. **2.** *a.* Offhand, curt, supercilious; hence ~LY[2] *adv.* [F, f. It. *cavaliere*, f. as CHEVALIER]

cavă'llў *n.* (arch.) Large sea-fish of genus *Caranx* etc. [f. Sp. *caballo* horse, *caballa* mare f. L (as foll.)]

că'valrў *n.* (usu. treated as *pl.*) Soldiers on horseback or in motor vehicles; ~ **sword,** sabre; ~ **twill,** strong fabric in double twill. [f. F *cavallerie* f. It. *cavalleria* (*cavallo* f. L *caballus* horse; see -ERY)]

căvati'na (-tē'-) *n.* Short simple song; similar piece of instrumental music, usu. slow and emotional. [It.]

cāve[1] *n.* Large natural underground hollow usu. with horizontal opening; ||(Polit.) dissident group (cf. ADULLAMITE); (*attrib.*) living in caves; **~-bear,** extinct species whose remains are found in caves; **~-dweller, ~-man,** (esp.) prehistoric man living in caves, (fig.) man of primitive or violent passions, instincts, and behaviour; **~-painting,** picture(s) of animals etc. on interior of cave esp. by prehistoric peoples. [ME f. OF, f. L *cava* (*cavus* hollow)]

cāve[2] *v.t.* & *i.* **1.** Hollow out, make into a cave; explore caves, whence **cā'**VER[1], **cā'**VING[1] (1), *ns.* **2.** ~ **in,** (cause to) subside or recede (of earth etc. over hollow, of wall yielding inwards); yield to pressure, submit, withdraw opposition. [sense 1 f. prec.; sense 2 prob. f. E. Anglian dial. *calve in*; cf. Flem. *inkalven*, Du. *afkalven*, in sim. sense]

||**cā'vė[3]** *int.* (school sl.) Look out! (as warning cry); **keep ~,** act as look-out. [L, = beware]

că'vėat *n.* (Law) process in court to suspend proceedings; warning, proviso; ~ ***emptor,*** let the buyer beware (he alone is responsible if he is disappointed). [L, = let him beware]

că'vendĭsh *n.* Tobacco softened, sweetened, and pressed into cakes. [prob. f. surname *C~*]

că'vern *n.* Underground hollow, (esp. vast) cave; dark hollow part; hence ~ED[2] (-nd), ~OUS, *adjs.* [ME, f. OF *caverne* or f. L *caverna* (*cavus* hollow)]

că'vėsson *n.* Strong nose-band used in taming troublesome horses. [f. F *caveçon* f. It. *cavezzone* augment. of *cavezza* halter f. Rom. **capitia* f. med. L *capitium* head-covering f. L *caput capitis* head]

cavĕ'tt|ō *n.* (*pl.* ~*i pr.* -ē). (Archit.) Hollowed moulding with quadrantal cross-section. [It., dim. of *cavo* hollow f. L *cavus*]

că'vĭāre, -âr, (*or* -âr') *n.* Pickled roe of sturgeon etc., eaten as delicacy; ~ **to the general,** [Shak. *Hamlet* II. ii. 457] good thing unappreciated by the ignorant. [early forms repr. It. *caviale* f. Turk. *ķāvyār*]

că'vĭl *v.i.* (||-ll-), & *n.* (Raise) captious objection (*at, about*); hence **~l**ER[1] *n.* [f. F *caviller* f. L *cavillari* (*cavilla* mockery)]

că'vĭtў *n.* Hollow place, hollow, empty space in a solid body; ~ **wall,** double wall with internal cavity; hence **căvĭt**A'TION *n.*, formation of cavity in a structure, or of bubbles in a liquid, or of a

vacuum in a liquid. [f. F *cavité* or f. LL *cavitas* f. L *cavus* hollow; see -ITY]
cavŏr′t *v.i.* (sl.) Prance. [U.S. wd, perh. f. CURVET]
cā′vȳ *n.* S. Amer. rodent of family Caviidae, esp. guinea-pig. [f. mod. L *cavia* f. Galibi *cabiai*]
caw *n.*, & *v.i.* (Make) cry of rook, crow, or raven. [imit.]
cay *n.* Insular bank or reef of coral, sand, etc.; cf. KEY[3]. [f. Sp. *cayo* shoal, reef f. F *quai*; see QUAY]
cayĕ′nne *n.* ~ (**pepper**), pungent red powder from capsicum plants, used for seasoning. [f. Tupi *kyynha*, assim. to *Cayenne* capital of French Guiana]
cay′man, cai′man, *n.* S. Amer. alligator, esp. of genus *Caiman*. [f. Sp. & Port. *caiman*, f. Carib *acayuman*]
***cay′ūse** (kī′-) *n.* Amer. Ind. pony. [Chinook]
ca′za (kah-) *n.* Turkish district under judge. [f. Turk. *kaza*, rel. to CADI]
C.B. *abbr.* ‖Companion (of the Order) of the Bath; confinement etc. to barracks.
***Cb** *symb.* columbium.
C.B.C. *abbr.* Canadian Broadcasting Corporation.
***CBD** *abbr.* cash before delivery.
‖**C.B.E.** *abbr.* Commander (of the Order) of the British Empire.
‖**C.B.I.** *abbr.* Confederation of British Industry.
***CBS** *abbr.* Columbia Broadcasting System.
‖**C.C.** *abbr.* County Council(lor); Cricket Club.
c.c. *abbr.* cubic centimetre(s).
C.C.C. *abbr.* Corpus Christi College.
‖**C.C.F.** *abbr.* Combined Cadet Force.
C.D. *abbr.* civil defence; *Corps Diplomatique*.
‖**Cd.** *abbr.* COMMAND[2] Paper (third series, 1900–1918).
cd *abbr.* candela.
Cd *symb.* cadmium.
Cdr. *abbr.* Commander.
Cdre. *abbr.* Commodore.
***CDT** *abbr.* Central Daylight Time.
C.E. *abbr.* Church of England; civil engineer; Common Era.
Ce *symb.* cerium.
cēanō′thus *n.* Shrub of genus *Ceanothus*, with usu. blue flowers. [mod. L, f. Gk *keanōthos* kind of thistle]
cease[1] *v.* **1.** *v.i.* (literary). Desist *from*; (of feelings, actions) come to an end. **2.** *v.t.* (literary). Stop do*ing*, be*ing*, etc. (or *to* do, be, etc.); bring to an end (strife, endeavours, etc.). **3.** (Mil.) ~ **fire**, discontinue firing; ~**-fire** *n.*, signal to do this, time or period when hostilities are discontinued. [ME, f. OF *cesser* f. L *cessare* frequent. of *cedere cess-* yield]
cease[2] *n.* (literary). **Without** ~, ~′LESS (-sl-) *a.*, not ceasing; hence ~**′lèss**LY[2] (-sl-) *adv.* [f. OF *ces* (*cesser*; see prec.)]
cē′citȳ *n.* (poet., usu. fig.) Blindness. [f. L *caecitas* (*caecus* blind; see -ITY)]
***cē′cum.** See CAECUM.
cē′dar *n.* Evergreen coniferous tree of genus *Cedrus*, with fragrant durable wood; one of various similar trees; ~(**wood**), wood of cedar, esp. of *Juniperus virginiana*; hence ~**n** [-EN[5]] *a.* (poet.). [ME f. OF *cedre*, f. L f. Gk *kedros*]
cēde *v.t.* Give up, grant, admit, surrender (territory). [f. F *céder* or f. L *cedere* yield]
cėdĭ′lla *n.* Mark written under *c* (*ç*) to show that it is sibilant; similar mark under *s* in Turkish, etc. [f. Sp. *cedilla*, dim. of *zeda* f. Gk *zēta* letter Z]
‖**C.E.G.B.** *abbr.* Central Electricity Generating Board.
ceilidh (kā′lĭ) *n.* (Sc. & Ir.) Informal gathering for music, dancing, song, and story. [Gael.]
cei′lĭng (sē′-) *n.* Lining of roof of room; top of room or other compartment; (Aeron.) maximum altitude a given aircraft can attain under specified conditions; altitude of base of cloud layer; upper limit of prices, wages, performance, etc.; (Naut.) inside planking of ship's bottom and sides. [f. *ceil* form ceiling for (perh. f. L *celare* hide) + -ING[1] (2)]
cĕ′ladŏn *n.* & *a.* Willow green; grey-green glaze used on some pottery; Chinese pottery thus glazed. [F, f. name of character in D'Urfé's *L'Astrée*]
cĕ′landīne *n.* One of two yellow-flowered plants, **greater** ~ (*Chelidonium majus*) and **lesser** ~ (*Ranunculus ficaria*). [ME and OF *celidoine* f. med. L *celidonia*, for L *chelidonia* (*herba* plant) f. Gk *khelidonion* (*khelidōn* the swallow); for *-n-* cf. *passenger*]
-cēle *comb. form.* (Path.) Tumour (of specified part), as *gastrocele*. [f. Gk *kēlē* tumour]
cĕ′lèbrant *n.* Officiating priest, esp. at Eucharist. [F, or f. L *celebrare* (see foll., -ANT)]
cĕ′lèbr|āte *v.* **1.** *v.t.* Perform publicly and duly (religious ceremony etc.); officiate at (Eucharist); observe (festival), honour, with rites, festivities, etc.; praise widely, extol; (in *p.p.*) widely known. **2.** *v.i.* Officiate at Eucharist; engage in festivities after success etc. **3.** So ~A′TION, ~**ātor**, *ns.*, ~**āt**ORY *a.* [f. L *celebrare* (*celeber -bris* frequented, renowned) + -ATE[3]]
cèlĕ′brĭtȳ *n.* Being famous; well-known person. [f. F *célébrité* or f. L *celebritas* (*celeber*; see prec., -ITY)]
cèlĕ′rĭăc *n.* Variety of celery with root like turnip. [f. CELERY; *-ac* unexplained]
cèlĕ′rĭtȳ *n.* Swiftness (of living movement or agency). [ME, f. F *célérité* f. L *celeritas -tatis* (*celer* swift; see -ITY)]
cĕ′lerȳ *n.* Plant (*Apium graveolens*) whose blanched stem is used as salad and vegetable; ~ **pine,** Austral. tree with branchlets like celery leaves. [f. F *céleri* f. It. dial. *selleri* f. L f. Gk *selinon* parsley]
cèlĕ′sta *n.* (Mus.) Small keyboard instrument with hammers striking metal bars, giving notes like those of glockenspiel. [pseudo-L, f. F *céleste* (see foll.)]
cèlĕ′ste *n.* Organ and harmonium stop with soft tremulous tone; =prec. [f. F *céleste* heavenly f. L *caelestis* (*caelum* heaven)]
cèlĕ′stĭal *a.* Of the sky (*celestial equator, globe, map,* SPHERE); heavenly, divine, divinely good, beautiful, etc., whence ~LY[2] *adv.*; **C**~ **Empire,** (Hist.) China [transl. of native title]; ~ **navigation** (using observed positions of heavenly bodies). [ME f. OF, f. med. L *caelestialis* f. L *caelestis* (see prec., -IAL)]
***cē′lĭăc.** See COELIAC.
cĕ′lĭbate *a.* & *n.* (Of) unmarried person, esp. one bound or resolved not to marry; so **cĕ′lĭb**ACY *n.* [f. F *célibat* or f. L *caelibatus* unmarried state (*caelebs -ibis* unmarried; see -ATE[1])]
cĕll *n.* **1.** Small room for one person in monastery; similar room in prison (**condemned** ~ for person condemned to death); compartment in bees' comb; (Electr.) vessel containing electrodes for current-generation or electrolysis; hermit's one-roomed dwelling; (Hist.) dependent monastery or nunnery. **2.** Enclosed cavity in organism or mineral; one of imaginary compartments of brain, assigned to various faculties; (Biol.) portion of protoplasm usu. enclosed in membrane, ultimate element of organic structures; (fig., of group of persons) centre or nucleus of political (esp. revolutionary or subversive) activities. **3.** Hence (-)~ED[2] (-ld) *a.* [ME f. OF *celle*, or f. L *cella* storeroom etc.]
cĕ′llar *n.*, & *v.t.* (Put or store in an) underground room; (**wine-**)~, place in which wine is kept, person's stock of wine (*keeps a good cellar*); hence ~AGE (1) *n.*, ~ER[1] *n.*, monastic officer in charge

of wine etc. [ME f. AF *celer*, OF *celier* f. LL *cellarium* storehouse (see prec., -AR², -ARY¹)]
cĕllarĕ't *n.* Case or sideboard for holding wine-bottles in dining-room. [f. prec. + -ET¹]
cĕ'll|ō (ch-) *n.* (*pl.* **~os**). Violoncello; hence ~IST (3) *n.* [abbr.]
cĕ'llophāne, C-, *n.* Transparent wrapping material made from viscose. [**P,** f. CELLULOSE + -O- + *-phane* (cf. DIAPHANOUS)]
cĕ'llūlar *a.* Of or having small compartments or cavities; porous; (Physiol.) of or consisting of cells; ~ **blanket, shirt,** etc., (of open texture); ~ **plant** (without distinct stem, leaves, etc.); hence **cĕllūlă'r**ITY *n.* [f. F *cellulaire* f. mod. L *cellularis*; see foll., -AR¹]
cĕ'llūl|e *n.* (Anat.) Small cell or cavity; hence or cogn. (as derivs. of CELL 2) ~ATE², ~OUS, *adjs.*, ~A'TION *n.* [F, or f. L *cellula* (*cella* cell; see -ULE)]
cĕllūlī'tĭs *n.* Inflammation of cellular tissue. [f. as prec. + -ITIS]
cĕ'llūloid *n.* Plastic made from camphor and cellulose nitrate; piece of this; (fig.) cinema films. [***P,** irreg. f. foll. + -OID]
cĕ'llūlōse (*or* -z) *n.*, & *v.t.* **1.** *n.* (Chem.) carbohydrate forming main constituent of plant-cell walls and textile fibres; (pop.) paint or lacquer consisting of esp. cellulose acetate or nitrate in solution; hence **cĕllūlō's**IC (-z-) *a.* **2.** *v.t.* Treat with cellulose. [F (as CELLULE; see -OSE²)]
***cē'lom.** See COELOM.
Cĕ'lsĭus *a.* Pertaining to the ~ **scale** of temperature, on which water freezes at 0° and boils at 100° under standard conditions. [f. A. ~, Sw. astronomer d. 1744]
Cĕlt¹ (*or* k-) *n.* Member of one of a group of W. Eur. peoples (incl. ancient Gauls and Britons; modern Bretons, Cornish, Gaels, Irish, Manx, Welsh). [f. L *Celtae* pl. f. Gk *Keltoi*]
cĕlt² *n.* (Archaeol.) Stone or metal chisel-edged prehistoric implement. [f. (?) L *celtes*]
Cĕ'ltĭc (*or* k-) *a.* & *n.* (Language) of the Celts and kindred peoples; ~ **cross,** Latin cross with circle round centre; ~ **fringe,** the Highland Scots, Irish, Welsh, and Cornish, in relation to the rest of Britain; ~ **Sea,** sea area S. of Ireland & W. of Cornwall; ~ **twilight,** romantic fairy-tale atmosphere of Ir. folklore [f. title of Yeats's anthology]; hence ~ISM (2, 4) *n.*, ~IZE (2, 3) *v.i.* & *t.* [f. L *celticus* (as CELT¹; see -IC) or F *celtique*]
cĕ'mbalō (ch-) *n.* (*pl.* **~s**). Harpsichord. [abbr. of CLAVICEMBALO]
cėmĕ'nt *n.*, & *v.t.* **1.** *n.* Substance applied as paste and hardening into stony consistency for binding together stones or bricks and for forming floors, walls, etc.; strong mortar of calcined lime and clay (**hydraulic** ~, kind hardening under water); any substance applied soft for sticking things together; substance for filling teeth; bony substance surrounding root of tooth; (fig.) principle that unites. **2.** *v.t.* Unite (as) with cement (lit. or fig.); apply cement to, line or cover with cement; hence **cēmĕnt**A'TION *n.*, (esp.) heating of iron with charcoal powder to form steel. [ME, f. OF *ciment* f. L *caementum* quarry stone (*caedere* hew; see -MENT)]
cĕ'mėterȳ (-trĭ) *n.* Place for burials, other than a churchyard. [f. LL f. Gk *koimētērion* dormitory (*koimaō* put to sleep)]
‖**C.Eng.** *abbr.* chartered engineer.
***cē'nobīte.** See COENOBITE.
cĕ'notaph (-ahf) *n.* Sepulchral monument to person whose body is elsewhere; ‖**the C~,** (esp.) that in London commemorating the dead of the 1914–18 and 1939–45 wars; empty tomb. [f. F *cénotaphe* f. LL *cenotaphium* f. Gk *kenos* empty + *taphos* tomb]
cĕnō'tė *n.* Natural underground reservoir used as sacrificial well by Mayas. [Mex. Sp., f. Maya *conot*]
***cēnozō'ĭc.** See CAINOZOIC.
cĕnse *v.t.* Perfume or worship with burning incense. [ME, f. OF *encenser* INCENSE²]
cĕ'nser *n.* Vessel in which incense is burnt, esp. one that is swung during religious ceremony. [ME f. AF; OF *censier* f. *encensier* (*encens* INCENSE¹; see -ER² (2))]
cĕ'nsor *n.*, & *v.t.* **1.** *n.* Person expressing opinions on others' morals and conduct. **2.** Official with power to suppress whole or parts of books, plays, films, letters, news, etc. on grounds of obscenity, seditiousness, etc. **3.** (Rom. Hist.) Magistrate who compiled censuses and supervised conduct. **4.** (Psych.) Power by which certain unconscious ideas and memories are prevented from emerging into the consciousness. **5.** Hence or cogn. **cĕnsōr'**IAL *a.*, ~SHIP *n.* **6.** *v.t.* Act as censor (sense 2) of; make deletions or changes in. [L, f. *censēre* assess (see -OR); in sense 4 mistransl. of G *zensur* censorship]
cĕnsōr'ĭous *a.* Fault-finding, severely critical; hence ~LY² *adv.*, ~NESS *n.* [f. L *censorius* (CENSOR; see -ORY) + -OUS]
cĕ'nsur|e (-sher) *n.*, & *v.t.* **1.** *n.* Adverse judgement, expression of disapproval, reprimand. **2.** *v.t.* Criticize harshly and unfavourably; reprove; hence ~ABLE *a.* [ME f. OF, f. L *censura* (*censēre* assess; see -URE); v. f. F *censurer*]
cĕ'nsus *n.* Official numbering of population with various statistics. [L (*censēre* assess)]
cĕnt *n.* **1.** See PER CENT. **2.** Hundredth of U.S. etc. dollar or other coin; typical small coin (*don't care a cent*). [F, or f. It. *cento* or L *centum* hundred]
cent. *abbr.* century.
‖**cĕ'ntal** *n.* Weight of 100 lb., esp. of corn. [f. L *centum* hundred + -AL]
cĕ'ntaur *n.* (Gk Myth.) Horse with human body, arms, and head, in place of its neck and head. [ME, f. L f. Gk *kentauros*, of unkn. orig.]
cĕ'ntaurȳ *n.* Plant of genus *Centaurium*, esp. *C. umbellatum*, formerly used in medicine. [f. LL *centauria*, *-ea*, f. L f. Gk *kentaur(e)ion* (*kentauros*, see prec.); said to have been discovered by the centaur Chiron]
cĕntėnār'ĭan *a.* & *n.* (Person) a hundred or more years old. [f. as foll. + -AN]
cĕntē'narȳ (*or* sĕ'ntĭ-) *a.* & *n.* (Festival) of the hundredth anniversary. [f. L *centenarius* (*centeni* a hundred each f. *centum* hundred; see -ARY¹)]
cĕntĕ'nnĭal *a.* & *n.* **1.** *a.* Lasting, occurring every, hundred years; ***C~ State,** Colorado. **2.** *n.* = prec. [f. L *centum* hundred, after *biennial*]
***cĕ'nter¹,².** See CENTRE¹,².
cĕ'ntering. See CENTRING.
cĕntĕ'sĭmal *a.* Reckoning or reckoned by hundredths; hence ~LY² *adv.* [f. L *centesimus* hundredth (*centum* hundred) + -AL]
cĕ'ntĭ- *comb. form.* Hundred; one-hundredth, esp. of a unit in the metric system, as: *centi*GRAM², *centi*LITRE, CENTIMETRE. [f. L *centum* hundred + -I-]
cĕ'ntĭgrāde *a.* Having a hundred degrees; esp. = CELSIUS. [F, f. L *centum* hundred + *gradus* step]
ce'ntime (sah'ntēm) *n.* One-hundredth of a franc. [F, f. L (as CENTESIMAL)]
cĕ'ntĭmētre (-ter), ***-mēter,** *n.* One-hundredth of a metre, about 0·4 inch; (as unit of rainfall or pressure, cf. INCH¹); **~-gram-second system** (using these as basic units of length, mass, and time). [f. CENTI- + METRE²]
cĕ'ntĭpēde *n.* Many-legged arthropod of class Chilopoda. [f. F *centipède* or f. L *centipeda* (*centum* hundred, *pes pedis* foot)]
cĕ'ntō *n.* (*pl.* **~s**). Composition made up of

quotations from other authors. [L, = patchwork garment]

CENTO (sĕ'ntō) *abbr.* Central Treaty Organization.

cĕ'ntral *a.* & *n.* **1.** *a.* Of, in, at, from, containing, the centre; leading, principal, dominant, essential; *central* BANK³; **~ heating,** method of warming a building by hot water or hot air or steam conveyed by pipes from central source, or by general system of radiators etc.; **~ nervous system,** brain and spinal cord; **C~ Powers,** Germany and Austria-Hungary before 1914; **C~ Time,** standard time used in central Canada and U.S.; hence **cĕntră'l**ITY, ~NESS, *ns.*, ~LY² *adv.* **2.** *n.* *Telephone exchange. [F, or f. L *centralis* (*centrum* CENTRE¹; see -AL)]

Cĕntrā'lia *n.* Remote central regions of Australia. [f. prec. + *Australia*]

cĕ'ntral|ĭsm *n.* Centralizing system; so ~IST (2) *n.* [f. CENTRAL + -ISM]

cĕ'ntralīz|e, -is|e (-īz), *v.i.* & *t.* Come or bring to a centre; concentrate (administration) at single centre; subject (State etc.) to this system; hence ~A'TION *n.* [f. CENTRAL + -IZE, or f. F *centraliser*]

cĕ'ntre¹ (-*ter*), ***cĕ'nter¹,** *n.* & *a.* **1.** *n.* Middle point (equidistant from ends of line or from extremities of regular surface or body, or from all points on circumference of arc or circle or sphere); DEAD *centre.* **2.** Point, pivot, axis, of revolution; (in lathe etc.) conical adjustable support for workpiece. **3.** Point of concentration or dispersion, nucleus, source. **4.** Place or group of buildings forming central point in district etc. or main area for an activity (*city,* DETENTION, HEALTH, *shopping, centre*). **5.** Filling within chocolates etc. **6.** = CENTRING. **7.** (Mil.) Main body of troops between wings. **8.** (Polit.) Party or group holding moderate opinions. **9.** (Footb. & Hockey). Middle player in line; kick or hit from wing to centre of pitch. **10. ~ of attraction,** (Phys.) point to which bodies tend by gravity, (fig.) person or thing drawing general attention; **~-bit,** boring tool with centre point and side cutters; **~-board** (for lowering through boat's keel to prevent leeway); **~-fold,** = *centre spread*; **~-forward, ~-half,** middle player or position in forward, half-back, line; *centre of* GRAVITY, *of* MASS²; **~-piece,** ornament for middle of table, principal item; **~ of pressure,** point at which single force can be applied to balance pressure over whole surface; **~-second,** (clock or watch with) seconds hand mounted on centre arbor; **~ spread,** two facing middle pages of newspaper etc.; **~ three-quarter,** (Rugby Footb.) one of two middle players in line of three-quarters. **11.** Hence **cĕ'ntr**IC(AL) *adjs.*, **cĕntrĭ'**CITY *n.* **12.** *a.* At or of the centre; hence ~MOST (-*erm*-) *a.* [ME, f. OF *centre* or f. L *centrum* f. Gk *kentron* sharp point]

cĕ'ntre² (-*ter*), ***cĕ'nter²,** *v.* **1.** *v.i.* Be concentrated *in, on, at,* (*a*)*round.* **2.** *v.t.* Place in centre; mark with a centre; concentrate *in* etc.; (Footb. & Hockey) kick or hit (ball) from wing to centre of pitch. [f. prec.]

centreing. See CENTRING.

-cĕ'ntrĭc *suf.* forming *adjs.* w. sense 'having a (specified) centre', as: ANTHROPO*centric,* CONCENTRIC, ECCENTRIC, HELIO*centric.* [after *concentric* etc. f. Gk *kentrikos* (as CENTRE¹; see -IC)]

cĕntrĭ'fūgal (*or* sĕ'-) *a.* Moving or tending to move from centre; **~ force** (with which body revolving round centre seems to tend to fly off); **~ machine** etc. (in which rotation causes centrifugal motion); hence ~LY² *adv.* [f. mod. L *centrifugus* (*centrum* CENTRE¹, *-fugus* -fleeing f. *fugere* flee) + -AL]

cĕ'ntrĭfūge *n.*, & *v.t.* **1.** *n.* Centrifugal machine rotating at very high speed, designed to separate solids from liquids, or liquids from other liquids (e.g. cream from milk). **2.** *v.t.* Subject to centrifugal motion; separate by centrifuge; hence **cĕntrĭfūg**A'TION *n.* [F, f. as prec.]

cĕ'ntrĭng, cĕ'ntreĭng, cĕ'nterĭng, (-*ter*-) *n.* Temporary framing used to support arch, dome, etc., while under construction. [f. CENTRE² + -ING¹]

cĕntrĭ'pėtal *a.* Moving or tending to move towards centre (opp. CENTRIFUGAL); hence ~LY² *adv.* [f. mod. L *centripetus* (*centrum* CENTRE¹, *-petus* -seeking f. *petere* seek) + -AL]

cĕ'ntr|ĭst *n.* (Polit. etc.) Holder of moderate views; so ~ISM (3) *n.* [f. CENTRE¹ + -IST]

cĕ'ntūple *a.*, *n.*, & *v.* **1.** *a.* & *n.* Hundredfold (amount). **2.** *v.t.* & *i.* Multiply by a hundred. [F, or f. eccl. L *centuplus, centuplex* f. L *centum* hundred]

cĕntūr'ĭon *n.* Commander of century in ancient Roman army. [ME, f. L *centurio -onis* (as foll.)]

cĕ'ntūrў (*or* -cherĭ) *n.* **1.** Company in ancient Roman army, orig. of 100 men; political division for voting in ancient Rome. **2.** A hundred of something; hundred runs at cricket; hundred-year period reckoned successively from an accepted epoch, esp. from birth of Christ (**first ~,** 1–100, **twentieth ~,** 1901–2000, **second century** B.C., 200–101 B.C., etc.); any hundred successive years; **~ plant,** agave, flowering only once in many years. [f. L *centuria* (*centum* hundred; see -Y¹)]

cĕp *n.* Edible mushroom of genus *Boletus.* [f. F *cèpe* f. Gascon *cep,* f. L *cippus* stake]

cėphă'lĭc *a.* Of or in the head; **~ index,** quantity expr. ratio of head's greatest breadth and length. [f. F *céphalique* f. L f. Gk *kephalikos* (*kephalē* head; see -IC)]

-cėphă'lĭc. See -CEPHALOUS.

cĕ'phalopŏd *n.* Mollusc of class Cephalopoda, with distinct tentacled head, e.g. cuttlefish and octopus. [f. Gk *kephalē* head + -O- + Gk *pous podos* foot]

cĕphalothôr'ăx *n.* Fused head and thorax of spider, crab, etc. [f. as prec. + THORAX]

-cĕ'phalous, -cėphă'lĭc, *comb. form.* (esp. Anthropol.) = -headed, as: BRACHY~, DOLICHO~. [f. Gk *kephalē* head + -OUS, -IC]

cē'phėĭd *n.* (Astron.) Variable star with typical curve of brightness change, used to measure distances. [f. δ *Cephei* orig. example (*Cepheus* constellation f. name of mythical king) + -ID³]

cėră'm|ĭc *a.* & *n.* **1.** *a.* Of (the art of) pottery; of (substances produced by) process of strong heating of clay etc. minerals. **2.** *n.* Article made of pottery; substance made by firing clay etc. minerals at high temperatures. **3.** Hence ~ICS, **cĕ'ram**IST (3), *ns.* [f. Gk *keramikos* (*keramos* pottery; see -IC)]

cėră'stēs (-z) *n.* Horned viper of N. Africa etc. [L f. Gk *kerastēs* (*keras* horn)]

cėră'stĭum *n.* Plant of genus *Cerastium,* with white flowers and often horn-shaped capsules. [mod. L, f. Gk *kerastēs* horned (*keras* horn)]

cĕrato-, kĕrato-, *comb. form.* Horn; cornea. [f. Gk *keras -atos* horn]

Cĕr'berus *n.* **Sop to ~,** something to propitiate an official, guard, etc. [L, f. Gk *Kerberos* three-headed dog guarding entrance to Hades]

cēre *n.* Naked waxlike membrane at base of some birds' beaks. [f. L *cera* wax]

cēr'ėal *a.* & *n.* **1.** *a.* Of corn or edible grain. **2.** *n.* (usu. in *pl.*) Kind(s) of grain used for human food; food made from wheat, maize, or other cereal (usu. as breakfast dish). [f. L *cerealis* (*Ceres* goddess of agriculture; see -AL)]

cĕrėbĕ'll|um *n.* Smaller (posterior) part of brain; hence ~AR *a.* [L, dim. of CEREBRUM]

cĕ′rėbral *a.* Of the brain; (of literature, music, etc.) appealing to the intellect rather than to the emotions; clever; intellectual; (Phonet.) cacuminal; ~ **palsy,** spastic paralysis from brain damage before or at birth, with jerky or uncontrolled movements. [f. L *cerebrum* brain + -AL]

cĕrėbrā′tion *n.* Working of the brain, esp. **unconscious** ~ (of results reached without conscious thought); hence **cĕ′rėbr**ATE[3] *v.i.* [f. as prec. + -ATION]

cĕrėbrō- *comb. form.* Brain, as: **~-spi′nal,** of brain and spine; **~to′nic,** like ectomorph in temperament, with predominantly intellectual interests; **~-vas′cular,** of the brain and its blood-vessels. [f. as foll. + -O-]

cĕ′rėbrum *n.* Principal (anterior) part of brain. [L]

cēr′eclŏth (sēr′k-; *or* -awth) *n.* Waxed cloth used as waterproof covering or (esp.) as winding-sheet. [earlier *cered cloth* f. *cere* to wax f. L *cerare* (*cera* wax)]

cer′ement (sēr′m-) *n.* (usu. in *pl.*; arch.) Grave-clothes. [first used by Shak. in *Hamlet* (1602); app. f. prec. + -MENT]

cĕrėmō′nĭal *a.* & *n.* **1.** *a.* With or of ritual or ceremony, formal; hence ~ISM (3), ~IST (2), *ns.*, ~LY[2] *adv.* **2.** *n.* System of rites; formalities proper to any occasion; observance of conventions; (R.C. Ch.) book containing order of ritual. [f. LL *caerimonialis* (as CEREMONY; see -AL)]

cĕrėmō′nĭous *a.* Addicted or showing addiction to ceremony, punctilious; hence ~LY[2] *adv.*, ~NESS *n.* [f. F *cérémonieux* or f. LL *caerimoniosus* (as foll.; see -OUS)]

cĕ′rėmon|y̆ *n.* Outward rite or observance; empty form; formalities; punctilious behaviour; **Master of C~ies,** person in charge of ceremonies that are observed on state or public occasions, person introducing speakers at banquet or entertainers in variety show; **stand on ~y,** insist on observance of formalities; **without ~y,** informally, casually. [ME, f. OF *ceremonie* or f. L *caerimonia* religious worship]

Cerenkov. See CHERENKOV.

cĕ′rėsĭn *n.* Hard whitish wax used with or instead of beeswax. [f. mod. L *ceres* f. L *cera* wax, + -IN]

ceri′se (-ē′z *or* -ē′s) *a.* & *n.* (Of) a light clear red. [F, = cherry]

cēr′ĭum *n.* (Chem.) Metallic element of lanthanide series. [f. *Ceres,* an asteroid discovered (1801) just previously, + -IUM]

cēr′mĕt *n.* Heat-resistant alloy of ceramic with metal. [f. CERAMIC + METAL]

CERN (sērn) *abbr.* European Organization for Nuclear Research. [f. F *Conseil Européen pour la Recherche Nucléaire,* former title]

cērо- *comb. form.* Wax, as: **~graphy** (-ŏ′g-), writing or designing on or with wax; **~pla′stic,** modelled in wax, of wax-modelling. [f. L *cera* or Gk *kēros* wax]

||**cērt** *n.* (sl.) Event or result certain to happen; horse certain to win race. [abbr. of CERTAIN(TY)]

cert. *abbr.* certificate; certified.

cēr′tain (-tan *or* -tĭn) *a.* **1.** Settled, unfailing; unerring, reliable; that may be relied on to happen (**for** ~, as a certainty; **make** ~ **of,** ensure that one will obtain); indisputable; confident, convinced, (*of, that*); destined, undoubtedly going, *to* do. **2.** That might but need not or should not be specified (*a certain person*; *lady of a certain age*); some though not much (*felt a certain reluctance*); existing but probably unknown to reader or hearer (*a certain John Smith*). [ME f. OF, f. Rom. **certanus* f. L *certus* settled]

cēr′tainlȳ (-tan-) *adv.* Indubitably; infallibly; confidently; admittedly; (in answers) I admit it, no doubt, yes. [f. prec. + -LY[2]]

cēr′taintȳ (-tan-) *n.* Undoubted fact (**bet on a** ~, usu. dishonestly with secret knowledge of result; MORAL *certainty*), indubitable prospect; thing in actual possession; absolute conviction (*of, that*); **for a** ~, beyond possibility of doubt. [ME f. AF *certainté,* OF *-eté* (as CERTAIN, -TY[1])]

Cert. Ed. *abbr.* Certificate in Education.

cēr′tės (-z) *adv.* (arch.) Assuredly; I assure you. [ME f. OF, prob. f. Rom. **ad certas* for a certainty f. L (as CERTAIN)]

cēr′tĭfīable *a.* Able to be certified, (esp.) insane. [f. CERTIFY + -ABLE]

certĭ′fĭcate *n.*, & *v.t.* **1.** *n.* Document formally attesting a fact, esp. birth, marriage, death, medical condition, abilities, fulfilment of requirements, ownership of shares, etc.; **C~ of Secondary Education,** examination set for secondary-school pupils in England and Wales, certificate gained by passing it. **2.** *v.t.* (-āt; esp. in *p.p.*) Provide with or license or attest by certificate; hence **cērtĭfĭc**A′TION *n.* [f. F *certificat* or f. med. L *certificatum* neut. p.p. (as n.) of *certificare* (see foll.)]

cēr′tĭf|ȳ *v.t.* Make formal statement of, declare by certificate; officially declare (person) insane; (arch.) inform with certainty; **~ied cheque** (value of which is guaranteed by bank); ***~ied mail** (whose delivery is recorded); **~ied milk** (guaranteed free from tuberculosis bácillus); ***~ied public accountant,** accountant holding certificate of professional competence. [ME, f. OF *certifier* f. med. L *certificare* f. L *certus* certain; see -FY]

certiorari (sērtĭerār′ī *or* sērshĭerār′ē) *n.* Writ from higher court for records of case tried in lower. [LL, pass. of *certiorare* inform (*certior* compar. of *certus* certain)]

cēr′tĭtūde *n.* Feeling certain or convinced. [ME, f. LL *certitudo* (*certus* certain; see -TUDE)]

ceru′lėan (-ōō′-) *a.* Deep-blue like clear sky. [f. L *caeruleus* sky-blue (*caelum* sky; see -EAN)]

ceru′m|ĕn (-ōō′-) *n.* Yellow waxy substance in outer ear; hence **~in**OUS *a.* [mod. L, f. L *cera* wax]

cēr′use (-ōōs; *or* sĭrōō′s) *n.* White LEAD[1]. [ME f. OF, f. L *cerussa,* perh. f. Gk (*kēros* wax)]

cēr′velat (-ah) *n.* Kind of smoked pork sausage. [obs. F, f. It. *cervellata*]

cēr′vĭcal *a.* (Anat.) Of neck; of cervix. [F, or f. mod. L *cervicalis,* f. L *cervix -icis* neck; see -AL]

cēr′vīne *a.* Of or like deer. [f. L *cervinus* (*cervus* deer; see -INE[1])]

cēr′vĭ|x *n.* (*pl.* **~ces** *pr.* -sēz). (Anat.) Neck; necklike structure, esp. that of womb. [L]

***Cesarean, -ian.** Vars. of CAESAREAN (in Med. sense).

Cėsă′rėvĭtch, -wĭtch, (-z-) *n.* (Hist.) eldest son of Tsar; ||(-*w*-) horse-race run annually at Newmarket. [f. Russ. *tsesarevich*]

***cesium.** See CAESIUM.

cĕss[1] *n.* (Sc., Ir., India, etc.) Tax, rate. [prop. *sess* for obs. *assess* n.; see ASSESS]

cĕss[2] *n.* (Ir.) **Bad ~ to,** may evil befall. [perh. f. prec.]

cĕssā′tion *n.* Ceasing; pause. [ME, f. L *cessatio* (*cessare* CEASE[1]; see -ATION)]

cĕ′sser *n.* (Law). Coming to an end, cessation, (*of* term, liability, etc.). [AF & OF, = CEASE[1]; see -ER[4]]

cĕ′ssion (-shon) *n.* Ceding, giving up, (*of* rights, property, or esp. *of* territory by State). [ME f. OF, or f. L *cessio* (*cedere cess-* go away; see -ION)]

cĕ′ssionarȳ (-shon-) *n.* = ASSIGN[2]. [f. LL *cessionarius* f. as prec.; see -ARY[1]]

cĕ′sspit *n.* Pit for disposal of refuse; = foll. [f. foll. + PIT[1]]

cĕ'sspōōl *n.* Underground chamber for temporary storage of liquid waste or sewage; (fig.) ~ (=SINK²) **of iniquity** etc. [perh. alt., after POOL¹, f. earlier *cesperalle*, f. *suspiral* vent, water-pipe, f. OF *souspirail* air-hole f. as SUSPIRE; see -AL 2]

cĕ'stōde, cĕ'stoid, *n.* (Zool.) Ribbon-like intestinal worm, esp. tapeworm. [f. L f. Gk *kestos* girdle + -ODE, -OID]

C.E.T. *abbr.* Central European Time.

cėtā'cean (-shan) *a.* & *n.* (Member) of the mammalian order Cetacea, containing whales; so **cėtA'**CEOUS *a.* [f. mod. L *Cetacea* f. L *cetus* f. Gk *kētos* whale; see -ACEAN]

cē'tāne *n.* (Chem.) Hydrocarbon ($C_{16}H_{34}$) of paraffin series, found in petroleum; ~ **number,** quantity measuring ignition properties of diesel oil. [f. SPERMACETI, after *methane* etc.]

cĕ'terăch (-k) *n.* Fern of genus *Ceterach*, having backs of fronds covered with scales. [med. L, f. Pers. *šaytarak* f. Arab. *šayṭaraj*]

ceteris paribus (kāterēs păr'ĭbus; *or* sĕt-) *adv.* Other things being equal or unchanged. [L]

Ceylŏ'n (sĭ-) *n.* ~ **moss,** E. Ind. red seaweed (*Gracilaria lichenoides*); hence ~E'SE (sĭlonē'z) *a.* & *n.* [island S. of India, now Sri Lanka]

||**C.F.** *abbr.* Chaplain to the Forces.

c.f. *abbr.* carried forward.

cf. *abbr.* compare. [f. L *confer* imper.]

Cf *symb.* californium.

||**C.G.M.** *abbr.* Conspicuous Gallantry Medal.

C.G.S. *abbr.* centimetre-gram-second; Chief of General Staff.

||**C.H.** *abbr.* Companion of Honour.

ch. *abbr.* chapter; chestnut; church.

||**cha** (-ah) *n.* (sl.) Tea. [f. as CHAR⁴]

Chă'blis (shă'blē) *n.* A white burgundy wine. [~ in E. France]

cha-cha-cha' (chahchahchah') *n.*, & *v.i.* (Perform) a ballroom dance with Latin-Amer. rhythm. [Amer. Sp.]

chacŏ'nne (sh-) *n.* (Mus.) (Dance to) music on ground bass; composition in this style. [F, f. Sp. *chacona*]

||**Chăd** *n.* (**Mr.**) ~, figure of a head above a wall, with caption protesting against shortages etc. [20th c.; orig. uncert.]

chae'tognăth (k-) *n.* Small planktonic worm of phylum Chaetognatha, with spined head. [f. mod. L *Chaetognatha* f. Gk *khaitē* long hair + *gnathos* jaw; see -A]

chae'topŏd (k-) *n.* Annelid of class Chaetopoda, with bristled feet. [f. as prec. + Gk *pous podos* foot]

chāfe *v.* & *n.* **1.** *v.t.* & *i.* Rub (skin, to restore warmth or sensation); make or become sore or damaged by rubbing; irritate; become annoyed, fret. **2.** *n.* (Sore made by) chafing; state of annoyance. [ME, f. OF *chaufer* f. Rom. **calefare* f. L *calefacere* (*calēre* be hot, *facere* make)]

chā'fer *n.* Large slow-moving beetle, esp. cockchafer. [OE *ceafor* & *cefer*, = OS *kever*, OHG *chevar*, f. Gmc **kabraz*, **kebraz*]

chaff (-ahf) *n.* & *v.* **1.** *n.* Husks of corn etc. separated by threshing or winnowing (**separate wheat from** ~, (fig.) distinguish good from bad); chopped hay and straw as cattle-food; spurious substitute (**caught with** ~, easily deceived or trapped); worthless stuff; strips of metal foil in air to obstruct radar detection; ~-**-cutter,** machine for chopping fodder; hence ~'Y² *a.* **2.** *v.t.* Chop (straw etc.). **3.** *v.t.* & *i.*, & *n.* Banter. [OE *ceaf*, *cæf*, = OHG *keva* husk, prob. f. Gmc **kaf-*, **kef-* gnaw; sense 3 perh. f. CHAFE]

chă'ffer *v.* & *n.* **1.** *v.i.* & *t.* Haggle, bargain; hence ~ER¹ *n.* **2.** *n.* Chaffering. [ME, f. OE *ceapfaru* (*ceap* bargain, *faru* journey)]

||**chă'ffĭnch** *n.* Common European finch (*Fringilla coelebs*). [f. OE *ceaffinc* (as CHAFF, FINCH)]

chā'fĭng-dĭsh *n.* Vessel with outer pan of hot water for keeping warm anything placed on it; dish with spirit-lamp etc. for cooking at table. [f. obs. sense of CHAFE = warm + -ING¹ + DISH¹]

Cha'gas (-ah'-) *n.* ~'(s) **disease,** form of sleeping sickness transmitted by blood-sucking bugs. [f. C. ~, Braz. physician d. 1934]

chagrin (shă'grĭn *or* shagrē'n) *n.*, & *v.t.* (Affect with) acute vexation or mortification. [f. F *chagrin(er)*, of uncert. orig.]

chain *n.*, & *v.t.* **1.** *n.* Connected flexible series of metal or other links; (in *pl.*) fetters, confinement, restraining force; ornament or badge of office in form of chain worn round neck etc.; = TYRE--*chain*, WATCH¹-*chain*. **2.** Sequence, series, set, (*of* proof, events, posts, mountains); group of associated shops, hotels, newspapers, etc.; figure in quadrille etc.; (Chem.) group of (esp. carbon) atoms joined in sequence in molecule. **3.** Jointed metal-rod measuring-line; its length (66 ft.). **4.** ~(**-shot**), (Hist.) two cannon-balls or half balls joined by chain for cutting masts etc. **5.** (Naut.) Device for widening basis of shrouds beyond ship's sides. **6.** ~**-armour** (made of interlaced rings); ~ **bridge,** suspension bridge on chains; ~ **drive** (Mech., with transmission by endless chains); ~**-gang** (of convicts, chained together, or forced to work in chains); ~**-gear** (transmitting motion by endless chain); ~**--letter,** letter of which recipient is asked to make copies to be sent to a (named) number of others (these being asked to do the like); ~**-link** *a.* (made of wire in diamond-shaped mesh); ~**--mail,** (erron.) chain-armour; ~ **reaction,** (Chem.) reaction forming intermediate products which react with the original substance and are repeatedly renewed, (Phys.) series of fission reactions each initiated by neutrons from previous one, (fig.) series of events each due to previous one; ~**-saw** (with teeth on endless chain); ~**-shot** (see sense 4); ~**-smoker,** one who smokes continually, esp. one who lights another cigarette or cigar from the end of the one last smoked; ~**-stitch,** ornamental crochet or embroidery stitch like chain; ~ **store,** one of a series of shops owned by one firm and selling the same class of goods; ~**-wale,** = CHANNEL²; ~**-wheel** (transmitting power by chain fitted to its edges). **7.** Hence ~'LESS *a.* **8.** *v.t.* Secure or confine with chain (lit. or fig.). [ME, f. OF *cha(e)ine* f. L *catena*]

chair *n.*, & *v.t.* **1.** *n.* Separate seat for one, of various forms (ARM¹-, BATH¹, DECK¹-, EASY, *chair*; **take a** ~, sit down). **2.** Seat of authority; professorship; ||mayoralty (*alderman* etc. **past** or **above the** ~, **below the** ~, who has, has not, been mayor). **3.** Seat or office of person presiding at meeting, public dinner, etc., (**be in the, take the** ~, be chairman); chairman (*address, appeal to, the chair*). **4.** Iron or steel socket holding railway rail in place. **5.** (Hist.) = SEDAN 1. **6.** * = ELECTRIC *chair*. **7.** ~**-bed,** chair that unfolds into a bed; ~**-borne,** (colloq.) administrative not active; ~**-car,** railway carriage with chairs instead of long seats, parlour car; ~**-lift,** series of chairs on endless cable for carrying passengers up mountain etc.; ~**'man** etc. (see foll.). **8.** *v.t.* Install in chair, esp. of authority; ||place (as if) in chair and carry aloft (winner of contest, election, etc.); act as chairman of, preside over, (meeting). [ME, f. AF *chaere*, OF *chaiere* f. L f. Gk *kathedra* (see CATHEDRAL)]

chair'man *n.* (*pl.* **chair'men;** *fem.* **chair'lady, chair'woman**). Person chosen to preside over meeting; permanent president of committee, board of directors, firm, country, etc.; master of ceremonies at entertainment; (Hist.) one of two sedan-bearers; hence ~SHIP *n.* [f. prec. + MAN[1]]

chaise (shāz) *n.* **1.** (esp. Hist.) Pleasure or travelling carriage, esp. light open carriage for one or two persons; POST[2]-*chaise*. **2.** ~ ***longue*** (-lŏ'ngg) [F, = long chair], kind of low chair with seat long enough to support user's legs; ~ ***percée*** (-pār'sā) [F, = pierced chair], chair incorporating chamber-pot. [F, var. of *chaire* f. as CHAIR]

chalā'za (k-) *n.* (*pl.* **~e**). One of two twisted membranous strips joining yolk to ends of egg. [mod. L f. Gk, = hailstone]

chălcĕ'donў (k-) *n.* Precious or semi-precious stone, a type of quartz, having many varieties such as agate, cornelian, chrysoprase. [ME, f. L *c(h)alcedonius* f. Gk *khalkēdōn*]

chălcĕ'nter|ĭc (k-) *a.* With bowels of bronze; tough; so ~OUS *a.* [f. Gk *khalkenteros* (as foll., ENTERO-) + -IC]

chălcolĭ'thĭc (k-) *a.* (Archaeol.) Of a period in which both stone and bronze implements were used. [f. Gk *khalkos* copper + *lithos* stone + -IC]

chălcopȳr'īte (k-) *n.* Copper-iron sulphide ore. [f. Gk *khalkos* copper + PYRITE]

Chăldē'an (k-) *a.* & *n.* **1.** (Native or language) of ancient Chaldea or Babylonia. **2.** (Exponent) of astrology. [f. L f. Gk *Khaldaios* f. Assyr. *kaldu*, + -AN]

Chăldee' (k-) *n.* = prec. 1; Aramaic as used in O.T. books. [ME, repr. L *Chaldaei* pl. (as prec.)]

cha'ldron (-aw'l-) *n.* Measure for coals, approx. 36 bushels. [f. OF *chauderon* augment. (see -OON) of *chaud(i)ere* pot f. LL *caldaria* f. L *cal(i)dus* hot]

chă'let (shă'lā) *n.* Swiss mountain cowherd's hut; Swiss peasant's wooden cottage; small villa; small house in holiday camp etc. [Swiss F]

chă'lĭce *n.* Goblet; Eucharistic wine-cup; (poet.) flower-cup. [ME f. OF, f. L *calix -icis* cup]

chalk[1] (-awk) *n.* White soft earthy limestone used for burning into lime and for writing and drawing; coloured preparation of like texture used in crayons for drawing; (Geol.) strata consisting mainly of chalk; **as different as ~ from cheese,** unlike in essentials; ||**by a long ~**, ||**by long ~s,** by far [f. use of chalk to mark score in games]. **2.** **~-pit,** quarry in which chalk is dug; **~-stone,** concretion of urates like chalk in tissues and joints esp. of hands and feet; **~-stripe(d),** (having) pattern of thin white stripes on dark background. [OE *cealc*, **cælc*, = OS *calc*, OHG *kalk*, WG f. L CALX]

chalk[2] (-awk) *v.t.* Rub, mark, draw, write, write *up*, with chalk; **~ it up,** charge it (*to* my account etc.); **~ out,** sketch, plan as thing to be accomplished; **~ up,** register (success etc.). [f. prec.]

cha'lk|ў (-aw'kĭ) *a.* Abounding in or white as chalk; like or containing chalk-stones; hence ~ĬNESS *n.* [f. CHALK[1] + -Y[2]]

chă'llĕnge[1] (-nj) *n.* Calling to respond, esp. sentry's call for password etc.; exception taken (e.g. to juryman); summons to trial or contest, esp. to duel; demanding or difficult task; (Sport) invitation to contest, esp. issued to reigning champion; (Med.) test of immunity after immunization treatment. [ME & OF *c(h)alenge*, f. L *calumnia* calumny]

chă'llĕng|e[2] (-nj) *v.t.* (Of sentry etc.) call to respond (lit. or fig.); take exception to (evidence, juryman), dispute, deny; claim (attention, admiration, etc.); invite to contest, game, discussion, or duel; (Med.) test by challenge; (abs., usu. in *part.*) offer interesting difficulties (*a challenging problem*); hence ~EABLE (-nja-) *a.*, ~ER[1] *n.* [ME, f. OF *c(h)alenger* f. L *calumniari* (*calumnia* calumny)]

chă'llĭs *n.* Lightweight soft clothing fabric. [perh. f. surname]

chalў'bėate (ka-) *a.* (Of mineral water or spring) impregnated with iron salts. [f. mod. L *chalybeatus* f. L *chalybs* f. Gk *khalups -ubos* steel; see -ATE[2]]

chăm (k-) *n.* **Great ~**, autocrat, dominant critic etc. (esp. Samuel Johnson). [F, f. Turki (as KHAN[1])]

chă'maephȳte (k-) *n.* (Bot.) Plant whose buds are on or near the ground. [f. Gk *khamai* on the ground + -PHYTE]

chā'mber *n.* **1.** (poet. or arch.) Room, esp. bedroom. **2.** (in *pl.*) Set of rooms in larger building, esp. in Inns of Court, let separately; judge's room for hearing cases not needing to be taken in court. **3.** (Hall used by) deliberative or judicial body, one of the houses of a parliament (esp. SECOND *chamber*, *Chamber of Deputies*). **4.** = *chamber-pot*. **5.** Cavity in body of animal or plant; enclosed space in machinery etc. (esp. part of gun-bore that contains charge); compartment in structure; (Phys.) apparatus designed to reveal tracks of ionizing particles by a visible effect (*bubble*, *cloud*, *spark*, *chamber*). **6.** **C~ of Commerce,** association to promote local commercial interests; **~ concert** (of chamber music); *Chamber of* HORRORS; **~maid,** housemaid at hotel etc., *housemaid; **~ music** (for small group of instruments); **~-pot,** receptacle for urine etc., used in bedroom. **7.** Hence (-)~ED[2] (*-erd*) *a.* (of tomb, containing a burial chamber). [ME f. OF *chambre* f. L *camera* f. Gk *kamara* vault]

chā'mberlain (-lĭn) *n.* Officer managing household of sovereign or great noble; treasurer of corporation etc.; ||**Lord Great C~ (of England),** hereditary holder of a ceremonial office; ||**Lord C~ (of the Household),** head of management of Royal Household, formerly licenser of plays; hence ~SHIP *n.* [ME, f. OF *chamberlain* etc., f. Frank. **kamerling* f. OS *kamara* f. L (see prec., -LING[1])]

Cha'mbertin (shah'ṅbertăṅ) *n.* A dry red burgundy wine. [~ in E. France]

chă'mbray (sh-) *n.* Linen-finished gingham with white weft and coloured warp. [irreg. f. *Cambrai* (see CAMBRIC)]

chamē'lė|on (k-) *n.* Small prehensile-tailed long-tongued lizard with power of changing colour according to its surroundings and of living long without food; variable or inconstant person; hence **~ŏ'nIC** *a.* [ME, f. L f. Gk *khamaileōn* (*khamai* on the ground, *leōn* lion)]

chă'mfer *v.t.*, & *n.* **1.** *v.t.* Bevel symmetrically (right-angled edge or corner). **2.** *n.* Surface so made. [back form. f. *chamfering* f. F *chamfrain* f. *chant* edge (CANT[1]) + *fraint* broken (OF *fraindre* break f. L *frangere*)]

chă'mois (shă'mwah; in sense 2 also shă'mĭ) *n.* (*pl.* same *pr.* -z). **1.** Wild antelope of goat size, found in mountains of Europe and Asia. **2.** ~**(-leather)**, soft pliable leather from sheep, goats, deer, etc., piece of this for polishing etc. [F; cf. Gallo-L *camox*]

chamomile. See CAMOMILE.

chămp[1] *v.t.* & *i.*, & *n.* Munch (fodder) noisily; work (bit) noisily in teeth (**~ing at the bit,** (fig.) restlessly impatient); (make) chewing action or noise. [prob. imit.]

chămp[2] *n.* (sl.) Champion. [abbr.]

chămpā'gne (shămpā'n) *n.* White (esp. sparkling) wine from Champagne or elsewhere; pale straw colour. [f. *C~*, former province in E. France]

chă'mpaign (-ān) *n.* (Expanse of) open country. [ME, f. OF *champagne* f. LL *campania*; cf. CAMPAIGN]

||**chă'mpers** (sh-; -z) *n.* (sl.) Champagne. [f. CHAMPAGNE + -ER[1] (5) + -S[1]]

chă'mpert|y̆ *n.* (Law) Action of assisting a party in a suit in which one is not naturally interested, with view to receiving share of disputed property; hence ~OUS *a.* [ME f. AF *champartie*, f. OF *champart* feudal lord's share of produce, f. L *campus* field + *pars* part]

chă'mpĭon *n.*, *a.*, *adv.*, & *v.t.* **1.** *n.* Person who fights, argues, etc., for another or for a cause (||**King's, Queen's, C~**, or **C~ of England,** hereditary official at coronations). **2.** Athlete, boxer, etc., animal, plant, etc., that has defeated all competitors (often attrib.: *champion boxer, turnip*); hence ~SHIP *n.* **3.** *a.* & *adv.* (colloq. or dial.) First-class, splendid(ly). **4.** *v.t.* Support the cause of, argue in favour of, defend. [ME f. OF, f. med. L *campio -onis* fighter f. L *campus* field]

champlevé (shah'ṅlevā) *a.* & *n.* (Enamel-work) in which hollows made in surface are filled with enamel colours. [F, = raised field]

chance[1] (-ah-) *n.* & *a.* **1.** *n.* Way things happen of themselves, fortune; undesigned occurrence; opportunity, esp. of escape etc.; (Cricket) opportunity of dismissing a batsman; possibility; probability (esp. in *pl.*; *the chances are against it, are even*). **2.** Absence of design or discoverable cause; course of events regarded as a power, fate; **game of ~** (decided by luck not skill). **3. By ~**, as it happens or happened, without design; *the* MAIN[3] *chance*; OFF *chance*; **on the ~**, in view of the possibility (*of, that*); **stand a ~**, have a prospect of success etc.; **take** one's **~**, let things go as they may, consent to take what comes; **take a ~, take ~s**, behave riskily. **4.** *a.* Fortuitous (*a chance companion, meeting*). [ME, f. AF *ch(e)aunce*, OF *chēance* (*chēoir* fall f. Rom. **cadēre* f. L *cadere*; see -ANCE)]

chance[2] (-ah-) *v.* **1.** *v.i.* Happen without intention (*that, to* do); **~ (up)on,** happen to find, meet, etc. **2.** *v.t.* (colloq.) Risk (esp. *chance it*); **~** one's **arm,** take one's (possibly slight) chance of doing something successfully. [ME, f. prec.]

cha'ncel (-ah'-) *n.* Part of church near altar, reserved for clergy, choir, etc., and usu. enclosed. [ME f. OF, f. L *cancelli* lattice]

cha'ncellerў (-ah'-) *n.* Position, staff, department, official residence, of a chancellor; office attached to embassy or consulate. [ME, f. OF *chancellerie* (*chancelier*; see foll., -ERY)]

cha'ncellor (-ah'-) *n.* **1.** State or law official of various kinds; ||*C~* (*of the* EXCHEQUER); ||**C~ of Duchy of Lancaster,** member of government (legally representative of Queen as Duke of Lancaster), often Cabinet Minister employed on non-departmental work; ||**Lord** (**High**) **C~** (presiding in House of Lords, Chancery Division, and Court of Appeal). **2.** Bishop's law officer; **C~ of Garter** or other order (who seals commissions etc.); non-resident head of university; *president of chancery court; (Germany, Austria) chief minister of the State. **3.** Hence ~SHIP *n.* [OE f. AF *c(h)anceler*, OF *-ier* f. LL *cancellarius* porter, secretary (*cancelli* lattice)]

chance-mĕ'dley (-ah-) *n.* (Law) action, esp. homicide, mainly but not entirely unintentional; inadvertency. [f. AF *chance medlee* (see MEDDLE) mixed chance]

cha'ncerў (-ah'-) *n.* ||(*C~*) Lord Chancellor's court, division of High Court of Justice (WARD[1] *in Chancery*); records office of order of knighthood; court of bishop's chancellor; *court of equity; chancellery of embassy; office for public records; **in ~**, (of boxer) with head held under opponent's arm being pummelled. [ME, contracted f. CHANCELLERY]

chă'ncre (shă'ngk*er*) *n.* Ulcer in venereal disease etc. [F, f. L CANCER]

chă'ncroid (shă'ngk-) *n.* Local form of chancre. [f. prec. + -OID]

cha'nc|y̆ (-ah'-) *a.* Uncertain, risky; hence ~ĬLY[2] *adv.*, ~ĬNESS *n.* [f. CHANCE[1] + -Y[2]]

chăndelier' (sh-) *n.* Branched hanging support for several lights. [F (*chandelle* f. as CANDLE)]

cha'ndler (-ah'-) *n.* (arch.) Dealer in candles, oil, soap, paint, and groceries (||**corn-~**, in corn; **ship('s)-~**, in cordage, canvas, etc.); hence **cha'ndl**ERY (1) (-ah'-) *n.* [ME, f. AF *chaundeler*, OF *chandelier* (*chandelle*, as CANDLE; see -ER[2])]

chānge[1] (-nj) *n.* **1.** Making or becoming different; substitution of one for another, variety (*for a change*); hence ~'FUL 1 (-jf-), ~'LESS (-jl-), *adjs.* **2.** ||**C~, 'C~** [as if f. EXCHANGE[1]], place where merchants meet (**on C~**, engaged there). **3.** (Of moon) arrival at fresh phase, esp. at new moon; **~ of air,** different climate; **~ (of clothes)**, second outfit in reserve; *change of* HEART; **~ (of life)**, menopause; SEA *change*. **4.** Money given for money in larger units or different currency; money returned as balance of that tendered in payment; **get no ~ out of,** (sl.) fail to get the better of (in business, argument, etc.) or information from; **give ~**, ***make ~**, select money from till etc. and give it to buyer as change; SMALL *change*. **5.** (Bell-ringing; usu. in *pl.*) Different orders in which peal of bells can be rung; **ring the ~s,** (fig.) vary ways of expressing or doing thing. [ME, f. AF *chaunge*, OF *change* (*changer*; see foll.)]

chānge[2] (-nj) *v.* **1.** *v.t.* Take or use another instead of (*change* one's *coat*); give up, get rid of, *for*; make different (often *to, into, from*); give or get money change for; put fresh clothes, coverings, etc., on (child, bed, etc.); go from one to another of (*change houses, sides, trains*); give and receive, exchange, (*change places with*; *we changed places*). **2.** *v.i.* Become different (often *to, into, from*); (of moon) arrive at fresh phase, esp. become new; change trains etc.; put on different (esp. evening) clothes. **3.** *Change* COLOUR[1]; **~ down,** engage lower gear in vehicle; **~** one's **feet,** (colloq.) put on other shoes etc.; *change* FRONT; **~ gear,** engage different gear in vehicle; *change* HAND[1]*s*; **~** one's MIND[1]; **~ over** *v.t.* & *i.*, **~-over** *n.*, change from one system or situation to another; *change* STEP[2]; *change the* SUBJECT[2]; change one's TUNE; **~ up,** engage higher gear in vehicle. [ME, f. OF *changer* f. LL *cambiare*, L *cambire* barter, prob. of Celt. orig.]

chā'nge|able (-nj*a*-) *a.* That can change or be changed; irregular, inconstant; hence ~ABI'LITY (-j*a*-), ~**able**NESS (-j*a*beln-), *ns.* [ME f. OF, f. as prec.; see -ABLE]

chā'ngeling (-njl-) *n.* Thing or child believed to be substituted for another by stealth, esp. elf-child thus left by fairies. [f. CHANGE[2] + -LING[1]]

chă'nnel[1] *n.*, & *v.t.* (||**-ll-**). **1.** *n.* Natural or artificial hollow bed of water; navigable part of waterway; piece of water, wider than strait, joining two larger pieces, usu. seas (||**the C~**, English Channel); tubular passage for liquid. **2.** Course in which anything moves, direction, line; medium of communication, agency, (*through the usual channels*); circuit for telegraphic communication; (Broadcasting) band of frequencies sufficiently wide for transmission of signal, esp. as used for a particular programme; path for information; lengthwise strip on recording tape etc.; groove, flute. **3.** *v.t.* Form channels in, groove; (fig.) guide, direct. [ME f. OF *chanel* f. L *canalis* CANAL]

chă'nnel[2] *n.* Broad thick plank projecting horizontally from ship's side abreast of mast to widen basis for shrouds. [for CHAIN-*wale* (WALE); cf. *gunnel* for *gunwale*]

chă'nnelize, -īse (-īz), *v.t.* Convey (as if) in a channel, guide. [f. CHANNEL[1] + -IZE]
chanson de geste (shahńsawń de zhĕ'st) *n.* (*pl.* ***-ns*** *pr.* -ńz). One of a group of medieval French epic poems. [F, = song of heroic deeds]
chant (-ah-) *n.* & *v.* **1.** *n.* Song; (Mus.) short musical passage in two or more phrases each beginning with reciting note, for singing unmetrical words (psalms, canticles); measured monotonous song, musical recitation of words; sing-song intonation in talk. **2.** *v.i.* & *t.* Sing; utter musically or rhythmically; intone, sing to a chant. [n. f. v., ME f. OF *chanter* sing, f. L *cantare* frequent. of *canere cant-* sing]
cha'nter (-ah'-) *n.* In vbl senses; melody-pipe, with finger-holes, of bagpipe. [f. prec. + -ER[1]]
chanterĕ'lle (shah-) *n.* **1.** Yellow funnel-shaped edible fungus, *Cantharellus cibarius*. **2.** (Mus.) Highest-pitched string of banjo etc. [F, in sense 1 f. mod. L *cantharellus* dim. of *cantharus* f. Gk *kantharos* drinking-vessel, in sense 2 f. as CHANT]
chanteuse (shahńtẽr'z) *n.* Female singer of popular songs. [F]
cha'nticleer (-ah'-) *n.* (Personal name for) domestic cock. [ME, f. OF *chantecler* (as CHANT, CLEAR[1]), name in *Reynard the Fox*]
Chanti'llȳ (shahńtē'yĭ) *n.* Delicate kind of bobbin-lace; sweetened whipped cream. [~ near Paris]
cha'ntrȳ (-ah'-) *n.* Endowment for priest(s) to sing masses for founder's soul; priests, chapel, altar, so endowed. [ME, f. AF *chaunterie*, OF *chanterie* (*chanter* CHANT; see -ERY)]
chanty. Var. of SHANTY[2].
Chanukkah. Var. of HANUKKAH.
chā'ŏs (k-) *n.* Formless primordial matter; utter confusion; hence **chāŏ'tic** (k-) *a.*, **chāŏ'tically** (k-) *adv.* [F or L, f. Gk *khaos*; *-otic* after *erotic* etc.]
chăp[1] *v.* (**-pp-**) & *n.* **1.** *v.t.* & *i.* Crack in fissures (usu. of skin or dry ground). **2.** *n.* (usu. in *pl.*) Crack, open seam, esp. in skin, whence **~'py**[2] *a.*; ***~'stick,** cylinder of cosmetic substance to prevent chaps. [ME, perh. rel. to MLG, MDu. *kappen* chop off]
chăp[2] *n.* Lower jaw or half of cheek, esp. of pig as food (*Bath chap*; **~-fallen,** with jaw hanging down, dispirited, dejected); see also CHOP[3]. [16th c., var. of CHOP[3]; orig. unkn.]
chăp[3] *n.* (colloq.) Man, boy, fellow. [short for CHAPMAN]
chap. *abbr.* chapter.
***chăpare'jōs** (-rā'hōs; *or* sh-) *n. pl.* Cowboy's leather overalls for legs. [Mex. Sp.]
***chăparră'l** (*or* sh-) *n.* Dense tangled brushwood; ~ **cock,** = ROAD[1]*runner*. [Sp. (*chaparra* evergreen oak)]
chapă't(t)ĭ. See CHUPATTY.
chă'p-bo͝ok *n.* (Hist.) Small pamphlet of tales, ballads, tracts, etc., hawked by chapmen. [19th c.; see CHAPMAN]
chāpe *n.* Metal cap of scabbard-point; back-piece of buckle attaching it to strap etc.; sliding loop on belt or strap. [ME f. OF, = cope, hood, f. as CAP[1]]
chapeau-bras (shapōbrah') *n.* (*pl.* ***chapeaux-bras*** *pr.* same). Three-cornered flat silk hat carried under arm. [f. F *chapeau* hat + *bras* arm]
chă'pel *n.* Place of Christian worship other than parish church or cathedral, esp. one attached to private house or institution (~ **royal,** of royal palace); place for private worship in larger building, with altar, esp. part of cathedral etc. separately dedicated (LADY *chapel*); Anglican church subordinate to parish church, esp. ~ **of ease** (for convenience of remote parishioners); ‖place of worship of Nonconformist bodies; chapel service, attendance at chapel; (Print.) journeyman printers' association or meeting (**father of the ~**, its president); so **~RY** *n.*, district served by chapel. [ME f. OF *chapele* f. med. L *capella* dim. of *cappa* cloak (CAP[1]); first chapel was sanctuary in which St. Martin's sacred cloak was kept by *cappellani* (see CHAPLAIN)]
chapelle ardente (shapĕl ârdah'ńt) *n.* Chamber prepared for lying-in-state of distinguished person and lit up with candles, torches, etc. [F, lit. 'burning chapel']
chă'perōn (sh-) *n.*, & *v.t.* **1.** *n.* Person who ensures propriety, esp. married or older woman accompanying young unmarried woman on social occasions; hence **~AGE** *n.* **2.** *v.t.* Act as chaperon to. [F, = hood, chaperon, dim. of *chape* cope f. as CAP[1]]
chă'plain (-lĭn) *n.* Clergyman officiating in private chapel of great person or institution, on board ship, or for regiment etc.; hence **~CY** *n.* [ME, f. AF & OF *c(h)apelain* f. med. L *cappellanus* (see CHAPEL)]
chă'plėt *n.* Wreath of flowers, leaves, gold, gems, etc., for head; string of beads for counting prayers (55, one-third of rosary number), or as necklace; bead-moulding. [ME f. OF *chapelet* dim. of *chapel* f. Rom. **cappellus* dim. of LL *cappa* CAP[1]]
‖**chă'p|man** *n.* (*pl.* **~men**). (Hist.) Pedlar. [OE *cēapman* (*cēap* barter; see CHEAP, MAN[1])]
chă'ppal *n.* Indian usu. leather sandal. [Hindi]
chă'ppĭe *n.* (colloq.) = CHAP[3]. [f. CHAP[3] + -IE]
chă'ppȳ. See CHAP[1].
***chăps** (*or* sh-) *n.* = CHAPAREJOS. [abbr.]
chă'pter *n.* **1.** Main division of a book (~ **and verse,** exact reference or authority); (fig.) limited subject, piece of narrative, etc. (*chapter of* ACCIDENTS); ‖Act of Parliament numbered as part of session's proceedings (Eliz. 2 1972 c. 60 = Gas Act, 1972). **2.** General meeting, or whole number, of certain appointed clergymen (canons) of collegiate or cathedral church or members of monastic or knightly order (~ **house,** building used for such meetings or *for meetings etc. of students); division of printers' guild; *local branch of a society. [ME f. OF *chapitre* f. L *capitulum* dim. of *caput -itis* head]
chăr[1]**, chărr,** *n.* (*pl.* same). Small trout of genus *Salvelinus*. [17th c.; orig. unkn.]
chăr[2] *n.*, & *v.i.* (**-rr-**). **1.** *n.* **~('woman),** ‖**~'lady,** woman hired by the hour or day to clean rooms in offices or ‖houses. **2.** *v.i.* Work as charwoman. [earlier *chare* f. OE *cerr* a turn, *cierran* to turn]
chăr[3] *v.t.* & *i.* (**-rr-**). Burn to charcoal; scorch, blacken with fire. [app. back form. f. CHARCOAL]
‖**chăr**[4] *n.* (sl.) Tea. [f. Chin. *ch'a*]
chă'rabănc (sh-; -ăng) *n.* (arch.) Motor coach. [f. F *char à bancs* seated carriage]
chă'racter (kă'rĭk-) *n.*, & *v.t.* **1.** *n.* Distinctive mark; (in *pl.*) inscribed letters or figures; graphic symbol, esp. denoting sound or idea; style of such symbols used in a language; (Computers) group of symbols representing letter etc. **2.** Characteristic (esp. Biol., of species etc.); collective peculiarities, sort, style; person's or race's idiosyncrasy, mental or moral qualities; distinction, individuality. **3.** Moral strength, esp. if highly developed or evident; reputation, good reputation (~ **assassination,** malicious destruction of person's reputation); ~ (**sketch,** brief) description of person's qualities; testimonial. **4.** Personage, personality; person portrayed in novel, drama, etc.; part played by actor or (arch.) hypocrite; **in, out of,** ~, appropriate to these or not, (of action etc.) in accord or not with person's character. **5.** Eccentric or noticeable person (*quite a character*); ~ **actor** (who plays eccentric characters). **6.**

Hence ~LESS *a.* **7.** *v.t.* (arch.) Inscribe; describe. [ME, f. OF *caractere* f. L f. Gk *kharaktēr* stamp, impress]

chăracteri'st|ic (kărĭk-) *a.* & *n.* Typical, distinctive, (trait, mark, quality); indicative of character; (Math.) integral part of logarithm; **~ic curve** (showing relation between interdependent quantities); **~ic radiation** (of wavelength peculiar to one substance); hence ~ICALLY *adv.* [f. F *caractéristique* or f. med. L f. Gk *kharaktēristikos* (see prec., -IST, -IC)]

chă'racteriz|e (kă'rĭk-), **-is|e** (-īz), *v.t.* Describe character of; describe *as*; be characteristic of, impart character to; hence ~A'TION *n.* [f. F *caractériser* or med. L *characterizare* f. Gk *kharaktērizō* (as CHARACTER; see -IZE)]

chăracterŏ'logy̆ (kărĭk-) *n.* (Psych.) Science of the development and variation of character. [f. G *characterologie* (as CHARACTER, -O-, -LOGY)]

chara'de (sharah'd) *n.* Game of guessing word from written or acted clue given for each syllable and for the whole; (fig.) absurd pretence. [F, f. mod. Prov. *charrado* conversation (*charra* chatter)]

char'as *n.* Narcotic resin from flower-heads of hemp, cannabis resin. [Hindi]

char'coal *n.* Black porous residue of partly burnt wood, bones, etc., a form of carbon; ~ **biscuit** (containing wood-charcoal to aid digestion); **~-burner,** maker of charcoal; ~ (**grey**), dark grey. [ME, conn. w. COAL in sense 'charcoal']

chard *n.* Kind of beet with edible leaves and stalks. [f. F *carde*, and *chardon* thistle; cf. CARDOON]

charge[1] *n.* **1.** Appropriate quantity of material to put into receptacle, mechanism, etc., at one time, esp. of explosive for gun; (fig.) load; (colloq.) dose of drugs; (Her.) device, bearing. **2.** Quantity of electricity carried by a body; energy stored chemically for conversion into electricity. **3.** Expense (*at his own charge*); price demanded for service or goods (*are his charges reasonable?*); obligation to pay. **4.** Task, duty, commission; care, custody, (*of*; *nurse in charge of child, child in the charge of nurse*; CURATE-*in-charge*; ||**give** person **in** ~, hand him over to police; **take** ~, assume control or direction *of*, (colloq., of things) get out of control, esp. with disastrous results); thing or person entrusted, minister's flock. **5.** Exhortation, directions, orders; formal instruction by bishop to clergy, judge to jury, etc. **6.** Accusation, esp. against prisoner brought for trial (**lay to** person's ~, accuse him of). **7.** Impetuous attack by soldiers, animal, etc. (**return to the** ~, begin again, esp. in argument); (Mil.) signal sounded for such attack; attack made by throwing oneself against opponent in football etc. **8.** ***~ account,** credit account at shop etc.; ||**~-hand,** workman in charge of a job; ||**~-nurse,** nurse in charge of ward etc.; **~-sheet,** record of cases and charges made at police station. [ME f. OF, f. Rom. **carrica* f. LL *car(ri)care*; see foll.]

charge[2] *v.* **1.** *v.t.* Load or fill to the full or proper extent (vessel, gun with explosive); saturate (air with vapour, water with chemicals); give electric charge to (body), store energy in (battery etc.). **2.** Entrust *with* (~ **oneself with,** undertake). **3.** Command *to* do, exhort. **4.** Accuse, impute, (person *with* action); make accusation *that*; debit (*charge it to my account*), debit to one's account (*I'd like to charge this dress*). **5.** Demand (price) *for*, demand (price) from (person). **6.** *v.t.* & *i.* Attack impetuously; throw oneself (against). **7.** Hence ~ABLE (-ar'ja-) *a.* [ME f. OF *charger* f. LL *car(ri)care* load f. L *carrus* CAR]

chargé (d'affaires) (shar'zhā dăfar') *n.* (*pl.* **-gés** *pr.* same). Ambassador's deputy; representative at minor court or government. [F, = in charge (of affairs)]

char'ger[1] *n.* (arch.) Large flat dish. [ME f. AF *chargeour*; see CHARGE[2], -OR]

char'ger[2] *n.* In vbl senses; (Mil.) cavalry horse; (poet.) any horse. [f. CHARGE[2] + -ER[1]]

chă'riot *n.*, & *v.t.* **1.** *n.* (poet.) Stately or triumphal vehicle. **2.** (Hist.) Four-wheeled carriage with back seats only; two-wheeled vehicle used in ancient fighting and racing, whence ~EER' *n.* **3.** *v.t.* (literary). Convey as or in chariot. [ME f. OF, augment. of *char* CAR]

chari'sma (k-; -z-) *n.* (*pl.* **~ta**). Divinely conferred power or talent; capacity to inspire followers with devotion and enthusiasm; hence **chărismă'tic** (k-; -z-) *a.* [eccl. L, f. Gk *kharisma* (*kharis* favour, grace)]

chă'ritable *a.* Generous in giving to the poor; connected with such giving; of or for charity; apt to judge favourably of persons, acts, and motives; hence ~NESS (-beln-) *n.*, **chă'ritab**LY[2] *adv.* [ME f. OF (*charité* = foll.; see -ABLE)]

chă'rity̆ *n.* **1.** Love of fellow men; kindness, affection; leniency in judging others. **2.** Beneficence, liberality to those in need or distress, alms-giving (in *pl.*, acts of this), alms; trust for advancement of education etc.; institution for helping those in need, help so given; ~ **begins at home** (is due first to one's own family and friends); **cold as** ~ (in allusion to unsympathetic administration); ||**C~ Commission(ers)**, board established to control charitable trusts; ~ **school** (supported by charitable contributions). [OE, f. OF *charité* f. L *caritas -tatis* (*carus* dear; see -ITY)]

charivar'i (sh-) *n.* Medley of sounds, hubbub. [F, = serenade with pans, trays, etc., to unpopular person]

||**char'lādy̆.** See CHAR[2].

char'latan (sh-) *n.* False pretender to knowledge or skill, esp. in medicine; hence ~ISM (2), ~RY (5), *ns.* [F, f. It. *ciarlatano* (*ciarlare* babble)]

Charles's Wai'n (-lzĭz-) *n.* Constellation Ursa Major or its seven bright stars. [OE *Carles wægn* the wain of Carl (Charles the Great, Charlemagne), perh. by assoc. of star Arcturus with legends of King Arthur and Charlemagne]

Char'leston (-ls- *or* -lz-) *n.*, & *v.i.* **1.** *n.* American dance with side-kicks from knee. **2.** *v.i.* Dance this, kick thus. [~ in S. Carolina, U.S.]

***char'ley horse** *n.* (sl.) Stiffness or cramp in arm or leg. [19th c.; orig. uncert.]

char'lie *n.* (sl.) Fool; person; (in *pl.*) woman's breasts; *inhabitant (esp. soldier) of (North) Vietnam. [dim. of name *Charles*; see -IE]

char'lock *n.* Wild mustard, a yellow-flowered weed. [OE *cerlic*, of unkn. orig.]

char'lotte (sh-) *n.* Pudding made of stewed fruit with casing or layers or covering of bread, biscuits, sponge-cake, or bread-crumbs, (*apple charlotte*); ~ **russe** (-rōō's), custard etc. enclosed in sponge-cake or sponge biscuits. [F]

charm[1] *n.* **1.** Word(s), act, or object supposedly having occult power (*against*), spell, (*work* **like a** ~, perfectly); thing worn to avert evil etc., amulet; trinket on bracelet etc. **2.** Quality or feature that excites love or admiration; attractiveness, indefinable power of delighting; (in *pl.*, esp.) woman's sexual attractiveness; ~ **school,** place where women are taught graceful behaviour; hence ~'LESS *a.* [ME f. OF *charme*, f. L *carmen* song]

charm[2] *v.t.* Bewitch, influence (as) by magic; bring (as) by magic (*charm secret, consent*, etc., *out of*); endow with seemingly magic power (*bear a charmed life*); captivate, delight, (*charmed with*); give pleasure to; hence ~'ING[2] *a.*, delightful. [ME, f. OF *charmer* (*charme*; see prec.)]

chār'mer *n.* In vbl senses; pleasant or attractive person; SNAKE-*charmer*. [f. prec. + -ER¹]

charmeu'se (shārmēr'z) *n.* Soft smooth silky dress-fabric. [F, fem. of *charmeur* (as CHARM², -ER¹)]

chār'nel-house *n.* House or vault in which dead bodies or bones are piled. [ME & OF *charnel* burying-place, f. med. L *carnale* f. LL *carnalis* CARNAL]

Chă'rollais, -olais, (shă'rolā) *n.* (Animal of) breed of large white beef-cattle. [f. Monts du ~ in E. France]

Chār'on (k-) *n.* (Gk Myth.) Ferryman conveying souls across Styx to Hades. [L, f. Gk *Kharōn*]

chār'poy *n.* (Ind.) Light bedstead. [f. Urdu *chārpāī*]

chārr. See CHAR¹.

chārt *n.*, & *v.t.* **1.** *n.* Navigator's sea map, showing coast outlines, rocks, shoals, etc.; outline map showing special features; set of curves on graph etc. showing fluctuations in temperature, prices, etc.; sheet of tabulated or diagrammatic information, esp. listing currently most popular gramophone records. **2.** *v.t.* Make chart of, map. [f. F *charte* f. L *charta* (CARD²)]

chār'ter¹ *n.* Written grant of rights by sovereign or legislature, esp. creation of borough, company, university, etc. (**Great C~**, Magna Charta); deed conveying land; = CHARTER-PARTY; privilege, admitted right(s), (fig.) licence to misbehave; ~ **flight** (by chartered aircraft); **~-member,** original member of society, corporation, etc. [ME f. OF *chartre*, f. L *chartula* dim. of *charta* (CARD²)]

chār'ter² *v.t.* Grant charter, give privilege, to (‖**~ed accountant, engineer, librarian, surveyor,** etc., member of professional body that has royal charter; **~ed libertine,** person allowed to do as he pleases); hire (ship, aircraft, vehicle, etc.); hence ~ER¹ *n.* [ME, f. prec.]

chār'ter-pārtў *n.* Deed between ship-owner and merchant for hire of ship and delivery of cargo. [f. F *charte partie* f. med. L *charta partita* divided charter, indenture]

Chār't|ism *n.* (Hist.) Principles of U.K. reform movement of 1837–48; hence ~IST (2) *n.* [f. L *charta* charter + -ISM; name taken from the manifesto 'People's Charter']

chārtreu'se (shārtrēr'z) *n.* Green or yellow liqueur of brandy and aromatic herbs etc.; dish of fruit enclosed in jelly etc.; apple-green colour. [f. La Grande *Chartreuse* (Carthusian monastery near Grenoble)]

chartulary. See CARTULARY.

charwoman. See CHAR².

chār'|ў *a.* Cautious; shy *of* or sparing *in doing*; ungenerous (*chary of praise*); hence ~ĭLY² *adv.*, ~ĭNESS *n.* [OE *cearig*, = OS *carag*, OHG *karag* f. WG **karag-* (**karō* CARE¹; see -Y²)]

Charў'bdĭs (k-) *n.* See SCYLLA.

Chas. *abbr.* Charles.

chāse¹ *n.* Pursuit (**give ~**, go in pursuit); hunting, esp. as sport (WILD-*goose chase*); steeplechase; unenclosed parkland; animal, ship, etc., pursued; (Hist.) **~, ~-gun, ~-port,** gun, port, in bow or stern for use while chasing or being chased. [ME f. OF *chace* f. Rom. **captia* (**captiare*; see foll.)]

chāse² *v.* **1.** *v.t.* Pursue; drive *from, out of, to,* etc.; (colloq.) try to attain; ~ **oneself,** (colloq., usu. in *imper.*) depart. **2.** *v.i.* Hurry (*after*, etc.). [ME, f. OF *chacier* f. Rom. **captiare* for L *captare* frequent. of *capere* take; cf. CATCH¹]

chāse³ *v.t.* Emboss, engrave, (metal). [app. f. earlier *enchase* f. F *enchâsser* (as EN-¹, CASE²)]

chāse⁴ *n.* Part of gun enclosing bore; trench or groove cut to receive pipe etc. [f. F *chas* enclosed space f. Prov. *ca(u)s* f. med. L *capsum* thorax]

chāse⁵ *n.* Iron frame holding composed type for page or sheet. [f. F *châsse* f. L *capsa* (CASE²)]

chā'ser *n.* In vbl senses; horse for steeplechasing; chase-gun; *amorous pursuer of women; (colloq.) drink following drink of another kind, e.g. spirits after coffee, water or beer after spirits. [f. CHASE² + -ER¹]

Chasid. Var. of HASID.

chă'sm (kă'zem) *n.* Deep fissure; wide difference of feeling, interests, etc., gulf; (arch.) hiatus. [f. L f. Gk *khasma* gaping hollow]

chasse (shahs) *n.* Liqueur taken after coffee etc. [F (*chasser* CHASE²)]

chassé (shă'sā) *n.*, & *v.i.* (Make) gliding step in dancing; ~ ***croisé*** (-krwah'zā), double *chassé*, (fig.) to-and-fro movement with change of position. [F, = chasing]

Chassid. Var. of HASID.

chă'ssis (shă'sĭ; *or* -sē) *n.* (*pl.* same *pr.* -z). Base-frame of gun-carriage, motor vehicle, etc.; metal frame to carry radio etc. equipment. [f. F *châssis* f. Rom. **capsicium* f. L *capsa* CASE²]

chāste *a.* Abstaining from unlawful or immoral or from all sexual intercourse, pure, virgin; decent (of speech); restrained, severe, pure in taste or style, unadorned, simple; **~-tree,** ornamental shrub (*Vitex agnus-castus*), with blue or white flowers; hence ~LY² (-tlĭ) *adv.* [ME f. OF, f. L *castus*]

chā'sten (-sen) *v.t.* Discipline, punish by inflicting suffering; moderate; restrain, subdue. [f. obs. *chaste* v. (f. OF *chastier* f. L *castigare* CASTIGATE) + -EN⁶]

chăstī'se (-z) *v.t.* Punish; thrash; hence ~MENT (-zm-; *or* chă'stĭzm-) *n.* [ME, app. irreg. f. obs. vbs. *chaste, chasty* (see prec.) + -ISE¹]

chă'stĭtў *n.* Being chaste; virginity, celibacy; simplicity of style or taste; ~ **belt,** garment designed to prevent woman from having sexual intercourse. [ME, f. OF *chasteté* f. L *castitas -tatis* (*castus* chaste; see -ITY)]

chă'sūble (-z-) *n.* Sleeveless vestment of celebrant at Mass or Eucharist, with colour regulated by the feast of the day. [ME f. OF *chesible*, later *-uble* f. F *chasuble* f. LL *casubla* irreg. f. L *casula* hooded cloak, little cottage, dim. of *casa* cottage]

chăt¹ *v.i.* & *t.* (-tt-), & *n.* (Indulge in) easy familiar talk; ~ (**up**), (sl.) chat to, esp. flirtatiously or with ulterior motive; ~ **show,** = TALK *show*. [ME, f. CHATTER]

chăt² *n.* Song-bird of genus *Saxicola, Epthianura,* or *Icteria*, esp. STONE*chat*, WHIN¹*chat*. [prob. imit.]

château (shah'tō) *n.* (*pl.* **-x** *pr.* -z). Large country house in France, esp. giving name to wine made near it. [F, f. OF *chastel* (CASTLE¹)]

chă'telaine (sh-) *n.* **1.** (Hist.) Set of short chains attached to woman's belt for carrying keys, watch, pencil, etc. **2.** Mistress of large house. [f. F *châtelaine*, fem. of *-ain* lord of a castle, f. med. L *castellanus* CASTELLAN]

chă'ttel *n.* Movable possession (usu. in *pl.*, esp. *goods and chattels*); *~ **mortgage,** conveyance of chattels by mortgage as security for debt. [ME f. OF *chatel*; see CATTLE]

chă'tter *v.i.*, & *n.* **1.** *v.i.* (Of bird) utter quick series of short notes; (of person) talk quickly, incessantly, foolishly, or inopportunely; (of teeth etc.) rattle together. **2.** *n.* Any of these sounds; vibration of tool; **~box,** talkative person, esp. child. [ME, imit.; see -ER⁵]

chă'tt|ў¹ *a.* Fond of chatting; resembling chat (*chatty letter*); hence ~ĭLY² *adv.*, ~ĭNESS *n.* [f. CHAT¹ + -Y²]

chă'ttў² *n.* (Ind.) Earthenware water-pot. [f. Hindi *chātī*]

chaud-froid (shōfrwah') *n.* Dish of cold cooked

meat or fish in jelly or sauce. [F (*chaud* hot, *froid* cold)]

chauffeur (shō′fer *or* shōfẽr′) *n.* (*fem.* **chauffeuse** *pr.* -ẽrz), & *v.t.* **1.** *n.* Person employed to drive a private or hired motor car. **2.** *v.t.* Drive (car) as chauffeur; convey (person) by car. [F, = stoker]

chaulmōō′gra *n.* E. Ind. tree of various species of family Flacourtiaceae, whose seeds yield an oil formerly used in treatment of leprosy. [Bengali]

***chautau′qua** (*or* sh-) *n.* Summer school or similar educational course. [f. *C*~ in New York State]

chau′vĭn|ĭsm (shō′v-) *n.* Bellicose patriotism; fervent support for a cause; so ~IST (2) *n.*, **~ĭ′stic** *a.* [f. *Chauvin*, Napoleonic veteran, in the Cogniards' *Cocarde Tricolore* (1831), + -ISM]

chaw *v.t.*, & *n.* (arch., dial., or vulg.) Chew; **~-bacon,** (derog.) bumpkin. [var. of CHEW]

Ch.B. *abbr.* Bachelor of Surgery. [f. L *Chirurgiae Baccalaureus*]

Ch.Ch. *abbr.* Christ Church.

cheap *a.* & *adv.* **1.** *a.* Low in price, value, or charge made (~ **and nasty,** of low cost and bad quality; **~′jack,** (*n.*) hawker at fair etc., (*a.*) inferior, shoddy; **dirt** ~, very cheap; **on the** ~, cheaply); worth more than its cost; easily got or made (*cheap gibes*); (of money) available at low interest; worthless, of little account, (**feel** ~, (sl.) feel ashamed or ill; **hold** ~, despise). **2.** *adv.* Cheaply (*got it cheap*; *going cheap*). **3.** Hence ~′ISH^{1} 2 *a.*, ~′LY^{2} *adv.*, ~′NESS *n.* [f. obs. phr. *good cheap* (*cheap* a bargain f. OE *cēap* barter, = OS *kōp*, OHG *kouf*, ON *kaup* f. Gmc **kaupaz* f. L *caupo* innkeeper)]

chea′pen *v.t.* & *i.* Make or become cheap, depreciate, degrade. [f. prec. + -EN^{6}]

cheat *n.* & *v.* **1.** *n.* Trick, fraud, deception; swindler, deceiver. **2.** *v.t.* Deceive, trick (person *into* or *out of* thing); (arch.) beguile (time etc.). **3.** *v.i.* Act fraudulently. [n. f. v., ME *chete* f. *achete*, var. of ESCHEAT^{2}]

chea′ter *n.* In vbl senses; *(in *pl.*, sl.) spectacles. [f. prec. + -ER^{1}]

chĕck^{1} *n.* **1.** (also as *int.*) (Announcement to opponent of) exposure of chess king to attack. **2.** Sudden stopping or slowing of motion; rebuff, repulse; crack or flaw in timber. **3.** (Hunting). Loss of the scent. **4.** Stoppage, pause; restraint on action (*keep* **in** ~, under control); person or thing that restrains. **5.** Control to secure accuracy; token of identification for left luggage, seat-holder, etc.; mark of verification; *bill in restaurant. **6.** *Counter at cards; **hand** or **pass in** one's **~s,** (colloq.) die. **7.** **~-action** (restraining piano hammer from striking string twice); **~-list,** (esp. complete) list for reference and verification; **~-nut,** LOCK^{2}-nut; **~-point** (where documents, vehicles, etc., are checked or inspected); **~-rein** (attaching one horse's rein to another's bit, or preventing horse from lowering head); ***~′room,** cloakroom in hotel or theatre, office for left luggage etc.; **~-valve** (allowing flow in one direction only); **~′weighman** (who checks weight of mined coal on behalf of miners). [ME, f. OF *eschec* f. med. L *scaccus* f. Arab. f. Pers. *šāh* king]

chĕck^{2} *v.* & *int.* **1.** *v.t.* Threaten (opponent's king) at chess. **2.** Suddenly stop or slow the motion of. **3.** *v.i.* (Of hounds) stop on losing scent, or to make sure of it. **4.** *v.t.* Restrain, curb; (colloq., of superior) find fault with, rebuke. **5.** *v.t.* & *i.* ~ (**on, up, up on, *out**), test (statement, account, figures, employees) by comparison etc., examine accuracy or condition of; *agree when compared; *mark with tick etc.; *deposit (luggage etc.); ~ **in,** register (prior to leaving by air) at airport; ~ **in, out,** arrive at, depart from, hotel or factory, record such arrival or departure of (person); **~-out,** act of checking out, final check, pay-desk in supermarket etc.; **~-up,** careful (esp. medical) examination. **6.** *int.* *expr. assent or agreement. [ME, f. OF *eschequier* play chess, give check to (*eschec*; see prec.)]

chĕck^{3} *n.* Cross-lined pattern of small squares; fabric woven or printed with this; hence ~ED^{2} (-kt) *a.* [ME, prob. f. CHEQUER^{1}]

***chĕck^{4}.** See CHEQUE.

chĕ′cker^{1,2}. See CHEQUER^{1,2}.

chĕ′ckerbĕrrȳ *n.* (Fruit of) the wintergreen *Gaultheria procumbens*. [f. *checkers* berries of service-tree + BERRY^{1}]

***chĕ′cker|s** (-z) *n. pl.* (usu. treated as *sing.*) The game of draughts; hence **~(man)**, draughtsman. [f. pl. of CHEQUER^{1}]

chĕ′ckmāte *n.*, & *v.t.* **1.** *n.* (also as *int.*) (Announcement to opponent of) inextricable check of king at chess; final defeat or deadlock. **2.** *v.t.* Give checkmate to; defeat, frustrate. [ME, f. OF *eschec mat* (cf. CHECK^{1}) f. Pers. *šāh māt* king is dead]

Chĕ′ddar *n.* Cheese made by piling curds and forming smooth mass. [~ in Somerset, where first made]

cheek *n.*, & *v.t.* **1.** *n.* Side-wall of mouth, side of face below eye; **~-bone,** that below eye; ~ **by jowl,** close together, intimate; **to** one's **own** ~, not shared with others; **turn the other** ~, accept attack etc. meekly, refuse to retaliate. **2.** Impertinent speech; cool confidence, effrontery, (*have the cheek to*). **3.** Side post of door etc.; (in *pl.*) jaws of vice, side-pieces of various parts of machines arranged in lateral pairs, (sl.) buttocks. **4.** *v.t.* Address saucily. [OE *cē(a)ce* f. WG **kækōn*, and OE *cēoce* f. WG **keuka*]

chee′k|ȳ *a.* Insolent, impudent; hence **~ĭly**^{2} *adv.*, **~ĭness** *n.* [f. prec. + -Y^{2}]

cheep *v.i.*, & *n.* (Utter) shrill feeble note as of young bird; **not a** ~, (colloq.) not the slightest sound etc. [imit.; cf. PEEP^{1}]

cheer^{1} *n.* **1.** Frame of mind (**what ~?,** how do you feel?; **be of good** ~, be stout-hearted or hopeful); food, fare, (**make good** ~, feast). **2.** Shout of encouragement or applause (**three ~s,** successive united hurrahs, often *for* person or thing honoured; **two ~s,** (iron.) mild enthusiasm); ||(in *pl.*, colloq.) = CHEERIO; **~-leader,** one who leads cheers of applause etc. [ME f. AF *chere* face etc., OF *chiere* f. LL *cara* face f. Gk *kara* head]

cheer^{2} *v.t.* & *i.* Comfort, gladden; incite, urge *on*, esp. by shouts; applaud; shout for joy; ~ **up,** comfort, take comfort. [ME, f. prec.]

cheer′ful *a.* Contented, in good spirits, hopeful; bright, pleasant; willing, not reluctant; hence ~LY^{2} *adv.*, ~NESS *n.* [f. CHEER^{1} + -FUL]

||**cheerĭō′** *int.* (colloq.) expr. encouragement on parting or before drinking; goodbye. [f. CHEER^{2}, CHEERY + O^{2}]

cheer′lėss *a.* Dull, gloomy, dreary, miserable; hence ~LY^{2} *adv.*, ~NESS *n.* [f. CHEER^{1} + -LESS]

cheer′lȳ *a.* & *adv.* **1.** *a.* (arch.) Cheerful. **2.** *adv.* (Naut.) Heartily, with a will. [f. CHEER^{1} + -LY^{1,2}]

cheer′|ȳ *a.* Lively, in good spirits; genial, cheering; hence **~ĭly**^{2} *adv.*, **~ĭness** *n.* [f. CHEER^{1} + -Y^{2}]

cheese^{1} (-z) *n.* **1.** Food made of pressed curds; complete cake etc. of this within rind; *bread and cheese*; CHALK^{1} *and cheese*; GREEN^{1} *cheese*; **hard** ~, (sl.) bad luck. **2.** Fruit of mallow; round flat object, e.g. heavy flat wooden disc used in skittles; (sl.) important person; DAMSON,

lemon, etc. ~, conserve of the fruit with shape or usu. consistency of (cream) cheese. **3. ~′board** (from which cheese is served); **~′burger,** hamburger with cheese in or on it; **~′cake,** tart(let) of pastry filled with sweetened curds, (sl.) display of shapely female body in advertisement etc.; **~′cloth,** BUTTER[1] muslin; **~-cutter,** knife with broad curved blade, device for cutting cheese by pulling a wire through it; **~-head,** squat cylindrical head of screw etc.; *cheese*-MITE; **~′monger,** dealer in cheese, butter, etc.; **~-paring,** stingy, stinginess; **~ straw,** thin cheese-flavoured strip of pastry; **~′wood,** (hard yellowish wood of) Austral. tree of genus *Pittosporum*. [OE *cēse* etc., = OS *kāsi, k(i)ēsi,* OHG *chāsi*, WG **kāsi* f. L *caseus*]

cheese[2] (-z) *v.t.* (sl.) (Esp. in *imper.*) stop *it*, leave off; **~d (off)**, bored, exasperated. [19th c.; orig. unkn.]

chee′s|ȳ (-zĭ) *a.* Like or tasting of cheese; (sl.) inferior, cheap and nasty; hence ~INESS *n.* [f. CHEESE[1] + -Y[2]]

chee′tah (-*a*) *n.* Swift-running spotted feline that can be trained to hunt deer etc. [f. Hindi *chītā*, perh. f. Skr. *chitraka* speckled]

chĕf (sh-) *n.* Man who is (usu. chief) cook in hotel etc. [F, = head]

chef-d'œuvre (shādėr′vr) *n.* (*pl.* ***chefs-*** *pr.* same). Masterpiece. [F]

cheiro-. Var. of CHIRO-.

che′la[1] (chā′-) *n.* Novice in course of qualifying for initiation in esoteric Buddhism; disciple, pupil. [Hindi, = servant]

chē′l|a[2] (k-) *n.* (*pl.* **~ae**). Prehensile claw of crabs, lobsters, scorpions, etc.; hence ~ATE[2] *a.*, (esp., Chem.) forming or having a group that loops round a central ion, whence ~ATE[3] *v.t.*, ~A′TION *n.* [mod. L, f. L *chele* or f. Gk *khēlē* claw]

Chĕ′llėan (sh-) *a.* (Archaeol.) = ABBEVILLIAN. [f. F *chelléen* (*Chelles* near Paris; see -AN)]

Chĕ′lsea (-sĭ) *n.* **~ bun,** kind of rolled currant-bun; **~ pensioner,** inmate of the Chelsea Royal Hospital for old or disabled soldiers; **~ ware,** kind of porcelain made at Chelsea in 18th c. [~ in London]

Chĕltō′nĭan *a.* & *n.* (Past or present member) of Cheltenham College. [f. mod. L *Cheltonia* Cheltenham + -IAN]

chĕ′mĭcal (k-) *a.* & *n.* **1.** *a.* Of, made by, relating to, chemistry; (of lavatory) effecting decomposition of waste by chemical process; *chemical* ENGINEER[1]; **~ engineering,** industrial application of chemistry; **~ warfare** (using poison gas and other chemicals); hence ~LY[2] *adv.* **2.** *n.* Substance obtained by or used in chemical process; **fine ~s,** those used in small amounts and fairly pure; **heavy ~s,** bulk chemicals used in industry and agriculture. [f. *chemic* alchemic f. F *chimique* or mod. L *chimicus*, *chymicus*, f. med. L *alchymicus* (as ALCHEMY; see -IC) + -AL]

chĕ′mĭcō- (k-) *comb. form.* Chemical (and), as: **~-physical,** pertaining to chemistry and physics. [f. *chemic* = prec. + -o-]

chĕmĭlūmĭnĕ′sc|ence (k-; *or* -lōō-) *n.* Emission of light accompanying chemical reaction; hence ~ENT *a.* [f. G (*-eszenz*) (as prec., LUMINESCENCE)]

chemin de fer (shemăṅdefār′) *n.* Form of baccarat. [F, = railway, lit. road of iron]

chėmi′se (shĭmē′z) *n.* Woman's loose-fitting undergarment or dress hanging straight from shoulders. [ME f. OF, f. LL *camisia* shirt]

chĕmĭsôr′ption (k-) *n.* Adsorption by chemical action. [f. CHEMICAL + ADSORPTION]

chĕ′mĭst (k-) *n.* Person skilled in chemistry; ||dealer in medicinal drugs. [earlier *chymist* f. F *chimiste* f. mod. L *chimista* (*alchimista* ALCHEMIST)]

chĕ′mĭstrȳ (k-) *n.* Science of the elements and compounds and their laws of combination and change resulting from interactions between substances in contact; (fig.) mysterious change or process. [f. prec. + -RY]

chĕmo- (k-) *comb. form.* Chemical, as: **~sy′nthesis,** formation of carbohydrates from inorganic compounds without sunlight; **~the′rapy,** treatment of disease by chemical means. [f. CHEMICAL + -o-]

***chĕ′murgȳ** (k-) *n.* Chemical and industrial use of organic raw materials. [f. prec., after *metallurgy*]

chėni′lle (shĭnē′l) *n.* Yarn with pile all round, used in trimming furniture; fabric made with it. [F, = hairy caterpillar f. L *canicula* dim. of *canis* dog]

chėŏngsă′m *n.* Chinese woman's garment with high neck and slit skirt. [Chin.]

||**chĕque** (-k), ***chĕck**[4], *n.* Written order to banker to pay named sum from drawer's account to bearer or (order of) named person; form on which such order is to be written; BLANK[1] *cheque*; **~-book,** book of forms for writing cheques, issued to bank's customer; **~ card** (issued by bank to guarantee honouring of any cheque up to stated value); ***checking account,** current account at bank. [f. CHECK[1] 5]

chĕ′quer[1] (-k*er*), **chĕ′cker**[1], *n.* (often in *pl.*) Pattern made of squares or with alternating colours; **~-board,** (pattern resembling) chess-board. [ME, f. EXCHEQUER]

chĕ′quer[2] (-k*er*), **chĕ′cker**[2], *v.t.* Mark with squares, esp. of alternate colours; variegate, break uniformity of, (lit., or fig., esp. (in *p.p.*) undergoing varied fortunes). [ME, f. prec.]

C(h)ĕrĕ′nkŏv (ch-; -f) *n.* **~ radiation** (emitted by particles moving in a medium at speeds faster than that of light). [f. P. A. ~, Russ. physicist b. 1904]

chĕ′rĭsh *v.t.* Foster, nurse; value, hold dear, cling to, (esp. hopes, feelings, etc.). [ME, f. OF *cherir* (*cher* f. L *carus* dear; see -ISH[2])]

cher′nozĕm (-ār′-) *n.* Fertile humus-rich black soil of S. Russia etc. [Russ. (*chernyĭ* black, *zemlya* earth)]

Chĕ′rokee (*or* -ē′) *n.* (Member of) Amer. Ind. tribe formerly inhabiting much of southern U.S.; **~ rose,** fragrant white wild rose of southern U.S. [f. Cherokee *Tsárăgĭ*]

cheroo′t (sh-) *n.* Cigar with both ends open. [f. F *cheroute* f. Tamil *shuruṭṭu* roll]

chĕ′rrȳ *n.* & *a.* **1.** *n.* Small stone-fruit; tree of genus *Prunus* bearing this or grown for its ornamental flowers; **~(-wood)**, its wood; **two bites at a ~,** unenterprising or hesitant action; **~-bob,** two cherries with joined stems (BOB[1]); **~ brandy,** dark-red liqueur of brandy in which cherries have been steeped; **~-laurel,** ||common laurel (*Prunus laurocerasus*), *evergreen shrub (*P. caroliniana*); **~-picker,** crane for raising and lowering persons; **~-pie,** (1) pie made with cherries, (2) garden heliotrope. **2.** *a.* Red, esp. of the colour of ripe cherries, (*cherry lips, ribbon*). [ME, f. ONF *cherise* (treated as pl.; cf. PEASE) f. med. L *ceresia* perh. f. L f. Gk *kerasos*]

chėr′sonēse (k-) *n.* (usu. poet. or rhet.) Peninsula, esp. of Thrace west of Hellespont. [f. L f. Gk *khersonēsos* (*khersos* dry, *nēsos* island)]

chėrt *n.* Flintlike form of quartz. [17th c.; orig. unkn.]

chĕ′rub *n.* (*pl.* **~s** *or* **-im**). Angelic being; one of the second ORDER[1] of ninefold celestial hierarchy, gifted with knowledge; (Art) winged (head of) child; beautiful or innocent child;

hence **cheru'bic** (-ōō'-) *a.* [ME, f. OE *cherubin* and f. Heb. *kᵉrūḇ*, pl. *kᵉrūḇîm*]

chĕr'vĭl *n.* Garden herb used to flavour soup, salad, etc. [OE *cerfille*, = OHG *kervela* f. L f. Gk *khairephullon*]

Ches. *abbr.* Cheshire.

Chĕ'shire (-*er or* -ēr) *n.* **Grin like a ~ cat** (broadly and fixedly); **~ cheese,** kind like Cheddar, orig. made in Cheshire. [county in England]

chĕss *n.* Game for two players with thirty-two **~-men,** on **~-board** chequered with sixty-four squares. [ME, f. OF *esches* pl. of *eschec* (CHECK¹)]

chĕ'ssel *n.* Cheese-making mould. [app. f. CHEESE¹ + WELL¹]

chĕst *n.* **1.** Large strong box; box for sailor's belongings; box for tools, medicines, etc.; treasury or coffer of institution, (fig.) the money in it; case of some commodity, esp. tea; **~ of drawers,** piece of furniture with set of drawers in frame; **~ of viols** (complete set, orig. kept in a chest). **2.** Part of human or animal body enclosed in ribs; front surface of body from neck to waist; **get** thing **off** one's ~, (colloq.) relieve one's anxiety by disclosing something; **play close to** one's ~, be cautious or secretive about; **~-protector,** flannel etc. worn on chest as protection against cold; **~-voice** (of lowest speaking or singing register); hence **-~'ED²** *a.*, **~'Y²** *a.*, (colloq.) inclined to, marked by, symptomatic of, chest disease, (colloq.) having a large chest or prominent breasts, *(sl.) arrogant. [OE *cest*, *cyst*, = OHG, ON *kista* f. Gmc **kistō(n)* f. L f. Gk *kistē*]

chĕ'sterfield *n.* Sofa with padded seat, back, and ends; plain overcoat usu. with velvet collar. [f. 19th-c. Earl of *C~*]

chĕ'stnŭt (-sn-) *n.* & *a.* **1.** *n.* Tree, *Castanea sativa*, (also **~-tree, Spanish ~,** or **sweet ~**); its hard brown edible fruit; **~(-wood),** its heavy wood; other tree of genus *Castanea*; = HORSE¹-*-chestnut*; small hard patch on horse's leg; stale joke or anecdote. **2.** *n.* & *a.* (Of) chestnut colour, deep reddish-brown; (horse) of reddish-brown or yellowish-brown colour (**liver ~,** dark kind). [f. obs. *chesten* (f. OF *chastaine* f. L f. Gk *kastanea*) + NUT]

chĕ'tnĭk *n.* Guerrilla fighter in Balkans. [f. Serbian *chetnik* (*cheta* band, troop)]

chĕvă'l-glass (sh-; -ahs) *n.* Tall mirror swung on upright frame. [f. F *cheval* horse, frame]

chĕvalier' (sh-) *n.* Member of certain orders of knighthood, or of French Legion of Honour etc.; (Hist.) title of Old and Young PRETENDERS; **~ *d'industrie*** (-dă'ṅdŏŏstrē), adventurer, swindler. [ME f. AF *chevaler*, OF *chevalier* f. med. L *caballarius* f. L *caballus* horse; see -IER, -EER]

chevaux de frise (shevōdefrē'z) *n. pl.* (occas. treated as *sing.*) Iron spikes set in timber etc. to repel cavalry etc. in war, or to guard fence or wall in peace. [F, lit. horses of Friesland; invented by 17th-c. Frisians who had no cavalry]

chevet (shevā') *n.* Apsidal end of church, with attached group of apses. [F, = pillow, f. L *capitium* (*caput* head)]

chĕ'vĭot *n.* (Animal of) breed of sheep from *Cheviot* Hills on border of England and Scotland; wool or cloth from it.

chĕ'vron (sh-) *n.* (Her. & Archit.) bent bar of inverted V shape; badge in V shape (inverted or not) on sleeve of uniform indicating rank or length of service. [ME f. OF, f. Rom. **caprione* f. L *caper* goat; cf. L *capreoli* pair of rafters]

chĕ'vrotain, -tĭn, (sh-) *n.* Small deerlike animal of genus *Tragulus*. [F, dim. of OF *chevrot* dim. of *chèvre* goat]

chĕ'vȳ. Var. of CHIVVY.

chew (-ōō) *v.* & *n.* **1.** *v.t.* & *i.* Work (food etc., or abs.) between the teeth, grind to pulp or indent by repeated biting; turn *over* in mind, meditate *on* or *over*; discuss, talk *over*; *chew the* CUD; ***~ out,** (colloq.) reprimand; **~ the rag** or **the fat,** (sl.) discuss a matter, esp. reiterate an old grievance, grouse; **like a piece of ~ed string,** (colloq.) weary and weak; **~'ing-gum,** preparation of sweetened and flavoured gums (esp. chicle), used for prolonged chewing; hence **~'ER¹** *n.* **2.** *n.* Act of chewing; quid of tobacco; chewy sweetmeat. [OE *cēowan*, = OHG *kiuwan* f. WG **kewwan*]

chew'ȳ (-ōō'ĭ) *a.* Suitable for chewing; needing to be chewed. [f. prec. + -Y²]

Cheyne–Stō'kes (-ānstō'ks) *a.* (Path.) **~ breathing** etc. (with gradual decrease of movement to complete stop, followed by gradual increase). [f. J. *Cheyne*, Sc. physician d. 1836, and W. *Stokes*, Ir. physician d. 1878]

chez (shā) *prep.* At the house or home of. [F, f. OF *chiese* f. L *casa* cottage]

chī (kī) *n.* Twenty-second Greek letter (X, χ) = kh, ch; **~-rho',** monogram of chi and rho as first two letters of Gk *Khristos* Christ; **~-square'e,** method of comparing observed and theoretical values in Statistics. [ME, f. Gk *khi*]

Chĭa'ntĭ (kĭah'-) *n.* Dry usu. red Italian wine. [~ in Tuscany, Italy]

chiâroscur'ō (kyâr-; -oor'ō) *n.* (*pl.* **~s**). Treatment of light and shade in painting; light and shade effects in nature; use of contrast in literature etc.; (*attrib.*) half-revealed. [It. (*chiaro* CLEAR¹; *oscuro* dark, OBSCURE)]

chīă'smus (kīă'z-) *n.* Inversion in second phrase of order followed in first (*To stop too fearful and too faint to go*); hence **chīă'stic** (kī-) *a.* [mod. L f. Gk *khiasmos* crosswise arrangement (*khiazō* mark with letter CHI)]

chĭbou'k, -que, (-ōō'k) *n.* Long Turkish tobacco-pipe. [f. Turk. *çubuk* tube]

chic (shēk) *n.*, & *a.* (**chic-er, chic-est**). **1.** *n.* Stylishness, elegance in dress; skill, effectiveness. **2.** *a.* Stylish, elegant. [F]

chĭcā'ne (sh-) *v.* & *n.* **1.** *v.i.* Use chicanery. **2.** *v.t.* Cheat (person) *into*, *out of*, etc. **3.** *n.* Chicanery; (Bridge) hand without trumps, or without cards of one suit; artificial barrier or obstacle on motor racecourse. [f. F *chicane(r)* quibble]

chĭcā'nerȳ (sh-) *n.* Legal trickery; deception; sophistry. [f. F *chicanerie* (as prec.; see -ERY)]

***chĭcā'nō** (*or* -ah'nō; *or* sh-) *n.* (*pl.* **~s**). American person of Mexican origin. [f. Sp. *mejicano* Mexican]

chi'chi (shē'shē) *a.* & *n.* Frilly or showy (thing); fussy or affected (person, behaviour). [F]

chĭck¹ *n.* Young bird before or after hatching; (sl.) young woman; **~abi'ddy,** term of endearment used of or to child; **~'weed,** small weed of genus *Stellaria* etc. [ME, f. CHICKEN]

chĭck² *n.* (Ind.) Screen for doorway etc., made from split bamboo and twine. [f. Hindi *chik*]

chĭ'ckadee *n.* Amer. titmouse of genus *Penthestes* or *Parus*, with dark-crowned head (lit., or fig. as term of endearment to woman). [imit.]

chĭ'ckėn *n.* (*pl.* **~s** *or* **~**), *a.*, & *v.i.* **1.** *n.* Young bird, esp. of domestic fowl; flesh of domestic fowl as food; youthful person (esp. *is no chicken*); (sl.) game testing courage in face of danger; **count** one's **~s before they are hatched,** be over-optimistic or precipitate; MOTHER *Carey's chicken*; **~-breast(ed),** (having) malformed projection of breastbone; *chicken* CHOLERA; **~-feed,** food for poultry, (colloq.) unimportant amount of money etc.; **~-heart(ed), ~-liver(ed),** (with) no courage; **~-pox,** mild eruptive disease esp. of children; **~-wire,** light wire netting with hexagonal mesh. **2.** *a.* (sl.) Cowardly. **3.** *v.i.* **~ out,** (sl.) withdraw through cowardice. [OE *cīcen, cȳcen,* f. Gmc **kiukīnam* cogn. w. COCK¹; cf. -EN¹]

chĭ'cklĭng *n.* Common cultivated vetchling (*Lathyrus sativus*). [earlier *chicheling* dim. of ME & F *chiche* f. L *cicer* chick-pea]

chĭ'ck-pea *n.* Dwarf pea (*Cicer arietinum*). [orig. *ciche pease,* f. as prec. + PEASE]

chĭ'cle (*or* chē'-; *or* -klē) *n.* Milky juice of the balata, sapodilla, or similar tree, the basis of chewing-gum. [Amer. Sp., f. Nahuatl *tzictli*]

chĭ'corȳ *n.* Blue-flowered plant (*Cichorium intybus*) cultivated for its salad leaves and its root; its root ground for use with or instead of coffee; *endive. [ME, f. obs. F *cicorée* endive f. med. L *cic(h)orea* f. L f. Gk *kikhorion* SUCCORY]

chīde *v.t.* & *i.* (**chī'ded** *or* **chid; chī'ded** *or* **chi'dden**). (arch. or literary). Scold, rebuke. [OE *cīdan,* of unkn. orig.]

chief¹ *n.* **1.** Leader, ruler; head man of tribe, clan, etc.; head of a department, highest official; **C~ of Staff,** senior staff officer of a service or commander; hence **~'**DOM, **~'**SHIP, *ns.*, **~'**LESS, **~'**LY¹, *adjs.* **2. In ~,** most of all, especially, (*for many reasons, and this one in chief*); **-in-~,** supreme (*Colonel, Commandant, Commander, Commodore, -in-Chief*). **3.** (Her.) Upper third of shield. [ME f. OF *ch(i)ef* f. Rom. **capum* f. L *caput* head]

chief² *a.* Formally leading or most important (*Chief Justice* etc.); first in importance, influence, etc.; prominent, leading; hence **~'**LY² *adv.*, above all, mainly but not exclusively. [ME, f. prec.]

chie'ftain (-tĭn *or* -tan) *n.* Captain of robbers; chief of tribe or clan; hence **~**CY, **~**ESS¹, **~**SHIP, *ns.* [ME f. OF *chevetaine* f. LL *capitaneus* CAPTAIN¹; assim. to CHIEF¹]

chĭ'ff-chăff *n.* Small European bird (*Phylloscopus collybita*) of warbler family. [imit.]

chĭ'ffŏn (sh-) *n.* & *a.* **1.** *n.* Light diaphanous plain-woven fabric of silk, nylon, etc. **2.** *a.* (Of fabric) lightweight; (of pie etc.) light-textured. [F (*chiffe* rag)]

chĭffonier' (sh-) *n.* Movable low cupboard with sideboard top. [f. F *chiffonnier, -ière* rag-picker, chest of drawers for odds and ends]

chĭ'gger (-g-) *n.* **1.** = CHIGOE. **2.** Harvest-bug. [var. of CHIGOE]

chi'gnon (shē'nyawṅ) *n.* Mass of hair on pad at back of head. [F, orig. = nape of neck]

chĭ'gōe *n.* Tropical flea, burrowing into skin. [Carib]

chĭhua'hua (chĭwah'wa) *n.* (Animal of) very small smooth-haired breed of dog, originating in Mexico. [*C~* state and city in Mexico]

chĭ'lblain *n.* Itching swelling on hand, foot, etc., from exposure to cold and poor circulation; hence **~**ED² (-nd) *a.* [f. CHILL¹ + BLAIN]

chīld *n.* (*pl.* **chĭ'ldren** *pr.* chĭ'-) **1.** Young human being, boy or girl; unborn or newborn human being (**with ~,** pregnant); person who has not reached age of discretion; childish person; **this ~,** (sl.) I, me. **2.** Son or daughter (at any age) *of* (or w. *my* etc.), offspring; descendant (lit. or fig.), follower, or adherent *of* (*Children of* ISRAEL; *child of nature, of* WRATH, *of God, of the Devil*); product *of.* **3. ~'birth,** (arch.) **~'bed,** parturition; **~ care,** local authority's care of children temporarily deprived of normal home life; **~ guidance,** supervision of children's welfare; **~-minder,** one who takes care of child esp. in absence of mother; **~-proof,** not able to be operated or damaged by child; **~'s play,** easy task. **4.** Hence **~'**LESS, **~'**LY¹ (poet.), *adjs.* [OE *cild* f. **kiltham*]

Childe *n.* (arch.) Youth of noble birth (*Childe Harold, Roland*). [var. of prec.]

Chĭ'ldermas *n.* (arch.) Festival of Holy Innocents, 28 Dec. [OE *cilderamæsse* (*cildra* gen. pl. of *cild* CHILD, *mæsse* MASS¹)]

chī'ldhood (-d-h-) *n.* State of being a child; time from birth to puberty; **second ~,** dotage. [OE *cildhād* (as CHILD, -HOOD)]

chī'ldĭsh *a.* Of or proper to a child; puerile, unsuitable for a grown person; hence **~**LY² *adv.*, **~**NESS *n.* [OE *cildisc* (as CHILD, -ISH¹)]

chī'ldlīke *a.* Having good qualities of child, as innocence, frankness, etc. [f. CHILD + -LIKE]

chĭ'ldren. See CHILD.

Chĭ'lė *n.* **~ pine,** monkey-puzzle; **~ nitre** or **saltpetre,** natural sodium nitrate; hence **~**AN *a.* & *n.* [**~** in S. America]

chĭ'lĭ. See CHILLI.

chĭ'lĭad (k-) *n.* A thousand; a thousand years. [f. LL f. Gk *khilias -ados*; see -AD 1]

chĭ'lĭăsm, chĭ'lĭăst, (k-) *ns.* Doctrine of or belief in, believer in, the millennium; hence **chĭlĭă'st**IC (k-) *a.* [f. Gk *khiliasmos* & LL *chiliastes,* f. as prec.]

chĭll¹ *n.* Cold sensation, lowered temperature of body, feverish shivering, feverish cold (*catch a chill*); unpleasant coldness of air, water, etc., (**take the ~ off,** warm slightly); depressing influence (*cast a chill over*); coldness of manner; hence **~'**SOME¹ *a.* (literary). [OE *c(i)ele* f. **kaliz* (**kalan* be cold); revived as f. CHILL³]

chĭll² *a.* (literary) Unpleasantly cold to feel; feeling cold; unfeeling, unemotional, austere; hence **~'**NESS *n.* [app. f. p.p. of foll., after *cool, cold*]

chĭll³ *v.t.* & *i.* Make or become cold; deaden or destroy with cold; depress, dispirit; harden (molten metal) by contact with cold material; preserve (meat etc.) at low temperature without freezing. [ME, of uncert. orig., though prob. rel. to CHILL¹]

chĭ'l(l)ĭ *n.* (*pl.* **~es**). Dried pod of capsicum (as relish, or made into cayenne); **~ con carne,** Mexican stew of chilli-flavoured minced beef. [f. Sp. *chile, chili* f. Aztec *chilli*]

chĭ'll|ȳ *a.* Somewhat cold to feel; feeling somewhat cold; sensitive to cold; not genial, cold-mannered; hence **~ĭ**NESS *n.* [f. CHILL¹ + -Y²]

||**Chĭltern Hŭ'ndreds** (-z) *n. pl.* Crown manor, administration of which is nominal office under Crown and so requires M.P. to vacate seat; **apply for the ~,** resign from House of Commons. [f. *Chiltern* Hills in S. England + HUNDRED 2 + -S¹]

chimaera. See CHIMERA.

chimb. See CHIME³.

chīme¹ *n.* Set of attuned bells; series of sounds given by this; agreement, correspondence. [ME, prob. f. *chym(b)e bell,* perh. f. **chimbel* f. OE *cimbal* f. L f. Gk *kumbalon* CYMBAL]

chīme² *v.* **1.** *v.t.* Make (bell) sound; ring chimes on (bells); show (hour) by chiming. **2.** *v.i.* (Of bells) ring chimes; be in agreement (*together, with,* or abs.); **~ in,** (1) join harmoniously, (2) interject remark. [ME, rel. to prec.]

chīme³, chīmb (-m), *n.* Projecting rim at end of cask. [ME; cf. MDu., MLG *kimme*]

chĭmēr'a, -aer'a, (kĭmēr'*a*) *n.* **1.** (Gk Myth.) Monster with lion's head, goat's body, and serpent's tail. **2.** Bogy; thing of hybrid character; fanciful conception; hence **chĭmĕ'r**ICAL (k-) *a.* **3.** (Biol.) Organism formed by grafting etc. from tissues of different genetic origin. **4.** (Zool.) Fish of family Chimaeridae. [f. L f. Gk *khimaira* she-goat, chimera]

chĭmēr'e *n.* Bishop's outer robe. [ME, perh. rel. to Sp. *zamarra* sheepskin cloak, It. *cimarra* long robe]

chĭ'mney *n.* **1.** Channel carrying off smoke or steam of fire, furnace, engine, etc.; part of this above roof; glass tube providing draught for lamp-flame; natural vent, e.g. of volcano; (Mountaineering) narrow cleft by which cliff may be climbed. **2. ~-breast,** projecting wall between chimney and room; **~-corner, ~-nook,** warm seat within old-fashioned fireplace; **~-piece,** mantelpiece; **~-pot,** earthenware or metal pipe added to chimney-top (*~-pot hat,* tall silk hat); *chimney*-STACK; **~-swallow, ~-swift,** the swift *Chaetura pelagica*; **~-sweep,** man whose business is to sweep chimneys to remove soot etc. [ME, f. OF *cheminée* f. LL *caminata* (? *camera*) (room) with a fireplace f. L f. Gk *kaminos* oven; see -Y[4]]

chĭmp *n.* (colloq.) = foll. [abbr.]

chĭmpanzee′ *n.* African ape of genus *Anthropopithecus,* animal most closely resembling man. [f. F *chimpanzé* f. Kongo]

chĭn *n.* **1.** Front of lower jaw; **keep** one's **~ up,** remain cheerful; STICK[1] one's *chin out*; **take on the ~,** (1) suffer severe blow from, (2) endure courageously; ***~ music,** talk, chatter; **~-strap** (for fastening hat etc. under chin); **~-wag** *n.,* & *v.i.,* (sl.) talk; hence **~′**LESS *a.,* (fig.) lacking firmness of character. **2.** *(sl.) Talk; insolence. [OE *cin(n),* = OS, OHG *kinni,* ON *kinn* chin, lower jaw, Goth. *kinnus* cheek f. Gmc **kinn*-]

Chī′na[1] *a.* From China (*China* CRÊPE, ASTER, etc.; **~ orange,** common orange, orig. from China; **~ silk,** light plain-woven silk fabric; **~ tea,** smoke-cured kind from small-leaved tea plant grown in China); **~town,** section of a town (esp. a seaport) in which the Chinese live as a colony. [~, country in Asia]

chī′na[2] *n.* Fine semi-transparent or white earthenware, porcelain; **~(ware),** things made of this; **~-closet** (for keeping or displaying one's china); **~ clay,** kaolin; **~ (plate),** (rhyming sl.) mate. [f. Pers. *chīnī* (as prec.)]

chī′nagraph (-ahf) *n.* Kind of pencil that can write on china, glass, etc. [f. prec. + -GRAPH]

Chī′naman *n.* (*pl.* **-men**). **1.** (arch. or derog.) A Chinese. **2.** (Cricket). Off-break or googly by left-handed bowler. **3.** *(colloq.) **~'s chance,** very slight chance. [f. CHINA[1] + MAN[1]]

***chĭnch** *n.* **~(-bug),** bedbug; small insect (*Blissus leucopterus*) destroying grain. [f. Sp. *chinche* f. L *cimex -icis*]

chĭncherĭnchee′ *n.* S. Afr. perennial white-flowered bulbous plant (*Ornithogalum thyrsoides*). [imit., f. the squeaky rubbing of its stalks]

chĭnchĭ′lla *n.* Small S. Amer. rodent of genus *Chinchilla*; its soft grey fur; breed of domestic cat or rabbit. [Sp., dim. of *chinche* bug, CHINCH (from supposed smell)]

‖**chĭn-chĭ′n** *int.* of greeting and farewell, and as toast. [f. Chin. *ts'ing ts'ing*]

Chĭ′ndĭt *n.* Allied fighter behind Japanese lines in Burma (1943–45). [f. Burm. *chinthé,* a mythical creature]

‖**chīne**[1] *n.* Deep narrow ravine in Isle of Wight and Dorset. [OE *cinu* chink etc., f. Gmc **ki-* burst open]

chīne[2] *n.,* & *v.t.* **1.** *n.* Backbone; joint of meat containing animal's backbone or part of it; ridge, arête. **2.** *v.t.* Cut through backbone of (carcass). [ME, f. OF *eschine* f. Rom. **skīna* f. Gmc **skin-* SHIN and L *spina* SPINE]

chīne[3] *n.* Join of side and bottom of ship etc. [= CHIME[3]]

chiné (shēnā′) *a.* (Of fabric) given mottled pattern of (supposedly) Chinese style by colouring warp before weaving. [F, p.p. of *chiner* (*Chine* China)]

Chīnee′ *n.* (sl.) Chinese person. [f. foll. taken as pl.]

Chīnē′se (-z) *a.* & *n.* (*pl.* same). (Native or language) of China; person of Chinese descent; **~ boxes** (nested together); **~ copy,** slavish imitation; **~ goose,** small brown or white domesticated goose; **~ gooseberry,** (N.Z.) vine with brown hairy fruit; **~ lantern,** (1) collapsible lantern of paper, (2) plant with inflated orange calyx; **~ puzzle,** intricate puzzle or problem; **~ wall,** (fig.) insurmountable barrier; **~ white,** white zinc oxide as pigment. [f. CHINA[1] + -ESE]

chĭnk[1] *n.* Long narrow opening, slit, peep-hole; place not fully closed and admitting light etc. [16th c., rel. to CHINE[1]]

chĭnk[2] *n.* & *v.* **1.** *n.* Sound as of glasses or coins striking together. **2.** *v.i.* Make this sound. **3.** *v.t.* Cause (coin etc.) to make this sound. [imit.]

Chĭnk[3] *n.* (sl., derog.) A Chinese. [abbr.]

chĭnkerĭnchee′. Var. of CHINCHERINCHEE.

***chi′nō** (-ē′-) *n.* (*pl.* **~s**). Cotton twill cloth, usu. khaki-coloured; (in *pl.*) garment made of it. [Amer. Sp., = toasted]

Chīno- *comb. form.* China, = SINO-. [f. CHINA[1] + -O-]

chinoi′serie (shĭnwah′z-) *n.* Imitation of Chinese motifs in furniture etc. [F]

chĭnōō′k *n.* Warm dry wind which blows east of the Rocky Mountains; warm wet southerly wind west of them; **~ salmon,** large salmon of N. Pacific. [Amer. Ind. name of a tribe]

chĭntz (-ts) *n.* & *a.* (Of) cotton cloth fast-printed with particoloured pattern and usu. glazed; hence **~′**Y[2] *a.,* (fig.) cheap, mean. [earlier *chints* pl. f. Hindi *chint* f. Skr. *chitra* variegated]

chīonodŏ′xa (k-) *n.* Blue-flowered early-blooming plant of genus *Chionodoxa,* glory-of-the-snow. [mod. L, f. Gk *khiōn* snow + *doxa* glory]

chĭp[1] *n.* **1.** Thin piece cut from wood or broken from stone etc. (*chip off the old* BLOCK[1]; **have a ~ on** one's **shoulder,** be touchy or embittered); thin slice of fruit, etc.; long slender piece of potato; small square of semiconductor used to make integrated circuit; ‖(in *pl.,* colloq.) potato chips fried (FISH[1] *and chips*); *(in *pl.*) potato CRISPS. **2.** Wood split into strips for making baskets, hats, etc.; **~ (basket),** basket made of these joined or woven. **3.** Place on china etc. from which chip has been knocked off. **4.** Counter, piece of money; **have had** one's **~s,** (sl.) be beaten etc.; **when the ~s are down,** when it comes to the point. **5. ~′board,** thin material made of compressed wood chips and resin; **~ (shot),** (Footb.) short upward kick, (Golf) short lofted approach-shot on to putting-green. [ME, f. OE *cipp, cyp* beam]

chĭp[2] *v.* (-pp-). **1.** *v.t.* Cut (wood), break (stone, crockery), at surface or edge, whence **~′**PING[1] (2) *n.*; shape thus; cut (potato) into chips; cut or break (piece etc.) *off, from*; carve (inscription); (colloq.) tease (a person); kick or hit with chip shot. **2.** *v.i.* Be apt to break at edge; play chip shot. **3.** *v.i.* & *t.* **~ in,** (colloq.) interrupt speaker, contribute (money etc.). [prob. repr. OE **cippian*; cf. MLG, MDu, *kippen* hatch out]

chĭ′pmŭnk, -ŭck, *n.* N. Amer. ground-squirrel. [Algonquian]

chĭpola′ta (-lah′-) *n.* Small spicy sausage. [F, f. It. *cipollata* dish of onions (*cipolla* onion)]

Chĭ′ppendāle *n.* Elegant style of ornamented furniture. [f. T. ~, Engl. cabinet-maker d. 1779]

***chĭ′pper** *a.* Cheerful. [perh. f. N. Engl. dial. *kipper* lively]

chĭ′pp|ȳ *a.* & *n.* **1.** *a.* (sl.) Unwell; irritable; hence **~**INESS *n.* **2.** *n.* (colloq.) Fish-and-chips shop; (sl.) promiscuous or delinquent young woman. [f. CHIP[1,2] + -Y[2]]

Chĭps *n.* (Naut. sl.) Ship's carpenter. [pl. of CHIP[1]]

chīr′al (k-) *a.* (Of crystal etc.) not superposable on its mirror image; hence **~**ITY (-ă′l-) *n.* [f. Gk *kheir* hand + -AL]

chīr'o- (k-) *comb. form.* Hand, as: **~graphy** (-ŏ'g-), handwriting; **~mancy,** palmistry. [f. Gk *kheir* hand + -o-]

chĭrŏ'pod|y̆ (kĭ- *or* shĭ-) *n.* Treatment given to feet, esp. for corns, bunions, etc.; hence **~IST** (3) *n.* [f. prec. + Gk *pous podos* foot + -Y[1]]

chīropră'ct|ic (k-) *n.* Manipulation of spinal column as method of curing disease; hence **~OR** *n.*, one who practises chiropractic. [f. CHIRO- + Gk *praktikos* (cf. PRACTICAL)]

chīrŏ'pter|an (k-) *n.* Member of mammal order Chiroptera, with membraned hands serving as wings, the bats; so **~OUS** *a.* [f. CHIRO- + Gk *pteron* wing + -AN]

chīrp *v.i.* & *t.*, & *n.* (Make) short sharp note (as) of small bird or of grasshopper etc.; utter (song), express (joy etc.), thus; talk merrily. [ME, earlier *chirk*, *chirt*; imit.]

chīr'p|y̆ *a.* (colloq.) Lively, cheerful; hence **~ĭLY**[2] *adv.*, **~ĭNESS** *n.* [f. prec. + -Y[2]]

chīrr *v.i.*, & *n.* (Make) prolonged trilling sound (as) of grasshopper. [imit.; cf. CHURR]

chĭ'rrup *v.i.*, & *n.* (Make) series of chirps, twittering. [trilled form of CHIRP]

chĭ'sel (-z-) *n.*, & *v.t.* (‖-ll-). **1.** *n.* Tool having square bevelled end for shaping wood, stone, or metal; **cold ~** (suitable for cutting cold metal). **2.** *v.t.* Cut or shape with chisel (**~led features** etc., clear-cut); (sl.) defraud, treat unfairly; hence **~LER**[1] *n.* [ME f. ONF, f. Rom. **cisellum* f. LL *cisorium* f. L *caedere caes-* cut]

chĭt[1] *n.* Young child; young, small, or slender woman (usu. derog.; *chit of a girl*). [ME, whelp, cub, kitten, perh. = dial. *chit* sprout]

chĭt[2] *n.* Note or written paper; note of order, sum owed, etc. [earlier *chitty*, Anglo-Ind. f. Hindi *chiṭṭhī* pass f. Skr. *chitra* mark]

chi'tal (-ē't-) *n.* Axis deer. [Hindi]

chĭ't-chăt *n.*, & *v.i.* (-tt-). (Hold) light conversation; gossip. [redupl. of CHAT[1]]

chī'tĭn (k-) *n.* Substance forming horny constituent in exoskeleton of arthropods; hence **~OUS** *a.* [f. F *chitine* irreg. f. Gk *khitōn*; see foll., -IN]

chī'ton (k-) *n.* **1.** Mollusc of genus *Chiton*, with shell or overlapping plates. **2.** Long woollen garment worn by ancient Greeks. [f. Gk *khitōn*]

chĭ'tterlĭng *n.* (usu. in *pl.*) Smaller intestines of pigs etc., esp. as cooked for food. [ME; orig. uncert.]

chĭv *n.*, & *v.t.* (-vv-) (sl.) Knife. [17th c.; orig. unkn.]

chĭ'valrous (sh-) *a.* Of or as of the Age of Chivalry; of or as of the ideal knight, gallant, honourable, courteous, disinterested; quixotic; hence **~LY**[2] *adv.* [ME, f. OF *chevalerous* (as CHEVALIER; see -OUS)]

chĭ'valr|y̆ (sh-) *n.* Medieval knightly system with its religious, moral, and social code (*Age of Chivalry*); ideal knight's characteristics, courage and courtesy; inclination to defend or help weaker party; (arch.) body of horsemen, knights, or gallant gentlemen; (arch.) knightly skill; hence **~IC** *a.* [ME f. OF *chevalerie* etc. f. med. L *caballerius* for LL *caballarius* horseman (as CAVALIER; see -RY)]

chīve *n.* Small culinary herb (*Allium schoenoprasus*) allied to onion and leek. [ME f. OF *cive*, dial. **chive*, f. L *cepa* onion]

chĭ'vvy̆, chĭ'vy̆, *v.t.* Pursue, harass. [f. *chevy* n. & v., prob. f. ballad of *Chevy Chase*, place on Scottish Border]

‖**chĭz(z)** *n.*, & *v.t.* (-zz-). (sl.) Cheat, swindle. [f. CHISEL]

chlămy̆domō'nas (kl-) *n.* Unicellular green freshwater alga of genus *Chlamydomonas*. [mod. L, f. Gk *khlamus -udos* cloak + *monos* single]

chlor-[1,2]. See **chloro-**[1,2].

chlôr'al (kl-) *n.* **~ (hydrate)**, white crystalline trichloroacetaldehyde hydrate, a hypnotic and anaesthetic. [F (*chlore* CHLORINE, *al*cool ALCOHOL)]

chlôrămphĕ'nĭcŏl (kl-) *n.* Antibiotic prepared from *Streptomyces venezuelae* or synthetically. [f. CHLORO-[2] + AMIDE + PHENO- + NITRO- + GLYCOL]

chlôr'āte (kl-) *n.* Salt of chloric acid. [f. CHLORIC + -ATE[1] (3)]

chlôrĕ'lla (kl-) *n.* Unicellular green alga of genus *Chlorella*. [mod. L, dim. of Gk *khlōros* green]

chlôr'ic (kl-) *a.* **~ acid,** a strong oxidizing acid, $HClO_3$. [f. CHLORO-[2] + -IC]

chlôr'īde (kl-) *n.* Binary compound of chlorine; bleaching agent containing chloride. [f. CHLORO-[2] + -IDE]

chlôr'in|āte (kl-) *v.t.* Impregnate or treat with chlorine; hence **~A'TION** *n.*, treatment with chlorine (esp. in disinfecting water, or in extraction of gold from ores). [f. foll. + -ATE[3]]

chlôr'ine (klôr'ēn) *n.* Non-metallic element, a yellowish-green heavy gas with irritant smell. [f. Gk *khlōros* green + -INE[5]]

chlôro-[1], (esp. bef. vowel) **chlôr-**[1], (kl-) *comb. form.* (Bot. & Min.) Green. [f. as prec. + -o-]

chlôro-[2], (esp. bef. vowel) **chlôr-**[2], (kl-) *comb. form.* (Chem.) Chlorine. [f. CHLORINE + -o-]

chlŏ'rofôrm (kl-) *n.*, & *v.t.* **1.** *n.* Anaesthetic, thin colourless liquid whose inhaled vapour produces unconsciousness. **2.** *v.t.* Treat (person) with or render unconscious by chloroform. [f. F *chloroforme* f. as CHLORO-[2] + *formyle* (cf. FORMIC)]

Chlôromy̆cē'tĭn (kl-) *n.* Trade name for CHLORAMPHENICOL. [f. CHLORO-[2] + Gk *mukēs -ētos* fungus + -IN]

chlŏ'rophy̆ll (kl-) *n.* Colouring-matter of green parts of plants. [f. F CHLORO[1](*phylle* f. Gk *phullon* leaf)]

chlŏ'roplăst (kl-) *n.* Plastid containing chlorophyll. [f. G *chloroplast*(*id*) (as CHLORO-[1], PLASTID)]

chlôr|ō'sĭs (kl-) *n.* (*pl.* **~oses** *pr.* -ō'sēz). (Hist.) green sickness, anaemic disease of young women, causing greenish complexion; (Bot.) blanching of green parts, or turning green of petal etc.; hence **~O'TIC** *a.* [f. CHLORO-[1] + -OSIS]

chlôrprō'mazīne (kl-) *n.* Bitter drug used as sedative and against vomiting. [F (as CHLORO-[2], PROMETHAZINE)]

Ch.M. *abbr.* Master of Surgery. [f. L *Chirurgiae Magister*]

‖**chŏc** *n.* (colloq.) Chocolate; **~-ice,** bar of ice cream enclosed in thin layer of chocolate. [abbr.]

chō'chō *n.* (*pl.* **~s**). (W. Ind.) = CHOKO.

chŏck[1] *n.* Block of wood, esp. wedge for stopping motion of cask or wheel. [prob. f. ONF **choque* etc., OF *ço(u)che*, of unkn. orig.]

chŏck[2] *v.t.*, & *adv.* **1.** *v.t.* Make fast with chocks. **2.** *adv.* Closely, tightly, close up; **~-a-block,** jammed together, crammed *with*; **~-full,** crammed full (*of*). [f. prec.]

‖**chŏ'cker** *a.* (sl.) Fed up, disgusted. [f. CHOCK[2]-*-a-block*]

chŏ'colate *n.* & *a.* **1.** *n.* Paste or solid block made from cacao seeds by roasting, grinding, etc.; sweetmeat made of or covered with chocolate; drink of chocolate in hot milk or water. **2.** *n.* & *a.* (Of) dark-brown colour. **3.** *a.* Flavoured with chocolate; **~ biscuit** (coated with chocolate); **~-box,** decorated box filled with chocolates, (fig.) stereotyped romantic style of pictures; **~ soldier,** (fig.) soldier unwilling to fight. [f. F *chocolat* or Sp. *chocolate* f. Aztec *chocolatl*]

Chŏ'ctaw *n.* (Skating). Step from either edge of skate to other edge on other foot in opposite direction. [name of Amer. Ind. tribe; cf. MOHAWK]

choice[1] *n.* **1.** Choosing, selection; **by** or **for ~,** preferably; **of** (one's) **~,** that one chooses; **take** one's **~,** decide between possibilities. **2.** Power, right, faculty, of choosing (**from ~,** willingly; **have no ~,** have no alternative; HOBSON'S *choice*). **3.** Élite, best, *of*; variety to choose from; thing or person chosen; alternative (*have no choice but*). [ME f. OF *chois* (*choisir* f. Gallo-Rom. **causire* f. Gmc **kausjan* CHOOSE)]

choice[2] *a.* Of picked quality; exquisite; carefully chosen; hence **~'LY**[2] (-slĭ) *adv.*, **~'NESS** (-sn-) *n.* [ME, f. prec.]

choir (kwīr), (arch.) **quīre**[2], *n.* **1.** Band of singers performing or leading in musical parts of church service; chancel of cathedral, minster, or large church; choral society, company of singers, birds, angels, etc. **2. ~'boy,** boy who sings in choir; **~'master,** conductor of a choir; **~ organ,** (Mus.) [corruption of *chair organ*] softest of three parts (GREAT, SWELL-, ~, *organ*) making up large compound organ, with lowest of three keyboards; **~ school,** school maintained by cathedral etc. for choirboys and other pupils; *choir*-STALL[1]. [ME, f. OF *quer* f. L CHORUS; cf. BRIER[1], FRIAR]

chōke[1] *v.* & *n.* **1.** *v.t.* Stop breath of, suffocate, temporarily or finally, by squeezing throat, blocking it up, or (of water, smoke, etc.) being unbreathable; (fig., of emotion) paralyse; smother, stifle, kill, (plant, fire, etc.) by deprivation of light, air, etc.; suppress (feelings); fill chock-full; block up wholly or partly (tube by narrowing part of it, channel with sand, stones, etc.); (in *p.p.*, colloq.) disgusted, disappointed; **~ back,** conceal (emotion etc.) with difficulty; **~ down,** swallow (food) with difficulty; **~ off,** dissuade, discourage, (person, attempt), esp. forcibly. **2.** *v.i.* Suffer temporary or permanent stoppage of breath; become speechless from emotion. **3.** *n.* Narrowed part of gun bore etc.; valve in petrol engine controlling inflow of air; (Electr.) inductance coil used to smooth variations of alternating current or to alter its phase. **4. ~'berry,** (scarlet fruit of) N. Amer. shrub of genus *Aronia*; **~-cherry,** astringent N. Amer. cherry; **~-damp,** carbon dioxide in mines, wells, etc. [ME, f. OE *āceocian* (A- 1, *ceoce, cēce* CHEEK)]

chōke[2] *n.* Centre part of artichoke. [prob. confusion of ending of *artichoke* w. prec.]

chō'ker *n.* In vbl senses; clerical or other high collar; woman's close-fitting necklace. [f. CHOKE[1] + -ER[1]]

||**chō'key.** See CHOKY[1].

chō'kō *n.* (*pl.* **~s**). (Austral. & N.Z.) Succulent vegetable like cucumber. [f. W. Ind. CHOCHO f. Braz. name]

||**chō'kў**[1], ||**chō'key,** *n.* (sl.) Prison. [orig. Anglo-Ind., f. Hindi *chaukī* shed]

chō'kў[2] *a.* Tending to choke or cause choking. [f. CHOKE[1] + -Y[2]]

chŏl(ė)- (k-) *comb. form.* (Med. & Chem.) Bile, as: **cholangio'graphy,** X-ray examination of gall-bladder and bile-ducts; **cholecysto'graphy,** X-ray examination of gall-bladder. [f. Gk *kholē* gall, bile]

chŏ'ler (k-) *n.* (Hist.) one of the four HUMOUR[1]s, bile; (poet. or arch.) anger, irascibility. [ME, f. OF *colere* bile, anger f. L f. Gk *kholera* diarrhoea, in LL = bile, anger (Gk *kholē* bile)]

chŏ'lera (k-) *n.* Infectious often fatal bacterial disease with severe intestinal symptoms; **chicken** or **fowl ~,** infectious disease of fowls; **~ belt,** flannel or silk waistband worn to prevent intestinal ailments; **~ morbus,** bilious disorder from over-eating etc.; hence **~IC** (-ā'ĭk) *a.* [ME f. L f. Gk *kholera*; see prec.]

chŏ'lerĭc (k-) *a.* Irascible; angry; *choleric* TEMPERAMENT; hence **cholĕ'rICALLY** (k-) *adv.* [ME, f. OF *cholerique* f. L f. Gk *kholerikos* (as CHOLER; see -IC)]

cholĕ'sterŏl (k-) *n.* (Chem.) Steroid alcohol found in body cells and fluids and thought to promote arteriosclerosis. [f. *cholesterin* f. Gk *kholē* bile + *stereos* stiff, + -OL]

chō'li (kō'lē) *n.* Indian woman's short-sleeved bodice. [f. Hindi *coli*]

chō'lĭămb (k-) *n.* (Pros.) = SCAZON; hence **~IC** (-ă'-) *a.* [f. LL f. Gk *khōliambos* (*khōlos* lame; see IAMBUS)]

chō'līne (k-; *or* -ēn) *n.* (Chem.) Strong base occurring widely in living matter. [f. G *cholin* f. Gk *kholē* bile; see -IN]

chŏmp *v.t.* = CHAMP[1]. [imit.]

chŏndrĭ-, chŏndro-, (k-) *comb. forms.* (Med. & Physiol.) Cartilage. [f. Gk *khondros* grain, cartilage + -I-, -O-]

chŏ'ndrīte (k-) *n.* Meteorite containing granules. [f. G *chondrit* f. Gk *khondros* granule; see -ITE[1]]

***chōō'-chōō** *n.* (colloq. or childish). Railway train or locomotive. [imit.]

chōōse (-z) *v.* (**chose** *pr.* chōz; **cho'sen** *pr.* chō'z-). **1.** *v.t.* Select out of greater number; (Theol., esp. in *p.p.*) destine to be saved (**the chosen people** or **race,** Jews); decide (*to* do one thing rather than another); think fit, be determined, *to* do; (w. compl.) select as (*was chosen king*); **nothing** etc. **to ~ between them** (nearly equal). **2.** *v.i.* **~ between** or **from,** take one or another of; **cannot ~ but,** (arch.) must, have to; PICK[2] *and choose.* **3.** Hence **chōō'SER**[1] (-z-) *n.*, **chōō's(e)Y**[2] (-zĭ) *a.*, (colloq.) fastidious. [OE *cēosan*, = OS, OHG *kiosan*, ON *kjósa*, Goth. *kiusan* f. Gmc **kiusan*]

chŏp[1] *v.* (**-pp-**). **1.** *v.t.* Cut by a blow usu. with axe (*off, away, down*, etc.; **~ up,** chop into small pieces, mince); (esp. in *p.p.*) cut (meat etc.) small; strike (ball) with short heavy edgewise blow. **2.** *v.i.* Make chopping blow (*at*); cut by chopping (*through* etc.) [ME, var. of CHAP[1]]

chŏp[2] *n.* **1.** Cutting stroke with axe etc.; (Austral. & N.Z., freq. in *pl.*) wood-chopping contest. **2.** Thick slice of meat, esp. pork or lamb, usu. including rib; **~-house,** (esp. cheap) restaurant. **3.** Broken motion of water usu. due to action of wind against tide; hence **~'PY**[2] *a.* **4.** Short heavy edgewise blow in boxing, cricket, tennis, etc.; **get the ~,** (sl.) be killed, be dismissed. [f. prec.]

chŏp[3] *n.* (usu. in *pl.*) Jaw of animal etc.; **lick** one's **~s** (with relish or anticipation); **~s of the Channel,** entrance from Atlantic Ocean to Engl. Channel; see also CHAP[2]. [16th c., var. of CHAP[2]; orig. unkn.]

chŏp[4] *v.* (**-pp-**). **~ and change** (emphatic for *change*, usu. as *v.i.*), vacillate, be inconstant; **~ round, about,** (esp. of wind) change direction suddenly; **~ logic,** bandy arguments. [ME, perh. rel. to *chap* f. OE *cēapian* (as CHEAP)]

||**chŏp**[5] *n.* Trade mark, brand of goods; **first, second, -~,** (colloq.) first, second, -class; **no ~, not much ~,** (Austral. & N.Z.) no good. [orig. in India & China, f. Hindi *chhāp* stamp]

chŏp-chŏ'p *adv.* & *int.* (pidgin Engl.) Quick, quickly. [f. Chin. *k'wâi-k'wâi*]

chŏ'pper *n.* In vbl senses; large-bladed short axe; butcher's cleaver; device for regularly interrupting light-beam etc.; (colloq.) helicopter; *(sl.) machine-gun. [f. CHOP[1] + -ER[1]]

chŏ'pstĭck *n.* One of a pair of sticks of wood, ivory, etc., held in one hand, used by Chinese etc. to lift food to mouth. [pidgin Engl. (*chop* = quick; STICK[2]) equivalent of Chin. *k'wâi-tsze* nimble ones]

chŏp-sū'ey (*or* -sōō'-) *n.* Chinese dish of meat or chicken fried in sesame oil with rice, onions, etc. [Chin., = mixed bits]

chōr'al[1] (k-) *a.* **1.** Of or sung by choir; ~ **service** (with canticles, anthems, etc., so sung); ~ **society** (of persons interested in choral music). **2.** (Read or said) by group of voices; of or with chorus. **3.** Hence ~LY[2] *adv.* [f. med. L *choralis* f. L CHORUS; see -AL]

chōra'le, chōra'l[2], (kōrah'l) *n.* (Metrical hymn to) simple tune usu. sung in unison, orig. in Lutheran church; harmonized form of this; group of singers. [f. G *choral(gesang)* f. med. L *cantus choralis*]

chōrd[1] (k-) *n.* **1.** (poet. or fig.) String of harp etc.; **strike a ~**, recall something to person's memory; **touch the right ~**, appeal skilfully to emotion. **2.** (Anat., arch.) = CORD (*vocal chord*; *spinal chord*). **3.** (Math., Aeron., etc.) Straight line joining ends of arc, wing, etc. [16th-c. refash. of CORD after L *chorda*]

chōrd[2] (k-) *n.* (Mus.) Group of notes sounded usu. together, combined according to some system (BROKEN *chord*; **common ~**, any note with its major or minor third, perfect fifth, and octave). [orig. *cord* f. ACCORD[2], later confused w. prec.]

chōr'dal (k-) *a.* Of or like a CHORD[1,2]. [f. CHORD[1,2] + -AL]

chōr'dāte (k-) *a.* & *n.* (Zool.) (Member) of the phylum Chordata, with developed notochord. [f. mod. L *Chordata* f. L *chorda* CHORD[1], after *Vertebrata* etc.]

chōre *n.* Odd job; recurrent, routine, or tedious task. [orig. dial. & U.S. form of CHAR[2]]

chorē'a (k-) *n.* St. Vitus's DANCE[2]. [L, f. Gk *khoreia* (as CHORUS)]

chŏrėŏ'graphў (k-) *n.* Arranging or designing of ballet or stage-dance; so **chŏrėŏ'**GRAPHER *n.*, **chŏ'rėograph** (-ahf) *v.t.* & *i.*, **chŏrėo**GRA'PHIC *a.*, (k-). [f. Gk *khoreia* choral dancing to music (see prec.) + -GRAPHY]

chŏrĭă'mb|us (k-) *n.* (*pl.* ~**i** *pr.* -ī). (Pros.) Foot consisting of two short syllables between two long; hence ~IC *a.* [LL, f. Gk *khoriambos* (*khoreios* of the dance; see IAMBUS)]

chōr'ĭc (k-) *a.* Of or like chorus in Greek play. [f. LL f. Gk *khorikos* (as CHORUS; see -IC)]

***chōr'ine** (kōr'ēn) *n.* Chorus-girl. [f. CHORUS + -INE[3,4]]

chōr'ĭon (k-) *n.* Outermost membrane enclosing foetus. [f. Gk *khorion*]

chŏ'rĭster (k-) *n.* Member of choir, esp. choir-boy (also fig. of angels, birds); *leader of choir. [ME, f. AF **cueristre*, OF *cueriste* (*quer* CHOIR)]

chorŏ'graph|ў (k-) *n.* Description of regions or districts of size between those involved in topography and in geography; hence ~ER[1] *n.*, **chōro**GRA'PHIC (k-) *a.* [f. F *chorographie* or f. L f. Gk *khōrographia* (*khōra* region; see -o-, -GRAPHY)]

chōr'oid (k-) *a.* & *n.* Like chorion in shape or vascularity; ~ (**coat** or **membrane**), membrane lining eyeball between retina and iris. [f. Gk *khoroeidēs* for *khorioeidēs* (as CHORION; see -OID)]

chorŏ'log|ў (k-) *n.* Study of geographical distribution of animals and plants; hence **chōro**LO'GICAL (k-) *a.*, ~IST (3) *n.* [f. Gk *khōra* region + -O- + -LOGY]

chōr'tle *v.i.*, & *n.* (Utter) loud gleeful chuckle. [portmanteau wd (Lewis Carroll) app. f. CHUCKLE + SNORT[1]]

chōr'us (k-) *n.* & *v.* **1.** *n.* Band of singers, choir; thing sung by many at once; any simultaneous utterance by many persons etc. (**in ~**, in unison, all speaking etc. together); group of singers and dancers in musical comedy etc. **2.** (Mus.) Composition in several (usu. four) parts each sung by several voices; refrain or main part of popular song. **3.** (Gk Ant.) Band of dancers and singers in religious ceremonies and dramatic performances; (one of) their utterances. **4.** Character speaking prologue etc. in play. **5.** **~-girl,** young woman who sings or dances in chorus of musical comedy etc.; **~-master,** conductor of chorus or choir. **6.** *v.t.* & *i.* Sing, speak, say, in chorus. [L, f. Gk *khoros*]

chose. See CHOOSE.

chose jugée (shōz zhōō'zhā) *n.* Thing it is idle to discuss, as already settled. [F]

chosen. See CHOOSE.

chou (shōō) *n.* (*pl.* ~**x** *pr.* same). Rosette or ornamental knot of ribbon, chiffon, etc., on woman's hat or dress; small round cake of pastry filled with cream etc. [F, f. L *caulis* cabbage]

choucroute (shōōkrōō't) *n.* Kind of pickled cabbage. [F, f. G dial. *surkrut* SAUERKRAUT]

chough (chŭf) *n.* Red-legged crow of genus *Pyrrhocorax*. [ME, prob. orig. imit.]

chou moe'llier (-mŏ'-) *n.* (Austral. & N.Z.) Coarse kind of kale grown as fodder. [F, = marrow-filled cabbage]

choux (shōō) *n.* = CHOU (sing. or pl.); **~ pastry,** very light pastry enriched with eggs. [F, pl. of CHOU]

chow *n.* Dog of a Chinese breed; (sl.) food. [shortened f. foll.]

chow'-chow *n.* Chinese preserve of orange-peel, ginger, etc.; = prec. [pidgin Engl.]

***chow'der** *n.* Stew or soup of fresh fish or clams with bacon, onions, biscuit, etc. [perh. f. F phr. *faire la chaudière* supply a pot etc. for cooking a stew of fish etc. (*chaudière* pot, CAULDRON)]

chow mei'n (-mā'n) *n.* Chinese dish of fried noodles usu. with shredded meat and vegetables. [Chin., = fried flour]

chrēmatĭ'st|ĭc *a.* (k-) Of money-making; hence ~ICS *n.*, study of wealth. [f. Gk *khrēmatistikos* (*khrēmatizō* make money f. *khrēma -matos* money; see -IC)]

chrĕstŏ'mathў (k-) *n.* Collection of choice passages, esp. to help in learning a language. [f. F *chrestomathie* or f. Gk *khrēstomatheia* (*khrēstos* useful, *-matheia* learning)]

chrĭ'sm (krĭ'zem) *n.* Consecrated oil, unguent, anointing, esp. in sacred rites. [OE *crisma* f. eccl. L f. Gk *khrisma* anointing]

chrĭ'som (k-) *n.* (Hist.) ~(**-cloth** etc.), child's white robe at baptism, used as shroud if it died within a month; **~-child** (less than a month old). [ME, f. pop. pronunc. of prec.]

Chrīst (k-) *n.* Messiah or Lord's anointed of Jewish prophecy; (title, now treated as name, given to) Jesus as fulfilling this prophecy; image or picture of Jesus; **the ~-child,** Christ as a child; hence ~'HOOD (-t-h-) *n.*, ~'LESS, ~'LIKE, *adjs.* [OE *Crīst*, = OS, OHG *Krīst*, f. L *Christus* f. Gk *khristos* anointed one (*khriō* anoint) transl. of Heb. *māšīaḥ* MESSIAH]

Chrĭstadĕ'lphĭan (k-) *a.* & *n.* (Member) of religious sect rejecting doctrine of Trinity and expecting second coming of Christ. [f. prec. + Gk *adelphos* brother + -IAN]

chrĭ'sten (krĭ'sen) *v.t.* Admit to Christian Church by baptism; give name to (person at baptism, or as nickname; *christen her*; *christen him John, Shorty*; also ship, bell, etc., with analogous ceremony); (colloq.) use etc. for first time. [OE *crīstnian* make Christian (*crīsten* a. Christian, = OS, OHG *kristīn* f. L *Christianus* CHRISTIAN)]

Chrĭ'stendom (krĭ'sen-) *n.* Christians; Christian countries. [OE *crīstendōm* (*crīsten* a.; see prec., -DOM)]

Chrĭ'stian (krĭ'styan) *a.* & *n.* (Person) believing in, professing, or belonging to, the religion of Christ; of Christ or his religion; (person) showing character consistent with Christ's teaching, of genuine piety, Christlike; (sl.) civilized, decent, (person); ~ **burial** (with the ceremonies of the church); ~ **era** (reckoned from birth of Christ); ~ **name,** name given (as) at baptism, personal name (cf. SURNAME); ~ **Science, Scientist,** (adherent of) a system of combating disease etc. without medical treatment by mental effect of patient's Christian faith; *Christian* SOCIALISM; *Christian* YEAR; hence ~IZE (2, 3) *v.i.* & *t.*, ~**iz**A'TION *n.* [f. L *Christianus* (*Christus* CHRIST; see -IAN)]

Chrĭstĭa'nĭa (k-; -ah'n-) *n.* (Skiing). Turn in which the skis are kept parallel, used for stopping short. [~ (now Oslo) in Norway]

Chrĭstĭă'nĭtȳ (k-) *n.* The Christian faith, doctrines of Christ and his apostles; being a Christian, Christian quality or character; Christendom. [ME *cristianite,* earlier *crist(i)ente* f. OF *crestienté* (*crestien* CHRISTIAN; see -ITY)]

Chrĭ'stĭe (k-) *n.* Christiania. [abbr.]

Chrĭ'stmas (krĭ'sm-) *n.* **1.** Festival of Christ's birth, celebrated on 25 Dec. (~ **Day**) and devoted esp. to family reunion and merry-making, (**Father** ~, old man dressed in red, personification of family festivity, = SANTA CLAUS); ~(**-tide**), period of some days beginning 24 Dec. (~ **Eve**). **2.** ||~**-box,** small present or gratuity given at Christmas esp. to employees of firms providing regular services; ~ **bush,** Austral. shrub with flower-like fruits at Christmas; ~ **card** (sent with greetings at Christmas); ~ **present,** gift given at Christmas; ||~ **pudding,** plum pudding eaten at Christmas; ~ **rose,** white-flowered hellebore blooming in winter; ~ **stocking** (hung up by children on Christmas Eve for Father Christmas to fill with presents); ~ **tree,** evergreen or artificial tree set up in room or in the open and hung with lights, presents, etc., (Austral.) Christmas bush. **3.** Hence ~**SY**[2] *a.* [OE *Cristes mæsse* (MASS[1])]

Chrĭsto- (k-) *comb. form.* Christ, as: ~LATRY (-ŏ'l-) *n.*; ~**logy** (-ŏ'l-), branch of theology relating to Christ; ~**phany** (-ŏ'f-), manifestation of Christ esp. after Resurrection. [f. L *Christus* or Gk *Khristos* + -O-]

Chrĭ'stȳ (k-) *n.* Christiania. [abbr.]

chrō'ma (k-) *n.* Purity or intensity of colour. [f. Gk *khrōma* colour]

chrō'māte (k-) *n.* (Chem.) Salt of chromic acid. [f. CHROMIC + -ATE[1] (3)]

chromă'tĭc (k-) *a.* **1.** Of, produced by, full of bright, colour; ~ **aberration,** failure of different colours to come to same focus after refraction. **2.** (Mus.) Of or having notes not included in diatonic scale; ~ **scale** (proceeding by semitones); ~ **semitone,** interval between note and its flat or sharp. **3.** Hence **chromă'tĭ**CALLY (k-) *adv.*, ~ISM (3) *n.* [f. F *chromatique* or f. L f. Gk *khrōmatikos* (*khrōma -atos* colour; see -IC)]

chrōmatĭ'cĭtȳ (k-) *n.* Quality of colour regarded independently of brightness. [f. prec. + -ITY]

chrō'matĭn (k-) *n.* (Biol.) Cell-nucleus constituent that can be readily stained. [G (as CHROMATO-, -IN)]

chrōmato-, chrōmo-[2], (k-) *comb. forms.* Colour, as: **chromato'psia,** abnormally coloured vision. [f. Gk *khrōma -atos* colour + -O-]

chrōmatŏ'graphȳ (k-) *n.* (Chem.) Separation of substances by slow passage through or over adsorbing etc. material; so **chrōmă'to**GRAM (k-) *n.*, result of this, **chrōmă'to**GRAPH (2, 3) (k-) *n.*, & *v.t.*, **chrōmatogră'phĭ**C (k-) *a.* [f. G *chromatographie* (as CHROMATO-, -GRAPHY)]

chrōme (k-) *n.* ~ (**yellow**), yellow pigment and colour got from lead chromate; ~ **leather** (tanned with chromium salts); ~**-nickel** *a.*, stainless (steel) containing chromium and nickel; ~ **steel,** hard fine-grained steel containing much chromium. [F, = chromium, f. Gk *khrōma* colour]

chrō'mĭc (k-) *a.* Of chromium; ~ **acid,** H_2CrO_4 forming yellow salts, or its anhydride, CrO_3. [f. prec. + -IC]

chrō'mĭnance (k-) *n.* Difference in colour quality, measured with respect to a reference colour of equal brightness. [f. Gk *khrōma* colour, after *luminance*]

chrō'mīte (k-) *n.* Mineral composed of chromium and iron oxides. [f. CHROME or foll. + -ITE[1]]

chrō'mĭum (k-) *n.* (Chem.) Metallic element, forming brilliantly coloured compounds; ~**-plate,** (*n.*) electrolytically deposited protective coating of chromium, (*v.t.*) coat thus; ~**-plated,** (fig.) pretentiously decorative. [f. CHROME + -IUM]

chrōmo-[1] (k-) *comb. form.* Chromium. [f. prec. + -O-]

chromo-[2]**.** See CHROMATO-.

chrōmolĭ'thograph (k-; -ahf) *n.*, & *v.t.* (Picture) print(ed) in colours by lithography; so **chrōmolĭthŏ'**GRAPHER, **chrōmolĭthŏ'**GRAPHY, *ns.*, **chrōmolĭtho**GRA'PHIC *a.*, (k-). [f. CHROMO-[2] + LITHOGRAPH]

chrō'mosōm|**e** (k-) *n.* (Biol.) Rodlike or threadlike structure occurring in pairs in the nucleus of animal and plant cells, carrying genes; hence ~AL *a.* [f. G *chromosom* (as CHROMO-[2], -SOME[3])]

chrō'mosphēre (k-) *n.* Reddish gaseous envelope of sun or other star; hence **chrōmosphĕ'**RIC (k-) *a.* [f. CHROMO-[2] + SPHERE]

Chron. *abbr.* Chronicles (O.T.).

chrŏ'nĭc (k-) *a.* Lingering, lasting, (of disease, cf. ACUTE); (of invalid) with chronic complaint; constant (*chronic doubt, rebellion*); ||(colloq.) bad, intense, severe; hence **chrŏ'nĭ**CALLY *adv.*, **chronĭ'**CITY *n.*, (k-). [f. F *chronique* f. L *chronicus* (in LL of disease) f. Gk *khronikos* (*khronos* time; see -IC)]

chrŏ'nĭcle (k-) *n.*, & *v.t.* (Enter or relate in a) continuous register of events in order of time; **C**~**s,** name of two historical books of O.T.; narrative, account; (*C*~) newspaper name; hence **chrŏ'nĭcl**ER[1] (k-) *n.* [ME, f. AF *cronicle* var. of OF *cronique* f. LL *chronica* sing. f. L f. Gk *khronika* neut. pl. annals (see prec.)]

chrŏ'nogrăm (k-) *n.* Phrase etc. of which the Roman-numeral letters added give a date, as LorD haVe MerCIe Vpon Vs = 50 + 500 + 5 + 1000 + 100 + 1 + 5 + 5 = 1666; hence **chrŏnogrammă'**TIC (k-) *a.* [f. Gk *khronos* time + -O- + -GRAM]

chrŏ'nograph (k-; -ahf) *n.* Instrument recording time with extreme accuracy; stop-watch; hence **chrŏno**GRA'PHIC (k-) *a.* [f. as prec. + -GRAPH]

chronŏ'log|**ȳ** (k-) *n.* Science of computing dates; arrangement of events according to dates or times of occurrence, table or treatise displaying this; hence ~ER[1], ~IST (3), *ns.*, **chrŏno**LO'GICAL (k-) *a.*, ~IZE (3) *v.t.* [f. mod. L *chronologia* (as prec.; see -LOGY)]

chronŏ'mèter (k-) *n.* Time-measuring instrument, esp. one keeping accurate time at all temperatures etc., used for navigation by astronomical observation at sea. [f. Gk *khronos* time + -O- + -METER]

chronŏ'mètrȳ (k-) *n.* Accurate time-measurement; hence **chrŏnomĕ'trĭ**C(AL) (k-) *adjs.* [f. as prec. + -METRY]

chrŏ'noscōpe (k-) *n.* Apparatus measuring velocity of projectiles, or person's reaction times. [f. as prec. + -SCOPE]

chrȳ'salĭs (k-) *n.* (*pl.* ~**es,** *or* **chrysalides** *pr.* krĭsă'lĭdēz). Pupa, esp. quiescent one of butterfly or moth; case enclosing it; (fig.) preparatory or transition state. [f. L f. Gk *khrusallis -idos* (*khrusos* gold)]

chrȳsă'nthèmum (k-) *n.* (Bot.) composite plant

of genus *Chrysanthemum*, e.g. corn marigold; (pop., colloq. abbr. **chrysa'nth**) one of the autumn-blooming cultivated varieties of this. [L, f. Gk *khrusanthemom* (*khrusos* gold, *anthemon* flower)]

chrȳsĕlėphă'ntīne (k-) *a.* Overlaid with gold and ivory as by ancient Greek sculptors. [f. Gk *khruselephantinos* (*khrusos* gold, *elephas* elephant, ivory; see -INE²)]

chrȳsobĕ'rȳl (k-) *n.* Yellowish-green gem, a compound of beryllium. [f. L *chrysoberyllus* f. Gk *khrusos* gold + *bērullos* beryl]

chrȳ'solīte (k-) *n.* Precious stone, a variety of olivine. [ME f. OF *crisolite* f. med. L *crisolitus* f. L f. Gk *khrusolithos* (*khrusos* gold, *lithos* stone)]

chrȳ'soprāse (k-; -z) *n.* Apple-green variety of chalcedony; (N.T. etc.) prob. a golden-green variety of beryl. [ME f. OF *crisopace* f. L *chrysopassus* var. of L f. Gk *khrusoprasos* (*khrusos* gold, *prason* leek)]

chthŏ'nĭc (k-) *a.* Dwelling in the underworld. [f. Gk *khthōn* earth + -IC]

chŭb *n.* (*pl.* same). Thick-bodied coarse-fleshed river fish (*Leuciscus cephalus*) of carp family. [15th c., of unkn. orig.]

Chŭbb *n.* ~ **(lock)**, patent lock with tumblers and device for fixing bolt immovably if attempt is made to pick the lock. [f. name of inventor, a 19th-c. London locksmith]

chŭ'bb|ȳ *a.* Plump-faced; plump; hence ~**ĭ**NESS *n.* [f. CHUB + -Y²]

chŭck¹ *v.t.*, & *n.* **1.** (Give) playful touch *under the chin*. **2.** Fling or throw (done) with contempt, carelessness, or ease; **the ~**, (sl.) dismissal (*give* person *the chuck*). **3.** (colloq.) = THROW¹ *away, out, up*, etc.; throw out, throw up; **~ it**, (sl.) stop, desist; **~ out**, expel (troublesome person) from meeting, public house, etc., whence ~ER¹-**-ou't** *n.* [16th c., perh. f. F *chuquer*, *choquer* to knock]

chŭck² *n.*, & *v.t.* **1.** *n.* Contrivance in lathe etc. for holding workpiece; cut of beef from neck to ribs. **2.** *v.t.* Fix (wood etc.) to chuck. [var. of CHOCK¹]

***chŭck³** *n.* (colloq.) Food; **~-wagon,** provision--cart on ranch etc. [19th c., perh. f. prec.]

chŭ'ckle *v.i.*, & *n.* (Make) suppressed sound(s) of glee etc.; exult *over*. [f. *chuck* cluck + -LE 3]

chŭ'ckle-head (-hĕd) *n.*, **chŭ'ckle-headėd** (-hĕd-) *a.* Stupid (fellow). [f. *chuckle* clumsy, prob. rel. to CHUCK²]

chŭff *v.i.* (Of engine etc.) work with regular sharp puffing sound. [imit.]

||**chŭffed** (-ft) *a.* (sl.) Pleased; displeased. [f. dial. *chuff*]

chŭg *n.*, & *v.i.* **(-gg-)**. (Make) muffled sound of slowly-running internal combustion engine or its exhaust. [imit.]

chukar' *n.* Red-legged Indian partridge (*Alectoris chukar*). [f. Hindi *chakor*]

chŭ'kker, chŭ'kka, *n.* Each of the periods into which game of polo is divided; **~ boot,** ankle--high leather boot as worn for polo. [f. Hindi *chakkar* f. Skr. *chakra* wheel]

chŭm *v.i.* **(-mm-)**, & *n.* (colloq.) **1.** *v.i.* Share rooms (*with*); **~ up,** form close friendship (*with*). **2.** *n.* Familiar friend (esp. among boys); **new ~,** (Austral. & N.Z.) recent immigrant, greenhorn; hence **~'my²** *a.* [17th c., prob. short for *chamber-fellow*]

chŭmp *n.* Short thick lump of wood; ||thick end, esp. of loin of lamb or mutton (so *chump chop*); (colloq.) head, esp. **off** one's ~, crazy, wild with excitement etc.; (sl.) foolish person. [18th c., blend of foll. w. LUMP¹ etc.]

chŭnk *n.* Thick lump cut or broken off (wood, bread, cheese, etc.); *small sturdy person or horse; hence ~'Y² *a.*, consisting of chunks, short and thick, small and sturdy. [prob. var. of CHUCK²]

||**Chŭ'nnel** *n.* (colloq.) Proposed tunnel under the English Channel. [portmanteau wd f. *Channel tunnel*]

chŭ'nter *v.i.* Mutter; grumble, complain. [prob. imit.]

chupă'ttȳ, -ĭ, chapă't(t)ĭ, *n.* (Ind.) Small flat thin cake of coarse unleavened bread. [f. Hindi *chapāti*]

chûrch¹ *n.* **1.** Building for public Christian worship, ||esp. according to established religion of country; public worship (*go to church*; *meet after church*). **2.** (*C~*). Body of all Christians (**C~ militant,** Christians on earth warring against evil; **C~ triumphant,** Christians at peace in heaven; *Church* VISIBLE); organized Christian society of any time (*primitive Church*), country (*Church of Scotland*), or distinguishing principle (*Reformed Church*); **C~ of England,** English branch of Western or Latin Church rejecting Pope's supremacy since Reformation; **Established C~** (recognized by State, as Church of England or Scotland). **3.** Organization, clergy and other officers, of a religious society or corporation; clerical profession (**go into the C~,** take holy orders); HIGH, LOW¹, BROAD, **Church,** parties with different views of Anglican doctrine and discipline. **4. C~ Army,** Church of England mission to poorer classes; **C~ Commissioners,** body managing finances of Church of England; **~-goer, -going,** attender, attendance, at public worship; **~'man, ~'manship,** member, membership, of clergy or church; **~ mouse** (proverbially poverty--stricken); **~ parade,** (Mil. etc.) attendance at worship; **~ service,** public worship; *Church* SLAVONIC; **~'warden,** elected lay representative of parish (usu. one of two, elected one by incumbent, one by parishioners), long clay pipe, *church administrator; **~'woman,** fem. of *churchman*; **~'yard,** (*n.*) enclosed ground in which church stands, esp. as used for burials, (*a.*, of cough) seeming to herald death; *Church* YEAR. [OE *cir(i)ce* etc., = OS *kirika*, OHG *chirihha* f. WG **kirika* f. med. Gk *kurikon* f. Gk *kuriakon* (sc. *dōma*) Lord's (house) f. *kurios* lord; cf. KIRK]

chûrch² *v.t.* Perform church service of thanksgiving for (esp. woman after childbirth). [ME, f. prec.]

Churchĭ'llĭan *a.* Of or relating to or characteristic of one of the Spencer-Churchill family, esp. Lord Randolph Churchill, Brit. statesman d. 1895, or his son Sir Winston Churchill, Brit. statesman d. 1965. [f. *Churchill* + -IAN]

chûr'ch|ȳ *a.* Obtrusively or intolerantly devoted to the Church or opposed to religious dissent; like a church; hence ~**ĭ**NESS *n.* [f. CHURCH¹ + -Y²]

chŭrĭ'nga (-ngga) *n.* (*pl.* ~**s** *or* same). Sacred amulet of Australian Aboriginals. [Aboriginal]

chûrl *n.* **1.** (arch.) Peasant; person of low birth. **2.** Ill-bred fellow; surly or niggardly person; hence ~'ISH¹ *a.* [OE *ceorl*, = MLG *kerle* f. WG **kerl-* man]

chûrn *n.* & *v.* **1.** *n.* Butter-making machine in which milk or cream is agitated; ||large milk-can (orig. shaped like butter-churn). **2.** *v.t.* Agitate (milk or cream) in churn; produce (butter thus); stir (liquid) about, cause to froth; **~ out,** (fig.) produce in quantity without quality. **3.** *v.i.* Operate butter-churn; (of liquid) wash to and fro, foam, seethe; hence ~'ING¹ (1, 2) *n.* [OE *cyrin*, **ci(e)rn*, = MDu., MLG *kerne*, ON *kirna* f. Gmc **kernjōn*]

chûrr *v.i.*, & *n.* (Make) deep trill as of nightjar. [imit.; cf. CHIRR]

Chŭrrĭguerĕ'sque (-*gerĕ'sk*) *a.* Lavishly orna-

mented in late Spanish baroque style. [f. J. *Churriguera*, Sp. architect d. 1723 + -ESQUE]
chuse. Var. (arch.) of CHOOSE.
chŭt *int.* expr. impatience. [imit.; cf. F *chut*]
chute (shōōt) *n.* **1.** Sloping channel or slide, with or without water, for conveying things to lower level; slope for shooting rubbish down. **2.** (colloq.) Parachute. [F *chute* fall (of water etc.), f. OF *cheoite* fem. p.p. (as n.) of *cheoir* fall f. L *cadere*; w. some senses of SHOOT²; sense 2 abbr.]
chŭ'tney *n.* Pungent orig. Indian condiment of fruits, vinegar, spices, etc. [f. Hindi *chaṭnī*]
chu'tzpah (hōō'tspa) *n.* (sl.) Shameless audacity. [Yiddish]
chȳle (k-) *n.* White milky fluid formed by action of pancreatic juice and bile on chyme. [f. LL f. Gk *khulos* juice]
chȳme (k-) *n.* Food converted by gastric secretion into acid pulp. [f. LL f. Gk *khumos* juice]
chypre (shē-) *n.* Heavy perfume made from sandalwood. [F, = Cyprus, perh. where first made]
||**C.I.** *abbr.* Channel Islands; Order of the Crown of India.
***C.I.A.** *abbr.* Central Intelligence Agency.
ciao (chow) *int.* (colloq.) Goodbye; hello. [It.]
cĭbōr'ĭ|um *n.* (*pl.* ~**a**). (Archit.) canopy, canopied shrine; receptacle for reservation of Eucharist, shaped like shrine, or cup with arched cover. [med. L, f. Gk *kibōrion* seed-vessel of water-lily, cup made from it]
cĭcā'da, cĭca'la, cĭga'la, (-ah'-), *n.* Transparent-winged shrill-sounding insect of genus *Cicada*. [L *cicada*, It. f. L *cicala*, It. *cigala*]
cĭ'catr|ĭce, cĭcā'tr|ĭx (*pl.* ~**ices** *pr.* sĭkatrī'sēz), *n.* Scar of healed wound; scar on tree bark; (Bot.) mark left on stem by fall of leaf etc., hilum of seed; hence **cĭcatrĭ'**CIAL (-shal) *a.* [ME f. OF *cicatrice* or f. L *cicatrix -icis*]
cĭ'catrīz|e, -īs|e (-iz), *v.t.* & *i.* Heal, skin over; mark with scars; hence ~A'TION *n.* [f. F *cicatriser* (*cicatrice*, see prec.; assim. to -IZE)]
cĭ'cely *n.* Umbelliferous plant esp. of genus *Myrrhis* or **Osmorhiza*; SWEET *cicely*. [app. f. L f. Gk *seselis*, w. assim. to the woman's name]
cĭcerō'n|ė (*or* chĭch-) *n.* (*pl.* ~**i** *pr.* -ē). Guide who understands and explains antiquities etc. [It., f. L *Cicero -onis* Roman orator d. 43 B.C.]
Cĭcerō'nĭan *a.* Eloquent, classical, or rhythmical, in the style of Cicero. [f. L *Ciceronianus* (as prec.; see -IAN)]
cĭ'chlĭd (-k-) *n.* Tropical freshwater fish of family Cichlidae, esp. kind kept in aquaria. [f. mod. L *Cichlidae* f. Gk *kikhlē* a kind of fish]
cicisbe|o (chĭchĭzbā'ō) *n.* (*pl.* ~*i* *pr.* -ē). (esp. Hist.) Married Italian woman's male companion or lover. [It.]
||**C.I.D.** *abbr.* Criminal Investigation Department.
-cīde *suf.* forming *ns.* meaning (1) person or substance that kills (*regicide, insecticide*), (2) killing of (*homicide, suicide*). [(1) f. or after F, f. L *-cida*, (2) f. or after F, f. L *-cidium*, both f. L *caedere* kill]
cī'der *n.* Fermented drink made from apple-juice; ~**-press** (for squeezing juice from apples). [ME, f. OF *sidre* f. eccl. L f. Gk *sikera* f. Heb. *šēkār* strong drink]
ci-devant (sēdevah'ṅ) *a.* or *adv.* Former(ly), that has been (w. person's earlier name or status). [F, = heretofore]
||**C.I.E.** *abbr.* Companion (of the Order) of the Indian Empire.
c.i.f. *abbr.* cost, insurance, freight.
cĭg *n.* (colloq.) Cigarette, cigar, etc. [abbr.]
cigala. See CICADA.
cigar' *n.* Roll of tobacco-leaf for smoking; ~**-holder,** mouthpiece holding cigar; ~**-lighter,** device (esp. in motor car) for lighting cigar, cigarette, etc.; ~**-shaped,** cylindrical with pointed end(s). [f. F *cigare* or f. Sp. *cigarro*]
cĭgarĕ'tte, *-ĕ't, *n.* Small cylinder of cut tobacco or of narcotic or medicated substance rolled in paper for smoking; ~**-card,** picture card included in packet of cigarettes; ~**-case** (for holding cigarettes before use); ~**-end,** unsmoked remainder of cigarette; ~**-holder,** mouthpiece holding cigarette; ~**-lighter,** mechanical device for lighting cigarettes; ~**-paper** (for rolling tobacco in to make cigarette). [F, dim. of *cigare*; see prec., -ETTE]
cĭgarĭ'llō *n.* (*pl.* ~**s**). Small cigar. [Sp., dim. of *cigarro* cigar]
C.I.G.S. *abbr.* (Hist.) Chief of Imperial General Staff.
cĭ'lĭce *n.* (Garment of) haircloth. [F, f. L f. Gk *kilikion* (*Kilikia* Cilicia in Asia Minor)]
cĭ'lĭ|um *n.* (*pl.* ~**a**). Eyelash; similar fringe on leaf, insect's wing, etc.; (Biol.) hairlike vibrating organ on animal or vegetable tissue, used by many aquatic lower animals for locomotion; hence ~ARY¹, ~ATE², ~**āt**ED¹, *adjs.*, ~A'TION *n.* [L, = eyelash]
cĭll. Var. of SILL.
cĭ'mbalom *n.* Dulcimer. [Magyar, f. It. *cembalo*; see CYMBALO]
Cĭmmēr'ĭan *a.* & *n.* **1.** *a.* (Of darkness, night, etc.) thick, gloomy. **2.** *n.* Member of nomadic people who overran Asia Minor in 7th c. B.C. [f. L f. Gk *Kimmerios* (of Cimmerii, people fabled to dwell in perpetual night) + -AN]
C.-in-C. *abbr.* Commander-in-Chief.
***cĭnch** *n.*, & *v.t.* **1.** *n.* Saddle-girth used in Mexico etc., usu. of twisted horsehair; firm hold; (sl.) sure thing, a certainty, easy task. **2.** *v.t.* Put cinch on; tighten as with cinch; secure grip on; (sl.) make certain of. [f. Sp. *cincha*]
cĭnchō'na (-ngk-) *n.* S. Amer. evergreen tree or shrub of genus *Cinchona*, with fragrant flowers, which yields cinchona bark and quinine; the bark, drug made from it containing quinine etc. and highly esteemed as tonic and febrifuge; hence **cĭ'nchon**INE⁵ (-ngk-) *n.* [mod. L, f. Countess of *Chinchón* d. 1641, introducer of drug into Spain]
cĭ'ncture *n.*, & *v.t.* (Surround with or as with) girdle, belt, or border; (Archit.) ring at end of column-shaft. [f. L *cinctura* (*cingere cinct-* gird; see -URE)]
cĭ'nder *n.* Slag; residue of coal, wood, etc., that has ceased to flame (whether cold or not) but has still combustible matter in it (**burnt to a** ~, made useless by burning); (in *pl.*) ashes; ~**-path,** ~**-track,** footpath or running-track laid with fine cinders; hence ~Y² *a.* [OE *sinder*, (= OHG *sintar*, ON *sindr*), w. assim. to the unconnected F *cendre* and L *cinis* ashes]
Cĭnderĕ'lla *n.* Person or thing of unrecognized or disregarded merit or beauty; neglected or despised member of group. [character in fairy-tale]
cĭ'nė *a.* Cinematographic (*cine camera, cine film, cine projector*); ***ciné-vérité*** = CINÉMA-*vérité*. [abbr.]
cĭ'nėăste, -ăst, *n.* Cinema enthusiast or devotee. [f. F *cinéaste* (as prec., ENTHUSIAST)]
cĭ'nėma *n.* Cinematography, moving pictures; production of these as an art or industry; theatre where these are shown; ~**-goer,** one who frequents such showings; ~ **organ,** (Mus.) kind with extra stops and effects; ***cinéma-vérité*** (-vĕ'rĭtā) [F], documentary films avoiding artificiality; hence **cĭnėmă'**TIC *a.*, relating to or having the qualities characteristic of the cinema. [f. F *cinéma*, abbr.; see foll.]
cĭnėmă'tograph (-ahf) *n.* Apparatus producing pictures of motion by rapid projection on a screen of many photographs taken successively

on a long film; hence **cĭnèmătoGRA′PHIC** *a.*, **cĭnèmatŏ′GRAPHY** *n.* [f. F *cinématographe* f. Gk *kinēma -atos* movement (*kineō* move); see -GRAPH]

cĭnerār′ĭa *n.* Bright-flowered composite plant, variety of *Senecio cruentus.* [mod. L, fem. of L *cinerarius* of ashes (*cinis -eris* ashes) f. ash-coloured down on leaves]

cĭnerār′ĭum *n.* Place where a cinerary urn is deposited. [LL, n. of *cinerarius*; see prec., -ARIUM]

cĭ′nerarў *a.* Of ashes; ~ **urn** (holding ashes of dead after cremation). [f. L *cinerarius* (see CINERARIA, -ARY[1])]

cinēr′ėous *a.* (Esp. of bird or plumage) ash-grey. [f. L *cinereus* (*cinis -eris* ashes) + -OUS]

Cĭngalē′se (-nggalē′z) *a.* & *n.* (arch.) Sinhalese. [f. F *cing(h)alais* f. as SINHALESE]

cĭ′ngŭl|um (-ngg-) *n.* (*pl.* ~**a**). (Anat.) Ridge round base of tooth-crown. [L, = belt]

cĭ′nnabār *n.* Red mercuric sulphide; vermilion; moth with reddish-marked wings. [ME, f. L *cinnabaris* f. Gk *kinnabari*, of Oriental orig.]

cĭ′nnamon *n.* S.E. Asian tree of genus *Cinnamomum*; its aromatic inner bark used as spice; ~ **bear,** cinnamon-coloured phase of N. Amer. black bear; ~**-colour(ed)**, yellowish-brown; ~ **toast,** buttered toast spread with ground cinnamon and sugar. [ME, f. OF *cinnamome* f. L f. Gk *kinnamōmon*, and L f. Gk *kinnamon*, f. Semitic (Heb. *ḳinnāmôn*)]

cĭnque, cĭnq, (sĭngk) *n.* The five on dice. [ME, f. OF *cinc, cink* f. L *quinque* five]

cĭnquėcĕ′nt|ō (chĭngkwĭchĕ′-) *n.* Italian style of art of the 16th c., with reversion to classical forms; hence ~IST (2, 3) *n.* [It., = 500, used w. ref. to years 15—]

cĭ′nq(ue)foil (sĭ′ngkf-) *n.* Plant of genus *Potentilla*, with compound leaf of five leaflets; (Archit.) five-cusped ornament in circle or arch. [ME, f. L *quinquefolium* (*quinque* five, *folium* leaf)]

Cĭnque Pōrts (sĭnk-) *n. pl.* Group of ports (orig. five only) on S.E. coast of England with ancient privileges. [ME, f. OF *cink porz*, L *quinque portus* five ports]

Cĭnza′nō (chĭnzah′-) *n.* (*pl.* ~**s**). An Italian vermouth. [**P**; f. name of manufacturer]

***C.I.O.** *abbr.* Congress of Industrial Organizations.

***cī′on.** Var. of SCION 1.

cī′pher[1], cȳ′pher[1], *n.* **1.** Arithmetical symbol (0) of no value in itself but used to occupy vacant place in decimal etc. numeration; person or thing of no importance; any Arabic numeral. **2.** Secret or disguised writing, thing so written, key to it; interlaced initials of person, company, etc., monogram. **3.** Continuous sounding of organ-pipe owing to mechanical defect. [ME, f. OF *cif(f)re* f. med. L *cif(e)ra* f. Arab. *ṣifr* (ZERO)]

cī′pher[2], cȳpher[2], *v.* **1.** *v.i.* (arch.) Do arithmetic. **2.** *v.t.* Work (usu. *out*) by arithmetic, calculate; put into secret writing, encipher. [f. prec.]

cĭ′polĭn *n.* Italian white-and-green marble. [F, or f. It. *cipollino* (*cipolla* onion)]

circa (sēr′ka) *prep.* About (w. dates). [L]

cīrcā′dĭan *a.* (Physiol.) Occurring or recurring about once per day. [irreg. f. L *circa* about + *dies* day + -AN]

Cīrcă′ssĭan *a.* & *n.* (Member or language) of tribes of Circassia in N. Caucasus, whose women are noted for their beauty. [f. *Circassia* (f. Russ. *cherkes*) + -AN]

Cīrcē′an *a.* Bewitching, dangerously attractive. [f. *Circe*, enchantress in Gk Myth. + -AN]

cīr′cĭnate *a.* (Bot. & Zool.) Rolled up with apex in centre. [f. L *circinatus* p.p. of *circinare* make round (*circinus* pair of compasses); see -ATE[2]]

circiter (sēr′sĭter) *prep.* About (w. dates). [L]

cīr′cle[1] *n.* **1.** (Line enclosing) perfectly round plane figure whose circumference is everywhere equidistant from its centre (SQUARE[3] *the circle*; ANTARCTIC, ARCTIC, POLAR, *Circle*; **great, small,** ~, circle on surface of sphere whose plane passes, does not pass, through sphere's centre). **2.** Roundish enclosure; ring; road, railway, etc., without ends, allowing traffic to circulate continuously, esp. (*C*~) London underground line; curved tier of rows of seats at theatre etc. (‖DRESS[2] *circle*); (Archaeol.) ring of stones; (Hockey) striking-circle; **go round in** ~**s,** make no progress despite effort; **run round in** ~**s,** (colloq.) be fussily busy with little result. **3.** Period, cycle, (**come full** ~, return to starting-point). **4.** (**Vicious**) ~, (1) fallacy of proving proposition from another that rests on it for proof, (2) unbroken sequence of reciprocal cause and effect, (3) action and reaction that intensify each other. **5.** Persons grouped round centre of interest; set, coterie, class, (*circles in which* one *moves*; *not done in the best circles*). [ME f. OF *cercle* f. L *circulus* dim. of *circus* ring]

cīr′cle[2] *v.* **1.** *v.i.* Move in a circle (*round, about*); ~ **back,** move in wide loop towards starting-point. **2.** *v.t.* Revolve round; form circle round. [ME, f. prec.]

cīr′clėt *n.* Small circle; circular band, esp. of gold, jewelled, etc., worn on head or elsewhere. [f. CIRCLE[1] + -ET[1]]

cīrcs *n. pl.* (colloq.) Circumstances. [abbr.]

cīr′cuĭt (-kĭt) *n.* **1.** Line enclosing an area, distance round; area enclosed; roundabout journey; motor-racing road. **2.** Sequence of sporting events (*the American golf circuit*); sequence of athletic exercises; chain of theatres, cinemas, etc., under a single management; journey of judge in particular district to hold courts, this district, lawyers making the circuit; group of local Methodist churches forming a minor administrative unit. **3.** (Electr.) Path of current (SHORT *circuit*); apparatus through which current passes; ~**-breaker,** device for interrupting circuit; CLOSED-*circuit*; hence ~RY *n.*, circuits collectively, equipment forming circuit(s). [ME f. OF, f. L *circuitus* f. CIRCUM(*ire it-* go)]

circū′ĭtous *a.* Roundabout, indirect; hence ~LY[2] *adv.*, ~NESS *n.* [f. med. L *circuitosus* (*circuitus* CIRCUIT; see -OSE[1])]

cīr′cūlar *a.* & *n.* **1.** *a.* Having form of circle; taking place along circle; (Logic etc.) of or using a vicious circle; addressed to a circle of persons, customers, etc. **2.** ~ **letter,** letter, notice, advertisement, etc., of which many copies are made for distribution; ~ **saw,** toothed disc rotated by machinery for sawing; ‖~ **tour,** one which brings traveller back to starting-place. **3.** Hence **cīrcūlă′rITY** *n.*, ~LY[2] *adv.* **4.** *n.* Notice or advertisement distributed as circular letter. [ME f. AF *circuler*, OF *circulier, cerclier* f. LL *circularis* (*circulus* CIRCLE[1]; see -AR[1])]

cīr′cūlarīze, -īse (-īz), *v.t.* Send circulars to. [f. prec. + -IZE]

cīr′cūlāt|e *v.i.* & *t.* Go round (*blood circulates through veins, water in pipes, wine on table, newspaper to readers*); cause to go round, give currency to, (book, report, scandal, etc.); ~**ing library** (with books taken by subscribers in succession); ~**ing medium,** notes, gold, etc., used in exchange; hence or cogn. ~IVE *a.*, ~OR *n.* [f. L *circulare* (*circulus* CIRCLE[1]) + -ATE[3]]

cīrcūlā′tion *n.* Movement of blood from and to heart; similar movement of sap etc.; movement to and fro (of water, atmosphere, currency, etc.; **in, out of,** ~, (fig.) participating, or not, in activities etc.); transmission, distribution, (of news, books, etc.); number of copies sold, esp. of newspapers; currency, coin, etc. [F, or f. L *circulatio* (*circulare*; see prec., -ATION)]

cîrcūlā'torÿ (*or* sẽr'-) *a.* Of circulation of blood or sap. [f. CIRCULATE + -ORY]

cîrcum- *pref.* Round, about, used (1) adverbially, as: **circumfu'se,** pour round or about; (2) prepositionally, as: **circumli'ttoral,** bordering the shore; **circumo'cular,** surrounding the eye. [f. or after L, f. *circum* prep. = round, about]

cîrcumă'mbĭ|ent *a.* (Esp. of air or other fluid) surrounding; hence ~ENCY *n.* [f. CIRCUM- (1) + AMBIENT]

cîrcumă'mbūl|āte *v.t.* & *i.* Walk round or about; hence ~A'TION *n.*, ~**at**ORY *a.* [f. CIRCUM- (1) + *ambulate* f. L *ambulare* walk + -ATE³]

cîrcumbě'ndĭbus *n.* (joc.) Roundabout method; circumlocution. [f. CIRCUM- (1) + BEND² + *-ibus* ending of L abl. pl. case]

cîr'cumcîrcle *n.* (Geom.) Circle passing through all vertices of triangle or polygon. [f. CIRCUM- (1) + CIRCLE¹]

cîr'cumcīse (-z) *v.t.* Cut off foreskin or clitoris of (as Jewish or Muslim rite, or surgically); (Bibl.) purify (heart etc.). [ME, f. OF *circonciser*, or *circoncis-* stem of *circoncire,* f. L CIRCUM(*cidere cis-* = *caedere* cut)]

cîrcumcĭ'sion (-zhon) *n.* Act or rite of circumcising; (Eccl.) feast of Circumcision of Christ, 1 Jan. [ME, f. OF *circoncision* f. LL *circumcisio -onis* (as prec.; see -ION)]

cîrcŭ'mference *n.* Enclosing boundary, esp. of circle or other figure enclosed by curve; distance round; so **cîrcumferě'nt**IAL (-shal) *a.* [ME, f. OF *circonference* f. L CIRCUM(*ferentia* f. *ferre* bear; see -ENCE)]

cîr'cumflěx *a.* & *n.* **1.** ~ (**accent**), mark (ˆ or ˆ) placed over vowel in some languages to indicate contraction, length, or special quality. **2.** *a.* (Anat.) Curved, bending round something else, (*circumflex artery, nerve,* etc.). [f. L CIRCUM(*flexus* p.p. of *flectere* bend) transl. of Gk *perispōmenos* drawn around]

circŭ'mflu|ent (-lōō-) *a.* Flowing round, surrounding; hence ~ENCE *n.* [f. L CIRCUM(*fluere* flow); see -ENT]

cîrcumjā'cent *a.* Situated around. [f. L CIRCUM(*jacēre* lie); see -ENT]

cîrcumlocū'tion *n.* Use of many words where a few would do; evasive talk; a roundabout expression; hence ~AL, ~ARY¹, **cîrcumlŏ'cūt**ORY, *adjs.*, ~IST (1) *n.* [ME f. F, or f. L CIRCUM(*locutio* LOCUTION) transl. of Gk PERIPHRASIS]

cîrcumlū'nar (*or* -lōō'-) *a.* Moving or situated around the moon. [f. CIRCUM- (2) + LUNAR]

cîrcumnă'vĭg|āte *v.t.* Sail round (esp. the world); hence ~A'TION, ~**āt**OR, *ns.* [f. L CIRCUM(*navigare* NAVIGATE)]

cîrcumpō'lar *a.* (Astron., of star, motion, etc.) above horizon at all times in a given latitude; (Geog.) around or near one of the earth's poles. [f. CIRCUM- (2) + POLAR]

cîr'cumscrībe *v.t.* Draw line round; (Geom.) describe (figure) round another meeting it at points, but not cutting it (cf. INSCRIBE); lay down limits of, confine, restrict; hence **cîrcumscrĭ'pt**ION *n.* [f. L CIRCUM(*scribere script-* write)]

cîrcumsō'lar *a.* Moving or situated around or near the sun. [f. CIRCUM- (2) + SOLAR]

cîr'cumspěct *a.* Cautious, wary, taking everything into account; hence **cîrcumspě'ct**ION, ~NESS, *ns.*, ~LY² *adv.* [ME, f. L CIRCUM(*spicere spect-* = *specere* look)]

cîr'cumstance *n.* **1.** (in *pl.*) Time, place, manner, cause, occasion, etc., surroundings, of an act or event; external conditions affecting or that might affect action (**in** or **under the ~s,** owing to or making allowance for them; **under no ~s,** not whatever happens, never); state of financial or material welfare (*in* REDUCED, STRAIT*ened, circumstances*). **2.** Full detail in narrative; ceremony, fuss, (*pomp and circumstance*); incident, occurrence, fact (esp. *the circumstance that*). **3.** Hence **cîr'cumstanc**ED² (-st) *a.* [ME, f. OF *circonstance* or f. L CIRCUM(*stantia* f. part. of *stare* stand); see -ANCE]

cîrcumstă'ntial (-shal) *a.* Depending on circumstances (~ **evidence,** evidence tending to establish a conclusion by inference from known facts otherwise hard to explain); adventitious, incidental; detailed (*circumstantial story*); hence **cîrcumstăntiă'l**ITY (-shĭ-) *n.*, ~LY² *adv.* [f. L *circumstantia* (see prec.) + -AL]

cîrcumterrě'strĭal *a.* Moving or situated around the earth. [f. CIRCUM- (2) + TERRESTRIAL]

cîrcumvă'llāte *v.t.* Surround (as) with rampart. [f. L CIRCUM(*vallare* f. *vallum* rampart) + -ATE³]

cîrcum|vě'nt *v.t.* Entrap by surrounding; evade (difficulty etc.); outwit; so ~**vě'nt**ION *n.* [f. L CIRCUM(*venire vent-* come)]

cîrcumvolu'tion (-lōō'-) *n.* Rotation; winding of one thing round another; sinuous movement. [ME, f. L CIRCUM(*volvere volut-* roll); see -ION]

cîr'cus *n.* **1.** Rounded or oval arena lined with tiers of seats for equestrian and other exhibitions; amphitheatre of hills; ‖open space in town with streets converging on it (*Piccadilly Circus*). **2.** Travelling show of horses, riders, acrobats, clowns, performing animals, etc.; (colloq.) disturbance, scene of lively action; (colloq.) group of persons performing in sports etc. together or in succession. [L, = ring]

ciré (sē'rā) *n.* & *a.* (Fabric) with smooth polished surface, obtained esp. by waxing and heating. [F, = waxed]

cire perdue (sẽrperdū') *n.* Method of bronze-casting by filling space between core and mould after wax coating of core has been melted away. [F, = lost wax]

cîrl *n.* ~ **bunting,** brightly-coloured species of bunting (*Emberiza cirlus*). [f. It. *cirlo*, prob. f. *zirlare* to whistle like thrush]

cîrque (-k) *n.* **1.** (Geog.) Bowl-shaped hollow at head of valley or on mountain-side. **2.** (poet.) Ring; arena, amphitheatre. [F, f. L CIRCUS]

cĭrrhō's|ĭs (sĭrō'-) *n.* (*pl.* ~**es** *pr.* -ēz). Chronic disease of liver, esp. suffered by alcoholics. [mod. L, f. Gk *kirrhos* tawny; see -OSIS]

cĭ'rrĭpěd, -ēde, *n.* Marine crustacean in valved shell, immobile when adult; barnacle. [f. mod. L *Cirripedia* f. L *cirrus* curl (from form of legs) + *pes pedis* foot]

cĭ'rr|us *n.* (*pl.* ~**i** *pr.* -ī). (Bot.) tendril; (Zool.) slender appendage, as beard of fish, foot of cirriped; (Meteorol.) form of cloud with diverging filaments like lock of hair or wool, whence ~**o-** *comb. form*; hence ~OSE¹, ~OUS, *adjs.* [L, = curl]

cĭs- *pref.* On this side of, opp. *trans-* or *ultra-*, retaining in some (orig. L) wds the Roman sense (**ci'spadane, cisa'lpine,** S. or Rome-wards of Po, Alps), but usu. w. ref. to user's or majority's position (**cisatla'ntic,** on one's own side of the Atlantic; **cislu'nar,** between earth and moon; **cispo'ntine,** in London, on north orig. better-known side of bridges or Thames); also of time (**cis-Elizabe'than**); (Chem.) having two atoms or groups on same side of plane of symmetry. [L prep.]

cĭ'scō *n.* (*pl.* ~**es**). N. Amer. white fish of genus *Leucichthys.* [19th c.; orig. unkn.]

For other words in *circum-* **see** CIRCUM-.

cĭ'ssȳ. See SISSY.
cist[1] (*or* k-) *n.* (Archaeol.) Prehistoric stone or hollowed-tree coffin or burial-chamber. [W, = CHEST]
cist[2] *n.* (Gk Ant.) Box used for sacred utensils. [f. L f. Gk *kistē* box]
Cĭstẽr'cian (-shan) *n.* & *a.* (Monk or nun) of order founded 1098 as stricter offshoot of Benedictines. [f. F *cistercien*, f. L *Cistercium* Cîteaux near Dijon in France (where founded); see -IAN]
cĭ'stern *n.* Reservoir for storing water, esp. one in roof-space supplying taps, or above water-closet; underground reservoir for rain-water. [ME, f. OF *cisterne* f. L *cisterna* (*cista*; see CIST[2])]
cĭ'stus *n.* Shrub of genus *Cistus*, with large white or red flowers. [mod. L, f. Gk *kistos*]
cĭ'tadel *n.* Fortress, esp. one guarding or dominating city; meeting-hall of Salvation Army. [f. F *citadelle* or f. It. *cittadella* dim. of obs. *cittade* f. L *civitas -tatis* CITY]
citā'tion *n.* Citing; mention in official dispatch; descriptive note accompanying announcement of award. [f. as foll. + -ATION]
cite *v.t.* Summon to appear in lawcourt; quote (passage, book, author) in support of a position; mention as example or in official dispatch. [ME, f. F *citer* f. L *citare* (*ciēre* set moving)]
cĭ'ther. Var. of foll.
cĭ'thern, cĭ'ttern, *n.* (Hist.) Wire-stringed lute-like instrument usu. played with plectrum. [f. L *cithara*, Gk *kithara* kind of harp, w. assim. to GITTERN]
cĭ'tĭfīed (-id) *a.* Made city-like or urban in appearance or behaviour. [p.p. of *citify*, f. CITY + -FY]
cĭ'tĭzen *n.* Inhabitant or freeman of city; townsman; *civilian; member, native or naturalized, of a State or Commonwealth (usu. *of*; ~ **of the world,** one who is at home everywhere, cosmopolitan); inhabitant *of*; hence ~HOOD, ~RY (1), ~SHIP, *ns.* [ME f. AF *citesein*, OF *citeain* f. Rom **civitatanus* f. L *civitas -tatis* CITY; cf. DENIZEN]
citō'le *n.* Small cithern. [ME f. OF, cogn. w. CITHERN + dim. suf.]
cĭ'tr|ic *a.* (Chem.) ~**ic acid,** sharp-tasting acid in juice of lemons etc.; hence ~ATE[1] (3) *n.* [f. F *citrique* f. L *citrus* citron; see -IC]
cĭ'trine *a.* Lemon-coloured. [ME f. OF *citrin* f. LL **citrinus* (*citrus* citron; see -INE[1])]
cĭ'tron *n.* (Tree, *Citrus medica*, bearing) fruit like lemon but larger, less acid, and thicker-skinned. [F, f. L CITRUS, after *limon* lemon]
cĭtronĕ'lla *n.* Fragrant S. Asian grass (*Cymbopogon nardus*); oil from it, used for keeping insects away. [mod. L, f. as prec. + dim. suf.]
cĭ'trous *a.* Belonging to genus *Citrus* (see foll.). [f. foll. + -OUS]
cĭ'trus *n.* Tree of genus *Citrus*, including citron, lemon, lime, orange, and grapefruit; ~ **(fruit)**, fruit from such a tree. [L, = citron-tree or thuja]
cĭ'ttern. See CITHERN.
cĭ'tȳ *n.* **1.** Large town; ||(strictly) town created city by charter, esp. as containing cathedral; *municipal corporation occupying a definite area; **Eternal C~, C~ of the Seven Hills,** Rome; **Heavenly C~, C~ of God,** Paradise; HOLY *City*; **the C~,** part of London governed by Lord Mayor and Corporation, business part of this, commercial circles. **2.** (*attrib.*) Of a city or the City; ||**C~ Company,** corporation representing ancient trade-guild; *~ **desk,** newspaper department for local news; ||**C~ editor,** one who deals with financial news in a daily or weekly journal; *~ **editor,** one who deals with local news; ~ **fathers,** persons responsible for administration of a city; *~ **hall,** municipal offices or officers; ~ **manager,** official directing administration of a city; ||~ **page** (in newspaper, dealing with financial and business news); *city of* REFUGE; ~**scape,** view of a city, city scenery; ~ **slicker,** (1) plausible rogue as usu. found in cities, (2) smart and sophisticated city-dweller; ~**-state,** (Hist.) city that is also an independent state. **3.** Hence ~WARD(s) *a.* & *adv.* [ME, f. OF *cité* f. L *civitas -tatis* (*civis* citizen; see -TY[1])]
cityfied. Var. of CITIFIED.
cĭ'vĕt *n.* ~**(-cat)**, carnivorous quadruped of family Viverridae, esp. *Civettictis civetta* of central Africa; strong musky perfume got from anal glands of this. [f. F *civette* f. It. *zibetto* f. med. L *zibethum* f. Arab. *azzabād*]
cĭ'vĭc *a.* Of or proper to citizens (~ **crown,** ancient-Roman garland of oak-leaves and acorns given to one who saved fellow citizen's life in war); of city, municipal, (~ **centre,** area where municipal offices and other public buildings are situated); of citizenship, civil, (*civic virtues*); hence **cĭ'**VICALLY *adv.*, **cĭ'**VICS *n.*, study of rights and duties of citizenship. [f. F *civique* or f. L *civicus* (*civis* citizen; see -IC)]
civies. See CIVVIES.
cĭ'vĭl (*or -il*) *a.* **1.** Of or proper to citizens. **2.** Polite, obliging, not rude. **3.** Not naval, military, etc. **4.** Not ecclesiastical. **5.** (Law). Not criminal or political; pertaining to civil law. **6.** (Of time measurement) fixed by custom or enactment, not natural or astronomical. **7.** ~ **aviation** (not military etc., and esp. commercial); ~ **commotion,** riot or similar disturbance; ~ **day** (as used for time reckoning in ordinary affairs); ~ **defence,** organization of civilians for dealing esp. with air raids; ~ **disobedience,** refusal to obey laws, pay taxes, etc., as part of political campaign; *civil* ENGINEER[1], so ~ **engineering;** ~ **law,** law concerning private rights only, (Hist.) Roman or non-ecclesiastical law; *civil* LIBERTY; ||~ **list,** annual allowance by Parliament for sovereign's household expenses; ~ **marriage** (solemnized as civil contract without religious ceremony); ~ **rights,** rights of each citizen, *esp. of Negroes, to liberty, equality, etc.; **C~ Service,** all non-military branches of State administration, whence ~ **servant;** ~ **state** (being single, married, divorced, etc.); ~ **war** (between citizens of same country, esp. in England (17th c.), U.S. (1861–65), or Spain (1936–39)); *civil* YEAR. **8.** Hence ~LY[2] *adv.* [ME f. OF, f. L *civilis* (*civis* citizen; see -IL)]
cĭvĭ'lian (-yan) *n.* & *a.* (Person) not in or of navy or army or air force; hence ~IZE (3) *v.t.*, convert (Service post) into a civilian one, **~īz**A'TION *n.* [f. prec. + -IAN]
cĭvĭ'lĭtȳ *n.* Politeness; (in *pl.*) acts of politeness. [ME, f. OF *civilité* f. L *civilitas -tatis* (as CIVIL; see -ITY)]
cĭvĭlīzā'tion, -īs- (-īz-), *n.* Making or becoming civilized; state reached in this process; stage, esp. advanced stage, in social development; civilized States. [f. foll. + -ATION]
cĭ'vĭlīz|e, -īs|e (-īz), *v.t.* Bring out of barbarism, enlighten; refine and educate; hence ~ABLE *a.*, ~ER[1] *n.* [f. F *civiliser* (CIVIL; see -IZE (3))]
cĭ'v(v)ĭes (-vĭz) *n. pl.* (sl.) Civilian clothes. [abbr.]
||**Cĭ'vvȳ Street** *n.* (sl.) Civilian life. [abbr.]
C. J. *abbr.* Chief Justice.
cl. *abbr.* centilitre(s); class.
Cl *symb.* chlorine.
clăck *n.*, & *v.i.* **1.** *n.* Sharp sound as of clogs on stone or of boards struck together; flap-valve in pumps etc.; noise of continual talking. **2.** *v.i.* Chatter loudly; make clack, clatter. [ME, =

to chatter, prate, prob. f. ON *klaka* chatter, twitter, of imit. orig.]

clăd[1]. See CLOTHE and IRON[1]*clad*.

clăd[2] *v.t.* (**-dd-**). Provide with cladding. [app. f. prec.]

clă'ddĭng *n.* Coating or covering on structure, material, etc. [f. prec. + -ING[1]]

clāde *n.* (Biol.) Group of organisms evolved from a common ancestor. [f. Gk *klados* branch]

clā'dōde *n.* (Bot.) Flattened leaflike stem. [f. Gk *kladōdēs* many-shooted (*klados* shoot)]

claim[1] *v.t.* Demand as one's due or property (recognition etc., *to* be, *that* one should be, recognized etc.); have as achievement or consequence (*the fire claimed many victims*); represent oneself as having (*claim the victory, accuracy*); profess *to* (*be* the owner, *have* told the truth); demand recognition of the fact *that*; contend, assert; (of things) deserve (esp. *attention*); hence ~'ABLE *a.*, ~'ANT *n.* [ME, f. OF *claim-* stressed st. of *clamer* f. L *clamare* call out]

claim[2] *n.* Demand for something as due (*lay claim to*); = PAY[1]-*claim*; right, title, *to* thing; right to make demand *on* person; statement of novel features in patent; contention, assertion; (Mining etc.) piece of land allotted (**stake a ~**, (fig.) make statement of one's rights); ***~-jumper,** one who appropriates a mining claim already taken by another. [ME, f. OF *claime* (*clamer*; see prec.)]

clairau'dĭ|ence *n.* Faculty of hearing mentally what is inaudible; so ~ENT *a.* & *n.* [f. F *clair* CLEAR + AUDIENCE, after foll.]

clairvoy'ance *n.* Faculty of seeing mentally what is happening or exists out of sight; exceptional insight. [F, f. *clairvoyant* (*clair* clear, *voyant* part. of *voir* see); cf. -ANCE, -ANT]

clairvoy'ant *n.* (occas. *fem.* **~e**) & *a.* (Person) having clairvoyance. [F, = clear-sighted; see prec.]

clăm *n.*, & *v.i.* (**-mm-**). **1.** *n.* Bivalve mollusc, esp. the N. Amer. hard or round clam (*Mercenaria mercenaria*) and soft or long clam (*Mya arenaria*), used for food; (sl.) taciturn person; ***~'bake,** social gathering for eating (esp. clams and fish) outdoors. **2.** *v.i.* Dig for clams; ***~ up,** become silent, cease talking. [16th c., app. f. *clam* a clamp]

clā'mant *a.* (literary). Noisy, insistent; urgent; hence ~LY[2] *adv.* [f. L *clamare* cry out; see -ANT]

clă'mber *v.i.*, & *n.* Climb with hands and feet; climb with difficulty or labour. [ME, prob. f. *clamb* (obs. past tense of CLIMB) + -ER[5]]

clă'mm|ȳ *a.* Moist, usu. cold, and sticky or slimy; (of weather) cold and damp; hence ~ĬLY[2] *adv.*, ~ĬNESS *n.* [ME, f. *clam* to daub + -Y[2]]

clă'mour (-m*er*), ***clă'mor,** *n.*, & *v.i.* & *t.* Shout(ing); (make) loud appeal, complaint, or demand (*for, against, to* do); (make) confused noise; so **clă'mor**OUS *a.* [ME, f. OF *clamour* f. L *clamor -oris* (*clamare* call out)]

clămp[1] *n.* & *v.* **1.** *n.* Brace, clasp, or band, usu. of iron, for strengthening other materials or holding things together; appliance or tool with screw connection of parts for holding or compressing. **2.** *v.t.* Strengthen or fasten (as) with clamp(s); place or hold firmly. **3.** *v.i.* **~ down on,** become stricter regarding, put a stop to. [ME, prob. f. MDu., MLG *klamp(e)*, f. **klamp-*, **klam-* press together]

clămp[2] *n.* Pile (of bricks for burning, ||potatoes etc. under straw and earth, turf, peat, garden rubbish, etc.). [16th c., prob. f. Du. *klamp* heap, in brick-making, rel. to CLUMP]

clăn *n.* Group of (esp. Highland) Scots with common ancestor, esp. while under patriarchal control (**~'sman,** member, fellow member, of clan); tribe; family holding together, whence ~'NISH[1] *a.*; party, coterie; genus, species, class; hence ~'SHIP *n.*, clan system or behaviour. [ME, f. Gael. *clann* f. L *planta* sprout]

clăndĕ'stĭne *a.* Surreptitious, secret; hence ~LY[2] (-nlĭ) *adv.* [f. F *clandestin* or f. L *clandestinus* (*clam* secretly)]

clăng *n.* & *v.* **1.** *n.* Loud resonant metallic sound (esp. of trumpet, armour, large bell, some birds). **2.** *v.i.* & *t.* Make, cause (thing) to make, clang; hence ~'ER *n.*, (esp., sl.) blunder (*drop a clanger*). [imit., but infl. by L *clangere* resound, *clangor* (of trumpets, birds)]

clă'ngour, *clă'ngor, (-ngg*er*) *n.* Succession or prevalence of clanging noises; hence **clă'ngor**OUS (-ngg-) *a.* [f. L *clangor* (see prec., -OR)]

clănk *n.* & *v.* **1.** *n.* Sound as of heavy pieces of metal meeting or chain rattling. **2.** *v.i.* & *t.* Make, cause (bucket, chain, etc.) to make, clank. [imit.; cf. CLANG, CLINK, Du. *klank*]

clannish, clanship, clansman. See CLAN.

clăp[1] *n.* Explosive noise (of thunder, of hand-palms struck together as applause); slap, pat, (*gave him a clap on the shoulder*). [ME, f. foll.]

clăp[2] *v.* (**-pp-**). **1.** *v.i.* & *t.* ~ (one's **hands**), show approval (of) by striking palms together loudly, (usu. w. *hands*) strike them for warmth, as signal, in delight, etc.; flap (wings) audibly; **~ on the back,** slap so in encouragement or congratulation. **2.** *v.t.* Put or place quickly or energetically (person *in(to)* prison, duty *on* goods; *clap on all sail*); **~ped out,** (sl.) exhausted; **~ eyes on,** catch sight of (esp. w. neg.); **~-net,** fowler's or entomologist's net shut by pulling string. [OE *clappian* throb, beat, = OHG *klapfōn*, ON *klappa*; OE *clæppan*, OHG *klepfen*, of imit. orig.]

clăp[3] *n.* (vulg.) Venereal disease, esp. gonorrhoea. [f. OF *clapoir* venereal bubo]

***clă'pboard** (*or* klă'b*erd*) *n.* = WEATHER-*board*. [anglicized f. LG *klappholt* cask-stave]

Clă'pham (-pam) *n.* **The man on the ~ omnibus,** the average man. [~ in S.W. London]

clă'pper *n.* In vbl senses; tongue or striker of bell; ~(**-board**), (Cinemat.) device for making sharp noise for synchronization of picture and sound; **like the ~s,** (sl.) very fast or very hard. [f. CLAP[2] + -ER[1]]

clă'ptrăp *n.* Language used or sentiments expressed only to gain applause; pretentious but empty assertions; nonsense. [f. CLAP[1] + TRAP[1]]

claque (-ahk) *n.* Hired body of applauders; so **claqueur** (klahkẽr') *n.*, member of claque. [F (*claquer* to clap)]

clă'rabĕlla (*or* -ār'-) *n.* Organ stop of flute quality. [f. fem. forms of L *clarus* clear, *bellus* pretty]

clă'rence *n.* (Hist.) Four-wheeled closed carriage with seats for four inside and two on box. [f. Duke of *C~*, afterwards William IV]

||**Clă'renceux** (-sū) *n.* Second KING[1] of Arms, with jurisdiction south of the Trent. [ME f. AF, f. Duke of *Clarence* (*Clare* in Suffolk)]

clă'rėt *n.* & *a.* Red wine from Bordeaux (or elsewhere); (sl.) blood (**tap** person's **~**, make his nose bleed with blow of fist); **~-colour(ed)**, reddish-violet. [ME, f. OF (*vin*) *claret* (orig. of light-red wines) f. *claré* clarified f. med. L *claratum* (*vinum*) (*clarare* f. L *clarus* clear)]

clă'rĭfȳ *v.* **1.** *v.t.* Make clear (difficult subject, obscure statement, mind, sight); free from impurities, make transparent, (butter, liquid, air, etc.). **2.** *v.i.* Become transparent; be made clear or pure (lit., or fig. of literary style etc.). **3.** Hence **clărĭ**FICA'TION *n.* [ME, f. OF *clarifier* f. LL *clarificare* f. L *clarus* clear; see -FY]

clărĭnĕ't *n.* Wood-wind instrument with single-reed mouthpiece, holes, and keys, whence

clărĭnĕ'ttIST (3), ***-ĕ'tĭst,** *n.*; its player; organ stop of like quality. [f. F *clarinette* dim. of *clarine* kind of bell]

clă'rĭon *n.* & *a.* **1.** *n.* (Hist.) shrill narrow-tubed war trumpet; rousing sound; organ stop of clarion quality. **2.** *a.* Clear and loud. [ME, f. med. L *clario -onis* f. L *clarus* clear]

clărĭonĕ't. Var. of CLARINET.

clă'rĭtў *n.* Clearness (esp. fig.). [ME, f. L *claritas* (*clarus* clear; see -ITY)]

clar'kĭa *n.* Annual plant of genus *Clarkia*, with showy white, pink, or purple flowers. [mod. L, f. W. *Clark*, U.S. explorer d. 1838 + -IA¹]

clar'ў *n.* Aromatic herb of genus *Salvia*. [ME, f. obs. F *clarie* repr. med. L *sclarea*]

clăsh *v.i.* & *t.*, & *n.* (Make) loud broken sound as of collision, striking weapons, cymbals, bells rung together; meet(ing) with force, conflict; disagree(ment); be(ing) at variance or incompatible *with*, (of colours) be(ing) discordant. [imit.; cf. *clack, clang, crack, crash*]

clasp¹ (-ah-) *n.* Contrivance of interlocking parts for fastening, buckle, brooch; metal fastening of book-cover; embrace, reach; grasp, handshake; bar of silver on medal-ribbon with name of battle etc. (in campaign commemorated by medal) at which wearer was present; **~-knife** (folding, with catch fixing blade when open). [ME; etym. unkn.]

clasp² (-ah-) *v.* **1.** *v.t.* & *i.* Fasten (clasp); fasten with or as clasp. **2.** *v.t.* Encircle, hold closely, embrace; grasp (another's hand; **~ hands,** shake hands with fervour or affection; ~ one's **hands,** interlace fingers). **3.** Hence ~'ER¹ *n.*, (esp., in *pl.*) appendages of some male fish and insects to hold female in copulation. [f. prec.]

class (-ahs) *n.*, & *v.t.* **1.** *n.* Rank or order of society (*upper, middle, lower, working, classes*; **~-conscious(ness)**, esp. realizing and usu. taking part in the conflict or **~ war** between one's own and other classes); (in *pl.*, arch.) *the* rich or educated; caste system; hence ~'LESS *a.*, making no distinction of classes. **2.** Set of students taught together, their time of meeting, their course of instruction, *all college students of same standing (**~ of 1970,** those graduating then); **~-fellow, -mate,** present or past member of same class as oneself; **~-room** (where class is taught). **3.** (In conscripted armies) all the recruits of a year (*the 1960 class*). **4.** ‖Division of candidates by merit in examination; **take a ~,** gain honours; **~-list** (issued by examiners). **5.** Division according to quality (FIRST, SECOND, etc., *class*); **in a ~ of** (or **on**) **its** (or **his**) **own,** unequalled; **no ~,** (colloq.) quite inferior. **6.** Group of persons or things having some characteristic in common. **7.** (Biol.) Group of animals or plants usu. next below phylum or division. **8.** Distinction, high quality, (also *attrib.*). **9.** *v.t.* Place in a class; hence ~'ABLE *a.* [f. L *classis* assembly]

clă'ssĭc *a.* & *n.* **1.** *a.* Of the first class, of acknowledged excellence; remarkably typical, outstandingly important, (*a classic case*). **2.** Of the standard ancient Latin and Greek authors, art, or culture; of Roman and Greek antiquity. **3.** (Of style) simple, harmonious, well-proportioned, and finished, in accordance with established forms (cf. ROMANTIC); having literary or historic associations (*classic ground*); (of clothes) made in simple style not much affected by changes of fashion; ‖**~ races,** Two and One Thousand Guineas, Derby, Oaks, St. Leger. **4.** *n.* Writer, artist, work, example, of acknowledged excellence or value; ancient Latin or Greek writer; (arch.) Latin and Greek scholar; follower of classic models (cf. ROMANTIC); garment in classic style; (in *pl.*) classical studies. [f. F *classique* or f. L *classicus* (*classis* class; see -IC)]

clă'ssĭcal *a.* **1.** Standard or first-class, esp. in literature. **2.** Of ancient Latin or Greek standard authors or art; learned in these; based on these (*classical education*); (of language) having form used by ancient standard authors (*classical* LATIN, *Hebrew*). **3.** In or following the restrained style of classical antiquity (as prec.; cf. ROMANTIC); pertaining to a long-established style etc.; (of music) serious or conventional, opp. *romantic*, or *folk, modern, popular*, etc.; (Phys.) relating to concepts preceding relativity, quantum theory, etc. **4.** Hence ~ISM (3), ~ITY (-ă'l-), *ns.*, ~LY² *adv.* [f. L *classicus* (see prec.) + -AL]

clă'ssĭc|ĭsm *n.* Following of classic style; classical scholarship; advocacy of classical education; Latin or Greek idiom; hence ~IST (2, 3) *n.* [f. CLASSIC + -ISM]

clă'ssĭcize, -ise (-īz), *v.* **1.** *v.t.* Make classic. **2.** *v.i.* Imitate the classical style. [f. CLASSIC + -IZE (2, 3)]

clă'ssĭ|fў *v.t.* Arrange in classes; assign to a class; designate as officially secret or not for general disclosure; hence or cogn. **~fīABLE, ~fĭcātORY,** *adjs.*, ~FICA'TION, **~fīER¹,** *ns.* [back form. f. *classification* f. F (as CLASS)]

cla'ssў (-ah'-) *a.* (sl.) Superior; stylish. [f. CLASS + -Y²]

clă'stĭc *a.* (Geol.) Composed of broken pieces of older rocks; **~ rocks,** conglomerates etc. [f. F *clastique* f. Gk *klastos* broken in pieces; see -IC]

clă'thrāte *n.* (Chem.) Compound in which one component is enclosed in structure of another. [f. L *clathratus* f. *clathri* f. Gk *klēthra* lattice-bars; see -ATE¹]

clă'tter *v.* & *n.* **1.** *v.i.* & *n.* (Make) rattling sound as of many plates or wooden objects struck together; (resound with) noisy talk; move, fall, etc., with clatter. **2.** *v.t.* Cause (plates etc.) to clatter. [OE *clatrian, of imit. orig.]

claudĭcā'tion *n.* (Med.) Limping. [f. L *claudicare* limp (*claudus* lame); see -ATION]

claus|e (-z) *n.* (Gram.) distinct part of a sentence including a subject and predicate; single statement in treaty, law, bill, or contract; hence ~'AL *a.* [ME f. OF, f. L *clausula* conclusion (*claudere claus-* shut; see -ULE)]

clau'stral *a.* Of the cloister, monastic; narrow-minded. [ME, f. LL *claustralis* (*claustrum* CLOISTER; see -AL)]

claustrophō'b|ia *n.* (Psych.) Morbid dread of confined places; hence ~IC *a.*, suffering from or inducing claustrophobia. [mod. L, f. L *claustrum* (see CLOISTER) + -O- + -PHOBIA]

clā'vāte *a.* (Bot.) Club-shaped. [f. mod. L *clavatus* f. L *clava* club; see -ATE²]

clāve¹ (*or* klahv) *n.* (Mus.) One of two hardwood sticks used to make a hollow sound. [Amer. Sp. f. Sp., = keystone f. L *clavis* key]

clāve². See CLEAVE².

clăvĭcĕ'mbalō (-chĕ'-) *n.* (*pl.* ~s). (Mus.) Harpsichord. [It.]

clă'vĭchord (-k-) *n.* (Hist.) Predecessor of piano, first stringed instrument with keyboard. [ME, f. med. L *clavichordium* (L *clavis* key, *chorda* string, CHORD¹)]

clă'vĭcle *n.* Collar-bone; so **clavĭ'cūl**AR¹ *a.* [f. L *clavicula* dim. of *clavis* key; from its shape]

clă'vĭer *n.* (Mus.) (Instrument with) keyboard. [F, or f. G *klavier* f. med. L *claviarius*, orig. = key-bearer, f. L *clavis* key; see -ER²]

clă'vĭform *a.* Club-shaped. [f. L *clava* club + -I- + -FORM]

claw¹ *n.* Pointed horny nail of animal's or bird's foot; foot so armed; pincers of shellfish; contrivance for grappling, holding, etc.; **~-and-ball,** (of furniture) having feet which represent claw holding ball; **~-hammer** (with bent split end for extracting nails); hence (-)~ED[2] (-awd) *a.* [OE *clawu* f. obl. cases of *clēa*, = OS *clāuua*, OHG *klāwa* f. WG **klāwa*]

claw[2] *v.t.* & *i.* Scratch, tear, seize or pull towards one, with claws or hands; (Naut.) beat to windward; (Sc.) scratch gently (**~ me and I'll ~ thee,** of mutual aid or flattery); **~ back,** regain gradually or laboriously, take back (allowance by added taxation etc.), whence **~-back** *n.* [OE *clawian* (as prec.)]

clay *n.* Stiff tenacious earth, material of bricks, pottery, etc. (*feet of clay*, see FOOT[1]; *clay* PIGEON[1]); (material of) human body; **~ (pipe)**, tobacco-pipe made of clay; **~-pan,** (Austral.) natural hollow in clay soil retaining water after rain; hence **~'ey**[2] *a.* [OE *clǣg*, = (M)Du., (M)LG *klei*, f. WG **klaija* (**klai-* etc., cogn. w. CLEAVE[2])]

clay'mōre *n.* (Hist.) Scottish two-edged broadsword; basket-hilted often single-edged broadsword; *type of anti-personnel mine. [f. Gael. *claidheamh mór* great sword]

-cle. See -CULE.

clean[1] *a.* **1.** Free from dirt or contaminating matter, unsoiled; clear, not or no longer having what is regarded as making defective or destroying original state; **~ air** (unpolluted); *clean* BILL[4] *of health*; *clean* BREAST[1]; **~ fingers,** (fig.) absence of corruption or bribery; **~ hands,** (fig.) absence of guilt; **show a ~ pair of heels,** escape by speed; **~ sheet** or **slate,** freedom from commitments or imputations; **~'skin,** (Austral.) unbranded animal, (sl.) person without police record; **come ~,** (colloq.) own up, confess everything. **2.** Free from ceremonial defilement or from disease; (of food) not prohibited. **3.** (Of atomic bomb etc.) producing relatively little fall-out. **4.** Cleanly; (of children and animals) trained to defecate in proper place. **5.** Well-formed, slender and shapely, (of joints, figure; so **~-limbed**); (of ship or aircraft) smooth, streamlined. **6.** Smart, adroit, not bungling, (*clean fielding*). **7.** Even, unobstructed, clear-cut, complete; **~ break** (quick and final); **make a ~ job of,** (colloq.) do thoroughly; *clean* SWEEP[2]; **~ timber** (without knots). **8.** (colloq.) Free from impropriety. **9.** Hence **~'NESS** (-n-n-) *n.* [OE *clǣne*, = OS *klēni*, OHG *kleini* f. WG **klaini*]

clean[2] *adv.* Completely, outright, simply, (*clean bowled*; *cut clean through*; *clean wrong*); in a clean manner (**~-cut,** sharply outlined; **~-living,** of upright character; **~-shaven,** without beard or whiskers or moustache). [OE *clǣne*, *clēne* (as prec.)]

clean[3] *v.* & *n.* **1.** *v.t.* & *i.* Make or become clean (*of* dirt etc.); eat all the food on (one's plate); make one*self*, make oneself, clean. **2. ~ down,** clean by brushing or wiping; **~ out,** empty, strip, (esp. sl., person of his money); **~ up,** make (oneself) clean, put things tidy, put (things) tidy, clear (mess) away, (colloq.) acquire as, or make, gain or profit, (fig.) deal with disorder, immorality, crime, etc., in (place), whence **~-up** *n.* **3.** Hence ~'ER[1] (1, 2) *n.*, (esp.) person who cleans rooms or clothes; **take to the ~ers,** (sl.) (1) rob or defraud (person) of all his money, (2) criticize strongly and adversely. **4.** *n.* Cleaning (*give it a clean*). [f. CLEAN[1]]

clea'nlÿ[1] *adv.* In clean way. [OE *clǣnlīce* (as CLEAN[1], -LY[2])]

clea'nl|ÿ[2] (-ĕ'n-) *a.* Habitually clean; attentive to cleanness; hence **~ĭLY**[2] *adv.*, **~ĭNESS** *n.* [OE *clǣnlic* (as CLEAN[1], -LY[1])]

cleans|e (-ĕnz) *v.t.* Purify (*of* sin etc.); (usu. formal or arch.) make clean; (Bibl.) cure (leper etc.); **~ing cream, tissue,** (for removing unwanted matter from face, hands, etc.); **~ing department,** local service of refuse collection etc.; hence ~'ER[1] (1, 2) *n.* [OE *clǣnsian* (*clǣne* CLEAN[1])]

clear[1] *a.* & *adv.* **1.** *a.* Unclouded, transparent, not turbid, lustrous, unblemished; *clear* CONSCIENCE; **~ soup** (containing little solid matter); **~-starch,** stiffen with colourless starch. **2.** Distinct, easily perceived; unambiguous, intelligible, (*make* thing *clear*; *make* one*self clear*); not confused or doubtful, manifest; **in ~,** not in cipher or code. **3.** Discerning, penetrating, (so **~-eyed, ~-headed, ~-sighted, ~-sightedness,** usu. fig.; *clear thinking*); confident, decided, certain, (*on* or *about* point, *of* fact, *that*). **4.** Without deduction, net; free *of* (**in the ~,** free of suspicion or difficulty); complete (*three clear days*). **5.** Open, unobstructed, (**coast is ~,** no one is near enough to see or interfere; ‖**~'way,** road on which vehicles must not stop); unengaged, free, unencumbered by debt. **6.** Hence ~'LY[2] *adv.*, ~'NESS *n.* **7.** *adv.* Clearly (*speak loud and clear*; **~-cut,** well defined); quite (*clear away, through*; *three feet clear*); *all the way *to*; apart, without contact, (*keep, hang,* STEER[1], *get, clear*; *stand clear of the doors*). [ME f. OF *cler* f. L *clarus*]

clear[2] *v.t.* & *i.* **1.** Make or become clear (*of*; **~ the air,** lit. of sultriness, fig. of suspicion, tension, etc.; ~ one's **throat,** by slight coughing; *clear the* WAY 4). **2.** Show or declare to be innocent (*of*); declare (person) fit to have secret information etc.; free from or *of* prohibition or obstruction (**~ the decks for action,** make ready to fight, lit. or fig.; **~ land,** cut down trees etc. before cultivating or building; **~ room** etc., cause persons to leave it); remove (obstruction, unwanted object, etc., esp. *clear out of the way*); pass (cheque) through clearing-house; make or become empty or unobstructed; (of mist etc.) disappear. **3.** Pass over or by without touching (esp. by jumping); pass through (customs office etc.). **4.** Make (sum) as net gain or to balance expenses. **5. ~ away,** remove, remove remains of meal from table, (of mist etc.) disappear; **~ off,** get rid of, go away; **~ out,** empty, make off; **~ up,** solve (mystery), make tidy, (of weather etc.) grow clear. [ME, f. prec.]

clear'ance *n.* **1.** Making clear; removal of obstructions, old buildings, etc.; removal of persons or objects so as to clear land. **2.** Clearing of cheques; (certificate of) clearing of ship at customs; permission (esp. for aircraft to land or take off, or for person to have secret information etc.); clear space allowed for the passing of two objects or parts. **3. ~ order** (for demolition of buildings); ‖**~ sale** (to effect clearance of superfluous stock). [f. prec. + -ANCE]

clear'cōle *n.*, & *v.t.* (Paint with) size and whiting or white lead as first coat in house-painting. [f. F *claire colle* clear glue]

clear'ĭng *n.* In vbl senses; piece of land in forest cleared for cultivation; **~ bank,** member of clearing-house; **~-house,** bankers' institution where cheques and bills are exchanged, so that only the balances need be paid in cash, (fig.) agency for collecting and distributing information etc. [ME, f. CLEAR[2] + -ING[1]]

***clear'stōrÿ.** Var. of CLERESTORY.

cleat *n.* Wedge; projecting piece bolted on spar, gangway, etc., to give footing or prevent rope from slipping; piece of wood or iron bolted on for securing ropes to, or to strengthen woodwork etc. [OE **clēat*, = OHG *klōz* lump f. WG **klaut-*; cf. CLOT]

clea'vage *n.* Way in which mineral, party, opinion, etc., tends to split; (colloq.) hollow between woman's breasts, esp. as exposed by low-cut garment. [f. foll. + -AGE]

cleave[1] *v.t.* & *i.* (**clove** *pr.* klōv *or* **cleft** *pr.* klĕft; **clo'ven** *or* **cleft**). **1.** (literary). Split; chop, break, or come, apart, esp. along grain or line of cleavage; make way through (water, air). **2.** Break apart (esp. of mineral); **cleft palate,** congenital fissure in roof of mouth; **in a cleft stick,** in tight place allowing neither retreat nor advance (also fig.); **cloven foot** or **hoof** (of ruminant quadrupeds, of god Pan, and so of Devil; *show the cloven hoof,* reveal one's evil nature). **3.** Hence **clea'**VABLE *a.* [OE *clēofan*, = OS *klioban*, OHG *kliuban*, ON *kljúfa* f. Gmc **kleubhan*]

cleave[2] *v.i.* (*past also* **clave** *pr.* klāv). (arch.) Stick fast, adhere, *to.* [OE *cleofian, clifian*, = OS *klibon*, OHG *klebēn* f. WG **klibhōjan* (**klibh-*; cf. CLAY)]

clea'ver *n.* In vbl senses; butcher's chopping-tool for carcasses. [f. CLEAVE[1] + -ER[1]]

clea'vers, clĭ'vers, (-z) *n.* (used as *sing.* or *pl.*) Goose-grass, creeper with prickly stem sticking to clothes etc. [OE *clife*, = OS, OHG *kliba* f. as CLEAVE[2]]

clĕf *n.* (Mus.) One of the several symbols (ALTO, BASS[3] or *F*, SOPRANO, TENOR, TREBLE or *G*, *clef*) indicating pitch of staff. [F, f. L *clavis* key]

clĕft[1] *n.* Space or division made by cleaving; fissure, split. [OE **clyft* (OHG, ON *kluft*), cogn. w. CLEAVE[1]; assim. to foll.]

clĕft[2]. See CLEAVE[1].

||**clĕg** *n.* Gadfly; horse-fly. [15th c., f. ON *kleggi*]

cleistogă'mĭc (klī-) *a.* (Bot., of flower) permanently closed and self-fertilizing. [f. Gk *kleistos* closed + *gamos* marriage]

clĕ'matĭs (*or* klemā'-) *n.* Climbing or erect plant of genus *Clematis*, e.g. *C. vitalba* (traveller's joy or old man's beard). [L, f. Gk *klēmatis* (*klēma* vine branch)]

clĕ'm|ent *a.* (Of temper or weather) mild; showing mercy; so ~ENCY *n.* [ME, f. L *clemens -entis*; see -ENT]

clĕ'mentīne (*or* -ēn) *n.* Kind of small orange, hybrid of tangerine and sour orange. [f. F *clémentine*]

clĕnch *v.t.*, & *n.* **1.** *v.t.* Secure (nail, rivet) by driving point sideways when through. **2.** Close (teeth, fingers) tightly; grasp firmly. **3.** *n.* Any of the above actions or the resulting state. [OE **clencan*, = OHG *klenken* f. Gmc **klankjan* (**klank-* etc.; cf. CLING)]

clĕ'psȳdra (*or* -sĭ'-) *n.* Ancient time-measuring device worked by flow of water. [L, f. Gk *klepsudra* (*kleptō* steal, *hudōr* water)]

clēr'estōrȳ (-ēr's-) *n.* Part of wall of cathedral or large church, with series of windows, above aisle roofs; *raised section of railway-carriage roof with windows or ventilators. [ME, f. CLEAR[1] + STOREY]

clēr'gȳ *n.* (usu. treated as *pl.*) The body of all persons ordained for religious service; clergymen (*30 clergy were present*); BENEFIT[1] *of clergy*; **~man,** ordained minister, ||esp. of Established Church (*clergyman's sore* THROAT). [ME, partly f. OF *clergé* f. eccl. L *clericatus,* partly f. OF *clergie* (*clerc* CLERK, *-ie* = -Y[1])]

clĕ'rĭc *n.* Clergyman. [orig. a. f. eccl. L f. Gk *klērikos* (*klēros* lot, heritage, as in Acts 1: 17)]

clĕ'rĭcal *a.* Of clergy, clergyman, or clergymen (**~ collar,** upright white collar fastening at back); of or made by clerk(s) (**~ error,** made in writing out); hence ~ISM (3), ~IST (2), *ns.*, ~IZE (3) *v.t.*, ~ITY (-ă'l-) *n.*, ~LY[2] *adv.* [f. eccl. L *clericalis* (as prec.; see -AL)]

clĕ'rĭhew *n.* Short witty, comic, or nonsensical verse, usu. in two rhyming couplets with lines of unequal length. [f. E. *Clerihew* Bentley, Engl. writer d. 1956, its inventor]

clĕ'rĭsȳ *n.* (arch.) Learned or literary persons as a class. [app. after G *klerisei*, ult. f. as CLERIC]

clerk (klârk) *n.*, & *v.i.* **1.** *n.* (arch. or Law) **~ (in holy orders),** clergyman; lay officer of parish church, university college chapel, etc.; *clerk* REGULAR. **2.** Officer in charge of records etc., secretary, agent, of town council (*town clerk*), corporation, court, etc.; ||senior official in Parliament; person employed in bank, office, shop, etc., to make entries, copy letters, keep accounts, etc.; *assistant in shop or hotel; **~ of the course,** judge's secretary etc. in horse or motor racing; **~ of the weather,** imaginary person supposed to control weather; **~ of (the) works,** overseer of building works etc.; hence ~'DOM, ~'ESS[1] (Sc.), ~'SHIP (1, 3), *ns.*, ~'LY[1] *a.* **3.** *v.i.* Work as clerk. [f. OE *cleric, clerc*, & OF *clerc*, f. eccl. L *clericus* CLERIC]

clĕ'ver *a.* Adroit, dextrous, neat in movement; skilful, talented; (of doer or thing done) ingenious; BOX[5] *clever*; **~ Dick, ~-sticks,** (colloq.) (would-be) smart or knowing person; hence ~LY[2] *adv.*, ~NESS *n.* [ME, perh. rel. to CLEAVE[2], w. sense 'apt to seize']

clĕ'ver-clĕver *a.* Ostentatiously clever; eagerly seeking to appear clever. [redupl. of prec.]

clĕ'vĭs *n.* U-shaped piece of metal at end of beam for attaching tackle etc.; connection in which bolt holds one part that fits between forked ends of another. [16th c., perh. f. OE **clyfes* (**klubisī*, rel. to CLEAVE[1])]

clew (-ōō) *n.*, & *v.t.* **1.** *n.* (arch.) Ball of thread or yarn; this as used in myth to guide through labyrinth; = CLUE. **2.** (Naut.) Small cords suspending hammock; lower or after corner of sail. **3.** *v.t.* (Naut.) **~ up,** draw lower ends of (sail) to upper yard or mast ready for furling. [OE *cliwen, cleowen*, = Du., MLG *kluwen*, corresp. to OHG *kliuwa, kliuwi* ball]

cliă'nthus *n.* Australian shrub or vine of genus *Clianthus*, with handsome drooping clusters of red flowers. [mod. L, app. f. Gk *klei-*, *kleos* glory + *anthos* flower]

cliché (klē'shā) *n.* Metal casting of stereotype or electrotype; hackneyed phrase or opinion; hence ~(')d *a.*, hackneyed, full of clichés. [F (*clicher* to stereotype, perh. imit.)]

clĭck *n.*, & *v.t.* & *i.* (Make) slight sharp sound (with *tongue, heels*, etc.) as of dropping latch (**~ beetle,** kind that makes such sound in recovering from capsized position); catch in machinery acting with this sound; (of horse) touch(ing of) shoes of fore and hind feet; (make) sharp non-vocal suction, used as speech-sound in some languages; (sl.) secure one's object, come to an agreement, be successful, be understood, become friendly *with* person of opposite sex; hence ~'ER[1] *n.*, foreman shoemaker who cuts out leather and gives out work, (Print.) foreman of companionship of compositors who distributes copy etc. [imit.; cf. Du. *klikken*, F *cliquer*]

clī'ent *n.* Person using services of professional man (lawyer, architect, social worker, etc.), customer; (Rom. Hist.) plebeian under protection of noble; (arch.) dependant, hanger-on; hence ~SHIP *n.* [ME, f. L *cliens -entis* (*cluere* hear, obey; see -ENT)]

clientè'le (klēŏn-) *n.* Customers (of shop); patrons (of theatre etc.); persons who seek professional advice (of lawyer etc.). [f. L *clientela* clientship & F *clientèle*]

clĭff *n.* Steep rock-face, usu. facing sea; **~-hanger, ~-hanging,** (story etc.) with outcome excitingly uncertain. [OE *clif*, = OS, ON *klif*, OHG *klep* f. Gmc **klibham*]

climă'ctĕrĭc (*or* -ĕ'r-) *a.* & *n.* **1.** *a.* Constituting a crisis, critical; (Med.) occurring at period of life (45–60) at which vital force begins to decline.

2. *n.* Supposed critical period in life (esp. occurring at intervals of seven years). [f. F *climatérique* or f. L f. Gk *klimaktērikos* f. *klimaktēr* critical period (*klimax -akos* ladder); see -IC]

clīmă'ctic. See CLIMAX.

clī'mate *n.* (Region with certain) prevailing conditions of temperature, humidity, wind, etc.; (fig.) prevailing trend of opinion or feeling in community or period; hence **clīmă'tic** *a.*, **clīmatŏ'**LOGY *n.*, **clīmato**LO'GICAL *a.* [ME, f. OF *climat* or f. LL f. Gk *klima -at-* (*klinō* slope)]

clī'măx *n.* & *v.* **1.** *n.* (Rhet.) series arranged in order of increasing importance etc.; last term in such series; event or point of greatest intensity or interest, culmination, apex; sexual orgasm; (Ecol.) state of equilibrium reached by plant community; hence **clīmă'ct**IC *a.* **2.** *v.i.* & *t.* Come or bring to a climax. [LL, f. Gk *klimax -akos* ladder, climax]

clīmb (-īm) *v.* (arch. *past* **clomb** *pr.* -ōm) & *n.* **1.** *v.t.* & *i.* Ascend, mount, go *up*, (often with help of hands); ~ **down,** descend (cliff etc., or abs.) similarly, retreat from position taken up, give in (so **~-down** *n.*). **2.** *v.i.* (Of sun, aeroplane, etc.) go upwards; (of plant) grow upwards with support by tendrils or twining from tree, trellis, etc.; slope upwards; rise by effort in social rank, intellectual or moral strength, etc. **3. ~'ing-frame,** structure of joined pipes etc. for children to climb on; **~'ing-iron,** spikes attachable to boot for climbing trees or ice slopes. **4.** Hence ~'ABLE (-ma-) *a.* **5.** *n.* Ascent by climbing; place (to be) climbed. [OE *climban*, = MDu., MLG *klimmen*, OHG *klimban* f. WG **klimban* f. nasalized var. of **klibhan* CLEAVE²]

clī'mber (-ī'm*er*) *n.* In vbl senses; climbing plant; one who climbs mountains; person climbing socially. [f. prec. + -ER¹]

clīme *n.* (literary). Tract, country; climate. [f. LL *clima*; see CLIMATE]

clĭnch *v.* & *n.* **1.** *v.i.* (Of boxers) come too close for full-arm blow; (colloq.) embrace. **2.** *v.t.* (Naut.) fasten (rope) with special half-hitch; confirm, settle (argument, bargain) conclusively; = CLENCH 1. **3.** *n.* Any of the above actions or the resulting state. [16th c. var. of CLENCH]

clĭ'ncher *n.* In vbl senses; remark or argument that clinches a matter; **~-built,** = CLINKER³-*-built.* [f. prec. + -ER¹]

clīne *n.* (Biol.) Graded sequence of differences within species etc. [f. Gk *klinō* to slope]

clĭng *v.i.* (**clung**). Stick, adhere *to*, (by stickiness, suction, grasping, or embracing; ~ **together,** remain in one body or in contact, resist separation); remain (stubbornly) faithful *to* (friend, habit, idea); **~'stone,** kind of peach or nectarine in which flesh adheres to stone. [OE *clingan*, = MDu. *klingen* stick, MHG *klingen* climb, f. Gmc **kling-*, **klang-*, **klung-* parallel to **klink-* etc.; cf. CLENCH]

clĭ'nĭc *n.* The teaching of medicine or surgery at the hospital bedside; private or specialized hospital; place or occasion for giving medical treatment or advice, esp. in a hospital and devoted to one topic (*fertility clinic, fracture clinic, welfare clinic*); *conference or short course on particular subject; hence **clĭnĭ'**CIAN *n.* [f. F *clinique* f. Gk *klinikē* CLINICAL art]

clĭ'nĭcal *a.* **1.** (Med.) Of or at the sick-bed (esp. of teaching so given); ~ **death** (judged by observation of person's condition); ~ **medicine** (based on observed symptoms); *clinical* THERMOMETER. **2.** Objective, dispassionate; coldly detached. **3.** Hence ~LY² *adv.* [f. L f. Gk *klinikos* (*klinē* bed); see -IC, -AL]

clĭnk¹ *n.*, & *v.i.* & *t.* (Make, cause (glasses etc.) to make) sharp ringing sound; **~'stone,** kinds of felspar (f. ringing like iron when struck); hence ~'ING² *a.* & *adv.*, (sl.) exceedingly (good etc.). [ME, prob. f. MDu. *klinken*; cf. CLANG, CLANK]

clĭnk² *n.* (sl.) Prison (esp. *in clink*). [16th c.; orig. unkn.]

clĭ'nker¹ *n.* In vbl senses; (sl.) excellent specimen; *(sl.) error in performance, blunder. [f. CLINK¹ + -ER¹]

clĭ'nker² *n.* Mass of slag or lava; stony residue from burnt coal. [earlier *clincard* etc. f. obs. Du. *klinkaerd* (*klinken* CLINK¹)]

clĭ'nker³ *n.* **~-built,** (of boat) made with external planks overlapping downwards and fastened with clenched copper nails. [f. *clink* N. Engl. var. of CLINCH + -ER¹]

clīnŏ'mėter *n.* Instrument for measuring slopes. [f. Gk *klinō* to slope + -O- + -METER]

clīomĕ'trĭcs *n. pl.* (usu. treated as *sing.*) Method of historical research making much use of statistical information and methods. [f. *Clio*, Muse of history + METRIC + -ICS]

clĭp¹ *v.t.* (-pp-), & *n.* **1.** *v.t.* Surround closely, grip tightly; fix with clip; **~-on** *a.*, attached by clip. **2.** *n.* Appliance for holding things together or for attachment to object as marker; piece of jewellery fastened by clip; set of attached cartridges for firearm; **~'board,** small board with sprung clip for holding papers etc. [OE *clyppan* embrace f. WG **kluppjan*]

clĭp² *v.t.* (-pp-), & *n.* **1.** *v.t.* Cut with shears or scissors, trim thus, take away part of (hair, wool) thus; ~ person's **wings,** prevent him from pursuing his ambition. **2.** Remove hair or wool of (sheep etc.) thus; remove small piece of (railway, bus, etc. ticket) to show that it has been used; *cut from newspaper etc.; (sl.) swindle, rob; pare edge of (coin). **3.** (colloq.) Hit smartly. **4.** Omit letters or syllables of (words); omit (letter etc.). **5.** *n.* Operation of shearing or hair-cutting; quantity of wool clipped from sheep, flock, etc.; extract from motion picture; smart blow with hand, cut with whip, etc.; (colloq.) rate of (esp. rapid) motion; **~-joint,** (sl.) club etc. charging exorbitant prices. [ME, f. ON *klippa*; prob. imit.]

clĭ'p-clŏp *n.*, & *v.i.* (-pp-). (Make) sound resembling beat of horse's hooves. [imit.]

clĭ'pper *n.* In vbl senses; (usu. in *pl.*) instrument for clipping hair; fast horse or ship, esp. fast sailing-ship with raking bows and masts. [ME, f. CLIP² + -ER¹]

‖**clĭ'ppie** *n.* (colloq.) Bus conductress. [f. CLIP² + -IE]

clĭ'ppĭng *n.* In vbl senses; piece clipped off; *newspaper cutting. [ME, f. CLIP² + -ING¹]

clique (-ēk) *n.* Small exclusive group; coterie; hence **cli'qu**ISH¹ (-ē'k-), **cli'qu(e)**Y² (-ē'kĭ), *adjs.*, **cli'qu**ISM (2) (-ē'k-) *n.* [F (*cliquer* CLICK)]

‖**C.Lit.** *abbr.* Companion of Literature.

clĭ'tor|ĭs *n.* Small internal part of female genitals analogous to penis; hence ~AL, **clĭtŏr'**IAL, *adjs.* [mod. L, f. Gk *kleitoris*]

clivers. See CLEAVERS.

‖**Cllr.** *abbr.* Councillor.

clōā'c|a *n.* (*pl.* **~ae** *pr.* -sē). Sewer; excretory cavity in birds, reptiles, etc.; hence ~AL *a.* [L]

cloak, (arch.) **clōke,** *n.*, & *v.t.* **1.** *n.* Loose usu. sleeveless outdoor upper garment (**~-and--dagger,** involving intrigue and espionage); covering (*cloak of snow*); pretence, pretext, (*under the cloak of*); **~'room,** room for leaving cloaks, coats, hats, etc., or any luggage, ‖(euphem.) (also **~s**), lavatory. **2.** *v.t.* Put cloak on (one*self* or another); conceal, disguise. [ME f. OF *cloke*, dial. var. of *cloche* bell, cloak (from its bell shape) f. med. L *clocca* bell; see CLOCK¹]

clŏ'bber¹ *n.* (sl.) Clothing, equipment. [19th c.; orig. unkn.]

clŏ'bber[2] *v.t.* (sl.) Hit, thrash; defeat; criticize severely. [20th c.; orig. unkn.]
clŏche (-sh) *n.* ~ **(hat)**, woman's bell-shaped hat; (orig. bell-shaped) small translucent esp. glass cover for forcing or protecting outdoor plants. [F, = bell, f. med. L *clocca* (see foll.)]
clŏck[1] *n.* & *v.* **1.** *n.* Time-measuring instrument with wheels etc. kept in motion by periodically wound up springs or weights or by electricity etc., and recording hours, minutes, etc., by hands on a dial or by displayed figures; **o'clock** = of the clock, usu. appended only to the hour itself (*six o'clock*, but *quarter to six, six fifteen, 7.25*; *what o'clock is it?*, what is the time?); **against the** ~, so as to finish a task by a certain time; **beat the** ~, complete a task before a stated time; **put the** ~ **back,** (fig.) go back to a past age or outmoded practice; **the** ~ **round, round the** ~, for all 12 or 24 hours; **watch the** ~, be eager to reach end of working day. **2.** Clocklike device showing readings on a dial; (colloq.) taximeter, speedometer, or odometer; (colloq.) stop-watch; (sl.) face; downy seed-head of dandelion etc. **3.** ~ **golf,** lawn game of holing ball with putter from successive points in circle; **~'wise, anti-** or **counter-~'wise,** *advs.* & *adjs.*, moving in curve from left to right, right to left, as seen from central position; **~'work,** mechanism on clock principle (**like ~work,** smoothly, regularly, automatically), (*attrib.*, fig.) regular, mechanical. **4.** *v.i.* (Of factory workers etc.) ~ **in, on,** ~ **out, off,** register arrival or departure by means of an automatic recording clock. **5.** *v.t.* (colloq.) Time (race) with stop-watch; ~ **(up)**, (colloq.) attain or register (stated time, distance, or speed in race etc.); (sl.) hit. [ME, f. MDu., MLG *klocke* (= OHG *glocka*, ON *klokka*), Gmc f. med. L *clocca* bell; perh. f. Celt.]
clŏck[2] *n.* Pattern used as ornament on side of sock or stocking. [16th c.; orig. unkn.]
clŏd *n.* Lump *of* earth etc.; lump of earth; ~**('hopper)**, **~'poll,** bumpkin, lout, (so **~'-hopping,** loutish), whence **~'dish**[1] *a.*; meat cut from neck of ox; **~'hopper,** (also, colloq.) large clumsy shoe. [ME, var. of CLOT]
clŏg[1] *n.* Wooden-soled shoe; block of wood to impede animal's movement; (arch.) impediment, encumbrance; **~-almanac** (Hist., cut on sides of square wooden block); **~-dance** (performed in clogs). [ME, of unkn. orig.]
clŏg[2] *v.* (-gg-). **1.** *v.t.* Impede, hamper; impede (animal) with clog; choke *up*, obstruct by stickiness. **2.** *v.t.* & *i.* Fill up or *up* with choking matter. [ME, f. prec.]
clŏ'ggy̆ (-gĭ) *a.* Lumpy, knotty; sticky. [f. CLOG[1] + -Y[2]]
cloisonné (klwah'zŏnā) *a.* & *n.* ~ **(enamel)**, enamel in which colours of pattern are kept apart by thin metal strips etc. [F]
cloi'ster *n.*, & *v.t.* (Enclose or shut up in) convent or monastic house; monastic life or seclusion; covered walk, often round quadrangle with wall on outer and colonnade or windows on inner side, esp. of convent, college, cathedral buildings; hence ~ED[2] (-*erd*) (lit., or fig. secluded, sheltered), **cloi'str**AL, *adjs.* [ME f. OF *cloistre* f. L *claustrum, clostrum* lock, enclosed place (*claudere claus-* CLOSE[3])]
clōke. See CLOAK.
clomb. See CLIMB.
clōne *n.*, & *v.t.* **1.** *n.* Group of plants produced vegetatively from one original seedling or stock; group of organisms formed asexually from one ancestor; hence **clō'n**AL *a.* **2.** *v.t.* Propagate as clone. [f. Gk *klōn* twig, slip]
clŏnk *v.* & *n.* (Make) abrupt heavy sound of impact; (colloq.) hit. [imit.]
clō'nus *n.* (Path.) Spasm with alternate muscular contractions and relaxations; hence **clŏ'n**IC *a.* [f. Gk *klonos* turmoil]
cloqué (klō'kā) *n.* Fabric with irregularly raised surface. [F, = blistered]
clōse[1] *a.* & *adv.* **1.** *a.* Shut; (of vowel) pronounced with relatively narrow opening of mouth; narrow, confined, contracted; (of air etc.) stifling. **2.** Covered, concealed, secret, given to secrecy, (**keep, lie,** ~, be in hiding); niggardly. **3.** Restricted, limited, (*close corporation* etc.); under prohibition. **4.** Near; in near relation or connection (*close friend, relative*); in intimate friendship or association; in or nearly in contact (*close combat, proximity*); fitting exactly (*close cap, copy, resemblance, translation*); nearly equal (*close contest*). **5.** Concentrated, searching, (*close examination, attention*); dense, compact, with no or only slight intervals, (*close texture, thicket, writing*); leaving no gaps or weaknesses (*close reasoning*). **6.** ||~ **borough,** (Hist.) = *pocket* BOROUGH; ~ **call,** (colloq.) narrow escape from death; **~-car'pet** *v.t.*, cover whole floor of (room) with carpet; **~-cropped,** (of hair) cut very short; **~-fisted,** niggardly; **~-grained,** without gaps between fibres etc.; ~ **harmony,** singing of parts within octave or twelfth; **~-hauled,** (of ship) with sails hauled aft to sail close to wind; **~-mouthed,** reticent; ~ **quarters,** direct contact or uncomfortable nearness (*at* ~ *quarters*, very near); ~ **scholarship** (open only to restricted range of candidates); ~ **score** (Mus., with more than one part on same staff); ||~ **season** (when something, esp. killing of game etc., is forbidden by law); ~ **shave,** (fig.) narrow escape from accident etc.; **~-stool,** chamber-pot mounted in stool with cover; ~ **thing,** = *close shave*; **~-up,** photograph or film taken at short range and showing subject on large scale, (fig.) intimate description. **7.** Hence ~'LY[2] (-slĭ) *adv.*, ~'NESS (-sn-) *n.* **8.** *adv.* In close manner (*shut close*; *close*-SET[3]); in near position (SAIL[2] *close to the wind*; *stand close*; **go** ~, (of racehorse) win or nearly win); ~ **by,** ~ **on,** ~ **to,** very near to; **~-fitting,** (of garment) fitting close to body. [ME f. OF *clos*, f. L *clausus* p.p. of *claudere* shut]
clōse[2] *n.* Enclosed place; street closed at one end; ||precinct of cathedral; ||school playing-field; (Sc.) entry from street to common stairway or to court at back. [ME f. OF *clos* f. L *clausum* enclosure (as prec.)]
clōse[3] (-z) *v.* & *n.* **1.** *v.t.* & *i.* Shut (of lid or box, door or room or house, etc.); (of place of business etc.) declare or be declared no longer open (**clo'sing-time,** time at which public houses, shops, etc., stop business); ~ **on,** (of hand, box, etc.) grasp or imprison; ~ one's **eyes,** (1) die, (2) pay no attention *to*. **2.** Conclude, bring or come to an end, complete, settle (bargain etc.); finish speaking (*with* the remark etc.). **3.** Bring or come closer or into contact (*close the ranks*); make (electric circuit etc.) continuous; come within striking distance, grapple *with*. **4.** Express agreement *with* (offer, terms, or person offering them). **5.** ~ **down,** (of shop, factory, etc.) close permanently, ||(of broadcasting station) end transmission till next day; ~ **in,** enclose, come nearer, (of days) get successively shorter; *~ **out,** discontinue, terminate, dispose of (business); ~ **up,** move closer *to*, block, fill, coalesce. **6.** *n.* Conclusion, end; (Mus.) cadence. [ME f. OF *clos-* st. of *clore* f. L *claudere* shut]
clōsed (-zd) *a.* In vbl senses; (of society, system, etc.) self-contained, not communicating with others; restricted to specified competitors etc.; *closed* BOOK[1]; **~-circuit,** (of television) for restricted number of receivers by use of wires

not waves for transmission; ~**-end,** having predetermined extent (cf. OPEN¹-*ended*); *~ **season,** = CLOSE¹ *season*; ~ **shop,** workshop or other establishment where only members of a trade union may be employed; ~ **syllable** (ending in consonant). [p.p. of prec.]

clŏ'sĕt (-z-) *n.* Private or small room, esp. for private interviews (||**Clerk of the C~,** sovereign's principal chaplain) or for study (~ **play,** play to be read not acted); *cupboard, recess for storage etc.; cupboard for special purpose, e.g. CHINA²-closet; = WATER¹-*closet*; hence ~ED¹ *a.*, in private consultation (*with*). [ME f. OF, dim. of *clos*; see CLOSE², -ET¹]

clō'sure (-zher) *n.*, & *v.t.* **1.** *n.* Closing; closed condition. **2.** (Parl. etc.) Decision by vote, or under rules, to put question without further debate. **3.** *v.t.* Apply closure to (motion, speakers, etc.). [ME f. OF, f. LL *clausura* (*claudere claus-* CLOSE³; see -URE)]

clŏt *n.* & *v.* (-tt-). **1.** *n.* Mass of material stuck together; semi-solid lump of coagulated liquid, esp. of blood exposed to air; (sl.) stupid person. **2.** *v.i.* & *t.* Form into clots; ~**ted cream** (got by scalding milk). [OE *clot(t)*, = MHG *kloz* f. WG **klutt-* (**klut-*, **klaut-*; cf. CLEAT)]

clŏth (*or* -awth w. *pl. pr.* -awdhz) *n.* **1.** (Piece of) woven or felted material; = TABLE-*cloth*. **2.** Woollen woven fabric as used for clothes; duster; ~ **of gold, silver,** tissue of gold or silver threads interwoven with silk or wool; **cut coat according to** ~, adapt expenditure to resources. **3.** Profession as shown by clothes, esp. clerical (*respect due to his cloth*; **the** ~, clergy). **4.** ~**-binding,** cover of book in linen or cotton cloth; ~**-cap** *a.*, pertaining to the working class; ~**-eared,** (colloq.) somewhat deaf; ~**-yard shaft,** (Hist.) arrow a yard long. [OE *clāth*, = MDu. *kleet*, MHG *kleit*, of unkn. orig.]

clōthe (-dh) *v.t.* (~**d** *or*, arch., tech., or formal, **clad**). Provide with clothes, put clothes upon; cover as with clothes or a cloth; endue *with* (qualities etc.). [OE **clāthian* (*clāth*; see prec.)]

clōthes (-dhz; *or* -ōz) *n. pl.* **1.** Things worn to cover the body and limbs; = BED¹*clothes*. **2.** ~**-bag, -basket,** (for holding or conveying clothes to be washed); *clothes*-HANGER²; ~**-horse,** frame for airing washed clothes, (fig.) affectedly fashionable person; ~**-line,** rope, wire, etc., for hanging washed clothes etc. to dry; ~**-moth** (with larva destructive to clothes); ||~**-peg,** ~**-pin,** wooden etc. clip or forked device to hold clothes on clothes-line; ~**-post,** ~**-prop,** support for clothes-line. [OE *clāthas* pl. of *clāth* CLOTH]

clō'thĭer (-dh-) *n.* Dealer in men's clothes. [ME *clother* f. CLOTH; see -ER¹, -IER]

clō'thĭng (-dh-) *n.* In vbl senses; clothes collectively. [f. CLOTHE + -ING¹]

***clō'ture** *n.*, & *v.t.* = CLOSURE 2, 3. [f. F *clôture* f. OF CLOSURE]

clou (kloo) *n.* Point of greatest interest, chief attraction; central idea. [F, = nail]

cloud *n.* & *v.* **1.** *n.* (Mass of) visible, condensed watery vapour floating in air high above general level of ground; **in the** ~**s,** mystical, unreal, imaginary, (of person) abstracted, inattentive; **with** one's **head in the** ~**s,** unrealistic(ally), living in a world of fantasy; **on** ~ **seven** or **nine,** (colloq.) extremely happy. **2.** Unsubstantial or fleeting thing; mass of smoke or dust; local dimness or vague patch of colour in or on liquid or transparent body; great number *of* birds, insects, etc., moving together. **3.** Obscurity; state of gloom, trouble, suspicion, frowning or depressed look, (*cloud on brow*; **under a** ~, out of favour, discredited). **4.** ~**'berry,** small mountain bramble with white flower and orange-coloured fruit; ~**'burst,** violent rainstorm; ~**-castle,** daydream; *cloud* CHAMBER; **C~-cuckoo-land,** fanciful or ideal realm [transl. of Gk *Nephelokokkugia* (*nephelē* cloud, *kokkux* cuckoo) in Aristophanes' *Birds*]; ~**-hopping,** (of aircraft) flying from cloud to cloud esp. for concealment; ~**-land,** utopia, fairyland; ~**'scape,** picture or picturesque grouping of clouds. **5.** Hence ~'LESS *a.*, ~'LET *n.*, ~'Y² *a.*, obscured by clouds, unclear. **6.** *v.t.* Overspread or darken with clouds, gloom, or trouble; make unclear; variegate with vague patches of colour (~**ed leopard,** mottled arboreal S. Asian feline, *Neofelis nebulosa*). **7.** *v.i.* Become overcast or gloomy (*cloud up, over*). [OE *clūd* mass of rock or earth, prob. cogn. w. CLOD]

clough (klŭf) *n.* Ravine, steep valley usu. with torrent bed. [OE *clōh*, = OHG *klinga*, f. Gmc **klanh-*]

clout *n.*, & *v.t.* **1.** *n.* Patch; piece of cloth or clothing; hit, esp. with open hand; (colloq.) influence, power of effective action esp. in politics; (Hist.) canvas on frame as mark at archery; nail with large flat head. **2.** *v.t.* Mend with patch; hit. [OE *clūt*, = MLG, MDu. *klūt(e)*, ON *klútr* kerchief; rel. to CLEAT, CLOT]

clōve¹. See CLEAVE¹.

clōve² *n.* One of small bulbs making up compound bulb of garlic, shallot, etc. [OE *clufu*, cogn. w. CLEAVE¹]

clōve³ *n.* (Pungent aromatic dried flower-bud of) tropical myrtle (**oil of** ~**s,** oil extracted from cloves and used in medicine); ~ (**gillyflower**), clove-scented pink, original of carnation and other double pinks. [ME, f. OF *clou* (*de girofle*) nail (of gillyflower), from its shape, GILLYFLOWER being orig. name of the spice; later applied to the similarly shaped bud of the pink]

clō've hĭtch *n.* Hitch by which rope is secured by passing twice round spar or rope that it crosses at right angles. [old p.p. of CLEAVE¹, as showing parallel separate lines]

clō'ven. See CLEAVE¹.

clō'ver *n.* Trefoil plant used for fodder; **in** ~, in ease and luxury; ~**-leaf,** junction of roads intersecting at different levels with connecting sections in shape like four-leaved clover. [OE *clāfre*, = MLG *klāver*, f. Gmc **klaibrōn*]

clown *n.*, & *v.i.* **1.** *n.* Jester, esp. in pantomime or circus, whence ~'ERY (4) *n.*; ignorant or ill-bred man, whence ~'ISH¹ *a.*; (arch.) rustic. **2.** *v.i.* Play the clown. [16th c., perh. of LG orig.]

cloy *v.t.* Satiate or weary by richness, sweetness, sameness, excess, of food or pleasure (usu. *with*). [ME, f. obs. *acloy* f. AF *acloyer*, OF *encloyer* f. Rom. **inclavare*; cf. ENCLAVE]

clŭb¹ *n.* **1.** Stick with one thick end as weapon etc. (INDIAN *clubs*); stick used in games, esp. golf. **2.** (Bot. etc.) Structure or organ with knob at end; ~**-foot,** congenitally distorted foot; ~**-moss,** pteridophyte with upright spikes of spore-cases; ~**-root,** disease of turnips etc. with swelling at base of stem. **3.** Playing-card of suit (~**s**) denoted by black trefoil. **4.** Association of persons united by some common interest, meeting periodically for shared activity (*Alpine, golf, yacht, club*) or socially (**in the** ~, (sl.) pregnant); body of persons combined for social purposes and having premises for resort, meals, temporary residence, etc., (||~**'land,** St. James's in London, where many clubs are; ~**-man,** member of one or more clubs; *~ **sandwich,** sandwich with two layers of filling between three slices of toast or bread); ~**('house),** premises used by club; group of persons, nations, etc., having something in common; group of persons in joint arrangement for saving etc. (BENEFIT[1]-*club*). [ME, f. ON *klubba* assim. form of *klumba* club, rel. to CLUMP]

clŭb[2] *v.* (**-bb-**). **1.** *v.t.* Beat (as) with club; contribute (money etc.) to a common stock. **2.** *v.i.* Combine *together*, *with*, for joint action, esp. making up a sum of money for a purpose. [f. prec.]

clŭ'bbable *a.* Fit for membership of a club; sociable. [f. CLUB[1] + -ABLE]

clŭck *n.*, & *v.i.* (Make) guttural cry of hen; DUMB *cluck*; hence ~'Y[2] *a.*, (of hen) sitting on eggs. [imit.]

clue (-ōō) *n.*, & *v.t.* **1.** *n.* Fact or principle that serves as guide, or suggests line of inquiry, in problem or investigation (**not have a ~**, (colloq.) be ignorant or incompetent); piece of evidence etc. in detection of crime; word(s) used to indicate word(s) for insertion in crossword; thread of story, train of thought; hence ~'LESS *a.*, (esp., colloq.) ignorant or stupid. **2.** *v.t.* Provide clue to; **~ in, up,** (sl.) inform. [var. of CLEW]

Clŭ'mber *n.* Kind of large spaniel. [~ in Nottinghamshire]

clŭmp *n.* & *v.* **1.** *n.* Cluster *of* trees or shrubs; agglutinated mass of blood-cells etc.; thick extra sole on boot or shoe. **2.** *v.i.* Tread heavily; form clump. **3.** *v.t.* Heap or plant together; (colloq.) hit. [f. MLG *klumpe*, MDu. *klompe*; see CLUB[1]]

clŭ'ms|ȳ (-zĭ) *a.* Awkward in movement or shape, ungainly; ill-contrived; without tact; hence **~ĭ**LY[2] *adv.*, **~ĭ**NESS *n.* [f. obs. *clumse* be numb with cold (prob. f. Scand.) + -Y[2]]

clŭng. See CLING.

Clu'n|ȳ (-ōō'-) *n.* **~y (lace)**, kind of bobbin-lace for clothing etc.; so **~ĭ**AC *a.* & *n.*, (member) of order of monks separated from Benedictines in 11th c. [~ in central France]

clŭ'ster *n.* & *v.* **1.** *n.* Group of similar things, esp. such as grow together, bunch (**~ pine,** Mediterranean pine with clustered cones); swarm, group, of persons, animals, faint stars, gems, etc. (**~ bomb,** anti-personnel bomb spraying pellets on impact); group of successive consonants or vowels. **2.** *v.t.* & *i.* Bring or come into, be in, cluster(s) (**~ed** *columns, pillars, shafts,* several close together, or disposed round or half detached from pier). [OE *clyster*, prob. f. Gmc **klut-*; cf. CLOT]

clŭtch[1] *v.* **1.** *v.t.* Seize eagerly, grasp tightly. **2.** *v.i.* Snatch *at*. [ME *clucche*, *clicche* f. OE *clyccan* crook, clench, f. Gmc **klukjan*]

clŭtch[2] *n.* Tight grasp; (in *pl.*) grasping hands, cruel grasp, relentless control; grasping *at*; (Mech.) arrangement for connecting or disconnecting working parts; (in motor vehicle) device for connecting engine to transmission, pedal operating this. [f. prec.]

clŭtch[3] *n.* Set of eggs; brood of chickens. [18th c.; prob. S. Engl. var. of *cletch* f. *cleck* to hatch f. ON *klekja*, assoc. w. CLUTCH[1]]

clŭ'tter *n.*, & *v.t.* **1.** *n.* Crowded confusion, confused mass, untidy state, litter. **2.** *v.t.* Litter *with*; **~ up,** crowd untidily *with*. [partly var. of *clotter* (CLOT, -ER[5]) coagulate, partly assoc. w. *cluster, clatter*]

Clȳ'desdāle (-dzd-) *n.* One of a breed of heavy draught-horses; kind of small terrier. [orig. bred near river *Clyde* in Scotland; see DALE]

clȳ'pė|us *n.* (*pl.* **~i** *pr.* -ī). Shieldlike part of insect's head; hence **~**AL, **~**ATE[2], *adjs.* [L, = round shield]

clȳ'ster *n.*, & *v.t.* (arch.) (Treat with) enema. [ME, f. OF *clystere* or f. L f. Gk *klustēr* syringe (*kluzō* wash out)]

cm *abbr.* centimetre(s).

Cm *symb.* curium.

||**Cmd.** *abbr.* COMMAND[2] Paper (fourth series, 1918–1956).

Cmdr. *abbr.* Commander.

Cmdre. *abbr.* Commodore.

||**C.M.G.** *abbr.* Companion (of the Order) of St. Michael & St. George.

||**Cmnd.** *abbr.* COMMAND[2] Paper (fifth series, 1956–).

||**C.M.S.** *abbr.* Church Missionary Society.

||**C.N.A.A.** *abbr.* Council for National Academic Awards.

C.N.D. *abbr.* Campaign for Nuclear Disarmament.

cnr. *abbr.* corner.

cō- *pref.*, orig. form of COM-, used (as in L) only before vowels, *h*, and *gn*; now before any letter. **1.** Prefixed to *vbs.*, = with other subjects (*co-operate*); to *adjs.* & *advs.*, = jointly (*co-belligerent*), mutually (*coequal*, *-ly*), and to *ns.* = joint (*co-author*, *co-precipitation*), mutual (*coequality*). **2.** (Math.) Of the complement (*cosine*); complement of (*co-latitude*, *coset*). [f. COM-]

C.O. *abbr.* Commanding Officer; conscientious objector.

Co. *abbr.* company; county; **and Co.** (-kō'), (colloq.) and the rest of them, and similar things.

c/o *abbr.* care of.

Co *symb.* cobalt.

cōăcervā'tion *n.* **1.** Heaping together; pile. **2.** (Chem.) Formation of viscous drops in colloidal solution; so **cōă'cerv**ATE[1] *n.* [f. L CO(*acervatio* f. *acervare* f. *acervus* heap; see -ATION)]

coach *n.* & *v.* **1.** *n.* State carriage; privately owned carriage; = STAGE[1]-*coach*. **2.** (Official name for) railway carriage; *daytime railway passenger carriage; chartered or long-distance single-decker bus; *economy-class seating in aircraft. **3.** Private tutor; instructor of athletic team etc. **4. Drive ~ and six** etc. **through,** render (legislation etc.) useless; **~-box,** coachman's seat; **~-built,** (of motor-car bodies) built of wood by craftsmen; **~-dog,** Dalmatian; **~-house,** outhouse for carriages; **~'man,** driver of any carriage; **~'whip,** whip used by coachman, (Austral.) whip-bird; **~'wood,** (Austral.) tree with close-grained wood suitable for cabinet-making; **~'work,** bodywork of road or rail vehicle. **5.** *v.i.* Travel in or go by stage-coach (*in the old coaching days*). **6.** *v.t.* Tutor, train, (pupil *for* examination, crew *for* race); give hints to, prime with facts. [f. F *coche* f. Magyar *kocsi* a. f. *Kocs* in Hungary]

cōă'djutor (-ōō-) *n.* Assistant esp. to bishop. [ME, f. OF *coadjuteur* f. LL CO(*adjutor* f. *adjuvare* *-jut-* help; see -OR)]

cōă'gūl|āte *v.t.* & *i.* Change from fluid to more or less solid state; clot, curdle; set, solidify; hence or cogn. **~**ABLE *a.*, **~**ANT, **~**A'TION, **~āt**OR, *ns.* [ME, f. L *coagulare* (*coagulum* rennet) + -ATE[3]]

cōă'gūl|um *n.* (*pl.* **~a**). Coagulated mass. [L; see prec.]

cōai'ta (kōī'-) *n.* Small S. Amer. red-faced spider-monkey of genus *Ateles*. [Tupi]

coal *n.* & *v.* **1.** *n.* Hard opaque black or blackish mineral, mainly carbonized plant matter, found in seams or strata below earth's surface and used as fuel and in manufacture of gas, tar, etc.; ||piece of this ready for burning in fire; red-hot piece of coal, wood, etc., in fire; **heap ~s of fire,** cause remorse by returning good for evil, cf. Prov. 25:22; **haul** or **call over the ~s,** reprimand; **~s to Newcastle,** thing brought where already plentiful, superfluous action. **2. ~-bed,** stratum of coal; **~-black,** quite black;

For other words in *co-* see CO-.

~-box, receptacle for coal to supply room fire; **~-bunker,** place for storing coal in ship etc.; **~-cellar,** basement storage place for coal; **~-dust,** powdered coal; **~-face,** exposed surface of coal in mine; **~'field,** district with series of coal strata; **~-fired,** heated or driven by coal; **~-fish,** saithe; **~ gas,** mixed gases extracted from coal and used for lighting and heating; **~-heaver,** man employed in moving coal; ||**~-hole,** small coal-cellar; **~-house,** building etc. for storage of coal; **~-master,** (Hist.) owner or lessee of coal-mine; **~ measures,** (Geol.) series of rocks formed by seams of coal and intervening strata; **~-merchant,** retail seller of coal; **~-mine** (in which coal is dug); ***~-oil,** paraffin; **~-owner,** (Hist.) = *coal-master*; **~-sack,** sack for carrying coal, black patch in Milky Way (esp. one near Southern Cross); **~-scuttle,** = *coal-box*; **~-seam,** stratum of coal; **~ tar,** tar extracted from bituminous coal, source of paraffin, naphtha, benzene, creosote, and aniline dyes; **~-tit,** = COALMOUSE. **3.** Hence ~'ER[1] *n.*, ship transporting coal; ~'Y[2] *a.* **4.** *v.t.* Put coal into (ship etc.). **5.** *v.i.* Take in supply of coal. [OE *col,* = MDu. *cole,* MLG *kole,* OHG *kol(o),* ON *kol* f. Gmc **kolam*]

cōalĕ'sc|e *v.i.* Come together and form one whole; combine in coalition; so ~ENCE *n.*, ~ENT *a.* [f. L co(*alescere alit-* grow f. *alere* nourish)]

cōalĭ'tion *n.* Union, fusion; ||(Polit.) temporary combination between parties that retain distinctive principles, whence ~IST (1) *n.* [f. med. L *coalitio* (as prec.; see -ITION)]

coa'lmouse, cō'le- (-lm-), *n.* (*pl.* **-mice**). Small greyish bird (*Parus ater*) with dark head. [OE *colmāse* (*col* COAL, *māse* as TITMOUSE)]

coa'mĭng *n.* Raised border round hatches etc. of ship to keep out water. [17th c.; orig. unkn.]

coarse *a.* Common, inferior, (**~ fish,** ||freshwater fish other than salmon and trout); rough, loose, or large, in texture, grain, or features; not delicate in perception, manner, or taste, unrefined; rude, uncivil, vulgar; (of language) obscene; hence ~LY[2] (-slĭ) *adv.*, **coar'sEN**[6] *v.t.* & *i.*, ~NESS (-sn-) *n.* [ME, of unkn. orig.]

coast[1] *n.* **1.** **(Sea-)~,** border of land near sea, sea-shore, (*the coast is* CLEAR[1]); ***the C~,** Pacific coast of U.S. **2.** *Toboggan slide; (usu. downhill) run on bicycle without pedalling or in motor vehicle with engine disconnected. **3.** **~'guard, ~ guard,** (one of a) body of men employed to keep watch on coasts and thus save life, prevent smuggling, etc.; **~'line,** the line of the sea-shore esp. with regard to its configuration (*the rugged coastline of the island*). **4.** Hence ~'AL *a.*, ~'WISE *a.* & *adv.* [ME f. OF *coste* f. L *costa* rib, flank, side]

coast[2] *v.i.* Sail along coast, trade between ports on same coast; *slide down hill on toboggan; ride down hill etc. without use of power (cf. prec. 2); (fig.) make progress without exertion. [ME, f. OF *costeier* (*coste*; see prec.)]

coa'ster *n.* Coasting vessel; silver tray for decanter; small mat for drinking-glass etc.; ||wooden stand for cheese; *sledge for coasting; * = ROLLER-*coaster*. [f. prec. + -ER[1]]

coat *n.*, & *v.t.* **1.** *n.* Man's sleeved usu. cloth outer garment (DRESS[2] *coat*; FROCK-*coat*; GREAT*coat*; OVERCOAT; RAIN[1]*coat*; RED*coat*); **~ of arms,** herald's tabard, person's or corporation's heraldic bearings or shield. **2.** **~ armour,** blazonry, heraldic arms; **~ dress,** woman's tailored dress resembling coat; *coat*-HANGER[2]; *cut coat according to* CLOTH; **on** person's **~-tails,** undeservedly benefiting from his progress etc.; **trail** one's **~(-tails)** (for someone to tread on), seek to pick quarrel; **turn** one's ~, change sides, desert. **3.** Woman's outdoor garment, overcoat; (esp. in *coat and skirt*) woman's tailored jacket worn with skirt. **4.** Covering comparable to garment; animal's hair, fur, etc.; (Physiol.) membrane etc. enclosing or lining organ; skin, rind, husk; layer of bulb etc.; covering of paint etc. laid on at one time. **5.** Hence (-)~'ED[2], ~'LESS, *adjs.* **6.** *v.t.* Put or be coat of paint, tin, etc., on; (in *p.p.*) covered over *with* dust, material to give smooth surface, etc. [ME f. OF *cote*, f. Rom. **cotta*, f. Frank. **kotta*, of unkn. orig.]

coatee' *n.* Woman's or infant's short coat; (arch.) close-fitting short coat. [f. prec. + -EE]

cōa'tĭ (-ah'-) *n.* Amer. carnivorous mammal of genus *Nasua*, like civet and racoon, with long flexible snout. [Tupi (*cua* belt, *tim* nose)]

cōatĭmŭ'ndĭ (kōah-) *n.* = prec. [f. as prec. + Tupi *mondi* solitary]

coa'tĭng *n.* In vbl senses; layer of paint etc.; material for coats. [f. COAT + -ING[1]]

cō-au'thor *n.*, & *v.t.* (Be) joint author (of). [f. CO- 1 + AUTHOR]

coax *v.t.* Persuade gradually or by flattery or by continued trial (*to* do, *into* doing or good temper etc.; *coax* thing *out of* person; *coax fire to light, key into lock,* etc.). [16th c., f. 'make a *cokes* of', f. obs. *cokes* simpleton, of unkn. orig.]

cōă'xĭal *a.* Having a common axis; **~ cable** (Electr., in which there are several coaxial lines, or = *coaxial line*); **~ line,** (Electr.) transmission line with two concentric conductors separated by insulator; hence ~LY[2] *adv.* [f. CO- 1 + AXIAL]

cŏb[1] *n.* Male swan; sturdy short-legged riding-horse; **~(-nut),** large kind of hazel-nut; roundish lump of coal etc.; round-headed loaf; CORN[1]-*cob*. [ME; orig. unkn.]

||**cŏb**[2] *n.* Composition of clay, gravel, and straw, used for building walls. [17th c.; orig. unkn.]

cō'balt (-awlt *or* -ŏlt) *n.* Silver-white metallic element similar in many respects to nickel; (deep-blue colour of) pigment made from it; **~ bomb,** (1) container of radioactive cobalt for medical use, (2) hydrogen bomb dispersing radioactive cobalt; hence ~IC, ~OUS, (kobaw'-) *adjs.* [f. G *kobalt* etc., prob. = *kobold* goblin of mines]

cŏ'bber *n.* (Austral. & N.Z. colloq.) Companion, mate, friend. [19th c.; perh. f. E dial. *cob* take a liking to]

cŏ'bble[1] *n.*, & *v.t.* **1.** *n.* **~(-stone),** water-worn rounded stone of size used for paving; ||(in *pl.*) coal in lumps of this size. **2.** *v.t.* Pave with cobbles. [ME *cobel(-ston)*, f. COB[1] + -LE 1]

cŏ'bble[2] *v.t.* Put together roughly; mend, patch up, (esp. shoes). [back form. f. foll.]

cŏ'bbler *n.* Mender of shoes; clumsy workman; iced drink of wine, sugar, and lemon, in tall glass (*sherry cobbler*); (in *pl.*, sl.) nonsense; *fruit pie with rich thick crust; (Austral. & N.Z. sl.) last sheep to be shorn; **~'s wax,** resinous substance used for waxing thread. [ME, of unkn. orig.]

Cŏ'bdenĭsm *n.* (Hist.) Policy of free trade, peace, and international collaboration. [f. R. *Cobden*, Engl. statesman d. 1865, its leading advocate, + -ISM]

cō-bellĭ'ger|ent *a.* & *n.* (Nation etc.) jointly waging war; hence ~ENCE, ~ENCY, *ns.* [f. CO- 1 + BELLIGERENT]

cō'ble *n.* Flat-bottomed fishing-boat in Scotland and N.E. England. [OE, perh. f. Celt.]

Cō'bŏl *n.* Computer language designed for use in business operations. [f. initial letters of *common business oriented language*]

cŏ'bra *n.* Venomous hooded Indian or African

snake of genus *Naja*, with neck dilated like hood when excited. [Port., f. L *colubra* snake]

cŏ'bwĕb *n.* Spider's network, material of it, thread of this; thing of flimsy texture; (in *pl.*) musty rubbish (esp. fig., *cobwebs of the law, of antiquity*; **blow away the ~s,** remove fustiness); insidious entanglement, mesh; hence **~BED**[2] (-bd), **~BY**[2], *adjs.* [ME *cop(pe)web* f. obs. *coppe* spider + WEB]

cō'ca *n.* S. Amer. shrub (*Erythroxylon coca*); its dried leaves, chewed as stimulant. [Sp., f. Quechua *cuca*]

Cōca-Cō'la *n.* Aerated non-alcoholic drink. [P]

cocai'n|e *n.* Drug from coca, used as local anaesthetic and as stimulant; hence **~ISM** (5) *n.* [f. COCA + -INE[5]]

cŏccĭdĭō's|ĭs *n.* (*pl.* **~es** *pr.* -ēz). Disease of birds and mammals caused by internal parasite of order Coccidia. [f. *coccidium* (mod. L f. Gk *kokkis* dim. of *kokkos* berry) + -OSIS]

cŏ'cc|us *n.* (*pl.* **~i** *pr.* -kī). (Roughly) spherical bacterium; hence **~AL, ~OID,** *adjs.* [mod. L, f. Gk *kokkos* berry]

cŏ'ccȳx (-ks-) *n.* Small triangular bone ending spinal column in man and some apes; analogous part in birds etc.; hence **cŏccȳ'gėAL** (-ks-) *a.* [L, f. Gk *kokkux -ugos* cuckoo (from being shaped like its bill)]

cŏ'chĭn(-chīna) *n.* & *a.* (Fowl) of Cochin China breed, with feathery legs. [place in S.E. Asia]

cŏ'chĭneal *n.* (Dried bodies of female of insect reared on cactus in Mexico etc., used for making) a scarlet dye. [f. F *cochenille* or f. Sp. *cochinilla* f. L *coccinus* scarlet (Gk *kokkos* kermes (oak))]

cŏ'chlėa (-k-) *n.* (*pl.* **~e** *pr.* -klĭē). Spiral cavity of internal ear. [L, = snail-shell, f. Gk *kokhlias*]

cŏck[1] *n.* **1.** Male bird, esp. of domestic fowl; woodcock; male lobster or crab or salmon; (**old**) ~ (vulg. form of address to man); ||(sl.) nonsense. **2. ~-and-bull story,** idle invention, incredible tale; **~-crow,** dawn; **~-a-doodle-doo,** crowing of cock, childish name for cock; **~-fighting,** setting cocks to fight as sport (*live like fighting ~s,* get best of fare; *that ~ won't fight,* that plea or plan will not do); **~-and-hen,** for both sexes; ||**~ of the north,** brambling; **~ of the rock,** crested orange S. Amer. bird (*Rupicola rupicola*); **~'scomb,** crest of cock, garden plant of genus *Celosia*, and see COXCOMB; **~'sfoot,** a pasture grass (*Dactylis glomerata*); **~-shy,** object set up to be thrown at with sticks, stones, etc., throw at this, (fig.) object of ridicule or criticism; **~ sparrow,** male sparrow, small lively pugnacious person; **~ of the walk,** dominant person; **~ of the wood,** capercaillie, *red-crested woodpecker. **3.** Tapped spout, tap, valve controlling flow; (vulg.) penis; lever in gun raised ready to be released by trigger (**at half ~,** (fig.) only half-ready). [f. OE *cocc*, and OF *coq*, prob. f. med. L *coccus* (imit.)]

cŏck[2] *v.t.,* & *n.* **1.** *v.t.* Erect, stick or stand up, jauntily or defiantly (**~ the ears,** raise them in attention; ~ one's **eye,** glance knowingly, wink; *cock a* SNOOK[2]); bend *knee, wrist,* etc., at an angle; **~-up,** ||(sl.) mistake, muddle. **2.** ~ one's **hat,** (1) set it on aslant, (2) turn up its brim (opp. *slouch*); **~ed hat,** (1) hat with brim fixed so, (2) brimless triangular hat pointed at front, back, and top (**knock into a ~ed hat,** defeat utterly). **3.** Raise cock of (gun) in readiness for firing. **4.** *n.* State of being cocked. [ME, f. prec.]

cŏck[3] *n.,* & *v.t.* **1.** *n.* Small conical heap of hay etc. in field. **2.** *v.t.* Pile into cocks. [ME, perh. of Scand. orig.]

cŏ'ckabullȳ (-bōō-) *n.* (N.Z.) Small blunt-nosed freshwater fish. [f. Maori *kokopu*]

cockā'd|e *n.* Rosette etc. worn in hat as badge of office or party or part of livery; hence **~ED**[2] *a.* [f. F *cocarde* orig. in *bonnet à la coquarde*, f. fem. of obs. *coquard* saucy (*coq* COCK[1]; see -ARD)]

cŏck-a-hōō'p *a.* & *adv.* Exultant(ly), with boastful crowing. [ME, of unkn. orig.]

Cockai'gne (-ā'n) *n.* Imaginary land of idleness and luxury; (punningly w. ref. to COCKNEY) London. [ME, f. OF (*pais de*) *cocaigne* lit. 'land of cakes' f. MLG *kokenje* sweet cake dim. of *koke* CAKE]

cŏck-a-lee'kĭe *n.* Scottish soup of cock boiled with leeks. [f. COCK[1] + LEEK + -IE]

cŏckalōr'um *n.* (colloq.) Self-important little man; (**hey** or **high**) ~, game like leap-frog. [18th c., arbitrary f. COCK[1]]

cŏckatie'l, -tee'l, *n.* (Austral.) Small delicately coloured crested parrot. [f. Du. *kaketielje*]

cŏckatōō' *n.* Parrot esp. of genus *Kakatoe*, with erectile crest; (Austral. & N.Z. colloq.) small farmer. [f. Du. *kaketoe* f. Malay *kakatua*, w. assim. to COCK[1]]

cŏ'ckatrīce *n.* = BASILISK; (Her.) fabulous animal, cock with serpent's tail. [ME f. OF *cocatris* f. med. L **calcatrix -cis* L *calcare* tread, track, rendering Gk *ikhneumōn* tracker (see ICHNEUMON)]

cŏ'ckboat *n.* Ship's small boat. [f. obs. *cock* small boat (f. OF *coque*) + BOAT[1]]

cŏ'ckchāfer *n.* Pale-brown nocturnal beetle flying with loud whirring sound. [perh. f. COCK[1] as expr. size or vigour + CHAFER]

cŏ'cker[1] *v.t.* ~ (**up**), indulge, pamper, coddle, (child, invalid, etc.). [ME, of uncert. orig.]

Cŏ'cker[2] *n.* **According to ~,** exact(ly), correct(ly). [f. E. ~, Engl. writer on arithmetic d. 1675]

cŏ'cker[3] *n.* (Breed of) small spaniel. [f. COCK[1] + -ER[1], as starting woodcock etc.]

cŏ'ckerel *n.* Young cock. [ME, dim. of COCK[1]; see -REL]

cŏ'ck-eyed (-īd) *a.* (sl.) Squinting; crooked, set aslant, not level; absurd; drunk. [19th c., app. f. COCK[2] + EYE[1] + -ED[2]]

cŏ'ck-hōrse *adv.* (Also **a-cock-horse;** see A[2]) astride, mounted. [16th c., = toy horse]

cŏ'ckle[1] *n.* (**Corn-**)~, purple-flowered plant formerly often growing among corn, esp. wheat; disease of wheat turning grains black. [OE *coccul*, perh. f. med. L **cocculus* dim. of LL COCCUS]

cŏ'ckle[2] *n.* Edible bivalve of genus *Cardium*; its shell; ~(**-shell**), small shallow boat; **~s of the heart,** one's feelings (*rejoice, warm, the cockles* etc.). [ME, f. OF *coquille* shell f. med. L **cochilia* f. med. Gk *kokhulia* f. Gk *kogkhulion* f. *kogkhē* (CONCH)]

cŏ'ckle[3] *v.* & *n* **1.** *v.i.* & *t.* (Cause to) bulge, curl up, pucker. **2.** *n.* Bulge or wrinkle in paper, glass, etc. [f. F *coquiller* blister (bread in cooking) f. *coquille*; see prec.]

cŏ'ck-lŏft *n.* Small upper loft. [16th c., orig. uncert.; perh. f. COCK[1] + LOFT]

cŏ'ckney *n.* & *a.* (Characteristic of a) native of London, esp. of the East End or speaking its dialect; this dialect; (Austral.) young snapper fish. [ME *cokeney* cock's egg (*cocene* gen. pl., *ey* f. OE *æg*), orig. sense prob. small or ill-shaped egg, later 'pampered child' and 'townsman']

cŏ'ckpĭt *n.* **1.** Place made for cock-fights. **2.** Arena for any struggle (**~ of Europe,** Belgium); (Aeron.) space for pilot etc. in fuselage of aeroplane or in spacecraft; driver's seat in racing car. [f. COCK[1] + PIT[1]]

For other words in *co-* see CO-.

cŏ'ckroach *n.* Insect of order Blattaria, esp. nocturnal voracious dark-brown beetle-like insect infesting kitchens. [f. Sp. *cucaracha*, w. assim. to COCK[1], ROACH[1]]

cŏcksur'e (-shoor') *a.* Quite convinced *of*, *about*; self-confident, dogmatic, presumptuous; hence ~NESS *n.* [f. *cock* = God + SURE]

cŏ'cktail *n.* Drink of spirits with bitters, sugar, etc.; appetizer containing shellfish etc.; finely--chopped fruit salad; ~ **stick,** small pointed stick for serving onion, small sausage, etc. [earlier senses 'docked horse', 'upstart', f. COCK[1,2] + TAIL[1]; tail like that of cock, or that cocks up]

cŏ'ck|ȳ[1] *a.* Conceited; saucy; hence ~ĬLY[2] *adv.*, ~ĬNESS *n.* [f. COCK[1] + -Y[2]]

cŏ'ckȳ[2] *n.* (Austral. & N.Z. colloq.) Small farmer. [f. COCKATOO + -Y[3]]

cŏckȳ-lee'kĭe. Var. of COCK-A-LEEKIE.

cō'cō (*pl.* ~s), **cō'coa**[1], *n.* ~(**nut**), tropical palm-tree (*Cocos nucifera*); ~**nut** (-kon-), its large ovate brown hard-shelled seed with edible white lining enclosing whitish liquid (~**nut milk**), (sl.) human head, (**that accounts for the milk in the ~nut,** (joc.) now all is explained; ~**nut butter,** solid oil obtained from lining of coconut, used in soap, candles, ointment, etc.; ~**nut ice,** sweet of sugar and desiccated coconut; ~**nut matting** (made from fibre of nut's outer husk); ~**nut shy,** fairground side-show where balls are thrown to dislodge coconuts; **double ~nut,** much larger nut of the coco-de-mer. [f. Port. & Sp. *coco* grimace, the base of the shell looking like a face]

cō'coa[2] *n.* Powder made from crushed cacao seeds often with other ingredients; drink made from this; ~ **bean,** cacao seed; ~ **butter,** fatty substance got from this; ~ **nib,** cotyledon of cocoa bean. [alt. of CACAO]

cōcō-de-mer' (-ār') *n.* Tall palm-tree of Seychelles. [F]

cō'conŭt. See COCO.

cocōō'n *n.* & *v.* **1.** *n.* Silky case spun by insect larva to protect it as chrysalis, esp. that of silkworm, whence ~ERY (3) *n.*; similar structure made by other animals; protective covering. **2.** *v.t.* & *i.* Form, or wrap (as) in, cocoon; spray with protective coating. [f. F *cocon* f. mod. Prov. *coucoun* dim. of *coca* shell]

cocŏ'tte *n.* **1.** (arch.) Fashionable prostitute. **2.** Small fireproof dish for cooking and serving one portion of food. [F]

cŏd[1] *n.* (*pl.* same). ~(**'fish**), large sea fish of family Gadidae, used as food, esp. *Gadus morrhua*; ~**-bank,** submarine bank frequented by cod; ~**-liver oil** (used as source of vitamins A and D). [ME, of unkn. orig.]

cŏd[2] *v.t.* & *i.* (**-dd-**), & *n.* (sl.) Hoax; parody. [19th c.; orig. unkn.]

cŏd[3] *n.* (sl.) Nonsense. [abbr. of CODS(WALLOP)]

C.O.D. *abbr.* cash on delivery, *collect on delivery; Concise Oxford Dictionary.

cō'da *n.* (Mus., or fig.) independent and often elaborate passage introduced after end of main part of a movement; (Ballet) concluding section. [It., f. L *cauda* tail]

cŏ'ddle *v.t.* Treat as invalid, keep from cold and exertion, feed *up*; cook (egg) lightly. [prob. dial. var. of CAUDLE]

cōde *n.*, & *v.t.* **1.** *n.* Systematic collection of statutes, body of laws so arranged as to avoid inconsistency and overlapping; set of rules on any subject; prevalent morality of a society or class (esp. *code of* HONOUR[1]); person's standard of moral behaviour. **2.** (Mil. etc.) system of signals, esp. used to ensure secrecy; system of letter or figure or word groups or symbols with arbitrary meanings for brevity or secrecy, or for machine processing of information; (Biol.) GENETIC *code.* **3.** ~**-book,** list of symbols etc. used in code; ~**-name,** ~**-number,** word or symbol, number, used for secrecy or convenience instead of ordinary name. **4.** *v.t.* Put (message etc.) into code; hence **cō'dER**[1] *n.* [ME f. OF, f. L CODEX]

cō'deine (-dēn *or* -dĭēn) *n.* Alkaloid got from opium, used as hypnotic and analgesic. [f. Gk *kōdeia* poppy-head + -INE[5]]

cō'dĕx *n.* (*pl.* **codices** *pr.* kŏ'dĭsēz). Manuscript volume, esp. of ancient texts; collection of pharmaceutical descriptions of drugs etc. [L, = wood block, tablet, book]

cŏ'dger *n.* (colloq.) Fellow, person, esp. strange one. [perh. var. of CADGER]

codices. See CODEX.

cŏ'dĭcil *n.* Supplementary addition, esp. modifying or revoking will; hence **cŏdĭcĭ'llARY**[1] *a.* [f. L *codicillus* (usu. in pl.), dim. of CODEX]

cōdĭcŏ'logȳ *n.* Study of manuscripts; hence **cōdĭcoLO'GICAL** *a.* [f. F *codicologie* f. L CODEX *codicis* + -O- + -LOGY]

cŏ'dĭ|fȳ *v.t.* Arrange (laws etc.) as code; hence ~FICA'TION, ~fĪER[1], *ns.* [f. CODE + -I- + -FY]

cŏ'dlĭng[1], **cŏ'dlĭn,** *n.* Cooking-apple of long tapering shape; moth whose larva feeds on apples; ~**s-and-cream,** willow-herb. [ME, f. AF *quer de lion* lion-heart]

cŏ'dlĭng[2] *n.* Small codfish. [f. COD[1] + -LING[1] 2]

cō'dŏn *n.* (Biol.) Group of three nucleotides forming unit of genetic code determining amino--acid sequence. [f. CODE + -ON]

cŏ'dpiece *n.* (Hist.) Bagged appendage to front of men's breeches. [ME, f. *cod* scrotum + PIECE[1]]

cō-drī'ver *n.* One who takes turns in driving a vehicle esp. in a race etc. [f. CO- 1 + DRIVER]

cŏ'ds(wallop) (-dzwŏ-) *n.* (sl.) Nonsense. [20th c.; orig. unkn.]

coecilian. Var. of CAECILIAN.

cō'ĕd *n.* & *a.* (colloq.) **1.** *n.* Girl or woman student at coeducational institution. **2.** *a.* Coeducational. [abbr.]

cōĕdūcā'tion *n.* Education of both sexes together; hence ~AL *a.* [f. CO- 1 + EDUCATION]

cōĕffĭ'cient (-shent) *n.* (Alg.) quantity placed before and multiplying another quantity; (Phys.) multiplier or factor that measures some property (*coefficient of friction, expansion*, etc.); DIFFERENTIAL *coefficient.* [f. mod. L CO*efficiens* (see EFFICIENT)]

coe'lacănth (sē'l-) *n.* Fish of family Coelacanthidae orig. thought to have hollow spine, extinct but for one species (*Latimeria chalumnae*). [f. mod. L *Coelacanthus* f. Gk *koilos* hollow + *akantha* spine]

coelĕ'nterāte (sēl-) *a.* & *n.* (Zool.) (Member) of the phylum Coelenterata, incl. jellyfish, sea anemones, and corals. [f. mod. L *Coelenterata* f. Gk *koilos* hollow + *enteron* intestine; see -ATE[2]]

coe'lĭăc (sē'l-), ***cē'lĭăc,** *a.* Of the belly; ~ **disease,** intestinal disease with defective digestion of fats. [f. L f. Gk *koiliakos* (*koilia* belly; see -AC)]

coe'lom (sē'l-), ***cē'lom,** *n.* (*pl.* ~**s,** *or* ~**ata** *pr.* -ō'mata). (Zool.) Body cavity or space between intestinal canal and body wall; hence ~ATE[2] *a.* & *n.*, (animal) having coelom. [f. Gk *koilōma* cavity]

coe'lostăt (sē'l-) *n.* (Astron.) Instrument with rotating mirror to photograph celestial objects without their diurnal motion. [f. L *caelum* sky + -O- + -STAT]

coe'nobite (sē'n-), ***cē'n-,** *n.* Member of monastic community; hence **c(o)enobĭ'tIC(AL)** (sēn-) *adjs.* [f. OF *cenobite* or eccl. L *coenobita* f. LL f. Gk *koinobion* convent (*koinos* common, *bios* life)]

cōē'qual *a.* & *n.* (arch. or literary). Equal; hence **cōėqua'lITY** (-kwŏ'l-) *n.*, ~LY[2] *adv.* [ME, f. L or eccl. L *coaequalis* (see CO-, EQUAL[1])]

coër'ce *v.t.* Forcibly constrain or impel (person) *into* obedience etc.; hence **coër'cIBLE** *a.* [ME, f. L CO(*ercēre ercit-* = *arcēre* restrain)]

coër'c|ion (-shon) *n.* Controlling of voluntary agent or action by force; government by force; hence ~IVE *a.* [f. OF *cohercion, -tion* f. L *coer(c)tio, coercitio -onis* (see prec., -ION)]

cōèssĕ'ntial (-shal) *a.* Of the same substance or essence. [ME, f. eccl. L *coessentialis* transl. Gk *homoousios*; see CO-, ESSENTIAL]

cōētā'nèous *a.* Coeval; hence ~LY² *adv.* [f. LL CO(*aetaneus* f. L *aetas* age) + -OUS]

cōètĕr'nal *a.* Alike eternal; hence ~LY² *adv.* [f. eccl. L CO(*aeternus* ETERNAL) + -AL]

cōē'val *a.* & *n.* (Person) having same age, existing at same epoch; of same duration or date of origin; hence ~ITY (-ă'l-) *n.*, ~LY² *adv.* [f. LL CO(*aevus* f. L *aevum* age) + -AL]

cōèxĭ'st (-gz-) *v.i.* Exist together (*with*); so ~ENT *a.*, ~ENCE *n.*; **peaceful ~ence** (of peoples with different political and social systems, living in mutual toleration). [f. LL CO(*existere* EXIST)]

cōèxtĕ'nsĭve *a.* Extending over same space or time. [f. CO- 1 + EXTENSIVE]

C. of E. *abbr.* Church of England.

cŏ'ffee (-fĭ) *n.* **1.** Shrub of genus *Coffea*; its seeds raw, or roasted and ground; drink made from the roasted and ground seeds; cupful of, light refreshments with, this drink; light brown colour. **2.** ~ **bar,** establishment serving coffee and light refreshments; **~-bean,** the seed; *coffee*-BREAK²; **~-cup** (of special shape or size); ~ **essence,** concentrated extract of coffee; **~--grounds,** sediment after infusion; **~-house,** (Hist.) refreshment house; ***~-maker,** device for brewing coffee; **~-mill** (for grinding roasted seeds); ~ **morning,** morning gathering with drinking of coffee; **~-pot** (for making or serving coffee in); *~ **shop,** small restaurant; ~ **stall,** movable structure serving as coffee bar; **~-table,** small low table (*~-table book,* large expensive illustrated book). [ult. f. Turk. *kahveh* f. Arab. *ḳahwa,* the drink]

cŏ'ffer *n.* Box, esp. strong-box for valuables; (in *pl.*) treasury, funds; sunk panel in ceiling etc.; ~**(-dam),** watertight case pumped dry in building bridges etc., or for repairing ship. [ME f. OF *coffre* f. L f. Gk *kophinos* basket]

cŏ'ffĭn *n.*, & *v.t.* **1.** *n.* Box in which corpse is buried or cremated (**nail in** one's ~, thing that slightly hastens one's death, by annoyance, over--indulgence, etc.); horse's hoof below coronet (**~-bone,** last phalangeal bone of foot; **~-joint,** joint at top of hoof); *~ **corner** (Footb., between goal-line and sideline); **~-nail,** (sl.) cigarette. **2.** *v.t.* Put in coffin. [ME, f. OF *cof(f)in* little basket etc. f. L *cophinus* (see prec.)]

cŏ'ffle *n.* Line of animals, slaves, etc., fastened together. [f. Arab. *ḳāfila* caravan]

cŏg *n.* One of series of projections on edge of wheel or side of bar transferring motion by engaging with another series; (fig.) unimportant member of organization etc.; **~-wheel** (with cogs); hence ~GED² (-gd) *a.* [ME, prob. of Scand. orig.]

cō'gent *a.* (Of argument, reasons, etc.) forcible, convincing; hence **cō'gENCY** *n.*, ~LY² *adv.* [f. L *cogere* compel (as CO-, *agere act-* drive); see -ENT]

cŏ'gĭtable *a.* Able to be grasped by the mind, conceivable. [f. L *cogitabilis* (as foll.; see -ABLE)]

cŏ'gĭt|āte *v.i.* & *t.* Ponder, meditate; so ~A'TION *n.*, ~ātIVE *a.* [f. L *cogitare* = CO(*agitare* AGITATE) think + -ATE³]

cogito (kō'gĭtō) *n.* (Philos.) Principle establishing existence of a being from fact of its thinking or awareness. [L, = I think, in Fr. philosopher Descartes's formula (1641) ~, *ergo sum* I think, therefore I exist]

cŏ'gnăc (kŏ'nyăk) *n.* French brandy, prop. that distilled from wine of Cognac. [f. *C~* in W. France]

cŏ'gnāte *a.* & *n.* **1.** Descended from common ancestor (cf. AGNATE); akin in origin, nature, or quality; a relative. **2.** (Philol.) Of same linguistic family; representing same original word or root; of parallel development in different allied languages (as E *father*, G *vater*, L *pater*); cognate word. **3.** (Gram.) ~ **object,** one whose meaning overlaps with that of its verb (*live a good life* = live virtuously). **4.** Hence ~LY² (-tlĭ) *adv.*, ~NESS (-tn-) *n.* [f. L CO(*gnatus* born); see -ATE²]

cŏgnĭ'tion *n.* (Philos.) Action or faculty of knowing, perceiving, conceiving, as opposed to emotion and volition; a perception, sensation, notion, or intuition; hence or cogn. ~AL, **cŏ'gnĭtIVE,** *adjs.* [f. L *cognitio* f. CO(*gnoscere gnit-* apprehend); see -ITION]

cŏ'gnĭzab|le (*or* kŏ'n-), **-ĭs-** (-z-), *a.* Perceptible; recognizable; within the jurisdiction of a court etc.; hence ~LY² *adv.* [f. foll. + -ABLE]

cŏ'gnĭzance (*or* kŏ'n-), **-ĭs-** (-z-), *n.* **1.** Being aware, notice, sphere of observation or concern; **have ~ of,** know, esp. in a legitimate or official way; **take ~ of,** attend to, not allow to go unobserved. **2.** (Right of) dealing with a matter legally or judicially. **3.** Distinctive device or mark. [ME, f. OF *conis(s)aunce, conois(s)ance*, f. Rom. **connoscentia* f. L *cognoscent-* part. st. of *cognoscere*; see COGNITION, -ANCE]

cŏ'gnĭzant (*or* kŏ'n-), **-ĭs-** (-z-), *a.* Having knowledge, being aware, *of*; (Philos.) having cognition. [f. prec.; see -ANT]

cŏ'gnīze, -īse (-īz), *v.t.* (Philos.) Have cognition of. [f. COGNIZANCE after *recognize* and other vbs. in -IZE]

cŏgnō'mĕn *n.* Nickname; (Rom. Ant.) third personal or family name (e.g. Marcus Tullius *Cicero*), or fourth name or personal epithet (e.g. Publius Cornelius Scipio *Africanus*); surname. [L]

cognoscent|e (kŏnyoshĕ'ntĭ) *n.* (*pl.* ~*i pr.* -ē *or* same). Connoisseur. [It., lit., one who knows]

cŏgnō'vĭt *n.* (Law). Defendant's acknowledgement, to save expense, that plaintiff's cause is just; acknowledgement of a debt. [L, = he has acknowledged]

cōhă'bĭt *v.i.* Live together, esp. as husband and wife (usu. of persons not married to each other); so ~A'TION *n.* [f. LL *cohabitare* f. L CO(*habitare* dwell frequent. of *habēre* hold)]

cōhēr'e *v.i.* (Of parts or whole) stick together, remain united; (of argument etc.) be consistent, be well-knit; hence **cōhēr'ER¹** *n.*, detector of radio waves consisting of glass cylinder containing loose metal filings etc. (which were thought to cohere when struck by a wave). [f. L CO(*haerēre haes-* stick)]

cōhēr'|ent *a.* Cohering; (of argument etc.) consistent, easily followed; (Phys., of radiation) having constant phase difference from other radiation, and so able to interfere with it; so ~ENCE, ~ENCY, *ns.*, **~ent**LY² *adv.*; **~ence theory,** (Philos.) theory that truth should be judged by mutual consistency of propositions. [f. L *cohaerēre* (see prec., -ENT)]

cōhē'sion (-zhon) *n.* Sticking together; force with which molecules cohere; tendency to remain united; so **cōhē'sIVE** *a.* [f. L *cohaes-* (see COHERE, -ION), after *adhesion*]

cō'hō, cō'hōe, *n.* (*pl.* ~s). N. Pacific silver salmon. [19th c., of unkn. orig.]

cō'hort *n.* Division of Roman army; band of

warriors; persons banded or grouped together; *assistant, colleague. [ME, f. F *cohorte* or f. L *cohors cohort-* enclosure, company]

||**C.O.I.** *abbr.* Central Office of Information.

coif *n.* (Hist.) Close cap covering top, back, and sides, of head; serjeant-at-law's white cap. [ME, f. OF *coife* f. LL *cofia* helmet]

coiffeur (kwahfẽr′) *n.* (*fem.* ***coiffeuse*** *pr.* -ẽr′z). Hairdresser. [F]

coiffure (kwahfūr′) *n.* Way hair is dressed. [F]

coign (koin) *n.* Projecting corner; ~ **of vantage,** place affording good view of something. [old form of COIN[1]; in Shak. *Macbeth* I. vi. 7]

coil[1] *v.t.* & *i.* Arrange (rope etc.) in concentric rings; twist (*up*) into circular or spiral shape; move sinuously. [f. OF *coillir* f. L *colligere* COLLECT[2]]

coil[2] *n.* Length of coiled rope, spring, etc.; arrangement, thing arranged, in concentric circles; single turn of coiled thing, e.g. snake; lock of hair twisted and coiled; wire, piping, etc., wound circularly or helically; flexible loop as contraceptive device in womb; roll of postage stamps; (Electr.) coiled wire for passage of current, esp. for ignition in internal combustion engine. [f. prec.]

coil[3] *n.* (arch. or poet.) Disturbance, noise; fuss; (esp.) **this mortal** ~, turmoil of life (Shak. *Hamlet* III. i. 67). [16th c.; orig. unkn.]

coin[1] *n.* Piece of metal made into money by official stamp; metal money (**false** ~, imitation in base metal etc., (fig.) anything spurious; **other side of the** ~, (fig.) opposite view of a matter; **pay** person **in his own** ~, give tit for tat); ~**-box,** telephone operated by inserting coins; ~**-op,** launderette etc. with automatic machines operated by coins. [ME f. OF, = wedge, stamping-die, f. L. *cuneus* wedge]

coin[2] *v.t.* Make (money) by stamping metal (~ **money,** (fig.) get money fast); make (metal) into money; invent, fabricate, (esp. new word); **to** ~ **a phrase** (iron., with banal remark); hence ~′ER[1] *n.*, (esp.) ||maker of counterfeit coins. [ME, f. OF *coignier* (*coin*; see prec.)]

coi′nage *n.* Coining; coins; system of coins in use (DECIMAL *coinage*); invention, coined word. [ME, f. OF *coigniage* (*coignier*; see prec., -AGE)]

cōinci′de *v.i.* Occupy same portion of space; occur at or during same time; agree together or *with*; concur in opinion etc. [f. med. L co(*incidere* fall upon; see INCIDENT[2])]

cōi′ncidence *n.* (Instance of) being coincident; notable concurrence of events or circumstances without apparent causal connection; (Phys.) presence of ionizing particles etc. in two or more detectors simultaneously, or of two or more signals simultaneously in a circuit. [f. med. L *coincidentia* f. as prec.; see -ENCE]

cōi′ncident *a.* Coinciding; hence ~LY[2] *adv.* [f. as COINCIDE; see -ENT]

cōincidĕ′ntal *a.* Of the nature of (a) coincidence; hence ~LY[2] *adv.* [f. prec. + -AL]

coi′ntreau (kwă′ntrō) *n.* Colourless orange-flavoured liqueur. [F; **P**]

coir (koi′*er*) *n.* Fibre from outer husk of coconut, used for ropes, matting, etc. [f. Malayalam *kāyar* cord (*kāyaru* be twisted)]

cōi′tion *n.* = foll. [f. L *coitio* f. co(*ire it-* go); see -ITION]

cō′ĭtus *n.* (Med.) Sexual intercourse; ~ **interru′ptus** (in which penis is withdrawn before ejaculation); ~ **reserva′tus** (in which orgasm is delayed or avoided); hence **cō′ĭt**AL *a.* [L, f. as prec.]

cojones (kōhō′nĕs) *n.pl.* Testicles; (fig.) courage. [Sp.]

cōke[1] *n.*, & *v.t.* (Convert into) solid substance left after heating coal, petrol, etc.; **go and eat** ~, (sl.) go away! [prob. f. N. Engl. dial. *colk* core, of unkn. orig.]

cōke[2] *n.*, & *v.t.* (sl.) (Drug with) cocaine. [abbr.]

Cōke[3] *n.* Coca-Cola. [abbr.; **P**]

cŏl *n.* **1.** Depression in mountain-chain. **2.** (Meteorol.) Low-pressure region between anticyclones. [F, = neck, f. L *collum*]

col- *pref.*, assim. form of COM- before *l.*

Col. *abbr.* Colonel; Colossians (N.T.).

col. *abbr.* column.

cō′la, kō′la, *n.* W. Afr. tree of genus *Cola*; its seed, used as condiment and tonic. [W. Afr.]

co′lander (kŭ′-) *n.* Perforated vessel used as strainer in cookery. [ME, perh. f. Prov. **colador* f. Rom. **colator* f. L *colare -at-* strain]

cō-lă′tĭtūde *n.* (Astron.) Complement of latitude, difference between it and 90°. [f. co- 2 + LATITUDE]

||**cŏlcă′nnon** *n.* Irish & Scottish dish of cabbage and potatoes boiled and pounded. [18th c.; perh. f. COLE]

cŏ′lchĭc|um (*or* -kĭ-) *n.* Plant of genus *Colchicum*, esp. meadow saffron; its dried corm or seed, used as drug etc.; hence ~INE[5] (-ēn) *n.*, poisonous yellow alkaloid present in colchicum, used esp. in plant-breeding. [L, f. Gk *kolkhikon* neut. a. (*Kolkhis* Colchis region E. of Black Sea; see -IC)]

cōld[1] *a.* & *adv.* **1.** *a.* Of or at low temperature, esp. when compared with human body or with that usual in things like the one in question (ICE[1]-*cold*, STONE-*cold*; BLOOD[1] *runs cold*). **2.** Not heated, or having cooled after heat, (*cold water*; *throw cold* WATER[1] *on*); dead; (sl.) unconscious; (colloq.) at one's mercy (*have* person *cold*); feeling cold; sexually frigid; (of soil) slow to absorb heat; *unrehearsed. **3.** Without ardour, friendliness (*cold reception*), or affection, undemonstrative, apathetic, (*idea* **leaves** one ~, does not move or impress one). **4.** Chilling, depressing (*cold facts*); uninteresting (*cold news*). **5.** (Of scent in hunting) weakened by passage of time; (in children's games) far from finding or guessing what is sought. **6.** *Cold* BLOOD[1]; ~**-blooded,** (of fish etc.) having blood temperature varying with that of surroundings, (fig.) sluggish, callous, deliberately cruel; ~ **cathode** (emitting electrons without being heated); *cold* CHISEL; ~ **colours,** blue or grey, as of cold or sunless day; ~ **comfort,** poor consolation; *cold* CREAM[1]; ~ **cuts,** sliced cold cooked meats; ~ **feet,** fear or cowardice; ~ **frame,** unheated frame for growing small plants; ~ **front** (of advancing mass of cold air); ~**-hearted,** lacking friendliness or affection; ~ **meat,** meat cooled after cooking, (sl.) corpse(s); ~ **shoulder,** (fig.) intentionally unfriendly treatment, so ~**-shou′lder** *v.t.*; *cold* SNAP; *cold* STEEL; ~ **storage,** storage in refrigerator, (fig.) state of abeyance; *cold* SWEAT; ~ **turkey,** *(sl.) blunt statements, (sl.) abrupt withdrawal of narcotics from addict; *cold* WAR[1], so ~ **warrior;** ~ **wave,** (1) kind of permanent hair-wave, (2) see WAVE[2] 4; ~**-work** *v.t.*, shape (metal) while cold. **7.** Hence ~′ISH[1] 2 *a.*, ~′LY[2] *adv.*, ~′NESS *n.* **8.** *adv.* In cold state; *(sl.) completely, absolutely. [OE *cald*, = OS *cald*, OHG *kalt*, ON *kaldr*, Goth. *kalds* f. Gmc **kaldaz* cogn. w. L *gelu* frost]

cōld[2] *n.* **1.** Prevalence of low temperature esp. in atmosphere, cold weather, (**left out in the** ~, (fig.) ignored, not looked after); cold condition. **2.** Inflamed state of mucous membrane of nose and throat, with hoarseness, running at nose, sore throat, etc., (CATCH[1] *cold*; often *common cold, cold in the head*); **catch a** ~, (fig.) encounter trouble or difficulties. [OE *cald* neut. adj.; see prec.]

cō′ld-shŏrt *a.* (Of metal) brittle in its cold state. [f. Sw. *kallskör* (*kall* cold, *skör* brittle), w. assim. to SHORT 6]

cōle *n.* Cabbage (usu. in *comb.*); ~**-seed,** rape,

plant from which colza oil is got; **~-slaw** [cf. SLAW], salad of sliced raw cabbage. [ME, f. ON *kál* (=OE *cāwel*, OHG *chōl(i)*), f. L *caulis* stem, cabbage]
colemouse. See COALMOUSE.
cŏlĕŏ'pter|ous *a.* Of the order Coleoptera (beetles and weevils), with front wings converted to sheaths for hinder wings; so **~IST** *n.*, one who studies beetles. [f. mod. L *Coleoptera* f. Gk *koleopteros* (*koleon* sheath, *pteron* wing) + -OUS]
cŏlĕŏ'ptīle *n.* (Bot.) Hollow organ containing first leaf of germinating cereal grain. [f. Gk *koleos* sheath + *ptilon* feather]
cō'le-tĭt. Var of *coal-tit* = COALMOUSE.
cō'lĕus *n.* Plant of genus *Coleus*, with variegated coloured leaves. [mod. L, f. Gk *koleos* sheath]
cō'ley *n.* Saithe; rock salmon. [perh. f. *coal-fish*]
cŏ'lic *n.* Severe spasmodic griping pain in belly; hence **~KY**² *a.* [ME, f. F *colique* f. LL *colicus* (COLON¹; see -IC)]
***cŏlĭsē'um** *n.* Large stadium etc. [med. L, f. neut. (as n., applied to a Roman amphitheatre) of L *colosseus* gigantic (COLOSSUS)]
coli'tĭs *n.* Inflammation of lining of colon. [f. COLON¹ + -ITIS]
Coll. *abbr.* College.
collă'bor|āte *v.i.* Work jointly (*with*, or abs.) esp. at literary or artistic production; co-operate traitorously with the enemy; hence **~A'TION**, **~ātOR**, *ns.* [f. L COL(*laborare* LABOUR²) + -ATE³]
cŏlla'g|e (-ah'zh) *n.* Abstract form of art, work of art, in which photographs, pieces of paper, string, matchsticks, etc. are placed in juxtaposition and glued to the pictorial surface; hence **~IST** (3) *n.* [F, = gluing]
cŏ'llagĕn *n.* Protein found in bone, tendons, etc., yielding gelatin on boiling. [f. F *collagène* f. Gk *kolla* glue + *-gène* = -GEN (1)]
collă'ps|e *n.* & *v.* **1.** *n.*, & *v.i.* (Undergo or experience a) falling in, sudden shrinking together, folding up, giving way, prostration by loss of nervous or muscular power, breakdown of mental energy, loss of courage. **2.** *v.t.* Cause to collapse; hence **~IBLE** *a.* [v. back form. f. *collapsed* f. L *collapsus* p.p. of COL(*labi laps-* slip); n. f. Med. L *collapsus* n.]
cŏ'llar¹ *n.* **1.** Neckband, upright or turned over, of coat, dress, shirt, etc., (**hot under the ~**, embarrassed); band of linen, lace, etc., completing upper part of costume; ‖neck-chain of order of knighthood; ‖**~ of SS** or **esses,** former badge of House of Lancaster, still used in some officials' costume. **2.** Leather etc. band round animal's (esp. dog's) neck (DOG¹-*collar*); (**horse-**)**~**, roll round draught-horse's neck bearing stress (GRIN *through a horse-collar*); restraining or connecting band, ring, pipe, in machines etc. **3.** Coloured stripe round animal's or bird's neck; piece of meat, brawn, fish, rolled and tied. **4. ~-beam,** horizontal beam connecting two rafters and forming with them an A-shaped roof-truss; **~-bone,** bone joining breastbone and shoulder-blade, clavicle; ***~-button,** ‖**~-stud,** (for fixing separate collar to shirt). **5.** Hence (-)**~ED**² (*-erd*), **~LESS**, *adjs.* [ME f. AF *coler*, OF *colier*, f. L *collare* (*collum* neck; see -AR¹)]
cŏ'llar² *v.t.* Seize (person) by collar, capture; (Rugby Footb.) lay hold of and stop (opponent holding ball); (sl.) appropriate. [f. prec.]
cŏllarĕ'tte *n.* Woman's collar of lace, fur, etc. [f. F *collerette* (*collier* COLLAR¹; see -ETTE)]
collāt|e *v.t.* Compare in detail (copies of text or document, one copy *with* another); (Bibliog.) verify order of (sheets) by signatures; put together (esp. information); (of Ordinary) appoint (clergyman) *to* benefice; so **~OR** *n.*, one who collates. machine for combining sets of punched cards. [f. L COL(*lat-* p.p. st. of *ferre* bring; see -ATE³)]
collă'teral *a.* & *n.* **1.** *a.* Side by side, parallel; subordinate but from same source; contributory, connected but aside from main subject, course, etc. **2.** *a.* & *n.* (Person) of common descent but by different line; **~ (security)**, property pledged as guarantee for repayment of money. **3.** Hence **~ITY** (-ă'l-) *n.*, **~LY**² *adv.* [ME, f. med. L COL(*lateralis* LATERAL)]
collā'tion *n.* **1.** Collating or being collated. **2.** (R.C. Ch.) light meal in evening of fast-day; light meal, esp. at unusual time. [ME f. OF, f. L *collatio -onis* (as COLLATE; see -ION); sense 2 f. Benedictine monastery readings of Cassian's *Lives of the Fathers* (*Collationes Patrum*) followed by light repast]
cŏ'lleague (-ēg) *n.* Fellow official or worker, esp. in a profession or business. [f. F *collègue* f. L COL(*lega* f. *legare* depute) partner in office]
cŏ'llĕct¹ (*or* -ĭkt) *n.* Short prayer of Anglican or R.C. Church, esp. one assigned to a particular day or season. [ME f. OF *collecte* f. L *collecta* fem. p.p. (as n.) of *colligere* (see foll.)]
collĕ'ct² *v.* **1.** *v.t.* & *i.* Assemble, accumulate, bring or come together; get (taxes, contributions, goods to be serviced, etc.) from a number of people (***~ on delivery,** = CASH¹ *on delivery*); (colloq.) receive money; (colloq.) call for, fetch. **2.** *v.t.* Obtain (specimens, books, stamps, etc.) for addition to others, esp. as hobby; regain control of, concentrate, recover, (one*self*, one's thoughts, energies, courage), (in *p.p.*) not distracted, cool; keep (horse) well in hand; (arch.) infer, gather, conclude; hence **~ABLE**, **~IBLE**, *adjs.* [f. F *collecter* or f. med. L *collectare*, f. L *collectus* p.p. of COL(*ligere* = *legere* pick)]
***collĕ'ct³** *a.* & *adv.* To be paid for by receiver (of telephone call, telegram, parcel, etc.). [imper. of prec.]
collectanea (kŏlĕktā'nĭa) *n. pl.* Collected passages, miscellany. [L, neut. pl. of *collectaneus* a. (as COLLECT²; cf. -ANEOUS)]
collĕ'ction *n.* Collecting or being collected; collecting of money, money collected, at meeting or Church service for charitable or religious purpose; regular removal of letters etc. for dispatch by post; accumulation *of* water, dust, etc.; group of things collected and belonging together (literary materials, specimens, fashionable clothes, works of art, etc.); ‖(in *pl.*) college terminal examination at Oxford etc. [ME f. OF, f. L *collectio -onis* (as COLLECT²; see -ION)]
collĕ'ctĭve *a.* & *n.* **1.** *a.* Formed by or constituting a collection, taken as a whole, aggregate; **~ fruit** (resulting from many flowers, as mulberry). **2.** Of or from many individuals, common; **~ bargaining,** negotiation of wages etc. by organized body of employees; **~ farm,** jointly operated amalgamation of several smallholdings; **~ ownership** (of land, means of production, etc., by all for benefit of all, whence **collĕ'ctĭvISM** (3), **collĕ'ctĭvIST** (2), *ns.*, **collĕ'ctĭvIZE** (3) *v.t.*); **~ security,** (Polit.) policy or principle of the alliance of several countries to guarantee the security of each one; **~ unconscious,** part of unconscious mind deriving from ancestral experience. **3.** (Gram. & Logic). **~ noun,** sing. noun denoting many individuals, e.g. *troop*. **4.** Hence **~LY**² (-vlĭ) *adv.*, **cŏllĕctĭ'vITY** *n.* **5.** *n.* Collective farm; collective noun. [f. F *collectif* or f. L *collectivus* (as COLLECT²; see -IVE)]

collĕ'ctor *n.* One who collects (specimens, books, stamps, railway tickets at station, money due, esp. taxes, rent, and subscriptions; **~'s item** or **piece,** thing of sufficient beauty or rarity to be placed in a collection); collecting-apparatus in various machines; region in transistor absorbing carriers of charge; hence ~SHIP *n.* [ME f. AF *collectour* f. med. L *collector* (as COLLECT²; see -OR)]

cŏllee'n *n.* (Ir.) Girl. [Ir. *cailín*, dim. of *caile* countrywoman; cf. -EEN]

cŏ'llège *n.* **1.** Organized body of persons with shared functions and privileges (**Sacred C~,** body of cardinals, (Hist.) the Pope's council of 70; *ELECTORAL *college*; ||**Heralds' C~,** or **C~ of Arms,** corporation recording lineage and granting arms; *College of Physicians, Preceptors,* etc.). **2.** ||Independent corporation in university, usu. with master, fellows, scholars, and students not on foundation; small university, esp. one not teaching beyond first degree; place of professional study (military, naval, agricultural, etc.; **C~ of Education,** place for training schoolteachers); ||public school; private school; buildings of any of these (*lives in college*). **3.** **~ living,** benefice in gift of a college; **~ pudding,** small plum pudding for one person. **4.** So **collē'g**IAL *a.* [ME f. OF, or f. L *collegium* (*collega* COLLEAGUE)]

collē'gĭan *n.* Member of a college. [f. med. L *collegianus* (as prec.; see -IAN)]

collē'gĭate *a.* Constituted as or belonging to a college, corporate; **~ church,** church endowed for chapter but without see, or (Sc. & U.S.) under joint pastorate; hence ~LY² (-tlĭ) *adv.* [f. LL *collegiatus* (as COLLEGE; see -ATE²)]

collĕ'nchy̆ma (-ngk-) *n.* (Bot.) Thickened tissue strengthening walls of young stems etc. [f. Gk *kolla* glue + *egkhuma* infusion]

Cŏ'llĕs *n.* **~ fracture,** (Med.) fracture of lower end of radius with backward displacement of hand. [f. A. ~, Ir. surgeon d. 1843]

cŏ'llĕt *n.* Encompassing band or ring on spindle etc.; socket; flange holding gem, bezel. [F, dim. of COL]

collī'de *v.i.* Come into collision; be in conflict. [f. L COL(*lidere lis-* = *laedere* strike and hurt)]

cŏ'llĭe *n.* Scottish sheep-dog with long pointed nose and usu. long hair. [perh. f. *coll* COAL (as being orig. black) + -IE]

cŏ'llĭ|er (-yer) *n.* Coal-miner; coal-ship; sailor on this; hence ~ERY (-yerĭ) *n.*, coal-mine and its buildings. [ME, f. COAL + -IER]

cŏ'llĭg|āte *v.t.* Bring into connection (esp. isolated facts by a generalization); so ~A'TION *n.* [f. L COL(*ligare* bind) + -ATE³]

cŏ'llĭm|āte *v.t.* Adjust line of sight of (telescope etc.); make (telescopes, rays) parallel; hence ~A'TION, **~ātor,** *ns.* [f. L *collimare*, false reading in Cicero for COL(*lineare* f. *linea* line) + -ATE³]

collĭ'nĕar *a.* In same straight line; hence ~ITY (-ă'r-) *n.*, ~LY² *adv.* [f. COL- + LINEAR]

||**Cŏ'llĭns**¹ (-z) *n.* (colloq.) Letter of thanks from guest after visit. [character in Jane Austen's *Pride & Prejudice*]

Cŏ'llĭns² (-z) *n.* Iced drink of gin, whisky, etc., with soda, lemon or lime juice, and sugar (JOHN or TOM *Collins*). [20th c.; orig. unkn.]

collĭ'sion (-zhon) *n.* Striking together, colliding; violent encounter of moving body, esp. ship or vehicle, with another or with fixed object; (fig.) clashing of opposed interests etc. (esp. *in collision, come into collision with*); **~ course,** course or action bound to end in collision (lit. or fig.); **~-mat** (Naut., ready for putting over hole made by collision); hence ~AL *a.* [ME, f. LL *collisio* (as COLLIDE; see -ION)]

cŏ'llŏc|āte *v.t.* Place together; arrange; set in particular place; so ~A'TION *n.* [f. L COL(*locare* f. *locus* place) + -ATE³]

cŏ'llocūtor *n.* Partaker in talk (**my ~,** the person talking to me). [LL, f. COL(*loqui locut-* talk); see -OR]

collō'dĭon *n.* Solution of pyroxylin in ether, used in photography and surgery. [f. Gk *kollōdēs* (*kolla* glue; cf. -ODE)]

collō'gue (-g) *v.i.* Talk confidentially *with.* [prob. alt. of obs. *colleague* conspire, by assoc. w. L COL(*loqui* speak) converse]

cŏ'lloid *a.* & *n.* **1.** Gluey (substance); (Path.) (substance) of homogeneous gelatinous consistency. **2.** *n.* (Chem.) Non-crystalline substance with very large molecules, forming viscous solution with special properties; finely divided substance dispersed in another; hence **colloi'd**AL *a.* [f. Gk *kolla* glue + -OID]

cŏ'llop *n.* Slice of meat, escalope. [ME (=fried bacon and eggs), of Scand. orig.]

collō'quĭal *a.* In or of talk, oral; belonging to familiar speech, not used in formal or elevated language; hence ~ISM (3, 4) *n.*, ~LY² *adv.* [f. L *colloquium* COLLOQUY + -AL]

collō'quĭ|um *n.* (*pl.* ~a). Academic conference or seminar. [L; see foll.]

cŏ'lloqu|y̆ *n.* Act of conversing; a conversation; judicial and legislative court in Presbyterian Church; so ~IZE *v.i.*, converse. [f. L COL(*loquium* f. *loqui* speak); see -Y¹]

cŏ'llotȳpe *n.* Thin plate of gelatin exposed to light, treated with reagents, and then printed from by lithography; print so made. [f. Gk *kolla* glue + -O- + TYPE¹]

collū'de (*or* -ōō'-) *v.i.* (arch.) Practise collusion. [f. L COL(*ludere lus-* play)]

collū'sion (-zhon; *or* -lōō'-) *n.* Fraudulent secret understanding, esp. between ostensible opponents as in lawsuit; hence **collu's**IVE (-ōō'-) *a.* [ME f. OF, or f. L *collusio* (as prec.; see -ION)]

collȳ'rĭ|um *n.* (*pl.* ~a). Eye-lotion. [L, f. Gk *kollurion* poultice (*kollura* coarse bread-roll)]

cŏ'llȳwŏbbles (-belz) *n.pl.* (colloq.) Rumbling in the intestines; stomach-ache; feeling of apprehension (with intestinal symptoms). [fanciful, f. COLIC + WOBBLE]

Colo. *abbr.* Colorado.

cŏ'lobus *n.* Short-thumbed African monkey of genus *Colobus.* [mod. L, f. Gk *kolobos* docked]

cŏ'locȳnth *n.* (Bitter-apple, gourd plant with bitter-pulped fruit used as) purgative drug. [f. L f. Gk *kolokunthis*]

colō'gne (-ō'n) *n.* Eau-de-Cologne. [abbr.]

cō'lon¹ (*or* -ŏn) *n.* (Anat.) Greater part of large intestine, from caecum to rectum; hence **colŏ'n**IC *a.*, ~I'TIS *n.* [ME, f. OF or f. L f. Gk *kolon*]

cō'lon² *n.* Punctuation-mark (:), used esp. to mark antithesis, illustration, listing, or (sometimes with dash:—) quotation, or between numbers in a proportion, Bibl. reference, etc. [f. L f. Gk *kōlon* limb, clause]

colonel (kẽr'nel) *n.* Highest regimental officer; = LIEUTENANT-*colonel*; *Colonel* BLIMP; *Colonel-in*-CHIEF¹; hence ~CY *n.* [f. obs. F *coronel* f. It. *colonnello* (*colonna* COLUMN)]

colō'nĭal *a.* & *n.* (Native or inhabitant) of a colony, esp. of a British Crown Colony; *(house etc.) built or designed in, or in style characteristic of, the period of the British colonies in America before they became the U.S.; **~ goose,** (Austral. & N.Z.) stuffed boned mutton; ||**C~ Office,** (Hist.) government department in charge of colonies; hence ~LY² *adv.* [F, or f. COLONY + -AL]

colō'nĭal|ĭsm *n.* Policy of maintaining colonies, (esp., derog.) alleged policy of exploitation of backward or weak peoples, whence ~IST (2) *n.*; colonial idiom. [f. prec. + -ISM]

cŏ'lonĭst *n.* Settler in or inhabitant of colony. [f. foll. + -IST]

cŏ'lonīz|e, -īs|e (-īz), *v.* **1.** *v.t.* Establish colony in; *(Polit.) plant voters in (a district) for party purposes. **2.** *v.i.* Establish or join a colony. **3.** Hence ~A'TION, ~ER¹, *ns.* [f. COLONY + -IZE]

cŏlonnā'd|e *n.* Series of columns with entablature; row of trees etc.; hence ~ED² *a.* [F (*colonne* COLUMN; see -ADE)]

cŏ'lonȳ *n.* **1.** Settlement or settlers in new country forming community fully or partly subject to mother State; their territory; people of one nationality or occupation in a city, esp. if living more or less in isolation or in a special quarter (so of animals, *colony of sparrows* etc.); segregated group (*leper colony, nudist colony*); (Biol.) aggregate of animals, plants, etc., connected or living close together. **2.** (Gk Hist.) independent city founded by emigrants; (Rom. Hist.) garrison settlement (usu. of veteran soldiers) in conquered territory. [ME, f. L *colonia* (*colonus* farmer f. *colere* cultivate; see -Y¹)]

cŏ'lophon *n.* Tailpiece in old manuscript or book, often ornamental, giving writer's or printer's name, date, etc. (**from title-page to ~**, from cover to cover); publisher's device on title-page, imprint. [LL f. Gk *kolophōn* summit, finishing touch]

colŏ'phonȳ *n.* Dark resin distilled from turpentine and water, rosin. [f. L *colophonia* (*resina* resin) of *Colophon* in Lydia]

cŏloquĭ'ntĭda. Var. of COLOCYNTH.

***color¹,².** See COLOUR¹,².

Cŏlora'dō (-rah'-) *n.* ~ **beetle,** yellow black-striped beetle, destructive to potato plant. [~ in U.S.]

cŏlo(u)rā'tion (-ler-; *or* kŭ-) *n.* Colouring, method of putting on or arranging colour; natural, esp. variegated, colour of living or other things. [F, or f. LL *coloratio* (*colorare* COLOUR²; see -ATION)]

cŏloratur'a (-ahtoor'*a*) *n.* Florid passages in vocal music; singer of these, esp. soprano. [It., f. L *colorare* COLOUR²; cf. -URE]

cŏlorĭ'fĭc (*or* kŭ-) *a.* Producing colour(s); highly coloured. [f. F *colorifique* or mod. L *colorificus* (as COLOUR¹; see -FIC)]

cŏlorĭ'|mèter (*or* kŭ-) *n.* Instrument for measuring intensity of colour; hence **~mĕ'tric** *a.*, ~METRY *n.* [f. L *color* COLOUR¹ + -I- + -METER]

colŏ'ssal *a.* Of or like a colossus; gigantic, huge; (colloq.) remarkable, splendid, delightful; (Archit., of order) more than one storey high; hence ~LY² *adv.* [F (*colosse* COLOSSUS; see -AL)]

colŏ'ss|us *n.* (*pl.* **~i** *pr.* -ī, *or* **~uses**). Statue of much more than life size; gigantic person or personified empire etc., esp. conceived (like Colossus of Rhodes) as standing astride over dominions. [L, f. Gk *kolossos*]

colŏ'stomȳ *n.* (Surg.) Incision in colon to provide artificial anus through abdominal wall in cases of stricture etc. [f. as COLON¹ + -O- + Gk *stoma* mouth + -Y¹]

colŏ'strum *n.* First milk of mammal after parturition. [L]

colŏ'tomȳ *n.* (Surg.) Incision in colon. [f. as COLON¹ + -O- + -TOMY]

co'lour¹, *co'lor¹, (kŭ'l*er*) *n.* **1.** Sensation produced on eye by rays of light when resolved by prism, selective reflection, etc. (cf. *black*, effect produced by no light or by surface reflecting no rays, and *white*, effect produced by rays of unresolved light). **2.** Particular hue; one, or any mixture, of the constituents into which light can be separated as in spectrum, including (loosely) black and white (**complementary ~,** colour that combined with given colour makes white; **primary ~s,** red, green, and violet, or for paints etc. red, blue, and yellow, giving all others by mixture; **secondary ~,** mixture of two primary colours); (Photog. etc.) use of all colours, not only black and white; *man* etc. **of ~,** of non-white race, esp. Negro; **see the ~ of** person's **money,** receive some evidence of forthcoming payment from him. **3.** Ruddiness of face (*lose, gain, colour*; **change ~,** turn pale or red; OFF *colour*). **4.** (usu. in *pl.*) Appearance, aspect, (*paint in bright, dark colours*; *see in its true colours*). **5.** (Art). Colouring, colour-system, -perception, effects as of colour got by light and shade in engraving, whence ~IST (3) *n.*; pigment, paint; blackness of printed type; conventional colour (gules, azure, etc.) used in heraldry. **6.** (in *pl.*) Coloured ribbon, dress, etc., worn as symbol of party, membership of club, etc. (||**get** one's, **give** person **his, ~s,** be included, include him, in sports team esp. as regular member; *show* one's **~s,** one's party or character); (in *sing.*) sportsman awarded colours. **7.** Flag of ship, pair of silken flags (**Queen's** or **King's ~, regimental ~**) carried by regiment, (TROOP*ing the colour* or *colours*; **with the ~s,** serving in army; *sail under* FALSE *colours*; **come off with flying ~s,** win credit; **nail ~s to mast,** persist, refuse to give in); (in *pl.*) national flag. **8.** Show of reason, pretext, false plea, (*lend colour to*; *under colour of*). **9.** (Mus.) Timbre, quality; variety of expression. **10.** Character, tone, quality, mood, shade of meaning, (*take* one's *colour from*). **11.** (In literature) picturesqueness, ornate style, (LOCAL² *colour*). **12.** ~ **atlas,** chart exemplifying shades of colour; ~ **bar,** legal or social discrimination between white and non-white persons; **~-blind,** unable to distinguish certain colours; **~-box** (of assorted artists'-paints); ***~cast,** broadcast of colour television; ~ **code,** use of colours as standard means of identification; **~-fast,** dyed in colours that will not fade or be washed out; ~ **line,** social demarcation between white and non-white persons; **~-man,** dealer in paints; ~ **scheme,** arrangement of colours esp. in design of room decoration or garden planting; **~-sergeant,** senior sergeant of infantry company; ~ **supplement** (with coloured illustrations, to newspaper etc. otherwise printed without colour); **~-wash** *n.*, & *v.t.*, (paint with) coloured distemper. **13.** Hence ~FUL *a.*, full of colour or interest, bright, gay, (lit. or fig.). [ME f. OF *color, -our* f. L *color*]

co'lour², *co'lor², (kŭ'l*er*) *v.* **1.** *v.t.* Give colour to; paint, stain, dye; disguise; misrepresent (*highly coloured details*); (fig.) imbue with its own colour (*emotion colours* one's *judgement*). **2.** *v.i.* Take on colour; ~ (**up**), blush. [ME, f. OF *colo(u)rer* f. L *colorare* (*color* COLOUR¹)]

co'lourab|le, *-or-, (kŭ'l*er*-) *a.* Specious, plausible, counterfeit; hence ~LY² *adv.* [ME, f. COLOUR¹ + -ABLE]

colouration. See COLORATION.

co'loured, *-or-, (kŭ'l*er*d) *a.* & *n.* Having colour(s); (person) wholly or partly of non-white descent; (**C~**; S. Afr.) (person) of mixed brown and white or black and white descent. [p.p. of COLOUR²]

co'louring, *-or-, (kŭ'l*er*-) *n.* In vbl senses; style in which thing is coloured, or in which artist employs colour; facial complexion. [f. COLOUR² + -ING¹]

co'lourist, *-or-, (kŭ'l*er*-) *n.* See COLOUR¹ 5.

co'lourlèss, *-or-, (kŭ'l*er*-) *a.* Without colour;

pale; dull-hued; lacking character or vividness; neutral, impartial, indifferent; hence ~LY² *adv.*, ~NESS *n.* [f. COLOUR¹ + -LESS]

co'loury̆, *-ory̆, (kŭ'lerĭ) *a.* Having colour, esp. indicative of good quality. [f. COLOUR¹ + -Y²]

cŏ'lpo- *comb. form.* Vagina, as: **~scope,** instrument for inspection of vagina; ~TOMY (-ŏ't-) *n.* [f. Gk *kolpos* womb]

cŏlpor̂teur' (-ter̂'; *or* kŏ'l-) *n.* Book-pedlar, esp. employed by a society to distribute Bibles. [F (*colporter* prob. f. *comporter* transport f. L COM-*portare*)]

cōlt¹ *n.* Young male horse from when it is taken from dam to age of usu. 4 or 5; (Bibl.) young camel; inexperienced person, esp. young cricketer etc. in junior team; **~'sfoot,** common large-leaved yellow-flowered weed; hence ~'HOOD (-t-h-) *n.*, ~'ISH¹ *a.* [OE, = young ass or camel, of unkn. orig.; perh. f. Scand.]

Cōlt² *n.* Type of automatic firearm, esp. repeating pistol. [P; f. S. ~, U.S. inventor d. 1862]

***cō'lter.** See COULTER.

cŏ'lūbrīne *a.* Snakelike; esp., of or like the Colubrinae, a subfamily of non-poisonous snakes. [f. L *colubrinus* (*coluber* snake; see -INE¹)]

cŏlumbār̂'ĭ|um *n.* (*pl.* **~a**). Building with niches for reception of cinerary urns. [L, = pigeon--house (*columba* pigeon; see -ARIUM)]

cŏ'lumbīne¹ *n.* Garden plant with flower like five clustered pigeons, aquilegia. [ME, f. OF *colombine* f. med. L *columbina* (*herba*) (*columba* pigeon; see -INE¹)]

Cŏ'lumbīne² *n.* Partner of Harlequin in pantomime. [f. F *Colombine* f. It. *Colombina* (*colombino* dovelike)]

***colŭ'mb|ium** *n.* (Chem.) Niobium; hence ~ITE¹ *n.*, native ore of iron and niobium. [f. *Columbia* (poet.) America = -IUM]

cŏ'lumn (-*u*m) *n.* **1.** (Archit.) Long vertical often slightly tapering cylinder usu. supporting entablature or arch, or alone as monument. **2.** Column-shaped object (e.g. part of animal body or plant, part of machine, etc.); vertical cylindrical mass of liquid or vapour. **3.** Vertical division of page, table, etc., for figures etc., or to reduce length of lines in printed matter (**~-inch,** quantity of print occupying one inch length of column); part of newspaper, sometimes more or less than one column, devoted to special subject, as *advertisement columns*, PERSONAL *column*; **our ~s, the ~s of** *The Times*, etc., contents of newspaper; hence ~IST (*or* -mn-) *n.*, journalist who regularly contributes to a newspaper a column esp. of miscellaneous comment on people and events. **4.** Narrow-fronted deep arrangement of troops or armoured vehicles in successive lines (**dodge the ~,** (colloq.) shirk duty, avoid work; FIFTH *column*); similar arrangement of ships; *party, faction. **5.** Hence or cogn. **colŭ'mn**AR¹, ~ED² (-md), *adjs.* [ME, f. OF *columpne* & f. L *columna* pillar]

colūr̂'e *n.* (Astron.) One of two great circles intersecting at right angles at poles and dividing celestial equator and ecliptic into four equal parts, one passing through equinoctial, and one through solstitial, points of ecliptic. [ME, f. LL f. Gk *kolouros* truncated]

cŏ'lza *n.* Rape plant; **~-oil** (made from it and used in lamps etc.). [f. F *kolza*(*t*) f. LG *kōlsāt* (see COLE, SEED)]

com- *pref.* meaning 'with', 'together', 'jointly', 'altogether'; used before *b*, *m*, *p*, and occas. before vowels and *f*, becoming co- before vowels, *h*, and *gn*, *col-* before *l*, *cor-* before *r*, and *con-* before other consonants. [f. L *com-*, *cum* with]

cō'ma¹ *n.* Unnatural heavy sleep, prolonged unconsciousness; hence **~to**SE¹ *a.* [f. med. L f. Gk *kōma -atos* deep sleep]

cō'ma² *n.* (*pl.* **~e**). (Bot.) tuft of silky hairs at end of seed; (Astron.) nebulous envelope round nucleus of comet. [L, f. Gk *komē* hair of head]

cōmb¹ (-m) *n.* **1.** Toothed strip of bone, metal, etc., for arranging, cleaning, or confining the hair; = CURRY²-*comb*. **2.** Thing of same shape, look, or purpose, in many machines, esp. for dressing wool, or collecting electricity, or in animal structure; red fleshy crest of fowl esp. cock, analogous growth in other birds; = HONEYCOMB. **3.** Hence (-)~ED² (-md) *a.* [OE *camb*, = OS *camb*, OHG *kamb*, ON *kambr* f. Gmc **kambaz*]

cōmb² (-m) *v.* **1.** *v.t.* Draw comb through (hair), curry (horse), dress (wool, flax) with comb; (colloq.) search (place) thoroughly; **~ out,** arrange (hair) with comb, search or attack systematically, separate for removal, so **~-out** *n.* **2.** *v.i.* (Of wave) curl over. [ME, f. prec.]

cŏ'mbat (*or* kŭ'-) *n.*, & *v.t.* & *i.* (Engage in) battle or contest (**single ~,** duel); oppose, strive against; **~ fatigue,** mental disorder due to stress in wartime combat. [f. F *combat* f. *combattre* f. LL (COM-, **battere* f. L *batuere* fight)]

cŏ'mbatant (*or* kŭ'-) *a.* & *n.* (Person) that fights. [OF part. (as prec.; see -ANT)]

cŏ'mbatĭve (*or* kŭ'-) *a.* Pugnacious; hence ~LY² (-vlĭ) *adv.*, ~NESS (-vn-) *n.* [f. COMBAT V. + -IVE]

||combe. See COOMB.

cō'mber¹ (-m*er*) *n.* In vbl senses; machine for combing cotton or wool very fine; long curling wave, breaker. [f. COMB² + -ER¹]

||cŏ'mber² *n.* Fish of sea-perch family, *Serranus cabrilla*. [18th c.; orig. unkn.]

cŏmbĭnā'tion *n.* **1.** Combining; combined state (*in combination with*); combined set of things or persons; small instrumental band; (Math.) group of things chosen from a larger number without regard to their arrangment. **2.** United action; (Chess) ingenious sequence of moves. **3.** (Chem.) Union of substances in compound whose properties differ from theirs. **4.** ||(in *pl.*) Single undergarment for body and legs. **5.** ||Motor cycle with side-car attached. **6.** Sequence of numbers etc. used to open **~ lock** (complicated locking arrangement used for safes, strong-rooms, etc.). **7.** **||~-room,** (Cambridge Univ.) = COMMON¹-*room*. **8.** Hence **cŏ'mbĭn**ATIVE *a.* [obs. F, or f. LL *combinatio* (as COMBINE; see -ATION)]

cŏmbĭnatōr̂'ĭal *a.* (Math.) Relating to combinations of items selected from larger groups. [f. prec. + -ORY + -AL]

combī'ne¹ *v.t.* & *i.* Join together, unite for common purpose; possess (esp, qualities usu. separate) together; (cause to) coalesce in one substance, form chemical compound; co-operate; **~d operation** (in which fighting services, or others, co-operate); **combining form,** (Gram.) special form of word used in combinations (e.g. *Anglo-* repr. *English*). [ME, f. OF *combiner* or f. LL COM(*binare* f. L *bini* two together)]

cŏ'mbīne² *n.* Combination of persons or firms to control prices etc.; **~ (harvester),** combined reaping and threshing machine. [f. prec.]

cō'mbĭng (-mĭ-) *n.* In vbl senses; (in *pl.*) hairs combed off; **~-wool** (long-stapled, suitable for combing and making into worsted). [f. COMB² + -ING¹]

cŏ'mbō *n.* (*pl.* **~s**). (sl.) Combination (esp. of jazz instruments). [abbr.; see -o]

||cŏmbs (-mz) *n. pl.* (colloq.) Combinations (undergarments). [abbr.]

combŭ'st *v.t.* Subject to combustion. [f. obs. *combust* adj. f. L *combustus* p.p. (as COMBUSTION)]

combŭ'st|ĭble *a.* & *n.* (Substance or thing) capable of or used for burning; excitable; hence

~IBI'LITY *n.* [F, or f. med. L *combustibilis* (as foll.; see -IBLE)]

combŭ'stion (-sch*o*n) *n.* **1.** Consumption by fire. **2.** (Chem. etc.) Development of light and heat with chemical combination (SPONTANEOUS *combustion*); oxidation of organic tissue. [ME f. F, or f. LL *combustio* f. L *comburere -ust-* burn up]

come (kŭm) *v.i.* (**came** *pr.* kām; **come**). **1.** Start or move towards, or arrive at, a point, time, or result, specified or obvious; *come of* AGE[1]; *come to* BLOW[5]*s*; EASY *come, easy go*; *come to an* END[1]; **~ and go,** pass to and fro, pay brief visit(s), be transitory (so **~-and-go** *n.*); **not know whether** one **is coming or going,** be utterly confused; *come to* GRIEF; *come to* HAND[1]; *come* HOME[1] *to*; *come to* LIGHT[1]; **~ to a point,** taper; *come* SHORT; *come into the* WORLD. **2.** (in *subj.*) **~ Friday,** when Friday comes; *two years* **~ Christmas,** including time from now to Christmas. **3.** Be brought (*the grocery order came*; *come to* one's *attention*; *came to no harm*); be available (*this dress comes in three sizes*); **as** (*tough* etc.) **as they ~,** supremely. **4.** Become perceivable e.g. by motion of beholder etc. (*church came into sight* or *view*; *news came as a surprise*). **5.** Reach or extend to specified point (*motorway comes within ten miles of us*). **6.** Occur, take or occupy specified position (*comes on page 20, within the scope of the inquiry*; *one comes before, after, another*; *ideas come into* one's *head*). **7.** Happen (*how comes it that . . .?*; *how did you come to break your leg?*); **how ~?,** (colloq.) how did that happen?; **to ~** *pred. a.*, future (*for a year to come*); **~ what may,** whatever happens. **8.** Become present instead of future (**~ to pass,** happen; *the time will come when*); **coming man,** person likely to be important in future; **coming week** etc., next following the present; **have it coming to** one, (colloq.) deserve what one suffers. **9.** Spring *of*, be the result *of*, (*that's what comes of grumbling*; *nothing came of it*; *come of noble parents*). **10.** Enter or be brought *into* (collision, play, prominence). **11.** Amount or be equivalent *to* (*total comes to £2*; *the idea came to nothing*; **if it ~s to that,** in that case). **12.** Take form (*the butter will not come*). **13.** Reach specified state (*have come to believe*; *has come to be used wrongly*; *string came undone, untied*; *all came right in the end*; *come* TRUE; *come expensive, easy, natural to* one); *come unstuck* (see UNSTICK). **14.** (w. cogn. obj.) Traverse, accomplish, (*have come 3 miles, a long way*). **15.** (sl.) Play a part (*come the bully over*; **~ it strong,** show vigour; **~ it too strong,** overdo something, exaggerate). **16.** (vulg.) Experience sexual orgasm. **17.** (in *imper.* as excl.) Now then (encouraging), think again, don't be hasty. **18.** (w. *advs.*): **~ about,** happen (and cf. ABOUT 9); **~ across,** (sl.) be perceived or effective, part *with* (money etc.); *come* AGAIN; **~ along,** (colloq., in *imper.*) make haste; *come* APART; **~ away,** become detached, be left *with* (impression etc.); **~ back,** return (*to* place, subject), recur to memory, *retaliate or retort; **~-back** *n.*, return to or reinstatement in one's former position (*stage a come-back*), (sl.) retort, (Austral. & N.Z.) sheep bred for both wool and meat; **~ by,** pass; **~ clean,** confess; **~ down,** come to place regarded as lower, be handed down by tradition, fall (esp. in price), (of aircraft) land, make decision (*in favour of* etc.), amount basically *to*, be humbled (esp. *in the world*, lose social status); **~-down** *n.*, downfall, degradation; **~ down on,** pounce on, rebuke, punish, exact reparation from; **~ down with,** pay (money), begin to suffer from (disease); *come* FORWARD[2]; **~-hi'ther** *a.*, enticing, flirtatious; **~ in,** enter house or room, (Cricket) begin innings, take specified place in race etc. (*come in third*), be elected, come to power, be received as income, begin radio transmission, become seasonable or fashionable, serve a purpose (esp. *come in useful*), find a place (*where does the joke come in?*; **where do I ~ in?,** what is my role?, how are my interests advanced?); **~ in for,** get share of, get; **this is where we came in,** this is the same point as we started from; **~ off,** be detached, extricate oneself from contest etc. (*with flying colours, badly*), be accomplished, fulfilled, or successful, (Cricket) cease bowling, (of play etc.) reach end of run, (vulg.) = *come* (sense 16); **~ on,** continue coming, advance esp. to attack, progress, thrive, begin, be heard or seen on television, telephone, etc., (of wind, storm, disease) supervene, arise to be discussed, appear on stage or scene, (Cricket) begin to bowl, (in *imper.*) hurry, follow me, please do what I ask, I defy you; **~-on** *n.*, (sl.) lure, swindler; **~ out,** go on strike, emerge from examination etc. with specified result, emerge from clouds, be revealed, declare oneself (*for* or *against*), be satisfactorily visible in photograph, be solved, become covered *in* (rash etc.), be published (*comes out on Saturdays*), make début on stage or in society; **~ out with,** utter; **~ over,** come from some distance or across obstacle (*came over with the Conqueror, over from London to see us*), change sides or opinion, (colloq.) undergo a feeling (*come over faint*); **~ round,** make informal or casual visit, recover from ill temper or unconsciousness, be converted to other person's opinion; **~ to,** cease moving, regain consciousness, revive; **~ up,** come to place regarded as higher, join university, approach person for talk, get abreast *with*, arise from out of ground, become fashionable, be discussed, present itself, be equal *to* standard etc.; **~ up with,** produce (idea etc.) in response to challenge; **coming up,** (colloq., of food etc.) ready, about to be served. **19.** (w. *preps.*): **~ across,** meet by chance; **~ at,** reach, get access to, (whence **~-a't-able** *a.*), attack; **~ before,** be dealt with by (judge etc.); **~ between,** interfere with relationship of (persons); **~ by,** obtain; **~ into,** receive esp. as heir, and see sense 10; **~ near doing** (narrowly escape or fail); **~ off it,** (colloq.) stop talking or acting like that; **~ on** = *come upon*; **~ over,** gain influence over (*what has come over you to behave like this?*); **~ to,** inherit, return to (one*self* or one's *senses*, from unconsciousness, folly, etc.), equal in total, amount to (see sense 11), be assigned by fate or by another to, arrive at (*what is the world coming to?*); **~ under,** be classed as or among, be subject to (influence or authority); **~ upon,** attack by surprise, make demand on, be burden to, meet by chance; **~ with,** (of things) (normally) accompany or be supplied together with (*this model comes with optional features*) (cf. sense 3). [OE *cuman*, = OS *cuman*, OHG *queman*, *coman*, ON *koma*, Goth. *qiman* f. Gmc **kweman*, **kuman*]

comē'dĭan *n.* Actor in comedy; humorous performer on stage, radio, etc. [f. F *comédien* (*comédie* COMEDY)]

comē'dĭc *a.* Of comedy. [f. L f. Gk *kōmōidikos* (as COMEDY; see -IC)]

comēdĭē'nne *n.* Woman comedian. [F, fem., as COMEDIAN]

cŏ'mėdĭst *n.* Writer of comedies. [f. COMEDY + -IST]

cŏ'mėdō *n.* (*pl.* **~nes** *pr.* -ō'nēz). (Med.) Blackhead. [L, = glutton (*comedere* eat up)]

For other words in *co-* see CO-.

cŏ'mĕdy̆ *n.* Stage-play of light, amusing, and often satirical character, chiefly representing everyday life, and with happy ending (cf. TRAGEDY; *comedy of* MANNERS); humorous or farcical incident in life; humour. [ME, f. OF *comedie* f. L f. Gk *kōmōidia* (*kōmōidos* comic poet f. *kōmos* revel]

co'mel|y̆ (kŭ'mlĭ) *a.* Pleasant to look at (usu. of personal appearance); hence **~ĭness** *n.* [ME *cumelich, cumli* prob. f. *becumelich* (BECOME, -LY[1])]

co'mer (kŭ'-) *n.* In vbl senses (usu. qualified, as *first comer*; **all ~s,** anyone who applies, takes up a challenge, etc.); *(colloq.) coming man. [f. COME + -ER[1]]

comĕ'stĭble *n.* (usu. in *pl.*) Thing to eat. [ME f. F, f. med. L *comestibilis* f. L *comedere -est-* eat up]

cŏ'mĕt *n.* (Astron.) Hazy object usu. with star-like nucleus and with tail pointing away from sun, moving in elliptical or nearly parabolic path about the sun; hence **~ARY[1]** *a.* [ME f. OF *comete* f. L *cometa* f. Gk *komētēs* long-haired (star); cf. -ET[2]]

come-ŭ'ppance (kŭm-) *n.* (sl.) One's deserts (for misbehaviour etc.). [f. COME + UP + -ANCE]

co'mfĭt (kŭ'-) *n.* (arch.) Sweet containing nut, seed, etc., in sugar. [ME, f. OF *confit* f. L CON(*fectum* = *factum* neut. p.p. of *facere* make)]

co'mfort (kŭ'-) *n.*, & *v.t.* **1.** *n.* Relief in affliction, consolation, being consoled (COLD[1] *comfort*); person who consoles one or saves one trouble; cause of satisfaction; physical well-being, being comfortable; possession of **~s,** things that make life easy (**creature ~s,** good food, clothes, etc.); *warm quilt; ***~ station,** public lavatory; hence **~LESS** *a.* **2.** *v.t.* Soothe in grief, console; make comfortable. [ME, f. OF *confort(er)* f. LL *confortare* strengthen (as CON-, L *fortis* strong)]

co'mfortab|le (kŭ'-) *a.* & *n.* **1.** *a.* Such as to obviate hardship, save trouble, and promote content, ministering to comfort; at ease, free from hardship, pain, and trouble; enjoying comfort, having ample money for one's needs; having an easy conscience; hence **~LY[2]** *adv.* **2. C~le Words,** four scriptural passages following and confirming the Absolution in the Communion Office. **3.** *n.* *Warm quilt. [ME, f. AF *confortable* (as prec.; see -ABLE)]

co'mforter (kŭ'-) *n.* One who comforts (**the C~,** Holy Spirit; JOB[4]'*s comforter*); ||baby's dummy teat of rubber etc.; ||woollen scarf; *warm quilt. [ME, f. AF *confortour*, OF *-ëor* (as prec.; see -ER[1])]

co'mfrey (kŭ'-) *n.* Tall rough-leaved ditch-plant of genus *Symphytum*, with clusters of usu. white or purple bells. [ME, f. AF *cumfrie*, OF *confi(e)re* f. med. L **confervia*, L *conferva* f. CON(*fervēre* boil)]

co'mfy̆ (kŭ'-) *a.* (colloq.) Comfortable. [abbr.; see -Y[3]]

cŏ'mĭc *a.* & *n.* **1.** *a.* Of, in the style of, comedy; causing or meant to cause laughter, facetious, burlesque, funny, (*comic paper, song*). **2.** *Comic* OPERA[1]; *comic* STRIP[2]. **3.** *n.* (colloq.) Theatre etc. comedian; amusing person; comic paper, e.g. (orig. children's) periodical with narrative mainly in pictures. [f. L f. Gk *kōmikos* (*kōmos* revel; see -IC)]

cŏ'mĭcal *a.* Causing laughter; hence **~ITY** (-ă'l-) *n.*, **~LY[2]** *adv.* [f. as prec. + -AL]

coming. See COME.

Cŏ'mĭntērn *n.* Third INTERNATIONAL. [f. Russ. *Komintern* (*kommunisticheskiĭ* communist, *internatsional'nyĭ* international)]

cŏmĭtă'dji *n.* Member of band of irregular soldiers in Balkans. [common Balkan form, f. Turk. *komitacı*, lit. 'member of a (revolutionary) committee']

cŏ'mĭty̆ *n.* Courtesy (**~ of nations,** friendly recognition as far as practicable of each other's laws and usages); association of nations etc. for mutual benefit. [f. L *comitas* (*comis* courteous; see -ITY)]

cŏ'mma *n.* Punctuation-mark (,) of the least separation indicated between parts of sentence, also used to separate (groups of) figures etc., (INVERT[1]*ed comma*); (Mus.) definite minute interval or difference of pitch; **~ bacillus** (comma-shaped kind causing cholera); **~ (butterfly),** kind with white comma-shaped mark on under-side of hind wings. [f. L f. Gk *komma* clause]

comma'nd[1] (-ah'-) *v.* **1.** *v.t.* Give command(s) to, order, bid, (*what God commands, commands us, commands us to do, commands that we should do, commands to be done*; *let us do as God commands*; *God commands and man obeys*); have authority over or control of; be in command of (ship, forces, etc.). **2.** Restrain, master, (passions, one*self*); have at disposal or within reach (money, skill, person; so **yours to ~,** (arch.) yours obediently); deserve and get (sympathy etc.); dominate (strategic position) from superior height, look down over. **3.** *v.i.* Be supreme; be in command. [ME, f. AF *comaunder*, OF *comander* f. LL *commandare* COMMEND]

comma'nd[2] (-ah'-) *n.* **1.** Authoritative statement that person must do something, order, bidding, (**at** or **by** person's **~,** in pursuance of his bidding; **word of ~,** customary order for movement in drill); description of operation in computer, signal initiating such operation. **2.** Exercise or tenure of authority, esp. naval or military (**in ~ of,** commanding; **under ~ of,** commanded by; HIGH *command*). **3.** Control, mastery, possession, (**great ~ of language,** skill in speech; **at ~,** ready to be used at will). **4.** Body of troops etc., district, under commander (*Bomber Command, Western Command*). **5. ~ module,** control compartment in spacecraft; **~ night, performance,** theatrical etc. performance given by royal command; ||**C~ Paper,** paper laid by command of the Crown before Parliament etc.; **~ post,** headquarters of military unit. [f. prec.]

cŏmmandă'nt *n.* Commanding officer, esp. of particular force, military academy, etc.; *Commandant-in-*CHIEF[1]; hence **~SHIP** (1) *n.* [F, or f. It. or Sp. *commandante* (see COMMAND[1], -ANT)]

cŏmmandeer' *v.t.* Seize (men or goods) for military service; take arbitrary possession of. [f. S. Afr. Du. *kommanderen* f. F *commander* COMMAND[1]]

comma'nder (-ah'-) *n.* **1.** One who commands (*Commander-in-*CHIEF[1]; **C~ of the Faithful,** title of Caliph); naval officer just below captain; ||WING *commander*; officer in charge of police district. **2.** Member of higher class in some orders of knighthood. **3.** Hence **~SHIP** (1) *n.* **4.** Large wooden mallet. [ME, f. OF *comandere*, *-ëor* f. Rom. **commandator* (as COMMAND[1]; see -OR)]

comma'ndĭng (-ah'-) *a.* In vbl senses; (of person, looks, ability, etc.) dignified, exalted, impressive; (of hill, position, etc.) giving wide view. [f. COMMAND[1] + -ING[2]]

comma'ndment (-ah'-) *n.* Divine command; **the Ten C~s,** those given by God to Moses on Mt. Sinai (Exod. 20: 1–17). [ME, f. OF *comandement* (as COMMAND[1]; see -MENT)]

comma'ndō (-ah'-) *n.* (*pl.* **~s**). Party called out for military service, body of troops; (member of) unit of British amphibious shock troops; (member of) similar troops elsewhere. [Port. (*commandar* COMMAND[1])]

commedia dell'arte (kŏmĕdĭa dĕl ar'tā) *n.* Improvised popular comedy in Italian theatres of 16th–18th c., with **stock characters.** [It., = comedy of art]

comme il faut (kŏm ēl fō′) *pred. a.*, & *adv.* Proper(ly), as it should be, (esp. of behaviour etc.). [F, = as is necessary]
commĕ′morāt|e *v.t.* Celebrate in speech or writing; preserve in memory by some celebration; (of thing) be a memorial of; hence ~IVE *a.* [f. L COM(*memorare* relate) + -ATE[3]]
commĕmorā′tion *n.* Act of commemorating; service or part of service in memory of saint or sacred event; ‖(Oxford Univ.) annual celebration in memory of founders and benefactors (~ **ball,** dance held at time close to this). [ME f. F, or f. L *commemoratio* (as prec.; see -ATION)]
commĕ′nce *v.t.* Begin (work, do*ing*, *to* do, or abs.); ‖take university degree of (M.A. etc.); (arch.) begin to act or work as (*commence author*). [ME, f. OF *com(m)encier* f. Rom. **cominitiare* (as COM-, L *initiare* INITIATE[1])]
commĕ′ncement (-sm-) *n.* Commencing; ceremony of degree conferment. [ME, f. OF (as prec.; see -MENT)]
commĕ′nd *v.t.* Entrust, commit, (thing *to* person's *care*; *dying man commends his soul to God*); praise (**highly ~ed** *competitor*, just missing prize-list); recommend (*I commend this method to you*; *method commends itself*); **~ me to,** (arch.) remember me kindly to, (often iron.) I prefer. [ME, f. L COM(*mendare* = *mandare* entrust; see MANDATE[1])]
commĕ′ndable *a.* Praiseworthy; hence ~NESS (-beln-) *n.*, **commĕ′ndab**LY[2] *adv.* [ME f. OF, f. L *commendabilis* (as prec.; see -ABLE)]
cŏmmĕndā′tion *n.* Praise; act of commending or recommending (esp. person to another's favour). [ME f. OF, f. L *commendatio* (as COMMEND; see -ATION)]
commĕ′ndatorў *a.* Commending, recommending. [f. LL *commendatorius* (as prec.; see -ORY)]
commĕ′nsal *a.* & *n.* (One) who eats at the same table; (animal or plant) living harmlessly with or in another and sharing its food; hence ~ISM (1), ~ITY (-ă′l-), *ns.* [ME f. F, or f. med. L COM(*mensalis* f. *mensa* table); see -AL]
commĕ′nsur|able (-sh*er- or* -sy*er*-) *a.* Measurable by the same standard (*with, to*); (of numbers) in ratio equal to ratio of integers; proportionate *to*; hence ~ABI′LITY, **~able**NESS (-beln-), *ns.*, **~ab**LY[2] *adv.* [f. LL COM(*mensurabilis*, as MEASURE[1]; see -ABLE)]
commĕ′nsurate (-sh*er- or* -sy*er*-) *a.* Coextensive (*with*); proportionate (*to, with*); hence ~LY[2] (-tlĭ) *adv.*, ~NESS (-tn-) *n.* [f. LL COM(*mensuratus*, as prec.; see -ATE[2])]
cŏ′mmĕnt[1] *n.* Explanatory note; remark; criticism; (fig., of event etc.) illustration (*the play is a comment on present-day values*); **no ~,** (colloq.) I decline to answer your question. [ME, f. L *commentum* contrivance (in LL also = interpretation), neut. p.p. of *comminisci* devise]
cŏ′mmĕnt[2] *v.i.* Write explanatory notes *on*; make (esp. unfavourable) remarks (*on, that*). [f. prec., or F *commenter* f. as prec.]
cŏ′mmentarў *n.* Expository treatise; series of comments on various points in book or remarks (esp. broadcast, or accompanying film) on event or performance; comment. [f. L *commentarius*, *-ium* a. used as n. (as COMMENT[1]; see -ARY[1])]
cŏ′mmentāte *v.i.* Act as commentator. [back form. f. foll.]
cŏ′mmentātor *n.* Writer or speaker of commentary; one who comments on current events. [L (*commentari* frequent. of *comminisci* devise; see -OR)]
cŏ′mmerce *n.* Exchange of merchandise or services, esp. on a large scale; CHAMBER *of Commerce*; (arch.) intercourse (esp. sexual). [F, or f. L COM(*mercium* f. *merx mercis* merchandise)]
commer′cial (-sh*a*l) *a.* & *n.* **1.** *a.* Of, engaged in, bearing on, commerce; interested in financial return rather than artistry; (of chemicals) unpurified. **2. ~ art,** art used in advertising etc.; **~ broadcasting** (in which advertisements are included to gain revenue); **~ college** etc. (giving instruction in commercial subjects); ‖**~ traveller,** firm's representative who visits shops etc. to show samples and get orders; **~ vehicle** (used for transport of goods or fare-paying passengers). **3.** Hence ~ISM (2, 3) *n.*, ~IZE (3) *v.t.*, make (purely) commercial, derive commercial profit from, ~LY[2] *adv.* **4.** *n.* Commercial announcement or broadcast programme; broadcast advertisement; (arch.) commercial traveller. [f. prec. + -IAL]
‖**cŏ′mmère** (-mār) *n.* Female compère. [F, fem. of COMPÈRE]
Cŏ′mmie *n.* (sl.) Communist. [abbr. + -IE]
cŏmmĭnā′tion *n.* Threatening of divine vengeance; recital of divine threats against sinners in Anglican Liturgy for Ash Wednesday, service that includes this. [ME, f. L *comminatio* (*comminari* threaten; see -ATION)]
cŏ′mmĭnatorў *a.* Threatening, denunciatory. [f. med. L *comminatorius* (as prec.; see -ORY)]
commĭ′ngle (-ngg*e*l) *v.t.* & *i.* Mingle together. [f. COM- + MINGLE]
cŏ′mmĭnūte *v.t.* Reduce to small fragments (**~d fracture,** one producing multiple fragments of bone); divide (property) into small portions; so **cŏmmĭnū′**TION *n.* [f. L COM(*minuere -ut-* lessen)]
cŏ′mmĭs (-mĭ) *n.* (*pl.* same *pr.* same *or* -ĭz). Junior waiter or chef. [orig. = deputy, clerk, f. F, p.p. of *commettre* entrust (as COMMIT)]
commĭ′ser|āte (-z-) *v.t.* & *i.* Feel or express pity for; condole *with*; hence or cogn. ~A′TION *n.*, **~at**IVE *a.* [f. L COM(*miserari* pity f. *miser* wretched) + -ATE[3]]
cŏmmĭssar′ *n.* (Hist.) Head of government department of U.S.S.R. [f. Russ. *kommissar* f. F *commissaire* (as COMMISSARY)]
cŏmmĭssār′ĭat *n.* Department (esp. Mil.) for supply of food etc.; (Hist.) government department of U.S.S.R. [F, & f. med. L *commissariatus* (as foll.; cf. -ATE[1])]
cŏ′mmĭssarў (*or* komĭ′-) *n.* Deputy, delegate; (Cambridge Univ.) assessor in Vice-Chancellor's court; representative of bishop in part of his diocese, or of absent bishop; (Mil.) officer charged with, *store for, supply of food etc. to soldiers; *restaurant in film studio etc.; hence **cŏmmĭssār′**IAL *a.*, ~SHIP (1) *n.* [ME, f. med. L *commissarius* person in charge (as COMMIT; see -ARY[1])]
commĭ′ssion[1] (-sh*o*n) *n.* **1.** Command, instruction; authority, body of persons having authority, to perform certain duties; office or department of Commissioner; ‖**~ of the peace,** (authority given to) Justices of the Peace; ‖**Royal C~,** commission of inquiry or committee appointed by the Crown at the instance of the Government. **2.** Warrant conferring authority, esp. that of officers in the army, navy, and air force, above a certain rank. **3. In ~,** (of warship etc.) manned, armed, and ready for sea; **out of ~,** not in service, not in working order. **4.** Entrusting of authority etc. to a person; charge or matter entrusted to person to perform. **5.** Authority to act as agent for another in trade (*have goods on commission*); pay of such agent, percentage on amount involved; **~-agent,** (esp.) bookmaker. **6.** Committing (*of* crime,

sin, etc.). [ME f. OF, f. L *commissio -onis* (as COMMIT; see -ION)]

commĭ'ssion[2] (-shon) *v.t.* Empower by commission; give (officer) command of ship; prepare (ship) for active service; bring (machine, equipment, etc.) into operation; give (artist etc.) a commission for piece of work. [f. prec.]

||**commĭssionair'e** (-shonār') *n.* Uniformed door-attendant at theatre, cinema, large shop, office, etc. [F, as foll.]

commĭ'ssioner (-sho-) *n.* One appointed by commission, esp. head of police department etc.; member of a commission, esp. of government boards etc. (*Charity, Civil Service, Commissioner*); representative of supreme authority in a district, department, etc. (**High C~**, chief representative of one Commonwealth country in another; **Lord (High) C~**, representative of the Crown at General Assembly of Church of Scotland); **C~ for Oaths,** solicitor authorized to administer oath to person making affidavit; PARLIAMENTARY *Commissioner for Administration.* [ME, f. med. L *commissionarius* (as COMMISSION[1], -ARY[1], -ER[2] (2))]

cŏ'mmĭssūre *n.* Junction, seam; joint between two bones; line where lips or eyelids meet; band of nerve tissue connecting hemispheres of brain, two sides of spinal cord, etc.; hence **cŏmmĭssūr'**AL *a.* [ME, f. L *commissura* junction (as foll.; see -URE)]

commĭ't *v.t.* (**-tt-**). **1.** Entrust or consign for treatment or safe keeping (*to* person, his care, *to* writing, memory, the earth, the waves, the flames); refer (bill etc.) to committee; **~ (to** prison), consign officially to custody, esp. until trial. **2.** Be doer of, perpetrate (crime, sin, blunder); expose to risk, involve, (character, honour, one*self*); pledge one*self* by implication, bind one*self*, (*to* a course of action). **3.** Hence **~**TABLE *a.*, **~**TAL *n.*, committing to prison, grave, etc., committing of oneself, **~**MENT *n.*, (esp.) engagement or involvement that restricts freedom of action. [ME, f. L COM(*mittere miss-* send) join, entrust]

commĭ'ttėd *a.* In vbl senses; morally dedicated (*to* doctrine or cause); obliged to adhere *to* (course of action); (Polit.) aligned. [p.p. of prec.]

committee *n.* **1.** (komĭ'tĭ). Body of persons appointed for special function by (and usu. out of) a (usu. larger) body (**standing ~**, one that is permanent during existence of appointing body); (esp.) such body appointed by Parliament etc. to consider details of proposed legislation; (*C~*) whole House of Commons when sitting as committee; **~-man, ~-woman,** member of a committee. **2.** (kŏmĭtē'). (Law). Person entrusted with charge of another or his property. [f. COMMIT + -EE]

commĭ'x *v.t.* & *i.* (arch. or poet.) Mix; so **~**TURE *n.* [ME, back form. f. *commixt* p.p. f. L COM*mixtus*; cf. MIX]

commō'de *n.* Chest of drawers; chiffonier; **(night-)~**, chamber-pot mounted in chair or box with cover. [F, a. (as n.) f. L COM(*modus* measure) convenient]

commō'dĭous *a.* Roomy and convenient; (arch.) convenient; hence **~**LY[2] *adv.*, **~**NESS *n.* [f. F *commodieux* or f. med. L *commodiosus* f. L *commodus* (see prec.)]

commŏ'dĭtў *n.* Useful thing; article of trade, esp. product as opp. to service. [ME, f. OF *commodité* or f. L *commoditas* (as COMMODE; see -ITY)]

cŏ'mmodōre *n.* Naval officer above captain and below rear-admiral; (in air force) *Commodore-in-*-CHIEF[1]; ||**air ~**, officer of air force just above group captain; commander of squadron or other division of fleet; president of yacht-club; senior captain of a shipping line. [prob. f. Du. *komandeur* f. F *commandeur* COMMANDER]

cŏ'mmon[1] *a.* (**~er, ~est**). **1.** Belonging equally to, coming from, or done by, more than one (*our common humanity*; *common* CAUSE[1]; *common consent*). **2.** Belonging to, open to, affecting, the public (*common hangman, lodging-house, scold*). **3.** Of ordinary occurrence (*a common experience*; **~ or garden,** (colloq.) ordinary); ordinary, of ordinary qualities, (*common honesty*; *no common mind*); without rank or position (*common* JURY, SOLDIER; *the common people*); of the most familiar type (*common* COLD[2], *nightshade, snake*). **4.** Of inferior quality; low-class, vulgar. **5.** (Math.) belonging to two or more quantities (*common denominator, factor, multiple*); (Gram., of noun) applicable to any one of a class (opp. PROPER), (of gender) indifferently masculine or feminine; (Pros., of syllable) that may be either short or long; (Mus.) (of time, measure) having two or four beats, esp. four crotchets, in bar; *common* CHORD[2]. **6. ~ carrier,** one legally obliged to serve the public; **C~ Era,** Christian era; *common* FORM[1]; **~ ground,** basis for argument etc. accepted by both sides; *common* INFORMER; **~ knowledge,** thing known to all; **~ law,** unwritten law of England, administered by the national courts, purporting to be derived from ancient usage (**~-law husband** or **wife,** one recognized by common law, usu. after cohabitation without ceremony of marriage); *Common* MARKET[1]; **~ metre,** hymn stanza of four lines with 8, 6, 8, and 6 syllables; **C~ Prayer,** Church of England liturgy set forth in *Book of Common Prayer* of Edward VI (1549); ||**~-room,** (in some colleges, schools, etc.) room to which members have common access for business or social purposes, members using this; *common* SALT; **~ seal** (of corporate body); **~ sense,** normal understanding, good practical sense in everyday affairs, general feeling (of mankind or community); **~se'nsical,** possessing or marked by common sense; *Common* SERJEANT; ***~ stock,** ORDINARY shares; **~ weal, ~weal,** (arch.) public welfare; *common* YEAR. **7.** Hence **~**LY[2] *adv.*, **~**NESS (-n-n-) *n.* [ME f. OF *comun*, f. L *communis*]

cŏ'mmon[2] *n.* **1.** Land belonging to a community, esp. unenclosed waste land; **(right of) ~**, a man's right over another's land, e.g. *common of pasturage.* **2.** (sl.) Common sense. **3. Out of the ~**, unusual; **in ~**, in joint use, shared; **in ~ with,** in the same way as. **4.** (in *pl.*) See COMMONS. [ME, f. F COMMUNE[1] and L *commune* neut. of *communis* (as prec.)]

cŏ'mmonable *a.* (Of animal) that may be pastured on common land; (of land) that may be held in common. [f. obs. *common* to exercise right of common + -ABLE]

cŏ'mmonage *n.* Right of common; (condition of) land held in common; commonalty. [f. COMMON[2] + -AGE]

cŏmmonă'lĭtў *n.* Sharing of an attribute; common occurrence. [var. of foll.]

cŏ'mmonaltў *n.* The common people; general body (of mankind etc.); corporate body. [ME f. OF *comunalté*, f. med. L *communalitas -tatis* (as COMMON[1]; see -AL, -ITY)]

cŏ'mmoner *n.* One of the common people (below the rank of peer); student without financial support from college, paying for his own commons; one who has right of common. [ME, f. med. L *communarius* (*communa*; see COMMUNE[1], -ER[2] (2))]

cŏ'mmonplāce *n.* & *a.* **1.** *n.* Notable passage, entered for use in a **~-book;** ordinary topic; everyday saying; platitude; anything usual or trite. **2.** *a.* Lacking originality, trite; hence

~NESS (-sn-) *n.* [transl. of L *locus communis* = Gk *koinos topos* general theme]
cŏ'mmons (-z) *n. pl.* **1.** The common people; third estate in British or other similar constitution, (**House of C~, the C~**, Lower House of Parliament, or its buildings). **2.** Provisions shared in common; daily fare (**short ~**, not enough food). [ME, pl. of COMMON²]
cŏ'mmonwealth (-wĕl-) *n.* Independent State or community; republic or democratic State (lit., or fig.: *commonwealth of learning*); (*C~*) republican government in England, 1649–60; (*C~*) title of federated Australian States; (**British**) **C~** (**of Nations**), association of U.K. with various independent States (previously subject to Britain) and dependencies; *State of the U.S. (esp. in titles of some of them); ||**C~ Day** (celebrated on Queen's official birthday); ||**C~ preference,** taxation system favouring imports from British Commonwealth countries. [f. COMMON¹ + WEALTH]
commō'tion *n.* Physical or mental disturbance; bustle, confusion; tumult, insurrection. [ME f. OF, or f. L *commotio* (see COM-, MOTION¹)]
commo've (-o͞o'v) *v.t.* (arch.) Move (lit. or fig.) violently, excite. [ME, f. OF COM*movoir*; see MOVE²]
cŏ'mmūnal *a.* Of or for the or a community, for the common use; of a commune, esp. that of Paris; hence ~IZE (3) *v.t.*, ~LY² *adv.* [F, f. LL *communalis* (as COMMUNE¹; see -AL)]
cŏ'mmūnal|ĭsm *n.* Principle of communal organization of society; so ~IST (3) *n.*, **~ĭ'st**IC *a.* [f. prec. + -ISM]
cŏ'mmūnâ͡rd *n.* Member of a commune; adherent of the Paris Commune. [F (as foll.; see -ARD)]
cŏ'mmūne¹ *n.* Communal settlement; group of persons not all of one family, sharing living accommodation and goods; French territorial division, smallest for administrative purposes; similar division elsewhere; **the C~**, communalistic government in Paris in 1871. [F, f. med. L *communia* neut. pl. of L *communis* common]
commū'ne² (*or* kŏ'm-) *v.i.* Have intimate discussion (*with* friend, one's heart, etc.; *together*); *receive Holy Communion. [ME, f. OF *comuner* share (*comun* COMMON¹)]
commū'nĭc|able *a.* That can be imparted (esp. of disease); (arch.) communicative; hence ~ABI'LITY, **~able**NESS (-beln-), *ns.*, **~ab**LY² *adv.* [ME f. OF, or f. LL *communicabilis* (as COMMUNICATE; see -ABLE)]
commū'nĭcant *n.* One who (esp. regularly) receives Holy Communion; one who imparts information. [f. as foll.; see -ANT]
commū'nĭcāt|e *v.* **1.** *v.t.* Impart, transmit, (heat, motion, feeling, news, a discovery, *to*); administer Holy Communion to. **2.** *v.i.* Receive Holy Communion; have social dealings *with*; succeed in conveying information; (of room etc.) have common door (*with*); hence ~OR *n.* [f. L *communicare* (as COMMON¹ + *ic* factitive suf.) + -ATE³]
commūnĭcā'tion *n.* **1.** Act of imparting (esp. news; **~ cord,** cord or chain for pulling by passenger to stop train in emergency); information given; paper read to learned society; social dealings, access; common door or passage or road or rail or telephone or other connection between places. **2.** (in *pl.*) Science and practice of transmitting information, (Mil.) means of transport between base and front; **~ theory,** study of language and other means of conveying information. [ME, f. as prec.; see -ATION]
commū'nĭcatĭve *a.* Ready to impart; open, talkative; hence ~LY² (-vlĭ) *adv.*, ~NESS (-vn-) *n.* [f. LL *communicativus* (as COMMUNICATE; see -IVE)]
commū'nion (-yon) *n.* Sharing, participation; fellowship (esp. between branches of Catholic Church; *communion of* SAINTS); body professing one branch of Christian faith; social dealings; (**Holy**) **C~**, participation in Eucharist (so **~-cloth, -cup, -table**); **~-rail** (at which Holy Communion is administered). [ME f. OF, or f. L *communio* (*communis* common; see -ION)]
commū'nĭqué (-kā) *n.* Official communication, esp. report. [F, = communicated]
cŏ'mmūn|ĭsm *n.* System of society with vesting of property in the community, each member working for the common benefit according to his capacity and receiving according to his needs; (usu. *C~ism*) movement or political party advocating communism esp. as derived from Marxism, communistic form of society established in 20th c. in U.S.S.R. and elsewhere; hence ~IST (2) *n.*, **~ĭ'st**IC *a.* [f. F *communisme* (*commun* COMMON¹; see -ISM)]
commūnĭtâr'ian *n.* & *a.* (Member) of a community practising co-operation and some communism. [f. foll. + -ARIAN, after *unitarian* etc.]
commū'nĭtȳ *n.* **1.** Joint ownership (*community of goods*) or liability; state of being shared or held in common; fellowship (*community of interest* etc.). **2.** Organized political, municipal, or social body; body of people living in same locality; body of people having religion, profession, etc., in common, (*the immigrant community*; *the mercantile community*; *the Jewish community*); *the* public; monastic, socialistic, etc., body practising community of goods; body of nations unified by common interests; (Ecol.) group of plants or animals growing or living together in a given area. **3. ~ centre,** place providing social, recreational, and educational facilities for a neighbourhood; ***~ chest,** fund for charity and welfare work in a community; ||**~ home,** centre for housing young offenders, replacing approved school and remand home; **~ singing** (in chorus by large gathering of people); **~ spirit,** feeling of membership of a community. [ME, f. OF *comuneté* f. L *communitas -tatis* (as COMMON¹; see -ITY)]
cŏ'mmūnĭz|e, -ĭs|e (-iz), *v.t.* Make (land etc.) common property; make communistic; hence ~A'TION *n.* [f. L *communis* COMMON¹ + -IZE]
commū't|able *a.* Exchangeable, convertible into money; that can be compounded for; hence ~ABI'LITY *n.* [f. L *commutabilis* (as COMMUTE; see -ABLE)]
cŏ'mmūtāte *v.t.* (Electr.) Regulate direction of (current), esp. to make it a direct current. [f. L *commutare* (as COMMUTE) + -ATE³]
cŏmmūtā'tion *n.* Commuting; commutating; (Math.) interchange of order of two quantities added etc.; ***~ ticket,** season-ticket. [F, or f. L *commutatio* (as COMMUTE; see -ATION)]
commū'tatĭve (*or* kŏ'mūtāt-) *a.* Relating to or involving substitution; (Math.) unchanged in result by interchange of order of quantities. [f. F *commutatif* or f. med. L *commutativus* (as COMMUTE; see -ATIVE)]
cŏ'mmūtātor *n.* Person or thing that commutes; device for commutating electric current. [as foll.; see -OR]
commū't|e *v.* **1.** *v.t.* Interchange (two things); make payment etc. to change (one obligation) *for*, *into*, another; change (punishment *to* another less severe); change (one kind of payment *into*, *for*, another); (Electr.) commutate. **2.** *v.i.* *Buy

and use season (commutation) ticket; travel esp. by train or car to and from one's daily work in city etc., whence ~ER[1] *n.*; (Math.) have commutative relation. [f. L COM(*mutare -tat-* change)]

cō'mōse *a.* (Of seeds etc.) hairy, downy. [f. L *comosus* (as COMA[2]; see -OSE)]

cŏmp *n.* & *v.* (colloq.) **1.** *n.* Accompaniment; competition; compositor. **2.** *v.t.* & *i.* Play accompaniment (to); work as compositor (on). [abbr.]

||**Comp**[a] *abbr.* (On banknotes) Company.

cŏ'mpăct[1] *n.* Agreement or contract between parties. [f. L *compactum* f. COM(*pacisci pact-* covenant); cf. PACT]

compă'ct[2] *a.* Closely or neatly packed together; made up *of*; (of style) condensed, terse; not wasteful of space; hence ~LY[2] *adv.*, ~NESS *n.* [ME, f. L COM(*pingere pact-* = *pangere* fasten)]

cŏ'mpăct[3] *n.* Small flat case for face-powder etc.; object formed by compacting of powder; *medium-sized motor car. [f. prec.]

compă'ct[4] *v.t.* Join or press firmly together; condense; devise, compose, (*of*); so **compă'ction**, ~OR, *ns.* [f. as COMPACT[2]]

compā'gēs (-z) *n.* (*pl.* same). Framework, complex structure (lit. or fig.). [L COM(*pages* f. *pangere* fix)]

compă'nion[1] (-yon) *n.* & *v.* **1.** *n.* One who accompanies another; associate *in*, sharer *of*, (~ **in arms,** fellow-soldier); ||member of lowest grade of some orders of knighthood (*Companion of the Bath*; ||**C~ of Honour, Literature,** member of orders founded 1917, 1961); woman paid to live with and accompany another. **2.** Handbook or reference-book; thing that matches another; star etc. that accompanies another; equipment combining several requisites; **~-set,** set of fireside implements on stand. **3.** Hence ~ATE[2], ~LESS, *adjs.* **4.** *v.t.* Accompany. **5.** *v.i.* Consort *with.* [ME, f. OF *compaignon* f. Rom. **companio -ōnis* (as COM-, L *panis* bread)]

compă'nion[2] (-yon) *n.* (Naut.) Raised frame on quarterdeck for lighting cabins etc. below; ~ **hatch,** wooden covering over companion-way; ~ **hatchway,** opening in deck leading to cabin; **~-ladder** (from deck to cabin); ~**(-way)**, staircase to cabin. [f. obs. Du. *kompanje* quarterdeck f. OF *compagne* f. It. (*camera della*) *compagna* pantry, prob. ult. rel. to prec.]

compă'nionab|le (-nyo-) *a.* Sociable, agreeable as companion; hence ~**le**NESS (-beln-) *n.*, ~LY[2] *adv.* [f. COMPANION[1] + -ABLE]

compă'nionship (-nyo-) *n.* State of being companion(s); ||(Print.) company of compositors working together. [f. COMPANION[1] + -SHIP]

co'mpany̆ (kŭ'm-) *n.* & *v.* **1.** *n.* State of being companion or fellow; **in** ~, not alone; **in** ~ **with,** together with; **bear** or **keep** person ~, accompany him; **keep** ~ **(with)**, associate habitually (with); **part** ~ **(with)**, (lit. or fig.) cease association (with). **2.** Number of persons assembled; social party, guests. **3.** One's associate(s) (*addicted to low company*; **good, bad,** ~, a pleasant, dull, companion; **I err in good** ~, better men have done the same). **4.** Body of persons combined for common (esp. commercial) object (JOINT[2] *-stock company*, ||*limited* LIABILITY *company*); partner(s) not named in title of firm (*Smith and Co.*); party of actors etc.; group of Guides; subdivision of infantry battalion usu. commanded by major or captain (~ **officer,** captain or lower commissioned officer; ~ **sergeant-major,** senior non-com. officer of company); **ship's** ~, entire crew. **5.** *v.t.* (arch.) Accompany. **6.** *v.i.* Consort *with.* [ME, f. AF *compainie*, OF *compai(g)nie* f. Rom. **compania* (**companio*; see COMPANION[1], -Y[1])]

cŏ'mpar|able *a.* That can be compared (*with*); fit to be compared (*to*); hence ~ABI'LITY, ~**able**NESS (-beln-), *ns.*, ~**ab**LY[2] *adv.* [ME f. OF, f. L *comparabilis* (as COMPARE[1]; see -ABLE)]

compă'ratĭst *n.* User of comparative methods in study of language or literature. [f. foll. + -IST]

compă'ratĭve *a.* & *n.* **1.** *a.* Of or involving comparison (esp. of sciences etc.: *comparative anatomy, philology*); (Gram.) ~ **adjective, adverb,** one in the ~ **degree,** expressing a higher degree of a quality (*braver*; *more absurdly*); estimated by comparison (*the comparative merits of the two proposals*); perceptible by comparison (*in comparative comfort*); hence ~LY[2] (-vlĭ) *adv.* **2.** *n.* (Gram.) Comparative degree or form. [ME, f. L *comparativus* (as COMPARE[1]; see -ATIVE)]

compă'rator *n.* Device for comparing product, output, etc., with a standard. [f. as foll. + -OR]

compār'e[1] *v.* **1.** *v.t.* Liken, pronounce similar, (*to*; esp. with negative: *not to be compared to*); estimate similarity or dissimilarity of (one thing *to* another in quality, *with* another in quantity or detailed nature; two things); observe similarity or relation between (passages of book etc.; ~ **notes,** exchange ideas or opinions); (Gram.) form comparative and superlative degrees of (adjective, adverb). **2.** *v.i.* Bear comparison (*this compares favourably with previous results*), be on terms of equality *with.* [ME, f. OF *comparer* f. L COM(*parare* f. *par* equal)]

compār'e[2] *n.* (literary). Comparison (*beyond, without, compare*). [app. f. (*without*) *compare* (obs. var. of COMPEER), assoc. w. prec.]

compă'rĭson *n.* Act of comparing (**bear** or **stand** ~, be able to be compared favourably *with*; **beyond** ~, totally different; **in** ~ **with,** compared to); simile, illustration; **degrees of** ~, (Gram.) positive, comparative, superlative, (of adjectives and adverbs). [ME, f. OF *comparesoun* f. L *comparatio -onis* (as COMPARE[1]; see -ATION, -ISON)]

compâr'tment *n.*, & *v.t.* **1.** *n.* Division separated by partitions, esp. of railway carriage; watertight division of ship. **2.** *v.t.* Put into compartments (lit. or fig.); hence ~A'TION *n.* [f. F *compartiment* f. It. *compartimento* f. LL COM(*partiri* share); see -MENT]

cŏmpârtmĕ'ntal *a.* Consisting of or pertaining to compartment(s); hence ~IZE (3) *v.t.*, ~LY[2] *adv.* [f. prec. + -AL]

co'mpass[1] (kŭ'm-) *n.* **1.** (usu. in *pl.*) Instrument for taking measurements and describing circles, with two legs connected at one end by movable joint; **beam-~(es)** (with beam connecting sliding sockets, for large circles); BOW[1]*-compass(es)*. **2.** Circumference, boundary; area, extent, scope, (lit. or fig.: *beyond my compass*); range of tones of voice or musical instrument; (arch.) roundabout way (*fetch* or *go a compass*). **3.** Instrument of navigation showing magnetic or true north and bearings from it (*mariners' compass, gyro-compass*); BOX[3] *the compass*; ~ **card,** card showing the 32 principal bearings (*points of the compass*; see POINT[1] 19); ~ **rose,** circle of the principal directions marked on chart; **~-saw,** narrow saw for cutting curves; ~ **window,** bay window with semicircular curve. [ME, f. OF *compas* (*compasser*; see foll.)]

co'mpass[2] (kŭ'm-) *v.t.* Go round; hem in; grasp mentally; contrive, accomplish; hence ~ABLE *a.* [ME, f. OF *compasser*, f. Rom. **compassare* measure (as COM-, L *passus* PACE[1])]

compă'ssion (-shon) *n.* Pity inclining one to be helpful or merciful. [ME f. OF, f. eccl. L *compassio -onis* f. COM(*pati pass-* suffer); see -ION]

compă'ssionate[1] (-sho-) *a.* Sympathetic, pitying; granted out of compassion; ||~ **allowance** (granted when an ordinary pension or allowance is not admissible under official rules); ||~ **leave** (granted on grounds of bereavement etc.); hence ~LY² (-tlĭ) *adv.* [f. obs. F *compassionné* (*compassionner* feel pity f. as prec.) + -ATE²]

compă'ssionāte² (-sho-) *v.t.* (arch.) Regard or treat with compassion. [f. prec. or obs. F *compassionner* (see prec.) + -ATE³]

compă't|ĭble *a.* Consistent, able to coexist, (*with*); mutually tolerant; (of equipment etc.) able to be used in combination; hence or cogn. ~IBI'LITY *n.*, ~**ĭb**LY² *adv.* [F, f. med. L *compatibilis* (see COMPASSION, -IBLE)]

compă'trĭot *n.* Fellow-countryman; hence ~IC (-ŏ't-) *a.* [f. F *compatriote* f. LL COM(*patriota* PATRIOT)]

compeer' *n.* Equal, peer; comrade. [ME f. OF *comper* (as COM-, PEER¹)]

compĕ'l *v.t.* (**-ll-**). Constrain, force, (*to* do, *to* a course of action); bring about (an action) by force (*compel submission*); (arch.) drive forcibly; (in *part.*) rousing strong interest or attention or feeling of admiration; hence ~**l**ABLE *a.* [ME, f. L COM(*pellere puls-* drive)]

compĕ'ndĭous *a.* Comprehensive but fairly brief; hence ~LY² *adv.*, ~NESS *n.* [ME, f. OF *compendieux* f. L *compendiosus* brief (as foll.; see -OUS)]

compĕ'ndĭ|um *n.* (*pl.* ~**ums** *or* ~**a**). Abridgement; summary, abstract; collection of table-games etc. [L, = what is weighed together, f. COM(*pendere* weigh)]

cŏ'mpĕnsāt|e *v.* **1.** *v.t.* Counterbalance; recompense (person *for* thing); (Mech.) provide (pendulum etc.) with arrangement to neutralize effects of temperature etc. **2.** *v.i.* Make amends (*for* thing, *to* person, or abs.); (Psych.) offset deficiency or frustration by developing another characteristic. **3.** Hence **compĕ'nsat**IVE *a.*, ~OR *n.*, **compĕ'nsat**ORY (*or* kŏmpensā'-) *a.* [f. L COM(*pensare* frequent. of *pendere pens-* weigh) + -ATE³]

cŏmpĕnsā'tion *n.* Compensating or being compensated; thing given as recompense; money given for requisitioned property; *salary or wages; (Psych.) act or result of compensating; ~ **pendulum** (designed so as to neutralize effects of temperature variation); hence ~AL *a.* [ME f. OF, f. L *compensatio* (as prec.; see -ATION)]

||**cŏ'mpère** (-pār) *n.*, & *v.t.* **1.** *n.* Organizer of variety entertainment who introduces the artistes, comments on the turns, etc. **2.** *v.t.* Act as compère to. [F, = godfather, f. Rom. **compater* (as COM-, L *pater* father)]

compē'te *v.i.* Strive (*with* or *against* another *for* thing, *in doing*, or abs.); strive for superiority *in* a quality. [f. L COM(*petere -tit-* seek), in late sense 'strive after or contend for (something)']

cŏ'mpėtence, -cy̆, *ns.* Sufficiency of means for living, easy circumstances; ability (*to* do, *for* a task); (of court, magistrate, etc.) legal capacity, right to take cognizance. [f. foll. + -ENCE, -ENCY]

cŏ'mpėtent *a.* Adequately qualified (*to* do, *for* a task); legally qualified (judge, court, witness); effective, adequate; (of action etc.) appropriate, legitimate; hence ~LY² *adv.* [ME f. OF, or f. L *competent-* (as COMPETE; see -ENT)]

cŏmpėtĭ'tion *n.* Act of competing (*for*), by examination, in trade, etc.; contest, event in which persons compete; those competing with one (*the competition is not very strong*); *competition-*-WALLAH. [f. LL *competitio* rivalry (as foll.; see -ITION)]

compĕ'tĭtive *a.* Of, by, offered for, involving, competition; (of prices etc.) comparable with those of rival sellers etc.; hence ~LY² (-vlĭ) *adv.* [f. p.p. st. of L *competere* (COMPETE) + -IVE]

compĕ'tĭtor *n.* One who competes, rival, esp. in trade. [f. F *compétiteur* or f. L *competitor* (as prec.; see -OR)]

cŏmpĭlā'tion *n.* Compiling or being compiled; thing compiled. [ME f. OF, f. L *compilatio -onis* (as foll.; see -ATION)]

compī'l|e *v.t.* Collect (materials) into a list, volume, etc.; make up (volume etc.) of such materials; accumulate (high score at cricket, etc.); hence ~ER¹ *n.*, (esp.) routine for putting program into form suitable for a particular computer. [ME, f. OF *compiler* or its app. source, L *compilare* plunder, plagiarize]

complā'cency̆ *n.* Tranquil pleasure, esp. self-satisfaction. [f. med. L *complacentia* f. L COM(*placēre* please); see -ENCY]

complā'cent *a.* Self-satisfied; hence ~LY² *adv.* [f. L *complacēre*; see prec., -ENT]

complai'n *v.i.* Express dissatisfaction (*at*, *that*); emit mournful sound, groan, creak; ~ **of,** express dissatisfaction with, announce that one is suffering from (headache etc.), state grievance concerning; hence ~ANT *n.*, plaintiff in certain lawsuits. [ME, f. OF *complaindre* (st. *-aign-*) f. Rom. COM(*plangere planct-* lament) bewail]

complai'nt *n.* Utterance of grievance; expression of grief; formal accusation; *plaintiff's case in civil action; subject or ground of complaint; bodily ailment. [ME, f. OF *complainte* (*complaint* p.p. of *complaindre*; see prec.)]

complai's|ance (-z-) *n.* Politeness; deference; willingness to please others; acquiescence; so ~ANT *a.* [F, f. *complaire* (st. *-plais-*) acquiesce to please, f. L *complacēre* (see COMPLACENCY)]

complea't. See COMPLETE¹.

cŏ'mplėment¹ *n.* That which completes; (Gram.) word(s) added to verb to complete the predicate; full number required (to man ship, fill conveyance, etc.); (Math.) ~ **of an angle,** its deficiency from 90° (cf. SUPPLEMENT¹); (Biol.) = ALEXIN; hence ~AL (-ĕ'n-) *a.* [ME, f. L *complementum* (as COMPLETE¹; see -MENT)]

cŏ'mplėmĕnt² *v.t.* Complete; form complement to. [f. prec.]

cŏmplėmĕ'ntar|y̆ *a.* Completing, forming a complement; (of two or more things) complementing each other; ~**y angles** (making up 90°); *complementary* COLOUR¹*s*; hence ~ĭLY² *adv.*, **cŏmplėmĕntă'r**ITY *n.*, (esp., Phys.) explainability of phenomena in terms of waves and particles jointly. [f. COMPLEMENT¹ + -ARY¹]

complē'te¹ *a.* Having all its parts, entire; finished; having the maximum extent (*it was a complete surprise*); accomplished (*a complete horseman*; also **compleat,** after Walton's *Compleat Angler*); hence ~LY² (-tlĭ) *adv.*, ~NESS (-tn-) *n.* [ME, f. OF *complet* or f. L *completus* p.p. of COM*plēre* fill up]

complē'te² *v.t.* Finish; make whole or perfect; make up the amount of; add what is required to (questionnaire etc.); so **complē'**TION *n.* [f. prec.]

cŏ'mplĕx¹ *n.* Complex whole; (Psych.) related group of usu. repressed ideas etc. causing abnormal behaviour or mental state (INFERIORITY *complex*, OEDIPUS *complex*), (pop.) obsession; (Chem.) complex substance. [f. L *complexus* embrace etc. (as foll.)]

cŏ'mplĕx² *a.* Consisting of parts, composite; complicated; (Gram., of sentence) containing subordinate clause(s); (Chem.) formed by combination of compounds; (Math.) containing real and IMAGINARY parts; hence **complĕ'x**ITY *n.*, ~LY² *adv.* [f. F *complexe* or f. L *complexus* p.p. of *complectere* embrace, assoc. w. *complexus* plaited]

For other words in *co-* see CO-.

complĕ'xion (-kshon) *n.* Natural colour, texture, and appearance, of the skin (esp. of face); (fig.) character, aspect, (*put a different complexion on the matter*); hence (-)~ED² (-nd) *a.*, ~LESS *a.*, pale-faced. [ME f. OF, f. L *complexio -onis* (as prec.; see -ION); orig. = combination of supposed qualities determining nature of a body]

complī'ance *n.* Action in accordance with request, command, etc. (**in ~ with,** according to (wish etc.)); unworthy submission; (Mech.) (degree of) yielding under applied force. [f. COMPLY + -ANCE]

complī'ant *a.* Disposed to comply, yielding; hence ~LY² *adv.* [f. COMPLY + -ANT]

cŏ'mplĭcacȳ *n.* Complexity; complicated structure. [f. foll. + -ACY]

cŏ'mplĭcāte *v.t.* Mix up (*with* other things); (esp. in *p.p.*) make complex or intricate. [f. L COM(*plicare* fold) + -ATE³]

cŏmplĭcā'tion *n.* Involved condition; entangled state of affairs; complicating circumstance (*here is a further complication*); (Path.) secondary disease or condition aggravating a previous one. [F, or f. LL *complicatio* (as prec.; see -ATION)]

complĭ'cĭtȳ *n.* Partnership in evil action. [f. *complice* (see ACCOMPLICE) + -ITY]

cŏ'mplĭment¹ *n.* Polite expression of praise; act implying praise; (in *pl.*) formal greetings (esp. as accompaniment to message, note, present, etc.); **the ~s of** (greeting appropriate to) **the season**; hence ~ARY¹ (-ĕ'n-) *a.*, expressing compliment(s), given free of charge by way of compliment. [F, f. It. *complimento* f. Rom. **complimentum* f. L (as COMPLEMENT¹)]

cŏ'mplĭmĕnt² *v.t.* Pay compliment to (person *on* thing); present (person *with* thing) as mark of courtesy. [f. F *complimenter* (as prec.)]

cŏ'mplĭne *n.* (Eccl.) (Office of) last of the canonical hours of prayer. [ME, f. OF *complie*, fem. p.p. (as n.) of obs. *complir* complete f. Rom. **complire* f. L COMplēre fill up]

complȳ' *v.i.* Act in accordance (*with* wish, command, etc., or abs.). [f. It. *complire* f. Cat. *complir*, Sp. *cumplir* f. L COMplēre fill up]

cŏ'mpō *n.* (*pl.* ~s). Composition, esp. = stucco, plaster; composite; ~ **rations** (in large pack designed to last several days). [abbr.]

compō'nent *a.* & *n.* **1.** *a.* Contributing to the composition of a whole. **2.** *n.* Component part, esp. of motor vehicle; (Math.) one of two or more vectors equivalent to given vector. [f. L COM(*ponere* put); see -ENT]

compôr't *v.t.* & *i.* Conduct or behave one*self*; ~ **with,** suit, befit. [f. L COM(*portare* carry)]

compos. See COMPOS MENTIS.

compō's|e (-z) *v.t.* **1.** (Of elements) make up, constitute, (esp. in *pass.*, *be composed of*). **2.** Construct in words, produce in literary form, (poem etc., or abs.); (Mus.) construct in notes, produce in written form, (song, symphony, etc., or abs.), set (words) to music; (Print.) set up (type) to form words and blocks of words, set up (article etc.) in type; put together to form a whole, arrange artistically. **3.** Settle (dispute etc.). **4.** Arrange in specified or understood manner, or for specified purpose, (*compose yourself to write*; *compose your countenance*; *compose your thoughts for action*); calm (one*self*, passions, etc.; esp. in *p.p.*, whence ~**ĕd**LY² *adv.*). [f. F *composer*, f. L COM(*ponere* put); see POSE¹]

compō'ser (-z-) *n.* One who composes (esp. music). [f. prec. + -ER¹]

cŏ'mposĭte (-z-) *a.* & *n.* (Thing) made up of various parts; (material) made of constituents that remain recognizable; (Archit.) fifth classical order, Ionic and Corinthian mixed; (Bot.) (plant) of family Compositae, in which the so-called flower is a head of many flowers (daisy, dandelion, etc.); hence ~LY² (-tlĭ) *adv.*, ~NESS (-tn-) *n.* [F, f. L *compositus* p.p. of COM(*ponere posit-* put); see -ITE²]

cŏmposĭ'tion (-z-) *n.* **1.** Act of putting together; formation, construction; formation of words into a compound word. **2.** Construction of sentences, art of literary production; act or art of composing music; setting-up of type. **3.** Mental constitution (*a touch of madness in his composition*); constitution of a substance, nature of its ingredients; arrangement (of parts of picture etc.). **4.** Thing composed, mixture; piece of music or writing; compound artificial substance, esp. one serving the purpose of a natural one. **5.** Compromise; agreement for payment of sum in lieu of larger sum or other obligation (*made a composition with his creditors*); sum thus paid. [ME f. OF, f. L *compositio -onis* (as prec.; see -ITION)]

compŏ'sĭtor (-z-) *n.* One who sets up type for printing. [ME, f. AF *compositour* f. L *compositor* (as COMPOSITE; see -OR)]

compos (mentis) (kŏ'mpŏs mĕ'ntĭs) *a.* Having control of one's mind, not mad. [L]

compŏ'ssĭble *a.* Able to coexist (*with*). [OF, f. med. L *compossibilis* (as COM-, POSSIBLE)]

cŏ'mpŏst *n.*, & *v.t.* (Treat with or make into) mixed manure of organic origin; (fig.) mixture of ingredients; ~ **heap** or **pile,** structure of alternate layers of garden refuse, soil, etc., for quick production of compost. [ME, f. OF *composte* f. L *compos(i)tum* (as COMPOSITE)]

compō'sure (-zher) *n.* Tranquil demeanour, calmness. [f. COMPOSE + -URE]

cŏ'mpōte *n.* Fruit preserved or cooked in syrup. [F, f. OF *composte*, f. **compos(i)ta* (as COMPOSITE)]

compou'nd¹ *v.* **1.** *v.t.* Mix (ingredients, lit. or fig.); combine (verbal elements) into a word; make up (a composite whole); increase, complicate, (difficulties etc.). **2.** Settle (matter by mutual concession, debt by partial payment, subscription by lump sum, or abs.). **3.** Condone (liability, offence) for money etc.; forbear prosecution of (felony) from private motives. **4.** Hence ~ABLE *a.* **5.** *v.i.* Come to terms (*with* person *for* forgoing claim etc., *for* offence). [ME *compoun(e)* f. OF *compondre* f. L COM(*ponere* put); *-d* as in *expound*]

cŏ'mpound² *a.* & *n.* **1.** *a.* Made up of several ingredients; consisting of several parts or (Zool.) individual organisms or (Bot.) simple parts; combined, collective; ~ **fracture** (complicated by skin wound); *compound* INTEREST¹; ~ **interval** (Mus., exceeding one octave); *compound* SENTENCE; ~ **time** (Mus., having more than one group of simple-time units in each bar). **2.** *n.* Mixture of elements, compound thing, esp. compound word; (Chem.) substance consisting of two or more elements chemically united in fixed proportions by weight. [ME, orig. p.p. of *compoun(e)*; see prec.]

cŏ'mpound³ *n.* (In India, China, etc.) enclosure in which house or factory stands; (in S. Afr.) enclosure in which miners live; large fenced-in space in prison etc.; = POUND². [f. Port. *campon* or Du. *kampoeng* f. Malay *kampong*]

cŏmpradôr'(e) *n.* Chinese chief agent of foreign business-house; (fig.) agent of a foreign power. [Port. *comprador* buyer f. LL *comparator* f. L *comparare* purchase]

cŏmprĕhĕ'nd *v.t.* Grasp mentally, understand, (person, thing); include, take in. [ME, f. OF *comprehender* or f. L COM(*prehendere -hens-* grasp)]

cŏmprĕhĕ'ns|ĭble *a.* That may be understood; that may be comprised; hence ~IBI'LITY *n.*, ~**ĭb**LY² *adv.* [f. F *compréhensible* or f. L *comprehensibilis* (as prec.; see -IBLE)]

cŏmprĕhĕ'nsion (-shon) *n.* Act or faculty of understanding; inclusion; (Eccl. Hist.) in-

clusion of Nonconformists in Anglican Church. [f. F *compréhension* or f. L *comprehensio* (as prec.; see -ION)]
cŏmprėhĕ'nsĭve *a.* & *n.* Of understanding (*comprehensive faculty*); including much or all (*comprehensive term*; *comprehensive grasp*, fig. or lit.); ~ (**school**), large secondary school providing courses for children of all abilities; hence ~LY² (-vlĭ) *adv.*, ~NESS (-vn-) *n.* [f. F *compréhensif -ive* or f. LL *comprehensivus* (as prec.; see -IVE)]
cŏ'mprĕss¹ *n.* Soft pad of lint etc. for compressing artery etc.; (**water**) ~, piece of wet cloth covered with waterproof bandage, for relief of inflammation. [f. F *compresse* (*compresser*; see foll.)]
comprĕ'ss² *v.t.* Squeeze together; bring (air, language, expressed thoughts) into smaller space; ~**ed air** (at more than atmospheric pressure); hence ~IBLE, ~IVE, *adjs.*, ~ION (-shon) *n.*, (also) (amount of) reduction in volume of fuel mixture in internal combustion engine before ignition. [ME, f. OF *compresser* or f. LL *compressare* frequent. of L COM(*primere press-* = *premere* press)]
comprĕ'ssor *n.* Machine for compressing air or other gases. [f. prec. + -OR]
comprī's|e (-z) *v.t.* Include, comprehend; consist of (*the house comprises three bedrooms etc.*); compose, make up; hence ~ABLE *a.* [ME f. F, fem. p.p. of *comprendre* COMPREHEND]
cŏ'mpromīse¹ (-z) *n.* Settlement of dispute by mutual concession; (finding of) intermediate way *between* conflicting opinions, courses, etc., by modification of each. [ME, f. OF *compromis* f. LL *compromissum* neut. p.p. (as n.) of COM(*promittere* PROMISE²)]
cŏ'mpromīse² (-z) *v.* **1.** *v.t.* Settle (dispute) by mutual concession; bring (person, one*self*) under suspicion or into danger by indiscreet action. **2.** *v.i.* Make a compromise. [f. prec.]
compte rendu (kawnt rahndū') *n.* (*pl.* ***-es -us*** *pr.* same). Report; review; statement. [F]
cŏmptŏ'mėter *n.* Type of calculating-machine. [P, app. f. F *compte* COUNT¹ + -O- + -METER]
comptrō'ller (kont-) *n.* Controller (sp. retained in some titles of financial officers, esp. *Comptroller and Auditor General*, **Comptroller General*). [var. of CONTROLLER by erron. assoc. w. COUNT¹, L *computus*]
compŭ'lsion (-shon) *n.* Constraint, obligation, (**under** ~, because one is compelled); (Psych.) irresistible urge to a form of behaviour esp. against one's normal wishes. [ME f. F, f. LL *compulsio -onis* (as COMPEL; see -ION)]
compŭ'lsĭve *a.* Tending to compel; resulting or acting (as if) from compulsion (*compulsive gambler*), esp. (Psych.) contrary to one's conscious wishes; irresistible (*the book is compulsive reading*); hence ~LY² (-vlĭ) *adv.* [f. med. L *compulsivus* (as COMPEL; see -IVE)]
compŭ'lsor|y̆ *a.* (Of action) enforced; compelling (*compulsory legislation* etc., opp. *permissive*); ~**y purchase** (by authority, of land etc. needed for public purposes); hence ~ĬLY² *adv.*, ~ĬNESS *n.* [f. med. L *compulsorius* (as COMPEL; see -ORY)]
compŭ'nct|ion *n.* Pricking of conscience; slight regret, scruple, (*without compunction*); hence ~IOUS (-shus) *a.* [ME, f. OF *componction* f. eccl. L *compunctio -onis* f. L COM(*pungere punct-* prick); see -ION]
cŏmpurgā'tion *n.* Clearing from charge or accusation, obtained by oaths of others; so **cŏ'mpurgāt**OR *n.*, (Hist.) witness who swore to innocence or good character of accused person, **compur'gat**ORY *a.* [f. med. L *compurgatio* f. L COM(*purgare* purify); see -ATION]
compū'te *v.* **1.** *v.t.* Reckon (number or amount, *that*). **2.** *v.i.* Make reckoning; use computer. **3.** Hence **compū'table** (*or* kŏ'-) *a.*, **cŏmpūta'tion** *n.* [f. F *computer* or f. L COM(*putare* reckon)]
compū'ter *n.* Reckoner, calculator; automatic electronic apparatus for making calculations or controlling operations that are expressible in numerical or logical terms; hence ~IZE *v.t.*, equip with, perform by, produce by, computer. [f. prec. + -ER¹]
cŏ'mrāde (*or* -rĭd; *or* kŭ'-) *n.* Mate or fellow in work or play or fighting, equal with whom one is on familiar terms, (usu. of males); fellow socialist, communist, etc., (also as *voc.*, or title before name); hence ~LY¹ (-dlĭ) *a.*, ~SHIP (-dsh-) *n.* [earlier *cama-*, *camerade* f. F, f. Sp. *camarada* room-mate (as CHAMBER; see -ADE)]
cŏ'msăt *n.* Satellite used for communication. [abbr.]
Cŏ'mt|ĭsm *n.* = POSITIVISM; so ~IST (2) *n.* [f. A. *Comte*, Fr. philosopher d. 1857 + -ISM]
cŏn¹ *v.t.* (**-nn-**) (arch.) ~ (**over**), study, learn by heart. [ME *cunn-*, *con*, forms of CAN²]
cŏn², ***cŏnn**, *v.t.* (**-nn-**). Direct steering of (ship, or abs.); **co'nning-tower**, armoured pilot-house of warship, superstructure of submarine from which steering, firing, etc., are directed when it is on or near the surface, and which contains periscope. [app. weakened form of obs. *cond*, *condie*, f. F *conduire* f. L *conducere* CONDUCT²]
cŏn³ *n.* (colloq. or sl.) Confidence (trick etc.); contra; convict. [abbr.]
cŏn⁴ *v.t.* (**-nn-**). (sl.) Persuade; swindle. [f. prec. = *confidence*]
con- *pref.*, assim. form of COM- before *c*, *d*, *f*, *g*, *j*, *n*, *q*, *s*, *t*, *v*, and occas. before vowels (*conurbation*).
cŏ'nācre (-ker) *n.* (Ir.) Letting by tenant of small portions of land prepared for crop or grazing. [f. CORN¹ + ACRE]
con amore (kŏn ămor'ā) *adv.* With devotion or zeal; (Mus.) with tenderness. [It., = with love]
conā'tion *n.* (Philos.) Desire to perform an action, volition, voluntary action; so **cŏ'nat**IVE *a.* [f. L *conatio* (*conari* try; see -ATION)]
con brio (kŏn brē'ō) *adv.* (Mus.) With spirit. [It.]
concă'tėn|āte (-n-k-) *v.t.* Link together (fig.); so ~A'TION *n.* [f. LL CON(*catenare* f. *catena* chain) + -ATE³]
cŏ'ncāve (-n-k-) *a.* With outline or surface curved like interior of circle or sphere (cf. CONVEX); hence or cogn. ~LY² (-vlĭ) *adv.*, **concă'v**ITY *n.* [f. L CON(*cavus* hollow), or thr. F *concave*]
concea'l *v.t.* Keep secret (*from*); not allow to be seen or noticed; so ~MENT *n.* [ME, f. OF *conceler* f. L CON(*celare* hide)]
concē'de *v.t.* Admit or allow (*that*, defeat, etc.); grant (right, privilege, points or start in game etc.; *to* person); (Sport) allow opponent(s) to score (goal), to win (match), etc.; admit defeat in (election etc.). [f. F *concéder* or L CON(*cedere cess-* yield)]
concei't (-sē't) *n.* Personal vanity; fanciful notion, far-fetched comparison, etc. esp. as affectation of style; (arch.) **in** one's **own** ~ (judgement), **out of** ~, no longer pleased *with*. [ME, f. CONCEIVE after *deceit*, *deceive*, etc.]
concei'tėd (-sē't-) *a.* Having too high an opinion of one's own beauty, ability, etc.; hence ~LY² *adv.* [f. prec. + -ED²]
concei'v|able (-sē'v-) *a.* That can be (mentally) conceived; hence ~ABI'LITY, ~**able**NESS (-beln-), *ns.*, ~**ably**² *adv.* [f. foll. + -ABLE]
concei've (-sē'v) *v.t.* & *i.* Become pregnant

(with); ~ (**of**), form in the mind (*conceive a dislike for*), imagine; fancy, think, (*that*); (usu. in *pass.*) formulate, express, (*conceived in plain terms*). [ME, f. OF *conceiv-* stressed st. of *concevoir* f. L CON(*cipere cept-* = *capere* take)]

concĕ'lėbr|āte *v.i.* (R.C. Ch., of two or more priests) celebrate mass together, (esp., of newly ordained priest) celebrate mass with ordaining bishop; hence ~ANT, ~A'TION, *ns.* [f. L CON(*celebrare* CELEBRATE) + -ATE[3]]

cŏ'ncentr|āte *v.* & *n.* **1.** *v.t.* Bring together to one point (troops, power, attention); (Chem.) increase strength of (liquid etc.) by removing water or other diluent; (fig., in *p.p.*, of hate etc.) intense. **2.** *v.i.* Employ all one's power or attention (*on*). **3.** Hence ~A'TION *n.* (**~ation camp,** for detention of political prisoners, internees, etc., esp. in Nazi Germany), **~ā**TIVE *a.*, **~ā**TOR *n.* **4.** *n.* Concentrated substance; concentrated form of something, esp. animal food. [f. after *concentre* f. F *concentrer* (f. as CON- + CENTRE[1]) + -ATE[3]]

concĕ'ntre (-t*er*), ***-ter,** *v.t.* & *i.* Bring or come to a common centre. [f. F *concentrer* (see prec.)]

concĕ'ntr|ic *a.* Having a common centre (*with*, or abs.); hence ~ICALLY *adv.*, **cŏncentri'**CITY *n.* [ME, f. OF *concentrique* or f. med. L CON(*centricus*, as CENTRE[1]; see -IC)]

cŏ'ncĕpt *n.* Idea of a class of objects; general notion (*the concept of evolution*); invention (*a new concept in caravans*). [f. LL *conceptus* f. *concept-* (see CONCEIVE)]

concĕ'ption *n.* Conceiving or being conceived; thing conceived, idea, (**no ~ of,** inability to imagine); hence ~AL *a.* [ME f. OF, f. L *conceptio -onis* (as prec.; see -ION)]

concĕ'ptĭve *a.* Conceiving (mentally); of conception. [f. L *conceptivus* (as prec.; see -IVE)]

concĕ'ptūal *a.* Of mental conceptions or concepts; hence ~IZE (3) *v.t.* [f. med. L *conceptualis* (*conceptus*, as prec.; see -AL)]

concĕ'ptūal|ĭsm *n.* (Philos.) doctrine that universals exist, but only as mental concepts; so ~IST (2) *n.* [f. prec. + -ISM]

concẽr'n[1] *v.t.* **1.** Relate to, affect; **to whom it may ~** (introducing testimonial etc.). **2.** Interest one*self* (*with, in, about*, matter; *to* do). [f. F *concerner* or f. LL CON(*cernere* sift, discern)]

concẽr'n[2] *n.* **1.** Relation, reference, (*with*); **have no ~** (nothing to do) **with; have a ~** (interest, share) **in. 2.** (Feeling of) anxiety or worry (*asked with deep concern*); (in Quaker use) conviction of divine will; matter that affects one (*no concern of mine*); (in *pl.*) affairs (*meddling in my concerns*); business, firm, (*sold as a* GOING[2] *concern*; see GO[1] 6); (colloq.) thing (*smashed the whole concern*). [f. prec.]

concẽr'ned (-nd) *a.* Involved, interested, (*spoke to the people concerned*; *concerned to prove, with proving, his innocence*); troubled, anxious, (*a concerned air*; *am concerned to hear, at, for* person, *about*); **be ~,** take part (*in*); **I am not ~,** it is not my business (*to*); **as** or **so far as I am ~,** as regards my interests. [p.p. of CONCERN[1]]

concẽr'nĭng *prep.* About, regarding. [f. CONCERN[1] + -ING[2]]

concẽr'nment *n.* Affair, business; importance; being concerned (*with*); anxiety. [f. CONCERN[1] + -MENT]

cŏ'ncert[1] *n.* **1.** Agreement, union, (*work in concert* (*with*); **C~ of Europe,** (Hist.) chief European powers acting together); combination of voices or sounds (*voices raised in concert*). **2.** Musical entertainment; **~-goer,** one who frequents concerts; **~ grand,** grand piano of largest size for concerts; **~-master,** leader of some orchestras; **~ overture,** (Mus.) piece like overture but for independent performance; **~ pitch,** slightly higher pitch than the ordinary, (fig.) state of unusual efficiency or readiness. [F, f. It. *concerto* (*concertare*; see foll.)]

concẽr't[2] *v.t.* Arrange (by mutual agreement or co-ordination). [f. F *concerter* f. It. *concertare* harmonize, of uncert. orig.]

concẽr'tėd *a.* In vbl senses; (Mus.) arranged in parts for voices or instruments. [p.p. of prec.]

cŏncerti'na (-tē'-) *n.* & *v.* **1.** *n.* Portable musical instrument consisting of a pair of bellows and reeds with set of finger-studs at each end to control valves. **2.** *v.t.* & *i.* Compress or collapse in folds like those of concertina. [f. CONCERT[1] + -INA]

cŏncẽrti'nō (-nchẽrtē'-) *n.* (*pl.* **~s**). (Mus.) Simple or short concerto; solo instrument(s) in concerto. [It., dim. of foll.]

concẽr't|ō (-nch-; *or* -ãr'-) *n.* (*pl.* **~os,** *or* **~i** *pr.* -ē). (Mus.) Composition (usu. in three movements) for solo instrument(s) accompanied by orchestra; **~o grosso** (grŏ'sō), composition with small group of solo instruments accompanied by orchestra. [It.; see CONCERT[1]]

concĕ'ssion (-sh*o*n) *n.* Act of conceding; thing conceded, esp. right to use land etc. (esp. for specific purpose) or sell goods; land or premises thus used; hence ~ARY[1] *a.* [F, or f. L *concessio* (as CONCEDE; see -ION)]

concĕssionair'e, -nnair'e, (-sh*o*nãr') *n.* Holder of concession or grant, esp. of use of land or trading rights. [F (*-nn-*) (as prec.; see -ARY[1])]

concĕ'ssĭve *a.* Of or tending to concession; (Gram.) expressing concession. [f. LL *concessivus* (as CONCEDE; see -IVE)]

cŏnch (*or* -ngk) *n.* Shellfish, esp. large gastropod; its shell; (Archit.) domed roof of semicircular apse; = foll. [f. L *concha* shell f. Gk *kogkhē* mussel etc.]

cŏ'ncha (-ngk*a*) *n.* (*pl.* **~e**). External ear or its central cavity. [L (see prec.)]

‖**cŏ'nchĭe, cŏ'nchy̆,** (-nshĭ) *n.* (sl.) Conscientious objector. [abbr.]

cŏnchoi'dal (-ngk-) *a.* (Min., of crystal fracture etc.) like the surface of a bivalve shell. [f. CONCH + -OID + -AL]

cŏnchŏ'log|y̆ (-ngk-) *n.* Study of shells and shellfish; so **cŏncho**LO'GICAL (-ngk-) *a.*, ~IST (3) *n.* [f. Gk *kogkhē* shell; see -LOGY]

co'ncierge (kaw'ṅsĭãrzh) *n.* (In France etc.) door-keeper, porter, (esp. of flats etc.). [F, f. Rom. *CON*servius* fellow slave]

concĭ'lĭar *a.* Of ecclesiastical councils. [f. med. L *consiliarius* counsellor; see -AR[2]]

concĭ'lĭ|āte *v.t.* Pacify; win over from hostility; reconcile (disagreeing parties etc.); gain (esteem, goodwill); hence **~at**IVE, **~at**ORY, (-ly*a*-), *adjs.*, **~āt**OR *n.* [f. L *conciliare* combine, gain (*concilium* COUNCIL) + -ATE[3]]

concĭlĭā'tion *n.* Reconcilement; use of conciliating measures. [f. L *conciliatio* (as prec.; see -ATION)]

concĭ'nnĭty̆ *n.* Elegance or neatness of literary style. [f. L *concinnitas* (*concinnus* well-adjusted; see -ITY)]

concī'se *a.* (Of speech, style, person) brief but comprehensive in expression; hence ~LY[2] (-slĭ) *adv.*, ~NESS (-sn-) *n.* [f. F *concis* or f. L *concisus* p.p. of CON(*cidere cis-* = *caedere* cut)]

concĭ'sion (-zh*o*n) *n.* Conciseness (esp. of style). [ME, f. L *concisio* (as prec.; see -ION)]

cŏ'nclāve (-n-k-) *n.* Meeting-place or assembly of cardinals for election of pope; private meeting. [ME f. OF f. L CON*clave* lockable room (*clavis* key)]

conclu'de (-n-klo͞o'd) *v.t.* & *i.* Bring or come to an end, make an end (of), (*conclude* one's *speech* etc., or *conclude, with* remark etc., *by* saying etc.); infer (*from* premisses etc.); settle, arrange, (treaty etc.); decide (*to* do). [ME, f. L CON-(*cludere clus-* = *claudere* shut)]

conclu'sion (-n-kloo͞'zhon) *n.* **1.** Termination; final result; decision; **in ~,** lastly, to conclude. **2.** Inference; (Logic) proposition deduced from previous ones, esp. last of three forming a syllogism; JUMP² *to conclusions*; **try ~s with,** engage in trial of skill etc. with. **3.** Settling, arrangement, (*of* peace etc.). [ME f. OF, or f. L *conclusio* (as prec.; see -ION)]

conclu'sive (-n-kloo͞'-) *a.* Decisive, convincing; hence ~LY² (-vlĭ) *adv.*, ~NESS (-vn-) *n.* [f. LL *conclusivus* (as prec.; see -IVE)]

concŏ'ct (-n-k-) *v.t.* Make up of mixed ingredients (soup, drink; story, plot); hence or cogn. ~ION, ~OR, *ns.* [f. L CON(*coquere coct-* cook)]

concŏ'mĭtance, -cy̆, (kon-k-) *n.* Coexistence, esp. doctrine of coexistence of body and blood of Christ in each of the Eucharistic elements (esp. in the bread). [f. med. L *concomitantia* (as foll.; see -ANCE, -ANCY)]

concŏ'mĭtant (-n-k-) *a.* & *n.* **1.** *a.* Going together (*concomitant circumstances*); hence ~LY² *adv.* **2.** *n.* Accompanying thing. [f. LL CON(*comitari* f. L *comes -mitis* companion); see -ANT]

cŏ'ncord¹ (*or* -n-k-) *n.* Agreement, harmony, between persons or things; treaty; (Mus.) chord pleasing or satisfactory in itself without others to follow; (Gram.) agreement between words in gender, number, etc. [ME f. OF *concorde* f. L *concordia* f. CON(*cors* f. *cor cordis* heart) of one mind]

***Cŏ'ncord²** (*or* -n-k-) *n.* ~ **grape** (large dark variety). [~ in Massachusetts]

concor'dance (kon-k-) *n.* Agreement; alphabetical arrangement of (chief) words occurring in a book (esp. the Bible) or author, with citations of the passages concerned. [ME f. OF, f. med. L *concordantia* (as foll.; see -ANCE)]

concor'dant (-n-k-) *a.* Agreeing, harmonious, (*with*, or abs.); in musical concord; hence ~LY² *adv.* [ME f. OF, f. L *concordare* (*concors*; see CONCORD¹, -ANT)]

concor'dăt (-n-k-) *n.* Agreement, esp. between Church and State. [F, or f. L *concordatum* neut. p.p. (as n.) of *concordare* (see prec.)]

concours d'élégance (kawnkoor dĕlĕgah'ns) *n.* Parade of vehicles with prizes for the most elegant-looking. [F, = contest of elegance]

cŏ'ncourse (-ors; *or* -n-k-) *n.* Crowd; coming together of things (*fortuitous concourse of atoms*); open central area in large public building, railway station, etc. [ME, f. OF *concours* f. L *concursus* (as CONCUR)]

concrĕ'sc|ence (kon-k-) *n.* (Biol.) Coalescence, growing together; so ~ENT *a.* [f. CON-, after *excrescence* etc.]

cŏ'ncrēte¹ (*or* -n-k-) *a.*, *n.*, & *v.t.* **1.** *a.* (Gram., of noun) denoting thing as opposed to quality, state, or action, not abstract; existing in material form, real, (**in the ~,** in sphere of reality); specific, definite; ~ **music** (constructed by rearrangement of recorded sounds); ~ **poetry** (using typographical devices to enhance visual effect); hence ~LY² (-tlĭ) *adv.* **2.** *n.* Composition of gravel, cement, etc., for building; **~-mixer,** machine (usu. with revolving drum) for mixing ingredients of concrete. **3.** *v.t.* Cover with concrete; embed in concrete. [f. F *concret* or f. L *concretus* p.p. of CON(*crescere cret-* grow)]

concrē'te² (-n-k-) *v.t.* & *i.* Form into a mass, solidify; make concrete instead of abstract. [f. prec.]

concrē'tion (-n-k-) *n.* Coalescence; concreted mass, esp. (Path.) morbid formation in the body, stone; (Geol.) mass formed of solid particles, whence ~ARY¹ *a.* [F, f. L *concretio* (as CONCRETE¹; see -ION)]

cŏ'ncrētīz|e, -īs|e, (-īz; *or* -n-k-) *v.t.* Make concrete instead of abstract; hence ~A'TION *n.* [f. CONCRETE¹ + -IZE]

concū'bĭn|age (-n-k-) *n.* Cohabiting of man and woman not legally married; having or being a concubine; so ~ARY¹ *a.* [ME f. F (as foll.; see -AGE)]

cŏ'ncūbīne *n.* Woman who cohabits with a man, not being his wife; (among polygamous peoples) secondary wife. [ME f. OF, f. L CON(*cubina* f. *cubare* lie; see -INE⁴)]

concū'pĭsc|ence (kon-k-) *n.* Sexual desire; so ~ENT *a.* [ME f. OF, f. LL *concupiscentia* f. L CON*cupiscere* begin to desire, incept. f. *cupere* desire; see -ENCE]

concur' (-n-k-) *v.i.* (**-rr-**). Happen together, coincide; (of cause etc.) combine in its action (*with*, or abs.); agree in opinion, express agreement, (*with*). [f. L CON(*currere* run)]

concŭ'rr|ent (-n-k-) *a.* Running in same direction, as parallel lines; (of three or more lines) meeting at or tending to one point; existing or acting together or at the same time (*with*); agreeing; hence ~ENCE *n.*, **~ent**LY² *adv.* [f. as prec.; see -ENT]

concŭ'ss (-n-k-) *v.t.* Subject to concussion; shake violently; (arch.) intimidate. [f. L CON(*cutere cuss-* = *quatere* shake)]

concŭ'ssion (-n-kŭ'shon) *n.* Violent shaking; shock; (Med.) injury to brain etc. caused by heavy blow etc. [f. L *concussio* (as prec.; see -ION)]

condĕ'mn (-m) *v.t.* **1.** Censure, blame. **2.** Give judgement against; bring about conviction of (*his looks condemn him*); sentence *to* punishment, esp. sentence to death; **~ed cell** (for person condemned to death). **3.** Pronounce forfeited (smuggled goods etc.), unfit for use, uninhabitable, incurable. **4.** Hence ~ABLE (-mn-) *a.* [ME, f. OF *condem(p)ner* f. L CON(*demnare* = *damnare* DAMN)]

cŏndĕmnā'tion *n.* Censure; judicial conviction; ground for condemning (*his own conduct is his condemnation*). [ME, f. LL *condemnatio* (as prec.; see -ATION)]

condĕ'mnatory̆ *a.* Expressing condemnation. [f. med. L *condemnatorius* (as CONDEMN; see -ORY)]

cŏ'ndensāte (*or* kondĕ'-) *n.* Product of condensation. [f. CONDENSE + -ATE¹]

cŏndĕnsā'tion *n.* Act of condensing; condensed material (esp. of water on cold windows etc.; ~ **trail,** trail of water from aircraft or rocket at high altitude, seen as white streak against sky); abridgement; (Chem.) combination of molecules with elimination of water etc. [f. LL *condensatio* (as foll.; see -ATION)]

condĕ'ns|e *v.t.* & *i.* Make denser or more compact (**~ed milk,** milk thickened by evaporation and sweetened); reduce or be reduced from gas or vapour to liquid; express in fewer words, make concise; hence ~ABLE *a.*, ~ERY (3) *n.*, factory for making condensed milk. [f. F *condenser* or L CON(*densare* f. *densus* thick)]

condĕ'nser *n.* In vbl senses; chamber in steam-engine in which steam is condensed on leaving cylinder; (Chem.) device for condensing vapour leaving flask etc.; (Electr.) = CAPACITOR; lens or system of lenses for concentrating light. [f. prec. + -ER¹]

cŏndėscĕ'nd *v.i.* Be gracious enough (*to* do) though showing one's feeling of dignity or superiority; disregard one's superiority (*to* a person). [ME, f. OF *condescendre* f. eccl. L CON(*descendere* DESCEND)]

cŏndėscĕ'nsion (-shon) *n.* Affability to inferiors;

patronizing manner. [obs. F, f. eccl. L *condescensio* (as prec.; see -ION)]

condi'gn (-ī'n) *a.* (Usu. of punishment) severe and well-deserved; hence ~LY[2] *adv.* [ME, f. OF *condigne* f. L CON(*dignus* worthy)]

cŏ'ndiment *n.* Substance used to give relish to food, seasoning. [ME, f. L *condimentum* (*condire* pickle; see -MENT)]

condi'tion[1] *n.* **1.** Stipulation, thing upon the fulfilment of which depends that of another, (**on ~ that,** with the condition that); (Gram.) clause expressing a condition; *subject in which student must pass examination within stated time to maintain provisionally granted status. **2.** (in *pl.*) Circumstances, esp. those essential to a thing's existence (*conditions of equilibrium*; *favourable conditions*; *under existing conditions*). **3.** State of being (*eggs arrived, machine is still, in good condition*; *not in a condition to be mended*; *all sorts and conditions of men*); **in, out of, ~,** in good, bad, condition; **~ powder,** medicine to keep animal in condition. **4.** State of being physically abnormal (*has a heart condition*). [ME, f. OF *condicion* f. L *condicio -onis* f. CON(*dicere* say) agree on; see -ION]

condĭ'tion[2] *v.t.* **1.** Govern, determine; impose conditions on (*they condition the universe anew*); be essential to (*the two things condition each other*); *subject to re-examination (cf. prec.). **2.** Bring into desired state or condition (*for*); make fit (esp. dogs, horses, etc.); teach, accustom, (*conditioned to respond to the stimulus*; **~ed reflex,** reflex response to non-natural stimulus, established by training); test condition of (textile etc.); AIR[1]-*conditioned*. **3.** Hence ~ER[1] *n.* [ME, f. OF *condicionner* or med. L *condicionare*, f. as prec.]

condĭ'tional *a.* & *n.* **1.** *a.* Not absolute, dependent (*on*, or abs.); (Gram.) **~ clause,** one expressing a condition, **~ mood** (used in apodosis); hence ~ITY (-ă'l-) *n.*, ~LY[2] *adv.* **2.** *n.* Conditional mood etc. [ME f. OF *condicionel* or f. LL *condicionalis* (as CONDITION[1]; see -AL)]

condō'latorў *a.* Expressing condolence. [f. foll., after *consolatory* etc.]

condō'l|e *v.i.* Express sympathy (*with*); hence ~ENCE *n.* [f. LL CON(*dolēre* suffer)]

cŏ'ndom *n.* Contraceptive or prophylactic sheath worn on penis in sexual intercourse. [18th c.; orig. unkn.]

cŏndomĭ'nĭum *n.* Joint control of a State's affairs vested in two or more other States; *set of flats, cottages, etc., rented or bought by a group of persons, unit of property so held. [mod. L (as CON-, L *dominium* DOMINION)]

condō'ne *v.t.* Forgive, overlook, (offence, esp. husband's or wife's adultery); (of action) atone for (offence); so **cŏndon**A'TION *n.* [f. L CON-(*donare* give)]

cŏ'ndor *n.* Large vulture of S. America or (**California ~**) N. America. [Sp., f. Quechua *cuntur*]

condottier|e (kŏndŏtyār'ĭ) *n.* (*pl.* ***~i*** *pr.* -ē). (Hist.) Leader of troop of mercenaries in Italy etc. [It. (*condotto* CONDUCT[1])]

condū'c|e *v.i.* (Usu. of event) lead or contribute *to* (result); hence ~IVE *a.* [f. L CON(*ducere duct-* lead)]

cŏ'nduct[1] *n.* **1.** Leading, guidance; SAFE[2] *conduct*; **~-money** (paid for travelling expenses). **2.** Manner of conducting (business etc.); (Art) mode of treatment; behaviour (esp. in its moral aspect); **~ sheet,** record of person's offences and punishments. [ME, f. L *conductus* (as prec.)]

condŭ'ct[2] *v.t.* & *i.* **1.** Lead or guide (*to*); **~ed tour** (led by guide on fixed itinerary). **2.** *v.t.* Be conductor of (orchestra, choir, concert, or abs.); direct, manage, (business etc.); **~ oneself,** behave (*well, with* judgement, etc.); (Phys.) transmit (heat, electricity, etc.) by conduction, whence ~ANCE *n.*, conducting power of specified conductor, ~IBLE *a.* [ME f. OF *conduite* p.p. of *conduire* f. L CON(*ducere duct-* lead); later assim. to L (see prec.)]

condŭ'ction *n.* Transmission (of heat or electricity by contact etc.); conducting (of liquid through pipe etc., esp. of natural processes); transmission of impulses along nerves. [F, or f. L *conductio* (as prec.; see -ION)]

condŭ'ctĭve *a.* Having the property of conducting; hence ~LY[2] (-vlĭ) *adv.*, **cŏnductĭ'v**ITY *n.*, conducting power of specified material. [f. CONDUCT[2] + -IVE]

condŭ'ctor *n.* Leader, guide; manager, director; director of orchestra, choir, etc., who indicates rhythm etc. by gestures; official in charge of bus, tram, or *train; thing that conducts or transmits (esp. heat or electricity; *good, bad, non-*, SEMI-, *conductor*; **~ rail** (transmitting current to electric train etc.); LIGHTNING-*conductor*); hence ~SHIP *n.*, **condŭ'ctr**ESS[1] *n.* (esp. in bus etc.). [ME, f. F *conducteur* f. L *conductor* (as CONDUCT[2]; see -OR)]

condŭ'ct|us *n.* (*pl.* ***~i*** *pr.* -ī). Musical composition of 12th–13th c., with Latin text. [med. L (see foll.)]

cŏ'ndŭĭt (*or* kŏ'ndĭt, kŭ'ndĭt) *n.* Channel or pipe for conveying liquids (lit. or fig.); tube or trough for protecting insulated electric wires, length of this. [ME f. OF *conduit* f. med. L *conductus* CONDUCT[1]]

||**Cŏ'ndў** *n.* **~'s fluid,** (colloq.) ~, strong solution of sodium (per)manganate as disinfectant. [f. H. B. ~, 19th-c. Engl. chemical manufacturer]

cŏ'ndўl|e *n.* (Anat.) Rounded process at end of bone, forming articulation with another bone; hence ~OID *a.* [F, f. L f. Gk *kondulos* knuckle]

cōne *n.*, & *v.t.* **1.** *n.* Solid figure with circular (or other curved) plane base, tapering to a point, so **cō'n**OID *a.* & *n.*; thing of similar shape, solid or hollow; cone-shaped structure in retina etc.; dry fruit of pine or fir; marine gastropod of family Conidae; ice-cream CORNET[1]; conical mountain, esp. of volcanic origin. **2.** *v.t.* Shape like cone; mark with cones. [f. F *cône* f. L f. Gk *kōnos* pine-cone etc.]

cō'ney. See CONY.

cŏ'nfăb *n.*, & *v.i.* (**-bb-**). (colloq.) = CONFABULATION or foll. [abbr.]

confă'bŭl|āte *v.i.* Converse, chat, (*with*, or abs.); (Psych.) devise imaginary experiences after loss of memory; so ~A'TION *n.*, **~at**ORY *a.* [f. L CON(*fabulari* f. *fabula* tale) + -ATE[3]]

confĕ'ction *n.* Mixing, compounding; thing compounded, esp. from sweet things, whence ~ARY[1] *a.*; fashionable article of women's dress. [ME f. OF, f. L *confectio -onis* f. CON(*ficere fect-* = *facere* make); see -ION]

confĕ'ction|er *n.* Maker or seller of sweetmeats, pastry, etc.; hence ~ERY (1, 2, 3) *n.* [f. *confection* prepare confections + -ER[1]]

confĕ'deracў *n.* League, alliance; conspiracy; collusion; body of confederate persons or States. [ME, AF, OF *confederacie* f. as foll.; see -ACY]

confĕ'derate[1] *a.* & *n.* **1.** *a.* Allied (lit. or fig.); **C~ States** (seceding from the U.S., 1861–5). **2.** *n.* Ally, esp. (in bad sense) accomplice; **C~,** supporter of the Confederate States. [f. LL *confoederatus* (as CON-; see FEDERATE)]

confĕ'der|āte[2] *v.t.* & *i.* Bring (person, State, one*self*) or come into alliance (*with*); so ~A'TION *n.*, (esp.) fairly permanent union of States. [prob. f. prec. + -ATE[3]]

confĕ'r *v.* (**-rr-**). **1.** *v.t.* Grant or bestow (title, degree, favour, etc., *on*). **2.** *v.i.* Converse, take counsel, (*with*, or abs.). **3.** Hence **cŏnfer**EE' *n.*, recipient of grant etc., participant in conference, ~MENT *n.*, ~rABLE *a.* [f. L CON(*ferre* bring)]

cŏ'nference *n.* Consultation (**in** ~, engaged in discussion); (esp. annual) meeting of any organization, association, etc., for consultation etc.; annual assembly of Methodist Church; PRESS[1] *conference*; association in commerce, sport, etc.; hence **cŏnferĕ'nti**AL (-shal) *a.* [f. F *conférence* or f. med. L *conferentia* (as prec.; see -ENCE)]

confĕ'ss *v.t.* & *i.* Acknowledge (*I confess my fault, that I did it, to doing it, to having done it, to a dread of spiders*); ~ (**oneself**), formally declare one's sins, esp. to a priest, whence ~ANT *n.*; (of priest) hear confession (of); hence ~**ėd**LY[2] *adv.* [ME, f. OF *confesser* f. Rom. **confessare* f. L *confessus* p.p. of CON(*fitēri* = *fatēri* declare, avow)]

confĕ'ssion (-shon) *n.* Acknowledgement (of offence, fact, etc.; of sins to priest, whence ~ARY[1] *a.*); thing confessed; body of persons sharing a ~ **of faith,** declaration of religious doctrine, creed, statement of one's principles in any matter, whence ~IST (2) *n.* [ME f. OF, f. L *confessio -onis* (as prec.; see -ION)]

confĕ'ssional (-sho-) *a.* & *n.* **1.** *a.* Of confession; denominational. **2.** *n.* Stall in which priest hears confession; act or practice of confessing to priest. [a. f. prec. + -AL; n. f. F, f. It. f. med. L *confessionale* neut. (as n.) of *confessionalis* (as prec.; see -AL)]

confĕ'ssor *n.* One who confesses; one who avows his religion in face of danger, but does not suffer martyrdom (*King Edward the Confessor*); (*or* kŏ'nfĕser) priest who hears confession. [ME, f. AF *confessur*, OF *-our*, f. eccl. L *confessor* (as CONFESS; see -OR)]

confĕ'ttĭ *n. pl.* Bits of coloured paper, thrown by wedding guests at bride and bridegroom. [It., = sweetmeats f. L (as COMFIT)]

cŏnfĭdă'nt (*or* kŏ'-) *n.* (*fem.* ~**e** *pr.* same). Person trusted with knowledge of one's private affairs. [18th c. for earlier CONFIDENT 2, prob. for sound of F *confidente* (as foll.); see -ANT]

confī'de *v.* **1.** *v.i.* Have confidence *in*; be trustful; ~ **in,** talk confidentially to. **2.** *v.t.* Impart (secret *to*); entrust (object of care, task, *to*). [f. L CON(*fidere* trust)]

cŏ'nfĭdence *n.* Firm trust; assured expectation; self-reliance; boldness, impudence; telling of private matters (**in** ~, as a secret; **in** person's ~, allowed to know his private thoughts or affairs); thing so told; *~ **game,** ||~ **trick,** theft by persuading victim to entrust valuables to one as sign of his confidence; ~ **man,** one who robs thus. [ME, f. L *confidentia* (as prec.; see -ENCE)]

cŏ'nfĭdent *a.* & *n.* **1.** *a.* Trusting, fully assured (*that, of,* or abs.); bold, impudent; hence ~LY[2] *adv.* **2.** *n.* Confidant. [F, f. It. *confidente* (as CONFIDE; see -ENT)]

cŏnfĭdĕ'ntial (-shal) *a.* Spoken or written in confidence; entrusted with secrets; charged with secret task; inclined to confide; hence ~ITY (-shĭă'l-), ~NESS, *ns.*, ~LY[2] *adv.* [f. prec. + -IAL]

confĭgūrā'tion *n.* Mode of arrangement, e.g. of equipment etc.; conformation, outline; (Astron.) relative position of planets etc.; (Psych.) = GESTALT; hence ~AL *a.* [f. LL *configuratio* f. L CON(*figurare* fashion); see -ATION]

cŏ'nfīne[1] *n.* (usu. in *pl.*) Borderland, esp. (fig.) between two classes of ideas etc.; boundary, limit. [ME, f. F *confins* pl. f. L CON(*finia* neut. pl. f. *finis* end, limit)]

confī'ne[2] *v.t.* Keep (person, thing, one*self*) *in* narrow place, *within* or *to* limits or defined area; imprison; (in *pass.*) be in childbirth. [f. F *confiner* (*confins*; see prec.)]

confī'nement (-nm-) *n.* Imprisonment; being confined, esp. in childbirth; limitation. [f. prec. + -MENT]

confir'm *v.t.* Establish more firmly (power, possession, person *in* possession); ratify (treaty, possession, title); certify, corroborate, (statement, evidence), whence ~ATIVE, ~**at**ORY, *adjs.*; establish, encourage, (person *in* habit, opinion, etc.), whence ~ED[1] (-md) *a.*, permanent, unlikely to change (*confirmed bachelor, invalid*); administer religious rite of confirmation to, whence **cŏ'nfirmănd** [-ND[1]] *n.*, candidate for confirmation. [ME, f. OF *confermer* f. L CON(*firmare* f. *firmus* firm)]

cŏnfirmā'tion *n.* **1.** Act of confirming; corroboration; (Sc. Law) grant of probate. **2.** Rite administered to baptized persons esp. at age of discretion in various Christian Churches; ceremony of confirming persons of similar age in Jewish faith. [ME f. OF, f. L *confirmatio -onis* (as prec.; see -ATION)]

cŏ'nfĭscāt|e *v.t.* Appropriate to the public treasury (by way of penalty); seize as by authority or summarily; so **confĭ'sc**ABLE, **confĭ'scat**ORY, *adjs.*, **cŏnfĭsc**A'TION, ~OR, *ns.* [f. L CON(*fiscare* f. *fiscus* treasury) + -ATE[3]]

cŏnflagrā'tion *n.* Great and destructive fire. [f. L *conflagratio* f. CON(*flagrare* blaze); see -ATION]

confl|ā'te *v.t.* Fuse together, blend, esp. (fig.) two variant texts or readings into one; so ~A'TION *n.* [f. L CON(*flare* blow) + -ATE[3]]

cŏ'nflĭct[1] *n.* Fight, struggle, (lit. or fig.; **in** ~, discrepant (*with*)); collision; clashing (*of* opposed principles etc.); (Psych.) (distress due to) opposition of incompatible wishes etc. in a person. [ME, f. L *conflictus* (as foll.)]

conflĭ'ct[2] *v.i.* Struggle (*with*, or abs., usu. fig.); clash, be incompatible; so ~ION *n.* [ME, f. L CON(*fligere flict-* strike)]

cŏ'nflu|ent (-ŏŏent) *a.* & *n.* **1.** *a.* Flowing together, uniting, (of streams, roads, etc., or fig.); so ~ENCE *n.* **2.** *n.* Stream joining another (prop. of same size). [f. L CON(*fluere* flow); see -ENT]

cŏ'nflŭx *n.* Confluence. [f. LL *confluxus* (as prec.)]

confor'm *v.* **1.** *v.t.* Form according to pattern, make similar (*to*). **2.** *v.i.* Be conformable (*to*, or abs.); comply with rules or general custom; ~ **to,** comply with. **3.** Hence ~ANCE, ~ER[1], *ns.* [ME, f. OF *conformer* f. L CON(*formare* f. *forma* shape)]

confor'm|able *a.* Similar (*to*); consistent, adapted, (*to*); tractable; (Geol., of strata in contact) lying in same direction; hence ~ABI'LITY *n.*, ~**ab**LY[2] *adv.* [f. med. L *conformabilis* (as prec.; see -ABLE)]

confor'mal *a.* (Of map) showing any small area in its correct shape; hence ~LY[2] *adv.* [f. LL *conformalis* (as CONFORM; see -AL)]

cŏnformā'tion *n.* Manner in which a thing is formed, structure; adaptation (*to*). [f. L *conformatio* (as CONFORM; see -ATION)]

confor'm|ist *n.* One who conforms to a practice or usage, esp. ||one who conforms to usages of Church of England; so ~ISM (3) *n.* [f. CONFORM + -IST]

confor'mĭtў *n.* Likeness (*to, with*); compliance (*with, to*), esp. with usages of Church of England. [ME, f. OF *conformité* or f. LL *conformitas* (as CONFORM; see -ITY)]

confou'nd *v.t.* **1.** Defeat (plan, hope); (in *subj.*, as mild oath) = DAMN 2; discomfit; throw into perplexity. **2.** Throw (things) into disorder; mix up; confuse (in one's mind). [ME, f. AF *conf(o)undre*, OF *confondre* f. L CON(*fundere fus-* pour) mix up]

confou'nded *a.* (colloq.) = DAMNED 2; hence ~LY[2] *adv.* [p.p. of prec.]
cŏnfratĕr'nĭtȳ *n.* Brotherhood (esp. religious or charitable). [ME, f. OF *confraternité* f. med. L CON(*fraternitas* FRATERNITY)]
cŏ'nfrère (-rār) *n.* Fellow member of profession, scientific body, etc. [ME f. OF, f. med. L *confrater* (as CON-, *frater* brother)]
confro'nt (-ŭ'nt) *v.t.* Meet face to face, stand facing; be opposite to; face in hostility or defiance; (of difficulties etc.) oppose; bring (person) face to face *with* (accusers etc.); make comparison of; hence **cŏnfront**A'TION *n.* [f. F *confronter* f. med. L CON(*frontare* f. *frons -ntis* face)]
Confū'cian (-shan) *a.* & *n.* (Follower) of Confucius; hence ~ISM (3) *n.* [f. *Confucius*, Chin. philosopher d. 479 B.C. (Latinization of *K'ung-fu-tse* K'ung the master) + -AN]
confū'se (-z) *v.t.* Throw into disorder; mix up in the mind; (usu. in *pass.*) abash, perplex; hence ~**d**LY[2] (-zĭd-) *adv.* [19th c. back form. f. *confused* (14th c.) f. OF *confus* f. L *confusus*; see CONFOUND]
confū'sion (-zhon) *n.* Act of confusing; confused state; tumult; ~ **of tongues** (cf. Gen. 11: 1–9); ~ **worse confounded** (made worse than it was). [ME f. OF, or f. L *confusio* (as prec.; see -ION)]
confū'te *v.t.* Prove (person) to be in error; prove (argument) to be false; so **cŏnfūt**A'TION *n.* [f. L *confutare* restrain]
cŏ'nga (-ngga) *n.*, & *v.i.* (~**ed** *or* ~**'d**, *pr.* -ad). (Perform) Cuban dance of Afr. origin, usu. with several persons in single line; ~ **drum,** tall, narrow, low-toned drum beaten with hands. [Amer. Sp., f. Sp. *conga* (fem.) of the Congo]
congé (kaw'n̄zhā) *n.* Unceremonious dismissal; leave-taking. [ME *congee*, f. OF *congié* f. L *commeatus* leave of absence f. COM(*meare* go) go and come; now usu. treated as mod. F]
congea'l (-nj-) *v.t.* & *i.* Freeze, solidify by cooling; (of blood etc., or fig.) coagulate; hence ~ABLE *a.*, ~MENT *n.* [ME, f. OF *congeler* f. L CON(*gelare* f. *gelu* frost)]
cŏngėlā'tion (-nj-) *n.* Congealing; congealed state; congealed substance. [ME f. OF, or f. L *congelatio* (as prec.; see -ATION)]
cŏ'ngėner (-nj-) *n.* One of the same kind as another (*the goldfinch is a congener of the canary*); *by-product giving distinctive character in whisky etc. [L (CON-, GENUS)]
cóngėnĕ'rĭc (-nj-) *a.* Of same genus, kind, or race; allied in nature or origin; so **congĕ'ner**OUS (-nj-) *a.* [f. prec. + -IC]
congē'nĭal (-nj-) *a.* (Of person, character, etc.) kindred, sympathetic, (*with*, *to*); suited, agreeable, (*to*); hence ~ITY (-ă'l-) *n.*, ~LY[2] *adv.* [f. CON- + GENIAL[1]]
congĕ'nĭtal (-nj-) *a.* (Esp. of disease, defect, etc.) existing from birth; that is such from birth (*congenital idiot*); hence ~LY[2] *adv.* [f. L CON(*genitus* p.p. of *gigno* beget) + -AL]
cŏ'nger (-ngg-) *n.* ~ (**eel**), large sea eel of family Congridae. [ME, f. OF *congre* f. L *conger*, *congrus*, f. Gk *goggros*]
congeries (-njēr'ēz; *or* -njĕ'rĭēz) *n.* (*pl.* same). Disorderly collection, mass, heap. [L, f. as foll.]
congĕ'st (-nj-) *v.t.* (esp. in *p.p.*) Affect with congestion; hence ~IVE *a.* [f. L CON(*gerere gest-* bring)]
congĕ'stion (-njĕ'schon) *n.* Abnormal accumulation (of blood in a part of the body; of population, traffic, etc.). [F, f. L *congestio -onis* (as prec.; see -ION)]
conglŏ'merate[1] (-n-g-) *a.* & *n.* Gathered into a round mass; (Geol.) (pudding-stone, water-worn fragments of rock) cemented into a mass (cf. AGGLOMERATE[2]); heterogeneous mixture; group or corporation formed by merging of unrelated firms. [f. L *conglomeratus* p.p. of CON(*glomerare* f. *glomus -eris* ball); see -ATE[2]]
conglŏ'mer|āte[2] (-n-g-) *v.t.* & *i.* Collect into a coherent mass (lit. or fig.); so ~A'TION *n.* [f. as prec. + -ATE[3]]
Cŏngolē'se (-nggolē'z) *a.* & *n.* (Native) of Congo region or republic. [f. F *congolais* (*Congo* river and region of central Africa); cf. -ESE]
cŏ'ngou (-nggōō; *or* -ō) *n.* Black China tea. [f. Chin. dial. *kung hu tē* tea laboured for]
congrā'ts, congrā'tters (-z), (-n-g-) *int.* (colloq.) Congratulations. [abbr.; see -ER[1](5)]
congrā'tūl|āte (-n-g-) *v.t.* Address (person) with expressions of sympathetic joy (*on* an event); ~**ate oneself,** think oneself fortunate; hence ~ANT *a.* & *n.*, ~**at**IVE, ~**āt**ORY, *adjs.*, ~**āt**OR *n.* [f. L CON(*gratulari* show joy f. *gratus* pleasing) + -ATE[3]]
congrătūlā'tion (-n-g-) *n.* Congratulating; (in *pl.*, esp. as *int.*) congratulatory expressions. [f. L *congratulatio* (as prec.; see -ATION)]
cŏ'ngrėgant (-ngg-) *n.* Member of a Jewish congregation. [f. L *congregare* (see foll., -ANT)]
cŏ'ngrėgāte (-ngg-) *v.t.* & *i.* Collect, gather, into a crowd (of persons) or mass (of things). [ME, f. L CON(*gregare* f. *grex gregis* flock) + -ATE[3]]
cŏngrėgā'tion (-ngg-) *n.* Collection into a crowd or mass; assemblage; ‖(Oxford etc.) general assembly of resident senior members of university; body assembled for religious worship or to hear preacher; body of persons regularly attending a particular church etc.; permanent committee of R.C. College of Cardinals. [ME f. OF, or f. L *congregatio* (as prec.; see -ATION)]
cŏngrėgā'tional (-ngg-) *a.* Of a congregation; (*C*~) of or adhering to Congregationalism. [f. prec. + -AL]
Cŏngrėgā'tional|ĭsm (-ngg-) *n.* System of ecclesiastical organization that leaves legislative, disciplinary, and judicial functions to the individual church and congregation (in England & Wales largely merged in UNITED Reformed Church from 1972); hence ~IST (2) *n.*, ~IZE (4) *v.t.* [f. prec. + -ISM]
cŏ'ngrĕss (-ngg-) *n.* Coming together, meeting; formal meeting of delegates for discussion, esp. of persons belonging to a particular body or engaged in special studies; (*C*~) national legislative body, esp. of U.S.; (*C*~) (Ind.) a political party; **C~man, C~woman,** member of Congress. [f. L *congressus* f. CON(*gredi gress-* = *gradi* walk]
congrĕ'ssional (-n-grĕ'sho-) *a.* Of a congress. [f. prec. & L *congressio* (as prec.; see -ION) + -AL]
cŏ'ngru|ence (-nggrōōens), ~|**encȳ**, *ns.* Agreement, consistency; (Geom.) state of being congruent. [ME, f. L *congruentia* (as foll.; see -ENCE)]
cŏ'ngruent (-nggrōō-) *a.* Suitable, accordant, (*with*); (Geom., of figures) coinciding exactly when superimposed; hence ~LY[2] *adv.* [ME, f. L *congruere* agree; see -ENT]
cŏ'ngruous (-nggrōō-) *a.* Accordant, conformable, (*with*); fitting; hence or cogn. **cŏngru'**ITY (-nggrōō'-) *n.*, ~LY[2] *adv.* [f. L *congruus* (as prec.) + -OUS]
cŏ'nĭc *a.* & *n.* **1.** *a.* Of a cone; ~ **section,** (Math.) figure formed by intersection of cone and plane. **2.** *n.* Conic section; (in *pl.*) study of conic sections. [f. mod. L f. Gk *kōnikos* (as CONE; see -IC)]
cŏ'nĭcal *a.* Cone-shaped; *conical* PROJECTION; hence ~LY[2] *adv.* [f. as prec. + -AL]
conĭ'dĭ|um *n.* (*pl.* ~**a**). Asexual spore of fungus or bacterium, not formed in a sporangium. [mod. L, dim. f. Gk *konis* dust]
cŏ'nĭfer *n.* Cone-bearing tree; hence **conĭ'**FEROUS *a.* [L (as CONE; see -FEROUS)]
cō'nĭfōrm *a.* Cone-shaped. [f. L *conus* cone + -I- + -FORM]

cō'nĭine (-ēn) *n.* Alkaloid forming poisonous principle of hemlock. [f. L *conium* f. Gk *kōneion* hemlock + -INE[5]]
conjĕ'ctural (-kch*er*-) *a.* Involving or given to conjecture; hence ~LY[2] *adv.* [F, f. L *conjecturalis* (as foll.; see -AL)]
conjĕ'cture[1] *n.* Formation of opinion on incomplete grounds; guessing, esp. in textual criticism, of a reading not in the text; guess, proposed reading. [ME f. OF, or f. L *conjectura* f. CON-(*jicere ject-* = *jacĕre* throw); see -URE]
conjĕ'ctur|e[2] *v.* **1.** *v.t.* Guess; propose (conjectural reading). **2.** *v.i.* Make guess. **3.** Hence ~ABLE *a.* [ME, f. OF *conjecturer* f. LL *conjecturare* (as prec.)]
conjoi'n *v.t.* & *i.* Join, combine. [ME, f. OF *conjoign-* pres. st. of *conjoindre* f. L CON(*jungere junct-* join)]
conjoi'nt *a.* United; associated; hence ~LY[2] *adv.* [ME f. OF, p.p. (as prec.)]
cŏ'njugal (-ŏŏ-) *a.* Of marriage (*conjugal* RITES; ~ **rights,** right of sexual intercourse with spouse); of mutual relation of husband and wife (*conjugal affection*); hence ~ITY (-ă'l-) *n.*, ~LY[2] *adv.* [f. L *conjugalis* f. CON(*jux -jugis* f. root of *jungere* join) consort; see -AL]
cŏ'njugāte[1] (-ŏŏ-) *v.* **1.** *v.t.* (Gram.) Inflect (verb) in voice, mood, tense, number, person. **2.** *v.i.* Unite sexually; (Biol., of gametes) become fused; (Chem., of protein) combine with non-protein. [f. L CON(*jugare* f. *jugum* yoke) yoke together + -ATE[3]]
cŏ'njugate[2] (-ŏŏ-) *a.* & *n.* **1.** *a.* Joined together, esp. coupled; (Gram.) derived from same root; (Math.) joined in a reciprocal relation, esp. having same real parts, and equal magnitudes but opp. signs of IMAGINARY parts; (Biol.) fused; hence ~LY[2] (-tlĭ) *adv.*, ~NESS (-tn-) *n.* **2.** *n.* Conjugate word or thing. [f. as prec.; see -ATE[2]]
cŏnjugā'tion (-ŏŏ-) *n.* Joining together; (Gram.) scheme of verbal inflexion; (Biol.) fusion of two gametes in reproduction; hence ~AL *a.* [f. L *conjugatio* (as prec.; see -ATION)]
conjŭ'nct *a.* Joined together; combined; associated, joint. [ME, f. L *conjunctus*; see CONJOIN]
conjŭ'nction *n.* **1.** Union, connection; **in ~,** together (*with*). **2.** (Astrol. & Astron.) Apparent proximity of two heavenly bodies. **3.** Combination of events or circumstances; number of associated persons or things. **4.** (Gram.) Uninflected word used to connect clauses or sentences, or to co-ordinate words in same clause. **5.** Hence ~AL *a.* [ME, f. OF *conjonction* f. L *conjunctio -onis* (as prec.; see -ION)]
cŏnjunctī'v|a *n.* Mucous membrane connecting inner eyelid and eyeball; hence ~AL *a.*, **conjŭnctĭvī'tis** *n.* [med. L (for *tunica* ~), f. as foll.]
conjŭ'nctĭve *a.* & *n.* **1.** *a.* Serving to join (*conjunctive tissue*). **2.** (Gram.) Of the nature of a conjunction. **3.** Hence ~LY[2] (-vlĭ) *adv.* **4.** *n.* Conjunctive word. [f. LL *conjunctivus* (as CONJOIN; see -IVE)]
conjŭ'ncture *n.* Combination of events; state of affairs. [obs. F f. It. *congiuntura* (as CONJOIN; see -URE)]
cŏnjurā'tion (-ŏŏ-) *n.* Solemn appeal; incantation. [ME f. OF, f. L *conjuratio -onis* (as foll.; see -ATION)]
conjure *v.* **1.** *v.t.* (k*o*njoor'). Appeal solemnly to (person *to* do). **2.** (kŭ'nj*er*). Constrain (spirit) to appear by invocation (~ **up,** bring into existence as if by magic, cause to appear to the eye or mind, evoke); effect, bring *out*, convey *away*, (as if) by magic. **3.** *v.i.* (kŭ'nj*er*). Produce magical effects by natural means (*conjuring trick*); perform marvels (*a name* **to ~ with,** of great importance); ***~ man, woman,** witch(-doctor). [ME, f. OF *conjurer* plot, exorcise, f. L CON(*jurare* swear) band together by oath]
co'njurer, co'njuror, (kŭ'nj*e*r*er*) *n.* One who practises sleight of hand. [f. prec. + -ER[1] & f. AF *conjurour* (OF *-eor*) f. med. L *conjurator* (as prec.; see -OR)]
cŏnk[1] *n.* (sl.) Nose; head; punch on nose etc. [19th c.; perh. = CONCH]
cŏnk[2] *v.i.* (colloq.) ~ **(out),** break down, give out (usu. of mechanism etc.), faint or die. [20th c.; orig. unkn.]
cŏ'nker *n.* Horse-chestnut; (in *pl.*) children's game played with horse-chestnuts on strings, each player seeking to break that held by opponent. [f. dial. *conker* snail-shell (orig. used in the game), assoc. w. CONQUER]
con moto (kŏn mō'tō) *adv.* (Mus.) With spirited movement. [It., = with movement]
***cŏnn.** See CON[2].
Conn. *abbr.* Connecticut.
cŏ'nnāte *a.* Born with a person, innate; formed at the same time; allied; congenial; (Bot. & Zool.) united from the start of life. [f. LL *connatus* p.p. of CON(*nasci* be born); see -ATE[2]]
connă'tural (-ch*er*-) *a.* Innate, belonging naturally (*to*); of like nature; hence ~LY[2] *adv.* [f. LL CON(*naturalis* NATURAL)]
connĕ'ct *v.* **1.** *v.t.* Join (two things, one *to* another); join in sequence or order; associate mentally or practically *with*; (usu. in *pass.* or *refl.*) unite *with* others in relationship etc. **2.** *v.i.* Join on (*with*); operate in connection *with* (*train connects with boat*); form logical sequence, be meaningful; (colloq.) hit target with blow etc.; **~ing-rod** (between piston and crankpin etc. in engine, or between wheels of locomotive). **3.** Hence ~ER[1] (2), ~OR, *ns.*, ~ABLE, ~IBLE, *adjs.* [f. L CON(*nectere nex-* bind)]
connĕ'ctėd *a.* In vbl senses; joined in sequence, coherent, whence ~LY[2] *adv.*, ~NESS *n.*; having relationships (**well ~,** associated with persons of good social position). [p.p. of prec.]
connĕ'ction, ‖connĕ'xion, (-ksh*o*n) *n.* **1.** Act of connecting; state of being connected (**cut the ~,** separate things, have no more to do with something; **in ~ with,** (of train etc.) meeting (another conveyance) for transfer of passengers); relation of ideas (**in this ~,** on a related matter); connecting part; connecting train, boat, etc., (*miss the* or one's *connection*). **2.** Personal dealings; (arch.) sexual relation or intercourse; family relationship; person connected with others by family relationship, marriage, etc.; (sl.) supplier of narcotics; religious body, esp. Methodist, whence ~AL *a.*; body of customers etc. (*business with a good connection*). [f. L *connexio* (as CONNECT; see -ION); sp. *-ct-* after CONNECT]
connĕ'ctĭve *a.* Serving or tending to connect; **~ tissue,** (Anat.) fibrous tissue connecting and supporting organs. [f. CONNECT + -IVE]
‖connexion. See CONNECTION.
conning-tower. See CON[2].
***connĭ'ption** *n.* (sl.) ~ **(fit),** fit of rage or hysteria. [19th c.; orig. unkn.]
connī'vance *n.* Conniving (*at, in*); tacit permission (*done with his connivance*). [f. F *connivence* or f. L *conniventia* (as foll.; see -ENCE, -ANCE)]
connī've *v.i.* **1.** ~ **at,** tolerate, disregard, (misbehaviour). **2.** Conspire (*with*). [f. F *conniver* or f. L *connivēre* shut the eyes (to)]
connoisseur' (kŏnosėr') *n.* Expert judge (*of* or *in* matters of taste, esp. in the fine arts); hence ~SHIP *n.* [F, obs. sp. of *connaisseur* f. pres. st. of *connaître* know + *-eur* -OR; cf. *reconnoitre*]

connō'tǀe *v.t.* (Of words) imply in addition to the primary meaning; (of fact etc.) imply as a consequence or condition; mean, signify; so **cŏnnot**A'TION *n.*, ~ATIVE *a.* [f. med. L CON(*notare* f. *nota* mark) mark in addition]

connū'bĭal *a.* Of marriage; of husband and wife; hence ~ITY (-ă'l-) *n.*, ~LY² *adv.* [f. L *connubialis* f. CON(*nubium* f. *nubere* marry); see -AL]

cō'noid. See CONE.

cŏ'nquer (-ngk*er*) *v.t.* Overcome (opponent, or abs.) by force; overcome (habit, passion, etc.) by effort of will; acquire, subjugate, (country); climb (mountain) successfully; hence ~ABLE *a.* [ME, f. OF *conquerre* f. Rom. **conquerere* f. L CON(*quirere = quaerere* seek, get)]

cŏ'nqueror (-ngk*erer*) *n.* One who conquers (**the C~**, William I of England); ǁconker. [ME, f. AF *conquerour* (OF *-eor*) f. *conquerre* (see prec., -OR)]

cŏ'nquĕst *n.* Subjugation (of country etc.); **the** (**Norman**) **C~**, acquisition of English crown by William of Normandy in 1066; conquered territory; person whose affections have been won. [ME, f. OF *conquest*(*e*) f. p.p. of Rom. **conquerere*; see CONQUER]

conquĭ'stadŏr (-n-kw-) *n.* (*pl.* ~**es** *pr.* -ŏrĕz, *or* ~**s**). Conqueror, esp. one of the Spanish conquerors of Mexico and Peru in 16th c. [Sp.]

cŏ'n-rŏd *n.* Connecting-rod. [abbr.]

Cons. *abbr.* Conservative.

cŏnsănguĭ'nǀėous (-nggw-) *a.* Having the same blood, akin; so ~ITY *n.* [f. L CON(*sanguineus* f. *sanguis -inis* blood) + -OUS]

cŏ'nscience (-sh*e*ns) *n.* Moral sense of right and wrong (**good** or **clear, bad** or **guilty,** ~, consciousness that one's actions are right, wrong; **have on** one's ~, feel guilty about; **in all** ~, by any reasonable standard; **for** ~ (or ~') **sake,** to satisfy one's conscience); **case of** ~, matter in which conscience has to decide conflict of principles; ~ **clause** in a law, one ensuring respect for the consciences of those affected; ~ **money** (sent to relieve the conscience, esp. in payment of evaded income-tax); **freedom** or **liberty of** ~, system allowing all citizens free choice of religion; **prisoner of** ~, person in prison for act of social protest; ~**-smitten, -stricken, -struck,** made uneasy by bad conscience; hence ~LESS *a.* [ME f. OF, f. L *conscientia* f. CON(*scire* know) be privy to; see -ENCE]

cŏnscĭĕ'ntious (-shĭĕ'nsh*u*s) *a.* (Of person or conduct) obedient to conscience, scrupulous; ~ **objector,** person who avails himself of conscience clause, esp. one who for reasons of conscience objects to military service etc.; hence ~LY² *adv.*, ~NESS *n.* [f. F *consciencieux* f. med. L *conscientiosus* (as prec.; see -OUS)]

cŏ'nscious (-sh*u*s) *a.* & *n.* **1.** *a.* Aware, knowing, (*of* fact, *of* external circumstances, *that*, or abs.); with mental faculties awake; self-conscious, affected; (of action, emotion, etc.) realized by the doer etc. (*with conscious superiority*; *a hardly conscious movement*); (as *suf.*) aware of, concerned with, (*class-conscious*; *clothes-conscious*); hence ~LY² *adv.* **2.** *n. The* conscious mind. [f. L *conscius* knowing with others or in oneself, f. CON(*scire* know); see -OUS]

cŏ'nsciousnėss (-sh*u*s-) *n.* State of being conscious; totality of a person's thoughts and feelings, or of a class of these (*moral consciousness*; STREAM *of consciousness*); perception (*of*, *that*). [f. prec. + -NESS]

conscrī'be *v.t.* = foll. [f. L *conscribere* (see CONSCRIPTION)]

conscrĭ'pt¹ *v.t.* Enlist by conscription. [back form. f. CONSCRIPTION]

cŏ'nscrĭpt² *n.* One enlisted by conscription. [f. F *conscrit* f. L *conscriptus* (as foll.)]

conscrĭ'ption *n.* Compulsory enlistment for State service, esp. military service. [F, f. LL *conscriptio* levying of troops f. L CON(*scribere script-* write) enrol]

cŏ'nsėcrātǀe *v.t.* Set apart as sacred (*to*); devote *to* (purpose); sanctify; hence ~OR *n.*, ~ORY *a.* [ME, f. L CON(*secrare = sacrare* dedicate f. *sacer* sacred) + -ATE³]

cŏnsėcrā'tion *n.* Act of consecrating, dedication, esp. of church, churchyard, etc., by bishop; ordination to sacred office, esp. of bishop; devotion *to* (a purpose). [ME f. OF, or f. L *consecratio* (as prec.; see -ATION)]

cŏnsėcū'tion *n.* Logical sequence; sequence of events. [f. L *consecutio* f. CON(*sequi secut-* pursue) overtake; see -ION]

consĕ'cūtĭve *a.* Following continuously; proceeding in logical sequence; (Gram.) expressing consequence (*consecutive clause*); ~ **intervals,** (Mus.) intervals of same kind, occurring adjacently between same two parts, esp. fifths or octaves; hence ~LY² (-vlĭ) *adv.*, ~NESS (-vn-) *n.* [f. F *consécutif -ive* f. med. L *consecutivus* (as prec.; see -IVE)]

consĕ'nsūal (*or* -shŏŏ-) *a.* Of or by consent or consensus; hence ~LY² *adv.* [f. L *consensus* (see foll.) + -AL]

consĕ'nsus *n.* Agreement (*of* opinion, testimony, etc.); majority view (*consensus government*). [L, = agreement (as foll.)]

consĕ'nt¹ *v.i.* Express willingness, agree, (*to* a thing, *to* do, *that*, or abs.); ~**ing adult,** (esp.) homosexual. [ME, f. OF *consentir* f. L CON(*sentire sens-* feel) agree]

consĕ'nt² *n.* Voluntary agreement, compliance; permission; **age of** ~ (at which consent, esp. of girl to sexual intercourse, is valid in law); **with one** ~, (arch.) unanimously. [ME f. OF *consente* f. *consentir* (see prec.)]

cŏnsĕntā'nėous *a.* Accordant, suited, (*to*, *with*); unanimous, concurrent. [f. L *consentaneus* (*consentire* CONSENT¹) + -OUS]

consĕ'ntĭent (-shĭ-; *or* -sh*e*nt) *a.* Agreeing; concurrent; consenting (*to*). [f. L (as CONSENT¹; see -ENT)]

cŏ'nsėquence *n.* **1.** Result (of something preceding; **in** ~, as a result (*of*); **take the** ~**s,** accept whatever results from one's choice or act); logical inference. **2.** Importance (**of no** ~, unimportant); social distinction, rank (*persons of consequence*). **3.** (in *pl.*, usu. treated as *sing.*) Round game in which narrative is made up by players each ignorant of what has already been contributed. [ME f. OF, f. L *consequentia* (as foll.; see -ENCE)]

cŏ'nsėquent *a.* & *n.* **1.** *a.* Following as a result (*on*); following logically; logically consistent; hence ~LY² *adv.* & *conj.*, as a result, therefore. **2.** *n.* Event that follows another; (Logic) the second part of a conditional proposition, dependent on the antecedent. [ME f. OF, f. L *consequi*; see CONSECUTION, -ENT]

cŏnsėquĕ'ntial (-sh*a*l) *a.* Following or required as a result or inference; following or resulting indirectly (*consequential damage*); self-important; hence ~ITY (-shĭă'l-) *n.*, ~LY² *adv.* [f. L *consequentia* CONSEQUENCE + -AL]

consêr'vancy̆ *n.* ǁCommission etc. controlling a port, river, etc., (*Thames Conservancy*); similar body concerned with other resources (*Nature Conservancy*); official preservation (of forests etc.). [18th c. alt. of obs. *conservacy* f. AF *conservacie* f. AL *conservatia* f. L *conservatio* (see foll., -ANCY)]

cŏnservā'tion *n.* Preservation, esp. of natural environment, whence ~IST (3) *n.*; ~ **of energy, momentum,** etc., (Phys.) principle that total quantity of energy etc. of any system of bodies not subject to external action remains constant.

[ME f. OF, or f. L *conservatio* (as CONSERVE²; see -ATION)]

consĕr′vatĭve *a.* & *n.* **1.** *a.* Tending to conserve; averse to rapid changes; **C~ Judaism** (allowing only minor changes in traditional ritual etc.); **~ surgery** (seeking to preserve parts as far as possible). **2.** ‖**C~ Party,** (Polit.) that which is disposed to maintain existing institutions and promote individual enterprise, whence **Consĕr′vat**ISM (3) *n.* **3.** (Of estimate etc.) moderate, cautious, purposely low; (of views, taste, etc.) avoiding extremes. **4.** Hence ~LY² (-vlĭ) *adv.* **5.** *n.* Conservative person or (arch.) thing; (*C~*) member of the Conservative Party. [ME, f. LL *conservativus* (as CONSERVE²; see -IVE)]

conservatoire (konsĕr′vatwâr) *n.* (Usu. Continental) school of music or other arts. [F, f. It. *conservatorio* (as CONSERVATORY)]

cŏ′nservātor (*or* konsĕr′va-) *n.* Preserver; official custodian (of museum etc.); member of conservancy. [ME, f. AF *conservatour*, OF *-ateur* f. L *conservator -oris* (as CONSERVE²; see -OR)]

consĕr′vatorў *n.* **1.** Greenhouse for tender plants. **2.** **Conservatoire*. [sense 1 f. LL *conservatorium*, neut. (as n.) of *conservatorius* (as CONSERVE²; see -ORY); sense 2 f. It. *conservatorio* (cf. CONSERVATOIRE)]

consĕr′ve¹ *n.* (*or* kŏ′-) (also in *pl.*) Jam, esp. made from fresh fruit and sugar. [ME f. OF, = med. L *conserva*, f. as foll.]

consĕr′ve² *v.t.* Keep from harm, decay, or loss, esp. with view to later use (*conserve one's energy, resources*); (Phys., esp. in *p.p.*) maintain quantity of (energy etc.) constant. [ME, f. OF *conserver* f. L CON(*servare* keep)]

consĭ′der *v.t.* Contemplate mentally; weigh merits of (course, claim, candidate, etc.); reflect (*that, whether*, etc., or abs.); reckon with, make allowance for; be of opinion (*that*); regard as (*I consider him* (*to be, as*) *a swindler*; *consider yourself under arrest*); (in *p.p.*) made after careful thought (*considered opinion*). [ME, f. OF *considerer* f. L *considerare* examine]

consĭ′derab|le *a.* Worth considering; (of person) notable, important; (of immaterial or *material things) much, no little, (trouble, annoyance, pleasure, *liquor); hence ~LY² *adv.* [f. med. L *considerabilis* (as prec.; see -ABLE)]

consĭ′derate *a.* Thoughtful for others; (arch.) careful; hence ~LY² (-tlĭ) *adv.*, ~NESS (-tn-) *n.* [f. L *consideratus* p.p. of *considerare* (as CONSIDER; see -ATE²)]

considerā′tion *n.* **1.** Act of considering; meditation; **in ~ of,** in return for, on account of; **take into ~,** make allowance for; **under ~,** being considered. **2.** Fact or thing regarded as a reason (*on no consideration*); compensation, reward, (*for a consideration*); (Law) thing given or done as equivalent by person to whom a promise is made; (act of) thoughtfulness for others; (arch.) importance. [ME f. OF, f. L *consideratio -onis* (as prec.; see -ATION)]

consĭ′dering *prep.* In view of (*it is excusable considering his age, how young he is,* (*that*) *he has no experience*; (ellipt.) *that is not so bad, considering* (the circumstances)). [f. CONSIDER + -ING²]

consī′gn (-ī′n) *v.t.* Hand over or deliver *to* (misery, watery grave, person, person's care); transmit, send by rail etc., *to* (person), whence ~EE′, ~OR, *ns.*; deposit (money in bank etc.). [ME, f. F *consigner* or f. L CON(*signare* SIGN²) mark with seal]

consī′gnment (-ī′n-) *n.* Consigning; goods consigned. [f. prec. + -MENT]

consĭ′st *v.i.* Be composed *of* (esp. material things); have its essential feature(s) *in* (*virtue consists in being uncomfortable*); harmonize *with*. [f. L CON(*sistere* stop) exist]

consĭ′stencў, -ce, *ns.* Degree of density, esp. of thick liquids; firmness, solidity, (lit. or fig.); state of being consistent. [f. F *consistence* or f. LL *consistentia* (as prec.; see -ENCE, -ENCY)]

consĭ′stent *a.* Compatible, not contradictory, (*with*); (of person) constant to same principles; hence ~LY² *adv.* [f. L *consistere* (see CONSIST, -ENT)]

consĭ′storў (*or* kŏ′n-) *n.* Senate of pope and cardinals; **C~** (**Court**), Anglican bishop's court for ecclesiastical causes and offences; Lutheran clerical board; court of presbyters; so **cŏnsĭstôr′ĭ**AL *a.* [ME, f. AF *consistorie*, OF *-oire* f. LL *consistorium* (as CONSIST; see -ORY)]

consō′cĭāte (-shĭ-) *v.t.* & *i.* Associate, esp. closely; so **consōcĭ**A′TION *n.*, (esp., Ecol.) part of association with one dominant species. [f. L CON(*sociare* f. *socius* fellow) + -ATE³]

cŏnsolā′tion *n.* Act of consoling; consoling circumstance; **~ prize** (given to competitor just missing main prizes). [ME f. OF, f. L *consolatio -onis* (as CONSOLE¹; see -ATION)]

consŏ′latorў *a.* Tending or intended to console. [ME, f. L *consolatorius* (as foll.; see -ORY)]

consō′l|e¹ *v.t.* Comfort, esp. in grief or depression; hence ~ABLE *a.*, ~ER¹ *n.* [f. F *consoler* f. L *consolari*]

cŏ′nsōle² *n.* (Archit.) slightly-projecting ornamented bracket or corbel; (Mus.) keyboards, stops, pedals, etc., of organ; panel for switches etc.; cabinet for television set etc.; **~ table,** one supported by bracket against wall. [F, perh. f. *consolider* (f. as foll.)]

consŏ′lĭdāt|e *v.t.* & *i.* **1.** Solidify. **2.** *v.t.* Strengthen (usu. fig., one's power etc.); combine (territories, estates, companies, statutes, debts) into one whole; ‖**~ed annuities,** = foll.; ‖**C~ed Fund,** united product of various taxes etc., whence interest of National Debt and other agreed regular charges are paid; hence **consŏlĭd**A′TION, ~OR, *ns.*, ~ORY *a.* [f. L CON(*solidare* f. *solidus* solid) + -ATE³]

consŏ′ls (-z; *or* kŏ′-) *n. pl.* Government etc. securities without maturity date. [abbr. of *consolidated annuities*]

consŏ′mmé (-mā) *n.* Clear meat soup. [F, p.p. (as n.) of *consommer* f. L *consummare* (see CONSUMMATE¹)]

cŏ′nsonance *n.* Recurrence of same or similar sounds (esp. consonants) in words, assonance; sounding of two notes in harmony; (Mus.) consonant interval, concord; (fig.) agreement, harmony. [ME f. OF, or f. L *consonantia* (as foll.; see -ANCE)]

cŏ′nsonant¹ *a.* Agreeable *to*, consistent *with*; harmonious; corresponding in sound; (Mus.) making concord; hence ~LY² *adv.* [ME f. F, f. L CON(*sonare* sound f. *sonus*); see -ANT]

cŏ′nsonant² *n.* Speech sound in which breath is at least partly obstructed, that in forming a syllable is combined with vowel; letter(s) representing it; hence **cŏnsonă′nt**AL *a.* [ME f. OF, f. L *consonans -ntis* (*littera* letter) sounding with another (as prec.)]

con sordino (kŏn sôrdē′nō) *adv.* (Mus.) with use of mute; (fig.) muted. [It.]

cŏ′nsôrt¹ *n.* **1.** Husband or wife; PRINCE *consort*; **queen ~,** king's wife. **2.** Ship sailing with another. [ME f. F, f. L CON(*sors sortis* lot) sharer, comrade]

consôr′t² *v.t.* & *i.* Class or bring together, keep company, (*with*); agree, harmonize, (*with*). [prob. f. SORT² 2]

cŏ′nsôrt³ *n.* (Mus.) Group of players or instruments. [earlier form of CONCERT¹]

For other words in *co-* see CO-.

consŏr'tĭ|um *n.* (*pl.* ~**a**). Association of several States, companies, etc.; (Law) right of association with husband or wife (*loss of consortium*). [L, = partnership (as CONSORT[1])]

cŏnspĕcĭ'fĭc *a.* Of same species. [f. CON- + SPECIFIC]

conspĕ'ctus *n.* General or comprehensive survey; summary, synopsis. [L, f. CON(*spicere spect-* look at)]

conspĭ'cūous *a.* Clearly visible, striking to the eye; attracting notice, remarkable, (*conspicuous by its absence, for his loyalty*); (of expenditure etc.) lavish; hence ~LY[2] *adv.*, ~NESS *n.* [f. L *conspicuus* (as prec.) + -OUS]

conspĭ'racy̆ *n.* Act of conspiring; combination for unlawful purpose, plot; ~ **of silence,** agreement to say nothing concerning a matter. [ME, f. AF *conspiracie*, alt. f. OF *-ation* f. L *conspiratio -onis* (as CONSPIRE; see -ATION)]

conspĭ'rator *n.* One engaged in a conspiracy; hence **conspĭratŏr'**IAL *a.* [ME, f. AF *conspiratour*, OF *-teur*, f. as foll.; see -OR]

conspīr'e *v.i.* Combine secretly (*with*) for unlawful purpose, esp. treason, murder, or sedition; combine, concur, (*to* do); (arch.) plot, devise. [ME, f. OF *conspirer* f. L CON(*spirare* breathe) agree, plot]

cŏ'nstable (*or* kŭ'n-) *n.* ‖Policeman (**Chief C**~, head of police force of county etc.; **police** ~, policeman or policewoman of lowest rank; **special** ~, person sworn in to act as constable on special occasion); governor or warden of royal fortress or castle; (Hist.) principal officer of household of king or noble, commander-in--chief in king's absence. [ME, f. OF *conestable*, *cun-*, f. LL *comes stabuli* count of the stable]

constă'būlary̆ *a.* & *n.* (Organized body) of constables or police. [f. med. L *con(e)stabularius* (as prec.; see -ARY[1])]

cŏ'nstancy̆ *n.* Firmness, endurance; faithfulness; unchangingness. [f. L *constantia* (as foll.; see -ANCY)]

cŏ'nstant *a.* & *n.* **1.** *a.* Unmoved; resolute; faithful (*to*); unchanging; unremitting, frequently occurring, (*constant attention, chatter*); hence ~LY[2] *adv.* **2.** *n.* (Math.) quantity that does not vary; (Phys.) number expressing relation, property, etc., and remaining same in all circumstances (*constant of gravitation*) or for same substance in same conditions (*dielectric constant*). [ME f. OF, f. L CON(*stare* stand); see -ANT]

cŏ'nstantăn *n.* Copper-nickel alloy used in electrical work. [f. prec.]

cŏnstatā'tion *n.* Ascertainment; thing ascertained. [F (*constater* verify f. L *constat* it is certain; see -ATION)]

cŏ'nstellāte *v.t.* Form into (group like) constellation; adorn as with stars. [f. as foll. + -ATE[3]]

cŏnstellā'tion *n.* Group of fixed stars within imaginary outline; (fig.) group of associated persons, ideas, etc. [ME f. OF, f. LL *constellatio -onis* (CON-, *stella* star; see -ATION)]

cŏ'nsternāte *v.t.* (usu. in *pass.*) Dismay. [f. L CON(*sternare* = *sternere* throw down) + -ATE[3]]

cŏnsternā'tion *n.* Amazement or dismay such as to cause mental confusion. [F, or f. L *consternatio* (as prec.; see -ATION)]

cŏ'nstĭpāte *v.t.* Affect (bowels) with constipation; (fig., esp. in *p.p.*) restrict, hinder. [f. L CON(*stipare* press) + -ATE[3]]

cŏnstĭpā'tion *n.* Irregular and difficult defecation; (fig.) restrictedness. [ME f. OF, or f. LL *constipatio* (as prec.; see -ATION)]

constĭ'tūency̆ *n.* Body of voters who elect a representative member; area so represented; body of customers, supporters, etc. [f. foll.; see -ENCY]

constĭ'tūent *a.* & *n.* **1.** *a.* Composing or making up a whole; appointing, electing; able to frame or alter a (political) constitution (*constituent assembly, power*). **2.** *n.* Component part; member of a constituency; one who appoints another his agent. [f. L *constituent-* (partly thr. F *-ant*), f. as foll.; see -ENT]

cŏ'nstĭtūte *v.t.* Appoint (*constitute him president*; *constitute oneself a judge*); establish, form, (*this does not constitute a precedent*); give legal form to (assembly etc.); frame, form, (esp. in *pass.* of bodily or mental constitution); make up, be the components of; hence **cŏ'nstĭtūt**OR *n.* [f. L CON(*stituere -ut-* = *statuere* set up)]

cŏnstĭtū'tion *n.* Act or mode of constituting; character of body as regards health, strength, etc.; mental character; mode in which State is organized; body of fundamental principles according to which a State or other organization is governed (**written** ~, document embodying these); (Hist.) decree, ordinance. [ME f. OF, or f. L *constitutio* (as prec.; see -ION)]

cŏnstĭtū'tional *a.* & *n.* **1.** *a.* Of, inherent in, affecting, bodily or mental constitution; essential. **2.** Of, in harmony with, authorized by, the political constitution; ~ **sovereign, monarchy, government,** (limited by constitutional forms); hence ~ITY (-ă'l-) *n.*, ~IZE (3) *v.t.* **3.** Hence ~LY[2] *adv.* **4.** Constitutional walk, taken regularly for health's sake. [f. prec. + -AL]

cŏnstĭtū'tional|ĭsm *n.* Constitutional government; adherence to constitutional principles; so ~IST (2) *n.* [f. prec. + -ISM]

cŏ'nstĭtūtive *a.* Constructive, formative; essential; component; hence ~LY[2] (-vlĭ) *adv.* [f. LL *constitutivus* (as CONSTITUTE; see -IVE)]

constrai'n *v.t.* Urge irresistibly or by necessity (person *to* do, *to* action or state, or abs.); bring about by compulsion; confine forcibly, imprison (lit. or fig.); (in *p.p.*) forced, embarrassed, (*constrained voice, manner*); hence ~**ĕd**LY[2] *adv.* [ME, f. OF *constraindre* (st. *constraign-*) f. L CON(*stringere strict-* tie)]

constrai'nt *n.* Constraining; being constrained (*under constraint*); confinement; restraint of natural feelings, constrained manner; limitation imposed on motion or action. [ME, f. OF *constreinte*, fem. p.p. (as n.); see prec.]

constrĭ'ct *v.t.* Make narrow, compress; cause (organic tissue) to contract; so ~ION *n.*, ~IVE *a.* [f. L, as CONSTRAIN]

constrĭ'ctor *n.* Muscle that draws together or narrows a part; snake that kills by compressing, esp. BOA *constrictor*. [mod. L (as prec.; see -OR)]

constrĭ'nge (-nj) *v.t.* Constrict. [f. L *constringere* (see CONSTRAIN)]

constrŭ'ct[1] *v.t.* Fit together, frame, build, (lit. or fig.); (Gram.) combine (words) syntactically; draw, delineate, esp. according to given conditions (*construct a triangle*); hence ~OR *n.* [f. L CON(*struere struct-* pile, build)]

cŏ'nstruct[2] *n.* Thing constructed, esp. by the mind; (Psych.) object of perception or thought constructed by combining sense-impressions; (Ling.) group of words in phrase. [f. prec.]

constrŭ'ction *n.* **1.** Act or mode of constructing; thing constructed; syntactical connection between words. **2.** Construing, explanation, (of words); interpretation (of conduct etc.; *put a good, bad, construction on his refusal*). **3.** Hence ~ISM *n.*, = CONSTRUCTIVISM. [ME f. OF, f. L *constructio -onis* (as CONSTRUCT[1]; see -ION)]

constrŭ'ctional *a.* Of or involving construction; structural, belonging to the original structure. [f. prec. + -AL]

constrŭ'ctive *a.* Of construction; tending to construct; helpful, opp. *destructive* (*constructive criticism*); belonging to the structure of a building; inferred, not directly expressed, virtual, (*constructive denial, permission, blasphemy, treason*); hence ~LY² (-vlĭ) *adv.* [f. LL *constructivus* (as CONSTRUCT¹; see -IVE)]

constrŭ'ctĭv|ĭsm *n.* Kind of art making use of various materials combined into forms that usu. do not depict anything; hence ~IST (2) *n.* [f. Russ. *konstruktivizm* (as prec.; see -ISM)]

construe' (-ōō') *v.t.* Combine (words *with* others) grammatically (*'rely' is construed with 'on'*); analyse (sentence), translate word for word; expound, interpret, (words, actions). [ME, f. L *construere* CONSTRUCT¹]

cŏnsubstă'ntial (-shal) *a.* Of the same substance, esp. of the three Persons of the Trinity; hence ~ITY (-shĭă'l-) *n.* [ME, f. eccl. L *consubstantialis* transl. Gk *homoousios*; see CON-, SUBSTANTIAL]

cŏnsubstă'ntĭāte (-shĭ-) *v.t.* & *i.* Unite as one substance. [f. LL *consubstantiatus* (as prec.; see -ATE²,³)]

cŏnsubstăntĭā'tion (-shĭ- *or* -sĭ-) *n.* (Doctrine of) real substantial presence of body and blood of Christ together with bread and wine in Eucharist. [f. mod. L *consubstantiatio*, after *trans(s)ubstantiatio* TRANSUBSTANTIATION]

cŏ'nsuètūde (-sw-) *n.* Custom, esp. as having legal force; so **cŏnsuètū'dĭnARY¹** (-sw-) *a.* [ME f. OF, or f. L *consuetudo -dinis* (*consuetus* accustomed; see -TUDE)]

cŏ'nsul *n.* One of two magistrates elected for one year and exercising supreme authority in Roman Republic; holder of corresponding title in Roman Empire; one of three chief magistrates of French Republic 1799–1804 (**First C~,** Napoleon); State agent residing in foreign town to protect subjects there and assist commerce; hence or cogn. **cŏ'nsūlAR¹** *a.*, ~SHIP *n.* [ME f. L, rel. to *consulere* take counsel]

cŏ'nsūlate *n.* Office or establishment of a (modern) consul; (period of) consular government in France; office of (Roman) consul. [ME, f. L *consulatus* (as prec.; see -ATE¹)]

consŭ'lt *v.* **1.** *v.i.* Have deliberations (*with* person, or abs.). **2.** *v.t.* Seek information or advice from (person, book, one's watch, etc.); take into consideration (feelings, interests); **~ing room** (in which doctor examines patients); hence ~ABLE, ~ATIVE, *adjs.* [f. F *consulter* f. L *consultare* frequent. of *consulere -sult-* take counsel]

consŭ'lt|ant *n.* One who consults; consulting physician etc.; hence ~ANCY *n.* [prob. F (as prec.; see -ANT)]

cŏnsultā'tion *n.* Act of consulting; deliberation; conference. [ME f. OF, or f. L *consultatio* (as prec.; see -ATION)]

consŭ'ltĭng *a.* In vbl senses; **~ architect, chemist, engineer,** etc., (whose business is to advise those doing work in his field); **~ physician** (who is consulted by colleagues or patients in special cases). [f. CONSULT + -ING²]

consū'm|e *v.* **1.** *v.t.* Destroy; use up; eat or drink; spend, waste, (time, trouble, etc.); (in *p.p.*) entirely preoccupied (*with* envy etc.); hence ~ABLE *a.* & *n.* (usu. in *pl.*), (article) intended for consumption. **2.** *v.i.* Waste away. [ME, f. L CON(*sumere sumpt-* take up); partly thr. F *consumer*]

consū'mèdlȳ *adv.* (arch.) Excessively. [f. p.p. of prec. + -LY²]

consū'mer *n.* In vbl senses; (Econ.) user of an article (opp. *producer*); purchaser of goods or services (**~ goods,** those used directly (esp. domestically), not in manufacturing etc.; **~ research,** investigation of such purchasers' needs and opinions; **~ resistance,** = SALES *resistance*); hence *~ISM (3) *n.*, protection of such purchasers' interests, *~IST (2) *n.* [f. CONSUME + -ER¹]

consŭ'mmate¹ *a.* Complete, perfect, (*consummate skill, folly*); fully accomplished (*a consummate general*); hence ~LY² (-tlĭ) *adv.* [f. L CON(*summare* complete f. *summus* utmost); see -ATE²]

cŏ'nsummāt|e² (*or* -sŭm-) *v.t.* Accomplish, complete, (esp. marriage by sexual intercourse); hence ~IVE *a.*, ~OR *n.* [f. as prec. + -ATE³]

cŏnsummā'tion *n.* Completion (esp. of marriage; see prec.); desired end, goal; perfection; perfected thing. [ME, f. OF *consommation* or f. L *consummatio* (as prec.; see -ATION)]

consŭ'mption *n.* Using up; destruction; waste; amount consumed; wasting disease, esp. pulmonary tuberculosis; purchase and use of goods etc. [ME, f. OF *consomption* f. L *consumptio* (as CONSUME; see -ION)]

consŭ'mptĭve *a.* & *n.* **1.** *a.* Tending to consume; tending to or affected with pulmonary tuberculosis; hence ~LY² (-vlĭ) *adv.* **2.** *n.* Consumptive patient. [f. med. L *consumptivus* (as prec.; see -IVE)]

cont. *abbr.* contents; continued.

cŏ'ntăct *n.*, & *v.t.* **1.** *n.* State or condition of touching (*be in contact with*; **come in(to) ~ with,** (fig.) come across, meet); (Electr.) connection for passage of current (*make, break contact*), device for providing this; (Math.) touching of straight line and curve, two curves, or two surfaces; (Med.) person likely to carry contagion through being near infected person; person who is or may be contacted for information, assistance, etc. **2. ~ lens,** small lens worn on eyeball or cornea to correct vision; **~ man,** intermediary; **~ print,** (Photog.) print made by placing negative directly on sensitized paper etc. and illuminating it. **3.** *v.t.* (*or* kontă'kt). Get into touch with (person); begin correspondence or personal dealings with. [f. L *contactus* f. CON(*tingere tact-* = *tangere* touch)]

contadin|o (kŏntahdē'nō) *n.* (*pl.* ***~i*** *pr.* -ē; *fem.* ***~a,*** *pl.* ***~e*** *pr.* -ā). Italian peasant. [It. (*contado* county)]

contā'gion (-jon) *n.* Communication of disease from body to body; contagious disease; moral corruption; (fig.) contagious influence. [ME, f. L CON(*tagio* f. *tangere* touch; see -ION)]

contā'gious (-jus) *a.* Communicating disease by contact (lit. or fig.); (of disease) so communicable (**~ abortion,** BRUCELLOSIS of cattle); (fig. of emotions etc.) infectious; hence ~LY² *adv.*, ~NESS *n.* [ME, f. LL *contagiosus* (as prec.; see -IOUS)]

contai'n *v.t.* **1.** Have or hold as contents; comprise, include; (of measure) be equal to (*pound contains 16 ounces*); (in *pass.*) be included (*within* a space, *between* limits); (Geom.) enclose, form boundary of; (of number) be divisible by (number) without remainder. **2.** Restrain (*could not contain himself for joy*; *contain your anger*); prevent from moving or extending. **3.** Hence ~ABLE *a.*, ~MENT *n.*, (esp.) policy of preventing expansion of hostile nation etc. [ME, f. OF *contenir* f. L CON(*tinēre tent-* = *tenēre* hold)]

contai'ner *n.* In vbl senses; vessel, box, etc., designed to contain some particular thing(s), esp. large boxlike receptable of standard design for transport of goods; **~ ship** etc. (carrying goods so packed); hence ~IZE *v.t.*, pack in or transport by container. [f. prec. + -ER¹]

contă'mĭn|āte *v.t.* Pollute, esp. with radioactivity; infect; hence ~ANT, ~A'TION, *ns.* [f. L *contaminare* (CON-, *tamen-* rel. to *tangere* touch) + -ATE³]

||**contă'ngō** (-nggō) *n.* (*pl.* **~s**). Percentage paid

by buyer of stock for postponement of transfer (cf. BACKWARDATION); ~ **day,** eighth day before settling day. [19th c.; orig. unkn.]

conte (kawnt) *n.* Short story (as a form of literary composition); medieval narrative tale. [F]

contě'mn (-m) *v.t.* (literary). Despise, treat with disregard; hence ~ER[1] (*or* -mn-) *n.* [ME, f. OF *contemner* or f. L CON(*temnere tempt-* despise)]

cŏ'ntempl|āte *v.* **1.** *v.t.* Gaze upon; view mentally; expect, regard as possible; intend, purpose. **2.** *v.i.* Meditate. **3.** So ~A'TION *n.* (**in ~ation,** intended), ~**āt**OR *n.* [f. L *contemplari* (CON-, *templum* place for observations) + -ATE[3]]

contě'mplative (*or* kŏ'ntemplā-) *a.* & *n.* **1.** *a.* Meditative, thoughtful; (of life) given up to religious contemplation, opp. *active*; hence ~LY[2] (-vlĭ) *adv.*, ~NESS (-vn-) *n.* **2.** *n.* Person devoted to religious contemplation. [ME, f. OF *contemplatif -ive*, or f. L *contemplativus* (as prec.; see -IVE)]

contĕmporā'nėous *a.* Existing or occurring at the same time (*with*); of the same period; hence **contĕmporanē'**ITY, ~NESS, *ns.*, ~LY[2] *adv.* [f. L CON(*temporaneus* f. *tempus -oris* time; see -ANEOUS)]

contě'mpor|arȳ *a.* & *n.* (Person, newspaper etc.) belonging to the same time, esp. as oneself; (person) equal in age; modern or ultra-modern in style or design; so ~IZE (3) *v.t.* [f. med. L *contemporarius* (as prec.; see -ARY[1])]

contě'mpt *n.* Act or mental attitude of despising; condition of being despised (**have** or **hold in ~,** despise; **bring, fall, into ~,** make, become, despised); (Law) disobedience to sovereign's lawful commands or to authority of Parliament or other body, esp. ~ **of court,** disobedience to, or interference with administration of justice by, courts of law. [ME, f. L *contemptus* (as CONTEMN)]

contě'mpt|ĭble *a.* Deserving contempt, despicable; **Old C~s,** (colloq.) British Army in France 1914 [w. ref. to German Emperor's alleged mention of a 'contemptible little army']; hence **contĕmpt**IBI'LITY, ~NESS (-beln-), *ns.*, ~**ĭb**LY[2] *adv.* [ME f. OF, or f. LL *contemptibilis* (as CONTEMN; see -IBLE)]

contě'mptūous *a.* Showing contempt (*of*); scornful; insolent; hence ~LY[2] *adv.*, ~NESS *n.* [f. med. L *contemptuosus* f. L *contemptus* (see CONTEMPT, -OUS)]

contě'nd *v.* **1.** *v.i.* Strive, fight, (*with* person *for* thing); struggle *with* or *against* (feelings, natural forces); compete, be in rivalry, (*contending passions*); argue (*with*). **2.** *v.t.* Maintain, assert, (*that*). [f. OF *contendre* or f. L CON(*tendere tent-* stretch, strive)]

cŏ'ntěnt[1] (*or* kontě'nt) *n.* **1.** (in *pl.*) **~s of,** what is contained in (vessel etc., book, document); (**table of**) **~s,** summary of subject-matter of book, usu. list of titles of chapters etc. **2.** Capacity (of vessel); volume (of solid). **3.** Constituent elements of a conception; substance (of cognition, art, etc.), opp. *form*; amount (of some particular constituent) contained (*ester content of an oil*), or yielded (*sugar content per acre of beet*). [ME, f. med. L *contentum*, pl. *-ta* (as CONTAIN)]

contě'nt[2] *n.* Contented state, satisfaction, esp. *to* one's *heart's content.* [16th c., perh. f. foll.]

contě'nt[3] *pred. a.* & *n.* **1.** *a.* Satisfied; willing (*to* do). **2.** *n.* ‖(In House of Lords) affirmative vote(r). [ME f. OF, f. L *contentus* satisfied, p.p. of *continēre* (see CONTAIN)]

contě'nt[4] *v.t.* Satisfy; ~ **oneself with,** be satisfied with, accept or do no more than; so ~MENT *n.*, satisfied state. [ME, f. OF *contenter* f. Rom. *contentare* f. L *contentus* (as prec.)]

contě'ntėd *a.* Satisfied; willing to be satisfied *with*; willing *to* do; hence ~LY[2] *adv.*, ~NESS *n.* [p.p. of prec.]

contě'ntion *n.* Strife, dispute, rivalry; point contended for in argument. [ME f. OF, or f. L *contentio* (as CONTEND; see -ION)]

contě'ntious (-shus) *a.* Quarrelsome; involving contention; hence ~LY[2] *adv.*, ~NESS *n.* [ME, f. OF *contentieux* f. L *contentiosus* (as prec.; see -IOUS)]

contěr'mĭnous *a.* Having a common boundary (*with, to*); coextensive (in space, time, or meaning), coterminous; hence ~LY[2] *adv.* [f. L CON(*terminus* boundary) + -OUS]

contě'ssa *n.* Italian countess. [It., f. LL *comitissa*; see COUNTESS]

cŏ'ntěst[1] *n.* Debate, controversy; strife; (friendly) competition. [f. foll., or f. F *conteste* (*contester*, f. as foll.)]

contě'st[2] *v.* **1.** *v.t.* Debate, dispute (point, statement, etc.); dispute by fighting (field, victory, issue, battle); contend or compete in (‖election) or for (seat in Parliament etc.); *dispute result of (election); hence ~ABLE *a.* **2.** *v.i.* Strive in argument (*with, against*). **3.** So ~ANT *n.* [f. L CON(*testari* f. *testis* witness)]

cŏntěstā'tion *n.* Disputation; assertion contended for. [(partly thr. F) f. L *contestatio* (as prec.; see -ATION)]

cŏ'ntěxt *n.* Parts that precede or follow a passage and fix its meaning (**out of ~,** without these and hence misleading); ambient conditions; **in this ~** (connection); hence **contě'xtūA**L *a.* [ME, f. L *contextus* f. CON(*texere text-* weave)]

contě'xture *n.* Structure; fabric. [F, prob. f. med. L *contextura* (as CON-, TEXTURE)]

cŏntĭgū'ĭtȳ *n.* Contact; proximity; (Psych.) proximity of ideas or impressions in place or time, as principle of association. [f. LL *contiguitas* (as foll.; see -ITY)]

contĭ'gūous *a.* ~ (**to**), touching, adjoining, next in order; neighbouring; hence ~LY[2] *adv.* [f. L *contiguus* f. CON(*tingere* = *tangere* touch) + -OUS]

cŏ'ntin|ent[1] *a.* Temperate; chaste; having normal control over one's excretions; hence or cogn. ~ENCE *n.*, ~**ent**LY[2] *adv.* [ME, f. L (as CONTAIN; see -ENT)]

cŏ'ntĭnent[2] *n.* Continuous land, mainland; one of the main continuous bodies of land (Europe, Asia, Africa, N. & S. America, Australia, Antarctica); **the C~,** mainland of Europe as distinct from British Isles. [f. L *terra continens* continuous land (as prec.)]

cŏntĭně'ntal *a.* & *n.* **1.** *a.* Of a continent; ~ **climate** (having wide variations of temperature); ~ **drift,** (Geol.) slow movement of the continents to their present positions, on a deep--lying plastic substratum; ~ **shelf,** bed of shallow sea area bordering continent. **2.** (*C~*). Belonging to or characteristic of the Continent; ~ **breakfast,** light breakfast of coffee, rolls, etc.; ~ **Sunday,** Sunday as a day of recreation rather than rest and worship; **C~ System,** Napoleon's plan to blockade England in 1806. **3.** Hence ~IZE (3) *v.t.*, ~LY[2] *adv.* **4.** *n.* Inhabitant of the Continent; (sl.) currency note of an early U.S. issue that rapidly depreciated, least possible amount (*don't care* or *give a continental*). [f. prec. + -AL]

contĭ'ngencȳ (-nj-) *n.* Uncertainty of occurrence; chance occurrence; thing that may happen at later time (~ **plan,** to take account of such); thing dependent on an uncertain event; thing incident to another, incidental expense etc. (~ **fund,** to deal with these). [earlier *-ence* f. LL *contingentia* (as foll.; see -ENCE, -ENCY)]

contĭ'ngent (-nj-) *a.* & *n.* **1.** *a.* Of uncertain occurrence; fortuitous; incidental *to*; true only under existing or specified conditions; non--essential; conditional; hence ~LY[2] *adv.* **2.** *n.* Troops contributed to form part of army etc.;

group contributed to larger one. [f. L CON(*tingere* = *tangere* touch); see -ENT]

conti'nūal *a.* Always happening; very frequent and without cessation; hence ~LY² *adv.* [ME f. OF *continuel* (*continuer*; see CONTINUE, -AL)]

conti'nūance *n.* Continuing, duration; remaining, stay, (*in* place, condition, etc.); *(Law) adjournment. [ME f. OF (as CONTINUE; see -ANCE)]

conti'nūant *a.* & *n.* (Phonet.) (Consonant) of which sound can be prolonged as desired (e.g. *f, r, s, v*). [F, & f. L *continuare* (as CONTINUE; see -ANT)]

continūā'tion *n.* Carrying on or resumption (of an action, course, story, book, etc.); ||(St. Exch.) carrying over an account to next settling day (~ **day** = CONTANGO *day*); that by which a thing is continued, additional part(s); ~ **school** (for additional teaching in spare time of those who have left full-time education). [ME f. OF, f. L *continuatio -onis* (as prec.; see -ATION)]

conti'nūative *a.* Tending or serving to continue. [f. LL *continuativus* (as prec.; see -IVE)]

conti'nūātor *n.* One who writes continuation to another's work. [f. as foll.; see -OR]

conti'nū|e *v.* **1.** *v.t.* Maintain, keep up, not stop (action etc.); take up, resume, (narrative, journey, etc., or abs.); *(Law) adjourn; hence ~ABLE *a.* **2.** *v.i.* Still be in existence; stay (*in, at,* place, *in* a state); not become other than (*weather continues fine*; *if you continue obstinate*); not cease (do*ing, to* do). [ME, f. OF *continuer* f. L *continuare* make or be CONTINUOUS]

cŏntinū'ĭtў *n.* State of being continuous; unbroken succession; logical sequence; detailed scenario of film (~ **girl** etc., person who ensures necessary agreement of detail between different filmings); script (esp. of linkage between broadcast items); **law of** ~ (that all changes in nature are continuous, not abrupt). [f. F *continuité* f. L *continuitas -tatis* (as CONTINUOUS; see -ITY)]

conti'nūō *n.* (*pl.* ~s). (Mus.) Figured BASS³; (usu. keyboard) accompaniment improvised from this; instrument(s) playing it. [f. *basso continuo* (It., = continuous bass)]

conti'nūous *a.* (Of material things) connected, unbroken; uninterrupted in time or sequence; (Gram.) progressive; ~ **creation,** creation of the universe or matter in it regarded as a continuous process; ~ **stationery** (with sheets joined together and folded alternately); ~ **wave,** (Phys.) electromagnetic wave of constant amplitude; hence ~LY² *adv.*, ~NESS *n.* [f. L *continuus* uninterrupted f. CON(*tinēre* = *tenēre* hold) + -OUS]

conti'nū|um *n.* (*pl.* ~**a**). Thing whose structure is continuous not discrete (*continuum of matter, sensation, events,* etc.; SPACE¹-*time continuum*). [L, neut. (as n.) of *continuus*; see prec.]

contŏr't *v.t.* Twist, distort. [f. L CON(*torquēre tort-* twist)]

contŏr'tion *n.* Twisting; twisted state (esp. of face or body). [f. L *contortio* (as prec.; see -ION)]

contŏr'tionist *n.* Acrobat who adopts unusual postures; one who contorts meanings etc. [f. prec. + -IST]

cŏ'ntour (-oor) *n.*, & *v.t.* **1.** *n.* Outline; line separating differently coloured parts of design; outline of coast, mountain mass, etc.; ~ **line,** one representing horizontal contour of earth's surface at given elevation, as in a ~ **map;** ~ **ploughing** (along lines of constant altitude to minimize soil erosion). **2.** *v.t.* Mark with contour lines; carry (road) round side of hill. [F, f. It. *contorno* f. *contornare* draw in outline (as CON-, *tornare* turn)]

cŏ'ntra *prep.* & *n.* See PRO¹. [L, adv. & prep. = against]

cŏntra- *pref.* **1.** Against, opposite, etc., (*contradict, contradistinguish*). **2.** (Mus., of instruments and organ-stops) denoting a pitch of an octave below (*contra-bassoo'n*). [f. or after L, as prec.]

cŏ'ntrabănd *n.* & *a.* **1.** *n.* Prohibited traffic, smuggling; smuggled goods; ~ **of war,** anything forbidden to be supplied by neutrals to belligerents; hence ~IST *n.*, smuggler. **2.** *a.* Forbidden to be imported or exported (*contraband goods*); concerned with these (*contraband trade, trader*). [f. Sp. *contrabanda* f. It. CONTRA(*bando* proclamation)]

cŏ'ntrabāss *n.* = DOUBLE¹-*bass.* [f. It. CONTRA-(*basso* BASS³)]

cŏntracĕ'ptive *a.* & *n.* Preventive of pregnancy; so **cŏntracĕ'ption** *n.*, use of contraceptives. [f. CONTRA- + CONCEPTIVE, CONCEPTION]

cŏ'ntrăct¹ *n.* **1.** Agreement between parties, States, etc.; business agreement for supply of goods or performance of work at specified price; agreement enforceable by law (NUDE *contract*). **2.** Accepted promise to do or not do; formal agreement for marriage; conveyance of property; (Bridge etc.) undertaking to make stated number of tricks; ~ (**bridge**), form of auction bridge in which only tricks bid and won count towards game. [ME f. OF, f. L *contractus* (as foll.)]

contră'ct² *v.t.* & *i.* **1.** Enter into business or legal engagement (*to* do, *for* piece of work, or abs.); arrange (work) to be done by contract; ~ (**oneself**) **out** (*of*), arrange for one's exemption or exclusion from provisions (*of* law etc.), refuse to take part (in). **2.** ~ (enter into) **marriage;** form (friendship, habit); become infected with (disease), whence ~ABLE *a.*; incur (debt). **3.** Draw together (muscles, brow, etc.), make smaller, whence ~IBLE *a.*; (Gram.) shorten (word) by combination or elision (as *do not* to *don't*); shrink, become smaller. **4.** Hence ~IVE *a.* [f. earlier *contract* adj. (= contracted) f. OF, f. L *contractus* (CON-, *trahere tract-* draw)]

contră'ctile *a.* Capable of or producing contraction (*contractile muscles, force*); hence **cŏntrăctĭ'lITY** *n.* [f. prec.; see -IL]

contră'ction *n.* Shrinking, contracting; shortening of word by combination or elision; contracted form of word(s); contracting (*of* debt, disease, habit). [F, f. L *contractio -onis* (as CONTRACT²; see -ION)]

contră'ctor *n.* Undertaker of contract, esp. for building to specified plans; contracting muscle. [LL (as CONTRACT²; see -OR)]

contră'ctūal *a.* Of (the nature of) a contract; hence ~LY² *adv.* [f. L *contractus* (CONTRACT¹) + -AL]

cŏntradĭ'ct *v.t.* Deny (statement, or abs.); deny statement made by (person); be contrary to (*these rumours contradict each other*); hence ~ABLE *a.*, ~OR *n.* [f. L CONTRA(*dicere dict-* say)]

cŏntradĭ'ction *n.* Denial; opposition; statement contradicting another; inconsistency; ~ **in terms,** self-contradictory statement or words ('*almost quite ready' is a contradiction in terms*). [ME f. OF, f. L *contradictio -onis* (as prec.; see -ION)]

cŏntradĭ'ctious (-shus) *a.* Inclined to contradict; disputatious; hence ~LY² *adv.*, ~NESS *n.* [f. CONTRADICT + -IOUS]

cŏntradĭ'ctor|ў *a.* Making denial; mutually opposed or inconsistent; inclined to contradict; (Logic, of two propositions) so related that one and only one must be true; hence ~ĬLY² *adv.*,

~ĭNESS *n.* [ME, f. LL *contradictorius* (as CONTRADICT; see -ORY)]

cŏntradĭstĭ'nction *n.* Distinction by contrast. [f. CONTRA- + DISTINCTION]

cŏntradĭstĭ'nguish (-nggw-) *v.t.* Distinguish (things, one *from* another) by contrast. [f. *contra-* + DISTINGUISH]

cŏ'ntrail *n.* Condensation trail. [abbr.]

cŏntra-ĭ'ndĭcāte *v.t.* (esp. Med.) Act as indication against (use of a particular treatment etc.). [f. CONTRA- + INDICATE]

contră'ltō *n.* (*pl.* ~s). (Mus.) Lowest female voice; singer with contralto voice; part written for contralto voice. [It. (CONTRA-, ALTO); cf. COUNTER-TENOR]

cŏntraposĭ'tion (-z-) *n.* Opposition, contrast; (Logic) conversion of proposition from *all A is B* to *all not-B is not-A*; so **cŏntrapŏ'sĭt**IVE (-z-) *a.* [f. LL *contrapositio* (CONTRA-, *ponere posit-* place; see -ION)]

contră'ption *n.* (colloq.) Strange machine; device, contrivance. [19th c.; perh. f. CONTRIVE (cf. *conceive, conception*), assoc. w. TRAP¹]

cŏntrapŭ'nt|al *a.* Of or in counterpoint; so ~IST *n.*, person skilled in counterpoint, ~**al**LY² *adv.* [f. It. *contrappunto* counterpoint + -AL]

cŏntrarī'etў *n.* Opposition in nature, quality, or action; disagreement, inconsistency. [ME, f. OF *contrarieté* f. LL *contrarietas -tatis* (as CONTRARY; see -TY¹)]

contrār'ious *a.* (arch.) Opposed; perverse; (of things) adverse; hence ~LY² *adv.*, ~NESS *n.* [ME f. OF, f. med. L *contrariosus* (as CONTRARY; see -OUS)]

contrār'iwise (-z) *adv.* On the other hand; in the opposite way; perversely. [ME, f. foll. + -WISE]

cŏ'ntrarў (see also sense 2) *a.*, *n.*, & *adv.* **1.** *a.* Opposed in nature or tendency (*to*); (of wind) impeding, unfavourable; opposite (of two things); opposite in position or direction; hence **cŏ'ntrarĭ**LY² *adv.* **2.** (kontrār'ĭ; colloq.) Perverse, self-willed; hence **contrār'ĭ**NESS *n.*, **contrār'ĭ**LY² *adv.* **3.** *n. The* opposite; **by contraries,** taking *Yes* for *No* etc., oppositely to logic or expectation; **on the** ~ (corroborating a denial expressed or understood: *Have you nearly finished?—On the contrary, I have only just begun*); **to the** ~, to the opposite effect (*there is no evidence to the contrary*). **4.** *adv.* In opposition *to* (*act contrary to nature*). [ME, f. AF *contrarie*, OF *contraire*, f. L *contrarius* (as CONTRA; see -ARY¹)]

contra'st¹ (-ah'-) *v.* **1.** *v.t.* Set (two things, one *with* another) in opposition, so as to show their differences. **2.** *v.i.* Show striking difference on comparison (*with*). [f. F *contraster* f. It. f. med. L CONTRA(*stare* stand)]

cŏ'ntrast² (-ah-) *n.* Juxtaposition (esp. of forms, colours, etc.) showing striking differences (*between*; *in contrast with*); thing or person having noticeably different qualities (*to*); degree of difference between tones in photograph or television picture, whence ~Y² *a.*, showing a high contrast; change of apparent brightness, colour, etc., of an object caused by adjacent objects; hence **contra'st**IVE (-ah'-) *a.* [f. F *contraste* f. It. *contrasto* (as prec.)]

cŏntra-suggĕ'stible (-suj-) *a.* (Psych.) Tending to respond to a suggestion by believing or doing the contrary. [f. CONTRA- + SUGGESTIBLE]

cŏ'ntrāte *a.* ~ **wheel,** = CROWN¹ *wheel.* [f. med. L & Rom. *contrata*; see COUNTRY]

cŏntravē'ne *v.t.* Infringe (law); (of things) conflict with. [f. LL CONTRA(*venire vent-* come)]

cŏntravĕ'ntion *n.* Infringement (**in** ~ **of,** violating). [F, f. med. L *contraventio* (as prec.; see -ION)]

contretemps (kaw'ntretahn) *n.* Unlucky or embarrassing occurrence; unexpected mishap. [F]

contrĭ'būte *v.t.* & *i.* Pay or furnish (*to* common fund etc.), pay or give jointly with others; supply (literary work etc. for publication with others); ~ **to,** help to bring about. [f. L CON(*tribuere -ut-* bestow)]

cŏntrĭbū'tion *n.* Act of contributing; thing, help, literary work, contributed; **lay under** ~, exact contributions from. [ME f. OF, or f. LL *contributio* (as prec.; see -ION)]

contrĭ'būtor *n.* One who contributes (esp. literary work). [f. AF *contributour* (as CONTRIBUTE; see -OR)]

contrĭ'būtorў *a.* & *n.* **1.** *a.* That contributes (~ **negligence,** (Law) by injured person who has failed to take proper precautions against accident); operated by means of contributions (*contributory pension scheme*). **2.** *n.* ||(Law). Person liable to contribute towards payment of wound-up company's debts. [f. med. L *contributorius* (as CONTRIBUTE; see -ORY)]

cŏ'ntrīte *a.* Crushed in spirit by sense of sin; completely penitent; (of action) showing a contrite spirit; hence ~LY² (-tlĭ) *adv.*, ~NESS (-tn-) *n.* [ME, f. OF *contrit* f. L *contritus* bruised (as CON-, *terere trit-* rub)]

contrĭ'tion *n.* Being contrite; thorough penitence. [ME f. OF, f. LL *contritio -onis* (as prec.; see -ION)]

contrī'vance *n.* Act of contriving; deceitful practice; invention; mechanical device; inventive capacity. [f. foll. + -ANCE]

contrī'v|e *v.t.* Devise, plan with skill; bring to pass, manage, (thing, *to* do; *contrive to open the window*; *contrive to make matters worse*); (abs.) manage household affairs etc. resourcefully; hence ~ABLE *a.*, ~ER¹ *n.* [ME, f. OF *controver* find, imagine f. med. L *contropare* compare]

contrō'l¹ *n.* **1.** Power of directing, command, (**out of** ~, no longer subject to guidance; **under** ~, (fig.) in proper order); restraint; means of restraint, check; (usu. in *pl.*) means of regulating prices etc. **2.** Standard of comparison for checking inferences deduced from experiment, esp. specimen, patient, etc., like those being investigated, but not specially treated etc. **3.** Personality directing actions of spiritualist medium; place where racing-cars etc. must stop for recording, inspection, etc., or where their speed is controlled; (usu. in *pl.*) various devices in aircraft or vehicle used to control direction, speed, etc., devices for operation of machine. **4.** ~ **panel** (containing switches, dials, etc., for remote control of apparatus); ~ **rod,** rod of neutron-absorbing material used to vary power of nuclear reactor; ~ **room,** room where an operation is controlled; ~ **tower,** high building at airport etc. from which air traffic is controlled by radio. [f. foll. or f. F *contrôle* (*contrôler*; see foll.)]

contrō'l² *v.t.* (**-ll-**). Dominate, command; exert control over (~**ling interest,** ownership of majority of stock or other means to determine policy of a business etc.); hold in check (one*self*, one's anger); check, verify; regulate (prices etc.); hence ~**l**ABLE *a.* [ME, f. AF *contreroller* keep copy of roll of accounts, f. med. L *contrarotulare* (as CONTRA-, *rotulus* ROLL¹)]

contrō'ller *n.* In vbl senses; one who checks expenditure, steward, COMPTROLLER; hence ~SHIP *n.* [ME *counterroller* f. AF *contrerollour* (as prec.; see -OR)]

cŏntrovēr'sial (-shal) *a.* Of, open to, given to, controversy; hence ~ISM (3), ~IST (2), *ns.*, ~LY² *adv.* [f. LL *controversialis* (as foll.; see -AL)]

cŏ'ntrovērsў (*or* kontrŏ'-) *n.* Disputation; argument, esp. conducted in writing; **beyond** ~, unquestionably. [ME, f. L *controversia* (as foll.; see -Y[1])]

cŏ'ntrovērt (*or* -vēr't) *v.t.* Dispute about, discuss; dispute, deny; hence ~IBLE *a.* [orig. p.p. for earlier *controversed* (cf. *converse*, *convert*) f. F *controvers(e)* f. L *controversus* (CONTRA-, *vertere vers-* turn)]

cŏntūmā'cious (-sh*u*s) *a.* Insubordinate, disobedient, esp. to order of court; hence or cogn. ~LY[2] *adv.*, ~NESS, **cŏ'ntūm**ACY, *ns.* [f. L *contumax* (perh. rel. to *tumēre* swell); see -ACIOUS]

cŏntūmē'lious *a.* Insolent; reproachful; hence ~LY[2] *adv.* [ME, f. OF *contumelieus* f. L *contumeliosus* (as foll.; see -OUS)]

cŏ'ntūmelў (*or* kontū'mĭlĭ) *n.* Insolent or reproachful language or treatment; disgrace. [ME, f. OF *contumelie* f. L *contumelia* (as CON-, *tumēre* swell)]

contū'se (-z) *v.t.* Injure by blow without breaking skin, bruise; so **contū'sI**ON (-zh*o*n) *n.* [f. L CON(*tundere tus-* thump)]

conŭ'ndrum *n.* Riddle; hard question. [16th c.; orig. unkn.]

cŏnūrbā'tion *n.* Aggregation of contiguous towns forming single community in some respects. [f. CON- + L *urbs urbis* city + -ATION]

cŏ'nūre *n.* Amer. parrot of genus *Aratinga* etc., resembling macaw. [f. mod. L *conurus* f. Gk *kōnos* cone + *oura* tail]

cŏnvalĕ'sce *v.i.* Regain health after illness. [ME, f. L CON(*valescere* incept. of *valēre* be well)]

cŏnvalĕ'sc|ent *a.* & *n.* (Person) recovering from illness; **~ent home** or **hospital** (for convalescents); so ~ENCE *n.* [f. prec. + -ENT]

convĕ'ct|ion *n.* Transport of heat by movement of heated substance; (Meteorol.) vertical movement of air; hence ~OR *n.*, heating appliance for circulating warm air, **~ion**AL, ~IVE, *adjs.* [f. LL *convectio* f. L CON(*vehere vect-* carry); see -ION]

convenance (kaw'n̈venahn̈s) *n.* (usu. in *pl.*) Conventional propriety. [F (*convenir* be fitting, f. as foll.; see -ANCE)]

convē'n|e *v.t.* & *i.* Assemble; convoke (assembly); summon (person *before* tribunal); hence ~ABLE *a.*, ~ER[1], ~OR, *ns.*, (esp.) person who arranges meetings of committee etc. [ME, f. L CON(*venire vent-* come) assemble, agree, fit]

convē'nience *n.* **1.** Suitableness; material advantage (FLAG[4] *of convenience*; **marriage of ~**, not primarily a love-match); personal pleasure (**at your ~**, in a way, at a time, convenient to you; **at your earliest ~**, as soon as you can); advantage (*a great convenience*; **make a ~ of** person, utilize his services without considering his feelings); **~ food** etc. (needing very little preparation and used whenever one wishes). **2.** Useful thing, esp. equipment or installation; water-closet; public lavatory. [ME, f. L *convenientia* (as prec.; see -ENCE)]

convē'nient *a.* Suitable; easily accessible; not troublesome (*if it is convenient to* or *for you*); available or occurring at a suitable moment (*went out and hailed a convenient taxi*); (colloq.) well situated as regards access (*convenient for station and shops*); hence ~LY[2] *adv.* [ME, f. as CONVENE; see -ENT]

cŏ'nvent *n.* Religious community (usu. of women; cf. MONASTERY) living together under discipline; building occupied by this; **~ school** (conducted by members of convent). [ME f. AF *covent*, OF *convent* f. L *conventus* assembly (as CONVENE)]

convĕ'nticle *n.* Clandestine religious meeting, esp. ‖(Hist.) of Nonconformists or Dissenters; building used for this. [ME, f. L *conventiculum* (place of) assembly, dim. of *conventus* (as CONVENE)]

convĕ'ntion *n.* **1.** Act of convening; formal assembly, whence *~EER' *n.*; (Hist.) meeting of Parliament without summons from sovereign. **2.** Agreement between parties; agreement between States, less formal than treaty; general (often implicit) consent; practice based on this, accepted social behaviour esp. if artificial or formal; (Cards) accepted method of play (in leading, bidding, etc.) used to convey information. [ME f. OF, f. L *conventio -onis* (as CONVENE; see -ION)]

convĕ'ntional *a.* Depending on convention(s); not natural, not spontaneous; following tradition; (of bomb, power source, etc.) other than nuclear; hence ~ISM (3), ~IST (2), ~ITY (-ă'l-), *ns.*, ~IZE (3) *v.t.*, ~LY[2] *adv.* [f. F *conventionnel* or f. LL *conventionalis* (as prec.; see -AL)]

convĕ'ntūal *a.* & *n.* (Member or inmate) of a convent; (member) of the less strict branch of Franciscans, living in large convents. [ME, f. med. L *conventualis* (as CONVENT; see -AL)]

convēr'ge *v.i.* (Of lines) tend to meet in a point; come together as if to meet or join; (Math., of series) approximate in the sum of its terms towards a definite limit. [f. LL CON(*vergere* incline)]

convēr'g|ent *a.* Converging; (Biol.) having tendency to become similar in same environment; (Psych., of thought) tending to reach only the most rational result; hence ~ENCE, ~ENCY, *ns.* [f. as prec.; see -ENT]

convēr's|ant (*or* kŏ'nver-) *a.* Having frequent dealings, well acquainted, (*with* person, subject, etc.); hence ~ANCE, ~ANCY, *ns.* [ME f. OF, part. of *converser* CONVERSE[1]; see -ANT]

cŏnversā'tion *n.* Informal exchange of ideas by spoken words, whence ~IST (1) *n.*; instance of this; **~ piece**, (1) kind of genre painting of group of figures, (2) thing that serves as topic of conversation owing to its unusualness etc. [ME f. OF, f. L *conversatio -onis* (as CONVERSE[1]; see -ATION)]

cŏnversā'tional *a.* Fond of, good at, pertaining to, conversation; hence ~IST (1) *n.*, ~LY[2] *adv.* [f. prec. + -AL]

cŏnversăziō'n|ĕ (-ăts-) *n.* (*pl.* **~es,** *or* **~i** *pr.* -ē). Social gathering held by learned or art society. [It., f. L (as CONVERSATION)]

convēr'se[1] *v.i.* Engage in conversation (*with* person, *on* or *about* subject). [ME, f. OF *converser* f. L *conversari* keep company (with), frequent. of *convertere* (CONVERT[1])]

cŏ'nvērse[2] *n.* (arch.) Conversation. [f. prec.]

cŏ'nvērse[3] *a.* & *n.* **1.** *a.* Opposite, contrary; hence **convēr'se**LY[2] (-slĭ) *adv.* **2.** *n.* Form of words produced by transposition of some terms of another (*he had learning without wealth* is the converse of *he had wealth without learning*); (Math.) proposition whose premiss and conclusion are the conclusion and premiss of another. [f. L *conversus*, p.p. of *convertere* (CONVERT[1])]

convēr'sion (-sh*o*n) *n.* **1.** Converting or being converted (see foll.). **2.** Transposition, inversion; (Theol.) change from sinfulness to holiness; (Psych.) change of unconscious conflict into physical disorder or disease; adaptation of building for new purposes, building so modified; transformation of fertile into fissile material in nuclear reactor. [ME f. OF, f. L *conversio -onis* (as foll.; see -ION)]

convēr't[1] *v.* **1.** *v.t.* Change (*into*); change in character or function; (Logic) interchange terms of (proposition); cause to turn, bring over, (*to* opinion, party, faith, etc.), change (moneys, stocks, etc.) into others of different kind;

(Rugby & Amer. Footb.) complete (a try, or abs.) by kicking goal; make structural alterations in (building; cf. prec.). **2.** *v.i.* Be able to be converted (*sofa converts into double bed*). **3.** Hence ~ER[1] *n.* [ME, f. OF *convertir* f. Rom. **convertire* for L CON(*vertere vers-* turn) turn about]

cŏ'nvêrt[2] *n.* Person converted (*to* opinion etc.), esp. to religious faith or life. [f. prec.]

convêr't|ĭble *a.* & *n.* **1.** *a.* That may be converted; (of terms) synonymous; (of currency etc.) that may be converted into gold or U.S. dollars; (of motor car etc.) with roof that can be folded down or removed; hence ~IBI'LITY *n.*, ~**ĭb**LY[2] *adv.* **2.** *n.* Convertible motor car etc. [OF, f. L *convertibilis* (as CONVERT[1]; see -IBLE)]

cŏ'nvĕx *a.* With outline or surface curved like exterior of circle or sphere (cf. CONCAVE); hence or cogn. **convĕ'**XITY *n.*, ~LY[2] *adv.* [f. L *convexus* vaulted]

convey' (-vā') *v.t.* Transport, carry; transmit (sound, smell, etc.); impart, communicate, (idea, meaning); (Law) transfer (property *to*, or abs.); hence ~ABLE *a.*, ~ER[1], ~OR, *ns.*, (esp.) endless belt etc. as mechanical contrivance for conveying articles or materials, esp. during manufacture. [ME, f. OF *conveier* f. med. L CON(*viare* f. *via* way)]

convey'ance (-ā'*a*-) *n.* Carrying; transmission; communication (of ideas etc.); (document effecting) transfer of property; means of transport, vehicle. [f. prec. + -ANCE]

convey'anc|er (-ā'*a*-) *n.* Lawyer who prepares documents for conveyance of property; so ~ING[1] *n.*, such work. [f. prec. + -ER[1]]

cŏ'nvĭct[1] *n.* Condemned criminal undergoing imprisonment. [f. obs. *convict* convicted f. L *convictus* (as foll.)]

convĭ'ct[2] *v.t.* Prove guilty (*of* offence); declare guilty by verdict of jury or decision of judge; cause (person) to admit he is guilty *of* (sin etc.); hence ~IVE *a.* [ME, f. L CON(*vincere vict-* conquer)]

convĭ'ction *n.* **1.** Proving or finding guilty; **summary** ~ (by judge or magistrates without jury). **2.** Act of convincing; settled belief (*have the* COURAGE *of* one's *convictions*; **carry** ~, be convincing); awakened consciousness of sin. [f. L *convictio* (as prec.; see -ION)]

convĭ'nc|e *v.t.* Firmly persuade (*of, that*); hence ~**e**MENT (-sm-) *n.* (esp. of religious conviction), ~IBLE *a.* [f. L (as CONVICT[2])]

convĭ'ncĭng *a.* Such as to convince; able to convince; hence ~LY[2] *adv.*, ~NESS *n.* [f. prec. + -ING[2]]

convĭ'vĭal *a.* Of or befitting a feast; festive, jovial; hence ~ITY (-ă'l-) *n.*, ~LY[2] *adv.* [f. L *convivialis* f. *convivium* feast (as CON-, *vivere* live); see -AL]

cŏnvocā'tion *n.* Calling together; assembly; ||synod of Anglican clergy of province of Canterbury or York; ||legislative or deliberative assembly of university; hence ~AL *a.* [ME, f. L *convocatio* (as foll.; see -ATION)]

convō'ke *v.t.* Call together; summon to assemble. [f. L CON(*vocare* call)]

cŏ'nvolutėd (-ōōt-) *a.* Coiled, twisted; complex. [p.p. of *convolute* f. L *convolutus* (as CON-, *volvere volut-* roll)]

cŏnvolu'tion (-ōō'-) *n.* Coiling, twisting; coil, twist; sinuous fold of brain surface. [f. med. L *convolutio* f. as prec.; see -ION]

convŏ'lve *v.t.* & *i.* (esp. in *p.p.*) Roll together; coil up. [f. L *convolvere* (see CONVOLUTED)]

convŏ'lvūlus *n.* Twining plant of genus *Convolvulus*, with trumpet-shaped flowers. [L]

cŏ'nvoy[1] *v.t.* (Of warship) escort (merchant or passenger vessel); escort, esp. with armed force. [ME, f. OF *convoyer*, var. of *conveier* CONVEY]

cŏ'nvoy[2] *n.* Act of convoying; company, supply of provisions, etc., under escort; number of merchant ships sailing in company under escort; group of vehicles travelling under escort or together. [f. F *convoi* (*convoier*; see prec.)]

convŭ'lsant *a.* & *n.* (Med.) (Drug etc.) that produces convulsions. [F, f. *convulser* (as foll.); see -ANT]

convŭ'lse *v.t.* Shake violently (lit. or fig.); (usu. in *pass.*) throw into convulsions; cause to be violently seized with laughter. [f. L CON(*vellere vuls-* pull)]

convŭ'lsion (-sh*o*n) *n.* Violent irregular motion of limb or body due to involuntary contraction of muscles (usu. in *pl.*, and esp. as disorder of infants); (in *pl.*) violent fit of laughter; violent social or political agitation; violent natural disturbance, esp. earthquake etc.; hence ~ARY[1] *a.* [F, or f. L *convulsio* (as prec.; see -ION)]

convŭ'lsĭve *a.* Attended or affected with, producing, convulsions (lit. or fig.); hence ~LY[2] (-vlĭ) *adv.*, ~NESS (-vn-) *n.* [f. CONVULSE + -IVE]

cō'nȳ, cō'ney, *n.* Rabbit; rabbit fur; (Bibl.) hyrax. [ME *cunin*(*g*) f. AF *coning*, OF *conin*, f. L *cuniculus*]

cōō *v.*, *n.*, & *int.* **1.** *v.i.*, & *n.* (Make) soft murmuring sound of or as of doves and pigeons; BILL[3] *and coo.* **2.** *v.t.* Say cooingly. **3.** *int.* (sl.) expr. surprise or incredulity. [imit.]

cōō'ee *n.*, & *v.i.* (esp. Austral. & N.Z.) (Make) sound used to attract attention, esp. at a distance; **within** (**a**) ~, (colloq.) very near. [imit. of signal used by Aboriginals and copied by settlers]

cŏŏk[1] *n.* **1.** One whose business is to cook food (**too many ~s spoil the broth,** one director is enough); (Chess) unintended solution to problem. **2.** ***~'book,** cookery book; ||**~-general,** servant who does both cooking and housework; **~'house,** camp kitchen, outdoor kitchen in warm countries, ship's galley; **~-shop,** eating-house, (N.Z.) sheep-station's kitchen; ***~-stove,** cooking-stove. [OE *cōc* f. pop. L *cocus* for L *coquus*]

cŏŏk[2] *v.* **1.** *v.t.* Prepare (food, or abs.) by heating (~ person's **goose,** ruin his chances); ~ (**up**), (fig.) concoct; (colloq.) falsify (accounts etc.), alter to produce desired result; ||(sl., esp. in *p.p.*) fatigue; (sl.) ruin, spoil; (Chess) find unintended solution to (problem); ***~'out,** excursion with open-air cooked meal. **2.** *v.i.* Undergo cooking; **what's ~ing?,** (colloq.) what is happening or planned? [ME, f. prec.]

Cŏŏk[3] *n.* **~'s tour,** extensive usu. rapid tour. [f. T. ~, Engl. travel agent d. 1892]

cŏŏ'ker *n.* Appliance or vessel for cooking food; fruit etc. that is better cooked than eaten raw. [f. COOK[2] + -ER[1]]

cŏŏ'kerȳ *n.* Art or practice of cooking; *place for cooking; ~ **book** (containing recipes for preparation of food). [ME, f. COOK[1,2] + -ERY]

cŏŏ'kie *n.* (Sc.) plain bun; *small sweet cake; (sl.) person; ***the way the ~ crumbles,** (colloq.) how things turn out, the unalterable situation of affairs. [f. Du. *koekje* dim. of *koek* cake]

cŏŏ'kĭng *n.* In vbl senses; suitable for or used in cooking (*cooking apple, sherry*). [f. COOK[2] + -ING[1]]

cōōl[1] *a.* & *n.* **1.** *a.* Of or at fairly low temperature, fairly cold; unexcited, calm, (*cool and collected*; **~-headed,** not easily excited); (Jazz) restrained, relaxed; unemotional, lacking zeal, lukewarm; lacking cordiality; (colloq.) excellent. **2.** Calmly audacious; (colloq., of large sums of money) *it cost me* **a** ~ (no less than a) **thousand. 3.** Hence ~'ISH[1] 2 *a.*, ~'LY[2] (-l-lĭ) *adv.*, ~'NESS *n.* **4.** *n.* Coolness; cool air or place; (sl.) composure (*keep, lose,* one's *cool*). [OE *cōl* f. Gmc *kōluz (*kōl-, *kal-; cf. COLD[1])]

coo͞l[2] *v.i.* & *t.* ~ (**down, off**), become or make cool (lit. or fig.); ~ **it,** (sl.) relax, calm down; ~ one's **heels,** be kept waiting; **~'ing tower,** industrial structure for cooling hot water before reuse. [OE *cōlian,* = OS *cōlon* f. Gmc **kōlōjan* (as prec.)]

coo͞'labah *n.* (Austral.) One of various gum-trees, esp. *Eucalyptus microtheca.* [Aboriginal]

coo͞'lant *n.* Cooling agent; fluid used to lessen friction of cutting-tool; fluid used to remove heat from internal combustion engine, nuclear reactor, etc. [f. COOL[2] + -ANT, after *lubricant*]

coo͞'ler *n.* Vessel in which a thing is cooled; *refrigerator; (sl.) prison cell. [f. COOL[2] + -ER[1]]

coo͞'lĭbah. Var. of COOLABAH.

coo͞'lĭe, coo͞'lȳ, *n.* Unskilled native labourer in Eastern countries; ~ **hat,** broad flat hat as worn by coolies. [perh. f. *Kulī,* aboriginal tribe of Gujarat, India]

coo͞lth *n.* (colloq.) Coolness. [f. COOL[1] + -TH[1]]

‖**coo͞mb,** ‖**combe,** (ko͞om) *n.* Valley on flank of hill; short valley running up from coast. [OE *cumb*; cf. CWM]

***coo͞n** *n.* Racoon; (sl., derog.) Negro; ~ **dog** (trained to hunt racoons); **~'skin,** (cap etc. of) racoon skin. [abbr.]

coo͞n-căn *n.* Simple card-game like rummy (orig. Mexican). [f. Sp. *con quién* with whom?]

coo͞p[1] *n.* Cage placed over sitting or fattening fowls; fowl-run (***fly the** ~, (sl.) depart abruptly); ‖basket used in catching fish; small place of confinement, esp. prison. [ME *cupe* basket f. MDu., MLG *kūpe,* ult. f. L *cupa* cask]

coo͞p[2] *v.t.* Put in coop; ~ (**in, up**), confine (person). [f. prec.]

cō'-ŏp *n.* (colloq.) ‖Co-operative society or store; *co-operative. [abbr.]

coo͞'per *n.,* & *v.t.* **1.** *n.* Maker of casks and similar vessels; (on ship) repairer of casks etc.; hence ~AGE (2, 4, 5) *n.* **2.** *v.t.* Make or repair (cask). [ME, f. MDu., MLG *kūper* (*kūpe* COOP[1]; see -ER[1])]

cō-ŏ'perāt|e, cōŏ'p-, *coöp-, *v.i.* Work together (*with* person *in* a work, *to* an end); (of things) concur in producing an effect; so ~OR *n.* [f. eccl. L co(*operari* f. *opus operis* work) + -ATE[3]]

cō-ŏperā'tion, cōŏp-, *coöp-, *n.* Working together to same end; (Econ.) co-operative combination. [ME, f. L *cooperatio* (as prec.; see -ION); partly thr. F *coopération*]

cō-ŏ'perative, cōŏ'p-, *coöp-, *a.* & *n.* **1.** *a.* Of, tending to, offering, co-operation; (Econ.) ~ **farm, society,** etc., (for production or distribution of goods, profits being shared by members), ~ **shop, store,** (belonging to co-operative society); hence ~LY[2] (-vlĭ) *adv.* **2.** *n.* Co-operative farm etc.; *dwelling jointly owned or leased by occupiers. [f. LL *cooperativus* (as prec.; see -IVE)]

cō-ŏ'pt, *coö-, *v.t.* Elect to committee etc. by votes of existing members; hence or cogn. ~A'TION, ~ION, *ns.,* ~IVE *a.* [f. L co(*optare* choose)]

cō-or'dĭnate[1]**, coor'-, *coör-,** *a.* & *n.* **1.** *a.* Equal in rank, esp. (Gram.) of parts of compound sentence (cf. SUBORDINATE[1]); consisting of co-ordinate things; hence ~LY[2] (-tlĭ) *adv.* **2.** *n.* Co-ordinate thing, esp. (Math., usu. *coor-*) each of a system of magnitudes used to fix position of point, line, or plane; (in *pl.*) women's outer clothes that can be worn together harmoniously. [f. co- + L *ordinare* (*ordo -inis* order); see -ATE[2]]

cō-or'dĭn|āte[2]**, coor'-, *coör-,** *v.t.* Make co-ordinate; bring (parts, movements, etc.) into proper relation; so ~A'TION, **~ātor,** *ns.,* ~ATIVE *a.* [f. as prec. + -ATE[3]]

coo͞t *n.* Aquatic bird of genus *Fulica,* esp. **bald** ~ (with base of upper mandible extended to form white plate on forehead, whence **bald as a** ~, entirely bald); (colloq.) stupid person. [ME, prob. f. LG]

coo͞'tie *n.* (sl.) Body-louse. [perh. f. Malay *kutu* a biting parasite]

cŏp[1] *n.* (Spinning). Conical ball of thread wound on spindle. [OE *cop* summit]

cŏp[2] *n.* (sl.) Policeman; **~-shop,** police station. [cf. foll. and COPPER[2]]

cŏp[3] *v.* (-pp-) & *n.* (sl.) **1.** *v.t.* Catch (~ **it,** get into trouble, be punished, die). **2.** **v.i.* ~ **out,** escape, give up attempt, go back on one's promise; **~-out** *n.,* (way of) escape, cowardly evasion, escapist. **3.** *n.* Capture (esp. *a fair cop*); **no ~, not much ~,** of little or no value or use. [perh. f. obs. *cap* arrest f. OF *caper* seize]

***cōpacĕ'tĭc** *a.* (sl.) Excellent, in good order. [20th c.; orig. unkn.]

copai'ba (-pī'-) *n.* Aromatic resin from S. Amer. plants of genus *Copaifera,* used in medicine and perfumery. [Sp. & Port., f. Guarani *cupauba*]

cō'pal *n.* Resin from various tropical trees, used for varnish. [Sp., f. Aztec *copalli* incense]

cōpar'cėnarȳ, cōpar'cėner, *ns.* (Law). = PARCENARY, PARCENER. [see CO-]

cōpar'tner *n.* Partner, sharer, associate; hence ~SHIP *n.* [f. CO- + PARTNER]

cōpe[1] *n.,* & *v.t.* **1.** *n.* (Eccl.) Long cloak worn in processions etc.; (fig., poet.) vault of heaven; **~-stone,** (fig.) finishing touch. **2.** *v.t.* Furnish with cope. [ME, repr. OE *-cāp,* **cāpe* (=ON *kápa*), f. med. L *capa* var. of LL *cappa* CAP[1], CAPE[1]]

cōpe[2] *v.i.* Contend successfully *with* (person, task); (colloq.) deal competently with situation or problem. [ME, f. OF *coper, colper,* (*cop, colp* blow f. med. L *colpus* f. L f. Gk *kolaphos* blow with fist)]

cō'pĕck *n.* Russian coin (hundredth part of a rouble). [f. Russ. *kopeika* dim. of *kopye* lance (from figure of Ivan IV bearing lance instead of sword 1535)]

cō'pėpŏd *n.* Small aquatic crustacean of sub-class Copepoda, with oarlike feet. [f. Gk *kōpē* oar-handle + *pous podos* foot]

cō'per *n.* Horse-dealer. [f. obs. *cope* buy, f. MDu., MLG *kōpen,* G *kaufen* (rel. to CHEAP) + -ER[1]]

Coper'nĭcan *a.* ~ **system, theory,** (that the planets, including the earth, move round the sun; cf. PTOLEMAIC). [f. *Copernicus* latinized f. N. *Koppernigk,* Polish astronomer d. 1543 + -AN]

cŏ'pier *n.* In vbl senses; person or machine that copies (esp. documents). [f. COPY[2] + -ER[1]]

cō'-pīlot, *cō'p-, *n.* Second pilot in aircraft. [f. CO- 1 + PILOT]

cō'pĭng[1] *n.* Top (usu. sloping) course of masonry in wall; **~-stone** (used for coping). [f. COPE[1] *v.* in sense 'cover with a coping' + -ING[1]]

cō'pĭng[2] *n.* ~ **saw** (for cutting wood into curves). [f. *cope* cut wood f. OF *coper* (see COPE[2]) + -ING[1]]

cō'pĭous *a.* Existing in large amounts; abounding in information; profuse in speech; hence ~LY[2] *adv.,* ~NESS *n.* [ME, f. OF *copieux* or f. L *copiosus* (*copia* plenty; see -OUS)]

copi'ta (-pē'-) *n.* Tulip-shaped sherry-glass; glass of sherry. [Sp., dim. of *copa* cup]

cōplā'nar *a.* (Math.) In same plane; hence **cōplană'**RITY *n.* [f. CO- 1 + PLANAR]

cōpŏ'lȳmer *n.* Polymer with units of more than one kind; so ~IZE (2, 3) *v.i.* & *t.* [f. CO- 1 + POLYMER]

For other words in *co-* see CO-.

cŏ'pper[1] *n.*, & *v.t.* **1.** *n.* Reddish malleable ductile metallic element; bronze coin; butterfly with copper-coloured wings; metal boiler, esp. for laundry; (*attrib.*) made of or coloured like copper. **2.** ~ **beech** (kind with copper-coloured leaves); ~ **belt,** copper-mining area of Central Africa; **~-bit,** soldering tool pointed with copper; **~-bottom** *v.t.*, sheathe bottom of (ship, pan, etc.) with copper, (in *p.p.*) (financially) reliable; **~head,** venomous Amer. or Austral. snake; **~plate,** polished copper plate for engraving or etching, print from this, (*a.*, of writing) careful and neat; *copper* PYRITES; **~-smith,** one who works in copper; *copper* VITRIOL. **3.** Hence ~Y[2] *a.*, (esp.) copper-coloured. **4.** *v.t.* Cover (ship's bottom, pan, etc.) with copper. [OE *copor, coper,* = ON *koparr* f. **kupar,* MDu. *coper* f. LL *cuprum* for L *cyprium aes* Cyprus metal]

||**cŏ'pper**[2] *n.* (sl.) Policeman. [f. COP[3] + -ER[1]]

cŏ'pperas *n.* Green iron-sulphate crystals. [ME *coperose* f. OF *couperose* f. med. L *cup(e)rosa,* perh. orig. *aqua cuprosa* copper water]

cŏ'ppĭce *n.* & *v.* **1.** *n.* Small wood of undergrowth and small trees, grown for periodical cutting; **~-wood,** undergrowth. **2.** *v.t.* & *i.* Grow as coppice. [f. OF *copeïz* f. Rom. **colpaticium* (**colpare* cut f. med. L *colpus*; see COPE[2])]

cŏ'pra *n.* Dried kernels of coconut. [Port., f. Malayalam *koppara* coconut]

cō-prĕcĭpĭtā'tion *n.* (Chem.) Simultaneous precipitation of more than one compound from a solution. [f. CO- 1 + PRECIPITATION]

cŏ'pro- *comb. form.* Dung, faeces, as: **~lite,** (piece of) fossil dung; **~logy** (-ŏ'l-), treatment of filthy subjects in literature etc.; **~phagous** (-ŏ'f-) *a.*, (of beetles) dung-eating; **~phi'lia,** undue interest in faeces and defecation. [f. Gk *kopros* dung + -O-]

coprŏ'sma (-z-) *n.* Small Australasian evergreen plant of genus *Coprosma.* [mod. L, f. Gk *kopros* dung + *osmē* smell]

cŏpse *n.*, & *v.t.* = COPPICE; **~'wood,** undergrowth; hence **cŏ'psy**[2] *a.* [shortened f. COPPICE]

Cŏpt *n.* Native Egyptian Christian, member of independent sect of Eastern Church. [f. F *Copte* or mod. L *Cop(h)tus* f. Arab. *al-kibt, al-kubt* Copts f. Copt. *Gyptios* f. Gk *Aiguptios* Egyptian]

Cŏ'ptĭc *a.* & *n.* **1.** *a.* Of the Copts. **2.** *n.* Medieval language of Egyptians, now used only in Coptic Church. [f. prec. + -IC]

cŏ'pūl|a *n.* (Logic & Gram.) Verb *be* (as mere sign of predication), or verb with similar function; hence ~AR[1] *a.* [L (co-, *apere* fasten); cf. -ULE]

cŏ'pūl|āte *v.i.* Have physical copulation (*with*); so **~at**ORY *a.* [f. L *copulare* fasten together (as prec.) + -ATE[3]]

cŏpūlā'tion *n.* Physical union of male and female persons or animals as in act of procreation; grammatical or logical connection. [ME f. OF, or f. L *copulatio* (as prec.; see -ION)]

cŏ'pūlātĭve *a.* Serving to connect; (Gram.) (1) connecting words or clauses that are joined in sense (cf. DISJUNCTIVE), (2) connecting subject and predicate; (Zool. & Anat.) relating to sexual union; hence ~LY[2] (-vlĭ) *adv.* [ME, f. OF *copulatif -ive,* or f. LL *copulativus* (as prec.; see -IVE)]

cŏ'pў[1] *n.* **1.** Thing made to look like another; reproduction (of writing, picture, etc.); imitation; written or printed specimen (of book etc.). **2.** Model to be copied; page written after model (of penmanship); **fair ~,** written matter transcribed after correction. **3.** Manuscript or matter to be printed (*incident* etc. **will make good ~,** lends itself to interesting narration in newspapers etc.); text of advertisement. **4. ~-book,** (*n.*) book containing copies for learners to imitate (BLOT[2] one's *copy-book*), (*a.*) (1) tritely conventional, (2) accurate, exemplary; *~ **desk** (where copy is edited for printing); **~-reader** (who reads and edits copy for printing); **~-taster,** one who selects copy for printing; **~-typist,** one who makes typewritten transcripts of documents; **~-writer,** one who writes or prepares copy for publication. [ME, f. OF *copie* f. L *copia* abundance etc., in med. L = transcript, f. phr. *facere copiam describendi* give permission to transcribe]

cŏ'pў[2] *v.t.* & *i.* Make copy (of); ~ **(out),** transcribe, whence ~IST (3) *n.*; imitate; **~-cat,** (colloq.) slavish imitator; **~ing-ink, -pencil,** (used for indelible writing). [ME, f. OF *copier* f. med. L *copiare* f. as prec.]

||**cŏ'pўhōld** *n.* (Hist.) Tenure in accordance with transcript of manorial records; land so held; hence ~ER[1] *n.*, such tenant. [f. COPY[1] + HOLD[2]]

cŏ'pўrīght (-rīt) *n.* & *a.*, & *v.t.* **1.** *n.* Exclusive right given by law for term of years to author, designer, etc., or his assignee to make copies or give performances of his original work. **2.** *a.* (Of book etc.) protected by copyright; ||~ **library** (entitled to free copy of each book published in U.K.). **3.** *v.t.* Secure copyright for (book etc.). [f. COPY[1] + RIGHT[3]]

coq au vin (kŏkōvă'ṅ) *n.* Chicken cooked in wine. [F]

cŏ'quĕtrў (-kĭ-) *n.* Coquettish behaviour or act; (fig.) trifling. [f. F *coquetterie* (*coqueter,* as foll.; see -ERY)]

coquĕ'tt|e (-kĕ't) *n.*, & *v.i.* **1.** *n.* Woman who trifles with men's affections to gain admiration; crested humming-bird of genus *Lophornis.* **2.** Hence ~ISH[1] *a.* **3.** *v.i.* Behave as coquette; flirt (*with*). [F, fem. of *coquet* wanton, dim. of *coq* cock]

***coqui'na** (-kē'-) *n.* Soft limestone of broken shells, used in road-making. [Sp., = cockle]

coqui'tō (-kē'-) *n.* (*pl.* ~s). Chilean palm-tree yielding palm-honey and fibre. [Sp., dim. of *coco* coconut]

||**Coȓ** *int.* (vulg.) God. [corrupt.]

cor- *pref.*, assim. form of COM- before *r.*

Cor. *abbr.* Corinthians (N.T.); *corner.

||**cŏ'racle** *n.* Small boat of wickerwork covered with watertight material, used on Welsh and Irish lakes and rivers. [f. W *corwgl* (*corwg* = Ir. *currach* boat; cf. CURRACH)]

cŏ'racoid *a.* & *n.* ~ **(process),** short projection from shoulder-blade in vertebrates. [f. mod. L *coracoides* f. Gk *korakoeidēs* raven-like (*korax -akos* raven; see -OID)]

cŏ'ral *n.* & *a.* **1.** *n.* Calcareous substance (red, pink, white, etc.) secreted by many kinds of marine polyps for support and habitation; unimpregnated roe of lobster. **2.** *a.* Like coral, esp. red; made of coral; ~ **island, reef,** (formed by growth of coral); ~ **rag,** limestone containing beds of petrified corals; **~-snake,** small brightly-coloured snake. [ME f. OF, f. L *corallum* f. Gk *korallion,* prob. of Semitic orig.]

cŏ'ralline[1] *n.* Seaweed of genus *Corallina,* with calcareous jointed stem; (pop.) name of various plantlike compound animals. [f. It. *corallina* dim. of *corallo,* f. as prec.]

cŏ'ralline[2] *a.* Coral-red; like or composed of coral. [f. F *corallin -ine* or f. LL *corallinus* (as CORAL; see -INE[1])]

cŏ'rallīte *n.* Fossil coral; coral skeleton of polyp. [f. L *corallum* CORAL + -ITE[1]]

cŏ'ralloid *a.* & *n.* (Organism) like or akin to coral. [f. CORAL + -OID]

coram populo (koȓam pŏ'pūlō) *adv.* In public. [L, = in the presence of the people]

coȓ anglais (koȓ ah'ṅglā *or* ŏ'ngglā) *n.* (Mus.) Instrument like oboe but lower in pitch; its player; organ stop of similar quality. [F, = English horn]

cŏr'bel *n.* & *v.* (‖-ll-). (Archit.) **1.** *n.* Projection of stone, timber, etc., jutting out from wall to support weight; short timber laid longitudinally under beam to help support it; **~-table,** projecting course resting on corbels. **2.** *v.t.* & *i.* **~ out, off,** (cause to) project on corbels. [ME f. OF, dim. of *corp* (see foll., -LE 2)]

cŏr'bĭe *n.* **1.** (Sc.) Raven; carrion crow. **2. ~-steps,** steplike projections on sloping sides of gable. [ME, f. OF *corb, corp* f. L *corvus* crow + -IE]

cŏrd *n.*, & *v.t.* **1.** *n.* (Piece of) long thin flexible material made from several twisted strands; (Anat.) similar structure in animal body (*spinal, umbilical, cord; vocal cords*); *electric flex, whence **~'LESS** *a.* **2.** Cordlike rib on cloth; ribbed cloth, esp. corduroy; (in *pl.*) corduroy breeches or trousers. **3.** Measure of cut wood (usu. 128 cubic ft.); **~'wood,** wood that is or can easily be so measured. **4.** (fig.) Moral or emotional tie (*cords of discipline, affection; fourfold cord of evidence*). **5.** *v.t.* Fasten or bind with cord; (in *p.p.*) furnished with cords, (of cloth) ribbed, (of muscles) standing out like taut cords. [ME, f. OF *corde* f. L f. Gk *khordē* gut, string of musical instrument]

cŏr'dage *n.* Cords or ropes, esp. in rigging of ship. [ME f. F (as prec.; see -AGE)]

cŏr'dāte *a.* Heart-shaped. [f. mod. L *cordatus* (*cor cordis* heart; see -ATE^2)]

cŏrdėlier' *n.* Franciscan friar of strict rule (wearing knotted cord round waist). [ME f. OF (*cordele* dim. of *corde* CORD; see -IER)]

cŏr'dĭal *a.* & *n.* **1.** (Medicine, food, drink) that stimulates the heart; flavoured and sweetened drink made from fruit. **2.** *a.* Hearty, sincere; warm, friendly; hence **~ITY^1** (-ă'l-) *n.*, **~LY^2** *adv.* [ME, f. med. L *cordialis* (*cor cordis* heart; see -IAL)]

cŏrdĭller'a (-lyār'*a*) *n.* Mountain ridge (one of parallel series), esp. of the Andes and in Central America and Mexico. [Sp. (*cordilla* dim. of *cuerda* CORD)]

cŏr'dīte *n.* Smokeless explosive made from gun-cotton, nitroglycerine, and vaseline. [f. CORD (from its appearance) + -ITE^1]

cŏr'don *n.*, & *v.t.* **1.** *n.* Chain of military posts; line or circle of police etc.; **~ (sanitaire,** *pr.* sănĭtār'), guarded line between infected and uninfected (lit. or fig.) districts. **2.** Ornamental cord or braid; ribbon of knightly order; **~ bleu** (*or* kŏrdawn blėr') first-class cook. **3.** Fruit-tree trained to grow as single stem; (Archit.) string-course. **4.** *v.t.* **~ (off),** enclose with (military, police, etc.) cordon. [f. It. *cordone* augment. of *corda* CORD, & F *cordon* (as CORD; see -OON)]

cŏr'dovan *n.* Kind of soft leather. [f. Sp. *cordovan* of Cordova, where orig. made]

cŏr'duroy (*or* -ūr-) *n.* Coarse thick ribbed cotton velvet; (in *pl.*) corduroy trousers; **~ road** (of tree-trunks laid across swamp). [18th c., prob. f. CORD ribbed fabric + obs. *duroy* coarse woollen fabric]

‖**cŏr'dwainer** *n.* (arch.) Shoemaker (now only as guild-name etc.). [f. obs. *cordwain* CORDOVAN + -ER^1]

cōre *n.*, & *v.t.* **1.** *n.* Horny capsule containing seeds of apple, pear, etc.; central part cut out (esp. of rock etc. in boring); piece of soft iron forming centre of electromagnet or induction coil; internal mould filling space to be left hollow in a casting; (Archaeol.) trimmed flint after removal of flakes; region of fissile material in nuclear reactor; unit of structure in computer, whose magnetization is reversible; central strand of rope, inner strand of electric cable. **2.** Central part of different character from what surrounds it; central region of the earth; innermost part (lit., or fig.: *rotten at the core; English to the core*). **3.** *v.t.* Remove core from; hence **cōr'ER^1** (2) *n.* [ME, of unkn. orig.]

***C.O.R.E.** *abbr.* Congress of Racial Equality.

cōrėlā'tion. Var. of CORRELATION.

cō-rėlĭ'gionĭst, *cōrė-, (-*jo*-) *n.* Adherent of same religion. [f. CO- 1 + RELIGION + -IST]

corĕ'lla *n.* (Austral.) White long-billed cockatoo that can be taught to talk. [app. Latinized f. Aboriginal *ca-rall*]

cŏrėŏ'psĭs *n.* Plant with rayed usu. yellow composite flowers. [mod. L, f. Gk *koris* bug + *opsis* appearance, w. ref. to shape of seed]

cō-rėspŏ'ndent, *cōrė-, *n.* Person (esp. man) proceeded against together with respondent in divorce suit; ‖**~ shoes,** (joc.) man's two-toned shoes. [f. CO- 1 + RESPONDENT]

‖**cŏrf** *n.* (*pl.* **corves** *pr.* -vz). Large basket formerly used in mining; basket in which fish are kept alive in water. [f. MDu., MLG *korf*, OHG *chorp, korb* f. L *corbis* basket]

cŏr'gĭ (-gĭ) *n.* **(Welsh) ~,** dog of short-legged breed with foxlike head. [W (*cor* dwarf, *ci* dog)]

cŏrĭā'ceous (-sh*us*) *a.* Like leather, leathery. [f. LL *coriaceus* (*corium* leather; see -ACEOUS)]

cŏrĭă'nder *n.* Annual plant (*Coriandrum sativum*) of S. Europe etc., with aromatic fruit (pop. called **~ seed**) used for flavouring. [ME, f. OF *coriandre* f. L *coriandrum* f. Gk *koriannon*]

Corĭ'nthĭan *a.* & *n.* (Native) of Corinth; (arch.) profligate; **~ order,** (Archit.) most ornate of the three Greek ORDER^{1}s, having bell-shaped capital with rows of acanthus leaves. [f. L f. Gk *Korinthios* + -AN]

cŏr'ĭum *n.* (Anat.) Dermis. [L, = skin]

cŏrk *n.*, & *v.t.* **1.** *n.* Bark of cork-oak; piece of cork used as float for fishing-line etc.; bottle-stopper of cork or other material; (Bot.) inner division of the bark in higher plants; (*attrib.*) made of cork. **2. ~-oak,** S. European oak (*Quercus suber*); **~'screw,** steel screw for drawing cork from bottle, thing spirally twisted, (*v.t.* & *i.*) move spirally; ‖**~-tipped** *a.*, (of cigarette) having end band or filter of corklike material; **~'wood,** (tree yielding) light porous wood. **3.** *v.t.* Stop (*up*) (as) with cork; bottle *up* (feelings etc.). [ME, f. Du. & LG *kork*, f. Sp. *alcorque* cork sole, perh. f. Arab.]

cŏr'kage *n.* Charge made by hotel or restaurant for serving wine etc. (esp. that brought from elsewhere). [f. prec. + -AGE]

cŏrked (-kt) *a.* Stopped with cork; blackened with burnt cork; (of wine) impaired by defective cork(ing). [f. CORK + -ED^1]

cŏr'ker *n.* (sl.) Astonishing or surpassingly good thing or person. [f. CORK + -ER^1]

***cŏr'kĭng** *a.* (sl.) Unusually large or excellent. [f. prec. + -ING^2]

cŏr'kў *a.* Corklike; (of wine) corked. [f. CORK + -Y^2]

cŏrm *n.* (Bot.) Bulblike underground stem, solid bulb. [f. mod. L f. Gk *kormos* trunk with boughs lopped off]

cŏr'morant *n.* Large lustrous-black voracious sea-bird. [ME, f. OF *cormaran* f. med. L *corvus marinus* sea-raven; for ending *-ant* cf. *peasant, tyrant*]

cŏrn^1 *n.* **1.** Grain or seed, esp. of cereal (also of pepper etc.); (collect. *sing.*) cereal(s) before or after harvesting, esp. wheat or oats or maize; (colloq.) something CORNY^2, esp. music. **2.** ‖*Corn*-CHANDLER; **~-cob,** cylindrical part to which grains are attached in ear of maize (**~-cob pipe,** tobacco-pipe made of this; **~ on the cob,** maize cooked and eaten in this form);

corn-COCKLE[1]; **~'crake,** bird (*Crex crex*) with harsh grating voice; **~ exchange** (for trade in corn); ||**~-factor,** dealer in corn; **~'field,** field in which corn is grown; **~'flakes,** breakfast cereal of toasted flavoured maize flakes; **~'flour,** (1) fine-ground maize, (2) flour of rice or other grain; **~'flower,** one of various plants growing among corn, esp. *Centaurea cyanus*; ||**~-laws** (regulating corn-trade, esp. English laws restricting importation, repealed 1846); **~ marigold,** daisy-like yellow-flowered cornfield weed; ***~ pone,** baked or fried maize bread; **~-salad,** lamb's-lettuce; ***~ silk** = SILK 4; *corn*-SPURRY; **~'starch,** = *cornflour*; ***~-whiskey,** whisky distilled from maize. [OE, = OS, OHG, ON *korn*, Goth. *kaurn* f. Gmc **kurnam* cogn. w. L *granum* grain]

cŏrn[2] *v.t.* (esp. in *p.p.*) Sprinkle or preserve with salt or brine; **~ed beef** (thus preserved and tinned). [f. prec.]

cŏrn[3] *n.* Horny place esp. on foot, extending into subcutaneous tissue; TREAD *on* person's *corns.* [ME f. AF, f. L *cornu* horn]

cŏr'nbrăsh *n.* (Geol.) Coarse calcareous sandstone. [f. CORN[1] + BRASH[1]]

cŏr'nė|a *n.* Transparent horny part of anterior covering of eyeball, over iris and pupil; hence **~**AL *a.* [mod. L, f. med. L *cornea* (*tela*) horny tissue, f. L *corneus* horny (*cornu* horn)]

cŏr'nel *n.* Plant of genus *Cornus*, e.g. cornelian cherry and dogwood. [16th c., thr. G, ult. f. L *cornus*]

cornē'lian[1], **car-,** *n.* Dull red or reddish-white chalcedony. [ME, f. OF *corneline*; *car-* after L *caro carnis* flesh]

cornē'lian[2] *n.* **~ cherry,** European berry-bearing tree (*Cornus mas*). [f. CORNEL + -IAN]

cŏr'nėous *a.* Hornlike, horny. [f. L *corneus* (*cornu* horn) + -OUS]

cŏr'ner *n.* & *v.* **1.** *n.* Place where converging sides or edges meet; projecting angle, esp. where two streets meet (**cut** (**off**) **a ~,** avoid it by a short cut, or pass round it as closely as possible; (fig.) scamp work; **just round the ~,** (colloq.) very near, imminent; **turn the ~,** pass round it into another street, (fig.) pass critical point (in illness etc.)); triangular piece from ham or gammon. **2.** Hollow angle enclosed by meeting walls etc.; (Boxing) angle of ring, esp. one where boxer rests between rounds; (fig.) **drive into a ~** (difficult position from which there is no escape), *in a* TIGHT *corner*; **within the four ~s of,** within the scope or extent of. **3.** Secluded or remote place (*done in a corner*; HOLE[1]-*-and-corner transactions*); region, quarter, esp. remote (*from the four corners of Britain, of the earth*). **4.** Buying up of the whole of any stock in the market, so as to compel speculative sellers to buy from one to fulfil their obligations; any combination to raise price by securing monopoly. **5.** (Hockey & Assoc. Footb.). **~(-hit, -kick),** free hit or kick from corner-flag after ball has been hit or kicked over his own goal-line by an opponent. **6. ~-boy, -man**[1], street rough, loafer; **~ cupboard** (fitted into corner of room); **~-man**[2] (at either end of row of Negro minstrels, playing bones or tambourine and contributing comic effects); **~ shop** (at corner of street, esp. as opp. supermarket etc.); **~-stone,** one in projecting angle of wall, foundation stone, (fig.) indispensable part, basis. **7.** *v.t.* Drive into corner (esp. fig.); force (dealers) or control (commodity) by means of corner. **8.** *v.i.* Move round corner (esp. of, or in, vehicle). [ME f. AF, f. Rom. **cornarium*, f. L *cornu* horn; see -ER[2] (2)]

cŏr'nėt[1] *n.* **1.** Brass musical instrument of trumpet family, with valves operated by pistons, whence **~(t)**IST (3) *n.*; its player; organ stop of similar quality; cornetto. **2.** Conically-rolled piece of paper for groceries etc.; ||conical wafer filled with ice cream. [ME f. OF, dim. of Rom. **corno* f. L *cornu* horn; see -ET[1]]

||**cŏr'nėt**[2] *n.* (Hist.) Fifth commissioned officer in cavalry troop, who carried the colours; hence **~**CY *n.* [earlier sense 'pennon, standard', f. F *cornette* dim. of *corne* f. Rom. **corna* horn f. L *cornua* horns]

cŏrnĕ'tt|ō *n.* (*pl.* **~i** *pr.* -ē). Old wood-wind instrument like flageolet. [It., dim. of *corno* horn (as CORNET[1])]

cŏr'nĭc|e *n.* (Archit.) horizontal moulded projection crowning a building or structure, esp. uppermost member of entablature of an order, surmounting frieze; ornamental moulding round wall of room just below ceiling; (Mountaineering) overhanging mass of hardened snow at edge of precipice; hence **~**ED[2] (-st) *a.* [f. F *corniche* etc. f. It. *cornice*, perh. f. L *cornix -icis* crow]

cŏr'nĭche (-sh; *or* -nē'sh) *n.* **~** (**road**), road along edge of cliff etc., coastal road with wide views. [F; see prec.]

Cŏr'nĭsh *a.* & *n.* **1.** *a.* Of Cornwall, England; **~ boiler,** cylindrical flue-boiler; **~ cream,** CLOTted cream; **~ pasty,** seasoned meat and vegetables baked in pastry without dish; *Cornish* RIVIERA. **2.** *n.* Ancient Celtic language of Cornwall. [f. *Cornwall* + -ISH[1]]

||**cŏr'nstōne** *n.* Mottled red and green limestone, subordinate bed in Old Red Sandstone. [f. CORN[1] + STONE]

cŏrnūcō'pĭ|a *n.* (Art) goat's horn represented as overflowing with flowers, fruit, and corn, horn of plenty; ornamental vessel shaped like this; overflowing store; hence **~**AN *a.* [LL, f. L *cornu copiae* horn of plenty]

cŏr'nȳ[1] *a.* Of or abounding in corn. [f. CORN[1] + -Y[2]]

cŏr'nȳ[2] *a.* (colloq.) Out of date, old-fashioned; trite; sentimental. [f. as prec.; orig. sense 'rustic']

corŏ'lla *n.* (Bot.) Whorl of modified leaves (petals), separate or combined, forming inner envelope of flower. [L, dim. of *corona* crown]

corŏ'llarȳ *n.* Proposition appended to one already demonstrated, as inference from it; immediate deduction; natural consequence, result. [ME, f. L *corollarium* money paid for garland, gratuity, neut. adj. f. prec.; see -ARY[1]]

corō'na[1] *n.* (*pl.* **~e** *or* **~s**). **1.** Small circle of light round sun or moon; rarefied gaseous envelope of sun, seen as halo of white light around disc of moon in total eclipse of sun. **2.** Circular chandelier hung from roof. **3.** (Archit.) Member of cornice, with broad vertical face, usu. of considerable projection. **4.** (Anat.) One of various crownlike parts of body. **5.** (Bot.) Appendage on top of seed or inner side of corolla. **6.** (Electr.) Glow around conductor at high potential. [L, = crown]

corō'na[2] *n.* Long straight-sided cigar. [f. Sp. *La Corona* (**P**) the crown]

cŏ'ronach (-k *or* -χ) *n.* Funeral-song, dirge, in Scottish Highlands and Ireland. [f. Ir. *coranach*, Gael. *corranach* (*comh-* together, *rànach* outcry)]

corō'nagraph (-ahf) *n.* Instrument for observing sun's corona, esp. other than during eclipse. [f. CORONA[1] + -GRAPH]

cŏ'ronal[1] *n.* Circlet (esp. of gold or gems) for the head; wreath, garland. [ME, app. f. AF **coronal* (*corone* CROWN[1]; see -AL)]

corō'nal[2] (*or* kŏ'ro-) *a.* (Anat.) **~ suture,** transverse suture of skull separating frontal bone (**~ bone**) from parietal bones; of the crown of the head; (Astron. & Bot.) of a corona. [F, or f. L *coronalis* (as CORONA[1]; see -AL)]

cŏ'ronarȳ *a.* & *n.* **1.** *a.* (Med.) Resembling, encircling like, a crown; ~ **arteries,** those that supply the tissues of the heart with blood; ~ **thrombosis** (in coronary artery). **2.** *n.* Coronary artery or thrombosis. [f. L *coronarius* (*corona* crown; see -ARY[1])]

cŏronā'tion *n.* Ceremony of crowning sovereign or sovereign's consort. [ME f. OF, f. med. L *coronatio -onis* (*coronare* to crown f. CORONA[1]; see -ATION)]

cŏ'roner *n.* Officer of county, district, or municipality, holding inquest on bodies of persons who may have died by violence or accident; official holding inquiry in cases of treasure trove; (Hist.) officer charged with maintaining rights of private property of Crown; hence ~SHIP *n.* [ME, f. AF *cor(o)uner* (*coro(u)ne* CROWN[1]; see -ER[2] (2))]

cŏ'ronėt *n.* Small crown (esp. as worn, or used as heraldic device, by peer or peeress); band of precious materials, esp. as decorative part of woman's head-dress; garland for the head; lowest part of horse's pastern; ring of bone at base of deer's antler. [f. OF *coronet(t)e* dim. of *corone* CROWN[1]]

cŏ'ronĕtėd *a.* Wearing a coronet (esp. as belonging to peerage). [f. prec. + -ED[2]]

corō'zō *n.* (*pl.* ~**s**). S. Amer. palm-tree, of various species; ~**-nut,** seed of one kind (*Phytelephas macrocarpa*) from which vegetable ivory is made. [Sp.]

Corp. *abbr.* Corporal; *Corporation.

cor'pora. See CORPUS.

cor'poral[1] *a.* Of the human body (*corporal punishment*); ~ **oath,** (arch.) one ratified by touching a sacred object; hence ~LY[2] *adv.* [ME f. OF, f. L *corporalis* (*corpus -oris* body; see -AL)]

cor'poral[2] *n.* Cloth on which consecrated elements are placed during celebration of Eucharist. [OE f. OF, or f. med. L *corporale* (*pallium*) body cloth (as prec.)]

cor'poral[3] *n.* Non-commissioned officer ranking just below sergeant (**the little C**~, Napoleon I); ||**ship's** ~, officer attending to police matters under master-at-arms; *fallfish. [obs. F, var. of *caporal* f. It. *caporale* prob. f. L *corporalis* (as prec.), confused w. It. *capo* head]

corporă'lĭtȳ *n.* Material existence; body. [ME, f. LL *corporalitas* (as CORPORAL[1]; see -ITY)]

cor'porate *a.* **1.** Forming a corporation (*corporate body, body corporate*); ~ **town** (having municipal rights). **2.** Forming one body of many individuals; of or belonging to a corporation or group (*corporate responsibility*). **3.** Hence **cor'poratISM** *n.*, corporativism, ~LY[2] (-tlĭ) *adv.* [f. L *corporare* form into a body (*corpus -oris*); see -ATE[2]]

corporā'tion *n.* United body of persons, esp. one authorized to act as an individual; artificial person created by charter, prescription, or act of the legislature, comprising many persons (~ **aggregate**) or one (~ **sole**); (**municipal**) ~, civic authorities of borough, town, or city; (colloq.) prominent abdomen. [f. LL *corporatio* (as prec.; see -ATION)]

cor'porativ|e *a.* Of a corporation; governed by or organized in corporations, esp. of employers and employed, whence ~ISM (3) *n.* [f. CORPORATE + -IVE]

corpor'ėal *a.* Bodily; material; (Law) consisting of material objects (*corporeal hereditament*); hence ~ITY (-ă'l-) *n.*, ~LY[2] *adv.* [f. LL *corporealis* f. L *corporeus* (*corpus -oris* body); see -AL]

corporē'ĭtȳ *n.* Quality of being or having a material body; bodily substance. [f. F *corporéité* or f. med. L *corporeitas* f. L *corporeus* (see prec., -ITY)]

cor'posant (-z-) *n.* Luminous electrical discharge sometimes seen on ship or aircraft during storm. [f. OSp., Port., It. *corpo santo* holy body]

corps (kor) *n.* (*pl.* same *pr.* korz). **1.** = ARMY *corps*. **2.** Body of troops for special (medical, ordnance, intelligence, etc.) service; body of persons engaged in same activity (DIPLOMATIC *corps, press corps*); students' society in German university. **3.** ~ ***de ballet*** (kordebă'lā), the company of ensemble dancers in a ballet; ~ ***d'élite*** (kordālē't), select group; ~ ***diplomatique*** (kordĭplōmătē'k), = DIPLOMATIC *corps*. [F (as foll.)]

corpse *n.* Dead (usu. human) body; ~**-candle,** (1) lambent flame seen in churchyard or over grave, regarded as omen of death, (2) lighted candle placed beside corpse before burial. [ME *corps*, var. sp. of *cors* (CORSE), f. OF *cors* f. L *corpus* body]

cor'pŭl|ent *a.* Bulky (of body); fat; so ~ENCE, ~ENCY, *ns.* [ME, f. L *corpulentus* (*corpus* body; see -ULENT)]

cor'pus *n.* (*pl.* **cor'pora**). **1.** Body or collection of writings etc. **2.** ~ ***delicti*** (dĭlĭ'ktī), all that goes to make a breach of law, (pop.) tangible evidence of crime, esp. corpse; ~ ***vile*** (vī'lĭ), thing worthless except as object of experiments. **3.** (Anat.) Structure of special character in the animal body; ~ **lu'teum** (lōō'tĭum), body developed in ovary after discharge of ovum, remaining in existence only if pregnancy has begun. **4. C**~ **Chri'sti** (krĭ'stĭ), Feast of the Body of Christ (Thursday after Trinity Sunday). [ME f. L, = body]

cor'puscle (-sel) *n.* Minute body forming distinct part of organism, esp. (in *pl.*) those constituting large part of blood in vertebrates; so **corpŭ'scūlAR**[1] *a.* [f. L *corpusculum* (as prec.; see -CULE)]

corra'l (-ah'l) *n.*, & *v.t.* (**-ll-**). **1.** *Pen for horses, cattle, etc.; defensive enclosure of wagons in encampment; enclosure for capturing wild animals. **2.** *v.t.* Form (wagons) into corral; confine in corral; *(colloq.) acquire. [Sp. & OPort., f. as KRAAL]

corrā'sion (-zhon) *n.* (Geol.) Local wearing away of earth's surface by movement of air, water, ice, etc. [f. L COR(*radere ras-* scrape); see -ION]

corrĕ'ct[1] *v.t.* **1.** Set right, amend; substitute right for (wrong); mark errors in (proof-sheet etc.) for amendment. **2.** Admonish (person; **stand** ~**ed,** accept correction from another person); punish (person, fault); counteract (harmful quality); bring (reading of barometer etc.) into accordance with standard; eliminate aberration etc. from (lens etc.). [ME, f. L COR(*rigere rect-* = *regere* guide)]

corrĕ'ct[2] *a.* True, accurate; (of conduct, manners, etc.) right, proper; in accordance with a good standard (of taste etc.); hence ~LY[2] *adv.*, ~NESS *n.* [F, f. as prec.]

corrĕ'ction *n.* Correcting (**I speak under** ~, I may be wrong); thing substituted for what is wrong; punishment (*house of correction*); hence ~AL *a.* [ME f. OF, f. L *correctio -onis* (as prec.; see -ION)]

corrĕ'ctitūde *n.* Correctness, esp. conscious correctness of conduct. [19th c., f. CORRECT[2] + RECTITUDE]

corrĕ'ctive *a.* & *n.* (Thing) serving or tending to correct or counteract what is harmful; hence ~LY[2] (-vlĭ) *adv.* [F *correctif -ive*, or f. LL *correctivus* (as CORRECT[1]; see -IVE)]

corrĕ'ctor *n.* One who corrects; censor, critic; ||~ **of the press,** proof-reader. [ME, f. AF *cor(r)ectour* f. L *corrector* (as CORRECT[1]; see -OR)]

For other words in *co-* see CO-.

cŏ'rrĕlāte[1] *n.* Each of two related things (esp. so related that one implies the other). [f. as foll.; see -ATE[1]]

cŏ'rrĕlāte[2] *v.* **1.** *v.i.* Have a mutual relation (*with, to*). **2.** *v.t.* Bring (thing) into mutual relation (*with* another). [back form. f. *correlation, correlative*; see -ATE[3]]

cŏrrĕlā'tion *n.* Mutual relation between two or more things; interdependence of variable quantities, quantity measuring extent of this; act of correlating; hence ~AL *a.* [f. med. L *correlatio*; see foll., -ATION]

corrĕ'lative *a.* & *n.* **1.** *a.* Having a mutual relation (*with, to*); (Gram., of words) corresponding to each other and regularly used together, e.g. *either* and *or*; hence ~LY[2] (-vlĭ) *adv.*, **corrĕlatĭ'**VITY *n.* **2.** *n.* Correlative word or thing. [f. med. L COR(*relativus* RELATIVE)]

cŏrrĕspŏ'nd *v.i.* **1.** Be in harmony (*with, to*); be similar or analogous (*to*); agree in amount, position, etc. (*to*); hence **~ing**LY[2] *adv.* **2.** Communicate by interchange of letters (*with*); **~ing member** (of learned society etc.), honorary non-resident member with no voice in the society's affairs. [f. F *correspondre* f. med. L COR(*respondere* RESPOND[1])]

cŏrrĕspŏ'ndence *n.* Agreement, harmony, (*with, to; between* two); communication by letters; letters; ~ **college, school,** (instructing by correspondence, and conducting ~ **courses**); ~ **column,** part of newspaper etc. with letters from its readers; ~ **theory,** (Philos.) theory that truth should be judged by accordance with external facts. [ME f. OF, f. med. L *correspondentia* (as prec.; see -ENCE)]

cŏrrĕspŏ'ndent *n.* & *a.* **1.** *n.* One who writes letters (to person or newspaper); person employed to contribute matter for publication esp. in newspaper (*our Moscow, chess, correspondent*); person or firm having regular business relations with another esp. in another country. **2.** *a.* (arch.) Corresponding (*to, with,* or abs.); hence ~LY[2] *adv.* [ME, f. OF *correspondant* or f. med. L (as prec.; see -ENT)]

cŏrrī'da (-ē'-) *n.* Bullfight(ing). [Sp. *corrida* (*de toros*) running (of bulls)]

cŏ'rrĭdŏr *n.* Main passage in large building, on which many rooms open (**~s of power,** (fig.) places where covert influence is exerted in government); outside passage connecting parts of building; (Polit.) strip of a State's territory that runs through that of another and secures access to the sea etc.; passage in railway carriage with door to each compartment; route to which aircraft are restricted. [F, f. It. *corridore* corridor for *corridojo* running-place (*correre* run) by confus. w. *corridore* runner]

cŏ'rrĭe *n.* (esp. Sc.) Circular hollow on mountainside, cirque. [f. Gael. *coire* cauldron]

cŏrrĭgĕ'nd|um *n.* (*pl.* **~a**). Thing to be corrected (esp. error in printed book). [L, neut. gerundive of *corrigere* (see CORRECT[1])]

cŏ'rrĭgĭble *a.* Capable of being corrected; (of person) submissive, or open, to correction. [ME f. F, f. med. L *corrigibilis* (as CORRECT[1]; see -IBLE)]

corrŏ'borant *a.* & *n.* (arch.) Strengthening (medicine); corroborating (fact). [F, or f. as foll.; see -ANT]

corrŏ'bor|āte *v.t.* Confirm formally (law etc.); confirm (person, statement) by evidence etc.; hence or cogn. **~at**IVE, **~at**ORY, *adjs.*, **~**A'TION, **~āt**OR, *ns.* [f. L COR(*roborare* f. *robur -oris* strength) strengthen + -ATE[3]]

corrŏ'boree *n.* Festive or warlike night-dance of Australian Aboriginals; noisy party. [Aboriginal dial.]

corrō'de *v.* **1.** *v.t.* (Of rust, chemical agent, disease, or fig.) wear away, destroy gradually. **2.** *v.i.* Be worn away, decay. **3.** So **corrō'**SION (-zhon) *n.* [ME, f. L COR(*rodere ros-* gnaw)]

corrō'sĭve *a.* & *n.* (Substance) tending to corrode (lit. or fig.); ~ **sublimate,** mercuric chloride, a strong acrid poison, used as fungicide etc.; hence ~LY[2] (-vlĭ) *adv.*, ~NESS (-vn-) *n.* [ME, f. OF *corosif -ive* (as prec.; see -IVE)]

cŏ'rrugāte (-ōō-) *v.t.* & *i.* Contract into wrinkles or folds; mark with or bend into ridges, esp. to produce stronger material (*corrugated iron, paper*); so **cŏrrug**A'TION (-ōō-) *n.* [f. L COR(*rugare* f. *ruga* wrinkle) + -ATE[3]]

cŏ'rrugātor (-ōō-) *n.* (Anat.) One of two muscles that contract the brow in frowning. [mod. L (as prec.; see -OR)]

corrŭ'pt[1] *a.* Rotten; depraved, wicked; influenced by bribery (~ **practices,** forms of bribery esp. at elections); (of language, text, etc.) vitiated by errors or alterations; hence ~LY[2] *adv.*, ~NESS *n.* [ME f. OF, or f. L *corruptus* p.p. of COR(*rumpere rupt-* break)]

corrŭ'pt[2] *v.* **1.** *v.t.* Infect, taint, (lit. or fig.); deprave; bribe; destroy purity of (language), vitiate (text). **2.** *v.i.* Become corrupt. **3.** So ~IBLE, ~IVE, *adjs.* [ME, f. prec., replacing obs. *corrump*]

corrŭ'ption *n.* Decomposition; moral deterioration; use of corrupt practices (bribery etc.); perversion (of language, text, etc.) from its original state; deformation (of word); ~ **of blood,** (Hist.) effect of attainder upon person attainted, depriving him and his heirs of all rank and titles. [ME f. OF, or f. L *corruptio* (as CORRUPT[1]; see -ION)]

cor'săc, -ăk, *n.* (Zool.) Small fox of Central Asia. [Turki]

corsa'ge (-ah'zh) *n.* Bodice of woman's dress; *bouquet (to be) worn on bodice. [ME f. OF (*cors* body; see CORPSE, -AGE)]

cor'sair *n.* (Hist.) privateer, privateering vessel, esp. of Barbary; pirate. [f. F *corsaire* f. med. L *cursarius* (*cursus* inroad, f. *currere* run; see -ARY[1])]

corse. Var. (arch. or poet.) of CORPSE.

cor'selĕt (-sl-). Var. of CORSELETTE, CORSLET.

cor'selĕtte (*or* -sl-) *n.* Woman's foundation garment combining corset and brassière. [f. CORSLET; ***P**]

cor'sĕt *n.*, & *v.t.* **1.** *n.* Woman's closely-fitting supporting undergarment; man's or woman's similar garment worn because of injury, weakness, or deformity; hence ~ED[2] *a.*, ~RY (1, 2) *n.* **2.** *v.t.* Provide with corset; (fig.) control closely. [ME f. OF, dim. of *cors* body; see CORPSE, -ET[1]]

cor'sĕtière (-tyar̄) *n.* Woman who makes or fits corsets. [F, fem. of *corsetier* (as prec., -IER)]

Cor'sĭcan *a.* & *n.* (Native, inhabitant, or Italian dialect) of Corsica; **the** ~ (**ogre** etc.), Napoleon I. [f. *Corsica*, island in the Mediterranean + -AN]

cor'slĕt *n.* (Hist.) piece of armour covering body; garment (usu. tight-fitting) covering body as distinct from limbs; (Zool.) hard part of fish's or insect's thorax. [f. OF *corselet*, dim. f. as CORSET; see -LET]

cortège (-tā'zh) *n.* Train of attendants; (esp. funeral) procession. [F]

Cor'tĕs (*or* -z) *n.* Legislative assembly of Spain or (Hist.) Portugal. [Sp. & Port., pl. of *corte* COURT[1]]

cor'tĕx *n.* (*pl.* **cor'tices** *pr.* -tĭsēz). Bark; outer grey matter of brain; outer part of kidney, adrenal gland, or hair; so **cor'tĭc**AL *a.* [L *cortex -icis* bark]

Cor'tĭ *n.* **Organ of** ~, structure in mammalian ear responsible for perception of sound. [f. A. ~, It. anatomist d. 1876]

cor'tĭcate, -ātĕd, *adjs.* Having bark or rind; barklike. [f. L *corticatus* (as CORTEX; see -ATE[2])]

cortĭcōtrŏ'p(h)ĭc, cortĭcōtrŏ'p(h)ĭn. Vars. of ADRENOCORTICOTROP(H)IC, -IN.

cor'tĭsōne (-z-) *n.* Steroid hormone produced by

the adrenal cortex or synthetically, used medicinally against inflammation and allergy. [f. Chem. name 17-hydroxy-11-dehydro*cortico*-ster*one*]

corŭ'ndum *n.* Crystallized alumina of various colours, with great hardness, used as abrasive and as gems. [f. Tamil *kurundam* f. Skr. *kuruvinda* ruby]

cŏ'rusc|āte *v.i.* Sparkle, flash, (lit., or fig. of wit etc.); so ~A'TION *n.* [f. L *coruscare* glitter + -ATE³]

cor̂vée (-vā') *n.* (Hist.) day's work of unpaid labour due by vassal; labour done in lieu of taxes; onerous task. [ME f. OF, f. Rom. **corrogata* (*opera*) requisitioned (work), f. COR-(*rogare* ask)]

||**corves.** See CORF.

cor̂vĕ'tte *n.* (Naut.) (Hist.) flush-decked war--vessel with one tier of guns; small fast naval escort-vessel. [F, f. MDu. *korf* kind of ship, + dim. -ETTE]

cor̂vi'na (-ē'-) *n.* Amer. or Afr. weakfish. [Sp. & Port., f. L (as foll.), perh. f. its black fins]

cor̂'vīne *a.* Of or akin to the raven or crow. [f. L *corvinus* (*corvus* raven; see -INE¹)]

cŏrўbă'ntĭc *a.* Wild, frenzied. [f. *Corybantes* priests of Cybele performing wild dances (L f. Gk *Korubantes*) + -IC]

cŏ'rўmb *n.* (Bot.) Type of inflorescence, raceme in which lower flower-stalks are proportionally longer, forming flattish top; hence ~OSE¹ *a.* [f. F *corymbe* or f. L f. Gk *korumbos* cluster]

cŏrўphae'|us *n.* (*pl.* ~**i** *pr.* -ē'ī). Leader of a chorus (lit. or fig.). [L, f. Gk *koruphaios* (*koruphē* head)]

cŏ'rўphée (-fā) *n.* A leading dancer in a *corps de ballet*. [F, as prec.]

corȳ'za *n.* Nasal catarrh; disease with this as symptom, esp. COLD² 2. [L, f. Gk *koruza* running at nose]

cōs¹ *n.* Kind of long-leaved lettuce. [f. *Cos*, island in the Aegean, where it originated]

cŏs², **'cŏs**, (-z) *adv.* & *conj.* (colloq.) Because. [abbr.]

cŏs³ (*or* -z) *abbr.* cosine.

***Cōsa Nŏ'stra** (-z*a*) *n.* Amer. branch of Mafia. [It., = our thing]

cō'sĕc *abbr.* = foll.

cōsĕ'cant *n.* (Math.) Secant of complement of given angle. [f. mod. L *cosecans* and F *cosécant* (as CO- 2, SECANT)]

cōsei'smal (-sī'z-) *a.* & *n.* (Line or curve connecting points) of simultaneous shock from earthquake wave. [f. CO- 1 + SEISMAL]

cō'sĕt *n.* (Math.) Set that when added to another forms a given larger set. [f. CO- 2 + SET²]

||**cŏsh¹** *n.*, & *v.t.* (sl.) **1.** *n.* Weighted stick or bludgeon; ~**-boy,** youth or man armed with cosh. **2.** *v.t.* Strike with cosh. [19th c.; orig. unkn.]

cŏsh² (*or* kŏsă'ch) *abbr.* hyperbolic cosine.

cŏ'sher *v.t.* Pamper. [19th c.; orig. unkn.]

cō-sĭ'gnatorў, *cōsĭ'-, *a.* & *n.* (Person or State) signing jointly with others. [f. CO- 1 + SIGNATORY]

cō'sīne *n.* (Math.) Sine of complement of given angle or quantity. [f. mod. L *cosinus* (as CO- 2, SINE)]

cŏ'smėa (-z-) *n.* = COSMOS². [mod. L, f. as COSMOS²; see -A 1]

cŏsmĕ't|ĭc (-z-) *a.* & *n.* **1.** *a.* Designed to beautify hair, skin, or complexion etc.; (of surgery or prosthetic device) imitating or restoring normal appearance; (fig.) intended to improve appearances; hence ~ICALLY *adv.*, *~I'CIAN, ~**ŏ'**LOGY, *ns.* **2.** *n.* Cosmetic preparation. [f. F *cosmétique* f. Gk *kosmētikos* (*kosmeō* adorn f. *kosmos* order, adornment; see -ETIC)]

cŏ'smĭc (-z-) *a.* **1.** Of the universe or cosmos (esp. as distinguished from the earth); ~ **dust,** minute particles of matter in or from outer space; ~ **radiation,** ~ **rays,** radiations from outer space etc. that reach earth from all directions, with high energy and penetrative power. **2.** Pertaining to space travel (*cosmic rocket* etc.). **3.** Hence ~AL *a.*, ~**al**LY² *adv.* [f. COSMOS¹ + -IC]

cŏsmŏ'gon|ў (-z-) *n.* (Theory of) the origin of the universe; hence **cŏsmogŏ'n**IC(AL) (-z-), *adjs.*, ~IST (3) *n.* [f. Gk *kosmogonia* (*kosmos* world, *-gonia* -begetting)]

cŏsmŏ'graphў (-z-) *n.* Description or mapping of general features of universe or earth; hence or cogn. **cŏsmŏ'**GRAPHER *n.*, **cŏsmo**GRA'PHIC(AL) *adjs.*, (-z-). [ME, f. F *cosmographie* or f. LL f. Gk *kosmographia* (as COSMOS¹; see -GRAPHY)]

cŏsmŏ'log|ў (-z-) *n.* Science of the universe; hence **cŏsmolŏ'g**ICAL (-z-) *a.*, ~IST (3) *n.* [f. F *cosmologie* or mod. L *cosmologia* (as COSMOS¹; see -LOGY)]

cŏ'smonaut (-z-) *n.* (Esp. Russian) astronaut. [f. COSMOS¹, after *astronaut*]

cŏsmŏ'polĭs (-z-) *n.* Cosmopolitan city. [f. Gk *kosmos* world + *polis* city]

cŏsmopŏ'lĭtan (-z-) *a.* & *n.* (Person, group of persons) belonging to many or all parts of the world; (person) free from national limitations; hence ~ISM (3) *n.*, ~IZE (2, 3) *v.t.* & *i.* [f. foll. + -AN]

cŏsmŏ'polīte (-z-) *n.* & *a.* **1.** *n.* Citizen of the world. **2.** *a.* Free from national attachments or prejudices. [F, f. Gk *kosmopolitēs* (*kosmos* world, *politēs* citizen)]

cŏsmŏs¹ (-z-) *n.* The universe as an ordered whole; ordered system of ideas, etc., sum-total of experience. [f. Gk *kosmos*]

cŏ'smŏs² (-z-) *n.* Plant of genus *Cosmos*, bearing single dahlia-like blossoms of various colours. [mod. L, f. Gk *kosmos* ornament]

COSPAR *abbr.* Committee on Space Research.

Cŏ'ssăck *n.* Member of a people of S.E. Russia, esp. (Hist.) as light horse in Russian army; ~ **hat,** brimless hat widening towards top. [f. F *cosaque* f. Russ. *kazak* f. Turki *quzzāq* nomad, adventurer]

cŏ'ssėt *v.t.* Pamper. [f. earlier n. = pet lamb, f. AF *coscet, cozet* f. OE *cotsǣta* cottager (as COT¹, SIT)]

cŏst¹ (*or* kaw-) *n.* **1.** Price (to be) paid for thing (*cost of* LIVING¹; **prime** ~, ~ **price,** that at which merchant etc. buys); (in *pl.*) law expenses, esp. those allowed in favour of winning party; expenditure of time, labour, etc. **2. At** ~, at the initial cost, at cost price; **at all** ~**s, at any** ~, no matter what it may cost [prob. orig. f. obs. *cost* manner]; **at the** ~ **of,** at the expense of losing; **count the** ~, consider the risks before action; **to** person's ~, to his loss (*I know to my* ~, I have learnt with loss or expense). **3.** ~ **accountant, clerk,** one who records costs and (esp. overhead) expenses in a business concern; ~**-benefit** *analysis* etc., assessing relation of cost of an operation to value of resulting benefits; ~**-effective** *a.*, effective in relation to its cost; ~**-plus** *a.*, calculated as basic cost plus profit factor; ~ **push,** factors other than demand that cause inflation. [ME f. AF, OF *coust* (*couster*; see foll.)]

cŏst² (*or* kaw-) *v.* (**cost**). **1.** *v.t.* (w. ind. obj.) Be acquirable at, involve expenditure of, (*cost him five pounds*; *cost the writer infinite labour*); result in the loss of (*cost him his life*); ~ person **dear(ly)**, involve a heavy penalty on him. **2.** (~**'ed**). Fix or estimate price of. **3.** *v.i.* & *t.* Be costly (to). [ME, f. OF *coster, couster* f. Rom. **costare* f. L CON(*stare* stand) stand firm, stand at a price]

For other words in *co-* see CO-.

cŏ'stal *a.* Of the ribs. [F, f. mod. L *costalis* f. L *costa* rib; see -AL]
cō'-stâr *n.* & *v.* (**-rr-**). **1.** *n.* Cinema or stage star appearing with other star(s) of equal importance. **2.** *v.i.* Perform as co-star. **3.** *v.t.* Include as co-star. [f. CO- 1 + STAR[1] 3]
‖**cŏ'stard** *n.* Large ribbed kind of apple; (arch., joc.) head. [ME f. AF (*coste* rib f. L *costa*; see -ARD)]
cŏ'stāte *a.* Ribbed, having ribs or ridges. [f. L *costatus* (*costa* rib; see -ATE[2])]
‖**cŏ'ster(monger)** (-ŭngg-) *n.* Man who sells fruit, vegetables, etc., from barrow in street. [f. COSTARD + MONGER]
cŏ'stĭve *a.* Constipated; (fig.) niggardly; hence ~LY[2] (-vlĭ) *adv.*, ~NESS (-vn-) *n.* [ME f. AF **costif*, OF *costivé* f. L *constipatus* CONSTIPATED]
cŏ'stl|ȳ (*or* kaw'-) *a.* Of great value; expensive; hence ~ĬNESS *n.* [f. COST[1] + -LY[1]]
cŏ'stmārȳ *n.* Aromatic perennial composite plant (*Chrysanthemum balsamita*), formerly used in medicine and for flavouring ale. [OE *cost* f. L f. Gk *kostos* f. Arab. *ķusț*, + (*St.*) *Mary* (with whom it was associated in medieval times)]
cŏ'stūme (*or* -tū'm) *n.*, & *v.t.* **1.** *n.* Style or fashion of dress or attire, esp. of a particular nation, class, or period; complete set of outer garments; garment(s) for a particular activity (*bathing-costume*); woman's matching jacket and skirt; ~ **jewellery,** artificial jewellery worn to decorate clothes; ~ **piece, play,** (in which actors wear historical costume). **2.** *v.t.* Provide with costume. [F f. It., f. L *consuetudo* CUSTOM]
cŏstū'mĭer, cŏ'stūmer, *n.* Maker of or dealer in costumes. [F *costumier* (as prec.; see -IER)]
cō's|ȳ (-zĭ), ***cō'z|ȳ,** *a.*, *n.*, & *v.* **1.** *a.* (Of person or place) comfortable, snug; warm and friendly; (derog.) complacent; hence ~ĬLY[2] *adv.*, ~ĬNESS *n.* **2.** *n.* Canopied corner seat for two [cf. F *causeuse*]; cover to retain heat in boiled egg, teapot, etc. **3.** *v.t.* (colloq.) ~**y** (**along**), reassure, delude. **4.** *v.i.* *(colloq.) ~**y up to,** snuggle up to, ingratiate oneself with. [18th c., orig. Sc.; etym. unkn.]
cŏt[1] *n.*, & *v.t.* (**-tt-**). **1.** *n.* Small erection for shelter, = COTE (*bell-cot*, *sheep-cot*); (poet.) cottage. **2.** *v.t.* Put (sheep) in cot. [OE, = MDu., MLG, ON *kot*, f. Gmc **kutam*, cogn. w. COTE]
cŏt[2] *n.* (Ind.) light bedstead; (Naut.) swinging bed; ‖small tall-sided bed esp. for child; *camp-bed; hospital bed; ~**-case,** person too ill to leave bed; ~**-death,** unexplained death of sleeping baby. [Anglo-Ind., f. Hindi *khāț* bedstead, hammock]
cŏt[3] *abbr.* cotangent.
cōtă'ngent (-nj-) *n.* (Math.) Tangent of complement of given angle. [f. CO- 2 + TANGENT]
cōte *n.* Shed, stall, shelter, esp. for birds and animals (DOVE[1]*cote*, *sheep-cote*). [OE, = LG *kote*, f. Gmc **kutōn*, cogn. w. COT[1]]
cōtĕ'mporarȳ etc. Var. of CONTEMPORARY etc.
cō'terĭe *n.* Circle or set of persons associated by exclusive interests; select circle in society. [F, orig. = association of tenants, f. **cote* hut f. MLG *kote* COTE; see -ERY]
cōtêr'mĭnous *a.* Having same boundaries or extent (in space, time, or meaning). [f. CO- 1 + TERMINUS + -OUS]
cŏth *abbr.* hyperbolic cotangent.
cothûr'n|us *n.* (*pl.* ~**i** *pr.* -ī). Buskin, thick-soled boot of Athenian tragic actor. [L, f. Gk *kothornos*]
cō-tī'dal *a.* ~ **line** (on map, connecting places at which high water occurs at same time). [f. CO- 1 + TIDAL]
cotĭ'llion (-lyon) *n.* One of various French dances with elaborate steps, figures, and ceremonial; *quadrille; *formal ball. [f. F *cotillon* petticoat, dim. of *cotte* f. OF *cote* COAT]
cŏtōnēă'ster *n.* Small tree or shrub of genus *Cotoneaster*, resembling hawthorn and bearing red or orange berries. [mod. L, f. L *cotoneum* QUINCE + -ASTER]
Cŏ'tswōld *n.* ~ (**sheep**), sheep of a long-woolled breed originating in the *Cotswold* Hills, Gloucestershire.
cŏ'tta *n.* Short surplice. [It., f. as COAT]
cŏ'ttage *n.* **1.** Labourer's or villager's small dwelling; small country or suburban house. **2.** ~ **cheese** (soft white kind, made from curds); ~ **hospital** (without resident medical staff); ~ **industry** (partly or wholly carried on at home); ~ **loaf** (of two round masses, smaller on top of larger); ~ **piano** (small upright); ~ **pie,** shepherd's pie. **3.** Hence ~Y[2] *a.* [ME, f. AF **cotage*, f. as COT[1], COTE; see -AGE]
cŏ'ttager (-tĭ-) *n.* Inhabitant of a cottage. [f. prec. + -ER[1]]
‖**cŏ'ttar, cŏ'tter**[1]**,** *n.* (Hist. & Sc.) peasant occupying cottage and labouring as required; (Ir. Hist.) = COTTIER. [f. COT[1] + -ER[1] (Sc. *-ar*)]
cŏ'tter[2] *n.* Key, wedge, bolt, for securing parts of machinery etc.; (esp.) split pin that opens after passing through hole; ~**-pin,** pin to keep cotter in place. [17th c., rel. to earlier *cotterel*; orig. unkn.]
‖**cŏ'ttĭer** *n.* Cottager; (Hist.) Irish peasant under ~ **tenure** (letting of land in small portions at rent fixed by competition). [ME, f. OF *cotier* (med. L *cotarius*), f. **cote*; see COTERIE, -IER]
cŏ'tton[1] *n.* **1.** White downy fibrous substance clothing seeds of ~**-plant** (*Gossypium*), used for making cloth, thread, etc.; cotton-plant; thread spun from cotton yarn, used for sewing etc.; cloth made of cotton; GUN-*cotton*. **2.** ~**-cake,** compressed cotton seed as food for cattle; *~ **candy,** candy-floss; *cotton*-GIN[1]; ~**-grass,** sedge of genus *Eriophorum* with long white silky hairs; *~**-picking** *a.*, (sl.) unpleasant, wretched; ~**-spinner,** worker who spins cotton, owner of cotton-mill; ~**tail,** common Amer. rabbit of genus *Sylvilagus*, with white fluffy tail; ~ **waste,** refuse yarn used for cleaning machinery etc.; ~**wood,** Amer. poplar with cottony seed-hairs, Austral. downy-leaved tree; ~ **wool,** raw cotton as prepared for wadding, *raw cotton. **3.** Hence ~Y[2] *a.* [ME, f. OF *coton* f. Arab. *ķuțn*]
cŏ'tton[2] *v.i.* Become attracted *to*; ~ **on to,** form liking for (person, thing); ~ **on** (**to**), (sl.) understand; ~ **up to,** make friendly advances to. [f. prec.]
cŏtȳlē'don *n.* Primary leaf in embryo of higher plants, seed-leaf; plant of genus *Cotyledon*, e.g. pennywort; hence ~ARY, ~OUS, *adjs.* [L, = pennywort, f. Gk *kotulēdōn* cup-shaped cavity (*kotulē* cup)]
cou'cal (ko͞o'-) *n.* Tropical bird of genus *Centropus*, allied to cuckoo and resembling pheasant. [F, perh. f. *coucou* cuckoo + *alouette* lark]
couch[1] *n.* **1.** (arch. or literary). Bed; thing one sleeps on. **2.** Piece of furniture like sofa, but with half-back and head-end only; piece of furniture on which doctor's or psychiatrist's patient reclines during examination. [ME f. OF *couche* (*coucher*; see foll.)]
couch[2] *v.* **1.** *v.t.* Lay (as) on couch; lower (spear etc.) to position of attack; treat (cataract, cataract-patient's eye) by displacement of lens; express (thought etc. *in* words). **2.** *v.i.* (Of animal) lie (esp. in lair); lie in ambush. [ME, f. OF *coucher* f. L COL(*locare* place)]
couch[3] (*or* ko͞o-) *n.* ~(**-grass**), weed with long creeping roots, esp. *Agropyron repens*. [var. of QUITCH]
cou'chant *a.* (Her.) (Of animal) lying with body

resting on legs and head raised. [F, part. as COUCH²; see -ANT]

couchě'tte (kōōsh-) *n.* (Berth in) railway carriage with seats convertible into sleeping-berths. [F, = little bed, dim. of *couche* COUCH¹]

coudé (kōōdā') *a.* & *n.* (Of or pertaining to) a telescope in which rays are bent to a focus off the axis. [F, p.p. of *couder* bend at right angles (*coude* elbow f. as CUBIT)]

Couéism (kōō'āĭ-) *n.* System of usu. optimistic auto-suggestion as psychotherapy. [f. E. *Coué*, Fr. psychologist d. 1926 + -ISM]

***cou'gar** (kōō'-) *n.* Puma. [F, repr. Guarani *guaçu ara*]

cough¹ (kŏf *or* kawf) *n.* Act of coughing; tendency to cough; condition of respiratory organs causing coughing; **~-drop,** medicated sweet to relieve cough, (fig., sl.) awkward or disagreeable person or thing; **~ mixture,** medicine to relieve cough. [f. foll.]

cough² (kŏf *or* kawf) *v.* **1.** *v.i.* Expel air from lungs with violent effort and noise produced by abrupt opening of glottis, to remove obstruction or congestion; (of engine, gun, etc.) make similar noise; (sl.) confess. **2.** *v.t.* **~ out, up,** eject by, or say with, cough; **~ up,** (sl.) bring out or produce reluctantly (esp. money), disclose. [ME *coghe*, *cowhe*, rel. to MDu. *kuchen*, MHG *kūchen*, of imit. orig.]

could, couldn't, etc. See CAN².

coulée (kōōlā' *or* kōō'lĭ) *n.* **1.** (Geol.) Lava-flow. **2.** *Deep ravine. [F, fem. p.p. of *couler* flow, f. L *colare* strain, filter]

coulisse (kōōlē's) *n.* (usu. in *pl.*) Wings in theatre; space between two of these; body of unofficial dealers on bourse; corridor; place of informal discussion or negotiation. [F, f. *coulis* sliding (see PORTCULLIS)]

cou'loir (kōō'lwar) *n.* Steep gully on mountainside. [F (*couler* glide; see COULÉE, -ORY)]

cou'lŏmb (kōō'lŏm) *n.* Unit of electric charge, quantity of electricity conveyed in one second by current of one ampere. [f. C. A. de *Coulomb*, Fr. physicist d. 1806]

coulŏ'mètrў (kōō-) *n.* (Chemical analysis by) measurement of number of coulombs used in electrolysis; hence **coulomě'tric** (kōō-) *a.* [f. prec. + -METRY]

cou'lter (kō'l-), ***cō'l-,** *n.* Vertical iron cutting blade fixed in front of ploughshare. [OE f. L *culter*]

cou'marĭn (kōō'-) *n.* Aromatic crystalline substance found in seeds of tonka bean etc. [f. F *coumarine* f. Tupi *cumarú* tonka bean; see -IN]

cou'marōne (kōō'-) *n.* Colourless organic liquid obtainable from coal tar or by synthesis; **~ resin,** thermoplastic resin formed by polymerization of coumarone. [f. prec. + -ONE]

cou'ncil *n.* **1.** Ecclesiastical assembly (*ecumenical, diocesan, council*); (N.T.) Sanhedrin. **2.** Advisory or deliberative assembly; body of persons chosen as advisers (PRIVY *Council*; **Queen** etc. **in C~,** Privy Council as issuing *Orders in Council* (ORDER¹ 15) or receiving petitions etc.; **~ of war,** assembly of officers called in special emergency, also fig.). **3.** Local administrative body of parish, district, town, city or administrative county. **4. ~-chamber,** room in which council meets; **~ estate, flat, house,** etc., dwelling-place(s) owned and let by local council; **~-house,** building in which council meets; **~man,** member of council (in City of London & in U.S.); **~ school** (supported by town or county council). [ME, f. AF *cuncile* f. L *concilium* convocation, assembly, (as CON-, *calare* summon); cf. COUNSEL¹]

cou'ncillor *n.* Member of a (town etc.) council; hence **~SHIP** *n.* [ME, alt. of COUNSELLOR; assim. to prec.]

cou'nsel¹ *n.* **1.** Consultation (**take ~,** consult (*with*, or abs.)); plan of action; advice (**~ of perfection,** advice guiding towards moral perfection, (fig.) advice that is ideal but impracticable; **keep** one's **own ~,** not confide in others). **2.** (Body of) legal adviser(s) in cause. **3.** (*pl.* same). Barrister; ||**Queen's, King's, C~,** counsel to the crown, taking precedence of other barristers. [ME, f. OF *c(o)unseil*, f. L *consilium* consultation, advice, rel. to *consulere* (cf. CONSUL), *consultare* consult; cf. COUNCIL]

cou'nsel² *v.t.* (||-**ll**-). Advise (person *to* do); give advice to (person) professionally on social problems etc.; recommend (thing, *that*). [ME, f. OF *conseiller* f. L *consiliari* (*consilium*; see prec.)]

cou'nsellor, *-elor, *n.* Adviser, *esp. of students; senior officer in diplomatic service; **~(-at-law),** *barrister, (Ir.) advising barrister; ||**C~ of State,** temporary regent during sovereign's absence. [ME, f. OF *conseiller* (f. L *consiliarius*), *conseillour, -eur* (f. L *consiliator*); see COUNSEL¹, -OR]

count¹ *n.* Counting; one's reckoning (**keep, lose, ~,** be aware, fail to know, how many there have been); sum total of things (BLOOD¹ *count*, POLLEN *count*); (Law) each charge in an indictment; (Boxing) counting of up to ten seconds by referee when boxer is knocked down (**out for the ~,** defeated by being unable to rise within ten seconds, also fig.; **take the ~,** be defeated); measure of fineness of yarn as number of threads per unit length; (Phys.) record of ionization event. [ME, f. OF *co(u)nte* f. LL *computus* (*computare*; see foll.)]

count² *v.* **1.** *v.t.* Find number of, esp. by assigning successive numerals; **~ out,** count while taking from a stock, complete count of ten seconds over (fallen boxer), (in children's games) select (player) for special role or dismissal by counting with words of rhyme etc., (colloq.) exclude from reckoning or plan, ||procure adjournment of (House of Commons) when fewer than 40 members are present; **~ up,** find sum of; hence **~'ABLE** *a.* **2. ~ (in),** include in reckoning or plan; **not ~ing,** excluding from reckoning. **3.** *v.t.* & *i.* Consider (thing or person) to be (lucky etc.); **~ on** or **upon,** depend or rely on, expect confidently. **4.** *v.i.* Repeat numerals in order; conduct reckoning (**~'ing-house,** place where accounts are kept); **~ down,** repeat numerals backwards to zero, esp. in procedure for launching rocket, etc.; so **~-down** *n.* **5.** Be included in reckoning (*that does not count*); **~ against,** be reckoned to disadvantage of; **~ for,** be worth (much etc.). [ME, f. OF *co(u)nter* f. L *computare* COMPUTE]

count³ *n.* Foreign noble corresp. to earl; *Count* PALATINE¹; hence **~'SHIP** *n.* [f. OF *conte* f. L *comes comitis* companion]

cou'ntènance¹ *n.* **1.** (Expression of) face; **change ~** (from emotion). **2.** Composure; **keep** (person) **in ~** (usu. by show of support); **keep** one's **~,** maintain composure, esp. refrain from laughing; **lose ~,** become embarrassed; **out of ~,** disconcerted. **3.** Moral support. [ME, f. AF *c(o)untenance*, OF *contenance* bearing (*contenir*; see CONTAIN, -ANCE)]

cou'ntènance² *v.t.* Give approval to (act); encourage (person, practice, person *in* practice). [f. prec.]

cou'nter¹ *n.* **1.** Small disc of metal, ivory, etc., used for keeping account in games, esp. cards; token representing coin; thing used in bargaining. **2.** Banker's or money-changer's table; table in shop on which money is counted out and across which goods are delivered (**~-jumper,** (derog.) shopman; **under the ~**, surreptitiously, esp. illegally); similar structure for service of goods in library, cafeteria, etc. **3.** Apparatus for counting manufactured products, ionization events, etc. [f. AF *count(e)our*, OF *conteo(i)r*, f. med. L *computatorium* (as COMPUTE; see -ORY (2))]

cou'nter² *n.* Part of horse's breast between shoulders and under neck; curved part of stern of ship; part of printing-type etc. enclosed by outline (e.g. loop of P). [17th c.; orig. unkn.]

cou'nter³ *n.* Back part of shoe or boot round heel. [abbr. of *counterfort* buttress]

cou'nter⁴ *a.* & *n.* Opposed; opposite; duplicate; ~(**-rocking-turn** or **-rocker**), skating figure (see ROCK³). [arising f. wds formed w. COUNTER-]

cou'nter⁵ *v.* **1.** *v.t.* Oppose, contradict; meet by countermove. **2.** *v.i.* Make countermove; (Boxing) give return blow while parrying. [ME, f. COUNTER- and COUNTER⁷]

cou'nter⁶ *adv.* In the opposite direction (**go, hunt, run, ~**, i.e. to direction taken by quarry); contrary; **act, go, ~, to,** disobey (instructions etc.); **run ~ to,** act contrary to. [ME, f. OF *countre* f. L *contra* against]

cou'nter⁷ *n.* Parry; countermove. [f. F *contre* (as prec.)]

counter- *pref.* w. senses (1) reciprocation, opposition, (*counter-threat*), frustration, rivalry (*counter-cheers*), (2) opposite direction (*counter-current*), (3) correspondence, match, (of things having naturally two opposite parts), (4) duplicate, substitute. [f. or after AF *countre-*, OF *contre* f. L *contra* against]

counterǎ'ct *v.t.* Hinder, defeat, by contrary action; neutralize; hence ~ION *n.*, ~IVE *a.* [f. COUNTER- (1) + ACT²]

cou'nter-attǎck *n.*, & *v.t.* & *i.* Attack (lit. or fig.) in reply to attack by enemy or opponent. [f. COUNTER- (1) + ATTACK¹,²]

cou'nter-attrǎction *n.* Attraction of contrary tendency; rival attraction. [f. COUNTER- (1) + ATTRACTION]

cou'nterbǎlance *n.*, & *v.t.* **1.** *n.* Weight (lit. or fig.) balancing another. **2.** *v.t.* Act as counterbalance to. [f. COUNTER- (1, 3) + BALANCE¹,²]

cou'nterblast (-ah-) *n.* Energetic declaration or action against something. [f. COUNTER- (1) + BLAST¹]

cou'nterchānge (-nj) *v.* **1.** *v.t.* Interchange; chequer, esp. with systematic contrast. **2.** *v.i.* Change places or parts. [f. F *contrechanger* (as COUNTER- (1), CHANGE²)]

cou'ntercharge *n.*, & *v.t.* Charge in opposition to another or against accuser. [f. COUNTER- (1) + CHARGE¹,²]

cou'ntercheck *n.* Check that opposes a thing; check that operates against another; (arch.) retort (*countercheck quarrelsome*, f. Shak. *As You Like It* v. iv. 85). [f. COUNTER- (1) + CHECK¹]

cou'nter-claim *n.*, & *v.t.* Claim against another claim; claim as defendant in suit. [f. COUNTER- (1) + CLAIM¹,²]

counter-clǒ'ckwise (-z). See CLOCK¹.

cou'nter-cǔlture *n.* Mode of life deliberately deviating from established social practices. [f. COUNTER- (1) + CULTURE]

counter-ě'spionage (*or* -ah'zh) *n.* Action against an enemy's spy system. [f. COUNTER- (1) + ESPIONAGE]

cou'nterfeit¹ (-fǐt *or* -fēt) *a.* & *n.* (Coin, writing, etc.) made in imitation, not genuine; pretended (claimant etc.). [ME, f. OF *countrefet, -fait*, p.p. of *contrefaire* f. Rom. *CONTRA(*facere* make)]

cou'nterfeit² (-fǐt *or* -fēt) *v.t.* Imitate fraudulently, forge, (coin, banknote, handwriting); make imitation of; simulate (feelings); (fig.) resemble closely; hence ~ER¹ *n.* [ME, f. AF *countrefeter* (*countrefet*, f. as prec.)]

cou'nterfoil *n.* Complementary part of bank cheque, official receipt, etc., with note of particulars, retained by person issuing such document. [f. COUNTER- (3) + FOIL¹]

cou'nter-intělligence *n.* Counter-espionage. [f. COUNTER- (1) + INTELLIGENCE 4]

counter-ǐ'rrǐt|ant *n.* Thing used to produce surface irritation and thus counteract symptoms of disease (also fig.); so ~A'TION *n.* [f. COUNTER- (1) + IRRITANT]

counterma'nd (-ah-) *v.t.*, & *n.* **1.** *v.t.* Revoke (command); recall (person, forces, etc.) by contrary order; cancel order for (goods etc.). **2.** *n.* Order revoking previous one. [ME, f. OF *contremander* f. med. L CONTRA(*mandare* order)]

cou'ntermarch *v.i.* & *t.*, & *n.* (Cause to) march in the contrary direction. [f. COUNTER- (2) + MARCH⁴,⁵]

cou'ntermeasure (-ězh*er*) *n.* Action taken to counteract danger, threat, etc. [f. COUNTER- (1) + MEASURE¹]

cou'ntermine *n.* & *v.* **1.** *n.* (Mil.) mine made to intercept that of besiegers; submarine mine sunk to explode enemy's mines by its own explosion; (fig.) counterplot. **2.** *v.t.* & *i.* Make countermine (against). [f. COUNTER- (1) + MINE¹]

cou'ntermove (-ōōv) *n.* Move or action in opposition to another. [f. COUNTER- (1) + MOVE¹]

cou'nter-offěnsive *n.* (Mil. etc.) Offensive action designed to allow escape from defensive situation. [f. COUNTER- (1) + OFFENSIVE]

cou'nterpāne *n.* Bedspread. [alt. (w. assim. to *pane* in obs. sense 'cloth') f. obs. *counterpoint* f. OF *contrepointe* alt. f. *cou(l)tepointe* f. med. L *culcita puncta* quilted mattress]

cou'nterpart *n.* Duplicate; person or thing forming natural complement to another (***~ funds** etc., in local currency and equivalent to goods etc. received from abroad); opposite part of indenture. [f. COUNTER- (3, 4) + PART¹, after OF *contrepartie*]

cou'nterplǒt *n.*, & *v.i.* (**-tt-**). (Make) plot contrived to defeat another plot. [f. COUNTER- (1) + PLOT]

cou'nterpoint *n.*, & *v.t.* **1.** *n.* (Mus.) Melody added as accompaniment to given melody; art or mode of adding melodies as accompaniment according to fixed rules; **strict ~** (acc. to code of rules as academic exercise, not as actual composition). **2.** *v.t.* Add counterpoint to; (fig.) set in contrast. [f. OF *contrepoint* f. med. L CONTRA*punctum* pricked or marked opposite, i.e. to the original melody (*pungere punct-* prick)]

cou'nterpoise¹ (-z) *n.* Counterbalancing weight; thing of equivalent force etc. on opposite side; equilibrium. [ME f. OF *countrepeis, -pois*, (*contre* COUNTER- (1), *peis, pois* f. L *pensum* weight; cf. POISE¹)]

cou'nterpoise² (-z) *v.t.* Counterbalance; compensate; bring into or keep in equilibrium. [ME, f. OF *contrepeser* (as prec.); later assim. to prec.]

counter-produ'ctive *a.* Having the opposite of the desired effect. [f. COUNTER- (2) + PRODUCTIVE]

counter-rěformā'tion *n.* Reformation running counter to another, esp. (Hist.; *C-, R-*) that in Church of Rome following on Protestant Reformation. [f. COUNTER- (1) + REFORMATION²]

counter-rěvolu'tion (-lōō'-) *n.* Revolution opposed to a former one or reversing its results; hence ~ARY¹ *a.* & *n.* [f. COUNTER- (1) + REVOLUTION 2]

cou'nterscarp *n.* Outer wall or slope of ditch in fortification. [f. F *contrescarpe* f. It. *contrascarpa* (as CONTRA-, SCARP)]

cou′ntershaft (-ah-) *n.* Intermediate shaft driven by main shaft and transmitting motion to particular machine etc.; *= LAY³*shaft.* [f. COUNTER- (4) + SHAFT]

cou′ntersign¹ (-in) *n.* Watchword, password, given to man on guard (cf. PAROLE); mark used for identification etc. [f. F *contresigne* f. It. *contrasegno* (as COUNTER- (3), SIGN¹)]

cou′ntersign² (-in) *v.t.* Add signature to (document already signed by another); ratify; so **countersi′gnature** *n.* [f. F *contresigner* (as prec.)]

cou′ntersink *v.t.* (**-sunk**). Bevel off (rim of hole) to receive head of screw or bolt; sink (screw-head) in such hole. [f. COUNTER- (3) + SINK¹]

cou′nterstrōke *n.* Stroke given in return. [f. COUNTER- (1) + STROKE¹]

counter-tĕ′nor *n.* (Mus.) Male voice higher than tenor, but with quality of tenor; singer with counter-tenor voice; part written for counter-tenor voice. [ME, f. F *contre-teneur* f. obs. It. *contratenore* (as CONTRA-, TENOR)]

cou′ntervail *v.t.* Counterbalance (**~ing duty,** one put on imports to offset subsidy in exporting country or tax on similar goods not from abroad); avail against. [ME, f. AF *countrevaloir* f. L *contra valēre* be of worth against]

cou′ntervălūe *n.* Equivalent value (esp. in strategy). [f. COUNTER- (3) + VALUE]

cou′nterweight (-wāt) *n.* Counterbalancing weight. [f. COUNTER- (1) + WEIGHT¹]

cou′ntĕss *n.* Wife or widow of count or earl; woman holding rank of count or earl in her own right. [ME, f. OF *contesse, cuntesse,* f. LL *comitissa* fem. of *comes* COUNT³; see -ESS¹]

cou′ntlĕss *a.* Too many to be counted. [f. COUNT¹ + -LESS]

cou′ntrĭfied, -rÿfied, (kŭ′ntrĭfīd) *a.* Rural, rustic, (in appearance, manners, etc.). [p.p. of *countrify* f. foll. + -FY]

cou′ntrÿ (kŭ′n-) *n.* **1.** Region; the region associated with a person (*the Hardy country*); territory of a nation; territory (lit. or fig.; **unknown ~,** unfamiliar place or topic); land of a person's birth, citizenship, etc., fatherland. **2.** Rural districts as opp. to towns, esp. the rest of a land as opp. to the capital (**across ~,** not keeping to main roads etc.; **in the ~,** (Cricket, sl.) far from the wickets; **up ~,** away from the capital or coast); ||national population, esp. as electors (*appeal,* GO¹ 24, *to the country*). **3. ~(-and-western),** rural or cowboy songs to guitar etc.; **~ club,** sporting and social club in a rural district; **~ cousin,** relation or person of countrified manners or appearance; **~ dance,** English rural, native, or traditional dance, esp. with couples face to face in long lines; **~ gentleman,** gentleman with landed property in rural area; **~ house,** rural residence, esp. of country gentleman; **~ music,** = *country-and-western*; **~ party,** political party supporting agricultural against manufacturing interests; *country* SEAT; **~side,** (inhabitants of) particular rural district, or rural areas generally; **~-wide** *a.*, extending throughout a nation. [ME, f. OF *cuntree,* f. med. L *contrata* (*terra*) (land) lying opposite (CONTRA); see -Y⁴]

countryfied. See COUNTRIFIED.

cou′ntrÿ|man (kŭ′n-) *n.* (*pl.* **~men**; *fem.* **~woman** *pr.* -wŏŏman, *pl.* **~women** *pr.* -wĭmĭn). Man of one's own (or a specified) country; person living in rural parts. [f. COUNTRY + MAN¹]

cou′ntÿ *n.* & *a.* **1.** *n.* ||Territorial division, chief unit for administrative, judicial, and political purposes; administrative division in Commonwealth; *political and administrative division next below State; people of a county, esp. county families; *County* PALATINE¹. **2. ~ borough,** (Hist.) large borough ranking as county for administrative purposes; **~ corporate,** (Hist.) city or town ranking as administrative county; **~ council,** representative governing body of administrative county; **~ court,** judicial court for civil (*and criminal) cases; ||**~ cricket** (between teams representing counties); **~ family** (with ancestral seat in a county); **~ school** (supported by county council); ***~ seat,** ||**~ town,** town in which business of county is or was transacted. **3.** *a.* Having social status or characteristics of county families. [ME, f. AF *counté,* OF *conté, cunté,* f. L *comitatus* (as COUNT³; see -ATE¹, -Y⁴)]

coup (kōō) *n.* (*pl. pr.* kōōz). **1.** Notable or successful stroke or move; (Billiards) direct pocketing of ball. **2. *~ d'état*** (-dātah′), violent or illegal change in government; ***~ de foudre*** (-defōō′dr), sudden unforeseen event, love at first sight; ***~ de grâce*** (-degrah′s), finishing stroke; ***~ de main*** (-demă′ṅ), sudden vigorous attack; ***~ d'œil*** (-dŭ′ē), comprehensive glance, general view; ***~ de théâtre*** (-detāah′tr), dramatically sudden or sensational action or turn of events. [F, f. med. L *colpus* blow (see COPE²)]

coupe¹ (kōōp) *n.* Shallow glass etc.; ice cream and fruit etc. served in glass. [F, = goblet]

coupé (kōō′pā), ***coupe²** (kōōp), *n.* Enclosed motor car, esp. one with two seats; (Hist.) four-wheeled closed carriage for two inside and driver. [F, p.p. (as n.) of *couper* cut (f. as COUP)]

cou′pla (kŭ′-) *n.* (colloq.) = couple of. [corrupt.]

cou′ple¹ (kŭ′-) *n.* **1.** (in *pl.*) Joined collars for holding two hounds together. **2.** (*pl.* same). Pair, brace, esp. of hunting dogs; **a ~ of,** two, approximately two, a few. **3.** Married or engaged pair; pair of partners in dance etc.; pair of rafters; (Mech.) pair of equal and parallel forces acting in opposite directions, and tending to cause rotation about an axis perpendicular to the plane containing them. [ME, f. OF *cople, cuple,* f. L COPULA]

cou′ple² (kŭ′-) *v.* **1.** *v.t.* Fasten or link together (esp. dogs in pairs); connect (railway carriages, oscillators, etc.) by a coupling; associate in thought or speech (two things *together,* one *with* another). **2.** *v.i.* Copulate. [ME, f. OF *copler, cupler* f. L *copulare* (see COPULATE)]

cou′pler (kŭ′-) *n.* In vbl senses; (Mus.) device in organ for connecting two manuals, or manual with pedals, or notes with their octaves above or below (*octave coupler*). [f. prec. + -ER¹]

cou′plĕt (kŭ′-) *n.* Pair of successive lines of verse, esp. when of same length and rhyming. [F, dim. of *couple* f. as COUPLE¹; see -ET¹]

cou′plĭng (kŭ′-) *n.* In vbl senses; link connecting railway carriages etc.; device for connecting parts of machinery; (Phys.) connection between two oscillating systems, causing one to oscillate when the other does so; arrangement of items on gramophone record(s), item so arranged. [f. COUPLE² + -ING¹]

cou′pŏn (kōō′-) *n.* Detachable ticket entitling holder to payment, goods, services, etc., or ration of food, clothes, etc.; form etc. to be completed and sent as application for information, gift, etc.; entry-form for football pool etc.; voucher given with retail purchase, a certain number of which entitle holder to a 'free gift'. [F, = piece cut off (*couper* cut; see COUPÉ, -OON)]

cou′rage (kŭ′-) *n.* Bravery, boldness, (*take, pluck up, lose, courage*); **take** one's **~ in both hands,** nerve oneself to a venture; **Dutch ~** (induced by drinking); ~ **of one's convictions,** courage to act up to what one believes. [ME f. OF *corage,* f. Rom. **coraticum* f. L *cor* heart; see -AGE]

courā'geous (kurā'jus) *a.* Brave, fearless; hence ~LY[2] *adv.*, ~NESS *n.* [ME f. AF *corageous,* OF *corageus* (as prec.; see -OUS)]

courgĕ'tte (koorzhĕ't) *n.* Small variety of vegetable marrow. [F, dim. of *courge* gourd]

cou'rier (kŏŏ'-) *n.* Special messenger; person employed to guide and assist group of tourists; (*C~*) title of some newspapers. [ME f. obs. F, f. It. *corriere,* & f. OF *coreor* f. Rom. **curritor,* both f. L *currere* run; see -ER[2], -OR]

cour'lan (koor-) *n.* Long-billed rail-like wading bird of tropical America, noted for its dismal cry. [F, f. Galibi *kurliri*]

course[1] (kōrs) *n.* **1.** Onward movement; direction taken (*change* one's *course; ship's course; course of events;* ~ **of nature,** ordinary events or procedure); correct or intended direction (*ship was off course*); line of conduct. **2.** Pursuit of game (esp. hares) with (grey)hounds. **3.** Ground on which race is run; channel in which water flows; golf links. **4.** Career (**run** or **take its course,** complete its natural development); series (of lectures etc.), book for or like such series; sequence of medical treatment etc. **5.** Each of successive divisions of meal (esp. soup, fish, meat, etc.). **6.** Continuous horizontal layer of stone etc. in building. **7.** (Naut.) **Fore, main,** ~, fore, main, -sail. **8. In the** ~ **of,** during (*in the* ~ *of time,* as time goes by); **in** ~ **of,** in the process of (construction, being constructed, etc.); **in due** ~, in the natural order; **of** ~, naturally, as was to be expected; **matter of** ~, natural or expected thing. [ME f. OF *cours* f. L *cursus* (*currere curs-* run), & f. corresp. fem. form OF *course* f. Rom. **cursa*]

course[2] (kōrs) *v.* **1.** *v.t.* Pursue (game, as prec. 2); use (hounds) in coursing. **2.** *v.i.* (Esp. of liquid) run about, run. [f. prec.]

cour'ser (kōr'-) *n.* **1.** (poet.) Swift horse. **2.** Fast-running African or Asian bird of genus *Cursorius* etc., akin to plover. [sense 1 ME, f. OF *corsier* f. Rom. **cursarius* (*cursus* COURSE[1]; see -ARY[1], -ER[2]); sense 2 f. LL *cursorius* adapted for running (see -ORY)]

court[1] (kōrt) *n.* **1.** ~(**'yard**), space enclosed by walls or buildings; ||(Cambridge Univ.) college quadrangle; subdivision of building open to the general roof; ||confined yard opening off street; (in town) yard surrounded by houses and communicating with street by an entry. **2.** Enclosed quadrangular area, open or covered, for games, (*tennis, croquet, fives, -court*); plot of ground marked out for lawn tennis; **ball is in your** ~, (fig.) you must be next to act. **3.** Sovereign's residence; his establishment and retinue; body of courtiers; sovereign and his councillors as ruling power (**C~ of St. James's,** British sovereign's court); assembly held by sovereign, state reception, (**hold** ~, (fig.) preside over admirers etc.). **4.** Assembly of judges or other persons acting as tribunal, (*court of law, lawcourt; court of justice, court of judicature, court* LEET[1], *court of* RECORD[2]; *court of* SUMMARY *jurisdiction*); place or hall in which justice is administered; **go to** ~, take legal action; **out of** ~, (of plaintiff) not entitled to be heard, (of settlement) before hearing or judgement, (fig.) not worthy of consideration. **5.** (Meeting of) qualified members of company, corporation, (in some friendly societies) = LODGE[1] 4. **6.** Attention paid to one whose favour, affection, interest, is sought (*pay court to*). **7.** ~-**-card,** playing-card that is king, queen, or jack [orig. *coat-card*]; ||~ **circular,** daily report of doings of royal court published in newspapers; ~ **cupboard,** 16th–17th c. sideboard usu. with cupboard in top part only; ~ **dress,** formal dress as worn at royal court; ~**-house,** building in which judicial court is held, *building containing administrative offices of county; ~ **martial** (pl. ~*s martial*), judicial court of naval, military, or air force officers; ~**-mar'tial** *v.t.* (||-*ll*-), try by this; ~ **plaster,** sticking-plaster for cuts etc. (formerly used by ladies at court for face-patches); ~ **roll,** (Hist.) manorial-court register of holdings; ~ **shoe,** woman's light shoe with low-cut upper; *~ **tennis,** = TENNIS 1; ~**'yard** (see sense 1). [ME, f. AF *curt,* OF *cort* f. Rom. **curte,* **corte* f. L *cohors -ortis* yard, retinue]

court[2] (kōrt) *v.t.* Pay court to; try to win favour or affection of, try to attract sexually, (person, or abs.); seek to win (applause etc.); unwisely invite (inquiry etc.; *you are courting disaster*). [f. OIt. *corteare,* OF *courtoyer* (*cort;* see prec.)]

court bouillon (koor bŏŏyaw'n) *n.* Stock made from wine, vegetables, etc., in which fish is boiled. [F (*court* short, BOUILLON)]

cour'tèous (kēr'-) *a.* Polite, kind, considerate, in manner or approach; hence ~LY[2] *adv.*, ~NESS *n.* [ME f. OF *corteis, curteis* f. Rom. **cortensis* (as COURT[1]; see -ESE); assim. to wds in -OUS]

courtèsă'n (kōrtĭză'n) *n.* Prostitute, esp. one whose clients are wealthy or upper-class. [f. F *courtisane* f. It. *cortigiana,* fem. of *cortigiano* courtier (*corte* COURT[1])]

cour'tesÿ (kēr'-) *n.* Courteous behaviour or disposition or act; (arch.) = CURTSY; **by** ~, by favour, not of right; **by** ~ **of,** with the kind permission of (person etc.); ~ **light,** light in motor car switched on by opening door; ~ **title,** one held by courtesy (usu. having no legal validity), ||e.g. of lower peerage given to heir of duke etc. [ME, f. OF *curtesie, co(u)rtesie* (*curteis* etc. COURTEOUS; see -Y[1])]

cour'tier (kōr'-) *n.* Attendant at or frequenter of sovereign's court. [ME, f. AF *courte(i)our,* f. OF **cortoyeur* (*cortoyer* be present at court); assim. to -IER]

cour'tl|ÿ (kōr'-) *a.* Polished, refined, in manners; obsequious; ~**y love,** conventional medieval tradition of knightly love and etiquette; hence ~**ĭ**NESS *n.* [f. COURT[1] + -LY[1]]

cour'tshĭp (kōr'-) *n.* Period of courting with view to marriage; courting of animals, birds, etc. [f. COURT[1] + -SHIP]

cou'scous (kŏŏ'skŏŏs) *n.* N. Afr. dish of crushed wheat or coarse flour steamed over broth, freq. with meat or fruit added. [F, f. Arab. *kuskus* (*kaskasa* to pound)]

cou'sin (kŭ'zin) *n.* **1.** ~ **(german), first** ~, child of one's uncle or aunt; **second** ~, one's parent's first cousin's child; **first** ~ **once** (*twice* etc.) **removed,** (1) one's first cousin's child (grandchild etc.), (2) one's parent's (grandparent's etc.) cousin. **2.** Title formerly used by sovereign in addressing another sovereign or a nobleman of same country. **3.** Hence ~HOOD, ~SHIP, *ns.*, ~LY[1] *a.* [ME, f. OF *cosin, cusin,* f. L *consobrinus* mother's sister's child]

couth (kōōth) *a.* Cultured; well-mannered. [back form. as antonym of UNCOUTH]

coutūr'e (kōō-) *n.* Dressmaking; design and making of fashionable garments; HAUTE *couture.* [F, = sewing, dressmaking]

coutūr'|ier (kōōtūr'yā) *n.* (*fem.* ~**ière** *pr.* -yār). Fashion designer. [F]

couva'de (kōōvah'd) *n.* Primitive people's custom by which husband feigns illness and is put to bed when his wife is giving birth to child. [F (*couver* hatch f. L *cubare* lie down)]

couvert (kōōvār') *n.* = COVER[2] 3. [F]

couvertūr'e (kōō-) *n.* Chocolate for covering sweets, cakes, etc. [F, = covering]

cōvā'l|ent *a.* (Chem.) Linking atoms by a bond in which a pair of electrons is shared; so ~ENCE, ~ENCY, *ns.*, ~**ent**LY² *adv.* [f. co- + *-valent,* after *trivalent* etc.]

cōve¹ *n.* Small bay or creek; sheltered recess; (Archit.) concave arch, curved junction of wall with ceiling or floor. [OE *cofa* chamber, = MLG *cove,* MHG *kobe* stable, ON *kofi* hut f. Gmc **kubon*]

cōve² *v.t.* Arch (esp. ceiling at junction with wall); slope (fireplace sides) inwards; hence **cō'v**ING¹ (2) *n.* [f. prec.]

cōve³ *n.* (sl.) Fellow, chap. [16th c. cant, of unkn. orig.]

co'ven (kŭ'-) *n.* Assembly of witches. [var. of *covent*; see CONVENT]

co'venant (kŭ'-) *n.* & *v.* **1.** *n.* Agreement, bargain; (Law) contract under seal, clause of this; (Bibl.) compact between God and the Israelites (ARK *of the Covenant*; **land of the C~**, Canaan); **Day of the C~**, (S. Afr.) 16 Dec.; **National C~** (in defence of Presbyterianism in Scotland, 1638); **Solemn League and C~** (establishing Presbyterianism in England and Scotland, 1643). **2.** *v.i.* & *t.* Agree, esp. by legal covenant, (*with* person *for* thing, *to* do, *that*); hence ~OR *n.* [ME f. OF, part. of *co(n)venir* f. as CONVENE]

co'venantėd (kŭ'-) *a.* Bound by a covenant. [p.p. of prec.]

co'venanter (kŭ'-) *n.* One who covenants, esp. (Sc. Hist., *C~*) adherent of the National COVENANT or the Solemn League and COVENANT. [f. COVENANT + -ER¹]

Cŏ'ventrȳ *n.* **Send to ~**, refuse to associate with or speak to (person). [~ in W. Midlands]

co'ver¹ (kŭ'-) *v.t.* **1.** Overspread, overlay, (*with* cloth, lid, etc., (fig.) *with* disgrace etc.); put cover on; strew thoroughly (*with*); ~ **in,** complete covering of. **2.** Lie over, be a covering to; (of stallion, bull, etc.) copulate with; extend over, occupy the surface of (*covered in dirt, with writing*); protect; clothe; ~ (**up**), conceal (traces, face, feelings, crime, etc., or abs.; so ~**-up** *n.*); travel (specified distance etc.); (in *p.p.*) wearing hat, having roof; ~**ing letter, note,** explanatory one with enclosure. **3.** (Of fortress, guns, etc.) command (territory); aim gun at; (Mil. & Cricket) stand behind (front-rank man, another player to stop balls he misses; ~**-point,** fieldsman covering point, his place). **4.** Include, comprise; deal with (subject); (Journalism) report (occurrences, proceedings of meeting, etc.), investigate as reporter; suffice to defray (expenses). **5.** Hence ~ING¹ (3) *n.* [ME, f. OF *covrir, cuvrir* f. L co(*operire opert-* cover)]

co'ver² (kŭ'-) *n.* **1.** Thing that covers (LOOSE¹ *cover*); lid; binding of book; either board of this (**from ~ to ~**, from beginning to end of a book); wrapper or envelope of letter (UNDER *separate cover*); outer case of pneumatic tyre; (in *pl.*) bedclothes. **2.** Hiding-place, shelter, (**take ~**, use natural or prepared shelter against attack); supporting force protecting from attack; = COVER¹*-point*; screen, pretence, (*under cover of humility*); woods or undergrowth sheltering game, COVERT², (**break ~**, leave such shelter); funds (esp. obtained by insurance) to meet liability or secure against contingent loss; state of being thus protected. **3.** Plate, napkin, etc., laid for each person at table. **4.** ~ **charge,** service charge usu. per person in restaurant etc.; ~ **crop** (grown for protection or enrichment of soil); ~**-drive,** (Cricket) drive past cover-point; ~ **girl,** girl or woman whose picture illustrates cover of magazine etc.; ~ **note** (certifying existence of current insurance policy). [f. prec.]

co'verage (kŭ'-) *n.* Area or amount covered; area reached by a particular broadcasting station or advertising medium; risk covered by insurance policy; reporting of events etc. for newspaper etc. [f. COVER¹ + -AGE]

co'verall (kŭ'verawl) *a.* & *n.* (Thing) covering entirely; (usu. in *pl.*) full-length protective outer garment. [f. COVER¹ + ALL]

co'verlėt (kŭ'-) *n.* Bedspread. [ME, f. AF *covrelet, -lit* f. OF *covrir* cover + *lit* bed]

co'vert¹ (kŭ'-) *a.* (Of threat, glance, etc.) secret, disguised; FEME *covert*; hence ~LY² *adv.* [ME f. OF, p.p. of *covrir* COVER¹]

co'vert² (kŭ'vert *or -er*) *n.* Shelter, esp. thicket hiding game; feather covering base of bird's wing feather or tail feather; ~ **coat,** short light overcoat worn for shooting, riding, etc. [ME, f. OF *covert* p.p. (as n.); see prec.]

co'verture (kŭ'-) *n.* Covering, cover; condition of married woman under husband's protection. [ME f. OF (as COVERT¹; see -URE)]

co'vėt (kŭ'-) *v.t.* Desire eagerly (usu. what belongs to another); hence ~ABLE *a.* [ME, f. OF *cu-, coveitier* f. Rom. **cupiditare* f. as CUPIDITY]

co'vėtous (kŭ'-) *a.* Eagerly desirous (*of* another's property etc.); grasping, avaricious; hence ~LY² *adv.*, ~NESS *n.* [ME, f. OF *coveitous* f. Gallo-Rom. **cupiditosus* (as CUPIDITY; see -OUS)]

co'vey (kŭ'-) *n.* Brood of partridges; party, group, *of* persons or things. [ME, f. OF *covee* f. Rom. **cubata* hatching f. L *cubare* lie; see -Y⁴]

co'vĭn (kŭ'-) *n.* (arch.) Fraud, deception; (Law) conspiracy, collusion. [ME, f. OF *covin(e)* f. med. L *convenium -ia* (*convenire*; see CONVENE)]

cō'vĭng. See COVE².

cow¹ *n.* (*pl.* ~**s,** arch. **kine**). **1.** Female of any bovine animal, esp. of the domestic species (*Bos taurus*) and esp. one that has calved; female elephant, rhinoceros, whale, seal, etc.; (vulg., derog.) woman, esp. coarse or unpleasant one; (Austral. & N.Z. sl.) unpleasant person, thing, situation, etc. **2.** ~**'bane,** water hemlock; ~**'bell** (worn round cow's neck or used as percussion instrument); ~**'boy,** (1) boy in charge of cows, (2) *man in charge of grazing cattle on ranch; *~**'catcher,** apparatus fixed in front of locomotive engine to remove cattle and other obstructions; ~**-fish,** (1) sea-cow, (2) Ind. and Amer. fish with hornlike spines over eyes; ~**-grass,** wild species of trefoil; ~**-heel,** foot of cow or ox stewed to jelly; ~**'herd,** one who tends cows at pasture; ~**'hide,** (leather, whip, made of) cow's hide; ~**'itch,** = COWAGE; ~**-lick,** projecting lock of hair; ~**'man,** = *cowherd*; ~**-parsley,** wild form of chervil; ~**-pat,** roundish patch of cow-dung; *~**'poke,** = *cowboy* (2); ~**'pox,** disease of cows of which the virus is used in vaccination against smallpox; *~**'puncher,** = *cowboy* (2); ~**'shot,** (Cricket, sl.) pull across ball to leg side; *~ **town,** small provincial town with cattle-dealers; ~**-tree,** S. Amer. tree with milk-like juice used as food. [OE *cū,* = OS *kō,* OHG *kuo,* ON *kýr* f. Gmc **kō(u)z,* cogn. w. L *bos,* Gk *bous*]

cow² *v.t.* Intimidate, dispirit. [prob. f. ON *kúga* oppress]

cow'age *n.* Tropical vine with stinging hairs on pod. [f. Hindi *kawānch*]

cow'ard *n.* & *a.* (Person) having little or no bravery; hence ~LY¹, (colloq.) ~Y², *adjs.*, ~LY² *adv.* [ME, f. OF *cuard, couard,* f. Rom. **coda* tail f. L *cauda*; see -ARD]

cow'ardĭce *n.* Lack of bravery; MORAL *cowardice.* [ME, f. OF *couardise* (as prec.; see -ICE)]

cow'er *v.i.* Stand or squat in bent position;

crouch, esp. from fear. [ME, f. MLG *kūren* lie in wait, of unkn. orig.]

cowl *n.* **1.** Monk's hooded garment; hood of this; hence ~ED² (-ld) *a.* **2.** Hood-shaped covering of chimney or ventilating shaft; hence ~'ING¹ (3) *n.*, removable cover of vehicle or aircraft engine. [OE *cugele*, *cūle*, = MDu. *cōghel*, OHG *cucula* etc. f. eccl. L *cuculla* f. L *cucullus* hood of cloak]

cō'-worker (-wer-) *n.* One who works in collaboration with another. [f. CO- 1 + WORKER]

cowr'ie, -ў, *n.* Small gastropod of Indian Ocean; its shell, used as money in Africa and S. Asia; gastropod of family Cypraeidae, with highly polished shell. [f. Urdu & Hindi *kaurī*]

cow'slĭp *n.* Wild plant (*Primula veris*) growing in pastures, with fragrant yellow flowers (~ **tea, wine,** made from these); *marsh marigold. [OE *cūslyppe* (*cū* cow¹, *slyppe* slimy substance, i.e. cow-dung)]

cŏx *n.* & *v.* (colloq.) **1.** *n.* = COXSWAIN, esp. of racing-boat. **2.** *v.i.* & *t.* Act as cox (of). [abbr.]

cŏ'x|a *n.* (*pl.* ~**ae**). (Anat.) hip; (Zool.) first segment of insect's leg; hence ~AL *a.* [L]

cŏ'xcōmb (-ōm) *n.* Conceited showy person; hence ~RY (5) *n.*, ~ICAL *a.* [= COCK¹'*s comb*; orig. (cap worn by) jester]

cŏ'xswain (-kswān *or* -ksan) *n.* & *v.* **1.** *n.* Helmsman of (esp. rowing-)boat; hence ~LESS *a.*, ~SHIP *n.* **2.** *v.i.* & *t.* Act as coxswain (of). [ME, f. *cock* (see COCKBOAT) + SWAIN; cf. BOATSWAIN]

coy *a.* (Esp. of girl) modest, shy; affectedly modest; archly reticent; hence ~'LY² *adv.*, ~'NESS *n.* [ME, f. OF *coi*, *quei*, f. Rom. **quetus* f. L *quietus* QUIET²]

Coy. *abbr.* (esp. Mil.) Company.

coyō'tė (ko-; *or* koi'ōt) *n.* N. Amer. prairie-wolf (*Canis latrans*). [Mex. Sp., f. Aztec *coyotl*]

coy'pu (-ōō) *n.* Aquatic beaver-like rodent, orig. from S. America. [Araucan]

coz (kŭz) *n.* (arch.) Cousin. [abbr.]

co'zen (kŭ'-) *v.* (literary). **1.** *v.t.* Cheat, defraud, (*of*, *out of*); beguile (*into* doing). **2.** *v.i.* Act deceitfully. **3.** Hence ~AGE (3) *n.* [16th c. cant, perh. rel. to COUSIN]

***cō'zў.** See COSY.

C.P. *abbr.* Cape Province; Communist Party; (Austral.) Country Party.

c.p. *abbr.* candle-power.

cp. *abbr.* compare.

Cpl. *abbr.* Corporal.

C.P.O. *abbr.* Chief Petty Officer.

C.P.R. *abbr.* Canadian Pacific Railway.

||**C.P.R.E.** *abbr.* Council for the Protection of Rural England.

c.p.s. *abbr.* cycles per second.

C.R. *abbr.* Community of the Resurrection.

Cr. *abbr.* Councillor; creditor.

Cr *symb.* chromium.

crăb¹ *n.* **1.** Ten-footed crustacean, esp. of group Brachyura, with first pair of legs modified into pincers; edible form of this found near most sea-coasts; its flesh as food; machine for hoisting heavy weights; (*C*~) *the* zodiacal sign Cancer; **catch a** ~, (Rowing) get oar jammed under water by faulty stroke, or miss the water with one's stroke. **2.** *~**-grass,** creeping grass infesting lawns; ~**(-louse)**, parasitical insect infesting human body; ~**-pot,** wicker trap for crabs. **3.** Hence ~'LIKE *a.* [OE *crabba*, = MDu. *krabbe*, ON *krabbi*, rel. to MLG *krabben*, ON *krafla* scratch]

crăb² *v.t.* & *i.* (**-bb-**). (colloq.) Criticize adversely or captiously; act so as to spoil. [orig. of hawks fighting, f. MLG *krabben* (cf. prec.)]

crăb³ *n.* ~**(-apple)**, wild apple (fruit or tree); sour person. [ME, perh. alt. (after CRAB¹ or foll.) of earlier *scrab*, prob. of Scand. orig.]

cră'bbėd *a.* **1.** Cross-grained, perverse; morose, irritable. **2.** (Of handwriting) ill-formed and hard to decipher; difficult to understand. **3.** Hence ~LY² *adv.*, ~NESS *n.* [ME, f. CRAB¹ + -ED², assoc. w. CRAB³]

cră'bbў *a.* = prec. 1. [f. CRAB³ + -Y²]

cră'bwise (-z) *adv.* (Moving) sideways or backwards like a crab. [f. CRAB¹ + -WISE]

crăck¹ *n.* & *a.* **1.** *n.* Sudden sharp or explosive noise (of whip, rifle, thunder); ~ **of doom,** thunder-peal of Day of Judgement; **fair** ~ **of the whip,** (colloq.) fair chance to participate etc. **2.** Sharp blow (*a crack on the head*); **have a** ~ **at,** (colloq.) attempt. **3.** ~ **of dawn,** (colloq.) daybreak. **4.** (colloq.) = WISE¹*crack*. **5.** Narrow opening formed by breaking or by opening door etc.; chink; partial fracture (the parts still cohering); hence ~'Y² *a.* **6.** Good player, horse, etc. **7.** *a.* (colloq.) First-rate (*crack regiment*, *shot*, *train*). [ME & MDu. *crak*, OHG *krach*; cf. foll.]

crăck² *v.t.* & *i.* **1.** (Cause to) make sudden sharp or explosive noise (*crack a whip*; *whips crack*); utter (joke etc.); ~ **down on,** (colloq.) take severe measures against, whence ~**-down** *n.*; ~ **up,** (colloq.) praise, collapse under strain, whence ~**-up** *n.*, (also) crash of vehicle. **2.** Break (nut, skull, etc.) with sudden sharp report; break into (safe etc.); find solution to (problem, code, etc.); ~ **a bottle,** drink its contents; ~ **a crib,** (sl.) break into a house; **get** ~**'ing,** (colloq.) start working. **3.** Break without complete separation of parts; (of voice, esp. boy's at age of puberty, or old person's) become dissonant; give way, yield, (under torture etc.); decompose (heavy oils) by heat and pressure with or without catalyst to produce lighter hydrocarbons (such as petrol); break (wheat) into coarse pieces. **4.** ~**-brained,** crazy; ~**'ing** *a.* & *adv.*, (sl.) outstanding(ly), very good; ~**-jaw,** (colloq.) (word) difficult to pronounce; ~**'pot,** (colloq.) eccentric or impractical (person); ~**-willow,** species of willow with brittle branches. [OE *cracian* resound, = MDu. *krāken*, OHG *krahhōn*]

crăcked (-kt) *a.* In vbl senses; (colloq.) crazy, infatuated. [p.p. of prec.]

cră'cker *n.* In vbl senses; firework exploding with sharp report; small paper toy containing paper hat etc. and made so as to explode when ends are pulled; instrument for cracking, (esp., in *pl.*) nutcrackers; thin dry biscuit; *biscuit; *(derog.) POOR-white person; *~**-barrel** *a.*, homespun (philosophy etc.); *~**jack,** (sl.) exceptionally fine or expert (thing or person); ~**s** *pred. a.*, (sl.) crazy, infatuated. [f. CRACK² + -ER¹]

cră'ckl|e *v.i.*, & *n.* **1.** *v.i.* Emit slight cracking sound. **2.** *n.* Such sound; (smooth surface of) paintwork, china, or glass with appearance of minute cracks. **3.** Hence ~Y² *a.* [f. CRACK² + -LE 3]

cră'cklĭng *a.* In vbl senses; crisp skin of roast pork; (**bit of**) ~, (colloq.) attractive woman. [f. prec. + -ING¹]

cră'cknel *n.* Light crisp biscuit. [ME, f. F *craquelin* f. MDu. *krākelinc* (*krāken* CRACK²)]

cră'cks|man *n.* (*pl.* ~**men**). Burglar. [f. CRACK¹ + MAN¹]

-cracў *suf.* forming *ns.*, meaning 'rule of, ruling body of, class influential by' (*aristocracy*, *bureaucracy*, *democracy*, *plutocracy*, *snobocracy*). [f. or after F *-cratie*, med. L *-cratia*, Gk *-kratia* power (*kratos* strength)]

cră'dle *n.*, & *v.t.* **1.** *n.* Bed or cot for infant, esp. one mounted on rockers (**from the** ~ (**to the grave**), from infancy (till death)); (fig.) place in which thing begins or is nurtured in earliest stage (*cradle of an art*, *of a nation*); framework resembling cradle, esp. that on which ship or boat rests during construction or repairs, or on which men are supported to work on vertical face of building, ship, etc.; part of telephone supporting receiver when not in use; CAT[1]'s-*-cradle*; ~**-snatcher,** (sl.) person amorously attracted to a much younger person; ~**-song,** lullaby. **2.** *v.t.* Place in cradle; contain or shelter (as) in cradle (*cradle in* one's *arms*). [OE *cradol*, perh. rel. to OHG *kratto* basket]

crā'dlĭng *n.* In vbl senses; (Archit.) wooden or iron framework esp. in ceiling. [f. prec. + -ING[1]]

craft (-ah-) *n.*, & *v.t.* **1.** *n.* Skill; cunning, deceit; art, trade, (esp. in comb., as *handicraft, priest-craft, statecraft*); *the* GENTLE *craft.* **2.** Members of a craft; **the C~,** brotherhood of Freemasons. **3.** (*pl.* same). Boat, vessel; aircraft or spacecraft. **4.** ~**-brother, -guild,** workman, guild of workmen, of same trade. **5.** *v.t.* *Make in skilful manner (*handcrafted jewelry*; *a superbly crafted novel*). [OE *cræft*,=OS, OHG *kraft*, ON *kraptr* strength]

cra'fts|man (-ah'-) *n.* (*pl.* ~**men**). One who practises a handicraft; skilled person; private soldier in R.E.M.E.; hence ~**man**SHIP (3) *n.* [ME, orig. *craft's man*]

cra'ft|ў (-ah-) *a.* Cunning, artful, wily; hence ~ĭLY[2] *adv.*, ~ĭNESS *n.* [OE *cræftig*,=OS *kraftag*, *-ig*, OHG *kreftig*, ON *kröptugr*; see -Y[2]]

crăg[1] *n.* Steep or rugged rock; ~**'sman** (-z-), skilled climber of crags; hence ~**'gy**[2] (-gĭ) *a.*, (esp., of person, face, etc.) rugged. [ME, of Celt. orig.]

crăg[2] *n.* (Geol.) Deposits of shelly sand found in E. Anglia; strata containing them. [18th c.; perh. f. prec.]

crāke *n.* Bird of family Rallidae, e.g. CORN*crake*; cry of corncrake. [ME, f. ON *kráka* (imit.); cf. CROAK]

crăm *v.* (**-mm-**). **1.** *v.t.* Fill overfull; force (thing *in, into, down*); ~**-full,** as full as cramming can make it. **2.** Feed to excess (poultry etc. *with* food). **3.** *v.t.* & *i.* Prepare for examination by intensive study; eat greedily. [OE *crammian* (= ON *kremja*, MLG *kremmen* squeeze), cogn. w. *crimman* cram, f. Gmc **kram-*, **krem-*]

cră'mbō *n.* (*pl.* ~**es**). Game in which player gives word or verse-line to which each of the others must find rhyme; **dumb ~,** game in which one side must guess word, a rhyme to which is given, by miming various possible answers. [earlier *crambe*, app. allus. L *crambe repetita* cabbage served up again]

cră'mmer *n.* In vbl senses; one who crams pupils for examinations. [f. CRAM + -ER[1]]

crămp[1] *n.*, & *v.t.* **1.** *n.* Painful involuntary contraction of muscle(s) from cold etc.; WRITER'*s cramp*; ~**-fish,** electric ray, torpedo. **2.** *v.t.* Affect with cramp. [ME, f. OF *crampe* f. MDu., MLG *krampe*, OHG *krampfo* f. adj. meaning 'bent'; cf. foll. and CRIMP[1]]

crămp[2] *n.* ~**(-iron)**, metal bar with bent ends for holding masonry etc. together; portable tool for pressing two planks etc. together; restraint. [ME, f. MDu. *krampe*, as prec.]

crămp[3] *v.t.* **1.** ~ **(up)**, confine narrowly; restrict (energies etc.); ~ person's **style,** prevent him from acting freely; (in *p.p.*, of handwriting) small and difficult to read. **2.** Fasten with cramp. [f. prec.]

cră'mpon, *crămpōō'n, *n.* Metal hook, grappling-iron; iron plate with spikes fixed to boot for walking on ice etc. [ME f. F, f. Frank. **krampo*, as CRAMP[2]; see -OON]

crăn *n.* (Sc.) Measure for fresh herrings (37½ gal.). [=Gael. *crann*, of uncert. orig.]

crā'nage *n.* Use of crane(s); money paid for this. [ME, f. CRANE[1] + -AGE]

crā'nberrў *n.* (Small red acid berry of) European or American shrub of genus *Vaccinium.* [17th c., named by Amer. colonists f. G *kranbeere*, LG *kranebere* crane-berry]

crāne[1] *n.* **1.** Large wading bird of family Gruidae, with long legs, neck, and bill. **2.** Machine for moving heavy weights, which are usu. suspended by rope or chain from JIB[1]; moving platform for camera; **(water-)~,** tube for supplying water to locomotive. **3.** ~**-fly,** long-legged two-winged fly of family Tipulidae; ~**'s-bill,** plant of genus *Geranium.* [OE *cran*,=OS, OHG *krano*, rel. to L *grus*, Gk *geranos*]

crāne[2] *v.t.* & *i.* Stretch (neck), stretch neck, like crane; move with crane; (of camera) change position etc. on crane. [f. prec.]

crā'nĭate *a.* & *n.* (Zool.) (Animal) having a skull. [f. mod. L *craniatus* f. CRANIUM; see -ATE[2]]

crānĭo- *comb. form.* = foll., as: ~LO'GICAL *a.*, ~LOGIST, ~LOGY, (-ŏ'l-) *ns.*, ~METRY (-ŏ'm-) *n.* [f. foll. + -O-]

crā'nĭ|um *n.* (*pl.* ~**a** *or* ~**ums**). Bones enclosing the brain; bones of the whole head, skull; hence ~AL *a.* (~**al index,** ratio of width and length of skull). [ME f. med. L, f. Gk *kranion* skull]

crănk[1] *n.*, & *v.t.* **1.** *n.* Part of axle or shaft bent at right angles for converting reciprocal into circular motion, or vice versa; elbow-shaped connection in bell-hanging. **2.** ~**'case,** case enclosing crankshaft; ~**'pin,** pin by which connecting-rod is attached to crank; ~**'shaft,** shaft driven by crank. **3.** *v.t.* Bend into crank shape, furnish or fasten with crank; turn with crank; ~ **up,** start (engine of motor car) by turning a crank, (sl.) increase (speed etc.) by intensive effort. [OE *cranc*, app. f. *crincan* by-form of *cringan* fall in battle, orig. 'curl up']

crănk[2] *n.* & *a.* Eccentric (person); fanciful turn of speech (*quips and cranks*). [back form. f. CRANKY]

crănk[3] *a.* (Naut.) Liable to capsize. [perh. f. *crank* weak, shaky or CRANK[1]]

cră'nk|ў *a.* Shaky; crotchety, eccentric; ill-tempered; hence ~ĭLY[2] *adv.*, ~ĭNESS *n.* [perh. f. obs. *crank* rogue feigning sickness + -Y[2]]

cră'nnog *n.* Lake-dwelling in Scotland or Ireland. [Ir. (*crann* tree, beam)]

cră'nn|ў *n.* Chink, crevice, crack; hence ~ĭED[2] (-ĭd) *a.* [ME, f. OF *crané* p.p. of **craner* (*cran* f. pop. L *crena* notch)]

crăp[1] *n.*, & *v.i.* (**-pp-**). (vulg.) **1.** *n.* Faeces; nonsense, rubbish. **2.** *v.i.* Defecate; ***~ out,** be unsuccessful, withdraw from game etc. [earlier senses 'chaff, refuse from fat-boiling', ME f. Du. *krappe*]

***crăp**[2] *n.* Losing throw of 2, 3, or 12 in craps; ~ **game,** game of craps. [f. as CRAPS]

crāpe *n.*, & *v.t.* **1.** *n.* Crêpe, usu. of black silk or imitation silk, esp. for mourning dress; band of this round hat etc. as sign of mourning; ~ **fern,** N.Z. fern with tall dark-green plumes; ~ **hair,** artificial hair for actor's false beard etc.; hence **crā'p**Y[2] *a.* **2.** *v.t.* Cover, clothe, drape, with crape. [earlier *crispe, crespe* f. F *crespe* CRÊPE]

cră'ppĭe *n.* N. Amer. freshwater sunfish of genus *Pomoxis.* [19th c.; orig. uncert.]

cră'ppў *a.* (vulg.) Rubbishy; disgusting. [f. CRAP[1] + -Y[2]]

***crăps** *n. pl.* Game of chance played with dice; **shoot ~,** play this. [19th c.; perh. f. *crab* lowest throw at dice]

cră'pūl|ent *a.* Given to or suffering from effects of, resulting from, intemperance; hence or cogn. ~ENCE *n.*, ~OUS *a.* [f. LL *crapulentus* very drunk f. L *crapula* inebriation f. Gk *kraipalē* drunken headache; see -ULENT]

cră'quelūre (-ă'kl-) *n.* Network of small cracks in a painting or its varnish. [F]

crăsh^1 *v.*, *adv.*, & *n.* **1.** *v.i.* Make a crash; move or go with a crash, collide violently with obstacle etc., run violently *into*, (of aircraft or airman) fall violently on land or sea. **2.** *v.t.* Throw or drive with a crash; cause (vehicle etc.) to crash; pass (red traffic-light etc.), (colloq.) enter without permission. **3.** *adv.* With a crash (*go*, *fall*, *crash*). **4.** *n.* Noise as of broken crockery, thunder, loud music, etc.; violent percussion or breakage; (fig.) ruin, esp. financial; violent impact or fall, esp. collision of vehicle or aircraft with another or with fixed object; (*attrib.*) done rapidly or urgently (*crash course*, *programme*). **5.** ~ **barrier,** barrier against car leaving road, etc.; **~-dive,** (of submarine) dive hastily and steeply in an emergency, (of aircraft) dive and crash; so **~-dive** *n.*; **~-halt,** sudden stop by vehicle; **~-helmet** (worn to protect head in case of crash); **~-land,** (of aircraft or airman) land hurriedly with a crash, usu. without lowering undercarriage; ~ **pad,** (sl.) place to sleep, esp. in emergency; **~-tackle,** (Footb.) vigorous tackle. [ME; imit.]

crăsh^2 *n.* Coarse plain linen, cotton, etc., fabric for towels etc. [f. Russ. *krashenina* coloured linen]

cră'shĭng *a.* In vbl senses; (colloq.) overwhelming (*a crashing bore*). [f. CRASH^1 + -ING^2]

crā's|ĭs *n.* (*pl.* **~es** *pr.* -ēz). (Gk Gram.) Contraction of two adjacent vowels into one long vowel or diphthong. [f. Gk *krasis* mixture]

crăss *a.* Thick, gross; (fig.) gross (*crass stupidity*); grossly stupid; hence **~'ĭ**TUDE *n.*, ~'LY^2 *adv.*, ~'NESS *n.* [f. L *crassus* solid, thick]

-crăt *suf.* forming *ns.*, meaning supporter or member of a -CRACY; hence **-cră'**TIC(AL) *adj. sufs.* [f. or after F *-crate* f. adjs. in *-cratique* (as -CRACY, -IC)]

crătch *n.* Rack for feeding animals out of doors. [ME, f. OF *creche* f. Rom. **creppja* f. Gmc **krippja* CRIB^1]

crāte *n.*, & *v.t.* **1.** *n.* Large open-work or wood-framed case or basket for carrying glass, crockery, fruit, etc.; (sl.) aeroplane or other vehicle; hence ~'FUL 2 (-tf-) *n.* **2.** *v.t.* Pack in crate. [ME, perh. f. Du. *krat* basket etc.]

crā'ter *n.*, & *v.t.* **1.** *n.* Mouth of volcano; bowl-shaped cavity, esp. that made by explosion of shell or bomb; (Astron.) raised bowl-shaped hollow on surface of moon etc.; (Gk Ant.) large bowl. **2.** *v.t.* Form crater in. [L, f. Gk *kratēr* mixing-bowl]

-cră'tĭc(al). See -CRAT.

cravă't *n.* Scarf; neck-tie; hence **~**TED^2 *a.* [f. F *cravate* f. G *Krawat*, *Kroat* f. Serbo-Croatian *Hrvat* Croat]

crāve *v.* **1.** *v.t.* Beg for; long for. **2.** *v.i.* Beg *for*, long *for*. **3.** Hence **crā'**VING^1 *n.*, strong desire, intense longing, (*for*). [OE *crafian*, rel. to ON *krefja*]

crā'ven *a.* & *n.* **1.** *a.* Cowardly, abject, (person, behaviour, etc.); hence ~LY^2 *adv.* **2.** *n.* Craven person. [ME *cravand* etc. perh. f. OF *cravanté* defeated, p.p. of *cravanter* f. Rom. **crepantare* f. L *crepare* burst; assim. to -EN^1]

craw *n.* Crop of bird or insect; **stick in** one's ~, be unacceptable. [ME, cogn. w. MDu. *crāghe*, MLG *krage*, MHG *krage* neck, throat]

craw'fĭsh *n.*, & *v.i.* **1.** *n.* Large marine spiny lobster. **2.** *v.i.* *Retreat, back *out*. [var. of CRAYFISH]

crawl *v.i.*, & *n.* **1.** *v.i.* Move slowly, dragging body along close to ground etc., or on hands and knees; walk or move slowly; (colloq.) behave abjectly or ingratiatingly *to*; (of ground etc.) be covered *with* crawling things; be filled *with*; feel creepy sensation, whence ~'Y^2 *a.*; swim with crawl stroke. **2.** *n.* Crawling; slow rate of movement; high-speed swimming stroke with alternate overhand arm-movements and rapid kicks with legs; PUB-*crawl*. [ME, of unkn. orig.; cf. Sw. *kravla*, Da. *kravle*]

craw'ler *n.* In vbl senses; (usu. in *pl.*) baby's overall for crawling in; crawling insect; tractor moving on endless chain. [f. prec. + -ER^1]

cray'fĭsh, (Austral. & N.Z.) **cray,** *n.* Small lobster-like freshwater crustacean; crawfish. [ME, f. OF *crevice*, *crevis*, Frank. **krabitja* = OHG *krebiz* CRAB^1; assim. to FISH^1]

cray'on *n.*, & *v.t.* **1.** *n.* Stick or pencil of coloured chalk or other material for drawing; drawing made with this. **2.** *v.t.* Draw with crayons, (fig.) sketch. [F, f. *craie* f. L *creta* chalk; see -OON]

crāze *v.* & *n.* **1.** *v.t.* Make insane (usu. in *p.p.*); produce small cracks on (pottery glaze etc.). **2.** *v.i.* Have such cracks. **3.** *n.* Insane fancy, mania, crazy condition; (object of) temporary enthusiasm. [ME, orig. = break, shatter, perh. f. ON **krasa* (Sw. *krasa* crunch)]

crā'z|ȳ *a.* (Of person, action, etc.) insane, mad; (colloq.) extremely enthusiastic (*about*; **like** ~, like MAD^1); (sl.) unrestrained, exciting, excellent; (of paving, quilt, etc.) made of irregular pieces fitted together; (of ship, building, etc.) unsound, shaky; ***~y bone,** funny bone; hence **~ĭ**LY^2 *adv.*, **~ĭ**NESS *n.* [f. prec. + -Y^2]

creak *n.*, & *v.i.* **1.** *n.* Harsh strident noise, as of unoiled hinge, new boots, etc. **2.** *v.i.* Make creak; move (as) with creaks. **3.** Hence ~'Y^2 *a.* [ME, imit.; cf. CRAKE, CROAK]

cream^1 *n.* **1.** Part of milk with high content of fat, which gathers on the top, and by churning is made into butter; CLOT*ted cream*; DAIRY *cream*. **2.** Best or choicest part of anything, esp. point of an anecdote, or group of persons outstanding in some way among a larger group. **3.** Part of a liquid that gathers at the top; ~ **of tartar,** purified and crystallized potassium bitartrate, used in medicine etc. **4.** Creamlike preparation, esp. cosmetic (**cold** ~, cooling skin-unguent); dish or sweet like or made of cream; soup or sauce containing cream or milk; full-bodied mellow sherry; sweet or biscuit with creamy filling. **5.** ~ **bun, cake,** (filled with cream); ~ **cheese,** soft rich kind made of unskimmed milk and cream; ~ **cracker,** crisp unsweetened biscuit; ~**(-coloured),** yellowish white; ||~ **ice,** ice cream; **~-laid, -wove,** laid, wove, cream-coloured (paper); ~ **puff,** puff pastry filled with cream, (fig.) unimportant person or thing; ~ **tea,** afternoon tea with jam and clotted cream. **6.** Hence ~'Y^2 *a.* [ME, f. OF *cre(s)me* f. LL *cramum* (perh. f. Gaulish) & eccl. L *chrisma* CHRISM]

cream^2 *v.* **1.** *v.i.* (Of milk or other liquid) form cream or scum. **2.** *v.t.* Take cream from (milk); ~ (**off**), take the best (or any specified) part of (anything); add cream to (tea etc.); treat (skin) with cosmetic cream; work (butter etc.) to creamy consistency. [ME, f. prec.]

crea'mer *n.* Flat dish for skimming cream off milk; machine for separating cream; *jug for cream. [f. prec. + -ER^1]

crea'merȳ *n.* Butter-factory; shop where milk, cream, etc., are sold. [f. CREAM^1 + -ERY, after F *crèmerie*]

crease^1 *n.* & *v.* **1.** *n.* Line caused by folding, fold, wrinkle; (Cricket) line defining position of bowler and batsman, as BOWLING-*crease*, POPPING-*crease*; (Ice Hockey, Lacrosse) area near goal into which puck or ball must precede players. **2.** *v.t.* Make creases in (material); (sl.) tire out, stun, kill. **3.** *v.i.* Fall into creases. [earlier *creast* = CREST ridge in material]

crease^2. See KRIS.

crèā'te *v.* **1.** *v.t.* Bring into existence, give rise to; originate (*actor creates a part*); invest (person) with rank (*create him a peer*; *create a peer*). **2.** *v.i.* (sl.) Make a fuss, grumble, (*about*). **3.** Hence **creā'**TABLE *a.* [ME, f. L *creare* + -ATE^{3}]

crē'atine *n.* Amino-acid found in muscles etc. of vertebrates. [f. Gk *kreas* meat + -INE^{5}]

creā'tion *n.* Act of creating (esp. the world); investing with title, rank, etc.; all created things; product of human (esp. designer's or actor's) intelligence, esp. of imaginative thought. [ME f. OF, f. L *creatio -onis* (as CREATE; see -ATION)]

creā'tion|ism *n.* Theory attributing origin of matter and biological species to special creation (not to evolution); so ~IST (2) *n.* [f. prec. + -ISM]

creā'tive *a.* Creating; able to create; inventive, imaginative; showing imagination as well as routine skill; hence ~LY^{2} (-vlĭ) *adv.*, ~NESS (-vn-), **crēati'**VITY, *ns.* [f. CREATE + -IVE]

creā'tor *n.* One who creates; **the C~**, God; hence **creā'tr**ESS^{1}, **creā'**TRIX, *ns.* [ME, f. OF *creat(o)ur* f. L *creator -oris* (as CREATE; see -OR)]

crea'ture *n.* Created thing; animate being; animal (often as distinct from man); human being, person, (esp. w. term of admiration, contempt, patronage, etc.); one who owes his fortune to, and remains subservient to, another; *creature* COMFORTS; *creature of* HABIT^{1}. [ME f. OF, f. LL *creatura* (as prec.; see -URE)]

crèche (krāsh) *n.* Day nursery for infants; model of the manger-scene at Bethlehem. [F (as CRATCH)]

crē'dal. See CREED.

crē'dence *n.* Belief (**give ~ to,** believe); **letter of ~** (INTRODUCTION, esp. of ambassador); **~ (table)**, small side-table, shelf, or niche for Eucharistic elements before consecration. [ME f. OF, f. med. L *credentia* (*credere* believe; see -ENCE)]

credĕ'ntial (-shal) *n.* (usu. in *pl.*) Letter(s) of INTRODUCTION; evidence of achievement or trustworthiness. [f. med. L *credentialis* (as prec.; see -AL)]

credĕ'nza *n.* Sideboard or cupboard. [It., f. as CREDENCE]

crĕ'd|ible *a.* (Of person or statement) believable, worthy of belief; (of threat etc.) convincing; hence or cogn. ~IBI'LITY *n.* (**~ibility gap,** seeming difference between official statements and the facts), **~ib**LY^{2} *adv.* [ME, f. L *credibilis* (*credere* believe; see -IBLE)]

crĕ'dit^{1} *n.* **1.** Belief, trust; **give ~ to,** believe (story). **2.** Good reputation; power derived from this; acknowledgement of merit (*get, give, have, take, the credit for*); (usu. in *pl.*) acknowledgement of contributor's services to film, book, etc., (**~ title,** this at beginning or end of cinema or television film); source of honour (*a credit to the school*). **3.** Trust in person's ability and intention to pay at a later time for goods etc. supplied (*give credit*; *deal on credit*; *long credit*); reputation of solvency and honesty; **~ account, ~ sale,** (for later payment by agreement); **~ card** (authorizing obtaining of goods on credit); **~ rating,** estimate of person's ability and intention to pay his debts in due course. **4.** Sum at person's disposal in books of a bank etc.; **letter of ~** (authorizing person to draw money from writer's correspondent in another place); (Bookk.) acknowledgement of payment by entry in account, (sum entered on) credit side of account; *certificate of completion of course by student; **get ~ for,** be given credit for; **give** person **~ for,** enter (sum) to his credit, (fig.) ascribe (usu. good quality) to him; **to** one's **~**, in one's favour. [f. F *crédit* f. It. *credito* or L *creditum* (*credere -it-* believe, trust)]

crĕ'dit^{2} *v.t.* Believe; enter on credit side of account (*credit* amount *to* person, person *with* amount); ~ person **with,** ascribe (usu. good quality) to him. [f. prec. or f. L *credere* (see prec.)]

crĕ'ditab|le *a.* That brings credit or honour (*to*); hence ~LY^{2} *adv.* [f. CREDIT^{1} + -ABLE]

crĕ'ditor *n.* One to whom a debt is owing; one who gives credit for money or goods. [ME f. AF *creditour* (OF *-eur*) f. L *creditor -oris* (as CREDIT^{1}; see -OR)]

crē'dō (*or* -ā'-) *n.* (*pl.* **~s**). Creed (esp. Apostles' and Nicene, beginning in Latin with *credo*); musical setting of Nicene Creed. [ME f. L, = I believe]

crĕ'dūlous *a.* Too ready to believe; (of behaviour) showing such readiness; hence or cogn. **credū'l**ITY, ~NESS, *ns.*, ~LY^{2} *adv.* [f. L *credulus* (*credere* believe; see -ULOUS)]

creed *n.* Brief formal summary of Christian doctrine, esp. APOSTLES' (also *the Creed*), NICENE, ATHANASIAN, *Creed*; this as part of Mass; system of religious belief; set of opinions or principles on any subject; hence ~'AL, **crē'd**AL, *adjs.* [OE *crēda* f. L CREDO]

creek *n.* ‖Inlet on sea-coast; small harbour; short arm of river; (Austral. & N.Z.) stream, brook; (U.S. etc.) tributary of river; **up the ~**, (sl.) (1) in difficulties or trouble, (2) crazy. [ME *crike* f. ON *kriki* nook (or partly f. OF *crique*, f. ON), & ME *crēke* f. MDu. *krēke* (or f. *crike* by lengthening); ult. orig. unkn.]

creel *n.* Large wicker basket for fish; angler's fishing-basket. [ME, orig. Sc.; ult. orig. unkn.]

creep *v.i.* (**crept**), & *n.* **1.** *v.i.* Move with body prone and close to ground; move timidly, slowly, or stealthily. **2.** Insinuate oneself *into*, come *in*, *up*, unobserved; proceed or exist abjectly; (of plant) grow along ground, wall, etc.; develop gradually (*creeping inflation*); (Metallurgy) undergo creep; (of flesh) feel as if things were creeping over it (result of fear, repugnance, etc.) **3.** *n.* Creeping; shrinking horror, as (colloq. in *pl.*) *gave me the creeps*; low arch under railway embankment, road, etc.; (sl.) disliked person; (Geol.) gradual movement of disintegrated rock due to atmospheric changes etc., or of strata by expansion, compression, etc.; (Metallurgy) gradual change of shape under stress. [OE *crēopan*, = OS *criopan*, ON *krjúpa* f. Gmc **kreupan* etc.]

cree'per *n.* In vbl senses; plant that creeps along ground or up wall; bird that climbs up trees, over bushes, etc., esp. TREE-*creeper*; (sl.) soft-soled shoe. [f. prec. + -ER^{1}]

cree'ping *a.* In vbl senses; **~ barrage** (moving ahead of advancing troops); **~ Jenny,** one of various creeping plants, esp. moneywort; **~ Jesus,** (sl.) abject or hypocritical person. [f. CREEP + -ING^{2}]

cree'pȳ *a.* Having a creeping of the flesh; producing this; given to creeping; **~-crawly** *a.* & *n.*, creeping and crawling (insect etc.). [f. CREEP + -Y^{2}]

creese. See KRIS.

crem|ā'te *v.t.* Consume (corpse) by fire; so ~A'TION *n.* [f. L *cremare* burn + -ATE^{3}]

crĕmator'i|um *n.* (*pl.* **~a** *or* **~ums**). Place for cremating corpses. [mod. L, f. as CREMATE; see -ORY]

crĕ'matorȳ *a.* & *n.* **1.** *a.* Of or pertaining to cremation. **2.** *n.* * = prec. [f. CREMATE + -ORY]

crème (krām) *n.* = CREAM^{1} 4; **~ *brûlée*** (broo'lā), cream or custard topped with caramelized sugar; **~ *de la* ~** (-dlah-), the very pick, élite; **~ *de menthe*** (demah'nt), peppermint liqueur. [F, = cream]

crē'n|āte *a.* (Bot. & Zool.) With notched edge or rounded teeth; so **~āt**ED^{1} *a.*, ~A'TION, **~at**URE, *ns.* [f. mod. L *crenatus* f. pop. L *crena* notch; see -ATE^{2}]

crĕ'nel, crĕnĕ'lle, *n.* Open space or indentation in embattled parapet, orig. for shooting through etc. [ME, f. OF *crenel*, f. Gallo-Rom. **crenellum* dim. of pop. L *crena* notch]

crĕ'nell|āte *v.t.* Furnish with battlements or loopholes; hence ~A'TION *n.* [f. F *créneler* (as prec.) + -ATE[3]]

Crē'ōle *n.* & *a.* **1.** *n.* Descendant of European settlers in W. Indies or Central or S. Amer.; white descendant of French settlers in southern U.S.; person of mixed European and Negro descent; creolized language. **2.** *a.* That is a Creole; of Creole(s); (*c*~) of local origin or production. [f. F *créole*, *criole* f. Sp. *criollo*, prob. f. Port. *crioulo* home-born slave (*criar* breed f. L *creare* CREATE)]

crē'olize, -īse (-īz), *v.t.* Make (language of dominant group, in modified form) into sole language of dominated group. [f. prec. + -IZE]

crē'osōte *n.*, & *v.t.* **1.** *n.* Colourless oily fluid distilled from wood tar, a strong antiseptic; ~ **(oil),** dark-brown oil distilled from coal tar, used as wood-preservative. **2.** *v.t.* Treat with creosote. [f. G *kreosote* f. Gk *kreas* flesh + *sōtēr* preserver, w. ref. to its antiseptic properties]

crêpe (-āp) *n.* **1.** Gauzelike fabric with wrinkled surface; ~ **de Chine** (deshē'n), **China** ~, fine silk crêpe; ~ **paper,** thin crinkled crêpelike paper; ~ **(rubber),** very durable wrinkled sheet rubber used for shoe-soles etc. **2.** Thin pancake; ~ **Suzette,** small dessert pancake served heated in sauce. [F, f. OF *crespe* curled f. L *crispus*]

crĕ'pĭt|āte *v.i.* Make crackling sound; (of beetle) eject pungent fluid with sharp report; so ~ANT *a.*, ~A'TION *n.*, (esp., Med.) crepitus. [f. L *crepitare* frequent. of *crepare* creak + -ATE[3]]

crĕ'pĭtus *n.* (Med.) Grating noise of ends of fractured bone; rattle of breath in pneumonia etc. [L (*crepare* rattle)]

crĕpt. See CREEP.

crĕpŭ'scūlar *a.* Of twilight; (Zool.) appearing or active in twilight; dim, not yet fully enlightened. [f. L *crepusculum* twilight + -AR[1]]

||**Cres.** *abbr.* Crescent.

crėscĕ'ndō (krĭsh-) *adv.*, *a.*, & *n.* (*pl.* ~**s**). (Mus.) (passage performed) with gradual increase of loudness; (fig.) progress towards a climax. [It., part. of *crescere* grow (as foll.)]

crĕ'scent *n.* & *a.* **1.** *n.* Waxing moon; figure of moon in first or last quarter; this as emblem of Turkey or Islam; **the C**~, the Muslim religion. **2.** Anything of crescent shape, esp. ||street of houses. **3.** *a.* Increasing; crescent-shaped. [ME f. AF *cressaunt*, OF *creissant*, f. L *crescere* grow; see -ENT]

crē'sŏl *n.* One of three isomeric phenols present in creosote and used as disinfectants. [f. CREOSOTE + -OL]

crĕss *n.* Cruciferous plant usu. with pungent edible leaves; **garden** ~, *Lepidium sativum*; INDIAN *cress*; WATER[1]*cress*. [OE *cresse* etc., = MLG *kerse*, OHG *kressa*, *-o*, f. WG **krasjō-*]

crĕ'ssėt *n.* (Hist.) Metal vessel for holding oil, coal, etc., for light, usu. mounted on pole. [ME f. OF *cresset*, *craisset*, f. *craisse* = *graisse* GREASE[1]]

crĕst *n.* & *v.* **1.** *n.* Comb or tuft on bird's or animal's head (~**'fallen,** with drooping crest, (fig.) dejected, abashed). **2.** Plume or tuft of feathers; (apex of) helmet. **3.** Head, top, esp. of mountain, roof, or wave; surface line of neck in animals; mane; **on the** ~ **of the** or **a wave,** (fig.) at most favourable moment in one's progress. **4.** (Anat.) Ridge along surface of bone, as **frontal, occipital,** ~ of skull. **5.** (Her.) Device above shield and helmet on coat of arms, or separately, as on seal, notepaper, etc. **6.** *v.t.* Furnish with crest; serve as crest to; reach crest of (hill, wave). **7.** *v.i.* (Of wave) form into a crest. [ME, f. OF *creste* f. L *crista* tuft]

crėtā'ceous (-shus) *a.* & *n.* Of (the nature of) chalk; (*C*~, Geol.) (of the) latest mesozoic period or system, above Jurassic, containing chalk. [f. L *cretaceus* (*creta* chalk; see -ACEOUS)]

Crē'tan *a.* & *n.* (Native) of Crete (at one time supposed to contain many liars). [f. L *Cretanus* (*Creta* f. Gk *Krētē* Crete, island in E. Mediterranean; see -AN)]

crē'tĭc *n.* (Pros.) Foot consisting of one short syllable between two long. [f. L f. Gk *Krētikos* (as prec.; see -IC)]

crĕ'tĭn *n.* Person with deformity and mental retardation caused by thyroid deficiency; (colloq.) stupid person; hence ~ISM (2) *n.*, ~IZE (3) *v.t.*, ~OUS *a.* [f. F *crétin* f. Swiss F *creitin*, *crestin* f. L *Christianus* CHRISTIAN]

crĕtŏ'nne (*or* -ĕ'-) *n.* Cotton cloth with pattern printed on one or both sides. [F, f. *Creton* in Normandy]

crėvă'sse *n.* Deep fissure in ice of glacier; *breach in river levee. [F, f. OF *crevace* (see foll.)]

crĕ'vĭce *n.* Narrow opening, fissure, esp. in rock, building, etc. [ME f. OF *crevace* (*crever* burst f. L *crepare*)]

crew[1] (-o͞o) *n.* & *v.* **1.** *n.* Body of persons manning ship, boat, aircraft, train, etc.; associated body, company, of persons; set, gang, mob; ~ **cut,** man's hair cut short all over; ~ **neck,** round close-fitting neckline. **2.** *v.i.* & *t.* Supply, act as, (member of) crew (for). [ME, f. OF *creüe* increase, fem. p.p. (as n.) of *croistre* grow f. L *crescere*]

crew[2]. See CROW[3].

crew'el (-o͞o'-) *n.* Thin worsted yarn for tapestry and embroidery; ~**-work,** design in worsted on linen or cloth ground. [ME *crule* etc.; orig. unkn.]

crĭb[1] *n.* **1.** Barred receptacle for fodder etc.; ~**-biting,** horse's habit of seizing manger in teeth and at same time noisily drawing in breath. **2.** Small bed for child, with barred or latticed sides; model of the manger-scene at Bethlehem; framework lining shaft of mine; ~**('work),** heavy crossed timbers used in foundations in loose soil etc. **3.** Set of cards given to dealer at cribbage by other player(s); (colloq.) cribbage. **4.** (colloq.) Plagiarism; translation for (esp. illegitimate) use of students. **5.** Small house; (sl.) brothel; CRACK[2] *a crib*. **6.** (Austral. & N.Z.) Food; light meal. [OE *crib(b)*, = OS *kribbia*, OHG *krippa*]

crĭb[2] *v.t.* (-bb-). Confine in small space; pilfer; copy unfairly or without acknowledgement; (colloq.) grumble. [f. prec.]

crĭ'bbage *n.* Card game for two, three, or four persons, in which dealer scores also from cards in CRIB[1] 3; ~**-board** (with pegs and holes for scoring at cribbage). [17th c.; orig. unkn.]

crĭ'bō *n.* (*pl.* ~**s**). Large harmless snake of tropical America. [19th c.; orig. unkn.]

crĭ'brĭfôrm *a.* (Anat. & Bot.) Having numerous small holes. [f. L *cribrum* sieve + -I- + -FORM]

crĭck *n.*, & *v.t.* **1.** *n.* Sudden painful stiffness of muscles of neck, back, etc. **2.** *v.t.* Produce crick in (neck etc.). [ME, of unkn. orig.]

crĭ'ckėt[1] *n.* Jumping chirping insect living in hearths etc.; MOLE[2]-*cricket*. [ME, f. OF *criquet* (*criquer* creak etc.; imit.)]

crĭ'ckėt[2] *n.*, & *v.i.* **1.** *n.* Open-air summer game played with ball, bats, and wickets, between two sides of 11 players each; ||**not** ~, (colloq.) infringing the codes of fair play between honourable opponents in any sphere; ~**-bag,** long bag for carrying cricketer's bat etc. **2.** *v.i.* Play cricket; hence ~ER[1] *n.* [16th c.; orig. uncert.]

crī'coid *a.* & *n.* Ring-shaped (cartilage of larynx). [f. mod. L *cricoides* f. Gk *krikoeidēs* (*krikos* ring; see -OID)]

cri de cœur (krē de kẽr') *n.* (*pl.* ***cris*** *pr.* same). Passionate appeal, complaint, or protest. [F, = cry from the heart]

crī'er *n.* One who cries; officer who makes public announcements in court of justice or (**town ~**) in a town. [ME f. AF *criour*, OF *criere* (*crier* CRY²; see -OR)]

crī'key *int.* (sl.) expr. astonishment. [euphem. for CHRIST]

crīme *n.*, & *v.t.* **1.** *n.* Act (usu. grave offence) punishable by law; evil act; such acts collectively; (colloq.) shameful act; **~-sheet,** record of soldier's offences against regulations; **~ wave,** sudden brief increase in number of crimes committed; **~-writer,** author who writes about fictional crimes. **2.** *v.t.* (Mil. etc.) Charge with or convict of offence. [ME f. OF, f. L *crimen -minis* judgement, offence]

crime passionnel (krēm păsyŏnĕ'l) *n.* (*pl.* ***-es -ls*** *pr.* same). Crime, esp. murder, due to sexual jealousy. [F, = crime of passion]

crĭ'mĭnal *a.* & *n.* **1.** *a.* Of (the nature of) crime; guilty of crime; **~ law** (concerned with punishment of offenders, opp. CIVIL *law*; so **~ code, court, lawyer**); *criminal* LIBEL; hence **~ITY** (-ă'l-) *n.*, **~LY²** *adv.* **2.** *n.* Person guilty of crime. [ME, f. LL *criminalis* (as CRIME; see -AL)]

crĭmĭnalĭ'st|ic *a.* Pertaining to (the habits of) criminals; so **~ICS** *n.*, use of physical sciences in investigating crimes. [f. prec. + -IST + -IC]

crĭ'mĭn|āte *v.t.* Charge with crime; prove guilty of crime; censure; hence or cogn. **~A'TION** *n.*, **~ātIVE, ~ātORY,** *adjs.* [f. L *criminari* (as CRIME) + -ATE³]

crĭmĭnŏ'log|ў *n.* Scientific study of crime; hence **~IST** (3) *n.* [f. L *crimen -minis* CRIME + -O- + -LOGY]

crĭ'mĭnous *a.* (arch.) **~ clerk,** clergyman guilty of crime. [AF; OF *crimineux* f. L *criminosus* (as prec.; see -OUS)]

crĭmp¹ *v.t.*, & *n.* **1.** *v.t.* Compress into pleats or folds, frill; make narrow wrinkles or flutings in, corrugate; make waves or curls in (hair) with hot iron. **2.** *n.* Crimped thing or form; ***put a ~ in,** (sl.) thwart, interfere with; hence **~'Y²** *a.* [ME, prob. f. MDu., MLG *krimpen*, OHG *krimphan*]

crĭmp² *n.*, & *v.t.* (Agent whose business is to) entrap for service in army or navy. [17th c.; orig. unkn.]

crĭ'mson (-z-) *a.*, *n.*, & *v.* **1.** *a.* & *n.* Deep-red (colour); *crimson* RAMBLER. **2.** *v.t.* & *i.* Turn crimson. [ME *cremesin*, *crimesin*, ult. f. Arab. *ḳirmizi* KERMES]

crĭnge (-nj) *v.i.*, & *n.* **1.** *v.i.* Cower; bow servilely; behave obsequiously (*to*). **2.** *n.* (arch.) Fawning obeisance, cringing. [ME *crenge*, *crenche*, OE *cringan*, *crincan*; see CRANK¹]

crĭ'ngle (-ngg*e*l) *n.* (Naut.) Eye of rope containing thimble for another rope to pass through. [f. LG *kringel* dim. of *kring* ring f. root of CRANK¹]

crĭ'nkl|e *v.t.* & *i.*, & *n.* Twist, wrinkle; hence **~Y²** *a.* [ME, frequent. f. st. of OE *crincan* yield; see CRINGE, CRANK¹, -LE 3]

crĭnkum-crā'nkum *n.* & *a.* (Thing) full of twists and turns (lit. or fig.). [18th c., playful f. CRANK¹]

crĭ'noid *a.* & *n.* (Zool.) Lily-shaped (echinoderm); hence **crĭnoi'dAL** *a.* [f. Gk *krinoeidēs* (*krinon* lily; see -OID)]

crĭ'nolĭne (*or* -ēn) *n.* Stiff fabric of horsehair etc. for linings, hats, etc.; (Hist.) hooped petticoat. [F, f. L *crinis* hair + *linum* thread]

crĭŏ'llō *n.* (*pl.* **~s**). High-quality kind of cocoa. [Sp., = local; see CREOLE]

crī'pes (-ps) *int.* (vulg.) expr. astonishment. [perversion of CHRIST]

crĭ'pple *n.*, & *v.t.* **1.** *n.* (Permanently) lame person; hence **~DOM** (-p*e*ld-), **~HOOD** (-p*e*lh-), *ns.* **2.** *v.t.* Lame; (fig.) disable, impair, have severe adverse effect on. [OE *crypel*, = OLG *krupil*, & OE *crēopel*, = MLG, MDu. *krēpel*, cogn. w. CREEP]

cris. Var. of KRIS.

crise de nerfs (krēz de nār') *n.* (*pl.* ***crises*** *pr.* same). Fit of hysterics. [F]

crī's|ĭs *n.* (*pl.* **~es** *pr.* -ēz). Turning-point, esp. of disease; time of danger or suspense in politics, commerce, etc. [L, f. Gk *krisis* decision (*krinō* decide)]

crĭsp *a.*, *n.*, & *v.* **1.** *a.* Hard but fragile, brittle, (**~'bread,** thin crisp biscuit of crushed rye etc. grains); bracing (*crisp air*); brisk, decisive, (*crisp manner, style,* etc.); (of hair etc.) curly; neat, clearly defined; hence **~'LY²** *adv.*, **~'NESS** *n.* **2.** *n.* Thing overdone in roasting etc.; (usu. in *pl.*) ||thin fried slice of potato (marketed in packets etc.). **3.** *v.t.* & *i.* Curl in short stiff folds or waves; make or become crisp. [OE *crisp*, *crips*, f. L *crispus* curled]

crĭ'spāte *a.* Crisped; (Bot. & Zool.) having wavy margin. [f. L *crispare* curl; see -ATE²]

crĭ'spў *a.* Curly; brittle; brisk; crisp. [ME, f. CRISP + -Y²]

crĭ'ss-crŏss (*or* -aws) *n.*, *a.*, *adv.*, & *v.* **1.** *n.* Crossing lines, currents, etc.; network of crossing lines. **2.** *a.* In cross lines (*criss-cross pattern, traffic*). **3.** *adv.* Crosswise, at cross purposes (*everything went criss-cross*). **4.** *v.i.* & *t.* Move crosswise; work or mark with criss-cross pattern; intersect repeatedly. [orig. (15th c.) f. *Christ's cross*; later treated as redupl. of *cross*]

crĭ'sta *n.* (*pl.* **~e**). (Anat. & Zool.) Ridge, crest; so **crĭ'stATE²** *a.* [L]

crĭstō'balīte *n.* (Min.) A principal form of silica, occurring in massive form as opals. [f. G *cristobalit* (Cerro San *Cristóbal* in Mexico; see -ITE¹ (2))]

crĭt *n.* (colloq.) Criticism; critique; critical mass. [abbr.]

critēr'ĭ|on *n.* (*pl.* **~a**). Principle or standard that a thing is judged by; hence **~AL** *a.* [f. Gk *kritērion* (as foll.)]

crĭ'tĭc *n.* One who pronounces judgement; censurer; judge of literary or artistic works, esp. professional reviewer of books etc.; one skilled in textual criticism. [f. L f. Gk *kritikos* (*kritēs* judge f. *krinō* decide; see -IC)]

crĭ'tĭcal *a.* **1.** Censorious, fault-finding, (*was critical of me, my efforts*); skilful at or engaged in criticism; providing textual criticism (*a critical edition of Ibsen*); belonging to criticism; **~ apparatus,** apparatus criticus. **2.** Pertaining to a crisis, involving risk or suspense, (*critical condition, operation*); decisive, crucial, (*arrive at the critical moment; matter of critical importance*). **3.** (Math. & Phys.) Marking transition from one state etc. to another (*critical angle*); (of nuclear reactor) maintaining a self-sustaining chain reaction, whence **~ITY** (-ă'l-) *n.*; **~ mass,** amount of fissile material needed to maintain nuclear chain reaction; **~ path,** sequence of stages determining minimum time needed for an operation; **~ temperature** (above which a gas cannot be liquefied). **4.** Hence **~LY²** *adv.* [f. L *criticus* (see prec.) + -AL]

crĭtĭcă'ster (*or* krĭ'-) *n.* Petty or inferior critic. [f. CRITIC + -ASTER]

crĭ'tĭcĭsm *n.* **1.** Work of a critic; critical article, essay, or remark; **textual ~** (dealing with and seeking correct reading of esp. MS. text of an author); **the higher ~** (dealing with origin, character, etc., of texts, esp. of Biblical writings);

the lower ~, textual criticism of Bible. **2.** Censure. [f. CRITIC or L *criticus* + -ISM]

crĭ'tĭcize, -īse (-īz), *v.t.* Discuss critically (work, or abs.); censure. [f. as prec. + -IZE]

crĭtī'que (-ē'k) *n.*, & *v.t.* **1.** *n.* Critical essay or analysis; art of criticism. **2.** *v.t.* Discuss critically. [f. obs. *critic* criticism, after its source F *critique* f. Gk *kritikē* (*tekhnē*) critical art]

crĭ'tter *n.* (dial. or joc.) Creature; (derog.) person. [var. of CREATURE]

croak *n.* & *v.* **1.** *n.* Deep hoarse sound uttered by frog or raven; sound resembling this; hence ~'Y[2] *a.* **2.** *v.i.* Utter croak; (sl.) die. **3.** *v.t.* Utter with croak or dismally; (sl.) kill. **4.** Hence ~'ER[1] *n.*, (esp.) prophet of evil. [ME, imit.]

Crō'ăt *n.* Native or inhabitant of Croatia in Yugoslavia; language of Croats; so **Crōā'tIAN** (-shan) *a.* & *n.* [f. mod. L *Croatae* pl. f. Serbo-Croatian *Hrvat*]

crŏc *n.* (colloq.) Crocodile. [abbr.]

crō'ceāte *a.* Saffron, saffron-coloured. [f. L *croceus* (CROCUS); see -ATE[2]]

crō'chet (-shā *or* -shĭ) *n.*, & *v.t.* **1.** *n.* Knitting (material or work) done with hooked needle forming intertwined loops. **2.** *v.t.* Make (shawl etc., or abs.) in crochet. [F, dim. of *croc* hook]

crōcĭ'dolīte *n.* Fibrous blue or green silicate of iron and sodium, blue asbestos. [f. Gk *krokis -idos* nap of cloth + -O- + -LITE]

crŏck[1] *n.* Earthenware pot or jar; broken piece of earthenware used for covering hole in flower-pot. [OE *croc(ca)*, rel. to Icel. *krukka*, & prob. to OE *crōg*, *crūce*]

crŏck[2] *n.* & *v.* **1.** *n.* (colloq. or dial.) Inefficient or broken-down or worn-out person; (sl.) worn-out vehicle, ship, etc. **2.** *v.i.* **~ up,** (colloq.) break down, collapse. **3.** *v.t.* **~ (up),** (colloq.) disable, cause to collapse. [orig. Sc., perh. f. Flem.]

crŏ'ckerў *n.* Earthenware vessels, esp. for household use. [f. obs. *crocker* potter (CROCK[1]); see -ERY]

crŏ'ckėt *n.* Small ornament (usu. bud or curled leaf) on inclined side of pinnacle etc. [ME, f. ONF var. of OF CROCHET]

Crŏ'ckford *n.* (colloq.) (Used for) 'Crockford's Clerical Directory' of Anglican clergy. [f. J. ~ d. 1865, nominal first publisher]

crŏ'codīle *n.* Large thick-skinned long-tailed amphibious tropical saurian of genus *Crocodilus* etc. (**~ tears,** hypocritical grief [from belief that crocodile wept while devouring, or to allure, its victim]); its skin; ||(colloq.) line of school-children etc. walking two and two; hence **crŏcodĭ'lIAN** (-yan) *a.* [ME f. OF *cocodrille* f. med. L *cocodrillus* f. L f. Gk *krokodilos*]

crō'cus *n.* Dwarf plant of genus *Crocus*, with corm and brilliant (often yellow or purple) flowers; AUTUMN *crocus*. [ME, = saffron, f. L, f. Gk *krokos* crocus, of Semitic orig.]

Croe'sus (krē's-) *n.* Wealthy person. [f. ~, king of Lydia in 6th c. B.C.]

||**crŏft** (*or* -aw-) *n.*, & *v.i.* **1.** *n.* Enclosed piece of (usu. arable) land; smallholding of crofter. **2.** *v.i.* Farm croft; live as crofter. [OE, of unkn. orig.]

||**crŏ'fter** (*or* -aw'-) *n.* One who rents a small-holding, esp. joint tenant of divided farm in parts of Scotland. [f. prec. + -ER[1]]

croi'ssant (krwah'sahṅ) *n.* Crescent-shaped bread roll. [F, f. as CRESCENT]

Crō-Mă'gnon (*or* -mă'nyon) *a.* Of a tall broad-faced European race of late palaeolithic times. [name of hill in Dordogne, France, where remains were found in 1868]

crŏ'mbĕc *n.* Afr. warbler of genus *Sylvietta*. [F, f. Du. *krom* crooked + *bek* beak]

crŏ'mlĕch (-k) *n.* Megalithic tomb, dolmen; circle of upright prehistoric stones. [W (*crom* fem. of *crwm* bent, *llech* flat stone)]

cromor̄'ne. Var. of KRUMMHORN.

crōne *n.* Withered old woman; old ewe. [ME, prob. f. MDu. *c(a)roonje* carcass f. ONF *carogne* CARRION]

crŏnk *a.* (Austral. colloq.) Unfit; unsound; fraudulent. [19th c.; cf. CRANK[3]]

crō'nў *n.* Intimate friend. [17th c. *chrony*, univ. sl. f. Gk *khronios* of long standing, chronic, (*khronos* time)]

crŏŏk *n.*, *a.*, & *v.* **1.** *n.* Hooked staff of shepherd or bishop; anything hooked; hook; bend, curve; act of bending. **2.** (colloq.) Rogue, swindler; professional criminal, whence ~'ERY (5) *n.*; *by* HOOK[1] *or by crook*; **on the ~,** dishonestly. **3.** *a.* Crooked; (Austral. & N.Z. colloq.) unsatisfactory, unpleasant, dishonest, bad-tempered (**go ~,** become angry, lose one's temper; **go ~ at** or **on,** become angry with, rebuke), unwell, injured; **~-back(ed),** hunchback(ed); ***~'neck,** kind of SQUASH[2] with curved neck. **4.** *v.t.* & *i.* Bend, curve; **~** one's **elbow,** one's **little finger,** (sl.) drink alcohol (esp. to excess). [ME, f. ON *krókr* hook etc.]

crooked *a.* **1.** (krŏŏ'kĭd; **~er, ~est**). Not straight, bent, twisted; deformed; bent with age; (fig.) not straightforward, dishonest; hence ~LY[2] *adv.*, ~NESS *n.* **2.** (krŏŏkt). (Of stick) having a transverse handle; (Austral. & N.Z. sl.) = CROOK 3. [ME, f. prec. + -ED[2], prob. after ON *krókóttr*]

Crŏŏkes (-ks) *n.* **~ glass,** type of glass protecting eyes from bright sunlight etc.; **~ tube,** vacuum tube for observation of stratified electric discharges. [f. Sir W. ~, Engl. scientist d. 1919]

crōōn *v.t.* & *i.*, & *n.* (Hum, sing, etc., in) low subdued voice; hence ~'ER[1] *n.*, esp. one who sings popular sentimental songs in low smooth voice. [ME, orig. Sc. and N. Engl., f. MDu., MLG *krōnen* groan, lament]

crŏp[1] *n.* **1.** Pouchlike enlargement of gullet in birds, where food is prepared for digestion (**~-full,** having a full crop or stomach, lit. or fig.). **2.** Stock or handle of whip; (**hunting-**)~, short whipstock with loop and (or instead of) lash. **3.** Produce of cultivated plants, esp. cereals (*crop*-DUSTING; **~-over,** W. Ind. celebration of end of sugar-cane harvest); season's total yield (of cereal etc.); group or amount appearing or produced at one time (*this year's crop of students*); entire hide of animal tanned. **4.** Cropping of hair; style of wearing hair cut short; NECK[1] *and crop*; **~-eared,** with ears (or hair) cut short. **5.** Piece cut off. [OE *crop(p)*, = MDu., MLG *kropp*, OHG *kropf*, ON *kroppr*]

crŏp[2] *v.* (**-pp-**). **1.** *v.t.* Cut off; (of animals) bite off (tops of plants); cut short (ears, tail, hair, nap of cloth, edges of book). **2.** Gather, reap; sow, plant, (land *with* barley etc.). **3.** *v.i.* Bear a crop; turn *up* unexpectedly; **~ up** or **out,** (Geol.) appear at surface. [ME, f. prec.]

crŏ'pper *n.* In vbl senses; **good, heavy, light,** ~, plant yielding good etc. crop; (sl.) heavy fall (lit. or fig.; *came a cropper*). [f. CROP[2] + -ER[1]]

crō'quet[1] (-kā *or* -kĭ) *n.* Game, played on lawn, in which wooden balls are driven with mallets through hoops; act of croqueting a ball. [perh. NF dial. form of F CROCHET hook]

crō'quet[2] (-kā *or* -kĭ) *v.t.* (Croquet). Drive away (opponent's ball, or abs.) with one's own by placing the two together and striking one's own (cf. ROQUET). [f. prec.]

croquĕ'tte (-kĕ't) *n.* Fried breaded ball of potato, meat, etc. [F (*croquer* crunch; see -ETTE)]

crōre *n.* (Ind.) Ten million; one hundred lakhs (of rupees, units of measurement, persons, etc.). [f. Hindi *k(a)rōr* f. Prakrit *kroḍi*, Skr. *koṭi* apex]

crō'sier, -zier, (-z-; *or* -zh*er*) *n.* Hooked staff symbolizing pastoral office of bishop etc., crook. [orig. = bearer of a crook, f. OF *crocier, crossier* (*croce, crosse* f. Rom. **croccia* f. *croccus* CROOK) & f. OF *croisier* cross-bearer (*crois* CROSS[1]; see -IER)]

crŏss[1] (*or* -aws) *n.* **1.** Stake (usu. with transverse bar) used for crucifixion of criminals, esp. (*C~*) that on which Christ was crucified; model of this as religious emblem; = SIGN[1] *of the cross*; staff surmounted by cross and borne before archbishop or in procession; monument in form of cross, esp. one in centre of town; **the C~**, the Christian religion. **2.** Trial, affliction, (*bear* one's *cross*); cause of trouble or vexation. **3.** Cross-shaped thing or mark; (**Southern**) **C~**, a southern constellation whose stars form a cross; CELTIC, FIERY, GREEK, LATIN, MALTESE, SAINT *Andrew's*, *Anthony('s)*, TAU, *cross*; *cross or* PILE[4]. **4.** Cross-shaped decoration in orders of knighthood (**Grand C~**, highest degree of this); decoration for personal valour (*Victoria, George, Distinguished Service, Military, Distinguished Flying, Cross*). **5.** Intermixture of breeds; animal resulting from this; mixture or compromise *between* two things; crosswise movement of actor, football, boxer's fist, etc. (**on the ~**, diagonally); (sl.) fraud, swindle, (**on the ~**, dishonestly). **6.** Hence ~'LET *n.*, ~'WAYS *adv.*, ~'WISE *a.* & *adv.* [OE *cros* f. ON *kross* f. OIr. *cros* f. L *crux crucis*]

crŏss[2] (*or* -aws) *v.* **1.** *v.t.* Place crosswise (*cross* one's *legs*); ~ one's **fingers, keep** one's **fingers ~ed,** crook one finger over another to bring good luck; ~ **swords,** (fig.) have fight or controversy or overt rivalry (*with*); ~ **wires,** make accidental telephone connection, (fig.) have misunderstanding. **2.** Make sign of cross on or over (esp. one**self,** as sign of awe, to invoke divine protection, etc.); ~ one's **heart** (in attestation of sincerity). **3.** Draw line across; ~ **out** or **off,** cancel; ||~ **a cheque** (with two parallel lines, usu. adding '& Co.' or name of bank through which or account to which cheque must be paid); ~ **fortune-teller's hand with,** give her (coin); *cross the t's* (see T). **4.** ~ (**over**), go across (road, river, sea, etc., or abs.); *cross a* BRIDGE[1] *when* one *comes to it*; ~ person's **mind,** occur to him; ~ **the path of,** meet with, thwart. **5.** Thwart (person, plans, etc.; *crossed in love*); (sl.) cheat. **6.** Cause to interbreed; cross-fertilize (plants). **7.** *v.i.* Meet and pass; **letters ~** (each being dispatched to the other's sender before receipt of the other). [ME, f. prec.]

crŏss[3] (*or* -aws) *a.* **1.** Passing from side to side, transverse; (Cricket, of bat) held aslant. **2.** Intersecting. **3.** Contrary, opposed, (*to* a purpose etc., or abs.; **at ~ purposes,** misunderstanding or conflicting with each other); (colloq.) peevish, out of humour, (*be cross with* person; *as cross as two sticks*); hence ~'LY[2] *adv.*, ~'NESS *n.* [f. CROSS[1] & f. obs. *cross* adv.]

crŏss- (*or* -aws) *comb. form.* (1) f. CROSS[1], objectively (*cross-bearer*), or *attrib.* = having a transverse part (*crossbow*); (2) f. CROSS[3], = crossing, transverse, (*crossbar, cross-beam, -current, -keys, -piece*), opposing (*cross-petition*); (3) f. *cross* adv. (*cross-breed, -examine, -fertilize, -fire*); (4) = ACROSS (*cross-Channel, -country, *-town*): **~'bar** (2), horizontal bar, esp. of bicycle or football goal; ||**~-bench** (2) (in Parliament for members not belonging to Government or official Opposition party), whence **~-bench**ER[1] (4) *n.*; **~'bill** (2), bird of genus *Loxia*, with mandibles crossing when bill is closed; **~-bones** (2), representation of two thigh-bones (see SKULL); **~'bow** (1), bow fixed across wooden stock, with groove for arrow etc. and mechanism for drawing and releasing string; **~-breed** (3), (*n.*) breed of animals or plants produced by crossing, individual of such breed, (*v.t.*) produce by such breeding; **~-buttock** (4), throw over hip in wrestling; **~-check** (3) *n.* & *v.*, check by alternative method of verification; **~-country** (4) *a.* & *adv.*, across fields etc., not following roads; **~-cultural** (4), of (comparison between) different cultures; **~-cut** (2), diagonal cut, path, etc. (*~-cut saw*, for cutting across grain of wood); **~-dating** (3), (Archaeol.) dating by correlation with another site or level; **~-examine** (3), examine (esp. witness in lawcourt) minutely to check or extend previous testimony; hence *~-examin*ATION *n.*; **~-eyed** (2), having one or both eyes turned permanently towards nose in squint; **~-fade** (3) *v.t.*, (Radio etc.) fade in one sound as another is faded out; **~-fertilize** (3), fertilize (animal or plant) from one of a different species, (fig.) help by interchange of ideas etc.; **~-fire** (3), firing in two crossing directions; **~-grain** (2), grain of timber running across regular grain (*~-grained* a., having such grain, (fig.) perverse, intractable); **~-hair** (2), fine wire at focus of optical instrument for use in measurement; **~-hatch** (3) *v.t.*, shade with intersecting sets of parallel lines; **~-head** (2), bar between piston-rod and connecting-rod in steam engine; **~-head(ing)** (2), heading printed across column before section of article in newspaper etc.; **~-legged** (3), squatting with legs crossed or sitting in chair with one leg laid across the other; **~-link(age)** (2), (Chem.) bond between chains of atoms in polymer etc.; **~-over** *n.* & *a.*, (having) point or place of crossing from one side to the other; **~-patch** (2), ill-tempered person; **~-piece** (2), transverse component of structure etc.; **~-ply** (2) *a.*, (of tyre) having fabric layers with cords lying crosswise; **~-pollinate** (3), pollinate (plant) from another; **~-question** (3) *v.t.*, = *cross-examine*; **~-reference** (2), (*n.*) reference from one part of book to another for further information, (*v.t.*) provide with this; **~'road(s)** (2), intersection of two roads (*at the ~roads*, (fig.) at critical turning-point in life etc.); **~-ruff** (3) *n.*, & *v.t.*, (Bridge etc.) (play by) alternate trumping of partners' leads; **~-section** (2), (drawing etc. of a) transverse SECTION, (fig.) representative sample, (Phys.) quantity expressing probability of interaction between particles; **~-stitch** (2), (needlework made with) stitch formed of two stitches crossing; **~-talk** (3), unwanted transfer of signals between communication channels, repartee; ***~-tie** (2), railway sleeper; **~-trees** (2), pair of horizontal timbers to support mast; **~-voting** (3), voting for a party not one's own or for more than one party; **~-wind** (2), wind blowing at right angles (or not parallel) to one's direction of travel; **~-wire** (2) = *cross-hair*.

crŏsse *n.* Netted crook used in lacrosse. [F, f. OF *croce, croc*, hook; see CROSIER]

crŏ'ssing (*or* -aw'-) *n.* In vbl senses; intersection of two roads, railways, etc. (*GRADE *crossing*; ||LEVEL *crossing*); intersection of church nave and transepts; place where street is crossed (PEDESTRIAN *crossing*; ZEBRA *crossing*); **~-sweeper,** (Hist.) one who sweeps this. [f. CROSS[2] + -ING[1]]

crŏ'ssword (-ērd; *or* -aw'-) *n.* Puzzle in which words crossing (usu. vertically and horizontally according to a chequered pattern) have to be filled in from clues. [f. CROSS- (2) + WORD[1]]

crŏtch *n.* Bifurcation, fork (esp. of human body). [perh. = ME & OF *croc(he)* hook f. as CROOK]

crŏ'tchet *n.* ||(Mus.) black-headed note with

stem, = two quavers, or half of minim; whimsical fancy, whence ~EER′ *n.*, ~Y² *a.*, whimsical, peevish; hook. [ME, f. OF *crochet* dim. of *croc* hook (see prec.)]

crō′ton *n.* Plant of genus *Croton*, akin to spurge; ~ **oil,** drastic purgative obtained from one species of this. [mod. L, f. Gk *krotōn* sheep-tick, croton]

crouch *v.i.*, & *n.* **1.** *v.i.* Stand or lie with legs bent close to body, e.g. for concealment or timidly or servilely. **2.** *n.* Crouching. [ME, perh. f. OF *crochir* be bent (*croc* hook f. ON *krókr*; cf. CROOK)]

croup¹ (-ōōp) *n.* Rump, hindquarters, (esp. of horse). [ME f. OF *croupe* f. Rom. **croppa* f. Gmc **kruppō*, rel. to CROP¹]

croup² (-ōōp) *n.* Inflammation of larynx and trachea of children, marked by hard cough and difficult breathing; hence ~′Y² *a.* [f. *croup* to croak (imit.)]

crou′pier (-ōō′-; *or* -ĭā) *n.* Raker-in and payer-out of money at gaming-table; assistant chairman at foot of table at public dinner. [F, orig. = rider on the CROUP¹]

croûton (krōō′tawṅ) *n.* Small piece of fried or toasted bread served with soup or used as garnish. [F (*croûte* CRUST)]

crow¹ (-ō) *n.* **1.** Bird of genus *Corvus* or family Corvidae, esp. ROOK¹, CARRION *crow*; **as the ~ flies,** in a straight line; **~ to pick** or **pluck,** (fig.) fault to find; ***eat ~**, submit to humiliation; **white ~** a rarity. **2.** ~(**′bar**), bar of iron (usu. with beaklike end) used as lever; **~′berry,** black flavourless edible fruit of a small heathlike shrub, *cranberry; **~-bill,** forceps for extracting bullets etc.; **~′foot,** name of various plants, esp. of genus *Ranunculus*, (Naut.) arrangement of small ropes for suspending awning; **~′s-foot,** (1, usu. in *pl.*) wrinkle at outer corner of person's eye, (2) caltrop; **~′s-nest,** barrel fixed at mast-head of sailing vessel as shelter for look-out man; **~ steps,** corbie-steps; **~-toe,** (arch. or dial.) bluebell (or other flower, e.g. buttercup). [OE *crāwe*, = OS *krāia*, OHG *krāja* etc., f. as CROW³]

crow² (-ō) *n.* Crowing of cock; joyful cry of infant. [ME, f. foll.]

crow³ (-ō) *v.i.* (‖*past* in sense 1 also **crew** *pr.* krōō). **1.** Utter loud cry of cock. **2.** (Of infant) utter joyful cry. **3.** Exult loudly (*over*). [OE *crāwan*, = OHG *krāen*, WG of imit. orig.]

crowd¹ *n.* Large number of persons gathered together without orderly arrangement (**follow the ~**, conform with the majority; **would pass in a ~**, is not conspicuously defective); mass of spectators, audience; *the* multitude; (colloq.) company, set, lot; (in *sing.* or *pl.*) large number (of things); actors representing a crowd. [f. foll.]

crowd² *v.* **1.** *v.i.* & *t.* Collect in a crowd. **2.** *v.t.* Fill, occupy, cram, (space etc. *with*); fill (place etc.) as a crowd does (lit. or fig.); come aggressively close to; *(colloq.) approach (specified age); force (thing, person) *into* etc.; **~ out,** exclude by crowding; **~ (on) sail,** hoist large number of sails. **3.** *v.i.* Force one's way *into*, *through*, etc. (confined space etc., or abs.). [OE *crūdan* press, drive, corresp. to MDu., MLG *kruden* press, push]

crown¹ *n.* **1.** Wreath of flowers etc. worn on head, esp. as emblem of victory, (also fig., as *martyr's crown, world heavyweight crown*). **2.** Monarch's head-covering of gold etc. and jewels; (*C~*, fig.) king or queen, regal power, supreme governing power in a monarchy. **3.** Crown-shaped thing, esp. device or ornament; bird's high crest. **4.** British coin worth 25p., formerly 5s.; foreign coin, esp. = KRONE. **5.** Top part, esp. of head, tree, etc.; upper part of cut gem above girdle; highest or central part of arch or arched structure (*crown of the road*); thing that completes or forms the summit; top of hat; part of tooth projecting from gum, artificial replacement for (outer part of) this (cf. foll. 3). **6.** Size of paper, 508×381 mm. **7. ~ and anchor,** gambling game played with dice marked with crowns, anchors, etc., and a corresponding board; **~ cap,** cork-lined metal cap for bottle-top; **C~ Colony,** British colony controlled by the Crown; **C~ Court,** court of criminal jurisdiction in England and Wales; **C~ Derby,** kind of china made at Derby and often marked with crown; **~ glass** (without lead or iron, used formerly in windows, now as optical glass of low refractive index); **~ green,** bowling-green with middle higher than sides; **~ imperial,** tall fritillary with flower-cluster at top of stalk; **~ jewels** (forming part of sovereign's regalia; also fig.); ‖**C~ Office** (transacting common-law business of Chancery); **C~ prince,** male heir to sovereign throne, (fig.) likely successor in any office; **C~ princess,** Crown prince's wife, female heir to sovereign throne; **~-roast,** roast of rib-pieces of pork or lamb in crownlike arrangement; **~ saw,** cylinder with toothed edge for making circular hole; **~ of thorns,** poisonous starfish of genus *Acanthaster*; **~ wheel** (with teeth at right angles to its plane). **8.** Hence (-)~ED² (-nd), ~′LESS, *adjs.* [ME, f. AF *corune*, OF *corone* f. L *corona*]

crown² *v.t.* **1.** Place crown on (person, head); invest (person) with regal crown or dignity (*crown him, crown him king*; **~ed heads,** kings and queens); occupy head of, form chief ornament to, (lit. or fig.); put finishing touch to (**to ~ all,** often iron. = to complete one's bad luck); bring (efforts) to happy issue; (sl.) hit on the head. **2.** (Draughts). Make (piece) a king. **3.** (Dent.) Protect remains of (tooth) with gold etc. cap cemented on. [ME, f. AF *coruner*, OF *coroner* f. L *coronare* (*corona* crown)]

crow′ner *n.* (joc., arch., or dial.) = CORONER. [pop. by-form of *coroner*, assim. to *crown*]

crozier. See CROSIER.

CRT *abbr.* cathode-ray tube.

cru (krōō) *n.* (Grade of wine from) French vineyard or wine-producing region. [F (*crû* grown)]

cruces. See CRUX.

cru′cial (krōō′shal) *a.* Decisive, critical, (case, point, test, etc.); (colloq.) very important; hence ~LY² *adv.* [F, f. L *crux crucis* cross + -AL]

cru′cian (krōō′shan) *n.* Yellow fish (*Carassius carassius*) allied to carp. [f. LG *karusse* etc. + -AN]

cru′ciāte (-ōō′sh-) *a.* (Zool. etc.) Cross-shaped. [f. mod. L *cruciatus* f. L (as foll.; see -ATE²)]

cru′cĭble (-ōō′-) *n.* Melting-pot (usu. of earthenware) for metals etc.; (fig.) severe trial. [ME, f. med. L *crucibulum* night-lamp, crucible, f. L *crux crucis* cross]

crucĭ′ferous (-ōō-) *a.* (Bot.) Of the family Cruciferae, having flowers with four equal petals arranged crosswise. [f. LL *crucifer* (as CRUCIAL; see -FEROUS)]

cru′cĭfĭx (-ōō′-) *n.* Model of (Christ on) the Cross. [ME f. OF, f. eccl. L *crucifixus* f. L *cruci fixus* fixed to a cross; see CROSS¹, FIX¹]

crucĭfĭ′xion (-ōō-; -kshon) *n.* Crucifying, esp. (*C~*) of Christ; picture of this. [f. eccl. L *crucifixio* (as prec.; see -ION)]

cru′cĭform (-ōō′-) *a.* Cross-shaped (esp. of church with transepts). [f. L *crux crucis* cross; see -FORM]

cru′cĭfȳ (-ōō′-) *v.t.* Put to death by fastening to a cross; (fig.) mortify (passions, sins, flesh); cause extreme mental pain to; torment, persecute. [ME, f. OF *crucifier* f. Rom. **crucificare* (see -FY) for LL *crucifigere* (as CRUCIFIX)]

||**crŭck** *n.* One of paired curved timbers extending to ground in framework of house-roof. [var. of CROOK]

crŭd *n.* (sl.) Unpleasant person; unwanted impurity etc.; illness; nonsense; hence **~'dy**² *a.* [var. of CURD]

crude (-ōōd) *a.* & *n.* **1.** *a.* In the natural or raw state; (fig.) ill-digested, rough, unpolished, lacking finish; (of action, statement, manners) rude, blunt; (Statistics) not adjusted or corrected (*crude death rate*); hence or cogn. ~LY² (-dlĭ) *adv.*, ~NESS (-dn-), **cru'd**ITY (-ōō'-), *ns.* **2.** *n.* Natural mineral oil. [ME, f. L *crudus* raw, rough]

cru'el (-ōō'-) *a.* (**-er, -est**; ||**-ll-**). Having or showing indifference to or pleasure in another's suffering; causing pain or suffering; hence or cogn. ~LY² *adv.*, ~TY¹ *n.* [ME f. OF, f. L *crudelis*, rel. to *crudus* (see prec.)]

cru'ėt (-ōō'-) *n.* Small stoppered glass bottle etc. for condiments at table; small vessel for wine or water in celebration of Eucharist; ~(**-stand**) (for cruets, mustard-pot, etc.). [ME, f. AF **cruet(e)* dim. of OF *crue* pot f. OS *krūka*, rel. to CROCK¹]

cruise (-ōōz) *v.i.*, & *n.* **1.** *v.i.* Sail to and fro for protection of shipping etc.; sail about for pleasure, making for no particular place or calling at series of places. **2.** (Of motor vehicle or aircraft) travel at **cruising speed** (economical travelling speed, less than top speed); (of vehicle or driver) travel at random, esp. slowly when patrolling, looking for passengers, etc. **3.** *n.* Cruising voyage; ||**~'way,** canal assigned for recreational use. [prob. f. Du. *kruisen* (*kruis* CROSS¹)]

crui'ser (-ōō'z-) *n.* Warship of high speed and medium armament; BATTLE¹-*cruiser*; = CABIN *cruiser*; *police patrol-car; **~weight,** (Boxing) see BOX⁵*ing-weights*. [f. Du. *kruiser* (as prec.; see -ER¹)]

***crŭ'ller** *n.* Small cake made of dough containing eggs, butter, sugar, etc., twisted or curled and fried in fat. [prob. f. Du. *krullen* curl]

crŭmb (-m) *n.*, & *v.t.* **1.** *n.* Small fragment, esp. of bread; (fig.) small particle, atom, (*of* comfort etc.); soft inner part of bread; (sl.) objectionable person; hence ~'Y² *a.* **2.** *v.t.* Cover or thicken with crumbs; break into crumbs. [OE *cruma*, = MDu. *crūme*, MDu., MLG *crōme*, MHG *krume*, Icel. *kr(a)umr*]

crŭ'mble *v.* & *n.* **1.** *v.t.* & *i.* Break or fall into crumbs or fragments (lit. or fig.). **2.** *n.* Crumbly or crumbled substance; dish, esp. of cooked fruit, with crumbly topping (*apple crumble*). [ME, f. OE **crymelan*]

crŭ'mblў *a.* Apt to fall into crumbs or fragments. [f. prec. + -Y²]

||**crŭmbs** (-mz) *int.* expr. dismay or surprise. [euphem. for *Christ*]

crŭ'mhōrn. Var. of KRUMMHORN.

crŭ'mmў *a.* (sl.) Dirty, unpleasant; inferior, worthless. [var. of CRUMBY]

crŭmp *v.t.*, & *n.* (Army sl.) (Sound of, make sound of) bursting bomb or shell. [imit.]

crŭ'mpėt *n.* Soft cake of yeast mixture, cooked on griddle etc. and eaten toasted with butter; (sl.) head; (sl.) sexually desirable woman, women collectively. [17th c., of uncert. orig.]

crŭ'mple *v.* **1.** *v.t.* Crush together or *up* into creased state; ruffle, wrinkle. **2.** *v.i.* Become creased; ~ (**up**), (fig.) collapse, give way. [f. obs. *crump* v. & a. (make or become) curved + -LE 3]

crŭnch *v.* & *n.* **1.** *v.t.* Crush with teeth, esp. noisily, whence ~'Y² *a.*; grind under foot (gravel etc.). **2.** *v.i.* Go (*up, through,* etc.) thus. **3.** *n.* Crunching (noise); decisive event (**when it comes to the ~, when the ~ comes,** in a show-down). [earlier *cra(u)nch*, imit.; assim. to *munch*]

crŭ'pper *n.* Strap buckled to back of saddle and looped under horse's tail; hindquarters of horse. [ME, f. AF *cropere*, OF *-iere*, f. Rom. **cropparia*, *-eria* (**croppa*; see CROUP¹, -ER²)]

crur'al (-oor'-) *a.* (Anat.) Of the leg. [F, or f. L *cruralis* (*crus cruris* leg; see -AL)]

crusā'd|e (-ōō-) *n.*, & *v.i.* **1.** *n.* (Hist.) One of several Christian expeditions to recover Jerusalem etc. from Muslims; war instigated by Church for alleged religious ends; (fig.) vigorous movement against poverty etc. **2.** *v.i.* Engage in crusade; hence ~ER¹ *n.* [earlier *croisade* (F, f. *croix* CROSS¹), *crusado*, *-ada* (Sp., f. *cruz* CROSS¹); see -ADE]

cruse (-ōōs *or* -ōōz) *n.* (arch.) Earthenware pot or jar; WIDOW'*s cruse*. [OE *crūse*, of unkn. orig.]

crŭsh¹ *v.t.* Compress with violence, so as to break, bruise, etc.; reduce to powder by pressure; crumple, crease (dress etc.) by rough handling; (fig.) subdue, overwhelm, (*a crushing defeat, reply*); *crushed* STRAWBERRY. [ME, f. AF *crussir*, *corussier*, OF *croissir*, *cruissir*, gnash (teeth), crack, f. Rom. **cruscire*, of unkn. orig.]

crŭsh² *n.* Act of crushing; crowded mass (esp. of persons); (colloq.) crowded social gathering; fenced passage with one narrow end for handling cattle etc.; drink made from juice of crushed fruit; (sl.) group of persons; (sl.) (object of) infatuation (**have a ~ on,** be infatuated with); **~ bar,** place for theatre audience to buy drinks in the intervals; **~-barrier,** (temporary) barrier for restraining a crowd; **~ hat,** opera-hat. [ME, f. prec.]

crŭst *n.* & *v.* **1.** *n.* Hard outer part of bread; similar casing of anything, e.g. harder layer over soft snow; UPPER *crust*. **2.** Hard dry scrap of bread; pastry covering pie; hard dry formation on skin, scab. **3.** (Geol.) Outer rocky portion of earth; hence ~'AL *a.* **4.** Coating or deposit on surface of anything; deposit on sides of wine-bottle; (fig.) superficial hardness of demeanour etc.; (sl.) impudence. **5.** *v.t.* Cover with or form into crust. **6.** *v.i.* Become covered with crust. [ME, f. OF *crouste* f. L *crusta* rind, shell]

crŭstā'cean (-shan) *a.* & *n.* (Member) of the Crustacea, a large class of arthropods with hard shells, mainly aquatic, e.g. crab, lobster, shrimp, wood-louse; hence **crŭstācėŏ'**LOGY *n.*, **crŭstā'ce**OUS (-shus) *a.* [f. mod. L *crustaceus* (*crusta*; see prec., -ACEOUS) + -AN]

crŭ'stėd *a.* Having a crust; (of wine) having deposited a crust; (fig.) antiquated, venerable, (*crusted prejudice, theory*). [f. CRUST + -ED¹,²]

crŭ'st|ў *a.* Crustlike, hard; having a crisp crust; irritable; curt; hence **~ĭLY**² *adv.*, **~ĭNESS** *n.* [ME, f. CRUST + -Y²]

crŭtch *n.* Staff (usu. with cross-piece at top) for lame person (usu. *pair of crutches*); support, prop, (lit. or fig.); fork of the human body, corresp. part of garment, (cf. CROTCH). [OE *cryc(c)*, = OS *krukka*, OHG *krucka*, ON *krykkja* f. Gmc **krukjō(n)* bend]

crŭx *n.* (*pl.* **~es,** *or* **cruces** *pr.* krōō'sēz). Difficult matter, puzzle; decisive point at issue; **~ ansata** (ănsā'ta), ankh (lit. = handled cross). [L, = cross]

cruzeir'ō (krōōzār'ō) *n.* (*pl.* **~s**). Monetary unit of Brazil. [Port., dim. of *cruz* cross]

crў¹ *n.* **1.** Loud inarticulate utterance of grief, pain, fear, joy, etc.; loud excited utterance of words; loud natural utterance of animal, esp. of excited hounds (**in full ~,** hotly pursuing); creaking of bent tin etc. **2.** Appeal, entreaty; proclamation of goods or business in streets; public demand (*for*); watchword (BATTLE¹-*cry*,

WAR¹-*cry*). **3.** Fit or spell of weeping (**~-baby,** person who weeps easily or without good reason). **4. A far ~,** (fig.) a long way. [ME f. OF *cri* (*crier* CRY²)]

crȳ² *v.* **1.** *v.t.* Utter loudly, exclaim, (*that*); announce for sale (*cry* one's *wares*; **~ stinking fish,** (fig.) condemn one's own wares). **2.** Weep (tears etc., or abs.); ~ one's **heart** or **eyes out,** weep bitterly; *cry over spilt* MILK¹; ~ **oneself to sleep,** weep till one falls asleep exhausted. **3.** *v.i.* Make loud utterance (*cry out*; *cry to* person; **for ~ing out loud** *int.*, (colloq.) expr. surprise or impatience); (of animal, esp. bird) make loud call. **4. ~ down,** disparage; **~ (out) for,** demand, ask for, (lit. or fig.; **~ for the moon,** ask for what is unattainable); **~ off,** withdraw from agreement, decline to keep promise; **~ up,** praise, extol; *cry* QUARTER¹, QUITS. [ME, f. OF *crier* f. L *quiritare* wail]

crȳ'er. Var. of CRIER.

crȳ'ing *a.* In vbl senses; (of evil) calling for notice, flagrant. [f. CRY² + -ING²]

crȳ'ō- *comb. form.* (Extreme) cold, as: **~bio'logy,** biology of materials below their normal operating temperature; **~gen,** freezing-mixture; **~ge'nic,** relating to very low temperatures; **~ge'nics,** branch of physics dealing with these and their effects; **~pump,** vacuum-pump using liquefied gases; **~stat,** apparatus for maintaining low temperature; **~sur'gery** (using local application of intense cold for anaesthesia or therapy). [f. Gk *kruos* frost + -O-]

crȳ'olite *n.* Lustrous mineral found in Greenland, consisting mainly of sodium-aluminium fluoride and used as source of aluminium. [f. as prec. + -LITE]

crȳpt *n.* Underground cell, vault, esp. one beneath church, used as burial-place etc. [ME, f. L f. Gk *kruptē* (*kruptos* hidden)]

crȳpt|ană'lȳsĭs *n.* Art of deciphering cryptograms by analysis; hence **~ă'nalȳst** *n.* [-IST (3)], **~ănalȳ'tic(al)** *adjs.* [f. CRYPTO- + ANALYSIS]

crȳ'pt|ĭc *a.* Secret, mystical; mysterious, enigmatic; obscure in meaning; (Zool., of coloration etc.) serving for concealment; hence **~ically** *adv.* [f. LL f. Gk *kruptikos* (as CRYPTO-; see -IC)]

crȳ'ptō *n.* (*pl.* **~s**). (colloq.) Person owing secret allegiance to a political creed etc.; (esp.) = *crypto-Communist.* [as foll.]

crȳ'ptō- *comb. form.* Concealed, secret; as: **~bra'nchiate,** having concealed gills; **~-Co'mmunist,** secret sympathizer with Communism; **~cry'stalline,** having crystalline structure visible only when magnified; **~zo'ic,** (Geol.) pre-Cambrian. [f. Gk *kruptos* hidden + -O-]

crȳ'ptogăm *n.* (Bot.) Plant that has no stamens or pistils, and therefore no proper flowers or seeds, e.g. fern, moss, fungus; hence **~ic** (-ă'm-), **crȳptŏ'gamous,** *adjs.* [f. F *cryptogame* f. mod. L *cryptogamae* (*plantae*) f. as CRYPTO- + Gk *gamos* marriage]

crȳ'ptogrăm *n.* Thing written in cipher; so **crȳptŏ'grapher, crȳptŏ'graphy,** *ns.*, **cryptogra'phic** *a.* [f. CRYPTO- + -GRAM]

crȳptomēr'ĭa *n.* Evergreen tree (*Cryptomeria japonica*) of the cypress type, Japanese cedar. [f. CRYPTO- + Gk *meros* part (because the seeds are enclosed by scales)]

crȳ'stal *n.* & *a.* **1.** *n.* Clear transparent icelike mineral; ROCK¹-*crystal.* **2.** Piece of this. **3. ~ ball,** globe-shaped crystal used for forecasting the future by **~-gazing,** concentrating one's gaze on a crystal to obtain a picture by hallucination etc.; **~ set,** simple form of receiving apparatus in early days of broadcasting using a crystal touching a metal wire as the rectifier. **4. ~ (glass),** highly transparent glass, flint glass; vessel etc. of this; glass over face of watch. **5.** (Chem. & Min.) Aggregation of molecules with definite internal structure and external form of solid enclosed by symmetrically arranged plane faces, solid with regular arrangement of atoms etc. **6.** *a.* Made of, like, clear as, crystal. [OE, f. OF *cristal* f. L f. Gk *krustallos* ice, crystal]

crȳ'stallīne *a.* Made of, clear as, like, crystal; (Chem. & Min.) having the structure and form of a crystal; **~ lens,** transparent body in membranous capsule behind iris of eye; hence **crȳstallĭ'nity** *n.* [ME, f. OF *cristallin* f. L f. Gk *krustallinos* (as prec.; see -INE²)]

crȳ'stallite *n.* Small crystal of no definite mineral; individual crystal or grain in metal etc.; region of cellulose etc. with crystal-like structure. [f. CRYSTAL + -ITE¹]

crȳ'stalliz|e, -is|e (-īz), *v.t.* & *i.* Form into crystals or (fig., often **~e out**) definite or permanent shape; **~ed fruit** (preserved by impregnation with sugar, and coated with sugar crystals); hence **~able** *a.*, **~a'tion** *n.* (**water of ~ation,** water forming essential part of structure of some crystals). [f. CRYSTAL + -IZE]

crȳstallŏ'graphȳ *n.* Science of crystal structure; hence **crȳstallŏ'grapher** *n.*, **crȳstallogra'phic** *a.* [f. Gk *krustallos* crystal + -O- + -GRAPHY]

crȳ'stalloid *a.* & *n.* Crystal-like; (body) with crystalline structure (cf. COLLOID). [f. CRYSTAL + -OID]

CS (sēē's) *n.* **~ gas,** irritant substance used as finely divided solid for riot-control etc. [f. B. B. *C*orson & R. W. *S*toughton, Amer. chemists]

C.S. *abbr.* ||chartered surveyor; Civil Service; Court of Session.

c/s *abbr.* cycles per second.

Cs *symb.* caesium.

csar'das, czar'das, (char'dahsh) *n.* (*pl.* same). Hungarian dance with slow start and quick wild finish. [f. Magyar *csárdás* (*csárda* inn)]

C.S.C. *abbr.* Civil Service Commission; ||Conspicuous Service Cross.

||**C.S.E.** *abbr.* Certificate of Secondary Education.

||**C.S.I.** *abbr.* Companion (of the Order) of the Star of India.

C.S.I.R.O. *abbr.* (Austral.) Commonwealth Scientific and Industrial Research Organization.

||**C.S.M.** *abbr.* Company Sergeant-Major.

***CST** *abbr.* Central Standard Time.

ct *abbr.* carat; cent.

||**C.T.C.** *abbr.* Cyclists' Touring Club.

ctē'noid (t-) *a.* & *n.* (Fish with scales or teeth) like a comb. [f. Gk *kteis ktenos* comb + -OID]

ctē'nophōre (t-) *n.* Marine animal of phylum Ctenophora, like jellyfish with ciliate swimming-organs. [f. mod. L *ctenophorus* (as prec., -PHORE)]

C.U. *abbr.* Cambridge University.

cu. *abbr.* cubic.

Cu *symb.* copper. [f. LL *cuprum*]

cŭb *n.* & *v.* (**-bb-**). **1.** *n.* Young of fox, bear, lion, tiger, etc.; young man lacking good manners etc.; *apprentice; **~ (reporter),** (colloq.) young or inexperienced newspaper reporter; **C~ (Scout),** member of junior branch of Scout Association; hence **~'hood** *n.* **2.** *v.t.* Bring forth (cubs, or abs.). **3.** *v.i.* Hunt fox-cubs. [16th c., of unkn. orig.]

Cūba li'bre (lē'brā) *n.* Drink of lime-juice and rum. [Amer. Sp., = free Cuba]

Cū'ban *n.* & *a.* (Native or inhabitant) of Cuba; **~ heel,** moderately high straight heel of shoe. [f. *Cuba* + -AN]

cŭ'bbȳ *n.* **~(-hole),** snug or confined place. [f. dial. *cub* stall, pen, of LG orig.]

cūbe *n.*, & *v.t.* **1.** *n.* Solid contained by six equal squares; block of anything so or similarly shaped; product of a number multiplied by its square (~ **root,** number which produces a given number when cubed). **2.** *v.t.* Find cube of (number); cut (food for cooking etc.) into small cubes. [F, or f. L f. Gk *kubos*]

cū'bĕb *n.* Pungent berry of a Javan shrub, *Piper cubeba,* crushed for use in medicated cigarettes. [ME, f. OF *cubebe, quibibe,* f. Rom. **cubeba* f. Arab. *kobāba, kubāba*]

cū'bĭc *a.* Cube-shaped; of three dimensions (~ **content** of solid, its volume expressed in cubic metres etc.; ~ **metre** etc., volume of a cube whose edge is one metre etc.); involving third and no higher power of unknown quantity or variable (*cubic equation*); (Cryst.) having three equal axes at right angles. [f. F *cubique* or f. L f. Gk *kubikos* (as CUBE; see -IC)]

cū'bĭcal *a.* Cube-shaped; hence ~LY² *adv.* [f. prec. + -AL]

cū'bĭcle *n.* Small separate sleeping-compartment; small partitioned space for dressing, private discussion, etc. [f. L *cubiculum* (*cubare* lie down; see -CULE)]

cū'bĭform *a.* Cube-shaped. [f. CUBE + -I- + -FORM]

cū'bĭsm *n.* Style of art (esp. painting) in which objects are so presented as to give the effect of an assemblage of geometrical figures; so **cū'bist** (3) *n.* [f. F *cubisme* (as CUBE, -ISM)]

cū'bĭt *n.* Ancient measure of length, approximately equal to length of forearm. [ME, f. L *cubitum* elbow, cubit]

cū'bĭtal *a.* Of the forearm; of the corresponding part in animals. [ME, f. L *cubitalis* (as prec.; see -AL)]

cū'boid *a.* & *n.* **1.** *a.* Cube-shaped, like a cube; ~ **bone** (of the tarsus). **2.** *n.* Cuboid bone; rectangular parallelepiped; hence **cūboi'dal** *a.* [f. mod. L *cuboides* f. Gk *kuboeidēs* (as CUBE; see -OID)]

cŭ'cking-stōōl *n.* (Hist.) Chair in which disorderly women etc. were ducked as punishment. [ME, f. obs. *cuck* defecate f. ON **kúka*]

cŭ'ckold *n.,* & *v.t.* **1.** *n.* Husband of adulteress; hence ~RY (2) *n.* **2.** *v.t.* Make cuckold of. [ME *cukeweld, cokewold,* f. AF **cucuald,* OF *cucuault,* pejorative form of *cucu* cuckoo]

cu'ckōō (kōō'-) *n.* & *pred. a.* **1.** *n.* Migratory bird with characteristic cry, depositing its eggs in nests of small birds (~ **in the nest,** unwanted intruder); bird of family Cuculidae, with or without this habit; simpleton. **2.** ~ **clock** (striking with sound like cuckoo's note); ~ **flower,** (1) meadow plant with pale lilac spring flower, lady-smock, (2) ragged robin; ~**-pint,** wild arum, lords-and-ladies; ~**-spit,** froth exuded by larvae of insects of family Cercopidae as a protection. **3.** *a.* (sl.) Crazy. [ME, f. OF *cucu,* imit.]

cū'cŭmber *n.* (Creeping plant with) long green fleshy fruit eaten in thin slices as salad; **cool as a** ~, quite cool, self-possessed; *~**-tree,** magnolia with fruit like small cucumber. [ME, f. OF *co(u)combre* f. L *cucumer*]

cūcur'bĭt *n.* = GOURD 1; hence ~A'CEOUS *a.* [f. L *cucurbita*]

cŭd *n.* Food that ruminating animal brings back from first stomach into mouth and chews at leisure; **chew the** ~, (fig.) reflect, ruminate. [OE *cwidu, cudu* what is chewed, corresp. to OHG *kuti, quiti* glue]

cŭ'dbear (-bār) *n.* Purple or violet dyeing-powder prepared from various lichens. [var. of *Cuthbert* Gordon, 18th-c. Sc. chemist, who patented it]

cŭ'ddl|e *v.* & *n.* **1.** *v.t.* Hug, embrace, fondle. **2.** *v.i.* Lie close and snug; nestle together. **3.** *n.* Hug, embrace. **4.** Hence ~ESOME¹ (-dels-), ~Y², *adjs.,* given to cuddling, tempting to cuddle. [16th c., perh. f. dial. *couth* snug + -LE 3]

cŭ'ddy̆ *n.* (Sc.) Donkey; stupid person. [perh. pet-form of *Cuthbert*]

cŭ'dgel *n.,* & *v.t.* (‖-ll-). **1.** *n.* Short thick stick used as weapon; **take up the** ~**s (for),** (fig.) defend vigorously. **2.** *v.t.* Beat with cudgel; ~ one's **brains,** think hard about a problem. [OE *cycgel,* of unkn. orig.]

cŭ'dweed *n.* Composite plant of genus *Gnaphalium,* with chaffy scales round flower-heads, given to cattle that have lost their cud. [f. CUD + WEED]

cūe¹ *n.,* & *v.t.* (~**'ing** *pr.* kū'ĭ-). **1.** *n.* Last words of speech in play, serving as signal to another actor to enter or speak; similar guide to other performer, e.g. singer or player; **on** ~, at the correct moment. **2.** Stimulus to perception etc.; signal for action; hint how to behave (**take** one's ~ **from,** follow the example or advice of); ~**-bid,** (Bridge) artificial bid to show particular card etc. in bidder's hand. **3.** *v.t.* Label so as to show proper choice; give cue to; ~ **in,** insert cue for, (fig.) give information to. [16th c., of unkn. orig.]

cūe² *n.* & *v.* **1.** *n.* Long straight tapering leather-tipped rod for striking ball in billiards etc.; ~**-ball** (that is to be struck with cue); hence ~'IST (3) (kū'ĭ-) *n.* **2.** *v.i.* & *t.* Use cue (on). [var. of QUEUE]

cuĕ'sta (kw-) *n.* (Geog.) Gentle slope, esp. ending in steep drop. [Sp., = slope, f. L *costa*; see COAST¹]

cŭff¹ *n.* End part of sleeve (**off the** ~, extempore, without preparation); separate band of linen worn round wrist; trouser turn-up; (in *pl.,* colloq.) handcuffs; ~**-link,** device of two joined buttons etc. to fasten sides of cuff together; hence (-)~ED² (-ft) *a.* [ME, of unkn. orig.]

cŭff² *v.t.,* & *n.* **1.** *v.t.* Strike with open hand. **2.** *n.* Such blow. [16th c., perh. imit.]

Cū'fĭc, Kū'fĭc, *a.* & *n.* (Of) early angular form of the Arabic alphabet found chiefly in decorative inscriptions. [f. *Cufa,* city S. of Baghdad + -IC]

cui bono? (kwē bō'nō) *n.* Question of who stood to gain (and therefore was likely to be responsible). [L, = to whom (is it) a benefit?]

cuĭră'ss (kw-) *n.* Body armour, breastplate and back-plate fastened together; device for artificial respiration. [ME, f. OF *cuirace,* **coirace* f. Rom. **coriacea* f. LL *coriaceus* (*corium* leather; see -ACEOUS)]

cuĭrassier' (kw-) *n.* Cavalry soldier wearing cuirass. [F (as prec.; see -IER)]

cuish. See CUISSE.

cuisi'ne (kwĭzē'n) *n.* (Style of) cooking. [F, f. L *coquina* (*coquere* cook)]

cuĭsse (kwĭs), **cuĭsh** (kw-), *n.* (Hist., usu. in *pl.*) Thigh armour. [ME, f. OF *cuisseaux* pl. of *cuissel* f. LL *coxale* (*coxa* hip)]

cŭ'l-de-săc (*or* kōō'-) *n.* (*pl.* **culs-** *pr.* same). Street, passage, etc., closed at one end; (Anat.) tube etc. open at one end only. [F, = sack-bottom]

-cūle, -cle, *suf.* forming (orig. dim.) *ns.* (*molecule, particle, article*). [f. F *-cule* or f. L *-culus -cula -culum*]

cŭ'lĭnary̆ *a.* Pertaining to a kitchen or cooking; fit for cooking (*culinary plants*). [f. L *culinarius* (*culina* kitchen; see -ARY¹)]

cŭll *v.t.,* & *n.* **1.** *v.t.* Pick (flower etc.); select; select from flock etc. and kill (surplus animals etc.). **2.** *n.* Act of culling; culled animal. [ME, f. OF *coillier* etc., f. Rom. **colgere* f. L *colligere* COLLECT²]

cŭ'llĕt *n.* Refuse glass added to new material in glass-making; broken glass. [var. of COLLET]

cŭ'lly̆ *n.* (sl.) Mate, pal. [17th c.; orig. unkn.]

cŭlm¹ *n.* Coal-dust (esp. of anthracite); (Geol.)

strata under coal measures in Europe. [ME, prob. rel. to COAL]

cŭlm[2] *n.* (Bot.) Stem of plant (esp. of grasses); so **~ĭ'**FEROUS *a.* [f. L *culmus* stalk]

cŭ'lminant *a.* At or forming the top; (Astron.) on the meridian. [f. as foll. + -ANT]

cŭ'lmin|āte *v.i.* Reach its highest point (*in*; lit. or fig.); (Astron.) be on the meridian; hence ~A'TION *n.* [f. LL *culminare* (*culmen* summit) + -ATE[3]]

cūlŏ'tte *n.* (usu. in *pl.*, pr. same). Women's trousers cut to resemble skirt. [F, = knee--breeches]

cŭ'lpab|le *a.* Blameworthy (*culpable negligence*; *hold him culpable*); hence **cŭlp**ABI'LITY, **~le**NESS (-beln-), *ns.*, ~LY[2] *adv.* [ME f. OF *coupable* f. L *culpabilis* (*culpare* f. *culpa* blame; see -ABLE)]

cŭ'lprĭt *n.* Person accused of or guilty of offence. [17th c.; orig. in formula *Culprit, how will you be tried?*, said by Clerk of Crown to prisoner pleading Not Guilty; said to be abbr. of AF *Culpable: prest d'averrer* etc. (You are) guilty: (I am) ready to prove etc.]

cŭlt *n.* System of religious worship; devotion or homage to person or thing (esp. derog. of transient fad); hence ~'IC *a.*, ~'ISM (3), ~'IST (2), *ns.* [f. F *culte* or f. L *cultus* worship (*colere cult-* inhabit, till, worship)]

cŭ'ltĭvar *n.* (Bot.) Variety produced by cultivation. [f. foll. + VARIETY]

cŭ'ltĭv|āte *v.t.* Prepare and use (soil) for crops; produce (crops) by tillage; culture (bacteria etc.); prepare (ground) with cultivator; (fig., esp. in *p.p.*) improve, develop, (person, mind, manners); pay attention to, cherish, (faculty, art, person, his acquaintance); so ~A'TION *n.* [f. med. L *cultivare* f. *cultiva* (*terra*) arable (land); see CULT, -IVE, -ATE[3]]

cŭ'ltĭvātor *n.* One who cultivates; implement or machine for breaking up ground and uprooting weeds. [f. prec. + -OR]

cŭ'lture *n.*, & *v.t.* **1.** *n.* Tillage of the soil; rearing, production, (of bees, oysters, fish, silk, bacteria); quantity of bacteria thus produced. **2.** Improvement by (mental or physical) training; intellectual development; particular form, stage, or type of intellectual development or civilization (**the two ~s,** literature and science); **~ vulture,** (joc.) person eager to acquire culture. **3.** Hence **cŭ'ltur**AL (-cher-) *a.*, (esp.) relating to culture of mind or manners. **4.** *v.t.* Cultivate (bacteria etc., or fig.), esp. in *p.p.* pr. -cherd; **~d pearl** (formed by oyster after insertion of suitable foreign body). [ME f. F, or f. L *cultura* (as CULT; see -URE); v. f. obs. F *culturer* or f. med. L *culturare*]

cŭ'ltus *n.* System of religious worship, cult. [L; see CULT]

cŭ'lverĭn *n.* (Hist.) Large cannon; small fire-arm. [ME, f. OF *coulevrine* (*couleuvre* snake f. Rom. **colobra* f. L *colubra*; see -INE[1])]

cŭ'lvert *n.* Channel or conduit carrying water across under road, canal, etc.; channel for electric cable. [18th c., of unkn. orig.]

cŭm *prep.* With; **~ dividend,** including dividend about to be paid; (indicating combined nature or function) *laboratory-cum-workshop*, *religious--cum-philosophical*; ||(in names of combined parishes) *Chorlton-cum-Hardy*. [L]

Cumb. *abbr.* Cumberland (former county in England).

cŭ'mber *v.t.*, & *n.* (literary). **1.** *v.t.* Hamper, hinder; burden (*with*). **2.** *n.* Hindrance, obstruction; burden. [ME, prob. f. ENCUMBER]

cŭ'mbersome *a.* Unwieldy, clumsy; hence ~LY[2] (-mlĭ) *adv.*, ~NESS (-mn-) *n.* [ME, f. prec. + -SOME[1]]

Cŭ'mbrĭan *a.* & *n.* (Native) of Cumberland or of the ancient British kingdom or modern county of Cumbria. [f. med. L *Cumbria* f. W *Cymry* Welshmen + -AN]

cŭ'mbrous *a.* = CUMBERSOME; hence ~LY[2] *adv.*, ~NESS *n.* [f. CUMBER + -OUS]

cum grano salis (kŭm grahnō sah'lĭs) *adv.* = *with a grain of* SALT. [L]

cŭ'mĭn, cŭ'mmĭn, *n.* Umbelliferous plant (*Cuminum cyminum*) like fennel, with aromatic seeds. [ME, f. OF *cumin, comin* f. L f. Gk *kuminon*, prob. of Semitic orig.]

cŭ'mmerbŭnd *n.* Waist sash. [f. Hindi & Pers. *kamar-band* loin-band]

cŭ'mmĭn. See CUMIN.

cŭ'mquat, kŭ'mquat, (-ŏt) *n.* Plum-sized orange-like fruit with sweet rind and acid pulp, used in preserves. [Cantonese dial. form of Chin. *kin kü* golden orange]

cū'mūlate[1] *a.* Heaped up, massed. [as foll.; see -ATE[2]]

cū'mūl|āte[2] *v.t.* & *i.* Accumulate; combine (catalogue entries etc.); so ~A'TION *n.* [f. L *cumulare* (*cumulus* heap) + -ATE[3]]

cū'mūlatĭve *a.* Tending to accumulate; increasing in force etc. by successive additions (*cumulative evidence, poison*); formed by successive additions; (of shares) entitling holder to arrears of interest before any other distribution is made; **~ voting,** system in which each voter has as many votes as there are representatives, and may give all to one candidate; hence ~LY[2] (-vlĭ) *adv.*, ~NESS (-vn-) *n.* [f. as prec. + -IVE]

cū'mūl|us *n.* (*pl.* **~i** *pr.* -ī). Heap; set of rounded masses of cloud heaped on each other and having horizontal base; hence ~O- *comb. form*, ~OUS *a.* [L]

cū'nėate *a.* Wedge-shaped. [f. L *cuneus* wedge + -ATE[2]]

cū'nėĭform (*or* kū'nĭf-) *a.* & *n.* **1.** *a.* Wedge--shaped. **2.** *n.* Writing in cuneiform impressed strokes usu. in clay in ancient inscriptions of Assyria, Persia, etc. [f. F *cunéiforme* or mod. L *cuneiformis* f. L *cuneus* wedge; see -FORM]

cŭ'njėvoi *n.* (Austral.) Green arum; sea-squirt. [Aboriginal]

cŭnnĭlĭ'ngus (-ngg-), **-lĭ'nctus,** *n.* Oral stimulation of vulva or clitoris. [L (*cunnus* vulva, *lingere* lick)]

cŭ'nnĭng[1] *n.* Artfulness, craft; (arch.) ability, dexterity. [ME, perh. f. ON *kunnandi* knowledge (*kunna* know; cf. CAN[2])]

cŭ'nnĭng[2] *a.* (~er, ~est). Artful, crafty; (arch.) skilful, ingenious; *attractively quaint, small, etc.; hence ~LY[2] *adv.* [ME, f. ON *kunnandi* knowing (as prec.)]

cŭnt *n.* (vulg.) Female genitals; (derog.) person, esp. woman. [ME, = ON *kunta*, MLG, MDu. *kunte* f. Gmc **kuntōn*]

cŭp[1] *n.* **1.** Drinking-vessel, with or without handle and stem (*teacup, coffee-cup*); ornamental vessel as prize for race etc. (**C~ Final,** (Footb. etc.) final match in competition for cup; *cup--*TIE[2]); small rounded open container; part of brassière to contain or support one breast. **2.** Cupful (**~ of tea,** (colloq., fig.) person or thing of specified kind; one's **~ of tea,** (colloq.) what interests or suits one); wine, cider, etc., with various flavourings; chalice used, wine taken, at Eucharist; fate, experience, (*a bitter cup*; **his ~ was full,** his happiness or misery was complete). **3. Between ~ and lip,** just before attainment; **in** one's **~s,** while (getting) drunk. **4.** Rounded cavity, esp. calyx of flower, socket of bone, etc. **5. ~'bearer,** one who serves wine, esp. officer of royal or noble household; **~-cake** (baked in paper cup or from ingredients measured in cupfuls); **~-moss,** lichen with cup-shaped processes arising from thallus.

6. Hence ~'FUL 2 *n.*, (*esp.) half-pint or 8-ounce measure in cookery. [OE *cuppe* f. med. L *cuppa* cup, prob. different. f. L *cupa* tub]

cŭp^2 *v.t.* (**-pp-**). Take or hold as in a cup; make cup-shaped; (Hist.) bleed (person) by means of a **~'ping-glass,** in which partial vacuum is formed by heating. [ME, f. prec.]

C.U.P. *abbr.* Cambridge University Press.

cŭ'pboard (kŭ'berd) *n.* Shelved recess or cabinet for crockery, provisions, etc.; **~ love** (simulated for sake of what one can get by it); SKELETON *in the cupboard.* [ME, f. CUP^1 + BOARD^1]

cū'pel *n.*, & *v.t.* (‖**-ll-**). **1.** *n.* Small flat circular vessel used in assaying gold or silver in the presence of lead. **2.** *v.t.* Assay or refine in cupel; hence **~LA'TION** *n.* [f. F *coupelle* f. LL *cupella* dim. of *cupa*; see CUP^1]

Cū'pĭd *n.* Roman god of love; representation of him as beautiful naked winged boy with bow and arrows; **~'s bow,** (upper edge of) upper lip etc., shaped like double-curved bow carried by Cupid. [ME, f. L *Cupido* (*cupere* desire)]

cūpĭ'dĭtў *n.* Greed for gain. [ME, f. OF *cupidité* or f. L *cupiditas* (*cupidus* desirous; see **-ITY**)]

cū'pola *n.* Small rounded dome forming or adorning roof; ceiling of dome; **~(-furnace)**, furnace for melting metals; revolving dome protecting mounted guns on warship. [It., f. LL *cupula* dim. of *cupa* cask]

cŭ'ppa, cŭ'pper, *n.* (colloq.) Cup of; cup of tea. [corrupt.]

cūprammō'nĭum *n.* Complex ion of copper and ammonium, solutions of which dissolve cellulose. [f. LL *cuprum* copper + AMMONIUM]

cū'prĕous *a.* Of or like copper. [f. LL *cupreus* (*cuprum* copper) + -OUS]

cū'prĭc *a.* Of copper; so **cūprĭ'**FEROUS, **cū'pr**OUS, *adjs.* [f. LL *cuprum* + -IC 1]

cū'prō- *comb. form.* Copper, as: **~-ni'ckel,** alloy of copper and nickel, esp. in proportions 3:1 as used in British 'silver' coins. [f. as prec. + -O-]

cū'pūle *n.* (Bot. & Zool.) Cup-shaped organ, receptacle, etc. [f. LL *cupula* (see CUPOLA)]

cûr *n.* Worthless, low-bred, or snappish dog; surly, ill-bred, or cowardly fellow. [ME, prob. orig. in *cur-dog*, perh. f. ON *kurr* grumbling]

cûr'able. See CURE^2.

cûr'açao, cûr'açoa, (-sō) *n.* (*pl.* **~s**). Liqueur of spirits flavoured with peel of bitter oranges. [f. F *Curaçao,* name of Caribbean island producing these oranges]

cûr'acў *n.* Curate's office; (Hist.) benefice of PERPETUAL curate. [f. CURATE; see **-ACY**]

cūrâr'ē *n.* Resinous bitter substance from S. Amer. plants of genus *Strychnos,* paralysing the motor nerves, used by Indians to poison arrows. [f. Carib]

cûr'ar|ine (-ēn) *n.* Alkaloid derived from curare and used to relax muscles; hence **~IZE** (5) *v.t.* [f. prec. + -INE^5]

cûr'assow (-ō) *n.* Turkey-like bird of Central and S. America, of family Cracidae. [anglicized f. CURAÇAO]

cûr'ate *n.* Assistant to parish priest; (arch.) ecclesiastical pastor; **~-in-char'ge,** clergyman appointed to take charge of parish during incapacity or suspension of incumbent; **~'s egg,** thing partly good and partly bad; PERPETUAL *curate.* [ME, f. med. L *curatus* f. L *cura* CURE^1]

cûr'ative *a.* & *n.* (Thing) tending to cure (esp. disease). [F *curatif -ive*, f. med. L *curativus* f. L *curare* CURE^2; see **-ATIVE**]

cūrā'tor *n.* Person in charge, manager; keeper or custodian of museum; ‖member of board managing property or having general superintendence in University; (Sc. Law) guardian of minor etc.; hence **cūratôr'**IAL *a.*, **~SHIP** *n.* [ME, f. AF *curatour* (OF *-eur*) or f. L *curator* (as prec.; see -OR)]

cûrb *n.*, & *v.t.* **1.** *n.* Chain or strap passing under lower jaw of horse, used as a check; (fig.) check, restraint; hard swelling on horse's leg. **2.** Frame round top of well; timber or iron plate round edge of circular structure; fender round hearth; = KERB; **~ roof** (of which each face has two slopes, the lower one steeper). **3.** *v.t.* Put curb on (horse); (fig.) restrain. [ME, f. OF *courber* f. L *curvare* bend, CURVE^1]

cûr'cūma *n.* Turmeric, substance used in curry--powder, as test for alkalis (*curcuma paper*), etc.; tuberous plant of genus *Curcuma,* yielding this and other commercial substances. [med. or mod. L, f. Arab. *kurkum* saffron, f. Skr. *kuṅkuma*^{m}]

cûrd *n.* Coagulated substance formed (naturally or artificially) by action of acids on milk, and made into cheese or eaten as food (often in *pl.*; **~s and whey,** milk thus treated); fatty substance found between flakes of boiled salmon flesh; edible head of cauliflower etc.; **~ soap** (white, of tallow and soda); hence **~'Y**^{2} *a.* [ME *crud(de)*, *crod(de)*, of unkn. orig.]

cûr'dle *v.t.* & *i.* Congeal, form into curd; (fig.) **~ the blood** (with horror). [frequent. f. *curd* v. (f. prec.) + -LE 3]

cūre^1 *n.* Thing that cures (*no cure for this disease*); restoration to health; course of medical or other treatment (REST^2-*cure*), success with this; spiritual charge (*cure of souls*); (degree of) vulcanization of rubber or curing of plastic. [ME f. OF, f. L *cura* care]

cūre^2 *v.* **1.** *v.t.* Restore to health, relieve (person *of* disease), (lit. or fig.; **~-all,** panacea); eliminate (an evil); preserve (meat, fruit, tobacco) by salting, drying, etc.; harden (concrete or plastic); vulcanize (rubber); hence **cûr'**ABLE *a.* **2.** *v.i.* Effect a cure; undergo process of curing. [ME, f. OF *curer* f. L *curare* take care of (*cura* care)]

curé (kūr'ā) *n.* Parish priest in France etc. [F, f. med. L *curatus*; see CURATE]

cūrĕ'ttage (*or* -ah'zh) *n.* Use of or operation with curette. [F (as foll.; see **-AGE**)]

cūrĕ'tte *n.* & *v.* **1.** *n.* Surgeon's small scraping--instrument. **2.** *v.t.* & *i.* Clean or scrape with curette. [F, f. *curer* cleanse (CURE^2)]

cûr'few *n.* **1.** (Hist.) Medieval regulation for extinction of fires at fixed hour in evening; hour for this; bell announcing it; ringing of bell at fixed evening hour. **2.** Signal or time after which persons must remain indoors until next day. [ME, f. AF *coeverfu*, OF *cuevrefeu*, f. st. of *couvrir* COVER^1 + *feu* fire]

Cûr'ĭ|a *n.* Papal court, government departments of Vatican; hence **~AL** *a.* [L, orig. division of ancient Roman tribe, senate-house at Rome, feudal court of justice]

cûr'ĭe *n.* Unit of radioactivity, corresp. to $3{\cdot}7 \times 10^{10}$ disintegrations per second; quantity of radioactive substance having this activity. [f. P. *Curie*, Fr. scientist d. 1906]

cûr'ĭō *n.* (*pl.* **~s**). Rare or unusual object or person. [19th-c. abbr. of CURIOSITY]

cūrĭō'sa *n. pl.* Curiosities; erotic or pornographic books. [neut. pl. of L *curiosus*; see CURIOUS]

cūrĭŏ'sĭtў *n.* Desire to know; inquisitiveness; strangeness; strange or rare object. [ME, f. OF *curiouseté* f. L *curiositas -tatis* (as foll.; see **-ITY**)]

cûr'ĭous *a.* **1.** Eager to learn; inquisitive. **2.** Strange, surprising, odd; (euphem. of books etc.) erotic, pornographic. **3.** Hence **~LY**^{2} *adv.*, **~NESS** *n.* [ME, f. OF *curios* f. L *curiosus* careful (*cura* care; see -IOUS)]

cûr'ĭum *n.* (Chem.) Artificially made transuranic radioactive metallic element. [f. M. *Curie* d.

1934 and P. *Curie* d. 1906, Fr. scientists + -IUM]

cūrl[1] *n.* **1.** Coiled lock of hair; **~-paper** (used for twisting hair into curls). **2.** Anything spiral or curved inwards. **3.** Act of curling (**~ of the lip,** expressing scorn); state of being curled (*keep the hair in curl*; **out of ~,** (fig.) lacking energy); disease of plants in which leaves are curled up. [f. foll.]

cūrl[2] *v.* **1.** *v.t.* & *i.* Bend or coil (*up*) into spiral shape; (cause to) form curls; **~** person's **hair** or **make his hair ~,** (fig.) horrify him. **2.** *v.i.* (Of smoke etc.) move in spiral form; play at curling; **~ up,** (fig.) writhe with horror, shame, etc., (colloq.) lie or sit with knees drawn up, (sl.) collapse. [ME; earliest form *crolled, crulled,* f. obs. adj. *crolle, crulle* curly, f. MDu. *krul*]

cūr'ler *n.* In vbl senses; pin, clip, etc., for curling the hair. [f. prec. + -ER[1]]

cūr'lew *n.* Wading bird of genus *Numenius*, with long slender curved bill. [ME, f. OF *courlieu, courlis* orig. imit., but assim. to OF *courliu* courier (*courre* run, *lieu* place)]

cūr'lĭcūe *n.* Decorative curl or twist. [f. CURLY + CUE[2] (= pigtail) or Q]

cūr'lĭng *n.* In vbl senses; game played on ice in Scotland and elsewhere with large flat round stones; **~-iron, ~-pins, ~-tongs,** (for use in curling the hair). [f. CURL[2] + -ING[1]]

cūr'l|ў *a.* Having, or arranged in, curls; *curly* KALE; hence **~ĭness** *n.* [f. CURL[1] + -Y[2]]

cūrmŭ'dgeon (-ŭ'jon) *n.* Churlish or miserly fellow; hence **~LY**[1] *a.* [16th c.; orig. unkn.]

cŭ'rrach, cŭ'rragh, (-r*a*) *n.* (Ir.) Coracle. [Ir.; cf. CORACLE]

cŭ'rrajŏng. Var. of KURRAJONG.

cŭ'rrant *n.* Dried fruit of seedless variety of grape grown in the Levant, much used in cookery; (fruit of) plant of genus *Ribes* (**red, white, black, ~; flowering ~,** N. Amer. species grown for ornament); *currant* TOMATO. [ME, *raysons of coraunce* f. AF, = grapes of Corinth (orig. source)]

cŭ'rrawŏng *n.* (Austral.) Small crowlike bird of genus *Strepera*, with resonant call. [Aboriginal]

cŭ'rrencў *n.* Time during which a thing is current; (of money) circulation; money in actual use in a country (HARD *currency*, SOFT *currency*); other commodity used as medium of exchange; prevalence (of words, ideas, reports). [f. foll.; see -ENCY]

cŭ'rrent[1] *a.* (Of money, opinion, rumour, word) in general circulation or use (*current* ACCOUNT[2]; **pass ~,** be generally accepted as true or genuine); (of time) now passing (*current week, month*); belonging to the current time (*current events*; *the current issue of this journal*); hence **~LY**[2] *adv.*, (esp.) at the present time. [ME, f. OF *corant*, part. of *courre* f. L *currere* run; see -ENT]

cŭ'rrent[2] *n.* Running stream; water, air, etc., moving in given direction; course, tendency, (of events, opinions, etc.); movement of electrically charged particles, quantity representing intensity of such movement. [ME, f. OF *corant* n. (as prec.)]

cŭ'rrĭcle *n.* (Hist.) Light open two-wheeled carriage (usu. with two horses abreast). [f. L *curriculum* (see foll.)]

cŭrrĭ'cŭl|um *n.* (*pl.* **~a**). Course (of study); **~*um vitae*** (-vē'tī), brief account of one's previous career; hence **~AR**[1] *a.* [L, = course, race-chariot (*currere* run); *vitae* of life]

cŭ'rrĭer *n.* One who dresses and colours tanned leather. [ME f. OF *corier*, f. L *coriarius* (*corium* leather; see -ARY[1], -ER[2])]

cūr'rĭsh *a.* Like a cur; snappish; ignoble; hence **~LY**[2] *adv.*, **~NESS** *n.* [f. CUR + -ISH[1]]

cŭ'rrў[1] *n.*, & *v.t.* **1.** *n.* Dish of meat, fish, eggs, etc., cooked with crushed spices and turmeric; **~-powder** etc., preparation of spices etc. for making curry. **2.** *v.t.* Prepare or flavour with curry-powder. [f. Tamil *kari* sauce]

cŭ'rrў[2] *v.t.* Rub down or comb (horse etc.) with **~-comb;** treat (tanned leather) to improve its properties; thrash; **~ favour** [orig. *favel* f. OF *fauvel* chestnut horse], ingratiate oneself (*with* person) by flattery etc. [ME, f. OF *correier* f. Rom. **conredare* f. Gmc **garædhjan* (as Y-, READY)]

cūrse[1] *n.* Utterance of deity or of person invoking deity, consigning person or thing to destruction, divine vengeance, etc. (*curses come home to* ROOST[1]; **under a ~,** feeling or liable to its effects); sentence of excommunication; profane oath, imprecation; accursed object; evil inflicted in response to a curse; great evil, bane; **the ~,** (colloq.) menstruation. [OE *curs*, of unkn. orig.]

cūrse[2] *v.* **1.** *v.t.* Utter curse against; (as oath) **~ it, you,** (= *may God curse*); excommunicate; (esp. in *pass.*) afflict *with.* **2.** *v.i.* Utter curses. [OE *cursian* (as prec.)]

cūr'sėd, (arch.) **cūrst,** *a.* In vbl senses; damnable, abominable; hence **~LY**[2] *adv.*, **~NESS** *n.* [ME, p.p. of prec.]

cūr'sĭve *a.* & *n.* (Writing) done with joined characters, opp. *block* or *uncial.* [f. med. L (*scriptura*) *cursiva* f. L *currere curs-* run; see -IVE]

cūr'sor *n.* Transparent slide engraved with hair-line and forming part of slide-rule. [L, = runner (as prec.; see -OR)]

cūrsōr'ĭal *a.* Having limbs adapted for running (*cursorial birds* etc.). [f. as prec. + -IAL]

cūr'sor|ў *a.* Hasty, hurried, (*cursory reader, inspection*); hence **~ĭLY**[2] *adv.*, **~ĭNESS** *n.* [f. L *cursorius* of a runner (as CURSOR; see -ORY)]

cūrt *a.* Discourteously brief; terse, concise; hence **~'LY**[2] *adv.*, **~'NESS** *n.* [f. L *curtus* cut short, abridged]

cūrtai'l *v.t.* Cut short (lit. or fig.); deprive *of*; hence **~MENT** *n.* [f. obs. *curtal* horse with docked tail f. F *courtault* (*court* short f. L *curtus*); assim. to *tail*]

cūr'tain (-t*a*n) *n.*, & *v.t.* **1.** *n.* Suspended cloth used as screen; = IRON[1] *curtain* or similar barrier to passage of information etc.; screen separating stage of theatre from auditorium, raised at start of action and lowered at end (SAFETY *curtain*); rise of curtain at start of play etc.; fall of curtain at end of scene; = *curtain-call*; (in *pl.*, sl.) the end. **2.** **~(-wall),** plain wall of fortified place, connecting two towers etc., piece of plain wall not supporting a roof; partition or cover. **3.** **~-call,** audience's summons to actor(s) to take bow after fall of curtain; **~-fire,** (Mil.) barrage; **~ lecture,** wife's private reproof to husband, orig. behind bed-curtains; **~-raiser,** short opening theatre-piece, (fig.) preliminary event. **4.** *v.t.* Furnish, cover, shut *off*, with curtain(s). [ME f. OF *cortine*, f. LL *cortina* transl. Gk *aulaia* (*aulē* court)]

cūrtā'na (*or* -ah'-) *n.* Unpointed sword borne before English sovereign at Coronation, as emblem of mercy. [ME, f. AL *curtana* (*spatha* sword), f. AF *curtain*, OF *cortain* name of Roland's similar sword (*cort* short f. as CURT)]

cūr'tĭlage *n.* Area attached to dwelling-house as part of its enclosure. [ME f. AF; OF *co(u)rtillage* (*co(u)rtil* small court f. *cort* COURT[1]; see -AGE)]

cūr'tsў, cūr'tsey, *n.*, & *v.i.* **1.** *n.* Woman's or girl's salutation made by bending knees and lowering body (*make* or *drop a curtsy*). **2.** *v.i.* Make curtsy (*to* person). [var. of COURTESY]

cūr'ule (-ōōl) *a.* (Rom. Ant.) **~ chair,** one shaped like camp-stool, inlaid with ivory; **~ magistrate,** one entitled to this. [f. L *curulis* f. *currus* chariot (*currere* run)]

cūrvā′ceous (-shus) *a.* (colloq.) Having many curves (esp. of shapely female figure). [f. CURVE[2] + -ACEOUS]
cūr′vature *n.* Curving; curved form; (Geom.) deviation of curve from straight line, or of curved surface from plane, quantity expressing this. [OF, f. L *curvatura* (as foll.; see -URE)]
cūrve[1] *v.t.* & *i.* Bend or shape so as to form a curve. [f. L *curvare* (as foll.)]
cūrve[2] *n.* Line of which no part is straight; surface of which no part is plane; curved form or thing; line showing diagrammatically a continuous variation of quantity, force, etc., graph; (Baseball) ball caused to deviate by pitcher's spin. [orig. *curve line*; *curve* a. f. L *curvus* bent]
cūrvě′t *n.*, & *v.i.* (**-tt-** *or* **-t-**). **1.** *n.* Horse's leap with forelegs raised together and hind legs raised with spring before forelegs reach ground. **2.** *v.i.* (Of horse or rider) make curvet. [f. It. *corvetta* dim. of *corva* curve, f. as prec.]
cūr′vi- *comb. form.* Curved, as: **~cau′date, ~co′state, ~de′ntate, ~ro′stral,** with curved tail, ribs, teeth, beak; **~fo′liate,** with leaves bent back; **~form,** of curved shape. [f. L *curvus* curved + -I-]
cūrvĭlĭ′nėar *a.* Contained by or consisting of curved line(s); hence **~**LY[2] *adv.* [f. prec. after *rectilinear*]
cŭ′scus[1] *n.* Aromatic fibrous root of Indian grass of genus *Andropogon*, used for fans etc. [f. Pers. *kaškaš* poppy]
cŭ′scus[2] *n.* Spotted phalanger of New Guinea and N. Australia. [f. native name]
cū′sěc *n.* (Flow of) one cubic foot (esp. of water) per second. [abbr.]
cush (ko͝osh) *n.* (colloq.) Cushion (esp. Bill.). [abbr.]
cŭ′shat *n.* (Sc.) Wood-pigeon, ring-dove. [OE *cūscute* etc., of unkn. orig.]
cu′sh-cush (ko͞o′shko͞osh) *n.* S. Amer. species of yam (*Dioscorea trifida*). [native name]
cu′shion[1] (ko͝o′shon) *n.* **1.** Mass of soft material, esp. stuffed into bag of cloth, silk, etc., for sitting, kneeling, reclining, on; PIN[1]*cushion.* **2.** Means of protection against shock; elastic lining of sides of billiard table, from which ball rebounds; body of air supporting hovercraft etc.; steam left in cylinders as buffer to piston; fleshy part of buttock (of pig etc.); frog of horse's hoof. **3.** Hence **~**Y[2] *a.* [ME, f. OF *co(i)ssin, cu(i)ssin,* f. Gallo-Rom. f. L *culcita* mattress, cushion]
cu′shion[2] (ko͝o′shon) *v.t.* Furnish or protect with cushions (lit. or fig.); mitigate effects of (as) with cushion (*cushion the blow*); quietly suppress; (Bill.) place, leave, rebound, (ball) against cushion. [f. prec.]
Cūshĭ′tĭc *a.* & *n.* (Of) group of E. Afr. languages of Hamitic type. [f. *Cush* ancient country in Nile valley + -ITE[1] (1) + -IC]
cu′shy̆ (ko͝o′-) *a.* (colloq.) (Of a post, task, etc.) easy, pleasant, comfortable. [Anglo-Ind., f. Hindi *khūsh* pleasant]
cŭsp *n.* Apex, peak; horn of crescent moon etc.; (Geom.) point at which two parts of a curve meet from same direction with common tangent and terminate; (Archit.) projecting point between small arcs in Gothic tracery; (Bot.) pointed end, esp. of leaf; (Astrol.) initial point of house; hence **~**ED[2] (-pt) *a.* [f. L *cuspis -idis* point, apex]
cŭ′spāte *a.* Cusp-shaped. [f. prec. + -ATE[2]]
cŭ′spĭd|al *a.* Of (the nature of) a cusp; so **~**ATE[2] *a.* [f. as CUSP + -AL]
***cŭ′spĭdŏr** *n.* Spittoon. [Port., = spitter (*cuspir* spit f. L *conspuere*; see -OR)]
cŭss *n.* & *v.* (colloq.) Curse (TINKER's *cuss*; ***~-word,** swear-word); (usu. derog.) person, creature. [vulg. pr. of CURSE[1,2]]
cŭ′ssėd *a.* (colloq.) Cursed; perverse, obstinate; hence **~**LY[2] *adv.*, **~**NESS *n.* [as prec. f. CURSED]
cŭ′stard *n.* **1.** Baked usu. sweetened mixture of eggs and milk. **2.** Sauce made of cooked sweetened mixture of milk with eggs or cornflour etc.; **~ powder,** preparation of cornflour etc. for making this. **3. ~-apple,** W. Ind. fruit with custard-like pulp; **~-pie,** (pie containing custard freq. thrown in) slapstick comedy acting. [ME, earlier *crusta(r)de* f. AF **crustade* (*cruste,* OF *crouste* CRUST; see -ADE)]
cŭstō′dĭal *a.* Relating to custody. [f. L *custodia* CUSTODY + -AL]
cŭstō′dĭan *n.* Guardian, keeper, esp. of public building etc. [f. foll. + -AN, after *guardian*]
cŭ′stody̆ *n.* Guardianship, care, (*parent has custody of child*; *child is in the custody of the father*); imprisonment (**take into ~,** arrest). [f. L *custodia* (*custos -odis* guardian; see -Y[1])]
cŭ′stom *n.* **1.** Usual way of behaving or acting; (Law) established usage having the force of law. **2.** (in *pl.*) Duty levied upon imports from foreign countries, (*C~s*) government department dealing with this; **~-house,** office (esp. in seaport) at which customs are collected; **~s union,** group of States with agreed common tariff, and usu. free trade with each other. **3.** Business patronage, regular dealings; regular customers; ***~ clothes** etc. (made to customer's order; so **~-built, -made,** etc.). [ME and OF *custume* f. Rom. **costumne* for **costudne* f. L *consuetudo -dinis*; see CONSUETUDE]
cŭ′stomar|y̆ *a.* & *n.* **1.** *a.* Usual; (Law) subject to or held by custom (of the manor etc.); hence **~**ĭLY[2] *adv.*, **~**ĭNESS *n.* **2.** *n.* Book etc. listing customs of a community. [f. med. L *custumarius* (*custuma* f. AF *custume* f. as prec.; see -ARY[1])]
cŭ′stomer *n.* One who buys, esp. regularly from one seller; account-holder of bank; person with whom one is concerned; (colloq.) **queer, awkward,** etc., **~** (person to deal with). [ME, f. AF *custumer* f. as prec., or f. CUSTOM + -ER[1]]
cŭ′stomīze, -ise (-iz), *v.t.* Make to order or according to individual requirements. [f. CUSTOM + -IZE]
cŭt[1] *n.* **1.** Act of cutting; stroke or blow with knife, sword, whip, etc.; **~ and thrust,** use of both edge and point of sword, (fig.) lively interchange of argument etc. **2.** Act or utterance that wounds the feelings; (Cricket, Lawn Tennis, Croquet, etc.) stroke made by cutting. **3.** Refusal to recognize a person. **4.** Way thing is cut; fashion, style, (of clothes, hair, etc.; *the cut of his* JIB[1]); **a ~ above,** noticeably superior to. **5.** Wound made by cutting; railway cutting; new channel made for river; excision of part of play, film, book, etc.; **short ~,** crossing that shortens the distance (lit. or fig.); =WOOD*cut*; piece (esp. of meat) cut off; reduction (in wages, prices, time, services, etc.), cessation (of power supply etc.); (sl.) commission, share of profits, etc. [ME, f. foll.]
cŭt[2] *v.* (**-tt-; cut**). **1.** *v.t.* & *i.* Penetrate, wound, with sharp-edged thing (lit. or fig.; *the knife cut his finger, he cut his finger with a knife*; *knife* **will not ~,** is blunt; *action* **~s both ways,** has good and bad effects, *argument* **~s both ways,** supports both sides; *a cutting wind*; *a cutting retort*; *it cut him to the heart*). **2.** *v.t.* Divide with knife, axe, etc. *in two, in* or *into* or *to pieces* (**~ no ice,** (sl.) have no influence or importance, achieve little or nothing; **~ the knot,** (fig.) solve problem in irregular but efficient way; cf. GORDIAN); meet and cross (*line cuts circle at two points*); (fig.) renounce (a connection), refuse to recognize (a person); detach by cutting, harvest (wheat etc.),

divide stalk for removal of (flower); castrate; carve (meat); divide (pack of cards, or abs.) to select dealer etc., select (card) thus; hit (ball, or abs.) with chopping motion. **3.** *v.i.* Cross, intersect, (*two lines cut*); pass *through*, *across*, etc., esp. as shorter way (~ **across,** (fig.) transcend (normal limitations); *cut* LOOSE¹); (sl.) run (~ **and run,** run away); (Cricket, of ball) turn sharply on pitching. **4.** *v.t.* Reduce by cutting (hair, nails, corns, hedge, etc.); reduce (wages, prices, time, services, etc.), cease (services, talk, etc.); switch off (engine etc.); absent oneself from (lecture etc.); *dilute, adulterate; *cut a* CORNER; *cut it* FINE²; ~ **a loss,** or one's **losses,** abandon a losing speculation in good time; ~ **short,** shorten by cutting (lit. or fig.), interrupt, terminate before the natural time; *cut down to* SIZE¹. **5.** Shape or fashion by cutting (coat, gem, glass, key, record, etc.); perform, execute, make, (*cut a caper, dash, sorry figure*); *cut coat according to* CLOTH; ~ **a tooth,** have it appear through gum (~ one's **teeth on,** (fig.) acquire experience from; *cut* one's EYE¹-*teeth*). **6.** *v.t.* & *i.* (Cinemat.) Edit (film); stop the cameras; go quickly *to* another shot. **7.** ~ **back,** reduce (expenditure etc.), prune, (Cinemat.) repeat, for dramatic effect, part of previous scene; so **~-back** *n.*; ~ **dead,** completely refuse to recognize (person); ~ **down,** bring or throw down by cutting, kill by sword or disease, (fig.) reduce (expenses); ~ **in,** come in abruptly, interpose (in conversation), join in card-game by taking place of player who cuts out, take dance-partner from another, obstruct path of vehicle one has just overtaken by returning to one's own side of the road too soon, connect (source of electricity), give share of profits etc. to (person); ~ **off,** remove by cutting, bring to abrupt end or (esp. early) death, intercept (supplies, communications), shut off (flow), exclude (*from* access etc.); ~ **off with a shilling,** disinherit (bequeathing only a shilling); **~-off** *n.*, device for stopping flow; ~ **out,** remove by cutting, omit, stop doing or using (something), (fig.) outdo or supplant (rival), fashion or shape (lit. or fig.; *have* one's WORK¹ *cut out*) *detach (animal) from the herd, be excluded from card-game as result of cutting, (usu. in *pass.*) make suitable for (*was not cut out to be a teacher*), (cause to) cease functioning; **~-out** *n.*, device for automatic disconnection, release of exhaust gases, etc., figure cut out of paper etc.; **~-out box*, = FUSE³-*box*; ~ **up,** cut in pieces, destroy utterly, (fig.) criticize severely, (usu. in *pass.*) distress greatly, *behave in comical or unruly manner; ~ **up rough,** show resentment; ~ **up well,** (sl.) bequeath large fortune. **8.** **~'away** *a.*, (of diagram etc.) with some parts of object absent to reveal interior, (of coat) with skirt cut back from waist; **~-and-come-again,** abundance; ~ **and dried,** completely decided, prearranged, (of opinions etc.) ready-made, lacking freshness; **~-line,** caption to illustration, (Rackets) line above which served ball must strike wall; **~-price** *a.*, selling or sold at reduced price; **~'purse,** (arch.) pickpocket, thief; **~-rate** *a.*, =*cut-price*; **~'throat,** (*n.*) murderer, *species of trout with red mark under jaw, (*a.*) (of competition) intense, merciless, (of card-game) three-handed, (of razor) having long blade set in handle; **~'water,** forward edge of ship's prow, wedge-shaped projection from pier or bridge; **~'worm,** caterpillar that cuts off young plants level with the ground. [ME *cutte, kitte, kette*, perh. f. OE **cyttan*]

cūtā'nėous *a.* Of the skin. [f. mod. L *cutaneus* f. L *cutis* skin; see -ANEOUS]

cŭtch. Var. of COUCH³.

cūte *a.* (colloq.) Clever, shrewd; ingenious; *attractive, quaint; hence ~'LY² (-tlĭ) *adv.*, ~'NESS (-tn-) *n.* [f. ACUTE]

cū'tĭcle *n.* Epidermis or other superficial skin; dead skin at base of finger-nail or toe-nail; (Bot.) thin surface film on plants; hence **cūtĭ'cūl**AR¹ *a.* [f. L *cuticula* dim. of *cutis* skin]

cū'tĭe *n.* (sl.) Attractive young woman. [f. CUTE + -IE]

cū'tĭs *n.* (Anat.) True skin or dermis, underlying the epidermis. [L, = skin]

cŭ'tlass *n.* Short sword with slightly curved blade, esp. (Hist.) that used by sailors; machete. [f. F *coutelas* f. Rom. **cultellaceum* augment. of L *cultellus* (see foll.)]

cŭ'tl|er *n.* One who makes or deals in knives and similar utensils; so ~ERY (1, 2) *n.*, (esp.) knives, forks, and spoons for domestic use. [ME, f. AF *cotillere*, OF *coutelier* f. *coutel* (f. L *cultellus* dim. of *culter* COULTER); see -ER² (2)]

cŭ'tlėt *n.* Neck-chop of mutton or lamb; small piece of veal etc. for frying; minced meat etc. in shape of cutlet. [f. F *côtelette*, OF *costelet* dim. of *coste* rib f. L *costa*]

cŭ'tter *n.* In vbl senses; tailor etc. who takes measurements and cuts cloth; boat belonging to ship of war, fitted for rowing and sailing; small one-masted vessel rigged like sloop, but with running bowsprit; *light horse-drawn sleigh. [ME, f. CUT² + -ER¹]

cŭ'ttĭng *n.* In vbl senses; ||excavation of high ground for railway, road, etc.; ||(**press**) ~, paragraph etc. cut from newspaper; piece cut from plant for propagation. [ME, f. CUT² + -ING¹]

cŭ'ttle *n.* ~(**fish**), mollusc of genus *Sepia*, ejecting black fluid when pursued; **~-bone,** its internal shell, crushed and used for polishing teeth etc. or as addition to diet of cage-bird. [OE *cudele*, corresp. to OFrank. *cudele*, Norw. dial. *kaule*, rel. to E *cod* bag, w. ref. to the ink-bag]

cŭ'ttȳ *a.* & *n.* (Sc. & N. Engl.) **1.** *a.* Cut short, abnormally short; **~-stool,** (Hist.) stool of repentance. **2.** *n.* Short tobacco-pipe. [f. CUT² + -Y²]

cūvĕ'tte *n.* Shallow vessel for liquid. [F, dim. of *cuve* cask f. L *cupa*]

||**C.V.O.** *abbr.* Commander of the Royal Victorian Order.

Cwlth. *abbr.* Commonwealth.

cwm (kōōm) *n.* **1.** Welsh var. of COOMB. **2.** Cirque. [W]

c.w.o. *abbr.* cash with order.

cwt. *abbr.* hundredweight.

-cȳ *suf.*, form of -Y¹ (esp. & orig. in -ACY, -ANCY, -CRACY, -ENCY, -MANCY) (*bankruptcy, captaincy, chaplaincy, colonelcy, idiocy*). [f. or after L *-cia, -tia*, Gk *-k(e)ia, -t(e)ia*]

cȳ'an *a.* & *n.* Greenish-blue (colour). [f. Gk *kuan(e)os* dark blue]

cȳā'namīde *n.* (Chem.) (Salt of) cyanogen amide, esp. its calcium salt used as fertilizer. [f. CYANOGEN + AMIDE]

cȳă'nĭc *a.* (Chem.) Of or containing cyanogen; ~ **acid,** colourless pungent unstable strong acid (HCNO). [f. CYANOGEN + -IC]

cȳ'anīde *n.* Salt or ester of hydrocyanic acid; highly poisonous such substance used e.g. in extraction of gold and silver. [f. CYANOGEN + -IDE]

cȳanōcōba'lamĭn (-baw'-) *n.* (Chem.) Vitamin B_{12}. [f. CYANOGEN + *cobalamin* f. COBALT + VITAMIN]

cȳă'nogėn *n.* (Chem.) Colourless inflammable highly poisonous gas, a compound of carbon and nitrogen. [f. F *cyanogène* f. Gk *kuanos* dark-blue mineral + -O- + -GEN, as being constituent of Prussian blue]

cȳanō′s|ĭs *n.* (*pl.* **~es** *pr.* -ēz). (Path.) Blue discoloration of skin due to presence of de-oxygenated blood. [mod. L f. Gk *kuanōsis* blueness (f. as prec.; see -OSIS)]

cȳbernā′tion *n.* Control by machines. [f. foll. + -ATION]

cȳbernĕ′tĭcs *n.* Science of systems of control and communications in animals and machines; hence **cȳbernĕ′tic** *a.* [f. Gk *kubernētēs* steersman + -ICS]

cȳ′cad *n.* (Bot.) Palmlike plant of family Cycadaceae (esp. of genus *Cycas,* yielding sago). [f. mod. L *cycas cycad-* f. supposed Gk *kukas,* scribal error for *koikas,* pl. of *koix* Egyptian palm]

Cȳclă′dĭc *a.* Of the Cyclades, esp. of the prehistoric civilization there. [f. *Cyclades,* circular group of islands in Aegean Sea (L, f. Gk *Kuklades* f. *kuklos* circle) + -IC]

cȳ′clamāte *n.* A sulphamate used as artificial sweetening agent. [f. Chem. name *cyclohexylsulphamate*]

cȳ′clamen *n.* European plant of genus *Cyclamen* with reflexed petals, often grown in pots. [med. L, f. L f. Gk *kuklaminos,* perh. f. *kuklos* circle, w. ref. to bulbous roots]

cȳ′cle *n.,* & *v.i.* **1.** *n.* Recurrent period (of events, phenomena, etc.); period of a thing's completion; (Electr.) = cycle per second, hertz. **2.** Recurring series of operations or states; complete set or series; series of poems, or of songs (**song-~**), composed round central event or idea. **3.** Bicycle, tricycle, or similar machine; **~-track, ~way,** road or path for cycles. **4.** *v.i.* Move in cycles; ride cycle. [ME f. OF, or f. LL f. Gk *kuklos* circle]

cȳ′clĭc *a.* **1.** Recurring in cycles; belonging to a chronological cycle. **2.** Of a cycle of poems etc.; (Bot., of flower) with its parts arranged in whorls; (Math.) of a circle or cycle; (Chem.) with constituent atoms forming ring. [f. F *cyclique* or f. L f. Gk *kuklikos* (as prec.; see -IC)]

cȳ′clĭcal *a.* = prec. 1; hence **~LY**² *adv.* [f. as prec. + -AL]

cȳ′clĭst *n.* Rider of a cycle. [f. CYCLE 3 + -IST]

cȳ′clo- *comb. form.* Circle, cycle, cyclic, as: **~graph,** instrument for tracing circular arcs; **~meter** (-ŏ′m-), instrument for measuring (1) circular arcs, (2) distance traversed by bicycle etc.; **~pa′raffin,** (Chem.) saturated cyclic hydrocarbon; **~ra′ma** (-ah′-), circular panorama, curved wall or cloth at rear of stage (esp. to represent sky). [f. Gk *kuklos* circle + -O-]

cȳ′clō-crŏss *n.* Cross-country racing on bicycles. [f. CYCLE + CROSS- (4)]

cȳ′cloid *n.* (Math.) Curve traced by point on circle rolling along straight line; hence **cȳcloi′dal** *a.* [f. Gk *kukloeidēs* (as CYCLE; see -OID)]

cȳ′clōne *n.* System of winds rotating inwards to area of low barometric pressure; violent hurricane of limited diameter; centrifugal machine for separating solids; hence **cȳclŏ′nic** *a.* [prob. repr. Gk *kuklōma* wheel, coil of snake, f. *kuklos* circle]

cȳclopae′d|ĭa, -pē′d|ĭa, *n.* Encyclopaedia; hence **~IC** *a.* [abbr. of ENCYCLOPAEDIA]

Cȳ′clŏps *n.* (*pl.* same *or* **~es,** *or* **Cyclopes** *pr.* -ō′pēz). (Gk Myth.) One-eyed giant; so **Cȳclope′an, Cȳclō′pian,** *adjs.,* (esp., of ancient masonry) made with large irregular blocks. [L, f. Gk *Kuklōps* (*kuklos* circle, *ōps* eye)]

cȳ′clostōme *n.* Primitive vertebrate with large sucking mouth, e.g. lamprey. [f. CYCLO- + Gk *stoma* mouth]

cȳ′clostȳle *n.,* & *v.t.* **1.** *n.* Apparatus printing copies of writing from stencil-plate cut by pen with small toothed wheel. **2.** *v.t.* Print or reproduce with this. [f. CYCLO- + STYLE]

cȳclothȳ′m|ĭa *n.* (Psych.) Condition with cyclic change from exhilaration to depression; hence **~IC** *a.* [f. CYCLO- + Gk *thumos* temper + -IA¹]

cȳ′clotrŏn *n.* (Phys.) Apparatus for acceleration of charged atomic particles revolving in magnetic field. [f. CYCLO- + -TRON]

cȳ′der. Var. of CIDER.

cȳ′gnėt *n.* Young swan. [ME, f. AF *cignet* dim. of OF *cigne* swan f. med. L *cicinus* f. L f. Gk *kuknos*; see -ET¹]

cȳ′lĭnder *n.* **1.** (Geom.) Solid shaped like rolling-pin, pencil, tree-trunk, etc., generated by straight line moving without change of direction and describing with one of its points any fixed curve, esp. circle. **2.** Roller-shaped body, hollow or solid; container for liquefied gas etc.; barrel-shaped object of baked clay covered with cuneiform writing and buried under Babylonian or Assyrian temple; small stone of similar shape used in antiquity as seal; **~ saw,** crown saw. **3.** Cylinder-shaped part of various machines, esp. chamber in which liquid or gas exerts pressure on piston etc.; metal roller used in printing; revolving roller in lock. [f. L f. Gk *kulindros* (*kulindō* to roll)]

cȳlĭ′ndrĭcal *a.* Cylinder-shaped; *cylindrical* PROJECTION; hence **~LY**² *adv.* [f. mod. L f. Gk *kulindrikos* (as prec.; see -IC) + -AL]

cȳ′ma *n.* **1.** Ogee moulding of cornice (**~ recta** with concave, **~ reversa** with convex, curve uppermost). **2.** = CYME. [mod. L, f. Gk *kuma* wave, wavy moulding]

cȳ′mbal *n.* Concave brass or bronze plate, struck with another or with stick etc. to make ringing sound; hence **~IST** (3) *n.* [ME, f. L f. Gk *kumbalon* (*kumbē* cup)]

cȳ′mbalō *n.* (*pl.* **~s**). Dulcimer. [f. It. *cembalo, cimbalo,* f. L *cymbalum* (see prec.)]

cȳmbĭ′dĭum *n.* Tropical orchid of genus *Cymbidium,* with recess in flower-lip. [mod. L, f. Gk *kumbē* cup]

cȳ′mbĭfōrm *a.* (Anat. & Bot.) Boat-shaped. [f. L f. Gk *kumbē* boat; see -FORM]

cȳme *n.* (Bot.) Inflorescence in which primary axis bears single terminal flower that develops first, system being continued by axes of secondary and higher orders each with flower (cf. RACEME); hence **cȳ′mose**¹ *a.* [F, var. of *cime* summit, f. pop. L **cima,* L f. Gk *kuma* wave]

Cȳ′mrĭc (k-) *a.* Welsh. [f. W *Cymru* Wales + -IC]

cyngha′nedd (kunghah′nĕdh) *n.* Intricate system of alliteration and rhyme in Welsh poetry. [W]

cȳ′nĭc *a.* & *n.* **1.** *a.* Of or characteristic of the Cynic philosophers; cynical. **2.** *n.* (*C~*) ancient Greek philosopher of sect founded by Antisthenes, marked by ostentatious contempt for ease and pleasure; one who sarcastically doubts human sincerity and merit; hence **~ISM** (2) *n.* [f. L f. Gk *kunikos* (*kuōn kunos* dog, nickname for Cynic; see -IC)]

cȳ′nĭcal *a.* Like a cynic, incredulous of human goodness; sneering; hence **~LY**² *adv.* [f. prec. + -AL]

cȳnocĕ′phalus *n.* Fabled dog-headed man; (Zool.) baboon. [ME f. L, f. Gk *kunokephalos* (*kuōn kunos* dog, *kephalē* head)]

cȳnoglŏ′ssum *n.* Tall plant of genus *Cynoglossum,* with tongue-shaped leaves. [mod. L, f. Gk *kunoglōsson* (as prec., *glōssa* tongue)]

cȳ′nosūre (-z-) *n.* Guiding star; centre of attraction or admiration. [F, or f. L f. Gk *kunosoura* dog's tail, Ursa Minor (as prec., *oura* tail)]

cȳ′pher¹,². See CIPHER¹,².

cy pres (sēprā′) *adv.* & *a.* (Law). As near as possible (to testator's or donor's intentions when these cannot be precisely followed). [AF, = F *si près* so near (as etc.)]

cȳʹprėss *n.* Coniferous tree of genus *Cupressus*, with hard wood and dark foliage, taken as symbol of mourning. [ME f. OF *cipres* f. LL *cypressus* f. Gk *kuparissos*]

Cȳʹprĭan, Cȳʹprĭot, Cȳʹprĭōte, *adjs.* & *ns.* (Native or inhabitant) of Cyprus. [f. L *Cyprius* + -AN, Gk *Kupriōtēs*, f. *Cyprus* (Gk *Kupros*) in E. Mediterranean]

cȳʹprĭnoid *a.* & *n.* (Fish) like or akin to carp. [f. L f. Gk *kuprinos* carp + -OID]

cȳprĭpēʹdĭum *n.* Orchid of genus *Cypripedium*, esp. lady's slipper. [mod. L, f. Gk *Kupris* Aphrodite + *pedilon* slipper]

cȳʹpsėla *n.* (*pl.* ~**e**). (Bot.) Achene with attached calyx, as in dandelion. [mod. L, f. Gk *kupselē* hollow vessel]

Cȳrėnāʹĭc *a.* & *n.* (Philosopher) of the hedonistic school of Aristippus of Cyrene. [f. L f. Gk *Kurēnaikos* (*Kurēnē* Cyrene in N. Africa)]

Cȳrĭʹllĭc *a.* Of alphabet used by Slavonic peoples of the Orthodox Church. [f. St. *Cyril* d. 869, reputed author, + -IC]

cȳst *n.* (Biol.) hollow organ, bladder, etc., in animal or plant, containing liquid secretion; (Path.) sac containing morbid matter, parasitic larva, etc.; cell containing embryo etc. [f. LL *cystis* f. Gk *kustis* bladder]

cȳʹstĭc *a.* Of the urinary bladder; of the gall-bladder; of the nature of a cyst. [f. F *cystique* or mod. L *cysticus* (as prec.; see -IC)]

cȳʹsto- *comb. form.* Bladder, esp. urinary bladder, as: **cȳstĭʹ**TIS, ~SCOPE, ~TOMY (-ŏʹt-), *ns.* [f. Gk *kustē*, *kustis* bladder + -O-]

-cȳte *suf.* (Biol.) Mature cell (*leucocyte*); cf. -BLAST. [f. Gk *kutos* vessel]

cȳʹtĭdine (-ēn) *n.* Crystalline nucleoside obtained from RNA by hydrolysis. [f. G *cytidin* (as prec.)]

cȳʹto- *comb. form.* (Biol.) Cell, as: ~**logy** (-ŏʹl-), study of cells; ~**plasm,** protoplasmic content of cell other than the nucleus; ~**sine,** crystalline base occurring as constituent of DNA. [f. as -CYTE + -O-]

czar etc. See TSAR etc.

czardas. See CSARDAS.

Czĕch (chĕk) *n.* & *a.* (Native or language) of Bohemia; = foll. [Pol. sp. of Bohemian *Čech*]

Czĕchōslōʹvăk, Czĕchōslovăʹkĭan, (chĕk-) *a.* & *n.* (Native) of Czechoslovakia. [f. prec. + -O- + SLOVAK; see -IAN]

D

D, d, (dē) *n.* (*pl.* **Ds** *or* **D's**). Fourth letter of alphabet; = DEE; (Mus.) second note in diatonic scale of C major; fourth highest class (of academic marks, population as regards affluence, etc.); (as Roman numeral) 500 (**dc** 600).

D. *abbr.* *Democrat; dimension (*3-D*).

d. *abbr.* daughter; deci-; delete; departs; died; ‖(former) penny [f. L DENARIUS].

D *symb.* deuterium.

'd[1] *v.* (colloq., chiefly after pronouns). = *had*, *would*. [abbr.]

-d, -'d[2], *suf.* (*heard*, *subpoena'd*, *toga'd*, etc.): see -ED[1,2].

D.A. *abbr.* deposit account; *District Attorney; duck-arse.

da *abbr.* deca-.

dăb[1] *v.* (-**bb**-). **1.** *v.t.* & *i.* Strike lightly or undecidedly, hit feebly (*at*), tap, peck. **2.** *v.t.* Press briefly but not rub (surface) with sponge etc., press (brush, sponge; colour etc.) on surface thus. [ME, imit.]

dăb[2] *n.* Slight or undecided blow, tap, peck; brief application of sponge, handkerchief, etc., to surface without rubbing; moisture, colour, etc., so applied; (in *pl.*, sl.) fingerprints. [ME, f. prec.]

dăb[3] *n.* Flat-fish of genus *Limanda*. [16th c., of unkn. orig.]

dăb[4] *n.* & *a.* (colloq.) Adept (*at* games etc., do*ing*; ~ **hand,** expert). [17th c., of unkn. orig.]

dăʹbbl|e *v.* **1.** *v.t.* Wet intermittently, slightly, or partly; soil, moisten, splash. **2.** *v.i.* Move feet, hands, bill, about in shallow water; engage *in* or *at* pursuit etc. as desultory hobby; hence ~ER[1] *n.* [16th c., f. Du. *dabbelen* or DAB[1] + -LE 3]

dăʹbchĭck *n.* Water-bird of grebe family, esp. little grebe. [16th c. *dap-*, *dop-*, later *dip-*; perh. cogn. w. OE *dūfedoppa*, DEEP[1], DIP[1]]

dăʹbster *n.* = DAB[4]; = DAUB*ster*; *one who dabbles. [f. DAB[4] + -STER]

da capo (dahkahʹpō) *adv.* (Mus.) Repeated from the beginning. [It.]

dāce *n.* (*pl.* same). Small freshwater fish allied to carp, esp. of genus *Leuciscus*. [ME, f. OF *dars*; see DART]

dăʹcha *n.* Small country villa in Russia. [Russ. = act of payment]

dăʹchshund (-ks-hŏŏ-) *n.* Short-legged long-bodied breed of dog. [G, = badger-dog]

dacoiʹt *n.* Member of Indian or Burmese armed robber band. [f. Hindi *ḍakait* (*ḍākā* gang-robbery)]

dacoiʹtȳ *n.* (Act of) gang-robbery. [f. Hindi *ḍakaitī* (as prec.)]

dăʹctȳl *n.* (Pros.) Foot consisting of one long syllable followed by two short. [ME, f. L f. Gk *daktulos* finger (w. its 3 bones), dactyl]

dăctȳʹlĭc *a.* & *n.* (Pros.) **1.** *a.* Of or using dactyls (*dactylic* HEXAMETER). **2.** *n.* (usu. in *pl.*) Dactylic verse. [f. L f. Gk *daktulikos* (as prec.; see -IC)]

***dăd**[1] *n.* (colloq., in oaths etc.) God. [corrupt.]

dăd[2] *n.* (colloq.) = DADDY 1. [perh. imit. of child's *da*, *da*]

Daʹda (dahʹdah) *n.* International movement in art and literature about 1915–20, repudiating conventions and intended to shock; hence ~ISM (3), ~IST (2), *ns.* [F, title of review (1916–), f. *dada* hobby-horse]

dăʹddȳ *n.* (colloq.) **1.** (Esp. as *voc.*) father; man. **2.** Oldest or most important person or thing. **3.** ~-**loʹng-legs,** crane-fly, *harvestman. [f. DAD[2] + -Y[3]]

dāʹdō *n.* (*pl.* ~**s**). Cube of pedestal between base and cornice; plinth of column; lower part of room-wall when faced or coloured differently from upper part. [It., = DIE[1]]

daeʹdal *a.* (literary). Skilful, inventive; complex, mysterious; (of the earth etc.) adorned with natural wonders. [f. L f. Gk *daidalos* skilful, variegated]

Daedāʹlĭan, -ėan, *a.* In the manner of Daedalus; intricate; labyrinthine. [f. L *Daedaleus*, Gk *daidaleos* (*Daidalos* Daedalus, who built the Cretan labyrinth; cf. prec.) + -IAN, -EAN]

daemon(ic). See DEMON(IC).

daff[1] (dahf) *v.t.* (arch.) Put aside, waive, (esp. *daff the world aside*, Shak. *1 Henry IV* IV. i. 96). [var. of DOFF]

dăff[2] *n.* (colloq.) = foll. [abbr.]

dă'ffodĭl *n.* Yellow-flowered narcissus; this as Welsh national emblem; pale-yellow colour. [f. earlier *affodill* (*d-* unexplained) f. med. L *affodilus* f. L f. Gk *asphodelos* asphodel]

dă'ffȳ *a.* (sl.) = foll. [f. *daff* simpleton + -Y[2]]

daft (dah-) *a.* Foolish, reckless, wild; crazy. [ME *daffte* = OE *gedæfte* mild, meek f. Gmc **gadhaftjaz* (**gadhafti* fitting, suitable)]

dă'geraad (-gerahd *or* -t) *n.* (S. Afr.) Brilliantly coloured sea-fish. [Afrik. f. Du., = daybreak]

dă'gga *n.* (S. Afr.) Hemp used as narcotic; similarly used plant of genus *Leonotis*. [Afrik., f. Hottentot *dachab*]

dă'gger (-g-) *n.* **1.** Stabbing-weapon with short pointed and edged blade (**at ~s drawn,** on the point of fighting, in bitter enmity, *with* person, or abs.; **look ~s,** stare angrily *at* person, or abs.). **2.** (Print.) (**double**) ~, = (*double*) OBELISK. [ME, perh. f. obs. *dag* pierce + -ER[1], infl. by OF *dague* long dagger]

dā'gō *n.* (*pl.* **~s** *or* **~es**). (sl., derog.) Spaniard, Portuguese, Italian; any foreigner. [f. Sp. *Diego* = James]

daguĕ'rreotȳpe (-gĕ'ro-) *n.* (Photograph taken by) early photographic process using iodine--sensitized silver(ed) plate and mercury vapour. [f. L. *Daguerre*, Fr. inventor d. 1851, + -O- + TYPE[1]]

dahabee'yah (dah-ha-), **-bi'ah** (-bē'-), *n.* Nile sailing-boat. [f. Arab. *dahabīya* = the golden, orig. used of gilded barge of Muslim rulers of Egypt]

dah'lĭa (dā'l-) *n.* Mexican composite plant of genus *Dahlia* cultivated for its many-coloured single or double flowers; **blue** ~, something impossible. [f. A. *Dahl*, Sw. botanist d. 1789 + -IA[1]]

Dáil (Éireann) (doil (ā'ran)) *n.* Lower house of Parliament in the Republic of Ireland. [Ir., = assembly (of Ireland)]

dai'lȳ *a.*, *adv.*, & *n.* **1.** *a.* & *adv.* (Produced or occurring) on every day or weekday; from day to day, constant(ly), often; *daily* BREAD; *daily* DOZEN. **2.** *n.* Daily newspaper; ‖(colloq.) charwoman coming daily. [ME, f. DAY + -LY[1,2]]

dai'mīō· (dī'-) *n.* (*pl.* **~s**). (Hist.) Japanese feudal vassal of the emperor. [Jap. (*dai* great, *myō* name)]

dai'm|ōn (dī'-) *n.* = DEMON 2; hence **~ŏ'nic** *a.* [Gk, = deity]

dai'ntȳ[1] *n.* Choice morsel, delicacy, (lit. or fig.). [f. AF *dainté*, OF *daintié*, *deintié* f. L *dignitas -tatis* (*dignus* worthy; see -ITY)]

dai'nt|ȳ[2] *a.* Delicate, choice; tasteful, pretty, of delicate beauty; having delicate tastes and sensitivity, fastidious; hence **~ĭLY**[2] *adv.*, **~ĭNESS** *n.* [ME, f. prec.]

dai'quĭrĭ (dī'k- *or* dă'k-) *n.* Cocktail of rum, lime-juice, etc. [f. *D~* in Cuba]

dair'ȳ *n.* **1.** Room or building for keeping milk and cream and making butter, cheese, etc.; shop for milk etc.; department of farm or farming concerned with dairy products. **2.** ~ **cattle** (kept for milk production); **~ cream,** real cream (not synthetic); **~ factory,** (N.Z.) factory making butter and cheese; **~ farm,** one chiefly concerned with dairy products; **~maid,** woman employed in dairy; **~man,** dealer in milk etc.; **~ products,** milk, cream, butter, cheese. [ME *deierie* (*deie* maidservant f. OE *dǣge* kneader of dough; see -ERY)]

dair'ȳing *n.* Dairy operations; production of milk, butter, etc. [f. *dairy* v. keep cows + -ING[1]]

dā'ĭs (*or* dās) *n.* Raised platform, esp. at end of hall for high table, throne, etc. [ME f. OF *deis* f. L *discus* disc, dish, in med. L = table]

dai'sȳ (-zĭ) *n.* **1.** Small European wild and garden flower (*Bellis perennis*), with yellow disc and white rays; other plant resembling it, esp. the larger ox-eye daisy, MICHAELMAS *daisy*, SHASTA *daisy*; (sl.) first-rate specimen of anything; **pushing up the daisies,** (sl.) dead and buried. **2. ~-chain,** string of daisies threaded together; **~-cutter,** horse lifting feet very little, (Cricket) ball travelling along ground. [OE *dæges ēage* day's eye, the disc being revealed in the morning]

dak. See DAWK.

Dak. *abbr.* Dakota.

dal. See DHAL.

Dalai. See LAMA[1].

dāle *n.* Valley (esp. in N. Engl.); HILL *and dale*; **~'sman** (-z-), inhabitant of dales in northern England. [OE *dæl*, = OS *dal*, OHG *tal*, ON *dalr*, Goth. *dal(s)* f. Gmc **dalam*, **dalaz*]

dă'llȳ *v.* **1.** *v.i.* Amuse oneself, sport or flirt or trifle (*with*, or abs.). **2.** Idle, loiter, delay. **3.** *v.t.* ~ **away,** consume (time, opportunity) to no purpose. **4.** Hence **dă'llĭANCE** *n.* [ME, f. OF *dalier* chat]

Dălmā'tian (-shan) *n.* Large short-haired white dog with dark spots. [f. *Dalmatia* in Yugoslavia + -AN]

dălmă'tĭc *n.* Wide-sleeved loose long vestment with slit sides worn by deacons and bishops on some occasions, and by kings and emperors esp. at coronation. [ME, f. OF *dalmatique* or LL *dalmatica* (*vestis* robe) of Dalmatia]

dal segno (dălsā'nyō) *adv.* (Mus.) Repeated from point indicated. [It., = from the sign]

Da'lton (daw'-) *n.* ~ **plan,** system of education in which pupils are made responsible for completion of assignments over fairly long periods at a time; hence **~IZE** (3) *v.t.* [~ in Massachusetts, location of first school to use the plan]

da'ltonĭsm (daw'l-) *n.* Colour-blindness, esp. congenital inability to distinguish green from red. [f. F *daltonisme* f. J. *Dalton*, Engl. chemist d. 1844, who suffered from it, + -ISM (5)]

dăm[1] *n.*, & *v.t.* (**-mm-**). **1.** *n.* Barrier constructed to hold back water and raise its level, to form a reservoir, or to prevent flooding; barrier constructed in stream by beavers; *(Dent.) rubber sheet to keep saliva from teeth during operation; causeway. **2.** *v.t.* Furnish or confine with dam; block *up*, hold *back*, obstruct, (lit. or fig.). [ME f. MLG, MDu.; MHG *tam*, of doubtful orig.]

dăm[2] *n.* Mother (esp. of animal). [ME, var. of DAME]

dăm[3]. Var. of DAMN 4, 5.

dă'mage *n.*, & *v.t.* **1.** *n.* Loss of what is desirable (*to* one's *great damage*); injury impairing value or usefulness; (Law, in *pl.*) sum of money claimed or adjudged in compensation for loss or injury; (sl.) cost (*what's the damage?*). **2.** *v.t.* Injure (usu. thing) so as to diminish value; detract from reputation of (person etc.; *trying to damage the Government*; *a damaging admission*); hence **~ABLE** (-ĭja-) *a.* [ME f. OF *damage* n., *damagier* v., f. *dam(me)* loss f. L *damnum*]

dămascē'ne *v.t.* Ornament (metal) with inlaid gold or silver; ornament (steel) with watered pattern produced in welding. [f. *Damascene* adj. of Damascus, f. L f. Gk *Damaskēnos*]

dă'mask *n.* & *a.*, & *v.t.* **1.** *n.* Figured woven material (orig. of silk) with pattern visible on either side; twilled table-linen with woven designs shown by reflection of light. **2.** (Hist.) Steel of or as of Damascus, with wavy surface--pattern due to special welding of iron and steel together. **3.** ~ **rose,** old sweet-scented variety grown esp. to make attar. **4.** *a.* Coloured like damask rose, velvety pink or light red; made of or resembling damask silk, linen, or steel. **5.** *v.t.* Weave with figured designs; = DAMASCENE;

ornament with pattern. [ME, f. AF **Damasc* f. L *Damascus*]

dāme *n.* **1.** (arch., poet., joc., or *sl.) Woman; (arch.) mistress of household. **2.** (*D~*). Title of woman of rank, or of thing personified as woman (*Dame Nature*); ‖(title of) woman Knight Commander or holder of Grand Cross in Order of the Bath, Order of the British Empire, Royal Victorian Order, or Order of St. Michael and St. George. **3.** Comic middle-aged woman in modern pantomime, usu. played by man; woman with administrative duties in Eton boarding-house. **4.** **~-school,** (Hist.) primary school of kind kept by elderly women; **~'s violet,** cruciferous plant with pale lilac flowers that have no scent until evening. [ME f. OF, f. L *domina* mistress]

dă'mfōōl *a.* & *n.* (colloq.) Foolish, stupid, (person). [f. DAMN 4 + FOOL¹]

dă'mmar *n.* (Resin used in varnish-making, obtained from) E. Asian tree esp. of genus *Agathis* or *Shorea*. [f. Malay *damar*]

dă'mmĭt *int.* etc. = DAMN *it.*

dămn (-m) *v.t.*, *n.*, *a.*, & *adv.* **1.** *v.t.* Condemn, censure, (*damn a person's character*; **~ with faint praise,** commend so frigidly as to suggest disapproval); bring condemnation upon, be the ruin of. **2.** Doom to hell, cause damnation of, curse (person or thing, or abs.; often in *subj.*, = *may God damn* person or thing, or without object); ‖**~ all,** (sl.) nothing at all; **I'll be ~ed,** (colloq.) I am astonished; **(I'm, I'll be) ~ed if I** (*know, will agree*, etc.), (colloq.) I certainly do not. **3.** *n.* Uttered curse; negligible amount (*don't care* or *give, not worth, a damn*; TINKER'*s damn*). **4.** *a.* = DAMNED 2. **5.** *adv.* = DAMNED 3. [ME, f. OF *dam(p)ner* f. L *damnare* inflict loss on (*damnum* loss)]

dă'mnab|le *a.* Subject to or deserving damnation; hateful, annoying; hence **~LY²** *adv.* [ME, f. OF *dam(p)nable* f. LL *dam(p)nabilis* (as prec.; see -ABLE)]

dămnā'tion *n.* & *int.* **1.** *n.* (Condemnation to) eternal punishment in hell. **2.** *int.* = may damnation take a person or thing. [ME, f. OF *dam(p)-nation* f. L *damnatio -onis* (as DAMN; see -ATION)]

dă'mnatorў *a.* Conveying or causing censure or damnation. [f. L *damnatorius* (as DAMN; see -ORY)]

dămned (-md) *a.* & *adv.* **1.** *a.* In vbl senses; **the ~,** souls in hell. **2.** Damnable; infernal, unwelcome; **do** one's **~est,** do one's utmost. **3.** *adv.* **~ (well)**, damnably, extremely, (*damned hot, funny*, etc.; *you can damned well do without it*). [p.p. of DAMN]

dă'mnĭ|fȳ *v.t.* (Law). Cause injury to; hence **~FICA'TION** *n.* [f. OF *damnifier* etc. f. LL *damnificare* injure f. L *damnificus* hurtful (*damnum* loss; see -FY)]

dă'mnĭng (-mĭ-) *a.* In vbl senses; (of evidence etc.) that proves guilt; hence **~LY²** *adv.* [f. DAMN + -ING²]

damnosa hereditas (dămnōsa hĭrĕ'dĭtăs) *n.* Inheritance that brings more burden than profit. [L, = insolvent inheritance]

dă'mnum *n.* (Law). Loss or wrong. [L, = hurt, harm]

Dă'moclēs (-z) *n.* **Sword of ~,** imminent danger esp. in midst of prosperity. [L f. Gk, name of flatterer whom Dionysius of Syracuse (4th c. B.C.) feasted while sword hung by a hair over him]

dă'mosĕl (-z-), **dă'mozĕl,** *n.* (arch.) Var. of DAMSEL.

dămp *n.*, *a.*, & *v.* **1.** *n.* Moisture in air, on surface, or diffused through solid; dejection, chill, discouragement, (*cast* or *strike a damp over* or *into*); *damp*-PROOF²; **~(-proof) course,** layer of damp-proof felt etc. in wall near ground to keep damp from rising. **2.** = CHOKE¹-*damp*; = FIRE¹-*damp*. **3.** *a.* Slightly or fairly wet (*damp* SQUIB); hence ***~'EN⁶** *v.t.* & *i.*, **~'LY²** *adv.*, **~'NESS** *n.* **4.** *v.t.* Stifle, choke, dull, extinguish, (**~ down,** heap (fire) with ashes etc. to retard combustion); (Mus. & Phys.) stop vibration of (string), reduce amplitude of (sound waves etc.); discourage, depress, (zeal, hopes); moisten. **5.** *v.i.* **~ off,** (of plant) die from fungus attack in damp conditions. [ME f. MLG, = vapour etc., OHG *dampf* steam f. WG **thamp-*]

dă'mper *n.* In vbl senses; (Mus.) pad silencing piano-string except when removed by pedal or by note's being struck; shock-absorber in vehicle; metal plate in flue controlling draught and combustion; device for moistening anything; (Austral., N.Z., etc.) unleavened bread or cake of flour and water baked in wood ashes. [f. prec. + -ER¹]

dă'msel (-z-) *n.* **1.** (arch. or literary). Young unmarried woman. **2.** **~fish,** small brightly-coloured fish of coral reefs; **~fly,** slender insect of order Odonata, like dragonfly but with wings folded over body when resting. [ME, f. OF *dam(e)isele*, earlier *danzele, donsele* f. Gallo-Rom. **dominicella* dim. of L *domina* mistress]

dă'mson (-z-) *n.* & *a.* **1.** *n.* Small dark-purple plum (**~ plum,** larger similar plum); tree (*Prunus insititia*) bearing it; **~ cheese,** solid preserve of damsons and sugar. **2.** *a.* Damson-coloured. [ME *dama(s)cene, damesene,* f. L *damascenum* (*prunum* plum) of *Damascus*; see DAMASCENE]

dăn¹ *n.* **~ (buoy)**, small buoy used as marker in deep-sea fishing, or showing limits of area cleared by minesweepers. [17th c.; orig. unkn.]

dăn² *n.* (Holder of) degree of proficiency in judo etc. [Jap.]

Dăn³ *n.* **From ~ to Beersheba,** over the whole extent. [~ in Palestine, f. name of a tribe of Israel]

Dan. *abbr.* Daniel (O.T.).

dance¹ (dah-) *v.* **1.** *v.i.* Move with rhythmical steps, glides, leaps, revolutions, gestures, etc., usu. to music, alone or with partner or set, (**~ to** person's **tune,** do as he demands; **dancing-girl,** female professional dancer, esp. member of a group); jump about, skip, (*dancing with rage, with joy*), (of heart, blood, etc.) move in lively way; bob up and down on water etc. **2.** *v.t.* Perform (minuet, waltz, polka, rumba, etc.; **~ attendance** (*on*), be deliberately kept waiting (by), follow about obsequiously); move up and down, dandle, (baby). [ME, f. OF *dancer, danser* f. Rom. **dansare*, of unkn. orig.]

dance² (dah-) *n.* **1.** Dancing motion; special form of this; single round or turn of one (**lead** person **a ~,** cause him much trouble); tune for dancing to, or in dance rhythm; dancing-party. **2.** **D~ of Death,** medieval representation of Death leading all to grave; **~-drama,** expression of dramatic situation by dance; **~-hall,** public hall for dancing; **St. Vitus's ~,** disorder chiefly in children, with convulsive involuntary movements. [ME, f. OF *dance, danse,* f. as prec.]

da'ncer (dah'-) *n.* In vbl senses; one who dances in public for money; ‖**merry ~s,** aurora borealis. [f. DANCE¹ + -ER¹]

dăncĕ'ttў *a.* (Her., of line) drawn with broad indentations. [alt. f. F *danché* etc. f. LL **denticatus* f. L *dens dentis* tooth]

d. and c. *abbr.* (Med.) dilatation and curettage.

dă'ndėlīon *n.* Yellow-flowered composite plant (*Taraxacum officinale*) with widely toothed leaves; **~ coffee,** (drink made from) dried dandelion roots. [f. F *dent-de-lion* f. med. L *dens leonis* lion's tooth]

dă'nder *n.* (colloq.) Temper, anger, indignation, (person's ~ **is up,** he is angry). [19th c.; orig. uncert.]

Dăndie Dĭ'nmont *n.* (Breed of) short-legged rough-coated terrier from Scottish Border. [character in Scott's *Guy Mannering*]

dă'ndle *v.t.* Dance (child) on one's knees or in one's arms; pamper, pet. [16th c., of unkn. orig.]

dă'ndrŭff *n.* Dead skin in small scales among the hair, scurf. [16th c.; *-ruff* perh. akin to ME *rove* scurfiness f. ON *hrufa* or MLG, MDu. *rōve*]

dă'ndȳ *n.* & *a.* **1.** *n.* Man unduly devoted to smartness esp. of clothes, whence **dăndī'**ACAL *a.*, **dă'ndĭ**FY *v.t.*, ~ISH[1] *a.*, ~ISM (2) *n.*; excellent thing. **2.** *a.* (colloq.) Very good of its kind, splendid, first-rate. **3.** **~-brush** (for cleaning horse); **~-roll(er)**, device for solidifying, and impressing watermark in, paper during manufacture. [18th c., perh. orig. = *Andrew*, in *Jack-a-dandy*]

Dāne *n.* Native or inhabitant of Denmark; (Hist.) Northman invader of England in 9th–11th c.; **(Great)** ~, powerful short-haired breed of dog. [ME, f. ON *Danir* pl., LL *Dani*]

Dā'negĕld (-n-g-) *n.* (Hist.) Annual tax prob. imposed orig. in 10th c. to provide funds to protect England against the Danes; tax; appeasement by bribery. [OE, f. as prec. + ON *gjald* payment]

Dā'nelaw (-nl-) *n.* (Hist.) Part of N. & E. England occupied by Danes in 9th–11th c. [OE *Dena lagu* Danes' law]

dăng. Var. of DAMN 2, 3.

dā'nger (-nj-) *n.* **1.** Liability or exposure to harm, risk, peril, (*of* one's *life, of death* or other evil; **in ~ of,** likely to incur etc.; **out of ~**, not likely to die from present illness etc.). **2.** Position of railway signal directing stoppage or caution (*signal is at danger*); thing that causes peril (*a danger to peace, to navigation*). **3.** **~ list,** list of dangerously ill hospital patients; **~ money,** payment above basic wages when dangerous work is done. [earlier sense 'jurisdiction, power', ME f. OF *dangier* f. Rom. **domniarium* f. L *dominus* lord]

dā'ngerous (-nj-) *a.* Causing danger, unsafe; **~ drug** (esp. that can cause addiction); hence ~LY[2] *adv.* [ME, f. AF *da(u)ngerous*, OF *dangereus* (as prec.; see -OUS)]

dă'ngle (-nggel) *v.* **1.** *v.i.* Be suspended and sway to and fro; (arch.) hover *after, round, about,* person as follower, lover, etc.; *lack proper grammatical connection (*dangling participle*). **2.** *v.t.* Hold or carry (thing) swaying loosely; hold (hopes etc.) as temptation *before* person. [16th c., imit.; cf. Sw. *dangla*, Da. *dangle*, and -LE 3]

Dă'niel (-yel) *n.* Upright judge, person of infallible wisdom. [*Susanna* (Apocr.) 45–64, and Shak. *Merchant of Venice* IV. i. 223, 333]

Dā'nĭsh *a.* & *n.* (Language) of Denmark or the Danes; **~ blue,** soft white cheese with blue veins; **~ modern,** simple plain and light style of furniture; **~ pastry,** yeast cake topped with icing, nuts, etc. [ME, f. AF *danes*, OF *daneis* f. med. L *Danensis*, assim. to -ISH[1]]

dănk *a.* Oozy; (of air, weather, etc.) unpleasantly or unwholesomely cold and damp. [ME, prob. f. Scand.; cf. Sw. *dank* marshy spot]

danse du ventre (dahṅs dū vah'ṅtr) *n.* Belly-dance. [F]

danse macabre (dahṅs makah'br) *n.* DANCE[2] of Death. [F; see DANCE[2], MACABRE]

danseur (dahṅsēr') *n.* (*fem.* ***danseuse*** *pr.* -sēr'z). Male ballet-dancer. [F, = dancer]

Dă'ntean (*or* -ē'an) *a.* & *n.* (Student) of Dante; in style of or reminiscent of Dante's writings; so **Dănt**E'SQUE *a.* [f. *Dante* Alighieri, It. poet. d. 1321 + -EAN]

dănthō'nĭa *n.* (Austral. & N.Z.) Tufted pasture grass of genus *Danthonia*. [mod. L, f. É. *Danthoine*, 19th-c. Fr. botanist + -IA[1]]

dăp *v.i.* & *t.* (-pp-). Fish by letting bait bob on water; dip lightly; make (ball) bounce, (of ball) bounce, on ground. [cf. DAB[1]]

dă'phnė *n.* Flowering shrub of genus *Daphne*, e.g. spurge laurel. [ME, = laurel, f. Gk *daphnē*]

dă'pper *a.* (Of person) neat, smart, in appearance or movement; sprightly. [ME, f. MLG, MDu. *dapper* strong, stout, = OHG *tapfar* weighty, ON *dapr* sad]

dă'pple *v.* & *n.* **1.** *v.t.* & *i.* Variegate or become variegated with rounded spots or patches of colour or shade. **2.** *n.* Dappled effect; dappled horse etc.; **~-grey,** (horse) of grey with darker spots. [ME *dappled, dappeld*, adj., of unkn. orig.]

||**dar'bies** (-bĭz) *n. pl.* (sl.) Handcuffs. [allus. use of *Father Darby's bands*, some rigid form of bond for debtors (16th c.)]

Dar'bȳ *n.* **~ and Joan,** devoted old married couple; ||**~ and Joan club,** club for elderly people. [18th c.; perh. f. poem 1735 in *Gentleman's Mag.*]

dare *v.t.* (3 *sing. pres.* usu. **dare** before expressed or implied inf. without *to*; *past* in this position (arch.) **durst**; *neg.* **dare not** or (colloq.) **daren't** *pr.* darnt), & *n.* **1.** *v.t.* Venture (to), have the courage or impudence (to), **(I ~ say,** I am prepared to believe, I do not deny, it is very likely; **I ~ swear,** I feel sure that; *dare he do it?*; *he dares to insult me*; *I would if I dared*; *they dared not come, did not dare to come*; (abs.) *how dare you?*). **2.** Attempt, take the risks of, (*dare all things*, person's *anger*); defy (person); challenge (person) *to* do, *to a fight*, etc.; **~'devil,** reckless (person). **3.** *n.* Act of daring; challenge. [OE *durran*, = OS *gidurran*, OHG *giturran*, Goth. *gadaursan*, preterite-present vbs. f. Gmc **ders-*, **dars-*, **durs-*, f. IE **dhers-* etc.; cf. Skr. *dhṛsh*, Gk *tharseō* be bold]

darg *n.* (Sc.) Day's work; definite amount of work, task. [ME, f. *daywerk* or *daywark* day-work]

dar'ĭng[1] *n.* In vbl senses; adventurous courage. [f. DARE + -ING[1]]

dar'ĭng[2] *a.* In vbl senses; adventurous, bold; fearless; hence ~LY[2] *adv.* [f. DARE + -ING[2]]

dă'rĭōle *n.* Savoury or sweet dish cooked and served in a small mould called a **~ (mould)**. [ME f. OF]

dark[1] *a.* **1.** With no or relatively little light, unilluminated; gloomy, sombre. **2.** (Of colour) more or less near black (esp. as pref. to adjs. of colour: *dark-brown* etc.); brown-complexioned, not fair. **3.** Evil, atrocious; cheerless (*dark side of things*); sad, sullen (*dark thoughts*); frowning. **4.** Obscure (*dark saying, dark oblivion*); secret, mysterious, (*keep* thing *dark*; **keep ~**, remain in hiding); little known of; unenlightened (*in the darkest ignorance*; **in ~est Africa,** with ref. to paucity of knowledge of Africa or to its relative unenlightenment, hence joc. of other places regarded as remote or uncivilized). **5. D~ Ages,** Middle Ages, esp. 5th–10th c., (fig.) period of relative unenlightenment; **D~ Age(s)**, time between end of Bronze Age and beginning of historical period in Greece etc.; *dark* BLUE[2]; **D~ Continent,** Africa; **~ current,** (Electr.) current in a photoelectric device when no radiation is incident; **~ glasses,** spectacles with dark-tinted lenses; **~ horse,** racehorse whose form is little known, (fig.) person who is little known yet successful in contest; **~ lantern,** one with means for covering its light; **~-room** (with actinic rays such as daylight excluded for photographic work). **6.** Hence or cogn. ~'LY[2] *adv.*, ~'NESS *n.*, (esp.) wickedness (*the powers of darkness*; PRINCE *of Darkness*). [OE *deorc*, prob. f. Gmc **derk-*, **dark-*]

dârk[2] *n.* Absence of light (esp. *in the dark*; **~-adapted,** (of eye) adjusted to low intensity of light); nightfall (*after dark*); dark colour (esp. in Art, *the lights and darks of a picture*); lack of knowledge (*am in the dark about it*; **leap in the ~,** rash step or enterprise; SHOT[1] *in the dark*); hence ~'SOME[1] *a.* (arch. or poet.). [ME, f. prec.]

dâr'ken *v.t.* & *i.* Make or become dark (lit. or fig.); ~ person's **door,** visit him (usu. w. neg.). [ME, f. DARK[1] + -EN[6]]

dâr'kĭe. Var. of DARKY.

dâr'kle *v.i.* Be seen darkly; become dark. [back form. f. foll.; cf. -ING[2]]

dâr'klĭng *adv.* & *a.* In the dark. [ME, f. DARK[1] + -LING[2]]

dâr'kȳ *n.* (colloq.) Negro. [f. DARK[1] + -Y[3]]

dâr'lĭng *n.* & *a.* Loved, best loved, lovable, especially favoured, (colloq.) pretty, (person or thing). [OE *dēorling* (as DEAR, -LING[1])]

dârn[1] *v.t.*, & *n.* **1.** *v.t.* Mend (esp. knitted material) by interweaving yarn with needle across hole, whence ~'ING[1] (5) *n.*; embroider with **~'ing-stitch** (large running stitch as used in darning material); **~'ing-egg** etc., curved piece of wood etc. to support material being darned. **2.** *n.* Place so mended. [16th c., perh. f. obs. *dern* hide; cf. MDu. *dernen* stop holes in (a dike)]

dârn[2] *v.t.*, *n.*, *a.*, & *adv.* (sl.) (Mild form of) DAMN 2, 3, 4, 5. [corrupt. of DAMN]

dârned (-nd) *a.* & *adv.* (sl.) (Mild form of) DAMNED 2, 3. [corrupt. of DAMNED]

dâr'nel *n.* Grass of genus *Lolium*, growing as weed among corn, or cultivated as ornament. [ME; cf. Walloon *darnelle*]

darshan (dâr'shahn) *n.* (Ind.) Seeing an august or holy personage. [f. Hindi *darśan* f. Skr. *darśana* view (*drś* see)]

dârt *n.* & *v.* **1.** *n.* Small pointed missile used as weapon; (in *pl.*, usu. treated as *sing.*) indoor game with light usu. feathered darts and target (**~'board**); sting of insect etc.; sudden rapid motion; tapering stitched tuck in garment. **2.** *v.t.* Throw (missile); direct suddenly (glance, flash). **3.** *v.i.* Throw missile; start rapidly in some direction. [ME, f. OF *darz*, *dars*, f. Frank. **daroth* spear, lance]

dâr'ter *n.* In vbl senses; tropical web-footed bird of genus *Anhinga*, snake-bird; small Amer. perchlike fish. [f. prec. + -ER[1]]

Dâr'tmoor (*or* -môr) *n.* **~ pony** (small and shaggy); **~ sheep,** hardy moorland sheep bred on Dartmoor. [~ in Devon]

dâr'tre (-*ter*) *n.* Generic name for various skin diseases, esp. herpes; hence **dâr'tr**OUS *a.* [F, f. med. L *derbita* f. Gaulish]

Dârwĭ'nĭan *a.* & *n.* (Adherent) of Darwin's doctrine of evolution of species; so **Dâr'wĭn**ISM (3), **Dâr'wĭn**IST (2), *ns.* [f. C. *Darwin*, Engl. naturalist d. 1882 + -IAN]

dăsh[1] *v.* **1.** *v.t.* Shatter; knock, drive, throw, or thrust, *away*, *off*, *out*, *down*, etc.; fling, drive, splash, (thing or person) *against* etc., bespatter *with* mud etc. (**~'board,** board of wood or leather in front of carriage to keep out mud, board beneath motor-car windscreen, in aircraft, etc., containing instruments and controls; **~'pot,** device for damping shock or vibration); frustrate (*dash* one's *hopes*), daunt, discourage, confound; dilute, mix. **2.** Write *down* or throw *off* rapidly (letter, composition, sketch); (sl.) bribe. **3.** (sl.) (Mild form of) DAMN 2. **4.** *v.i.* Fall, move, throw oneself, with violence; come into collision *against* etc.; ride, run, or drive *up*, move about, behave, with spirit or display, whence ~'ING[2] *a.* **5.** Hence ~'ER[1] *n.* [ME, prob. imit.]

dăsh[2] *n.* **1.** Sound of water striking or struck; splash of colour; slight admixture *of* liquid etc. (*dash of brandy, of good blood*); =DASH[1]*board*. **2.** Hasty pen-stroke; horizontal stroke in writing or printing to mark a break in sense, (in pairs) a parenthesis, omitted letters or words, etc.; (Mus.) short vertical stroke indicating 'extremely staccato'; longer signal of the two used in Morse code. **3.** Rush, onset, sudden advance (**make a ~ for,** try to reach by quickness); *sprinting-race; (capacity for) vigorous action; showy appearance or behaviour (**cut a ~,** make a brilliant show); (sl.) bribe. [ME, f. prec.]

da'shĭkĭ (dah'-) *n.* Loose brightly-coloured shirt worn by Amer. Negroes. [W. Afr.]

dă'ssĭe (*or* dah'-) *n.* (S. Afr.) Cape rock-badger; small coastal fish with black tail-spot. [Afrik., f. Du. *dasje* dim. of *das* badger]

dă'stard *n.* Mean, base, or despicable coward; hence ~LY[1] *a.* [ME, prob. f. *dazed* p.p. + -ARD, or obs. *dasart* dullard and *dotard*]

dă'sȳūre *n.* (Austral.) Small ferocious arboreal catlike carnivorous marsupial of genus *Dasyurus*. [F, f. mod. L *dasyurus* f. Gk *dasus* rough + *oura* tail]

daṭa. See DATUM.

dāte[1] *n.* ~(**-palm**), W. Asian and N. Afr. tree (*Phoenix dactylifera*); its oblong single-stoned fruit. [ME f. OF, f. L f. Gk *daktulos* finger, from its leaf-shape]

dāte[2] *n.* **1.** Statement in document, letter, book, or inscription, of the time (and often place) of execution, writing, publication, etc.; time at which thing happens or is to happen; (colloq.) engagement, appointment; *(colloq.) person of opposite sex with whom one has a social engagement. **2.** Period to which antiquities etc. belong; duration, term of life. **3. Out of ~,** old-fashioned, obsolete; **to ~,** until now; **up to ~,** meeting, according to, the latest requirements or knowledge, whence **up-to-~** *attrib. a.* **4. ~-line,** (1) line from north to south pole partly along meridian 180° from Greenwich, east and west of which the date differs, (2) line in newspaper at head of dispatch, special article, etc., giving date and place of writing; **~-stamp,** (1) adjustable rubber stamp etc. used to record date of delivery, receipt, etc., (2) impression made by this. [ME f. OF, f. med. L *data*, fem. p.p. of *dare*, = (letter) given (at specified time and place)]

dāte[3] *v.* **1.** *v.t.* Mark (letter etc.) with date; refer (event, thing) *to* a time (*pottery dated to 1500* B.C.); (colloq.) make evidently belonging to a past time (*dated fashions*); ~ (**up**), *(colloq.) make social engagement with; hence **dā't**ABLE *a.* **2.** *v.i.* Count time, reckon; bear date, be dated; **~ back to, ~ from,** have existed since (*church dates from the 14th c.*). **3.** Be recognizable as belonging to a past or particular period; (colloq.) be or become out of date. [ME, f. prec.]

dā'telėss (-tl-) *a.* Having no date; of immemorial age; not likely to become out of date; hence ~NESS *n.* [f. DATE[2] + -LESS]

dā'tĭve *a.* & *n.* **1.** (Gram.) ~ (**case**), case of nouns etc. expressing indirect object or recipient, = *to* or *for* w. the noun etc.; hence **datī'v**AL *a.*, ~LY[2] (-vlĭ) *adv.* **2.** *a.* (Sc. Law, of executor) named by court, not by testator. [ME, f. L (*casus*) *dativus* (*dare dat-* give; see -IVE), in sense 1 transl. Gk (*ptōsis*) *dotikē*]

dā't|um (*or* dah'-) *n.* (*pl.* **~a**). **1.** Thing known or granted, assumption or premiss from which inferences may be drawn (SENSE-*datum*); fixed starting-point of scale etc. (*datum-line*; ORDNANCE *datum*). **2.** (in *pl.*, also treated as *sing.*)

Facts or information, esp. as basis for inference; quantities or characters operated on by computers etc. and stored or transmitted on punched cards etc.; **~a bank,** place where data are stored in large amounts; **~a processing,** automatic performance of operations on data; **~a sheet,** leaflet summarizing information on a subject. [L, neut. p.p. of *dare* give]

datū́r'a *n.* Poisonous plant of genus *Datura.* [mod. L, f. Hindi *dhatura*]

daub *v.* & *n.* **1.** *v.t.* Coat (wall etc.) with plaster, clay, etc.; smear (surface), lay on (greasy or sticky stuff); soil, stain. **2.** *v.t.* & *i.* Paint crudely and inartistically, lay (colours) on crudely and clumsily; hence ~'ER[1], ~'STER, *ns.* **3.** *n.* Plaster, clay, etc., for surface-coating esp. mixed with straw etc. and applied to laths or wattles to form wall; crude painting; smear of paint etc.; hence ~'Y[2] *a.* [ME, f. OF *dauber* f. L DE(*albare* f. *albus* white) whitewash]

daube (dōb) *n.* Braised meat (usu. beef) stew with wine etc. [F]

dau'ghter (daw't-) *n.* Female child in relation to her parents; female descendant, female member of family, nation, etc.; woman who is the spiritual or intellectual product of person or thing; product personified as female (*Carthage, daughter of Tyre*; *Fortune and its daughter Confidence*); (Phys.) nuclide formed by disintegration of another; (Biol.) cell etc. formed by division etc. of another; **~-in-law,** son's wife; **D~s of the American Revolution,** patriotic Amer. women's society; hence ~HOOD *n.*, ~LY[1] *a.* [OE *dohtor,* = OS *dohtar,* OHG *tohter,* ON *dóttir,* Goth. *dauhtar* f. Gmc **dohtēr*, **dhuktēr* f. IE **dhughetēr*]

daunt *v.t.* Discourage, intimidate. [ME, f. AF *daunter,* OF *danter, donter* f. L *domitare* frequent. of *domare* tame]

dau'ntlėss *a.* Intrepid, persevering; hence ~LY[2] *adv.*, ~NESS *n.* [f. prec. + -LESS]

dau'phĭn *n.* (Hist.) King of France's eldest son; hence ~ESS[1] *n.*, wife of dauphin. [ME f. F, f. Prov. *dalfin* f. med. L *dalphinus,* L *delphinus* DOLPHIN, as name of lords of Viennois or Dauphiné]

dă'venpōrt *n.* ||Escritoire with drawers and hinged writing-slab; *large sofa. [19th c.; f. maker's name]

Dā'vĭs *n.* ~ **apparatus,** means of escaping from submarine. [f. Sir R. H. ~, Engl. inventor d. 1965]

dă'vĭt *n.* Crane on board ship, used for hoisting anchor, torpedo, etc. inboard or outboard; one of pair of cranes for suspending or lowering ship's boat. [f. AF & OF *daviot* dim. of *Davi* David]

Dā'vȳ *n.* ~ **(lamp),** miner's safety lamp with wire gauze to prevent explosion of gas. [f. Sir H. ~, Engl. chemist d. 1829, who invented it]

Dāvȳ Jō'nes (-nz) *n.* (Naut. sl.) Evil spirit of the sea; **~'s locker,** the deep, a watery grave (in the sea). [18th c., of unkn. orig.]

daw *n.* = JACK[1]*daw.* [ME, corresp. to OE **dāwe,* OHG *tāha*]

daw'dle *v.* & *n.* **1.** *v.i.* Idle, dally. **2.** *v.t.* **~ away,** waste (time etc.). **3.** *n.* Act of dawdling; dawdling person. [cf. dial. *daddle, doddle,* sense 1]

dawg. Var. (colloq.) of DOG[1].

dawk, dak (dawk), *n.* (Ind. Hist.) (Post or transport by) relay of men or horses; ~ **bungalow,** house for travellers at place on route of dawk. [f. Hindi & Marathi *ḍāk*]

dawn *v.i.*, & *n.* **1.** *v.i.* (Of day, daylight, morning, country shone upon, thing becoming evident to mind, intelligence, civilization, etc.) begin to appear or grow light; **~ (up)on,** begin to be perceptible to; hence ~'ING[1] *n.*, daybreak, (fig.) first beginning of something. **2.** *n.* First light of day, daybreak, rise or incipient gleam of anything; ~ **chorus,** early-morning bird-song. [n. f. v., back form. f. *dawning,* ME f. earlier *dawing* after Scand., as DAY]

day *n.* **1.** Time during which sun is above horizon, interval of light between two nights; daylight (*by day*; *was broad day*; *clear as day*); time during which work is customarily done (*works an 8-hour day*); day of notable eventfulness etc. **2.** Time for one rotation of earth, period of 24 hours as unit of time (CIVIL, SIDEREAL, SOLAR, *day*). **3.** Civil day as point of time, date, etc. **4.** Date of specified festival etc. (BIRTH*day*, CHRISTMAS *Day*, LAST[3] *Day*). **5.** Date agreed upon; day for regular event (being at home to guests, etc.). **6.** Victory (*carry, lose, save, win, the day*). **7.** (in *sing.* or *pl.*) Period (*in the days of Queen Victoria*; *in the days of old*; *in days to come*; *men of other days*; *at, to, this day*); *the* current period (*questions of the day*). **8.** (in *sing.* or *pl.*) One's lifetime, period of prosperity, activity, or power. **9. All (the) ~,** throughout the day (sense 1); **all in the** (or **a**) **~'s work,** part of normal routine; **any ~,** at any time, under any conditions; **better ~s,** time when one was or will be better off; **call it a ~,** consider that one has done a day's work and cease working, (fig.) rest content, cease one's action; **(in) this ~ and age,** (at) the present time; *day* IN[2], *day out*; ~ **off** (away from work etc.); ~ **out** (away from home or lodgings); *days of* GRACE; *day of* RECKONING; ~ **and night,** throughout these or in both alike; ~ **of rest,** the Sabbath; *day* BY[1] *day*; ~ **to ~,** continuous(ly), routine(ly); **every dog has his ~,** no one is always unlucky; **at the end of the ~,** in the final reckoning; **end** one's **~s,** die, pass last part of one's life; EVIL *day*(*s*); **if he's** etc. **a ~,** (of time, age, etc.) at least; **late in the ~,** (fig.) too late to be useful; SEE[1] *the light of day*; MAKE[1] one's *day*; MAKE[1] *a day of it*; **not** one's **~,** time when things go badly for one; **on** one's **~,** at time of one's best achievement etc.; ONE *day*; **one of these (fine) ~s,** before long; ORDER[1] *of the day*; *the* OTHER *day*; **some ~** *adv.*, in the future; **that will be the ~,** it will be worth waiting for, (iron.) it will never happen; **(in) these ~s** *adv.*, nowadays; **those were the ~s,** past times were better or (iron.) worse; **one of those ~s,** a day of misfortune; TIME[1] *of day*; *a good day's* WORK[1]. **10. ~-bed,** bed for daytime sleep or rest; **~-book,** account-book in which esp. sale transactions are entered at once for later transfer to ledger; ||**~-boy,** schoolboy in boarding-school but living at home; **~'break,** dawn, first light of day; **~-dream** *n.*, & *v.i.*, (indulge in) fancy or reverie while awake; **~-fly,** insect living only a few hours or days; ||**~-girl,** schoolgirl in boarding-school but living at home; **~-labourer** (hired by the day); *~ **letter,** low-priority telegram sent by day; ~ **lily,** plant of genus *Hemerocallis,* with flowers lasting only a day; **~-long** *a.* & *adv.*, (lasting) for whole day; ~ **nursery,** (1) room for children in daytime, (2) place where children are looked after while mothers work; **~-owl,** hawk-owl hunting by day; ~ **release,** system of allowing employees days off work for education; **~-return,** (ticket) at reduced rate for journey both ways in one day; **~-room** (used by day only, esp. common living-room at boarding-schools); **~-school,** opp. Sunday, evening, or boarding school; ~ **shift,** opp. *night shift*; **~-spring,** (arch. or poet.) dawn; **~-star,** sun or morning star; **~'time,** not night, esp. *in the daytime*; **~'work** (paid for according to time worked). [OE *dæg,* = OS *dag,* OHG *tac,* ON *dagr,* Goth. *dags* f. Gmc **dagaz*]

Dayak. Var. of DYAK.

day'light (-līt) *n.* Light of day; openness, publicity; dawn (*before, at, daylight*); (in *pl.*, sl.) internal organs (esp. *beat, scare*, etc. *the daylights out of*); visible interval, e.g. between boats in race, wine and glass-rim, or rider and saddle; **burn ~,** (arch.) use artificial light in daytime; **see ~,** (fig.) understand what was previously puzzling; **~ robbery,** unashamed swindling; **~ saving,** use of modified time to give longer evening daylight in summer, by making clocks show later time. [ME, f. DAY + LIGHT[1]]

dāze *v.t.*, & *n.* **1.** *v.t.* Stupefy, bewilder. **2.** *n.* (State of) stupefaction or bewilderment. [ME *dased* p.p., f. ON *dasathr* weary]

dă'zzle *v.* & *n.* **1.** *v.t.* Confuse or dim (sight, eye, person) with excess of light, intricate motion, incalculable number, etc.; delude or surprise (mind, person) by brilliant display or prospect; confuse or impress *by* or *with* brilliance etc.; hence **~MENT** (-zelm-) *n.* **2.** *v.i.* (arch.) (Of eyes) be dazzled. **3.** *n.* Bright confusing light; **~ paint** (patterned on ship to deceive enemy about her type or course). [ME, f. prec. + -LE 3]

dB *abbr.* decibel(s).

||**D.B.E.** *abbr.* Dame Commander (of the Order) of the British Empire.

D.C. *abbr. da capo*; (*or* **d.c.**) direct current; District of Columbia; District Commissioner.

||**D.C.B.** *abbr.* Dame Commander (of the Order) of the Bath.

D.C.L. *abbr.* Doctor of Civil Law.

D.C.M. *abbr.* Distinguished Conduct Medal.

||**D.C.M.G.** *abbr.* Dame Commander (of the Order) of St. Michael & St. George.

||**D.C.V.O.** *abbr.* Dame Commander of the Royal Victorian Order.

D.D. *abbr.* Doctor of Divinity.

D-Day (dē'dā) *n.* Day (6 June 1944) on which British and American forces invaded N. France; day (in Britain 15 Feb. 1971) on which decimal currency came into use; day on which any operation is scheduled to begin. [f. *D* for *day* + DAY]

D.D.T. (dēdētē') *n.* White chlorinated hydrocarbon used as insecticide. [f. Chem. name *d*ichloro*d*iphenyl*t*richloroethane]

de- *pref.* meaning (1) down (*depend, descend*), away (*defend, deduct*), removal (*decapitate*), completely (*declare, denude*), in a bad sense (*deceive, defame, deride*); (2) [thr. OF *des-* f. L *dis-*] removal or reversal, forming compd. vbs. (w. derivs.) from vbs. (*de-acidify, decentralize, decentralization, de-escalate, demoralize, demoralization, depressurize, desegregate*) and ns. (*defuse, dehorn, de-ice, delouse, detrain*). [f. or after L *de* adv. & prep. = off, from]

***dea'con**[1] *v.t.* Read aloud each line of (hymn etc.) before it is sung; deceive to slight extent. [f. foll.]

dea'con[2] *n.* **1.** (In Episcopal churches) member of third order of ministry, below bishop and priest. **2.** (In Nonconformist churches) lay officer attending to congregation's secular affairs. **3.** (In early Church) appointed minister of charity. **4.** Hence **~ATE**[1], **~SHIP**, *ns.* [OE *diacon* f. eccl. L f. Gk *diakonos* servant]

dea'coness *n.* Woman in early and some modern Churches with functions analogous to deacon's. [f. prec., after LL *diaconissa* (see -ESS[1])]

dēă'ctĭv|āte *v.t.* Render inactive or less reactive; hence **~A'TION**, **~ātor**, *ns.* [f. DE- + ACTIVATE]

dead (dĕd) *a., adv.,* & *n.* **1.** *a.* That has ceased to live (**the ~**, dead person or persons, all who have ever died; **from the ~**, from among these); **~ as a doornail, ~ as mutton,** quite dead; FLOG *dead horse*; **~ from the neck up,** (colloq.) brainless; **wouldn't be seen ~ in** etc., (colloq.) shall have nothing to do with, refuse to wear etc.; *dead men's* SHOE[1]*s*. **2.** Benumbed, insensible, (hands etc.; **~ to,** unconscious or unappreciative of, hardened against: **~ to the world,** unconscious or fast asleep); extremely tired or ill; without spiritual life. **3.** Obsolete, past, not effective, (**~ as the** or **a dodo,** entirely obsolete). **4.** Inanimate; extinct, dull, lustreless, without force, muffled, (of champagne etc.) no longer effervescent, flat; (of coal) no longer red-hot; (of match) already struck and burnt out; (of sound) not resonant. **5.** Inactive (*the dead season*), motionless, idle; (of microphone, telephone, etc.) not transmitting sounds; (of ball in games) out of play. **6.** Abrupt, complete, unrelieved, exact, (*come to a dead stop*; *a dead loss*; *a dead faint*; *on a dead level*; *a dead calm*; *in dead silence*; (colloq.) *in dead trouble*; *be in dead earnest*; *a dead certainty*; **a ~ shot,** unerring). **7.** (Golf, of ball) very close to hole, within sure holing distance. **8. ~-(and-)alive,** (of place, work, etc.) dull, monotonous, (of person) spiritless; **~ bat,** (Cricket) bat held loosely so that ball strikes it and immediately falls to the ground; **~ centre,** exact centre, position of crank etc. in line with connecting-rod and not exerting torque; **~ duck,** (sl.) unsuccessful or useless person or thing; **~ end,** closed end of passage etc.; **~-end** *a.*, (fig., of job, policy, etc.) having no prospects of advancement (**~-end kid,** young slum-dwelling tough); **~-eye,** (Naut.) round flat three-holed block for extending shrouds; ***~'fall,** trap with falling weight to kill animal (also fig.); **~-fire,** corposant as presaging death; **~ hand,** posthumous control (esp. fig., of undesirable persisting influence); **~'head,** faded flower-head, non-paying theatre-goer etc. or passenger, useless or unenterprising person; **~ heat,** race in which two or more competitors finish exactly level (so *~-heat* v.i.); **~ language,** one no longer ordinarily spoken, e.g. Latin; **~ letter,** law no longer observed, unclaimed or undelivered letter; **~ lift,** exertion of utmost strength to lift something; **~'light,** (Naut.) shutter inside porthole; **~'line,** line beyond which it is not permitted or possible to go, time-limit; **~'lock,** (1) lock that opens and shuts only with key, (2) complete standstill or lack of progress (so as *v.t.*, bring to standstill); **~ loss,** complete loss, (colloq.) worthless person or thing; **~ man's fingers,** (1) kind of orchis, (2) soft coral of genus *Alcyonium*, (3) finger-like divisions of lobster's or crab's gills; **~ man's handle, pedal,** etc., controlling-device on electric and other trains, disconnecting power supply if released; **~ march,** marchlike funeral music; **~ men,** (colloq.) emptied bottles; **~ nettle,** plant of genus *Lamium*, with nettle-like leaves but not stinging; **~ pan,** (colloq.) expressionless (face); **~ reckoning** (Naut., of ship's position by log, compass, etc., when observations are impossible); *dead* SET[2]; **~'s part,** (Sc. Law) part of estate whose disposal is decidable by testator; **~'stock,** farm machinery; **~ time,** (Phys.) period after recording of pulse etc. when detector is unable to record another; **~ weight,** inert mass, (fig.) debt not covered by assets, weight of cargo, fuel, crew, and passengers carried by ship; **~ wood,** wood no longer alive, (fig.) useless person(s) or thing(s). **9.** Hence **~'NESS** *n.* **10.** *adv.* Profoundly, absolutely, exactly, completely, (*dead asleep, drunk, easy, level,*

For other words in *de-* see DE-.

on the target etc., *slow, straight, tired*); CUT² person *dead*; ~ **against,** directly opposed or opposite to; **~-beat,** (person) completely exhausted or without money, (Phys., of instrument) without recoil; **~-on** *a.*, exactly right. **11.** *n.* Inactive or silent time (*the dead of night, winter*). [OE *dēad*, =OS *dōd*, OHG *tōt*, ON *dauthr*, Goth. *dauths* f. Gmc **daudhaz* f. **dhautós* p.p. of **dhau-* DIE²]

dea'den (dĕ'd-) *v.t.* & *i.* Deprive of or lose vitality, force, brightness, feeling, etc.; make insensitive *to*. [f. prec. + -EN⁶]

dea'dl|ȳ¹ (dĕ'd-) *a.* Causing fatal injury or serious damage; (of aim etc.) accurate; of poisonous nature (*deadly* NIGHTSHADE); entailing damnation (*deadly* SIN¹); implacable, internecine; deathlike (*deadly paleness, faintness, gloom*); intense (*deadly dullness*); hence **~ĭNESS** *n.* [OE *dēadlic* (as DEAD, -LY¹)]

dea'dlȳ² (dĕ'd-) *adv.* As if dead (*deadly pale, faint*); extremely (*deadly tired, dull*). [OE *dēadlīce* (as DEAD, -LY²)]

dē-aer'|āte (-ār'-) *v.t.* Remove air from; hence **~A'TION** *n.* [f. DE- + AERATE]

deaf (dĕf) *a.* **1.** Wholly or partly without hearing (**the ~,** deaf people; *deaf in one ear*). **2.** Insensitive to harmony, rhythm, etc. (TONE¹-*deaf*); not giving ear *to*, uncompliant; **turn a ~ ear,** be unresponsive (*to* appeal etc.); **fall on ~ ears,** be ignored. **3. ~-aid,** hearing aid; **~-and-dumb alphabet, language,** etc., signs for communication with the deaf; **~ mute,** deaf and dumb person; **~ nut,** one with no kernel. **4.** Hence **~'LY²** *adv.*, **~'NESS** *n.* [OE *dēaf*, =OS *dōf*, OHG *toup*, ON *daufr*, Goth. *daufs* f. Gmc **daubhaz*]

dea'fen (dĕ'f-) *v.t.* Deprive of hearing by noise, temporarily or permanently. [f. prec. + -EN⁶]

deal¹ *n.* **A great, good, ~,** (colloq.) **a ~,** large or considerable amount, (*adv.*) to a large or considerable extent, (esp. w. compar. or superl.) by much, considerably. [OE *dǣl*, =OS *dēl*, OHG *teil*, Goth. *dails* f. Gmc **dailiz*; cf. DOLE¹]

deal² *v.* (**~t** *pr.* dĕlt) & *n.* **1.** *v.t.* Distribute, give *out*, (gifts etc.) among several; (esp. of Providence etc.) deliver as share or deserts to person (*dealt him happiness, good measure*); cause to be received, administer, (esp. **~ a blow,** lit. or fig.). **2.** *v.t.* & *i.* Distribute (cards) to players for a game or round. **3.** *v.i.* Associate *with* (esp. w. neg.; *refuse to deal with*); do business *with* person, *in* goods (lit. or fig.). **4.** Occupy oneself *with* (esp. with view to discussion or refutation), take (esp. corrective or punitive) measures *with*; (w. *adv.*) behave (*deal honourably, cruelly*, etc., esp. *with* or *by* person). **5.** Hence **~'ING¹** (1) *n.* (**have ~ings with,** associate with). **6.** *n.* Distribution of cards by dealing, player's turn for this (*it is my deal*), round of play following this; (colloq.) bargain, transaction (BIG *deal*; **it's a ~,** (colloq.) I agree to the terms you propose; **new ~,** new and improved arrangement, esp. (*New Deal*) of U.S. reforms 1932–; **raw** or **rough ~,** harsh or unfair treatment; **fair** or SQUARE² *deal*); *secret or dishonest bargain. [OE *dǣlan*, =OS *dēljan*, OHG *teilen*, ON *deila*, Goth. *dailjan* f. Gmc (as prec.)]

deal³ *n.* Piece of sawn fir or pine wood of standard size; a quantity of these; fir or pine timber. [ME, f. MLG *dele* plank, OHG *dil* etc., ON *thilja* f. Gmc **thelaz* etc.]

dea'ler *n.* In vbl senses; player dealing at cards; trader, usu. in comb., as *horse-dealer*; jobber on Stock Exchange. [f. DEAL² + -ER¹]

dealt. See DEAL².

dēămbūlā'tion *n.*, **dēă'mbūlatorȳ** *a.* Walking about. [f. L *deambulatio, deambulatorius*, f. DE(*ambulare* walk); see -ATION, -ORY]

dean¹ *n.* Head of cathedral or collegiate-church chapter; ‖(**rural**) **~,** clergyman exercising supervision over group of parochial clergy within division of archdeaconry; (in college or university) resident fellow, or one of several, with disciplinary and advisory functions; head of university faculty or department; = DOYEN; **D~ of Faculty,** president of the Faculty of Advocates in Scotland. [ME, f. AF *de(e)n*, OF *d(e)ien* f. LL *decanus* (*decem* ten); orig. = chief of group of 10]

‖**dean²,** ‖**dēne,** *n.* Vale (esp. as ending of place-names); narrow wooded valley of stream. [f. OE *denu*, cogn. w. DEN]

dea'nerȳ *n.* Office or house of dean; ‖group of parishes presided over by rural dean. [f. DEAN¹ + -ERY]

dear *a.*, *n.*, *adv.*, & *int.* **1.** *a.* Beloved (often as merely polite or even iron. form in talk, esp. **my ~ sir, my ~ Jones**; now used as part of polite formula at beginning of most letters: *Dear Sir*; *Dear Mr. Jones*; *Dear Jones* or — ‖less formally, *more formally — *My dear Jones*; *Dear Jane*; *Dear Father*). **2.** Precious *to*; cherished (**for ~ life,** as though life itself were at stake); earnest (*his dearest desire is for your happiness*). **3.** High-priced relative to its value; having high prices; (of money) available as loan only at high rate of interest. **4.** Hence **~'LY²** *adv.* (**love ~ly** or **~ly love,** love very much), **~'NESS** *n.* **5.** *n.* (esp. in *voc.*; also **~'est**). Dear person. **6.** *adv.* At high price relative to value (*buy*, COST² one, *pay, sell, dear*). **7.** *int.* (usu. **~, ~!** or **~ me!** or **oh ~!**) expr. surprise, distress, sympathy, etc.; **~ knows,** = GOD *knows*. [OE *dēore*, =OS *diuri*, OHG *tiuri*, ON *dýrr* f. Gmc **deurjaz*]

dear'ie *n.* (usu. in *voc.*) Darling; **~ me!,** = prec. 7. [f. prec. + -IE]

dearth (dēr-) *n.* Scarcity and dearness of food; scanty supply *of*. [ME, f. as DEAR; see -TH¹]

death (dĕth) *n.* **1.** Dying, final cessation of vital functions; DIE² *the death*; **as sure as ~,** quite certain. **2.** Event that terminates life (**civil ~,** ceasing to have citizen's privileges through outlawry, banishment, etc.; **catch** one's **~,** (colloq.) catch fatal chill etc.). **3.** Being killed or killing (**be the ~ of,** cause death of; *bleed, drink oneself, put, stone, work*, etc., *to death*; *war to the death*); **be in at the ~,** see fox killed, or (fig.) any enterprise ended; **be ~ on,** (sl.) be skilful at killing game, prey, etc., or (fig.) at doing anything; **do to ~,** kill, (fig.) overdo; **fate worse than ~,** (joc.) being raped; **scared to, sick to, tickled to, tired to, ~** (to utmost limit); **worked** etc. **to ~,** (fig.) hackneyed. **4.** Ceasing to be, annihilation, (*death of* one's *hopes*); (*D~*) personified power that annihilates; **at ~'s door,** close to death; **like ~ warmed up,** (sl.) very tired or ill; *hold on* **like grim ~,** with all one's force. **5.** Being dead (*eyes closed in death*; LIVING² *death*). **6.** Lack of spiritual life (**everlasting ~,** damnation). **7. Black D~,** (mod. name, transl. f. G for) great epidemic of plague in Europe in 14th c. **8.** Hence or cogn. **~'LESS, ~'LIKE,** *adjs.*, **~LY¹** *a.* & *adv.* **9. ~ adder,** venomous Austral. snake; **~'bed,** bed on which person dies (*~bed repentance* etc., last-minute change of conduct or policy); **~-blow,** blow that causes death (lit. or fig.); **~ cap,** a poisonous toadstool (*Amanita phalloides*); **~ cell** (for person condemned to death); **~ certificate,** official statement of cause and date and place of person's death; **~-dealing,** lethal; ‖**~ duty,** tax levied on property after owner's death; ***~ house,** group of death cells; **~-knell,** tolling of bell to mark person's death, (fig.) event that heralds the end of something; **~-mask,** cast taken of dead person's face; **~ penalty,** capital punishment; **~ rate,** number of deaths per thousand of population per year; **~-rattle,** sound in dying person's throat; **~-ray,** (imaginary) ray that causes death; **~-roll,** list or number of those killed in accident, battle, etc.; **~'s head,** skull as emblem of mortality (**~'s head moth,** large dark hawk-moth with skull-like markings on back of thorax); ***~ tax** = *death duty*; **~-trap,** unsuspectedly unwholesome or dangerous place or structure; **~-warrant** (for execution of criminal or (fig.) abolition of custom, etc.); **~-watch (beetle),** small beetle whose larva bores in old wood and which makes sound like watch ticking, once supposed to portend death; **~-wish,** (Psych.) (usu. unconscious) wish for death of oneself or another. [OE *dēath*, = OS *dōth*, OHG *tōd*, ON *dauthr*, Goth. *dauthus* f. Gmc **dauthuz* (**dau* DIE²; see -TH¹)]

dĕb *n.* (colloq.) Débutante. [abbr.]

débâcle (dābah'kl) *n.* **1.** Break-up of ice in river; sudden rush of water carrying along blocks of stone and other debris. **2.** Sudden collapse; downfall, e.g. of a government; confused rush or rout, stampede. [F (*débâcler* unbar)]

dēbă'g *v.t.* (-gg-). (sl.) Remove the trousers of (person) as punishment or joke. [f. DE- + BAG¹]

dėbar' *v.t.* (-rr-). Exclude *from* admission or right. [ME, f. F *débarrer*, OF *desbarrer* (*des-* DE-, *barrer* BAR²)]

dėbar'k¹ *v.t.* & *i.* = DISEMBARK; hence **dēbarka'tion** *n.* [f. F *débarquer* (as DE-, BARK³)]

dēbar'k² *v.t.* Remove bark from (tree). [f. DE- + BARK¹]

dēbar'k³ *v.t.* Operate on (dog) to prevent it from barking. [f. DE- + BARK⁴]

dėbā'se *v.t.* Lower in quality, value, or character; depreciate (coin) by alloying etc.; hence **~MENT** (-sm-) *n.* [f. DE- + obs. *base* for ABASE]

dėbā'table *a.* Questionable, subject to dispute; capable of being debated; **~ ground,** borderland (lit. or fig.) claimed by both sides. [OF, or f. AL *debatabilis* (as foll.; see -ABLE)]

dėbā't|e *v.* & *n.* **1.** *v.t.* & *i.* Dispute about, discuss, (a question); hold formal argument, esp. in legislature or public meeting; consider, ponder; (arch.) contest; hence **~ER¹** *n.* **2.** *n.* Debating, discussion; public argument. [ME; (n. f. OF *debat*) f. OF *debatre* f. Rom. **desbattere* (as DE-, BATTLE¹)]

dėbā'ting *n.* In vbl senses; **~ club, society,** (for practice in debating); **~ point,** inessential matter used to gain advantage in debate. [f. prec. + -ING¹]

dėbau'ch *v.t.*, & *n.* (literary). **1.** *v.t.* Pervert from virtue or morality; make intemperate or sensual; seduce (woman); vitiate (taste, judgement); (in *p.p.*) dissolute. **2.** *n.* Bout or habit of sensual indulgence; hence **~ERY** (4) *n.* [f. F *débauche(r)*, OF *desbaucher*, of unkn. orig.]

dėbauchee' *n.* Excessively sensual person; person addicted to sensual indulgence. [f. F *débauché* p.p.; see prec., -EE]

dēbea'k *v.t.* Remove upper part of beak of (bird) to prevent fighting etc. [f. DE- + BEAK¹]

dėbĕ'nture *n.* **1.** ‖Sealed bond of corporation or company acknowledging sum on which interest is due, esp. as prior charge on assets (**~ stock,** stock comprising debentures, with only interest secured); ***~ (bond),** fixed-interest bond of corporation or company; (arch.) voucher for payment from government department. [ME, f. L *debentur* are owing (*debēre* owe); assim. to -URE]

dėbĭ'lĭtāte *v.t.* Enfeeble (constitution etc.). [f. L *debilitare* (as foll.) + -ATE³]

dėbĭ'lĭtȳ *n.* Feebleness (of health, purpose, etc.). [ME, f. OF *debilité* f. L *debilitas -tatis* (*debilis* weak; see -ITY)]

dĕ'bĭt *n.*, & *v.t.* **1.** *n.* (Bookk.) Record of sum owing by entry in account; (sum entered on) debit side of account. **2.** *v.t.* Enter on debit side of account (amount *against* or *to* person, person *with* amount). [f. F *débit* f. L *debitum* DEBT]

dĕbonair' *a.* Having pleasant manners; cheerful, carefree, unembarrassed. [ME, f. OF *debonaire* = *de bon aire* of good disposition]

dėbou'ch (*or* -ōō'sh) *v.i.* (Of troops, stream) issue from ravine, wood, etc., into open ground; (of river, road, etc.) merge into larger body or area (sea, square, etc.); hence **~MENT** *n.* [f. F *déboucher* (*dé-*, DE-, *bouche* mouth)]

‖**Dėbrĕ'tt** *n.* (colloq.) (Used for) 'Debrett's Peerage etc.' [f. J. ~, compiler d. 1822]

dēbrie'f *v.t.* (colloq.) Interrogate (person) after completion of mission etc. [f. DE- + BRIEF²]

dĕ'bris (-rē; *or* dā'-) *n.* Scattered fragments, wreckage, drifted accumulation. [f. F *débris* f. obs. *débriser* break down (as DE-, *briser* break)]

dĕbt (dĕt) *n.* **1.** Money, goods, or service, owing; BAD *debt*; **~-collector,** one whose business it is to collect debts for creditors; **~ of honour** (not legally recoverable, esp. of sum lost in gambling); **~ of nature,** necessity of death; **floating ~** (repayable on demand, or at stated time); **National D~,** money owed by State because of loans to it. **2.** Being under obligation to pay something (*in, out of, get into, debt*); **in** person's **~,** under obligation to him. [ME *det(te)* f. OF *dette* (later *debte*) f. Rom. **debita* f. L *debitum* p.p. of *debēre* owe]

dĕ'btor (dĕ't-) *n.* One who owes money or an obligation or duty. [ME f. OF *det(t)o(u)r* f. L *debitor* (as prec.; see -OR)]

dēbŭ'g *v.t.* (-gg-). Remove bugs (lit., or fig. = defects or microphones) from. [f. DE- + BUG]

dēbŭ'nk *v.t.* (colloq.) Remove false reputation from (person, institution, cult, etc.); expose falseness of (claim etc.). [f. DE- + BUNK³]

dēbŭ's *v.t.* & *i.* (-ss-). (esp. Mil.) Unload (men, stores) or alight from motor vehicles. [f. DE- + BUS]

début, *debut, (dā'bōō; *or* -bū) *n.* First appearance in society, or on stage, in sport, etc. as performer. [F (*débuter* lead off)]

débutante, *deb-, (dĕ'būtahnt; *or* dā'-) *n.* Woman performer making début; young woman making social début. [F, fem. part. of *débuter* (see prec.)]

Dec. *abbr.* December.

dec. *abbr.* deceased; declared.

dĕ'ca- *comb. form.* **1.** Tenfold, having ten, as: **deca'gynous** (-ă'j-), having ten pistils; **~HE'DRAL,** having ten faces (**~HE'DRON,** such solid); **deca'ndrous,** having ten stamens; **~style,** ten-columned (portico). **2.** Ten, esp. of a unit in the metric system (*deca*GRAM², *deca*LITRE, *deca*METRE²). [f. Gk *deka* ten]

dĕ'cāde (*or* dĭkā'd) *n.* Set or series of ten; ten years; so **dĕ'cadAL, dėcă'dIC,** *adjs.* [ME, f. F *décade* f. LL *decas -adis* f. Gk (*deka* ten); see -AD, -ADE]

dĕ'cadence *n.* Falling away, decline, deterioration, (esp. of a period of art or literature after culmination). [f. F *décadence* f. med. L *decadentia* (*decadere* DECAY¹; see -ENCE)]

dĕ'cadent *a.* & *n.* **1.** *a.* Declining, decaying; self-indulgent; of a period of decadence. **2.** *n.* Decadent person; 19th-c. writer or artist with artificial and obscure style, whence **~ISM** (3) *n.* [f. F *décadent* (as prec.; see -ENT)]

dėcă'ffeināte (-fĭn-) *v.t.* Remove caffeine from or reduce quantity of caffeine in (coffee). [f. DE- + CAFFEINE + -ATE³]

For other words in *de-* see DE-.

dĕ′cagon *n.* Plane figure with ten sides and angles; hence **dėcă′gon**AL *a.* [f. med. L f. Gk *dekagōnon* (as DECA-, -GON)]
***dē′căl** *n.* Picture transferred to and permanently fixed on china or other material. [abbr. of *decalcomania* f. F *décalcomanie* (*décalquer* transfer; see -MANIA)]
dēcă′lcĭ|fȳ *v.t.* Deprive (bone etc.) of lime or calcareous matter; hence ~FICA′TION *n.* [f. DE- + CALCIFY]
Dĕ′calŏgue (-ŏg) *n.* *The* Ten COMMANDMENTS collectively. [ME f. OF, or f. eccl. L f. Gk *dekalogos* (after *hoi deka logoi* the ten commandments)]
dėcă′mp *v.i.* Break up or leave camp; go away suddenly, take oneself off, abscond; hence ~MENT *n.* [f. F *décamper* (as DE-, CAMP[1])]
dėcā′nal (*or* dĕ′ka-) *a.* Of dean or deanery; of S. side (on which dean sits) of choir (cf. CANTORIAL). [f. med. L *decanalis* f. LL *decanus* DEAN[1]; see -AL]
dėcā′nī *a.* (Mus.) To be sung by decanal side in antiphonal singing (cf. CANTORIS). [L, gen. of *decanus* DEAN[1]]
dėcă′nt *v.t.* Pour off (liquid or solution) by gradual inclination of vessel without disturbing sediment; pour (wine) similarly from bottle into decanter; (fig.) move or transfer as if by pouring. [f. med. L DE(*canthare* f. L f. Gk *kanthos* canthus, used of lip of beaker)]
dėcă′nter *n.* Stoppered glass bottle in which wine or spirit is brought to table. [f. prec. + -ER[1]]
dėcă′pĭt|āte *v.t.* Behead (esp. as legal punishment); cut the head or end from; *dismiss abruptly from office; so ~A′TION *n.* [f. LL DE(*capitare* f. *caput -itis* head)]
dĕ′capŏd *n.* Ten-footed crustacean (crab, lobster, etc.). [f. F *décapode* f. mod. L *decapoda* f. Gk *deka* ten + *pous podos* foot]
dēcar′bonīz|e, -īs|e (-īz), *v.t.* Remove carbon from (internal combustion engine etc.); hence ~A′TION *n.* [f. DE- + CARBON + -IZE]
dēcă′sualīz|e (-zhŏŏ-; *or* -zū-), **-īs|e** (-īz), *v.t.* Do away with casual employment of (labour) by introducing permanent jobs; hence ~A′TION *n.* [f. DE- + CASUAL + -IZE]
dĕcasўllă′bĭc *a.* & *n.*, **dĕ′casўllable** *n.* (Metrical line) of ten syllables. [f. DECA- + SYLLABIC, SYLLABLE]
dėcă′thlon *n.* Athletic contest comprising ten different events for competitor. [f. DECA- + Gk *athlon* contest]
dėcay′[1] *v.i.* & *t.* (Cause to) become rotten; (cause to) deteriorate, lose quality, decline in power, wealth, energy, beauty, etc.; (Phys.) decrease in amplitude or intensity of radioactivity, (of substance etc.) change by radioactivity *into* another. [ME, f. OF *decair* f. Rom. *DE(*cadere* fall)]
dėcay′[2] *n.* Decline in health, loss of quality; rotten or ruinous state, wasting away; decayed tissue; (Phys.) loss of amplitude or intensity of radioactivity, change into another substance etc. by radioactivity. [ME, f. prec.]
dėcea′s|e *n.*, & *v.i.* (Esp. in legal and formal use for) death, die; hence ~ED[1] (2) (-ē′st) *a.* & *n.* (with or without *the*), (person) who has died (esp. recently). [ME, f. OF *deces* f. L DE(*cessus* n. f. *cedere cess-* go)]
***dėcē′dent** *n.* Deceased person. [f. L *decedere* die; see prec., -ENT]
dėcei′t (-sē′t) *n.* Misrepresentation, deceiving; trick, stratagem; willingness to deceive, deceitfulness; hence ~FUL *a.* [ME f. OF, f. p.p. of *deceveir* f. L DE(*cipere cept-* = *capere* take) deceive]
dėcei′ve (-sē′v) *v.* **1.** *v.t.* Persuade of what is false, mislead purposely, (~ one**self, be** ~**d,** be mistaken or deluded); disappoint (esp. hopes). **2.** *v.i.* Use deceit. **3.** Hence or cogn. **dėcei′v**ABLE *a.*, **dėcei′v**ER[1] *n.*, (-sē′-). [ME, f. OF *deceivre* or *deceiv-* stressed st. of *deceveir* (as prec.)]
dēcĕ′ler|āte *v.* **1.** *v.t.* Make slower (*decelerated motion*); cause to move more slowly. **2.** *v.i.* Begin to move more slowly. **3.** Hence ~A′TION, ~**ā**TOR, ~**ŏ′**METER, *ns.* [f. DE-, after ACCELERATE]
Dėcĕ′mber *n.* Twelfth month of year. [ME, f. OF *decembre* f. L *December* (*decem* ten; orig. tenth month of Roman year)]
dē′cencȳ *n.* Propriety of behaviour; what is accepted as being required by good taste or delicacy; avoidance of obscene language and gestures and of undue exposure of person; respectability; (in *pl.*) requirements of respectable behaviour. [f. L *decentia* (*decēre* be fitting; see -ENCY)]
dėcĕ′nnĭal *a.* Lasting, recurring every, ten years; hence ~LY[2] *adv.* [f. L (as foll.) + -AL]
dėcĕ′nnĭ|um *n.* (*pl.* ~**ums** *or* ~**a**). Period of ten years. [L, f. *decennis* of ten years (*decem* ten, *annus* year)]
dē′cent *a.* Seemly, not immodest or obscene or indelicate; respectable; passable, good enough, tolerable; ‖(colloq.) kind, generous, obliging; hence ~LY[2] *adv.* [f. F *décent* or f. L *decēre* be fitting; see -ENT]
dēcĕ′ntralīz|e, -īs|e (-īz), *v.t.* Do away with centralization of; confer local government on; distribute (administrative powers etc.) among local centres; hence ~A′TION *n.* [f. DE- + CENTRALIZE]
dėcĕ′ption *n.* Deceiving or being deceived; thing that deceives, trick, sham. [ME f. OF, or f. LL *deceptio* (*decipere*; see DECEIT, -ION)]
dėcĕ′ptĭve *a.* Apt to deceive, easily mistaken for something else; hence ~LY[2] (-vlĭ) *adv.*, ~NESS (-vn-) *n.* [f. OF *deceptif -ive* or f. LL *deceptivus* (as prec.; see -IVE)]
dēcĕ′rėbrate *a.* Having had the cerebrum removed. [f. DE- + CEREBRUM + -ATE[2]]
dĕ′cĭ- *comb form.* One-tenth, esp. of a unit in the metric system (DECIBEL, *deci*GRAM[2], *deci*LITRE, *deci*METRE[2]). [f. L *decimus* tenth]
dĕ′cĭbĕl *n.* Unit (=one-tenth of a bel) used in comparison of power levels in electrical communication or intensities of sound, one of the compared values often being an understood standard. [f. prec. + BEL]
dėcī′d|e *v.t.* & *i.* Settle (question, issue, dispute) by giving victory to one side; give judgement (*between*, *for*, *in favour of*, *against*, *that*, or abs.); bring or come to a resolution (*that decides me*; *decide to* do, *on*, *for*, or *against* thing or do*ing*, *that*); hence ~ABLE *a.* [ME, f. F *décider* or f. L DE(*cidere cis-* = *caedere* cut)]
dėcī′dėd *a.* In vbl senses; definite, unquestionable, (*a decided difference*); (of person) having clear opinions or vigorous initiative, not vacillating; hence ~LY[2] *adv.* [p.p. of prec.]
dėcī′der *n.* In vbl senses; game, race, etc., to decide between competitors with equal scores. [f. DECIDE + -ER[1]]
dėcĭ′dūous *a.* (Of leaves, teeth, horns, etc.) shed periodically or normally; (of tree) shedding its leaves annually; (of ant etc.) shedding its wings after copulation; (fig.) fleeting, transitory. [f. L *deciduus* f. DE(*cidere* = *cadere* fall) + -OUS]
dĕ′cĭmal *a.* & *n.* **1.** *a.* Of tenths or ten, reckoning or proceeding by tens; ~ **arithmetic** (counting in tens); ~ **coinage, currency,** (in which units are decimal multiples or fractions of each other); ~ **fraction,** one whose denominator is a power of ten, esp. when expressed by figures written to right of the ~ **point** or dot placed after the unit figure; *decimal* SCALE[3]; ~ **system** (in which each denomination (weight, measure)

is ten times the value of the one before it, or in which each class is divided into ten subclasses). **2.** Of decimal coinage; **go ~**, adopt decimal coinage. **3.** Hence ~IZE *v.t.*, express as decimal, convert to decimal system, ~LY[2] *adv.* **4.** *n.* Decimal fraction (RECURring *decimal*). [f. mod. L *decimalis* f. L *decimus* tenth (*decem* ten; see -AL)]

dě'cim|āte *v.t.* **1.** (Hist.) Put to death one in ten of (mutinous or cowardly soldiers). **2.** (Of epidemic etc.) destroy tenth or large proportion of. **3.** So ~A'TION *n.* [f. L *decimare* take the tenth man (*decimus*; see prec.) + -ATE[3]]

dėcī'pher *v.t.* Turn into ordinary writing or make out by means of key (text written in cipher); make out meaning of (bad writing, hieroglyphics, anything perplexing); hence ~ABLE *a.*, ~MENT *n.* [f. DE- + CIPHER[2]]

dėcĭ'sion (-zhon) *n.* Settlement (*of* question etc.), conclusion, formal judgement; making up one's mind, resolve, (*come to, make, take, a decision*); resoluteness, decided character. [ME f. OF, or f. L *decisio* (as DECIDE; see -ION)]

dėcī'sĭve *a.* Deciding, conclusive, (esp. *decisive battle*); = DECIDED (*decisive character, decisive preference*); hence ~LY[2] (-vlĭ) *adv.*, ~NESS (-vn-) *n.* [f. F *décisif -ive* f. med. L *decisivus* (as DECIDE; see -IVE)]

děck[1] *n.* **1.** Platform of planks or wood-covered iron extending from side to side of ship or part of it (**below ~(s)**, in or into space under main deck; CLEAR[2] *the decks*; LOWER[3] *deck*; **on ~**, not below deck, (fig.) available for work etc.). **2.** Floor of pier; floor or compartment of bus etc.; platform for sunbathing etc.; device for carrying and moving (and playing etc., or transferring information to or from) magnetic tape in recorder; similar arrangement in record-player; (sl.) ground. **3. ~-chair,** folding chair of wood and canvas, used in passenger ships and elsewhere; **~-hand,** man employed on vessel's deck in cleaning and odd jobs; **~-house,** room erected on deck; **~ passenger** (having no cabin); **~ quoits** (played with rope quoit and peg); **~ tennis,** game of tossing quoit etc. to and fro over net. **4.** *Pack of cards; *packet of narcotics. [ME = 'covering', f. MDu. *dec* roof, cloak]

děck[2] *v.t.* **1. ~ (out)**, array, adorn. **2.** Furnish with or cover as a deck. [f. MDu. *dekken* cover; cf. THATCH]

-děcker *comb. form.* Having (so many, such) decks (*double-decker bus*); **three-~** (= three-volume) **novel.** [f. DECK[1] + -ER[1]]

dě'ckle *n.* Frame in paper-making machine for limiting size of sheet (**~-edge,** rough uncut edge formed by deckle). [f. G *deckel* dim. of *decke* cover; cf. -LE 1]

dėclai'm *v.i.* & *t.* Speak or utter rhetorically; inveigh *against*; practise speaking or recitation; deliver impassioned (rather than reasoned) speech; hence ~ER[1] *n.* [ME, f. F *déclamer* or f. L *declamare*; see DE- 1, CLAIM[1]]

děclamā'tion *n.* Act or art of declaiming; rhetorical exercise, set speech; impassioned speech, harangue; so **dėclă'mat**ORY *a.* [f. F *déclamation* or f. L *declamatio* (as prec.; see -ATION)]

dėclār'ant *n.* One who makes legal declaration. [f. F *déclarant* part. of *déclarer*, f. as DECLARE]

děclarā'tion *n.* Stating or announcing openly or formally; emphatic, solemn, or legal assertion, announcement, or proclamation (**~ of the poll,** public official announcement of vote-totals of election-candidates; **~ of war,** announcement before beginning hostilities); written public announcement of intentions, terms of agreement, etc.; (Cricket) act of declaring (see foll.); (Law) plaintiff's statement of claim, affirmation in lieu of oath; (Cards) naming of trumps by player in turn or by winning bid, announcement of combination held. [ME, f. L *declaratio* (as foll.; see -ATION)]

dėclār'e *v.* **1.** *v.t.* Make known, announce openly or formally, (*declare* WAR[1], *a dividend*); state explicitly; (of things) make evident, prove, (*the heavens declare the glory of God*); (abs.) **Well, I (do) ~** (excl. of incredulity, surprise, or vexation). **2.** *v.t.* & *i.* Pronounce (person etc.) to be something (*declare him (to be) a villain*); **~ oneself,** avow intentions, reveal character; **~ for** or **against,** openly side with or against; **~ (innings closed)**, (Cricket) elect to cease batting before all wickets have fallen; (in *p.p.*) who is such by his own admission (*a declared atheist*). **3.** *v.t.* Acknowledge possession of (dutiable goods, income, etc.). **4.** (Cards). Name the trump suit (see prec.); announce that one holds (certain combinations of cards etc.). **5.** Hence or cogn. **dėclă'rat**IVE, **dėclă'rat**ORY, *adjs.*, **dėclār'**ER[1] *n.* (esp. at cards; in Bridge, player in pair making highest bid who first made bid in same suit or no-trumps). [ME, f. L DE(*clarare* f. *clarus* clear)]

déclassé (dāklă'sā) *a.* (*fem.* **~e** *pr.* same). That has fallen in social status. [F]

dēclă'ssĭfȳ *v.t.* Cease to designate (information etc.) as secret. [f. DE- + CLASSIFY]

dėclě'nsion (-shon) *n.* **1.** Declining, deterioration. **2.** (Gram.) Variation of form of noun etc. to give its cases; class in which noun etc. is put according to this variation. [f. OF *declinaison* (*decliner* DECLINE[1]), after L *declinatio*, assim. to *ascension* etc.]

dėclinā'tion *n.* Downward bend or turn; *declining, refusal; (Astron.) angular distance of star etc. north or south of celestial equator; (Phys.) angular deviation of compass needle, E. or W. from true north; hence ~AL *a.* [ME, f. L *declinatio* (as foll.; see -ATION)]

dėclī'ne[1] *v.* **1.** *v.i.* Slope downwards; bend down, droop; (of day, life, etc.) draw to close (**declining years,** old age); fall off, decay, deteriorate; decrease in price etc. **2.** *v.t.* Bend down, bow; turn away from, refuse, (discussion, challenge, battle; *decline to* do, do*ing*, *to be made use of* etc.); say politely that one cannot accept (invitation etc., or abs.; **~ with thanks,** freq. iron., reject scornfully). **3.** (Gram.) Inflect, state the case-forms of; so **dėclī'n**ABLE *a.* [ME, f. OF *decliner* f. L DE(*clinare* bend)]

dėclī'ne[2] *n.* Sinking, gradual loss of vigour or excellence (*on the decline*); decay, deterioration; (arch.) tuberculosis or similar disease; fall in price; setting, last part of course, (of sun, life, etc.). [ME, f. prec.]

děclinŏ'mėter *n.* Instrument for measuring astronomical or magnetic declination. [irreg. f. L *declinare* (see DECLINE[1]) + -O- + -METER]

dėclĭ'vĭt|ȳ *n.* Downward slope; sloping ground; hence ~OUS *a.* [f. L *declivitas* f. DE(*clivis* f. *clivus* slope); see -ITY]

dēclŭ'tch *v.i.* Disengage clutch of motor vehicle; **double-~,** release and re-engage clutch twice when changing gear. [f. DE- + CLUTCH[2]]

dėcŏ'ct *v.t.* Make decoction of. [ME, f. L *decoquere* boil down; see foll.]

dėcŏ'ction *n.* Boiling down so as to extract essence; liquor resulting from this. [ME f. OF, or f. LL DE(*coctio* f. *coquere coct-* boil; see -ION)]

dēcō'd|e *v.t.* Decipher (coded message); hence ~ER[1] *n.*, (esp.) device for analysing stereophonic signals and feeding separate amplifier-channels. [f. DE- + CODE]

For other words in *de-* see DE-.

||**dēcō'ke** *v.t.*, & *n.* (colloq.) **1.** *v.t.* Remove carbon from (internal combustion engine). **2.** *n.* Process of decoking. [f. DE- + COKE¹]

dėcŏ'll|āte *v.t.* Behead; truncate; so ~A'TION *n.* [f. L DE(*collare* f. *collum* neck) + -ATE³]

décolletage (dākŏ'ltahzh) *n.* (Exposure of neck and shoulders by) low-cut neck of dress. [F (DE-, *collet* collar of dress; see -AGE)]

décolleté (dākŏ'ltā) *a.* (*fem.* ~*e pr.* same). (Of dress) low-necked; (of woman) wearing low-necked dress. [F, as prec.]

dēcŏlonizā'tion *n.* Withdrawal of a State from its former colonies, leaving them independent; acquisition of such independence. [f. DE- + COLONIZATION]

dēco'loriz|e, -our-, (-kŭ'ler-), **-īs|e** (-īz), *v.t.* & *i.* Remove colour from; lose colour; hence ~A'TION *n.* [f. DE- + COLOUR¹ + -IZE]

dēcompō's|e (-z) *v.t.* & *i.* Separate (substance, light, etc.) into its elements or simpler constituents; disintegrate, break up; rot, decay; hence ~ABLE *a.*, **dēcŏmposi'**TION (-z-) *n.* [f. F *décomposer* (as DE-, COMPOSE)]

dēcŏ'mposite (-z-) *a.* & *n.* = foll. [f. LL *decompositus* (transl. Gk *parasunthetos*; as DE-, COMPOSITE)]

dē'compound *a.* & *n.* (Substance, word, etc.) that is a compound of something itself a compound (e.g. *gentlemanly* from *gentleman*). [f. DE- + COMPOUND²]

dēcomprĕ'ss *v.t.* Relieve or reduce pressure on (e.g. underwater or other worker by means of an air-lock); hence **dēcomprĕ'ss**ION (-ĕ'shon) *n.* (~**ion sickness,** caisson disease), ~OR *n.*, device for reducing pressure in motor-vehicle engine. [f. DE- + COMPRESS²]

dēcongĕ'stant (-nj-) *a.* & *n.* (Drug etc.) that relieves congestion. [f. DE- + CONGEST + -ANT]

dēcŏ'nsėcr|āte *v.t.* Transfer from sacred to secular use; hence ~A'TION *n.* [f. DE- + CONSECRATE]

dēcontă'mĭn|āte *v.t.* Remove (risk of) contamination from (esp. area, clothes, person, etc., affected by poison gas or by radioactivity); hence ~A'TION *n.* [f. DE- + CONTAMINATE]

dēcontrō'l *v.t.* (-ll-), & *n.* **1.** *v.t.* Release (commodity etc.) from (esp. Government) control. **2.** *n.* Act of decontrolling. [f. DE- + CONTROL¹,²]

décor (dā'kor) *n.* Furnishing and decoration of room or stage. [F (*décorer*, as foll.)]

dĕ'cor|āte *v.t.* Furnish with adornments (esp. church with flowers, street with flags, house or room with new paint, etc.); serve as adornment to; invest with order, medal, etc.; hence ~**at**IVE *a.* [f. L *decorare* (*decus -oris* beauty) + -ATE³]

dĕ'corātėd *a.* In vbl senses; **D**~ **style,** (Archit.) second stage of English Gothic (14th c.), with increasing decoration and geometrical tracery. [p.p. of prec.]

dĕcorā'tion *n.* In vbl senses; medal, cross, etc., conferred and worn as honour (***D**~ **Day,** Memorial Day); (in *pl.*) flags etc. put up on occasion of public rejoicing. [f. F *décoration* or f. LL *decoratio* (as DECORATE; see -ATION)]

dĕ'corātor *n.* In vbl senses; tradesman who papers, paints, etc., houses. [f. DECORATE + -OR]

dĕ'corous *a.* Not violating good taste or propriety; dignified and decent; hence ~LY² *adv.*, ~NESS *n.* [f. L *decorus* seemly + -OUS]

dēcor'tĭc|āte *v.t.* Remove bark, rind, or husk from; remove cerebral cortex from; hence ~A'TION *n.* [f. L DE(*corticare* f. *cortex -icis* bark) + -ATE³]

dėcor'um *n.* Seemliness, propriety, etiquette; particular usage required by politeness or decency. [L, neut. (as n.) of *decorus* seemly]

découpage (dākōōpah'zh) *n.* Decoration of surfaces with paper cut-outs. [F, = action of cutting out]

dēcou'ple (-kŭ'-) *v.t.* (Electr.) Make coupling between (oscillators etc.) so weak that there is little transfer of energy between them. [f. DE- + COUPLE²]

dėcoy' *n.*, & *v.t.* **1.** *n.* Pond with narrow netted arms into which wild duck may be tempted and caught; bird etc. trained to entice others; swindler's confederate, tempter; bait, enticement. **2.** *v.t.* Entice into decoy; allure *into*, *out of*, etc., ensnare. [17th c., perh. f. Du. *de kooi* the decoy (*de* THE, *kooi* f. L *cavea* cage)]

dėcrea'se¹ *v.i.* & *t.* Lessen, diminish. [ME, f. OF *de(s)creiss-*, pres. st. of *de(s)creistre* f. Rom. **discrescere* f. L DE(*crescere cret-* grow)]

dē'crease² *n.* Diminution, lessening. [ME, f. OF *de(s)creis* f. st. of *de(s)creistre* (see prec.)]

dėcree' *n.*, & *v.t.* **1.** *n.* Ordinance or edict set forth by authority; judgement in court of equity, admiralty, probate, or divorce (~ **nisi** *pr.* nī'sī, provisional order for divorce, made absolute unless cause to the contrary is shown within fixed period); will, as shown by result, of God, Providence, Nature, etc. **2.** *v.t.* Ordain by decree. [ME, f. OF *decré* f. L DE(*cretum* neut. p.p. of *cernere* sift) thing decided]

dĕ'crėment *n.* Decrease, amount lost by diminution or waste; (Phys.) ratio of amplitudes in successive cycles of damped oscillation. [f. L *decrementum* (as DECREASE¹; see -MENT)]

dėcrĕ'pĭ|t *a.* Wasted, worn out, enfeebled with age and infirmities; dilapidated; so ~TUDE *n.* [ME, f. L DE(*crepitus* p.p. of *crepare* creak)]

dėcrĕ'pĭt|āte *v.t.* & *i.* Calcine (mineral or salt) till it ceases to crackle in fire; crackle under heat; hence ~A'TION *n.* [prob. f. mod. L *decrepitare* f. DE- + L *crepitare* crackle; see -ATE³]

decrĕscĕ'ndō (dākrĕsh-) *adv.*, *a.*, & *n.* (*pl.* ~**s**). = DIMINUENDO. [It., part. of *decrescere* DECREASE¹]

dėcrĕ'scent *a.* (Usu. of moon) waning, decreasing. [f. L *decrescere* (see DECREASE¹, -ENT)]

dėcrē'tal *n.* Papal decree; (in *pl.*) collection of these, forming part of canon law. [ME, f. med. L *decretale* f. LL (*epistola*) *decretalis* (letter) of decree f. L *decernere* (see DECREE, -AL)]

dėcrȳ' *v.t.* Disparage, depreciate. [f. DE- + CRY², after F *décrier*; cf. *cry down*]

dēcrȳ'pt *v.t.* Decipher (cryptogram), with or without knowledge of its key. [f. DE- + CRYPTOGRAM]

dĕ'cūman *a.* **1.** (Esp. of wave) very large. **2.** (Rom. Ant.) Of tenth cohort; ~ **gate,** main gate of camp, where this cohort was quartered. [f. L *decumanus*, *decimanus* of the tenth (*decimus*), large; see -AN]

dėcŭ'mbent *a.* (Bot. & Zool.) (Of plant, shoot, bristles) lying along ground or surface of body. [f. L DE(*cumbere* lie); see -ENT]

dĕ'cūple *a.*, *n.*, & *v.* **1.** *a.* & *n.* Tenfold (amount). **2.** *v.t.* & *i.* Multiply by ten. [ME, f. LL *decuplus* f. L *decem* ten]

dĕ'cūplėt *n.* Set of ten things of same kind. [f. prec., after *triplet*]

dėcŭ'ssate¹ *a.* X-shaped; (Bot.) with pairs of opposite leaves etc. each at right angles to pair below. [f. L *decussatus* p.p. of *decussare* divide in cross shape (*decussis* numeral ten or shape X f. *decem* ten); see -ATE²]

dėcŭ'ssāte² *v.t.* & *i.* Arrange or be arranged in decussate form; intersect; so **dĕcŭss**A'TION *n.* [f. as prec. + -ATE³]

deda'ns (-ah'ṅ) *n.* (Tennis). Open gallery at end of service-side of a court; spectators watching a tennis match. [F, = inside]

dĕ'dĭcāt|e *v.t.* Devote with solemn rites (*to* God or *to* sacred use; of church etc. esp. without certain forms necessary for legally consecrating ground or buildings); give up (*to* special purpose); put words in (book etc.) as compliment *to* friend, patron, etc.; hence or cogn. ~EE′, ~OR, *ns.*, ~IVE, ~ORY, *adjs.* [f. L DE(*dicare* declare) + -ATE³]

dĕ′dĭcātėd *a.* In vbl senses; (of person) devoted to aims or vocation, having single-minded loyalty or integrity. [p.p. of prec.]

dĕdĭcā′tion *n.* In vbl senses; dedicatory inscription on building etc. or in book etc. [ME, f. OF *dedicacion* or f. L *dedicatio* (as DEDICATE; see -ATION)]

dėdū′c|e *v.t.* Infer, draw as conclusion, (*from*); (arch.) trace course or derivation of; hence ~IBLE *a.* [f. L DE(*ducere duct-* lead)]

dėdŭ′ct *v.t.* Take away, put aside, (amount, portion, etc., *from*, or abs.); hence ~IBLE *a.*, (esp.) that may be deducted from one's tax or taxable income. [f. L, as prec.]

dėdŭ′ction *n.* **1.** Deducting; amount deducted. **2.** Deducing, inference from general to particular (cf. *induction*); thing deduced. [ME f. OF, or f. L *deductio* (as DEDUCE; see -ION)]

dėdŭ′ctĭve *a.* Of, or reasoning by, deduction; hence ~LY² (-vlĭ) *adv.* [f. med. L *deductivus* (as DEDUCE; see -IVE)]

dee *n.* (Thing shaped like) letter D; (Phys.) hollow semicircular electrode in cyclotron; (euphem.) damn. [name of the letter]

deed *n.*, & *v.t.* **1.** *n.* Thing done intentionally or responsibly; brave, skilful, or conspicuous act; actual fact, performance, (*in word and deed*; *in deed and not in name*, whence INDEED; (arch.) *in very deed*); (Law) written or printed instrument effecting legal disposition and bearing disposer's signature and seal; **~-box,** strong box for keeping deeds and other documents; **~ poll,** deed made and executed by one party only (paper polled or cut even, not indented). **2.** *v.t.* *Convey or transfer by legal deed. [OE *dēd*, = OS *dād*, OHG *tāt*, ON *dath*, Goth. *-dēths* f. Gmc **dǣdiz* (**dhētis* f. IE **dhē-*, **dho-*; cf. DO¹)]

dee′dȳ *a.* Active, industrious; earnest. [f. prec. + -Y²]

deejay′ *n.* (sl.) Disc jockey. [f. abbr. *D.J.*]

deem *v.t.* Believe, consider, judge, or count, to be (*deem it* one's *duty*; *was deemed sufficient*; *shall be deemed to have given his assent*; abs. in parenth.: *it was, I deemed, time to go*). [OE *dēman*, = OS *dōmian*, OHG *tuomen*, ON *dœma*, Goth. *domjan* f. Gmc **dōmaz* DOOM¹]

dē-ĕ′mphasize, -īse (-īz), *v.t.* Remove emphasis from; reduce emphasis on. [f. DE- + EMPHASIZE]

dee′mster *n.* One of two justices of Isle of Man. [f. DEEM + -STER]

deep¹ *a.* **1.** Extending far down from top (lit. or fig.; *deep breath, hole, water, draught, drink, drinker*; *go (in) off the deep* END¹; *in deep* WATER¹(*s*)); going far in from surface or edge (*deep wound, plunge, shelf, border*; (fig.) *deep insight, thinker*); **~ breathing** (esp. as form of physical exercise); **~-freeze [*P],** refrigerator etc. in which food can be quickly frozen and kept for long periods at very low temperature, (fig.) suspension of activity; so *~-freeze* v.t.; **~ kiss** (with contact between partners' tongues); **~ mourning** (expressed by wearing only black clothes); **~ therapy,** curative treatment with short-wave X-rays of high penetrating power. **2.** Lying far down, back, or inwards; (Cricket) distant from batsman; (Football) distant from front line of one's team; difficult to understand, profound, not superficial, penetrating, (*the deeper causes*; *deep learning, study*); **a ~ one,** (sl.) cunning or secretive person; **~ sea,** deeper parts of ocean; **Deep* SOUTH; **~ space,** regions beyond solar system or earth's atmosphere. **3.** Heartfelt, absorbing, absorbed (*deep affection, feelings, interest*); **~ in,** giving all one's attention to (a pursuit etc.). **4.** Intense, vivid, extreme, (*deep disgrace, sleep, night, sin, colour*; *deep-red* etc.). **5.** (*pred.*) Going or placed (so) far down, back, or inwards (*water 6 ft. deep*; *ankle-deep in mud*; *ship deep in the water*; *hands deep in pockets*; *deep in debt, deep in thought*); in (so many) ranks one behind another (*soldiers drawn up six deep*). **6.** Brought from far down (*deep sigh*); low-pitched, full-toned, not shrill, (*deep note, bell, voice*); **~-mouthed,** (esp. of dog) having deep voice. **7.** Hence ~′EN⁶ *v.t.* & *i.*, ~′LY² *adv.*, ~′NESS *n.* [OE *dēop*, = OS *diop*, *diap*, OHG *tiuf*, ON *djúpr*, Goth. *diups* f. Gmc **deupaz*; cogn. w. DIP¹]

deep² *n.* Deep part(s) of the sea; abyss, pit, cavity; (poet. or rhet.) mysterious region of thought or feeling; (poet.) *the* sea; **the ~,** (Cricket) deep position of fieldsmen. [f. as prec. (neut. a. in OE)]

deep³ *adv.* **1.** Deeply, far down or in, (*read deep into the night*; **still waters run ~,** quiet manner covers depths of feeling or knowledge or cunning). **2. ~-drawn,** (of metal etc.) shaped by forcing through die while cold; **~-fried,** (of food) fried in fat etc. covering it; **~-laid,** (of scheme) secret and elaborate; **~-rooted** (esp. of convictions); **~-seated** (of disease, emotion, etc.). [OE *dīope*, *dēope*, (as DEEP¹)]

||**dee′pĭng** *n.* Section, one fathom deep, of fishing-net. [f. DEEP¹ + -ING³]

deer *n.* (*pl.* same). **1.** Ruminant quadruped of family Cervidae, the male usu. with deciduous branching horns; **small ~,** (arch.) insignificant animals or things collectively. **2. ~-forest,** wild land reserved for stalking of deer; **~-hound,** large rough-haired greyhound; **~-lick,** spring or damp spot impregnated with salt etc. where deer come to lick; **~′skin,** (made of) deer's skin; **~′stalker,** sportsman stalking deer, cloth cap peaked in front and behind. [OE *dēor* animal, deer, = OS *dior*, OHG *tior*, ON *dýr*, Goth. **dius* f. Gmc **deuzam* f. IE **dheusóm* creature that breathes]

dē-ĕ′scal|āte *v.t.* Reduce level or intensity of; so ~A′TION *n.* [f. DE- + ESCALATE]

dėfā′ce *v.t.* Spoil appearance or beauty of, disfigure; make illegible; hence ~ABLE (-sa-) *a.*, ~MENT (-sm-) *n.* [ME, f. F *défacer* f. OF *desfacier* (as DE-, FACE¹)]

de facto (dē fă′ktō *or* dā f-) *a.* & *adv.* (Existing) in fact, whether by right or not. [L]

dē′faecāte etc. Var. of DEFECATE etc.

dē′falcāt|e *v.i.* Commit defalcations, misappropriate property in one's charge; so ~OR *n.* [f. med. L DE(*falcare* lop f. L *falx -cis* sickle) + -ATE³]

dēfalcā′tion *n.* Defection, shortcoming; misappropriation of money; amount misappropriated. [ME, f. med. L *defalcatio* (as prec.; see -ATION)]

dėfā′me *v.t.* Attack the good reputation of, speak ill of; so **dĕfam**A′TION *n.*, **dėfă′mat**ORY *a.* [ME, f. OF *diffamer* etc. f. L *diffamare* spread evil report (as DIS-, *fama* report); see DE-]

dēfă′t *v.t.* (-tt-). Remove fat(s) from. [f. DE- + FAT]

dėfau′lt¹ (*or* -ŏ′lt) *n.* **1.** Lack, absence; **in ~ of,** if or since thing is lacking. **2.** Failure to act or appear, neglect, (*make default*); **go by ~,** be absent, be ignored because of absence; **judgement by ~** (given for plaintiff on defendant's failure to plead). **3.** Failure to pay, defaulting. [ME, f. OF *defaut(e)* f. *defaillir* fail f. Rom. *DE(*fallire*); see FAIL²]

For other words in *de-* see DE-.

dėfau'lt[2] (*or* -ŏ'lt) *v.* **1.** *v.i.* Fail to act or appear, esp. in lawcourt; fail to meet pecuniary or other obligation; hence ~ER[1] *n.*, (esp., ||Mil.) soldier guilty of military offence. **2.** *v.t.* Declare (party) in default and give judgement against him. [ME, f. prec. & f. OF *defaillir* (3 sing. *defaut*); see prec.]

dėfea'sance (-z-) *n.* Rendering null and void. [ME, f. OF *defesance* f. *de(s)faire* undo (as DE-, *faire* make f. L *facere*; see -ANCE)]

dėfea's|ĭble (-z-) *a.* Capable of annulment, liable to forfeiture; hence ~IBI'LITY *n.*, **~ĭbLY**[2] *adv.* [AF, f. as prec.; see -IBLE]

dėfea't *v.t.*, & *n.* **1.** *v.t.* Overcome in battle or other contest, matter decided by voting, etc.; frustrate, baffle; (Law) annul. **2.** *n.* Defeating; being defeated. [ME, f. AF *defeter* f. *defet* f. OF *deffait, desfait* p.p. of *desfaire* f. med. L *disfacere* (as DIS-, L *facere* do)]

dėfea't|ĭsm *n.* Conduct tending to bring about acceptance of defeat; so ~IST (2) *n.* [f. F *défaitisme* (*défaite* defeat, as prec.; see -ISM)]

dĕ'fĕc|āte *v.* **1.** *v.i.* Discharge faeces from body. **2.** *v.t.* Clear of dregs, refine, purify, (lit. or fig.). **3.** Hence ~A'TION, **~ātOR**, *ns.* [f. obs. *defecate* purified f. L DE(*faecare* f. *faex faecis* dregs); see -ATE[2]]

dėfĕ'ct *n.*, & *v.i.* **1.** *n.* (*or* dĕ'fĕkt). Lack of something essential to completeness; shortcoming, failing, (*has* **the ~s of his qualities,** the particular ones that often accompany his particular virtues); blemish; amount by which thing falls short. **2.** *v.i.* Desert, esp. to another country etc.; hence ~OR *n.* [f. L *defectus* n. f. DE(*ficere fect-* =*facere* do) desert, fail]

dėfĕ'ction *n.* Falling away from allegiance to leader, party, religion, or duty; desertion, esp. to another country etc. [f. L *defectio* (as prec.; see -ION)]

dėfĕ'ctive *a.* & *n.* **1.** *a.* Having defect(s), (in some respect) incomplete, faulty; lacking or deficient (*in*); mentally DEFICIENT; (Gram.) not having all the usual inflexions; hence ~LY[2] (-vlĭ) *adv.*, ~NESS (-vn-) *n.* **2.** *n.* Mentally defective person. [ME, f. OF *defectif -ive* or f. LL *defectivus* (as prec.; see -IVE)]

||**dėfĕ'nce, *dėfĕ'nse,** *n.* **1.** Defending from or resistance against attack (cf. OFFENCE; **best ~ is offence,** advantage goes with the initiative); (Cricket) guarding of one's wicket, batting as opposed to bowling; ~ **mechanism,** body's reaction against disease organisms, (Psych.) usu. unconscious mental process avoiding conscious conflict or anxiety. **2.** Military resources of a country; (in *pl.*) fortifications; *defence in* DEPTH. **3.** Thing that protects; means of resisting attack; justification, vindication, speech or writing used to this end; (Law) accused party's denial, pleading, and proceedings, counsel for the accused party; (Lacrosse, Netball) player in defending position. **4.** Hence ~LESS (-sl-) *a.* [ME f. OF *defens(e)*, f. LL *defensum, -a*, p.p. of *defendere* (see foll.)]

dėfĕ'nd *v.* **1.** *v.t.* Ward off attack made on, keep safe, protect (*against, from*; person, thing, or abs. for *refl.*); uphold by argument, vindicate, speak or write in favour of; (Law) make defence of in court (~ **oneself,** conduct one's own defence). **2.** *v.i.* Make defence; (arch.) forbid, avert (*God* or *heaven defend*). [ME, f. OF *defendre* f. L DE(*fendere fens-*; cf. OFFEND)]

dėfĕ'ndant *n.* Person etc. sued or accused in court of law. [ME f. OF, part. of *defendre* (see prec., -ANT)]

dėfĕ'nder *n.* One who defends (**D~ of the Faith,** title of Engl. sovereigns from Henry VIII, who received it from Pope Leo X in 1521 for writing against Luther); (Sport) holder of championship etc. defending the title (opp. *challenger*). [ME f. AF *defendour*, OF *-eor* (as DEFEND; see -OR)]

dēfĕnĕstrā'tion *n.* Action of throwing (esp. person) out of a window. [f. mod. L *defenestratio* f. as DE- + L *fenestra* window + -ATION]

***dėfĕ'nse.** See DEFENCE.

dėfĕ'ns|ĭble *a.* Easily defended (in war or argument); justifiable; hence ~IBI'LITY *n.*, **~ĭbLY**[2] *adv.* [ME, f. LL *defensibilis* (as DEFEND; see -IBLE)]

dėfĕ'nsĭve *a.* & *n.* **1.** *a.* Serving, used, done, for defence, protective, not aggressive; hence ~LY[2] (-vlĭ) *adv.* **2.** *n.* State or position of defence (esp. *be, stand, act, on the defensive*). [ME, f. F *défensif -ive* f. med. L *defensivus* (as DEFEND; see -IVE)]

dėfēr'[1] *v.t.* (**-rr-**). Put off to later time, postpone, (**~red annuity,** one not beginning immediately; **~red payment** (by instalments); **~red shares, stock,** (on which smaller dividend may be paid than on ordinary shares)); *postpone date of call-up of (person); hence ~MENT, **~rAL**, *ns.* [ME, orig. same as DIFFER]

dėfēr'[2] *v.i.* (**-rr-**). Submit or make concessions in opinion or action *to* (person). [ME, f. F *déférer* f. L DE(*ferre* bring)]

dĕ'ference *n.* Compliance with advice etc. of one superior in wisdom or position (*pay* etc. *deference to*); respect, manifestation of desire to comply, courteous regard, (**in ~ to,** out of respect for authority of). [f. F *déférence* (as prec.; see -ENCE)]

dĕferĕ'ntial (-sh*a*l) *a.* Showing deference, respectful; hence ~LY[2] *adv.* [f. prec., after *prudential* etc.]

dėfī'ance *n.* Challenge to fight or maintain cause, assertion, etc.; open disobedience, bold resistance, (*bid defiance to, set at defiance*); **in ~ of,** disregarding, in conflict with. [ME f. OF (as DEFY; see -ANCE)]

dėfī'ant *a.* Openly disobedient; showing defiance; hence ~LY[2] *adv.* [f. prec. + -ANT]

dėfĭ'ciencў (-ĭ'sh*e*n-) *n.* Being deficient; lack; thing lacking; amount by which thing, esp. revenue, falls short; ~ **disease** (caused by lack of some essential or important element in the diet); ~ **payment** (by Government to farmers to ensure guaranteed minimum price). [f. foll. + -ENCY]

dėfĭ'cient (-ĭ'sh*e*nt) *a.* Incomplete, lacking (*in*) a specified quality; insufficient in quantity, force, etc.; (**mentally**) ~, incapable of adequate social or intellectual behaviour through imperfect mental development; hence ~LY[2] *adv.* [f. L *deficiens* part. of *deficere*; see DEFECT, -ENT]

dĕ'fĭcĭt *n.* Amount by which thing (esp. sum of money) is too small (opp. *surplus*); excess of liabilities over assets; ~ **spending** (of funds raised by borrowing, not by taxation). [f. F *déficit* f. L *deficit* 3 sing. pres. of *deficere* (see DEFECT)]

dėfī'er. See DEFY.

dĕfĭlā'de *v.t.*, & *n.* **1.** *v.t.* Secure (fortification) against enfilading fire. **2.** *n.* This precaution or arrangement. [f. foll. + -ADE]

dėfī'le[1] *v.i.*, & *n.* **1.** *v.i.* March in file(s). **2.** *n.* (*or* dē'fīl). Narrow way through which troops can only march in file; gorge. [f. F *défiler* and *défilé* p.p. (as DE-, FILE[3])]

dėfī'le[2] *v.t.* Make dirty, befoul; pollute, corrupt; desecrate, profane; deprive of virginity; make ceremonially unclean; hence ~MENT (-lm-) *n.* [ME *defoul* f. OF *def(o)uler* trample down, outrage (as DE-, *fouler* see FOIL[2]), altered after obs. *befile* f. OE *befȳlan* (BE-, *fūl* FOUL)]

dėfī'n|e *v.t.* Mark out limits of; make clear, esp. in outline (*well-defined image*; **~e** one's **position,**

state it precisely); set forth essence of, declare exact meaning or scope of, (abs.) frame definitions; (of properties) make up total character of; hence ~ABLE *a.* [ME, f. OF *definer* f. Rom. **definare* for L DE(*finire* finish f. *finis* end)]

dĕ'fĭnĭte *a.* Having exact limits; determinate, distinct, precise, not vague; *definite* ARTICLE[1]; *definite* INTEGRAL; PAST[1] *definite*; hence ~LY[2] (-tlĭ) *adv.*, & *int.* (colloq.) yes, certainly, ~NESS (-tn-) *n.* [f. L *definitus* p.p. of *definire* (see prec.)]

dĕfĭnĭ'tion *n.* Stating precise nature of thing or meaning of word; form of words in which this is done; making or being distinct, degree of distinctness, in outline (esp. of image given by lens or shown in photograph or on cinema or television screen). [ME f. OF, f. L DE(*finitio* f. as DEFINE; see -ITION)]

dėfĭ'nĭtĭve *a.* (Of answer, treaty, verdict, etc.) decisive, unconditional, final; (of edition of book etc.) most authoritative; (Philately, of series of stamps) for permanent use, not commemorative etc.; hence ~LY[2] (-vlĭ) *adv.* [ME, f. OF *definitif -ive* f. L *definitivus* (as prec.; see -IVE)]

dĕ'flagr|āte *v.t.* & *i.* Burn away with sudden flame; hence or cogn. ~A'TION, ~**ātor**, *ns.* [f. L DE(*flagrare* blaze) + -ATE[3]]

dėflā'te *v.* **1.** *v.t.* Let inflating air or gas out of (tyre, balloon, etc.); (Econ.) subject (currency) to deflation; reduce importance of, depreciate; cause to lose one's conceitedness or confidence. **2.** *v.i.* Be deflated; lose confidence; pursue policy of deflation. [f. DE- + INFLATE]

dėflā'tion *n.* Deflating; (esp., Econ.) reverse or reversal of INFLATION (of currency etc.); (Geol.) removal of particles of rock etc. by wind; hence ~ARY[1] *a.*, ~IST (2) *n.* [f. prec. + -ATION]

dėflĕ'ct *v.t.* & *i.* Bend or turn aside from straight course; (cause to) deviate (*from*); hence ~OR *n.*, (esp.) device for deflecting flow of air etc. [f. L DE(*flectere flex-* bend)]

dėflĕ'xion (-kshon), **-ĕ'ction,** *n.* Lateral bend or turn, deviation, (lit. or fig.); (Phys.) movement of instrument's pointer from its zero position. [f. LL *deflexio* (as prec.; see -ION)]

dēflorā'tion *n.* Deflowering. [ME f. OF, or f. LL *defloratio* (as foll.; see -ATION)]

dēflow'er *v.t.* Deprive (woman) of virginity, ravish; ravage, spoil; strip of flowers. [ME, f. OF *de(s)flo(u)rer* f. Rom. **disflorare* for LL DE*florare* (*flos floris* flower)]

dēfō'cus *v.t.* & *i.* (**-s-** *or* **-ss-**). (Cause to) go out of focus. [f. DE- + FOCUS]

dēfō'lĭ|āte *v.t.* Remove leaves from, esp. as military tactic; hence ~ANT *a.* & *n.*, ~A'TION *n.* [f. LL DE*foliare* (*folium* leaf) + -ATE[3]]

dēfŏ'rėst *v.t.* Remove forest(s) from; hence ~A'TION *n.* [f. DE- + FOREST]

dėfôr'm *v.* **1.** *v.t.* Make ugly, deface; put out of shape, misshape, (esp. in *p.p.*, of person with misshapen body or limb). **2.** *v.i.* Undergo deformation. [ME, f. OF *deformer* etc. f. med. L *difformare*, Rom. **disformare* f. L DE(*formare* f. *forma* shape)]

dēfôrmā'tion *n.* Disfigurement; perverted form of word (*dang* for *damn*, etc.); (Phys.) change in shape *of*, quantity representing amount of this, whence ~AL *a.* [ME f. OF, or f. L *deformatio* (as prec.; see -ATION)]

dėfôr'mĭtў *n.* Being deformed, ugliness, disfigurement, (physical or moral); malformation, esp. of body or limb. [ME, f. OF *deformité* etc. f. L *deformitas -tatis* f. DE(*formis* f. *forma* shape); see -ITY]

dėfrau'd *v.t.* Cheat (person, person *of*, or abs.). [ME, f. OF *defrauder* or f. L DE*fraudare* (*fraus* FRAUD)]

dėfray' *v.t.* Provide money to pay (cost, expense); hence ~ABLE *a.*, ~AL 2 *n.* [f. F *défrayer* f. as DE- + obs. *frai(t)* cost, f. med. L *fredum, -us* fine for breach of peace]

dēfrŏ'ck *v.t.* = UNFROCK. [f. F *défroquer* (as DE-, FROCK)]

dēfrŏ'st (*or* -aw'-) *v.t.* Remove frost from, unfreeze, (esp. frozen food, interior of refrigerator, or windscreen). [f. DE- + FROST]

dėft *a.* Dextrous, (esp. manually) skilful, handling things neatly; hence ~'LY[2] *adv.*, ~'NESS *n.* [ME, var. of DAFT in obs. sense 'meek']

dėfŭ'nct *a.* Dead; no longer existing; no longer used or in fashion. [f. L DE(*functus* p.p. of *fungi* perform) dead]

dēfū'se *v.t.* Remove fuse from (explosive); (fig.) reduce likelihood of trouble arising from (crisis etc.). [f. DE- + FUSE[2]]

dėfȳ' *v.t.* Challenge *to* do or prove something; resist openly, refuse to obey; (of thing) present insuperable obstacles to (*defies definition, capture*, etc.); (arch.) challenge to combat; hence **dėfī'**ER[1] *n.* [ME, f. OF *defier* f. Rom. *DIS(*fidare* f. *fidus* faithful, *fides* faith)]

deg *abbr.* degree.

dégagé (dāgah'zhā) *a.* (*fem.* **~e** *pr.* same). Easy, unconstrained. [F, p.p. of *dégager* set free]

dēgă's *v.t.* (**-ss-**). Remove unwanted gas from. [f. DE- + GAS[1]]

dēgau'ss (-gow's) *v.t.* Demagnetize (television receiver, ship esp. as precaution against magnetic mines, etc.) with encircling current-carrying conductor. [f. DE- + GAUSS]

dėgĕ'nerate[1] *a.* & *n.* **1.** *a.* Having lost the qualities that are normal and desirable or proper to its kind, fallen from former excellence; (Biol.) having reverted to lower type; hence **dėgĕ'ner**ACY *n.* **2.** *n.* Degenerate person or animal. [f. L *degeneratus* p.p. (as foll.; see -ATE[2])]

dėgĕ'nerāte[2] *v.i.* Become degenerate. [f. L *degenerare* f. DE(*gener* f. *genus -eris* race) ignoble + -ATE[3]]

dėgĕnerā'tion *n.* Becoming degenerate; (Path.) morbid deterioration of tissue or change in its structure. [ME, f. F *dégéneration* or f. LL *degeneratio* (as prec.; see -ATION)]

dēglutĭ'tion (-gloo-) *n.* (arch.) Swallowing. [f. F *déglutition* or mod. L *deglutitio* f. L DE(*glutire* swallow); see -ITION]

dėgrā'd|e *v.* **1.** *v.t.* Reduce to lower rank, esp. as punishment; bring into dishonour or contempt, whence ~ING[2] *a.*; (Biol.) reduce to lower organic type; (Chem.) reduce to simpler molecular structure; (Phys.) reduce (energy) to less convertible form; (Geol.) wear down (rocks etc.) by disintegration. **2.** *v.i.* Degenerate; (Chem.) disintegrate. **3.** So **dĕgrad**A'TION *n.*, ~ATIVE *a.* [ME, f OF *degrader* f. eccl. L DE*gradare* f. L *gradus* step]

dēgrea'se *v.t.* Remove grease or fat from. [f. DE- + GREASE[1]]

dėgree' *n.* **1.** Thing placed like step in series, tier, row; stage in ascending or descending scale or process (**by ~s,** a little at a time; SONG *of Degrees*); step in direct genealogical descent (**forbidden** or **prohibited ~s,** number of these too few to allow of marriage between two related persons). **2.** Social or official rank; relative condition (*each good in its degree*); stage in intensity or amount (*in some degree*; *to a high* or *the last degree*; **to a ~**, (colloq.) considerably); (Law) grade of crime or criminality (*murder, principal, in the first* etc. *degree*); (Gram.) *degrees of* COMPARISON; *degree of* FREEDOM; (Math.) highest power of unknowns or variables (*of equation* etc.); **third ~**, (1) rank of master freemason,

(2) *severe and protracted interrogation by police to extract confession etc., (3) extent of burns characterized by much destruction of skin. **3.** Academic rank conferred as mark of proficiency, or (**honorary ~**) on distinguished person, (**~ day,** when these are formally awarded); masonic rank (**third ~**; see above). **4.** (Math.) unit of angular or circular-arc measurement, 1/90 of right angle or 1/360 of circumference (symbol °, as *45°*; *degree of* LATITUDE, LONGITUDE, etc.); (Phys.) unit in scale of temperature, hardness, etc., (symbol ° or deg, or omitted where letter indicating scale used serves as symbol). [ME, f. OF *degré* f. Rom. *DE(*gradus* step)]

dėgrĕ'ssīve *a.* Descending; (of taxation) at successively lower rates on low amounts. [f. L DE(*gredi gress-* = *gradi* walk); see -IVE]

dégringolade (dāgrăṅgōlah'd) *n.* Rapid fall or deterioration. [F (*dégringoler* fall rapidly; see -ADE)]

de haut en bas (deōtahṅbah') *adv.* In a condescending or superior manner. [F, = from above to below]

dėhī'sc|e *v.i.* Gape, burst open, (esp. in Bot. of seed-vessel, and in Physiol.); so ~ENCE *n.*, ~ENT *a.* [f. L DE(*hiscere* incept. of *hiare* gape)]

dēhor'n *v.t.* Remove horns from (animal). [f. DE- + HORN[1]]

dēhū'manīze, -ise (-īz), *v.t.* Divest of human characteristics; make impersonal or machine-like. [f. DE- + HUMAN + -IZE]

dēhȳ'drāte *v.* **1.** *v.t.* Remove water from (esp. foods for preservation and reduction of bulk); make dry (lit or fig.). **2.** *v.i.* Lose water. [f. DE- + Gk *hudōr* water + -ATE[3]]

dē-ī'c|e *v.t.* Remove, or prevent formation of, ice on aircraft, windscreen, etc.; so ~ER[1] (2) *n.* [f. DE- + ICE[1]]

dē'icīde *n.* Killer or killing of a god. [f. eccl. L *deicida* f. L *deus* god; see -CIDE]

deī'ctic (dī'k-) *a.* & *n.* (Philol. & Gram.) Pointing, demonstrative, (word). [f. Gk *deiktikos* (*deiktos* capable of proof f. *deiknumi* show; see -IC)]

dē'ifōrm *a.* Godlike in form or nature. [f. med. L *deiformis* (*deus* god; see -FORM)]

dē'ifȳ *v.t.* Make a god of; treat as a god, worship; so **dēIFICA'TION** *n.* [ME, f. OF *deifier* f. eccl. L *deificare* (*deus* god; see -FY)]

deign (dān) *v.t.* Think fit, condescend, *to* do; (arch., usu. w. neg.) condescend to give (answer etc.). [ME, f. OF *degnier*, *deigner*, *daigner* f. L *dignare*, *-ari* deem worthy (*dignus*)]

Dei gratia (dāī grah'tĭa *or* -shĭa) *adv.* By God's grace. [L]

dēī'onīz|e, -is|e (-īz), *v.t.* Remove ions or ionic constituents from (water etc.); hence ~A'TION, ~ER[1] (2), *ns.* [f. DE- + IONIZE]

deipnŏ'sophĭst (dī-) *n.* Person skilled in dining and table-talk. [f. Gk *deipnosophistēs* (in pl. as title of work by Athenaeus (3rd c.) describing long discussions at a banquet; *deipnon* dinner, *sophistēs* wise man; see SOPHIST)]

dē'|ĭsm *n.* Belief in the existence of a god without accepting revelation (cf. THEISM), natural religion; so ~IST (2) *n.*, **~ĭ'stic(AL)** *adjs.* [f. L *deus* god + -ISM]

dē'ĭtȳ (*or* dā'-) *n.* Divine status, quality, or nature; god; **the D~**, the Creator, God. [ME, f. OF *deité* f. eccl. L *deitas -tatis* transl. Gk *theotēs* (*theos* god); see -ITY]

déjà vu (dāzhahvū') *n.* (Psych.) illusory feeling of having already experienced a present situation; something tediously familiar. [F, = already seen]

dėjĕ'ct *v.t.* (esp. in *p.p.*) Make sad or gloomy. [ME, f. L DE(*jicere ject-* = *jacĕre* throw)]

dėjĕ'ction *n.* Dejected state, low spirits. [ME, f. L *dejectio* (as prec.; see -ION)]

de jure (dē joor'ĭ *or* dā yoor'ā) *a.* & *adv.* Rightful(ly), by right. [L]

dĕ'kkō *n.* (*pl.* **~s**). (sl.) A look (*let's have a dekko*). [f. Hindi *dekho* imper. of *dekhnā* look]

Del. *abbr.* Delaware.

dėlai'ne *n.* Light woollen dress-fabric. [f. F (*mousseline*) *de laine* woollen (MUSLIN) f. *de* of + *laine* f. L *lana* wool]

dėlā'te *v.t.* (arch.) Inform against, impeach, (person); report (offence); so **dėlā'TION**, **dėlā'TOR**, *ns.* [f. L DE(*lat-* p.p. st. of *ferre* carry)]

dėlay' *v.* & *n.* **1.** *v.t.* Postpone, defer; make late; hinder; **~ed-action** *a.*, operating after an interval of time. **2.** *v.i.* Loiter, be late; wait. **3.** *n.* Act or process of delaying; hindrance; time lost by inaction or inability to proceed; **~ line,** (Electr.) device producing desired delay in transmission of signal. [ME, f. OF *delayer* v., *delai* n., prob. f. *des-* DIS- + *laier* leave; see RELAY[2]]

dĕl cre'derė (-ā'd-) *a.*, *adv.*, & *n.* (Commerc.) Subject to, charge made for, selling-agent's guarantee that buyer is solvent. [It., = of trust]

dē'lė *v.t.* (Print.) Delete (letter, word, etc., struck out or otherwise indicated). [L, imper. of *delēre* (see DELETE)]

dėlĕ'ctab|le *a.* (literary or iron.) Delightful, pleasant; hence ~LY[2] *adv.* [ME f. OF, f. L *delectabilis* (*delectare* DELIGHT; see -ABLE)]

dēlĕctā'tion *n.* Enjoyment (usu. *for* one's *delectation*). [ME f. OF (as prec.; see -ATION)]

dĕ'lėgacȳ *n.* System of delegating; appointment as delegate; body of delegates. [f. foll. + -ACY]

dĕ'lėgate[1] *n.* Deputy; member of committee: elected representative sent to conference; member of deputation. [ME, f. L *delegatus* (as foll.; see -ATE[2])]

dĕ'lėgāte[2] *v.t.* Depute (person), send as representative(s); commit (authority, powers, etc.) to or *to* agent. [f. L DE(*legare* depute) + -ATE[3]]

dĕlėgā'tion *n.* Entrusting of authority to deputy; body of delegates; deputation. [f. L *delegatio* (as prec.; see -ATION)]

dėlē'te *v.t.* Strike out, obliterate, (letter, word, passage); so **dėlē'TION** *n.* [f. L *delēre -let-* efface]

dĕlėtēr'ious *a.* Harmful (to mind or body); hence ~LY[2] *adv.* [f. med. L *deleterius* f. Gk *dēlētērios* noxious + -OUS]

dĕlf, dĕlft, *n.* Glazed earthenware made at *Delft* (earlier *Delf*) in Holland.

dėlĭ'berate[1] *a.* Intentional; fully considered, not impulsive; slow in deciding, cautious; (of movement etc.) leisurely, not hurried; hence ~LY[2] (-tlĭ) *adv.*, ~NESS (-tn-) *n.* [f. L *deliberatus* p.p. (as foll.; see -ATE[2])]

dėlĭ'berāte[2] *v.* **1.** *v.i.* Think carefully; take counsel, consult, hold debate. **2.** *v.t.* Consider (question, *what to do*, etc.). [f. L DE(*liberare* = *librare* weigh f. *libra* balance) + -ATE[3]]

dėlĭberā'tion *n.* Weighing in mind, careful consideration; discussion of reasons for and against, debate; care, avoidance of precipitancy; unhurriedness of movement. [ME f. OF, f. L *deliberatio -onis* (as prec.; see -ATION)]

dėlĭ'berative *a.* Of, appointed for purpose of, deliberation or debate (*deliberative assembly* or *functions*); hence ~LY[2] (-vlĭ) *adv.* [f. F *délibératif -ive* or f. L *deliberativus* (as DELIBERATE[2]; see -IVE)]

dĕ'lĭcacȳ *n.* **1.** Fineness of texture, graceful slightness, tender beauty. **2.** Weakliness, susceptibility to disease or injury, need of care, discretion, or skill; (of person, sense, or instrument) accuracy of perception, sensitiveness. **3.** Consideration for others' feelings; avoidance of what is immodest or offensive. **4.** Choice kind of food, dainty. [ME, f. foll. + -ACY]

dĕ'lĭcate *a.* **1.** Fine in texture, soft, slender, slight; of exquisite quality or workmanship; (of food) dainty and palatable; (of colour) subdued; subtle, hard to appreciate. **2.** Easily injured, liable to illness (**in a ~ condition,** (arch.) pregnant); requiring careful handling (lit. or fig.), critical, ticklish; (of person or instrument) highly sensitive. **3.** Deft (*a delicate touch*); avoiding the offensive or immodest; (esp. of actions) considerate. **4.** Hence ~LY² (-tlĭ) *adv.* [ME, f. OF *delicat* or f. L *delicatus*, of unkn. orig.; see -ATE²]

dĕlĭcatĕ'ssen *n.* (Shop selling) prepared delicacies or relishes for the table. [f. G *delikatessen* or Du. *delicatessen* f. F *délicatesse* (*délicat*, as prec.)]

dėlĭ'cious (-sh*u*s) *a.* Highly delightful, esp. to taste, smell, or sense of humour; hence ~LY² *adv.*, ~NESS *n.* [ME f. OF, f. LL *deliciosus* f. L *deliciae* delight; see -OUS]

dėlĭ'ct *n.* (arch.) Violation of law, offence. [f. L *delictum* neut. p.p. (as n.) of DE(*linquere* leave) offend]

dėlī'ght (-ī't) *v.* & *n.* **1.** *v.t.* Please greatly (*shall be delighted to accept the invitation*; *was delighted with* or *at the result*); hence ~**ėd**LY² *adv.* **2.** *v.i.* Take or find great pleasure *in*; be highly pleased *to* do. **3.** *n.* Great pleasure; thing that causes it; hence ~FUL *a.*, ~**ful**LY² *adv.*, ~SOME¹ *c* (literary). [ME, f. OF *delitier*, *delit*, f. L *delectare* frequent. of *delicere*; alt. after *light* etc.]

Dėlī'lah (-l*a*) *n.* Temptress, seductive and wily woman. [f. ~, betrayer of Samson (Judges 16)]

dėlĭ'mĭt *v.t.* Determine limits or territorial boundary of; so ~ATE³ *v.t.*, ~A'TION *n.* [f. F *délimiter* f. L DE(*limitare* f. *limes -itis* boundary)]

dėlĭ'nė|āte *v.t.* Show by drawing or description, portray; hence or cogn. ~A'TION, ~**ā**TOR, *ns.* [f. L DE(*lineare* f. *linea* line) + -ATE³]

dėlĭ'nquencў *n.* Neglect of duty; guilt (esp. *juvenile delinquency*); misdeed. [f. eccl. L *delinquentia* (L *delinquens* part. of *delinquere*; see DELICT, -ENCY)]

dėlĭ'nquent *a.* & *n.* **1.** *a.* Defaulting, guilty; *in arrears. **2.** *n.* Offender (esp. *juvenile delinquent*). [f. L *delinquens* (as prec.; see -ENT)]

dĕlĭquĕ'sc|e *v.i.* Become liquid, melt, (fig.) melt away; (Chem.) dissolve in water absorbed from the air; so ~ENT *a.*, ~ENCE *n.* [f. L DE(*liquescere* incept. of *liquēre* be liquid); see -ESCE]

dėlĭ'rĭous *a.* Affected with delirium, temporarily or apparently mad, raving; wildly excited, ecstatic; betraying delirium or ecstasy; hence ~LY² *adv.* [f. as foll. + -OUS]

dėlĭ'rĭum *n.* Disordered state of mind with incoherent speech, hallucinations, and frenzied excitement; great excitement, ecstasy; ~ **tremens** (trē'mĕnz), special form of delirium with tremors and terrifying delusions due to prolonged consumption of alcohol. [L, f. DE*lirare* be deranged (*lira* ridge between furrows)]

dėlĭ'ver *v.t.* **1.** Save, rescue, set free, (*from*). **2.** Assist in giving birth; give birth to; (in *pass.*) give birth (lit. or fig.; *was delivered of a child, a sonnet*); unburden one*self* (*of* opinion etc.) in discourse. **3.** Give *up* or *over*, abandon, resign, hand on *to* another; distribute (letters, parcels, ordered goods) to addressee or purchaser (~ **the goods** or ~, (fig.) carry out one's part of agreement); present, render, (account); (Law) hand over formally (esp. sealed deed to grantee). **4.** Launch, aim, (blow, ball, attack); (of judge) pronounce (judgement); utter, recite, (*well-delivered sermon*). **5.** Hence ~ABLE *a.*, ~ER¹ *n.* [ME, f. OF *delivrer* f. Gallo-Rom. **deliberare* (as DE-, L *liberare* LIBERATE)]

dėlĭ'verance *n.* Rescue; formally expressed opinion, (in jurors' oath) verdict. [ME, f. OF *delivrance* (as prec.; see -ANCE)]

dėlĭ'verў *n.* **1.** Childbirth. **2.** Surrender *of*. **3.** Delivering of letters etc., a periodical performance of this; **take ~ of,** receive (thing purchased). **4.** (Law). Formal handing over of property, transfer of deed to grantee or third party. **5.** Sending forth of missile, esp. of cricket-ball or baseball; action shown in doing this (*a good, high, delivery*); uttering of speech etc. (*its delivery took two hours*), manner of doing this (*a telling delivery*). [ME, f. AF *delivree* fem. p.p. (as n.) of *delivrer* (see DELIVER, -Y⁴)]

dĕll *n.* Small usu. wooded hollow or valley. [OE, = MLG, MDu. *delle*, MHG *telle* f. Gmc **daljō* (**dal-*; cf. DALE)]

Dĕlla Crŭ'scan *a.* & *n.* (Member) of academy in Florence concerned with purity of Italian; (member) of school of English poets with artificial style in late 18th c. [f. It. (*Accademia*) *della Crusca* (Academy) of the bran (w. ref. to sifting) + -AN]

dēlou'se *v.t.* Rid of lice, or (fig.) of undesirable things. [f. DE- + LOUSE]

Dĕ'lphĭan, Dĕ'lphĭc, *adjs.* (As) of the ancient Greek oracle of Delphi; obscure, ambiguous, enigmatic. [f. *Delphi* + -AN, -IC]

dĕlphĭ'nĭum *n.* Ranunculaceous usu. blue-flowered plant of genus *Delphinium*, e.g. larkspur. [mod. L, f. Gk *delphinion* larkspur (*delphin* dolphin)]

dĕ'lphĭnoid *n.* & *a.* (Animal) like dolphin; (member) of the family including dolphins, porpoises, grampuses, etc. [f. Gk *delphinoeidēs* (*delphin* dolphin; see -OID)]

dĕ'lta *n.* Fourth Greek letter (Δ, δ) = d; (Astron.) fourth star in a constellation; fourth-class mark in examination; triangular alluvial tract at mouth of river enclosed or traversed by its diverging branches, whence **dĕltā'**IC *a.*; ~ **connection,** (Electr.) triangular arrangement of three-phase windings with circuit wire from each angle; ~ **rays,** rays of low penetrative power consisting of slow electrons knocked from an atom by other particles, esp. alpha rays; ~ **wing,** triangular swept-back wing of aircraft. [ME f. Gk, f. Phoen. *daleth*]

dĕltĭŏ'|logў *n.* Hobby of collecting postcards; hence ~LOGIST *n.* [f. Gk *deltion* dim. of *deltos* writing-tablet + -O- + -LOGY]

dĕ'ltoid *a.* & *n.* Triangular; ~ (**muscle**), muscle of shoulder lifting upper arm; like a river delta. [f. F *deltoïde* or f. mod. L *deltoides* f. Gk *deltoeidēs* (DELTA; see -OID)]

dėlū'de (*or* -ōō'd) *v.t.* Impose on, deceive. [ME, f. L DE(*ludere lus-* play) mock]

dĕ'lūge *n.*, & *v.t.* **1.** *n.* Great flood, inundation, (**the D~**, Noah's flood, Gen. 6–8); heavy fall of rain; flood of words etc. **2.** *v.t.* Flood, inundate, (lit. or fig.). [ME f. OF, f. L *diluvium*, rel. to *lavare* wash]

dėlū'sion (-zh*o*n; *or* -lōō'-) *n.* Imposing or being imposed on; false impression (*was under the delusion that*) or opinion, esp. as symptom or form of madness (**~s of grandeur,** hallucinatory exaggeration of one's own personality or status), whence ~AL *a.* [ME, f. LL *delusio* (as DELUDE; see -ION)]

dėlū'sĭve (*or* -lōō'-) *a.* Deceptive, disappointing, unreal; hence ~LY² (-vlĭ) *adv.*, ~NESS (-vn-) *n.* [f. as DELUDE + -IVE]

dēlŭ'stre, *-ster, *v.t.* Remove lustre from (textile). [f. DE- + LUSTRE¹]

de lŭ'xe (*or* lōō'ks) *a.* Luxurious, sumptuous; of superior kind. [F, = of luxury]

For other words in *de-* see DE-.

dĕlve *v.* **1.** *v.t.* & *i.* (poet.) Dig. **2.** *v.i.* Make laborious research in documents etc. [OE *delfan*, = OS *-delban*, OHG *-telban* f. WG **delbh-* etc.]

***Dem.** *abbr.* Democrat.

dēmă'gnėtīz|e, -īs|e (-īz), *v.t.* Remove magnetization of; hence ~A'TION *n.* [f. DE- + MAGNETIZE]

dĕ'magŏgue (-g), ***-gŏg,** *n.* Leader of the populace; political agitator appealing to desires or prejudices of the mob; hence or cogn. **dĕmagŏ'gIC** (-gĭk) *a.*, **dĕ'magŏguERY** (4) (-gerĭ), **dĕ'magŏgY**[1] (-gĭ), *ns.* [f. Gk *dēmagōgos* (*dēmos* the people, *agōgos* leading)]

dėma'nd[1] (-ah'-) *n.* **1.** Request made as of right or peremptorily (~ **note,** ||request for payment, *bill payable at sight; *payable* etc. **on** ~, as soon as the demand is made). **2.** Desire of would-be purchasers or users for commodity (~ **pull,** available money as factor causing economic inflation; **in** ~, sought after; SUPPLY[1] *and demand*); urgent claim (*many demands on me, on my time*). [ME, f. OF *demande* (*demander*; see foll.)]

dėma'nd[2] (-ah'-) *v.t.* Ask for (thing) as of right or peremptorily or urgently (*of* or *from* person; *demand an answer, to know, that* one *be told*); require, need (*piety demands it; task demands skill*); ask to be, insist on being, told (*demand* person's *business, what he wants*); (in *part.*, abs.) making demands, requiring skill, effort, etc.; hence ~ABLE *a.*, ~ANT *n.* [ME, f. OF *demander* f. L DE(*mandare* order; cf. MANDATE) entrust]

dėmă'ntoid *n.* Lustrous green garnet. [G]

dēmārcā'tion *n.* Marking of boundary or limits, esp. between work considered by trade unions to belong to different trades (*demarcation dispute*); hence (as back form.) **dē'mārcATE**[3] *v.t.* [f. Sp. *demarcación* (*demarcar* mark bounds of; as DE-, MARK[2]); see -ATION]

démarche (dā'mārsh) *n.* (Diplom.) Political step or proceeding, esp. initiating fresh policy. [F (*démarcher* take steps; as DE-, MARCH[5])]

dēmatēr'ĭalīz|e, -īs|e (-īz), *v.t.* & *i.* Make or become non-material or spiritual; hence ~A'TION *n.* [f. DE- + MATERIALIZE]

dēme *n.* (Gk Hist.) township of ancient Attica; administrative division in modern Greece; (Ecol.) local population of closely related plants and animals. [f. Gk *dēmos* the people]

dėmea'n[1] *v. refl.* (w. *adv.* or *adv. phr.*) Behave, conduct oneself. [ME, f. OF *demener* f. Rom. **deminare* (as DE-, L *minare* drive animals f. *minari* threaten)]

dėmea'n[2] *v.t.* (usu. *refl.*) Lower the dignity of; ~ **oneself,** condescend *to* do. [f. DE- + MEAN[3], after *debase*]

dėmea'nour (-ner), ***-or,** *n.* Bearing, outward behaviour. [f. DEMEAN[1], prob. after obs. *havour* behaviour]

dėmĕ'nt *n.* Demented person. [orig. a. f. F *dément* or f. L *demens* (see foll.)]

dėmĕ'ntėd *a.* Driven mad, crazy; hence ~LY[2] *adv.* [p.p. of *dement* v. f. OF *dementer* or f. LL *dementare* f. DEmens out of one's mind (*mens mentis*)]

démenti (dāmah'ṅtē) *n.* Official denial of rumour etc. [F (*démentir* accuse of lying)]

dėmĕ'ntĭa (*or* -sha) *n.* (Med.) Insanity consisting in loss of intellectual power, due to brain disease or injury; ~ ***praecox*** (prē'kŏks), schizophrenia. [L (*demens*; see DEMENTED)]

dĕmerār'a (*or* -ār'*a*) *n.* Brown raw cane sugar brought orig. and chiefly from *Demerara* in Guyana.

dēmĕ'rĭt *n.* Quality or action deserving blame; fault, defect; *mark awarded to offender; hence **~ōr'ĭous** [-ORY, -OUS] *a.* [ME, f. OF *de(s)merite* or f. L *demeritum* neut. p.p. of *demerēri* deserve; orig. sense DESERT[1] (good or bad)]

dėmēr'sal *a.* Being or living near sea-bottom. [f. L *demersus* p.p. of DE(*mergere* plunge) + -AL]

dėme'sne (-ē'n *or* -ā'n) *n.* **1.** (Law). Possession (of real property) as one's own (*estate* **held in** ~, occupied by owner, not by his tenants). **2.** Sovereign's or State's territory, domain; landed property, estate; land attached to mansion etc.; region, sphere, (*of*). [ME, f. AF, OF *demeine* (later AF *demesne*) belonging to a lord, f. L *dominicus* (see DOMINICAL)]

dĕ'mĭ- *pref.* Half-size, half, imperfect, partial(ly), semi-. [ME f. F, f. med. L *dimedius* half, for L *dimidius*]

dĕ'mĭgŏd *n.* (*fem.* **~dess**). Partly divine being, offspring of god and mortal; person who seems to have godlike powers. [f. DEMI- + GOD]

dĕ'mĭjŏhn (-jŏn) *n.* Bulging narrow-necked bottle of 3–10 gal., usu. cased in wicker and with wicker handles. [prob. corrupt. of F *dame-jeanne* Lady Jane, assim. to DEMI-, JOHN]

dēmĭ'lĭtarīz|e, -īs|e (-īz), *v.t.* Remove military organization or forces from (frontier, zone, etc.); hence ~A'TION *n.* [f. DE- + MILITARY + -IZE]

demi-mond|e (dĕ'mĭmawṅd) *n.* Women of doubtful reputation and social standing; group behaving with doubtful legality or propriety; so ***~aine*** *n.*, woman of the *demi-monde*. [F, = half-world]

dēmĭ'neralīz|e, -īs|e (-īz), *v.t.* Remove salts from (sea-water etc.); hence ~A'TION *n.* [f. DE- + MINERALIZE]

demi-pension (demĭpah'ṅsyawṅ) *n.* Accommodation at hotel etc. with bed, breakfast, and one main meal per day. [F (as DEMI-, PENSION 2)]

dĕ'mĭ-rĕp *n.* (arch.) Woman of doubtful reputation esp. as regards chastity. [abbr. of *demi-reputable* (DEMI-, REPUTABLE)]

dėmī'se (-z) *v.t.*, & *n.* **1.** *v.t.* Convey or grant (estate) by will or lease; transmit (title etc.) by death or abdication. **2.** *n.* Conveyance or transfer by demising; death (lit. or fig.). [v. f. n., AF use of p.p. of OF *de(s)mettre* DISMISS, in refl. abdicate]

||**dĕmĭsĕ'mĭquāver** (*or* dĕ'-) *n.* (Mus.) Note, with three-hooked symbol, equal to half a semiquaver. [f. DEMI- + SEMI*quaver*]

dēmĭ'st *v.t.* Clear mist from (windscreen etc.); so ~ER[1] (2) *n.* [f. DE- + MIST]

dėmĭ't *v.t.* (**-tt-**). Resign, abdicate, (office, or abs.); so **dėmĭ'ssION** (-shon) *n.* [f. F *démettre* f. L DE(*mittere miss-* send)]

dĕ'mĭtăsse *n.* Small coffee-cup; its contents. [F, = half-cup]

dĕ'mĭūrge *n.* (In Platonic philosophy) creator of world; (in Gnosticism etc.) a being subordinate to Supreme being; hence **dĕmĭūr'gIC** *a.* [f. eccl. L f. Gk *dēmiourgos* craftsman (*dēmios* public f. *dēmos* people, *-ergos* working)]

demi-vierge (demĭvyār'zh) *n.* Woman who behaves licentiously but retains her physiological virginity. [F, = half-virgin]

dĕ'mō *n.* (*pl.* **~s**). (colloq.) = DEMONSTRATION 4. [abbr.]

dēmŏ'b *v.t.* (**-bb-**), & *n.* (colloq.) Demobilize, demobilization. [abbr.]

dēmō'bĭlīz|e, -īs|e (-īz), *v.t.* Release from mobilized state, disband, (troops, ships); hence ~A'TION *n.* [f. F *démobiliser* (as DE-, MOBILIZE)]

dėmŏ'cracy̆ *n.* (A State having) government by all the people, direct or representative; form of society ignoring hereditary class distinctions and tolerating minority views; *principles or members of Democratic Party. [f. F *démocratie* f. LL f. Gk *dēmokratia* (*dēmos* the people; see -CRACY)]

dĕ'mocrăt *n.* Advocate of democracy; *(*D~*) member of Democratic Party; hence **dėmŏ'cratISM** (3) *n.* [f. F *démocrate* f. as prec., after *aristocrate*]

dĕmocră'tĭc *a.* Of, like, practising, advocating, constituting, (a) democracy; favouring social equality; ***D~ Party** (opposed to Republican Party and supporting social reform and international commitment); so **dĕmocră'tically** *adv.*, **dėmŏ'cratize** (3) *v.t.* & *i.* [f. F *démocratique* f. med. L f. Gk *dēmokratikos* (*dēmokratia* DEMOCRACY; see -IC)]

démodé (dāmō'dā) *a.* Out of fashion. [F, p.p. of *démoder* (as DE-, *mode* fashion)]

dēmŏdūlā'tion *n.* (Radio etc.) Process of extracting modulating signal from modulated wave etc. [f. DE- + MODULATION]

dėmŏ'graphy̆ *n.* Study of statistics of births, deaths, disease, etc., as illustrating conditions of life in communities; hence **dėmŏ'grapher** *n.*, **dĕmogra'phic(al)** *adjs.* [f. Gk *dēmos* the people + -O- + -GRAPHY]

dĕmoisĕ'lle (-mwaz-) *n.* (Zool.) Small crane of Asia & N. Africa; damselfish; damselfly; (arch.) young lady. [F, = DAMSEL]

dėmŏ'lĭsh *v.t.* Pull or throw down (building), destroy; overthrow (institution), refute (theory); (joc.) eat up; so **dĕmolĭ'tion** *n.* [f. F *démolir* (-ISH²) f. L DE(*moliri -it-* construct f. *moles* mass)]

dē'mon *n.* **1.** Evil spirit or devil (esp. possessing a person); malignant supernatural being; cruel, malignant, destructive, forceful, or fierce, person (~ **bowler,** (Cricket) very fast bowler; **is a ~ for work,** works strenuously); personified evil passion. **2.** (Also **daemon,** *pr.* same.) Supernatural being in Gk Myth.; attendant or indwelling spirit. **3.** Hence **~ŏ'latry, ~ŏ'logy,** *ns.* [ME f. med. L, f. L f. Gk *daimōn* deity]

dēmo'nĕtĭz|e (-mŭ'n-), **-īs|e** (-īz), *v.t.* Withdraw (coin etc.) from use as money; hence **~a'tion** *n.* [f. F *démonétiser* (as DE-, L *moneta* MONEY, -IZE)]

dėmō'nĭăc *a.* & *n.* (Person) possessed by an evil spirit; of such possession; of or like demons; fiercely energetic, frenzied; so **dĕmonī'acal** *a.* [ME, f. OF *demoniaque* f. eccl. L *daemoniacus* (*daemonium* f. Gk *daimonion* dim. of *daimōn*; cf. DEMON)]

dēmŏ'nĭc, dae-, *a.* Demoniac; having supernatural genius or power. [f. LL f. Gk *daimonikos* (as DEMON; see -IC)]

dē'monĭsm *n.* Belief in the power of demons. [f. DEMON + -ISM]

dē'monize, -īse (-īz), *v.t.* Make into or like, represent as, demon. [f. DEMON + -IZE]

dĕ'monstr|able (*or* dĭmŏ'n-) *a.* Capable of being shown or logically proved; hence **~abi'lity** *n.*, **~ably²** *adv.* [ME, f. L *demonstrabilis* (as foll.; see -ABLE)]

dĕ'monstrāte *v.* **1.** *v.t.* Show evidence of (feelings etc.); describe and explain by help of specimens or experiments; logically prove the truth of; be proof of the existence of. **2.** *v.i.* Act as demonstrator; make, take part in, a demonstration by public meeting etc. [f. L DE(*monstrare* show) + -ATE³]

dĕmonstrā'tion *n.* **1.** Outward exhibition *of* feeling etc. **2.** Logical proving, clear proof, argument etc. serving as proof. **3.** Exhibition and explanation of specimens or experiments as way of teaching. **4.** Exhibition of opinion on political or other question; public meeting or procession for such purpose; show of military force. **5.** Hence **~al** *a.* [ME f. OF, or f. L *demonstratio* (as prec.; see -ATION)]

dėmŏ'nstratĭve *a.* & *n.* **1.** *a.* Serving to point out or exhibit; (Gram.) indicating person or thing referred to (*demonstrative* PRONOUN). **2.** Giving proof *of*; logically conclusive; concerned with proof. **3.** Given to or marked by open expression of feelings (*demonstrative person, behaviour, affection*, etc.). **4.** Hence **~ly²** (-vlĭ) *adv.*, **~ness** (-vn-) *n.* **5.** *n.* (Gram.) Demonstrative word. [ME, f. OF *demonstratif -ive* f. L *demonstrativus* (as prec.; see -IVE)]

dĕ'monstrātor *n.* One who demonstrates; one who teaches by demonstration, esp. in laboratory etc.; person who explains working of machine etc. to prospective customers; one who takes part in demonstration by public meeting etc. [L (as DEMONSTRATE; see -OR)]

dėmŏ'ralīz|e, -īs|e (-īz), *v.t.* Destroy morale of; (arch.) corrupt morals of; hence **~a'tion** *n.* [f. F *démoraliser* (as DE-, MORAL, -IZE)]

Dē'mŏs *n.* Personification of the populace, esp. in a democracy. [Gk, = the people]

dēmō'te *v.t.* Reduce to lower rank or class; hence **dēmō'tion** *n.* [f. DE- + PROMOTE]

dėmŏ'tĭc *a.* & *n.* Popular, vulgar, (language etc.); (of) the popular simplified form (opp. *hieratic*) of ancient Egyptian writing; (of) the popular form of modern Greek. [f. Gk *dēmotikos* f. *dēmotēs* one of the people (*dēmos*); see -IC]

dēmou'nt *v.t.* Take (apparatus etc.) from its mounting; dismantle for later reassembly. [f. F *démonter*; cf. DISMOUNT]

dėmŭ'lcent *a.* & *n.* Soothing (medicine). [f. L DE(*mulcēre* soothe); see -ENT]

dėmûr' *v.i.* (-rr-), & *n.* **1.** *v.i.* Raise scruples or objections *to* or *at*; (Law) put in a demurrer, whence **dėmŭ'rrant** *n.* **2.** *n.* Objecting, objection, (usu. *without, with no, demur*). [ME, f. OF *demeure(r)* f. Rom. *DE(*morare* f. L *morari* delay)]

dėmūr'e *a.* Sober, grave, composed; affectedly or artificially quiet and serious; decorous; hence **~ly²** (-ūr'lĭ) *adv.*, **~ness** (-ūr'n-) *n.* [ME; perh. f. AF *demuré* f. OF *demoré* p.p. of *demorer* remain f. as prec. (cf. STAID), infl. by OF *meür* f. L *maturus* ripe]

dėmŭ'rrable *a.* (esp. Law). That may be demurred to; open to objection. [f. DEMUR + -ABLE]

dėmŭ'rrage *n.* Rate or amount payable to shipowner by charterer for failure to load or discharge ship within time allowed; similar charge on railway trucks or goods; such detention, delay. [f. OF *demo(u)rage* (*demorer*, as DEMUR; see -AGE)]

dėmŭ'rrer *n.* Legal objection to relevance of opponent's point even if granted, which stays action till relevance is settled; exception taken. [AF, inf. as n., = DEMUR; see -ER⁴]

dėmȳ' *n.* Size of paper, 216 × 138 mm; ‖scholar of Magdalen College, Oxford (orig. with half Fellow's allowance), whence **~ship** *n.* [ME, var. of DEMI-]

dēmȳ'stĭ|fȳ *v.t.* Clarify (obscure beliefs etc.); reduce or remove irrationality etc. of (person); hence **~fica'tion** *n.* [f. DE- + MYSTIFY]

dēmȳthŏ'logize, -īse (-īz), *v.t.* Remove mythical elements from (legend etc.); reinterpret mythological elements in (Bible). [f. DE- + MYTHOLOGIZE]

dĕn *n.* Wild beast's lair; resort of criminals etc. (*opium den*; *den of vice*); small room in which person secludes himself to work etc. [OE *denn*, = MLG, MDu. *denne*, OHG *tenni*, f. Gmc **danjam*, *danjō*; cogn. w. DEAN²]

dėnār'ĭ|us *n.* (*pl.* **~i** *pr.* -ī). Ancient Roman silver coin. [L, = (coin) of ten asses (as foll.; see AS²)]

dē'narȳ *a.* Of ten, decimal; *denary* SCALE³. [f. L *denarius* containing ten (*deni* by tens, distrib. of *decem* ten; see -ARY¹)]

dēnă'tionalīz|e, -īs|e (-īz), *v.t.* Deprive (nation) of its status or characteristics, (person) of membership or characteristics of his nation; transfer (institution, industry, etc.) from national to private ownership; hence ~A'TION *n.* [f. F *dénationaliser* (as DE-, NATIONAL, -IZE)]

dēnă'turalīz|e, -īs|e, (-ch*er*alīz) *v.t.* Change nature or properties of, make unnatural; deprive (esp. one*self*) of citizenship; make (alcohol etc.) unfit for drinking; hence ~A'TION *n.* [f. DE- + NATURAL + -IZE, or f. DE- + NATURALIZE]

dēnā'tur|e *v.t.* Denaturalize; change properties of (protein) by heat etc.; so ~ANT, ~A'TION, (-ch*er*-) *ns.* [f. F *dénaturer* (as DE-, NATURE)]

dēna'zĭ|fȳ (-ah'tsĭ-) *v.t.* Remove (Nazis or their supporters) from Nazi allegiance; remove Nazis from (official positions etc.); hence ~FICA'TION *n.* [f. DE- + NAZI + -FY]

dĕ'ndrīte *n.* (Stone or mineral with) natural treelike or mosslike marking; (Zool.) branching process conducting signals to nerve-cell. [F, f. Gk *dendritēs* a. (*dendron* tree); see -ITE[1]]

dĕndrĭ't|ĭc *a.* Of or like a dendrite; treelike in shape or markings; hence ~ICALLY *adv.* [f. prec. + -IC]

dĕndrōchronŏ'log|ȳ (-k-) *n.* Study of chronology by means of annual growth rings in timber; hence ~IST (3) *n.* [f. Gk *dendron* tree + -o- + CHRONOLOGY]

dĕ'ndroid *a.* Tree-shaped. [f. Gk *dendrōdēs* treelike + -OID]

dĕndrŏ'logȳ *n.* Study of trees. [f. Gk *dendron* tree + -o- + -LOGY]

||**dēne**[1] *n.* Bare sandy tract, low sand-hill, by sea. [perh. rel. to LG *düne*, Du. *duin*; cf. DUNE]

||**dēne**[2]. See DEAN[2].

dēnėgā'tion *n.* (arch.) Denial. [f. LL DE(*negatio* f. L *negare* deny); see -ATION]

||**dēne-hōle** *n.* (Archaeol.) Artificial cave in chalk entered by vertical shaft. [18th c.; orig. uncert., perh. f. DANE + HOLE[1]]

dĕ'nguė (-nggĭ) *n.* Infectious eruptive tropical fever causing acute pains in joints. [W. Ind. Sp., f. Swahili *denga, dinga*, w. assim. to Sp. *dengue* fastidiousness, w. ref. to stiffness of patient's neck and shoulders]

dėnī'able. See DENY.

dėnī'al *n.* Refusal of request or wish (SELF-*-denial*); statement that thing is not true (*meet charge with flat denial*) or existent, contradiction; disavowal of person as one's leader etc. [f. DENY + -AL 2]

dĕ'nier (-ny*er*) *n.* Unit of weight by which fineness of silk, rayon, or nylon yarn is estimated. [orig. name of a small coin; ME f. OF, f. L *denarius* (see DENARY)]

dĕ'nĭgr|āte *v.t.* Blacken (fig.), defame; hence ~**āt**OR, ~A'TION, *ns.*, ~**āt**ORY *a.* [f. L DE(*nigrare* f. *niger* black) + -ATE[3]]

dĕ'nĭm *n.* Twilled hard-wearing cotton fabric used for overalls, jeans, etc.; (in *pl.*) garment made of this. [for *serge de Nim* (*Nîmes* in S. France)]

dēnī'trĭ|fȳ *v.t.* Remove nitrates or nitrites from (soil etc.); so ~FICA'TION *n.* [f. DE- + NITRIFY]

dĕ'nĭzen *n.* Inhabitant or occupant (*of* place); foreigner admitted to residence and certain rights; naturalized foreign word, animal, or plant; hence ~SHIP *n.* [ME, f. AF *deinzein* f. OF *deinz* within (L *de* from, *intus* within) + *-ein* (L *-aneus*; see -ANEOUS)]

dėnŏ'mĭnāte *v.t.* Give name to; call or describe (person or thing) as. [f. L DE(*nominare* NOMINATE) + -ATE[3]]

dėnŏmĭnā'tion *n.* Name, designation, esp. characteristic or class name; class of units in numbers, weights, money, etc., (*reduce to the same denomination*; *money of small denominations*); class or kind having specific name; rank of playing-card within suit; Church or religious sect, whence ~AL *a.* (**~al education,** according to principles of a Church or sect). [ME f. OF, or f. L *denominatio* (as prec.; see -ATION)]

dėnŏ'mĭnatĭve *a.* Serving as or giving a name. [f. LL *denominativus* (as prec.; see -ATIVE)]

dėnŏ'mĭnātor *n.* Number below line in vulgar fraction, divisor; (**least, lowest**) **common ~,** (least) common multiple of denominators of several fractions, (fig.) common feature of members of a group. [f. F *dénominateur* or f. med. L *denominator* (as DENOMINATE; see -OR)]

de nos jours (denōzhoor') *a.* (placed after *n.*) Of the present time. [F, = of our days]

dėnō't|e *v.t.* Distinguish, be the sign of; indicate, give to understand, (esp. *that*); stand as name for, designate; signify; so **dēnot**A'TION *n.*, ~ATIVE *a.* [f. F *dénoter* or f. L DE(*notare* mark f. *nota* NOTE[1])]

dénouement, de-, (dānōō'mahṅ) *n.* Unravelling of plot or complications; final resolution in play, novel, etc. [f. F *dénouement* (*dénouer* unknot, f. as DE-, L *nodare* f. *nodus* knot; see -MENT)]

dėnou'nce *v.t.* Inform against, accuse publicly, openly inveigh against; give notice of termination of (armistice, treaty); hence ~MENT (-sm-) *n.* [ME, f. OF *denoncier* f. L DE(*nuntiare* make known f. *nuntius* messenger)]

de nouveau (de nōōvō') *adv.* Afresh, starting again. [F]

de novo (dē nō'vō; *or* dā-) *adv.* = prec. [L]

dĕnse *a.* Closely compacted in substance (*dense fog, forest*); crowded together; crass, stupid; hence ~LY[2] (-slĭ) *adv.*, ~'NESS (-sn-) *n.* [F, or f. L *densus*]

dĕnsĭtŏ'mėter *n.* Instrument for measuring photographic density. [f. foll. + -o- + -METER]

dĕ'nsĭtȳ *n.* Closeness of substance; (Phys.) degree of consistency measured by quantity of mass in unit volume; (Photog.) opaqueness of image; crowded state; stupidity. [f. F *densité* or f. L *densitas* (as DENSE; see -ITY)]

dĕnt *n.*, & *v.t.* **1.** *n.* Surface impression (as) from blow of blunt-edged instrument. **2.** *v.t.* Mark with dent; (fig.) have (esp. adverse) effect on. [ME, prob. f. INDENT[1]]

dĕ'ntal *a.* Of tooth, teeth, or dentistry; (Phonet., of consonant) pronounced with tongue-tip against upper front teeth (as *th*) or ridge of teeth (as *n, s, t*), whence ~IZE (3) *v.t.*; **~ floss,** threads of floss silk etc. used to clean between teeth; **~ mechanic,** person who makes and repairs artificial teeth; **~ surgeon,** dentist. [f. LL *dentalis* f. L *dens dentis* tooth; see -AL]

dĕntā'lĭ|um *n.* (*pl.* **~a**). Tooth-shell of genus *Dentalium*, used as ornament or currency. [mod. L, f. LL *dentalis* (see prec.)]

dĕ'ntāte *a.* (Bot. & Zool.) Toothed, with toothlike notches. [f. L *dentatus* (*dens dentis* tooth; see -ATE[2])]

dĕntĭ- *comb. form.* Tooth, teeth, as: **~lĭ'ngual,** formed by teeth and tongue. [f. L *dens dentis* tooth; see -I-]

dĕ'ntĭcle *n.* (Zool.) Small tooth or toothlike projection. [ME, f. L *denticulus* dim. of *dens dentis* tooth; see -CULE]

dĕ'ntĭfrĭce *n.* Powder, paste, etc., for tooth--cleaning. [F, f. L *dentifricium* (*dens dentis* tooth, *fricare* rub)]

dĕ'ntĭl *n.* One of series of small rectangular blocks under bed-moulding of cornice in classical architecture. [f. obs. F *dentille* dim. of *dent* tooth f. L *dens dentis*]

dĕ'ntine (-ēn), ***dĕ'ntĭn,** *n.* Hard dense tissue forming main part of teeth. [f. L (as prec.) + -INE[4]]

dĕ'ntĭst *n.* One whose profession is to treat diseases and malformations of the teeth, extract

them, insert artificial ones, etc.; hence ~RY (5) *n.* [f. F *dentiste* (*dent* tooth; see DENTIL, -IST)]
dĕnti'tion *n.* Cutting of teeth, teething; characteristic arrangement of teeth in species etc. [f. L *dentitio* (*dentire* to teethe; see -ITION)]
dĕ'nture *n.* Set of (esp. artificial) teeth. [F (*dent* tooth; see DENTIL, -URE)]
dēnū'clėarīz|e, -īs|e (-īz), *v.t.* Remove nuclear armaments from; hence ~A'TION *n.* [f. DE- + NUCLEAR + -IZE]
dėnū'd|e *v.t.* Make naked; strip *of* clothing, covering, possession, attribute; (Geol.) lay (rock, formation) bare by removal of what lies above; so **dēnūd**A'TION *n.*, ~ATIVE *a.* [f. L DE(*nudare* f. *nudus* naked)]
dėnū'mer|able *a.* (Math.) Able to be counted by correspondence with infinite set of integers; hence ~ABI'LITY *n.* [f. LL DE(*numerare* NUMBER²) + -ABLE]
dėnŭnciā'tion *n.* Denouncing; invective; so **dėnŭ'nciat**IVE, **dėnŭ'nciat**ORY, (-sha-) *adjs.*, **dėnŭ'nciāt**OR (-shĭ-) *n.* [f. F *dénonciation* or f. L *denunciatio* (as DENOUNCE; see -ATION)]
dėnȳ' *v.t.* Declare untrue or non-existent (*deny the charge, the possibility, having lied, that it is so, this to be the case*); disavow, repudiate, (*deny* one's *word, signature, faith, leader*); refuse (person, thing, person a thing, thing *to* person; *I was denied this, this was denied me* or *to me*); refuse access to (person sought); ~ one**self,** be abstinent; hence **dėnī'**ABLE *a.* [ME, f. OF *denier* f. L DE(*negare* say no)]
deoch an doris (dŏχandŏ'rĭs; *or* dŏk-) *n.* (Sc. & Ir.) Drink taken at parting, stirrup-cup. [f. Gael. *deoch an doruis* drink at the door]
‖**dē'odănd** *n.* (Hist.) Thing forfeited to Crown for religious or charitable use, as having caused a human death. [f. AF *deodande* f. AL *deodanda* f. L *Deo dandum* thing to be given to God (*Deus* God, *dare* give)]
dē'odār *n.* Himalayan cedar. [f. Hindi *dē' odār* f. Skr. *deva-dāru* divine tree]
dēō'dorant *a.* & *n.* (Substance) that removes or conceals unwanted odours. [f. as foll. + -ANT]
dēō'dorīz|e, -īs|e (-īz), *v.t.* Destroy odour of; hence ~A'TION *n.* [f. DE- + L ODOR smell + -IZE]
Deo gratias (dāō grah'tĭas *or* -shĭas) *int.* Thanks be to God. [L, = (we give) thanks to God]
dėŏ'ntĭc *a.* Of or relating to duty or obligation. [f. as foll. + -IC]
dēŏntŏ'logȳ *n.* Science of duty, ethics; hence **dēŏnto**LO'GICAL *a.*, **dēŏntŏ'**LOGIST *n.* [f. Gk *deont-* part. st. of *dei* it is right + -O- + -LOGY]
Deo volente (dāō volĕ'ntā) *adv.* God being willing; if nothing prevents it. [L]
dē-ŏ'xȳgenāte *v.t.* Remove (the free) oxygen from. [f. DE- + OXYGENATE]
dēŏxȳrībonūclē'ĭc *a.* ~ **acid,** substance in chromosomes of higher organisms, storing genetic information. [f. DE- + OXYGEN + RIBONUCLEIC]
dep. *abbr.* departs; deputy.
dėpār't *v.i.* & *t.* (formal or literary). Go away (*from*), take one's leave; set out, start, leave, (*for* place; esp. of public transport); die, leave by death, (*depart from life, depart this life*); diverge, deviate, (*depart from accepted view, custom*). [ME, f. OF *departir* f. Rom. **departire*, **dispartire* for L *dispertire* divide]
dėpār'tėd *a.* & *n.* Bygone (*departed greatness*); deceased (person(s); esp. *the departed*). [p.p. of prec.; see -ED¹ (2)]
dėpār'tment *n.* Separate part of complex whole, branch, esp. of municipal or State administration, university, shop; administrative district in France etc.; area of activity; ~ **store,** large shop supplying many kinds of goods from various departments. [f. F *département* (as DEPART; see -MENT)]
dēpārtmĕ'ntal *a.* Of or belonging to a department; ~ **store,** = *department store*; hence ~ISM (3) *n.*, ~IZE (3) *v.t.*, ~LY² *adv.* [f. prec. + -AL]
dėpār'ture *n.* Going away; deviation *from* (truth, standard); starting of train, aircraft, etc., (*the departure platform, lounge*); setting out on course of action or thought (esp. *new departure*); (Naut.) amount of ship's change of longitude. [f. OF *departeüre* (as DEPART; see -URE)]
dėpa'stur|e (-ah'-) *v.t.* & *i.* (Of cattle) graze upon, graze; put (cattle) to graze; (of land) give pasturage to (cattle); hence ~AGE *n.* [f. DE- + PASTURE]
dépaysé (dāpā'zā) *a.* (*fem.* ~*e pr.* same). Removed from one's habitual surroundings. [F, = removed from one's own country]
dėpĕ'nd *v.i.* **1.** (poet., arch., etc.) Hang down (*from*). **2.** Be contingent (**that ~s,** the question can only be answered conditionally); ~ **(up)on,** be controlled or determined by (**it ~s upon himself,** i.e. upon his efforts, skill, wisdom, etc.); be grammatically dependent (*up*)*on*. **3.** ~ **(up)on,** be obliged to use, be unable to do without, (*she depends upon her own efforts, her pen, her mother, my help*), rely on (esp. in *imper.*: ~ **upon it,** you may be sure). [ME, f. OF *dependre* f. Rom. **dependere* for L DE(*pendēre* hang)]
dėpĕ'nd|able *a.* That may be relied on; hence ~ABI'LITY, **~able**NESS (-beln-), *ns.*, **~ab**LY² *adv.* [f. prec. + -ABLE]
dėpĕ'ndant, -ent¹, *n.* One who depends on another for support; retainer, servant. [f. F *dépendant* part. of *dépendre* (see DEPEND, -ANT, -ENT)]
dėpĕ'ndence *n.* Depending; being dependent; reliance, confident trust. [f. F *dépendance* (as prec.; see -ANCE, -ENCE)]
dėpĕ'ndencȳ *n.* Subordinate or dependent thing, esp. country or province controlled by another. [f. as prec.; see -ENCY]
dėpĕ'ndent¹. See DEPENDANT.
dėpĕ'ndent² *a.* Depending (*on*), contingent, subordinate, subject; unable to do without something (esp. a drug); maintained at another's cost; (Gram., of clause, phrase, or word) in subordinate relation to a sentence or word; (Math., of variable) having value determined by that of another quantity. [ME, earlier *-ant* = DEPENDANT]
dēpēr'sonalīz|e, -īs|e (-īz), *v.t.* Deprive of personality; make impersonal; hence ~A'TION *n.* (esp., Psych.) morbid loss of sense of identity. [f. DE- + PERSONAL + -IZE]
dėpĭ'ct *v.t.* Represent in drawing or colours; portray in words, describe; hence or cogn. ~ER¹, ~ION, ~OR, *ns.*, ~IVE *a.* [f. L DE(*pingere pict-* paint)]
dĕ'pĭl|āte *v.t.* Remove hair from; hence ~A'TION *n.*, **dėpĭ'lat**ORY *a.* & *n.* [f. L DE(*pilare* f. *pilus* hair) + -ATE³]
dēplā'ne *v.i.* & *t.* Descend or remove from aeroplane. [f. DE- + PLANE³]
dėplē'te *v.t.* Empty out, exhaust; reduce numbers of (*depleted forces*); so **dėplē'ti**ON *n.* [f. L DE(*plēre plet-* fill)]
dėplōr'|e *v.t.* Bewail, grieve over, regret; be scandalized by; hence ~ABLE *a.*, (esp.) exceedingly bad, **~ab**LY² *adv.* [f. F *déplorer* or It. f. L DE(*plorare* bewail)]
dėploy' *v.* **1.** *v.t.* & *i.* (Mil.) Spread (troops) out, (of troops) be spread out, from column into line. **2.** *v.t.* Bring (forces, arguments, etc.) into

effective action. **3.** So ~MENT *n.* [f. F *déployer* f. L DIS(*plicare* fold) & LL DE*plicare* explain]

dėplu'me (-ōō'm) *v.t.* Strip of feathers or (fig.) honour etc. [ME, f. F *déplumer* or f. med. L DE(*plumare* f. L *pluma* feather)]

dēpō'larīz|e, -īs|e (-īz), *v.t.* (Phys.) Reduce or remove polarization of; hence ~A'TION *n.* [f. DE- + POLARIZE]

dēpolĭ'tĭcīz|e, -īs|e (-īz), *v.t.* Make non-political; remove from political activity or influence; hence ~A'TION *n.* [f. DE- + POLITICIZE]

dēpŏ'lўmerīz|e, -īs|e (-īz), *v.t.* & *i.* (Chem.) (Cause to) break down into monomers or other smaller units; hence ~A'TION *n.* [f. DE- + POLYMERIZE]

dėpō'nent *a.* & *n.* **1.** *a.* (L & Gk Gram., of verb) passive (or, in Gk, middle) in form but active in sense [named from notion that it had laid aside the passive sense]. **2.** *n.* Deponent verb; person making deposition under oath or giving written testimony for use in court etc. [f. L DE(*ponere posit-* place); see -ENT]

dēpŏ'pūl|āte *v.t.* & *i.* Reduce population of; decline in population; hence ~A'TION *n.* [f. L DE(*populari* lay waste f. *populus* people) + -ATE[3]]

dėpor't *v.t.* **1.** Bear or conduct *oneself* (in specified manner). **2.** Remove, esp. into exile, banish; hence **dēport**A'TION *n.*, **dēport**EE' *n.*, person who is or has been deported. [sense 1 f. OF *deporter* (as DE-, *porter* carry f. L *portare*); sense 2 f. F *déporter* f. L DE(*portare* carry)]

dėpor'tment *n.* Bearing, demeanour, manners, esp. of cultivated kind. [f. F *déportement* (as prec. 1; see -MENT)]

dėpō's|e (-z), *v.* **1.** *v.t.* Remove from office, esp. dethrone; hence ~ABLE *a.* **2.** *v.i.* Bear witness *that*, testify *to*, esp. on oath in court. [ME, f. OF *deposer* after L *deponere* (see DEPONENT, POSE[1])]

dėpŏ'sĭt[1] (-z-) *n.* Thing stored or entrusted for safe keeping; sum placed in bank, ‖usu. at interest and not to be drawn on without notice (**on ~**, so placed; *has a current and a* ~ **account**); sum required and paid as pledge or first instalment; layer of precipitated matter, natural accumulation. [f. L DE(*positum* neut. p.p. (as n.) of *ponere* place)]

dėpŏ'sĭt[2] (-z-) *v.t.* Lay down in a (usu. specified) place; (of water or natural agency) leave (matter) lying; store or entrust for keeping (esp. sum in bank ‖at interest); pay as pledge for fulfilment of contract or further payment. [f. obs. F *dépositer* or f. med. L *depositare* frequent. of L *deponere*; see prec.]

dėpŏ'sĭtarў (-z-) *n.* Person to whom thing is entrusted, trustee. [f. LL *depositarius* (as DEPOSIT[1]; see -ARY[1])]

dĕposĭ'tion (-z-) *n.* Deposing from office, esp. dethronement; (giving of) sworn evidence, allegation; depositing; (picture of) taking down of Christ from the Cross. [ME f. OF, f. L *depositio -onis* (*deponere*; see DEPOSIT[1], -ION)]

dėpŏ'sĭtor (-z-) *n.* Person who deposits money, property, etc. [f. DEPOSIT[2] + -OR]

dėpŏ'sĭtorў (-z-) *n.* Storehouse (lit. or fig.); = DEPOSITARY. [f. LL *depositorium* (as DEPOSIT[1]; see -ORY)]

dĕ'pōt (-ō) *n.* **1.** (Mil.) Place for stores; headquarters of regiment. **2.** Storehouse, emporium; bus or *railway station. [f. F *dépôt*, OF *depost* f. L (as DEPOSIT[1])]

dėprā've *v.t.* Make bad, deteriorate; pervert, corrupt, esp. in moral character or habits; so **dĕprav**A'TION *n.* [ME, f. OF *depraver* or f. L DE(*pravare* f. *pravus* crooked)]

dėprā'vĭtў *n.* Moral corruption, wickedness; (Theol.) innate corruptness of human nature. [f. DE- + obs. *pravity* f. L *pravitas* (as prec.; see -ITY), after prec.]

dĕ'prĕc|āte *v.t.* Plead against (~ person's **anger,** entreat him not to be angry); express wish against or disapproval of (*deprecate war, hasty action, panic*); so ~A'TION *n.*, ~ATIVE, **~ātory,** *adjs.* [f. L DE(*precari* pray) + -ATE[3]]

dėprē'cĭāt|e (-shĭ-) *v.* **1.** *v.t.* & *i.* Diminish in value. **2.** *v.t.* Lower market price of; reduce purchasing power of (money); disparage, belittle. **3.** Hence ~ORY (-sha-) *a.* [f. LL DE(*pretiare* f. *pretium* price) + -ATE[3]]

dėprēcĭā'tion (-shĭ-) *n.* Depreciating or being depreciated; (allowance made in valuations, estimates, and balance sheets, for) wear and tear. [f. prec. + -ATION]

dĕprėdā'tion *n.* (usu. in *pl.*) Despoiling, ravages. [f. F *déprédation* f. LL DE(*praedatio -onis* f. L *praedari* plunder; see -ATION)]

dĕ'prėdātor *n.* Despoiler, pillager. [f. LL *depraedator* (as prec.; see -OR)]

dėprĕ'ss *v.t.* Push or pull down, lower; reduce activity of (esp. trade); dispirit, deject; **~ed area,** area of economic depression; **~ed classes,** (Ind.) persons of the lowest castes, 'untouchables'; hence ~IBLE *a.* [ME, f. OF *depresser* f. LL DE(*pressare* frequent. of *premere* press)]

dėprĕ'ssant *a.* & *n.* (Influence) that depresses; (Med.) sedative (drug etc.). [f. prec. + -ANT]

dėprĕ'ssion (-sh*o*n) *n.* Lowering, sinking; (Astron. etc.) angular distance of object below horizon or horizontal plane; sunk place, hollow, on surface; reduction in vigour (esp. of trade; **the D~**, the slump of 1929–), vitality, or spirits; (Meteorol.) lowering of barometer level or atmospheric pressure, esp. centre of minimum pressure or system of winds round it; (Psych.) state of morbidly excessive melancholy, mood of hopelessness and feelings of inadequacy, often with physical symptoms. [ME f. OF, or f. L DE(*pressio* f. *premere press-* press; see -ION)]

dėprĕ'ssive *a.* & *n.* **1.** *a.* Tending to depress (lit. or fig.); (Psych.) involving or characterized by depression. **2.** *n.* (Psych.) Person suffering from depression. [f. F *dépressif -ive* or f. med. L *depressivus* (as prec.; see -IVE)]

dėprĕ'ssor *n.* (Anat.) ~ (**muscle**), one pulling down some organ etc.; (Surg.) instrument for pressing down some organ etc. [L (as prec.; see -OR)]

dēprĕ'ssurīze, -īse, (-sher*ī*z) *v.t.* Cause appreciable drop of pressure in (enclosed gas, esp. to natural level). [f. DE- + PRESSURIZE]

dĕprĭvā'tion (*or* dēprī-) *n.* Loss, being deprived, *of*; deposition from esp. ecclesiastical office; loss of desired thing (*that is a great deprivation*). [f. med. L *deprivatio* (as foll.; see -ATION)]

dėprī'v|e *v.t.* Strip, bereave, debar from enjoyment, *of*; depose (esp. clergyman) from office; (esp. in *p.p.*) prevent (child etc.) from having normal home life; hence ~ABLE *a.*, ~AL 2 *n.* [ME, f. OF *depriver* f. med. L *deprivare* f. as DE- + L *privare* deprive]

de profundis (dā profōō'ndĭs) *n.* & *adv.* (Cry) from the depths (of sorrow etc.). [initial L wds of Ps. 130]

Dept. *abbr.* Department.

dĕpth *n.* **1.** Being deep; measurement from top down, from surface inwards, or from front to back. **2.** Abstruseness; sagacity; intensity of colour, darkness, etc. **3.** (in *pl.*) Deep water, deep place, abyss; low moral condition; lowest or inmost part (*lives in the depths of the country*). **4.** Middle (*in the depth of winter*); deep or mysterious region of thought, feeling, etc. **5. In** ~ *adv.* & *a.*, comprehensive(ly), profound(ly), thorough(ly) (**defence in ~**, system of defence with successive areas of resistance); **out of** one's **~,** in water too deep to stand in, (fig.) engaged on task or subject beyond one's powers. **6. ~-bomb, ~-charge,** bomb exploding under water, for dropping on submerged submarine etc.; **~ psychology,** psycho-analysis to reveal hidden motives etc. [ME, f. as DEEP[1] + -TH[1]]

dĕ'pūr|āte *v.t.* & *i.* Make or become free from impurities; so ~A'TION, **~ātor**, *ns.*, **dėpūr'**ATIVE *a.* & *n.* [f. med. L DE(*purare* f. L *purus* pure)]

dĕpūtā'tion *n.* Body of persons appointed to represent others. [ME, f. LL *deputatio* (as foll.; see -ATION)]

dėpū'te[1] *v.t.* Commit (task, authority) to or *to* substitute; appoint as deputy. [ME, f. OF *deputer* f. L DE(*putare* think) regard as, allot]

dĕ'pūte[2] *n.* (Sc.) Deputy. [ME, f. OF *deputé*, p.p. of *deputer* (see prec.)]

dĕ'pūtīze, -īse (-īz), *v.i.* Act as deputy or understudy (*for*). [f. foll. + -IZE]

dĕ'pūtў *n.* Person appointed or delegated to act for another or others (**by ~**, by proxy); parliamentary representative (**Chamber of Deputies,** lower house in some parliaments); coal-mine overseer responsible for safety; (*attrib.*) deputed, acting (||**~ lieutenant,** deputy of Lord Lieutenant of county); hence ~SHIP (l) *n.* [ME, var. of DEPUTE[2]; see -Y[4]]

dėră'cĭn|āte *v.t.* (literary). Tear up by the roots (lit. or fig.); hence ~A'TION *n.* [f. F *déraciner* (as DE-, *racine* f. LL *radicina* dim. of *radix* root) + -ATE[3]]

déraciné (dārā'sĭnā) *a.* & *n.* (*fem.* *~e pr.* same). (Person) 'uprooted' from natural environment. [F, p.p. (as prec.)]

dėrai'l (*or* dē-) *v.t.* (usu. in *pass.*) Cause (train etc.) to leave the rails; hence ~MENT *n.* [f. F *dérailler* (as DE-, RAIL[1])]

dėrā'nge (-nj) *v.t.* Throw into confusion, put out of order, disorganize, cause to act irregularly; (esp. in *p.p.*) make insane; disturb, interrupt; so ~MENT (-jm-) *n.* [f. F *déranger* (as DE-, *rang* RANK[1])]

dērā'te *v.t.* & *i.* Remove part or all of burden of rates (RATE[1] 2) (from). [f. DE- + RATE[1]]

dērā'tion *v.t.* Remove (food etc.) from rationing. [f. DE- + RATION]

Der'bў (dâr'-) *n.* **1.** Annual horse-race at Epsom (**~ Day,** that of the race); similar race elsewhere. **2.** Any important sporting contest; **local ~** (between two teams from same district). **3.** (*d~*). Low-heeled shoe; *bowler hat. [f. 12th Earl of ~ d. 1834, founder of the horse-race]

dērĕ'gĭster *v.t.* Remove from register; hence **dērĕgĭstr**A'TION *n.* [f. DE- + REGISTER[1]]

de règle (derā'gl) *pred. a.* Customary, proper. [F, = of rule]

dĕ'rėlĭct *a.* & *n.* **1.** *a.* Abandoned, ownerless, (esp. of ship at sea or decrepit property); *negligent. **2.** *n.* Abandoned property, esp. ship; socially forsaken person, one not established in society. [f. L *derelictus* p.p. of DE(*relinquere* leave)]

dĕrėlĭ'ction *n.* Abandoning, being abandoned; neglect *of duty*; failure in duty, shortcoming; retreat of sea exposing new land. [f. L *derelictio* (as prec.; see -ION)]

dērĕquĭsĭ'tion (-z-) *v.t.* Return (requisitioned property) to its former owner. [f. DE- + REQUISITION]

dērėstrĭ'ct *v.t.* Remove restrictions from, (esp.) remove or not impose speed limit on traffic in a specified road etc.; so ~ION *n.* [f. DE- + RESTRICT]

dėrī'de *v.t.* Laugh scornfully at; treat with scorn. [f. L DE(*ridēre ris-* laugh)]

de rigueur (derĭgėr') *pred. a.* Required by custom or etiquette (*evening dress is de rigueur*). [F, = of strictness]

dėrĭ'sion (-zhon) *n.* Ridicule, mockery, (*bring into derision*); **hold, have, in ~**, (arch.) mock at. [ME f. OF, f. LL *derisio -onis* (as DERIDE; see -ION)]

dėrī'sĭve *a.* = foll. (*derisive cheers*); hence ~LY[2] (-vlĭ) *adv.* [f. prec. + -IVE]

dėrī'sorў (*or* -z-) *a.* Scoffing; ironical; so small or unimportant as to be ridiculous (*derisory offer, result*). [f. LL *derisorius* (as DERISION; see -ORY)]

dĕrĭvā'tion *n.* Obtaining from a source; extraction, descent; formation of word from word or root, tracing or statement of this; hence ~AL *a.* [f. F *dérivation* or f. L *derivatio* (as DERIVE; see -ATION)]

dėrĭ'vatĭve *a.* & *n.* **1.** (Thing, word, chemical substance) derived from a source, not primitive or original; hence ~LY[2] (-vlĭ) *adv.* **2.** *n.* (Math.) Quantity measuring rate of change of another. [f. F *dérivatif -ive* f. L *derivativus* (as foll.; see -IVE)]

dėrī'v|e *v.* **1.** *v.t.* Get or obtain or form (*from* a source); have *origin* etc. *from*; gather, deduce, (knowledge, truth, ideas, etc.) *from*; trace, show, or assert, descent, origin, or formation of (person, thing, word) *from*; hence ~ABLE *a.* **2.** *v.i.* Be descended, originate, *from*. [ME, f. OF *deriver* or f. L *derivare* (as DE-, *rivus* stream)]

dẽrm, dẽr'ma. Vars. of DERMIS.

dẽrmatī'tĭs *n.* Inflammation of the skin. [f. Gk *derma -atos* skin + -ITIS]

dẽrmat|ŏ'logў *n.* Study of skin and its diseases; hence ~OLO'GICAL *a.*, ~ŏ'LOGIST *n.* [f. as prec. + -O- + -LOGY]

dẽr'm|ĭs *n.* (Anat.) Skin; true skin or layer of tissue below epidermis; so ~AL, ~IC, *adjs.* [mod. L, after *epidermis*]

***dẽrn, *dẽrned** (-nd). Var. of DARN[2], DARNED.

dernier cri (dãrnyākrē') *n.* The very latest fashion. [F, lit. 'last cry']

dĕ'rogāte *v.i.* Detract, take away part, *from* (a merit, right, etc.); deviate *from* (correct behaviour etc.). [f. L DE(*rogare* ask) + -ATE[3]]

dĕrogā'tion *n.* Lessening or impairment *of* law, authority, position, dignity, etc.; deterioration, debasement. [ME, f. F *dérogation* or f. L *derogatio* (as prec.; see -ATION)]

dėrŏ'gator|ў *a.* Tending to detract *from*, involving impairment, disparagement, or discredit, *to*; lowering, unsuited to one's dignity or position; depreciatory; hence ~ĬLY[2] *adv.* [f. LL *derogatorius* (as DEROGATE; see -ORY)]

dĕ'rrĭck *n.* Contrivance for moving or hoisting heavy weights, kind of crane with adjustable arm pivoted at foot to central post, deck, or floor; framework over oil-well or similar boring. [obs. senses *hangman, gallows*, f. name of London hangman *c.* 1600]

derrière (dĕrĭãr') *n.* (colloq.) Buttocks. [F]

dĕrrĭng-do' (-dōō') *n.* (literary). Heroic courage or action. [ME, = *daring to do*, misinterpreted by Spenser and by Scott]

dĕ'rrĭnger (-nj-) *n.* Small large-bore pistol. [f. H. *Deringer*, Amer. inventor d. 1868]

dĕ'rrĭs *n.* Tall woody tropical climbing plant of genus *Derris*; insecticide made from powdered tuberous root of some kinds of derris. [mod. L f. Gk, = leather covering (w. ref. to its pod)]

dĕ'rrў *n.* (Austral. & N.Z.) Dislike, prejudice, (*have a derry on a person*). [app. f. song-refrain *derry down*]

dẽrv *n.* Fuel oil used in heavy road-vehicles. [f. *d*iesel-*e*ngined *r*oad *v*ehicle]

dẽr'vĭsh *n.* Muslim religious man vowed to poverty and austerity; **dancing** or **whirling ~**, **howling ~**, (according to the practice of his order). [f. Turk. *derviş* f. Pers. *darvēsh* poor, a mendicant]

For other words in *de-* see DE-.

dēsă'lĭn|āte *v.t.* Remove salt from (esp. sea-water); hence ~A'TION *n.* [f. DE- + SALINE + -ATE[3]]

dēsa'lt (-sŏ'lt *or* -saw'lt) *v.t.* = prec. [f. DE- + SALT]

dĕ'scant[1] *n.* **1.** (poet.) Melody, song. **2.** (Mus.) Melodic independent treble accompaniment; ~ **recorder** (highest-pitched of standard kinds). [ME, f. OF *deschant* f. med. L DIS(*cantus* CHANT)]

dėscă'nt[2] *v.i.* Talk lengthily, dwell freely, *upon* (esp. in praise, *descant upon the beauties of*); sing descant. [f. prec.]

dėscĕ'nd *v.* **1.** *v.i.* Go or come down; (of thing) sink, fall; (Print., of letter) have tail below line; slope downwards, lie along descending slope. **2.** Make sudden attack or (fig.) unexpected visit (*on*); sink in thought, rank, or degree of quality; (of sound) become lower in pitch; go forward in point of time; go from greater to less or from general to particular; behave so unworthily as *to* do; (of qualities, property, privileges) be transmitted by inheritance *from*, pass (*to* heir). **3.** *v.t.* Go down (hill, stairs); go along (river) towards sea etc. [ME, f. OF *descendre* f. L DE(*scendere* = *scandere* climb)]

dėscĕ'ndant *n.* ~ (**of**), person or thing descended (from). [F, part. of *descendre* (as prec.; see -ANT)]

dėscĕ'ndėd *a.* Sprung, having origin, *from* (ancestor or stock). [p.p. of DESCEND; see -ED[1] (2)]

dėscĕ'ndĭble *a.* That may be descended; that may descend by inheritance. [f. OF *descendable* (as DESCEND; see -ABLE, -IBLE)]

dėscĕ'nt *n.* **1.** Act of descending; downward motion; way by which one may descend; downward slope; sudden attack. **2.** Decline, sinking in scale, fall; being descended, lineage; transmission (of qualities, property, privileges) by inheritance. [ME, f. OF *descente* (*descendre* DESCEND)]

dėscrī'be *v.t.* Set forth in words, recite the characteristics of, (~ **as**, assert to be, call); mark out, draw, (esp. figure in Geom.); move in (specified line, curve); hence **dėscrī'b**ABLE *a.* [f. L DE(*scribere script-* write)]

dėscrĭ'ption *n.* Describing, verbal portrait(ure), of person, object, or event, (**answers** (**to**) or **fits the** ~, has the qualities specified); more or less complete definition; sort, kind, class, (*no food of any description*; *tyrant of the worst description*). [ME f. OF, f. L *descriptio -onis* (as prec.; see -ION)]

dėscrĭ'ptĭve *a.* Serving or seeking to describe (*descriptive touches, writer*); not expressing feelings or judgements; (Ling.) describing a language factually as it is, without drawing comparisons; hence ~LY[2] (-vlĭ) *adv.* [f. LL *descriptivus* (as DESCRIBE; see -IVE)]

dėscrĭ'ptor *n.* Expression, word, etc., used to describe or identify. [L, = describer (as DESCRIBE; see -OR)]

dėscrȳ' *v.t.* Catch sight of, succeed in discerning (lit. or fig.). [ME, earlier senses 'proclaim, DECRY', f. OF *descrier*; prob. confused w. var. of obs. *descrive* f. OF *descrivre* DESCRIBE]

dĕ'sėcr|āte *v.t.* Deprive of sacred character; outrage, profane, (sacred thing); hence ~A'TION, ~ātOR, *ns.* [f. DE- + CONSECRATE]

dēsĕ'grėg|āte *v.t.* Abolish racial segregation in (schools etc.) or of (persons etc.); hence ~A'TION *n.* [f. DE- + SEGREGATE[1]]

dēsĕ'nsĭtīz|e, -is|e (-īz), *v.t.* Reduce or destroy the sensitiveness of (photographic materials, allergic person, etc.); hence ~A'TION *n.* [f. DE- + SENSITIZE]

dėsẽr't[1] (-z-) *n.* Deserving, being worthy of reward or punishment; (in *pl.*) acts or qualities deserving good or bad recompense, such recompense, (*reward him according to, give him, he has got, his deserts*). [ME f. OF (*deservir* DESERVE)]

dĕ'sert[2] (-z-) *a.* & *n.* **1.** *a.* Uninhabited, desolate; uncultivated, barren. **2.** *n.* Waterless and treeless region, (fig.) uninteresting or barren subject, period, etc.; ~ **boot,** suède etc. boot reaching to or just above ankle; ~ **island,** remote and presumably uninhabited island; ‖~ **rat,** (colloq.) soldier of 7th British armoured division (with jerboa as badge) in N. Afr. desert campaign 1941–2. [ME f. OF, f. L *desertus* (eccl. L *desertum* n.) p.p. of *deserere* leave, forsake]

dėsẽr't[3] (-z-) *v.* **1.** *v.t.* Abandon, give up, (thing); depart from (place, haunt), leave (place) empty; forsake (person or thing having claims on one; *desert* one's *wife, husband, post, ship*); fail (*his presence of mind deserted him*). **2.** *v.i.* Run away (esp. from service in armed forces), whence ~ER[1] *n.* **3.** So **dėsẽr'**TION (-z-) *n.* [f. F *déserter* f. LL *desertare* f. L *desertus* (see prec.)]

dėsẽr'v|e (-z-) *v.* **1.** *v.t.* Be entitled by conduct or qualities to (reward or treatment; *to* be or do); hence ~**ėd**LY[2] *adv.* **2.** *v.i.* Have established a claim to be *well* or *ill* treated at the hands *of.* [ME, f. OF *deservir* f. L DE(*servire* serve)]

dėsẽr'vĭng (-z-) *a.* Meritorious; worthy (*of* praise, censure, help, etc.); hence ~LY[2] *adv.* [f. prec. + -ING[2]]

dē-sĕ'x *v.t.* Castrate or spay; deprive of sexual qualities or attractions. [f. DE- + SEX]

dēsĕ'xūalize, -ise (-īz), *v.t.* Deprive of sex or sexual characters or qualities. [f. DE- + SEXUAL + -IZE]

déshabillé (dāzăbē'ā) *n.* (State of) being only partly or not carefully dressed. [F, = undressed]

dĕ'sĭcc|āte *v.t.* Remove moisture from, dry up, (esp. foodstuffs for preservation); hence or cogn. ~ANT, ~A'TION, *ns.*, ~ATIVE *a.* [f. L DE(*siccare* f. *siccus* dry) + -ATE[3])]

dĕ'sĭccātor *n.* Apparatus for desiccating; (Chem.) apparatus containing drying agent for removing moisture from specimens. [f. prec. + -OR]

dėsĭ'derāte *v.t.* (arch.) Feel to be missing, regret absence of, wish to have. [f. L DE(*siderare*; see CONSIDER) + -ATE[3])]

dėsĭ'deratĭve *a.* & *n.* (Gram.) (Verb, conjugation, etc.) formed from another verb etc. and denoting desire to perform the action of that verb etc. [f. LL *desiderativus* (as prec.; see -IVE)]

dėsĭderā't|um *n.* (*pl.* ~**a**). Thing lacking but needed or desired. [L, neut. p.p. (as n.); see DESIDERATE]

dėsī'gn[1] (-zī'n) *n.* **1.** Mental plan; scheme of attack (**have** ~**s on,** plan to harm or appropriate). **2.** Purpose (**by** ~, on purpose; *whether by accident or design*); end in view; adaptation of means to ends (**argument from** ~, deducing existence of a God from evidence of such adaptation in the universe). **3.** Preliminary sketch for picture, plan of building, machine, etc.; delineation, pattern; art of making these. **4.** Established form of a product; general idea, construction from parts. [f. obs. F *desseing* (*desseigner* f. L *designare* DESIGNATE[2])]

dėsī'gn[2] (-zī'n) *v.* **1.** *v.t.* Set (thing) apart *for* person; destine (person, thing) *for* a service. **2.** Contrive, plan; purpose, intend, (*designs an attack, to* do, *doing, that*; *design* thing or person *to* be or do something). **3.** Make preliminary sketch of (picture); draw plan of (future building etc.). **4.** *v.i.* Be a designer. [f. F *désigner* appoint & f. L *designare* DESIGNATE[2]]

dĕ'sĭgnate[1] (-z-) *a.* (placed after *n.*) Appointed to office but not yet installed (*bishop designate* etc.). [f. L *designatus* p.p. (as foll.; see -ATE[2])]

dĕ'sĭgnāte[2] (-z-) *v.t.* Specify, particularize; serve as name or distinctive mark of; style, describe *as*; appoint to office (*as*, *to*, *for*). [f. L DE(*signare* f. *signum* mark) + -ATE³]

dĕsĭgnā'tion (-z-) *n.* Appointing to office; name, description, title. [ME f. OF, or f. L *designatio* (as prec.; see -ATION)]

dėsī'gnėdlў (-zī'n-) *adv.* By design, on purpose. [f. p.p. of DESIGN² + -LY²]

dėsī'gner (-zī'n-) *n.* In vbl senses; draughtsman who makes plans for manufacturers; person who prepares designs for clothing, stage-productions, etc. [f. DESIGN² + -ER¹]

dėsī'gnĭng (-zī'n-) *a.* In vbl senses; crafty, artful, scheming; hence ~LY² *adv.* [f. DESIGN² + -ING²]

dėsīr'|able (-z-) *a.* Worth having or wishing for; causing desire; hence ~ABI'LITY, **~able**NESS (-beln-), *ns.*, **~ab**LY² *adv.* [ME f. OF (as DESIRE²; see -ABLE)]

dėsīr'e¹ (-z-) *n.* Unsatisfied longing, feeling that one would derive pleasure or satisfaction from attaining or possessing something; expression of this, request; thing desired; lust. [ME, f. OF *desir* (*desirer*: see foll.)]

dėsīr'e² (-z-) *v.t.* Long for, want earnestly (thing, *to* do, *that*); ask for (**leaves much to be ~d,** is very imperfect); (arch.) pray, entreat, command, (*desire him to wait*; *she desired they would wait*). [ME, f. OF *desirer* f. L *desiderare* DESIDERATE]

dėsīr'ous (-z-) *pred. a.* Wishful *to* do, *that*; ambitious *of* (success etc.); having the desire *of* doing. [ME f. AF; OF *desireus* f. Rom. **desiderosus* (as prec.; see -OUS)]

dėsĭ'st (*or* -zĭ'-) *v.i.* (literary). Abstain *from* continuing (action etc.). [f. OF *desister* f. L DE(*sistere* stop, redupl. f. *stare* stand)]

dĕsk *n.* Fixed or movable piece of furniture or box having flat or sloped surface serving as rest for writing or reading at; compartment for cashier, receptionist, etc.; music-stand; section of newspaper office etc. dealing with specified topics or *editorial work; **~-bound,** obliged to remain working at a desk. [ME, f. med. L *desca* f. L DISCUS disc]

dĕ'sman *n.* Aquatic insectivorous shrewlike mammal of two species, one in Russia and one in Pyrenees. [F & G, f. Sw. *desman-råtta* musk-rat]

dĕ'solate¹ *a.* Left alone, solitary; uninhabited; ruinous, neglected, barren, dreary; forlorn, wretched; hence ~LY² (-tlĭ) *adv.*, ~NESS (-tn-) *n.* [ME, f. L *desolatus* p.p. of DE(*solare* f. *solus* alone); see -ATE²]

dĕ'solāt|e² *v.t.* Depopulate; devastate; make (person) wretched; hence ~OR *n.* [ME, f. as prec. + -ATE³]

dĕsolā'tion *n.* Desolating; neglected, ruined, solitary, or barren state; being forsaken, loneliness; grief, wretchedness. [ME, f. LL *desolatio* (as prec.; see -ATION)]

dēsōr'ption *n.* Release of substance from surface on which it is adsorbed; hence (as back form.) **dēsōr'b** *v.t.* & *i.*, **dēsōr'b**ENT *a.* & *n.* [f. DE- + ADSORPTION]

dėspair' *n.*, & *v.i.* **1.** *n.* Complete loss or absence of hope; thing that causes this, whether by badness or unapproachable excellence. **2.** *v.i.* Lose hope, be without hope, (*of*); **~ of,** lose hope that person or thing will succeed, be maintained, etc. (*his life is despaired of*). [ME, f. OF *desespeir*, *desperer* f. L DE(*sperare* hope)]

||**dėspă'tch**¹·². See DISPATCH¹·².

dĕsperа'dō (-ah'dō) *n.* (*pl.* ~es *or* *~s). Desperate or reckless person, esp. criminal. [after foll. (as obs. n.) & wds in -ADO]

dĕ'sperate *a.* **1.** Leaving no or little room for hope, extremely dangerous or serious (*desperate situation*). **2.** Reckless from despair, violent, lawless; staking all on a small chance (*desperate remedy*); so **dĕsper**A'TION *n.* **3.** Extremely bad (*a desperate night*, *storm*, etc.). **4.** Hence ~LY² (-tlĭ) *adv.*, ~NESS (-tn-) *n.* [ME, f. L *desperatus* p.p. of DE(*sperare* hope); see -ATE²]

dėspĭ'cab|le (*or* dĕ'-) *a.* Vile, morally contemptible; hence ~LY² *adv.* [f. LL *despicabilis* f. DE(*spicari* cogn. w. *specere* look at); see -ABLE]

dėspī'se (-z) *v.t.* Regard as inferior or worthless; feel contempt for. [ME, f. *despis-* pres. st. of OF *despire* f. L DE(*spicere* = *specere* look at)]

dėspī'te *n.* & *prep.* **1.** *n.* (arch.) Outrage, injury; malice, hatred, (*died of mere despite*); **(in) ~ of,** in spite of; hence ~FUL (-tf-) *a.* **2.** *prep.* In spite of or (arch.) *of.* [ME, f. OF *despit* f. L *despectus* n. f. *despicere* (see prec.)]

dėspoi'l *v.t.* (literary). Plunder, rob, deprive, (person or place *of*); hence or cogn. ~ER¹, ~MENT, **dėspōlĭ**A'TION, *ns.* [ME, f. OF *despoil-l(i)er* f. L DE(*spoliare* SPOIL²)]

dėspŏ'nd *v.i.*, & *n.* **1.** *v.i.* Lose heart or hope, be dejected; hence ~ENCY *n.*, ~ENT *a.*, **~ent**LY² *adv.* **2.** *n.* (arch.) **Slough of D~,** state of despondency (f. name of bog in Bunyan's *Pilgrim's Progress*). [f. L DE(*spondēre* promise) give up, abandon]

dĕ'spot *n.* Absolute ruler; tyrant, oppressor; so **dėspŏ'tIC** *a.*, **dėspŏ'tICALLY** *adv.*, ~ISM (3) *n.* [f. F *despote* f. med. L *despota* f. Gk *despotēs* master, lord]

dĕ'squam|āte *v.i.* Come off in scales; hence ~A'TION *n.*, **dėsquă'mat**IVE, **dėsquă'mat**ORY, *adjs.* [f. L DE(*squamare* f. *squama* scale) + -ATE³]

dėssĕr't (-z-) *n.* Sweet (course of meal); ||course of fruit, nuts, etc., at end of dinner; *dessert*-SPOON¹; **~ wine** (for drinking with dessert or after meal). [F, p.p. of *desservir* (as DIS-, *servir* SERVE) clear the table]

dĕstĭnā'tion *n.* Place to which person or thing is going. [OF, or f. L *destinatio* (as foll.; see -ATION)]

dĕ'stĭne *v.t.* Appoint, foreordain, devote, set apart, (person or thing *to* do, *to* or *for* a service, achievement, etc.); **was ~d to,** later (as we now know) did. [ME, f. F *destiner* f. L DE(*stinare* = **stanare* settle f. *stare* stand)]

dĕ'stĭnў *n.* Predetermined events; what is destined to happen to person, country, etc.; power that foreordains, invincible necessity. [ME, f. OF *destinee* f. Rom. **destinata* fem. p.p. (as n.) of *destinare*; see prec., -Y⁴]

dĕ'stĭtūte *a.* Without resources, in great need of food, shelter, etc.; devoid *of*; so **dĕstĭtū'tION** *n.* [ME, f. L *destitutus* p.p. of DE(*stituere* -*tut*- = *statuere* place) forsake]

dĕ'strĭer *n.* (Hist.) War-horse. [ME f. AF *destrer*, OF *destrier* f. Rom. **dextrarius* (*caballus* horse) f. L DEXTER¹ (as knight's horse was led by squire with right hand)]

dėstroy' *v.t.* Pull or break down, demolish; make useless; kill, annihilate; nullify, neutralize effect of; hence ~ABLE *a.* [ME, f. OF *destruire* f. Rom. **destrugere* for L DE(*struere struct-* build)]

dėstroy'er *n.* In vbl senses; fast warship designed to protect other ships by attacking submarines etc. with guns and torpedoes. [f. prec. + -ER¹]

***dėstrŭ'ct** *v.t.*, & *n.* **1.** *v.t.* Bring about deliberate destruction of (one's own rocket etc.). **2.** *n.* Action of destructing. [f. L *destruere* (see DESTROY), or as back form. f. DESTRUCTION]

dėstrŭ'ct|ĭble *a.* Able to be destroyed; hence ~IBI'LITY *n.* [F, or f. LL *destructibilis* (as DESTROY; see -IBLE)]

dėstrŭ'ction *n.* Destroying or being destroyed;

what destroys, cause of ruin, (*is our destruction*). [ME f. OF, f. L *destructio -onis* (as DESTROY; see -ION)]

dėstrŭ'ctĭve *a.* Destroying; tending to destroy; deadly *to*, causing destruction *of*; merely negative, refuting etc. without amending, opp. *constructive* (*destructive criticism*); hence ~LY[2] (-vlĭ) *adv.*, ~NESS (-vn-) *n.* [ME, f. OF *destructif -ive*, f. LL *destructivus* (as DESTROY; see -IVE)]

‖**dėstrŭ'ctor** *n.* Refuse-burning furnace. [f. as prec. + -OR]

dėsū'ėtūde (*or* dĕ'swĭ-) *n.* (Passing into) state of disuse. [f. F *désuétude* or f. L DE(*suetudo* f. *suescere suet-* be accustomed; see -TUDE)]

dĕ'sultor|ȳ *a.* Going constantly from one subject to another; disconnected, unmethodical; hence ~ĬLY[2] *adv.*, ~ĬNESS *n.* [f. L *desultorius* superficial f. *desultor* vaulter f. DE(*sult-* = *salt-* p.p. st. of *salire* leap)]

dėtă'ch *v.t.* Unfasten and remove (*from*) (lit. or fig.; ~**ed** *mind, view*, etc., regarding things impartially, unemotional; ~**ed house,** one not joined to another on either side); send (ship, regiment, officer, etc.) on separate mission; hence ~ABLE *a.*, ~**ėd**LY[2] *adv.* [f. F *détacher* (as DE-, ATTACH)]

dėtă'chment *n.* Detaching; portion of army etc., or large body, separately employed; being aloof from or unaffected by surroundings, public opinion, etc.; independence of judgement. [f. F *détachement* (as prec.; see -MENT)]

dē'tail[1] *n.* Dealing with things item by item (*in detail*; *in great* or *much detail*; **go into** ~, give the items separately); account of separate small items, number of particulars; item, small or subordinate particular, (**but that is a** ~, often iron. to call special attention); minor decoration in building, picture, etc., way of treating this; part of picture etc. shown alone; (Mil.) distribution of orders of the day; small detachment for special duty. [f. F *détail* (*détailler*; see foll.)]

dē'tail[2] *v.t.* **1.** Give particulars of, relate circumstantially; (in *p.p.*) described item by item. **2.** (Mil.) Assign for special duty. [f. F *détailler* (as DE-, *tailler* cut f. as TAIL[2])]

dėtai'n *v.t.* Keep in confinement or under restraint; keep waiting, delay; hence ~EE' *n.*, person detained in custody, usu. on political grounds. [ME, f. OF *detenir* f. Rom. **detenēre* for L DE(*tinēre tent-* = *tenēre* hold)]

dėtai'ner *n.* (Law). Detaining of goods taken from owner for distraint etc.; keeping of person in confinement; writ by which person already arrested may be detained on another suit. [f. AF *detener* f. OF *detenir*; see prec., -ER[4]]

dėtĕ'ct *v.t.* Reveal guilt of, discover, (person, person *in* doing); discover existence or presence of; (Phys.) use instrument to observe (signal, radiation, etc.); hence ~ABLE *a.* [f. L DE(*tegere tect-* cover)]

dėtĕ'ction *n.* Detecting; work of a detective; (Electr.) extraction of desired signal, demodulation. [f. LL *detectio* (as prec.; see -ION)]

dėtĕ'ctĭve *a.* & *n.* **1.** *a.* Serving to detect. **2.** *n.* Policeman or other person employed to investigate crimes e.g. by eliciting evidence or information (**private** ~, person undertaking special inquiries for pay); ~ **story** etc. (describing crime and detection of criminals). [f. DETECT + -IVE]

dėtĕ'ctor *n.* In vbl senses; (Electr.) device for detection or demodulation of signals. [f. DETECT + -OR]

dėtĕ'nt *n.* Catch by removal of which machinery is allowed to move; (in clock etc.) catch that regulates striking. [f. F *détente* f. OF *destente* f. *destendre* slacken (as DE-, *tendre* stretch f. L *tendere*)]

détente (dātah'ṅt) *n.* Easing of strained relations esp. between States. [F, = relaxation]

dėtĕ'ntion *n.* Detaining or being detained; military imprisonment; confinement of aliens etc.; compulsory delay; (at schools) keeping in as punishment; ‖~ **centre,** institution for brief detention of young offenders. [f. F *détention* or f. LL *detentio* (as DETAIN; see -ION)]

détenu (dātenōō') *n.* Person detained in custody. [F, p.p. of *détenir* DETAIN]

dėtẽr' *v.t.* (-rr-). Discourage or hinder (*from*) by fear, dislike of trouble, etc.; hence ~MENT *n.* [f. L DE(*terrēre* frighten)]

dėtẽr'gent *a.* & *n.* Cleansing (agent), esp. substance used with water for removing dirt etc. (usu. a synthetic substance other than soap). [f. L DE(*tergēre ters-* wipe); see -ENT]

dėtēr'ior|āte *v.t.* & *i.* Make or become worse; hence or cogn. ~A'TION *n.*, ~ātIVE *a.* [f. LL *deteriorare* f. L *deterior* worse, + -ATE[3]]

dėtẽr'mĭnant *a.* & *n.* Determining; decisive, conditioning, defining, (agent, factor, element, word); (Math.) quantity obtained by adding products of elements of a square matrix according to a certain rule. [f. L *determinare* (see DETERMINE, -ANT)]

dėtẽr'mĭn|ate *a.* Limited; definite, distinct; finite; definitive; hence ~ACY *n.*, ~**ate**LY[2] (-tlĭ) *adv.*, ~**ate**NESS (-tn-) *n.* [ME, f. L *determinatus* p.p. (as DETERMINE; see -ATE[2])]

dėtẽrmĭnā'tion *n.* **1.** Delimitation, definition; exact ascertainment *of* amount etc. **2.** Fixing of purpose, fixed intention; resoluteness. **3.** (Law) cessation of estate or interest; conclusion of debate; judicial decision or sentence; fixing of date etc. **4.** (arch.) Tendency to move in fixed direction. [ME (in sense 3) f. OF, f. L *determinatio -onis* (as DETERMINE; see -ATION)]

dėtẽr'mĭnatĭve *a.* & *n.* (Thing) that serves to define, qualify, or direct. [f. F *déterminatif* (as foll.; see -IVE)]

dėtẽr'mĭne *v.* **1.** *v.t.* & *i.* Settle, decide, (dispute, person's fate, *what is to be done, that, whether*, etc.), come to a conclusion, give decision; be the decisive factor in regard to (*demand determines supply*); ascertain precisely, fix; (arch.) direct, impel *to*. **2.** Decide (person) *to* do; resolve (*to* do, *that, on* doing, *on* a course of action; **be** ~**d,** have resolved). **3.** *v.t.* & *i.* (esp. Law). Bring or come to an end. **4.** *v.t.* Limit in scope, define; fix (date) beforehand. **5.** Hence **dėtẽr'mĭn**ABLE *a.* [ME, f. OF *determiner* f. L DE(*terminare* f. *terminus* end)]

dėtẽr'mĭned (-nd) *a.* In vbl senses; resolute, unflinching; hence ~LY[2] *adv.*, ~NESS *n.* [p.p. of prec.]

dėtẽr'mĭn|ĭsm *n.* Doctrine that human action is not free but determined by motives regarded as external forces acting on the will; so ~IST (2) *n.*, ~ĭ'stIC *a.* [f. DETERMINE + -ISM]

dėtĕ'rr|ent *a.* & *n.* **1.** *a.* That deters; hence ~ENCE *n.* **2.** *n.* Thing that deters, esp. nuclear weapon of a State or alliance as deterring attack by another. [f. as DETER; see -ENT]

dėtĕ'st *v.t.* Abhor, dislike intensely; so ~ABLE *a.*, intensely hateful, abominable, ~**ab**LY[2] *adv.* [f. L DE(*testari* call to witness f. *testis* witness)]

dētĕstā'tion *n.* Abhorrence, intense dislike; detested person or thing. [ME f. OF, f. L *detestatio -onis* (as prec.; see -ATION)]

dēthrō'ne *v.t.* Remove from throne, lit. or fig. (ruler, dominant influence); hence ~MENT (-nm-) *n.* [f. DE- + THRONE]

dĕ'tĭnūe *n.* (Law). (Suit against) wrongful detention of personal chattel. [f. OF *detenue* fem. p.p. (as n.) of *detenir* DETAIN]

dĕ'ton|āte *v.i.* & *t.* (Cause to) explode with loud report; hence ~ātIVE *a.* [f. L DE(*tonare* thunder) + -ATE[3]]

dĕtonā'tion *n.* Detonating; premature combustion of fuel in internal combustion engine, causing it to PINK[6]. [f. F *détonation* (*détoner* f. as prec.; see -ATION)]

dĕ'tonātor *n.* Detonating contrivance, esp. as part of bomb or shell; railway fog-signal that detonates. [f. DETONATE + -OR]

dē'tour (-oor; *or* dā'-) *n.*, & *v.t.* **1.** *n.* Deviation, roundabout way, digression, (esp. *make a detour*). **2.** *v.t.* Cause to make a detour. [f. F *détour* change of direction (*détourner* turn away f. as DE-, TURN[1])]

dētŏ'xic|āte *v.t.* Remove poison from; hence ~A'TION *n.* [f. DE- + L *toxicum* poison, after *intoxicate*]

dētŏ'xi|fȳ *v.t.* = prec.; hence ~FICA'TION *n.* [f. as prec. + -FY]

dètră'ct *v.t.* Take away (*much*, *something*, etc., or abs.) *from* a whole; ~ **from,** reduce credit due to, depreciate; so ~ION, ~OR, *ns.*, ~IVE *a.* [f. L DE(*trahere tract-* draw)]

dētrai'n *v.t.* & *i.* Discharge or alight from railway train; hence ~MENT *n.* [f. DE- + TRAIN]

détraqué (dātrah'kā) *a.* & *n.* (*fem.* ~*e pr.* same). Deranged or psychopathic (person). [F, p.p. of *détraquer* derange]

dētrī'balīz|e, -īs|e (-īz), *v.t.* Make (person) no longer member of tribe; destroy tribal habits of; hence ~A'TION *n.* [f. DE- + TRIBAL + -IZE]

dĕ'trĭment *n.* Harm, damage, (esp. *without detriment to*); thing that causes harm or damage. [ME f. OF or f. L DE(*trimentum* f. *terere trit-* rub, wear; see -MENT)]

dĕtrĭmĕ'ntal *a.* Harmful, causing loss; hence ~LY[2] *adv.* [f. prec. + -AL]

dètrī'tèd *a.* Worn down; (Geol.) disintegrated, formed as detritus. [f. L *detritus* p.p. of *deterere* (see DETRIMENT) + -ED[1]]

dètrī'tion *n.* Wearing away by rubbing. [f. med. L *detritio* f. as DETRIMENT; see -ITION]

dètrī't|us *n.* Matter produced by detrition, as gravel, sand, silt; debris; hence ~AL *a.* [after F *détritus* f. L *detritus* n. = wearing down, f. as DETRIMENT]

de trop (detrō') *pred. a.* Not wanted, unwelcome, in the way. [F, = excessive]

dētūmĕ'scence *n.* Subsidence from swollen state. [f. L DE(*tumescere* swell); see -ENCE]

deuce[1] *n.* The two on dice or (arch.) cards; (Tennis) state of score (40 all, or five or more games all) at which either side must gain two consecutive points or games to win. [f. OF *deus* f. L *duo* (acc. *duos*) two]

deuce[2] *n.* Misfortune, mischief; the Devil (*deuce take it*); **who, where, what,** etc., **the ~?** (imprecations expr. annoyance or complete ignorance); **the ~!** (excl. of annoyance or surprise); **the ~ to pay,** trouble to be expected; **a** (or **the**) **~ of a,** a very bad or very remarkable (mess, fellow, etc.). [f. LG *duus*, = G *daus*, f. as prec., two aces at dice being the worst throw]

deu'cèd (*or* dūst) *a.* & *adv.* (arch.) = DAMNED 2, 3; hence ~LY[2] *adv.* [f. prec. + -ED[2]]

deus ex machina (dāŏos ĕks mă'kĭna; *or* dē'us) *n.* Power or event that comes in the nick of time to solve difficulty; providential interposition, esp. in novel or play. [mod. L transl. Gk *theos ek mēkhanēs*, = god from the machinery (by which in Gk theatre the gods were shown in the air)]

Deus misereatur (dēus mĭzĕrĭā'ter) *n.* Canticle 'God be merciful', Ps. 67. [L]

Deut. *abbr.* Deuteronomy (O.T.).

deuteră'gonĭst *n.* Person of next importance to PROTAGONIST in drama. [f. Gk *deuteragōnistēs* (as DEUTERO-, *agōnistēs* actor)]

deu'ter|āte *v.t.* Replace ordinary hydrogen in (substance) by deuterium; hence ~A'TION *n.* [f. DEUTERIUM + -ATE[3]]

deutēr'ĭum *n.* (Chem.) Heavy isotope of hydrogen with mass about double that of ordinary hydrogen; so **deu'ter**ON *n.*, nucleus of deuterium atom, consisting of proton and neutron. [mod. L, f. as foll. + -IUM]

deu'terō- *comb. form.* Second, as: **D~-Isaiah,** supposed later author of Isaiah 40–55. [f. Gk *deuteros* second + -O-]

Deuterŏ'nom|ȳ *n.* Fifth book of Pentateuch; hence **Deuteronŏ'mic**(AL) *adjs.*, ~IST *n.*, (joint) writer of Deuteronomy. [ME, f. eccl. L f. Gk DEUTERO(*nomion* f. *nomos* law) second law (Deut. 17:18), mistranslation f. Heb.]

Deu'tschmârk (doi'ch-) *n.* Currency unit in Federal Republic of Germany. [G, = German MARK[3]]

deu'tzĭa (-ts-; *or* doi'ts-) *n.* Ornamental shrub of genus *Deutzia*, with usu. white flowers. [mod. L, f. J. *Deutz* 18th-c. Du. patron of botany + -IA[1]]

dēvă'lū|e *v.t.* Reduce value of; (Econ.) reduce value of (currency) relative to that of other currencies or gold; hence ~A'TION *n.* [f. DE- + VALUE]

Devana'garī (dāvanah'-) *n.* Alphabet used for Sanskrit, Hindi, and other Indian languages. [Skr., = divine town script]

dĕ'vast|āte *v.t.* Lay waste, ravage; **~ating** *a.*, (fig.) very effective, overwhelming, (criticism, handicap, loveliness); hence or cogn. ~A'TION, **~āt**OR, *ns.* [f. L DE(*vastare* lay waste) + -ATE[3]]

dèvĕ'lop *v.* **1.** *v.t.* & *i.* Unfold, reveal or be revealed, bring or come from latent to active or visible state; *make or become known; make or become fuller, more elaborate or systematic, or bigger. **2.** *v.t.* Construct buildings etc. on (land), convert (land) to new use, so as to realize its potentialities; treat (photographic material) so as to make picture visible; (Mus.) elaborate (theme) by modification of melody, harmony, rhythm, etc.; (Chess) bring (piece) into position for effective use. **3.** *v.t.* & *i.* Make progress; begin to exhibit or suffer from (*develop a habit*, *measles*, *a squeak*); come or bring to maturity; **~ing country,** poor or primitive country that is developing better economic and social conditions. **4.** Hence ~ABLE *a.* (**~able surface,** one that can be flattened into a plane without overlap or separation, e.g. cylinder), ~ER[1] (1, 2) *n.* [f. F *développer* f. Rom. v. f. as DIS- + **volup-*, **velup-*, of unkn. orig.]

dèvĕ'lopment *n.* **1.** Gradual unfolding, fuller working out; developing of land etc. (‖**~ area,** one where new industries are encouraged in order to counteract severe unemployment there); growth; evolution (of animal and plant races); full-grown state; stage of advancement; developing of photograph; (Mus.) elaboration of theme, esp. in second part of sonata movement; (Chess) developing of pieces from original position. **2.** Product; more elaborate form; developed land. [f. prec. + -MENT]

dèvĕlopmĕ'ntal *a.* Incidental to growth (*developmental diseases*); evolutionary; hence ~LY[2] *adv.* [f. prec. + -AL]

dē'vĭ|ant *a.* & *n.* (Thing or person) that deviates from normal behaviour; hence ~ANCE, ~ANCY, *ns.* [ME, f. as foll.; see -ANT]

dē'vĭāte[1] *v.i.* Turn aside, diverge, (*from* course of action, rule, truth, etc.); digress. [f. LL DE(*viare* f. *via* way) + -ATE[3]]

dē'vĭate[2] *n.* = DEVIANT, esp. sexual pervert. [f. prec.]

dēvĭā'tion *n.* Deviating; deflexion of compass-needle by iron in ship etc.; (Statistics) amount by which single measurement differs from mean (**standard ~**, quantity calculated to indicate extent of this difference for group as a whole); (Polit.) departure from (esp. Communist) party doctrine, whence ~AL *a.*, ~ISM (3), ~IST (2), *ns.* [f. F *déviation* f. med. L *deviatio -onis* (as DEVIATE[1]; see -ION)]

dėvī′ce *n.* **1.** Plan, scheme, trick; contrivance, invention, thing adapted for a purpose or designed for a particular function. **2.** Drawing, design, figure; emblematic or heraldic design; motto. **3.** (in *pl.*) Fancy, will; **left to** one's **own ~s,** allowed to do whatever one is able or wishes without assistance or advice. **4.** (arch.) Make, look, (*things of rare device*). [ME f. OF *devis* f. Rom., f. L as DIVIDE[1]]

dĕ′vĭl[1] *n.* **1. The D~,** supreme spirit of evil, tempter of mankind, enemy of God, Satan. **2.** Heathen god; demon, evil spirit supposed to be in a demoniac; one of Satan's followers, superhuman malignant being. **3.** Wicked or cruel person; mischievously energetic, clever, or self-willed person; luckless or wretched person (usu. *poor devil*); vicious animal; awkward problem etc. **4.** Junior legal counsel working for a principal. **5.** Literary hack doing what his employer takes the credit and pay for; **printer's ~,** (Hist.) errand-boy in printing-office. **6.** Personified evil quality (*the devil of greed* etc.); fighting-spirit, energy or dash in attack. **7.** = TASMANIAN *devil*; instrument or machine for tearing etc.; **(dust) ~,** (S. Afr.) violent dust-storm. **8.** (or *D~*). = DEUCE[2] (q.v. for phrases); **the (very) ~,** a great difficulty or nuisance; **go to the ~,** be damned, (in *imper.*) depart at once; **like the ~,** with great energy etc.; **~ a bit,** not at all; **~ a one,** not even one. **9.** (or *D~*). **Between the ~ and the deep (blue) sea,** in a dilemma; **~ take the hindmost** (motto of selfish competition); *give the Devil his* DUE[2]; **play the ~ with,** cause severe damage to; RAISE *the devil*; **speak** or **talk of the ~ (and he will appear)** (said when person comes just after being mentioned). **10. ~'s advocate,** official who puts the case against beatification or canonization by R.C. Church, (transf.) one who indicates shortcomings so as to cause discussion; **~'s bit,** plant whose root looks bitten off, esp. species of scabious or blazing-star; ‖**~'s coach-horse,** large rove-beetle; **~'s darning-needle,** dragonfly or damselfly; *devil's* DOZEN; **~'s own,** very difficult or unusual (*devil's own problem, luck,* etc.); *devil's* PATERNOSTER, TATTOO[1]. **11. ~-fish,** angler-fish, *large ray; **~-may-care,** reckless, rollicking; **~s-on--horseback** (see ANGEL 3); ***~wood,** small hard-wooded tree. **12.** Hence ~DOM, ~ISM (2), *ns.* [OE *dēofol,* = OS *diubul, -al,* OHG *tiufal,* ON *djöfull,* f. LL f. Gk *diabolos* accuser, slanderer (*dia* across, *ballō* to throw), in Septuagint rendering Heb. *śāṭān* SATAN]

dĕ′vĭl[2] *v.* (‖-ll-). **1.** *v.i.* Work as lawyer's or author's devil (usu. *for* principal). **2.** *v.t.* Cook with peppery condiments; *(colloq.) worry, harass. [f. prec.]

dĕ′vĭlish *a.* & *adv.* **1.** *a.* Like or worthy of the Devil; damnable; hence ~LY[2] *adv.* **2.** *adv.* (arch. colloq.) Very. [f. DEVIL[1] + -ISH[1]]

dĕ′vĭlment *n.* Mischief, wild spirits; devilish or strange phenomenon. [f. DEVIL[1] + -MENT]

dĕ′vĭlrў, dĕ′vĭltrў, *n.* Diabolical art, black magic; the Devil and his works; wickedness, cruelty; reckless mischief, daring, or hilarity. [f. DEVIL[1] + -RY; *-try* wrongly after *harlotry* etc.]

dē′vĭous *a.* Remote, sequestered; winding, circuitous, erratic; erring; unscrupulous, insincere; hence ~LY[2] *adv.*, ~NESS *n.* [f. L DE(*vius* f. *via* way) + -OUS]

dėvī′s|e (-z) *v.t.*, & *n.* **1.** *v.t.* (Law) assign, give (realty; cf. BEQUEATH) by will, whence ~EE′, ~OR, *ns.*; plan, invent, plot, scheme, (thing, *how*, or abs.); hence or cogn. ~ABLE *a.*, ~ER[2] (4) *n.* **2.** *n.* (Law). Devising act or clause. [ME, f. OF *deviser* f. Rom. **divisare* frequent. of L *dividere -vis-* DIVIDE; n. f. OF *devise* f. med. L *divisa* fem. p.p. of *dividere*]

dēvī′talīz|e, -īs|e (-īz), *v.t.* Make lifeless or effete; hence ~A′TION *n.* [f. DE- + VITALIZE]

dēvĭ′trĭ|fў *v.t.* Deprive of vitreous quality, make (glass or vitreous rock) opaque and crystalline; hence ~FICA′TION *n.* [f. DE- + VITRIFY]

dėvoi′d *a.* **~ of,** quite lacking or free from. [ME, p.p. of obs. *devoid* f. OF DE(*voidier* f. *voider* VOID)]

dĕ′voir (-vwâr) *n.* (arch.) Duty, one's best, (*do* one's *devoir*); (in *pl.*) courteous or formal attentions (*pay* one's *devoirs to*). [ME f. AF *dever* = OF *deveir* f. L *debēre* owe]

dē′volūte (*or* -ōōt) *v.t.* Transfer by devolution. [f. as OF DEVOLVE]

dēvolu′tion (-lōō′-) *n.* **1.** Descent through a series of changes; descent of property by due succession; lapse of unexercised right to ultimate owner; (Biol.) degeneration. **2.** Deputing, delegation, of work or power (esp. by House of Parliament to bodies appointed by and responsible to it, or by central government to local or regional administration). [f. LL *devolutio* (as foll.; see -ION)]

dėvŏ′lve *v.t.* & *i.* Throw (duty, work), (of duties) be thrown, fall, descend, *upon* (deputy, or one who must act for want of others); descend, fall by succession, (*to, upon*). [ME, f. L DE(*volvere volut-* roll)]

Dėvō′nĭan *a.* & *n.* (Native) of Devon(shire); (Geol.) (of) palaeozoic period or system, above Silurian and below Carboniferous. [f. med. L *Devonia* Devonshire + -AN]

Dĕ′vonshire (*-er or* -ēr) *n.* **~ cream,** CLOTted cream. [~ (now Devon) in England]

dévot (dāvō′) *n.* (*fem.* ~*e pr.* -ŏ′t). Devotee. [F, f. OF as DEVOUT]

dėvō′te *v.t.* Consecrate, give up exclusively, (*oneself*, person, thing, esp. one's life, abilities, etc.) *to* (God, person, pursuit, purpose); (arch.) doom to destruction; hence ~MENT (-tm-) *n.* [f. L DE(*vovēre vot-* vow)]

dėvō′tėd *a.* In vbl senses; zealously loyal or loving (*devoted friend*), whence ~LY[2] *adv.* [p.p. of prec.]

dĕvotee′ *n.* Votary *of*, one devoted *to*; zealously or fanatically pious person; enthusiast *of* sport etc. [f. DEVOTE + -EE]

dėvō′tion *n.* Devoutness; devoting; divine worship, (in *pl.*) prayers, worship, (*was at his devotions*), whence ~AL *a.*; enthusiastic addiction or loyalty (*to*). [ME f. OF, or f. L *devotio* (as DEVOTE; see -ION)]

dėvour′ (-owr′) *v.t.* (Of animal) eat; eat like a beast or ravenously; (of fire etc.) engulf; take in greedily with ears or eyes (book, story, beauty or beautiful person); (esp. in *pass.*) absorb the attention of (*devoured by anxiety*); hence ~ER[1] *n.* [ME, f. OF *devorer* f. L DE(*vorare* swallow)]

dėvou′t *a.* (Of person, act, etc.) reverential, earnestly religious, pious, whence ~NESS *n.*; earnest, hearty, genuine (*devout hope*); hence ~LY[2] *adv.* [ME f. OF *devot* f. L *devotus* p.p. (as DEVOTE)]

dew[1] *n.* **1.** Atmospheric vapour condensing in small drops on cool surfaces between evening and morning; freshness, refreshing quality; beaded or glistening moisture, esp. tears or sweat; MOUNTAIN *dew.* **2. ~′berry,** bluish fruit like blackberry; **~-claw,** rudimentary inner toe of some dogs, false hoof of deer etc.; **~-fall,** time when dew begins to form, evening;

~-point, temperature at which dew forms; ||**~-pond,** shallow, usu. artificial, pond once supposed fed by atmospheric condensation. [OE *dēaw*, = OS *dau*, OHG *tou*, ON *dögg* f. Gmc **dauwaz*, *-am*]

dew[2] *v.* **1.** *v.t.* Wet (as) with dew. **2.** *v.i.* (arch., impers.) Form or fall as or like dew (*it is beginning to dew*). [ME, f. OE **dēawian*, = OS **daujan*, OHG *touwōn*, ON *döggva* f. Gmc **dauwōjan* (as prec.)]

D.E.W. *abbr.* distant early warning.

dėwa'n (-wah'n) *n.* Prime minister or finance minister of Indian state. [f. Arab. & Pers. *diwān* fiscal register]

dew'ar *n.* Double-walled flask with evacuated interspace to reduce transfer of heat. [f. Sir J. *Dewar*, Brit. physicist d. 1923]

Dew'ey *n.* ~ **system,** decimal system of library classification. [f. M. ~, Amer. librarian d. 1931, its deviser]

dew'lăp *n.* Fold of loose skin hanging from throat of cattle (transf., of other animals, birds, or men). [ME, f. DEW[1] + LAP[1], perh. after ON **döggleppr*]

dew'|ỹ *a.* Wet with or affected by dew; **~y(--eyed),** innocently trusting, naïvely sentimental; hence **~ĭLY**[2] *adv.*, **~ĭNESS** *n.* [OE *dēawig* (as DEW[1], -Y[2])]

dĕ'xter[1] *a.* (Her.) Of or on right-hand side of shield etc. (i.e. to the spectator's left). [L, = on the right]

dĕ'xter[2] *n.* (Animal of) small hardy breed of Irish cattle. [19th c., perh. f. name of breeder]

dĕxtĕ'rĭtỹ *n.* Manual or mental adroitness, skill, neatness of handling; right-handedness, using of right hand. [f. F *dextérité* f. L DEXTER[1] (*itas* -ITY)]

dĕ'xterous. See DEXTROUS.

dĕ'xtral *a.* & *n.* **1.** Right-handed (person). **2.** *a.* Of or on the right; (of flat-fish) with right side uppermost; (of spiral shell) with whorls rising to right. **3.** Hence **~ITY** (-ă'l-) *n.*, **~LY**[2] *adv.* [f. med. L *dextralis* f. L *dextra* right hand; see -AL]

dĕ'xtrăn *n.* (Chem.) Amorphous gum formed by fermentation of sucrose etc.; degraded form of this used as substitute for blood-plasma. [G, f. as DEXTRO- + *-an* as in various Chem. names]

dĕ'xtrĭn *n.* (Chem.) Soluble gummy substance obtained from starch and used as adhesive. [f. F *dextrine* f. L *dextra* on the right; see foll., -IN]

dĕ'xtrō- *comb. form.* (Chem.) Having the property of causing plane of polarized light ray to rotate to right (opp. LAEVO-, which see for compounds). [f. L *dexter, dextra* on or to the right + -O-]

dĕ'xtrorse *a.* Rising towards the right (esp. Bot. of spiral stem). [f. L *dextrorsus* (as prec.)]

dĕ'xtrōse *n.* (Chem.) Dextro-rotatory form of glucose. [f. as DEXTRO- + -OSE[2]]

dĕ'xtrous, dĕ'xterous, *a.* Handling things neatly; skilful; mentally adroit, clever; using right hand by preference; hence **~LY**[2] *adv.* [f. L DEXTER[1] + -OUS]

dey (dā) *n.* (Hist.) Ruler of Algiers 1710–1830; governor of Tunis or Tripoli. [F, f. Turk. *dayı* mother's brother, used as friendly title of older people by janizaries]

D.F. *abbr.* Defender of the Faith [f. L *Defensor Fidei*]; direction-finder.

||**D.F.C.** *abbr.* Distinguished Flying Cross.

||**D.F.M.** *abbr.* Distinguished Flying Medal.

D.G. *abbr.* *Dei gratia*; *Deo gratias*; director--general.

dhal, dal, (dahl) *n.* Split pulse, a common food-stuff in India. [Hindi]

dhar'ma (dar'-; *or* der'-) *n.* (Ind.) Social custom; right behaviour, virtue, justice; the Buddhist truth; the Hindu moral law. [Skr., = decree, custom]

dhō'bĭ (dō'-) *n.* (Ind. etc.) Washerman or washerwoman; **~('s) itch,** troublesome tropical dermatitis. [f. Hindi *dhōbī* (*dhōb* washing)]

dhō'tĭ (dō'-) *n.* Loincloth worn by male Hindus. [f. Hindi *dhōtī*]

dhow (dow) *n.* Lateen-rigged Arabian-Sea ship. [19th c.; orig. unkn.]

dhurra. See DURRA.

di-[1] *pref.* Form of DIS-, occurring before *b, d, l, m, n, r, s* + cons., *v*, usu. *g*, and sometimes *j*. [L var. of *dis-*]

di-[2] *pref.* Twice, two-, double-; (Chem., forming names of compounds) containing two atoms or groups of a specified kind (*dichromate, dioxide*). [Gk (*dis* twice)]

di-[3] *pref.* = DIA- before vowel (*dioptric*).

||**D.I.** *abbr.* Defence Intelligence.

dia- *pref.* w. sense 'through' (*diaphanous*), 'apart' (*diacritical*), 'across' (*diameter*). [Gk (*dia* through)]

dia. *abbr.* diameter.

dīabē'tēs (-z) *n.* ~ **insipidus,** pituitary disease with excessive thirst and urination; ~ **(mellitus),** disease in which sugar and starch are not properly absorbed, with thirst, emaciation, and excessive urine containing glucose. [orig. = siphon, L f. Gk (*diabainō* go through)]

dīabĕ'tic *a.* & *n.* Of diabetes; (person) suffering from diabetes; (of food) made especially for diabetes patients. [f. prec. + -IC]

dĭa'blerie (-ah'-) *n.* Devil's work; sorcery; wild recklessness. [F (*diable* f. L *diabolus* DEVIL[1]; see -ERY)]

dīabŏ'lĭc(al) *adjs.* Of, having to do with, proceeding from, externally like, the Devil; devilish, inhumanly cruel or wicked; hence **diabŏ'lical**LY[2] *adv.* [ME, f. OF *diabolique* or LL *diabolicus* f. L *diabolus* (as DEVIL[1]; see -IC)]

dīă'bol|ĭsm *n.* Sorcery; devilish conduct or nature; belief in or worship of the Devil; hence **~IST** (2) *n.* [f. Gk *diabolos* DEVIL[1] + -ISM]

dīă'bolize, -ise (-īz), *v.t.* Make into or represent as a devil. [f. as prec. + -IZE]

dĭă'bolō *n.* (*pl.* **~s**). Game with two-headed top thrown up and caught with string stretched between two sticks; the top itself. [It., = DEVIL[1]; formerly called *devil on two sticks*]

dīachrŏ'n|ĭc (-k-) *a.* (Ling. etc.) Concerned with historical development of a subject (esp. a language; opp. *synchronic*); hence **~ICALLY** *adv.*, **dīă'chron**ISM (3), **dīă'chron**Y[1] (1), (-k-) *ns.*, **dīăchronĭ'st**IC, **dīă'chron**OUS, (-k-) *adjs.* [f. F *diachronique* (as DIA-, Gk *khronos* time, -IC)]

dīă'conal *a.* Of a deacon. [f. eccl. L *diaconalis* (*diaconus* DEACON[2]; see -AL)]

dīă'conāte (*or* -*at*) *n.* Office of, one's time as, deacon; body of deacons. [f. eccl. L *diaconatus* (as prec.; see -ATE[1])]

dīacrĭ'tĭc *a.* & *n.* = foll. [as foll.]

dīacrĭ'tĭcal *a.* & *n.* Distinguishing, distinctive; ~ **(mark** or **sign),** sign used to indicate different sounds or values of a letter (accent, diaeresis, cedilla, etc.). [f. Gk DIA(*kritikos*; see CRITIC) + -AL]

dīadĕ'lphous *a.* (Bot.) With stamens united in two bundles (cf. *monadelphous, polyadelphous*). [f. DI-[2] + Gk *adelphos* brother + -OUS]

dī'adĕm *n.*, & *v.t.* **1.** *n.* Crown, or plain or jewelled head-band, as badge of sovereignty; wreath of leaves or flowers worn round head; sovereignty; crowning distinction or glory. **2.** *v.t.* (esp. in *p.p.*) Adorn (as) with diadem. [ME, f. OF *diademe* f. L f. Gk DIA(*dēma* f. *deō* bind)]

dīaer'ės|ĭs (-ēr'-), ***dīēr'ės|ĭs,** *n.* (*pl.* **~es** *pr.*

-ēz). Mark (as in *Brontë, naïve*) over vowel indicating that it is separately sounded; (Pros.) break where foot ends at end of word. [LL, f. Gk DI³(*airesis* f. *haireō* take) separation]

diagnō'se (-z) *v.t.* Make diagnosis of (disease, mechanical fault, etc.); infer presence of (specified disease etc.) from symptoms. [f. foll.]

diagnō's|is *n.* (*pl.* **~es** *pr.* -ēz). Identification of disease by means of patient's symptoms etc., formal statement of this; ascertainment of cause of mechanical fault etc.; distinctive characterization of species etc. [mod. L f. Gk (DIA-, *gignōskō* recognize)]

diagnŏ'st|ic *a.* & *n.* **1.** *a.* Of or assisting diagnosis. **2.** *n.* Symptom. **3.** Hence **~ICALLY** *adv.*, **~I'CIAN, ~ICS**, *ns.* [f. Gk DIA(*gnōstikos* f. as prec.; see -IC)]

diă'gonal *a.* & *n.* (Straight line) joining two non-adjacent angles of rectilinear figure or solid contained by planes, or opposite corners of a thing; (line) obliquely placed like the diagonal of a parallelogram; inclined at other than a right angle, having some part so inclined; hence **~LY²** *adv.* [f. L *diagonalis* f. Gk DIA(*gōnios* f. *gōnia* angle); see -AL]

dī'agrăm *n.*, & *v.t.* (||**-mm-**). **1.** *n.* Sketch showing the features of an object needed for exposition; graphical or symbolic representation, by lines, of process, force, etc.; (Geom.) figure made of lines used in proving theorem etc.; hence or cogn. **~mA'TIC** *a.*, **diagră'mmatIZE** (1) *v.t.* **2.** *v.t.* Represent in diagram. [f. L f. Gk DIA-(*gramma -atos* f. *graphō* write; cf. -GRAM)]

dī'agrĭd *n.* Supporting structure of diagonally intersecting ribs of metal etc. [f. DIAGONAL + GRID]

dī'al *n.* & *v.* (||**-ll-**). **1.** *n.* Face of clock or watch, marked to show hours etc.; plate in steam-gauge, gas-meter, etc., on which pressure, consumption, etc., are indicated by pointer; (**su'n**)**~**, instrument showing time by shadow of pointer, cast by sun on graduated plate; circular plate on telephone with numbers etc. and movable disc with finger-holes for effecting connection with other telephones; (illuminated) plate etc. showing wavelength selected on radio receiver or channel selected on television set; (sl.) person's face. **2.** *v.t.* Measure or indicate (as) with dial. **3.** *v.i.* & *t.* Make telephone call by using dial; ring up (number etc.) thus; **~(ling) tone,** sound given by automatic-exchange telephone to show that caller may start to dial. [ME, = sundial, f. med. L *diale* clock-dial f. **dialis* f. L *dies* day; see -AL]

dī'alĕct *n.* Form of speech peculiar to a district or class; subordinate variety of a language with non-standard vocabulary, pronunciation, or idioms; hence **dialĕ'ctAL** *a.*, **~ŏ'LOGY, ~ŏ'LOGIST**, *ns.* [f. F *dialecte* or f. L f. Gk *dialektos* discourse (DIA*legomai* converse)]

dialĕ'ctĭc¹ *n.* **1.** (Also **~s,** occas. treated as *sing.*) Art of investigating the truth of opinions, testing of truth by discussion, logical disputation. **2.** Criticism dealing with metaphysical contradictions and their solutions; existence or action of opposing social forces etc. **3.** So **dialĕcti'CIAN** *n.* [ME, f. OF *dialectique* or f. L f. Gk *dialektikē* (*tekhnē* art) of debate (as prec.; see -IC)]

dialĕ'ctĭc² *a.* & *n.* Logical, of disputation; (person) skilled in critical inquiry by discussion; dialectal. [f. L or Gk *dialektikos* (see prec.)]

dialĕ'ctical *a.* = prec.; belonging to DIALECTIC¹ (sense 2); **~ materialism,** Marxist theory of political events as due to conflict of social forces caused by man's material needs; hence **~LY²** *adv.* [f. prec. + -AL]

dialŏ'gĭc *a.* In or of dialogue. [f. LL f. Gk *dialogikos* (as DIALOGUE; see -IC)]

diă'logĭst *n.* Speaker in or writer of dialogue. [f. LL f. Gk *dialogistēs* (as foll.; see -IST)]

dī'alŏgue (-ŏg), ***dī'alŏg,** *n.* Conversation; piece of written work in conversational form, this kind of composition (*written in dialogue; play contains much dialogue*); conversational part in a novel; discussion between representatives of two groups etc., exchange of proposals. [ME, f. OF *dialoge* f. L f. Gk *dialogos* (DIA*legomai* converse)]

diă'lÿs|ĭs *n.* (*pl.* **~es** *pr.* -ēz). **1.** (Chem.) Separation of particles in liquid by differences in their ability to pass through membrane into another liquid. **2.** (Med.) Purification of blood by flow past suitable membrane. **3.** Hence or cogn. **dī'alÿse** (-z) *v.t.*, separate thus, **dialÿ'tIC** *a.* [f. L f. Gk DIA(*lusis* f. *luō* set free)]

diamăgnĕ't|ĭc *a.* & *n.* (Body or substance) tending to become magnetized so as to lie transversely to a magnetic field force; hence **diamă'gnĕtISM** (2) *n.* [f. DIA- + MAGNETIC]

diamanté (dēamah'ńtā) *a.* & *n.* (Material) scintillating with powdered crystal etc. [F, p.p. of *diamanter* set with diamonds (*diamant* DIAMOND)]

diamănti'ferous *a.* Diamond-yielding. [f. F *diamantifère* (*diamant* DIAMOND; as -I-, -FEROUS)]

diamă'ntīne *a.* Of or like diamonds. [f. F *diamantin* (as prec.; see -INE¹)]

diă'mĕt|er *n.* Straight line passing from side to side of any body or figure through centre; transverse measurement, width, thickness; unit of linear measurement of magnifying-power (*lens magnifying 2000 diameters*); so **~RAL** *a.* [ME, f. OF *diametre* f. L f. Gk DIA*metros* (*grammē* line) measuring across f. *metron* measure]

diamĕ'trĭcal *a.* Of or along a diameter, diametral; (of opposition, difference, etc.) direct, complete, like that between opposite ends of diameter; hence **~LY²** *adv.* [f. Gk *diametrikos* (as prec.; see -IC) + -AL]

dī'amond *n.*, *a.*, & *v.t.* **1.** *n.* Colourless or tinted brilliant precious stone of pure carbon crystallized in octahedrons and allied forms, hardest naturally-occurring substance; **black ~,** (1) dark-coloured diamond, (2, in *pl.*) coal; **rough ~,** diamond not yet cut, (fig.) person of intrinsic worth but rough manners; **~ cut ~,** wit or cunning is met by its like. **2.** Glittering particle or point (of frost etc.). **3.** Tool with small diamond for glass-cutting. **4.** Figure shaped like cross-section of diamond, rhomb, (**~ panes,** small panes so shaped set in lead); playing-card of suit (**~s**) denoted by red rhomb. **5.** (Baseball). Space enclosed by bases; entire field. **6. ~-back,** moth, *snake, or terrapin with diamond-shaped markings; **~-bird,** (Austral.) pardalote; **~-cement** (for setting diamonds); **~-drill** (set with diamonds for boring hard substance); **~-field,** tract yielding diamonds; **~ jubilee,** 60th (or 75th) anniversary of sovereign's accession or other event; **~-point,** (1) diamond-tipped stylus for engraving, (2) place where two railway lines intersect obliquely; **~-snake,** (Austral.) greenish-black carpet-snake with diamond-shaped markings; **~ wedding,** 60th (or 75th) anniversary of wedding. **7.** Hence **~ĭ'FEROUS** *a.* **8.** *a.* Made of or set with diamond or diamonds; rhomb-shaped. **9.** *v.t.* Adorn (as) with diamonds. [ME f. OF *diamant* f. med. L *diamas -mant-* var. of L f. Gk *adamas* ADAMANT]

Diă'na *n.* Horsewoman, huntress. [ME f. L, name of goddess of hunting]

diă'ndrous *a.* Having two stamens. [f. DI-² after *monandrous*]

diă'nthus *n.* Flowering plant of genus *Dianthus*, e.g. carnation or pink. [f. Gk *Dios* of Zeus + *anthos* flower]

dīapā'son (or -z-) *n.* **1.** Compass of voice or instrument; range, scope; fixed standard of musical pitch; **open, stopped,** ~, two chief foundation-stops in organ, extending through its whole compass. **2.** Combination of notes or parts in harmonious whole; melody, strain, esp. grand swelling burst of harmony. [ME in sense 'octave' f. L, f. Gk *dia pasōn* (*khordōn*) through all (notes)]

dī'apause (-z) *n.* Period of retarded or suspended development in some insects. [f. DIA- + PAUSE]

dī'aper *n.*, & *v.t.* **1.** *n.* Linen or cotton fabric with small diamond pattern; baby's napkin (orig. of this material); ornamental design of diamonds etc. for panels, walls, etc. **2.** *v.t.* Decorate with diaper design. [ME, f. OF *diapre* f. med. L *diasprum* f. med. Gk *diaspros* adj. (DIA-, *aspros* white)]

dīă'phanous *a.* (Of fabric etc.) light and delicate, and so almost transparent; hence ~LY² *adv.* [f. med. L *diaphanus* f. Gk DIA(*phanēs* -showing f. *phainō* show) + -OUS]

dīaphorĕ'tĭc *a.* & *n.* (Drug) inducing perspiration. [f. LL f. Gk *diaphorētikos* (*diaphorēsis* perspiration f. DIA*phoreō* carry through; see -ETIC)]

dī'aphrăgm (-ăm) *n.* **1.** Muscular partition separating thorax from abdomen in mammals; partition in shellfish and plant tissues. **2.** Thin sheet used as partition etc. (~ **pump,** pump in which flexible diaphragm replaces piston); disc pierced by one or more holes in optical and acoustic systems etc.; device for varying effective aperture of lens in camera etc.; thin contraceptive cap fitting over cervix. **3.** Hence **dīaphrăgmă'tɪc** *a.* [ME, f. LL f. Gk DIA(*phragma* -*atos* f. *phrassō* fence in)]

dīapŏ'sĭtĭve (-z-) *n.* Positive photographic slide or transparency. [f. DIA- + POSITIVE]

dī'ar̄chў (-kĭ) *n.* Government by two independent authorities (esp. in India 1921–37); hence **dīar̄'chAL, dīar̄'chIC,** (-k-) *adjs.* [f. DI-² + Gk *-arkhia* rule, after *monarchy*]

dī'arĭst *n.* One who keeps a diary; hence **dīarĭ'stIC** *a.* [f. DIARY + -IST]

dī'arīze, -īse (-īz), *v.i.* & *t.* Keep, enter in, a diary. [f. DIARY + -IZE]

dīarrhoe'|a, *dīarrhē'|a, (-rē'*a*) *n.* Excessive evacuation of too fluid faeces; (fig.) excessive flow of words etc.; hence ~AL, ~IC, *adjs.* [ME f. LL f. Gk DIA(*rrhoia* f. *rheō* flow)]

dī'arў *n.* Daily record of events, journal; book prepared for keeping this in; book etc. with daily memoranda esp. for persons of a particular profession. [f. L *diarium* (*dies* day; see -ARY¹)]

dī'ascōpe *n.* Optical projector giving images of transparent objects. [f. DIA- + -SCOPE]

Dīă'spora *n.* The Dispersion (of the Jews); Jews so dispersed; (situation of) any group of people similarly dispersed. [Gk, f. DIA(*speirō* scatter)]

dī'astāse *n.* (Chem.) Enzyme converting starch to sugar, important in digestion; hence or cogn. **dīastā'sIC, dīastă'tIC,** *adjs.* [F, f. Gk *diastasis* separation (DIA-, *stasis* placing)]

dīă'stolē *n.* (Physiol.) Dilatation of heart rhythmically alternating with systole to form pulse; hence **dīastŏ'lIC** *a.* [LL f. Gk, f. DIA-(*stellō* place)]

dīatĕ'ssarŏn *n.* Arrangement of the four Gospels as one narrative. [ME, f. LL f. Gk *dia tessarōn* composed of four]

dīather̄'mancў *n.* Quality of transmitting radiant heat; so **dīather̄'manOUS, dīather̄'mIC,** *adjs.* [f. F *diathermansie*, f. Gk DIA- through + *thermansis* heating, assim. to -ANCY]

dī'ather̄mў *n.* Application of high-frequency electric currents to produce heat in deeper tissues of body. [f. G *diathermie* f. Gk *dia* through + *thermon* heat + -Y¹]

dīă'thĕs|ĭs *n.* (*pl.* ~es *pr.* -ēz). **1.** (Med.) Constitutional predisposition to disease etc. **2.** (Gram.) Voice of verb. [mod. L f. Gk (DIA*tithēmi* arrange)]

dī'atŏm *n.* Microscopic unicellular alga with silicified cell-wall, found as plankton and forming fossil deposits; hence **dīatomA'CEOUS** *a.* [f. mod. L *Diatoma* (genus-name) f. Gk DIA(*tomos* f. *temnō* cut)]

dīatŏ'mĭc *a.* (Chem.) Consisting of two atoms; having two replaceable atoms or radicals. [f. DI-² + ATOM + -IC]

dīă'tomīte *n.* Substance composed of siliceous skeletons of diatoms. [f. DIATOM + -ITE¹]

dīatŏ'nĭc *a.* (Mus.) (Of scale or interval) involving only notes proper to key without chromatic alteration; (of melody or harmony) constructed from such a scale. [f. F *diatonique* or f. LL f. Gk DIA(*tonikos* TONIC) at intervals of a tone]

dī'atrībe *n.* Piece of bitter criticism; invective, denunciation. [F, f. L f. Gk *diatribē* spending of time, discourse, f. DIA(*tribō* rub)]

dīă'zō *n.* **1.** (Chem.) ~ **compound,** one containing two nitrogen atoms joined by usu. double bond. **2.** ~(**type**), copying or colouring process using diazo compound decomposed by light. [f. DI-² + AZO-]

dĭb *v.i.* (-bb-). = DAP. [var. of DAB¹]

dībā'sĭc *a.* (Chem.) Having two replaceable hydrogen atoms. [f. DI-² + BASE¹ 5 + -IC]

dĭ'bber *n.* Instrument for dibbling, dibble. [f. DIB in sense of foll. + -ER¹]

dĭ'bble *n.* & *v.* **1.** *n.* Pointed instrument for making holes in ground for bulbs etc. **2.** *v.t.* Prepare (soil) with this; sow or plant thus. **3.** *v.i.* Use dibble. [ME, perh. rel. to DIB]

dĭbs (-z) *n.pl.* (sl.) Money. [earlier sense 'pebbles for game', also *dib-stones*, perh. f. DIB]

dīce¹. See DIE¹.

dīce² *v.* **1.** *v.i.* & *t.* Play dice (see DIE¹); gamble *away* at dice; take great risks (*dicing with death*); hence **dī'cER¹** *n.* **2.** *v.t.* Chequer, mark with squares; (Cookery) cut into small cubes. [ME, f. prec.]

dī'cey *a.* (sl.) Risky, unreliable. [f. DICE¹ + -Y²]

dĭchŏ'tom|ў (-k-) *n.* Division (esp. sharply defined) into two; result of such division; binary classification; (Bot. & Zool.) repeated bifurcation; so **dĭchotŏ'mIC** (-k-), ~OUS, *adjs.*, ~IZE (1, 3) *v.t.* & *i.* [f. mod. L f. Gk *dikhotomia* (*dikho-* apart; see -TOMY)]

dīchrō'|ĭc (-k-) *a.* (Esp. of doubly refracting crystals) showing two colours; so ~ISM (2) *n.* [f. Gk DI²(*khroos* f. *khrōs* colour) + -IC]

dīchromă'tĭc (-k-) *a.* Two-coloured; (of animal species) having individuals that show different colorations; having vision sensitive to only two of three primary colours, whence **dīchrō'matISM** (5) (-k-) *n.* [f. DI-² + Gk *khrōmatikos* (*khrōma -atos* colour; see -IC)]

‖**dĭck¹** *n.* (sl.) **Take** one's ~, swear, affirm, (*that*). [abbr. of *declaration*]

dĭck² *n.* (sl.) Detective. [perh. abbr.]

dĭck³ *n.* **1.** CLEVER *Dick*; TOM, *Dick, and Harry*. **2.** (vulg.) Penis. [f. *Dick* = *Richard*]

dĭ'ckēns (-z) *n.* (colloq., in imprecations etc.) Devil, deuce. [16th c.; prob. use of surname *Dickens*]

Dĭckĕ'nsĭan (-z-) *a.* & *n.* **1.** *a.* Of Dickens or his works; having similarities to the situations described by Dickens (*Dickensian squalor, working conditions*). **2.** *n.* Admirer or student of Dickens('s works). [f. C. *Dickens*, Engl. novelist d. 1870 + -IAN]

dĭ'cker *v.i.* Trade by barter; haggle; dither, hesitate. [perh. f. *dicker* set of ten (hides), as unit of trade]

dĭ'ckȳ¹, dĭ'ckey, *n.* (colloq.) ~(**-bird**), small bird; false shirt-front; ‖driver's seat in carriage; ‖extra folding seat at back of vehicle. [some senses f. *Dicky* dim. of *Richard*]

dĭ'ckȳ² *a.* (sl.) Unsound, shaky. [19th c., perh. f. 'as queer as Dick's hatband']

dĭ'cŏt *n.* = foll. [abbr.]

dīcŏtȳlē'don *n.* Flowering plant having two cotyledons; hence ~OUS *a.* [f. mod. L *dicotyledones* (as DI-², COTYLEDON)]

dīcrŏ'tĭc *a.* (Of pulse) with double beat. [f. Gk *dikrotos* + -IC]

dĭ'cta. See DICTUM.

dĭ'ctaphōne *n.* Machine that records and later reproduces for transcription or rehearing what is spoken into it. [**P**; f. DICTATE² + -PHONE]

dĭ'ctāte¹ *n.* (usu. in *pl.*) Authoritative instruction (esp. *of* reason, conscience, nature, etc.). [f. L *dictatum* neut. p.p. (as n.) of *dictare*; see foll.]

dĭctā'te² *v.t.* & *i.* **1.** Say or read aloud (matter to be written down, *to* writer). **2.** (Of person, motive, etc.) prescribe, lay down authoritatively, (terms, thing to be done); lay down the law, give orders, (*will not be dictated to*). **3.** So **dĭct**A'TION *n.*; **dictation speed,** rate of speech used by person dictating (sense 1). [f. L *dictare* frequent. of *dicere dict-* say + -ATE³]

dĭctā'tor *n.* **1.** Absolute ruler, usu. temporary or irregular, of a State, esp. one who suppresses or succeeds a democratic government; (Rom. Ant.) chief magistrate with absolute power, appointed in emergencies; person with absolute authority in any sphere; hence ~SHIP *n.*, (esp.) State ruled by a dictator. **2.** One who dictates for transcription. [ME f. L (as prec.; see -OR)]

dĭctatōr'ĭal *a.* Of a dictator; imperious, overbearing; hence ~LY² *adv.* [f. L *dictatorius* (as prec.) + -AL]

dĭ'ction *n.* **1.** Choice of words and phrases in speech or writing. **2.** Manner of enunciation in speaking or singing. [F, or f. L *dictio* (*dicere dict-* say; see -ION)]

dĭ'ctionarȳ *n.* Book explaining, usu. in alphabetical order, the words of a language or words and topics of some special subject, author, etc., wordbook, lexicon, (**French–English** etc. ~, list of French etc. words with English etc. translation or explanation; *dictionary of Americanisms, of architecture, of the Bible, of proverbs, Dictionary of National Biography, Shakespeare dictionary*, etc.). [f. med. L *dictionarium* (*manuale* manual) & *dictionarius* (*liber* book) f. L *dictio* (see prec., -ARY¹)]

dĭ'ctograph (-ahf) *n.* Apparatus reproducing in one room the sounds made in another, loud-speaking internal telephone. [**P**; f. DICTATION + -O- + -GRAPH]

dĭ'ct|um *n.* (*pl.* ~**a** *or* **-ums**). Formal saying, pronouncement; (Law) = OBITER DICTUM; maxim, current saying. [L, neut. p.p. of *dicere* say]

***dĭ'ctȳ** *a.* (sl.) Conceited; stylish. [20th c.; orig. unkn.]

dĭd. See DO¹.

dĭ'dachē (-kē) *n.* Instructional element in early Christian theology (opp. *kerygma*). [Gk *didakhē* teaching; cf. foll.]

dĭdă'ct|ĭc *a.* Meant to instruct; having the manner of an authoritarian teacher; hence ~ICALLY *adv.*, ~**ĭ**CISM (2) *n.* [f. Gk *didaktikos* (*didaskō* teach; see -IC)]

didakai, diddicoy, etc. Vars. of DIDICOI.

dĭ'dăpper *n.* Dabchick. [for *dive-dapper* f. earlier *divedap* f. OE *dūfedoppa* (*dūfan* dive, *doppa* cf. DIP)]

dĭ'ddle *v.t.* (sl.) Cheat, swindle. [prob. back form. f. Jeremy *Diddler* in Kenney's *Raising the Wind* (1803)]

dĭdgerĭdōō', -dj-, *n.* Australian Aboriginal musical instrument of long tubular shape. [imit.]

dĭ'dĭcoi *n.* (sl.) Gipsy; itinerant tinker. [Romany]

didn't. See DO¹.

***dī'dō** *n.* (colloq.) (*pl.* ~**es** *or* ~**s**). Antic, caper, prank (esp. *cut* (*up*) *didoes*). [19th c.; orig. unkn.]

dĭdst. See DO¹.

dĭdȳ'mĭum *n.* Mixture of praseodymium and neodymium, orig. regarded as element. [mod. L, f. Gk *didumos* twin (from being closely associated with lanthanum) + -IUM]

dīe¹ *n.* **1.** (*pl.* **dice,** also colloq. as *sing.*) Small cube with faces bearing usu. 1–6 spots used in games of chance; (in *pl.*) game played with these; (in *pl.*) small cubes of meat etc. for cooking; **the ~ is cast,** irrevocable step is taken; **no dice,** (colloq.) no success or prospect of it; **as straight** or **true as a ~,** (fig.) entirely honest or loyal. **2.** (*pl.* ~**s**). (Archit.) cube of pedestal between base and cornice; plinth of column; engraved stamp for coining, striking medal, embossing paper, etc.; hollow mould for shaping extruded metal etc. **3.** **~-casting,** process or product of casting from metal moulds; **~-sinker,** engraver of dies; **~-stamping,** embossing paper etc. with die. [ME f. OF *de* f. L *datum* neut. p.p. (as n.) of *dare* give, play]

dīe² *v.i.* (*part.* **dy'ing** *pr.* dī'ĭ-). **1.** (Of person or animal) cease to live, expire, (*of* illness, hunger, etc., *by* violence, the sword, one's own hand, *from* wound etc., *through* neglect, *on* scaffold, *at* the stake, *in* battle, *for* friend, cause, etc., *in* poverty; *die a beggar, a martyr*; *die a glorious, a dog's, death*). **2.** ~ **the death,** (arch. or joc.) be put to death; ~ **game** (fighting, not tamely); ~ **hard** (not without struggle); **~-hard** *n.*, conservative or stubborn person; ~ **in** one's **bed** (of age or illness), **in** one's **boots** or **shoes** (by violence), **in harness** (while still at work), **in the last ditch** (desperately defending something); **never say ~,** not give in, keep up courage. **3. Be dying** *for*, *to* do, have great desire; **be dying of** *boredom* etc., find it exceedingly vexatious; ~ **(of) laughing,** laugh to exhaustion. **4.** (Of plant etc.) lose vital force, decay (~ **back,** from tip towards root); come to an end, cease to exist or function; (of flame, fame, sound, etc.) go out, disappear, be forgotten, fade away, (*away, down, off*); **~-away** *a.*, languishing; ~ **out,** become extinct; *secret* etc. **~s with** person, he dies without revealing it. [ME, prob. f. ON *deyja* = OS *dōian*, OHG *touwen*, f. Gmc **dawjan*; cf. DEAD, DEATH]

die'ldrĭn *n.* Crystalline insecticide got by oxidation of aldrin. [f. O. *Diels*, Ger. chemist d. 1954 + ALDRIN]

dīĕlĕ'ctrĭc *a.* & *n.* (Electr.) Insulating (medium or substance); ~ **constant,** permittivity. [f. DI-³ + ELECTRIC = through which electricity is transmitted (without conduction)]

dī'ēne *n.* (Chem.) Organic compound with two double bonds between carbon atoms. [f. DI-² + -ENE]

***dīēr'ėsĭs.** See DIAERESIS.

die'sel (-z-) *n.* **1.** ~ **(engine),** internal combustion engine in which ignition of fuel is produced by heat of air highly compressed; vehicle driven by, fuel for, diesel engine; hence ~IZE (4) *v.t.* **2.** **~-electric,** driven by electric current from generator driven by diesel engine; ~ **oil,** heavy petroleum fraction used in diesel engines. [f. R. *Diesel*, Ger. engineer d. 1913]

Dies irae (dīēz ĭr'ē) *n.* Latin hymn sung in Mass for the dead. [L (its first words), = day of wrath]

dies non (dīēz nŏ'n) *n.* (Law) day on which no legal business is done; day that does not count or cannot be used. [L, short for *dies non juridicus* non-judicial day]

dī'et[1] *n.* & *v.* **1.** *n.* Way of feeding; prescribed course of food, whence **~ī'tIAN**, ~I'CIAN, (-shan) *n.*, one versed in or practising dietetics; one's habitual food. **2.** *v.i.* Restrict oneself to special food, esp. in order to control one's weight; hence ~ER[1] *n.* **3.** *v.t.* Feed, esp. on special food as treatment or punishment. [ME, f. OF *diete(r)* f. L f. Gk *diaita* way of life]

dī'et[2] *n.* Conference, congress, on national or international business; meeting of the estates of the realm or confederation (esp. as English name for some foreign parliamentary assemblies); (Sc.) session of court. [ME, f. med. L *dieta* day's work, wages, etc.]

dī'ètarў *n.* & *a.* **1.** *n.* (Course of) diet; allowance or nature of food in hospital, prison, etc. **2.** *a.* Of diet(ary). [ME, f. med. L *dietarium* (as DIET[1]; see -ARY[1])]

dīètĕ't|ĭc *a.* Of diet; hence ~ICALLY *adv.*, ~ICS *n.* [f. L f. Gk *diaitētikos* (as DIET[1]; see -ETIC)]

dif- *pref.* Form of DIS-, occurring before *f.* [L var. of DIS-]

dĭ'ffer *v.i.* Be unlike; be distinguishable *from*; disagree, be at variance, (*from, with*); AGREE *to differ*. [ME, f. OF *differer* f. L DIF(*ferre* bear, tend), all used in senses (a) *differ*, (b) DEFER[1]]

dĭ'fference *n.*, & *v.t.* **1.** *n.* Being different, dissimilarity, non-identity (DISTINCTION *without difference*). **2.** Point in which things differ (**make all the ~**, be very important or significant; **make a ~ between,** treat differently; *make a great difference, make no difference*; **with a ~**, in a special way); characteristic mark distinguishing individual or species; quantity by which amounts differ, remainder after subtraction, (**split the ~**, take average of two proposed amounts). **3.** Disagreement in opinion, dispute, quarrel. **4.** *n.*, & *v.t.* (Her.) (Make) alteration in (coat of arms) to distinguish members of same family. [ME f. OF, f. L *differentia* (as foll.; see -ENCE)]

dĭ'fferent *a.* Able to be distinguished, unlike, of other nature, form, or quality, (*from, to, than*); distinct, separate, (*several different people, colours*); unusual; hence ~LY[2] *adv.* [ME f. OF, f. L (as DIFFER; see -ENT)]

dĭfferĕ'ntĭa (-shĭa) *n.* (*pl.* **~e**). Distinguishing mark, esp. of species within a genus. [L; see DIFFERENCE]

dĭfferĕ'ntial (-shal) *a.* & *n.* **1.** *a.* Of, exhibiting, depending on, a difference; varying according to circumstances. **2.** Constituting a specific difference, distinctive, relating to specific differences (*differential diagnosis*); (Math.) relating to infinitesimal differences (**~ calculus,** for finding rates of change, maximum and minimum values, etc.; cf. INTEGRAL). **3.** (Phys. & Mech.) Concerning the difference of two or more motions, pressures, etc.; ~ (**gear**), gear enabling motor vehicle's rear wheels to revolve at different speeds in rounding corners. **4.** Hence ~LY[2] *adv.* **5.** *n.* (Math.) infinitesimal difference between successive values of a variable (**~ coefficient,** = DERIVATIVE; **~ equation,** one involving derivatives); difference between rates of interest etc.; difference in wage between industries or between different classes of workers in same industry. [f. med. & mod. L *differentialis* (as DIFFERENCE; see -AL)]

dĭfferĕ'ntĭ|āte (-shĭ-) *v.t.* & *i.* Constitute difference between, of, or in; make or become different in process of growth or development (species, word-forms, organs, functions, synonyms); discriminate, discriminate between; (Math.) calculate derivative of; hence ~A'TION (-shĭ- *or* -sĭ-) *n.* [f. med. L *differentiare* (as DIFFERENCE) + -ATE[3]]

dĭ'ffĭcult *a.* Needing much labour to do or practise; troublesome, perplexing, (*difficult of access, to answer*, etc.); unaccommodating, stubborn. [ME, back form. f. foll.]

dĭ'ffĭcult|ў *n.* Being difficult (**with ~y,** not easily) or obscure; difficult thing or problem (**make ~ies,** be unaccommodating); hindrance; (often in *pl.*) trouble, esp. shortage of money. [ME, f. L DIF(*ficultas* = *facultas* FACULTY)]

dĭ'ffĭd|ent *a.* Lacking self-confidence, excessively modest; hence or cogn. ~ENCE *n.*, **~ent**LY[2] *adv.* [f. L DIF(*fidere* trust); see -ENT]

dĭffră'ct *v.t.* (Phys.) (Of edge of opaque body, narrow slit, etc.) break up (beam of light) into series of dark and light bands or coloured spectra, or (beam of radiation or particles) into series of alternately high and low intensities; so ~ION *n.*, ~IVE *a.*, **~ŏ'**METER *n.*, instrument for measuring diffraction esp. in crystallographic work. [f. L DIF(*fringere fract-* = *frangere* break)]

dĭffū'se[1] *a.* (Of light, inflammation, etc.) spread out, diffused, not concentrated; not concise, long-winded, verbose; hence ~LY[2] (-slĭ) *adv.*, ~NESS (-sn-) *n.* [ME, f. F *diffus* or L DIF(*fusus* p.p. of *fundere* pour) extensive]

dĭffū's|e[2] (-z) *v.t.* & *i.* **1.** Disperse or be dispersed from a centre; (be) spread widely (light, particles, heat, geniality, knowledge, rumour). **2.** (Phys., esp. of fluids) intermingle by diffusion. **3.** So ~IBLE, ~IVE, *adjs.* [f. L, as prec.]

dĭffū'sion (-zhon) *n.* Diffusing or being diffused; (Phys.) interpenetration of substances by natural movement of their particles; (Anthrop.) spread of elements of culture etc. to another region or people, whence ~IST (2) *n.* [ME, f. L *diffusio* (as DIFFUSE[1]; see -ION)]

dĭg *v.* (**-gg-; dug,** arch. **~ged** *pr.* -gd), & *n.* **1.** *v.i.* Use spade or pick, claws, hands, or snout, in excavating or turning over ground; excavate archaeologically; make search (*for* information, *into* book etc.); make way by digging *into, through, under.* **2.** *v.t.* Excavate or turn up (ground) with spade etc. or for archaeological purposes; make (hole, grave, etc.) by digging (**~ a pit for,** fig., try to entrap); obtain by digging (potatoes etc.); (sl.) understand, experience, or admire. **3.** Thrust (spurs, one's nails, feet, point of weapon) *into* something or *in* (**~** one's **feet, heels,** or **toes in,** be obstinate); poke (person *in the ribs*). **4. ~** (**oneself**) **in,** prepare defensive trench or pit, establish one's position; **~ in** or **into,** mix (thing) with the soil by digging, (colloq.) begin eating; **~ out** or **up,** get or find by digging (lit. or fig.); **~ up,** break up soil of (fallow land). **5.** *n.* Piece of digging; (colloq.) archaeological excavation; thrust, poke, (esp. *in the ribs*; (fig.) **~ at,** remark directed against); ||(in *pl.*, colloq.) lodgings. [ME, perh. f. OE **dicigian* (*dic* DITCH)]

dĭgă'mma *n.* Sixth letter (F, ϝ) of original Greek alphabet (prob. pronounced w), later disused but philologically important. [L f. Gk (as DI-[2], GAMMA)]

dĭ'gam|ў *n.* Second marriage, after divorce or death of first spouse; hence or cogn. ~IST (1) *n.*, ~OUS *a.* [f. LL f. Gk DI[2](*gamia* f. *gamos* marriage)]

dĭgă'strĭc *a.* & *n.* (Anat.) **1.** *a.* (Of muscle) having two wide parts with tendon between. **2.** *n.* Muscle that opens the jaw. [f. mod. L DI[2](*gastricus* f. Gk *gastēr* belly)]

dī'gĕst[1] *n.* Methodical compendium or summary esp. of a body of laws (**the D~**, that of Roman laws compiled by order of Justinian); periodical synopsis of current literature or news. [ME, f. L *digesta* things methodically arranged, neut. pl. p.p.; see foll.]

dĭgĕ'st[2] *v.t.* **1.** Reduce to a systematic or

convenient form, classify; summarize; think over, arrange in the mind. **2.** Assimilate (food) in stomach and bowels; treat (substance) with heat or solvent in order to decompose it, extract essence, etc., whence ~ER¹ (2) *n.*; endure (insults etc.); understand and assimilate mentally. **3.** So ~IBI'LITY *n.*, ~IBLE *a.* [ME, f. L DI¹(*gerere gest-* carry) distribute, dissolve, digest]

dĭgĕ'stion (-schon) *n.* Digesting of physical or mental food; power of digesting (*a good, weak, digestion*); digesting of substance by heat or solvent. [ME f. OF, f. L *digestio -onis* (as prec.; see -ION)]

dĭgĕ'stĭve *a.* & *n.* Of or promoting digestion; substance aiding digestion; ||kind of wholemeal (biscuit); hence ~LY² (-vlĭ) *adv.* [ME, f. OF *digestif -ive* or f. L *digestivus* (as DIGEST²; see -IVE)]

dĭ'gger (-g-) *n.* In vbl senses; (colloq.) Australian or New Zealander, esp. private soldier; member of 17th-c. Engl. religious group cultivating commons; hippie believing in free sharing of property and food; **~'s delight,** (Austral.) kind of speedwell thought to indicate presence of gold; ~(**-wasp**), burrowing wasp of family Sphecidae. [f. DIG + -ER¹]

dĭ'gging (-g-) *n.* In vbl senses; (in *pl.*) mine or goldfield, ||(colloq.) lodgings; **~-stick,** pointed stick as primitive digging implement. [f. DIG + -ING¹]

dight (dīt) *a.* (arch.) Clothed, arrayed. [p.p. of *dight* v. f. OE *dihtan* f. L *dictare* DICTATE²]

dĭ'git *n.* **1.** (Zool. & Anat., or joc.) Finger or toe. **2.** Any numeral from 0 to 9, esp. when forming part of number; hence ~IZE (3) *v.t.* **3.** Finger's breadth as unit of length, ¾ inch. [ME, f. L *digitus*]

dĭ'gĭtal *a.* Of digit(s); ~ **clock** (showing time by displayed digits, not by hands); ~ **computer** (making calculations with data represented by digits or in similar discrete form); hence ~IZE (3) *v.t.* [f. L *digitalis* (as prec.; see -AL)]

dĭgĭtā'l|ĭs *n.* Drug prepared from dried foxglove leaves, used as heart-stimulant; hence ~IN *n.*, steroid poison extracted from foxglove leaves. [mod. L, genus-name of foxglove after G *fingerhut* thimble; see prec.]

dĭ'gĭtate *a.* (Zool. & Bot.) Having separate fingers or toes; having deep radiating divisions; hence **dĭgĭt**A'TION *n.* [f. L *digitatus* (as DIGIT; see -ATE²)]

dĭ'gĭtigrāde *a.* & *n.* (Animal) that walks on its toes not touching ground with heels, e.g. lion (cf. PLANTIGRADE). [F, f. L *digitus* + -I- + -*gradus* -walking]

dĭ'gnĭfīed (-īd) *a.* Having or showing dignity; self-respecting, stately. [p.p. of foll.]

dĭ'gnĭfȳ *v.t.* Make worthy or illustrious; confer dignity on, ennoble; make stately; give high-sounding title to (*school dignified with name of college*). [f. obs. F *dignifier* f. OF *dignefier* f. LL *dignificare* (*dignus* worthy; see -FY)]

dĭ'gnĭtarȳ *n.* Person holding high rank or office, esp. ecclesiastical. [f. foll. + -ARY¹, after *proprietary*]

dĭ'gnĭtȳ *n.* True worth, excellence, (*the dignity of labour*); high rank or estimation (**beneath** one's ~, unfitting for one to do); honourable office, rank, or title; elevated manner, proper stateliness (**stand on** one's ~, insist on respectful treatment). [ME f. OF *digneté, dignité* f. L *dignitas -tatis* (*dignus* worthy; see -ITY)]

dĭ'graph (-ahf) *n.* Group of two letters representing one sound (*ph, ea*). [f. DI-² + -GRAPH]

dĭgrĕ'ss *v.i.* Diverge from the track, stray; depart from the main subject temporarily in speech or writing (*to digress for a moment; must not digress from the point at issue*); so ~ION (-shon) *n.*, ~IVE *a.* [f. L DI¹(*gredi gress-* = *gradi* walk)]

dīhē'dral *a.* & *n.* **1.** *a.* Having or contained by two plane faces; ~ **angle,** (esp.) angle formed by aircraft wing with horizontal. **2.** *n.* Dihedral angle. [f. *dihedron* (DI-², -HEDRON) + -AL]

dīhȳ'drĭc *a.* (Chem.) Containing two hydroxyl groups. [f. DI-² + HYDRIC]

dĭ'k-dĭk *n.* Small Afr. antelope of genus *Madoqua* or *Rhynchotragus*. [name in E. Africa & in Afrik.]

dīke, dȳke, *n.*, & *v.t.* **1.** *n.* Ditch; ||natural watercourse; low wall esp. of turf. **2.** Embankment, long ridge, dam, against flooding, esp. one of those in Holland against sea; causeway; (fig.) barrier, obstacle, defence; (Mining & Geol.) intrusion of igneous rock across strata; (sl.) lavatory. **3.** *v.t.* Provide or defend with dike(s). [ME, f. ON *dík* or f. MLG *dīk* dam, MDu. *dijc* ditch, dam; cf. DITCH]

dĭ'kkŏp *n.* (S. Afr.) Stone-curlew. [Afrik. (*dik* thick, *kop* head)]

dĭ'ktăt *n.* Imposition of severe terms by victor; dictate, categorical statement. [G, = DICTATE¹]

dĭlă'pĭdātėd *a.* (Of building, furniture, clothing) in disrepair or decay. [p.p. of *dilapidate* f. L DI¹(*lapidare* f. *lapis* stone) squander + -ATE³]

dĭlăpĭdā'tion *n.* Bringing or coming into, being in, disrepair; ||(Eccl.) sum charged against incumbent for wear and tear during his tenancy. [ME, f. LL *dilapidatio* (as prec.; see -ATION)]

dĭlā't|e *v.* **1.** *v.t.* & *i.* Make or become wider or larger, expand, widen, enlarge, (*with dilated eyes*); hence or cogn. ~ABLE *a.*, **dĭlat**A'TION *n.*, (esp., Med.) widening of cervix e.g. for curettage, **dĭl**A'TION *n.* **2.** Expatiate, speak or write at length (*upon*). [ME, f. OF *dilater* f. L DI¹(*latare* f. *latus* wide) spread out]

dĭlā'tor *n.* (Anat.) Muscle that dilates an organ; (Surg.) instrument for dilating tube or cavity in body. [f. prec. + -OR]

dĭ'lator|ȳ *a.* Tending to, designed to cause, given to, delay; hence ~ĬLY² *adv.*, ~ĬNESS *n.* [f. LL *dilatorius* (DI¹*lat-* p.p. st. of *differre* DEFER¹; see -ORY)]

dĭ'ldō *n.* (*pl.* ~s). Artificial penis used by women for sexual pleasure. [17th c.; orig. unkn.]

dĭlĕ'mma *n.* Argument forcing opponent to choose one of two alternatives (**horns of the** ~) both unfavourable to him; position that leaves only a choice between equally unwelcome possibilities. [L, f. Gk DI²(*lēmma* assumption, premiss)]

dĭlėttă'nt|ė *n.* (*pl.* ~**i** *pr.* -ē, *or* ~**es**) & *a.* **1.** *n.* Lover of the fine arts; amateur; one who toys with subject or studies it without seriousness; hence ~ISH¹ *a.*, ~ISM (1) *n.* **2.** *a.* Trifling, not thorough; amateur. [It., f. part. of *dilettare* f. L *delectare* DELIGHT; see -ANT]

dĭ'lĭgence¹ *n.* Persistent effort or work; industrious character. [ME f. OF, f. L *diligentia* (as DILIGENT; see -ENCE)]

dĭ'lĭgence² (*or* dēlēzhah'ṅs) *n.* (Hist.) Public stage-coach, esp. in France. [F, for *carrosse de diligence* coach of speed]

dĭ'lĭgent *a.* Steady in application, industrious, attentive to duties; hence ~LY² *adv.* [ME f. OF, f. L *diligens* assiduous, part. of DI¹(*ligere lect-* = *legere* choose) love, take delight in; see -ENT]

dĭll *n.* Umbelliferous annual yellow-flowered herb (*Anethum graveolens*); ~ **pickle,** pickled cucumber etc. flavoured with dill; **~-water,** distillate of dill as carminative. [OE *dile,* = OS *dilli*, OHG *tilli*, ON *dylla*, of unkn. orig.]

dĭ'llȳ *n.* (sl.) Remarkable or excellent person or thing. [f. *dilly* a. f. DELIGHTFUL OR DELICIOUS; see -Y³]

dĭ'llȳ-dăllȳ *v.i.* (colloq.) Vacillate; dawdle, loiter. [redupl. of DALLY]

dĭ'lūent *a.* & *n.* Diluting (agent). [f. L *diluere* DILUTE²; see -ENT]

dīlū'te¹ (*or* dĭ'-) *a.* Weakened by addition of water or other solvent; (of colour) washed-out, faded; (fig.) watery, watered down. [f. L *dilutus* p.p. of *diluere* (see foll.)]

dīlū'te² *v.t.* Reduce strength of (fluid) by adding water or other solvent; diminish brilliance of (colour); make (doctrine, zeal) less strict or forceful; substitute a proportion of unskilled for skilled (workers); hence **dīlūt**EE' *n.*, unskilled person thus substituted, **dīlū'**TION (*or* -ōō'-) *n.* [f. L DI¹(*luere lut-* wash)]

dĭlū'vĭal (*or* -ōō'-) *a.* **1.** Of a flood, esp. of the Flood in Genesis. **2.** (Geol.) Of the drift formation now called Glacial Drift; ~ **theory** etc. (postulating general deluge or catastrophic water-action, whence ~IST (2) *n.*). [f. LL *diluvialis* (*diluvium* DELUGE; see -AL)]

dĭlū'vĭum (*or* -ōō'-) *n.* (Geol.) = DRIFT¹. [L (see prec.)]

dĭm *a.* & *v.* (-mm-). **1.** *a.* Faintly luminous or visible; not bright (lit. or fig.), clear, or well-defined; (colloq.) stupid; obscure; seeing or seen, hearing or heard, apprehending or apprehended, indistinctly; **take a ~ view of,** (colloq.) regard with disfavour or pessimism; **~-wit(ted)**, (colloq.) stupid (person); hence ~'LY² *adv.*, **~'mish**¹ 2 *a.*, ~'NESS *n.* **2.** *v.i.* & *t.* Become or make dim, becloud, outshine; *dip (headlights); ~ **out,** reduce brightness of (lights on stage, or street lights etc. esp. in wartime); so **~-out** *n.* [OE *dim(m)*, = ON *dimmr*, cogn. w. OHG *timbar*, of unkn. orig.]

dim. *abbr.* diminuendo.

***dīme** *n.* Silver coin, 1/10 of dollar (**a ~ a dozen,** commonplace; ~ **novel,** cheap sensational novel). [ME, orig. = tithe, f. OF *disme* f. L *decima* (*pars* part) fem. of *decimus* tenth]

dĭmĕ'nsion (-shon) *n.* **1.** Measurable extent of any kind, as length, breadth, thickness, area, volume, (often in *pl.*; **of great ~s,** very large); **the three ~s,** length, breadth, and thickness (point has no dimensions, line one, surface two, solid body three); **fourth ~,** property of bodies that would make them be to solids as solids are to planes, (Phys.) time viewed as lengthlike quantity. **2.** (Alg.) number of unknown or variable quantities contained as factors in a product (*x^3, x^2y, xyz, are all of three dimensions*); (Phys.) power of length, time, mass, etc., contained in a quantity. **3.** Extent in a particular aspect (*gave the problem a new dimension*). **4.** Hence (-)~AL *a.* (TWO-*dimensional* etc.), ~LESS *a.* **5.** *v.t.* Give dimensions or measurements to. [ME f. OF, f. L DI¹(*mensio -onis* f. *metiri mensus* measure; see -ION)]

dī'mer *n.* (Chem.) Compound whose molecule contains twice the numbers of atoms in another compound (the *monomer*); hence **dīmĕ'r**IC *a.* [f. DI-² + *-mer* after POLYMER]

dĭ'merous *a.* (Bot. & Entom.) Having two parts in whorl, tarsus, etc. [f. mod. L *dimerus* f. Gk *dimerēs* bipartite; see -MEROUS]

dĭ'mèter *n.* (Pros.) Verse of two measures. [f. LL f. Gk *dimetros* (as DI-², -METER)]

dĭmĭ'dĭate *a.* Halved, split in two. [f. L *dimidiatus* p.p. of *dimidiare* f. DI¹(*midium* f. *medius* mid) half; see -ATE²]

dĭmĭ'nĭsh *v.t.* & *i.* Make or become smaller or less (in fact or in appearance); lessen the reputation of (person); **law of ~ing returns,** (Econ.) fact that expenditure, taxation, etc., beyond a certain point does not produce proportionate yield; hence ~ABLE *a.* [ME, blending of earlier *minish* f. OF *menusier* f. as MINCE², and *diminue* f. OF *diminuer* f. L DI¹*minuere -minut-* break up small]

dĭmĭ'nĭshed (-sht) *a.* In vbl senses; (Mus., of interval) less by a semitone than corresp. minor or perfect interval; ~ **responsibility,** (Law) limitation of criminal responsibility on ground of mental weakness or abnormality. [p.p. of prec.]

dĭmĭnūĕ'ndō *adv.*, *a.*, & *n.* (*pl.* ~s). (Mus.) (Passage performed) with gradual decrease of loudness. [It., part. of *diminuire* DIMINISH]

dĭmĭnū'tion *n.* Diminishing, amount of it; (Mus.) repetition of passage in notes shorter than those previously used. [ME f. OF, f. L *diminutio -onis* (as DIMINISH; see -ION)]

dĭmĭ'nūtĭve *a.* & *n.* Remarkably small, tiny; (Gram.) (word) describing small or liked or despised specimen of the thing denoted by corresponding radical word (*ringlet*; *duckling*; *wifie*; *princeling*), whence **dĭmĭnūtī'v**AL *a.*; hence ~LY² (-vlĭ) *adv.*, ~NESS (-vn-) *n.* [ME f. OF (*-if -ive*), f. LL *diminutivus* (as DIMINISH; see -IVE)]

dĭ'missorў *a.* Sending away; permitting to depart; **letters ~,** (Eccl.) bishop's authorization of candidate's ordination outside the bishop's own see. [ME, f. LL *dimissorius* (DI¹*mittere -miss-* send away; see -ORY)]

dĭ'mĭtў *n.* Cotton fabric woven with raised stripes or checks. [ME, f. It. *dimito* or f. med. L *dimitum* f. Gk DI²(*mitos* warp-thread)]

dĭ'mmer *n.* In vbl senses; device for dimming lights in theatre etc. [f. DIM + -ER¹]

dīmôr'phĭc, dīmôr'phous, *adjs.* (Biol., Chem., & Min.) Exhibiting, or occurring in, two distinct forms; hence **dīmôr'ph**ISM (2) *n.* [f. Gk DI²(*morphos* f. *morphē* form) + -IC, -OUS]

dĭ'mple *n.* & *v.* **1.** *n.* Small hollow or dent, esp. in cheek or chin; ripple in water; hence **dĭ'mpl**Y² *a.* **2.** *v.t.* Produce dimples in. **3.** *v.i.* Show dimples. [ME, prob. f. OE **dympel*, = OHG *tumphilo* deep place in water, perh. nasalized form f. as DEEP¹]

dĭn *n.* & *v.* (-nn-). **1.** *n.* Continued confused stunning or distracting noise. **2.** *v.t.* Get (thing to be learnt) *into* person or person's *ears* by incessant repetition; assail with din. **3.** *v.i.* Make a din. [OE *dyne, dynn, dynian* v., = OHG *tuni*, ON *dynr*, *dynja* rumble down f. Gmc **dunjaz*, **dunjan* v.]

DIN *abbr.* German Standard. [G (*D*eutsche *I*ndustrie-*N*orm)]

dĭ'nâr (dē'-) *n.* Unit of currency in Yugoslavia and in several countries of Middle East and N. Africa. [f. Arab. & Pers. *dīnār* f. Gk *dēnarion* f. L *denarius* (see DENIER)]

dīne *v.i.* & *t.* Eat dinner; entertain (persons) at dinner; ~ **out** (away from home); ~ **out on,** be invited to dinner mainly because of one's knowledge of (interesting event etc.). [ME, f. OF *di(s)ner* f. Rom. **dis(je)junare* break one's fast f. DIS- + LL *jejunare* (*jejunus* fasting)]

dī'ner *n.* In vbl senses; railway dining-car; *restaurant; (small) dining-room; **~-out,** one who often dines away from home, esp. one much invited for his social qualities. [f. prec. + -ER¹]

dī'nĕtte (*or* -ĕ't) *n.* Small room or part of room used for meals; compactly designed set of furniture for dining. [f. DINE + -ETTE]

Ding an sich (dĭng ahn zĭ'χ) *n.* (Philos.) Thing in itself. [G]

dĭ'ngbăt *n.* **1.** *Piece of money; *tramp; *'thingummy'. **2.** (Austral. & N.Z., in *pl.*) Discomfort; madness. [19th c., perh. f. *ding* to beat + BAT²]

dĭng-dŏ'ng *adv.*, *n.*, & *a.* (With) alternating strokes as of two bells; with great energy (*hammer away at it ding-dong*); ~ **race** etc. (in which each has the better of it alternately); sound of bell(s); (colloq.) riotous party, heated argument. [16th c.; imit.]

dĭnge[1] (-nj) *n.* Dinginess. [f. DINGY or f. *dinge* make dingy]

***dĭnge**[2] (-nj) *n.* (sl., derog.) Negro (esp. *attrib.* of Negro jazz style). [f. DINGY]

dĭ'nghy̆ (-nggĭ *or* -ngĭ) *n.* Small boat of ship; small pleasure-boat; aircraft's small inflatable rubber boat for emergency use. [orig. native rowing-boat on Indian rivers, f. Hindi *ḍiṅgī, ḍēṅgī*]

dĭ'ngle (-nggel) *n.* Deep dell, usu. shaded with trees. [ME; orig. unkn.]

dĭ'ngō (-nggō) *n.* (*pl.* ~es). Wild or half-domesticated Australian dog; (Austral. sl.) cheat, traitor, coward. [Aboriginal]

dĭ'ngus (-ngg-) *n.* (colloq.) Gadget; what's-its-name. [f. Du. *ding* thing]

dĭ'ng|y̆ (-njĭ) *a.* Dull-coloured, drab; grimy, dirty-looking; hence ~ĭLY[2] *adv.*, ~ĭNESS *n.* [perh. rel. to DUNG; see -Y[2]]

dī'nĭng *n.* In vbl senses; **~-car,** railway carriage in which meals are served; **~-room,** room in house where meals are eaten; **~-table** (on which meals are served in dining-room etc.). [f. DINE + -ING[1]]

dĭ'nkel *n.* = SPELT[1]. [G]

dĭ'nkum *a.* & *n.* (Austral. & N.Z. colloq.) **1.** *a.* Genuine, real; ~ **oil,** the honest truth. **2.** *n.* Work, toil; the truth. [19th c.; orig. unkn.]

dĭ'nky̆ *a.* (colloq.) ||Pretty, neat; small, dainty; *trifling. [f. Sc. *dink* neat, trim (of unkn. orig.) + -Y[2]]

dĭ'nner *n.* Chief meal of day, whether at midday or evening (formal meal with several courses); public banquet in honour of person or event; **~-dance,** dinner followed by dancing; ||**~-jacket,** man's short usu. black coat for evening wear; *dinner*-SERVICE[1] or *-set*; **~-table** (at which dinner is eaten); **~-wagon,** trolley with tiers for holding dishes etc.; hence ~LESS *a.* [ME, f. *di(s)ner*; see DINE, -ER[4]]

dīnôr'nĭs *n.* Ostrich-sized New Zealand flightless bird of genus *Dinornis* now extinct, moa. [f. Gk *deinos* terrible + *ornis* bird]

dī'nosaur *n.* Reptile (freq. huge) of mesozoic era; hence **dinosaur'**IAN *a.* & *n.* [f. mod. L *dinosaurus* f. Gk *deinos* terrible + *sauros* lizard]

dī'nothēre *n.* Huge elephant-like animal of extinct genus *Deinotherium*. [f. mod. L *dinotherium* f. Gk *deinos* terrible + *thērion* wild beast]

dĭnt *n.*, & *v.t.* **1.** *n.* (arch.) Blow, stroke. **2.** **By ~ of,** by force or means of. **3.** Mark made by blow or pressure, dent. **4.** *v.t.* Mark with dints, dent. [ME, f. OE *dynt*, and partly f. cogn. ON *dyntr*; ult. orig. unkn.]

dīŏ'cēsan *a.* & *n.* **1.** *a.* Of a diocese. **2.** *n.* Bishop in relation to diocese or its clergy; ||member of diocese in relation to bishop. [ME, f. F *diocésain* f. LL *diocesanus* (as foll.; see -AN)]

dī'ocēse *n.* District under pastoral care of bishop. [ME f. OF *diocise* f. LL *diocesis* f. L f. Gk DI[3](*oikēsis* f. *oikeō* inhabit) administration]

dī'ōde *n.* Thermionic valve having two electrodes; semiconductor rectifier having two terminals. [f. DI-[2] + ELECTRODE]

dīoe'cious (-ē'shus) *a.* (Bot.) with male and female organs on separate plants; (Zool.) having the two sexes in separate individuals. [f. DI-[2] + Gk *-oikos* -housed + -OUS]

Dīony̆'sĭăc, -ĭan, *adjs.* Of Dionysus, the Greek god of wine, or his worship. [f. L *Dionysius* a. f. L f. Gk *Dionusos*, + -AN]

Dīophă'ntīne *a.* (Math.) ~ **equations** (containing more unknowns than there are equations, but usu. to be solved for rational numbers). [f. *Diophantus*, Alexandrian mathematician of 3rd c. + -INE[1]]

||**dīŏ'ptre** (-ter), ***dīŏ'pter,** *n.* Refractive power of lens having focal length of one metre; unit of refractive power when this is expressed as reciprocal of focal length in metres. [F *dioptre* f. L f. Gk *dioptra* (see foll.)]

dīŏ'ptr|ĭc *a.* Serving as medium for sight, assisting sight by refraction, (*dioptric glass, lens, system*); of refraction, refractive; hence ~ICS *n.*, part of optics dealing with refraction. [f. Gk *dioptrikos* (DI[3]*optra* kind of theodolite; see -IC)]

dīora'ma (-rah'-) *n.* Scenic painting in which changes in colour and direction of illumination simulate sunrise etc.; small representation of scene with three-dimensional figures, viewed through window etc.; small-scale model or film-set; hence **dīoră'mIC** *a.* [f. DI-[3] + Gk *horama -atos* (*horaō* see)]

dī'or|īte *n.* Variety of GREEN[1]*stone* (1); hence ~ĭ'TIC *a.* [F, irreg. f. Gk *diorizō* distinguish + -ITE[1]]

dīŏ'xīde *n.* (Chem.) Oxide formed by combination of two atoms of oxygen with one of metal or non-metal (*carbon dioxide* etc.). [f. DI-[2] + OXIDE]

dĭp[1] *v.* (-pp-). **1.** *v.t.* Put or let down into liquid, immerse; dye thus; make (candles) by immersing wick in hot tallow; wash (sheep) in vermin-killing liquid; take *up* (liquid, grain, etc.) in scoop, pan, etc., take *out of* (liquid etc.) thus. **2.** Lower (esp. flag, sail) for a moment; ||lower (beam of vehicle's headlight) to reduce its brightness; ||(colloq.) involve in debt, mortgage. **3.** *v.i.* Go under water and emerge quickly; put hand, ladle, etc., *into* to take something out (~ **into** one's **pocket, purse, reserves,** etc., spend therefrom); go below any surface or level (*sun dips below horizon; bird dips and rises in flight; balance-scale dips*). **4.** Extend downwards; have downward slope (esp. of magnetic needle, and of strata; **~'ping-needle,** one so mounted as to measure magnetic dip). **5.** Look cursorily *into* (book etc.). [OE *dyppan* f. Gmc **dupjan*, cogn. w. DEEP[1]]

dĭp[2] *n.* **1.** Dipping (LUCKY[1] *dip*); quantity dipped up; (colloq.) bathe in sea etc.; (sl.) pickpocket. **2.** (Astron. & Surv.) Apparent depression of horizon due to observer's elevation; (Phys.) angle made by magnetic needle with horizon. **3.** Downward slope of stratum, road, etc.; depression in skyline etc. **4.** Tallow candle. **5.** Washing-preparation for SHEEP etc. **6.** Sauce or dressing into which food is dipped before eating. **7.** **~-circle,** dipping-needle with graduated vertical circle; **~-needle,** = *dipping-needle* (see prec.); **~-net,** small fishing-net with long handle; ~ **pen,** pen that has to be dipped in ink, not fountain-pen; **~-stick,** rod for measuring depth of liquid; ||**~-switch,** switch for dipping vehicle's headlight beams. [f. prec.]

Dip. *abbr.* Diploma.

||**Dip. A. D.** *abbr.* Diploma in Art and Design.

Dip. Ed. *abbr.* Diploma in Education.

dīpĕ'ptīde *n.* (Chem.) Peptide formed by combination of two amino-acids. [f. DI-[2] + PEPTIDE]

dĭphthēr'ĭa *n.* Acute infectious bacterial disease with inflammation of a mucous membrane esp. of throat, and formation of false membrane; hence **dĭphthēr'ĭAL, dĭphthĕ'rIC, dĭphtherĭ'tIC, dĭ'phtherOID,** *adjs.* [mod. L, f. F *diphthérie*, earlier *diphthérite* f. Gk *diphthera* skin, hide; see -IA[1], -ITIS]

dĭ'phthŏng *n.* Union of two vowels (letters or sounds) pronounced in one syllable (as in *coin, loud, side*); two vowel characters representing sound of single vowel (as in *feat*); compound vowel character, ligature, (as *æ*); hence **dĭphthŏ'ngAL** *a.*, ~IZE (3) *v.t.* & *i.*, (-ngg-). [f. F *diphtongue* f. LL f. Gk DI[2](*phthoggos* -sounded f. *phthoggos* voice)]

dĭplo- *comb. form.* Double, as: **~co'ccus,** coccus

occurring mainly in pairs; **diplo′docus** (-ŏ′d-) [Gk *dokos* wooden beam], giant herbivorous dinosaur. [f. Gk *diplous* double + -o-]

dĭ′ploid *a.* & *n.* (Biol.) (Organism or cell) having chromosomes in homologous pairs; hence ~Y[1] *n.*, condition of being diploid. [G, f. as DIPLO- + -OID]

dĭplō′ma *n.* **1.** State paper, official document, charter. **2.** Document conferring honour or privilege; (certificate of) university or college degree or qualification, whence ~′D[2], ~ED[2] (-mad), *a.* [L, f. Gk *diplōma -atos* folded paper (*diploō* fold f. *diplous* double)]

dĭplō′macy̆ *n.* Management of, skill in managing, international relations; adroitness in personal relations, tact. [f. F *diplomatie* (*diplomatique* DIPLOMATIC after *aristocratie*; see -ACY)]

dĭ′plomăt *n.* One engaged in diplomacy, esp. accredited to court or seat of government; adroit negotiator. [f. F *diplomate,* back form. f. *diplomatique* (see DIPLOMATIC)]

dĭ′plomāte *n.* Holder of diploma. [f. DIPLOMA + -ATE[1]]

dĭplomă′tic *a.* & *n.* **1.** *a.* Of diplomas (sense 1); of diplomacy (~ **bag,** bag containing official mail from embassy etc.; ~ **corps,** ambassadors and their staff at a court or seat of government; ~ **immunity,** exemption of diplomatic staff etc. abroad from arrest, taxation, etc.; ~ **service,** branch of public service concerned with representation of country abroad); skilled in diplomacy, tactful; proceeding by negotiation; (of statement etc.) uncandid, subtle; (of edition etc.) exactly reproducing the original; hence **dĭplomă′t**ICALLY *adv.* **2.** *n.* (in *sing.* or *pl.*) Palaeographic and critical study of diplomas (sense 1). [f. mod. L *diplomaticus* and F *-ique* f. L DIPLOMA; see -IC]

dĭplō′matĭst *n.* = DIPLOMAT. [f. as DIPLOMAT + -IST]

dĭplō′matīze, -īse (-īz), *v.i.* Act as diplomat; use diplomatic skill. [f. DIPLOMAT + -IZE]

dī′pōle *n.* (Phys.) object oppositely charged or magnetized at two points or poles; (Chem.) molecule in which positive and negative charges are separated; (Radio etc.) aerial of two equal rods in line, metal strip serving as reflector for a certain wavelength; hence **dīpō′l**AR[1] *a.*, having two poles, as a magnet. [f. DI-[2] + POLE[2]]

dĭ′pper *n.* In vbl senses; Anabaptist or Baptist; diving bird, esp. water OUZEL; ladle; BIG *dipper,* LITTLE *dipper.* [ME, f. DIP[1] + -ER[1]]

dĭ′ppy̆ *a.* (sl.) Crazy. [20th c.; orig. uncert.]

dĭ′psō *n.* (*pl.* ~**s**). (colloq.) = DIPSOMANIAC. [abbr.]

dĭpsomā′nĭa *n.* Morbid craving for alcoholic liquor; hence **dĭpso**MA′NIAC *n.* [f. Gk *dipso-* (*dipsa* thirst; see -o-) + -MANIA]

dĭ′pteral *a.* (Archit.) With double peristyle. [f. L f. Gk DI[2](*pteros* -winged f. *pteron* wing) + -AL]

dĭ′pteran *a.* & *n.* (Member) of the order Diptera (see foll.). [f. mod. L f. Gk *diptera* neut. pl. of *dipteros* two-winged (as DI-[2], *pteron* wing) + -AN]

dĭ′pterous *a.* (Entom.) Two-winged, belonging to the order Diptera (insects with one pair of membranous wings, e.g. fly, gnat, mosquito); (Bot.) having two winglike appendages. [f. mod. L f. Gk *dipteros* (see prec.) + -OUS]

dĭ′ptȳch (-ĭk) *n.* Ancient hinged two-leaved writing-tablet with inner sides waxed; painting, esp. altar-piece, with two leaves closing like book. [f. LL *diptycha* f. Gk DI[2](*ptukha* neut. pl. of *-ptukhos* f. *ptukhē* fold)]

dīre *a.* Dreadful, calamitous; ominous; urgent (*in dire need*); hence ~′LY[2] (dīr′lĭ) *adv.* [f. L *dirus*]

dĭrĕ′ct[1] *v.t.* **1.** Give indications for delivery of (letter etc. *to* person or place); utter or write *to* or to be conveyed *to* (*I direct my remarks to you*); aim (remark, blow, etc., *at, towards*); turn (thing, person, eyes, attention) straight *to* or *towards* something; tell (person) the way (*to*); assign (worker) to particular industry etc. **2.** Control, govern movements of; guide as adviser, principle (*duty directs my actions*), etc.; order (person) *to* do, thing *to be* done; supervise acting etc. of (film, play, etc.); give orders (*that*, or abs.). [ME, prob. f. foll.]

dĭrĕ′ct[2] *a.* & *adv.* **1.** Straight, not crooked(ly) or oblique(ly) or round about (*the direct road; went direct to heaven*); (of descent) lineal(ly), not collateral(ly); (of argument) following uninterrupted chain of cause and effect etc.; without intermediaries (*prefer direct dealings, to deal with him direct*). **2.** Straightforward, frank(ly), going straight to the point, not ambiguous(ly); immediate(ly), personal(ly), not by proxy. **3.** *a.* Diametrical (*direct contradiction, contrary, opposite*). **4.** (Astron.) Proceeding from west to east, not retrograde. **5.** (Mus., of interval or chord) not inverted. **6.** ~ **action,** exertion of pressure on the community by action (e.g. strike or sabotage) seeking immediate effect, rather than by Parliamentary means; ~ **current,** (Electr.) current flowing in one direction only; ~ **dye** (not needing mordant); ‖~ **grant** (of money given to certain schools by Government not local authority); ~ **hit** (without ricochet, or exactly on target); ~ **labour** (by employees without intervention of contractor); ~ **method,** teaching foreign language without use of native language or study of formal grammar; ~ **object** (Gram., expressing primary object of action of verb); ~ **proportion,** relation between quantities whose ratio is constant; ~ **ray** (not reflected or refracted); ~ **speech,** words quoted as actually spoken, not as modified in reporting; ~ **tax** (levied on person who bears the ultimate burden of the tax, e.g. income tax, but not value-added tax). **7.** Hence ~NESS *n.* [ME, f. L *directus* p.p. of DI[1](*rigere rect-* = *regere* put straight)]

dĭrĕ′ction *n.* **1.** Directing, aiming, guiding, managing; (usu. in *pl.*) instruction what to do, order. **2.** (arch.) Address on letter or parcel. **3.** Course pursued by moving body, point to or from which person or thing moves or looks, (*in the direction of London*; **sense of** ~, ability to know without guidance the places towards which one is walking, etc.; ~**-finder,** receiver of radio waves that determines the direction from which they come; ~**-indicator,** device showing direction in which driver is about to take motor vehicle); scope, sphere, subject (*new directions of inquiry; improvement in many directions*); hence ~AL *a.* (esp. of radio transmission within a narrow angle). [ME f. F, or f. L *directio* (as prec.; see -ION)]

dĭrĕ′ctĭve *a.* & *n.* **1.** *a.* Serving to direct. **2.** *n.* General instruction for procedure or action. [ME, f. med. L *directivus* (as DIRECT[2]; see -IVE)]

dĭrĕ′ctly̆ *adv.* & *conj.* **1.** *adv.* In a direct manner; exactly (*directly in front of*); at once, without delay; presently, in no long time. **2.** *conj.* ‖(colloq.) As soon as (*went directly I knew*). [ME, f. DIRECT[2] + -LY[2]]

Dĭrĕ′ctoire (-twâr) *a.* (Dressmaking & Art). In imitation of styles prevalent during the French Directory (~ **knickers,** straight knee-length kind). [F, as DIRECTORY]

dĭrĕ′ctor *n.* Superintendent, manager, esp. member of managing-board of commercial company, (~**-general,** chief administrator); person who directs film, play, etc.; (Eccl.) priest acting as spiritual adviser; (Fr. Hist.) member of Directory; hence **dĭrĕctôr′**IAL *a.*,

~SHIP *n.* [f. AF *directour* f. LL *director* governor (as DIRECT²; see -OR)]

dīrĕ'ctorate *n.* Office of director; board of directors. [f. prec. + -ATE¹]

dīrĕ'ctorў *n.* Book with list of telephone subscribers, inhabitants of district, members of profession etc., with various details; (Fr. Hist., *D~*) revolutionary executive of five persons in power 1795–9; book of rules, esp. for order of public or private worship. [f. LL *directorium* neut. (as n.) of *directorius* adj. (as DIRECT²; see -ORY)]

dīrĕ'ctrėss, dīrĕ'ctrice (-ēs), *ns.* Woman director. [f. DIRECTOR + -ESS¹, F *directrice* f. as foll.]

dīrĕ'ctr|ix *n.* (*pl.* **~ices** *pr.* -īsēz). (Geom.) Fixed line used in describing curve or surface. [med. L, f. LL DIRECTOR; see -TRIX]

dīr'eful (dīr'f-) *a.* Terrible, dreadful; hence ~LY² *adv.* [f. DIRE + -FUL]

dirge *n.* Song of mourning sung at burial, or in commemoration of the dead; slow mournful song; lament. [ME, f. L *dirige* imper. of *dirigere* DIRECT¹, first wd in Latin antiphon in Matins part of Office of the Dead]

dīr'hăm *n.* Small coin of Morocco etc. [Arab., f. L DRACHMA]

dĭ'rĭgĭble (*or* -rī'-) *a.* & *n.* **1.** *a.* (Esp. of balloon) capable of being guided. **2.** *n.* Dirigible balloon or airship. [f. as DIRECT²; see -IBLE]

dirig|isme (dērēzhē'zm) *n.* Policy of State direction and control in economic and social matters; hence ***~i'ste*** (-ē'st) *a.*, pertaining to such policy. [F (*diriger* DIRECT¹; see -ISM)]

dĭ'rĭment *a.* Nullifying; **~ impediment** (making marriage null and void from the first). [f. L *dirimere* (*dir-* = DIS-, *emere* take); see -ENT]

dirk *n.* Kind of long dagger (esp. of Sc. Highlander). [17th c. *durk*, of unkn. orig.]

dīr'ndl *n.* Woman's dress imitating Alpine peasant costume with bodice and full skirt; **~ (skirt)**, full skirt with tight waistband. [G dial., dim. of *dirne* girl]

dirt *n.* **1.** Unclean matter that soils; wet mud; excrement; dirtiness; foul or scurrilous talk; anything worthless; **treat** person **like ~** (entirely without respect); **~ cheap,** very cheap. **2.** Earth, soil, (***~ farmer** (raising crops on his own land); ***~ road,** road without made surface); **do** person **~,** (sl.) harm or injure him maliciously; **eat ~,** put up with insult etc., *make humiliating confession; *PAY¹ *dirt.* **3. ~-eating,** disease with morbid craving to eat earth; **~-track,** course made of rolled cinders, brick-dust, etc., for motor-cycle racing, or of earth for flat-racing; ***~-wagon,** dust-cart. [ME, f. ON *drit* excrement]

dīr'tў *a.*, *adv.*, & *v.* **1.** *a.* Soiled, foul, like or connected with dirt; (colloq., of nuclear weapon) causing considerable fall-out; obscene, lewd; sordid, mean, despicable; ill-gotten; (of weather) rough, squally; (of colour) not pure or clear, tinged with black or brown. **2.** Hence **dīr'tĭ**LY² *adv.*, **dīr'tĭ**NESS *n.* **3. ~ dog,** (sl.) despicable or untrustworthy person; **~ end of the stick,** (colloq.) difficult or unpleasant part; **~ look,** (colloq.) look of disapproval or disgust; **~ money** (paid to those who must handle dirty materials); **~ trick,** despicable act; **~ word,** (1) obscene word, (2) word denoting concept regarded as discreditable; **~ work,** dishonourable or illicit behaviour; **do the ~,** play a mean trick *on.* **4.** *adv.* (sl.) Very (*big, great*, etc.). **5.** *v.t.* & *i.* Make or become dirty. [f. prec. + -Y²]

dĭs- *pref.* forming *ns.*, *adjs.*, and *vbs.*, meaning: apart (*distinguish*), away (*dispose*), utterly (*disannul, disembowel, disgruntled*), not (*dishonest*), reverse of action (*disabuse*), absence of action (*disbelieve*) or state (*disaccord*), removal of thing (*disarm*) or quality (*disable*), expulsion from (*disbar*). [f. or after OF *des-*, or LL *dis-* (L DE-), or L *dis-*, cogn. w. *bis* twice; cf. DI-¹, DIF-]

dĭsabĭ'lĭtў *n.* Thing or lack that prevents one's doing something; legal disqualification; physical incapacity caused by injury or disease. [f. DIS- + ABILITY]

dĭsā'ble *v.t.* Make unable, incapacitate *from* doing or *for* work etc.; (esp. in *p.p.*) cripple, deprive of or reduce power of acting, walking, etc.; disqualify legally; hence ~MENT (-bělm-) *n.* [ME, f. DIS- + ABLE]

dĭsabū'se (-z) *v.t.* Undeceive, disillusion, (person, mind); relieve *of* illusion etc. [f. DIS- + ABUSE²]

dĭsaccōr'd *n.*, & *v.i.* Disagree(ment), (be at) variance. [ME, f. F *désaccorder* v. (as DIS-, ACCORD¹)]

dĭsadva'ntage (-vah'-) *n.* Unfavourable condition (*taken at a disadvantage*); loss or injury to reputation etc. [ME, f. OF *desavantage* (as DIS-, ADVANTAGE¹)]

dĭsadva'ntaged (-vah'ntĭjd) *a.* Placed in unfavourable conditions (esp. of person lacking normal social opportunities etc.). [p.p. of *disadvantage* v., f. prec.]

dĭsădvantā'geous (-jus) *a.* Involving disadvantage or discredit; derogatory; hence ~LY² *adv.* [f. DIS- + ADVANTAGEOUS]

dĭsaffĕ'ctėd *a.* Estranged, unfriendly; disloyal, esp. to one's superiors. [p.p. of *disaffect* v., orig. = dislike, disorder (DIS-, AFFECT¹,²)]

dĭsaffĕ'ction *n.* Political discontent, disloyalty. [f. DIS- or prec., after AFFECTION]

dĭsaffĭ'lĭ|āte *v.t.* & *i.* Cease affiliation (of); detach; hence ~A'TION *n.* [f. DIS- + AFFILIATE]

dĭsaffīr'm *v.t.* (Law). Reverse (previous decision); repudiate (settlement); hence **dĭsăffirm**A'TION *n.* [f. DIS- + AFFIRM]

||**dĭsaffŏ'rėst** *v.t.* Reduce from legal status of forest to that of ordinary land; clear of forests; hence ~A'TION *n.* [ME, f. AL DIS(*afforestare* AFFOREST)]

dĭsagree' *v.i.* **~ (with),** differ in nature (from), be unlike, not correspond (to); **~ (with),** differ in opinion (from), dissent (from), quarrel (with); **~ with,** (of food, climate, etc.) prove unsuitable for, have bad effects on, (person, his health, digestion, etc.); hence ~MENT *n.* [ME, f. OF *desagreer* (as DIS-, AGREE)]

dĭsagree'ab|le (*or* -grī'a-) *a.* & *n.* **1.** *a.* Not to one's taste, unpleasant; unamiable, bad-tempered; hence **~le**NESS (-běln-) *n.*, ~LY² *adv.* **2.** *n.* (in *pl.*) Disagreeable things or experiences. [ME, f. OF *desagreable* (as DIS-, AGREEABLE)]

dĭsallow' *v.t.* Refuse to sanction or accept as reasonable or admit, prohibit. [ME, f. OF *desalouer* (as DIS-, ALLOW)]

dĭsămbĭ'gū|āte *v.t.* Remove ambiguity from; so ~A'TION *n.* [f. DIS- + AMBIGUOUS + -ATE³]

dĭsamĕ'nĭtў *n.* Disadvantage, unpleasant feature (of place etc.). [f. DIS- + AMENITY]

dĭsannŭ'l *v.t.* (-ll-). Cancel, annul. [f. DIS- + ANNUL]

dĭsappear' *v.* **1.** *v.i.* Cease to be visible, vanish, pass from sight or existence. **2.** *v.t.* Cause to disappear. **3.** Hence ~ANCE *n.* [ME, f. DIS- + APPEAR]

dĭsappoi'nt *v.t.* Fail to fulfil desire or expectation of, break appointment with, (person, or abs.; *disappointed at* failure, *in* thing, *of* one's expected gain, *with* person; **agreeably** etc. ~**ed,** glad to find one's fears groundless); frustrate (hope, purpose, etc.; person *in love*); hence ~MENT *n.*, event etc. that disappoints, resulting distress. [ME, f. F *désappointer* (as DIS-, APPOINT)]

dĭsăpprobā'tion *n.* Disapproval; so **dĭsă'pprobātIVE, dĭsă'pprobātORY,** *adjs.* [f. DIS- + APPROBATION]

dĭsappro'v|e (-ōō'v) *v.t.* & *i.* Have or express unfavourable opinion (of or *of*); hence ~AL 2 *n.* [f. DIS- + APPROVE]

dĭsar̂'m *v.* **1.** *v.t.* Deprive of or *of* weapons; deprive of weapon (esp. in Fencing); deprive (city, ship) of means of defence; reduce (army) to peace footing; deprive of power to injure; remove fuse of (bomb etc.); pacify hostility or suspicions of, whence ~ING[2] *a.* **2.** *v.i.* (Of nation etc.) disband or reduce its armed forces, whence **dĭs**AR'MAMENT *n.* [ME, f. OF *desarmer* (as DIS-, ARM[3])]

dĭsarrā'nge (-nj) *v.t.* Bring into disorder, disorganize; hence ~MENT (-jm-) *n.* [f. DIS- + ARRANGE]

dĭsarray' *n.*, & *v.t.* (Throw into) disorder. [ME, f. or after DIS- + ARRAY[1,2]]

dĭsar̂tĭ'cūl|āte *v.t.* & *i.* Separate or be separated at the joints; hence ~A'TION *n.* [f. DIS- + ARTICULATE[2]]

dĭsassĕ'mble *v.t.* Take (machine etc.) to pieces; so **dĭs**ASSE'MBLY *n.* [f. DIS- + ASSEMBLE]

dĭsassōcĭā'tion *n.* = DISSOCIATION (esp. Psych.). [f. *disassociate* v. (DIS-, ASSOCIATE[2]) + -ATION]

dĭsa'st|er (-zah'-) *n.* Sudden or great misfortune, calamity; complete failure (*a record of disaster*); ~**er area** (in which major disaster has recently occurred); so ~ROUS *a.* [orig. 'unfavourable aspect of star', f. F *désastre* or f. It. *disastro* (as DIS-, *astro* f. L *astrum* star)]

dĭsavow' *v.t.* Say one does not know or have responsibility for or approve of; disclaim, repudiate; hence ~AL 2 *n.* [ME, f. OF *desavouer* (as DIS-, AVOW)]

dĭsbă'nd *v.t.* & *i.* Discontinue organized state (of), disperse, (troops etc.); hence ~MENT *n.* [f. obs. F *desbander* (as DIS-, BAND[1] 4)]

dĭsbar̂' *v.t.* (**-rr-**). Expel from membership of the bar, deprive of status of barrister; hence ~MENT *n.* [f. DIS- + BAR[1] 5]

dĭsbėlie'v|e *v.* **1.** *v.t.* Refuse to believe (person, statement, etc.). **2.** *v.i.* Be a sceptic; have no faith *in.* **3.** So **dĭs**BELIE'F, ~ER[1], *ns.* [f. DIS- + BELIEVE]

||**dĭsbĕ'nch** *v.t.* Deprive of status of bencher. [f. DIS- + BENCH]

dĭsbou'nd *a.* (Of pamphlet etc.) removed from bound volume. [f. DIS- + p.p. of BIND[1]]

dĭsbŭ'd *v.t.* (**-dd-**). Remove (esp. superfluous) buds of. [f. DIS- + BUD[1]]

dĭsbûr'den *v.t.* Relieve of or *of* a burden; get rid of, discharge, (load, anxieties, etc.). [f. DIS- + BURDEN[1]]

dĭsbûr'se *v.* **1.** *v.t.* Expend (money); defray (cost). **2.** *v.i.* Pay money. **3.** Hence **dĭsbûr'**SAL, ~MENT (-sm-), *ns.* [f. OF *desbourser* (as DIS-, BOURSE)]

dĭsc, dĭsk, *n.* **1.** Thin circular plate of any material (e.g. medal, coin); round flat or apparently flat surface (*sun's disc*) or mark; round flattened part in body, plant, etc., esp. layer of cartilage between vertebrae (**slipped** ~, one that has become displaced and causes lumbar pain by pressure on nerves); gramophone record. **2.** ~ **brake** (using disc-shaped friction surfaces); ~ **harrow** (with row(s) of concave discs at an oblique angle); ~ **jockey,** (colloq.) compère of broadcast programme of gramophone records; ~ **parking,** system in which parked vehicles must display disc showing time of arrival or latest permitted time of departure. [f. F *disque* or f. L DISCUS]

dĭscă'lced (-st) *a.* (Of friar or nun) barefooted or only sandalled. [var. of *discalceated* (after F *déchaux*) f. L DIS(*calceatus* f. *calceus* shoe); see -ATE[2], -ED[1]]

dĭscar̂'d[1] *v.t.* Cast aside, give up, (clothes, unwanted material, habit, belief, friend, etc.); throw out or reject from hand at cards (specified card, or abs. of playing non-trump that does not follow lead). [f. DIS- + CARD[2]]

dĭ'scar̂d[2] *n.* Discarded card(s) or thing(s). [f. prec.]

dĭscar̂'nate *a.* Disembodied, separated from the flesh. [f. DIS- + L *caro carnis* flesh + -ATE[2]]

dĭscêr'n *v.t.* **1.** Perceive clearly with mind or senses, make out by thought or by gazing, listening, etc.; hence ~IBLE *a.*, ~ING[2] *a.*, (esp.) having quick or true insight; ~MENT *n.*, (esp.) insight, keen perception. **2.** (arch.) Distinguish (good *and* or *from* bad, *between* good and bad). [ME, f. OF *discerner* f. L DIS(*cernere cret-* separate)]

dĭscêr'pt|ĭble *a.* (literary). That can be plucked apart, not indestructibly one; hence ~IBI'LITY *n.* [f. L DIS(*cerpere cerpt-* = *carpere* pluck) + -IBLE]

dĭscêr'ption *n.* (arch.) Pulling apart, severance; severed piece. [f. LL *discerptio* (as prec.; see -ION)]

dĭschar̂'g|e[1] *v.* **1.** *v.t.* Relieve (ship etc.) of load; fire (gun). **2.** Release electric charge from; hence ~ER[1] *n.* **3.** Dismiss, cashier, (*was discharged from the service*); release (prisoner), relieve (bankrupt) of residual liability, let go (patient, jury). **4.** Put forth, get rid of, send out, emit, (missile, liquid, purulent matter, abuse); unload from ship; (Law) cancel (order of court); acquit oneself of, pay, perform, (duty, debt, vow). **5.** *v.i.* Undergo discharge of contents; (of river) flow *into* sea etc. [ME, f. OF *descharger* (as DIS-, CHARGE[2])]

dĭ'schar̂ge[2] (*or* -ar̂'j) *n.* Discharging or being discharged; unloading (of ship or cargo); firing of gun etc.; emission (of liquid, purulent matter); release of electric charge esp. with emission of light; release, exoneration, exemption, acquittal, written certificate of these; dismissal; liberation; payment (*of* debt); performance (*of* obligation). [ME, f. prec.]

dĭscī'ple *n.* **1.** One of Christ's personal followers, esp. one of the twelve Apostles; any early believer in Christ. **2.** Follower or adherent of any leader of thought, art, conduct, etc. **3.** Hence ~SHIP (-pelsh-) *n.*, **dĭscĭ'pūl**AR[1] *a.* [OE *discipul* f. L *discipulus* (*discere* learn)]

dĭscĭplĭnar̂'ian *n.* Maintainer of discipline (sense 2) (*strict, good, poor, no, disciplinarian*). [f. as foll. + -AN]

dĭ'scĭplĭnarў (*or* -lĭ'n-) *a.* Of or promoting discipline (sense 2). [f. med. L *disciplinarius* (as foll.; see -ARY[1])]

dĭ'scĭplĭn|e[1] *n.* **1.** Branch of instruction or learning; mental and moral training, adversity as effecting this; system of rules for conduct; behaviour according to established rules. **2.** Order maintained among schoolchildren, soldiers, prisoners, etc.; control exercised over members of church or other organization. **3.** Chastisement; (Eccl.) mortification by penance. **4.** Hence ~AL *a.* [ME f. OF, f. L *disciplina* (*discipulus* DISCIPLE; see -INE[4])]

dĭ'scĭplĭn|e[2] *v.t.* Bring under control, train to obedience and order, drill; punish; chastise; hence ~ABLE *a.* [ME, f. OF *discipliner* or f. LL & med. L *disciplinare*, f. as prec.]

dĭsclai'm *v.t.* Renounce legal claim to (thing, or abs.); disown, disavow, deny one's connection with, (*responsibility* etc.). [ME, f. AF *desclaim-* stressed st. of *desclamer* (as DIS-, CLAIM[1])]

dĭsclai'mer *n.* Act of disclaiming, renunciation, disavowal. [ME f. AF (=prec. as n.; see -ER⁴)]
dĭsclō'se (-z) *v.t.* Remove cover from, expose to view; make known, reveal. [ME, f. OF *desclos-* st. of *desclore* f. Gallo-Rom. **disclaudere* (as DIS-, CLOSE³)]
dĭsclō'sure (-zh*er*) *n.* Disclosing; thing disclosed. [f. prec. + -URE, after *closure*]
dĭ'scō *n.* (*pl.* **~s**). (colloq.) Discothèque; party at which records are played for dancing. [abbr.]
dĭscŏ'bol|us *n.* (*pl.* **~i** *pr.* ~-ī). Ancient discus-thrower; statue of one in act of throwing. [L, f. Gk *diskobolos* (*diskos* DISCUS, *-bolos* -throwing f. *ballō* to throw)]
dĭscŏ'graphy̆ *n. Catalogue raisonné* or study of gramophone records. [f. DISC + -O- + -GRAPHY]
dĭ'scoid *a.* Disc-shaped. [f. Gk *diskoeidēs* (*diskos* DISCUS; see -OID)]
dĭsco'lour, *dĭsco'lor, (-ŭ'l*er*) *v.t.* & *i.* Change or spoil colour of, stain, tarnish; become stained etc.; so **dĭscolor**A'TION, **-our-,** (-ŭl*er*-) *n.* [ME, f. OF *descolorer* or med. L *discolorare* f. as DIS- + L *colorare* COLOUR²]
***dĭscombŏ'būlāte** *v.t.* (joc.) Disturb, disconcert. [prob. based on *discompose* or *discomfit*]
dĭsco'mfĭt (-ŭ'm-) *v.t.* Baffle, thwart, disconcert; (arch.) defeat in battle; so ~URE *n.* [ME, f. *disconfit* f. OF p.p. of *desconfire* f. Rom. **disconficere* (as DIS-, L *conficere* put together; see CONFECTION)]
dĭsco'mfort (-ŭ'm-) *n.*, & *v.t.* **1.** *n.* Uneasiness of body or mind; lack of comfort. **2.** *v.t.* Make uneasy. [ME, f. OF *desconfort(er)* (as DIS-, COMFORT)]
dĭscommō'd|e *v.t.* Put to inconvenience; so ~IOUS *a.* [f. obs. F *discommoder* var. of *incommoder*; see DIS-, INCOMMODE]
dĭscompō'se (-z) *v.t.* Disturb composure of, ruffle, agitate; hence **dĭscompō's**URE (-zh*er*) *n.* [f. DIS- + COMPOSE]
dĭsconcer̂'t *v.t.* Spoil, upset, (plan, concerted measures); disturb self-possession of, ruffle, fluster; hence ~ION, ~MENT, *ns.* [f. obs. F *desconcerter* (as DIS-, *concerter* CONCERT²)]
dĭsconfir̂'m *v.t.* (Tend to) disprove (hypothesis etc.); so **dĭscŏnfirm**A'TION *n.* [f. DIS- + CONFIRM]
dĭsconnĕ'ct *v.t.* Break the connection of (things, one thing *from* another); (Electr.) put (apparatus) out of action by disconnecting parts. [f. DIS- + CONNECT]
dĭsconnĕ'ctėd *a.* In vbl senses; (of speech or writing) incoherent, with bad connection; hence ~LY² *adv.*, ~NESS *n.* [p.p. of prec.]
dĭsconnĕ'ction, ‖dĭsconnĕ'xion, (-kshon) *n.* Disconnecting; lack of connection, disconnectedness. [f. DISCONNECT after *connection*]
dĭscŏ'nsolate *a.* Forlorn, inconsolable; unhappy, disappointed; hence ~LY² (-tlĭ) *adv.*, ~NESS (-tn-) *n.* [ME, f. med. L DIS(*consolatus* p.p. of L *consolari* console)]
dĭscontĕ'nt *n.*, & *v.t.* **1.** *n.* Dissatisfaction, lack of contentment; grievance. **2.** *v.t.* (esp. in *p.p.*) Make dissatisfied; hence ~MENT *n.* [f. DIS- + CONTENT²,⁴]
dĭscontĭ'nū|e *v.t.* & *i.* (Cause to) cease; cease from, give up, (do*ing*, habit, etc.); cease taking, paying, (newspaper, subscription); so ~ANCE *n.* [ME, f. OF *discontinuer* f. med. L DIS(*continuare* CONTINUE)]
dĭscontĭ'nūous *a.* Lacking continuity in space or time, having interstices or breaks, intermittent; hence or cogn. **dĭscŏntinū'**ITY *n.*, ~LY² *adv.* [f. med. L DIS(*continuus* CONTINUOUS) + -OUS]
dĭ'scor̂d¹ *n.* **1.** Disagreement, opposition of views, strife; harsh noise, clashing sounds. **2.** (Mus.) Lack of harmony between notes sounded together; chord unpleasing or unsatisfactory in itself and requiring to be resolved by another; any interval except unison, octave, perfect fifth and fourth, major and minor third and sixth, and their octaves; single note dissonant with another. [ME, f. OF *descord, discord*, f. as foll.]
dĭscor̂'d² *v.i.* Disagree, quarrel, be different or inconsistent, (*with*); be dissonant, jar, clash. [ME, f. OF *descorder, discorder* f. L *discordare* f. DIS(*cors -cord-* -hearted f. *cor cordis* heart) discordant]
dĭscor̂'d|ant *a.* Not in harmony, dissonant, disagreeing, (*to, from, with*); hence or cogn. ~ANCE *n.*, **~ant**LY² *adv.* [ME f. OF, part. of *discorder* (see prec., -ANT)]
dĭ'scothèque (-tĕk) *n.* Club, café, etc., where records are played for dancing. [F, = record-library]
dĭ'scount¹ *n.* Deduction from amount due or price of goods in consideration of its being paid promptly or in advance, or for special class of buyers; deduction from amount of bill of exchange etc. by one who gives value for it before it is due; discounting; **at a ~,** below nominal or usual price (cf. PREMIUM), (fig.) depreciated, not in demand; **~ shop** etc., one that sells goods at less than normal retail price. [f. obs. F *descompte, -conte* (as foll.)]
dĭscou'nt² *v.t.* Give or get present worth of (bill not yet due); disregard or disbelieve partly or wholly; lessen, detract from; reduce effect of (event etc.) by previous action; hence ~ABLE *a.* [f. obs. F *descompter* or f. It. *(di)scontare* (as DIS-, COUNT²)]
dĭscou'ntėnance *v.t.* Refuse to countenance; discourage, show disapproval of. [f. DIS- + COUNTENANCE¹]
dĭscou'rage (-kŭ'-) *v.t.* Deprive of courage, confidence, or energy; dissuade *from*; show disapproval of; so ~MENT (-rĭjm-) *n.* [ME, f. OF *descouragier* (as DIS-, COURAGE)]
dĭ'scourse¹ (-ôrs) *n.* (literary). Talk, conversation; dissertation, treatise, sermon. [ME, f. L DIS(*cursus* COURSE¹)]
dĭscour'se² (-ôr's) *v.i.* Talk, converse; speak or write at length on a subject (*of*, *(up)on*, or abs.); (arch.) give forth (music etc.). [f. prec., partly after F *discourir*]
dĭscour'tėous *a.*, **dĭscour'tesy̆** *n.*, (-kêr'-). Impolite(ness), rude(ness); hence **dĭscour'tėous**LY² (-kêr'-) *adv.* [f. DIS- + COURTEOUS, COURTESY]
dĭsco'ver (-kŭ'-) *v.t.* **1.** Expose to view, reveal; make known; exhibit, manifest; (arch.) disclose, betray; (Chess) give (check) by removing one's own obstructing man. **2.** Find out (fact etc., *that* etc., unknown country); become aware *that*. **3.** Hence ~ABLE *a.*, ~ER¹ *n.* [ME, f. OF *descovrir* f. LL DIS(*cooperire* COVER¹)]
dĭsco'very̆ (-kŭ'-) *n.* Revealing, disclosure; (Law) compulsory disclosure, by party to action, of facts or documents on which he relies; finding out, making known; thing found out. [f. prec., after *recover, recovery*]
dĭscrĕ'dĭt¹ *n.* Loss of repute (*bring discredit on*; *bring into discredit*); person or thing causing loss of repute; doubt, lack of credibility, (*throws discredit on*); loss of commercial credit. [f. DIS- + CREDIT¹]
dĭscrĕ'dĭt² *v.t.* Refuse to believe; bring disrepute to; cause to be disbelieved. [f. DIS- + CREDIT²]
dĭscrĕ'dĭtab|le *a.* Bringing discredit, shameful; hence ~LY² *adv.* [f. DIS- + CREDITABLE]
dĭscree't *a.* (**~er, ~est**). Judicious, prudent; circumspect in speech or action; unobtrusive;

For other words in *dis-* see DIS-.

hence ~LY² *adv.* [ME, f. OF *discret -ete* f. L DIS(*cretus* p.p. of *cernere* sift) separate, w. LL sense f. its derivative *discretio* discernment]

discrĕ'p|ant *a.* Differing, inconsistent; so ~ANCY *n.* [f. L DIS(*crepare* creak); see -ANT]

discrē'te *a.* Separate, individually distinct, discontinuous; hence ~LY² (-tlĭ) *adv.*, ~NESS (-tn-) *n.* [ME, f. L *discretus*; see DISCREET]

discrĕ'tion *n.* **1.** Liberty of deciding as one thinks fit, absolutely or within limits, (**use** one's ~, make such decision; *it is within* one's *discretion to*; **at the ~ of,** to be settled or disposed of according to the judgement or choice of; **at ~,** as one pleases); (Law) court's degree of freedom to decide sentence etc.; hence ~ARY¹ *a.* **2.** Discernment, prudence, judgement, (**years** or **age of ~,** age at which one is fit to manage one's own affairs). [ME f. OF, f. L *discretio -onis* (as DISCREET; see -ION)]

discrĭ'mĭn|āte *v.t.* & *i.* Be, set up, or act on the basis of, a difference between or *between*, distinguish *from* another; make a distinction, esp. on grounds of race or colour, (**~ate against,** select for unfavourable treatment by taxation etc.); observe distinctions carefully, have good judgement; so ~A'TION *n.*, ~ATIVE, ~**at**ORY, *adjs.* [f. L *discriminare* (*discrimen -minis* distinction f. *discernere* DISCERN) + -ATE³]

discrĭ'mĭnātĭng *a.* In vbl senses; discerning, acute; hence ~LY² *adv.* [f. prec. + -ING²]

discrow'n *v.t.* Take crown from, depose (sovereign; lit. or fig.). [f. DIS- + CROWN¹,²]

discûr'sĭve *a.* Rambling, digressive, expatiating; proceeding by argument or reasoning, not intuitive; hence ~LY² (-vlĭ) *adv.*, ~NESS (-vn-) *n.* [f. med. L *discursivus* f. L DIS(*currere curs-* run); see -IVE]

dĭ'scus *n.* Heavy thick-centred disc thrown in ancient and modern athletic sports. [L, f. Gk *diskos*]

discŭ'ss *v.t.* Examine by argument, debate, whence ~ANT *n.*; hold conversation about; (arch.) consume (food, wine, meal) with leisurely enjoyment; hence ~ABLE, ~IBLE, *adjs.* [ME, f. L DIS(*cutere cuss-* = *quatere* shake) disperse]

discŭ'ssion (-sh*o*n) *n.* Examination by argument; a debate; a conversation; (arch.) consumption *of* food etc. with leisurely enjoyment. [ME f. OF, f. LL *discussio -onis* (as prec.; see -ION)]

disdai'n *n.*, & *v.t.* **1.** *n.* Scorn, contempt. **2.** *v.t.* Regard with disdain; think beneath oneself or one's notice (thing, *to* do, do*ing*). [ME, f. OF *desdeign*(*ier*) f. Rom. **disdignare* f. L DE(*dignari* f. *dignus* worthy)]

disdai'nful *a.* Showing disdain, scornful, contemptuous; hence ~LY² *adv.*, ~NESS *n.* [f. prec. + -FUL]

disea'se (-zē'z) *n.* Unhealthy condition of body, mind, plant, or some part thereof, illness, sickness; particular kind of this with special symptoms or location. [ME, f. OF *desaise* (as DIS-, EASE¹)]

disea'sed (-zē'zd) *a.* Affected with disease; abnormal, disordered. [ME, p.p. of *disease* v. f. OF *desaaisier* (as prec.)]

disėcŏ'nomў *n.* Absence or reverse of economy, increase of costs, esp. in large-scale operation. [f. DIS- + ECONOMY]

disėmbâr'k *v.t.* & *i.* Put or go ashore from ship; hence **disėmbârk**A'TION *n.* [f. F *désembarquer* (as DIS-, EMBARK)]

disėmbă'rrass *v.t.* Free from embarrassment, rid or relieve (*of*); hence ~MENT *n.* [f. DIS- + EMBARRASS]

disėmbŏ'd|ў *v.t.* Separate, free, (soul, idea, etc.) from body or the concrete form; (arch.) disband (troops); hence ~ĭMENT *n.* [f. DIS- + EMBODY]

disėmbō'gue (-g) *v.i.* & *t.* (Of river etc.) pour (*itself*) forth at mouth; (fig.) discharge, pour forth. [f. Sp. *desembocar* (as DIS-, *en* in, *boca* mouth)]

disėmbow'el *v.t.* (‖-ll-). Remove entrails of; rip up so as to cause bowels to protrude; hence ~MENT *n.* [f. DIS- 'utterly' + EMBOWEL]

disėmbroi'l *v.t.* Extricate from confusion or entanglement. [f. DIS- + EMBROIL]

disėncha'nt (-ah'-) *v.t.* Free from enchantment or illusion; hence ~MENT *n.* [f. F *désenchanter* (as DIS-, ENCHANT)]

disėncŭ'mber (-n-k-) *v.t.* Free from encumbrance. [f. DIS- + ENCUMBER]

disėndow' *v.t.* Strip (esp. Church) of endowments; hence ~MENT *n.* [f. DIS- + ENDOW]

disėnfră'nchise (-z) *v.t.* Disfranchise. [f. DIS- + ENFRANCHISE]

disėngā'ge (-n-g-) *v.* & *n.* **1.** *v.t.* Detach, liberate, loosen; remove (troops) from (area of) fighting. **2.** *v.i.* Become detached; (Fencing) pass point of sword to other side of opponent's. **3.** *n.* Fencer's movement to disengage. [f. DIS- + ENGAGE]

disėngā'ged (-n-gā'jd) *a.* In vbl senses; at leisure to attend to any visitor or business that comes; vacant, not bespoken; uncommitted. [p.p. of prec.]

disėngā'gement (-n-gā'jm-) *n.* Disengaging; freedom from ties, detachment; ease of manner or behaviour; dissolution of engagement to marry; (Fencing) = DISENGAGE. [f. DISENGAGE + -MENT]

disėntai'l *v.t.* (Law). Free from entail, break the entail of. [f. DIS- + ENTAIL²]

disėntă'ngle (-ngg*e*l) *v.* **1.** *v.t.* Extricate, free from complications; unravel, untwist; hence ~MENT *n.* **2.** *v.i.* Become disentangled. [f. DIS- + ENTANGLE]

disėnthra'l, *-ll, (-aw'l) *v.t.* (-ll-). Free from enthralment; hence **disėnthra'l(l)**MENT (-aw'l-) *n.* [f. DIS- + ENTHRAL]

disėnto'mb (-ōō'm) *v.t.* Remove from tomb, disinter; unearth; hence ~MENT (-m-m-) *n.* [f. DIS- + ENTOMB]

disēquilĭ'brĭum *n.* Lack or loss of equilibrium, instability. [f. DIS- + EQUILIBRIUM]

disėstă'blish *v.t.* Terminate establishment of; deprive (Church) of State connection; depose from official position; hence ~MENT *n.* [f. DIS- + ESTABLISH]

diseur (dēzer') *n.* (*fem.* ***diseuse*** *pr.* dēzer'z). Artiste entertaining with spoken monologue. [F, = talker (*dire dis-* say)]

disfā'vour (-v*e*r), ***disfā'vor,** *n.*, & *v.t.* **1.** *n.* Dislike, disapproval; being disliked (*fall into, be in, disfavour*). **2.** *v.t.* Regard or treat with disfavour. [f. DIS- + FAVOUR¹,²]

disfĭ'gure (-g*e*r) *v.t.* Spoil beauty of, deform, deface; hence ~MENT *n.* [ME, f. OF *desfigurer* f. Rom. *DIS*figurare* (L *figura* FIGURE¹)]

disfŏ'rėst *v.t.* = DISAFFOREST; clear of forests. [f. AL **disforestare* (as DIS-, *foresta* FOREST)]

disfră'nchise (-z) *v.t.* Deprive of rights as citizen or of franchise held; deprive (place) of right of sending, (person) of right of voting for, parliamentary representative; hence ~MENT (-zm-) *n.* [ME, f. DIS- + obs. *franchise* = enfranchise]

disfrŏ'ck *v.t.* Unfrock. [f. DIS- + FROCK]

disgôr'ge *v.t.* Eject (as) from throat (what has been swallowed, lit. or fig., esp. wrongfully taken, or abs.); (of river etc.) discharge (waters, or abs.). [ME, f. OF *desgorger* (as DIS-, GORGE¹)]

disgrā'ce¹ *n.* Loss of favour or respect, downfall from position of honour, ignominy, shame, (*is in disgrace*); thing or person involving dishonour, cause of reproach. [f. F *disgrâce* f. It. *disgrazia* (as DIS-, GRACE)]

dĭsgrā′ce² *v.t.* Dismiss from favour, degrade from position of honour; bring shame or discredit on, be a disgrace to. [f. F *disgracier* f. It. *disgraziare* (as prec.)]

dĭsgrā′ceful (-sf-) *a.* Shameful, dishonourable; degrading; hence ~LY² *adv.*, ~NESS *n.* [f. DISGRACE¹ + -FUL]

dĭsgrŭ′ntle|d (-teld) *a.* Discontented, moody, sulky; hence ~MENT *n.* [f. DIS- + *gruntle* obs. frequent. of GRUNT]

dĭsguī′se¹ (-gī′z) *v.t.* Conceal identity of (*disguise oneself*, person or thing, *as* someone or something else, *with* false beard etc.); misrepresent, show in false colours; conceal, cover up, (*disguise* one's *intentions, opinion*); hence ~MENT *n.* [ME, f. OF *desguis(i)er* (as DIS-, Rom. **guisa* GUISE)]

dĭsguī′se² (-gī′z) *n.* (Use of) changed dress or appearance for concealment or deception; disguised condition (BLESSING *in disguise*). [ME, f. prec.]

dĭsgŭ′st¹ *n.* Repugnance, strong aversion, indignation, (*at, for*); **in ~,** as a result of such feeling (*I left in disgust*). [f. OF *degoust* f. *desgouster*, or f. It. *disgusto* f. *disgustare* (as DIS-, GUSTO)]

dĭsgŭ′st² *v.t.* Cause disgust in (*disgusted with, at, by*). [f. OF *desgouster* or It. *disgustare* (see prec.)]

dĭsgŭ′stful *a.* Disgusting, repulsive; (of curiosity etc.) caused by disgust. [f. DISGUST¹ + -FUL]

dĭsh¹ *n.* **1.** Shallow usu. flat-bottomed vessel of earthenware, glass, metal, etc., for holding food at meals or for cooking. **2.** Food so held, particular kind of food (MADE *dish*, SIDE¹-*dish*); (colloq.) attractive person, esp. woman; (sl.) thing that suits one's taste etc. **3.** ‖(arch.) Cup, esp. **~ of tea,** cup of tea, tea-drinking. **4.** Dish-shaped receptacle, object, or cavity; concave aerial for microwaves. **5. ~′cloth, ~′rag,** (for washing dishes and plates); **~cloth gourd,** loofah; **~-cover** (of metal etc. for keeping food in dish hot); **~′washer,** (1) water wagtail, (Austral.) restless flycatcher, (2) machine for automatically washing dishes etc.; **~-water** (in which dishes have been washed). [OE *disc* plate, bowl, = OS *disk*, OHG *tisc*, ON *tiskr* f. L *discus* DISC]

dĭsh² *v.t.* **1.** Put (food) into dish ready for serving; circumvent, outmanœuvre; **~ out,** (sl.) distribute, esp. carelessly or indiscriminately; **~ up,** dish (food), prepare to serve (meal, or abs.), (fig.) present (facts, argument) attractively. **2.** Make concave or dish-shaped. [f. prec.]

dĭshabi′lle (-sabē′l). Var. of DÉSHABILLÉ.

dĭshar′mon|ȳ (-s-h-) *n.* Lack of harmony; discord; so **dĭsharmō′nĭ**OUS (-s-h-) *a.*, ~IZE (1) *v.t.* [f. DIS- + HARMONY]

dĭshear′ten (-s-har′-) *v.t.* Make despondent, cause to lose courage or confidence; hence ~MENT *n.* [f. DIS- + HEARTEN]

‖**dĭshĕ′velled, *-veled,** (-ld) *a.* (Of hair) loose, disordered; (of person) untidy, ruffled; hence **dĭshĕ′vel**MENT *n.* [ME *dischevelee*, f. OF *deschevelé* p.p. (as DIS-, *chevel* hair f. L *capillus*) + -ED¹]

dĭshŏ′nėst (-sŏ′-) *a.* (Of person, act, statement) fraudulent, insincere; hence ~LY² *adv.* [ME, f. OF *deshoneste* (as DIS-, HONEST)]

dĭshŏ′nėstȳ (-sŏ′-) *n.* Lack of honesty; deceitfulness, fraud. [ME, f. OF *deshon(n)esté* (as prec.; see -Y¹)]

dĭshŏ′nour¹, ***dĭshŏ′nor**¹, (-sŏ′ner) *n.* State of shame or disgrace, discredit; thing that causes such state. [ME, f. OF *deshonor* f. Rom. *DIS-(*honor* HONOUR¹)]

dĭshŏ′nour², ***dĭshŏ′nor**², (-sŏ′ner) *v.t.* Treat without honour or respect; (arch.) violate chastity of; disgrace; refuse to accept or pay (cheque, bill of exchange). [ME, f. OF *deshonorer* f. med. L DIS(*honorare* HONOUR²)]

dĭshŏ′nourab|le, *-nor-, (-sŏ′ner-) *a.* Causing disgrace, ignominious; unprincipled, base, against dictates of honour; hence ~**le**NESS (-beln-) *n.*, ~LY² *adv.* [f. prec. + -ABLE or DIS- + HONOURABLE]

dĭshor′n (-s-h-) *v.t.* Dehorn. [f. DIS- + HORN¹]

dĭ′shȳ *a.* (sl.) Very attractive. [f. DISH¹ 2 'attractive person' + -Y²]

dĭsillū′sion (-zhon; *or* -lōō′-) *n.*, & *v.t.* Disenchant(ment), free(dom) from illusions; hence ~MENT *n.* [f. DIS- + ILLUSION]

dĭsincĕ′ntive *a.* & *n.* (Thing) that tends to discourage a particular (esp. economic) action etc. [f. DIS- + INCENTIVE]

dĭsinclĭnā′tion (-n-k-) *n.* Absence of liking or willingness (*for* course of action, *to* do). [f. DIS- + INCLINATION]

dĭsinclī′ne (-n-k-) *v.t.* Make unwilling (*to* do, *for* course of action). [f. DIS- + INCLINE¹]

dĭsincor′porāte (-n-k-) *v.t.* Dissolve (corporate body). [f. DIS- + INCORPORATE]

dĭsinfĕ′ct *v.t.* Cleanse (room, clothes, etc.) of infection; hence or cogn. **dĭsinfĕ′ct**ANT *a.* & *n.*, **dĭsinfĕ′ct**ION *n.* [f. F *désinfecter* (as DIS-, INFECT)]

dĭsinfĕ′st *v.t.* Rid (person, building, etc.) of infesting insects, vermin, etc.; so ~A′TION *n.* [f. DIS- + INFEST]

dĭsinflā′tion *n.* (Econ.) Policy designed to counteract inflation without producing disadvantages of deflation; hence ~ARY¹ *a.* [f. DIS- + INFLATION]

dĭsingĕ′nūous (-nj-) *a.* Insincere, having secret motives, not candid; hence ~LY² *adv.*, ~NESS *n.* [f. DIS- + INGENUOUS]

dĭsinhĕ′rĭt *v.t.* Reject as one's heir, deprive of right of inheritance; hence ~ANCE *n.* [ME, f. DIS- + INHERIT in obs. sense 'make heir']

dĭsĭ′ntėgr|āte *v.t.* & *i.* Separate into component parts or fragments; deprive of or lose cohesion; (Phys.) (cause to) undergo disintegration; hence ~A′TION *n.*, (e.g., Phys.) process in which nucleus emits particle(s) or divides into smaller nuclei, **~āt**OR *n.* [f. DIS- + INTEGRATE²]

dĭsinter′ *v.t.* (-rr-). Remove (buried object, corpse, etc.) from ground; unearth (lit. or fig.); hence ~MENT *n.* [f. F *desenterrer* (as DIS-, INTER¹)]

dĭsĭ′nterėst (*or* -tr-) *n.* Absence of interest, unconcern. [f. DIS- + INTEREST¹]

dĭsĭ′nterėstėd (*or* -tr-) *a.* Not influenced by one's own advantage, impartial; (colloq.) uninterested; hence ~LY² *adv.*, ~NESS *n.* [p.p. of *disinterest* v. divest of interest]

dĭsinvĕ′stment *n.* Realization of invested assets of a person, institution, etc. [f. DIS- + INVESTMENT]

disjecta membra (dĭsjĕkta mĕ′mbra) *n. pl.* Fragments, scattered remains. [L, alt. of Horace's *disjecti membra poetae* limbs of a dismembered poet]

dĭsjoi′n *v.t.* Separate, disunite, part. [ME, f. OF *desjoindre* f. L DIS(*jungere junct-* join)]

dĭsjoi′nt *v.t.* Dislocate, disturb working or connection of; (in *p.p.*, esp. of talk) incoherent, desultory; take to pieces at the joints. [ME, f. obs. *disjoint* adj. f. p.p. of OF *desjoindre*, as prec.]

dĭsjŭ′nction *n.* Disjoining, separation. [ME f. OF, or f. L *disjunctio* (as DISJOIN; see -ION)]

dĭsjŭ′nctive *a.* Disjoining, involving separation; (Logic, of proposition) expressing an alternative; (Gram.) expressing choice between two words etc. (cf. COPULATIVE); hence ~LY² (-vlĭ) *adv.* [ME, f. L *disjunctivus* (as DISJOIN; see -IVE)]

For other words in *dis-* see DIS-.

dĭsk. See DISC.

dĭslī'ke *v.t.*, & *n.* **1.** *v.t.* Not like, have aversion or objection to, (do*ing*, person, thing). **2.** *n.* Feeling that thing etc. is unattractive, unpleasant, etc.; object of this. [f. DIS- + LIKE²]

dĭ'slocāte *v.t.* Disturb normal connection of (esp. joint in the body); put (machinery, affairs) out of order or normal course; (Geol.) make (strata) discontinuous; displace. [prob. back form. f. foll.]

dĭslocā'tion *n.* Act or result of dislocating; (Phys.) displacement of crystal lattice structure. [ME f. OF, or f. med. L *dislocatio* f. DIS(*locare* place); see -ATION]

dĭslŏ'dge *v.t.* Remove from established or fixed position; hence ~MENT, **dĭslŏ'dg**MENT, (-jm-) *n.* [ME, f. OF *dislog(i)er* (as DIS-, LODGE²)]

dĭsloy'al *a.* Unfaithful to or *to* friend(ship) etc.; untrue to allegiance, disaffected to government, whence ~IST (2) *n.*; hence or cogn. ~LY² *adv.*, ~TY¹ *n.* [ME, f. OF *desloial* (as DIS-, LOYAL)]

dĭ'smal (-z-) *a.* Causing or showing gloom, miserable, sombre, dreary; (colloq.) feeble, inept; ~ **science,** (arch.) economics; **the ~s,** melancholy; hence ~LY² *adv.*, ~NESS *n.* [orig. n. = unlucky days, ME f. AF *dis mal* f. med. L *dies mali* two days in each month held to be unpropitious]

dĭsmă'ntle *v.t.* Strip *of* covering, protection, etc.; pull down, take to pieces; deprive of defences, equipment, etc.; hence ~MENT (-telm-) *n.* [f. OF *desmanteler* (as DIS-, MANTLE¹)]

dĭsma'st (-ah'-) *v.t.* Remove mast(s) from (ship). [f. DIS- + MAST¹]

dĭsmay' *v.t.*, & *n.* (Fill with) consternation, discourage(ment), (reduce to) despair. [ME, f. OF **de(s)maier* f. Rom. **dismagare* make powerless f. as DIS- + Gmc **mag-* be able; cf. MAY¹]

dĭsmĕ'mber *v.t.* Tear or cut limbs from; partition (empire, country), divide up; hence ~MENT *n.* [ME, f. OF *desmembrer* f. Rom. **desmembrare* f. as DIS- + L *membrum* limb]

dĭsmĭ'ss *v.t.* **1.** Send away, disperse, disband, (assembly, army); (Mil. in *imper.*) word of command at end of drilling; allow to go. **2.** Send away (esp. dishonourably) from service or office (*was dismissed the*, or *from the, army*); send away from one's presence. **3.** Put out of one's thoughts, cease to feel or discuss; treat (subject) summarily; (Law) send out of court, refuse further hearing to, (case); (Cricket) put (batsman, side) out (usu. *for* score). **4.** Hence ~AL 2 *n.*, ~IBLE, ~IVE, *adjs.*, ~ION (-sh*o*n) *n.* [ME, orig. as p.p. after OF *desmis* f. med. L *dismissus* (DIS-, L *mittere miss-* send)]

dĭsmou'nt *v.i.* & *t.* (Cause to) alight or fall from or *from* horseback etc.; remove (thing) from its mount (esp. gun from carriage). [f. DIS- + MOUNT²]

Dĭsneyĕ'sque (dĭznĭĕ'sk) *a.* Like the animated cartoons of Disney. [f. W. E. *Disney*, Amer. cartoonist d. 1966 + -ESQUE]

dĭsobē'dĭ|ent *a.* Disobeying (**~ent to** orders, master, etc.); rebellious, rule-breaking; so ~ENCE *n.* (CIVIL *disobedience*), **~ent**LY² *adv.* [ME, f. OF *desobedient* (as DIS-, OBEDIENT)]

dĭsobey' (-bā') *v.t.* Disregard (orders), break (rules); fail or refuse to obey (person, law, etc., or abs.). [ME, f. OF *desobeir* f. Rom. **desobedire* (as DIS-, OBEY)]

dĭsoblī'ge *v.t.* Refuse to consider convenience or wishes of. [f. F *désobliger* f. Rom. **desobligare* (as DIS-, OBLIGE)]

dĭsŏr'der¹ *n.* Lack of order, confusion; tumult, riot, commotion; disturbance of normal state of body, organ, etc., ailment, disease. [f. foll.]

dĭsŏr'der² *v.t.* Disarrange, throw into confusion; put out of good health, upset. [ME assim. to ORDER² of earlier *disordain* f. OF *desordener* (as DIS-, ORDAIN)]

dĭsŏr'derl|ȳ *a.* **1.** Untidy, confused; irregular, unruly, riotous; hence ~**ĭ**NESS *n.* **2.** Contrary to public order or morality (**~y house,** brothel). [f. DISORDER¹ + -LY¹]

dĭsŏr'ganiz|e, -is|e (-īz), *v.t.* Destroy system, order, etc. of; throw into confusion; (in *p.p.*) lacking organization or system; so ~A'TION *n.* [f. F *désorganiser* (as DIS-, ORGANIZE)]

dĭsŏr'ient (*or* -ŏ'r-) *v.t.* = foll. [f. F *désorienter* (as DIS-, ORIENT²)]

dĭsŏ'rient|āte (*or* -ŏr'-) *v.t.* Confuse (person) as to his bearings or (fig.) sense of what is correct; hence ~A'TION *n.* [f. DIS- + ORIENTATE]

dĭsow'n (-ō'n) *v.t.* Refuse to recognize, repudiate, disclaim; renounce connection with or allegiance to; hence ~ER⁴ *n.* [f. DIS- + OWN²]

dĭspă'rage *v.t.* Bring discredit on; speak slightingly of, depreciate; so ~MENT (-ĭjm-) *n.* [ME, f. OF *desparagier* marry unequally (as DIS-, *parage* equality of rank f. Rom. **paraticum* f. L *par* equal; see -AGE)]

dĭ'sparate *a.* & *n.* **1.** Essentially different, diverse in kind, incommensurable, without comparison or relation; hence ~LY² (-tlĭ) *adv.*, ~NESS (-tn-) *n.* **2.** *n.* (in *pl.*) Things so unlike that there is no basis for their comparison. [f. L DIS(*paratus* p.p. of *parare* prepare) separated, infl. in sense by L *dispar* unequal]

dĭspă'rĭtȳ *n.* Inequality, difference, incongruity. [f. F *disparité* f. LL *disparitas -tatis* (as DIS-, PARITY)]

dĭspar'k *v.t.* Convert (parkland) to other uses. [f. DIS- + PARK¹]

dĭspar't *v.t.* & *i.* (arch.) Separate, divide. [f. It. or f. L *dispartire* (as DIS-, PART²)]

dĭspă'ssionate (-sh*o*-) *a.* Free from emotion, calm, impartial; hence ~LY² (-tlĭ) *adv.*, ~NESS (-tn-) *n.* [f. DIS- + PASSIONATE]

dĭspă'tch¹, dėspă'tch¹, *v.t.* Send off to a destination or for a purpose; give the death-blow to, kill; get (task, business) promptly done, settle, finish off; eat (food, meal) quickly; hence ~ER¹ *n.*, (esp.) one who gives orders for departure of goods, vehicles, etc. [f. It. *dispacciare* or Sp. *despachar* expedite (as DIS-, It. *impacciare* and Sp. *empachar* hinder, of uncert. orig.)]

dĭspă'tch², dėspă'tch², *n.* **1.** Sending off (of messenger, letter, etc.); putting to death (**happy ~**, hara-kiri); prompt settlement of business, promptitude, efficiency, rapidity. **2.** Written message, esp. official communication on State or military affairs (**mention in ~es,** distinction given by having one's actions etc. commended in these; **~-box, ~-case,** container for carrying these or other documents; **~-rider,** esp. motor-cyclist or horseman carrying military messages). [f. prec., or It. *dispaccio*, Sp. *despacho*, as prec.]

dĭspĕ'l *v.t.* (-**ll**-). Dissipate, disperse, scatter, (suspicions, fears, darkness). [f. L DIS(*pellere* drive)]

dĭspĕ'nsable *a.* Not necessary, that can be done without; (of law etc.) that can be relaxed in special cases. [f. med. L *dispensabilis* (as DISPENSE; see -ABLE)]

dĭspĕ'nsarȳ *n.* Place where medicines etc. are dispensed; public or charitable institution for medical advice and dispensing. [f. med. L *dispensarius* (as DISPENSE; see -ARY¹)]

dĭspĕnsā'tion *n.* **1.** Distributing, dealing out. **2.** Ordering, management, esp. of the world by Providence; arrangement made by Nature or Providence; special dealing of Providence with community or person; religious system regarded as divinely ordained for a nation or period (*Mosaic, Christian, dispensation*). **3.** Exemption *from* penalty or duty; ~ **with,** doing without.

[ME f. OF, or f. L *dispensatio* (as foll.; see -ATION)]

dĭspĕ'ns|e *v.* **1.** *v.t.* Distribute, deal out; administer (sacrament, justice); make up (and give out) (medicine etc.) according to prescription (**~ing chemist,** one qualified to do this); hence ~ER[1] *n.*, (esp.) person who dispenses something, device that dispenses a selected quantity at a time. **2.** Grant dispensation to (person *from* obligation). **3.** *v.i.* **~e with,** relax, give exemption from, (rule), render needless (usu. *the need of* or *for* etc.), do without. [ME, f. OF *despenser* f. L *dispensare* frequent. of DIS- (*pendĕre pens-* weigh) weigh or pay out]

dĭspeo'ple (-pē'p-) *v.t.* Depopulate. [ME, f. OF *despeupler* (as DIS-, PEOPLE)]

dĭspêr's|e *v.* **1.** *v.t.* & *i.* Scatter; drive, go, throw or send, in different directions. **2.** *v.t.* Send to or station at separate points; put in circulation, disseminate; (Phys.) distribute (small particles) uniformly in fluid (whence ~ANT *n.*), divide (white light) into its coloured constituents. **3.** Hence ~AL 2 *n.*, ~IVE *a.* [ME, f. L DI[1](*spergere spers-* = *spargere* scatter)]

dĭspêr'sion (-shon) *n.* Dispersing; **the D~**, the Jews dispersed among Gentiles after Captivity; (Phys.) mixture of one substance dispersed in another, separation of white light into colours or of any radiation according to wavelength etc.; (Statistics) extent to which values of a variable differ from the mean. [ME, f. LL *dispersio* (as prec.; see -ION) transl. Gk DIASPORA]

dĭspĭ'rĭt *v.t.* (esp. in *p.p.*) Make despondent, deject. [f. DIS- + SPIRIT[1]]

dĭsplā'ce *v.t.* **1.** Shift from its place (**~d person,** one who has had to leave his home country as a result of war, persecution, etc.); remove from office. **2.** Oust, take the place of, put something else in the place of. [f. DIS- + PLACE[1,2] or obs. F *desplacer*]

dĭsplā'cement (-sm-) *n.* **1.** Displacing or being displaced; amount by which thing is shifted from its place. **2.** Ousting, replacement by something else; (Psych.) substitution of one idea or impulse for another, unconscious transfer of strong unacceptable emotions. **3.** Amount or weight of fluid displaced by solid floating or immersed in it (*a ship with a displacement of 11,000* TON[1]*s*). [f. prec. + -MENT]

dĭsplay'[1] *v.t.* Exhibit, expose to view, show; show ostentatiously; reveal, betray, allow to appear; present as a display (see foll.). [ME, f. OF *despleier* f. L DIS(*plicare* fold); cf. DEPLOY]

dĭsplay'[2] *n.* Displaying; exhibition, show, (*is on display*); ostentation; (Print.) arrangement and choice of type with a view to calling attention; presentation of signals or data on screen of cathode-ray tube etc.; bird's special pattern of behaviour as means of visual communication [f. prec.]

dĭsplea's|e (-z) *v.t.* Offend, annoy, make indignant or angry, be disagreeable to; **be ~ed** (*at, with*, or abs.), disapprove, be indignant or dissatisfied; hence ~ING[2] *a.* (*to*). [ME, f. OF *desplaisir* (as DIS-, L *placēre* please)]

dĭsplea'sure (-lĕ'zher) *n.*, & *v.t.* **1.** *n.* Displeased feeling, dissatisfaction, disapproval, anger. **2.** *v.t.* (arch.) Cause displeasure to, annoy. [ME, f. OF as prec., assim. to PLEASURE]

dĭspôr't *v.* & *n.* (literary). **1.** *v.i.* & *refl.* Frolic, gambol, enjoy one*self*. **2.** *n.* Relaxation, pastime. [ME, f. AF *desporter* v., OF *desport* n. f. *desporter* (as DIS-, *porter* carry f. L *portare*)]

dĭspō's|able (-za-) *a.* & *n.* **1.** *a.* That can be disposed of, got rid of, made over, or used; at one's disposal; that is designed to be thrown away after one use; hence ~ABI'LITY *n.* **2.** *n.* Article that is disposable (esp. in last sense). [f. DISPOSE + -ABLE]

dĭspō'sal (-zal) *n.* Disposing *of*, getting rid *of*; settling, dealing with; bestowal, assignment; sale; control, management, (**at** one's ~, available for one's use, subject to one's orders or decisions); placing, disposition, arrangement. [f. foll. + -AL 2]

dĭspō'se (-z) *v.* **1.** *v.t.* Place suitably, at intervals, or in order; bring (person, mind) into certain state (esp. in *pass.*, have a specified tendency of mind: *be well* or *ill disposed*); incline, make willing or desirous, *to* something or *to* do; give (thing) tendency *to*. **2.** *v.i.* Determine course of events (*man proposes, God disposes*); ~ **of,** do what one will with, get rid of, sell, settle, finish, kill, prove (claim, argument, opponent) to be incorrect, consume (food). [ME, f. OF DIS(*poser*; see POSE[1]), confused with L *disponere* thr. such derivs. as foll.]

dĭsposĭ'tion (-zĭ'-) *n.* Setting in order, arrangement, relative position of parts; (usu. in *pl.*) plan, preparations, stationing of troops ready for attack, defence, etc.; ordinance, dispensation, (*a disposition of Providence* etc.); bestowal by deed or will; control, disposal; bent, temperament, natural tendency; inclination *to*. [ME f. OF, f. L DIS(*positio -onis* f. *ponere posit-* place)]

dĭspossĕ'ss (-oz-) *v.t.* Oust, dislodge, (person); deprive *of*; hence **dĭspossĕ'ss**ION (-zĕ'shon) *n.* [f. OF *despossesser* (as DIS-, POSSESS)]

dĭsprai'se (-z) *v.t.*, & *n.* Disparage(ment), censure. [ME; n. f. DIS- + PRAISE or v., f. OF *despreisier* f. Rom. ***despretiare* f. LL *depretiare* DEPRECIATE]

dĭsprōō'f *n.* Refutation; thing that disproves. [f. DIS- + PROOF[1]]

dĭspropôr'tion *n.* Lack of proportion; being out of proportion. [f. DIS- + PROPORTION]

dĭspropôr'tionate *a.* Lacking proportion; relatively too large or small; hence ~LY[2] (-tlĭ) *adv.* [f. DIS- + PROPORTIONATE]

dĭspro've (-ōō'v) *v.t.* Prove false, show fallacy of, refute. [ME, f. OF *desprover* (as DIS-, PROVE)]

dĭspū'tab|le (*or* dĭ'-) *a.* Open to question, uncertain; hence ~LY[2] *adv.* [F, or f. L *disputabilis* (as DISPUTE[1]; see -ABLE)]

dĭspūtā't|ion *n.* Argument, controversy; debate; formal attack on and defence of set question or thesis; hence ~IOUS (-sh*us*) *a.*, fond of argument. [ME f. F, or f. L *disputatio* (as foll.; see -ATION)]

dĭspū'te[1] *v.* **1.** *v.i.* Argue, hold disputation, (*with, against*, person; *on, about*, subject), whence **dĭspū't**ANT *n.*; quarrel, have altercation. **2.** *v.t.* Discuss esp. heatedly (*whether, how*, etc.; point, question); controvert, call in question, (statement, fact); resist (landing, advance, etc.); contend for, strive to win, (pre-eminence, possession, victory, ground fought over). [ME, f. OF *desputer* f. L DIS(*putare* reckon) estimate]

dĭspū'te[2] (*or* dĭ'-) *n.* Controversy, debate, (**in ~**, being argued about; **beyond, past, without,** ~, certainly, indisputably); heated contention, quarrel, difference of opinion. [f. prec.]

dĭsqualĭfĭcā'tion (-ŏl-) *n.* In vbl senses; thing that disqualifies. [f. foll. + -FICATION]

dĭsqua'lĭfȳ (-ŏ'l-) *v.t.* Make unfit, disable, (*for* some purpose or office); incapacitate legally, pronounce unqualified; debar from competition because of infringement of rules. [f. DIS- + QUALIFY]

dĭsquī'et *v.t.*, & *n.* **1.** *v.t.* Deprive of peace; worry. **2.** *n.* Anxiety, unrest. [f. DIS- + QUIET[1,3]]

dĭsquī'ètūde *n.* State of uneasiness, anxiety. [f. *disquiet* adj. (DIS-, QUIET[2]) + -TUDE]

For other words in *dis-* see DIS-.

dĭsquĭsĭ'tion (-zĭ'-) *n.* Long or elaborate treatise or discourse on subject; hence ~AL *a.* [F, f. L DIS(*quisitio* f. *-quirere -quisit-* = *quaerere* seek; see -ION)]

dĭsrā'te *v.t.* Reduce (sailor) to lower rating or rank. [f. DIS- + RATE[1]]

dĭsrėgar'd *v.t.*, & *n.* **1.** *v.t.* Pay no attention to, ignore, treat as of no importance. **2.** *n.* Indifference, neglect (*of, for*); hence ~FUL *a.* [f. DIS- + REGARD[1,2]]

dĭsrĕ'lĭsh *n.*, & *v.t.* Dislike, (regard with) distaste. [f. DIS- + RELISH[1,2]]

dĭsrėmĕ'mber *v.t.* & *i.* (esp. dial.) Fail to remember. [f. DIS- + REMEMBER]

dĭsrėpair' *n.* Bad condition due to lack of repairs (*is in disrepair, in a state of disrepair*). [f. DIS- + REPAIR[3]]

dĭsrĕ'pūtab|le *a.* Discreditable; of bad repute, not respectable in character or appearance; hence ~**le**NESS (-beln-) *n.*, ~LY[2] *adv.* [f. DIS- + REPUTABLE, after foll.]

dĭsrėpū'te *n.* Lack of good repute, discredit. [f. DIS- + REPUTE]

dĭsrėspĕ'ct *n.* Lack of respect; discourtesy; so ~FUL *a.* [f. DIS- + RESPECT[1]]

dĭsrō'be *v.t.* & *i.* Divest (oneself) of robe or garment (lit. or fig.); undress (oneself). [f. DIS- + ROBE]

dĭsrŭ'pt *v.t.* Shatter, separate forcibly; interrupt flow or continuity of; hence ~ION *n.* (**the D~ion,** split in Church of Scotland 1843), ~IVE *a.* [f. L DIS(*rumpere rupt-* break)]

dĭssă'tĭsfȳ *v.t.* Fail to satisfy, make discontented (*dissatisfied with* or *at*); so **dĭs**SATISFA'CTION *n.* [f. DIS- + SATISFY]

dĭssā've *v.i.* Spend more than one's income, by drawing on savings or capital. [f. DIS- + SAVE[1]]

dĭssĕ'ct *v.t.* Cut into pieces; cut up (animal, plant) to show its parts, structure, etc.; examine part by part, analyse, criticize in detail; hence or cogn. ~ION, ~OR, *ns.* [f. L DIS(*secare sect-* cut)]

dĭssei'se, -ze, (-sē'z) *v.t.* (Law). Dispossess (esp. wrongfully) *of.* [ME, f. AF *disseisir*, OF *dessaisir* dispossess (as DIS-, SEIZE)]

dĭssei'sĭn (-ē'z-) *n.* (Law). Wrongful dispossession of estates etc. [ME, f. AF *disseisine*, OF *dessaisine* (as DIS-, SEISIN)]

dĭssĕ'mbl|e *v.* **1.** *v.t.* Cloak, disguise, conceal, (character, feeling, intention, act). **2.** *v.i.* Conceal one's motives etc.; talk or act hypocritically. **3.** Hence ~ER[1] *n.* [ME, alt. after *semblance* of obs. *dissimule* f. OF *dissimuler* f. L DIS(*simulare* SIMULATE)]

dĭssĕ'mĭn|āte *v.t.* Scatter about, sow in various places, (esp. fig. of doctrines, sedition, disease, etc.); *disseminated* SCLEROSIS; hence or cogn. ~A'TION, ~**āt**OR, *ns.* [f. L DIS(*seminare* f. *semen -inis* seed) + -ATE[3]]

dĭssĕ'nsion (-shon) *n.* Discord arising from difference in opinion. [ME f. OF, f. L DIS(*sensio -onis* f. *sentire sens-* feel; see -ION)]

dĭssĕ'nt[1] *v.i.* Refuse to assent; disagree, think differently or express such difference (*from*), esp. in religious doctrine from an established, national, or orthodox church. [ME, f. L DIS(*sentire* feel)]

dĭssĕ'nt[2] *n.* (Expression of) difference of opinion; refusal to accept doctrines of established, national, or orthodox church, nonconformity. [f. prec.]

dĭssĕ'nter *n.* In vbl senses; ‖(*D~*) member of a sect that has separated itself from the Church of England, Nonconformist. [f. DISSENT[1] + -ER[1]]

dĭssĕ'ntient (-shĭ- *or* -shent) *a.* & *n.* (Person) disagreeing with a majority or official view. [f. L DIS(*sentire* feel); see -ENT]

dĭssĕ'pĭment *n.* (Bot. & Zool.) Partition, septum. [f. L DIS(*saepimentum* f. *saepire* to shut in f. *saepes* hedge; see -MENT)]

dĭssertā'tion *n.* Detailed discourse on a subject, esp. as submitted for higher degree in university. [f. L *dissertatio* (*dissertare* discuss, frequent. of *disserere -sert-* examine (as DIS-, *serere* join)]

dĭsser've *v.t.* Do an ill turn to, esp. when intending to help; serve (person) badly or imperfectly; so **dĭs**SER'VICE[1] *n.* [f. DIS- + SERVE]

dĭssĕ'ver *v.t.* & *i.* Sever, divide; hence or cogn. ~ANCE, ~MENT, *ns.* [ME, f. AF *des(c)everer*, OF *dessevrer* f. LL *disseparare* (as DIS-, SEPARATE[2])]

dĭ'ssĭdence *n.* Disagreement, dissent. [F, or f. L *dissidentia* (as foll.; see -ENCE)]

dĭ'ssĭdent *a.* & *n.* (Person) disagreeing, at variance, esp. with established government etc.; dissentient. [F, or f. L DIS(*sidēre* = *sedēre* sit) disagree; see -ENT]

dĭssĭ'mĭlar *a.* Unlike (*to*); hence **dĭssĭmĭlă'rity** *n.*, ~LY[2] *adv.* [f. DIS- + SIMILAR]

dĭssĭ'mĭl|āte *v.t.* (Philol.) Make (sounds in a word) unlike each other, as in *cinnamon*, orig. *cinnamom*; hence ~A'TION *n.*, ~**at**ORY *a.* [f. L DIS(*similis* like), after *assimilate*]

dĭssĭmĭ'lĭtūde *n.* Unlikeness. [f. L *dissimilitudo* (as prec.; see -TUDE)]

dĭssĭ'mūl|āte *v.t.* & *i.* Dissemble; hence or cogn. ~A'TION, ~**āt**OR, *ns.* [f. L DIS(*simulare* SIMULATE) + -ATE[3]]

dĭ'ssĭpāt|e *v.t.* & *i.* Disperse, dispel, (cause to) disappear, (cloud, vapour, care, fear, darkness); break up entirely, bring or come to nothing; squander (money); fritter away (energy, attention); hence ~IVE *a.* [f. L DIS(**sipare* throw) + -ATE[3]]

dĭ'ssĭpātėd *a.* In vbl senses; given to dissipation, dissolute. [p.p. of prec.]

dĭssĭpā'tion *n.* Scattering, dispersion, disintegration; wasteful expenditure *of*; frivolous amusement; intemperate or dissolute living. [F, or f. L *dissipatio* (as DISSIPATE; see -ATION)]

dĭssō'cĭ|āte (*or* -shĭ-) *v.* **1.** *v.t.* Disconnect, separate, in thought or in fact (*from*; **~ate oneself from,** declare oneself unconnected with); (Chem.) decompose, esp. reversibly, e.g. by heat; (Phys.) cause (person's mind) to develop more than one centre of consciousness (**~ated personality,** pathological coexistence of two or more distinct personalities in the same person). **2.** *v.i.* Become dissociated. **3.** Hence or cogn. ~A'TION (-sĭ-) *n.*, ~ATIVE *a.* [f. L DIS(*sociare* f. *socius* companion) + -ATE[3]]

dĭssŏ'l|ūble *a.* That can be disintegrated, loosened, or disconnected; hence ~UBI'LITY *n.*, ~**ūb**LY[2] *adv.* [F, or f. L DIS(*solubilis* SOLUBLE)]

dĭ'ssolūte (*or* -ōōt) *a.* Lax in morals, licentious; hence ~LY[2] (-tlĭ) *adv.*, ~NESS (-tn-) *n.* [ME, f. L *dissolutus* p.p. of *dissolvere* DISSOLVE]

dĭssolū'tion (*or* -lōō'-) *n.* Disintegration, decomposition; undoing or relaxing *of* bond, partnership, marriage, or alliance; dismissal or dispersal of assembly, esp. of parliament for new election; death; coming or being brought to an end, fading away, disappearance. [ME f. OF, or f. L *dissolutio* (as foll.; see -ION)]

dĭssŏ'lv|e (-z-) *v.* & *n.* **1.** *v.t.* & *i.* Make or become liquid, esp. by immersion or dispersion in liquid (**~e into tears,** begin to weep copiously); (cause to) vanish; (Cinemat.) change gradually (*into* a different picture); dismiss or disperse (assembly, esp. parliament; cf. prec.); put an end to (partnership etc.), annul; hence ~ABLE *a.* **2.** *n.* Act or process of dissolving a picture. [ME, f. L DIS(*solvere solut-* loosen)]

dĭssŏ'lvent (-z-) *a.* & *n.* (Thing) that dissolves or tends to dissipate. [f. L *dissolvere* (see prec., -ENT)]

dĭ'sson|ant *a.* Not in harmony, harsh-toned,

incongruous; so ~ANCE *n.*, **~ant**LY² *adv.* [ME f. OF, or f. L DIS(*sonare* sound); see -ANT]

dĭssuā'de (-swā'd) *v.t.* Give advice or exercise influence to discourage or divert (person *from*); so **dĭssuā'**SION (-wā'zhon) *n.*, **dĭssuā'**SIVE (-swā'-) *a.* [f. L DIS(*suadēre suas-* persuade)]

dĭssȳ'llable etc. See DISYLLABLE etc.

dĭssȳmmĕ'trical *a.*, **dĭssȳ'mmĕtrȳ** *n.* (Having) no symmetry; (having) symmetry as of mirror images or the two hands (esp. of crystals with two corresponding forms). [f. DIS- + SYMMETRICAL, SYMMETRY]

dĭ'staff (-ahf) *n.* Cleft stick holding wool or flax wound for spinning by hand; corresp. part of spinning-wheel; woman's work; **~ side,** female branch of family. [OE *distæf*, f. as STAFF¹, the first element being app. = LG *diesse*, MLG *dise(ne)* bunch of flax]

dĭ'stal *a.* (Anat. & Bot.) Situated away from centre of body or point of attachment, terminal; hence ~LY² *adv.* [f. DISTANT + -AL]

dĭ'stance *n.*, & *v.t.* **1.** *n.* Being far off, remoteness; avoidance of familiarity, aloofness, reserve, (esp. *keep* one's, or *at a, distance*). **2.** Extent of space between, interval, (**within hailing, walking,** etc., **~**, near enough to reach easily by that means); distant point (*to, from, a distance*; **at a ~,** far off, not very near); remoter field of vision (*in the distance*; **middle ~**, in painted or actual landscape, between foreground and far part); space of time (*at this distance of time*); (Racing) length of 240 yds. or thereabouts (orig. between winning-post and **~-post,** used to disqualify slower runners in heats); (Boxing) scheduled duration of fight (**go the ~**, complete this without previous knock-out etc.). **3.** *v.t.* Place or make seem far off; leave far behind in race or competition. [ME f. OF *distance, destance* f. L *distantia* (DI¹*stare* stand apart: see -ANCE)]

dĭ'stant *a.* Far, or at a specified distance, away or *from* (*three miles distant*); remote, far apart, in position, time, resemblance, etc., (*a distant prospect, relation, connection, likeness*; *distant ages*; **~ early warning,** N. Amer. radar system for detection of missile attack; **~ signal** on railway, one in advance of home signal to give warning of latter's setting); not intimate, reserved, cool; hence ~LY² *adv.* [ME f. OF, or f. L *distant-* part. st. of *distare* (see prec., -ANT)]

dĭstā'ste *n.* Dislike, repugnance, (slight) aversion, (*for*); hence ~FUL (-tf-) *a.* (*to*). [f. DIS- + TASTE²]

dĭstĕ'mper¹ *v.t.* (arch., usu. in *p.p.*) Upset, derange, in health or sanity (*a distempered fancy*). [ME, f. LL DIS(*temperare* mingle correctly)]

dĭstĕ'mper² *n.* Derangement or ailment of body or mind; dog-disease with catarrh, cough, and weakness; similar disease of other animals; (arch.) political disorder. [f. prec.]

dĭstĕ'mper³ *n.*, & *v.t.* **1.** *n.* Method of painting on plaster or chalk with powder colours mixed with yolk or white of egg, size, etc., instead of oil, used for scene-painting and internal walls (*paint in distemper*); paint so used. **2.** *v.t.* Paint (wall etc., or abs.) thus. [n. f. v., f. OF *destremper* or f. LL *distemperare* soak, macerate (see DISTEMPER¹)]

dĭstĕ'nd *v.t.* & *i.* Swell out (balloon, vein, nostril, etc.) by pressure from within; so **dĭstĕ'ns**IBLE *a.*, **dĭstĕns**IBI'LITY, **dĭstĕ'ns**ION (-shon), *ns.* [ME, f. L DIS(*tendere tens-* stretch)]

dĭ'stĭch (-k) *n.* (Pros.) Pair of verse lines, couplet. [f. L f. Gk DI²(*stikhon* f. *stikhos* line) neut. a. (as n.)]

dĭ'stĭchous (-k-) *a.* (Bot.) Arranged in two vertical rows. [f. L *distichus* (as prec.) + -OUS]

dĭstĭ'l, *dĭstĭ'l|l, *v.i.* & *t.* (-ll-). Trickle down; come or give forth in drops, exude; turn to vapour by heat, condense by cold, and re-collect (liquid, esp. to remove dissolved impurities or to separate mixed liquids boiling at different temperatures); extract essence of (plant etc., or (fig.) doctrine etc.); drive (volatile constituent) *off* or *out* by heat; make (whisky, essence) by distilling raw materials; undergo distillation; so **~la'**TION *n.*, **~lat**ORY *a.* [ME, f. L *distillare* f. DE(*stillare* f. *stilla* drop)]

dĭ'stillāte *n.* Product of distillation. [f. prec.; see -ATE¹]

dĭstĭ'll|er *n.* In vbl senses; one who manufactures alcoholic liquor by distilling, whence ~ERY (3) *n.* [f. DISTIL + -ER¹]

dĭstĭ'nct *a.* Not identical, separate, individual, different in quality or kind, unlike, (*from*, or abs.); clearly perceptible, plain, definite; unmistakable, decided, positive; hence ~LY² *adv.*, ~NESS *n.* [ME, f. L *distinctus* p.p. of *distinguere* DISTINGUISH]

dĭstĭ'nction *n.* Making of a difference, discrimination; the difference made (**~ without a difference,** a merely nominal or artificial one); being different; thing that differentiates, mark, name, title; showing of special consideration, mark of honour; distinguished character, excellence, eminence. [ME f. OF, f. L *distinctio -onis* (as DISTINGUISH; see -ION)]

dĭstĭ'nctive *a.* Distinguishing, characteristic; hence ~LY² (-vlĭ) *adv.*, ~NESS (-vn-) *n.* [f. as prec. + -IVE]

distingué (dĭstă'nggā) *a.* (*fem.* **~e** *pr.* same). Having distinguished air, features, manners, etc. [F, p.p. of *distinguer* (see foll.)]

dĭstĭ'nguĭsh (-nggw-) *v.* **1.** *v.t.* Divide *into* classes etc.; be, see, or point out, the difference of (thing, thing *from* another); make out by listening, looking, etc.; differentiate, draw distinctions between. **2.** Characterize, be a mark or property of; make one*self* prominent or noteworthy (*by* gallantry etc.). **3.** Hence ~ABLE *a.* **4.** *v.i.* Make distinction *between*. [f. F *distinguer* or f. L DI¹(*stinguere stinct-* extinguish) w. irreg. use of -ISH²; cf. *extinguish*]

dĭstĭ'nguĭshed (-nggwĭsht) *a.* In vbl senses; remarkable (*for* or *by* quality of excellence etc.), eminent, famous, of high standing; *distingué*. [p.p. of prec.]

dĭstȯr't *v.t.* Put out of shape, make crooked or unshapely, (actually or, as by curved mirror etc., apparently); misrepresent (motives, facts, statements). [f. L DIS(*torquēre tort-* twist)]

dĭstȯr'tion *n.* Distorting or being distorted; (Electr.) change in form of signal during transmission etc., usu. with impairment of quality; hence ~AL, ~LESS, *adjs.* [f. L *distortio* (as prec.; see -ION)]

dĭstră'ct *v.t.* Draw (attention, the mind, etc.) away *from* or in different directions; divide or confuse the attention of, bewilder, perplex; (usu. in *p.p.*) make mad or angry (*distracted with, by, at*). [ME, f. L DIS(*trahere tract-* draw)]

dĭstră'ction *n.* **1.** Diversion of, thing that diverts, the mind; interruption; lack of concentration; amusement, relaxation from work. **2.** Confusion, perplexity, internal conflict, dissension; frenzy, madness, (**to ~**, almost to a state of madness). [ME f. OF, or f. L *distractio* (as prec.; see -ION)]

dĭstrai'n *v.i.* (Law). Levy distraint (*upon* person, his goods, or abs.); hence ~EE', ~ER¹, ~MENT, ~OR, *ns.* [ME, f. OF *destreindre* f. L DI¹(*stringere strict-* draw tight)]

dĭstrai'nt *n.* (Law). Seizure of chattels to make

person pay rent etc. or meet obligation, or to obtain satisfaction by their sale. [f. prec., after *constraint*]

distrait (dĭstrā′) *a.* (*fem.* **~e** *pr.* -ā′t). Absent-minded, not paying attention; distraught. [ME, f. OF *destrait* p.p. of *destraire* f. as DISTRACT]

dĭstrau′ght (-aw′t) *a.* Much agitated in mind; nearly crazy with worry etc. [ME, alt. of obs. *distract* adj. (f. as DISTRACT) after *straught* obs. p.p. of STRETCH]

dĭstrĕ′ss[1] *n.* Severe pressure of pain, sorrow, etc., anguish; lack of money or necessaries; damage or danger to ship etc. (*in distress*); exhaustion, being tired out, breathlessness; misfortune, calamity; (Law) distraint; **~-signal** (from ship in danger); **~-warrant** (authorizing distraint); hence ~FUL *a.* [ME, f. OF *destresse* etc. f. Gallo-Rom. **districtia* f. as DISTRAIN]

dĭstrĕ′ss[2] *v.t.* Subject to distress; exhaust; afflict; cause anxiety to, vex, make unhappy. [ME, f. AF *destresser*, OF *-ecier*, f. as prec.]

dĭstrĕ′ssed (-ĕ′st) *a.* In vbl senses; impoverished (*distressed gentlefolk*); (of furniture) with simulated marks of age and wear; ‖~ **area,** region of high unemployment. [p.p. of prec.]

dĭstrĭ′būtarў *n.* River or glacier branch that does not return to main stream after leaving it (as in a delta). [f. foll. + -ARY[1]]

dĭstrĭ′būt|e *v.t.* Deal out, give share of to each of a number; spread about, scatter, put at different points; divide into parts, arrange, classify; (Print.) separate (type that has been set up) and return each letter to its proper box in the case; (Logic) use (term) in its full extension so that it includes every individual of the class; hence ~ABLE *a.* [ME, f. L DIS(*tribuere tribut-* assign)]

dĭstrĭbū′tion *n.* Distributing, apportionment; (esp., Econ.) dispersal among consumers effected by commerce, extent to which individuals or classes share in aggregate products of community; (Statistics) way in which a characteristic is spread over members of a class; hence ~AL *a.* [ME f. OF, or f. L *distributio* (as prec.; see -ION)]

dĭstrĭ′būtĭve *a.* & *n.* **1.** *a.* Of, concerned with, produced by, distribution; (Logic & Gram.) referring to each individual of a class, not to the class collectively (*distributive* PRONOUN); hence ~LY[2] (-vlĭ) *adv.* **2.** *n.* (Gram.) Distributive word (*each, neither, every*). [ME, f. F (*-if -ive*), or f. LL *-ivus* (as DISTRIBUTE; see -IVE)]

dĭstrĭ′būtor *n.* Person or thing that distributes; agent who markets goods; electric cable from which lines run to individual premises; device in internal combustion engine for passing current to each sparking-plug in turn. [f. DISTRIBUTE + -OR]

dĭ′strĭct *n.*, & *v.t.* **1.** *n.* Territory marked off for special administrative purpose; ‖division of county; tract of country with common characteristics, region. **2.** ***~ attorney,** prosecuting officer of a district; ***~ court,** Federal court of first instance; **~ heating,** supply of heat or hot water from one source to a district or group of buildings; ‖**~ nurse,** nurse serving rural or urban area; ‖**~ visitor,** person working under clergyman's direction in section of parish. **3.** *v.t.* *Divide into districts. [F, f. med. L *districtus* (territory of) jurisdiction f. as DISTRAIN]

dĭstrĭ′ngăs (-ngg-) *n.* (Law). = STOP[2]*-order*; (Hist.) writ ordering distraint by sheriff etc. [L (first word of writ) = you shall distrain]

dĭstrŭ′st[1] *n.* Lack of trust; doubt, suspicion; hence ~FUL *a.* (*of*). [f. DIS- + TRUST 1]

dĭstrŭ′st[2] *v.t.* Have no confidence in; doubt, not rely on. [ME, f. DIS- + TRUST 10]

dĭstûr′b *v.t.* Break the rest or quiet or calm of; agitate, worry; move from settled position (*nothing has been disturbed; don't let me disturb you, don't disturb yourself*); (Psych., in *p.p.*) emotionally or mentally unstable or abnormal. [ME, f. OF *desto(u)rber* f. L DIS(*turbare* f. *turba* tumult)]

dĭstûr′bance *n.* Interruption of tranquillity; agitation; tumult, uproar; (Law) molestation, interference with rights or property. [ME, f. OF *desto(u)rbance* (as prec.; see -ANCE)]

dĭsū′nion (-yon) *n.* Separation, lack of union; dissension; so **dĭs**UNI′TE *v.t.* & *i.*, **dĭs**U′NITY *n.* [f. DIS- + UNION]

dĭsū′se[1] *n.* Discontinuance, lack of use or practice; disused state (*fall into disuse*). [f. DIS- + USE[1]]

dĭsū′se[2] (-z) *v.t.* Cease to use. [ME, f. OF *desuser* (as DIS-, USE[2])]

dĭsў′ll|able, dĭss-, *n.* Word or metrical foot of two syllables; so **~ă′bɪc** *a.* [f. F *disyllabe* f. L f. Gk *disullabos* (as DI-[2], SYLLABLE)]

dĭtch *n.* & *v.* **1.** *n.* Long narrow excavation, esp. to hold or conduct water or serve as boundary; watercourse; **last ~,** place of final desperate defence (DIE[2] *in last ditch*); **~-water** (stagnant in ditch; esp. *dull as ditch-water*). **2.** *v.i.* & *t.* Make or repair ditches (esp. *hedging and ditching*), whence ~′ER[1] (1, 2) *n.*; provide with ditches, drain; (sl.) abandon, discard, leave in the lurch; (sl.) defeat, frustrate; (sl.) make forced landing on sea, bring (aircraft) down thus; drive (vehicle) into ditch, *derail (train). [OE *dīc*, = OS *dik*, MHG *tich*, ON *diki*, of unkn. orig.; cf. DIKE]

dĭthē′|ĭsm *n.* Religious dualism, belief in independent principles of good and evil; hence ~IST (2) *n.* [f. DI-[2] + THEISM]

dĭ′ther (-dh-) *v.i.*, & *n.* **1.** *v.i.* Tremble, quiver; vacillate, hesitate. **2.** *n.* State of dithering; (colloq.) state of tremulous excitement or apprehension (*all of a dither*); hence ~Y[2] *a.* [var. of *didder*, DODDER[2]]

dĭ′thўrămb (-ăm) *n.* Greek choric hymn, wild in character; Bacchanalian song; passionate or inflated poem, speech, or writing; so **dĭthўră′mbɪc** *a.* [f. L f. Gk *dithurambos*]

dĭ′ttanў *n.* Herb of genus *Dictamnus*, formerly of medicinal repute. [ME, f. OF *dita(i)n* f. med. L *dictamus* f. L f. Gk *diktamnon* perh. f. *Diktē* in Crete]

dĭ′ttō *n.* (*pl.* **~s**), & *v.t.* **1.** *n.* The aforesaid, the same, (in accounts, inventories, etc., or colloq.); duplicate, similar thing; ‖(in *pl.*, arch.) clothes all of same material and colour; **~ marks,** inverted commas etc. representing the word 'ditto'; **say ~ to,** agree with, endorse opinion of. **2.** *v.t.* Repeat (another's action or words). [It. dial., f. L *dictus* p.p. of *dicere* say]

dĭttŏ′graphў *n.* Copyist's mistaken repetition of letter, word, or phrase; hence **dĭttogră′phɪc** *a.* [f. Gk *dittos* double + -GRAPHY]

dĭ′ttў *n.* Short simple song. [ME, f. OF *dité* composition f. L *dictatum* neut. p.p. (as n.) of *dictare* DICTATE[2]]

dĭ′ttў-băg, -bŏx, *ns.* Sailor's or fisherman's receptacle for odds and ends. [19th c.; orig. unkn.]

diūrē′s|ĭs *n.* (*pl.* **~es** *pr.* -ēz). (Med.) Increased excretion of urine. [mod. L f. Gk (as DI-[3], *ourēsis* urination)]

diūrĕ′tĭc *a.* & *n.* (Drug) causing increased excretion of urine. [ME, f. OF *diuretique*, or f. LL f. Gk *diourētikos* f. DI[3](*oureō* urinate); see -ETIC]

diûr′nal *a.* Of the day, not nocturnal; (Astron.) occupying one day; daily, of each day; (Zool.) active in daytime; hence ~LY[2] *adv.* [ME, f. LL *diurnalis* f. L *diurnus* (*dies* day); see -AL]

dĭ′va (dē′-) *n.* Great woman singer, prima donna. [It. f. L, = goddess]

dī'vag|āte *v.i.* (literary). Stray, digress; hence ~A'TION *n.* [f. L DI[1](*vagari* wander) + -ATE[3]]

dī'valent (*or* dīvā'-) *a.* (Chem.) Having a valence of two. [f. DI-[2] + *valent-* part. st. f. as VALENCE[2]]

dīvă'n (*or* dĭ'văn) *n.* Long seat against room-wall; couch or bed without head- or foot-board; oriental council of State; oriental council-chamber, court of justice; (arch.) (smoking-room attached to) cigar-shop. [f. F *divan* or It. *divano* f. Turk. *dīvān* f. Arab. *dīwān* f. Pers. *dīvān* anthology, register, court, bench]

dīvă'ric|āte *v.i.* (literary & Biol.) Diverge, branch, separate widely; hence or cogn. ~A'TION *n.*, ~ATE[2] *a.* [f. L DI[1](*varicare* f. *varicus* straddling) + -ATE[3]]

dīve *v.i.* (~**d,** *or* ***dove** *pr.* dōv), & *n.* **1.** *v.i.* Plunge, esp. head foremost, into water etc., esp. as sport; (of aircraft) plunge steeply downwards at increasing speed, (of submarine) submerge; go down or out of sight suddenly; put one's hand *into* water, vessel, pocket, handbag, etc.; penetrate or search mentally *into*; **dī'ving-bell,** open-bottomed box or bell with air supplied by tube, in which person can be let down into deep water; **dī'ving-board,** elevated board for diving from; **dī'ving-suit,** watertight suit usu. with helmet and air-supply for work under water. **2.** *n.* Act of diving, plunge, header; submerging of submarine, aircraft's steep descent; sudden darting movement; (colloq.) drinking-den, disreputable place of resort; (Boxing, sl.) pretended knock-out. **3.** ~**-bomber,** aircraft designed to aim and release bombs while diving towards target; so ~**-bomb** *v.t.* [OE *dūfan* v.i. dive, sink, and *dȳfan* v.t. immerse, f. Gmc **dubh-* etc. cogn. w. DEEP[1], DIP[1]]

dī'ver *n.* In vbl senses; person who dives for pearls, (esp. in diving-suit) to examine sunken ships, etc.; diving bird, esp. loon. [f. prec. + -ER[1]]

dīvēr'ge *v.* **1.** *v.i.* Proceed in different directions from point; take different courses from each other; go aside *from* track (lit. or fig.); differ; (Math., of series) become indefinitely large in the sum of a sufficient number of its terms. **2.** *v.t.* Cause to diverge, deflect. [f. med. L *divergere* f. as DI-[1] + L *vergere* incline]

dīvēr'g|ent *a.* Diverging; (Psych., of thought) tending to reach a variety of possible solutions when analysing a problem; so ~ENCE, ~ENCY, *ns.*, ~**ent**LY[2] *adv.* [f. prec. + -ENT]

dī'vers (-z) *a.* (arch.) Sundry, several, more than one. [ME f. OF, f. L DI[1](*versus* p.p. of *vertere* turn) = foll.]

dīvēr'se (*or* dĭ'-) *a.* Unlike in nature or qualities; varied, changeful; hence ~LY[2] (-slĭ) *adv.* [ME, as prec.]

dīvēr'sĭ|fȳ *v.t.* Make diverse, vary, modify, variegate; spread (investment) over several enterprises or products, esp. to guard against loss; so ~FICA'TION *n.* [ME, f. OF *diversifier* f. med. L *diversificare* (as DIVERS; see -FY)]

dīvēr'sion (-shon) *n.* Deflecting, deviation; diverting of attention, manœuvre to secure this, feint; recreation, pleasant mental distraction, pastime; ‖alternative route when road is temporarily closed to traffic; hence ~ARY[1] *a.*, ~IST (2) *n.*, (esp., in Communist use) saboteur, conspirator against State. [f. LL *diversio* (as DIVERT; see -ION)]

dīvēr'sĭtȳ *n.* Being diverse, unlikeness; different kind; variety. [ME, f. OF *diversité* f. L *diversitas* -*tatis* (as DIVERS; see -ITY)]

dīvēr't *v.t.* Turn aside, deflect, (stream etc., *from, to,* or abs.); turn elsewhere, get rid of, ward off; draw attention of (away *from* one thing *to* another), distract; entertain, amuse, whence ~ING[2] *a.* [ME, f. F *divertir* f. L DI[1](*vertere* turn)]

dīvertĭ'cūl|um *n.* (*pl.* ~**a**). (Anat.) Blind tube forming side-branch of cavity or passage; hence ~I'TIS *n.* [med. L, var. of L *deverticulum* byway f. DE(*vertere* turn); see -CULE]

dīvertĭmĕ'nt|ō (-vār-) *n.* (*pl.* ~**i** *or* ~**os**). (Mus.) Composition primarily for entertainment, esp. suite for chamber orchestra. [It., = diversion]

divertissement (dēvĕrtē'smahṅ) *n.* Short ballet etc. between acts or longer pieces; diversion, entertainment. [F, f. *divertiss-* st. of *divertir* DIVERT; see -MENT]

Dī'vēs (-z) *n.* Rich man. [L, in Vulgate transl. of Luke 16]

dīvĕ'st *v.t.* Unclothe; strip *of* garment etc.; deprive or rid *of* (~ one**self of,** abandon); hence ~**ĭt**URE, ~MENT, *ns.* [f. earlier *devest* f. OF *desvestir* etc. (as DIS-, L *vestire* f. *vestis* garment)]

dĭ'vĭ. See DIVVY.

dīvī'de[1] *v.t.* & *i.* **1.** Separate into or *in*(*to*) parts, split or break up (*~**d highway,** dual carriageway; ~**d skirt,** culotte); separate, part, cut off or *off,* (things, thing *from*); mark out into parts, specify different kinds of; cause to disagree, set at variance (*opinion is divided*; ~**d against itself,** formed into factions). **2.** Distribute, deal *out,* (*among, between*); share *with* others; find how many times number contains another (*divide 20 by 3*), do DIVISION, (of number) be contained in (number) without remainder; part (legislative assembly etc.) into two sets in voting, be thus parted. [ME, f. L DI[1](**videre vis-*)]

dīvī'de[2] *n.* Watershed; (fig.) dividing line; **the Great D~** (between life and death). [f. prec.]

dĭ'vĭdĕnd *n.* **1.** (Math.) Number to be divided by divisor. **2.** Sum payable as profit of joint-stock company or to creditors of insolvent estate; individual's share of it (EX[2] *dividend,* CUM *dividend*; ~ **stripping,** evasion of tax on dividends by arrangement between company liable to pay tax and another able to claim repayment of tax; ‖~**-warrant,** authority for shareholder to receive dividend). **3.** Benefit from any action (*his long training paid dividends*). [f. AF *dividende* f. L *dividendum* (as DIVIDE[1]; see -ND[1])]

dīvī'der *n.* In vbl senses; screen, piece of furniture, etc., to divide room into two parts; (in *pl.*) measuring-compasses, esp. with screw for setting to small intervals. [f. DIVIDE[1] + -ER[1]]

dĭ'vi-dĭvĭ *n.* Curved pods of a small tropical-Amer. tree (*Caesalpinia coriaria*), used in tanning; this tree. [Carib]

dĭvĭnā'tion *n.* Divining, insight into or discovery of the unknown or future by supernatural means; skilful forecast, good guess; hence **dĭvī'nat**ORY *a.* [ME f. OF, or f. L *divinatio* (as DIVINE[2]; see -ATION)]

dĭvī'ne[1] *a.* (~**r,** ~**st**) & *n.* **1.** *a.* Of, from, like, God or a god (~ **right of kings,** doctrine that kings have authority independently of their subjects' will); devoted to God, sacred, (*divine* OFFICE; ~ **service,** meeting for worship); superhumanly excellent, gifted, or beautiful; (colloq.) excellent, delightful; hence or cogn. **dĭ'vĭn**IZE (3) *v.t.*, ~LY[2] (-nlĭ) *adv.*, ~NESS (-n-n-) *n.* **2.** *n.* Person (usu. cleric) skilled in theology. [ME, f. OF *devin -ine* f. L *divinus* (*divus* godlike; see -INE[1])]

dĭvī'n|e[2] *v.* **1.** *v.t.* Discover by inspiration, magic, intuition, or guessing; foresee, predict, conjecture. **2.** *v.i.* Practise divination; ~**ing-rod** (see DOWSE[2]). **3.** Hence ~ER[2] (1) *n.* [ME, f. F *deviner* f. OF *devin* (see prec.)]

dĭvĭ'nĭtȳ *n.* Being divine, godhood; a god, godhead; theology, university theological faculty; ~ **calf,** dark brown bookbinding style with blind tooling. [ME, f. OF *divinité* f. L *divinitas -tatis* (as DIVINE[1]; see -ITY)]

dĭvĭ'sĭ|ible (-z-) *a.* Capable of being divided actually or in thought; **~ible by,** (Math.) containing (a number) some number of times without remainder; hence ~IBI'LITY *n.* [F, or f. LL *divisibilis* (as DIVIDE[1]; see -IBLE)]

dĭvĭ'sion (-zhon) *n.* **1.** Dividing or being divided, severance; distribution, sharing, (**~ of labour**, improvement of efficiency by giving different parts of manufacturing process etc. to different persons). **2.** Disagreement, discord, (*division of opinion*). **3.** (Math.) Process of dividing number by another; **~ sign,** ÷; **long ~** (writing down details of calculation); **short ~** (writing quotient directly). **4.** Separation of legislative assembly etc. into two sets for counting votes; **~-bell** (announcing this). **5.** Dividing line, boundary; part, section. **6.** Administrative etc. district; definite part, under single command, of army or navy, police, governmental or industrial organization, High Court, etc., (*airborne, armoured, parachute, division; Chancery Division*); ||part of county or borough returning a Member of Parliament. **7.** (Bot.) major taxonomic grouping equivalent to phylum; (Zool.) subsidiary category between major levels of classification; (Logic) classification of kinds, parts, or senses. **8.** Hence ~AL *a.* [ME, f. OF *divisiun* f. L *divisio -onis* (as DIVIDE[1]; see -ION)]

dĭvī'sĭve *a.* Tending to divide, esp. in opinion etc.; hence ~LY[2] (-vlĭ) *adv.*, ~NESS (-vn-) *n.* [f. LL *divisivus* (as DIVIDE[1]; see -IVE)]

dĭvī'sor (-z-) *n.* (Math.) Number by which dividend is to be divided; number that divides another without remainder. [ME, f. F *diviseur* or f. L *divisor* (as DIVIDE[1]; see -OR)]

dĭvŏr'ce[1] *n.* Legal dissolution of marriage; judicial separation of married pair; decree of nullity of marriage; (fig.) severance, separation. [ME f. OF, f. L *divortium* f. DI[1](*vortere = vertere* turn)]

dĭvŏr'ce[2] *v.t.* Legally dissolve marriage between; separate (spouse) by divorce *from*; obtain divorce from (spouse); detach, separate, (things, thing *from*; esp. fig.); (arch.) dissolve (union); hence **dĭvŏrc**EE' *n.* (also **divorcé** *masc.*, **divorcée** *fem.*, (dĭvŏr'sā) [F]), ~MENT (-sm-) *n.* [ME, f. OF *divorcer* f. LL *divortiare* (as prec.)]

dĭ'vot *n.* (Sc.) piece of turf, sod; (Golf) piece of turf cut out by club-head in making a stroke. [16th c.; orig. unkn.]

dĭvŭ'lg|e *v.t.* Disclose, reveal, (secret etc.); hence or cogn. **dĭvŭlg**A'TION, ~EMENT (-jm-), ~ENCE, *ns.* [f. L DI[1](*vulgare* publish f. *vulgus* common people)]

dĭ'vvў, dĭ'vĭ, *n.*, & *v.t.* (colloq.) **1.** *n.* Dividend, share; distribution. **2.** *v.t.* ~ (**up**), divide, share out. [abbr. of DIVIDEND]

Dĭ'xĭe[1] *n.* Southern States of U.S.; ***~crat,** (colloq.) member of seceding group of Democrats in Dixie; **~land,** (1) Dixie, (2) kind of jazz with strong two-beat rhythm and collective improvisation. [19th c.; orig. uncert.]

||**dĭ'xĭe**[2] *n.* Large iron pot in which stew, tea, etc., are made or carried by soldiers etc. [f. Hind. *degchī* cooking-pot f. Pers. *degcha* dim. of *deg* pot]

D.I.Y. *abbr.* do-it-yourself.

dĭzz|ў *a.*, & *v.t.* **1.** *a.* Giddy, dazed, unsteady, tottering, confused; making giddy (*dizzy heights, speed*); (of mountain, tower, etc.) very high; whirling rapidly; hence ~ĬLY[2] *adv.*, ~ĬNESS *n.* **2.** *v.t.* Make dizzy, bewilder. [OE *dysig*, = MDu. *dosech*, LG *dusig, dösig*, OHG *tusic* weak f. WG **dus-*; see -Y[2]]

D.J. *abbr.* dinner-jacket; disc jockey.

djĕ'llaba. Var. of JELLABA.

djibba(h). Var. of JIBBA(H).

djĭnn. Var. of JINN.

||**D.L.** *abbr.* Deputy Lieutenant.

dl *abbr.* decilitre(s).

D-layer (dē'lāer) *n.* Lowest stratum of ionosphere. [f. *D* (arbitrary) + LAYER]

D.Litt. *abbr.* Doctor of Letters. [f. L *Doctor Litterarum*]

dm *abbr.* decimetre(s).

DM, D-mark, *abbr.* Deutschmark.

D.Mus. *abbr.* Doctor of Music.

***D.M.Z.** *abbr.* demilitarized zone.

DNA *abbr.* deoxyribonucleic acid.

D.N.B. *abbr.* Dictionary of National Biography.

||**D-notice** (dē'nōtĭs) *n.* Official request to news editors not to publish items on specified subjects, for reasons of security. [f. *d*efence + NOTICE]

do[1] (dōō *or* do) *v.t., i.,* & *aux.* (*sing. pres.* 2 (arch.) **doest** *pr.* dōō'ist as *t.* & *i.*, **dost** *pr.* dŭst as *aux.*, 3 **does** *pr.* dŭz or doz, (colloq.) **'s,** (arch.) **doth** *pr.* dŭth, (arch.) **doeth** *pr.* dōō'ĭth; *past* **did,** (2 *sing.* arch.) **didst**; *part.* DOING; p.p. DONE; *neg.* **do not** *or* (colloq.) **don't** *pr.* dōnt, **does not** *or* (colloq.) **doesn't** *pr.* dŭ'zent *or* (vulg.) **don't, did not** *or* (colloq.) **didn't** *pr.* dĭ'dent). **1.** *v.t.* Bestow, impart, grant, give, (*does him credit, does credit to his intelligence; do me a favour; does me good, harm; do justice to; did a service to his country*). **2.** Perform, carry out, effect, complete, bring to pass, (thing, work, good, right, wrong, duty, bidding, penance; *do* one's BEST[1]; *easier said than done*); *do* BATTLE[1], one's BIT[2]; **do a degree,** study for and obtain it; DO-GOODER; *do the* HONOUR[1]*s*; **do a play,** give performance(s) of it; **do something for** or **to,** (colloq.) enhance appearance or quality of; *do the* TRICK; *do 30 miles to the gallon, do 100 m.p.h.*; **that's done it,** excl. of achievement or dismay; **do a,** (colloq.) act like (*Garbo* etc.); **do-it-yourself** *a.*, (to be) made etc. by amateur handyman. **3.** Produce, make, (*copies, omelette, painting, translation*); provide (*we do bed and breakfast*). **4.** Operate on, deal with, repair, set in order, (*do to* DEATH; **do the dishes,** wash up; **do the flowers,** arrange them; **do** one's **head** or **nut,** (sl.) be very worried or angry; **do a room,** clean it or paint it etc.); cook, esp. to right degree (*do it in the oven, done to a* TURN[2], *overdone; do* BROWN[1]); solve (problem); translate or transform (*into* English, book *into* film, etc.); work at (lesson, subject); play the part of, act like, (*did Lear, do the cicerone*, hence *do the affable* etc.); (sl.) rob (*did a shop in Soho*); (sl.) prosecute, convict; (sl.) have sexual intercourse with. **5.** Exhaust, tire out; ~ (**in the eye**), (sl.) swindle, cheat, (*out of*); (sl.) defeat, ruin, kill. **6.** Traverse (distance); (colloq.) visit, see sights of, (place, entertainment, etc.); (sl.) undergo (term of punishment). **7.** (colloq.) ||Provide food etc. for (*they do* one *very well here*; **do oneself well,** make liberal provision for one's own comfort); ||satisfy (*that will do me nicely*); *do* PROUD. **8.** *v.i.* (w. *adv.* etc.) Act, proceed, (*do as they do in Rome; would do wisely to withdraw*); perform deeds (**do or die,** be undeterred by danger); make an end (*have* DONE *with*); (of person or thing) fare, get on, (well, badly, etc.; **do well for oneself,** prosper; **do well out of,** profit by; *mother and child doing well*; **how do you do?,** conventional greeting on being introduced); be suitable or acceptable, serve purpose, suffice (**that will do!,** stop it; *it doesn't do to worry*; MAKE[1] *do*); be in progress (**nothing doing,** nothing happening, no prospect of success; **what is to do,** what is happening, what is the matter; TO-DO). **9.** *v. substitute.* (*a*) replacing v. and taking its construction (*I treat him as he does me*), (*b*) replacing v. and obj. etc. (*if you knew him as well as I do*), (*c*) as ellipt. aux. (*did you see him?—yes, I did; why don't you answer?—but I did!*), (*d*) with *so, it, which,* etc. (*I wanted to see him, and I did so* or *and so I did; when visiting London, which I seldom do; if you want to tell him, do it now*), (*e*) in emphatic repetition (*tell me, do!; you don't know me, do you?*). **10.** *v. aux.* w. inf. as pres. or past (*a*) for special emphasis (*I do so wish I could*), esp. in contrast with what precedes or follows (*but I did see him; I did go, but she wasn't in*), (*b*) for inversion (*rarely does it happen that; little did I imagine that; did he but know it*), (*c*) in questions and negations exc. with *be,* CAN², DARE, *have* v. aux. & ||sometimes v.t., *may, must,* sometimes NEED², *ought, shall, will*; in neg. commands also with *be, have* (**don't-care** *n.*, person who is careless or indifferent; **don't-know** *n.*, person who does not answer definitely to questionnaire item etc.); w. inf. as imper. for emphasis, urgency, etc., (*do tell me*). **11.** (w. *preps.*) **Do by,** treat, deal with, in specified way; **do for,** be satisfactory or sufficient for, (colloq.) ruin, destroy, kill, ||(colloq.) act as housekeeper etc. for; **do to** or (arch.) **unto,** = *do by*; **do with,** accept, find useful or sufficient; *could do with,* (colloq.) would be glad to have; *to do with,* concerned with, related to; *have to do with,* be concerned with, have dealings with; *not know what to do with* one*self,* be embarrassed or bored; **do without,** manage without, complete one's task in the absence of, (thing expressed or implied). **12.** (w. *advs.*) **Do away with,** abolish; **do down,** (colloq.) overcome, cheat, swindle; **do in,** (sl.) ruin, kill, (colloq.) exhaust, tire out; **do out,** clean or redecorate (room); **do over,** (sl.) attack, beat, *(colloq.) do again; **do up,** fasten, adorn (one*self*), (sl.) ruin, beat. [OE *dōn,* = OS *dōn,* OHG *tuon,* f. WG **do-* f. IE **dhō-* etc. (Skr. *dádhāmi* put, Gk *tithēmi* place, L *facere* do)]

do² (dōō) *n.* (*pl.* **dos** *or* **do's**). **1.** (sl.) Swindle, imposture, hoax. **2.** ||(colloq.) Entertainment, jollification, elaborate operation etc.; (in *pl.*) share (**fair dos!,** share fairly). **3. Dos and don'ts,** rules of behaviour. [f. prec.]

dō³. See DOH.

do. *abbr.* ditto.

D.O.A. *abbr.* dead on arrival (at hospital etc.).

do'able (dōō'-) *a.* That can be done. [ME, f. DO¹ + -ABLE]

doat. Var. of DOTE.

dŏ'bbĭn *n.* Draught-horse; farm horse. [pet-form of *Robert*]

***dō'bė** *n.* Adobe. [abbr.]

Dō'bermănn *n.* ~ (**pinscher** *pr.* pĭ'nsher), (breed of) German hound with smooth coat and docked tail. [f. L. ~, 19th-c. Ger. dog-breeder; G *pinscher* terrier]

dŏc *n.* (colloq.) Doctor. [abbr.]

Docē't|ĭsm *n.* Heresy that Christ's body was only apparently human; so ~IC *a.*, ~IST (2) *n.* [f. med. L f. Gk *Dokētai* adherents of the heresy (*dokeō* seem) + -ISM]

doch an dorris. Var. of DEOCH AN DORIS.

dō'cīle *a.* Teachable; submissive; easily managed; hence or cogn. ~LY² (-l-lĭ) *adv.*, **docĭ'lITY** *n.* [ME, f. L *docilis* (*docēre* teach; see -IL)]

dŏck¹ *n.* Coarse weed of genus *Rumex,* with leaves used to cure nettle-stings. [OE *docce*; cf. MDu. *dockeblaederen*]

dŏck² *n.* Solid fleshy part of animal's tail; crupper of saddle or harness. [ME, perh. f. OE **docca,* MLG *dokke* bundle of straw, OHG *tocka* doll]

dŏck³ *v.t.* Cut short (tail of animal), cut short tail of (animal); lessen, deduct, deprive *of,* put limits on (person, wages, supplies etc.); ~**-tailed,** with tail docked. [ME, f. prec.]

dŏck⁴ *n.* & *v.* **1.** *n.* Artificial enclosed body of water in which ships may be loaded, unloaded, or repaired (**dry** or **graving** ~, dry enclosure for repairing or building, water being pumped out; **floating** ~, floating structure usable as dry dock; **in** ~, (colloq.) in hospital or repair-shop); (usu. in *pl.*) range of dock basins with wharves and offices, dockyard; *ship's berth, wharf; (Theatr.) = SCENE-*dock*; hence ~'AGE (4) *n.* **2.** ~**-glass,** large glass for wine-tasting; ~**'land,** district near docks; ~**'yard,** area with docks and all shipbuilding and repairing appliances, esp. for naval use. **3.** *v.t.* & *i.* Bring (ship), (of ship) come, into dock; furnish with dock(s); join (spacecraft) together in space, be thus joined. [f. MDu. *docke,* of unkn. orig.]

dŏck⁵ *n.* Enclosure in criminal court for prisoner; **in the** ~, on trial (lit. or fig.); ||~ **brief** (handed direct in court to barrister selected by prisoner in dock). [16th c., prob. orig. cant = Flem. *dok* cage, of unkn. orig.]

dŏ'cker *n.* Labourer in docks. [f. DOCK⁴ + -ER¹]

dŏ'ckėt *n.*, & *v.t.* **1.** *n.* ||Document recording payment of customs duties, nature of goods delivered, jobs done, etc.; voucher, order form; endorsement of document to indicate its contents; label attached to goods etc. **2.** *List of causes for trial or persons having causes pending; *list of things to be done. **3.** *v.t.* Label with docket. [15th c., of unkn. orig.]

dŏ'ctor¹ *n.* **1.** (arch.) Teacher, learned man, (*who shall decide when doctors disagree?*; **D~s of the Church,** certain, esp. four Eastern and four Western, early Fathers of the Church). **2.** Holder of the highest university degree in any faculty (often honorary; used as prefix to surname); **D~s' Commons,** (Hist.) London building in which various legal business was done. **3.** Physician; *dentist or veterinary surgeon; (colloq.) one who carries out repairs (lit. or fig.; *company doctor; tree doctor*); (sl.) cook on board ship or in camp; **what the** ~ **ordered,** (colloq.) something beneficial or desirable; **you're the** ~, (colloq.) the decision is up to you; ~**-bird,** W. Ind. humming-bird; ~**s' stuff,** (derog.) medicines. **4.** Mechanical appliance for regulating, adjusting, etc.; artificial fishing-fly. **5.** Hence or cogn. ~AL, **dŏctōr'IAL** *adjs.*, ~ATE¹, ~HOOD, ~SHIP (1, 3), *ns.* [ME, f. OF *doctour* f. L *doctor* (*docēre doct-* teach; see -OR)]

dŏ'ctor² *v.* (colloq.) **1.** *v.t.* Confer degree of doctor on; treat (patient, one*self*) medically; castrate or spay; patch up (machinery etc.); adulterate; falsify. **2.** *v.i.* Practise as physician (esp. ~ING¹ (1) *n.*). [f. prec.]

dŏctrĭnair'|e *n.* & *a.* **1.** *n.* Pedantic theorist, person who applies principle without allowance for circumstances; hence ~ISM (2) *n.* **2.** *a.* Theoretical and unpractical. [F, f. *doctrine* DOCTRINE + *-aire* -ARY¹]

dŏctrī'nal (*or* dŏ'ktrĭnal) *a.* Of or inculcating doctrine(s); hence ~LY² *adv.* [f. LL *doctrinalis* (as foll.; see -AL)]

dŏ'ctrĭn|e *n.* What is taught, body of instruction; religious, political, scientific, etc., belief, dogma, or tenet; hence ~ISM (1), ~IST (1), *ns.* [ME f. OF, f. L *doctrina* teaching (as DOCTOR¹; see -INE⁴)]

dŏ'cūment¹ *n.* Thing, esp. title-deed, writing, or inscription, that furnishes evidence (esp. in law and commerce); hence ~AL (-ĕ'n-) *a.*, **dŏcūmĕ'ntalIST** *n.*, person engaged in documentation. [ME f. OF, f. L *documentum* proof (*docēre* teach; see -MENT)]

dŏ'cūmĕnt² *v.t.* Prove by or provide with

documents or evidence; hence ~A'TION *n.*, (esp.) accumulation, classification, and dissemination of information, material thus collected. [f. prec.]

dŏcūmĕ'ntarў *a.* & *n.* **1.** *a.* Pertaining to or consisting of documents; factual, based on real events. **2.** *n.* Documentary film etc. [f. DOCUMENT¹ + -ARY¹]

***DOD** *abbr.* Department of Defense.

dŏ'dder¹ *n.* Slender leafless threadlike twining parasitic plant of genus *Cuscuta*. [ME, = MLG *dod(d)er*, MHG *toter*]

dŏ'dder² *v.i.* Tremble or nod owing to frailty, palsy, etc. (**~-grass**, quaking-grass); totter, be feeble; hence ~ER¹ *n.*, infirm, feeble, or inept person, ~Y² *a.* [17th c., var. of obs. dial. *dadder*]

dŏ'ddered (*-erd*) *a.* (Of oaks and other trees) having lost top or branches. [prob. f. obs. *dod* poll, lop]

dŏ'ddle *n.* (colloq.) Easy task. [perh. f. *doddle* = toddle]

dōdĕ'ca- *comb. form.* Twelve, as: **~gon,** plane figure with twelve sides and angles; ~HE'DRON, solid figure with twelve faces; **~pho'nic,** = TWELVE-*note*; **~sy'llable,** metrical line of twelve syllables. [f. Gk *dōdeka* twelve]

dŏdge¹ *v.* **1.** *v.i.* Move to and fro, change position, shuffle; move quickly *round, about,* or *behind*, obstacle so as to elude pursuer, blow, etc.; quibble, prevaricate; (of bell in change-ringing) move one place contrary to the normal sequence. **2.** *v.t.* Baffle by artfulness, trifle with; elude (pursuer, opponent, blow) by sideward deviation etc.; evade by trickery (*dodge paying* one's *fare*; *dodge the* COLUMN). [16th c.; orig. unkn.]

dŏdge² *n.* Piece of dodging, quick side-movement; trick, artifice, clever expedient; dodging of bell in change-ringing. [f. prec.]

dŏ'dgem *n.* Small electrically-powered car at fun-fair, in which driver bumps into similar cars in enclosure. [f. DODGE¹ + 'EM]

dŏ'dger *n.* In vbl senses; artful or elusive person; screen on ship's bridge etc. as protection from spray etc.; *small handbill; *maize-flour cake (*corn dodger*); (sl.) sandwich, bread, food. [f. DODGE¹ + -ER¹]

dŏ'dgў *a.* Cunning, artful; (colloq.) awkward, unreliable, tricky. [f. DODGE¹ + -Y²]

dō'dō *n.* (*pl.* **~s** *or* **~es**). Large extinct bird of Mauritius etc.; old-fashioned, stupid, or inactive person; **as dead as the** or **a** ~, entirely obsolete. [f. Port. *doudo* simpleton]

dōe *n.* Female of fallow deer, reindeer, hare, or rabbit; **~'skin** (dō's-), skin of doe fallow deer, leather of this, fine cloth resembling it. [OE *dā*, of unkn. orig.]

‖**D.O.E.** *abbr.* Department of the Environment.

doek (do͝ok) *n.* (S. Afr.) Cloth, esp. head-cloth. [Afrik.]

do'er (do͞o'-) *n.* In vbl senses; one who acts rather than merely talking or thinking; (Austral.) eccentric person. [ME, f. DO¹ + -ER¹]

does, doesn't, doest, doeth. See DO¹.

dŏff *v.t.* Take off (hat, clothing). [ME, = *do off*]

dŏg¹ *n.* **1.** Carnivorous quadruped of genus *Canis*, of many breeds wild and domesticated; one used for hunting (*dogs of* WAR¹); male of dog, wolf (also **~-wolf**), or fox (also **~-fox**). **2.** Despicable person (esp. *dirty dog*); (colloq.) fellow (*sly, lucky, gay, dull, dog*; SEA-*dog*); *(sl.) something poor, a failure. **3.** Mechanical device for gripping etc.; = FIRE¹*dog*. **4.** BOTTOM¹ *dog*; **not a ~'s chance,** not even the least chance; *every dog has his* DAY; **die like a ~** (miserably or shamefully); **like a ~'s dinner,** (colloq.) smartly or flashily (dressed, arranged, etc.); **give a ~ a bad name and hang him,** nicknaming or slander is effective; **go to the ~s,** be ruined; **hair of the ~ that bit one,** further drink to cure effects of drink; **help lame ~ over stile,** be friend in time of need; HOT¹ *dog*; **love me, love my ~,** accept my friends as yours; **~ in the manger,** one who prevents others from enjoying what is useless to him; **put on ~,** (colloq.) behave pretentiously; *rain* CAT¹*s and dogs*; *let* SLEEP²*ing dogs lie*; **like a ~ with two tails,** delighted; ‖**the ~s,** (colloq.) greyhound racing; TOP¹ *dog*; **try it on the ~,** experiment so that only inferior or unimportant person or thing may be harmed. **5. ~'berry,** fruit of dogwood; **~-biscuit** (for feeding dogs); **~'cart,** two-wheeled driving-cart with cross seats back to back (orig. with compartment for dogs); **~-clutch** (with teeth of one part engaging in slots in other part); **~-collar,** lit., and fig. of person's straight high collar divided at back, (joc.) clerical collar; **~ days,** hottest period of year [reckoned in antiquity from heliacal rising of dog-star]; **~-ear,** corner of book-page turned down through use; **~-eat-~,** ruthlessly competitive; **~-end,** (sl.) cigarette-end; **~-faced,** epithet of kind of baboon (*Cynocephalus*); **~-fall** (in which wrestlers touch ground together); **~-fennel,** stinking camomile; **~'fight,** fight (as) between dogs, general uproar, (colloq.) fight between aircraft; **~'fish,** small shark; **~'house,** *dog's kennel; *in the ~house*, (sl.) in disgrace; **~ Latin,** incorrect or mongrel Latin; **~-leg(ged),** bent like dog's hind leg; **~-paddle** *n.*, & *v.i.*, (use) elementary swimming-stroke; **~'rose,** wild hedge-rose; **~'s age,** (sl.) a long time; **~'s-body,** (Naut. sl.) junior officer, (colloq.) drudge; **~'s breakfast,** (sl.) mess; **~'shore,** temporary wooden support for ship just before launching; **~'skin,** leather of or imitating dog's skin used for gloves; **~'s life,** life of misery or wretched servitude; **~'s meat,** horse's or other flesh as food for dogs, carrion; **~'s nose,** drink of beer mixed with gin or rum; **~('s)-tail,** grass of genus *Cynosurus*; **~-star,** chief star of constellation Canis Major or Minor, esp. Sirius; **~'s-tongue,** cynoglossum; **~'s-tooth,** violet of genus *Erythronium*, esp. one with speckled leaves, purple flowers, and toothed perianth; **~-tag,** dog's or *(sl.) soldier's metal identity-disc; **~-tired,** tired out; **~-tooth,** small pointed ornament or moulding esp. in Norman and Early English architecture; **~-violet,** scentless wild kind; **~-watch,** (Naut.) short half-watch of two hours (4–6 or 6–8 p.m.); **~'wood,** wild cornel or its wood, one of various similar trees. **6.** Hence **~'GISH¹** (-g-), ~'LIKE, *adjs.*, ~'HOOD *n.* [OE *docga*, of unkn. orig.]

dŏg² *v.t.* (**-gg-**). Follow closely, pursue, track, (person, his *steps*); (Mech.) grip with dog. [f. prec.]

dō'gāte *n.* Office of doge. [f. F *dogat* f. It. *dogato* (as foll.; see -ATE¹)]

dōge *n.* (Hist.) Chief magistrate of Venice or Genoa. [F f. It., f. Venetian *doze* f. L *dux ducis* leader]

dŏ'ggėd (-g-) *a.* Obstinate, tenacious, persistent, unyielding; **it's ~ as does it,** (colloq.) persistence succeeds; hence ~LY² *adv.*, ~NESS *n.* [ME, f. DOG¹ + -ED²]

dŏ'gger¹ (-g-) *n.* Two-masted bluff-bowed Dutch fishing-boat. [ME f. MDu., = fishing-boat]

dŏ'gger² (-g-) *n.* (Austral.) Dingo-hunter. [f. DOG¹ + -ER¹]

Dŏ'gger³ *n.* (Geol.) Middle section of European Jurassic strata. [dial., = kind of iron-stone, perh. f. DOG¹]

dŏ'ggerel (-g-) *a.* & *n.* Trivial, worthless, or irregular, (verse). [ME, app. f. DOG[1] (as in *dog Latin* etc.); cf. -REL]

dŏ'ggie (-gĭ) *n.* Little dog; (pet-name for) dog. [f. DOG[1] + -IE]

dŏ'ggō *adv.* (sl.) **Lie ~** (motionless or hidden, making no sign). [prob. f. DOG[1]; cf. -O]

dŏ'ggŏne *a.*, *adv.*, & *v.t.* (sl.) **1.** *a.* & *adv.* = DAMNED 2, 3. **2.** *v.t.* = DAMN 2. [prob. f. *dog on it* = *God damn it*]

doggy[1]. Var. of DOGGIE.

dŏ'gg|y̆[2] (-gĭ) *a.* Of dogs; devoted to dogs; hence **~iness** *n.* [f. DOG[1] + -Y[2]]

***dō'gie** (-gĭ) *n.* Motherless or neglected calf. [19th c.; orig. unkn.]

dŏ'gma *n.* Principle, tenet, doctrinal system, esp. as laid down by authority of Church; arrogant declaration of opinion. [L f. Gk *dogma -matos* opinion (*dokeō* seem)]

dŏgmă't|ic *a.* Of dogma(s), doctrinal, (*dogmatic theology*); based on a priori principles, not on induction; asserting dogmas or opinions (*about*), authoritative, arrogant; hence **~ics** *n.*, **~ically** *adv.* [f. LL f. Gk *dogmatikos* (as prec.; see -IC)]

dŏ'gmat|ize, -t|ise (-īz), *v.* **1.** *v.i.* Make positive unsupported assertions, speak authoritatively. **2.** *v.t.* Express (principle etc.) as a dogma. **3.** So **~ism** (1), **~ist** (1), *ns.* [f. F *dogmatiser* or f. LL f. Gk *dogmatizō* (as DOGMA; see -IZE)]

do-goo'd|er (dōō-) *n.* Well-meaning but unrealistic philanthropist or reformer; so **do'-good** (dōō'-) *a.* & *n.*, **~ism** (2) *n.*, **~y**[2] *a.* [f. DO[1] + GOOD + -ER[1]]

doh (dō), **dō**[3], *n.* (Mus.) Keynote of scale (*movable doh*), or the note C (*fixed doh*), in systems of SOLMIZATION. [18th c., f. It. *do*]

doi'ly̆, doy'ley, *n.* Small ornamental mat of paper, linen, etc., on plate for cakes etc. [orig. name of a fabric, f. surname]

do'ing (dōō'-) *n.* In vbl senses; activity, effort; (colloq.) scolding, beating; (in *pl.*, sl.) adjuncts, things needed. [f. DO[1] + -ING[1]]

doit *n.* (arch.) Very small amount of money. [f. MLG *doyt*, MDu. *duit*, of unkn. orig.]

dō'jō *n.* (*pl.* **~s**). Room or hall, mat, for practising judo. [Jap.]

dol. *abbr.* dollar(s).

dolce far niente (dŏlchā fâr nĭĕ'ntĭ) *n.* Pleasant idleness. (It., = sweet doing nothing]

dolce vita (dŏlchā vē'ta) *n.* Life of pleasure and luxury. [It., = sweet life]

dŏ'ldrums (-z) *n. pl.* Dullness, low spirits; becalmed state of ship; (fig.) state of stagnation; region of calms, sudden storms, and light unpredictable winds near equator. [prob. after *dull* and *tantrum*]

dōle[1] *n.*, & *v.t.* **1.** *n.* Charitable distribution; charitable (esp. sparing, niggardly) gift of food, clothes, or money; ‖**the ~,** (colloq.) benefit claimable by the unemployed from State (*on the ~*, receiving this). **2.** (arch.) Lot, destiny. **3.** *v.t.* Deal *out* sparingly, esp. as alms. [OE *dāl* f. Gmc ***dailaz**; cf. DEAL[1]]

dōle[2] *n.* (poet.) Grief, woe; lamentation. [ME, f. OF *do(e)l* etc. f. pop. L *dolus* f. L *dolēre* grieve]

dō'leful (-lf-) *a.* Dreary, dismal; sad, discontented, melancholy; hence **~ly**[2] *adv.*, **~ness** *n.* [ME, f. prec. + -FUL]

dŏ'lerite *n.* Coarse basaltic rock. [f. F *dolérite* f. Gk *doleros* deceptive (because its constituents are difficult to distinguish); see -ITE[1]]

dŏlĭchocĕphă'lic, -cĕ'phalous, (-ko-) *adjs.* Having a long or narrow head. [f. Gk *dolikhos* long + -CEPHALIC, -CEPHALOUS]

doli'na, doli'ne, (-ē'-) *n.* (Usu. large) sink-hole. [Russ. *dolina* valley]

dŏll *n.* & *v.* **1.** *n.* Small model of human figure, esp. of child as toy (**~'s house, *~'house,** miniature toy house for dolls, diminutive dwelling-house); ventriloquist's dummy; pretty but silly woman; (sl.) young woman; (sl.) attractive person. **2.** *v.t.* & *i.* (colloq.; esp. in *p.p.*) Dress *up* smartly. [pet-form of *Dorothy*]

dŏ'llar *n.* Unit of U.S. currency (**~ mark** or **~ sign,** $); unit of currency in other countries; (Hist.) German thaler, piece of eight; **~ area** (in which currency is linked to U.S. dollar); **~-bird,** (Austral.) roller with round white patch on wing; **~-diplomacy** (seeking to advance country's financial and commercial interests abroad, and hence its international influence); **~ gap,** excess of country's import trade with dollar area over corresp. export trade; **~ spot,** (discoloured patch caused by) fungal disease of lawns etc. [f. LG *daler* f. G *taler* (*Joachimstaler*, coin from silver-mine of the *Joachimstal* in Germany)]

dŏ'llop *n.*, & *v.t.* (colloq.) **1.** *n.* Clumsy or shapeless lump of food etc. **2.** *v.t.* Serve *out* in large quantities. [perh. f. Scand.]

dŏ'lly̆ *n.*, *a.*, & *v.* **1.** *n.* (Pet-name, esp. in *voc.*, for) doll; stick for stirring in clothes-washing; movable platform for cine camera; (colloq.) easily hit or caught ball at cricket; **~(-bird),** (colloq.) attractive young woman; **~ mixture** (of tiny variously shaped and coloured sweets). **2.** *a.* (colloq.) Attractive, fashionable, (girl, etc.); (Cricket) easily hit or caught. **3.** *v.t.* Dress *up* smartly. **4.** *v.i.* Move cine camera (*in* or *up* to subject, *out* from it). [f. DOLL + -Y[3]]

Dŏlly̆ Vâr'den *n.* CHAR[1] (*Salvelinus malma*) of western N. America; woman's large hat with one side drooping and with floral trimming. [character in Dickens's *Barnaby Rudge*]

dŏ'lman *n.* Long Turkish robe open in front; hussar's jacket worn with sleeves hanging loose; woman's mantle with capelike or dolman sleeves; **~ sleeve,** loose sleeve cut in one piece with body of coat etc. [ult. f. Turk. *dolama*]

dŏ'lmĕn *n.* Megalithic tomb with large flat stone laid on upright ones. [F, perh. f. Cornish *tolmēn* hole of stone]

dŏ'lomite *n.* Mineral or rock of calcium magnesium carbonate; hence **dŏlomĭ'tic** *a.* [F, f. S. G. de *Dolomieu*, Fr. geologist d. 1802; see -ITE[1]]

***dŏ'lor.** See DOLOUR.

dŏ'lorous *a.* (literary or joc.) Distressing, painful; dismal, doleful; distressed; hence **~ly**[2] *adv.* [ME, f. OF *doleros* f. LL *dolorosus* (as DOLOUR; see -OUS)]

dŏ'lour (-ler), ***dŏ'lor,** *n.* (literary). Sorrow, distress. [ME f. OF, f. L *dolor -oris* pain, grief]

dŏ'lphĭn *n.* Cetaceous mammal (*Delphinus delphis*), resembling porpoise but larger and with beaklike snout, whence **~ar'ium** *n.*, aquarium for dolphins; (pop.) dorado; curved fish in heraldry, sculpture, etc.; bollard, pile, or buoy, for mooring; structure for protecting pier of bridge. [ME, also *delphin* f. L *delphinus* f. Gk *delphis -inos*]

dōlt *n.* Stupid person; hence **~'ish**[1] *a.* [app. related to *dol*, *dold*, obs. vars. of DULL, DULLED]

Dŏm *n.* Title prefixed to names of some R.C. dignitaries, and Benedictine and Carthusian monks; Portuguese equivalent of DON[1] 1. [f. L *dominus* master, in second sense thr. Port.]

D.O.M. *abbr.* To God, the best and greatest. [f. L *Deo optimo maximo*]

-dom *suf.* forming *ns.* denoting (1) rank, condition, domain, f. *ns.* or *adjs.* (*earldom*, *freedom*, *kingdom*), (2) collective pl. or the ways of, f. *ns.* (*officialdom*). [OE *-dōm*, = OS *-dōm*, OHG *-tuom* orig. an independent n. = DOOM[1]]

domai'n *n.* Estate, lands, dominions; district

under rule, realm, sphere of influence; scope, field, province, of thought or action; (Math.) set of possible values of an independent variable; (Phys.) elementary region of magnetism in ferro-magnetic material; **eminent ~,** lordship of the sovereign power over all property in a State, with right of expropriation; hence **domā'n**IAL *a.* [ME, f. F *domaine*, OF *demeine* DEMESNE, assoc. w. L *dominus* lord]

domai'ne *n.* Vineyard. [F; see prec.]

dōme *n.*, & *v.t.* **1.** *n.* Rounded vault as roof, with circular, elliptical, or polygonal base, large cupola; revolving openable hemispherical roof of observatory; (Geol.) dome-shaped structure; natural vault, canopy, (of sky, trees, etc.); rounded summit of hill etc.; (sl.) head; (poet.) stately building; hence **dōm**ED² (-md), **dō'm**IC(AL), ~'LIKE (-ml-), **dō'm**Y², *adjs.* **2.** *v.t.* Cover with or shape as dome. [f. F *dôme* f. It. *duomo* cathedral, dome, f. L *domus* house]

Do'mesday (dōō'mzdā) *n.* ~ **(Book),** record of lands in England made in 1086 by order of William I. [ME var. of DOOM¹*sday*, as being book of final authority]

domĕ'stĭc *a.* & *n.* **1.** *a.* Of the home, household, or family affairs, (~ **science,** study of household management); of one's own country, not foreign or international (*domestic* TRADE); native, home-made; (of animal) kept by or living with man; fond of home life; hence **domĕ'st**ICALLY *adv.* **2.** *n.* Household servant. [f. F *domestique* f. L *domesticus* (*domus* home)]

domĕ'stĭc|āte *v.t.* Naturalize (plant, animal); make fond of home life; bring (animal) under human control, tame; hence ~ABLE *a.*, ~A'TION *n.* [f. med. L *domesticare* (as prec.) + -ATE³]

dŏmĕstĭ'cĭtȳ *n.* Being domestic; home life or privacy. [f. DOMESTIC + -ITY]

dŏ'mĭcīle, dŏ'mĭcĭl, *n.*, & *v.t.* **1.** Dwelling-place, home; (Law) place of permanent residence, fact of residing. **2.** *v.t.* Establish, settle, in a place; make (bill of exchange) payable *at* place. [ME f. OF, f. L *domicilium* (*domus* home)]

dŏmĭcĭ'liarȳ (-lyerĭ) *a.* Of a dwelling-place (~ **visit,** visit of doctor, officials, etc., to person's home). [f. F *domiciliaire* f. med. L *domiciliarius* (as prec.; see -ARY¹)]

dŏ'mĭn|ant *a.* & *n.* **1.** *a.* Ruling, prevailing, most influential; (of high place) outstanding, overlooking others. **2.** *n.* (Mus.) Fifth note of diatonic scale of any key; reciting note in church mode, usu. fifth from final. **3.** *a.* & *n.* (Genetics). (Characteristic) appearing in offspring even when a corresponding opposite characteristic is also inherited. **4.** Hence ~ANCE *n.*, **~ant**LY² *adv.* [F, f. L *dominari* (as foll.; see -ANT)]

dŏ'mĭnāte *v.t.* & *i.* Have commanding influence over or *over*; (of person, power, sound, feature of scene) be the most influential or conspicuous; (of high place) overlook, hold commanding position *over*. [f. L *dominari* (*dominus* lord) + -ATE³]

dŏmĭnā'tion *n.* **1.** Ascendancy, sway, control. **2.** (in *pl.*) Fourth ORDER¹ of ninefold celestial hierarchy. [ME f. OF, f. L *dominatio -onis* (as prec.; see -ATION)]

dŏmĭneer' *v.i.* Act imperiously, tyrannize, be overbearing. [f. Du. *domineren* f. F *dominer* (as DOMINATE; see -EER)]

domĭ'nĭcal *a.* Of the Lord's day, Sunday-, (~ **letter,** the one of the seven A–G indicating dates of Sundays in a year); of the Lord (Christ). [F, or f. LL *dominicalis* f. L *dominicus* (*dominus* lord; see -IC) + *-alis* -AL]

Domĭ'nĭcan *a.* & *n.* **1.** Of St. Dominic or his order of preaching friars, founded 1215. **2.** *n.* Black or Dominican friar. [f. med. L *Dominicanus* (*Dominicus* L name of *Domingo* de Guzmán (St. Dominic) + -AN)]

dŏ'mĭnĭe *n.* (Sc.) Schoolmaster. [later sp. of *domine* sir, voc. of L *dominus* lord]

domĭ'nion (-yon) *n.* Lordship, sovereignty, control; domains of feudal lord, territory of sovereign or government; (Hist.) title of self-governing territories of British Commonwealth. [ME f. OF, f. med. L *dominio -onis* f. L *dominium* (*dominus* lord)]

dŏ'mĭnō *n.* (*pl.* ~**es**). **1.** Loose cloak with mask for upper part of face, worn to conceal identity esp. at masquerade; hence ~ED² (-ōd) *a.* **2.** One of usu. 28 small oblong pieces marked with usu. 0–6 pips in each half, used in game of ~**es** (usu. treated as *sing.*); ~ **theory** (that political event etc. in one place will cause similar events in others, like row of falling dominoes). [F, prob. f. L *dominus* lord, but unexplained]

dŏn¹ *n.* **1.** (*D*~) Spanish title prefixed to Christian name (**Don Juan,** rake, libertine; *Don Quixote*); Spanish gentleman, Spaniard. **2.** Head, fellow, or tutor, of college, esp. at Oxford or Cambridge; (arch.) person of distinction. [Sp., f. L *dominus* lord]

dŏn² *v.t.* (-**nn**-). Put on (clothing). [=*do on*]

‖**dō'na(h)** *n.* (sl.) Woman, sweetheart. [f. Sp. *doña* or Port. *dona* f. L (as DONNA)]

donā'te *v.t.* Make donation of. [back form. f. foll.]

donā'tion *n.* Bestowal, presenting; thing presented, gift (esp. of money given to institution). [ME f. OF, f. L *donatio -onis* (*donare* give f. *donum* gift; see -ATION)]

dŏ'natĭve *a.* & *n.* (Given as) donation or bounty; (Hist., of benefice) given directly, not presentative. [ME, f. L *donativum* gift, largess (*donare*; see prec., -IVE)]

done (dŭn) *a.* In vbl senses; (colloq.) socially acceptable (*the done thing; it isn't done*); ~ **(in, up)**, (colloq.) tired out; (esp. as *int.* in reply to offer etc.) accepted; **be ~ with,** have (been) finished with; **have ~,** cease; **have ~ with,** finish dealing with. [p.p. of DO¹]

dōnee' *n.* Recipient of gift. [f. DONOR + -EE]

dŏng *v.i.*, & *n.* (Make) deep sound of large bell; (Austral. & N.Z. colloq.) heavy blow. [imit.]

dŏ'nga (-ngga) *n.* (S. Afr. etc.) Gully, ravine. [Bantu]

dŏ'njon (*or* dŭ'-) *n.* Great tower of castle, keep. [arch. sp. of DUNGEON]

dŏ'nkey *n.* = ASS¹ (**talk the hind leg off a ~,** talk incessantly); stupid person; ~ **engine,** small auxiliary engine; ~ **jacket,** workman's thick weatherproof jacket; **~'s years,** (colloq.) a very long time; **~-work,** drudgery, laborious part of an enterprise. [18th c., perh. f. DUN¹, or proper name *Duncan* (cf. *dicky, neddy*)]

dŏ'nna *n.* (*D*~, title of) Italian or Spanish or Portuguese lady. [It., f. L *domina* mistress fem. of *dominus*; cf. DON¹]

donnée, donné, (dŏ'nā) *n.* Subject or theme of story etc.; basic fact or assumption. [F, fem. or masc. p.p. of *donner* give]

dŏ'nnĭsh *a.* Like a college don; pedantic; hence ~LY² *adv.*, ~NESS *n.* [f. DON¹ + -ISH¹]

Dŏ'nnȳbrŏŏk *n.* Scene of uproar, free fight. [~ near Dublin, Ireland, formerly site of annual fair]

dō'nor *n.* Giver of gift; person or animal providing blood for transfusion, semen for insemination, organ for transplantation, etc.; (Chem. & Phys.) atom or molecule that gives an electron to another or to a crystal. [ME, f. AF *donour*, OF *doneur* f. L *donator -oris* (*donare* give; see -OR)]

dōn't¹. See DO¹.

dōn't² *n.* Prohibition (DO²*s and don'ts*). [f. prec.]

***dōō'dăd** *n.* Fancy article; trivial ornament; gadget. [20th c.; orig. unkn.]

dōō'dah *n.* (sl.) = prec.; **all of a ~,** excited, dithering. [f. refrain of song *Camptown Races*]

dōō'dle *v.i.*, & *n.* **1.** *v.i.* Scrawl or draw absent-mindedly; hence **dōō'dlER**[1] *n.* **2.** *n.* Scrawl or drawing so made; **~-bug,** *(larva of) tiger-beetle,*unscientific device for locating minerals, (colloq.) flying bomb. [orig. = foolish person; cf. LG *dudelkopf*]

***dōō'hĭckey** *n.* (colloq.) Small object, esp. mechanical. [f. DOODAD + HICKEY]

dōōm[1] *n.* **1.** Fate, destiny, (usu. evil); ruin, death; **~'watch,** observation to prevent destruction of the environment. **2.** (Hist.) Statute, law, decree. **3.** (arch.) Decision, sentence, condemnation. **4.** The Last Judgement (*crack, day, of doom*; *doo'msday*; **~sday machine,** hypothetical weapon able to annihilate mankind; **till ~sday,** for ever; cf. DOMESDAY). [OE *dōm*, = OS *dōm*, OHG *tuom*, ON *dómr*, Goth. *dōms* f. Gmc **dōmaz* that which is set, f. as DO[1]]

dōōm[2] *v.t.* Pronounce sentence against, condemn *to* some fate, *to* do; (esp. in *p.p.*) consign to misfortune or destruction. [ME, f. prec.]

door (dōr) *n.* **1.** Hinged or sliding barrier usu. of wood or metal for closing entrance to building, room, safe, etc. (FRONT *door*; *lives* etc. **next ~,** in next house or room; so **three ~s away** etc.; **next ~ to,** (fig.) nearly, almost, near to; *at* DEATH's *door*); **~-to-~** *a.*, (of selling etc.) done at each house in turn, (of journey) from start to finish. **2.** Entrance, access, exit, (**close the ~ to,** make impossible; **foot in the ~,** chance of ultimate success; **leave the ~ open,** preserve possibility; **open the ~ to,** create opportunity for; **packed to the ~s,** entirely full; **show** person **the ~,** dismiss him); doorway. **3. Out of ~s,** in or into the open air; DARKEN *door*; **lay, lie, at the ~ of,** impute, be imputable, to. **4. ~'bell,** bell in house rung by handle or button outside door; **~-case, -frame,** structure in which door is fitted; **~-head,** upper part of door-case; **~-keeper,** person who guards door, janitor, porter; **~'knob** (for turning to release latch of door); **~'man,** = *door-keeper*; **~'mat,** mat for wiping mud from shoes, (fig.) despised passive person; **~'nail** (with which doors were studded for strength or ornament; DEAD *as a doornail*); **~-plate** (usu. of brass, bearing occupant's name); **~'post,** upright of door-case; **~'step,** step leading up to usu. outer door (*on* one's or *the ~step*, (fig.) very near), (sl.) thick slice of bread; **~'stop,** device for keeping door open or to prevent it from striking wall etc.; **~'way,** opening filled by door; ***~'yard,** yard or garden near house-door. **5.** Hence (-)~ED[2] (dōrd), **~'LESS,** *adjs.* [OE *duru*, *dor*, = OS *duru*, *dor*, OHG *tor*, Goth. *daur* f. Gmc **dur-*]

dŏp *n.* (S. Afr.) Cheap brandy; tot of liquor. [Afrik.]

dō'pa *n.* Crystalline amino-acid used in treatment of Parkinsonism. [G, f. *dioxyphenylalanine*]

dōpe *n.* & *v.* **1.** *n.* Thick liquid used as food or lubricant; varnish used esp. in aeroplane manufacture; (sl.) narcotic, stupefying drug (**~-fiend,** drug addict); drug etc. given to horse or greyhound to affect its performance; (sl.) information about a subject, esp. if not generally known; (sl.) misleading information; (colloq.) stupid person. **2.** *v.t.* Administer dope to, drug; add impurity to (semiconductor etc.), whence **dō'pANT** *n.*; **~ out,** (sl.) discover. **3.** *v.i.* Indulge in narcotics etc. [f. Du. *doop* sauce (*doopen* to dip)]

dō'pey *a.* (sl.) Stupefied (as) by a drug; stupid. [f. prec. + -Y[2]]

doppelgänger (dŏ'pelgĕnger) *n.* Wraith of living person. [G, = double-goer]

Dŏ'pper *n.* (S. Afr.) Member of the Gereformeerde Kerk, usu. regarded as old-fashioned in ideas etc. [Afrik.]

Dŏ'ppler *n.* **~ effect** or **shift,** apparent increase (decrease) in frequency of sound, light, or other waves when source and observer become closer (more distant). [f. C. J. ~, Austrian physicist d. 1853]

dōr *n.* Insect flying with loud humming noise. [OE *dora*; prob. imit.]

dora'dō (-ah'-) *n.* (*pl.* **~s**). Blue and silver sea-fish of genus *Coryphaena*, showing brilliant colours when dying out of water; S. Amer. carplike fish of genus *Salminus*. [Sp., f. L DE(*auratus* gilt f. *aurum* gold; see -ADO)]

Dōr'ian *a.* & *n.* **1.** (Inhabitant) of or from Doris in ancient Greece. **2.** *a.* **~ mode,** (Mus.) (1) ancient Greek MODE, reputedly simple and solemn in character, (2) first of church modes (with D as final and A as dominant). [f. L f. Gk *Dōrios* (*Dōris*; cf. foll.) + -AN]

Dŏ'rĭc *a.* & *n.* **1.** *a.* (Of dialect) broad, rustic; **~ order,** (Archit.) oldest, sturdiest, and simplest of the Greek ORDER[1]s. **2.** *n.* Dialect of Dorians in ancient Greece; rustic English or esp. Scots; Doric order. [f. L f. Gk *Dōrikos* (as prec.; see -IC)]

Dōr'kĭng *a.* & *n.* (Fowl) of the Dorking breed (large, white, with five toes). [~ in Surrey]

dōrm *n.* (colloq.) Dormitory. [abbr.]

dōr'm|ant *a.* Lying inactive as in sleep (of some animals through winter, undeveloped buds, potential faculties); (Her., of beast) lying with head on paws; not acting or in use, in abeyance, (*lie dormant*); hence **~ANCY** *n.* [ME f. OF, part. of *dormir* f. L *dormire* sleep; see -ANT]

dōr'mer *n.* **~ (window),** projecting upright window in sloping roof. [f. OF *dormēor* (as prec.; see -ER[2] (3))]

dōr'mĭtorȳ *n.* Sleeping-room with several beds and sometimes cubicles; suburban or country district of city workers' residences; *university or college hall of residence or hostel. [ME, f. L *dormitorium* (*dormire -it-* sleep; see -ORY)]

dōr'mouse *n.* (*pl.* **-mice** *pr.* -mīs). Small hibernating rodent of family Gliridae, resembling mouse and squirrel. [ME; orig. unkn.]

dōr'mȳ *a.* (Golf). (Of player or side) as many holes ahead in score as there are holes left to play (*dormy one, five*, etc.). [19th c.; orig. unkn.]

||**Dŏ'rothȳ** *n.* **~ bag,** woman's open-topped handbag closed by draw-string and slung by loops from wrist. [fem. name]

dōrp *n.* (S. Afr.) Village, small township. [Du., as THORP]

dōr'sal *a.* (Anat., Zool., & Bot.) of, on, near, the back; ridge-shaped; hence **~LY**[2] *adv.* [F, or f. LL *dorsalis* f. L *dorsum* back; see -AL]

dōr'ter, dōr'tour (-ter), *n.* (Hist.) Bedroom, dormitory, esp. in monastery. [ME, f. OF *dortour* f. L *dormitorium* DORMITORY]

dōr'ȳ[1] *n.* (Also **John D~**) yellow European marine food-fish (*Zeus faber*). [ME, f. F *dorée* fem. p.p. of *dorer* gild (as DORADO)]

dōr'ȳ[2] *n.* Flat-bottomed skiff, esp. *fishing-vessel's boat. [18th c.; orig. unkn.]

dos-à-dos (dōzahdō') *adv.*, *n.* (*pl.* same), & *a.* **1.** *adv.* (arch.) Back to back. **2.** *n.* Seat, carriage, etc., in which occupants sit back to back. **3.** *a.* (Of two books) bound together with shared central board and facing in opposite directions. [F]

dō'sage *n.* Giving of medicine in doses; size of dose. [f. foll. + -AGE]

dōse *n.*, & *v.t.* **1.** *n.* Amount of medicine to be taken at once (lit., or fig. of flattery, punishment, etc.; **like a ~ of salts,** (sl.) very fast); amount of radiation received by person or thing exposed to it, whence **dōsĭ'METER, dōsĭ'METRY,**

ns., **dōsĭmĕ'tr**IC *a.*; (sl.) venereal infection. **2.** *v.t.* Give medicine to (person); adulterate, blend, (esp. wine with spirit). [F, f. LL f. Gk *dosis* gift (*didōmi* give)]

‖**dŏss** *n.*, & *v.i.* (sl.) **1.** *n.* Bed, esp. in **~-house** = cheap lodging-house. **2.** *v.i.* Sleep, esp. in doss-house; **~ down,** sleep on makeshift bed; hence **~'**ER[1] *n.* [prob. = *doss* ornamental covering for seat-back etc., f. OF *dos* f. pop. L *dossum* f. L *dorsum* back]

dŏ'ssal *n.* Hanging cloth behind altar or round a chancel. [f. med. L *dossale* f. LL *dorsalis* DORSAL]

dŏ'ssier (*or* dŏ'syā) *n.* Set of documents, esp. record of information about a person or event. [F, so called f. label on back (*dos* f. L *dorsum*; see -ER[2] (2))]

dost. See DO[1].

dŏt[1] *n.* Small spot, speck, roundish pen-mark; such mark written or printed as part of *i* or *j*, or as diacritical mark; (Mus.) such mark used to denote lengthening of note or rest, or to indicate staccato; decimal point; tiny object; shorter signal of the two used in Morse code; **on the ~,** exactly on time; ‖**the year ~,** (colloq.) very long ago. [16th c., perh. repr. OE *dott* head of boil]

dŏt[2] *v.t.* (-tt-). Mark with dot(s); place dot over (letter; **~ the i's and cross the t's,** (fig.) be minutely accurate, emphasize details); (Mus.) mark (note or rest) to show time value increased by half; diversify as with dots (*sea dotted with ships*); scatter (*about, all over*) like dots; (sl.) hit (*dotted him one in the eye*); **~ and carry** (**one**), child's formula for remembering to carry in addition sum, (joc., also **~ and go one,** *n.*, *a.*, & *adv.*) limp, limping(ly); **~ted line,** (esp.) line of dots on document to show place left for signature (*sign on the ~ted line*, give formal agreement). [f. prec.]

dot[3] (dŏt) *n.* Woman's dowry. [F, f. L *dos dotis* (**do-* give)]

dō'tage. See DOTE.

dō'tard *n.* One in his dotage. [ME, f. foll. + -ARD]

dōte *v.i.* Be silly, deranged, infatuated, or feeble-minded, esp. from age, whence **dō'**TAGE (2) *n.*; **~ on,** be excessively fond of. [ME, corresp. to MDu. *doten* be silly]

doth. See DO[1].

dŏ'tterel *n.* Small plover, *Eudromias morinellus*. [ME, f. DOTE + -REL, named from the ease with which it is caught, taken to indicate stupidity]

dŏ'ttle *n.* Remnant of unburnt tobacco in pipe. [f. DOT[1] + -LE 1]

dŏ'tt|ў *a.* (colloq.) Feeble-minded; silly; absurd; hence **~ĭ**NESS *n.* [f. DOT[1] + -Y[2]]

Dou'ai, Dou'ay, (dōō'ā *or* dow'ā) *n.* **~ version, Bible,** English translation of the Bible used in R.C. Church., completed at ~ in France early in 17th c.

doua'ne (dōōah'n) *n.* Foreign custom-house. [F, f. It. *do*(*g*)*ana* f. Turk. *duwan*, Arab. *dīwān*; cf. DIVAN]

dou'ble[1] (dŭ'-) *a.* & *adv.* **1.** *a.* Consisting of two members, things, layers, sets, etc., forming a pair, twofold; folded, bent, stooping. **2.** Having some part double; (of flower) with petals multiplied by conversion of stamens etc.; (of domino) with same number of pips on each half. **3.** Having twofold relation, dual, ambiguous; twice as much or as many (*double the amount*); of twofold or extra size, strength, value, etc., (*a double whisky*); (Mus.) lower in pitch by an octave (*double bassoon* etc.); deceitful, hypocritical (*playing a double game*). **4.** Hence **~**NESS (-beln-) *n.*, **dou'b**LY[2] (dŭ'-) *adv.* **5.** *adv.* To twice the amount etc. (**see ~,** seem to see two thing when there is only one; esp. of drunken person); two together (*sleep double*). **6.** *Double* ACROSTIC; **~-acting** (in two ways, directions, etc., esp. of engine in which steam acts on both sides of piston); **~ agent,** one who spies for two rival countries etc.; **~ axe** (with two blades); **~-banking,** (1) = *double-parking*, (2) (Austral. & N.Z.) riding two on a horse etc.; **~-barrel,** double-barrelled (gun); **~-barrelled,** (of gun) having two barrels, (fig.) twofold, (of surname) having two parts; **~-bass,** lowest-pitched instrument of violin family; **~ bed** (for two persons); **~ bill,** programme with two principal items; **~ bind,** dilemma; **~-bitt** *v.t.*, (Naut.) pass (cable) twice round bitts or round two pairs of bitts; **~-blind** *a.* & *n.*, (test etc.) in which neither tester nor subject has knowledge of identities etc. that might lead to bias; **~ boiler,** saucepan with detachable upper compartment heated by boiling water in lower; **~ bond,** (Chem.) pair of bonds between two atoms; **~-breasted,** (of coat etc.) having two fronts overlapping across body; **~-check** *v.t.*, verify twice or in two ways; **~ chin,** chin with fold of flesh under it; **~ concerto** (for two solo instruments); **~ cream,** thick cream with high fat-content; **~-cross** *n.*, & *v.t.*, (subject to) act of treachery or cheating; *double* DAGGER; **~-dealer,** deceiver; **~-dealing** *n.* & *a.*, deceit(ful); *double*-DECKER; *double*-DECLUTCH; **~ decomposition,** (Chem.) simultaneous decomposition of two compounds in reaction; **~ drummer,** (Austral.) noisy kind of cicada; *double* DUMMY; *double* DUTCH[1]; **~-dyed,** dyed twice (usu. fig., deeply stained with guilt); *double* EAGLE; **~-edged,** having two cutting edges, (fig.) damaging to user as well as his opponent; *double* ENTRY; **~ exposure,** (Photog.) accidentally or deliberately repeated exposure of film etc.; **~-faced,** insincere; *double* FAULT; **~ feature,** cinema programme with two full-length films; *double figures* (FIGURE[1] 5); ‖**~ first,** (person winning) first-class honours in two subjects or examinations at university; **~ fleece,** (Austral. & N.Z., from sheep that has missed a shearing); **~-ganger,** = DOPPELGÄNGER; **~ glazing,** (provision of) two sheets of glass in a window to reduce heat loss etc.; **~ harness,** harness for two horses, (fig.) matrimony or close partnership; ***~ header,** two games etc. in succession between same opponents; **~ helix,** pair of parallel helices with common axis, esp. in structure of DNA molecule; **~-jointed,** having joints that allow unusual bending of fingers, limbs, etc.; **~ life,** sustaining of two different characters in one's life, esp. one virtuous and the other not; **~-lock** *v.t.*, lock by double turn of key; **~ meaning,** = DOUBLE ENTENDRE; *double* OBELISK; *double* PADDLE[1]; **~-parking,** parking of vehicle alongside one that is already parked at roadside; **~ play,** (Baseball) putting out two runners; **~ pneumonia** (of both lungs); **~-quick** *a.* & *adv.*, at running pace (lit. or fig.); **~-reef** *v.t.*, (Naut.) reduce spread of (sail) by two reefs; *double* REFRACTION, RHYME[1]; **~ room,** bedroom for two persons; **~ salt,** (Chem.) salt composed of two simple salts and having different crystal properties from either; **~ saucepan,** = *double boiler*; *double* SHUFFLE; **~ standard,** (1) rule etc. applied more strictly to some persons than to others, (2) bimetallism; **~ star,** two stars actually or apparently very close together; **~-stopping,** (Mus.) sounding of two notes at once on stringed instrument; **~ take,** delayed reaction to situation etc. immediately after one's first reaction; **~-talk,** verbal expression that is (usu. deliberately) ambiguous; **~-think,** mental capacity to accept contrary opinions etc. at same time; *double* TIDE¹*s*; **~ time,** payment of employee at twice normal rate, (Mil.) regulation running-pace; *double* TRACK¹; **~ wedding** (of two couples at same time). [ME, f. OF *doble, duble* f. L *duplus* DUPLE]

dou'ble² (dŭ'-) *n.* **1.** Double quantity or thing, double measure of spirits etc., twice as much or many (**~ or quits,** game, throw, toss, deciding whether person shall pay either twice his loss or debt, or nothing); counterpart of thing or person, understudy, wraith; **at the ~**, running, hastening. **2.** Pair of victories over same team, pair of championships at same game, etc.; (Bridge) doubling of a bid; (Lawn Tennis etc., in *pl.*) game between two pairs; (Darts) throw on narrow ring enclosed by two outer circles of dartboard, scoring double; (Racing) bet on two horses etc. in different races, winnings and stake from one race being bet on the second; sharp turn of hunted animal, or of river. [f. prec. and foll.]

dou'ble³ (dŭ'-) *v.* **1.** *v.t.* Make double, increase twofold, multiply by two; (Bridge) make call increasing value of points to be won or lost on (opponent's bid); amount to twice as much as; (Mus.) add same note in higher or lower octave to; (of actor) play (two parts) in same piece; (of musician) play as second (instrument) besides one's main instrument. **2.** ~ (**up**), put (passenger etc.) in same quarters as another, bet twofold (stake). **3.** Bend or turn (paper, cloth) over upon itself; clench (fist). **4.** (Naut.) Get round (headland). **5.** *v.t.* & *i.* **~ up,** bend one's body into stooping or curled-up position (fig., be convulsed with laughter or pain), cause (another) to do this by blow, fold (paper, leaf, etc.) or become folded. **6.** (Bill.) (Cause to) rebound. **7.** *v.i.* Move at double pace, run. **8.** Turn sharply in flight or pursuit, take tortuous course (**~ back,** take direction opposite to previous one). **9.** Play twofold part (*as*). [ME, f. OF *dobler, dubler* f. LL *duplare* (L *duplus* DOUBLE¹)]

double entendre (dōōblahṅtah'ṅdr) *n.* Ambiguous expression, phrase with two meanings, one usu. indecent; use of such phrases. [obs. F, = double understanding]

double entente (dōōblahṅtah'ṅt) *n.* = prec. [F]

dou'blėt (dŭ'-) *n.* **1.** (Hist.) Man's close-fitting body-garment with or without sleeves and short skirts (**~ and hose,** masculine attire, light attire without cloak). **2.** One of a pair, esp. one of two words of same derivation but different sense (*fashion* and *faction*, *cloak* and *clock*). **3.** (in *pl.*) Same number on two dice thrown at once. **4.** Pair of associated lines close together in spectrum. **5.** Combination of two simple lenses. [ME f. OF (*double*; see DOUBLE¹, -ET)]

dou'bleton (dŭ'belton) *n.* Two cards only of a suit (dealt to a player). [f. DOUBLE¹, after *singleton*]

doublōō'n (dŭ- *or* du-) *n.* (Hist.) Spanish gold coin, double pistole; (sl., in *pl.*) money. [f. F *doublon* or f. Sp. *doblón* (as DOUBLE¹; see -OON)]

doublure (dōōblūr') *n.* Ornamental usu. leather lining inside book-cover. [F, = lining (*doubler* to line; see -URE)]

doubt¹ (dowt) *n.* **1.** Feeling of uncertainty (*about*), undecided frame of mind, inclination to disbelieve (*of, about*), hesitation, (*be in no doubt about*; *have* or *make no doubt that; have* one's *doubts about*; **no ~**, certainly, probably, admittedly). **2.** Uncertain state of things, lack of full proof (BENEFIT¹ *of the doubt*) or of clear signs of the future (**beyond ~, without (a) ~,** certainly). [ME, f. OF *d(o)ute* (*douter*; see foll.)]

doubt² (dowt) *v.i.* & *t.* Feel undecided or uncertain (about); be undecided about or *about*, hesitate to believe or trust, call in question, (person, thing, *whether, if*, (neg. or interrog.) *that, but, but that*); have doubts *of* (esp. w. neg.; *never doubted of success*); ||(arch. or dial.) be afraid, rather think, suspect, that (*I doubt we are late*); **~ing Thomas,** incredulous or sceptical person (after John 20: 24–29); hence ~'ER¹ *n.* [ME f. OF *doter, duter, douter*, f. L *dubitare* hesitate; mod. sp. after L]

dou'btful (dow't-) *a.* Feeling or causing doubt; uncertain in meaning, character, truth, or result; undecided, ambiguous, questionable; unreliable (*doubtful ally*); giving reason to suspect evil; unsettled in opinion, uncertain, hesitating; hence ~LY² *adv.*, ~NESS *n.* [ME, f. DOUBT¹ + -FUL]

dou'btlėss (dow't-) *adv.* Certainly, no doubt; probably; admittedly. [f. DOUBT¹ + -LESS]

douce (dōōs) *a.* (Sc.) Sober, gentle, sedate. [ME, f. OF *dous douce* f. L *dulcis* sweet]

douceur (dōō'sėr) *n.* Gratuity; bribe. [F, f. Rom. **dulçōre* f. LL *dulcor* sweetness]

douche (dōōsh) *n.* & *v.* **1.** *n.* Jet of liquid applied to body as form of bathing or for medicinal purpose; device for producing such jet. **2.** *v.t.* Administer douche to. **3.** *v.i.* Take douche. [F, f. It. *doccia* pipe (*docciare* pour by drops f. Rom. **ductiare* f. L *ductus*; see DUCT)]

dough (dō) *n.* Kneaded moistened flour, bread-paste; (sl.) money; **~'boy,** boiled dumpling, (colloq.) U.S. infantryman; hence ~Y² (dō'ĭ) *a.* [OE *dāg*, = OHG *teic*, ON *deig*, Goth. *daigs* f. Gmc **daigaz* (**daig-* f. IE **dhoigh-* etc. knead)]

dou'ghnŭt (dō'n-) *n.* Sweetened and fried cake of dough, often ring-shaped; ring-shaped object, esp. (Phys.) vacuum chamber for acceleration of particles in betatron etc. [f. prec. + NUT]

dou'ght|ȳ (dow'tĭ) *a.* (arch. or joc.) Valiant, stout, formidable; hence ~ĭLY² *adv.*, ~ĭNESS *n.* [OE *dohtig* var. of *dyhtig* = MLG, MDu. *duchtich*, MHG *tühtic* f. Gmc **dug-* be strong]

Dou'glas (dŭ'-) *n.* ~ **fir, pine,** or **spruce,** large conifer of genus *Pseudotsuga*, of western N. America. [f. D. ~, Sc. botanist d. 1834]

Dou'khobōr (dōō'ko-) *n.* Member of Russian religious sect, with some likeness in doctrines to Quakers, of which large numbers migrated from Russia to Canada in 1899 after persecutions for refusing military service. [f. Russ. *dukhobor* spirit-wrestler]

doum (*or* dōōm) *n.* ~(**-palm**), Egyptian palm-tree (*Hyphaene thebaica*) with edible fruit. [f. Arab. *dawm, dūm*]

dour (door) *a.* (Sc.) Severe, stern, obstinate; hence ~'LY² *adv.*, ~'NESS *n.* [ME, prob. f. Gael. *dúr* dull, obstinate, perh. f. L *durus* hard]

douroucou'lĭ (doorōōkōō'-) *n.* Nocturnal Amer. monkey of genus *Aotus*, with large staring eyes. [f. Indian name]

douse, dowse¹, *v.t.* (Naut.) lower (sail), close (porthole); extinguish (light); throw water over, drench. [16th c., perh. rel. to MDu., LG *dossen* strike]

dove¹ (dŭv) *n.* Bird of family Columbidae, pigeon, (esp. RING¹-*dove*, STOCK*dove*, TURTLE¹-*dove*); Holy Spirit; gentle or innocent person, beloved person; (Polit.) person advocating negotiation rather than violence; **~-colour(ed)**, (of) warm grey; **~'cot(e)**, pigeon-house (*flutter the ~cots*, alarm quiet people); **~-hawk,** hen-harrier (from its colour); **~'s-foot,** kind of crane's-bill; **~-tree,** Chinese tree (*Davidia involucrata*) with dovelike flowers. [ME, f. ON *dúfa*, = OS *dūba*, OHG *tūba*, Goth. *dūbo* f. Gmc **dūbhōn*, perh. imit.]

dōve². See DIVE.

do'vekĭe (dŭ'vkĭ) *n.* Little AUK. [Sc. dim. of DOVE¹]

Dō′ver *n.* **~'s powder,** medicine of opium and ipecacuanha. [f. T. ~, Engl. physician d. 1742]

do′vetail (dŭ′vt-) *n.* & *v.* **1.** *n.* Tenon shaped like dove's spread tail or reversed wedge, fitting into corresponding mortise and forming joint; such a joint. **2.** *v.t.* & *i.* Put together with dovetails; (fig.) fit together compactly or neatly (*into, with*). [f. DOVE¹ + TAIL¹]

dow′ager *n.* Woman with title or property derived from her late husband (often in comb., *Queen dowager, dowager countess* or *countess dowager, dowager duchess*); (colloq.) dignified elderly lady. [f. OF *douag(i)ere* (*douage*, as DOWER; see -ER² (2))]

dow′d|y̆ *n.* & *a.* (Woman) shabbily, badly, or unfashionably dressed; (of dress etc.) unattractively dull, unfashionable; hence **~ĭLY²** *adv.*, **~ĬNESS** *n.* [f. ME *dowd* slut, of unkn. orig.]

dow′el *n.*, & *v.t.* (‖-ll-). **1.** *n.* Headless pin of wood, metal, etc., for keeping two pieces of wood, stone, etc., in proper relative position; hence **~(l)ING¹** (3) *n.* **2.** *v.t.* Fasten with dowel. [ME, f. MLG *dovel*, = OHG *tubili*; cf. THOLE²]

dow′er *n.*, & *v.t.* **1.** *n.* Widow's share for life of husband's estate; (arch. or poet.) dowry; endowment, gift of nature, talent; ‖**~ house,** smaller house near big one, forming part of widow's dower; hence **~LESS** *a.* **2.** *v.t.* Give dowry to; endow *with* talent etc. [ME, f. OF *douaire* f. med. L *dotarium* f. L *dos dotis*; see -ARY¹]

Dow-Jō′nes (-nz) *n.* **~ index** etc., figure indicating relative price of shares on N.Y. Stock Exchange. [f. C. H. *Dow* d. 1902 & E. D. *Jones* d. 1920, Amer. economists]

dow′las *n.* Strong coarse calico or (Hist.) linen. [f. *D(a)oulas* in Brittany]

down¹ *n.* Open high land, esp. (in *pl.*) treeless undulating chalk uplands of S. England and elsewhere, used for pasture; **the D~s,** part of sea (opposite North Downs) off E. Kent. [OE *dūn*, = OS *dūna*, perh. f. OCelt. **dūnom*]

down² *n.* First covering of young birds; bird's under-plumage, used in cushions etc.; fine short hair, esp. first hair on youth's face; similar substance on plant, fruit, etc.; fluffy substance (THISTLE*down*). [ME, f. ON *dúnn*]

down³ *adv.* (*superl.* **~′most**). **1.** Denoting motion: from above, to lower place, to ground, from bedroom etc., (*knock, fall, down*; BRING *down*, COME *down*, GET¹ *down*, GO¹ *down*, PUT¹ *down*, SET¹ *down*, TURN¹ *down*; *brought down by river*; **cash ~, pay ~,** (at once, as though on counter); WRITE, **copy, ~,** (on paper); *meeting is ~ for next week, he is ~ to speak at the meeting*, (on programme)); to place regarded as lower, into helpless position, with current or wind, southwards, ‖from capital or university, (of ship's helm) with rudder to windward, (BEAR³ *down*; SEND¹ *down*; UP *and down*; **run, ride, hunt, ~,** overtake and trap; **howl, shout, ~** (into silence); *down to Norfolk from Scotland, to Scotland* or *the country from London*); (as *int.*) lie, get, put, bring, etc., down (*down, Bonzo!*; and w. *with, down with the aristocrats!*). **2.** Denoting position: in lower place (*blinds were down*; *is not ~ yet*, i.e. out of bedroom etc.); in place regarded as lower, ‖not in capital or university (*down in Devon, in the country, in the south*; **~ south, ~ east,** *in southern, eastern, States); in fallen posture, prostrate, at low level, in depression, humiliation, restraint, etc., (*hit a man who is down*; *many down with colds*; *river, sun, temperature, tide, is down*; *down to* one's *last penny*, one's *underwear*; KEEP¹ *down*; *bread is ~*, now cheaper). **3.** Denoting order, time, quality: inclusively of lower limit in series (*from King down to cobbler*); from earlier to later time (*custom handed down*); to finer consistency or smaller size (*boil, grind, thin, wear, down*); into quiescence (*calm down*); in position of lagging or loss (*team was three goals down*; *£5 down on the transaction*). **4. Be ~ on,** disapprove of; DO¹ *down*; **~ to the ground,** (colloq.) completely; **~-hearted,** dejected; *down at* HEEL¹; *down on* one's LUCK; **~ in the mouth,** down-hearted; **~ and out,** unable to resume fight in boxing, (fig.) beaten in the struggle of life, completely without resources or means of livelihood (so **~-and-out** *n.*); **~-to-earth,** practical, realistic; **~ under,** at the antipodes, in Australia etc. [OE *dūn(e)* (*adūne* ADOWN)]

down⁴ *prep.* Downwards along, through, or into; from top to bottom of; at or in a lower part of (*situated down the river*); UP *and down*; along (*walk down the road*; *cut down the middle*); **~ stage,** at or to front of theatre stage; **~ town,** into town from higher or outlying part, *to or in business part of city; **~ (the) wind,** in direction in which it is blowing (*let go ~ the wind*, abandon, discard). [f. prec.]

down⁵ *a.* (*superl.* **~′most**). Directed downwards; **~ beat,** (Mus.) accented beat; **~ draught,** downward draught, esp. one down chimney into room; **~ grade,** descending slope of road or railway, (fig.) deterioration; **~ payment** (made in cash, esp. initially and to be followed by instalments); **~-stroke** (made or written downwards); **~ train,** train going or coming from capital or place regarded as higher (**~ platform,** for such train's departure or arrival). [f. DOWN³]

down⁶ *v.t.* (colloq.) Knock, bring, swallow, (person, aeroplane, drink) down; **~ tools,** cease work for the day etc., go on strike. [f. DOWN³]

down⁷ *n.* Act of putting down (esp. in Wrestling, Amer. & Can. Footb.); reverse of fortune (usu. **ups and ~s,** UP 10); (Dominoes) play of first piece; **have a ~ on,** (colloq.) dislike, have grudge against. [f. DOWN³]

Down⁸ *n.* **~'s syndrome,** mongolism. [f. J. L. H. ~, Engl. physician d. 1896]

dow′nbeat *a.* Pessimistic, gloomy; relaxed, unemphatic. [f. DOWN⁵ *beat*]

dow′ncast¹ (-n-kah-) *n.* Shaft for introducing fresh air into mine. [f. DOWN³ + CAST²]

dow′ncast² (-n-kah-) *a.* (Of look) directed downwards; dejected. [f. DOWN³ + p.p. of CAST¹]

dow′ncomer (-n-kŭ-) *n.* Pipe for downward transport of water or gas. [f. DOWN³ + COMER]

dow′ner *n.* (sl.) Depressant drug; a depressing experience. [f. DOWN⁶ + -ER¹]

dow′nfall (-awl) *n.* Great fall of rain etc.; fall from prosperity, ruin. [ME, f. DOWN³ + FALL²]

dow′ngrāde (-n-g-) *v.t.* Lower in rank etc. [f. DOWN⁵ *grade*]

downhĭll *n.*, *a.*, & *adv.* **1.** *n.* (dow′-). Downward slope, decline, (**~ of life,** later half); downhill race in skiing. **2.** *a.* (dow′-). Sloping down, descending, declining. **3.** *adv.* (-ĭ′l). In descending direction, on a decline. [f. DOWN³,⁴ + HILL]

Dow′nĭng Street *n.* British Government, Prime Minister, or Foreign (etc.) Office. [street in London containing Foreign & Commonwealth Office and (No. 10; cf. NUMBER¹) official residence of Prime Minister, f. Sir G. *Downing*, Brit. diplomat d. 1684 + STREET]

dow′nlănd *n.* = DOWN¹. [f. DOWN¹ + LAND¹]

dow′nmōst. See DOWN³,⁵.

dow′npīpe *n.* Pipe to carry rain-water from roof to drain. [f. DOWN⁵ + PIPE¹]

dow′npour (-pôr) *n.* Heavy fall of rain etc. [f. DOWN³ + POUR]

dow′nright (-rīt; downrī′t as *a.* after *n.*) *a.* & *adv.* **1.** *a.* Plain, definite, straightforward, blunt, whence **~NESS** *n.*; not short of being, out-and-out, (*a downright lie, atheist*; *downright nonsense*).

2. *adv.* Thoroughly, positively, quite, (*downright scared, insolent*). [ME, f. *adownright* (ADOWN, RIGHT[1,4])]
downstair's *adv.* & *n.*, **dow'nstair(s)** *a.*, (-z). Down the stairs; (to, on, of) lower floor of house etc. [f. DOWN[3] + STAIR]
***dow'nstāte** *a.*, *adv.*, & *n.* (Pertaining to, in) part of state remote from large cities, esp. southern part. [f. DOWN[4] + STATE[1]]
dow'nstream *a.* & *adv.* In the direction in which a stream or river flows. [f. DOWN[4] + STREAM]
dow'nthrow (-ō) *n.* (Geol.) Downward dislocation of strata. [f. DOWN[3] + THROW[2]]
***dow'ntown** *a.*, *adv.*, & *n.* (Pertaining to, in) lower or more central part or business part of town or city. [f. DOWN[4] *town*]
dow'ntrŏdden *a.* Oppressed, kept under. [f. DOWN[3] + TRODDEN]
dow'ntûrn *n.* Decline, esp. in economic or business activity. [f. DOWN[3] + TURN[2]]
dow'nward *a.* & *adv.*, **dow'nward|s** (-z) *adv.* (Moving, extending, pointing, leading) towards what is lower, inferior, less important, or later; hence ~LY[2] *adv.* [ME, f. ADOWN + -WARD(s)]
dow'nwarp (-ôrp) *n.* (Geol.) Broad surface depression, syncline. [f. DOWN[3] + WARP[2]]
dow'nwĭnd *a.* & *adv.* In the direction in which the wind is blowing. [f. DOWN[4] + WIND[1]]
dow'nȳ[1] *a.* Of or like downs. [f. DOWN[1] + -Y[2]]
dow'n|ȳ[2] *a.* Of, like, covered with, down; (sl.) aware, knowing; hence **~ĭLY**[2] *adv.*, **~ĭNESS** *n.* [f. DOWN[2] + -Y[2]]
dow'rȳ (dow'erĭ) *n.* Property or money brought by bride to her husband; talent, natural gift. [ME, f. AF *dowarie*, OF *douaire* DOWER]
dowse[1]. See DOUSE.
dows|e[2] (-z) *v.i.* Search for hidden water or minerals with forked twig (**~'ing-rod,** or *divining-rod*) which dips suddenly when held over the right spot; hence ~'ER[1] *n.* [17th c.; orig. unkn.]
dŏxŏ'|grapher *n.* Writer who collected and recorded the opinions of the ancient Greek philosophers; hence **dŏxo**GRA'PHIC *a.*, ~GRAPHY *n.* [f. mod. L *doxographus* f. Gk (see foll., -GRAPHER)]
dŏxŏ'logȳ *n.* Liturgical formula of praise to God. [f. med. L f. Gk *doxologia* (*doxa* glory; see -LOGY)]
dŏ'xȳ[1] *n.* (arch.) Beggar's wench; paramour. [16th c. cant, of unkn. orig.]
dŏ'xȳ[2] *n.* (arch. joc.) Opinion, esp. on theological matters. [f. *orthodoxy*, *heterodoxy*]
doy'en (*or* dwah'yăṅ) *n.* (*fem.* **doyenne** *pr.* dwahyĕ'n). Senior member *of* a body of colleagues, esp. senior ambassador at a court. [F, f. as DEAN[1]]
doy'ley. See DOILY.
doz. *abbr.* dozen.
dōze *v.i.*, & *n.* **1.** *v.i.* Sleep lightly, be half asleep; **~ off,** fall lightly asleep. **2.** *n.* Short light sleep. [17th c.; cf. Da. *døse* make drowsy]
do'zen (dŭ'-) *n.* (*pl.* ~ *or* **~s;** for pl. usage see HUNDRED). Twelve; set of twelve (*pack them in dozens*); **~s of,** (colloq.) very many; **by the ~,** in large quantities; **daily ~,** (colloq.) physical exercises done daily on rising; BAKER'*s*, **devil's, long, ~,** thirteen; **half a ~,** (about) six; ||**talk nineteen to the ~** (incessantly). [ME, f. OF *dozeine*, ult. f. L *duodecim* twelve]
dō'zer *n.* (colloq.) Bulldozer. [abbr.]
dō'zȳ *a.* (colloq.) Stupid; lazy. [f. DOZE + -Y[2]]
D.P. *abbr.* displaced person.
D.P.H. *abbr.* Diploma in Public Health.
D.Phil. *abbr.* Doctor of Philosophy.
D.P.M. *abbr.* Diploma in Psychological Medicine.
||**D.P.P.** *abbr.* Director of Public Prosecutions.
Dr. *abbr.* debtor; Doctor; Drive.
dr. *abbr.* drachm(s); drachma(s); dram(s).
drăb[1] *n.* Slut, slattern; prostitute. [perh. rel. to LG *drabbe* mire, Du. *drab* dregs]
drăb[2] *a.* & *n.* (Of) dull light-brown colour; dull, monotonous; monotony; hence ~'LY[2] *a.*, ~'NESS *n.* [prob. f. obs. *drap* cloth f. OF, f. LL *drappus*, perh. of Celt. orig.]
dră'bble *v.i.* & *t.* Become or make dirty and wet with water or mud. [ME, f. LG *drabbelen* paddle in water or mire; cf. DRAB[1]]
drăchm (-ăm) *n.* Apothecaries' weight of 60 grains, ⅛ ounce; (**fluid**) ~, apothecaries' measure of 60 minims, ⅛ fluid ounce; avoirdupois weight, one-sixteenth ounce; (arch.) small quantity. [ME *dragme* f. OF, or f. LL *dragma* f. L f. Gk *drakhmē* Attic weight and coin]
dră'chma (-k-) *n.* (*pl.* **~s** *or* **~e**). Ancient Greek silver coin; modern Greek monetary unit and coin. [L, f. Gk *drakhmē*]
dră'cōne *n.* Large flexible container for liquids, towed on surface of sea. [f. L, as DRAGON]
Drācō'nĭan, Drācŏ'nĭc, (*or* dra-) *adjs.* (Of laws) rigorous, harsh, cruel. [f. *Drakōn* Athenian legislator *c.* 620 B.C. + -IAN, -IC]
drăff (*or* -ahf) *n.* Dregs, lees; refuse. [ME, perh. f. OE **dræf* = MLG, MDu. *draf*, OHG **trab*, ON **draf*]
draft[1] (-ah-) *n.* **1.** (Selection of) detachment from larger body for special duty or purpose; contingent, reinforcement; *(Mil.) conscription. **2.** Drawing of money by written order, (fig.) demand made *on* person's confidence, friendship, etc.; bill or cheque drawn, esp. by one branch of bank on another. **3.** Sketch of work to be executed; preliminary copy of document. **4.*** = DRAUGHT[1]. [phonetic sp. of DRAUGHT[1]]
draft[2] (-ah-) *v.t.* **1.** Draw off (part of larger body) for special duty or purpose; *conscript (lit. or fig.), whence ~EE' *n.* **2.** Prepare, make preliminary copy of, (document, e.g. Parliamentary Bill), whence ~'ER[1] *n.* [f. prec.]
dra'fts|man (-ah'f-) *n.* (*pl.* **~men**). One who drafts documents; = DRAUGHTSMAN. [phonetic sp. of DRAUGHTSMAN]
***dra'ftȳ** (-ah'-) *a.* = DRAUGHTY.
drăg[1] *v.* (-gg-). **1.** *v.t.* Pull along with force, difficulty, or friction; allow (feet, tail, etc.) to trail; (colloq.) take (person *to* place etc., esp. against his will); **ship ~s her anchor,** anchor fails to hold; search bottom of (river etc.) with grapnels or drags. **2.** *v.i.* Trail, go or pass heavily or slowly or laboriously; use grapnel or drag (*for* drowned person or lost object); (colloq.) suck *on* or *at* (cigarette). **3.** ~ one's **feet** or **heels,** (fig.) be deliberately slow or reluctant; **~ in,** introduce (subject) needlessly; **~ on,** continue tediously; **~ out,** protract; **~ up,** (colloq.) rear (child) roughly and without proper training. [ME, f. OE *dragan* or ON *draga* DRAW[1]]
drăg[2] *n.* **1.** (Hist.) Four-horsed private vehicle like stage-coach. **2.** = *drag-net*; apparatus for dredging or recovering drowned persons etc. from under water; strong-smelling lure for hounds in lieu of fox (so **~-hounds**), club for pursuing this sport. **3.** Obstruction to progress; slow motion, impeded progress; iron shoe for retarding coach etc. downhill; boring or dreary performance, person, etc.; (Aeron.) longitudinal retarding force exerted by air. **4.** Act of dragging; (sl.) pull at cigarette; *(sl.) influence, pull. **5.** (sl.) Motor car; acceleration race between cars usu. over quarter-mile distance (**~'ster,** car modified to take part effectively in this). **6.** *(sl.) Street, road, (esp. *main drag*). **7.** (sl.) Women's clothes worn by men; party at which clothes are so worn; clothes in general. **8. ~-anchor,** = SEA *anchor*; **~-line,** excavator with bucket pulled in by wire rope; **~-net,** net

drawn through river or across ground to trap fish or game, (fig.) means of systematically discovering criminals, etc. [ME, f. prec.]

dragée (drahʹzhā) *n.* Sugar-coated almond etc.; small silver ball for decorating cake; chocolate-coated sweet. [F; see DREDGE[2]]

drăʹggle *v.* **1.** *v.t.* Make wet, limp, and dirty, by trailing. **2.** *v.i.* Hang trailing; lag, straggle in rear; **~-tail(ed)**, (woman) with draggled or untidily trailing skirts. [f. DRAG[1] + -LE 3]

drăʹggy̆ (-gĭ) *a.* (colloq.) Tedious; unpleasant. [f. DRAG[1] + -Y[2]]

drăʹgom|an *n.* (*pl.* **~ans** *or* **~en**). Interpreter or guide, esp. in countries using Arabic, Turkish, or Persian. [F, f. It. *dragomano* f. med. Gk *dragomanos* f. Arab. *tarjumān* (*tarjama* interpret, f. Aram. *targēm* f. Assyr. *targumânu* interpreter)]

drăʹgon *n.* **1.** Mythical monster like reptile, usu. with wings and claws and often breathing fire; (w. allus. to legends) watchful guardian of treasure etc.; fierce person; **the (old) D~**, Satan; lizard of genus *Draco* with winglike structures; KOMODO *dragon*. **2.** **~-fly,** neuropterous insect with long slender body and two pairs of large wings usu. spread while resting; **~'s blood,** red gum that exudes from fruit of some palms, esp. **~-tree** (*Dracaena draco*); **~'s teeth,** (colloq.) anti-tank etc. obstacles resembling teeth pointed upwards. [ME f. OF, f. L *draco -onis* f. Gk *drakōn* serpent]

drăʹgonėt *n.* Brightly-coloured spiny fish of family Callionymidae. [ME f. F, dim. of prec.]

drăgonnāʹde *n.*, & *v.t.* **1.** *n.* Persecution by use of troops, esp. (in *pl.*) of French Protestants under Louis XIV by quartering dragoons on them. **2.** *v.t.* Subject to dragonnade. [F (*dragon*; see foll., -ADE)]

dragōōʹn *n.*, & *v.t.* **1.** *n.* Cavalryman (orig. mounted infantryman armed with carbine); rough fierce fellow; variety of pigeon. **2.** *v.t.* Set dragoons upon, persecute; force *into* a course of action by persecution. [orig. = carbine, f. F *dragon* DRAGON, so named as breathing fire; see -OON]

drail *n.* Fish-hook and line weighted with lead for dragging at depth through water. [app. var. of TRAIL]

drain[1] *v.* **1.** *v.t.* Draw (liquid) *off* or *away* by pipe etc. (lit. or fig.; *drain the wealth of England*); drink (liquid), empty (vessel), to the dregs; make (land etc.) dry by providing outflow for moisture; (of river) carry off superfluous water of (district); remove purulent matter from (abscess); deprive (person, thing) *of* property, strength, etc. **2.** *v.i.* Trickle *through*, flow *off* or *away*; (of wet cloth, vessel, etc.) get rid of moisture by its flowing away (*set it there to drain*). **3.** ‖**~ʹing-board, *~ʹboard,** sloping usu. grooved board on which washed dishes etc. are put to drain. [OE *drē(a)hnian*, prob. f. **drēag-* f. Gmc **draug-*; cf. DRY[1]]

drain[2] *n.* Channel carrying off liquid, artificial conduit for water, sewage, etc., (**down the ~,** (colloq.) lost, wasted; **laugh like a ~,** (colloq.) guffaw); tube for drawing off discharge from abscess etc.; constant outlet, withdrawal, demand, or expenditure (*a great drain on my resources*; BRAIN *drain*); (sl.) a drink; **~-pipe,** pipe for carrying off surplus water or liquid sewage from a building, (*attrib.*, colloq., of trousers etc.) very narrow; **~-pipes,** (colloq.) such trousers. [f. prec.]

draiʹnage *n.* Draining; system of drains, artificial or natural; what is drained off, sewage. [f. DRAIN[1] + -AGE]

draiʹner *n.* In vbl senses; thing in or on which things are put to drain, e.g. DRAIN[1]ing-board. [f. DRAIN[1] + -ER[1]]

drāke[1] *n.* Mayfly, esp. as used in fishing. [OE *draca*, = MLG, MDu. *drake*, OHG *trahho*, WG **drako* f. L *draco* DRAGON]

drāke[2] *n.* Male duck (*play* DUCK[1]*s and drakes*). [ME, corresp. to LG *drake*, *drache*, WG **drako*, corresp. to second element in OHG *antrehho*]

drăm *n.* = DRACHM; small drink of spirit etc. (**~-drinker,** tippler); ***~-shop,** (arch.) = BAR[1] 7. [ME, f. OF *drame* or med. L *drama*, *dragma*; cf. DRACHM]

draʹma (-ah-) *n.* Play for acting on stage, radio, etc.; **the ~,** dramatic art, composition and presentation of plays; dramatic series of events. [LL, f. Gk *drama -atos* (*draō* do)]

dramăʹt|ĭc *a.* Of (the study of) drama; as of a play-actor, theatrical; fit for theatrical representation, sudden, striking, impressive; **~ic irony,** = TRAGIC *irony*; hence **~ICALLY** *adv.*, **~ICS** *n.*, dramatic performance or behaviour. [f. LL f. Gk *dramatikos* (as prec.; see -IC)]

drămatĭs persōʹnae *n. pl.* (often treated as *sing.*) (List of) characters in a play. [L, = persons of the drama]

drăʹmatĭst *n.* Writer of dramas. [f. Gk DRAMA + -IST]

drăʹmatiz|e, -īs|e (-īz), *v.t.* & *i.* Convert (novel etc.) into a play, admit of such conversion; make a drama or dramatic scene of, behave dramatically; hence **~AʹTION** *n.* [f. as prec. + -IZE]

drăʹmatûrg|e *n.* Dramatist; so **drămatûrʹgic(al)** *adjs.*, **~y**[1] *n.* [F, f. Gk *dramatourgos* (as DRAMA, *-ergos* worker)]

Drămbūʹie (*or* -bōōʹĭ) *n.* Scotch whisky liqueur. [P]

drănk. See DRINK[1].

drāpe *v.t.*, & *n.* **1.** *v.t.* Cover, hang, adorn, with cloth etc.; arrange (clothes, hangings) in graceful folds. **2.** *n.* Piece of drapery, *curtain; **~ suit,** (sl.) man's suit of long jacket and narrow trousers. [ME, f. OF *draper* (*drap* f. LL *drappus* cloth)]

‖**drāʹper** *n.* Retailer of textile fabrics. [ME f. AF, OF *drapier* (as prec.; see -ER[2] (2))]

drāʹpery̆ *n.* ‖Cloth, textile fabrics; ‖draper's trade; arrangement of clothing in sculpture etc.; clothing or hangings disposed in folds; *curtain. [ME, f. OF *draperie* (*drap* cloth; see -ERY)]

drăʹst|ĭc (*or* -ahʹ-) *a.* Acting strongly or severely; vigorous, violent, (esp. of purgative); hence **~ICALLY** *adv.* [f. Gk *drastikos* (*draō* do; see -IC)]

drăt *v.t.* (**-tt-**; esp. in 3 *sing. subj.*) (As mild imprecation) confound, curse, bother; hence **~ʹTED**[1] *a.* [for 'od (= God) *rot*]

draught[1] (-ahft) *n.* **1.** Drawing, traction; **~horse** etc. (for drawing cart, plough, etc.). **2.** Drawing of net for fish etc.; fish taken at one drawing. **3.** Drawing of liquor from cask etc.; **~ beer** (not bottled). **4.** Single act of drinking, amount so drunk; dose of liquid medicine. **5.** (Naut.) Depth of water ship draws or requires to float her. **6.** (in *pl.*, usu. treated as *sing.*) ‖Game for two, with initially 24 pieces of equal value on **~-board** (same as chess-board). **7.** Current of air in confined space (room, chimney, etc.); **feel the ~,** (sl.) suffer from adverse (usu. financial) conditions; **forced ~** (provided by blower etc.); hence **~ʹY**[2] *a.* **8.** = DRAFT 1, 2, 3. [ME *draht*, perh. f. ON *drahtr*, *dráttr*, = MDu. *dragt*, OHG *traht* f. Gmc **dragan* DRAW[1]]

draught[2] (-ahft) *v.t.* = DRAFT[2]. [f. prec.]

drauʹghtsman (-ahʹft-) *n.* (*pl.* **-men**). One who makes drawings, plans, or sketches (**good, bad, no, ~,** one who draws well etc.), whence **~SHIP** (3) *n.*; = DRAFTSMAN; piece in game of draughts. [f. *draught's* + MAN[1]]

Dravĭʹdĭan *a.* & *n.* (Member or language) of a

dark-skinned people of S. India and Sri Lanka (including Tamils and Kanarese). [f. Skr. *Dravida*, a province of S. India + -IAN]

draw[1] *v.* (**drew** *pr.* drōō; DRAWN). **1.** *v.t.* Pull (boat up from water, hat over face, belt tighter, pen across paper, friend aside); pull after one (plough, cart, cart-load, etc.); (Hist.) drag (criminal) on hurdle etc. to execution. **2.** Haul in (net); bend (bow; *draw a* BEAD[1] *on*); *draw in* one's HORN[1]*s*; pull at (~ **bit, bridle, rein,** check horse, or (fig.) oneself); pull (curtain, veil) open or shut; (of ship) need (specified depth of water) for floating; (Bowls) cause (bowl) to travel in curve to desired point; (Cricket) divert (ball) to on-side with bat; (Golf) drive (ball) too much to left (of right-handed player). **3.** Attract, bring to oneself or to something, take in, (*drew a deep breath*; *I felt drawn to him*; *drew my attention to the matter*; *draw him into conversation*; *display draws customers*), (abs.) *chimney*, *pipe*, **~s well,** promotes or allows draught; induce *to* do; bring about, entail, (*drew after it great consequences*; *draw criticism*, *ruin*, *upon* one*self*; ~ person's **fire,** deflect it from more important target). **4.** Take out (cork, tooth, gun-charge, nail, cricket-stumps from ground (at close of play), card from pack; pistol, sword from sheath); (abs.) = draw one's sword or pistol; ~ one's **sword against,** attack; *draw* LOTS; (abs.) = draw lots; obtain by lot (*drew the winner*; *draw (a)* BLANK[2]); drag (badger, fox) from hole; haul up (water) from well; bring out (liquid from vessel, blood from body; ~ **it mild,** [orig. of beer] = be moderate, not exaggerate); extract liquid essence of; leave (game, battle) undecided. **5.** Take or get from a source (*draw inspiration*, one's *salary*, *money from bank*); elicit, evoke; (Cards) cause to be played (*draw all the trumps*); bring (person) out, make (him) reveal information, talent, irritation, etc.; deduce, infer, (conclusion). **6.** Disembowel (criminal is **hanged, ~n, and quartered;** ~ **fowl** before cooking). **7.** (Hunt.) Search (cover) for game (~ **blank,** find none; cf. sense 4 and BLANK[2]). **8.** Protract, stretch, elongate, (*long drawn agony*); make (wire) by pulling piece of metal through successively smaller holes. **9.** Trace (furrow, figure, line; ~ **the line at,** refuse to go as far as or beyond); delineate, make (picture), represent (object), by drawing lines, (abs.) practise this; frame (document) in due form, compose; formulate, institute, (comparisons, distinctions); write out (bill, cheque, draft, *on* banker etc.), (abs.) make call *on* person or his faith, memory, one's imagination, etc., for money or service. **10.** *v.i.* Make one's way, move, *towards*, *round*, *into*, *near*, *off*, *back*, etc. (*draw to an end* or *close*); (Racing) get farther *away* to the front, come *level*, gain *on*; (of tea) infuse; (of sail) swell tightly in wind. **11.** ~ **back,** withdraw from undertaking; ~ **in,** entice, persuade to join, (of day) close in, (of successive days) become shorter, (of train etc.) enter station etc.; ~ **off,** withdraw (troops); ~ **on,** lead to, bring about, allure, come nearer, put (gloves, boots, etc.) on; ~ **out,** lead out, detach, or array (troops), prolong, elicit, induce to talk, write out in proper form, (of days) become longer, (of train etc.) leave station etc.; ~ **up,** come up *with* or *to* = overtake, come to a halt, bring or come into regular order, compose (document etc.), make one*self* stiffly erect. **12. ~-hoe** (used with pulling action); **~-sheet** (that can be taken from under patient without remaking bed); **~-string** (that can be pulled to tighten mouth of bag, waist of garment, etc.); **~-well,** deep well with rope and bucket. [OE *dragan*, = OS *dragan*, OHG *tragan*, ON *draga*, Goth. *gadragan* f. Gmc **dragan*]

draw[2] *n.* Act of drawing; strain, pull; *suck on cigarette etc.; attractive effect, person or thing that draws custom, attention, etc.; drawing of lots, raffle; drawn game; act of whipping out revolver in order to shoot (*quick on the draw*, lit. or fig.); *movable part of drawbridge. [f. prec.]

draw'băck *n.* Amount of excise or import duty paid back or remitted on goods exported; deduction *from*; thing that impairs satisfaction, disadvantage; ~ **lock** (with spring bolt that can be drawn back by inside knob). [f. DRAW[1] + BACK[3]]

draw'brĭdge *n.* Bridge hinged at one end for drawing up to prevent passage or to open channel. [ME, f. DRAW[1] + BRIDGE[1]]

Drawcă'nsir *n.* Person formidable to both friend and foe; fierce swashbuckler. [name of character in Villiers's *Rehearsal* (1672), perh. intended to suggest *draw can* (of liquor)]

drawee' *n.* Person on whom draft or bill is drawn. [f. DRAW[1] + -EE]

draw'er *n.* In vbl senses; (arch.) tapster; (*pr. also* draw) receptacle sliding in and out of frame (**~s** or **chest of ~s**) or of table etc., for holding clothes, papers, etc. (BOTTOM[1] *drawer*; TOP[1] *drawer*), whence ~FUL 2 *n.*; (in *pl.*) knickers or other garment worn next to body below waist. [f. DRAW[1] + -ER[1]]

draw'ĭng *n.* In vbl senses; art of representing by line, delineation without colour or with single colour (**out of** ~, incorrectly depicted); product of this, black-and-white or monochrome sketch; ~ **account,** account from which money can be drawn, esp. against credited future earnings; **~-board,** board for spreading drawing-paper on (**back to the ~-board,** (colloq.) the enterprise has failed, we must begin afresh); **~-paper** (stout, for drawing pictures etc. on); ||**~-pin** (for fastening paper to drawing-board etc.). [f. DRAW[1] + -ING[1]]

draw'ĭng-rōōm (*or* -ŏŏm) *n.* Room for formal reception of company, to which ladies retire after dinner, (*attrib.*) restrained, observing social proprieties; (Hist.) levee, formal reception esp. at court; *private compartment in train. [f. earlier WITHDRAW*ing-room*]

drawl *v.* & *n.* **1.** *v.i.* & *t.* Speak or utter with indolent or affected slowness. **2.** *n.* Drawling utterance. [16th c., prob. orig. cant, f. LG, Du. *dralen* delay, linger]

drawn *a.* In vbl senses; (of face etc.) distorted with pain or fear; (of butter) melted; (of position in chess etc.) resulting in draw if both players make best moves; **~-(thread-)work,** ornamental work on linen etc. done by drawing out threads, usu. with additional needlework. [p.p. of DRAW[1]]

dray[1] *n.* **1.** Low esp. brewer's cart without sides for heavy loads; **~-horse** (large and powerful); **~'man,** brewer's driver. **2.** (Austral. & N.Z.) Two-wheeled cart. [ME, f. OE *dræge* drag-net, *dragan* DRAW[1]]

dray[2]. Var. of DREY.

dread[1] (-ĕd) *v.t.*, & *n.* **1.** *v.t.* Be in great fear of; shrink from, look forward to with terror; fear greatly (*that*, *to* learn etc.), be afraid (*to* do). **2.** *n.* Great fear, awe, apprehension; object of fear or awe. [OE *ādrǣdan*, *ondrǣdan*, = OS *antdrādan*, OHG *intrātan*, f. *and-* (cf. ANSWER[1]) + WG base of uncert. orig.]

dread[2] (-ĕd) *a.* Dreaded, dreadful; (arch.) awful, revered. [ME, p.p. of prec.]

drea'dful (-ĕ'd-) *a.* Terrible, awe-inspiring (||**penny** ~, cheap story-book full of horrors); troublesome, disagreeable, boring, very bad or long, horrid; hence ~LY² *adv.*, ~NESS *n.* [ME, f. DREAD¹ + -FUL]

drea'dnought (-ĕ'dnawt) *n.* **1.** (arch.) (Cloth used for) thick coat for stormy weather; fearless person. **2.** (Hist.; *D*~). Type of battleship greatly superior in armament to all predecessors (f. name of first, launched 1906). [f. DREAD¹ + NOUGHT]

dream¹ *n.* Series of pictures or events in mind of sleeping person (**like a** ~, (colloq.) easily, effortlessly; WET *dream*); act or time of seeing such vision; (**waking**) ~, similar experience of one awake; = DAY-*dream*; ideal, (esp. national) aspiration or ambition; person, dress, dish, etc., of dreamlike goodness, beauty, or refinement; **~-boat,** (colloq.) very attractive person or thing; **~-land,** ideal or imaginary land; **~-time,** (Austral.) alcheringa; hence ~'FUL, ~'LESS, ~'LIKE, *adjs.* [ME, corresp. to OE **drēam*, OS *drōm*, OHG *troum*, ON *draumr*]

dream² *v.* (~**t** *pr.* -ĕmt, *or* ~**ed**). **1.** *v.i.* Have visions etc. (as) in sleep; (w. neg. etc.) think *of* even in a dream, so much as contemplate possibility *of*, (*would not dream of upsetting them*), have any conception *of*; fall into reverie; be inactive or unpractical. **2.** *v.t.* See, hear, etc., in sleep; imagine as in a dream, believe possible (*never dreamt that he would behave so badly*); spend (time) *away* unpractically; ~ **up,** imagine, invent. **3.** Hence ~'ER¹ *n.* [ME, as prec.]

drea'm|ȳ *a.* Given to reverie, fanciful, unpractical; dreamlike, vague, misty; (poet.) full of dreams; (colloq.) delightful; hence ~**ĭ**LY² *adv.*, ~**ĭ**NESS *n.* [f. DREAM¹ + -Y²]

drear *a.* (esp. poet.) = foll. [abbr.]

drear'|ȳ *a.* Dismal, gloomy, dull; hence ~**ĭ**LY² *adv.*, ~**ĭ**NESS *n.* [OE *drēorig* (*drēor* gore), cogn. w. *drēosan* to drop, f. Gmc **dreuzaz*]

drĕdge¹ *n.* & *v.* **1.** *n.* Apparatus for bringing up oysters, specimens, etc., or clearing out mud etc., from river or sea bottom. **2.** *v.t.* Bring *up*, clear *away* or *out*, (as) with dredge; clean out (harbour, river) with dredge. **3.** *v.i.* Use dredge. [15th c. Sc. *dreg*, perh. rel. to MDu. *dregghe*]

drĕdge² *v.t.* Sprinkle with flour or other powder; sprinkle (flour etc.) *over*. [f. obs. *dredge* sweetmeat, f. OF *dragie*, *dragee*, perh. f. L f. Gk *tragēmata* spices]

drĕ'dger¹ *n.* In vbl senses; (boat with) machine used for dredging rivers etc. [f. DREDGE¹ + -ER¹]

drĕ'dger² *n.* Container with perforated lid for sprinkling flour etc. [f. DREDGE² + -ER¹]

dree *v.t.* (arch. or Sc.) Endure (~ one's **weird,** submit to one's destiny). [OE *drēogan* f. Gmc **dreug-* etc.]

dreep *n.* (colloq.) Ineffective or lugubrious person. [f. obs. v. *dreep* drip]

drĕg *n.* (usu. in *pl.*) Sediment, grounds, lees, (*drink*, *drain*, **to the** ~**s**, leaving nothing); worthless part, refuse; (in *sing.*) small remnant (esp. *not a dreg*); hence ~'**gy²** (-gĭ) *a.* [ME, prob. f. ON *dreggjar*]

drĕnch¹ *n.* Draught or dose administered to animal; (arch.) medicinal or poisonous draught; a soaking or downpour. [OE *drenc* f. Gmc **drank-* (**drink-* DRINK¹)]

drĕnch² *v.t.* Force (animal) to take draught of medicine; wet thoroughly (by immersion or by falling liquid); saturate, steep, as if in liquid; (arch.) cause to drink. [OE *drencan*, = OS *drenkian*, OHG *trenchen*, ON *drekkja*, Goth. *dragkjan* f. Gmc **drankjan*]

Drĕ'sden (-z-) *n.* ~ **china, porcelain,** kind made at Meissen near Dresden, with elaborate decoration and delicate colourings; (*attrib.*, fig.) delicately pretty. [~ in Germany]

drĕss¹ *v.t.* & *i.* **1.** Array, clothe (*dressed in black*, *dressed in rags*, etc.); provide oneself with clothes (*dress well* etc.); put on one's clothes; put on evening dress (esp. *dress for dinner*); ~ **out,** attire conspicuously; ~ **up,** attire oneself, attire (another), elaborately or in masquerade, (fig.) disguise by embellishment. **2.** Deck, adorn, (ship with flags, shop-window with attractive goods). **3.** Treat (wound) with remedies; apply dressing to. **4.** Subject to cleansing, trimming, smoothing, etc.; prepare (bird, crab, etc.) for cooking or eating; brush, comb, do up, (hair); curry (horse, leather); manure; ~ **down,** (fig.) thrash or scold. **5.** Finish surface of (textile fabrics, building-stone). **6.** (Mil.) Correct the alignment of (companies etc. in relation to each other, or men in line), come into correct place in line etc. [ME, f. OF *dresser* f. Rom. **directiare* f. L *directus* DIRECT²]

drĕss² *n.* **1.** Clothing, esp. the visible part of it, formal or ceremonial costume (EVENING *dress*, FULL¹ *dress*, MORNING *dress*); woman's or girl's garment of bodice and skirt. **2.** External covering, outward form, (*birds in their winter dress*; *French book appearing in English dress*). **3.** ||~ **circle,** first gallery in theatres, in which evening dress was at one time required; ~ **coat** (swallow-tailed for evening dress); **~-improver,** (Hist.) = BUSTLE³; ~ **length,** piece of material sufficient to make a dress; **~'maker, ~'making,** (woman) making women's dresses; ~ **parade,** (1) display of clothes by mannequins, (2) military parade in full dress uniforms; **~-preserver,** = *dress-shield*; ~ **rehearsal,** (esp. final) rehearsal in costume; **~-shield,** piece of waterproof material fastened under armpit of dress to protect it from perspiration. [f. prec.]

drĕ'ssage (-ahzh) *n.* Training of horse in obedience and deportment. [F (*dresser* train)]

drĕ'sser¹ *n.* Kitchen sideboard with shelves for dishes etc.; *dressing-table. [ME, f. OF *dresseur* (*dresser* prepare; see -ER²); cf. med. L *directorium*]

drĕ'sser² *n.* In vbl senses; surgeon's assistant in hospital operations; one who helps to dress actors or actresses, looks after costumes, etc. [f. DRESS¹ + -ER¹]

drĕ'ssĭng *n.* In vbl senses; seasoning, sauce, stuffing, etc. for food; manure etc. spread over land; bandage, ointment, etc., for wound; size or stiffening used in finishing textile fabrics; **~-case** (of toilet necessaries); ~ **down,** scolding or thrashing; **~-gown,** loose robe worn while one is resting, not fully dressed, etc.; **~-room,** place for dressing or changing clothes, esp. in theatre, sports-ground, etc., or attached to bedroom; **~-station,** place for giving emergency treatment to wounded; **~-table,** table with mirror etc. for use while dressing. [ME, f. DRESS¹ + -ING¹]

drĕ'ss|ȳ *a.* Fond of or smart in dress; (of clothes) stylish; (fig.) over-elaborate; hence ~**ĭ**NESS *n.* [f. DRESS² + -Y²]

drew. See DRAW¹.

drey (drā) *n.* Squirrel's nest. [17th c.; orig. unkn.]

drĭb *n.* **~s and drabs,** small scattered amounts. [*drib* f. v. (see foll.); *drab* redupl.]

drĭ'bble *v.* & *n.* **1.** *v.i.* & *t.* (Let) flow in drops or trickling stream; (of child etc.) run at the mouth. **2.** (Footb., Hockey, etc.) Move (ball) forward with slight touches of feet or of stick. **3.** *n.* Act or process of dribbling; small trickling stream. **4.** Hence **drĭ'bbly²** *a.* [frequent. of obs. *drib* var. of DRIP¹; see -LE 3]

drĭ'blĕt *n.* Small quantity, petty sum; **in** or **by ~s,** a little at a time. [f. *drib* (see prec.) + -LET]

dried (drīd). See DRY².

drī'er¹, drī'ĕst. See DRY¹.

drī'er², drȳ'er, *n.* In vbl senses; machine for

drying hair, laundry, etc.; substance mixed with oil-paint or ink to promote drying. [f. DRY[2] + -ER[1]]

drĭft[1] *n.* **1.** Being driven by current; slow movement or variation; ship's deviation from course, due to currents; projectile's deviation due to its rotation; aircraft's deviation due to side-wind; controlled slide of racing car etc. **2.** ||Driving of cattle in forest, esp. to one place on appointed day to determine ownership etc. **3.** Awaiting events, inaction, (esp. derog.; *the policy of drift*). **4.** Intention, meaning, tenor, or scope, of person or his words. **5.** Shower, driving mass; snow, sand, etc., accumulated by wind; ~(**-ice, ′wood,** etc.), material driven by water; (Geol.) material deposited by wind, current of water, etc. (**D~**, Pleistocene ice detritus, boulder clay); large mass of flowering plants. **6.** ~(**-net**), large net for herrings etc., allowed to drift with tide. **7.** (Mining). Horizontal passage following mineral vein. **8.** (S. Afr.) Ford. **9.** Tool for enlarging or shaping hole in metal. [ME f. ON & MDu., MHG *trift* movement of cattle cogn. w. DRIVE[1]]

drĭft[2] *v.i.* & *t.* Be carried (as) by current of air or water, (of current) carry; move passively, casually, or aimlessly; pile or be piled by wind into drifts; cover (field, road) with drifts; form or enlarge (hole) with drift; hence ~′AGE (1) *n.*, ~′ER[1] *n.*, (esp.) aimless person, boat used in drift-net fishing. [f. prec.]

drĭll[1] *n.* & *v.* **1.** *n.* Pointed steel etc. (esp. revolving) tool, or machine, for boring holes or sinking wells; shellfish that bores into shells of young oysters. **2.** Instruction or training in military exercises; (fig.) rigorous discipline, (exact) routine, (colloq.) recognized procedure. **3.** *v.t.* & *i.* (Of person or tool) make hole with drill through (metal etc.), make (hole) with drill; subject to or undergo discipline by drill; impart (knowledge etc.) by strict method. [n. f. v., f. MDu. *drillen* bore, of unkn. orig.]

drĭll[2] *n.*, & *v.t.* **1.** *n.* Small furrow for sowing seed in; ridge with such furrow on top; row of plants so sown. **2.** Machine for furrowing, sowing, and covering seed. **3.** *v.t.* Sow (seed) thus, plant (ground) in drills. [perh. f. obs. *drill* rill, 17th c., of unkn. orig.]

drĭll[3] *n.* W. Afr. baboon (*Mandrillus leucophaeus*) akin to mandrill. [prob. native name; cf. MANDRILL]

drĭll[4] *n.* Coarse twilled linen or cotton fabric. [earlier *drilling* f. G *drillich* f. L *trilix -licis* (*tri-* three-, *licium* thread)]

drī′lȳ. See DRY[1].

drĭnk[1] *v.* (**drank; drunk**). **1.** *v.t.* Swallow (liquid); swallow contents of (vessel); ~ **off,** drink the whole (contents) of at once; ~ **up,** drink the whole or remainder of. **2.** (Of plant, porous material, etc.) absorb (moisture; ~ **in,** (fig.) contemplate or listen to with delight or eagerness); bring (one*self to death* etc.) by drinking (~ **under the table,** outlast (person) in ability to continue drinking liquor etc.); wish good etc. to by drinking (*drink* person's *health*); spend (wages etc. *away*) on drink. **3.** *v.i.* Swallow liquid, take draught, (*of* or *from* a source; ~ **deep,** take large draught(s); ~ **up,** empty one's glass etc.; **~′ing-song,** song about (and usu. sung at time of) drinking; **~ing-u′p time,** short period legally allowed for consumption of drinks bought before closing-time in public house; **~′ing-water,** water reserved, or pure enough, for drinking); take alcoholic liquor esp. to excess, tipple, be a drunkard, (*drink hard, heavily, like a* FISH[1]; *drinking-bout*); ~ **to,** pledge, toast, wish success to. **4.** Hence ~′ABLE *a.*, (-)~′ER[1] *n.* [OE *drincan*, = OS *drinkan*, OHG *trinkan*, ON *drekka*, Goth. *drigkan* f. Gmc **drenkan*].

drĭnk[2] *n.* Liquid swallowed or absorbed; liquid for drinking; (**strong**) ~, intoxicating liquor, excessive indulgence in it, intemperance (**in** ~, drunk); glass etc. or portion of liquid for drinking (*have* or *take a drink*), esp. alcoholic; **the** ~, (colloq.) the sea; hence ~′LESS *a.* [OE *drinc(a)* (*drincan*; see prec.)]

drĭp[1] *v.i.* & *t.* (**-pp-**). Fall or let fall in drops; let drops fall, be so wet (*with* blood etc.) as to shed drops (**~′ping wet,** very wet); **~-dry,** (*v.i.* of fabric etc.) dry when hung up to drip, without wringing or ironing, (*a.*) that will drip-dry. [f. MDa. *drippe* f. Gmc **drupp-* (cf. DROP[1])]

drĭp[2] *n.* Act of dripping; dripping liquid; (Archit.) projection keeping rain from parts below (so **~-moulding, ~′stone**); (sl.) stupid or dull person; (sl.) grumble; (sl.) flattery, drivel; **~-feed,** feeding (esp. intravenously) by liquid a drop at a time; ~ **mat,** small mat under glass etc.; hence ~′PY[2] *a.* [f. prec.]

drĭ′pping *n.* In vbl senses; fat melted from roasted meat, and used for cooking or as food; (in *pl.*) water, grease, etc., dripping from anything. [ME, f. DRIP[1] + -ING[1]]

drīve[1] *v.t.* & *i.* (**drove** *pr.* drōv; **driven** *pr.* drĭ′ven). **1.** Urge in some direction by blows, threats, violence, etc., (usu. w. adv. or prep.: *away, back, in, out, from, to, through,* etc.; ~ **out,** oust, take place of). **2.** Chase or frighten (game, wild beasts, enemy esp. in guerrilla warfare) from large area into small in order to kill or capture; ||hold DRIFT[1] (sense 2). **3.** (Urge and) direct course of (animal drawing vehicle or plough); operate and direct course of (vehicle etc., or locomotive); convey in vehicle; direct course of vehicle; be competent to direct course of motor vehicle etc. (**driving-licence, driving test,** etc., concerned with such competence); travel or go in private car or carriage (cf. RIDE 1); **~-in** *a.* & *n.*, (bank, cinema, etc.) that can be used without getting out of one's car; **~-on** *a.*, (of ship) on to which motor vehicle can be driven. **4.** Impel forcibly, constrain, compel, (*to, into, to* do); force into state of being (*mad* etc.); overwork (*was very hard driven*; *tends to drive himself*). **5.** Impel, (of wind, water) carry along; throw, propel, send, cause to go, in some direction, (inanimate thing); (Cricket) return (ball) from freely swung bat to or past bowler; (Golf) strike (ball, or abs.) with driver from tee; (Tennis) hit (ball) with freely swung racket. **6.** Force (stake, nail, etc.) *into* ground etc. by blows; bore (tunnel, horizontal cavity); (**let**) ~, aim blow or missile (*at*). **7.** (Of steam or other power) set or keep (machinery) going (**driving-wheel,** wheel communicating motive power in machinery, large wheel of locomotive); (of person) ~ **a quill, a pen,** write. **8.** Carry on, effect, conclude, (*drove a roaring trade, a good bargain*). **9.** Postpone (*drive it to the last minute*). **10.** Dash, rush, hasten; work hard *at*. **11.** Float along, drift, tend; be moved by wind etc., esp. rapidly (*driving rain*); ~ **at,** seek, intend, mean (*what is he driving at?*). [OE *drīfan*, = OS *drīban*, OHG *trīban*, ON *drífa*, Goth. *dreiban* f. Gmc **drībhan*]

drīve[2] *n.* **1.** Excursion or journey in vehicle; driving of game or enemy; stroke made by driving at cricket, golf, etc. **2.** Transmission of power to machinery, wheels of motor vehicle, etc., (*belt drive*; *front-wheel drive*); position of steering-wheel of motor vehicle (*left-hand drive*). **3.** Energy, capacity to achieve things; (Psych.) inner urge to attain a goal or satisfy a need. **4.** Organized effort to achieve a special purpose; game of whist, bingo, etc., with many players.

5. Street or road, esp. scenic one; ~(**'way**), road for vehicles, esp. private one leading to house. [f. prec.]

drĭ'vel *v.* (||-ll-) & *n.* **1.** *v.i.* Run at mouth or nose like child; talk childishly or idiotically. **2.** *v.t.* Fritter *away*. **3.** Hence ~**ler**¹ *n.* **4.** *n.* Silly nonsense, twaddle. [OE *dreflian*; cf. DRAFF]

drĭ'ven. See DRIVE¹.

drī'ver *n.* In vbl senses; person who drives vehicle (*bus-driver, cab-driver, engine-driver, taxi-driver*, etc.; **in the ~'s seat,** in charge); (Golf) straight-faced wooden-headed club for driving from tee; (Electr.) device or part of circuit providing power for output; (Mech.) wheel etc. receiving power directly and transmitting motion to other parts; hence ~LESS *a.* [f. DRIVE¹ + -ER¹]

drĭ'zzle *n.*, & *v.i.* **1.** *n.* Spraylike rain. **2.** *v.i.* (Of rain, *it*) fall in drizzle. **3.** Hence **drĭ'zzly**² *a.* [prob. f. ME *drēse*, OE *drēosan* fall + -LE 3]

drōgue (-ōg) *n.* Buoy at end of harpoon line; sea anchor; (Aeron.) truncated cone of fabric used as brake, target for gunnery, wind-sock, etc. [18th c., of unkn. orig.]

droit (*or* drwah) *n.* Right, due, legal perquisite; **~s of Admiralty,** proceeds of enemy's ships, wrecks, etc.; **~ de** or **du seigneur** (de-, dūsānyer̂'), alleged right of feudal lord to copulate with vassal's bride on her wedding-night. [ME f. OF, f. L *directum* n. f. *directus* DIRECT²]

drŏll *a.* & *n.* **1.** *a.* Amusing (esp. through quaintness); queer, odd, surprising; hence or cogn. **drō'lly**² (-ō'l-lĭ) *adv.*, ~'ERY (4), ~'NESS, *ns.* **2.** *n.* (arch.) Jester, wag; droll person. [f. F *drôle*, perh. f. MDu. *drolle* little man]

drōme *n.* (colloq.) Aerodrome. [abbr.]

-drōme *suf.* forming *ns.* denoting (1) place for running etc. (*aerodrome, hippodrome*), (2) thing that runs (*palindrome, syndrome*). [f. or after Gk *dromos* course, running]

drŏ'mėdarȳ (*or* -ŭ'm-) *n.* Light fast-moving (esp. Arabian or one-humped) camel bred for riding. [ME, f. AF **dromedarie*, OF *dromedaire*, or f. LL *dromedarius* f. L f. Gk *dromas -ados* runner; see -ARY¹]

drŏ'mond *n.* (Hist.) Large medieval ship for war or commerce. [ME f. AF; OF *dromon(t)* f. LL *dromo -onis* f. late Gk *dromōn* light vessel]

drōne *n.* & *v.* **1.** *n.* Male of honey-bee, which does not work in hive but may impregnate queen; idler; remotely-controlled pilotless aircraft or missile. **2.** Deep humming sound; monotonous speech or speaker; low-pitched pipe (as of bagpipe) or string; fixed continuous note emitted by this. **3.** *v.i.* & *t.* Buzz like bee or bagpipe; talk or utter monotonously; be idle; idle *away* (life etc.). [OE *drān, drǣn*, = OS *drān, dreno*, OHG *treno*, prob. f. WG **dran-*, **dren-*, **drun-* boom]

drŏ'ngō (-nggō) *n.* (*pl.* ~s *or* ~es). Black bird of India, Africa, or Australia, of family Dicruridae; (Austral. sl.) simpleton. [Malagasy]

drōōl *v.i.*, & *n.* Drivel, slobber. [contr. of *drivel*]

drōōp *v.* & *n.* **1.** *v.i.* Hang down, slope, incline, as in weariness; (of eyes) look downwards; (poet., of sun etc.) sink; languish, decline, flag, lose heart. **2.** *v.t.* Let (head, face, eyes) fall forward or down. **3.** *n.* Drooping attitude, loss of spirit; **~-snoot,** (colloq.) (aircraft with) adjustable nose or leading-edge flap. [ME, f. ON *drúpa* hang the head f. Gmc **drūp-* (cf. foll.)]

drŏp¹ *n.* **1.** Round, pear-shaped, or hemispherical portion of liquid (water, tears, sweat, dew, rain, blood) such as hangs or falls separately or adheres to surface; (Med.) smallest separable quantity of a liquid, (in *pl.*) liquid medicine to be measured by drops; minute quantity (**~ in a bucket** or **the ocean,** infinitesimal factor); glass etc. of intoxicating liquor (*take a drop*; **has had a ~ too much,** is drunk); pendant, hanging ornament, (of glass chandelier etc.; **ear-~s,** ear-rings); sweet, lozenge, (ACID¹, *pear* etc., *drops*); hence ~'LET *n.* **2.** Act of dropping, fall, social come-down, descent in prices, temperature, etc., (*at the drop of a* HAT; **get** or **have the ~ on,** (colloq.) have the advantage over); thing that drops or is dropped; ~(**-curtain** or **-scene**), (Theatr.) painted curtain or scenery let down on to stage; (in gallows) platform or trapdoor withdrawn from under feet of condemned person; distance dropped; abrupt fall or steep slope of surface, amount of this; ~(**-kick**), kick at football made by dropping ball and kicking it as it touches ground; (sl.) hiding-place for stolen or illicit goods, secret letters, etc.; (sl.) bribe; *box for letters etc. **3. ~-forging,** system of forcing piece of white-hot metal by heavy weight through open-ended die of required shape; **~-hammer,** forging-machine using power of dropped weight; ||**~-head,** adjustable canvas roof of car; **~-leaf,** (of table etc.) having hinged flap; ||**~ scone** (made by dropping spoonful of batter on cooking surface); **~-shot,** (Lawn Tennis) shot dropping abruptly after clearing net; **~-test** *n.*, & *v.t.*, test by dropping under standard conditions; **~'wort,** plant (*Filipendula hexapetala*) with tuberous root fibres. [OE *dropa*, = OS *dropo*, ON *dropi* f. Gmc *dropon*, & OE **droppa* f. Gmc **droppon* f. **drup-*; cf. DRIP¹, DROOP]

drŏp² *v.* (-pp-). **1.** *v.i.* Fall in drops; give off moisture in drops. **2.** Fall by force of gravity from not being held etc., (fig.) be uttered casually (*the remark dropped from him*; *he let drop a remark*); (of card) be played in same trick as higher card. **3.** Sink to ground esp. because exhausted, wounded, etc. (**~ dead!**, sl. excl. of intense scorn; **~ on** one's **knee(s)**, kneel; **fit** or **ready to ~**, (colloq.) tired out). **4.** Fall naturally *asleep*, (*back*) *into* habit etc.; die; cease, lapse, (*affair was allowed to drop*; *the correspondence dropped*). **5.** Fall in direction, condition, amount, degree, pitch, (*price, voice, wind, drops*); go *down* stream, hillside, etc.; fall *behind, to the rear*, etc. **6.** Come or go casually *by* or *in* as visitor, *into* place, *across* person. **7.** *v.t.* Let fall (liquid, tears) in drops, shed; let go, relinquish, cease to hold, (**~ anchor,** anchor ship; *drop a* BRICK¹, *a* STITCH); give birth to (esp. lamb). **8.** Utter casually as if unconsciously (esp. *drop a hint*); send casually (*postcard, line, note*). **9.** Lose (money, esp. in gambling). **10.** Fell with axe, blow of fist, or bullet; cause (card) to drop (sense 2). **11.** Set down (passenger, parcel); allow (supplies etc.) to fall by parachute. **12.** Omit (*letter*, one's *h's, syllable*) in speech. **13.** Let (eyes) droop; lower (voice); *drop* CURTSY; place in lower than usual position (*dropped handlebars* of bicycle, *dropped waist* of garment). **14.** (Footb.) Send (ball), make (goal), by DROP¹-kick. **15.** Cease to associate with, have done with, abandon, (**~ it!**, stop that). **16. ~ away,** decrease or depart gradually; **~ in,** come in gradually or casually; **~ off,** (1) = *drop away*, (2) fall asleep, (3) = sense 11; **~ on,** reprimand or punish; **~ out,** cease to appear or participate, esp. in course of study or in conventional society; **~-out** *n.*, (colloq.) one who drops out, (Rugby Footb.) restarting of game by drop-kick after defender's touch-down etc.; **~ to,** (sl.) become aware of. [OE *drop(p)ian* (as prec.)]

drŏ'pper *n.* In vbl senses; device for administering liquid in drops; (Austral., N.Z., & S. Afr.) light vertical member of fence etc. [f. prec. + -ER¹]

drŏ'ppĭngs (-z) *n. pl.* What falls or has fallen in drops, e.g. wax from candles; dung of animals or birds. [f. DROP[2] + -ING[1] + -S[1]]

drŏ'ps|y̆ *n.* **1.** Disease in which watery fluid collects in cavities or tissue of the body; hence ~ICAL *a.* **2.** (sl.) Tip or bribe. [ME, f. HYDROPSY]

drŏ'shky̆ *n.* Russian low four-wheeled open carriage. [f. Russ. *drozhki* dim. of *drogi* wagon (*droga* shaft)]

drosŏ'phĭla *n.* Fruit-fly of genus *Drosophila*, used extensively in genetic research. [mod. L, f. Gk *drosos* dew, moisture + *philos* loving]

drŏss *n.* Scum separated from metals in melting; foreign matter mixed with anything, impurities; refuse, rubbish; hence ~'Y[2] *a.* [OE *drōs*, = MDu. *droese* dregs; cf. MLG *drōsem*, OHG *truosana*]

drought (-owt), (poet., Sc., Ir., & U.S.) **drouth,** *n.* Continuous dry weather, absence of rain; (fig.) prolonged lack of something; (arch.) dryness, lack of moisture, thirst; hence **drou'ghty**[2] (-ow'tĭ), **drou'thy**[2], *a.* [OE *drūgath* (*drȳge* DRY[1]; see -TH[1])]

drōve[1] *n.* Herd or flock being driven or moving together; crowd, multitude, shoal, large number, esp. as moving together; **~-road,** ancient unmetalled track for cattle. [OE *drāf* (*drīfan* DRIVE[1])]

drōve[2]. See DRIVE[1].

drō'ver *n.* Driver of droves to market, cattle-dealer; hence (by back form.) **drōve**[3] *v.t.*, **drō'ving**[1] *n.* [ME, f. DROVE[1] + -ER[1]]

drown *v.* **1.** *v.i.* Suffer death by suffocation in liquid. **2.** *v.t.* (Of person, liquid, etc.) suffocate (person, animal) by submersion; submerge, flood, drench, (esp. fig.; *like a drowned* RAT[1]; **~ed valley** etc., one partly or wholly submerged by change in land-levels; **~ out,** drive out by flood). **3.** Deaden (grief etc.) with or *in* drink; overpower (esp. of louder sound making voice etc. inaudible). [ME (orig. north.) *drun(e)*, *droun(e)*, perh. f. OE **drūnian*, rel. to ON *drukna* be drowned; cogn. w. DRINK[1]]

drowse (-z) *v.* & *n.* **1.** *v.i.* Be dull and sleepy, or half asleep; (arch.) be sluggish. **2.** *v.t.* Make drowsy; pass *away* (time) in drowsing. **3.** *n.* Half-asleep condition. [back form. f. foll.]

drow's|y̆ (-zĭ) *a.* Sleepy, half asleep, dozing; lulling, soporific; sluggish; **~y-head,** sleepy person; hence **~ĭ**HEAD (arch.), **~ĭ**NESS, *ns.*, **~ĭ**LY[2] *adv.* [prob. rel. to OE *drūsian* be languid or slow, cogn. w. *drēosan* fall; cf. DREARY]

drŭb *v.t.* (-bb-). Cudgel, thump, belabour; beat in fight; beat (notion) *into*, *out of*, person; hence **~'bing**[1] *n.* [ult. f. Arab. *ḍaraba* beat]

drŭdg|e *n.*, & *v.i.* **1.** *n.* Servile worker, slave, hack; hence ~'ERY (2, 5) *n.* **2.** *v.i.* Work slavishly *at* laborious, dull, or distasteful work. [15th c., perh. rel. to DRAG[1]]

drŭg *n.* & *v.* (-gg-). **1.** *n* Medicinal substance, used alone or as ingredient; (esp.) narcotic, hallucinogen, or stimulant, (*drug addict, habit, traffic*; DANGEROUS *drug*); unsaleable commodity, thing no longer in demand (usu. ~ **on the market**); ***~'store,** chemist's shop also selling miscellaneous articles, light refreshments, etc.; hence **~'gy**[2] (-gĭ) *a.* **2.** *v.t.* Add drug, esp. narcotic or poison, to (food or drink); administer drugs, esp. narcotics, to; (arch.) nauseate, cloy. **3.** *v.i.* Indulge in narcotics etc. [ME *drogges*, *drouges*, f. OF *drogue*, of unkn. orig.]

drŭ'ggėt (-g-) *n.* (Floor-covering etc. of) coarse woven fabric used for floor or table covering. [f. F *droguet*, of unkn. orig.]

drŭ'ggĭst (-g-) *n.* Dealer in drugs, pharmaceutical chemist. [f. F *droguiste* (as DRUG; see -IST)]

Dru'ĭd (-ōō'-) *n.* **1.** Priest, magician, soothsayer, among Celts of ancient Gaul, Britain, and Ireland. **2.** Officer of Welsh etc. Gorsedd. **3.** Hence ~ESS[1], ~ISM (3), *ns.*, **Druĭ'dic**(AL) (-ōō-) *adjs.* [f. F *druide* or f. L pl. *druidae*, *-des*, Gk *druidai* f. Gaulish *druides*]

drŭm[1] *n.* **1.** Musical instrument sounded by striking and made of hollow cylinder or hemisphere with skin or parchment stretched over opening(s) (*bass, tenor, big*, SIDE[1]-, KETTLE-, etc., *drum*); its player; (in *pl.*) percussion section of jazz band etc. **2.** (Zool. & Anat.) Natural organ giving resonance, e.g. howler monkey's hyoid bone; membrane of middle ear. **3.** Sound (as) of drum. **4.** Cylindrical structure or object; cylinder or barrel in machinery on which something is wound or for other purposes; solid part of Corinthian or composite capital; stone block forming section of shaft; cylindrical receptacle for packing dried fruit, holding oil, etc. **5.** (Hist.) Evening or afternoon-tea party. **6.** **~(-fish)**, Amer. fish able to make drumming noise. **7.** (sl.) House, night-club, brothel. **8.** **~ brake,** one in which shoes on vehicle press against drum on wheel; **~'fire,** heavy continuous rapid artillery fire usu. heralding infantry attack, (fig.) barrage of criticism etc.; **~'head,** skin or membrane of drum (*~head court martial, service*, etc., improvised or summary), ear-drum, circular top of capstan; **~ major,** leader of marching band, (arch.) N.C.O. commanding drummers of regiment; **~ majorette,** female drum major; **~'stick,** stick with knob or pad for beating drum, lower joint of cooked fowl's leg. [f. obs. *drombslade*, *drombyllsclad*, f. LG *trommelslag* drum-beat (*trommel* drum, *slag* beat)]

drŭm[2] *v.* (**-mm-**). **1.** *v.i.* Play the drum; beat, tap, or thump, continuously on something (*on* piano, *at* door; *feet drum on floor*; *a drumming in the ears*); (of bird, insect) make loud hollow noise with quivering wings; **~ up,** (sl.) make tea in billycan etc. **2.** *v.t.* Summon, beat *up*, (as) by drumming (**~ out,** cashier by beat of drum, dismiss with ignominy); drive (lesson) *into* person by persistence; strike (hands etc.) repeatedly (*up*)*on* something; play (tune etc.) (as) on drum. [f. prec.]

drŭm[3], **drŭ'mlĭn,** *ns.* (Geol.) Long oval mound of drift or diluvial formation; hence **drŭ'mlĭn**OID *n.* [f. Gael. & Ir. *druim* ridge; *-lin* perh. for -LING[1]]

drŭ'mmer *n.* In vbl senses; commercial traveller; (sl.) thief. [f. DRUM[2] + -ER[1]]

drŭnk *a.* & *n.* **1.** *a.* Deprived of proper control of oneself by alcoholic liquor, (*blind, dead, half*, etc., *drunk*; *drunk as a fiddler* or *lord*; *Philip drunk to Philip* SOBER); (fig.) overcome *with* joy, success, etc.; hence ~'ARD *n.*, ***~ŏ'meter** *n.*, breathalyser. **2.** *n.* (sl.) Drinking-bout, period of drunkenness; drunken person. [p.p. of DRINK[1]]

drŭ'nken *a.* (usu. *attrib.*) = prec.; fond of drinking, often drunk; caused by or exhibiting drunkenness (*drunken frolic, brawl*); hence ~LY[2] *adv.*, ~NESS (-n-n-) *n.* [as prec.; see -EN[1]]

drup|e (-ōōp) *n.* Stone-fruit, fleshy or pulpy fruit enclosing stone or nut with kernel, e.g. olive, plum, cherry; hence ~A'CEOUS *a.* [f. L f. Gk *druppa* olive]

dru'pel (-ōō'-), **dru'pelėt** (-ōō'pl-), *ns.* Small drupe in aggregate fruit, e.g. blackberry. [f. prec. + -EL, -LET]

druse[1] (-ōōz) *n.* Crust of crystals lining rock-cavity; cavity so lined. [F f. G, = weathered ore]

Druse[2] (-ōōz) *n.* Member of political and religious sect of Muslim origin living near Mt. Lebanon. [F, f. Arab. *durūz* pl., prob. f. their founder *al-Darazī* (11th c.)]

drȳ[1] *a.* (**drī'er, drī'est,** *pr.* -ī'-). **1.** Without moisture; (of eyes) free from tears; (of shampoo) for use without water; (of shave) with electric etc. razor; not rainy, with deficient rainfall, (*dry* *spell, climate,* SEASON); *dry* STEAM^1; HIGH *and dry.* **2.** Parched, dried up, (colloq.) thirsty; (of liquid) having disappeared by evaporation, draining, wiping, etc.; (of country, state, legislation, etc.) teetotal, prohibiting sale of alcoholic liquor at some or all times (**go ~**, enact such legislation). **3.** Not yielding water, milk, etc., (*well, cow, is dry*). **4.** Without butter etc. (*dry bread, toast*). **5.** Solid, not liquid, (*dry provisions*). **6.** (Of wine etc.) free from sweetness. **7.** Unconnected with liquid (*dry distillation*; **die a ~ death,** not by drowning or bloodshed; **~ cough,** without phlegm; *dry*-BOB^5). **8.** Impassive, unsympathetic, stiff, hard, cold; (of jest, sarcasm, humour) expressed in matter-of-fact tone with pretended unawareness. **9.** Meagre, plain, bare, not enlarged upon, (*dry facts, thanks*); uninteresting, dull, unprofitable, (*dry as dust*); unprejudiced. **10. ~ battery, ~ cell,** (Electr.) battery or cell in which electrolyte is absorbed in a solid and cannot be spilt; **~-clean,** clean (clothes etc.) by means of organic solvents without using water; **~-cure,** cure (meat etc.) without pickling in liquid; *dry* DOCK^4; **~-fly** *a.* & *v.i.*, (fish) with artificial fly floating lightly on water; **~ goods,** non-liquid goods, e.g. corn, *drapery and haberdashery; *dry* ICE^1; **~ land,** land as opp. sea, river, etc.; **~ measure,** measure of capacity for dry goods; **~-nurse** (tending but not suckling child); **~-plate,** photographic plate with sensitized film hard and dry for convenience of keeping, developing at leisure, etc.; **~-point,** needle for engraving without acid on bare copper plate, engraving so produced; **~ rot,** decayed state of wood when not well ventilated, caused by certain fungi, these fungi, (fig.) unsuspected moral or social decay; **~ run,** (colloq.) rehearsal; **~-salt** *v.t.*, = *dry-cure*; **~-salter,** dealer in drugs, dyes, gums, oils, pickles, tinned meats, etc.; **~-shod** *a.* & *adv.*, without wetting the shoes; **~'stone, ~-walling,** (without mortar). **11.** Hence **~'**ISH^1 2 *a.*, **drī'**LY^2, **~'**LY^2, *adv.* (esp. in fig. senses), **~'**NESS *n.* [OE *drȳge*, rel. to MLG *dröge*, MDu. *drōghe* f. Gmc **draug*- etc.]

drȳ^2 *v.t.* & *i.* Make or become dry by wiping, evaporation, draining, etc.; preserve food by removal of moisture (*dried egg, fruit*); **~ (off)**, (cause to) cease yielding milk; **~ out,** become fully dry, (of drug addict etc.) undergo treatment to cure addiction; **~ up,** make utterly dry, dry washed dishes, (of moisture) disappear utterly, (of well etc.) cease to yield water, (colloq., esp. in *imper.*) cease talking or doing something; **~ (up)**, (Theatr.) forget one's lines. [OE *drygan* (as prec.)]

drȳ'ăd *n.* (Myth.) Nymph inhabiting tree, wood-nymph. [ME, f. OF *dryade* f. L f. Gk *druas* -*ados* (*drus* tree)]

Drȳ'asdŭst (-*az*-) *n.* & *a.* **1.** *n.* Dull laborious antiquary or historian. **2.** *a.* (*d~*). Very dry, uninteresting. [Dr. ~, fictitious person (*dry as dust*) to whom Scott dedicated novels]

drȳ'er. See DRIER^2.

D.S. *abbr. dal segno*; disseminated sclerosis.

D.S.C. *abbr.* Distinguished Service Cross.

D.Sc. *abbr.* Doctor of Science.

D.S.M. *abbr.* Distinguished Service Medal.

‖**D.S.O.** *abbr.* Distinguished Service Order.

D.T.(s) *abbr.* delirium tremens.

dū'al *a.* & *n.* **1.** *a.* Of two, twofold, divided in two, double, (*dual ownership*; ‖**~ carriageway,** road with dividing strip between traffic in opposite directions; **~ control** (esp. of vehicle or aircraft controlled by instructor as well as by learner); **~-purpose** *a.*, (of vehicle) usable for passengers or goods); shared by two, joint. **2.** *a.* & *n.* (Gram.) **~ (number)**, (form of noun, verb, etc.) denoting two persons or things (additional to singular and plural). **3.** So **dūă'l**ITY *n.*, **~**IZE (3) *v.t.*, **~**LY^2 *adv.* [f. L *dualis* (*duo* two; see -AL)]

dū'al‖ism *n.* Duality; theory recognizing two independent principles (mind and matter, cf. *idealism* and *materialism*; good and evil in the universe; two personalities in Christ); so **~**IST (2) *n.*, **~ĭ'st**IC *a.* [f. DUAL + -ISM]

dŭb^1 *n.* (sl.) Inexperienced or unskilful person. [perh. f. foll. in sense 'beat flat']

dŭb^2 *v.t.* (-bb-). **1.** Make (person) a knight by touching his shoulders with sword; give title of, name, nickname, (person or thing, with complement: *dubbed me Doctor, a crank*). **2.** ‖Dress (artificial fishing-fly). **3.** Smear (leather) with grease. [OE **dubbian*, f. AF *duber, aduber*, OF *adober* equip with armour, repair, of unkn. orig.]

dŭb^3 *v.t.* (-bb-). Make another sound-track of (film) esp. in a different language; add (sound effects or music) to a film or broadcast; combine (sound-tracks) into one. [abbr. of DOUBLE^3]

dŭb^4 *v.i.* (-bb-). (sl.) **~ in, up,** pay up, contribute money. [19th c.; orig. uncert.]

dŭ'bbĭn *n.*, & *v.t.* **1.** *n.* Prepared grease for softening and waterproofing leather. **2.** *v.t.* Apply dubbin to. [f. foll.]

dŭ'bbĭng *n.* In vbl senses; = prec. [f. DUB^{2,3} + -ING^1]

dūbī'etȳ *n.* Feeling of doubt; doubtful matter. [f. LL *dubietas* (*dubium* doubt; see -TY^1)]

dū'bĭous *a.* Hesitating, doubting; unreliable (*dubious friend*); of questionable value or truth (*a dubious claim, compliment*); of doubtful result (*dubious undertaking*); of suspected character (*dubious gains, company*); hence **~**LY^2 *adv.*, **~**NESS *n.* [f. L *dubiosus* (*dubium* doubt; see -OUS)]

dūbĭtā'tion *n.* Doubt, hesitation. [ME f. OF, or f. L *dubitatio* (*dubitare* DOUBT^2; see -ATION)]

dū'bĭtatĭve *a.* Of, expressing, inclined to, doubt or hesitation; hence **~**LY^2 (-vlĭ) *adv.* [f. F *dubitatif -ive* or f. LL *dubitativus* (as prec.; see -IVE)]

Dŭ'blĭn *n.* **~ (Bay) prawn,** Norway lobster, (in *pl.*) scampi. [~ in Ireland]

dū'cal *a.* Of, like, bearing title of, duke. [F (*duc* DUKE; see -AL)]

dŭ'cat *n.* (Hist.) Gold coin, current in most European countries; coin, (in *pl.*) money. [ME, f. It. *ducato* or f. med. L *ducatus* DUCHY]

dŭ'chĕss *n.* **1.** Duke's wife or widow; woman holding rank of duke in her own right; imposing woman. **2.** ‖(sl.) Costermonger's wife; (sl.) mother, wife, woman. [ME, f. OF *duchesse*, f. med. L *ducissa* (as DUKE; see -ESS^1)]

dŭ'chĕsse (*or* dōōshĕ's) *n.* Soft heavy kind of satin; **~ lace,** kind of Brussels pillow-lace; **~ potatoes,** mashed potatoes mixed with egg, baked or fried, and served as small cakes; **~ set,** cover or set of covers for dressing-table. [F, = prec.]

dŭ'chȳ *n.* Territory of duke or duchess; royal dukedom of Cornwall or Lancaster, each with certain estates, revenues, and jurisdiction of its own. [ME, f. OF *duché(e)* f. med. L *ducatus* & Rom. **ducitas* f. L *dux* (see DUKE)]

dŭck^1 *n.* (*pl.* **~s** *or* collect. **~**). **1.** Swimming-bird of family Anatidae, esp. the domesticated form of the mallard or wild duck; female of this; its flesh as food. **2. Like a (dying) ~ in a thunderstorm,** with upturned eyes, looking flabbergasted, distressed, etc.: LAME *duck*; **like water off a ~'s back,** producing no effect; **take to** thing **like a ~ to water** (very readily). **3.** ‖**~**('Y^3), **~s,** (colloq.) darling (esp. in *voc.*), attractive thing. **4.** (Cricket). **~('s egg)**, batsman's score of 0; **break** one's **~**, score one's first run in the innings. **5.** BOMBAY DUCK; **~(s)**

and drake(**s**), game of making flat stone skip along water (*make ~s and drakes of*, *play ~s and drakes with*, squander); **~-arse,** (sl.) haircut with back hair shaped like duck's tail; **~'bill,** = *duck-billed* PLATY*pus*; **~-boards,** narrow path of wooden slats in trench or over mud; **~-hawk,** ||marsh harrier, *peregrine; ***~'pin,** short squat bowling pin; **~'s disease,** (joc.) short legs; ***~ soup,** (sl.) easy task; **~'weed,** plant that carpets surface of still water. **6.** Hence ~'LING¹ 2 *n.* (UGLY *duckling*). [OE *duce*, *dūce* (**dūcan* dive; see foll.)]

dŭck² *v.* & *n.* **1.** *v.i.* Plunge, dive, dip head, under water and emerge; bend quickly, bob, to avoid blow etc. or by way of bow or curtsy; (colloq.) withdraw, abscond; (Bridge) lose trick deliberately by playing low card. **2.** *v.t.* Plunge (person etc.) momentarily in or *in* water, whence ~'ING¹ (1) *n.* (**~ing-stool,** chair at end of rising and falling pole, formerly used for ducking scolds and other objectionable persons); lower (head) suddenly; (colloq.) avoid, dodge. **3.** *n.* Quick dip below water in bathing, or lowering of head. [f. OE **dūcan* (= MLG, MDu. *dūken*, OHG *tūhhan*)]

dŭck³ *n.* Strong untwilled linen or cotton fabric for small sails and outer clothing esp. of sailors; (in *pl.*) trousers of this. [f. MDu. *doek*, = OS *dōk*, OHG *tuoh*, of unkn. orig.]

dŭck⁴ *n.* (colloq.) Amphibious landing-craft. [f. *DUKW*, official designation]

dŭ'cklĭng. See DUCK¹ 6.

dŭ'ckȳ¹. See DUCK¹ 3.

dŭ'ckȳ² *a.* (colloq.) Sweet, pretty; splendid. [f. DUCK¹ + -Y²]

dŭct *n.*, & *v.t.* **1.** *n.* Channel or tube for conveying liquid, gas, cable, etc.; tube in body conveying secretions etc. (**~'less gland,** one secreting directly into bloodstream); vessel of plant's vascular tissue holding air, water, etc.; hence ~'ING¹ (6) *n.* **2.** *v.t.* Convey through duct. [f. L *ductus* leading, aqueduct (*ducere duct-* lead)]

dŭ'ctīle *a.* Capable of being drawn out into wire, tough; (of clay etc., or of person or character) pliable, tractable, docile; hence **dŭctĭ'l**ITY *n.* [ME f. OF, or f. L *ductilis* (*ducere duct-* lead; see -IL)]

dŭd *n.* & *a.* (sl.) **1.** *n.* Counterfeit article; shell etc. that fails to explode; futile plan or person; (in *pl.*) clothes, rags. **2.** *a.* Counterfeit; useless, worthless, unsatisfactory, futile. [ME; orig. unkn.]

***dūde** (*or* dōōd) *n.* (sl.) Fastidious aesthetic person; foppish person; holiday-maker in western U.S., esp. on ranch; **~ ranch,** cattle ranch converted to holiday centre for tourists etc.; hence **dū'd**ISH¹ (*or* dōō'-) *a.* [19th c., prob. f. G dial. *dude* fool]

dudee'n, dudhee'n, (dōōdē'n) *n.* (Ir.) Short clay pipe. [f. Ir. *dúidín*, dim. of *dúd* pipe; cf. -EEN]

dŭ'dgeon (dŭ'jen) *n.* Resentment, feeling of offence; **in** (**high**) ~, (very) angr(il)y. [16th c.; orig. unkn.]

dūe¹ *a.* & *adv.* **1.** *a.* Owing, payable, as a debt or obligation; **fall, become,** ~, (e.g. of bill reaching maturity). **2.** That ought to be given *to* person (*first place is due to Milton*: *it is due to him to say*); merited, appropriate, (*has his due reward*); rightful, proper, adequate, (*after due consideration*); to be looked for, calculated or foreseen (*in due time*); *in due* COURSE¹. **3.** To be ascribed *to* cause, agent, etc., (*the difficulty is due to our ignorance*; *the discovery is due to Newton*); under engagement *to* do something (*is due to speak tonight*) or to arrive at certain time (*train due at 7.30*). **4.** *adv.* (Of point of compass) exactly, directly, (*went due east*; *a due north wind*); **~ to,** because of (*was late due to an accident*). [ME, f. OF *dĕu* f. Rom. **debutus* f. L *debitus* p.p. of *debēre* owe]

dūe² *n.* Person's right, what is owed him, (**give** person, esp. **the Devil, his** ~, not be unjust to him, however undeserving); what one owes (*pay* one's *dues*); (usu. in *pl.*) toll, fee, legally demandable (*harbour*, *light*, *tonnage*, *university*, *dues*). [ME, f. F *du* p.p. (as n.) of *devoir* owe f. L *debēre*]

dū'el *n.*, & *v.i.* (||**-ll-**). **1.** *n.* Fight with deadly weapons between two persons, in presence of two seconds, to settle quarrel; any contest between two persons, animals, parties, causes; hence ~**l**IST (1) *n.* **2.** *v.i.* Fight duel(s). [f. It. *duello* or L *duellum* (arch. form of *bellum* war), in med. L = single combat]

duĕ'ndė (dōō-) *n.* Evil spirit; inspiration. [Sp.]

dūĕ'nna *n.* Older woman acting as governess and companion in charge of girls (orig. and esp. in Spanish family); chaperon. [f. Sp. *dueña* f. L *domina* mistress]

dūĕ't *n.* (Mus.) (composition for) two voices or performers; (fig.) dialogue; hence **dūĕ'tt**IST (1) *n.* [f. G *duett* or f. It. *duetto* dim. of *duo* duet f. L *duo* two]

dŭff¹ *n.* Boiled pudding (PLUM *duff*). [N. Engl. form of DOUGH]

dŭff² *v.t.* (sl.) (Austral.) steal and alter brands on (cattle); ||(Golf) mishit (shot, ball); bungle; **~ up,** (sl.) beat, thrash. [perh. back form. f. DUFFER]

dŭff³ *n.* & *a.* (sl.) Worthless, counterfeit, useless, (thing). [perh. = DUFF¹]

dŭ'ffer *n.* Inefficient, useless, or stupid person; (Austral.) one who duffs cattle. [perh. f. Sc. *doofart* stupid person (*douf* spiritless)]

dŭ'ffle, dŭ'ffel, *n.* Coarse woollen cloth with thick nap; *sportsman's or camper's kit; **~ bag,** cylindrical canvas bag closed by draw-string; **~-coat,** hooded overcoat of duffle with toggle fastenings instead of buttons. [f. *Duffel* in Belgium]

dŭg¹ *n.* Udder or breast, teat, nipple, (of female mammal, or derog. of woman). [16th c., of unkn. orig.]

dŭg². See DIG.

dū'gŏng (*or* dōō'-) *n.* (*pl.* **~s** *or* **~**). Large aquatic herbivorous mammal (*Dugong dugon*) of Asian seas and coasts. [ult. f. Malay *dūyong*]

dŭ'g-out *n.* Canoe made by hollowing tree-trunk; roofed shelter esp. for troops in trenches; (sl.) retired officer etc. recalled to service. [f. DUG² + OUT]

dui'ker¹, duy'ker, (dī'k-) *n.* Small Afr. antelope of genus *Cephalophus*. [f. Du. *duiker* diver, from plunging through bushes when pursued]

duiker² (dī'k-) *n.* (S. Afr.) Cormorant of genus *Phalacrocorax*. [Afrik., f. as prec.]

dūke *n.* **1.** (fem. **duchess**). Person holding highest hereditary title of nobility (**royal ~,** one who is also royal prince); sovereign prince ruling duchy or small State. **2.** (sl., usu. in *pl.*) Hand, fist. **3.** Cherry intermediate between sweet and sour kinds. [ME, f. OF *duc* f. L *dux ducis* leader]

dū'kedom (-kd-) *n.* Territory ruled by, rank of, duke. [f. prec. + -DOM]

DUKW *n.* = DUCK⁴.

dŭ'lcėt *a.* (Esp. of sound) sweet, soothing. [ME, earlier *doucet* f. OF dim. of *doux* f. L *dulcis* sweet]

dŭ'lcĭ|fȳ *v.t.* Sweeten, make gentle; hence ~FICA'TION *n.* [f. L *dulcificare* (*dulcis* sweet; see -FY)]

dŭ'lcimer *n.* Musical instrument with strings of graduated length over sounding-board or box struck with hammers, prototype of piano. [f. OF *doulcemer*, said to repr. L **dulce melos* sweet song]

Dŭlcinē'a (*or* -sĭ'nĭa) *n.* Idolized and idealized lady. [f. ~ del Toboso, object of Don Quixote's devotion in Cervantes' romance]

dŭ'lcĭtōne *n.* (Mus.) Keyboard instrument with steel tuning-forks struck by hammers. [f. L *dulcis* sweet + TONE¹]

dū'lĭa *n.* (R.C. Ch.) Reverence paid to saints and angels. [med. L, f. Gk *douleia* servitude (*doulos* slave)]

dŭll *a.* & *v.* **1.** *a.* Slow of understanding, obtuse, stupid, whence ~'ARD *n.*; (of ears, eyes, etc.) without keen perception. **2.** (Of pain etc.) indistinctly felt, not acute; (of person, animal, trade) sluggish, slow-moving, stagnant; (of goods, stocks) not easily saleable, not in demand; listless, depressed. **3.** Tedious, monotonous; (esp. of edge) blunt; (of colour, light, sound, taste) not bright, vivid, or keen; (of weather) overcast, gloomy. **4.** Hence ~'ISH¹ 2 *a.*, **dŭ'l(l)-**NESS *n.*, **dŭ'l**LY² (dŭ'l-lĭ) *adv.* **5.** *v.t.* Make dull (~ **the edge of,** blunt, make less sensitive, interesting, or effective). **6.** *v.i.* Lose force, intensity, clearness, or keenness. [ME, f. MLG, MDu. *dul*, = OE, OS *dol* stupid, OHG *tol*]

dŭlse *n.* Edible kind of red seaweed. [f. Ir. & Gael. *duileasg*]

dū'lȳ *adv.* Rightly, properly, fitly; sufficiently; punctually. [ME, f. DUE¹ + -LY²]

du'ma (dōō'-) *n.* (Hist.) Russian council of state. [Russ., orig. elective municipal council]

dŭmb (-m) *a.* (~'**er** *pr.* -mer, ~'**est** *pr.* -mĭst). **1.** Unable to speak, either abnormally (of human beings; *the dumb*, *the deaf and dumb*, as *ns.*) or normally (~ **animals, our ~ friends,** term of pity or contempt; ~ **chum,** ~ **friend,** a domestic animal); inarticulate, having no voice in government etc., (*the dumb millions*); silenced by surprise, shyness, etc., (esp. *strike dumb*); taciturn, reticent. **2.** Stupid, ignorant [G *dumm*]; ~ **blonde,** pretty but stupid blonde woman. **3.** (Of action) performed without speech (*dumb* CRAMBO; ~ **show,** significant gestures, part of play given in early drama without words). **4.** Unheard, giving no sound; without voice, sound, or other property, usual in things of the name (~ **piano,** set of keys for exercising fingers; ~ **waiter,** movable table esp. with revolving shelves making waiter unnecessary in dining-room, lift for food etc.). **5.** ~**-bell,** short bar with weight at each end used in pairs for exercising muscles, (sl.) stupid person; ~ **cluck, *~'head,** (sl.) stupid person; ~**-iron,** curved side-piece of motor-vehicle chassis, joining it to front springs. **6.** Hence ~'LY² (-mlĭ) *adv.*, ~'NESS (-mn-) *n.* [OE, = OS *dumb*, OHG *tumb* stupid, ON *dumbr*, Goth. *dumbs* mute, of unkn. orig.]

dŭm(b)fou'nd (-mf-) *v.t.* Strike dumb; confound, nonplus. [f. DUMB + CONFOUND]

dŭ'mdŭm *a.* & *n.* ~ (**bullet**), kind of soft-nosed bullet that expands on impact and inflicts laceration. [f. *Dum-Dum* in India, where first produced]

dŭ'mmȳ *n.*, *a.*, & *v.i.* **1.** *n.* (Whist) imaginary fourth player whose hand is turned up and played by partner; (Bridge) partner of declarer, whose cards are exposed after first lead, this player's hand (**double ~,** play with two hands exposed, allowing every card to be located). **2.** Person taking no real part, or present only for show, figure-head; stupid person. **3.** Counterfeit object, sham package etc., object serving to replace real or normal one; tailor's model of body to hang clothes on; ventriloquist's model of person, or animal, which he can make seem to talk etc.; baby's indiarubber teat; **sell the** or **a ~,** (Rugby Footb., colloq.) deceive opponent by feigning to pass ball. **4.** *a.* Sham; ~ **run,** practice attack etc., trial run, rehearsal. **5.** *v.i.* (Footb.) use feigned pass or swerve etc.; ***~ up,** (sl.) keep quiet, give no information. [f. DUMB + -Y³]

dŭmp¹ *n.* Heap of refuse; place for depositing refuse; accumulated pile of ore, earth, etc.; temporary deposit of ammunition, provisions, etc.; (colloq.) unpleasant or dreary place; ~ **truck** etc. (with body that tilts or opens at back for unloading). [f. foll.]

dŭmp² *v.* **1.** *v.t.* Shoot, deposit, (rubbish); let fall with bump; leave (ammunition etc.) in dump; send (goods unsaleable at high price in home market) to foreign market for sale at low price, to avoid lowering home price and to capture new market; (colloq.) abandon. **2.** *v.i.* Fall with thud. **3.** Hence ~'ER¹ (1, 2) *n.* [ME, perh. f. Norse; cf. Da. *dumpe*, Norw. *dumpa* fall suddenly]

dŭ'mplĭng *n.* Mass of dough boiled or baked either plain or enclosing apple etc.; small fat person. [app. dim. (-LING¹) of *dump* small round object, but recorded very much earlier]

dŭmps *n. pl.* (colloq.) Depression, melancholy, (*in the dumps*). [prob. f. LG or Du., fig. use of MDu. *domp* exhalation, haze, mist, rel. to DAMP]

dŭ'mp|ȳ *a.* Short and stout; hence ~**ĭNESS** *n.* [f. *dump* (cf. DUMPLING) + -Y²]

dŭn¹ *a.* & *n.* **1.** (Of) dull greyish-brown colour as of ass or mouse (~**-bird,** pochard; ~ **diver,** female or young male of goosander). **2.** *a.* (poet.) Dark, dusky. **3.** *n.* Dun horse; dark fishing-fly. [OE *dun(n)*, = OS *dun* nut-brown]

dŭn² *n.*, & *v.t.* (-nn-). **1.** *n.* Importunate creditor; debt-collector; demand for payment. **2.** *v.t.* Importune for payment of debt; pester. [abbr. of obs. *dunkirk* privateer, f. *Dunkirk* in France]

dŭnce *n.* One slow at learning, dullard, (~**'s cap,** paper cone formerly put on head of dunce at school as mark of disgrace). [f. John *Duns* Scotus, schoolman d. 1308, whose followers were ridiculed by 16th-c. humanists and reformers as enemies of learning]

Dŭndee' *n.* ~ **cake,** rich fruit-cake usu. decorated with almonds; ~ **marmalade,** special kind orig. made in Dundee. [~ in Scotland]

dŭ'nderhead (-ĕd) *n.*, **dŭ'nder-headĕd** (-ĕd-) *a.* Stupid (person). [17th c., perh. rel. to dial. *dunner* resounding noise]

Dŭndrear'ȳ *n.* ~ **whiskers,** (arch.) long side-whiskers worn without beard. [f. Lord ~, character in T. Taylor's *Our American Cousin* (1858)]

dūne *n.* Mound or ridge of loose sand etc. formed by wind; *dune* BUGGY². [F, f. MDu. *dūne*; cf. DOWN¹]

dŭng *n.* & *v.* **1.** *n.* Faeces of animal, occas. of man; manure; ~**-beetle** (whose larvae develop in dung); ~**-cart, -fork,** (for conveying, loading, and spreading, manure); ~**-fly** (feeding in dung); ~**'hill,** heap of dung or refuse in farmyard; ~**-worm** (found in cow-dung and used as bait). **2.** *v.t.* Apply dung to (land). **3.** *v.i.* Excrete dung. [OE, = OHG *tunga*, Icel. *dyngja*, of unkn. orig.]

dŭngaree' (-ngg-) *n.* Coarse Indian calico; (in *pl.*) overalls etc. of dungaree or similar material. [f. Hindi *dungrī*]

dŭ'ngeon (-njon) *n.*, & *v.t.* **1.** *n.* Strong subterranean cell for prisoners; (arch.) donjon. **2.** *v.t.* (arch.) Shut *up*, imprison in dungeon. [orig. = *donjon*; ME, f. OF *donjon* f. Gallo-Rom. **domnio -onis* f. L *dominus* lord]

du'nĭwăssal (dōō'-) *n.* (Sc.) Highland gentleman of secondary rank. [f. Gael. *duine* man, *uasal* noble]

dŭnk *v.t.* Dip (bread, cake, etc.) into soup or beverage while eating; immerse (lit. or fig.). [f. Pennsylvanian G *dunke* to dip (G *tunken*)]

Dŭnkīr'k (-n-k-) *n.* Scene of crisis or withdrawal; ~ **spirit,** refusal to surrender or despair in time of crisis. [~ in France, whence British forces were evacuated in 1940]

dŭ'nlĭn *n.* Red-backed sandpiper. [prob. f. **dunling* f. DUN¹ + -LING¹]

dŭ'nnage *n.* Mats, brushwood, gratings, etc., stowed under or among cargo to prevent wetting and chafing; (colloq.) miscellaneous baggage. [=AL *dennagium*, of unkn. orig.]

dŭnnō' (*or* dŭ'-) *v.i.* & *t.* (colloq.) (I) do not know. [corrupt.]

‖**dŭ'nnock** *n.* HEDGE¹-sparrow. [app. f. DUN¹ + -OCK, f. its brown and grey plumage]

dŭ'nnӯ *n.* (Sc.) underground passage or cellar esp. in tenement; (esp. Austral. & N.Z.) earth-closet, outdoor privy. [20th c.; orig. uncert.]

dū'ō *n.* (*pl.* ~**s**). Pair of artistes (*comedy duo*); (Mus.) duet. [L, = two]

dūodĕ'cĭmal *a.* Of twelfths or twelve; reckoning or reckoned by twelves; hence ~LY² *adv.* [f. L *duodecimus* twelfth (*duodecim* twelve) + -AL]

dūodĕ'cĭmō *n.* (*pl.* ~**s**). Book-size in which each leaf is 1/12 of printing-sheet; book of this size; (arch.) diminutive thing or person. [f. L (*in*) *duodecimo* in a twelfth (as prec.)]

dūodē'narӯ *a.* Proceeding by twelves, in sets of twelve. [f. L *duodenarius* (*duodeni* distrib. of *duodecim* twelve; see -ARY¹)]

dūodē'n|um *n.* (Anat.) First portion of small intestine immediately below stomach; hence ~AL *a.*, ~Ī'TIS *n.* [ME f. med. L (*duodeni*; see prec.) from its length of 12 fingers' breadth)]

dū'olŏgue (-ŏg) *n.* Conversation between two persons; dramatic piece with two actors. [irreg. f. L or Gk *duo* two, after *monologue*]

duō'mō (dw-) *n.* (*pl.* ~**s**). Italian cathedral. [It., = DOME]

dūŏ'polӯ *n.* Possession of trade in a commodity etc. by only two sellers. [f. Gk *duo* two + *pōleō* sell, after *monopoly*]

dū'otōne *n.* & *a.* **1.** *n.* (Process of making) half-tone illustration in two colours from same original with different screen angles. **2.** *a.* In two colours. [f. L *duo* two + TONE¹]

dūp|e *n.*, & *v.t.* **1.** *n.* Victim of deception; hence ~'ERY (2) *n.* **2.** *v.t.* Cheat, make a fool of; hence ~'ABLE *a.*, ~'ER¹ *n.* [F, f. dial. F *dupe* hoopoe, from the bird's stupid appearance]

dū'pĭon *n.* Rough silk fabric from threads of double cocoons; imitation of this with other fibres. [f. F *doupion* f. It. *doppione* (*doppio* double)]

dū'ple *a.* ~ **ratio,** (Math.) that of 2 to 1; ~ **time,** (Mus., with two beats to the bar). [f. L *duplus* (*duo* two)]

dū'plĕx *a.* & *n.* **1.** *a.* Having two elements, two-fold; two-storey (flat), two-family (house). **2.** *n.* Duplex house etc.; dwelling forming part of this. [L *duplex duplicis* (*duo* two, *plic-* fold)]

dū'plĭcate¹ *a.* & *n.* **1.** *a.* Having two corresponding parts, existing in two examples; doubled, twice as large or many (~ **ratio,** proportion of squares of two numbers); exactly like a thing already existing (with any number of copies or specimens); ~ **bridge** or **whist,** form where same hands are played successively by different players. **2.** *n.* One of two things exactly alike, esp. that made after the other; second copy, with equal legal force, of letter or document; (arch.) pawnbroker's ticket; one of two or more specimens of thing exactly or virtually alike; exact correspondence between two things (*made in duplicate*); = *duplicate bridge* etc. [ME, f. L *duplicatus* p.p. of *duplicare* (see foll., -ATE²)]

dū'plĭc|āte² *v.t.* Double, multiply by two; make in duplicate, make or be exact copy of, produce or supply copies of; repeat (action etc.), esp. unnecessarily; hence ~Ā'TION *n.*, ~**ātor** *n.*, (esp.) machine for making copies of documents etc. [f. L *duplicare* (as DUPLEX) + -ATE³]

dūplĭ'cĭt|ӯ *n.* Double-dealing, deceitfulness; (arch.) doubleness; hence ~OUS *a.* [ME, f. OF *duplicité* or f. LL *duplicitas* (as DUPLEX; see -ITY)]

dŭ'ppӯ *n.* (W. Ind.) Malevolent ghost or spirit. [perh. of Afr. orig.]

dura. See DURRA.

dūr'ab|le *a.* & *n.* **1.** *a.* Capable of lasting, not transitory; (of goods) remaining useful for a period, not immediately consumed; resisting wear, decay, etc.; hence **dūr**ABI'LITY, ~**le**NESS (-beln-), *ns.*, ~LY² *adv.* **2.** *n.* (in *pl.*) Durable goods. [ME f. OF, f. L *durabilis* (*durare* endure f. *durus* hard; see -ABLE)]

Dūră'lūmĭn *n.* Aluminium alloy with copper etc., remarkable for its strength and hardness combined with lightness. [P; perh. f. *Düren* in the Rhineland or L *durus* hard + ALUMINIUM]

dūra mā'ter *n.* (Anat.) Tough outer membrane enveloping brain and spinal cord. [med. L, = hard mother, transl. of Arab. *al-'umm al-jāfiya* ('mother' in Arab. indicating relationship of things)]

dūrā'mĕn *n.* Heartwood of exogenous tree. [L (*durare* harden)]

dūr'ance *n.* (arch.) Imprisonment (esp. *in durance vile*). [ME f. F f. *durer* last f. L *durare* (see DURABLE, -ANCE)]

dūrā'tion *n.* Continuance in, length of, time; time for which thing, esp. war, continues (**for the** ~, until end of war, (fig.) for a very long time). [ME f. OF, f. med. L *duratio -onis* (as prec.; see -ATION)]

dūr'atĭve *a.* (Gram.) Denoting continuing action. [f. prec. + -IVE]

dûr'bar *n.* (Hist.) Court of Indian ruler; public levee of Indian prince or Anglo-Ind. governor or viceroy. [Urdu, f. Pers. *darbār* court]

dūrĕ'ss (*or* dūr'ĕs) *n.* Forcible restraint, imprisonment; compulsion, esp. imprisonment, threats, or violence, illegally used to force person to do something (*under duress*). [ME, f. OF *duresse* f. L *duritia* (*durus* hard; see -ESS²)]

dur'ĭan (door'-) *n.* (S.E. Asian tree, *Durio zibethinus*, bearing) large oval fruit containing pulp notable for its fetid smell and agreeable taste. [f. Malay *durian* (*dūri* thorn)]

dūr'ĭng *prep.* Throughout the continuance of; at some point in the duration of. [ME, part. of obs. *dure* continue, after OF *durant* and L abl. abs. constr., as *durante vita* (or *vita durante*) while life continues]

dûr'mast (-ah-) *n.* Sessile-flowered species of oak, *Quercus petraea*. [f. *dur-* (perh. erron. for DUN¹) + MAST²]

***dûrn,** ***dûrned** (-nd). Var. of DARN², DARNED.

du'rra, du'ra, dhu'rra, (dŏŏ'-) *n.* Kind of sorghum (esp. *Sorghum vulgare*) grown in Asia, Africa, and U.S. [f. Arab. *dur*(*r*)*a*]

dûrst. See DARE.

dūr'um *n.* Species of wheat with hard seeds. [L, neut. of *durus* hard]

dûr'zi (-zē) *n.* Indian tailor. [f. Hindi f. Pers. *darzi* (*darz* sewing)]

dŭsk *n.*, *a.*, & *v.* **1.** *n.* Shade, gloom; darker stage of twilight. **2.** *a.* (poet.) Shadowy, dim, dark-coloured. **3.** *v.t.* & *i.* (poet.) Make or become shadowy or dim. [ME *dosk*, *dusk*, f. OE *dox* dark, swarthy, *doxian* darken in colour]

dŭ'sk|ӯ *a.* Shadowy, dim; dark-coloured; hence ~ĬLY² *adv.*, ~ĬNESS *n.* [f. prec. + -Y²]

dŭst¹ *n.* **1.** Finely powdered earth or other matter lying on ground or on surfaces or carried about by wind (BITE¹ *the dust*; ~ **and ashes,** something very disappointing; **in the** ~, humiliated; **shake the** ~ **off** one's **feet,** depart indignantly or disdainfully; **throw** ~ **in**

person's **eyes,** mislead him by misrepresentation or diverting attention from point). **2.** ||Household refuse. **3.** Pollen; fine powder of any material (*gold dust*; *pyrethrum dust*). **4.** Cloud of dust (RAISE *a dust*); (fig.) confusion, turmoil. **5.** Dead person's remains (*honoured dust*; **in the ~,** dead); (arch.) the human body, man. **6. ~-bath,** bird's rolling in or sprinkling itself with dust to freshen its feathers; ||**~'bin,** container for household refuse; **~ bowl,** area denuded of vegetation by drought and erosion and so reduced to desert; ||**~-cart,** vehicle for collecting household refuse; **~-coat, -cloth,** (worn or put over objects to keep off dust); **~-colour,** dull light brown; **~-cover,** removable cloth to keep dust off furniture etc., paper jacket of book; *dust* DEVIL[1] 7; **~-jacket,** book's dust-cover (see JACKET 3); ||**~'man,** (1) man who removes refuse from dustbins, (2) = SAND*man*; **~'pan** (into which dust is brushed from floor); **~-sheet,** dust-cover for furniture; **~-shot,** smallest-sized shot; **~-trap,** something on which dust readily collects; **~-up,** (colloq.) fight, disturbance; **~-wrapper,** book's dust-cover. **7.** Hence **~'**LESS *a.* [OE *dūst*, = MDu. *donst, dūst*, ON *dust*; cf. LG *dunst* vapour]

dŭst[2] *v.* **1.** *v.t.* Sprinkle with dust or powder; make dusty; sprinkle (dust, powder). **2.** Clear of dust by brushing, wiping, or beating (**~** person's **jacket,** (colloq.) thrash him); clear away (dust etc.). **3.** *v.i.* Clear furniture etc. of dust; (of bird) take dust-bath. [ME, f. prec.]

dŭ'ster *n.* Cloth for dusting furniture etc.; person who does this; woman's light loose casual full-length coat. [f. prec. + -ER[1]]

dŭ'stĭng *n.* In vbl senses; **crop-~,** sprinkling of powdered insecticide or fertilizer on crops, esp. from the air; **~-powder,** (esp.) talcum powder. [f. DUST[2] + -ING[1]]

dŭ'st|ȳ *a.* Full of, strewn with, finely powdered like, dust; dry as dust, uninteresting; (of colour) dull; vague, indefinite, unsatisfactory, (*dusty answer*); ||**not so ~y,** (sl.) fairly good; **~y miller,** auricula plant [from white dust on leaves and flowers], artificial fishing-fly, *speckled moth; hence **~ĭLY**[2] *adv.*, **~ĭNESS** *n.* [OE *dūstig* (as DUST[1], -Y[2])]

Dŭtch[1] *a.* & *n.* **1.** *a.* (Of the language or people) of the Netherlands. **2.** Originating in the Netherlands, made or invented by the Dutch, (*Dutch chair, cheese*). **3.** Characteristic of or attributed to the Dutch; *Dutch* AUCTION; **~ bargain** (concluded by drinking together); **~ barn,** roof on poles over hay etc.; **~ cap,** (1) woman's lace cap with triangular piece turned back on each side, (2) contraceptive diaphragm; *Dutch* COURAGE; **~ doll,** jointed wooden doll; **~ elm disease,** fungous disease of elms, first found in the Netherlands; *Dutch* HOE; **~ interior,** painting of interior of Dutch room or house, esp. by P. de Hooch (d. 1683); **~ metal,** copper-zinc alloy imitating gold leaf; *Dutch* OVEN; **~ treat** etc., party where each person pays for his own share (**go ~,** share expenses thus); **talk to** person **like a ~ uncle,** lecture him with kindly severity; **~ wife,** frame of cane etc. for resting the limbs in bed, long bolster similarly used. **4.** (arch.) Of Germany incl. Netherlands (**High ~,** of S. Germany; **Low ~,** of N. Germany and Netherlands). **5.** *(sl.) German; (S. Afr.) of Dutch descent. **6.** *n.* (**High**) **~,** language of the Netherlands (**double ~,** gibberish); (**Cape**) **~,** Afrikaans; **the ~,** (*pl.*) people of the Netherlands (***beat the ~,** (colloq.) do something remarkable); **in ~,** (sl.) in disgrace. **7.** (arch.) Language of Germany incl. Netherlands (**High ~,** German). **8. Low ~,** Low German or language of the Netherlands. [f. MDu. *dutsch* etc. Hollandish, Netherlandish, German, OHG *diutisc* national]

||**dŭtch**[2] *n.* = DUCHESS 2. [abbr.]

Dŭ'tchman *n.* (*pl.* **-men;** *fem.* **-woman**). Native of the Netherlands (**or I'm a ~, I'm a ~ if,** forms of asseveration); Dutch ship (**Flying ~,** spectral ship or its captain); ***~'s breeches,** herb (*Dicentra cucullaria*) with white flowers and finely divided leaves. [f. DUTCH[1] + MAN[1]]

dū'tėous *a.* (literary). (Of person or conduct) dutiful, obedient; hence **~**LY[2] *adv.*, **~**NESS *n.* [f. DUTY + -OUS (cf. *beauteous*)]

dū'tĭable *a.* Liable to customs or other duties. [f. DUTY + -ABLE]

dū'tĭful *a.* Regular or willing in obedience and service; hence **~**LY[2] *adv.*, **~**NESS *n.* [f. foll. + -FUL]

dū'tȳ *n.* **1.** Behaviour due to superior, deference, expression of respect. **2.** Payment to public revenue levied on import, export, manufacture, or sale, of goods (CUSTOMS, EXCISE[1], *duty*), transfer of property (DEATH, PROBATE, *duty*), licences, legal recognition of documents, etc. **3.** Moral or legal obligation, what one is bound or ought to do (**~-bound,** obliged by duty; **~ visit** etc., thing that one would rather not, but feels bound to, do); binding force of what is right. **4.** Business, office, function, performance of or engagement in these (HEAVY-*duty*; **on, off, ~,** actually so engaged or not), (Eccl.) performance of church services; **~ officer** etc., the one currently on duty; **do ~ for,** serve as or pass for (something else). **5.** Measure of engine's effectiveness in units of work done per unit of fuel. **6. ~-paid, -free,** (of goods) on which customs or excise duty has been paid, is not leviable; **~-free shop,** one at which duty-free goods can be bought. [f. AF *deweté, dueté* (as DUE[1]; see -TY[1])]

dūŭ'mvir *n.* (Rom. Hist.) One of two coequal magistrates or officials; hence **~**ATE[1] *n.* [L, f. *duum virum* of the two men]

du'vet (dōō'vā) *n.* Thick soft quilt used instead of bedclothes. [F]

dŭx *n.* (Sc., N.Z., S. Afr., etc.) Top pupil in class or school. [L, = leader]

duyker. See DUIKER[1].

D.V. *abbr. Deo volente.*

Dvr. *abbr.* Driver.

dwāle *n.* = BELLADONNA 1. [prob. f. Scand.]

dwarf (-ôrf) *n.* (*pl.* **~s,** *or* **dwarves** *pr.* -vz), *a.*, & *v.t.* **1.** *n.* Person, animal, or plant, much below ordinary size of species, whence **~'**ISH[1] *a.*; small dense star. **2.** Small supernatural being in Gmc (esp. Scand.) mythology, skilled in metal-working. **3.** *a.* Undersized (esp. in plant-names); puny, stunted, (naturally or deliberately). **4.** *v.t.* Stunt in growth, or in intellect etc.; make look small by contrast or distance. [OE *dweorg, dweorh*, = MDu. *dwerch*, OHG *twerg*, ON *dvergr* f. Gmc **dwergaz*]

dwar'fĭsm (-ôr'-) *n.* Condition or character of being a dwarf. [f. prec. + -ISM (5)]

dwĕll *v.i.* (**dwelt**), & *n.* **1.** *v.i.* Keep one's attention fixed, write or speak at length, (*up*)*on* subject; **~ upon,** prolong (note, syllable, etc.). **2.** (literary). Make one's abode, spend one's time, live, *in, at, near, on*, etc. **3.** (Of horse) be slow in raising feet, pause before taking fence. **4.** Hence (-)**~'**ER[1] *n.*, (esp.) inhabitant. **5.** *n.* Slight regular pause in motion of machine. [OE *dwellan* lead astray, = MDu. *dwellen* stun, OHG *twellan*, ON *dvelja* delay, etc., f. Gmc **dwel-* etc.]

dwĕ'llĭng *n.* In vbl senses; **~(-place),** place of residence, house; **~-house** (used as residence, not as office, warehouse, etc.). [ME, f. prec. + -ING[1]]

dwĕlt. See DWELL.

dwi'ndle *v.i.* Become gradually smaller, shrink, waste away; lose importance, decline, degenerate. [f. *dwine* fade away f. OE *dwinan*, ON *dvina*, + -LE 3]

dwt. *abbr.* pennyweight.

d.w.t. *abbr.* deadweight tonnage.

dy̆ *n.* Sediment rich in organic matter, deposited in unproductive lakes. [Sw., = mire]

Dy *symb.* dysprosium.

dy̆'ăd *n.* The number two; group of two, couple; hence **dyă'dIC** *a.* [f. LL f. Gk *duas duados* (*duo* two; see -AD 1)]

Dy̆'ăk *n.* Aboriginal of Borneo or Sarawak. [f. Malay *dayak* up-country]

dyarchy. Var. of DIARCHY.

dy̆'bbuk (-ŏŏk) *n.* (*pl.* **~im** *or* **~s**). Malevolent spirit in Jewish folklore. [f. Heb. *dibbūḳ* (*dāḇaḳ* cling)]

dȳe[1] *n.* **1.** Colour produced by or as by dyeing, tinge, hue, (lit., or fig.: *crime, scoundrel, of (the) blackest, deepest, dye*). **2.** **~('stuff)**, substance used for dyeing, colouring-matter in solution. **3.** **~-line,** (print made by) diazo process; **~'wood,** wood yielding dye. [f. foll.]

dȳe[2] *v.t.* (*part.* **~ing** *pr.* dī'ĭ-). Colour, stain, tinge; impregnate with colouring-matter (**~d in the wool, in grain,** while material is in raw state, giving more permanent result, (fig.) unchangeable); make (thing) a specified colour (*dye cloth red* etc.). [OE *deagian*, of unkn. orig.]

dy̆'er *n.* One who dyes cloth etc.; **~'s broom, bugloss, oak, weed,** etc., names of plants yielding dyes. [f. prec. + -ER[1]]

dy̆'ing *n.* In vbl senses; connected with, at time of, death (*dying words, declaration, wish*; **to** one's **~ day,** for the rest of one's life; **~ oath,** made at, or with solemnity proper to, death). [f. DIE[2] + -ING[1]]

dy̆ke. See DIKE.

dyn *abbr.* dyne.

dy̅nă'mĭc *a.* & *n.* **1.** *a.* Of motive force (opp. *static*); of force in actual operation (opp. *potential*); active, potent, energetic; of dynamics; (Med.) affecting function (opp. *organic*); (Philos.) relating to dynamism; (Mus.) relating to volume of sound; *dynamic* VISCOSITY. **2.** *n.* Energizing or motive force; (Mus.) = DYNAMICS 3. [f. F *dynamique* f. Gk *dunamikos* (*dunamis* power; see -IC)]

dy̅nă'mĭcal *a.* Of dynamics; of force or mechanical power actively operative; (Theol., of inspiration) endowing with divine power, not impelling mechanically; of dynamism; hence **~LY**[2] *adv.* [f. as prec. + -ICAL]

dy̅nă'mĭcs *n. pl.* (usu. treated as *sing.*) **1.** Branch of mechanics that treats of motion in itself, and of the motion of bodies or matter under the influence of forces (including *kinematics* and *kinetics*; opp. *statics*), whence **dy̅nă'mĭcIST** (3) *n.*; branch (of any science) in which forces or changes are considered (now often with a specific prefix: *aerodynamics, population dynamics*). **2.** Motive forces, physical or moral, in any sphere. **3.** (Mus.) Variation or amount of volume of sound. [f. DYNAMIC + -ICS]

dy̆'nam|ĭsm *n.* Energizing or dynamic action or power; (Philos.) theory that phenomena of matter and mind are due merely to the action of forces, whence **~IST** (2) *n.* [f. Gk *dunamis* power + -ISM]

dy̆'namite *n.*, & *v.t.* **1.** *n.* High explosive of nitroglycerine mixed with inert absorbent; potentially dangerous person or thing; (sl.) heroin or similar narcotic. **2.** *v.t.* Charge or shatter with dynamite. [f. as prec. + -ITE[1]]

dȳ'namō *n.* (*pl.* **~s**). Machine converting mechanical into electric energy by electric induction, e.g. by rotating conductor in magnetic field; (fig.) energetic person. [abbr. of *dynamo-electric machine*, f. Gk *dunamis* power + -O-]

dy̅namŏ'mèter *n.* Instrument measuring energy expended by animal, engine, or mechanical force. [f. F *dynamomètre* f. Gk *dunamis* force; cf. -METER]

dy̆'nast *n.* Ruler; member of a dynasty. [f. L f. Gk *dunastēs* (*dunamai* be able)]

dy̆'nasty̆ *n.* Line of hereditary rulers; succession of leaders in any field; hence **dy̆nă'stIC** *a.*, **dy̆nă'stICALLY** *adv.* [f. F *dynastie* or f. LL f. Gk *dunasteia* lordship (as prec.)]

dy̆'natrŏn *n.* (Electr.) Thermionic valve with four electrodes, used to generate continuous oscillations. [f. Gk *dunamis* power + -TRON]

dȳne *n.* (Phys.) Unit of force, the force that, acting for one second on one-gram mass, gives it velocity of one centimetre per second. [F, f. Gk *dunamis* force]

dy̆s- *comb. form.* (esp. Med. etc.) Bad, difficult, as: **dysgra'phia,** inability to write coherently; **dysmenorrhoe'a,** painful menstruation. [f. Gk *dus-* bad]

dy̆'sentery̆ *n.* Disease with inflamed intestinal mucous membrane and glands, griping pains, diarrhoea, and evacuation of mucus and blood; so **dy̆sentĕ'rIC** *a.* [f. OF *dissenterie* or f. L f. Gk DYS(*enteria* f. *entera* bowels); see -Y[1]]

dy̆sfŭ'nction *n.* Abnormality or impairment of function; hence **~AL** *a.* [f. DYS- + FUNCTION]

dy̆sgĕ'nĭc *a.* Exerting a detrimental effect on later generations. [f. DYS- + -GENIC]

dy̆slĕ'x|ĭa *n.* Word-blindness; hence **~IC** *a.* & *n.* [f. G *dyslexie* (as DYS-, Gk *lexis* speech, -IA[1])]

dy̆slogĭ'st|ĭc *a.* (Of sense in which term is used) disapproving, opprobrious; hence **~ICALLY** *adv.* [f. DYS- + EULOGISTIC]

dy̆spĕ'psĭa *n.* Indigestion; so **dy̆spĕ'ptIC** *a.* & *n.*, (person) subject to dyspepsia or the resulting depression. [L, f. Gk DYS(*pepsia* f. *peptos* cooked, digested)]

dy̆'sphèmĭsm *n.* (Substitution of) unpleasant or derogatory word etc. for pleasant or inoffensive one. [f. DYS- + EUPHEMISM]

dy̆sphôr'ĭa *n.* State of unease or mental discomfort; hence **dy̆sphŏ'rIC** *a.* [f. Gk *dusphoria* (*dusphoros* hard to bear, f. as DYS- + *pherō* bear; see -IA[1])]

dy̆splā'sĭa (-zĭa) *n.* (Path.) Abnormal growth of tissues etc.; so **dy̆splă'stIC** *a.* [mod. L, f. as DYS- + Gk *plasis* formation; see -IA[1]]

dy̆spnoe'|a (-nē'*a*), ***dy̆spnē'|a,** *n.* (Path.) Difficult or laboured breathing; hence **~IC** *a.* [L, f. Gk DYS(*pnoia* f. *pneō* breathe)]

dy̆sprō'sĭum (-zĭ-) *n.* (Chem.) Metallic element of lanthanide series. [mod. L, f. Gk *dusprositos* hard to get at + -IUM]

dy̆'stōpĭa *n.* Imaginary place where everything is as bad as possible. [mod. L, f. DYS- + UTOPIA]

dy̆'strophy̆ *n.* Defective nutrition; **muscular ~,** hereditary progressive weakening and wasting of muscles. [f. mod. L *dystrophia* f. as DYS- + Gk *-trophia* nourishment; see -Y[1]]

dy̆sūr'ĭa *n.* Painful urination. [LL, f. Gk DYS(*ouria* f. *ouron* urine)]

dzhō, dzō, *n.* (*pl.* **~s** *or* **~**). Hybrid of cow and yak. [f. Tibetan *ṃdso*]

dzĭ'ggetai (jĭ'getī) *n.* = KIANG. [Mongolian (*tchikki* ear)]

E

E, e, (ē) *n.* (*pl.* **Es** *or* **E's**). Fifth letter of alphabet; (Mus.) third note in diatonic scale of C major.

E. *abbr.* east(ern); Egyptian (*£E*); Engineering (*M.I.Mech.E.*, etc.).

e- *pref.*, form of EX-[1] 1 bef. consonants exc. *c, f, h, p, q, s,* and in *adjs.* w. sense 'not having' (*ecaudate* tailless).

ea. *abbr.* each.

each *a.* & *pron.* (Of two or more) every (one) taken separately (*each man has two votes, each of us has two votes, we have two votes each; they cost a penny each; each is worse than the one before;* **sides of two triangles are equal ~ to ~,** each side of one equals the corresponding side of the other); **~ and every,** every single; **~ other** (used as compound reciprocal pron.; **they hate ~ other,** each hates the other(s); **they wore ~ other's hats,** each wore the hat of the (*or* an) other); ‖**~ way,** (of bet) backing horse etc. to win or be placed. [OE *ǣlc,* = MLG, MDu. *elk,* OHG *eogilīh* f. WG **aiwō galīkaz* ever alike (as AYE, ALIKE)]

ea'ger (-g-) *a.* Full of keen desire (*eager* BEAVER[1]); strongly desirous (*to* do, *for*, etc.); (of passions etc.) keen, impatient; (arch., of air) cold; hence **~**LY[2] *adv.*, **~**NESS *n.* [ME, f. AF *egre,* OF *aigre* keen, f. Rom. **acrum* f. L *acer acris*]

ea'gle *n.* **1.** Large bird of prey of family Accipitridae, with keen vision and powerful flight; figure of this, esp. as (Hist.) ensign of Roman or French army, as symbol of State (esp. U.S.), or as lectern in church; *coin worth ten dollars. **2.** (Golf). Hole played in two strokes under par or bogey. **3. Double ~,** figure of eagle with two heads, *(Golf) = ALBATROSS, *coin worth twenty dollars; **~ eye,** keen sight; **~-owl,** large horned owl, or other owl of genus *Bubo.* [ME, f. AF *egle,* OF *aigle* f. L *aquila*]

ea'glĕt *n.* Young eagle. [f. prec. + -ET[1]]

ea'gre (ā'ger *or* ē'ger) *n.* = BORE[5]. [17th c.; orig. unkn.]

-ean (-ē'an *or* -ĭan) *suf.* forming *adjs.* and *ns.*, orig. = -AN + end of stem (*Achaean, antipodean, empyrean, Epicurean, European, Herculean, Jacobean*). [f. or after L *-aeus, -eus,* Gk *-aios, -eios* + -AN]

E. & O. E. *abbr.* errors and omissions excepted.

ear[1] *n.* **1.** Organ of hearing in man and animals, esp. external part of this; faculty of discriminating sound (*an ear for music*); listening, attention (**give ~,** listen *to*); ear-shaped thing, esp. handle of jug. **2.** *Bring* (storm, hornets' nest, etc.) **about** one's **~s,** down upon oneself; **all ~s,** listening attentively; *not* BELIEVE one's *ears*; one's *ears* BURN[2]; *turn a* DEAF *ear*; *with a* FLEA *in* one's *ear*; **give** one's **~s,** make any sacrifice (*for* a thing, *to* do, *if*); **~ to the ground,** alertness regarding rumours or trend of opinion; **have** person's **~,** have his favourable attention; **over head and ~s, head over ~s,** deeply immersed (lit. or fig.); **in (at) one ~ and out (at) the other,** heard but leaving no impression; **out on** one's **~,** dismissed ignominiously; *play by ear* (PLAY[1] 6); PRICK[2] *up* one's *ears*; **set by the ~s,** cause to quarrel; **up to the ~s,** (colloq.) very deeply involved *in*; **wet behind the ~s,** immature, inexperienced; **a word in your ~** (in private). **3. ~'ache,** pain in ear-drum; **~-drops,** (1) medicinal drops for the ear, (2) hanging ear-rings; **~-drum,** DRUM[1] 2 of ear, tympanum; **~'mark,** (*n.*) mark on ear of sheep etc. as sign of ownership, (fig.) mark of ownership, (*v.t.*) mark (sheep etc.) thus, (fig.) assign (money etc.) to definite purpose; **~-muff** (protecting ears against cold, noise, etc.); **~'phone,** device worn on ear to aid hearing or to listen to radio or telephone communication; **~-piece,** apparatus to be applied to ear as part of telephone etc.; **~-piercing,** shrill; **~-plug,** piece of wax etc. placed in ear to protect against cold air, water, or noise; **~-ring** (worn in or on lobe of ear for ornament); **~'shot,** distance over which something can be heard (*within, out of, earshot*); **~-splitting,** very loud; **~-trumpet,** tube used by partly deaf person; **~-wax,** yellow waxy secretion in ear. **4.** Hence (-)**~**ED[2] (ērd) *a.* (*eared* SEAL[1]), **~'**FUL 2 *n.*, (colloq.) large amount of talk etc., strong reprimand, **~'**LESS *a.* [OE *ēare,* = OS, OHG *ōra,* ON *eyra,* Goth. *ausō* f. Gmc **auson* etc. cogn. w. L *auris,* Gk *ous*]

ear[2] *n.* Spike or head of corn, containing its flowers or seeds. [OE *ēar,* = OS *ahar,* OHG *ahir,* ON *ax,* Goth. *ahs* f. Gmc **ahuz,* **ahiz*]

ear'ĭng *n.* (Naut.) Small rope (one of several) fastening upper corner of sail to yard. [f. EAR[1] + -ING[1] or RING[1]]

earl (ērl) *n.* (*fem.* **countess**). British nobleman ranking between marquis and viscount (cf. COUNT[3]); ‖**E~ Marshal,** officer presiding over College of Arms, with ceremonial duties on various royal occasions; hence **~'**DOM *n.* [OE *eorl,* = OS, OHG *erl,* ON *jarl,* of unkn. orig.]

ear'lȳ (ēr'-) *a.* & *adv.* **1.** Before the due or usual time (*was early for his appointment; it is too early to look for blackberries;* **~ riser,** one who gets up unusually early from bed); forward in flowering, ripening, etc., (*early peaches*); not far on in day or night, or in time (*seek an early opportunity for discussion; on Wednesday* **at earliest,** not before then); not far on in a period, development, etc., (*the early part of the century; the early spring; the early morning, chapters, Christians*); of the distant past (*early man*). **2. ~ bird,** (joc.) person who arrives, rises, etc., early; **~ closing,** shutting of business premises on the afternoon of one particular day of the week; **~ days,** early in time for something (to happen, etc.); **E~ English style,** (Archit.) first stage of English Gothic (13th c.), with pointed arches, lancet windows, and simple tracery; **keep ~ hours,** rise and go to bed early; **~ on,** at an early stage [f. *earlier on,* formed by anal. w. *later on*]; **~ Victorian,** of the early years of Queen Victoria's reign; **~ warning** (esp. of aerial etc. attacks). **3.** Hence **ear'lĭ**NESS (ēr'-) *n.* [orig. adv., f. OE *ǣrlīce, ārlīce* (*ǣr* ERE; see -LY[2])]

earn (ērn) *v.t.* (Of person, action, conduct, etc.) obtain or be entitled to as reward of labour or merit; incur (reproach etc.); bring in as income or interest; (Baseball) score (run) without help from opponent. [OE *earnian,* = OHG *arnēn, arnōn* reap f. WG **aznōjan* (*aznu,* rel. to OE *esne,* Goth. *asneis* labourer)]

ear'nĕst[1] (ēr'-) *a.* & *n.* **1.** *a.* Serious, zealous, not trifling; ardent (desire etc.); hence **~**LY[2] *adv.*, **~**NESS *n.* **2.** *n.* Seriousness; **in (real) ~,** serious(ly), not joking(ly). [OE *eornust, eornost,* = OHG *ernust* f. **ern-* (cf. ON *ern* vigorous)]

ear'nĕst[2] (ēr'-) *n.* Money paid as instalment, esp.

to confirm contract etc.; foretaste, presage, token, (*is an, in, earnest of what is to come*). [ME *ernes*, prob. var. of *erles, arles* prob. f. med. L **arrhula* dim. of L *arr(h)a* pledge]

ear′nĭng (ẽr′-) *n.* In vbl senses; (in *pl.*) money earned. [f. EARN + -ING[1]]

earth[1] (ẽr-) *n.* **1.** Dry land; soil, mould; ground (*it fell to earth*); **come back to ~**, return to realities; DOWN[3]-*to-earth*. **2.** Hole of badger, fox, etc.; **gone to ~**, (fig.) in hiding; **run to ~**, (fig.) find after long searching. **3.** Land and sea, opp. sky; (or *E~*) the planet on which we live; present abode of man, opp. heaven or hell as places of future existence; **on ~**, existing anywhere (*happiest man on earth; looked like nothing on earth; what on earth do you mean?*); (colloq.) huge sum etc. (*cost the earth*). **4.** (Chem.) One of several naturally occurring metallic oxides; RARE[1] *earth* **5.** ‖(Electr.) Connection to earth as completion of circuit. **6. ~-born,** of mortal race, (Myth.) emerging from earth at birth; **~-bound,** (1) attached (lit. or fig.) to the earth, (2) moving towards the earth; ‖**~-closet** (like water-closet, but with dry earth used to cover excreta); **~-light,** partial illumination of dark part of moon by light reflected from earth; **~ mother,** (Myth.) spirit symbolizing earth, (fig.) sensual and maternal woman; **~-moving,** excavation of large quantities of soil; **~-nut,** (edible roundish tuber of) one of various plants, esp. (1) an umbelliferous woodland plant (*Conopodium denudatum*), (2) PEA*nut*; **~′quake,** convulsion of earth's surface due to faults or volcanic action, (fig.) social etc. disturbance; **~ sciences,** those dealing with the earth or part of it (e.g. geology, oceanography); **~-shaking** *a.*, (fig.) having a violent effect; **~-shine,** = *earth-light*; *earth* TREMOR; **~′work,** (raising of) bank of earth in fortification or construction of road etc.; **~′worm,** annelid worm living in ground. **7.** Hence **~′**WARD(s) *a.* & *adv.* [OE *eorthe*, = OS *ertha*, OHG *erda*, ON *jörth*, Goth. *airtha* f. Gmc **erthō*]

earth[2] (ẽr-) *v.* **1.** *v.t.* Cover (roots of plants *up*) with heaped-up earth; drive (fox) to earth; ‖(Electr.) connect to earth. **2.** *v.i.* (Of fox etc.) run to its earth. [ME, f. prec.]

ear′then (ẽr′-) *a.* Made of earth; made of baked clay. [ME, f. EARTH[1] + -EN[5]]

ear′thenwāre (ẽr′-) *n.* & *a.* (Vessels etc.) made of baked clay, esp. coarser kind (opp. porcelain); baked clay. [f. prec. + WARE[1]]

ear′thlĭng (ẽr′-) *n.* Inhabitant of the earth. [f. EARTH[1] + -LING[1]]

ear′thl|ȳ (ẽr′-) *a.* Of the earth, terrestrial, (opp. *celestial*); **no ~y** *use, reason, chance*, (colloq.) no use etc. at all; **not an ~y,** (sl.) no chance whatever; hence **~ĭ**NESS *n.* [OE *eorthlic* (as EARTH[1], -LY[1])]

ear′th|ȳ (ẽr′-) *a.* Like or of earth or soil; (fig.) grossly material, coarse (*earthy jokes*); hence **~ĭ**NESS *n.* [f. EARTH[1] + -Y[2]]

ear′wĭg *n.*, & *v.t.* (**-gg-**). **1.** *n.* Insect of order Dermaptera, with large terminal forceps; *small centipede. **2.** *v.t.* (arch.) Influence (person) by secret communications. [OE *ēarwicga* (*ēare* EAR[1], *wicga* earwig, prob. rel. to *wiggle*; once thought to enter head through ear)]

ease[1] (ēz) *n.* **1.** Freedom from pain or trouble (**set** person **at ~**, relieve his anxiety). **2.** Freedom from constraint (*at* one's *ease*; ILL *at ease*; **put** or **set** person **at his ~**, avoid undue formality); relief from pain; **at ~**, (Mil.) in relaxed attitude, with feet apart; CHAPEL *of ease*. **3.** Facility (**with ~**, without difficulty). **4.** Hence **~′**LESS (-zl-) *a.* [ME, f. AF *ese*, OF *eise, aise* f. Rom. **adjaces* f. L *adjacens* ADJACENT]

ease[2] (ēz) *v.* **1.** *v.t.* Relieve from pain etc. or *of* burden; give mental ease to (person, one*self*, one's mind); **~ nature, ~ oneself,** urinate or defecate; (joc.) rob (person *of* his purse etc.); relax, adjust, (what is too tight); (Naut.) slacken (rope, sail, *away, down, off*); cause to move by gentle force. **2.** *v.i.* **~ (off)**, become less burdensome (*pain, rain, is easing*), begin to take it easy; (of shares etc.) descend in price. [ME, f. OF *(a)aisier* (*a aise* at ease), & f. prec.]

ea′seful (ē′zf-) *a.* (arch.) Comfortable, soothing; at rest; slothful; hence **~**LY[2] *adv.*, **~**NESS *n.* [ME, f. EASE[1] + -FUL]

ea′sel (ē′z-) *n.* Wooden frame to support picture, blackboard, etc. [f. Du. *ezel* = G *esel* ASS[1]]

ea′sement (ē′zm-) *n.* (Law) right of way or similar right over another's ground or property; (arch.) supplementary building, shed, etc.; (arch.) relief from pain or burden. [ME, f. OF *aisement* (as EASE[2]; see -MENT)]

east *adv.*, *n.*, & *a.* **1.** (Towards, at, near) point of horizon where sun rises at the equinoxes (cardinal point 90° to right of North); **(to the) ~ (of)**, in an eastward direction (from); *lie* **~ and west,** lengthwise along line from east to west; **~ wind,** wind blowing from the east. **2.** *n.* (usu. *E~*). Part of the world lying east of Europe; part of country or town lying to the east; Communist States of eastern Europe; eastern part of late-Roman world; altar-end of church (whether truly oriented or not); card-player occupying position designated 'east'; ***the E~**, (esp.) north-east region of the U.S.; **Far E~**, China, Japan, etc.; **Middle E~**, (esp.) countries from Egypt to Iran inclusive; **Near E~**, (1) = *Middle East*, (2) (arch.) Turkey and Balkan countries. **3. ~′about,** eastwards; **~′bound,** travelling eastwards; *east* BY[1] *north* or *south*; ‖**E~ End,** eastern part of London including docks (*E~-Ender*, inhabitant thereof); **E~ Indiaman,** (Hist.) large ship engaged in trade with East INDIES; *East* INDIAN; **~-north-~**, compass point midway between east and north-east (so **~-south-~**); ***E~ Side,** eastern part of Manhattan. **4.** Hence **~′**WARD *a.* & *n.*, **~′**WARD(s) *adv.* [OE *ēast-*, = OS, OHG *ōst*, ON *aust-* f. Gmc **austo-*, **austro-* f. IE **aus-*]

Ea′ster *n.* Christian festival commemorating Christ's resurrection, corresponding to Passover, and observed on a variable Sunday (**~ day, ~ Sunday**) in March or April; **~ (week),** week commencing with Easter day; **~ egg,** edible artificial (esp. chocolate) or hard-boiled egg as gift at Easter; **~ offering**(s), customary payments made to the incumbent on Easter day (now usu. the collection-proceeds); **~tide,** (arch.) Easter. [OE *ēastre*, pl. *ēastron*, = OHG *ōstarūn* app. f. *Ēostre* goddess with festival in spring, f. Gmc **Austrōn* (see prec.)]

ea′sterlȳ *a.*, *adv.*, & *n.* In an eastern position or direction; (wind) blowing (nearly) from the east. [prob. f. obs. *easter* (perh. compar. of EAST) + -LY[1]]

ea′stern *a.* Of or (dwelling) in the east; lying or directed towards the east; **E~ Church,** Orthodox Church; **E~ Empire** (cf. ROMAN[2] *Empire*); *Eastern* HEMISPHERE; **E~ Time,** standard time used in eastern Canada and U.S. or in eastern Australia; hence **~**ER[1] (4) *n.*, **~**MOST *a.* [OE *ēasterne* (as EAST, -ERN)]

ea′stĭng *n.* (Naut. etc.) Distance travelled or measured eastward; easterly direction. [f. EAST + -ING[1]]

ea′sȳ (ē′zĭ) *a.* & *adv.* **1.** *a.* Free from pain, discomfort, annoyance, anxiety, etc. (**~ circumstances,** (colloq.) **E~ Street,** affluence). **2.** Free from embarrassment, constraint, strictness, etc., (*easy manners*; FREE[1] *and easy*).

3. Not difficult (*to* do, or abs.; ~ **of access,** easily got at; ~ **on the eye** etc., pleasant to look at). 4. Easily persuaded, compliant; **of ~ virtue,** (of woman) sexually promiscuous; **I'm ~,** (colloq.) I have no preference. 5. *adv.* In easy manner; with ease; *come easy to* (COME 13); ~ **come ~ go,** what is easily got is soon lost or spent; ~ **does it,** go carefully; **go ~,** be sparing or cautious *with*; **take it ~,** proceed comfortably or carefully, do only what is necessary. 6. (As command) **~!,** move gently, ~ **all!,** stop (prop. rowing), ||**stand ~!,** (Mil.) permission to squad standing at ease to relax attitude further. 7. ~ **chair,** one designed for comfort, usu. with arms; **~-going,** (of horse) having an easy gait, (of person) fond of comfort, not strict, indolent, taking things as they are; ~ **mark, meat,** TOUCH², (colloq.) person or thing easily overcome, persuaded, etc.; ~ **money,** money got without effort (esp. illicitly). 8. Hence **ea'sĭ**LY² *adv.*, **ea'sĭ**NESS *n.*, (-z-). [ME, f. AF *aisé*, OF *aisié* p.p. of *aisier* EASE²; see -Y⁴]

eat *v.* (**ate** *pr.* ĕt *or* āt; **ea'ten**). 1. *v.t.* & *i.* Take into mouth, chew and swallow (solid food); swallow (soup etc.); *eat the* BREAD *of*; *eat* DIRT; ~ **out of** person's **hand,** be entirely submissive to him; *eat* one's HAT; ~ **its head off,** (of animal) cost more to feed than it is worth; ~ person **out of house and home,** ruin him by eating (lit. or fig.) all he has; *eat* HUMBLE *pie*; ||~ one's **terms,** be studying for the Bar (and so have to dine a certain number of times at Inn of Court); **what's ~ing you?,** (colloq.) why are you vexed?; ~ one's **words,** retract them in humiliating manner. 2. Destroy, consume, (*eat* one's HEART *out*); make (hole) by corrosion etc.; ~ **away,** destroy gradually (lit. or fig.); ~ **into,** begin to consume (fig.); ~ **up,** consume completely, finish eating, waste, (lit. or fig.), absorb (*eaten up with pride*), traverse (distance) rapidly. 3. *v.i.* Consume food, take a meal; ~ **of,** (arch.) eat (some of); ~ **out,** take a meal other than at home. 4. Hence **ea't**ABLE *a.* & *n.* (usu. in *pl.*), ~'ERY (3) *n.* (colloq.). [OE *etan*, = OS *etan*, OHG *ezzan*, ON *eta*, Goth. *itan* f. Gmc **etan* f. IE **ed*-]

ea'ter *n.* In vbl senses (**big ~,** one who eats much food); fruit suitable for eating raw. [f. prec. + -ER¹]

ea'tĭng *n.* In vbl senses; ~ **apple** etc. (suitable for eating raw); **~-house,** restaurant. [ME, f. EAT + -ING¹]

eats *n. pl.* (colloq.) Food. [pl. of obs. *eat*, something edible (OE *ǣt*), or f. EAT]

eau (ō) *n.* **~-de-Cologne** (ōd*e*k*o*lō'n), perfume made orig. at Cologne; ~ **de Javelle** (ōd*e*zh*a*vĕ'l), JAVELLE water; ***~-de-Nil*** (ōd*e*nē'l), greenish colour (supposed to resemble Nile water); ***~-de-vie*** (ōd*e*vē'), brandy; ~ ***sucrée*** (ōsōō'krā), water and sugar. [F, = water]

eaves (ēvz) *n. pl.* Overhanging edge of roof or thatch; **~'drop** *v.i.*, (orig.) stand under this to listen to secrets, (fig.) listen secretly to private conversation; **~'dropper,** one who does this (usu. fig.). [orig. sing., f. OE *efes*; cf. OHG *obasa*, ON *ups*, Goth. *ubizwa* porch, f. Gmc **obhaswa* etc., prob. rel. to OVER]

ĕbb *n.*, & *v.i.* 1. *n.* Outward movement of tide (*ebb and flow*; *ebb*-TIDE¹); decline, decay, (*at a low ebb*). 2. *v.i.* Flow back; recede, decline, decay. [OE (*ebbian* v. f.) *ebba* n. f. WG **abhigo* (**abh*- OFF)]

E'-boat (ē'-) *n.* (Hist.; in war of 1939–45) enemy torpedo-boat. [f. *e*nemy + BOAT¹]

ĕ'bon *a.* (poet.) Made of or black as ebony. [ME f. OF *eban*, f. med. L *ebanus* f. L f. Gk *ebenos* ebony tree, of Semitic origin]

ĕ'bonīte *n.* = VULCANITE. [f. foll. + -ITE¹]

ĕ'bonȳ *n.* & *a.* 1. *n.* Hard heavy black wood from tropical tree esp. of genus *Diospyros*. 2. *a.* Made of or black as ebony. [earlier *hebeny* f. (*h*)*eben*(*e*) = EBON, perh. after *ivory*]

ėbŭ'llĭ|ent (*or* -ōō'-) *a.* Boiling; exuberant; hence ~ENCE, ~ENCY, *ns.*, **~ent**LY² *adv.* [f. L E(*bullire* -*it*- boil); see -ENT]

ĕbullĭ'tion *n.* Boiling; (fig.) sudden outburst (*of* passion, war, etc.). [f. LL *ebullitio* (as prec.; see -ITION)]

E.C. *abbr.* East Central.

ē'căd *n.* (Ecol.) Organism modified by its environment. [f. Gk *oikos* house + -AD]

écarté (āka̅r'tā) *n.* Card-game for two persons in which cards may be exchanged for others; (Ballet) position with one arm and leg extended. [F, p.p. of *écarter* discard]

Ecce Hō'mō (ĕksĭ- *or* ĕkĭ- *or* ĕchā-) *n.* Picture of Christ wearing crown of thorns. [L, = behold the man (John 19:5)]

ėccĕ'ntr|ic (ĭks-) *a.* & *n.* 1. *a.* (Of circle etc.) not concentric (*to* another); not placed, not having its axis etc. placed, centrally; (of orbit) not circular; irregular. 2. Odd, whimsical; differing from the usual in behaviour etc. 3. Hence ~ICALLY *adv.*, **ĕccentrĭ'**CITY (ĕks-) *n.* 4. *n.* Eccentric person; (Mech.) eccentric contrivance for changing rotatory into backward-and--forward motion, esp. for slide-valve of steam--engine. [f. LL *eccentricus* f. Gk *ekkentros* (*ek* out of, *kentron* CENTRE¹); see -IC]

||**E'ccles** (ĕ'k*e*lz) *n.* ~ **cake,** round cake of pastry filled with currants etc. [~ in Greater Manchester]

Eccles. *abbr.* Ecclesiastes (O.T.).

ėcclē'sĭa (-z-) *n.* (Gk Ant.) General assembly of citizens, esp. at Athens. [f. Gk *ekklēsia* (see ECCLESIASTES)]

ėcclē'sĭal (-z-) *a.* Pertaining to the Church. [f. Gk *ekklēsia* (see foll.) + -AL]

Ecclēsĭă'stēs (ĭklēzĭă'stēz) *n.* O.T. book, traditionally ascribed to Solomon. [ME, f. Gk *ekklēsiastēs* public speaker, preacher (*ekklēsia* assembly, church f. *ekklētos* summoned out f. *ek* out + *kaleō* call)]

ėcclēsĭă'stĭc (-zĭ-) *n.* Clergyman. [f. F *ecclésiastique* or f. LL f. Gk *ekklēsiastikos* f. as prec.]

ėcclēsĭă'stĭc|al (-zĭ-) *a.* Of the Church or the clergy; *ecclesiastical* YEAR; hence or cogn. **~al**LY² *adv.*, ~ISM (3) *n.* [f. prec. + -AL]

Ecclēsĭă'stĭcus (ĭklēzĭ-) *n.* Book of the Apocrypha, containing moral and practical maxims. [LL, as ECCLESIASTIC, = of (i.e. to be read in) church]

ėcclēsĭŏ'log|ȳ (-zĭ-) *n.* Science of churches, esp. of church building and decoration; hence **ėcclēsĭolŏ'**GIC(AL) (-zĭ-) *adjs.*, ~IST (3) *n.* [f. Gk *ekklēsia* (see ECCLESIASTES) + -O- + -LOGY]

Ecclus. *abbr.* Ecclesiasticus (Apocrypha).

ĕ'ccrīne *a.* (Of gland) secreting without loss of cell material. [f. Gk *ek* out of + *krinō* sift]

ĕ'cdȳs|ĭs *n.* (*pl.* **~es** *pr.* -ēz). Casting off (of shell or outer skin). [mod. L, f. Gk *ekdusis* (*ekduō* put off)]

E.C.G. *abbr.* electrocardiogram.

ĕ'chelon (ĕ'sh-; *or* ā'-) *n.*, & *v.t.* 1. *n.* Arrangement of troops in parallel groups each with its end clear of those ahead and behind; similar arrangement of things (e.g. ships); **in ~,** so drawn up. 2. Division of main supply service in warfare; group of persons at a particular level in an organization. 3. *v.t.* Arrange in echelon. [(v. f. n. or f. F *échelonner*) f. F *échelon* (*échelle* ladder f. L *scala*; see -OON)]

ĕchėvēr'ĭa *n.* Tropical Amer. succulent plant of genus *Echeveria*. [f. M. *Echeveri*, 19th-c. Mex. botanical draughtsman + -IA¹]

ėchĭ'dna (ĭk-) *n.* Australian toothless burrowing

egg-laying animal like hedgehog, spiny ant-eater. [mod. L, f. Gk *ekhidna* viper]

ĕ'chĭnite (ĕ'k-) *n.* Fossil echinoderm. [f. *echinus* + -ITE[1]]

ėchī'noderm (ĭk-; *or* ĕ'kĭn-) *n.* Animal of phylum Echinodermata, incl. starfish and sea-urchins, some having spiny skins. [f. as foll. + Gk *derma -atos* skin]

ėchī'noid (ĭk-) *n.* Sea-urchin. [f. as foll + -OID]

ėchī'nus (ĭk-) *n.* Sea-urchin of genus *Echinus*, incl. common European kind; (Archit.) rounded moulding below abacus. [ME f. L, f. Gk *ekhinos* hedgehog, sea-urchin]

ĕ'chō[1] (ĕ'kō) *n.* (*pl.* **~es**). **1.** Repetition of sound by reflection of sound-waves, secondary sound so produced, (*cheer* person etc. **to the ~,** loudly); (*E~*) cause of this personified; reflected radio or radar wave. **2.** Close imitation or imitator; (Bridge etc.) conventional mode of play to show number of cards held in suit led etc. **3.** **~gram,** record of **~-sounder** (apparatus for determining depth of sea beneath ship from time taken to receive echo from bed); **~graph,** device for automatic recording of echograms; **~loca'tion,** location of objects by reflected sound; **~ verse** (in which a line is made to repeat the last syllables of the previous line). **4.** Hence ~LESS *a.* [ME, f. OF or f. L f. Gk *ēkhō*, conn. w. *ēkhē* a sound]

ĕ'chō[2] (ĕ'kō) *v.* **1.** *v.i.* (Of place) resound with echo; (of sound) be repeated, resound; (Bridge etc.) play an echo (see prec.). **2.** *v.t.* Repeat (sound) by echo; repeat (another's words), imitate words or opinions of (person). [f. prec.]

ĕ'chōism (ĕ'k-) *n.* = ONOMATOPOEIA; so **ĕchō'**IC (ĕk-) *a.* [f. ECHO[1] + -ISM]

ĕchōlā'lia (ĕk-) *n.* (Path.) meaningless repetition of speech; repetition of speech by child learning to talk. [mod. L, f. Gk *ēkhō* echo + *lalia* talk]

ĕ'chō-vīrus (ĕ'k-) *n.* Type of enterovirus sometimes causing mild meningitis. [f. *e*nteric *c*ytopathogenic *h*uman *o*rphan (because not originally assignable to any known disease) + VIRUS]

echt (ĕχt) *a.* Authentic, genuine, typical. [G]

éclair (āklār' *or* āklār') *n.* Small finger-shaped cake of choux pastry filled with cream and iced, esp. with chocolate icing. [F, = lightning]

éclaircissement (āklārsē'smahṅ) *n.* (arch.) Explanation (of conduct etc.). [F (*éclaircir* clear up; see -MENT)]

ėclă'mp|sĭa *n.* Kind of epileptic convulsion caused by anatomical lesion to which pregnant women are especially liable; so **~t**IC *a.* [mod. L, f. F *eclampsie* f. Gk *eklampsis* sudden development (*eklampō* shine forth)]

éclat (ĕklah' *or* ā'klah) *n.* Conspicuous success, general applause, (*with great éclat*); social distinction; brilliant display. [F (*éclater* burst out)]

ėclĕ'ct|ĭc *a.* & *n.* (Ancient philosopher) selecting from each school of thought such doctrines as pleased him; (person, doctrine) borrowing freely from various sources; not exclusive in opinion, taste, etc.; hence ~ICALLY *adv.*, **~ĭ**CISM (3) *n.* [f. Gk *eklektikos* (*eklegō* pick out; see -IC)]

ėclĭ'pse[1] *n.* Interception of the light of a luminous body (sun, moon, etc.), by intervention of another body between it and the eye or between the luminous body and what illuminates it (ANNULAR, PARTIAL, TOTAL, *eclipse*); deprivation of light; loss of brilliance or splendour (**in ~,** (of bird) having lost the courting plumage); periodical obscuration of lighthouse light. [ME f. OF, f. L f. Gk *ekleipsis* vbl n. f. *ekleipō* fail to appear, be eclipsed (*leipō* leave)]

ėclĭ'pse[2] *v.t.* (Of heavenly body) obscure (another) by passing between it and spectator or between it and the source of its light; intercept (light, esp. of lighthouse); (fig.) deprive of lustre, outshine, surpass. [ME, f. prec.]

ėclĭ'ptĭc *n.* & *a.* **1.** *n.* Sun's apparent path among stars during year. **2.** *a.* Of eclipse or ecliptic. [ME, f. L f. Gk *ekleiptikos* (as ECLIPSE[1]; see -IC)]

ĕ'clŏgue (-g) *n.* Short poem, esp. pastoral dialogue, such as those of Virgil. [f. L f. Gk *eklogē* selection (*eklegō* pick out)]

ėclō'sion (-zhon) *n.* Emergence of insect from pupa-case or of larva from egg. [f. F *éclosion* (*éclore* hatch f. as EX-[1] + L *claudere* to close)]

ē'co- *pref.* Ecology, ecological, as: **~climate,** climate as an ecological factor; **~sphere,** region of space where living things can exist; **~system,** system of interacting organisms in a particular habitat. [f. ECOLOGY]

ēcŏ'log|ȳ *n.* Branch of biology dealing with organisms' relations to one another and to their surroundings; (**human**) **~y,** study of interaction of persons with their environment; hence **ēco**LO'GICAL *a.*, ~IST (3) *n.* [f. G *ökologie* f. Gk *oikos* house; see -LOGY]

Econ. *abbr.* Economics.

ēcŏnomĕ'tr|ĭcs *n.* Branch of economics concerned with application of mathematical economics by use of statistics; hence or cogn. ~IC(AL) *adjs.*, **ēcŏnomĕtrĭ**'CIAN *n.* [f. ECONOMY + METRIC + -ICS]

ĕconŏ'mĭc *a.* & *n.* **1.** *a.* Of economic; maintained for profit, on a business footing; paying (at least) the expenses, (of rent) high enough to compensate builder, owner, etc.; **~ botany, geography,** etc., botany etc. studied from the utilitarian standpoint. **2.** *n.* (in *pl.*, treated as *sing.*) Practical and theoretical science of the production and distribution of wealth; application of this to a particular thing (*the economics of publishing*); condition of a country as regards material prosperity. [ME, f. OF *economique* or f. L f. Gk *oikonomikos* (as ECONOMY; see -IC)]

ĕconŏ'mĭcal *a.* Saving, thrifty, avoiding waste (*of*). [f. as prec. + -AL]

ĕconŏ'mĭcallȳ *adv.* In adj. senses. [f. ECONOMIC or prec.; see -ICALLY]

ėcŏ'nomĭst *n.* Manager (*of* money etc.); thrifty person; student of or writer on economics. [f. Gk *oikonomos* (see ECONOMY) + -IST]

ėcŏ'nomīz|e, -īs|e (-īz), *v.* **1.** *v.t.* Use sparingly. **2.** *v.i.* Practise economy, reduce expenses; **~e on,** use sparingly. **3.** Hence ~'ATION *n.* [f. as prec. + -IZE]

ėcŏ'nomȳ *n.* **1.** (Administration or condition of) concerns and resources of a community; **political ~,** study of economic problems of government, (arch.) economics. **2.** Careful use of resources, frugality; instance of this; cheapest class of air travel; **~-size,** (of goods etc.) so large as to be economically advantageous to the customer. **3.** (arch.) Organized system. [f. F *économie* or f. L f. Gk *oikonomia* f. *oikonomos* steward (*oikos* house, *-nomos* f. *nemō* manage)]

écossai'se (ĕkŏsā'z) *n.* (Dance to) lively tune in duple time. [F, fem. of *écossais* Scotch]

ecru (ā'krōō) *n.* Colour of unbleached linen, light fawn. [f. F *écru* unbleached]

ĕ'cstasīze, -īse (-īz), *v. t.* & *i.* Throw or go into ecstasies. [f. foll. + -IZE]

ĕ'cstas|ȳ *n.* Exalted state of feeling, rapture, (esp. of delight; **in ~ies,** extremely delighted etc.); trance; poetic frenzy. [ME, f. OF *extasie* f. LL f. Gk *ekstasis* vbl n. f. *existēmi* put (person) out of (his senses) (EX-[2], *histēmi* place)]

ėcstă't|ĭc *a.* & *n.* **1.** *a.* Of, subject to, producing, ecstasy (esp. of joy); hence ~ICALLY *adv.* **2.** *n.*

Person subject to (religious) ecstasy. [f. F *extatique* f. Gk *ekstatikos* (as prec.; see -IC)]

E.C.T. *abbr.* electroconvulsive therapy.

ĕ'cto- *comb. form.* Outside, as: **~blast,** (Biol.) outer membrane of cell; **~derm,** (Biol.) outermost layer of embryo in early development; **~plasm,** (1) = EXO*plasm*, (2) supposed viscous substance exuding from body of spiritualistic medium during trance; **~zoon,** external parasite. [f. Gk *ekto-* st. of *ektos* outside]

ĕctogĕ'nėsĭs *n.* (Biol.) Production of structures outside the organism; hence **ĕctogėnĕ'tɪc,** **ĕctogĕ'nɪc, ĕctŏ'gėnous,** *adjs.* [mod. L, f. as prec. + GENESIS]

ĕ'ctomôrph *n.* Lean-bodied person (with predominance of structures formed from ectoderm of embryo); hence ~IC *a.* [f. ECTO- + Gk *morphē* form]

-ĕ'ctomȳ *suf.* forming *ns.*, denoting surgical operation in which some part is removed, as: **appendice'ctomy,** removal of the appendix; **hystere'ctomy,** removal of the womb. [f. Gk *ektomē* excision]

ĕctŏ'pĭc *a.* (Path.) In abnormal place or position. [f. *ectopia* (mod. L f. Gk *ektopos* out of place) pathological displacement + -IC]

ēcūmĕ'nĭcal *a.* Of or representing the whole Christian world; seeking world-wide Christian unity; world-wide; hence ~ISM (3), **ēcūmenĭ'cɪty, ē'cūmenɪsm** (3), *ns.* [f. LL f. Gk *oikoumenikos* of the inhabited earth (*oikoumenē*) + -AL]

ĕ'czėma (*or* ĕ'ks-) *n.* Inflammation of the skin, with itching and discharge from vesicles; hence **ĕczĕ'matous** *a.* [mod. L, f. Gk *ekzema -atos* (*ek* out, *zeō* boil)]

-ed¹ *suf.* (1) forming *past* and *p.p.* of weak vbs. (also *-d, -'d, -t* as in *sold, subpoena'd, bought*; see notes on Verb forms p. xvi); (2) forming *adjs.* f. such *p.p.* (also occas. f. *v.i.*) meaning: (*a*) that has been subject to vbl action, (*b*) (f. *v.i.*) that has performed vbl action (*vanished hand, fallen idol, escaped prisoner, am finished with it*), (*c*) that habitually performs vbl action in stated manner (*outspoken, well-behaved*). [OE *-ed, -ad, -od*; *-d* f. Gmc **-dhaz* f. IE **-tos*]

-ed² *suf.* forming *adjs.* f. *ns.*, meaning 'having, wearing, affected with, etc.' (*diseased, moneyed, tuxedoed, talented, wooded*), having the habits of (*bigoted, dogged*); esp. used to form *adj.* f. phr. of *adj.* & *n.* (*quick-witted, good-humoured, stout-hearted, three-cornered*); see notes on Verb forms, p. xvi. [OE *-ede*, = OS *-ōdi* f. Gmc **-ōdhja*]

Ed. *abbr.* Edward.

ed. *abbr.* edited (by); edition; editor; educated.

ėdā'cious (-sh*us*) *a.* (literary or joc.) Of eating; greedy; so **ėdă'cɪty** *n.* [f. L *edax -acis* (*edere* eat; see -ACIOUS)]

E'dăm (ē'-) *n.* Spherical Dutch cheese, usu. yellow with red rind. [~ in Holland, where orig. made]

ėdă'phĭc *a.* (Bot.) Of the soil; (Ecol.) produced or influenced by the soil. [f. G *edaphisch* f. Gk *edaphos* floor; see -IC]

E.D.C. *abbr.* European Defence Community.

E'dda (ĕ'-) *n.* **Elder, Poetic,** ~, collection of ancient Icelandic poems; **Younger, Prose,** ~, miscellaneous handbook (*c.* 1230) to Icelandic poetry. [perh. f. a name in ON poem or f. ON *óthr* poetry]

ĕ'ddȳ *n.* & *v.* **1.** *n.* Small whirlpool; wind, fog, smoke, moving like this; ~ **current,** (Electr.) circulating current induced in conductor by varying magnetic field. **2.** *v.t.* & *i.* Whirl round in eddies. [prob. f. OE *ed-* again, back]

e'delweiss (ā'delvīs) *n.* Alpine plant with woolly leaves and white flowers, growing in rocky places. [G (*edel* noble, *weiss* white)]

F·

***ēdē'ma.** See OEDEMA.

E'den (ē'-) *n.* Abode of Adam and Eve at their creation; delightful abode; state of supreme happiness; hence ~IC (ēdĕ'-) *a.* [ME, f. LL f. Gk *Edēn* f. Heb. *'eden*, orig. = delight]

ėdĕ'ntāte *a.* & *n.* (Animal, esp. mammal of order Edentata) having few or no teeth. [f. L E(*dentatus* f. *dens dentis* tooth; see -ATE²)]

ĕdge¹ *n.* **1.** Sharpened side of blade of cutting instrument or weapon; sharpness of this (*the knife has no edge*), (fig.) effectiveness; **be on ~,** be excited or irritable; **take the ~ off,** blunt, weaken, dull, (appetite, argument, etc.); **set** person's **teeth on ~**, cause him revulsion as from eating sour fruit; **rough** or **sharp ~ of** one's **tongue,** reviling. **2.** Edge-shaped thing, esp. crest of a ridge; meeting-line of two surfaces of a solid; narrow surface of thin object. **3.** Boundary line of region or surface; brink (of precipice); **on the ~ of,** (fig.) almost involved in or affected by; **have the ~ on,** (colloq.) have an advantage over. **4. ~-tool,** cutting-tool (in fig. sense also *edged tool*). **5.** Hence ~'LESS (-jl-) *a.* [OE *ecg*, = OS *eggia*, OHG *ekka*, ON *egg* f. Gmc **agjō* (**ag-* f. IE **ak-* be sharp)]

ĕdge² *v.* **1.** *v.t.* Sharpen (tool etc., also fig.); ~ **on,** = EGG² *on*; furnish with or *with* border, form border to; insinuate, push, (thing, one*self*) *into, in, out, off*, etc.; (Cricket) strike (ball) with edge of bat. **2.** *v.i.* Advance, esp. gradually and obliquely. [ME, f. prec.]

ĕ'dgeways (-jwāz), **ĕ'dgewise** (-jwīz), *advs.* With edge uppermost or foremost; (fig.) **get a word in ~** (in talkative person's silent interval); (of two things) edge to edge. [f. EDGE¹ + -WAYS, -WISE]

ĕ'dgĭng *n.* In vbl senses; border, fringe; **~-shears** (for trimming edges of lawn). [f. EDGE² + -ING¹]

ĕ'dg|ȳ *a.* Sharp-edged; having one's nerves on edge, irritable; hence ~ĬLY² *adv.* [f. EDGE¹ + -Y²]

ĕdh, ĕth, *n.* Name of OE & Icel. letter, = th. [Icel. *eth*]

ĕ'dĭble *a.* & *n.* (Thing) fit to be eaten; hence **ĕdɪʙɪ'ʟɪᴛʏ** *n.* [f. LL *edibilis* (*edere* eat; see -IBLE)]

ē'dĭct *n.* Order proclaimed by authority; so **ėdĭ'ctal** *a.* [ME, f. L *edictum* f. E(*dicere dict-* say) proclaim]

ĕ'dĭfĭce *n.* Building (esp. large one; also fig.). [ME f. OF f. L *aedificium* (*aedis* dwelling + *-ficium* f. *facere* make)]

ĕ'dĭfȳ *v.t.* Benefit spiritually; improve morally; so **ĕdɪꜰɪᴄᴀ'ᴛɪᴏɴ** *n.* [ME, f. OF *edifier* f. L *aedificare* (as prec.; see -FY)]

ĕ'dĭt *v.t.* Prepare an edition of (another's work); set in order for publication (material chiefly provided by others); take extracts from and collate (films, tape-recordings, etc.) to form a unified sequence; act as editor of (newspaper etc.); reword for a purpose. [f. F *éditer* f. as foll.; partly back form. f. EDITOR]

ėdĭ'tion *n.* Form in which a literary work is published (*first, paperback, pocket, edition*); one copy in such form (*this is a first edition*); whole number of copies of book, newspaper, etc., issued from same types, or = IMPRESSION; (fig.) product of the same kind, person etc. resembling another (*a more charming edition of her sister*). [f. F *édition* f. L *editio -onis* f. E(*dere dit-* = *dare* give) put out]

editio princeps (ĭdĭshĭō prĭ'nsĕps) *n.* (*pl.* ***editiones principes*** *pr.* -ōnēz -sĭpēz). First printed edition of a book. [L]

ĕ'dĭtor *n.* One who prepares the work of others for publication, broadcasting, etc.; one who conducts a newspaper or periodical, or a section of one (*financial editor*); head of department of publishing house; one who edits films etc.; hence ~SHIP, **ĕ'dĭtress**[1], *ns.* [L (as EDIT; see -OR)]

ĕdĭtŏr'ial *a.* & *n.* **1.** *a.* Of an editor; written by or as by the editor, opp. news and advertising matter; hence ~LY[2] *adv.* **2.** *n.* Newspaper article written by or under responsibility of the editor; hence ~IST (3) *n.*, ~IZE *v.i.*, writer of, write, editorials. [f. prec. + -IAL]

-edly (usu. *pr.* -ĭdlĭ) *suf.* forming *advs.* f. *vbs.*, meaning 'in manner characterized by performance of or undergoing of vbl action' (*allegedly, discontentedly, disgustedly, heatedly, hurriedly*). [f. -ED[1] + -LY[2]]

EDP *abbr.* electronic data processing.

***EDT** *abbr.* Eastern Daylight Time.

ĕ'dūc|āte *v.t.* Bring up (young person); give intellectual and moral training to; provide schooling for; train (person, one*self*, a physical or mental faculty, *to* do); **~ated guess** (based on experience); hence ~ABI'LITY, **~ātor**, *ns.*, ~ABLE, ~ATIVE, *adjs.* [f. L *educare* conn. w. EDUCE + -ATE[3]]

ĕdūcā'tion *n.* Educating, being educated; systematic instruction; course of this (*classical, commercial*, FURTHER, *education*); development of character or mental powers; COLLEGE *of Education*; hence ~AL *a.*, ~(**al**)IST (3) *ns.* [f. F *éducation* or f. L *educatio* (as prec.; see -ATION)]

ėdū'c|e *v.t.* Bring out, develop, from latent or potential existence; elicit, evoke; infer (number, principle, *from* data); hence ~IBLE *a.*, **ėdŭ'ct**ION *n.* [ME, f. L E(*ducere duct-* lead)]

ėdŭ'lcor|āte *v.t.* Free from acid properties or from soluble particles, purify; hence ~A'TION *n.* [f. med. L *edulcorare*, f. as E- + LL *dulcor* sweetness (*dulcis* sweet); see -ATE[3]]

Edw. *abbr.* Edward.

Edwar̂'dĭan (ĕ-; *or* -ôr'-) *a.* & *n.* **1.** *a.* Of the time of any of the Kings Edward. **2.** (esp.) Characteristic of Edward VII's reign (1901–10). **3.** *n.* Person belonging to this period. [f. *Edward* + -IAN]

-ee' *suf.* forming *ns.* expr. (1) person affected by vbl action, corresp. to agent *ns.* in *-or*, orig. in legal terms after AF (*appellor, appellee*), extended to indirect obj. (*lessee, vendee*) and non-tech. wds without corresp. *-or* (*employee, payee*), (2) person concerned with or described as (*absentee, bargee, dilutee, escapee, refugee*), (3) object of smaller size (*bootee, coatee*). [f. or after AF p.p. in *-é* f. L *-atus*]

E.E. *abbr.* Early English.

E.E.C. *abbr.* European Economic Community.

E.E.G. *abbr.* electroencephalogram.

eel *n.* Snakelike fish of order Apodes; (fig.) slippery or evasive person or thing; **~-grass,** marine plant with long narrow leaves; **~-pout,** burbot or blenny; **~'worm,** nematode worm infesting plants; hence ~'Y[2] *a.* [OE *ǣl*, = OS, OHG *āl*, ON *áll* f. Gmc **ǣlaz*, of unkn. orig.]

e'en[1,2]. See EVEN[1,3].

-een *suf.* (Ir.) forming dim. *ns.* (*colleen, dudeen, poteen, spalpeen*). [f. Ir. *-ín* dim. suf.]

e'er. See EVER.

-eer *suf.* forming (1) *ns.* denoting 'person concerned with' (*auctioneer, mountaineer*; often derog., *profiteer, sonneteer*), (2) *vbs.* denoting 'be concerned with' (*electioneer*), by back form. f. *electioneering* etc. [f. or after F *-ier* f. L *-arius*; cf. -IER, -ARY[1]]

eer'|ĭe *a.* Gloomy; strange, weird; hence **~ĭly**[2] *adv.*, **~ĭ**NESS *n.* [ME, orig. 'timid', f. OE *earg*]

ef- *pref.*, assim. form of EX-[1] 1 before f.

ĕff *v.* (sl.) **1.** *v.t.* & *i.* = FUCK (*eff off*). **2.** *v.i.* Say *fuck* or similar taboo word; **~ and blind,** use strong expletives. [name of letter *F*, as euphem. abbr.]

ėffā'ce *v.t.* Rub out; (fig.) obliterate, wipe out; utterly surpass, eclipse; treat or regard one*self* as unimportant; hence ~ABLE (-sa-) *a.*, ~MENT (-sm-) *n.* [f. F *effacer* (*es-* EX-[1], *face* FACE[1])]

ėffĕ'ct[1] *n.* **1.** Result, consequence, (**in ~,** for practical purposes; **to that ~,** having that result or implication); efficacy (*of no effect*); combination of colour or form in picture etc. (*a pretty effect*). **2.** (in *pl.*) Property (*personal effects*; **'no ~s',** written by banker on dishonoured cheque); lighting, sounds, etc., used to accompany play, film, or broadcast. **3.** Impression produced on spectator, hearer, etc., (*did it only* **for ~**, to impress hearers etc.); (Phys.) phenomenon, usu. named after discoverer (*Doppler effect*). **4.** Operativeness (**bring** or **carry into ~,** accomplish; **give ~ to,** make operative; **take ~,** become operative; **with ~ from,** coming into operation at (stated time)). **5.** Hence ~LESS *a.* [ME f. OF, or f. L *effectus* f. EF(*ficere fect-* = *facere* make)]

ėffĕ'ct[2] *v.t.* Bring about, accomplish; cause to exist or occur. [f. prec.]

ėffĕ'ctive *a.* & *n.* **1.** *a.* Having an effect; powerful in effect; striking, remarkable; coming into operation (*effective as from 1 September*); actual, existing; actually usable, equivalent in its effect; hence ~LY[2] (-vlĭ) *adv.*, ~NESS (-vn-) *n.* **2.** *a.* & *n.* (Soldier etc.) fit for work or service. [ME, f. L *effectivus* (as EFFECT[1]; see -IVE)]

ėffĕ'ctor *n.* & *a.* (Biol.) (Organ) acting in response to stimulus. [f. EFFECT[2] + -OR]

ėffĕ'ctūal *a.* Answering its purpose, sufficient to produce an effect; valid; hence ~LY[2] *adv.*, ~NESS *n.* [ME, f. med. L *effectualis* (as EFFECT[1]; see -AL)]

ėffĕ'ctū|āte *v.t.* Cause to happen; accomplish; hence ~A'TION *n.* [f. med. L *effectuare* (as EFFECT[1]) + -ATE[3]]

ėffĕ'mĭn|ate *a.* Womanish, unmanly; hence ~ACY *n.*, **~ate**LY[2] (-tlĭ) *adv.* [ME, f. L *effeminatus* p.p. of EF(*feminare* f. *femina* woman); see -ATE[2]]

ĕffĕ'ndĭ *n.* Person of education or standing in E. Mediterranean or Arab country; (Hist.) title of respect or courtesy in Turkey. [f. Turk. *efendi* f. mod. Gk *afentēs* f. Gk *authentēs* lord, master (as AUTHENTIC)]

ĕ'fferent *a.* (Physiol.). Conducting outwards (*efferent nerves, vessels*) (opp. *afferent*). [f. L EF(*ferre* carry); see -ENT]

ĕffervĕ'sc|e *v.i.* Give off bubbles of gas, bubble, (lit., or fig. of persons); hence ~ENCE, ~ENCY, *ns.*, ~ENT *a.* [f. L EF(*fervescere* incept. of *fervēre* be hot); see -ESCE]

ĕffē'te *a.* Exhausted, worn out; feeble, incapable; hence ~NESS (-tn-) *n.* [f. L EF*fetus* worn out by bearing young (cf. FOETUS)]

ĕffĭcā'cious (-shus) *a.* (Of thing) producing, sure to produce, desired effect; hence or cogn. ~LY[2] *adv.*, ~NESS, **ĕ'ffĭc**ACY, *ns.* [f. L *efficax* (as EFFICIENT; see -ACIOUS)]

ėffĭ'ciencў (-shensĭ) *n.* State or quality of being efficient; (Mech. & Phys.) ratio of useful work done to total energy expended or heat taken in; ***~ (apartment),** one with limited facilities for washing and cooking; **~ bar,** restriction of salary subject to proof of efficiency; **~ expert,** one who advises on efficiency of an organization or production process. [f. L *efficientia* (as foll.; see -ENCY)]

ėffĭ'cient (-shent) *a.* Productive of effect; (of person) competent, capable; **~ cause,** that which makes a thing what it is; hence ~LY[2] *adv.* [ME, f. L EF(*ficere* = *facere* make) accomplish; see -ENT]

ĕ'ffĭgў *n.* Portrait, image; **burn** etc. (person) **in ~,** burn etc. a figure representing him. [f. L *effigies* (EF*fingere* to fashion)]

ĕfflorĕ'sc|e *v.i.* Burst out into flower (lit. or fig.); (Chem., of crystalline substance) turn to fine powder on exposure to air, (of salts) come to the surface and there crystallize, (of ground or wall) become covered with salt particles; so ~ENCE *n.*, ~ENT *a.* [f. L EF(*florescere* incept. of *florēre* bloom f. *flos floris* flower); see -ESCE]

ĕ'ffluence (-lōō-) *n.* Flowing out (of light, electricity, etc., or fig.); that which flows out. [F, or f. med. L *effluentia* (as foll.; see -ENCE)]

ĕ'ffluent (-lōō-) *a.* & *n.* **1.** *a.* Flowing forth or out. **2.** *n.* Stream flowing from larger stream, lake, sewage tank, industrial process, etc. [f. L EF(*fluere flux-* flow); see -ENT]

ĕfflu'v|ĭum (-lōō'-) *n.* (*pl.* ~**ia**). Exhaled substance (esp. unpleasant) affecting lungs or sense of smell etc. [L, f. as prec.]

ĕ'fflŭx *n.* Flowing out (of liquid or gas, or fig.); that which flows out; hence **ĕfflŭ'x**ION (-kshon) *n.* [f. med. L *effluxus* f. as EFFLUENT]

ĕ'ffort *n.* Strenuous exertion; vigorous attempt (*at, to* do); force exerted; special activity; (colloq.) something accomplished involving concentration or special activity (*that's a pretty good effort*); hence ~FUL *a.* [F, f. OF *esforcier* f. Rom. *EX¹(*fortiare* f. L *fortis* strong)]

ĕ'ffortlĕss *a.* (Of skill etc.) without effort, easy; (arch.) making no effort, passive; hence ~LY² *adv.*, ~NESS *n.* [f. prec. + -LESS]

ėffro'nterȳ (-ŭ'-) *n.* Shameless insolence. [f. F *effronterie* f. *effronté* f. Rom. **exfrontatus* f. LL EF(*frons -ntis* forehead) shameless; see -ERY]

ĕffŭ'lg|ent *a.* Radiant (lit. or fig.); hence or cogn. ~ENCE *n.*, ~**ent**LY² *adv.* [f. L EF(*fulgēre* shine); see -ENT]

ĕffū'se¹ *a.* (Bot., of inflorescence etc.) spreading loosely; (of shell) with lips separated by groove. [f. L *effusus* p.p. of EF(*fundere fus-* pour)]

ĕffū'se² (-z) *v.t.* Pour forth (liquid, air, light, smell; or fig.). [ME, f. L (as prec.)]

ėffū'sion (-zhon) *n.* Pouring forth (lit. or fig.; ~ **of blood,** bloodshed); unrestrained utterance (often derog. of literary work). [ME f. OF, or f. L *effusio* (as EFFUSE¹; see -ION)]

ėffū'sĭve *a.* (Of speech or emotion) exuberant, demonstrative; (Geol., of igneous rock) poured out when molten and later solidified; hence ~LY² (-vlĭ) *adv.*, ~NESS (-vn-) *n.* [f. as EFFUSE¹; see -IVE]

ĕft *n.* Newt. [OE *efeta*, of unkn. orig.]

E'fta (ĕ'-), **E.F.T.A.,** *n.* European Free Trade Association. [abbr.]

ĕftsōō'ns (-z) *adv.* (arch. or joc.) Soon afterwards; occasionally. [OE *eftsōna* (*eft* again, *sōna* SOON) + -S³]

e.g. *abbr.* for example. [f. L *exempli gratia*]

ėgă'd *int.* (arch.) By God. [prob. orig. *a* ah + GOD]

ėgălĭtār'ĭan *a.* & *n.* Of, relating to, (person) holding, the principle of equal rights etc. for all persons; hence ~ISM (3) *n.* [f. F *égalitaire* (*égal* EQUAL¹) + -IAN]

Egēr'ĭa (ĭ-) *n.* Patroness and adviser. [L, name of Roman goddess said to have instructed Numa Pompilius]

ĕgg¹ *n.* **1.** Spheroidal body produced by female of birds etc., containing germ of a new individual; (esp.) that of domestic fowl, for eating; **bad ~,** person or scheme that comes to no good; **have all** one's **~s in one basket,** risk all on a single venture; **teach** one's **grandmother to suck ~s,** presume to advise those who are more experienced; **as sure as ~s is** or **are ~s,** undoubtedly. **2.** (Zool.) ovum; (pop.) pupa of ant etc.; (sl.) person or thing (*good, tough,* etc., *egg*); (sl.) bomb, mine. **3.** ~ **and anchor, dart, tongue,** (Archit.) kinds of moulding with egg-shaped and triangular figures; **~-and-spoon race** (in which runners carry egg in spoon); **~-beater,** device for beating eggs, *(sl.) helicopter; ||*egg*-COSY 2; **~-cup** (for holding egg boiled in shell); ~ **custard,** = CUSTARD 1; **~-flip,** hot or cold beer, cider, wine, etc., with eggs and usu. milk stirred in; **~'head,** (colloq.) intellectual person; **~-nog,** = *egg-flip*; **~-plant,** (fruit of) purple- or white-fruited *Solanum melongena*, aubergine; **~-plum,** small egg-shaped yellow plum; *egg* SAUCE; **~'shell,** shell of egg, fragile thing (~*shell china*, very thin kind), (of paint etc.) slightly glossy; **~-slice,** utensil for taking omelette from pan; **~-spoon,** small spoon for eating boiled egg; **~-timer,** device for timing cooking of egg; **~-tooth,** protuberance on bill-sheath of embryo bird or reptile for cracking shell; **~-whisk,** utensil for beating eggs; **~-white,** WHITE² of egg. **4.** Hence ~'LESS, ~'Y², *adjs.* [ME, f. ON; OS, OHG *ei*, Goth. **addi-* f. Gmc **ajjaz*]

ĕgg² *v.t.* Urge (person) *on* (*to* an act, *to* do). [ME, f. ON *eggja* = EDGE²]

ĕ'gger, ĕ'ggar, *n.* Kind of large moth with egg-shaped cocoon. [prob. f. EGG¹ + -ER¹]

ĕ'glantīne *n.* Sweet-BRIER¹. [ME, f. F *églantine* f. OF *aiglent* f. Rom. **aculentus* f. L *acus* needle; see -LENT]

ĕ'gō *n.* (*pl.* ~**s**). (Metaphys.) conscious thinking subject; (Psych.) part of the mind that reacts to reality and has sense of individuality; self-esteem; **~-ideal,** (Psych.) part of mind developed from ego by awareness of social standards, (pop.) idealization of oneself; **~-trip,** activity etc. devoted entirely to one's own interests or feelings. [L, = I]

ĕgocĕ'ntrĭc *a.* Centred in the ego; self-centred, egoistic; hence **ĕgocĕntrĭ'c**ITY *n.* [f. EGO + CENTRIC, after *geocentric* etc.]

ĕ'gō|ĭsm *n.* Ethical theory that treats self-interest as foundation of morality; systematic selfishness; self-opinionatedness; = EGOTISM; hence ~IST (2) *n.*, **~ĭ'st**IC(AL) *adjs.* [f. F *égoïsme* f. mod. L *egoismus* (as EGO; see -ISM)]

ĕgōmā'nĭ|a *n.* Morbid egotism; hence ~AC *n.* [f. EGO + -MANIA]

ĕ'got|ĭsm *n.* Too frequent use of 'I' and 'me'; practice of talking about oneself; self-conceit; selfishness; hence ~IST (2) *n.*, **~ĭ'st**IC(AL) *adjs.*, ~IZE (2) *v.i.* [f. EGO + -ISM, w. intrusive *-t-*]

ėgrē'gious (-jus) *a.* Shocking (*egregious folly, blunder, ass*); (arch.) remarkable; hence ~LY² *adv.*, ~NESS *n.* [f. L E(*gregius* f. *grex gregis* flock) illustrious, lit. 'standing out from the flock']

ĕ'grĕss *n.* (Right of) going out; (Astron.) end of eclipse or transit; way out (lit. or fig.). [f. L *egressus* f. L E(*gredi gress-* = *gradi* step)]

ėgrĕ'ssion (-shon) *n.* Going out or forth. [f. *egress* v. (f. prec.) + -ION]

ĕ'grĕt *n.* Lesser white heron. [ME; var. of AIGRETTE]

Egȳ'ptian (ĭjĭ'pshan) *a.* & *n.* (Native or inhabitant) of Egypt; Hamitic language used in Egypt until 3rd c.; ~ **lily,** calla lily; hence ~IZE (3) *v.t.* [ME, f. *Egypt* + -IAN]

Egȳptŏ'|logȳ (ē-) *n.* Study of Egyptian antiquities; so ~LOGIST *n.* [f. *Egypt* + -O- + -LOGY]

eh (ā) *int.* (colloq.) expr. inquiry or surprise, or inviting assent, or asking for something to be repeated or explained. [ME *ey*, instinctive excl.]

-eian *suf.* = *-ey* or *-y* + -AN (*Bodleian, Rugbeian*).

ei'der (ī'-) *n.* ~ (**duck**), large northern duck, esp. of genus *Somateria*, yielding ~(**-down**), small soft feathers from its breast; **~down,** quilt stuffed with eider-down or other soft material. [f. Icel. *aethr*]

eidĕ'tĭc (ī-) *a.* & *n.* **1.** *a.* (Psych., of mental image) having unusual vividness and detail, as if actually visible. **2.** *n.* Person able to see eidetic images. [f. G *eidetisch* f. Gk *eidētikos* (*eidos* form; see -ETIC)]

eidō'l|on (ī-) *n.* (*pl.* **~ons** *or* **~a**). Spectre, phantom; idealized figure. [f. Gk *eidōlon* (see IDOL)]

ei'gen- (ī'g-) *comb. form.* (Math. & Phys.) Proper, characteristic; **~frequency,** one of the frequencies causing resonance of a system; **~value,** value of a parameter for which a differential equation has a non-zero solution satisfying given conditions. [f. G *eigen* OWN[1]]

eight (āt) *a.* & *n.* One more than seven; symbol for this (8, viii, VIII); (**figure of**) **~,** 8-shaped figure; card with eight pips; time of eight o'clock; size etc. denoted by eight; set of eight, esp. crew of eight in rowing-boat (**~s,** boat-races at Oxford etc. between such crews); eight-oared boat; **have one over the ~,** (sl.) get slightly drunk; ***behind the ~ ball,** baffled, at a disadvantage [f. high-valued ball in game of pool]; hence **~'**FOLD *a.* & *adv.*, **eigh**TH[2] (ātth) *a.* & *n.* (***~h-note,** (Mus.) quaver), **~h**LY[2] (ā'tth-) *adv.* [OE *e(a)hta*, = OS, OHG *ahto*, ON *átta*, Goth. *ahtau* f. Gmc **ahtō* f. IE **oktō*]

eightee'n (āt-; *or* ā'tēn) *a.* & *n.* One more than seventeen; symbol for this (18, xviii, XVIII); size etc. denoted by eighteen; set of eighteen, esp. persons forming side at Australian Rules football; **~mo,** OCTODECIMO; hence **~**TH[2] *a.* & *n.* [OE *e(a)htatēne*, = OS *ahtotian*, OHG *ahtozehan*, ON *áttján* (as prec., -TEEN)]

ei'ghtsome (ā't-) *n.* & *a.* **~ (reel),** lively Scottish reel for eight dancers. [f. EIGHT + -SOME[2]]

ei'ghtў (ā'tĭ) *a.* & *n.* **1.** Eight times ten; symbol for this (80, lxxx, LXXX); (in *pl.*) numbers etc., esp. years of a century or a life, from 80 to 89; hence **~**FOLD *a.* & *adv.*, **eightĭ**ETH[1] (āt-) *a.* & *n.* **2. ~-one** etc., (arch.) **one-and-~** etc., eighty plus one etc., w. corresp. ordinals **~-first** etc. [OE *-eahtatig* (as EIGHT, -TY[2])]

ei'nkōrn (ī'n-k-) *n.* Species of wheat (*Triticum monococcum*). [G (*ein* one, *korn* seed)]

einstei'nĭum (īnstī'-) *n.* (Chem.) Artificially made transuranic radioactive metallic element. [mod. L, f. A. *Einstein*, Ger.-Amer. physicist d. 1955 + -IUM]

eirenic. Var. of IRENIC.

eirē'nĭcŏn (īrē-) *n.* Proposal tending to make peace. [Gk, neut. of *eirēnikos* adj. (*eirēnē* peace; see -IC)]

eisteddfod (īstĕ'dhvod) *n.* (*pl.* **~s,** *or* **~au** *pr.* -ī). Congress of Welsh bards; national or local gathering for musical competitions etc.; hence **~**IC (-ŏ'd-) *a.* [W, lit. = session (*eistedd* sit)]

ei'ther (ī'dh-; *or* ē'-) *a.*, *pron.*, & *adv.* or *conj.* **1.** *a.* & *pron.* Each of two (*at either end was a lamp*; *either view is tenable*; *either is tenable*); one or other of two (*put the lamp at either end*; *there is no lamp at either end*; *either of you can go*); *either* WAY 12. **2.** *adv.* or *conj.* On one or other supposition, which way you will, (*he is either drunk or mad*; *either come in or go out*); (w. neg. or interrog.) any more than the other (*if you do not go, I shall not either*); **~-or,** (involving) unavoidable choice between alternatives. [OE *ǣgther*, *ǣg(e)hwæther*, = OHG *eogihwedar* f. Gmc **aiwo gihwatharaz* ever each of two; cf. AYE[2], EACH, WHETHER[1]]

ėjă'cūl|āte[1] *v.t.* Utter suddenly (words esp. of prayer or other emotion, or abs.); eject (fluid etc., esp. semen) from the body; hence **~**A'TION *n.*, **~āt**ORY *a.* [f. L E(*jaculari* f. *jaculum* javelin) to dart + -ATE[3]]

ėjă'cūlate[2] *n.* Ejaculated semen. [f. prec.]

ėjĕ'ct *v.t.* Expel (*from* place, office, property; spent cartridge *from* gun, pilot *from* aircraft or spacecraft esp. in emergency); dispossess (tenant) by legal process; dart forth, emit; hence or cogn. **~**ION, **~**MENT, **~**OR, *ns.*, **~**IVE *a.*; **~ion** or **~or seat** (for ejection of pilot). [f. L E(*jicere ject-* = *jacĕre* throw)]

ē'ka- *pref.* (Chem.) denoting predicted element occupying place in periodic system directly beneath specified element (*eka-tantalum*). [f. Skr. *eka* one]

ēke[1] *v.t.* **~ out,** supplement, make best use of, (defective means etc. *with*, *by*), contrive to make (livelihood) or support (existence). [OE **ēacan*, = OS *ōkian*, ON *auka*, Goth. *aukan*, cogn. w. L *augēre* increase]

ēke[2] *adv.* (arch.) Also. [OE *ē(a)c*, = OS *ōk*, OHG *ouh*, ON, Goth. *auk*, perh. f. IE **au* again, or as prec.]

ėkĭ'st|ĭcs *n.* Study of human settlements and their development; hence **~**IC *a.*, **~**I'CIAN *n.* [f. mod. Gr. *oikistikē* f. Gk *oikistikos* (*oikizō* settle a colony f. *oikos* house); see -ICS]

ĕ'kka *n.* (Ind.) Small one-horse vehicle. [f. Hindi *ekkā* unit]

***ĕl** *n.* (colloq.) Elevated railway. [abbr.]

-el. See -LE 1, 2.

ėlă'borate[1] *a.* Carefully or minutely worked out; highly developed or complicated; hence **~**LY[2] (-tlĭ) *adv.*, **~**NESS (-tn-) *n.* [f. L *elaboratus* p.p. of E(*laborare* f. *labor* work); see -ATE[2]]

ėlă'bor|āte[2] *v.* **1.** *v.t.* Produce by labour; work out (invention, theory, etc.) in detail; (of natural agency) produce (substance etc.) from its elements or sources. **2.** *v.i.* Discuss something in detail (*I need not elaborate*). **3.** Hence or cogn. **~**A'TION *n.*, **~at**IVE *a.* [f. as prec. + -ATE[3]]

élan (ā'lahṅ) *n.* Vivacity; impetuous rush; **~ *vital*** (-vētah'l), life-force in Bergson's philosophy, mysterious vital principle. [F (*élancer* launch)]

ē'land *n.* Large Afr. antelope of genus *Taurotragus*. [Du., = elk]

ėlă'pse *v.i.* (Of time) pass away. [f. L E(*labi laps-* glide)]

ėlă'smobrănch (-z-; -ngk) *n.* Fish of class Chondrichthyes (shark, skate, etc.). [f. mod. L *elasmobranchii* f. Gk *elasmos* beaten metal + *bragkhia* gills]

ėlăsmosaur'us (-zm-) *n.* Large extinct marine reptile. [mod. L, f. as prec. + Gk *sauros* lizard]

ėlă'st|ĭc (*or* -ah'-) *a.* & *n.* **1.** *a.* Spontaneously resuming its normal bulk or shape after contraction, dilatation, or distortion, (*elastic* STOCKING; **~ic band,** = RUBBER[2] *band*); springy; (of feelings or person) buoyant; flexible, adaptable (*elastic conscience*); hence **~**ICALLY *adv.*, **ĕlăstĭ'**CITY *n.*, **~ĭ**CIZE (3) *v.t.* **2.** *n.* Elastic cord or fabric, usu. woven with strips of rubber. [f. mod. L *elasticus*, f. Gk *elastikos* propulsive (*elaunō* drive)]

ėlă'stĭcātėd (*or* ĭlah'-) *a.* (Of fabric) made elastic by weaving with rubber thread. [f. prec. + -ATE[3] + -ED[1]]

ėlă'sto|mĕr *n.* Natural or synthetic rubber or rubber-like plastic; hence **~mĕ'r**IC *a.* [f. ELASTIC, after *isomer*]

ėlā'te *v.t.*, & *a.* **1.** *v.t.* Inspirit, stimulate, (esp. in *p.p.*); make proud. **2.** *a.* (arch.) In high spirits, exultant, proud. **3.** So **ėlā't**ION *n.* [ME, f. L EF*ferre* ELAT- raise]

ĕ'later *n.* Click beetle. [mod. L, f. Gk *elatēr* driver (*elaunō* drive)]

E-layer (ē'lāer) *n.* = HEAVISIDE *layer*. [f. *E* (arbitrary) + LAYER]

ĕ'lbow[1] (-ō) *n.* **1.** Joint between forearm and upper arm, corresponding part in animal; elbow-shaped bend or corner, short piece of piping bent through right angle; part of garment covering elbow. **2. At** one's **~,** close at hand; **bend** or **lift** one's **~,** drink too much liquor; **out at ~s,** (of coat) worn-out, (of person) ragged, poor; **up to the ~s,** busily engaged *in*. **3.** ***~-chair,** armchair; **~-grease,** (joc.) vigorous polishing, hard work; **~-room,** plenty of room to move or work in. [OE *el(n)boga*, = OHG *elinbogo*, ON *öllnbogi* f. Gmc **alinobogon* (as ELL, BOW[1])]

ĕ'lbow[2] (-ō) *v.t.* & *i.* Thrust, jostle, (as) with elbows (person *aside*, one*self into*, *in*, one's *way*, etc.). [f. prec.]

ĕld *n.* (arch. or poet.) Old age; olden time. [OE *(i)eldu*, = OS *eldi*, OHG *elti*, ON *elli* f. Gmc **aldh-*; cf. OLD]

ĕ'lder[1] *a.* (*attrib.*) & *n.* **1.** (The) senior (of two related or indicated persons; *his elder brother*; *which is the elder?*); ||**~ brother** (pl. ~ *brethren*), one of thirteen senior members of Trinity House; **~ hand,** (Cards) first player; *elder* STATESMAN. **2.** *n.* (in *pl.*) Persons of greater age (*respect your elders*) or venerable because of age. **3.** Person advanced in life; (Hist.) member of a senate or governing body; official in early-Christian, Presbyterian, or Mormon Church, whence ~SHIP *n.* [OE *eldra*, = OS *aldira*, OHG *altiro*, *eltiro*, ON *ellri*, Goth. *althiza* (as OLD, -ER[3])]

ĕ'lder[2] *n.* Low white-flowered dark-fruited tree of genus *Sambucus*; **~(-berry) wine** (made from fruit of this). [OE *ellærn*, = MLG *ellern*, *elderne*, etc., prob. orig. adj.]

ĕ'lderlȳ *a.* Somewhat old; (of person) past middle age. [f. ELDER[1] + -LY[1]]

ĕ'ldėst *a.* First-born or oldest surviving (member of family, son, daughter, etc.); **~ hand,** (Cards) first player. [OE, = OHG *altist*, ON *ellztr*, Goth. *altista* (as ELDER[1], -EST[1])]

E.L.D.O. (ĕ'ldō) *abbr.* European Launcher Development Organization.

ĕldora'dō (-ah'-) *n.* (*pl.* **~s**). Fictitious country or city abounding in gold; place of great abundance. [f. Sp. *el dorado* the gilded]

ĕ'ldrĭtch *a.* (Sc.) Weird; hideous. [16th c., perh. f. OE **elfrīce* fairy realm]

Eleă'tĭc (ĕl-) *a.* & *n.* **1.** *a.* Relating to Elea, an ancient Greek city in S.W. Italy, or the school of philosophers who were born or lived there about the 6th c. B.C., esp. Xenophanes, Parmenides, and Zeno. **2.** *n.* An Eleatic philosopher. [f. L *Eleaticus* (*Elea*; see -ATIC)]

ĕlėcămpā'ne *n.* Perennial plant (*Inula helenium*), with bitter aromatic leaves and root; sweetmeat flavoured with this. [corrupt. of med. L *enula* (for L *inula* f. Gk *helenion*) *campana* (prob. = of the fields)]

ėlĕ'ct[1] *a.* Chosen; select, choice; (Theol.) chosen by God; (after *n.*) chosen to office etc. (*president elect*). [ME, f. L *electus* p.p. of E(*ligere lect-* = *legere* pick)]

ėlĕ'ct[2] *v.t.* Choose (thing, *to* do); choose (person) by vote, (*elect a chairman*, *elect him to the chair*, *elect him* (*to be*) *chairman*); (Theol., of God) choose (persons) in preference to others for salvation. [f. as prec.]

ėlĕ'ction *n.* Electing or being elected; **general ~** (of representatives, esp. members of House of Commons, throughout the country etc.); **by-~** (of M.P. etc. to fill vacancy). [ME f. OF, f. L *electio -onis* (as prec.; see -ION)]

ėlĕctioneer' *v.i.*, & *n.* **1.** *v.i.* Busy oneself in political elections. **2.** *n.* One who electioneers. [f. prec. + -EER]

ėlĕ'ctĭve *a.* & *n.* **1.** *a.* (Of official, office, authority) appointed by, filled up by, derived from, election; having power to elect; (of course of study) chosen by student, optional; having tendency to act on or be concerned with some things rather than others (*elective affinity*); (of surgical operation etc.) optional, not urgently necessary; hence ~LY[2] (-vlĭ) *adv.* **2.** *n.* *Elective course of study. [f. F *électif -ive* f. LL *electivus* (as ELECT[1]; see -IVE)]

ėlĕ'ctor *n.* One who has right of voting to elect M.P. etc.; (Hist.; *E~*) German prince entitled to share in election of Emperor; *member of electoral college; hence ~SHIP *n.* [ME, f. F *électeur* f. L *elector* (as ELECT[1]; see -OR)]

ėlĕ'ctoral *a.* Relating to or ranking as electors; ***~ college,** body of persons representing states of U.S. who cast votes for election of President. [f. prec. + -AL]

ėlĕ'ctorate *n.* Body of electors; (Hist.) dignity or dominions of German Elector. [f. ELECTOR + -ATE[1]]

Elĕ'ctra (ĭ-) *n.* **~ complex,** (Psych.) daughter's feelings of attraction to father and hostility to mother. [f. ~ in Gk tragedy, who caused her mother to be killed for having murdered ~'s father]

ėlĕ'ctrėss *n.* (Hist.) Wife of German Elector. [f. ELECTOR + -ESS[1]]

ėlĕ'ctrėt *n.* Permanently polarized piece of dielectric material, analogous to permanent magnet. [f. ELECTRICITY + MAGNET]

ėlĕ'ctrĭc *a.* & *n.* **1.** *a.* Of, charged with, capable of generating, operated or produced by, electricity; suddenly exciting, as if caused by electricity (*had an electric effect*). **2.** *Electric* BLANKET[1]; **~ blue,** steely or brilliant light blue; **~ chair** (used in electrocution of criminals); ***~ cord,** = FLEX[2]; **~ eel,** eel-like fish able to give electric shock; **~ eye,** photoelectric cell operating relay when beam of light is broken; **~ fence** (charged with electricity; often of one strand); *electric* FIELD 6; **~ fire,** electrically operated incandescent (esp. domestic) heater; *electric* GUITAR; **~ hare,** dummy hare propelled by electricity, used in greyhound racing; **~ organ,** (1) organ giving electric shock in some fishes, (2) (Mus.) electrically-operated organ; **~ ray,** RAY[3] that can give electric shock; **~ shock,** effect of sudden discharge of electricity on person or animal, usu. with stimulation of nerves and contraction of muscles; **~ storm,** violent disturbance of electrical condition of atmosphere; ||*electric* TORCH. **3.** Hence **ėlĕ'ctr**ICALLY *adv.*, **ėlĕctrĭ'**CIAN (*or* ĕlĭ-) *n.* **4.** *n.* Electric circuit, light, motor car, etc.; (in *pl.*) electrical equipment. [f. mod. L *electricus* f. L f. Gk *ēlektron* amber, rubbing of which causes electrostatic phenomena; see -IC]

ėlĕ'ctrĭcal *a.* Relating to, connected with, of the nature of, electricity; *electrical* ENGINEER[1] 4; suddenly exciting, as if produced by electricity (*the effect was electrical*). [f. prec. + -AL]

ėlĕctrĭ'cĭtȳ (*or* ĕ-) *n.* **1.** Form of energy occurring as two types (see NEGATIVE[1] 4, POSITIVE 9) in elementary particles (cf. ELECTRON, PROTON) and hence in macroscopic bodies, either statically (see CHARGE[1]) or dynamically (see CURRENT[2]). **2.** Branch of science concerned with this. **3.** Supply of electric current for lighting, heating, etc. [f. ELECTRIC + -ITY]

ėlĕ'ctrĭ|fȳ *v.t.* Charge (body) with electricity; convert (railway, factory, farm, etc.) to electric working; (fig.) startle, excite, as if by electric shock; hence ~FICA'TION *n.* [f. ELECTRIC + -FY]

ėlĕ'ctrō *n.* (*pl.* **~s**), & *v.t.* (colloq.) = ELECTROPLATE, ELECTROTYPE. [abbr.]

ėlĕctrō- *comb. form.* Of, pertaining to, caused by, electricity, as: **~bio'logy,** science of the electrical phenomena of living beings; **~che'mical, ~che'mistry,** (study) of electricity as applied to chemistry; **~dyna'mic, ~dyna'mics,** (study) of electricity in motion; **~mecha'nical,** pertaining to application of electricity to mechanical process, device, etc.; **~ne'gative, ~po'sitive,** of negative, positive, electricity, (of element) tending to acquire, lose, electrons; **~the'rapy,** treatment of diseases by use of electricity, whence **~the'rapist; ~ther'mal,**

relating to heat electrically derived. [f. Gk *ēlektron* amber (see ELECTRIC) + -O-]

ėlĕctrōcar'dīō|grăm *n.* Record of electric currents generated by person's heartbeats; so ~GRAPH (2), **ėlĕctrōcardĭŏ'**GRAPHY, *ns.* [f. G *electrocardiogramm* (as ELECTRO-, CARDIO-, -GRAM)]

ėlĕctrōconvŭ'lsĭve *a.* (Esp. of therapy) making use of convulsive response to application of electric shocks. [f. ELECTRO- + CONVULSIVE]

ėlĕ'ctrocūte *v.t.* Kill by electricity (as capital punishment); cause death of (person etc.) by electricity in any way; hence **ėlĕctrocū'**TION *n.* [f. ELECTRO-, after *execute*]

ėlĕ'ctrōde *n.* Conductor through which electricity enters or leaves an electrolyte, gas, vacuum, or other medium. [f. ELECTRIC + Gk *hodos* way]

ėlĕctrōėncĕ'phalō|grăm *n.* Record of electrical activity of brain; so ~GRAPH (2), **ėlĕctrōėncĕphalŏ'**GRAPHY, *ns.* [f. G *elektrenkephalogramm* (as ELECTRO-, ENCEPHALO-, -GRAM)]

ėlĕctrolier' *n.* Cluster of electric lamps. [f. ELECTRO-, after *chandelier*]

ėlĕ'ctrolȳse (-z), ***-ȳze,** *v.t.* Subject to or treat by electrolysis. [f. foll. after *analyse* etc.]

ėlĕctrŏ'lȳs|ĭs (*or* ĕ-) *n.* (*pl.* **~es** *pr.* -ēz). Chemical decomposition by electric action; (Surg.) breaking up of tumours, hair-roots, etc., by electric action; hence **ėlĕctrolȳ'**TIC *a.* [f. ELECTRO- + -LYSIS]

ėlĕ'ctrolȳte *n.* (Substance that can dissolve to give a) solution able to conduct electric current, esp. in electric cell or battery. [f. ELECTRO- + Gk *lutos* released (*luō* loosen)]

ėlĕctrōmă'gnėt *n.* Magnet consisting of material surrounded by coil etc. carrying electric current. [f. ELECTRO- + MAGNET]

ėlĕctrōmăgnĕ'tĭc *a.* Having both electrical and magnetic character; ~ **radiation** etc., kind of radiation including visible light, radio waves, gamma rays, etc., in which electric and magnetic fields vary simultaneously; ~ **units** (based primarily on magnetic properties of electric currents). [f. prec. + -IC]

ėlĕctrōmă'gnėtĭsm *n.* (Study of) magnetic forces produced by electricity. [f. as prec. + -ISM]

ėlĕctrŏ'mėter (*or* ĕ-) *n.* Instrument for measuring electrical potential by means of forces between charges; hence **ėlĕctromĕ'tr**IC *a.* [f. ELECTRO- + -METER]

ėlĕctromō'tĭve *a.* Producing or tending to produce electric current; ~ **force** (set up by difference of potential in electric circuit). [f. ELECTRO- + MOTIVE[1]]

ėlĕ'ctrŏn *n.* **1.** Stable elementary particle with indivisible charge of negative electricity, found in all atoms and acting as carrier of electricity in solids. **2.** (**Positive**) ~, positron. **3.** ~ **beam,** stream of electrons; ~ **gun,** device for producing narrow stream of electrons from heated cathode; ~ **lens,** device for focusing stream of electrons by electric and magnetic fields; ~ **microscope,** microscope with high magnification and resolution using electron lenses; *electron* OPTICS; ~ **pair,** electron and positron; **~-volt,** unit of energy, amount gained by electron when accelerated through potential difference of one volt. [f. ELECTRIC + -ON]

ėlĕctrŏ'nĭc (*or* ĕ-) *a.* Pertaining to electrons or to electronics; (of music) produced electronically or electrically without pipes, strings, etc., (of musical instrument) operating thus; ~ **brain** (colloq.), ~ **computer,** computer operated by electronic means; ~ **flash** (from gas-discharge tube, used in high-speed photography). [f. prec. + -IC]

ėlĕctrŏ'nĭcs (*or* ĕ-) *n. pl.* (treated as *sing.*) Branch of physics and technology concerned with phenomena associated with movement of electrons in vacuum, gas, semiconductor, etc. [f. prec.; see -ICS]

ėlĕctrophŏ'nĭc *a.* (Of music etc.) = ELECTRONIC. [f. ELECTRO- + -PHONE + -IC]

ėlĕctrōphor|ē'sĭs *n.* (*pl.* **~eses** *pr.* -ē'sēz). (Phys.) Movement of colloidal particles in a fluid under the influence of an electric field; hence **~E'TIC** *a.* [f. ELECTRO- + Gk *phorēsis* being carried]

ėlĕctrŏ'phorus (*or* ĕ-) *n.* Device for repeatedly generating static electricity by induction. [mod. L, f. ELECTRO- + Gk *-phoros* bearing]

ėlĕ'ctrōplāte *v.t.*, & *n.* **1.** *v.t.* Coat (utensil etc.) with chromium, silver, etc., by electrolysis. **2.** *n.* Objects thus produced. [f. ELECTRO- + PLATE[2]]

||**ėlĕ'ctroplĕxȳ** *n.* Electroconvulsive therapy. [f. ELECTRO- + APOPLEXY]

ėlĕ'ctroscōpe *n.* Instrument for detecting and measuring electricity, esp. as indication of ionization of air by radioactivity. [f. ELECTRO- + -SCOPE]

ėlĕctrō-shŏ'ck *n.* Electric shock; ~ **treatment,** medical treatment by means of electric shocks. [f. ELECTRO- + SHOCK[1]]

ėlĕctrōstă't|ĭc *a.* Of electricity at rest; **~ic unit** (based primarily on forces between electric charges); hence ~ICS *n.*, study of electricity at rest. [f. ELECTRO- + STATIC, after *hydrostatic*]

ėlĕctrōtĕchn|ŏ'logȳ (-tĕk-) *n.* Science of the application of electricity in technology; so ~IC(AL) *adjs.*, ~ICS *n.*, (-tĕ'k-). [f. ELECTRO- + TECHNOLOGY]

ėlĕ'ctrōtȳpe *n.*, & *v.t.* (Make) copy formed by electrolytic deposition of copper on mould, esp. for printing. [f. ELECTRO- + TYPE[1]]

ėlĕctrōvā'l|ent *a.* (Chem.) Linking ions by a bond resulting from electrostatic attraction; so ~ENCE, ~ENCY, *ns.* [f. ELECTRO- + *-valent* after *trivalent* etc.]

ėlĕ'ctrum *n.* Alloy of silver and gold used by the ancients; (Min.) native argentiferous gold ore. [ME f. L, f. Gk *ēlektron* amber, electrum]

ėlĕ'ctūarȳ *n.* Medicinal powder etc. mixed with honey or other sweet substance. [ME, f. LL *electuarium*, prob. f. Gk *ekleikton* (*ekleikhō* lick up)]

ĕlēēmŏ'sȳnarȳ (*or* -z-) *a.* Of or dependent on alms; charitable; gratuitous. [f. med. L *eleemosynarius* f. LL *eleemosyna* (see ALMS, -ARY[1])]

ĕ'lėg|ant *a.* (Of movements, style, author, manners) graceful; tasteful; refined; (of mode of life etc.) of refined luxury; ingeniously simple and effective; (vulg.) excellent; hence or cogn. ~ANCE *n.*, **~ant**LY[2] *adv.* [f. F *élégant* or L *elegant-* f. **elegare* rel. to *eligere* (cf. ELECT[1])]

ĕlėgī'ac *a.* & *n.* **1.** *a.* (Of metre) used for elegies, esp. ~ **couplet,** (usu. Gk or L) dactylic hexameter and pentameter, ~ **stanza,** four iambic pentameters rhyming *abab*; mournful. **2.** *n.* (in *pl.*) Elegiac verses. [f. F *élégiaque* or f. LL f. Gk *elegeiakos* (as ELEGY; see -AC)]

ĕ'lėgīze, -īse (-īz), *v.* **1.** *v.i.* Write an elegy (*upon*); write in mournful strain. **2.** *v.t.* Write an elegy upon. [f. foll. + -IZE]

ĕ'lėgȳ *n.* Song of lamentation, esp. for the dead (sometimes vaguely used of other poems); poem in elegiac metre. [f. F *élégie* or f. L f. Gk *elegeia* (*elegos* mournful poem; see -Y[1])]

ĕ'lėment *n.* **1.** Component part (**reduced to its ~s,** analysed; *the elements of national wealth*; *there was an element of cant, cant was a notable element, in his style*). **2.** (Chem.) Any of the (about 100) substances that cannot be resolved by chemical means into simpler substances. **3.** Any of **the four ~s** (earth, water, air, fire) in ancient and medieval philosophy; one of these as a being's natural abode or sphere, (usu. fig.: **in** one's ~, in one's accustomed or preferred surroundings). **4.** (in *pl.*) Atmospheric agencies, esp. wind and storm. **5.** (Electr.) Resistance wire in an electric heater, cooker, etc.; electrode. **6.** (in *pl.*) Rudiments of learning (i.e. the ABC) or of an art or science; **Euclid's E~s** (of Geometry). **7.** (in *pl.*) Bread and wine used in Eucharist. **8.** (Math. and Logic). Entity that is a member of a set. [ME f. OF, f. L *elementum*]

ĕlėmĕ'ntal *a.* & *n.* **1.** *a.* Of the four elements; of the powers of nature (*elemental worship*), whence ~ISM (3) *n.*; comparable to these (*elemental grandeur, tumult*); uncompounded (*elemental oxygen*); essential. **2.** *n.* Entity or force thought to be physically manifested by occult means. [f. med. L *elementalis* (as prec.; see -AL)]

ĕlėmĕ'ntar|ў *a.* Rudimentary, introductory, simple; (Chem.) not decomposable; **~y particle,** (Phys.) one of several subatomic particles not known to be composed of simpler particles; **~y school** (in which elementary subjects are taught to young children); hence **~ĭLY²** *adv.*, **~ĭNESS** *n.* [ME, f. L *elementarius* (as ELEMENT; see -ARY¹)]

ĕ'lėmĭ *n.* Fragrant resin of tropical tree, used in ointments, varnish, etc. [prob. f. Arab. *al-lami*]

ėlĕ'nch|us (-ngk-) *n.* (*pl.* **~i** *pr.* -ī). Logical refutation; **Socratic ~us,** mode of eliciting truth by short question and answer; so **ėlĕ'nctIC** *a.* [L, f. Gk *elegkhos*]

ĕ'lėphant *n.* **1.** Largest living land animal, of which two species survive, with trunk and long curved ivory tusks; **pink ~s,** hallucinations due to excessive indulgence in alcohol etc.; **white ~,** (fig.) burdensome or unwanted possession [from cost of maintenance]. **2. ~ bird,** aepyornis; **~ seal,** = SEA *elephant*; **~'s-ear,** begonia or taro. **3.** Size of paper, 711 × 584 mm. **4.** Hence **ĕlėphă'ntOID** *a.* [ME, orig. *olifaunt* etc. f. OF *oli-, elefant,* f. Rom. **olifantus* f. L *elephantus, elephans* f. Gk *elephas -antos* ivory, elephant]

ĕlėphantī'asĭs *n.* Skin disease due to nematode parasite, causing gross enlargement of limb etc.; (fig.) undue expansion or enlargement. [L f. Gk (as prec.; see -ASIS)]

ĕlėphă'ntīne *a.* Of elephants; huge; clumsy, unwieldy, (*elephantine movements, humour*). [f. L f. Gk *elephantinos* (as ELEPHANT.; see -INE²)]

Eleusĭ'nĭan (ē-) *a.* Of Eleusis in Attica; **~ mysteries,** (Gk Ant.) annual celebrations there in honour of Demeter. [f. L f. Gk *Eleusinios* + -AN]

ĕ'lėvāt|e *v.t.* **1.** Bring to higher position; (Eccl.) hold up (the Host) for adoration; raise (one's eyes, voice, hopes); raise axis of (gun); raise (railway etc.) above ground level. **2.** Exalt in rank etc.; (esp. in *p.p.*) raise morally or intellectually (aims, style); (in *p.p.*, colloq.) slightly drunk. **3.** Hence **~ORY** *a.* [f. L E(*levare* lift f. *levis* light) + -ATE³]

ĕlėvā'tion *n.* Elevating or being elevated; angle (esp. of gun or direction of heavenly body) with the horizontal; height above given (esp. sea) level; drawing or diagram made by projection on vertical plane (cf. PLAN), flat drawing of front, side, or back, of house etc., whence **~AL** *a.*; grandeur, dignity; (Ballet) leap from ground, action of tightening muscles and uplifting the body. [ME f. OF, or f. L *elevatio* (as prec.; see -ATION)]

ĕ'lėvātor *n.* Person, thing, device, that elevates; muscle that raises limb etc.; machine for hoisting grain etc.; * = LIFT 4; (Aeron.) movable part of tailplane, used to change aircraft's attitude. [mod. L (as prec.; see -OR)]

ėlĕ'ven *a.* & *n.* One more than ten; symbol for this (11, xi, XI); time of eleven o'clock; size etc. denoted by eleven; set of eleven, esp. eleven persons forming side at cricket, football, etc.; **the E~** (Apostles, without Judas); **~s(es)** *n.*, light refreshment about 11 a.m.; ||**~-plus,** examination taken at age 11–12 before entering secondary school; hence **~TH²** *a.* & *n.* (**the ~th hour,** latest possible time). [OE *endleofon* etc., = OS *elleban*, OHG *einlif*, ON *ellifu*, Goth. *ainlif* f. Gmc **ainaz* ONE + **-lif*, perh. = one *left* over (ten)]

ĕ'lėvŏn *n.* (Aeronaut.) Movable part of trailing edge of delta wing. [f. ELEVATOR + AILERON]

ĕlf *n.* (*pl.* **elves** *pr.* -vz). (Gmc Myth.) a supernatural being; mischievous creature; dwarf, little creature; **~-arrow, ~-bolt, ~-dart,** (arch.) flint arrowhead; **~-land,** Fairyland; **~-lock,** tangled mass of hair; hence **ĕ'lfISH¹, ĕ'lvISH¹,** *adjs.* [OE, = MDu. *elf* f. Gmc **albhiz*]

ĕ'lfĭn *a.* & *n.* **1.** *a.* Of elves, elfish. **2.** *n.* (arch.) Dwarf, child. [f. prec., perh. infl. by ME *elvene* gen. pl. of *elf*, and *Elphin* in Arthurian romance]

ėlĭ'cĭt *v.t.* Draw forth (what is latent; usu. fig.); draw out, evoke, (admission, answer *from* person). [f. L E(*licere licit-* = *lacere* deceive)]

ėlī'de *v.t.* Omit (vowel, syllable) by ELISION. [f. L E(*lidere lis-* = *laedere* dash) crush out]

ĕ'lĭg|ĭble *a.* Fit or entitled to be chosen (*for* office etc.); desirable, suitable, esp. as partner in marriage (*eligible bachelor*); hence **~IBI'LITY** *n.*, **~ĭbLY²** *adv.* [f. F *éligible* f. LL *eligibilis* (as ELECT¹; see -IBLE)]

ėlĭ'mĭn|āte *v.t.* Remove, get rid of; (Physiol.) discharge (waste matter *from* body); (Chem.) remove (simpler substance *from* a compound); ignore as irrelevant; exclude from competition etc. by defeat; (Alg.) get rid of (quantity) by combining equations; hence **~ABLE** *a.*, **~A'TION, ~ātOR,** *ns.* [f. L E(*liminare* f. *limen liminis* threshold) + -ATE³]

ėlĭ'sion (-zhon) *n.* Omission of vowel or syllable in pronouncing, (*I'm; let's; e'en*), or of passage in book etc. [f. LL *elisio* (as ELIDE; see -ION)]

élit|e (ālē't) *n.* **1.** *The* choice part, *the* best, (of a group); size of letters in typewriting (12 per inch); select group or class. **2.** Hence **~ISM** *n.*, advocacy of or reliance on leadership or dominance of a select group; so **~IST** (2) *n.* [F, f. p.p. of *élire* f. Rom. **exlegere* ELECT²]

ėlĭ'xir *n.* Alchemist's preparation designed to change metals into gold or (**~ of life**) to prolong life indefinitely; sovereign remedy; (Pharm.) aromatic solution used as medicine or flavouring. [ME f. med. L, f. Arab. *al-iksīr* (*al* the, *iksīr* prob. f. Gk *xērion* desiccative powder for wounds f. *xēros* dry)]

Elĭzabē'than (ĭ-) *a.* & *n.* (Person, writer) of the time of Queen Elizabeth I or II. [f. *Elizabeth* + -AN]

ĕlk *n.* (*pl.* **~s** *or* **~**). Large species of deer (*Alces alces*) in N. Europe and Asia; moose; *wapiti; IRISH *elk*; *(*E~*) member of a social and charitable organization; **~-hound,** large Scandinavian shaggy-coated hunting dog. [ME, prob. repr. OE *e(o)lh*]

ĕll *n.* (Hist.) measure of length (**English ~,** = 45 in.); **give him an inch** (a little) **and he'll take an ~** (much). [OE *eln*, = OS, OHG *elina*, ON *öln*, Goth. *aleina* orig. 'forearm', cogn. w. L ULNA]

ėllĭ'pse¹ *n.* Regular oval, traced by point moving in plane so that the sum of its distances from two other points is constant, or produced when a cone is cut by a plane making smaller angle with base than side of cone makes (cf. HYPERBOLA). [F, f. L f. Gk *elleipsis* f. *elleipō* come short (*en* in, *leipō* leave)]

ėllĭ'psĭs, ėllĭ'pse², *n.* (*pl.* **ellĭ'pses** *pr.* -ēz). Omission from sentence of words needed to complete construction or sense; omission of sentence at end of paragraph; set of three dots etc. indicating such omission. [f. as prec.]

ėllĭ'psoid *n.* Solid of which all plane sections through one axis are ellipses and all other plane sections are ellipses or circles; hence **ĕllĭpsoi'dal** *a.* [f. ELLIPSE[1] + -OID]

ėllĭ'ptĭc(al) *adjs.* Of or relating to an ellipse or ellipsis; hence **ėllĭ'ptĭcal**LY[2] *adv.*, **ĕllĭptĭ'c**ITY *n.* [f. Gk *elleiptikos* defective f. *elleipō* (see ELLIPSE[1])]

ĕlm *n.* Tree of genus *Ulmus*, esp. *U. procera* with rough doubly serrated leaves; ~(**'wood**), its wood; hence ~'Y[2] *a.* [OE, = OHG *elm*, cogn. w. ON *álmr*, L *ulmus*]

ĕ'locūte *v.i.* (joc.) Practise elocution; declaim. [back form. f. foll., after *execute* etc.]

ĕlocū'tion *n.* Art of expressive oral delivery; style of speaking; hence ~ARY[1] *a.*, ~IST (3) *n.* [f. L *elocutio* f. E(*loqui locut-* speak); see -ION]

éloge (ĕlŏ'zh) *n.* Discourse in honour of deceased person (esp. member of French Academy, pronounced by his successor). [F, f. L *elogium* epitaph]

Elō'hĭst (ĕ-) *n.* Author(s) of parts of Hexateuch where God is called 'Elohim' (cf. JEHOVIST). [f. *Elohim* (Heb., pl. of *'elōah* god) + -IST]

ĕ'lŏngāte (-ngg-) *v.* & *a.* **1.** *v.t.* Lengthen, prolong. **2.** *v.i.* (Bot.) Be of slender or tapering form. **3.** *a.* (Bot. & Zool.) Long in proportion to its width. [f. LL E(*longare* f. L *longus* long) + -ATE[3,2]]

ēlŏngā'tion (-ngg-) *n.* Lengthening; part (of line etc.) formed by lengthening; (Astron.) angular distance of planet from sun or of satellite from planet; (Mech.) amount of extension under stress. [ME, f. LL *elongatio* (as prec.; see -ATION)]

ėlō'pe *v.i.* (Of woman) run away from husband, or from home for secret marriage, (*with* her lover); (of couple) run away together to get married; abscond; hence ~MENT (-pm-) *n.* [f. AF *aloper* perh. f. ME **alope* p.p. of **alepe* run away (A- 1, LEAP[1])]

ĕ'loquence *n.* Fluent, forcible, and apt use of language; rhetoric. [ME f. OF, f. L *eloquentia* f. E(*loqui* speak); see -ENCE]

ĕ'loquent *a.* Possessing or showing eloquence; (fig.) clearly indicative (*of*); hence ~LY[2] *adv.* [ME f. OF, f. L *eloqui* (as prec.; see -ENT)]

||**E'lsăn** (ĕ'-) *n.* Type of lavatory in which chemicals are used for deodorization etc. **[P,** app. f. *E. L.* Jackson (manufacturer) + SANITATION]

ĕlse *adv.* **1.** (following indef. or interrog. pron.) Besides, in addition, (*someone, anybody, nowhere, else; who else?; who else's?, whose else?*); instead (*what else could I say?*). **2.** Otherwise, if not, (*run,* (*or*) *else you will be late*); **or** ~ (colloq., expr. warning or threat; *hand over the money or else*); **~'where,** in or to some other place. [OE *elles*, = OHG *elles*, OSw. *äljes* gen. sing. cogn. w. Goth. *aljis* other, L *alius*, Gk *allos*]

ĕ'lūant. See ELUENT.

ĕ'lūāte *n.* (Chem.) Solution obtained by elution. [f. as ELUENT + -ATE[1]]

ėlū'cĭd|āte (*or* -ōō'-) *v.t.* Throw light on, explain; hence ~A'TION, **~ātor**, *ns.*, **~āt**IVE, **~āt**ORY, *adjs.* [f. LL E(*lucidare* f. *lucidus* bright, LUCID) + -ATE[3]]

ėlū'de (*or* -ōō'd) *v.t.* Escape adroitly from (blow, danger, difficulty, person's grasp, person, inquiry, observation); avoid compliance with (law, request) or fulfilment of (obligation); escape from, baffle, (person's memory, understanding); so **ėlū's**ION (-zh*on*), **ėlū'sĭve**NESS (-vn-), *ns.*, **ėlū's**IVE, **ėlū's**ORY, (*or* -ōō'-) *adjs.* [f. L E(*ludere lus-* play)]

ĕ'lūent, ĕ'lūant, *n.* (Chem.) Fluid used for elution. [f. L E(*luere lut-* wash); see -ENT, -ANT]

elusion etc. See ELUDE.

ėlū'tion *n.* (Chem.) Removal of adsorbed substance by washing; so **ėlū'te** *v.t.* [G, f. LL *elutio* (as ELUENT; see -ION)]

ėlū'trĭ|āte *v.t.* (Chem.) Separate lighter and heavier particles in a mixture by washing or gas flow; hence ~A'TION *n.* [f. L E(*lutriare* wash) + -ATE[3]]

ĕ'lver *n.* Young eel. [var. of *eel*-FARE[1] = brood of young eels]

elves, ĕ'lvĭsh. See ELF.

Elȳ'sĭ|um (ĭlĭ'z-) *n.* (Gk Myth.) abode of the blessed after death; place or state of ideal happiness; hence ~AN *a.* [f. L f. Gk *Elusion* (*pedion* plain)]

ĕ'lȳtr|ŏn *n.* (*pl.* ~**a**). Outer hard wing-case of coleopterous insect. [f. Gk *elutron* sheath]

E'lzėvir (ĕ-) *a.* & *n.* (Book) printed by *Elzevier* family at Amsterdam etc. in 17th c.

ĕm *n.* (Print.) Unit for measuring amount of printed matter in line, equal to space occupied by m; measure-unit of 12 points; *em* QUADRAT, RULE. [name of letter *M*]

'em *pron.* (colloq.) Them (*let 'em all come*). [orig. a form of ME *hem*, dat. & acc. 3rd pers. pl. pron.; now regarded as abbr. of THEM]

em-[1,2] *pref.*, assim. form of EN-[1,2] bef. *b, p*.

ėmā'cĭ|āte (*or* -shĭ-) *v.t.* (esp. in *p.p.*) Make (person, face, etc.) thin; make feeble; hence ~A'TION *n.* [f. L E(*maciare* f. *macies* leanness) + -ATE[3]]

ĕ'manāte *v.* **1.** *v.i.* Issue, originate, (*from* source, person, etc.); (of gas, light, etc.) proceed, issue, (*from*). **2.** *v.t.* Cause to emanate, send forth. [f. L E(*manare* flow) + -ATE[3]]

ĕmanā'tion *n.* Issuing (*from*); thing proceeding from a source (esp. fig., of virtues, qualities, moral powers); (Chem.) radioactive gas formed by radioactive decay of solid; hence **ĕ'manā**TIVE *a.* [f. LL *emanatio* (as prec.; see -ATION)]

ėmă'ncĭpāt|e *v.t.* Free from legal, social, political, intellectual, or moral restraint (*emancipate from slavery; emancipated people ignoring social conventions*); (Rom. Law) release (child, wife) from power of paterfamilias; hence ~OR *n.*, ~ORY *a.* [f. L E(*mancipare* transfer property f. *manus* hand + *capere* take) + -ATE[3]]

ėmăncĭpā'tion *n.* Emancipating; setting free, esp. from slavery or from legal disabilities, whence ~IST (2) *n.*; setting free, freedom, from intellectual or moral restraint. [f. L *emancipatio* (as prec.; see -ATION)]

ėmă'ncĭpĭst *n.* (Austral. Hist.) Ex-convict who had served his term. [f. EMANCIPATE + -IST]

ėmă'scūlate[1] *a.* Castrated; effeminate. [f. L *emasculatus* p.p. of E(*masculare* f. *masculus* dim. of *mas* male); see -ATE[2]]

ėmă'scūl|āte[2] *v.t.* Castrate; weaken, make effeminate; impoverish (language); weaken (literary composition) by excisions, (legislation) by amendments etc.; hence ~A'TION *n.*, **~at**ORY *a.* [f. as prec. + -ATE[3]]

ėmba'lm (-ah'm) *v.t.* Preserve (corpse) from decay orig. with spices, now by means of arterial injection; preserve from oblivion; endue with balmy fragrance; hence ~MENT (-m-m-) *n.* [ME, f. OF EM[1](*baumer*, as BALM)]

ėmbă'nk *v.t.* Shut in or confine (river etc.) by banks, raised stone structure, etc. [f. EM-[1] + BANK[2]]

ėmbă'nkment *n.* Bank etc. for confining a river etc.; long bank or mound of earth etc. carrying road or railway. [f. prec. + -MENT]

ĕmbar̂'gō (*or* ĭ-) *n.* (*pl.* ~**es**), & *v.t.* **1.** *n.* Order forbidding ships of a foreign power to enter, or any ships to leave, the country's ports; suspension of (a branch of) commerce or other activity (*be under an embargo*); impediment. **2.** *v.t.* Place (ships, trade, etc.) under embargo; seize (ship, goods) for State service. [Sp., f. *embargar* arrest f. Rom. **imbarricare* (as IM-¹, *barra* BAR¹)]

ėmbâr′k *v.t.* & *i.* Put or go on board ship (*for* destination), whence **ĕmbârk**A′TION *n.*; engage (*in*, *on*, *upon*, undertaking, war, etc.). [f. F EM¹(*barquer* f. *barque* BARK³)]

embarras de choix, de richesse(s), (ahṅbahrah deshwah′, derēshĕ′s) *n.* More alternatives, wealth, than one knows how to deal with. [F, = embarrassment of choice, of riches]

ėmbă′rrass *v.t.* Encumber, impede; make (person) feel awkward or ashamed; complicate (question etc.); perplex; (in *p.p.*) encumbered with debts; hence ~MENT *n.* [f. F *embarrasser* f. Sp. *embarazar* f. It. *imbarrazzare* (*imbarrare* bar in, f. as IM-¹, BAR²)]

ĕ′mbassў *n.* Ambassador's function, office, or residence; deputation to a sovereign etc. [earlier *ambassy* f. OF *ambassée* etc. f. med. L *ambasciata* f. Rom. **ambactiare*; see AMBASSADOR]

ėmbă′ttle¹ *v.t.* Set (army etc.) in battle array; fortify against attack. [ME, f. OF EM¹(*bataillier* f. *bataille* BATTLE¹)]

ėmbă′ttle² *v.t.* Furnish (building, wall) with battlements; (in *p.p.*, Her.) like battlements in form. [ME, f. EM-¹ + OF *bataillier*; see BATTLEMENT]

ėmbay′ *v.t.* Enclose (as) in a bay, shut in; form (coast) into bays; hence ~MENT *n.* [f. EM-¹ + BAY²]

ėmbĕ′d, ĭmbĕ′d, *v.t.* (**-dd-;** esp. in *p.p.*) Fix firmly in surrounding mass; (of mass) surround thus; place (as) in a bed. [f. EM-¹, IM-¹ + BED¹]

ėmbĕ′llĭsh *v.t.* Beautify, adorn; heighten (narrative) with fictitious additions; hence ~MENT *n.* [ME, f. OF EM¹(*bellir* f. *bel* f. L *bellus* handsome); see -ISH²]

ĕ′mber¹ *n.* (usu. in *pl.*) Small piece of live coal or wood in dying fire; (fig.) almost extinct residue of activity etc. [OE *ǣmyrge*, = OHG *eimuria* pyre, ON *eimyrje* embers f. Gmc **aimuzjōn*; for *-b-* cf. SLUMBER]

ĕ′mber² *a.* ~ **days,** days of fasting and prayer (esp. in Anglican & R.C. Ch.), the Wed., Fri., and Sat., after (1) 1st Sun. in Lent, (2) Whit Sunday, (3) Holy Cross Day (14 Sept.), and (4) St. Lucy's day (13 Dec.). [OE *ymbren* n., perh. f. *ymbryne* period (*ymb* about, *ryne* course)]

ĕ′mber³ *n.* ~**(-goose)**, a sea-bird, species of LOON² (*Gavia immer*). [f. Norw. *emmer*]

ėmbĕ′zzle *v.t.* Divert (money etc., or abs.) fraudulently to one's own use; hence ~MENT (-zelm-) *n.* [f. AF *embesiler* (as EM-¹, *besiler* = OF *besillier* maltreat, ravage, of unkn. orig.)]

ėmbĭ′tter *v.t.* Make bitter (fig.); aggravate (evil); exasperate (person, feeling); hence ~MENT *n.* [f. EM-¹ + BITTER]

ėmblā′zon *v.t.* Portray conspicuously, as on heraldic shield; adorn (shield) with heraldic devices; adorn; celebrate, extol; hence ~MENT *n.* [f. EM-¹ + BLAZON²]

ėmblā′zonrў *n.* Blazonry. [f. prec. + -RY]

ĕ′mblem *n.* Symbol, typical representation (~ **book,** of drawings with allegorical explanations); (of person) type (*of* a quality); heraldic device or symbolic object as distinctive badge; so **ĕmblėm**A′TIC(AL) (*of*), *adjs.* [ME, f. L f. Gk *emblēma -matos* insertion f. EM²(*ballō* throw)]

ėmblĕ′matize, -ise (-īz), *v.t.* Serve as emblem of; represent by an emblem. [f. as prec. + -IZE]

ĕ′mblėment *n.* (Law, usu. in *pl.*) Profits of sown land; natural products of soil. [ME, f. OF *emblaement* (EM¹*bla(i)er* f. *blé* corn; see -MENT)]

ėmbŏ′d|ў *v.t.* Clothe (spirit) with body; give concrete form to (ideas etc.); express tangibly (principles *in* actions etc.); (of thing or person) be an expression of (ideas etc.); form into a body; include, comprise; hence ~ĬMENT *n.* [f. EM-¹ + BODY¹]

ėmbō′lden *v.t.* Make bold, encourage (*to* do). [f. EM-¹ + *bolden* (BOLD, -EN⁶)]

ĕ′mbolĭsm *n.* Obstruction of artery etc. by clot of blood, air-bubble, etc., esp. as cause of paralysis; embolus. [ME, = 'intercalation' f. LL f. Gk *embolismos* (EM²*ballō* throw in; see -ISM)]

ĕmbolĭ′smĭc (-z-) *a.* (Of year, in Jewish calendar) containing an intercalated month. [f. prec. + -IC]

ĕ′mbol|us *n.* (*pl.* ~*i pr.* -ī). Object causing embolism of artery etc. [L, = piston, f. Gk *embolos* peg, stopper]

embonpoint (ahṅbawṅpwă′ṅ) *n.* Plumpness (of person). [f. F phr. *en bon point* in good condition]

ėmbo′som (-ŏŏ′z-) *v.t.* (literary). Embrace; enclose, surround. [f. EM-¹ + BOSOM]

ėmbŏ′ss *v.t.* Carve or mould in relief; cause figures etc. to stand out on (surface); make protuberant; hence ~MENT *n.* [ME, f. OF **embocer* (as EM-¹, BOSS¹)]

embouchure (ahṅbōōshoor′) *n.* Mouth of river; opening of valley; (Mus.) part of musical instrument applied to mouth, mode of applying mouth to this. [F, f. *s'emboucher* discharge itself by mouth (as EM-¹, *bouche* mouth); see -URE]

ėmbow′el *v.t.* (‖-ll-). (arch.) Disembowel. [f. OF *emboweler* f. *esboueler* (*es-* EX-¹, *bouel* BOWEL)]

ėmbow′er *v.t.* Enclose as in bower. [f. EM-¹ + BOWER¹]

ėmbrā′ce *v.t.*, & *n.* **1.** *v.t.* Hold (person etc.; in *pl.* abs. = embrace one another) closely in the arms, usu. as sign of affection; clasp, enclose; accept eagerly (offer, opportunity, etc.); adopt (course of action, doctrine, party, cause); include, comprise, (thing *in* another); take in with eye or mind; hence ~ABLE *a.* (-*sa*-), ~MENT (-sm-) *n.* **2.** *n.* Folding in the arms; (euphem.) sexual intercourse. [ME, f. OF *embracer* f. Rom. **imbracchiare* f. L *in-* IN-¹ + *bracchium* arm]

ėmbra′nchment (-ah′-) *n.* Branching out (of arm of river etc.). [f. F *embranchement* (as EM-¹, BRANCH¹, -MENT)]

ėmbră′ngle (-nggel) *v.t.* Entangle, confuse; hence ~MENT (-gelm-) *n.* [f. EM-¹ + obs. *brangle* wrangle]

ėmbrā′sure (-zh*er*) *n.* Bevelling of wall at sides of door or window, splaying; opening in parapet, widening from within, for gun. [F (*embraser* splay, of unkn. orig.; see -URE)]

ėmbrĭ′ttle *v.t.* Make brittle; hence ~MENT (-telm-) *n.* [f. EM-¹ + BRITTLE]

ĕmbrocā′tion *n.* Liquid used for rubbing on body to relieve muscular pain etc. [F, or f. med. L *embrocatio* (*embrocare* f. LL f. Gk *embrokhē* lotion; see -ATION)]

ėmbroi′der *v.t.* Ornament (cloth etc., or abs.) with needlework; heighten (narrative) with fictitious additions; hence ~ER¹ *n.* [ME, f. AF *enbrouder* (as EN-¹, OF *brouder, broisder* f. Gmc **brusdan*)]

ėmbroi′derў *n.* Embroidering; embroidered work; inessential ornament. [ME, f. AF *enbrouderie* (as prec.; see -ERY)]

ėmbroi′l *v.t.* Bring (affairs, narrative, etc.) into state of confusion; involve (person) in hostility (*with* another); hence ~MENT *n.* [f. F EM¹-(*brouiller* f. Rom. **brodiculare*)]

ėmbrow′n *v.t.* Make brown or dark. [f. EM-¹ + BROWN¹]

ĕ′mbrўō *n.* (*pl.* ~*s*) & *a.* **1.** *n.* Offspring of animal before birth (or emergence from egg); human offspring in first eight weeks from conception; rudimentary plant contained in seed; thing in rudimentary stage (**in** ~, undeveloped); hence **ĕmbrўŏ′n**IC *a.* **2.** *a.* Undeveloped; immature. [LL *embryo -onis* erron. f. Gk EM²-(*bruon* f. *bruō* swell, grow)]

ĕmbrўo- *comb. form.* = prec., as: **~ge′nesis,**

formation of embryo; ~**logy** (-ŏ′l-), science of the embryo. [f. Gk *embruon* (see prec.) + -O-]

||**ėmbŭ′s** *v.t.* & *i.* (-ss-). (Mil. etc.) Put (men, stores) or get into motor vehicle. [f. EM-[1] + BUS, after *embark*]

embusqué (ahṅbōō′skā) *n.* One who avoids military service by obtaining government work etc. [F, p.p. of *embusquer* ambush]

ĕmcee′ *n.* & *v.* (sl.) **1.** *n.* Master of ceremonies; compère of show etc. **2.** *v. t.* & *i.* Act as emcee (of). [f. letters *M.C.*]

-ēme *suf.* (Ling.) forming *ns.* denoting units of structure etc. (*grapheme, morpheme*). [f. F *-ème* unit f. Gk *-ēma*]

ėmĕ′nd *v.t.* (Seek to) remove errors from (text of book etc.); so **ēmĕnd**A′TION, **ē′mĕndāt**OR, *ns.*, ~**at**ORY *a.* [ME, f. L E(*mendare* f. *menda* fault)]

ĕ′merald *n.* Bright-green precious stone, variety of beryl; ~ **(green),** colour of this; **E~ Isle,** Ireland; hence ~INE[1] *a.* [ME, f. OF *e(s)meraude* f. Rom. **smaralda* f. L f. Gk *smaragdos*]

ėmer′g|e *v.i.* Come up out of a liquid; come into view (*from* enclosed space etc.); come out (*from* state of suffering etc.); (of facts etc.) become known as result of inquiry or trial; (of question, difficulty, etc.) crop up; so ~ENCE *n.*, ~ENT *a.*, (esp., of nation) newly independent. [f. L E(*mergere mers-* dip)]

ėmer′gency *n.* & *a.* **1.** *n.* Sudden state of danger etc.; (patient with) condition needing immediate treatment; (Polit.) condition approximating to that of war. **2.** *a.* Used or arising in an emergency. [f. med. L *emergentia* (as prec.; see -ENCY)]

ėmĕ′ritus *a.* Honourably discharged from service; retired and holding honorary title (*emeritus professor, professor emeritus*). [L, p.p. of E(*merēri* earn)]

ĕ′merŏds (-z) *n. pl.* (arch.) Haemorrhoids. [ME var.]

ėmer′sion (-shon) *n.* Emerging; (Astron.) reappearance of celestial body after eclipse or occultation. [f. LL *emersio* (as EMERGE; see -ION)]

ĕ′merў *n.* Coarse corundum used for polishing metal, stones, etc.; **~-board,** emery-coated nail-file; **~-cloth, -paper, -wheel,** (covered with emery powder). [f. F *émeri(l)* f. It. *smeriglio* f. Rom. **smericulum* f. Gk *smiris, smēris* polishing powder]

ėmĕ′tĭc *a.* & *n.* (Medicine) that causes vomiting. [f. Gk *emetikos* (*emeō* vomit; see -ETIC)]

émeute (ĭmū′t) *n.* Popular uprising. [F, f. Rom. **exmovita* (**exmovēre*; cf. EMOTION)]

E.M.F. *abbr.* electromotive force.

***-ē′mĭa.** See -AEMIA.

ĕ′mĭgr|āte *v.* **1.** *v.i.* Leave one country to settle in another. **2.** *v.t.* Assist (person) to emigrate. **3.** Hence or cogn. ~ANT *a.* & *n.*, ~A′TION *n.*, ~**āt**ORY *a.* [f. L E(*migrare* MIGRATE) + -ATE[3]]

émigré (ĕ′mĭgrā) *n.* Emigrant, esp. political exile. [F, p.p. of *émigrer*, = prec.]

ĕ′mĭnence *n.* **1.** Piece of rising ground. **2.** Distinguished superiority (social, intellectual, etc.); important person; (*E~*) cardinal's title. [f. L *eminentia* (as EMINENT; see -ENCE)]

éminence grise (āmēnahṅs grē′z) *n.* Confidential agent, esp. one who exercises power unofficially. [F, = grey cardinal (see prec. 2; orig. applied to Cardinal Richelieu's private secretary, Père Joseph d. 1638)]

ĕ′mĭnent *a.* Exalted, distinguished, (*eminent* DOMAIN); (of qualities) remarkable in degree, whence ~LY[2] *adv.* [ME, f. L *eminēre* jut; see -ENT]

ĕmir′ (-ēr′) *n.* Title of various Muslim rulers; (arch.) male descendant of Muhammad; hence ~ATE[1](1) *n.* [f. F *émir* f. Sp. *emir* f. Arab. *'amir* (cf. AMIR)]

ĕ′mĭssarў *n.* Person sent on special (occas. odious or underhand) mission. [f. L *emissarius* scout, spy (as EMIT; see -ARY[1])]

ėmĭ′ssion (-shon) *n.* Giving off or out (*of* radiation, heat, smell, noise, fluid from body, etc.); thing thus given off or out; so **ėmĭ′ss**IVE *a.*, **ēmĭssĭ′v**ITY *n.*, power of radiating light, heat, etc. [f. L *emissio* (as foll.; see -ION)]

ėmĭ′t *v.t.* (-tt-). Give out, send forth, (stream, light, heat, sound; (arch.) opinion, paper currency, etc.); hence ~**t**ER[1] *n.*, (e.g.) region in transistor producing carriers of current. [f. L E(*mittere miss-* send)]

E′mment(h)al (ĕ′mentahl) *n.* Kind of Swiss cheese with many holes. [f. G *Emmentaler* f. ~ in Switzerland]

ĕ′mmer *n.* Species of wheat (*Triticum dicoccum*). [G dial.]

ĕ′mmėt *n.* (arch. or dial.) Ant. [OE *ǣmete*; see ANT]

***E′mmў** (ĕ′-) *n.* Statuette awarded to outstanding television programme or performer. [perh. f. *Immy* f. *image* (*orthicon tube*) + -Y[3]]

ėmŏ′llient (-lye-) *a.* & *n.* (Substance) that softens skin etc.; soothing (agent). [f. L E(*mollire* f. *mollis* soft); see -ENT]

ėmŏ′lūment *n.* Profit from office or employment, salary. [ME f. OF, or f. L *emolumentum*, orig. prob. 'payment for corn-grinding', f. E(*molere* grind); see -MENT]

ėmō′te *v.i.* Act emotionally. [back form. f. foll.]

ėmō′tion *n.* Disturbance of mind; mental sensation or state; instinctive feeling as opposed to reason; hence ~LESS *a.* [f. F *émotion* (*émouvoir* excite, after *mouvoir* MOVE[2], *motion* MOTION[1])]

ėmō′tional *a.* Of or relating to the emotions; expressing emotion; liable to excessive emotion, whence ~ISM (1), ~IST (2), ~ITY (-ă′l-), *ns.*, ~IZE (3) *v.t.*, ~LY[2] *adv.* [f. prec. + -AL]

ėmō′tĭve *a.* Of emotion; tending to excite emotion; arousing feeling, not purely descriptive; hence ~LY[2] (-vlĭ) *adv.*, **ēmōtĭ′v**ITY *n.* [f. L E(*movēre mot-* MOVE[2]); see -IVE]

ėmpă′nel, ĭm-, *v.t.* (||-ll-). Enter on panel, enrol, (jury). [f. AF EM[1](*paneller* f. as PANEL[1])]

ėmpă′radise. Var. of IMPARADISE.

ĕ′mpath|ў *n.* (Psych.) Power of projecting one's personality into (and so fully comprehending) object of contemplation; hence ~E′TIC, **ĕmpă′th**IC, *adjs.*, ~IST (2) *n.*, ~IZE (1, 2) *v.t.* & *i.* (*with*). [transl. G *einfühlung* (*ein* in, *fühlung* feeling), after Gk *empatheia* (as EM-[2]; see SYMPATHY)]

ĕmpĕ′nnage *n.* (Aeron.) Arrangement of stabilizing surfaces at tail of aircraft. [F (*empenner* feather (an arrow); cf. -AGE)]

ĕ′mperor *n.* (*fem.* EMPRESS). Sovereign of higher rank than king; sovereign of an empire; **~ penguin,** largest known species of penguin, confined to Antarctic; PURPLE *emperor*; hence ~SHIP *n.* [ME, f. OF *emperere, empereor*, f. L *imperator -oris* f. IM[1](*perare* = *parare* prepare, order) command; see -OR]

ĕ′mperў *n.* (poet.) Dominion(s). [ME f. OF *emperie*, f. L (as EMPIRE)]

ĕ′mphas|ĭs *n.* (*pl.* ~es *pr.* -ēz). Stress laid on word(s) to indicate special meaning or importance; vigour or intensity of expression, feeling, action, etc.; importance assigned to fact, idea, etc.; prominence, sharpness of contour. [L f. Gk f. EM[2](*phainō* show) exhibit]

ĕ′mphasīze, -īse (-īz), *v.t.* Lay stress on (word in speaking); bring (fact etc.) into special prominence. [f. prec. + -IZE]

ėmphă'tĭc *a.* (Of language, tone, gesture) forcibly expressive; (of words) bearing the stress; (of person) expressing himself with emphasis; (of action or process) forcible, significant; hence ~ICALLY *adv.* [f. LL f. Gk *emphatikos* (as EMPHASIS; see -IC)]

ĕmphȳsē'ma *n.* (Path.) Enlargement of air vesicles of the lungs; swelling caused by presence of air in connective tissues of body. [LL, f. Gk *emphusēma* (*emphusaō* puff up)]

ĕ'mpīre *n.* Supreme and extensive (political) dominion; (arch.) absolute control (*over*); (period of) government in which sovereign is called emperor; territory of an emperor; (Hist.) **the E~,** (usu.) British Empire or Holy Roman Empire; large commercial organization etc. owned or directed by one person or group; **~-builder,** one who deliberately acquires extra territory, authority, etc., esp. unnecessarily; **E~ Day,** former name of COMMONWEALTH *Day*, orig. 24 May; ***E~ City, State,** (of New York); (*attrib.*, *E~*) denoting a style of furniture or dress fashionable during the first (1804–14) or second (1852–70) French Empire, or ||wine etc. from the Commonwealth. [ME f. OF, f. L *imperium* conn. w. *imperare*; see EMPEROR]

ėmpĭ'rĭc *a.* & *n.* **1.** *a.* = foll.; hence ~ISM (3), ~IST (2), *ns.* **2.** *n.* (arch.) Person relying solely on experiment; quack doctor. [f. L f. Gk *empeirikos* (*empeiria* experience f. *empeiros* skilled; see -IC)]

ėmpĭ'rĭcal *a.* Based or acting on observation or experiment, not on theory; regarding sense-data as valid information; deriving knowledge from experience alone; ~ **formula,** (Chem.) formula showing constituents of a compound but not their configuration; hence ~LY² *adv.* [f. prec. + -AL]

ėmplā'cement (-sm-) *n.* Situation; placing; platform for gun(s). [F (as EM-¹, PLACE¹, -MENT)]

ėmplā'ne *v.i.* & *t.* Go or put on board aeroplane. [f. EM-¹ + PLANE³]

ėmploy' *v.t.*, & *n.* **1.** *v.t.* Use (thing, one's power, time, etc., *for*, *in*, *on*, a purpose); use services of (person); keep (person) in one's service; busy, keep occupied, (one*self*, others, do*ing*, *in*, etc.); hence ~ABLE *a.*, ~ER¹ *n.* **2.** *n.* Being employed, esp. for wages; **in the ~ of,** employed by. [ME, f. OF *employer* f. Rom. *implicare* f. L *implicari* be involved (*implicare* enfold; see IMPLICATE¹)]

employé (ŏmploi'ā) *n.* (*fem.* **-ée** *pr.* same). = foll. [F, p.p. of *employer* (as prec.)]

ėmployee', *ėmployē', (*or* -oi'ē) *n.* Person employed for wages. [f. EMPLOY + -EE]

ėmploy'ment *n.* In vbl senses; one's regular trade or profession; ~ **agency,** business that finds employers or employees for those seeking them; ~ **exchange,** State office performing similar function; **full ~,** condition in which there is no idle capital or labour of kind that is in demand. [f. EMPLOY + -MENT]

ėmpoi'son (-z-) *v.t.* (arch. or literary). Put poison into; taint; (fig.) corrupt; embitter (feelings). [ME, f. OF EM¹(*poisonner* POISON)]

ėmpō'lder. Var. of IMPOLDER.

ĕmpōrĭ|um *n.* (*pl.* **~ums** *or* **~a**). Centre of commerce, market; shop. [f. L f. Gk *emporion* (*emporos* merchant)]

ėmpow'er *v.t.* Authorize, license, (person *to* do); give power to, make able, (person *to* do). [f. EM-¹ + POWER]

ĕ'mprėss *n.* Wife of emperor; woman emperor. [ME, f. OF *emperesse* fem. of *emperere* EMPEROR; see -ESS¹]

empressement (ahṅprĕ'smahṅ) *n.* Display of cordiality or eagerness. [F]

ĕmprī'se (-z) *n.* (arch.) (Chivalrous) enterprise. [ME f. OF, f. Rom. **imprensa*, fem. p.p. (as n.) of *IM¹(*pre(he)ndere* take)]

ĕ'mptȳ¹ *a.* & *n.* **1.** Containing nothing (**on an ~ stomach,** after not having eaten for some time); devoid *of* (qualities); (colloq.) hungry; (of house etc.) devoid of furniture or occupants; (of van, ship, etc.) without load; foolish, unsatisfactory; meaningless. **2.** *n.* Empty truck, bottle, box, etc., after removal of contents. **3. ~-handed,** bringing no gift, carrying nothing away; **~-headed,** lacking common sense. **4.** Hence **ĕ'mptĭ**LY² *adv.*, **ĕ'mptĭ**NESS *n.* [OE *ǣm(e)tig* (*ǣmetta* leisure; see -Y²)]

ĕ'mptȳ² *v.* **1.** *v.t.* Remove contents of (vessel etc.), deprive (vessel etc.) *of* its contents; transfer (contents of one thing *into* etc. another). **2.** *v.i.* (Of river) discharge itself (*into*); become empty. [f. prec.]

ėmpûr'ple *v.t.* Make purple, redden. [f. EM-¹ + PURPLE]

ĕmpȳē'ma *n.* (Path.) Collection of pus in cavity, esp. in pleura. [LL, f. Gk *empuēma* (EM²*pueō* suppurate f. *puon* pus)]

ĕmpȳrē'an *a.* & *n.* (Of) the highest heaven, as the sphere of fire in ancient cosmology or as the abode of God; (of) the visible heavens; so **ĕmpȳ'rė**AL (*or* -ē'al) *a.* [f. med. L *empyreus* f. Gk EM²(*purios* f. *pur* fire) + -EAN]

ē'mū *n.* Large flightless fast-running Australian bird allied to the cassowary. [earlier *emia*, *eme*, f. Port. *ema*]

e.m.u. *abbr.* electromagnetic unit(s).

ĕ'mūl|āte *v.t.* Try to equal or excel; rival; imitate zealously; hence or cogn. ~A'TION, **~āt**OR, *ns.*, **~āt**IVE *a.* [f. L *aemulari* (as foll.) + -ATE³]

ĕ'mūlous *a.* Eagerly or jealously imitative (*of*); actuated by spirit of rivalry; hence ~LY² *adv.* [ME, f. L *aemulus* rival + -OUS]

ėmŭ'lsĭ|fȳ *v.t.* Convert into an emulsion; hence **~fī**ABLE *a.*, ~FICA'TION, **~fī**ER¹ (1, 2), *ns.* [f. as foll. + -FY]

ėmŭ'lsion (-shon) *n.* Fine dispersion of one liquid in another, esp. as paint, medicine, etc.; (Photog.) mixture of silver compound suspended in gelatin etc. for coating plates or films; hence or cogn. ~IZE (3) *v.t.*, **ėmŭ'ls**IVE *a.* [f. F *émulsion* or f. mod. L *emulsio* f. E(*mulgēre muls-* to milk); see -ION]

ĕn *n.* (Print.) Unit of width, half an EM; *en* QUADRAT, RULE. [name of letter *N*]

en-¹ *pref.* = IN-¹, forming *vbs.* (1) f. *ns.*, w. sense 'put into or on' (*enamour*, *embed*, *engulf*, *entrust*), (2) f. *ns.* or *adjs.*, w. sense 'bring into condition of' (*enslave*), often w. *suf.* -EN⁶ (*embolden*, *enlighten*), (3) f. *vbs.*, w. sense 'in, into, on' (*enfold*) or intensively (*entangle*). [f. or after F *en-* f. L *in-*]

en-² *pref.* In, inside, (*energy*, *enthusiasm*). [Gk]

-en¹, -n¹, *suf.* forming *p.p.* of strong *vbs.* (*spoken*, *sworn*), sometimes w. only restricted use (*drunken*, *gotten*); cf. -ED¹ (2). [OE, = OS, OHG *-an*, ON *-inn*, *-enn*, Goth. *-ans*]

-en² *suf.* forming dims. of *ns.* (*chicken*, *maiden*). [f. Gmc *-*īnam*, neut. of *-*īnaz* -EN⁵]

-en³ *suf.* forming *fem. ns.* (*vixen*), or abstract *ns.* (*burden*). [f. WG *-*innja* f, Gmc *-*inī*]

-en⁴ *suf.* forming *pl. ns.* (*children*, *oxen*). [orig. part of stem in weak-decl. nouns, but retained only in *pl.*, and added to other plurals (*children* earlier *childer*). [ME, f. OE *-an*]

-en⁵, -n², *suf.* forming *adjs.* f. *ns.*, usu. expr. material (*wooden*); often arch. (*silvern*) or metaph. (*golden*). [f. Gmc *-*īnaz*]

-en⁶ *suf.* forming *vbs.* f. *adjs.* (*deepen*, *fasten*, *moisten*) or f. *ns.* (*happen*, *heighten*, *hearten*, *listen*). [f. or after OE *-an*]

ėnā'bl|e *v.t.* Authorize, empower, (person *to* do); supply (person etc.) with means *to* (do); make possible; **~ing act,** statute empowering person or body to take certain action, *statute legalizing something otherwise unlawful. [ME, f. EN-¹ + ABLE]

ėnă'ct *v.t.* **1.** Ordain, decree, (thing, *that*); make (bill etc.) a law; hence ~ION, ~MENT, *ns.*, ~IVE, ~ORY, *adjs.* **2.** Play (scene, part, on stage or in life). [ME, f. EN-¹ + ACT¹,²]

ėnă'mel¹ *n.* Glasslike opaque or semi-transparent coating of metallic surfaces for ornament or as preservative lining (also fig.); smooth hard coating, cosmetic simulating this; hard glossy natural coating of teeth; painting done in enamel; (poet.) smooth bright surface colouring, verdure, etc. [ME, f. foll.]

ėnă'mel² *v.t.* (||**-ll-**). Inlay, encrust, (metal etc.) with enamel; portray (figures etc.) with enamel; (arch.) adorn with varied colours. [ME, f. AF EN¹*ameler*, *-amailler*, f. OF *esmail* f. Gmc **smalt-*]

ėnă'mour (-mer), ***ėnă'mor,** *v.t.* (esp. in *p.p.*) Inspire with love or liking (*of*); charm, delight. [ME, f. OF EN¹(*amourer* f. AMOUR love)]

ĕnanthē'ma *n.* (Path.) Disease with eruptions on mucosa. [mod. L, f. Gk EN²*anthēma* eruption (as EXANTHEMA)]

ĕnă'ntĭomŏrph *n.* Mirror image, form (esp. crystal) related to another as an object is to its image in a mirror; hence ~IC, ~OUS, (-ŏr'-) *adjs.*, ~ISM (2) (-ŏr'-) *n.* [G, f. Gk *enantios* opposite + *morphē* form]

ĕnarthrō's|is *n.* (*pl.* **~es** *pr.* -ēz). (Anat.) Ball-and-socket joint. [Gk, f. EN²(*arthros* f. *arthron* joint); see -OSIS]

en attendant (ahn attah'ndahn) *adv.* While waiting. [F]

en bloc (ahn blŏ'k) *adv.* In a block, wholesale, all at the same time. [F]

en brosse (ahn brŏ's) *a.* (Of hair) cut short and bristly. [F]

ĕncae'nĭa (-sē'n-) *n.* Dedication festival; ||(Oxf. Univ.) = COMMEMORATION. [L, f. Gk *egkainia* (EN-², *kainos* new)]

ėncā'ge (ĭn-k-) *v.t.* Confine (as) in cage. [f. EN-¹ + CAGE]

ėncă'mp (ĭn-k-) *v.t.* & *i.* Settle in military camp; lodge in the open in tents. [f. EN-¹ + CAMP¹]

ėncă'mpment (ĭn-k-) *n.* In vbl senses; place where troops etc. are encamped. [f. prec. + -MENT]

ėncă'psūl|āte (ĭn-k-) *v.t.* Enclose (as) in a capsule; (fig.) summarize or isolate as if in capsule; hence ~A'TION *n.* [f. EN-¹ + L *capsula* CAPSULE + -ATE³]

ėncā'se (ĭn-k-) *v.t.* Put into a case; surround as with a case; hence ~MENT (-sm-) *n.* [f. EN-¹ + CASE²]

||**ėncă'sh** (ĭn-k-) *v.t.* Convert (bills etc.) into cash; receive in form of cash, realize; hence ~ABLE *a.*, ~MENT *n.* [f. EN-¹ + CASH¹]

ėncau'stĭc (ĭn-k-) *a.* & *n.* (Painting, art of painting) by burning-in wax paint etc.; **~ brick, tile,** (inlaid with differently coloured clays burnt in). [f. L f. Gk *egkaustikos* (as EN-², CAUSTIC)]

-ence *suf.* forming *ns.* of quality (or instance of it) (*congruence*, *sapience*; *an impertinence*) or action (*reference*, *reminiscence*). [f. or after F *-ence* f. L *-entia*, *-antia* (cf. -ANCE) f. part. st. *-ent-*, *-ant-*]

enceinte (ahnsă'nt) *a.* & *n.* **1.** *a.* (arch.) (Of woman) pregnant. **2.** *n.* Enclosure (in fortification). [F, 1 f. med. L IN²*cincta* ungirded, 2 f. L IN¹*cincta* girded in; cf. CINCTURE]

ĕncėphă'lĭc (*or* ĕn-k-) *a.* Of the brain. [f. Gk *egkephalos* brain (as EN-², *kephalē* head) + -IC]

ĕncĕphalī'tĭs (*or* ĕn-k-) *n.* Inflammation of the brain; **~ lethargica,** infectious encephalitis caused by virus, usu. with extreme drowsiness, sleepy sickness. [f. as prec. + -ITIS]

ĕncĕ'phalo- (*or* ĕn-k-) *comb. form.* Brain, as: **~gram,** X-ray photograph of the brain; **~graph,** instrument for recording electrical activity of brain. [f. Gk *egkephalos* brain (see ENCEPHALIC) + -O-]

ėnchai'n *v.t.* Chain up, fetter; hold fast (attention, emotions); hence ~MENT *n.* [ME, f. F *enchaîner* f. Gallo-Rom. *IN¹(*catenare* f. L *catena* chain)]

ėncha'nt (-ah'-) *v.t.* Bewitch (lit. or fig.); charm, delight; hence or cogn. ~ER¹, ~MENT, ~RESS¹, *ns.*; *enchanter's* NIGHTSHADE. [ME, f. F *enchanter* f. L IN¹(*cantare* frequent. of *canere cant-* sing)]

ėnchā'se *v.t.* Place (jewel) *in* setting; set (gold etc.) *with* gems; inlay with gold etc.; adorn with figures in relief; engrave; enclose. [ME, f. F *enchâsser* (as EN-¹, CHASE⁵)]

ĕnchĭla'da (-ah'-) *n.* Tortilla with meat etc. and chilli sauce. [Amer. Sp., fem. p.p. (as n.) of *enchilar* season with chilli]

ĕnchīrī'dĭon (ĕn-k-) *n.* Handbook. [f. LL f. Gk *egkheiridion* (as EN-², *kheir* hand, *-idion* dim. suf.)]

ėncī'pher *v.t.* Write (message etc.) in cipher. [f. EN-¹ + CIPHER¹]

ėncīr'cle *v.t.* Surround, encompass, (*with*); form a circle round; hence ~MENT (-kelm-) *n.* (esp. by supposedly hostile nations). [ME, f. EN-¹ + CIRCLE¹]

encl. *abbr.* enclosed; enclosure.

en clair (ahn klār') *a.* & *adv.* (Of telegram, official message, etc.) in ordinary language (not in code or cipher). [F, lit. 'in clear']

ėncla'sp (ĭn-klah'-) *v.t.* Hold in clasp or embrace. [f. EN-¹ + CLASP¹,²]

ĕ'nclāve (ĕ'n-k-) *n.* Foreign territory surrounded by one's own territory. [F, f. *enclaver* f. Rom. *IN¹(*clavare* f. *clavis* key)]

ĕnclĭ't|ĭc (ĕn-k-) *a.* & *n.* (Gram.) (Word) so unemphatic as to be pronounced as if part of preceding word, e.g. *not* in *cannot*, *-que* in L *virginibus puerisque*; hence ~ICALLY *adv.* [f. LL f. Gk *egklitikos* (EN-², *klinō* lean; see -IC)]

ėnclō'se, ĭnclō'se, (ĭn-klō'z) *v.t.* Surround, fence in, (land etc. *with*, *in*, walls etc.; esp. of common land, see foll.); shut up in receptacle (esp. something besides letter in envelope); bound on all sides, contain, (esp. Math.); hem in on all sides; seclude (religious community) from the outside world. [ME, f. OF *enclos* p.p. of *enclore* f. Rom. **inclaudere* f. L (as INCLUDE)]

ėnclō'sure (ĭn-klō'zher) *n.* Enclosing (esp. of common land, to make it private property); enclosing fence etc.; enclosed place, esp. for special class of persons at racecourse; paper etc. enclosed with letter in envelope. [AF & OF (as prec.; see -URE)]

ėncō'd|e (ĭn-k-) *v.t.* Write (message etc.) in code or cipher; hence ~ER¹ *n.* [f. EN-¹ + CODE 2]

ĕncō'mĭăst (ĕn-k-) *n.* Composer of an encomium; flatterer; so ~IC (-ă'-) *a.* [f. Gk *egkōmiastēs* f. as foll.]

ĕncō'mĭ|um (ĕn-k-) *n.* (*pl.* **~ums** *or* **~a**). Formal or high-flown praise. [L, f. Gk *egkōmion* (EN-², *kōmos* revelry)]

ėnco'mpass (ĭn-kŭ'm-) *v.t.* Surround, form circle about, esp. to protect or attack; contain; hence ~MENT *n.* [f. EN-¹ + COMPASS¹]

encore (ŏngkōr'; *or* ŏ'-) *int.*, *n.*, & *v.t.* **1.** *int.* & *n.* (Spectators' or audience's demand for song etc. to be sung etc.) again, once more; further item given in response to such demand. **2.** *v.t.* Call for repetition of (song etc.); summon (performer) for this. [F, = once again]

ėncou'nter (ĭn-k-) *v.t.*, & *n.* **1.** *v.t.* Meet as adversary; meet, esp. by chance or unexpectedly. **2.** *n.* Meeting in combat or by chance. [ME; (n. f. OF *encontre*) f. OF *encontrer* f. Rom. *IN¹(*contrare* f. L *contra* against)]

ėncou'rage (ĭn-kŭ'-) *v.t.* Give courage to; urge, advise, (person *to* do); stimulate by help, reward, etc.; promote, assist, (commerce, opinion, etc.); hence or cogn. ~MENT (-kŭ'rĭjm-) *n.* [ME, f. F *encourager* (as EN-¹, COURAGE)]

ĕ'ncrĭnīte (ĕ'n-k-) *n.* Fossil crinoid. [f. mod. L *encrinus* f. Gk *en* EN-² + *krinon* lily + -ITE¹]

ėncroa'ch (ĭn-k-) *v.i.* Intrude usurpingly (*on* others' territory, rights, etc., or abs.); (fig.) make gradual inroads *on*; hence ~MENT *n.* [ME, f. OF EN¹(*crochier* f. *croc* hook; see CROOK)]

ėncrŭ'st, ĭncrŭ'st, (ĭn-k-) *v.* **1.** *v.t.* Cover with crust; overlay (surface) with ornamental crust of precious material. **2.** *v.i.* Form into a crust. **3.** Hence ~MENT *n.* [f. F *incruster* f. L IN¹(*crustare* f. *crusta* CRUST)]

encrustation. Var. of INCRUSTATION.

ėncŭ'mber (ĭn-k-) *v.t.* Hamper (person, movement, action, *with* burden, difficulty, etc.); burden (person, estate, *with* debts, esp. mortgages); fill, block, (place *with* lumber etc., lit. or fig.); hence ~MENT *n.* [ME, f. OF *encombrer* block up f. Rom. *IN*combrare*]

ėncŭ'mbrance (ĭn-k-) *n.* Burden; annoyance; impediment (**without ~,** having no children); claim, mortgage, etc., on property. [ME, f. OF *encombrance* (as prec.; see -ANCE)]

-ency̆ *suf.* forming *ns.* denoting quality (*efficiency, fluency*) or state (*presidency*), but not action (cf. -ENCE). [f. L *-entia* (cf. -ANCY)]

ĕncy̆'clĭc(al) *adjs.* & *ns.* (Pope's letter) for extensive circulation. [f. LL *encyclicus* f. Gk *egkuklios* (EN-², *kuklos* circle)]

ĕncy̆clopae'd|ĭa, -pē'd|ĭa, (*or* ĭ-) *n.* Literary work giving information on all branches of knowledge or of one subject, usu. arranged alphabetically; (*E~*; Hist.) *the* French encyclopaedia of Diderot, D'Alembert, and others; WALKING² *encyclopaedia*; hence ~IC *a.*, ~ISM (3), ~IST (3), *ns.* [mod. L, f. spurious Gk *egkuklopaideia* for *egkuklios paideia* all-round education (cf. prec.)]

ėncy̆'st *v.t.* & *i.* Enclose (itself) in a cyst; hence ~A'TION, ~MENT, *ns.* [f. EN-¹ + CYST]

ĕnd¹ *n.* **1.** Extreme limit, point beyond which a thing does not continue; extremity of line, or of greatest dimension of object; farthest point (*to the ends of the earth*); **the ~,** (colloq.) the limit of endurability; ||EAST *End*, WEST *End*; *at* one's *wits' end* (WIT²); WRONG *end of the stick*. **2.** Surface bounding a thing at either extremity, head of cask etc.; remnant (*candle ends, cigarette end*; ODDS *and ends*; ROPE'*s end*); portion, part, side (*no problem at my end*); BIG *end*; LITTLE *end*; *at a* LOOSE¹ *end*. **3.** Half of sports pitch or court occupied by one team or player; (U.S. & Can.) football player at extremity of line or team; (Bowls) unit of play from one side of green towards the other; **deep ~,** end of swimming-pool where water is deeper; **go (in) off the deep ~,** (colloq.) give way to emotion or anger. **4.** Conclusion (of period, action, state, book, etc.; *end of the* WORLD; WORLD *without end*); latter or final part; destruction, downfall, death; ultimate state or condition. **5.** Result, purpose, (*to gain his ends*; *to what end?*); object for which a thing exists. **6. All ~s up,** completely; **at an ~,** exhausted or completed; **come to an ~,** become exhausted, be completed or finished; **come to a bad ~,** meet with ruin or disgrace; **~ for ~,** so as to interchange position of ends; *end of* one's TETHER; **~ on,** with end facing one, or with end adjoining end of next object etc.; **~ to ~,** lengthwise continuously; **in the ~,** finally, after all; **keep** one's **~ up,** sustain one's part in undertaking or performance; **make an ~ of,** put a stop to; **make (both) ~s meet,** live within one's income; **no ~,** (colloq.) to a great extent; **no ~ of,** (colloq.) much or many of; **on ~,** (1) (place, stand) upright, (2) continuously (*for three weeks on end*); **put an ~ to,** stop, abolish, destroy; **~ of the road,** (fig.) point at which survival etc. becomes impossible; WITHOUT *end*. **7. ~-game,** final stage of game in chess, bridge, etc., when few men or cards remain; **~-man,** CORNER-*man*²; **~-note,** note put at end of book, chapter, etc.; **~-paper,** blank leaf at beginning or end of book; **~-play,** (Bridge) method of play in last few tricks to force opponent to make disadvantageous lead; **~-point,** final stage of process, esp. point at which effect is observed in titration, dilution, etc.; **~-product,** final product of manufacture, radioactive decay, etc.; **~-stopped,** (of verse) having pause at end of each line. [OE *ende*, = OS *endi*, OHG *enti*, ON *endi(r)*, Goth. *andeis* f. Gmc **andja-* f. IE **antjó*]

ĕnd² *v.* **1.** *v.t.* Bring (action, speech, life, etc.) to an end; put an end to, destroy; **~ it (all),** (colloq.) commit suicide. **2.** *v.i.* Come to an end; **~ by doing,** eventually do (*will end by marrying a millionaire*); result *in*; **~ up,** conclude, finish, arrive finally. [OE *endian*, = OS *endion*, OHG *entōn*, ON *enda*, f. as prec.]

-ĕnd *suf.* See -ND¹.

ėndă'mage *v.t.* = DAMAGE. [ME, f. EN-¹ + DAMAGE, or f. OF **endamagier*]

ėndā'nger (-nj-) *v.t.* Cause danger to; hence ~MENT *n.* [ME, f. EN-¹ + DANGER]

ėndear' *v.t.* Render (person, thing, one*self*) dear (*to*); hence ~ING² *a.*, inspiring affection, ~MENT *n.*, (esp.) action or utterance expressing affection. [f. EN-¹ + DEAR]

ėndea'vour, *-vor, (-dĕ'ver) *v.* & *n.* **1.** *v.t.* & *i.* Try (*to* do); (arch.) strive *after*. **2.** *n.* Attempt (*to* do, *at* doing). [ME, f. *put oneself in* DEVOIR]

ĕndĕ'm|ĭc *a.* & *n.* **1.** *a.* Regularly or only found among (specified) people or in (specified) country; hence ~ICALLY *adv.*, **ĕndėmĭ'city** *n.* = foll. **2.** *n.* Endemic disease or plant. [f. F *endémique* or mod. L *endemicus* f. Gk *endēmos* native (as EN-², *dēmos* the people); see -IC]

ĕ'ndėmĭsm *n.* Character of quality of being endemic. [f. prec. + -ISM]

ĕndėr̄'mĭc *a.* Acting on or through the skin. [f. EN-² + Gk *derma* skin + -IC]

ĕ'ndĭng *n.* In vbl senses; latter or final part (of word, story, etc.). [OE (as END¹, -ING¹)]

ėndĭ'stance *v.t.* (Theatr. etc.) Produce alienation of (audience). [f. EN-¹ + DISTANCE]

ĕ'ndīve *n.* Salad plant (*Cichorium endivia*); *chicory crown. [ME f. OF, f. LL *endivia* f. med. Gk *indibi* f. L *intibum* f. Gk *entubon*]

ĕ'ndlėss *a.* Infinite; eternal; incessant; (colloq.) innumerable; **~ band, belt, cable, chain,** etc., (with ends joined for continuous action over wheels etc.); **~ screw,** short length of screw revolving to turn cog-wheel; hence ~LY² *adv.*, ~NESS *n.* [OE *endelēas* (as END¹, -LESS)]

ĕ'ndmōst *a.* Nearest the end. [f. END¹, after *hindmost*]

ĕ'ndō- *comb. form.* Internal, as; **~car'dium,** lining membrane of heart; **~cardī'tis,** inflammation of this; **~carp,** innermost layer of pericarp; **~crine** (-krīn), (of gland) secreting directly into the blood, ductless [Gk *krinō* sift]; **~derm,** (Biol.) innermost layer of embryo in early development; **~gamous, ~gamy,** (-ŏ'g-), (of) marrying within the tribe,

(Bot.) (of) pollination from same plant; **~gen,** plant that develops wood in interior of stem; **~genous** (-ŏ'j-), growing or originating from within; **~lymph,** fluid in membranous labyrinth of ear; **~me'trium, ~metri'tis,** (inflammation of) lining membrane of womb; **~morph,** mineral enclosed in another, person of pyknic build; **~pa'rasite,** internal parasite; **~plasm,** inner fluid layer of cytoplasm; **~radiosonde,** encapsulated device placed in the body to give radio signals to indicate conditions there; **~scope,** instrument for viewing internal parts of body; **~skeleton,** internal skeleton, as of vertebrates etc.; **~sperm,** albumen enclosed with germ in seeds; **~spore,** inner coat of spore, spore formed in a case; **~the'lium,** layer of cells lining blood-vessels etc.; **~ther'mic,** occurring or formed with absorption of heat. [f. Gk *endon* within + -o-]

ėndor̂'se, ĭndor̂'se, *v.t.* **1.** Write on back of (document), esp. sign one's name on back of (bill, cheque, etc.); write (explanation, comment, *on* back of document); transfer one's rights in (bill, etc. *to* another person). **2.** Confirm (statement, opinion); declare one's approval of. **3.** ‖Make official entry regarding offence on (motorist's, publican's, licence). **4.** Hence ~MENT (-sm-) *n.* [f. med. L IN[1](*dorsare* f. *dorsum* back)]

ėndow' *v.t.* Bequeath or give permanent income to (person, institution); invest (person) *with* (privileges etc.); (esp. in *p.p.*) furnish (person) *with* (ability etc.). [ME, f. AF *endouer* f. *en* EN-[1] + OF *douer* f. L *dotare* (*dos dotis* DOWER)]

ėndow'ment *n.* Act of endowing; property etc. with which person or body is endowed; talent etc. with which person is endowed; ~ **assurance** or **insurance,** form of life insurance with payment of fixed sum to insured person on specified date, or to his estate on earlier death. [f. prec. + -MENT]

ėndūe', ĭndūe', *v.t.* Put on (clothes etc., lit. or fig.); clothe (person) *with*; (usu. in *pass.*) furnish (person *with* powers, qualities, etc.). [ME, f. OF *enduire* f. L IN[1](*ducere* lead, draw), assoc. in sense w. L *induere* put on (clothes)]

ėndūr'ance *n.* Habit or power of enduring (*beyond endurance*); act of enduring; ability to withstand prolonged strain (*endurance test*). [OF (*endurer*; see foll., -ANCE)]

ėndūr'|e *v.* **1.** *v.t.* Undergo (pain etc.); tolerate (*cannot endure that fellow*); submit to; (esp. w. neg.) bear *to* do; hence ~ABLE *a.* **2.** *v.i.* Remain in existence, last. [ME, f. OF *endurer* f. L IN[1](*durare* harden f. *durus* hard)]

ĕ'ndways, ĕ'ndwīse, (-z) *adv.* With its end turned towards the spectator or uppermost or foremost; end to end. [f. END[1] + -WAYS, -WISE]

-ēne *suf.* **1.** (Chem.) Forming names of unsaturated hydrocarbons (*benzene*, *ethylene*). **2.** Forming names of natives or inhabitants of places (*Cairene*, *Gadarene*, *Nazarene*). [f. or after Gk *-ēnos*]

E.N.E. *abbr.* east-north-east.

ĕ'nėma (*or* ĭnē'-) *n.* (*pl.* **~s,** *or* **~ta** *pr.* ĭnĕ'mata). Injection of liquid or gas into rectum esp. to expel its contents; fluid or syringe so used. [LL, f. Gk *enema* (EN[2]*iēmi* inject f. *hiēmi* send)]

ĕ'nemy̆ *n.* & *a.* **1.** *n.* Person who hates one and eagerly seeks one's defeat etc.; opponent (*of*, *to*, another; **the E~,** the Devil); member of hostile army or nation; hostile force or ship; thing that harms or injures; **how goes the ~?,** (colloq.) what is the time?; **be** one's **own worst ~, be nobody's ~ but** one's **own,** be responsible for one's own misfortunes. **2.** *a.* Of or belonging to the enemy (*enemy ships*, *aircraft*, *alien*; *destroyed by enemy action*). [ME, f. OF *enemi* f. L IN[2](*imicus* = *amicus* friend)]

ĕnergĕ't|ĭc *a.* & *n.* Strenuously active; forcible, vigorous; powerfully operative; hence ~ICS *n.*, science of energy, ~ICALLY *adv.* [f. Gk *energētikos* f. EN[2](*ergeō* f. *ergon* work); see -IC]

ĕ'nergīze, -īse (-īz), *v.* **1.** *v.t.* Infuse energy into (person, work); provide energy for operation of (device). **2.** *v.i.* (arch.) Be in active operation. [f. ENERGY + -IZE]

ĕnẽrgū'mĕn *n.* Demoniac; enthusiast, fanatic. [f. LL f. Gk *energoumenos* p.p. of *energeō* (see ENERGETIC)]

ĕ'nergy̆ *n.* **1.** Force, vigour, (of speech, action, person, etc.); active operation; (in *pl.*) individual powers in use (*devote your energies to this*); (arch.) (latent) ability. **2.** (Phys.) Ability of matter or radiation to do work; CONSERVATION *of energy*; **kinetic ~,** body's ability to do work by virtue of its motion; **mass** or **rest ~,** body's ability to do work by virtue of its mass, released in nuclear fission etc.; **potential ~,** body's ability to do work by virtue of its position relative to others, stresses within itself, electric charge, etc. [f. F *énergie* or f. LL f. Gk EN[2]*ergeia* (*ergon* work; see -Y[1])]

ėnẽr'vate[1] *a.* Lacking (physical, moral, literary, artistic) vigour. [f. L *enervatus* p.p. of E(*nervare* f. *nervus* sinew); see -ATE[2]]

ĕ'nerv|āte[2] *v.t.* Weaken (physically etc., as prec.); so ~A'TION *n.* [f. as prec. + -ATE[3]]

en face (ahṅ fah's) *a.* Facing forwards; on facing page of book etc. [F, = opposite]

en famille (ahṅ fămē'ye) *adv.* At home; in or with one's family. [F, = in family]

enfant gâté (ahṅfahṅ gah'tā) *n.* Person given undue flattery or indulgence. [F, = spoilt child]

enfant terrible (ahṅfahṅ tĕrē'bl) *n.* Child who asks awkward questions, embarrassingly repeats what he has heard, etc.; (fig.) person or thing causing embarrassment by unruliness. [F, = terrible child]

ėnfee'ble *v.t.* Make feeble; hence ~MENT (-belm-) *n.* [ME, f. OF EN[1](*feblir* f. *feble* FEEBLE)]

ėnfeo'ff (-fē'f) *v.t.* Invest (person) with FEUD[2]; (arch., fig.) surrender; hence ~MENT *n.* [ME, f. AF *enfeoffer*, OF *enfeffer* (as EN-[1], FIEF)]

en fête (ahṅ fā't) *adv.* & *pred. a.* Engaged in, attired etc. for, holiday-making. [F, = in festival]

ėnfĕ'tter *v.t.* Bind in fetters (lit. or fig.); enslave (person *to*). [f. EN-[1] + FETTER]

ĕnfĭlā'de *n.*, & *v.t.* **1.** *n.* Fire from guns etc. sweeping line from end to end. **2.** *v.t.* Subject (troops, road, etc.) to enfilade. [F, f. EN[1](*filer* f. *fil* thread); see -ADE]

ėnfō'ld *v.t.* Wrap up (person etc. *in*, *with*); clasp, embrace; shape into folds. [f. EN-[1] + FOLD[1,2]]

ėnfor̂'ce *v.t.* Urge, press home, (argument, demand); impose (action, conduct, (*up*)*on* person etc.); compel observance of (law etc.); hence or cogn. ~ABLE (-sa-) *a.*, ~MENT (-sm-) *n.* [ME, f. OF *enforci(e)r* f. Rom. *IN[1](*forti(a)re* f. L *fortis* strong)]

ėnfrā'nch|īse (-z) *v.t.* Invest (town) with municipal rights, esp. that of representation in parliament; admit (person) to electoral franchise; release (slave, villein, etc.) from bondage; hence **~īse**MENT (-zm-) *n.* [f. OF EN[1](*franchir* f. *franc franche* FRANK[2]); see -ISH[2]]

ėngā'ge (ĭn-g-) *v.* **1.** *v.t.* Bind by contract (*to* perform, lecture, etc.). **2.** Bind by promise (esp. of marriage). **3.** Hire (servant, employee); arrange beforehand to occupy (seat, cab, etc.). **4.** (Archit.) Fasten (pillar) into wall; (Mech.) interlock (thing *with* another), cause (part) to interlock thus; (of fencers etc.) interlock (weapons, or abs.). **5.** Hold fast (attention); (usu. in *pass.*) employ busily. **6.** Bring (troops) into conflict; enter into conflict with (enemy etc.). **7.** *v.i.* Take part *in* (politics etc.). **8.** Pledge oneself (*to* do, *that*); ~ **for,** (arch.) guarantee, promise. **9.** (Of mechanical part) interlock *with* another; (of troops etc.) come into conflict *with* enemy etc. [f. F *engager* f. Rom. *IN¹(*wadiare* f. **wadium* GAGE¹)]

engagé (ahngah'zhā) *a.* (Of writer etc.) morally committed. [F, p.p. of *engager* (see prec.)]

ėngā'ged (ĭn-gā'jd) *a.* In vbl senses; under promise to marry; occupied by person, with business, etc.; (of telephone line) unavailable because already in use (~ **signal** etc., indicating this condition); = prec. [p.p. of ENGAGE]

ėngā'gement (ĭn-gā'jm-) *n.* Action of engaging; state of being engaged; appointment made with another person; moral commitment; battle; ~ **ring,** finger-ring given by man to woman when they promise to marry. [F (*engager*; see ENGAGE)]

ėngā'gĭng (ĭn-g-) *a.* In vbl senses; attractive, charming; hence ~LY² *adv.* [f. ENGAGE + -ING²]

en garçon (ahn gar'sawn) *adv.* & *pred. a.* As a bachelor. [F]

ėngar'land (ĭn-g-) *v.t.* Put a garland on; wreathe *with* (flowers etc.). [f. EN-¹ + GARLAND]

ėngĕ'nder (ĭnj-) *v.t.* Give rise to, bring about; (arch.) beget (lit. or fig.). [ME, f. OF *engendrer* f. L IN¹(*generare* GENERATE)]

ĕ'ngĭne (ĕ'nj-) *n.*, & *v.t.* **1.** *n.* Mechanical contrivance consisting of several parts working together, esp. as source of power; = STEAM¹-*-engine*, locomotive; FIRE¹-*engine*. **2.** (arch.) Machine or instrument used in war; instrument, means. **3.** ~**-driver** (of engine, esp. railway locomotive); ~**-room,** room containing engines (esp. of ship); ~**-turning,** engraving of symmetrical patterns on metals by machine. **4.** *v.t.* Fit (ship etc.) with engine(s). [f. OF *engin* f. L *ingenium* talent, device (cf. INGENIOUS)]

ĕngĭneer'¹ (ĕnj-) *n.* **1.** One who designs and constructs military works; soldier trained for this purpose (ROYAL *Engineers*). **2.** **(Civil)** ~, one who designs or maintains works of public utility (roads, bridges, canals, gas-works, etc.). **3.** Maker of engines. **4.** One who works in a branch of engineering (*chemical, electrical, mechanical, engineer*), esp. as qualified professional. **5.** One who has charge of engine; *engine--driver. **6.** Person with special skill in treatment of human problems (*human engineer*); skilful or artful contriver (*of* plan etc.). **7.** Hence ~SHIP *n.* [ME f. OF *engigneor* f. med. L *ingeniator -oris* (*ingeniare* as ENGINE; see -OR); ending later assim. to -EER]

ĕngĭneer'² (ĕnj-) *v.* **1.** *v.i.* Act as engineer. **2.** *v.t.* Construct, manage, (bridge, work, etc.) as engineer; (colloq.) arrange, contrive, bring about, esp. artfully. [f. prec.]

ĕngĭneer'ĭng (ĕnj-) *n.* Application of science for the control and use of power, esp. by means of machines; ~ **science,** engineering as a field of study. [f. prec. + -ING¹]

ĕ'ngĭnerў (ĕ'njĭnrĭ) *n.* Engines; machinery (lit. or fig.). [f. ENGINE + -RY]

ėngir'd(le) (ĭn-g-) *vbs. t.* Surround (as) with girdle. [f. EN-¹ + GIRD¹, GIRDLE¹]

E'nglander (ĭ'ngg-) *n.* **Little** ~, (Hist.) one opposed to British imperial policy. [f. *England* + -ER¹]

E'nglĭsh¹ (ĭ'ngg-) *a.* & *n.* **1.** *a.* Of England; ~**man,** ~**woman,** one who is English by birth, descent, or naturalization; EARLY *English*. **2.** Of, written or spoken in, the English language. **3.** *n.* The language of England (now used in U.K., U.S. and in most Commonwealth countries, and often internationally); **the King's, Queen's,** ~, the English language as correctly written or spoken; **Middle** ~ (*c.* 1150–1500); **Old** ~ (before about 1150); **in plain** ~, in plain words. **4.** *(Bill.) = SIDE¹ 12; **the** ~, (*pl.*) people of England. **5.** *English* BOND¹ 5; ~ **flute,** recorder; ~ **horn,** cor anglais; *English* MUSTARD. [OE *englisc*, *ænglisc* (as ANGLE⁴, -ISH¹)]

english² (ĭ'ngg-) *v.t.* (arch. or pedantic). Render into English. [ME, f. prec.]

ėngor'ge (ĭn-g-) *v.t.* Devour greedily; (in *pass.*) be crammed, (Path.) be congested with blood; hence ~MENT (-jm-) *n.* [f. F EN¹(*gorger* GORGE²)]

ėngra'ft, ĭngra'ft, (ĭn-grah'-) *v.t.* Insert (scion of one tree *into, upon,* another); implant (principles etc. *in* the mind etc.); incorporate (thing *into* another). [f. EN-¹, IN-¹ + GRAFT¹]

ėngrai'l (ĭn-g-) *v.t.* Indent the edge of, give serrated appearance to, (esp. Her.). [ME, f. OF EN¹(*gresler* f. *gresle* HAIL¹)]

ėngrai'n (ĭn-g-) *v.t.* (usu. fig.) Cause (dye etc.) to sink deeply into a thing; (in *p.p.*; cf. INGRAINED) inveterate (*an engrained rogue*). [ME, f. OF *engrainer* dye in grain (*en graine*); see GRAIN 4]

ĕ'ngrăm (ĕ'n-g-) *n.* Memory-trace, supposed permanent change in brain accounting for existence of memory; hence ~**ma**'TIC *a.* [f. G *engramm* f. Gk *en* in + *gramma* letter]

en grande tenue (ahn grahnd tenū') *adv.* In full dress. [F]

ėngrā'v|e (ĭn-g-) *v.t.* Inscribe, ornament, (hard surface *with* incised marks); carve (figures etc. *on* surface); (fig.) impress deeply (*on* memory etc.); cut (figures etc.) as lines on metal plates for printing; hence ~ER¹ *n.* [f. EN-¹ + GRAVE²]

ėngrā'vĭng (ĭn-g-) *n.* In vbl senses; copy of picture etc. from engraved plate. [f. prec. + -ING¹]

ėngrō'ss (ĭn-g-) *v.t.* **1.** Write (document) in large letters; express in legal form. **2.** (arch.) Monopolize (conversation etc.). **3.** Fully occupy (person, his attention, time, etc.; esp. in *p.p.*, *engrossed in subject* etc.); hence ~ING² *a.* **4.** Hence ~MENT *n.* [ME, f. AF *engrosser*; 1 f. *en* in, *grosse* large writing; 2, 3 f. *en gros* wholesale]

ėngŭ'lf (ĭn-g-) *v.t.* Plunge into, swallow up (as) in, a gulf; hence ~MENT *n.* [f. EN-¹ + GULF]

ėnha'nce (-hah'-) *v.t.* Heighten, intensify, (qualities, powers, value, etc.); (arch.) exaggerate; hence ~MENT (-sm-) *n.* [ME, f. AF *enhauncer*, prob. alt. f. OF *enhaucier* f. Rom. *IN¹(*altiare* f. L *altus* high)]

ĕnharmŏ'n|ĭc *a.* (Mus.) Of or having intervals smaller than semitone (esp. such intervals as that between G sharp and A flat, these notes being made the same in a scale of equal temperament); hence ~ICALLY *adv.* [f. LL f. Gk EN²*armonikos* (*harmonia* HARMONY; see -IC)]

ėnĭ'gma *n.* Riddle; puzzling person or thing; hence or cogn. **ĕnĭgmă'tic**(AL) *adjs.*, ~**tize** (3) *v.t.* [f. L f. Gk *ainigma -matos* f. *ainissomai* speak allusively (*ainos* fable)]

ėnĭ'sle (-ī'l) *v.t.* (literary). Make into or place on island. [f. EN-¹ + ISLE]

ĕnjă'mbment, -bem-, (-m-m-) *n.* (Pros.) Continuation of sentence beyond end of line, couplet, or stanza. [f. F *enjambement* f. EN¹(*jamber* f. *jambe* leg); see -MENT]

ėnjoi'n *v.t.* Prescribe, impose, (action, conduct, *on* person); command (person *to* do); issue instructions (*that*); (Law) prohibit by injunction (*from* doing). [ME, f. OF *enjoindre* (st. *-joi(g)n-*) f. L IN¹(*jungere* join)]

ėnjoy' *v.t.* Take delight or pleasure in, whence ~ABLE *a.*, ~ABLY *adv.*; have use of (advantages etc.); (arch.) copulate with (woman); experience (*enjoy poor health*); ~ **oneself,** experience pleasure; hence ~MENT *n.* [ME, f. OF EN[1](*joier* f. *joie* JOY[1]) give joy to, (refl.) enjoy, or f. OF EN[1](*joïr* f. L *gaudēre* rejoice)]

ėnki'ndle (ĭn-k-) *v.t.* Cause (flame, passions, war, etc.) to blaze up; inflame with passion. [f. EN-[1] + KINDLE]

ėnlā'ce *v.t.* Encircle tightly; enfold; entwine; hence ~MENT (-sm-) *n.* [ME, f. OF *enlacier* f. Rom. *IN[1](*laciare* f. **lacium* f. L *laqueus* noose)]

ėnlar'ge *v.* **1.** *v.t.* Make larger or wider (lit. or fig.); (Photog.) reproduce on larger scale; (arch.) liberate; hence ~ABLE (-ja-) *a.* **2.** *v.i.* Grow larger; expatiate *upon*. **3.** Hence ~MENT (-jm-) *n.*, (esp.) photographic reproduction on larger scale, **ėnlar'g**ER[1] *n.*, apparatus for enlarging or reducing photographic negatives or positives. [ME, f. OF EN[1](*large*r f. *large* LARGE)]

ėnlī'ghten (-ī't-) *v.t.* Instruct, inform, (person *on* subject); (rhet. or poet.) shed light on (object), give light to (person); (esp. in *p.p.*) free (person) from prejudice or superstition; hence ~MENT *n.* (**the E~ment,** 18th-c. philosophy allegedly placing too much emphasis on reason and individualism against tradition). [ME, f. EN-[1] + LIGHTEN[2]]

ėnlĭ'st *v.* **1.** *v.t.* & *i.* Engage for military service (***~ed man,** soldier or sailor below rank of officer). **2.** *v.t.* Secure as means of help or support. **3.** Hence ~MENT *n.* [f. EN-[1] + LIST[1]]

ėnlī'ven *v.t.* Animate, inspirit, (persons, feelings, trade, etc.); brighten (picture, scene); hence ~MENT *n.* [f. EN-[1] + LIFE + -EN[6]]

en masse (ahṅ mă's) *adv.* In a mass; all together. [F]

ėnmĕ'sh *v.t.* Entangle (as) in a net; hence ~MENT *n.* [f. EN-[1] + MESH[1]]

ĕ'nmĭtȳ *n.* Hatred; state of being an enemy. [ME, f. OF *enemi(s)tié* f. Rom. **inimicitas -tatis* (as ENEMY; see -TY[1])]

ĕ'nnėăd *n.* Group of nine. [f. Gk *enneas enneados* (*ennea* nine; see -AD)]

ėnnō'ble *v.t.* Make (person) a noble; make noble, elevate; hence ~MENT (-belm-) *n.* [f. F EN[1](*noblir*, as NOBLE)]

ennui (ŏ'nwē) *n.* Mental weariness from lack of occupation or interest; so ***ennuyé*** (ŏnwē'yā; *fem.* ***-ée,*** *pl.* ***-és, -ées,*** *pr.* same) *a.* [F, f. L *in odio*; cf. ODIUM]

***ēnŏ'logȳ.** See OENOLOGY.

ėnor'mĭtȳ *n.* Monstrous wickedness; dreadful crime; serious error; enormousness. [ME, f. F *énormité* f. L *enormitas -tatis* (*enormis*; see foll., -ITY)]

ėnor'mous *a.* Very large, huge, (*enormous animal, difference*); hence ~LY[2] *adv.*, ~NESS *n.* [f. L E(*normis* f. *norma* pattern, standard) + -OUS]

ĕ'nosĭs (*or* -ō'-) *n.* Proposed political union of Cyprus and Greece. [f. mod. Gk *henōsis* (*heis hen-* one)]

ėnou'gh (ĭnŭ'f) *a.*, *n.*, & *adv.* Not less than the required number, quantity, degree, as: (a.) *we have apples enough, enough apples, beer enough, enough beer, he made enough noise* (to justify supposition etc.), *enough noise to wake the dead, for his purpose*; (n.) *we have enough of everything except beer, enough of* (stop) *this folly, enough!* (say no more), *enough said* (no more need be said), *enough is as good as a feast, cry 'enough'* (acknowledge defeat), *I have had enough* (am tired) *of him, I had enough to do* (no easy task) *to catch the train, you have done more than enough* or *enough and to spare*; (pred. a. or n.) *five men are enough, five quarts is not enough*; (adv.) *it is boiled (just) enough, he does not advertise enough, are you warm enough?, he is willing enough* (but incapable), *she sings well enough* (tolerably but not excellently), *you know well enough* (very well) *what I mean*; **oddly** etc. ~ (to justify the term *oddly* etc.); **sure ~,** undeniably as was (or might have been) expected. [OE *genōg*, = OS *ginōg*, OHG *ginuog*, ON *gnógr*, Goth. *ganōhs* f. Gmc **ganōgaz*]

ėnou'nce *v.t.* Enunciate; pronounce (words); hence ~MENT (-sm-) *n.* [f. F *énoncer* (as ENUNCIATE), after *announce, pronounce*]

ėnow'. Var. (poet.) of ENOUGH *a.* & *adv.*

en pantoufles (ahṅ pahṅtōō'fl) *adv.* In a free and easy manner; in relaxed atmosphere. [F, lit. 'in slippers']

en passant (ahṅ pă'sahṅ) *adv.* By the way; **take ~,** (Chess) take (opponent's pawn that advances two squares at once) with one's own pawn that could have taken it if it had advanced only one. [F, = in passing]

en pension. See PENSION 2.

ėnplā'ne. Var. of EMPLANE.

en plein (ahṅ plă'ṅ) *a.* (Of gambling bet) placed wholly on one number etc. [F, = in full]

en poste (ahṅ pŏ'st) *a.* (Of diplomat) occupying official position (at specified place). [F]

en prise (ahṅ prē'z) *a.* (Chess). In a position to be taken. [F]

enquire, enquiry. See INQUIRE, INQUIRY.

ėnrā'ge *v.t.* Make furious (*enraged at, by, with*). [f. F EN[1](*rager* f. as RAGE[1])]

en rapport (ahṅ răpor') *adv.* In harmony or rapport (*with*). [F; see RAPPORT]

ėnră'pture *v.t.* Delight intensely. [f. EN-[1] + RAPTURE]

en règle (ahṅ rā'gl) *adv.* In due form. [F, = in rule]

ėnrĭ'ch *v.t.* Make rich; add to contents of (collection, museum, book); make richer in quality, flavour, nutritive value, etc.; increase content of an isotope in (material); hence ~MENT *n.* [ME, f. OF EN[1](*richir* f. *riche* RICH)]

ėnrō'be *v.t.* Put a robe on. [f. EN-[1] + ROBE]

ėnrō'l, *-ll, *v.* (-ll-). **1.** *v.t.* Write name of (person) on list, esp. of army; incorporate (person) as member (*in* society etc.); (Hist.) enter (deed etc.) among rolls of court of justice; record, celebrate. **2.** *v.i.* Enter one's name on list etc. **3.** Hence **ėnrō'l**MENT, ***-ll-,** *n.* (esp. *number of students in a school etc.). [ME, f. OF EN[1](*roller* f. *rolle* ROLL[1])]

en route (ahṅ rōō't) *adv.* On the way (*to, for,* place etc., or abs.). [F]

ĕns (-z) *n.* (*pl.* **entia** *pr.* ĕ'nshĭa). Entity (esp. as abstract notion). [LL *ens ent-* part. of *esse* be (after *absens*), transl. Gk *on* being]

ėnsa'mple (-ah'-) *n.* (arch.) Example. [ME, f. AF *ensa(u)mple*, OF *essemple* f. L (as EXAMPLE)]

ėnsă'nguĭned (-nggwĭnd) *a.* (literary). Blood-stained, bloody, (lit. or fig.). [f. EN-[1] + L *sanguis -inis* blood + -ED[1]]

ėnscŏ'nce *v.t.* Establish (one*self* etc. in secret, safe, snug, etc., place). [f. EN-[1] + SCONCE[3]]

en secondes noces (ahṅ zegawṅd nŏ's) *adv.* By a second marriage. [F]

ensemble ahṅsah'ṅbl) *n.* **1.** (*or* TOUT ENSEMBLE). Thing viewed as a whole; general effect. **2.** (Mus.) Concerted passage in which all performers unite (**good ~,** accurate and balanced performance of such passage); group of musicians performing thus. **3.** Group of subsidiary dancers in ballet, musical comedy, etc. **4.** (Math.) Group of systems with same constitution but possibly in different states. **5.** Woman's outfit of harmonizing items. [F, f. Rom. **insemul* f. L *insimul* (*in* IN-[1], *simul* at same time)]

ėnshrī'ne *v.t.* Enclose (relic etc.) in shrine; serve as shrine for (precious thing; lit. or fig.); hence ~MENT (-nm-) *n.* [f. EN-[1] + SHRINE]

ėnshrou'd *v.t.* Cover completely, hide from view. [f. EN-[1] + SHROUD]

ĕ'nsĭform *a.* Sword-shaped; = XIPHOID. [f. L *ensis* sword + -FORM]

ĕ'nsign (-īn *or* -in) *n.* **1.** Banner, flag, (esp. Naut.); ‖flag with union in corner (**blue** ~ of government departments and formerly of naval reserve etc., **red** ~ of merchant service, **white** ~ of Royal Navy and Royal Yacht Squadron). **2.** Standard-bearer; *lowest commissioned officer in navy; (Hist.) lowest commissioned infantry officer, whence ~CY *n.* **3.** (arch.) Badge (of office etc.). [ME, f. OF *enseigne* f. L INSIGNIA]

ĕ'nsĭlage *n.*, & *v.t.* **1.** *n.* Preservation of green fodder in silo or pit without drying; fodder thus preserved. **2.** *v.t.* Treat (fodder) by ensilage. [F (as foll.; see -AGE)]

ėnsī'le *v.t.* Put (fodder) into silo; preserve (fodder) in silo. [f. F *ensiler* f. Sp. *ensilar* (as EN-[1], SILO)]

ėnslā've *v.t.* Make (person etc.) a slave (lit., or fig. *to* habit, superstition, etc.); hence ~MENT (-vm-) *n.* [f. EN-[1] + SLAVE]

ėnsnār'e *v.t.* Entrap (lit. or fig.). [f. EN-[1] + SNARE]

ėnsou'l (-sō'l) *v.t.* Infuse a soul into. [f. EN-[1] + SOUL]

ėnsphēr'e *v.t.* (literary). Encircle or enclose (as) in a sphere. [f. EN-[1] + SPHERE]

ėnsūe' *v.* **1.** *v.i.* Happen afterwards; result (*from, on*). **2.** *v.t.* (arch.) Seek after. [ME, f. OF *ensuivre* f. Rom. *IN[1](*sequere* = L *sequi* follow)]

en suite (ahṅ swē't) *adv.* Forming a single unit (*bedroom with bathroom en suite*). [F, = in sequence]

ėnsur'e (-shoor') *v.t.* Make (person, thing) safe (*against* risks); make certain (thing, *that*); secure (thing *to, for*, person etc.). [ME, f. AF EN[1]*seürer* f. OF *aseürer* ASSURE]

ėnswā'the (-dh) *v.t.* Bind or wrap in bandage (lit. or fig.); hence ~MENT (-dhm-) *n.* [f. EN-[1] + SWATHE[2]]

-ent *suf.* forming *adjs.* denoting existence of action (*consequent, effluent*), and *ns.* denoting agent (*coefficient, president*), usu. f. *vbs.* [f. or after F *-ent* or f. L *-ent-* part. st. of vbs. (cf. -ANT)]

E.N.T. *abbr.* ear, nose, and throat.

ėntă'blature *n.* (Archit.) The part of an order above the column, including architrave, frieze, and cornice. [f. It. *intavolatura* f. IN[1](*tavolare* f. *tavola* table) board up; see -URE]

ėntā'blement (-belm-) *n.* Horizontal platform(s) supporting statue, above dado and base. [F, f. EN[1](*tabler* f. TABLE); see -MENT]

ėntai'l[1] *n.* Settlement of succession of landed estate so that it cannot be bequeathed at pleasure; estate so secured; (fig.) inalienable inheritance (of qualities, beliefs, etc.). [ME, f. foll.]

ėntai'l[2] *v.t.* **1.** Settle (land etc.) by entail; bestow (thing) as inalienable possession (*on* person). **2.** Impose (expense, labour, *on* person); necessitate. **3.** Hence ~MENT *n.* [ME, f. EN-[1] + AF *taile* TAIL[2]]

ėntă'ngle (-nggel) *v.t.* Catch in snare or among obstacles; involve (person etc.) in difficulties or illicit activities; make (thing) tangled or intricate (lit. or fig.). [f. EN-[1] + TANGLE[1]]

ėntă'nglement (-nggelm-) *n.* In vbl senses; compromising (esp. amorous) relationship; thing that entangles, esp. (Mil.) extensive barrier erected to obstruct enemy's movements (esp. one made of stakes and interlaced barbed wire). [f. prec. + -MENT]

ĕ'ntasĭs *n.* (Archit.) Slight convexity of column shaft (introduced to correct visual illusion of concavity). [mod. L f. Gk (*enteinō* to stretch)]

ėntĕ'lechў (-kĭ) *n.* (Philos.) Realization, the becoming or being actual of what was potential. [f. LL f. Gk *entelekheia* (*en telei ekhō* be in perfection; see -Y[1])]

ėntĕ'llus *n.* = HANUMAN. [name in Virgil's *Aeneid*]

ente'nte (ahṅtah'ṅt) *n.* Friendly understanding, esp. between States; group of States in such relation; ~ **cordiale,** = entente, esp. of Great Britain and France 1904, or of these with Russia 1908. [F, = understanding (as INTENT[1])]

ĕ'nter *v.* **1.** *v.i.* Go or come in (*into* place, room, etc., or abs.); (3rd pers. subjunctive as stage direction) come on stage (*Enter Macbeth*); announce oneself as competitor in race etc. **2.** ~ **into,** engage in (conversation, relations, agreement, inquiry, etc.), sympathize with (person's feelings etc.), form part of (calculations, plans, etc.), bind oneself by (recognizances, treaty, contract). **3.** ~ **(up)on,** assume possession of (property) or functions of (office), begin (process etc.), begin to deal with (subject). **4.** *v.t.* Go or come into (place etc.); penetrate (flesh etc.); become member of (a society, army, church, etc.); admit, procure admission for, (pupil, person as member of a society); write (name, details etc.) in list, book, etc.; record in due form before court of law or in minutes of debate etc.; make known (a protest etc.); record name of (person etc.) as competitor *for* (contest, race, etc.); ~ **up,** complete series of entries in (account-books etc.); hence ~ABLE *a.* [ME, f. OF *entrer* f. L *intrare* (*intra* within)]

ĕntĕ'rĭc *a.* & *n.* Of the intestines; ~ **(fever),** typhoid; so **ĕnterī'TIS** *n.* [f. Gk *enterikos* (as foll.; see -IC)]

ĕ'ntero- *comb. form.* Intestine, as: ~**stomy** (-ŏ's-), making of permanent opening in intestine; ~**tomy** (-ŏ't-), cutting open the intestine; ~**vir'us,** virus infecting intestine and sometimes other organs. [f. Gk *enteron* intestine + -o-]

ĕ'nterprīse (-z) *n.* Undertaking, esp. bold or difficult one, (FREE[1] *enterprise*, PRIVATE *enterprise*); courage, readiness, to engage in enterprises (*he has no enterprise*). [ME, f. OF *entreprise* fem. p.p. (as n.) of *entreprendre* var. of *emprendre* f. L IM[1](*pre*(*he*)*ndere* take)]

ĕ'nterprīsĭng (-z-) *a.* Ready to engage in enterprises; showing courage or imaginativeness; hence ~LY[2] *adv.* [part. of arch. v. *enterprise* (f. prec.)]

ĕntertai'n *v.t.* Amuse, occupy agreeably, (person etc.; often iron.), whence ~ING[2] *a.*; receive with hospitality (guest, or abs.; *entertained me at* or ‖*to lunch*; *they entertain a great deal*); harbour, cherish, welcome or consider, (idea, feeling, proposal). [ME, f. F *entretenir* f. Rom. *INTER-(*tenēre* hold)]

ĕntertai'ner *n.* In vbl senses; professional provider of amusement. [f. prec. + -ER[1]]

ĕntertai'nment *n.* In vbl senses; hospitality; amusement (*much to my entertainment*); diversions or amusements for guests etc.; public performance or show. [f. ENTERTAIN + -MENT]

ĕ'nthalpў (*or* -ă'-) *n.* (Phys.) Total heat content of a system. [f. Gk EN[2](*thalpō* make hot); see -Y[1]]

ėnthra'l, *-ll, (-aw'l) *v.t.* (**-ll-**). Enslave (usu. fig.); please greatly; hence **ėnthra'lMENT, *-ll-,** (-aw'l-) *n.* [f. EN-[1] + THRALL]

ėnthrō'ne *v.t.* Place (king, bishop, etc.) on throne, esp. with ceremony; exalt; hence ~MENT (-nm-) *n.* [f. EN-[1] + THRONE]

ĕnthrōnīzā'tion, ĭn-, -is- (-z-), *n.* Enthronement (lit. or fig.). [f. obs. *enthronize* f. OF *introniser* f. LL *inthronizare* f. Gk EN[2](*thronizō* as THRONE; see -IZE) + -ATION]

ėnthū'se (-z; *or* -ōō'z) *v.i.* & *t.* (colloq.) Show, or fill with, enthusiasm. [back form. f. foll.]

ėnthū'sĭăsm (-zĭ-; *or* -ōō'-) *n.* Ardent zeal (*for, about*, a person, purpose, cause, etc.); great eagerness; object of enthusiasm; (arch.) extravagant religious emotion. [f. F *enthousiasme* or f. LL f. Gk *enthousiasmos* (*enthousiazō* f. EN[2](*theos* god) possessed by a god, inspired)]

ėnthū'siăst (-zĭ-; *or* -ōō'-) *n.* One who is full of enthusiasm (*for* cause etc.); visionary, self--deluded person; hence ~IC (-ă'-) *a.* [f. F *enthousiaste* or f. eccl. L f. Gk *enthousiastēs* (as prec.)]

ĕ'nthȳmēme *n.* (Logic). Syllogism in which one premiss is not explicitly stated. [f. L f. Gk *enthumēma* f. EN²(*thumeomai* f. *thumos* mind) consider]

ėnti'ce *v.t.* Persuade by offer of pleasure etc. (person etc. *from* place, course of action, etc., *into* another; *to* do); so ~MENT (-sm-) *n.* [ME, f. OF *enticier* prob. f. Rom. *IN¹(*titiare* f. **titius* firebrand)]

ėntīr'e *a.* & *n.* **1.** *a.* Whole, complete; not broken or decayed; not castrated; unqualified (*an entire delusion, success*); all in one piece, continuous; pure, unmixed; hence ~NESS (-īr'n-) *n.* **2.** *n.* Uncastrated animal; ‖(arch.) kind of mixed beer. [ME, f. AF *enter*, OF *entier* f. Rom. **integro* f. L IN²(*teger* f. **tag-*, *tangere* touch)]

ėntīr'elȳ (-īr'lĭ) *adv.* Wholly (*stock is entirely exhausted*); solely (*did it entirely for my benefit*). [f. prec. + -LY²]

ėntīr'etȳ (*or* -īr'tĭ) *n.* Completeness (**in its ~,** in its complete form); sum total (*of*). [ME, f. OF *entiereté* f. L *integritas -tatis* f. *integer* (see ENTIRE, -TY¹)]

ėnti'tle *v.t.* Give (book etc.) the title of (*War and Peace* etc.); (arch.) give (person) the title of (sultan etc.); (of circumstances, qualities, etc.) give (person etc.) a rightful claim (*to* a thing, *to* do); hence ~MENT (-telm-) *n.* [ME, f. AF *entitler*, OF *entiteler* f. LL IN¹(*titulare* f. *titulus* TITLE)]

ĕ'ntĭtȳ *n.* Thing's existence, as opp. to its qualities or relations; thing that has real existence; so **ĕ'ntĭt**ATIVE *a.* [f. F *entité* or f. med. L *entitas*, f. LL ENS; see -ITY]

ĕ'ntō- *comb. form.* Within, as: **~pa'rasite,** = ENDO*parasite*; **~phyte,** plant growing inside a plant or animal. [f. Gk *entos* within + -O-]

ėnto'mb (-ōō'm) *v.t.* Place in tomb (lit. or fig.); serve as tomb for; hence ~MENT (-m-m-) *n.* [f. OF EN¹(*tomber* f. *tombe* TOMB)]

ėntŏ'mĭc *a.* Of insects. [f. as foll. + -IC]

ĕntomo- *comb. form.* Insect, as: **~phagous** (-ŏ'f-), insect-eating; **~philous** (-ŏ'f-), (Bot.) pollinated by insects. [f. Gk EN²(*tomos* f. *temnō* cut) cut up, in neut. = INSECT]

ĕntomŏ'log|ȳ *n.* Study of insects; hence **ĕntomolŏ'g**ICAL *a.*, ~IST (3) *n.*, ~IZE (2) *v.i.* [f. F *entomologie* or mod. L *entomologia* (as prec.; see -LOGY)]

entourage (ŏntoorah'zh) *n.* Surroundings; attendant persons. [F (*entourer* surround; see -AGE)]

en-tout-cas (ahṅ tōō kah') *n.* (*pl.* same). Umbrella-sunshade; (**P**) all-weather hard lawn--tennis court. [F, = in any case]

entr'acte (ŏ'ntrăkt) *n.* (Performance in) interval between acts of play. [F (*entre* between, *acte* act)]

ĕ'ntrails (-z) *n. pl.* Bowels, intestines; (fig.) inner parts (*of* the earth etc.). [ME, f. OF *entrailles* f. med. L *intralia* alt. f. L *interanea* neut. pl. of *interaneus* internal (*inter* among)]

ėntrai'n¹ *v.t.* Drag along; (of fluid) carry (particles etc.) along in its flow, whence ~MENT *n.* [f. F EN¹(*trainer* drag f. as TRAIN)]

ėntrai'n² *v.t.* & *i.* Put (esp. troops) or get into a train. [f. EN-¹ + TRAIN 12]

***entrain*³** (ahṅtră'ṅ) *n.* Enthusiasm, animation. [F]

ėntră'mmel *v.t.* (‖**-ll-**). Entangle, hamper. [f. EN-¹ + TRAMMEL]

ĕ'ntrance¹ *n.* Going or coming in; coming of actor on stage; entering *into* or *upon* (office etc.); right of admission; ~ (**fee**), fee paid for admission to society, club, exhibition, etc.; door, passage, etc., one enters by. [OF (as ENTER, -ANCE)]

ėntra'nc|e² (-ah'-) *v.t.* Throw into a trance; overwhelm (*with* joy, fear); carry away as in trance, whence ~ING² *a.*, (esp.) delightful; hence ~EMENT (-sm-) *n.* [f. EN-¹ + TRANCE]

ĕ'ntrant *n.* One who enters room, profession, etc., or *for* race etc. [F, part. of *entrer* (see ENTER, -ANT)]

ėntră'p *v.t.* (**-pp-**). Catch (as) in trap; beguile (person *to* destruction etc., *into* doing); hence ~MENT *n.* [f. OF EN¹(*traper* f. *trappe* TRAP¹)]

ėntrea't *v.t.* Ask (person) earnestly (*to* do, *that*); (arch.) treat, act towards, (person). [ME, f. OF EN¹(*traitier* TREAT)]

ėntrea'tȳ *n.* Earnest request. [f. prec., after *treaty*]

entrechat (ŏ'ntreshah) *n.* Dancer's leap with one or more crossings of legs while in air. [F, f. It. (*capriola*) *intrecciata* complicated (caper)]

entrecôte (ŏ'ntrekōt) *n.* Boned steak cut off sirloin. [F (*entre* between, *côte* rib)]

entrée (ŏ'ntrā *or* ah'ṅtrā) *n.* Right or privilege of admission, esp. at Court; ‖dish served between fish and meat courses; *main dish of meal. [F, = ENTRY]

entremets (ŏ'ntremā) *n.* Side dish; sweet dish. [F (*entre* between, *mets* dish)]

ėntrĕ'nch, ĭntrĕ'nch, *v.* **1.** *v.t.* Surround (post, army, town) with trench; establish firmly in defensible position; apply extra safeguards to (rights etc. guaranteed by legislation); ~ one**self**, adopt well-defended position (lit. or fig.). **2.** *v.i.* Entrench oneself; encroach, trespass, *upon*. **3.** Hence ~MENT *n.* [f. EN-¹, IN-¹ + TRENCH]

entre nous (ŏntre nōō') *adv.* Between you and me; in private. [F, = between ourselves]

entrepôt (ŏ'ntrepō) *n.* Storehouse for deposit; commercial centre for import and export, and collection and distribution. [F, f. *entreposer* store (*entre-* INTER-, *poser* place)]

entrepreneur (ŏntreprenẽr') *n.* Person in effective control of commercial undertaking; one who undertakes a business or enterprise, with chance of profit or loss; contractor acting as intermediary; hence ~IAL (*or* -ūr'-) *a.*, ~SHIP *n.* [F (*entreprendre* undertake; see ENTERPRISE)]

entresol (ŏ'ntresŏl) *n.* Low storey between first and ground floor. [F (*entre* between, *sol* ground)]

ĕ'ntropȳ *n.* **1.** (Phys.) Measure of the unavailability of a system's thermal energy for conversion into mechanical work; measure of the degradation or disorganization of the universe. **2.** (Math.) Measure of the rate of transfer of information in a message etc. [f. G *entropie* f. as EN-² + Gk *tropē* transformation; see -Y¹]

ėntrŭ'st, ĭntrŭ'st, *v.t.* Charge (person) *with* (duty, object of care); confide (duty, person thing, its safety, *to* person). [f. EN-¹, IN-¹ + TRUST]

ĕ'ntrȳ *n.* **1.** Going or coming in; liberty to do this (~ **permit** etc., authorization to enter a particular country); ceremonial entrance; (Law) taking possession; coming of actor on stage; place of entrance, door, gate, lobby, mouth of river; passage between buildings; start or resumption of performer's part in concerted music; (Bridge) (card providing) transfer of lead to partner's hand. **2.** Registration in records, account-books, diary, etc.; item so entered; **double, single,** ~ (in which each item is entered twice, once, in ledger); list of competitors for race etc.; person or thing competing in race, contest, etc. [ME f. OF *entree* f. Rom. **intrata* fem. p.p. (as n.) of L *intrare* ENTER]

ėntwī'ne *v.t.* Interweave (lit. or fig.); wreathe (thing, *with*, *about*, *round*, another); (arch.) embrace like twining plant. [f. EN-¹ + TWINE]

ėntwĭ'st *v.t.* (arch.) Clasp with or form into a twist; twist (thing) in *with* (another). [f. EN-¹ + TWIST]

ėnū'clė|āte *v.t.* (Surg.) extract (tumour etc.) from shell, (eye) from socket, etc.; (arch.) explain; hence ~A'TION *n.* [f. L E(*nucleare* f. NUCLEUS kernel) + -ATE³]

ėnū'mer|āte *v.t.* Count; specify, mention one by one, (items); hence or cogn. ~ABLE *a.*, ~A'TION *n.*, **~āt**OR *n.* (esp. person employed in census-taking), **~āt**IVE *a.* [f. L E(*numerare* NUMBER²) + -ATE³]

ėnŭ'ncĭ|āte *v.t.* Express (proposition, theory) in definite terms; proclaim; pronounce (words); hence or cogn. ~A'TION, **~āt**OR, *ns.*, ~ATIVE (*or* -sha-) *a.* [f. L E(*nuntiare* announce f. *nuntius* messenger) + -ATE³]

ėnūr'e *v.i.* = INURE 2. [var. of INURE]

ĕnūr|ē'sĭs *n.* (Path.) Involuntary urination; hence ~E'TIC *a.* & *n.* [mod. L, f. Gk *enoureō* urinate in (as EN-², *ouron* urine)]

ėnvĕ'lop *v.t.* Wrap up (person, thing, subject, etc., *in* garment, flames, clouds, mystery); (of garment etc.) cover closely on all sides; (Mil.) effect the surrounding of (enemy); hence ~MENT *n.* [ME, f. OF *envoluper* (as EN-¹; cf. DEVELOP)]

ĕ'nvelōpe (*or* ŏ'n-) *n.* Wrapper, covering, (lit. or fig.); folded and gummed cover for letter; gas container of balloon or airship; outer vessel of vacuum-tube; (Electr.) curve joining successive peaks of modulated wave; (Bot.) calyx or corolla or both; (Math.) line or curve tangent to each line or curve of a given family. [f. F *enveloppe* (as prec.)]

ėnvĕ'nom *v.t.* Put poison on or into (weapon, air, etc.); infuse venom or bitterness into (feelings, words, actions). [ME, f. OF EN¹-(*venimer* f. *venim* VENOM)]

ĕ'nvĭab|le *a.* Such as to excite envy (of desirable thing or its possessor); hence ~LY² *adv.* [f. ENVY² + -ABLE]

ĕ'nvĭous *a.* Full of envy; feeling envy *of* (person, thing); hence ~LY² *adv.* [ME f. AF; OF *envieus* (*envie* ENVY¹; see -OUS)]

ėnvīr'on *v.t.* (Of persons or things) form a ring, be stationed, round; surround (person, place, etc.) hostilely, protectively, etc.; surround (person or thing *with* others). [ME, f. OF *environer* (*environ* surroundings; see ENVIRONS)]

ėnvīr'onment *n.* Surrounding; surrounding objects, region, or conditions, esp. circumstances of life of person or society, whence ~AL (-mĕ'n-) *a.* [f. prec. + -MENT]

ėnvīronmĕ'ntalĭst *n.* One who is concerned with protection of the environment; one who considers that environment has primary influence on person's or group's development. [f. ENVIRONMENTAL + -IST]

ėnvīr'ons (-z; *or* ĕ'nvĭronz) *n. pl.* District surrounding town etc. [F, f. OF *environ* n. f. adv. (*en* in, *viron* circuit, neighbourhood, f. *virer* turn, VEER²)]

ėnvĭ'sage (-z-) *v.t.* **1.** (arch.) Look in the face of; face (danger, facts). **2.** Contemplate, esp. under particular aspect; imagine (thing or conditions not yet existing). **3.** Hence ~MENT (-jm-) *n.* [f. F EN¹(*visager* f. as VISAGE)]

ėnvĭ'sion (-zhon) *v.t.* = prec. 2. [f. EN-¹ + VISION]

ĕ'nvoy¹, ĕ'nvoi, *n.* (arch.) (Author's concluding words, esp.) short stanza concluding ballade etc. [ME, f. OF *envoi* f. *envoyer* send (*en voie* on the way f. L *via*)]

ĕ'nvoy² *n.* Messenger, representative, esp. on diplomatic mission; ~ (**extraordinary**), minister plenipotentiary, ranking below ambassador and above chargé d'affaires; hence ~SHIP *n.* [f. F *envoyé* p.p. (as prec.)]

ĕ'nvȳ¹ *n.* Resentful or admiring contemplation (*of* more fortunate person, *of*, *at*, his advantages, or abs.); object or ground of this (*his car is the envy of the neighbourhood*). [ME f. OF *envie* f. L *invidia* f. IN¹(*vidēre* see) envy]

ĕ'nvȳ² *v.t.* Feel envy of (*I envy him, envy his impudence, envy him his impudence*). [ME, f. OF *envier* (*envie*; see prec.)]

ėnwea've. See INWEAVE.

ėnwī'nd *v.t.* (**enwou'nd**). (Of thing) wind itself or be wound round (another). [f. EN-¹ + WIND³]

ėnwo'mb (-ōō'm) *v.t.* (arch.) Enclose (as) in womb. [f. EN-¹ + WOMB]

ėnwrā'p (ĭnr-) *v.t.* (**-pp-**). Wrap, enfold, (*in*; lit. or fig.). [ME, f. EN-¹ + WRAP]

Enzĕ'd (ĕ-) *n.* (Austral. & N.Z. colloq.) New Zealand(er); hence ~**d**ER¹ *n.*, New Zealander. [pr. of *N.Z.*]

ĕnzōō'tĭc *a.* & *n.* (Disease) regularly affecting animals in a particular district or at a particular season (cf. ENDEMIC). [f. Gk *en* in + *zōion* animal + -IC]

ĕ'nzȳm|e *n.* (Chem.) Protein catalyst of a specific biochemical reaction; hence ~A'TIC, **ĕnzȳ'm**IC, *adjs.*, **~ŏ'**LOGY *n.* [f. Gk *en* in + *zumē* leaven]

E'ocēne (ē'-) *a.* & *n.* (Geol.) (Of) second lowest division of tertiary period or system. [f. Gk *ēōs* dawn + *kainos* new]

ēōhĭ'ppus *n.* Extinct small primitive horse of genus *Eohippus*. [f. as prec. + Gk *hippos* horse]

***ēō'lĭan.** See AEOLIAN.

ē'olĭth *n.* (Archaeol.) Flint object found in tertiary strata, possibly an early artefact. [f. Gk *ēōs* dawn + *lithos* stone]

ēolĭ'thĭc *a.* (Archaeol.) Of the period preceding the palaeolithic age, possibly with earliest use of worked flint implements. [f. F *éolithique* (as prec.; see -IC)]

ē'on. See AEON.

E'onĭsm (ē'-) *n.* Transvestism, esp. by a man. [f. C. d'*Éon*, Fr. adventurer d. 1810 + -ISM]

ē'osĭn *n.* Red fluorescent dyestuff used (esp.) as stain in microscopy; hence **ēosĭ'no**PHIL *a.* & *n.*, (cell) readily stained by eosin. [f. Gk *ēōs* dawn + -IN]

-ėous *suf.* forming *adjs.* meaning 'of the nature of' (*ligneous* like wood, *vitreous* like glass). [f. or after L *-eus* + -OUS; cf. -ACEOUS, -ANEOUS]

ep- *pref.* See EPI-.

E.P. *abbr.* electroplate; extended-play (record).

e.p. *abbr.* (Chess) en passant.

Ep. *abbr.* Epistle.

ē'pāct *n.* Age of moon on 1 Jan. [f. F *épacte* f. LL f. Gk *epaktai* (*hēmerai*) intercalated (days) f. EP(*agō* bring) intercalate]

ĕ'pārch (-k) *n.* Governor or bishop of diocese in Orthodox Church; so ~Y¹ *n.*, his diocese. [f. Gk EP(*arkhos* ruler)]

épatant (āpahtah'ṅ) *a.* Shockingly unconventional. [F, part. of *épater* (see foll.)]

épater les bourgeois (āpahtā lā boor'zhwah) *v.i.* Startle or shock those bound by conventional beliefs. [F, = flabbergast the ordinary citizens]

ĕ'paulĕtte, *ĕ'paulĕt, (*or* -ōl-; *or* ĕpelĕ't) *n.* Ornamental shoulder-piece of uniform. [f. F *épaulette* dim. of *épaule* shoulder f. L SPATULA; see -ETTE]

épée (āpā') *n.* Sharp-pointed duelling-sword,

used (blunted) in fencing; hence ~IST (3) *n.* [F, = sword, f. OF *espee* (see SPAY)]

ĕpeirogĕ'nėsĭs, ĕpeirŏ'gėnȳ, (ĕpīr-) *n.* (Geol.) Process of making continents. [f. Gk *ēpeiros* mainland + GENESIS, -GENY]

ėpĕ'nthės|is *n.* (*pl.* ~*es pr.* -ēz). Insertion of a letter or sound within a word, e.g. *b* in THIMBLE; so **ĕpĕnthĕ'tɪc** *a.* [LL f. Gk (*epentithēmi* insert f. as EPI- + EN-² + *tithēmi* place)]

ėpĕr'gne (ĭpĕr'n) *n.* Centre ornament (esp. in branched form) for dinner-table, holding flowers or fruit. [18th c.; orig. unkn.]

ĕpĕxėg|ē'sĭs *n.* (*pl.* ~*eses pr.* -ē'sēz). Additional, addition of, words to make meaning clear (e.g. 'difficult *to do*'); hence **~ĕ'tɪc(AL)** *adjs.* [f. Gk *epexēgēsis* (as EP-, EXEGESIS)]

Eph. *abbr.* Ephesians (N.T.).

ĕphē'be *n.* (Gk Ant.) Young man of 18–20 undergoing military training. [f. L f. Gk *ephēbos* (as EPI-, *hēbē* early manhood)]

ĕphĕ'dra *n.* Evergreen trailing shrub of genus *Ephedra.* [mod. L, f. Gk *ephedra* sitting upon]

ĕ'phedrĭne *n.* Alkaloid drug found in some ephedras, used to relieve asthma, hay fever, etc. [f. prec. + -INE⁵]

ėphĕ'mera *n.* (*pl.* **~s** *or* **~e**). Insect living only a day or a few days; insect of order Ephemeroptera, e.g. mayfly; short-lived thing; thing of short-lived usefulness. [mod. L, f. LL f. Gk *ephēmeros* lasting only a day (*epi* on, *hēmera* day)]

ėphĕ'meral *a.* Lasting only a day; (of insect, flower, etc.) lasting a day or a few days; short-lived, transitory; hence ~ITY (-ă'l-) *n.* [f. Gk *ephēmeros* (see prec.) + -AL]

ėphĕ'mer|ĭs *n.* (*pl.* ~*ides pr.* ĕfĭmĕ'rĭdēz). Astronomical almanac or table of predicted positions. [L, f. Gk *ephēmeris* diary (as prec.)]

ėphĕ'mer|on *n.* (*pl.* **~ons** *or* **~a**). = EPHEMERA. [f. as EPHEMERA]

ĕ'phod *n.* Jewish priestly vestment. [ME, f. Heb. *'ēp̄ōd*]

ĕ'phor *n.* (Gk Ant.) One of five magistrates controlling kings of Sparta; hence ~ATE¹, ~SHIP, *ns.* [f. Gk EP(*horos* f. *horaō* see) overseer]

ĕpĭ- *pref.* (usu. **ep-** bef. vowel or *h*) w. sense 'upon' (*epicycle*), 'above' (*epicotyl*), 'in addition' (*epiphenomenon*). [f. Gk *epi* prep.]

ĕ'pĭblăst *n.* (Biol.) Outermost layer of gastrula etc.; ectoderm. [f. EPI- + -BLAST]

ĕ'pĭc *a.* & *n.* (Poem) narrating continuously achievements of one or more heroes, e.g. the *Iliad*, *Paradise Lost*; (subject) fit for recital in an epic; (book, film, etc.) of heroic type or scale; **folk ~, national ~,** poem of any form, embodying nation's conception of its past history; hence ~AL *a.*, **~al**LY² *adv.* [f. L f. Gk *epikos* (as EPOS; see -IC)]

ĕ'pĭcărp *n.* (Bot.) Outermost layer of pericarp. [f. EPI- + Gk *karpos* fruit]

ĕpĭcē'dĭ|um *n.* (*pl.* ~**a**). Funeral ode. [L, f. Gk EPI(*kēdeion* f. *kēdos* care)]

ĕ'pĭcēne *a.* & *n.* For or used by both sexes; (person) with characteristics of both sexes; (person) without sexual characteristics; effete, effeminate, (person); (Gram.) denoting either sex without change of gender. [ME, f. LL f. Gk EPI(*koinos* common)]

ĕ'pĭcĕntre (-*ter*), ***-ter**, *n.* Point at which earthquake reaches earth's surface (also fig.). [f. Gk EPI(*kentros* a. f. as CENTRE¹)]

ĕpĭclē'sĭs *n.* (*pl.* ~*es pr.* -ēz). (Eccl.) Invocation of Holy Spirit to consecrate and transubstantiate Eucharistic elements. [f. Gk EPI(*klēsis* f. *kaleō* to call)]

ĕpĭcŏ'tȳl *n.* (Bot.) Part of embryo or seedling above cotyledon(s). [f. EPI- + COTYLEDON]

ĕ'pĭcūr|e *n.* Person with refined tastes in food, literature, etc.; hence ~ISM (2) *n.* [f. med. L *epicurus* one preferring sensual pleasures, appellative use of L f. Gk *Epikouros* Epicurus, Athenian philosopher d. 270 B.C.]

ĕpĭcūrē'an *a.* & *n.* **1.** (*E*~). (Follower) of Epicurus (cf. prec.), who taught that highest good was calmness of mind. **2.** (Person) devoted to pleasure, esp. refined sensuous enjoyment. **3.** Hence ~ISM (3) *n.* [f. F *épicurien* or f. L *epicureus* f. Gk *epikoureios* (as prec.; see -EAN)]

ĕ'pĭcȳcle *n.* (Geom.) Small circle moving round circumference of a larger one; hence **ĕpĭcȳ'cl**IC *a.* [ME f. OF, or f. LL f. Gk EPI(*kuklos* circle)]

ĕpĭcȳ'cloid *n.* (Math.) Curve traced by point on circumference of circle rolling on exterior of another circle; hence ~AL (-oi'd-) *a.* [f. prec. + -OID]

ĕpĭdei'ctĭc (-dī'-) *a.* Meant for effect or display. [f. Gk EPI(*deiktikos* f. *deiknumi* show; see -IC)]

ĕpĭdĕ'mĭc *a.* & *n.* (Disease, lit. or fig.) prevalent among community at special time (cf. ENDEMIC); hence ~AL *a.*, **~al**LY² *adv.* [f. F *épidémique* (*épidémie* f. LL f. Gk *epidēmia* prevalence of disease f. *epidēmios* a. f. as EPI- + *dēmos* the people)]

ĕpĭdēmĭŏ'logȳ *n.* Science of epidemics. [f. Gk *epidēmios* (see prec.) + -LOGY]

ĕpĭdĕr'm|ĭs *n.* Outer layer of skin of animals, cuticle; outer chitinous integument of shell; true skin of (esp. young) plant below cuticle; hence ~AL, ~IC, ~OID, *adjs.* [LL f. Gk (as EPI-, DERMIS)]

ĕpĭdī'ascōpe *n.* Optical projector giving images of both opaque and transparent objects. [f. EPI- + DIA- + -SCOPE]

ĕpĭdĭ'dȳmĭs *n.* (Anat.) Coil of efferent duct behind testis. [f. Gk EPI(*didumis* f. *didumoi* testicles)]

ĕpĭdūr'al *a.* (Anat.) On or affecting the dura mater. [f. EPI- + DURA MATER + -AL]

ĕ'pĭfauna *n.* Animals living on a marine deposit or on aquatic animal or plant. [Da. (as EPI-, FAUNA)]

ĕpĭgă'str|ĭum *n.* Part of abdomen immediately over stomach; hence ~IC *a.* [LL, f. Gk EPI*gastrion* neut. adj. (*gastēr* belly)]

ĕpĭgē'al *a.* (Bot.) Having cotyledon(s) above ground; growing above ground. [f. Gk EPI(*geios* f. *gē* earth) + -AL]

ĕ'pĭgēne *a.* (Geol.) produced on surface of earth; (of crystal) chemically altered since its formation. [f. F *épigène* f. Gk EPI(*genēs* born)]

ĕpĭglŏ'tt|ĭs *n.* Erect cartilage at root of tongue, depressed during swallowing to cover glottis; hence ~AL, ~IC, *adjs.* [Gk EPI(*glōttis* f. *glōtta* tongue)]

ĕ'pĭgōne *n.* (*pl.* **~s,** *or* **epigoni** *pr.* ĕpĭ'gonī). One of a later (and less distinguished) generation. [pl. f. F *épigones* f. L f. Gk *epigonoi* those born afterwards (as EPI-, root of *gignomai* be born)]

ĕ'pĭgrăm *n.* Short poem ending in witty turn of thought; pointed saying or mode of expression; so **ĕpĭgrammă'tɪc** *a.*, **ĕpĭgră'mmat**IST (3) *n.*, **ĕpĭgră'mmat**IZE (1, 2) *v.t.* & *i.* [f. F *épigramme* or f. L f. Gk EPI(*gramma -atos*); cf. -GRAM]

ĕ'pĭgraph (-ahf) *n.* Inscription on stone, statue, coin, at head of chapter, etc.; hence **ĕpĭgră'ph**IC *a.*, **ĕpĭ'graph**IST (3), **ĕpĭ'**GRAPHY (1, 2), *ns.* [f. Gk EPI(*graphē* f. *graphō* write)]

ĕ'pĭl|āte *v.t.* Remove hair from; hence ~A'TION *n.* [f. F *épiler*, after DEPILATE, + -ATE³]

ĕ'pĭlĕpsȳ *n.* Nervous disorder in which patient suffers mild or severe convulsions with or without loss of consciousness. [f. F *épilepsie* or f. LL f. Gk *epilēpsia* f. EPI(*lambanō* take) attack]

ĕpĭlĕ'ptĭc *a.* & *n.* Of epilepsy; (person) subject to epilepsy. [f. F *épileptique* f. LL f. Gk *epilēptikos* (as prec.; see -IC)]

ĕpĭlĭ'mnĭ|on *n.* (*pl.* ~**a**). Upper layer of water in stratified lake. [f. EPI- + Gk *limnion* dim. of *limnē* lake]

ėpĭ'logĭst *n.* Writer or speaker of epilogue. [f. foll. + -IST]

ĕ'pĭlŏgue (-g) *n.* Concluding part, appendix, of literary work; speech or short poem addressed to spectators by actor at end of play (cf. PROLOGUE). [ME, f. F *épilogue* f. L f. Gk EPI(*logos* speech)]

ĕ'pĭmer *n.* (Chem.) One of two isomers with different configurations of atoms about one of several asymmetric carbon atoms present; hence **ĕpĭmĕ'r**IC *a.*, **ĕpĭ'mer**ISM (2) *n.*, **ĕpĭ'mer**IZE (3) *v.t.*, convert (one epimer) into the other. [G, f. as EPI- + -MER]

ĕ'pĭnăstў *n.* (Bot.) Tendency in plant-organs to grow more rapidly on upper side. [f. EPI- + Gk *nastos* pressed + -Y[1]]

ĕpĭnĕ'phrĭne *n.* (Chem.) = ADRENALIN. [f. Gk *epi* upon + *nephros* kidney + -INE[5]]

ėpĭ'phanў *n.* **1.** (*E*~). Manifestation of Christ to the Magi; festival of this (6 Jan.). **2.** Manifestation of a superhuman being. **3.** Hence **ĕpĭphă'n**IC *a.* [ME: sense 1 f. OF *epiphanie* f. eccl. L f. Gk *epiphania* neut. pl. adj. f. EPI(*phainō* show), sense 2 f. Gk *epiphaneia* manifestation (*epiphanēs* manifest)]

ĕpĭphėnŏ'mėn|on *n.* (*pl.* ~**a**). **1.** (Med. & Philos.) Secondary symptom, mere concomitant of something else not regarded as its cause or result. **2.** (Psychol.) Consciousness regarded as a by-product of brain activity. **3.** Hence ~AL *a.*, ~**al**ISM (3) *n.* [f. EPI- + PHENOMENON]

ĕpĭ'phўs|ĭs *n.* (*pl.* ~**es** *pr.* -ēz). (Anat.) End part of long bone during growth; pineal gland. [mod. L, f. Gk EPI(*phusis* growth)]

ĕ'pĭphўte *n.* Plant growing on (usu. not fed by) another; vegetable parasite on animal body; hence **ĕpĭphў'**TAL, **ĕpĭphў'**TIC, *adjs.* [f. EPI- + Gk *phuton* plant]

Epīr'ot, -ōte, (ī-) *n.* Native or inhabitant of Epirus. [f. Gk *ēpeirōtēs* (*ēpeiros* mainland; see -OT[2])]

ėpĭ'scopacў *n.* Government of church by bishops; **the** ~, the bishops. [f. as EPISCOPATE + -ACY, after *prelacy*]

ėpĭ'scopal *a.* Of bishop(s); ~ **church** (constituted on principle of prec., esp. *Episcopal Church*, Church of England in U.S. and Scotland); hence ~ISM (3) *n.*, ~LY[2] *adv.* [ME, f. F *épiscopal* or f. eccl. L *episcopalis* (*episcopus* BISHOP; see -AL)]

ėpĭscopā'lĭan *a.* & *n.* (Adherent) of episcopacy; (*E*~) (member) of episcopal church; hence ~ISM (3) *n.* [f. prec. + -IAN]

ėpĭ'scopate *n.* Office, position, tenure, of bishop; **the** ~, the bishops. [f. eccl. L *episcopatus* (*episcopus* BISHOP; see -ATE[1])]

ĕ'pĭscōpe *n.* Optical projector giving images of opaque objects. [f. EPI- + -SCOPE]

ĕpĭsėmă'tĭc *a.* (Zool.) (Of coloration, markings, etc.) serving to help recognition by other members of same species. [f. EPI- + Gk *sēma sēmatos* sign + -IC]

ĕ'pĭsōde *n.* Incidental narrative or series of events forming digression in poem etc.; incident in narrative, part of serial story; incident, event, viewed as part of sequence; (Mus.) passage introducing new subject; part between two choric songs in Gk tragedy (orig. interpolated); hence **ĕpĭsŏ'd**IC(AL) *adjs.*, (also) sporadic, irregularly occurring. [f. Gk *epeisodion* f. as EPI- + *eisodos* entry (*eis* into, *hodos* way)]

ĕpĭstă'xĭs *n.* Nose-bleeding. [mod. L f. Gk (as EPI-, *stazō* drip)]

ĕpĭstĕ'm|ĭc *a.* (Philos.) Relating to knowledge or degree of acceptance; hence ~ICALLY *adv.* [f. Gk *epistēmē* knowledge + -IC]

ĕpĭstėmŏ'log|ў *n.* Theory of the method or grounds of knowledge; hence **ĕpĭstėmolŏ'gĭc**AL *a.*, ~IST (3) *n.* [f. as prec. + -O- + -LOGY]

ėpĭ'stle (-sel) *n.* Letter in N.T., written by apostle; (*E*~) extract from this read in church service (**E~ side,** S. side of altar, at which Epistle is read); (usu. joc.) = LETTER 2; literary work, usu. verse, in form of letter. [ME f. OF, f. L f. Gk *epistolē* f. EPI(*stellō* send)]

ėpĭ'stolarў *a.* Of, carried on by, suited to, letters. [f. F *épistolaire* or f. L *epistolaris* (as prec.; see -ARY[2])]

ėpĭ'stoler *n.* (Eccl.) Reader of the Epistle. [f. OF *epistelier* or f. med. L *epistolari(u)s* (as EPISTLE; see -ER[2] (1, 2))]

ėpĭ'strophė *n.* Repetition of word at end of successive clauses. [Gk EPI(*strophē* turning; see STROPHE)]

ĕ'pĭstўle *n.* (Archit.) = ARCHITRAVE. [f. F *épistyle* or f. L f. Gk EPI(*stulion* f. *stulos* pillar)]

ĕ'pĭtaph (-ahf) *n.* Words (composed as if to be) inscribed on tomb. [ME, f. OF *epitaphe* f. L f. Gk EPI(*taphion* f. *taphos* tomb) funeral oration]

ĕ'pĭtăxў (*or* -ă'-) *n.* Growth of crystals on an underlying crystal that determines their orientation; hence **ĕpĭtă'xĭ**AL *a.* [f. F *épitaxie* f. as EPI- + Gk *taxis* arrangement; see -Y[1]]

ĕpĭthalā'mĭ|um *n.* (*pl.* ~**ums** *or* ~**a**). Nuptial song or poem; hence ~AL, **ĕpĭthală'm**IC, *adjs.* [f. L f. Gk EPI(*thalamion* f. *thalamos* bridal chamber)]

ĕpĭthē'lĭ|um *n.* (*pl.* ~**ums** *or* ~**a**). Tissue forming outer layer of body surface or lining of cavity that opens to body surface; (Bot.) epidermis formed of young cells; hence ~AL *a.* [mod. L, f. EPI- + Gk *thēlē* teat; see -IUM]

ĕ'pĭthĕt *n.* Adjective expressing quality or attribute; this as term of abuse or profanity; title, significant appellation; hence ~IC(AL) (-ĕ't-) *adjs.* [f. F *épithète* or L f. Gk *epitheton* f. EPI(*tithēmi* place)]

ėpĭ'tom|ė *n.* Summary or abstract of book; condensed account; (fig.) thing that represents another in miniature, person who embodies a quality etc.; hence ~IST (1) *n.*, ~IZE (3) *v.t.* [f. L f. Gk *epitomē* f. EPI(*temnō* cut) abridge]

ĕpĭzō'|ŏn *n.* (*pl.* ~**a**). External parasite or commensal. [mod. L f. as EPI- + Gk *zōion* animal]

ĕpĭzōŏ'tĭc *a.* & *n.* (Disease) temporarily prevalent among animals (cf. ENZOOTIC, EPIDEMIC). [f. F *épizootique* (*épizootie* f. as EPI- + Gk *zōion* animal); see -IC]

E.P.N.S. *abbr.* electroplated nickel silver.

ĕ'pŏch (-k) *n.* Beginning of era in history, science, life, etc., (**~-making,** marking the beginning of a new era, remarkable); date; period in history or life marked by special events; (Geol.) division of a PERIOD, corresp. to a SERIES in rocks; hence ~AL *a.* [f. mod. L f. Gk *epokhē* stoppage f. EP(*ekhō* hold)]

ĕ'pōde *n.* **1.** Form of lyric poem with long line followed by shorter one. **2.** See STROPHE. [f. F *épode* or f. L *epodos* f. Gk *epōidos* (as EPI-, ODE)]

ĕ'ponўm *n.* One who gives his name to a people, place, or institution; so **ėpŏ'nўm**OUS *a.* [f. Gk EP(*ōnumos* f. *onoma* name)]

ĕ'popee *n.* Epic (poem or poetry). [f. F *épopée* f. Gk *epopoiia* (as foll., *poieō* make)]

ĕ'pŏs *n.* Early unwritten epic poetry; epic poem. [L, f. Gk *epos* word, song]

ėpŏ'xide *n.* (Chem.) Compound in which oxygen atom and two carbon atoms form ring. [f. EPI- + OXIDE]

ėpŏ'xў *a.* & *n.* Pertaining to or derived from an epoxide; ~ (**resin**), synthetic thermosetting resin containing epoxide rings. [f. EPI- + OXY- (2)]

épris (āprē') *a.* (*fem.* ***éprise*** *pr.* āprē'z). Enamoured (*of*, *with*). [F]

ĕpsī'lon *n.* Fifth Greek letter (Ε, ε) = ĕ (cf. ETA¹). [ME f. Gk, = bare E (*psilos* bare)]

E'psom (ĕ'-) *n.* ~ **salt(s)**, magnesium sulphate used as purgative etc. [~ in Surrey]

ĕpy̆'llĭ|on *n.* (*pl.* ~**a**). Miniature epic poem. [f. Gk *epullion* dim. of EPOS]

ĕ'qu|able *a.* Uniform, even, not easily disturbed; uniform and moderate (*equable climate*); hence or cogn. ~ABI'LITY *n.*, ~**ab**LY² *adv.* [f. L *aequabilis* (as EQUATE; see -ABLE)]

ē'qual¹ *a.* & *n.* **1.** *a.* The same in number, size, value, degree, rank, musical pitch, etc., (*to*, *with*, or abs.; *twice three is equal to six*; *the totals are equal*; *speaks French and Dutch with equal ease*; *came equal second with Jones in the race*; *the two are equal in ability*; *met his rival on equal terms*); ~(**s**) **sign,** =. **2.** Having strength, courage, ability, etc., adequate *to* (*the occasion, a ten-mile walk, doing*, etc.). **3.** Uniform in operation etc. (*equal laws*); evenly balanced (fight etc.); ~ **pay** (for same work done, esp. by either sex); *equal* TEMPERAMENT. **4.** Hence ~LY² *adv.* **5.** *n.* Person equal to another in rank etc. (*mix with* one's *equals*) or in power etc. (*he has no equal*); (in *pl.*) equal things (*if equals be added to equals*). [ME, f. L *aequalis* (*aequus* even; see -AL)]

ē'qual² *v.t.* (‖-**ll**-). Be equal to (person, thing, *in* quality, number, etc.; *twice three equals six*); do something equal to (feat etc.). [f. prec.]

ēqualĭtār'ĭan (-ŏl-) etc. Var. of EGALITARIAN etc.

ėqua'lĭty̆ (-ŏ'l-) *n.* Condition of being equal (*between* two or more; *with* person etc. *in* or *of* quality etc.; or abs.); ***E~ State,** Wyoming. [ME, f. OF *equalité* f. L *aequalitas -tatis* (as EQUAL¹; see -ITY)]

ē'qualīz|e, -īs|e (-īz), *v.* **1.** *v.t.* Make (thing etc.) equal (*to*, *with*). **2.** *v.i.* Become equal; (Footb. etc.) bring score to equality with opponent's. **3.** Hence ~A'TION *n.*, ~ER¹ *n.*, (esp.) goal that equalizes, (sl.) revolver or other weapon. [f. EQUAL¹ + -IZE]

ĕquanĭ'mĭty̆ *n.* Evenness of mind or temper; composure; resignation, acceptance of fate. [f. L *aequanimitas* (*aequanimis* f. *aequus* even + *animus* mind; see -ITY)]

ėquā't|e *v.t.* State equality of (thing *to*, *with*, another); treat or regard as equivalent (*with*); hence ~ABLE *a.* [ME, f. L *aequare* (*aequus* equal) + -ATE³]

ėquā'tion (-ā'zhon) *n.* **1.** Making equal, equating, balancing, (of demand and supply etc.). **2.** (Amount or process of) correction for inaccuracy; **personal** ~, (Astron.) allowance for person's time of reaction in making observations, (fig.) bias or prejudice. **3.** (Math.) Formula affirming equivalence of two expressions connected by the sign =. **4.** (Chem.) Formula indicating reaction by use of symbols. **5.** Hence ~AL *a.* [ME f. OF, or f. L *aequatio* (as prec.; see -ATION)]

ėquā'tor *n.* Great circle of the earth, sun, etc., equidistant from the poles; great circle of sky in plane perpendicular to earth's axis; **magnetic** ~, aclinic line. [ME, f. OF *equateur* or f. med. L *aequator* (as prec.; see -OR)]

ĕquatŏr'ial *a.* Of or near the equator; ~ **telescope** (attached to axis perpendicular to plane of equator); hence ~LY² *adv.* [f. prec. + -IAL]

ĕ'querry̆ (*or* ĭkwĕ'rĭ) *n.* (Hist.) officer of prince or noble, charged with care of horses; officer of British royal household, attending sovereign etc. [earlier *esquiry* etc. f. obs. F *escu(i)rie* stable, of unkn. orig.; in E wrongly assoc. w. L *equus* horse]

ėquĕ'strĭan *a.* & *n.* **1.** *a.* Of horse-riding (~ **statue,** of person on horse); of knights. **2.** *n.* (fem. **equestrie'nne**). Rider or performer on horseback; hence ~ISM (2) *n.* [f. L *equestris* (*eques* horseman, knight, f. *equus* horse) + -AN]

ēquĭ- *comb. form.* Equal, as: ~**a'ngular,** having equal angles; ~**di'stant,** separated by equal distances; ~**la'teral,** having all sides equal, (of hyperbola) rectangular. [f. L *aequi-* (*aequus* equal; see -I-)]

ėquĭ'lĭbr|āte (*or* ēkwĭlĭ'-) *v.t.* & *i.* Cause (two things) to balance; balance; so ~A'TION *n.* [f. LL *aequilibrare* (*aequi-* EQUI-, *libra* balance) + -ATE³]

ėquĭ'lĭbrĭst *n.* Rope-walker, acrobat. [f. foll. + -IST]

ēquĭlĭ'brĭ|um *n.* (*pl.* ~**a** *or* ~**ums**). State of balance (lit. or fig.); mental state of uncertainty or equanimity; **stable, unstable, neutral,** ~**um** (in which body when disturbed tends to return to equilibrium, to move farther from equilibrium, or has neither tendency). [L (*aequi-* EQUI-, *libra* balance)]

ĕ'quīne *a.* Of or like a horse. [f. L *equinus* (*equus* horse; see -INE¹)]

ĕquĭnŏ'ctial (-shal) *a.* & *n.* **1.** *a.* Of equal day and night; ~ **line,** celestial EQUATOR; ~ **point** (at which ecliptic crosses equator); *equinoctial* YEAR. **2.** Happening at or near time of equinox (*equinoctial gales*). **3.** At or near the (terrestrial) equator. **4.** *n.* Equinoctial line. [ME f. OF, or f. L *aequinoctialis* (as foll.; see -AL)]

ĕ'quĭnŏx *n.* Time or date at which sun crosses equator and day and night are equal (**spring** or **vernal** ~, about 20 Mar.; **autumn** or **autumnal** ~, about 22 Sept.); equinoctial point; PRECESSION *of equinoxes*. [ME, f. OF *equinoxe* or f. med. L *equinoxium* for L *aequinoctium* (as EQUI-, *nox noctis* night)]

ėquĭ'p *v.t.* (-**pp**-). Furnish (ship, army, person, *with* requisites); furnish (*oneself* etc.) with what is needed for journey etc. [f. F *équiper*, prob. f. ON *skipa* man (ship) f. *skip* SHIP¹]

ĕ'quĭpage *n.* Requisites for an undertaking; outfit for journey etc.; carriage and horses with attendants. [f. F *équipage* (as prec.; see -AGE)]

ēquĭpârtĭ'tion *n.* (Phys.) Equal division of energy between degrees of FREEDOM of a system in thermal equilibrium. [f. EQUI- + PARTITION]

ėquĭ'pment *n.* Equipping or being equipped; manner in which person or thing is equipped; outfit, tools, apparatus, necessary for expedition, job, warfare, etc.; intellectual resources. [f. F *équipement* (as EQUIP; see -MENT)]

ĕ'quĭpoise (-z) *n.*, & *v.t.* **1.** *n.* Equilibrium (usu. fig.); counterbalancing thing. **2.** *v.t.* Counterbalance. [f. EQUI- + POISE¹]

ēquĭpŏ'll|ent *a.* & *n.* **1.** *a.* Equal in power, force, etc., practically equivalent; so ~ENCE, ~ENCY, *ns.* **2.** *n.* Equipollent thing. [ME, f. OF *equipolent* f. L *aequipollens -entis* of equal value (as EQUI-, *pollēre* be strong)]

ēquĭpŏ'nder|āte *v.t.* Counterbalance; so ~ANT *a.* & *n.* [f. med. L *EQUI(*ponderare* weigh f. L *pondus -eris* weight) + -ATE³]

ēquĭpotĕ'ntial (-shal) *a.* & *n.* (Phys.) (Surface, line, etc.) such that the potential of a force is the same or constant at all its points. [f. EQUI- + POTENTIAL]

ēquĭprŏ'b|able *a.* (Logic). Equally probable; hence ~ABI'LITY *n.* [f. EQUI- + PROBABLE]

ĕ'quĭtab|le *a.* Fair, just, whence ~**le**NESS (-beln-) *n.*, ~LY² *adv.*; (of claim etc.) valid in equity as opposed to law. [f. F *équitable* (as EQUITY; see -ABLE)]

ĕquĭtā'tion *n.* Riding on horseback; horsemanship. [f. F *équitation* or f. L *equitatio* (*equitare* ride horse f. *eques -itis* horseman f. *equus* horse; see -ATION)]

ĕ'quĭty̆ *n.* **1.** Fairness; recourse to principles of justice to correct or supplement law; system of justice supplementing or prevailing over common and statute law. **2.** ||(*E*~). Actors' trade union. **3.** (in *pl.*) Stocks and shares not bearing fixed interest. **4.** Value of shares issued by a company; net value of mortgaged property after deduction of charges. [ME, f. OF *equité* f. L *aequitas -tatis* (*aequus* fair; see -ITY)]

ėquĭ'val|ent *a.* & *n.* **1.** *a.* Equal in value, amount, or importance, (*to*); (of words) meaning the same; (Chem.) equal in combining value (*to*); having same result; corresponding. **2.** *n.* Equivalent thing, amount, word, etc. **3.** So ~ENCE, ~ENCY, *ns.* [ME f. OF, f. LL *aequi(valēre* be worth); see EQUI-, -ENT]

ėquĭ'vocal *a.* **1.** Of double meaning, ambiguous; of uncertain nature. **2.** (Of person, character, etc.) questionable, suspicious. **3.** Hence ~ITY (-ă'l-), ~NESS, *ns.*, ~LY² *adv.* [f. LL *aequivocus* (as EQUI-, *vocare* call) + -AL]

ėquĭ'voc|āte *v.i.* Use ambiguous words to conceal the truth, prevaricate; hence or cogn. ~A'TION, ~**ātor**, *ns.* [ME, f. LL *aequivocare* (as prec.) + -ATE³]

ĕ'quĭvōque (-k), **-vōke,** *n.* Pun; ambiguity. [ME in sense 'equivocal', f. OF *equivoque* or f. LL *aequivocus* EQUIVOCAL]

ẽr *int.* expr. hesitation. [imit.]

-er¹ *suf.* forming *ns.* f. *ns.*, *adjs.*, and *vbs.*, meaning (1) person or animal that does (*lover, maker, pointer, executioner, probationer*), person or thing that has or is (*foreigner, fiver, four-wheeler, three-decker, second-rater*), (2) instrument, machine, occurrence, action, etc., (*poker, computer, deodorizer, eye-opener, header*), (3) person concerned with thing (*hatter, geographer*), (4) person belonging to place etc. (*Londoner, Merseysider, Britisher, Hamburger, villager, sixth-former, *fourth-grader*), (5) sl. distortion of word with other ending (*rugger, soccer*). [orig. 'one who has to do with', f. OE *-ere* f. Gmc **-arjaz*]

-er² *suf.* forming *ns.* and *adjs.* (1) ME f. OF, f. L *-aris*, now usu. -AR¹ (SAMPLER²); (2) ME f. AF (OF *-ier*) f. L *-arius, -arium* (*butler, carpenter, danger*); (3) f. OF *-eüre* f. L *-atura* or OF *-eör* f. L *-atorium* (COUNTER¹); (4) = -OR.

-er³ *suf.* forming *compar.* of *adjs.* and *advs.* esp. of one or sometimes two syllables (*wider, narrower*); see notes on Comparatives, p. xv. [OE *-ra* adj., *-or* adv. f. Gmc *-iz(on)-, -ōz(on)-*]

-er⁴ *suf.* forming *ns.* (esp. Law) meaning (single instance of) the vbl action, document effecting this, (*cesser, disclaimer, misnomer*; *dinner, supper*). [AF inf. ending of vbs.]

-er⁵ *suf.* forming frequent. *vbs.* f. *vbs.* (*wander* f. *wend*) or on sound-imitations (*twitter*); *clamber, mutter, shudder, slumber.* [OE *-(e)rian,* = OS, OHG *-arōn*, ON *-ra* f. Gmc **-rōjan*]

E.R. *abbr.* East RIDING²; King Edward [f. L *Edwardus Rex*]; Queen Elizabeth [f. L *Elizabetha Regina*].

Er *symb.* erbium.

ēr'a *n.* System of chronology starting from some particular point of time (*Christian era*); historical or other period; date forming commencement of this; (Geol.) major division of time. [f. LL *aera* number expressed in figures (pl. of *aes aeris* money, treated as fem. sing.)]

ėră'dĭc|āte *v.t.* Tear up by roots; extirpate, remove, get rid of; hence ~ABLE *a.*, ~A'TION, ~**ātor**, *ns.* [ME, f. L E(*radicare* f. *radix -icis* root) + -ATE³]

ėrā's|e (-z) *v.t.* Rub out; obliterate, remove all traces of (*from* memory etc.); remove recorded signal from (magnetic tape etc.); hence **ėrā'sable** (-z-) *a.*, ~ER¹ (2), ~URE (-zher), *ns.* [f. L E(*radere ras-* scrape)]

Eră'stĭan (ĭ-) *a.* & *n.* (Hist.) (Adherent) of the supposed doctrines of Erastus, subordinating ecclesiastical to secular power; hence ~ISM (3) *n.*, ~IZE (3) *v.t.* & *i.* [f. *Erastus*, Swiss physician d. 1583 + -IAN]

ẽr'bĭum *n.* (Chem.) Metallic element of lanthanide series. [mod. L, f. *Ytterby* in Sweden + -IUM]

ere (ār) *prep.* & *conj.* (poet. or arch.) Before (of time); **~whi'le,** (arch.) formerly. [OE *ǣr,* = OS, OHG *ēr*, Goth. *airis* f. Gmc **airiz* compar. of **air* adv. early]

ėrĕ'ct¹ *a.* Upright, not stooping, (lit. or fig.); vertical; (of hair etc.) set up, bristling; (of part of the body) enlarged and rigid, esp. from sexual excitement; hence ~LY² *adv.*, ~NESS *n.* [ME, f. L E(*rigere rect-* = *regere* direct) set up]

ėrĕ'ct² *v.t.* Raise, set upright, (*oneself*, body, etc.); build, establish, (lit. or fig.); form or elevate *into* (principle, system, etc.); hence ~OR *n.* [ME, f. as prec.]

ėrĕ'ctile *a.* That can be erected or become erect; **~ tissue** in animals (capable of being distended and becoming rigid upon excitement). [f. F *érectile* (as ERECT¹; see -IL)]

ėrĕ'ction *n.* Erecting; building, structure, (lit. or fig.); (occurrence of) erect state of part of body, esp. of penis. [f. F *érection* or f. L *erectio* (as prec.; see -ION)]

ĕ'rėmite *n.* Hermit (esp. Christian recluse); hence **ĕrėmĭ'tic(al)** *adjs.* [ME f. OF, var. of (*h*)*ermite* HERMIT]

ĕ'rėthism *n.* (Path.) Abnormal excitement (of organ or tissue; fig. of mind). [f. F *éréthisme* f. Gk *erethismos* (*erethizō* irritate; see -ISM)]

ẽrg¹ *n.* (Phys.) Unit of work or energy, work done by force of one dyne when its point of application moves one centimetre in the direction of action of the force. [f. Gk *ergon* work]

ẽrg² *n.* (*pl.* **~s** *or* **areg**). Area of shifting sand dunes in the Sahara. [F, f. Arab. *'irj*]

ẽr'gō *adv.* Therefore. [L]

ẽrgonŏ'm|ĭcs *n.* Study of efficiency of persons in their working environment; hence ~IC *a.*, **ẽrgŏ'nomist** (3) *n.* [f. Gk *ergon* work; cf. ECONOMICS]

ẽrgŏ'sterŏl *n.* Steroid present in ergot etc., a source of vitamin D_2. [f. foll., after CHOLESTEROL]

ẽr'got *n.* (Disease of rye etc. caused by) fungus of genus *Claviceps*; dried mycelium of the fungus, used in medicine. [F, f. OF *argot* cock's spur, f. appearance produced]

ẽr'gotism *n.* Disease produced by bread made from flour affected by ergot. [f. prec. + -ISM]

ĕ'rĭca (*or* ĭrī'ka) *n.* Heath of genus *Erica.* [L, f. Gk *ereikē* heath]

ĕrĭ'gerŏn *n.* Hardy composite herb of genus *Erigeron*, with daisy-like flowers. [f. Gk *ērigerōn* (*ēri* early, *gerōn* old man), some species bearing grey down]

Erin (ĕ'rĭn *or* ẽr'ĭn) *n.* (Ancient or poet. name of) Ireland. [Ir.]

Erī'nȳ|s (ĕ-) *n.* (*pl.* **~es** *pr.* ĕrĭ'nĭēz). (Gk Myth.) A Fury. [Gk]

ĕrĭ'stĭc *a.* & *n.* (Art or exponent) of disputation; (of argument or arguer) aimed or aiming at victory rather than truth. [f. Gk *eristikos* (*erizō* wrangle f. *eris* strife; see -IC)]

||**ẽrk** *n.* (sl.) Naval rating; aircraftman; disliked person. [20th c.; orig. unkn.]

Er'lăng (ẽr'-) *n.* **~ unit,** measure of intensity of traffic flow, corresponding to full occupation of capacity. [f. A. K. ~, Da. mathematician d. 1929]

ẽr'l-kĭng *n.* (Gmc Myth.) Bearded golden-crowned giant who lures little children to land of death. [f. G *erlkönig* alder-king, a mistransl. of Da. *ellerkonge* king of the elves]

ẽr'mĭn|e *n.* **1.** Carnivorous animal (*Mustela erminea*) of weasel family, whose fur is brown in summer and white (except black tail-tip) in winter. **2.** Its winter fur, used in robes of judges, peers, etc.; emblem of honour and purity; hence ~ED[2] (-nd) *a.* **3.** (Her.) white fur marked with black spots; ~ **moth** (having white wings with black spots). [ME, f. OF *(h)ermine*, prob. f. med. L *(mus) Armenius* Armenian (mouse)]

-ern *suf.* forming *adjs.* (*northern* etc.). [OE *-erne*, = OS, OHG *-roni*, ON *-rænn*, f. Gmc **-rōnja*]

ẽrne, *ẽrn, *n.* Sea eagle. [OE *earn*, = OHG *arn*, ON *örn* f. Gmc **arnuz*]

||**Er'nie** (ẽr'-) *n.* Device for drawing prize-winning numbers of Premium Bonds. [f. initial letters of *electronic random number indicator equipment*]

ėrō'd|e *v.* **1.** *v.t.* (Of acid, current, course of events, etc.) eat away, destroy gradually, wear out. **2.** *v.i.* Become eroded. **3.** So ~IBLE *a.*, **ėrō'**SION (-zhon) *n.*, **ėrō'**SIVE *a.* [f. F *éroder* or f. L E(*rodere ros-* gnaw)]

ėrŏ'gėnous *a.* Giving rise to sexual desire or excitement. [irreg. f. as foll. + -GENOUS]

Er'ŏs (ẽr'-) *n.* Earthly or sexual love; god of love, Cupid. [L, f. Gk *Erōs*, as foll.]

ėrŏ'tĭc *a.* Of sexual love, amatory, esp. tending to arouse sexual desire or excitement; hence or cogn. ~A *n. pl.*, erotic literature or art, **ėrŏ'**TICALLY *adv.*, ~ISM *n.*, erotic spirit or character. [f. F *érotique* f. Gk *erōtikos* (*erōs erōtos* sexual love; see -IC)]

ĕ'rotĭsm *n.* Sexual desire or excitement; eroticism. [f. Gk *erōs* (see prec.) + -ISM]

ėrŏtogĕ'nĭc, ĕrotŏ'gėnous, *adjs.* = EROGENOUS. [f. as foll. + -GENIC, -GENOUS]

ĕrotŏ'logy̆ *n.* Description of methods of love-making. [f. Gk *erōs erōtos* sexual love + -O- + -LOGY]

ėrōto|mā'nĭa *n.* Excessive or morbid erotic desire; preoccupation with sexual passion; hence ~MA'NIAC *n.* [f. as prec. + -MANIA]

ẽrr *v.i.* Make mistake(s); (of statement etc.) be incorrect; sin; ~ **on the right side,** avoid the more dangerous of possible errors. [ME, f. OF *errer* f. L *errare*, rel. to Goth. *airzei* error, *airzjan* lead astray]

ĕ'rrand *n.* **1.** Short journey on which person goes or is sent to carry message, deliver goods, etc. (*run, go, (on) errands; errand-boy, errand-girl;* ~ **of mercy,** journey to relieve distress etc.). **2.** Object of journey; purpose. [OE *ǣrende*, = OS *ārundi*, OHG *ārunti* f. Gmc **ǣrundjam*]

ĕ'rrant *a.* **1.** Roaming in quest of adventure, esp. KNIGHT *errant*; (of official) itinerant. **2.** Erring, deviating from correct standard; hence **ĕ'rr**ANCY *n.* [ME; sense 1 f. OF *errer* f. Rom. **iterare* f. L *itinerare* (*iter* journey), sense 2 f. as ERR; see -ANT]

ĕ'rrantry̆ *n.* Condition, conduct, notions, of a knight errant. [f. prec. + -RY]

ėrră't|ĭc *a.* Uncertain in movement; irregular in conduct, habit, opinion; ~**ic block,** (Geol.) large rock brought from a distance by glacier; hence ~ICALLY *adv.* [ME, f. OF *erratique* f. L *erraticus* (as ERR; see -ATIC)]

ĕrrā't|um (*or* -ah'-) *n.* (*pl.* ~**a**). Error in printing or writing, esp. (in *pl.*) errors shown in list attached to book etc. [L, neut. p.p., f. as ERR]

ėrrō'nėous *a.* Mistaken, incorrect; hence ~LY[2] *adv.*, ~NESS *n.* [ME, f. OF or L *erroneus* (*erro -onis* vagabond, f. as ERR) + -OUS]

ĕ'rror *n.* **1.** Mistake (*make, commit, an error;* CLERICAL *error*); condition of erring in opinion or conduct (*error of judgement; realize the error of* one's *ways*); wrong opinion; **in** ~, mistaken(ly), by mistake. **2.** (Math. etc.) Amount of deviation from correct or accurate result. **3.** Hence ~LESS *a.* [ME f. OF *errour* f. L *error -oris* (as ERR; see -OR)]

ẽr'sătz (-zăts) *n.* & *a.* Substitute, imitation, (esp. of inferior kind). [G, = replacement]

Erse (ẽrs) *a.* & *n.* Highland Gaelic or Irish Gaelic (language). [early Sc. form of IRISH]

ẽrst *adv.* (arch.) Formerly, of old. [OE *ǣrest* superl. of *ǣr*; see ERE]

ẽr'stwhīle *a.* & *adv.* **1.** *a.* Former, previous. **2.** *adv.* (arch.) = prec. [f. prec. + WHILE[1]]

ĕrubĕ'scent (ĕroo-) *a.* Reddening, blushing. [f. L E(*rubescere* incept. of *rubēre* be red); see -ESCENT]

ērŭctā'tion *n.* Belching (lit. or fig., esp. of volcano). [f. L *eructatio* f. E(*ructare* belch); see -ATION]

ĕ'rūd|īte (*or* -rŏŏ-) *a.* (Of person or writings) learned; hence or cogn. ~**īte**LY[2] (-tlĭ) *adv.*, ~I'TION *n.* [ME, f. L *eruditus* p.p. of Erudire instruct, train (*rudis* untrained); see -ITE[2]]

ėrŭ'pt *v.i.* Break out or through (lit., or fig. of anger etc.); (of volcano) emit rocks, lava, etc.; (of geyser) spurt water; (of rash etc.) appear on skin; (of teeth) break through gums. [f. L E(*rumpere rupt-* break)]

ėrŭ'ption *n.* Erupting, outbreak, (of volcano, geyser, disease, war, passion, mirth, wit); (Path.) breaking out (of rash etc.); (of teeth) breaking through gums. [OF, or f. L *eruptio* (as prec.; see -ION)]

ėrŭ'ptĭve *a.* Bursting forth; tending to burst forth; of, formed by, forced up by, volcanic eruption; hence ~LY[2] (-vlĭ) *adv.*, ~NESS (-vn-), **ērupti'**VITY, *ns.* [f. ERUPT + -IVE]

-ery̆, -ry̆, *suf.* forming *ns.* meaning (1) class of goods (*drapery*) or things (*greenery, machinery*), body of persons (*citizenry*), (2) employment or condition (*archery, slavery*), (3) place of work or cultivation or breeding or *obtaining (*brewery, orangery, piggery, eatery*), (4) conduct (*foolery*), (5) (often derog.) all that has to do with (*popery*), thing of the nature of. [ME, f. or after F *-erie* (a) f. Rom. *-aria* f. L *-ario-*, (b) f. OF *-ere* (f. L *-ator*) + *-ie* -Y[1]]

ĕry̆'ngō (-nggō) *n.* Sea holly. [f. It. or Sp. *eringio* f. L f. Gk *ēruggion* dim. of *ēruggos* sea holly]

ĕry̆sĭ'pėlas *n.* Local inflammation caused by streptococcus, producing deep red colour on skin. [ME f. L, f. Gk *erusipelas*]

ĕry̆thē'ma *n.* Superficial inflammation of the skin in patches; hence **ĕry̆'thėm**AL *a.* [mod. L, f. Gk *eruthēma* f. *eruthainō* be red (*eruthros*)]

ėry̆'throblăst *n.* Immature erythrocyte. [G, f. as foll. + -BLAST]

ėry̆'throcy̆te *n.* Red blood-corpuscle. [f. Gk *erythros* red + -O- + -CYTE]

-es[1] *suf.* Var. of -s[1]; see notes on Plurals, p. xv.

-es[2] *suf.* Var. of -s[2]; see notes on Verb forms, p. xvi.

Es *symb.* einsteinium.

ĕscadrĭ'lle *n.* French squadron of aeroplanes. [F]

ĕscalā'de *n.* Scaling of walls with ladders. [F, f. Sp. *escalada, -ado*, f. med. L *scalare* (*scala* ladder); see -ADE]

ĕ'scal|āte *v.t.* & *i.* Increase or develop by successive stages; hence ~A'TION *n.* [back form. f. foll.]

ĕ'scalātor *n.* Staircase with endless chain of steps moving continuously up or down; ~ **clause** etc. (providing for change in price etc. under stated conditions). [f. *escalade* v. 'climb wall by ladder' + ELEVATOR]

ĕscallō'nia *n.* Flowering shrub of genus *Escallonia*, orig. S. Amer. [f. *Escallon*, 18th-c. Sp. traveller + -IA[1]]

ėscă'llop *n.* = SCALLOP 1, 2; (Her.) scallop-shell as device; = foll.; (in pl.) = SCALLOP 4. [f. as foll.]

ĕ'scalōpe *n.* Slice of boneless meat, esp. from leg of veal. [F; in OF = shell; see SCALLOP]

ĕscapā'de *n.* Breaking loose from restraint; piece of irresponsible or unorthodox conduct. [F, f. Prov. or Sp. *escapada* (as ESCAPE²; see -ADE)]

ėscā'pe¹ *n.* **1.** Act of escaping; fact of having escaped (*a narrow escape*). **2.** Means of escaping (FIRE¹-*escape*); distraction or relief from reality, esp. given by literature etc. **3.** Leakage (of gas etc.); garden plant growing wild. **4.** ~ **clause** (specifying conditions under which contracting party is free from an obligation); **~-hatch,** means of emergency exit (from ship etc., or fig.); **~-pipe** (for escape of steam or water); ~ **road** (for vehicle unable to make turn on race-track, hill, etc.); **~-shaft** (for escape of miners when other shaft is blocked); ~ **velocity,** minimum velocity needed to escape from gravitational field of a body; ~ **wheel,** toothed wheel in escapement of watch or clock. [f. foll.]

ėscā'pe² *v.* **1.** *v.i.* Get free of restriction or control by fleeing (*from* prison, person, etc.); (of gas or liquid or granular solid) get out of container etc.; get off safely, go unpunished. **2.** *v.t.* Get clear away from (person, his grasp, etc.), avoid (unpleasant thing, do*ing*); not be noticed or recollected by (*his name escapes, had escaped, me*); not be recalled or detected by (person's memory, attention, etc.); (of words, sigh, etc.) issue unawares from (person, his lips); hence **ėscā'p**ABLE *a.* **3.** Hence **ĕscāp**EE' (*or* ĕskā'pē), **ėscā'p**ER¹, *ns.*, one who has escaped. [ME, f. AF, ONF *escaper* f. Rom. *EX(*cappare* f. med. L *cappa* cloak; see CAP¹)]

ėscā'pement (-pm-) *n.* (Of watch or clock) mechanism connecting motive power and regulator; (of piano) space between strings and raised hammer; (arch.) means of escape. [f. F *échappement* (*échapper* escape f. as prec.; see -MENT)]

ėscā'p|ism *n.* Tendency to seek distraction or relief from reality; so ~IST (2) *n.* & *a.* [f. ESCAPE¹ + -ISM]

ĕscapŏ'|logy̆ *n.* Methods and technique of escaping, esp. from captivity, confinement in box, etc.; so ~LOGIST *n.*, performer skilled in these. [f. ESCAPE¹ + -O- + -LOGY]

ĕscar̂'gōt (-gō) *n.* Edible snail. [F]

ėscar̂'p(ment) *n.* (Geog.) Long steep face of plateau etc. [f. F *escarpement* (*escarpe* SCARP; see -MENT)]

-ĕsce *suf.* forming usu. incept. *vbs.* (*deliquesce, effervesce, fluoresce*). [f. or after L *-escere*]

-ĕ'scence *suf.* forming *ns.* corresp. to *adjs.* f. foll. (*deliquescence, effervescence, fluorescence, iridescence*). [f. or after F *-escence* or L *-escentia* (as foll.; see -ENCE)]

-ĕ'scent *suf.* forming *adjs.* denoting onset of a state or variation of colour etc. (*deliquescent, effervescent, fluorescent, iridescent*). [f. or after F *-escent* or L *-escent-* part. st. of (usu. incept.) vbs. in *-escere*]

ĕschatŏ'|logy̆ (ĕsk-) *n.* (Theol.) Doctrine of death, judgement, heaven, and hell; (**realized**) **~logy,** present significance of this in Christian life; hence **ĕschato**LO'GICAL (ĕsk-) *a.*, ~LOGIST *n.* [f. Gk *eskhatos* last + -O- + -LOGY]

ėschea't¹ *n.* (Hist.) Lapsing of property to government or lord of manor on owner's dying intestate without heirs; property so lapsing. [ME f. OF *eschete*, f. Rom. **excadecta* p.p. (as n.) of **excadēre* f. L EX(*cidere* = *cadere* fall)]

ėschea't² *v.* **1.** *v.t.* Confiscate; hand over (property) as an escheat (*to* person, *into* his hands). **2.** *v.i.* Revert by escheat (*to*, or abs.). [ME, f. prec.]

ėschew' (-o͞o') *v.t.* Avoid, abstain from, (action, conduct, kind of food, etc.); hence ~AL *n.* [ME, f. OF *eschiver* f. Rom. **skivare* f. Gmc **skeuh*(*w*)*an* (**skeuh*(*w*)*az* SHY¹)]

eschschŏ'ltzia (ĭskŏ'lsh*a* *or* ĕshŏ'ltsĭa) *n.* Herb of genus *Eschscholtzia*, esp. yellow-flowered Californian poppy. [f. J. F. von *Eschscholtz*, Ger. botanist d. 1831 + -IA¹]

ĕ'scôrt¹ *n.* Body of armed men acting as guard to persons, baggage, etc.; person(s), ship(s), etc., accompanying another on journey for protection or guidance, or for courtesy's sake; man accompanying woman socially. [f. F *escorte* f. It. *scorta* fem. p.p. (as n.) of *scorgere* conduct]

ėscôr't² *v.t.* Act as escort to. [f. F *escorter* f. It. *scortare* (*scorta*; see prec.)]

ĕscrī'be *v.t.* (Math.) Describe (circle) so as to touch one side of triangle exteriorly and the other two sides produced. [f. E- + L *scribere* write]

ĕ'scrĭtoire (-twar̂) *n.* Writing-desk with drawers etc. [F, f. L SCRIPTORIUM]

ĕscrow' (-ō') *n.*, & *v.t.* **1.** *n.* Written legal engagement to do something, kept in third person's custody until some condition has been fulfilled; *money or goods so kept; ***in** ~, so kept. **2.** *v.t.* *Place in escrow. [f. AF *escrowe*, OF *escroe* scrap, scroll, f. med. L *scroda* f. Gmc **skraudh-*; cf. SHRED]

ĕscū'dō *n.* (*pl.* **~s**). Monetary unit of Portugal, Portuguese territories, and Chile. [Sp. and Port., f. L *scutum* shield]

ĕ'scūlent *a.* & *n.* (Thing) fit for food. [f. L *esculentus* (*esca* food; see -ULENT)]

ėscŭ'tcheon (-ch*o*n) *n.* Shield with armorial bearings (**blot on** one's ~, stain on one's reputation); middle of ship's stern where name is placed; pivoted keyhole cover. [f. AF & ONF *escuchon* f. Rom. **scutio -onis* f. L *scutum* shield]

Esd. *abbr.* Esdras (Apocrypha).

-ēse (ēz) *suf.* forming *adjs.* and *ns.* (*pl.* same) (1) f. names of foreign countries and towns (*Japanese, Milanese, Viennese*), meaning '(inhabitant or language) of', (2) f. *ns.* or names of writers (*officialese, Carlylese*), denoting 'style of writing'. [f. OF *-eis* f. Rom. *-*ese* f. L *-ensis*]

E.S.E. *abbr.* east-south-east.

ĕ'sker, ĕ'skar, *n.* (Geol.) Long ridge of post-glacial gravel in river valleys. [f. Ir. *eiscir*]

E'skĭmō (ĕ'-) *n.* (*pl.* **~s** *or* same) & *a.* (Member or language) of people inhabiting arctic coast of America and of E. Siberia; ~ (**dog**), breed of powerful dog used by Eskimos to pull sledges etc. [Da., f. F *Esquimaux* pl., f. Algonquian]

E.S.N. *abbr.* educationally SUBNORMAL.

***ēsŏ'phagus.** See OESOPHAGUS.

ĕsotĕ'rĭc *a.* (Of philosophical doctrine etc.) meant only for the initiated, not generally intelligible; private, confidential; hence ~AL *a.*, **~al**LY² *adv.*, ~ISM (2, 3), ~IST (2), *ns.* [f. Gk *esōterikos* (*esōterō* compar. of *esō* within; see -IC)]

E.S.P. *abbr.* extra-sensory perception.

ĕspadrĭ'lle *n.* Light canvas shoe with plaited fibre sole, alpargata. [F, f. Prov. *espardillo* (*espart* ESPARTO)]

ėspă'lier *n.* Lattice-work on which fruit-trees or ornamental shrubs are trained; tree etc. so trained. [F, f. It. *spalliera* (*spalla* shoulder)]

ĕspar̂'tō *n.* ~ (**grass**), species of grass (*Stipa tenacissima*) growing in Spain and N. Africa, used in paper-making. [Sp., f. L f. Gk *sparton* rope]

ėspĕ'cial (-sh*a*l) *a.* Pre-eminent, exceptional, (*my especial friend*; *thing of especial importance*); belonging chiefly to one person or thing (*for your especial benefit*); hence ~LY² *adv.* [ME f. OF, f. L *specialis* SPECIAL]

Esperă'nt|ō (ĕ-) *n.* Artificial language designed in 1887 as medium for persons of all nations; hence ~IST (3) *n.* [pen-name (f. L *sperare* hope) of its inventor, L. L. Zamenhof, Pol. physician d. 1917]

ėspī'al *n.* Acting as a spy; espying; being espied. [ME, f. OF *espiaille* (*espier*; see ESPY, -AL 2)]
ĕ'spĭonage (*or* -ah'zh) *n.* Practice of spying or using spies, esp. to obtain secret information. [f. F *espionnage* (*espionner* f. *espion* SPY; see -AGE)]
ĕsplanā'de (*or* -ah'd) *n.* Level piece of ground, esp. one used for public promenade; level space separating citadel of fortress from town. [F, f. Sp. *esplanada* f. *esplanar* f. L EX*planare* make level (*planus*); see -ADE]
ėspou'sal (-zal) *n.* **1.** (arch.; usu. in *pl.*) Marriage or betrothal. **2.** (fig.) Espousing *of* (cause etc.). [ME, f. OF *espousailles* f. L *sponsalia* neut. pl. of *sponsalis* (*sponsus* p.p., as foll.; see -AL)]
ėspou'se (-z) *v.t.* (Usu. of man) marry; give (woman) in marriage (*to*); (fig.) adopt, support, (doctrine, cause, etc.). [ME, f. OF *espouser* f. L *sponsare* (*sponsus* p.p. of *spondēre* betroth)]
ĕsprĕ'ssō *n.* (*pl.* **~s**). Apparatus for making coffee under steam pressure; coffee so made; place where such coffee is sold. [It., = pressed out]
esprit (ĕ'sprē *or* ĕsprē') *n.* Sprightliness, wit; ***~ de corps*** (-dekôr'), regard for honour and interests of body one belongs to; ***~ de l'escalier*** (-delĕskah'lyā), clever remark that occurs to one after opportunity to make it is lost. [F, f. L *spiritus* SPIRIT[1]; *corps* body, *escalier* stairs]
ėspȳ' *v.t.* Catch sight of; detect (flaw etc.). [ME, f. OF *espier*; see SPY]
Esq. *abbr.* Esquire.
-ĕ'sque (ĕ'sk) *suf.* forming *adjs.* meaning 'in the manner of' (*arabesque, burlesque, Daliesque, romanesque*). [F, f. It. *-esco* f. med. L *-iscus*]
E'squĭmau (ĕ'skĭmō) *n.* (*pl.* **~x** *pr.* -z). = ESKIMO. [F]
ėsquīr'e *n.* ||Title appended to name of one regarded as gentleman by birth, position, or education, or to name of any man in formal use or in address of letter where there is no prefixed title; *title of law officer etc.; (arch.) = SQUIRE. [ME, f. OF *esquier* f. L *scutarius* shield-bearer (*scutum* shield; see -ARY[1])]
E.S.R.O. (ĕ'zrō) *abbr.* European Space Research Organization.
-ėss[1] *suf.* forming *ns.* denoting females (*actress, adulteress, authoress, countess, goddess, lioness*; sometimes w. sense 'wife of', as *mayoress*). [f. or after F *-esse* f. Rom. *-essa* f. LL f. Gk *-issa*]
-ess[2] *suf.* forming abstract *ns.* f. *adjs.* (*duress*). [ME f. F *-esse* f. L *-itia*; cf. -ICE]
ĕ'ssay[1] *n.* **1.** Attempt (*at, in*). **2.** Literary composition (usu. in prose and short) on any subject; hence **~**IST (3) *n.* [f. F *essai* (*essayer*; see foll.)]
ĕssay'[2] *v.t.* Attempt (task, *to* do, or abs.); (arch.) try, test, (person, thing). [ME, f. ASSAY[2], assim. to F *essayer* f. Rom. **exagiare* weigh, f. LL *exagium* weighing (*exigere* weigh; see EXACT[2])]
ĕ'ssence *n.* **1.** All that makes a thing what it is; intrinsic nature (**in ~**, fundamentally); indispensable quality or element (**of the ~**, indispensable). **2.** Extract obtained by distillation etc. (lit. or fig.); perfume, scent, etc., esp. as alcoholic solution of volatile substances. **3.** Abstract entity; reality underlying phenomena. [ME f. OF, f. L *essentia* f. **essens -ntis* fictitious part. of *esse* be, repr. Gk *ousia*]
Essē'ne (ĕ-; *or* ĕ'-) *n.* Member of ancient Jewish ascetic sect, living communally. [f. L f. Gk pl. *Essēnoi*]
ėssĕ'ntial (-shal) *a.* & *n.* **1.** *a.* Of or constituting a thing's essence; fundamental; indispensable (*to*); exceedingly important; (of disease) idiopathic; that is or resembles an essence (**~ oil,** volatile OIL with characteristic odour etc.); hence **~**ITY (-shĭă'l-) *n.*, **~**LY[2] *adv.* **2.** *n.* (esp. in *pl.*) Indispensable or fundamental element or thing. [ME, f. LL *essentialis* (as ESSENCE; see -IAL)]
-ėst[1] *suf.* forming superl. of *adjs.* and *advs.* esp. of one or sometimes two syllables (*widest, narrowest*); see notes on Superlatives, p. xv. [OE *-ost-, -ust-, -ast-* f. Gmc **-ōstaz*, & OE *-est-, -st-* f. Gmc **-istaz*]
-ėst[2], **-st,** *suf.* (arch.) forming 2nd pers. sing. of *vbs.* (*canst, doest, dost, findest, gavest*); see notes on Verb forms, p. xvi. [OE *est, -ast, -st,* = OHG *-ist* etc., Goth. *-is* etc.]
EST *abbr.* Eastern Standard Time; electro-shock treatment.
ėstă'blĭsh *v.t.* Set up (government, business, etc.) on permanent basis; settle (person, one*self*, *in* office, status, etc.); appoint (civil servant etc.) to permanent (opp. temporary) post; secure permanent acceptance for (custom, precedent, belief, etc.); place beyond dispute (fact, *that*); make (church, religion) officially national. [ME, f. OF *establir* (st. *-iss-*; see -ISH[2]) f. L *stabilire* (*stabilis* STABLE[1])]
ėstă'blĭshment *n.* Establishing; church system established by law; organized body of men maintained for a purpose, (*army, navy, civil service, establishment*; **peace, war, ~**, reduced, increased, army etc. in time of peace, war); household, staff of servants etc.; public institution, house of business; ||(esp. **the E~**) social group exercising authority or influence, and generally seeking to resist changes. [ME, f. prec. + -MENT]
ėstăblĭshmentār'ĭan *a.* & *n.* (Person) adhering to, or advocating the principle of, an established Church. [f. prec. + -ARIAN]
estaminet (ĕstă'mĭnā) *n.* Small French café etc. selling alcoholic liquor. [F, f. Walloon *staminé* byre (*stamo* pole for tethering cow, prob. f. G *stamm* stem)]
ėstā'te *n.* **1.** Order or class forming part of body politic and sharing in government; **the Three E~s (of the Realm)** (in England, Lords Spiritual, Lords Temporal, Commons); **third ~**, (usu.) French bourgeoisie before Revolution; **fourth ~**, (joc.) the PRESS[1] 6; **E~s General,** = STATE[1]*s General.* **2.** Person's interest in landed property (**real ~**) or movables (**personal ~**); person's collective assets and liabilities; ||**~ duty,** ***~ tax,** = DEATH *duty.* **3.** Landed property; ||**~ agent,** (1) steward of estate, (2) one who conducts business in sale of houses and land; ||**~ (car),** light saloon motor car constructed or adapted to carry both passengers and goods in one compartment, usu. with rear door. **4.** Property where rubber, tea, grapes, etc., are cultivated. **5.** Residential, industrial, etc., district planned by one owner or local council. **6.** (arch.) Condition (*come to man's estate*; *holy estate of matrimony*). [ME, f. OF *estat* f. L STATUS]
ėstee'm *v.t.*, & *n.* **1.** *v.t.* Think favourably of, regard as valuable; consider (*I shall esteem it* (*as*) *a favour*). **2.** *n.* Favourable opinion, regard, respect. [ME, f. OF *estimer* f. L *aestimare* fix price of]
ĕ'ster *n.* (Chem.) Compound formed by replacing the hydrogen of an acid by an alkyl, aryl, etc., radical; hence **ĕstĕ'rĭ**FY *v.t.* [G, prob. f. *essig* vinegar + *äther* ether]
Esth. *abbr.* Esther (O.T. & Apocrypha).
***ē'sthēte** etc. Var. of AESTHETE etc.
ĕ'stĭmable *a.* Worthy of esteem. [F, f. L *aestimabilis* (as ESTEEM; see -ABLE)]
ĕ'stĭmate[1] *n.* Approximate judgement (of number, amount, etc.); quantity assigned by this (||**the E~s,** forecasts of national expenditure, presented annually to Parliament); contractor's statement of sum for which he will undertake specified work; judgement of character or

qualities. [f. foll., or f. L *aestimatus* f. *aestimare* fix price of; see -ATE[1]]

ĕ'stĭm|āte[2] *v.t.* Form an estimate of or *that*; fix (number etc.) by estimate *at* (so much); form an opinion of or *that*; hence or cogn. **~ative** *a.*, **~ātor** *n.* [f. L *aestimare* fix price of + -ATE[3]]

ĕstĭmā'tion *n.* Judgement of worth (*in my estimation*; (arch.) esteem (*hold in estimation*; *be in estimation*). [ME f. OF, or f. L *aestimatio* (as prec.; sec -ATION)]

estival etc. See AESTIVAL etc.

Estō'nĭan (ĕ-) *n.* & *a.* (Native, Finno-Ugric language) of Estonia. [f. *Estonia*, republic of U.S.S.R. + -AN]

ėstŏ'p *v.t.* (-pp-). (Law). Bar or preclude esp. by estoppel (*from* thing, *from* doing); hence **~page** *n.* [ME, f. AF, OF *estoper* f. LL *stuppare* stop up f. L *stuppa* tow (cf. STOP[1], STUFF)]

ėstŏ'ppel *n.* (Law). Being precluded from a course of action by one's own previous behaviour. [f. OF *estoup(p)ail* bung (*estoper*, as prec.; see -AL 2)]

ėstō'vers (-z) *n. pl.* Necessaries allowed by law (as wood for repairs or fuel taken by a tenant from his holding); right of common whereby wood etc. may be taken from another's property. [f. AF *estover*, OF *-eir* be necessary, f. L *est opus*; see -ER[4]]

ĕstra'de (-ah'd) *n.* Raised platform, dais. [F, f. Sp. *estrado* carpeted floor f. L *stratum* neut. p.p. (as n.) of *sternere* spread]

ėstrā'nge (-nj) *v.t.* Cause (person) to turn away in feeling or affection (*from* another); hence **~MENT** (-jm-) *n.* [ME, f. AF *estraunger*, OF *estranger* f. L *extraneare* treat as a stranger (*extraneus*; cf. EXTRANEOUS)]

ėstrea't *v.t.*, & *n.* (Law). (Make) copy of court record of (fine etc.) for use in prosecution; enforcement of fine or forfeiture of recognizance. [ME, f. AF *estrete*, OF *estraite* fem. p.p. (as n.) of *estraire* f. L *extrahere* EXTRACT[2]]

***ē'strogėn.** See OESTROGEN.

***ē'strum, -us.** See OESTRUS.

ĕ'stūar|ў *n.* Tidal mouth of large river; hence **~INE**[1] *a.* [f. L *aestuarium* tidal channel, neut. a. (as n.) f. *aestus* tide; see -ARY[1]]

e.s.u. *abbr.* electrostatic unit(s).

ėsūr'ĭ|ent *a.* (joc. or arch.) Hungry; impecunious and greedy; hence **~ENCE**, **~ENCY**, *ns.* [f. L *esurire*, desiderative f. *edere es-* eat; see -ENT]

-ėt[1] *suf.* forming *ns.* (orig. dim.) (*bullet*, *fillet*, *hatchet*, *pullet*, *sonnet*). [f. OF *-et -ete* f. Rom. *-itto -itta*]

-ėt[2], **-ēte,** *suf.* forming *ns.* usu. denoting persons (*athlete*, *comet*, *poet*). [f. Gk *-ētēs*]

ē'ta[1] *n.* Seventh Greek letter (H, η) = ē (cf. EPSILON). [Gk]

e'ta[2] (ā'-) *n.* Member of outcast class in Japan. [Jap.]

E.T.A. *abbr.* estimated time of arrival.

ĕtaer'īō (-ēr'-) *n.* (*pl.* **~s**). (Bot.) Aggregate fruit (e.g. strawberry, raspberry). [f. F *etairion*, *-ium*, f. Gk *hetaireia* association]

ĕt ăl. *abbr.* and others. [f. L *et alii*, *et alia*, etc.]

ĕ'talŏn *n.* (Phys.) Device of two reflecting plates producing interfering light-beams. [f. F *étalon* standard]

étatisme (ātahtē'zm) *n.* Extreme authority of State over individual citizens. [F (*état* STATE[1], *-isme* -ISM)]

etc. *abbr.* = foll.

ĕt cĕ'tera, ėtcĕ'tera, *phr.* & *n.* **1.** *phr.* And the rest, and so on; and the customary continuation (*I remain yours etc.*); and similar things; or similar things. **2.** *n.* (in *pl.*) (The usual) extras, sundries. [ME f. L]

ĕtch *v.* & *n.* **1.** *v.t.* Reproduce (picture etc.) by engraving metal plate etc. with acids or corrosives, esp. for purpose of printing copies; engrave (plate) thus; (fig.) impress deeply *on*. **2.** *v.i.* Practise this craft. **3.** Hence **~'ER**[1] *n.* **4.** *n.* Action or process of etching. [f. Du *etsen* f. G *ätzen* etch f. OHG *azzen* cause to eat or be eaten f. Gmc **atjan* causative of **etan* EAT]

ĕ'tchant *n.* Corrosive used in etching. [f. prec. + -ANT]

ĕ'tchĭng *n.* In vbl senses; copy from etched plate. [f. ETCH + -ING[1]]

-ēte. See -ET[2].

ėtėr'nal (*or* ē-) *a.* That always (has existed and) will exist (*eternal life*, *punishment*; **the E~**, God; *Eternal* CITY); unchanging; (colloq.) incessant, too frequent, (*these eternal arguments*); **~ triangle,** two men and a woman or two women and a man, with problems resulting from conflict of sexual attractions; hence or cogn. **ėtėrn(al)IZE** (3) *vbs. t.*, **~LY**[2] *adv.* [ME f. OF, f. LL *aeternalis* f. L *aeternus* (= *aeviternus* f. *aevum* age); see -AL]

ėtėr'nĭtў (*or* ē-) *n.* Being eternal; (in *pl.*) eternal truths; infinite time, past or future; the future life; (colloq.) very long time; **~ ring,** finger-ring with gems set all round it, symbolizing eternity. [ME, f. OF *eternité* f. L *aeternitas -tatis* (*aeternus*; see prec., -ITY)]

Etē'sian (ĭtē'zhan) *a.* **~ winds** (blowing annually in Mediterranean from N. for about 40 days in summer). [f. L f. Gk *etēsios* (*etos* year) + -AN]

ĕth. See EDH.

-ėth[1]**.** See -TH[2].

-ėth[2]**, -th**[3]**,** *suf.* (arch.) forming 3rd pers. pres. sing. of *vbs.* (*doeth*, *doth*, *findeth*, *saith*); see notes on Verb forms, p. xvi. [OE *-eth*, *-ath*, *-th*, = OHG *-it* etc., Goth. *-ith* etc.]

ĕ'thāne *n.* (Chem.) Hydrocarbon of the paraffin series, C_2H_6. [f. ETHER + -ANE]

ĕ'thanŏl *n.* (Chem.) Ethyl ALCOHOL. [f. prec. + ALCOHOL]

ē'ther *n.* **1.** Clear sky, upper regions beyond clouds. **2.** (Phys.) Medium formerly assumed to permeate space and fill interstices between particles of matter; medium in which electromagnetic waves were formerly thought to be transmitted; (colloq.) radio; hence **~IC** *a.* **3.** (Chem.) Colourless volatile liquid produced by action of acids on alcohol, used as solvent or anaesthetic; compound with structure similar to this, having oxygen atom joined to two alkyl etc. groups. [ME f. OF, or f. L f. Gk *aithēr* f. root of *aithō* burn, shine]

ėthēr'ėal, -ial, *a.* **1.** Light, airy; heavenly; of unearthly delicacy of substance, character, or appearance, whence **~ITY** (-ă'l-) *n.*, **~IZE** (3) *v.t.*, **~LY**[2] *adv.* **2.** (Phys. & Chem.). Of or like ether; **~ oil,** essential or volatile oil. [f. L *aethereus*, *-ius* f. Gk *aitherios* (as prec.) + -AL]

ē'therīz|e, -īs|e (-īz), *v.t.* Put (patient) under influence of ether; hence **~A'TION** *n.* [f. ETHER 3 + -IZE]

ĕ'thĭc *a.* & *n.* **1.** *a.* Relating to morals, treating of moral questions; morally correct, honourable; **~ dative,** (Gram.) dative of person indirectly interested (*answer* me *the telephone*); hence **~IZE** (3) *v.t.* **2.** *n.* Set of principles of morals (*the Quaker ethic*); (in *pl.*, also treated as *sing.*) science of morals, moral principles, rules of conduct, whole field of moral science. [ME, f. OF *éthique* or f. L f. Gk *ēthikos* (as ETHOS; see -IC)]

ĕ'thĭcal *a.* = prec. 1, whence **~ITY** (-ă'l-) *n.*; (of medicine or drug) not advertised to the general public, and usu. available only on doctor's prescription. [f. prec. + -AL]

ĕ'thĭcallў *adv.* In adj. senses. [f. ETHIC or prec.; see -ICALLY]

Ethĭō'pĭan (ē-) *a.* & *n.* (Native or inhabitant) of

Ethiopia; (arch.) Negro. [f. *Ethiopia* f. L *Aethiops* (as foll.) + -AN]

Ethiŏ'pĭc (ē-) *a.* & *n.* (Of the) Christian liturgical language of Ethiopia. [f. L f. Gk *aithiopikos* (*Aithiops* Ethiopian f. *aithō* burn + *ōps* face; see -IC)]

ĕ'thmoid *a.* Sievelike; ~ **bone,** square bone at root of nose, with many perforations through which olfactory nerves pass to nose; hence **ĕthmoi'dAL** *a.* [f. Gk *ēthmoeidēs* (*ēthmos* sieve; see -OID)]

ĕ'thnârch (-k) *n.* Governor of a people or province; so ~Y[1] *n.* [f. Gk *ethnarkhēs* (*ethnos* nation, *-arkhēs* ruler)]

ĕ'thnĭc *a.* & *n.* **1.** *a.* Pertaining to race, ethnological, whence **ĕthnĭ'cITY** *n.*; (arch.) gentile, heathen; *originating from a specified racial, linguistic, etc., group (usu. a minority); hence **ĕ'thnICALLY** *adv.* **2.** *n.* *Member of ethnic group; (in *pl.*, usu. treated as *sing.*) ethnology. [ME, f. eccl. L f. Gk *ethnikos* heathen (*ethnos* nation; see -IC)]

ĕ'thnĭcal *a.* Ethnological. [f. prec. + -AL]

ĕthnocĕ'ntr|ĭc *a.* Regarding one's own race as the most important; so **~ĭ'cITY,** ~ISM (2), *ns.* [f. Gk *ethnos* nation + -CENTRIC]

ĕthnŏ'graphy̆ *n.* Scientific description of races of men; hence **ĕthnŏ'GRAPHER** *n.*, **ĕthnogră'phIC(AL)** *adjs.* [f. Gk *ethnos* nation + -GRAPHY]

ĕthnŏ'logy̆ *n.* Science of human races and their relations to one another and their characteristics; hence **ĕthnolŏ'gIC(AL)** *adjs.*, **ĕthnŏ'LOGIST** *n.* [f. as prec. + -LOGY]

ĕthnomūsĭcŏ'log|y̆ (-z-) *n.* Study of music of one or more cultures; so ~IST (3) *n.* [f. Gk *ethnos* nation + MUSICOLOGY]

ēthŏ'log|y̆ *n.* Science of character-formation; science of animal behaviour; hence **ētho-LO'GICAL** *a.*, ~IST (3) *n.* [f. L f. Gk *ēthologia* (as ETHOS; see -LOGY)]

ē'thŏs *n.* Characteristic spirit and beliefs of community, people, system, literary work, or person. [mod. L, f. Gk *ēthos* nature, disposition]

ĕ'thy̆l (*or* ē'thīl) *n.* (Chem.) Radical, C_2H_5, derived from ethane, present in (*ethyl*) ALCOHOL and in ether. [G, f. as ETHER + -YL]

ĕ'thy̆lēne *n.* Hydrocarbon of olefin series, C_2H_4; ~ **glycol,** colourless liquid used as antifreeze etc.; hence **ĕthy̆lē'nIC** *a.* [f. prec. + -ENE]

-ĕ'tĭc *suf.* forming *adjs.* and *ns.* (*ascetic, emetic, genetic, synthetic*). [f. or after Gk *-ētikos* or *-ētikos*; cf. -IC]

ē'tĭol|āte *v.t.* Make (plant) pale by excluding light; give sickly hue to (person); hence ~A'TION *n.* [f. F *étioler* f. Norm. *étieuler* make into haulm (*éteule* f. pop. L **stupila* f. L *stipula* straw), + -ATE[3]]

***ētĭŏ'logy̆.** See AETIOLOGY.

ĕtĭquĕ'tte (-kĕ't; *or* ĕ'-) *n.* Conventional rules of personal behaviour in polite society; ceremonial of court; unwritten code restricting professional men in what concerns interests of their brethren or dignity of their profession (esp. *medical, legal, etiquette*). [f. F *étiquette* TICKET, etiquette]

ĕ'tna *n.* (Hist.) Vessel for heating small quantity of liquid by burning spirit. [f. *E*~, volcano in Sicily]

E'ton (ē'-) *n.* ~ **blue,** = CAMBRIDGE *blue*; ~ **collar** (broad and stiff, worn outside coat-collar); ~ **crop,** cutting of woman's hair short all over; *Eton* FIVES; ~ **jacket,** short coat reaching only to waist; hence **Etō'nIAN** (ē-) *a.* & *n.*, (past or present member) of Eton College. [f. ~ College, school in Berkshire]

étrier (ā'trĭā) *n.* (Mount.) Short rope ladder with a few rungs of wood or metal. [F, = stirrup]

Etrŭ'scan (ĭ-) *a.* & *n.* (Native or language) of ancient Etruria; so **Etrŭscŏ'LOGY** (ĭ-) *n.* [f. L *Etruscus* + -AN]

et seq(q)., **et sq(q).,** *abbrs.* and the following (pages, matter, etc.). [f. L *et sequentia*]

-ĕ'tte *suf.* forming *ns.*, meaning (1) small (*cigarette, kitchenette, roomette*), (2) imitation or substitute (*flannelette, leatherette*), (3) female (*suffragette, usherette*). [f. or after OF *-ette* fem. (as -ET[1])]

étude (ā'tūd *or* ātū'd) *n.* Short musical composition or exercise. [F, = study]

étui (ĕtwee') *n.* Small case for needles etc. [f. F *étui* f. OF *estui* prison (*estuier* shut up)]

-ē'tum *suf.* forming *ns.* denoting collection of trees or other plants (*arboretum, pinetum*). [L]

ĕty̆mŏ'logīze, -īse (-īz), *v.* **1.** *v.t.* Give or trace the etymology of. **2.** *v.i.* Study etymology. [f. med. L *etymologizare* f. L *etymologia* (see foll., -IZE)]

ĕty̆mŏ'logy̆ *n.* Account of or facts relating to formation of word and development of its meaning; branch of linguistic science concerned with this; FOLK *etymology*; hence or cogn. **ĕty̆mŏ'LOGER, ĕty̆mŏ'LOGIST,** *ns.*, **ĕty̆molŏ'gIC(AL)** *adjs.* [f. OF *ethimologie* f. L f. Gk *etumologia* (as foll.; see -LOGY)]

ĕ'ty̆m|on *n.* (*pl.* ~**a**). Primary word that gives rise to a derivative or borrowed or later form. [L, f. Gk *etumon* (neut. of *etumos* true) literal sense or original form of a word]

eu- *comb. form.* Well, easily. [Gk]

Eu *symb.* europium.

eucaly̆'ptus, eu'caly̆pt, *n.* Austral. etc. evergreen tree of genus *Eucalyptus*; **eucalyptus (oil),** essential oil from leaves of this used as antiseptic etc. [mod. L, f. EU- + Gk *kaluptos* covered (*kaluptō* cover), unopened flower being protected by cap]

eu'charĭs (ū'k-) *n.* S. Amer. bulbous plant of genus *Eucharis*, with white umbellate flowers. [Gk EU(*kharis* grace) pleasing]

Eu'charĭst (ū'k-) *n.* Christian sacrament in which bread and wine are consecrated and consumed; consecrated elements, esp. the bread, (*give, receive, the Eucharist*); hence ~IC(AL) (-ĭ's-) *adjs.* [ME, f. OF *eucariste* f. eccl. L f. eccl. Gk *eukharistia* thanksgiving f. Gk EU-(*kharistos* f. *kharizomai* offer willingly) grateful]

eu'chre (-*ker*) *n.*, & *v.t.* **1.** *n.* Amer. card game for 2, 3, or 4 persons. **2.** *v.t.* Gain advantage over (opponent) by his failure to take three tricks at euchre; (fig.) deceive, outwit. [19th c.; orig. unkn.]

Euclĭ'dėan *a.* Of Euclid; ~ **geometry,** that of ordinary experience, based on postulates used by Euclid; ~ **space** (for which Euclidean geometry is valid). [f. L *Euclideus* f. Gk *Eukleideios* (*Eukleidēs* Euclid, Alexandrian geometrician *c.* 300 B.C.) + -AN]

eudėmŏ'nĭc, -daem-, (-dĭm-) *a.* Conducive to happiness. [f. Gk *eudaimonikos* (as foll.; see -IC)]

eudē'mon|ĭsm, -dae'm-, *n.* System of ethics basing moral obligation on likelihood of actions to produce happiness; so ~IST (2) *n.*, **~ĭ'stIC** *a.* [f. Gk *eudaimonismos* f. *eudaimonia* happiness f. EU(*daimōn* guardian spirit) happy; see -ISM]

eudĭŏ'mėter *n.* Graduated glass tube in which gases may be chemically combined by electric spark, used in chemical experiments; hence **eudĭomĕ'trIC(AL)** *adjs.*, **eudĭŏ'METRY** *n.* [f. Gk *eudios* clear (weather) + -METER; orig. used to measure amount of oxygen, thought to be greater in clear air]

eugĕ'n|ĭc *a.* Of the production of fine (esp. human) offspring by improvement of inherited qualities; hence ~ICALLY *adv.*, ~ICS, **eu'gėn**IST (2), *ns.* [f. EU- + Gk *gen-* produce + -IC]

euhē'mer|ism *n.* Explanation of myths on historical basis; so ~IST (2) *n.*, **~ĭ'st**IC *a.*, ~IZE (4) *v.t.* & *i.* [f. *Euhemerus*, Sicilian author of 4th c. B.C. + -ISM]

eulō'gĭ|um *n.* (*pl.* **~a** *or* **~ums**). = EULOGY. [med. L; see EULOGY]

eu'log|ize, ~ise (-iz), *v.t.* Extol, praise, in speech or writing; so ~IST (1) *n.*, **~ĭ'st**IC *a.* [f. foll. + -IZE]

eu'logy̆ *n.* Speech or writing in praise of person etc., *esp. funeral oration; (expression of) praise. [f. med. L *eulogium* f. (app. by confus. w. L *elogium* epitaph) LL f. Gk *eulogia* praise (as EU-, -LOGY)]

Eumĕ'nĭdēs (-ēz) *n. pl.* (Euphemistic name for) the Furies. [Gk, = kindly ones]

eu'nuch (-k) *n.* Castrated man, esp. one employed in harem, or as court official (esp. in the Orient or under Roman Empire); (fig.) person lacking effectiveness (*political eunuch*); hence ~OID *a.* & *n.* [ME, f. L f. Gk *eunoukhos* lit. bedchamber attendant (*eunē* bed, **okh-* cogn. w. *ekhō* hold)]

euŏ'ny̆mus *n.* Plant of genus *Euonymus*, e.g. spindle-tree. [L, f. Gk EU(*ōnumos* f. *onoma* name) of lucky name]

eupĕ'ptĭc *a.* Of or having good digestion. [f. Gk EU(*peptos* f. *peptō* digest) + -IC]

eu'phėm|ĭsm *n.* Substitution of mild or vague or roundabout expression for harsh or blunt or direct one; expression thus substituted (*'intimacy' is a euphemism for 'sexual intercourse'*); so **~ĭ'st**IC *a.*, ~IZE (1, 2) *v.t.* & *i.* [f. Gk *euphēmismos* f. EU(*phēmos* f. *phēmē* speaking); see -ISM]

euphō'nĭum *n.* (Mus.) Wind instrument of saxhorn family, tenor tuba. [mod. L, f. Gk *euphōnos*; see foll.]

eu'phony̆ *n.* Pleasing sound; (usu. of word, phrase, etc.) quality of having this; tendency to phonetic change for ease of pronunciation; hence **euphŏ'n**IC, **euphō'nĭ**OUS, *adjs.*, **eu'phon**IZE (3) *v.t.* [f. F *euphonie* f. LL f. Gk *euphōnia* f. EU(*phōnos* f. *phōnē* sound)]

euphôr'bĭa *n.* Herb or shrub of genus *Euphorbia*, spurge. [ME, f. L *euphorbea* f. *Euphorbus* physician to Juba II of Mauritania (1st C. A.D.) + -IA[1]]

euphôr'ĭa *n.* Feeling of well-being, esp. one based on over-confidence or over-optimism; hence **euphŏ'r**IC *a.* [Gk, f. EU(*phoros* f. *pherō* bear) well-bearing; see -IA[1]]

euphôr'ĭant *a.* & *n.* (Drug) inducing euphoria. [f. prec. + -ANT]

eu'phrasy̆ *n.* Plant of genus *Euphrasia*, eyebright. [f. med. L f. Gk *euphrasia* cheerfulness f. EU(*phrainō* f. *phrēn* mind) gladden]

eu'phrōe. Var. of UPHROE.

eu'phū|ĭsm *n.* Artificial or affected style of writing; high-flown style; so ~IST (2) *n.*, **~ĭ'st**IC *a.* [orig. of writing in imit. of Lyly's *Euphues* (16th c.; Gk, = well endowed by nature); see -ISM]

Eurā'sian (ūrā'zhan) *a.* & *n.* **1.** (Person) of mixed European and Asian parentage. **2.** *a.* Of Europe and Asia. [f. *Europe* + *Asia* + -AN]

Eură'tom (ūr-) *n.* European Atomic Energy Community. [abbr.]

eurē'ka (ūr-) *int.* & *n.* (The exulting exclamation) 'I have (found) it!' [f. Gk *heurēka* 1st pers. sing. perf. of *heuriskō* find; orig. of ARCHIMEDES]

eurhy̆'thm|ĭc (ūrĭ'-) *a.* In or of harmonious proportion (esp. in architecture); hence ~ICS *n. pl.*, harmony of bodily movement, esp. as developed with music and dance into a system of education. [f. *eurhythmy* harmony of proportions etc. f. L f. Gk *euruthmia* (as EU-, *rhuthmos* proportion, rhythm) + -IC]

eur'ō (ūr'ō) *n.* (*pl.* **~s**). (Austral.) Large reddish kangaroo. [Aboriginal]

Eur'ō- (ūr'ō) *comb. form.* Europe, European, as: **~crat,** bureaucrat of European Communities; **~dollar,** dollar held in bank in Europe etc., not in U.S.; **~vision,** television of European range. [abbr.]

Europē'an (ūr-) *a.* & *n.* (Native or inhabitant) of Europe; (person) descended from natives of Europe; happening in or extending over Europe (*a European reputation*); (person) concerned with Europe as a whole rather than its individual countries; ***~ plan** (charging for hotel-room without meals); hence ~ISM (2, 3, 4), **~īz**A'TION, *ns.*, ~IZE (3) *v.t.* [f. F *européen* f. L *europaeus* (L f. Gk *Eurōpē* Europe) + -EAN]

eurō'pĭum (ūr-) *n.* (Chem.) Metallic element of lanthanide series. [mod. L, f. *Europe* + -IUM]

Eustā'chian (-shan) *a.* **~ tube,** canal leading from pharynx to cavity of middle ear. [f. L *Eustachius* = B. *Eustachi*, It. anatomist d. 1574 + -AN]

eu'stasy̆ *n.* Uniform change of sea level throughout the world; so **eustă'tĭ**C *a.* [back form. f. G *eustatisch* a. (as EU-, STATIC)]

eutĕ'ctĭc *a.* & *n.* (Phys.) ~ **(mixture),** mixture whose constituents are in such proportions as to melt and solidify at one temperature (**~ temperature** or **point**) like a pure substance. [f. Gk EU(*tēktos* f. *tēkō* melt) + -IC]

euthanā'sĭa (-z-) *n.* Gentle and easy death; bringing about of this, esp. in case of incurable and painful disease. [Gk (as EU-, *thanatos* death)]

eutrŏ'phĭc *a.* (Of lake etc.) rich in nutrients and hence having excessive plant growth, which kills animal life by deprivation of oxygen; hence ~ATE[3] *v.t.*, make eutrophic, ~A'TION *n.* [f. foll. + -IC]

eu'trophy̆ *n.* State of being eutrophic. [f. Gk EU(*trophia* f. *trephō* nourish) + -Y[1]]

eV *abbr.* electron-volt.

E.V.A. *abbr.* extra-vehicular activity.

ėvă'cū|āte *v.t.* **1.** Empty (esp. bowel or other bodily organ *of* contents, whence ~ANT *a.* & *n.*; vessel *of* air etc.); discharge (faeces etc., or abs.; lit. or fig.). **2.** Withdraw from, remove occupants of, (place; esp. of troops); remove (person) esp. from place considered to be dangerous *to* safer place, whence ~EE' *n.*, person so removed. **3.** So ~A'TION *n.* [f. L E(*vacuare* f. *vacuus* empty) + -ATE[3]]

ėvā'de *v.t.* Escape from, avoid, (attack, pursuit, designs, adversary, blow, obstacle, etc.); avoid doing (duty etc.), answering (question), paying (tax due), yielding to (argument etc.); defeat intention of (law etc., esp. while complying with its letter); (of thing) elude, baffle; hence **ėvā'd**ABLE *a.* [f. F *évader* f. L E(*vadere vas-* go)]

ėvă'gĭn|āte *v.t.* (Physiol.) Turn (tubular organ) inside out; hence ~A'TION *n.* [f. L E(*vaginare* f. VAGINA) + -ATE[3]]

ėvă'lū|āte *v.t.* Ascertain amount of; find numerical expression for; appraise, assess; hence or cogn. ~A'TION *n.*, **~at**IVE *a.* [back form. f. *evaluation* f. F *évaluation* (*évaluer* f. as E-, VALUE)]

ĕvanĕ'sce *v.i.* Fade out of sight; become effaced; disappear. [f. L E(*vanescere* f. *vanus* empty); see -ESCE]

ĕvanĕ'sc|ent *a.* (Of impression, appearance, etc.) quickly fading; hence ~ENCE *n.*, **~ent**LY[2] *adv.* [f. as prec.; see -ENT]

ėvă'ngel (-nj-) *n.* (arch.) The gospel; any of the four Gospels; doctrine, principle, (of politics etc.). [ME, f. OF *evangile* f. eccl. L f. Gk EU(*aggelion*; cf. ANGEL) good news]

evangelic. Var. (arch.) of foll.

ēvăngĕ'lĭcal (-nj-) *a.* & *n.* Of or according to the teaching of the gospel or the Christian religion; (member) of the Protestant school maintaining that the essence of the gospel consists in doctrine of salvation by faith in Atonement, whence ~ISM (3) *n.*; hence ~LY² *adv.* [f. eccl. L f. eccl. Gk *euaggelikos* (as EVANGEL; see -IC, -AL)]

ėvă'ngelĭsm (-nj-) *n.* Preaching or promulgation of the gospel; = EVANGELICALISM. [f. EVANGEL + -ISM]

ėvă'ngelĭst (-nj-) *n.* Writer of one of the four Gospels; preacher of the gospel; layman doing missionary work. [ME, f. OF *evangeliste* f. eccl. L *evangelista* f. Gk *euaggelistēs* (as EVANGELIZE; see -IST)]

ėvăngelĭ'stĭc (-nj-) *a.* Of the four evangelists; of preachers of the gospel; = EVANGELICAL. [f. prec. + -IC]

ėvă'ngeliz|e (-nj-), **-īs|e** (-īz), *v.t.* Preach the gospel to (persons, or abs.); win over (person) to Christianity; hence ~A'TION *n.* [ME, f. eccl. L *evangelizare* f. eccl. Gk *euaggelizomai* (as EVANGEL; see -IZE)]

ėvă'nĭsh *v.i.* (literary). Vanish; die away; hence ~MENT *n.* [ME, f. OF *evanir* (st. *-iss-*; see -ISH²) f. Rom. **exvanire* = L *evanescere* EVANESCE]

ėvă'por|āte *v.t.* & *i.* Turn from solid or liquid into vapour; (cause to) lose moisture as vapour; (fig.) (cause to) be lost or disappear; **~ated milk,** unsweetened milk concentrated by partial evaporation of its liquid content; hence or cogn. ~ABLE, **~at**IVE, *adjs.*, ~A'TION, **~āt**OR, *ns.* [f. L E(*vaporare* f. as VAPOUR) + -ATE³]

ėvā'sion (-zhon) *n.* Act or means of evading; subterfuge, prevaricating excuse. [ME f. OF, f. L *evasio -onis* (as EVADE; see -ION)]

ėvā'sĭve *a.* Seeking to evade, addicted to evasion; tending to evasion; **~ action** (to avoid trouble etc.); hence ~LY² (-vlĭ) *adv.*, ~NESS (-vn-) *n.* [f. as prec. + -IVE]

Eve¹ (ēv) *n.* First woman, in Hebrew tradition; **daughter of ~,** woman (often w. allus. to feminine curiosity etc.). [OE *Ēfe* f. LL *Eva* f. Heb. *Ḥavvāh*, orig. = life, living]

ēve² *n.* Evening or day before (*of*) church festival or any date or event; time just before anything (*on the eve of an election*); (arch.) evening. [ME, =EVEN¹; for loss of *-n* cf. MAID]

ėvĕ'ction *n.* Perturbation of moon's motion by sun's attraction. [f. L E(*vectio* f. *vehere vect-* carry); see -ION]

ē'ven¹, **e'en**¹ (Sc.; ēn), *n.* **1.** (poet.) Evening. **2. ~song,** evening prayer in Church of England. [OE *ǣfen*, =OS, OHG *āband*]

ē'ven² *a.* (**~er, ~est**). **1.** Level (**on an ~ keel,** of ship or aircraft, or fig.); smooth; uniform in quality; (of temper etc.) equable, unruffled; in same plane or line (*with*; **be** or **get ~ with,** have one's revenge on). **2.** Equally balanced (*even-handed justice*); **~ money,** ‖**~s,** equal stakes in betting, so **~ chance** etc. (of success as likely as not). **3.** Equal in number or amount; (Law & Commerc.) **of ~** (same) **date. 4.** (Of number) integrally divisible by two, opp. *odd*; (of money, time, etc.) not involving fractions, exact (*dozen* etc.). **5.** Hence ~LY² *adv.*, ~NESS (-n-n-) *n.* [OE *efen*, = OS, OHG *eban*, ON *jafn*, Goth. *ibns* f. Gmc **ebhnaz*]

ē'ven³, (poet.) **e'en**² (ēn), *adv.* **1.** (Inviting comparison of the assertion, negation, etc., with a less strong one that might have been made:) *he disputes even the facts* (not merely the inferences from them); *I never even opened* (and certainly did not read) *the letter*; *does he even suspect* (not to say realize) *the danger?*; *even if my watch is right we shall be late* (later if it is slow); **~ now** (as well as previously); **~ so** (in that case as well as in others); *this applies even more* (not merely equally) *to French* (*than to English*). **2.** (arch. or rhet.) Neither more nor less than, just, simply, (*even as I was deploring his absence, he came in*; **~ now,** at this very moment; **~** (quite) **so**); (emphasizing identity) that is (*God, even our own God*). [OE *efne*, = OS *efno*, OHG *ebano* f. WG **ebhnō*]

ē'ven⁴ *v.t.* & *i.* Make or become even; (arch.) treat as equal or comparable (*to*); **~ up,** make or become equal or uniform. [OE *efnan*, *efnian* (as EVEN²)]

ē'venĭng (ē'vn-) *n.* Close of day, esp. from sunset to bedtime (*in* or *during the evening*; *on Wednesday evening*); this time spent in a particular way (*musical evenings*); (fig.) decline of life, closing period; **~ dress,** that prescribed by fashion to be worn in the evening, esp. at dinner or theatre; **~ paper,** newspaper published after (usu.) midday; *evening* PRAYER¹; **~ primrose,** plant of genus *Oenothera* with pale yellow flowers that open in the evening; **~-school,** night-school; **~ star,** planet, esp. Venus, when seen in west after sunset. [OE *ǣfnung* vbl n. (cf. -ING¹) f. *ǣfnian* (as EVEN¹)]

ėvĕ'nt *n.* **1.** Fact of a thing's happening (**in the ~ of his death, of his coming, *that he dies, comes,** if he dies, comes); thing that happens, esp. important thing (*quite an event*), whence ~FUL, ~LESS, *adjs.*; any of several possible but mutually exclusive occurrences (**double ~,** combined occurrence of two events, esp. as subject of bet); (Sport) something on the result of which money is staked, item of programme; (Phys.) single occurrence of process, e.g. ionization of one atom. **2.** Result, outcome; **in any** or **either ~, at all ~s,** in any case; **in the ~,** as things turn(ed) out; WISE¹ *after the event*. [f. L *eventus* f. E(*venire vent-* come)]

ē'ventīde *n.* **1.** (arch.) Evening. **2.** ‖**~ home** (for old people, orig. run by Salvation Army). [OE *ǣfentīd* (as EVEN¹, TIDE¹)]

ėvĕ'ntūal *a.* That will happen under certain circumstances; ultimately resulting, whence ~LY² *adv.* [f. as EVENT + -AL, after *actual*]

ėvĕntūă'lĭtȳ *n.* Possible event. [f. prec. + -ITY]

ėvĕ'ntūāte *v.i.* Turn out (*well, ill,* etc.) as the result; result (*in*, or abs.). [f. as EVENT + -ATE³, after *actuate*]

ĕ'ver, (poet.) **e'er** (ār), *adv.* **1.** (arch.) Always, at all times; **~ and again, ~ and anon,** occasionally. **2. For ~ (and ~, and a day), *fore'ver(mor'e),** for all future time, incessantly, (colloq.) for a very long time, (*the Stars and Stripes* etc. **for ~!**, as expression of support); **(for) ~more,** always; *ever after, ever since*; **~ yours** or **yours ~** (in ending letter to close friend etc.); (in comb. w. participles etc.) constantly (*ever-recurring, ever-present*). **3.** (w. negative, question, condition, comparison). At any time (*nothing ever happens in this town*; *did you ever hear such nonsense?*; (colloq.) **did you ~?** (i.e. see or hear the like); *if I ever catch him*; *the best thing I ever heard*; *his best performance ever*; *as good as ever*; *better than ever*; *(sl.) **is he ~** (he is very) *conceited* etc.; (strengthening *as*) *be as quick as ever you can*). **4.** (Emphasizing question, colloq.) *what ever* (or *whatever*) *does he want?*; *who ever can it be?*; *which ever Brown do you mean?*; *when, where, how, ever did I drop it?*; *why ever didn't you say so?*; **~ so** [f. earlier *never so*] to any possible extent, (colloq.) very (*it is ever so easy, so much easier*), (vulg.) very much (*thanks ever so*) **~ such a,** (vulg.) a very (*he is ever such a nice man*). [OE *ǣfre*, of unkn. orig.]

ĕver-dūr'ĭng *a.* (arch.) Everlasting. [f. EVER + as DURING]

E'verėst (ĕ'-) *n.* Highest peak of attainment etc.

[Mount ~ in Nepal and Tibet, world's highest mountain, f. Sir G. ~, Surveyor-General of India d. 1866]

***ĕ'verglāde** *n.* Marshy tract of land, esp. (in *pl.*) swamp in S. Florida. [prob. f. EVER + GLADE]

ĕ'vergreen *a.* & *n.* **1.** *a.* Always green or fresh (lit. or fig.). **2.** *a.* & *n.* (Tree or shrub) having leaves all the year round (cf. DECIDUOUS). [f. EVER + GREEN¹]

ĕverla'stĭng (-ah'-) *a.* & *n.* **1.** *a.* Lasting for ever; lasting long; lasting too long, repeated too often; (of plant) keeping shape and colour when dried; ~ **pea,** plant of genus *Lathyrus* with ornamental coloured flowers; hence ~LY² *adv.*, ~NESS *n.* **2.** *n.* Eternity (*from everlasting*); strong twilled woollen stuff; immortelle. [ME, f. EVER + LASTING]

ėvĕr't *v.t.* (Physiol.) Turn (organ etc.) outwards or inside out; so **ėvĕr'sION** *n.* [f. L E(*vertere vers-* turn)]

ĕ'verȳ (ĕ'vrĭ) *a.* **1.** Each single (*every word of it is false*; *it engaged his every thought*); (of succession or alternation) *he comes* ~ **day,** ~ **other day** (with one day between each two days of coming, (fig.) on a high proportion of days), ~ **three days,** ~ **third day,** (with two days between each two days of coming); ~ **now and again,** ~ **now and then,** ~ **so often,** from time to time (cf. NOW). **2.** *Every* BIT² *as*; ~**body (else),** every (other) person; ~**day** *a.*, occurring daily, worn or used on ordinary days, commonplace; ~ **last,** (sl.) each without any exception; ~ **one,** each one (*every one of them is wrong*); ~**one** (or ~ **one**), everybody (*everyone likes to have his way*); ~**thing,** all things (*everything depends on that*; **have** ~**thing,** (colloq.), possess every attraction etc.), thing of first importance (*speed is everything*); ~ **time,** (colloq.) without exception, without any hesitation; ~**way,** in every way, in every respect; ~**where,** in every place, (colloq.) in many places; *~ **which way,** in every direction. [OE *ǣfre ǣlc* ever each]

E'verȳmăn (ĕ'vr-) *n.* The ordinary or typical human being, the 'man in the street'. [character in 15th-c. morality play, f. prec. + MAN¹]

ėvĭ'ct *v.t.* Expel (person; esp. tenant *from* land etc.); recover (property, title to it, *of*, *from*, person) by legal process; hence or cogn. ~ION, ~OR, *ns.* [f. L E(*vincere vict-* conquer)]

ĕ'vĭdence *n.*, & *v.t.* **1.** *n.* Clearness, obviousness; **in** ~, conspicuous. **2.** Indication, sign, (*of* quality, treatment, etc.); testimony, facts, in support *of* (or *for*) a conclusion; INTERNAL, EXTERNAL, *evidence*. **3.** (Law). Information (given personally or drawn from documents etc.) tending to establish fact; statements or proofs admissible as testimony in court; *call* (person) **in** ~, as a witness; CIRCUMSTANTIAL, PRESUMPTIVE, *verbal*, *evidence*; *turn* ‖**King's** or ‖**Queen's** or ***State's** ~ (of accomplice in crime testifying for prosecution). **4.** So **ĕvĭdĕ'ntIAL** (-shal), **ĕvĭdĕ'ntiARY**¹ (-sherĭ), *adjs.* **5.** *v.t.* Serve to indicate, attest. [ME f. OF, f. L *evidentia* (as foll.; see -ENCE)]

ĕ'vĭdent *a.* Obvious (to eye or mind); hence ~LY² *adv.* [ME f. OF, or f. L E(*vidēre* see); see -ENT]

ē'vĭl (*or* -*ĭl*) *a.* & *n.* **1.** *a.* Bad, harmful, (**the E~ One,** the Devil); *of evil* (bad) *repute*, *an evil* (slanderous) *tongue*, *an evil* (disagreeable) *smell*; ~ **days,** time when one suffers misfortune; ~ **day** or **hour,** time of ill luck, disaster, etc.; ~ **eye,** malicious look (superstitiously believed to do material harm), ability to cast such looks; hence ~LY² *adv.* **2.** *n.* Evil thing, sin, harm, (*the lesser of two evils*; *evil-doer*); KING¹'*s evil*; **speak** ~ **of,** slander. [OE *yfel*, = OS, OHG *ubil*, Goth. *ubils* f. Gmc **ubhilaz*]

ėvĭ'nc|e *v.t.* Show, indicate, (quality etc., *that* etc.); show that one has (quality); hence ~IVE *a.* [f. as EVICT]

ėvĭ'scer|āte *v.t.* Disembowel; (fig.) empty (thing) of vital contents; hence ~A'TION *n.* [f. L Eviscerare (VISCERA) + -ATE³]

ėvō'ke *v.t.* Call up (spirit from the dead, response, feelings, memories, energies); so **ĕvocA'TION** *n.*, **ėvŏ'catIVE**, **ėvŏ'catORY**, *adjs.* [f. L E(*vocare* call)]

évolué (āvŏ'lūā) *n.* & *a.* (African) with European education or modes of thought. [F, p.p. of *évoluer* EVOLVE]

ĕ'volūte¹ (*or* -ōōt) *a.* & *n.* (Math.) ~ **(curve),** locus of centres of curvature of another curve that is its involute. [f. L *evolutus* p.p. (as EVOLVE)]

ē'volūte² (*or* -ōōt) *v.i.* & *t.* Develop by evolution. [back form. f. foll.]

ĕvolu'tion (-lōō'-) *n.* **1.** Opening out (of roll, bud, etc.; usu. fig.); appearance (of events etc.) in due succession; evolving, giving off, (of gas, heat, etc.). **2.** Unfolding of curve; (Math.) extraction of root from any given power (cf. INVOLUTION). **3.** Development (of organism, human society, the universe, design, argument, etc.); origination of species by development from earlier forms, not by special creation; hence ~ISM (3), ~IST (2), *ns.*, ~**ĭ'st**IC *a.* **4.** Change in disposition of troops or ships; wheeling about, movement, in dancing etc. **5.** Hence ~AL, ~ARY¹, *adjs.* [f. L *evolutio* unrolling (as EVOLVE; see -ION)]

ĕ'volutĭve (-lōō-) *a.* Tending to evolution. [f. prec. + -IVE]

ėvŏ'lve *v.t.* & *i.* Unfold, open out; give off (gas, heat, etc.); develop, deduce, (theory, facts, etc.); develop by natural process; hence ~MENT (-vm-) *n.* [f. L E(*volvere volut-* roll)]

ėvŭ'lsion (-shon) *n.* Forcible extraction. [f. L *evulsio* f. E(*vellere vuls-* pluck); see -ION]

ĕ'vzōne *n.* Member of select Greek infantry regiment. [f. mod. Gk *euzōnos* f. Gk EU(*zōnos* a. f. *zōnē* girdle) dressed for exercise]

ewe (ū) *n.* Female (esp. adult) sheep; ~ **lamb,** one's most cherished possession [2 Sam. 12]; ~**-necked,** (of horse) having thin concave neck. [OE *ēowu*, = OS *ewwi*, OHG *ouwi*, ON *ær* f. Gmc **awi* f. IE **owi*]

ew'er *n.* Pitcher; water-jug with wide mouth. [ME, f. AF **ewere*, ONF *eviere*, OF *aiguiere* f. Rom. **aquaria*, fem. adj. as n. (L *aqua* water; see -ARY¹)]

ewigkeit (ā'vĭgkīt) *n.* (joc.) **Into, in, the** ~, into thin air, in the unknown. [G, = eternity]

ĕx¹ *a.* & *n.* (colloq.) **1.** *a.* Former; outdated. **2.** *n.* Former occupant of specified position etc., esp. former husband or wife. [f. EX-¹ 2]

ĕx² *prep.* (Commerc.) (Of goods) out of, sold from, (*ship*, *store*, *works*, etc.); (of stocks or shares) without, excluding, (**ex dividend,** not including next dividend). [L, = out of]

ex-¹ *pref.* **1.** Forming *vbs.* w. sense 'out', 'forth', (*exclude*, *exit*), 'upward' (*extol*), 'thoroughly' (*excruciate*), 'bring into a state' (*exasperate*), 'remove, expel, or free, from' (*expatriate*, *exonerate*, *excoriate*), and *adjs.* w. sense 'not having', usu. in form *e-* (*ecaudate* tailless). **2.** Forming *ns.* f. titles of office, status, etc., in sense 'formerly' (*ex-convict*, *ex-president*, *ex-Prime-Minister*, *ex-wife*); ‖**ex-ser'vice** *a.*, having belonged to one of the fighting services, pertaining to former servicemen and -women. [f. L *ex* out of]

ex-² *pref.* meaning 'out' (*exodus*). [f. Gk *ex*]

ĕxă'cerb|āte *v.t.* Aggravate (pain, disease,

anger); irritate (person etc.); so ~A'TION *n.* [f. L EX¹(*acerbare* f. *acerbus* bitter) + -ATE³]

ėxă'ct¹ (ĭgz-) *a.* Precise, rigorous, (rules, order, etc.); (of person, judgement, description, report, answer, etc.) accurate, strictly correct; **~ science** (admitting of absolute or quantitative precision); hence or cogn. ~ĬTUDE, ~NESS, *ns.* [f. L *exactus* p.p. (as foll.)]

ėxă'ct² (ĭgz-) *v.t.* Demand and enforce payment of (money, fees, etc.; *from* or *of* person); demand, insist on, (act, conduct, *from*, *of*), (of circumstances) require urgently, whence ~ING² *a.*; hence or cogn. ~ABLE *a.*, ~OR *n.* [f. L EX¹(*igere act-* = *agere* drive)]

ėxă'ction (ĭgz-) *n.* Exacting (*of* money etc.); illegal or exorbitant demand, extortion; sum or thing thus exacted. [ME, f. L *exactio* (as prec.; see -ION)]

ėxă'ctlȳ (ĭgz-) *adv.* In adj. senses (*exactly when, when exactly, did it happen?*); (as answer or confirmation) quite so, just as you say; **not ~**, (colloq., iron.) by no means. [f. EXACT¹ + -LY²]

ėxă'gger|āte (ĭgză'j-) *v.t.* Enlarge (thing described, or abs.) beyond limits of truth; intensify, aggravate; (arch.) make (physical features etc.) of abnormal size; hence or cogn. ~A'TION, **~āt**OR, *ns.*, **~at**IVE *a.* [f. L EX¹-(*aggerare* heap up f. *agger* heap) + -ATE³]

ėxa'lt (ĭgzaw'lt) *v.t.* Raise, place high in rank, power, etc.; praise, extol, (*exalt to the skies*); dignify, ennoble. [ME, f. L EX¹(*altare* f. *altus* high)]

ĕxaltā'tion (-awl-; *or* ĕgz-) *n.* Raising, lifting up, (usu. fig.); elation, rapturous emotion; **E~ of the Cross,** (festival on 14 Sept. commemorating) reputed apparition of Cross to Constantine and later recovery of Cross from Persians. [ME f. OF, or f. LL *exaltatio* (as prec.; see -ATION)]

exalté (ĕgzah'ltā) *a.* & *n.* (*fem.* ***exaltée*** *pr.* same). Excited or elated (person). [F, p.p. of *exalter* EXALT]

ėxă'm (ĭgz-) *n.* (colloq.) = foll. 2. [abbr.]

ėxămĭnā'tion (ĭgz-) *n.* **1.** Detailed inspection (*of, into*). **2.** Testing of knowledge or ability (of pupils, candidates) by oral or written questions; **~-paper,** series of such questions or of examinee's answers to them. **3.** (Law). Formal questioning of witness or accused; **~-in-chief** (by party calling witness). **4.** Hence ~AL *a.* [ME f. OF, f. L *examinatio -onis* (as foll.; see -ATION)]

ėxă'mĭn|e (ĭgz-) *v.* **1.** *v.t.* Investigate, scrutinize, test, (accounts, person *in* or *on* subject, bodily organ, baggage for contraband goods, theory, statement, one's own conscience, *whether*); (Law) formally question (witness or accused). **2.** *v.i.* Inquire *into*. **3.** Hence **~atôr'**IAL *a.*, ~EE', ~ER¹, *ns.* [ME, f. OF *examiner* f. L *examinare* (*examen -minis* for **exagmen* tongue of balance, examination, as EXACT²)]

ėxa'mple (ĭgzah'-) *n.* Fact or thing illustrating general rule (**for ~**, by way of such illustration); problem or exercise designed to do this; specimen of workmanship, picture, etc.; instance of punishment etc. as warning to others (*make an example of him*); precedent (*beyond, without, example*); conduct as object of imitation (*give, set, a good example*; cf. EXEMPLARY). [ME f. OF, f. L *exemplum* (as EXEMPT¹)]

ėxă'nĭmate (ĭgz-) *a.* Dead; lacking animation, spiritless. [f. L *exanimatus* p.p. of EX¹*animare* deprive of life (*anima*); see -ATE²]

ĕxanthē'ma (ĕgz-) *n.* (Path.) Disease (esp. feverish) with eruptions on skin. [LL, f. Gk *exanthēma* eruption (EX²*antheō* f. *anthos* blossom)]

ĕ'xârch (-k) *n.* Head of autocephalous Orthodox Church; bishop ranking between patriarch and metropolitan; (Hist.) governor of Byzantine province; so ~ATE¹ *n.* [f. eccl. L f. Gk *exarkhos* (as EX²-, *-arkhos* ruler)]

ėxă'sper|āte (ĭgz-; *or* -ah'-) *v.t.* Make worse (ill feeling, disease, pain); irritate (person; *exasperated at* or *by*); provoke (person *to* anger etc., *to* do); so ~A'TION *n.* [f. L EX¹(*asperare* f. *asper* rough) + -ATE³]

ex cathedra (ĕkskathē'dra *or* -kă'thĭ-) *adv.* & *a.* Authoritative(ly); (of papal pronouncement) given as infallible judgement. [L, = from the (teacher's) chair]

ĕ'xcav|āte *v.t.* Make hollow; make (hole, channel) by digging; dig out (soil) leaving a hole; reveal or extract by digging; hence or cogn. ~A'TION, **~āt**OR, *ns.* [f. L EX¹(*cavare* f. *cavus* hollow) + -ATE³]

ėxcee'd *v.t.* Do more than is warranted by, go beyond the limit set by, (one's instructions, rights, etc.); be greater than (quantity, thing, *by* so much); surpass (person etc. *in*). [ME, f. OF *exceder* f. L EX¹(*cedere cess-* go)]

ėxcee'dĭng *a.* & (arch.) *adv.* Surpassing(ly) in amount or degree; pre-eminent(ly); hence ~LY² *adv.* [f. prec. + -ING²]

ėxcĕ'l *v.* (**-ll-**). **1.** *v.t.* Be superior to (others *in* quality, *in* doing). **2.** *v.i.* Be pre-eminent (*in, at*, thing, *in* quality, *in* doing). [ME, f. L EX¹(*cellere*; cf. *celsus* lofty)]

ĕ'xcellence *n.* Surpassing merit; thing in which person etc. excels. [ME f. OF, or f. L *excellentia* (as prec.; see -ENCE)]

ĕ'xcellencȳ *n.* Title of ambassadors, governors, and their wives, and some other officers. [ME, f. L *excellentia* (as EXCEL; see -ENCY)]

ĕ'xcellent *a.* Pre-eminent; very good; hence ~LY² *adv.* [ME f. OF (as EXCEL; see -ENT)]

ėxcĕ'lsĭor *int.* & *n.* **1.** *int.* Higher (as motto, trade mark, etc.). **2.** *n.* Shavings of soft wood for stuffing. [L, compar. of EX¹*celsus* lofty]

ĕxcĕ'ntrĭc *a.* = ECCENTRIC (esp. in sense 1). [f. as ECCENTRIC; see EX-¹]

ėxcĕ'pt¹ *v.t.* Exclude (thing) from enumeration, statement, etc., (*present company excepted*; *except him from the general amnesty*); so ~IVE *a.* [ME, f. L EX¹(*cipere cept-* = *capere* take)]

ėxcĕ'pt² *prep.* & *conj.* **1.** *prep.* Not including, but, (*we all failed except him*; *he is everywhere except in the right place*; *never to be found except in the wrong place*; *it is right except that the accents are omitted*, *except for the omission of accents*). **2.** *conj.* (esp. arch.) Unless (*except he be born again*). [ME, orig. p.p. f. L *exceptus* (as prec.)]

ėxcĕ'ptĭng *prep.* & *conj.* = prec. [f. EXCEPT¹ + -ING²]

ėxcĕ'ption *n.* Excepting; thing excepted, thing that does not follow the rule; **the ~ proves the rule,** the excepting of some cases shows that the rule exists, or that it applies to those not excepted; **with the ~ of,** except; **take ~,** object *to*, whence ~ABLE *a.*, open to objection. [ME f. OF, f. L *exceptio -onis* (as EXCEPT¹; see -ION)]

ėxcĕ'ptional *a.* Forming an exception; unusual (*exceptional advantages*); hence ~ITY (-ă'l-) *n.*, ~LY² *adv.* [f. prec. + -AL]

exceptis excipiendis (ĕksĕptĭs ĕksĭpĭĕ'ndĭs) *adv.* With appropriate exceptions. [LL, f. abl. pl. of *exceptus* p.p., *excipiendus* gerundive, of *excipere* (see EXCEPT¹)]

ĕ'xcêrpt¹ *n.* Extract from book, manuscript, musical work, etc. [f. L *excerptum* neut. p.p. (as n.) of *excerpere* (see foll.)]

ėxcêr'pt² *v.t.* Extract, quote, (passage *from* book etc., or abs.); hence ~IBLE *a.*, ~ION *n.* [f. L EX¹(*cerpere cerpt-* = *carpere* pluck)]

ėxcĕ'ss *n.* **1.** Overstepping of due limits; intemperance in eating or drinking. **2.** Fact of exceeding (**in ~ of,** more than). **3.** Amount by which one number or quantity exceeds another; agreed amount subtracted by insurer from insured person's claim in determining payment to be made; ~ **fare,** payment due for travelling farther or in higher class than ticket allows; ~ **baggage** or **luggage** (over the weight for free carriage); ~ **postage,** payment due when stamps on letter etc. are insufficient. **4.** Superabundance, extreme degree, (*of* cruelty etc.); exceeding of the proper amount or degree, esp. *in* or *to excess*. **5.** So ~IVE *a.*, ~**ive**LY[2] (-vlĭ) *adv.* [ME, f. OF *exces* f. L *excessus* (as EXCEED)]

ėxchā'nge[1] (-nj) *n.* **1.** Act or process of exchanging (*of* goods, prisoners of war, blows, words, etc.); (**fair**) ~ **is no robbery,** lit., or joc. excuse for unfair exchange; HEAT[1]-, ION, *exchange*; **in** ~, as a thing exchanged (*for*); ~ **student,** one who is given free tuition etc. at another school etc. in consideration of reciprocal treatment of a student from that school; similarly ~ **teacher. 2.** Exchanging of money for its equivalent in money of same or another country; money-changer's trade; PAR[1] *of exchange*; (**rate of**) ~, price at which (bills drawn in a) foreign currency may be bought, or difference between this and par; foreign currency got by exchange; system of settling debts between persons (esp. in different countries) without use of money, by bills of exchange (see BILL[4]). **3.** (Chess). Possession of superior piece (esp. rook) against inferior one. **4.** Building where merchants, brokers, etc., assemble to transact business (*corn exchange, stock exchange*); place where potential employers and employees are made known (EMPLOYMENT *exchange*, LABOUR[1] *Exchange*). **5.** Central telephone office of a district where connections are made between lines concerned in calls. [ME f. AF *eschaunge*, OF *eschange* (*eschangier*; see foll.)]

ėxchā'ng|e[2] (-nj) *v.* **1.** *v.t.* Give (thing) in place of (*for*) another; give and receive (blows, words, glances, positions, prisoners, etc.); hence ~**e**ABLE (-nj*a*-) *a.* **2.** *v.i.* Take part in exchange of positions etc. (*with* another). **3.** Hence ~ER[1] (1, 2) *n.* [ME, f. OF *eschangier* f. Rom. **excambiare* (as EX-[1], CHANGE[2])]

ėxchě'quer (-k*er*) *n.* ||Department of public service charged with receipt and custody of revenue (||**Chancellor of the E**~, finance minister of United Kingdom); royal or national treasury; money of private person etc.; ||(**Court of**) **E**~, (Hist.) court of law now merged in Queen's Bench Division or Court of Session. [orig. = 'chess-board', then w. ref. to keeping of accounts on chequered table-cloth; ME, f. AF *escheker*, OF *eschequier*, *eschaquier*, f. med. L *scaccarium* chess-board, CHEQUER[1]; *ex-* by erron. assoc. w. EX-[1] in *exchange* etc.]

ĕ'xcīse[1] (-z) *n.*, & *v.t.* **1.** *n.* Duty or tax levied on goods and commodities produced or sold within the country, and on various licences etc.; ||(Hist.) government office collecting excise (now *Board of Customs and Excise*); ||~**man,** (Hist.) officer collecting excise and preventing infringement of excise laws. **2.** *v.t.* Force (person) to pay excise; charge excise on (goods); (arch.) overcharge (lit. or fig.); hence **ėxcī'**SABLE (-z-) *a.* [f. MDu. *excijs*, *accijs*, perh. f. Rom. **accensum* f. *ACC*ensare* tax (CENSUS)]

ėxcī'se[2] (-z) *v.t.* Cut out or away (passage of book, limb, organ, etc.); so **ėxci'**SION (-zh*o*n) *n.* [f. L EX[1](*cidere cis-* = *caedere* cut)]

ėxcī't|e *v.t.* **1.** Bring into play, rouse up, (feelings, faculties, etc.); provoke, bring about, (action, active condition); promote activity of (bodily organ etc.) by stimulus; move (person) to strong emotion. **2.** (Electr. & Magn.) induce activity in (substance), cause (current) to flow; (Phys.) cause emission of (spectrum), cause (substance) to emit radiation, put (atom etc.) into state of higher energy; hence ~A'TION, ~ER[1] (2), *ns.* **3.** Hence or cogn. ~ABI'LITY, ~**e**MENT (-tm-), *ns.*, **ĕ'xcĭt**ANT *a.* & *n.*, ~ABLE (esp., of person, easily excited, unbalanced), ~**at**IVE, ~**at**ORY, *adjs.*, ~**ėd**LY[2] *adv.* [ME, f. OF *exciter* or f. L *excitare* frequent. of EX[1](*ciēre* set in motion)]

ėxcī'ting *a.* In vbl senses; causing great interest or eagerness; hence ~LY[2] *adv.*, ~NESS *n.* [f. prec. + -ING[2]]

ĕ'xcĭtŏn (*or* ĕksī'tŏn) *n.* (Phys.) Combination of excited electron and hole, having some properties of a particle. [f. EXCITATION + -ON]

ėxclai'm *v.* **1.** *v.i.* Cry out, esp. from pain, anger, etc.; ~ **against,** (arch.) accuse loudly. **2.** *v.t.* Utter (words, *that*) thus. [f. F *exclamer* or f. L EX[1](*clamare* cf. CLAIM[1])]

ĕxclamā'tion *n.* Exclaiming; words exclaimed; ~ **mark, *point,** punctuation mark (!) indicating exclamation; so **ėxclă'mat**ORY *a.* [ME f. OF, or f. L *exclamatio* (as prec.; see -ATION)]

ĕ'xclāve *n.* Territory surrounded by foreign territory. [f. EX-[1] + ENCLAVE]

ĕxclō'sure (-zh*er*) *n.* (Forestry etc.) Area from which unwanted animals are excluded. [f. EX-[1] + ENCLOSURE]

ėxclu'd|e (-lōō'd) *v.t.* Shut out (person, thing, *from* place, society, privilege, etc.); prevent the occurrence of, make impossible, (doubt, etc.); expel and shut out; hence ~ER[1] (1, 2) *n.* [ME, f. L EX[1] (*cludere clus-* = *claudere* shut)]

ėxclu'sion (-lōō'zh*o*n) *n.* Excluding, shutting out; **to the** ~ **of,** so as to exclude; ~ **principle,** (Phys.) assertion that no two particles of same kind can be in same quantum state; hence ~ARY[1] *a.* [f. L *exclusio* (as prec.; see -ION)]

ėxclu'sive (-lōō'-) *a.* & *n.* **1.** *a.* Shutting out; not admitting *of*; desirous of excluding others, (of social circles etc.) chary of admitting members, select; (of article in shop or newspaper, etc.) not to be had, not published, elsewhere; high-class, expensive; (of terms etc.) excluding all but what is specified; employed or followed or held to the exclusion of all else (*his exclusive occupation*; *exclusive rights*); (as *adv.*) not counting (*20 men, exclusive of our own*); hence ~LY[2] (-vlĭ) *adv.*, ~NESS (-vn-), **ĕxclusĭ'v**ITY (-lōō-), *ns.* **2.** *n.* Article etc. published by only one newspaper or periodical. [f. med. L *exclusivus* (as EXCLUDE; see -IVE)]

ĕxcŏ'gĭt|āte *v.t.* Think out, contrive; hence ~ABLE *a.*, ~A'TION *n.*, ~**āt**IVE *a.* [f. L EX[1](*cogitare* COGITATE) + -ATE[3]]

ĕxcommū'nĭcāt|e[1] *v.t.* (Eccl.) Cut off (person) from participation in sacraments, or from all communication with the Church; hence or cogn. **ĕxcommūnĭc**A'TION, ~OR, *ns.*, ~IVE, ~ORY, *adjs.* [f. eccl. L EX[1](*communicare* f. *communis* COMMON[1]) + -ATE[3]]

ĕxcommū'nĭcate[2] *a.* (arch.) Excommunicated. [f. L *excommunicatus* p.p. (as prec.); see -ATE[2]]

ĕxcor'ĭ|āte *v.t.* Remove part of skin of (person etc.) by abrasion etc.; strip, peel off, (skin); (fig.) censure severely; so ~A'TION *n.* [f. L EX[1](*coriare* f. *corium* hide) + -ATE[3]]

ĕ'xcrėment *n.* (in *sing.* or *pl.*) Faeces; hence ~AL (-ĕ'n-), ~I'TIOUS[1], *adjs.* [f. F *excrément* or f. L *excrementum* (as EXCRETE; see -MENT)]

ėxcrĕ'scence *n.* Abnormal or morbid outgrowth (on animal or vegetable body, or fig.); so **ĕxcrėscĕ'nt**IAL (-sh*a*l) *a.* [f. L *excrescentia* (as foll.; see -ENCE)]

ėxcrĕ'scent *a.* Growing abnormally; redundant;

For other words in *ex-* **see** EX-[1], EX-[2].

(Gram., of sound or letter in word) due merely to euphony, not to derivation. [f. L EX[1](*crescere* grow); see -ENT]

ėxcrē'ta *n. pl.* Waste discharged from body, esp. faeces and urine. [L, neut. pl. (as n.) of p.p. (as foll.)]

ėxcrē't|e *v.t.* (Of animal or plant) separate and expel (waste matter, or abs.) from system; hence or cogn. **ėxcrē'tION** *n.*, ~IVE, ~ORY, *adjs.* [f. L EX[1](*cernere cret-* sift)]

ėxcru'cĭ|āte (-krōō'shĭ-) *v.t.* Torment acutely (person's senses; esp. in *part.* as *a.*, also joc. of pun, comedy, etc.); torture mentally; hence ~**ĭng**LY[2] *adv.*, ~A'TION *n.* [f. L EX[1](*cruciare* torment f. *crux crucis* cross) + -ATE[3]]

ĕ'xculpāte *v.t.* Free from blame; clear (person *from* charge etc.); hence **ĕxculp**A'TION *n.*, **ĕxcŭ'lpat**ORY *a.* [f. med. L EX[1](*culpare* f. *culpa* blame) + -ATE[3]]

ėxcûr'sion (-shon) *n.* Journey or ramble with intention of returning to starting-point (lit. or fig.); pleasure-trip of number of persons, whence ~IST (3) *n.*, ~ **train** (for excursionists, usu. at reduced rates); (arch.) sortie (ALARUMS *and excursions*); (Astron.) deviation from regular path; hence ~AL, ~ARY[1], *adjs.* [f. L *excursio* f. EX[1](*currere curs-* run); see -ION]

ėxcûr'sĭve *a.* Making or tending to make excursions; diverse; digressive; hence ~LY[2] (-vlĭ) *adv.*, ~NESS (-vn-) *n.* [f. as prec. + -IVE]

ėxcûr'sus (*or* ĕ-) *n.* Detailed discussion of special point in book, usu. in appendix at end; digression in narrative. [L, vbl n. f. as EXCURSION]

ėxcū's|e[1] (-z) *v.t.* Attempt to lessen the blame attaching to (person, act, fault); obtain exemption for (person, one*self*, *from* duty etc.; ~**e oneself,** ask permission or apologize before leaving); (of thing) serve as exculpation of (person, act, person *for* act); release (person (*from*) duty etc.); forgive (fault or offence, person *for* this); not insist upon (what is due); ~**e me** (as apology for lack of ceremony, interruption, etc., or as form of dissent); ~**e-me dance** (in which one may take another dancer's partner); so ~ABLE, ~**at**ORY, *adjs.*, ~**ab**LY[2] *adv.* [ME, f. OF *escuser* f. L EX[1]*cusare* (*causa* CAUSE[1], accusation)]

ėxcū'se[2] *n.* Apology offered, exculpation; ground of this; ~ **for,** poor or scanty specimen of. [ME, f. OF (as prec.)]

ĕx-dĭrĕ'ctorў *a.* (Of telephone number or subscriber) deliberately not listed in the directory. [f. EX[2] + DIRECTORY]

ex div. *abbr.* EX[2] dividend.

ĕ'xĕăt *n.* ||Permission for temporary absence from school etc.; bishop's permission to priest to move to another diocese. [L, 3rd sing. pres. subj. of EX[1](*ire* go)]

ĕ'xĕcrab|le *a.* Abominable, detestable; hence ~LY[2] *adv.* [ME f. OF, f. L *execrabilis* (as foll.; see -ABLE)]

ĕ'xĕcrāt|e *v.t.* & *i.* Express or feel abhorrence for; utter curses; hence or cogn. **ĕxĕcr**A'TION *n.*, ~IVE, ~ORY, *adjs.* [f. L EX[1](*s*)*ecrari* (*sacrare* devote f. *sacer* sacred, accursed) + -ATE[3]]

ėxĕ'cūtant (ĭgz-) *n.* One who executes (sense 1), performer (esp. *of* music etc.). [f. F *éxécutant*, part. f. as foll.]

ĕ'xĕcūt|e *v.t.* **1.** Carry (plan, command, law, judicial sentence, order for goods etc., a will) into effect; carry out design for (product of art or skill); perform (action, operation, etc.); make (legal instrument) valid by signing, sealing, etc.; perform (duty, function, musical composition). **2.** Inflict capital punishment on. **3.** Hence ~ABLE *a.* [ME, f. OF *executer* f. med. L *executare* f. L EX[1](*sequi secut-* follow)]

ĕxĕcū'tion *n.* **1.** Carrying out, performance; dexterity in performing music; **do** ~, (of weapon, or fig. of argument etc.) have destructive effect. **2.** Seizure of property or person of debtor in default of payment. **3.** Infliction of capital punishment; hence ~ARY[1] *a.*, ~ER[1] *n.* [ME f. OF, f. L *executio -onis* (as prec.; see -ION)]

ėxĕ'cūtĭve (ĭgz-) *a.* & *n.* **1.** *a.* Pertaining to or having the function of executing. **2.** *a.* & *n.* (Branch of government or organization) concerned with executing laws, agreements, etc.; *~ **session,** private meeting (orig. of Senate for executive business). **3.** *n.* Person having executive authority; person in executive position in business organization etc. [f. med. L *executivus* (as EXECUTE; see -IVE)]

executor *n.* **1.** (arch.; ĕ'ksĭ-). One who carries out or performs. **2.** (ĭgzĕ'k-). Person appointed by testator to execute his will; **literary** ~, person entrusted with writer's unpublished works etc.; hence **ėxĕcūtôr'**IAL (ĭgz-) *a.*, ~SHIP, **ėxĕ'cūtr**IX (ĭgz-), *ns.* [ME, f. AF *execut*(*o*)*ur* f. L *executor -oris* (as EXECUTE; see -OR)]

ĕxėg|ē'sĭs *n.* (*pl.* ~**eses** *pr.* -ē'sēz). Exposition esp. of Scripture; hence or cogn. ~ETE *n.*, ~**ē'**TIC(AL) *adjs.*, ~**ē'**TIST (3) *n.* [f. Gk *exēgēsis* f. EX[2](*ēgeomai* lead) interpret]

ėxĕ'mplar (ĭgz-) *n.* Model, pattern; typical member (of a class); parallel instance. [ME f. OF *exemplaire*, f. LL *exemplarium* (as EXAMPLE; see -ARY[1])]

ėxĕ'mplar|ў (ĭgz-) *a.* Fit to be imitated; (arch.) typical; illustrative; serving as a warning (~**y damages** in Law, exceeding amount needed for simple compensation); hence ~ĭLY[2] *adv.*, ~ĭNESS *n.* [f. LL *exemplaris* (as EXAMPLE; see -ARY[2])]

ėxĕ'mplĭ|fў (ĭgz-) *v.t.* Illustrate by example; be an example of; make attested copy of (document) under official seal; so ~FICA'TION *n.* [ME, f. med. L *exemplificare* (as EXAMPLE; see -FY)]

exempli gratia (ĕgzĕmplĭ grā'sha) *adv.* For the sake of example. [L]

ĕxĕ'mpl|um (ĕgz-) *n.* (*pl.* ~**a**). Example or model, esp. moralizing or illustrative story. [L (see EXAMPLE)]

ėxĕ'mpt[1] (ĭgz-) *a.* & *n.* **1.** Freed (*from* taxation, liability, risk, duty, control, failings, etc.); not subject to risk etc. *from*. **2.** *n.* Person exempted, esp. from tax; ||=EXON. [ME, f. L *exemptus* p.p. of EX[1](*imere empt-* =*emere* take)]

ėxĕ'mpt[2] (ĭgz-) *v.t.* Free *from* (as prec.); so ~ION *n.* [f. as prec.]

ĕxequā'tur *n.* Recognition of a country's consul by a foreign government; temporal sovereign's authorization of bishop under papal authority, or of publication of papal bulls. [L, =let him perform, 3rd sing. pres. subj. of *exequi* = *exsequi* (see EXECUTE)]

ĕ'xequĭes (-kwĭz) *n. pl.* Funeral rites. [ME f. OF, f. L *exsequiae* f. EX[1](*sequi* follow)]

ĕ'xercise[1] (-z) *n.* **1.** Employment, application, (*of* organ, faculty, power, right); practice (*of* virtue, profession, function, religious rite); act of worship. **2.** Exertion of muscles, limbs, etc., esp. for health's sake; bodily, mental, or spiritual training. **3.** Task set for such training (**object of the** ~, essential purpose of action etc.); problem, piece of music, etc., used as such task; (in *pl.*) military drill, athletics, etc. academical declamation etc. required for degree, *(in *pl.*) ceremony of conferment of degree etc. [ME, f. OF *exercice* f. L *exercitium* f. EX[1](*ercēre -cit-* = *arcēre* restrain) keep at work; see -ISE[2]]

ĕ'xercĭs|e[2] (-z) *v.* **1.** *v.t.* Employ or apply (faculty, right, influence, restraint, etc.); train (person etc.); tax the powers of; perplex, worry; perform (functions); give (horse etc.) exercise; hence ~ABLE *a.* **2.** *v.i.* Take exercise (sense 2). [ME, f. prec.]

ėxêrcĭtā'tion (ĭgz-) *n.* (arch.) Practice, training;

literary or oratorical exercise. [ME, f. L *exercitatio* (*exercitare* frequent. of *exercēre*; see EXERCISE[1], -ATION)]

ĕ'xĕrgue (-g; *or* ĕgzĕ̄r'g) *n.* Small space usu. on reverse of coin or medal, below principal device; inscription there; hence **ĕxĕ̄r'gu**AL (-gal; *or* ĕgz-) *a.* [F, f. med. L *exergum* f. Gk EX-[2] + *ergon* work]

ėxĕ̄r't (ĭgz-) *v.t.* Exercise, bring to bear, (quality, force, influence); ~ one**self,** use efforts or endeavours, strive, (*to* do, *for* object); hence ~ION *n.* [f. L EX[1](*serere sert-* bind) put forth]

ĕ'xĕs (-z) *n. pl.* (colloq.) Expenses. [abbr.]

exeunt (ĕ'ksĭunt) *v.i.* (Stage direction): (actors) leave the stage; ~ ***omnes*** (ŏ'mnēz), all leave the stage. [L, = they (all) go out, f. as EXIT[2]]

ĕxfō'lĭ|āte *v.i.* (Of bone, skin, mineral, etc.) come off in scales or layers; (of tree) throw off layers of bark; hence ~A'TION *n.* [f. LL EX[1](*foliare* f. *folium* leaf) + -ATE[3]]

ex gratia (ĕks grā'sha) *adv.* & *a.* (Done etc.) as an act of grace, without acceptance of liability etc. [L, = from favour]

ĕxhalā'tion (ĕksa-) *n.* Expiration of air; puff of breath; mist, vapour; emanation, effluvium. [ME, f. L *exhalatio* (as foll.; see -ATION)]

ėxhā'le *v.* **1.** *v.t.* Give off (as) in vapour; breathe out (air, life, soul, words, etc.); (arch.) get rid of (anger etc.) as if by blowing. **2.** *v.i.* Be given off in vapour (*from, out of*). [ME, f. OF *exhaler* f. L EX[1](*halare* breathe)]

ėxhau'st[1] (ĭgzaw'-) *n.* (Expulsion or exit of) motive fluid, steam, or gaseous products of combustion from engine cylinder after completion of power stroke by piston; (similar exit of) spent fluid or gas from turbine; ~(**-pipe** etc.) (for this); (apparatus for) production of outward current of air by creating partial vacuum. [f. foll.]

ėxhau'st[2] (ĭgzaw'-) *v.t.* **1.** Draw off (air, or fig.); empty (vessel) of contents. **2.** Consume entirely; account for or use the whole of; find out or say all that is worth knowing of (subject); (esp. in *p.p.*) drain (person, kingdom, etc.) of strength, resources, etc.; tire out; hence ~IBI'LITY *n.*, ~IBLE *a.* [f. L EX[1](*haurire haust-* draw (water), drain)]

ėxhau'stion (ĭgzaw'schon) *n.* Exhausting or being exhausted; total loss of strength; process of establishing conclusion by eliminating alternatives. [f. LL *exhaustio* (as prec.; see -ION)]

ėxhau'stive (ĭgzaw'-) *a.* Tending to exhaust, esp. a subject; thorough, comprehensive; hence ~LY[2] (-vlĭ) *adv.*, ~NESS (-vn-) *n.* [f. EXHAUST[2] + -IVE]

ėxhĭ'bĭt[1] (ĭgzĭ'-) *n.* **1.** Document or thing produced in lawcourt and referred to in written evidence; ~ **A,** first such document etc., (fig.) thing or person regarded as (important) piece of evidence. **2.** Thing or collection of things sent by person, firm, etc., to an exhibition. [f. L *exhibitum*, neut. p.p. (as foll.)]

ėxhĭ'bĭt[2] (ĭgzĭ'-) *v.t.* Show, display; submit for consideration; manifest (quality); show publicly (for amusement, in competition, etc.): hence or cogn. ~OR *n.*, ~ORY *a.* [f. L EX[1](*hibēre hibit-* = *habēre* hold)]

ĕxhĭbĭ'tion (ĕksĭ-) *n.* **1.** Showing, display, (of thing); **make an ~ of oneself,** behave so as to appear ridiculous or contemptible. **2.** Public display of works of art, industrial products, etc. **3.** ||Scholarship (SCHOLAR 5), esp. from funds of school, college, etc.; hence ~ER[1] *n.* [ME f. OF, f. LL *exhibitio -onis* (as prec.; see -ION)]

ĕxhĭbĭ'tion|ĭsm (ĕksĭ-) *n.* Tendency towards display or extravagant behaviour; (Path.) perverted mental condition characterized by indecent exposure of one's genitals; so ~IST (1) *n.*, **~ĭ'st**IC *a.* [f. prec. + -ISM]

ėxhĭ'lar|āte (ĭgzĭ'-) *v.t.* Enliven, gladden, (person, spirits); hence or cogn. ~ANT *a.* & *n.*, ~A'TION *n.*, **~at**IVE *a.* [f. L EX[1](*hilarare* f. *hilaris* cheerful) + -ATE[3]]

ėxhŏ̄r't (ĭgzŏ̄r't) *v.t.* Admonish earnestly; urge (person *to* do, *to* a course of action); hence **~at**IVE, **~at**ORY, *adjs.* [ME, f. OF *exhorter* or f. L EX[1](*hortari* exhort)]

ĕxhŏ̄rtā'tion (ĕksŏ̄r-; *or* ĕgz-) *n.* Exhorting; formal or liturgical address. [ME f. OF, or f. L *exhortatio* (as prec.; see -ATION)]

ėxhūm|e (ĭgzū'm) *v.t.* Dig out, unearth, (esp. buried corpse; lit. or fig.); so ~A'TION (ĕksū-) *n.* [f. F *exhumer* f. med. L EX[1](*humare* f. *humus* ground)]

ex hypothesi (ĕks hīpŏ'thĭsī) *adv.* According to the hypothesis (made). [mod. L]

ĕ'xĭgence, ĕ'xĭgencў, (*or* ĕgz-) *ns.* Urgent need or demand; emergency. [f. F *exigence* & f. LL *exigentia* (as foll.; see -ENCE, -ENCY)]

ĕ'xĭgent (*or* ĕ'gz-) *a.* Urgent, pressing; requiring much, exacting. [ME, f. L *exigere* EXACT[2]; see -ENT]

ĕ'xĭgĭble *a.* That may be demanded or exacted (*against* or *from* person). [F (*exiger* f. as EXACT[2]; see -IBLE)]

exĭ'gūous (ĕgz- *or* ĭgz-) *a.* Scanty, small; hence or cogn. **ĕxĭgū'**ITY, ~NESS, *ns.* [f. L *exiguus* scanty (*exigere* weigh exactly; see EXACT[2]) + -OUS]

ĕ'xīle[1] (*or* ĕ'gz-) *n.* (State of) being expelled or long absence from one's native land (lit. or fig.); **the E~,** captivity of Jews in Babylon (6th c. B.C.). [ME, f. OF *exil, essil* f. L *exilium* banishment (*exul* = foll.)]

ĕ'xīle[2] (*or* ĕ'gz-) *n.* Exiled person (lit. or fig.). [ME, prob. f. OF *exilé* p.p. of *exiler* (see foll.), infl. by L *exul*]

ĕ'xīle[3] (*or* ĕ'gz-) *v.t.* Condemn to exile (person *from*; lit. or fig.). [ME, f. OF *exil(i)er, essilier* f. LL *exiliare* (as EXILE[1])]

ĕxĭ'lĭc (*or* ĕgz-) *a.* Of exile, esp. the Exile in Babylon. [f. EXILE[1] + -IC]

ėxĭ'st (ĭgz-) *v.i.* Have place as a part of objective reality; have being under specified conditions (~ **as** (in the form of)); (of circumstances etc.) occur, be found; live, esp. under adverse conditions; continue in being. [prob. back form. f. foll.; cf. LL *existere*]

ėxĭ'stence (ĭgz-) *n.* Being, existing, (esp. *in existence*); life, esp. under adverse conditions (*a wretched, precarious, existence*); mode of existing; existing thing; all that exists. [ME f. OF, or f. LL *existentia* f. L EX[1](*sistere* redupl. of *stare* stand); see -ENCE]

ėxĭ'stent (ĭgz-) *a.* Existing, actual, current. [f. as prec. + -ENT]

ĕxĭstĕ'ntial (ĕgz-; -shal) *a.* Of or relating to existence; (Logic, of a proposition) predicating existence; (Philos.) concerned with existence, esp. with human existence as viewed by existentialism; hence ~LY[2] *adv.* [f. LL *existentialis* (as EXISTENCE; see -AL)]

ĕxĭstĕ'ntialĭsm (ĕgz-; -shal-) *n.* Philosophical theory emphasizing existence of the individual person as free and responsible agent determining his own development; hence ~IST (2) *n.* [f. G *existentialismus* (as prec.; see -ISM)]

ĕ'xĭt[1] (*or* ĕ'gz-) *n.* Departure of actor from stage (lit. or fig.); death; going out or forth; liberty to do this (~ **permit** etc., authorization to leave a particular country); (Cards) (means of) deliberately losing the lead; passage or door to go out by; *place where vehicles can leave motorway etc. [partly f. L *exitus* going out (as foll.), partly f. foll.]

exit[2] (ĕ'ksĭt) *v.i.* (Stage direction): (actor) leaves the stage (lit. or fig.; *Exit Macbeth*). [L, 3rd sing. pres. ind. of EX(*ire* go)]

ĕ'xĭt[3] (*or* ĕ'gz-) *v.i.* Make one's exit; die; (Cards) deliberately lose lead. [f. EXIT[1]]

ĕx-lĭ'brĭs *n.* (*pl.* same). Book-plate, label with arms, design, etc., and owner's name, pasted into front of book. [f. L *ex libris* out of the books of (+owner's name)]

ex nihilo (ĕks nī'hĭlō) *adv.* Out of nothing (*creation ex nihilo*). [L]

ĕ'xō- *comb. form.* External, as: **~bio'logy,** study of life outside the earth; **~crine** (-krĭn), (of gland) secreting through a duct [Gk *krinō* sift]; **~derm,** ectoderm; **~gamous, ~gamy,** (-ŏ'g-), (of, following) custom compelling man to marry outside his own tribe; **~gen,** plant that develops by external growth of stem; **~genous** (-ŏ'j-), growing or originating from outside; **~plasm,** outermost layer of cytoplasm; **~skeleton,** external integument, bony or leathery; **~sphere,** layer of atmosphere farthest from the earth; **~ther'mal, ~ther'mic,** occurring or formed with evolution of heat. [f. Gk *exō* outside]

Exod. *abbr.* Exodus (O.T.).

ĕ'xodus *n.* Departure, going forth, of many persons (esp. of emigrants); departure of Israelites from Egypt, (*E~*) book of O.T. relating this. [eccl. L, f. Gk EX[2]*odos* (*hodos* way)]

ex officio (ĕks ofĭ'shĭō) *adv.* & *a.* By virtue of one's office (*ex officio members of committee*). [L]

‖**ĕ'xŏn** *n.* One of four officers acting as commanders of Yeomen of the Guard. [repr. F pr. of EXEMPT[1]]

ėxŏ'ner|āte (ĭgz-) *v.t.* Free (person *from* blame etc.); release (person *from* duty etc.); hence **~A'TION** *n.*, **~ātIVE** *a.* [f. L EX[1](*onerare* f. *onus oneris* burden) + -ATE[3]]

ĕxŏphthă'lm|us, ~|os, *n.* Protrusion of eyeball; hence **~IC** *a.* [mod. L, f. Gk EX[2](*ophthalmos* eye) having prominent eyes]

exor. *abbr.* executor (sense 2).

ėxŏr'bĭt|ant (ĭgz-) *a.* (Of price, demand, ambition, person) grossly excessive; hence **~ANCE** *n.*, **~antLY**[2] *adv.* [f. LL EX[1](*orbitare* f. *orbita* ORBIT); see -ANT]

ĕ'xŏrc|ise (-īz), **-īze,** *v.t.* Expel (evil spirit *from, out of,* person or place) by invocation or use of holy name; free (person, place, *of* evil spirits); so **~isA'TION** (-z-), **~ISM** (1), **~IST** (1), *ns.* [f. F *exorciser* or f. eccl. L *exorcizare* f. Gk EX[2]*orkizō* (*horkos* oath)]

ĕxŏr'dĭ|um *n.* (*pl.* **~ums** *or* **~a**). Beginning, introductory part, esp. of discourse or treatise; hence **~AL** *a.* [L, f. EX[1](*ordiri* begin)]

ĕxotĕ'rĭc *a.* (Of philosophical doctrine, mode of speech, etc.) intelligible to outsiders (cf. ESOTERIC); (of disciple) not admitted to esoteric teaching; commonplace, ordinary, popular; hence **~AL** *a.*, **~alLY**[2] *adv.*, **~ISM** (3), **~IST** (2), *ns.* [f. LL f. Gk *exōterikos* (*exōterō* compar. of *exō* outside; see -IC)]

ėxŏ'tĭc (ĭgz-) *a.* & *n.* **1.** *a.* (Of plant, word, fashion) introduced from abroad; strange, bizarre; attractively strange or unusual; (of fuel, metal, etc.) of kind newly brought into use; **~ dancer,** strip-tease dancer. **2.** *n.* Exotic plant, word, dancer, etc. [f. L f. Gk *exōtikos* (as EXO-; see -IC)]

ėxŏ'tĭca (ĭgz-) *n. pl.* Exotic objects. [L, neut. pl. of *exoticus* (see prec.)]

ėxpă'nd *v.* **1.** *v.t.* & *i.* Spread out flat; develop (*into*); swell, dilate, increase in bulk or importance. **2.** *v.t.* Set forth, write out, in full (what is condensed or abbreviated, algebraical expression, etc.). **3.** *v.i.* Become genial, throw off reserve. **4. ~ed metal,** sheet metal slit and stretched into a lattice, used (esp.) to reinforce concrete; **~ing universe,** the universe regarded as continually expanding and carrying the galaxies farther apart. **5.** Hence or cogn. **~ABLE** *a.*, **ėxpănsIBI'LITY** *n.*, **ėxpă'nsIBLE** *a.* [ME, f. L EX[1](*pandere pans-* spread)]

ėxpă'nse *n.* Wide area or extent; amount of expansion. [f. mod. L *expansum* neut. p.p. (as prec.)]

ėxpă'nsīle *a.* (Capable) of expansion. [f. as EXPAND; see -IL]

ėxpă'nsion (-shon) *n.* Expanding; enlargement of scale of operations in commerce etc.; increase of amount of territory etc., whence **~ISM** (3), **~IST** (2), *ns.*; increase in bulk of steam etc. in cylinder of engine; hence **~ARY**[1] *a.* [f. LL *expansio* (as EXPAND; see -ION)]

ėxpă'nsĭve *a.* Able or tending to expand; extensive, wide-ranging; (of person, feelings, speech) effusive, open; hence **~LY**[2] (-vlĭ) *adv.*, **~NESS** (-vn-), **ĕxpănsĭ'vITY**, *ns.* [f. as EXPAND + -IVE]

ex parte (ĕkspar'tĭ) *adv.* & *a.* (Law or transf.) (Made or said) on, or in the interests of, one side only, or by person having interest in proceedings but not being a party to them. [L]

ėxpā'tĭ|āte (-shĭ-) *v.i.* Speak or write copiously (*on* subject); (usu. fig.) wander unrestrained; hence **~A'TION** *n.*, **~atORY** (-sha-) *a.* [f. L EX[1](*spatiari* walk about, f. *spatium* SPACE[1]) + -ATE[3]]

ĕxpă'trĭ|āte[1] *v.t.* Expel, remove one*self,* from homeland; withdraw one*self* from citizenship or allegiance; hence **~A'TION** *n.* [f. med. L EX[1]-(*patriare* f. *patria* native land) + -ATE[3]]

ĕxpă'trĭate[2] *a.* & *n.* Expatriated (person); (person) living abroad. [as prec.; see -ATE[1,2]]

ėxpĕ'ct *v.t.* **1.** Look forward to, regard as likely, assume as future event, (*I expect a storm, expect to see him, expect him to come, expect* (*that*) *he will come, expect him next week, don't expect me* (*to come*), *expect payment today, not so bad as I expected* (*it to be*), *just what I expected of him*); **shall not ~ you till I** etc. **see you,** allow you to arrive when you please; **~ me when you see me,** (colloq.) I do not know when I shall return. **2.** Look for as due (*I expect you to be punctual, that you will be punctual*; *do you expect payment for this?*); (colloq.) think, suppose, (*that*); **be ~ing** *a baby, a child,* etc., or abs., be pregnant. [f. L EX[1](*spectare* look, frequent. of *specere* see)]

ėxpĕ'ctancy̆ *n.* State of expectation; prospect, esp. of future possession; prospective chance (*of*). [f. L *ex*(*s*)*pectantia* (as prec.; see -ANCY)]

ėxpĕ'ctant *a.* & *n.* **1.** *a.* Expecting (*of,* or abs.; **~ mother,** pregnant woman); having the prospect, in normal course, of possession, office, etc.; characterized by waiting for events, esp. (Med.) *expectant method*; hence **~LY**[2] *adv.* **2.** *n.* One who expects; candidate for office etc. [ME, f. as EXPECT; see -ANT]

ĕxpĕctā'tion *n.* Awaiting; anticipation (*beyond, contrary to, expectation*); (in *pl.*) prospects of inheritance; thing expected; *expectation of* LIFE 4; probability of a thing's happening. [f. L *expectatio* (as EXPECT; see -ATION)]

ėxpĕ'ctorant *a.* & *n.* (Medicine) that promotes expectoration. [f. as foll.; see -ANT]

ėxpĕ'ctor|āte *v.t.* Eject (phlegm etc.) from chest or lungs by coughing or spitting; (abs.) spit; hence **~A'TION** *n.* [f. L EX[1]*pectorare* (*pectus -oris* breast) + -ATE[3]]

ėxpē'dĭ|ent *a.* & *n.* **1.** *a.* (usu. *pred.*) Advantageous, suitable, (*do whatever is expedient*; *it is expedient that he should go*); politic rather than just; hence or cogn. **~ENCE, ~ENCY,** *ns.*, **~entLY**[2] *adv.* **2.** *n.* Resource, means of attaining one's end. [ME, f. L *expedire* (see foll., -ENT)]

ĕ'xpėdite *v.t.* Assist progress of, hasten, (action, process, etc.); accomplish (business). [f. L EX[1]*pedire -dit-* (*pes pedis* foot) extricate, put in order + -ITE[2]]

ĕxpėdĭ'tion *n.* **1.** Warlike enterprise; journey, voyage, for definite purpose; men or fleet sent on this; hence ~ARY[1] *a.*, ~IST (3) *n.* **2.** Promptness, speed. [ME f. OF, f. L *expeditio -onis* (as prec.; see -ION)]

ĕxpėdĭ'tious (-sh*u*s) *a.* Doing or done speedily; suited for speedy performance; hence ~LY[2] *adv.*, ~NESS *n.* [f. prec.; see -IOUS]

ėxpĕ'l *v.t.* (-ll-). Cause to depart or emerge (person *from* place, bullet *from* gun, etc.) by use of force; compel departure of (person; *from* a country, community, school, etc.); hence ~**l**EE' *n.*, ~**l**ENT *a.* [ME, f. L EX[1](*pellere puls-* drive)]

ėxpĕ'nd *v.t.* Spend (money, care, time, *on* object, *in doing*); use up; (Naut.) wind (spare rope) round spar etc. [ME, f. L EX[1](*pendere pens-* weigh)]

ėxpĕ'ndable *a.* That may be expended; not regarded as worth preserving or saving; not normally reused; unimportant, that may be sacrificed to gain one's ends. [f. prec. + -ABLE]

ėxpĕ'ndĭture *n.* Spending (*of* money etc.); using up, consuming; amount expended. [f. EXPEND, after obs. *expenditor*, med. L f. *expenditus* irreg. p.p. of L *expendere*; see -URE]

ėxpĕ'nse *n.* **1.** Spending of money (**go to the ~ of,** spend money on; **put to ~**, cause to spend money); **at** person's ~, causing him to spend money or (fig.) suffer injury, ridicule, etc.; **at the ~ of,** so as to cause loss, damage, or discredit to. **2.** Amount of money spent; (usu. in *pl.*) amount spent in executing commission etc., amount paid to reimburse this, (*he paid my expenses, offered me £10 and expenses*); **~ account,** list of employee's expenses payable by employer. [ME f. AF; OF *espense* f. LL *expensa* (*pecunia* money), fem. p.p. of L *expendere* EXPEND]

ėxpĕ'nsĭve *a.* Of high price, dear; making a high charge; causing much expense; hence ~LY[2] (-vlĭ) *adv.*, ~NESS (-vn-) *n.* [f. as EXPEND + -IVE]

ėxpēr'ĭenc|e[1] *n.* Actual observation of or practical acquaintance with facts or events; knowledge or skill resulting from this, whence ~ED[2] (-st) *a.*; event that affects one (*an unpleasant experience*); fact or process of being so affected (*I learnt by experience*); state or phase of religious emotion. [ME f. OF, f. L *experientia* f. EX[1]*periri -pert-* try; see -ENCE]

ėxpēr'ĭence[2] *v.t.* Meet with, feel, undergo, (pleasure, treatment, fate, etc.); hence ~ABLE (-s*a*-) *a.* [f. prec.]

ėxperĭĕ'ntial (-sh*a*l) *a.* Of experience; **~ philosophy** (treating all knowledge as based on experience), whence ~ISM (3), ~IST (2), *ns.*; hence ~LY[2] *adv.* [f. EXPERIENCE[1] + -IAL, after *inferential* etc.]

ėxpĕ'rĭment[1] *n.* Test or trial (*of*); procedure adopted on chance of its succeeding, for testing hypothesis etc., or to demonstrate known fact. [ME f. OF, or f. L *experimentum* (as EXPERIENCE[1]; see -MENT)]

ėxpĕ'rĭmĕnt[2] *v.i.* Make experiment (*on, with*); hence ~A'TION, ~ER[1], *ns.* [f. prec.]

ėxpĕrĭmĕ'ntal *a.* Based on experience, not on authority or conjecture; based on or making use of experiment (*experimental philosophy, physicist, physics, psychologist, psychology*), whence ~ISM (3), ~IST (2), *ns.*; tentative; used in experiments; hence ~IZE (2) *v.i.*, ~LY[2] *adv.* [ME, f. med. L *experimentalis* (as EXPERIMENT[1]; see -AL)]

ĕ'xpērt[1] *a.* Trained by practice, skilful, (*at, in*); hence ~LY[2] *adv.*, ~NESS *n.* [ME f. OF, f. L *expertus* p.p. of *experiri* (see EXPERIENCE[1])]

ĕ'xpērt[2] *n.* Person having special skill or knowledge (*at, in*; *mining expert*); (*attrib.*) of or being an expert (*expert evidence, expert witness*). [F, f. adj. f. as prec.]

|**ĕxpērti'se**[1] (-ē'z) *n.* Expert opinion or skill or knowledge. [F]

ĕ'xpertīze, -īse[2] (-īz), *v.i.* & *t.* Give expert opinion (concerning). [f. EXPERT[2] + -IZE]

ĕ'xpĭ|āte *v.t.* Pay the penalty of, make amends for, (sin); hence or cogn. ~ABLE, ~**ā**TORY, *adjs.*, ~A'TION, ~**ā**TOR, *ns.* [f. L EX[1](*piare* seek to appease f. *pius* devout) + -ATE[3]]

ĕxpirā'tion *n.* Breathing out (*of* air etc.); termination (*of* period, truce, etc.). [f. L *expiratio* (as foll.; see -ATION)]

ėxpīr'e *v.* **1.** *v.t.* Breathe out (air *from* lungs, or abs.), whence **ėxpīr'at**ORY *a.* **2.** *v.i.* Die; (of period) come to an end; (of law, patent, truce, etc., or of right granted for a certain period) become void, reach its term; (of title etc.) cease, become extinct. [ME, f. OF *expirer* f. L EX[1]- (*spirare* breathe)]

ėxpīr'ȳ *n.* Termination (*of* period, truce, etc.). [f. prec. + -Y[1]]

ėxplai'n *v.t.* Make known in detail (thing, *that, how*, etc.); make intelligible (meaning, difficulty, etc., or abs.); say (*that*) as explanation; account for (conduct etc.); **~ away,** modify, remove force of, (esp. offensive language, awkward facts) by explanation; ~ one**self,** (1) make one's meaning clear, (2) give an account of one's motives or conduct; hence ~ABLE *a.* [f. L EX[1](*planare* f. *planus* flat); assim. to PLAIN[1]]

ĕxplanā'tion *n.* Explaining; declaration made with view to mutual understanding or reconciliation; statement or circumstance that explains. [ME, f. L *explanatio* (as prec.; see -ATION)]

ėxplă'nator|ȳ *a.* Serving, or intended to serve, to explain; hence ~ĭLY[2] *adv.* [f. LL *explanatorius* (as EXPLAIN; see -ORY)]

ĕxpla'nt[1] (-ah'-) *v.t.* (Biol.) Transfer (living tissue) from body, esp. to nutrient medium; hence ~A'TION *n.* [f. mod. L EX[1](*plantare* PLANT[2])]

ĕ'xplant[2] (-ah-) *n.* (Biol.) Explanted tissue, organ, etc. [f. prec.]

ėxplē'tĭve (*or* ĕ-) *a.* & *n.* **1.** *a.* Serving to fill out (esp. sentence, line of verse, etc.). **2.** *n.* Expletive thing, word, etc., esp. oath or meaningless exclamation. [f. LL *expletivus* f. EX[1](*plēre plet-* fill); see -IVE]

ĕ'xplĭc|āte *v.t.* Develop meaning or implication of (notion, principle, etc.); make clear, explain, whence ~ABLE, ~**at**IVE, ~**ā**TORY, *adjs.*; hence ~A'TION *n.* [f. L EX[1](*plicare plicat-* or *plicit-* fold) unfold + -ATE[3]]

ĕ'xplĭcĭt[1] *n.* Last words (of book etc., or fig.). [LL, = 'here ends', formerly used by scribes to mark end of book or section]

ėxplĭ'cĭt[2] *a.* Stated in detail, leaving nothing merely implied; definite; (of person, book, etc.) outspoken; **~ faith,** acceptance of doctrine with clear understanding of all it involves (cf. IMPLICIT); hence ~LY[2] *adv.*, ~NESS *n.* [f. F *explicite* or f. L *explicitus* (as EXPLICATE)]

ėxplō'de *v.* **1.** *v.i.* & *t.* (Of gas, gunpowder, bomb, boiler, etc.) expand suddenly with loud noise owing to release of internal energy, cause (gas etc.) to do this; give vent suddenly to emotion; (of population etc.) increase suddenly or rapidly; **~d view** etc. (showing components of machine etc. as if separated by explosion but in same relative positions). **2.** *v.t.* Bring (theory, fallacy, etc.) into disrepute by showing it to be baseless. [orig. sense 2, f. L EX[1](*plodere plos-* = *plaudere* clap) hiss off the stage]

ĕ'xploit[1] *n.* Brilliant or daring achievement. [ME, f. OF *esplait, esploit(e)* f. Gallo-Rom. **explictum*, **explicta* f. L neut. and fem. p.p. (as EXPLICATE)]

ėxploi't[2] *v.t.* Work, turn to account, (mine etc.); utilize (person etc.) for one's own ends, esp. (derog.) thus utilize workers, colonial possessions, etc.; hence or cogn. ~ABLE *a.*, **ĕxploit**A'TION, *n.*, ~(**at**)IVE *adjs.* (esp. derog.). [ME, f. OF *exploiter* f. Gallo-Rom. **explicitare* frequent. of L *explicare* (see EXPLICATE)]

ėxplōr'|**e** *v.t.* Inquire into, investigate; examine (wound etc.) by touch; examine (country etc.) by going through it; hence or cogn. **ĕxplor**A'TION, ~ER[1], *ns.*, ~**at**IVE, ~**at**ORY, (*or* -ŏ'r-) *adjs.* [f. F *explorer* f. L *explorare*]

ėxplō'sion (-zh*o*n) *n.* Exploding; loud noise due to this; sudden outbreak (of anger etc.); rapid or sudden increase (of population etc.); (Phonet.) plosion. [f. L *explosio* scornful rejection (as EXPLODE; see -ION)]

ėxplō'sĭve (*or* -z-) *a.* & *n.* **1.** *a.* Tending to expand suddenly with loud noise; (of consonant sound) plosive; tending to cause explosion (lit. or fig.); hence ~LY[2] (-vlĭ) *adv.*, ~NESS (-vn-) *n.* **2.** *n.* Explosive substance (**high** ~, explosive substance with very violent shattering effect and used in shells, bombs, etc.); plosive consonant, STOP[2] 5. [f. prec. + -IVE]

ėxpō'nent *a.* & *n.* (Person or thing) that sets forth or interprets; executant (of music etc.); person who favours or advocates the use *of*; type, representative; (Math.) symbol indicating what power of a factor is to be taken, usu. written at upper right of factor symbol. [f. L EX[1](*ponere posit-* put); see -ENT]

ĕxponĕ'ntial (-sh*a*l) *a.* (Math.) Pertaining to an exponent, indicated by an exponent (~ **function,** one which increases as a quantity raised to a power determined by the variable on which the function depends); (of increase etc.) more and more rapid. [f. F *exponentiel* (as prec.; see -IAL)]

ėxpōr't[1] (*or* ĕ'-) *v.t.* Send out (goods) esp. to another country; hence or cogn. ~ABLE *a.*, ~A'TION (ĕ-), ~ER[1], *ns.* [f. L EX[1](*portare* carry)]

ĕ'xpōrt[2] *n.* Exported article; (usu. in *pl.*) amount exported; exportation (~ **reject,** article sold in its country of manufacture, as being below standard for export); (*attrib.*) suitable for export, esp. of better quality. [f. prec.]

ėxpō'se (-z) *v.t.* **1.** Leave (person, thing) unprotected (esp. from weather); subject *to* (risk etc.); (Photog.) subject (film etc.) to light; (Hist.) leave (child) out of doors to perish; (in *p.p.*) open *to* (the east etc.). **2.** Exhibit, display; put up for sale; ~ one**self,** expose one's body indecently. **3.** Disclose (secret, project, etc.); reveal (villain, villainy). [ME, f. OF *exposer*, after L *exponere* (see EXPONENT, POSE[1])]

exposé (ĕkspō'zā) *n.* Orderly statement of facts; revealing (of discreditable thing). [F, p.p. of *exposer* (see prec.)]

ĕxposĭ'tion (-z-) *n.* Setting forth, description; (Mus.) presentation of principal theme(s); explanation; commentary; (arch.) exposure; exhibition of goods etc. [ME f. OF, or f. L *expositio* (as EXPONENT; see -ION)]

ėxpŏ'sĭt|**ĭve** (-z-) *a.* Descriptive; explanatory; so ~OR *n.*, ~ORY *a.* [f. prec. + -IVE]

ex post facto (ĕks pōst făʹktō) *a.* & *adv.* (Acting) retrospectively (*ex post facto law*). [f. LL *ex postfacto* from what is done afterwards]

ėxpŏ'stūl|**āte** *v.i.* Make protest, remonstrate (*with* person *about, on*); hence or cogn. ~A'TION *n.*, ~**āt**ORY *a.* [f. L EX[1](*postulare* demand) + -ATE[3]]

ėxpō'sure (-zh*e*r) *n.* Exposing or being exposed (*to* air, cold, danger, etc.; **indecent** ~, intentional act of publicly and indecently exposing one's body); unmasking of imposture etc.; aspect (*southern exposure*); (Photog.) action of exposing plate or film to the light, duration of this action, area of film etc. affected by it, (~ **meter,** device to measure illumination and indicate correct duration of exposure). [f. EXPOSE, after *enclosure* etc.; see -URE]

ėxpou'nd *v.t.* Set forth in detail (doctrine etc.); explain, interpret, (esp. Scripture). [ME, f. OF *espondre* f. as EXPONENT]

ėxprĕ'ss[1] *a.*, *adv.*, & *n.* **1.** *a.* Definitely stated, not merely implied; (arch., of likeness) exact; hence ~LY[2] *adv.* **2.** Done, made, sent, for special purpose; (of messages or goods) delivered by special messenger or service. **3.** Operating at high speed; ~ **lift** (not stopping at every floor); ~ **rifle** (discharging bullet at high speed); ~ **train** (fast, stopping at few intermediate stations); ~**way,** urban motorway. **4.** *adv.* At high speed; by express messenger or train. **5.** *n.* Express train, messenger, rifle, etc.; *company undertaking transport of parcels etc. [ME, f. OF *expres* f. L *expressus* distinctly shown, p.p. of EX[1](*primere press-* = *premere* press)]

ėxprĕ'ss[2] *v.t.* **1.** Squeeze out (juice, air, *from, out of*; milk etc. from breast). **2.** Represent by symbols, as (Math.) *express* (quantity) *in terms of* (another). **3.** Reveal, betoken, (feelings, qualities); put (thought) into words; ~ one**self,** say what one means (*strongly* etc. *on* subject, *well, aptly*, etc.). **4.** Hence ~IBLE *a.* [ME, f. OF *expresser* f. Rom. EX[1](*pressare*; see PRESS[2])]

ėxprĕ'ss[3] *v.t.* Send by express (messenger or delivery). [f. EXPRESS[1]]

ėxprĕ'ssion (-sh*o*n) *n.* **1.** Expressing; wording, diction, word, phrase; (Math.) collection of symbols expressing a quantity. **2.** Aspect (of face), intonation (of voice), esp. as indicating emotion, whence ~LESS *a.*; (Art) mode of expressing action etc.; (Mus.) execution that expresses the feeling of a passage (~**-mark,** sign or word indicating expression required; ~**-stop** in harmonium, stop allowing expression by varied air-pressure). **3.** Hence ~AL *a.* [ME f. OF, or f. L *expressio* f. *exprimere* (see EXPRESS[1], -ION)]

ėxprĕ'ssion|**ĭsm** (-sh*o*n-) *n.* Style of painting, drama, music, etc., subordinating realism to symbolic or stylistic expression of the artist's etc. inner experience; so ~IST (2) *n.*, ~**ĭ'st**IC *a.* [f. prec. + -ISM]

ėxprĕ'ssĭve *a.* Serving to express (*expressive of* motion etc.); (of word, gesture, etc.) significant; hence ~LY[2] (-vlĭ) *adv.*, ~NESS (-vn-), **ĕxprĕssĭ'v**ITY, *ns.* [ME, f. F *expressif -ive* or f. med. L *expressivus* (as EXPRESSION; see -IVE)]

ĕxprĕ'ssō. Var. of ESPRESSO.

ĕxprō'prĭ|**āte** *v.t.* Dispossess (*from* estate etc.); (esp. of State) take away (property); so ~A'TION *n.* [f. med. L EX[1](*propriare* f. *proprium* property); see PROPER, -ATE[3]]

ėxpŭ'ls|**ion** (-sh*o*n) *n.* Expelling, being expelled; so ~IVE *a.* [ME, f. L *expulsio* (as EXPEL; see -ION)]

ėxpŭ'nge (-nj) *v.t.* Erase, omit, (name *from* list, passage *from* book, etc.); so **ėxpŭ'nct**ION *n.* [f. L EX[1](*pungere punct-* prick)]

ĕ'xpurg|**āte** *v.t.* Purify (book etc.) by removing matter thought objectionable; remove (such matter); hence or cogn. ~A'TION, ~**āt**OR, *ns.*, **ĕxpurgatōr'**IAL, **ėxpūr'gat**ORY, *adjs.* [f. L EX[1](*purgare* cleanse) + -ATE[3]]

ĕ'xquĭsĭte (-z-; *or* -ĭ'z-) *a.* & *n.* **1.** *a.* Of great excellence or beauty; acute, keenly felt, (*exquisite pain, pleasure*); keen (*exquisite sensibility* etc.); hence ~LY² (-tlĭ) *adv.*, ~NESS (-tn-) *n.* **2.** *n.* Coxcomb, dandy. [ME, f. L EX¹(*quirere quisit-* = *quaerere* seek)]

exrx. *abbr.* executrix.

ĕxsă'nguĭnāte (-nggwĭn-) *v.t.* Drain of blood. [f. L EX¹(*sanguinatus* f. *sanguis -inis* blood) + -ATE³]

ėxscĭ'nd *v.t.* Cut out, excise, (lit. or fig.). [f. L EX¹(*scindere* cut)]

ėxsẽr't *v.t.* (Biol.) Put forth. [f. L *exserere*; see EXERT]

ĕx-sẽr'vĭce. See EX-¹ 2.

ĕ'xsĭccāte *v.t.* Dry up; drain dry. [f. L EX¹-(*siccare* f. *siccus* dry) + -ATE³]

ex silentio (ĕks sīlĕ'nshĭō) *adv.* By absence of contrary evidence. [L, = from silence]

ext. *abbr.* exterior; external.

ĕxtă'nt (*or* ĕ'kstant) *a.* (Esp. of document etc.) still existing. [f. L EX¹(*stare* stand); see -ANT]

ėxtĕ'mpor|ė *adv.* & *a.* (Spoken or done) without preparation; offhand; **speak ~e** (without notes); hence or cogn. ~A'NEOUS, ~ARY¹, *adjs.* [L *ex tempore* on the spur of the moment, lit. out of the time (*tempus* time)]

ėxtĕ'mporiz|e, -īs|e (-iz), *v.* **1.** *v.t.* Compose or produce extempore. **2.** *v.i.* Speak extempore. **3.** Hence ~A'TION *n.* [f. prec. + -IZE]

ėxtĕ'nd *v.* **1.** *v.t.* Lay out (esp. body, limbs, etc.) at full length; write out at full length. **2.** Cause to be continuous *over* space, *to* point, etc.; prolong (period; **~ed-play** *a.*, containing a recording longer than that of a gramophone record etc. that is taken as 'normal'); enlarge (scope, meaning of word, etc.); (usu. in *pass.* or *refl.*) tax powers of (horse, athlete, etc.) to the utmost. **3.** Stretch forth (hand, arm); accord (kindness, patronage, *to*); offer (invitation, welcome, *to*). **4.** *v.i.* Stretch (*to* point; *over*, *across*, etc., space). **5.** Hence or cogn. ~IBI'LITY, **ėxtĕnsi**BI'LITY, *ns.*, **ėxtĕ'nd**IBLE, **ėxtĕ'ns**IBLE, *adjs.* [ME, f. L EX¹(*tendere tens-* or *tent-* stretch)]

ėxtĕ'nsīle *a.* Capable of being stretched out or protruded. [f. as prec.; see -IL]

ėxtĕ'nsion (-shon) *n.* **1.** Extending or being extended; extent, range; (Logic) group of things denoted by a term; prolongation; enlargement. **2.** Additional part (of railway, plan, theory, etc.); (number of a) subsidiary telephone distant from main instrument; extramural instruction by university or college (*extension course*). **3.** Hence ~AL *a.* [ME, f. LL *extensio* f. as EXTEND; see -ION]

ėxtĕ'nsĭve *a.* (Of space, purchase, operation, etc.) large; far-reaching, comprehensive; (of agricultural production etc.) depending on extension of area (cf. INTENSIVE); hence ~LY² (-vlĭ) *adv.*, ~NESS (-vn-) *n.* [f. F *extensif -ive* or f. LL *extensivus* (as prec.; see -IVE)]

ĕxtĕnsŏ'mėter *n.* Instrument for measuring deformation of metal under stress; instrument using such deformation to record elastic strains in other materials. [f. L *extensus* p.p. of *extendere* (see EXTEND) + -O- + -METER]

ėxtĕ'nsor *n.* ~ **(muscle)**, muscle that extends or straightens out part of the body. [mod. L (as EXTEND; see -OR)]

ėxtĕ'nt *n.* Space over which a thing extends; width or limits of application, scope, (*to a great extent*; *to the full extent of his power*); large space (*a vast extent of marsh*). [ME, f. AF *extente* f. med. L *extenta* fem. p.p. (as n.) of L *extendere* (see EXTEND)]

ėxtĕ'nūāte *v.t.* Lessen seeming seriousness of (guilt, offence) by partial excuse (*we must not extenuate, nothing can extenuate, his behaviour; there were extenuating circumstances*), whence **ėxtĕ'nūāt**ORY *a.*; (arch.) make thin or weak; hence ~A'TION *n.* [f. L EX¹(*tenuare* f. *tenuis* thin) + -ATE³]

ėxtẽr'ior *a.* & *n.* **1.** *a.* Outer (opp. *interior*); situated on the outside (relative *to*); coming from outside; (Cinemat.) outdoor; ~ **angle** (between side of rectilineal figure and adjacent side produced); hence ~ITY (-ŏ'r-) *n.*, ~IZE (3) *v.t.*, ~LY² *adv.* **2.** *n.* Outward aspect or surface or demeanour; (Cinemat.) outdoor scene. [L, compar. of *exterus* outside]

ėxtẽr'mĭn|āte *v.t.* Destroy utterly (species, race, sect, opinion); hence or cogn. ~A'TION, **~ātor**, *ns.*, **~āt**ORY *a.* [f. L EX¹(*terminare* f. *terminus* boundary) + -ATE³]

ėxtẽr'nal *a.* & *n.* **1.** *a.* Of, or situated on, the outside or visible part (opp. *internal*); (of remedy etc.) applied to the outside of the body; of the foreign affairs of a State; pertaining to students taking examinations of, but not attending, a university; belonging to the ~ **world** of phenomena, outside the conscious subject; ~ **evidence** (derived from source independent of the thing discussed); hence **ĕxtẽrnă'l**ITY *n.*, ~IZE (3) *v.t.*, ~LY² *adv.* **2.** *n.* (in *pl.*) Outward features or aspect; external circumstances; non-essentials. [f. med. L **externalis* f. L *externus* (*exterus* outside); see -AL]

ĕxterŏcĕ'ptĭve *a.* (Biol.) Relating to stimuli produced outside an organism. [irreg. f. L *externus* exterior + -O- + RECEPTIVE]

ĕxtĕrrĭtŏr'ĭal *a.* = EXTRATERRITORIAL; so ~ITY (-ă'l-) *n.* [f. EX-¹ + TERRITORIAL]

ėxtĭ'nct *a.* (Of fire etc.) no longer burning; (of volcano) that no longer erupts (~ **volcano,** (fig.) person no longer having remarkable energy etc.); (of life, hope, etc.) terminated, quenched; (of family, class, species) that has died out; (of office etc.) obsolete; (of title of nobility) having no qualified claimant. [ME, f. L EX¹(*stinguere stinct-* quench)]

ėxtĭ'nct|ion *n.* Extinguishing, being extinguished; making, being, becoming, extinct; abolition, wiping out (of debt), annihilation; (Phys.) reduction in intensity of radiation by absorption, scattering, etc.; hence ~IVE *a.* [f. L *extinctio* (as prec.; see -ION)]

ėxtĭ'nguish (-nggw-) *v.t.* Make extinct, terminate (light, hope, life, faculties); (arch.) eclipse, obscure, (person) by superior brilliancy, reduce (opponent) to silence; destroy; abolish, wipe out (debt), annihilate; hence ~ABLE *a.*, ~MENT *n.* [irreg. f. L *extinguere* (as EXTINCT) + -ISH²; cf. *distinguish*]

ėxtĭ'nguisher (-nggw-) *n.* In vbl senses; hollow conical cap for extinguishing flame of candle etc.; (**fire**) ~, apparatus with jet for discharging liquid chemicals or foam to extinguish fire. [f. prec. + -ER¹]

ĕ'xtĭrp|āte *v.t.* Destroy, root out, (tree, weed, species, nation, tumour, heresy, etc.); hence or cogn. ~A'TION, **~ātor**, *ns.* [f. L EX¹(*stirpare* f. *stirps* stem) + -ATE³]

ėxtŏ'l *v.t.* (**-ll-**). Praise enthusiastically (*extol him to the skies*). [f. L EX¹(*tollere* raise)]

ėxtŏr't *v.t.* Obtain (money, promise, etc.) by violence, intimidation, persistent demands, etc. (*from*); extract forcibly (meaning, inference, *from* words, data); hence ~IVE *a.* [f. L EX¹-(*torquēre tort-* twist)]

ėxtŏr'tion *n.* Extorting, esp. of money; illegal exaction; hence ~ER¹ *n.* [ME, f. LL *extortio* (as prec.; see -ION)]

ėxtŏr'tionate *a.* Using or given to extortion; (of price etc.) exorbitant. [f. prec. + -ATE²]

For other words in *ex-* see EX-¹, EX-².

ĕ'xtra *a.*, *adv.*, & *n.* **1.** *a.* Additional; more than is usual or necessary; ~ **cover,** (Cricket) fieldsman on line between cover-point and mid-off but beyond these, his place. **2.** *adv.* More than usually (*extra strong*); additionally; ~ **dry** or **sec,** (of champagne) very slightly sweetened. **3.** *n.* Extra thing; thing for which extra charge is made (*dancing is an extra*); (Cricket) run not scored from hit with bat; special issue of newspaper etc.; (Cinemat.) person engaged temporarily for minor part or to be one of a crowd. [prob. for EXTRAORDINARY, after sim. forms in F and G]

ĕxtra- *pref.* forming *adjs.* usu. f. *adjs.*, w. senses 'situated outside', 'not coming within the scope of', as: **~-atmosphe'ric,** of the space beyond the atmosphere; **~-corpor'eal,** outside the body; **~cra'nial,** outside the skull; **~-curri'cular,** not coming within the normal curriculum; **~gala'ctic,** situated outside the Galaxy; **~-i'llustrate,** add pictures to (book) from another source; **~judi'cial,** not belonging to the case before the court, not legally authorized, (of confession) not made in court; **~-ma'rital,** of sexual relationships outside marriage; **~mu'ndane,** outside our world or the universe; **~phy'sical,** not subject to physical laws; **~-se'nsory,** derived by means other than the known senses (e.g. telepathy); **~terre'strial,** outside the earth or its atmosphere; **~-vehi'cular,** outside a vehicle, esp. a spacecraft. [med. L, f. L *extra* outside]

ĕ'xtrăct[1] *n.* Substance got by treating another with solvents and then evaporating them; preparation containing active principle of a substance in concentrated form; passage from book, music, etc. [f. L *extractum*, neut. p.p. (as n.) of *extrahere* (see foll.)]

ėxtră'ct[2] *v.t.* **1.** Copy out (passage in book etc.); take passages from (book etc.). **2.** Take out by force (tooth, anything firmly fixed); draw forth (money, admission, etc.) against person's will; obtain (juice etc.) by suction, pressure, etc.; obtain extract from (substance); derive (pleasure etc. *from*); (arch.) deduce (principle etc. *from*); (Math.) find (root of a number). **3.** Hence ~ABLE *a.*, ~OR *n.* (**~or fan,** ventilating fan in window etc. to remove stale air). [f. L EX[1](*trahere tract-* draw)]

ėxtră'ction *n.* Extracting; lineage, descent, (*of Indian extraction*). [ME f. F, f. LL *extractio -onis* (as prec.; see -ION)]

ėxtră'ctĭve *a.* & *n.* (Thing) of the nature of an extract; ~ **industries** (obtaining coal, ore, oil, etc.). [f. EXTRACT[2] + -IVE]

ĕxtradī'table *a.* Liable to, (of crime) warranting, extradition. [f. foll. + -ABLE]

ĕ'xtradīte *v.t.* Give up (fugitive foreign criminal or accused person) to proper authorities; obtain the extradition of. [back form. f. foll.]

ĕxtradĭ'tion *n.* Delivery of fugitive foreign criminal or accused person to proper authorities; (Psych.) localizing of sensation at distance from the centre of sensation. [F (as EX[1], TRADITION)]

ėxtrā'dŏs *n.* Upper or outer curve of arch. [F EXTRA(*dos* back f. L *dorsum*)]

ĕxtramūr'al *a.* Outside walls or boundaries (of town or city); additional to ordinary university teaching or studies, esp. for non-resident students. [f. L *extra muros* outside the walls + -AL]

ėxtrā'nėous *a.* Of external origin; foreign *to* (object to which it is attached etc.); not belonging (*to* matter in hand, class); hence ~LY[2] *adv.*, ~NESS *n.* [f. L *extraneus* (*extra* outside) + -OUS]

ĕxtraor'dinar|y̆ (*or* ĭkstror'-) *a.* **1.** Out of the usual course; (of official etc.) additional, specially employed (ENVOY[2] *extraordinary*). **2.** Exceptional, surprising; unusually great. **3.** Hence ~ĬLY[2] *adv.*, ~ĬNESS *n.* [f. L *extraordinarius* (*extra ordinem* outside the usual order; see -ARY[1])]

ėxtră'pol|āte *v.t.* & *i.* (Math. etc.) Estimate from known values, data, etc., (others which lie outside the range of those known); so ~A'TION *n.* [f. EXTRA- + INTERPOLATE]

ĕxtratĕrrĭtor'ĭal *a.* (Of ambassador etc.) free from jurisdiction of the territory in which one resides; so ~ITY (-ă'l-) *n.* [f. L *extra territorium* outside the territory + -AL]

ėxtră'vag|ance (*or* -vĭg-) *n.* Being extravagant; extravagant thing; absurd statement or action; so ~ANCY *n.* [F (as foll.; see -ANCE)]

ėxtră'vagant (*or* -vĭg-) *a.* Immoderate; exceeding the bounds of reason; profuse, wasteful; (of price etc.) exorbitant; hence ~LY[2] *adv.* [ME, f. med. L EXTRA(*vagari* wander); see -ANT; infl. in sense by F *extravagant*]

ėxtrăvagă'nza *n.* Fanciful composition (literary, musical, or dramatic); extravagant language or behaviour. [f. It. *estravaganza*, after EXTRA-]

ėxtră'vag|āte *v.i.* (arch.) Wander away (*from* right course, *into* error etc.); exceed due bounds; hence ~A'TION *n.* [f. as EXTRAVAGANT + -ATE[3]]

ėxtră'vasāte *v.* **1.** *v.t.* Force out (fluid, esp. blood) from its proper vessel. **2.** *v.i.* (Of blood, lava, etc.) flow out. **3.** Hence **ĕxtrăvas**A'TION *n.* [f. L *extra* outside + *vas* vessel + -ATE[3]]

ĕ'xtravert etc. Var. of EXTROVERT etc.

ėxtrē'me *a.* & *n.* **1.** *a.* Outermost, farthest from centre, situated at either end (*extreme and mean ratio*, cf. GOLDEN *section*); utmost; last; ~ **unction,** (R.C. & Orthodox Ch.) anointing of dying person by priest. **2.** Reaching a high or the highest degree (*extreme old age*; *in extreme danger*); **an ~ case** (having some characteristic in the utmost degree). **3.** (Of action, measure) severe, stringent; (of opinion, person, etc.) going to great lengths, advocating severe measures, not moderate, whence **ėxtrē'm**ISM (3), **ėxtrē'm**IST (2), *ns.* **4.** Hence ~LY[2] (-mlĭ) *adv.*, ~NESS (-mn-) *n.* **5.** *n.* Thing at either end of anything, esp. (in *pl.*) things as remote or as different as possible (*extremes meet*); (Logic) subject or predicate in proposition, major or minor term in syllogism; (Math.) first or last term of ratio or series; **go to ~s,** take an extreme course of action; **go to the other ~,** take a diametrically opposite course of action; **in the ~,** to an extreme degree. [ME f. OF, f. L *extremus* superl. of *exterus* outward]

ėxtrĕ'mĭty̆ *n.* Extreme point, very end; (in *pl.*) hands and feet; extreme adversity, embarrassment, etc., (*driven to extremity*; *what can we do in this extremity?*); (arch., usu. in *pl.*) extreme measure(s). [ME, f. OF *extremité* or f. L *extremitas* (as prec.; see -ITY)]

ĕxtrē'm|um *n.* (*pl.* ~*a or* ~**ums**). (Math.) Maximum or minimum value of a function; hence ~AL *a.* [L, neut. of *extremus* EXTREME]

ĕ'xtrĭc|āte *v.t.* Disentangle, release, (person, thing, *from* confinement, difficulty); hence ~ABLE *a.*, ~A'TION *n.* [f. L EX[1](*tricare* f. *tricae* perplexities) + -ATE[3]]

ĕxtrĭ'ns|ĭc *a.* Lying outside, not belonging, (*to*); originating or operating from without; not inherent or essential; hence ~ICALLY *adv.* [f. LL *extrinsicus* f. L *extrinsecus* adv. (*exter* outside + *-im* (as *interim*) + *secus* beside)]

ĕxtrover'sion *n.* (Psych.) Direction of thoughts and interests to things outside oneself (opp. INTROVERSION); so **ĕ'xtrovert** *n.* & *a.*, **ĕ'xtrovert**ED[1] *a.*, (person) characterized by extroversion, sociable or unreserved (person). [f. as EXTRA- (after *intro-*) + VERSION]

ėxtru′|de (-rōō′d) *v.t.* Thrust out (person, thing, *from*); shape (metal, plastics, etc.) by forcing through die; hence or cogn. ~SION (-zhən) *n.*, ~SILE, ~SIVE, *adjs.* [f. L EX¹(*trudere trus-* thrust)]

ėxū′ber|ant (ĭgz-) *a.* Luxuriantly prolific (lit. or fig.); growing luxuriantly; (of health, emotion, etc.) overflowing, abounding; (of person, action, etc.) effusive, overflowing with high spirits; (of language) copious, lavish in ornament; abundant; hence or cogn. ~ANCE *n.*, **~ant**LY² *adv.* [f. F *exubérant* f. L EX¹(*uberare* be fruitful f. *uber* fertile); see -ANT]

ėxū′berāte (ĭgz-) *v.i.* Be exuberant; (arch.) abound, overflow, indulge freely *in*. [f. L (as prec.) + -ATE³]

ėxū′de (ĭgz-) *v.i.* & *t.* Ooze out, give off (moisture etc.), emit (smell), (fig.) show (pleasure etc.) abundantly; so **ĕ′xūd**ATE¹ (5), **ĕxūd**A′TION, *ns.*, **ėxū′d**ATIVE (ĭgz-) *a.* [f. L EX¹(*sudare* sweat)]

ėxŭ′lt (ĭgz-) *v.i.* Rejoice exceedingly (*at*, *in*, thing, *to* find etc.); triumph (*over* person); hence or cogn. ~ANCY, **ĕxŭlt**A′TION (*or* ĕgz-), *ns.*, ~ANT *a.* [f. L EX¹(*sultare* = *saltare* frequent. of *salire salt-* leap)]

ĕ′xûrb *n.* District outside city or town, esp. prosperous area beyond suburbs; so **ĕxûr′b**AN *a.*, **ĕxûr′ban**ITE¹ (1) *n.* [f. L *ex* out of + *urbs* city, or back form. f. *exurban* f. EX-¹ + URBAN, after *suburban*]

ĕxûr′bĭa *n.* Exurbs collectively, region beyond suburbs. [f. EX-¹, after *Suburbia*]

ĕxū′vĭ|ae *n. pl.* Animal's cast skin, shell, or covering, (recent or fossil, or fig.); hence ~AL *a.* [L, = animal's skins, spoils of enemy, f. EX¹*uere* divest oneself of]

ĕxū′vĭ|āte *v.t.* & *i.* Shed (exuviae, or fig.), slough; hence ~A′TION *n.* [f. prec. + -ATE³]

ex voto (ĕks vō′tō) *adv.* & *n.* (Offering made) in pursuance of a vow. [L, = out of a vow]

-ey. See -Y³.

ey′as (ī′*a*s) *n.* Young hawk in nest, or taken from nest for training, or not yet completely trained. [orig. *nyas* f. F *niais* f. Rom. **nid(i)ax -acis* f. L *nidus* nest; for loss of *n-* cf. ADDER]

eye¹ (ī) *n.* **1.** Organ of sight in man and animals; iris of this (*blue, brown, eyes*); region of the eyes (BLACK¹ *eye*). **2. All ~s,** watching intently; **all my ~,** (sl.) nonsense; *turn a* BLIND¹ *eye*; CATCH¹ *the eye*; CLAP² *eyes on*; CRY² one's *eyes out*; **~ of day,** sun; **do** (person) **in the ~,** defraud or thwart; *throw* DUST¹ *in* person's *eyes*; EASY *on the eye*; EVIL *eye*; **~ for an ~,** retaliation in kind (Exod. 21:24); **~s and no ~s** (said of or to one who is unobservant); **~s front, left, right,** (Mil.) turn them in direction stated; GLAD *eye*; **have ~s for,** be interested in; **have an ~ to,** have as one's object; **hit** person **in the ~,** (fig.) be very obvious; **in** or **through the ~s of,** from the point of view of, in the judgement of; **keep an ~ on,** direct one's attention (lit. or fig.) to; **keep an ~ open** or **out, keep** one's **~s open** or **skinned** etc., watch carefully (*for*); *keep* one's *eye on the* BALL¹; **look** person **in the ~** (directly or unashamedly at him); **make (sheep's) ~s,** look amorously (*at*); MEET² *the eye*; *in the* MIND¹*'s eye*; **my ~,** (sl.) nonsense; NAKED *eye*; **one in the ~,** disappointment or discomfiture *for* (person); OPEN² one's, person's, *eyes*; **with** one's **~s open,** (fig.) deliberately, with full awareness; *pore* etc. one's **~s out,** tire them; **cast** or **run an** or one's **~ over,** examine cursorily; PIPE² one's *eye*; *in the* PUBLIC *eye*; **see ~ to ~,** be in full agreement *with* (person); SET¹ *eyes on*; SHUT one's *eyes to*; **with** one's **~s shut,** (fig.) (1) without full awareness, (2) with great ease; SMACK² *in the eye*; **up to the ~s,** deeply (engaged, involved, etc.); *in the* WIND¹*'s eye*; WIPE one's or person's *eye(s)*; **with a** *friendly, jealous*, etc., **~,** (view) with feeling of friendship, jealousy, etc.; **with an ~ to,** with a VIEW *to*. **3.** Faculty of seeing, sight; (in *sing.* or *pl.*) look, gaze, glance; **have an ~ for,** be capable of perceiving or appreciating; **a good ~ for,** sound appreciation of; **half an ~,** the slightest degree of perceptiveness; **get** one's **~ in,** become accustomed to conditions of batting etc., so as to judge speed etc.; **lose an ~,** become unable to see with it; *a* STRAIGHT *eye*. **4.** Thing like an eye, e.g. spot on peacock's tail or insect's wing, **~ of needle** etc. (hole for thread etc.); hole in head of axe etc. for insertion of handle; calm region in centre of hurricane etc., centre of flower, loop of cord or rope, leaf bud of potato; BULL¹*'s-eye*; ELECTRIC *eye*; **glass ~** (artificial, of glass etc.); HOOK¹ *and eye*; MAGIC *eye*; APPLE *of the eye*. **5. ~′ball,** pupil of the eye, eye itself within lids and socket (*~ball to ~ball*, (colloq.) confronting closely); **~-bath,** small glass etc. for applying lotion etc. to eye; **~′black,** mascara; **~-bolt,** bolt or bar with eye at end for hook etc.; **~′bright,** plant of genus *Euphrasia*, formerly used as remedy for weak eyes; **~′brow,** hair growing on ridge over eye (*raise an ~brow* or one's *~brows*, show surprise; *up to the ~brows*, deeply engaged); **~-cup,** = *eye-bath*; **~′glass,** lens for correcting or assisting defective sight, (in *pl.*) pair of these held in position by hand or frame or by spring on nose; **~′hole,** hole containing eye, hole to look through; **~′lash,** hair or row of hairs on edge of eyelid; **~-level,** level seen by eyes looking straight ahead; **~′lid,** upper or lower fold of skin that can cover eye (*hang on by the ~lids*, (fig.) have only slight hold); **~-liner,** cosmetic applied as line round eye; **~-opener,** enlightening or surprising circumstance etc., *drink taken on awakening; **~′piece,** lens(es) at eye-end of telescope etc.; **~-rhyme,** correspondence of words in spelling but not in pronunciation (*love, move*); **~-service,** (arch.) service performed only when one is watched by employer; **~-shade,** device to protect eyes from strong light; **~-shadow,** cosmetic applied to skin round eyes; **~′shot,** seeing-distance (*beyond, in, out of, eyeshot*); **~′sight,** power or faculty of seeing; **~′sore,** ugly object, thing that offends the sight; **~-stalk,** (Zool.) movable stalk carrying eye; **~-strain,** weariness of eyes from excessive or incorrect use; **~-tooth,** canine tooth just under or next to eye, in upper or lower jaw (*cut* one's *~-teeth*, attain worldly wisdom); **~′wash,** lotion for eye, (sl.) bunkum, mere pretentious concealment; **~′water,** tears, lotion for eye, aqueous or vitreous humour of eye; **~′witness,** one who can bear witness from his own observation. **6.** Hence (-)**eye**D² (īd), **~′**LESS (ī′l-), *adjs.*, **~′**FUL 2 (ī′f-) *n.*, (esp., colloq.) thorough look, remarkable or attractive thing or person. [OE *ēage*, = OS *ōga*, OHG *ouga*, ON *auga*, Goth. *augo* f. Gmc **augon*]

eye² (ī) *v.t.* (**~ing** *or* **eying,** *pr.* ī′ĭng). Observe, watch, (jealously, narrowly, with disgust, askance, etc.). [f. prec.]

eye′lėt (ī′l-) *n.* Small eye; small hole in leather, cloth, sail, etc., for lace, ring, rope, etc.; loophole; **~-hole,** small hole to look or shoot through. [ME, f. OF *oillet* dim. of *oil* eye f. L *oculus*]

Eye′tie (ī′tī) *n.* & *a.* (sl., derog.) Italian. [repr. vulg. or joc. pr. (ītă′lyən)]

For other words in *ex-* see EX-¹, EX-².

eyot. See AIT.
eyr'a (ār'a) *n.* Red form of jaguarundi. [f. Tupi *(e)irara*]
eyre (ār) *n.* (Hist.) Circuit, circuit court, (*Justices in Eyre*). [ME, f. OF *eire* f. L *iter* journey]
eyr'ĭe, aer'ĭe, (ār'ĭ, ēr'ĭ, *or* īr'ĭ) *n.* Nest of bird of prey, esp. eagle, or of other bird that builds high up; human residence perched high on mountain. [f. med. L *aeria, aerea,* etc., prob. f. OF *aire* lair f. Rom. f. L *agrum* piece of ground]
Ezek. *abbr.* Ezekiel (O.T.).

F

F, f, (ĕf) *n.* (*pl.* **Fs** *or* **F's**). Sixth letter of alphabet; (Mus.) fourth note in diatonic scale of C major.
F. *abbr.* Fahrenheit; farad(s); Fellow of; (Biol.) filial generation; fine (pencil-lead).
f. *abbr.* female; feminine; femto-; filly; focal length (cf. F-NUMBER); folio; following page etc.; FORTE2.
F *symb.* fluorine.
fa. See FAH.
F.A. *abbr.* FANNY ADAMS 2; ‖Football Association.
făb *a.* (colloq.) Marvellous. [abbr. of FABULOUS]
Fā'bĭan *a.* & *n.* **1.** *a.* Employing cautious and dilatory strategy to wear out an enemy (esp. *Fabian policy*); ~ **Society** (of socialists aiming at gradual social change; so ~ISM (3), ~IST (2), *ns.*). **2.** *n.* Member of or sympathizer with Fabian Society. [f. L *Fabianus* (Q. *Fabius* Cunctator (= delayer), Roman general d. 203 B.C.; see -AN)]
fā'ble1 *n.* Story, esp. of supernatural character, not founded on fact; (collect.) myths, legendary tales; false statement, lie; thing only supposed to exist; short story, esp. with animals as characters, conveying a moral; (arch.) plot of play etc. [ME f. OF, f. L *fabula* discourse (*fari* speak)]
fā'ble2 *v.* (arch. or poet.) **1.** *v.i.* Tell fictitious tales, whence **fā'bler1** *n.* **2.** *v.t.* Describe fictitiously; (in *p.p.*) celebrated in fable, legendary, fictitious. [ME, f. OF *fabler* f. L *fabulari* (*fabula*; see prec.)]
fă'blĭau (-ō) *n.* (*pl.* **~x** *pr.* -z). Metrical tale in early French poetry, often coarsely humorous. [F, f. OF dial. *fablia(u)x* pl. of *fablel* dim. as FABLE1]
fă'brĭc *n.* Thing put together; frame, structure, (lit. or fig.); walls, floor, and roof of building; woven, knitted, or felted material; construction, texture, tissue; (arch.) edifice, building. [ME, f. F *fabrique* f. L *fabrica* (*faber* metal-worker etc.)]
fă'brĭc|āte *v.t.* **1.** Construct, manufacture, (esp. product in final shape from semi-finished metal stock etc.). **2.** Invent (story), forge (document). **3.** Hence or cogn. ~A'TION, ~**ātor**, *ns.* [f. L *fabricare* (as prec.) + -ATE3]
fă'būlĭst *n.* Composer of fables; liar. [f. F *fabuliste* f. L *fabula* (see FABLE1, -IST)]
fă'būlous *a.* Celebrated in fable; unhistorical, legendary; incredible, absurd, exaggerated; (colloq.) marvellous; hence or cogn. **făbūl**O'SITY, ~NESS, *ns.*, ~LY2 *adv.* [f. F *fabuleux* or f. L *fabulosus* (as FABLE1; see -OUS)]
façа'de (-sah'd) *n.* Face of building (esp. principal front) towards street or open space; frontal or outward appearance, esp. deceptive one. [F (as foll.; see -ADE)]
fāce1 *n.* **1.** Front of head from forehead to chin; corresponding part of animal's head; **~ to ~,** confronted; **~ to ~ with,** confronting; **fly in the face ~ of,** openly disobey; **in (the) ~ of,** despite; **in** one's **~,** straight against one, as one approaches; **look** person **in the ~,** confront him steadily; **put** one's **~ on,** (colloq.) apply make-up to one's face; **set** one's **~ against,** steadfastly oppose; **show** one's ~, let oneself be seen; SMACK2 *in the face*; **to** person's **~,** openly in his presence. **2.** What is shown by one's face, expression of countenance; grimace (*make* or *pull a face* or *faces*); LONG1 *face*. **3.** Composure, coolness, effrontery; **have the ~,** be shameless enough; **save** person's or one's **~,** forbear from or evade shaming him or oneself openly. **4.** Outward show, aspect, (**on the ~ of it,** to judge by appearances; **put a new ~ on,** alter aspect of; **put a good** or **bold ~ on** (a matter), make it look well, show courage in facing it); **lose ~,** be humiliated, lose one's credit or good name [transl. of Chin. *tiu lien*]. **5.** Surface (*from the face of the earth*); front, façade, right side, obverse, dial-plate of clock etc., distinctive side of playing-card, working surface of implement etc.; (Geom.) each surface of a solid; = TYPE1-*face*; = COAL-*face*. **6. ~-ache,** neuralgia, (sl.) mournful-looking person; **~ card,** = COURT1-*card*; **~-cloth,** (1) cloth for washing face, (2) smooth-surfaced woollen cloth; **~-cream,** cream applied to face to improve complexion; ‖**~-flannel,** = *face-cloth* (1); **~-fungus,** (colloq.) beard; **~-lift,** face-lifting, (fig.) improvement in appearance; **~-lifting,** operation for removing wrinkles by tightening skin of face; **~-saving,** that saves one's face (see sense 3); **~ value,** nominal value as stated on coin, note, etc.; **~-worker,** miner who works at coal-face. **7.** Hence **-fāced2** (-st) *a.* [ME f. OF, f. Rom. **facia* f. L *facies*]
fāce2 *v.* **1.** *v.t.* Meet confidently or defiantly (~ *matter* **out,** carry it through by effrontery; ~ *opponent* **down,** overcome him by show of determination or browbeating); not shrink from (*face the facts*), stand fronting (**~ the music,** be resolute in face of difficulty or unpleasant consequences); present itself to (*the problem that faces us, that we are faced with*). **2.** Turn (card) face upwards. **3.** *v.i.* (Of person etc.) look, (of thing) be situated with front, in a certain direction (*on, to,* or *north, eastwards,* etc.); **~ up to,** confront. **4.** *v.t.* Front towards, be opposite to, (*to face page 20*). **5.** *v.t.* & *i.* (Lacrosse, Ice Hockey, etc.) Place (ball, puck, etc.) between crosses, sticks, etc., of two opposing players as preliminary to commencement of play, start or restart play thus, (also **~ off**); so **~-off** *n.*, act of doing this. **6.** (Mil.) (Cause to) turn in certain direction while remaining in same place (*left, about, face*; *he faced his men about*). **7.** *v.t.* Supply (garment) with facings; cover (surface) with layer of other material; dress surface of. [ME, f. prec.]
fā'celėss (-sl-) *a.* Without a face; without identity; purposely not identifiable; hence ~NESS *n.* [f. FACE1 + -LESS]
fā'cer *n.* Blow in the face; great and sudden difficulty. [f. FACE1 + -ER1]

fă′cĕt *n.* One side of many-sided body, esp. of cut gem; one segment of compound eye; particular aspect of thing (*another facet of his genius*); hence ~ED[2] *a.* [f. F *facette* dim. f. as FACE[1]; see -ETTE]
facē′tiae (-shiē) *n. pl.* Pleasantries, witticisms; (in bookselling) pornography. [L, pl. of *facetia* jest (*facetus* witty)]
facē′tious (-shus) *a.* Addicted to or marked by pleasantry or joking; hence ~LY[2] *adv.*, ~NESS *n.* [f. F *facétieux* (*facétie* f. L *facetia*; see prec.)]
fā′cia (-sha) *n.* Plate over shop-front with occupier's name etc.; instrument panel of motor vehicle. [var. of FASCIA]
fā′cial (-shal) *a.* & *n.* **1.** *a.* Of the face; ~ **angle,** that formed by two lines from nostril to ear and to forehead. **2.** *n.* Beauty treatment for the face. [f. med. L *facialis* (as FACE[1]; see -AL)]
-fā′cient (-shent) *suf.* forming *adjs.* & *ns.* w. sense '(substance etc.) producing an action or state' (*abortifacient, liquefacient, rubefacient*). [f. or after L *-faciens -entis* part. (*facere* make; see -ENT)]
fā′cies (-shēz) *n.* (*pl.* same). (Med.) appearance or expression of face; (Geol.) character of rock etc. expressed by composition, fossil content, etc. [L, = FACE[1]]
fă′cĭle *a.* **1.** (often derog.) Easily done or won, working easily, ready, fluent. **2.** (arch.) Of easy temper, gentle, flexible, yielding. [F, or f. L *facilis* (*facere* do; see -IL)]
facile princeps (făsĭlĭ prĭ′nsĕps) *a.* & *n.* (One who is) easily first; the acknowledged leader or chief. [L]
facĭ′lĭt|āte *v.t.* Make easy, promote, help forward, (action or result); hence ~A′TION *n.* [f. F *faciliter* f. It. *facilitare* (*facile* easy f. L *facilis*) + -ATE[3]]
facĭ′lĭtȳ *n.* Being easy, absence of difficulty, unimpeded opportunity (*give facilities for* action or do*ing*, *of* do*ing*); (esp. in *pl.*) equipment or physical means for doing something (*washing, conference, facilities*); ease or readiness of speech etc., aptitude, dexterity, fluency; (arch.) pliancy. [f. F *facilité* or f. L *facilitas* (as FACILE; see -ITY)]
fā′cĭng *n.* In vbl senses; material covering part of garment etc. for contrast or strength; (in *pl.*) cuffs, collar, etc., of military(-style) jacket, differently coloured from rest; coating of different material, esp. of stone etc. on wall. [f. FACE[2] + -ING[1]]
façon de parler (fahsawṅ de pār′lā) *n.* Manner of speaking; mere formula. [F]
făcsĭ′mĭlė *n.* & *v.* **1.** *n.* Exact copy, esp. of writing, printing, picture, etc., (*reproduced* **in** ~, exactly); system of producing this by radio etc. transmission of signal from scanning of writing etc. **2.** *v.t.* & *i.* Make or be facsimile (of). [mod. L, f. L *fac* imper. of *facere* make + *simile* neut. of *similis* like]
făct *n.* **1.** Thing certainly known to have occurred or be true, datum of experience, (often with explanatory clause or phrase: *the fact that fire burns, the fact of my having seen him*); **~s and figures,** precise information; ~ **of life,** something whose existence cannot be ignored; **the ~s of life,** (colloq., euphem.) knowledge of human sexual functions. **2.** Thing assumed as basis for inference (*his facts are disputable*). **3.** What is true or existent, reality; **in** ~, in reality, (in summarizing) in short; MATTER[1] *of fact.* **4.** Perpetration of wrongful act (*before* or *after the fact*; *confess the fact*). **5. ~-finding** *a.*, engaged in finding out facts. [f. L *factum* neut. p.p. (as n.) of *facere* do]
fă′ctĭce *n.* Rubber-like substance got by vulcanizing unsaturated vegetable oils. [f. G *faktis* f. L *facticius* FACTITIOUS]
fă′ction *n.* Self-interested, turbulent, or unscrupulous party or group, esp. in politics; prevalence of party spirit; hence ~AL *a.* [F, f. L *factio -onis* (*facere fact-* do; see -ION); cf. FASHION]
-fă′ction *suf.* forming *ns.* of action f. *vbs.* in -FY (*petrifaction, satisfaction*). [f. or after L *-factio -onis* (*-facere* make)]
fă′ctious (-shus) *a.* Characterized by or pertaining to faction(s); hence ~LY[2] *adv.*, ~NESS *n.* [f. F *factieux* or f. L *factiosus* (as FACTION; see -OUS)]
făctĭ′tious (-shus) *a.* Made for a special purpose, not genuine; not natural, artificial; hence ~LY[2] *adv.*, ~NESS *n.* [f. L *facticius* (*facere fact-* make) + -OUS; see -ITIOUS[1]]
fă′ctĭtĭve *a.* (Gram.) ~ **verb,** one with sense of making, calling, or thinking, that takes obj. and compl. (*appointed him captain, called it a swindle, thought her mad*). [f. mod. L *factitivus*, irreg. f. L *factitare* frequent. of *facere fact-* make; see -IVE]
fă′ctor *n.* & *v.* **1.** *n.* Merchant buying and selling on commission, whence ~AGE (4) *n.*; (Sc.) land-agent, steward; agent, deputy. **2.** (Math.) one of the numbers etc. that make up a number or expression by multiplication; (Biol.) gene etc. determining hereditary character; *factor of* SAFETY. **3.** Circumstance, fact, or influence, contributing to a result. **4.** ~ **cost** cost of product to producer. **5.** *v.t.* Resolve into factors or components. **6.** *v.i.* Buy at discount the debts owed to another, in order to profit by collecting them. [f. F *facteur* or f. L *factor* (as prec.; see -OR)]
făctōr′ĭal *n.* & *a.* (Math.) **1.** *n.* Product of series of factors in arithmetical progression; product of an integer and all lower integers. **2.** *a.* Of factor(s) or factorial(s); ~ **4,** = product of 4, 3, 2, and 1 (denoted by '4!'). [f. prec. + -IAL]
fă′ctorĭz|e, -ĭs|e (-īz), *v.* (Math.) **1.** *v.t.* Resolve into factors. **2.** *v.i.* Be capable of resolution into factors. **3.** Hence ~A′TION *n.* [f. FACTOR + -IZE]
fă′ctorȳ *n.* Building(s) and equipment for manufacturing, workshop; (Hist.) merchant company's foreign trading station; ||**F~ Acts** (regulating operation of factories for benefit of employees); ~ **farm** (organized on industrial lines); ||~ **ship,** base-ship of whaling fleet. [f. Port. *feitoria* & f. LL *factorium*]
făctō′tum *n.* One who does all kinds of work; servant managing his master's affairs. [med. L, f. L *fac* imper. of *facere* make + *totum* neut. of *totus* whole]
fă′ctūal *a.* Concerned with or of the nature of fact(s); hence ~ITY (-ă′l-), ~NESS, *ns.*, ~LY[2] *adv.* [f. FACT, after *actual*]
fă′ctūal|ĭsm *n.* (Philos.) Theory maintaining that facts are pre-eminent and fundamental; so ~IST (2) *n.* [f. prec. + -ISM]
fă′ct|um *n.* (*pl.* **~ums** *or* **~a**). (Law). Act, deed; statement of facts. [F, f. L (see FACT)]
fă′cture *n.* Quality of execution of (esp. surface of) a painting. [ME f. OF, f. L *factura* (*facere fact-* make; see -URE)]
fă′cūl|a *n.* (*pl.* **~ae**). (Astron.) Bright spot or streak on sun; hence ~AR[1], ~OUS, *adjs.* [L, dim. of *fax facis* torch]
fă′cultatĭve *a.* Permissive; optional; contingent; (Biol.) not restricted to a particular function, mode of life, etc.; of a faculty. [f. F *facultatif -ive* f. as foll.; see -IVE]
fă′cultȳ *n.* **1.** Aptitude or competence for any special kind of action; power inherent in the body or in an organ; a mental power (e.g. the will, reason). **2.** Branch of art or science, those qualified to teach it, department of University teaching, *staff of university or college; members of a particular profession, esp. medicine. **3.** (esp. Eccl.) Liberty to do something

given by law or a superior, authorization, licence. [ME, f. OF *faculté* f. L *facultas -tatis* (*facilis* easy; see -TY¹)]

făd *n.* Peculiar notion or rule of action; craze; hence **~'dish¹**, **~'dy²**, *adjs.*, **~'dism** (3), **~'dist** (2), *ns.* [19th c., orig. dial., prob. f. *fidfad* f. FIDDLE-FADDLE]

fāde *v.* & *n.* **1.** *v.i.* ~ **(away, out)**, droop, wither, lose freshness and vigour, disappear gradually, depart, (of colour, light, etc.) grow pale or dim, (of sound) grow faint; (of brake) gradually lose power; (of radio signal) vary irregularly in intensity; (of golf-ball etc.) deviate from straight course. **2.** *v.t.* Cause to lose freshness or colour; (Cinemat.) cause (picture) to come gradually *in* or *out* (of view on the screen); bring (sound) *up* or *in*, *away* or *out* (of audibility); cause (golf-ball etc.) to fade. **3.** So **~-away, ~-in, ~-out,** *ns.* **4.** *n.* Action or process of fading; **do a ~**, (sl.) depart; hence **~'less** (-dl-) *a.* [ME, f. OF *fader* (*fade* dull, insipid f. Rom. **fatidus*, prob. f. L *fatuus* silly + *vapidus* VAPID)]

fado (fah'dō) *n.* (*pl.* ~*s*). Melancholy Portuguese folk-song. [Port., = fate]

fae'cēs, *fē'cēs, (-z) *n. pl.* Waste matter discharged from bowels; hence **fae'cal, *fē'cal,** *a.* [L, pl. of *faex* dregs]

fā'erĭe, fā'erў, *n.* (arch.) Fairyland, the fairies, esp. as represented by Spenser; (*attrib.*) visionary, fancied. [var. of FAIRY]

‖**făff** *v.i.*, & *n.* (colloq.) Fuss, dither. [imit.]

făg¹ *v.* (-gg-) & *n.* **1.** *v.i.* & *t.* Toil; (of occupation) tire, make weary; ‖(at schools, of senior) use the service of (junior), (of junior) do service for senior; fray (end of rope). **2.** *n.* ‖Drudgery, unwelcome task (*what a fag!*); ‖exhaustion (*brain-fag*); ‖(at schools) junior who has to fag; (sl.) cigarette; **~-end,** inferior or useless remnant, (sl.) cigarette-end. [orig. unkn.; cf. FLAG⁵]

făg² *n.* (sl.) Homosexual (usu. male). [abbr. of foll.]

fă'ggot, *fă'got, *n.* & *v.* **1.** *n.* Bundle of sticks or twigs bound together as fuel; bundle of iron rods for heat treatment; bunch of herbs; (usu. in *pl.*) dish of liver etc. chopped, seasoned, and baked as ball or roll; unpleasant woman; (sl.) homosexual (usu. male), whence **~y²** *a.*; **~-stitch** (used in FAGGOTING); **~-vote,** (Hist.) vote manufactured by transferring sufficient property to unqualified person. **2.** *v.t.* & *i.* Bind in faggots, make faggot(s); use, join by, FAGGOTING. [ME, f. OF *fagot* f. It. *fagotto*, dim. of Rom. **facus*]

fă'ggotĭng *n.* Embroidery in which threads are fastened together like faggot; joining of materials in similar manner. [f. prec. + -ING¹]

Fā'gĭn (-g-) *n.* Person who receives stolen goods or trains thieves. [character in Dickens's *Oliver Twist*]

***fă'got.** See FAGGOT.

fah, fa (fah), *n.* (Mus.) Fourth note of scale in movable-doh system; the note F in fixed-doh system. [ME *fa* f. L *famuli*; see GAMUT]

Fahr. *abbr.* = foll.

Fah'renheit (fă'rĕnhīt) *a.* Pertaining to the ~ **scale** of temperature, on which water freezes at 32° and boils at 212° under standard conditions. [f. G. ~, Ger. physicist d. 1736]

faience (fah'yahṅs *or* fīah'ṅs) *n.* Decorated earthenware and porcelain. [f. F *faïence* f. *Faenza* in Italy]

fail¹ *n.* Failure in an examination; **without ~,** for certain, irrespective of hindrances, (emphasizing injunction or promise). [ME, f. OF *fail(l)e* (*faillir* FAIL²)]

fail² *v.* **1.** *v.i.* & *t.* Be absent, be or become insufficient, not suffice for needs of (person), run short, (**words ~ me,** I cannot adequately describe etc.; *his heart failed him*). **2.** *v.t.* Neglect, not remember or not choose or not be able, *to* (*he failed to appear*; *don't fail to let me know*; *I fail to see the reason*). **3.** *v.i.* Become extinct, die away; flag, break down, (*engine, health, fails*; ~ **safe,** revert to danger-free condition in event of breakdown etc.); become weaker or less efficient. **4.** *v.i.* & *t.* Prove misleading, disappoint hopes of, (*the prophecy failed*; *the wind failed us*); be insufficiently equipped *in*, not succeed in the attainment *of*; not succeed (*in* doing or *to* do; hence **~ed¹** (2) (-ld) *a.*, unsuccessful); miscarry, come to nothing; become bankrupt. **5.** Be rejected as candidate; reject (candidate), be unsuccessful in (examination). [ME, f. OF *faillir* f. Rom. **fallire* = L *fallere* deceive]

fai'lĭng¹ *n.* In vbl senses; foible, shortcoming, weakness in character. [f. prec. + -ING¹]

fai'lĭng² *prep.* In default of (~ **this,** if this does not happen); **whom ~** or **~ whom,** or in his absence (in proxy appointments). [f. FAIL² + -ING²]

fai'lure (-yer) *n.* Failing; non-occurrence, non-performance; running short, breaking down; (Med.) cessation or impairment of vital function (*heart failure*; *renal failure*); lack of success; unsuccessful person, thing, or attempt; bankruptcy. [earlier *failer* f. AF, = OF *faillir* FAIL²; cf. -ER⁴, -URE]

fain¹ *pred. a.*, & *adv.* (arch.) **1.** *a.* Willing under the circumstances *to*; left with no alternative but *to*. **2.** *adv.* **Would ~**, would be glad to. [OE *fægen*, = OS *fagan*, ON *feginn* f. Gmc **fagin-*]

‖**fain², fains** (-z), **fĕn²(s)** (-z), *v.t.* Forbid, not want, (usu. in child's formulae **fains I** etc. claiming exemption from unwelcome duty etc.). [f. FEND in obs. sense 'forbid']

fainéant (fā'nāahṅ) *n.* & *a.* Idle(r), inactive (official etc.); hence **~ism(e)** (fā'nāahṅtizm) *n.* [F (*fait* does, *néant* nothing)]

faint¹ *a.* **1.** Timid (~ **heart,** cowardly spirit; **~-heart,** coward); feeble (*a faint show of resistance*; *faint praise*). **2.** Dim, indistinct, pale (~ or **feint lines, ruled ~** or **feint,** of paper with inconspicuous lines to guide writing); (of idea etc.) inadequate; giddy or languid through fear, hunger, etc., inclined to faint; (arch., of air, scent, etc.) sickly, oppressive. **3.** Hence **~'ness** *n.* [ME f. OF, p.p. of *faindre* FEIGN]

faint² *v.i.*, & *n.* **1.** *v.i.* Lose consciousness (esp. through syncope); (arch.) lose courage, give way. **2.** *n.* Act or state of fainting (**in a dead ~,** completely unconscious). [ME, f. prec.]

fai'ntlў *adv.* Feebly; indistinctly; very slightly. [f. FAINT¹ + -LY²]

fair¹ *n.* Periodical gathering for sale of goods, often with shows and entertainments, at place and time fixed by charter, statute, or custom, (**a day after the ~,** too late); exhibition, esp. to publicize specified product(s); = FUN-*fair*. [ME, f. OF *feire* f. LL *feria* sing. f. L *feriae* holiday]

fair² *a.*, *n.*, & *v.* **1.** *a.* Beautiful (**the ~ sex,** women); (arch.) kind (*fair sir* etc., in courteous address). **2.** Considerable, satisfactory, (*a fair heritage*); specious (*fair speeches*); complimentary (*fair words*). **3.** Blond, not dark, (*a fair man, complexion*; *fair hair*); hence **~-haired** *a.*, blond, (fig.) favourite (person). **4.** Clean, clear, unblemished, (*fair water*; *fair* COPY¹); **~-faced** *a.*, (of brickwork etc.) not plastered. **5.** Just, unbiased, equitable, legitimate, in accordance with rules; **~ and square** *a.* & *adv.*, (1) without finesse, above-board, (2) exactly (*in the middle* etc.); *fair* or SQUARE² *deal*; *fair* DO²*s!*; ~ **enough!,** (colloq.) I agree to your conditions; *a fair* FIELD *and no favour*; *fair* GAME¹ 8; *all's fair in love and war*; *by fair means or foul*; ~ **play,**

equal conditions for all. **6.** Of (only) moderate quality, not bad, pretty good, whence **~'**ISH[1] 2 *a.*; **~-to-middling,** slightly above average. **7.** Favourable, promising, gentle, unobstructed, (*fair* WIND[1]; *fair or foul weather*); **~-weather friend** (not good in a crisis); **in a ~ way** (likely) *to succeed*; **by ~ means,** without violence or fraud; **~'way,** navigable channel, regular course or track of ship, prepared part of golf-links free from rough grass between tee and green. **8.** (Austral., N.Z., & sl.) complete, unquestionable; **a ~ treat,** (colloq.) very enjoyable or attractive thing or person. **9.** Hence **~'**NESS *n.* **10.** *n.* Fair thing; (arch.) beautiful woman; **for ~,** *(sl.) completely; **~'s ~,** (colloq.) (reciprocal) fairness is desirable. **11.** *v.i.* (Of weather) become fair. **12.** *v.t.* Make (surface of ship etc.) smooth and regular (**~'water,** structure on ship etc. assisting its passage through water). [OE *fæger*, = OS, OHG *fagar*, ON *fagr*, Goth. *fagrs* f. Gmc **fagraz*]

fair[3] *adv.* **1.** In a fair manner; **speak** person **~,** address him courteously; **~-spoken,** (of person) courteous, bland; **write out ~** (as fair COPY[1]); **fight ~** (according to the rules); BID[1] *fair.* **2.** Exactly, completely; **~ and square** (see FAIR[2] 5). [OE *fægre* (as prec.)]

‖**fair'ĭng**[1] *n.* Present bought at a fair. [f. FAIR[1] + -ING[1]]

fair'ĭng[2] *n.* Making surface of ship, aircraft, motor vehicle, etc., smooth and streamlined; structure added for this purpose. [f. FAIR[2] 12 + -ING[1]]

Fair' Isle (-īl) *n.* & *a.* (Jersey etc.) knitted in characteristic particoloured design. [~ in the Shetlands]

fair'lў̆ *adv.* In adj. senses; utterly, completely, (*fairly beside himself*); tolerably (*fairly good*); actually (*fairly jumped for joy*); **~ and squarely,** = FAIR[2] 5 *and square.* [ME, f. FAIR[2] + -LY[2]]

fair'ў̆ *n.* & *a.* **1.** *n.* Mythical small being with magical powers; (sl.) male homosexual. **2.** **~-cycle,** low small-wheeled bicycle for children; **~ godmother,** (fig.) benefactress; **F~land,** home of fairies, enchanted region; **~ lights,** small coloured lights for esp. outdoor decoration; **~ ring,** circular band of darker grass caused by fungi and attributed to dancing of fairies; **~ story, ~-tale,** tale about fairies, of strange incident, coincidence, marvellous progress, etc., fabrication, fib. **3.** Hence **~**ISM (2) *n.* **4.** *a.* Of fairies; fairy-like, beautiful and delicate or small. [ME, f. OF *faerie* f. *fae* FAY; see -ERY]

faisandé (fā'zahṅdā) *a.* Affected, theatrical. [F, p.p. of *faisander* hang (game) till high]

fait accompli (fātahkaw'ṅplē *or* -kŏ'mplĭ) *n.* Thing done and no longer worth arguing against. [F]

faith *n.* **1.** Reliance or trust *in*; belief founded on authority (**pin** one's **~ on, put** one's **~ in,** believe implicitly). **2.** (Theol.) belief in religious doctrines, esp. such as affects character and conduct, spiritual apprehension of divine truth apart from proof; system of religious belief (*the Christian, Jewish, faith*; DEFENDER *of the Faith*; **the ~,** the true religion); things (to be) believed; (arch.) **in ~, by my ~,** etc. (in asseveration). **3.** Promise, engagement, (*give, keep,* one's *faith*; *break faith with*); (observance of) duty to fulfil trust, promise, etc., (**good ~,** honesty of intention; **bad ~,** intent to deceive; **Punic ~,** treachery). **4.** **~-cure, -curer, -healing, -healer,** (acting by prayer, not drugs etc.). [ME, f. AF *fed*, f. OF *feid* (pr. fāth) f. L *fides*]

fai'thful *a.* Showing faith; loyal, constant, (*to* person, one's word), conscientious; trustworthy; true to fact, the original, etc., accurate; **the ~,** (*pl.*) true believers, esp. Muslims (COMMANDER *of the Faithful*); hence **~**NESS *n.* [ME, f. prec. + -FUL]

fai'thfullў̆ *adv.* In adj. senses; **yours ~,** customary formula for closing business or formal letter; (colloq.) emphatically (*promise faithfully*). [f. prec. + -LY[2]]

fai'thlėss *a.* Unbelieving; perfidious, false to promises; unreliable; hence **~**LY[2] *adv.*, **~**NESS *n.* [ME, f. FAITH + -LESS]

fāke[1] *v.t.*, & *n.* (Naut.) **1.** *v.t.* Coil (rope). **2.** *n.* One round of a coil of rope. [ME; cf. Sc. *faik* fold]

fāk|e[2] *v.t.*, *n.*, & *a.* **1.** *v.t.* **~e** (**up**), make presentable or plausible; alter so as to deceive; contrive out of poor or sham material; feign; hence **~'**ER[1], **~'**ERY (5), *ns.* **2.** *n.* Piece of faking, thing faked up (esp. sham antique); trick; spurious person or thing. **3.** *a.* Spurious, counterfeit. [f. obs. *feak, feague* thrash, f. G *fegen* sweep, thrash]

fă'kir (-ēr; *or* fakēr') *n.* Muslim (or Hindu) religious mendicant or ascetic. [f. Arab. *faḳīr* poor man]

Fala'ng|e (-lah'nj *or* -lah'nhā) *n.* Spanish Fascist and right-wing political party; hence **~**ISM (3), **~**IST (2), *ns.* [Sp., = PHALANX]

fă'lbala *n.* Flounce or trimming on dress. [F, 17th c., of unkn. orig.; cf. FURBELOW]

fă'lcāte *a.* (Anat. etc.) Curved like a sickle. [f. L *falcatus* (*falx falcis* sickle; see -ATE[2])]

fa'lchion (faw'lchon) *n.* (Hist.) Broad curved convex-edged sword. [ME *fauchoun* f. OF *fauchon* f. Rom. **falcio -onis* f. L *falx falcis* sickle]

fă'lcĭfōrm *a.* (Anat.) Curved like a sickle. [f. L *falx falcis* sickle + -I- + -FORM]

fa'lcon (faw'- *or* fŏ'-) *n.* Small long-winged diurnal bird of prey, esp. as trained to hunt game-birds for sport; (in falconry) female of this (cf. TERCEL). [ME f. OF *faucon* f. LL *falco -onis*, perh. f. L *falx* scythe or Gmc **falkon*]

fa'lconer (faw'- *or* fŏ'-) *n.* Keeper and trainer of hawks; one who hunts with hawks. [ME f. AF *fauconer*, OF *fauconier* (as prec.; see -ER[2] (2))]

fa'lconėt (faw'- *or* fŏ'-) *n.* **1.** (Hist.) Light cannon. **2.** Pygmy falcon. [sense 1 f. It. *falconetto* dim. of *falcone* FALCON; sense 2 f. FALCON + -ET[1]]

fa'lconrў̆ (faw'- *or* fŏ'-) *n.* Breeding and training of hawks. [f. F *fauconnerie* (as FALCON; see -ERY)]

fă'lderăl *n.* Gewgaw, trifle; *nonsense. [cf. FAL-LAL]

fa'ldstōōl (faw'l-) *n.* Bishop's backless folding chair; ‖movable desk for kneeling at; small desk for litany to be said from. [OE *fældestōl*, f. med. L *faldistolium* f. WG **faldistōl* (as FOLD[2], STOOL)]

Falēr'nĭan *a.* & *n.* (Famous wine) of Falernus in ancient Campania, Italy. [f. L *Falernus* + -IAN]

fall[1] (fawl) *v.i.* (**fell; ~'en,** conjugated with *have* or *be*, see -ED[1] (2), or used as *a.*). **1.** Go or come down freely (**~ing star,** meteor) or (as) from previously fixed place (*he let fall a remark*; **hair ~s** (is lost from head to cause baldness); **lambs ~** (are born); *rain, darkness, falls*); come down, lose high position (*statesman falls*; *fall from* GRACE; **~en angel,** one of those cast out of heaven; **~en arch** of foot); swoop (*vengeance fell*). **2.** Become detached, hang down; sink to lower level (*barometer, demand, price, falls*); decline, slope down; (of river) discharge *into*; subside, ebb, abate; show dismay (*face falls*); (of eyes, glance) look downwards. **3.** Cease to stand (**~ing sickness,** (arch.) epilepsy), become prostrate, come to the ground, be overthrown, sin, perish esp. by violence; (of fortress) be captured; (of woman) (1) lose chastity, (2) become pregnant; (of house) tumble in ruins; *fall a prey or sacrifice to*; *fall into error*; *fall to pieces, in two, apart*; **~ on evil times,** suffer misfortune;

~ **to the ground,** (of plan etc.) be abandoned, fail; **wicket ~s,** (Cricket) batsman is out. **4.** Take specified direction (*his eye fell upon me*), have specified place (*accent falls on first syllable*), alight, come by chance, duty, etc., (*the lot fell upon me; it fell to my lot, to me, to; it fell in my way; fall amongst thieves; subject falls into three divisions*). **5.** Pass into specified state (*fell into a rage, in love*), become (*fall asleep, dumb, due, ill*); lapse, revert, (*revenues fall to the Crown*). **6.** Occur, have date, (*Easter falls early*), find place (*what now falls to be described*). **7.** (w. *preps.*): ~ **a-doing,** (arch.) begin to do (*fell a-sighing and a-sobbing*); ~ **behind,** be outstripped by; ~ **for,** (colloq.) be captivated or deceived by, admire, yield to the charms or merits of; ~ **from,** (of words) be spoken by; ~ **into,** (*line*) take one's place in the ranks, collaborate with others, (*conversation with*) begin talking to, (*habit* etc.) adopt it; ~ **on,** assault, come across; ~ *on* one's *face*, fail ridiculously; ~ *on* one's *feet*, get well out of difficulty; ~ *on* one's *sword*, kill oneself with sword; ~ **over,** stumble at; ~ **over oneself,** (colloq.) be very awkward or hasty or eager; ~ **to,** be killed etc. by; ~ **to doing,** (arch.) begin to do (*fell to quarrelling among themselves*); ~ **under,** be classed among, be subjected to (observation etc.); ~ **within,** be included in. **8.** (w. *advs.*): ~ **about,** be helpless esp. with mirth; ~ **astern,** (of ship) drop behind; ~ **away,** desert, revolt, apostatize, decay, become few or thin, vanish; ~ **back,** retreat (~ *back on*, have recourse to); ~*-back* a., emergency, esp. minimum (wage) paid when no work is available; ~ **behind,** lag; ~ **down (on),** (colloq.) fail (*in*); *fall* FLAT² 1; ~ **foul of,** come into collision with, quarrel with; ~ **in,** (Mil.) take place in line, (of building etc.) collapse inwards, (of debt etc.) become due, (of land etc.) become available, (of lease) run out; ~ **in with,** happen to meet, accede to (views, plans), agree with (person), coincide with, humour; ~ **off,** withdraw, decrease in size or number, deteriorate, (of ship) deviate to leeward; so ~*-off* n.; ~ **out,** quarrel, come to pass, result *well* etc., (Mil.) leave the ranks; ~*-out* n., airborne radioactive debris from nuclear explosion, (fig.) side-effects; ~ **out of,** give up (habit) etc.; ~ **over,** not stay upright; *fall over* BACKWARDS; ~ **short,** be or become insufficient or inadequate, (of missile) not go far enough; ~ **short of,** fail to obtain or reach; ~ **through,** miscarry, fail; ~ **to,** begin working, eating, fighting, etc.; ~ **together,** (Phonet., of sounds) become identical. [OE *f(e)allan*, = OS, OHG *fallan*, ON *falla* f. Gmc **fallan*]

fall² (fawl) *n.* **1.** Act or manner of falling (RIDE *for a fall*); overthrow; succumbing to temptation; **the F~ (of man),** Adam's sin and its results; ~ **guy,** (sl.) (1) easy victim, (2) scapegoat. **2.** Amount of rain etc. that falls; downward trend, amount of descent. **3.** *Autumn; ***~'fish,** N. Amer. freshwater fish like chub. **4.** Cataract, cascade, (esp. in *pl.*; *Niagara Falls*). **5.** Wrestling-bout, throw in this; **try a ~,** contend *with* (lit. or fig.). **6.** Rope of hoisting-tackle; loosely hanging attachment to garment. **7.** (Number at a) birth of lambs etc. [ME, partly f. ON, partly f. prec.]

fă'llacy̆ *n.* Misleading argument, sophism; (Logic) flaw that vitiates syllogism, one of the types of such flaws; delusion, error, (PATHETIC *fallacy*); unsoundness, delusiveness, disappointing character, (of arguments, or beliefs); so **fallA'**CIOUS *a.* [f. L *fallacia* (*fallax -acis* deceiving f. *fallere* deceive); see -ACY]

făl-lă'l *n.* (arch.) Piece of finery; hence **fällă'l-(l)**ERY (5) *n.* [perh. f. FALBALA]

fallen. See FALL¹.

fă'll|ĭble *a.* Liable to err or be erroneous; hence ~IBI'LITY *n.* [f. med. L *fallibilis* (*fallere* deceive; see -IBLE)]

Fallō'pĭan *a.* ~ **tube,** oviduct in female mammals. [f. G. *Fallopius*, Latinized name of *Fallopio*, It. anatomist d. 1562 + -AN]

fă'llow¹ (-ō) *n., a.,* & *v.t.* **1.** *n.* & *a.* (Ground) ploughed and harrowed but left uncropped for a year; uncultivated (land). **2.** *a.* (Of sow) not pregnant; potentially useful but not yet in use (*ideas lying fallow*); inactive. **3.** *v.t.* Break up (land) for sowing or to destroy weeds. [ME, f. OE *fealh* n., *fealgian* v.]

fă'llow² (-ō) *a.* Of pale brownish or reddish yellow; ~ **deer,** species (*Dama dama*) of deer smaller than red deer, white-spotted in summer. [OE *f(e)alu*, = OS *falu*, OHG *falo*, ON *fölr* f. Gmc **falwaz*]

false (fawls *or* fŏls) *a.* & *adv.* **1.** *a.* Wrong, incorrect, (*false idea, verdict, weights*); illegal (*false imprisonment*); ~ **concord,** breach of agreement rules in grammar; ~ **note** (in music); ~ **position,** one in which person must seem to act against his principles; ~ **pride, shame,** (based on wrong notions); ~ **quantity,** incorrect length of vowel in verse or pronunciation; ~ **start,** incorrect start (in racing, or fig.); ~ **step,** stumble, transgression; *false* SYLLOGISM. **2.** Lying, deceitful, treacherous, unfaithful *to*; deceptive; spurious, sham, artificial, (*false* COIN¹, *god, hair, prophet,* SCENT, *teeth,* WINDOW); improperly so called, pseudo-, (*false acacia, false* RIB, *false* TOPAZ); ~ **alarm** (given without valid cause, either to deceive or under misapprehension of danger); ~ **bottom,** (disguised) horizontal partition in vessel, drawer, suitcase, etc.; ~ **card,** one played contrary to usual custom, in order to mislead opponents (so ~*-card* v.i.); ~ **ceiling,** dummy ceiling below real one; ~ **colours,** flag one has no right to (lit. or fig.); ~ **dawn,** transient light in east before dawn; *false* KEEL¹; ~ **pretences,** misrepresentations made with intent to deceive; **~'work,** temporary framework used during building. **3.** Hence or cogn. ~'LY² (-slĭ) *adv.*, ~'NESS (-sn-), **fa'ls**ITY (fawl- *or* fŏl-), *ns.* **4.** *adv.* **Play** person ~, cheat or betray him. [f. OE *fals* and OF *fals, faus*, f. L *falsus* p.p. of *fallere* deceive]

fa'lsehōōd (faw'ls-h-; *or* fŏ'l-) *n.* Falseness; untrue thing; lying, lie(s). [ME, f. prec. + -HOOD]

falsĕ'ttō (fawl- *or* fŏl-) *n.* (*pl.* ~s). High-pitched artificial voice esp. when used by male singers; singer using falsetto. [It., dim. of *falso* FALSE]

fa'lsĭes (faw'lsĭz *or* fŏ'lsĭz) *n. pl.* (colloq.) Padded brassière; shaped padding etc. to increase apparent size of breasts. [f. FALSE + -IE + -S¹]

fa'lsĭ|fy̆ (faw'l- *or* fŏ'l-) *v.t.* Fraudulently alter (document); misrepresent; make wrong, pervert; show to be false; disappoint (hope, fear, etc.); so ~FICA'TION *n.* [ME, f. F *falsifier* or f. med. L *falsificare* f. L *falsificus* making false (*falsus*); see -FY]

Falstă'ffĭan (fawl- *or* fŏl-) *a.* Like or characteristic of Falstaff; fat, jovial, and humorous. [f. Sir John *Falstaff* in Shakespeare's 'Henry IV' etc. + -IAN]

fa'lter (faw'l- *or* fŏ'l-) *v.* **1.** *v.i.* Stumble, stagger, go unsteadily; waver, lose courage, flinch. **2.** *v.t.* & *i.* Stammer, speak hesitatingly; ~ **out,** utter or say thus. [ME, perh. f. *falde* (FOLD²) in obs. sense 'falter', after *totter* etc.]

fāme¹ *n.* **1.** Renown, celebrity. **2.** (arch.) Public report, rumour. **3.** Reputation (**ill ~,** disrepute; **house of ill ~,** (arch.) brothel); good reputation. [ME f. OF, f. L *fama*]

fāme² *v.t.* (In *p.p.*) famous, much spoken of, (*for* valour etc.); (arch., in *pass.*) be currently reported *as*, *for*, *to* be or do. [ME, f. OF *famer* (*fame*; see prec.)]

famĭ'lial (-lyal) *a.* Of, occurring in, characteristic of, (members of) a family. [F, f. L *familia* FAMILY; see -AL]

famĭ'liar (-lyer) *a.* & *n.* **1.** *a.* Well acquainted or intimate (*with*), in close friendship, (~ **spirit,** demon attending and obeying witch etc.); closely acquainted *with* (subject); well known, no longer novel, (*to*); common, current, usual; unceremonious, informal; excessively informal, impertinent; sexually intimate (*with*); hence ~LY² *adv.* **2.** *n.* (R.C. Ch.) person rendering certain services in pope's or bishop's household; intimate friend or associate; =*familiar spirit.* [ME, f. OF *familier* f. L *familiaris* (as FAMILY; see -AR¹)]

famĭliă'rĭtў *n.* Close relationship; close acquaintance with person or subject; sexual intimacy, (in *pl.*) caresses etc.; unceremonious action or behaviour, treating of inferiors or superiors as equals, (*familiarity breeds contempt*). [ME, f. OF *familiarité* f. L *familiaritas -tatis* (as prec.; see -ITY)]

famĭ'liariz|e, -īs|e, (-lyerīz), *v.t.* Make (thing) well known; make (person, person's *mind* etc., one*self*) well acquainted *with*; hence ~A'TION *n.* [f. F *familiariser* (*familiaire*, as FAMILIAR; see -IZE)]

famille (fămē'y) *n.* ~ ***jaune*** (zhōn), ***noire*** (nwâr), ***rose*** (rōz), ***verte*** (vârt), Chinese enamelled porcelain with predominant colour yellow, black, red, green. [F, =family]

fă'mĭlў *n.* **1.** Members of a household, parents, children, servants, etc.; set of parents and children, or of relations, living together or not (HOLY *Family*; ROYAL *family*); person's children. **2.** All descendants of common ancestor, house, lineage, (**of good** ~, descended from noble or worthy persons); race or group of peoples from common stock. **3.** Brotherhood of persons or nations united by political or religious ties. **4.** Group of objects distinguished by common features; (Math.) group of curves etc. obtained by varying one quantity. **5.** (Biol.) Group of allied genera of animals or plants, usu. subdivision of order. **6.** ~ **allowance** (paid by State or employer to parent of family); ~ **Bible,** large Bible with pages for recording births etc.; ~ **butcher** etc. (supplying meat to families as opp. to institutions etc.); ‖**F**~ **Division** (of High Court, dealing with adoption, divorce, etc.); ~ **doctor,** general practitioner regularly consulted by a family; ~ **hotel** (with special terms for families); ~ **likeness,** that between relations, vague resemblance; ~ **man,** one with family, domestic person; ~ **name,** surname (also when used as Christian name); ~ **planning,** birth control; ~ **tree,** genealogical chart; **in a** ~ **way,** without ceremony; **in the** or **a** ~ **way,** (colloq.) pregnant. [ME, f. L *familia* household (*famulus* servant; see -Y¹)]

fă'mĭne *n.* Extreme scarcity of food in a district etc.; dearth of something specified (*water famine*; ~ **prices,** prices raised by scarcity); (arch.) hunger, starvation (*die of famine*). [ME f. OF (*faim* f. L *fames* hunger)]

fă'mĭsh *v.t.* & *i.* Reduce or be reduced to extreme hunger; **be** ~**ing** or ~**ed,** (colloq.) feel very hungry. [ME, f. obs. *fame* (f. OF *afamer* f. Rom. *AF*famare* f. L *fames* hunger) + -ISH²]

fā'mous *a.* Celebrated (*for* quality etc.), well known; (colloq.) excellent; hence ~LY² *adv.* [ME f. AF, OF *fameus* f. L *famosus* (*fama* fame; see -OSE¹)]

fă'mūl|us *n.* (*pl.* ~**i** *pr.* -ī). Attendant on magician or scholar. [L, =servant]

făn¹ *n.* **1.** Device (usu. folding, and sector-shaped when spread out) for moving air to cool one's face etc.; anything so spread out, as bird's tail, wing, leaf, kind of ornamental vaulting (*fan tracery*). **2.** Rotating apparatus giving current of air for ventilation etc.; small sail for keeping head of windmill towards wind. **3.** Device for winnowing grain. **4.** Fan-shaped deposit of alluvium esp. where stream begins to descend gentler slope. **5.** ~ **belt** (transmitting torque from engine of motor car to fan that cools radiator); ~ **dance** (in which dancer is nude but partly concealed by fans); ~ **heater** (in which electric fan drives air over electric heater into room etc.); ~**-jet,** jet engine with additional thrust from cold air drawn in by fan; ~**'light,** fan-shaped window over door; ~ **palm,** palm-tree with fan-shaped leaves; ~**'tail,** fan-shaped tail or end, fan of windmill, projecting part of boat's stern, broad-tailed pigeon, fly-catcher of genus *Rhipidura.* [OE *fann* (in sense 3) f. L *vannus* winnowing-fan]

făn² *v.* (**-nn-**). **1.** *v.t.* Move (air) with fan; drive current of air (as) with fan upon, to cool (face etc.) or to kindle (flame etc.; ~ **the flame,** (fig.) increase excitement etc.); (of breeze) blow gently on, cool. **2.** Winnow (grain), whence ~**'nER¹** (2) *n.*; winnow away (chaff), sweep away (as) by wind from fan; (sl.) search (person) for weapons etc.; (Baseball) strike out (batter). **3.** *v.t.* & *i.* Spread *out* in fan shape. [f. OE *fannian* (as prec.)]

făn³ *n.* Devotee of a specified amusement, performer, etc., (*film fans*; *football fans*); ~ **club,** organized group of person's devotees; ~ **mail,** letters from fans; hence ~'DOM *n.* [abbr. of foll.]

fană'tĭc *a.* & *n.* (Person) filled with excessive and mistaken enthusiasm, esp. in religion; hence ~AL *a.*, ~**al**LY² *adv.*, ~ISM (1) *n.*, ~IZE (2, 3) *v.i.* & *t.* [f. F *fanatique* or f. L *fanaticus* (*fanum* temple; see -ATIC)]

fă'ncier *n.* Connoisseur of some article or animal (*rose-fancier, dog-fancier*). [f. FANCY² + -ER¹]

fă'ncĭful *a.* Indulging in fancies, whimsical, capricious; fantastically designed, ornamented, etc., odd-looking; imaginary, unreal; hence ~LY² *adv.*, ~NESS *n.* [f. foll. + -FUL]

fă'ncў¹ *n.* & *attrib. a.* **1.** *n.* Delusion, unfounded belief. **2.** Faculty of calling up things not present, of inventing imagery; mental image. **3.** Arbitrary supposition; caprice, whim; individual taste, inclination, (*take a fancy to* or *for*; **catch** or **take the** ~ **of,** please; ~**-free,** not in love); fancy cake. **4.** Those who have a certain hobby, fanciers, esp. patrons of boxing; art of breeding fancy animals. **5.** *a.* Ornamental, not plain, (*fancy bread, cake*; ~ **dress,** fanciful costume esp. representing animal, character in history or fiction, etc.; ~ **goods,** ornamental novelties etc.; ~**-work,** ornamental sewing etc.); *(of foods etc.) above average quality; (of flowers etc.) particoloured. **6.** Capricious, whimsical, extravagant, (*at a fancy price*; ~ **franchise,** (Hist.) based on complicated or arbitrary qualifications); (of animal) bred for particular points of beauty etc. **7.** Based on imagination, not fact. **8.** ~ **man,** (sl., derog.) (1) woman's lover, (2) man living on earnings of prostitute, pimp; ~ **woman,** (sl., derog.) =MISTRESS 4. [contraction of FANTASY]

fă'ncў² *v.t.* **1.** Picture to oneself, conceive, imagine, (*fancy one*self *dead*; *fancy a blue dahlia*; *fancy him to be here, that he is here*; (in *imper.* as excl. of surprise) *fancy!*, *fancy that!*, *fancy his believing it!*. **2.** Be inclined to suppose, rather think. **3.** Take a fancy to, like; (colloq.) have unduly high opinion of (one*self*, one's ability, etc.). **4.** Breed, grow, (animals, plants) with attention to certain points. [f. prec.]

făndă'ngle (-ă'ngg*e*l) *n.* Fantastic ornament; nonsense, tomfoolery. [perh. f. foll., after *newfangle*]

făndă'ngō (-nggō) *n.* (*pl.* ~**es** *or* ~**s**). Lively Spanish dance for two; music for it; nonsense, tomfoolery. [Sp., perh. of Negro orig.]

fāne *n.* (poet.) Temple. [ME, f. L *fanum*]

fă'nfāre *n.* Short showy or ceremonious sounding of trumpets, bugles, etc. [F, imit.]

fănfăronā'de *n.* Arrogant talk, brag; fanfare. [f. F *fanfaronnade* (*fanfaron* braggart f. as prec., -OON; see -ADE)]

făng[1] *n.* Canine tooth, esp. of dog or wolf; serpent's venom-tooth; tang of tool; (prong of) root of tooth; (colloq.) tooth; hence (-)~ED[2] (-ngd), ~'LESS, *adjs.* [OE f. ON (=OS, OHG) *fang* f. Gmc **fang-*, **fanh-* to catch]

făng[2] *v.t.* Strike with fang; prime (pump) by pouring in water to start it. [f. prec.]

fă'nnȳ[1] *n.* (Naut.) Tin container for drink. [20th c., perh. f. woman's name *Fanny*]

fă'nnȳ[2] *n.* **1.** *(sl.) Buttocks. **2.** ||(vulg.) Female genitals. [20th c.; orig. unkn.]

fă'nnȳ[3] *n.*, & *v.t.* (sl.) (Deceive or persuade by) glib talk. [20th c.; orig. unkn.]

Fănnȳ A'dams (-ă'd*a*mz) *n.* (sl.) **1.** (Naut.) Tinned meat; stew. **2.** (**Sweet**) ~, nothing at all. [f. name of murder victim *c.* 1870]

făntă'būlous *a.* (sl.) Of almost incredible excellence. [f. FANTASTIC + FABULOUS]

fă'n-tăn *n.* Chinese gambling game in which players try to guess remainder after division by four of number of coins etc. hidden under bowl; card-game with play of sevens and sequences on them. [f. Chin. *fan t'an* repeated divisions]

făntā'sĭa (-z-; *or* -tazē'*a*) *n.* Musical or other composition in which form is of minor importance, or which is based on several familiar tunes. [It., = FANTASY]

fă'ntas|ize, -|ise (-īz), *v.t.* & *i.* Have fantasy or fanciful vision (of); so ~IST (1) *n.* [f. FANTASY + -IZE]

fă'ntăst *n.* Visionary, dreamer. [f. med. L f. Gk *phantastēs* boaster (*phantazomai* make a show f. *phainō* to show)]

făntă'stĭc *a.* Extravagantly fanciful, capricious, eccentric, (*light fantastic* TOE); grotesque or quaint in design etc.; (colloq.) excellent, extraordinary; hence ~ISM (2) *n.*, [f. obs. *fantastical*] ~ă'lITY, ~alNESS, *ns.*, ~alLY[2] *adv.* [ME, f. OF *fantastique* f. med. L *fantasticus* f. LL f. Gk *phantastikos* (as prec.; see -IC)]

făntă'stĭc|āte *v.t.* Make fantastic; hence ~A'TION *n.* [f. prec. + -ATE[3]]

fă'ntasȳ, phă'ntasȳ, *n.*, & *v.t.* **1.** *n.* Image-inventing faculty, esp. when extravagant or visionary; mental image, day-dream; fantastic invention or composition, fantasia; whimsical speculation. **2.** *v.t.* Imagine in visionary manner. [ME, f. OF *fantasie* f. L f. Gk *phantasia* appearance (see FANTAST, -Y[1])]

Fă'ntĭ, Fă'ntė, Fă'ntee, *n.* Member or language of a Negro tribe inhabiting Ghana; **go** ~, (of European) conform to native habits. [native name]

fantoccini (făntŏchē'nē) *n. pl.* Mechanically worked puppets; marionette show. [It., pl. of dim. of *fantoccio* puppet (*fante* boy)]

fă'ntŏd *n.* Crotchety behaviour; state of alarm or worry; (in *pl.*) state of restlessness, fidgets. [19th c.; orig. uncert.]

||**F.A.N.Y.** *abbr.* First Aid Nursing Yeomanry.

fă'nzine (-ēn) *n.* Magazine for (esp. science-fiction) fans. [f. FAN[3] + MAGAZINE]

F.A.O. *abbr.* Food and Agriculture Organization.

F.A.Q. *abbr.* fair average quality.

faquir. Var. of FAKIR.

far[1] *adv.* (FARTHER, FURTHER; FARTHEST, FURTHEST). **1.** At, to, by, a great distance, a long way (off), in space or time, or fig., (*far away, off, out*, etc.; *driven far into the ground, talked far into the night*; *far different, better, the best*). **2. As ~ as,** (1) right to, not short of, (place), (2) to whatever extent (*travel as far as you like*); ~ **and away,** by a very large amount (*better* etc.); ~ **and near,** everywhere; ~ **and wide,** over a large area; ~ **be it from me to,** I would on no account; **by** ~, by a great amount; ~ **from,** more nearly the opposite of than the same as (*problem is far from easy*; (*so*) *far from seeking help he offered it*); **from** ~, from a considerable distance; **go** ~, (fig.) achieve much, contribute greatly *to*(*wards*); **not go** ~, be soon spent or used; **go too** ~, (fig.) go beyond limits of what is reasonable, polite, etc.; **how** ~, to what extent; (**in**) **so** ~ **as,** to the extent that; **so** ~, to such an extent or distance, until now; **so** ~ **so good,** progress has been satisfactory. **3.** ~**-away,** remote, long-past, (of look etc.) absent, dreamy, (of voice) sounding as if from a distance; ~ **between,** infrequent; *Far* EAST; ~**-famed,** widely known; ~**-fetched,** (of simile, illustration etc.) carefully but unnaturally sought out, not obvious, strained; ~**-flung,** (rhet.) widely extended; ~ **gone,** advanced in time, very ill or mad or drunk or much in debt; ~**-off,** remote; ~**-out,** distant, (fig.) avant-garde or excellent; ~**-reaching,** widely applicable, carrying many consequences; ~**-seeing,** prescient, prudent; ~**-sighted,** (1) far-seeing, (2) seeing distant things more clearly than near ones; *Far* WEST. [OE *feor*(*r*), = OS, OHG *fer*, ON *fjarri*, Goth. *fairra* f. Gmc **ferrō* compar. of **fer-* f. IE **per-*]

far[2] *a.* (compar. & superl. as prec.). Situated at or extending over a great distance in space or time, remote, (*a far* CRY[1]); more distant (*the far end of the hall*); hence ~'NESS *n.* [OE *feorr*, = OS, OHG *fer* f. WG **ferro-*]

F.A.R. *abbr.* Federation of Arab Republics.

fă'rad *n.* (Electr.) Unit of capacitance, such that one coulomb of charge causes a potential difference of one volt. [f. M. *Faraday*, Engl. physicist d. 1867]

făradā'ĭc, fară'dĭc, *adjs.* (Electr.) Inductive, induced. [f. as prec. + -IC]

fă'raday *n.* (Electr.) Quantity of charge needed to form one gram-equivalent of an element in electrolysis; **F~ cage,** earthed metal screen excluding electrostatic influence; **F~'s constant,** =*faraday*; **F~ effect,** rotation of plane of polarization of electromagnetic waves in certain substances in a magnetic field. [f. as FARAD]

fărandō'le *n.* Lively Provençal dance; music for it. [F, f. mod. Prov. *farandoulo*]

farce *n.* Dramatic work meant merely to cause laughter, often by presenting ludicrously improbable events; this branch of drama; absurdly futile proceedings, pretence, mockery. [F, orig. = stuffing, f. OF *farsir* f. L *farcire* to stuff, used metaph. of interludes etc.]

farceur (farser') *n.* Joker, wag; actor or writer of farces. [F (*farcer* act farces)]

far'cĭcal *a.* Of or like farce; extremely ludicrous or futile; hence ~ITY (-ă'l-) *n.*, ~LY[2] *adv.* [f. FARCE + -ICAL]

far'cȳ *n.* Glanders (~ **bud, button,** small lymphatic tumour in this); bacterial disease of cattle. [ME, f. earlier & OF *farcin* f. LL *farciminum* (*farcire* stuff)]

far'dėd *a.* (Of face etc.) painted with cosmetics. [p.p. of obs. *fard* f. OF *farder*]

far'del *n.* (arch.) Bundle, burden. [ME f. OF, dim. of Rom. **fardum* f. Arab. *fard*(*a*) camel-load; see -LE 2]

fāre[1] *n.* **1.** Price of passenger's conveyance, passage-money; passenger in hired vehicle; *fare*-STAGE[1]. **2.** Food provided (*good, bad, plentiful*, etc., *fare*; BILL[4] *of fare*). [OE *fær* and *faru* journeying, both f. same root as foll.]

fāre[2] *v.i.* **1.** (poet. or literary). Journey, go, travel; ~ **forth,** start. **2.** (arch.) Happen, turn out, (*how fares it?*). **3.** Get on *well, ill*, etc., have good, bad, etc., luck; (arch.) be entertained, be fed or feed oneself, *well* etc. [OE *faran*, = OS, OHG, Goth. *faran* f. Gmc **faran* (**far-* f. IE **por-*)]

fārewĕ'll (fārw-) *int.* & *n.* **1.** *int.* Goodbye!, Adieu!, (~ **to,** there will be no more of). **2.** *n.* Leave-taking, departure; parting good wishes. [ME, f. imper. of prec. + WELL[3]]

***fār'e-you-wĕll** (fār'ūwĕl) *n.* (colloq.) **To a** ~, to the utmost degree, to perfection. [f. *fare you well* = prec. (FARE[2] 3)]

farī'na (*or* -ē'-) *n.* Flour or meal of cereal, nuts, or starchy roots; powdery substance; (Bot.) pollen; ||(Chem.) starch; so **fărin**A'CEOUS *a.* [L (*far* corn; see -INE[4])]

fārl *n.* (Sc.) Thin cake, orig. quadrant-shaped, of oatmeal or flour. [f. obs. *fardel* quarter (as FOURTH, DEAL[1])]

fārm[1] *n.* **1.** Tract of land used under one management for cultivation (||**home** ~, reserved and worked by owner of estate containing other farms); ~(**'house**), dwelling-place attached to farm; tract of water used as a preserve (*fish-farm; oyster-farm*); place for storage of oil etc.; place where animals are bred for fur etc. (*mink farm*); place where children are farmed (see foll.). **2.** ~**-hand,** worker on farm; ~**'stead,** farm with buildings on it; ~**'yard,** yard or enclosure attached to farmhouse. [ME f. OF *ferme* f. med. L *firma* fixed payment (L *firmare* fix f. *firmus* FIRM[2]; orig. applied only to leased land)]

fārm[2] *v.* **1.** *v.t.* & *i.* Cultivate, till; till the soil, be farmer; (Cricket) contrive to receive most of (balls bowled). **2.** *v.t.* Take proceeds of (tax, office, etc.) on payment of fixed sum; ~ (**out**), let out proceeds of (tax etc.) to person for fixed sum, delegate (work) to sub-contractor etc., arrange for (person) to be farmed (see next sense). **3.** Let the labour of (person) for hire; contract to maintain and care for (person, esp. child) for fixed sum. **4.** Hence ~'ING *n.* [ME in sense 'rent land', f. prec.]

fār'mer *n.* One who cultivates a farm; one who undertakes collection of taxes after paying fixed fee (~**-general,** of districts in France before the Revolution); one who farms children etc. [ME, f. AF *fermer*, OF *fermier*, f. med. L *firmarius*, *firmator*, (*firma* FIRM[1])]

fār'ō *n.* Gambling card-game, with bets on order of appearance of cards. [f. F *pharaon* PHARAOH (said to have been name of king of hearts)]

Fārōē'se (-z; *or* făr-) *a.* & *n.* (*pl.* same). (Native, inhabitant, or Norse language) of Farōe Islands. [f. *Farōe* + -ESE]

farou'che (-ōō'sh) *a.* Sullen, shy; hence ~LY[2] (-shlĭ) *adv.* [F, f. OF *faroche, forache* f. med. L *forasticus* f. L *foras* out of doors]

farra'gō (-rah'-) *n.* (*pl.* ~**s** *or* *~**es**). Medley, hotchpotch; hence **farrā'ginous** *a.* [L *farrago farraginis* mixed fodder (*far* corn)]

||**fă'rrier** *n.* Smith who shoes horses; horse-doctor; hence **fă'rri**ERY (2) *n.* [f. OF *ferrier* f. L *ferrarius* (*ferrum* iron, horseshoe; see -ER[2] (2))]

fă'rrow (-ō) *n.* & *v.* **1.** *n.* Giving birth to, litter of, pigs (*20 at one farrow*). **2.** *v.t.* & *i.* (Of sow) produce (pigs). [OE *fearh, færh*, = OS **farh*, OHG *farah* f. WG **farha* f. IE **porkos*]

farru'ca (-ōō'-) *n.* Type of flamenco dance. [Sp.]

fārt *v.i.*, & *n.* (vulg.) **1.** *v.i.* Emit wind from anus; fool *about* or *around*. **2.** *n.* Emission of wind from anus; contemptible person. [OE **feortan*, = OHG *ferzan*, ON *freta* f. Gmc **fertan* etc.]

fār'ther (-dh-) *adv.* & *a.* (used as compar. of FAR[1,2]). **1.** *adv.* To or at a more advanced point or greater extent or distance; = FURTHER 1. **2.** *a.* More extended, additional, more; more distant or advanced; = FURTHER 2; hence ~MOST *a.* [ME *ferther* var. of FURTHER]

fār'thėst (-dh-) *a.* & *adv.* (used as superl. of FAR[1,2]). **1.** *a.* Most distant; = FURTHEST 1. **2.** *adv.* To or at the greatest distance; = FURTHEST 2. [ME, var. of FURTHEST]

fār'thing (-dh-) *n.* (Hist.) quarter of a penny, lowest-valued coin recently current in Britain; least possible amount (*doesn't matter a farthing*; BRASS *farthing*). [OE *fēorthing* (*fēortha* fourth; see -ING[3])]

fār'thingāle (-dhĭngg-) *n.* (Hist.) Hooped petticoat or stiff curved roll to extend woman's skirt. [earlier *vard-, verd-*, f. F *verdugale* f. Sp. *verdugado* (*verdugo* rod; see -ADO)]

fār'tlĕk *n.* (Athl.) Method of training for middle- and long-distance running, in which athlete runs over country, mixing fast with slow work. [Sw. (*fart* speed, *lek* play)]

f.a.s. *abbr.* free alongside ship.

fă'scēs (-z) *n. pl.* (Rom. Hist.) bundle of rods with projecting axe-blade, carried by lictor before high magistrate; emblems of authority. [L, pl. of *fascis* bundle]

fa'scia (fă'shĭa *or* fā'sha) *n.* (Archit.) long flat surface of wood or stone under eaves or cornice; (Anat.) thin sheath of fibrous tissue; stripe, band, fillet, belt; = FACIA. [L, = band, door-frame, etc.]

fă'sciāte, fă'sciātėd, (-shĭ-) *a.* **1.** (Bot.) (Of contiguous parts) compressed or growing into one; so **făsci**A'TION *n.* **2.** Striped or banded. [f. L *fasciatus*, p.p. of *fasciare* swathe (as prec.); see -ATE[2], -ED[1]]

fă'scicle, fă'scicūle, fasci'cūlus (*pl.* **-li** *pr.* -lī), *ns.* (Bot. etc.) bunch, bundle, whence **fă'scicl**ED[2] (-keld), **fasci'cūl**AR[1], **fasci'cūl**ATE[2], *adjs.*, **fascicūl**A'TION *n.*; one part of book published in instalments. [f. L *fasciculus* dim. of *fascis* (see FASCES, -CULE)]

fă'scin|āte *v.t.* (Esp. of serpent) deprive (victim) of power of escape or resistance by look or presence; attract irresistibly, enchant, charm, whence ~**āt**ED[1] *a.* (*with* or *by*), ~**āt**ING[2] *a.*; hence or cogn. ~A'TION, ~**āt**OR (esp. woman's head-scarf of light material), *ns.* [f. L *fascinare* (*fascinum* spell) + -ATE[3]]

făsci'ne (-sē'n) *n.* Long faggot used for engineering purposes and (esp. in war) for lining trenches, filling ditches, etc. [F, f. L *fascina* (*fascis* bundle; see -INE[1])]

Fă'sc|ism (*or* fă'shĭ-) *n.* Principles and organization of Italian nationalist and anti-communist dictatorship (1922–43); similar nationalist and authoritarian movement in other countries; (fig.) system of extreme right-wing or authoritarian views; so ~IST (2) *n.*, ~**i'st**IC *a.* [f. It. *fascismo* (*fascio* bundle, (politically organized) group, f. L *fascis* bundle)]

făsh *v.t.* (or *refl.*), & *n.* (Sc.) Bother, trouble, inconvenience. [f. obs. F *fascher* f. Rom. **fastidicare* f. L *fastus* disdain]

fă'shion (-shon) *n.*, & *v.t.* **1.** *n.* Make, shape, style, pattern, manner; **after the** ~ **of,** like; **after** or **in a** ~, not satisfactorily, but somehow or other; (as *suf.*) = -WISE (*walk crab-fashion*). **2.** Prevailing (usu. transient) custom, esp. in dress; ~**-plate,** picture showing style of dress, (fig.) person who dresses in the current fashion. **3.** Conventional usages of society; *man* etc. **of** ~, of high social standing esp. as shown by dress and behaviour; OLD-*fashioned*; **the ~**, whatever is in accord with these usages for the time being; **in, out of, (the) ~**, agreeing or not with current usages; **set the ~**, give the example in changing them. **4.** *v.t.* Give shape to, form, mould, (*into*); shape (stocking) to fit contour of leg. [ME, f. AF *fasun*, OF *façon*, f. L *factio -onis* (*facere fact-* make; see -ION)]

fă'shionab|le (-shon-) *a.* & *n.* **1.** *a.* Following or suited to the fashion; characteristic of, treating of, or patronized by, those who are in the fashion; hence **~le**NESS (-beln-) *n.*, ~LY[2] *adv.* **2.** *n.* Fashionable person. [f. prec. + -ABLE]

fast[1] (fah-) *v.i.* **1.** Abstain from all or some kinds of food as religious observance or in sign of mourning. **2.** Go without food. [OE *fæstan*, = OHG *fastēn*, ON *fasta*, Goth. *fastan* f. Gmc **fastējan* (as FAST[3])]

fast[2] (fah-) *n.* Act of, season or day appointed for, fasting (see prec. 1); going without food (**break** one's ~ = BREAKFAST *v.*). [ME, f. ON *fasta* (OS, OHG *fasta*) f. as prec.]

fast[3] (fah-) *a.* **1.** Firmly fixed or attached (BED[1]*fast*); **~ colour** (unfading, not affected by washing etc.); **~ friend** or **friendship** (steady, close); **make ~**, fasten; **play ~ and loose,** ignore obligations, be unreliable, trifle; **take ~ hold of,** hold tightly. **2.** Rapid, quick-moving, producing or allowing quick motion (*fast and* FURIOUS); (of cricket-pitch, tennis-court, putting-green, etc.) on which ball bounces or runs quickly; (of clock etc.) showing too advanced time; (of person) immoral, dissipated; (of photographic film) needing only short exposure, (of lens) having large aperture; **~'back,** (motor car with) rear sloping continuously down to bumper; *fast* BUCK[8]; **~ lane** (on road, for overtaking by fast-moving vehicles); **~ neutron** (with high kinetic energy, esp. not slowed by moderator etc.); **~ one,** (sl.) unfair action to gain advantage (*pull a fast one*); **~ reactor,** nuclear reactor using mainly fast neutrons; **~ worker,** one who makes rapid progress (esp. in amatory activities). [OE *fæst*, = OS *fast*, OHG *festi*, ON *fastr*, prob. f. Gmc **fastuz*]

fast[4] (fah-) *adv.* Firmly, fixedly, tightly, securely, (*stand, sit, stick, fast*; **~ bind ~ find,** lock up what you would not lose; *eyes fast shut*); soundly *asleep*; (arch. or poet) close *beside, by,* etc.; quickly, in quick succession; ***~-talk,** (colloq.) persuade by rapid or deceitful talk. [OE *fæste*, = OS, OHG *fasto*, ON *fast* f. Gmc **fastō* (as prec.)]

fa'sten (fah'sen) *v.* **1.** *v.t.* Make fast, attach, fix, secure by some tie or bond, (*to, on* adv. or prep., *together, up, in* adv. or prep., or abs.; *fasten parcel, garment, door,* etc., or *string, button, bolt,* etc.; *fasten off thread* etc., secure with knot or otherwise); hence ~ING[1] (4) *n.* **2.** Direct (look, thoughts, etc.) keenly (*up*)*on*; fix (nickname, imputation, etc.) (*up*)*on*. **3.** *v.i.* Become fast (*door will not fasten*); **~ (up)on,** lay hold of, single out for attack, seize upon (pretext). **4.** Hence ~ER[1] (2) (fah'sner) *n.* [OE *fæstnian*, = OS *fastnon*, OHG *fastinōn* f. Gmc **fastinōjan* (**fastuz* FAST[3]; see -EN[6])]

făsti'dĭous *a.* Easily disgusted, carefully selective, hard to please; hence ~LY[2] *adv.*, ~NESS *n.* [ME, f. L *fastidiosus* (*fastidium* loathing; see -OUS)]

făstĭ'gĭate *a.* (Bot.) With conical or tapering outline. [f. L *fastigium* gable-top + -ATE[2]]

fa'stnĕss (fah'-) *n.* In adj. senses; stronghold, fortress. [OE *fæstnes* (as FAST[3], -NESS)]

făt *a.*, *n.*, & *v.* (**-tt-**). **1.** *a.* Well-fed, plump, corpulent; (of animal) made plump for slaughter, fatted; ***~ cat,** (sl.) wealthy person, esp. as contributor of funds; **~ hen,** = GOOD *King Henry*; **~'stock,** livestock made fat for slaughter. **2.** Thick, substantial, (esp. of printing-type); containing much fat; greasy, oily, unctuous, (Theatr., of actor's part) giving opportunity for skill or display, (of coal) bituminous, (of clay etc.) sticky. **3.** Fertile, rich, yielding abundantly, (*fat lands, benefice, job*); **~ lime,** nearly pure lime, slaking easily; **a ~ lot,** (sl.) a great deal (usu. iron. = very little, so *a fat chance* etc.). **4.** Slow-witted, indolent; **~-head,** stupid person. **5.** Hence ~'TISH[1] 2 *a.*, ~'NESS *n.* **6.** *n.* The fat part of anything (**live off the ~ of the land,** have the best of everything). **7.** Oily or greasy substance composing fat parts of animal bodies; **a bit of ~,** (colloq.) piece of good luck; CHEW *the fat*; **the ~ is in the fire,** (usu. fig.) there will be an explosion of anger. **8.** (Chem.) Natural ester of glycerol and acid. **9.** Hence ~'LESS *a.* **10.** *v.t.* & *i.* Fatten; **kill the fatted calf for,** receive (returned prodigal) with joy (Luke 15). [OE *fæt(t)* a., *fattian* v., = MDu., MLG *vett*, OHG *feizzit* f. WG **fæitidha* p.p., f. Gmc **faitjan* fatten (*faitaz* fat)]

fā'tal *a.* **1.** Like fate, inevitable, necessary; of or appointed by destiny (**F~ Sisters,** the Fates; **~ thread,** allotted length of life); fateful, important, decisive. **2.** Destructive, ruinous, ending in death, (*to*); deadly, sure to kill; disastrous, ill-advised, (*made the fatal mistake of being over-confident*). **3.** Hence ~LY[2] *adv.*, ~NESS *n.* [ME f. OF, or f. L *fatalis* (as FATE; see -AL)]

fā'tal|ĭsm *n.* Belief that all events are predetermined by arbitrary decree; submission to all that happens as inevitable; so ~IST (2) *n.*, **~ĭ'stic** *a.* [f. prec. + -ISM]

fată'lĭtȳ *n.* Subjection to or supremacy of fate, predestined liability to disaster; fatal influence; misfortune, calamity; death by accident, in war, etc. [f. F *fatalité* or f. LL *fatalitas* (*fatalis* FATAL; see -ITY)]

fata mŏrga'na (fah-; -gah'-) *n.* Kind of mirage seen esp. in S. Italy; illusion. [It. (*fata* FAY, *Morgana* sister of King Arthur)]

fāte *n.*, & *v.t.* **1.** *n.* Power predetermining events unalterably from eternity; (Myth., usu. *F~*) goddess, esp. one of the three Greek or Scandinavian goddesses, of destiny. **2.** What is destined to happen (**as sure as ~,** quite certain); appointed lot of person etc.; person's or thing's ultimate condition (*decide, fix, seal,* person's *fate*; *fate worse than* DEATH 3); death, destruction. **3.** *v.t.* (usu. in *pass.*) Preordain (*he was fated to do* or *be*; *it was fated that*); (in *p.p.*) doomed to destruction. [ME, f. It. *fato* & f. L *fatum* that which is spoken, neut. p.p. (as n.) of *fari* speak]

fā'teful (-tf-) *a.* Fraught with destiny, important, decisive; controlled by or showing power of fate; prophetic; hence ~LY[2] *adv.* [f. prec. + -FUL]

fa'ther[1] (fah'dh-) *n.* **1.** Male parent (lit., or fig.: **the wish is ~ to the thought,** one believes because one wishes to; **the child is ~ of the man,** tendencies in childhood foreshadow adult development); (**adoptive**) **~**, man who has adopted a child; **the ~ and mother of a,** (colloq.) an extremely large, severe, etc. **2.** Progenitor, forefather; originator, designer, early leader, (**~ of English poetry,** Chaucer; **F~ of History,** Herodotus; **F~ of lies,** the Devil; **F~s (of the Church)**, Christian writers esp. of first five centuries). **3.** One who deserves filial reverence (*father of his country*); religious teacher. **4.** (*F~*). God; First Person of the Trinity. **5.** Confessor; priest belonging to religious order, superior of monastic house; **Right, Most, Reverend F~ in God,** titles of C.E. bishop, archbishop; **Holy F~,** the Pope; (*F~*, as prefixed title) priest; venerable person, god, (*Father* CHRISTMAS, *Thames*, TIME[1], etc., as personifications). **6.** Oldest member, doyen, (*father of the* CHAPEL; **F~ of House of Commons,** member with longest continuous service; ***F~ of Waters,** the Mississippi); (in *pl.*) leading men, elders, (CITY *fathers*); (**Conscript**) **F~s,** Roman senators. **7. ~-figure,** older person regarded as a trusted leader; **~-in-law,** father of one's wife or husband; **~land,** one's native land (esp. of Germany); **F~'s Day,** day (usu. third Sunday in June) established for special tribute to fathers. **8.** Hence ~HOOD, ~SHIP, *ns.*, ~LESS *a.*, ~LIKE, ~LY[1,2], *adjs.* & *advs.* [OE *fæder*, = OS *fadar*, OHG *fater*, ON *fathir*, Goth. *fadar* f. Gmc **fadēr* f. IE **p'tēr*]

fa'ther[2] (fah'dh-) *v.t.* Beget; be father of; produce by education etc.; originate (statement etc.); appear as or confess oneself father or author of (child, book); (arch.) govern paternally; fix paternity of (child, book) *on.* [ME, f. prec.]

fă'thom[1] (-dh-) *n.* (*pl.* often same when used with number). Measure of six feet, chiefly used in soundings; ‖quantity of wood 6 ft. square in cross-section, whatever the length. [OE *fæthm* the outstretched arms, cogn. w. OS *fathmos*, OHG *fadum* cubit, ON *fathmr* embrace f. Gmc **fathmaz*]

fă'thom[2] (-dh-) *v.t.* Measure (depth of water) with sounding-line; (fig.) get to the bottom of, comprehend, whence ~LESS *a.*; (arch.) encircle with arms as in measuring. [OE *fæthmian* (as prec.)]

făthŏ'mėter (-dh-) *n.* Type of ECHO[1]-sounder. [f. FATHOM[1] + -METER; ***P**]

fatĭ'dĭcal *a.* Gifted with prophetic power. [f. L *fatidicus* (*fatum* FATE, *-dicus* -saying) + -AL]

fati'gue (-ē'g) *n.*, & *v.t.* **1.** *n.* Weariness after exertion; weakness in metals etc. after repeated variations of stress; reduction of efficiency of muscle, organ, etc., after prolonged activity; task etc. that wearies; soldier's non-military duty (**~-party** or ~, party told off for this; **~-dress** or **~s,** garments worn for it). **2.** *v.t.* Tire, exhaust, cause fatigue in. [f. F *fatigue*(*r*) f. L *fatigare* exhaust as by riding or working]

Fa'tĭha(**h**) (fah'tĭhah) *n.* Short first sura of Koran, used as Muslim prayer. [f. Arab. *fātiḥa* opening (*fataḥa* to open)]

fă'tlĭng *n.* Young fatted animal. [f. FAT 10 + -LING[1]]

Fă'tsō *n.* (*pl.* ~**es**). (sl. joc. or derog.) Fat person. [prob. f. FAT = fat person + -S[1] + -O]

fă'tten *v.* **1.** *v.t.* Make fat (esp. animals for slaughter); enrich (soil). **2.** *v.i.* Become fat. [f. FAT + -EN[6]]

fă'ttỹ *a.* & *n.* **1.** *a.* Like fat, unctuous, greasy; consisting of fat, adipose; with morbid deposition of fat (**~ degeneration** of heart or kidney); **~ acid,** (Chem.) member of a series of acids occurring in or derived from natural fats, waxes, etc. **2.** *n.* Fat person (esp. as nickname). [ME, f. FAT + -Y[2]]

fă'tūous *a.* Vacantly silly, purposeless, idiotic; hence or cogn. **fatū'**ITY *n.*, ~LY[2] *adv.*, ~NESS *n.* [f. L *fatuus* foolish + -OUS]

faubourg (fō'boorg) *n.* Suburb, esp. of Paris. [F; cf. med. L *falsus burgus* not the city proper]

fau'cēs (-z) *n. pl.* (Anat.) Cavity at back of mouth. [L, = throat]

fau'cėt *n.* Tap for barrel etc.; *any kind of tap. [ME, f. OF *fausset* vent-peg f. Prov. *falset* (*falsar* to bore)]

faugh (faw) *int.* expr. disgust. [spontaneous utterance]

fault (*or* fŏlt) *n.* & *v.* **1.** *n.* Defect, imperfection, blemish, of character or of structure, appearance, etc. (*generous* etc. **to a ~,** excessively so; **with all ~s,** at buyer's risk); break or other defect in electric circuit. **2.** Transgression, offence, thing wrongly done, (Tennis, etc.) ball wrongly served (**double ~,** two consecutive faults losing point); **find ~** (**with**), make adverse criticism (of), complain (of); **~'finder** *n.*, **~'finding** *n.* & *a.*, (esp. of captious criticism). **3.** Responsibility for something wrong (*the fault was mine*; *it will be our own fault*); defect that causes something undesirable; **at ~,** (arch.) **in ~,** guilty, to blame. **4.** (Hunt.) Loss of scent, check so caused, (**be at ~,** lit., or fig. = be puzzled, not know what to do). **5.** (Geol.) Break in continuity of strata or vein. **6.** *v.t.* Find fault with, blame; declare to be faulty; (Geol.) break continuity of (strata or vein). **7.** *v.i.* Commit fault; (Geol.) show fault. **8.** Hence ~'LESS *a.*, ~'Y[2] *a.*, **~'ĭ**LY[2] *adv.*, **~ĭ**NESS *n.* [ME f. OF *faut*(*e*) f. Rom. **fallita* fem. p.p. (as n.) of *fallere* FAIL[2]]

faun *n.* Latin rural deity with horns and tail. [ME, f. OF *faune* or f. L *Faunus* Latin god identified w. Gk Pan]

fau'n|a *n.* (*pl.* **~ae** *or* **~as**). Animals of a region or epoch; treatise on or list of these; hence ~AL *a.*, ~IST (3) *n.*, **~ĭ'st**IC(AL) *adjs.* [mod. L, f. name of rural goddess, sister of Faunus (see prec.)]

faute de mieux (fōt de myėr') *adv.* & *a.* (Used) for want of any better alternative. [F]

fauteuil (fōtŭ'ē) *n.* Theatre stall, seat in bus, etc., resembling armchair; seat or rank of member of French Academy; (arch.) armchair. [F, f. OF *faudestuel*, *faldestoel* FALDSTOOL]

fau'v|ĭsm (fō'-) *n.* Style of painting with vivid use of colour; so ~IST (2) *n.* [f. F *fauve* wild beast, applied to painters of Matisse's school; see -ISM]

faux bonhomme (fō bŏnŏ'm) *n.* Seemingly good-natured but actually sly person. [F, = false good-natured man]

faux-naïf (fōnahē'f) *a.* & *n.* (Person) pretending to be ingenuous; self-consciously unaffected (person). [F (*faux* false, *naïf* NAÏVE)]

faux pas (fō pah') *n.* (*pl.* same *pr.* -ah'z). Act that compromises one's, esp. a woman's, reputation; offence against social convention, indiscreet speech or action. [F, = false step]

favela (fahvā'la) *n.* Brazilian shack or slum. [Port.]

fā'vour[1] (-ver), ***fā'vor**[1], *n.* **1.** Friendly regard, goodwill, (**find ~ in the eyes of,** be liked by; CURRY[2] *favour*); approval (*look with favour on*); esteem, liking, (*be* or *stand high* etc. *in* person's *favour*); kindness beyond what is due or usual (*should esteem it a favour*; *do me the favour of accepting*; *woman* **bestows her ~s,** allows sexual intercourse); (arch., Commerc.) letter (*your favour of yesterday*). **2.** (arch.) Leave, pardon, (*by your favour*; **under ~,** if one may venture to say so). **3.** Partiality, too lenient or generous treatment (FEAR[1] *or favour*). **4.** Aid, support, furtherance, (*under favour of night*); **in ~ of,** on behalf or in support of, on the side of, to the advantage or account of, (*am in favour of a five-day week*; *cheques to be drawn in favour of the treasurer*). **5.** Thing given or worn as mark of favour, knot of ribbons, rosette, cockade, badge. **6.** (arch.) Looks, countenance; hence *well*, *ill*, *hard*, etc., -~ED[2] (-*erd*) *a.* [ME f. OF, f. L *favor -oris* (*favēre* show kindness to; see -OR)]

fā'vour[2] (-ver), ***fā'vor**[2], *v.t.* **1.** Look kindly upon, approve; treat kindly, countenance; oblige *with.* **2.** Treat with partiality, be unjust on behalf of. **3.** Aid, support; tend to confirm (theory etc.); prove advantageous to (person), facilitate (process etc.), whence ~ING[2] *a.* **4.**

(colloq.) Resemble in features (*favour* one's *father*). **5.** (in *p.p.*) Having unusual advantages (**most ~ed nation,** nation to which a State accords lowest scale of import duties). [ME, f. OF *favorer* f. med. L *favorare* f. L *favor* (see prec.)]

fā'vourab|le (-ver-), ***fā'vorab|le,** *a.* Well-disposed, propitious; commendatory, approving; giving consent (*favourable answer*); promising, auspicious, satisfactory, (*favourable aspect*); helpful, suitable, (*to*); hence **~le**NESS (-beln-) *n.*, ~LY² *adv.* [ME, f. OF *favorable* f. L *favorabilis* (as FAVOUR¹; see -ABLE)]

fā'vourĭte (-ver-), ***fā'vorĭte,** *n.* & *a.* (Person or thing) preferred above others (*the favourite of*; *a favourite with* or *of*); (Sport) competitor generally expected to win, horse etc. at shortest odds; person chosen as intimate by king or superior and unduly favoured; ***~ son,** person preferred as presidential candidate by delegates from his own state. [f. obs. F *favorit* f. It. *favorito*, p.p. of *favorire* FAVOUR²; see -ITE²]

fā'vourĭtism (-ver-), ***fā'vorĭtism,** *n.* Unfair favouring of one person or group at expense of another. [f. prec. + -ISM]

fawn¹ *n.*, *a.*, & *v.t.* **1.** *n.* Young fallow etc. deer; buck or doe of first year; **in ~,** (of deer) pregnant. **2.** *n.* & *a.* ~ or **~-colour(ed),** (of) light yellowish brown. **3.** *v.t.* (Of deer) bring forth (young, or abs.). [ME, f. OF *faon* etc. f. Rom. **feto -onis* f. L *fetus* offspring (cf. FOETUS)]

fawn² *v.i.* (Of animal, esp. dog) show affection by tail-wagging, grovelling, etc. (**~ on, upon,** lavish caresses on); (of person) behave servilely, cringe (*on* or *upon*, or abs.), whence ~'ING² *a.* [OE *fagnian*, *fægnian*, f. as FAIN¹]

fay *n.* (literary). Fairy. [ME, f. OF *fa(i)e* f. L *fata* pl. the FATES]

fāze *v.t.* (usu. w. neg.) Disconcert, perturb. [var. of *feeze* drive off, f. OE *fēsian*, of unkn. orig.]

F.B.A. *abbr.* Fellow of the British Academy.

***F.B.I.** *abbr.* Federal Bureau of Investigation.

F.C. *abbr.* Football Club.

***F.C.C.** *abbr.* Federal Communications Commission.

||**F.C.O.** *abbr.* Foreign & Commonwealth Office.

fcp. *abbr.* foolscap.

F.D. *abbr.* Defender of the Faith. [f. L *Fidei Defensor*]

***F.D.A.** *abbr.* Food & Drugs Administration.

F.D.C. *abbr.* first-day cover; *fleur de coin.*

Fe *symb.* iron. [f. L *ferrum*]

fē'altȳ *n.* Feudal tenant's or vassal's (acknowledgement of obligation of) fidelity to his lord (*do, make, receive, swear, fealty*); allegiance. [ME, f. OF *feau(l)té* f. L *fidelitas -tatis* (*fidelis* faithful f. *fides* faith; see -TY¹)]

fear¹ *n.* **1.** Painful emotion caused by impending danger or evil, state of alarm (*was in fear*), dread *of*, *that*, or *lest*; **for ~ of, (that), lest,** to avoid the risk of; **without ~ or favour,** impartially; hence ~'LESS *a.* (*fearless of danger*). **2.** Dread and reverence (*the fear of God*; **put the ~ of God into,** terrify); anxiety for the safety of (*in fear of his life*); **no ~,** (colloq.) it is not likely. [OE *fǣr* sudden calamity, danger, = OS *vār* ambush, OHG *fāra*, ON *fár* misfortune f. Gmc **fǣraz*]

fear² *v.* **1.** *v.i.* Be afraid; (*refl.*, arch.) *I fear me* (used in parenthesis); **never ~,** there is no danger of that. **2.** *v.t.* Be afraid of; hesitate *to* do, shrink from do*ing*; revere (God); apprehend, have uneasy expectation of; be afraid (*that*) (*need not* etc. *fear but* or *that*). [OE *fǣran*, = OS *fāron* lie in wait, OHG *fārēn*, ON *færa* taunt; cf. prec.]

fear'ful *a.* Terrible, awful; (colloq.) annoying, extreme, etc. (*in a fearful mess*); frightened, timid; apprehensive *of*, *lest*, (*that*); lacking resolution *to*; reverential; hence ~LY² *adv.*, ~NESS *n.* [ME, f. prec. + -FUL]

fear'some *a.* Appalling, awe-inspiring, esp. in appearance; hence ~LY² (-mlĭ) *adv.*, ~NESS (-mn-) *n.* [f. FEAR¹,² + -SOME¹]

fea's|ĭble (-z-) *a.* Practicable, possible; (colloq.) manageable, convenient, serviceable, plausible; hence ~IBI'LITY *n.*, **~ĭb**LY² *adv.* [ME, f. OF *faisable*, *-ible* f. *fais-* st. of *faire* f. L *facere* do; see -IBLE]

feast *n.* & *v.* **1.** *n.* Joyful religious anniversary (**movable, immovable, ~,** one that recurs on different, same, date; **movable ~,** (joc.) meal taken at no regular time); annual village festival; sumptuous meal, esp. public one given to many guests; (fig.) gratification to the senses or mind (**~ of reason,** intellectual talk); **~-day** (on which feast is held). **2.** *v.i.* Partake of feast, eat and drink sumptuously; hence ~'ER¹ *n.* **3.** *v.t.* Pass (night etc.) *away* in feasting; regale (guests, one's *eyes on* beauty etc.). [ME, f. OF *feste(r)* f. pop. L *festa* neut. pl. of *festus* joyous]

feat¹ *n.* Noteworthy act, esp. deed of valour (esp. *feat of arms*); action showing dexterity or strength, surprising trick. [ME, f. OF *fait*, *fet* f. as FACT]

||**feat²** *a.* (arch. or dial.) Adroit, smart, dextrous, neat; hence ~'LY² *adv.* [ME, f. OF *fet* (as prec.)]

fea'ther¹ (fĕ'dh-) *n.* **1.** One of the appendages growing from bird's skin, consisting of quill, shaft, and two vanes of barbs, (**show the white ~,** betray cowardice, white feather in game-bird's tail being mark of bad breeding); (collect.) plumage (**in high** or **full ~,** in good spirits etc.; BIRDS *of a feather*); game-birds (**fur and ~,** game animals and birds). **2.** Piece(s) of feather attached to arrow; plume worn in hat etc. (**~ in** one's **cap,** achievement one may be proud of); very light object (**you could have knocked me down with a ~,** I was astonished); fringe of long hair on dog's leg etc. **3.** (Rowing). Action of feathering (see foll.). **4.** **~ bed,** mattress stuffed with feathers; **~-bed** *v.t.* (*-dd-*), make things easy for (esp. in economic or financial respects), pamper; **~-brain(ed),** = *feather-head(ed)*; **~ duster,** dusting-brush made of feathers; **~-edge,** fine edge of wedge-shaped board; **~-head(ed), ~-pate(d),** silly (person); **~-stitch,** ornamental zigzag sewing; **~weight,** very light thing or person, esp. boxer (see BOX⁵-*ing-weights*). **5.** Hence (-)~ED² (-*erd*), ~LESS, ~Y², *adjs.*, ~INESS, ~LET, *ns.* [OE *fether*, = OS *fethara*, OHG *fedara*, ON *fjöthr* f. Gmc **fethrō* f. IE **petra*]

fea'ther² (fĕ'dh-) *v.* **1.** *v.t.* Furnish, adorn, line, coat, (as) with feathers (*feather an arrow*; **~** one's **nest,** enrich oneself when opportunity occurs; TAR *and feather*). **2.** *v.t.* & *i.* Turn (oar) so as to pass through air edgeways; (Aeron. & Naut.) make (propeller blades) rotate in such a way as to lessen air or water resistance; vary angle of incidence of (helicopter blades). **3.** *v.i.* Float, move, or wave, like feathers. **4.** (Hunt., of hound) make quivering motion of body and tail while seeking scent. [f. OE *gefithrian* & f. prec.]

fea'therĭng (fĕ'dh-) *n.* In vbl senses; plumage; feathers of an arrow; feather-like structure in animal's coat; (Archit.) cusps in tracery. [f. prec. + -ING¹]

fea'ture *n.* & *v.* **1.** *n.* (usu. in *pl.*) Part of face, esp. with regard to shape and visible effect. **2.** Distinctive or characteristic part of a thing, part that arrests attention; distinctive or prominent article etc. in newspaper etc.; ~

(**film**), one of some length forming main item in cinema programme, whence **featur**E'TTE (-cher-) *n.*; ~ (**programme**), broadcast based on one specific theme. **3.** *v.t.* Be feature of; (arch.) portray, sketch the prominent points of; make special display or attraction of, give special prominence to, (esp. in film etc.). **4.** *v.i.* Be feature; be (important) participant *in*. **5.** Hence **-featur**ED² (-cherd), ~LESS (-cherl-), *adjs.* [ME, f. OF *feture, faiture* form f. L *factura* formation (see FACTURE)]

Feb. *abbr.* February.

fĕ'brĭfūge *n.* Medicine to reduce fever, cooling drink; hence **fĕbrĭ'fūg**AL *a.* [f. F *fébrifuge* f. L *febris* fever; see -FUGE]

fē'brīle *a.* Of fever, feverish; hence **fēbrĭ'l**ITY *n.* [f. F *fébrile* or f. med. L *febrilis* f. L *febris* fever; see -IL]

Fĕ'bruarȳ (-rōō-) *n.* Second month of year; ~ **fill-dike** (name referring to its rain and snow). [ME, f. OF *feverier* f. Rom. *febrarius* f. L *februarius* (*februa* purification feast held in this month)]

***fē'cal, *feces.** See FAECAL, FAECES.

fĕ'cklėss *a.* Feeble, futile, inefficient, aimless; hence ~LY² *adv.*, ~NESS *n.* [f. Sc. *feck* (*effeck* var. of EFFECT¹) + -LESS]

fĕ'cūl|ent *a.* Turbid; fetid; containing sediments or dregs; hence ~ENCE *n.* [f. F *féculent* or f. L *faeculentus* (as FAECES; see -ULENT)]

fĕ'cund *a.* Prolific, fertile; fertilizing; so **fėcŭ'nd**ITY *n.* [ME, f. F *fécond* or f. L *fecundus*]

fĕ'cund|āte *v.t.* Make fruitful; = FERTILIZE 2; so ~A'TION *n.* [f. L *fecundare* (*fecundus* fruitful) + -ATE³]

fĕd¹. See FEED¹.

***Fĕd²** *n.* (sl.) Federal official, esp. member of Federal Bureau of Investigation. [abbr. of FEDERAL]

fĕdayee'n (-a-y-) *n. pl.* Arab guerrillas operating esp. against Israel. [f. colloq. Arab. *fidā'iyīn* pl. f. Arab. *fidā'ī* adventurer]

fĕ'deral *a.* **1.** Of a system of government in which several States form a unity but remain independent in internal affairs; concerning this whole and not the separate parts. **2.** Relating to or favouring central government, as dist. from government by separate provinces etc.; *of the Northern States in the Civil War; ~ **district, territory,** etc., region used as seat of federal government; *~ **reserve,** national system of reserve cash available to banks. **3.** (Theol.) Based on doctrine of God's covenants with Adam and Christ. **4.** Comprising an association of largely independent units (‖*federal university*). **5.** Hence or cogn. ~ISM (3), ~IST (2), *ns.*, ~IZE (3) *v.t.*, ~LY² *adv.* [f. mod. L **foederalis* f. L *foedus -eris* covenant + -AL; in sense 1 orig. of dispositions by treaty]

fĕ'der|āte *v.t.* & *i.* Band together in league for some common object; organize (States) on federal basis; so ~ATE², ~ATIVE, *adjs.* [f. LL *foederare* (as prec.) + -ATE³]

fĕderā'tion *n.* Federating, whence ~IST (2) *n.*; federated society; federal group of States etc. [f. F *fédération* f. LL *foederatio* (as prec.; see -ATION)]

fėdŏr'a *n.* Low soft felt hat with crown creased lengthways. [f. *Fédora*, drama by V. Sardou (1882)]

fee *n.*, & *v.t.* (~**'d** *or* ~**d**). **1.** *n.* (Hist.) Fief, feudal benefice. **2.** Inherited estate; ~ **simple** (without limitation to particular class of heirs); ~**-tail** (with such limitation [TAIL²]); **hold in** ~ (**simple**), have as absolute property. **3.** Sum payable to public officer for performing his function; remuneration of lawyer, physician, or any professional person, for consultation etc. (RETAIN*ing fee*); money paid to another employer for transfer of footballer etc.; entrance money for examination, society, etc.; (in *pl.*) regular payment for instruction at school, university, etc.; gratuity. **4.** *v.t.* Pay fee to; engage for a fee. [ME f. AF, = OF *feu, fieu*, etc. f. med. L *feodum, feudum*, Rom. **feudum*, perh. f. Frank. **fehu-ōd* cattle-property; cf. FEUD², FIEF]

***feeb** *n.* (sl.) Feeble-minded or stupid person. [abbr. of foll.]

fee'b|le *a.* Weak, infirm; deficient in character or intelligence (~**le-minded,** mentally deficient, esp. with mental age of 8 or 9); lacking energy, force, or effect; dim, indistinct; hence ~**le**NESS (-beln-) *n.*, ~LISH¹ 2 *a.*, ~LY² *adv.* [ME, f. AF & OF *feble, fieble, fleible* f. L *flebilis* lamentable (*flēre* weep)]

feed¹ *v.* (**fed**). **1.** *v.t.* Supply with food; put food into mouth of (*cannot feed himself*); graze (cattle). **2.** Gratify (vanity etc.); comfort (person) *with* hope etc. **3.** Serve as food for; nourish, make grow; ~ (**up**), (1) fatten, (2) satiate, whence **fed up, fed to death, fed to the** (**back**) **teeth,** etc., (sl.) having had too much of something, bored *with*. **4.** Keep (reservoir, fire, etc.) supplied; supply (machine) with material; give out (fodder) to animals; use (land) as pasture; supply (material) (*in*)*to* machine; (Theatr. sl.) supply (actor etc.) with cues; (Footb. etc.) give passes to; ~**'ing-bottle** (with teat, for hand-fed infants); ~**'ing-cup** (with spout, for invalids); ~**'ing-time** (at which captive animals etc. are fed). **5.** *v.i.* Take food, eat, (esp. of animal, or colloq.); ~ **on,** consume, be nourished by. **6.** *v.t.* & *i.* ~ **back,** return by or as FEEDBACK. [OE *fēdan*, = OS *fōdean*, OHG *fuoten*, ON *fœtha*, Goth. *fōdjan* f. Gmc **fōdjan* (**fōdhon* FOOD)]

feed² *n.* **1.** Act or instance of feeding, giving of food; **off** one's ~, with no appetite; **on the** ~, (of fish) feeding or looking out for food; **out at** ~, turned out to graze. **2.** Pasturage, green crops; horse's allowance of oats etc.; fodder; (colloq.) meal, feast; feeding of machine, material supplied, charge of gun, (*feed-cock, -pipe, -shaft*, etc.). **3.** (Theatr. sl.) Actor who supplies another with cues. **4.** ~**'lot,** area of land where animals are fed; ~**'stock,** raw material supplied to machine etc.; ~**-tank** (holding water for locomotive or for drinking). [f. prec.]

feed³. See FEE.

fee'dbăck *n.* **1.** (Electr.) Return of fraction of output signal from one stage of circuit, amplifier, etc., to input of same or a preceding stage (**positive, negative,** ~, tending to increase, decrease, the amplification etc.); signal so returned. **2.** (Biol., Psych., etc.) Modification or control of a process or system by its results or effects, esp. by difference between desired and actual result. **3.** Information about result of experiment etc.; response. [f. FEED¹ + BACK³]

fee'der *n.* In vbl senses; one who eats in specified manner; child's feeding-bottle; ‖child's bib; tributary stream (lit. or fig.); hopper or feeding apparatus in machine; branch road, railway line, etc., linking outlying districts with main communications system; main carrying electricity to distribution point; (Theatr. sl.) = FEED² 3. [ME, f. FEED² + -ER¹]

feel *v.* (**felt**) & *n.* **1.** *v.t.* Explore by touch (~ **the pulse of,** lit. to ascertain state of health, or fig. = cautiously ascertain intentions or sentiments of; ~ one's **way,** find it by groping, or fig. = proceed carefully); try to ascertain by touch *whether, if, how*; perceive by touch, have sensation of, (*feel a hard substance, heat, pain, a* *blow; I felt him move, moving, that he was cold; feel* one's OATS*)*; ~ **(up)**, (sl.) caress genitals of. **2.** Be conscious of (sensation, emotion, conviction; *feel the* DRAUGHT[1] 7; ~ **no pain,** (sl.) be very drunk; **make** one's **presence felt,** have effect on others). **3.** Experience, undergo, (*he shall feel my vengeance; felt the storm severely*); be affected by. **4.** Behave as if conscious of (*ship feels her helm*); be emotionally affected by (*feel the censure keenly*); have vague or emotional conviction (*that*; esp. *feel in* one's BONE[1]*s*); consider, think, (*I feel it necessary to make a correction*). **5.** *v.i.* Search (*about*) with hand etc. *after* or *for*; have sensation of touch (*can you feel in your fingers?*). **6.** Be consciously (*well, warm, angry,* CHEAP 1); ~ **like,** (colloq.) desire (thing), have inclination towards do*ing*; ~ **(quite)** one**self,** be fit, self-possessed, etc.; ~ **up to,** be ready to face (*work* etc.). **7.** Be emotionally affected (*feel strongly about it*); have sympathy *with* or compassion *for*. **8.** Be consciously perceived as, produce impression of being, (*air feels chilly; this feels like velvet*). **9.** *n.* Sense of touch (*firm to the feel*); act of feeling, testing by touch; sensation characterizing a material, a situation, etc. [OE *fēlan*, =OS *-fōlian*, OHG *fuolen* f. WG **fōljan*]

fee'ler *n.* In vbl senses; organ in certain animals for testing things by touch or for searching for food; tentative proposal or hint, *ballon d'essai*; ~ **gauge** (equipped with blades for measuring gaps etc.). [f. prec. + -ER[1]]

fee'lĭng[1] *n.* **1.** In vbl senses; sense of touch; physical sensation. **2.** Emotion (*of* hope, fear, etc.); (in *pl.*) susceptibilities, sympathies, (*strong feelings on the matter*; **hurts my ~s,** offends me); readiness to feel, tenderness for others' sufferings, (**good** ~, avoidance of unkindness etc.); consciousness of (*had a feeling of safety*); belief not based solely on reason; sentiment (*the general feeling was against it*); general emotional effect produced by work of art. [ME, f. FEEL[2] + -ING[1]]

fee'lĭng[2] *a.* In vbl senses; sensitive; sympathetic; showing emotion; hence ~LY[2] *adv.* [ME, f. FEEL[2] + -ING[2]]

fee'lthy̆ *a.* (sl.) Obscene. [joc. imit. of foreigners' pr. of FILTHY]

feet. See FOOT[1].

feign (fān) *v.t.* & *i.* **1.** Simulate, pretend, (*feign that* one *is mad, to be mad,* one*self mad, madness; feign innocence, ignorance*); practise simulation. **2.** (arch.) Invent (excuse, story, accusation), forge (document); represent in fiction, imagine. [ME, f. *feign-* st. of OF *feindre* f. L *fingere* mould, contrive]

feijō'a (fā- *or* fī-) *n.* Evergreen shrub or tree of genus *Feijoa*; its guava-like fruit. [mod. L, f. J. da Silva *Feijo*, 19th-c. Sp. naturalist + -A 1]

feint[1] (fā-) *n.*, & *v.i.* **1.** *n.* Sham attack (blow, cut, thrust, or military assault) to divert attention or deceive opponent; pretence (*make a feint of* doing). **2.** *v.i.* Make feint (*at, upon, against*). [f. F *feinte*, fem. p.p. (as n.) of *feindre* FEIGN]

feint[2] (fā-) *a.* (Commerc.) = FAINT[1] (*feint lines; ruled feint*). [ME f. OF, p.p. of *feindre* FEIGN]

feis (fĕsh *or* fāsh) *n.* (*pl.* **~'eanna** *pr.* *-ana*). Early Celtic parliament of kings etc.; Irish or Scottish arts festival like eisteddfod. [Ir., = assembly]

***fei'st|y̆** (fī'-) *a.* (sl.) Aggressive, exuberant; touchy; hence ~ĬNESS *n.* [f. *feist* (= FIST) small dog + -Y[2]]

fĕla'fel (-ah'-) *n.* (Israel etc.) Flat bread roll stuffed with seasoned vegetables. [f. Arab. *falāfil*]

fĕ'ldscher (-sh*er*) *n.* Russian medical auxiliary without professional qualifications. [f. Russ. *fel'dsher* f. G *feldscher* field surgeon (*feld* FIELD)]

fĕ'ldspâr. See FELSPAR.

Félibre (fālē'br) *n.* Member of the Félibrige, society of Provençal poets and writers founded 1854; so **Fe'lĭbr**ISM (3) (fā'-) *n.* [F, f. Prov. *felibre* teacher in the temple (Luke 2:46), prob. f. LL *fellibris* nursling (of the Muses) f. L *fellare* suck]

fēlĭcĭ'fĭc *a.* (Eth.) Tending to produce happiness. [f. L *felix -icis* happy + -I- + -FIC]

fėlĭ'cĭt|āte *v.t.* Congratulate (usu. *on*); hence ~A'TION *n.* (usu. in *pl.*). [f. LL *felicitare* make very happy f. L *felix* happy, + -ATE[3]]

fėlĭ'cĭtous *a.* (Of expression, quotation, civilities, or person in these connections) strikingly apt, pleasantly ingenious; hence ~LY[2] *adv.* [f. foll. + -OUS]

fėlĭ'cĭty̆ *n.* **1.** Being happy; intense happiness; thing causing happiness. **2.** Fortunate trait; happy faculty in expression, appropriateness; well chosen phrase. [ME, f. OF *félicité* f. L *felicitas -tatis* (*felix felicis* happy; see -ITY)]

fē'līne *a.* & *n.* **1.** *a.* Of cats; catlike esp. in beauty or slyness; hence **fėlĭ'n**ITY *n.* **2.** *n.* Animal of cat family Felidae. [f. L *felinus* (*feles* cat; see -INE[1])]

fĕll[1] *n.* Animal's hide or skin with hair; human skin (FLESH[1] *and fell*); thick or matted hair or wool, fleece; **~'monger,** one who prepares skins for leather-making, (arch.) dealer in hides and skins. [OE *fel(l)*, =OS, OHG *fel*, ON *-fjall*, Goth. *-fill* f. Gmc **fellam* f. IE **pello-*]

||**fĕll**[2] *n.* Hill, mountain, (in names, as *Scafell*); stretch of high moorland. [ME, f. ON *fjall, fell* hill, prob. cogn. w. OS, OHG *felis* rock]

fĕll[3] *a.* (poet. or rhet.) Fierce, ruthless, terrible, destructive; **at one ~ swoop,** in a single (deadly) action. [ME, f. OF *fel* f. Rom. **fel(l)o* FELON[1]]

fĕll[4] *v.t.*, & *n.* **1.** *v.t.* Strike (person, animal) down by blow or cut; cut down (tree); stitch down (edge of seam) to lie flat. **2.** *n.* Amount of timber cut. [OE *fellan*, =OS *fellian*, OHG *fellen*, ON *fella* f. Gmc **falljan* causative of **fallan* FALL[1]]

fĕll[5]. See FALL[1].

fĕ'lla, fĕ'llah[1], *n.* = FELLOW 5. [repr. affected or vulg. pronunc.]

fĕ'llah[2] (-*a*) *n.* (*pl.* ~**in** *pr.* *-a*-hēn). Egyptian peasant. [f. Arab. *fallāḥ* husbandsman (*falaḥa* till the soil)]

fĕllā'tĭo (*or* -shĭō) *n.* (*pl.* **~s**). Sucking or licking of penis; hence **fĕllā'te** *v.t.*, perform fellatio on (person), **fĕllā'**TOR, **fĕllā'**TRIX, *ns.* [mod. L, f. L *fellare* suck; cf. -ATION]

fĕ'ller[1] *n.* In vbl senses. [f. FELL[4] + -ER[1]]

fĕ'ller[2] *n.* = FELLOW 5; **young ~-me-lad,** frivolous young man. [repr. affected or vulg. pronunc.]

fĕ'llōe, fĕ'lly̆, *n.* Outer circle (or one piece of it) of wheel, attached by spokes. [OE *felg*, = MLG, MDu. *velge*, OHG *felga*, of unkn. orig.]

fĕ'llow (-ō) *n.* & *a.* **1.** *n.* One associated with another, comrade, (usu. in *pl.*; *separated from his fellows*); **~-feeling,** sympathy; **good** ~, congenial companion; HAIL[3]-*fellow-well-met.* **2.** Counterpart, match, other of pair; equal, one of same class; contemporary. **3.** Incorporated senior member of college (~ **commoner,** (Hist.) undergraduate privileged to dine at fellows' table); elected graduate receiving stipend for period of research. **4.** Member of governing body in some universities; member of learned society. **5.** (colloq.) Man, boy, (*poor fellow!*; *my dear* or *good fellow, old fellow*; STOUT *fellow*); (derog.) despised person; **young ~-my-lad** (cf. FELLER[2]). **6.** *attrib.* or *a.* Belonging to same class (~ **creature,** person or animal also created by God), associated in joint action (*fellow soldier*), in same relation to same object (*fellow-countryman*); ~**-traveller,** (1) one who travels with another, (2) non-Communist who sympathizes with aims and general policy of Communist Party. [OE *fēolaga* f. ON *félagi* (*fé* cattle, property, money; see LAY[3])]

fĕ'llowship (-lō-) *n.* Participation, sharing, community of interest; companionship, intercourse, friendliness; body of associates, company, (**right hand of** ~, sign of admission); guild, corporation; brotherhood, fraternity; dignity or emoluments of fellow of college or society. [ME, f. prec. + -SHIP]

fĕ'llў. See FELLOE.

fĕlō dē sē' *n* (*pl.* **felones** *pr.* fĭlōnēz-, *or* **felos, de se**). Self-murderer; self-murder. [AL (*felo* FELON[1], *de se* of himself)]

fĕ'lon[1] *a.* & *n.* **1.** *a.* (arch.) Cruel, wicked, murderous. **2.** *n.* One who has committed felony; hence ~RY (1) *n.* [ME f. OF, f. med. L *fel(l)o -onis*, of unkn. orig.]

fĕ'lon[2] *n.* Whitlow. [ME, perh. as prec.; cf. med. L *fel(l)o* in same sense]

fĕlō'nious *a.* Criminal; (Law) of or involving felony; who has committed felony; hence ~LY[2] *adv.* [f. foll. + -OUS]

fĕ'lonў *n.* Crime regarded by the law as grave, and usu. involving violence. [ME, f. OF *felonie* (as FELON[1]; see -Y[1])]

fĕ'l(d)spâr *n.* Widely distributed white or flesh-red mineral containing aluminium and other silicates in various proportions; hence **fĕl(d)spă'th**IC *a.*, **fĕ'l(d)spath**OID *n.* [f. G *feldspat(h)* (*feld* FIELD, *spat(h)* SPAR[2]); ‖usu. *felspar*, by false deriv. f. G *fels* rock]

fĕlt[1] *n.* & *v.* **1.** *n.* Kind of cloth made by rolling and pressing wool etc., or by weaving and shrinking wool etc.; similar material made from other fibres; ~**(-tipped) pen,** pen with point made of felt; hence ~'Y[2] *a.* **2.** *v.t.* Make into felt, mat together; cover with felt. **3.** *v.i.* Become matted. [OE, = OS *filt*, OHG *filz* f. WG **felta*, **felti*]

fĕlt[2]. See FEEL.

fĕlŭ'cca *n.* Small Mediterranean coasting vessel with oars or lateen sails or both. [f. It. *feluc(c)a* f. obs. Sp. *faluca* f. Arab. *fulk*, perh. f. Gk *efolkion* sloop]

fē'māle *a.* & *n.* **1.** *a.* Of the sex that can bear offspring or produce eggs (*female child, slave, dog, ostrich, salmon, wasp*); (of plants or their parts) fruit-bearing, having pistil and no stamens, or thought of as female because of colour etc., (~ **fern,** tall slender kind; *female bamboo, myrtle*); of women (*female sex, education,* SUFFRAGE; ~ **impersonator,** male performer dressed and acting as woman) or female animals; *female* RHYME[1]. **2.** (In instruments etc.) designed to receive corresponding male part; ~ **screw** (as in nut). **3.** *n.* Female person or animal; (derog. or joc.) woman, girl. [ME, f. OF *femelle* n. f. L *femella* dim. of *femina* woman, w. assim. to *male*]

fēme *n.* (Law). Woman, wife; ~ **covert** (kŭ'-), married woman; ~ **sole,** woman without husband (esp. if divorced). [ME f. AF & OF, f. L *femina* woman]

fĕ'mĭnal *a.* Womanly; hence ~ITY (-ă'l-) *n.* [f. med. L *feminalis* f. L *femina* woman; see -AL]

fĕmĭnē'ĭtў *n.* Womanliness; womanishness. [f. L *femineus* womanish (*femina* woman) + -ITY]

fĕ'mĭnĭne *a.* & *n.* **1.** *a.* Of women; womanly (*feminine intuition*). **2.** (Gram.) Having gender proper to women's names. **3.** (Pros.) ~ **caesura** (not immediately following stress); ~ **rhyme** (of two syllables, the second being unstressed; orig. in F verse, of feminine wds ending in mute *-e*). **4.** ~ **ending** (of verse line or phrase of music with unaccented syllable or note after final stress). **5.** Hence ~LY[2] (-nlĭ) *adv.*, ~NESS (-n-n-), **fĕmĭnĭ'n**ITY, *ns.* **6.** *n.* Feminine gender or word. [ME, f. OF *feminin -ine* or f. L *femininus* (*femina* woman; see -INE[1])]

fĕ'mĭn|ism *n.* Advocacy of women's rights on ground of equality of the sexes, whence ~IST (2) *n.*; (Path.) development of female characteristics in male person. [f. F *féminisme*, or f. L *femina* woman + -ISM]

fĕmĭ'nĭtў *n.* = FEMININITY. [ME, f. OF *feminité* f. med. L *feminitas -tatis* f. L *femina* woman; see -ITY]

fĕ'mĭnĭz|e, -ĭs|e (-īz), *v.t.* & *i.* Make or become feminine or female; hence ~A'TION *n.* [f. L *femina* woman + -IZE]

femme fatale (făm fătah'l) *n.* Dangerously attractive woman. [F]

fĕ'mtō- *pref.* denoting factor of 10^{-15}, as ~METRE[2]. [f. Da. or Norw. *femten* fifteen + -O-]

fē'mur *n.* (*pl.* ~**s,** *or* **femora** *pr.* fĕ'-). Thigh-bone; corresponding part of insect; so **fĕ'mor**AL *a.* [L *femur femoris* thigh]

fĕn[1] *n.* **1.** Low marshy or flooded tract of land (**the F~s,** low-lying districts in Cambs. etc.). **2.** ~**-berry,** cranberry; ~**-fire,** will-o'-the-wisp; ~**'man,** inhabitant of Fens. **3.** Hence ~'NY[2] *a.* [OE *fen(n)*, = OS *fen(n)i*, OHG *fenna*, *fenni*, ON *fen*, Goth. *fani* f. Gmc **fanjam*]

fĕn[2], **fens.** See FAIN[2].

fĕnce[1] *n.* **1.** Hedge, railing, bank, etc., preventing entry to or exit from field etc.; **sunk** ~ (placed along bottom of ditch, or formed by ditch); **mend** one's ~**s,** make peace with person; **sit on the** ~, remain neutral in contest, not take sides, not commit oneself. **2.** Guard, guide, gauge, in various machines. **3.** Receiver, receiving-house, of stolen goods. **4.** (arch.) Art of fencing; means of defence. [ME, f. DEFENCE]

fĕnce[2] *v.* **1.** *v.i.* Practise sword-play, use the sword scientifically; (fig.) ~ **with** *question* or *questioner*, parry, evade answering. **2.** *v.t.* Screen, shield, protect, (*from, against*); repel, keep *off* or *out*. **3.** Surround (as) with fence, enclose, fortify, (*about, in, round, up*). **4.** *v.i.* (Of horse etc.) leap fences. **5.** *v.i.* & *t.* Deal in (stolen goods). **6.** Hence **fĕ'nc**ER[1] *n.* (esp. of swordsman or horse). [f. prec.]

fĕ'ncelėss (-sl-) *a.* Unenclosed; (poet. or arch.) unfortified, defenceless. [f. FENCE[1] + -LESS]

fĕ'ncĭble *n.* (Hist.) Soldier liable only for home service. [ME, f. DEFENSIBLE]

fĕ'ncĭng *n.* In vbl senses; enclosure, railing; fences; material for fences. [f. FENCE[2] + -ING[1]]

fĕnd *v.* **1.** *v.t.* Ward *off*, keep *away*, repel *from*. **2.** *v.i.* Provide *for* (usu. *oneself*). [ME, f. DEFEND]

fĕ'nder *n.* Thing used to keep something off, prevent collision, etc.; (Naut.) piece of old cable, matting, etc., hung over vessel's side to protect it against impact; *bumper or mudguard of motor car etc.; guard, esp. metal frame for fire to keep coals from rolling into room; ~**-stool,** long footstool before fender. [ME, f. prec. + -ER[1]]

fĕnėstĕ'lla *n.* (Archit.) Niche in wall S. of altar holding piscina and often credence. [L, dim. of *fenestra* window]

fėnĕ'stra *n.* (*pl.* ~e). Small hole or opening in bone etc., esp. one of two (~ **ovalis** and ~ **rotunda**) in inner ear; perforation in surgical instrument; (Surg.) hole made by fenestration. [L, = window]

fėnĕ'strāte *a.* (Bot. & Zool.) Having small window-like perforations or transparent areas. [f. L *fenestratus* p.p. of *fenestrare* (*fenestra* window); see -ATE[2]]

fėnĕ'strātėd *a.* Having windows; perforated; = prec.; (Surg.) having fenestrae. [f. as prec. + -ED[1]]

fĕnėstrā'tion *n.* (Archit.) arrangement of windows in a building; (Bot. & Zool.) being fenestrate; (Surg.) (operation of making) artificial 'window' in labyrinth of ear, used in some cases of deafness. [f. as prec. + -ATION]

Fē'nĭan *n.* & *a.* **1.** *n.* (Hist.) Member of 19th-c. league among Irish in U.S. & Ireland for promoting revolution and overthrowing British government in Ireland; hence ~ISM (3) *n.* **2.** *a.* Of Fenians or Fenianism. [f. OIr. *féne* name of ancient Irish people, confused w. *fiann* guard of legendary kings]

fĕnks *n. pl.* Fibrous parts of whale's blubber, refuse of blubber when melted. [19th c.; orig. unkn.]

fĕ'nnĕc *n.* Small N. Afr. fox notable for its huge pointed ears. [f. Arab. *fanak*]

fĕ'nnel *n.* Yellow-flowered fragrant umbelliferous herb used in salads and sauces; plant related or similar to this. [f. OE *finugl* etc. & f. OF *fenoil* f. L *feniculum* (*fenum* hay; see -CULE)]

Fĕnnōscă'ndĭ|a *n.* Region of Scandinavia and Finland as political unit or (Geol.) ancient land-mass; hence ~AN *a.* [f. G *fennoskandisch* a., f. L *Fenni* Finns + *Scandia* Scandinavia]

fĕ'nūgreek *n.* Leguminous plant (*Trigonella foenumgraecum*) with aromatic seeds. [ME, f. OF *fenugrec* f. L *fenugraecum* (*fenum* hay, *Graecus* Greek); used by Romans as fodder]

feoff (fĕf) *n.* = FEUD². [AF var. of FIEF]

feoffee (fĕfē') *n.* (Hist.) Person to whom freehold estate in land is conveyed by feoffment; ~ **in** or **of trust,** trustee invested with such estate. [ME, f. AF *feoffé* p.p. of *feoffer* f. OF *fie(u)ffer* (as FIEF)]

feo'ffment (fĕ'f-) *n.* (Hist.) Mode of conveying freehold estate by formal transfer of possession. [ME, f. AF *feoffement* (as prec.; see -MENT)]

feo'ffor, feo'ffer, (fĕ'f-) *n.* (Hist.) One who makes feoffment to another. [ME, f. AF *feoffour* (as FEOFFEE; see -OR)]

ferae naturae (fērē natūr'ē) *a.* (*pred.* or placed after *n.*) Not domesticated, living in a wild state, (*hares are, the hare is, ferae naturae*; *animals ferae naturae*). [L, = of wild nature]

fēr'al *a.* Wild, untamed, uncultivated; in wild state after escape from captivity; brutal. [f. L *ferus* wild + -AL]

fer de lance (fārdelah'ńs) *n.* Large and very venomous snake of tropical S. America. [F, = iron (head) of lance]

fĕ'rėtorў *n.* Shrine for saint's relics; chapel in which this was deposited. [ME, f. OF *fiertre* f. L *feretrum* f. Gk *pheretron* (*pherō* bear), w. assim. to wds in *-tory*]

fēr'ĭal *a.* (Eccl.) (Of day) ordinary, not appointed for festival or fast; (of service etc.) for use on ferial day. [ME f. OF, or f. med. L *ferialis* (*feriae*; see FAIR¹, -AL)]

ferma't|a (-mah'-) *n.* (*pl.* **~as,** *or* **~e** *pr.* -ā). (Mus.) (Sign indicating) unspecified prolongation of note or rest. [It.]

fēr'mĕnt¹ *n.* Leaven, fermenting-agent; (arch.) enzyme; fermenting, fermentation; agitation, excitement, tumult. [ME f. OF, or f. L *fermentum* (*fervēre* boil; see -MENT)]

fermĕ'nt² *v.i.* & *t.* Undergo or subject to fermentation; (cause to) effervesce; excite, stir up, foment; hence ~ABLE *a.* [ME, f. OF *fermenter* f. L *fermentare* (as prec.)]

fērmĕntā'tion *n.* Process like that induced by leaven in dough, with effervescence, evolution of heat, and change of properties; agitation, excitement; so **fermĕ'ntATIVE** *a.* [ME, f. LL *fermentatio* (as prec.; see -ATION)]

fēr'mĭ *n.* (Phys.) Unit of length equal to 10^{-15} metre. [f. E. *Fermi*, Ital.-Amer. physicist d. 1954]

fēr'mĭŏn *n.* (Phys.) Particle obeying relations stated by Fermi and Dirac, with half-integral spin. [f. as prec. + -ON]

fēr'mĭum *n.* (Chem.) Artificially made transuranic radioactive metallic element. [f. as FERMI + -IUM]

fērn *n.* Vascular cryptogam of order Filicales, usu. with feathery fronds; (collect.) quantity of ferns; **~-owl,** nightjar; hence ~'LESS, ~'Y², *adjs.*, ~'ERY (3) *n.* [OE *fearn*, = MDu. *væren*, OHG *farn* f. WG **farno*]

ferō'cious (-shus) *a.* Fierce, savage, cruel; hence ~LY² *adv.*, ~NESS *n.* [f. L *ferox -ocis* + -OUS]

ferŏ'citў *n.* Ferocious character or act. [f. F *férocité* or f. L *ferocitas* (as prec.; see -ITY)]

-ferous *suf.* forming *adjs.* (usu. w. intermediate -I-) w. sense 'bearing, having' (*auriferous, odoriferous*); hence ~LY² *adv. suf.*, ~NESS *n. suf.* [f. or after F *-fère* or L *-fer* producing (*ferre* bear) + -OUS]

fĕ'rrāte *n.* (Chem.) Salt of (hypothetical) ferric acid, H_2FeO_4. [f. L *ferrum* iron + -ATE¹ (3)]

fĕ'rrel. See FERRULE.

fĕ'rrėt¹ *n.* Half-tamed variety or species of polecat kept for driving rabbits from burrows, killing rats, etc.; searcher, detective; hence ~Y² *a.* [ME, f. OF *fu(i)ret* alt. f. *fu(i)ron* f. LL *furo -onis* f. L *fur* thief]

fĕ'rrėt² *v.* **1.** *v.i.* Hunt with ferrets (*go ferreting*); rummage, search about, (*for*). **2.** *v.t.* Clear out (holes, ground), take or drive away (rabbits etc.), with ferrets (*about, away, out*, etc.); search *out* (secrets, criminals, etc.). [f. prec.]

fĕ'rrėt³ *n.* (arch.) Stout cotton or silk tape. [f. It. *fioretti* floss silk pl. of *fioretto* dim. of *fiore* f. L *flos floris* flower]

fĕrrĭ- *comb. form.* Containing iron, esp. in ferric compounds. [f. L *ferrum* iron + -I-]

fĕ'rrĭage *n.* Conveyance by or charge for using ferry. [f. FERRY + -AGE]

fĕ'rrĭc *a.* Of iron; (Chem.) containing iron in trivalent form (cf. FERROUS). [f. L *ferrum* iron + -IC]

fĕrrĭmă'gnėtĭsm *n.* Form of ferromagnetism with non-parallel alignment of neighbouring atoms or ions; hence **fĕrrĭmăgnĕ'tIC** *a.* [f. F *ferrimagnétisme* (as FERRI-, MAGNETISM)]

Fĕ'rrĭs *n.* ~ **wheel,** giant revolving vertical wheel with passenger cars on its periphery, used at amusement parks etc. [f. G. W. G. *Ferris*, Amer. engineer d. 1896]

fĕ'rrīte *n.* **1.** (Chem.) Salt of (hypothetical) acid, $H_2Fe_2O_4$, often with magnetic and insulating properties. **2.** Allotrope of pure iron occurring as solvent in low-carbon steel; hence **fĕrrĭ'tIC** *a.* [f. L *ferrum* iron + -ITE¹]

fĕrrō- *comb. form.* Containing iron, esp. in ferrous compounds; (of alloys) containing iron and (*chromium, manganese*, etc.). [f. L *ferrum* iron + -O-]

fĕrrōcŏ'ncrēte (*or* -n-k-) *n.* & *a.* (Made of) reinforced concrete. [f. FERRO- + CONCRETE¹ 2]

fĕrrōėlĕ'ctrĭc *a.* & *n.* (Phys.) Exhibiting permanent electric polarization and hysteresis when subjected to electric field; hence **fĕrrōėlĕctrĭ'CITY** *n.* [f. ELECTRIC after *ferromagnetic*]

fĕrrōmă'gnėtĭsm *n.* Form of magnetism with high variable permeability and with hysteresis, as found in iron etc.; hence **fĕrrōmăgnĕ'tIC** *a.* [f. FERRO- + MAGNETISM]

fĕ'rrous *a.* Containing iron (*ferrous and non-ferrous metals*); (Chem.) containing iron in divalent form (cf. FERRIC). [f. L *ferrum* iron + -OUS]

ferru'gĭnous (-rōō'-) *a.* Of or containing iron-rust, or iron as a chemical constituent; rust-coloured, reddish-brown. [f. L *ferrugo -ginis* rust (*ferrum* iron) + -OUS]

fĕ'rrule (*or* -ōōl), **fĕ'rrel,** *n.* Metal ring or cap strengthening end of stick or tube; band strengthening or forming joint. [earlier *verrel* etc. f. OF *virelle*, *virol(e)*, f. L *viriola* dim. of *viriae* bracelet; assim. to L *ferrum* iron]

fĕ'rrȳ *v.* & *n.* **1.** *v.t.* & *i.* Convey or pass in boat, work (boat), (of boat) pass to and fro, over river, lake, etc.; transport (persons or things) from one place to another, esp. as regular service. **2.** *n.* Place for or means of or service of ferrying; right to operate ferry service; means of transporting astronaut from surface of planet etc. to spacecraft. [ME, f. ON *ferja* n. & v. f. Gmc **farjōn*, **farjan* (**far-* go)]

fer'tile *a.* Bearing abundantly, fruitful, (lit. or fig.); (of seed, egg, etc.) capable of developing into new individual; able to become a parent; (of nuclear material) able to become fissile by capture of neutrons; **F~ Crescent,** semicircular region from E. Mediterranean to Persian Gulf; so **fertĭ'lity** *n.* [ME f. F, f. L *fertilis*]

fer'tĭlĭz|e, -ĭs|e (-īz), *v.t.* **1.** Make (esp. soil) fertile or productive. **2.** Make (egg etc., female individual or organ) develop new individual by introduction of male reproductive material. **3.** Hence ~ABLE *a.*, ~A'TION, ~ER[1] (1, 2), *ns.* [f. prec. + -IZE]

fĕ'rula (-ōō-) *n.* Giant fennel or other plant of genus *Ferula*. [ME f. L, = giant fennel, rod]

fĕ'rule (-ōōl) *n.*, & *v.t.* (Strike with) flat ruler with widened pierced end for punishing boys. [ME, f. as prec.]

fer'vent *a.* Hot, glowing; ardent, intense, (*fervent soul, lover, hatred*); hence or cogn. **fer'vency** *n.*, ~LY[2] *adv.* [ME f. OF, f. L *fervēre* boil; see -ENT]

fer'vĭd *a.* **1.** Ardent, intense. **2.** (poet.) Hot, glowing. **3.** Hence ~LY[2] *adv.* [f. L *fervidus* (as prec.; see -ID[1])]

fer'vour (-*er*), ***fer'vor,** *n.* Glowing condition, intense heat; vehemence, passion, zeal. [ME f. OF, f. L *fervor -oris* (as FERVENT; see -OR)]

Fĕ'scĕnnine *a.* Obscene or scurrilous (songs, remarks, etc.). [f. L *Fescenninus* (*Fescennia* in Etruria, famous for scurrilous verse; see -INE[1])]

fĕ'scūe *n.* Small stick, teacher's pointer; grass of genus *Festuca*, valuable for pasture and fodder. [ME *festu(e)* f. OF *festu* f. Rom. **festucum* f. L *festuca* stalk, straw]

fĕss *v.i.* ~ (**up**), (colloq.) = CONFESS. [abbr.]

fĕsse *n.* (Her.) Horizontal stripe across middle of shield; **in ~**, arranged horizontally. [ME f. OF, f. L *fascia* band]

***fĕst** *n.* Festival or special occasion (*filmfest, shooting fest*). [G, = festival]

fĕ'stal *a.* Of a feast; engaging in holiday activities; gay; hence ~LY[2] *adv.* [OF, f. LL *festalis* (as FEAST; see -AL)]

fĕ'ster *v.* **1.** *v.i.* (Of wound or sore) become purulent or ulcerated; (of poison, disease, grief) cause suppuration, rankle; putrefy, rot. **2.** *v.t.* Cause festering in. [ME, f. obs. *fester* n. or OF *festrir*, f. OF *festre* f. L FISTULA]

fĕ'stĭval *n.* & *attrib. a.* **1.** *n.* Feast day, celebration, merry-making; periodic musical etc. performance(s) of special importance. **2.** *a.* Of a feast(-day). [n. f. a., ME f. OF, f. med. L *festivalis* (as foll.; see -AL)]

fĕ'stĭve *a.* Of a feast; joyous; fond of feasting, jovial; hence ~LY[2] (-vlĭ) *adv.* [f. L *festivus* (*festum*, as FEAST; see -IVE)]

fĕstĭ'vĭtȳ *n.* Gaiety, rejoicing; festive celebration, (in *pl.*) festive proceedings. [ME, f. OF *festivité* or f. L *festivitas* (as prec.; see -ITY)]

fĕstōō'n *n.*, & *v.t.* **1.** *n.* Chain of flowers or leaves, or ribbons etc., hung in curve between two points; carved or moulded ornament representing this. **2.** *v.t.* Adorn (as) with or form into festoons. **3.** Hence ~ERY (5) *n.* [f. F *feston* f. It. *festone* (*festa* FEAST; see -OON)]

Fĕ'stschrĭft (-shr-) *n.* (*pl.* **~en** *or* **~s**). Collection of writings presented to scholar to mark an occasion in his life. [G, = festival-writing]

fĕtch[1] *v.* & *n.* **1.** *v.t.* & *i.* (Go for and) bring back (person or thing; (*go and*) *fetch a doctor*); FAR[1]-*fetched*; ~ **and carry,** run backwards and forwards with things, be a mere servant; *fetch a* COMPASS[1]; ~ **up,** come to rest. **2.** *v.t.* Cause to come, draw forth, (blood, tears; ~ **up,** vomit); bring in, realize, be sold for, (a price); heave (sigh), draw (breath); deal (blow; usu. w. ind. obj., *fetch him a box on the ears*). **3.** Move feelings of, delight, whence ~'ING[2] *a.*; irritate. **4.** *n.* Act of fetching; dodge, trick; (Naut.) line of continuous extent of water from point to point, e.g. of a bay or of open sea. [OE *fecc(e)an* var. of *fetian*, prob. cogn. w. *fatian*, OHG *fazzōn* grasp]

fĕtch[2] *n.* Person's wraith or double. [18th c.; orig. unkn.]

fête (fāt) *n.*, & *v.t.* **1.** *n.* Festival, great entertainment, (**~-day,** appointed for fête); saint's day; bazaar-like function to raise money for charity. **2.** *v.t.* Entertain, make much of, (person). [f. F *fête* (as FEAST)]

fête champêtre (fāt shahṅpā'tr) *n.* Outdoor entertainment, rural festival. [F (as prec., *champêtre* rural)]

fĕ'tĭd, foe'tĭd (fē'-), *a.* Stinking; hence ~LY[2] *adv.*, ~NESS *n.* [f. L *fetidus* (*fetēre* stink; see -ID[1])]

fĕ'tĭsh *n.* Inanimate object worshipped by primitive peoples for its supposed inherent magical powers or as being inhabited by a spirit; principle etc. irrationally reverenced; (Psych.) abnormal stimulus, or object, of sexual desire; hence ~ISM (3), ~IST (2), *ns.*, **~ĭ'stic** *a.* [f. F *fétiche* f. Port. *feitiço* charm, orig. adj. = made by art, f. L *factitius* FACTITIOUS]

fĕ'tlŏck *n.* Part of horse's leg where tuft of hair grows behind pastern-joint. [ME *fet(e)lak* etc. corresp. to MHG *vizzeloch*; rel. to G *fessel* & Gmc **fet-* f. IE **ped-*; cf. FOOT[1]]

fē'tor *n.* Stench. [L (as FETID; see -OR)]

fĕ'tter *n.*, & *v.t.* **1.** *n.* Shackle for the feet; bond, (in *pl.*) captivity; check, restraint; **~lock,** (heraldic representation of) D-shaped fetter for tethering horse by leg. **2.** *v.t.* Bind (as) with fetters; impede, restrain. [OE *feter*, = OS *feteros*, OHG *fezzera*, ON *fjöturr* f. Gmc **feterō*, **feteraz* (**fet-*; cf. FOOT[1])]

fĕ'ttle *n.*, & *v.t.* **1.** *n.* Condition, trim, (*in good, fine*, etc. *fettle*). **2.** *v.t.* Trim, clean, (rough edge of metal casting, pottery before firing, etc.). [n. f. v., f. dial. n. = girdle, f. OE *fetel*, OHG *fezzil* chain, ON *fetill* bandage f. Gmc **fatilaz* (**fat-* hold)]

***fē'tus.** See FOETUS.

feu *n.*, & *v.t.* (Sc.) **1.** *n.* Perpetual lease at fixed rent; piece of land so held. **2.** *v.t.* Grant (land) on feu. [OF (see FEE)]

feud[1] *n.*, & *v.i.* **1.** *n.* Lasting mutual hostility (*be at feud with*), esp. between two tribes, families, etc., with murderous assaults in revenge for previous injury. **2.** *v.i.* Conduct feud, whence *~'IST (1) *n.* [ME *fede*, f. OF *feide*, *fede* f. MDu., MLG *vēde* = OHG *fēhida*, OE *fǣhthu* enmity f. Gmc **faihithō* (**faih-*; cf. FOE)]

feud[2] *n.* Feudal benefice, territory held in fee, fief. [f. med. L *feudum* (see FEE)]

feu'dal *a.* Of a feud or fief; ~ **system,** medieval European form of government based on relation of vassal and superior arising from holding of lands in FEUD[2]; of, resembling, according to, this system; hence ~ISM (3), ~IST (2), *ns.*, **~ĭ'stic** *a.*, ~IZE (3) *v.t.*, ~LY[2] *adv.* [f. med. L *feudalis*, *feodalis* (*feudum*, *feodum* FEE 1, perh. f. Gmc; see -AL)]

feudă'lĭtў *n.* Feudal system or principles; feudal holding, fief. [f. F *féodalité* (*féodal* f. as prec.; see -ITY)]

feu'datorў *a.* & *n.* **1.** *a.* Feudally subject *to*, under overlordship. **2.** *n.* Feudal vassal. [f. med. L *feudatorius* f. *feudare* enfeoff (as FEUD²; see -ATE³, -ORY)]

feu de joie (fẽrdezhwah') *n.* Salute by firing rifles etc. on ceremonial occasion. [F, = fire of joy]

feuilleton (fẽr'yetawṅ) *n.* (Part of newspaper etc. devoted to) fiction, criticism, light literature, etc. [F, = leaflet]

fē'ver *n.*, & *v.t.* **1.** *n.* (Path.) Abnormally high temperature with excessive change and destruction of tissues; disease so characterized (*scarlet, typhoid, fever*); nervous excitement, agitation; ~ **heat,** high temperature of body in fever, (fig.) fever pitch; ~ **pitch,** state of abnormal excitement; ~ **therapy,** treatment of disease by artificially causing fever. **2.** *v.t.* Throw into fever; affect with fever (*fevered brow*). [f. OE *fēfor* & f. AF *fevre*, OF *fievre* f. L *febris*]

fē'verfew *n.* Feathery-leaved herb (*Chrysanthemum parthenium*) formerly used as febrifuge. [f. OE *feferfuge* f. L *febrifuga* (as FEBRIFUGE)]

fē'verĭsh *a.* Having symptoms of fever; excited, fitful, restless; (of place) infested by fever, feverous; hence ~LY² *adv.*, ~NESS *n.* [ME, f. FEVER + -ISH¹]

fē'verous *a.* Infested with or apt to cause fever; (arch.) feverish. [ME, f. FEVER + -OUS]

few *a.* & *n.* **1.** Not many (*few words, only a few words; man of few* WORD¹*s; many are called but few are chosen; visitors are few*); **every** ~ *days* etc., once in every small group of days etc.; **in** ~, (arch.) in few words, briefly; **not a** ~, a considerable number; **the** ~, the minority, the elect, etc.; hence ~'NESS *n.* **2.** **A** ~, some, not none, (*a few words should be added; a few of his friends were there*); **a good** ~, (colloq.) a fairly large number; **have a** ~, (colloq.) take several alcoholic drinks; **some** ~, some but not at all many. [OE *fēawe, fēawa,* = OS, OHG *fao*, ON *fár*, Goth. pl. *fawai* f. Gmc **faw-* f. IE **pau-*]

fey (fā) *a.* (Sc.) fated to die, at point of death; disordered in mind (often with over-confidence etc.) like person about to die; clairvoyant, other-worldly; elfin; whimsical; hence ~'NESS *n.* [OE *fǣge,* = OS *fēgi*, OHG *feigi*, ON *feigr* f. Gmc **faigjaz*]

fĕz *n.* (*pl.* **~'zes**). Muslim man's flat-topped conical red cap with tassel; hence ~ZED² (-zd) *a.* [Turk., perh. f. *Fez* in Morocco]

ff. *abbr.* folios; following pages etc.; fortissimo.

fia'cre (fēah'kr) *n.* Small four-wheeled cab. [f. the Hôtel de St. *F*~, Paris]

fiancé (fēah'ṅsā) *n.* (*fem.* **~e** *pr.* same). Person who is betrothed to another (esp. *my, your,* etc., *fiancé*). [F, p.p. of *fiancer* betroth f. OF *fiance* a promise]

fianchĕ'ttō *n.* (*pl.* **~es**), & *v.t.* (Chess). Develop(ment of) bishop on long diagonal of board. [It., dim. of *fianco* FLANK]

fiă'scō *n.* (*pl.* **~s**). Failure or breakdown (orig. in dramatic etc. performance); ignominious result. [It., = bottle (w. unexplained allusion); see FLASK]

fī'ăt (*or -at*) *n.* Authorization; decree, order; *~ **money,** inconvertible paper-money made legal tender by Government decree. [L, = let it be done]

fĭb *n.*, & *v.i.* (**-bb-**). (Tell) trivial or venial lie; hence ~'**b**ER¹, ~'STER, *ns.* [perh. f. obs. *fible-fable* nonsense, redupl. of FABLE¹]

***fī'ber.** See FIBRE.

Fibona'ccĭ (fēbonah'chĭ) *n.* ~ **numbers, series,** (in which each is the sum of the two preceding, esp. 1, 1, 2, 3, 5, 8, etc.). [f. L. ~, Tuscan mathematician *c.* 1200]

fī'bre (-ber), ***fī'ber,** *n.* **1.** Threadlike cell or filament forming with others animal or vegetable tissue or textile substance; threadlike piece of glass etc. (~ **optics,** transmission of images through glass etc. fibres by total internal reflection). **2.** Substance consisting of fibres; substance that can be spun, woven, or felted. **3.** Fibrous structure; structure, grain, character, (*lacks moral fibre; man of coarse fibre*). **4.** **~board,** building material made of wood or other plant fibres compressed into boards; **~glass,** (1) fibrous glass woven as fabric or used as insulator etc., (2) plastic containing this. **5.** Hence **(-)fī'br**ED², ***(-)fī'ber**ED², (-berd), ~LESS (-erl-), **fī'brĭ**FORM, **fī'br**OUS, *adjs.* [ME f. F, f. L *fibra*]

fī'brĭl *n.* Small fibre; subdivision of fibre; ultimate subdivision of root; hence ~LAR, ~LARY¹, *adjs.* [f. mod. L *fibrilla* dim. of L *fibra* fibre]

fī'brĭll|āte *v.* **1.** *v.i.* (Of fibre) split up into fibrils; (of muscle, esp. in heart) undergo quivering movement in fibrils. **2.** *v.t.* Break (fibre) into fibrils. **3.** Hence ~A'TION *n.* [f. as prec. + -ATE³]

fī'brĭn *n.* Insoluble protein formed in blood-clotting from the soluble blood-plasma protein **fībrĭ'no**GEN *n.*; hence ~OID *n.*, substance with same staining-behaviour as fibrin. [f. FIBRE + -IN]

fī'brō *n.* (*pl.* **~s**). (Austral.) (House constructed mainly of) fibro-cement. [abbr.]

fī'brō- *comb. form.* Fibre (‖**~-cement,** mixture of asbestos and cement used in sheets for building etc.); fibrous tissue. [f. FIBRE + -O-]

fī'broid *a.* & *n.* **1.** *a.* (esp. Path.) Of or characterized by fibrous structure or appearance. **2.** *n.* Fibroid uterine tumour. [f. FIBRE + -OID]

fī'brōĭn *n.* Chemical substance of which silk (etc.) mainly consists. [f. FIBRO- + -IN]

fībrō'ma *n.* (*pl.* **~s** *or* **~ta**). Fibrous tumour. [mod. L, f. L *fibra* fibre + -OMA (2)]

fībrō's|ĭs *n.* (*pl.* **~es** *pr.* -ēz). (Path.) Development of excessive fibrous tissue; hence **fībro**'TIC *a.* [mod. L, f. L *fibra* fibre + -OSIS]

fībrosī'tĭs *n.* Rheumatic painful inflammation or disorder of fibrous tissue; hence **fībrosĭ'**TIC *a.* [mod. L (*fibrosus* FIBROUS; see -ITIS)]

fī'brous. See FIBRE.

fĭ'būl|a *n.* (*pl.* **~ae** *or* **~as**). (Anat.) Outer and usu. smaller of two bones from knee to ankle; (Ant.) brooch or clasp; hence ~AR¹ *a.* [L, perh. cogn. w. *figere* fix]

-fĭc *suf.* forming (usu. w. intermediate -I-) *adjs.* w. sense 'producing, making' (*beatific, horrific, malefic, pacific, scientific*); hence ~FICALLY *adv. suf.* [f. or after F *-fique* or L *-ficus* (*facere* make)]

-fĭcā'tion *suf.* forming (usu. w. intermediate -I-) *ns.* of action etc. (cf. -ATION) f. *vbs.* in -FY (*acidification, beautification, purification*). [f. or after F, or L *-ficatio -onis* (*-ficare*; see -FY)]

fiche (fēsh) *n.* (*pl.* same). = MICRO*fiche*. [F, = slip of paper]

fĭ'chu (-shōō) *n.* Woman's small triangular shawl of lace etc. for shoulders and neck. [F]

fĭ'ckle *a.* Inconstant, changeable; hence ~NESS (-keln-) *n.*, **fĭ'ck**LY² *adv.* [OE *ficol*; cf. *befician* deceive, *fǣcne* deceitful, -LE 1]

fĭ'ctĭle *a.* Made of earth or clay by potter; of pottery. [f. L *fictilis* (*fingere fict-* fashion; see -IL)]

fĭ'ction *n.* Feigning, invention; thing feigned or imagined, invented statement or narrative; literature consisting of such narrative, esp. novels, whence ~EER', ~IST (3), *ns.*; conventionally accepted falsehood (esp. LEGAL, *polite, fiction*); hence ~AL *a.*, ~al1ZE (3) *v.t.* [ME f. OF, f. L *fictio -onis* (as prec.; see -ION)]

fĭctĭ'tious (-shus) *a.* Counterfeit, not genuine; (of name or character) assumed; imaginary, unreal; of or in novels; regarded as what it is called by legal or conventional fiction; hence ~LY[2] *adv.*, ~NESS *n.* [f. L *ficticius* (as FICTILE; see -ITIOUS[1])]

fĭ'ctĭve *a.* Creating or created by imagination; not genuine. [f. F *fictif -ive* or f. med. L *fictivus* (as FICTILE; see -IVE)]

fĭd *n.* **1.** (Naut.) Conical wooden pin used in splicing; square wooden or iron bar to support topmast. **2.** Small thick piece or wedge or heap of anything. [17th c.; orig. unkn.]

||**Fid. Def.** *abbr.* Defender of the Faith. [f. L *Fidei Defensor*]

fĭ'ddle *n.* & *v.* **1.** *n.* (colloq. or derog.) Violin; **fit as a ~**, in good condition and spirits; **hang up** one's **~ when** one **comes home,** be witty only when away from home; **face as long as a ~**, dismal face; **play first, second, ~**, take leading, subordinate, position. **2.** Other instrument of viol family; (Naut.) contrivance for stopping things from rolling or sliding off table in bad weather. **3.** (sl.) Piece of cheating, swindle. **4. ~-back,** fiddle-shaped back of chair or front of chasuble; **~-de-dee'** *int.* & *n.*, nonsense; **~-head,** scroll-like carving at ship's bows; **~ pattern** (of spoons and forks with fiddle-shaped handles); **~stick,** bow for fiddle, (usu. in *pl.*, as *int.*) nonsense! **5.** *v.i.* & *t.* Play the fiddle, play (tune etc.) on fiddle; be idle or frivolous, make aimless movements, (*about, at, with*, etc.); (sl.) cheat, swindle, falsify, get by cheating. [OE *fithele*, = OHG *fidula*, ON *fithla* f. Gmc **fithula* f. Rom. **vitula* VIOL]

fĭ'ddle-făddle *n.*, *a.*, *v.i.*, & *int.* **1.** *n.* Trifling or trivial matter(s). **2.** *a.* (Of person or thing) petty, fussy. **3.** *v.i.* Fuss, trifle. **4.** *int.* Nonsense! [redupl. of prec.]

fĭ'ddler *n.* Player on fiddle (**F~'s Green,** sailor's Elysium); (sl.) swindler, cheat; small crab of genus *Uca*, the male having one large claw held in position like violinist's arm. [OE *fithelere* (as prec.; see -ER[1])]

fĭ'ddlĭng *a.* In vbl senses; petty; futile, contemptible, inconsiderable. [f. FIDDLE + -ING[2]]

fĭ'ddlȳ *a.* (colloq.) Awkward or tiresome to do or use. [f. FIDDLE + -Y[2]]

fī'dė|ism *n.* Doctrine that knowledge depends on faith or revelation; so ~IST (2) *n.*, **~ĭ'stic** *a.* [f. L *fides* faith + -ISM]

Fĭdĕ'l|ĭsm *n.* = CASTROISM; hence ~IST (2) *n.* [f. Sp. *Fidelismo* (*Fidel* Castro Ruz; see -ISM)]

fĭdĕ'lĭtȳ *n.* Faithfulness, loyalty, (*to*); strict conformity to truth or fact; exact correspondence to the original; (Radio etc.) precision of reproduction (HIGH *fidelity*); **~ insurance** (by employer against losses by employees' fault). [f. F *fidélité* or f. L *fidelitas* (see FEALTY)]

fĭ'dgėt[1] *n.* **1.** (in *sing.* or *pl.*) Bodily uneasiness seeking relief in spasmodic movements; restless mood. **2.** One who fidgets or causes others to; act of bustling etc. **3.** Hence ~Y[2] *a.* [sense 1 f. obs. or dial. *fidge* to twitch; sense 2 f. foll.]

fĭ'dgėt[2] *v.* **1.** *v.i.* Move restlessly (*about*); be uneasy, worry. **2.** *v.t.* Make uncomfortable, worry, (person). [f. prec.]

Fī'dō *n.* Device for enabling aircraft to land by dispersing fog by means of petrol-burners on ground. [f. initials of *Fog Investigation Dispersal Operation*]

fĭdū'cial (-shal) *a.* **~ line, point,** etc., (Surv., Astron., etc.) one assumed as fixed basis of comparison. [f. LL *fiducialis* (*fiducia* trust f. *fidere* to trust; see -AL)]

fĭdū'ciarȳ (-sherĭ) *a.* & *n.* **1.** *a.* Of trust or trustee(ship); held or given in trust; (of paper currency) depending for its value on public confidence or securities. **2.** *n.* Trustee. [f. L *fiduciarius* (as prec.; see -ARY[1])]

fidus Achates (fīdus akā'tēz) *n.* Faithful friend, devoted follower. [L, = faithful Achates (companion of Aeneas in Virgil's 'Aeneid')]

fie *int.* expr. disgust or pretence of outraged propriety. [ME, f. OF f. L *fi* excl. of disgust at stench]

fief (fēf) *n.* = FEUD[2]; one's sphere of operation or control; hence ~'DOM *n.* [F, f. as FEE]

field *n.* & *v.* **1.** *n.* (Piece of) ground, esp. one used for pasture or tillage, and usu. bounded by hedges etc.; tract abounding in some natural product (*coalfield, diamond field, gas field, oilfield*); = AIR[1]*field*, playing-field, etc. **2.** Ground on which battle is fought, battlefield (lit., or fig., *left his rival in possession of the field*; **a fair ~ and no favour,** equal conditions in contest; **hold the ~**, not be superseded); scene of campaign (**in the ~**, campaigning, (fig.) working etc. outside headquarters, laboratory, etc.; **take, keep, the ~**, begin, continue, campaign); battle. **3.** Ground for playing cricket, football, etc.; part of this as area of attack or defence; player(s) stationed in such area; players or partakers in outdoor contest or sport; all competitors or all except specified one(s) (**a good ~**, many and good competitors; ***play the ~**, (colloq.) avoid exclusive commitment to one person etc.); (Cricket) side not batting, one of this side (LONG[1] *field*). **4.** Large stretch, expanse, of sea, sky, ice, snow, etc., (lit., or fig., *the whole field of history*). **5.** (Her.) surface of escutcheon or of one of its divisions; groundwork of picture, coin, flag, etc. **6.** Area or sphere of operation, observation, intellectual activities, etc., (*each supreme in his own field; filled the field of the telescope; field of view; wide field of vision*); region of electric, gravitational, magnetic, etc., influence, presence of such influence, force exerted by it on standard object. **7.** *attrib.* (Of animal etc.) found in the open country (*field-mouse*); carried out in the natural environment (*field test*); (of artillery etc.) light and mobile for use with armies in the field. **8. ~-book** (used in field by surveyor for technical notes); **~ boot** (knee-length and close-fitting); **~-cornet,** magistrate of township in Cape Province etc.; **~-day,** (Mil.) manœuvring-exercise or review, (fig.) great occasion, important debate, great triumph; **~ events,** athletic sports such as weight-putting, jumping, discus-throwing, etc. (i.e. other than races); **~-glasses,** binocular telescope for outdoor use; **~ goal,** (Amer. Footb., Basketball) goal scored when ball is in normal play; ***~ hockey,** = HOCKEY; **~ hospital,** temporary hospital near battlefield; ||**F~ Marshal,** army officer of highest rank; **~ mustard,** charlock; **~ officer, ~ rank,** (rank of) army officer above captain and below general; **~'sman** (-z-), (Cricket & Baseball) member of side not batting; **~ sports,** outdoor sports, esp. hunting, shooting, fishing; **~ telegraph** (movable kind for use on campaign); **~-work,** (1) temporary fortification, (2) outdoor work of surveyor, collector of scientific data, sociologist, etc.; so **~-worker. 9.** *v.i.* Act as fieldsman in cricket, baseball, etc. **10.** *v.t.* Stop (and return) (ball); put (football team etc.) into the field; (fig.) deal with (succession of questions etc.). **11.** Hence ~'ER[1] *n.*, ~'WARD(s) *adv.* [OE *feld*, = OS, OHG *feld* f. WG **felthu*]

fie'ldfāre *n.* Species of thrush (*Turdus pilaris*) spending winter, not summer, in Britain etc. [ME *feldefare*, perh. f. as FIELD + FARE[2]]

fiend *n.* *The* Devil; evil spirit, demon; person of superhuman wickedness, esp. cruelty; person causing mischief or annoyance; (w. qualifying wd) devotee or addict (*fresh-air fiend, dope fiend, camera fiend*); hence ~'ISH[1], ~'LIKE, *adjs.* [OE *fēond*, = OS *fīond*, OHG *fīant*, ON *fjándi*, Goth. *fijands* part. of Gmc **fijējan* hate; cf. FRIEND]

fierce *a.* Violent in hostility, angrily combative; raging, vehement; (of mechanism) violent, not smooth or easy in action; ardent, eager; unpleasantly strong or intense; hence ~′LY² (-slĭ) *adv.*, ~′NESS (-sn-) *n.* [ME, f. AF *fers*, OF *fiers* *fier* proud f. L *ferus* savage]

fieri fā′ciăs (-shĭ-) *n.* (Law). Writ to sheriff for executing judgement. [L, = cause to be made]

fier′ȳ (fīr′ĭ) *a.* Consisting of or flaming with fire (~ **cross,** wooden cross charred or set on fire as rallying-signal in Scotland or *intimidating symbol); (of arrow etc.) fire-bearing; looking like fire, blazing-red; (of eyes) flashing, ardent; hot as fire; acting like fire, producing burning sensation, inflaming, (*fiery taste*, *condiment*, etc.); eager, pugnacious, spirited, irritable; (of horse) mettlesome; (of gas, mine, etc.) inflammable, liable to explosions; (of cricket-pitch) making ball rise dangerously; hence **fier′ĭ**LY² *adv.*, **fier′ĭ**NESS *n.*, (fīr′-). [ME, f. FIRE¹ + -Y¹]

fiĕ′sta (fēĕ′-) *n.* Religious festival in Spanish-speaking countries; festivity, holiday. [Sp., = feast]

FIFA (fē′fa) *abbr.* International Football Federation. [f. F *Fédération Internationale de Football Association*]

fi. fa. *abbr.* fieri facias.

fīfe *n.* & *v.* **1.** *n.* Kind of small shrill flute used with drum in military music; its player. **2.** *v.i.* & *t.* Play the fife; play (air etc.) on the fife; hence **fī′f**ER¹ *n.* [f. G *pfeife* PIPE¹, or F *fifre* f. Swiss G *pfifre* piper]

fī′fe-rail (-fr-) *n.* (Naut.) Rail round mainmast with belaying-pins. [18th c., of unkn. orig.]

fĭftee′n (*or* fĭ′f-) *a.* & *n.* One more than fourteen; symbol for this (15, xv, XV); size etc. denoted by fifteen; (Rugby Footb.) side of fifteen players; **the F~**, Jacobite rebellion of 1715; hence ~TH² *a.* & *n.* [OE *fīftēne*, = OS *fīftein*, OHG *fimfzehan*, ON *fimtán*, Goth. *fimftaihun* (as FIVE, -TEEN)]

fĭfth *a.* & *n.* **1.** *a.* Next after fourth; ~ **part,** one of five equal parts into which thing is or might be divided. **2.** *n.* Fifth part, thing, etc.; (Mus.) interval of which the span involves five alphabetical notes, harmonic combination of notes thus separated; *(colloq.) (bottle containing) fifth of a gallon of liquor. **3.** ~ **column,** organized body sympathizing with and working for the enemy within a country at war etc. [f. Gen. Mola's ref. to such support in besieged Madrid 1936]; **~-co′lumnist,** member of fifth column, traitor, spy; ~ **day,** Thursday; *fifth* FORM¹ 6; **fifth* GRADE 1; **F~ Monarchy,** last of the five great empires (Dan. 2: 44); **F~-monarchy-man,** 17th-c. zealot expecting immediate second coming of Christ and repudiating all other government; **smite under the ~ rib,** (arch.) kill; ~ **wheel,** (1) extra wheel of coach, (2) superfluous person or thing, (3) horizontal turntable over front axle of carriage as extra support to prevent its tipping. **4.** Hence ~′LY² *adv.*, in the fifth place. [earlier & dial. *fift* f. OE *fīfta*, OS *fīfto*, OHG *fimfto*, ON *fimti* f. Gmc **fimfton* f. IE **penqto-*; assim. to *fourth*]

fĭ′ftȳ *a.* & *n.* **1.** Five times ten; symbol for this (50, l, L); set of fifty persons or things; (in *pl.*) numbers etc., esp. years of a century or life, from 50 to 59; large indefinite number (*have fifty things to tell you*); ~-~, half and half, equal shares (*go fifty-fifty*; *on a fifty-fifty basis*); hence **fĭ′ftĭ**ETH¹ *a.* & *n.*, ~FOLD *a.* & *adv.* **2.** **~-one** etc., (arch.) **one-and-~** etc., fifty plus one etc., w. corresp. ordinals **~-first** etc. [OE *fīftig*, = OS *fīftich*, OHG *fimzug*, ON *fimmtigr*, Goth. *fimftigjus* (as FIVE, -TY²)]

fĭg¹ *n.* **1.** ~**(-tree)**, broad-leaved tree, esp. *Ficus carica*, bearing soft pear-shaped many-seeded fruit eaten fresh or dried; fruit of this tree. **2.** Valueless thing (*don't care a fig for*; *a fig for—!*, as excl.). **3.** **~-bird,** Austral. oriole feeding on figs etc.; **~-leaf,** device for concealing something, esp. genitals (Gen. 3: 7); **~′wort,** brown-flowered herb of genus *Scrophularia*, formerly thought useful against scrofula. [ME, f. OF *figue* f. Prov. *fig(u)a* f. Rom. **fica* f. L *ficus*]

fĭg² *n.* Dress, equipment, (*in full fig*); condition, form, (*in fine* or *good fig*). [f. foll.]

fĭg³ *v.t.* (-gg-). ~ **out** or **up,** make (horse) lively; ~ **out,** dress up (person). [var. of obs. *feague* f. G *fegen*; see FAKE²]

fig. *abbr.* figure.

fīght¹ (fīt) *v.* (**fought** *pr.* fawt). **1.** *v.i.* Contend in war or battle or single combat (*against*, *with*; ~ **for,** fight on behalf of (person) or to secure (thing)); ~ **back,** resist; ~ **shy of,** be unwilling to approach (person, task, etc.); *that* COCK¹ *won't fight*. **2.** *v.t.* Maintain (cause, suit at law, quarrel) against opponent, contend over (question, election), make one's *way* by fighting; contend with in war or battle or duel, or with the fists; strive to overcome (disease, fire, fear, etc.); cause (cocks, dogs) to fight; handle (troops, ship) in battle; ~ **off,** repel with effort; ~ (dispute etc., or *it*) **out,** settle by fighting. [OE *feohtan*, = OS, OHG *fehtan* f. WG **fehtan*]

fīght² (fīt) *n.* Act of fighting; battle (**make a ~ of it, put up a ~**, offer resistance); combat, esp. unpremeditated, between two or more persons, animals, or parties (**running ~**, fight kept up while one party flees and one pursues; SHAM *fight*; STAND¹-*up fight*); boxing-match; (fig.) strife, conflict; appetite or ability for fighting (*has fight in him yet*; **show ~**, not yield tamely). [OE *feoht(e)* (as prec.)]

fī′ghter (fī′t-) *n.* In vbl senses; fast military aircraft designed mainly for aerial combat; **~-bomber,** aircraft serving as both fighter and bomber. [ME, f. FIGHT¹ + -ER¹]

fī′ghtĭng (fī′t-) *a.* & *n.* In vbl senses; *~ **chair,** fixed chair on boat for person catching large fish; ~ **chance,** opportunity of succeeding by great effort; *fighting* COCK¹; ~ **drunk,** (colloq.) drunk and quarrelsome; ~ **fish,** Siamese fish of genus *Betta*; ~ **fit,** fit enough to fight, at peak of fitness; ~ **fund,** money raised to support campaign etc.; ~ **mad,** furiously angry; **~-top,** (Naut.) circular gun-platform high on warship's mast; *in fighting* TRIM; ~ **words,** (colloq.) words indicating willingness to fight. [f. FIGHT¹ + -ING¹,²]

fĭ′gment *n.* Invented statement; thing that has no existence except in imagination. [ME, f. L *figmentum* (*fig-* see FIGURE¹, -MENT)]

figura (fĭgūr′a) *n.* Person or thing representing or symbolizing fact etc.; (Theol.) type of a person etc. [mod. L, f. L, = FIGURE¹]

fĭ′gūral *a.* Figurative; pertaining to figures or shapes; (Mus.) florid, with rapid repetitive accompaniment. [OF, or f. LL *figuralis* (*figura* FIGURE¹; see -AL)]

figurant (fĭ′gūrant) *n.* (*fem.* ***figurante***¹ *pr.* same). Ballet-dancer appearing only in a group. [F, part. of *figurer* FIGURE²]

figurant|e² (fĭgūră′ntĭ) *n.* (*pl.* **~i** *pr.* -ē). = prec. [It., part. of *figurare* FIGURE²]

fĭgūrā′tion *n.* Assignment to a certain form; the resulting form; shape, outline; allegorical representation; ornamentation by designs; (Mus.) use of florid counterpoint. [ME f. F, or f. L *figuratio* (as FIGURE²; see -ATION)]

fĭ′gūrative (*or* -ger-) *a.* Emblematic, typical; of pictorial or sculptural representation; metaphorical, not literal; metaphorically so called; abounding in or addicted to figures of speech;

hence ~LY² (-vlĭ) *adv.*, ~NESS (-vn-) *n.* [ME, f. LL *figurativus* (as prec.; see -ATIVE)]

fĭ'gure¹ (-*ger*) *n.* **1.** External form, shape; (Geom.) two-dimensional space enclosed by line(s) or three-dimensional space enclosed by surface(s), or any of the classes of these, as triangle, sphere; bodily shape (*has a well-developed figure*; **keep** one's ~, not grow stout). **2.** Person as seen (*saw a figure leaning against the door*; ~ **of fun,** grotesque person); person as contemplated mentally (*the most terrible figure in our history*; FATHER¹-*figure*; **public** ~, person known to many); conspicuous appearance (**make** or **cut a brilliant, poor,** etc., ~, produce such impression). **3.** Image, likeness; representation of human form, statue, person in picture, emblem, type, simile. **4.** Diagram, illustrative drawing; horoscope; decorative pattern (*figure in the* CARPET); evolution in dancing, division of set dance; (Skating) movement, series of movements, beginning and ending at centre. **5.** Numerical symbol, esp. one of the ten in Arabic notation (**double ~s,** number between 9 and 100; **three, four,** etc., **~s,** number between 99 and 1000, 999 and 10,000, etc., whence **three** etc. **-figure** *a.*; *figure of* EIGHT); number so expressed, amount of money, value; (in *pl.*) arithmetical calculations. **6.** ~ (**of speech**), recognized form of rhetorical expression giving variety, force, etc., esp. hyperbole or metaphor. **7.** (Gram.) Permitted deviation from rules of construction, e.g. ellipsis. **8.** (Logic). Particular form of syllogism according to position of middle term. **9.** (Mus.) Short succession of notes producing single impression, brief melodic or rhythmic formula out of which longer passages are developed. **10. ~-head,** (1) carving, usu. bust or full-length figure, over ship's cutwater, (2) nominal leader or president without real authority. **11.** Hence ~LESS (-gerl-) *a.* [ME f. OF, f. L *figura* (**fig-* st. of *fingere* fashion; see -URE)]

fĭ'gure² (-*ger*) *v.* **1.** *v.t.* Represent in diagram or picture; picture mentally, imagine; be symbol of, represent typically; embellish with pattern (*figured satin*) or (Mus.) figures; mark with numbers (*figured* BASS³) or prices; calculate; *understand, *ascertain; ~ **out,** work out by arithmetic, *estimate, *understand. **2.** *v.i.* Do arithmetic; make appearance, appear, be conspicuous; *(colloq.) be likely or understandable (*that figures*); *~ **on,** count on, expect. [ME, f. OF *figurer* f. L *figurare* (as prec.)]

fĭ'gūrine (-ēn) *n.* Statuette. [F, f. It. *figurina* dim. of *figura* FIGURE¹]

fĭ'lagree. Var. of FILIGREE.

fĭ'lament *n.* Slender threadlike body, fibre, (esp. in animal or vegetable structure); not easily fusible conducting wire or thread in electric bulb or thermionic valve, heated or made incandescent by current; (arch., of air, light, etc.) imaginary portion of stream, row of particles following each other; (Bot.) part of stamen that supports anther; hence ~ARY¹ (-ĕ'n-), ~ED², ~OUS (-ĕ'n-), *adjs.* [F, or f. mod. L *filamentum*, f. LL *filare* spin f. L *filum* thread; see -MENT]

fĭlar'ĭ|a *n.* (*pl.* **~ae**). Parasitic nematode worm introduced into the blood by certain flies and mosquitoes; hence ~AL *a.*, **fĭlarī'**ASIS *n.* [mod. L, f. L *filum* thread (see -AR¹, -IA¹)]

fĭ'lature *n.* (Establishment for) reeling silk from cocoons. [F, f. It. *filatura* (*filare* spin; see -URE)]

fĭ'lbert *n.* (Nut of) cultivated hazel. [ME *philliberd* etc. f. AF *philbert*, dial. F *noix de filbert*, nut ripe about St. Philibert's day (20 Aug.)]

fĭlch *v.t.* Steal, pilfer. [16th-c. thieves' sl., of unkn. orig.]

fīle¹ *n.*, & *v.t.* **1.** *n.* Instrument usu. of steel with roughened surface(s) for shaping or smoothing objects; (sl.) (esp. artful) person; **~-fish** (with skin like surface of file). **2.** *v.t.* Smooth or shape with file; elaborate to perfection (esp. literary work); ~ **away,** remove (roughness etc.) with file. [OE *fīl*, = OS, OHG *fila* f. WG **fīhalā*]

fīle² *n.*, & *v.t.* **1.** *n.* Stiff pointed wire on which documents etc. are run for keeping; folder etc. for holding papers arranged for reference; set of papers so kept, esp. in office, or in lawcourt referring to a cause; series of issues of a newspaper etc. in order; collection of records stored for use by computer. **2.** *v.t.* Place (papers) on file or among public records; submit (application for patent, petition for divorce, etc.) to appropriate authority; (of reporter) send (information, story, etc.) to newspaper. [f. F *fil* f. L *filum* thread]

fīle³ *n.*, & *v.i.* **1.** *n.* (Mil. etc.) Line of men one behind another (**single, Indian,** ~, arrangement of marchers etc. in file, with no two abreast); small detachment *of* men (now usu. two); row of persons or things one behind another; (Chess) line of squares from player to player (cf. RANK¹). **2.** *v.i.* March in file; ~ **off, away,** go off by files. [f. F *file* f. LL *filare* spin or f. L *filum* thread]

fĭ'lèmŏt *a.* & *n.* (arch.) Dead-leaf colour(ed), brownish yellow. [f. F *feuille morte* dead leaf]

fĭ'lèt *n.* Kind of net or lace with square mesh; fillet of meat. [F, = thread]

fĭ'lĭal *a.* Of or due from son or daughter; (Biol.) resulting from cross-breeding; hence ~LY² *adv.* [ME f. OF, or f. LL *filialis* (*filius* son, *filia* daughter; see -AL)]

fĭlĭā'tion *n.* Being child of specified parent(s); descent, transmission, (*from*); formation of offshoots; branch of a society or language; genealogical relation or arrangement. [F, f. LL *filiatio -onis* f. L *filius* son; see -ATION]

fĭ'lĭbĕg *n.* (Sc.) Kilt. [f. Gael. *feileadh-beag* little fold]

fĭ'lĭbŭster *n.*, & *v.i.* **1.** *n.* One who engages in unauthorized warfare against foreign State; *obstruction(ist) in legislative assembly, esp. by prolonged speaking. **2.** *v.i.* Act as filibuster; hence ~ER¹ *n.* [ult. f. Du. *vrijbuiter* FREEBOOTER, infl. by F *flibustier*, Sp. *filibustero*]

fĭ'lĭgree *n.* Ornamental work of gold or silver or copper as fine wire formed into delicate tracery, fine metal open-work; anything delicate resembling this; hence **fĭ'lĭgree**ED² *a.* [earlier *filigreen*, *filigrane* f. F *filigrane* f. It. *filigrana* (L *filum* thread, *granum* seed)]

fī'lĭng *n.* In vbl senses; (usu. in *pl.*) particle(s) rubbed off by file. [f. FILE¹ + -ING¹]

Fĭlĭpi'n|ō (-pē'-) *n.* (*pl.* **~os,** *fem.* **~a**) & *a.* (Native or inhabitant) of the Philippine Islands. [Sp., = Philippine]

fĭll *v.* & *n.* **1.** *v.t.* & *i.* Make or become full (*with*); (of sail) be distended by wind. **2.** *v.t.* Stock abundantly; occupy whole capacity or extent of, spread over, pervade, (~ **the bill,** do all that is required, suffice); (of dentist) block up (hollow tooth, cavity) with cement, amalgam, gold, etc.; satisfy, satiate, (esp. in *part.*, of food); (Poker etc.) complete (holding) by drawing necessary cards. **3.** Hold (position), discharge duties of (office); execute (order, commission, etc.); occupy (vacant time); appoint person to (vacant post). **4.** ~ **in,** add material to occupy space within (cavity, outline), add what is wanted to complete (unfinished document, blank cheque, etc.), find occupation during (time of inactivity), *(colloq.) inform (person) more fully, act as substitute; ~ **out,** enlarge, become enlarged, or plumper, to the proper limit, * = fill in (document etc.); ~ **up,** fill completely, provide what is needed to occupy vacant parts or places or deal with deficiencies in, fill in (document etc.), do away with (pond etc.) by filling, fill tank of motor car with petrol, become full; ~-*up* n., thing that fills up. **5.** *n.* As much as one wants of food etc. (*drink, have*, etc., one's *fill*; *weep her fill*); enough to fill something (*a fill of ink, tobacco*); earth etc. used to fill cavity. [OE *fyllan*, = OS *fullian*, OHG *fullen*, ON *fylla*, Goth. *fulljan* f. Gmc **fulljan* (**fullaz* FULL[1])]

fille (fē'ye) *n.* ~ ***de chambre*** (-de shah'nbr), (arch.) chamber-maid; ~ ***de joie*** (-de zhwah'), prostitute. [F, = daughter]

fi'ller *n.* In vbl senses; object or material used to fill cavity or increase bulk; ~ **cap** (closing filling-pipe leading to petrol tank of motor vehicle). [f. FILL + -ER[1]]

fi'llėt *n.*, & *v.t.* **1.** *n.* Headband, ribbon, string, or narrow band, for binding the hair or worn round head; band, bandage; thin narrow strip of anything. **2.** Fleshy boneless piece of meat from near loins or ribs; ~ **(steak),** undercut of sirloin; thick boneless half or quarter of fish. **3.** (Archit.) Narrow flat band separating two mouldings; small band between flutes of column. **4.** (Her.) Horizontal division of shield, quarter of CHIEF[1] in depth. **5.** Raised rim or ridge on any surface; plain line impressed on cover of book; added structure to round off interior angle. **6.** *v.t.* Bind (hair), provide (person for hair), with fillet; encircle with ornamental band; divide (meat, fish) into fillets; remove bones from (fish etc.). [ME f. OF *filet* f. Rom. dim. of L *filum* thread; see -ET[1]]

fi'lling *n.* In vbl senses; material used to fill tooth-cavity, sandwich, etc.; *weft; ~ **station,** establishment selling petrol etc. to motorists. [f. FILL + -ING[1]]

fi'llip *n.* & *v.* **1.** *n.* Sudden release of finger or thumb when it has been bent and checked by thumb or finger; slight smart stroke thus given; stimulus, incentive. **2.** *v.t.* Propel (coin, marble, etc.) with a fillip; stimulate (*fillip* one's *memory* or *wits*); strike slightly and smartly. **3.** *v.i.* Make a fillip. [imit.]

fi'llister *n.* Rabbet(ing-plane) for window-sashes etc. [19th c.; perh. f. F *feuilleret*]

fi'lly *n.* Young female horse (cf. COLT[1]); (sl.) young woman, esp. lively one. [ME, prob. f. ON *fylja* f. Gmc **fuljōn-* (as FOAL)]

film *n.* & *v.* **1.** *n.* Thin skin, sheet, coating, or layer. **2.** (Photog.) Coating of emulsion on plastic or other support in form of sheet or rolled strip, single roll of this; **~'setting,** (Print.) photographic composing; **~-strip,** series of transparencies for projection, esp. in teaching. **3.** Story, drama, episode, etc., recorded on cinematographic film and shown in cinemas etc.; (in *pl.*) the cinema industry; **~-goer,** one who frequents the cinema; ~ **star,** star actor or actress in films; hence **~ŏ'**GRAPHY *n.*, list of films by one director etc. or on one subject, ~'IC *a.* **4.** Dimness or morbid growth affecting eyes; slight veil of haze etc.; fine thread or filament. **5.** Hence ~'Y[2] *a.* **6.** *v.t.* & *i.* Cover or become covered (as) with film; photograph (scene etc., or abs.) for the cinema; make cinema film of (book etc., or abs.); be (well or ill) suited for reproduction on film. [OE *filmen* membrane = OFris. *filmene* skin, f. WG **filminja* ult. f. **fellam* FELL[1]]

fi'loselle *n.* Floss silk. [F]

fils (fēs) *n.* The son, junior, (appended to name to distinguish between father and son of same names; cf. PÈRE). [F, = son]

fi'lter *n.* & *v.* **1.** *n.* Device for freeing liquids from suspended matter, esp. by passing them through unsized paper or stratum of sand, charcoal, etc.; screen for absorbing light of some or all colours, or X-rays etc.; (Electr.) circuit that attenuates signals outside specified frequency range; arrangement for filtering of traffic. **2.** **~-bed,** tank or pond containing layer of sand etc. for filtering large quantities of liquid; **~-paper,** porous paper for filtering; **~-tip,** (cigarette) having filter at mouth end to purify the smoke. **3.** *v.t.* & *i.* Pass (liquid, electrical signal, etc.) or flow through filter; make way gradually *through, into*, etc., percolate, (of news etc.) leak *out* or come *through*; (of road traffic) join traffic coming from another direction at junction, esp. when other traffic from one's own direction has to stop; ~ **out,** separate or hold back (as) by filtering. **4.** Hence ~ABLE *a.*, (esp., of virus) able to pass through a filter that retains bacteria. [f. F *filtre* f. med. L *filtrum* f. WG **filtir* FELT[1] (earliest filters being of felt)]

filth *n.* Loathsome dirt; corruption, vileness, pollution, obscenity; foul language. [OE *fylth*, = OS *fūlitha*, OHG *fūlida* (as FOUL, -TH[1])]

fi'lth|y̆ *a.* & *adv.* **1.** *a.* Loathsomely dirty; vile; obscene; (of weather) very unpleasant; **~y lucre,** dishonourable gain (Tit. 1:11), (joc.) money; hence ~ĭLY[2] *adv.*, ~ĭNESS *n.* **2.** *adv.* Filthily (*filthy dirty, rich*). [ME, f. prec. + -Y[2]]

fi'ltrable. Var. of FILTERABLE.

fi'ltrāte[1] *n.* Filtered liquid. [f. as foll. + -ATE[1] (5)]

fi'ltr|āte[2] *v.t.* & *i.* = FILTER 3; so ~A'TION *n.* [f. mod. L *filtrare* (f. as FILTER) + -ATE[3]]

fi'mbrĭate, fi'mbrĭātėd, *adjs.* **1.** (Bot. & Zool.) Fringed, bordered with hairs etc. **2.** (Her.) Having a narrow border. [f. L *fimbriatus* (*fimbriae* fringe); see -ATE[2], -ED[1]]

fin *n.* & *v.* **(-nn-). 1.** *n.* Organ for propelling and steering, growing on fish and cetaceans at various parts of body (*anal, caudal, dorsal, pectoral, ventral*, etc., *fin*); underwater swimmer's rubber flipper. **2.** Sharp lateral projection on share or coulter of plough; small projecting surface on aircraft or rocket for ensuring stability; similar projection on other devices to improve heat transfer etc.; projecting attachment on motor car (esp. *tail-fin*). **3.** **~-back,** ~ **whale,** rorqual. **4.** *v.t.* Provide with fins. **5.** *v.i.* Swim under water. **6.** Hence (-)~NED[2] (-nd), ~'LESS, *adjs.* [OE *fin(n)*, = MLG *finne*, MDu. *vinne*]

fi'nable. See FINE[1].

fĭnā'gle *v.i.* & *t.* (colloq.) Act or obtain dishonestly or by trickery. [f. dial. *fainaigue* cheat]

fi'nal *a.* & *n.* **1.** *a.* At the end, coming last, ultimate (~ **drive,** last part of transmission system in motor vehicle); putting an end to doubt, conclusive, definitive, unalterable. **2.** Concerned with the purpose or end aimed at (~ **cause,** ultimate purpose of a thing; ~ **clause,** (Gram.) one expressing purpose, introduced by *in order that, lest*, etc.). **3.** Hence ~LY[2] *adv.* **4.** Last or deciding heat or game in sports or competition (CUP[1] *Final*), whence ~IST *n.*, competitor in this; (in *sing.* or *pl.*) last of a series of examinations; edition of newspaper published latest in the day; (Mus.) principal note in any mode. [ME f. OF, or f. L *finalis* (*finis* end; see -AL)]

fina'lė (-nah'-) (Mus.) last movement of instrumental composition, piece of music closing act in opera; close of drama etc.; conclusion. [It., f. as prec.]

fi'nalism *n.* Doctrine that natural evolution etc. is directed towards some goal; so **finalĭ'st**IC *a.* [f. FINAL + -ISM]

fīnă'lĭtў *n.* Quality or fact of being final; belief that something is final; final act, state, or utterance; principle of final cause viewed as operative in the universe. [f. F *finalité* f. LL *finalitas -tatis* (as FINAL; see -ITY)]

fī'nalīz|e, -is|e (-īz), *v.t.* Complete, bring to an end; put in final form; approve final form or details of; hence ~A'TION *n.* [f. FINAL + -IZE]

fĭnă'nce (*or* fī'-) *n.*, & *v.t.* **1.** *n.* (in *pl.*) Money resources of State, company, or person. **2.** Management of (esp. public) money, science of revenue; money support for an undertaking; **~ company, house,** company mainly concerned with providing money for hire-purchase transactions. **3.** *v.t.* Provide with money, esp. capital. [ME f. OF (*finer* settle debt f. *fin* end; see FINE¹, -ANCE)]

fĭnă'ncial (-shal) *a.* Of revenue or money matters (*financial* YEAR); (Austral. & N.Z. sl.) possessing money; hence ~LY² *adv.* [f. prec. + -IAL]

fĭnă'ncĭer¹ *n.* One skilled in establishing and managing public funds; capitalist. [F (as FINANCE; see -IER)]

fĭnăncier'² *v.i.* (usu. derog.) Conduct financial operations. [f. prec.]

fĭnch *n.* Small passerine bird esp. of genus *Fringilla* (usu. w. defining wd: BULL¹*finch*, GOLD*finch*). [OE *finc*, = OHG *finc(h)o* f. WG **finki, *finkjo(n)*]

find *v.t.* (**found**), & *n.* **1.** *v.t.* Become aware of or get possession of by chance (*was found dead; we find St. John saying; found a treasure*); (sl.) steal. **2.** Obtain, receive; **~ favour,** prove acceptable; ~ one's **feet,** get the use of them, develop one's powers. **3.** Recognize as present, acknowledge or discover to be so-and-so, (*I find no sense in it, find the terms reasonable; woke to find myself in hospital; found herself agreeing to this absurd idea; word is not found in the Bible*); **must take us as you ~ us,** put up with us as we are; **how do you ~ yourself?** how are you? **4.** Discover by trial to be or do or (*that*) or *to* (*has been found inadequate; finds rest agreeable; is found to pay; I find it pays, pay,* or *to pay,* or *that it pays; find it impossible* or *necessary to reply* etc.); discover by search; discover (game, or abs.) in hunting; reach by natural or normal process (*water finds its own level*). **5.** Succeed in obtaining (money, bail, sureties; *can't find time to read; found courage to protest* etc.; *find it in* one's HEART (*to* do); *find expression, place, vent*); (arch.) reach the conscience of; ascertain by study or calculation or inquiry (~ one's **way to,** contrive to reach, arrive at; ~ **its way,** be brought or get *into* etc.). **6.** (Law, of jury etc.) determine and declare (*it*, i.e. the offence, *murder*; person *guilty* etc.; *that* or abs.). **7.** Supply, provide, furnish; **~ in,** provide with (*they found him in clothes*); **all found,** (of servants' wages) with board and lodging provided free. **8.** ~ **oneself,** (1) provide for one's own needs, (2) discover one's vocation; **~ out,** discover, devise, solve, detect in offence. **9.** Hence ~'ABLE *a.* **10.** *n.* Finding of fox; discovery of treasure, minerals, etc.; thing found; person who comes usefully to notice; **~-spot,** (Archaeol.) place where object is found. [OE *findan*, = OS, OHG *findan*, ON *finna*, Goth. *finthan* f. Gmc **finthan*]

fī'nder *n.* In vbl senses; small telescope attached to large one to locate object for observation; viewfinder of camera; **~s keepers,** (colloq.) whoever finds a thing is entitled to keep it. [f. prec. + -ER¹]

fin de siècle (făňdesyā'kl) *a.* Characteristic of end of nineteenth century; decadent. [F, = end of century]

fī'ndĭng *n.* In vbl senses; conclusion reached by judicial or other inquiry; *(in *pl.*) small parts or tools used by workmen. [f. FIND + -ING¹]

fīne¹ *n.*, & *v.t.* **1.** *n.* Sum of money fixed as penalty for offence; (Hist.) sum of money paid by incoming tenant in consideration of only small rent. **2. In ~,** to sum up, finally, in short. **3.** *v.t.* Punish by a fine (*fined him £5*); hence **fī'nABLE** *a.* [ME, f. OF *fin* f. med. L *finis* sum paid on settling lawsuit (L *finis* end)]

fīne² *a., n., adv.,* & *v.* **1.** *a.* Of high quality; clear, pure, refined, (of gold or silver) containing specified proportion of pure metal; delicate, subtle, exquisitely fashioned, (of feelings) refined, elevated. **2.** Of slender thread, in small particles, thin, sharp (*not to put too fine a* POINT¹ *on it*), (of pen) narrow-pointed; (Cricket) behind wicket and near ball's line of flight; (of print) small-sized (cf. SMALL *print*); **cut** or **run it ~,** allow only minimum margin, time, amount, etc. **3.** Capable of delicate perception or discrimination; perceptible only with difficulty (*a fine distinction*). **4.** Excellent, of striking merit, good, satisfactory, fortunate, of good effect, (*had fine sport; has been a fine thing for him*; (iron.) *a fine friend you have been!, all very fine, but . . .*); well conceived or expressed; of handsome appearance or size, dignified, (*fine potatoes; a man of fine presence*); in good health. **5.** (Of weather etc.) bright and clear, free from precipitation or thick fog and with some sunshine, (**one ~ day,** once upon a time; **one of these ~ days,** some day in the future). **6.** Ornate, showy, smart, (**~ feathers,** gaudy plumage, lit. or fig.: *fine feathers make fine birds*). **7.** Fastidious, dainty, affecting refinement, (of speech or writing) affectedly ornate. **8.** Complimentary, euphemistic, (*say fine things about person; call things by fine names*). **9. ~ arts,** those appealing to mind or to sense of beauty, as poetry, music, and esp. painting, sculpture, architecture; *fine* CHEMICAL*s*; **~-draw,** sew together (two pieces of cloth, edges of rent, parts of garment) so that join is imperceptible; **~-drawn,** subtle, extremely thin; **~ gentleman, lady,** person of fashion, person who thinks himself or herself above working; **~-spun,** delicate, flimsy, (of theory, etc.) excessively subtle, unpractical; **~-tooth comb,** comb with narrow close-set teeth, (fig.) detailed search. **10.** Hence ~'LY² (-nlĭ) *adv.*, ~'NESS (-n-n-) *n.* **11.** *n.* Fine weather (*in rain or fine*); (in *pl.*) very small particles in mining, milling, etc. **12.** *adv.* Finely; (colloq.) very well (*that will suit me fine*). **13.** *v.t.* & *i.* ~ **(down),** make (beer) clear; (of liquid) become clear; **~ away, down, off,** make or become finer, thinner, less coarse, (make) dwindle, taper. [ME, f. OF *fin* f. Rom. **finus*, f. L *finire* finish, after *grossus, grossire* (GROSS²)]

fine³ (fēn) *n.* = foll. [abbr.]

fine champagne (fēn shahňpah'nye) *n.* Old liqueur brandy. [F, = fine (brandy from) Champagne (vineyards in Charente)]

fī'nerў¹ *n.* Showy dress or decoration. [f. FINE² 6 + -ERY, after *bravery*]

fī'nerў² *n.* Hearth where cast iron is made malleable or steel made from pig-iron. [f. F *finerie* (*finer* refine, FINE² 13; see -ERY)]

fines herbes (fēnzār'b) *n. pl.* Mixed herbs used in cooking, esp. chopped as omelette-flavouring. [F, = fine herbs]

fĭnĕ'sse *n.* & *v.* **1.** *n.* Delicate manipulation, subtle discrimination; artfulness, cunning strategy; (Cards) attempt to take trick with card that is not the highest and might lose to an opponent's card. **2.** *v.i.* Use finesse; (Cards) make a finesse. **3.** *v.t.* Play (card) by way of finesse; achieve by finesse; trick by finesse. [F, f. Rom. **finitia* (**finus* FINE²; see -ESS²)]

fĭ'nger (-ngg-) *n.*, & *v.t.* **1.** *n.* One of five

terminal members of hand (*thumb, fore-* or *index finger, middle finger, ring finger, little finger*), or four excluding thumb; **little ~,** (fig.) smallest part of body (*more wit in his little finger than you in your whole body*). **2.** BURN² one's *fingers*; CROSS² one's *fingers*; one's **~s itch,** one is longing or impatient (*to* do); **lay a ~ on,** touch however slightly; **lift, move, raise, a ~,** make the least effort; **get, pull, take,** one's **~ out,** (sl.) hurry up, begin work in earnest; *finger in* PIE²; **point ~ at** (esp. in scorn); **put the ~ on,** (sl.) inform against, identify as victim; **put** one's **~ on,** point with precision to (cause of trouble etc.); **shake** or **wag** one's **~ at** (in reproof etc.); **let slip through** one's **~s,** lose hold of, (fig.) miss opportunity of having; one's **~s are (all) thumbs,** one is clumsy; **twist** or **wind round** one's **(little) ~,** persuade (person) without difficulty, dominate (person) completely; *work* one's *fingers to the* BONE¹. **3.** Part of glove etc. that holds finger; finger-like object (FISH¹ *finger*), esp. such part of a fruit etc., and in various machines; long narrow structure; (sl.) amount of liquor one finger-breadth deep in glass; (sl.) policeman, informer, pickpocket, etc. **4. ~ alphabet,** conventional signs for communicating with the deaf; **~-board,** part of neck of violin etc. where strings are pressed by fingers; **~-bowl, -glass,** (for rinsing fingers after dessert); *finger* LANGUAGE; **~-mark,** mark left on surface by (dirty) finger; *finger*-NAIL¹; **~-paint** *n.*, & *v.i.*, (use) paint that can be applied with the fingers; **~-plate** (fastened on door to prevent finger-marks); **~-post,** signpost at junction of roads; **~print,** impression of person's finger, esp. as used for identifying criminals etc., (fig.) distinctive characteristic; **~-stall,** cover of leather or rubber to protect finger in handicraft etc. or when injured; **~-tight,** as tight as it can be made by the hand; **~tip,** end of finger (**have at** one's **~tips,** be fully conversant with; **to the ~tips,** completely). **5.** Hence (-)~ED² (-nggerd), ~LESS, *adjs.* **6.** *v.t.* Touch with, turn about in, the fingers; play upon (instrument) with the fingers, play (passage) with fingers used in particular way, mark (music) with signs showing which fingers are to be used; *(sl.) indicate (victim, or criminal to police). [OE, = OS, OHG *fingar*, ON *fingr*, Goth. *figgrs* f. Gmc **fingraz*]

fĭ'ngerĭng¹ (-ngg-) *n.* In vbl senses; (Mus.) action or method of using fingers to play an instrument, indication of this by numerals etc. [f. prec. 6 + -ING¹]

fĭ'ngerĭng² (-ngg-) *n.* Fine wool for knitting. [earlier *fingram*, perh. f. F *fin grain*, as GROGRAM f. *gros grain*]

‖**fĭ'ngerlĭng** (-ngg-) *n.* Parr. [f. FINGER + -LING¹]

fĭ'nĭal *n.* (Archit.) Ornament finishing off apex of roof, pediment, gable, tower-corner, canopy, etc.; topmost part of pinnacle. [ME, f. AF **finial* or AL **finialis* f. OF *fin* f. L *finis* end; see -AL]

fĭ'nĭcal *a.* Over-particular, precise, fastidious; (arch.) too much elaborated in details; hence ~LY² *adv.*, ~ITY (-ă'l-), ~NESS, *ns.* [16th c., prob. orig. univ. sl. f. FINE² + -ICAL]

fĭ'nĭckĭng *a.* = prec. [f. prec. + -ING²]

fĭ'nĭckȳ *a.* Finical; needing much attention to detail. [var. of prec.; see -Y²]

fī'nĭs *n.* (At end of book) the end; end of anything, esp. of life. [L]

fĭ'nĭsh *v.* & *n.* **1.** *v.t.* Bring to an end, come to the end of, (thing, or do*ing*; **~ off,** provide with an ending), complete; consume, get through, the whole or remainder of (food, book); **~ (off),** kill, dispatch, overcome completely; make perfect or highly accomplished, put final touches to, (*finished manners, gentleman*; *finishing* STROKE¹ 1, 5); complete education of (girl); complete manufacture of (woodwork, cloth, etc.) by surface treatment. **2.** *v.i.* Reach the end, cease; come to end of horse-race etc. (*finishing*-POST¹); **~ (up),** end *in* something or *by* doing; **~ with,** complete one's use of or association with (*be ~ed with*, have or have been finished with). **3.** *n.* Last stage, termination, esp. of a fox-hunt (*be in at the finish*, lit. or fig.); point at which race etc. ends (**fight to a ~,** till one party is completely beaten); what serves to give completeness; accomplished or completed state; mode of finishing (esp. furniture, as *mahogany finish*). [ME, f. OF *fenir* f. L *finire* (*finis* end); see -ISH²]

fĭ'nĭsher *n.* In vbl senses; workman or machine doing last operation in manufacture; (colloq.) discomfiting thing, crushing blow, etc. [f. prec. + -ER¹]

fī'nīte *a.* Bounded, limited, not infinite or infinitesimal; (Gram., of verb) limited by number and person; hence ~LY² (-tlĭ) *adv.*, ~NESS (-tn-) *n.* [f. L *finitus* p.p. of *finire* FINISH]

fī'nīt|ĭsm *n.* Belief in finiteness of world, God, etc.; so ~IST (2) *n.* [f. prec. + -ISM]

fĭnk¹ *n.* (S. Afr.) Weaver-bird. [f. Afrik. *vink* FINCH]

***fĭnk**² *n.*, & *v.i.* (sl.) **1.** *n.* Unpleasant person; informer; detective; strike-breaker. **2.** *v.i.* Inform *on*. [20th c.; orig. unkn.]

Fĭnn *n.* Native or inhabitant of Finland. [OE *Finnas* pl., = ON *Finnr*]

fĭ'nnan *n.* **~ (haddock),** haddock cured with smoke of green wood, turf, or peat. [f. *Findhorn* or *Findon*, Scotland]

fĭ'nner *n.* Rorqual, fin whale. [f. FIN + -ER¹]

fĭ'nneskō *n.* (*pl.* same). Boot of tanned reindeer skin with hair on outside. [f. Norw. *finnsko* (as FINN, *sko* SHOE¹)]

Fĭ'nnĭc *a.* Of the group of peoples allied to the Finns; of the group of languages allied to Finnish. [f. FINN + -IC]

Fĭ'nnĭsh *a.* & *n.* (Language) of the Finns. [f. FINN + -ISH¹]

Fĭnnō-U'grĭc (-ōō'g-) *a.* & *n.* (Belonging to) group of Ural-Altaic languages including Finnish, Estonian, Lapp, and Magyar; so **Fĭnnō-U'grĭan** (-ōō'g-) *a.* & *n.* [f. FINN + -O- + UGRIAN, UGRIC]

fĭ'nnȳ *a.* Having fins; like a fin; of or teeming with fish. [f. FIN + -Y²]

fi'nō (fē'-) *n.* (*pl.* **~s**). Light-coloured dry sherry. [Sp., = fine]

fiôrd, fjôrd, (fy-) *n.* Long narrow arm of sea between high cliffs as in Norway. [Norw., f. ON *fjörthr* f. Gmc **ferthuz*; cf. FIRTH, FORD]

fĭ'pple *n.* Plug at end of whistle etc.; **~ flute,** flute played by blowing endwise. [17th c.; cf. Icel. *flipi* horse's lip]

fīr *n.* **~(-tree),** evergreen coniferous tree esp. of genus *Abies*, with needles placed singly on the shoots (cf. PINE¹; SCOTCH¹, SILVER¹, SPRUCE², *fir*); its wood; **~-cone,** its fruit; hence **~'rȳ**² *a.* [ME, prob. f. ON *fyri*- f. Gmc **furhjōn*]

fīre¹ *n.* **1.** Active principle operative in combustion, in which substances join chemically with oxygen in air and usu. give out bright light and heat; flame, incandescence; **set ~ to,** cause to start burning, kindle; **strike ~,** elicit sparks by friction or blow; **no smoke without ~,** rumour is never entirely baseless. **2.** State of combustion; **on ~,** burning, (fig.) excited; **catch ~, take ~,** (Sc. & Ir.) **go on ~,** begin to burn; **set on ~,** ignite, kindle; ‖**set the Thames on ~, set the world on ~,** (usu. w. neg.) do something remarkable. **3.** Burning fuel in grate, furnace, etc.; = ELECTRIC *fire*, GAS¹ *fire*, etc.; *heap* COALS *of fire*; *the* FAT *is in the fire*; **~ in**

one's **belly,** ambition, enthusiasm; *out of the frying-pan into the fire* (see FRY[2]); **play with ~,** trifle with dangerous matters. **4.** Conflagration, destructive burning; **~!,** call for aid at a fire; **~ and brimstone,** torment in hell; **~ and sword,** burning and slaughter esp. by invading army; **go through ~ and water,** face all perils; **Greek ~,** (Hist.) combustible composition for igniting enemy's ships etc. **5.** Luminosity, glow, (SAINT *Elmo's fire*); burning heat, fever, (SAINT *Anthony's fire*). **6.** Vehement emotion, fervour, spirit, lively imagination, vivacity, poetic inspiration. **7.** Firing of guns (lit or fig.); CEASE[1] *fire,* HANG[1] *fire;* **line of ~,** path of bullet etc. about to be shot; MISS[2] *fire,* OPEN[2] *fire;* **running ~,** successive shots from line of troops etc. (esp. fig., of criticism, objections, etc.); **between two ~s,** shot at from two directions; **under ~,** being shot at, adversely criticized, etc. **8. ~-alarm,** automatic arrangement for giving warning of fire; **~'arm,** (usu. in *pl.*) rifle, gun, pistol, etc.; **~'back,** (1) (iron sheet for) back wall of fireplace, (2) S.E. Asian pheasant of genus *Lophura;* **~-ball,** large meteor, ball of flame from nuclear explosion, globular lightning, energetic person, (Mil. Hist.) ball filled with combustibles; **~-balloon** (made buoyant by heat of fire burning at its mouth); **~-bird,** small orange or red bird; **~-blast, ~-blight,** diseases of plants causing scorched appearance; **~-bomb,** incendiary bomb; **~-box,** fuel-chamber of steam-boiler; **~'brand,** piece of burning wood, person or thing kindling strife; **~-break,** obstacle to spread of fire in forest etc.; **~-brick** (proof against fire, used in grates etc.); **~ brigade,** organized body of men trained and employed to extinguish fires; **~-bug,** (colloq.) incendiary, pyromaniac; **~-clay** (kind used for fire-bricks); **~ company,** (1) fire brigade, (2) fire-insurance company; **~-control,** system of regulating fire of ship's or fort's guns; **~'crest,** warbler very similar to goldcrest; **~'damp,** miners' name for methane, which is explosive when mixed in certain proportion with air; ***~ department,** fire brigade; **~'dog,** metal support for burning wood or for grate or fire-irons; **~-drake,** (Gmc Myth.) fiery dragon; **~-drill,** (1) primitive device for kindling fire with stick and wood, (2) rehearsal of procedure to be used in case of fire; **~-eater,** conjurer who (allegedly) eats fire, person fond of fighting or quarrelling; **~-engine,** vehicle carrying equipment used to extinguish large fires; **~-escape,** apparatus or emergency staircase for saving people in burning building; *fire* EXTINGUISHER; **~-eyed,** (poet.) with glowing eyes; **~-fighter,** one whose task is to extinguish fires; **~'fly,** beetle emitting phosphorescent light; **~-guard,** (1) protective frame or grating in front of fire in room, (2) *=*fire-watcher,* (3) *=*fire-break;* **~-hose,** hose-pipe for extinguishing fires; **~ insurance** (against losses by fire); **~-irons,** tongs, poker, and shovel, for tending domestic fire; **~'light,** light from fireplace; ||**~-lighter,** piece of inflammable material to help start fire in grate; **~'lock,** (Hist.) musket in which priming was ignited by sparks; **~'man,** one who tends furnace or steam-engine fire, man employed to extinguish fires, member of fire brigade; **~-new,** (arch.) brand-new; **~-office** (insuring against fire); **~-opal,** girasol; **~'place,** grate or hearth for domestic fire; **~-plug,** connection in water-main for fire-hose, hydrant; **~-policy,** fire-office's certificate guaranteeing compensation in case of fire; **~-power,** ability of guns etc. to inflict destruction; **~-practice,** =*fire-drill* (2); *fire'*PROOF[2] *a.,* & *v.t.;* ||**~-raising,** arson; **~-screen,** (1) screen to keep off direct heat of fire, (2) *=*fire-guard* (1); **~-ship,** (Hist.) ship freighted with combustibles and sent adrift to ignite enemy's ships etc.; **~'side,** space round fireplace, home (esp. as place of informal talk etc.); **~ station,** headquarters of fire brigade; **~-step,** =FIRING-*step;* **~-stone,** kind that resists fire, used for furnaces etc.; **~-storm,** high wind or storm following fire caused by bombs; *fire-*TONGS; **~-trap,** building without proper exits in case of fire; **~-tree,** pohutukawa; **~-walking,** (religious) ceremony of walking barefoot over white-hot stones, wood-ashes, etc.; **~ wall,** fireproof wall to prevent spread of fire; ***~ warden,** person employed to prevent or extinguish fires; **~-watcher,** person keeping watch for fires esp. those caused by bombs; **~-water,** alcoholic spirits; **~'wood,** wood prepared for fuel; **~'work,** device giving spectacular effects by use of combustibles etc., squib, rocket, etc., (fig., in *pl.*) display of wit, passion, etc.; **~-worship,** treatment of fire as a deity, (pop.) Zoroastrianism. **9.** Hence **~'LESS** (fīr'l-) *a.* [OE *fȳr,* = OS, OHG *fiur,* f. WG **fūir*]

fīre[2] *v.* **1.** *v.t.* Set fire to with intention of destroying; kindle (explosives); (fig.) stimulate (the imagination), fill (person) with enthusiasm; cause to glow or redden. **2.** Bake (pottery, bricks), cure (tea, tobacco) by artificial heat; (Farriery) cauterize. **3.** Supply (furnace, engine, boiler, power-station) with fuel. **4.** Cause (explosive) to explode; discharge (gun); produce (broadside, salute, etc.) by discharge of guns; propel (missile) from gun etc. (lit. or fig.); **~ (*out),** expel, dismiss, reject, (person). **5.** *v.i.* (Of explosive etc.) catch fire; (of cylinder in internal combustion engine) undergo ignition of its fuel; become heated or excited. **6.** Shoot, discharge gun etc. (*at, into, on,* etc.); (of gun etc.) be discharged; **~ away,** (fig.) begin, go ahead. **7.** Hence **fīr'ER**[1] *n.* [OE *fȳrian* (as prec.)]

fīr'ing *n.* In vbl senses; material for a fire, fuel; discharge of guns; **~-line,** front line of battle (lit. or fig.); **~-party, ~-squad,** group detailed to fire salute at military funeral or perform military execution; **~-step,** step on which soldier in trench stands to fire. [f. prec. + -ING[1]]

fir'kin *n.* Small cask for liquids, butter, fish, etc.; (as measure) half of kilderkin. [ME *ferdekyn,* prob. f. MDu. **vierdekijn* dim. of *vierde* fourth; see -KIN]

firm[1] *n.* Partners carrying on business; group of persons working together, esp. of hospital doctors and assistants. [earlier = signature, style, f. Sp. and It. f. med. L *firma* (L *firmare* confirm f. *firmus* FIRM[2]); cf. FARM[1]]

firm[2] *a., adv.,* & *v.* **1.** *a.* Of solid or compact structure; fixed, stable; steady, not shaking; established, immutable, (of offer etc.) not liable to cancellation after acceptance; steadfast, unflinching, resolute; constant *to;* (Commerc., of prices, goods) maintaining their level or value; hence **~'LY**[2] *adv.,* **~'NESS** *n.* **2.** *adv.* Firmly (*stand firm; hold firm to*). **3.** *v.t.* & *i.* Solidify, make or become firm or compact; fix firmly (plants in soil). [ME, f. OF *ferme* f. L *firmus*]

fir'mament *n.* Vault of HEAVEN with its clouds and stars; hence **~AL** (-ĕ'n-) *a.* [ME f. OF, f. L *firmamentum* (*firmare,* as FIRM[1]; see -MENT)]

fir'man *n.* Oriental sovereign's edict; grant, permit. [f. Pers. *fermān,* Skr. *pramāṇam* right measure]

first *a., n.,* & *adv.* **1.** *a.* Earliest or earlier in time or order (**come in ~,** win race; **in the ~ place,** to begin with; *shall do it* etc. **~ thing,** (colloq.) before anything else; **the two** etc. **~, the ~ two** etc., (1) the two etc. equally first, (2) the first and second etc.); basic or evident (*first* *principles*). **2.** Foremost in position, rank, or importance (*head, feet,* etc., *first,* with the head etc. in front); most willing, likely, etc., (*should be the first to admit the difficulty*); (Mus.) performing highest or chief of two or more parts for same instrument or voice; **F~ Lord, F~ Secretary,** etc., (titles of chief officers); **~ things ~,** the most important things before any others. **3.** Coming next after a specified or implied time (*shall take the first train; the first cuckoo*). **4. The ~,** even one elementary (*he doesn't know the first thing about it*). **5. ~ aid,** help given to injured person before doctor comes; *first* BASE[1] 9; *first* BLOOD[1]; *First* CAUSE[1]; *first*-CHOP[5]; **~ class,** set of persons or things grouped together as better than others, best accommodation in train, ship, etc., mail given preferential treatment, (place in) highest division in examination-list; **~-class,** (*a.*) belonging to or travelling by the first class, of best quality, very good, (*adv.*; -ah's) by the first class (*travels first-class*); **~ coat,** first layer of paint; ||**~ cost,** = *prime* COST[1]; *first* COUSIN; **~ day,** Sunday; **~-day cover,** envelope with stamps postmarked on first day of issue; *first* EDITION; *first* FLOOR; **~-foot** *n.*, & *v.i.* (Sc.) (be) first person to cross threshold in the New Year; *first* FORM[1] 6; **~-fruit,** (usu. in *pl.*) first products of agriculture for the season esp. as offered to God, (fig.) first results of work etc., (Hist.) payment to a superior by new holder of office; *first* GEAR; **first* GRADE 1; **~'hand,** direct, without intermediate agency (*at first hand,* directly); *first* INTENTION; ***F~ Lady,** wife of U.S. President; *first* LESSON; **first* LIEUTENANT; **~ light,** time when light first appears in the morning; **~ name,** personal or Christian name; **~ night, ~-ni'ghter,** (habitual attender of) first performance of plays; **~ offender** (against whom no previous conviction is recorded); **~ officer,** mate on merchant ship; *first* PERSON 5, 6; *first* POST[4]; *first* PROOF[1] 6; **~-rate,** of the highest class, excellent, (colloq.) very well, (*a first-rate machine; feeling first-rate*); *first* READING; ***~ sergeant,** highest-ranking n.c.o. in company; *first* STRING; *first* WATER[1] 5. **6.** *n.* **The ~,** person or thing first mentioned or occurring (**at ~,** at the beginning; **from the ~,** from the beginning; **from ~ to last,** throughout); first day of month; first form; first gear; (person having) place in first class in examination; (winner of) first place in race; (in *pl.*) best quality of goods. **7.** *adv.* Before anyone or anything else (*first of all, first and foremost; first come first served*); **~ and last,** taking one thing with another, on the whole; **~ or last,** sooner or later); before some specified or implied event, time, etc., (*must get this done first*); in preference, rather, (*will see him damned first*); for the first time (*when did you first see her?*); first-class (*I usually travel first*); **~-born** *a.* & *n.*, eldest (child). [OE *fyrst,* = OS, OHG *furist,* ON *fyrstr* f. Gmc **furistaz,* superl. f. **fur-,* **for-* f. IE **pr-*]

fir'stling *n.* (usu. in *pl.*) First result of anything, first-fruits; first offspring, first born in a season. [f. prec. + -LING[1]]

fir'stly *adv.* In the first place, first, (in enumerating topics, arguments, etc.). [f. FIRST + -LY[2]]

firth, frith, *n.* Arm of sea; estuary. [ME, orig. Sc., f. ON *fjörthr* FIORD]

fisc *n.* Public treasury of ancient Rome, Roman emperor's privy purse. [F, or f. L *fiscus* rush-basket, purse, treasury]

fi'scal *a.* & *n.* **1.** *a.* Of public revenue; *fiscal* YEAR; hence **~LY[2]** *adv.* **2.** *n.* Legal official in some countries; (Sc.) = PROCURATOR *fiscal.* [F, or f. L *fiscalis* (as prec.; see -AL)]

fish[1] *n.* (*pl.* usu. same). **1.** Vertebrate cold-blooded animal having gills throughout life and limbs (if any) modified into fins (FLAT[2]-*fish,* FLYING *fish,* GOLD*fish,* SUN*fish,* SWORD*fish,* etc.); any animal living in water (CUTTLE*fish,* JELLY*fish,* SHELL[1]*fish*). **2. Cry stinking ~,** disparage one's own efforts; **drink like a ~** (excessively); **feed the ~es,** (1) be drowned, (2) be seasick; **~ out of water,** person not in his element; **there's as good ~ in the sea as ever came out of it,** no fear of scarcity; *pretty* KETTLE *of fish.* **3.** (colloq.) Person (*cool, queer,* etc., *fish*). **4.** Flesh of fish (*fish, flesh, and fowl*); **neither ~, flesh, nor good red herring,** of indefinite character; **other ~ to fry,** more important business to attend to. **5.** (in *pl.*; *F~(es)*). *The* zodiacal sign Pisces. **6. ~ and chips,** fried fish and fried chipped potatoes; *fish* BALL[1] 5; **~-bowl,** glass bowl for keeping fish in; **~ cake,** small cake of shredded fish and mashed potato; **~-carver,** knife for serving fish; **~ eagle,** osprey; **~-eye,** (of lens) wide-angled with curved front; **~-farm,** place where fish are bred for food; **~ finger,** small oblong piece of fish in batter or bread-crumbs; **~-fork** (for eating or serving fish); **~-glue,** isinglass; **~-hawk,** osprey; *fish*-HOOK[1]; **~-kettle,** oval pan for boiling fish; **~-knife** (for eating or serving fish); **~ louse,** small crustacean parasitic on fish; **~-meal,** ground dried fish as fertilizer etc.; ||**~'monger,** dealer in fish; **~-net,** (of fabric) open-meshed; **~-pond, ~-pool,** pond in which fish are kept; **~-pot,** wicker trap for eels, lobsters, etc.; **~-slice,** carving-knife for fish, cook's implement for turning or taking out fish; **~-sound,** fish's swimming-bladder; **~-tail,** (*n.*) thing shaped like fish's tail (*fish-tail burner,* with jet of gas so shaped), (*v.i.*) move tail of vehicle etc. from side to side; **~'wife,** woman selling fish. [OE *fisc,* = OS, OHG *fisk,* ON *fiskr,* Goth. *fisks* f. Gmc **fiskaz* f. IE **piskos*]

fish[2] *v.* **1.** *v.i.* Try to catch fish (**~ in troubled waters,** make one's profit out of disturbances), whence **~'ERY** (2, 3) *n.* **2.** Search *for* something in or under water or in concealed place; seek by indirect means *for* (secrets, compliments, etc.). **3.** *v.t.* Try to catch (fish) or get (coral etc.) from below water; (colloq.) draw *out* (*of* water, pocket, etc.); draw flukes of (anchor) up to gunwale; try to catch fish in (pool etc.; **~ out,** exhaust the fish in); get (fact, opinion, secret) *out.* **4.** Hence **~'ING[1]** (1) *n.*; **~'ing expedition,** (fig.) search etc. made in hope of coming across incriminating evidence; **~'ing frog,** angler-fish; **~'ing-rod,** long tapering usu. jointed rod to which fishing-line is attached; **~'ing story,** exaggerated account of an incident. [OE *fiscian,* = OS *fiskon,* OHG *fiskōn,* ON *fiska,* Goth. *fiskōn* f. Gmc **fiskōjan* (as prec.)]

fish[3] *n.*, & *v.t.* **1.** *n.* (Naut.) piece of wood, convex and concave, used to strengthen mast etc.; flat plate of iron, wood, etc. to strengthen beam or joint (**~-plate,** one of two holding rails together and fastened with **~-bolt**). **2.** *v.t.* Mend or strengthen (spar etc.), join (rails), with fish. [n. f. v., f. F *ficher* fix f. Rom. **figicare* f. L *figere*]

fish[4] *n.* Piece of ivory etc. used as counter in games. [f. F *fiche* (*ficher*; see prec.)]

fi'sher *n.* Fishing animal, esp. pekan; (arch.) fisherman (**~ of men,** evangelist, Matt. 4: 19); **~man,** man who lives by fishing, angler, fishing-boat. [OE *fiscere,* = ON, OS *fiskari,* OHG *fiscāri* f. Gmc **fiskarjaz* (as FISH[1]; see -ER[1])]

fi'shery. See FISH[2] 1.

fi'sh|y *a.* Like that of fish; (of eye) dull, vacant-looking; smelling or tasting like fish; (joc. or poet.) abounding in fish; consisting of fish (*a fishy repast*); (sl.) of dubious character, questionable; hence ~ĭLY[2] *adv.*, ~ĭNESS *n.* [f. FISH[1] + -Y[2]]

fĭsk *n.* (Sc.) State treasury, exchequer. [var. of FISC]

fĭ'ssile *a.* Cleavable, tending to split; capable of undergoing nuclear fission; hence **fĭssĭ'lITY** *n.* [f. L *fissilis* (as FISSURE; see -IL)]

fĭ'ssion (-sh*o*n) *n.* & *v.* **1.** *n.* (Biol.) Division of cell etc. into new cells etc. as mode of reproduction. **2.** (Phys.) Splitting of heavy atomic nucleus spontaneously or on impact of another particle, with release of energy; ~ **bomb,** atomic bomb. **3.** *v.t.* & *i.* (Cause to) undergo fission. **4.** Hence ~ABLE *a.* [f. L *fissio* (as FISSURE; see -ION)]

fĭssĭ'parous *a.* (Biol. or fig.) Reproducing by fission; hence ~NESS *n.* [f. L *fissus* p.p. (as foll.) after *viviparous*]

fĭ'ssure (-sh*er*) *n.* & *v.* **1.** *n.* Opening, usu. long and narrow, made esp. by cracking, splitting, or separation of parts; (Bot. & Anat.) narrow opening in organ etc., esp. depression between convolutions of brain; cleavage. **2.** *v.t.* & *i.* Split, crack. [ME f. OF, or f. L *fissura* (*findere fiss-* cleave; see -URE)]

fĭst *n.*, & *v.t.* **1.** *n.* Clenched hand, esp. as used in boxing; (joc.) hand (**give us your ~,** shake hands), handwriting (*writes a good fist*; *I know his fist*); HAND[1] *over fist*; **make a** (*good, poor*) ~ **at** or **of,** (colloq.) make a (good, poor) attempt at; hence -~'ED[2] *a.* **2.** *v.t.* Strike with fist; (Naut.) handle (sail, oar, etc.). [OE *fȳst*, = MLG, OHG *fūst* f. WG **fūsti*]

fĭ'stĭc(al) *adjs.* (joc.) Pugilistic. [f. prec. + -IC, -ICAL]

fĭ'stĭcŭffs *n. pl.* Fighting with the fists. [prob. f. obs. *fisty* a. = prec., + CUFF[2]]

fĭ'stūl|a *n.* Long pipelike ulcer etc. with narrow mouth; surgically made body-passage; natural pipe or spout in whales, insects, etc.; hence ~AR[1], ~OUS, *adjs.* [L, = pipe, flute]

fĭt[1], fȳtte, *n.* (arch.) Section of a poem. [OE *fitt*, = OS **fittia*, perh. = OHG *fizza* edge of cloth, ON *fit* hem]

fĭt[2] *n.* **1.** Sudden transitory or recurring attack of an illness; sudden seizure (with loss of consciousness or convulsions) of hysteria, apoplexy, fainting, paralysis, or epilepsy; (fig.) attack of strong feeling (**give** person **a ~,** surprise or outrage him; **have a ~,** be greatly surprised or outraged). **2.** Sudden transitory state (*a fit of energy, idleness, devotion, indifference, pique,* etc.); **by** or **in ~s (and starts),** spasmodically. **3.** Capricious impulse, mood, (*when the fit was on him*). [ME, = position of danger, perh. = OE *fitt* conflict (?); orig. unkn.]

fĭt[3] *a.* & *adv.* **1.** *a.* Well adapted or suited (*for* some purpose or status, *to* do or be; SURVIVAL *of the fittest*); good enough *for* (*a dinner fit for a king*); becoming, proper, right, (*it is fit that*); **see** or **think ~,** decide or choose (*to* do esp. arbitrary or foolish thing). **2.** Qualified, competent, worthy, *to* do (*not fit to hold a* CANDLE *to*); in suitable condition, ready, *to* do or *for*; angry troubled, or exhausted enough *to* (do something violent, sink to the ground, etc.). **3.** In good athletic condition or health (*fit as a* FIDDLE). **4.** Hence ~'LY[2] *adv.*, ~'NESS *n.* **5.** *adv.* (vulg.) In a suitable manner *to* (*was laughing fit to bust*). [ME, of unkn. orig.]

fĭt[4] *v.t.* (**-tt-**), & *n.* **1.** *v.t.* Be in harmony with, become, befit; (esp. of dress) be of right measure, shape, and size for (person, or abs.: *the* CAP[1] *fits*). **2.** Fill up, exactly correspond to, be in accordance with, (receptacle, counterpart, etc.; or abs., often *in, into, in with*); cause to do this; **~ted carpet,** carpet cut to fit floor exactly; **~ted coat** etc. (shaped to fit a person's figure). **3.** Make suitable, adapt, *for, to* thing or person, *to* do; make competent *for* or *to*; ~ **on,** try on (garment). **4.** Supply, furnish, (ship etc. *with*); ~ **out, up,** equip; **~-up,** (Theatr. sl.) temporary stage etc., travelling company. **5.** Hence ~'TER[1] *n.*, one who supervises cutting, fitting, altering, etc., of garments, mechanic who fits (up) all kinds of machinery. **6.** *n.* Adaptation, adjustment, style in which garment or machine-part fits (*a tight, bad, excellent, fit*). [ME, perh. f. prec.]

fĭtch *n.* Polecat; (brush made of) polecat's or similar hair. [f. MDu. *fisse* etc.; cf. foll.]

fĭ'tchew (-ōō) *n.* Polecat. [14th c., f. OF *ficheau, fissel*, dim. of MDu. *fisse*]

fĭ'tful *a.* Having irregular periods of activity or strength; spasmodic, capricious; hence ~LY[2] *adv.*, ~NESS *n.* [f. FIT[2] + -FUL]

fĭ'tment *n.* (usu. in *pl.*) Piece of fixed furniture. [f. FIT[4] + -MENT]

fĭ'ttĭng[1] *n.* In vbl senses; action of having a garment fitted; (usu. in *pl.*) fixture(s), apparatus, furniture; **~-shop,** place where machine-parts are put together. [f. FIT[4] + -ING[1]]

fĭ'ttĭng[2] *a.* In vbl senses; becoming, proper, right, whence ~LY[2] *adv.* [f. FIT[4] + -ING[2]]

FĭtzGĕ'rald (-ts-) *n.* **~(–Lorentz) contraction** or **effect,** (Phys.) shortening of moving body in direction of its motion, small except at speeds comparable with that of light. [f. G. F. ~, Ir. physicist d. 1901]

five *a.* & *n.* **1.** One more than four; symbol for this (5, v, V); card etc. with five pips; time of five o'clock; size etc. denoted by five; set of five; hit at cricket scoring five runs; (in *pl.*) gloves, shoes, etc., of fifth size; ‖**bunch of ~s,** (sl.) hand. **2. ~-corner(s),** (Austral.) (pentagonal fruit of) shrub of genus *Styphelia*; *five-day* WEEK; **~-eighth,** (Austral. & N.Z. Rugby Footb.) player between half-back and three-quarter; **~-finger exercise,** exercise on piano for exercising all fingers, (fig.) easy task; ~ **hundred,** form of euchre in which 500 points make a game; ~ **o'clock shadow,** beard-growth visible on man's face about 5 p.m.; *five* ORDER[1]*s*; **~-star,** of highest class; ‖**~-stones,** jacks played with five stones; **~-year plan** (for the economic development of U.S.S.R. in 5 years, inaugurated in 1928, later of other countries and repeated in U.S.S.R.). **3.** Hence ~'FOLD (-vf-) *a.* & *adv.* [OE *fīf*, = OS *fīf*, OHG *fimf, finf*, ON *fimm*, Goth. *fimf* f. Gmc **fimfi* f. IE **pempe*, **penqwe*]

fī'ver *n.* £5 or $5 note. [f. prec. + -ER[1]]

fives (-vz) *n.* Ball-game played with gloved hands or with bat in court with three (**Eton ~**) or four (**Rugby ~**) walls. [*pl.* of FIVE used as *sing.*; significance unkn.]

fĭx[1] *v.* **1.** *v.t.* Make firm or stable, fasten, secure, implant (principles, memory, etc.), (*in, on, to,* etc.); attach (bayonet) to muzzle of rifle etc. **2.** Direct steadily, set, (eyes, gaze, affection, attention) *on* or *upon*; (of object) attract and hold (attention, eyes, etc.). **3.** Make (eyes, features) rigid; deprive of volatility or fluidity, congeal; (of plant etc.) assimilate (nitrogen or carbon dioxide) by formation of non-gaseous compound; make (colour, microscope-specimen, photographic image) fast or permanent; single out (person) *with* one's eyes etc. **4.** Place definitely or permanently, station, establish; assign precise position of; refer (thing, person) to definite place or time. **5.** Determine incidence of (liability etc.); settle, determine, specify, (price, date, place). **6.** Arrest changes or development in (language, literature). **7.** Mend, repair; ~ **(up),** arrange, organize, prepare; (sl.) deal with, silence, kill, (person); obtain support of (person) esp. by bribery etc.; arrange (result of match etc.) fraudulently; castrate or spay (animal); (sl.) inject one*self* with narcotic. **8.** *v.i.* Become rigid or congealed, lose volatility or fluidity; (arch.) take up one's position; settle one's choice, decide, *on* or *upon*; (sl.) take injection of narcotic. [ME, partly f. obs. *fix* fixed f. OF *fix* or f. L *fixus* p.p. of *figere* fix, fasten, partly f. med. L *fixare* f. *fixus*]

fĭx[2] *n.* Dilemma, position hard to escape from; finding position, position found, by bearings or astronomical observations (**radio ~**, position of aircraft, ship, etc., found by radio); (sl.) dose of narcotic drug; *(sl.) bribery. [f. prec.]

fĭxā'te *v.t.* Direct one's gaze on; (Psych.) arrest (part of libido) at immature stage, causing abnormal attachment to persons or things, cause (person) to undergo this process. [f. L *fixus* (see FIX[1]) + -ATE[3]]

fĭxā'tion *n.* Fixing, being fixed; process of rendering solid, coagulation; process of combining a gas with a solid; act or process of being fixated; (pop.) obsession, concentration on one idea. [ME, f. med. L *fixatio* (*fixare*; see FIX[1], -ATION)]

fĭ'xatĭve *a.* & *n.* **1.** *a.* Tending to fix. **2.** *n.* Substance used to fix colours or drawings, hair, microscope-specimens, volatile components of perfumes, etc. [f. FIX[1] + -ATIVE]

fĭxed (-kst) *a.* In vbl senses; (*pred.*, colloq.) situated as regards money etc.; **~ capital,** machinery etc. that remains in owner's use; **~ focus,** camera focus at distance from lens that is not adjustable; **~ idea,** *idée fixe*; **~ income** (from pension, investment at fixed interest, etc.); **~ odds** (predetermined, in betting); **~ oil** (non-volatile); **~ point,** (Phys.) well-defined reproducible temperature; *fixed* STAR[1]; hence **fĭ'xĕd**LY[2] *adv.*, **fĭ'xĕd**NESS *n.* [p.p. of FIX[1]]

fĭ'xer *n.* In vbl senses; substance for fixing photographic image etc.; one who makes (esp. illicit) arrangements. [f. FIX[1] + -ER[1]]

***fĭ'xings** (-z) *n. pl.* Apparatus, equipment; trimmings of dress or dish, adjuncts. [f. FIX[1] + -ING[1] + -S[1]]

fĭ'xĭtў *n.* Fixed state; stability, permanence. [f. obs. *fix* fixed (see FIX[1]) + -ITY]

fĭ'xture *n.* Thing fixed or fastened in position; (Law, in *pl.*) accessory articles annexed to house or land and regarded as legally part of it; person or thing confined to or established in one place (chiefly in pred.; *seems to be a fixture*); (Sport) (date appointed for) match, race, etc. [alt. of obs. *fixure* f. LL *fixura* f. L *figere fix-* fix; see -URE]

fĭ'zgĭg (-g-) *n.* & *a.* (arch.) **1.** *n.* Giddy flirtatious young woman; kind of small firework, cracker. **2.** *a.* Flighty. [prob. f. foll. + obs. *gig* flighty girl]

fĭzz *v.i.*, & *n.* (Make) hissing or spluttering sound, whence ~'Y[2] *a.*; effervescence; (colloq.) effervescent drink, esp. champagne. [imit.]

fĭ'zzle *v.i.*, & *n.* (Make) feeble hissing or spluttering sound; **~ out,** come to lame conclusion. [f. as prec. + -LE 3]

fjord. See FIORD.

fl. *abbr.* floor; floruit; fluid.

Fla. *abbr.* Florida.

flăb *n.* (sl.) Fat, flabbiness. [imit., or back form. f. FLABBY]

flă'bbergast (-gah-) *v.t.* (colloq.) Dumbfound, overwhelm with astonishment. [18th c., perh. f. foll. + AGHAST]

flă'bb|ў *a.* (Of flesh etc.) hanging down, flaccid, limp; (of language or character) feeble; hence **~ĭ**NESS *n.* [alt. f. earlier *flappy* f. FLAP + -Y[2]]

flă'ccĭd (-ks-) *a.* (Of flesh etc.) hanging loose or wrinkled, limp, flabby; relaxed, drooping; lacking vigour, feeble; hence ~ITY (-ĭ'd-) *n.* [f. F *flaccide* or f. L *flaccidus* (*flaccus* flabby)]

***flăck** *n.* (sl.) Publicity agent. [20th c.; orig. unkn.]

flăg[1] *n.* Plant with bladed leaf esp. of genus *Iris* growing on moist ground; long slender leaf of a plant; hence **~'gy**[2] (-gĭ) *a.* [ME; cf. MDu. *flag*, Da. *flæg*]

flăg[2] *n.*, & *v.t.* (-gg-). **1.** *n.* ~(**'stone**), flat slab of rock for paving, (in *pl.*) pavement made of these. **2.** *v.t.* Pave with flags. [ME, = sod; cf. Icel. *flag* spot whence sod has been cut out, ON *flaga* slab of stone, and FLAKE[2]]

flăg[3] *n.* ~(**-feather**), quill-feather of bird's wing. [perh. rel. to obs. *fag* loose flap; cf. FLAG[5]]

flăg[4] *n.*, & *v.t.* (-gg-). **1.** *n.* Piece of bunting or other material, usu. oblong or square, attached by one edge to staff or halyard and used as standard, ensign, or signal; **black ~,** (1) pirate's ensign, (2) flag formerly hoisted outside prison to announce execution of criminal; **red ~,** (1) symbol of revolution, (2) danger-signal on shooting-range, railway, etc.; **white ~,** flag of truce, flag disclaiming hostile intention; **yellow ~,** flag displayed by ship with infectious disease on board, hospital ship, or ship in quarantine. **2. ~ of convenience,** foreign flag under which a ship is registered to avoid financial charges etc.; **~ of truce,** white flag indicating desire to parley; **hoist the ~** (as claim to discovered territory); **keep the ~ flying,** (usu. fig.) continue the fight; **put the ~ out,** celebrate victory etc.; **show the ~,** make official visit to foreign port etc., (fig.) ensure that notice is taken of oneself, one's own country, etc. **3.** (Naut.) Flag carried by flagship as emblem of admiral's rank afloat. **4.** Oblong strip of metal etc. used as signal that taxi is for hire; small paper etc. device resembling flag. **5. ~-boat** (serving as mark in sailing-matches); **~-captain,** captain of flagship; ||**~-day** (on which money is raised for a cause by sale to passers-by etc. of small paper etc. flags to be worn as evidence of having given); ***F~ Day,** 14 June, anniversary of the adoption of the Stars and Stripes in 1777; **~-lieutenant,** admiral's A.D.C.; ||**~-list,** roll of flag-officers; **~'man,** signaller at races etc.; **~-officer,** admiral, vice-admiral, or rear-admiral, or commodore of yacht club; **~-pole,** = *flagstaff*; **~-rank** (of flag-officers); **~'ship,** ship having admiral on board; **~'staff,** pole on which flag is hoisted; **~-station** (where trains stop only if signalled); **~-wagging,** (sl.) signalling with hand-held flags; **~-waver,** chauvinist, political agitator. **6.** *v.t.* Place flag on or over; mark out (as) with flag(s); inform (person), communicate (information, *that*), by flag-signals; **~ (down)**, signal to (vehicle or driver) to stop. [16th c., perh. f. obs. *flag* drooping]

flăg[5] *v.i.* (-gg-). Hang down, flap loosely; droop, fade, become limp; lag, lose vigour, grow languid; become uninteresting. [16th c., as prec.]

flă'gellant (*or* flajĕ'-) *n.* & *a.* (One) who scourges himself, (one) who engages in flogging, esp. as religious discipline or sexual stimulus. [f. L *flagellare* whip (FLAGELLUM); see -ANT]

flă'gell|āte[1] *v.t.* Scourge, flog, (cf. prec.); hence or cogn. ~A'TION, **~ā**TOR, *ns.*, **~ā**TORY *a.* [f. as prec. + -ATE[3]]

flă'gellate[2] *a.* & *n.* (Protozoan) having flagella (see foll.). [f. foll. + -ATE[2]]

flagĕ'll|um *n.* (*pl.* ~**a**). (Bot.) runner, creeping shoot; (Biol.) lashlike appendage; hence ~AR, ~**ĭ**FORM, *adjs.* [L, = whip, dim. of *flagrum* scourge]

flăgeolĕ't[1] (-jol-; *or* flă'j-) *n.* Small flute blown at end, like recorder but with thumb-holes; organ stop of like quality. [F, dim. of OF *flag(e)ol* f. Prov. *flajol*, of unkn. orig.; see -ET[1]]

flăgeolĕ′t[2] (-jol-; *or* -lā′) *n.* French kidney-bean. [F]

flagĭ′tious (-shus) *a.* Deeply criminal; utterly villainous; hence ~LY[2] *adv.*, ~NESS *n.* [ME, f. L *flagitiosus* (*flagitium* shameful crime; see -OUS)]

flă′gon *n.* Large vessel usu. with handle, spout, and lid, to hold liquor for table; similar vessel for Eucharist; flattened globular glass wine-bottle holding nearly twice as much as ordinary bottle. [ME *flakon* f. AF **flagon*, OF *flacon*, **flascon* f. LL *flasco -onis* FLASK]

flā′grant *a.* (Of offence or offender) glaring, notorious, scandalous; hence or cogn. **flā′gr**ANCY *n.*, ~LY[2] *adv.* [F, or f. L *flagrare* blaze; see -ANT]

flail *n.* & *v.* **1.** *n.* Hand threshing-implement, wooden staff at end of which a short heavy stick hangs swinging. **2.** *v.t.* Beat or strike (as) with flail. **3.** *v.i.* Wave or swing wildly or erratically. [OE **flegil*, = OS *flegil*, OHG *flegel*, WG **flagil*-prob. f. L FLAGELLUM]

flair *n.* Instinct for selecting or performing what is excellent, useful, etc. [F (*flairer* to smell f. Rom. **flagrare* = L *fragrare*; see FRAGRANT)]

flăk *n.* Anti-aircraft fire; (fig.) barrage of criticism; ~ **jacket,** protective jacket of heavy fabric reinforced with metal. [abbr. of G *fliegerabwehrkanone*, lit. aviator-defence-gun]

flāke[1] *n.* Rack for storing oatcake etc.; stage for drying fish etc [ME, perh. f. ON *flaki, fleki* wicker shield]

flāke[2] *n.* & *v.* **1.** *n.* Light fleecy piece, esp. of snow; portion of ignited matter thrown off; thin broad piece peeled off, chiplike piece (CORN[1]*flakes*; *soap flakes*); (Archaeol.) piece of hard stone chipped off and used as tool; natural division of fish's flesh; dogfish or other shark as food. **2.** *v.i.* & *t.* Fall like, sprinkle as with, snow; take or come away or off in flakes; ~ **out,** (colloq.) faint, fall asleep from exhaustion etc. [ME; orig. unkn.; cf. ON *flakna* flake off]

flā′kў *a.* Of or like flakes; (of pastry) consisting of thin flakes after baking. [f. prec. + -Y[2]]

flăm *n.* Sham story; trick, deception. [perh. f. FLIMFLAM]

flambé (flah′ṅbā) *a.* (Of food) covered with spirit and served alight. [F, p.p. of *flamber* singe (as foll.)]

flă′mbeau (-bō) *n.* (*pl.* ~**s** *or* ~**x**, *pr.* -z). Flaming torch, esp. of several thick waxed wicks. [F (*flambe* f. L *flammula* dim. of *flamma* flame)]

flămboy′|ant *a.* (Archit.) marked by wavy flamelike lines; floridly decorated; gorgeously coloured; ostentatious, showy; hence ~ANCE, ~ANCY, *ns.*, ~**ant**LY[2] *adv.* [F, part. of *flamboyer* (*flambe*; see prec.)]

flāme[1] *n.* **1.** (Portion of) ignited gas (**the** ~**s**, fire, esp. as consuming); visible combustion (*in flames*; *burst into flame* or *flames*). **2.** Bright light, brilliant colouring; red colour of flame. **3.** Passion, esp. of love, (FAN[2] *the flame*); (joc.) sweetheart (*an old flame of mine*). **4.** ~ **gun** (throwing flames to destroy weeds etc.); *flame*-PROOF[2]; ~**-projector, -thrower,** weapon for throwing spray of flame; ~**-tree,** one of several trees with brilliant red or yellow flowers. **5.** Hence ~′LESS (-ml-), **flā′m**Y[2], *adjs.* [ME, f. AF **flaume*, OF *flame* f. L *flamma*]

flāme[2] *v.* **1.** *v.i.* Emit flames, blaze, (*away*, *forth*, *out*, *up*); (of passion) burst out; (of person) break *out*, blaze *up*, into anger; shine or glow like flame; (poet.) move like flame; ~ **out,** (of jet aircraft engine) lose power through extinction of flame in combustion chamber. **2.** *v.t.* Subject to action of flame; send (signal) by means of flame. [ME, f. OF *flam(m)er* (as prec.)]

flā′mĕn *n.* (Rom. Ant.) Priest serving a particular deity. [ME f. L]

flamĕ′ncō *n.* (*pl.* ~**s**). Spanish gipsy style of song or dance. [Sp., = FLAMINGO]

flā′mĭng *a.* In vbl senses; very hot (*flaming June*; *a flaming sun*); bright-coloured; (arch.) exaggerated, over-laudatory, (*a flaming description*); (colloq.) passionate (*had a flaming row about it*); (colloq.) = DAMNED 2, 3, (*that flaming dog*). [f. FLAME[2] + -ING[2]]

flamĭ′ngō (-nggō) *n.* (*pl.* ~**s** *or* ~**es**). Tall long-necked web-footed (sub)tropical bird with pink, scarlet, and black plumage. [f. Port. *flamengo* f. Prov. *flamenc* (*flama* flame, *-enc* = -ING[3])]

flă′mm|able *a.* Inflammable; hence ~ABI′LITY *n.* [f. L *flammare* (*flamma* flame) + -ABLE]

flăn *n.* Pastry or sponge cake filled or spread with jam, fruit, cheese, etc.; disc of metal from which coin etc. is made. [F, orig. = round cake, f. OF *flaon* f. med. L *flado -onis* f. Frank. **flado* flat cake]

flanch (-ah-) *v.i.* & *t.* (Cause to) slope inwards towards the top (esp. of chimney); hence ~′ING[1] (2) *n.* [perh. f. OF *flanchir* (*flanche*, *flanc* FLANK)]

flânerie (flah′nrē) *n.* Idling; so ***flâneur*** (flahnẽr′) *n.*, idler. [F (*flâner* lounge)]

flănge (-nj) *n.*, & *v.t.* **1.** *n.* Projecting flat rim, collar, or rib, used for strengthening or attachment. **2.** *v.t.* Provide with flange. [17th c., perh. f. *flange* widen out f. OF *flangir* (as FLANCH)]

flănk *n.*, & *v.t.* **1.** *n.* Fleshy part of side of body between ribs and hip; side of building, mountain, etc.; right or left side of army or other body of persons (**in** ~, at the side; TURN[1] *flank of*); ~ **forward,** (Rugby Footb.) wing forward. **2.** *v.t.* Guard or strengthen on the flank; menace flank of; enfilade, rake; be posted or situated at flank of. [ME, f. OF *flanc* f. Frank. **hlanca* side]

flă′nker *n.* Fortification guarding or menacing flank; thing that flanks anything; (Rugby Footb.) flank forward; (sl.) trick, swindle. [f. prec. + -ER[1]]

flă′nnel[1] *n.* **1.** Woven woollen stuff, usu. without nap; (in *pl.*) garments (esp. trousers) of flannel, whence ~**l**ED[2], *~ED[2], (-ld) *a.*; hence ~′ETTE (2) *n.*, cotton fabric imitating flannel, ~**l**Y[2] *a.* **2.** ‖Piece of flannel etc. used in washing hands, face, etc., or cleaning floor. **3.** (sl.) Nonsense; flattery, bragging. **4.** Hence ~**board,** ~**graph,** sheet of flannel for attachment of paper or cloth cut-outs esp. in teaching; *~**-mouth,** flatterer, braggart. [perh. f. W *gwlanen* (*gwlān* wool)]

flă′nnel[2] *v.t.* (‖-**ll**-). Use flannel to wash or clean; (sl.) flatter. [f. prec.]

flăp *v.* (-**pp**-) & *n.* **1.** *v.t.* Strike with something broad, drive (flies etc.) *away* or *off* thus; move (wings) up and down. **2.** *v.i.* Swing or sway about, flutter, oscillate; (of wings) move up and down; beat the wings; (colloq., of ears) be listening intently; (colloq.) become agitated or panicky. **3.** *n.* Light blow with something broad; up-and-down motion of wing etc.; (colloq.) state of agitation or fuss (*be in*, *get into*, *a flap*). **4.** Broad hanging piece hinged or attached by one side only, e.g. trapdoor, pocket-cover, envelope-seal, table-leaf, valve, fish's gill-cover; open mushroom-top; (Aeronaut.) aileron, hinged or sliding section used to control lift. [ME, prob. imit.]

flăpdōō′dle *n.* (colloq.) Nonsense. [19th c.; orig. unkn.]

flă′pjăck *n.* Pancake; sweet oatcake; vanity case for face-powder. [f. FLAP + JACK[1]]

flă'pper *n.* **1.** Instrument that is flapped to kill flies, scare birds, etc.; young wild-duck or partridge; (arch. sl.) girl in late teens. **2.** Hinged or hanging piece, flap; broad fin; crustacean's tail. [f. FLAP + -ER[1]]

flāre *v.* & *n.* **1.** *v.i.* (Of ship's sides, wineglass, woman's skirt, etc.) widen gradually in upward or downward direction. **2.** Blaze with bright spreading unsteady flame, glow as with flame, (*away, out*); ~ **up,** burst into sudden blaze or anger or activity, whence **~-up** *n.* **3.** *v.t.* Cause to flare. **4.** *n.* Dazzling irregular light, unshaded flame in open air; sudden outburst of flame; (Astron.) sudden outburst of radiation from sun or star; signal light used at sea; bright light used as signal; container of combustible material, dropped from aircraft to illuminate target etc. (**~-path,** area illuminated to enable aircraft to land or take off); (Photog.) extraneous illumination caused by internal reflection etc. **5.** Upward bulge in ship's sides; gradual widening (esp. of skirt). [16th c., of unkn. orig. (perh. Scand.)]

flăsh[1] *v.* **1.** *v.i.* Break suddenly into flame, give out flame or sparks, (~ **in the pan,** cf. foll.; **~'ing-point,** = FLASH[2]-*point*; ~ **over,** make electrical contact by sparking across gap, whence **~-over** *n.*); emit or reflect light, gleam, (*lighthouse flashes once a minute*); ~ **out** or **up,** show sudden passion. **2.** Burst suddenly into view or perception (*idea flashed upon me*); move swiftly; (of water) rush along, rise and flow; **~'back,** (Cinemat. etc.) scene returning to or changing to earlier time; **~-board** (for sending more water from mill-dam into mill--race); **~-flood,** sudden local flood due to heavy rain etc. **3.** *v.t.* Send or reflect like a flash or in flashes (*eyes flash fire, flash back defiance*); cause to gleam or shine briefly (*flashed his sword; had a torch flashed in my face; flash headlights of car*); signal to (person) by causing (head)lights to shine briefly; show suddenly or ostentatiously; send (news etc.) by radio, telegraph, etc. [ME, orig. app. imit. of sea etc.; cf. *splash*]

flăsh[2] *n.* **1.** Sudden transitory blaze, esp. of lightning or (fig.) of wit, (~ **in the pan,** failure after showy start [from priming of old guns]); (Photog.) =*flashlight* (2). **2.** Very brief time, instant, (*in a flash*); brief news dispatch by radio, telegraph, etc.; sudden short access of feeling (*a flash of hope*). **3.** (Cinemat.) Momentary exposure of a scene. **4.** Rush of water, esp. down weir to take boat over shallows, contrivance for producing this. **5.** ||(Mil.) Coloured patch of cloth on uniform etc. as distinguishing emblem of unit etc. **6.** ~ **bulb** (giving light for flashlight photograph); ~ **burn** (caused by sudden intense heat esp. from nuclear explosion); ~ **card** (with words etc. for brief inspection during learning); **~-gun,** device to operate camera flashlight; **~-lamp,** portable flashing electric lamp; **~'light,** (1) flashing light used for signals and in lighthouses, (2) illuminating device for photographing by night etc., picture so taken, (3) *electric TORCH; **~-point,** temperature at which vapour from oil etc. will ignite, (fig.) point at which indignation etc. begins. [f. prec.]

flăsh[3] *a.* Gaudy, showy; counterfeit (*flash notes, money*); cant, slang; connected with thieves, tramps, etc. [f. prec.]

flă'sher *n.* In vbl senses; automatic device for switching lights rapidly on and off; sign or signal using this. [f. FLASH[1] + -ER[1]]

flă'shĭng *n.* Strip of metal to prevent flooding or leakage at joint of roofing etc. [f. dial. *flash* seal with lead sheets or obs. *flash* flashing, + -ING[1]]

flă'sh|y̆ *a.* Brilliant but shallow or transitory, cheaply attractive; showy, gaudy; given to display; hence **~ĭLY**[2] *adv.*, **~ĭNESS** *n.* [f. FLASH[1,2] + -Y[2]]

flask (-ah-) *n.* Narrow-necked bottle for wine or oil, or for use in chemistry; traveller's pocket bottle of metal or (usu. leather-covered) glass for wine, spirit, etc.; = VACUUM *flask*; (Hist.) = POWDER-*flask*. [f. F *flasque* & (prob.) It. *fiasco* f. med. L *flasca, flasco*; cf. FLAGON]

||**flăt**[1] *n.* Rooms on one floor as residence; hence **~'LET** *n.* [alt. f. obs. *flet* = OE & ON *flet* floor, dwelling f. Gmc **flatjam* (as foll.)]

flăt[2] *a., adv., n.,* & *v.t.* (**-tt-**). **1.** *a.* Horizontal, level; spread out, lying at full length, (*fell flat; flat against the wall; with the flat hand*). **2.** Even, smooth, unbroken, without projection, (of tint) uniform; with broad level surface and little depth (*flat cap, heel, nose*). **3.** Unqualified, plain, downright, (*flat denial, refusal; flat nonsense, blasphemy;* **that's ~,** let there be no doubt about it); dull, lifeless, monotonous, (**fall ~,** prove a failure, not win applause); (of market, prices, etc.) inactive, sluggish; (Photog.) lacking contrast; (of paint etc.) not glossy; dejected, without energy, (of drink) that has lost its effervescence; (of accumulator etc.) unable to generate any more electric current. **4.** (Mus.) Below true pitch (**B, E,** etc., **~,** a semitone lower than B, E, etc.); (of key) having flat(s) in signature. **5.** ~ **arch** (with flat intrados); **~(-bottomed) boat** (with flat bottom for transport in shallow water); ***~'car,** railway wagon without raised sides or ends; **~-fish,** fish of order Heterosomata, including sole, turbot, plaice, etc.; **~ foot,** foot with less than normal arch; **~'foot,** (sl.) policeman; **~-footed,** having flat feet, (colloq.) downright, resolute, uninspired, unprepared; **~-four** *a.,* (of engine) having four cylinders all horizontal, two on each side of crankshaft; **~-head,** snake with flat head of genus *Heterodon,* (sl.) foolish person; **~-iron** (for ironing clothes etc., usu. triangular and heated by external means); ~ **race** (over level ground, opp. hurdle-race or steeplechase); ~ **rate** (same in all cases, not proportional etc.); ~ **spin,** (Aeron.) nearly horizontal spin, (colloq.) agitation or panic; ***~-top,** (sl.) aircraft-carrier; ~ **tyre** (deflated or punctured); **~'ware,** plates, saucers, etc. (opp. *hollow-ware*), *domestic cutlery; **~'worm,** worm of phylum Platyhelminthes (tapeworm, fluke, etc.). **6.** Hence **~'LY**[2] *adv.*, **~'NESS** *n.*, **~'TISH**[1] 2 *a.*, **~'WAYS, ~'WISE,** *advs.* **7.** *adv.* In a flat manner (*lies flat; turned it down flat; sings flat*); (colloq.) completely (*flat broke*), exactly or not exceeding (*ten seconds flat*); **~ out,** at top speed, using all one's strength or resources. **8.** *n.* What is flat; flat part of anything (*the flat of the hand; with the flat of his sword*); level ground, plain, low land, swamp; flat tyre; *the* season of flat races for horses; (Theatr.) section of scenery mounted on frame (**join the ~s,** (fig.) make a thing into a coherent whole, preserve appearance of a consistent attitude); (sl.) foolish person. **9.** (Mus.) Note lowered a semitone below natural pitch; sign indicating this lowering; **sharps and ~s,** black keys on piano. **10.** *v.t.* Make flat (esp. tech. & *Mus.). [ME, f. ON *flatr,* OHG *flaz* f. Gmc **flataz*]

flă'tten *v.t.* & *i.* Make or become flat; humiliate; ~ **out,** (Aeronaut.) bring aircraft parallel to ground. [f. prec. + -EN[6]]

flă'tter *v.t.* Pay obsequious attention to; compliment unduly, overpraise; gratify vanity of, make feel honoured; inspire (person, or abs.) with (esp. unfounded) hope; please or delude one*self* with the belief (*that*); gratify (eye, ear, etc.; **~ing unction,** salve one administers to one's own conscience or self--esteem [Shakespeare's *Hamlet* III. iv. 145]); (of portrait, painter, etc.) exaggerate good looks of, represent too favourably; hence or cogn. ~ER[1], **flă'tt**ERY (4, 5), *ns.* [ME, perh. rel. to OF *flater* to smooth]

flă'ttie *n.* (colloq.) Flat-heeled shoe; flat--bottomed boat; policeman. [f. FLAT[2] + -IE]

flă'tūl|ent *a.* Causing formation of gas in the alimentary canal; caused by, accompanied by, troubled with, accumulation of such gas; inflated, puffed up, windy, pretentious; hence or cogn. ~ENCE, ~ENCY, *ns.*, **~ent**LY[2] *adv.* [F, f. mod. L *flatulentus* (as foll.; see -ULENT)]

flā'tus *n.* Wind in or from stomach or bowels. [L, = blowing (*flare* blow)]

flaunch. Var. of FLANCH.

flaunt *v.i.* & *t.* Wave proudly; display oneself or one's finery; show off, parade, (one*self*, finery, etc.); hence ~'Y[2] *a.* [16th c.; orig. unkn.]

flau'tist *n.* Flute-player. [f. It. *flautista* (*flauto* FLUTE)]

flavĕ'scent *a.* Turning yellow, yellowish. [f. L *flavescere* (*flavus* yellow; see -ESCENT)]

flā'vine (-ēn) *n.* Yellow dye got from dyer's oak; antiseptic derived from acridine. [f. L *flavus* yellow + -INE[5]]

flāvōprō'tein (-tēn) *n.* (Biol.) One of group of conjugated proteins concerned in oxidation and reduction reactions in cells. [f. as prec. + -o- + PROTEIN]

flā'vour (-v*er*), ***flā'vor,** *n.*, & *v.t.* **1.** *n.* Aroma, mingled sensation of smell and taste; distinctive taste; undefinable characteristic quality; slight admixture *of* (usu. undesirable) quality; hence ~FUL, **flā'vorous,** ~LESS, ~SOME[1], *adjs.* **2.** *v.t.* Give flavour to, season; hence ~ING[1] (3) *n.* [ME, f. OF *flaor*, perh. f. Rom. **flator* f. L *flatus* blowing & *foetor* stench; assim. to *savour*]

flaw[1] *n.* & *v.* **1.** *n.* Crack, breach, rent; imperfection, blemish; (Law) invalidating defect in document, procedure, evidence, etc.; hence ~'LESS *a.* **2.** *v.t.* & *i.* Crack; damage; spoil. [ME, perh. f. ON *flaga* slab f. Gmc **flah-*, **flag-*; cf. FLAKE[2], FLAG[2]]

flaw[2] *n.* Squall of wind; short storm. [prob. f. MDu. *vlāghe*, MLG *vlāge*, perh. = stroke]

flăx *n.* Blue-flowered plant (*Linum usitatissimum*) cultivated for its textile fibre and its seeds (LINSEED); similar plant (*toadflax*; **New Zealand ~,** = *flax-lily*); fibres of flax, dressed or not; (arch.) cloth of flax, linen; **~-lily,** N.Z. plant of genus *Phormium* yielding valuable fibre; **~-seed,** linseed. [OE *flæx*, = OHG *flahs* f. WG **flahsa*]

flă'xen *a.* Of flax; (of hair) coloured like dressed flax, pale yellow. [f. prec. + -EN[5]]

flay *v.t.* Strip off skin or hide of; peel off (skin, bark, peel); (fig.) criticize severely; (arch.) pillage, plunder, (person); **~-flint,** (arch.) extortioner, miser. [OE *flēan*, = MDu. *vlae(gh)en*, ON *flá* f. Gmc **flahan*]

F-layer (ĕ'flāer) *n.* Highest and most strongly ionized region of ionosphere. [f. *F* (arbitrary) + LAYER]

flea *n.* **1.** Small wingless jumping insect of order Siphonaptera, feeding on human and other blood (*send* person *away* **with a ~ in his ear,** discomfited by reproof or repulse); small jumping crustacean; = *flea-beetle*. **2. ~-bag,** (sl.) sleeping-bag, unattractive place (esp. lodgings); **~'bane,** one of various composite plants supposed to drive away fleas; **~-beetle,** jumping beetle infesting hops, cabbages, etc.; **~-bite,** (1) bite of flea, (2) (fig.) slight inconvenience or expense, mere trifle, (3) small reddish or brown or black spot in animal's coloration (so **~--bitten,** sprinkled with these on lighter ground); ***~-bug,** = *flea-beetle*; **~-circus,** show of performing fleas; **~-dock,** butterbur; **~-louse,** jumping plant-louse of family Psyllidae; **~ market,** (joc.) street market; **~-pit,** (sl.) allegedly verminous place of public assembly, e.g. cinema; **~-wort,** one of various plants supposed to drive away fleas. [OE *flēa(h)*, = MLG, MDu. *vlō*, OHG *flōh*, ON *fló* f. Gmc **flauh-* or **thlauh-*; cf. FLEE]

fleam *n.* Lancet for bleeding of horses. [f. OF *flieme* f. Rom. **fleutomum* f. LL *phlebotomus* f. Gk *phlebotomon* (see PHLEBOTOMY)]

flèche (flāsh) *n.* Slender spire perforated with windows, esp. at intersection of nave and transept. [F, orig. = arrow]

flĕck *n.*, & *v.t.* **1.** *n.* Spot in the skin, freckle; patch of colour or light; small particle, speck; hence ~'LESS *a.* **2.** *v.t.* Mark with flecks, dapple, variegate. [perh. f. ON *flekkr* n., *flekka* v., or MLG, MDu. *vlecke*, OHG *flec*, *fleccho*]

flĕ'cker *v.t.* Dapple, variegate; scatter in patches. [f. prec. + -ER[5]]

***flĕ'ction.** See FLEXION.

flĕd. See FLEE.

flĕdge *v.t.* **1.** Provide (bird, arrow) with feathers or plumage; wing for flight; deck with feathers or down. **2.** Bring up (young bird) till it can fly; (in *p.p.*) able to fly, (fig.) mature, independent. [f. obs. *fledge* a. 'fit to fly', f. OE **flecge*, **flycge*, MDu. *vlugghe*, OHG *flucchi* f. WG **fluggja* (**flug-* FLY[2])]

flĕ'dglĭng, flĕ'dgelĭng, (-jl-) *n.* Young bird; inexperienced person. [f. as prec. + -LING[1]]

flee *v.* (**fled**). **1.** *v.i.* Run away, seek safety in flight, (*from, before*); vanish, cease, pass away. **2.** *v.t.* Run away from, leave abruptly; eschew, shun. [OE *flēon*, = OS, OHG *fliohan*, ON *flý(j)a*, Goth. *thliuhan* f. Gmc **thleuhan*]

fleece *n.*, & *v.t.* **1.** *n.* Woolly covering of sheep or similar animal (**Golden F~,** (Gk Myth.) fleece of gold sought and won by Jason); (Her.) representation of this suspended from ring; quantity of wool shorn from a sheep at one time; rough, abundant, or woolly head of hair; thing like fleece (white cloud, falling snow, etc.); soft silky textile fabric used for lining etc.; hence (-)**fleec**ED[2] (-ēst), **flee'c**Y[2], *adjs.* **2.** *v.t.* Strip (person) of or *of* money, property, etc., whence ~'ABLE (-sa-) *a.*; overspread as with fleece (*sky fleeced with clouds*). [OE *flēos*, = Du. & MHG *vlies* f. WG **fleusa*, & OE *flēs* f. WG **fleusi*]

fleer *v.i.*, & *n.* **1.** *v.i.* Laugh impudently or mockingly, gibe, jeer, sneer. **2.** *n.* Mocking look or speech. [ME, prob. f. Scand.; cf. Norw. & Sw. dial. *flira* to grin]

fleet[1] *n.* **1.** Naval force, number of warships under one commander-in-chief, *the* navy; number of ships or boats sailing in company; similar force of aircraft; **~ of buses, lorries, taxis,** etc., (owned by one proprietor). **2.** **Fleet* ADMIRAL; **F~ Air Arm,** (Hist.) aviation service of Royal Navy. [OE *flēot* ship, shipping (*flēotan* float, FLEET[5])]

fleet[2] *n.* **1.** (dial.) Creek, inlet. **2. The F~,** (1) stream (now covered) running into Thames E. of Fleet Street in London, (2) (Hist.) prison that stood near it; **F~ marriage,** (Hist.) wedding performed by disreputable clergyman (**F~ parson**) in or near the Fleet Prison ready to conduct weddings clandestinely; **F~ Street,** the London press, London journalism. [OE *flēot*, = MDu. *vliet*, MHG *vliez*, ON *fljót* f. Gmc **fleut-* FLEET[5]]

fleet[3] *a.* (poet. or literary). Swift, nimble; hence ~'LY[2] *adv.*, ~'NESS *n.* [prob. f. ON *fljótr* f. Gmc **fleut-* FLEET[5]]

||**fleet**[4] *a.* & *adv.* (dial.) **1.** *a.* (Of water) shallow. **2.** *adv.* At or to a small depth (*plough* or *sow*

fleet). [perh. f. OE **flēat*; cf. Du. *vloot* shallow, f. as foll.]

fleet[5] *v.i.* Glide away, vanish, be transitory; pass rapidly, slip *away*; move swiftly, fly; hence ~′ING[2] *a.*, **~′ĭng**LY[2] *adv.* [OE *flēotan* float, swim, = OS *fliotan*, OHG *fliozan*, ON *fljóta* f. Gmc **fleutan*]

Flĕ′mĭng *n.* Native of Flanders. [OE f. ON *Flæmingi* & MDu. *Vlāming*, f. root of *Vlaanderen* Flanders; see -ING[3]]

Flĕ′mĭsh *a.* & *n.* (Language) of Flanders; *Flemish* BOND[1] 5. [f. MDu. *Vlāmisch* (as prec.; see -ISH[1])]

flĕnch, flĕnse, flĭnch[1], *v.t.* Cut up (whale or seal); flay (seal). [f. Da. *flense*; cf. Norw. *flinsa, flunsa* flay]

flĕsh[1] *n.* **1.** Soft substance between skin and bones, esp. muscular part of animal bodies. **2.** Body as opp. to mind or soul; **all ~**, whatever has bodily life (*the way of all flesh*, experience common to all men); **~ and blood,** (*n.*) the body or its material, mankind, human nature with its emotions and infirmities, (*a.*) actually living, not supernatural or imaginary; one's **own ~ and blood,** near relatives, descendants; **~ and fell,** (*n.*) the whole body, (*adv.*) entirely; **in the ~**, in bodily form, in life; **make** person's **~ creep,** frighten or horrify him esp. with dread of the supernatural; **one ~**, united as one personality [Gen. 2:24]; PROUD *flesh*; **sins of the ~**, unchastity. **3.** Pulpy substance of fruit or plant. **4.** Plumpness, fat, (**lose, put on, ~**, grow thinner, fatter). **5.** Tissue of animal bodies (excluding fish and sometimes fowl) as food, meat, esp. muscle with or without fat (*flesh-eater* etc.; *neither* FISH[1], *flesh, nor* etc.). **6.** Visible surface of human body, w. ref. to its colour or appearance; **~-colour**(**ed**), yellowish pink. **7.** **~-brush** (for stimulating circulation by rubbing); **~-fly** (depositing eggs or larvae in dead flesh); **~-pots,** luxurious living [Exod. 16:3]; **~ (side),** side of a hide that adjoined the flesh; **~ tints,** (esp.) painter's rendering of flesh-colours; **~-wound,** one not reaching bone or vital organ. **8.** Hence ~′LESS *a.* [OE *flǣsc*, = OS *flēsk*, OHG *fleisc*, ON *flesk* pork f. Gmc **flaiskaz, -iz*]

flĕsh[2] *v.* **1.** *v.t.* Incite (hound etc.) by taste of blood; initiate in bloodshed; inflame by fore-taste of success; use (sword etc.) for first time on flesh (or fig. of pen, wit, etc.); embody in flesh. **2.** *v.t.* & *i.* **~ out,** make or become substantial. [f. prec.]

flĕ′sher *n.* (Sc.) Butcher. [ME, f. FLESH[1] + -ER[1]]

flĕ′shĭngs (-z) *n. pl.* Actor's flesh-coloured tights. [f. FLESH[1] + -ING[1] + -S[1]]

flĕ′shl|y̆ *a.* (Of desire etc.) bodily, lascivious, sensual; mortal, material, not divine or spiritual; worldly; hence **~ĭ**NESS *n.* [OE *flǣsclic* (as FLESH[1], -LY[1])]

flĕ′sh|y̆ *a.* Plump, fat; of flesh, without bone; (of plant or fruit tissue) pulpy; like flesh; hence **~ĭ**NESS *n.* [ME, f. FLESH[1] + -Y[2]]

flĕ′tcher *n.* (arch.) Maker or seller of arrows. [ME, f. OF *flech(i)er* (*fleche* arrow)]

Flĕ′tton *n.* Type of brick made by semi-dry process. [~ in Cambs., near where clay was orig. taken for this process]

fleur de coin (flẽrdekwă′ṅ) *n.* Mint or perfect condition of a coin. [F, = bloom of the minting-die]

fleur-de-lis (flẽrdelē′) *n.* (*pl.* **fleurs-** *pr.* same). Iris flower; heraldic lily; (in *sing.* or *pl.*) former royal arms of France. [ME f. OF *flour de lys* flower of lily]

fleur′ĕt (-oor′-) *n.* Ornament like small flower. [f. F *fleurette* (*fleur* flower; see -ET[1])]

fleuron (flẽraw′ṅ) *n.* Flower-shaped ornament in architecture or printing, on coin, etc. [ME, f. OF *floron* (*flour* FLOWER)]

fleur′y̆ (-oor′ĭ), **flôr′y̆,** *a.* (Her.) Decorated with fleurs-de-lis. [ME, f. OF *flo(u)ré* (as prec.; see -Y[4])]

flew. See FLY[2].

flews (-ōōz) *n. pl.* Hanging lips of bloodhound etc. [16th c.; orig. unkn.]

flĕx[1] *v.t.* (Anat.) bend (joint, limb); move (muscle) to bend joint; (Geol.) distort (strata); (Archaeol.) place (corpse) with legs drawn up under chin. [f. L *flectere flex-* bend]

||**flĕx**[2] *n.* Flexible insulated wire used for carrying electric current to lamp, iron, etc. [abbr. of foll.]

flĕ′x|ĭble *a.* That will bend without breaking, pliable, pliant; easily led, manageable; adaptable, versatile; supple, complaisant; hence or cogn. **~**IBI′LITY *n.*, **~ĭb**LY[2] *adv.* [ME f. OF or f. L *flexibilis* (as FLEX[1]; see -IBLE)]

flĕ′xĭle *a.* (arch.) Supple, mobile; tractable; versatile; hence **flĕxĭ′l**ITY *n.* [f. L *flexilis* (as FLEX[1]; see -IL)]

flĕ′xion (-kshon), ***flĕ′ction,** *n.* Bending, curvature, bent state, (esp. of limb or joint); bent part, curve; (Gram.) inflexion, whence **~**AL, **~**LESS, *adjs.*; (Math.) =FLEXURE. [f. L *flexio* (as FLEX[1]; see -ION)]

flĕ′xor *n.* **~ (muscle)**, muscle that bends part of the body. [mod. L (as FLEX[1]; see -OR)]

flĕ′xūous *a.* Full of bends, winding; hence or cogn. **flĕxūo**′SITY *n.*, **~**LY[2] *adv.* [f. L *flexuosus* (*flexus* bending f. as FLEX[1]) + -OUS]

flĕ′xure (-ksher) *n.* Bending, curvature, bent state; bend, curve, turn; (Math.) curving of line or surface or solid (esp. from straight line, plane, etc.); (Geol.) bending of strata under pressure. [f. L *flexura* (as FLEX[1]; see -URE)]

flĭbbertĭgĭ′bbĕt *n.* Gossiping, flighty, frivolous, or restless person. [imit. of chatter]

flĭck *n.* & *v.* **1.** *n.* Light sharp blow with whip-lash etc. shot out and withdrawn, or with finger-nail; sudden movement, jerk; quick turn of wrist in playing games; slight sharp sound; (colloq.) cinema film, (in *pl.*) cinema performance; **~-knife,** weapon with blade springing out when button is pressed. **2.** *v.t.* Strike or move with a flick; dash or jerk (dust etc.) *away, off*; give a flick with (whip, towel, etc.). **3.** *v.i.* Make flicking movement; **~ through,** turn over (cards, pages, etc.) by rapid movement of fingers. [ME, imit.]

flĭ′cker[1] *v.i.*, & *n.* **1.** *v.i.* (Of flag, leaf, serpent's tongue, wind, etc.) quiver, vibrate, move or wave to and fro, blow lightly and unsteadily; (of flame, or fig. of hope, etc.) burn up and die away by turns; (of light) undergo transient increase or decrease of brightness. **2.** *n.* Flickering movement or light. [OE *flicorian, flycerian*]

flĭ′cker[2] *n.* N. Amer. woodpecker of genus *Colaptes*. [imit. of its note]

flī′er. See FLYER.

flīght[1] (-īt) *n.*, & *v.t.* **1.** Act or manner of flying through air (**take** one's **~**, fly); pursuit of game by hawk; migration, migrating body, flock, of birds or insects. **2.** Swift movement of projectiles etc.; passage of projectile from gun to target; trajectory and pace of ball in games; (of time) swift passage; soaring, excursion, sally, (*of* wit, fancy, ambition, etc.); distance that bird, aircraft, or missile, can fly. **3.** Series (*of* stairs in straight line or between two landings, or *of* hurdles or rails for racing over); volley (*of* arrows etc.); tail of dart; **in the first** or **top ~**, taking a leading place. **4.** Act or technique of travelling in aircraft, spacecraft, etc.; movement of such craft; regular journey by airline; R.A.F. unit of about six aircraft. **5. ~ control,** system (internal or external) directing movement of aircraft; **~-deck,** (1) deck of aircraft-carrier for take-off and landing, (2) accommodation for pilot, navigator, etc., in aircraft; **~ lieutenant, sergeant,** ranks in R.A.F.; **~ officer,** rank in W.R.A.F., corresp. to *flight lieutenant*; **~ path,** planned course of aircraft or spacecraft; **~-recorder,** device in aircraft to record technical details during flight for use in case of accident; **~-test** *v.t.*, test (aircraft, rocket, etc.) during flight. **6.** *v.t.* Shoot (wildfowl, or abs.) in flight; vary trajectory and pace of (cricket-ball etc.). [OE *flyht*, = OS *fluht* f. WG **fluhti* (**fleugan* FLY²)]

flight² (-īt) *n.* Act or manner of fleeing, hasty retreat, (**take, take to, ~**, run away; **put to ~**, rout); (Econ.) selling of currency, investments, etc., in anticipation of fall in value (*flight from sterling*). [OE **flyht*, = OS, OHG *fluht*, ON *flótti* f. Gmc **thluhtiz* (**thleuhan* FLEE)]

flī′ghtlėss (-ī′t-) *a.* (Of bird etc.) unable to fly. [f. FLIGHT¹ + -LESS]

flī′ght|y̆ (-ī′tĭ) *a.* Guided by whim or fancy, fickle; crazy; hence **~ĭLY²** *adv.*, **~ĭNESS** *n.* [f. FLIGHT¹ + -Y²]

flĭ′mflăm *n.*, & *v.t.* (**-mm-**). **1.** *n.* Trifle, nonsense, idle talk; piece of humbug, deception. **2.** *v.t.* Cheat, deceive; hence **~MER¹**, **~MERY** (4), *ns.* [imit. redupl.]

flĭ′ms|y̆ (-zĭ) *a.* & *n.* **1.** *a.* Easily destroyed, frail, lightly put together; paltry, trivial; frivolous, superficial; hence **~ĭLY²** *adv.*, **~ĭNESS** *n.* **2.** *n.* Flimsy thing or material; (document on) thin paper. [17th c., prob. f. prec.; cf. TIPSY]

flĭnch¹. See FLENCH.

flĭnch² *v.i.* Give way, draw back, (*from* duty, course, etc.); wince. [f. OF *flenchir*, *flainchir* f. WG **hlankjan*]

flĭ′nders (-z) *n. pl.* Fragments, splinters. [ME, prob. f. Scand.]

flĭng *v.* (**flung**) & *n.* **1.** *v.i.* Rush, go angrily or violently (*fling out of the room*; *flung away in a rage*); (of horse etc.) kick and plunge (*out*). **2.** *v.t.* Throw, hurl, (*about, aside, away, out, up, at*; rejected thing, missile, foam, dice); throw oneself *into* person's arms, a boat, etc. *on* person's compassion etc., or *into* an enterprise (i.e. take it up with all one's might); utter (words) forcefully; suddenly spread *out* (arms), kick *up* (heels); put *on*, take *off*, (clothes) carelessly; (arch.) send, emit, (sound, smell, light). **3.** Put (person) suddenly or violently *into* prison; launch (troops etc.) *on* enemy or *against* fortress or enemy; *fling* thing *in* person's *teeth* (see TOOTH). **4.** *n.* Throw, cast, (**have a ~ at,** make an attempt at, jeer at); impetuous dance (esp. **Highland ~**); violent movement, plunge; spell of indulgence in pleasure (*have* one's *fling*). [ME, perh. f. ON **flinga*, rel. to *flengja* flog]

flĭnt *n.* **1.** Hard stone of nearly pure silica found in pebbly lumps steel-grey within and encrusted with white; piece of flint, esp. as flaked or chipped by prehistoric man to form tool or weapon, (**set** one's **face like a ~**, be steadfast; SKIN² *a flint*); anything hard and unyielding. **2.** Piece of flint used with steel to produce fire (*flint and steel*) esp. in flintlock gun; piece of hard alloy of rare-earth metals used in cigarette-lighter as the spark-producing element. **3. ~ corn,** variety of maize having very hard kernels; **~ glass** (pure lustrous kind orig. made with flint); **~′lock,** (Hist.) (lock of) gun discharged by spark from flint. **4.** Hence **~′Y²** *a.* [OE, = MDu. *vlint*, OHG *flins*]

flĭp¹ *v.* (**-pp-**) & *n.* **1.** *v.t.* Put (pellet, coin, etc.) in motion with a fillip or flick; fillip or flick (person's ear, cheek, etc.), strike lightly; turn over (**~** one's **lid** etc., (sl.) lose self-control). **2.** *v.i.* Make a fillip with fingers; move (fan, whip, etc.) about with sudden jerk(s); strike smartly *at* with whip etc.; (sl.) become excited or enthusiastic; **~ through,** = FLICK *through*; hence **~′PING²** *a.* & *adv.*, (sl.) = DAMNED 2, 3. **3.** *n.* Smart light blow, fillip, flick; (colloq.) (short) flight in aeroplane; quick tour etc.; turning over (**~ side,** reverse side of gramophone record). [prob. f. FILLIP]

flĭp² *n.* Beer and spirit mixed, sweetened, and heated with hot iron; EGG¹-*flip*. [perh. f. prec. in sense *whip up*]

flĭp³ *a.* (**-pp-**). Glib, flippant. [f. FLIP¹]

flĭ′p-flŏp *n.*, & *v.i.* (**-pp-**). **1.** *n.* Somersault; electronic switching circuit changed from stable state to another, or via an unstable state back to its stable state, by triggering pulse; plastic or rubber sandal of sole and straps. **2.** *v.i.* Go or act in way suggested by 'flip-flop'. [imit.]

flĭ′ppant *a.* Lacking in seriousness, treating serious things lightly, disrespectful; hence **flĭ′ppANCY** *n.*, **~LY²** *adv.* [f. FLIP¹ + -ANT]

flĭ′pper *n.* Limb used to swim with, as in turtle and penguin; rubber attachment to foot for underwater swimming; (sl.) hand. [f. FLIP¹ + -ER¹]

flirt *v.* & *n.* **1.** *v.t.* Fillip, send with a jerk; wave or move briskly (fan, bird's tail). **2.** *v.i.* Pretend courtship or love-making (*with*); toy *with* (idea etc.); move with a jerk; hence **~A′TION** *n.*, **~ā′tiOUS** (-sh*us*) *a.* **3.** *n.* Sudden jerk, quick motion quickly checked; woman who invites or accepts man's attentions merely for amusement, whence **~′Y²** *a.* [imit.]

flĭt *v.i.* (**-tt-**), & *n.* **1.** *v.i.* Migrate, depart; (esp. Sc. & N. Engl.) change one's abode, move; pass lightly, softly, or rapidly, (*about, by, to and fro*); (of bat or bird) fly lightly, make short flights. **2.** *n.* Change of abode, esp. to evade creditor etc. [ME, f. ON *flytja*, cogn. w. FLEET⁵]

flĭtch *n.* Side of pork salted and cured (**Dunmow ~**, flitch given yearly at Dunmow in Essex to any couple proving conjugal harmony for year and day); slab (usu. outside one) of timber from tree-trunk; **~-beam,** compound beam, esp. of iron plate between two slabs of wood; **~(-plate)**, strengthening plate in beam etc. [OE *flicce*, = MLG *vli(c)ke*, ON *flikki* f. Gmc **flikkjam* (**flik-* rag)]

flĭ′tter *v.i.* Flit about, flutter; **~-mouse,** BAT¹. [f. FLIT + -ER⁵]

***flĭ′vver** *n.* (sl.) Cheap motor car or aeroplane; failure. [20th c.; orig. uncert.]

float¹ *n.* **1.** Raft; cork or quill used on fishing-line as indicator; cork supporting edge of fishing-net; hollow or inflated part or organ supporting fish etc. in water; structure to enable aircraft to float on water; floating device to control flow of water, petrol, etc. **2.** (Theatr., in *sing.* or *pl.*) footlights; **~(-board)**, one of the boards of water-wheel or paddle-wheel; low-bodied cart, esp. ||MILK¹-*float*; platform on wheels with display in processions; tool for smoothing plaster; sum of money made available for minor expenditures or change-giving. **3. ~ process,** making **~ glass** by drawing it continuously on to surface of molten metal for hardening from the molten state. [partly f. OE & ON *flot* floating state, OE *flota* ship, ON *floti*; partly f. foll.]

float² *v.* **1.** *v.i.* Rest or move on surface of liquid without sinking; (of stranded ship) get afloat; move with moving liquid, drift; move or be suspended freely *in* liquid or gas; (sl.) move in leisurely or casual way; hover *before* eye or mind; (Commerc., of acceptance) be in circulation; (Finance, of currency) be allowed to have fluctuating exchange rate. **2.** *v.t.* (Commerc.) bring (company, scheme) into favour, launch;

(arch.) cover with liquid, inundate; (of water etc.) support, bear along, (buoyant object); set afloat; cause (currency) to float; circulate (rumour); waft through air. **3. ~-stone,** light porous stone that floats. [OE *flotian*, = OS *floton*, ON *flota* cogn. w. FLEET[5]; in ME infl. by OF *floter* f. Rom. **flottare*, prob. also f. Gmc]

floa'tage *n.* Floating; ||(right of appropriating) flotsam; ships etc. afloat on river; floating masses; buoyancy; part of ship above water-line. [f. FLOAT[1] + -AGE]

floatā'tion. Var. of FLOTATION.

floa'ter *n.* In vbl senses; ||(St. Exch.) government stock certificate etc. recognized as security; floating voter; one who frequently changes his job; (sl.) mistake, gaffe. [f. FLOAT[2] + -ER[1]]

floa'ting *a.* In vbl senses (*floating* DEBT, DOCK[4], RIB); fluctuating, variable, not settled in a definite place, (*the floating population*); **~ anchor,** sea-anchor; **~ bridge,** (1) bridge on pontoons etc., (2) ferry working on chains; **~ kidney,** abnormal condition in which the kidneys are movable, such kidney; **~ light,** lightship, life-buoy with lantern; **~ point,** (in computer) decimal etc. point that does not occupy fixed position in numbers processed; **~ voter** (not attached to any political party). [f. FLOAT[2] + -ING[2]]

flŏc *n.* Flocculent mass of fine particles. [abbr. of FLOCCULUS]

flŏccĭnaucĭnĭhĭlĭpĭlĭfĭcā'tion (flŏksĭ-) *n.* (joc.) Act or habit of estimating as worthless. [f. L *flocci, nauci, nihili, pili*, wds denoting 'at little value' + -FICATION]

flŏ'ccūl|āte *v.t.* & *i.* Form into flocculent masses; hence **~A'TION** *n.* [f. FLOCCULUS + -ATE[3]]

flŏ'ccūle *n.* Small portion of matter like flock of wool. [f. FLOCCULUS; see -ULE]

flŏ'ccūl|ent *a.* Like tufts of wool; in or showing tufts; hence **~ENCE** *n.* [f. L *floccus* FLOCK[1] + -ULENT]

flŏ'ccūl|us *n.* (*pl.* **~i** *pr.* -ī). Floccule; (Anat.) small lobe in under-surface of cerebellum; (Astron.) small cloudy wisp on sun's surface. [mod. L, dim. of foll.]

flŏ'cc|us *n.* (*pl.* **~i** *pr.* -ŏ'ksī). Tuft of woolly hairs or filaments. [L, = foll.]

flŏck[1] *n.* Lock or tuft of wool, cotton, etc.; (in *pl.*) material for quilting and stuffing made of wool-refuse or torn-up cloth; powdered wool or cloth; (Chem., in *pl.*) light loose masses precipitated; **~-bed, ~-mattress,** (stuffed with flocks); **~-paper,** wallpaper sized and then sprinkled with powdered wool; hence **~'Y**[2] *a.* [ME, f. OF *floc* f. L *floccus*]

flŏck[2] *n.*, & *v.i.* **1.** *n.* Number of animals of one kind, esp. birds, feeding or travelling together; number of domestic animals, usu. sheep, goats, or geese, kept together (**~-master,** sheep-farmer; **~s and herds,** sheep and cattle); large number of persons. **2.** Christian body, congregation esp. in relation to its pastor; family of children, number of pupils, etc. **3.** *v.i.* Congregate, go in great numbers, troop, (*about, after, into, to, in, out, together*). [OE *flocc*, = MLG *vlocke*, ON *flokkr*)

flōe *n.* Sheet of floating ice. [prob. f. Norw. *flo* f. ON *fló* layer]

flŏg *v.* (**-gg-**). **1.** *v.t.* Beat with birch, cane, whip, etc.; drive (learning etc.) *into* or (laziness etc.) *out of* person; urge (horse etc.) on with whip (**~ a dead horse,** waste energy on something unalterable); (sl.) defeat, excel; (sl.) sell; (sl.) steal. **2.** *v.i.* (sl.) Proceed by violent or painful effort. [17th-c. cant; prob. imit., or f. L *flagellare* to whip]

flŏng *n.* Prepared paper for making stereotype moulds. [f. F *flan* FLAN]

flood (flŭd) *n.* & *v.* **1.** *n.* Inflow of tide; (poet.) river, stream, sea (**~ and field,** sea and land). **2.** Irruption of water over land, inundation, (**the F~,** that described in Genesis); outpouring (as) of water, torrent, downpour, (*flood of rain*; *a flood of abuse* or *light* or *tears* or *words*); (colloq.) = *floodlight*. **3. ~'gate,** gate opened and closed to admit or exclude water, esp. lower gate of lock, (fig.) barrier against rain, tears, etc.; **~'light** *n.*, & *v.t.*, (illuminate with, lamp used for) copious artificial light projected from many directions, eliminating all shadows on surface illuminated; *flood-*TIDE[1]. **4.** *v.t.* Overflow in or cover with a flood (lit. or fig.; *market was flooded with foreign goods*; *I was flooded with letters*); irrigate; deluge (burning house, mine) with water; overfill (carburettor) with petrol; (of rain) fill (river) to overflowing; drive *out* (of home etc.) because of flood. **5.** *v.i.* Come (*in*) in great quantities; become flooded; have uterine haemorrhage. [OE *flōd*, = OS *flōd*, OHG *fluot*, ON *flóth*, Goth. *flōdus* f. Gmc **flōdhuz*, **flōdham* (**flō-* f. IE **plō-*)]

floor (-ōr) *n.*, & *v.t.* **1.** *n.* Lower surface of room, boards etc. of which it is made, (*mop* or WIPE *the floor with*); bottom of sea, cave, cavity, etc.; level area; part of legislative assembly where members sit and speak; right to speak next in debate (*have* or *be given the floor*); (Cricket colloq.) *the* ground; minimum of prices, wages, etc.; **cross the ~,** join opposing side in debating-assembly; **from the ~,** given by individual member at meeting, not by those on platform etc.; **take the ~,** (1) begin to dance on dance-floor etc., (2) *speak in debate. **2.** Set of rooms etc. on same level in building (GROUND[1] *floor*, ***first ~,** on ground level; ||**first ~,** ***second ~,** above this), storey. **3. ~-cloth** (for washing floors); ***~-lamp,** standard lamp; ***~-leader,** leader of party in legislative assembly; **~ manager,** stage manager of a television production, shopwalker; **~ plan,** diagram of rooms etc. on one storey of building; **~-polish,** manufactured substance for making floors glossy; **~ show,** entertainment presented not on stage but on floor of night-club etc.; ***~-walker,** shopwalker. **4.** Hence **~'ING**[1] (3) *n.*, **~'LESS** *a.* **5.** *v.t.* Furnish with floor, pave; serve as floor of; bring to the floor or ground, knock down; confound, nonplus, baffle; overcome, get the better of. [OE *flōr*, = MDu. *vloer*, MHG *vluor*, ON *flór* f. Gmc **floruz*]

flōō'zĭe, flōō'sĭe, (-zĭ) *n.* (colloq.) Girl or woman, esp. disreputable one. [20th c.; cf. FLOSSY and dial. *floosy* fluffy]

flŏp *v.i.* (**-pp-**), *n.*, & *adv.* **1.** *v.i.* Sway about heavily and loosely; move in ungainly way; sit, kneel, lie, fall, *down* awkwardly or suddenly; change one's behaviour etc. suddenly; make dull sound of soft body falling or of flat thing slapping water; (sl.) sleep; (sl.) fail, collapse; hence **~'PY**[2] *a.* **2.** *n.* Flopping motion, sound made by it; (sl.) thing or person that fails; *(sl.) bed; **~-house,** (sl.) doss-house. **3.** *adv.* With a flop. [var. of FLAP]

flor. *abbr.* floruit.

flor'a *n.* (*pl.* **~e** *or* **~s**). Plants of a region, epoch, or environment; treatise on or list of these. [mod. L, f. name of goddess of flowers (*flos floris* flower)]

flor'al (*or* -ŏ'r-) *a.* Of flowers; decorated with or depicting flowers; of flora(e). [f. L *floralis* or *flos floris* flower; see -AL]

flŏ'rėāt *v.i.* May (he etc.) flourish. [L, 3rd sing. pres. subj. of *florēre* flourish]

Flŏ'rentīne *a.* & *n.* (Native or inhabitant) of Florence in Italy. [f. F *Florentin -ine* or f. L *Florentinus* (*Florentia* Florence; see -INE[1])]

florĕ'scence (*or* flŏr-) *n.* Flowering time or state

(lit. or fig.). [f. mod. L *florescentia* f. L *florescere* (*florēre* bloom; see -ESCENCE)]

flŏr'ĕt *n.* (Bot.) one of small flowers making up a composite flower (~ **of the disc, of the ray,** of the flower's centre or circumference); small flower, floweret. [f. L *flos floris* flower + -ET[1]]

flŏr'iāte *v.t.* Decorate with flower-designs etc. [f. as prec. + -ATE[3]]

flŏrĭbŭ'nda (*or* flŏr-) *n.* Plant, esp. rose, bearing dense clusters of flowers. [mod. L (*floribundus* freely flowering f. L *flos floris* flower + *-bundus*; cf. MORIBUND; infl. by L *abundus* copious)]

flŏr'ĭcultur|e (*or* flŏ'r-) *n.* Cultivation of flowers; hence ~AL *a.*, ~IST (3) *n.*, (-ŭ'lcher-). [f. L *flos floris* flower + CULTURE, after *horticulture*]

flŏ'rĭd *a.* Profusely adorned as with flowers, (of literary, artistic, or musical style) elaborately ornate; ostentatious, showy; ruddy, flushed, high-coloured; hence **flori'd**ITY, ~NESS, *ns.*, ~LY[2] *adv.* [f. F *floride* or f. L *floridus* (*flos floris* flower; see -ID[1])]

Flŏ'rĭda *n.* ~ **water,** perfume like eau-de--Cologne; hence **Flori'd**IAN *a.* & *n.* [~ in U.S.]

florĭ'ferous (*or* flŏr-) *a.* (Of seed or plant) producing many flowers. [f. L *florifer* (*flos floris* flower) + -OUS; see -FEROUS]

florĭlē'gĭ|um *n.* (*pl.* ~**a** *or* ~**ums**). Anthology. [mod. L (L *flos floris* flower, *legere* gather), transl. of Gk *anthologion* ANTHOLOGY]

flŏ'rĭn *n.* Foreign coin of gold or silver, esp. Dutch guilder; (Hist.) English gold coin (6s. 8d.) of 14th c. and silver coin (2s.) of 19th–20th c. [ME f. OF, f. It. *fiorino* dim. of *fiore* flower f. L *flos floris*, orig. coin having figure of lily on it]

flŏ'rĭst *n.* One who deals in or grows flowers; hence ~RY (5) *n.* [f. L *flos floris* flower + -IST]

flŏrĭ'st|ĭc *a.* Relating to study of distribution of plants; hence ~ICALLY *adv.*, ~ICS *n.* [f. FLORA + -IST + -IC]

flor'uĭt (-ŏŏ-; *or* flŏ'r-) *n.* Period or date at which person was alive or working. [L, = he or she flourished]

flor'ȳ. See FLEURY.

flŏ'scŭlar, flŏ'scŭlous, *adjs.* Having florets, composite-flowered. [f. L *flosculus* dim. of *flos* flower (see -CULE) + -AR[1], -OUS]

flŏss *n.* Rough silk enveloping silkworm's cocoon; untwisted silk thread for embroidery; CANDY--*floss*; DENTAL *floss*; ~ **silk,** rough silk used in cheap goods. [f. F (*soie*) *floche* floss(-silk) f. OF *flosche* down, nap of velvet]

flŏ'ssȳ *a.* Of or like floss; (colloq.) fancy, showy. [f. prec. + -Y[2]]

flōtā'tion *n.* Floating (**centre of** ~, centre of gravity in floating body); starting of company or enterprise; separation of components of crushed ore etc. by their different capacities to float. [alt. of *floatation* (FLOAT[2], -ATION) after *rotation* etc.]

flotĭ'lla *n.* Small fleet; fleet of boats or small ships. [Sp., dim. of *flota* fleet, OF *flote* multitude]

flŏ'tsam *n.* Wreckage found floating; ~ **and jetsam,** (fig.) vagrants etc. [f. AF *floteson* (*floter* FLOAT[2])]

flounce[1] *v.i.*, & *n.* **1.** *v.i.* Go with agitated or violent motion, flop, plunge, throw the body about, (*away, out, about, down, up*). **2.** *n.* Fling or jerk of body or limb(s). [16th c., of unkn. orig.; perh. imit., as *bounce, pounce*]

flounce[2] *n.*, & *v.t.* **1.** *n.* Ornamental wide strip gathered and sewn by upper edge esp. round woman's skirt, and with lower edge hanging. **2.** *v.t.* Trim with flounce(s). [alt. of earlier *frounce* fold, pleat, f. OF *fronce* (*froncir* wrinkle f. Frank. **hrunkjan*)]

flou'nder[1] *n.* Flat-fish, esp. of small edible species. [ME, f. AF *floundre*, OF *flondre*, prob. of Scand. orig.]

flou'nder[2] *v.i.*, & *n.* **1.** *v.i.* Struggle and plunge (as) in mud or when wading; make mistakes, manage business badly or with difficulty. **2.** *n.* Act of floundering. [imit., perh. assoc. w. *founder, blunder*]

flour (-owr) *n.*, & *v.t.* **1.** *n.* Finer part of meal of grain, obtained by bolting; wheat meal; CORN[1]-*flour*; fine soft powder, esp. from seeds, farinaceous roots, etc.; hence ~'Y[2] *a.* **2.** *v.t.* Sprinkle with flour; *grind into flour. [ME, different. sp. of FLOWER in sense 'finest part']

flou'rĭsh[1] (flŭ'-) *v.* **1.** *v.i.* Grow vigorously; thrive, prosper, be successful; be in one's prime; be in good health; spend one's life, be active, *in, at, about*, etc., a certain time (cf. FLORUIT). **2.** *v.t.* Show ostentatiously; wave (weapon) about; move (limbs) about vigorously. [ME, f. OF *florir* (-ISH[2]) f. Rom. **florire* f. L *florēre* (*flos floris* flower)]

flou'rĭsh[2] (flŭ'-) *n.* Ornament of flowing curves about letter or word in handwriting; rhetorical embellishment, florid expression; ostentatious waving of weapon, hand, etc. (*removed his hat with a flourish*); (Mus.) fanfare of brass instruments, florid passage, extemporized addition or prelude; prosperity, flourishing; hence ~Y[2] *a.* [f. prec.]

flout *v.* & *n.* **1.** *v.t.* Mock, insult, express contempt for by word or act. **2.** *v.i.* Mock or scoff *at.* **3.** *n.* Flouting speech or act. [perh. f. Du. *fluiten* whistle, hiss (cf. FLUTE)]

flow (-ō) *v.i.*, & *n.* **1.** *v.i.* Glide along as a stream; (of blood, money, electric current) circulate; (of persons or things) come or go in large numbers or smoothly; (of talk, literary style, etc.) proceed smoothly; (of garment, hair, etc.) hang easily, undulate; (of solid) undergo permanent change of shape under stress. **2.** Gush out, spring; (of blood) be spilt; result *from*; run full, be in flood (*ebb and flow*; **swim with the ~ing tide,** be on the winning side); (of wine) be poured out without stint; (arch.) be plentifully supplied *with* (*land flowing with milk and honey*). **3.** *n.* Flowing movement in stream; gradual deformation of solid under stress; amount that flows; manner in which a thing flows; flowing liquid; outpouring, stream, copious supply; rise of tide (*ebb and flow*) or river; ~ **chart, ~-sheet,** diagram of movement of things or persons in a complex activity; ~ **of soul,** genial conversation (as complement to FEAST *of reason*); ~ **of spirits,** habitual cheerfulness; **~'stone,** (Geol.) rock deposited by flow of water in thin sheet. [OE *flōwan*, cogn. w. ON *flóa*, Du. *vloeien*, f. Gmc **flō-* (FLOOD)]

flow'er (*or* flowr) *n.* & *v.* **1.** *n.* Coloured (usu. not green) part of plant from which fruit or seed is later developed; (Bot.) reproductive organ in plant containing one or more pistils or stamens or both, and usu. a corolla and calyx; a blossom apart from the plant, esp. as used in groups for decoration or as mark of honour or respect (**No ~s,** intimation that wreaths etc. are not desired at funeral); state of blooming (*in flower*); plant cultivated or esteemed for its flowers. **2.** (in *pl.*) Ornamental phrases (*flowers of speech*). **3.** *The* pick or choice *of*; *the* best part, essence; *the* choicest embodiment *of*; prime (*in the flower of his age*). **4.** (in *pl.*) Powder obtained by sublimation (*flowers of sulphur*); scum formed by fermentation; **~s of tan,** a mould (*Fuligo septica*) found on dead wood, bark, etc.; *flowers of* ZINC. **5. ~-bed,** garden bed in which flowers are grown; **~-de-luce,** (arch.) fleur-de-lis, *iris flower; **~-girl,** woman who sells flowers esp. in street; **~-pecker,** Austral. etc. bird of family Dicaeidae; ~ **people,** young people carrying flowers as symbols of peace and love; **~pot,** pot of red earthenware, plastic, etc., holding soil in which plant may be set; **~-show,** competitive or other exhibition of flowers. **6.** Hence (-)~ED[2] (-*erd*), ~LESS (esp. of cryptogam), *adjs.*, ~ET[1] *n.* **7.** *v.i.* Produce flowers, bloom or blossom (lit. or fig.), whence ~ER[1] *n.*, plant that flowers at specified time etc., ~ING[2] *a.* (**~ing cherry, currant,** etc., tree grown mainly for its flowers; **~ing fern,** osmund). **8.** *v.t.* Cause or allow (plant) to flower; decorate with worked flowers or floral design. [ME f. AF *flur*, OF *flour*, *flor*, f. L *flos floris*]

flow'er|ȳ *a.* Abounding in flowers; full of fine words, compliments, figures of speech, etc., whence ~ĭNESS *n.* [ME, f. prec. + -Y[2]]

flow'ĭng (-ō'ĭ-) *a.* In vbl senses; (of style) fluent, easy; (of line, curve, contour) smoothly continuous, not abrupt; (of hair, garment, sail, etc.) unconfined; *flowing* SHEET[3]; hence ~LY[2] *adv.* [f. FLOW + -ING[2]]

flown[1] (-ōn) *a.* (arch.) Swollen, puffed up, (*flown with insolence and wine*). [obs. p.p. of FLOW, used by Milton (*Paradise Lost* I. 502)]

flown[2]. See FLY[2].

F.L.Q. *abbr.* Front de Libération du Québec.

Flt. Lt., Flt. Off., Flt. Sgt., *abbrs.* Flight Lieutenant, Officer, Sergeant.

flu (flōō) *n.* (colloq.) Influenza. [abbr.]

***flŭb** *v.* (-bb-) & *n.* **1.** *v.t.* & *i.* Botch, bungle. **2.** *n.* Thing badly or clumsily done. [20th c.; orig. unkn.]

***flŭ'bdŭb** *n.* Bombastic or inept language. [19th c., prob. fanciful formation]

flŭ'ctū|āte *v.i.* Vary irregularly, rise and fall, move to and fro, be unstable; vacillate, waver; so ~A'TION *n.* [f. L *fluctuare* (*fluctus* flow, wave f. *fluere fluct-* flow) + -ATE[3]]

flue (flōō) *n.* Smoke-duct in chimney; channel for conveying heat, esp. hot-air passage in wall, tube for heating water in some kinds of boiler; **~-cure,** cure (tobacco) by artificial heat from flues; **~-pipes,** (Mus.) organ-pipes other than reed-pipes. [16th c.; orig. unkn.]

flu'ence (flōō'-) *n.* Influence; **put the ~ on,** apply hypnotic etc. power to (person). [f. INFLUENCE]

flu'encȳ (flōō'-) *n.* Smooth easy flow, esp. in speech; ready utterance. [f. foll. + -ENCY]

flu'ent (flōō'-) *a.* Flowing easily; (arch.) not settled, liable to change; (of motion, curve, etc.) graceful, easy; (of speech or style) copious, coming easily, ready; expressing oneself quickly and easily; hence ~LY[2] *adv.* [f. L *fluere* flow; see -ENT]

flŭff *n.*, & *v.t.* **1.** *n.* Light feathery stuff given off by blankets etc.; soft fur; soft downy mass or bunch (**bit of ~,** (arch. colloq.) young woman); (sl.) theatrical part imperfectly known, mistake in speaking, playing game, playing music, etc.; hence ~'Y[2] *a.* **2.** *v.t.* Put soft surface on (flesh side of leather); make into fluff; shake (*oneself*, its feathers etc.) up or out into fluffy mass; (sl.) blunder in (theatrical part), mispronounce, misplay, etc. **3.** *v.i.* Become fluffy; (sl.) make mistake in speaking, playing game, playing music, etc. [prob. dial. alt. of *flue* fluff]

flu'gelhōrn (flōō'g-) *n.* Brass wind instrument of bugle family. [f. G *flügelhorn* (*flügel* wing, *horn* horn)]

flu'ĭd (flōō'-) *a.* & *n.* **1.** *a.* Consisting of particles that move freely among themselves and yield to the slightest pressure; moving or changing readily, not solid or rigid or stable, (*situation is fluid*); hence **fluĭ'dĭ**FY *v.t.*, **fluĭ'd**ITY *n.*, (flōō-). **2.** *n.* Fluid substance (including gases and liquids); liquid constituent or secretion; ~ **clutch, coupling, flywheel,** etc., (using liquid to transmit power); *fluid* DRACHM; *fluid* OUNCE[1]. [f. F *fluide* or f. L *fluidus* (*fluere* flow; see -ID[1])]

fluĭ'd|ĭcs (flōō-) *n. pl.* (usu. treated as *sing.*) Technique of using small interacting flows and fluid jets for amplification, switching, etc.; hence ~IC *a.* [f. prec. + -ICS]

flu'ĭdīz|e, -īs|e, (flōō'ĭdīz) *v.t.* Cause (finely divided solid) to acquire characteristics of fluid by upward passage of gas etc.; hence ~A'TION *n.* [f. FLUID + -IZE]

***flu'ĭdounce** (flōō'-) *n.* Fluid OUNCE[1]. [contr.]

***flu'ĭdrăm** (flōō'-) *n.* Fluid DRACHM. [contr.]

fluke[1] (flōōk) *n.* Flat-fish, flounder; trematode worm found in sheep's liver. [OE *flōc*, = ON *flóki*; cf. MLG, MDu. *flac* flat, OHG *flah*]

fluke[2] (flōōk) *n.* Broad triangular plate on arm of anchor; barbed head of lance, harpoon, etc.; lobe of whale's tail. [16th c., perh. f. prec.]

fluk|e[3] (flōōk) *n.* & *v.* **1.** *n.* Lucky accidental stroke; chance breeze; hence ~'Y[2] *a.* **2.** *v.i.* Make fluke. **3.** *v.t.* Get, hit, etc., by fluke. [19th c., perh. f. dial. *fluke* guess]

flume (flōōm) *n.* & *v.* **1.** *n.* Artificial channel conveying water etc. for industrial use; ravine with stream. **2.** *v.i.* Build flumes. **3.** *v.t.* Convey down a flume. [ME f. OF *flum*, *flun*, f. L *flumen* river (*fluere* flow)]

flŭ'mmerȳ *n.* Sweet dish made with flour, milk, eggs, honey, etc.; empty compliments, trifles, nonsense. [f. W *llymru*, of unkn. orig.]

flŭ'mmox *v.t.* (sl.) Confound, bewilder, disconcert. [19th c.; prob. dial., imit.]

flŭmp *v.* & *n.* (colloq.) **1.** *v.i.* & *t.* Fall or move heavily, set or throw *down*, with dull noise. **2.** *n.* Action or sound of flumping. [imit.]

flŭng. See FLING.

***flŭnk** *v.* (colloq.) **1.** *v.i.* Fail, esp. in examination; ~ **out,** be dismissed from school etc. because of flunking. **2.** *v.t.* Fail (examination); reject (examination candidate). [cf. FUNK and obs. *flink* be coward]

flŭ'nkey, flŭ'nkȳ, *n.* (usu. derog.) Liveried servant, footman; toady, snob; *cook, waiter, etc.; hence ~DOM, ~ISM (3), (-kĭ-) *ns.* [18th c., orig. Sc.; perh. f. FLANK, w. sense 'sidesman, flanker']

fluō- (flōōō) *comb. form.* Fluorine, as: **~boric acid** (containing fluorine and boron). [f. FLUORINE + -O-]

fluor|ĕ'scence (flōō-) *n.* Visible or invisible radiation produced from certain substances by incident radiation of shorter wavelength, electrons, etc., esp. by violet and ultraviolet light and X-rays; property of absorbing light of short (invisible) wavelength and emitting light of longer (visible) wavelength; hence ~E'SCE *v.i.*, exhibit fluorescence, ~E'SCENT *a.* (**~escent lamp,** lamp radiating largely by fluorescence, esp. tubular lamp in which phosphor on inside surface of tube is made to fluoresce by ultraviolet radiation from mercury vapour; **~escent screen,** screen coated with fluorescent material to show images from X-rays etc.). [f. FLUORSPAR (which fluoresces) after *opalescence*]

fluorĭd|ā'tion (flōō-) *n.* Addition of traces of fluoride to drinking-water to prevent or reduce tooth-decay, whence **~ā'tion**IST (2) *n.*; application of fluoride to teeth for similar purpose; hence ~ATE[3] (-ōō'-) *v.t.* [f. foll. + -ATION]

flu'orīde (flōō'-) *n.* Binary compound of fluorine. [f. FLUORINE + -IDE]

fluorĭdīzā'tion (flōō-). Var. of FLUORIDATION.

flu'orĭn|āte (flōō'-) *v.t.* = FLUORIDATE; (Chem.) introduce fluorine into (compound; *fluorinated hydrocarbons*); hence ~A'TION *n.* [f. foll. + -ATE[3]]

flu'orine (flōō'erēn) *n.* Non-metallic element, a

pale yellow highly reactive gas. [F (as FLUORSPAR; see -INE⁵)]

flu'orīte (flōō'-) *n.* = FLUORSPAR. [It. (as FLUORSPAR; see -ITE¹ (2))]

flu'orō- (flōō'-) *comb. form.* **1.** (Chem.) Fluorine, as: **~car'bon,** synthetic compound of carbon and fluorine; **~form,** compound analogous to chloroform but with fluorine in place of chlorine. **2.** Fluorescence, as: **~scope,** instrument with fluorescent screen used instead of dark room to show X-ray effects. [f. FLUORINE & FLUORESCENCE + -O-]

fluorō'sĭs (flōō-) *n.* Poisoning by fluorine or its compounds. [f. F *fluorose* (as FLUORO- 1; see -OSIS)]

flu'orspār (flōō'-) *n.* Calcium fluoride as mineral. [f. *fluor* flow, mineral used as flux (sense 4), fluorspar, f. L *fluor* (*fluere* flow) + SPAR²]

flŭ'rrȳ *n.*, & *v.t.* **1.** *n.* Gust, squall; commotion, excitement; nervous hurry, agitation; sudden burst of activity. **2.** *v.t.* Confuse by haste or noise, agitate. [imit.; cf. obs. *flurr* ruffle, *hurry*]

flŭsh¹ *v.* **1.** *v.i.* (Of bird) fly up and away. **2.** *v.t.* Cause to do this, put up, (birds); reveal, drive *out.* [ME, imit.; cf. *fly, rush*]

flŭsh² *v.* **1.** *v.i.* Spurt, rush out; (of plant) throw out fresh shoots; glow with warm colour; (of blood) rush into and redden face; (of face) become red or hot, blush; (of plant) throw out fresh shoots. **2.** *v.t.* Cleanse (drain, lavatory, etc.) by flow of water; dispose of thing thus (*away, down*); flood (meadow); (usu. in *p.p.*) cause to glow or blush, suffuse with warm colour, inflame with pride or passion, encourage, (*flushed with exercise, joy, victory, insolence,* etc.). [perh. = prec., infl. by *flash* and *blush*]

flŭsh³ *n.* **1.** Rush of water; sudden abundance; cleansing of drain, lavatory, etc., by flushing. **2.** Rush of emotion, elation produced by it or by victory etc. **3.** Freshness, vigour; fresh growth of grass etc. **4.** Glow of light or colour; rush of blood to face, reddening caused by it; hot fit in fever, menopause, etc. [ME, f. prec.]

flŭsh⁴ *a.*, & *v.t.* **1.** *a.* Full to overflowing, in flood; (usu. *pred.*) having plentiful supply of or *of* money etc., (of money) abundant. **2.** Even, in same plane, level *with*, without projections or raised edges. **3.** *v.t.* Make level; fill in (joint) level with surface. [prob. f. FLUSH²]

flŭsh⁵ *n.* Hand of cards all of one suit; **straight ~,** flush that is also a sequence; **royal ~,** (Poker) straight flush headed by ace. [f. OF *flus, flux* f. L *fluxus* FLUX]

flŭ'ster *v.* & *n.* **1.** *v.t.* Confuse with drink, half-intoxicate; flurry, make nervous. **2.** *v.i.* Be agitated, bustle. **3.** *n.* Flurry, flutter, agitation. [ME, orig. unkn.; cf. Icel. *flaustr(a)* hurry, bustle]

flute (flōōt) *n.* & *v.* **1.** *n.* Wood-wind instrument without reed, having holes along it stopped by fingers or keys, and blow-hole in side near end, whence **flu'tER¹** (1) (arch.), ***flu'tIST** (3), (flōō'-) *ns.*; its player; organ stop of like quality. **2.** Semicylindrical vertical groove in pillar, similar groove elsewhere, e.g. in frills, whence **flu'tING¹** (6) (flōō'-) *n.*; tall wineglass. **3.** *v.i.* Play flute; whistle, sing, or speak, in flutelike tones. **4.** *v.t.* Play (tune etc.) on flute; make flutes or grooves in. [ME, f. OF *flëute, flaüte, flahute,* prob. f. Prov. *flaüt*]

flŭ'tter *v.* & *n.* **1.** *v.i.* Flap wings without flying or in short flights; come or go with quivering motion (usu. to the ground); go about restlessly, flit, hover; quiver, vibrate, (of pulse) beat feebly and irregularly; tremble with excitement, be agitated. **2.** *v.t.* Flap (wings) without flying or in short flights; move (flag etc.) irregularly, agitate, ruffle; throw (person) into confusion or agitation (*flutter the* DOVE¹*cots*). **3.** *n.* Fluttering; tremulous excitement (*be* or *put in a flutter*); vibration, esp. undesired oscillation in part of aircraft etc. under stress; (Med.) abnormal rapid but regular contractions of muscle; (Mus.) rapid movement of tongue by player of wind instrument (esp. *flutter-tonguing* etc.); rapid variation of pitch or loudness of sound; ||(sl.) small bet or speculation. [OE *floterian, flotorian,* frequent. form cogn. w. FLEET⁵; see -ER⁵]

flu'tȳ (flōō'-) *a.* Like flute in tone, soft and clear. [f. FLUTE + -Y²]

flu'vĭal (flōō'-) *a.* Of or found in river(s). [ME, f. L *fluvialis* (*fluvius* river f. *fluere* flow; see -AL)]

flu'vĭatīle (flōō'-) *a.* Of, found in, produced by, river(s). [F, f. L *fluviatilis* (*fluviatus* moistened f. *fluvius*; see prec., -IL)]

flu'vĭō- (flōō'-) *comb. form.* River, as: **~-gla'cial,** of or caused by streams from glacial ice, or combined action of rivers and glaciers; **~METER** (-ŏ'm-), instrument for measuring rise and fall of rivers. [f. L *fluvius* river (*fluere* flow) + -O-]

flŭx *n.* & *v.* **1.** *n.* Flowing out, issue; flowing; inflow of tide (*flux and reflux*; usu. fig.); (arch.) morbid or excessive discharge of blood, excrement, etc., (**bloody ~,** dysentery). **2.** Flood *of* talk etc.; continuous succession of changes (*in a state of flux*). **3.** (Phys.) Rate of flow of any fluid across given area, amount crossing area in given time, (**~-line,** line representing direction and rate of flow at each point); amount of radiation or particles incident on area in given time; total electric or magnetic field passing through a surface. **4.** Substance mixed with metal etc. to promote fusion. **5.** *v.i.* Issue in a flux, flow copiously. **6.** *v.t.* Make fluid, fuse; treat with a fusing flux. [ME f. OF, or f. L *fluxus* (*fluere flux-* flow)]

flŭ'xion (-kshon) *n.* (arch.) Flowing; (Math.) rate at which a variable quantity increases, derivative, (**method of ~s,** the Newtonian calculus); hence **~AL, ~ARY¹,** *adjs.* [F, or f. L *fluxio* (as prec.; see -ION)]

flȳ¹ *n.* **1.** Two-winged insect; **~ in amber,** curious relic; **~ in the ointment,** trifling circumstance that spoils enjoyment; **~ on the wall,** unperceived observer; **~ on the wheel,** person who overestimates his own influence; *die* etc. **like flies** (in large numbers); (**there are**) **no flies on him,** (sl.) he is very astute. **2.** Winged insect (BUTTERFLY, FIRE¹*fly*, MAY³*fly*). **3.** Disease of plants or animals, caused by one of various flies. **4.** Natural or artificial fly used as fishing-bait; DRY¹-*fly*. **5. ~ agaric,** poisonous mushroom (*Amanita muscaria*); **~-blow,** fly's egg in meat etc.; **~-blown,** tainted (lit. or fig.); **~-book,** case for keeping fishing-flies in; **~'catcher,** (1) trap for flies, (2) bird that catches insects in the air; **~-fish** *v.i.*, fish with fly; **~-flap** (for driving away flies); **~-net,** net or fringe protecting horse from flies; **~-paper** (for catching or poisoning flies); **~-specked,** marked with flies' excrement; **~-spray,** liquid for killing flies, to be sprayed from canister etc.; **~-strip,** impregnated plastic strip for poisoning flies; **~-swatter,** device for killing flies by hitting them; **~-trap,** (1) trap for catching flies, (2) plant able to catch flies, esp. VENUS'*s fly-trap*; **~'weight** (see BOX⁵*ing-weights*); **~-whisk** (for driving away flies). [OE *flȳge, flēoge,* = OS, OHG *flioga* f. WG **fleug(j)ō* f. Gmc **fleugan* (cf. foll.)]

flȳ² *v.* (**flew** *pr.* flōō; **flown** *pr.* flōn). **1.** *v.i.* Move through air with wings (*about, away, off, out*; **bird is flown,** person wanted has escaped; *as the* CROW¹ *flies*; **~ high,** (1) be ambitious, (2) prosper; HIGH-*flown*); move through air or space in or as aircraft or spacecraft; **~ in, ~ out,**

arrive, depart, by aircraft. **2.** (Hawk.) Soar by way of attack *at*; ~ **at higher game,** (fig.) have nobler ambitions. **3.** Pass or rise quickly through air; jump clear over or *over* fence etc. **4.** (Of flag, hair, garment, etc.) wave. **5.** Travel swiftly, rush along, pass rapidly (*time flies*); spring, start, hasten, (~ **to arms,** take up arms eagerly; *fly in the* FACE[1] *of*; ~ **at, upon,** attack violently; ~ **into** a passion, raptures, etc.); be driven or forced off suddenly (*made sparks* or *feathers* or FUR *fly*; *send flying*; **make the money ~**, spend it quickly; *door flew open*; **glass** etc. **flies,** breaks in pieces; *fly off the* HANDLE[1]); **let ~**, discharge (missile), (abs.) shoot, hit, or use strong language, *at* (person etc. *with* missile etc.). **6.** Run away, flee; (colloq.) depart hastily. **7.** *v.t.* Control flight of (aircraft); transport (passengers etc.) in aircraft; traverse (distance, region) in or as aircraft. **8.** Make (pigeon, hawk) fly; make (kite) rise and stay aloft; ~ **a kite,** (1) raise money by accommodation bill, (2) make announcement or take step so as to test public opinion; ***go ~ a kite,** (colloq.) go away. **9.** Set or keep (flag) flying. **10.** Flee from (*must fly the country*); ***~ the coop,** (colloq.) depart suddenly. **11.** **~-away,** (of garment) streaming, loose, (of person) flighty; **~-by,** (1) =*fly-past*, (2) close approach of spacecraft to planet etc.; **~-by-night,** (*n.*) one who makes night excursions or decamps by night, (*a.*) *(of enterprise etc.) shady; **~'over,** (1) =*fly-past*, (2) bridge for carrying railway or road over another; **~-past,** ceremonial flight of aircraft past some person or place; **~'under,** passage of road or railway under another; **~'way,** birds' customary migration-route. [OE *flēogan*, =OS, OHG *fliogan*, ON *fljúga* f. Gmc **fleugan*]

flȳ[3] *n.* **1.** Flying; **on the ~**, on the wing, while in motion in the air. **2.** (*pl.* usu. **~s**). ||(Hist.) One-horse hackney carriage. **3.** Lap on garment (esp. trousers) to contain or cover fastening; flap at entrance of tent; TENT[1]-*fly*; part of flag farthest from staff; breadth of flag from staff to end. **4.** (Theatr., in *pl.*) Space over proscenium. **5.** Speed-regulating device in clockwork and machinery. **6.** **~ ash** (from burning of powdered coal); **~-half,** (Rugby Footb.) stand-off half; **~'leaf,** blank leaf at beginning or end of book, blank leaf of circular etc.; **~-post,** display (handbills etc.) rapidly in unauthorized places; **~'sheet,** 2 or 4 page circular etc.; **~'wheel,** heavy-rimmed wheel on revolving shaft to regulate machinery or accumulate power. [f. prec.]

flȳ[4] *a.* (sl.) Knowing, wide awake. [19th c.; orig. unkn.]

flȳ'er, flī'er, *n.* In vbl senses; bird etc. that flies (HIGH, *poor*, etc., *flyer*); (colloq.) ambitious or outstanding person; animal, vehicle, etc., going with exceptional speed; airman or airwoman; aircraft; *small handbill; *speculative investment; flying jump. [ME, f. FLY[2] + -ER[1]]

flȳ'ĭng[1] *n.* In vbl senses; ~ **field,** airfield; ~ **machine,** (esp. heavier-than-air) machine able to fly in the air; ~ **officer,** rank in R.A.F.; ~ **school,** place for learning to fly aircraft. [f. FLY[2] + -ING[1]]

flȳ'ĭng[2] *a.* In vbl senses; hanging loose, fluttering; passing, hasty (*flying visit*); temporary (*flying bridge*); designed for rapid movement; ~ **bedstead,** experimental aircraft shaped like bedstead for tests of vertical take-off; ~ **boat,** seaplane with boatlike fuselage; ~ **bomb,** pilotless aircraft with explosive warhead; ~ **buttress** (slanting from column etc. up to wall, usu. on arch); *with flying* COLOUR[1]*s*; ~ **column,** military force capable of rapid movement and independent operation; ~ **doctor** (using aeroplane to visit distant patients); *Flying* DUTCHMAN; ~ **fish,** tropical fish able to rise into air by winglike pectoral fins; ~ **fox,** fruit-eating bat of genus *Pteropus*; ~ **jib,** light sail set on extension of jib-boom; ~ **jump, leap,** (with running start); ~ **lemur,** nocturnal animal of genus *Cynocephalus* able to make long leaps by means of folds of skin from neck to tail; ~ **lizard,** lizard of genus *Draco* able to make long leaps by means of membranes on extended ribs; ~ **mare,** a throw in wrestling; ~ **phalanger,** small phalanger able to make long leaps by means of skin joining fore and hind legs; ~ **saucer,** unidentified saucer-shaped object reported as seen in the sky; ~ **squad,** police detachment or other body organized for rapid movement; ~ **squadron,** military detachment or other body organized for rapid movement; ~ **squirrel,** (1) squirrel esp. of genus *Pteromys* able to make long leaps by means of skin joining fore and hind legs, (2) =*flying phalanger*; ~ **start,** start in which starting-point is passed at full speed, (fig.) initial advantage; ~ **tackle** (Footb. etc., made while running or jumping); ~ **wing,** aircraft without fuselage or tailplane. [f. FLY[2] + -ING[2]]

flȳ'tĭng *n.* (Hist.) Contest of invective between two persons. [f. *flyte* wrangle f. OE *flītan* contend + -ING[1]]

F.M. *abbr.* Field Marshal; frequency modulation.

fm. *abbr.* fathom(s).

Fm *symb.* fermium.

f-nŭmber (ĕ'f-) *n.* (Photog.) Quantity giving ratio of focal length and effective diameter of lens. [f. *f* (denoting focal length) + NUMBER[1]]

F.O. *abbr.* Flying Officer; ||(Hist.) Foreign Office.

fo. *abbr.* folio.

foal *n.*, & *v.t.* **1.** *n.* Young horse, ass, etc., colt or filly; **in** or **with ~**, (of mare etc.) pregnant. **2.** *v.t.* (Of mare etc.) bring forth (young, or abs.). [OE *fola*, =OS, OHG *folo*, ON *foli*, Goth. *fula* f. Gmc **folon*; cf. FILLY]

foam *n.* & *v.* **1.** *n.* Collection of small bubbles formed in liquid by agitation, fermentation, etc.; froth of saliva or perspiration; (poet.) the sea; rubber or plastic in cellular mass (**~'back,** thin layer of synthetic foam on fabric); ~ **extinguisher,** fire-extinguisher generating mass of foam; hence ~'LESS, ~'Y[2], *adjs.* **2.** *v.i.* Emit foam, froth at the mouth, (colloq.) be very angry; (of water etc.) froth, gather foam, run foaming *along*, *down*, *over*, etc., pass off or away in foam; (of cup etc.) be filled with foaming liquor. **3.** *v.t.* (in *p.p.*) Having or given cellular structure like that of foam (*foamed slag*). [OE *fām*, = OHG *feim* f. WG **faim-* f. IE **poimo-*]

fŏb[1] *n.*, & *v.t.* (**-bb-**). **1.** *n.* Small pocket for watch etc. in waistband of trousers; ~(**-chain**), chain attached to watch carried in fob. **2.** *v.t.* Put in one's fob, pocket. [orig. cant, prob. f. G]

fŏb[2] *v.t.* (**-bb-**). Cheat; palm (something inferior) *off on* (person); put (person) *off with* (something inferior). [16th c.; cf. obs. *fop* to dupe, G *foppen* to banter]

f.o.b. *abbr.* free on board.

fō'cal *a.* Of, situated or collected at, a focus; ~ **distance** or **length,** distance between centre of mirror or lens and its focus; ~ **plane,** plane through focus perpendicular to axis of mirror or lens. [f. mod. L *focalis* (as FOCUS; see -AL)]

fō'calīz|e, -īs|e (-īz), *v.t.* = FOCUS 4; hence ~A'TION *n.* [f. prec. + -IZE]

fo'c's'le. See FORECASTLE.

fō'cus *n.* (*pl.* **foci** *pr.* -sī, *or* **~es**), & *v.* (**-s-** *or* **-ss-**). **1.** *n.* (Geom.) one of points such that their distances from any point of given curve or solid have constant sum, difference, etc., or are in constant ratio to distance of directrix from that point. **2.** (Phys.) Point at which rays or waves meet after reflection or refraction, point from which rays etc. appear to proceed, point at which object must be situated for image given by lens or mirror to be well defined (*in, out of, bring into, focus*); focal length of lens; adjustment of eye or lens necessary to produce clear image; (fig.) state of clear definition (*in* or *into focus*). **3.** Principal seat (of disease, activity, etc.); place of origin of earthquake. **4.** *v.t.* & *i.* Converge or make converge to a focus; adjust focus of (lens, eye); bring into focus; concentrate or be concentrated *on*. [L, = hearth]

fŏ'dder *n.*, & *v.t.* **1.** *n.* Dried food, hay, straw, etc., for stall-feeding cattle; CANNON[1]-*fodder*. **2.** *v.t.* Give fodder to. [OE *fōdor*, = OHG *fuotar*, ON *fōthr* f. Gmc **fōdhram* (**fōdh-*; cf. FOOD)]

fōe *n.* (poet. or rhet.) Enemy, adversary, opponent, ill-wisher; **~'man,** (arch. or literary) enemy in war (lit. or fig.). [OE *fāh* adj. f. WG **faiha* and OE *gefā* n. (*gefāh* a. at feud, OHG *gifēh* f. WG **gafaiha*); cf. FEUD[1]]

foehn. Var. of FÖHN.

foetid. See FETID.

foe't|us (fē't-), ***fē't|us,** *n.* Unborn or unhatched offspring, esp. human embryo more than 8 weeks after conception; hence **~**AL *a.*, **~**ĭCIDE (2) *n.* [ME, f. L *fetus* offspring]

fŏg[1] *n.*, & *v.t.* (**-gg-**). **1.** *n.* Aftermath; long grass left standing in winter; a fodder-grass (*Holcus lanatus*). **2.** *v.t.* Leave (land) under fog; feed (cattle) on fog. [ME, of unkn. orig.]

fŏg[2] *n.* & *v.* (**-gg-**). **1.** *n.* Thick cloud of water droplets or smoke suspended in atmosphere at or near earth's surface; obscurity caused by this (**in a ~**, puzzled, at a loss); (Photog.) cloud on developed negative etc. obscuring image. **2. ~-bank,** mass of fog at sea; **~-bound,** unable to proceed because of fog; **~-bow** (like rainbow, produced by light on fog); **~-horn,** sounding instrument for warning ships in fog, (fig.) loud penetrating voice; **~-lamp** (used to improve visibility in fog); **~-signal,** detonator placed on railway line in fog to warn driver. **3.** *v.t.* Envelop (as) with fog; bewilder, perplex; (Photog.) make (negative etc.) obscure or cloudy. **4.** *v.i.* Become covered with fog or condensed vapour. [perh. back form. f. FOGGY]

fogey. See FOGY.

fŏ'gg|y̆ (-gĭ) *a.* (Of air) thick, murky; of, like, having much, FOG[2]; obscure, dull, confused, (*has only a foggy idea of it*; **not the ~iest,** (colloq.) no idea at all); beclouded, indistinct; hence **~**ĭLY[2] *adv.*, **~**ĭNESS *n.* [f. FOG[1] + -Y[2]; earlier senses 'covered with coarse grass, boggy, flabby (of flesh)']

fŏ'gle *n.* (arch. sl.) Silk handkerchief. [19th c., of unkn. orig.]

fō'gy̆, fō'gey, (-gĭ) *n.* (**Old**) **~**, old-fashioned person, person with antiquated ideas; hence **~**DOM, **fō'gy̆**ISM (2), *ns.*, **fō'gy̆**ISH[1] *a.*, (-g-). [18th c., rel. to sl. *fogram*, of unkn. orig.]

föhn (fern) *n.* Hot southerly wind on N. slope of the Alps; warm dry wind on lee side of mountains. [G, ult. f. L *Favonius* mild west wind]

foi'ble *n.* Weak point, weakness of character, quality on which one mistakenly prides oneself; (Fenc.) part of sword-blade from middle to point (cf. FORTE[1]). [F, obs. form of *faible* (as FEEBLE)]

foie gras (fwah grah') *n.* (colloq.) = PÂTÉ *de foie gras*. [abbr.]

foil[1] *n.* **1.** (Archit.) Arc or space between cusps of window. **2.** Metal hammered or rolled into thin sheet (*gold, silver, tin*, etc., *foil*); sheet of this, or of tin amalgam, placed behind mirror-glass as reflector; sheet of it used to wrap or cover food; leaf of it placed under precious stone etc. to brighten or colour it or enhance its brightness by contrast. **3.** Anything that sets something off by contrast. [ME f. OF, f. L *folium* leaf, and f. OF *foille* f. L *folia* pl.]

foil[2] *v.t.*, & *n.* **1.** *v.t.* (Hunt.) run over or cross (scent, ground) so as to baffle hounds; (abs., of deer etc.) spoil the scent thus; beat off, repulse; frustrate, parry, baffle. **2.** *n.* Track of hunted animal; (arch.) repulse, defeat, check. [ME, perh. f. AF **fuler*, OF *fouler* to full cloth, trample f. Rom. **fullare* f. L *fullo* FULLER[1]]

foil[3] *n.* Blunt-edged sword with button on point used in fencing; hence **~**'IST (3) *n.* [16th c., of unkn. orig.]

foil[4] *n.* Hydrofoil. [abbr.]

foi'son (-z-) *n.* (arch.) Plenty, abundance. [ME f. OF, f. Rom. **fusio -onis* f. L *fusio* (*fundere fus-* pour; see -ION)]

foist *v.t.* Introduce surreptitiously or unwarrantably *into* (thing) or *in*; palm (*off*) *on* or *upon*, falsely fix authorship of (composition) *upon*. [orig. of palming false die, f. Du. dial. *vuisten* take in the hand (*vuist* FIST)]

fol. *abbr.* folio.

fōld[1] *n.*, & *v.t.* **1.** *n.* = SHEEP-*fold*; (fig.) church, body of believers. **2.** *v.t.* Enclose (sheep etc.) in fold; place sheep in fold or folds on (land) to manure it. [OE *fald*, = MLG *valt*]

fōld[2] *v.* & *n.* **1.** *v.t.* Double (flexible thing) over upon itself (*in, over, together*; **~ away, up,** make more compact by folding); bend portion of (thing) *back, down*. **2.** Wind, clasp, (arms etc.) *about, round*; embrace *in* arms or *to* breast; lay (one's arms) together across chest, clasp (one's hands); swathe, envelop, (*fold it in paper*; *hills folded in mist*); **~ in,** (Cookery) add (ingredient) gently with spoon etc. so as to mix it in without stirring or beating. **3.** *v.i.* Become folded; be able to be folded (*folding stool*; **~ing door**(**s**)**,** pair of doors with jambs on each side of opening, the doors themselves often able to be folded; ***~'ing money,** (colloq.) paper money); **~ out,** be able to be unfolded; **~** (**up**)**,** collapse (lit. or fig.), cease to function, go bankrupt; **~'away,** adapted to be folded away; **~-out,** oversize page in book etc. to be unfolded by reader; **~-up,** adapted to be folded up. **4.** *n.* Doubling of folded object; hollow between two thicknesses (*carried it in a fold of her dress*), hollow or nook in mountain etc.; coil of serpent, string, etc.; act of folding; line made by folding; (Geol.) folding or curvature of strata; **~'boat,** collapsible boat. [OE *f(e)aldan*, = OHG *faltan*, ON *falda*, Goth. *falthan* f. Gmc **falthan*]

-fōld *suf.* forming *adjs.* and *advs.* f. cardinal numerals, w. sense 'multiplied by', 'in an amount multiplied by', (*a twofold charm*; *repaid tenfold*; MANIFOLD), & sim. *ns.* f. numerals used with *a* (*repaid a hundredfold*). [OE *-f(e)ald*, = OS *-fald*, OHG *-falt*, ON *-faldr*, Goth. *-falths*, cogn. w. prec.; orig. sense 'folded in so many layers etc.']

fō'lder *n.* In vbl senses; folded circular etc.; folding cover or holder for loose papers. [f. FOLD[2] + -ER[1]]

fŏ'lderŏl. Var. of FALDERAL.

fōlĭā'ceous (-shus) *a.* Leaflike; having organs like leaves; of leaves; laminated. [f. L *foliaceus* leafy (*folium* leaf; see -ACEOUS)]

fō'lĭage *n.* Leaves, leafage, (lit., or as represented in art); **~ leaf** (opp. petals etc.); **~ plant** (cultivated for foliage, not for flowers). [ME, f. F *feuillage* (*feuille* leaf f. OF *foille*; see FOIL[1], -AGE)]

fō'lĭar *a.* Of leaves. [f. mod. L *foliaris* f. L *folium* leaf; see -AR[1]]

fō'lĭate[1] *a.* Leaflike; having leaves; having specified number of leaflets (*1*, *5*, etc., *-foliate*). [f. L *foliatus* (*folium* leaf; see -ATE[2])]

fō'lĭ|āte[2] *v.* **1.** *v.i.* Split into laminae. **2.** *v.t.* Decorate (arch, door-head) with foils; number leaves (not pages) of (volume) consecutively. **3.** Hence ~A'TION *n.* [f. L *folium* leaf + -ATE[3]]

fŏ'lĭc *a.* ~ **acid,** B-group vitamin, deficiency of which causes human anaemia. [f. L *folium* leaf (because found especially in green leaves) + -IC]

folie (fŏ'lē) *n.* Madness, insanity; ~ ***à deux*** (ahdėr'), delusion shared by two emotionally associated persons; ~ ***de grandeur*** (degrahṅdėr'), DELUSIONS of grandeur. [F, = FOLLY]

fō'lĭō *n.* (*pl.* ~**s**) & *a.* **1.** *n.* Leaf of paper, parchment, etc., esp. if not numbered as two separate pages; leaf-number or page-number of printed book. **2.** Number of words (72 or 90 or 100) taken as unit in reckoning length of document. **3.** Sheet of paper folded once; **in** ~, (of book) on such paper. **4.** *n.* & *a.* (Book) made of such sheets, largest-sized (volume). [L, abl. of *folium* leaf, f. use in refs. = *on leaf 50* etc.]

fō'lĭōle *n.* Division of compound leaf, leaflet. [F, f. LL *foliolum* dim. of L *folium* leaf]

folk (fōk) *n.* (*pl.* ~ *or* ~**s**). **1.** A people, nation, race (BEAKER *Folk*); = *folk-music*. **2.** (in *pl.* exc. arch.) People in general; people of specified class; one's relatives. **3.** (*attrib.*) Of the people; traditional; **~-dance,** (music for) dance of popular origin; ~ **etymology,** popular modifying of word's form to make it seem to be derived from familiar words (*sparrowgrass* for *asparagus*); **~'lore,** traditional beliefs etc., study of these, whence **~'lor**IST (3) *n.*; **~-memory,** recollection of past persisting among a people; **~-music,** music of popular origin or style; **~'nik,** devotee of folk-music [after *beatnik*]; **~-singer,** singer of folk-songs; **~-song, ~-tale,** song, tale, of popular or traditional origin; **~'-ways,** traditional behaviour of a people; **~'weave,** rough loosely woven fabric. **4.** Hence **~'**SY[2], ~'Y[2], *adjs.*, friendly, sociable, informal, having characteristics of folk art. [OE *folc*, = OS, OHG *folc*, ON *folk* f. Gmc **folkam*]

fŏ'llĭcle *n.* Small sac or vesicle; small sac-shaped secretory gland or cavity containing hair-root; (Bot.) single-carpelled fruit opening on one side only; hence **fŏllĭ'cūl**AR[1], **fŏllĭ'cūl**ATE[2], **fŏllĭ'cūlāt**ED[2], *adjs.* [f. L *folliculus* dim. of *follis* bellows; see -CULE]

fŏ'llow (-ō) *v.* **1.** *v.t.* & *i.* Go or come after or *after* (moving thing or person); ~ **the hounds,** go hunting; **~-my-leader, *~-the-leader,** game in which each player must do as leader does; *follow* one's NOSE; ~ **the plough,** be ploughman. **2.** *v.t.* Go along (path); come after in order or time; accompany, serve; provide *with* sequel or successor; go after as admirer or suitor; attend (funeral, corpse to grave). **3.** Result from, be the necessary consequence of, be involved in. **4.** Strive after, aim at. **5.** Treat or take as guide or leader, obey, espouse opinions or cause of; conform to, act upon, (*follow advice*, *the fashion*, SUIT); practise (profession etc.; ~ **the sea,** be sailor). **6.** Keep up with mentally, grasp the meaning of, (argument, speaker); be aware of the present state or progress of (events, football team, etc.). **7.** *v.i.* Go or come after person or thing (*follow in his steps*; *follow in the wake of*); come next in order (*his arguments are as follows*); happen after something else, ensue; result, be deducible, (*from*). **8.** ~ **on,** provide continuation, (Cricket, of side) bat a second time immediately after making score less than that of opponents by certain number (so *~-on* n. & a.); ~ **out,** pursue to the end, carry out (instructions etc.) precisely; ~ **through,** (Golf etc.) carry stroke through to fullest extent possible after striking ball (so *~-through* n.); ~ **up,** pursue steadily, add another blow, action, etc., to (previous blow etc.), make further investigation of, (Footb. etc.) keep near (player with) ball to support; **~-up,** continuation of an action, esp. second advertisement, letter, etc., referring to earlier one. [OE *folgian*, = OS *folgon*, OHG *folgēn*, & OE *fylgan*, = ON *fylgja* f. Gmc **fulg-*]

fŏ'llower (-ōer) *n.* In vbl senses; adherent, disciple; (arch.) man courting maidservant. [f. prec. + -ER[1]]

fŏ'llowĭng[1] (-ō-) *n.* In vbl senses; body of adherents, followers. [f. FOLLOW + -ING[1]]

fŏ'llowĭng[2] (-ō-) *a.* & *prep.* **1.** *a.* In vbl senses; now to be mentioned (thing, or abs.: *the following is* or *are noteworthy*); (of wind) blowing in one's direction of travel. **2.** *prep.* As a sequel to, coming after in time. [f. FOLLOW + -ING[2]]

fŏ'llў̆ *n.* Being foolish, lack of good sense, unwise conduct; foolish act, idea, or practice, ridiculous thing; costly structure that is (considered) useless; (Theatr., in *pl.*) (revue with) glamorous female performers. [ME, f. OF *folie* (*fol* mad, FOOL[1]; see -Y[1])]

fomĕ'nt (*or* fō-) *v.t.* Bathe with warm or medicated lotions, apply warmth to; foster, stimulate, or instigate (sentiment, conduct, sedition, etc.), whence ~ER[1] *n.* [ME, f. F *fomenter* f. LL *fomentare* f. L *fomentum* poultice, lotion (*fovēre* heat, cherish; see -MENT)]

fōmĕntā'tion *n.* In vbl senses; (application of) warm cloths etc. for fomenting. [ME f. OF, or f. LL *fomentatio* (as prec.; see -ATION)]

fŏnd *a.* Foolishly credulous or sanguine (*fond hopes of success*); over-affectionate, doting; tender, loving; ~ **of,** having much love for, much inclined to; hence ~'LY[2] *adv.*, ~'NESS *n.* [ME, p.p. of obs. *fon* be foolish, or f. obs. *fon* fool + -ED[2] (cf. *wretched*)]

fŏ'ndant *n.* Soft sweetmeat of flavoured sugar. [F, part. of *fondre* melt f. L *fundere* pour; see -ANT]

fŏ'ndle *v.* **1.** *v.t.* Touch or stroke lovingly. **2.** *v.i.* Dally amorously (*with*, *together*). [back form. f. *fondling* fondled person (FOND, -LING[1])]

fŏ'ndūe *n.* Dish of flavoured melted cheese. [F, fem. p.p. of *fondre* melt f. L *fundere* pour]

fons et origo (fŏnz ĕt ŏrī'gō) *n.* Source and origin (*of*). [L]

fŏnt[1] *n.* Receptacle for baptismal water (**~-name,** baptismal name); receptacle for holy water; oil-reservoir of lamp. [OE *font*, *fant* f. OIr. *fant*, *font* f. L *fons fontis* fountain, baptismal water]

***fŏnt**[2]. See FOUNT[2].

fŏ'ntal *a.* Primary, original, of the fountain-head; baptismal. [OF, or f. med. L *fontalis* (as prec.; see -AL)]

fŏntanĕ'lle, *fŏntanĕ'l, *n.* Membranous space in infant's skull at angles of parietal bones. [f. F *fontanelle* f. mod. L *fontanella* f. OF *fontenelle* dim. of *fontaine* FOUNTAIN; see -LE 2]

fōōd *n.* **1.** Substance(s) (to be) taken into the body to maintain life and growth; **be ~ for fishes** (drowned); ~ **for powder,** soldiers; **be ~ for worms** (dead). **2.** Solid food (*food and drink*). **3.** Particular kind of food; nutriment for plants, skin, etc.; material for mental work (*food for thought* etc.). **4.** **~-chain,** (Ecol.) series of organisms dependent on one another for supply of food; ~ **poisoning,** illness due to bacteria or toxins in food; **~'stuff,** substance used as food; ~ **value,** relative nourishing power of a food. [OE *fōda* f. Gmc **fōdhon*; cf. FEED[1]]

fōōl[1] *n.*, *a.*, & *v.* **1.** *n.* Person who acts or thinks unwisely or imprudently; **be a ~ to,** (arch.) be nothing in comparison with; **a ~'s bolt is soon shot,** his stock of argument is soon exhausted; **no ~, nobody's ~,** prudent person. **2.** Jester or clown in medieval great household; **act** or **play the ~,** indulge in buffoonery, act foolishly. **3.** Dupe (*make a fool of*); **be a ~ for,** be unable to resist attractions of. **4.** ALL *Fools' Day*; APRIL *fool*; **~'s errand** (fruitless); **~'s gold,** pyrite; *fool's* MATE[1]; **~'s paradise,** illusory happiness; **~'s parsley,** species of hemlock resembling parsley. **5.** Hence ~'ERY (4, 5) *n.*, ~'PROOF[2] *a.* (of rules etc. so plain or simple as to be incapable of misuse or misinterpretation), (of machinery etc.) that cannot break down. **6.** *a.* *(colloq.) Foolish, silly. **7.** *v.i.* Play the fool, idle, trifle, (*about*, **around*); *~ **along,** proceed at leisure. **8.** *v.t.* Cheat (person) *out of* money etc. or *into doing*; throw (time, money) *away* foolishly; make a fool of, dupe, play tricks on. [ME f. OF *fol* f. L *follis* bellows, empty-headed person]

fōōl[2] *n.* Creamy liquid of fruit stewed, crushed, and mixed with milk, cream, custard, etc. (esp. *gooseberry fool*). [16th c., perh. f. prec.]

fōō'lhardy̆ *a.* Foolishly venturesome, delighting in needless risks; hence ~INESS *n.* [ME, f. OF *folhardi* (*fol* foolish, cf. FOOL[1]; *hardi* HARDY[1])]

fōō'lĭsh *a.* Lacking good sense or judgement; indicative of folly; ridiculous; hence ~LY[2] *adv.*, ~NESS *n.* [ME, f. FOOL[1] + -ISH]

fōō'lscăp (*or* -z-) *n.* Size of paper, about 330 × 200 (or 400) mm. [f. use as watermark of *fool's cap* = jester's cap with bells (FOOL[1] 2)]

fŏŏt[1] *n.* (*pl.* **feet;** cf. senses 6 and 11). **1.** Terminal part of leg beyond ankle. **2.** Step, pace, tread, (*swift of foot*; *has a light foot*). **3.** ||(Hist.) Infantry (*the 4th Foot*; *regiment of foot*; *a captain of foot*). **4.** Lower end of table, bed, grave, couch, etc. (opp. HEAD[1] 12); part of stocking etc. covering foot. **5.** Metrical unit with varying number of syllables one of which is stressed; similar unit of speech etc. **6.** (*pl.* also **foot**). Linear measure of 12 in., 30·48 cm (*10 feet long*; *a ten-foot pole*; *six foot* or *feet three*; *six feet three inches*; SQUARE[2] *foot*, CUBIC *foot*). **7.** Lower (usu. projecting) part, base; part of sewing-machine that holds material steady. **8.** (Zool.) Locomotive or adhesive organ of invertebrates. **9.** (Bot.). Part by which petal is attached; root of hair. **10.** Lowest part, bottom, of hill, ladder, staircase, wall, list, page, class, etc. **11.** (*pl.* ~**s**). Dregs, oil refuse; coarse sugar. **12. At ~,** (of foal) accompanying its mother; **at** person's **feet,** as his disciple, subject, or suppliant; BALL[1] *at* one's *feet*; BEST[1] *foot forward*; **have ~ in both camps,** belong to each of two opposing factions etc.; CHANGE[2] one's *feet*; **feet of clay,** fundamental weakness [cf. Dan. 2:33]; DRAG[1] one's *feet*; FALL[1] *on* one's *feet*; FIND one's *feet*; **feet first** or **foremost,** being carried to burial; *foot in the* DOOR; **have one ~ in the grave,** be near death; **have** one's **feet on the ground,** be practical; **keep** one's **feet,** not fall; **my ~!,** colloq. excl. of contemptuous contradiction; **~ on neck of,** complete dominance over; OFF one's *feet*; **on ~,** walking not riding etc.; **set on ~,** start (action etc.); **on** one's **feet,** (1) standing, (2) in good health; **put** one's **~ down,** (1) be firmly insistent or repressive, (2) accelerate motor vehicle; **put** one's **~ in it,** blunder; **put** one's **feet up,** take a rest; **on the right ~,** in an advantageous position; **set ~ in** or **on,** enter, go to, (place etc.); **stand on** one's **own feet,** be independent; **to** one's **feet,** to a standing position; **under ~,** on the ground (*wet under foot*); **tread under ~,** (fig.) oppress; **under** one's **feet,** obstructing one's progress; **get** one's **feet wet,** (fig.) begin to participate; **on the wrong ~,** in a disadvantageous position; **not put a ~ wrong,** make no mistakes. **13. ~-and-mouth (disease),** contagious virus disease of cattle etc. with ulceration of mouth, around hooves, etc.; **~-bath,** washing of feet, small bath used for this; **~'board** (in or on vehicle, for resting or placing feet); **~-brake,** foot-operated brake on vehicle; **~-bridge,** bridge for foot-passengers only; **~-candle,** illumination given by source of one candela at distance of one foot; **~'fall,** sound of footstep; **~-fault,** (Lawn Tennis) (make) fault consisting in overstepping baseline or running etc. while serving; **~-gear,** = *footwear*; ||**F~ Guards,** Grenadier, Coldstream, Scots, Irish, and Welsh Guards; **~'hill** (lying at base of mountain or range); **~'hold,** support for feet, surface for standing on, (lit. or fig.); **~'lights,** screened lights in front of stage at level of actors' feet (cf. GET[1] *across*); **~'loose,** free to act as one pleases; **~'man,** (1) infantryman, (2) liveried servant for carriage, door, and table, (3) trivet to hang on grate bars; **~'mark,** footprint; **~-muff** (for keeping feet warm); **~'note** (inserted at foot of page); **~-pace, ~'s pace,** walking pace; **~'pad,** (Hist.) unmounted highwayman; **~-passenger,** one who walks, not rides or drives; **~'path** (for walkers, esp. ||pavement at side of road); **~'plate,** driver's and fireman's platform in locomotive; **~-pound,** quantity of energy that will raise 1 lb. to height of 1 foot; **~-pound-second system** (using these as basic units of length, mass, and time); **~'print,** impression left by foot; **~-race,** race between persons on foot; **~-rope** (below yard, for sailors to stand on when furling or reefing); **~-rot,** disease of foot in sheep and cattle; **~-rule,** rigid measure 1 foot long; **~-slog** *v.i.*, & *n.*, (colloq.) walk, march; **~-soldier,** infantryman; **~'sore,** having sore feet, esp. from walking; **~'stalk,** (Bot.) stalk of leaf or peduncle of flower, (Zool.) attachment of barnacle etc.; **~'step,** tread, footprint, (*follow* or *tread in* person's *footsteps*, (fig.) do as he did); **~'stool** (for resting feet on); **~'sure,** sure-footed; **~'-warmer,** thing to warm feet; **~'way,** path for foot-passengers only; **~'wear,** shoes, socks, etc.; **~'work,** use of feet in sports, dancing, etc., agility. **14.** Hence (-)~'ED[2], ~'LESS, *adjs.*; (sense 6) ~'AGE (1) *n.* (esp. of cinema or television film), -~'ER[1] (1) *n.* (*six-footer*). [OE *fōt*, = OS *fōt*, OHG *fuoz*, ON *fōtr*, Goth. *fōtus* f. Gmc **fōt-* f. IE **pŏd-* etc.]

fŏŏt[2] *v.* **1.** *v.t.* Walk etc. on; **~ it,** dance, walk not ride. **2.** Put new foot to (stocking). **3.** Add up or *up* (account); pay (bill). **4.** *v.i.* (Of bill, items, etc.) mount *up to*. [ME, f. prec.]

fŏŏ'tball (-awl) *n.*, & *v.i.* **1.** *n.* Large round or elliptical inflated leather ball; (fig.) person or thing continually kicked or tossed or bandied about. **2.** Open-air game played with such ball by two sides each seeking to move it across opponents' goal-line by kicking or other permitted means; *football* POOL[2]. **3.** *v.i.* Play football; hence ~ER[1] *n.* [ME, f. FOOT[1] + BALL[1]]

||**fŏŏ'ter** *n.* (sl.) = prec. 2. [f. FOOT[1] + -ER[1] (5)]

fŏŏ'ting *n.* Placing of feet, foothold; surface for standing on, secure position, (lit. or fig.); conditions, relations, position, status, in which person or organization stands towards others, degree of intimacy etc.; entrance on new position, admittance to trade, society, etc., (**pay** (**for**) one's ~, pay customary fee for it); projecting course at foot of wall etc. [ME, f. FOOT[2] + -ING[1]]

foo'tl|e *v.i.* (sl.) Trifle (*about*), play the fool; hence ~ING² *a.*, trivial, silly. [19th c., perh. f. dial. *footer* idle, bungle, assoc. w. -LE 3]

foo'tsie *n.* (colloq.) Amorous play with the feet. [joc. dim. of FOOT¹; see -IE]

foo'ty *n.* **1.** (colloq.) = FOOTSIE. **2.** (Austral. & N.Z. colloq.) = FOOTBALL 2. [joc. dim. of FOOT¹; see -Y³]

foo'zle *v.t.*, & *n.* (sl., esp. in Golf). **1.** *v.t.* Do clumsily, bungle, make a mess of. **2.** *n.* Clumsy failure. [f. G dial. *fuseln* work badly; cf. FUSEL]

fŏp *n.* = DANDY; hence ~'LING¹ 2, ~'**pERY** (4, 5), *ns.*, ~'**pISH**¹ *a.* [17th c., perh. f. earlier *fop* fool]

for (*or, when stressed,* fôr; occas. fŏr) *prep.* & *conj.* **1.** *prep.* Representing, in place of, in exchange against, as price or penalty of, in requital of, (*sits for, member for, Liverpool*; ONCE *for all*; *A for Andrew*; *substituted for*; *agent for*; *got it for £1*; *thrashed for his pains*; *fined for speeding*; *do you take me for a fool?*); in defence or support or favour of, on side of, (*take* etc. *my* WORD¹ *for it*; *hurrah for* person or thing; *am for abandoning the attempt*; *arguments for and against*); with a view to, in order to be, conducive(ly) to, (*go for a walk*; (arch.) *went for a soldier*; *is, did it, for her good*; *for* SALE); to obtain, win, or save, (*send, go, for a doctor*; *would not do it for the world*; *not paid for*; *play for penny points*; *was tried for his life*; *cannot do it for the life of me*; *run for* IT¹); to reach, arrive at, be received by, or belong to, (*left, sailed, for India*; *made for shelter*; *meeting is at 7.30 for* (so as to start promptly at) *8*; *getting on for two o'clock*; *bought shoes for the children*; *won a name for himself*); **there's** or **that's** (*courage, gratitude,* etc.) **for you!** (expr. enthusiasm or resignation). **2.** (after *vbs.*, *adjs.*, *ns.*, & *ints.* of emotion, faculty, or fitness, after *adjs.* & *advs.* with *too*, *enough*, after expressions implying fitness etc.). As regards, in the direction of, (*don't care for games*; *a longing for praise*; *an eye for colour*; *fit for nothing*; *ready for dinner*; O² *for wings!*; NOW *for it!*; *too beautiful for* WORD¹*s*; *good enough for me*; *time for school*; **is not long ~ this world,** will soon die; **nothing ~ it but to submit,** submission is the only course open; **be ~ it,** (sl.) be involved in punishment or trouble; *is the man for the job*; *it is for you to make the move*; *the motive for retreating*). **3.** With the result of, at the cost of, to the amount of, (*all out for 44*; *150 for 5 wickets*; *a bill for £100*; *drew on him for £100*); to affect or as affecting, beneficially or the reverse, (*they live for each other*; *can shift for myself*; *things look bad for you*; *it is bad for him to smoke*); hence *for* with *n.* or *pron.* & *inf.* as noun-phrase: **it is wicked ~ him to smoke** (his smoking is wicked), **it is usual ~ hats to be worn** (that hats should be worn). **4.** In the character of, as, as being, (*hold it for certain*; *was often mistaken for Churchill*; *be hanged for a pirate*; *take for* GRANTED; *I for one do not believe it*; *did it for the second time*; **for* FREE¹ 6; *for one* THING; *for* GOOD); by reason of, under influence of, because of, on account of, (*did it for pure wantonness*; *avoid it for fear of accidents*; *I* TREMBLE *for him*; *famous for cider*; *notorious for parsimony*; *do it for my sake*; *alas for him!*); in spite of (*for all his bragging, for all that, for all (that) you say, for all (that) he seems to dislike me, I still like him*); on account of the hindrance of (*can't see* WOOD *for trees*; *could not speak for laughing*; *were it not for, but for, except for, one thing I might be happy*). **5.** Corresponding to, in contrast with, (*for one enemy he has a hundred friends*; *bulk for bulk,* taking equal bulk of each; WORD¹ *for word*); so far as concerns, regarding, (*for the rest*; *for all the* WORLD; *for my part*; *for all* or *aught I know*; *hard up for money*; *wants for nothing*); considering, or making the allowance required by, the usual nature of (*quite active for a man of 80*; *very bright for a winter day*). **6.** During, over, to the extent of, (*has been so for months*; *walk for two miles, for two hours*; *made comfortable for life, for the present*; *left him alone for once, for* EVER). **7.** *conj.* (Introducing new clause or series of clauses containing proof of or reason for believing what has been previously stated) seeing that, since, (*something fell in, for I heard a splash*); in order to be convinced of this observe or remember that . . . (*the angles are equal*; *for ABC is isosceles*). [OE, = OS *for*, Goth. *faur*, prob. shortened f. Gmc **fora* FORE²]

for- *pref.* forming *vbs.* etc., meaning (1) away, off, apart, (*forbye, forget, forgive*), (2) prohibition (*forbid, forfend*), (3) abstention, neglect, (*forbear, forgo, forsake, forswear*), (4) bad effect (*fordo*), (5) excess, intensity, (*forlorn*). [OE *for-*, *fær-*, = OS *for-*, *far-*, OHG *fir-*, *far-*, Goth. *fair-*, *faur-*, *fra-* f. IE pref. with many senses]

f.o.r. *abbr.* free on rail.

fŏ'rage *n.* & *v.* **1.** *n.* Food for horses and cattle, esp. for horses in army; foraging (*on the forage* etc.); **~-cap,** infantry undress cap. **2.** *v.t.* Collect forage from, ravage; supply with forage; get by foraging. **3.** *v.i.* Search for forage; search *for* (thing), rummage. **4.** So **fŏ'rag**ER² (-ĭj-) *n.*, one who forages. [ME, f. OF *fourrage(r)* (*fuerre* f. Frank. **fōder* FODDER)]

forā'm|ĕn *n.* (*pl.* ~*ina*). (Anat. etc.) Orifice, hole, passage; so **forā'mĭn**ATE² *a.* [f. L *foramen -minis* (*forare* bore a hole)]

forāmĭnĭ'ferous *a.* Of the order Foraminifera of protozoans, usu. marine organisms with perforated shells. [f. as prec. + -I- + -FEROUS]

fŏrasmŭ'ch (-z-) *adv.* ~ **as,** (conj.) seeing that, since. [= *for as much*]

fŏ'ray *n.*, & *v.i.* (Make, go on) incursion, raid, inroad. [ME, prob. n. f. v. back form. f. *forayer* f. OF *forrier* forager f. Rom. **fodrarius* (**fodro* FODDER)]

forbad(e). See FORBID.

fôr'bear¹, fôr'ebear, (fôr'bâr) *n.* (usu. in *pl.*) Ancestor. [f. FORE- + obs. *bear*, *beer* (BE, -ER¹)]

forbear'² (-bâr') *v.t.* & *i.* (**forbor'e; forbor'ne**). Abstain or refrain from or *from*; not use or mention; be patient; hence ~ANCE *n.* [OE *forberan*, = OHG *farberan*, Goth. *frabairan* (as FOR- (3), BEAR³)]

forbĭ'd *v.t.* (**-dd-; forba'd** *pr.* -ăd, *or* **forba'de** *pr.* -ăd; FORBIDDEN). **1.** Command (person etc.) not *to* do, (person etc.) not to go to (place), (*forbid him to go, him the court*); not allow (person etc. something; person or thing to exist or happen; *forbid him wine*; *forbid duels*; *was forbidden wine*; *wine was forbidden him*). **2.** (Of circumstances, hindrance, etc.) exclude, prevent, make undesirable, (**God ~!,** may it not happen!). [OE *forbēodan*, = OHG *farbiotan*, Goth. *faurbiudan* (as FOR- (2), BID¹)]

forbĭ'dden *a.* In vbl senses; *forbidden* DEGREES; **~ fruit,** thing desired because not allowed; **~ line,** (Phys.) spectral line occurring with low probability but observable in certain conditions. [f. prec. + -EN¹]

forbĭ'dding *a.* Repellent, of uninviting appearance; stern; hence ~LY² *adv.*, ~NESS *n.* [f. FORBID + -ING²]

forbôr'(n)e. See FORBEAR².

forbȳ'e, forbȳ', *prep.* & *adv.* (arch. or Sc.) **1.** *prep.* Besides. **2.** *adv.* In addition. [ME, f. FOR- (1) + BY¹]

fôrce¹ *n.* **1.** Strength, power, impetus, violence, intense effort; military strength. **2.** Body of armed men, army, (in *pl.*) troops, fighting strength of a nation or commander; body of police (**the ~,** the police); body of workers etc. (*labour force*); **join ~s,** combine efforts. **3.**

Strength exerted on an object, coercion, (**by ~**, by compulsion). **4.** Mental or moral strength; influence, controlling power, efficacy, power to convince, vividness of effect, (*the force of circumstances, force of* HABIT[1], *brought it about*; *there is force in what you say*; *described with much force*). **5.** Binding power, validity, (*has the force of law*; *comes into force*; **put in ~**, enforce). **6.** Real import, precise meaning (*what is the force of* 'but' *here?*). **7.** (Phys.) measurable and determinable influence tending to cause motion of a body, intensity of this; (fig.) agency likened to this (*considers himself a force in the world*); (Bridge) forcing bid. **8. By ~ of,** by means of; **in ~,** (1) in large numbers, (2) (of law etc.) valid, effective. **9. ~ cup,** rubber cup on handle, clearing blocked drain by vacuum; **~-feed,** feed (prisoner etc.) by force; **~ field,** (esp.) invisible barrier of force (in science fiction etc.); **~-out,** (Baseball) putting-out of runner displaced from base by next runner; **~-pump** (that forces water beyond range of atmospheric pressure). [ME f. OF, f. Rom. **fortia* f. L *fortis* strong]

fo͡rce[2] *v.* **1.** *v.t.* Constrain, compel; **~** person's **hand,** compel him to act prematurely or adopt policy unwillingly; **~d-choice** *a.*, (of question) in which choice must be made between two alternatives; *force the* ISSUE[1]; **~d labour,** compulsory labour usu. under rigorous conditions; **~d landing,** unavoidable landing of aircraft in an emergency (so **~-land** *v.t.* & *i.*). **2.** Compel (person) *to* do, *into* doing, or *into* course of action; (Phys.) modify by external action; put strained sense upon (words); compel (card-player) to trump etc., compel play of (card); rape (woman); **~ down,** compel (aircraft) to land. **3.** Strain to the utmost, urge; overstrain (analogy etc.); **~ the bidding** (at auction), raise price rapidly; **~ the game,** run risks to score quickly; **~ the pace,** adopt high speed in race to tire adversary out quickly; **~** one's **voice,** strain to get notes beyond usual compass or degree of loudness beyond what is easy or natural; *forced* DRAUGHT[1]; **~d march** (by troops etc., requiring special effort). **4.** Overpower, capture, make way through, break open, (stronghold, defences, pass, lock, door) by force. **5.** Drive or propel violently or against resistance. **6.** Impose, press, (thing) *on* person (**~ a card,** in conjuring, make person choose a particular card unconsciously). **7.** Cause or produce by effort (**~ a smile,** make oneself smile; **~** one's **way,** make a passage); take by force, extort, wring, (*force it out of his hands*; *forced loan*; *forced tears from his eyes, the facts out of him*). **8.** Artificially hasten the growth or maturity of (plant, scholar, child); **for'cing-house,** place where this is done. **9.** *v.i.* (Of card-player or his action) compel particular (type of) bid or play by another player. [ME, f. OF *forcer* (as prec.)]

fo͡rce[3] *n.* (N. Engl.) Waterfall. [f. ON *fors*]

fo͡r'ceful (-sf-) *a.* Powerful, vigorous; (of speech etc.) impressive, effective; hence **~**LY[2] *adv.*, **~**NESS *n.* [f. FORCE[1] + -FUL]

force majeure (fo͡rs mahzhe͡r') *n.* Irresistible compulsion or coercion, unforeseeable course of events excusing from fulfilment of contract. [F, =superior strength]

fo͡r'cemeat (-sm-) *n.* Meat etc. chopped, spiced, and seasoned for stuffing or garnish. [f. obs. *force, farce* stuff f. OF *farsir* (see FARCE)]

fo͡r'cĕps *n.* (*pl.* same). Surgical pincers (also **pair of ~**); (Anat. & Zool.) organ resembling forceps, whence **fo͡r'cĭp**ATE[2] *a.* [L *forceps forcipis*]

fo͡r'cĭble *a.* Done by or involving force; forceful; **~-feeble,** disguising feebleness under show of force; hence **~**NESS (-beln-) *n.*, **fo͡r'cĭb**LY[2] *adv.* [ME f. AF & OF (as FORCE[2]; see -IBLE)]

fo͡rd *n.* & *v.* **1.** *n.* Shallow place where river etc. may be crossed by wading or in vehicle. **2.** *v.t.* & *i.* Cross (water), cross water, by wading. **3.** Hence **~'**ABLE, **~'**LESS, *adjs.* [OE,=OS *-ford*, OHG *furt* f. WG **furdu* f. Gmc **fer-* etc.; cf. FARE[2]]

fordo' (-o͞o') *v.t.* (**fordi'd; fordo'ne** *pr.* -dŭ'n; cf. DO[1]). (arch.) Kill, destroy; spoil; (in *p.p.*) exhausted, tired out. [OE *fordōn*, = OS *fardōn*, OHG *fartuon* (as FOR- (4), DO[1])]

fo͡re[1] *a.* & *n.* **1.** *a.* Situated in front (opp. *hind, back, aft*); *fore* COURSE[1]. **2.** *n.* Fore part, bow of ship; **to the ~**, conspicuous (*come to the* **~**, take leading part), available. [ME; developed f. compounds w. FORE-]

fo͡re[2] *adv.* & *prep.* **1.** *adv.* **~ and aft,** at bow and stern, all over ship, backwards and forwards or lengthwise in ship etc.; **~-and-aft cap** (with peak at each end); **~-and-aft rigged,** having mainly fore-and-aft sails (i.e. sails set lengthwise, not on yards), opp. to *square-rigged*. **2.** *prep.* In presence of (in adjurations; *fore God*). [OE, = OS, OHG *fora*, Goth. *faura* f. Gmc **for-*; *prep.* often regarded as *'fore* abbr. of *before*]

fo͡re[3] *int.* (Golf). (To person in probable line of flight of ball) look out! [prob. for *before* or *afore*]

fo͡re- *pref.* **1.** To *vbs.* and their derivatives, meaning (1) in front (*foreshorten*), (2) beforehand, in advance, (*foreordain*). **2.** To *ns.*, meaning (3) in front, front-, (*forecourt, fore-paw*), (4) front part of (*forearm*), (5) of, near, or towards bow of ship or connected with foremast (*forecastle, forehold*), (6) anticipatory, precedent, (*forefather*). [f. FORE[2]]

fo͡r'ea͡rm[1] (fo͡r'a͡rm) *n.* Arm from elbow to wrist or finger-tips; corresponding part in foreleg or wing. [f. FORE- (4) + ARM[1]]

forea͡r'm[2] (fora͡r'm) *v.t.* Arm beforehand (usu. fig.). [f. FORE- (2) + ARM[3]]

forebear. See FORBEAR[1].

forebō'de (fo͡rb-) *v.t.* Betoken, portend; have presentiment of (usu. evil) or *that*. [f. FORE- (2) + BODE]

forebō'dĭng (fo͡rb-) *n.* Presage or omen, presentiment, (esp. of evil). [ME, f. prec. + -ING[1]]

fo͡r'ecast[1] (fo͡r'kahst) *v.t.* (**~** *or* **~ed**). Estimate or conjecture beforehand, predict. [ME, f. FORE- (2) + CAST[1]]

fo͡r'ecast[2] (fo͡r'kahst) *n.* Conjectural estimate of something future, esp. of coming weather; prediction. [f. prec.]

forecastle, fo'c's'le, (fō'ksel) *n.* (Naut.) Forward part of ship where sailors live; (Hist.) short raised deck at bow, forward part of upper deck. [ME in second sense, f. FORE- (5) + CASTLE[1]]

foreclō's|e (fo͡rklō'z) *v.t.* Bar, preclude, prevent, shut out from enjoyment (*of*); bar (person entitled to redeem mortgage) upon non-payment of money due, bar (right of redemption), take away power of redeeming (mortgage), whence **~**URE (fo͡rklō'zher) *n.*; settle (arguable point etc.) by anticipation. [ME, f. OF *forclos* p.p. of *forclore* (*for-* out f. L *foris*; see CLOSE[3])]

forecŏ'nscious (fo͡rkŏ'nshus) *a.* & *n.* (Psych.) (Of) part of mind below threshold of immediate conscious attention, from which memories etc. can easily become consciously recalled. [after G *vorbewusst* (*vor-* FORE-, *bewusst* conscious)]

fo͡r'ecourt (fo͡r'kort) *n.* Enclosed space in front of building, outer court; part of filling station where petrol is supplied; part of lawn-tennis

For other words in *fore-* see FORE-.

court between service-line and net. [f. FORE- (3) + COURT¹]

forėdōō'm (fŏrd-) *v.t.* Doom or condemn beforehand (*to*). [f. FORE- (2) + DOOM²]

fŏr'e-ĕdge (fŏr'ĕj) *n.* Front or outer edge (esp. of pages of book); ~ **painting,** decoration of spread fore-edges with coloured design. [f. FORE- (3) + EDGE¹]

fŏr'efather (fŏr'fahdher) *n.* (usu. in *pl.*) Person from whom one's father or mother is descended, ancestor; member of past generations of a family or race; ***F~s' Day,** 21 Dec., anniversary of first settlers' landing at Plymouth, Massachusetts. [ME, f. FORE- (6) + FATHER¹]

forefee'l (fŏrf-) *v.t.* (**forefe'lt**). Feel beforehand, have presentiment of. [f. FORE- (2) + FEEL]

fŏr'efĭnger (fŏr'fĭngger) *n.* Finger next to thumb. [ME, f. FORE- (3) + FINGER]

fŏr'efōōt (fŏr'f-) *n.* (*pl.* **for'efeet**). Front foot of animal; (Naut.) foremost piece of keel. [ME, f. FORE- (3, 5) + FOOT¹]

fŏr'efront (fŏr'frŭnt) *n.* Very front, foremost part, van, (*in the forefront of the battle*). [ME, f. FORE- (3) + FRONT]

foregather. Var. of FORGATHER.

foregō'¹ (fŏrgō') *v.t.* & *i.* (**forewe'nt; forego'ne** *pr.* -gŏ'n *or* -gaw'n *or attrib.* fŏr'-; cf. GO¹). Precede in place or time; **~ne conclusion,** (1) decision or opinion come to in advance of the evidence or necessary facts, (2) result that can be or could have been foreseen; so ~ER¹ *n.*, predecessor. [OE *foregān* (as FORE², GO¹)]

forego². Var. of FORGO.

fŏr'egōĭng (fŏr'g-; *or* -gō'-) *a.* In vbl senses; previously mentioned (thing, or abs.). [f. FOREGO¹ + -ING²]

fŏr'eground (fŏr'g-) *n.* Part of view, esp. in picture, nearest observer; (fig.) most conspicuous position. [f. Du. *voorgrond* (as FORE- (3), GROUND¹)]

fŏr'ehănd (fŏr'h-) *n.* & *a.* **1.** *n.* Part of horse in front of rider. **2.** *n.* & *a.* (Tennis etc.) (Stroke) played with palm of hand towards opponent; (of part of court) where forehand stroke is used. [f. FORE- (3) + HAND¹]

fŏr'ehănded (fŏr'h-) *a.* = prec. 2; *thrifty. [f. as prec. + -ED²]

forehead (fŏ'rĭd *or* fŏr'hĕd) *n.* Part of face above eyebrows and between temples. [OE *forhēafod* (as FORE- (4), HEAD¹)]

fŏr'ehŏck (fŏr'h-) *n.* Foreleg cut of pork or bacon. [f. FORE- (3) + HOCK¹]

fŏr'ehōld (fŏr'h-) *n.* (Naut.) Hold in fore part of ship. [f. FORE- (5) + HOLD³]

fŏ'reign (-rĭn) *a.* **1.** Belonging to or proceeding from other persons or things; alien, irrelevant, dissimilar, or inappropriate, *to*; introduced from outside (esp. ~ **body** or **substance** in the tissues etc.). **2.** Situated outside, coming from another district, society, etc.; outside the country, not of one's own land; of, in, characteristic of, coming from, dealing with, some country or language other than one's own (*foreign and home* TRADE). **3.** ~ **aid,** money or goods given by one State to another; ~ **devil,** (Chinese derog.) foreigner, esp. European; ~ **exchange,** (dealings in) currency of other countries; **~-going,** (of ship) going to foreign countries; *foreign* LEGION; **F~ Minister,** equivalent of ||*Foreign Secretary* in most countries other than U.K.; ||**F~ and Commonwealth Office,** ||**F~ Office** (Hist.), government department dealing with matters concerning other countries (**F~ Secretary,** head of this). **4.** Hence ~ISM (2, 4) *n.*, ~IZE (3) *v.t.* & *i.* [ME, f. OF *forein, forain* f. Rom. **foranus* f. L *foras* outside; for *-g-* cf. *sovereign*]

fŏ'reigner (-rĭn-) *n.* Person born or dwelling in foreign country or place or habitually speaking foreign language; foreign ship, imported animal or article. [ME, f. prec. + -ER¹]

forejŭ'dge (fŏrj-) *v.t.* Judge or determine before hearing the evidence. [f. FORE- (2) + JUDGE²]

foreknow' (fŏrnō') *v.t.* (**foreknew'** *pr.* fŏrnū'; **foreknown'** *pr.* fŏrnō'n). Know beforehand, have prescience of; so **fore**KNOW'LEDGE (fŏrnŏ'lĭj) *n.* [f. FORE- (2) + KNOW¹]

***fŏr'elādy̆** (fŏr'l-) *n.* = FOREWOMAN 2. [f. FORE- (3) + LADY]

fŏr'eland (fŏr'l-) *n.* Cape, promontory; piece of land in front of something. [ME, f. FORE- (3) + LAND¹]

fŏr'elĕg (fŏr'l-) *n.* Front leg of animal. [ME, f. FORE- (3) + LEG]

fŏr'elŏck (fŏr'l-) *n.* Lock of hair growing just above forehead (**take time** etc. **by the ~,** not let chance slip). [ME, f. FORE- (3) + LOCK¹]

fŏr'e|man (fŏr'm-) *n.* (*pl.* **~men**). **1.** President and spokesman of jury. **2.** Principal workman superintending others. [ME, f. FORE- (3) + MAN¹]

fŏr'emast (fŏr'mahst) *n.* Forward (lower) mast of ship (**~ man** etc., sailor below rank of petty officer). [f. FORE- (5) + MAST¹]

fŏr'emōst (fŏr'm-; *or* -ost) *a.* & *adv.* **1.** *a.* Most advanced in position, front, (**head, end,** etc., **~,** with head etc. in front); most notable, best, chief, (*foremost authority on Dickens*). **2.** *adv.* Before anything else in position, in the first place, (*first and foremost*). [earlier *formost, formest* superl. of OE *forma* first, assim. to FORE¹ and -MOST; cf. FORMER¹]

fŏr'enāme (fŏr'n-) *n.* First or Christian name. [f. FORE- (3) + NAME¹]

fŏr'enōōn (fŏr'n-) *n.* (Naut., Law, or arch.) The day till noon, morning. [f. FORE² + NOON]

forĕ'ns|ic *a.* Of or used in courts of law (*forensic science*) or in forensic science etc. (*forensic laboratory*); **~ic medicine,** application of medical knowledge to legal problems; hence ~ICALLY *adv.* [f. L *forensis* (FORUM) + -IC]

foreordai'n (fŏrŏr-) *v.t.* Predestinate, ordain beforehand; hence **fore**ORDINA'TION (fŏrŏr-) *n.* [ME, f. FORE- (2) + ORDAIN]

fŏr'epeak (fŏr'p-) *n.* (Naut.) End of forehold in angle of bows. [f. FORE- (5) + PEAK¹]

fŏr'eplay (fŏr'p-) *n.* Stimulation preceding sexual intercourse. [f. FORE- (6) + PLAY²]

forerŭ'n (fŏr-r-) *v.t.* (**-nn-; forera'n; foreru'n**). Go before; indicate the coming of, foreshadow; hence **fŏr'erŭnn**ER¹ (1, 2) (fŏr-r-) *n.* [ME, f. FORE- (1) + RUN¹]

fŏr'esail (fŏr's-; *or* -sal) *n.* Principal sail on foremast (lowest square sail, or fore-and-aft bent on mast, or triangular before mast). [ME, f. FORE- (5) + SAIL¹]

foresee' (fŏrsē') *v.t.* (**foresaw'; foresee'n**). See or be aware of beforehand (thing, or *that*); **~able future,** period during which general course of events can reasonably be predicted. [OE *foresēon* (as FORE- (2), SEE¹)]

foreshă'dow (fŏrshă'dō) *v.t.* Prefigure, serve as type or presage of, indicate (future event). [f. FORE- (2) + SHADOW²]

fŏr'e-sheets (fŏr'sh-) *n. pl.* Inner part of bows of boat with gratings for bowman to stand on. [f. FORE- (5) + SHEET¹ + -S¹]

fŏr'eshōre (fŏr'sh-) *n.* Part of shore between high- and low-water marks, or between water and land cultivated or built on. [f. FORE- (4) + SHORE¹]

foreshŏr'ten (fŏrsh-) *v.t.* Show or portray (object) with the apparent shortening due to visual perspective. [f. FORE- (1) + SHORTEN, prob. after Du. *verkorten*]

foreshow' (fŏrshō') *v.t.* (*p.p.* **~n**). Foretell;

foreshadow, portend, prefigure. [f. FORE- (2) + SHOW¹]

fŏr'esīght (fŏr'sīt) *n.* Foreseeing; care for the future; front sight of gun. [ME, prob. after ON *forsjá, forsjó* (as FORE-, SIGHT¹)]

fŏr'eskĭn (fŏr's-) *n.* Loose skin covering end of penis. [f. FORE- (3) + SKIN¹, after G *vorhaut*]

fŏ'rĕst *n.*, & *v.t.* **1.** *n.* Large tract covered with trees and undergrowth sometimes mixed with pasture; trees growing in it (lit. or fig.; *a forest of masts*); DEER-*forest*; district formerly forest but now cultivated (*Sherwood Forest*); ||(Hist.) unenclosed woodland district kept for hunting and usu. owned by sovereign; **~-tree** (of large growth suitable for forest). **2.** *v.t.* Plant with trees; convert into forest. [ME f. OF, f. LL *forestis* (*silva* wood) outside (walls of park) f. L *foris* outside]

fŏresta'l|l (fŏrstaw'l) *v.t.* Anticipate the action of; anticipate and so baffle; deal with before the regular time, anticipate (action of another, or event); (Hist.) buy up (goods) in order to profit by enhanced price; hence ~MENT *n.* [ME in last sense; cf. AL *for(e)stallare* f. OE *for(e)steall* an ambush (as FORE- (6), STALL¹)]

fŏr'estay (fŏr's-) *n.* Stay from head of foremast to ship's deck to support foremast. [ME, f. FORE- (5) + STAY²]

fŏ'rĕster *n.* Officer in charge of forest, or of growing timber; dweller in forest; (*F~*) member of the Ancient Order of Foresters (friendly society); bird or animal of forest, e.g. New Forest pony, forest-dwelling moth, great kangaroo. [ME, f. OF *forestier* (as FOREST, -IER)]

fŏ'rĕstrў *n.* Wooded country, forests; science or art of managing forests. [f. FOREST + -RY]

fŏr'etāste¹ (fŏr't-) *n.* Partial enjoyment or suffering (*of*) in advance, anticipation. [ME, f. FORE- (2) + TASTE²]

fŏretā'ste² (fŏrt-) *v.t.* Taste beforehand, anticipate enjoyment etc. of. [ME, f. FORE- (2) + TASTE¹]

fŏretĕ'll (fŏrt-) *v.t.* (**foreto'ld**). Tell of (event etc.) before it takes place, predict, prophesy; presage, be precursor of. [ME, f. FORE- (2) + TELL¹]

fŏr'ethought (fŏr'thawt) *n.* Previous thinking or devising; deliberate intention; care for the future. [ME, f. FORE- (6) + THOUGHT¹]

fŏr'etīme (fŏr't-) *n.* (arch.) The past, early days, old times. [f. FORE- (6) + TIME¹]

fŏr'etōken¹ (fŏr't-) *n.* Sign of something to come. [OE *foretācn* (as FORE- (6), TOKEN)]

fŏretō'ken² (fŏrt-) *v.t.* Portend, indicate beforehand. [f. prec.]

fŏr'etŏp (fŏr't-) *n.* Top of foremast (TOP¹ 7); **foretop-gallant mast,** mast above **fore-topmast** (mast above foremast); **foretop-gallant-sail,** sail above **fore-topsail** (sail above foresail). [ME, f. FORE- (5) + TOP¹]

***forĕ'ver, *forĕvermŏr'e.** See *for ever* (EVER 2).

fŏrewar'n (fŏrwŏr'n) *v.t.* Warn beforehand (*forewarned is forearmed*). [ME, f. FORE- (2) + WARN]

fŏr'e|woman (fŏr'wŏŏman) *n.* (*pl.* **~women** *pr.* -wĭmĭn). **1.** Woman foreman of jury. **2.** Chief workwoman supervising others. [f. FORE- (3) + WOMAN]

fŏr'eword (fŏr'wĕrd) *n.* Preface; introductory remarks, esp. by person other than the author of the book etc. [f. FORE- (3) + WORD¹, after G *vorwort*]

fŏr'eyard (fŏr'yard) *n.* Lowest yard on foremast. [f. FORE- (5) + YARD¹]

fŏr'feit (-fĭt) *n.*, *a.*, & *v.t.* **1.** *n.* & *a.* (Thing) lost owing to crime or fault. **2.** *n.* Penalty for breach of contract or neglect, fine; trivial fine for breach of rules in clubs etc. or in games; article surrendered by player in game of **~s** to be redeemed by performing ludicrous task; forfeiting. **3.** *v.t.* Lose right to, be deprived of, have to pay, as penalty of crime, neglect, etc., or as necessary consequence of something; hence ~ABLE *a.*, ~URE *n.* [ME, f. OF *forfet, forfait* p.p. of *forfaire* transgress (*for(s)* beyond (what is right) f. L *foris* outside, *faire* f. L *facere* do)]

fŏrfĕ'nd *v.t.* (arch.) Avert, keep off, (*God, Heaven, forfend!*); *protect by precautions. [ME, f. FOR- (2) + FEND]

fŏrgă'ther (-dh-) *v.i.* Assemble, meet together, associate. [16th c. Sc., f. Du. *vergaderen*, assim. to FOR- (5), GATHER]

forgā've. See FORGIVE.

fŏrge¹ *n.* Smithy; blacksmith's hearth or fireplace with bellows; furnace or hearth for melting or refining metal, workshop containing it. [ME f. OF, f. Rom. **faurga* f. L *fabrica* trade, workshop, FABRIC]

fŏrge² *v.t.* Shape by heating in fire and hammering (lit. or fig.); fabricate, invent, (tale, lie); make (money etc.) in fraudulent imitation, esp. write (document, signature) in order to pass it off as written by another, whence **fŏr'gER¹** *n.*; hence ~ABLE (-ja-) *a.* [ME, f. OF *forger* f. L *fabricare* FABRICATE]

fŏrge³ *v.i.* Make one's way, advance, gradually or steadily; ~ (**ahead**), take lead in race, move forward rapidly. [18th c., perh. alt. f. FORCE²]

fŏr'gerў *n.* Forging, counterfeiting, or falsifying, of document etc.; spurious thing, esp. document or signature. [f. FORGE² + -ERY]

forgĕ't (-g-) *v.* (**-tt-; forgo't; forgo'tten,** U.S. or arch. or poet. **forgo't**). **1.** *v.t.* & *i.* Lose remembrance of or *about* (thing, person, *that, how to, where*, etc., or abs.); neglect (*to* do), inadvertently omit to bring or mention or attend to; put out of mind, cease to think of, (*forgive and forget*); ~ (**about**) **it!**, (colloq.) take no more notice of it, there is no need for apology or thanks. **2.** *v.t.* Disregard, slight. **3.** ~ **oneself,** (1) neglect one's own interests, (2) act unbecomingly or unworthily, (3) (arch.) lose consciousness. **4.** **~-me-not,** plant of genus *Myosotis*, esp. of species with small yellow-eyed bright blue flowers. **5.** Hence ~TABLE *a.* [OE *forgietan*, = OS *fargetan*, OHG *firgezzan* f. WG (as FOR- (1), GET¹)]

forgĕ'tful (-g-) *a.* ~ (**of**), apt to forget, forgetting, neglectful (of); (poet.) causing one to forget; hence ~LY² *adv.*, ~NESS *n.* [ME, f. prec. + -FUL]

forgĭ'v|e (-g-) *v.t.* (**forga've; forgi'ven**). Remit, let off, (debt, person debt); cease to resent, pardon, (offence, offender, offender offence, or abs.; *forgive us our trespasses*); hence ~ABLE, ~ING², *adjs.* [OE *forgiefan*, = OS, OHG *fargeban*, ON *fyrirgefa*, Goth. *fragiban* grant; as FOR- (1), GIVE¹]

forgĭ'venĕss (-gĭ'vn-) *n.* Act of forgiving; state of being forgiven. [OE *forgief(e)nes* (as prec., -NESS)]

forgō' *v.t.* (**forwe'nt; forgo'ne** *pr.* -gŏ'n *or* -gaw'n; cf. GO¹). Abstain from, go without, let go; omit or decline to take or use (pleasure, advantage, etc.); relinquish. [OE *forgān* (as FOR- (3), GO¹)]

forgŏ't(ten). See FORGET.

fŏ'rĭnt *n.* Principal monetary unit of Hungary. [Magyar, f. It. *fiorino* (see FLORIN)]

fŏrk *n.* & *v.* **1.** *n.* Pronged agricultural implement used for digging, lifting, carrying, or throwing; two, three, or four, -pronged instrument used in eating at table or cooking; TUNING-*fork*;

For other words in *fore-* **see** FORE-.

pronged device pushed under load to be lifted; forked support for bicycle wheel; stick with forked end used as support for vines etc. **2.** Forking bifurcation, e.g. that of human legs, of diverging roads, or of branches; one such branch; flash of forked lightning; (Chess) simultaneous attack on two men by one. **3.** ~-**-lift** (*truck* etc.), vehicle with fork in front for lifting and carrying loads; ~ **lunch, supper,** etc., (eaten with fork at buffet etc.). **4.** *v.i.* Form fork, have or develop branches; take one or other road etc. at fork (*fork left for Banbury*). **5.** *v.t.* Dig, lift, carry, or throw with fork; (Chess) attack (two men) at once. **6.** *v.i.* & *t.* (sl.) ~ **out** or **over** or **up,** hand over, pay. [OE *forca, force,* = OS *furka,* OHG *furcha,* ON *forkr* f. L *furca*]

fŏrked (-kt) *a.* Having fork or forklike end or branches; divergent, cleft, (**three-~** etc., having three etc. prongs). [ME, f. prec. + -ED²]

forlŏr'n *a.* Desperate, hopeless; abandoned, forsaken, (poet.) deprived *of*; in pitiful condition, of wretched appearance; ~ **hope,** desperate enterprise, faint hope. [p.p. of obs. *forlese* f. OE *forlēosan* (as FOR- (5), LOSE); *forlorn hope* f. Du. *verloren hoop* lost troop (*hoop* company, HEAP¹), orig. of storming-party etc.]

fŏrm¹ *n.* **1.** Shape, arrangement of parts, visible aspect (esp. apart from colour), shape of body. **2.** Person or animal as visible or tangible (*saw a form, the form of my son, before me*). **3.** (Philos.) Essential nature of a species or thing. **4.** Mode in which thing exists or manifests itself (*in, under, take, the form of*); species, kind, variety; cf. CONTENT¹. **5.** (Gram.) One of the ways in which a word may be spelt or pronounced or inflected; external characteristics of words apart from meaning. **6.** Class in schools (usu. numbered from SIXTH downwards). **7.** Arrangement and style in literary or musical composition. **8.** Customary method (*in due form*; *that is* **common** ~, what is usually done and of no special significance; **matter of** ~, mere routine); set order of words, formula; regularly drawn document; document with blanks to be filled up. **9.** Formality, mere piece of ceremony. **10.** Behaviour according to rule or custom (**good, bad,** ~, complying with or offending against current social conventions); correct procedure (*he knows the form*). **11.** (Of horse, athlete, etc.) condition of health and training (**in, out of,** ~, fit or not for racing etc.; **in good** or **top** ~, **on** ~, playing, performing, etc., well; **off** ~, not playing etc. well); details of previous performances in racing etc.; (sl.) criminal record; good spirits (*was in great form*). **12.** Long seat without back, bench. **13.** (Print.) = FORME. **14.** Hare's lair. **15.** ~(**'work**), temporary structure to hold concrete during setting. **16.** ~ **criticism,** textual analysis of Bible etc. by tracing history of its content of proverbs, myths, and other forms; ~ **letter,** standardized letter to deal with frequently occurring matters. [ME, f. OF *forme* f. L *forma* mould, shape, beauty]

fŏrm² *v.* **1.** *v.t.* Fashion, mould, (*into* certain shape; *after, by, from, on,* pattern; or abs.). **2.** Mould by discipline, train, instruct, (person, or faculty etc.); embody, organize, *into* a company etc. **3.** Frame, make, produce; articulate (word); conceive (idea, judgement); develop (habit); enter into (alliance); be material of, make up, be *one of* or *part of.* **4.** (Gram.) Construct (new word) by derivation, inflexion, etc. **5.** *v.i.* Take shape, be formed. **6.** *v.t.* & *i.* (Mil. etc.). Draw up or *up* in order, assume specified formation (*form line, column*), take up arrangement in a formation (*right, left, form*). [ME, f. OF *fo(u)rmer* f. L *formare* (as prec.)]

-fŏrm *suf.* forming *adjs.* (usu. w. intermediate -I-) (1) w. sense 'having the form of' (*cruciform, cuneiform*), (2) referring to number of forms (*uniform, multiform*). [f. or after F *-forme* f. L *-formis* (*forma* FORM¹)]

fŏr'mal *a.* & *n.* **1.** *a.* Of the outward form, shape, appearance, arrangement, or external qualities; (Philos.) of the essence of a thing, essential not material; (Logic) concerned with the form, not the matter, of reasoning. **2.** Valid or correctly so called in virtue of its form, explicit and definite, not merely tacit or accepted as equivalent; in accordance with recognized forms or rules of art etc. **3.** Ceremonial, required by convention (*a formal call*); perfunctory, having the form without the spirit; observant of forms or rules, precise, regular, (*formal garden*); prim, excessively regular or symmetrical, stiff, methodical. **4.** Hence ~LY² *adv.* **5.** **n.* Evening dress; occasion on which evening dress is worn. [ME, f. L *formalis* (as FORM¹; see -AL)]

fŏrmă'ldėhȳde *n.* Aldehyde of formic acid, HCHO, used as disinfectant and preservative and in manufacture of synthetic resins. [f. FORMIC + ALDEHYDE]

fŏr'malĭn *n.* Aqueous solution of formaldehyde. [f. prec. + -IN]

fŏr'mal|ĭsm *n.* **1.** Excessive adherence to prescribed forms; use of forms without regard to inner significance. **2.** Treatment of mathematics as manipulation of meaningless symbols; (Theatr.) symbolic and stylized manner of production; (derog.) artist's concentration on form at expense of content. **3.** Hence ~IST (2) *n.*, **~ĭ'stIC** *a.* **4.** (Phys.) Mathematical description of physical situation etc. [f. FORMAL + -ISM]

fŏrmă'lĭtў *n.* Conformity to rules, propriety; ceremony, elaborate procedure; formal or ceremonial act, requirement of etiquette, regulation, or custom, (often with implied lack of real significance); being formal, precision of manners, stiffness of design. [f. F *formalité* or f. med. L *formalitas* (as FORMAL; see -ITY)]

fŏr'malīz|e, -īs|e (-īz), *v.t.* Give definite shape or legal formality to; make ceremonious, precise, or rigid, imbue with formalism; hence ~A'TION *n.* [f. FORMAL + -IZE]

fŏr'mant *n.* Characteristic pitch-constituent of vowel; morpheme occurring only in combination in word or word-stem. [G, f. L *formare*; see FORM², -ANT]

fŏr'măt *n.*, & *v.t.* (**-tt-**). **1.** *n.* Shape and size (of book etc.); style or manner of arrangement or procedure; arrangement of data etc. for processing or storage by computer. **2.** *v.t.* Arrange in format, esp. for computer. [F f. G, f. L *formatus* (*liber*) shaped (book), p.p. of *formare* FORM²]

fŏr'māte. See FORMIC.

fŏrmā'tion *n.* Forming, being formed; thing formed; arrangement of parts, structure, (Mil.) disposition of troops; a number of aircraft flying in company; (Geol.) assemblage of rocks or series of strata having some common characteristic; hence ~AL *a.* [ME f. OF, or f. L *formatio* (as FORM²; see -ATION)]

fŏr'matĭve *a.* & *n.* **1.** *a.* Serving to fashion, of formation; (Gram., of flexional or derivative suffix or prefix) used in forming words. **2.** *n.* Formative element. [ME, f. OF *formatif -ive* or f. med. L *formativus* (as FORM²; see -ATIVE)]

‖**fŏrme** *n.* (Print.) Body of type secured in chase for printing at one impression; quantity of film arranged for making plate etc. [var. of FORM¹]

fŏr'mer¹ *attrib. a.* Of the past or an earlier period (*in former times*; *more like her former self*; *our former haunts*), whence ~LY² *adv.*; * = EX-¹ 2; **the** ~ (w. noun, or abs.), the first or first mentioned of two (opp. *latter*). [ME, f. *forme* first + -ER³, after FOREMOST]

for'mer² *n.* In vbl senses; (Electr.) frame or core for winding coil; (Aeron.) transverse strengthening member in wing or fuselage. [f. FORM² + -ER¹]

for'm|ic *a.* (Chem.) **~ic acid,** colourless irritant volatile acid contained in fluid emitted by ants; hence ~ATE¹ (3) *n.* [f. L *formica* ant + -IC]

Formi'ca *n.* Hard durable plastic laminate used on surfaces. [P]

formicā'tion *n.* Sensation as of ants crawling over the skin. [f. L *formicatio* (*formica* ant; see -ATION)]

for'midab|le *a.* To be dreaded or viewed with respect; likely to be hard to overcome, resist, or deal with; hence **~le**NESS (-bəln-) *n.*, ~LY² *adv.* [F, or f. L *formidabilis* (*formidare* fear; see -ABLE)]

for'mless *a.* Shapeless, without determinate or regular form; hence ~LY² *adv.*, ~NESS *n.* [f. FORM¹ + -LESS]

for'mūla *n.* (*pl.* **~e** *or* **~s**). **1.** Fixed form of words as definition or enunciation of principle or as occurring in literary composition; statement prescribed or accepted for use on ceremonial or social occasion etc.; rule unintelligently followed, conventional usage or belief; list of ingredients, recipe; *infant's food made up from recipe; principle serving to reconcile difference of aim or opinion (*diplomats seeking a formula*). **2.** (Math.) rule or statement in algebraic symbols; (Chem.) expression by symbols of substance's constituents; tabulation of certain facts by symbols and figures; classification of racing car esp. by engine capacity. **3.** Hence **formūlā'**IC *a.*, **for'mūl(ar)**IZE (3) *v.t.* [L, dim. of *forma* FORM¹; see -ULE]

for'mūlary *n.* & *a.* **1.** *n.* Collection of formulae; document or book of set forms esp. for religious use. **2.** *a.* Using formulae; in or of formulae. [n. f. F *formulaire* or f. med. L *formularius* (*liber* book) f. L (as prec.); a. f. prec. + -ARY¹]

for'mūl|āte *v.t.* Reduce to or express in a formula; set forth systematically; hence ~A'TION *n.* [f. FORMULA + -ATE³]

for'mūl|ism *n.* Adherence to or dependence on conventional formulas; so ~IST (2) *n.* [f. FORMULA + -ISM]

for'nicāt|e *v.i.* Commit fornication; so ~OR *n.* [f. eccl. L *fornicari* (L *fornix -icis* brothel) + -ATE³]

fornicā'tion *n.* Voluntary sexual intercourse between unmarried persons or (esp. Bibl.) other than between husband and wife. [ME f. OF, f. eccl. L *fornicatio -onis* (as prec.; see -ATION)]

fŏ'rrader. See FORWARD².

forsā'ke *v.t.* (**forsoo'k** *pr.* -ŏŏ'k; **~n**). Give up, break off from, renounce; withdraw one's help, friendship, or companionship from, desert, abandon. [OE *forsacan* deny, renounce, refuse, = OS *forsakan*, OHG *firsahhan* f. WG (as FOR- (3); cf. OE *sacan* quarrel)]

forsoo'th *adv.* (arch., iron., or derog.) Truly, in truth, no doubt. [OE *forsōth* (as FOR, SOOTH)]

forspĕ'nt *a.* (arch.) Tired out. [p.p. of obs. *forspend* f. OE *forspendan* (as FOR- (5), SPEND)]

forswear' (-wār') *v.t.* (**forswor'e; forswor'n**). Abjure, renounce on oath; **~ oneself,** swear falsely, perjure oneself; (in *p.p.*) perjured. [OE *forswerian* (as FOR- (3, 1), SWEAR)]

forsȳ'thia *n.* Spring-flowering ornamental shrub of genus *Forsythia* bearing bright-yellow flowers. [mod. L, f. W. *Forsyth*, Engl. botanist d. 1804 + -IA¹]

fort *n.* Fortified building or position; (Hist.) trading-station, orig. fortified; **hold the ~,** act as temporary substitute, cope with emergency. [F, or f. It. *forte*, abs. uses of adj. = strong f. L *fortis*]

for'talice *n.* (arch.) Fortress; small outwork of fortification, small fort. [ME, f. med. L *fortalitia* f. L *fortis* strong]

forte¹ (*or* -tĭ) *n.* Person's strong point; (Fenc.) part of sword-blade from hilt to middle (cf. FOIBLE). [f. F *fort* abs. use of adj. = strong; for substitution of fem. form cf. *morale, locale*]

for'tė² *a., adv.,* & *n.* (Mus.) (Passage to be) performed loudly; **~ piano,** loud(ly) and then immediately soft(ly). [It., = strong, loud]

forth *adv.* & *prep.* (arch. exc. in set phrs.) **1.** Forwards (**back and ~,** to and fro); onwards in time (*from this time forth*; *henceforth* etc.); forward, into view, (*bring, come,* HOLD¹, SET¹, *show,* etc., *forth*); out from home etc. (*set* etc. *forth*); **and so ~,** and so on, and the like. **2.** *prep.* From out of. [OE, = OS *forth*, MHG *vort* f. Gmc **furtha* f. IE **pr̥to*]

for'thcoming (-kŭ-; *or* -kŭ'-). *a.* About or likely to come forth or appear; approaching; produced when wanted (*no reply was forthcoming*); (of person) informative, responsive, whence ~NESS *n.* [f. prec. + COME + -ING²]

forthright (-rīt) *adv., a.,* & *n.* **1.** *adv.* (-rī't). Straight forward, in a direct manner; (arch.) immediately. **2.** *a.* (for'-). Going straight; outspoken; unswerving; decisive, unhesitating. **3.** *n.* (for'-; arch.) Straight course (*forthrights and meanders*). [OE *forthriht(e)* (as FORTH, RIGHT¹·⁴)]

forthwi'th (*or* -dh) *adv.* Immediately, without delay. [f. earlier *forthwithal* (FORTH, WITH, ALL)]

for'tieth. See FORTY.

fortificā'tion *n.* Fortifying; strengthening of wine with alcohol; (Mil.) (art or science of) providing with defensive works, (usu. in *pl.*) defensive work(s), wall(s), earthwork(s), tower(s), etc. [ME f. F, f. LL *fortificatio -onis* act of strengthening (as foll.; see -ATION)]

for'tif|ȳ *v.* **1.** *v.t.* Strengthen structure of; impart vigour or physical strength or endurance to, strengthen mentally or morally, encourage; increase nutritive value of (food, esp. with vitamins); strengthen (wine) with alcohol; (arch.) corroborate, confirm, (statement); provide (town, army, etc.) with defensive works; hence **~i**ABLE *a.* **2.** *v.i.* Erect fortifications. [ME, f. OF *fortifier* f. LL *fortificare* f. L *fortis* strong; see -FY]

forti'ssim|ō *a., adv.,* & *n.* (*pl.* **~os,** *or* **~i** *pr.* -ē). (Mus.) (Passage to be) performed very loudly. [It., superl. of FORTE²]

for'titūde *n.* Courage in pain or adversity. [ME f. F, f. L *fortitudo -dinis* (*fortis* strong; see -TUDE)]

for'tnight (-īt) *n.* Period of two weeks; **today, this day, Monday,** etc., **~, a ~ (from) today, a ~ on Monday,** etc. a fortnight before or esp. after today etc. [OE *fēowertiene niht* fourteen nights]

for'tnightlȳ (-īt-) *a., adv.,* & *n.* **1.** *a.* & *adv.* (Produced or occurring) once every fortnight. **2.** *n.* Fortnightly magazine etc. [f. prec. + -LY¹·²]

For'trăn *n.* Computer language used esp. for scientific calculations. [f. FORMULA + TRANSLATION]

for'trėss *n.,* & *v.t.* **1.** *n.* Military stronghold, esp. strongly fortified town fit for large garrison. **2.** *v.t.* (arch.) Serve as fortress to; protect. [ME, f. OF *forteresse* f. Rom. **fortaritia* f. L *fortis* strong]

fortū'it|ism *n.* Belief that adaptation in nature is due to mere chance; so ~IST (2) *n.* [f. foll. + -ISM]

fortū'itous *a.* Due to or characterized by chance, accidental, casual; hence ~LY² *adv.*, ~NESS *n.* [f. L *fortuitus* (*forte* by chance) + -OUS]

fortū'itȳ *n.* Fortuitousness; a chance occurrence; accident. [irreg. f. as prec. + -ITY]

for'tūnate (*or* -chu- *or* -chŏŏ-) *a.* Favoured by fortune, lucky, prosperous; auspicious, favourable. [ME, f. L *fortunatus* (as FORTUNE[1]; see -ATE[2])]

fŏr'tūnatelȳ (-tlĭ; *or* -chu- *or* -choo-) *adv.* Luckily, successfully, (qualifying whole sentence) it is fortunate that. [f. prec. + -LY[2]]

fŏr'tune[1] (-chun *or* -choon) *n.* **1.** Chance or luck as a power in human affairs (**F~**, this power personified as goddess; *Fortune's* WHEEL[1]; SOLDIER *of fortune*). **2.** (in *sing.* or *pl.*) Luck good or bad that falls to anyone or to an enterprise etc. **3.** Person's destiny; (of gipsies etc.) *tell person his fortune, tell fortunes,* **~-teller, ~-telling;** ***~ cookie,** baked dough cake enclosing prediction etc. on slip of paper. **4.** Good luck; prosperity, prosperous condition, wealth, (**make** one's **~**, prosper; **make a ~**, become rich); (**small**) **~**, large sum of money; **marry a ~**, (arch.) marry rich heiress; **~-hunter,** man seeking rich wife for himself. [ME f. OF, f. L *fortuna* luck, chance]

fŏr'tune[2] (-chun *or* -choon) *v.i.* (arch. or poet.) Chance, occur, (esp. impers., *it fortuned that*); come by chance *upon.* [ME, f. OF *fortuner* f. L *fortunare* make fortunate (as prec.)]

fŏr'tȳ *a.* & *n.* **1.** Four times ten; symbol for this (40, xl, XL); (in *pl.*) numbers etc., esp. years of a century or life, from 40 to 49; **~ winks,** short sleep esp. after dinner; HUNGRY *Forties*; **roaring forties,** stormy ocean tracts between lat. 40° and 50° S.; ||**the Forties,** sea area between N.E. coast of Scotland and S.W. coast of Norway [so named from its depth of forty fathoms or more]; hence **~**FOLD *a.* & *adv.*, **fŏr'tĭeth[1]** *a.* & *n.* **2. ~-one** etc., (arch.) **one--and-~** etc., forty plus one etc., w. corresp. ordinals **~-first** etc.; **the F~-fi've,** Jacobite rebellion of 1745; ***~-ni'ner,** seeker for gold etc., esp. in California (1849). [OE *fēowertig,* = OS *fiwartig,* OHG *fiorzug,* ON *fjórir tigir,* Goth. *fidwor tigjus* (as FOUR, -TY[2])]

fŏr'um *n.* **1.** (Rom. Ant.) Public place, market--place, place of assembly for judicial and other business, esp. at Rome. **2.** Place of or meeting for public discussion; periodical etc. giving opportunity for debate etc.; court, tribunal, (lit. or fig., *the forum of conscience* etc.). [L]

fŏr'ward[1] *a.* & *n.* **1.** *a.* (Naut.) belonging to fore part of ship; lying in one's line of motion (*the forward horizon*), onward or towards the front (*the forward path*); (Cricket) of playing FORWARD[2]; (Rugby Footb. etc., of pass) towards opponents' goal-line; (of opinions etc.) advanced or extreme. **2.** (Commerc.) Relating to future produce, delivery, etc., (*forward contract*). **3.** Advanced, progressing to maturity or completion; (of plant, crop, season) well advanced or early; (arch.) ready, prompt, eager, (*to* do); precocious; presumptuous, pert. **4.** Hence **~**LY[2] *adv.*, **~**NESS *n.* **5.** *n.* (Position of) an attacking player in football, hockey, etc. [f. foll.]

fŏr'ward[2] *adv.* **1.** Towards the future, continuously onwards, (*from this time forward;* CARRIAGE *forward;* **date ~**, post-date). **2.** Towards the front in the direction one is facing; in normal direction of motion or traversal; BACKWARD(s) *and forward(s)*; with continuous forward motion (*rushing forward*). **3.** (Cricket). **Play ~**, reach forward to play short-pitched ball. **4.** In advance, ahead, (*send him forward;* BRING *forward;* CARRY[1] *forward;* **~-looking,** progressive); to the front, into prominence, (BRING *forward;* **come ~**, offer oneself for task, post, etc.; PUT[1] *forward;* SET[1] *forward*). **5.** (Naut. & Aeron.) In or near or to or towards bow or nose. **6.** Onward so as to make progress; **go ~**, be going on, progress; **can't get any forwarder** or (colloq.) **forrader,** can make no progress. [OE *forweard,* var. of *forthweard* (as FORTH; see -WARD)]

fŏr'ward[3] *v.t.* Help forward, promote; accelerate growth of; send (letter etc.) on to further destination; dispatch (goods etc.; *forwarding agent*). [f. prec.]

fŏr'wards (-dz) *adv.* = FORWARD[2] 2. [ME, f. FORWARD[2]; see -S[3], -WARD(S)]

forwear'ĭed (-ĭd), **forwŏr'n,** *adjs.* (arch.) Tired out. [f. FOR- (4); see WEARY, WEAR[1]]

fŏrwĕ'nt. See FORGO.

fŏ'ssa *n.* (*pl.* **~e**). (Anat.) Shallow depression or cavity. [L, = ditch, fem. p.p. of *fodere* dig]

fŏsse *n.* Long narrow excavation, canal, ditch, trench, esp. in fortification; (Anat.) = prec.; **F~ Way,** Roman road in Britain with fosse on each side. [ME f. OF, f. L FOSSA]

fŏ'ssick *v.i.* (Austral. & N.Z. sl.) Rummage, search *about*; search for gold etc. in abandoned workings. [19th c.; cf. dial. *fossick* bustle about]

fŏ'ssĭl *a.* & *n.* **1.** *a.* Found buried, dug up, (**~ fuel,** coal etc. formed in geological past, esp. opp. *nuclear fuel*). **2.** *a.* & *n.* (Thing) preserved in strata of earth and recognizable as remains or vestiges of plant or animal of past (usu. prehistoric) ages (*fossil bones, shells,* IVORY; *hunting for fossils*); (person or thing) belonging to the past, antiquated, incapable of further development; (word etc.) that has become obsolete except in set phrases or forms, e.g. *hue* in *hue and cry*; hence **~ĭ'**FEROUS *a.*, **~**IZE (3) *v.t.* & *i.*, **~īzA'**TION *n.* [f. F *fossile* f. L *fossilis* (*fodere foss-* dig; see -IL)]

fŏssŏr'ĭal *a.* (Zool.) Burrowing; used in burrowing. [f. med. L *fossorius* (*fossor* digger f. as prec.; see -OR) + -AL]

fŏ'ster[1] *a.* Having a specified relationship not by blood, but in virtue of nursing or bringing up (*foster-brother, -child, -daughter, -father, -mother, -parent, -sister, -son*); concerning care of orphans etc. (*foster care; foster home*); ||**~-mother,** apparatus for rearing chickens hatched in incubator. [orig. 'food', f. OE *fōster* (as FOOD)]

fŏ'ster[2] *v.t.* Promote growth of; encourage or harbour (feeling); (of circumstances) be favourable to; nurse or bring up as foster-child; (arch.) tend affectionately, cherish, keep warm (in bosom). [OE *fōstrian* (as prec.)]

fŏ'sterage *n.* Fostering; custom of employing foster-mothers. [f. prec. + -AGE]

fŏ'sterlĭng *n.* Foster-child, nursling, protégé. [f. OE *fōsterling* (as FOSTER[1], -LING[1])]

Fou'cault (fōō'kō) *n.* **~ current,** (Electr.) eddy current; **~('s) pendulum** (showing rotation of earth by turning of its plane of motion relative to floor etc.). [f. J.B.L. ~, Fr. physicist d. 1868]

fouetté (fwĕtā') *n.* (Ballet). Quick whipping movement of raised leg. [F, p.p. of *fouetter* whip]

fouga'sse (fōōgah's) *n.* Improvised mortar excavated in the ground, charged with stones, bits of iron, etc., and fired by gunpowder. [F, alt. of *fougade* f. It. *fogata*]

fought. See FIGHT[1].

foul *a.*, *n.*, *adv.*, & *v.* **1.** *a.* Offensive to the senses, loathsome, stinking; dirty, soiled, (*foul linen*), filthy; (sl.) revolting, disgusting; defaced with corrections (*foul copy*). **2.** Containing noxious matter (*foul air, water*); clogged, choked, (*foul gun-barrel*); (of ship's bottom) overgrown with weed, barnacles, etc.; morally polluted, obscene, disgustingly abusive, (*foul deed, motive, talk; foul-mouthed, -tongued*); ugly (*fair or foul*). **3.** Unfair, against rules of game etc., (*foul blow, stroke*); (of weather) wet, rough, stormy; in collision (FALL[1] or *run foul of,* lit. or fig.); entangled (*foul anchor; rope is foul*). **4. ~ brood,** bacterial disease of larval bees; **~ fiend,** the Devil; **~ line** (marking boundary of playing area etc.); ~ **play,** unfair play in games, (fig.) treachery or murder or violence. **5.** Hence ~'LY[2] (-l-lĭ) *adv.*, ~'NESS *n.* **6.** *n.* Foul thing; collision, entanglement, esp. in riding, rowing, or running; foul stroke or piece of play. **7.** *adv.* In foul way (*hit him foul*; **play** person ~, deal treacherously with him). **8.** *v.i.* Become foul, get clogged or entangled. **9.** *v.t.* Make foul or dirty (*foul* one's *own* NEST; *dog fouls pavement*, esp. with excrement); pollute with guilt, dishonour; ~ (**up**), cause (anchor, cable, etc.) to become entangled or muddled, jam or block (crossing, railway line, traffic); commit foul against (player); run foul of, collide with; ~**-up** *n.*, state of muddle or confusion. [OE *fūl*, = OS, OHG *fūl*, ON *fúll*, Goth. *fuls* stinking f. Gmc **fūlaz* (**fū-* f. IE **pū-*)]

foular'd (fōōl-) *n.* (Handkerchief etc. of) thin soft material of silk or silk and cotton. [F]

fou'mart (fōō'-) *n.* Polecat. [ME *fulmert* etc. (as FOUL, *mart* MARTEN)]

found[1] *v.* **1.** *v.t.* Lay base of (building etc.); be original builder, begin building, of (town, edifice); set up, establish (esp. with endowment), originate, initiate, (institution). **2.** Construct, base, (tale, one's fortunes, classification, rule, etc.) (*up*)*on* or *in* some ground, support, principle, etc., (WELL, **ill,** etc., **-~ed,** reasonable or justified, baseless, etc.). **3.** *v.i.* Rely, base oneself, (of argument etc.) be based, (*up*)*on.* **4.** **~ing father,** person associated with a founding, esp. Amer. statesman at time of Revolution. [ME, f. OF *fonder* f. L *fundare* (*fundus* bottom)]

found[2] *v.t.* Melt and mould (metal), fuse (materials for glass); make (thing of metal, glass) thus; hence ~'RY (3) *n.* [ME, f. OF *fondre* f. L *fundere fus-* pour]

found[3]. See FIND.

foundā'tion *n.* **1.** Establishing, constituting on permanent basis, esp. of an endowed institution; such institution, e.g. monastery, college, or hospital, (**on the** ~, entitled to benefit by its funds, whence ||~ER[1] *n.*), or its revenues. **2.** Solid ground or base, natural or artificial, on which building rests, lowest part of building usu. below ground-level; basis, groundwork, underlying principle, (*report has no foundation*; *base religion on a moral foundation*); body or ground on which other parts are overlaid; base for application of cosmetics. **3.** ~ (**garment**), woman's supporting undergarment, e.g. corset; ~**-school** (endowed); ~**-stone,** (esp.) stone laid with ceremony to celebrate founding of edifice, (fig.) basis. [ME, f. OF *fondation* f. L *fundatio -onis* (as FOUND[1]; see -ATION)]

fou'nder[1] *n.* In vbl senses; one who founds an institution (*founder-member*; ~**'s kin,** relatives of founder entitled to election or preference); hence ~SHIP, **fou'ndr**ESS[1], *ns.* [f. FOUND[1] + -ER[1]]

fou'nder[2] *n.* In vbl senses. [f. FOUND[2] + -ER[1]]

fou'nder[3] *v.* & *n.* **1.** *v.i.* (Of earth, building, etc.) fall down or in, give way; (or horse or its rider) fall to the ground, fall from lameness, stick fast in bog etc.; (of ship) fill with water and sink; (of plan etc.) fail. **2.** *v.t.* Cause (horse) to break down, esp. with founder; cause (ship) to founder. **3.** *n.* Inflammation of horse's foot from overwork; rheumatism of chest-muscles in horses. [ME, f. OF *fondrer*, *esfondrer* submerge, collapse, f. Rom. ***(EX[1]) *fundorare* f. L *fundus* bottom]

fou'ndlĭng *n.* Deserted infant of unknown parents. [ME, perh. f. obs. *funding* (as FIND, -ING[3]), assim. to -LING[1]]

fou'ndrў. See FOUND[2].

fount[1] *n.* Reservoir of oil in lamp or of ink in pen; (poet. or rhet.) spring, source, fountain. [back form. f. FOUNTAIN[1], after MOUNT[1]]

||**fount**[2] (*or* fŏnt), ***fŏnt**[2], *n.* (Print.) Set of type of same face and size. [f. F *fonte* (*fondre* FOUND[2])]

fou'ntain[1] (-tĭn) *n.* Water-spring; source *of* river etc. (lit., or fig., *the Crown is the fountain of honour*; *poison the fountains of trust*); jet of water made to spout, structure provided for it; structure for constant public supply of drinking-water; = SODA-*fountain*; reservoir in lamp, printing-press, etc., for oil, ink, etc., (~**-pen,** pen having this); ~**-head,** original source; hence (-)~ED[2] (-ĭnd) *a.* [ME, f. OF *fontaine* f. LL *fontana* (*aqua* water) fem. of L *fontanus* a. (*fons fontis* a spring; see -AN)]

fou'ntain[2] (-tĭn) *v.i.* & *t.* (Cause to) rise like waters of fountain. [f. prec.]

four (fōr) *a.* & *n.* **1.** One more than three; symbol for this (4, iv, IV, rarely iiii, IIII); card etc. with four pips; time of four o'clock; size etc. denoted by four; set of four, esp. horses, card-players, or crew of four in rowing-boat (~**s,** boat-races between such crews); hit at cricket scoring four runs; (in *pl.*) gloves, shoes, etc., of fourth size, candles weighing four to the pound; **on all ~s,** (1) crawling on hands and knees, (2) completely analogous or corresponding (*the examples are not on all fours*). **2.** ||~**-ale,** (Hist.) ale sold at 4d. a quart; ~**-ball,** golf match between two pairs with each person using a separate ball; ~**-colour problem** (to prove that any plane map can be coloured with only four different colours so that no two same-coloured regions have a common boundary); ~**-cycle,** = four-stroke; *four-*DIMENSIONAL; ***~-flush,** almost worthless poker hand having four (not five) cards of same suit; ***~-flusher,** bluffer, humbug; ~**-footed,** having four feet (esp. opp. biped); ***~-H,** of clubs etc. for instruction of young people in agriculture and citizenship [improving head, heart, hands, and health]; ~**-handed,** (of monkey) quadrumanous, (of game) for four persons, (of piece of keyboard music) for two players; ***~ hundred,** highest social group of a locality; ~**-in-hand,** (1) vehicle with four horses driven by one person on the box, (2) *necktie worn with knot and two hanging ends superposed; ~**-leaf** or ~**-leaved clover,** clover leaf with four leaflets thought to bring good luck; ~**-letter word,** vulgar monosyllable referring to sexual or excretory functions; ~ **o'clock,** the plant marvel of Peru; ~**-part,** arranged for four voices to sing; ||~**'pence,** sum of 4p. or 4d.; ||~**'penny,** costing 4p. or 4d. (*fourpenny one,* (colloq.) hit, blow); ~**-post,** (of bed) having four posts to support canopy (~**-poster,** such bed); ~**-pounder,** gun throwing 4-lb. shot; ~**-rowed barley** (with four rows of awns); ~**'score,** (arch.) eighty; ~**-square,** square-shaped, solidly based or steady, resolute; ~**-stroke,** (of internal combustion engine) having a cycle of four strokes (intake, compression, combustion, and exhaust); ~**-wheel,** having four wheels, acting on all four wheels of a vehicle (*four-wheel drive*); ~**-whee'ler,** (Hist.) four-wheeled hackney carriage. **3.** Hence ~'FOLD *a.* & *adv.* [OE *fēower*, = OS *fiwar* etc., OHG *fior*, *fier*, ON *fjórir*, Goth. *fidwōr* f. Gmc **petwor-* f. IE **quetwōr-*]

fourchĕ'tte (foorshĕ't) *n.* (Anat.) Membrane at posterior junction of labia minora. [F, dim. of *fourche* (as FORK); see -ETTE]

Fourdrĭ'nier (foor-; *or* -ĭā) *n.* ~ (**machine**), machine for making paper as continuous sheet by drainage on wire mesh belt. [f. H. & S. ~, Brit. printers d. 1854, 1847]

fourgon (foor'gawn) *n.* Luggage-van. [F]

Four'ĭer (foor'ĭā) *n.* (Math.) ~ **analysis, series,** etc., (relating to resolution of vibrations etc. into combinations of simple harmonic functions). [f. J. B. J. ~, Fr. mathematician d. 1830]

Four'ĭerĭsm (foor'-) *n.* System for reorganization of society (cf. PHALANX 2). [f. C. *Fourier*, Fr. socialist d. 1837 + -ISM]

four'some (fōr'-) *n.* Golf match between two pairs with partners playing same ball; a company, party, or dance of four persons. [f. FOUR + -SOME[2]]

fourtee'n (fōrt-; *or* fōr'tēn) *a.* & *n.* One more than thirteen; symbol for this (14, xiv, XIV); size etc. denoted by fourteen; hence ~ER[1] *n.*, (Pros.) line of fourteen syllables, ~TH[2] *a.* & *n.* [OE *fēowertiene*, = OS *fiertein*, OHG *fiorzehan*, ON *fjórtán*, Goth. *fidwōrtaihun* (as FOUR, -TEEN)]

fourth (fōr-) *a.* & *n.* **1.** *a.* Next after third; ~ **part,** quarter. **2.** *n.* Quarter, fourth part; fourth thing etc.; player who completes a group of four; fourth day of month; (person having) place in fourth class in examination; fourth gear; (Mus.) interval of which the span involves four alphabetical notes, harmonic combination of notes thus separated; ||**F~ of June,** principal annual celebration at Eton College; ***F~ of July,** anniversary of Declaration of Independence (1776). **3.** ~ **day,** Wednesday; *fourth* DIMENSION; *fourth* ESTATE; *fourth* FORM[1] 6; **fourth* GRADE 1; ~ **wall,** (Theatr.) proscenium opening through which audience sees performance. **4.** Hence ~'LY[2] *adv.*, in the fourth place. [OE *fēo(we)rtha*, = OS *fiortho*, OHG *fiordo*, ON *fjórthi* f. Gmc **fi(dh)-worthon* f. IE **qweturto-*]

fō'vė|a *n.* (*pl.* **~ae**). (Anat.) Small depression or pit; hence ~AL, ~ATE[2], *adjs.* [L]

fōvē'ola *n.* (*pl.* **~e**). (Anat.) Small fovea; hence **fō'vėol**ATE[2] *a.* [L, dim. of prec.]

fowl *n.* (*pl.* **~s** *or* ~), & *v.i.* **1.** *n.* Domestic cock or hen of genus *Gallus* (*fowl* CHOLERA; ~ **pest,** ~ **plague,** ~ **pox,** infectious virus diseases of fowls; **~-run,** place where fowls may run, breeding establishment for fowls); its flesh as food. **2.** Bird (GAME[1]*fowl*, GUINEA-*fowl*, WILD-*fowl*); flesh of birds as food (*fish, flesh, and fowl*). **3.** *v.i.* Catch, hunt, shoot, or snare, wildfowl; hence ~'ER[1], ~'ING[1], *ns.* (**~ing piece,** light gun used in fowling). [OE *fugol*, = OS *fugal*, OHG *fogal*, ON *fugl*, Goth. *fugls* f. Gmc **foglaz*, **fuglaz*, f. **flug-* FLY[2]]

fŏx[1] *n.* **1.** Red-furred sharp-snouted bushy-tailed carnivorous quadruped preserved in England etc. as beast of chase and proverbial for cunning; its fur; (fig.) crafty person, *(sl.) attractive woman. **2.** Animal of species related to this; FLYING[2] *fox.* **3.** **~'glove,** tall plant with purple or white flowers like glove-fingers; **~'hole,** (Mil.) hole in ground used as shelter against missiles or as firing-point, (fig.) place of refuge or concealment; **~'hound,** kind of hound bred and trained to hunt foxes; **~-hunt** *n.*, & *v.i.*, chasing of, chase, fox with hounds, whence **~-hunter** *n.*, **~-hunting** *a.* & *n.*, (given to) this sport; **~-mark,** brown spot or stain caused by damp in book etc.; ~ **shark,** thresher; **~'tail,** (1) fox's tail, (2) grass with brushlike spikes; **~-terrier** (short-haired for unearthing fox, but kept chiefly as pet); **~'trot** *n.*, & *v.i.*, (perform) ballroom dance with slow and quick steps. [OE, = OS *vuhs*, OHG *fuhs* f. WG **fuhs*]

fŏx[2] *v.* **1.** *v.i.* Act craftily, dissemble. **2.** *v.t.* Deceive, puzzle, trick; (esp. in *p.p.*) discolour (leaves of book, engraving, etc.) with fox-marks, whence ~'ING[1] (2) *n.* [f. prec.]

fŏ'x|ȳ *a.* Foxlike, crafty(-looking); reddish-brown; damaged by mildew etc.; hence **~ĭ**NESS *n.* [f. FOX[1] + -Y[2]]

foyer (foi'ā *or* fwah'yā) *n.* Large room in theatre etc. for audience's use during interval; entrance hall of hotel etc. [F, = hearth, home, f. Gallo-Rom. **focarium* f. L *focus* fire]

F.P. *abbr.* former pupil; freezing point.

fp *abbr.* forte piano.

||**F.P.A.** *abbr.* Family Planning Association.

F.P.S. *abbr.* foot-pound-second.

Fr. *abbr.* Father; French.

fr. *abbr.* franc(s).

Fr *symb.* francium.

Fra (-ah) *n.* = FRATE (as prefixed title). [It.]

fră'bjous *a.* Delightful, joyous; hence ~LY[2] *adv.* [made by Lewis Carroll perh. on FAIR[2], JOYOUS]

fră'cas (-kah) *n.* (*pl.* same *pr.* -kahz). Noisy quarrel, row. [F (*fracasser* f. It. *fracassare* make uproar)]

fră'ction *n.* **1.** Numerical quantity that is not a whole number, one or more aliquot parts, (DECIMAL, IMPROPER, PROPER, VULGAR, *fraction*). **2.** Small part, piece, or amount. **3.** Portion of mixture obtainable by physical separation, e.g. by distillation. **4.** Dividing of Eucharistic bread. **5.** Hence ~ARY[1] *a.*, ~IZE (3) *v.t.* [ME f. OF, f. LL *fractio -onis* f. L *frangere fract-* break; see -ION]

fră'ctional *a.* Of fraction(s); being a fraction; ~ **crystallization, distillation,** etc., separation of parts of a mixture by making use of their different physical properties; hence ~IZE (3) *v.t.* [f. prec. + -AL]

fră'ction|āte *v.t.* Break up into parts; separate (mixture) by fractional distillation etc.; hence ~A'TION *n.* [f. FRACTION + -ATE[3]]

fră'ctious (-shus) *a.* Unruly; peevish; hence ~LY[2] *adv.*, ~NESS *n.* [f. FRACTION in obs. sense 'brawling' + -OUS, prob. after *factious* etc.]

fră'ctō- *comb. form.* (Meteorol., of cloud form) broken, fragmentary, (*fracto-cumulus, fracto-nimbus*). [f. L *fractus* broken (see FRACTION) + -O-]

fră'cture *n.* & *v.* **1.** *n.* Breaking, breakage, esp. of bone or cartilage (COMMINUTE*d*, COMPOUND[2], *fracture*); surface shown by mineral when broken with hammer. **2.** Substitution of diphthong, diphthong substituted, for simple vowel owing to influence esp. of following consonant. **3.** *v.t.* Cause fracture in, break continuity of; *(sl.) impress, amuse greatly. **4.** *v.i.* Undergo fracture. [ME f. F, or f. L *fractura* (as FRACTION; see -URE)]

frae'nūl|um, frē'nūl|um, *n.* (*pl.* **~a**). Small fraenum. [mod. L, dim. of foll.]

frae'n|um, frē'n|um, *n.* (*pl.* **~a**). Small ligament checking motion of organ. [L, = bridle]

fră'gīle *a.* Easily snapped or shattered, weak, perishable, of delicate frame or constitution; hence or cogn. ~LY[2] (-l-lĭ) *adv.*, **fragĭ'l**ITY *n.* [F, or f. L *fragilis* (**frag-* root of *frangere* break; see -IL)]

fră'gment *n.* & *v.* **1.** *n.* Part broken off, detached piece; isolated or incomplete part, remainder of otherwise lost or destroyed whole, esp. extant remains or unfinished portion of writing or work of art; hence ~IZE (3) *v.t.* **2.** *v.t.* & *i.* (*or* -ĕ'nt). Break or separate into fragments. [ME f. F, or f. L *fragmentum* (as prec.; see -MENT)]

fră'gmentar|ȳ *a.* Consisting of fragments; disconnected; (Geol.) composed of fragments of previously existing rocks; hence **~ĭ**LY[2] *adv.* [f. prec. + -ARY[1]]

frăgmentā'tion *n.* Breaking into fragments; ~ **bomb** etc. (designed to break up into small rapidly-moving fragments when exploded). [f. FRAGMENT + -ATION]

frā'grance *n.* Sweetness of smell; sweet scent. [F, or f. L *fragrantia* (as foll.; see -ANCE)]

frā′grant *a.* Sweet-smelling (lit. or fig.). [ME f. F, or f. L *fragrare* smell sweet; see -ANT]

′fraid *a.* (colloq.) Afraid; **~(′y) cat,** coward. [f. AFRAID]

frail[1] *n.* Rush basket for packing figs, raisins, etc.; quantity (e.g. 32 lb.) contained in this. [ME f. OF *fraiel*, of unkn. orig.]

frail[2] *a.* & *n.* **1.** *a.* Fragile; transient (*frail life, bliss*, etc.); in weak health; morally weak, unable to resist temptation, (arch. euphem., of woman) unchaste; hence **~′**NESS *n.* **2.** *n.* *(sl.) Woman. [ME, f. OF *fraile, frele* f. L *fragilis* FRAGILE]

frai′ltў *n.* Liability to err or yield to temptation; fault, weakness, foible. [ME, f. OF *fraileté* f. L *fragilitas -tatis* (as FRAGILE; see -ITY)]

fraise (-z) *n.* Tool for enlarging circular hole, or cutting teeth in watch-wheels. [F (*fraiser* enlarge hole)]

Fră′ktur (-oor) *n.* German style of black-letter type. [G]

frămboe′sĭa, *frămbē′sĭa, (-bē′z-) *n.* = YAWS. [mod. L, f. F *framboise* raspberry f. L *fraga ambrosia* ambrosial strawberry + -IA[1]]

frām|e[1] *v.t.* **1.** Shape, direct, dispose, (thoughts, acts, (arch.) person) to a purpose (*for, to, to* do, or w. *adv.*); adapt, fit, *to* or *into*; construct by combination of parts or adaptation to design, contrive, devise, invent, compose, express, (complex article, plot, rule, story, theory); articulate (words); (arch.) conceive, imagine. **2.** [f. foll.] Set in or provide with a frame, serve as frame for (*landscape framed in an archway*), whence **~′**ING[1] (3) *n.*; (sl.) concoct false charge or evidence against, devise plot with regard to; **~e up,** *(sl.) prearrange (event) with sinister intent, fake result of (race, election, etc.); hence **~e-up** *n.*, (colloq.) conspiracy. **3.** Hence **~′**ABLE *a.*, **~′**ER[1] *n.* [OE *framian* be helpful (*fram* forward; see FROM)]

frāme[2] *n.* **1.** Construction, constitution, build; established order, plan, system, (*the frame of society* or *government*; **~ of reference,** system of geometrical axes for defining position, set of standards etc. governing behaviour); temporary state (*of mind*). **2.** Framed work or structure (*the frame of heaven* or *earth*), human or animal body (*sobs shook her frame*; *man of gigantic frame*); skeleton of building, underlying or surrounding support or essential substructure of anything; rigid part of bicycle, spectacles, umbrella, etc.; supporting skeleton of motor vehicle, aircraft, etc. **3.** Case or border enclosing picture, pane of glass, door, etc., whence **~′**LESS (-ml-) *a.*; single complete image or picture on cinema film or transmitted in series of lines by television; single picture in comic strip; (Hort.) glazed portable boxlike structure protecting plants from cold; removable box of slats for building of honeycomb in beehive; triangular frame for setting up snooker etc. balls or skittles, balls so set up, round of play during which skittles are thrown at or balls are pocketed; *(sl.) = FRAME[1]-*up*. **4. ~ aerial,** revolving aerial composed of rectangle or loop or wire, adapted for directional reception; **~-house** (of wooden skeleton covered with boards etc.); **~-saw** (stretched in frame to make it rigid); **~′work,** frame, structure, upon or into which casing or contents can be put (lit. or fig.). [f. prec.]

frănc *n.* Monetary unit of France, Belgium, Switzerland, and other countries. [ME, f. OF, f. *Francorum Rex* king of the FRANK[1]s, legend on earliest gold coins so called (14th c.)]

fră′nchīse (-z) *n.*, & *v.t.* **1.** *n.* Right of voting at public elections esp. for Parliament etc.; principle of qualification for this (FANCY[1] *franchise*). **2.** Full membership of corporation or State, citizenship. **3.** Authorization to sell company's goods or services in a particular area. **4.** (Hist.) Legal immunity or exemption from burden or jurisdiction. **5.** Right or privilege granted to person or corporation. **6.** *v.t.* Grant franchise to. [ME f. OF (*franc, franche* free, FRANK[2]; see -ISE[2])]

Frănci′scan *a.* & *n.* (Friar) of order (also *Grey Friars* f. their grey cloak) founded 1209 by St. Francis of Assisi; of the Franciscans. [f. F *franciscain* f. mod. L *Franciscanus* (*Franciscus* Francis; see -AN)]

fră′ncĭum *n.* (Chem.) Radioactive metallic element, heaviest alkali metal. [mod. L, f. *France* + -IUM]

Fră′ncō- *comb. form.* French (and), as: **~-Ger′man,** French and German; **~**MA′NIA *n.*, **~**PHIL(E), **~**PHOBE, *ns.* & *adjs.*, **~**PHO′BIA *n.* [f. med. L *Francus* FRANK[1] + -O-]

fră′ncolĭn *n.* Partridge of genus *Francolinus*. [F, f. It. *francolino*]

fră′ncophōne *n.* & *a.* French-speaking (person). [f. FRANCO- + Gk *phōnē* voice]

franc tireur (frahṅ tērẽr′) *n.* (*pl. -cs -rs pr.* same). (Hist.) member of irregular light-infantry corps; guerrilla fighter. [F, = free shooter]

fră′ngĭble (-nj-) *a.* Breakable, fragile. [OF, or f. med. L *frangibilis* f. L *frangere* to break; see -IBLE]

fră′ngĭpāne (-nj-) *n.* = foll.; flavoured almond cream or paste. [F, prob. f. *Frangipani*, Italian inventor of the perfume]

frăngĭpă′nĭ (-nj-; *or* -pah′-) *n.* (Perfume of) fragrant shrub or tree of genus *Plumeria*. [var. of prec.]

franglais (frah′ṅglā) *n.* Corrupt version of French with indiscriminate use of words etc. borrowed from English. [F (*français* French, *anglais* English)]

Frănk[1] *n.* Member of the Germanic nation or coalition that conquered Gaul in 6th c.; (in Levant) person of Western nationality; hence **~′**ISH[1] *a.* [f. OE *Franca*, OHG *Franko*, perh. f. weapon (cf. OE *franca* javelin)]

frănk[2] *a.* Ingenuous, open, (*a frank face*); candid, outspoken, (*a frank opinion*); undisguised, avowed, (*frank admiration*); (Med.) unmistakable; hence **~′**LY[2] *adv.* (also ellipt., = 'to speak frankly': *frankly, you haven't a chance*), **~′**NESS *n.* [ME, f. OF *franc* f. med. L *francus* free, f. prec. (since only Franks had full freedom in Frankish Gaul)]

frănk[3] *v.t.*, & *n.* **1.** *v.t.* (Hist.) superscribe (letter etc.) with signature ensuring conveyance without charge, send without charge; (arch.) facilitate coming and going of (person), give social passport to; (Hist.) exempt from future payment etc. (*a franking duty, imposition*); put stamp on or mark (letter) to record payment of postage; ‖**~′ing-machine** (for so marking letters etc. and recording cost of postage incurred). **2.** *n.* Franking signature or mark; franked cover. [f. prec. in obs. sense 'free of charge']

***frănk**[4] *n.* (colloq.) Frankfurter. [abbr.]

Fră′nkenstein (-tīn) *n.* **~('s monster)**, thing that becomes formidable to the person who has created it. [character in & title of novel (1818) by M. W. Shelley]

fră′nkfŭrter, *fră′nkfurt, *n.* Highly seasoned smoked sausage. [f. G *Frankfurter wurst* Frankfurt sausage]

fră′nkĭncĕnse *n.* Aromatic gum resin from trees of genus *Boswellia* used for burning as incense; turpentine from conifers. [ME, f. OF *franc encens* (as FRANK[2] in obs. sense 'high-quality', INCENSE[1])]

fră'nklĭn[1] *n.* (Hist.) Land-owner of free but not noble birth in 14th–15th c. [ME *francoleyn* etc., f. AL *francalanus* (*francalis* held without dues f. *francus* free, FRANK[2])]

***Fră'nklĭn**[2] *n.* ~ **stove,** free-standing stove for heating room. [f. B. ~, Amer. inventor etc. d. 1790]

fră'nk-plĕdge *n.* (Hist.) System by which each member of tithing was responsible for good behaviour of every other. [f. med. L *franciplegium* f. AF *frauncplege* (as FRANK[2], PLEDGE[1]), mistransl. of OE *frithborh* peace-pledge (not free-pledge)]

fră'nt|ic *a.* Wildly excited, distraught with rage, pain, grief, joy, haste, etc.; showing frenzy, uncontrolled, violent, (*frantic effort*); (colloq.) extreme, very great; hence ~ICALLY, ~ĭcLY[2], *advs.* [ME *frentik, frantik* f. OF *frenetique* f. L *phreneticus* (see PHRENETIC)]

frăp *v.t.* (**-pp-**). (Naut.) Bind tightly. [f. F *frapper* bind, strike]

frappé (fră'pā) *a.* & *n.* **1.** *a.* (Esp. of wine) iced, cooled. **2.** *n.* Iced drink; soft water-ice. [F, p.p. of *frapper* strike, ice (drinks)]

frăss *n.* Excrement of larvae; refuse left by boring insects. [G (*fressen* devour f. as FRET[2])]

***frăt**[1] *n.* (sl.) (Member of) students' fraternity. [abbr.]

frăt[2] *n.*, & *v.i.* (**-tt-**). (sl.) **1.** *n.* Fraternization by troops; woman with whom soldier fraternizes. **2.** *v.i.* (Of troops) fraternize. [abbr.]

fră'tchȳ *a.* (colloq.) Irritable, quarrelsome. [imit.]

frat|e (frah'tā) *n.* (*pl.* **~*i*** *pr.* -ē). Friar. [It., = brother]

frā'ter *n.* (Hist.) Refectory. [ME, f. OF *fraitur* (*refreitor* f. med. L *refectorium* REFECTORY)]

fratẽr'nal *a.* (As) of brother(s), brotherly; *~ **order,** = FRATERNITY 3; ~ **twins** (developed from separate ova and not necessarily closely similar). [f. med. L *fraternalis* f. L *fraternus* (*frater* brother; see -AL)]

fratẽr'nĭtȳ *n.* **1.** Being fraternal, brotherliness. **2.** Religious brotherhood. **3.** Guild, company with common interests, set of men of same class etc. **4.** *Male students' society in university or college. [ME, f. OF *fraternité* f. L *fraternitas -tatis* (as prec.; see -ITY)]

fră'ternīz|e, -īs|e (-īz), *v.i.* Associate, make friends, behave as intimates, (*with, together*, or abs.); (of troops) enter into friendly relations *with* (enemy troops, or inhabitants of an occupied country); so ~A'TION *n.* [f. F *fraterniser* & med. L *fraternizare* f. L *fraternus* (see FRATERNAL, -IZE)]

fră'trĭcīd|e *n.* Killing of one's brother or sister; one who kills his brother or sister; hence ~AL *a.* [F, or f. LL *fratricidium*, L *fratricida*, (*frater fratris* brother; see -CIDE)]

Frau (frow) *n.* (*pl.* **~'*en***). Title of German wife or widow = Mrs.; German woman. [G]

fraud *n.* Criminal deception, use of false representations to gain unjust advantage; dishonest artifice or trick (**pious ~,** deception intended to benefit those deceived, and esp. to strengthen religious belief); person or thing not fulfilling expectation or description; (arch.) deceitfulness. [ME, f. OF *fraude* f. L *fraus fraudis*]

frau'dūl|ent *a.* Guilty of, of the nature of, characterized or effected by, fraud; hence or cogn. ~ENCE *n.*, **~ent**LY[2] *adv.* [ME f. OF, or f. L *fraudulentus* (as prec.; see -ULENT)]

fraught (frawt) *a.* **1.** ~ **with,** involving, attended with, full of (meaning etc.), threatening or promising, destined to produce, (sorrow, danger, etc.). **2.** (colloq.) Causing or suffering anxiety or distress. **3.** (poet.) Stored or equipped *with*. [ME, p.p. of obs. v. *fraught* load with cargo, f. MDu. *vrachten* (*vracht* FREIGHT)]

Fräulein (froi'līn) *n.* Title of German spinster = Miss (also as *voc.*); German spinster; German governess. [G, dim. of FRAU]

Frau'nhōfer (frow'n-) *n.* ~ **lines,** dark lines in solar and stellar spectra. [f. J. von ~, Bavarian physicist d. 1826]

frăxĭnĕ'lla *n.* Perennial herb (*Dictamnus albus*), species of dittany. [mod. L, dim. of L *fraxinus* ash-tree]

fray[1] *n.* Noisy quarrel, brawl; fight, conflict, (lit. or fig.; *eager* or *ready for the fray*). [ME, f. *fray* to quarrel f. *affray* v. f. as AFFRAY]

fray[2] *v.t.* & *i.* Wear through by rubbing, ravel out edge or end of, (usu. woven material); become ragged at edge (lit., or fig. of nerves, temper, etc.); ~ (**its head**), (of deer) rub velvet off new horns. [f. F *frayer*, **freiier* f. L *fricare* rub]

frā'zil *n.* (Can. & U.S.) Ice crystals in a stream or on its bed. [f. Can. F *frasil* snow floating in the water; cf. F *fraisil* cinders]

fră'zzle *n.* Worn or exhausted state (esp. *worn, beaten*, etc. *to a frazzle*). [perh. f. FRAY[2] + dial. *fazzle* tangle]

freak[1] *n.* **1.** Caprice, vagary; capriciousness. **2.** Product of sportive fancy; ~ (**of nature**), monstrosity, abnormally developed individual, abnormal or irregular thing. **3.** One who freaks out; drug addict; unconventional person, whence ~'Y[2] *a.* **4.** Hence ~'ISH[1] *a.* [16th c., prob. f. dial.]

freak[2] *v.i.* & *t.* (sl.) ~ (**out**), (cause to) undergo narcotic etc. hallucinations or strong emotional experience, adopt unconventional life-style; hence **~-out** *n.*, such experience. [f. prec.]

freaked (-kt) *a.* Oddly flecked or streaked. [f. FREAK[1] + -ED[2]]

frĕ'ckle *n.* & *v.* **1.** *n.* Light brown spot on skin, usu. from exposure to sun. **2.** *v.t.* & *i.* Spot or be spotted with freckles. [ME *fracel* etc. f. dial. *freken* f. ON *freknur* pl.]

free[1] *a.* (**freer** *pr.* frē'er; **freest** *pr.* frē'ĭst) & *adv.* **1.** *a.* Not in bondage to another, having personal rights and social and political liberty; (of State, its citizens or institutions) subject neither to foreign domination nor to despotic government, having national and civil liberty, (*free press, society*; **it's a ~ country,** (colloq.) the action proposed is not illegal). **2.** Loose, unrestricted; at liberty, not confined, released from ties or duties, unimpeded; unfettered in action (*go free*; *set free*); permitted *to* do, independent; unconstrained (*free step, gestures*); (of literary style) not observing strict laws of form; (of translation) not literal; (arch.) allowable (*for* or *to* person *to* do). **3.** Open to all comers; clear of obstructions, clear *of* or *from* something undesirable, clear of engagements etc. (*are you free on Monday?*), not occupied or in use (*the bathroom is free now*). **4.** Not fixed, not in contact; (Chem.) not combined (*free radical*); (Phys.) not bound in an atom or molecule; (of power or energy) disengaged or available. **5.** Spontaneous, unforced; (Phys.) not modified by external force; unearned, gratuitous; willing; lavish, profuse, unstinted, copious, (*free of* or *with his money*; *free flow of water*); frank, unreserved; forward, familiar, impudent, (**make** or **be ~,** take liberties *with*); (of talk, stories, etc.) slightly indecent. **6.** Released or exempt *from* (*free from the ordinary rules, from disease, difficulty*, etc.); not subject to tax, duty, trade-restrictions, or fees; (***for**) ~, provided without payment; **~ of,** having right to enter and use. **7.** *Free* AGENT; **~ association,** (Psych.) association of ideas by person under test without suggestion or control by tester;

~'board, part of ship's side between water-line and deck; **~-born,** inheriting citizen's rights and liberty; **F~ Church,** (1) Church free from State control, (2) nonconformist Church; **F~ Church of Scotland** (seceding from Presbyterian establishment 1843–1929); **~ and easy,** unceremonious; **~ enterprise,** freedom of private business from State control; **~ fall,** movement under force of gravity only, esp. (1) part of parachute descent before parachute opens, (2) movement of spacecraft in space without thrust from engines; **~ fight** (in which all present may join); **~-for-all** *n.* & *a.*, free (fight), unrestricted (discussion), etc.; **~ gift** (not in return for anything, esp. object given away to promote sales); **~ hand,** right of acting at discretion; **~-hand,** (of drawing) done without artificial aid to the hand; **~-ha'nded,** generous; **~'hold,** (*n.*) (estate held by) tenure in fee simple or fee-tail or for life, (office held by) similar tenure, (*a.*) held by freehold; **~'holder,** possessor of freehold estate; ||**~ house,** inn or public house selling more than one brewer's liquor; **~ kick,** (Footb.) kick allowed to be taken without interference by opponents, as minor penalty against them; **~ labour,** (1) labour of freemen not slaves, (2) labour of workmen not in trade unions; **~ lance,** (1) medieval mercenary, (2) person working for no fixed employer (so **~-lance** *v.i.*); *free* LIBRARY; **~ list,** list of persons or things to be admitted free of payment, duty, etc.; **~-li'ver,** one who indulges in pleasures esp. of eating; **~-loa'der,** (sl.) one who eats or drinks at others' expense, sponger; **~ love,** (doctrine permitting) sexual relations irrespective of marriage; **~'man,** (1) person not slave or serf, (2) one who has freedom of city, company, etc.; **~ market** (in which prices are determined by unrestricted competition); **F~'-mason,** member of a fraternity for mutual help called *Free and Accepted Masons* and having elaborate secret rituals; **~'masonry,** (*F~*) system and institutions of Freemasons, (fig.) instinctive sympathy or understanding; **~ on board, rail,** etc., without charge for delivery to ship, railway wagon, etc.; **~ pass,** authority to travel on railway etc. or enter place of entertainment etc. without payment; **~ port,** (1) port open to all traders, (2) port area where goods are exempt from customs duty during loading and unloading; **~-range,** (of hens etc.) given freedom of movement in seeking food; *free* REIN; **~ school** (with no fees charged); **~ speech,** right to express opinions of any kind; **~-spoken,** not concealing one's opinions; **~-standing,** not supported by a structural framework; **~ state,** State not subject to another, *State of U.S. in which slavery did not exist; **~-stone,** (1) fine-grained easily sawn sandstone or limestone, (2) kind of peach with stone loose when fruit is ripe; **~-style,** (of swimming-race) in which any stroke may be used, (of wrestling) all-in; **~ thinker,** rejector of authority in religious belief, rationalist etc. (so **free-thinking** *n.* & *a.*, **free thought**); **~ trade** (left to its natural course without restriction on imports etc.); **~ verse,** = VERS LIBRE; **~ vote,** Parliamentary vote not subject to party discipline; **~'way,** express highway esp. with limited access; **~ wheel,** driving-wheel of bicycle able to revolve with pedals at rest; **~-wheel** *v.i.*, ride bicycle without pedalling, coast, (fig.) move or act without constraint or effort; *free* WILL² 1, 3; **~-will** *attrib. a.*, voluntary; **~ world,** non-Communist countries' collective name for themselves. **8.** Hence **~'LY** *adv.* **9.** *adv.* Freely; without cost or payment; (Naut.) not close-hauled. [OE *frēo*, = OS, OHG *frī*, ON **frīr*, Goth. *freis* f. Gmc **frijaz* f. IE **prijos* dear]

free² *v.t.* Make free, set at liberty, (**~'dman,** emancipated slave); relieve *from*, rid or ease *of*; clear, disengage, disentangle. [OE *frēon*, *freog(e)an*, = ON *fría*, *friá* f. Gmc **frijējan* (as prec.)]

-free *comb. form.* Free of or from (*disease-free*; POST²-*free*). [f. FREE¹]

***free'bĭe** *n.* & *a.* (colloq.) (Thing provided) free of charge. [arbitr. f. FREE¹]

free'boōter *n.* Pirate, piratical adventurer (lit. or fig.); hence [by back form.] **free'boōt** *v.i.* [f. Du. *vrijbuiter* (as FREE¹, BOOTY, -ER¹); cf. FILIBUSTER]

free'dom *n.* **1.** Personal liberty, non-slavery, (*freedom of* CONSCIENCE); civil liberty, independence, (*freedom of the* PRESS¹); liberty of action, right *to* do, (**the four ~s,** freedom of speech and religion, freedom from fear and want; *freedom of the* WILL²); power of self-determination, independence of fate or necessity. **2.** Frankness, outspokenness, undue familiarity; facility or ease in action; boldness of conception; **degree of ~,** (Phys.) independent direction etc. in which motion can occur, (Chem. etc.) independent manner in which a system can vary without fundamental change of constituents. **3.** Exemption *from* defect, disadvantage, burden, duty, etc.; privilege possessed by city or corporation; participation in privileges of membership *of* company etc. or citizenship *of* city (often given as honour to distinguished persons); unrestricted use *of* (*has the freedom of the library*). **4. ~ fighter,** one who takes part in resistance to established political system etc.; ***~ ride,** organized ride in buses etc. as demonstration against racial segregation. [OE *frēodōm* (as FREE¹, -DOM)]

free'mărtĭn *n.* Hermaphrodite or imperfect female calf etc. [17th c., of unkn. orig.]

freer, freest. See FREE¹.

free'sĭa (-z-) *n.* Bulbous Afr. plant of genus *Freesia*. [mod. L, f. F. H. T. *Freese*, Ger. physician d. 1876 + -IA¹]

freeze *v.* (**froze; fro'zen;** *pr.* frō-), & *n.* **1.** *v.i.* (impers.) **It ~s, it is freezing,** etc., there is etc. frost. **2.** Be converted into or covered (*over, up*) with ice; become rigid as result of cold (**~ to death,** die by frost); become fastened *to* or *together* by frost (**~ on to,** (sl.) take or keep tight hold of); be or feel very cold (lit. or fig.); be chilled by fear; make oneself suddenly motionless. **3.** *v.t.* Cause to congeal, form ice in or on (fluid or thing containing it); preserve (food) by refrigeration below freezing-point; **~-dry,** freeze and dry by evaporation of ice in high vacuum; **~ up,** obstruct by formation of ice; so **~-up** *n.* **4.** Make (credits, assets, etc.) temporarily or permanently unrealizable; fix or stabilize (prices, wages, etc.); determine (details), arrest (action) at a certain stage of development; arrest (movement in film) by repeating a frame. **5.** Render (person) powerless, chill (feelings), paralyse (powers); stiffen, harden, injure, kill, by chilling (*frozen to death*); **~** person's **blood,** terrify him; ***~ out,** (sl.) exclude from business, society, etc., by competition or boycotting etc. **6. Freezing-mixture,** salt and snow or other mixture used to freeze liquids; **freezing-point,** temperature at which liquid, esp. water, freezes; **freezing works,** (Austral. & N.Z.) place where animals are slaughtered and carcasses frozen for export; **frozen limit,** (colloq.) the extreme of what is objectionable or unendurable; **frozen* MITT.

7. *n.* State, coming, or period, of frost; fixing or stabilization of prices, wages, etc.; film-shot in which movement is arrested by repetition of a frame. [OE *frēosan*, = OHG *friosan*, ON *frjósa*, Goth. **friusan* f. Gmc **freusan* (**freus-* etc. f. IE **preus-* etc.)]

free'zer *n.* In vbl senses; refrigerated room or compartment esp. for keeping food frozen, deep-freeze. [f. prec. + -ER¹]

freight (frāt) *n.*, & *v.t.* **1.** *n.* Hire of ship or aircraft for transporting goods; transport of goods in containers or by water (or *by land), charge for this; cargo, shipload, (*freight* TON¹); load, burden; **~'liner,** train carrying goods in containers; ***~ train,** goods train. **2.** *v.t.* Load (ship) with cargo; hire or let out (ship) for carriage of goods and passengers. [f. MDu., MLG *vrecht* var. of *vracht*; cf. FRAUGHT]

frei'ghtage (-ā't-) *n.* Hire of ship for, or cost of, conveyance of goods; freighting or hiring of ship; cargo. [f. prec. + -AGE]

frei'ghter (-ā't-) *n.* **1.** One who (charters and) loads ship; one who consigns goods for carriage inland; one whose business is to receive and forward freight. **2.** Cargo ship, freight-carrying aircraft; *freight-wagon. [f. FREIGHT + -ER¹]

Frĕnch *a.* & *n.* **1.** *a.* Of France or its language or people; having the qualities attributed to French people, esp. culturedness or slight impropriety. **2.** ||**~ bean,** kidney or haricot bean (*Phaseolus vulgaris*) used as vegetable both in unripe sliced pods and as ripe seeds; **~ bread,** bread in long crisp loaf; **~ Canadian** *a.* & *n.*, (native or inhabitant) of French-speaking area of Canada; **~ chalk,** kind of steatite used for marking cloth and removing grease and as dry lubricant; **~ cricket,** informal type of cricket using batsman's legs as stumps; **~ cuff** (of double thickness); **~ curve,** template used for drawing curved lines; **~ drain** (of rubble, letting water soak away); **~ dressing,** salad dressing of vinegar and oil, usu. seasoned; ***~ fried potatoes,** ***~ fries,** potato chips; **~ grey,** grey with lavender tint; *French* HORN¹; **~ kiss,** = DEEP¹ *kiss*; **~ knickers** (wide-legged); **take ~ leave,** depart or act without having permission or giving notice; **~ letter,** (colloq.) condom; **~'man,** man of French birth or nationality, French ship, ||red-legged partridge; *French* MOROCCO; ||*French* MUSTARD; **~ polish,** shellac polish for wood (**~-polish** *v.t.*, polish with this); **~ roof,** mansard; **~ seam** (with raw edges enclosed); **~ toast,** bread (1) buttered on one side and toasted on the other, (2) dipped in egg and milk and fried; **~ vermouth** (dry); **~ window,** glazed door in outside wall, serving as window and door; **~'woman,** woman of French birth or nationality. **3.** Hence ~'NESS *n.*, ~'Y²,³ *a.* & *n.* **4.** *n.* The French language; (euphem.) bad language (*excuse my French*); dry vermouth (*gin and French*); (sl.) fellatio; **the ~,** (*pl.*) the French people. [OE *frencisc* f. Gmc **frankiskaz* (**Frankon* FRANK¹; see -ISH¹)]

Frĕ'nchĭ|fȳ, f-, *v.t.* (usu. in *p.p.*) Make French in form, character, or manners; hence ~FICA'TION *n.* [f. prec. + -I- + -FY]

frĕnĕ'tĭc *a.* Frantic; fanatic. [ME, f. OF *frenetique* f. L *phreneticus* f. Gk *phrenitikos* (*phrenitis* delirium f. *phrēn phrenos* mind); see -ITIS, -IC]

frē'nūlum, frē'num. See FRAENULUM, FRAENUM.

frĕ'nz|ȳ *n.*, & *v.t.* **1.** *n.* Mental derangement, temporary insanity, paroxysm of mania; delirious fury or agitation, wild folly. **2.** *v.t.* (usu. in *p.p.*) Drive to frenzy, infuriate, (**~ied rage,** that of a frenzied person). [ME, f. OF *frenesie* f. med. L *phrenesia* f. L *phrenesis* f. Gk *phrēn* mind]

frē'quencȳ *n.* **1.** Frequent occurrence; commonness of occurrence (*word frequency*); being repeated at short intervals. **2.** (Of pulse) number of beats per minute; (Phys.) rate of recurrence (of vibration etc.), number of repetitions in given time esp. per second, number of cycles of carrier wave per second, band or group of frequency values; (Statistics) ratio of number of actual to possible occurrences of an event; **~ modulation** (in which frequency of carrier wave is varied); **~ response,** dependence on signal-frequency of output-input ratio of amplifier etc. [f. L *frequentia* (as foll.; see -ENCY)]

frē'quent¹ *a.* **1.** Found near together, numerous, abundant; often occurring, common, (*it is a frequent practice to*); happening in close succession, (of pulse) rapid; hence ~LY² *adv.* **2.** Habitual, constant, (*a frequent caller*). [f. F *fréquent* or f. L *frequens -entis* crowded; see -ENT]

frėquĕ'nt² *v.t.* Go often or habitually to (place, meetings, company, house); hence **frēquĕntA'TION,** ~ER¹, *ns.* [f. F *fréquenter* or f. L *frequentare* (as prec.)]

frėquĕ'ntatĭve *a.* & *n.* (Gram.) (Verb or verbal form or conjugation) expressing frequent repetition or intensity of action (*chatter, dribble, twinkle*). [f. F *fréquentatif -ive* or f. L *frequentativus* (as prec.; see -ATIVE)]

frĕ'scō *n.* (*pl.* **~s** *or* **~es**), & *v.t.* **1.** *n.* Method of painting (esp. *in fresco*), or picture done, in water-colour laid on wall or ceiling before plaster is dry; **~ secco,** = SECCO. **2.** *v.t.* Paint (wall etc., picture or subject) in fresco. [It., = cool, fresh]

frĕsh *a.*, *adv.*, & *n.* **1.** *a.* New, novel, not previously known, used, met with, or introduced, (*break fresh* GROUND¹ 7); additional, other, different, further, (*begin a fresh chapter*). **2.** Recent, lately made or arrived, just come *from*; raw, inexperienced, (**~'man,** first-year student at university or *high school). **3.** Not preserved by salting, pickling, smoking, tinning, freezing, etc., (*fresh herrings, butter, meat, fruit*; see also 4 and 6). **4.** Not salt or bitter (*fresh butter, water*); **~'water** *a.*, of fresh water, not of the sea, (*freshwater fish, fishing, sailor*; ***~water college,** rustic or provincial college). **5.** (Of air, wind, water) pure, untainted, invigorating, refreshing, cool. **6.** Not stale, musty, or vapid (*fresh eggs, fish, meat, fruit*; see also 3); newly made (*fresh tea*); not faded (*fresh flowers, memories*). **7.** Unsullied, bright and pure in colour (*a fresh complexion*), looking healthy or young. **8.** Not weary, brisk, vigorous, fit, (*never felt fresher*; **as ~ as a daisy, as paint,** quite brisk); **a ~ wind** (of fair strength). **9.** Presumptuous, forward, cheeky, amorously impudent, [perh. infl. by G *frech* saucy]. **10.** Hence ~'EN⁶ *v.t.* & *i.*, ~'LY² *adv.*, ~'NESS *n.* **11.** *adv.* Newly, esp. in comb. (*fresh-caught, -coined*); **~-run,** (of salmon) lately come up from the sea. **12.** *n.* Fresh part of the day, year, etc. (*in the fresh of the morning*); rush of water in river, flood. [ME, f. OF *freis fresche* f. Rom. **friscus* f. Gmc **friskaz*]

||**frĕ'sher** *n.* (sl.) = FRESH*man*. [f. prec. + -ER¹]

frĕ'shėt *n.* Rush of fresh water flowing into sea; flood of river from heavy rain or melted snow. [prob. f. OF *freschete* f. *frais* FRESH]

frĕt¹ *n.*, & *v.t.* (**-tt-**). **1.** *n.* (**Greek**) **~,** ornamental pattern made of continuous combinations of straight lines joined usu. at right angles. **2.** (Her.) Device of narrow bands and diamond interlaced. **3.** *v.t.* Variegate, chequer; adorn (esp. ceiling) with carved or embossed work; **~'saw,** very narrow saw stretched on frame for cutting thin wood in ornamental patterns; **~'work,** (1) carved work in decorative patterns esp. of straight lines, (2) wood cut with fretsaw. [ME, f. OF *frete* trellis-work and *freter* v.]

frĕt[2] *v.* (**-tt-**), & *n.* **1.** *v.t.* Gnaw, wear or consume or torment by gnawing, (lit. of moth etc., horse champing bit, action of frost, rust, corrosives, friction, etc., or fig. of emotions); make (passage etc.) by wearing away; chafe, irritate, annoy; worry, distress, (person, one*self*); ruffle (water). **2.** *v.i.* Distress oneself with regret or discontent (*at*; ~ **and fume,** show angry impatience); (of stream etc.) flow or rise in little waves, chafe. **3.** Hence ~′FUL *a.* **4.** *n.* Irritation, vexation, querulousness, (*in a fret*; *fret and fume*; *on the fret*). [OE *fretan*, = OHG *frezzan*, Goth. *fraïtan* f. Gmc **fra-* FOR- (5) + **etan* EAT]

frĕt[3] *n.* Bar or ridge on finger-board of some stringed instruments fixing positions of fingers to produce required notes. [15th c.; orig. unkn.]

Freu′dĭan (froi′d-) *a.* & *n.* (Disciple) of Freud or his methods of psycho-analysis; ~ **slip,** unintentional error that seems to reveal subconscious feelings. [f. S. *Freud*, Austrian psychologist d. 1939 + -IAN]

Fri. *abbr.* Friday.

frī′able *a.* Easily crumbled; hence **frīABI′LITY,** ~NESS (-beln-), *ns.* [F, or f. L *friabilis* (*friare* crumble; see -ABLE)]

frī′ar *n.* Member of one of certain religious orders of men, esp. the four mendicant orders of Franciscans (*Grey Friars, Friars Minor*), Augustinians (*Austin Friars*), Dominicans (*Black Friars, Friars Major*), and Carmelites (*White Friars*); ~(**-bird**), (Austral.) honey-eater of genus *Philemon* etc.; **~'s** or **~s' balsam,** tincture of benzoin etc. used esp. as inhalant; hence ~LY[1] *a.* [ME & OF *frere* f. L *frater fratris* brother]

frī′arў *n.* Convent of friars. [f. prec. + -Y[1]]

frĭ′bble *v.i.*, & *n.* **1.** *v.i.* Trifle, be frivolous. **2.** *n.* Trifler. [earlier senses 'stammer, totter'; imit.]

frĭ′candeau (-dō) *n.* (*pl.* **~x** *pr.* -z), & *v.t.* **1.** *n.* (Slice of) fried or stewed meat, esp. veal, served with sauce. **2.** *v.t.* Make into fricandeaux. [F]

frĭ′cassee (*or* -ē′) *n.*, & *v.t.* **1.** *n.* Meat cut up, fried or stewed, and served with sauce, esp. ragout of birds or small animals cut up. **2.** *v.t.* Make fricassee of. [F, fem. p.p. (as n.) of *fricasser* cut up and stew in sauce]

frĭ′catĭve *a.* & *n.* (Phonet.) (Consonant) made by friction of breath in narrow opening, as *f, th,* Scots *ch.* [f. mod. L *fricativus* f. L *fricare* rub; see -ATIVE]

frĭ′ction *n.* Rubbing of two bodies; (Phys. & Mech.) resistance body encounters in moving over another (**angle of** ~, maximum angle at which one will remain on another without sliding); rubbing the body for therapeutic purposes; massage of scalp; (fig.) clash of wills, temperaments, opinions, etc., (usu. between two persons); **~-ball** (used in bearings to lessen friction); **~-clutch, -cone, -coupling, -disc, -gear**(**ing**), contrivances for transmitting motion by frictional contact; hence ~AL, ~LESS, *adjs.* [F, f. L *frictio -onis* (*fricare frict-* rub; see -ION)]

Frī′day (*or* -dĭ) *n.* & *adv.* **1.** *n.* Day of week, following Thursday; **Good** ~, Friday before Easter day, commemorating Crucifixion; **girl** ~, **man** ~ [f. Man F~ in Defoe's *Robinson Crusoe*], assistant doing general duties in office etc. **2.** *adv.* (colloq.) On Friday (*see you Friday*); **~s,** on Fridays, each Friday. [OE *frīgedæg*, = OHG *frīatag*, day of *Frigg* (wife of Odin) cogn. w. FREE[1]; WG transl. of LL *Veneris dies* day of planet Venus]

||**frĭdge** *n.* (colloq.) Refrigerator. [abbr.]

friend (frĕnd) *n.*, & *v.t.* **1.** *n.* One joined to another in intimacy and mutual benevolence independently of sexual or family love (**be** or **keep, make, ~s,** be, become, friendly (*with*); BOY-*friend*, GIRL-*friend*; hence ~′ED[2] *a.*); person who acts for one, e.g. as second in duel; acquaintance, stranger that one comes across or has occasion to mention again, (*my friend in the brown hat now left me*; used in *voc.* as polite form or in irony, and by Quakers as ordinary address; preceding a name, *friend Jones, friend Dick*; ||**my honourable** ~, **my noble** ~, used of another member of same party in House of Commons, House of Lords; **my learned** ~, of another lawyer in court); (in *pl.*) one's near relatives, those responsible for one; (*F~*) member of the Society of Friends, Quaker. **2.** Sympathizer, helper, patron, (*no friend of* or *to order, virtue*, etc.; **a** ~ **at court,** one whose influence may be made use of); helpful thing (*my shyness was here my best friend*); one who is not an enemy, one who is on the same side; (usu. in *pl.*) regular contributor of help, money, etc., to support an institution. **3.** Hence ~′LESS *a.* **4.** *v.t.* (arch. or poet.) Befriend, help. [OE *frēond*, = OS *friund*, OHG *friunt*, ON *frændi*, Goth. *frijonds*, part. of Gmc **frijōjan* love (**frijaz* beloved; cf. FREE[1])]

frie′ndlў (frĕ′-) *a.*, *n.*, & *adv.* **1.** *a.* Acting or disposed to act as friend; characteristic of friends, expressing, showing, or prompted by, kindness; not hostile, on amicable terms (*with*), (*a friendly nation*; ~ **action,** (Law) action brought merely to get a point decided; ~ **match,** match played for pleasure merely, not in competition for cup etc.); favourably disposed, ready to approve or help, (of thing) serviceable, convenient, opportune; ||**F~ Society,** = BENEFIT[1] society; hence **frie′ndlĭLY**[2] (rare) *adv.*, **frie′ndlĭNESS** *n.*, (frĕ′-). **2.** *n.* Friendly match etc. **3.** *adv.* In friendly manner. [f. prec. + -LY[1,2]]

frie′ndshĭp (frĕ′-) *n.* Being friends, relation between friends; friendly disposition felt or shown. [f. OE *frēondscipe* (as FRIEND, -SHIP)]

frī′er. See FRYER.

Frie′sĭan (-z-; *or* frē′zhan) *a.* & *n.* (Of, one of) a breed of usu. black and white large Friesland dairy cattle. [var. of FRISIAN]

frieze[1] *n.* Coarse woollen cloth with nap usu. on one side only. [ME, f. F *frise* f. med. L *(*lana*) *frisia* Frisian (wool)]

frieze[2] *n.* Part of entablature coming between architrave and cornice; horizontal broad band of sculpture filling this; band of decoration elsewhere, esp. along wall near ceiling. [f. F *frise* f. med. L *frisium, frigium* f. L *Phrygium* (*opus* work) of Phrygia]

||**frĭg**[1] (-j) *n.* (colloq.) Refrigerator. [abbr.]

frĭg[2] *v.* (**-gg-**) & *n.* (vulg.) **1.** *v.i.* & *t.* Copulate (with); masturbate; = DAMN 2; mess, fool, *about* or *around*; make *off*. **2.** *n.* Act of frigging. [perh. imit.; orig. senses 'move about, rub']

frĭ′gate *n.* Corvette, sloop, small destroyer; (Hist.) warship next in size and equipment to ships of the line; ~(**-bird**), large swift tropical marine bird of prey. [f. F *frégate* f. It. *fregata*, of unkn. orig.]

frīght (frīt) *n.*, & *v.t.* **1.** *n.* Sudden fear, violent terror, (**take** ~, become frightened); instance of this (*gave me a fright*); grotesque or ridiculous-looking person or thing. **2.** *v.t.* (poet.) Frighten. [OE *fryhto*, metathetic form of *fyrhto* = Goth. *faurhtei* (OS, OHG *foraht*) f. Gmc **furhtīn* (**furhtaz* afraid)]

frī′ghten (-ī′t-) *v.t.* Throw into a fright, terrify, (*out of* or *into doing*); drive *away, out of* (place etc.), or *into* (submission etc.), by fright; *frightened at* or *of* (*at* usu. w. ref. to a particular occasion). [f. prec. + -EN[6]]

frī′ghtful (-ī′t-) *a.* **1.** Dreadful, shocking, revolting; ugly, hideous; hence ~NESS *n.* (esp. to render G *schrecklichkeit* terrorizing of civilian population as military resource). **2.** (sl.) Very great, extreme. **3.** Hence ~LY² *adv.* [ME, f. FRIGHT + -FUL]

fri'gid *a.* Cold (esp. of climate or air; *frigid* ZONE); without ardour, apathetic, formal, forced; (of woman) sexually unresponsive; chilling, depressing; dull, flat, insipid; hence or cogn. **frigi'd**ITY, ~NESS, *ns.*, ~LY² *adv.* [f. L *frigidus* (*frigēre* be cold f. *frigus* n. cold)]

frijoles (frēhō'lās) *n. pl.* Beans. [Sp., pl. of *frijol* bean ult. f. L *phaseolus*]

frill *n.*, & *v.t.* **1.** *n.* Ornamental edging of woven material, one side of strip being gathered and the other left loose with fluted appearance; similar paper ornament on ham-knuckle etc.; natural fringe of feathers, hair, etc., on bird, animal, or plant; ~**(ed) lizard,** large N. Austral. lizard with erectile membrane round neck. **2.** (in *pl.*) Airs, affectation, (*put on frills*); useless embellishments, showy accomplishments. **3.** Hence ~ED² (-ld) *a.*, ~'ERY (5), ~'ING¹ (3 ,6), *ns.* **4.** *v.t.* Decorate with a frill. [16th c.; orig. unkn.]

fri'll|ÿ *a.* & *n.* **1.** *a.* Having frill(s); resembling a frill; hence ~**i**NESS *n.* **2.** *n.* (in *pl.*, colloq.) Frilled underwear. [f. prec. + -Y²]

fringe (-nj) *n.*, & *v.t.* **1.** *n.* Ornamental bordering of threads left loose or formed into tassels or twists; such bordering made separately; border, edging; front hair allowed to hang over forehead; natural border of hair etc. in animal or plant. **2.** Outer edge or margin; outer limit of area, population, etc. (~ **benefits,** perquisites or benefits supplementing money wage or salary; **lunatic** ~, fanatical or eccentric or visionary minority of polit. party etc.); band of contrasting brightness or darkness produced by diffraction or interference of light; strip of false colour in optical image. **3.** Hence ~'LESS (-njl-), **fri'ngy**² (-njĭ), *adjs.* **4.** *v.t.* Adorn or encircle with fringe, serve as fringe to, whence **fri'ng**ING¹ (3) (-nj-) *n.*; **fringing reef,** coral reef that fringes shore. [ME & OF *frenge* f. Rom. **frimbia* f. LL *fimbria* fibres, fringe]

fri'ppery *n.* & *a.* **1.** *n.* Finery, needless or tawdry adornment esp. in dress; empty display esp. in literary style; knick-knacks, trifles. **2.** *a.* Frivolous; contemptible. [f. F *friperie* f. OF *freperie* (*frepe* rag; see -ERY)]

fri'ppet *n.* (sl.) Frivolous or showy young woman. [20th c.; orig. unkn.]

fri'sbee (-zbĭ) *n.* Concave plastic disc thrown in air as game. [***P**; said to be f. *Frisbie* bakery (Bridgeport, Conn.), whose pie-tins could be used similarly]

***Fri'scō** *n.* (sl.) San Francisco. [abbr.]

Fri'sian (-z-) *a.* & *n.* (Native or language) of Friesland. [f. L *Frisii* pl. f. OFris. *Frisa, Frēsa* + -AN]

frisk *v.* & *n.* **1.** *v.i.* Leap or skip playfully. **2.** *v.t.* Feel over or search (person) for weapon etc. (usu. rapidly). **3.** *n.* Playful leap or skip, whence ~'Y² *a.*; frisking of person. [f. obs. *frisk* a. f. OF *frisque* lively, of unkn. orig.]

fri'sket *n.* (Print.) Thin iron frame keeping sheet in position while printing on hand-press. [f. F *frisquette* f. Prov. *frisqueto* f. Sp. *frasqueta*]

frisson (frē'sawn) *n.* Emotional thrill. [F, = shiver]

frit *n.*, & *v.t.* (-tt-). **1.** *n.* Calcined mixture of sand and fluxes as material for glass-making; vitreous composition from which soft porcelain, enamel, etc., are made. **2.** *v.t.* Make into frit, partially fuse, calcine. [f. It. *fritta* fem. p.p. of *friggere* FRY²]

fri't-fly *n.* Small fly destructive to wheat. [19th c.; orig. unkn.]

frith. See FIRTH.

friti'llary (*or* fri't-) *n.* Plant of genus *Fritillaria*, esp. wild snake's-head; spotted butterfly, esp. of genus *Argynnis.* [f. mod. L *fritillaria* f. L *fritillus* dice-box; see -ARY¹]

fri'tter¹ *n.* Piece of fried batter often containing (a slice of) fruit, meat, etc., (*apple, oyster,* etc., *fritter*). [ME, f. OF *friture* f. Rom. **frictura* f. L *frigere frict-* FRY²; see -URE, -ER² (3)]

fri'tter² *v.t.* Throw (time, money, energy, etc.) *away* triflingly and wastefully on divided aims; (arch.) subdivide. [f. obs. n. *fritter(s)* = obs. *fitters* n. pl., perh. rel. to MHG *vetze* rag]

fritto misto (frĭtō mĭ'stō) *n.* Mixed grill. [It., = mixed fry]

***fritz** (-ts) *n.* (sl.) **On the** ~, out of order, unsatisfactory. [20th c.; orig. unkn.]

fri'vol *v.* (||-ll-). **1.** *v.i.* Be a trifler, trifle. **2.** *v.t.* Throw (money, time) *away* foolishly. [back form. f. foll.]

fri'volous *a.* Paltry, trumpery, trifling, futile; given to trifling, not serious, silly; hence or cogn. **frivŏ'l**ITY, ~NESS, *ns.*, ~LY² *adv.* [f. L *frivolus* silly, trifling + -OUS]

frizz *v.t.*, & *n.* **1.** *v.t.* Curl, crisp, form into mass of small curls, (hair); frizz hair of (person); dress (wash-leather etc.) with pumice or scraping-knife. **2.** *n.* Frizzed state, frizzed hair, row of curls; hence ~'Y² *a.* [f. F *friser*, perh. f. st. of *frire* FRY²]

fri'zzle¹ *v.* & *n.* **1.** *v.t.* & *i.* Curl (*up*, of hair etc.) in small crisp curls. **2.** *n.* Frizzled hair; hence **fri'zzl**Y² *a.* [16th c.; orig. unkn.; earlier than FRIZZ]

fri'zzle² *v.i.* & *t.* Fry, toast, or grill, with sputtering noise. [f. *frizz* v. in same sense (FRY², w. imit. ending) + -LE 3]

Frl. *abbr. Fräulein.*

frō *adv.* See TO². [ME, f. ON *frá* FROM]

frŏck *n.*, & *v.t.* **1.** *n.* Woman's or girl's dress; monk's or priest's long gown with loose sleeves, (fig.) priestly character; sailor's woollen jersey; = SMOCK-*frock*; ~**(-coat)**, man's long-skirted coat not cut away in front; military coat of like shape. **2.** *v.t.* Invest with priestly office (cf. UNFROCK). [ME, f. OF *froc* f. Frank. **hrok*]

***frōe, *frow,** (frō) *n.* Cleaving tool with handle at right angles to blade. [abbr. of *frower* f. FROWARD 'turned away']

Frō'ebel (-ō'b-) *n.* ~ **system** etc., education of children by use of kindergarten; hence ~IAN (-bē'-) *a.*, ~ISM (3) *n.* [f. F. W. A. *Fröbel*, Ger. teacher d. 1852]

frŏg¹ *n.* Tailless smooth-skinned leaping amphibian of order Anura, developing from tadpole; ~**(-eater)**, (derog.) Frenchman; ~**-fish,** angler-fish; ~ **in the** or one's **throat,** (colloq.) hoarseness; ~**'man,** person equipped with rubber suit and flippers etc. and oxygen supply for underwater operations orig. against enemy shipping; ~**('s)-march,** (*n.*) carrying of prisoner face downwards by four men each holding a limb, (*v.t.*) carry thus or hustle forward after seizing from behind and pinning arms; ~**-spawn,** spawn of frog, (fig.) alga or pudding resembling it. [OE *frogga*, pet name for *forsc, frosc, frox* = OHG *frosc*, ON *froskr* f. Gmc **froskaz*]

frŏg² *n.* Elastic horny substance in middle of sole of horse's foot. [perh. f. prec.]

frŏg³ *n.* Attachment to waist-belt to support sword, bayonet, etc.; ornamental coat-fastening of spindle-shaped button and loop, whence ~GED² (-gd) *a.*, ~'GING¹ (6) (-g-) *n.* [18th c.; orig. unkn.]

frŏg⁴ *n.* Grooved piece of iron at place in railway where tracks cross. [19th c.; orig. unkn.]

frŏ'ggy (-gĭ) *a.* & *n.* **1.** *a.* Of or like frog(s); cold as a frog; abounding in frogs; (derog.) French.

2. *n.* (*F*~). (derog.) Frenchman. [f. FROG¹ + -Y²]

frŏ'lĭc *a.*, *v.i.* (**-ck-**), & *n.* **1.** *a.* (arch.) Joyous, mirthful, sportive, full of pranks. **2.** *v.i.* Play pranks, gambol. **3.** *n.* Outburst of gaiety, prank, merriment, merry-making, merry party; hence ~SOME¹ *a.* [f. Du. *vrolijk* adj. (*vro* glad, *-lijk* -LY¹)]

from (*or, when stressed*, frŏm) *prep.* expr. separation or origin, followed by: **1.** Person, place, etc., that is the starting-point of motion (*comes from the clouds*; *repeated from mouth to mouth*). **2.** Starting-point of extent in space or time (*from title-page to colophon*; *from 2 July*; ~ **now on,** henceforward; ~ **day to day,** daily; ~ **time to time,** occasionally; ~ **year to year,** each year, as years pass; ~ **a child,** since childhood). **3.** Lower limit (*saw from 10 to 20 boats*). **4.** Object etc. whose distance or remoteness is reckoned or stated (*ten miles from Rome*; *am far from saying*; ~ **home,** out, away; *absent*, *away*, *from home*; *apart from its moral aspect*). **5.** Thing or person got rid of, escaped, avoided, of which one is deprived etc., person or thing deprived, (*took his sword from him*; *released him from prison*; *cannot refrain from laughing*; *appeal from lower court*; *dissuade from folly*). **6.** State changed for another (*from being attacked he became the aggressor*; *raise penalty from banishment to death*). **7.** Thing distinguished (*doesn't know black from white*). **8.** Source (*dig gravel from pit*; *a man from Italy*; *draw conclusion from premisses*; *quotations from the Fathers*). **9.** Place of one who observes etc. (*saw it from the roof*; ~ **his point of view,** as he sees things). **10.** Giver, sender, etc., (*gifts from Providence*; *clothes from Selfridges*; *have had no news from him*). **11.** Model (*painted from* NATURE). **12.** Reason, cause, motive, (*died from fatigue*; *suffering from shingles*; *from his looks you might suppose*). **13.** Advs. or adv. phrs. of place or time (*from long ago, of old, above, abroad, within*, etc.), or prepositions (*from behind her spectacles*; *from among the nettles*; *took a live coal from off the altar*). [OE *fram*, *from*, = OS, OHG, Goth. *fram*, ON *frá* f. Gmc **fra-* forward]

frŏnd *n.* (Bot.) leaflike organ formed by union of stem and foliage in certain flowerless plants, esp. ferns, and differing from leaf in usu. bearing fructification; (Zool.) leaflike expansion; hence ~'AGE (1) *n.*, ~'OSE¹ *a.* [f. L *frons frondis* leaf]

frŏndeur' (-ẽr') *n.* Political rebel. [F, = slinger, applied to party (the Fronde) rebelling during minority of Louis XIV of France]

front (-ŭnt) *n.*, *a.*, & *v.* **1.** *n.* Side or part normally nearer or towards spectator or direction of motion (*front of car, chair, door, house, mouth*). **2.** (Archit.) Any face of building, esp. that of main entrance. **3.** (Mil.) foremost line or part of army etc., line of battle, part of ground towards real or imaginary enemy, scene of actual fighting (**go to the** ~, join troops on campaign), direction in which formed line faces (*change front*); (fig.) sector of activity regarded as resembling military front. **4.** Outward appearance; bluff; pretext; person etc. serving to cover subversive or illegal activities. **5.** (Meteorol.) Forward edge of advancing mass of cold or warm air. **6.** *The* promenade of a seaside resort; *the* auditorium of a theatre. **7.** Breast of man's shirt; false shirt-front. **8.** (poet. or rhet.) Forehead. **9.** Face; bearing, demeanour, (*show a bold front*). **10.** Forward position; **come to the** ~, become conspicuous; **in** ~, advanced or facing spectator; **in** ~ **of,** (1) before, in advance of, (2) confronting, in the presence of. **11.** Hence ~'WARD *a.* & *adv.*, ~'WARDS *adv.* **12.** *a.* Of the front; situated in front; (Phonet.) formed at front of mouth; ||~ **bench,** foremost seats of Government and Opposition parties in Parliament (so ~**-be'ncher,** occupant of such seat); ~ **door,** chief entrance of house or (fig.) of country, situation, etc.; ~ **line,** = sense 3; ~ **man,** person acting as front (sense 4); ~ **matter,** (Print.) title-page, preface, etc., preceding the text; ~ **office,** main office, esp. police headquarters; ~ **page,** first page of newspaper, esp. as containing important or remarkable news; *front* PASSAGE¹; ~ **runner,** leading contestant. **13.** *v.i.* Have one's or its front directed *to*, *towards*, (*up*)*on*; (sl.) act as front (sense 4) *for*. **14.** *v.t.* Stand opposite to, front towards; have front on side of (street etc.); lead (band); (arch.) confront, meet, oppose; furnish with front (*fronted with stone*). [ME, f. OF *front* n., *fronter* v. f. L *frons frontis*]

fro'ntag|e (-ŭn-) *n.* Land abutting on street or water, land between front of building and road, whence ~ER¹ (4) *n.*; extent of front; front of building; facing a certain way, exposure, outlook; *~**e road,** service road. [f. prec. + -AGE]

fro'ntal¹ (-ŭ'n-) *n.* Covering for front of altar; façade. [ME, f. OF *frontel* f. L *frontale* (as FRONT; see -AL)]

fro'ntal² (-ŭ'n-) *a.* Of forehead (*frontal bone, artery*); of or on front (~ **attack,** delivered direct, not on flank or rear); of person facing spectator (*frontal picture*); hence ~LY² *adv.* [f. mod. L *frontalis* (as FRONT; see -AL)]

fro'ntier (-ŭ'n-) *n.* Part of a country that borders on another; *borders of civilization; limits of attainment in science etc.; ~**sman** (-z-), one living on or beyond the borders of civilization. [ME, f. AF *frounter*, OF *frontiere*, f. Rom. deriv. of L *frons frontis* FRONT]

fro'ntispiece (-u'n-) *n.* **1.** Illustration facing title-page of book or one of its divisions. **2.** (Archit.) Principal face of building, decorated entrance, pediment over door etc. [f. F *frontispice* or f. LL *frontispicium* façade f. L *frons frontis* FRONT + *-spicium* f. *specere* look; assim. to PIECE¹]

fro'ntlėt (-ŭ'n-) *n.* Band worn on forehead; = PHYLACTERY; animal's forehead; cloth hanging over upper part of altar frontal. [f. OF *frontelet* (as FRONTAL¹; see -LET)]

frontōgĕ'nėsĭs (frŭ-) *n.* (Meteorol.) Formation or development of fronts; hence **frontōgėnĕ'tic** (frŭ-) *a.* [f. G *frontogenese* (as FRONT, -O-, GENESIS)]

fro'nton (frŭ'-) *n.* Pediment. [F, f. It. *frontone*, augment. of *fronte* forehead (see FRONT, -OON)]

frōre *a.* (poet.) Frozen, frosty. [arch. p.p. of FREEZE]

frŏst (*or* -aw-) *n.*, & *v.t.* **1.** *n.* Freezing, prevalence of temperature below freezing-point of water (||**ten degrees of** ~, 22° Fahrenheit; **hard, sharp,** ~ (severe); **white, black,** ~, with, without, hoar-frost; **Jack F**~, frost personified); frozen state or consistency (*there is still frost in the ground*); frozen dew or vapour (*windows covered with frost*); hence ~'LESS *a.* **2.** Influence that chills, makes grey, etc.; (sl.) failure. **3.** ~**-bite,** inflammation or gangrene of and below skin from severe cold (~**-bitten,** affected with this); ~**-fish,** (N.Z.) scabbard-fish; ~**-flower,** flower-like ice crystal; ~**-work,** tracery made by frost on glass etc. **4.** *v.t.* Injure (plant etc.) with frost; cover (as) with rime, powder (cake etc.) with frostlike coating of sugar etc., whence ~'ING (3) *n.*; give roughened or finely granulated surface to (glass, metal). [OE, = OS, OHG, ON *frost* f. Gmc **frustaz*, **frustam* (**fruesan* FREEZE)]

frŏ'st|ȳ (*or* -aw'-) *a.* Cold with frost; cold, chilling, frigid, lacking in warmth of feeling; (seeming to be) covered with hoar-frost; hence ~ĭLY² *adv.*, ~ĭNESS *n.* [f. prec. + -Y²]

frŏth (*or* -aw-) *n.* & *v.* **1.** *n.* Collection of small bubbles in liquid, caused by shaking, fermenting, etc., foam; impure matter on liquid, scum; worthless matter, idle talk, light substance, etc.; ||**~-blower,** (joc.) beer-drinker (esp. as designation of member of a charitable organization); hence ~'Y² *a.* **2.** *v.i.* Emit or gather froth (*frothing at the mouth*). **3.** *v.t.* Cause (beer etc.) to foam. [ME, f. ON *frotha, frauth* f. Gmc **freuth-* etc.]

frŏtta'ge (-ah'zh) *n.* **1.** (Psych.) Abnormal desire for contact between clothed bodies of oneself and another. **2.** (Art). Technique or process of taking rubbing from uneven surface to form basis of work of art. [F, = rubbing (*frotter* rub f. OF *froter*; see -AGE)]

frou'-frou (froo'froo) *n.* Rustling, esp. of dresses. [F, imit.]

frow¹ *n.* Dutchwoman; housewife. [ME, f. Du. *vrouw* woman]

***frow².** See FROE.

frō'ward *a.* (arch.) Perverse, refractory; hence ~LY² *adv.*, ~NESS *n.* [ME, f. FRO + -WARD]

frown *v.* & *n.* **1.** *v.i.* Knit brows esp. to express displeasure or concentrate one's attention; (of thing) present gloomy aspect; express disapprobation (*at, on, upon*). **2.** *v.t.* Drive *away, into* silence, etc., with frown; express (defiance etc.) with frown. **3.** *n.* Vertically furrowed or wrinkled state of brow; look expressing severity, disapproval, or deep thought. [ME, f. OF *frongnier, froignier* (*froigne* surly look f. Celt.)]

frowst *n.*, & *v.i.* (colloq.) **1.** *n.* Fusty warmth in room. **2.** *v.i.* Stay in or enjoy frowst. [back form. f. foll.]

frow'st|ȳ *a.* Fusty, stuffy; hence ~ĬNESS *n.* [var. of foll.]

frow'z|ȳ *a.* Ill-smelling, fusty, musty, close; slatternly, unkempt, dingy; hence ~ĬNESS *n.* [17th c., of unkn. orig.; cf. earlier *frowy*]

frō'ze(n). See FREEZE.

F.R.S. *abbr.* Fellow of the Royal Society.

F.R.S.E. *abbr.* Fellow of the Royal Society of Edinburgh.

frŭctĭ'ferous *a.* Bearing fruit. [f. L *fructifer* (*fructus* FRUIT; see -FEROUS)]

frŭctĭfĭcā'tion *n.* (Bot.) Fructifying; reproductive parts of plant, esp. of ferns and mosses. [f. LL *fructificatio* (as foll.; see -FICATION)]

frŭ'ctĭfȳ *v.* **1.** *v.i.* Bear fruit (lit. or fig.). **2.** *v.t.* Make fruitful, impregnate. [ME, f. OF *fructifier* f. L *fructificare* (*fructus* FRUIT; see -FY)]

frŭ'ctōse *n.* (Chem.) Sugar found in fruit juice, honey, etc. [f. L *fructus* FRUIT + -OSE²]

frŭ'ctūous *a.* Full of or producing fruit (lit. or fig.). [ME f. OF, or f. L *fructuosus* (as FRUIT; see -OUS)]

fru'gal (froo'-) *a.* Careful, sparing (*of*), economical, esp. as regards food; sparingly used or supplied, costing little; hence or cogn. **frugă'lity** *n.* (froo-), ~LY² *adv.* [f. L *frugalis* (*frugi* economical; see -AL)]

frugĭ'vorous (froo-) *a.* Feeding on fruit. [f. L *frux frugis* fruit + -VOROUS]

fruit (froot) *n.* & *v.* **1.** *n.* Plant's or tree's edible product of seed with its envelope, quantity of these (*feeds on fruit*); vegetable seed with envelope as means of reproduction; (usu. in *pl.*) vegetable products fit for food (*fruits of the earth*), so ~'AGE (1) *n.*; *old fruit* (see OLD 5); (sl.) male homosexual. **2.** (Bibl.) offspring (usu. *fruit of the body, loins, womb*); produce of action, (in *pl.*) revenues produced (*the fruits of industry*); result, issue, consequence. **3.** **~-bat,** fruit-eating bat, esp. flying fox; **~-body,** spore-bearing part of fungus; **~-cake** (containing currants etc.); **~ cocktail,** finely-chopped fruit salad; **~-knife** (with silver etc. blade unaffected by acid); ||**~ machine,** gaming machine operated by coins etc., in which a player is successful who gets a certain combination of different symbols often representing fruit; **~ salad,** various fruits cut up and mixed in bowl and often eaten with cream etc., (sl.) display of military decorations; **~ salts,** effervescent health salts (SALT 4); **~ sugar,** fructose; **~-tree** (grown for its fruit); **~-wood** (of fruit-tree, esp. when used in furniture). **4.** Hence (-)~'ED² *a.* **5.** *v.i.* & *t.* Bear or make bear fruit. [ME f. OF, f. L *fructus* enjoyment (*frui* enjoy)]

fruitār'ĭan (froo-) *n.* One who eats only fruit. [f. prec. + -ARIAN]

frui'ter (froo'-) *n.* Tree producing fruit (*good, poor, fruiter*); ||fruit-grower; ship carrying fruit. [ME, f. OF *fruitier* (as FRUIT, -ER²); later f. FRUIT + -ER¹]

frui'terer (froo'-) *n.* Dealer in fruit. [ME, f. prec. + -ER¹]

frui'tful (froo'-) *a.* Productive, fertile, causing fertility; productive of offspring, prolific, (lit., or fig., *a long and fruitful career*); beneficial, remunerative; hence ~LY² *adv.*, ~NESS *n.* [ME, f. FRUIT + -FUL]

frui'tion (froo-) *n.* Enjoyment, attainment of thing desired, realization of hopes etc.; bearing of fruit (lit. or fig.). [ME f. OF, f. LL *fruitio -onis* (*frui* enjoy; see -ION) erron. assoc. w. FRUIT]

frui'tlėss (froo'-) *a.* Not bearing fruit; yielding no profit, ineffectual, useless, empty, vain; hence ~LY² *adv.*, ~NESS *n.* [ME, f. FRUIT + -LESS]

frui'tlėt (froo'-) *n.* (Bot.) = DRUPEL. [f. FRUIT + -LET]

frui't|ȳ (froo'-) *a.* Of fruit; (of wine) tasting of the grape; (colloq.) full of rich quality, suggestive, full of rough humour or (usu. scandalous) interest; hence ~ĬNESS *n.* [f. FRUIT + -Y²]

fru'mentȳ (froo-), **fūr'mėtȳ,** *n.* Hulled wheat boiled in milk and seasoned with cinnamon, sugar, etc. [ME f. OF *frumentee* (*frument* f. L *frumentum* corn); see -Y⁴]

frŭmp *n.* Old-fashioned dowdily-dressed woman; hence ~'ISH¹, ~'Y², *adjs.* [16th c., perh. f. dial. v. *frumple* wrinkle f. MDu. *verrompelen* (as FOR-, RUMPLE)]

frŭ'strāte¹ *a.* (arch.) Frustrated. [ME, f. L *frustratus* p.p. of *frustrari* (see foll., -ATE²)]

frŭstr|ā'te² (*or* frŭ's-) *v.t.* Balk, baffle, neutralize, counteract, disappoint; (in *p.p.*) discontented through inability to achieve one's desires; so ~A'TION *n.* [ME, f. L *frustrari* (*frustra* in vain) + -ATE³]

frŭ'stūle *n.* Two-valved shell of diatom. [F, f. L *frustulum* (as foll.; see -ULE)]

frŭ'st|um *n.* (*pl.* **~a** *or* **~ums**). Remainder of cone or pyramid whose upper part has been cut off by plane parallel to base, or part intercepted between two planes. [L, = piece cut off]

frutė'scent (froo-) *a.* (Bot.) Of the nature of a shrub. [irreg. f. L *frutex* bush + -ESCENT]

fru't|ĕx (froo'-) *n.* (*pl.* **~ices** *pr.* -ĭsēz). (Bot.) Woody-stemmed plant smaller than tree, shrub. [L *frutex fruticis*]

fru'tĭcōse (froo'-) *a.* (Bot.) shrubby; resembling a shrub. [f. L *fruticosus* (as prec.; see -OSE¹)]

frȳ¹ *n.* Young fishes fresh from the spawn; young of salmon in second year; young of other creatures produced in large numbers, e.g. bees or frogs; **small ~,** young or insignificant beings, children etc. [ME, f. ON *frjó* = Goth. *fraiw* seed]

frȳ² *v.* & *n.* **1.** *v.t.* & *i.* Cook in hot fat (*other* FISH¹ *to fry*; **~'ing-pan,** shallow pan used in frying; **out of the ~ing-pan into the fire,** from bad to worse); (in *p.p.*, sl.) drunk. **2.** *v.t.* **~ up,** heat or reheat (food) in frying-pan (hence **~-up** *n.*); (sl.) electrocute. **3.** *v.i.* (sl.) Be electrocuted. **4.** *n.* Fried meat etc.; various internal parts of animals usu. fried, esp. LAMB's *fry*; *social gathering to eat fried food; ~-**pan,** frying-pan. [ME, f. OF *frire* f. L *frigĕre*]

frȳ'er, frī'er, *n.* Vessel for frying fish; one who fries (fish); *chicken suitable for frying. [f. prec. + -ER[1]]

F.S.A. *abbr.* Fellow of the Society of Antiquaries.

F.S.S.U. *abbr.* Federated Superannuation Scheme for Universities.

ft. *abbr.* feet; foot.

***F.T.C.** *abbr.* Federal Trade Commission.

‖**fŭ'bsy̆** (-zĭ) *a.* Fat or squat. [f. obs. *fubs* small fat person + -Y[2]]

fū'chsia (fū'sha) *n.* Drooping-flowered shrub of genus *Fuchsia.* [mod. L, f. L. *Fuchs,* Ger. botanist d. 1566 + -IA[1]]

fu'chsīne (fōōk- *or* fyōō'k-) *n.* Deep red aniline dye. [f. prec. (f. resemblance to colour of flower) + -INE[5]]

fŭck *v.* & *n.* (vulg.) **1.** *v.t.* Copulate with; = DAMN 2; mess *up.* **2.** *v.i.* Copulate; mess, fool, *about* or *around*; make *off.* **3.** Hence ~'ER[1] *n.* (often as general term of abuse), ~'ING[2] *a.* & *adv.* (often as mere intensive). **4.** *n.* Act of copulation; person as partner in copulation; slightest amount (*not care* or *give a fuck*). [16th c.; orig. unkn.]

fū'c|us *n.* (*pl.* ~**i** *pr.* -sī). Seaweed of genus *Fucus,* with flat leathery fronds; hence ~OID *a.* [L, = rock-lichen, f. Gk *phukos,* of Semitic orig.]

fŭ'ddle *v.* & *n.* **1.** *v.i.* Tipple, booze. **2.** *v.t.* Intoxicate; stupefy, confuse. **3.** *n.* Spell of drinking (*on the fuddle*), intoxication; confusion. [16th c.; orig. unkn.]

fŭ'ddy̆-dŭddy̆ *a.* & *n.* (sl.) Old-fashioned (person), ineffectual (old fogy). [20th c.; orig. unkn.]

fŭdge[1] *int.* & *n.* **1.** *int.* Expr. disbelief or annoyance. **2.** *n.* Nonsense; piece of late news inserted in newspaper page; soft-grained toffee-like sweetmeat made with milk, sugar, butter, etc. [f. foll.]

fŭdge[2] *v.* & *n.* **1.** *v.t.* Fit together, patch, make up, in a makeshift or dishonest way, cook, fake. **2.** *v.i.* Practise such methods. **3.** *n.* Piece of fudging. [perh. f. obs. *fadge* v.i. fit]

fuehr'er, führ'er, (fūr'er) *n.* Leader, esp. tyrannical one. [f. G *führer* leader; part of title assumed 1934 by HITLER]

fū'el *n.* & *v.* (‖-**ll**-). **1.** *n.* Material for burning as fire or source of heat or power; food as source of energy; material used as source of nuclear energy; thing that sustains or inflames passion etc. **2.** ~ **cell,** primary cell producing electricity direct from chemical reaction; ~ **element,** assemblage of nuclear fuel etc. for use in reactor; ~ **injection,** direct introduction of fuel under pressure into combustion unit of internal combustion engine; ~-**value,** amount of energy available from a fuel. **3.** *v.t.* Supply (fire, engine, etc.) with fuel. **4.** *v.i.* Get fuel. [ME, f. AF *fuaille, fewaile,* OF *fouaille* f. Rom. **focalia* f. L *focus* hearth]

fŭg *n.,* & *v.i.* (-**gg**-). (colloq.) **1.** *n.* Fustiness of air in room; hence ~'**g**Y[2] (-gĭ) *a.* **2.** *v.i.* Stay in or enjoy fug. [19th c.; orig. unkn.]

fūgā'cious (-shus) *a.* Fleeting, evanescent, hard to capture or keep; so **fūg**A'CITY *n.* [f. L *fugax fugacis* (*fugere* flee; see -ACIOUS)]

fū'gal *a.* Of the nature of a fugue; hence ~LY[2] *adv.* [f. FUGUE + -AL]

-fūge *suf.* forming *adjs.* & *ns.* w. sense '(agent) dispelling or expelling' (*febrifuge, vermifuge*). [f. or after mod. L *-fugus* f. L *fugare* put to flight]

fū'gĭtive *a.* & *n.* **1.** *a.* Fleeing, running away, that has taken flight; flitting, shifting; transient, evanescent, of short duration, quickly fading; (of literature) of passing interest, ephemeral, occasional. **2.** *n.* One who flees, esp. *from* danger, enemy, justice, or master; exile, refugee. [ME, f. OF *fugitif -ive,* f. L *fugitivus* (*fugere fugit-* flee; see -IVE)]

fū'gle|man (-gelm-) *n.* (*pl.* ~**men**). **1.** (Hist.) Soldier placed in front of regiment etc. while drilling to show the motions and time. **2.** Leader, organizer, spokesman; hence [by back form.] **fū'gle** *v.i.* [f. G *flügelmann* (*flügel* wing, *mann* man)]

fūgue (fūg) *n.,* & *v.i.* **1.** *n.* (Mus.) Polyphonic composition in which short melodic theme ('subject') is introduced by one part and successively taken up by others and developed by interweaving the parts; hence **fū'gu**IST (1) (-gĭ-) *n.* **2.** (Psych.) Loss of awareness of one's identity, often coupled with disappearance from one's usual environment. **3.** *v.i.* (Mus.) Compose or perform fugue (**fuguing** or ~**d,** in the form of a fugue). [F, or f. It. f. L *fuga* flight]

führer. See FUEHRER.

-ful *suf.* **1.** Forming *adjs.* f. *ns.,* w. sense 'full of' (*beautiful*), 'having qualities of' (*masterful*), or f. *adjs.* or L adj. stems (*direful, grateful*) w. little change of sense (perh. after older synonyms in *-ful*), or f. *vbs.* w. sense 'apt to, able to, accustomed to' (*forgetful, mournful*), occas. w. passive force (*bashful*). **2.** (fōōl). Forming *ns.* (*pl.* occas. **-sful**), w. sense 'amount needed to fill' (*handful, houseful, mouthful, spoonful*). [f. FULL[1]]

fŭ'lcr|um (*or* fōō'-) *n.* (*pl.* ~**a**). (Mech.) point against which lever is placed to get purchase or on which it turns or is supported; means by which influence etc. is brought to bear. [L, = post of couch (*fulcire* to prop)]

fulfĭ'l, *fulfĭ'll, (fōōl-) *v.t.* (-**ll**-). Bring to consummation, carry out (prophecy, promise), satisfy (desire, prayer); perform, execute, do, (command, law); answer (purpose), comply with (conditions); bring to an end, finish, complete, (period, work); ~ **oneself,** develop one's gifts and character to the full; hence ~MENT *n.* [OE *fullfyllan* (as FULL[1], FILL)]

fŭ'lgent *a.* (poet. or rhet.) Shining, brilliant. [ME, f. L *fulgēre* shine; see -ENT]

fŭlgūrā'tion *n.* (Med.) Destruction of tumours etc. by means of electric sparks. [f. L *fulguratio* sheet lightning (*fulgurare* f. *fulgur* lightning; see -ATION)]

fŭ'lgūrite *n.* (Geol.) Rocky substance of sand fused or vitrified by lightning. [f. L *fulgur* lightning + -ITE[1] (2)]

fūlĭ'gĭnous *a.* Sooty, dusky. [f. LL *fuliginosus* (*fuligo -ginis* soot; see -OUS)]

full[1] (fōōl) *a., n., adv.,* & *v.* **1.** *a.* Holding all (*of,* or abs.) its limits will allow, replete, (*full to the brim*; *full of water*; (colloq.) *full up*); (of heart etc.) overcharged with emotion; (sl.) drunk. **2.** Holding or having abundance *of,* crowded, showing marked signs *of* (*full of vitality*). **3.** Engrossed with the thought *of* (*full of himself, of his subject*; ~ **of the news** etc., unable to keep from talking of it). **4.** Replete with food (*full stomach*; arch. or vulg. of persons); (chiefly Bibl.) having had plenty *of* (*full of years and honours*). **5.** Abundant, sufficient, copious, satisfying, (*a full meal*; *turned it to full account*; *give full details*; *he is very full on this point*). **6.** Complete, entire, perfect, answering in every way to its name or description, reaching the specified or usual limit, entirely visible, (*full daylight, membership, orchestra*; *waited a full hour*; *it was full summer*; *in full bloom*); used for entire cover in bookbinding (*full leather*). **7.** (Of light) intense, (of colour) deep, (of motion etc.) vigorous (*a full pulse*; *full gallop, speed,* etc., used as *adv.* with *come* etc.). **8.** Swelling, plump, protuberant; (of garment) containing much material arranged in folds etc. **9.** ~ **age,**

adult status (esp. w. ref. to legal rights and duties); ~ **back,** (position of) player behind half-backs in football etc.; ~ **blood,** pure descent; **~-blooded,** (1) not hybrid, (2) vigorous, hearty, sensual; ~ **board,** provision of bed and all meals at hotel etc.; **~-bodied,** rich in quality, tone, etc.; **~-bottomed,** (of wig) long at back; ~ **brother** (born of same father and same mother); ~ **and by,** close-hauled; *full* CIRCLE[1]; **~-cream** *a.*, of or made from unskimmed milk; ~ **dress,** dress worn on great occasions; **~-dress** *a.*, (of debate etc.) of major importance; *full* EMPLOYMENT; ~ **face** (entirely visible to spectator); ~ **hand,** (Poker) hand with three of a kind and a pair; **~-hearted,** zealous, confident, courageous; ~ **house,** (1) = *full hand*, (2) maximum or large attendance in Parliament, at theatre, etc.; **~-length,** not shortened or abbreviated, (of mirror, portrait, etc.) showing whole height of human figure; **at ~ length,** (1) lying stretched out, (2) without abridgement; *full* LOCK[2] 6; ~ **marks,** maximum award in examination, in assessment of person, etc.; *full* MEASURE[1]; ~ **moon,** moon with whole disc illuminated, time when this occurs; **~-mouthed,** (of cattle) having full set of teeth, (of dog) baying loudly, (of oratory etc.) sonorous, vigorous; ~ **page,** entire page of newspaper etc.; ~ **pay** (amount allowed on active service); ~ **pitch,** (Cricket) ball pitched right up to batsman, (*adv.*) without ball's having touched ground; ~ **point,** = *full stop* (1); ~ **professor,** professor of highest grade in university etc.; **~-scale,** not reduced in size, complete; ~ **score,** (Mus.) score giving parts for all performers on separate staves; *full* SERVICE[1] 6; ~ **sister** (born of same father and same mother); ~ **speed ahead!** (order to pursue course of action energetically); ~ **stop,** (1) punctuation-mark (.) for pause at end of sentence or to show end of abbreviation, (2) complete cessation; *in full* SWING; *full* TERM[1]; *full* TILT[1]; ~ **time,** (1) total normal duration of work etc. (so *~-time* a., occupying or using all one's working time, *~-timer* n.), (2) end of football etc. match; ~ **toss,** = *full pitch*; *full* TREATMENT; **in ~ view,** entirely visible. **10.** *n.* Whole (*cannot tell you the full of it*; **in ~,** without abridgement, to or for the full amount (*paid in full*); **to the ~,** to the utmost extent, quite); height, acme, (*season, moon, is past the full*). **11.** *adv.* Very (*know it full well*); quite, fully, (*full six miles*; *full ripe*; esp. in comb., as **~-blown,** (of flowers) quite open, (fig.) fully developed, complete, (*full-blown dignity* etc.); ~ **fashioned,** = FULLY *fashioned*; **~-fledged,** mature; **~-grown,** having reached maturity); exactly (*hit him full on the nose*); more than sufficiently (*full early*; *this chair is full high*); ~ **out,** complete, at full power, (Print.) flush with margin. **12.** *v.i.* & *t.* Be or become or make (esp. dress) full. [OE, = OS *ful*, OHG *foll*, ON *fullr*, Goth. *fulls* f. Gmc **fullaz* f. IE **pḷnŏs*]

full[2] (fŏŏl) *v.t.* Cleanse and thicken (cloth). [ME, back form. f. foll.; cf. OF *fouler* (FOIL[2])]

fu'ller[1] (fŏŏ'-) *n.* One who fulls cloth; **~'s earth,** type of clay used in fulling cloth and as adsorbent. [OE *fullere*, f. L *fullo* + -ER[1]]

fu'ller[2] (fŏŏ'-) *n.*, & *v.t.* **1.** *n.* Grooved or rounded tool on which iron is shaped; groove made by this esp. in horseshoe. **2.** *v.t.* Stamp with fuller. [19th c.; orig. unkn.]

fu'llnėss, fu'lnėss, (fŏŏ'l-) *n.* **1.** Being full; **the ~ of the heart,** (Bibl.) emotion, genuine feelings; **the ~ of time,** the destined time. **2.** (Of sound, colour, etc.) richness, volume, body; all that is contained (in the world etc.). [ME, f. FULL[1] + -NESS]

fu'llў (fŏŏ'-) *adv.* Completely, without deficiency; quite as many as (esp. w. numbers); ~ **fashioned,** (of women's stockings etc.) seamed and shaped to fit the body. [OE *fullīce* (as FULL[1], -LY[2])]

-fullў *suf.* forming *advs.* corresp. to *adjs.* in -FUL (*beautifully, distrustfully, gratefully, masterfully, mournfully*). [f. -FUL + -LY[2]]

fu'lmar (fŏŏ'-) *n.* Arctic herring-gull-sized sea-bird related to petrels. [orig. Hebridean dial., perh. f. ON *fúll* FOUL (w. ref. to its smell) + *már* gull (cf. MEW[1])]

fŭ'lmĭnant *a.* Fulminating; (Path., of disease) developing suddenly. [F, or f. L (as foll.; see -ANT)]

fŭ'lmĭnāt|e[1] *v.* **1.** *v.i.* Flash like lightning, explode, detonate, (**~ing gold, mercury,** etc., various explosive fulminates; see foll.); (Path., of disease) develop suddenly; issue censures *against*. **2.** *v.t.* Thunder forth, utter or publish, (censure). **3.** Hence or cogn. **fŭlmĭn**A'TION *n.*, ~ORY *a.* [f. L *fulminare* (*fulmen -minis* lightning) + -ATE[3]]

fŭ'lmĭnāte[2] *n.* (Chem.) Salt of hypothetical *fulminic acid*, an isomer of cyanic acid. [f. L *fulmen* (see prec.) + -ATE[1] (3), many fulminates being explosive]

fulness. See FULLNESS.

-fulnėss *suf.* forming *ns.* corresp. to *adjs.* in -FUL (*distrustfulness, forgetfulness, hopefulness*). [f. -FUL + -NESS]

fu'lsome (fŏŏ'-) *a.* Cloying, excessive, disgusting by excess (of flattery, servility, exaggerated affection); hence ~LY[2] (-mlĭ) *adv.*, ~NESS (-mn-) *n.* [ME, f. FULL[1] + -SOME[1]]

fŭ'lvous *a.* Reddish-yellow, tawny; so **fŭlv**E'SCENT *a.* [f. L *fulvus* + -OUS]

fū'marōle *n.* Crevice in or near volcano, through which hot vapour issues; hence **fūmarŏ'l**IC *a.* [f. F *fumarolle*]

fŭ'mbl|e *v.* & *n.* **1.** *v.i.* Use the hands awkwardly, grope about (*at* or *with* fastening etc.; *for* or *after* thing sought). **2.** *v.t.* Handle or deal with awkwardly or nervously; (Games) not stop (ball) cleanly. **3.** Hence ~ER[1] *n.* **4.** *n.* Bungling attempt. [f. LG *fummeln, fommeln*, Du. *fommelen*]

fūme *n.* & *v.* **1.** *n.* (Esp. malodorous or harmful) smoke, vapour, or exhalation; noxious vapour supposed to rise from stomach to brain (*the fumes of wine* etc., or (fig.) of excitement, enthusiasm, etc.); fit of anger (*in a fume*); ‖**~-chamber** etc., laboratory structure with ventilator for removal of noxious gases; hence **fū'm**Y[2] *a.* **2.** *v.t.* Fumigate; perfume with incense; subject to chemical fumes esp. those of ammonia (photographic film, oak, to darken tints). **3.** *v.i.* Emit fumes; (of vapour etc.) rise, be emitted; be angry or irritated (*at*). [ME, f. OF *fum* f. L *fumus* smoke & OF *fume* (*fumer* f. L *fumare* to smoke)]

fū'mĭg|āte *v.t.* Apply fumes to; disinfect or purify with fumes; hence or cogn. ~ANT, ~A'TION, **~āt**OR, *ns.* [f. L *fumigare* (*fumus* smoke) + -ATE[3]]

fū'mĭtorў *n.* Herb of genus *Fumaria*, formerly used against scurvy. [ME, f. OF *fumeterre* f. med. L *fumus terrae* earth-smoke; assim. to -ORY]

fŭn *n.* & *a.* **1.** *n.* Sport, amusement, jocularity, drollery, (**make ~ of, poke ~ at,** ridicule; **for** or **in ~,** as a joke, not seriously; **for ~, for the ~ of it,** not for a serious purpose; FIGURE[1] *of fun*; **have ~,** (1) enjoy oneself, (2) engage in sexual intercourse; **like ~,** vigorously, quickly, much, (iron.) not at all; **what ~!,** how amusing!). **2.** Source of amusement (**is good** or **great ~,** is very amusing). **3.** ~ **(and games),** (colloq.) exciting goings-on. **4.** ‖**~-fair,** (part of) fair devoted to amusements and side-shows.

5. *a.* Amusing, entertaining, enjoyable. [f. obs. v. *fun* var. of *fon* befool; cf. FOND]

fūnă'mbūlĭst *n.* Rope-walker. [f. F *funambule* or f. L *funambulus* (*funis* rope, *ambulare* walk) + -IST]

fŭ'nction *n.*, & *v.i.* **1.** *n.* Activity proper to person or institution; mode of action or activity by which thing fulfils its purpose; office-holder's duty, employment, profession, calling; religious or other public ceremony or occasion, social meeting of formal or important kind; (Math.) variable quantity in relation to other(s) in terms of which it may be expressed or on which its value depends; basic operation in computer; hence ~LESS *a.* **2.** *v.i.* Fulfil a function, operate, act. [f. F *fonction* f. L *functio -onis* (*fungi funct-* perform; see -ION)]

fŭ'nctional *a.* Of function(s); (Physiol., esp. of disease) of or affecting the functions of an organ etc. only, not structural or organic, (of mental disorder) having no discernible organic cause, (of organ) having a function, not functionless or rudimentary; (Math.) of a function; (of building etc.) shaped or constructed with regard mainly to its function rather than to aesthetic considerations, whence ~ISM (3), ~IST (2), *ns.*; practical, utilitarian; hence ~LY² *adv.* [f. prec. + -AL]

fŭ'nctionarȳ *n.* Person who has to perform functions or duties; official. [f. FUNCTION + -ARY¹]

fŭ'nctionāte *v.i.* = FUNCTION 2. [f. FUNCTION + -ATE³]

fŭnd *n.*, & *v.t.* **1.** *n.* Permanent stock of something ready to be drawn upon (*a fund of common sense, tenderness, labour, knowledge*); stock of money, esp. one set apart for a purpose (SINKING-*fund*); (in *pl.*) pecuniary resources (**in ~s,** having money to spend); ||**the ~s,** stock of National Debt (as mode of investment). **2.** *v.t.* Convert (floating debt) into more or less permanent debt at fixed interest; provide with money; put into a fund. [f. L *fundus* bottom, piece of land]

fŭ'ndament *n.* Buttocks; anus. [ME, f. OF *fondement* f. L *fundamentum* (as FOUND¹; see -MENT)]

fŭndamĕ'ntal *a.* & *n.* **1.** *a.* Of the groundwork, going to the root of the matter, serving as base or foundation, essential, primary, original, from which others are derived, (*a fundamental change*; *the fundamental rules*; *the fundamental form*); **~ particle,** = ELEMENTARY *particle*. **2.** (Mus.) **~ note,** lowest note of chord in its original (uninverted) form; **~ tone** (produced by vibration of whole sonorous body, opp. *harmonics* produced by that of its parts). **3.** Hence ~ITY (-ă'l-) *n.*, ~LY² *adv.* **4.** *n.* (usu. in *pl.*) Principle, rule, article, serving as groundwork of system. **5.** (Mus.) Fundamental note or tone. [ME, f. F *fondamental* or f. LL *fundamentalis* (as prec.; see -AL)]

fŭndamĕ'ntal|ĭsm *n.* Strict maintenance of traditional orthodox religious beliefs such as the inerrancy of Scripture and literal acceptance of the creeds as fundamentals of Protestant Christianity; so ~IST (2) *n.* [f. prec. + -ISM]

fŭ'nd|us *n.* (*pl.* **~i** *pr.* -ī). (Anat.) Lowest or farthest part of stomach or other hollow organ. [L, = bottom]

fūnē'brĭal *a.* Of funeral(s) (*custom is funebrial in origin*); melancholy. [f. L *funebris* (*funus*; see foll.) + -AL]

fū'neral *attrib. a.*, & *n.* **1.** *a.* Of, or used etc. at, burial or cremation of the dead (*funeral oration*); *funeral* HONOUR¹*s*; **~ pile, pyre,** pile of wood etc. on which corpse is burnt; **~ urn** (holding ashes of cremated body). **2.** *n.* Burial of the dead with its ceremonies, obsequies; burial *service or procession; (sl.) one's (unpleasant) concern (*that's your funeral*). [ME; a. OF, f. LL *funeralis* (L *funus -eris* funeral + -AL); n. f. OF *funeraille* f. med. L *funeralia* neut. pl. of *funeralis*; see -AL 2]

fū'nerarȳ *a.* Of funeral(s). [f. LL *funerarius* (as prec.; see -ARY¹)]

fūnē̆r'ėal *a.* Appropriate to a funeral; gloomy, dismal, dark; hence ~LY² *adv.* [f. L *funereus* (as FUNERAL) + -AL]

fŭ'ngĭble (-nj-) *a.* (Law). That can serve for, or be replaced by, another answering to the same definition (of goods etc. contracted for, when an individual specimen is not meant). [f. med. L *fungibilis* f. *fungi* (*vice*) serve (in place of); see -IBLE]

fŭ'ngĭcīde (-nj-) *n.* Fungus-destroying substance; hence **fŭngĭcī'd**AL (-nj-) *a.* [f. FUNGUS + -I- + -CIDE]

fŭngĭstă'tĭc (-nj-) *a.* Inhibiting growth of fungi. [f. FUNGUS + -I- + -STATIC]

fŭ'ngoid (-ngg-) *a.* & *n.* **1.** *a.* Resembling a fungus in texture or in rapid growth; ||of a fungus or fungi. **2.** *n.* Fungoid plant. [f. FUNGUS + -OID]

fŭ'ngous (-ngg-) *a.* Of fungi, having nature of a fungus; springing up like a mushroom, transitory. [ME, f. L *fungosus* (as foll.; see -OUS)]

fŭ'ng|us (-ngg-) *n.* (*pl.* **~i** *pr.* -nggī *or* -njī, *or* **~uses**). Mushroom, toadstool, or allied plant including moulds; (Bot.) cryptogamous plant without chlorophyll feeding on organic matter; thing of sudden growth; (Path.) spongy morbid growth or excrescence; skin-disease of fish; (sl.) beard; hence ~AL, **~ĭ**FORM (-nj-), **~ĭ'**VOROUS (-nj-), *adjs.* [L, perh. f. Gk *sp(h)oggos* SPONGE¹]

fūnĭ'cūlar *a.* & *n.* **1.** *a.* Of a rope or its tension; **~ railway,** cable railway with ascending and descending cars counterbalanced. **2.** *n.* Funicular railway. [f. L *funiculus* (*funis* rope; see -CULE) + -AR¹]

fŭnk *n.* & *v.* (sl.) **1.** *n.* Fear, panic, (**blue ~,** terror); coward; ||**~-hole,** (1) trench dug-out, (2) employment used as pretext for evading military service. **2.** *v.i.* Flinch, shrink, show cowardice. **3.** *v.t.* (Try to) evade (undertaking), shirk; be afraid of. [18th c. Oxford sl.; perh. = sl. *funk* tobacco-smoke]

fŭ'nkĭa *n.* = HOSTA. [mod. L, f. H. C. *Funck*, Prussian botanist d. 1839 + -IA¹]

fŭ'nkȳ¹ *a.* (sl.) Terrified, cowardly. [f. FUNK + -Y²]

fŭ'nkȳ² *a.* (sl.) (Of jazz etc.) uncomplicated, emotional; fashionable; strong-smelling. [f. *funk* strong smell + -Y²]

fŭ'nnel *n.* & *v.* (||-**ll**-). **1.** *n.* Narrowing tube, or truncated cone and tube, for guiding liquid, powder, etc., into small opening; metal chimney of steam engine or ship; hence (-)**fŭ'nnel(l)**ED² (-ld) *a.* **2.** *v.t.* & *i.* (Cause to) move (as) through funnel. [ME, f. Pr. *fonilh* f. LL *fundibulum* f. L *infundibulum* f. IN¹(*fundere* pour)]

fŭ'nnĭment *n.* Joke, drollery. [f. FUNNY + -MENT]

fŭnnĭŏ'sĭtȳ *n.* (joc.) Comicality; comical thing. [f. foll. + -OSITY]

fŭ'nnȳ *a.* & *n.* **1.** *a.* Affording fun, comical. **2.** Curious, perplexing, hard to account for; (colloq.) slightly unwell, insane, etc. **3. ~-bone,** part of elbow over which ulnar nerve passes; **~ business,** comic behaviour, jesting, (sl.) misbehaviour or deception; **~-face** (joc. & colloq., as form of address); **~ farm,** (sl.) mental hospital; **~-ha-ha',** (colloq.) = sense 1; **~ man,** professional clown or jester; **~ paper,** newspaper etc. containing humorous matter; **~-pecu'liar,** (colloq.) = sense 2. **4.** Hence

fŭ'nniLY[2] *adv.*, **fŭ'nni**NESS *n.* **5.** *n.* (esp. in *pl.*) Comic strip in newspaper; joke. [f. FUN + -Y[2]]

fûr *n.* & *v.* (**-rr-**). **1.** *n.* Trimming or lining made of dressed coat of certain animals, e.g. ermine, beaver, or of material imitating this; coat of such animals, as material for trimming etc.; garment of or trimmed or lined with fur. **2.** Short fine soft hair of certain animals distinguished from the longer hair, (in *pl.*) skins of such animals with the fur; (Her.) representation of tufts on plain ground; (collect.) furred animals (esp. *fur and* FEATHER[1]); **make the ~ fly,** make a disturbance, stir up trouble; **~-seal,** eared seal with valuable undercoat. **3.** Crust adhering to surface, e.g. deposit from wine; coating formed on tongue in sickness; coating formed by hard water in kettle etc. **4.** *v.t.* (esp. in *p.p.*) Provide (garment, animal), clothe (person), coat (tongue, inside of kettle), with fur; (Carpent.) level (floor-timbers) by inserting strips of wood. **5.** *v.i.* ~ (**up**), (of kettle etc.) become coated with fur. [ME; n. f. v. f. AF **furrer*, OF *forrer* (*forre, fuerre* sheath f. Gmc **fōdhram*)]

fur. *abbr.* furlong(s).

fûr'bèlow (-ō) *n.*, & *v.t.* **1.** *n.* Gathered strip or pleated border of skirt or petticoat; (in *pl.*, derog.) showy ornaments. **2.** *v.t.* Adorn with furbelow(s). [18th c. var. of FALBALA]

fûr'bĭsh *v.t.* Remove rust from, polish *up*, burnish; ~ (**up**), give new look to, renovate, revive, (something antiquated). [ME, f. OF *forbir* (-ISH[2]) f. Gmc **furbjan*]

fûr'cāte[1] (*or -at*) *a.* Forked, branched. [f. LL *furcatus* f. L *furca* fork; see -ATE[2]]

fûr'c|āte[2] *v.i.* Form a fork, divide; so ~A'TION *n.* [f. L *furca* fork + -ATE[3]]

fûrfurā'ceous (-sh*u*s) *a.* Scurfy; (Bot.) covered with branlike scales. [f. *furfur* scurf f. L *furfur* bran + -ACEOUS]

fūr'ious *a.* Full of fury, raging, frantic, violent, intense; **fast and** ~, (of mirth etc.) eager(ly), uproarious(ly); hence ~LY[2] *adv.* [ME, f. OF *furieus* f. L *furiosus* (as FURY; see -OUS)]

fûrl *v.* **1.** *v.t.* Roll up and bind (sail on yard or boom; umbrella, flag); close (fan), fold up (wings), draw away (curtain), relinquish (hopes). **2.** *v.i.* Become furled. [f. F *ferler* f. OF *fer*(*m*) FIRM[2] + *lier* bind f. L *ligare*]

fûr'lŏng *n.* Eighth of mile, 220 yds. [OE *furlang* (*furh* FURROW, *lang* LONG[1]; orig. = length of furrow in common field)]

fûr'lough (-lō) *n.* & *v.* **1.** *n.* Leave of absence, esp. granted to soldier. **2.** *v.t.* *Grant furlough to. **3.** *v.i.* *Spend furlough. [f. Du. *verlof* (after G *verlaub*; as FOR-, LEAVE[1])]

fûr'mėtў. See FRUMENTY.

fûr'nace (-ĭs) *n.*, & *v.t.* **1.** *n.* Apparatus including combustion chamber in which minerals, metals, etc., may be subjected to continuous intense heat (BLAST[1]-*furnace*); very hot place; (fig.) severe test (*tried in the furnace*); closed fireplace for heating water to warm building etc. by hot pipes. **2.** *v.t.* Heat in furnace. [ME, f. OF *fornais* f. L *fornax -acis* (*fornus* oven)]

fûr'nĭsh *v.t.* **1.** ~ **with,** cause to have possession or use of. **2.** Fit up (house, room) with all necessary appliances, esp. movable furniture (~**ed house, rooms,** etc., esp. premises let with furniture); hence ~ING[1] (3) *n.* (esp. in *pl.*). **3.** Provide, afford, yield. [f. OF *furnir* (-ISH[2]) f. Rom. **fornire* ult. f. WG **frumjan* supply, promote, (**frum-*; cf. FRAME[1], FROM)]

fûr'nĭture *n.* **1.** Movable contents of house or room, tables, chairs, etc.; ~ **beetle,** *Anobium punctatum*, boring in furniture; ~ **van,** large van used to move furniture from one house to another. **2.** (Print.) Pieces of wood or metal placed round or between type to make blank spaces and fasten the matter in the chase. **3.** (Naut.) Ship's equipment, esp. tackle etc. **4.** (arch.) Contents of receptacle; things occupying a place. **5.** Accessory equipment, e.g. handles and lock of door. [f. F *fourniture* (*fournir*, f. as prec.; see -URE)]

fūrōr'ė, *fūr'ŏr, *n.* Enthusiastic admiration; rage, craze; uproar, fury. [It., f. L *furor -oris* (*furere* be mad; see -OR)]

fûr'phў *n.* (Austral. sl.) False report or rumour; absurd story. [f. water and sanitary *F~ carts* of 1914–18 war, made at foundry set up by F~ family]

fŭ'rrĭ|er *n.* Dealer in or dresser of furs; hence ~ERY (2) *n.* [ME *furrour* f. OF *forreor* (*forrer* trim with fur), assim. to -IER]

fŭ'rrĭn(er). Joc. or dial. var. of FOREIGN(ER).

fŭ'rrow (-ō) *n.*, & *v.t.* **1.** *n.* Narrow track made by plough (PLOUGH[2] *a lonely furrow*); ship's track; rut, track, groove, long indentation, deep wrinkle, hollow between ridges; **~-slice,** slice of earth turned up by mould-board of plough; hence ~LESS, ~Y[2], *adjs.* **2.** *v.t.* Plough; make furrows, grooves, etc., in; mark with wrinkles. [OE *furh*, = OHG *furuh*, ON *for* trench f. Gmc **furh-* f. IE **pṛk-*]

fûr'rў *a.* Of or like fur; covered with or wearing fur. [f. FUR + -Y[2]]

fûr'ther (-dh-) *adv.* & *a.* (used as *compar.* of FAR[1,2]), & *v.t.* **1.** *adv.* To or at more advanced point in space or time (*unsafe to proceed further*; *and then to lapse unless further continued*); to greater extent, more, (*inquire further*); ~(**more**), in addition (esp. introducing fresh consideration in argument); at greater distance (*nothing was further from his thoughts*); (euphem.) in hell (*I'll see you further first*, as strong refusal of request). **2.** *a.* Going beyond what exists or has been dealt with, additional, (*threats of further punishment*; ||~ **education,** formal education for persons above school age; **till ~ notice** or **orders,** to continue until explicitly changed); more distant (*on the further side*); hence ~MOST *a.* **3.** *v.t.* Help on, promote, favour, (undertaking, movement, cause); hence ~ANCE *n.*, (arch.) ~SOME[1] *a.* [OE *furthor* adv., *furthra* adj., *fyrthrian* v., f. as FORTH, -ER[3]]

fûr'thėst (-dh-) *a.* & *adv.* (used as *superl.* of FAR[1,2]). **1.** *a.* Most distant; **at (the)** ~, at the greatest distance, at latest, at most. **2.** *adv.* To or at the greatest distance. [ME, superl. formed f. prec.; see -EST[1]]

fûr'tĭve *a.* Done by stealth, clandestine, meant to escape notice; sly, stealthy; stolen, taken secretly; thievish, pilfering; hence ~LY[2] (-vlĭ) *adv.*, ~NESS (-vn-) *n.* [f. F *furtif -ive* or f. L *furtivus* (*furtum* theft; see -IVE)]

fūr'ŭnc|le *n.* = BOIL[1]; hence **~ūl**AR, **~ūl**OUS, (-ŭ'ngk-) *adjs.* [f. L *furunculus* (*fur* thief; see -UNCLE)]

fūrŭncūlō's|ĭs *n.* (*pl.* **~es** *pr.* -ēz). **1.** Diseased condition in which boils appear. **2.** Bacterial disease of salmon and trout. [mod. L, f. as prec. + -OSIS]

fūr'ў *n.* **1.** Fierce passion, wild anger, rage, (**in a** ~, in a fit of rage); impetuosity in battle etc.; violence of weather, disease, etc.; **like** ~, (colloq.) furiously, hard. **2.** (usu. in *pl.*; *F~*) snake-haired goddess of Gk myth (esp. Alecto, Tisiphone, or Megaera) sent from Tartarus to punish crime; (fig.) avenging spirit, remorseful pang, (*haunted by the furies of her father's blood*). **3.** Virago, angry or malignant woman. [ME, f. OF *furie* f. L *furia* (*furere* be mad; see -Y[1])]

||**fûrze** *n.* Spiny yellow-flowered evergreen shrub growing esp. on European waste lands, gorse, whin; hence **fûr'**ZY[2] *a.* [OE *fyrs*, of unkn. orig.]

fŭ'scous *a.* Sombre, dark-coloured. [f. L *fuscus* dusky + -OUS]

fūse[1] (-z) *v.t.* & *i.* Melt with intense heat; blend or amalgamate into one whole (as) by melting (of metals, living bones, institutions, motives, etc.); hence **fū'**SIBLE *a.*, **fū**SIBI'LITY *n.*, (-z-). [f. L *fundere fus-* pour, melt]

fūse[2] (-z), ***fūze,** *n.*, & *v.t.* **1.** *n.* Tube, casing, cord, etc., filled or saturated with combustible matter for igniting bomb, blasting-charge, etc., component in shell, mine, etc., designed to detonate explosive charge after an interval (*time-fuse*) or on impact or when subjected to magnetic or vibratory stimulation. **2.** *v.t.* Fit fuse to. [f. It. *fuso* f. L *fusus* spindle]

fūse[3] (-z) *n.* & *v.* (Electr.) **1.** *n.* (Device containing) strip or wire of easily melted metal placed in circuit so as to interrupt current by melting when current exceeds safe value; **~-box,** small cupboard or box containing fuses for circuits in house etc. **2.** *v.t.* Provide (circuit etc.) with fuse(s); cause (appliance etc.) to fuse. **3.** *v.i.* (Of appliance etc.) cease to function, owing to melting of fuse.[f. FUSE[1]]

fūsee' (-z-), ***fūzee',** *n.* Conical pulley or wheel esp. in watch or clock; large-headed match for lighting cigar or pipe in wind; *railway signal-flare. [f. F *fusée* spindle f. LL **fusata* f. L *fusus*]

fū'sel (-z-) *n.* **~ oil,** mixture of several alcohols, chiefly amyl alcohol, produced, usu. in small amounts, during alcoholic fermentation and making alcoholic liquors harmful or poisonous. [f. G *fusel* bad brandy etc.; cf. *fuseln* FOOZLE]

fū'selage (-z-; *or* -ahzh) *n.* Body of aeroplane. [F (*fuseler* cut in spindle form f. *fuseau* spindle f. OF *fusel* f. Rom. **fusellus* dim. of L *fusus*; see -AGE)]

fū'sĭfôrm (-z-) *a.* (Bot. & Zool.) Shaped like spindle or cigar, tapering at both ends. [f. L *fusus* spindle + -I- + -FORM]

fū'sĭl (-z-) *n.* (Hist.) Light musket. [F, f. LL **focile* f. L *focus* hearth, fire; see -IL]

fūsĭlier', *fūsĭleer', (-z-) *n.* (usu. in *pl.*) (Hist.) soldier armed with fusil; (member of) one of several British regiments formerly armed with fusils. [F (as prec.; see -IER)]

fūsĭllā'de (-z-) *n.*, & *v.t.* **1.** *n.* (Wholesale execution by) continuous discharge of firearms; sustained outburst of criticism etc. **2.** *v.t.* Assault (place), shoot down (persons), by fusillade. [F (*fusiller* shoot; see -ADE)]

fū'sion (-zhon) *n.* **1.** Fusing, melting; fused mass; blending of different things into one; coalition, whence ~IST (2) *n.* **2.** (Phys.) Union of atomic nuclei to form heavier one, usu. with release of energy; this process as source of energy; **~ bomb** (using this process, esp. hydrogen bomb). [F, or f. L *fusio* (as FUSE[1]; see -ION)]

fŭss *n.* & *v.* **1.** *n.* Bustle, excessive commotion, ostentatious or nervous activity; **make a ~,** complain vigorously; **make a ~ of** or **over,** treat (person) with display of affection or attention. **2.** Treatment of trifles as important; abundance of petty detail. **3.** **~(-pot), ~'budget,** (colloq.) person who continually makes a fuss. **4.** *v.i.* Make fuss; busy oneself restlessly with trifles; move fussily *about, up and down,* etc. **5.** *v.t.* Agitate, worry, (person). [18th c., perh. Anglo-Ir.]

fŭ'ss|ȳ *a.* Fond of fussing; full of unnecessary detail or decoration; hence **~ĭLY**[2] *adv.*, **~ĭNESS** *n.* [f. prec. + -Y[2]]

fŭstanĕ'lla *n.* Man's stiff white kilt worn in Albania and Greece. [It. dim. of mod. Gk *phoustani* prob. f. It. *fustagno* FUSTIAN]

fŭ'stian *n.* & *a.* **1.** *n.* Thick twilled short-napped cotton cloth usu. dyed dark; turgid speech or writing, bombast. **2.** *a.* Made of fustian, (fig.) bombastic, worthless. [ME, f. OF *fustaigne* (med. L *fustaneus* adj. ref. to cloth from *Fostat* suburb of Cairo)]

fŭ'stĭc *n.* One of two kinds of wood yielding yellow dye (**young ~,** from Venetian sumac; ~ or **old ~,** from tropical Amer. tree *Chlorophora tinctoria*); dye from these. [f. F f. Sp. *fustoc* f. Arab. *fustuk* f. Gk *pistakē* pistachio]

fŭ'stĭg|āte *v.t.* (joc.) Cudgel; hence **~A'TION** *n.* [f. LL *fustigare* (*fustis* cudgel) + -ATE[3]]

fŭ'st|ȳ *a.* Stale-smelling, musty, mouldy; close, stuffy; antiquated, old-fashioned; hence **~ĭLY**[2] *adv.*, **~ĭNESS** *n.* [ME, f. OF *fusté* smelling of the cask (*fust* cask,tree-trunk,f. L *fustis* cudgel)]

fu'thôrc (fōō'-) *n.* Scandinavian runic alphabet. [f. its first six letters *f, u, th, ö, r, k*]

fū'tĭle *a.* Useless, ineffectual, vain, frivolous; hence or cogn. **fūtĭ'lĭTY** *n.*, **~LY**[2] (-l-lĭ) *adv.* [f. L *futilis* leaky, futile, (**fud-* st. of *fundere* pour; see -IL)]

fūtĭlĭtār'ian *a.* & *n.* (Person) devoted to futile pursuits. [joc. f. prec. after *utilitarian*]

fŭ'ttock *n.* One of ship's middle timbers between floor and top timbers; **~ plates,** iron plates in a ship's top to which the **~ shrouds** (lower ends of which are fastened to ring on mast below) are fixed, as well as the dead-eyes of the topmast rigging. [ME *votekes* etc. pl. f. MLG (*fōt* FOOT[1], *-ken* -KIN)]

fū'ture *a.* & *n.* **1.** *a.* About to happen or be or become; that will be hereafter (**~ life, state,** existence after death); that will be something specified (*my future wife*); of time to come, (Gram., of participle or tense) describing event yet to happen (*future* PERFECT[1]). **2.** *n.* Time to come (**for the ~, in ~,** from now onwards; *past, present, and future*); what will happen in the future; person's, country's, etc., prospective condition; prospective condition of success etc. (*that idea has no future*); (Gram.) future tense; (Commerc., in *pl.*) goods and stocks sold for future delivery, contracts for these; hence **~LESS** (-cherl-) *a.* [ME f. OF *futur -ure* f. L *futurus* fut. part. of *esse* be f. st. *fu-* be]

fū'turĭsm (-cher-) *n.* Movement in art, literature, music, etc., with violent departure from traditional forms so as to express movement and growth. [f. FUTURE + -ISM, after It. *futurismo,* F *futurisme*]

fū'turĭst (-cher-) *n.* **1.** (Theol.) One who believes that the prophecies of the Apocalypse etc. are still to be fulfilled. **2.** (Art etc.) Adherent of futurism. **3.** Student of the future; believer in human progress. [f. FUTURE + -IST]

fūturĭ'stĭc (-cher-) *a.* **1.** Having characteristics of futurism, ultra-modern. **2.** Pertaining to the future. [f. prec. + -IC]

fūtūr'ĭtȳ *n.* Future time; (in *sing.* or *pl.*) future events; future condition, existence after death; ***~ stakes,** stakes raced for long after entries or nominations are made. [f. FUTURE + -ITY]

fūturŏ'|logȳ (-cher-) *n.* Systematic forecasting of future esp. from present trends in society; hence **~LOGIST** *n.* [f. FUTURE + -O- + -LOGY]

***fūze, *fūzee'.** See FUSE[2], FUSEE.

fŭzz *n.* Loose volatile matter, fluff; fluffy or frizzed hair; (sl.) police(man) [perh. diff. wd]; **~-ball,** puff-ball fungus. [17th c., prob. f. LG or Du.]

fŭ'zz|ȳ *a.* Like fuzz; frayed, fluffy; blurred, indistinct; frizzy; **~y-wuzzy,** (colloq.) Sudanese soldier, (sl.) coloured native of other countries; hence **~ĭLY**[2] *adv.*, **~ĭNESS** *n.* [f. prec. + -Y[2]]

f.w.d. *abbr.* four-wheel drive; front-wheel drive.

fwd. *abbr.* forward.

-fȳ *suf.* forming (usu. w. intermediate -I-) *vbs.* (1) f. *ns.* w. sense 'make, produce' (*pacify, satisfy*), 'make into' (*deify, petrify*), 'make like' (*countrify*), (2) f. *adjs.* w. sense 'bring or come into state' (*Frenchify, sanctify, solidify*), (3) f. *vbs.* w. causative sense (*horrify, stupefy*). [f. or after F *-fier* f. L *-ficare* (cf. -FICATION) and *-facere* (cf. -FACTION)]

***f.y.** *abbr.* fiscal year.

fȳ'lfot *n.* Swastika. [perh. f. *fill-foot*, pattern to fill the foot of a painted window]

fȳtte. See FIT[1].

G

G, g, (jē) *n.* (*pl.* **Gs** *or* **G's**). Seventh letter of alphabet; (Mus.) fifth note in diatonic scale of C major.

G *abbr.* gauss; giga-.

g. *abbr.* gelding; gram(s); (acceleration due to) gravity.

Ga. *abbr.* Georgia (U.S.).

Ga *symb.* gallium.

găb *n.* (colloq.) Talk, prattle, twaddle; **gift of the ~,** (1) talent for speaking, (2) loquacity; **stop your ~,** be silent. [17th-c. var. of GOB[3]]

gă'bardine (-ēn) *n.* Smooth durable twill-woven cloth esp. of worsted or cotton; garment of this. [var. of GABERDINE]

gă'bble *v.* & *n.* **1.** *v.i.* Talk volubly or inarticulately; read aloud too fast. **2.** *v.t.* Utter too fast esp. in reading aloud. **3.** *n.* Voluble confused unintelligible talk. [f. MDu. *gabbelen*; imit.]

gă'bbrō *n.* (*pl.* **~s**). Dark granular igneous rock of crystalline texture resembling dolerite and granite; hence **gă'bbr**OID *a.* [It., f. L *glaber* smooth]

gă'bbȳ *a.* (colloq.) Talkative. [f. GAB + -Y[2]]

gabĕ'lle *n.* (Hist.) Tax (usu. foreign tax, esp. the French pre-Revolution salt-tax). [ME f. F, f. It. *gabella* f. Arab. *al-ḳabāla* the tribute]

ga'berdine (-ēn) *n.* (Hist.) loose long upper garment esp. of Jews and almsmen; gabardine. [f. OF *gauvardine* perh. f. MHG *wallevart* pilgrimage]

***gă'bfĕst** *n.* (sl.) Gathering for conversation; prolonged spell of talking. [f. GAB + FEST]

gā'bĭon *n.* Cylinder of wicker or woven metal bands to be filled with earth or stones for use in engineering or (Hist.) fortification; hence **~**A'DE *n.*, line of gabions. [F, f. It. *gabbione* (*gabbia* CAGE; see -OON)]

gā'ble *n.* Triangular upper part of wall at end of ridged roof; **~(-end),** gable-topped wall; gable-shaped canopy over window or door, whence **gā'bl**ET[1] *n.*; hence **(-)gā'bl**ED[2] (-beld) *a.* [ME *gavel* f. ON *gafl*; ME *gable* f. OF f. ON *gafl*]

gā'bȳ *n.* (arch. or dial.) Simpleton. [18th c.; orig. unkn.]

găd[1] *int.* (*or* **by ~**) expr. surprise, asseveration, etc. [= *God*]

găd[2] *v.i.* **(-dd-),** & *n.* **1.** *v.i.* Go about idly or in search of pleasure, rove, wander, (*about, abroad, out*); (of plant, esp. in *part.*) straggle; **~'about** *n.* & *a.*, (person) given to gadding. **2.** *n.* **(Up)on the ~,** going about, on the move. [back form. f. obs. *gadling* companion f. OE *gædeling* (*gæd* fellowship; see -LING[1])]

Gă'darēne *a.* Of Gadara in ancient Palestine; involving or engaged in headlong rush or flight. [f. LL f. Gk *Gadarēnos* (cf. -ENE 2), w. ref. to Matt. 8:28 ff.]

ga'ddĭ (gŭ'-) *n.* (Hist.) Cushioned throne of Indian ruler; power as sovereign. [f. Hind. *gaddī*, lit. cushion]

gă'dflȳ *n.* Cattle-biting fly, esp. horse-fly or bot-fly; irritating or harassing person. [f. obs. *gad* spike f. ON *gaddr*, cogn. w. YARD[1]]

gă'dgėt *n.* Small fitting or contrivance in machinery etc.; adjunct; (mere) knick-knack; hence **~**EER', **~**RY (5), *ns.*, **~**Y[2] *a.* [19th c. Naut.; orig. unkn.]

Gadhĕ'lic (-dĕ'-) *a.* & *n.* = GAELIC 2. [f. Ir. *Gaedheal* Gael + -IC]

gā'doid *a.* & *n.* (Fish) of the cod family Gadidae. [f. mod. L *gadus* f. Gk *gados* cod + -OID]

gă'dolĭnite *n.* Dark mineral containing silicates of rare-earth elements. [f. J. *Gadolin*, Finnish mineralogist d. 1852 + -ITE[1] (2)]

gădolĭ'nĭum *n.* Metallic element of lanthanide series, found in gadolinite. [mod. L, f. prec. + -IUM]

gadrōō'n *n.* Convex curves in series forming ornamental edge like inverted fluting on silverware etc. [f. F *godron*; cf. *goder* pucker, -OON]

gă'dwall (-awl) *n.* Brownish-grey freshwater duck (*Anas strepera*). [17th c.; orig. unkn.]

gădzōō'ks *int.* (arch.) expr. asseveration etc. [f. GAD[1] + *zooks* of unkn. orig.]

Gael (gāl) *n.* Scottish Celt; Gaelic-speaking Celt; hence **~'**DOM *n.* [f. Gael. *Gaidheal*]

Gae'lĭc (gă'l-) *a.* & *n.* **1.** (Language) of Scottish Celts. **2.** (Language) of Scottish and Irish and Manx Celts. **3. ~ coffee** (with cream and Irish whisky). [f. prec. + -IC]

Gaeltacht (gā'ltaχt) *n.* Region in Ireland where vernacular language is Irish. [Ir.]

găff[1] *n.*, & *v.t.* **1.** *n.* Barbed fishing-spear; stick with iron hook for landing large fish; spar extending top of fore-and-aft sail not set on stays; **~-rigged,** having gaff on mainsail; **~ topsail,** small sail having foot on gaff. **2.** *v.t.* Seize (fish) with gaff. [ME, f. Prov. *gaf* hook]

găff[2] *n.* (sl.) **Blow the ~,** let out plot or secret; ***stand the ~,** endure difficulties. [19th c.; orig. unkn.]

‖**găff**[3] *n.* (arch. sl.) Public place of amusement; **(penny) ~,** low theatre or music-hall. [18th c.; orig. unkn.]

găffe *n.* Blunder, indiscreet act or remark, *faux pas.* [F]

gă'ffer *n.* Elderly rustic, old fellow, (also as title or in *voc.*); ‖foreman of gang of workmen. [prob. contr. of GOD*father*; *ga-* by assoc. w. *grandfather*; cf. GAMMER, GOSSIP]

găg *n.* & *v.* **(-gg-). 1.** *n.* Thing thrust into mouth to prevent speech or outcry or (Surg.) hold it open for operation; (Parl.) closure or guillotine. **2.** Actor's interpolations in dramatic dialogue; (Theatr.) carefully prepared comic effect or business introduced into music-hall sketch, stage-play, etc.; **~-man, ~'**STER, professional deviser of gags. **3. ~-bit,** specially powerful bit for horse-breaking; **~-rein** (arranged to make the bit more powerful). **4.** Joke, hoax; humorous action or situation; imposture, deception. **5.** *v.t.* Apply gag to; silence, deprive of free speech; apply gag-bit to (horse); cause to choke or retch. **6.** *v.i.* (Theatr.) make gags; choke, retch. [n. f. v., ME, perh. imit. of choking]

gă'ga (*or* gah'gah) *a.* (sl.) Fatuous, senile; slightly crazy. [F, = senile (person)]

gāge[1] *n.*, & *v.t.* **1.** *n.* Pledge, thing deposited as security; (glove thrown down as, any symbol of) challenge to fight. **2.** *v.t.* (arch.) Stake, pledge, offer as guarantee. [ME; n. f. OF *gage* f. Rom. **gwadjo* f. Gmc **wadhjam* (cf. WED); v. f. F *gager* (*gage*), or f. ENGAGE]

gāge[2,3]. See GAUGE[1,2].

gāge[4] *n.* Greengage. [abbr.]

gă'ggle *n.*, & *v.i.* **1.** *n.* Flock (of geese); (derog.) company (of women); (disorderly) group. **2.** *v.i.* (Of geese) cackle. [ME, n. f. v., imit.; cf. *gabble, cackle*]

gai'etў, *gay'etў, *n.* Being gay, mirth (~ **of nations,** cheerfulness or pleasure of numerous people); merry-making, amusement; bright appearance. [f. F *gaieté* (as GAY, -TY[1])]

gaillar'dĭa *n.* Showy-flowered composite plant of genus *Gaillardia.* [mod. L, f. *Gaillard* de Marentonneau, 18th-c. Fr. botanist + -IA[1]]

gai'lў. See GAY.

gain[1] *n.* Increase of possessions etc., profit, advance, improvement; acquisition of wealth; (in *pl.*) sums acquired by trade etc., emoluments, winnings; increase in amount; (Electr.) (logarithm of) factor by which power etc. is increased. [OF (*gaaignier* GAIN[2])]

gain[2] *v.* **1.** *v.t.* Obtain or secure (usu. desired or desirable thing; *gain advantage, recognition*; ~ **time,** obtain delay by pretexts or slow methods); win (sum) as profits or as result of changed conditions, earn, whence **~'ĭngs** (-z) *n. pl.* [-ING[1] (2)]; obtain as increment or addition (*gain momentum, weight*). **2.** Win (land from sea, battle, victory; *gain* GROUND[1]; *gain the* UPPER *hand*); bring over or *over* to one's interest or views; reach, arrive at, (desired place); (of clock etc.) become fast by (amount of time). **3.** *v.i.* Make a profit, be benefited, improve or advance *in* some respect; be enhanced *by* comparison or contrast; (of clock etc.) become fast, indicate time ahead of correct time; ~ **(up)on,** come closer to (what is pursued). **4.** Hence ~'ABLE *a.*, ~'ER[1] *n.* [f. OF *gaigner, gaaignier* to till, acquire, f. Rom. **gwadanjare* f. Gmc **waithanjan* (**waithō* pasture)]

gai'nful *a.* Lucrative, remunerative; bent on gain; paid (employment); hence ~LY[2] *adv.* [f. GAIN[1] + -FUL]

gainsay' *v.t.* (**gainsai'd** *pr.* -ā'd *or* -ĕ'd). (arch. or literary). Deny, contradict; hence ~ER[1] *n.* [ME, f. obs. *gain-* pref. against, f. ON *gegn* straight, f. Gmc **gagan-*, **gagin-* + SAY[2]]

'gainst *prep.* (poet.) = AGAINST. [abbr.]

gait *n.* Manner of walking, bearing or carriage as one walks (**go** one's **(own)** ~, pursue one's own course); manner of forward motion of runner, horse, vehicle, etc. [var. of GATE[2]]

gai'ter *n.* Covering of cloth, leather, etc., for leg below knee, for ankle, for part of machine, etc.; hence ~ED[2] (-*erd*) *a.* [f. F *guêtre*, perh. cogn. w. WRIST]

găl[1] *n.* (vulg.) Girl. [repr. variant pr.]

găl[2] *n.* (Phys.) Unit of acceleration due to gravity, one centimetre per second per second. [f. *Galileo* (see GALILEAN[1])]

Gal. *abbr.* Galatians (N.T.).

gal. *abbr.* gallon(s).

gā'la (*or* gah'-) *n.* Festive occasion, fête; ‖festive gathering for sports. [F, or f. It. f. Sp., f. Arab. *ḵil'a* presentation garment]

gală'ctĭc *a.* Of the Galaxy; of a galaxy or galaxies. [f. Gk *galaktias*, var. of *galaxias* (see GALAXY) + -IC]

gală'cto- *comb. form.* (Med. etc.) Milk, as: **~gogue** (-ŏg), (substance) inducing a flow of milk. [f. Gk *gala galaktos* milk]

galā'gō *n.* (*pl.* **~s**). Small African tree-climbing lemur of genus *Galago.* [mod. L]

galah' *n.* (Austral.) Rose-breasted grey-backed cockatoo; (sl.) fool, simpleton. [Aboriginal]

Gă'lahăd (-*a*-h-) *n.* Person characterized by nobility, integrity, courtesy, etc. [f. noblest knight of Round Table in Arthurian legend]

gă'lantine (-ēn) *n.* White meat boned, cooked, pressed, and served cold in aspic etc. [ME f. OF, alt. f. *galatine* jellied meat f. med. L *galatina*]

gală'ntў *n.* ~ **show,** (Hist.) pantomime made by shadows of puppets on screen. [perh. f. It. *galanti* pl. of *galante* GALLANT]

gă'laxў *n.* **1.** (*G*~) the irregular luminous band of stars indistinguishable to naked eye encircling the heavens, Milky Way; one of many independent systems of stars, gas, dust, etc., existing in space, esp. (*G*~) the one which contains the earth. **2.** Brilliant company (*of* beauties, talent, etc.). [ME, f. OF *galaxie* f. med. L *galaxia*, LL f. Gk *galaxias* (*gala galaktos* milk)]

gă'lbanum *n.* Gum resin from kinds of ferula. [ME f. L, f. Gk *khalbanē*, prob. of Semitic orig.]

gāle[1] *n.* (**Sweet-**)~, bog myrtle. [OE *gagel* (*le*), = MDu. *gaghel*]

gāle[2] *n.* Very strong wind, esp. (on Beaufort scale) of 35–50 m.p.h.; (Naut.) storm; outburst, esp. of laughter; (poet.) gentle breeze. [16th c.; orig. unkn.]

gā'lė|a *n.* (Bot. & Zool.) Structure like helmet in shape, function, or position; so ~ATE[2], **~āt**ED[1], *adjs.* [L, = helmet]

galē'na *n.* Commonest lead ore, lead sulphide. [L, = lead ore (in partly purified state)]

galĕ'nĭc *a.*, **galĕ'nĭcal** *a.* & *n.* Of or according to Galen; (remedy) made of vegetable, not synthetic, components. [f. *Galen*, Gk physician of 2nd C. A.D. + -IC(AL)]

galère (galar') *n.* Coterie, (usu. undesirable) group of people; unexpected situation. [F, = galley, used fig. in Molière's *Scapin*]

Gălĭlē'an[1] *a.* Of Galileo; ~ **satellite,** one of Jupiter's four largest moons; ~ **telescope** (with bi-convex objective and bi-concave eyepiece). [f. *Galileo* Galilei, It. astronomer d. 1642 + -AN]

Gălĭlē'an[2] *a.* & *n.* **1.** *a.* Of Galilee; Christian. **2.** *n.* Native or inhabitant of Galilee; Christian; (derog.) Christ. [f. *Galilee* in Palestine + -AN]

gă'lilee *n.* Porch or chapel at entrance of church. [f. OF *galilée* f. med. L *galilea*, w. some ref. to *Galilee* in Palestine]

gălĭmă'tĭas (*or* -ā'shas) *n.* Confused or meaningless talk, rigmarole. [F, of unkn. orig.]

gă'lĭngāle (-ngg-) *n.* Aromatic rhizome of E. Asian plant of genus *Alpinia* or *Kaempferia*, formerly used in cookery and medicine; **(English)** ~, sedge (*Cyperus longus*) having root with similar properties. [OE *gallengar*, & f. OF *galingal* f. Arab. *ḵalanjān* f. Chin. *ko-liang-kiang* mild ginger from Ko in Canton]

gă'lĭot. See GALLIOT.

gă'lĭpŏt *n.* Hardened turpentine formed on stem of cluster pine. [F, of unkn. orig.]

gall[1] (gawl) *n.* **1.** Bile of animals; gall-bladder and its contents. **2.** (fig.) Anything bitter, bitterness, (*gall and wormwood*); asperity, rancour, (**dip** one's **pen in** ~, write virulently); (sl.) impudence. **3.** **~-bladder,** vessel containing bile after secretion by liver; **~'stone,** calculous formation in gall-bladder. [ON, = OE *gealla*, OS, OHG *galla* f. Gmc **gallam* etc.]

gall[2] (gawl) *n.* Sore produced by chafing; mental soreness, exasperation or its cause; place rubbed bare, flaw; bare spot in field or coppice. [ME, f. MLG, MDu. *galle* (OE *gealla* sore on horse, ON *galli* fault)]

gall[3] (gawl) *v.t.* Rub sore, injure by rubbing; vex, annoy, harass, humiliate, whence ~'ING[2] *a.* [ME, f. prec., orig. as back form. f. *gall*ED[2]]

gall[4] (gawl) *n.* ~(**'nut**), excrescence produced by insect, fungus, or bacterium, on plant, esp. on oak; **~-fly, ~-mite, ~-wasp,** (producing galls). [ME, f. OF *galle* f. L *galla*]

gall. *abbr.* gallon(s).

Gă'lla *n.* & *a.* (Member or language) of group of Hamitic peoples in equatorial Africa. [perh. f. Arab. *galiẓ* wild]

gă'llant (*or* in senses 3, 5, 6, 7, gală'nt) *a., n.,* & *v.* **1.** *a.* (Of ship, horse, etc.) grand, fine, stately; (arch.) finely dressed. **2.** Brave, chivalrous; (used as conventional epithet of Member of Parliament who was in the Services: *the honourable and gallant member*). **3.** Markedly attentive to women; concerned with sexual love, amatory. **4.** Hence ~LY[2] *adv.* **5.** *n.* (arch.) Man of fashion, fine gentleman; ladies' man, lover, paramour. **6.** *v.t.* Flirt with; escort, act as cavalier to, (lady). **7.** *v.i.* Play the gallant; flirt *with.* [ME, f. OF *galant* part. of *galer* make merry (*gale* rejoicing); see -ANT]

gă'llantrў *n.* Bravery, dashing courage; courtliness, devotion to women; polite act or speech; conduct of a gallant, sexual intrigue, immorality. [f. F *galanterie* (as prec.; see -ERY)]

gă'llėon *n.* (Hist.) Vessel shorter and higher than galley; ship of war (usu. Spanish); large Spanish ship used in American trade. [f. MDu. *galjoen* f. F *galion* (*galie* galley), or f. Sp. *galeón*; see -OON]

gă'llerў *n.,* & *v.t.* **1.** *n.* Covered space for walking in partly open at side, portico, colonnade; balcony; long narrow passage in thickness of wall or supported on corbels, open towards interior of building. **2.** Platform projecting from inner wall of church, hall, etc., providing extra room for spectators etc. or reserved for musicians etc. (*minstrels' gallery*); (Theatr.) highest balcony thus constructed, persons there seated, least refined part of audience (**play to the ~,** appeal to unrefined tastes); group of spectators at golf-match etc. **3.** Long narrow room (e.g. SHOOTING-*gallery*), passage, corridor; room or building used for showing works of art; (Mil & Mining) horizontal underground passage; **~ tray,** silver tray with raised rim, used to carry glasses etc. **4.** *v.t.* Provide, pierce, etc., with gallery or galleries. [f. F *galerie* f. It. *galleria* f. med. L *galeria*, perh. alt. of *galilea* GALILEE]

gă'lley *n.* **1.** (Hist.) Low flat single-decked vessel using sails and oars, and usu. rowed by slaves or criminals; ancient Greek or Roman warship with one or more banks of oars; large open rowing-boat, e.g. that used by captain of man-of-war; **in this** etc. **~** (unexpected situation; after Molière, see GALÈRE). **2.** Ship's or aircraft's kitchen. **3.** (Print.) Oblong tray for set type; corresponding part of composing-machine; ~ (**proof**), proof in form of long single-column strips from type in galley, not in sheets or pages. **4. ~-slave,** person condemned to row in galley, (fig.) drudge. [ME, f. OF *galie* f. med. L *galea*, med. Gk *galaia*]

***gă'lley-wĕst** *adv.* (colloq.) **Knock ~,** knock askew, confuse, defeat. [f. E dial. *colly-west*(*on*), perh. f. village in Northamptonshire]

găllĭă'mbĭc *a.* & *n.* (Verse) in metre of Tennyson's *Boadicea*, etc., formed of two iambic dimeters. [f. L *galliambus* song of *Galli* or priests of Cybele; see IAMBUS, -IC]

gă'llĭard *n.* (Hist.) Quick and lively dance in triple time for two persons; music for it. [ME, f. OF *gaillard* valiant, perh. f. Rom. **gallia* strength, of Celt. orig.]

gă'llĭc[1] *a.* (Chem.) ~ **acid** (obtained from gall-nuts etc. and used in making ink). [f. F *gallique* (*galle* GALL[4]; see -IC)]

Gă'llĭc[2] *a.* Of the Gauls, Gaulish; (often joc.) French, whence **Gă'llĭc**ISM (4) *n.*, **Gă'llĭc**IZE (2, 3) *v.t.* & *i.* [f. L *Gallicus* (*Gallus* a Gaul; see -IC)]

Gă'llĭcan *a.* & *n.* **1.** (Adherent) of the school of Roman Catholics (orig. in France) claiming partial autonomy with regard to pope (opp. ULTRAMONTANE); hence ~ISM (3), ~IST (2), *ns.* **2.** *a.* Of the ancient church of Gaul or France. [F, or f. L *Gallicanus* (as prec.; see -AN)]

gă'llĭcė *adv.* In French. [L, = in Gaulish]

găllĭgă'skĭns (-z) *n. pl.* (joc.) Breeches, trousers. [orig. wide hose of 16th–17th c., f. obs. F *garguesque* for *greguesque* f. It. *grechesca* fem. of *grechesco* Greek (see -ESQUE)]

găllĭmau'frў *n.* Heterogeneous mixture, jumble, medley. [f. F *galimafrée*, of unkn. orig.]

găllĭnā'ceous (-sh*u*s) *a.* Of the order Galliformes, incl. domestic poultry, pheasants, partridges, etc. [f. L *gallinaceus* (*gallina* hen f. *gallus* cock; see -ACEOUS)]

gă'llĭnūle *n.* Small aquatic bird of genus *Gallinula*. [f. mod. L *gallinula*, dim. of L *gallina* hen (see prec., -ULE)]

Gă'llĭō *n.* (*pl.* **~s**). Indifferent easy-going person. [name of Roman proconsul (Acts 18:17)]

gă'llĭot, gă'lĭot, *n.* Dutch cargo-boat or fishing--vessel; small (usu. Mediterranean) galley. [ME, f. OF *galiote* f. It. *galeotta* f. med. L *galea* galley]

gă'llĭpŏt *n.* Small pot of earthenware, metal, etc., used for ointments etc. [prob. f. GALLEY, as being brought in galleys from the Mediterranean, + POT[1]]

gă'llĭum *n.* Soft bluish-white metallic element. [mod. L, perh. f. L *gallus* cock, transl. of *Lecoq* de Boisbaudran, name of its discoverer (1875) + -IUM]

găllĭvă'nt *v.i.* (colloq.) Gad about; flirt. [perh. corrupt. of GALLANT 7]

gă'llĭwasp (-ŏsp) *n.* W. Ind. lizard (*Diploglossus monotropis*). [18th c., of unkn. orig.]

Găllō- *comb. form.* **1.** French, as: ~MA'NIA *n.*, ~MA'NIAC *a.* & *n.*, ~PHIL(E), ~PHOBE, *ns.* & *adjs.*, ~PHO'BIA *n.* **2.** Gaul, as: **~-Ro'man** *n.* & *a.*, (inhabitant or language) of Gaul when under Roman rule. [f. L *Gallus* a Gaul + -O-]

gă'llon *n.* Measure of capacity, = 8 pints (‖**imperial ~**, ‖~, 4546 c.c.; ‖**wine ~**, ***~**, 3785 c.c.) for liquids, ‖corn, etc., whence ~AGE (1) *n.*; (colloq., usu. in *pl.*) large amount. [ME, f. ONF *galon*, OF *jalon*, f. Rom. **gallone*; cf. med. L *galletum*, *galleta*, OF *jaloie* liquid measure]

gallōō'n *n.* Narrow close-woven braid of gold, silver, silk, cotton, nylon, etc., for binding dresses etc. [f. F *galon* (*galonner* trim with braid, of unkn. orig.)]

gă'llop *n.* & *v.* **1.** *n.* Horse's or other quadruped's fastest pace, with all feet off ground together in each stride (**full ~, at a ~,** going thus); ride at this pace; track or ground for such riding. **2.** *v.i.* (Of horse or its rider, or of other quadruped) go at a gallop; read, recite, or talk, fast (*through*, *over*); move or progress rapidly (*galloping consumption, inflation*). **3.** *v.t.* Make (horse etc.) gallop. **4.** Hence ~ER[1] *n.* [f. OF *galop*(*er*); see WALLOP]

Gă'llophĭl etc. See GALLO-.

gă'lloway (-*o*-) *n.* Horse of small strong breed from Galloway; small horse; one of a breed of cattle from Galloway. [f. *G~*, area in S.W. Scotland]

gă'llows (-ōz) *n. pl.* (usu. treated as *sing.*) Structure, usu. of two uprights and cross-piece, for the hanging of criminals; punishment by hanging; **~-bird,** person fit to be hanged; **~ humour** (grim and ironical); **~-tree,** gallows. [ME, f. ON *gálgi* = OE *gealga*, OS, OHG *galgo*, Goth. *galga* f. Gmc **galgon*]

Gă'llup *n.* **~ poll,** assessment of public opinion by questioning representative sample, esp. as basis of forecasts of voting etc. [f. G. H. ~, Amer. statistician b. 1901]

gă'llusės (-z) *n. pl.* (dial. & U.S.) Trouser--braces. [pl. of *gallus* var. of GALLOWS]

galōō't *n.* (colloq.) (Strange or clumsy) person. [19th c. Naut. sl.; orig. unkn.]

gă'lop *n.*, & *v.i.* **1.** *n.* Lively dance in duple time; music for it. **2.** *v.i.* Perform this dance. [F; see GALLOP]

galōr'e *adv.* In abundance (*whisky galore*). [f. Ir. *go leór* to sufficiency]

galŏ'sh, ||golŏ'sh, *n.* Overshoe usu. of rubber to keep shoe clean or dry. [ME, f. OF *galoche* f. LL *gallicula* small Gallic shoe]

galŭ'mph *v.i.* (colloq.) Go prancing in triumph; move noisily or clumsily. [made by Lewis Carroll perh. after GALLOP, TRIUMPHANT]

gălvă'n|ic *a.* **1.** Of, produced by, as of, galvanism (**~ic battery, pile,** former names for types of primary battery; **~ic electricity,** electricity from a primary battery). **2.** (fig.) Sudden and remarkable (*had a galvanic effect*); stimulating; full of energy (*a galvanic performance*). **3.** Hence ~ICALLY *adv.* [f. foll. + -IC]

gă'lvan|ĭsm *n.* (Hist.) electricity from a primary battery; use of this or other direct--current electricity for medical purposes; hence ~IST (3) *n.* [f. F *galvanisme* (L. *Galvani*, It. physiologist d. 1798); see -ISM]

gă'lvanīz|e, -īs|e (-īz), *v.t.* **1.** Stimulate by or as if by electricity; (fig.) rouse (*into* action etc.) by shock or excitement. **2.** Coat (iron) with zinc (usu. without the use of electricity) to protect it from rust; hence ~A'TION *n.* [f. F *galvaniser* (as prec.; see -IZE)]

gălvanŏ'mėter *n.* Instrument for detecting and measuring small electric currents. [f. GALVANISM + -O- + -METER]

gă'lvō *n.* (*pl.* ~s). (colloq.) = prec. [abbr.]

gă'mba *n.* ~ **(stop)**, organ stop with string tone. [abbr. f. (earlier sense) VIOLA[1] *da gamba*]

gămbā'de, gămbā'dō (*pl.* **-os** *or* **-oes**), *n.* Horse's leap or bound; fantastic movement; escapade. [*-ade* F f. It. *gambata* (*gamba* leg; see -ADE 1); *-ado* f. Sp. *gambada* (*gamba* leg; see -ADO)]

gă'mbĭer *n.* Astringent extract of Eastern plant used in tanning etc. [f. Malay *gambir* name of the plant]

gă'mbĭt *n.* **1.** Chess opening in which player sacrifices pawn or piece to secure advantage. **2.** (fig.) Opening move in discussion etc.; trick, device. [earlier *gambett* f. It. *gambetto* tripping up (*gamba* leg); *-it* = F *gambit*, Sp. *-ito*]

gă'mbl|e *v.* & *n.* **1.** *v.i.* Play games of chance for money, esp. for high stakes; take great risks to secure great results in war, finance, etc.; **~e on,** act in hope of (*gamble on its being fine tomorrow*); hence ~ER[1] *n.* **2.** *v.t.* **~e away,** lose by gambling. **3.** *n.* Gambling; risky undertaking or attempt. [f. obs. *gamel* to sport, *gamene* GAME[3]]

gămbo'ge (-ōō'zh *or* -ō'zh) *n.* Gum resin from various E. Asian trees used as yellow pigment and as purgative. [f. mod. L *gambaugium* f. *Cambodia*]

gă'mbol *n.*, & *v.i.* (||-ll-). Caper, frisk. [f. GAMBADE]

gă'mbrel *n.* ~ **(roof)**, roof like mansard but with gable-like ends. [f. ONF *gamberel* (*gambier* forked stick f. *gambe* leg), f. resemblance to shape of horse's hind leg]

gāme[1] *n.* **1.** (Form of) contest played according to rules and decided by skill, strength, or luck; ROUND[1] *game*; SQUARE[2] *game*; **be on, off,** one's ~, be playing well, badly; **beat** person **at his own ~**, outdo him in his chosen procedure; *the* NAME[1] *of the game*; **not in the ~**, unlikely to succeed; **play the ~**, (lit. or fig.) observe the rules, behave honourably; **~ that two can play,** behaviour that can be copied to its originator's disadvantage; **play a good, poor, ~**, be skilful or not. **2.** (in *pl.*) (In antiquity) athletic, dramatic, and musical contests, gladiatorial etc. shows; athletic contests (*Highland Games*, OLYMPIC *Games*); athletics or sports as organized in school etc. **3.** Scheme, undertaking, etc., followed up like a game (*was playing a deep, double, winning, losing,* etc., *game*; *so that's your* LITTLE *game*; *spoilt my game*); **the ~ is up,** success is now impossible; **play** person's **~**, advance his schemes unintentionally; *game not worth the* CANDLE; **give the ~ away,** reveal intentions. **4.** Policy, line of action; **the ~**, (sl.) prostitution or thieving. **5.** (in *pl.*) Dodges, tricks, (*none of your games!*). **6.** Single portion of play forming a scoring unit in some contests, e.g. bridge or tennis, (**~ all,** one game scored to each side); equipment for a game; winning score in game (**~ and,** short for *game and set* in tennis); state of score in game (*the game is four all, love three,* etc.). **7.** Jest (**make ~ of,** ridicule); diversion, spell of play (*a game of ball*); piece of fun (*was only playing a game with you*). **8.** Hunted animal, quarry, object of pursuit or attack (**fair ~**, legitimately to be pursued or attacked); (collect.) wild animals, birds, fish, etc., hunted for sport or food, flesh of these, (**big ~**, lions, elephants, etc.). **9.** Kept flock (of swans). **10. ~ act, law,** (usu. in *pl.*), enactment regulating killing and preservation of game; **~'bag, ~'book,** (for holding, recording, game killed by sportsman); **~ ball,** state of game in fives etc. at which one point may win; **~ chips,** thin round potato chips served with game; **~'cock, ~'fowl,** (of kind bred for cock-fighting); **~'keeper,** man employed to breed and take care of game, prevent poaching, etc.; **~ law,** = *game act*; **~ licence** (to kill, or deal in, game); **~ point,** state of game when one side needs only one more point to win it; **~-preserver,** landowner etc. who breeds game and applies game laws strictly; **~-tenant,** lessee of shooting or fishing; **~(s) theory,** mathematical analysis of conflicts in war, economics, games of skill, etc.; **~-warden,** person locally supervising game and hunting. [OE *gamen*, = OS, OHG, ON *gaman*]

gāme[2] *a.* Like a gamecock, spirited (DIE[2] *game*; **as ~ as Ned Kelly,** (Austral. colloq.) very brave); having the spirit or energy *to* do; valiantly ready *for*; hence ~'LY[2] (-mlĭ) *adv.*, ~'NESS (-mn-) *n.* [f. GAME[1] in obs. sense 'fighting spirit']

gāme[3] *v.i.* Play at games of chance for money, gamble; **gaming-house, -table,** (frequented for gambling); hence ~'STER (-ms-) *n.* [ME, f. GAME[1]]

gāme[4] *a.* (Of leg, arm, etc.) lame, crippled. [18th c. dial., of unkn. orig.]

gă'melăn *n.* E. Ind. orchestra, mainly of percussion instruments; kind of xylophone used in this. [Jav.]

gā'mes|man (-mzm-) *n.* (*pl.* **~men**). Exponent of gamesmanship; hence **~man**SHIP *n.*, art or practice of winning games or other contests by psychological means rather than skill. [f. GAME[1] + *-sman* as in SPORTSMAN]

gā'mesome (-ms-) *a.* Merry, sportive; hence ~LY[2] (-mlĭ) *adv.*, ~NESS (-mn-) *n.* [ME, f. GAME[1] + -SOME[1]]

gămėtă'ngĭ|um (-nj-) *n.* (*pl.* **~a**). Organ in which gametes are formed. [f. as foll. + Gk *aggeion* vessel]

gamē'te (*or* gă'mēt) *n.* (Biol.) Mature germ-cell, which unites with another in sexual reproduction; hence **gamĕ'**TIC *a.* [f. mod. L f. Gk *gametē* wife (*gamos* marriage)]

gamē'to|phȳte *n.* Gamete-producing form of plant with alternation of generations; hence **~phȳ'tic** *a.* [f. prec. + -O- + -PHYTE]
gă'min (*or* gă'măṅ) *n.* (Street) urchin; impudent child. [F]
gami'ne (-ē'n) *n.* Girl gamin; small attractively informal, mischievous or elfish young woman. [F]
gă'mma *n.* Third Greek letter (Γ, γ) = g; (Astron.) third brightest star in a constellation; third-class mark in examination (**~ plus, ~ minus,** rather better, worse, than average third-class); species of Y-moth with γ-shaped markings; **~ radiation, ~ rays,** X-rays of very short wavelength emitted by radioactive substances. [ME, f. Gk]
gammā'dĭon *n.* Arrangement of shapes of capital gamma (Γ), esp. of four as swastika or as hollow Greek cross. [late Gk (as prec.)]
gă'mmer *n.* (arch.) (Rustic name for) old woman. [prob. contr. of GODmother; *ga-* by assoc. w. *grandmother*; cf. GAFFER, GOSSIP]
gă'mmon¹ *n.*, & *v.t.* **1.** *n.* Bottom piece of flitch of bacon including hind leg; ham of pig cured like bacon. **2.** *v.t.* Cure (bacon). [f. ONF *gambon* (*gambe* leg; cf. JAMB)]
gă'mmon² *n.*, & *v.t.* **1.** *n.* Kind of victory scoring two games at backgammon. **2.** *v.t.* Defeat thus. [app. = ME *gamen* GAME¹]
gă'mmon³ *n.* & *v.* **1.** *n.* Humbug, deception. **2.** *v.i.* Talk speciously; pretend. **3.** *v.t.* Hoax, deceive. [perh. as prec.]
gă'mmon⁴ *v.t.*, & *n.* (Naut.) **1.** *v.t.* Lash (bowsprit) to stem. **2.** *n.* **~(ing)**, rope etc. used in such lashing. [perh. f. GAMMON¹, w. ref. to tying-up of ham]
gă'mmȳ *a.* (sl.) = GAME⁴. [f. dial. form of GAME⁴]
||**gămp** *n.* (colloq.) Umbrella, esp. large untidy one. [f. Mrs. *Gamp* in Dickens's *Martin Chuzzlewit*]
gă'mut *n.* **1.** (Mus.) Lowest note in medieval sequence of hexachords, = modern G on lowest line of bass staff; whole series of notes used in medieval or modern music; major diatonic scale; people's or period's recognized scale; voice's or instrument's compass. **2.** Whole series or range or scope of anything (*the whole gamut of crime; run up and down the gamut*). [f. med. L *gamma ut* (GAMMA taken as name for note one tone lower than A of classical scale, *ut* first of six arbitrary names of notes forming hexachord, being the italicized syllables of a 7th-c. Latin hymn: *Ut* queant laxis *re*sonare fibris *Mi*ra gestorum *fa*muli tuorum, *Sol*ve polluti *la*bii reatum, Sancte Iohannes)]
gā'm|ȳ *a.* = GAME²; having flavour or scent of game kept till it is high; *scandalous, sensational; hence **~ĭly**² *adv.*, **~ĭness** *n.* [f. GAME¹,² + -Y²]
gă'nder *n.*, & *v.i.* **1.** *n.* Male goose (**sauce for the goose is sauce for the ~**, used in retorting an argument etc. on its first user); fool, simpleton. **2.** *n.*, & *v.i.* (sl.) Look, glance. [OE *gan(d)ra*, = MLG *ganre*, LG, Du. *gander*; cogn. w. GANNET]
gă'ndȳ *a.* **~ dancer,** (sl.) railway maintenance workman. [20th c.; orig. uncert.]
găng¹ *n.* & *v.* **1.** *n.* Company of workmen, or of slaves or prisoners; band of persons acting or going about together, esp. for criminal purpose or (colloq.) other purpose causing disapproval; set *of* tools etc. arranged to work simultaneously; **~-bang, ~-shag,** (sl.) successive copulation of group of men with one woman on same occasion; **~'board, ~'plank,** movable plank usu. with cleats nailed on it for walking into or out of boat etc.; **~'land,** domain of gangsters. **2.** *v.i.* Join *up with*, act in concert *with*; **~ up on,** (colloq.) combine against; **~-up** *n.*, (colloq.) act of ganging up. **3.** *v.t.* Arrange (tools etc.) to work in co-ordination. [f. ON *gangr*, *ganga* GOING¹, = OE, OS, OHG *gang*, Goth. *gaggs*, Gmc f. **gangan* GO¹]
găng² *v.i.* (Sc.) Go; **~ agley,** (of plan etc.) go wrong. [OE *gangan*; cf. GANG¹, GO¹]
||**gă'nger** (-ng-) *n.* Foreman of gang of workmen. [f. GANG¹ + -ER¹]
Găngĕ'tĭc (-nj-) *a.* Of the Ganges. [f. L *Gangeticus* f. Gk *Gaggēs*; see -IC]
gă'ng-găng *n.* (Austral.) Small grey cockatoo, the male being red-crested. [Aboriginal]
gă'ngle (-nggel) *v.i.* Move ungracefully. [back form. f. foll.]
gă'nglĭng, gă'nglȳ, (-ngg-) *a.* (Of person) loosely built, lanky. [f. **gangle* frequent. of GANG²]
gă'nglĭ|on (-ngg-) *n.* (*pl.* **~a** *or* **~ons**). Enlargement or knot on nerve, containing assemblage of nerve-cells; mass of grey matter in central nervous system forming a nerve-nucleus; (Med.) cyst esp. on tendon-sheath; (fig.) centre of force, activity, or interest; hence **~onātED**¹, **gănglĭŏ'nIC** (-ngg-), **~FORM,** *adjs.* [f. Gk *gagglion*]
gă'ngrēne (-ngg-) *n.* & *v.* **1.** *n.* Necrosis, usu. with decomposition, of part of the body, usu. caused by obstructed circulation; (fig.) moral corruption; hence **gă'ngrėnOUS** (-ngg-) *a.* **2.** *v.i.* & *t.* Become affected, affect, with gangrene. [f. F *gangrène* f. L f. Gk *gaggraina*]
gă'ngster *n.* Member of a gang of violent criminals; hence **~ISM** (1) *n.* [f. GANG¹ + -STER]
găngue (-ng) *n.* Valueless earth etc. in which ore is found. [F, f. G *gang* lode = GANG¹]
gă'ngway *n.* & *int.* **1.** *n.* ||Passage esp. between rows of seats (in House of Commons, cross-passage half-way down giving access to back benches; members **above, below, ~** are more, less, closely associated with official policy of their party); passage etc. on ship, esp. platform connecting quarterdeck and forecastle; opening in bulwarks by which ship is entered or left; bridge laid from ship to shore, on building site, etc. **2.** *int.* Make way! [17th c., f. GANG¹ + WAY]
gă'nĭster *n.* Close-grained hard siliceous stone found in the lower coal-measures of South Yorkshire, and used for furnace-linings. [19th c.; orig. unkn.]
gă'nja *n.* Marijuana. [f. Hindi *gānjhā*]
gă'nnėt *n.* Sea-bird of genus *Sula*, esp. solan goose, *Sula bassana*, whence **~RY** (3) *n.*; (sl.) greedy person. [OE *ganot*, = MHG *ganiz, genz*, OHG *ganazzo* f. Gmc **ganitaz*, **ganoton*; cogn. w. GANDER]
gă'noid *a.* & *n.* **1.** *a.* (Of fish-scale) enamelled, smooth and bright; having ganoid scales. **2.** *n.* Ganoid fish. [f. F *ganoïde* f. Gk *ganos* brightness; see -OID]
***gă'ntlėt.** See GAUNTLET².
gă'ntrȳ *n.* Structure supporting travelling crane, railway signals, equipment to prepare rocket for launching, etc.; (also **gau'ntry**) wooden stand for barrels. [prob. f. dial. form of GALLON + TREE]
||**gaol** (jāl), **jail,** *n.*, & *v.t.* (**g-** in official use, **g-** and **j-** in literary use, **j-** in U.S.). **1.** *n.* Public prison for detention of persons committed by process of law; confinement in this; **~'bird,** prisoner, habitual criminal, rogue; **~'break,** escape from gaol; **~ delivery,** clearing of gaol esp. formerly at assizes by trying all prisoners awaiting trial; **~ fever,** virulent typhus formerly endemic in gaols. **2.** *v.t.* Put in gaol. [ME, f. ONF *ga(i)ole* & OF *jaiole, jeole* f. Rom. dim. of L *cavea* CAGE]
||**gao'ler** (jā'l-), **jai'ler, jai'lor,** *n.* (see prec.) Man in charge of gaol or prisoners in it. [f. as prec. + -ER² (2)]

găp *n.* Breach in hedge or wall; gorge, pass; unfilled space or interval, blank, break in continuity (**bridge, close, fill, stop, a ~,** make up deficiency; **~-toothed** *a.*, having gaps between teeth); wide (usu. undesirable) divergence in views, sympathies, development, etc., (CREDIBILITY *gap*, GENERATION *gap*); hence **~PED**[2] (-pt), **~'PY**[2], *adjs.* [ME, f. ON, = chasm, cogn. w. foll.]

gāpe *v.i.*, & *n.* **1.** *v.i.* Open mouth wide, (of mouth, oyster, wound, chasm, etc.) open or be open wide; split, part asunder; stare, gaze curiously, *at*; yawn. **2.** *n.* Yawn; open-mouthed stare; **the ~s,** disease of birds with gaping as symptom, caused by nematode **~'worm** in windpipe, (joc.) fit of yawning. **3.** Expanse of open mouth or beak; part of beak that opens; rent, opening. [ME, f. ON *gapa* cogn. w. MHG *gaffen*]

gā'per *n.* In vbl senses; the comber fish, which gapes when dead; bivalve mollusc of genus *Mya*, with shell open at one or both ends; (colloq.) easy catch at cricket. [f. GAPE + -ER[1]]

gar. See GARFISH.

gă'rage (*or* -ahzh *or* -ahj) *n.*, & *v.t.* **1.** *n.* Building or shed for storage of motor vehicle(s); establishment selling petrol etc., often also repairing and selling motor vehicles. **2.** *v.t.* Put or keep (motor vehicle) in garage. [F (*garer* shelter; see -AGE)]

garb *n.*, & *v.t.* **1.** *n.* Dress, costume, esp. of distinctive kind; way one is dressed. **2.** *v.t.* Attire; (usu. in *pass.* or *refl.*) put (esp. distinctive) clothes on (person). [f. obs. F *garbe* f. It. *garbo* f. Gmc, cogn. w. GEAR]

gar'bage *n.* Refuse, filth; domestic waste (***~ can,** dustbin); foul or rubbishy literature etc. [AF; orig. unkn.]

gar'ble *v.t.* Make (usu. unfair or malicious) selections from (facts, statements, etc.); mutilate in order to misrepresent; unintentionally distort or confuse (facts, statement, message, etc.). [f. It. *garbellare* f. Arab. *ġarbala* sift (cf. *ġirbāl* sieve), perh. f. LL *cribellare* to sieve f. L *cribrum* sieve]

gar'board (-berd) *n.* **~ (strake),** first range of planks laid on ship's bottom next to keel; corresponding plates in iron ship. [f. Du. *gaarboord* (perh. as GATHER, BOARD[1])]

garçon (gar'sawn) *n.* Waiter in French restaurant, hotel, etc. [F, lit. 'boy']

gar'den *n.*, & *v.i.* **1.** *n.* Piece of ground devoted to growing flowers, fruit, or vegetables (KITCHEN *garden*; ||MARKET[1] *garden*); **everything in the ~ is lovely,** (colloq.) all is well; **lead up the ~ (path),** (colloq.) entice, mislead. **2.** Ornamental grounds for public resort (*botanical, zoological,* etc., *garden* or *gardens*); similar place with service of refreshments (*beer, tea, garden*); *large public hall; especially fertile region (**the ~ of England,** Kent, Vale of Evesham, etc.); ||(usu. in *pl.* w. name prefixed, as *Onslow, Spring, Gardens*) street, square, etc.; **the G~,** philosophy or school of Epicurus (cf. ACADEMY, LYCEUM, PORCH). **3.** (*attrib.*, with or without hyphen) Cultivated, not wild (*garden plants*; *garden-cress*); **common or ~,** (colloq.) ordinary; **~ centre,** establishment where gardening tools, plants, etc., are sold; **~ chair, ~ roller, ~ seat,** (for use in a garden); **~ city,** industrial or other town laid out systematically with spacious and garden-like surroundings; so **||~ suburb, ||~ village**; **~ party,** social event on lawn or in garden; ***G~ State,** New Jersey; **~ stuff,** vegetables etc. from garden; **~ warbler,** a woodland bird (*Sylvia borin*). **4.** Hence **~E'SQUE** *a.* **5.** *v.i.* Cultivate, work in, a garden; hence **~ING**[1] (1) *n.* [ME, f. ONF *gardin* (OF *jardin*) f. Rom. **gardino* f. Gmc **gardon*; cf. YARD[2]]

gar'dener *n.* Person who gardens; person employed to tend a garden; (**jobbing**) **~,** employee working in garden at intervals; **~-bird,** bower-bird making 'garden' of moss etc. in front of bower; **~'s garters,** ribbon-grass. [ME, f. ONF **gardinier* (OF *jard-*), f. as prec. + -ER[2] (2)]

gardē'nia *n.* Tree or shrub of genus *Gardenia*, with large white or yellow flowers and usu. fragrant scent; flower of this. [mod. L, f. name of Dr. A. *Garden*, Sc. naturalist d. 1791 + -IA[1]]

gar'efowl (gar'f-) *n.* The great AUK. [f. Icel. *geirfugl* (*geir* of doubtful meaning; see FOWL)]

gar'fish *n.* (*pl.* same). Fish with long spearlike snout, of genus *Belone* (needlefish), **Lepisosteus* (gar), or (Austral. & N.Z.) *Hyporhynchus* (halfbeak). [app. f. OE *gār* spear + *fisc* FISH[1]]

gar'ganey *n.* A duck (*Anas querquedula*). [f. It., dial. var. of *garganello*]

gargă'ntūan *a.* Enormous, gigantic. [f. *Gargantua* giant in Rabelais's book so named + -AN]

gar'gėt (-g-) *n.* Inflammation of cow's or ewe's udder; *pokeweed. [perh. f. obs. *garget* throat f. OF *gargate, -guete*]

gar'gle *v.* & *n.* **1.** *v.t.* & *i.* Wash (mouth and throat), esp. for medicinal purposes, with liquid kept in motion by breath; make sound as when doing this. **2.** *n.* Liquid used thus. [f. F *gargouiller* (*gargouille*; see foll.)]

gar'goyle *n.* Grotesque spout usu. in form of human or animal mouth, head, or body, projecting from gutter of (esp. Gothic) building to carry water clear of wall. [f. OF *gargouille* throat, gargoyle]

găriba'ldi (-baw'l-) *n.* Kind of woman's or child's loose blouse, orig. of bright red material; ||biscuit containing layer of currants; *small Californian fish (*Hypsypops rubicundus*). [f. (red shirts of) G. *Garibaldi* (It. patriot d. 1882) and his followers]

gar'ish *a.* Obtrusively bright, showy; gaudy, over-decorated; hence **~LY**[2] *adv.*, **~NESS** *n.* [16th c. *gaurish* app. irreg. f. obs. *gaure* stare + -ISH[1]]

gar'land *n.*, & *v.t.* **1.** *n.* Wreath of flowers, leaves, etc., worn on head or hung on something as decoration; distinction, palm, prize, for victory etc.; anthology, miscellany; metal etc. object resembling garland. **2.** *v.t.* Crown with garland; deck with garlands; serve as garland to. [ME, f. OF *ger-, garlande*, of unkn. orig.]

gar'lic *n.* (Plant of genus *Allium* with) bulbous strong-smelling pungent-tasting root used as flavouring in cookery; hence **~KY**[2] *a.* (esp. of smell). [OE *gārleac* (*gār* spear; see LEEK)]

gar'ment *n.*, & *v.t.* **1.** *n.* Article of dress; (in *pl.*) clothes; outward and visible covering of anything. **2.** *v.t.* (rhet., usu. in *p.p.*) Attire. [ME f. OF *garnement* (as GARNISH; see -MENT)]

garn *int.* (colloq.) expr. disbelief or ridicule. [repr. Cockney pr. of *go on*]

gar'ner *v.t.*, & *n.* **1.** *v.t.* Store, deposit; collect. **2.** *n.* (literary). Storehouse, granary, (lit. or fig.). [ME, v. f. n. f. OF *gernier* f. L *granarium* GRANARY]

gar'nėt[1] *n.* Vitreous silicate mineral, of which transparent deep-red kind is used as gem. [ME, f. OF *grenat* f. med. L *granatum* POMEGRANATE, f. resemblance to the pulp of the fruit]

Gar'nėt[2] *n.* (**All**) **Sir ~,** (sl.) satisfactory. [f. Sir ~ Wolseley, Brit. mil. commander d. 1913]

gar'nish *v.t.*, & *n.* **1.** *v.t.* Decorate, embellish, (esp. dish for table); (Law) serve notice on (person) for purpose of legally seizing money belonging to debtor or defendant, summon (person) as party to litigation started between others; hence **~MENT** *n.* **2.** *n.* **~(ing),** decorative or savoury addition, esp. to dish for table, or (fig.) of literary embellishments. [ME, f. OF *garnir* (-ISH²) f. Gmc **warnjan* guard]

gar̂nĭshee′ *n.*, & *v.t.* (Law). **1.** *n.* Person garnished. **2.** *v.t.* Garnish (person); attach (money etc.) by way of garnishment. [f. prec. + -EE]

gar̂′nĭture *n.* Appurtenances, accessories; adornment, trimmings esp. of dish. [F (as GARNISH; see -URE)]

garŏ′tte. See GARROTTE.

gar̂′pīke *n.* Needlefish or gar (see GARFISH). [f. *gar* + PIKE³]

gă′rrėt *n.* Room (esp. wretched) on top floor or partly or entirely in roof; attic; hence ~EER′ *n.*, dweller in garret, esp. literary hack. [ME, f. OF *garite* watch-tower (*garir* f. Gmc **warjan* defend)]

gă′rrĭson *n.*, & *v.t.* **1.** *n.* Troops stationed in fortress, town, etc., to defend it; **~ town** (having permanent garrison). **2.** *v.t.* Furnish with or occupy as garrison; place (troops, soldier) on garrison duty. [ME, f. OF *garison* (*garir*; see GARRET, -ISON) defence, w. sense of F & obs. E *garnison* (GARNISH)]

gar(r)ŏ′tt|e, *garrŏ′t|e, *n.*, & *v.t.* **1.** *n.* Spanish method of capital punishment by strangulation; apparatus used in it; highway robbery in which victim is throttled. **2.** *v.t.* Execute or kill by strangulation; throttle in order to rob. [f. F *garrotter* or Sp. *garrotear* (*garrote* a cudgel, of unkn. orig.)]

gă′rrulous (-rōō-) *a.* Given to talk, esp. on unimportant matters; loquacious, wordy; (of bird, stream, etc.) chattering, babbling; hence or cogn. **garru′**LITY (-rōō′-), ~NESS, *ns.*, ~LY² *adv.* [f. L *garrulus* (*garrire* chatter) + -OUS]

Gă′rrȳ *n.* **~ oak,** a N. Amer. oak (*Quercus garryana*). [f. N. ~, Hudson's Bay Co. officer d. 1856]

gă′rrȳa *n.* Ornamental catkin-bearing evergreen shrub of genus *Garrya*. [mod. L, f. as prec. + -A 1]

gar̂′ter *n.*, & *v.t.* **1.** *n.* Band worn to keep a stocking up (‖**the G~,** (badge of) highest order in English knighthood, membership of this); ‖(*G~*) = *Garter King of Arms* (KING¹ 7); *suspender for sock or stocking; ***~-belt,** suspender belt; **~-snake,** striped snake of N. Amer. (*Thamnophis*) or S. Afr. (*Elaps*); **~ stitch,** plain knitting stitch or pattern, forming ridges in alternate rows. **2.** *v.t.* Fasten (stocking), encircle (leg), with garter. [ME, f. OF *gartier* (*garet* bend of knee, perh. f. Celt.)]

‖**gar̂th** *n.* **1.** (arch. or prov.) Close, yard; garden, paddock. **2.** Open space within cloisters. [ME, f. ON *garthr* = OE *geard* YARD²]

gar′uda (gar̂′ŏŏdah) *n.* Fabulous partly human bird of Indian myth; national emblem of Indonesia. [f. Skr. *garudá*]

găs¹ *n.* (*pl.* **~es** *pr.* gă′sĭz). **1.** Any airlike or completely elastic fluid (esp. one that does not become liquid or solid at ordinary temperatures, other gases being usu. called 'vapours'); such fluid, esp. COAL *gas*, or **natural ~** (found in earth's crust, not manufactured), used for lighting, heating, or cooking. **2.** *(colloq.) Petrol, gasoline [abbr.]; **step on the ~,** accelerate motor vehicle by pressing down accelerator pedal with foot, (fig.) hurry. **3.** (Mining) explosive mixture of firedamp with air; hydrogen, helium, etc., used to fill balloon or airship; nitrous oxide or other gas as (esp. dental) anaesthetic; (**poison**) ~, substance used to disable enemy in war. **4.** Jet of gas used for lighting. **5.** Empty talk, boasting, humbug, windbag eloquence. **6.** (sl.) Very attractive or impressive person or thing. **7.** Hence **gă′s**EOUS *a.*, **~′**ĬFY *v.t.*, **~**ĬFICA′TION *n.* **8.** **~′bag,** bag for holding gas, balloon's or airship's gas-container, (derog.) empty talker; **~ bracket,** pipe with gas-burner(s) projecting from wall; **~ chamber** (used to kill animals or prisoners by gas poisoning); **~ chromatography** (using carrier gas as moving medium); **~ cooker** (heated by gas); **~-cooled,** (of engine etc.) cooled by current of gas; **~ engine, motor,** internal combustion engine using mixture of gas and air as fuel; **~ fire,** domestic heater (usu. fixed) burning gas; **~-fitter,** workman providing house with **~-fittings,** apparatus for heating etc. with gas; **~ gangrene** (rapidly spreading, with evolution of gas); **~ helmet, ~ mask,** kinds of appliance including respirator worn as defence against poison gas; **~′holder,** large receptacle for storing gas, gasometer; **~′light,** light given by esp. coal gas, jet of burning gas; **~ lighter,** (1) device for igniting gas, (2) lighter for cigarettes etc. with gaseous fuel; **~ main,** main pipe supplying gas; **~′man,** man employed in manufacture of gas, collector of sums due for gas-supply, gas-fitter; **~ mask** (as *gas helmet*); **~ meter,** apparatus registering amount of gas consumed; **~ motor** (as *gas engine*); **~ oven,** = *gas cooker* or *gas chamber*; **~ poker,** hollow poker through which gas flows to be ignited and kindle fire; *gas*-PROOF²; ***~ range,** = *gas cooker*; **~ ring** (perforated, hollow, and fed with gas for cooking etc.); ***~ station,** petrol filling-station; **~ stove** (heated by gas); *gas*-TIGHT; **~ turbine** (driven by gas flow or by gas from combustion); **~′works,** manufactory of gas. [wd invented by J. B. van Helmont, Belgian chemist d. 1644, after Gk *khaos* chaos]

găs² *v.* (**-ss-**). **1.** *v.t.* Expose to gas; pass (thread, lace) through gas-flame to remove loose fibres; ***~ (up),** (colloq.) fill (motor-vehicle tank) with petrol; (in *p.p.*) killed or disabled by gas, (sl.) drunk. **2.** *v.i.* Talk emptily or boastfully; hence **~′**SER¹ *n.*, empty talker, (sl.) very attractive or impressive person or thing. [f. prec.]

Gă′scon *n.* Native of Gascony; braggart; so **gă̆scon**A′DE *n.*, boasting. [F, f. L *Vasco -onis*]

gă′sėous. See GAS¹ 7.

găsh¹ *n.*, & *v.t.* **1.** *n.* Long and deep slash, cut, or wound; cleft such as might be made by slashing cut; act of making such cut. **2.** *v.t.* Make gash in, cut. [16th c., var. of ME *garse* v. & n., f. OF **garce* (*garcer* scarify, wound)]

‖**găsh²** *a.* (sl.) Spare, extra. [20th c. Naut. sl.; orig. unkn.]

gă′sĭfȳ etc. See GAS¹ 7.

gă′skėt *n.* Small cord for securing furled sail to yard; strip of tow etc. for packing piston or caulking joint; flat sheet or ring of rubber, asbestos, etc., to seal junction of metal surfaces. [perh. alt. of obs. *gassit* f. F *garcette* little girl, thin rope]

gă′skĭn *n.* Hinder part of horse's thigh. [perh. erron. f. GALLIGASKINS]

gă′soline (-ēn), **gă′solēne,** *n.* **1.** Volatile inflammable liquid got by distilling petroleum and used for heating and lighting. **2.** *Petrol. [f. GAS¹ + -OL + -INE⁵, -ENE]

găsŏ′mėter *n.* Large reservoir in which gas is stored for distribution by pipes; (Chem.) vessel for holding gas. [f. F *gazomètre* (*gaz* GAS¹, *-mètre* -METER)]

gasp (gah-) *v.* & *n.* **1.** *v.i.* Catch breath, strain *for* air or breath, with open mouth as in exhaustion or astonishment. **2.** *v.t.* **~ life** etc. **away** or **out,** expire; **~ (out),** utter with gasps. **3.** Hence **~′**ER¹ *n.*, (esp., ‖sl.) (cheap) cigarette. **4.** *n.* Convulsive catching of breath; **at** one's **last ~,** at point of death, (fig.) exhausted. [ME, f. ON *geispa*; cf. *geip* idle talk]

gă′spereau (-rō; *or* -rō′) *n.* (*pl.* **-s** *or* **-x,** *pr.* -z).

(Can.) The alewife fish. [f. Can. F *gaspareau, gasparot*]

gă'ssў *a.* Of, full of, like, gas; (of talk etc.) empty, verbose. [f. GAS¹ + -Y²]

gă'steropŏd. Var. of GASTROPOD.

ga'sthaus (gah'st-hows) *n.* Small German inn or hotel. [G (*gast* GUEST, *haus* HOUSE¹)]

gă'strĭc *a.* Of the stomach; *gastric* INFLUENZA; ~ **juice,** thin clear nearly colourless acid fluid secreted by stomach glands, agent in digestion. [f. mod. L *gastricus* f. Gk (as foll.; see -IC)]

găstrō- *comb. form.* Stomach, as: **~-ente'ric,** of stomach and intestines; *gastro-enterI'TIS*; *gastrE'CTOMY*; *gastrI'TIS*; *ga'stroSCOPE*. [f. Gk *gastēr* -(*e*)*ros* stomach + -O-]

gă'stronōme *n.* Judge of good eating and drinking. [F, back form. f. *gastronomie*; see foll.]

găstrŏ'nomў *n.* Art and science of good eating and drinking; hence or cogn. **găstronŏ'mIC** *a.* [f. F *gastronomie* f. Gk *gastronomia* (GASTRO-, *-nomia* f. *nomos* law)]

gă'stropŏd *n.* Mollusc (e.g. snail, limpet) of class Gastropoda, with locomotive organ placed ventrally; hence **găstrŏ'podOUS** *a.* [f. F *gastéropode* f. mod. L *gasteropoda* f. as GASTRO- + Gk *pous podos* foot]

gă'stroscōpe. See GASTRO-.

gă'strula (-rōō-) *n.* (*pl.* ~*e*). (Zool.) Embryonic stage developing from blastula. [mod. L, f. Gk *gastēr* belly; see -ULE]

găt *n.* (sl.) Revolver or other firearm. [abbr. of GATLING]

gāte¹ *n.,* & *v.t.* **1.** *n.* Opening in wall of city, enclosure, or large building, made for entrance and exit and capable of being closed with barrier; mountain pass; means of entrance or exit; numbered place of access to aircraft at airport; (sl.) mouth; *(sl.) dismissal; ~ **of ivory, horn,** by which false, true, dreams come. **2.** Barrier closing the opening of a wall, road, or passage; wooden or iron framework, solid or of bars or gratings, hung on hinges, turning on pivots, or sliding, single or double; arrangement of slots into which motor-vehicle gear lever moves to engage different gears; device for holding frame of cine film momentarily in position behind lens of camera or projector; electrical signal that causes or controls passage of other signals; contrivance regulating passage of water in lock etc.; number entering by payment at gates to see football match etc.; **~(-money),** amount of money thus taken. **3.** **~'crasher,** uninvited intruder at party etc.; so **~'crash** *v.*; **~'fold,** folded oversize page in magazine etc.; **~'house,** lodge of park etc., entrance building of castle, (Hist.) room over city gate often used as prison; **~'keeper,** (1) attendant at gate, (2) large brown species of butterfly; **~'leg(ged),** (of table) having legs in gatelike frame swinging back to allow top to fold down; **~'man,** = *gatekeeper* (1); **~'post** (on which gate is hung or against which it shuts; *between you and me and the ~post*, in strict confidence); **~'way,** = gate (first sense), frame of or structure built over gate, means of entrance or exit (lit. or fig.). **4.** *v.t.* ‖Confine to college or school entirely or after certain hours. [OE *gæt, geat*, pl. *gatu*, = OS, ON *gat* f. Gmc **gatam*]

gāte² *n.* (With prefixed name in N. England etc.) street. [ME, f. ON *gata*, = OHG *gazza*, Goth. *gatwō* f. Gmc **gatwōn*]

gă'teau (-tō) *n.* (*pl.* **-s** *or* **-x,** *pr.* -z). Large rich cream-cake. [f. F *gâteau* cake]

gă'ther (-dh-) *v.* **1.** *v.t.* Bring together, cause to assemble; **be ~ed to** one's **fathers,** die. **2.** Acquire by gradually collecting, amass; pluck (flowers etc.); collect (grain etc.) as harvest; pick *up* from ground; infer, deduce, (*that*); receive addition of (*rolling stone gathers no* MOSS; *unread books gathering dust*; *train gathered speed*; *invalid gathers strength*; ~ **way,** (of ship) begin to move). **3.** Summon up (energy); gain or recover (breath); draw (garment, fabric, brow) together in folds or wrinkles, esp. pucker (part of dress) by running thread through; draw *up* (limbs, one*self*) into smaller compass; sum *up* (scattered facts); summon *up* (thoughts, strength, etc.) for an effort. **4.** Hence(-)~ER¹ *n.* **5.** *v.i.* Come together, congregate, form a mass; receive additions; come to a head, develop purulent swelling. [OE *gaderian*, = MLG *gadern*, f. WG **gadurōjan* (**gaduri* together)]

gă'thering (-dh-) *n.* In vbl senses; assembly, meeting, e.g. in Scottish Highlands, cf. Highland GAME¹s; purulent swelling; group of leaves taken together in bookbinding. [f. GATHER + -ING¹]

gă'thers (-dh*erz*) *n. pl.* Part of garment that is gathered or drawn in. [f. GATHER + -S¹]

Gă'tling *n.* ~ **(gun),** machine-gun with clustered barrels. [f. R.J. ~, Amer. inventor d. 1903]

***'gā'tor** *n.* (colloq.) Alligator. [abbr.]

G.A.T.T. (găt) *abbr.* General Agreement on Tariffs and Trade.

gauche (gōsh) *a.* Tactless; without ease or grace, socially awkward; hence **~'NESS** *n.* [F, = left(-handed), awkward]

gau'cherie (gō'sh*erē*) *n.* Gauche manners; a gauche action. [F]

gau'chō (*or* gow'-) *n.* (*pl.* **~s**). One of a mixed European and Amer. Ind. people of mounted herdsmen in S. America. [Sp., f. Quechua]

gaud *n.* Gaudy thing, showy ornament; (in *pl.*) showy ceremonies. [perh. thr. AF f. OF *gaudir* rejoice f. L *gaudēre*]

‖**gau'dў¹** *n.* Annual feast or entertainment, esp. college dinner for old members etc. [f. L *gaudium* joy or *gaude* rejoice!]

gau'd|ў² *a.* Tastelessly or inappropriately fine, showy, or brilliant (of dress, decoration, literary style, etc.); hence **~ĭLY²** *adv.*, **~ĭNESS** *n.* [prob. f. GAUD + -Y²]

gauge¹ (gāj), ***gāge²** (also ‖ in sense 2), *n.* **1.** Standard measure to which things must conform, esp. measure of capacity or contents of barrel, fineness of textile, diameter of bullet, or thickness of sheet metal; capacity, extent, scope (**take the ~ of,** estimate); distance between pair of rails or opposite wheels. **2.** (Naut.; usu. *gage.*) Relative position with respect to wind; **have the weather ~ of,** be to windward of, (fig.) have advantage of. **3.** Graduated instrument measuring force or quantity of rainfall, stream, tide, wind, etc. (**~ pressure,** amount by which pressure exceeds that of atmosphere); contrivance attached to vessel to show height of its contents; instrument for testing and verifying dimensions of tools, wire, etc.; carpenter's adjustable tool for marking parallel lines; (Print.) strip regulating depth of margin etc.; means of estimating, criterion, test. [ME, f. ONF *gauge* (OF *jauge*), of unkn. orig.]

gauge² (gāj), ***gāge³,** *v.t.* Measure exactly (esp. objects of standard size, as wire, bolts; fluctuating quantities or forces, as rainfall, wind; depth of liquid content); find capacity or content of (cask etc.) by measurement and calculation; estimate, take measure of, (person, character); make uniform, bring to standard size or shape; hence **~'ABLE** (-*ja*-) *a.*, **gau'gER¹** (1, 2) *n.* (gā'j-), (esp.) exciseman. [ME, f. ONF *gauger* (prec.)]

Gaul *n.* Inhabitant of ancient Gaul. [f. *Gaul* the country f. F *Gaule* f. Gmc **walhoz* foreigners]

gau'leiter (gow'lîter) *n.* Nazi district political leader; (fig.) local or petty tyrant. [G (*gau* administrative district, *leiter* leader)]

Gau'lish *a.* & *n.* (Language) of ancient Gauls. [f. GAUL + -ISH¹]

Gau'll|ism (gō'-) *n.* (Adherence to) principles and policies of Charles de *Gaulle*, Fr. military and political leader (d. 1970); so ~IST (2) *n.* [f. F *Gaullisme*; see -ISM]

Gau'loise (gō'lwahz) *n.* Brand of French cigarettes. [F (*gaulois* Gallic); **P**]

gault *n.* (Geol.) Series of clay and marl beds between upper and lower greensand in S. England; clay obtained from these. [16th c., of unkn. orig.]

gaulther'ia *n.* Evergreen aromatic plant of genus *Gaultheria*, some species of which yield medicinal oil. [f. J.-F. *Gaultier*, Can. botanist d. 1756 + -IA¹]

gaunt *a.* Lean, haggard; grim or desolate looking; hence ~'NESS *n.* [ME, of unkn. orig.]

gau'ntlet¹ *n.* Stout glove with long loose wrist for driving, fencing, wicket-keeping, etc.; wide wrist-part of glove; (Hist.) armoured glove; (fig.) **fling, throw, down the** ~, issue challenge, **pick, take, up the** ~, accept challenge. [ME, f. OF *gantelet* (*gant* glove f. Gmc **want-*; see -LET)]

gau'ntlet², *gă'ntlet, *n.* **Run the** ~, pass between rows of persons who strike one with sticks, cords, etc., as military, naval, or school punishment (also fig., of being subjected to criticism). [earlier *gantlope* f. Sw. *gatlopp* (*gata* lane, *lopp* course), w. assim. to prec.]

gau'ntry. See GANTRY.

gaur (gowr) *n.* Wild ox (*Bibos gaurus*) of E. Asia. [Hindi]

gauss (gows) *n.* (*pl.* same *or* ~**'es**). Electromagnetic unit of magnetic induction. [f. K. *Gauss*, Ger. mathematician d. 1855]

gauz|e *n.* Thin transparent fabric of silk, cotton, etc.; fine mesh of wire, etc.; slight haze; hence ~'Y² *a.* [f. F *gaze* f. *Gaza* in Palestine]

gāve. See GIVE¹.

gă'vel *n.*, & *v.i.* (||-ll-). **1.** *n.* Auctioneer's hammer; chairman's or judge's hammer for calling attention etc. **2.** *v.i.* Use gavel. [19th c., of unkn. orig.]

||**gă'velkind** *n.* (Hist.) Form of land-tenure (esp. in Kent) with equal division of intestate's property among sons. [ME, f. OE **gafolgecynd* (*gafol* tribute, *gecynd* KIND¹)]

gā'vial *n.* Long-snouted Asian crocodile. [F, f. Hind.]

gavŏ'tte *n.* Medium-paced dance of 18th c.; music for it; piece of music in common time, each phrase beginning on third beat of bar. [F, f. Prov. *gavoto* (*Gavot* native of region in Alps)]

Gawd *n.* (vulg. or sl. pr. of) God.

gawk¹ *n.* Awkward or bashful person. [rel. to obs. *gaw* gaze (f. ON *gá* heed) and GAWK²]

gawk² *v.i.* (colloq.) Stare stupidly. [rel. to obs. *gaw* (see prec.) and GAWK¹]

gaw'k|ȳ *a.* & *n.* Awkward, ungainly, bashful, (person); hence ~ĭLY² *adv.*, ~ĭNESS *n.* [f. GAWK¹ or GAWK² + -Y²]

gawp *v.i.* = GAWK². [earlier *gaup*, *galp* f. ME *galpen* yawn, cogn. w. YELP]

gay *a.* **1.** Full of or disposed to or indicating mirth; light-hearted, carefree, sportive; airy, offhand. **2.** (euphem.) Dissolute, immoral; (sl.) homosexual, frequented by homosexuals. **3.** Showy, brilliant, bright-coloured; finely dressed or decorated *with*. **4.** Hence **gai'**LY² *adv.* ~'NESS *n.* [ME, f. OF *gai*, of unkn. orig.]

***gay'etȳ.** See GAIETY.

***gazā'bō, *gazē'bō²,** *n.* (*pl.* ~**s**). (sl., often derog.) Person. [19th c.; orig. unkn.]

gazā'nia *n.* S. Afr. herb of genus *Gazania*, with showy yellow or orange flowers. [18th c., f. Theodore of *Gaza*, Greek scholar d. 1478 + -IA¹]

gāze *v.i.*, & *n.* **1.** *v.i.* Look fixedly (*at, on, upon*). **2.** *n.* Intent look; **at** ~, gazing in wonder etc. [ME, orig. unkn., but cf. obs. *gaw* (GAWK¹)]

gazē'bō¹ *n.* (*pl.* ~**s** *or* ~**es**). Structure whence a view may be had; belvedere, turret, balcony, etc. [perh. joc. formation f. prec. on L future (cf. LAVABO)]

***gazē'bō².** See GAZABO.

gazĕ'lle *n.* Small graceful soft-eyed Asian or African antelope, esp. of genus *Gazella*. [F, prob. f. Sp. *gacela* f. Arab. *ġazāl*]

gazĕ'tte *n.*, & *v.t.* **1.** *n.* (Hist.) news-sheet, periodical publication giving current events; ||**London G~, Edinburgh G~, Belfast G~,** official journals with lists of government appointments, bankruptcies, and other public notices; newspaper (used in titles, as *Isle of Thanet Gazette*, *Oxford University Gazette*). **2.** *v.t.* ||Publish in official gazette (esp. in *pass.*, of official etc. with status so announced). [F, f. It. *gazzetta* (*gazeta*, a Venetian small coin)]

găzėtteer' *n.* Geographical index. [so called as first provided for 'gazetteers' in earlier sense 'journalists', f. F *gazettier* f. It. *gazzettiere* (as prec.; see -EER)]

gazpa'chō (gahspah'-) *n.* (*pl.* ~**s**). Spanish cold vegetable soup. [Sp.]

gazŭ'mp *v.t.* (sl.) Swindle; raise price of house etc. after accepting offer by (intending buyer, or abs.). [20th c.; orig. uncert.]

G.B. *abbr.* Great Britain.

||**G.B.E.** *abbr.* Knight (or Dame) Grand Cross (of the Order) of the British Empire.

||**G.C.** *abbr.* George Cross.

||**G.C.B.** *abbr.* Knight (or Dame) Grand Cross (of the Order) of the Bath.

||**G.C.E.** *abbr.* General Certificate of Education.

||**G.C.I.E.** *abbr.* Knight Grand Commander (of the Order) of the Indian Empire.

||**G.C.M.G.** *abbr.* Knight (or Dame) Grand Cross (of the Order) of St. Michael & St. George.

||**G.C.S.I.** *abbr.* Knight Grand Commander (of the Order) of the Star of India.

||**G.C.V.O.** *abbr.* Knight (or Dame) Grand Cross of the Royal Victorian Order.

Gd *symb.* gadolinium.

Gdn(s). *abbr.* Garden(s).

G.D.R. *abbr.* German Democratic Republic.

Ge *symb.* germanium.

||**gean** (g-) *n.* Mazard cherry. [f. F *guine*, of unkn. orig.]

gear (g-) *n.*, & *v.t.* **1.** *n.* Equipment; apparel, esp. (colloq.) for young people, and cf. HEAD¹ 23; harness of draught animals. **2.** Apparatus, appliances (*aircraft's landing gear*); tackle, tools. **3.** Combination of wheels, levers, etc., usu. for special purpose (*winding-gear*); wheels working on one another by teeth etc.; arrangements connecting motor or engine with its work (**in** ~, connected or working; **out of** ~, with connection interrupted or not working, (fig.) out of order); particular state of adjustment of such connection (**high, low,** ~, by which driven part of bicycle, motor car, etc., revolves faster, slower, relatively to driving part; similarly ||**top,** ||**bottom** or ||**first,** ~, the available extremes; CHANGE² *gear*. **4.** Rigging. **5.** Goods, household utensils. **6.** ~**'box,** ~**'case,** (enclosing gearing of motor car, bicycle, etc.); ~**-lever,** *~**-shift,** (used to engage or change gear); ~**'wheel,** cogwheel, esp. that in bicycles which is driven directly by pedals. **7.** *v.t.* Harness (draught animal; often *up*); put (machinery) in gear, provide with gear (~ **up, down,** provide with high, low, gear); make (industry or factory) subservient or ancillary *to* another, or *to* a programme; adjust or adapt *to*. [ME, f. ON *gervi*, OS *gerwi*, OHG *garawī* f. Gmc **garwin-* prepare]

gear'ing (g-) *n.* Set or arrangement of gears in machine; ||(fig., Finance) allocation of part of dividend to preferred recipients, amount of this part. [f. prec. + -ING[1]]

gĕ'ckō (g-) *n.* (*pl.* **~s** *or* **~es**). House lizard found in warm climates, able to climb walls by its adhesive toes. [f. Malay *gēkoq*, imit. of its cry]

||**gee**[1], **gee'-gee,** *n.* (colloq.) Horse. [orig. child's wd, f. foll.]

gee[2], **gee'-hō, gee'-ŭp,** *ints.* of command to horse etc.: go on, go faster; (occas.) turn to right. [17th c., of unkn. orig.]

gee[3], **gee whĭ'llĭkĭns** (-nz), **gee whĭ'z,** *ints.* expr. asseveration, discovery, etc. [perh. abbr. of JESUS]

***gee**[4] *n.* (sl.) Person, fellow. [f. first letter of GUY[2]]

geese. See GOOSE.

gee'-strĭng. Var. of G-STRING 2.

gee'zer (g-) *n.* (sl.) Old man; person. [dial. pronunc. of GUISER]

Gėhĕ'nna (g-) *n.* Hell; place of burning, torment, or misery. [eccl. L, f. Hellenistic Gk *geenna* f. Heb. *gê' hinnōm* hell, orig. valley of Hinnom near Jerusalem where children were sacrificed]

Gei'ger (gī'ger) *n.* ~ **counter,** cylindrical device for detecting and counting ionizing particles in order to measure radioactivity etc. [f. H. ~, Ger. physicist d. 1945]

gei'sha (gā'-) *n.* (*pl.* **~s** *or* same). Japanese hostess entertaining men with dance and song; Japanese prostitute. [Jap.]

Gei'ssler (gī'-) *n.* ~ **tube,** sealed glass or quartz tube with central constriction, filled with vapour for production of luminous electrical discharge. [f. H. ~, Ger. mechanic d. 1879]

geist (gīst) *n.* (Individual) spirit; intellectuality, intelligence. [G, as GHOST]

gĕl *n.*, & *v.i.* (**-ll-**). (Form) semi-solid colloidal solution or jelly, of solid dispersed in liquid. [abbr. of foll.]

gĕ'latĭn, ||**gĕ'latine** (-ēn), *n.* Almost colourless transparent tasteless water-soluble substance derived from animal skin, tendons, ligaments, etc., and used in food preparation, photography, etc.; **blasting ~,** an explosive nitro-glycerine solution of collodion cotton; ~ **paper** (coated with sensitized gelatin for photography); hence or cogn. **gėlă'tĭn**IZE (3) *v.t.* & *i.*, **gėlă'tĭn**OUS *a.*, (esp.) of jelly-like consistency. [f. F *gélatine* f. It. *gelatina* (*gelata* JELLY; see -IN, -INE[5])]

gėlā'tion[1] *n.* Solidification by freezing. [f. L *gelatio* (*gelare* freeze; see -ATION)]

gėlā'tion[2] *n.* Formation of a gel. [f. GEL + -ATION]

gĕld (g-) *v.t.* Deprive (usu. male animal) of ability to reproduce; castrate or spay, excise testicles or ovaries of. [ME, f. ON *gelda* (*geldr* barren, OHG *galt*, f. Gmc **galduz*)]

gĕ'ldĭng (g-) *n.* Gelded animal, esp. male horse. [ME, f. ON *geldingr* (as prec.; see -ING[3])]

gĕ'lĭd *a.* Icy, ice-cold; chilly, cool. [f. L *gelidus* (*gelu* frost; see -ID[1])]

gĕ'lĭgnīte *n.* Explosive based on blasting-GELATIN. [f. GELATIN + L *ignis* fire + -ITE[1] (2)]

gĕ'llў *n.* (sl.) Gelignite. [abbr.]

gĕm *n.*, & *v.t.* (**-mm-**). **1.** *n.* Precious stone, esp. when cut and polished; object of great beauty or worth; choicest part *of*; prized thing; precious or semiprecious stone with engraved design; hence **~'**LIKE, **~'my**[2], *adjs.* **2.** *v.t.* Adorn (as) with gems. [ME, f. OF *gemme* f. L *gemma* bud, jewel]

Gėmar̂'a (g-) *n.* Rabbinical commentary on Mishnah, forming second part of Talmud. [f. Aram. *g^emārâ* completion]

gĕ'mĭnate[1] *a.* Combined in pairs. [f. L *geminatus* p.p. of *geminare* (*geminus* twin); see -ATE[2]]

gĕ'mĭn|āte[2] *v.t.* Double, repeat; arrange in pairs; so **~**A'TION *n.* [f. as prec. + -ATE[3]]

Gĕ'mĭnī *n.* Sign of the ZODIAC, the Twins. [L, = twins]

gĕ'mma *n.* (*pl.* **~e**). (In cryptogams) small cellular body that separates from mother-plant and starts a new one. [L; see GEM]

gĕmmā'tion *n.* Reproduction by gemmae. [F (*gemmer* to bud, *gemme* bud; see -ATION)]

gĕmmĭ'ferous *a.* Producing precious stones; bearing buds. [f. L *gemmifer* (as GEMMA, -I-, -FEROUS)]

gĕmmĭ'parous *a.* Of, or propagating by, gemmation. [f. mod. L *gemmiparus* (*gemma* bud, *parĕre* bring forth) + -OUS]

gĕmmŏ'|logў *n.* Science of gems; hence **~**LOGIST *n.* [f. L *gemma* GEM + -O- + -LOGY]

gĕ'mmūle *n.* Encysted embryonic cell-cluster in sponges. [F, or f. L *gemmula* little bud (as GEM; see -ULE)]

gĕ'mmў. See GEM.

gemü'tlich (gemo͞o'tlĭk *or* -mū'-) *a.* Cheerful; cosy; genial; so **~keit** (-kīt) *n.*, cheerfulness, cosiness, geniality. [G]

||**gĕn** *n.* & *v.* (**-nn-**). (sl.) **1.** *n.* Information. **2.** *v.t.* & *i.* ~ **up,** provide (oneself) with information. [perh. f. first syl. of *general information*]

-gėn *suf.* forming *ns.* (1) (Chem.) in *oxygen* and later formations *-gen* has the sense 'that which produces' (*hydrogen, nitrogen, cyanogen, antigen*); (2) (Bot.) in *endogen, exogen*, etc., *-gen* = 'growth' (*acrogen, thallogen*). [f. F *-gène* f. Gk *-genēs* -born, of a specified kind, (*gen-*, root of *gi-gn-omai* be born, become)]

Gen. *abbr.* General; Genesis (O.T.).

ge'ndar̂me (zhŏ'n-) *n.* **1.** Soldier, mounted or on foot, employed in police duties esp. in France; so **~rie** (zhŏndar̂'merē) *n.*, force of gendarmes, gendarmes' headquarters. **2.** Rock-tower on mountain, occupying and blocking arête. [F, f. *gens d'armes* men of arms]

gĕ'nder *n.* Grammatical classification (or one of the classes) of objects roughly corresponding to the two sexes and sexlessness (see MASCULINE, FEMININE, NEUTER, COMMON[1]); (of nouns and pronouns) property of belonging to such class, (of adjectives) appropriate form for accompanying a noun of one such class; (joc.) one's sex. [ME, f. OF *gendre* f. Rom. **genero* f. L GENUS]

gēne *n.* (Biol.) Unit of heredity in chromosome, controlling a particular inherited characteristic of an individual. [mod. formation in G (*gen*); cf. -GEN]

gĕnėalŏ'gĭcal *a.* Of genealogy; tracing family descent; ~ **tree,** chart like inverted branching tree showing descent of family or of animal species; hence **~**LY[2] *adv.* [f. F *généalogique* f. Gk *genealogikos* (as GENEALOGY; see -IC) + -AL]

gēnėă'log|ў *n.* Account of descent from ancestor by enumeration of intermediate persons, pedigree; investigation of pedigrees; plant's or animal's line of development from earlier forms; hence **~**IST (3) *n.*, **~**IZE (1, 2) *v.t.* & *i.* [ME, f. OF *genealogie* f. LL f. Gk *genealogia* (*genea* race; see -LOGY)]

gĕ'nera. See GENUS.

gĕ'neral *a.* & *n.* **1.** *a.* Completely or almost universal; including or affecting all or nearly all parts or cases or things; not partial, particular, local, or sectional; **G~ American,**

U.S. speech not markedly dialectal or regional; *general* AVERAGE[1]; **G~ Certificate of Education,** examination set esp. for secondary-school pupils in England and Wales, certificate gained by passing it; **~ confession** (to be made by whole congregation); ***~ delivery** (of letters to callers at post office); *general* ELECTION; **~ headquarters** (of Commander-in-Chief); **~ meeting** (open to all members of a society etc.); **~ post,** (1) first morning delivery, (2) an indoor game, (3) (fig.) general and rapid exchange of positions etc.; ||**G~ Post Office,** chief post office in city or town; **~ staff** (assisting military commander in planning and administration); **~ strike** (of workers in all or most trades, esp. in Britain in 1926); *General* SYNOD. **2.** Prevalent, widespread, usual; **in a ~ way,** ordinarily. **3.** Not limited in application; relating to whole class of objects, occasions, etc.; true of all or (opp. *universal*) nearly all cases (**as a ~ rule,** in most cases); including points common to individuals of a class and neglecting differences (*general word, term, notion*). **4.** Not restricted to one department, not specialized; **~ dealer,** trader in many kinds of article; **~ hospital,** (1) hospital not specializing in any particular disease or age or sex, (2) large military hospital receiving sick and wounded from field hospitals; **~ knowledge** (of miscellaneous facts); **~ practice,** work of **~ practitioner,** doctor treating cases of all kinds (opp. *consultant* or *specialist*); **~ reader** (of miscellaneous literature). **5.** Roughly corresponding or adequate; sufficient for practical purposes; not detailed (*general resemblance, idea*). **6.** Vague, indefinite, (*spoke only in general terms*). **7.** (Mil., of officer) above rank of colonel. **8.** Chief, head, having unrestricted authority, (*general manager, secretary*; often appended to titles: ATTORNEY-*General*, SECRETARY-*General*, SOLICITOR-*General*). **9. In ~,** generally, in all ordinary cases, barring special exceptions, for the most part. **10.** *n.* Chief of religious order, e.g. of Jesuits, Dominicans, Salvation Army; (Mil.) officer next below Field Marshal or *general of the army or air force (see below) (also, by courtesy, of lieutenant-general and major-general; ***~ of the army** or **air force,** officer of highest rank); commander of army; tactician or strategist of specified merit (*a good, bad, great, general; no general*); ||(colloq.) General Post Office; ||(colloq.) servant for general work; (arch.) *the* public. [ME f. OF, f. L *generalis* (as GENUS; see -AL)]

gĕneralĭ'ssĭmō *n.* (*pl.* **~s**). Commander of combined military and naval and air force, or of several armies. [It., superl. of *generale* GENERAL]

gĕ'neralĭst *n.* Person competent in several different fields (opp. *specialist*). [f. GENERAL + -IST]

gĕneră'lĭtў *n.* Being general; applicability to whole class of instances; vagueness, lack of detail; general point, principle, law, or statement; main body, bulk, majority, *of*. [f. F *généralité* f. LL *generalitas -tatis* (as GENERAL; see -ITY)]

gĕneralīzā'tion, -īsā'tion (-z-), *n.* (Forming of) general notion or proposition obtained by induction (often derog., esp. **hasty ~**, one based on too few instances). [f. F *généralisation* (as foll.; see -ATION)]

gĕ'neralīz|e, -īs|e (-īz), *v.* **1.** *v.t.* Reduce to general laws; form into a general notion; give a general character to; call by a general name. **2.** Infer (law, conclusion) by induction; base general statement on (facts etc.). **3.** (Math. & Philos.) express in general form, extend application of; form general notions by abstraction; make vague; (Paint.) render only the typical characteristics of. **4.** Bring into general use. **5.** *v.i.* Use generalities, speak vaguely. **6.** Hence **~ER**[1] *n.* [f. F *généraliser* (as GENERAL; see -IZE)]

gĕ'nerallў *adv.* For the most part, extensively; in a general sense, without regard to particulars, not specially, (**~ speaking,** in general); as a general rule, usually. [f. GENERAL + -LY[2]]

gĕ'neralshĭp *n.* Office of a general; strategy, military skill; skilful management, tact, diplomacy. [f. GENERAL + -SHIP]

gĕ'nerāte *v.t.* Bring into existence, produce, evolve, (heat, force, light, friction, electricity, etc.; result, state of things, state of mind, etc.); (Math., of point, line, surface, conceived as moving) make (line, surface, solid). [f. L *generare* beget (as GENUS) + -ATE[3]]

gĕnerā'tion *n.* **1.** Procreation, propagation of species, begetting or being begotten. **2.** Production by natural or artificial process, esp. production of electricity. **3.** Single step in descent or pedigree (*have known them for three generations; his descendant in the tenth generation*); whole body of persons born about same time (*my generation; the rising generation*; **~ gap,** differences of opinion between those of different generations; **first ~** *Americans, university students*, etc., whose parents were not so); average time in which children are ready to take place of parents (usu. reckoned at about 30 years); stage in development (*third-generation computers*). **4.** Hence **~AL** *a.* [ME f. OF, f. L *generatio -onis* (as prec.; see -ATION)]

gĕ'neratĭve (*or* -āt-) *a.* Of procreation; able to produce, productive; **~ grammar,** set of rules whereby permissible sentences may be generated from elements of a language. [ME, f. OF (*-if*) or f. LL *generativus* (as prec.; see -ATIVE)]

gĕ'nerātor *n.* Apparatus for producing gases, steam, etc.; machine for converting mechanical into electrical energy, dynamo; originator. [f. GENERATE + -OR]

gėnĕ'r|ĭc *a.* Characteristic of a genus or class; applied to (any individual of) a large group or class; general, not specific or special; hence **~ICALLY** *adv.* [f. F *générique* f. L GENUS; see -IC]

gĕ'ner|ous *a.* **1.** Magnanimous, noble-minded; not mean or prejudiced; free in giving, munificent; so **~O'SITY** *n.* **2.** Ample, abundant, copious; (of wine) rich and full. **3.** Hence **~ousLY**[2] *adv.* [f. OF *genereus* f. L *generosus* (as GENUS; see -OUS) noble, magnanimous]

gĕ'nėsĭs *n.* **1.** (*G~*). First book of O.T., with account of the creation of the world. **2.** Origin, mode of formation or generation. [L, f. Gk (*gen-* be produced)]

gĕ'nėt, gėnĕ'tte, *n.* (Fur of) civet-cat of genus *Genetta*. [ME, f. OF *genete* f. Arab. *jarnayṭ*]

gėnĕ'tĭc *a.* **1.** Of, in, concerning, origin; causal. **2.** Of genetics or genes; **~ code,** system of storage of genetic information in chromosomes. **3.** Hence **gėnĕ'tICALLY** *adv.* [f. GENESIS after *antithesis -etic*]

gėnĕ'tĭc|s *n.* Study of heredity and variation in animals and plants; hence **~IST** (3) *n.* [pl. of prec. used as n.; see -ICS]

gėnē'va[1] *n.* Hollands gin. [f. Du. *genever* f. OF *genevre* f. L *juniperus* juniper, w. assim. to foll.]

Gėnē'va[2] *n.* **~ bands,** clerical BAND[1]s like those of Swiss Calvinists; **~ Conventions** (of 1864 and later, governing status of wounded, hospitals, ambulances, etc., in war); **~ cross,** red Greek cross on white ground distinguishing hospitals, ambulances, etc., in war; **~ gown,**

black gown worn by Calvinists and other clergy in pulpit; ~ **Protocol** (of 1925, against use of poison gas and bacteria in war); hence **Gĕnève**'SE *a.* & *n.* [~ in Switzerland]

gē'nial[1] *a.* **1.** (Of air, climate, etc.) conducive to growth, mild, pleasantly warm; cheering, enlivening; jovial, kindly, sociable, whence ~ITY (-ă'l-) *n.*, ~IZE (3) *v.t.* **2.** Of or showing genius. **3.** Hence ~LY[2] *adv.* [f. L *genialis* (as GENIUS; see -AL)]

gėnī'al[2] *a.* (Anat.) Of the chin. [f. Gk *geneion* chin (*genus* jaw) + -AL]

gē'nĭc *a.* Pertaining to genes. [f. GENE + -IC]

-gĕ'nĭc *suf.* forming *adjs.* meaning (1) producing (*carcinogenic*, *pathogenic*); (2) well suited to (*photogenic*, *radiogenic*); (3) produced by (*iatrogenic*); hence **-gĕ'nICALLY** *adv. suf.* [f. -GEN + -IC]

gē'nĭe *n.* (*pl.* usu. **genii** *pr.* jē'nĭī). Jinnee, sprite or goblin of Arabian tales. [f. F *génie* f. L GENIUS; cf. JINNEE]

gē'nĭī. See GENIE, GENIUS.

gėnĭ'sta *n.* Flowering shrub of genus *Genista*, e.g. dyer's broom. [L]

gĕ'nĭtal *a.* & *n.* **1.** *a.* Of animal reproduction. **2.** *n.* (in *pl.*) External organs of reproduction. [OF, or f. L *genitalis* (*gignere genit-* beget; see -AL)]

gĕnĭtā'lĭa *n. pl.* = prec. 2. [L, neut. pl. (as n.) of *genitalis* (see prec., -IA[2])]

gĕ'nĭtive *a.* & *n.* (Gram.) ~ **(case),** case of nouns etc. in inflected languages, corresponding to *of*, *from*, and other prepositions with noun representing source, possessor, etc.; *genitive* ABSOLUTE; hence **gĕnĭtī'vAL** *a.*, **gĕnĭtī'valLY**[2] *adv.* [ME, f. OF *genetif* or *-ive* or f. L *genitivus* (*casus* case), transl. Gk *genikē* (*ptōsis* case), as GENITAL; see -IVE]

gĕ'nĭtō- *comb. form.* = GENITAL, as: **~-urinary,** of the genital and urinary organs. [f. GENITAL + -O-]

gē'nĭus *n.* (*pl.* **~es,** *or* **ge'nii** *pr.* -ĭī). **1.** Tutelary spirit of person, place, or institution; **good, evil,** ~, one of two opposed spirits or angels supposed to attend each person, person who powerfully influences one for good or ill. **2.** Nation's, age's, etc., prevalent feeling, opinions, or taste; character, spirit, drift, method, of a language, law, etc.; associations or inspirations of a place. **3.** Natural ability or tendency; special mental endowments; exalted intellectual power; instinctive and extraordinary imaginative, creative, or inventive capacity; (*pl.* **~es**) person having this. **4.** ~ ***loci*** (lō'sī; *pl.* ***genii loci***), presiding deity, associations, etc., of a place. [L, in sense 1, f. root of *gignere* beget]

geni'zah (gĕnē'*z*a) *n.* Room attached to synagogue, housing damaged, discarded, or heretical books etc. and sacred relics. [Heb. *gĕnīzāh*, lit. hiding-place (*gānaz* hide, set aside)]

Gĕ'nōa *n.* ~ **cake,** rich fruit-cake with almonds on top; ~ **(jib),** large jib on racing-yacht; hence **Gĕnōē**'SE *a.* & *n.* [~ in Italy]

gĕ'nocid|e *n.* Deliberate extermination of a race, nation, etc.; hence ~AL (*or* -sī'-) *a.* [f. Gk *genos* race + -CIDE (2)]

gĕ'no|tȳpe *n.* (Biol.) Genetic constitution of an individual; hence **~tȳ'pIC** *a.* [f. G *genotypus* (as GENE, -O-, TYPE[1])]

-gėnous *suf.* forming *adjs.* w. sense 'produced' (*endogenous*). [f. -GEN + -OUS]

genre (zhahnr) *n.* Kind or style, esp. of art or literature; **~(-painting),** portrayal of scenes etc. from ordinary life. [F, = kind; see GENDER]

gĕns (-z) *n.* (*pl.* **ge'ntes** *pr.* -ēz). **1.** (Rom. & Gk Ant.) Group of families with supposed common origin, sharing name and religious rites; clan. **2.** (Biol.) Group of related organisms. **3.** Line of descent through father. [L, f. ***gen-*** root of *gignere* beget]

gĕnt *n.* Gentleman (vulg. or joc.); **~s,** (in shops) men (*gents' hairdresser*); ‖**the G~s,** (colloq.) men's public lavatory. [abbr. of GENTLEMAN]

gĕntee'l *a.* **1.** (arch., iron., or vulg.) Appropriate to, characteristic of, belonging to, the upper classes. **2.** Stylish, fashionable, well-dressed, elegant; SHABBY-*genteel*. **3.** Hence ~ISM (4) *n.*, word used because thought to be more genteel than the usual one (e.g. *perspire* for *sweat*), ~LY[2] (-l-lĭ) *adv.* [earlier *gentile*, readoption of F *gentil* GENTLE]

gĕ'ntian (-sh*a*n *or* -shĭ*a*n) *n.* Plant of genus *Gentiana* or *Gentianella* (usu. blue-flowered), found esp. in mountain regions; ~ **(bitter),** liquor extracted from its root; ~ **violet,** a dye, used as antiseptic, esp. in treatment of burns. [OE f. L *gentiana* (*Gentius* king of Illyria; see -AN)]

gĕ'ntile *a.* & *n.* **1.** (Person) not Jewish; hence ~DOM (-ld-) *n.* **2.** Of a nation or tribe; (Gram.) (word) indicating nationality; heathen, pagan. [ME, f. L *gentilis* (GENS *gentis* family; see -IL)]

gĕntĭlĭ'tial (-sh*a*l) *a.* Of a nation or family; of the gentry. [f. L *gentilicius* national (GENS) + -AL]

gĕntĭ'lĭtȳ *n.* Social superiority, good manners, upper-class habits; SHABBY-*gentility*; (arch.) gentle birth, gentlefolk. [ME, f. OF *gentilité* (as foll.; see -ITY)]

gĕ'ntle *a.* (**~r, ~st**), *n.*, & *v.t.* **1.** *a.* (Of birth, family, pursuits, etc.) honourable, belonging to or fit for the class of gentlemen; (in *comb.*, as GENTLEMAN) well-born. **2.** (arch.) Generous, noble, courteous, (~ **reader,** author's formula of address). **3.** Tame, quiet, (**the ~ art** or **craft,** angling or other activity requiring patience or (iron.) force); easily managed; not stormy, rough, or violent, (*a gentle breeze*; *has a gentle nature*); (of medicine) mild, not drastic; (of rule etc.) not severe; moderate (*a gentle heat*); gradual (*a gentle slope*); kind, mild, tender, (*a gentle hint* (also iron.); **the ~ sex,** women); **~folk(s),** people of good position and family. **4.** *n.* Maggot, larva of meat-fly or bluebottle, used as fishing-bait [f. obs. sense *soft* of adj.]. **5.** *v.t.* Make gentle; break in (horse), handle (horse etc.) firmly but gently. [ME, f. OF *gentil* f. L *gentilis* GENTILE]

gĕ'ntleman (-telm-) *n.* (*pl.* **-men**). **1.** Man of chivalrous manners and good breeding; man of good social position, man of wealth and leisure (*country gentleman*); (Hist.) non-professional cricketer; (euphem.) smuggler; *gentleman at* LARGE; **~'s ~,** valet. **2.** (Courteous synonym for) man, esp. in Parliament, Congress, etc.; **old ~,** the Devil (OLD 5); (in *pl.* as *voc.*) male members of audience, (also as *pl.* of SIR 1, and in letter = *Dear* SIRS); ‖**the Gentlemen('s),** (as *sing. n.*) men's public lavatory. **3.** Man of gentle birth attached to household of sovereign or great person (*gentleman in waiting* etc.). **4.** **~-at-arms,** one of sovereign's bodyguard; ~ **farmer,** country gentleman who farms; ~ **usher,** gentleman acting as usher to great person; **~'s** or **gentlemen's agreement** (binding in honour, but not enforceable at law). **5.** Hence ~LY[1] *a.*, feeling, behaving, or looking, like a gentleman, befitting a gentleman. [f. GENTLE + MAN[1], after OF *gentilz hom*]

gĕ'ntlenėss (-teln-) *n.* Kindliness, mildness; freedom from severity, suddenness, violence, steepness, etc. [f. GENTLE + -NESS]

gĕ'ntle|woman (-t*e*lwŏŏm*a*n) *n.* (*pl.* **~women** *pr.* -wĭmĭn). (arch.) Woman of good birth or breeding; lady. [f. GENTLE + WOMAN]

gĕ'ntlȳ *adv.* Quietly, moderately, softly, slowly;

(as *int.* expr. remonstration) do not go so fast etc.; mildly, tenderly, kindly; ~ **born,** of gentle birth. [f. GENTLE + -LY²]

gĕ'ntōō *n.* Kind of penguin (*Pygoscelis papua*). [perh. f. Anglo-Ind. *Gentoo* = Hindu, f. Port. *gentio* GENTILE]

gĕ'ntrȳ *n. pl.* People next below the nobility in position and birth; (derog., esp. *these gentry*) people. [prob. f. obs. *gentrice* f. OF *genterise* var. of *gentelise* nobility (*gentil* GENTLE)]

gĕ'nūflĕct *v.i.* Bend the knee, esp. in worship; hence or cogn. ~OR, **gĕnūflĕ'x**ION, ~ION (-kshon), *ns.*, ~ORY *a.* [f. eccl. L *genuflectere -flex-* f. L *genu* knee + *flectere* bend]

gĕ'nūĭne *a.* Of the original stock, pure-bred; really proceeding from its reputed source or author; having the supposed character, not sham or feigned; properly so called; hence ~LY² (-nlĭ) *adv.*, ~NESS (-n-n-) *n.* [f. L *genuinus* (*genu* knee, w. ref. to father's acknowledging new-born child by placing on knee; see -INE¹); later assoc. w. GENUS]

gē'nus *n.* (*pl.* **ge'nera** *pr.* jĕ'-). (Logic) kinds of things including subordinate kinds or species; (Biol.) group of animals or plants having common structural characteristics distinct from those of all other groups, and usu. containing several species; (pop.) kind, class, order, tribe. [f. L *genus -eris* birth, race, stock]

-gėnȳ *suf.* forming *ns.* w. sense 'mode of production or development of' (*anthropogeny, ontogeny, pathogeny*). [f. F *-génie* (as -GEN, -Y¹)]

gēo- *comb. form.* Earth, as: **geobo'tany,** study of geographical distribution of plants; **ge'omancy,** divination from configuration of handful of thrown earth or random dots, whence **geoma'ntic** *a.* [f. Gk *geō-* (*gē* earth)]

Geo. *abbr.* George.

gēocĕ'ntrĭc *a.* Considered as viewed from the earth's centre (~ **latitude,** that at which planet would appear to observer at earth's centre); having or representing the earth as centre, not heliocentric. [f. GEO- + -CENTRIC]

gēochĕ'm|istrȳ (-k-) *n.* The chemistry of the earth; hence ~ICAL *a.*, ~IST (3) *n.* [f. GEO- + CHEMISTRY]

gēochronŏ'log|ȳ (-k-) *n.* Measurement of geological time; ordering of geological events; hence **gēochrŏnolŏ'g**ICAL (-kr-) *a.*, ~IST (3) *n.* [f. GEO- + CHRONOLOGY]

gē'ōde *n.* (Rock containing) cavity lined with crystals or other mineral matter; hence **gēŏ'd**IC *a.* [f. L f. Gk *geōdēs* earthy (*gē* earth; see -ODE)]

gēŏ'd|ėsȳ *n.* Branch of mathematics dealing with figure and area of the earth or large portions of it; so **gēodĕ's**IC, **gēodĕ't**IC, *adjs.*; ~**esic** (or ~**etic**) **dome** (built of short struts along geodesic lines); ~**esic** (or ~**etic**) **line,** shortest possible line on surface between two points; ~**ė**SIST (3) *n.* [f. mod. L f. Gk GEO-(*daisia* f. *daiō* divide)]

gēogră'phĭc, -ĭc|al, *adjs.* Of geography; ~**(al) latitude,** angle made with plane of equator by perpendicular to earth's surface at any point; ~**al mile** = 1′ of longitude on equator, or of latitude, about 1850 metres; hence ~**al**LY² *adv.* [f. F *géographique* or f. LL f. Gk GEO(*graphikos* -GRAPHIC) + -AL]

gėŏ'graphȳ *n.* Science of the earth's surface, form, physical features, natural and political divisions, climate, productions, population, etc. (**mathematical, physical, political,** ~, the science in these aspects); subject-matter of geography; features, arrangement, of place, esp. (colloq.) location of w.c. or other rooms in house; so **gėŏ'**GRAPHER *n.* [f. F *géographie* or f. L f. Gk GEO(*graphia* -GRAPHY)]

gē'oid *n.* Earth's figure; shape formed by mean sea-level and its imagined extension under land areas. [f. Gk *geoeidēs* (as GEO-; see -OID)]

gėŏ'logȳ *n.* Science of the earth's crust, its strata, and their relations and changes; geological features of district; corresponding study of moon etc.; hence **gēolŏ'g**IC(AL) *adjs.*, **gēolŏ'g**ICALLY *adv.*, **gėŏ'**LOGIST *n.*, **gėŏ'log**IZE (1, 2) *v.t.* & *i.* [f. mod. L *geologia* (as GEO-; see -LOGY)]

gēomă'gnėtĭsm *n.* Study of earth's magnetic properties; hence **gēomăgnĕ't**IC *a.* [f. GEO- + MAGNETISM]

gėŏ'mėter *n.* Person skilled in geometry; moth esp. of family Geometridae (from its caterpillar's seeming to measure ground by its mode of walking). [ME, f. LL *geometra* f. L f. Gk GEO(*metrēs* measurer)]

gēomĕ'trĭc, -ĭc|al, *adjs.* Of, according to, like, geometry; ~**al architecture** (with figures of geometric form, as circles, trefoils, etc.); *geometric* MEAN¹; **G~ pottery** (of ancient Greece, using geometric forms in decoration); ~**al progression** (with constant ratio between successive quantities, as 1:3:9:27:81); ~ **spider** (constructing web of geometric pattern); *geometric* TRACERY; hence ~**al**LY² *adv.* [f. F *géometrique* f. L f. Gk *geōmetrikos* (as prec.; see -IC) + -AL]

gėŏ'mėtr|ȳ *n.* Science of properties and relations of magnitudes (as lines, surfaces, solids) in space; relative arrangement of objects or parts; hence or cogn. **gēomėtrɪ'**CIAN *n.*, ~IZE (1) *v.t.* [ME, f. OF *geometrie* f. L f. Gk (as GEO-; see -METRY)]

gēomôrphŏ'log|ȳ *n.* Study of the physical features of the earth's surface and their relation to its geological structures; hence **gēomôrpholŏ'g**ICAL *a.*, ~IST (3) *n.* [f. GEO- + MORPHOLOGY]

gē'ophōne *n.* Device for detecting vibrations in ground. [f. GEO- + -PHONE]

gēophȳ'sĭc|s (-z-) *n.* The physics of the earth; hence ~AL *a.*, ~IST (3) *n.* [f. GEO- + PHYSICS]

gēopŏ'lĭtics *n.* Politics of a country as determined by its geographical features; hence **gēopolĭ'tĭc**AL *a.* [f. GEO- + POLITICS]

||**Geor'dĭe** (jôr'-) *n.* Native of Tyneside. [f. foll. + -IE]

George (jôrj) *n.* **1.** Man's name; SAINT *George.* **2.** Jewel forming part of Garter insignia. **3.** ||(sl.) Automatic pilot of aircraft. **4. By ~,** oath or exclamation of surprise or approval; ||**~ Cross, Medal,** decorations for (esp. civilian) gallantry, instituted 1940 by King George VI. [f. L f. Gk *Geōrgios* d. 303, perh. a supposed prince of Lydda and dragon-slayer, martyred under Diocletian]

georgĕ'tte (jôr-) *n.* A thin silk or other crêpe dress-material. [f. dressmaker's name]

Geor'gĭan¹ (jôr'-) *a.* Of the time of the first four Kings George (1714–1830); of the time of Kings George V and VI (1910–52), esp. of literature of 1910–20. [f. GEORGE + -IAN]

Geor'gĭan² (jôr'-) *a.* & *n.* (Native, inhabitant, or language) of Georgia in the Caucasus; (native or inhabitant) of Georgia in U.S. [f. *Georgia* + -AN]

gē'osphēre *n.* Solid surface of earth; any of the almost spherical concentric regions of the earth and its atmosphere. [f. GEO- + -SPHERE]

gēostā'tionarȳ *a.* (Of artificial satellite of earth) moving so as to remain always above same point on earth's surface. [f. GEO- + STATIONARY]

gēostrŏ'phĭc *a.* (Meteorol.) Depending on the rotation of the earth. [f. GEO- + Gk *strophē* a turning (*strephō* to turn) + -IC]

gēother'mal *a.* Pertaining to the earth's internal heat. [f. GEO- + THERMAL]

gėŏ'tropĭsm *n.* Plant-growth in relation to gravity; **positive ~,** tendency of roots etc. to grow towards, **negative ~**, tendency of stems etc. to grow away from, centre of earth; so **gēotrŏ'p**IC *a.* [f. GEO- + Gk *tropikos* (*tropē* a turning f. *trepō* to turn; see -IC) + -ISM]

Ger. *abbr.* German.

gerā'nĭum *n.* Crane's-bill, herb or shrub of genus *Geranium* bearing fruit shaped like bill of crane; (pop.) cultivated pelargonium; colour of the scarlet geranium. [L, f. Gk *geranion* (*geranos* crane)]

gēr'bera (*or* g-) *n.* African or Asian herb of genus *Gerbera*, esp. Transvaal daisy. [f. T. *Gerber*, Ger. naturalist d. 1743 + -A 1]

gēr'bĭl, jēr'bĭl, *n.* Mouselike desert rodent of subfamily Gerbillinae, with long hind legs. [f. F *gerbille* f. mod. L *gerbillus* dim. of *gerbo* JERBOA]

gerfalcon. Var. of GYRFALCON.

gĕrĭă'tr|ĭc *a.* Relating to ~ICS *n. pl.*, branch of medical or social science dealing with health and welfare of old people; so **gĕrĭătrĭ'**CIAN, ~IST (3), *ns.* [f. Gk *gēras* old age + *iatros* physician + -IC]

gērm *n.*, & *v.i.* **1.** *n.* Portion of organism capable of developing into a new one, rudiment of animal or plant; embryo of seed (*wheat germ*). **2.** Micro-organism or microbe, esp. one of those supposed to cause disease, whence ~'Y² *a.* **3.** (fig.) That from which something may spring, elementary principle (**in ~**, not yet developed). **4. ~-cell,** cell in body of an organism which is specialized for reproductive purposes, and which, when united to one of the opposite sex, forms a new individual; **~-plasm,** nuclear part of germ-cell by which, according to Weismann's theory, hereditary characteristics are transmitted; **~ warfare** (using germs to spread disease). **5.** *v.i.* (fig.) Germinate, sprout. [f. F *germe* f. L *germen germinis* sprout]

gēr'man¹ *a.* **1.** (placed after *brother, sister, cousin*). In the fullest sense of relationship, not half-brother etc. **2.** (arch.) = GERMANE. [ME, f. OF *germain* f. L *germanus* genuine, of same parents]

Gēr'man² *a.* & *n.* **1.** *a.* Of or characterizing Germany or its people or language. **2. ~ band** (of street musicians); **~ measles,** contagious disease like mild measles, rubella; **~ Ocean,** (arch.) North Sea; **~ sausage,** large sausage stuffed with spiced partly cooked meat; ***~ shepherd (dog)**, Alsatian; **~ silver,** silver-like white alloy of nickel, zinc, and copper. **3.** *n.* Native or language of Germany (**High ~**, form of German orig. spoken in South, but now in literary and cultured use throughout Germany; **Low ~**, (1) dialects of Germany that are not High German, (2) all forms of West Germanic, including English and Dutch, except High German). **4.** Hence ~ISH¹ *a.*, ~ISM (2, 3, 4), ~IST (1, 3), *ns.*, ~IZE (2, 3, 4) *v.t.* & *i.*, **~iz**A'TION, **~īz**ER¹, *ns.*, **Gēr'măno-** *comb. form*, **Gēr'măno**MA'NIA *n.*, **Gērmă'no**PHIL(E), **Gērmă'no**PHOBE, *ns.* & *adjs.*, **Gērmă'no**PHO'BIA *n.* [f. L *Germanus* a. & n. of related peoples of central and N. Europe, name perh. given by Celts to their neighbours (cf. OIr. *gair* neighbour)]

gērmă'nder *n.* Plant of genus *Teucrium*; **~ speedwell,** blue-flowered speedwell with germander-like leaves. [ME, f. med. L *germandra* ult. f. Gk *khamaidrus* (*khamai* on the ground, *drus* oak)]

gērmā'ne *a.* Relevant or pertinent *to* the matter or subject. [var. of GERMAN¹]

Gērmă'nĭc¹ *a.* & *n.* **1.** *a.* (Hist.) Of the Germans (*Germanic Confederation, Empire*). **2.** Of the Scandinavians, Anglo-Saxons, or Germans. **3.** *a.* & *n.* (Of) the primitive language of the Germanic peoples; **East ~**, Gothic and some almost lost languages, as Burgundian and Vandal; INDO-*Germanic*; **North ~**, Scandinavian; **West ~**, High and Low German, English, Frisian, Dutch, etc. **4.** Having German characteristics; hence ~ISM (2, 4) *n.* [f. L *Germanicus* (as GERMAN²; see -IC)]

gērmă'nĭc² *a.* (Chem.) Of or containing germanium, esp. in quadrivalent state. [f. foll. + -IC]

gērmā'nĭum *n.* Brittle greyish-white semi-metallic element. [mod. L, f. *Germanus* GERMAN² + -IUM]

gērmā'nous *a.* (Chem.) Containing germanium in the bivalent state. [f. prec. + -OUS]

gēr'mĕn *n.* (Bot.) Rudiment of seed-vessel. [L, = sprout]

gēr'mĭcīd|e *n.* Substance having power to destroy (esp. disease-)germs; hence ~AL *a.* [f. GERM + -I- + -CIDE (1)]

gēr'mĭnal *a.* Of germs, of the nature of a germ, (GERM 1); in the earliest stage of development; productive of new ideas etc.; hence ~LY² *adv.* [f. as GERM + -AL]

gēr'mĭn|āte *v.* **1.** *v.i.* Sprout, bud, put forth shoots, (lit. or fig.); so ~ANT *a.* (fig.). **2.** *v.t.* Cause to shoot or sprout, develop, produce. **3.** Hence or cogn. ~A'TION, **~ātor**, *ns.*, ~ATIVE *a.* [f. L *germinare* (as GERM) + -ATE³]

gēr'mon *n.* = ALBACORE 1. [F]

gĕrŏnt|ŏ'cracȳ *n.* Government by, governing body of, old men; hence **~o**CRA'TIC *a.* [f. Gk *gerōn -ontos* old man + -O- + -CRACY]

gĕrŏntŏ'|logȳ *n.* Scientific study of old age and process of ageing, and of old people's special problems; hence **gĕrŏnto**LO'GICAL *a.*, ~LOGIST *n.* [f. as prec. + -O- + -LOGY]

gĕrŏntophĭ'lĭa, gĕrŏntŏ'phĭlȳ, *n.* Desire for sexual relations with old people; so **gĕrŏ'nto**PHIL(E) *n.* & *a.*, **gĕrŏntophĭ'l**IC *a.* [f. as GERONTOCRACY + -PHIL + -IA¹, -Y¹]

-gerous *suf.* forming *adjs.* (usu. w. intermediate -I-), w. sense 'bearing' (*lanigerous, setigerous*). [f. or after L *-ger* bearing (*gerere* bear) + -OUS]

gĕrrȳmă'nder *v.t.*, & *n.* **1.** *v.t.* Manipulate boundaries of (constituency etc.) unfairly so as to secure disproportionate influence at election for some party or class; hence ~ER¹ *n.* **2.** *n.* Such manipulation. [v. f. n., orig. U.S., by substitution of name of governor *Gerry* of Massachusetts (1812) for *sala-* in *salamander*]

gēr'tcha (g-) *int.* (vulg.) Get away with you! (expr. disbelief). [corrupt.]

gĕ'rund *n.* **1.** Form of Latin verb (*-ndum -ndi -ndo*) serving as cases of infinitive used as noun, construed as noun but able to govern object etc. like the verb; **~-grinder,** (arch.) teacher of Latin. **2.** English verbal noun in ~ING¹ when used distinctly as part of verb (*what is the use of my scolding him?*). **3.** Hence **gerŭ'nd**IAL *a.* [f. LL *gerundium* f. *gerundum* var. of *gerendum* gerund of L *gerere* do]

gerŭ'ndĭve *a.* & *n.* **1.** *a.* Of or like the gerund. **2.** *n.* Latin verbal adjective (*-ndus*) from gerund stem having sense 'that should be done' etc.; hence **gĕrundī'v**AL *a.*, ~LY² (-vlĭ) *adv.* [f. LL *gerundivus* (*modus* mood) f. *gerundium* (see prec.)]

gĕ'ssō *n.* (*pl.* **~es**). Plaster of Paris or gypsum prepared for use in painting or sculpture. [It., f. L GYPSUM]

gĕ'stagĕn *n.* (Med.) Substance having hormonal effects similar to those of ovulation; hence **gĕstagĕ'n**IC *a.* [f. GESTATION + -GEN]

Gesta'lt, g-, (geshtah'lt) *n.* (Psych.) Perceived organized whole that is more than sum of its parts, e.g. a melody as distinct from the separate notes of it; **~ psychology** (holding that perceptions, reactions, etc., are Gestalts); hence ~ISM (3), ~IST (2), *ns.* [G, = form, shape]

Gesta'pō (gestah'-; *or* gĕ-) *n.* German secret state police of Nazi regime; organization comparable to this. [G, f. *Ge*heime *Sta*ats*po*lizei]

gĕstā'te *v.t.* Carry (as) in gestation. [f. as foll. + -ATE[3]]

gĕstā'tion *n.* Carrying or being carried in the womb between conception and birth; this period. [f. L *gestatio* (*gestare* frequent. of *gerere* carry; see -ATION)]

gĕstatŏr'ial *a.* ~ **chair** (for carrying pope on certain occasions). [f. L *gestatorius* (*gestator* carrier f. as prec. + -OR; see -ORY) + -AL]

gĕstĭ'cūl|āte *v.* **1.** *v.i.* Use expressive motion of limbs or body with or instead of speech. **2.** *v.t.* Express thus. **3.** Hence or cogn. ~A'TION, ~**ā**TOR, *ns.*, ~ATIVE, ~**ā**TORY, *adjs.* [f. L *gesticulari* (*gesticulus* dim. of *gestus* GESTURE) + -ATE[3]]

gĕ'stur|e *n.* & *v.* **1.** *n.* Significant movement of limb or body; use of such movements as expression of feeling or as rhetorical device; (fig.) step or move calculated to evoke response from another or to convey (esp. friendly) intention; hence ~AL *a.* **2.** *v.i.* & *t.* = prec. [ME, f. med. L *gestura* (L *gerere gest-* wield; see -URE)]

gesundheit (gezōō'nt-hīt) *int.* expr. wish of good health, esp. to person who sneezes. [G, = health]

gĕt[1] (g-) *v.* (**-tt-;** *past* **got;** *p.p.* **got,** in comb. or arch. or U.S. **go'tten;** *got* also colloq. abbr. of *has got* or *have got*). **1.** *v.t.* Come into possession of, obtain, procure, by effort or contrivance, extract (coal from mine), prepare (meal etc.), earn (*cannot get a living*), gain (*got little by it*), win (*get the* UPPER *hand, the advantage, the* BETTER[1], *of* a person; *get the* BEST[1] *of it*; *get fame, credit, glory,* etc.; *get knowledge* or WIND[1] *of*, learn, hear rumours of; *get runs* or *wickets* at cricket, *tricks* at cards etc.). **2.** Learn *by heart* or *by rote.* **3.** Obtain as result of calculation (*we get 9·5 as the average*). **4.** Receive as gift, wages, etc.; extract by prayer, demand, inquiry, etc., (*from, out of*; *could not get leave, any supper*); come to have (desired thing, as *rest*, one's *way, a sight of, possession of*; *get* RELIGION); contract (idea etc.; **get it into** one's **head,** be convinced *that*; *get measles, the giggles*; *get* person or thing *on the* BRAIN; **have got it bad**(**ly**), (sl.) be infatuated); have inflicted on one, suffer, receive as one's lot or penalty, (*fall, blow, the worst of it, six months in prison*; **get his, theirs,** etc., (sl.) be killed; **get it,** be punished, scolded, etc.; *get it in the* NECK[1]; *get the* BOOT[1], *the* SACK[1]). **5.** (with *for* or ind. obj.) Procure, provide, (*got him a place, some dinner*; *we can get it for you*). **6.** Catch (fish, train, etc.); (deliberately) kill or injure; bring in, carry home, (crop); pick up (broadcast signal); communicate with (person or place) by telephone; (esp. in *perf.* and *past*, colloq.) corner, puzzle, catch in argument; (colloq.) understand (person or thing); (colloq.) annoy; (colloq.) attract, obsess; (colloq.) take, eat, (dinner etc.). **7.** (in *perf.*, colloq.) Have (*have not got a penny*; *I've got it!*; **have got to** = *have to*, see HAVE[1] 13). **8.** (Usu. of animals) beget. **9.** (w. compl.) Succeed in bringing, placing, etc., (*got it over* or *across, through door, into room*, etc., (fig.) *flattery will get you nowhere*); bring into some state (**get with child,** make pregnant; *get them ready*; *get your hair cut*; *get ship* etc. *under* WAY; *get it done, got himself elected*); suffer injury etc. to some part of one (*got my elbow dislocated*; *shall get my feet wet*); induce, prevail upon, (person) *to* do. **10.** *v.i.* Succeed in coming or going *to, from, into, out of, through, over, here, nowhere* (lit. or fig.), *as far as*, etc. (*where has it got to?*, what has become of it?; ***get to** do, succeed in doing); (sl.) be off, clear out; (w. *inf.*) acquire habit (*one soon gets to like it*); come to be do*ing* or *to* do (*they got talking, got to know her quite well*; *get* CRACK[2]*ing*); become (*get tired, hot, excited, drunk*; **get well, better,** recover from illness; *get clear, rid,* or *quit, of*; **get-rich-quick,** attempting to acquire wealth rapidly; *get* ROUND[3] *to*; *get under* WAY; **get* WISE[1] *to*; *get married, used to it, caught in the rain, shelved*). **11.** (w. *preps.*): ~ **across,** (sl.) annoy; *~ **around,** = *get round*; ~ **at,** reach (whence ~**-a't-able** *a.*), get hold of, ascertain, (colloq.) imply (*what are you getting at?*), (sl.) tamper with, bribe, etc., (sl.) attack, banter, (*who are you getting at?*); ~ **into,** (colloq.) put on (boots, clothes), become interested in, take possession of (*what's got into you tonight?*), (of liquor) affect, confuse, (one's *head*); ~ **off,** dismount from, obtain release from (engagement etc.), not remain on (the grass etc.); ~ **on,** place oneself on, climb on to, (horse, bicycle, etc.; *get on* person's NERVES), rise on one's *feet* or *legs* to speak in public, (colloq.) discover *something* etc. incriminating about (person); ~ **outside** (**of**), (sl.) eat; ~ **over,** surmount (difficulty), show (evidence, argument) to be unconvincing, recover from (illness) or from surprise at, accomplish (distance, task, etc.); ~ **round,** (1) cajole, (2) evade; ~ **through,** bring to an end, (of Bill etc.) be passed by (Lords, Commons, etc.), spend (money), while away (time etc.); ~ **to,** arrive at, begin (business etc.). **12.** (w. *advs.*): ~ **about,** go from place to place, begin walking after illness etc., (of news) be circulated, esp. orally; ~ **across,** (colloq.) be or make effective or acceptable; ~ **along,** advance, meet with success, fare *ill* or *well* etc., manage *without* something, live harmoniously (*together* or *with*); ~ *along with you!*, (colloq.) be off!, nonsense!; *~ **around,** visit many places; ~ **away,** escape (*from*), start, (colloq., in *imper.*) be off! nonsense!, (usu. w. neg.) escape *from* (fact etc.); ~*-away* n., escape esp. after committing crime; ~ *away with it*, succeed in what one tries to do, escape retribution, act with impunity; ~ **back,** come home etc., recover (lost thing); ~ *back at*, (colloq.) retaliate on; ~ (*some of*) one's *own back*, (sl.) have revenge; ~ **by,** (colloq.) be (just) adequate, manage *without* etc.; ~ **down,** alight, swallow, record in writing, (colloq.) depress, weary; ~ *down to*, begin work on; ~ **in,** be elected as M.P. etc., obtain place at college etc., enter vehicle, arrive at destination, bring home (crop), collect (money owed etc.), fit (work etc.) into given time, become friendly *with*, succeed in placing (blow); *get a word in* EDGEWAYS; ~ **off,** escape (from), alight from public vehicle (*tell* person *where he gets off*, (colloq.) rebuke his presumption etc.), start, (cause to) go to sleep, be acquitted or pardoned, be let off *with* or *for* specified penalty, procure acquittal or slight penalty for (person), dispatch (letter etc.); ~ *off with*, (colloq.) become on friendly or amorous terms with member of opposite sex; ~ **on,** display (pace; *get a* MOVE[1] *on*), advance, make progress, prosper, fare, manage *without* something, agree or live sociably (*with*); *getting on*, becoming old or (of time) late; *getting on for*, approaching (an age, time, etc.); ~ *on to*, (colloq.) succeed in understanding, become aware of (fact), communicate with (person); ~ **out,** transpire, elicit, succeed in uttering, publishing, etc., finish (puzzle etc.), dismiss or be dismissed at cricket, leave one's house, alight from vehicle, (in *imper.*) be off!, nonsense!; ~ *out of*, issue or escape from (*got out of* BED[1] *on wrong side*; *get out of sight*, disappear; *get out of* one's DEPTH; *get out of hand*, break from control), abandon (habit) gradually, evade do*ing*, elicit (information) or obtain (money) from (person); ~*-out* n., (colloq.) means of evasion (*for* or *like all get-out*, (sl.) with utmost vigour etc.); ~ **over,** = *get across* adv.; ~ **over** (**with**), bring (troublesome task) to an end; ~ **round,** (of news) = *get about*; ~ *round to*, find time etc. to deal with;

~ **there,** (sl.) succeed, understand what is meant; ~ **through,** bring to or reach destination, (of Bill) be passed in Parliament, succeed in an examination, make contact by radio or telephone; ~ *through to,* (colloq.) reach attention or understanding of; ~ *through with,* succeed in doing or enduring; ~ **together,** collect (*t.* & *i.*), unite in discussion, promotion of plan, etc., (sl.) put in order; ~*-together* n., (colloq.) (social) assembly; ~ **under,** subdue (fire); ~ **up,** rise esp. from bed, mount esp. on horseback, (of fire, wind, sea) begin to be violent, (of game) rise from cover, (of cricket-ball) rise sharply from pitch, organize, set on foot, make presentable, arrange the appearance of (hair, one*self,* mounting of play, binding and print of book), make rise (*get* person's BACK[1] *up*), produce (*get up speed,* STEAM[1]; *get the* WIND[1] *up*), work up (factitious emotion, subject for examination etc.; *got-up,* artificially produced or adorned to impress or deceive); ~*-up* n., style of equipment, costume, production of book, etc.; ~ *up to,* indulge in (prank etc.). **13.** Hence ~'TABLE *a.* [ME, f. ON *geta* obtain, beget, guess, = OE *-gietan* (cf. BEGET, FORGET) f. Gmc **getan* etc. f. IE **ghed-* seize]

gĕt² (g-) *n.* Begetting, offspring, (of animals); (sl.) fool, idiot. [ME, f. prec.]

ge'ta (gā'-) *n. pl.* Japanese wooden shoes with thong between big toe and other toes. [Jap. (*ge* under, *ta* footwear)]

gĕ'tter (g-) *n.*, & *v.t.* **1.** *n.* In vbl senses; (Phys.) substance used to remove residual gas from evacuated vessel. **2.** *v.t.* Remove (gas), evacuate (vessel), by means of getter. [ME, f. GET[1] + -ER[1]]

gē'um *n.* Rosaceous plant of genus *Geum,* incl. herb bennet. [mod. L, var. of L *gaeum*]

GeV *abbr.* gigaelectron-volt.

gew'gaw (g-) *n.* Gaudy plaything or ornament, bauble; paltry showy trifle. [ME, of unkn. orig.]

gey (gā) *a.* & *adv.* (Sc.) **1.** *a.* Considerable; ~ **and,** = sense 2. **2.** *adv.* Very, considerably. [var. of GAY]

gey'ser *n.* **1.** (gī'z- *or* gā'z-). Intermittent hot spring throwing up column of water. **2.** ||(gē'z-). Apparatus for quickly heating water for washing etc. [f. Icel. *Geysir* name of a particular spring in Iceland (*geysa* to gush)]

G.G. *abbr.* Governor-General.

Ghanai'an (gah-) *a.* & *n.* (Native or inhabitant) of Ghana. [f. *Ghana* in W. Africa + -IAN]

ghar̄'ial (gar̄'-). Var. of GAVIAL.

ghă'rrȳ (gă'-) *n.* Indian carriage (usu. horse-drawn and plying for hire). [f. Hindi *gāṛī*]

gha'stl|ȳ (gah'-) *a.* & *adv.* **1.** *a.* Horrible, frightful, shocking; (colloq.) objectionable, unpleasant; deathlike, pale, wan, lurid; (of smile etc.) painfully forced; hence ~ĭLY[2] *adv.*, ~ĭNESS *n.* **2.** *adv.* Ghastlily (pale etc.). [ME *gastlich* f. obs. *gast* terrify + -LY[1]; *gh-* after *ghost*]

ghat, ghaut, (gawt) *n.* (Ind.) **1.** Flight of steps leading to river; landing-place; **burning-~,** level area at top of river ghat on which Hindus burn their dead. **2.** Mountain pass, defile; **Eastern, Western, G~s,** mountain chains parallel to east and west coasts of S. India. [f. Hindi *ghāṭ*]

Gha'zi (gah'-) *n.* Muslim fighter against non-Muslims. [f. Arab. *al-ġāzī* part. of *ġazā* raid]

ghee, ghi, (gē) *n.* Indian clarified butter from milk of buffalo or cow. [f. Hindi *ghī* f. Skr. *ghṛitá-* sprinkled]

gherao' (gĕrow') *n.* (*pl.* ~**s**). (India & Pakistan). Harassment of employers etc. by workers' preventing them from leaving premises until claims are granted. [f. Hindi *gherna* besiege]

gher̄'kĭn (gẽr̄'-) *n.* Young green, or small kind of, cucumber used for pickling. [f. Du. **gurkkijn* dim. of (*a*)*gurk* f. Slavonic, ult. f. med. Gk *aggourion*]

ghĕ'ttō (gĕ'-) *n.* (*pl.* ~**s**), & *v.t.* **1.** *n.* (Hist.) Jews' quarter in city. **2.** Part of city, esp. slum area, occupied by minority group(s); isolated or segregated group or area. **3.** *v.t.* Put or keep (people) in ghetto. [perh. f. It. *getto* foundry (applied to site of first ghetto in Venice 1516)]

ghi. See GHEE.

Ghĭ'bellĭn|e (gĭ'-) *n.* & *a.* **1.** *n.* Member of emperor's faction (opp. GUELPH) in medieval Italian States; hence ~ISM (3) *n.* **2.** *a.* Adhering to Ghibellines. [f. It. *Ghibellino* supposed to be f. G *Waiblingen* estate belonging to Hohenstaufen emperors]

ghillie. Var. of GILLIE.

ghōst (gō-) *n.* & *v.* **1.** *n.* Soul of dead person in Hades etc.; spectre esp. of dead person appearing to the living (**raise, lay,** ~, cause it to appear or to cease appearing); emaciated person; shadowy outline or semblance (**not the ~ of a chance,** no chance at all). **2. Give** or (arch.) **yield up the** ~, die, (fig.) give up hope; HOLY *Ghost.* **3.** Bright spot or secondary image in field of telescope due to defect of lens; faint duplicated image in television picture. **4.** ~ (**writer**), artistic or literary hack doing the work for which his employer takes credit. **5.** ~ **moth,** hovering white nocturnal moth; ~ **town,** town with few or no remaining inhabitants; **~-word,** word originating from writer's or printer's error or popular etymology, as *tweed*; **the ~ walks,** (Theatr. sl.) salaries are, or will soon be, paid. **6.** Hence ~'HOOD (-t-h-) *n.*, ~'LIKE *a.* **7.** *v.t.* & *i.* Haunt, prowl, act, as a ghost; act or write as a ghost writer etc. (*for*). [OE *gāst,* = OS *gēst,* OHG *geist* f. WG **gaista*; sp. *gh-* first in Caxton, prob. due to Flem. *gheest*; sense 2 f. obs. meanings 'principle of life, spirit']

ghō'stl|ȳ (gō'-) *a.* **1.** As of a ghost, spectral. **2.** (arch.) Spiritual, incorporeal, concerned with sacred or ecclesiastical matters. **3.** Hence ~ĭNESS *n.* [OE *gāstlic* (as prec., -LY[1])]

ghoul (go͞ol *or* gowl) *n.* Spirit preying on corpses in Muslim superstition; (fig.) person unnaturally interested in death etc.; hence ~'ISH[1] *a.* [f. Arab. *ġūl* protean desert demon]

G.H.Q. *abbr.* General Headquarters.

||**ghyll.** Var. of GILL[2].

G.I. (jē'ī *or* jēī') *a.* & *n.* **1.** *a.* For or pertaining to U.S. armed forces or servicemen; ~ **bride,** foreign woman married to U.S. serviceman on duty abroad; ~ **Joe,** (colloq.) American private soldier. **2.** *n.* American private soldier. [abbr. of *government* (or *general*) *issue*]

giallo antico (jahlō ahntē'kō) *n.* Rich-yellow marble found in Italian ruins. [It., = ancient yellow]

gī'ant *n.* & *a.* **1.** *n.* Legendary being of human form but superhuman stature; (Gk Myth.) one of the sons of Gaea (Earth) and Uranus (Heaven) or Tartarus (Hell) who warred against the Gods; abnormally tall person, animal, or plant; large diffuse star. **2.** Agency of enormous power; person of extraordinary ability, courage, strength, etc., (**there were ~s in those days,** our forefathers were superior to us). **3. ~-killer,** one who defeats a seemingly much more powerful opponent; **~-powder,** kind of dynamite; **~('s)-stride,** gymnastic apparatus of pole with revolving head and hanging ropes enabling user to take huge strides round pole. **4.** Hence ~ESS[1] *n.*, ~ISM *n.* = GIGANTISM, ~-LIKE *a.* **5.** *a.* Of extraordinary size or force, gigantic, monstrous; (of plant) unusually large (*the giant fennel*); *giant* PANDA; *giant* SLALOM. [ME *geant* (later infl. by L) f. OF, f. Rom. **gagante* f. L f. Gk *gigas gigantos*]

giaour (jowr) *n.* (Turkish derog. name for) non--Muslim, esp. Christian. [f. Pers. *gaur, gōr*]
gĭb (*or* g-) *n.* Piece of wood or metal used to keep some part of machine etc. in place; bolt, pin, or wedge. [18th c.; orig. unkn.]
Gĭb. *n.* (colloq.) Gibraltar. [abbr.]
gĭ'bber¹ (g-) *n.* (Austral.) Boulder, (large) stone. [Aboriginal]
gĭ'bber² (*or* g-) *v.i.*, & *n.* **1.** *v.i.* Speak fast and inarticulately, chatter like an ape. **2.** *n.* Such speech or sound. [imit.]
gĭbberĕ'llĭn *n.* One of a group of compounds acting as growth-regulators in many plants. [f. *Gibberella* genus of fungi, dim. of genus-name *Gibbera* f. L *gibber* hump + -IN]
gĭ'bberĭsh (*or* g-) *n.* Unintelligible speech, meaningless sounds; blundering or ungrammatical talk. [perh. f. GIBBER² (but found earlier) + -ISH¹ as used in *Spanish, Swedish*, etc.]
gĭ'bbėt *n.*, & *v.t.* **1.** *n.* (Hist.) Gallows; upright post with arm on which bodies of executed criminals were hung up. **2.** Death by hanging. **3.** *v.t.* Put to death by hanging; expose on gibbet; hang up as on gibbet; hold up to infamy or contempt. [ME, f. OF *gibet* gallows dim. of *gibe* club, prob. f. Gmc]
gĭ'bbon (g-) *n.* Long-armed S.E. Asian ape of genus *Hylobates*. [F, f. aboriginal name]
gĭ'bbous (g-) *a.* Convex, protuberant; (of moon or planet) having bright part greater than semicircle and less than circle; humped, hunchbacked; hence or cogn. **gĭbbo**'SITY (g-) *n.*, ~LY² *adv.* [ME, f. LL *gibbosus* (*gibbus* hump; see -OUS)]
gībe, jībe², *v.* & *n.* **1.** *v.i.* & *t.* Flout, jeer, mock, (at or *at*); hence **gī'b**ER¹ *n.* **2.** *n.* Act of gibing, taunt. [perh. f. OF *giber* handle roughly]
gĭ'blėt|s *n. pl.* Edible parts of bird taken out or cut off before cooking, as liver, gizzard; ~ **soup** (made with these). [f. OF *gibelet* game stew, perh. f. **giberet* (*gibier* game)]
gĭ'ddăp (g-; *or* -ă'p) *int.* (colloq.) of command to horse etc.: go on, go faster. [f. *get up*]
gĭ'ddȳ (g-) *a.* & *v.* **1.** *a.* Having sensation of whirling and tendency to fall, stagger, or spin round (*with* sickness, success, etc.); making dizzy (*a giddy precipice, maze, success*); circling with bewildering speed; mentally intoxicated, incapable of attention, excitable, frivolous (**play the ~ goat** or **ox,** fool about); inconstant, flighty, (also as intensive, esp. iron.); **my ~ aunt,** excl. of surprise; hence **gĭ'ddĭ**LY² *adv.*, **gĭ'ddĭ**NESS *n.*, (g-). **2.** *v.t.* & *i.* Make or become giddy. [OE *gidig* insane (as GOD, -Y²), lit. 'possessed by a god']
Gĭ'dėon (g-) *n.* Member of organization placing Bibles in hotel rooms etc. [f. ~ in Judges 6:11ff.]
gĭft (g-) *n.*, & *v.t.* **1.** *n.* Giving (*the living* **is in the ~ of** *the Bishop*, is his to bestow; *came to me by free gift*); (Law) voluntary transference of property with compensation. **2.** Thing given, present, donation, (FREE¹ *gift*; *would not have it* **as a ~,** (arch.) **at a ~,** even gratis); faculty miraculously bestowed, virtue looked upon as emanation from heaven etc., (*gift of* TONGUE¹*s*); natural endowment (*gift of the* GAB), talent, whence ~'ED² *a.*; easy task etc. **3. ~-book,** book given or suitable for giving as present; ~ **coupon,** voucher issued with certain commodities, a specified number of which entitles holder to a gift; **~-horse,** horse given as present (*look a ~-horse in the mouth*, find fault with a gift); ~ **shop,** shop selling articles suitable for gifts; ~ **token** or **voucher,** voucher for money to buy something, used as gift; **~-wrap** *v.t.*, wrap attractively (as gift). **4.** Hence ~'IE *n.* (Sc.; *the giftie gie us to see oursels as others see us*). **5.** *v.t.* Endow with gifts, present *with* as gift; bestow as gift (*to* person; *away*). [ME, f. ON *gipt* = OE, OS, OHG *gift*, Goth. *-gifts* f. Gmc **geftiz* (**gebh-* GIVE¹)]
gĭg¹ (g-) *n.* **1.** Light two-wheeled one-horse carriage. **2.** Light narrow clinker-built ship's--boat for rowing or sailing; rowing-boat chiefly used for racing. [ME in var. senses; prob. imit.]
gĭg² (g-) *n.* Kind of fish-spear. [short for *fizgig, fishgig*; cf. Sp. *fisga* harpoon]
gĭg³ (g-) *n.*, & *v.i.* (colloq.) **1.** *n.* Engagement of musician(s) to play jazz etc., esp. for one night only; place of such performance. **2.** *v.i.* Perform gig. [20th c.; orig. unkn.]
gĭ'ga- (*or* g-) *pref.* denoting factor of 10^9 (*giga*METRE²). [f. Gk *gigas* giant]
gīgă'nt|ĭc *a.* Giant-like in size, stature, etc., abnormally large, huge; hence or cogn. ~E'SQUE *a.*, ~ICALLY *adv.* [f. L *gigas gigantis* GIANT + -IC]
gĭ'gantĭsm *n.* Abnormal largeness, esp. (Path.) excessive growth due to hormonal imbalance, or to polyploidy in plants. [f. as prec. + -ISM]
gĭ'ggle (g-) *v.* & *n.* **1.** *v.i.* Laugh in affected or silly manner, titter, have small bursts of half--suppressed laughter. **2.** *v.t.* Utter thus. **3.** *n.* Such laugh, freq. in *pl.* (*fit of*) *the giggles*; (colloq.) amusing person or thing, a joke (*did it for a giggle*); hence **gĭ'ggl**Y² *a.* [imit.; cf. Du. *gi(e)chelen*, G *gickeln*]
gĭ'glėt, gĭ'glot, (g-) *n.* Giggling girl. [ME, perh. f. obs. *gig* flighty girl (GIG¹), later assoc. w. prec.]
gĭgmă'nĭtȳ (g-) *n.* Respectable unimaginative middle classes, Philistines. [made by Carlyle 1831, f. *gigman* (GIG¹, MAN¹) + -ITY]
gĭ'golō (*or* zhĭ'-) *n.* (*pl.* ~s). Professional male dancing-partner or escort; young man paid by older woman for his attentions. [F, formed as masc. of *gigole* dance-hall woman]
gĭ'got *n.* Leg of mutton etc.; ~ **sleeve** = LEG--*of-mutton* sleeve. [F, dim. of dial. *gigue* leg]
gigue (zhēg) *n.* = JIG¹ 1; (Mus.) lively dance with two sections each repeated. [F; see JIG¹]
Gi'la (hē'la) *n.* ~ (**monster**), large venomous lizard of S.W. United States. [River ~ of New Mexico & Arizona]
gĭ'lbert (g-) *n.* Electromagnetic unit of magnetomotive force. [f. W. *Gilbert*, Engl. physician d. 1603]
Gĭlber̄'tĭan (g-; *or* -shan) *a.* (Of situation etc.) ludicrous or paradoxical, as in Gilbert and Sullivan opera. [f. W. S. *Gilbert*, Engl. librettist d. 1911 + -IAN]
gĭld¹ (g-) *v.t.* (*p.p.* sometimes **gilt** as *adj.* in lit. sense, otherwise **~'ed**). Cover with thin layer of gold laid on as gold leaf or otherwise (*gild the* LILY; ~ **the pill,** soften down unpleasant necessity), whence ~'ER¹, ~'ING¹ (2, 4), *ns.*; tinge or adorn with golden colour or light; give specious brilliance to by fair words; **~ed** or **gilt spurs,** (arch.) emblem of knighthood; **~ed youth,** young men of fashion and wealth; **gĭ'ltwood** *a.*, made of wood and gilded. [OE *gyldan*, = ON *gylla* f. Gmc **gulthjan* (**gultham* GOLD)]
gild². See GUILD.
Gĭ'lderoy (g-) *n.* *(colloq.) **Higher than ~'s kite,** very high, out of sight. [name of Scottish robber]
gĭ'lgai (gĭ'lgī) *n.* (Austral.) Saucer-like natural reservoir for rain-water. [Aboriginal]
gĭll¹ (g-) *n.* (usu. in *pl.*), & *v.t.* **1.** *n.* Respiratory organ in fishes and other water-breathing animals; wattles or dewlap of fowls; vertical radial plate on under side of mushroom etc.; flesh below person's jaws and ears (**rosy, green, about the ~s,** healthy-looking, sickly--looking). **2. ~-cover,** bony case protecting fish's gills; **~-net** (for entangling fishes by the gills). **3.** Hence (-)~ED² (-ld) *a.* **4.** *v.t.* Gut (fish);

cut off gills of (mushroom); catch in gill-net. [ME, f. ON *gil f. Gmc *geliz]

||**gill²** (g-) *n.* Deep usu. wooded ravine; narrow mountain torrent. [ME, f. ON *gil* glen]

gill³ *n.* Quarter-pint liquid measure; ||(dial.) half-pint. [ME, f. OF *gille*, med. L *gillo* f. LL *gello, gillo* water-pot]

gill⁴ *n.* **1.** (derog.) Young woman. **2.** (colloq.) Female ferret. [ME, abbr. of *Gillian* f. OF *Juliane* f. L *Juliana* (*Julius*)]

gillaroō' (g-) *n.* Irish species of trout. [f. Ir. *giolla* fellow, *ruadh* red]

gĭ'llĭe (g-) *n.* **1.** Man or boy attending sportsman in Scotland. **2.** (Hist.) Highland chief's attendant. [f. Gael. *gille* lad, servant]

gĭ'llion (-yon) *n.* A thousand million; large number. [f. GIGA- + MILLION]

gĭ'llȳflower *n.* **1.** (**Clove**) ~, clove-scented pink (CLOVE³). **2.** Other similarly scented flower, as wallflower or white stock. [ME *gilofre, gerofle*, f. OF *gilofre, girofle* f. med. L f. Gk *karuophullon* (*karuon* nut, *phullon* leaf) clove-tree; assim. to FLOWER]

gilt¹ (g-). See GILD¹.

gilt² (g-) *n.* **1.** Gilding (**take the ~ off the gingerbread,** strip thing of adventitious attractions); **~-edged,** (of securities, stocks, etc.) having high degree of reliability as investment. **2.** Gilt-edged security. [f. prec.]

gilt³ (g-) *n.* Young sow. [ME, f. ON *gyltr*]

gĭ'mbal|s (-z; *or* g-) *n. pl.* Contrivance (usu. of rings and pivots) for keeping articles (esp. compass and chronometer) horizontal at sea; **~-ring,** (ring in) gimbals. [var. of earlier *gimmal* f. OF *gemel* double finger-ring, f. L *gemellus* dim. of *geminus* twin]

gĭ'mcrăck *n.* & *a.* **1.** *n.* Trumpery article, knick-knack, useless ornament; hence ~ERY (5) *n.*, ~Y² *a.* **2.** *a.* Showy and flimsy, worthless, trumpery. [ME *gibecrake* (? inlaid work), of unkn. orig.]

gĭ'mlėt (g-) *n.* Kind of small boring-tool (usu. with wooden crosspiece as handle and screw at pointed end); cocktail usu. of gin and lime-juice; ~ **eye,** eye with sharp or piercing glance. [ME, f. OF *guimbelet*, dim. of *guimble*, whence obs. E *wimble*]

gĭ'mmė (g-) *v.t.* (colloq.) = *give me*. [contr.]

gĭ'mmĭck (g-) *n.* (sl.) Tricky device, esp. one adopted for the purpose of attracting attention or publicity; hence ~RY (5) *n.*, ~Y² *a.* [20th c. U.S.; orig. unkn.]

gĭmp¹, gȳmp, (g-) *n.* Silk, worsted, or cotton twist with cord or wire running through it, used esp. as trimming; fishing-line of silk etc. bound with wire; coarser thread outlining design of lace. [Du., of unkn. orig.]

gĭmp² (g-) *n.* (sl.) Courage. [20th c.; orig. uncert.]

gĭn¹ *n.*, & *v.t.* (**-nn-**). **1.** Snare, net, trap. **2.** *n.* Hoisting apparatus, kind of crane or windlass. **3.** Machine for separating cotton from its seeds. **4.** *v.t.* Remove seeds of (cotton) with gin. [ME, f. OF *engin* ENGINE]

gĭn² *n.* **1.** Spirit distilled from grain or malt and flavoured with juniper berries, GENEVA¹; *gin and* IT²; **pink ~,** gin flavoured with angostura bitters. **2.** ***~-mill,** drinking-saloon; **~-palace,** gaudily decorated public house; **~ rummy,** form of RUMMY² where player with cards totalling less than ten may terminate play; *gin* SLING². [abbr. of GENEVA¹]

gĭn³ (g-) *conj.* (Sc. & dial.) If. [app. rel. to *gif* (as IF, perh. after GIVE¹)]

gĭn⁴ *n.* (Austral.) Aboriginal woman. [Aboriginal]

gĭ'nger (-nj-) *n.*, *a.*, & *v.t.* **1.** *n.* (Plant esp. of genus *Zingiber* with) hot spicy root used in cooking and medicine and preserved in syrup or candied as sweet (**black ~,** unscraped, **white ~,** scraped, ginger). **2.** Mettle, spirit; stimulation; ||**~ group,** group that urges party or movement to more decided action. **3.** *n.* & *a.* (Of) light reddish-yellow colour. **4. ~-ale, -beer,** kinds of aerated ginger-flavoured drink (*~-beer plant*, mixture of yeast and bacteria to ferment sugar solution in making ginger-beer); **~bread,** (*n.*) a cake made with treacle and flavoured with ginger (*~bread nut*, small button-like cake of it; *take the* GILT² *off the gingerbread*), (*a.* & *n.*, w. allus. to fancy and often gilded shapes in which it was made) gaudy, showy, tawdry, (ornaments, e.g. Archit.); **~-nut,** gingerbread nut; **~-pop,** (colloq.) = *ginger-ale*; **~-race,** a root of ginger; **~-snap,** thin brittle cake flavoured with ginger; **~ wine,** drink of fermented sugar, water, and bruised ginger. **5.** Hence ~Y² *a.* **6.** *v.t.* Flavour with ginger; (fig., from treatment of horses) rouse *up* (person). [ME f. OE *gingiber* & OF *gingi(m)bre*, both f. med. L *gingiber* f. L *zingiber* f. Gk *ziggiberis* f. Skr. *çrngavēram* (*çrngam* horn, *vēra* body, f. antler-shape of root)]

||**gingerā'de** (-nj-) *n.* = GINGER-*beer*. [f. prec., after *lemonade*]

gĭ'ngerlȳ (-nj-) *adv.* & *a.* With or showing extreme caution so as to avoid making a noise or injuring oneself or what is touched or trodden on. [perh. f. OF *gensor* delicate, compar. of *gent* graceful f. L *genitus* (well-)born + -LY¹,²]

gĭ'ngham (gĭ'ngam) *n.* Plain-woven cotton cloth of dyed yarn often in stripes or checks. [f. Du. *gingang* f. Malay *ginggang* (orig. adj. = striped)]

gĭ'ngĭlĭ (-nj-) *n.* Sesame (oil). [f. Hindi *jinjalī* f. Arab. *juljulān*]

gĭngī'val (-nj-) *a.* Of the gums; so **gĭngĭvī'tis** (-nj-) *n.* [f. mod. L *gingivalis* f. L *gingiva* GUM¹; see -AL]

gĭ'ngkō (g-). Var. of GINKGO.

gĭ'nglȳm|us (-nggl-; *or* g-) *n.* (*pl.* **~i** *pr.* -ī). (Anat.) Hingelike joint in body with motion only in one plane (e.g. elbow). [mod. L, f. Gk *gigglumos* hinge]

gĭnk (g-) *n.* (sl., usu. derog.) Fellow, man. [20th c. U.S.; orig. unkn.]

gĭ'nkgō (g-; *or* -ngkō) *n.* (*pl.* **~s** *or* **~es**). Tree with fan-shaped leaves and yellow flowers, orig. from China and Japan. [f. Jap. *ginkyo* f. Chin. *yinhsing* silver apricot]

gĭ'nsĕng *n.* (Root of) medicinal plant of genus *Panax* found in E. Asia and N. America. [f. Chin. *jen shen* perh. = man-image, w. allus. to forked root]

Giocŏ'nda (jo-) *a.* (Of smile etc.) enigmatic. [f. painting *La Gioconda* by L. da Vinci; It., fem. of *giocondo* (as JOCUND)]

gĭ'ppȳ *n.* (sl.) Egyptian soldier; Egyptian cigarette; gipsy; **~ tummy,** diarrhoea of visitors to hot countries. [f. foll. & *Egyptian* + -Y³]

gĭ'psȳ, gȳ'psȳ, G-, *n.* **1.** Member of a wandering race (called by themselves *Romany*) of Hindu origin with dark skin and hair, living esp. by basket-making, horse-dealing, fortune-telling, etc., and speaking a language related to Hindi; person resembling or living like a gipsy. **2. ~ bonnet** (with large side flaps); **~ moth,** kind of tussock-moth very destructive to foliage; **~ rose,** scabious; **~'s warning,** cryptic or sinister warning; **~ table,** light round table on three crossed sticks. **3.** Hence ~DOM, ~HOOD, ~ISM (2), *ns.*, ~ISH¹ *a.*, ~FY *v.t.* (usu. in *p.p.*). [earlier *gipcyan, gipsen*, f. EGYPTIAN, f. supposed orig. of the race when it appeared in England in early 16th c.]

gira'ffe (*or* -ah'f) *n.* African ruminant quadruped,

tallest living animal, with spotted skin and long neck and forelegs. [f. F *girafe*, ult. f. Arab. *zarāfa*]

gi'randōle *n.* Revolving firework, discharge of rockets from revolving wheel; revolving jet of water; branched candle-bracket or candlestick; ear-ring or pendant with large central stone surrounded by small ones. [F, f. It. *girandola* (*girare* GYRATE²)]

gi'rasŏl, -sōle, *n.* Kind of opal reflecting reddish glow, fire-opal. [orig. = sunflower, f. F *girasol* or f. It. *girasole* (*girare* as prec., *sole* sun)]

gird¹ (g-) *v.t.* (~'**ed** *or* **girt**). (literary). **1.** ~ (**up**), encircle (waist), encircle waist of (person), with belt esp. to confine clothes (~ **oneself,** (**up**) one's **loins,** prepare for action); (arch.) invest *with* strength, power, etc. **2.** Equip *with* sword in belt; fasten (sword etc.) on or *on* with belt (*to* or *upon* or *on*); secure (clothes) on body with girdle or belt; put (cord etc.) *round*; encircle (town etc.) *with* besiegers or siege-works; (of belt, fence, sea, etc.) encircle. [OE *gyrdan*, = OS *gurdian*, OHG *gurten*, ON *gyrtha* f. Gmc **gurdhjan* (as GIRTH)]

gird² (g-) *v.i.*, & *n.* Jeer or gibe *at*. [ME = 'strike' etc.; orig. unkn.]

gir'der (g-) *n.* Beam supporting joists of floor; iron or steel beam for like use; latticed or other compound structure of steel etc. forming span of bridge, roof, etc. [f. GIRD¹ + -ER¹]

gir'dle¹ (g-) *n.*, & *v.t.* **1.** *n.* Belt, cord, etc. used to gird waist; corset, esp. one not extending above waist; thing that surrounds like a girdle; part of cut gem dividing crown from base and embraced by the setting; (Anat.) bony support for upper or lower limb (*shoulder* or *pectoral*, *pelvic* or *hip*, *girdle*); ring round tree made by removal of bark. **2.** *v.t.* Surround with girdle (*about*, *in*, *round*); kill (tree) or make it more fruitful by removing ring of bark round trunk. [OE *gyrdel*, = OHG *gurtil*, ON *gyrthill* (as GIRD¹, -LE 1)]

gir'dle² (g-) *n.* (Sc. & N. Engl.) Circular iron plate placed over fire or heated electrically for baking, toasting, etc.; **~-cake** (made on girdle). [var. of GRIDDLE]

gir'dler (g-) *n.* (arch.) Maker of girdles (now only as guild-name). [ME, f. GIRDLE¹ + -ER¹]

girl (g-) *n.* **1.** Female child; young woman; *old girl* (see OLD 5, 6); woman working in office, shop, factory, etc., woman secretary or other assistant; female servant; man's sweetheart. **2.** *Girl* FRIDAY; **~-friend,** female friend, esp. boy's or man's usual or preferred female companion; ~ **guide,** = GUIDE¹ 4; **les ~s** (lā-; after F *les* the), girls collectively, esp. chorus-girls; **the ~s,** group of women esp. with similar interests, grown-up daughters of a family; ***~ scout,** = GUIDE¹ 4. **3.** Hence ~'DOM, ~'HOOD, *ns.*, ~'ISH¹ *a.* [ME *gurle, girle, gerle*, perh. cogn. w. LG *gör* child]

gir'lie (g-) *n.* & *a.* **1.** *n.* Little girl (as term of endearment). **2.** *a.* (Of publication etc.) containing many pictures of young women usu. with little or no clothing. [f. prec. + -IE]

gir'lȳ-girlȳ (g-; -g-) *a.* Exaggeratedly or affectedly girlish. [redupl. f. *girly* (GIRL, -Y²)]

gir'ō *n.* (*pl.* ~**s**). System of credit transfer between banks, post offices, etc. [G f. It., = circulation (of money)]

girt¹ (g-). See GIRD¹.

girth, girt², (g-) *n.* & *v.* **1.** *n.* Leather or cloth band tightened round body of horse etc. to secure saddle etc.; measurement round any more or less cylindrical thing. **2.** *v.t.* Surround; encircle (horse etc.), secure (saddle etc.), with girth. **3.** *v.i.* Measure (so much) in girth. [ME, f. ON *gjörth*, Goth. *gairda* f. Gmc **gerdō*, cogn. w. GARTH, GIRD¹, GIRDLE¹]

***gi'smō, *gi'zmō,** (gĭ'z-) *n.* (*pl.* ~**s**). (sl.) Gadget, gimmick. [20th c.; orig. unkn.]

gist *n.* (Law) real ground of action etc.; substance or essence of a matter. [OF, 3rd sing. pres. of *gesir* lie f. L *jacēre*]

git (g-) *n.* (sl., derog.) Worthless person. [var. of GET²]

gi'ttern (g-) *n.* Gut-stringed instrument, kind of early guitar. [ME, f. OF *guiterne*; cf. CITHERN, GUITAR]

give¹ (g-) *v.t.* & *i.* (**gave** *pr.* gāv; GIVEN). **1.** *v.t.* Transfer possession of gratuitously, hand over as present, (*to* recipient); confer ownership of with or without actual delivery, render (benefit etc.) without payment; (abs.) bestow alms or donations (*to*); confer, grant, (favour, honour, etc.); accord (one's heart, affection, confidence); (of God etc.) grant (faculty etc., or *to* be or do; ~ **me,** (in *imper.*) I prefer or admire: *give me the good old times*); bequeath; sanction marriage of (daughter etc.; usu. *in marriage*); ~ **oneself,** (of woman) yield sexually. **2.** Deliver, hand over, (without reference to ownership), put (food etc.) for person to consume, administer (medicine, *the* BOOT¹, *the* SACK¹; ~ **it him** etc. (**hot**), administer punishment; ~ *child* etc. **something to cry for,** chastise for causeless crying; ~ person **what for,** (sl.) punish or scold him severely); deliver (message, LOVE¹, compliments, etc.); commit, consign, entrust, (*give into custody* or ‖*in* CHARGE¹); pledge, assign as guarantee, (one's WORD¹, *honour*, etc.). **3.** Make over in exchange or payment, pay, sell *for* price, (~ **as good as** one **gets,** retort adequately in words or blows; *give a* ROLAND *for an Oliver*; *not give a* DAMN etc.; *give* person *his* DUE²; *would give the* WORLD or one's EAR¹*s*). **4.** Devote, dedicate, addict, (*gave his life to it*; *give* one's *mind to a matter*; *much given to these pursuits*). **5.** Exert (some action or effort) esp. to affect another (*give him a kick, a kiss, a sly look*; *give a jump, cry*, etc.; *give orders*; *give* person one's *blessing*; *give* BIRTH, CHASE¹, RISE², TONGUE¹; *give you joy, good day*, [prob. orig. w. ellipsis of *God*, now taken as = *wish* with *I* expressed or omitted]); (colloq.) tell, offer, (esp. something unacceptable); deliver (judgement etc.) authoritatively (*give the case*, or *it*, *for* or *against* person; of umpire in cricket, *give batsman out* or *not out*); (in *p.p.*, of document) dated; provide (party, dinner) as host. **6.** Present, offer, expose, hold out, show, (*give* person one's *hand* or *arm*, *a* BACK¹, EAR¹; '*The Times*' *gives the facts*; *gives no sign of life*; *thermometer gives 80° in the shade*); read, recite, sing, act, perform, (play, lecture, etc.). **7.** Make partaker of, impart, be source of, (*gave me his sore throat*; *gave its name to the battle*; *she gave him four sons*; *give a piece of* one's MIND¹; *give to the* WORLD; ~ person *to understand, know*, etc., inform or assure him). **8.** Allot, assign, ascribe, grant, assume, (*he was given the contract, the name of John, quarters*; *under the given conditions*; *given health, the thing can be done*). **9.** Yield as product or result (*lamp gives a bad light*; *analysis gives the following figures*). **10.** Cause or allow to have (*solitude gives it its only charm*; *gave me much pain*; *this gives him a right to complain*; *give* oneself AIR¹*s*; *give* person BEST¹; *give* GROUND¹, PLACE¹ 12, WAY; *can give you five minutes before I must go*; *gave myself an hour to get there*; *give him thirty seconds start*; *was given a rest*); ~ **and take,** (*v.i.*) exchange words, blows, or concessions, (*n.*) exchange of words etc., compromise; ~ **or take,** (colloq.) add or subtract in estimating. **11.** *v.i.* Collapse, lose firmness, yield to pressure, become relaxed, make room, shrink. **12.** (Of window, passage, etc.) look, lead, (*up*)*on, on to, into.* **13.** (colloq.) Be happening, (*what gives?*). **14.** (w. *advs.*): ~ **away,** transfer by gift, hand over (bride) to bridegroom, betray or expose to ridicule or detection (*give the* GAME[1] or SHOW[2] *away*), distribute (prizes); ~*-away* n., (colloq.) act of giving away, free gift, low price, inadvertent betrayal; ~ **back,** return (thing) to previous owner or in exchange; ~ **down,** (of cow) let (milk, or abs.) flow; ~ **forth,** emit, publish, report; ~ **in,** yield, cease fighting or arguing, hand in (document) to proper official; ~ **off,** emit (vapour etc.); ~ **out,** announce, emit, distribute, cease or break down from exhaustion etc., run short; ~ **over,** cease from do*ing*, abandon (habit etc.), desist, hand over, devote; ~ **up,** resign, surrender, part with (*give up the* GHOST), deliver (fugitive etc.) into hands of pursuers etc., abandon one*self to* a feeling etc., cease to have to do with, cease from effort or do*ing*, (in *refl.* or *p.p.*) devote or addict *to*, divulge (names of accomplices etc.), pronounce incurable or insoluble, renounce hope (of). **15.** Hence ~'ABLE (-va-) *a.*, **gĭ'**VER[1] (g-) *n.* [OE *g(i)efan*, = OS, OHG *geban*, ON *gefa*, Goth. *giban* f. Gmc **gebhan*]

gĭve[2] (g-) *n.* Yielding to pressure, elasticity, (*there is no give in a stone floor*). [f. prec.]

gĭ'ven (g-) *a.* & *n.* **1.** *a.* In vbl senses; *~ **name,** name given (as) at baptism. **2.** *n.* Known fact or situation. [p.p. of GIVE[1]]

***gizmo.** See GISMO.

gĭ'zzard (g-) *n.* Bird's second stomach for grinding food mixed in the first with gastric juice; specially muscular stomach of some fish, insects, molluscs, etc.; **stick in** one's ~, be distasteful. [ME *giser* f. OF *giser, gesier* etc. f. Rom. **gicerium* f. L *gigeria* cooked entrails of fowl]

glabĕ'lla *n.* (*pl.* ~**e**). (Anat.) Smooth part of forehead above line of eyebrows. [mod. L, f. L *glabellus* a. dim. of *glaber* smooth]

glā'brous *a.* (Anat. & Bot.) Free from hair or down, smooth-skinned. [f. L *glaber glabri* hairless + -OUS]

gla'cé (-ah'sā; *or* -ă'-) *a.* (Of cloth, leather, etc.) smooth, polished; (of fruit) iced, sugared. [F, p.p. of *glacer* to ice, gloss (*glace* ice; see GLACIER)]

glā'cĭal (*or* -shal) *a.* **1.** Of ice, icy, (lit. or fig.); (Chem.) forming icelike crystals on freezing. **2.** (Geol.) Characterized or produced by the presence or agency of ice; ~ **epoch** or **period** (when unusually large area was covered with ice-sheet). **3.** Hence ~LY[2] *adv.* [F, or f. L *glacialis* icy (*glacies* ice; see -AL)]

glă'cĭātėd *a.* Marked or polished by ice-action; covered with glaciers or ice-sheet; so **glăcĭ**A'TION *n.* [p.p. of *glaciate* f. L *glaciare* freeze (*glacies* ice) + -ATE[3]]

glă'cĭer *n.* Slowly moving river or mass of ice formed by accumulation of snow on higher ground. [F (*glace* ice f. Rom. **glacia* f. L *glacies*)]

glācĭŏ'log|y̆ *n.* Science of geological action of ice; hence **glācĭolŏ'**GICAL *a.*, ~IST (3) *n.* [f. L *glacies* ice + -O- + -LOGY]

glă'cĭs (*or* -sē) *n.* (*pl.* same *pr.* -sĭz *or* -sēz). Bank sloping down from fort, on which attackers are exposed to defenders' missiles etc. [F, f. OF *glacier* to slip (*glace* ice; see GLACIER)]

glăd[1] *a.*, & *v.t.*, (**-dd-**). **1.** *pred. a.* Pleased (*I am glad, glad of it, glad to hear it, glad* (*that*) *it is so, shall be glad to come* etc., (iron.) *should be glad to know*). **2.** *a.* (Of looks, feelings, etc.) marked by, filled with, expressing, joy; (of news or event) giving joy; (of person's nature etc.) bright, beautiful. **3. The** ~ **eye,** (sl.) amorous or festive glance; ~ **hand,** the hand of welcome; ~**-ha'nd** *v.t.*, greet cordially; ~ **rags,** (colloq.) best clothes, evening dress. **4.** Hence ~'DEN[6] *v.t.*, ~'LY[2] *adv.*, ~'NESS *n.*, (poet.) ~'SOME[1] *a.* **5.** *v.t.* (arch.) Make glad. [OE *glæd*, = OS *glad*, ON *glathr*, OHG *glat* smooth f. Gmc **gladhaz*]

glăd[2] *n.* (colloq., usu. in *pl.*) Gladiolus. [abbr.]

glāde *n.* Clear open space or passage between forest trees. [16th. c.; orig. unkn.]

glă'dĭātor *n.* Man trained to fight with sword or other weapon at ancient Roman shows; political etc. champion in argument, controversialist; hence **glădĭatôr'**IAL *a.* [L (*gladius* sword)]

glădĭō'l|us *n.* (*pl.* ~**i** *pr.* -ī, *or* ~**uses**). Iridaceous plant with sword-shaped leaves and bright-coloured flower-spikes. [L, dim. of *gladius* sword]

Glă'dstone *n.* & *a.* ~ **(bag),** light portmanteau opening into two equal compartments. [f. W. E. ~, Engl. statesman d. 1898]

Glăgolĭ'tĭc *a.* Of alphabet ascribed to St. Cyril and formerly used in writing some Slavonic languages. [f. mod. L *glagoliticus* f. Serbo-Croatian *glagolica* Glagolitic alphabet f. OSlav. *glagol* word]

glair *n.* White of egg; adhesive preparation made from it; any similar viscous substance; hence ~'EOUS, ~'Y[2], *adjs.* [ME, f. OF *glaire*, ult. f. L *clara* fem. of *clarus* clear]

glaive *n.* (arch. or poet.) Broadsword, sword. [ME f. OF, app. f. L *gladius* sword]

glăm *n.*, *a.*, & *v.t.* (**-mm-**). (colloq.) **1.** *n.* Glamour. **2.** *a.* Glamorous. **3.** *v.t.* Glamorize. [abbr.]

Glam. *abbr.* Glamorgan(shire).

glă'morīz|e, -īs|e (-īz), **-our-** (-*er*-), *v.t.* Make glamorous or attractive; hence ~A'TION *n.* [f. foll. + -IZE]

glă'mour (-*er*), ***glă'mor,** *n.*, & *v.t.* **1.** *n.* Magic, enchantment, (**cast a** ~ **over,** enchant); delusive or alluring beauty or charm; (esp. feminine) physical attractiveness (~ **girl,** young woman possessing this; so ~ **boy**); hence **glă'mor**OUS *a.* **2.** *v.t.* Affect with glamour, bewitch, enchant; (colloq.) make glamorous. [18th c., var. of GRAMMAR in sense GRAMARYE]

glance[1] (-ah-) *v.* & *n.* **1.** *v.i.* & *t.* (Of weapon) glide off or *off* object instead of striking it full; (Cricket) deflect (ball) with glance-stroke; (of talk or talker) pass quickly *over*, glide *off* or *from*, subject; ~ **at,** make passing and usu. sarcastic allusion to. **2.** *v.i.* (Of bright object or light) flash, dart, gleam; (of eye) cast momentary look (*down, up*, etc.; ~ **at,** give brief look at; ~ **over,** read cursorily). **3.** *v.t.* ~ one's **eye,** direct it *at, over*, etc. **4.** *n.* Swift oblique movement or impact; (Cricket) stroke with bat's face turned slantwise to deflect ball; (sudden movement producing) flash or gleam; brief look (*at, into, over*, etc.); **at a** ~, immediately upon looking. [ME *glence* etc., prob. a nasalized form of obs. *glace* in same sense, f. OF *glacier* to slip (see GLACIS)]

glance[2] (-ah-) *n.* Lustrous sulphide ore (*copper glance, lead glance*). [f. G *glanz* lustre]

glănd[1] *n.* Organ in animal body secreting substances for use in the body or for ejection; (Bot.) secreting cell or group of cells on surface of plant-structure; so ~'ULE *n.* [f. F *glande* f. OF *glandre* f. L *glandulae* throat-glands]

glănd[2] *n.* (Mech.) Sleeve used to press a packing tight on a piston. [19th c., perh. var. of earlier *glam, glan* a vice, rel. to CLAMP[1]]

glă'nder|s (-z) *n. pl.* (sometimes treated as *sing.*) Contagious horse-disease with swellings below jaw and mucous discharge from nostrils; this disease communicated to man or to other animals; hence ~ED[2] (-*erd*), ~OUS, *adjs.* [f. OF *glandre* (see GLAND[1])]

glă'ndūlar *a.* Of or pertaining to gland(s) or glandule(s); ~ **fever,** infectious disease with swelling of lymph-glands. [f. F *glandulaire* (as GLAND¹*ule*; see -AR)]

glăn|s (-z) *n.* (*pl.* **~'des** *pr.* -dēz). (Anat.) Conical part forming end of penis or clitoris. [L, = acorn]

glār|e¹ *v.* & *n.* **1.** *v.i.* Shine dazzlingly or disagreeably; be over-conspicuous or obtrusive, whence ~'ING² *a.*; look fixedly or fiercely (*at, upon*). **2.** *v.t.* Express (hate, defiance) by look. **3.** *n.* Strong fierce light, oppressive unrelieved sunshine; tawdry brilliance; fierce or fixed look; hence ~'Y² *a.* [ME, = MDu. and MLG *glaren* gleam, glare]

***glāre²** *a.* (Esp. of ice) smooth and glassy. [perh. f. *glare* frost (16th c., of uncert. orig.)]

glass¹ (-ahs) *n.* **1.** Substance, usu. transparent, lustrous, hard, and brittle, made by fusing sand with soda or potash or both and other ingredients (CROWN¹, FLINT, PLATE¹, *glass*); substance of similar properties or composition (WATER¹-*glass*). **2.** Glass utensils, ornaments, windows, greenhouse(s); glass vessel esp. for drinking from; ~('FUL), amount of liquid contained in this, drink (*a friendly glass*; *fond of his glass*; **has had a ~ too much,** is rather drunk); = HOUR*glass*, SAND-*glass*; plate of glass covering picture; glass disc covering watch-face; glazed frame for plants. **3.** = LOOK*ing-glass*; (esp. in *pl.*) = EYE¹*glass*; lens, esp. one that magnifies; telescope; (esp. in *pl.*) = FIELD-*glasses*, OPERA¹-*-glass*; microscope; barometer. **4.** **~-blower,** one who blows and shapes semi-molten glass; **~ case** (chiefly of glass, for exhibiting or protecting objects); **~-cloth,** (1) linen cloth for drying glasses, (2) cloth covered with powdered glass like glass-paper; **~ cloth,** woven fabric of fine-spun glass; **~-cutter,** workman or tool cutting glass; *glass* EYE¹ 4; **~ fibre,** filament(s) of glass esp. as woven into fabric or embedded as reinforcement in plastic; **~-gall,** sandiver; **~'house,** building where glass is made, greenhouse, (sl.) military prison; **~-making,** manufacture of glass; **~-paper** (covered with glass-dust); **~ snake,** snakelike lizard of Southern U.S. etc., with very brittle tail; **~'ware,** articles made of glass; **~ wool,** glass in form of fine fibres for packing and insulation; **~'wort,** plant of genus *Salicornia* or *Salsola* formerly burnt for use in glass-making. [OE *glæs*, = OS, OHG *glas* f. WG var. of Gmc **glazam*]

glass² (-ahs) *v.t.* **1.** (usu. in *p.p.*) Fit with glass, glaze. **2.** Reflect as in mirror. **3.** Look at or for with field-glasses. [f. prec.; cf. GLAZE]

gla'ssine (-ah'sēn) *n.* Glossy transparent paper. [f. GLASS¹ + -INE⁵]

gla'ss|ȳ (-ah'-) *a.* Having properties of or resembling, glass; (of eye etc.) lacking fire, dull, fixed; (of water) lustrous and transparent, or smooth, as glass (so *glassy calm, surface*, etc.); hence **~ĭLY²** *adv.*, **~ĭNESS** *n.* [ME, f. GLASS¹ + -Y²]

Glăswē'gĭan (*or* -z-; *or* -jan) *a.* & *n.* (Native or inhabitant) of Glasgow. [f. *Glasgow* after *Norwegian* etc.]

Glau'ber (*or* -ow'-) *n.* **~'s salt(s),** crystalline (hydrated) sodium sulphate used esp. as laxative. [f. J. R. ~, Ger. chemist d. 1668]

glaucō'ma *n.* Eye-disease with increased pressure within eyeball and gradual loss of sight; hence **~tous** *a.* [L, f. Gk *glaukōma -atos* (*glaukos*; see foll.)]

glau'cous *a.* (esp. Bot.) Of dull greyish green or blue; covered with bloom as of grapes. [f. L f. Gk *glaukos* + -OUS]

glāze *v.* & *n.* **1.** *v.t.* Fit (window, picture) with glass, furnish (building) with glass windows (~ **in,** enclose thus). **2.** Cover (pottery etc.) with glaze; fix (paint) on pottery thus; overlay (cloth, paper, leather, pastry, meat, etc.) with glaze. **3.** Cover (eye) with film. **4.** Cover (painted surface) with glaze. **5.** Give glassy surface to, e.g. by rubbing. **6.** *v.i.* (Esp. of eye) become glassy; **~d frost,** = SILVER¹ *thaw*. **7.** Hence **glā'zER¹** (1, 2) *n.*, **glā'zY²** *a.* **8.** *n.* Vitreous substance used to glaze pottery; smooth lustrous coating on materials, e.g. edible coating of gelatin etc. on food; thin top-coat of transparent paint to modify tone of underlying colour; smooth surface formed by glazing; *thin coating of ice. [ME, f. obl. form of GLASS¹]

glā'zi|er (*or* -zh*er*) *n.* One whose trade is to glaze windows etc.; hence **~ERY** (2) *n.* [ME, f. prec.; see -IER]

glā'zĭng *n.* In vbl senses; windows (DOUBLE *glazing*); material used to produce glaze. [ME, f. GLAZE + -ING¹]

||**G.L.C.** *abbr.* Greater London Council.

gleam *n.*, & *v.i.* **1.** *n.* Subdued or transient light; faint, temporary, or intermittent show of some quality etc. (*an occasional gleam of humour*; *not a gleam of hope*); hence ~'Y² *a.* **2.** *v.i.* Emit gleams; shine with subdued or interrupted brightness. [OE *glǣm*, cogn. w. OS *glīmo*, MHG *glīmen* shine, OHG *gleimo* glow-worm, WG **glaimiz*; cf. GLIMMER]

glean *v.* **1.** *v.i.* Gather ears of corn left by reapers. **2.** *v.t.* Gather (such remains); strip (field etc.) thus; collect in small quantities, scrape together, (news, facts, etc.); hence ~'ER¹, ~'ING¹ (1, 2), *ns.* [ME, f. OF *glener* f. LL *glennare*, prob. f. Gaulish **glenn-* f. Celt. **glendn-*]

glēbe *n.* **1.** Portion of land going with clergyman's benefice. **2.** (poet.) Earth, land; a field. [ME, f. L *gl(a)eba* clod, soil]

glēde *n.* (arch. or dial.) = KITE 1. [OE *glida*, = ON *gletha* f. Gmc**glidhon* (as GLIDE)]

glee *n.* **1.** Musical composition for three or more (prop. adult male) voices, one to each part, set to words grave or gay, often with contrasted movements and prop. without accompaniment; ~ **club,** society for singing glees and other part-songs; **~'man,** (Hist.) travelling minstrel etc. **2.** Mirth, lively and manifest delight; hence ~'FUL, ~'SOME¹, *adjs.* [OE *glīo*, *glēo*, = ON *glý* f. Gmc **gliujam*]

Gleichschaltung (glī'kshahltoo͝ng) *n.* Standardization of political etc. institutions among authoritarian States. [G]

glĕn *n.* Narrow valley. [f. Gael. & Ir. *gleann*]

glĕngă'rrȳ (-n-g-) *n.* Highland cap with pointed front and usu. pair of ribbons attached at back. [f. *G~* in Highland, Scotland]

glē'noid *a.* (Anat.) ~ **cavity** etc., shallow cavity on bone (esp. scapula and temporal bone) receiving projection of other bone to form joint. [f. F *glénoïde* f. Gk *glēnoeidēs* (*glēnē* socket; see -OID)]

gley (-ā) *n.* Blue-grey waterlogged soil. [Ukrainian, = sticky blue clay, cogn. w. CLAY]

glī'|a *n.* = NEURO*glia*; hence **~AL** *a.* [Gk, = glue]

glĭb *a.* (Of speaker, speech, etc.) fluent, ready, more voluble than sincere or thoughtful; (arch.) smooth, unimpeded; hence ~'LY² *adv.*, ~'NESS *n.* [rel. to obs. *glibbery* slippery = MLG *glibberich*, Du. *glibberig* f. Gmc **glibh-*, perh. imit.]

glīde *v.* & *n.* **1.** *v.i.* (Of liquid, ship, bird, train, snake, person skating, etc.) pass, change position, by smooth continuous movement; (of aircraft) fly without engine-power; go quietly or stealthily; (of time etc.) pass gently and imperceptibly; pass gradually, shade off insensibly, *into*. **2.** *v.t.* Cause to glide (*light airs* *glided the ship on her course*); traverse in glider. **3.** *n.* Act of gliding; (Mus.) succession of sounds made in passing from one note to another without silence of voice or instrument; (Phonet.) gradually changing sound made in passing from one position of speech-organs to another; (Cricket) = GLANCE[1]; gliding dance or dance-step; flight in glider; **~ path,** aircraft's line of descent to land, esp. as indicated by ground radar. [OE *glīdan,* = OS *glīdan,* OHG *glītan* f. WG **glīdhan*]

glī'der *n.* In vbl senses; engineless aeroplane; (expert) user of this. [f. prec. + -ER[1]]

glĭm *n.* Faint light; (arch. sl.) candle, lantern, (*douse the glim*). [17th c., perh. abbr. of GLIMMER or GLIMPSE]

glĭ'mmer *v.i.,* & *n.* **1.** *v.i.* Shine faintly or intermittently. **2.** *n.* Feeble or wavering light; faint gleam *of* hope or understanding; glimpse, half-view. [ME, prob. f. Scand. f. WG **glim-*, **glaim-* (see GLEAM)]

glĭ'mmerĭng *n.* In vbl senses; = prec. 2. [ME, f. prec. + -ING[1]]

glĭmpse *n.* & *v.* **1.** *n.* Faint and transient appearance, momentary or imperfect view *of.* **2.** *v.t.* Catch glimpse of, see faintly or partly. **3.** *v.i.* Shine faintly or intermittently; (poet.) appear faintly, dawn. [ME *glimse,* corresp. to MHG *glimsen* f. WG **glimisōjan* (as prec.)]

glĭnt *v.* & *n.* **1.** *v.i.,* & *n.* Flash, glitter, sparkle. **2.** *v.t.* Make flash, reflect, (light). [alt. of ME *glent,* prob. of Scand. orig.]

glĭssā'de (*or* -ah'd) *n.,* & *v.i.* **1.** (Mountaineering). Slide down steep slope esp. of ice or snow usu. on the feet with support of ice-axe etc. **2.** (Dancing). (Make) gliding step. [F (*glisser* slip, slide; see -ADE)]

glĭssă'nd|ō *n.* (*pl.* **~i** *pr.* -ē, *or* **~os**). (Mus.) = GLIDE. [It., f. F *glissant* sliding (as prec.)]

glissé (glĭsā') *n.* (Ballet). (**Pas**) **~**, sliding step in which flat of foot is often used. [F, p.p. of *glisser* (see GLISSADE)]

glĭ'sten (-ĭ'sen) *v.i.,* & *n.* **1.** Glitter, sparkle. **2.** *v.i.* Shine fitfully. [OE *glisnian* (*glisian* shine; see -EN[6])]

glĭ'ster *v.i.,* & *n.* (arch.) Sparkle, glitter. [ME, f. MLG *glistern,* MDu. *glisteren,* cogn. w. prec.]

glĭtch *n.* (sl.) Sudden irregularity or malfunction of equipment etc. [20th c.; orig. unkn.]

glĭ'tter *v.i.,* & *n.* **1.** (Shine with) brilliant tremulous light, gleam, sparkle. **2.** *v.i.* Be showy or splendid (*with* jewels etc., or fig., *glittering rhetoric, prospects*). [ME, f. ON *glitra* f. Gmc **glit-*]

gloa'mĭng *n.* Evening twilight. [OE *glōmung* (*glōm* twilight cogn. w. GLOW; see -ING[1])]

gloat *v.i.,* & *n.* **1.** *v.i.* Feast eyes or mind lustfully, avariciously, malignantly, triumphantly, etc., (*up*)*on* or *over.* **2.** *n.* Act of gloating; look or expression of triumphant satisfaction. [16th c.; orig. unkn., but perh. cogn. w. ON *glotta* grin, MHG *glotzen* stare]

glō'bal *a.* World-wide; pertaining to or embracing the whole of a group of items etc.; total; hence **~**LY[2] *adv.* [F, f. as foll. + -AL]

glōbe *n.* & *v.* **1.** *n.* Spherical body; *the* earth; planet, star, sun. **2.** Spherical chart of the earth or the constellations: **use of the ~s,** (arch.) teaching of geography and astronomy by these. **3.** Golden orb as emblem of sovereignty; (Anat.) eyeball; approximately spherical glass vessel, esp. lampshade, fish-bowl, or electric-light bulb. **4.** *Globe* ARTICHOKE; **~-fish,** tropical fish of family Tetraodontidae, able to inflate itself into globular form; **~-flower,** ranunculaceous plant of genus *Trollius* with globular yellow flowers; **~ lightning** (rare globular form); **~-trotter, -trotting,** hurried traveller, hurried travelling, through foreign countries esp. for sightseeing. **5.** Hence or cogn. **glō'b**OID *a.* & *n.,* **glō'b**OSE[1] *a.* **6.** *v.t.* & *i.* Make (usu. in *pass.*) or become globular. [F, or f. L *globus*]

glōbĭgerī'na (*or* -ē'na) *n.* Foraminiferous organism of genus *Globigerina,* living near surface of sea. [mod. L, f. as prec. + *-ger* carrying + -INA]

glŏ'būlar *a.* Globe-shaped, spherical; composed of globules; hence **~**ITY (-ă'r-) *n.,* **~**LY[2] *adv.* [f. as foll. + -AR[1]]

glŏ'būle *n.* Small globe or round particle, drop, pill. [F, or f. L *globulus* (as GLOBE; see -ULE)]

glŏ'būlĭn *n.* Protein found usu. associated with albumin in animal and plant tissues. [f. prec. + -IN]

glŏ'ckenspiel (*or* -nshp-) *n.* Musical instrument consisting of a series of bells or metal bars or tubes struck by hammers. [G, = bell-play]

***glŏm** *v.t.* & *i.* (**-mm-**). (sl.) **~** (**on to**), steal, grab. [var. of Sc. *glaum* (18th c., of unkn. orig.)]

glŏ'merate *a.* (Bot. & Anat.) Compactly clustered. [f. L *glomeratus* p.p. of *glomerare* (*glomus -eris* ball); see -ATE[2]]

glŏ'merule (-ōōl) *n.* Clustered flower-head; = foll. [f. as foll.; see -ULE]

glomĕ'rul|us *n.* (*pl.* **~i** *pr.* -ī). Cluster of small organisms, tissues, blood-vessels, etc., esp. of capillaries in kidney; hence **~**AR *a.* [mod. L, dim. of L *glomus glomeris* ball]

glōōm[1] *n.* Darkness, obscurity; melancholy, despondency; (poet.) dark place. [perh. back form. f. GLOOMY]

glōōm[2] *v.* **1.** *v.i.* Look sullen, frown, be gloomy or melancholy; (of sky etc.) lour, be dull or threatening; appear darkly or obscurely. **2.** *v.t.* Cover with gloom, make dark or dismal. [ME *gloum*(*b*)*e,* of unkn. orig.; cf. GLUM]

glōō'm|ȳ *a.* Dark, unlighted; depressed, sullen; dismal, depressing; hence **~ĭ**LY[2] *adv.,* **~ĭ**NESS *n.* [f. obs. *gloom* a frown f. prec. + -Y[2]]

***glŏp** *n.* (sl.) Liquid or viscous substance, esp. unattractive food. [imit.; cf. obs. *glop* swallow greedily]

glôr'ĭa *n.* **1. G~** (**Patri**), doxology *Glory be to the Father* etc.; **G~** (**tibi**), response *Glory be to thee* etc.; **G~** (**in excelsis**), hymn *Glory be to God on high,* as part of Mass etc. **2.** Aureole. [L, = glory]

glôr'ĭ|fȳ *v.t.* Make glorious, exalt to the glory of heaven; invest with radiance; transform into something more splendid; (try to) make (common or inferior thing) seem more splendid than it really is; extol, praise; so **~**FICA'TION *n.* [ME, f. OF *glorifier* f. eccl. L *glorificare* f. LL *glorificus* f. L *gloria* glory; see -FY]

glôr'ĭōle *n.* Aureole, halo. [F, f. L *gloriola* dim. of *gloria* glory]

glôr'ĭous *a.* Possessing glory, illustrious; conferring glory, honourable; splendid, magnificent, intensely delightful, (*a glorious view, day*; *glorious fun*; (iron.) *the glorious uncertainty of cricket, a glorious muddle*); (colloq.) ecstatically happy with drink; hence **~**LY[2] *adv.* [ME f. AF; OF *glorios, -eus* f. L *gloriosus* (as foll.; see -OUS)]

glôr'ȳ[1] *n.* **1.** Exalted renown, honourable fame; adoring praise and thanksgiving; **~** (**be**)**!,** devout ejaculation or (vulg.) excl. of surprise or delight. **2.** Resplendent majesty, beauty, or magnificence, effulgence of heavenly light, imagined unearthly beauty; bliss and splendour of heaven (**go to ~**, (sl.) die, be destroyed); state of exaltation, prosperity, etc., (*is in his glory*). **3.** Thing that brings renown, special distinction, (*OLD *Glory*); circle of light round head or figure of deity or saint, aureole, halo; anthelion; **~-box,** (Austral. & N.Z.) box for woman's clothes etc. stored in preparation for marriage;

~-hole, *open quarry, (sl.) untidy room, drawer, or receptacle; **~-of-the-snow,** chionodoxa. [ME, f. AF & OF *glorie* f. L *gloria*; see -Y¹]

glŏr'ȳ² *v.i.* Exult, pride oneself, *in* thing or doing, *to* do. [ME, f. L *gloriari* boast (*gloria* glory)]

Glos. *abbr.* Gloucestershire.

glŏss¹ *n.* & *v.* **1.** *n.* Word inserted between lines or in margin to explain word in text; comment, explanation, interpretation, paraphrase; misrepresentation of another's words; glossary, interlinear translation, or annotations. **2.** *v.t.* Insert glosses in (text etc.) or concerning (word etc.); read different sense into, explain away. **3.** *v.i.* Write glosses; make (esp. unfavourable) comments *on*. [alt. of GLOZE after med. L *glossa*]

glŏss² *n.*, & *v.t.* **1.** *n.* Superficial lustre; deceptive external appearance; ~ **paint** etc. (containing varnish to give glossy finish). **2.** *v.t.* Make glossy; ~ **(over)**, give specious appearance to, seek to conceal. [16th c., of unkn. orig.]

glŏ'ssal *a.* (Anat.) Of the tongue, lingual. [f. Gk *glōssa* tongue + -AL]

glŏ'ssar|ȳ *n.* Collection of glosses; list and explanations of abstruse, obsolete, dialectal, or technical terms, partial dictionary; hence **glŏssār'**IAL *a.*, ~IST (1) *n.* [f. L *glossarium* (*glossa* GLOSS¹; see -ARY¹)]

glŏssā'tor *n.* Writer of glosses, commentator, esp. on medieval law-texts. [ME f. med. L (*glossare* f. *glossa* GLOSS¹; see -OR)]

glŏ'ssēme *n.* Feature of a language that carries meaning and does not consist of smaller meaningful units. [f. Gk *glōssēma* (*glōssa* GLOSS¹; see -EME)]

glŏssī'tĭs *n.* Inflammation of the tongue. [f. Gk *glōssa* tongue + -ITIS]

glŏssō- *comb. form.* **1.** Tongue, as: **~-lary'ngeal,** of tongue and larynx. **2.** = GLOSS¹, as: **glŏssŏ'**-GRAPHER *n.*, commentator, **glŏssŏ'**LOGY *n.*, terminology. [sense 1 f. Gk *glōssa* tongue, sense 2 f. GLOSS¹, + -O-]

glŏ'ssolā'lia *n.* Gift of TONGUE¹s. [mod. L, f. as prec. 1 + Gk *-lalia* speaking]

glŏ'ss|ȳ *a.* & *n.* **1.** *a.* Having a gloss; (of paper etc.) smooth and shiny; (of magazine etc.) printed on such paper; hence ~ĭLY² *adv.*, ~ĭNESS *n.* **2.** *n.* (colloq.) Photograph with glossy surface; glossy magazine. [f. GLOSS² + -Y²]

glŏ'ttal *a.* Of or produced by the glottis; ~ **stop,** sound produced by sudden opening or shutting of glottis; hence ~IZE *v.t.*, articulate with glottis wholly or partly closed. [f. foll. + -AL]

glŏ'tt|ĭs *n.* Opening at upper end of windpipe and between vocal cords, affecting modulation of voice by contracting or dilating; hence ~IC *a.* [mod. L, f. Gk *glōttis* (*glōtta* var. of *glōssa* tongue)]

Glou'cester (glŏ'st*er*) *n.* Kind of hard cheese made in Gloucestershire (**double** ~ with richer milk than **single** ~). [~ in England]

glove (-ŭv) *n.*, & *v.t.* **1.** *n.* Covering to protect hand or keep it warm or clean, usu. with separated fingers; **fit like a** ~ (exactly); HAND¹ *and* or *in glove*; **throw down, take up, the** ~, issue, accept, challenge. **2.** = BOX⁵*ing-glove*; **with the ~s off** etc. (of arguing or contending in earnest, mercilessly, etc.). **3.** ~ **box,** (1) box for gloves, (2) = *glove compartment*, (3) closed chamber with sealed-in gloves for handling radioactive material etc.; ~ **compartment,** recess for small articles in motor-car dashboard; ~ **puppet** (made to fit on hand like a glove). **4.** Hence ~'LESS (-vl-) *a.*, **glo'v**ER¹ (3) (-ŭ'v-) *n.* **5.** *v.t.* Cover with glove; provide with gloves. [OE *glōf*, = ON *glófi*, perh. f. Gmc **galōfō* (**ga*-Y-; cf. ON *lófi*, Goth. *lofa* hand)]

glow (-ō) *v.i.*, & *n.* **1.** *v.i.* Be heated to incandescence, throw out light and heat without flame; shine like thing intensely heated; show warm colour; burn *with* or be indicative of bodily heat, emotional fervour, etc., (*glowing cheeks*; *gave me a glowing account of the achievement*). **2.** *n.* Glowing state (**in a** ~, hot or flushed); brightness and warmth of colour, e.g. red of cheeks; ardour, passion. **3.** **~-discharge,** luminous sparkless electrical discharge from pointed conductor or in gas; **~-worm,** beetle whose wingless female emits light from end of abdomen. [OE *glōwan*, = OS *glōjan*, OHG *gluoen*, ON *glóa* f. Gmc **glō*-]

glow'er *v.i.* Stare or scowl (*at*). [orig. uncert.; perh. Sc. var. of ME *glore* f. LG or Scand., or f. obs. (ME) *glow* stare + -ER⁵]

glŏxĭ'nĭa *n.* American tropical plant of genus *Gloxinia*, with large bell flowers of various colours. [mod. L, f. B.P. *Gloxin*, 18th-c. Ger. botanist + -IA¹]

glōze *v.* **1.** *v.i.* (arch.) Comment (*up*)*on*; talk speciously, fawn. **2.** *v.t.* ~ **(over)**, palliate, explain away, extenuate. [ME, f. OF *gloser* (*glose* f. med. L *glosa*, *gloza* f. L *glossa* tongue, GLOSS¹)]

glu'cagon (gloo͞'-) *n.* Polypeptide hormone formed in pancreas, which aids breakdown of glycogen. [f. Gk *glukus* sweet + *agōn* leading]

glu'cōse (gloo͞'-) *n.* **1.** (Chem.) Sugar found widely in its dextro-rotatory form (*dextrose*) in fruit juice, blood, etc., and obtainable from carbohydrates by hydrolysis. **2.** Syrup containing glucose etc. from incomplete hydrolysis of starch. [F, f. Gk *gleukos* sweet wine, rel. to *glukus* sweet; see -OSE²]

glu'cosīde (gloo͞'-) *n.* (Chem.) Compound giving glucose and other product(s) on hydrolysis. [f. prec. + -IDE]

glue (gloo͞) *n.*, & *v.t.* **1.** *n.* Hard brittle brownish gelatin made by boiling hides and bones and used warm for uniting substances; adhesive or viscous substance got from other sources (*fish*, *vegetable*, *casein*, *resin*, *glue*). **2.** **~-pot,** pot with outer vessel holding water to heat glue, (colloq.) area of ground sticky because of wet or mud; **~-sniffer,** person who inhales fumes of plastic cement as narcotic. **3.** Hence ~'Y² (gloo͞'ĭ) *a.* (**glu'ier, glu'iest**). **4.** *v.t.* Fasten or join (as) with glue; apply or attach tightly or closely (*eye, ear, glued to the keyhole*). [ME, f. OF *glu* n., *gluer* v. f. LL *glus glutis* f. L *gluten*]

glŭm *a.* Sullen, looking or feeling dejected or displeased; hence ~'LY² *adv.*, ~'NESS *n.* [rel. to dial. *glum* v. frown, var. of *gloume* GLOOM²]

glum|e (gloo͞m) *n.* (Bot.) Chafflike bract in spikelet of grasses and sedges; husk of grain; hence or cogn. ~A'CEOUS, ~'OSE¹, *adjs.* [f. L *gluma* husk]

glŭt *v.t.* (**-tt-**), & *n.* **1.** *v.t.* Feed (person, stomach) or indulge (appetite, desire) to the full, overload with food (lit. or fig.), satiate, cloy; choke up, fill to excess; overstock (market) with goods. **2.** *n.* Full indulgence, one's fill, surfeit; supply exceeding demand (*a glut in the market*). [n. f. v., ME prob. f. OF *gloutir* swallow f. L *gluttire*; cf. GLUTTON]

glu'tamāte (gloo͞'-) *n.* (Chem.) Salt or ester of glutamic acid, esp. the sodium salt used to flavour food. [f. foll. + -ATE¹ (3)]

glută'mĭc (gloo͞-) *a.* (Chem.) ~ **acid,** amino--acid normally found in proteins. [f. foll. + AMINE + -IC]

glu'ten (gloo͞'-) *n.* **1.** Viscous animal-secretion; nitrogenous part of flour remaining as viscid substance when starch is washed out; ~ **bread** (with high gluten content). **2.** (arch.) Sticky substance. [F, f. L *gluten glutinis* glue]

glu'tė|us (gloo͞'-) *n.* (*pl.* **~i** *pr.* -ī). One of three muscles of each buttock; hence ~AL *a.* [mod. L, f. Gk *gloutos* buttock]

glu'tĭnous (gloo'-) *a.* Sticky, gluelike, viscid; hence ~LY² *adv.*, ~NESS *n.* [f. F *glutineux* or f. L *glutinosus* (as GLUTEN; see -OUS)]

glŭ'tton *n.* **1.** Excessive eater, gormandizer; greedy reader (*of books*), person insatiably eager (*for work*). **2.** Voracious animal (*Gulo gulo*) of weasel family. **3.** Hence or cogn. ~IZE (2) *v.i.*, ~OUS *a.*, ~Y¹ *n.* [ME, f. OF *gluton, gloton* f. L *glutto -onis* (*gluttire* swallow, *gluttus* greedy)]

glȳ'cer|ine (-ēn), ***glȳ'cer|in,** *n.* Colourless sweet viscous liquid formed as by-product in saponification of fats, used as ointment, as vehicle for drugs, in explosives, etc.; hence ~IDE *n.* [f. F *glycerin* f. Gk *glukeros* sweet; see -INE⁵, -IN]

glȳ'cerŏl *n.* (chem.) Glycerine. [f. GLYCERINE + -OL 1]

glȳ'cine (-ēn) *n.* Simplest amino-acid, a general constituent of proteins. [f. G *glycin* f. Gk *glukus* sweet; see -INE⁵]

glȳco- *comb. form.* Sugar, as: **~pro'tein,** protein with short side-chain(s) of carbohydrates. [irreg. f. Gk *glukus* sweet + -O-]

glȳ'co|gėn *n.* Polysaccharide serving to store carbohydrates in animal tissues and yielding glucose on hydrolysis; so ~GE'NIC (1) *a.*, **~ge'nesis,** formation of glycogen from sugar. [f. prec. + -GEN]

glȳ'cŏl *n.* Aliphatic dihydric alcohol, esp. ethylene glycol; hence **glȳcŏ'l(l)**IC *a.* [f. GLYCERINE + -OL 1, orig. as being intermediate between glycerine and alcohol]

glȳcŏ'lȳs|ĭs *n.* (*pl.* **~es** *pr.* -ēz). Breakdown of sugars etc. by enzymes to release energy in animal tissues or in fermentation etc. [f. GLYCO- + -LYSIS]

glȳ'coside *n.* (Chem.) Compound giving sugar and other product(s) on hydrolysis. [f. GLYCO-, after GLUCOSIDE]

glȳ'cosūr'|ĭa *n.* (Path.) Diseased condition with sugar present in the urine; hence ~IC *a.* [f. F *glycose* glucose + -URIA]

glȳph *n.* Sculptured character or symbol; hence ~'IC *a.* [f. F *glyphe* f. Gk *gluphē* carving (*gluphō* carve)]

glȳ'ptăl *n.* Alkyd resin, esp. one formed from glycerine and phthalic acid or anhydride. [**P**; perh. f. *glycerol* + *phthalic*]

glȳ'ptĭc *a.* Of carving esp. on precious stones. [f. F *glyptique* or f. Gk *gluptikos* (*gluptēs* carver f. *gluphō* carve; see -IC)]

glȳ'ptodŏn *n.* Extinct S. Amer. quadruped allied to armadillos, with fluted teeth. [mod. L, f. Gk *gluptos* carved (as prec.) + *odous odontos* tooth]

glȳptŏ'graphȳ *n.* Art and science of gem--engraving. [f. as prec. + -O- + -GRAPHY]

||**G.M.** *abbr.* George Medal.

gm. *abbr.* gram(s).

***G-man** (jē'măn) *n.* (*pl.* **G-men**). (sl.) Federal criminal-investigation officer. [f. *G*overnment + MAN¹]

G.M.T. *abbr.* Greenwich mean time.

gnar̄led (nar̄ld), **gnar̄'lȳ** (n-), *adjs.* (Of tree, hands, etc.) covered with protuberances, twisted, rugged. [var. of **knurled* (KNURL; see -ED², -Y²)]

gnăsh (n-) *v.* **1.** *v.i.* (Of teeth) strike together; grind the teeth. **2.** Grind (the teeth). [var. of obs. *gnacche* or *gnast* rel. to ON *gnastan* a gnashing (imit.)]

gnăt (n-) *n.* Small two-winged biting fly of genus *Culex*, esp. mosquito; insignificant annoyance, tiny thing; STRAIN¹ *at a gnat.* [OE *gnætt*, cogn. w. LG *gnatte*, G dial. *gnatze*]

gnă'thĭc (n-) *a.* Of the jaws. [f. Gk *gnathos* jaw + -IC]

gnaw (n-) *v.t.* & *i.* (*p.p.* **~ed** *or* **~n**). Bite persistently, wear away thus, (*away, off, in two,* etc.; *at, into*); (of destructive agents, pain, etc.) corrode, waste away, consume, torture. [OE *gnagan*, = OS, OHG *gnagan*, ON *gnaga*; ult. imit.]

gneiss (gnīs *or* nīs) *n.* (Geol.) Coarse-grained metamorphic rock of quartz, felspar, and mica; hence ~'IC, ~'OID, ~'OSE¹, *adjs.* [G]

gnŏ'cchĭ (nŏ'kĭ *or* nyŏ'kĭ) *n. pl.* Small dumplings cooked and served with cheese etc. [It., pl. of *gnocco* (*nocchio* knot in wood)]

gnō'mē¹ (n-; *or* nōm) *n.* Maxim, aphorism. [f. Gk *gnōmē* opinion (*gignōskō* know)]

gnōme² (nōm) *n.* (Myth.) dwarfish spirit of subterranean race guarding treasures of earth; goblin, dwarf; figure of gnome esp. in garden; (colloq., esp. in *pl.*) person with sinister influence, esp. in international finance; hence **gnō'm**ISH¹ (n-) *a.* [F, f. mod. L *gnomus* (wd invented by Paracelsus)]

gnō'm|ĭc (n-) *a.* Of, consisting of, using, gnomes (GNOME¹), sententious; (Gram., of tense) used without implication of time to express a general truth, e.g. *men were deceivers ever*; hence ~ICALLY *adv.* [f. Gk *gnōmikos* (as GNOME¹; see -IC)]

gnō'mon (n-) *n.* Pillar, rod, pin, or plate, of sundial, showing time by its shadow on marked surface; column etc. used in observing sun's meridian altitude; (Geom.) part of parallelogram left when similar one has been taken from its corner; hence **gnōmŏ'n**IC (n-) *a.* [F, or f. L f. Gk *gnōmōn* indicator etc. (*gignōskō* know)]

gnō's|ĭs (n-) *n.* (*pl.* **~es** *pr.* -ēz). Knowledge of spiritual mysteries. [f. Gk *gnōsis* knowledge (as prec.)]

gnŏ'stĭc (n-) *a.* & *n.* **1.** *a.* Relating to knowledge, cognitive; having esoteric spiritual knowledge; (*G~*) of the Gnostics, occult, mystic. **2.** *n.* (*G~*; usu. in *pl.*) Christian heretic of 1st–3rd c. claiming gnosis; hence ~ISM (3) *n.*, ~IZE (2, 3, 4) *v.i.* & *t.* [f. eccl. L f. Gk *gnōstikos* (as prec.; see -IC)]

G.N.P. *abbr.* gross national product.

||**Gnr.** *abbr.* Gunner.

||**gns.** *abbr.* guineas.

gnū (nū) *n.* Oxlike antelope of genus *Connochaetes.* [ult. f. Kaffir *nqu*]

gō¹ *v.* (**went;** GONE; *part.* GOING²; *sing. pres.* 2 (arch.) **goest** *pr.* gō'ĭst, 3 **goes** *pr.* gōz, (arch.) **goeth** *pr.* gō'ĭth). **1.** *v.i.* Start, depart, move, continue moving, with self-originated or imparted motion, from some place, position, time, etc., specified or obvious; ***to go,** (of refreshments etc.) for taking away from place of supply before consumption. **2.** Journey, travel, proceed, progress, (*go* FAR¹, *the* PACE¹, WEST; *go easy, straight*; *go by car, train, air*; *went miles round*; *go (for) a walk, (on) a journey*; *go the same way, the shortest way*); **go slow,** (esp.) work at deliberately slow pace; **go-slow** *n.*, such action as industrial protest. **3.** (Of line etc.) lie, point, in certain direction. **4.** Be guided *by*, act in harmony *with*, judge or act (*up*)*on*, (*a good rule to go by*; *have nothing to go upon*; *always goes with his party*; *promotion goes by favour*); **go with the tide** or **times,** do as others do. **5.** Be habitually in specified state (*go hungry*, SHORT 3, *armed*, *in rags, in fear of* one's *life*; *six months* etc. **gone with child,** having spent that time in gestation). **6.** Be moving, acting, working, etc., (**Who goes there?** (sentry's challenge); *clock does not go, goes well*; *tongue goes nineteen to the* DOZEN). **7.** Make specified motion (*go like this with your left foot*). **8.** (Of bell, striking clock, gun, or other source of sound) emit sound; make sound of specified kind (*go bang, go crack*). **9.** (Of time) pass, elapse, (*ten days to go before Easter*); (of distance etc.) be traversed or accomplished (*ten miles to go*). **10.** Be current or accepted (*the gold sovereign went anywhere*; *the* STORY[1] *goes*); be known *by*, or *under*, *the name of*; be on the average (*is a good actor as actors go nowadays*). **11.** (Of document, verse, tune, etc.) run, have specified content or wording. **12.** (Of verse, song) be rhythmical, be adaptable *to* a tune. **13.** (Of events) turn out *well*, *ill*, HARD, etc., (of decision, election, etc.) result *for* or *against*, (of constituency, politician, voter) take certain course or views, (*Liverpool went Labour*; *go* DRY[1]; *case goes by* DEFAULT[1]; *goes without* SAYING; **how goes it, how is it going, how are things going?,** what progress is being made?); be successful (*make the party go*); (colloq.) be acceptable or permitted (*anything goes*), be accepted without question (*what he says goes*). **14.** Begin motion; **Go!** (starter's word in race); **from the word go,** (colloq.) from the very beginning; LET[2] *go*; HERE *goes!*. **15.** Get away *free*, *unpunished*, etc. **16.** Be sold (*go cheap*, *for £1*, etc.); **going!, gone!** (auctioneer's announcement that bidding is almost, quite, closed). **17.** (Of money) be spent (*in* or *on* thing). **18.** Be relinquished, dismissed, abolished, or lost (*the car*, *the cook*, *must go*; *my sight*, *our trade*, *is going*; *my headache has gone*; *next wicket went for nothing*). **19.** Die (esp. in *p.p.*, and in many phrs.: *go the way of all the earth* or *of all flesh*, *to a better world*, *to* one's *account* or *reward*, (sl.) *aloft*, etc.). **20.** Fail, give way, succumb, break down, crack; LET[2] one*self go*. **21.** Make one's way *to*, *towards*, *into*, etc., (*go to* BLAZE[1]*s*, HELL, JERICHO, *the* DEVIL[1]; *go* HANG[1] 5; *go* PLACE[1]*s*; *which road goes to Bristol?*; **go to** *a ball*, *to church*, *to market*, etc., attend it; *go to* SCHOOL[1]; **go to the bar, to sea,** become barrister, sailor; **go on the stage, the streets,** become actor, prostitute; *go to* STOOL). **22.** Proceed *to* do (*went to find him*), *and* do (esp. colloq. = be so foolish as to do; **have been and gone and done it,** (vulg.) have made a blunder etc.), *on pilgrimage*, *on an errand*, *on the spree*, etc.; (colloq. or U.S.) proceed to (do) (*go jump in the lake*); be about *to* do; **go do*ing*,** (arch.) **a-do*ing*,** make an expedition to do (*went shopping*, *fishing*), (colloq.) be so foolish as to do (*don't go making him angry*). **23.** Act as (BAIL[1] *for* person). **24.** Have recourse, refer, appeal, *to* (‖**go to the country,** test opinion by general election; *go to war*, *work*, etc.). **25.** Carry action to certain point (*went to any* or *all lengths*; *will go so far as to say*; *will go as high as £100* (in bidding or offering price); *go halves* or SHARE[1]*s*, share equally (*with*); *went to great expense*, *trouble*, etc.; *go the whole* HOG[1]; *go one* BETTER[1]). **26.** Penetrate, sink, (*ship went to the bottom*; *goes to* one's HEART); find room, (of number) be capable of being contained in another either without remainder or at all, (*will not go into* or *in the basket*; *6 into 12 goes twice*, *into 5 will not go*, *into 13 goes twice and one over*; *thread is too thick to go through needle*). **27.** Belong *in* receptacle, *on* shelf, etc. **28.** (Of prize, victory, inheritance, office, etc.) pass, be allotted, etc., *to* person; be applied *to* purpose, contribute *to* or *towards* result, amount together *to* (*12 inches go to the foot*), tend *to show* etc. **29.** Reach, extend, (*the difference goes deep*); **as** (or **so**) **far as it goes** (caution against taking statement too widely); **goes a long** etc. **way,** *goes* FAR[1], (1) has great etc. effect *towards*, (2) (of food, money, etc.) lasts long etc., buys much etc. **30.** Pass into specified condition (*go absent*, *blind*, *brown*, *mad*, *to seed*, *to sleep*; *go* HOT[1] *and cold*; *go* NATIVE[2]; *go to* PIECE[1]*s*; *go* SICK[1]). **31.** *v.t.* Bid, declare, (*go* NAP[3], *two spades*). **32. Go it,** (sl.) act vigorously, furiously, etc., indulge in dissipation; *go it* ALONE. **33.** (w. *preps.*): **go about,** set to work at; **go at,** attack, take in hand energetically; **go for,** go to fetch, pass or be accounted as or achieve *nothing*, *little*, etc., be applicable to, strive to attain, prefer, choose, (sl.) attack; **go into,** enter (profession, Parliament), frequent (society), take part in, be a part of, allow oneself to pass into (hysterics etc.), dress oneself in (mourning etc.), investigate; **go off,** begin to dislike; **go on,** become chargeable to (parish, relief fund, etc.), (colloq.) use as evidence, (colloq., esp. neg.) concern oneself (*much* etc.) about; **go over,** inspect details of, rehearse, retouch; **go through,** discuss in detail, scrutinize, perform, (ceremony, recitation, etc.), undergo, (of book) be successively published in (so many editions), make holes in, use up, spend (money); **go to it,** (colloq., esp. in *imper.*) begin work; **go with,** be concomitant of, take same view as, agree to, match, follow the drift of; **go without,** not have, put up with lack of, (thing expressed or implied). **34.** (w. *advs.*): **go about,** move from place to place, endeavour *to* do, be in the habit of do*ing*, (Naut.) change to opposite tack; **go ahead,** proceed without hesitation; **go along with,** = *go with*; **go around,** be regularly in company *with*, be in the habit of do*ing*; **go away,** depart esp. from home for holiday etc.; **go back on** one's *word* etc., fail to keep it; **go by,** pass; **go down,** (of ship) sink, (of sun) set, be continued *to* specified point, fall *before* conqueror, deteriorate, fail, be recorded in writing, be swallowed, find acceptance *with*, leave university, (sl.) be sent to prison; **go down with,** begin to suffer from (disease); **go in,** enter as competitor (*go in and win!*, excl. of encouragement), (Cricket) take or begin innings, (of sun etc.) become obscured by cloud; **go in for,** take as one's object, pursuit, style, principle, etc.; **go off,** leave the stage, begin, explode, die, gradually cease to be felt, deteriorate, become unconscious in sleep, faint, etc., be got rid of by sale, succeed *well*, *badly*, etc.; **go on,** continue, persevere, (do*ing*, *with*, *in*, or abs.), talk at undue length, make it one's next step *to* do, happen, conduct oneself (*shamefully* etc.), (colloq.) rail *at*, appear on stage, (Cricket) begin bowling, (of garment etc.) be large enough for wearer, take one's turn to do something, (colloq., in *imper.*) don't talk nonsense!; **go out,** leave room or house, fight duel, be broadcast, be extinguished, (of Government) leave office, cease to be fashionable, depart *to* colony etc., *(colloq.) lose consciousness, mix in society, (of workmen) strike, (of heart etc.) expand with love etc. *to* person, play first 9 holes in round of golf; **go over,** change one's allegiance or religion, (of play etc.) be successful; **go round,** pay informal visit *to*, be long enough to encompass, (of food etc.) suffice for the whole party, = *go around*; **go through with,** complete, not leave unfinished; **go to,** (*imper.*, arch.) excl. of remonstrance, incredulity, impatience, etc.; **go together,** be concomitant, match, be courting; **go under,** sink, fail, succumb; **go up,** enter university, increase in price, explode, burn. **35. Go-ahead,** (*a.*) enterprising, (*n.*) permission to proceed; **go-as-you-please,** unfettered by regulations; **go-between,** intermediary, negotiator; **go-by,** passing (usu. in *give the go-by to*, outstrip, leave behind, elude, disregard, cut, slight); **go-cart,** handcart, push-chair, (arch.) baby-walker; ***go-devil,** movable contrivance used to clean interior of pipes etc.; **go-getter,** (colloq.) enterprising person; **go-go,** (colloq.) unrestrained, energetic, (of investment) speculative; **go-kart,** miniature racing car with skeleton body; **go-off,** start (usu. *at the first go-off*); **go-to-meeting,** (of hat, clothes, etc.) fit or kept for going to church in. [OE *gān*, = OS, OHG *gan* f. Gmc **gai-*, **gǣ-*; *went* orig. past of WEND¹]

gō² *n.* (*pl.* **goes** *pr.* gōz). **1.** Act of going; mettle, spirit, dash, animation; (colloq.) vigorous activity (*it's all go*); (colloq.) embarrassing turn of affairs (*here's, what, a go!*; *a rum go*); (colloq.) success (*make a go of it*); (colloq.) turn or attempt at doing something (*have a go at*; *scored seven at one go*); (colloq.) quantity of liquor etc. served at one time; attack of an illness. **2. All the go,** (colloq.) in fashion; **it's a go,** (colloq.) the bargain is agreed; **it's no go,** (colloq.) the task is impossible, the situation is hopeless; **near go,** (colloq.) narrow escape; **on the go,** (colloq.) in constant motion. [f. prec.]

gō³ *a.* (colloq.) Functioning properly; fashionable, progressive. [f. GO¹]

gō⁴ *n.* Japanese board game of territorial possession and capture. [Jap.]

goad *n.*, & *v.t.* **1.** *n.* Spiked stick used for urging cattle; thing that torments, incites, or stimulates. **2.** *v.t.* Urge with goad; irritate; ~ (**on**), instigate, drive, by annoyance (*to* do, *into* doing, *to* or *into* fury etc.). [OE *gād*, cogn. w. Lombard *gaida* arrowhead f. Gmc **gaidō*]

goal *n.* **1.** Point marking end of race; object of effort or ambition; destination. **2.** Pair of posts between which ball is to be driven in football etc., cage or basket used similarly in other games, point(s) so won (DROP², *kick*, *make*, *score*, *a goal*). **3.** ~ **average,** ratio of numbers of goals scored by and against a team in a series of matches; **~'keeper,** player stationed to protect goal; **~-kick,** (Assoc. Footb.) kick by defending side after attackers send ball over goal-line, (Rugby Footb.) attempt to kick a goal; **~-line,** line between each pair of goal-posts, extended to form end-boundary of field of play (cf. TOUCH²-*line*); **~-mouth,** space between or near goal-posts; ***~-tender,** goalkeeper at ice hockey. **4.** Hence ~'IE *n.*, (colloq.) goalkeeper, ~'LESS (-l-l-) *a.* [16th c., of unkn. orig., perh. identical with ME *gol* boundary]

gōă'nna *n.* (Austral.) Large monitor lizard of genus *Varanus*. [corrupt. of IGUANA]

goat *n.* **1.** Hardy lively frisky usu. horned and (in the male) bearded ruminant of genus *Capra* (SHEEP *and goats*); related animal (MOUNTAIN *goat*). **2.** (*G~*). *The* zodiacal sign Capricorn. **3.** Licentious person; (colloq.) foolish person; *scapegoat; **get** person's ~, (sl.) irritate him; *play the* GIDDY *goat*. **4. ~-antelope,** antelope-like member of goat family; **~-god,** Pan; **~'herd** (-t-h-), one who tends goats; **~'s-beard,** (1) meadowsweet, (2) meadow plant of genus *Tragopogon*, (3) fungus of genus *Clavaria*; ~ **moth,** large moth of family Cossidae; **~'skin,** (garment or bottle made of) skin of goat; **~'sucker,** = NIGHT*jar*. **5.** Hence ~'ISH¹, ~'Y², *adjs.*, ~'LING¹ *n.* [OE *gāt* she-goat, = OS *gēt*, OHG *geiz*, ON *geit*, Goth. *gaits* f. Gmc **gaitaz* f. IE **ghaidos*]

goatee' *n.* Chin-tuft like goat's beard. [f. prec. + -EE]

gŏb¹ *n.*, & *v.i.* (**-bb-**). (vulg.) **1.** *n.* Clot of slimy substance etc. **2.** *v.i.* Spit. [ME, f. OF *go(u)be* mouthful]

gŏb² *n.* (sl.) American sailor. [20th c.; cf. GOBBY]

gŏb³ *n.* (sl.) Mouth; **~-stopper,** large hard sweet for sucking. [perh. f. Gael. & Ir., = beak, mouth]

gōbă'ng *n.* Game played on board marked with squares, each player seeking to place five men in line. [f. Jap. *goban* perh. f. Chin. *k'i pan* GO⁴-board]

H•

gŏ'bbĕt *n.* **1.** (arch.) Piece, lump, esp. of raw flesh or food. **2.** Extract from a text esp. set for translation or comment in examination. [ME, f. OF *gobet* (as GOB¹; see -ET¹)]

gŏ'bble¹ *v.t.* & *i.* Eat hurriedly and noisily. [prob. dial., f. GOB¹ + -LE 3]

gŏ'bble² *n.* (Golf). Rapid straight putt into the hole. [prob. f. prec.]

gŏ'bble³ *v.i.* (Of turkey-cock) make characteristic sound in throat; make such sound when speaking, from rage etc. [imit.; perh. based on GOBBLE¹]

gŏ'bbledėgōōk, -dўg-, (-beldĭ-; *or* -ōōk) *n.* Pompous official, or professional, jargon. [prob. imit. of turkey-cock]

gŏ'bbler *n.* In vbl senses; turkey-cock. [f. GOBBLE¹,³ + -ER¹]

gŏ'bbў *n.* (sl.) Coastguard; American sailor. [perh. f. GOB¹ + -Y²]

Gŏ'belĭn *n.* ~ **tapestry** (made, or imitated from that made, at the Gobelins). [f. name of State factory in Paris, called *Gobelins* after its orig. owners]

gŏ'bemouche (gŏ'bmōōsh) *n.* (*pl.* **~s** *pr.* same). Credulous hearer of news. [f. F *gobe-mouches*, = fly-catcher (*gober* swallow, *mouches* flies)]

gŏ'blėt *n.* Glass having foot and stem; (arch.) metal or glass drinking-cup, bowl-shaped and without handles, sometimes with foot and cover; (poet.) drinking-cup. [ME, f. OF *gobelet*, dim. of *gobel* cup, of unkn. orig.; see -ET¹]

gŏ'blĭn *n.* Mischievous ugly demon. [ME, prob. f. AF **gobelin*, med. L *gobelinus*, prob. f. name dim. of *Gobel*, rel. to *Kobold* (see COBALT)]

gō'bў *n.* Small fish with ventral fins joined into a disc or sucker. [f. L *gobius*, *cobius* f. Gk *kōbios* GUDGEON¹]

G.O.C.(-in-C.) *abbr.* General Officer Commanding(-in-Chief).

gŏd *n.* **1.** Superhuman being worshipped as having power over nature and human fortunes, deity; ~ **from machine,** *deus ex machina*; **Ye ~s (and little fishes)!,** mock-heroic excl.; **feast** or **sight for the ~s,** something exquisite etc.; **on the knees** or **in the lap of the ~s,** beyond human control. **2.** Image, animal, or other object, worshipped as symbolizing, being the visible habitation of, or itself possessing, divine power; an idol (TIN *god*). **3.** Adored, admired, or influential person. **4.** (Theatr., in *pl.*) (Occupants of) gallery. **5.** (**God**). Supreme being, Creator and Ruler of universe; **God the Father, Son, Holy Ghost,** Persons of Trinity. **6. Act of God,** operation of uncontrollable natural forces; **God knows,** (1) it is beyond mortal or my knowledge, (2) I call God to witness that; *God save the* MARK¹; **God's Acre,** churchyard; **God's book,** Bible; **God's earth,** the whole earth; **God's gift,** a godsend; **God's (own) country,** earthly paradise, esp. the United States regarded as such; **God's plenty, quantity,** (colloq.) abundance; **God's truth,** the absolute truth; **God willing,** if Providence allows; **God wot,** (arch.) God knows; MAN¹ *of God*; **play God,** seek to be all-powerful; **under God** (qualifying attribution of full agency to man); **with God,** dead and in heaven. **7.** (In excl.:) (of asseveration) **by God,** *so* HELP¹ *me God*, (of astonishment etc.) *God* BLESS *me*, *my soul*, etc., (of imprecation) **God damn** (*you*, *him*, etc.), (of pain, grief, or anger) **God in Heaven, good God, my God, oh God,** (of pleasure or relief) **thank God,** (of prayer) **God bless** (*you*, *him*, etc.), **God forbid, God grant** (*that* etc.), **God help** *you*, *him*, etc., (of urgent supplication) **for God's sake,** *in God's* NAME¹. **8. God-awful,** (sl.) extremely unpleasant; **~'child,** child sponsored at baptism;

~-dam(n), **~-damned,** accursed, damnable; **~-daughter,** female godchild; **~'father,** male godparent, (fig.) person after whom person or thing is named; *my ~fathers!*, (euphem.) my God!; **God-fearing,** sincerely religious; **God-forsaken,** devoid of all merit, dismal; **Go'dman,** Christ; **~'mother,** female godparent; **~'parent,** sponsor at baptism; **~'send,** unexpected welcome event or acquisition; **~'son,** male godchild; **Godspee'd,** wish of 'God speed you!' to departing person. **9.** Hence ~'HOOD (-d-h-), ~'SHIP, *ns.*, ~'WARD *adv.* & *a.*, ~'WARDS *adv.* [OE, = OS, ON *god*, OHG *got*, Goth. *guth* f. Gmc **gudh-* f. IE **ghut-*]

gŏ'ddėss *n.* Female deity in polytheism; woman one adores. [ME, f. prec. + -ESS¹]

gō'det (-dā) *n.* Triangular piece of material inserted in a dress, glove, etc. [F]

godē'tia (-sh*a*) *n.* Showy-flowered hardy annual plant of genus *Godetia*. [mod. L, f. C. H. *Godet*, Swiss botanist d. 1879 + -IA¹]

gŏ'dhead (-d-hĕd) *n.* Being God or a god, divine nature; deity; **the G~,** God. [ME, f. GOD + -HEAD]

gŏ'dlėss *a.* Without a god; not recognizing God; impious, wicked; hence ~NESS *n.* [f. GOD + -LESS]

gŏ'dlīke *a.* Resembling God or a god in some quality; fit for, or like that of, a god. [f. GOD + -LIKE]

gŏ'dl|ȳ *a.* Religious, pious, devout; hence ~ĬNESS *n.* [ME, f. GOD + -LY¹]

godow'n *n.* Warehouse in parts of E. Asia, esp. in India. [f. Port. *gudão* f. Malay *godong*, *gadong*, perh. f. Telugu *giḍaṅgi* place where goods lie (*kiḍu* lie)]

gŏ'dwĭt *n.* Wading bird like curlew but with bill straight or slightly curved upwards. [16th c.; orig. unkn.]

Gŏdwŏ'tterȳ *n.* Affected or over-elaborate treatment of gardens. [f. *God wot* (in poem on gardens, by T. E. Brown 1876) + -ERY]

gō'er *n.* Person or thing that goes (*good*, *slow*, etc., *goer*; *comers and goers*); person who goes to (*church-goer*, *theatre-goer*); lively or persevering person. [ME, f. GO¹ + -ER¹]

goes, goest, goeth. See GO¹.

Goe'thĭan, -ėan, (gẽr'tĭ-) *a.* & *n.* (Admirer or follower) of Goethe. [f. J. W. von *Goethe*, Ger. writer d. 1832 + -IAN, -EAN]

gŏ'ffer *v.t.*, & *n.* **1.** *v.t.* Make wavy, flute, crimp, (lace edge, trimming, etc.) with heated irons; (in *p.p.*) embossed (edges of book). **2.** *n.* Iron used for goffering; ornamental plaiting used for frills etc. [f. F *gaufrer* stamp with patterned tool (*gaufre* honeycomb, cogn. w. WAFER, WAFFLE¹)]

gŏ'ggle *v.*, *a.*, & *n.* **1.** *v.i.* Squint, roll eyes about; look with wide-open eyes; (of eyes) be rolled or project. **2.** *v.t.* Turn (eyes) sideways or from side to side. **3.** *a.* (Of eyes) protuberant, full and rolling; so **~-eyED²** (-gelīd) *a.* **4.** *n.* (in *pl.*) Spectacles for protecting eyes from glare, dust, etc., often with side shields and coloured glass, wire gauze, etc.; a sheep disease, staggers. **5.** **~-box,** (sl.) television set; **~-dive,** underwater dive by person wearing goggles. [ME, prob. frequent. f. imit. base **gog* (cf. JOG) + -LE 3]

gŏ'glėt *n.* (India). Long-necked vessel usu. of porous ware for keeping water cool. [f. Port. *gorgoleta*]

Goi'del *n.* Member of GAELIC (sense 2) peoples; hence **Goidĕ'lɪc** *a.* & *n.* [f. OIr. *Góidel*]

gō'ing¹ *n.* In vbl senses; condition of ground for walking, riding, etc. (esp. for horse-racing); progress as helped or hindered by this (**heavy ~,** slow or difficult progress; **while the ~ is good,** while conditions are favourable); **~ away,** (esp.) departure for honeymoon; **~s-o'n,** (usu. *strange*, *such*, etc.) behaviour; **~-over,** (colloq.) inspection or overhaul, (sl.) thrashing, *(colloq.) scolding. [f. GO¹ + -ING¹]

gō'ing² *a.* In vbl senses; in or into action (*set the clock going*); existing, to be had, (*one of the best fellows going*; *there is cold beef going*); currently valid (*the going rate*); **~ concern,** business already in operation; **get ~** *v.t.* & *i.*, start talking, working, etc.; **~ (on) fifteen,** etc., approaching one's fifteenth etc. birthday; **~ for** one, (colloq.) in one's favour; *going great* GUNS; **~ on for,** approaching (a time, age, etc.); **to be ~ on with,** to start with, for the time being; *going* STRONG; **~ to,** about to, intending or intended to, likely to. [f. GO¹ + -ING²; in some senses f. earlier *a-going* (A³, prec.)]

goi'tre (-t*er*), ***goi'ter,** *n.* Morbid enlargement of thyroid gland, often showing as large pendulous swelling in neck; hence or cogn. **goi'trED²**, ***goi'terED²**, (-t*er*d), **goi'trOUS**, *adjs.* [F, back form. f. *goitreux*, or f. Prov. *goitron*, ult. f. L *guttur* throat]

Gŏlcŏ'nda *n.* Mine of wealth (lit. or fig.). [city near Hyderabad, India]

gōld *n.* & *a.* **1.** *n.* Precious yellow non-rusting malleable ductile metallic element of high specific gravity, used as a fundamental monetary medium (*as* GOOD *as gold*; **go off ~,** abandon the gold STANDARD; **worth** one's **weight in ~,** exceedingly helpful etc.); coins made of this, money in large sums, wealth; the metal as used for coating surface or as pigment, gilding; the colour of the metal; bull's-eye of archery target (usu. gilt); = *gold medal*. **2.** (fig.) Brilliant, beautiful, or precious things, material, etc. (*all that glisters* or *glitters is not gold*; *a heart, voice*, etc., *of gold*; *she is pure gold*); **age of ~,** = GOLDEN *age*. **3.** *a.* Made wholly or chiefly of gold; coloured like gold; (of money) reckoned at undepreciated value according to gold standard. **4.** **~ amalgam,** plastic combination of gold with mercury; **~-beater,** one who beats gold out into gold leaf; **~-beater's skin,** membrane used to separate leaves of gold during beating, or as covering for slight wounds; **~ bloc** (of countries having gold STANDARD); **~ brick,** (sl.) thing with only a surface appearance of value, sham, fraud, *(sl.) lazy person; **~'crest,** very small bird with golden crest; **~-digger,** one who digs for gold, (sl.) coquette who wheedles money out of men; **~-dust,** (1) gold in fine particles as often found naturally, (2) plant (*Alyssum saxatile*) with many small yellow flowers; **~-fever,** rage for going in search of gold; **~-field,** district in which gold is found as mineral; **~'finch,** bright-coloured song-bird with patch of yellow on wings; **~'fish,** small red Chinese carp kept for ornament (*~fish bowl*, (fig.) situation lacking privacy); **~ foil, ~ leaf,** gold beaten into thin sheet, *gold foil* being the thicker; **~ medal,** medal of gold (usu. awarded as first prize); **~-mine,** source of wealth (lit. or fig.); **~ of pleasure,** annual yellow-flowered plant (*Camelina sativa*); **~ plate,** (1) vessels made of gold, (2) material plated with gold; *~-plate* v.t., plate with gold; **~ reserve** (of gold coin or bullion held by central bank etc.); **~-rush,** a rush to some new gold-field; **~'smith,** worker in gold (*~smith beetle*, beetle with gold-coloured wing-covers); *gold* STANDARD; ‖**Gold Stick,** (bearer of) gilt rod borne on State occasions by colonel of Life Guards or captain of Gentlemen-at-arms; *gold* THREAD¹. [OE, = OS, OHG *gold*, ON *gull*, Goth. *gulth* f. Gmc **gultham* f. IE **ghl̥tom* (**ghel-* yellow)]

***gŏldar̃'n** *v.t.*, *a.*, & *adv.* (sl.) = DAMN 2, DAMNED 2, 3. [euphem. corrupt. of *God damn*]

gō'lden *a.* **1.** Made or consisting of gold; abounding in or yielding gold; coloured or shining like gold (*golden hair*); precious, excellent, important, (*a golden opportunity, remedy*). **2.** ~ **age,** (1) past time when men were happy and innocent, (2) period of nation's greatest prosperity or literary etc. merit; ***~-a'ger,** old person; ~ **balls,** pawnbroker's sign; ~ **boy,** popular or successful boy or man; *golden* CALF[1]; ~ **chain,** laburnum; ~ **disc,** award to artiste after sale of a million copies of gramophone record made by him or her; ~ **eagle,** large eagle with yellow-tipped head-feathers; **~-eye,** duck of genus *Bucephala*; *Golden* FLEECE; ~ **girl,** popular or successful girl or woman; *golden* HAMSTER; ~ **handshake,** gratuity as compensation for dismissal or compulsory retirement; **G~ Horde,** Tartar horde that overran E. Europe in 13th c. [f. richness of leader's tent]; **G~ Horn,** harbour of Istanbul; ~ **jubilee,** 50th anniversary of sovereign's accession or other event; *Golden* LEGEND; ~ **mean,** (1) neither too much nor too little, principle of moderation, (2) = *golden section*; **~-mouthed,** eloquent; ~ **number,** (of year in Metonic lunar cycle, from its importance in fixing Easter); ~ **opinions,** high regard; ~ **perch,** (Austral.) edible freshwater fish (*Plectroplites ambiguus*); ~ **retriever,** retriever dog with thick golden-coloured coat; ~ **rod,** plant of genus *Solidago* with rodlike stem and spike of small bright-yellow flowers; *golden* ROSE[1]; ~ **rule,** (1) 'do as you would be done by', (2) basic principle of action; ~ **section,** division of line so that whole is to one part as that part to other part; ***G~ State,** California; ‖*golden* SYRUP; ~ **wedding,** 50th anniversary of wedding. [ME, f. prec. + -EN[5]]

gō'ldĭlŏcks *n.* Person with golden hair; species of buttercup (*Ranunculus auricomus*); composite plant (*Linosyris vulgaris*) like golden rod. [f. *goldy* (GOLD, -Y[2]) + LOCK[1]*s*]

gō'lĕm *n.* Clay figure supernaturally brought to life (in Jewish legend); automaton, robot. [f. Yiddish *goylem* f. Heb. *gōlem* shapeless mass]

gŏlf *n.*, & *v.i.* **1.** *n.* Game in which small hard ball is struck in fewest possible strokes with clubs having wooden or metal heads into each of a series of (usu. 18 or 9) holes on smooth greens at varying distances apart and separated by fairways, rough ground, hazards, etc. **2. ~-bag** (for carrying clubs and balls); ~ **ball,** (1) ball used in golf, (2) (colloq.) spherical ball used in some electric typewriters to carry the type; ~ **cart,** (1) trolley for carrying clubs in golf, (2) motorized cart for golfers and equipment; **~-club,** (1) club used in golf, (2) (premises of) association for playing golf; **~-course, ~-links,** area of land on which golf is played; ~ **widow,** woman whose husband spends much leisure time at golf. **3.** *v.i.* Play golf. [15th c. Sc., of unkn. orig.]

gŏ'lfer *n.* Golf-player; cardigan. [f. prec. + -ER[1]]

Golī'ath *n.* Giant; ~ **beetle,** very large African black white-striped beetle; ~ (**crane**), powerful travelling crane; ~ (**heron**), African giant heron. [LL, f. Heb. *golyat̲* giant slain by David (1 Sam. 17)]

gŏ'llĭwŏg *n.* Black-faced grotesquely-dressed doll with fuzzy hair. [19th c., perh. f. GOLLY[1] + POLLIWOG]

gŏ'llop *v.t.*, & *n.* (colloq.) (Swallow with) greedy or hasty gulp. [perh. f. GULP, infl. by GOBBLE[1]]

gŏ'llȳ[1] *int.* = (*By*) *God.* [euphem. for GOD]

gŏ'llȳ[2] *n.* = GOLLIWOG. [abbr.]

‖**golŏ'sh.** See GALOSH.

golŭ'ptious (-sh*us*) *a.* (joc.) Luscious, delightful. [perh. f. *voluptuous*]

G.O.M. *abbr.* Grand Old Man.

gŏmbee'n *n.* (Ir.) Usury (**~-man,** money-lender). [f. Ir. *gaimbín* perh. f. same OCelt. source as med. L *cambire* CHANGE[2]]

-gon *suf.* forming *ns.* denoting plane figures with specified number of angles (*hexagon, polygon, n-gon*). [f. Gk *-gōnos* -angled]

gō'năd *n.* Animal organ producing gametes, e.g. testis or ovary; hence **gōnā'd**AL *a.* [f. mod. L *gonas -adis* f. Gk *gonē, gonos,* generation, seed; see -AD]

gōnadotrō'phĭc, -trŏ'pĭc, *a.* (Physiol.) Regulating activity of gonads. [f. prec. + -o- + TROPHIC, TROPIC]

gŏ'ndola *n.* Light flat-bottomed boat with cabin amidships and high point at each end worked by one oar at stern, used on Venetian canals; car suspended from airship; ***~ (car),** flat-bottomed open railway goods wagon; car attached to ski-lift; island shelves to display goods in self-service shop. [It., f. Rhaeto-Rom., = rock, roll]

gŏndolier' *n.* Rower of gondola. [F, f. It. *gondoliere* (as prec.; see -IER)]

gŏne (*or* gawn) *a.* In vbl senses; lost, hopeless; dead; (of time) past (*not until gone nine*); **be ~,** depart (cf. BEGONE), (colloq.) be temporarily absent; FAR[1] *gone*; ~ **away!** (huntsman's indication that fox has been started); ~ **goose** or **gosling,** (colloq.) person or thing beyond hope; ~ **on,** (sl.) infatuated with. [p.p. of GO[1]]

gŏ'ner *n.* (sl.) Person or thing that is doomed, ended, irrevocably lost, etc. [f. prec. + -ER[1]]

gŏ'nfalon *n.* Banner, often with streamers, hung from crossbar, esp. (Hist.) as standard of some Italian republics; so ~IER[1] *n.* [f. It. *gonfalone* f. Frank. **gundfano* f. Gmc **gund-* war + Frank. **fano* banner (cf. VANE)]

gŏng *n.*, & *v.t.* **1.** *n.* Metal disc with turned rim giving resonant note when struck; saucer-shaped bell; (sl.) medal or decoration. **2.** *v.t.* Summon with gong; (of traffic police) sound gong etc. to direct (motorist) to stop. [f. Malay *gong, gung,* of imit. orig.]

gŏ'ngorĭsm (-ngg-) *n.* Spanish literary style marked by inversion, antithesis, and classical allusion, corresponding to euphuism in England. [f. L. de *Góngora* y Argote, Sp. poet d. 1627 + -ISM]

gōnĭŏ'mèter *n.* Instrument for measuring angles; hence or cogn. **gōnĭŏ'**METRY *n.*, **gōniomĕ'tric**(AL) *adjs.* [f. F *goniomètre* f. Gk *gōnia* angle; see -METER]

‖**gŏnk** *n.* Egg-shaped doll. [20th c., of unkn. orig.]

gŏ'nna (vulg., or U.S. colloq.) = GOING[2] *to.* [corrupt.]

gŏnocŏ'cc|us *n.* (*pl.* **~i** *pr.* -ki). Micro-organism causing gonorrhoea. [f. Gk *gonos* generation, semen + COCCUS]

gŏnorrhoe'|a, ***gŏnorrhē'|a,** (-orē'*a*) *n.* Venereal disease with inflammatory discharge of mucus from urethra or vagina; hence **~AL** *a.* [LL, f. Gk *gonorrhoia* (*gonos* semen, *rhoia* flux)]

goo *n.* (sl.) Viscous or sticky substance; (fig.) sickly sentiment. [20th c.; perh. f. BURGOO]

good *a.* & *adv.* (BETTER[1], BEST[1]), & *n.* **1.** *a.* Having the right qualities, satisfactory, adequate; *a good fire* (not too small or dull); *meat keeps good* (untainted); *good soil* (fertile); *good theatre* etc., entertainment suited to specified medium; **not ~ enough,** (colloq.) not worth doing, accepting, etc.; **in ~ time,** with no risk of being late; **all in ~ time,** in due course but without haste; (used as conventional epithet in) *the good ship* —, *the good town of* —; *good law* (valid, sound); *is good eating* etc. (pleasant to eat etc.). **2.** Commendable (*good and true*); *a good leg* (well shaped); ~ **for you** etc., ~ **man,** ~ **old** —, (Austral. & N.Z.)

~ o'n you etc., (colloq. forms of approval); **a ~ one,** (sl.) incredible lie or exaggeration, excellent joke etc.; (used in courteous, patronizing, ironically polite, or indignant address, as) *my good friend, man, sir*; (used in polite or indulgently contemptuous description, as) *your good lady, the good man.* **3.** Right, proper, expedient, (*it is good to be here*; *I thought, it seemed, good to* do something; or abs. as excl. of approval or consent). **4.** Morally excellent, virtuous, (*do* one's *good deed for the day*). **5.** Kind, benevolent, (so of God etc.; in excl. of surprise etc.: *good God!, good gracious!, good heavens!*); *how good of you!*; *did me a good turn*; *has always been good to me*; **be so ~ as, be ~ enough, to** do, please do; **put in** or **say a ~ word for,** commend, defend. **6.** (Esp. of child) well behaved, not giving trouble, (*as good as gold*). **7.** Gratifying, agreeable, favourable, advantageous, beneficial, wholesome, (*good news*; *it's good to be alive*); (used in forms of greeting or parting, as) *good day, evening, morning, night*; *have a good* NIGHT; *a good saying* or *story, as good as a play,* (amusing); *oil is good for burns*; *beer is not good for him* or *for his health*; *are acorns good to eat?*; **take in ~ part,** not be offended at; **~ times,** period of prosperity; **have a ~ time,** enjoy oneself. **8.** Adapted to a purpose, efficient, suitable, competent, (*a good actor, correspondent, driver*; *good English*; *good at describing* etc.; *has been a good wife to him*). **9.** Reliable, safe, sure; financially sound, able to meet liabilities; *good debts* (sure to be paid); **~ for** an amount, safely to be trusted to pay it, (of draft etc.) drawn for so much; **~ for,** able to perform, inclined for, (*good for a ten-mile walk*). **10.** Valid, sound, thorough, ample, considerable, (*gave her a good beating*; *did it for good reasons*; *rule holds good*; *a good excuse*); *a good* DEAL[1], FEW, MANY; *have a good* MIND[1]; *a good* WHILE[1]; (as intensive before adj., as) *went a good round pace, will take a good long time.* **11.** Not less than (*played for a good hour*; *it is a good three miles from the station*). **12. As ~ as,** practically (*he as good as told me so*; *as good as dead*; *it is as good as done*); **make ~,** compensate for, pay (expense), fulfil (promise), effect (purpose, intended action), demonstrate (statement), substantiate (charge), gain and hold (position), replace or restore (thing lost or damaged), (abs.) accomplish what one has attempted. **13.** *Good* BOOK[1](*s*); **~ breeding,** correct or courteous manners; *good* BUY; *good* CAUSE[1]; *good* FAITH; **of ~ family,** well-born; **~ fellow,** virtuous man, sociable person, agreeable companion; **~-fe'llowship,** conviviality, sociability; *good* FORM[1]; **~-for-nothing, ~-for-nought,** *adjs.* & *ns.*, worthless (person); *Good* FRIDAY; *with a good* GRACE; **~-hearted,** kindly or well-meaning; **~ humour,** cheerful mood or disposition, amiability; **~-humoured,** cheerful, amiable; *good* JOB[1]; **G~ King Henry,** kind of goose-foot used in cooking; *good* LIVER[2] (1, 2), LIVING[1]; **~-loo'ker,** handsome person; **~-loo'king,** handsome; **~'-looking,** of virtuous appearance; **~ looks,** personal beauty; **~ luck,** being fortunate, happy chance; *good luck to you!* (as wish); ||**~'man,** (arch.) head of household, husband, father, etc.; **~ money,** genuine money, money that might have been spent usefully elsewhere (*throw good money after bad*), (colloq.) high wages; ||**~ morrow,** (arch.) = *good morning* (see sense 7); **~ nature,** kindly disposition, willingness to subordinate one's own interests; **~-natured,** kindly, willing to please; **~ neighbour,** one who acts in friendly manner; *good* OFFICES; **the ~ people,** fairies; **~ question** (not answerable immediately or easily); **~ sense,** soundness of judgement, practical wisdom; **in ~ spirits,** not depressed; **~-tempered,** having good TEMPER[2]; **~ thing,** anything one approves of, advantageous bargain or speculation, witty saying, (in *pl.*) dainties or luxuries; **~ time** (see senses 1 and 7); **~-time,** recklessly pursuing pleasure; **~'wife,** (Sc.) mistress of house; **~ will,** virtuous intent (cf. GOODWILL); **~ works,** charitable acts. **14.** Hence **~'**ISH[1] 2 *a.* **15.** *adv.* (colloq.) *Well, properly, (*doing pretty good*); **~ and,** (colloq., as intensive: *raining good and hard, *I was good and angry*). **16.** *n.* What is good or beneficial, well-being, profit, benefit, advantage, (*is a power for good*; *deceive him for his (own) good*; *what good is it, what is the good of it, what good will it do?*; *much good may it do you!* (often iron.)); **be any, much, no, some, ~,** be of any etc. use; **come to (no) ~,** yield (no) good result; **do ~,** show kindness *to,* act philanthropically, be beneficial *to*; **for ~ (and all),** permanently or finally; **in ~,** (colloq.) in favour *with*; **to the ~,** as net profit, advantage, something extra, etc. **17.** Desirable end or object, thing worth attaining; **no ~,** some mischief (*is up to, after, no good*). **18.** (as *pl.*) Virtuous persons (*the good and the bad alike respect him*). **19.** (*in pl.*) Movable property; merchandise, wares, (**piece of ~s,** (joc.) person); ||things for transmission by rail etc. (opp. *passengers*; so *goods agent, station, train,* etc.; **by ~s,** by goods train). **20.** (in *pl.*, colloq.) Objects etc. one has undertaken to supply (*deliver the goods*, lit. or fig.); the real thing, the genuine article; information etc. to one's own advantage (*have the goods on a person*). [OE *gōd*, = OS *gōd*, OHG *guot*, ON *góthr*, Goth. *gōths* f. Gmc **gōdhaz* cogn. w. **gadh-* in GATHER]

goo͝dbȳe', *goo͝dbȳ', *int.* & *n.* (*pl.* **goodbyes** *or* ***goodbys**). (Saying of) farewell (expressing good wishes on parting, ending telephone conversation, etc., or fig. w. ref. to thing got rid of or irrevocably lost). [contr. of *God be with you!*, w. *good* substituted after *good night* etc.]

goo͝'dl|y̆ *a.* Comely, handsome; of considerable size etc.; hence **~ĭness** *n.* [OE *gōdlic* (as GOOD, -LY[1])]

goo͝'dness *n.* **1.** Virtue; positive or comparative excellence; benevolence, kindness, generosity, (**have the ~,** be kind enough *to*); what is good in thing, its essence or strength. **2.** (In excl., substituted for) God (*goodness knows*; *for goodness' sake*; THANK *goodness!*; *I wish to goodness*; **~ gracious!, ~ me!,** excl. of surprise or indignation). [OE *gōdnes* (as GOOD, -NESS)]

goo͝dwi'll *n.* Kindly feeling to person, favour; cheerful acquiescence, heartiness, zeal; established custom or popularity of business etc.; privilege granted by seller of established business, of trading as recognized successor; amount paid for this. [f. GOOD + WILL[2]]

goo͝'dy̆[1] *n.* (arch.) Elderly woman of humble station; (as prefix to surname) *Goody Blake* etc. [for GOOD*wife*; cf. HUSSY]

goo͝'dy[2] *n.* Something good or attractive, esp. to eat; (colloq.) hero etc., opp. *baddy* (BAD 3). [f. GOOD + -Y[3]]

goo͝'dy̆[3], **goo͝'dy̆-goo͝dy̆,** *a.* & *n.* (Person who is) primly, affectedly, obtrusively, weakly, or sentimentally virtuous; hence **(goo͝dy̆-)goo͝'dĭ-ness** *n.* [f. GOOD + -Y[3]]

goo͝'dy̆[4] *int.* expr. childish delight or surprise. [f. GOOD + -Y[3]]

goo͞'ey *a.* (**goo'ier, goo'iest**). (sl.) Viscous or sticky; (fig.) sentimental. [f. GOO + -Y[2]]

goo͞f[1] *n.* (sl.) Foolish or stupid person; mistake; **~'ball,** (1) marijuana or other drug tablet, (2) foolish or stupid person; hence **~'**Y[2] *a.*, (sl.) silly. [var. of dial. *goff* f. F *goffe* f. It. *goffo* f. med. L *gufus* coarse]

goof[2] *v.* (sl.) **1.** *v.i.* Idle; blunder. **2.** *v.t.* Bungle, mess up; (in *p.p.*) stupefy with drug. [f. prec.]

goo'glỹ *n.* (Cricket). Off-break ball bowled with apparent leg-break action. [20th c.; orig. unkn.]

***gook** (*or* gŏŏk) *n.* (sl., derog.) Foreigner, esp. coloured person from E. Asia etc. [20th c.; orig. unkn.]

goon *n.* (sl.) Stupid person; person hired by racketeers etc. to terrorize workers. [perh. f. dial. *gooney* booby; infl. by subhuman cartoon character 'Alice the *Goon*']

goop *n.* (sl.) Stupid or fatuous person; hence ~'Y[2] *a.* [20th c.; cf. GOOF[1]]

goosă'nder *n.* Duck (*Mergus merganser*) with sharp serrated bill. [app. f. foll.; cf. *bergander* sheldrake]

goose *n.* (*pl.* **geese** *pr.* gēs, exc. in sense 3), & *v.t.* **1.** *n.* Large web-footed bird of genus *Anser* etc., between duck and swan in size; female of this (opp. *gander*); flesh of goose as food; **all his geese are swans,** he overestimates the merits of his own schemes, friends, etc.; **kill the ~ that lays the golden eggs,** sacrifice future profit to greed of the moment; COOK[2] person's *goose*; GONE *goose*; *say* BOO *to goose*; *sauce for goose is sauce for* GANDER. **2.** Simpleton. **3.** (*pl.* ~s). Tailor's smoothing-iron (with handle like goose's neck). **4.** *~ **bumps,** = *goose-flesh*; ***~-egg,** zero score in game; **~-flesh,** rough bristling state of skin produced by cold or fright; **~-foot** (*pl.* *~-foots*), plant esp. of genus *Chenopodium,* named from shape of leaves; **~-girl** (employed to tend geese); **~-grass,** cleavers; **~'herd,** one who tends geese; **~-neck,** thing shaped like neck of goose; **~-pimples, ~-skin,** = *goose-flesh*; **~ step,** (1) balancing-drill taught to army recruits, (2) balance step of marching soldiers with knees kept stiff. **5.** *v.t.* (sl.) Poke person in sensitive (esp. genital or anal) region. [OE *gōs,* = OHG *gans,* ON *gás* f. Gmc **gans-* f. IE **ghans-*]

goo'seberrỹ (-zb-) *n.* **1.** (Edible berry of) any thorny species of *Ribes*; (arch.) wine made of gooseberries; **play ~,** act as chaperon, or be unwelcome companion, for pair of lovers. **2.** **~ bush** (w. ref. to source of babies in explanation sometimes given to children); *gooseberry* FOOL[2]. [perh. f. prec., but cf. dial. *groser* (F *groseille*)]

||**goo'segŏg** (-zg-) *n.* (colloq.) Gooseberry. [joc. corrupt.]

***G.O.P.** *abbr.* Grand Old Party (the Republican Party).

gō'pher[1] *n.* (Bibl.) tree from wood of which Noah's ark was made; **~(-wood),** tree yielding yellowish timber. [f. Heb. *gōper*]

gō'pher[2] *n.* **1.** American bŭrrowing rodent of family Geomyidae. **2.** N. Amer. ground-squirrel of genus *Citellus.* **3.** Nocturnal burrowing tortoise of Southern U.S. **4.** **~ snake,** cribo; ***G~ State,** Minnesota. [18th c.; said to be f. Can. F. *gaufre* honeycomb, w. ref. to burrowing]

gor'al *n.* Indian antelope of genus *Naemorhedus.* [native name]

||**gorblī'mey** *int.* (vulg.) expr. surprise, indignation, etc. [corrupt. of *God blind me*]

gor'cŏck *n.* (Sc. & N. Engl.) Male of the red grouse. [f. *gor-* (of unkn. orig.) + COCK[1]]

Gor'dĭan *a.* **~ knot,** intricate knot, difficult problem or task; **cut the ~ knot,** solve problem by force or by evading the conditions. [f. *Gordius,* who tied a knot later cut by Alexander the Great, + -AN]

Gor'don *n.* **~ (setter),** black and tan setter used as gun dog. [f. 4th Duke of ~ d. 1827, promoter of the breed]

gore[1] *n.* Blood shed and thickened or clotted; hence **gor'**Y[2] *a.*, **gor'**ĭLY[2] *adv.* [OE *gor* dung, dirt, = OHG, ON *gor* slimy matter]

gore[2] *n.*, & *v.t.* **1.** Wedge-shaped piece of cloth inserted to adjust width of a garment; triangular or lune-shaped piece in umbrella, balloon, dome, globe, etc. **2.** *v.t.* Shape or narrow with gore. [OE *gāra* triangular piece of land, = OHG *gēro,* ON *geiri,* cogn. w. OE *gār* spear, w. ref. to shape of spearhead]

gore[3] *v.t.* Pierce with horn, tusk, etc. [ME, of unkn. orig.]

gorge[1] *n.* **1.** What has been swallowed, contents of stomach, (**cast the ~ at,** reject with loathing; one's **~ rises at,** one is sickened or disgusted by); (rhet.) internal throat. **2.** (Fortif.) neck of bastion or other outwork, rear entrance to a work; narrow opening, usu. with stream, between hills; *mass of ice etc. blocking narrow passage. [ME f. OF, f. Rom. **gurga* for L *gurges* whirlpool]

gorge[2] *v.* & *n.* **1.** *v.i.* Feed greedily. **2.** *v.t.* Satiate, glut; swallow, devour greedily; fill full, distend, choke up. **3.** *n.* Act of gorging, surfeit. [ME, f. OF *gorger* (as prec.)]

gor'geous (-jus) *a.* Richly coloured, sumptuous, magnificent; (colloq.) very pleasant, splendid, (*had a gorgeous time*); hence ~LY[2] *adv.*, ~NESS *n.* [earlier *gorgayse, -yas* f. OF *gorgias* fine, elegant, of unkn. orig.]

gor'gĕt *n.* **1.** (Hist.) Piece of armour for throat; woman's wimple. **2.** Patch of colour on throat of bird etc. [f. OF *gorgete* (as GORGE[1]; see -ET[1])]

Gor'gĭō *n.* (*pl.* ~s). (Gipsy name for) non-gipsy. [Romany]

gor'gon *n.* (Gk Myth.) one of three snake-haired sisters (esp. Medusa) whose looks turned any beholder to stone; terrible or ugly person, repellent woman; hence **gorgō'n**IAN *a.* [f. L *Gorgo -onis* f. Gk *Gorgō* (*gorgos* terrible)]

gorgō'nĭ|a *n.* Polyp of genus *Gorgonia,* e.g. sea-fan; hence ~AN *a.* & *n.* [mod. L, f. as prec. + -IA[1], w. ref. to its petrifaction]

gor'gonīze, -īse (-īz), *v.t.* Stare at like gorgon; paralyse with terror etc. [f. GORGON + -IZE]

Gorgonzō'la *n.* Type of rich blue-veined cheese. [~ in Italy]

gorĭ'lla *n.* Large powerful arboreal anthropoid ape, with reputation for fierceness. [perh. Afr. for 'wild man', in Gk account of Hanno's voyage 5th or 6th c. B.C., adopted as specific name 1847]

gor'mandiz|e, -īs|e (-īz), *n.* & *v.* **1.** *n.* = GOURMANDISE. **2.** *v.i.* & *t.* Eat or devour voraciously; hence ~ER[1] *n.* [f. as GOURMANDISE]

gor'mlĕss *a.* (colloq.) Foolish, lacking sense; hence ~NESS *n.* [orig. *gaumless* f. dial. *gaum* understanding + -LESS]

gorse *n.* = FURZE; hence **gor'**SY[2] *a.* [OE *gors(t)* cogn. w. OHG *gersta,* L *hordeum,* barley]

Gor'sĕdd (-ĕdh) *n.* Meeting of Welsh etc. bards and druids (esp. as daily preliminary to the eisteddfod). [W, lit. 'throne']

gor'ў. See GORE[1].

gŏsh *n.* (In excl. etc., substituted for) God (*gosh, my gosh, gosh-awful,* etc.). [euphem.]

gŏ'shawk (-s-h-) *n.* Large short-winged hawk. [OE *gōs-hafoc* (as GOOSE, HAWK[1])]

gŏ'slĭng (-z-) *n.* Young goose; GONE *gosling.* [ME, orig. *gesling* f. ON *gæslingr* (as GOOSE, -LING[1])]

gŏ'spel *n.* **1.** Glad tidings preached by Christ; religious doctrine of Christ and his apostles, Christian revelation. **2.** (*G~*). Record of Christ's life and teaching in first four books of N.T. (Matthew, Mark, Luke, John); one of these books; portion from one of them read at

Communion service. **3.** Thing that may safely be believed (*takes his dreams for gospel*); principle that one acts upon, believes in, or preaches, (*the gospel of efficiency, laissez-faire, soap and water*). **4.** ~ **oath** (sworn on the Gospels); **G~ side,** N. side of altar, at which Gospel is read; ~ (**song**), fervent or evangelical singing esp. as style of jazz; ~ **truth,** truths contained in Gospel, something as true as Gospel. [OE *gōdspel* (*gōd* GOOD, *spel* news, SPELL¹), rendering eccl. L *bona annuntiatio, bonus nuntius* = *evangelium* EVANGEL; assoc. w. GOD]

gŏ'speller *n.* Reader of Gospel in Communion service; **hot** ~, zealous puritan, rabid propagandist. [f. prec. + -ER¹]

gŏ'ssamer *n.* & *a.* **1.** *n.* Light filmy substance, the webs of small spiders, floating in calm air or spread over grass; *a* thread of this; something flimsy; delicate gauze; hence ~ED² (-*erd*), ~Y², *adjs.* **2.** *a.* Light and flimsy as gossamer. [ME *gos(e)somer(e)*, app. f. GOOSE + SUMMER¹ (*goose summer* = St. Martin's summer, i.e. early November when geese were eaten, gossamer being most seen then)]

gŏ'ssip *n.*, & *v.i.* **1.** *n.* ||(arch., esp. of woman). Familiar acquaintance, friend. **2.** Idle talker, newsmonger, tattler. **3.** Idle talk, groundless rumours, tittle-tattle, whence ~-MONGER *n.*; easy unconstrained talk or writing esp. about persons or social incidents (~ **column,** section of newspaper etc. containing this); hence ~RY (4, 5) *n.*, ~Y² *a.* **4.** *v.i.* Talk idly or lightly, tattle; write in gossipy style; hence ~ER¹ *n.* [earlier sense 'godparent', f. OE *godsibb* person related to one in GOD; see SIB]

gŏssōō'n *n.* (Ir.) Lad. [earlier *garsoon* f. F *garçon* boy]

gŏt. See GET¹.

Gŏth *n.* Uncivilized or ignorant person. [f. name of Gmc tribe invading Eastern & Western Empires in 3rd–5th c.; f. LL *Gothi* pl. f. Gk *Go(t)thoi* f. Goth. **Gutos* or **Gutans*]

Gŏ'tham (-t*a*m) *n.* **1.** Town proverbial for folly (**wise man of** ~, fool). **2.** (*or* gō'th*a*m). *(colloq.) New York City. **3.** Hence ~ITE¹ (1) *n.* [ME, perh. f. the village in Notts.]

Gŏ'thĭc *a.* & *n.* **1.** *a.* Of the Goths or their language. **2.** (Archit.) In the pointed-arch style prevalent in churches etc. of Western Europe in 12th–16th c., including in England the Early English, Decorated, and Perpendicular; ~ **Revival,** reversion to this in 19th c. **3.** (arch.) Barbarous, rude, uncouth. **4.** (Print.) Old-fashioned German, black letter, or sanserif, (type). **5.** (Of novel etc.) in style popular in 18th–19th c., with supernatural or horrifying events. **6.** Hence **Gŏ'thi**CALLY *adv.*, ~ISM (2, 3, 4) *n.*, ~IZE (2, 3) *v.i.* & *t.* **7.** *n.* Gothic language; Gothic architecture; Gothic type. [f. F *gothique* or f. LL *gothicus* (*Gothi*; see GOTH, -IC)]

gŏ'tta (colloq. or vulg.) = (*have*) *got a* or (*have*) *got to.* [corrupt.]

gŏ'tten. See GET¹.

Götterdämmerung (gẽr'terdĕ'merŏŏng) *n.* Twilight of the gods; (fig.) complete downfall of regime etc. [G, esp. as title of opera by Wagner]

gouache (gŏŏah'sh) *n.* (Way of painting in) opaque colours ground in water and thickened with gum and honey; picture thus painted [F, f. It. *guazzo*]

Gou'da *n.* Flat round cheese. [~ in Holland, where orig. made]

gouge (*or* gōōj) *n.* & *v.* **1.** *n.* Concave-bladed chisel used in carpentry, sculpture, and surgery; *(colloq.) swindle. **2.** *v.t.* Cut with gouge; cut *out* (a cork, a channel) (as) with gouge; force (*out*, esp. person's eye with thumb) (as) with gouge; force out eye of; *(colloq.) swindle, extort money from. **3.** *v.i.* (Austral.) Dig for opal. [F, f. LL *gubia*, perh. of Celt. orig.]

gou'lăsh (gōō'-; *or* -ahsh) *n.* **1.** Highly seasoned stew of meat and vegetables. **2.** (Contract Bridge). Re-deal, several cards at a time, of the four hands (unshuffled, but with each hand arranged in suits and order of value) when no player has bid. [f. Magyar *gulyás-hús* (*gulyás* herdsman, *hús* meat)]

gour'amĭ (goor'-; *or* -ah'-) *n.* Large S.E. Asian freshwater food-fish (*Osphronemus goramy*); smaller fish of same family, freq. kept in aquaria. [f. Malay *gurāmi*]

gourd (goord) *n.* **1.** (Fleshy usu. large fruit of) trailing or climbing plant of family Cucurbitaceae. **2.** Rind of gourd-fruit emptied, dried, and used as bottle etc.; hence ~'FUL 2 *n.* [ME, f. AF *gurde*, OF *gourde* ult. f. L *cucurbita*]

gour'mand (goor'-) *a.* & *n.* **1.** *a.* Gluttonous, fond of eating. **2.** *n.* Greedy feeder, glutton; gourmet; hence ~ISM (2) *n.* [ME f. OF, of unkn. orig.]

gourmandise (goor'mahṅdēz) *n.* Habits of a gourmand, indulgence in good eating, gluttony. [F (as prec.; cf. -ISE²)]

gour'met (goor'mā) *n.* Connoisseur of table delicacies; judge of good eating. [F, = wine-taster; sense infl. by GOURMAND]

gout *n.* **1.** Paroxysmal disease with inflammation of smaller joints, esp. that of big toe, and chalk-stones; hence ~'Y² *a.* **2.** Wheat-disease caused by ~-**fly** (*Chlorops*). **3.** Drop, esp. of blood; splash, spot. [ME, f. OF *goute* f. L *gutta* drop, w. ref. to medieval theory of flowing down of humours]

Gov. *abbr.* Government; Governor.

go'vern (gŭ'-) *v.* **1.** *v.t.* Rule with authority, conduct the policy, actions, and affairs, of (State, subjects) either despotically or constitutionally; regulate proceedings of (corporation etc.; ~**ing body,** managers of hospital, school, etc.); be in military command of (fort, town). **2.** Sway, rule, influence, regulate, determine, (person, his acts, course or issue of events). **3.** Conduct one*self* in some way; curb, bridle, (one's passions, one*self*). **4.** Constitute a law, rule, standard, or principle, for; serve to decide (case). **5.** (Gram., esp. of *v.* or *prep.*) have (noun or pronoun, case) depending on it, require (a certain case of dependent word). **6.** Hence ~ABLE *a.* **7.** *v.i.* Exercise function of government in person; *king reigns but does not govern* (merely selects those who are to govern). **8.** Be predominating influence. [ME, f. OF *governer* f. L *gubernare* steer, rule f. Gk *kubernaō* steer]

go'vernance (gŭ'-) *n.* Act, manner, fact, or function, of governing; sway, control. [ME f. OF (as prec.; see -ANCE)]

go'vernĕss (gŭ'-) *n.* **1.** Female teacher, usu. of children in private household; hence ~Y² *a.* (esp. prim). **2.** ||~-**car(t)**, (Hist.) light two-wheeled tub-shaped cart with rear entrance, and side seats face to face. [earlier *governeress* f. OF *governeresse* (as GOVERNOR; see -ESS¹)]

go'vernment (gŭ'-) *n.* **1.** System of governing, form of organization of State. **2.** Body or successive bodies of persons governing a State; the State as an agent; an administration or ministry; **form a G~** (of Prime Minister selecting colleagues); **G~ House,** official residence of governor; *~ **issue,** (equipment) provided by the government; **G~ paper, securities,** bonds etc. issued by the government; ~ **surplus,** unused equipment sold by the government. **3.** (Gram.) Relation between governing and governed word. **4.** Act, manner, or fact, of governing. **5.** Hence ~AL (-ĕ'n-) *a.* [ME, f. OF *governement* (as GOVERN; see -MENT)]

go'vernor (gŭ'-) *n.* **1.** One who governs, ruler; official appointed to govern province, town, etc., representative of Crown in Commonwealth country (*Governor-General*) or colony; executive head of each State of U.S.; officer commanding fortress or garrison; head, or one of governing body, of institution; official in charge of prison. **2.** (sl.) One's employer, one's father; (as *voc.*) sir. **3.** (Mech.) Automatic regulator of supply of gas, steam, water, etc., to machine, ensuring uniform motion. **4.** Hence ~ATE[1] (1) ~SHIP (1, 2), *ns.* [ME, f. AF *governour* OF *governēo(u)r* f. L *gubernator -oris* (as GOVERN; see -OR)]

Govt. *abbr.* Government.

gow'an *n.* (Sc.) Daisy; white or yellow field-flower. [prob. var. of dial. *gollan* ranunculus etc., and cogn. w. mari*gold*]

gowk *n.* (dial.) Cuckoo; awkward or half-witted person, fool. [ME, f. ON *gaukr* = OE *gēac*, OHG *gouh* f. Gmc **gaukaz*]

gown *n.*, & *v.t.* **1.** *n.* Loose flowing outer garment, esp. woman's dress (now usu. of dress with some pretension to elegance), frock; ancient Roman toga; surgeon's overall; official or uniform robe of various shapes worn by alderman, judge, lawyer, clergyman, member of university, college, or school, etc., (**town and ~**, non-members and members of university at Oxf. and Camb.); **~'sman** (-z-), wearer of gown, member of university. **2.** *v.t.* (usu. in *p.p.*) Attire in gown. [ME, f. OF *goune, gon(n)e* f. LL *gunna* fur garment (cf. med. Gk *gouna* fur)]

goy *n.* (*pl.* **~s** *or* **~'im**). (Jewish name for) GENTILE 1. [f. Heb. *gōy* people, nation]

G.P. *abbr.* general practitioner; Grand Prix.

Gp. Capt. *abbr.* Group Captain.

G.P.O. *abbr.* General Post Office; *Government Printing Office.

G.R. *abbr.* King George. [f. L *Georgius Rex*]

gr. *abbr.* grain(s); gram(s); gross.

Graa'fĭan (grah'f-) *a.* **~ follicle** or **vesicle,** one of small sacs in mammal ovary in which ova are matured. [f. R. de *Graaf*, Du. anatomist d. 1673 + -IAN]

grăb *v.* (**-bb-**) & *n.* **1.** *v.t.* Seize suddenly; appropriate rapaciously; capture, arrest; (sl.) attract attention of, impress. **2.** *v.i.* Make sudden snatch *at*; (of brakes of motor vehicle) act harshly or jerkily. **3.** Hence (-)~'BER[1] *n.* **4.** *n.* Sudden clutch, grasp, seizure, or attempt to seize (***up for ~s,** (sl.) easily obtainable, inviting capture); practice of grabbing, rapacious proceedings esp. in politics or commerce; (Mech.) device or implement for clutching; children's card-game in which certain cards may be snatched from the table; **~-bag,** lucky dip; **~ handle, ~ rail,** etc., (to steady passengers in moving vehicle). [f. MLG, MDu. *grabben*; cf. GRIP[2], GRIPE, GROPE]

gră'bble *v.i.* Grope about, feel for something; sprawl on all fours, scramble (*for* something). [f. Du. & LG *grabbeln* scramble for a thing (as prec.; see -LE 3)]

gră'bbў *a.* (colloq.) Having tendency to grab; greedy. [f. GRAB + -Y[2]]

gra'ben (-ah'-) *n.* (*pl.* **~s** *or* **~**). (Geol.) Depression of earth's surface between faults. [G, orig. = ditch]

grāce *n.*, & *v.t.* **1.** *n.* Pleasing quality, attractiveness, charm, esp. that belonging to elegant proportions or ease and refinement of movement, action, expression, or manner. **2.** Becomingness (*cannot with any grace ask him*; **have the ~ to,** be sufficiently conscious of duty or decency to); air with which thing is done (**with a good ~,** as if willingly; **with a bad** or **ill ~,** reluctantly, ungraciously). **3.** Attractive feature, accomplishment, ornament, (*social graces*); **airs and ~s,** behaviour put on with a view to effect or attraction. **4.** (Mus.) **~(-note), -notes,** embellishment of extra note(s) not essential to harmony or melody. **5.** (Gk Myth.; *G~*). One of three beautiful goddess sisters, bestowers of beauty and charm. **6.** Favour, benignant regard or its manifestation, on part of superior; **be in** person's **good ~s,** enjoy his favour or liking; **~ and favour** *house* etc., occupied by permission of sovereign etc. **7.** Unconstrained goodwill as ground of concession; **act of ~,** privilege or concession that cannot be claimed as right (and see 11); **by the ~ of God,** (esp. in royal titles) through God's favour. **8.** ‖Permission to take university degree; dispensation from university statutes. **9.** (Theol.) Unmerited favour of God, divine regenerating, inspiring, and strengthening influence; (**state of**) **~,** condition of being so influenced (**fall from ~,** lapse into sin or disgrace from good behaviour etc.); divinely given talent etc.; SAVING[1] *grace*; **year of ~,** date A.D. **10.** Favour shown by granting delay (*give a day's, year's*, etc., *grace*); **days of ~,** time allowed by law for payment of bill of exchange or insurance premium after it falls due. **11.** Mercy, clemency; **Act of ~,** formal, esp. general, pardon by Act of Parliament (and see 7). **12.** Short thanksgiving before or after meal (**~-cup,** cup of wine etc. passed round after grace, parting draught). **13. His, Her, Your, G~** (forms of description or address for duke, duchess, or archbishop). **14.** *v.t.* Add grace to, adorn, enhance *with*; confer honour or dignity on, honour *with* title etc.; do credit to. [ME f. OF, f. L *gratia* (*gratus* pleasing; cf. GRATEFUL)]

grā'ceful (-sf-) *a.* Pleasing, attractive, esp. in form, movement, or action; hence ~LY[2] *adv.*, ~NESS *n.* [ME, f. prec. + -FUL]

grā'celėss (-sl-) *a.* **1.** (arch. or joc.) Unregenerate, depraved; **~ florin** (of 1849, from which the letters *D.G.* were omitted). **2.** Lacking sense of decency, unabashed. **3.** Lacking charm or elegance. **4.** Hence ~LY[2] *adv.*, ~NESS *n.* [ME, f. GRACE + -LESS]

gră'cĭle *a.* Slender; gracefully slender; hence **gracĭ'l**ITY *n.*, slenderness, (of literary style) unornamented simplicity. [f. L *gracilis* slender]

grā'cious (-shus) *a.* & *int.* **1.** *a.* (Of exalted person, or iron. or joc.) kind, indulgent and beneficent to inferiors; (esp. as polite epithet of royal persons or their acts: *the gracious speech from the throne*); **~ living,** elegant way of life with observance of proprieties etc. **2.** (Of God) dispensing grace, merciful, benignant; (arch.) agreeable, pleasing; (poet.) kindly, courteous. **3.** Hence or cogn. ~LY[2] *adv.*, ~NESS, **grācĭo**'SITY, *ns.* **4.** *int.* (orig. ellipt. for *gracious God* in excl. of indignation or surprise) *gracious!, good gracious!, gracious me!* [ME f. OF, f. L *gratiosus* (as GRACE; see -OUS)]

gră'ckle *n.* **1.** Asian bird of mina family, esp. of genus *Gracula*. **2.** Amer. oriole, esp. of genus *Quiscalus*. [f. mod. L *Gracula* f. L *graculus* jackdaw]

grăd *n.* (colloq.) = GRADUATE[1] 1. [abbr.]

gradā'te *v.i.* & *t.* (Cause to) pass by imperceptible degrees from one shade of colour to another; arrange in steps or grades of size etc. [back form. f. foll.]

gradā'tion *n.* **1.** (usu. in *pl.*) Stage of transition or advance; degree in rank, merit, intensity, divergence, etc. **2.** Such degree; arrangement in such degrees. **3.** (Paint. etc.) Gradual passing from one shade, tone, etc., to another. **4.** (Philol.) Ablaut. **5.** Hence ~AL *a.* [f. L *gradatio* (*gradus* step; see -ATION)]

grāde *n.* & *v.* **1.** *n.* Degree in rank, proficiency, quality, value, etc., class of persons or things alike in these; *class or form in school (*~ **school,** elementary school); mark indicating quality of student's work. **2.** Variety of cattle produced by crossing native stock with superior breed. **3.** Group of animals at similar level of development. **4.** (Philol.) Relative position in ablaut-series. **5.** Gradient, slope, rate of ascent or descent; ***at** ~, on same level; *~ **crossing,** LEVEL crossing; **on the up** or **down** ~, rising or falling (lit. or fig.); **make the** ~, reach desired standard. **6.** *v.t.* Arrange in grades, class, sort; give grade to (student); blend so as to affect grade of colour with tints passing into each other. **7.** Reduce (road, canal, etc.) to easy gradients. **8.** Cross (cattle) with better breed (~ **up,** improve thus). **9.** Hence **grā'd**ER[1] (1, 2) *n.* **10.** *v.i.* Pass gradually (*down, up,* etc.) from one grade into another. [F, or f. L *gradus* step]

||**grā'delў** (-dlĭ) *a.* (dial.) Excellent, thorough; handsome, comely; real, true, proper. [ME *graythly* f. ON *greithligr* (*greithr* = OE *gerǣde* ready; see -LY[1])]

Grăʹdgrīnd *n.* Person without warm feelings, interested only in facts. [character in Dickens's *Hard Times*]

grā'dĭent *n.* **1.** Amount of slope, inclination to the horizontal, in road, railway, etc.; inclined part of road etc. **2.** (Rate of) rise or fall of temperature, pressure, etc. in passing from one region to another. [prob. formed on GRADE after *salient*]

gradi'ne (-ē'n), **grā'dĭn,** *n.* One of series of low steps or tier of seats; ledge at back of altar. [f. It. *gradino* dim. of *grado* GRADE]

grăʹdūal[1] *n.* Response sung between Epistle and Gospel in the service of the Mass; book of music for Mass service. [so called as being sung at steps of altar or while deacon mounted ambo; f. med. L *graduale* neut. adj. (as n.), see foll.]

grăʹdūal[2] *a.* **1.** Taking place by degrees, slowly progressive, not rapid, steep, or abrupt; hence ~ISM (3), ~IST (2), *ns.*, (advocate of) policy of gradual not sudden change, ~LY[2] *adv.*, ~NESS *n.* **2.** ~ **psalm,** = SONG *of Degrees.* [f. med. L *gradualis* (L *gradus* step; see -AL)]

||**grăʹdūănd** *n.* One about to receive an academic degree. [f. med. L *graduandus* gerundive of *graduare* GRADUATE[2]; see -ND[1]]

grăʹdūate[1] *n.* **1.** One who holds academic degree; *one who has completed a school course; *~ **nurse,** trained nurse; ~ **school,** department of university for advanced work by graduates. **2.** Chemist's graduated measuring-glass. [f. med. L *graduatus* p.p. of *graduari* (see foll., -ATE[2])]

grăʹdū|āte[2] *v.i.* & *t.* **1.** Take or *admit to academic degree or *certificate of completion of school studies; *send out or come as graduate *from* (university etc.); move up *to* (higher grade of activity etc.); gain qualifications *as.* **2.** *v.t.* Mark out in degrees or portions; arrange in gradations, apportion incidence of (tax) according to a scale. **3.** *v.i.* Pass by degrees (*into* or *away*). **4.** Hence ~A'TION, ~**ātor**, *ns.* [f. med. L *graduari* f. L *gradus* step, + -ATE[3]]

grā'dus *n.* (Hist.) Dictionary of Latin prosody used in schools to help in writing Latin verse. [abbr. of its title '*Gradus ad Parnassum*' steps to Parnassus]

Grae'cĭsm *n.* A Greek idiom, esp. as imitated in another language; Greek spirit, style, mode of expression, etc.; imitation of these. [f. F *grécisme* or f. med. L *Graecismus* (*Graecus* GREEK; see -ISM)]

Grae'cīze, -īse (-īz), *v.t.* Give a Greek character or form to. [f. L *Graecizare* (as prec.; see -IZE)]

Grae'cō- *comb. form.* Greek (and), as: ~MA'NIA(C) *ns.*, ~PHIL(E) *n.* & *a.*; **~-Roman,** of the Greeks and Romans (esp. of wrestling style attacking only upper part of body). [f. L *Graecus* GREEK + -O-]

graffi't|o (-fē'-) *n.* (*pl.* ~**i** *pr.* -ē). **1.** Drawing or writing scratched or scribbled on wall etc. **2.** Decoration by scratches through plaster showing different-coloured under-surface. [It. (*graffio* scratching)]

graft[1] (-ah-) *n.* & *v.* **1.** *n.* Shoot or scion inserted in slit of another stock, from which it receives sap; (Surg.) piece of transplanted living tissue; process of grafting; place where graft is inserted; (sl.) hard work. **2.** *v.t.* Insert (scion) as graft (*in, into, on, upon, together*); (fig.) insert or fix *in* or *on* so as to produce vital or indissoluble union; insert graft(s) on (stock); sew together (two pieces of knitted material); (Surg.) transplant (living tissue). **3.** *v.i.* Insert graft(s); (sl.) work hard. **4.** **~'ing-clay, -wax,** composition for covering united parts of graft and stock. [ME, earlier *graff* n. & v. f. OF *grafe, grefe* f. L f. Gk *graphion* stylus (*graphō* write)]

graft[2] (-ah-) *n.*, & *v.i.* (colloq.) **1.** *n.* Illicit gain esp. in connection with politics or business; practices intended to secure this, esp. bribery. **2.** *v.i.* Seek or make graft; hence ~'ER[1] *n.* [19th c.; orig. unkn.]

***grā'ham** (-ā'am) *n.* ~ **bread** etc. (made from ~ **flour,** unbolted wheat flour). [f. S. *Graham,* Amer. dietitian d. 1851]

grail[1] *n.* (arch.) = GRADUAL[1]. [ME f. OF *grael,* f. med. L *gradale* var. of *graduale* GRADUAL[1]]

Grail[2] *n.* (**Holy**) ~, cup or platter used (according to legend) by Christ at Last Supper, and in which Joseph of Arimathea received Christ's blood at the Cross; this as object of prolonged quest (by medieval knights, or fig.). [ME, f. OF *graal* etc. f. med. L *gradalis* dish, of unkn. orig.]

grain *n.* & *v.* **1.** *n.* Fruit or seed of a cereal; (collect.) wheat or the allied food-grasses or their fruit, corn; a particular species of corn; *grain* ELEVATOR; **~s of Paradise,** capsules of W. Afr. plant (*Aframomum melegueta*) used as spice and drug. **2.** Small hard particle of sand, gold, SALT, gunpowder, incense, etc.; (usu. small) discrete particle or crystal in rock or metal; piece of solid propellant used in rocket engine. **3.** Smallest unit of weight in some systems, 1/480 of oz. troy, 1/437·5 of oz. avoirdupois; smallest possible quantity (*without a grain of vanity, love,* etc.). **4.** (Hist.) kermes or cochineal, or dye made from either of these (**dye in** ~, dye in kermes, dye in any fast colour, dye in the fibre or thoroughly; **in** ~, thorough, genuine, by nature, downright, indelible); (poet.) dye, colour. **5.** Granular texture, roughness of surface, mottling; texture, arrangement and size of constituent particles, in flesh, skin, wood, stone, etc.; lines of fibre in wood or paper giving a pattern; lamination or planes of cleavage in coal, stone, etc.; (fig.) nature, temper, tendency, (**against the** ~, contrary to inclination). **6.** **~-leather** (dressed with the grain-side out); **~-side** (of hide, on which the hair was). **7.** Hence (-)~ED[2] (-nd), ~'LESS, ~'Y[2], *adjs.* **8.** *v.t.* & *i.* Form into grains. **9.** *v.t.* Dye in grain; give granular surface to; remove hair from (hides); paint in imitation of grain of wood or marble; hence ~'ER[1] (1, 2) *n.* [ME f. OF, f. L *granum,* and (sense 4) f. OF *graine* f. Rom. **grana* collect. fem., orig. neut. pl. of L *granum*]

graip *n.* (Sc.) Three- or four-pronged fork used

for lifting dung or digging potatoes etc. [f. ON *greip* corresp. to OE *grāp* grasp; cf. GRIP[1], GROPE]

grăllatōr'ĭal *a.* (Zool.) Of the long-legged wading birds. [f. mod. L *grallatorius* f. L *grallator* stilt-walker (*grallae* stilts) + -AL]

gră'lloch (-ok) *n.*, & *v.t.* **1.** *n.* Dead deer's viscera. **2.** *v.t.* Disembowel (deer etc.). [f. Gael. *grealach* intestines]

grăm[1] *n.* Chick-pea; any pulse used as horse-fodder. [f. Port. *grão* f. L *granum* grain]

grăm[2], **grămme,** *n.* Unit of mass in metric system, now defined as thousandth part of the KILOGRAM; **~-atom,** quantity of chemical element whose mass in grams numerically equals its atomic weight; **~-force,** unit of force, equal to weight of one gram under standard attraction of gravity; **~-molecule,** quantity of substance whose mass in grams numerically equals its molecular weight. [f. F *gramme* f. Gk *gramma* small weight]

Grăm[3] *n.* **~ method** (of staining bacteria with iodine solution); **~-positive, ~-negative,** that can, cannot, be stained by this method. [f. H. C. J. ~, Da. physician d. 1938]

-grăm *suf.* forming *ns.*: (1) prepositional compds. f. Gk w. ref. to writing (*anagram, diagram, epigram*), (2) denoting thing written or recorded (*chromatogram, chronogram, logogram, telegram*), (3) compds. w. Gk numerals (*monogram, pentagram*). [f. or after Gk *gramma -atos* thing written, letter of alphabet (*graphō* write)]

grā'ma, gră'mma, *n.* ~ **(grass),** pasture grass of genus *Bouteloua* in W. and S.W. parts of U.S. [f. Sp. *grama*]

gră'marўe *n.* (arch.) Magic, necromancy. [ME, f. AF *gramarie*, OF *gramaire* learning, GRAMMAR]

gramēr'cў *int.* (arch.) Thank you. [ME, f. OF *grant merci* (God give you) great reward (as GRAND, MERCY)]

grămĭnā'ceous (-sh*us*), **gramĭ'nėous,** *adjs.* Of or like grass, grassy. [f. L *gramen -inis* grass + -ACEOUS, and L *gramineus* (see -EOUS)]

grămĭnĭ'vorous *a.* Feeding on grass, cereals, etc. [f. as prec. + -I- + -VOROUS]

gră'mmalŏgue (-ŏg) *n.* Word represented by single shorthand sign; logogram. [irreg. f. Gk *gramma* letter of alphabet + *logos* word]

gră'mmar *n.* **1.** Art and science dealing with a language's inflexions or other means of showing relation between words as used in speech or writing, and its phonetic system, and the established rules for using these, (**historical ~,** study of the development of a language's inflexions and syntax). **2.** Treatise or book on grammar. **3.** Person's manner of using grammatical forms; speech or writing regarded as good or bad by the rules of grammar; what is correct according to those rules. **4.** Body of forms and usages in a language (*Latin grammar*). **5.** Elements or rudiments of an art or science. **6.** ‖(colloq.) = *grammar school.* **7. ~ school,** (1) ‖school founded in or before 16th c. for teaching Latin, later becoming secondary school teaching languages, history, science, etc., (2) ‖secondary school with similar curriculum, (3) *school intermediate between primary school and high school. **8.** Hence **~**LESS *a.* [ME, f. AF *gramere*, OF *gramaire* f. **gramadie* f. L f. Gk *grammatikē* (*tekhnē* art) of letters (*gramma -atos* letter of alphabet)]

grammār'ian *n.* One versed in grammar or linguistics, philologist. [ME, f. OF *gramarien* (as prec.; see -IAN)]

-grammă'tic *suf.* forming *adjs.* corresp. to *ns.* in -GRAM (1, 3). [f. as -GRAM + -ATIC]

grammă'tical *a.* **1.** Of grammar; **~ gender** (determined by form etc. of word, not by sex of what it denotes); **~ sense** (literal, irrespective of considerations other than the rules of grammar). **2.** Conforming to the rules of grammar, or to the formal principles of an art. **3.** Hence **~**IZE (3) *v.t.*, express by or adopt in grammar, **~**LY[2] *adv.* [F, or f. LL *grammaticalis* f. L f. Gk *grammatikos* (as GRAMMAR, -IC); see -AL]

grammă'ticize, -ise (-īz), *v.t.* = GRAMMATICALIZE. [f. *grammatic* earlier form of prec. + -IZE]

grămme. See GRAM[2].

gră'mophōne *n.* Instrument for reproduction of recorded sound by vibrations of stylus resting in irregular spiral groove on rotating disc (cf. RECORD[2]-*player*); hence **grămophŏ'nic** *a.* [formed by inversion of PHONOGRAM]

gră'mpus *n.* Blowing spouting blunt-headed dolphin-like cetacean, esp. *Grampus griseus*; person breathing heavily and loudly. [earlier *graundepose, grapeys* f. OF *grapois* etc. f. med. L *craspiscis* f. L *crassus piscis* fat fish]

grăn *n.* (colloq. or childish). Granny, grandmother. [abbr.]

grănadĭ'lla, grĕ-, *n.* Passion-fruit. [Sp., dim. of *granada* pomegranate]

gră'narў *n.* Storehouse for threshed grain; region producing, and esp. exporting, much corn. [f. L *granarium* (*granum* grain; see -ARY[1])]

grănd *a.* & *n.* **1.** *a.* (In official titles) chief over others, of highest rank (*Grand* CROSS[1]; *grand* LODGE[1]; *grand* VIZIER). **2.** (Law). Great, principal, (opp. *petit* or *petty* or *common*; *grand* LARCENY). **3.** Of most or great importance (*that is the grand question*; *made a grand mistake*; *grand* SLAM); final, summing up minor constituents, (*grand total*; *grand finale*; *the grand sum* or *result of his achievements*). **4.** (Distinguishing parts of large building) main (*the grand staircase, entrance,* etc.). **5.** [In F phrases or imitations] great (*grand army, Grand Hotel*; **G~ Monarch,** Louis XIV). **6.** Conducted with solemnity, splendour, etc.; fine, splendid, gorgeous. **7.** Belonging to high society, distinguished, (**do the ~,** put on airs); imposing, impressive, great and handsome. **8.** Dignified or lofty in conception, treatment, or expression; morally imposing, noble, admirable. **9.** (colloq.) Very enjoyable, excellent, (*had a grand run*; *ground was in grand condition*). **10.** (In names of relationships) in the second degree of ascent or descent; **~'parent,** one's parent's parent; so **~'father, ~'mother,** (*~father clock*, clock worked by weights in tall wooden case; *~mother clock*, similar clock in smaller case; *teach one's grandmother to suck* EGG[1]*s*); (colloq. or childish) **~-dad(dy), ~'ma(ma), ~'pa(pa)**; **~'child,** one's child's child; so **~'daughter, ~'son; ~'aunt, ~'uncle,** one's parent's aunt, uncle; **~'nephew, ~'niece,** one's nephew's or niece's son or daughter. **11. ~ air,** distinguished appearance; **~ duke,** (1) ruler of State called **~ duchy,** (2) (Hist.) son of Russian Emperor; *grand* INQUEST; *Grand* INQUISITOR; **~ jury,** (Hist. or U.S.) group of persons selected to examine validity of accusation prior to trial; **~ manner,** style suited to noble subjects; **~ master,** (1) head of military order of knighthood, of Freemasons, etc., (2) chess-player of highest class; ‖**G~ National,** annual steeplechase at Liverpool; **~ old man,** venerated person, esp. Gladstone or Churchill; ***G~ Old Party,** the Republican Party; **~ opera,** serious opera without spoken dialogue; **~ passion,** = GRANDE *passion*; **~ piano,** large full-toned piano with horizontal strings; **~'sire,** (1) sire of animal's sire, (2) (arch.) grandfather, ancestor, old man, (3) method of change-ringing; **~'stand,** principal stand for spectators at races etc. (*~stand finish*, close and exciting finish in sport; **~stand play*, way of playing with view to gaining applause); ~ **style,** = *grand manner*; ~ **tour,** (arch.) tour of chief towns etc. of Europe completing education, (fig.) extensive tour, flight to several planets, etc. **12.** Hence ~′LY² *adv.*, ~′NESS *n.* **13.** *n.* Grand piano. **14.** (sl.; *pl.* usu. same). Thousand pounds, *dollars, etc. [ME f. AF *graunt*, OF *grant* f. L *grandis* full-grown]

gră′ndăd. Var. of *grand-dad* (GRAND 10).

gră′ndăm *n.* **1.** (arch.) Grandmother; ancestress; old woman. **2.** Animal's dam's dam. [ME, f. AF *graund dame* (as GRAND, DAME)]

gră′ndāme. Var. of prec. 1.

grande (grahṅd) *a.* ~ ***amoureuse*** (ahmoorer̄′z), passionate or amorous woman; ~ ***dame*** (dahm), dignified lady of high rank; ~ ***passion*** (pă′syawṅ), overwhelming love affair; ~ ***tenue*** (tenū′), full dress. [F, fem. of *grand* great (see GRAND)]

grăndee′ *n.* Spanish or Portuguese nobleman of highest rank; person of high rank or eminence. [f. Sp. & Port. *grande* (*grande* a. GRAND), assim. to -EE]

gră′ndeur (-nj*er* or -ndy*er*) *n.* Great power, rank, or eminence; great nobility of character; sublimity or majesty of appearance or effect; conscious dignity, splendour of living, surroundings, etc. (DELUSIONS *of grandeur*). [F (*grand* great, GRAND)]

Grand Guignŏ′l (grahṅ gēnyŏ′l) *n.* Dramatic entertainment in which short sensational or horrific pieces are played successively. [name (= Great PUNCH⁴) of theatre in Paris]

grăndĭflōr′a *a.* Bearing large flowers. [mod. L (often used in specific names of large-flowered plants) f. L *grandis* great + FLORA]

grăndĭ′loqu|ent *a.* Pompous in language; given to boastful talk; hence ~ENCE *n.*, ~**ent**LY² *adv.* [f. L *grandiloquus* (as GRAND, *-loquus* -speaking f. *loqui* speak), after *eloquent* etc.]

gră′ndiōse *a.* Producing, intended or trying to produce, an impression of greatness; planned on a magnificent scale; pompous; hence **grăndĭo**′SITY *n.*, ~LY² (-slĭ) *adv.* [F, f. It. *grandioso* (as GRAND; see -OSE¹)]

Grăndĭsō′nĭan *a.* Marked by stately courtesy and chivalric magnanimity. [f. Sir C. *Grandison* in Richardson's novel + -IAN]

grand mal (grahṅ mah′l) *n.* Serious form of epilepsy with loss of consciousness. [F, = great sickness]

Grand Prix (grahṅ prē′) *n.* Motor-racing championship event held in various countries under international rules. [F, = great or chief prize]

grand siècle (grahṅ syĕ′kl) *n.* Classical or golden age, esp. 17th c. in France. [F, = great century or age]

grā′nge (-nj) *n.* Country house with farm-buildings attached; (arch.) barn. [ME, f. AF *graunge*, OF *grange* f. med. L *granica* (*villa*) (**granicus* f. L *granum* GRAIN)]

grā′nger|ize (-nj-), **-|ise** (-īz), *v.t.* Illustrate (book) by inserting prints etc. often cut from other books; hence ~**īz**A′TION, ~**īz**ER¹, ~ISM (1), ~ITE¹ (1), *ns.* [f. J. *Granger*, Engl. biographer d. 1776, whose *History of England* (1769) had blank pages for this purpose, + -IZE]

granĭ′ferous *a.* Producing grain or grainlike seed; so **gră′nĭ**FORM *a.* [f. L *granum* GRAIN + -I- + -FEROUS]

grănĭ′t|a (-ē′-) *n.* (*pl.* ~**e** *pr.* -ā). Coarse Italian water-ice. [It., fem. of *granito* (see foll.)]

gră′nĭte *n.* Granular crystalline rock of quartz, orthoclase felspar, and mica or hornblende, used for building; (fig.) unyieldingness; **bite on** ~, waste pains, persist in vain; **the** ~ **city,** Aberdeen; ~**-ware,** (1) speckled pottery imitating appearance of granite, (2) kind of enamelled ironware; hence **granĭ′t**IC *a.*, **gră′nĭt**OID *a.* & *n.* [f. It. *granito*, lit. grained (*grano* f. L *granum* GRAIN)]

granĭ′vorous *a.* Feeding on grain. [f. L *granum* GRAIN + -I- + -VOROUS]

gră′nnў, gră′nnĭe, *n.* **1.** (colloq. or childish). Grandmother. **2.** ~ (**knot**), reef-knot crossed the wrong way and therefore insecure; **G~ Smith,** Australian green variety of apple [f. Maria Ann ('Granny') Smith d. 1870]. [f. obs. *grannam* for GRANDAM + -Y³]

grănolĭ′thĭc *a.* & *n.* (Of) concrete made with crushed granite. [f. L *granum* grain + Gk *lithos* stone + -IC]

grant (-ah-) *v.t.*, & *n.* **1.** *v.t.* Consent to fulfil (request etc.). **2.** Concede as indulgence, allow (person) to have (thing or *that*). **3.** Give (possession, right) formally, transfer (property) legally, whence ~EE′, ~OR′, *ns.* **4.** Concede (proposition) as basis for argument (**I** ~ **you,** I admit; **take for** ~**ed,** regard as necessarily true or certain to happen). **5.** Hence ~′ABLE *a.* **6.** *n.* Granting (*the grant or refusal of*); formal conferment, legal assignment; thing, esp. sum of money, granted (~**-in-aid,** sum granted esp. by government to school etc.); conveyance by written instrument; ‖~**-aided school,** school receiving some financial assistance from public funds. [ME, f. OF *gr*(*e*)*anter* var. of *creanter* f. Rom. **credentare* f. part. of L *credere* entrust]

Granth (grŭnt) *n.* Sacred scriptures of the Sikhs. [Hindi, = book, code f. Skr. *grantha* tying, literary composition]

gran turismo (grăn toorĭ′zmō) *n.* (*pl.* ~*s*). Touring-car. [It., = great touring]

gră′nūlar *a.* Of or like grains or granules; having granulated surface or structure; hence ~ITY (-ă′r-) *n.*, ~LY² *adv.* [f. LL *granulum* GRANULE + -AR¹]

gră′nūl|āte *v.* **1.** *v.t.* & *i.* Form into grains (*granulated sugar*). **2.** *v.t.* Roughen surface of. **3.** *v.i.* (Of wound etc.) form small prominences as beginning of healing or junction; heal, join. **4.** Hence ~A′TION, ~**āt**OR, *ns.* [f. as prec. + -ATE³]

gră′nūle *n.* Small grain. [f. LL *granulum*, dim. of L *granum* grain; see -ULE]

gră′nūlo|cўte *n.* (Med.) Cell having conspicuous granules in its cytoplasm; hence ~**cў′t**IC *a.* [f. GRANULE + -O- + -CYTE]

grănūlomĕ′trĭc *a.* Pertaining to distribution of grain sizes in sand etc. [f. F *granulométrique* (as GRANULE, -O-, METRIC)]

grāpe *n.* **1.** Berry (usu. green, purple, or black) growing in clusters on vine, eaten as fruit or used in making wine; (**the juice of**) **the** ~, wine; **sour** ~**s** (said when person disparages what he desires but cannot attain). **2.** = *grape-shot*; (in *pl.*) diseased growth like bunch of grapes on pastern of horse etc., or on pleura in cattle. **3.** ~**-brandy** (distilled from grapes, or wine, alone); ~**′fruit,** large round yellow citrus fruit growing in clusters, with acid juicy pulp; ~ **hyacinth,** small herb of genus *Muscari* with raceme of usu. blue flowers; ~**-scissors** (for thinning grape-bunches at early stage of growth, or for dividing bunches at table); ~**-shot,** (Hist.) small balls put several together in bag etc. to make scattering charge for cannon; ~**-sugar,** dextrose; ~**-vine,** (1) vine, (2) skating figure in which both feet are on ice together and form interlacing lines, (3) means of transmission of rumour or (secret) information. **4.** Hence **grā′p**ERY (3) *n.*, **grā′p**EY², **grā′p**Y², *adjs.* [ME, f. OF, bunch of grapes, prob. f. *graper* gather (grapes) f. *grap*(*p*)*e* hook f. Rom. **grap*(*p*)*o* f. Gmc **krappon*]

grăph[1] (*or* -ahf) *n.*, & *v.t.* **1.** *n.* Diagram showing relation between two variable quantities each measured along one of a pair of axes usu. at right angles; ~ **paper** (printed with network of lines to assist in drawing graphs). **2.** *v.t.* Plot or trace on a graph. [abbr. of *graphic formula*]

grăph[2] (*or* -ahf) *n.* (Philol.) Visual symbol, esp. letter(s), representing phoneme or other feature of speech. [f. Gk *graphē* writing]

-graph (-ahf) *suf.* forming *ns.* & *vbs.* denoting: (1) thing written, drawn, etc., in specified way (*autograph, photograph, pictograph*), (2) instrument that records something or by some means (*heliograph, seismograph, telegraph*), (3) write in specified way (*hectograph*). [f. or after F *-graphe* f. L f. Gk *-graphos* written, writing]

gră'phēm|e *n.* (Ling.) Class of letters etc. representing a phoneme; feature of written expression that cannot be analysed into smaller meaningful units; hence ~A'TIC, **graphē'mic**, *adjs.* [f. GRAPH[2] + -EME]

-grapher *suf.* forming *ns.* denoting person skilled in -GRAPHY (*geographer, radiographer*). [f. or after Gk *-graphos* writer + -ER[1]]

gră'phĭc *a.* & *n.* **1.** *a.* Of drawing, painting, engraving, etching, etc.; vividly descriptive, lifelike; of writing; (of minerals) showing marks like writing on surface or in fracture; graphical; ~ **arts,** arts of writing, printing, decorating, etc., on flat media. **2.** *n.* Product of graphic arts; cf. GRAPHICS. [f. L f. Gk *graphikos* (*graphē* writing; see -IC)]

-gră'phĭc(al) *sufs.* forming *adjs.* denoting 'of or by -GRAPH or -GRAPHY' (*geographical, photographic*); hence **-gră'phically** *adv. suf.* [f. or after Gk *-graphikos* (as prec.) + -IC]

gră'phĭcal *a.* Of GRAPH[1]S. [f. as GRAPHIC + -ICAL]

gră'phĭcallŷ *adv.* In adj. senses. [f. GRAPHIC or GRAPHICAL; see -ICALLY]

gră'phĭcs *n. pl.* (usu. treated as *sing.*) Use of diagrams in calculation and design; production of diagrams etc. by computer; design and decoration involving or accompanying typographic work. [f. GRAPHIC + -ICS]

gră'phīte *n.* Crystalline allotropic form of carbon used in pencils, as lubricant, etc.; hence **graphĭ'tic** *a.*, **gră'phĭtize** (3) *v.t.* & *i.* [f. G *graphit* f. Gk *graphō* write; cf. -ITE[1]]

gră'phīūre *n.* S. Afr. rodent with tail ending in pencil of hairs. [f. mod. L *graphiurus* f. Gk *grapheion* pencil + *oura* tail]

graphŏ'|logŷ *n.* Study of, or art of inferring character from, handwriting; system of graphic formulae, notation for GRAPH[1]S; (Ling.) study of systems of writing; hence **gră'pholo'gical** *a.*, ~LOGIST *n.* [f. Gk *graphē* writing + -O- + -LOGY]

gră'phŷ *n.* (Philol.) = GRAPH[2]. [f. F *graphie* writing-system]

-graphŷ *suf.* forming *ns.* denoting: (1) style or method of writing, drawing, etc., (*calligraphy, lithography, stenography*), (2) descriptive science (*bibliography, geography*). [f. or after F or G *-graphie* f. L f. Gk *-graphia* writing]

gră'pnel *n.* Iron-clawed instrument thrown with rope attached to seize object, esp. enemy's ship; small anchor with several flukes used for boats and balloons. [ME, f. AF **grapenel* f. OF *grapon* f. Gmc **krāppon*; cf. GRAPE]

gră'ppa *n.* Brandy distilled from refuse of grapes after wine-making. [It.]

gră'ppl|e *n.* & *v.* **1.** *n.* Clutching-instrument, grapnel. **2.** Hold or grip (as) of wrestlers, contest at close quarters. **3.** *v.t.* Seize or fasten (as) with grapnel; take hold of or grip with the hands, come to close quarters with. **4.** *v.i.* Contend (*with, together*, or abs.) in close fight, battle *with*; ~**e with,** (fig.) try to overcome, accomplish, or deal with. **5.** ~**ing-hook** or **-iron,** grapnel. [f. OF *grapil* f. Prov., dim. of *grapa* hook f. as GRAPNEL]

gră'pplĭng *n.* In vbl senses; grappling-iron, grapnel. [f. prec. + -ING[1]]

gră'ptolīte *n.* Extinct marine animal found as fossil in lower palaeozoic rocks. [f. Gk *graptos* marked with letters + -LITE]

grasp (-ah-) *v.* & *n.* **1.** *v.i.* ~ **at,** try to seize, accept with avidity. **2.** *v.t.* Clutch at, seize greedily; hold firmly (~ **the nettle,** tackle difficulty or danger boldly), grip; get mental hold of, comprehend; hence ~'ABLE *a.* **3.** *n.* Firm hold, grip; control, mastery; mental hold, comprehensiveness of mind; **within, beyond,** one's ~, close, not close, enough to be grasped (lit. or fig.). [ME *graspe, grapse* perh. f. OE **græpsan* f. Gmc **graip-* GROPE; but cf. LG *grapsen*]

gra'spĭng (-ah'-) *a.* In vbl senses; avaricious, miserly, whence ~LY[2] *adv.*, ~NESS *n.* [f. prec. + -ING[2]]

grass (-ahs) *n.* & *v.* **1.** *n.* Herbage of which blades or leaves and stalks are eaten by cattle, horses, sheep, etc. (**not let the ~ grow under** one's **feet,** be quick to act or seize opportunity); any species of this; (Bot.) plant of family Gramineae, incl. also cereals, reeds, and bamboos; (sl.) marijuana; (sl.) asparagus. **2.** Grazing, pasture, (*be at, go, put, send, turn out, to grass*; **at ~,** (fig.) out of work, on holiday, etc.); pasture land; grass-covered ground, lawn, (*keep off the grass*); (Mining) earth's surface, pit-head; (sl.) police informer. **3. ~-box,** receptacle for cut grass on lawn-mower; **~-cloth,** linen-like cloth woven from ramie etc.; **~ court,** grass-covered lawn-tennis court; **~'hopper,** jumping and chirping insect of sub-order Saltatoria; **~'land,** area of land covered with grass, esp. if used for grazing; **~ parakeet,** (Austral.) parakeet frequenting grassland; **~ of Parnassus,** saxifrage of genus *Parnassia*; **~ roots,** fundamental level or source, esp. (Polit.) the voters themselves; **~ skirt** (made of long grass and leaves fastened to waistband); **~ snake,** ||common ringed snake (*Natrix natrix*), *common green snake (*Ophiodrys vernalis*); **~ widow(er),** person whose husband or wife is absent for a period; **~ wren,** (Austral.) small bird of genus *Amytornis*. **4.** Hence ~'LESS, ~'Y[2], *adjs.* **5.** *v.t.* Cover with turf; *provide with pasture; knock down, fell, (opponent); bring (fish) to bank, (bird by shot) to ground; (sl.) betray. **6.** *v.i.* (sl.) Inform police. [OE *græs*, = OS, OHG, ON, Goth. *gras* f. Gmc **grasam*, cogn. w. GREEN[1], GROW]

grāte[1] *n.* (Frame of metal bars for confining fuel in) fireplace or furnace; hence ~'LESS (-tl-) *a.* [ME = grating, f. OF, f. Rom. **grata*, **crata* f. L *cratis* hurdle]

grāt|e[2] *v.* **1.** *v.t.* Reduce to small particles by rubbing on rough surface, whence (-)~'ER[1] (2) *n.*; utter in harsh tone; grind (teeth). **2.** *v.t.* & *i.* Rub with harsh scraping noise *against* or (*up*)*on* something else. **3.** *v.i.* Have irritating effect (*up*)*on*; sound harshly or discordantly (*a grating laugh, voice*); (of hinge etc.) creak. [ME, f. OF *grater* f. Rom. **grattare* f. WG **krattōn* scratch]

grā'teful (-tf-) *a.* **1.** Acceptable, comforting, refreshing. **2.** Thankful, feeling or showing gratitude (*to* person, *for* thing). **3.** Hence ~LY[2] *adv.*, ~NESS *n.* [f. obs. *grate* a. f. L *gratus* + -FUL]

gră'tĭcūle *n.* **1.** Fine lines or fibres incorporated in telescope or other optical instrument as measuring scale or as aid in locating objects. **2.** (Surv.) Network of lines on paper representing meridians and parallels. [F, f. med. L *graticula* for *craticula* gridiron (L *cratis* hurdle; see -ULE)]

grăʹtĭfȳ *v.t.* **1.** Please, satisfy, oblige, delight, whence ~ING[2] *a.* (*to*); please by compliance, assent to wish of, give free scope to or indulge (desire, feeling, impulse). **2.** (arch.) Remunerate, make present usu. of money to; bribe. **3.** So **grătiFICAʹTION** *n.* [f. F *gratifier* or f. L *gratificari* do a favour to, make a present of (*gratus* pleasing; see -FY)]

gratin (grăʹtăṅ) *n.* Way of cooking, dish cooked, with crisp brown crust usu. of breadcrumbs or grated cheese; ***au*** ~ (ō-), (dish) so prepared. [F (*gratter* GRATE[2])]

grāʹting *n.* Framework of parallel or crossed wooden or metal bars; (Opt.) set of parallel wires, or surface of glass etc. ruled with parallel lines, for producing spectra by diffraction. [f. GRATE[1] + -ING[1]]

grăʹtĭs (*or* -ahʹ-) *adv.* & *a.* Gratuitous(ly); (given, done) for nothing, without charge, free. [L, contr. abl. pl. of *gratia* favour]

grăʹtĭtūde *n.* Being thankful, appreciation of and inclination to return kindness. [f. F, or f. med. L *gratitudo* (*gratus* thankful; see -TUDE)]

gratūʹĭtous *a.* Got or given free, not earned or paid for; uncalled for, unwarranted, motiveless, done or acting without good or assignable reason (*a gratuitous lie* or *liar*); hence ~LY[2] *adv.*, ~NESS *n.* [f. L *gratuitus* spontaneous; cf. *fortuitous*]

gratūʹĭtȳ *n.* Money present of amount fixed by giver in recognition of an inferior's good offices, tip; ‖bounty to soldiers etc. on demobilization or retirement or some other occasions. [f. OF *gratuité* or f. med. L *gratuitas* gift (L *gratus* grateful; see -ITY)]

grăʹtūl|āte *v.t.* (arch.) = CONGRATULATE; so ~AʹTION *n.* [f. L *gratulari* (*gratus* pleasing) + -ATE[3]]

grăʹtūlātorȳ *a.* Expressing joy at another's success etc., complimentary, congratulatory. [f. LL *gratulatorius* (as prec.; see -ORY)]

graunch *v.t.* & *i.* (Cause to) make crunching or grinding sound; damage (mechanism) thus. [imit.]

gravāʹmĕn *n.* (*pl.* ~**s** *or* **gravaʹmina**). **1.** Grievance; memorial from Lower House of Convocation to Upper on disorders or grievances of Church. **2.** Essence, worst part, of accusation. [LL, = inconvenience (L *gravare* to load f. *gravis* heavy)]

grāve[1] *n.* **1.** Excavation to receive corpse, mound or monument over it; **dig ~ of,** cause downfall of; *one* FOOT[1] *in the grave*; **make** person **turn in his** ~ (of act etc. that would have shocked him while alive); **someone walking on my** ~ (said when one shivers unaccountably); hence ~ʹLESS (-vl-) *a.* **2.** Being dead, death, (*carry the scar to* one's *grave*); hence ~ʹWARD (-vw-) *adv.* & *a.* **3.** Receptacle of or for what is dead (**~ of reputations,** place where many reputations have been lost). **4. ~-clothes,** wrappings in which corpse is buried; **~-digger,** (1) person who digs graves, (2) beetle that buries bodies of insects etc. as food for its larvae; **~-goods,** objects found with corpses in ancient graves; **~ʹstone,** stone over grave, inscribed stone at head or foot of grave; **~ʹyard,** (1) burial-ground (*~yard cough,* = CHURCH[1]yard cough), (2) = sense 3. [OE *græf,* = OS *graf,* OHG *grap* f. WG **grabha*]

grāve[2] *v.t.* (*p.p.* **graʹven** *or* **~d**). **1.** (arch.) Carve, sculpture, engrave, (material, representation; **~n image,** idol). **2.** (fig.) Fix indelibly (*on* or *in* mind etc.). [OE *grafan* dig, engrave, = OHG *graban,* ON *grafa,* Goth. *graban* dig f. Gmc **grabhan* (as prec.; cf. GROOVE)]

grāve[3] *a* & *n.* **1.** *a.* Important, weighty, needing serious thought; (of faults, difficulties, responsibilities, symptoms) formidable, threatening, serious; dignified, solemn, slow-moving, not gay; sombre, plain, not showy; hence ~ʹLY[2] (-vlĭ) *adv.* **2.** (Of sound) low-pitched, not acute. [F, or f. L *gravis* heavy, serious]

grāve[4] *v.t.* Clean (ship's bottom) by burning off accretions and tarring while aground or in *graving* DOCK[4]. [perh. f. F dial. *grave* = OF *greve* shore f. Celt. **gravo-* gravel, pebbles]

grāve[5] (*or* grahv) *a.* & *n.* ~ (**accent**), mark (\`) placed over vowels in some languages to show quality etc., orig. indicating low or falling pitch. [f. GRAVE[3]]

grăʹvel *n.*, & *v.t.* (‖-**ll**-). **1.** *n.* Coarse sand and small water-worn or pounded stones, used for paths and roads; (Geol. & Mining) stratum of this, esp. one containing gold; (Path.) (disease with) aggregations of visible urinary crystals; **~-blind,** almost completely blind (orig. joc. = more than sand-blind, Shakespeare's *Merchant of Venice* II. ii. 38); hence **~ly**[2] *a.* (of voice, deep and rough-sounding). **2.** *v.t.* Lay or strew with gravel; perplex, puzzle, nonplus, (f. obs. sense *run aground*). [ME, f. OF *gravel*(*e*) dim. of *grave* (as GRAVE[4])]

grāʹver *n.* In vbl senses; burin. [ME, f. GRAVE[2] + -ER[1]]

Graves[1] (grahv) *n.* (*pl.* same *pr.* -z). Light white or occas. red wine produced in the Graves district. [~ in S.W. France]

Grāves[2] (-vz) *n.* **~' disease,** exophthalmic goitre. [f. R. J. ~, Ir. physician d. 1853]

Gravĕʹttian *a.* & *n.* (Culture) of a palaeolithic period in Europe, upper Aurignacian. [f. La *Gravette* in S.W. France + -IAN]

grăʹvĭd *a.* (literary or Zool.) Pregnant. [f. L *gravidus* (*gravis* heavy)]

gravĭʹmèter *n.* Instrument measuring difference in force of gravity between two places. [f. F *gravimètre* f. L *gravis* heavy; cf. -METER]

grăvĭmĕʹtrĭc *a.* Pertaining to gravimeters or gravimetry. [f. prec.]

gravĭʹmètrȳ *n.* Measurement of weight. [f. as GRAVIMETER + -METRY]

gravitas (grăʹvĭtahs) *n.* Solemn demeanour, seriousness. [L (as GRAVE[3]; see -ITY)]

grăʹvĭtāte *v.* **1.** *v.t.* & *i.* Move or tend by force of gravity *towards* a body; sink (as) by gravity, tend to low level, settle down. **2.** *v.i.* Move because, or be, strongly attracted *to*(*wards*) some centre of influence. [f. mod. L *gravitare* (after GRAVITAS) + -ATE[3]]

grăvĭtāʹtion *n.* Falling of bodies to earth; (movement or tendency towards centre of) attraction exercised by every particle of matter on every other; **law of** ~ (specifying force of this attraction in terms of masses concerned and their distance apart); hence ~AL *a.* [f. mod. L *gravitatio* (as prec.; see -ATION)]

grăʹvĭtȳ *n.* **1.** Being serious, solemnity; importance, seriousness; staidness, sobriety, serious demeanour. **2.** Weight (**centre of ~,** centre of MASS[2] of rigid body, (fig.) point of chief importance; **specific ~,** relative weight of any kind of matter, expressed by ratio of given volume to same volume of a standard—usu. water for liquid or solid, and air for gas). **3.** Attractive force by which bodies tend to centre of earth etc.; degree of intensity of this measured by acceleration; gravitational force. **4. ~ feed,** supply of material by its fall under gravity; **~ wave,** (1) wave on liquid surface caused mainly by gravity, (2) hypothetical periodic variation of gravitational field, propagated as wave. [f. F *gravité* or f. L GRAVITAS]

gravūrʹe *n.* Photogravure. [abbr.]

grāʹvȳ *n.* **1.** Juices that exude from meat during

and after cooking; dressing for food, made from these with other materials; (sl.) unearned or unexpected money. **2. ~-boat,** boat-shaped vessel for serving gravy; **~ train,** source of easy financial benefit. [ME, perh. f. misreading as *gravé* of OF *grané*, prob. f. *grain* spice, GRAIN]

***gray.** See GREY.

gray'lĭng *n.* Silver-grey freshwater fish with long high dorsal fin; butterfly with grey under-side to wings. [f. prec. + -LING[1]]

***graywacke.** See GREYWACKE.

grāz|e[1] *v.* **1.** *v.t.* Feed (sheep or cattle) on growing grass; feed on (grass). **2.** *v.i.* (Of sheep or cattle) eat growing grass; tend grazing cattle; pasture cattle. **3.** Hence **~'ING[1]** (3) *n.* [OE *grasian* (*græs* GRASS)]

grāze[2] *v.* & *n.* **1.** *v.t.* Touch lightly in passing; abrade (skin etc.) in rubbing past; suffer slight abrasion of (part of body). **2.** *v.i.* Go with passing contact *against, along, through, by, past,* etc. **3.** *n.* Grazing abrasion. [perh. by transf. f. prec. 'take off the grass close to the ground' (of a bullet etc.)]

grā'zĭ|er (*or* -zher) *n.* One who feeds cattle for market; (Austral.) sheep-farmer; hence **~ERY** (2) *n.* [f. GRASS + -IER]

grease[1] *n.* **1.** Oily or fatty matter, esp. semi-solid as lubricant; oily matter in wool, uncleansed wool, (**wool in the ~,** wool in fleeces). **2.** Fat of deer or other game (**in ~, in pride** or **prime of ~,** fit for killing, fat); melted fat of dead animals, esp. when soft. **3. ~-box** (attached to train-wheel for lubrication); **~-gun,** small pump for applying grease as lubricant to bearings etc.; **~ monkey,** (sl.) a mechanic; **~-paint,** composition for painting actors' faces; *grease*-PROOF[2] (esp. of paper); **~-trap,** appliance for catching grease in drains. [ME, f. AF *grece, gresse,* OF *graisse* f. Rom. **crassia* (L *crassus* a. fat)]

grease[2] (*or* -ēz) *v.t.* Anoint, soil, or lubricate, with grease; smear (e.g. cooking-pan) with fat; **like ~d lightning,** (sl.) very fast; **~ palm of,** bribe; **~ the wheels,** make affairs go smoothly, esp. by use of money. [ME, f. prec.]

grea'ser (*or* -z-) *n.* In vbl senses; engineer on ship; *(sl., derog.) native Mexican or Spanish-American; (sl.) objectionable person; (sl.) member of gang of young motor-cyclists. [f. prec. + -ER[1]]

grea's|ȳ (*or* -zĭ) *a.* Smeared or covered with, containing, made of, like, with too much, grease; (of wool) uncleansed; slimy with mud or moisture; (of manners or expression) disagreeably unctuous; **~y pole** (greased for climbing or walking on in sports); **~y spoon,** (sl.) cheap inferior eating-house; hence **~ĭLY[2]** *adv.*, **~ĭNESS** *n.* [f. GREASE[1] + -Y[2]]

great (grāt) *a.* & *n.* **1.** *a.* Occupying much space, extending far, large, big, (usu. with implied surprise, admiration, contempt, indignation, etc.; *made a great blot, look at that great wasp,* (colloq.) *a great big loaf* or *thick stick*); **~('er)** (as distinctive epithet of the larger species or individual: *great St. John's wort, greater celandine* etc., *great titmouse, Great* BEAR[1], *Great* DANE, *Great* LAKE[1]*s, Great Malvern* etc., *Great Portland Street* etc.); capital (A etc.); *a great* DEAL[1], *many*; **Greater London** etc. (including adjacent urban areas); **the ~ majority,** much the larger part; *greatest common* MEASURE[1]; *a great* MIND[1]; *lived a great* WHILE[1] *ago*; **~ with child,** (arch.) pregnant. **2.** Beyond the ordinary (*take great care; lived to a great age; shows great ignorance; are great friends*). **3.** Important, worthy of consideration, elevated, distinguished, critical, *the* chief, pre-eminent, (*it is a great thing to have courage; to a great extent; a great occasion; the great attraction; in great* SPIRIT[1]*s*); (in excl.) *Great God!, Caesar!, Scott!*; **the G~** (appended in sense *historically important and most distinguished of the name,* as *Alexander the Great,* or prefixed in titles, *the Great Mogul,* etc., and burlesqued in *the great* ||UNPAID, UNWASHED). **4.** Of remarkable ability, genius, intellectual or practical qualities, or loftiness or integrity of character, (*a great judge, painter,* etc.; *the truly great man; great thoughts*). **5.** *pred.* Having much skill *at* or information *on*. **6.** (colloq.) Highly satisfactory (*wouldn't it be great if we won?; had a great time in Monte Carlo*). **7.** Fully deserving the name of, (with agent-nouns) doing a thing much or on a large scale, (*a great scoundrel, fiasco; is not a great one for travelling; is a great believer in fresh air, reader, landowner*). **8.** (Prefixed once or more to *uncle, aunt, nephew, niece,* and kinship words compounded with GRAND) one degree further removed upwards or downwards. **9. G~ Assize,** Judgement Day; **G~ Bible** (Coverdale's version 1539); **G~ Britain,** England, Wales, and Scotland; *Great* CHARTER[1]; *great* CIRCLE[1]; **~'coat,** heavy overcoat; *Great* DIVIDE[2]; **~ game,** (1) golf, (2) spying; **~ gross,** twelve gross; **~-hearted,** having noble or generous mind; **~ house,** chief house in village etc.; **~ hundred,** 120; *great* INQUEST; **~ organ,** chief manual with its related pipes and mechanism in an organ having two or more manuals; **G~ Power,** State having military or political influence and great international importance; *Great* REBELLION; **G~ Russian,** (member or language) of principal ethnic group of U.S.S.R.; ||*Great* SEAL[2]; **~ toe,** big toe; *great* VASSAL; **G~ War** (of 1914–18); ***G~ White Way,** theatre area of Broadway in New York. **10.** Hence **~'EN[6]** *v.t.* & *i.* (arch.), **~'NESS** *n.* **11.** *n.* Great (sense 3) person or thing; **the ~,** (as *pl.*) great persons; **the ~est,** (sl.) extremely remarkable person. **12. Greats,** Oxford B.A. course or final examination esp. in classics and philosophy. [OE *grēat,* = OS *grōt,* OHG *grōz* f. WG **grauta*]

grea'tlȳ (grā't-) *adv.* Much, by much, (usu. w. verbs, participles, or comparatives; *greatly esteemed, superior; should greatly prefer*); nobly, loftily. [ME, f. prec. + -LY[2]]

greave *n.* (usu. in *pl.*) Piece of armour for shin. [ME, f. OF *greve* shin, greave, of unkn. orig.]

greaves (-vz) *n. pl.* Fibrous refuse of tallow as dog-food etc. [f. LG *greven,* = OHG *griubo*]

grēbe *n.* Short-bodied lobe-footed almost tailless diving bird esp. of genus *Podiceps.* [f. F *grèbe,* of unkn. orig.]

Grē'cian (-shan) *a.* & *n.* **1.** *a.* (Of architecture or facial outline, or arch.) Greek; ||**~ bend,** affected attitude in walking prevalent *c.* 1870; **~ gift,** = GREEK *gift*; ||**~ knot,** way of dressing woman's hair at back of head as ancient Greeks did; **~ nose** (straight, and continuing forehead line without dip); ||**~ slipper,** soft slipper with low sides. **2.** *n.* Person skilled in Greek; ||boy in highest class at Christ's Hospital. [f. OF *grecien* or f. med. L **graecianus* f. L *Graecia* Greece; see -IAN]

Grē'cĭsm, Grē'cīze, Grē'cō-. Vars. of GRAECISM etc.

greed *n.* Insatiate longing esp. for wealth or food. [back form. f. foll.]

gree'd|ȳ *a.* Having inordinate appetite for food or drink, gluttonous, (*of*); avaricious, covetous, (*of* or *for*); eager, keen, intensely desirous, (*to* do); **~y-guts,** (vulg.) gluttonous person; hence **~ĭLY[2]** *adv.*, **~ĭNESS** *n.* [OE *grǣdig,* = OS *grādag,* OHG *grātac,* ON *gráthugr,* Goth. *grēdags* f. Gmc **grǣdhagaz* (**grǣdhuz* hunger)]

gree'gree *n.* African charm or fetish. [17th c., of native orig.]

Greek *n.* & *a.* **1.** *n.* Native or inhabitant of Greece; ~ **meets** ~ (said of encounter between equals). **2.** Member of Orthodox Church. **3.** (arch.) Cunning person, sharper. **4.** The Greek language (~ **to me,** beyond my comprehension), whence ~′LESS *a.* **5.** *a.* Of Greece or its people, Hellenic; of, according to, written or spoken in, Greek (*Greek alphabet, letter, philology*). **6.** *Greek* CALENDS; ~ **Church,** ORTHODOX Church; ~ **cross** (with four equal arms); ~ **Fathers,** Fathers of the Church who wrote in Greek; *Greek* FIRE[1], FRET[1] or *key*; ~ **gift,** one given with intent to harm (Virgil's *Aeneid* ii. 49); ~ **god,** (fig.) paragon of male beauty. **7.** Hence ~′NESS *n.* [OE *Grēcas* (pl.), = ON *Grikkir* (pl.), OHG *Chrēch*, Goth. *Krēks* f. Gmc **Krēkaz* f. L *Graecus* Greek f. Gk *Graikoi* prehistoric name of Hellenes (in Aristotle)]

green[1] *a.* & *n.* **1.** *a.* Of the colour between blue and yellow in the spectrum, coloured like grass, sea-water, emerald, olive, etc. **2.** Covered with herbage, verdant, in leaf; **a** ~ **Christmas, winter, Yule,** (mild, without snow). **3.** (Of complexion) pale, sickly-hued; (fig.) jealous, envious. **4.** Vegetable (*green food, green salad*). **5.** (Of fruit etc.) unripe, young and tender, flourishing, not dried. **6.** Full of vitality, not withered or worn out, (*a green old age*). **7.** Immature, undeveloped, inexperienced, naïve, gullible. **8.** Not dried, seasoned, smoked, or tanned. **9.** (arch.) Fresh, not healed, (*a green wound*). **10.** ***~′back,** (1) U.S. legal-tender note, (2) green-backed animal; ~ **belt,** area of open land round city, designated for preservation; **G~ Beret,** (colloq.) British or American commando; **~-blind,** having retina insensitive to green rays; ~ **card,** international insurance document for motorists; ~ **cheese,** (1) whey cheese, (2) cheese coloured green with sage; ‖(*Board of*) **G~ Cloth,** Lord Steward's department of Royal Household; ~ **crop** (used for food in green state, opp. *hay* etc.); ~ **drake,** mayfly; ~ **earth,** hydrous silicate of potassium, iron, and other metals; ~ **eye, ~-eyed monster,** jealousy; **~-eyed,** (fig.) jealous; ~ **fat** (of turtle, esteemed by epicures); **~′finch,** finch with yellow and green plumage; ~ **fingers,** (colloq.) skill in making plants grow; ‖**~′fly,** green aphid; **~′gage,** roundish green fine-flavoured plum [Sir W. *Gage c.* 1725]; ~ **goose** (killed under four months old and eaten without stuffing); ‖**~′grocer(y),** (business of, things sold by) retail dealer in fruit and vegetables; **~′head,** (1) biting fly of family Tabanidae, (2) Austral. ant with painful sting; **~′heart,** (hard greenish wood of) one of several tropical Amer. trees; **~′horn,** ignoramus, raw recruit, simpleton; **~′house** (of glass for rearing delicate plants or hastening growth of plants); **~′keeper,** keeper of golf course; ~ **leek,** green-faced Austral. parakeet; ~ **light,** signal to proceed on road, railway, etc., (colloq.) permission to go ahead with some project; ~ **linnet,** = *greenfinch*; ~ **manure,** growing plants ploughed into soil as fertilizer; *green* MEAT; ***G~ Mountain State,** Vermont; ‖**G~ Paper,** tentative report of Government proposals, without commitment; ~ **plover,** lapwing; ~ **revolution,** greatly increased crop production in developing countries; **~-room** (accommodating actors and actresses when off stage); **~′sand,** (1) = *green earth*, (2) kind of sandstone largely composed of this earth, (3) stratum largely formed of this sandstone; **~′shank,** large sandpiper (*Tringa nebularia*); **~′sick(ness),** (affected with) chlorosis; **~-stick,** (of bone-fracture, esp. in children) in which one side of bone is broken and one only bent; **~′stone,** (1) green eruptive rock containing felspar and hornblende, (2) variety of jade found in N.Z., used for tools, ornaments, etc.; **~′stuff,** vegetation, green vegetables; **~′sward,** grassy turf; ~ **tea** (made from steam-dried, not fermented, leaves); ~ **thumb,** = *green fingers*; ~ **turtle,** green-shelled species of turtle esteemed as food; *green* VITRIOL; **~′weed,** dyer's broom; **~′wood,** woodlands in summer, esp. as scene of outlaw life; ‖**~′yard,** enclosure for stray animals, pound. **11.** Hence ~′ISH[1] 2, ~′Y[2] (in comb.: *greeny-yellow*), *adjs.*, ~′LY[2] *adv.*, ~′NESS (-n-n-) *n.* **12.** *n.* Green colour (**do you see any** ~, i.e. sign of gullibility, **in my eye?**); green pigment; green clothes or material (*dressed in green*); green ball in snooker etc.; colour symbolizing Ireland; green light. **13.** Vigour, youth, virility, (*in the green*). **14.** Verdure, vegetation. **15.** (in *pl.*) Green vegetable leaves before or after cooking. **16.** Piece of public or common grassy land (*village green*); grass-plot used for special purpose (*bleaching, bowling,* PUTTing, *-green*); (Golf) (1) putting-green, (2) fairway (**through the green,** between tee and putting-green). **17.** (sl.) Money; low-grade marijuana; (in *pl.*) sexual intercourse. [OE *grēne*, = OS *grōni*, OHG *gruoni*, ON *grœnn* f. Gmc **grōnjaz* (**grō-*; see GROW)]

green[2] *v.* **1.** *v.i.* Become green, esp. with verdure. **2.** *v.t.* Make green, soil etc. with green; (sl.) hoax, take in. [OE *grēnian* (as prec.)]

gree′nerÿ *n.* Verdure, vegetation. [f. GREEN[1] + -ERY]

gree′nĭng *n.* Kind of apple, green when ripe. [prob. f. MDu. *groeninc* (as GREEN[1]; see -ING[3])]

Gree′nland *n.* ~ **whale,** Arctic species of whale (*Balaena mysticetus*); hence ~ER[1] (4) *n.* [~, large island in Arctic Ocean]

Greenlă′ndĭc *a.* & *n.* (Dialect or language) of Greenland. [f. prec. + -IC]

gree′nlėt *n.* = VIREO. [f. GREEN[1] + -LET]

greenth *n.* (literary). Verdure. [f. GREEN[1] + -TH[1]]

Gree′nwich (grĭ′nĭj *or* grĕ′n-; *or* -ĭch) *n.* ~ **(mean) time,** (mean) time on the meridian of Greenwich, used as international basis of time-reckoning. [~ in London, former site of Royal Observatory]

greet[1] *v.t.* Accost with salutation; salute *with* words or gestures, receive on meeting or arrival *with* speech or action (friendly or not); (of cheers etc.) hail; (of sight, sound, etc.) meet (eye, ear); hence ~′ING[1] (1, and, often in *pl.*, 2) *n.* [OE *grētan* handle, attack, salute, etc., = OS *grōtian* call on, OHG *gruozzen* address, attack, f. WG **grōtjan* cry out etc.]

greet[2] *v.i.* (Sc.) Weep. [OE *grētan*, = OS *grātan*, ON *gráta*, Goth. *grētan* f. Gmc **grǣtan* cogn. w. prec., & OE *grēotan*, = OS *griotan*, of uncert. orig.]

grĕ′ffier *n.* Registrar, notary, (in Channel Islands etc.). [F, f. med. L *graphiarius* f. *graphium* register; see GRAFT[1]]

grėgār′ĭous *a.* Living in flocks or communities; fond of company; (Bot.) growing in clusters; of flocks, of crowds; hence ~LY[2] *adv.*, ~NESS *n.* [f. L *gregarius* (*grex gregis* flock; see -ARY[1]) + -OUS]

grège (grāzh) *a.* & *n.* (Of) colour between beige and grey. [F, = raw (silk)]

Grėgōr′ĭan *a.* & *n.* **1.** *a.* Of or according to the plainsong ritual music named after Pope Gregory I; ~ **tones,** eight plainsong melodies prescribed for psalms in R.C. Ch. **2.** ~ **calendar,** correction of the Julian calendar, established by Pope Gregory XIII in 1582. **3.** ~ **telescope,** reflecting telescope in which light reflected from secondary mirror passes through hole in primary mirror, devised by J. Gregory, Sc.

mathematician d. 1675. **4.** *n.* Gregorian chant. [f. med. L *Gregorianus* f. LL f. Gk *Grēgorios* Gregory + -AN]

grĕ'gorȳ-powder *n.* Compound powder of rhubarb, magnesia, and ginger, used as aperient. [f. J. *Gregory*, Sc. physician d. 1822 + POWDER]

greige. Var. of GRÈGE.

grē'mĭal *n.* Silk apron placed on bishop's lap at Mass etc. [f. med. L *gremiale* f. L *gremium* lap; see -AL]

grĕ'mlĭn *n.* (sl.) Mischievous sprite alleged to cause mishaps to machinery etc. [20th c.; orig. unkn., but prob. after *goblin*]

grėnā'de *n.* Small explosive shell thrown by hand (**hand-~**) or shot from rifle-barrel (**rifle-~**); glass receptacle thrown to disperse chemicals for testing drains, extinguishing fires, etc. [F, f. OF *grenate* & Sp. *granada* POMEGRANATE]

grĕnadier' *n.* **1.** (Hist.) Soldier who threw grenades. **2.** ‖**G~s** or **G~ Guards,** first regiment of household infantry. **3.** S. Afr. weaver-bird with red and black plumage. **4.** Deep-sea fish of family Macrouridae, with long tapering body and pointed tail. [F (as prec.; see -IER)]

grĕnadĭ'lla. See GRANADILLA.

grĕ'nadīne^{1} *n.* Dish of veal or poultry fillets, trimmed, larded, and glazed. [f. F *grenadin*]

grĕ'nadīne^{2} *n.* Dress-fabric of loosely woven silk or silk and wool. [F, earlier *grenade* grained silk (*grenu* grained f. *grain*; see GRAIN, -INE^{4})]

grĕ'nadine^{3} (-ēn) *n.* French cordial syrup of pomegranates etc. [F, f. *grenade* (see GRENADE)]

Grĕ'sham *n.* **~'s law,** (Econ.) tendency for money of lower intrinsic value to circulate more freely than money of higher intrinsic and equal nominal value. [f. Sir T. ~, Engl. financier d. 1579]

grĕssôr'ĭal *a.* (Zool.) Walking; adapted for walking. [f. mod. L *gressorius* f. L *gradi gress-* walk; see -OR, -IAL]

Grĕtna Gree'n *n.* (Hist.) ~ **marriage** etc. (contracted by runaway couples from England immediately after entering Scotland, where parental consent was not necessary). [~ in Scotland, close to the border with England]

grew. See GROW.

grey (grā), ***gray,** *a.*, *n.*, & *v.* **1.** *a.* Intermediate between black and white, coloured like ashes or lead. **2.** Between light and dark, dull, clouded, depressing, dismal; (of hair) turning white with age etc., (of person) having grey hair; ancient, immemorial; belonging to old age, experienced, mature; (of person) anonymous, unidentifiable; less extreme than 'black' (*grey market*, *grey-out*). **3. ~-back,** grey-backed animal or bird, *(Hist.) Confederate soldier; **~'beard,** old man, large stoneware jug for spirits, ‖clematis; **~ cells,** = *grey matter*; **~ crow,** hooded crow; ‖**~ drake,** species of mayfly; **~ eminence,** = ÉMINENCE GRISE; **G~ Friar,** Franciscan; **~ goose,** greylag; **~-headed,** old, of long service *in*, ancient, time-worn; **~-hen,** female of black grouse (cf. BLACK^{1}*cock*); **~ mare,** (fig.) wife who dominates husband; **~ matter,** material of active part of brain and spinal cord; **~ monk,** Cistercian; *grey* NURSE^{3}; **~ squirrel,** Amer. squirrel (*Sciurus carolinensis*) brought to Europe in 19th c.; **~'stone,** grey volcanic rock. **4.** Hence **~**'ISH^{1} 2 *a.*, **~**'LY^{2} *adv.*, **~**'NESS *n.* **5.** *n.* Grey clothes or material (*dressed in grey*); cold sunless light; grey colour; grey pigment; grey horse (‖**the Greys** or **Scots Greys,** 2nd Dragoons); *(Negro sl.) white person. **6.** *v.i.* & *t.* Become or make grey. [OE *grǣg*, = OHG *grāo*, ON *grár* f. Gmc **grǣwaz*]

grey'hound (grā'-) *n.* Slender long-legged keen-sighted swift dog used in coursing hares etc.; **~-racing,** sport in which mechanical hare is coursed by greyhounds on track as opportunity for betting; OCEAN *greyhound.* [OE *grīghund* (corresp. to ON *greyhundr*) f. **grieg* bitch (ON *grey* f. Gmc **graujam*) + *hund* dog, HOUND^{1}]

grey'lăg (grā'-) *n.* ~ **(goose),** common European wild goose. [f. GREY + LAG^{1} (f. its staying long in England for a migrant)]

grey'wacke, *gray'wacke, (grā'wăke *or* -ăk) *n.* (Geol.) Conglomerate rock consisting of rounded pebbles and sand cemented together. [Anglicized f. G *grauwacke* (*grau* grey; see WACKE)]

grĭd *n.* **1.** Frame of spaced parallel bars, grating; perforated or ridged plate carrying active substance in accumulator; wire network between filament and anode of thermionic valve, or other perforated electrode with same function of controlling flow of electrons. **2.** System of numbered squares printed on map and forming basis of map references. **3.** Network of lines, electric-power connections, gas-supply lines, etc. **4.** = GRIDIRON 1, 2, 3. **5.** Pattern of lines marking starting-places on car-racing track. **6.** Arrangement of town streets in rectangular pattern. **7.** Hence **~'d**ED^{2} *a.* [back form. f. GRIDIRON]

grĭ'ddle *n.*, & *v.t.* **1.** *n.* = GIRDLE^{2}. **2.** Miner's wire-bottomed sieve. **3.** *v.t.* Sieve with griddle. [ME, f. OF *gredil*, *gridil* gridiron f. Rom. **graticulum*, **craticulum* f. L *craticula* dim. of *cratis* hurdle; cf. GRATE^{1}, GRILL^{2}]

grīde *v.i.*, & *n.* **1.** *v.i.* Cut or scrape *along*, *through*, etc., with strident or grating sound. **2.** *n.* Grating sound. [orig. sense *pierce*, by metath. f. GIRD^{2}]

grĭ'diron (-īern) *n.* **1.** Cooking utensil of metal bars for broiling or grilling. **2.** Frame of parallel beams for supporting ship in dock. **3.** *Football field (with parallel lines marking out area of play). **4.** (Theatr.) Plank structure over stage supporting mechanism for drop-scenes etc. **5. ~(-pendulum),** compensation pendulum with parallel rods of different metals. **6.** = GRID 6. [ME *gredire*, var. of *gredil* GRIDDLE, later assoc. w. IRON^{1}]

grief *n.* **1.** Deep or violent sorrow, keen regret; **come to ~,** meet with disaster, fail, fall. **2. Good** or **great ~** (excl. of surprise, alarm, etc.). [ME f. AF *gref*, OF *grief* (*grever* GRIEVE^{1})]

grie'vance *n.* Real or fancied ground of complaint. [ME, = injury, f. OF *grevance* (as prec.; see -ANCE)]

grieve^{1} *v.* **1.** *v.t.* Give deep sorrow to. **2.** *v.i.* Feel grief (*at*, *for*, *about*, *over*). [ME, f. OF *grever* f. Rom. **grevare* f. L *gravare* (*gravis* heavy)]

grieve^{2} *n.* (Sc.) Farm-bailiff, overseer. [OE *grǣfa*; cf. REEVE^{1}]

grie'vous *a.* Bringing serious trouble, injurious, (**~ bodily harm,** (Law) serious injury); (of pain etc.) severe; flagrant, heinous; causing grief; hence **~**LY^{2} *adv.* [ME, f. OF *grevos* (as GRIEVE^{1}; see -OUS)]

‖**grĭff** *n.* (sl.) News; reliable information. [abbr. of foll.]

‖**grĭ'ffĭn^{1}** *n.* (sl.) Betting tip; hint. [19th c.; orig. unkn.]

grĭ'ffĭn^{2}, grȳ'phon, *n.* Fabulous creature with eagle's head and wings and lion's body. [ME, f. OF *grifoun* f. Rom. **grypho -onis* augment. of LL *gryphus* f. L f. Gk *grups*]

grĭ'ffon^{1} *n.* = prec.; **~ (vulture),** large vulture of genus *Gyps*. [var. of prec.]

grĭ'ffon^{2} *n.* European coarse-haired terrier-like (breed of) dog. [F, = GRIFFIN^{2}]

***grĭft** *n.*, & *v.i.* (sl.) = GRAFT^{2}; hence **~**'ER^{1} *n.* [perh. corrupt.]

grig *n.* Small eel; grasshopper or cricket; **merry** or **lively as a ~,** full of fun, extravagantly lively. [ME, orig. = 'dwarf', of unkn. orig.]

gri-gri. Var of GREEGREE.

grill¹ *v.* & *n.* **1.** *v.t.* & *i.* Cook on gridiron or under grill; (fig.) subject to or undergo torture or great heat; hence **~'ER¹** (1, 2) *n.* **2.** *v.t.* Subject to severe questioning (esp. by police). **3.** *n.* (Dish of) grilled food; **~(-room)**, informal restaurant. [f. F *griller* (as foll.)]

grill² *n.* Gridiron (sense 1); device on cooker for downward emission of radiant heat. [f. F *gril* = OF *grail, greil* masc. form of *grille* (see GRILLE)]

grill³. See GRILLE.

gri'llage *n.* Heavy framework of cross-timbering as foundation for building in treacherous soil. [F (as foll.; see -AGE)]

grille, grill³, *n.* Grating, latticed screen, esp. in door for observing callers, in convent separating nuns from visitors, (Hist.) in front of Ladies' Gallery in House of Commons, etc.; (Tennis) square opening in wall; metal grid to protect radiator of motor vehicle; hence **grill**ED² (-ld) *a.* [F, f. OF *graïlle* f. med. L *graticula, craticula*; see GRIDDLE]

grilse *n.* Young salmon that has been only once to the sea. [ME; orig. unkn.]

grim *a.* **1.** Stern, unrelenting, merciless, severe; of forbidding or harsh aspect; **hold on like ~ death** (with great determination). **2.** Sinister, ghastly, mirthless, (*has a grim truth in it*; *a grim smile*); unpleasant, unattractive. **3.** Hence **~'**LY² *adv.*, **~'**NESS *n.* [OE, = OS, OHG *grim*, ON *grimmr* f. Gmc **grimmaz*]

grimā'c|e *n.*, & *v.i.* **1.** *n.* Distortion of face expressing annoyance etc. or meant to cause laughter; affected look; use of such looks, affectation. **2.** *v.i.* Make grimace; hence **~**ER¹ *n.* [F, f. Sp. *grimazo* (*grima* fright)]

grimă'lkin (*or* -aw'l-) *n.* Old she-cat; spiteful old woman. [f. GREY + *Malkin* dim. of fem. name *Matilda* (see -KIN)]

grime *n.*, & *v.t.* **1.** *n.* Soot or dirt ingrained in some surface, esp. the skin; hence **gri'm**Y² *a.* **2.** *v.t.* Blacken with grime, befoul. [n. f. v., f. MLG, MDu. **grimen*]

Grimm *n.* **~'s law** (specifying regular consonantal differences between related words in different Indo-European languages). [f. J. L. C. ~, Ger. philologist d. 1863]

grin *v.* **(-nn-)** & *n.* **1.** *v.i.* Show teeth esp. in amusement or pain or in forced or unrestrained or vacant smile (*at*); **~ and bear it,** take pain etc. stoically; *grin like a* CHESHIRE *cat*; **~ through a horse-collar** (in grimacing-match at rustic sports). **2.** *v.t.* Express (contempt, satisfaction) by grinning. **3.** *n.* Act or action of grinning. [OE *grennian*, rel. to OHG *grennan* mutter, *granōn* grunt, ON *grenja* howl f. Gmc **gran-*; cogn. w. GROAN]

grind *v.* **(ground)** & *n.* **1.** *v.t.* Reduce to small particles or powder by crushing between millstones, teeth, etc., (*down, small, to pieces, into dust*, etc.). **2.** Oppress, harass with exactions, (*grinding poverty, tyranny*; *grind the faces of the poor* etc.). **3.** Produce (flour) by grinding; sharpen or smooth by friction (*has an* AXE *to grind*; *grind lenses, diamonds*, etc.; *grind engine-valve in*, or *into its seat*; **ground glass,** glass made non-transparent by grinding etc.); work (hand-mill); turn handle of (barrel-organ etc.); produce or bring *out* with effort. **4.** *v.i.* Toil monotonously, study hard. **5.** *v.t.* & *i.* Rub gratingly *on, into, against*, etc., (*ground his heel into it*; *ground to a halt*; *ship was grinding on rocks*); rub (teeth) hard together. **6.** **~'stone,** thick revolving stone disc for grinding, sharpening, and polishing (**hold** or **keep** person's **nose to the ~stone,** make him work incessantly), kind of stone used for these. **7.** *n.* Grinding; size of ground particles; hard monotonous work or task (**the daily ~**, (colloq.) one's usual day's work); *student who works hard; (sl.) (act of) sexual intercourse; (sl.) dancer's rotatory movement of hips. [OE *grindan*, of unkn. orig.]

gri'nder *n.* Molar tooth; grinding-machine; upper millstone; person who grinds (esp. in comb., as *organ, knife, -grinder*); *student who works hard. [ME, f. prec. + -ER¹]

gri'ngō (-nggō) *n.* (*pl.* **~s**). Foreigner (esp. Briton or American) in Spanish-speaking country. [Sp., = gibberish]

grip¹ *n.* **1.** Firm hold, tight grasp or clasp; **at ~s, come** or **get to ~s with,** (of close combat, or purposeful approach to a subject). **2.** Grasping power; way of clasping hands; way of grasping or holding (*overlapping grip*; **shorten, lengthen,** one's **grip,** hold bat, club, etc., nearer, farther from, point of impact). **3.** Control, mastery, intellectual hold, (*get a grip on oneself*; *lose* one's *grip*); power of arresting attention. **4.** Part in machinery etc. that clips, part of weapon etc. that is held; hair-grip; = GRIP²*sack*. [OE *gripe* grasp & *gripa* handful, both f. as GRIPE]

grip² *v.* **(-pp-). 1.** *v.t.* Seize, grasp, or hold, tightly; compel attention of; ***~'sack,** suitcase or travelling-bag; hence **~'P**ER¹ (2) *n.* **2.** *v.i.* Take firm hold esp. by friction. [OE *grippa*, = MHG *gripfen*, f. as GRIPE]

gripe *v.* & *n.* **1.** *v.t.* & *i.* Clutch, grip. **2.** *v.t.* Oppress, pinch; affect with colic; (Naut.) secure with gripes. **3.** *v.i.* (Naut., of ship) turn to face wind in spite of helm; (sl.) complain. **4.** *n.* Act of griping, clutch; (arch.) hold, control; (in *pl.*) colic; handle of implement or weapon; (Naut., in *pl.*) lashings securing boat in its place; (sl.) complaint; **~-water,** carminative esp. for babies. [OE *gripan*, = OS *gripan*, OHG *grifan*, ON *grípa*, Goth. *greipan* f. Gmc **grip-*; cf. GROPE]

grippe *n.* Influenza. [F (*gripper* seize)]

grisai'lle (-z-; *or* -zī') *n.* Method of decorative painting in grey monochrome representing figures and objects in relief; stained-glass window of this kind. [F (*gris* grey)]

griseofu'lvin (-z-) *n.* Antibiotic used esp. against ringworm. [f. mod. L *griseofulvum* f. med. L *griseus* grey + L *fulvus* reddish yellow, + -IN]

grise'tte (-z-) *n.* Young Frenchwoman of working class. [F, orig. = grey dress-material (*gris* grey; see -ETTE)]

gris-gris. Var. of GREEGREE.

‖**gri'skin** *n.* Lean part of loin of bacon pig. [app. f. obs. *gris, grice* young pig f. ON *gríss*, + -KIN]

gri'sl|y (-z-) *a.* Causing horror, terror, or superstitious dread; hence **~i**NESS *n.* [OE *grislic* (**grisan* terrify; see -LY¹)]

gri'son (-z-) *n.* S. Amer. carnivore of weasel family, resembling glutton. [F, app. f. adj. = grey (*gris* grey)]

grissi'ni (-ē'nē) *n. pl.* Crisp bread in long thin sticks. [It.]

grist¹ *n.* Corn for grinding (**brings ~ to the mill,** is profitable; **all is ~ that comes to his mill,** he utilizes everything); malt crushed for brewing. [OE, f. Gmc **grinst-* (**grindan* GRIND)]

grist² *n.* Size or thickness of yarn or rope. [perh. cogn. w. GIRD¹]

gri'stle (-sel) *n.* Whitish tough flexible tissue in vertebrates, cartilage; hence **gri'stl**Y² (-slĭ) *a.* [OE, = OFris. & MLG *gristel*; cf. OHG *chrustila*, of unkn. orig.]

grit¹ *n.* Small particles of stone or sand, esp. as causing discomfort or clogging machinery etc.; ~(**'stone**), coarse sandstone; grain or texture of stone; (colloq.) strength of character, pluck, endurance; hence **~'ty**[2] *a.* [OE *grēot*, = OS *griot*, OHG *grioz*, ON *grjót* f. Gmc **greutam*; cf. GRITS, GROATS]

grĭt[2] *v.i.* & *t.* (**-tt-**). Produce, or move with, grating sound; grind or clench (teeth); spread grit on (icy roads etc.). [f. prec.]

grĭts *n. pl.* Husked but unground oats; coarse oatmeal. [OE *grytt(e)*, = OHG *gruzzi* f. WG **grutjō*; cf. GRIT[1], GROATS]

||**grĭ'zzle** *v.i.* (colloq.) (Esp. of child) whimper, cry fretfully. [19th c.; orig. unkn.]

grĭ'zzled (-zeld) *a.* Grey(-haired). [f. *grizzle* grey f. OF *grisel* (*gris* grey; see -LE 2) + -ED[2]]

grĭ'zzlў *a.* & *n.* **1.** *a.* Grey, greyish, grey-haired; **~ bear,** large fierce N. Amer. bear. **2.** *n.* Grizzly bear. [f. as prec. + -Y[2]]

groan *v.* & *n.* **1.** *v.i.*, & *n.* (Make) deep inarticulate sound expressing pain, grief, or disapproval, (**~ inwardly,** be distressed). **2.** *v.t.* Utter with groans. **3.** *v.i.* Be oppressed or loaded *under*, *beneath*, *with*, (*groan under injustice*; *shelf groans with books*; **~ing board,** well-loaded dining-table); (arch.) long *for*. [OE *grānian* f. Gmc **grain-*, cogn. w. GRIN]

||**groat** *n.* (Hist.) Silver coin issued 1351–1662, equal in value to four pennies; fourpenny piece 1836–56; (arch.) small sum (*don't care a groat*). [ME, f. MDu. *groot*, orig. = great, in sense thick (penny); cf. GROSCHEN]

groats *n. pl.* Hulled (sometimes also crushed) grain, esp. oats. [OE *grotan* pl.; cf. *grot* fragment, *grēot* GRIT[1], *grytt* bran]

Grō'bĭan *n.* Coarse slovenly person. [G, or f. med. L *Grobianus* imaginary typical German boor f. G *grob* coarse (as GRUFF)]

grō'c|er *n.* Dealer in tea, butter, flour, sugar, spices, tinned foods, and miscellaneous household stores; hence **~ERY** (2, and, usu. in *pl.*, 1) *n.* [ME & AF *grosser*, orig. one who sells in the gross, f. OF *grossier* f. med. L *grossarius* (as GROSS[2], -ARY[1])]

***grōcetēr'ia** *n.* Self-service grocery shop. [f. GROCERY after *cafeteria*]

grŏg *n.* & *v.* (**-gg-**). **1.** *n.* Drink of spirit and water; (Austral. & N.Z. colloq.) alcoholic liquor; **~-blossom,** pimple or redness on nose from intemperance. **2.** *v.i.* Drink grog. **3.** *v.t.* Extract spirit from (empty cask) by pouring in hot water. [reputedly from GROGRAM, nickname (from his cloak) of Adm. Vernon, who in 1740 first had grog served out to sailors instead of neat rum]

grŏ'gg|ў (-gĭ) *a.* Unsteady, tottering; (of horse) weak in forelegs; (arch.) drunk; hence **~ĭLY**[2] *adv.*, **~ĭNESS** *n.* [f. prec. + -Y[2]]

grŏ'gram *n.* Coarse fabric of silk, mohair, and wool, or these mixed, often stiffened with gum. [f. F *gros grain* coarse grain (as GROSS[2], GRAIN)]

groin[1] *n.*, & *v.t.* **1.** *n.* Depression between belly and thigh. **2.** (Archit.) Edge formed by intersecting vaults, arch supporting vault; hence **~'ING**[1] (6) *n.* **3.** *v.t.* Build with groins. [ME *grynde*, perh. f. OE *grynde* depression]

***groin**[2]. See GROYNE.

grŏ'mmĕt. See GRUMMET.

grŏ'mwĕll *n.* Plant of genus *Lithospermum*, with hard seeds formerly used in medicine. [ME f. OF *gromil*, prob. f. med. L **gruinum milium* crane's millet (*grus* CRANE[1] 1)]

grōōm (*or* -ŏŏm) *n.*, & *v.t.* **1.** *n.* ||One of certain officers of Royal Household. **2.** Person employed to take care of horses. **3.** Bridegroom; **~'sman** (-z-), best man or other unmarried male friend officially attending bridegroom at wedding. **4.** *v.t.* Curry, tend, etc., (horse); give neat appearance to (person etc.); prepare (person) *as* political candidate, *for* career, etc. [ME, orig. = 'boy', of unkn. orig.]

grōōve *n.* & *v.* **1.** *n.* Channel or hollow, esp. one made to direct motion or receive corresponding ridge; spiral cut in gramophone record for needle; **in the ~,** (sl.) performing excellently, appreciative of such performance, excellent. **2.** Piece of routine, undeviating course. **3.** (sl.) Well-played jazz; something excellent or very satisfying. **4.** *v.t.* Make groove(s) in; (sl.) give pleasure to (person). **5.** *v.i.* Settle *into* (routine etc.). **6.** (sl.) Be 'in the groove'; enjoy well-played jazz; make progress; get on well *with* (person). [ME, = mine-shaft, f. obs. Du. *groeve* furrow, OHG *gruoba*, ON *gróf*, Goth. *grōba* f. Gmc **grōbh-*; cf. GRAVE[1]]

grōō'v|ў *a.* Of or resembling a groove; (sl.) = *in the* GROOVE; hence **~ĭLY**[2] *adv.*, **~ĭNESS** *n.* [f. prec. + -Y[2]]

grōpe *v.* **1.** *v.i.* Feel about as in dark (*for*, *after*, or abs.), search blindly (lit. or fig.). **2.** *v.t.* Find one's *way* by feeling or tentatively. [OE *grāpian*, = OHG *greifōn* f. WG **graipōjan* f. Gmc **graip-*; cogn. w. GRIP[2], GRIPE]

grō'per *n.* (esp. Austral. & N.Z.) = GROUPER. [var. of GROUPER]

grō'sbeak *n.* = HAW[1]*finch*. [f. F *grosbec* (as GROSS[2], BEAK[1])]

grō'schen (-shen) *n.* **1.** (Hist.) Small German silver coin. **2.** Smallest Austrian coin, 1/100 of schilling. **3.** (colloq.) German 10-pfennig piece. [G, f. MHG *gros(se)* f. med. L (*denarius*) *grossus* thick (penny); cf. GROAT]

grō'sgrain (-ō'gr-) *n.* Corded silk etc. fabric. [F, = coarse grain (as GROSS[2], GRAIN)]

gros point (grō' pwăṅ) *n.* Embroidery on canvas using cross-stitches. [F (as GROSS[2], POINT[1])]

grōss[1] *n.* (*pl.* same). Twelve dozen; **by the ~,** in large quantities, wholesale. [ME, f. F *grosse* (*douzaine* dozen) fem. of *gros* great, GROSS[2]]

grōss[2] *a.* **1.** Luxuriant, rank; overfed, bloated, repulsively fat. **2.** Flagrant, glaring, (*gross negligence*). **3.** Total, without deductions, not net, (*gross* TON[1], *tonnage*, *weight*; **~ national product,** annual total value of goods produced and services provided in a country). **4.** Dense, thick, solid; not ethereal, transparent, or impalpable; (of food) coarse, greasy, uncleanly, repulsive, (**~ feeder,** one who likes such food); (of senses etc.) not delicate, dull. **5.** Coarse in manners or morals, unrefined, indecent. **6.** Hence **~'LY**[2] *adv.*, **~'NESS** *n.* [ME, f. OF *gros grosse* big, f. LL *grossus*]

grōss[3] *v.t.* Produce or earn as gross profit; **~ up,** increase (net amount) to its value before deduction of tax etc. [f. prec.]

grosso modo (grŏsō mō'dō) *adv.* Roughly, approximately. [It.]

grŏt *n.* (poet.) Grotto. [f. F *grotte* f. It. *grotta* GROTTO]

grōtĕ'sque (-sk) *n.* & *a.* **1.** *n.* Decoration with fantastic interweaving of human and animal forms with foliage; comically distorted figure or design; sanserif type. **2.** *a.* (Archit.) in the style of a grotesque; distorted, bizarre; ludicrous from incongruity, absurd. **3.** Hence **~LY**[2] *adv.*, **~NESS, grōtĕ'squerĭe** (-skerĭ) [-ERY (5)], *ns.* [earlier *crot-* f. F *crotesque* f. (w. assim. to OF *crote* grotto), It. *grottesca* grotto-like (painting etc.) fem. of *grottesco* (as foll.; see -ESQUE)]

grŏ'ttō *n.* (*pl.* **~es** *or* **~s**). Picturesque cave; artificial ornamental cave, room etc. adorned with shells etc. in imitation of cave, as pleasant retreat; hence **~ED**[2] (-ōd) *a.* [f. It. *grotta* f. Rom. **grupta*, **crupta* f. L f. Gk *kruptē* CRYPT]

||**grŏ'ttў** *a.* (sl.) Unpleasant, dirty, ugly, etc. [f. GROTESQUE + -Y[2]]

grouch *v.i.*, & *n.* **1.** *v.i.* Grumble. **2.** *n.* Discontented person; cause of discontent; fit of grumbling or bad temper or the sulks; hence ~'Y[2] *a.* [var. of *grutch*; see GRUDGE]

ground[1] *n.* & *a.* **1.** *n.* Bottom of sea; **touch** ~, (fig.) come to something solid after vague talk etc.; (in *pl.*) dregs, esp. of coffee. **2.** (Electr.) = EARTH[1] 5. **3.** Base, foundation, motive, valid reason, (**on the** ~ **of,** by reason or under pretext of; *on public* etc. *grounds*). **4.** Substratum, underlying part, surface worked upon in embroidery, painting, etc., undecorated part, prevailing colour or tone. **5.** Surface of earth (esp. Aeron., opp. *air*: *ground-based, ground crew*, etc.); **above** ~, (fig.) alive; **below** ~, (fig.) dead and buried; **cut** ~ **from under** person's **feet,** anticipate and defeat his arguments or plans; **down to the** ~, (colloq.) completely; **fall** etc. **to the** ~, (of scheme, hope, etc.) be abandoned, fail; *feet on the ground* (see FOOT[1]); **from the** ~ **up,** (colloq.) completely; **get off the** ~, start successfully; **go to** ~, (of dog, fox, etc.) enter burrow, (of person) withdraw from public notice; **into the** ~, to exhaustion etc.; **on the** ~, on the spot, in practical conditions; **on firm, solid,** etc., ~, using soundly-based reasoning; **run to** ~, (fig.) = *run to* EARTH[1]; **thin on the** ~, not numerous; **to the** ~, completely. **6.** (in *pl.*) Enclosed land for ornament or recreation attached to house. **7.** Position, area, or distance, on earth's surface; **break** (**fresh** or **new**) ~, begin work on previously untouched ground (lit. or fig.); **cover much** ~, (of inquiry, report, etc.) be wide-ranging; **cover the** ~, deal adequately with subject; **gain** or **make** ~, advance, catch up *on* (person pursued); **give** or **lose** ~, retreat, decline; **hold** one's ~, = *hold* one's OWN[1]; **meet** person **on his own** ~ (in his own territory or on his own terms); SHIFT[1], STAND[1], one's *ground*. **8.** Area of special kind or use (*camping-ground, cricket-ground, fishing-grounds*); COMMON[1] *ground*; **forbidden** ~, subject that must be avoided. **9.** ||Floor of room etc. **10.** (Cricket). Area where player may lawfully stand, esp. that of batsman behind popping-crease (*in, out of, his ground*); = *ground-staff* (2). **11.** *a.* (In names of birds) terrestrial, (of animals) burrowing or lying on ground, (of plants) dwarfish or trailing. **12.** ~**-ash,** ash sapling, walking-stick of this; ~**-bait** *n.*, & *v.t.*, (prepare with) bait thrown to bottom of intended fishing-ground to attract fish, (lit. or fig.); ~ **bass,** (Mus.) short passage in bass of composition, repeated many times with upper part of music varied; ~**-box,** small BOX[1] used to edge garden beds; ~**-cherry,** (1) dwarf cherry, (2) plant of genus *Physalis*; ~**-colour,** first coat of paint, prevailing colour on which design is done; ~ **control,** directing of aircraft-landing from ground; ~**-fish** (living at bottom of water); ~**-fishing** (with bait near bottom); *ground* FLOOR (**get in on the** ~ **floor,** be admitted to project, company, etc., as one of the initiators); ~ **frost** (on surface of ground or in top layer of soil); ||~ **game,** hares, rabbits, etc.; ~**'hog,** (1) aardvark, (2) Amer. marmot, woodchuck, (**G~hog Day*, usu. 2 Feb., when sunny weather is supposed to foretell continuing cold); ~**-ice** (formed at bottom of water); ~ **ivy,** creeping herb with bluish-purple flower and kidney-shaped leaf; *~**'-keeper,** = *groundsman*; ||~ **landlord,** owner of ground leased for building; ~ **level,** also (Phys.) lowest energy state of atom etc.; ~**'man,** = *groundsman*; ~**-note** (on which a common chord is built, fundamental bass); ~**-nut,** (1) (edible tuber of) N. Amer. wild bean, (2) ||peanut; ~**-pine,** (1) yellow-flowered herb with resinous smell, (2) club-moss; ~**-plan,** plane drawing of divisions of building at ground level, outline or general design of anything; ~**-rent,** rent paid to ground landlord; ~ **rule,** basic principle; ~ **sea,** heavy sea without apparent cause; ~**'sheet,** waterproof sheet for spreading on ground; ~**'sman** (-z-), man keeping cricket-ground etc. in order; ~ **speed,** (Aeron.) aircraft's speed relative to ground; ~**-squirrel,** terrestrial squirrel-like rodent, e.g. chipmunk, gopher, etc.; ~ **staff,** (1) non-flying members of aerodrome staff, (2) ||paid staff of players employed by cricket-club; ~ **state,** (Phys.) = *ground level*; ~ **stroke,** (Lawn Tennis) stroke played near ground after ball has bounced; ~ **swell,** heavy sea caused by distant or past storm or earthquake; ~ **water** (in surface soil); ~**'work,** foundation or basis (usu. fig.), chief ingredient, general surface of thing showing where not overlaid with embroidery or other ornament; ~ **zero,** point on ground under exploding bomb. [OE *grund*, = OS *grund*, OHG *grunt*, Goth. **grundus* f. Gmc **grunduz*]

ground[2] *v.* **1.** *v.t.* & *i.* Run ashore, strand. **2.** *v.t.* Base, establish, (institution, principle, belief) *on* some fact or authority (in *pass.* also *in*; in *p.p.*, *well, ill*, etc., founded, or abs. = well founded); instruct thoroughly (*in* elements of subject), whence ~'ING[1] (1) *n.*; place or lay (esp. Mil. arms) on ground; (Electr.) connect with earth as conductor; prevent (aircraft, airman) from flying. **3.** *v.i.* Alight on ground. [ME, f. prec.]

ground[3]. See GRIND.

||**grou'ndage** *n.* Duty levied on ship entering a port or lying on a shore. [f. GROUND[1] + -AGE]

grou'nder *n.* In vbl senses; (Cricket etc.) ball hit along ground. [ME, f. GROUND[2] + -ER[1]]

grou'ndlĕss *a.* Without basis, authority, or support; unfounded; hence ~LY[2] *adv.*, ~NESS *n.* [OE *grundlēas* (as GROUND[1], -LESS)]

grou'ndlĭng *n.* **1.** = GROUND[1]-*fish*; creeping or dwarf plant. **2.** (literary). Spectator or reader of inferior taste (w. ref. to Shakespeare's *Hamlet* III. ii. 12). **3.** Person on the ground, opp. one in aircraft. [f. GROUND[1] + -LING[1]]

grou'ndsel[1] *n.* Plant of genus *Senecio*, of which the commonest species is used as food for cage-birds. [OE *grundeswylige, gundæswelgiæ* (perh. f. *gund* pus, **swulg-* SWALLOW[1], = pus-absorber, as being used for poultices)]

grou'ndsel[2] *n.* (arch.) Timber serving as foundation, lowest part of wooden framework; threshold. [ME, app. f. GROUND[1] + SILL]

group (-ōōp) *n.*, & *v.t.* **1.** *n.* Number of persons or things standing near together, knot, cluster; number of persons or things belonging or classed together or forming a whole; number of commercial companies under one owner; (Polit.) smaller unit than a party; division of air force or air-fleet; = POP[3] *group*. **2.** (Math.) Set of elements with operation for combining any pair to give another element in the set. **3.** (Chem.) Set of ions or radicals giving characteristic qualitative reaction; set of elements having similar properties; combination of atoms having recognizable identity in a number of compounds. **4.** ~ **captain,** officer in Royal Air Force; ~ **practice,** medical practice in which several doctors are associated; ~ **sex,** sexual activity in which more than two persons take part simultaneously; ~ **therapy,** therapy in which patients with similar condition are brought together to assist one another psychologically; ~ **velocity,** speed of travel of energy of wave(-group). **5.** *v.t.* Form into a group; place in a group (*with*); form (colours, figures, etc.) into well-arranged and harmonious whole; classify; hence ~'AGE (3), ~'ING (1, 2), *ns.* [f. F *groupe* f.

It. *gruppo* f. Gmc **kruppaz* round mass, cogn. w. CROP[1]]

grou'per (-ōō'-) *n.* Marine food-fish of family Serranidae. [f. Port. *garupa*, prob. f. native name in S. Amer.]

grou'pĭe (-ōō'-) *n.* (sl.) **1.** Group captain. **2.** Girl who follows touring pop groups. [f. GROUP + -IE]

grouse[1] *n.* (*pl.* same). Wild bird of family Tetraonidae with feathered feet, esp. ||(**red**) ~, reddish European game-bird (*Lagopus scoticus*); its flesh as food. [16th c., perh. pl. of **grue* f. med. L *gruta* or W *grugiar* (*grug* heath, *iar* hen)]

grous|e[2] *v.i.*, & *n.* (sl.) Grumble; hence ~'ER[1] *n.* [19th c.; orig. unkn.]

grout[1] *n.*, & *v.t.* **1.** *n.* Thin fluid mortar for filling interstices. **2.** *v.t.* Fill up or finish with grout. [perh. f. foll., but cf. F dial. *grouter* grout a wall]

grout[2] *n.* Sediment, dregs. [OE *grūt*, cogn. w. GRITS, GROATS]

grout[3] *v.i.* & *t.* (Of pigs, or fig.) turn up earth, turn up (earth etc.), with snout. [var. of *groot* f. ME *groot* mud, rel. to OE *grēot* GRIT]

grōve *n.* Small wood, group of trees; hence **grō'**VY[2] *a.* [OE *grāf*, rel. to *grǣfa* brushwood]

grŏ'vel *v.i.* (||**-ll-**). Lie prone in abject humility, humble oneself; hence ||~**l**ER[1], *~ER[1], *n.* [back form. f. foll.]

grŏ'vellĭng, *grŏ'velĭng, *a.* Abject, base, sordid; prone; hence ~LY[2] *adv.* [f. obs. *grovelling(s)* adv. (*gruf* face down f. *on grufe* f. ON *á grúfu*; see -LING[2]); later taken as part. (-ING[2])]

grow (-ō) *v.* (**grew** *pr.* grōō; **~n** *p.p.* w. *have* or *be*, cf. -ED[1] (2), or as *a.*). **1.** *v.i.* Develop or exist as living plant (~ **into one, together,** etc., coalesce); germinate, sprout, spring up; be produced, come naturally into existence, arise, (*grow on* TREE*s*). **2.** Increase in or *in* size, height, quantity, degree, power, etc.; ~ **downwards,** extend downwards, (fig.) diminish; *habit, person, picture,* etc., **~s on** person, becomes more influential with or admired by him; ~ **out of,** become too large to wear (garment; see also sense 3); **~'ing pains,** neuralgic pain in children's legs due to fatigue etc., (fig.) early difficulties in development of an enterprise etc.; **~ing season,** time of year when weather promotes growth of plants; **~n man** etc., adult. **3.** Become gradually (*grow rich, less*); come by degrees *to* do; ~ **out of,** become too mature to retain (childish habit etc.; see also sense 2); ~ **up,** advance to maturity, (esp. in *imper.*) begin to behave sensibly, (of custom) arise, become common; **~n-up** *a.* & *n.*, adult. **4.** *v.t.* Produce (plants, fruit, wool, etc.) by cultivation, bring forth, let (beard etc.) develop, whence ~'ABLE *a.* **5.** (in *pass.*) Be covered (*up* or *over*) with some growth. [OE *grōwan*, = OHG *gruoan*, ON *gróa* f. Gmc **grō-* cogn. w. GRASS, GREEN[1]]

grow'er (-ō'*er*) *n.* Plant that grows in specified way (*fast, free,* etc., *grower*); person growing produce (often in comb., as *fruit-grower*). [f. prec. + -ER[1]]

growl *v.i.* & *t.*, & *n.* (Make) guttural sound of anger (*at*); rumble; murmur angrily, angry murmur, complain(t); utter with a growl (*out*). [prob. imit.]

grow'ler *n.* In vbl senses; ||(Hist.) four-wheeled cab; small iceberg. [f. prec. + -ER[1]]

grown. See GROW.

growth (-ōth) *n.* Growing, development, increase in size or value, (**of foreign** etc. ~, grown abroad etc.; **full** ~, size ultimately attained); cultivation of produce; what has grown or is growing; crop or yield of grapes; (Path.) morbid formation; ~ **industry,** one developing faster than most other industries; ~ **stock** etc. (tending to increase in capital value rather than yield high income). [f. GROW + -TH[1]]

groyne, *groin[2], *n.*, & *v.t.* **1.** *n.* Timber framework or low broad wall run out to check drifting of beach and so stop encroachment of sea. **2.** *v.t.* Supply (beach) with groynes. [f. (dial.) *groin* snout f. OF *groign* f. LL *grunium* pig's snout f. L *grunnire* grunt]

grŭb[1] *n.* Larva of insect, caterpillar, maggot; (arch.) dull drudge, literary hack, sloven; (sl.) food, a feed; **~-screw** (headless); ***~-stake** *v.t.*, & *n.*, (sl.) (supply with) outfit, provisions, etc., given in return for share in profits (orig. in prospecting for ore). [ME, prob. f. foll.]

grŭb[2] *v.* (**-bb-**). **1.** *v.t.* & *i.* Dig superficially. **2.** *v.t.* Clear (ground) of roots and stumps, clear away (roots etc.), fetch *up* or *out* by digging (lit., or fig. in books etc.). **3.** *v.i.* Search, rummage; plod, toil, *on, along, away*; (sl.) feed [perh. f. prec.]. **4.** **~-axe, -hoe, -hook,** (for grubbing up stumps). **5.** Hence (**-**)**~'b**ER[1] (1, 2) *n.* [ME, perh. repr. OE **grybban* f. Gmc **grubh-*, **grabh-* GRAVE[2]]

grŭ'bb|ȳ *a.* Of or infested with grubs; dirty, grimy, slovenly, whence ~ĭLY[2] *adv.*, ~ĭNESS *n.* [f. GRUB[1] + -Y[2]]

Grŭ'b Street *n.* & *a.* (Typical of) the tribe of needy authors and literary hacks. [name of a London street (later Milton St., Moorgate), inhabited by such in 17th c.]

grŭdge *v.t.*, & *n.* **1.** *v.t.* Be unwilling to give, grant, or allow (thing; *to* person); show reluctance in do*ing* or *to* do. **2.** *n.* Feeling of resentment or ill will (*have a* or **hold a grudge against*; *bear* or *owe* person *a grudge*). [f. ME *grutch* f. OF *grouc(h)ier* murmur, of unkn. orig.]

grŭ'dgĭng *a.* Reluctant, not willing; hence ~LY[2] *adv.* [f. prec. + -ING[2]]

gru'el (-ōō'-) *n.*, & *v.t.* (||**-ll-**). **1.** *n.* Liquid food of oatmeal etc. boiled in milk or water chiefly for invalids; ||(arch.) punishment, defeat. **2.** *v.t.* Exhaust, punish, (esp. ~(**l**)ING[1,2] *n.* & *a.*). [ME f. OF, f. Gallo-Rom. **grutellum* f. Frank. **grūt*; cf. GROUT[2], -LE 2]

grue'some (-ōō's-) *a.* Horrible, grisly, disgusting; hence ~LY[2] (-mlĭ) *adv.*, ~NESS (-mn-) *n.* [f. Sc. *grue* to shudder (f. Scand.) + -SOME[1]]

grŭff *a.* Surly, laconic, rough-mannered, rough-voiced; hence ~'LY[2] *adv.*, ~'NESS *n.* [f. Du., MLG *grof* coarse, = OHG *grob* f. WG **gahrubha* (as Y-, ROUGH)]

grŭ'mbl|e *v.i.* & *t.*, & *n.* (Utter) dull inarticulate sound, murmur, growl faintly; rumble; complain(t) (*at, about, over*); be discontented; utter complainingly (*out*); hence ~ER[1] *n.*, ~ING[2] *a.* (**~ing appendix,** (colloq.) one that causes intermittent discomfort without developing appendicitis). [f. obs. *grumme* + -LE 3; cf. MDu. *grommen*, MLG *grommelen*, f. imit. Gmc **grum-*]

grum|e (-ōōm) *n.* Thick or viscous fluid, esp. clotted blood; hence ~'OUS *a.* [f. L *grumus* small heap]

grŭ'mmėt, grŏ'mmėt, *n.* **1.** (Naut.) Ring usu. of twisted rope as fastening, rowlock, wad, etc. **2.** Insulating washer placed round electric conductor passing through hole in metal etc. **3.** Stiffening ring in serviceman's cap. [f. obs. F *grom(m)ette* (*gourmer* to curb, of unkn. orig.)]

grŭmp *n.* (colloq.) Grumpy person; (in *pl.*) fit of sulks; hence ~'ISH[1] *a.* [imit.]

grŭ'mp|ȳ *a.* Ill-tempered, surly; hence ~ĭLY[2] *adv.*, ~ĭNESS *n.* [f. prec. in sense 'ill-humour' + -Y[2]]

Grŭ'ndȳ *n.* (**Mrs.**) ~, person embodying conventional propriety and prudery; hence ~ISM (2) *n.* [person repeatedly mentioned in T. Morton's *Speed the Plough* 1798]

grŭ'nion (-nyon) *n.* Small Californian sea-fish coming ashore to spawn. [prob. f. Sp. *gruñón* grunter]

grŭnt *v.i.* & *t.*, & *n.* **1.** (Utter) low guttural sound characteristic of pigs; express discontent, dissent, fatigue, etc., by this; utter with grunt (*out*). **2.** *n.* Amer. fish of family Pomadasidae, grunting when caught. [OE *grunnettan*, = OHG *grunnizōn*, intensive f. imit. **grun-*]

grŭ'nter *n.* In vbl senses; pig; grunting fish, esp. = prec. 2 [ME, f. prec. + -ER[1]]

Grunth. Var. of GRANTH.

grŭ'ntled (-teld) *a.* (colloq.) Pleased, satisfied. [back form. f. DISGRUNTLED]

gru'yère (grōō'yār) *n.* Swiss pale cows'-milk cheese with many cavities. [f. *G~* district in Switzerland]

grȳ'phon. See GRIFFIN[2].

grȳ'sbŏk *n.* Small grey S. Afr. antelope. [S. Afr. Du., f. Du. *grijs* grey + *bok* BUCK[1]]

||**gs.** *abbr.* guineas.

G-strĭng (jē'-) *n.* **1.** (Mus.) String on violin etc. sounding note G. **2.** Narrow strip of cloth etc. covering genitals, attached to string round waist, as worn by American Indian, chorus-girl, etc. [f. G + STRING]

G-suit (jē'sūt *or* -ōōt) *n.* Garment to enable wearer to withstand high acceleration. [f. *g* (= *gravity*) + SUIT]

G.T. *abbr. gran turismo.*

Gt. *abbr.* Great.

gua'charō (gwah'ch-) *n.* (*pl.* **~s**). The oil-bird of S. America. [S. Amer. Sp.]

guai'ăc (gwī'-) *n.* = foll. 2, 3. [Anglicized form of foll.]

guai'acum (gwī'-) *n.* **1.** Tropical Amer. tree of genus *Guaiacum*. **2.** Brownish-green wood of two species of this used in medicine, lignum vitae. **3.** Resin from these; drug made from it. [mod. L, f. Sp. *guayaco* of Haitian orig.]

guan (gwahn) *n.* Tropical Amer. bird of family Cracidae, allied to curassow. [prob. f. native name]

gua'na (gwah'-) *n.* Iguana; goanna. [var. of IGUANA]

guana'cō (gwanah'-) *n.* (*pl.* **~s**). Wild llama with reddish-brown wool. [f. Quechua *huanaco*]

gua'nine (gwah'nēn) *n.* (Chem.) White base obtained from guano and found as constituent of DNA. [f. foll. + -INE[5]]

gua'nō (gwah'-) *n.* (*pl.* **~s**), & *v.t.* **1.** *n.* Excrement of sea-fowl, found esp. in islands off Peru and used as manure; artificial manure esp. that made from fish. **2.** *v.t.* Fertilize with guano. [Sp., f. Quechua *huanu* dung]

guar'anĭ (gw-) *n.* **1.** (*G~*). Language or member of a S. Amer. Indian ethnic group. **2.** Monetary unit of Paraguay. [Sp.]

guărantee' (gă-) *n.*, & *v.t.* **1.** *n.* Person making guaranty or giving security; guaranty; thing (esp. document) given or existing as security for fulfilment of conditions or permanence etc. of something; ~ **fund,** sum pledged as contingent indemnity for loss. **2.** *v.t.* Be guarantee for, answer for due fulfilment of (contract etc.) or genuineness etc. of (article), assure permanence etc. of; give one's word *that* something has happened or will happen or *to* do; secure possession of *to* person; secure *against* or *from* (risk etc.), or *in* (possession etc.); hence **guă'rant**OR (gă'-; *or* -ōr') *n.* [earlier *garante*, perh. f. Sp. *garante* = F *garant* WARRANT[1]; later infl. by F *garantie* guaranty]

guă'rantȳ (gă'-) *n.* Written or other undertaking to answer for payment of debt or performance of obligation by another person liable in first instance; ground or basis of security. [f. AF *guarantie*, var. of *warantie* WARRANTY]

guard[1] (gard) *n.* **1.** Defensive posture or motion in fencing, boxing, etc.; (Cricket) position of bat to defend wicket (**take, give,** ~, (of batsman, umpire) ascertain correct spot on ground for this). **2.** Watch, vigilant state, (**keep ~, be on ~, stand ~,** act as sentry etc.; **on, off,** one's ~, prepared, unprepared, against attack, surprise, or one's own impulses etc.). **3.** Protector, defender, sentry; ||official in general charge of train or (Hist.) stage-coach; *prison warder; defensive player in basketball or Amer. football. **4.** (in *pl.*) ||Household troops (including FOOT[1] *Guards*, HORSE[1] *Guards*, LIFE *Guards*, and by extension some (orig. seven) regiments of *Dragoon Guards*). **5.** Body of soldiers etc. serving as protectors of place or person, escort, separate portion of army, etc., (*advance, rear, -guard*; *guard of honour*; HOME[1] *Guard*; OLD *guard*; **mount, relieve,** ~, take up, take others' place on, sentry duty). **6.** Thing that protects or defends; contrivance to prevent injury or accident (often in comb., as *fire-guard, mudguard*); part of sword-hilt that protects user's hand. **7. ~-boat,** (1) boat going rounds of fleet in harbour to see that good watch is kept, (2) official harbour boat enforcing quarantine or customs regulations; **~-book** (arranged for the reception of additional leaves, letters, etc.); **~-chain** (securing watch, brooch, etc.); **~'house** (accommodating military guard or securing prisoners); **~-rail,** hand or other rail to prevent falling, derailment, etc.; **~-ring** (preventing other ring from slipping off finger); **~'room** (as *guardhouse*); **~-ship,** warship protecting harbour and receiving seamen till they can join their ships; **~'sman** (-z-), soldier belonging to guard or Guards; **~-tent** (as *guardhouse*). **8.** Hence **~'**LESS *a.* [ME, f. OF *garde* (*garder* f. Rom. **wardare* f. WG **wardho* WARD[1])]

guard[2] (gard) *v.* **1.** *v.t.* Keep safe, stand guard over, keep (door etc.) so as to control entry or exit; protect, defend, (*from, against*); secure by explanations or stipulations etc. from misunderstanding or abuse. **2.** Keep (thoughts, speech) in check. **3.** *v.i.* Use a fencing guard; take precautions *against*; (Curling, Bowling) protect (stone, bowl) by placing one's own between it and later player; (Chess, Cards) protect (man, card) with another. **4.** So **~'**ANT *a.*, (Her.) depicted with body sideways but face towards spectator. [f. prec., or f. OF *garder* (see prec.)]

guar'dėd (gar'-) *a.* In vbl senses; (of speech etc.) cautious; hence **~**LY[2] *adv.*, **~**NESS *n.* [p.p. of prec.]

||**guardee'** (gar-) *n.* (colloq.) Guardsman, esp. as representing smartness and elegance. [f. GUARD[1] + -EE (2)]

guar'dĭan (gar'-) *n.* Keeper, defender, protector; ||(Hist.) member of board elected to administer poor-laws in parish or district; (*G~*) title of newspaper; (Law) one having custody of person or property (or both) of WARD[1] (minor, lunatic, etc.); superior of Franciscan convent; ~ **angel,** spirit conceived as watching over person or place; hence **~**SHIP *n.* [ME f. AF *gardein*, OF *garden* f. Frank. **warding* (as WARD[1], -ING[3]); cf. WARDEN[1]]

Guarnēr'ius (gw-) *n.* Violin or violoncello made by member of *Guarnerius* family of Cremona in 17th–18th c.

gua'va (gwah'-) *n.* (Tropical Amer. tree yielding) edible orange-coloured acid fruit. [f. Sp. *guayaba* prob. f. S. Amer. name]

guayu'lė (gwiōō'lĭ) *n.* (Silver-leaved Mexican plant the sap of which furnishes) a rubber substitute. [Amer. Sp., f. Nahuatl *cuauhuli*]

gŭ'bbĭns (-z) *n.* Trash; valueless thing; gadget; ||(colloq.) foolish person. [orig. = 'fragments', f. obs. *gobbon*, perh. rel. to GOBBET]

***gūbernatŏr'ial** *a.* Of a governor. [f. L *gubernator* governor + -IAL]

gŭ'ddl|e *v.* (Sc.) **1.** *v.t.* Catch (fish) with the hands, by groping under the stones or banks of a stream. **2.** *v.i.* Grope for fish thus. **3.** Hence ~'ER[1] *n.* [19th c.; orig. unkn.]

gŭ'dgeon[1] (-jon) *n.* Small freshwater fish used as bait; credulous person. [ME, f. OF *goujon* f. L *gobio -onis* GOBY]

gŭ'dgeon[2] (-jon) *n.* Pivot at end of beam, axle, etc., on which bell, wheel, etc., works; ring of gate fitting on hook of post; socket in which rudder works; pin holding two blocks of stone etc. together; **~-pin,** (esp.) pin holding piston-rod and connecting-rod together. [ME, f. OF *goujon* dim. of *gouge* GOUGE]

guĕ'lder (gĕ'-) *n.* **~ rose,** deciduous shrub with round bunches of creamy-white flowers, snowball-tree. [f. Du. *geldersch* (*Gelderland* province in Holland)]

Guĕlph, Guĕlf, (gwĕ-) *n.* Member of medieval Italian party supporting Pope against Emperor (opp. GHIBELLINE); hence ~'IC *a.*, ~'ISM (3) *n.* [f. It. *Guelfo* f. MHG *Welf* name of founder of princely family of Guelphs, ancestors of British Royal Family]

gueno'n (genaw'ṅ) *n.* Long-tailed Afr. monkey of genus *Cercopithecus* etc. [F, of unkn. orig.]

guer'don (gêr'-) *n.*, & *v.t.* (poet.) Reward, recompense. [ME, f. OF *guer(e)don* f. med. L *widerdonum* f. WG *widarlōn* (as WITH, LOAN[1]) w. assim. to L *donum* gift]

guéridon (gĕ'rĭdon) *n.* Small ornamental table or stand. [F]

Guer'nsey (gêr'nzĭ) *n.* (Animal of) breed of dairy cattle from Guernsey; (*g*~) thick knitted woollen usu. blue outer tunic or jersey, (Austral.) football jersey; **~ lily,** kind of amaryllis orig. from S. Africa, with large red lily-like flowers. [~ in Channel Islands]

guerrĭ'lla, guerĭ'lla, (ger-) *n.* Person taking part in irregular fighting (**~ war, warfare**) by small independently acting groups; URBAN *guerrilla.* [f. Sp. *guerrilla*, dim. of *guerra* war]

guess (gĕs) *v.* & *n.* **1.** *v.t.* & *i.* Estimate without measurement or detailed calculation. **2.** *v.t.* Think likely, think one divines nature of, form hypothesis as to, conjecture, hazard opinion about, (thing, *that, how, when, whether*, etc., thing *to be*, or abs.); conjecture (answer to riddle, solution of problem, or abs.) rightly. **3.** *v.i.* **~ at,** make guess concerning; ***I ~,** I think it likely, I suppose; **keep** person **~'ing,** (colloq.) let him remain uncertain. **4.** *n.* Rough estimate, conjecture, hypothesis, (**by ~**, haphazard, also *by guess and by God(frey)*; ANYBODY'*s* or *anyone's guess*; **my ~ is,** I am fairly sure; ***miss** one's ~, make wrong assumption; **have another ~ coming,** be mistaken); **~'work,** (procedure based on) guessing; OTHER*guess.* [ME *gesse*, of uncert. orig.; cf. OSw. *gissa*, MLG, MDu. *gissen*; f. root of GET[1]]

guĕ's(s)tĭmate (gĕ'-) *n.* (colloq.) Estimate based on guesswork combined with reasoning. [f. prec. + ESTIMATE[1]]

guest (gĕst) *n.* **1.** Person invited to visit another's house or have meal etc. at his expense (**paying ~**, boarder); person lodging at hotel, boarding-house, etc.; occasional performer from outside regular company etc. **2. ~-chamber** (kept for guests); **~-house,** superior boarding-house; **~-night** (on which guests are entertained at club, college, mess, etc.); **~-room** (kept for guests). **3.** Hence ~'SHIP *n.* [ME, f. ON *gestr*, = OS, OHG *gast*, Goth. *gasts* f. Gmc **gastiz* f. IE **ghostis*]

guĕ'st-rōpe, guĕss-, (gĕ's-) *n.* Second rope fastened to boat in tow to steady it; rope slung outside ship to give hold for boats coming alongside. [17th c.; orig. uncert.]

gŭff *n.* (sl.) Empty talk, nonsense. [19th c., orig. = 'puff'; imit.]

gŭ'ffaw (*or* -aw') *n.* & *v.* **1.** *n.* Coarse or boisterous laugh. **2.** *v.i.* & *t.* Make, say with, guffaw. [orig. Sc.; imit.]

gŭ'ggle. Var. of GURGLE.

gui'chet (gē'shā) *n.* Grating, hatch; ticket-office window. [F]

guidance. See GUIDE[2].

guide[1] (gīd) *n.* **1.** One who shows the way; hired conductor of traveller or tourist; (esp. in Switzerland etc.) professional mountain-climber. **2.** Soldier, vehicle, or ship enabling others to regulate their movements. **3.** Adviser; directing principle or standard (*the feelings are a bad guide*; *Scripture is our guide*). **4.** (*G*~). ||Member of girls' organization similar to Scouts; **King's** or **Queen's G~** (who has reached highest rank of proficiency). **5.** Book of rudiments, manual; **~('book)**, book of information for tourists (*to* cathedral, city, district, etc.). **6.** (Mech.) Bar, rod, etc., directing motion of something, gauge etc. controlling tool. **7.** Thing marking a position or guiding the eye. **8. ~'-book** (see sense 5); **~-dog** (trained to guide blind person); **~-line,** (fig.) directing principle; **~-post,** signpost; **~-rope,** (1) small rope attached to load of crane to guide it, (2) rope trailed along ground by balloon or small airship to assist in preserving altitude by drag of rope, (3) one of several ropes steadying an airship before flight; **~'way,** groove, track. [ME f. OF (*guie* f. *guider*; see foll.)]

guīde[2] (gīd) *v.t.* **1.** Act as guide to, go before, lead, direct course of; arrange course of (events); be the principle, motive, or ground, of (action, judgement, etc.); conduct affairs of (State etc.); **~d missile** (under remote control or directed by equipment within itself); **~d tour** (accompanied by guide). **2.** Hence **guī'd**ABLE *a.*, **guī'd**ANCE *n.*, (gī'-); **Guī'd**ER[1] (gī'-) *n.*, adult leader of Guides (sense 4). [ME, f. OF *guider*, earlier *guier* f. Rom. **widare* f. Gmc **witan*, cogn. w. WIT[1]]

guī'don (gī'-) *n.* Pennant narrowing to point or fork at free end (used as standard of dragoons or *cavalry). [F, f. It. *guidone* (*guida* GUIDE[1])]

Guignŏ'l (gēnyŏ'l) *n.* = GRAND GUIGNOL; Punch and Judy show; hence ~E'SQUE *a.* [see GRAND GUIGNOL]

guĭld, gĭld[2], (gĭ-) *n.* Society for mutual aid or prosecution of common object; **G~-hall,** (1) hall in which a medieval guild met, (2) (from being used as meeting-place of Corporation) town hall; ||(*the*) **G~'hall,** hall of the Corporation of the City of London, used for State banquets, municipal meetings, etc.; **~ socialism,** system by which the resources, methods, and profits, of each industry should be controlled by a council of its members. [ME, prob. f. MLG, MDu. *gilde* f. Gmc **geldhjōn*; rel. to OE *gi(e)ld* payment, sacrifice, guild, OS *geld*, OHG *gelt*, ON *gjald*, Goth. *gild* tribute f. Gmc **geldham*, & ON *gildi* f. Gmc **geldhjam*]

guĭ'lder (gĭ'-) *n.* Monetary unit of Netherlands; (Hist.) gold coin of Netherlands and Germany. [ME, alt. of Du. GULDEN]

guile (gīl) *n.* Treachery, deceit, cunning devices; hence ~'FUL, ~'LESS (-l-l-), *adjs.* [ME f. OF, f. Scand. **wihl-* WILE]

guĭ'llĕmot (gĭ'-) *n.* Auk of genus *Uria* or *Cepphus.* [F, f. *Guillaume* William]

guĭllō'che (gĭlō'sh) *n.* Architectural or metal-work ornament imitating braided ribbons. [f. F *guillochis*, or f. F *guilloche* the tool used]

guĭ'llotine (gĭ'lotēn; *or* -tē'n) *n.*, & *v.t.* **1.** *n.*

Machine with knife-blade sliding in grooves for beheading; surgical instrument for excising uvula etc.; machine for cutting paper, metal, etc.; ||(Parl.) method of preventing obstruction, by fixing times at which parts of Bill must be voted on. **2.** *v.t.* Use the guillotine upon. [F, f. J.-I. *Guillotin*, Fr. physician d. 1814, who recommended its use for executions in 1789]

guilt (gĭ-) *n.* Fact of having committed a specified or implied offence; (feeling of) culpability; ~ **complex,** (Psych.) mental obsession with idea of having done wrong. [OE *gylt*, of unkn. orig.]

guĭ'ltlėss (gĭ'-) *a.* Innocent (*of* offence); not having knowledge or possession *of* (*guiltless of Greek, soap*, etc.); hence ~LY² *adv.*, ~NESS *n.* [OE *gyltlēas* (as prec., -LESS)]

guĭ'lt|ȳ (gĭ'-) *a.* Criminal, culpable; conscious of or promoted by guilt (*guilty conscience, behaviour, look*); having committed a particular offence (*of*); **~y, not ~y,** (verdicts in criminal trials); hence **~ĭLY**² *adv.*, **~ĭ**NESS *n.* [OE *gyltig* (as GUILT, -Y²)]

guimp. Var. of GIMP¹.

guĭ'nea (gĭ'nĭ) *n.* **1.** (Hist.) Former British gold coin first coined for African trade. **2.** ||Money of account (£1.05) used in stating professional fees, amount of subscriptions, and prices of pictures, horses, estates, etc. **3. ~-corn,** durra; **~-fowl, -hen,** gallinaceous bird of genus *Numida*, esp. *Numida meleagris*, with slate-coloured white-spotted plumage; **G~ grains,** = GRAINS *of Paradise*; **~-pig,** S. Amer. rodent of genus *Cavia* kept as pet or for research in biology, person or thing used as subject for experiment, ||(arch.) person receiving guinea fees, esp. company director or deputy clergyman; **G~ worm,** tropical nematode infecting human and animal skin. [f. *G~* in W. Africa]

gui'pure (gē'poor) *n.* Heavy lace of linen pieces joined by embroidery. [F (*guiper* cover with silk etc. f. Gmc **wīpan* wind round)]

guīse (gīz) *n.* External appearance; semblance, assumed appearance, pretence, (*under* or *in the guise of*); (arch.) style of attire, garb. [ME f. OF, f. Rom. **guisa* f. Frank. **wisa* f. Gmc *wīsō* (WISE²)]

guī'ser (gī'z-) *n.* (Sc. & N. Engl.) Mummer, esp. at Hallowe'en. [f. *guise* v. masquerade (f. prec.) + -ER¹]

guĭtar' (gĭ-) *n.*, & *v.i.* (**-rr-**). **1.** *n.* Six-stringed musical instrument played with fingers or plectrum; **electric ~** (with built-in microphone); hence ~IST (3) *n.* **2.** *v.i.* Play guitar. [f. (F *guitare* f.) Sp. *guitarra* f. Gk *kithara*; cf. CITHERN, GITTERN]

Gujara'tĭ (gōōjerah'-) *n.* & *a.* (Inhabitant or language) of state of Gujarat in W. India. [Hind. (see -I)]

***gŭlch** *n.* Ravine, esp. one with torrent. [perh. f. dial. *gulch* to swallow]

gu'lden (gŏŏ- *or* gōō'-) *n.* = GUILDER. [Du. & G, = GOLDEN]

gūles (-lz) *n.*, & *a.* (usu. placed after *n.*) (esp. Her.) Red. [ME, f. OF *go(u)les* (pl. of *gole* throat) red-dyed fur neck-ornaments]

gŭlf *n.*, & *v.t.* **1.** *n.* (Geog.) portion of sea, proportionally narrower at mouth than bay, partly surrounded by coast; deep hollow, chasm, abyss, (poet.) profound depth of the sea; (arch.) whirlpool, what swallows up anything; impassable gap (Luke 16: 26); wide difference of feelings, opinion, etc.; **G~ Stream,** oceanic warm current flowing from Gulf of Mexico to Europe; **~-weed,** sargasso. **2.** *v.t.* Engulf, swallow up. [ME, f. OF *golfe* f. It. *golfo* f. Rom. **colp(h)us* f. Gk *kolpos* bosom, gulf]

gŭll¹ *n.* Long-winged web-footed aquatic bird of family Laridae, usu. white with mantle varying from pearly-grey to black, and bright bill; **~-wing,** (of door of motor car) opening upwards, (of aeroplane wing) with upward-sloping short inner part and horizontal long outer part; hence ~'ERY (3) *n.* [ME, prob. f. W *gwylan*, Corn. *guilan* f. OCelt. **voilenno-*]

gŭll² *n.*, & *v.t.* (arch. or dial.) Dupe, fool. [perh. f. obs. *gull* yellow f. ON *gulr*]

gŭ'llėt *n.* Food-passage from mouth to stomach, oesophagus; throat. [ME, f. OF dim. of *go(u)le* throat f. L *gula*; see -ET¹]

gŭ'll|ĭble *a.* Easily cheated or duped; hence ~IBI'LITY *n.* [f. GULL² + -IBLE]

gŭ'llȳ¹ *n.*, & *v.t.* **1.** *n.* Water-worn ravine; deep artificial channel, gutter, drain, sink; (Austral. & N.Z.) river valley. **2.** (Cricket). (Position of) fieldsman between point and slips. **3. ~-hole,** opening in street to drain or sewer. **4.** *v.t.* Make gullies in, form (channels) by water action. [f. F *goulet* bottle-neck, f. as GULLET]

||**gŭ'llȳ**² *n.* Large knife. [16th c.; orig. unkn.]

gūlŏ'sĭtȳ *n.* (literary). Gluttony. [f. LL *gulositas* f. L *gulosus* gluttonous (*gula* throat)]

gŭlp *v.* & *n.* **1.** *v.t.* Swallow (*down*) hastily, greedily, or with effort; ~ **back** or **down** *sobs, tears*, suppress. **2.** *v.i.* Perform act of swallowing only with difficulty, gasp, choke. **3.** *n.* Act of gulping (*drained it at one gulp*); effort to swallow; large mouthful of a drink; hence ~'Y² *a.* [ME, prob. f. MDu. *gulpen* (imit.)]

gŭm¹ *n.* (usu. in *pl.*) Firm flesh around roots of teeth; **~'boil,** small abscess on gum; **~-shield,** pad protecting boxer's teeth and gums. [OE *gōma*, = OHG *guomo*, ON *gómr* roof or floor of mouth]

gŭm² *n.* & *v.* (**-mm-**). **1.** *n.* Viscous secretion of some trees and shrubs that hardens on drying but is soluble in water (cf. RESIN), used to stick paper etc. together and stiffen linen etc. **2.** Secretion collecting in inner corner of eye; hard transparent sweet made of gelatin etc.; *= CHEW*ing-gum*; waxy substance round raw-silk filaments; solid deposit in petroleum etc.; = *gum-tree*; *rubber boot. **3.** *Gum* ARABIC; **~'boot,** rubber boot; ~ **dragon,** tragacanth; ~ **juniper,** sandarac; ~ **resin,** vegetable secretion of resin mixed with gum, e.g. gamboge; ***~'shoe,** (1) galosh, (2) (colloq.) stealthy action, (3) (colloq.) detective or policeman; **~-tree,** tree exuding gum, esp. eucalyptus (*up a ~-tree*, in great difficulties). **4.** *v.t.* Stiffen, smear, or cover with gum; fasten *down, together, up, in*, etc., with gum; ~ **up,** interfere with smooth running of, spoil, (esp. *gum up the works*). **5.** *v.i.* Exude gum. [ME, f. OF *gomme* f. Rom. **gumma* f. L *gummi, cummi* f. Gk *kommi* f. Egypt. *kemai*]

gŭm³ *n.* (vulg.) God (in oaths, as *by gum!*). [corrupt. of *God*]

***gŭ'mbō** *n.* (*pl.* **~s**). = OKRA; soup thickened with okra pods; (*G~*) patois of Negroes and Creoles esp. in Louisiana. [Negro wd]

gŭ'mma *n.* (Path.) Morbid growth of gummy tissue in late stage of syphilis; hence **~t**OUS *a.* [mod. L, f. L *gummi* GUM²]

gŭ'mm|ȳ¹ *a.* Viscous, sticky; abounding in or exuding gum; (of ankle or leg) puffy, swollen; hence **~ĭ**NESS *n.* [ME, f. GUM² + -Y²]

gŭ'mm|ȳ² *a.* & *n.* **1.** *a.* Toothless; hence **~ĭ**LY² *adv.* **2.** *n.* (Austral.) small shark (*Mustelus antarcticus*); (Austral. & N.Z.) toothless sheep. [f. GUM¹ + -Y²]

gŭmp *n.* (colloq.) = foll. [abbr.]

gŭ'mption *n.* (colloq.) Resource, enterprising spirit; ready practical sense. [18th c.; Sc., of unkn. orig.]

gŭn *n.* & *v.* (**-nn-**). **1.** *n.* Metal tube for throwing missiles with gunpowder or other propellant;

piece of ordnance, cannon, rifle, carbine, pistol; **big ~,** (sl.) important person; **blow great ~s,** (of wind) blow violently; **give** (engine, motor vehicle) **the ~,** (colloq.) cause acceleration of; **going great ~s,** proceeding vigorously towards success; **son of a ~,** (colloq.) contemptible person (also joc.); SPIKE[1] person's *guns* **stick to** one's **~s,** maintain one's position under attack (lit. or fig.). **2.** Starting-pistol; **beat** or **jump the ~,** start before the signal is given, (fig.) act before permitted or agreed or proper time. **3.** Device for discharging insecticide, grease, electrons, etc., in desired direction. **4.** Member of shooting-party; *gunman. **5. ~'boat,** small vessel of shallow draught and with relatively heavy guns (*~boat diplomacy*, diplomacy supported by use or threat of military force); *gun*-CARRIAGE; **~-cotton,** explosive used for blasting, made by steeping cotton in nitric and sulphuric acids; **~ crew,** team manning gun; **~ dog,** dog trained to follow sportsmen who use guns; ***~-fight,** (colloq.) fight with firearms; **~-fire,** firing of gun(s), esp. (Mil. & Naut.) of morning or evening gun to show time, or independent firing by each gun of a battery; **~-harpoon** (propelled from gun, not by hand); **~-layer,** one whose task is to aim large gun; **~-lock,** mechanism by which charge of gun is exploded; **~'man,** man armed with gun, assassin using gun; **~-metal,** alloy of copper and tin or zinc (formerly used for guns), dull bluish-grey colour; **~ moll,** (sl.) gangster's mistress, woman criminal with gun; **~-pit,** excavation to protect guns and gun crews; **~-play,** use of firearms, gun-fight; **at ~'point,** under threat of injury by a gun; **~'powder,** (1) explosive of saltpetre, sulphur, and charcoal, (*Gunpowder Plot*, 5 Nov. 1605 to blow up Parliament), (2) fine green tea of granular appearance; ||**~'room,** (1) room for sporting-guns etc. in house, (2) compartment in warship fitted up for junior officers or as lieutenants' mess-room [orig. for gunner and his mates]; **~-runner, -running,** (person engaged in) illegal introduction of firearms into country; **~'shot,** (1) shot fired from gun, (2) range of gun (*out of, within, gunshot*); **~-shy,** (esp. of sporting dog) frightened at report of gun; **~-site,** (usu. fortified) emplacement for gun; **~-slinger,** gunman; **~'smith,** maker and repairer of small firearms; **~-stock,** wooden mounting of gun-barrel. **6.** Hence (*heavily* etc.) **~NED**[2] (-nd), ~'LESS, *adjs.* **7.** *v.t.* Shoot at; shoot (*down*); accelerate (engine etc.). **8.** *v.i.* Go shooting; **~ for,** seek with gun, (fig.) seek to attack, harm, or destroy. [ME *gunne, gonne*, perh. f. **Gunna* pet-form of Scand. *Gunnhildr* woman's name]

gŭng-hō' *a.* Enthusiastic, eager. [f. Chin. *kung ho* work together, slogan adopted by U.S. Marines 1942]

gŭnk *n.* (sl.) Viscous or liquid material. [20th c.; orig. **P**]

gŭ'nnel[1] *n.* Small eel-shaped sea-fish (*Pholis gunnellus*). [17th c.; orig. unkn.]

gŭ'nnel[2]. See GUNWALE.

gŭ'nner *n.* Artillery soldier (esp. as official term for private; **Master G~,** R.A. warrant officer in charge of equipment etc. in a fort, or similarly employed); (Naut.) warrant officer in charge of battery, magazine, etc. (**~'s daughter,** (joc.) gun to which sailors were lashed for flogging); member of aircraft crew who operates gun; game-shooter. [ME, f. GUN; see -ER[2] (2)]

gŭ'nnera *n.* Ornamental foliage plant of genus *Gunnera*, with large leaves. [f. J. E. *Gunnerus*, Norw. botanist d. 1773 + -A 1]

gŭ'nnerȳ *n.* Construction and management of large guns; firing of guns. [f. GUN + -ERY]

gŭ'nnȳ *n.* Coarse sacking, sack, usu. of jute fibre. [f. Hindi & Marathi *gōnī* f. Skr. *gōṇi* sack]

gŭ'nter *n.* **1.** Flat 2-ft. rule with scales, logarithmic lines, etc., used for solving mechanically problems in surveying and navigation. **2.** Topmast, or its sail, sliding up and down lower mast on rings [from resemblance to sliding gunter]. **3. G~'s chain,** 66-ft. surveying chain; **G~'s scale,** = sense 1. [f. E. *Gunter*, Engl. mathematician d. 1626]

gŭ'nwale (-nal), **gŭ'nnel**[2], *n.* Upper edge of ship's or boat's side (**~ to, under,** level with, below, surface of water). [f. GUN + WALE (because formerly used to support guns)]

gŭ'nyah *n.* (Austral.) Aboriginal hut, bush hut. [Aboriginal]

gŭp *n.* (colloq.) Silly talk, nonsense. [orig. Anglo-Ind., f. Hindi, = gossip]

gŭ'ppȳ[1] *n.* Small W. Ind. fish freq. kept in aquaria. [f. R. J. L. *Guppy*, 19th-c. Trinidad clergyman who sent first specimen to British Museum]

gŭ'ppȳ[2] *n.* Streamlined submarine with schnorkel. [f. *g*reater *u*nderwater *p*ropulsive *p*ower + -Y[3]]

gûrgĭtā'tion *n.* Surging, bubbling motion or sound. [f. mod. L **gurgitatio* f. LL *gurgitare* to surge f. L *gurges gurgitis* whirlpool; see -ATION]

gûr'gle *v.i.* & *t.*, & *n.* (Make) bubbling sound as of water from bottle or among stones; utter with such sound. [imit., or f. Du. *gorgelen*, G *gurgeln*, or med. L *gurgulare* f. L *gurgulio* gullet]

gûr'jun *n.* E. Ind. tree of genus *Dipterocarpus* yielding an oleo-resin (**~ balsam**) used medicinally or as varnish. [f. Bengali *garjan*]

gûrk *n.*, & *v.i.* & *t.* (colloq.) Belch. [imit.]

Gûr'kha (-ka; *or* goor'-) *n.* Member of dominant Hindu race in Nepal, forming regiments in British army. [native name, f. Skr. *gāus* cow + *raksh* protect]

gûr'nard, gûr'nėt, *n.* Sea-fish of family Triglidae, with large head, mailed cheeks, and three finger-like pectoral rays. [ME, f. OF *gornart*, **gronart* (*gron*(*d*)*ir* to grunt f. L *grunnire*)]

gu'ru (go͞o'ro͞o) *n.* Hindu spiritual teacher or head of religious sect; influential teacher; revered mentor. [f. Hindi *gurū* teacher f. Skr. *gurús* grave, dignified]

gŭsh *v.i.* & *t.*, & *n.* **1.** (Issue in, send forth) sudden or copious stream (lit., or fig. of speech, tenderness, etc.); emit (water) copiously; (speak or behave with) effusiveness or sentimental affectation. **2.** Hence ~'ER[1] *n.*, (esp.) oil-well from which oil flows without being pumped, ~'ING[2], ~'Y[2], *adjs.* [ME *gosshe, gusche*, prob. imit.]

gŭ'ssėt *n.* Piece let into garment etc. to strengthen or enlarge some part; iron bracket strengthening angle of structure; hence ~ED[2] *a.* [ME, f. OF *gousset* (*gousse* pod, shell) flexible piece filling up joint in armour]

gŭ'ssȳ *v.t.* (sl.) Smarten *up*. [perh. f. *Augustus*]

gŭst[1] *n.*, & *v.i.* **1.** *n.* Sudden violent rush of wind; burst of rain, fire, smoke, sound, or passion. **2.** *v.i.* Blow in gusts. [f. ON *gustr*, cogn. w. *gjósa* to gush]

gŭst[2] *n.* (arch. or poet.) Sense of taste; keen relish (**have a ~ of,** appreciate); flavour. [ME, f. L *gustus* taste]

gŭstā'tion *n.* Tasting; so **gŭ'st**ATIVE, **gŭ'sta**TORY, *adjs.* [F, or f. L *gustatio* (*gustare* f. *gustus* taste; see -ATION)]

gŭ'stō *n.* (*pl.* ~es). **1.** Zest, enjoyment with which something is done. **2.** (arch.) Relish or liking *for*; style of artistic execution. [It., f. as GUST[2]]

gŭ'st|ȳ *a.* **1.** Characterized by, blown by, gusts. **2.** Characterized by gusto. **3.** Hence ~ĭLY[2] *adv.*, ~ĭNESS *n.* [f. GUST[1] + -Y[2]]

gŭt *n.*, *a.*, & *v.t.* (**-tt-**). **1.** *n.* (in *pl.*) Bowels or entrails (esp. of animals); contents of anything (**has no ~s in it,** is of no real value or force; **hate** person's **~s,** (colloq.) dislike him intensely; **sweat** or **work** one's **~s out,** (colloq.) work extremely hard). **2.** (Particular part of) lower alimentary canal, intestine; **~-rot,** (colloq.) = ROT²-*gut*. **3.** (in *pl.*, vulg.) Belly as seat of appetite. **4.** (in *pl.*, colloq.) Pluck, force of character, staying power. **5.** Material for violin or racket strings or surgical use made from intestines of animals; material for fishing-lines made from intestines of silkworm. **6.** Narrow water-passage, sound, straits; defile, narrow passage. **7.** Hence **~′**LESS *a.*, lacking energy or determination. **8.** *a.* Fundamental (*a gut issue*); instinctive (*a gut reaction*). **9.** *v.t.* Take out guts of, clean, (fish); remove or destroy (esp. by fire) internal fittings of (house etc.); extract essence of (book etc.). [OE *guttas* pl., prob. cogn. w. *gēotan* pour]

gŭts *v.i.* (colloq.) Eat greedily. [f. prec.]

gŭ′tser *n.* (Austral., N.Z., & colloq.) Heavy fall. [f. GUTS + -ER¹]

gŭ′ts|ȳ *a.* **1.** Greedy. **2.** Courageous. **3.** Hence **~**ĬLY² *adv.*, **~**ĬNESS *n.* [f. GUTS + -Y²]

gŭtta-per′cha (*or* -ka) *n.* Tough greyish-black plastic substance got from latex of various Malayan trees. [f. Malay *getah* gum + *percha* name of tree]

gŭ′ttāte *a.* (Biol.) Having droplike markings. [f. L *guttatus* speckled (*gutta* drop; see -ATE²)]

gŭ′tter *n.* & *v.* **1.** *n.* Track made by flow of water. **2.** Shallow trough below eaves, or channel at side of street, carrying off rain-water; **the ~,** place of low breeding or vulgar behaviour. **3.** Open conduit for outflow of fluid; groove; hence **~**ING¹ (3) *n.* **4. ~ press,** journalism catering for depraved or vulgar tastes; **~snipe,** street urchin. **5.** *v.t.* Furrow, channel. **6.** *v.i.* Flow in streams; (of candle) melt away by becoming channelled so that wax etc. runs down. [ME f. AF *gotere*, OF *gotiere* f. Rom. **guttaria* f. L *gutta* drop; see -ER²]

gŭ′ttle *v.t.* & *i.* Eat gluttonously. [f. GUT, after *guzzle*]

gŭ′ttural *a.* & *n.* **1.** *a.* Of the throat; (of sound) coming from the throat. **2.** *n.* & *a.* (Phonet.) (Consonant) produced in throat or by back of tongue and palate (as *k*, *g*). **3.** Hence **~**IZE (3) *v.t.*, **~**ISM (1) *n.*, **~**LY² *adv.* [F, or f. med. L *gutturalis*, f. L *guttur* throat; see -AL]

||**gŭv,** ||**gŭ′v′nor,** *ns.* (vulg. or colloq.) = GOVERNOR. [corrupt.]

guy¹ (gī) *n.*, & *v.t.* **1.** *n.* Rope, chain, etc., to steady load of crane etc. or hold tent etc. in place. **2.** *v.t.* Secure with guy(s). [prob. of LG orig.; cf. LG, Du. *gei* brail etc.]

guy² (gī) *n.*, & *v.t.* **1.** *n.* ||Effigy of Guy Fawkes in ragged clothing, burnt on 5 Nov.; ||grotesquely dressed person; (sl.) man, fellow; ||(sl.) act of decamping (**give the ~ to,** escape from; **do a ~,** disappear). **2.** *v.t.* Exhibit in effigy; ridicule. [f. *Guy* Fawkes, conspirator in GUNpowder Plot]

gŭ′zzle *v.* **1.** *v.i.* & *t.* Drink or eat greedily. **2.** *v.t.* Consume (money etc.; *away*) in guzzling. **3.** Hence **gŭ′zzl**ER¹ *n.* [perh. f. OF *gosiller* chatter, vomit (*gosier* throat)]

gwȳ′nĭad *n.* White-fleshed fish found in Lake Bala, Wales. [W (*gwyn* white)]

gȳbe, ***jībe**², *v.i.* & *t.*, & *n.* (Of fore-and-aft sail or boom) swing across, make (sail) do this, in wearing or running before wind; (of ship, crew, etc.) change (of) course so that this happens. [f. obs. Du. *gijben*]

gȳm *n.* (colloq.) Gymnasium, gymnastics; **~-slip, ~t′unic,** schoolgirl's sleeveless usu. belted garment reaching from shoulder to thigh. [abbr.]

gȳmkha′na (-kah′-) *n.* (orig. Anglo-Ind.) Public place with facilities for athletics; athletic-sports display; meeting for competition between horse-riders, vehicle-drivers, etc. [f. Hindi *gendkhāna* ball-house, racket-court, assim. to foll.]

gȳmnā′sĭ|um (-z-) *n.* (*pl.* **~ums** *or* **~a**). **1.** Place, room, or building, with appliances for practice in gymnastics. **2.** (*or* gĭmnah′ziŏŏm). Continental, esp. German, school of highest grade, preparing pupils for universities; hence **~**AL *a.* [L, f. Gk *gumnasion* (*gumnazō* exercise f. *gumnos* naked)]

gȳ′mnăst *n.* Expert in gymnastics. [f. F *gymnaste* or f. Gk *gumnastēs* athlete-trainer (*gumnazō*; see prec.)]

gȳmnă′st|ĭc *a.* & *n.* **1.** *a.* Of gymnastics, involving bodily or mental exercise, discipline, effort, or activity; hence **~**ICALLY *adv.* **2.** *n.* Course of instruction regarded as discipline; gymnastic feat. **3.** Hence **~**ICS *n. pl.* (occas. treated as *sing.*), exercises developing the muscles (esp. such as are performed in gymnasium) or the mind. [f. L f. Gk *gumnastikos* (as GYMNASIUM; see -IC)]

gȳ′mno- *comb. form.* (Biol.) Bare, as: **~sperm, ~sper′mous,** (plant) having seeds unprotected by seed-vessels, opp. *angiosperm*(*ous*). [f. Gk *gumnos* naked + -O-]

gȳmnŏ′soph|ĭst *n.* One of ancient Hindu philosophic sect going nearly naked and given up to contemplation; so **~**Y¹ *n.* [ME, f. F *gymnosophiste* f. L f. Gk *gumnosophistai* pl. (as prec., SOPHIST)]

gymp. See GIMP¹.

gȳnaecē′um (*or* g-; *or* -nĭs-) *n.* **1.** (Gk & Rom. Ant.) Women's apartments in house. **2.** (Bot.) = GYNOECIUM. [L, f. Gk *gunaikeion* (*gunē gunaikos* woman)]

gȳnaeco- (g-) *comb. form.* Woman, women, as: **gynaecŏ′**CRACY (gīnĭ-) *n.*, **~ma′stia,** condition of man's breasts when they resemble woman's in size and function. [f. Gk *gunē gunaikos* woman + -O-]

gȳnaecŏ′|logȳ (gīnĭ-) *n.* Science of physiological functions and diseases of women; hence ***~**LO′GIC, **~**LO′GICAL, (-olŏ′-) *adjs.*, **~**LOGIST *n.* [f. prec. + -LOGY]

gȳnă′ndromôrph (g-) *n.* (Biol.) Individual (esp. insect) having some parts male and others female; hence **~**IC *a.*, **~**ISM (2) *n.*, (-ôr′-). [f. as foll. + Gk *morphē* form]

gȳnă′ndrous (g-) *a.* (Bot.) With stamens and pistil united in one column as in orchids. [f. Gk *gunandros* (*gunē* woman, *anēr andros* man) of doubtful sex + -OUS]

gȳ′no- (g-) *comb. form.* **1.** = GYNAECO- (*gyno′*-CRACY, *gyno*PHO′BIA). **2.** (Bot.) Of pistils or ovaries, as: **~base,** enlarged part of receptacle supporting gynoecium. [abbr. of GYNAECO-]

gȳnoe′cĭ|um (gīnē′-) *n.* (*pl.* **~a**). (Bot.) Carpels taken collectively. [orig. GYNAECEUM, infl. by Gk *oikion* house; cf. ANDROECIUM]

-gȳnous (g- *or* j-) *suf.* (Bot.) forming *adjs.* = having specified female organs or pistils (*monogynous*, *androgynous*). [f. mod. L f. Gk *-gunos* (*gunē* woman) + -OUS]

||**gȳp**¹ *n.* College servant at Cambridge and Durham (cf. SCOUT¹ 5). [perh. for obs. *gippo* scullion, orig. man's short tunic, f. obs. F *jupeau*]

gȳp² *n.* (colloq.) **Give** person **~,** scold or punish or defeat him unmercifully, pain him. [19th c., perh. f. GEE-UP]

gȳp³ *v.t.* (**-pp-**), & *n.* Cheat, swindle. [19th c.; perh. f. GYP¹]

gȳ′ppȳ. Var. of GIPPY.

gȳpsŏ′phĭla *n.* Garden plant of genus *Gypsophila*,

with profusion of small usu. white composite flowers. [mod. L, f. Gk *gupsos* chalk + *philos* loving]

gў'ps|um *n.* Hydrated calcium sulphate, mineral used to make plaster of Paris or as dressing for crop-land; hence ~EOUS, ~ĭ'FEROUS, *adjs.* [L, f. Gk *gupsos*]

gў'psў. See GIPSY.

gȳr'ate[1] *a.* (Bot.) Arranged in rings or convolutions. [f. L *gyratus* (as GYRE; see -ATE[2])]

gȳr|ā'te[2] *v.i.* Go in circle or spiral, revolve, whirl; hence or cogn. ~A'TION *n.*, **gȳr'at**ORY *a.* [f. LL *gyrare* (as foll.) + -ATE[3]]

gȳr'e *v.i.*, & *n.* (esp. poet.) Gyrate; gyration. [(v. f. LL *gyrare*) f. L f. Gk *guros* ring]

gyr'falcon (jẽr'faw-; *or* -fŏ-) *n.* Large northern falcon of subgenus *Hierofalco.* [ME, f. OF *gerfaucon* f. Frank. *gērfalco* f. ON *geirfálki*; see FALCON]

gȳr'ō *n.* (*pl.* **~s**). **1.** (colloq.) = GYROSCOPE or *gyro-compass.* **2. ~-compass,** compass giving true north and bearings from it by means of a gyroscope; **~-pilot,** gyro-compass used for automatic steering; **~-stabilizer,** gyroscopic device for keeping ship in equilibrium position. [abbr.]

gȳr'o- *comb. form.* Rotation, as: **~graph,** instrument recording revolutions; **~magne'tic,** of the magnetic and mechanical properties of a rotating charged particle, (of compass) combining gyroscope and normal magnetic compass; **~plane,** form of aircraft deriving its lift mainly from freely rotating overhead vanes. [f. Gk *guros* ring + -o-]

gȳr'oscōpe *n.* Rotating wheel whose axis is free to turn but maintains fixed direction in absence of perturbing forces, esp. as used for stabilization or to replace compass in ship etc.; hence **gȳroscŏ'p**IC *a.* [F (as prec., -SCOPE)]

gȳr'|us *n.* (*pl.* **~i** *pr.* -ī). Fold or convolution, esp. of brain. [L, f. Gk *guros* ring]

gў'ttja (yĭ'cha) *n.* (Geol.) Lake deposit of usu. black sediment containing much organic material. [Sw., = mud, ooze]

gȳve *n.* (usu. in *pl.*), & *v.t.* (poet.) Shackle, fetter. [ME *give*, of unkn. orig.]

H

H, h, (āch) *n.* (*pl.* **Hs** *or* **H's,** *pr.* ā'chĭz). Eighth letter of alphabet; DROP[2] one's *h's*; **H-iron,** girder of H-shaped section.

H. *abbr.* hardness; hard (pencil-lead); henry(s).

h. *abbr.* hecto-; horse; hot; hour(s); husband.

H *symb.* hydrogen.

ha[1] (hah) *int.* expr. surprise, joy, suspicion, hesitation, triumph, etc.; cf. HA HA. [ME]

ha[2] (hah) *v.i.*, & *n.* (*pl.* **ha's**). See HUM[1,2]. [f. prec.]

ha. *abbr.* hectare(s).

haar (har̄) *n.* Cold sea-fog on E. coast of England or Scotland. [perh. f. ON *hárr* hoar(y)]

Hab. *abbr.* Habakkuk (O.T.).

habaner'a (ahbanar̄'*a*) *n.* Cuban dance in slow duple time. [Sp., fem. of *habanero* of Havana in Cuba]

hābėas cor̄'pus *n.* Writ requiring person to be brought before judge or into court, esp. to investigate lawfulness of his restraint; **Habeas Corpus Act** (of Charles II, 1679, facilitating use of this). [L, = you must have the body]

hă'berdăsh|er *n.* ||Dealer in small articles of dress etc.; *dealer in men's wear; hence ~ERY (1, 3) *n.* [ME, prob. f. AF **haberdasser*, **hapertasser* (*hapertas* perh. name of fabric, of unkn. orig.)]

hă'bergeon (-jon) *n.* (Hist.) Sleeveless coat of mail. [ME, f. OF *haubergeon* (as HAUBERK; see -OON)]

hă'bĭle *a.* (literary). Skilful, dextrous. [ME, var. of ABLE]

habĭ'lĭment *n.* **1.** (in *pl.*) Dress suited to any office or occasion (joc. of ordinary clothes). **2.** (arch.) Equipment, attire. [ME, f. OF (*h*)*abillement* (*habiller* fit out f. *habile* ABLE; see -MENT)]

habĭ'lĭt|āte *v.i.* Qualify for office (esp. as teacher in German Univ.); hence ~A'TION *n.* [f. med. L *habilitare* (as ABILITY) + -ATE[3]]

hă'bĭt[1] *n.* **1.** Settled tendency or practice (*he is in, has* (*fallen into*), *the* or *a* (*bad*) *habit of contradiction*); **creature of ~,** one whose behaviour is guided by his habits; **from** (**force of**) **~, out of ~,** because it has been one's custom; **make a ~ of,** do regularly; **get out of the ~ of,** cease to do regularly. **2.** Mental constitution, esp. *habit of mind*; bodily constitution (*a man of corpulent habit*); (Biol. & Cryst.) mode of growth. **3.** Dress of particular class etc., esp. religious order; (**riding-**)**~,** woman's riding-dress; (arch.) dress. **4.** (Psych.) Automatic reaction to a specific situation. **5.** (colloq.) The practice of taking drugs as addict; hence **~-forming** *a.* [ME f. OF *abit*, f. L *habitus* (*habēre habit-* have, (refl.) be constituted)]

hă'bĭt[2] *v.t.* **1.** (usu. in *p.p.*) Clothe. **2.** (arch.) Inhabit. [f. OF *habiter* f. L *habitare* inhabit (as prec.)]

hă'bĭt|able *a.* That can be inhabited; hence ~ABI'LITY, **~able**NESS (-beln-), *ns.*, **~ab**LY[2] *adv.* [ME f. OF, f. L *habitabilis* (as prec.; see -ABLE)]

hă'bĭtant *n.* **1.** Inhabitant. **2.** (*pr.* ăbētah'ṅ). (Descendant of) early French settler in Canada etc. [F (as HABIT[2]; see -ANT)]

hă'bĭtăt *n.* Natural home of plant or animal; habitation. [L, 3rd sing. pres. (as HABIT[2])]

hăbĭtā'tion *n.* Inhabiting (*fit for human habitation*); place of abode, house or home. [ME f. OF, f. L *habitatio -onis* (as HABIT[2]; see -ATION)]

habĭ'tūal *a.* Customary; constant, continual; given to (specified) habit (*habitual drunkard*); hence ~LY[2] *adv.*, ~NESS *n.* [f. med. L *habitualis* (as HABIT[1]; see -AL)]

habĭ'tū|āte *v.t.* Accustom (*to* thing, *to* doing); so ~A'TION *n.* [f. LL *habituare* (as HABIT[1]) + -ATE[3]]

hă'bĭtūde *n.* Mental or bodily disposition; custom, tendency. [ME f. OF, f. L *habitudo -dinis* (*habēre habit-* have; see -TUDE)]

habitué (habĭ'tūā) *n.* Habitual visitor or resident. [F, p.p. of *habituer* (as HABITUATE)]

habutai' (hahbōōtī') *n.* Soft Japanese silk fabric. [f. Jap. *habutae*]

||**H.A.C.** *abbr.* Honourable Artillery Company.

hăchur'es (-shūr') *n. pl.* Lines used in hill-shading on maps to indicate steepness of slope by their closeness. [F (*hacher* HATCH[3]; see -URE)]

hăciĕ'nda *n.* Estate or plantation with dwelling-house, or factory, in Spanish-speaking country. [Sp., f. L *facienda* things to be done]

hăck[1] *n.* Mattock; miner's pick; (gash, wound, esp. from) kick with toe of boot. [ME, partly f. MLG *hakke* (as foll.), partly f. foll.]

hăck² *v.* **1.** *v.t.* Cut, notch, mangle; kick shin of (opponent at football). **2.** *v.i.* Deal cutting blows (*at*); **a ~'ing** (short dry frequent) **cough**; **~-saw** (for metal-cutting). [OE *haccian* cut in pieces, = MLG, MDu., MHG *hacken* f. WG **hakkon* (**hak-*, imit.)]

hăck³ *n.* Board on which hawk's meat is laid; (of eyas hawk) **at ~**, not allowed to prey for itself. [var. of HATCH¹, perh. assoc. w. HECK¹]

hăck⁴ *n.* & *a.* **1.** *n.* Horse let out for hire; = JADE¹ 1; horse for ordinary riding; common drudge, uninspired writer or other worker; *taxi. **2.** *a.* Used as a hack; typical of a hack, commonplace. [abbr. of HACKNEY]

hăck⁵ *v.* **1.** *v.t.* Make common, hackney. **2.** *v.t.* & *i.* Ride (horse), ride on horseback, on road at ordinary pace; **~'ing coat** or **jacket** (with slits at sides or back and slanting pockets). [f. prec.]

***hă'ckberrÿ** *n.* (Purple edible berry of) N. Amer. tree of genus *Celtis*. [var. of *hagberry*, of Norse orig.]

hă'ckerÿ *n.* (Ind.) Bullock-cart. [f. Hindi *chhakrā* two-wheeled cart]

hă'ckle¹ *n.*, & *v.t.* **1.** *n.* Steel flax-comb. **2.** Long feathers on neck of domestic cock and other birds; **with his ~s rising** or **up,** (lit. of cock, fig. of dog, man) angry, ready to fight. **3.** Artificial fly dressed with hackle. **4.** Feather in Highland soldier's bonnet. **5.** *v.t.* Dress (flax, fly) with hackle. [ME *hechele, hakele*, f. OE **hæcel* f. WG **hakila* (**hak* HOOK¹)]

hă'ckle² *v.t.* Hack, mangle. [f. HACK² + -LE 3]

hă'cklÿ *a.* Rough, jagged. [f. prec. + -Y²]

hă'ckmatăck *n.* Amer. larch; its wood. [Amer. Ind.]

hă'ckney *n.*, & *v.t.* **1.** *n.* Horse of middle size and quality for ordinary riding; **~ cab, carriage, coach,** (kept for hire). **2.** *v.t.* (esp. in *p.p.*) Make common or trite by indiscriminate use. [ME, perh. f. pastures at *Hackenei* (Hackney) in Middlesex, whence horses may have been taken to Smithfield market]

had. See HAVE¹.

hă'ddock, (esp. Sc.) **hă'ddĭe,** *n.* Food-fish (*Melanogrammus aeglefinus*) of N. Atlantic, allied to cod but smaller. [ME, prob. f. AF *hadoc*, OF (*h*)*adot*, of unkn. orig.]

hāde *n.*, & *v.i.* (Geol. & Mining). Incline from the vertical. [17th c., perh. dial. form of *head*]

Hā'dēs (-z) *n.* (Gk Myth.) lower world, abode of departed spirits; (euphem.) = HELL 2. [f. Gk *haidēs* (orig. a name of Pluto), transl. Heb. *šᵉʼôl*]

Hă'dĭth *n.* Body of traditions relating to Muhammad. [f. Arab. *ḥadīṯ* tradition]

hădj, hăjj, *n.* Pilgrimage to Mecca. [f. Arab. *ḥājj* pilgrimage]

hă'djĭ, hă'jjĭ, *n.* Muslim who has been to Mecca; (*H~*) title of such person. [f. Pers. & Turk. *ḥāj*(*j*)*i* pilgrim (as prec.)]

hadn't. See HAVE¹.

hă'drŏn *n.* (Phys.) Strongly interacting elementary particle; hence **hădrŏ'nic** *a.* [f. Gk *hadros* bulky + -ON]

hădst. See HAVE¹.

haeccē'ĭtÿ (hěks-) *n.* (Philos.) Quality of being describable as 'this'; individuality. [f. med. L *haecceitas* (*haec* fem. of *hic* this; see -ITY)]

haem, hēme, *n.* Red compound containing iron and forming non-protein part of haemoglobin. [f. Gk *haima* blood or f. HAEMOGLOBIN]

hae'mal, *hē'mal, *a.* (Anat.) Of the blood; situated on same side of body as the heart and great blood-vessels, ventral. [f. Gk *haima* blood + -AL]

haemă'tĭc, *hēm-, *a.* Of or containing blood. [f. Gk *haimatikos* (as foll.; see -IC)]

hae'matĭn, *hě'm-, *n.* Bluish-black amorphous substance, constituent of haemoglobin. [f. Gk *haima -matos* blood + -IN]

hae'matīte, *hě'm-, *n.* Ferric oxide as ore. [f. L f. Gk *haimatitēs* (*lithos*) bloodlike stone (as prec.; see -ITE¹)]

hae'mato-, *hě'mato-, *comb. form.* Blood, as: **~cele, h(a)emato'ma,** tumour containing extravasated blood; **~crit** [f. Gk *kritēs* judge], (instrument for determining) ratio of volume of red cells to total volume of blood sample; **~logy** (-ŏ'l-), study of physiology of blood; **h(a)ematur'ia,** (Path.) presence of blood in urine. [f. Gk *haimat-* (*haima* blood)]

-hae'mĭa. Var. of -AEMIA.

hae'mo-, *hě'mo-, *comb. form.* = HAEMATO-. [abbr.]

haemocȳ'anĭn, *hēm-, *n.* Oxygen-carrying substance containing copper, present in blood plasma of arthropods and molluscs. [f. prec. + *cyanin* blue pigment (as CYAN; see -IN)]

haemoglō'bĭn, *hēm-, *n.* Oxygen-carrying substance containing iron, present in red blood--cells of vertebrates. [f. *haematoglobulin*, compound of HAEMATIN and GLOBULIN]

haemŏ'lÿ|sĭs, *hēm-, *n.* (*pl.* **~ses** *pr.* -sēz). Loss of haemoglobin from red blood-cells; so **~TIC** (-ĭ'tĭk) *a.* [f. HAEMO- + -LYSIS]

haemophĭ'l|ĭa, *hēm-, *n.* (Med.) (Hereditary) tendency to severe bleeding from even a slight injury, through failure of blood to clot quickly; hence **~ĬAC** *n.*, sufferer from haemophilia, **~IC** *a.* [mod. L, f. as HAEMO- + -PHILIA]

hae'morrhage, *hě'm-, (hě'merĭj) *n.* Escape (esp. profuse) of blood from blood-vessels, bleeding. [earlier *haemorrhagy* f. F *hémorr*(*h*)*agie* f. L f. Gk *haimorrhagia* (*haima* blood, st. of *rhēgnumi* burst)]

hae'morrhoid, *hě'm-, (hě'meroid) *n.* (usu. in *pl.*) Swollen venous tissue near anus. [ME *emeroudis* (Bibl. *emerods*) f. OF *emeroyde*, & f. L f. Gk *haimorrhoides* (*phlebes*) bleeding (veins) (*haima* blood, *-rhoos* -flowing)]

haemŏ'sta|sĭs, *hēm-, *n.* (*pl.* **~ses** *pr.* -sēz). Stoppage of flow of blood; so **~TIC** (hěmostă'tĭk) *a.* [f. HAEMO- + -STASIS]

haer'ēmai (hīr'ĭmī) *int.* (N.Z.) Welcome. [Maori, lit. 'come hither']

ha'fĭz (hah'-) *n.* Muslim who knows Koran by heart. [Pers., f. Arab. *ḥāfiẓ* guardian]

hă'fnĭum *n.* (Chem.) Metallic element resembling and usu. accompanying zirconium. [mod. L, f. *Hafnia*, Da. (*København*)*havn*, Copenhagen + -IUM]

haft (hah-) *n.*, & *v.t.* **1.** *n.* Handle (of dagger, knife, etc.). **2.** *v.t.* Furnish (knife etc.) with haft. [OE *hæft*(*e*), = OHG *hefti*, ON *hepti* f. Gmc **haftjam* (**haf-* HEAVE¹)]

hăg¹ *n.* Ugly old woman; witch; **~('fish)**, parasite fish allied to lamprey; **~'ridden,** afflicted by nightmare, mentally harassed; hence **~'GISH¹** (-g-) *a.* [ME *hegge, hagge*, perh. f. OE *hægtesse*, OHG *hagazissa*, of unkn. orig.]

hăg² *n.* (Sc. & N. Engl.) Soft place in moor; firm place in bog. [cf. ON *högg* gap, cogn. w. HEW]

Hag. *abbr.* Haggai (O.T.).

Hagga'dah (-gah'da) *n.* Legendary illustrative part of the Talmud; book recited at Seder. [Heb., = tale (*higgîḏ* tell)]

hă'ggard *a.* & *n.* **1.** *a.* Wild-looking (esp. as result of fatigue, privation, worry, etc.). **2.** (Of hawk) caught when in the adult plumage, untamed. **3.** Hence **~LY²** *adv.*, **~NESS** *n.* **4.** *n.* Haggard hawk. [f. F *hagard*, perh. cogn. w. HEDGE¹]

‖hă'ggĭs (-g-) *n.* Minced heart, lungs, and liver, of sheep etc., boiled in maw or artificial bag with suet, oatmeal, etc. [ME; orig. unkn.]

hă'ggle *v.i.*, & *n.* Dispute, wrangle, (*about* or *over* price etc.). [earlier sense 'hack' f. f. ON *höggva* HEW + -LE 3]

hă'gio- (-g-) *comb. form.* Saint(ly), as: **~cracy** (-ŏ'k-), government by holy persons; **H~-grapha** (-ŏ'g-), 12 books of the Hebrew Scriptures not included under Law and Prophets; **~grapher** (-ŏ'g-), **~gra'phic,** (writer) of any of these, or of saints' lives; **~graphy** (-ŏ'g-), writing of saints' lives; **~latry** (-ŏ'l-), worship of saints; **~logy** (-ŏ'l-), literature treating of lives and legends of saints; **~scope,** = SQUINT 4. [f. Gk *hagios* holy + -o-]

hah. Var. of HA[1,2].

ha ha (hah hah') *int.* repr. laughter. [OE; cf. HA[1]]

ha-ha (hah'hah) *n.* Sunk fence bounding park or garden. [F, perh. from cry of surprise at discovering the obstacle]

hai(c)k (*or* hah'ĭk) *n.* Arab's outer wrapper for head and body. [f. Moroccan Arab. *ḥā'ik*]

hai'ku (hī'ko͞o) *n.* (*pl.* same). (English imitation of) Japanese three-line poem of 17 syllables. [Jap.]

hail[1] *n.* Pellets of frozen rain falling in shower or **~'storm**; shower *of* missiles, curses, questions, etc.; **~'stone,** pellet of hail; hence **~'**Y[2] *a.* [OE *hagol, hægl,* = OS, OHG *hagal,* ON *hagl* f. Gmc **hag(a)laz, -am*]

hail[2] *v.* **1.** *v.i. impers.* **It ~s** or **is ~ing,** hail falls. **2.** *v.t.* & *i.* (fig.) Pour down (blows, words, etc.), come down violently. [OE *hagalian* (as prec.)]

hail[3] *int.* of greeting (*to*); ALL *hail*; **~-fellow, ~-fellow-well-met,** (too) intimate *with* (person); **H~ Mary,** = AVE *Maria.* [ellipt. use of obs. *hail* a. f. ON *heill* sound, HALE[1], WHOLE]

hail[4] *v.* & *n.* **1.** *v.t.* Salute; greet (person etc. (*as*) king etc.; *hail him king*). **2.** Call to (ship, person) to attract attention (**within ~ing distance,** close enough to do this, lit. or fig.); LOUD *hailer.* **3.** *v.i.* (Of ship, person) have come *from* (place). **4.** *n.* Salutation (**within ~,** close enough to be hailed). [ME, f. prec.]

hair *n.* **1.** One of the fine filaments growing from skin of animals, esp. from human head; (collect. *sing.* or arch. *pl.*) all such filaments on person's head etc.; mass of hairs used in manufacture etc.; elongated cell growing from epidermis of plant; hairlike thing; very small quantity. **2. Against the ~,** (fig.) against the grain; *hair of the* DOG[1] *that bit* one; **~ on end** (standing erect with fright or horror); **in** person's **~,** (colloq.) encumbering or annoying him; **keep** one's **~ on,** (sl.) remain calm; **let** one's **~ down,** (of woman) release it from chignon etc., (fig., colloq.) cease to be formal, behave unconventionally or unrestrainedly; *make* person's *hair* CURL[2]; **not turn a ~,** show no sign of exhaustion or discomposure; **put up** one's **~,** (of woman) arrange it in dressed state, not loose or in ringlets etc.; *get* or *have by the* SHORT *hairs*; SPLIT[1] *hairs*; TEAR[1] one's *hair*; **to a ~,** exactly. **3. ~'breadth** or **~'s breadth,** minute distance (*~breadth escape*, very narrow); **~'brush,** brush for smoothing the hair; **~'cloth** (made of hair, for various purposes); **~ crack,** short narrow crack in metal; **~'cut,** (style of) cutting of the hair; **~-do,** (colloq.) style or process of woman's hairdressing; **~'dresser,** one whose business is to dress and cut (*women's) hair; **~-grass** (of genus *Aira* etc., with slender stems); ||**~-grip,** flat hairpin with ends close together; **~-line,** (1) line or rope made of hair, (2) thin up-stroke in writing, thin stroke in printed letter, (3) edge of person's hair on forehead etc., (4) very narrow line, crack, stripe, etc.; **~-piece,** quantity of false hair augmenting person's natural hair; **~'pin** (U-shaped, for fastening the hair; *~pin bend*, very sharp doubling-back of road); **~-raising,** enough to make hair stand on end through fear or excitement; **~-restorer,** substance used to promote growth of hair; **~ shirt** (of haircloth, for penitents or ascetics); ||**~-slide,** hinged clip of horn or tortoise-shell or plastic for keeping hair in position; **~-space,** (Typogr.) very thin space between words or letters; **~-splitting** *a.* & *n.*, over-subtle(ty); **~'spring,** fine spring regulating balance-wheel in watch; **~-streak,** butterfly of genus *Strymon* etc. with fine streaks on wings; **~-stroke,** thin up-stroke in writing; **~-style,** particular way of dressing the hair; **~-stylist,** one who chooses (and constructs) hair-styles for individual persons; **~-trigger,** secondary trigger releasing main one by slight pressure. **4.** Hence (-)**~**ED[2] (hārd), **~'**LESS, **~'**LIKE, *adjs.* [OE *hǣr, hēr,* = OS, OHG *hār,* ON *hár* f. Gmc **hǣram*]

hair'|ȳ *a.* Having much hair; made of hair; (sl.) difficult, unpleasant, crude, clumsy; **~y-heeled,** (sl.) uncouth, ill-bred; hence **~ĭ**NESS *n.* [ME, f. prec. + -Y[2]]

hă'jj(ĭ). See HADJ(I).

hāke[1] *n.* Edible fish of genus *Merluccius* like cod. [ME, perh. f. **hakefish* f. dial. *hake* hook + FISH[1]]

hāke[2] *n.* Wooden frame for drying cheeses, bricks, etc. [cogn. w. or var. of HECK[1]]

hakenkreuz (hah'ken-kroits) *n.* Swastika, esp. as Nazi symbol. [G (*haken* hook, *kreuz* CROSS[1])]

haki'm[1] (-ē'm) *n.* (In India and Muslim countries) physician. [f. Arab. *ḥakīm* wise man, physician]

ha'kĭm[2] (hah'-) *n.* (In India and Muslim countries) judge, ruler, governor. [f. Arab. *ḥākim* governor]

Hă'kka *n.* & *a.* (People or dialect) of S.E. China, esp. Canton. [Cantonese]

Hala'chah (-ah'χa) *n.* Body of Jewish law in Mishnah. [f. Aram. *hᵃlāḵāh* law]

hal(l)al (hahlah'l) *v.t.*, & *n.* **1.** *v.t.* Kill (meat) as prescribed by Muslim law. **2.** *n.* Meat thus prepared. [f. Arab. *ḥalāl* lawful]

halā'tion *n.* (Photog.) Spreading of light beyond its proper boundary in a developed image, caused by internal reflection in the support of the emulsion. [irreg. f. HALO + -ATION]

hă'lberd, -rt, *n.* (Hist.) Combined spear and battle-axe. [ME, f. F *hallebarde* f. It *alabarda* f. MHG *helmbarde* (*helm* handle, *barde* hatchet)]

hălberdier' *n.* Man armed with halberd. [f. F *hallebardier* (as prec.; see -IER)]

hă'lcȳon *n.* & *a.* **1.** *n.* Bird said by the ancients to breed in floating nest on sea at winter solstice, and to charm wind and waves into calm for the purpose; (Zool.) Australasian kingfisher. **2.** *a.* Calm, peaceful, esp. **~ days** (orig. 14 days about winter solstice); (of period) happy, prosperous. [ME, f. L *(h)alcyon* f. Gk *(h)alkuōn* kingfisher]

hāle[1] *a.* (Esp. of old person) robust, vigorous, (*hale and hearty*); hence **~'**NESS (-ln-) *n.* [north. repr. of OE *hāl* WHOLE]

hāle[2] *v.t.* Drag or draw forcibly (lit. or fig.). [ME, f. OF *haler* f. ON *hala* = OS *halon,* OHG *halōn*]

half (hahf) *n.* (*pl.* **halves** *pr.* hahvz), *a.*, & *adv.* **1.** *n.* One of two equal or corresponding parts or groups into which a thing is or might be divided (*half of 10 is 5*; *cut it in half* or *into halves*; *your half is bigger than mine*; *two hours and a half (hour)* or *two and a half hours*; *half of it is, half of them are, rotten*; see also sense 2); (colloq.) = *half-back, half-pint*; one of two equal periods constituting football etc. match; ||school term (the school year being formerly divided into two portions); (Golf) halved hole; half-price ticket. **2. And a ~,** (fig., colloq.) of unusual excellence etc. (*that was a game and a half*); BETTER[1] *half*; **by halves,** imperfectly or incompletely (*never does things by halves*); **too** *clever* etc. **by ~** (far more than would be satisfactory); **cry halves,** claim equal share; **go halves,** share equally (*with* person *in* thing); **how the other ~ lives,** other people's mode of life; **the ~ of it,** the more important part (usu. w. neg.). **3.** *a.* Forming a half (*a half length*; *a half share*); of amount or quantity equal to a half (*half the men*; *half your time*; *stays at home half the time*; *half the batch is rotten*; *half a pint*); used in half-binding (*half calf* etc.); *half the* BATTLE[1]; **a ~ dozen, ~ a dozen,** six; *half an* EYE[1]; **~-hour, -inch, -pint,** etc., (unit half as large); *half a* LOAF[1]; *half a* MIND[1]. **4.** *adv.* To the extent of half, (loosely) to a considerable extent, (*it is only half cooked*; *a half-cooked potato*; *half-buried*; *half dead*; *I half wish*; *am half inclined to agree*); **not ~,** not nearly (*not half long enough*), (colloq.) not at all (*not half bad*; *not half a bad fellow*), (sl.) to the greatest possible extent (*he didn't half get angry*). **5.** By the amount of half (an hour etc.); **~ after** or **past two,** thirty minutes after two o'clock; **~ three,** (Naut.) 3½ (fathoms); **east ~-south,** half a point south of east. **6. ~-and-~,** (what is) half one thing and half another, esp. (arch.) mixture of ale and porter; *half as much* or *many* AGAIN; **~-back,** (Footb. & Hockey) (position of) player immediately behind forwards, (Amer. Footb.) flank back; **~-baked,** (fig.) not thorough(ly planned), not earnest, half-witted; **~-ball,** (Bill. etc.) with moving ball directed at edge of object-ball; **~-beak,** fish with lower jaw projecting beyond upper; **~-binding** (of book, with leather back and corners, cloth or paper sides); **~-blood,** (1) person having one parent in common with another, (2) this relationship, (3) person of mixed race; **~-blooded,** born from parents of different races; ‖**~-blue,** (holder of) award (see BLUE[2]) made to second string or to representative in minor sports; **~-boot** (reaching up to the calf); **~-breed,** half-blooded person; *half-*BROTHER; **~-butt,** (Bill.) cue of length between ordinary cue and long butt; **~-caste** *a.* & *n.*, (that is a) half-breed, esp. (child) of European father and Indian mother; *half* COCK[1] 3; ***~-co'cked,** = *at half cock*; ‖**~-crow'n,** ‖**~ a crown,** (Hist.) coin or amount of 2s. 6d.; **~-deck,** (esp.) quarters of cadets and apprentices on merchant vessel; **~-hardy,** (of plant) able to grow in the open air at all times except in severe frost; **~-hearted,** lacking courage or zeal; *half* HITCH[2]; **~ holiday,** day of which (usu. the latter) half is taken as holiday; *half-*-HOSE; **~-hourly,** at intervals of thirty minutes; *half-*HUNTER; **~-inch,** (sl.) steal [rhyming sl. for *pinch*]; **~-integral,** equal to half an odd integer; **~-landing** (half-way up flight of stairs); *half-*LAP[3]; **~-length,** portrait of upper half of person; **~-life,** (Phys.) time during which radioactivity or other property of substance falls to half of its original value; **~-light,** dim imperfect light; **at ~-ma'st, ~-mast high,** (of flag) lowered to half height of mast as mark of respect for the dead; **~ measures,** compromise, policy etc. lacking thoroughness; **~-miler,** runner whose distance is half a mile; **~ moon,** moon when only half disc is illuminated, time when this occurs, semicircular object; **~ mourning,** black relieved by grey etc.; **~(-)nelson,** a hold in wrestling with arm under opponent's arm and behind his back (*get a ~ nelson on,* hold in a crippling position, gain complete mastery over); ***~-note,** (Mus.) minim; **~ pay,** reduced allowance to army etc. officer when retired or not in actual service; **~-plate,** photographic plate 16·5 by 10·8 cm, photograph reproduced from it; **~-price,** reduced price (of admission etc.); **~-seas-over,** (sl.) half drunk; **~-shell** (of oyster, esp. for serving food on); **~ shot,** (Golf) shot played with about half full swing; *half-*SISTER; **~-sole,** sole of boot or shoe from shank to toe; ‖**~-so'vereign,** (Hist.) British gold coin worth ten shillings; ***~-staff,** = *half-mast*; ***~-step,** (Mus.) semitone; ‖**~-ter'm,** period about half-way through school term, esp. as occasion of short holiday; **~-timbered,** having walls with timber frame and brick or plaster filling; **~-ti'me,** time at which half of a game or contest is completed, interval then occurring; **~-title,** (1) title or short title of a book, printed on recto of leaf preceding the title-leaf or at head of first page, (2) title of section of a book printed on recto of leaf preceding it; **~-tone,** illustration printed from a block (produced by photographic means) in which lights and shades of original are represented by small and large dots, *(Mus.) semitone; **~-track,** (vehicle having) propulsion system with wheels at front and endless driven belt at back; **~-truth,** statement that (esp. deliberately) conveys only part of the truth; *half-*VOLLEY; **~-way,** *a.* & *adv.*, at point equidistant between two others (MEET[2] person *half-way*); *~-way house,* inn midway between two towns etc., (fig.) compromise; **~-wit(ted),** stupid or foolish (person); **~-year'ly,** at intervals of six months. [OE *h(e)alf*, = OS *half*, *halbha*, OHG *halb(a)*, ON *hálfr*, *hálfa*, Goth. *halbs*, *halba*, f. Gmc **halbhaz*; orig. = 'side']

hā'lfpennȳ (hā'pnĭ) *n.* (*pl.* usu. **halfpennies** *pr.* hā'pnĭz for separate coins, **halfpence** *pr.* hā'pens for sum of money). British bronze coin worth half a penny; **three halfpence,** a penny and a halfpenny; **~worth** (usu. *pr.* hā'perth), **hā'p'orth,** as much as can be bought for a halfpenny, a very small amount. [ME, f. HALF + PENNY]

hă'lĭbut *n.* Large flat-fish (*Hippoglossus vulgaris*) used for food. [ME, f. *haly* HOLY + BUTT[2] flat-fish, perh. because eaten on holy days]

hă'līde *n.* (Chem.) Binary compound of a HALOGEN. [f. HALOGEN + -IDE]

hă'lĭdom *n.* (arch.) Holy thing, esp. (as oath) **by my ~.** [OE *hāligdom* (as HOLY, -DOM)]

hălĭeu'tĭc *a.* & *n.* **1.** *a.* Of fishing. **2.** *n.* (in *pl.*, usu. treated as *sing.*). Art of fishing. [f. L f. Gk *halieutikos* (*halieutēs* fisherman; see -IC)]

hălĭō'tĭs *n.* Gastropod of genus *Haliotis*, with ear-shaped shell lined with mother-of-pearl. [f. Gk *hals hali-* sea + *ous ōt-* ear]

hă'līte *n.* Rock-salt. [f. mod. L *halites* f. Gk *hals* salt; see -ITE[1]]

hălĭtō's|ĭs *n.* (*pl.* **~es** *pr.* -ēz). (Med.) Foul breath. [mod. L, f. L *halitus* breath + -OSIS]

hall (hawl) *n.* **1.** Large public room in palace etc.; principal living-room of medieval house; SERVANTS' *hall*. **2.** Mansion, large residence esp. of landed proprietor; university building set apart for residence or instruction of students, (in Engl. colleges etc.) common dining-room, dinner in this; building of guild (*Fishmongers' Hall*). **3.** Large room for public gathering; (in *pl.*) music-halls. **4.** Entrance-passage of house; *corridor or passage in a building. **5.** LIBERTY *Hall*; ***H~ of Fame,** building with memorials of celebrated persons; **~'mark,** (*n.*) mark used at Goldsmiths' Hall (and by U.K. assay offices) for marking standard of gold, silver, and platinum, (fig.) token of excellence, (*v.t.*) stamp with this; ||~ **porter** (esp. carrying luggage etc. in hotel); **~-stand** (in hall of house, with mirror, hat-pegs, etc.); **~'way,** entrance-hall or corridor. [OE *h(e)all,* = OS, OHG *halla,* ON *höll* f. Gmc **hallō* (**hal-* cover, cogn. w. HELL)]

hallal. See HALAL.

hallelujah. See ALLELUIA.

halliard. See HALYARD.

hallō', halloa', *int., n.* (*pl.* ~s), & *v.i.* **1.** *int.* calling attention or expr. ||surprise or ||informal greeting or ||beginning telephone conversation. **2.** *n.,* & *v.i.* (The) cry 'hallo'. [var. of earlier HOLLO]

hallōō'[1] *int.* & *n.* **1.** *int.* inciting dogs to the chase, calling attention, or expr. surprise. **2.** *n.* The cry 'halloo'; VIEW *halloo.* [as foll.]

hallōō'[2] *v.i.* & *t.* Cry 'halloo!', esp. to dogs; urge on (dogs etc.) with shouts; shout to attract attention (*don't halloo till you are out of the* WOOD). [perh. f. *hallow* pursue with shouts f. OF *halloer* (imit.)]

hă'llow[1] (-ō) *n.* **1.** (arch.) Holy person, saint. **2. All H~s, H~mas,** = ALL *Saints' Day;* **H~e'en,** (Sc. & U.S.) eve of this. [OE *hālga,* form of *hālig* HOLY]

hă'llow[2] (-ō) *v.t.* Make holy; honour as holy. [OE *hālgian,* = OS *hēlagon,* OHG *heilagōn,* ON *helga* f. Gmc (**hailag-* HOLY)]

Ha'llstatt (hah'lshtaht) *a.* Relating to the civilization of a phase of the early Iron Age. [~ in Upper Austria, where remains of this period were discovered]

hallu'cĭn|āte (-lōō'-) *v.t.* Produce illusions in the mind of (person); hence ~ANT *a.* & *n.* [f. L *(h)al(l)ucinari* wander in mind f. Gk *alussō* be uneasy, + -ATE[3]]

hallucinā'tion (-lōō-) *n.* Illusion; apparent perception of external object not actually present; so **hallu'cĭnatory** (-lōō'-) *a.* [f. L *hallucinatio* (as prec.; see -ATION)]

hallu'cĭnogĕn (-ōō'-) *n.* Drug causing hallucinations; hence ~IC (-ĕ'n-) *a.* [f. prec. + -O- + -GEN]

hă'll|ŭx *n.* (*pl.* ~**uces** *pr.* -ūsēz). Big toe; innermost digit of hind foot. [mod. L, f. L *allex*]

halm. See HAULM.

hă'lma *n.* Game played by two or four persons on board of 256 squares, with men moved by leaping over other men into vacant squares beyond, from one corner to the opposite corner. [Gk, = leap]

hā'lō *n.* (*pl.* ~es), & *v.t.* **1.** *n.* Circle of white or coloured light round luminous body, esp. sun or moon; circle, ring; disc of light surrounding head of saint, nimbus; (fig.) glory around idealized person etc.; ~ **hat,** woman's hat worn at back of head with brim framing face. **2.** *v.t.* Surround with halo. [med. L, f. L f. Gk *halōs* threshing-floor, disc of sun or moon]

hă'logĕn *n.* (Chem.) Any of the group of non-metallic elements fluorine, chlorine, bromine, iodine, and astatine, which form halides (e.g. sodium chloride or common salt) by simple union with a metal etc.; hence ~A'TION *n.,* introduction of halogen atom into molecule. [f. Gk *hals halos* salt + -O- + -GEN]

halt[1] (hawlt *or* hŏlt) *n.* & *v.* **1.** *n.* Temporary stoppage on march or journey; interruption of progress (*call a halt to; come, grind, to a halt*); ||railway stopping-place used for local services only and without regular station buildings etc. **2.** *v.i.* Make a halt. **3.** *v.t.* Cause (troops etc.) to halt. [orig. in phr. *make halt* f. G *halt machen* (*halt* hold)]

halt[2] (hawlt *or* hŏlt) *a.* (arch.) Lame; crippled. [OE *h(e)alt,* = OS *halt,* OHG *halz,* ON *haltr,* Goth. *halts* f. Gmc **haltaz*]

halt[3] (hawlt *or* hŏlt) *v.i.* Walk hesitatingly; hesitate (*halt between two opinions*); (of argument, verse, etc., esp. in *part.*) be defective; (arch.) be lame. [OE *healtian* (as prec.)]

ha'lter (haw'l- *or* hŏ'l-) *n.,* & *v.t.* **1.** *n.* Rope, strap, with noose or headstall for horses or cattle; rope with noose for hanging a person; death by hanging; (woman's dress-top held by) strap round back of neck leaving shoulders bare; **~-break** *v.t.,* accustom (horse) to halter. **2.** *v.t.* Fasten (*up*) with halter; hang (person) with halter. [OE *hælftre,* = OLG *heliftra,* WG **halftra-* f. root **halbh-*; cf. HELVE]

hăltēr'ēs (-z) *n. pl.* Balancing-organs of dipterous insects. [Gk, = weights used to aid leaping (*hallomai* to leap)]

halva(h) (hahlvah') *n.* Sweetmeat of sesame flour and honey. [Yiddish, f. Turk. *helva* f. Arab. *ḥalwa*]

halve (hahv) *v.t.* Divide into halves; share equally; reduce to half; (Golf) play (hole) in same number of strokes as other player, win same number of holes in (match); fit (crossing timbers) together by cutting out half thickness of each. [ME *halfen,* f. HALF I]

halves. See HALF.

hă'lyard, hă'llĭard, hau'lyard, *n.* (Naut.) Rope or tackle for raising or lowering sail, yard, etc. [ME *halier* f. HALE[2] + -IER, assoc. w. YARD[1]]

hăm[1] *n.* **1.** Back of thigh, thigh and buttock; (arch.) bend of the knee. **2.** Thigh of pig salted and dried in smoke or otherwise for food. **3.** (sl.) Amateur (**radio ~,** operator of an amateur radio station), inexpert performer, inexperienced or ineffective acting or actor, one who rants and overacts; **~-fisted, -handed,** (sl.) heavy-handed, clumsy. [OE *ham, hom,* = OHG *ham(m)a,* ON *höm* f. Gmc **ham(m)-* be crooked]

hăm[2] *v.i.* & *t.* (**-mm-**). (sl.) Overact. [f. prec.]

hămadrȳ'ăd *n.* **1.** (Gk & Rom. Myth.) Nymph living and dying with the tree she inhabited. **2.** King cobra; large Arabian baboon, held sacred in ancient Egypt. [ME f. L, f. Gk *hamadruas* (*hama* with, *drus* tree)]

hămamē'lĭs *n.* Shrub of genus *Hamamelis,* e.g. wych-hazel. [mod. L, f. Gk *hamamēlis* medlar]

Hă'mbûrg *n.* ||Small variety of domestic fowl; ~ **parsley,** variety of parsley with edible parsnip-like root. [~ in N. Germany]

hă'mbûrger (-ger) *n.* **1.** (*H~*). Native or inhabitant of Hamburg. **2.** Cake of minced beef usu. fried and eaten with onions, often in soft bread roll. [G (*Hamburg* in N. Germany; see -ER[1])]

hāmes (-mz) *n. pl.* Two curved pieces of iron or wood forming (part of) collar of draught-horse, to which traces are attached. [ME, f. MDu. *hame*]

Hă'mīte *n.* (Supposed) descendant of Ham, second son of Noah (Gen. 10:6 ff.); member of Egyptian or other African people; hence **Hamĭ'tic** *a.,* (esp.) of group of African languages incl. ancient Egyptian, Berber, and Cushitic. [f. *Ham* + -ITE[1]]

hă'mlĕt *n.* Small village, esp. one without church. [ME, f. AF *hamelet(t)e,* OF *hamelet* dim. of *hamel* dim. of *ham* f. MLG *hamm*; see -LE 2, -ET[1]]

hă'mmăm (*or* hŭmah'm *or* hŭ'mŭm) *n.* Turkish bath(s). [f. Arab. *ḥammām* bath]

hă'mmer[1] *n.* **1.** Instrument for beating, breaking, driving nails, etc., with hard solid (usu. steel) head at right angles to handle; machine with metal block serving same purpose; similar contrivance, as for exploding charge in gun (whence ~LESS *a.*), striking string of piano, etc.; (Anat.) a bone of the ear, the malleus; auctioneer's mallet indicating by rap that article is sold (**come under the ~,** be sold by auction); metal ball of about 7 kg, attached to wire in athletic contest of **throwing the ~**; **~ and sickle,** symbols of worker and peasant, esp. as emblem on national flag of U.S.S.R.; **~ and tongs,** with great energy (and noise). **2. ~-beam** (projecting from wall at foot of principal rafter); **~-blow,** stroke (as) with hammer; **~-cloth** (covering driver's seat in coach; orig. unexpl.); **~-head,** (1) head of hammer, (2) shark with lateral extensions of head bearing the eyes, (3) Afr. bird with thick bill and occipital crest, (4) *stupid person; **~-lock,** hold in which wrestler's arm is bent behind his back; **~man, ~-smith,** smith who works with hammer; **~-toe** (permanently bent downwards). [OE *hamor*, *hamer*, = OS *hamur*, OHG *hamar*, ON *hamarr* hammer, back of axe, crag]

hă'mmer[2] *v.* **1.** *v.t.* Strike, beat, drive, (as) with hammer (*hammer home the nail*, one's *advantage*; *hammer idea into* person's *head*); (colloq.) inflict heavy defeat(s) on in war or games; **~ out,** (fig.) devise laboriously, work hard at. **2.** (St. Exch.) Declare (person or firm) a defaulter with three taps of hammer on rostrum. **3.** *v.i.* Beat (as) with hammer, (fig.) work hard, (*at*). [ME, f. prec.]

hă'mmock *n.* Hanging bed of canvas or netting suspended by cords at ends, used esp. on board ship. [earlier *hamaca* f. Sp., of Carib orig.]

Hă'mmond *n.* **~ organ,** (Mus.) type of electronic organ. [f. ~ Electric Co. of Chicago]

hă'mmy̆ *a.* **1.** Containing or resembling ham. **2.** (sl.) Of or like ham actors. [f. HAM[1] + -Y[2]]

hă'mper[1] *n.* Basketwork packing-case; consignment of eatables, wines, etc., however packed (usu. as a present: *Christmas hamper*). [ME, f. obs. *hanaper*, AF f. OF *hanapier* case for goblet (*hanap* f. Frank. **hnap*)]

hă'mper[2] *v.t.*, & *n.* **1.** *v.t.* Obstruct movement of (person etc.) with material obstacles; (fig.) impede, hinder. **2.** *n.* (Naut.) Necessary but cumbersome part of equipment of vessel (TOP[1]-*-hamper*). [ME, of unkn. orig.]

hă'mster *n.* Ratlike hibernating rodent of genus *Cricetus* etc., with short tail, and cheek-pouches for carrying grain to its winter store; **golden ~,** tawny species (*Mesocricetus auratus*) much kept as pet or laboratory animal. [G, f. OHG *hamustro* corn-weevil]

hă'mstrĭng *n.*, & *v.t.* (**ha'mstrung** *or* **~ed**). **1.** (In man) one of five tendons at back of knee; (in quadruped) great tendon at back of hock. **2.** *v.t.* Cripple (person, animal) by cutting the hamstrings; (fig.) destroy activity or efficiency of. [f. HAM[1] + STRING]

hă'mūl|us *n.* (*pl.* **~i** *pr.* -ī). (Anat., Zool., & Bot.) Hooklike process. [L, dim. of *hamus* hook]

hănd[1] *n.* **1.** Terminal part of human arm beyond wrist; similar member of all four limbs of monkey; forefoot of quadruped; forehock of pork. **2.** Authority, custody, disposal, (*child is in good hands*); agency (*by the hands of*; *pass through many hands*; *the hand of God*); share in action (*have a hand in it*; **bear, give, lend, take, a ~,** take part *in* action). **3.** Pledge of marriage (*ask for* or *seek woman's hand*; *give* one's *hand to*). **4.** Manual worker in factory, farm, etc. **5.** Person who does something (*a picture by the same hand*; **all ~s,** the whole crew; **a good ~,** person skilful *at*; OLD *hand*); person or source from which thing comes (FIRST, SECOND, etc., *hand*). **6.** Skill (*a hand for pastry*); style of workmanship; TRY one's *hand*. **7.** Style of handwriting (*a legible hand*); signature (*witness the hand of A.B.*). **8.** Handlike thing, esp. pointer of clock or watch; *hand of* BANANAS. **9.** RIGHT[1] or LEFT[1] side relative to thing or person; side or direction. **10.** Linear measure of horse's height, = 4 in. **11.** Playing-cards dealt to a player; player holding these (*first, third, hand*); FORCE[2] person's *hand*; PLAY[1] *into* person's *hands*; SHOW[1] one's *hand*. **12.** (colloq.) Applause (*got a big hand*). **13. At ~,** close by, about to happen soon; **at the ~(s) of,** through the action of, from; **by ~,** by manual labour, in handwriting (not typed etc.), by messenger (not by post etc.); *brought up by* **~,** (of child etc.) fed from bottle; **for** one's **own ~,** on one's own account; *live* **from ~ to mouth,** improvidently; **in ~,** held in the hand, at one's disposal, still unused, under control, receiving attention; **in** person's **~s,** to be dealt with by him, subject to his control (so **fall into the ~s of**); **man of his ~s,** practical person; OFF-HAND; **off** one's **~s,** no longer on one's hands, no longer one's responsibility etc.; **on ~,** in one's possession, in attendance; **on** one's **~s,** resting on one as a responsibility; **on every ~, on all ~s,** to or from all quarters; **on the one ~, on the other ~,** (of contrasted points of view etc.); **out of ~,** (1) at once, extempore, (2) out of control; **to ~,** within reach; **to** one's **~,** ready for one without exertion on one's own part. **14. Change ~s,** (1) pass to different owner, (2) use opposite hands for a task; CLEAN[1] *hands*; **come to ~,** turn up, be received; **do a ~'s turn,** make the slightest effort (usu. w. neg.); **~ and foot,** (bind) completely, (serve) assiduously; **~ and** or **in glove,** on intimate terms (*with*); **~ in ~,** with hands mutually clasped, (fig.) in close association; **~ over ~** or **fist,** with each hand successively passing above the other as in climbing rope etc., (fig.) with steady or rapid progress; **~ to ~,** (of fighting etc.) at close quarters; **get** or **have** or **keep** one's **~ in,** become or be in PRACTICE[1] (2); **~s down,** (win etc.) easily; **~s off!,** do not touch (lit. or fig.); one's **~s are tied,** (fig.) one is powerless to act; **~s up!** (ordering persons to raise their hands to signify assent or surrender); **have** one's **~s full,** be fully occupied; **hold** one's **~,** refrain from punishment etc.; **hold** person's **~,** (fig.) give him close guidance or moral support; **hold** or **join ~s,** be hand in hand; LAY[3] *hands on*; **lay** or **put** one's **~ on,** find; **put** or SET[1] one's *hand to*; SHAKE[1] *hands*; SIT *on* one's *hands*; TAKE[1] *in hand*; **turn** one's **~ to,** undertake (task of new kind); UPPER *hand*; WASH[1] one's *hands* (*of*); **with a heavy ~,** oppressively; **with a high ~,** arrogantly. **15.** *attrib.* Operated by hand (*hand-brake*, *hand-mill*, *hand-press*, *hand-pump*, *hand-wheel*); held or carried in the hand (*hand-baggage*, *-mirror*); done by hand not by machine (*hand-knitted*, *-sewn*, *-painted*). **16. ~'bag,** (1) small bag carried by woman to hold purse and other personal articles, (2) travelling-bag; **~'ball,** ball for throwing with hand, game played with this in walled court or between two goals; **~-barrow,** frame for loads etc. carried by two persons; **~'bell,** bell rung by hand, esp. one of a set for musical performance; **~'bill,** printed notice circulated by hand; **~'book,** (usu. short) treatise, manual, guidebook; **~('s)-breadth,** width of average adult hand as measure of distance; **~'cart** (pushed or drawn by hand); **~'clap,** clapping of hands (SLOW *handclap*); **~'craft,** (make by) handicraft; **~ cream,** emollient for the hands; **~'cuff** *v.t.*, secure with **~'cuffs** (pair of metal rings joined by short chain, for securing prisoner's hands); **~-gallop,** easy gallop; **~'glass,** (1) magnifying glass held in hand, (2) small mirror with handle; *hand*-GRENADE; **~'grip** *n.*, grasp, seizure with the hand (friendly or hostile), handle; **~'guard** (on sword); **~-gun** (held and fired with one hand); **~'hold,** something for the hands to grip on (in climbing etc.); **~'line,** fishing-line worked without rod; **~'list** (of books etc., for reference); **~'made,** (of paper etc.) made by hand (esp. opp. to *machine-made*); **~'maid(en),** (arch. or fig.) female servant; **~ of glory,** charm made from mandrake root or dried hand of executed felon [transl. of F *main de gloire*, corrupted f. *mandragore* mandrake]; **~-organ,** barrel-organ with crank turned by hand; **~-picked,** (of supporters etc.) carefully chosen; **~'rail,** railing along edge of stairs etc.; **~'saw,** saw held with one hand (cf. HAWK¹); **~'set,** telephone mouthpiece and ear-piece as one unit; **~'shake,** shake of person's hand with one's own (see SHAKE¹ 1; GOLDEN *handshake*); **~'spike,** wooden lever shod with iron, used on shipboard and by artillery; **~'spring,** somersault in which one lands first on hands and then on feet; **~'stand,** feat of supporting body on hands only; **~-towel,** small towel for wiping hands after washing; **~'writing,** writing by hand with pen or pencil, esp. as done by particular person. **17.** Hence (-)~'ED², ~'LESS, *adjs.* [OE *hand, hond,* = OS *hand*, OHG *hant*, ON *hönd*, Goth. *handus*]

hănd² *v.t.* Help (person) with the hand (*into, out of*, carriage etc.); (Naut.) furl (sail); deliver, transfer by hand or otherwise (*over to* person, *down* or *on to* succeeding generations, *in* at office, *on, up*, etc.); offer (food) at meal; **~ down,** transmit (decision) from superior court etc.; **~-me-down,** ready-made or second-hand (clothing, or fig.); **~ off,** (Rugby Footb.) push off (tackling opponent) with hand (so *~-off* n.); **~-out,** information given to the press etc., food or clothes or money given to beggar; **~ it to,** (colloq.) acknowledge merit of (person). [f. prec.]

h. & c. *abbr.* hot and cold (water).

hă'ndĕdnĕss *n.* Tendency to, or preference for, use of right, or left, hand. [f. HAND¹*ed* + -NESS]

hă'ndful (-ŏŏl) *n.* Quantity that fills the hand; small number (*of* men etc.); (colloq.) troublesome person or task. [OE *handfull* (as HAND¹, -FUL)]

hă'ndĭcăp *n.*, & *v.t.* (**-pp-**). **1.** *n.* Race or competition in which chances of competitors are made more nearly equal by conceding start, difference in weight to be carried (in horse-race), etc.; extra weight or other condition imposed or advantage conferred on competitor, number of strokes by which golfer normally exceeds par for course; (fig.) hindrance, thing that prevents one from doing something. **2.** *v.t.* Impose handicap on (competitor); (fig., of circumstances) place (person) at disadvantage; (in *p.p.*) suffering from physical or mental disability; hence **~PER¹** *n.* [app. f. phr. *hand i'* (= in) *cap* describing a kind of sporting lottery]

hă'ndĭcraft (-ahft) *n.* Manual skill; manual art or trade or occupation; **~sman,** man skilled in a handicraft. [ME, alt. of older (f. OE) *handcraft*, after foll.]

hă'ndĭwork (-wêrk) *n.* Work done, thing made, by the hands or by anyone's personal agency. [OE *handgeweorc* (as HAND¹ + collect. form (see Y-) of *weorc* WORK¹)]

hă'ndkerchief (hăngkerchĭf *or* -ēf) *n.* (*pl.* **~s,** *or* **-ieves** *pr.* -ēvz). Square of linen, cotton, silk, etc., carried in pocket (**pocket-~**) for wiping nose etc., or worn round neck (**neck ~,** NECK¹*erchief*). [f. HAND¹ + KERCHIEF]

hă'ndle¹ *n.* Part of a thing by which it is to be held; fact that may be taken advantage of (*gave a handle to his critics*); **~bar,** (1) steering-bar of bicycle etc., with handle at each end, (2) long heavy moustache with curved ends; **fly off the ~,** (colloq.) lose self-control; **~ to** one's **name,** (colloq.) title of nobility etc. [OE *handle* (as HAND¹; see -LE 1)]

hă'ndle² *v.t.* Touch or feel with the hands; manipulate; manage (thing, person); put (thing, person) through stated process; treat (person *roughly, kindly*, etc.); discuss (subject); deal in (goods); hence **hă'ndlER¹** *n.*, (esp.) person in charge of trained police-dog etc. [OE *handlian* (as prec.)]

hă'ndle³ *n.* Feel of goods, esp. textiles, when handled. [f. prec.]

hă'n(d)sel (-ns-) *n.*, & *v.t.* (||**-ll-**). **1.** *n.* Gift at beginning of New Year, or on coming into new circumstances; earnest-money; foretaste. **2.** *v.t.* Give handsel to, inaugurate, be the first to try. [ME, corresp. to OE *handselen* giving into a person's hands, ON *handsal* giving of the hand (esp. in promise), f. as HAND¹ + OE *sellan* SELL]

hă'ndsome (-ns-) *a.* (**~r, ~st**). Of fine form or figure; (of conduct etc.) generous (*a handsome present*; *handsome treatment*; **~ is that ~ does,** one is judged by behaviour not appearance); (of price, fortune, etc.) considerable; hence ~LY² (-mlĭ) *adv.*, ~NESS (-mn-) *n.* [ME, = 'easily handled', f. HAND¹ + -SOME¹]

hă'nd|ȳ *a.* Ready to hand, conveniently placed; convenient to handle or use (*the legacy will come in handy*); clever with the hands; **~y-dandy,** child's game in which one player guesses which of other player's hands conceals some object; **~yman,** man able to do various odd jobs; hence ~ĬLY² *adv.*, ~ĬNESS *n.* [f. HAND¹ + -Y²]

hăng¹ *v.* (**hung,** exc. sense 5 or arch. **hanged**). **1.** *v.t.* Support from above and otherwise allow to take form determined by action of gravity etc., attach loosely, (*from, to*, hook, etc.); place (meat, game) thus to dry (**hung beef,** so cured) or become tender or high. **2.** Place (picture) on wall (*hung on the* LINE²). **3.** Attach (wallpaper) to wall; fit up (bells in belfry). **4.** Rest (door on hinges, coach on springs) in free swinging position. **5.** *v.t.* & *i.* Suspend or be suspended by neck as capital punishment; kill one*self* thus; (as imprecation) = DAMN, be damned, (*I'll be hanged if I can see it*; *well, I'm hanged!*; *do it and hang the expense*; *let everything go hang*). **6.** *v.t.* Let droop (*hang* one's *head in shame*). **7.** *v.i.* Remain, or be, hung (lit. or fig.; *sword, punishment, hangs over his head*; *dress hangs badly*; *curtain hangs loose, in folds*, etc.); **~ in the balance,** remain uncertain; THERE*by hangs a tale*; *hang by a* THREAD¹. **8.** *v.t.* Decorate *with* (things hung on). **9.** *Prevent (jury, by disagreement) from reaching decision. **10. ~ about** or **around,** loiter about, not move away or disperse; **~ back,** show reluctance to act or move; **~ fire,** (of firearm) be slow in going off, (fig.) be delayed in action; **~ heavily** or **heavy,** (of time) pass slowly; **~ on,** depend or rely on, attend closely to, stick closely (*to*), remain in office, stick to duty etc., (sl.) attach blame for (thing) to, (sl.) wait for a short time, (colloq., in telephoning) not ring off; **~ out,** hang from window, clothes-line, etc., (cause to) protrude downwards, (sl.) reside; *~-out* n., (sl.) place of residence; HANGOVER; **hung-over,** (sl.) having hangover; **~ together,** be coherent, be or remain associated; **~ up,** hang from hook etc., put aside, postpone indefinitely, end telephone conversation, cause delay or difficulty to; *~-up* n., (sl.) difficulty, obsession, inhibition, **11. ~'dog** *n.* & *a.*, sneaking shamefaced (person); **~-glider** (controlled and stabilized by movements of operator suspended upright in it); **~'man,** executioner esp. by hanging; **~'nail,** = AGNAIL. [f. ON *hanga* v.t., OE *hōn*, = OS, OHG, Goth. *hāhan*, & f. OE *hangian* v.i., = OS *hangon*, OHG *hangēn*, f. Gmc **hang-*]

hăng² *n.* Downward droop or bend; way a thing hangs; **get the ~ of,** (colloq.) get the knack of, understand; **not** (*care* etc.) **a** ~, (colloq.) not at all. [f. prec.]

hă'ngar (*or* -ngg-) *n.* Shed for housing aircraft etc.; hence ~AGE (4) *n.* [F]

hă'nger[1] *n.* Wood on side of steep hill. [OE *hangra* (*hangian* HANG[1])]

hă'nger[2] *n.* In vbl senses; loop etc. by which thing is hung; chain, rod, to which pot is hung in fireplace by pot-hook; (**clothes-, coat-**)~, shaped piece of wood etc. from which clothes may be hung in normal shape; short sword, orig. hung from belt; **~-o'n,** follower, dependant. [ME, f. HANG[1] + -ER[1]]

hă'nging[1] *n.* In vbl senses; (usu. in *pl.*) drapery with which walls etc. are hung; ~ **committee** (deciding on hanging of pictures in exhibition); **a** ~ **matter** (resulting in capital punishment). [ME, f. HANG[1] + -ING[1]]

hă'nging[2] *a.* In vbl senses; ~ **gardens** (placed on steep slope); ~ **lie,** (Golf) position of ball on ground sloping downhill in direction of play; ~ **paragraph** (with all lines except first indented); ~ **valley** (ending in abrupt descent to another valley); ~ **wardrobe** (for clothes to hang in at full length). [ME, f. HANG[1] + -ING[2]]

hă'ngōver *n.* **1.** (sl.) Unpleasant after-effects of (esp. alcoholic) dissipation. **2.** Remainder, surviving part. [f. HANG[1] + OVER]

hănk *n.* (Circular) loop or coil, skein; definite length of cotton yarn (840 yds.), worsted (560 yds.), etc.; (Naut.) ring of rope, iron, etc., for securing staysails to stays. [ME, f. ON *hönk*, **hanku*; cf. Sw. *hank* string, Da. *hank* handle]

hă'nker *v.i.* ~ **after,** crave or long for; hence ~ING[1] *n.* [rel. to syn. obs. *hank* (-ER[5]), prob. cogn. w. HANG[1]]

hă'nkȳ *n.* (colloq.) Handkerchief. [abbr.; see -Y[3]]

hă'nkȳ-pănkȳ *n.* (sl.) Trickery; underhand dealing; questionable behaviour. [arbitr., perh. after *hocus-pocus*]

Hă'nōver *n.* **House of** ~, British sovereigns from George I to Victoria; hence **Hănovēr'**IAN *a.* & *n.* [~ in Germany, whose Elector became George I in 1714]

Hă'nsard *n.* Official report of proceedings in British and other Parliaments; hence ~IZE *v.t.*, (arch.) confront (M.P.) with his former utterances recorded in Hansard, prove (person) to have formerly expressed different opinion. [f. L. ~, Engl. printer d. 1828, whose firm orig. compiled it]

Hănse *n.* (Hist.) Guild of merchants; political and commercial league of Germanic towns, whence **Hănseă'**TIC *a.*; entrance-fee of guild. [f. MHG *hanse*, OHG, Goth. *hansa* company]

hă'nsel. See HANDSEL.

hă'nsom *n.* ~ (**cab**), two-wheeled cabriolet for two inside, with driver mounted behind and reins going over roof. [f. J. A. *Hansom*, Engl. architect d. 1882, who designed such a cab]

Hănts. *abbr.* Hampshire. [f. OE *Hantescire*]

Ha'nukkah (hah'nuka; *or* χ-) *n.* Jewish festival of lights, commemorating purification of the Temple in 165 B.C. [f. Heb. *ḥănukkāh* consecration]

hanuma'n (-ōōmah'n) *n.* Indian langur venerated by Hindus; (Hindu Myth., *H*~) semi-divine monkey-like creature. [Hindi]

hăp[1] *n.* (arch.) Chance, luck, lot; chance occurrence. [ME, f. ON *happ*]

hăp[2] *v.t.* (**-pp-**). (arch.) Come about by chance; happen (*to* do). [ME, f. prec.]

hapax legomen|on (hăpăks lĭgŏ'mĭnŏn) *n.* (*pl.* ~*a*). Word of which only one instance is recorded (*'hugger-mugger' is hapax legomenon in Shakespeare*). [Gk, = thing said once]

ha'penny. Var. of HALFPENNY.

hăphă'zard (-p-h-) *n.*, *a.*, & *adv.* **1.** *n.* Mere chance (*at* or *by haphazard*). **2.** *a.* & *adv.* Casual(ly), (at) random. [f. HAP[1] + HAZARD]

hă'plĕss *a.* Unlucky; hence ~LY[2] *adv.* [f. HAP[1] + -LESS]

hăplŏ'graphȳ *n.* Mistake of writing once what should be written twice (e.g. *philogy* for *philology*). [f. Gk *haplous* single + -o- + -GRAPHY]

hă'ploid *a.* & *n.* (Biol.) (Cell) having a single set of unpaired chromosomes; (organism) having this in somatic cells. [G, f. Gk *haplous* single + *eidos* form]

hăplŏ'logȳ *n.* Mistake of uttering once what should be spoken twice (e.g. *Feb'ry* for *February*). [f. as HAPLOGRAPHY + -LOGY]

hă'plȳ *adv.* (arch.) By chance; perhaps. [ME, f. HAP[1] + -LY[2]]

‖**ha'p'orth.** See HALFPENNY.

hă'ppen *v.i.* **1.** Occur, come to pass, (by chance or otherwise). **2.** Chance, have the (good or bad) fortune, *to* (do). **3.** Come by chance (*up*)*on* (person, thing), *by*, *in*, etc.; ~ **to,** be experienced by (*something* etc. ~*s to* person, he dies etc.). [ME, f. HAP[1] + -EN[6]]

hă'ppening (-pn-) *n.* In vbl senses; (usu. in *pl.*) occurrence, event; improvised or spontaneous theatrical etc. performance. [f. prec. + -ING[1]]

***hă'ppenstance** *n.* Thing that happens by chance. [f. HAPPEN + CIRCUMSTANCE]

hă'ppĭ *n.* Loose informal Japanese coat. [Jap.]

hă'ppȳ *a.* **1.** (Of person or circumstance) lucky, fortunate; contented with one's lot; glad or pleased (*to* help another etc.); (of language or conduct) apt, felicitous; (colloq.) slightly drunk. **2.** ~ **birthday, Christmas,** (expr. greetings at these times); *happy* DISPATCH[2]; ~ **event,** birth of child; **~-go-lucky,** taking things cheerfully as they happen; *happy* HUNTING-*-ground*(*s*); ~ **land,** (esp.) heaven; ~ **medium,** something that achieves satisfactory avoidance of extremes, golden mean; ~ **pill,** (colloq.) tranquillizer; ~ **release,** (esp.) death; *happy* RETURN[2]*s*; ~ **ship,** ship whose crew work together in harmony, (fig.) organization whose members do likewise; *happy* THOUGHT[1]. **3.** (as *suf.*) Excited or dazed or nervous from, behaving irresponsibly over, inclined to use excessively, (*bomb-happy*, TRIGGER-*happy*). **4.** Hence **hă'ppi**LY[2] *adv.*, **hă'ppi**NESS *n.* [ME, f. HAP[1] + -Y[2]]

hă'ptic *a.* Pertaining to the sense of touch. [f. Gk *haptikos* able to touch (*haptō* fasten; see -IC)]

hăra-kĭ'rĭ *n.* Suicide by disembowelment, as practised by samurai in Japan when in disgrace or sentenced to death. [colloq. Jap. (*hara* belly, *kiri* cutting)]

har'am. Var. of HAREM.

hară'ngue (-ng) *n.* & *v.* **1.** *n.* Speech to an assembly; loud or vehement address. **2.** *v.i.* & *t.* Make harangue (to). [ME f. F, f. OF *arenge* f. med. L *harenga*, perh. f. Gmc **harihring*- assembly (**harjaz* crowd, **hringaz* RING[1])]

hă'rass *v.t.* Vex by repeated attacks; trouble, worry; hence ~MENT *n.* [f. F *harasser*, pej. f. OF *harer* set a dog on]

har'binger (-nj-) *n.*, & *v.t.* **1.** *n.* One who announces another's approach, forerunner; (Hist.) one sent as purveyor of lodgings for army, royal party, etc. **2.** *v.t.* Announce approach of. [ME, f. AF & OF *herbergere -geour* f. *herbergier* to lodge f. *herberge* lodging f. OS *heriberga* (*heri* army, **berg*- protect); *-n-* as in *messenger* etc.]

har'bour (-ber), ***har'bor,** *n.* & *v.* **1.** *n.* Place of shelter for ships; shelter; **~-master,** officer in charge of harbour; ***~ seal,** small Atlantic seal (*Phoca vitulina*); hence ~LESS *a.* **2.** *v.t.* Give shelter to (esp. vermin, criminal, evil thoughts). **3.** *v.i.* Come to anchor in harbour. [OE *herebeorg(ian)*, (perh. f.) ON *herbergi*, cogn. w. prec.]

hâr'bourage (-ber-), ***hâr'borage,** *n.* (Place of) shelter. [f. prec. + -AGE]

hârd *a.*, *n.*, & *adv.* **1.** *a.* Firm, unyielding to pressure, solid, not easily cut; (of data etc.) reliable; (of radiation) highly penetrating; ~ **facts** (not disputable like opinions etc.). **2.** Difficult (*to* do), not easily allowing one *to* do (*she is hard to please*; *this is hard to believe*; ~ **nut to crack,** difficult problem, person or thing not easily understood or overcome or influenced; ~ **of hearing,** somewhat deaf); difficult to understand or explain (*hard question*); (of person or conduct) unfeeling, harsh, (*hard as* NAIL[1]*s*); involving undue or unfair suffering (*hard luck*; *hard cases make bad law*); stingy. **3.** Difficult to bear (*hard life, times,* LINE[2]*s*); (of season or weather) severe, esp. frosty; (of bargain) without concession; harsh or unpleasant to eye or ear (*hard colours, voice*). **4.** (Of liquor) alcoholic; (of drug) potent and addictive; (of water) difficult to use soap with, owing to its mineral salts; (of markets and prices) high, unyielding; (of pornography) highly obscene. **5.** (Phonet.) Surd (k, t, *and* p, *are hard as opposed to* g, d, *and* b); guttural (*c is hard in 'cat', and g in 'go'*). **6.** Strenuous (*a hard drinker, fight, worker*; *try* one's *hardest*); ~ **row to hoe,** difficult task; do thing **the ~ way,** by one's unaided efforts or bitter experience. **7.** *n.* ‖Sloping roadway across foreshore; (sl.) = *hard labour* (*got 2 years hard*). **8.** *adv.* Strenuously, severely, with effort, (Naut.) to full extent, (*try hard*; *raining hard*; *freezing hard*; *look hard at*; *hard a-port!*); ~ **pressed,** closely pursued. **9.** With difficulty (*hard-earned*). **10.** So as to be hard (*hard-baked*); **~-boiled,** (of egg) boiled to solidify white and yolk, (fig.) tough, callous, shrewd. **11.** ~ **at it,** working hard; **be ~ put to it,** be in difficulties; **die ~** (only after hard struggle; cf. DIE[2]-*hard*); **go ~ with** person, turn out to his disadvantage; **it shall go ~ but** (unless there are overpowering difficulties) *I will find them*; ~ **by,** close by; ~ **(up)on,** too severe in criticism or treatment of (*don't be too hard on him*), (of circumstances) bearing with undue severity on, close to (*was hard on my* HEEL[1]*s*); ~ **up,** lacking money etc., at a loss *for*; **run** person ~, pursue him closely. **12.** ~ **and fast,** (of distinction made, or rule of behaviour etc.) strict; **~'back** *n.* & *a.*, (book) bound in durable covers; **~'bake,** almond toffee; **~'bitten,** tough in fight etc.; **~'board,** stiff board of compressed and processed wood-pulp fibre used in place of wood; *hard-boiled* (see sense 10); ~ **case,** (1) instance of hardship, (2) intractable person, (3, Austral. & N.Z.) amusing person; ~ **cash,** (1) coins as opp. paper money, (2) money as opp. mere promises of payment; *hard* CHEESE[1]; ~ **coal,** anthracite; ~ **copy,** legible permanent record of matter stored on microfilm etc.; ~ **core,** irreducible nucleus of resistance etc., ‖heavy material forming foundation of road etc.; ~ **court,** lawn-tennis court made of asphalt, concrete, etc., (opp. *grass court*); ~ **cover,** stiff durable binding-case of book; ~ **currency** (not likely to depreciate suddenly or fluctuate greatly in value; cf. SOFT *currency*); **~-favoured, -featured,** having harsh or ugly features; **~-fisted,** stingy; ~ **hat,** (1) bowler hat, (2) protective headgear worn on building-sites etc., (3) reactionary person; **~-head,** knapweed; **~-headed,** practical, not sentimental; **~-hearted,** unfeeling; ~ **hit,** severely troubled; **~-hitting,** vigorous, not sparing feelings; ~ **labour,** (orig.) stone-breaking etc. by prisoners, (until 1948 in U.K.) compulsory labour by prisoners, with loss of privileges during first few weeks of sentence; **~-laid,** (of string, fabric, etc.) tightly twisted or woven; ~ **landing** (in which spacecraft etc. is destroyed on impact); ~ **line,** unyielding adherence to firm policy; **~-lying money,** extra pay to naval men serving in small craft; ***~ money,** coins; **~-mouthed,** (of horse) not easily controlled by bit; **~-nose(d),** (colloq.) obdurate, uncompromising; ~ **pad,** form of distemper of dogs etc.; ~ **palate,** front part of palate; ~ **pan,** firm subsoil of clay etc., hard unbroken ground; ~ **roe** (of female fish); ~ **rubber,** ebonite; ~ **sauce** (of butter and sugar, often with brandy etc. added); ***~-scrabble** *a.* & *n.*, (land) yielding subsistence only with difficulty; ~ **sell,** aggressive salesmanship; ~ **set,** set so as to be hard, (of egg) that has been subjected to incubation, (of person) hungry; **~'shell,** having a hard shell, (fig.) rigid, uncompromising, (esp. **Hardshell Baptists*); ~ **shoulder,** hardened land beside motorway for vehicles to leave road in emergency; ~ **soap** (made with sodium compounds); *hard* SOLDER; **~sta'nding,** area of hard material for vehicle to stand on when not in use; ~ **swearing,** (euphem.) unabashed perjury; ~ **tack,** ship biscuit; **~-top,** motor car with metal roof; **~'ware,** (1) ironmonger's goods, (2) weapons, machinery, (3) physical components of computer etc., opp. SOFT*ware*; **~-wearing,** able to stand much wear; ~ **wheat** (with hard grain rich in gluten); **~'wood** (of deciduous tree); ~ **words,** (1) words difficult to understand, (2) angry talk; **~-working,** diligent. **13.** Hence **~'ISH**[1] 2 *a.*, **~'NESS** *n.* [OE *h(e)ard*, = OS *hard*, OHG *hart*, ON *harthr*, Goth. *hardus* f. Gmc **hardhuz* f. IE **kratus*]

hâr'den *v.t.* & *i.* Make or become hard, callous (esp. in *p.p.*), or robust; ~ **off,** inure (plant) to cold by gradual increase of exposure; hence **~ER**[1] (1, 2) *n.* [ME, f. prec. + -EN[6]]

hâr'die. Var. of HARDY[2].

hâr'dihŏŏd *n.* Boldness, audacity. [f. HARDY[1] + -HOOD]

hâr'dlў *adv.* In a hard manner; (only) with difficulty; harshly; scarcely, only just. [ME, f. HARD + -LY[2]]

hâr'dship *n.* Hardness of fate or circumstance; severe suffering or privation. [ME, f. HARD + -SHIP]

hâr'd|ў[1] *a.* **1.** Bold, audacious; hence **~ĭLY**[2] *adv.* **2.** Robust, capable of endurance; (Hort., of plant) able to grow in the open air all the year; HALF-*hardy*; **~y annual,** annual plant that may be sown, or sows itself, in the open, (fig., joc.) subject that comes up at regular intervals. **3.** Hence **~ĭNESS** *n.* [ME, f. OF *hardi* p.p. of *hardir* become bold, f. Gmc **hardjan* make hard (**hardhuz* HARD)]

hâr'dў[2] *n.* Blacksmith's edged blade of hard iron for shaping metal on. [prob. f. prec. or f. HARD]

hāre *n.*, & *v.i.* **1.** *n.* Mammal of genus *Lepus* like large rabbit, with tawny fur, long ears, short tail, and hind legs longer than forelegs, inhabiting fields, hills, etc.; BELGIAN *hare*; = ELECTRIC *hare*. **2. Mad as a March ~** (hare in breeding season); **first catch your ~** (before trying to cook it; usu. fig.); **hold** (or **run**) **with the ~ and run** (or **hunt**) **with the hounds,** try to remain on good terms with both sides; **start a ~,** raise topic of discussion. **3.** ~ **and hounds,** paper-chase; ~ **and tortoise,** defeat of ability by persistence; **~'bell,** bell-flower with rounded basal leaves (Scottish bluebell), (orig.) wild hyacinth (English bluebell); **~-brained,** rash, wild; **~'lip,** congenital fissure of upper lip; **~'s-ear,** thoroughwax; **~'s-foot,** (1) species of clover (*Trifolium arvense*) with soft hair about flowers, (2) corkwood tree, (3) hare's foot formerly used for applying rouge etc. to face. **4.** *v.i.* Run with great speed. [OE *hara*, = OHG *haso*, ON *heri* f. Gmc **hason*, **hazon*]

hār'em (*or* hahrē'm) *n.* Women's part of Muslim dwelling-house; its occupants; Muslim sacred place. [f. Arab. *ḥarām, ḥarīm* prohibited, sanctuary, women's apartment (*ḥarama* prohibit)]

hār'ewood (hār'w-) *n.* Stained sycamore-wood used in cabinet-making. [f. G. dial. *ehre* f. Rom. **acre* f. L *acer* maple, + WOOD]

hă'rĭcōt (-kō) *n.* Ragout (usu. of mutton or lamb); ~ (**bean**), (white dried seed of) bean of genus *Phaseolus*. [F]

hă'rĭjăn *n.* Indian Untouchable. [Skr., = person dedicated to Vishnu (*Hari* Vishnu, *jana* person)]

hark *v.* **1.** *v.i.* Listen (*to* or *at* or abs. in *imper.*); ‖(as call to hounds) go *forward, away, off,* etc. **2.** *v.i.* & *t.* ~ **back,** (of hounds) retrace course to find scent, (fig.) revert (*to* subject), recall (hounds). [ME *herkien* f. OE **he(o)rcian*, = MLG, MDu. *horken*, OHG *hōrechen*; cf. HEARKEN]

har'ken. Var. of HEARKEN.

harl[1] *v.* & *n.* (Sc.) **1.** *v.t.* Drag along the ground. **2.** *v.i.* Drag oneself along. **3.** *v.t.*, & *n.* Roughcast with lime and small gravel. [ME, of unkn. orig.]

harl[2], **harle,** *n.* Barb or fibre of feather; fibre of flax or hemp. [app. f. MLG *herle, harle* fibre of flax or hemp]

har'lèquin *n.* & *a.* **1.** *n.* Stock character of witty servant in Italian comedy; mute character in English pantomime, invisible to clown and pantaloon, usu. wearing mask and particoloured tights; buffoon. **2.** ~ (**duck**), northern duck with variegated plumage. **3.** *a.* Gaily coloured; variegated. [F, f. earlier *Herlequin* leader of legendary nocturnal troop of demon horsemen]

harlèquinā'de *n.* Part of pantomime in which harlequin plays chief part; piece of buffoonery. [f. F *arlequinade* (as prec.; see -ADE)]

‖**Har'ley Street** *n.* Medical specialists. [~ in London, associated with eminent physicians and surgeons]

har'lot *n.*, & *v.i.* (arch.) Prostitute (oneself); hence ~RY (4) *n.* [ME f. OF *harlot, herlot* lad, knave, vagabond, of unkn. orig.]

harm *n.*, & *v.t.* Damage, hurt, (**out of ~'s way,** in safety); hence ~'FUL *a.* [OE *hearm(ian)*, = OS, OHG *harm*, ON *harmr* grief, f. Gmc **harmaz*]

harmă'ttan *n.* Parching dusty land-wind on W. Afr. coast from Dec. to Feb. [f. Fanti or Twi *haramata*]

har'mlèss *a.* Doing no harm; suffering no harm or loss (**save** or **hold** ~, indemnify); hence ~LY[2] *adv.*, ~NESS *n.* [ME, f. HARM + -LESS]

harmŏ'nĭc *a.* & *n.* **1.** *a.* Harmonious, concordant. **2.** (Mus.) Relating to harmony; ~ **minor,** scale with minor 6th and major 7th both ascending and descending; ~ **tones** (produced by vibration of aliquot parts of strings etc.). **3.** (Math.) In the relation of quantities whose reciprocals are in arithmetical progression (*harmonic progression, quantities, series*); (**simple**) ~ **motion,** oscillatory motion under a retarding force proportional to amount of displacement from equilibrium position; ~ **function** (representing harmonic motion). **4.** Hence **harmŏ'n**ICALLY *adv.* **5.** *n.* Harmonic tone, usu. accompanying the fundamental; component frequency of wave motion. [f. L f. Gk *harmonikos* (as HARMONY; see -IC)]

harmŏ'nĭca *n.* Musical glasses; mouth-organ. [L, fem. sing. or neut. pl. (as n.) of *harmonicus* (see prec.)]

harmō'nĭous *a.* Forming a consistent or orderly or pleasing or agreeable whole, concordant; free from dissent or ill-feeling; sweet-sounding; singing or playing tunefully; hence ~LY[2] *adv.* [f. HARMONY + -OUS]

har'mon|ist *n.* Person skilled in harmony; (arch.) musician; collator of parallel narratives, whence ~ĭ'STIC *a.*; harmonizer. [f. HARMONY + -IST]

harmō'nĭum *n.* Keyboard instrument in which notes are produced by air blown through reeds. [F, f. L (as HARMONY)]

har'moniz|e, -is|e (-iz), *v.t.* & *i.* Bring into or be in harmony (*with*); make or be agreeable in artistic effect; add notes to (melody) to form chords; hence ~A'TION *n.* [f. F *harmoniser* (as foll.; see -IZE)]

har'monȳ *n.* State of being harmonious; agreeable effect of apt arrangement of parts; (Mus.) (study of) combination of simultaneous notes to form chords (cf. MELODY); sweet or melodious sound (*harmony of the* SPHERES); collation of parallel narratives etc., esp. of the four Gospels. [ME, f. OF *harmonie* f. L f. Gk *harmonia* joining, concord (*harmos* joint)]

har'nèss *n.*, & *v.t.* **1.** *n.* Equipment of draught-horse or other animal, by which it is fastened to cart etc. and controlled; (fig.) working equipment; DOUBLE[1] *harness*; **in** ~, in the routine of daily work; DIE[2] *in harness*; ~**-racing** (in which horse pulls two-wheeled vehicle and driver). **2.** Arrangement for fastening thing to person, resembling horse's harness; arrangement of straps fitted to dog in place of a collar; apparatus in loom for shifting warp-threads; (Hist.) defensive armour; ~**-cask,** (Naut.) tub of salt meat for current consumption. **3.** *v.t.* Put harness on (horse etc. *to* cart etc.); (fig.) utilize (river, waterfall, natural forces) for motive power. [ME; (v. f. OF *harneschier*) f. OF *harneis* military equipment f. ON **hernest* (*herr* army, *nest* provisions)]

harp[1] *n.* Stringed musical instrument, roughly triangular, played by plucking with the fingers, esp. traditionally by those in heaven, or as large vertical orchestral instrument resting on floor and equipped with pedals to alter pitch of strings; ~(**-seal**), Greenland seal with harp-shaped dark mark on back. [OE *hearpe*, = OS, ON *harpa*, OHG *harfa* f. Gmc **harpōn*]

harp[2] *v.i.* Play on harp, whence ~'ER[1], ~'IST (3), *ns.*; dwell tediously *on* (subject). [OE *hearpian* (as prec.)]

harpoō'n *n.*, & *v.t.* **1.** *n.* Spearlike missile with rope attached, for catching whales etc.; ~**-gun** (for firing this). **2.** *v.t.* Strike or spear with harpoon. [(v. f. n.) f. F *harpon* (*harpe* clamp f. L f. Gk *harpē* sickle)]

har'psĭchord (-k-) *n.* Double-keyboard instrument like piano but with strings plucked by quill or leather points, used esp. in 16th–18th c. [f. obs. F *harpechorde* f. LL *harpa* harp + *chorda* string; -*s*- of uncert. orig.]

har'pȳ *n.* (Gk & Rom. Myth.) rapacious monster with woman's face and body and bird's wings and claws; rapacious person; ~(**-eagle**), S. Amer. crested bird of prey. [f. F *harpie* or f. L f. Gk *harpuiai* snatchers (cf. *harpazō* snatch)]

(h)ar'quèbus *n.* (Hist.) Early type of portable gun, supported on tripod by hook or on forked rest; so ~IER' *n.* [f. F *(h)arquebuse*, ult. f. MLG *hakebusse* or MHG *hakenbühse* (*haken* hook, *busse* gun)]

hă'rrĭdan *n.* Haggard or ill-tempered old woman. [17th c. cant; perh. f. F *haridelle* old horse]

hă'rrĭer[1] *n.* One who harries. [f. HARRY + -ER[1]]

hă'rrĭer[2] *n.* Hound used for hunting hares; (in *pl.*) pack of these with huntsmen, group of

cross-country runners. [f. HARE + -IER, assim. to prec.]
hă'rrĭer³ *n.* Falcon of genus *Circus.* [f. *harrower* (HARROW³, -ER¹), assim. to HARRIER¹]
Hă'rrĭs *n.* ~ **tweed** (hand-woven kind made in Harris). [~ in Outer Hebrides]
Harrō'vĭan *a.* & *n.* (Past or present member) of Harrow School; (inhabitant) of Harrow. [f. mod. L *Harrovia* Harrow near London + -AN]
hă'rrow¹ (-ō) *n.* Heavy frame with iron teeth for breaking clods or removing weeds on ploughed land, covering seed, etc.; **under the** ~, in distress. [ME, f. ON *hervi*, **harwjan*; cf. MLG & MDu. *harke* rake]
hă'rrow² (-ō) *v.t.* Draw harrow over (land); lacerate, wound, (lit., or fig. the feelings etc.), distress greatly, whence ~ING² *a.* [ME, f. prec.]
hă'rrow³ (-ō) *v.t.* Harry, rob, esp. (of Christ rescuing righteous souls) *harrow hell.* [ME, var. of HARRY]
***harrŭ'mph** *n.*, & *v.i.* (Speak with) guttural rasping sound. [imit.]
hă'rrȳ *v.t.* Ravage, lay waste, (land, or abs.); despoil (person); harass, worry. [OE *her(g)ian*, = OS *herion*, OHG *heriōn*, ON *herja* f. Gmc **harjō(ja)n* (**harjaz* army)]
har͡sh *a.* Rough to the touch, taste, eye, or ear; repugnant to feelings or judgement; cruel, unfeeling; hence ~'EN⁶ *v.t.* & *i.*, ~'LY² *adv.*, ~'NESS *n.* [f. MLG *harsch* (as HAIR; see -ISH¹)]
har͡t *n.* Male of (esp. red) deer, esp. after fifth year; ~ **of ten** (branches on horns); **~'s--tongue,** fern with narrow undivided fronds. [OE *heor(o)t*, = OS *hirot*, OHG *hir(u)z*, ON *hjörtr* f. Gmc **herutaz*]
har͡'tal *n.* Closing of Indian shops and offices as mark of protest or sorrow. [f. Hind. *hartāl*, *haṭṭāl* f. Skr. *haṭṭa* shop + *tālaka* lock]
har͡'tėbeest *n.* Large Afr. antelope of genus *Alcelaphus*, with ringed horns bent back at tips. [Afrik., f. Du. *hert* HART, *beest* BEAST]
har͡'tshor͡n (-s-h-) *n.* Substance got from horns of hart, formerly chief source of ammonia; (**spirit of**) ~, (arch.) aqueous solution of ammonia. [OE (as HART, 's 1, HORN¹)]
har͡'um-scar͡um *a.* & *n.* (colloq.) Reckless (person, conduct). [rhyming form. on HARE, SCARE]
harŭ'sp|ĕx *n.* (*pl.* **~ices** *pr.* -ĭsēz). (Rom. Ant.) Soothsayer divining from inspection of entrails etc. [L]
har͡'vėst *n.*, & *v.t.* **1.** *n.* (Season for) reaping and gathering-in of grain or other products; corn--crop; season's yield of any natural product; (fig.) product of any action. **2.** **~-bug,** larval mite troublesome during harvest; ~ **festival,** thanksgiving service for completion of harvest, in church usu. decorated with grain, fruit, etc.; ~ **home,** (festival to mark) close of harvesting; **~man,** arachnid with very long thin legs; ~ **moon** (full within fortnight of 22 or 23 Sept., and rising at almost same time for several nights); ~ **mouse,** very small mouse species nesting in stalks of growing grain. **3.** *v.t.* Reap and collect (crop, or abs.) as harvest; take (wild animals) for food, sport, etc.; lay up, husband. [OE *hærfest*, = OHG *herbist*, ON *haust* f. Gmc **harbhistaz* (**harbh-* reap f. IE **karp-*)]
har͡'vėster *n.* Reaper; reaping-machine (esp. with sheaf-binding). [f. prec. + -ER¹]
has. See HAVE¹.
hă's-been (-z-) *n.* (colloq.) Person who, thing which, has lost a quality or proficiency formerly possessed, out-of-date person or thing. [f. prec. + BEEN]
hăsh¹ *v.t.* ~ (**up**), cut (meat, or fig.) into small pieces, make into hash, mutilate, mangle, (lit. or fig.). [f. F *hacher* (*hache* HATCHET)]
hăsh² *n.* Dish of hashed (esp. previously cooked) meat; old matter served up in new form; medley; **make a ~ of,** spoil in dealing with; **settle** person's ~, (colloq.) make an end of or subdue him; ***~-slinger,** (sl.) waiter or waitress. [f. prec.]
hăsh³ *n.* (colloq.) Hashish. [abbr.]
Hă'shėmīte, Hă'shĭmīte, *a.* & *n.* (Member) of Arab princely family related to Muhammad. [f. *Hāšim*, great-grandfather of Muhammad + -ITE¹]
hă'shĭsh *n.* Top leaves and tender parts of HEMP 1, dried for smoking or chewing as narcotic. [f. Arab. *ḥašīš* dry herb, powdered hemp--leaves]
Hă'sĭd *n.* (*pl.* **~im**). Member of any of several mystical Jewish sects (esp. one founded in 18th c.); hence **Hasĭ'dɪc** *a.* [f. Heb. *ḥāsīḏ* pious]
hā'slėt *n.* Piece of meat to be roasted, esp. pig's pluck. [ME f. OF *hastelet* dim. of *haste* roast meat, spit, f. OLG, OHG *harst* roast; see -LET]
hasn't. See HAVE¹.
hasp (hah-) *n.*, & *v.t.* **1.** *n.* Fastening contrivance, esp. hinged clasp passing over staple and secured by pin or padlock. **2.** *v.t.* Fasten with hasp. [OE *hæpse*, *hæsp*, = MLG *haspe*, OHG *haspa*, ON *hespa*]
Hă'ssĭd etc. Var. of HASID etc.
hă'ssle *n.*, & *v.i.* (colloq.) Quarrel, struggle, wrangle. [20th c.; orig. dial.]
hă'ssock *n.* Thick firm cushion for kneeling on esp. in church; tuft of matted grass etc. [OE *hassuc*, of unkn. orig.]
hăst. See HAVE¹.
hă'stāte *a.* (esp. Bot.) Triangular like spearhead. [f. L *hastatus* (*hasta* spear; see -ATE²)]
hāste *n.*, & *v.i.* **1.** *n.* Urgency of movement; hurry, precipitancy, (**more ~, less speed,** best results are obtained by proceeding with deliberation); **in** ~, (1) quickly, (2) hurriedly; **make** ~, act quickly (*to* do, *and* do). **2.** *v.i.* Make haste (*to* do, or abs.); go or come quickly. [ME; (v. f. OF *haster*) f. OF *haste* f. WG **haisti-* violence]
hā'sten (-sen) *v.* **1.** *v.t.* Cause (person) to make haste; accelerate (work etc.). **2.** *v.i.* = prec. [f. prec. + -EN⁶]
hā'st|ȳ *a.* Hurried; speedy; rash, inconsiderate; quick-tempered; **~y pudding** (of ‖wheat flour or *maize flour stirred to thick batter in boiling milk or water); hence ~ɪLY² *adv.*, ~ɪNESS *n.* [ME, f. OF *hasti(f)* (as HASTE; see -IVE)]
hăt *n.*, & *v.t.* (-tt-). **1.** *n.* Man's, woman's, or child's esp. outdoor head-covering, usu. with brim; ‖**bad** ~, (sl.) immoral or dishonest person; **black as** one's ~, completely black; **at the drop of a** ~, promptly, immediately; **eat** one's ~, perform repulsive task (*if*; expr. one's conviction that condition will not be fulfilled); **hang up** one's ~, take up one's quarters; ~ **in hand,** (fig.) servilely or humbly; **~s in the ring,** indications of persons' willingness to be contestants; **my ~!,** excl. of astonishment; **old** ~, (colloq.) something tediously familiar; **out of a** ~, by random selection or as if by magic; **pass** or **send the ~ round,** solicit contributions; **take off** one's ~ **to,** applaud as admirable; **talk through** one's ~, (sl.) exaggerate, bluff, talk wildly or nonsensically; **under** one's ~, in secrecy; **wear** one's . . . ~, **wear two ~s,** present oneself in one specified, or two, capacities at a particular time. **2.** **~'band,** ribbon etc. put round hat; **~-peg** (for hanging hat on); **~-pin** (used to fasten hat in position); ~ **trick,** (Cricket) taking 3 wickets by successive balls from same bowler, (Footb. etc.) scoring of 3 goals by same player in same match, winning of 3 races at one meeting, etc. **3.** *v.t.* Cover, furnish, with hat. **4.** Hence ~'FUL 2 *n.*, (fig., considerable number), ~'LESS *a.*,

~'TER[1] (3) *n.* [OE *hætt,* = ON *höttr* hood f. Gmc **hattuz* (**hadnús*; cf. HOOD[1])]

hā'table. See HATE[2].

hătch[1] *n.* Lower half of divided door; aperture in door, wall, ceiling, floor, or deck; (Naut.) hatchway, trapdoor covering this (**down the ~,** (sl.) down the throat (in drinking); **under ~es,** below deck, (fig.) down out of sight, brought low, dead); floodgate; opening or door in aircraft or spacecraft; **~'way,** opening in ship's deck for lowering cargo. [OE *hæcc,* = MLG *heck,* f. Gmc **hak-*]

hătch[2] *v.* & *n.* **1.** *v.t.* Bring forth (young bird etc., or abs.) from egg; incubate (egg); contrive and develop (plot etc.). **2.** *v.i.* Emerge from egg; (of egg) produce young. **3.** *n.* Hatching; brood hatched; hence ~'LING[1] *n.,* bird or fish just hatched. [ME *hacche,* perh. f. OE **hæccan,* rel. to MHG *hecken,* Sw. *häcka,* Da. *hække,* of unkn. orig.]

hătch[3] *v.t.,* & *n.* **1.** *v.t.* Mark (usu. close parallel) lines on (surface); **~ed moulding** (Archit., with two crossing sets of parallel lines); hence ~'ING[1] (2) *n.* **2.** *n.* Hatched line. [ME, f. F *hacher* (*hache* HATCHET)]

hă'tcherӯ *n.* Place for hatching eggs esp. of fish or poultry. [f. HATCH[2] + -ERY]

hă'tchėt *n.* Light short-handled axe; **~ face** (narrow, sharp-featured); **~ man,** one who makes a business of killing, maliciously attacking (so **~ job**), etc.; BURY *the hatchet*; **throw the helve after the ~,** add new loss to that already incurred. [ME, f. OF *hachette* dim. of *hache* axe f. med. L *hapia* f. Gmc **hapja*; see -ET[1]]

hă'tchment *n.* Large (usu. diamond-shaped) tablet with deceased person's armorial bearings, affixed to his house or elsewhere. [contr. of ACHIEVEMENT]

hāte[1] *n.* Hatred; (colloq.) hated person or thing. [ME, partly f. foll., partly f. ON *hatr*]

hāte[2] *v.t.* Have strong dislike of or strong aversion to; dislike greatly *to* do or do*ing*; hence **hā'**TABLE *a.,* **hā'**TER[1] *n.* [OE *hatian,* = OS *haton,* OHG *hazzōn,* ON *hata,* Goth. *hatan* f. Gmc **hatōjan*]

hā'teful (-tf-) *a.* Exciting hatred; hence ~LY[2] *adv.,* ~NESS *n.* [ME, f. HATE[1] + -FUL]

hăth. See HAVE[1].

hătha yō'ga (*or* hŭ'ta-) *n.* System of physical exercises and breathing-control used in yoga. [f. Skr. *haṭha* force; see YOGA]

hā'trėd *n.* Active dislike; enmity; rejection and ill will. [ME, f. HATE[1] + *-red* f. OE *rǣden* condition]

hă'tter. See HAT.

hau'berk *n.* Coat of mail. [ME, f. OF *hau(s)berc* f. Frank. **halsberg* (*hals* neck, **berg-* protect)]

haugh (haw *or* hahχ) *n.* Piece of flat alluvial land by river. [ME, prob. f. OE *healh* corner, rel. to HOLLOW[2]]

hau'ght|ȳ (haw'tĭ) *a.* Proud; lofty and disdainful; dignified; hence ~ĬLY[2] *adv.,* ~ĬNESS *n.* [extension of *haught* a., earlier *haut* f. OF *haut* f. L *altus* high; see -Y[2]]

haul *v.* & *n.* **1.** *v.t.* Pull, drag, forcibly; transport by cart or other conveyance; bring *up* for reprimand or trial. **2.** *v.i.* Pull *at* or *on* (rope etc.); (Naut.) turn ship's course (**~ to** or **upon the wind,** bring ship round to sail closer to wind); (of wind) shift. **3.** *n.* Act of hauling; (fig.) amount gained, acquisition; distance to be traversed; hence ~'AGE *n.* [var. of HALE[2]]

hau'ler, ||**hau'lĭer,** *n.* One who hauls (e.g. tubs in coal-mine to bottom of shaft); jobbing carter; firm or person engaged in road transport of goods. [f. prec. + -ER[1], -IER]

||**ha(u)lm** (hawm *or* hahm) *n.* Stalk, stem; (collect.) stems, stalks, of peas, beans, potatoes, etc., without the pods etc. [OE *h(e)alm,* = OS, OHG *halm,* ON *hálmr* f. Gmc **halmaz* f. IE **kolmos*]

hau'lyard. See HALYARD.

haunch *n.* Part of body (esp. of sheep or deer) on side of spine between last ribs and thigh; fleshy part of buttock and thigh; leg and loin of deer etc. as food; side of arch between crown and pier. [ME, f. OF *hanche,* of Gmc orig.; cf. LG *hanke* hind leg of horse]

haunt *v.* & *n.* **1.** *v.t.* Frequent (place); frequent company of (person); (of thoughts, memories, etc.) visit (person) persistently or frequently; (in *p.p.*) visited or frequented by ghosts. **2.** *v.i.* Stay habitually (*in* or *about* place; *with* person). **3.** *n.* Place of frequent resort; usual feeding-place of animals; place frequented by criminals. [ME, f. OF *hanter* f. Gmc **haimatjan* (**haimaz* HOME[1])]

Hau'sa (how'-) *n.* (Member) of Negroid people in Sudan etc.; their Hamitic language, widely used in W. Africa. [native name]

hausfrau (how'sfrow) *n.* (German) housewife. [G (*haus* house, *frau* woman)]

hautboy. See OBOE.

haute couture (ōt kōōtūr') *n.* High-class dressmaking; leading dressmakers collectively, or their products. [F]

haute cuisine (ōt kwīzē'n) *n.* High-class (traditional French) cooking. [F]

haute école (ōt ākŏ'l) *n.* The more difficult feats of horsemanship. [F, = high school]

hauteur (ōtēr') *n.* Haughtiness of manner. [F (*haut* high)]

haute vulgarisation (ōt vōōlgarīzah'syawṅ) *n.* Popularization of abstruse or complex matters. [F, = high vulgarization]

haut monde (ōmaw'ṅd) *n.* Fashionable society. [F, = high world]

Havă'na *n.* Cigar made at Havana or elsewhere in Cuba. [~ in Cuba]

hăve[1] (*or, when unstressed,* hav *or* av) *v.t., i.,* & *aux.* (*sing. pres.* 2 (arch.) **hast,** 3 **has** *pr.* hăz *or* haz *or* az, (colloq.) 's, (arch.) **hath;** colloq. 'VE; *past* **had** *pr.* hăd *or* had *or* ad, (colloq.) 'D, (2 *sing.* arch.) **hadst;** *p.p.* **had;** *neg.* **have not** *or* (colloq.) **haven't** *pr.* hă'vent, **has not** *or* (colloq.) **hasn't** *pr.* hă'zent, (vulg.) **ain't, had not** *or* (colloq.) **hadn't** *pr.* hă'dent). **1.** *v.t.* Hold in possession as one's property or at one's disposal (*all the money that I had; have no* TIME[1] *for*); know (a language; *he has no Latin; she has the Gaelic*). **2.** Experience the possession of (persons etc. in various relations; *I have two sons, no uncle, no equals*); give birth to (baby); gain advantage over (*I had him there*); ||(sl.) cheat, deceive, (*you were had*); have sexual intercourse with. **3.** Possess or contain as appendage, part, quality, etc., (*June has 30 days; has blue eyes; trees have leaves; it has its advantages*); *have an* EYE[1] *to,* EYE[1]*s for; have it in* MIND[2], *have a good* etc. MIND[2], *to; have what it* TAKE[1]*s.* **4.** Enjoy (*I had that pleasure; never had it so good; have a good time!*), suffer (*had a toothache, an accident, a shock, my leg broken*); *have it coming to one* (see COME 8); *have a* TIME[1] (*of it*). **5.** Permit (to), accept, (*am not having any of that behaviour here; I won't have it; I will not have you say such things*); *is not having* ANY. **6.** Be under burden or obligation of (*I had my work to do; I had to do my work*); be provided with (*have nothing to do, say, wear*). **7.** Let (feeling etc.) be present in the mind (*have no doubt; have no fear!; has a grudge against me; have nothing against drink in moderation*). **8.** Show by action that one is influenced by (quality etc.; *have the impudence to disobey; have mercy on us; have the goodness* or *kindness to*); *have a* CARE[1]. **9.** Engage in, carry on, (*had some conversation, breakfast,* SEX, *a game, a* TRY, *a wash; she had an affair with him; have a look at* *this*); *have to* DO[1] *with.* **10.** Obtain, receive, (*we had news*; *there is not a loaf to be had*); eat, drink, etc., (*have an egg, a cup of tea, a cigarette*). **11.** Cause, instruct, invite, (person or thing to do, be, etc.; *have her make a copy*; *had me guessing*; *have him dismissed*; *have them to stay with us, to dinner*; *have* one's *hair cut*, one's *shoes mended*). **12.** ~ **it,** express or be aware of the view *that*, win decision in vote etc. (*the ayes have it*), (colloq.) possess advantage *on* or *over*, receive punishment etc. (*let him have it*); ~ **had it,** (colloq.) have missed one's chance, passed one's prime, been killed, etc.; ~ **it (away** or **off**), (sl.) copulate; *have it* IN[1] *one*; *have it* BOTH *ways*; *have it* (*all*) one's *own* WAY; **I ~ it,** (colloq.) I have found the answer etc.; *have it* IN[2] *for*; *as* LUCK *would have it*; *have* NOTHING *on*; ~ **it so good,** (colloq.) possess so many advantages. **13.** ~ **at,** make attack on; ~ **on,** wear (clothes), be committed to (engagement), (colloq.) play trick on or tease (person); ~ **out,** settle (dispute) by discussion (*with* person), get (tooth) extracted, complete full duration of (one's sleep etc.); ~ **to,** (colloq.) ~ **got to,** be obliged to, MUST[4]; ||~ **up,** bring (person) before court of justice, interviewer(s), etc. **14.** *v. aux.* w. *p.p.* of *vbs.*, forming past tenses (*I have, had, shall have, seen*; *had I known I would have gone*); HAS-BEEN; *have* DONE; *have got to* (see sense 13); **had** = would (*had* BETTER[1], RATHER, *as soon*). [OE *habban*, = OS *hebbian*, OHG *habēn*, ON *hafa*, Goth. *haban* f. Gmc **habhēn*, prob. cogn. w. HEAVE[1]]

hăve[2] *n.* One who has (esp. wealth or resources; **~s and ~-nots,** rich and poor); (sl.) swindle. [f. prec.]

***hă'velock** (-vl-) *n.* Cloth cap-cover with neck-flap to protect wearer against sun etc. [f. Sir H. *Havelock*, Brit. commander in India d. 1857]

hā'ven *n.* Harbour, port; (fig.) refuge. [OE *hæfen* f. ON *höfn*, corresp. to MLG, MDu. *havene*]

have-not. See HAVE[2].

haven't. See HAVE[1].

||**hā'ver** *v.i.*, & *n.* **1.** *v.i.* Talk foolishly, babble; vacillate, hesitate. **2.** *n.* (usu. in *pl.*) (Sc.) Foolish talk, nonsense. [18th c.; orig. unkn.]

hă'versăck *n.* Stout canvas bag for provisions, carried on back or over shoulder by soldier etc. [f. F *havresac* f. G *habersack* (*haber* oats, *sack* SACK[1])]

hă'vildar *n.* Indian n.c.o. corresponding to sergeant. [f. Hind. *ḥavildār* f. Pers. *ḥawāldār* trust-holder]

hă'ving *n.* In vbl senses; (usu. in *pl.*) property, belongings. [ME, f. HAVE[1] + -ING[1]]

hă'voc *n.*, & *v.t.* (**-ck-**). **1.** *n.* Devastation, destruction, confusion, disorder, (*make havoc of*; *play havoc among*); **cry ~,** predict imminent disaster, (orig.) give signal to army to seize spoil. **2.** *v.t.* Devastate (land etc., or abs.). [ME, f. AF *havok* f. OF *havo*(*t*), of unkn. orig.]

haw[1] *n.* (Fruit of) hawthorn; (Hist.) hedge, enclosure; **~'finch,** thick-beaked species of finch. [OE *haga*, = OS *hago*, ON *hagi* f. Gmc **hagon-* (**hag-*; cf. HEDGE[1])]

haw[2] *n.* Nictitating membrane of horse, dog, etc., esp. when inflamed. [16th c.; orig. unkn.]

haw[3] *v.i.*, & *n.* See HUM[1,2]. [f. foll.]

haw[4] *int.* expr. hesitation. [imit.; cf. HA[1]]

haw'-haw[1] *int.* & *n.* (expr.) boisterous laugh or sound of repeated hesitation or affected pausing in speech. [imit.]

haw-haw[2]. Var. of HA-HA.

hawk[1] *n.* & *v.* **1.** *n.* Diurnal bird of prey once much used in falconry, with rounded wings shorter than falcon's; **know a ~ from a handsaw** [perh. corrupt. of *hernshaw* heron f. OF *heronceau* dim.], have ordinary discernment (Shak. *Hamlet* II. ii. 397). **2.** Rapacious or aggressive person, (Polit.) person advocating warlike action. **3.** ***H~'eye State,** Iowa; **~-eyed,** keen-sighted; **~ monitor, ~-moth,** large hovering and darting moth; **~-nosed,** with aquiline nose; **~-owl,** diurnal owl somewhat like hawk; **~'s-bill,** kind of turtle; **~'weed,** plant of genus *Hieracium*, with yellow flowers. **4.** Hence **~'**ISH[1], **~'**LIKE, *adjs.* **5.** *v.i.* Hunt game with hawk. **6.** *v.i.* & *t.* ~ (**at**), attack as hawk does, (of swallows etc.) hunt on the wing for insects. [OE *h*(*e*)*afoc*, *hæbuc*, = OS *habuk*, OHG *habuh*, ON *haukr* f. Gmc **habhukaz*]

hawk[2] *v.t.* Carry (goods) about for sale (lit. or fig.). [back form. f. HAWKER[1]]

hawk[3] *v.* **1.** *v.i.* Clear the throat noisily. **2.** *v.t.* Bring (phlegm etc.) *up* from throat. [prob. imit.]

hawk[4] *n.* Plasterer's square board with handle underneath. [17th c.; orig. unkn.]

haw'ker[1] *n.* One who hawks goods about. [16th c., prob. f. LDu.; cf. MLG *hoker*, LG *höker*, Du. *heuker*; cf. HUCKSTER]

haw'ker[2] *n.* Falconer. [OE *hafocere* (as HAWK[1], -ER[1])]

hawse (-z) *n.* (Naut.) Part of ship's bows in which **~-holes** or **~-pipes** are placed for cables to run through; space between head of anchored vessel and anchors; arrangement of cables when ship is moored with port and starboard forward anchors; ATHWART-*hawse*. [ME *halse*, prob. f. ON *háls* neck, ship's bow]

haw'ser (-z-) *n.* (Naut.) Large rope or small cable; **~-laid,** = CABLE[1]-*laid*. [ME, f. AF *haucer*, *-eour* f. OF *haucier* hoist f. Rom. **altiare* f. L *altus* high; see -ER[2]]

haw'thorn *n.* Thorny shrub or tree of genus *Crataegus*, with white, red, or pink blossom and small dark red berry or haw; **~ china** (Oriental, with pattern of plum-blossom on dark background). [OE *hagathorn* (as HAW[1], THORN)]

hay[1] *n.* & *v.* **1.** *n.* Grass mown and dried for fodder; **hit the ~,** (sl.) go to bed; *look for a* NEEDLE *in a bottle of hay* (= *haystack*); **make ~,** mow grass and turn it over for exposure to sun; **make ~ of,** throw into confusion, overthrow; **make ~ (while the sun shines),** seize opportunities for profit; ***not ~,** (colloq.) a large amount of money; **roll in the ~,** (colloq.) make love. **2. ~'box** (stuffed with hay, in which heated food is left to continue cooking); **~'cock,** conical heap of hay in field; **~ fever,** summer disorder with catarrhal and freq. asthmatic symptoms, caused by pollen or dust; **~'field** (where hay is being or is to be made); **~-fork** (for turning over or loading hay); **~'maker,** one who lifts, tosses, and spreads hay after mowing, apparatus for shaking and drying hay, (sl.) swinging blow or punch; **~-mow,** hay in stack or barn; **~'-rick, ~'stack,** regular pile of hay with pointed or ridged top (NEEDLE *in haystack*); **~'seed,** grass seed from hay, *(colloq.) a rustic; **~'wire,** poorly or roughly contrived [f. use of hay-baling wire in makeshift repairs], (colloq.) tangled, in disorder, distracted. **3.** *v.t.* Put (land) under grass for hay; make into hay. **4.** *v.i.* Make hay. [OE *hēg*, *hīeg*, *hīg*, = OS *hōi*, OHG *hewi*, *houwi*, ON *hey*, Goth. *hawi* f. Gmc **haujam* (**hauwan* HEW)]

hay[2], **hey**[2], (hā) *n.* (Figure in) country dance with interweaving steps. [f. obs. f. *haie*]

hay'ward (-ŏrd) *n.* Officer of parish etc. in charge of fences and enclosures. [ME, f. obs. *hay* hedge f. OE *hege* (as HAW[1]) + WARD[1]]

hă'zard *n.*, & *v.t.* **1.** *n.* Dice game with complicated chances; chance; (source of) danger; **at ~,** (arch.) at random; **at all ~s,** despite all risks. **2.** Each of winning openings in real-tennis court; (Bill.) **winning ~**, striking object-ball into pocket, **losing ~**, pocketing own ball off another; (Golf) obstruction in playing a shot, e.g. bunker, water, road, etc. **3.** *v.t.* Expose to hazard; run the risk of; venture on (action, statement, guess). [n. ME, v. f. F *hasarder*, f. OF *hasard* f. Sp. *azar* f. Arab. *al-zahr* chance, luck]

hă'zardous *a.* Risky; dependent on chance; hence ~LY[2] *adv.*, ~NESS *n.* [f. F *hasardeux* (as prec.; see -OUS)]

hāze[1] *n.*, & *v.t.* **1.** *n.* Obscuration of atmosphere near earth by fine particles of water, smoke, or fine dust; (fig.) mental obscurity or confusion. **2.** *v.t.* Make hazy. [prob. back form. f. HAZY]

hāze[2] *v.t.* **1.** (Naut.) Harass with overwork. **2.** *Bully, seek to disconcert. [cf. obs. F *haser* tease, insult]

hā'zel *n.* Bush of genus *Corylus* whose fruit is the **~-nut**; (stick of) its wood; reddish-brown or greenish-brown or light brown colour (esp. of eyes); **~-grouse, -hen,** species of grouse (*Tetrastes bonasia*); *witch-* or WYCH-*hazel.* [OE *hæsel*, = OHG *hasal*, ON *hasl* f. Gmc **hasalaz* f. IE **kosolos*]

hā'z|ў *a.* Misty; vague, indistinct; (arch.) slightly drunk; hence ~ĭLY[2] *adv.*, ~ĭNESS *n.* [17th c., Naut., also *hawsey, heysey*, of unkn. orig.]

HB *abbr.* hard black (pencil-lead).

Hb *symb.* haemoglobin.

H.B.M. *abbr.* Her or His Britannic Majesty('s).

H-bomb (ā'chbŏm) *n.* Hydrogen bomb. [f. H (for HYDROGEN) + BOMB]

H.C. *abbr.* Holy Communion; House of Commons.

h.c. *abbr. honoris causa.*

H.C.F. *abbr.* highest common factor; ||Honorary Chaplain to the Forces.

hē[1] (*or, when unstressed,* hĭ) *pron.* (*obj.* **him** *pr.* ĭm *or, when stressed,* hĭm; *refl.* HIMSELF *or* arch. **him,** *poss.* HIS, *pl.* THEY etc.), *n.*, & *a.* **1.** *pron.* The male (or thing personified as male, e.g. tree, sun, or person of unknown or unspecified sex) previously mentioned or implied or easily identified; the or any male person *who*; = IT[1] 8; **him** (colloq.; cf. HER[1] 2). **2.** *n.* Male, man, (cf. SHE). **3.** *a.* (usu. w. hyphen). Male (*he-goat*); **~-man,** masterful or virile man. [OE *he, hē*, dat. *him*, = OS *hi(e), he* f. Gmc dem. st. **hi-*]

hē[2]**(-hē')** *int.* expr. amusement or derision. [OE; natural excl.]

H.E. *abbr.* high explosive; His Eminence; His or Her Excellency.

He *symb.* helium.

head[1] (hĕd) *n.* **1.** Foremost part of body of animal, upper part of human body, containing mouth, sense-organs, and brain; (as measure) length of head (*taller by a head*; *horse won by a* (SHORT) *head*); *cannot* **make ~ or tail of,** understand at all; **count ~s,** (merely) determine number present, voting, etc. **2.** Seat of intellect or imagination; natural aptitude or talent (*a good head for business*); **~ for heights,** ability to be close to edge of high cliff, roof, etc., without giddiness. **3.** (colloq.) Headache, esp. as result of blow or intoxication. **4.** Life (*it cost him his head*; a PRICE *on his head*). **5.** Image of head on one side of coin; (usu. in *pl.*) this side turned upwards after toss (cf. TAIL[1]). **6.** Antlers of deer; **deer of the first ~** (when antlers are first developed). **7.** Person with ... head (*crowned heads*; HOT[1]*head*); individual (*£1 a* or *per head*); individual animal of cattle, (collect.) cattle (*twenty head*), whence ~'AGE (1) *n.*; ||number of animals (*large head of game*); (sl.) drug-addict, one who takes drugs. **8.** Thing like head in form or position, e.g. cutting or striking part of tool, golf-club, etc., knobbed end of NAIL[1], pin, screw, etc., rounded part of musical note; (of plant) compact mass of leaves or flowers at top of stem; ||roof of motor car; flat surface of cask, drum, etc.; closed end of cylinder in pump or engine; device for converting electrical signals into record on magnetic tape etc. or vice versa. **9.** Foam on top of liquor; cream on top of milk. **10.** Top (of mast, staircase, list, page, etc.); ||**~ of the river,** leading position in bumping-races. **11.** Fully developed part of boil etc., where it tends to break; **come to a ~**, (fig.) reach a climax or crisis. **12.** Upper end; end of table occupied by host; end of lake at which river enters it; end of bed, couch, grave, etc., at which one's head rests. **13.** Body of water kept at height for mill etc.; pressure exerted by this; pressure of confined body of steam etc. **14.** Front (of procession, army, etc.); front part of plough, holding the share; bows of ship (BY[1] *the head*); (colloq.) headlight. **15.** Promontory (in names, as *Beachy Head*). **16.** Underground passage for working in coal-mine. **17.** Ruler, chief; master etc. of college; headmaster of school; (*attrib.*) occupying leading position with regard to others (*head boy, clerk, girl, office, waiter*); hence ~'SHIP *n.* **18.** Position of command (*at the head of*). **19.** Main division in discourse; category. **20.** Culmination, crisis, (*bring to a head*; cf. sense 11). **21.** (Naut.; in *sing.* or *pl.*) Seamen's latrine in ship's bows. **22. Above** one's **~**, = *over* one's *head* (1, 2); **come into** or **enter** one's **~**, (of idea) be thought of; **from ~ to foot,** all over a person; **get** one's **~ down,** (sl.) go to bed; GET[1] *it into* one's *head that*; **give** (**horse,** or fig. person) **his ~, let him have his ~**, allow him to go freely; **go to** person's **~**, (of liquor, success, etc.) impair his mental acuteness or his modesty; HANG[1] one's *head*; **~ and front,** (arch.) essence *of* offence or leader *of* action, (Shak.) highest extent; **~ and shoulders,** (*taller* etc.) by measure of head and shoulders or (fig.) considerably; **drag in** (irrelevant topic) **by the ~ and shoulders; ~ first** or **foremost,** (of plunge etc.) with the head foremost, (fig.) precipitately; *head in the air* or CLOUD*s*; *head in the* SAND; **~ of hair,** the hair on person's head, esp. as noticeable feature; one's or person's **~ off,** (fig.) into a state of exhaustion (*beat* or *talk* person's *head off*; BITE[1] person's *head off*; EAT *its head off*; *laugh* one's *head off*); **~ over ears** or **heels,** = *over head and* EAR[1]*s*; **~ over heels,** topsy-turvy, so as to turn completely over in somersault etc.; **~s will roll,** (fig.) there will be some persons dismissed or disgraced; HOLD[1] one's *head high*; **hold up** one's **~**, not be ashamed; **in** one's **~**, by thought, mental calculation, etc.; **keep** one's **~**, remain calm; **keep** one's **~ above water,** (fig.) keep out of debt; **keep** one's **~ down,** avoid distraction or danger; ||KNOCK[1] *on the head*; **lay** or **put ~s together,** consult one another; **lose** one's **~**, (1) be beheaded, (2) become agitated or confused; **make ~**, make progress or resistance; **off** one's **~**, crazy; **off the top of** one's **~**, (sl.) impromptu; *old head on young* SHOULDER*s*; **on** one's **~**, supported by head and arms with feet off ground, (sl.) with great ease (*could do it on my head*); **on** one's (**own**) **~**, (of vengeance, guilt, responsibility, etc.) falling on one; **out of** one's **~**, (1) from one's own invention, (2) forgotten by one, (3) *crazy; *over head and* EAR[1]*s*; **over** one's **~**, (1) above one, esp. fig. of impending danger etc., (2) beyond one's comprehension, (3) (of another's promotion etc.) when one has prior or stronger claim; **put into** person's **~**, suggest (idea etc.) to him; **put ~s together,** = *lay heads together*; *head* SCREWED *on the right way*; SWELL*ed* or *swollen head*; **take it into** one's ~, conceive notion (*that* or *to*); TURN[1] person's *head*; **two ~s are better than one,** combination of two persons' ideas is superior to those of either separately. **23. ~'ache,** continuous pain in head, (colloq.) troublesome or annoying thing; **~'achy,** suffering from or causing headache; **~'band,** band worn round head; **~'board** (forming head of bed etc.); **~'borough,** (Hist.) petty constable; ***~ cheese,** brawn made from pig's head etc.; **~-cloth,** cloth or covering for head; **~-dress,** covering (esp. ornamental attire) for the head; **~'fast,** rope or chain securing head of vessel to quay etc.; **~'gear,** (1) hat, cap, head-dress, (2) machinery etc. at top of mine-shaft; **~-hunter,** savage who collects heads of his enemies as trophies; **~'lamp,** = *headlight*; **~'land,** (1) promontory, (2) strip left (at first) unploughed at end of field; **~'light,** (beam from) powerful lamp carried on front of locomotive, motor vehicle, etc.; **~'line,** line at top of page containing title etc., title or sub-title in large type in newspaper, (in *pl.*) summary at beginning of broadcast news bulletin (*hit* or *make the ~lines*, be very important news); ***~'liner,** star performer; **~'lock,** wrestling hold with arm round opponent's head; **~'man,** chief man, chief of tribe etc.; **~ma'ster, ~mi'stress,** principal master, mistress, of school; **~-money** (paid for or by each person); **~-note** (inserted at head of page or document); **~-on** *a.*, involving the meeting of two vehicles head to head (*a head-on collision*), or of the head of a vehicle with a stationary object, (fig.) with direct opposition; **~-o'n** *adv.*, with the head pointed directly towards some object; **~'phone,** radio or telephone receiver held by band fitting over head; **~'piece,** (1) helmet, (2) intellect, man of intellect, (3) ornamental engraving at head of chapter etc.; **~quar'ters,** (as *pl.* or *sing.*), central or chief place of business etc., (Mil.) quarters of officer commanding army, corps, division, etc.; **~-race,** part of mill-race bringing water to wheel; **~-rest,** support for head of person sitting in vehicle etc.; **~'room,** overhead space; **~-sail** (on foremast or bowsprit); **~'scarf** (worn instead of hat); **~ sea,** waves from forward direction; **~-set,** attachment for fixing earphones and microphone to head; **~-shrinker,** head-hunter who shrinks enemies' heads, (sl.) psychiatrist; **~'spring,** main source of stream (lit. or fig.); **~'square,** scarf for head; **~'stall,** part of bridle or halter that fits round horse's head; **~ start,** = START[2] 3 (in race, or fig.); **~'stock,** bearings of revolving parts in machine; **~'stone,** (1) gravestone, (2) chief stone in foundation (lit. or fig.); ***~ tax,** poll-tax; **~-up,** (of instrument-readings in aircraft, vehicle, etc.) shown so as to be visible without lowering one's eyes from view ahead; **~-voice,** high register of voice in speaking or singing; **~'water(s),** streams from sources of river; **~'way,** (1) progress, (of ship) rate of progress, (2) headroom, (3) interval between successive buses etc. on route; **~ wind** (blowing from directly in front); **~'word,** word forming a heading (of entry in dictionary etc.), (Ling.) word qualified in phrase; **~-work,** mental work. **24.** Hence (-)~'ED, ~'LESS, *adjs.* [OE *hēafod*, = OS *hōbid*, OHG *houbit*, ON *haufuth*, Goth. f. Gmc **haubhudham*]

head² (hĕd) *v.* **1.** *v.t.* Furnish with head or heading; ~ (**down**), lop off head of (plant, tree); be or form the head of; place inscription, (of name etc.) be placed, at head of (chapter, list, etc.); lead; precede; surpass; ~ (***up**), be, put oneself, at the head of (a company etc.); (Footb.) strike (ball) with head; direct course of *towards* etc.; ~ **back, off,** get ahead of so as to force to turn back, aside. **2.** *v.i.* Face (in specified direction); ~ **for,** (of ship etc.) be moving towards (place, point, or fig. disaster etc.). [ME, f. prec.]

-head (hĕd) *suf.* Var. of -HOOD (*godhead, maidenhead*). [f. ME *-hed(e)* -HOOD]

hea'der (hĕ'd-) *n.* In vbl senses; one who puts heads on casks etc.; brick or stone laid at right angles to face of wall (cf. STRETCHER); (colloq.) dive or plunge head first; (Footb.) act of heading the ball. [ME, f. HEAD[1,2] + -ER[1]]

hea'dĭng (hĕ'd-) *n.* In vbl senses; (Footb.) striking ball with head; material for making cask-heads; title etc. at head of page etc.; horizontal passage in preparation for tunnel. [ME, f. HEAD[2] + -ING[1]]

hea'dlŏng (hĕ'd-) *adv.* & *a.* Head foremost (in falling etc.); precipitate(ly); impetuous(ly). [ME *headling* (HEAD[1], -LING[2]), assim. to -LONG]

hea'dmost (hĕ'd-; *or* -ō-) *a.* (Esp. of ship) foremost. [f. HEAD[1] + -MOST]

hea'ds|man (hĕ'dz-) *n.* (*pl.* **~men**). Executioner who beheads; man in command of whaling boat. [ME, f. HEAD[1] + -'s 1 + MAN[1]]

hea'dstrŏng (hĕ'd-) *a.* Violently self-willed; obstinate; hence ~NESS *n.* [ME, f. HEAD[1] + STRONG, = strong in head]

hea'd|ȳ (hĕ'dĭ) *a.* (Of person, thing, action) impetuous, violent; (of liquor etc., or fig. of triumph etc.) apt to intoxicate; hence ~ĬLY[2] *adv.*, ~ĬNESS *n.* [ME, f. HEAD[1] + -Y[2]]

heal¹ *v.* **1.** *v.t.* Restore (person, injured part) to health (lit. or fig.); cure (person, wound; *of* disease); **~-all,** (1) universal remedy, (2) (pop. name of various medicinal plants). **2.** *v.i.* ~ (**over, up**), (of wound or part) become healed. **3.** Hence ~'ER[1] *n.* (*time is a great healer*). [OE *hǣlan*, = OS *hēlian*, OHG *heilen*, ON *heila*, Goth. *hailjan* f. Gmc **hailjan* (**hailaz* WHOLE)]

heal². See HELE.

heald *n.* = HEDDLE. [app. f. OE *hefel(d)*, = OS *hevild*, ON *hafald* f. Gmc **hafjan* raise]

health (hĕl-) *n.* **1.** Soundness of body (lit. or fig.; **for** one's ~, in order to attain or maintain good health; **not for** one's ~, for one's material advantage); condition of body (*good, poor, bad, ill, health*; BILL[4] *of health*); toast drunk in person's honour. **2.** ~ **centre,** local headquarters of medical services; ~ **certificate** (stating person's fitness for work etc.); ~ **food** (chosen for its dietary or health-giving or unmodified natural qualities); ~ **officer** (charged with administering health laws etc.); ~ **physics,** study of health of persons exposed to radiation from radioactive materials; ~ **resort,** place visited for benefit of one's health; ~ **salts,** mild aperient; ~ **service,** public medical services collectively; ||~ **visitor,** trained person visiting sick or old people etc. at their homes. [OE *hǣlth*, = OHG *heilida* f. WG **hailitha* f. Gmc **hailaz* WHOLE; see -TH[1]]

hea'lthful (hĕ'l-) *a.* Health-giving; conducive to moral or spiritual welfare; hence ~LY[2] *adv.*, ~NESS *n.* [ME, f. prec. + -FUL]

hea'lth|ȳ (hĕ'l-) *a.* Having good health (lit. or fig.); conducive to good health (*healthy climate*); beneficial (*a healthy interest in, respect for*); hence ~ĬLY[2] *adv.*, ~ĬNESS *n.* [f. HEALTH + -Y[2]]

heap¹ *n.* Group of things lying one on another; (in *sing.* or *pl.*, colloq.) large number or quantity (*a heap of people*; *there is heaps of time*; *have seen it heaps of times*; *he is heaps better*); (colloq.) battered old motor vehicle; *knock* or STRIKE *all of a heap*; **top, bottom, of the ~,**

(colloq., fig.) winner, loser. [OE *hēap*, = OS *hōp*, OHG *houf*, *hūfo*, f. Gmc **haup-*, **hūp-*]

heap[2] *v.t.* Pile (things *up*, *together*, etc.) in a heap; load (cart, person, etc. esp. above normal level *with* goods, benefits, etc.); place large quantities of (insults etc. *upon*). [OE *hēapian* (as prec.)]

***hea'pĭng** *a.* (Of spoonful etc.) heaped; (fig.) mounting up. [f. prec. + -ING[2]]

hear *v.* (**heard** *pr.* hẽrd). **1.** *v.t.* Perceive (sound etc., or abs.) with the ear (*I heard a groan, him groaning, him groan; he was heard groaning* or *to groan*). **2.** Listen to (*hear him, his lesson, a sermon*); listen judicially to (case, plaintiff, etc.); grant (prayer), obey (order); ~ **out,** listen to whole of (what is said by). **3.** Learn by being told (*that*); ~ **say,** ~ **tell** (**of**), (arch. or dial.) be told (about). **4.** *v.i.* Be told (*about*); ~ **from,** receive letter or message from; ~ **of,** be told about, (w. neg.) be willing to consider (*will not hear of my paying for it*); ~ (**more**) **of,** (fig.) be reprimanded etc. for. **5.** **~!, ~!** (as form of cheering a speaker or iron. derision etc.); **~'say,** what one hears (but does not certainly know to be true), gossip, (often *attrib.*; *hearsay evidence*). **6.** Hence ~'ABLE *a.*, ~'ER[1] *n.* [OE *hīeran*, = OS *hōrian*, OHG *hōrren*, ON *heyra*, Goth. *hausjan* f. Gmc **hauzjan*]

heard. See prec.

hear'ing *n.* In vbl senses; faculty of perception by response of brain to action of sound on ear (**hard of** ~, somewhat deaf); **within, out of,** ~, near enough, too far off, to be heard; **in** one's ~, so that one can hear; **a fair** ~, impartial listening to statement of case; **~-aid,** small sound-amplifier worn by deaf person to improve hearing. [f. HEAR + -ING[1]]

hear'ken (har'-) *v.i.* (arch. or literary). Listen (*to*). [OE *he(o)rcnian* (as HARK, -EN[6])]

hearse (hẽrs) *n.* Vehicle for carrying coffin at funeral; (arch.) framework supporting pall at great person's funeral and carrying tapers and other decorations. [ME, f. OF *herse* harrow f. med. L *erpica* f. Rom. **herpica* f. L *(h)irpex -picis* large rake f. Samnite *(h)irpus* wolf, w. ref. to its teeth]

heart (hart) *n.*, & *v.i.* **1.** *n.* Hollow muscular organ keeping up circulation of blood by contracting and dilating; disease of this (*I believe he has a heart*). **2.** Breast, bosom, (*pressed her to his heart*); mind, intellect; seat of inmost thoughts, = SOUL 2 (~ **to** ~, with candour); **after** one's **own** ~, just such as one likes or desires; one's ~ **is not in it,** one is not really interested in succeeding etc. **3.** Seat of the emotions, esp. of love, opp. *head* as seat of intellect, (**give** or **lose** one's ~ **to,** fall in love with; *win the heart of*). **4.** Susceptibility to emotion (*he has no heart*); courage (*pluck up* or *take, lose, heart*). **5.** (As term of endearment to person: *dear, sweet, heart*); (Naut. etc.) brave fellow. **6.** Central or innermost part, e.g. of tree (~ **of oak,** courageous man); close compact head of cabbage, lettuce, etc.; vital part, essence, (*the heart of the matter*). **7.** (Of land) fertility (**in good** ~, in prime condition; **out of** ~, in poor condition). **8.** Heart-shaped thing; conventional symmetrical figure of a heart with two equal curves meeting in point and cusp; playing-card of suit (**~s**) denoted by red figure of this kind; (in *pl.*) card-game in which players try not to take tricks containing card of this suit. **9.** **At** ~, in one's inmost feelings; **have at** ~, be deeply interested in; **bless his** etc. ~ (excl. of pleasure); **bless my** ~ (excl. of surprise); **from** or **to the bottom of** one's ~, genuinely, profoundly; **break** person's ~, overwhelm him with sorrow; **by** ~, in or from memory (*learn* or *say by heart*); **change of** ~, conversion to different frame of mind; **find it in** one's ~, (esp. w. neg.) prevail upon oneself (*to* do); **from** one's or **the** ~, sincerely; **go to** one's or **the** ~, deeply touch or grieve one; **do** one's ~ **good,** cheer or rejoice one; **have a** ~, (sl.) be merciful; **have the** ~, (esp. w. neg.) be hard-hearted enough (*to* do); *heart* BLEEDS; *to* one's *heart's* CONTENT[2]; one's ~ **goes out to,** one feels strong affection or sympathy for; one's ~ **is in** one's **boots,** one is terrified or dejected; *heart of* GOLD; **take** ~ **of grace,** pluck up one's courage; one's ~ **is in** one's **mouth,** one is violently alarmed or startled; one's ~ **is in the right place,** one has good intentions; **wear** one's ~ **on** one's **sleeve,** let one's feelings be quite obvious; ~ **and soul,** with all one's energy or devotion; one's ~ **stands still,** one is momentarily paralysed with fright; **in** ~, in good spirits; **in** one's ~, secretly, in one's inmost feelings; **in** one's ~ **of** **~s,** in one's inmost feelings; **lay to** ~, think over seriously; **near**(**est**) one's ~, dear(est) to one, affecting one (most) deeply; **out of** ~, in low spirits (and see sense 7); *cry, play,* etc., one's ~ **out,** to exhaustion, with utmost effort; **eat** one's ~ **out,** pine away with vexation or longing; SET[1] one's *heart on*; **take to** ~, be much affected by; **with all** one's ~, sincerely, with the utmost goodwill. **10.** **~'ache,** mental anguish; ~ **attack,** = *heart failure*; **~'beat,** pulsation of heart, (fig.) emotion; **~-block,** failure of parts of heart to beat together, caused by muscular defect; **~('s)-blood,** life-blood, life; **~-break,** overwhelming distress (**~-breaking, -broken,** causing, crushed by, this); **~'burn,** pyrosis; **~-burn**(**ing**), jealousy, grudge; **~-cherry,** heart-shaped cultivated sweet cherry; **~-disease** (of heart); ~ **failure,** deranged action of heart, esp. if fatal; **~'felt,** sincere (emotion etc.); **~'land,** central or most important part of an area; **~-lung machine** (providing means to by-pass these organs in blood circulation during an operation); **~-rending,** distressing; **~-searching,** examination of one's own feelings; **~'s-ease,** pansy; **~'sick,** despondent; **~'sore,** grieved at heart; **~-strings,** (fig.) deepest affections; **~-throb,** beating of heart, (sl.) object of one's infatuation; **~-warming,** emotionally moving and encouraging; **~-whole,** (1) undismayed, (2) not in love, (3) sincere; **~'wood,** dense inner part of tree-trunk yielding hardest timber. **11.** Hence -~'ED[2] *a.* **12.** *v.i.* (Of cabbage etc.) form a heart. [OE *heorte*, = OS *herta*, OHG *herza*, ON *hjarta*, Goth. *hairtō* f. Gmc **herton* f. IE **k(e)rd-*]

hear'ten (har'-) *v.* **1.** *v.t.* Inspirit, cheer (*up* or *on*). **2.** *v.i.* Cheer *up*. [f. prec. v.t. in same sense + -EN[6]]

hearth (har-) *n.* **1.** Floor of fireplace; ~ **and home,** home and its comforts; **~-money,** 17th-c. tax on hearths in England & Wales; **~'rug** (laid before fireplace); **~'stone,** (1) flat stone forming hearth, (2) stone etc. for whitening hearths etc. **2.** Bottom of blast-furnace where molten metal collects. [OE *heorth*, = OS *herth*, OHG *hert* f. WG **hertha*]

hear'tĭlў (har'-) *adv.* In adj. senses; with goodwill, courage, or appetite; very (*am heartily sick of it*). [ME, f. HEARTY + -LY[2]]

hear'tless (har'-) *a.* Unfeeling, pitiless, cruel; hence ~LY[2] *adv.*, ~NESS *n.* [ME, f. HEART + -LESS]

hear't|ў (har'-) *a.* & *n.* **1.** *a.* Cordial, genial; (of feelings) sincere; vigorous (*hearty laugh*); (of meal) abundant; hence **~ĭNESS** *n.* **2.** *n.* Hearty person (as *voc.* to sailors: *my hearties*); ‖(at university) sportsman, athlete (opp. AESTHETE). [ME, f. HEART + -Y[2]]

heat[1] *n.* **1.** Being hot; sensation or perception of this; (high) temperature; RED, WHITE[1], *heat.* **2.** (Phys.) Form of energy arising from random motion of molecules of bodies, capable of transmission by conduction, convection, or radiation, (formerly thought to be an elastic material fluid); amount of this needed to cause a specified process, or evolved in a process, (*heat of formation; heat of solution*); **latent ~,** heat required to convert a solid into liquid or vapour, or a liquid into vapour, without change of temperature; **specific ~,** heat required to raise temperature of unit mass of a given substance by given amount (usu. one degree), usu. calculated relatively to water. **3.** Hot weather. **4.** (Normal or abnormal) high temperature of body. **5.** Pungency of flavour. **6.** Redness of skin with sensation of heat; PRICKLY *heat.* **7.** Single run in race etc.; (**trial**) **~s,** races or contests the winners of which compete in FINAL (*heat*). **8.** Warmth of feeling, anger; most vigorous stage (of debate etc.); (sl.) pursuit by police etc.; **in the ~ of the moment,** without pause for thought, as a result of the vigorous action etc. then in progress. **9.** Sexual excitement of (esp. female) animals during breeding season (**on, in,** or **at ~,** undergoing this). **10. ~ barrier,** limitation of speed of aircraft etc. by heat resulting from air friction; **~ bump,** skin-protuberance thought to be due to heat; **~ capacity,** thermal capacity; **~ death,** (Phys.) state of uniform distribution of energy to which universe seems to be tending; **~-engine** (producing motive power from heat); **~-exchange(r),** (device for) transfer of heat from one medium to another; **~ pump,** reversed heat-engine, using mechanical energy to transfer heat to hotter place; **~-resistant,** = *heat*-PROOF[2]; **~ shield,** device to protect from excessive heat (esp. on spacecraft during re-entry); **~ sink,** device for removing unwanted heat; **~-stroke,** prostration from excessive heat; **~ treatment,** use of heat to modify properties of metal etc.; *heat* WAVE[2]. [OE *hǣtu,* = MDu. *hēte,* OHG *heizī* f. WG **haitī(n)* f. Gmc **haitaz* HOT[1]]

heat[2] *v.* **1.** *v.t.* Make hot or warm; inflame (blood etc.); (esp. in *p.p.*) inflame with rage or passion, excite. **2.** *v.i.* Become hot or warm (lit. or fig.). [OE *hǣtan,* = OHG *heizen,* ON *heita* f. Gmc **haitjan* (**haitaz* HOT[1])]

hea'ter *n.* In vbl senses; stove; warming device; (sl.) firearm. [f. prec. + -ER[1]]

heath *n.* Open flat waste tract of land, esp. if covered with shrubs; shrub growing on such land, esp. of genus *Erica* or *Calluna*; butterfly frequenting heath; **~-bell,** bell-shaped flower of heath; **~-cock,** blackcock; **~-hen,** grey-hen; hence **~'Y**[2] *a.* [OE *hǣth,* = OS *hētha,* OHG *heida,* ON *heithr,* Goth. *haithi* f. Gmc **haithiz*]

hea'then (-dh-) *a.* & *n.* **1.** (One who is) not an adherent of any of the world's chief religions, esp. (one who is) neither Christian, Jew, nor Muslim; (O.T.) Gentile; **the ~,** (collect.) heathen people. **2.** *n.* Unenlightened person; person regarded as lacking culture or moral principles. **3.** Hence **~DOM, ~ISM** (2), **~RY** (2), *ns.,* **~ISH**[1] *a.,* **~IZE** (3) *v.t.* & *i.* [OE *hǣthen,* = OS *hēthin,* OHG *heidan,* ON *heithinn,* Goth. *haithnō* Gentile, f. Gmc **haithanaz* savage (**haith*-HEATH, perh. rendering L *paganus* PAGAN; see -EN[5])]

hea'ther (hĕ'dh-) *n.* Plant or shrub of genus *Erica, Calluna,* or *Daboecia,* esp. *Calluna vulgaris*; **take to the ~,** (Sc. Hist.) become outlaw; **~-bell,** (flower of) *Erica tetralix* or *cinerea*; **~ mixture,** (fabric) of mixed hues supposed to resemble heather; hence **~Y**[2] *a.* [ME, Sc. & N. Engl. *hathir* etc., of unkn. orig.; assim. to *heath*]

Heath Rŏ'bĭnson *a.* Absurdly ingenious and impracticable in construction. [f. W. ~, Engl. cartoonist d. 1944, who drew many such contrivances]

heave[1] *v.* (**~d** *or,* esp. Naut., **hove** *pr.* hōv). **1.** *v.t.* Lift (heavy thing); utter (groan, sigh) with effort; (Naut. or colloq.) throw (*heave the* LEAD[1]); (Naut.) haul up, haul, by rope. **2.** *v.i.* Rise, swell up; rise with alternate falls, as waves; pant; retch; pull (*at* rope etc.). **3. ~ down,** turn (ship) over on one side for cleaning etc.; **~ to,** bring (vessel, or abs.) to standstill with head to wind; **~ in sight,** become visible; **~ ho** (*int.,* cry of sailors in heaving anchor up), (*n.,* sl.) snub, dismissal. [OE *hebban,* = OS *hebbian,* OHG *heffen,* ON *hefja,* Goth. *hafjan* f. Gmc **habhjan* cogn. w. L *capere* take]

heave[2] *n.* Heaving; **~ of the sea,** force exerted by swell of sea on ship's course; (in *pl.*) disease of horses with laboured breathing, broken wind. [f. prec.]

hea'ven (hĕ'-) *n.* **1.** (usu. *pl.* exc. poet.) Apparent vault over the earth, in which sun, moon, and stars are seen (*the spangled heavens*); region of the atmosphere in which clouds float, winds blow, and birds fly, (**the ~s opened,** there was a downpour). **2.** (Hist.) = SPHERE 3. **3.** Abode of immortals; habitation of God and his angels and the beatified spirits, usually regarded as beyond sky (opp. *hell*); **seventh ~, ~ of ~s,** highest of seven heavens recognized by Muslims and some Jews, abode of God; **in the seventh ~,** in a state of extreme delight or exaltation; **move ~ and earth,** make every possible effort (*to* do). **4.** (usu. *H~*). God, Providence, (*it is Heaven's will*); (in asseverations and exclamations: **by H~!,** GOOD *heavens!,* **H~s above!, H~ forbid** or FORFEND!, **H~ (only) knows,** *in Heaven's* NAME[1], *for Heaven's* SAKE[1], THANK *heaven(s)!,* (cf. phrs. at GOD). **5.** Place or state of supreme bliss or great delight. **6. ~-born,** of divine origin; **~-sent,** providential. **7.** Hence **~WARD** *a.,* **~WARD(s)** *adv.* [OE *heofon, hefen, heben,* = OS *heban,* ON *himinn hifn-,* Goth. *himins*]

hea'venlў (hĕ'-) *a.* Of heaven, divine, (**the H~ City,** Paradise; *the heavenly* HOST[1]); of the sky (*heavenly* BODY[1]); of more than earthly or human excellence; (colloq.) attractive, excellent, (*what a heavenly day!*); **~-minded,** holy, devout; hence **hea'venlĭNESS** (hĕ'-) *n.* [OE *heofonlic* (as prec., -LY[1])]

hea'ver *n.* In vbl senses; COAL-*heaver.* [f. HEAVE[1] + -ER[1]]

Hea'vĭsīde (hĕ'-) *n.* **~ layer,** layer of ionosphere able to reflect long radio waves. [f. O. ~, Engl. physicist d. 1925]

hea'vў (hĕ'-) *a., n.,* & *adv.* **1.** *a.* Of great weight; of great density; weighty because abundant (*a heavy crop*); laden *with*; (of ordnance) of the larger kind (*heavy guns, artillery*); (Mil.) carrying heavy arms (*the heavy brigade*). **2.** (Phys.) Having a greater than the usual mass (esp. of isotopes and compounds containing them; **~ hydrogen,** DEUTERIUM; **~ water,** substance composed entirely or mainly of deuterium oxide). **3.** Severe, intense, extensive, (*heavy fighting, frost, losses*); acting in this manner (*heavy drinker, loser*); (of jazz etc.) serious, forceful. **4.** Striking or falling with force (*heavy blows, rain, sea, storm*); causing strong impact (*heavy fall*). **5.** (Of ground) clinging, difficult to travel over; (of bread etc.) dense from not having risen; (of food or fig. of writings) hard to digest. **6.** (Of sky) overcast, gloomy. **7.** Clumsy or ungraceful in appearance or effect (*heavy features*); (of person) intellectually slow; unwieldy; (of artistic or literary production) dull, tedious; (of newspaper etc.) serious in tone; (Theatr.) serious, sombre, (*heavy villain*); ponderously dignified, sternly repressive, (*heavy father*). **8.** Oppressive, grievous, (*a heavy fate*); sad (*heavy news*); despondent; doleful; drowsy; **lie ~**, make its weight felt; *time* HANG[1]*s heavy*. **9. Heavier-than-air′,** (of aircraft) weighing more than the air it displaces; **~-armed,** bearing heavy weapons or armour; *heavy* CHEMICAL*s*; **~-duty,** intended to be unusually resistant to stresses in use; **~-footed,** ponderous; **~-handed,** ungraceful, oppressive; **~-hearted,** melancholy, doleful; **~ industry** (concerned with production of metal, machines, etc.); **~ metal,** (1) heavy guns, (fig.) formidable opponent(s), (2) metal of high density; **~ oil,** a heavier-than-water oil obtained from coal tar by distillation at high temperature; **~ spar,** barytes; **~ swell,** strong swell of sea, (arch. colloq.) man who emphasizes his real or imagined importance by overdressing etc.; **~ traffic,** (1) lorries and other large vehicles, (2) large quantity of vehicles; **~ type,** printed characters with unusually thick strokes; *heavy* WEATHER[1]; **~weight,** jockey, boxer (see BOX[5]), etc., of more than average weight, (fig.) person of unusual ability or importance. **10.** Hence ~ISH[1] 2 *a.*, **hea′vĭ**LY[2] *adv.*, **hea′vĭ**NESS *n.*, (hĕ′-). **11.** *n.* (Theatr.) heavy character (see sense 7); (usu. in *pl.*) heavy vehicle, serious newspaper; (in *pl.*) heavy artillery. **12.** *adv.* Heavily (esp. in *comb.*: *heavy-laden*). [OE *hefig*, = OS *hebig*, OHG *hebīg*, ON *höfugr*, *höfigr* f. Gmc **habhuza-* (**habhiz* weight, cogn. w. HEAVE)]

Heb. *abbr.* Hebrew; Hebrews (N.T.).

hĕ′bdomăd *n.* Week (esp. in reference to Dan. 9:27). [f. LL f. Gk *hebdomas -ados* (*hepta* seven; see -AD)]

hĕbdŏ′madal *a.* Weekly; **H~ Council,** (Oxf. Univ.) representative board meeting weekly. [f. LL *hebdomadalis* (as prec.; see -AL)]

hĕ′bėtāte *v.t.* & *i.* (literary). Make or become dull. [f. L *hebetare* (*hebes -etis* blunt) + -ATE[3]]

hĕ′bėtūde *n.* (literary). Dullness, lethargy. [f. LL *hebetudo* (as prec.; see -TUDE)]

Hēbrā′|ĭc *a.* Of Hebrew or the Hebrews; hence ~ICALLY *adv.* [f. LL f. Gk *Hebraikos* (as HEBREW; see -IC)]

Hē′brā|ĭsm *n.* Attribute of the Hebrews; Hebrew system of thought or religion; Hebrew idiom or expression esp. in the Greek of the Bible; so ~IZE (3) *v.t.* & *i.*, **~ĭ′st**IC *a.* [f. F *hébraïsme* or f. mod. L f. late Gk *Hebraïsmos*; see HEBREW, -ISM]

Hē′brāĭst *n.* Person skilled in Hebrew. [f. HEBRAIC + -IST]

Hē′brew (-ōō) *n.* & *a.* **1.** *n.* Member of Semitic people in ancient Palestine; Israelite, Jew. **2.** Semitic language of the ancient Jews; modern form of this used esp. in Israel; (colloq.) unintelligible speech (cf. GREEK). **3.** *a.* Of or in Hebrew; of the Hebrews or the Jews. [ME, f. OF *Ebreu* f. med. L *Ebreus* f. L f. Gk *Hebraios* f. Aram. *ʻibray* f. Heb. *ʻibrî* one from the other side (of the river)]

Hĕbrĭdē′an (*or* hĭbrĭ′dĭan) *a.* & *n.* (Native or inhabitant) of the Hebrides. [f. *Hebrides* islands off W. Scotland + -AN]

hĕ′catomb (-ōōm) *n.* (Gk & Rom. Ant.) great public sacrifice (prop. of 100 oxen); (fig.) sacrifice of many victims. [f. L f. Gk *hekatombē* (*hekaton* hundred, *bous* ox)]

hĕck[1] *n.* (Sc. & N. Engl.) Frame obstructing passage of fish in river. [ME; northern form of HATCH[1]]

hĕck[2] *n.* (colloq., euphem.) = HELL 2. [alt. f. HELL]

hĕ′ckelphōne *n.* (Mus.) Baritone oboe. [f. G *heckelphon* (W. *Heckel*, 20th-c. Ger. instrument--maker); see -PHONE]

hĕ′ckl|e *v.t.*, & *n.* **1.** (Dress flax or hemp with) HACKLE[1]. **2.** *v.t.* Interrupt (public speaker) with aggressive questions or abuse. **3.** Hence ~ER[1] *n.* [ME, northern and eastern form of HACKLE[1]]

hĕ′ctâre *n.* Metric unit of square measure, 100 ares (2·471 acres). [F (as HECTO-, ARE[1])]

hĕ′ct|ĭc *a.* & *n.* **1.** *a.* **~ic fever,** that which accompanies consumption and similar diseases, with flushed cheeks and hot dry skin. **2.** Having hectic fever; morbidly flushed (lit. or fig.); (colloq.) exciting, feverishly active; hence ~ICALLY *adv.* **3.** *n.* Hectic fever, patient, or flush. [ME *etik* f. OF *etique* f. LL f. Gk *hektikos* habitual (*hexis* habit), assim. to F *hectique* or LL]

hĕ′cto- *comb. form.* Hundred, esp. of a unit in the metric system (*hecto*GRAM[2], *hecto*LITRE, *hecto*METRE[2]). [F, irreg. f. Gk *hekaton* hundred]

hĕ′ctograph (-ahf) *n.*, & *v.t.* **1.** *n.* Apparatus for copying documents by use of gelatin plate. **2.** *v.t.* Copy with hectograph. [f. prec. + -GRAPH]

hĕ′ctor *n.*, & *v.t.* & *i.* Bluster(er), bully. [f. *Hector*, L f. Gk *Hektōr*, son of Priam and Hecuba, Trojan hero in Homer's 'Iliad' (*hektōr* holding fast)]

hĕ′ddle *n.* One of sets of small cords or wires between which warp is passed in loom before going through the reed. [app. f. OE **hefedl*, *hefeld* (see HEALD)]

hĕdge[1] *n.* **1.** Fence of bushes or low trees, esp. forming boundary of field, garden, or road; similar boundary of turf, stone, etc. **2.** Line of things or persons forming barrier; (fig.) barrier; act or means of hedging bet or speculation. **3.** (in *comb.*) Living, working, done, etc., by the wayside, inferior. **4. ~-hop,** fly at low altitude; **~-priest,** (Hist., derog.) illiterate priest of low status; **~′row,** row of bushes forming hedge; **~-school,** (Hist.) low-class school, (orig.) open--air school esp. in Ireland; **~-sparrow,** common British and European thrushlike bird (*Prunella modularis*). [OE **hecg*, *hegg*, = MDu. *hegghe*, OHG *hegga*, *hecka* f. Gmc **hagja*; cf. HAW[1]]

hĕdg|e[2] *v.* **1.** *v.t.* Surround with hedge (lit. or fig.); fence *off*; hem *in*. **2.** *v.i.* Make or trim hedges; hence ~′ER[1] *n.* **3.** *v.t.* Secure oneself against loss on (bet, speculation, or abs.) by compensating transactions on the other side. **4.** *v.i.* Avoid committing oneself. [ME, f. prec.]

hĕ′dgehŏg (-jh-) *n.* Small spiny nocturnal pig--snouted insectivorous mammal of genus *Erinaceus*, rolling itself up into ball for defence; porcupine, sea-urchin, or other animal similarly armed with spines; (Mil.) small self-contained defensive position bristling with fortifications on all sides; prickly seed-vessel of some plants, e.g. corn crowfoot; person hard to get on with, whence **~gy**[2] (-gĭ) *a.* [ME, f. HEDGE[1] (from its habitat) + HOG[1] (from its snout)]

hēdŏ′n|ĭc *a.* Of pleasure; (Psych.) of pleasant or unpleasant sensations; hence ~ICS *n.*, doctrine of pleasure. [f. Gk *hēdonikos* (as foll.; see -IC)]

hē′don|ĭsm *n.* Doctrine that pleasure is the chief good or the proper aim; behaviour based on this; so ~IST (2) *n.*, **~ĭ′st**IC *a.* [f. Gk *hēdonē* pleasure + -ISM]

-hĕ′dr|on *suf.* (*pl.* ~a) forming *ns.* naming geometrical solids with various numbers or shapes of faces (*dodecahedron*, *rhombohedron*); hence ~AL *adj. suf.* [f. Gk *hedra* seat]

hee′bĭe-jeebĭes (-ĭz) *n. pl.* (sl.) **The ~**, state of nervous depression or apprehension. [20th c., of unkn. orig.]

heed *v.t.*, & *n.* **1.** *v.t.* Concern oneself about, take notice of. **2.** *n.* Careful attention (*take heed*; *pay* or *give heed to*); hence ~'FUL, ~'LESS, *adjs.* [OE *hēdan*, = OS *hōdian*, OHG *huoten* f. WG **hōdjan* (**hōda* care)]

hee'-haw *n.*, & *v.i.* **1.** *n.* Ass's bray; loud coarse laugh. **2.** *v.i.* Give hee-haw. [imit.]

heel[1] *n.* **1.** Hinder part of human foot below ankle (**Achilles' ~**, only vulnerable spot, weak point); (Zool.) corresponding part of hind limb in quadruped, often raised above ground; (of quadruped) hinder part of hoof, (in *pl.*) hind feet. **2.** Part of stocking that covers heel; part of boot or shoe that supports heel. **3.** Thing like heel in shape or position, e.g. handle end of violin bow, crook in head of golf-club, part of palm next to wrist; rear end of ski; bottom or end crust of loaf; (Hort.) irregularly shaped piece of plant attached to a cutting. **4.** (sl.) Untrustworthy or despicable person. **5. At ~** = *to heel*; **at the ~s of,** close behind (person, event, etc.); **back on** one's **~s,** into state of discomfiture or astonishment; **show a clean pair of ~s,** run away; COOL[2] one's *heels*; DIG one's *heels in*; **down at** (***the**) **~,** (of shoe) with heel crushed down by wear, (of person) wearing such shoes, slovenly, shabby; DRAG[1] one's *heels*; *heel-and-toe* WALKING[1]; **~s over head,** (arch.) = HEAD[1] *over heels*; **his ~s,** (Cribbage) score of two points by dealer turning up a jack; **kick** one's **~s,** be kept waiting; **lay by the ~s,** arrest, overthrow; **on** (=*at*) **the ~s of; take to** one's **~s,** run away; **to ~,** (of dog, or fig.) close behind, under control (*bring* or *come to heel*; as command to dog, *heel!*); **turn on** one's **~,** turn sharply round; **under the ~ of,** dominated by; **upon** (=*at*) **the ~s of. 6. ~'ball,** (1) shoemaker's polishing mixture of hard wax and lampblack, (2) this or similar composition for taking rubbings of monumental brasses etc.; **~-plate,** metal plate protecting heel of shoe; **~'tap,** (1) a thickness of leather in heel, (2) liquor left at bottom of glass after drinking. **7.** Hence ~'LESS (-l-l-) *a.* [OE *hēla*, *hǣla*, = OFris. *hēla*, MDu. *hiele*, ON *hæll* f. Gmc **hāhil-*, cogn. w. HOUGH]

heel[2] *v.* **1.** *v.i.* Touch ground with heel, e.g. in dancing. **2.** *v.t.* & *i.* Furnish (boot etc.) with heel; (Rugby Footb.) pass ball *out* at back of scrummage with the heels; (Golf) strike (ball) with heel of club; (in *p.p.*, colloq.), armed with revolver, supplied with money (WELL-*heeled*); hence *(**ward-**)~'ER[1] *n.*, local worker for professional politician. [f. prec.]

heel[3] *v.* **1.** *v.i.* (Of ship etc.) lean over owing to pressure of wind or uneven load (cf. LIST[3]). **2.** *v.t.* Cause (ship etc.) to do this. [prob. f. obs. *heeld*, *hield* incline, f. OE *hieldan*, OS *-heldian* f. Gmc **halthjan* (**haltha* inclined)]

heel[4] *n.* (Naut.) Inclination of heeling ship. [f. prec.]

heel[5]. See HELE.

hěft *n.*, & *v.t.* **1.** *n.* (dial. or U.S.) Weight. **2.** *v.t.* Lift, esp. to judge weight. [prob. f. HEAVE, after *cleft*, *weft*]

hě'ft|ў *a.* Sturdy, stalwart, (*a battalion of hefty fellows*); bulky, heavy, powerful; hence ~ILY[2] *adv.*, ~INESS *n.* [f. prec. + -Y[2]]

Hěgē'lian (*or* hā-; *or* -g-) *a.* & *n.* (Adherent) of Hegel or his philosophy of objective idealism; hence ~ISM (3) *n.* [f. G. W. F. *Hegel*, Ger. philosopher d. 1831 + -IAN]

hěgėmŏ'nĭc (*or* -g-) *a.* Ruling, supreme. [f. Gk *hēgemonikos* (as foll.; see -IC)]

hėgě'monў (*or* -g-; *or* hě'jĭ-) *n.* Leadership esp. by one State of a confederacy. [f. Gk *hēgemonia* (*hēgemōn* leader f. *hēgeomai* lead); cf. -MONY]

hě'gĭra, hě'jĭra, *n.* **1.** (*H~*). Muhammad's flight from Mecca to Medina (A.D. 622); Muslim era reckoned from this. **2.** General exodus or departure. [med. L *hegira* f. Arab. *hijra* departure from one's country (*hajara* separate)]

heh (hā) *int.* expr. inquiry or surprise. [imit.]

hei'fer (hě'f-) *n.* Young cow, esp. one that has not had more than one calf; female calf; (sl., derog.) woman. [OE *heahfore*, of unkn. orig.]

heigh (hā) *int.* expr. encouragement or inquiry; **~-ho,** *int.* expr. boredom, disappointment, etc. [var. of HEH]

height (hīt) *n.* Measurement from base to top; (Print.) distance from foot to face of type; elevation above ground or recognized (esp. sea) level; considerable elevation (*situated at a height*); high point; top; rising ground; ***~ of land,** watershed; **the ~,** utmost degree (*of* folly, fashion, luxury, etc.); **at its ~** (highest degree). [OE *hēhthu*, = OHG *hōhida*, Goth. *hauhitha* f. Gmc **hauhithō* (as HIGH, -TH[1])]

hei'ghten (hī't-) *v.* **1.** *v.t.* Make high(er); intensify; strengthen details of (description, story). **2.** *v.i.* Rise (usu. fig.), become more intense. [f. prec. + -EN[6]]

heil (hīl) *int.* Hail! (as used in Nazi greeting *Heil Hitler!*). [G]

hei'nous (hā'n-) *a.* (Of crime or criminal) utterly odious, atrocious; hence ~LY[2] *adv.*, ~NESS *n.* [ME, f. OF *haïneus* (*haïne* hatred f. *haïr* to hate f. Frank. **hatjan*; see -OUS)]

heir (ār) *n.* Person receiving or entitled to receive property or rank as legal successor of its former owner; (fig.) one to whom something (joy, punishment, etc.) is morally due; *heir* APPARENT; **~-at-law** (by right of blood, esp. to intestate's real property); **~ in tail** (to entailed estate); **~ of the** or one's **body** (direct descendant); *heir* PRESUMPTIVE; hence ~'DOM, ~'SHIP, *ns.*, ~'LESS *a.* [ME f. OF *eir* f. LL *herem* f. L *heres heredis*]

heir'ėss (ār'-) *n.* Female heir, esp. to great wealth. [f. prec. + -ESS[1]]

heir'lōōm (ār'-) *n.* Chattel that follows devolution of real estate; piece of personal property or (fig.) quality that has been in family for generations. [f. HEIR + LOOM[1] in sense 'tool']

***heist** (hī-) *n.*, & *v.t.* (sl.) Rob(bery). [repr. local pr. of HOIST[1]]

hei-tĭ'kĭ (hā-) *n.* (N.Z.) Greenstone neck-ornament worn by Maoris. [Maori (*hei* hang, TIKI)]

hě'jĭra. See HEGIRA.

Hē'La *a.* Of a strain of human epithelial cells maintained in culture. [f. *Hen*rietta *La*cks, whose cervical carcinoma provided the original cells]

hěld. See HOLD[1].

Heldentenor (hě'ldentěnōr) *n.* (Singer with) powerful tenor voice suitable for heroic operatic roles. [G (*held* hero)]

hēle, heal[2]**, heel**[5]**,** *v.t.* Set (plant) in the ground and cover its roots *in*. [OE *helian*, = OS *-hellian*, OHG *-hellen* f. WG **haljan* causative of Gmc **helan* (**hel-* conceal; cf. HELL)]

hě'lĭ- *comb. form.* Helicopter (*heliborne*, *heliport*). [abbr.]

hēlĭ'acal *a.* (Astron.) Relating to or near the sun; **~ rising, setting,** first rising of a star after, last setting before, a period of invisibility due to conjunction with the sun. [f. LL f. Gk *hēliakos* (*hēlios* sun; see -AC) + -AL]

hēlĭă'nthus *n.* Plant of genus *Helianthus*, e.g. common sunflower. [mod. L, f. Gk *hēlios* sun + *anthos* flower]

hě'lĭc|al *a.* Having form of helix; hence or cogn. **~al**LY[2] *adv.*, ~OID *a.* & *n.* [f. as HELIX + -AL]

hělĭchrȳ'sum (-k-) *n.* Composite Afr. or Austral. plant of genus *Helichrysum*, with flowers retaining their appearance when dried. [L, f. Gk *helikhrusos* (*helix* spiral, *khrusos* gold)]

Hě'lĭcon *n.* **1.** Source of poetic inspiration; so

Hĕlĭcō'nIAN *a.* **2.** (*h*~). Large spiral saxhorn encircling body of player. [L, f. Gk *Helikōn* Boeotian mountain sacred to Muses]

hĕ'lĭcŏpter *n.* Aircraft deriving both lift and propulsive power from horizontally revolving usu. engine-driven blades or rotors, and capable of ascending and descending vertically. [f. F *hélicoptère* f. Gk HELIX + *pteron* wing]

hē'lĭo- *comb. form.* Sun, as: **~ce'ntric,** as viewed from centre of sun, taking sun as centre; **~gram,** message by *heliograph* (3); **~graph,** (*n.*) (1) engraving obtained chemically by exposure to light, (2) apparatus for photographing sun, (3) signalling apparatus reflecting sunlight in flashes from movable mirror, (4) message thus sent, (*v.t.*) send (message) by heliograph; **~graphy** (-ŏ'g-), (1) description of the sun, (2) process of engraving heliographs, (3) signalling by heliograph; **~gravure,** photogravure; **~li'thic,** (of civilization) characterized by sun-worship and megaliths; **~meter** (-ŏ'm-), instrument for finding angular distance between two stars (orig. for measuring diameter of sun); **~scope,** apparatus for observing sun without injury to eye; **~stat,** apparatus with mirror driven by clockwork to reflect sunlight in fixed direction; **~the'rapy,** use of sun-baths in treating disease; **~tro'pic, ~tropism** (-ŏ't-), (of plant etc.) turning, property of turning, towards or away from (esp. sun)light; **~type,** picture obtained from sensitized gelatin film exposed to light. [f. Gk *hēlios* sun + -o-]

hēlĭō's|ĭs *n.* (*pl.* **~es** *pr.* -ēz). Sunstroke. [mod. L, f. Gk *hēliōsis* (*hēlios* sun; see -OSIS)]

hē'lĭotrōpe *n.* Herb or shrub of genus *Heliotropium*, with fragrant purple flowers; colour or scent of these; bloodstone. [f. L f. Gk *hēliotropion* plant turning flowers to the sun (*hēlios* sun, *-tropos* f. *trepō* turn)]

hĕ'lĭport *n.* Place for helicopters to take off and land. [f. HELI-, after *airport*]

hē'lĭum *n.* Colourless odourless light inert gaseous element, inferred as existing in sun's atmosphere in 1868, first obtained in 1895; **~ II,** form of liquid helium with very low viscosity. [f. Gk *hēlios* sun + -IUM]

hē'l|ix *n.* (*pl.* **~ices** *pr.* -ĭsēz). Spiral (like corkscrew, or in one plane like watch-spring); (Archit.) spiral ornament; rim of external ear. [L *helix -icis* f. Gk *helix -ikos*]

hĕll *n.* **1.** Abode of the dead; abode of devils and of condemned spirits in torment; place or state of wickedness or misery; den for captives in prisoners' base and other games; gaming-house. **2.** (in colloq. imprecations etc.) = *the* DEUCE², *the* DEVIL¹, (*a* or **one* or ||*the hell of a* or *helluva*; *go to hell*; *hell take it*; *hell to pay*; *play* (*merry*) *hell with*; RAISE *hell*; *who* etc. *in* or *the hell?*); **all ~ let loose,** utter pandemonium; (*tired* etc.) **as ~,** exceedingly; **beat** or **knock ~ out of,** pound heavily; **come ~ or high water,** no matter what the obstacles; **for the ~ of it,** solely for amusement; **get ~,** be severely reprimanded; **give** person **~,** make him very uncomfortable; **like ~,** recklessly, exceedingly, (iron.) not at all; **not a hope in ~,** no chance at all; **the ~ you say,** that is very surprising; **to** or **the ~,** away to perdition (*to hell with it*; *get the hell out of here*); **what the ~** (dismissing a difficulty; *what the hell, I can go tomorrow instead*). **3.** ***~'bender,** large salamander; **~-bent,** recklessly determined (*for* or *on*); **~-box,** (printer's sl.) receptacle for refuse type; **~-cat,** spiteful or furious person (esp. woman); **~-fire,** fire(s) of hell; **~ for leather,** at full speed (usu. of rider); **~-hound,** fiend; **~'s angel,** violent lawless young motor-cyclist; **~'s bells** (excl. of anger or annoyance); **~-weed,** dodder or corn crowfoot. **4.** Hence **~'**WARD *adv.* & *a.* [OE *hel(l)*, = OS *hell(j)a*, OHG *hella*, ON *hel*, Goth. *halja* f. Gmc **haljō* (**hal-*, **hel-* cover, conceal)]

Hĕllă'dĭc *a.* Of Bronze Age culture of mainland Greece. [f. Gk *Helladikos* (*Hellas -ados* Greece; see -IC)]

hĕ'llèbōre *n.* **1.** Ancient name of various plants supposed to cure madness. **2.** Plant of genus *Helleborus*, e.g. Christmas rose. [ME, f. OF *ellebre*, *elebore* or f. med. L *eleborus* f. L f. Gk *helleboros*]

hĕ'llèborīne *n.* Orchid of genus *Epipactis* or *Cephalanthera*. [F, or f. L f. Gk *helleborinē* plant like hellebore (as prec.; see -INE¹)]

Hĕ'llēne *n.* Ancient Greek of genuine Grecian descent; subject of modern nation of Greece; so **Hĕllē'n**IC *a.* [f. Gk *Hellēn* a Greek]

Hĕ'llėn|ĭsm *n.* Greek idiom or construction; imitation of the Greeks; Greek character or culture; Greek nationality; so **~**IZE (3) *v.t.* & *i.* [f. Gk *Hellēnismos* (*Hellēnizō* speak Greek, make Greek, f. as prec.; see -ISM)]

Hĕ'llėn|ĭst *n.* One who used the Greek language but was not a Greek; person skilled in Greek; hence **~ĭ'st**IC *a.* (of Greek history etc. after Alexander). [f. Gk *Hellēnistēs* (as prec.; see -IST)]

***hĕ'llgrammīte** *n.* Aquatic larva of an Amer. fly, much used as bait. [19th c., of unkn. orig.]

***hĕ'llĭon** *n.* (colloq.) Mischievous or troublesome person, esp. child. [perh. f. dial. *hallion* worthless fellow, assim. to HELL]

hĕ'llĭsh *a.* & *adv.* **1.** *a.* Of or like hell; infernal; hence **~**LY² *adv.*, **~**NESS *n.* **2.** *adv.* Infernally (esp. as mere intensive: *hellish expensive*). [f. HELL + -ISH¹]

hellō' (*or* hĕ-) *int.*, *n.* (*pl.* **~s**), & *v.i.* **1.** *int.* expr. surprise or informal greeting or beginning telephone conversation. **2.** *n.*, & *v.i.* (The) cry 'hello'. [var. of HALLO]

hĕ'lluva. See HELL.

hĕlm¹ *n.* (arch.) Helmet; hence **~**ED² (-md) *a.* [OE, = OS, OHG *helm*, ON *hjálmr*, Goth. *hilms* f. Gmc **helmaz* f. IE **kelmos* (**kel-* cover)]

hĕlm² *n.*, & *v.t.* **1.** *n.* Tiller or wheel by which rudder is controlled; space through which helm is turned (*more, little, helm*); **down (with the) ~, up (with the) ~,** place helm so as to bring rudder to windward, to leeward; **weather, lee, ~,** helm put up, down. **2.** (fig.) Government, guidance; **take the ~,** assume control. **3.** **~'sman** (-z-), steersman. **4.** *v.t.* Steer (usu. fig.). [OE *helma*, corresp. to ON *hjalm*; prob. rel. to HELVE]

hĕ'lmėt *n.* Defensive or protective head-cover of soldier, policeman, fireman, diver, fencer, motor-cyclist, Amer. footballer, etc.; felt or pith hat for hot climates; (Bot.) arched upper part of corolla in some flowers; shell of mollusc of genus *Cassis*; hence **~**ED² *a.* [ME f. OF, dim. of *helme* f. WG (as HELM¹); see -ET¹]

hĕ'lmĭnth *n.* Worm (esp. intestinal); hence **~ī'**ASIS *n.*, disease characterized by presence of worms in the body, **hĕlmĭ'nth**IC, **hĕlmĭ'nth**OID, *adjs.*, **~ŏ'**LOGY *n.* [f. Gk *helmins -inthos* intestinal worm]

hĕ'lot *n.* **1.** (*H*~). One of a class of serfs in ancient Sparta; **drunken H~** (made drunk as warning to young Spartans). **2.** Serf. **3.** Hence **~**ISM (2), **~**RY (1, 2), *ns.*, **~**IZE (3) *v.t.* [f. L *Helotes* pl. f. Gk *Heilōtes*, *-ōtai* (pl. of *Heilōs*, *-ōtes*) taken as = inhabitants of *Helos*, Laconian town]

hĕlp¹ *v.t.* (**~ed** or arch. *past* **holp** and *p.p.* **ho'lpen**). **1.** Provide (person etc.) with means towards what is needed or sought, be of use or service to (person, or abs.), (*help me*; *help me* (*to*) *lift it*; *help me in lifting it*; *help me with my work*, *to an answer*; *help the work on* or *forward*; *help me over the stile*); enable to come or go more easily *down, up*, etc.; ~ person **on, off,** *with coat* etc., help him put it on, take it off; ~ person **out** (of a difficulty); ~ (person) **to,** serve him with (food). **2.** Distribute (food at meal). **3.** Remedy, prevent, (*it can't be helped*; *I can't help that*); **more than** one **can** ~, more than is unavoidable. **4.** (w. neg.) Refrain from or avoid (*cannot help but admire her*; *cannot help laughing*). **5.** (In invocation or oath) **so ~ me God** (as I keep my word, as I speak the truth, etc.). **6.** ~ **oneself,** (w. neg.) be able to avoid an undesired action; ~ one**self** (**to,** or abs.), take without seeking assistance or permission of another; **~-yourself,** (of restaurant etc.) self-service. **7.** Hence ~'ER[1] *n.*, ~'ING[2] *a.* (**a ~ing hand,** (fig.) assistance). [OE *helpan*, = OS *helpan*, OHG *helfan*, ON *hjalpa*, Goth. *hilpan* f. Gmc **help-*, **halp-*, **hulp-*]

hĕlp[2] *n.* Action of helping (*we need your help*) or being helped (*come to our help*); person or thing that helps; domestic servant(s) or employee(s) (‖**home** ~, one who helps in household work; ‖**lady** ~, (arch.) assistant and companion to mistress of house; ‖**mother's** ~, one who gives help in house with children); remedy or escape (*there is no help for it*); helping (of food). [OE, f. as prec.]

hĕ'lpful *a.* (Of person or thing) useful, serviceable; hence ~LY[2] *adv.*, ~NESS *n.* [ME, f. prec. + -FUL]

hĕ'lpĭng *n.* In vbl senses; portion of food served. [ME, f. HELP[1] + -ING[1]]

hĕ'lplĕss *a.* Lacking help; unable to act without help; hence ~LY[2] *adv.*, ~NESS *n.* [ME, f. HELP[2] + -LESS]

hĕ'lpmāte *n.* Helpful companion or partner (usu. husband or wife). [f. HELP[1,2] + MATE[2], prob. infl. by foll.]

hĕ'lpmeet *n.* = prec. [formed by misunderstanding of Gen. 2: 18, 20, *help meet* (i.e. suitable helper) being taken as one word]

hĕ'lter-skĕlter *adv.*, *a.*, & *n.* **1.** (In) disordered haste. **2.** *n.* Tower-shaped structure in fun-fair etc. with external spiral track down which persons may slide on mat. [imit., perh. f. ME *skelte* hasten; cf. HARUM-SCARUM]

hĕlve *n.* Handle of weapon or tool; *throw the helve after the* HATCHET. [OE *h(i)elfe*, = OS *helfi*, OHG *halp* f. WG **halbh-*; cf. HALTER, HELM[2]]

Hĕlvē'tian (-shan) *a.* & *n.* Swiss. [f. L *Helvetia* Switzerland + -AN]

hĕm[1] *n.* Border or edge of cloth etc., esp. border made by turning edge in and sewing it down; **~-line,** lower edge of skirt etc.; **~-stitch** *n.*, & *v.t.* (to hem with) ornamental stitch like drawn-work. [OE, perh. rel. to dial. *ham* enclosure]

hĕm[2] *v.t.* (**-mm-**). Turn down and sew in edge of (cloth etc., or abs.); ~ **in, up,** etc., enclose, confine. [ME, f. prec.]

hĕm[3] (*or* hem) *int.*, *n.*, & *v.i.* (**-mm-**). **1.** *int.* calling attention or expressing hesitation by slight cough or clearing of throat. **2.** *n.* Utterance of this. **3.** *v.i.* Utter sound of *hem*, clear throat, hesitate in speech; ~ **and ha**(**w**) (cf. HUM[1]). [imit.]

***hē'mal, *hĕ'mato-,** etc. See HAEMAL, HAEMATO-, etc.

hēme. See HAEM.

hĕmerōcă'llĭs *n.* = DAY *lily*. [mod. L, f. L f. Gk *hēmerokallēs* a kind of lily (*hēmera* day, *kallos* beauty)]

hĕ'mĭ- *pref.* Half-, affecting one half, etc., as: **~ano'p(s)ia,** blindness over half of field of vision; **~cycle,** semicircular figure; ‖**~demisemiquaver,** half a demisemiquaver; ~-HE'DRAL, (Cryst.) having half number of planes given by complete symmetry; **~pterous** (-ĭ'p-), of the insect order including aphids, bugs, and cicadas, with base of front wings thickened. [Gk *hēmi-* = L SEMI-]

***-hē'mĭa.** Var. of -AEMIA.

hĕmĭplē'g|ĭa *n.* (Path.) Paralysis of one side of the body; hence ~IC *a.* & *n.* [mod. L, f. Gk HEMI(*plēgia* f. *plēgē* stroke) paralysis; see -IA[1]]

hĕ'mĭsphēre *n.* Half sphere; half the celestial sphere, esp. as divided by the equator or by the ecliptic; half the earth, containing (**Eastern** ~) Europe, Asia, and Africa, or (**Western** ~) America, or as divided by equator (**Northern, Southern,** ~); (Anat.) each half of cerebrum; **Magdeburg ~s,** pair of brass hemispheres exhausted of air to show atmospheric pressure by their cohesion; hence **hĕmĭsphĕ'r**IC(AL) *adjs.* [f. OF *emisp(h)ere* & f. L *hemisphaerium* f. Gk HEMI(*sphaira* SPHERE)]

hĕ'mĭstĭch (-k) *n.* Half of line of verse. [f. LL f. Gk HEMI(*stikhion* f. *stikhos* line)]

hĕ'mlŏck *n.* **1.** Poisonous umbelliferous plant (*Conium maculatum*) whose juice or dried fruit or leaves are used as powerful sedative; poisonous potion got from this. **2.** *~ (**fir** or **spruce**), conifer of genus *Tsuga*. [OE *hymlic(e)*, of unkn. orig.]

***hĕ'mo-** etc. See HAEMO- etc.

hĕmp *n.* **1.** (**Indian**) ~, herbaceous plant, *Cannabis sativa*, native of Asia. **2.** Its cortical fibre used for rope and stout fabrics; (joc.) rope for hanging a person. **3.** Narcotic drug made from hemp plant. **4.** Other plant yielding similar fibre (MANILA *hemp*). **5.** ~ **agrimony,** perennial composite plant with pale-purple flowers and hairy leaves; **~-nettle,** nettle-like plant of genus *Galeopsis*. **6.** Hence ~'EN[5] *a.* [OE *henep*, *hænep*, = OS *hanap*, OHG *hanaf*, ON *hampr* f. Gmc **hanipiz* cogn. w. Gk *kannabis*]

hĕn *n.* **1.** Female bird, esp. of domestic fowl; (in *pl.*) domestic fowls of either sex; **as scarce as ~'s teeth,** very scarce; **like a ~ with one chicken,** absurdly fussy; ~ **and chickens,** name of a cultivated compound daisy, and other plants. **2.** Female lobster or crab or salmon. **3.** **~'bane,** (drug got from) narcotic and poisonous plant (*Hyoscyamus niger*); **~-coop** (for keeping poultry in); **~-harrier,** European falcon (*Circus cyaneus*); ***~-hawk,** large hawk attacking poultry; **~-hearted,** lacking courage; **~-party** (colloq., of women only); **~'pecked,** domineered over by one's wife; **~-roost,** place where fowls roost at night; **~-run,** enclosure for fowls; **~'wife,** (arch.) woman who keeps fowls. [OE *henn*, = OHG *henna* f. WG **hannja* dim. of **hanon* cock]

hĕnce *adv.* **1.** (arch.) (**From**) ~, from here, from this place; ~!, (poet. or rhet.) go away; **go** ~, die; ~ **with,** away with, take away. **2.** From this time (**five years** ~, in five years' time from now); **~for'th, ~for'ward,** from this time onwards. **3.** As a result from this; from this source; as an inference from this (*hence it appears that*), therefore. [ME *hens*, *hennes*, (*henne* adv. f. OE *heonan* f. root of HE[1]) + -S[3]]

hĕ'nch|man *n.* (*pl.* **~men**). **1.** (Hist.) Squire, page of honour. **2.** Chief attendant of Highland chief. **3.** Trusty follower; political supporter. [ME *henxman*, *hengestman*, f. OE *heng(e)st* male horse + MAN[1]]

hĕndĕ'ca- *comb. form.* Eleven, as: **~gon,** plane figure with eleven sides and angles; **~sylla'bic** *a.* & *n.*, (metrical line) of eleven syllables; **~sy'llable,** such a line. [f. Gk *hendeka* eleven]

hĕndī'adȳs *n.* Expression of a complex idea by two words connected with *and* (e.g. *in goblets and gold* for *in golden goblets*; *nice and warm* for *nicely warm*). [med. L, f. Gk *hen dia duoin* one thing by two]

hĕ'nèquĕn (-k-) *n.* (Sisal-like fibre from) species of agave grown in Mexico etc. [f. Sp. *jeniquen*]

hĕnge (-nj) *n.* Monument of wood or stone resembling the circle of stones at Stonehenge. [f. *Stonehenge* in Wiltshire]

hĕ'nna *n.* Tropical shrub (*Lawsonia inermis*); its shoots and leaves used as reddish dye esp. for the hair. [f. Arab. *ḥinnā'*]

hĕ'nothēĭsm *n.* Belief in god (of one's tribe etc.) without asserting that he is the only God. [f. Gk *heis henos* one + *theos* god + -ISM]

hĕ'nr|ў *n.* (*pl.* **~ies** *or* **~ys**). (Electr.) Unit of inductance which gives an e.m.f. of one volt in a closed circuit with rate of change of current one ampere per second. [f. J. *Henry*, Amer. physicist d. 1878]

hēortŏ'logў *n.* Study of church festivals. [f. G *heortologie*, F *héortologie* f. Gk *heortē* feast; see -LOGY]

hĕp[1]. See HIP[2].

hĕp[2] *a.* (sl.) Well-informed; stylish; **~ to,** aware of; **~-cat,** hep person, jazz or swing addict, HIPSTER[1]. [20th c., of unkn. orig.]

hĕ'parĭn *n.* Substance extracted from animal livers and used to prevent blood-clotting; hence ~IZE (1) *v.t.* [f. L *hepar* liver + -IN]

hėpă'tĭc *a.* Of, good for, the liver; liver-coloured, dark brownish-red. [ME, f. L f. Gk *hēpatikos* (*hēpar -atos* LIVER[1]; see -IC)]

hėpă'tĭca *n.* Plant of genus *Hepatica*, closely related to anemone, with lobed leaves resembling the liver. [med. L, fem. (as n.) of *hepaticus* (see prec.)]

hĕpatī'tĭs *n.* Inflammation of the liver. [mod. L, f. as HEPATIC; see -ITIS]

hĕpato- *comb. form.* Liver, as: **~me'galy,** abnormal enlargement of the liver. [f. Gk *hēpato-* (as HEPATIC; see -O-)]

Hĕ'pplewhīte (-pelwīt) *n.* Light and graceful style of furniture. [f. G. ~, Engl. cabinet-maker d. 1786]

hĕ'pta- *comb. form.* Seven, as: **~chord** (-k-), 7-stringed musical instrument, 7-note scale; **~glot** *a.* & *n.*, (book) in seven languages; **~gon,** plane figure with seven sides and angles; so **~gonal** (-ă'g-) *a.*; ~HE'DRON, solid figure with seven faces; **~merous** (-ă'm-), having seven parts; **~meter** (-ă'mĭ-), verse of seven measures; **~sylla'bic** *a.* & *n.*, (metrical line) of seven syllables; **H~teuch** (-k), first seven books of O.T.; **~va'lent,** (Chem.) having a valence of seven. [f. Gk *hepta* seven]

hĕ'ptăd *n.* Group of seven. [f. Gk *heptas -ados* set of seven (*hepta*); see -AD 1]

hĕ'ptāne *n.* (Chem.) Hydrocarbon of the paraffin series, C_7H_{16}. [f. HEPTA- + -ANE]

hĕ'ptar͡chў (-kĭ) *n.* Government by seven rulers; supposed seven kingdoms of Angles and Saxons in Britain in 7th–8th c.; so **hĕptar͡'ch**IC(AL) (-k-) *adjs.* [f. HEPTA-, after *tetrarchy*]

her͡[1] (*or, when unstressed,* her) *pron.* **1.** Obj. case of SHE; (arch.) = HERSELF 2. **2.** (colloq.) = SHE (*it's her all right*; *am older than her*); **not quite ~,** garment etc. that does not suit her. [OE *hire* dat. of *hīo, hēo* fem. of HE[1]]

her͡[2] (*or, when unstressed,* her) *poss. pron. attrib.* Of HER[1] or herself (*it is her hat*; *shook her head*; *her father and mine, her and my father*); (in titles) that she is (*Her Majesty*). [OE *hi(e)re* gen. of *hīo* (see prec.)]

hĕ'rald[1] *n.* **1.** Officer who made State proclamations, and bore messages between princes, or officiated in the TOURNAMENT 1, or arranged various State ceremonials, or regulated use of armorial bearings, or settled questions of precedence, or recorded names and pedigrees of those entitled to armorial bearings; ‖official of *Heralds'* COLLEGE. **2.** Messenger (often as title of newspaper); forerunner. **3.** Hence ~IST *n.*, expert in heraldry. [ME, f. OF *herau(l)t* f. Gmc **hariwald-* (**harjaz* army, **wald-* rule)]

hĕ'rald[2] *v.t.* Proclaim the approach of; usher in. [ME, f. OF *herauder* (as prec.)]

hĕră'ldĭc *a.* Of heraldry. [f. HERALD[1] + -IC]

hĕ'raldrў *n.* Science or art of a herald, esp. in dealings with armorial bearings; armorial bearings; heraldic pomp. [f. HERALD[1] + -RY]

her͡b *n.* **1.** Plant of which the stem is not woody or persistent and which dies down to ground after flowering; plant of which leaves etc. are used for food, medicine, scent, flavour, etc. **2.** **~ beer,** drink made from herbs; **~ bennet,** common yellow-flowered avens (*Geum urbanum*) [prob. f. med. L *herba benedicta* blessed herb, as having expelled the Devil]; **~ Christopher,** white-flowered baneberry; **~ Gerard,** white-flowered plant (*Aegopodium podagraria*); **~-grace, ~ of grace,** (arch.) RUE[2]; **~ Paris,** plant with single flower and four leaves in cross shape; **~ Robert,** common wild crane's-bill; **~-tea, -water,** medicinal infusion of herbs; **~ tobacco,** mixture of herbs smoked as substitute for tobacco or as medicine. **3.** So **~'ĭ**CIDE *n.*, substance toxic to plants and used to destroy unwanted vegetation, **~ĭ'**FEROUS, ~'LESS, *adjs.* [ME, f. OF *erbe* f. L *herba* grass, green crops, herb]

her͡bā'ceous (-sh*us*) *a.* Of the nature of herbs; **~ border** (in garden, containing esp. perennial flowering plants); **~ perennial,** plant whose growth dies down annually but whose roots etc. survive. [f. L *herbaceus* grassy (as prec.; see -ACEOUS)]

her͡'bage *n.* Herbs collectively; succulent parts of herbs; (Law) right of pasture on another's ground. [ME, f. OF *erbage* f. med. L *herbaticum, herbagium* right of pasture, f. L *herba* herb; see -AGE]

her͡'bal *a.* & *n.* (Book with descriptions and account of properties) of herbs. [f. med. L *herbalis* (as prec.; see -AL)]

her͡'balĭst *n.* One skilled in herbs, esp. early botanical writer; dealer in medicinal herbs. [f. prec. + -IST]

her͡bār'ĭ|um *n.* (*pl.* **~a**). (Book, case, room, for) systematically arranged collection of dried plants. [LL (as HERB; see -ARIUM)]

her͡'bĭvōre *n.* Animal of group Herbivora, feeding on plants; so **her͡bĭ'**VOROUS *a.* [f. L *herba* herb + -I- + -VORE]

her͡'bў *a.* Abounding in herbs; of the nature of a herb. [f. HERB + -Y[2]]

Her͡cū'lėan (*or* -ē'an) *a.* Of Hercules; strong as Hercules; difficult as his labours. [f. L *Herculeus* (as foll.) + -AN]

Her͡'cūlēs (-z) *n.* **1.** (Gk & Rom. Myth.) hero of prodigious strength, who performed 12 immense tasks (LABOUR[1] *of Hercules*); **Pillars of ~,** rocks on either side of Strait of Gibraltar, (fig.) ultimate limit. **2.** Very strong man; **~ beetle** (S. Amer., 5 in. long). [ME f. L, f. Gk *Hēraklēs* (*Hēra* wife of Zeus, *kleos* glory)]

Her͡cў'nĭan *a.* (Geol.) Of an episode of mountain-formation in E. hemisphere in late palaeozoic era. [f. L *Hercynia silva* forested mountains of central Germany]

herd[1] *n.* **1.** Company of animals, esp. cattle, feeding or travelling together; ***ride ~,** (fig.) keep watch *on.* **2.** (derog.) Large number of people (*the herd*; *the common herd*). **3.** **The ~ instinct,** gregariousness and mutual influence as a psychological factor; **~-book,** pedigree-book of cattle or pigs; **~'sman** (-z-), owner or keeper of herds. [OE *heord*, = OHG *herta*, ON *hjörth*, Goth. *hairda* f. Gmc **herdhō*]

hĕrd[2] *n.* Keeper of herds, herdsman, (esp. in comb.: *cowherd, swine-herd*). [OE *hirdi*, = OS *hirdi*, OHG *hirti*, ON *hirthir*, Goth *hairdeis* f. Gmc **herdhjaz* (as prec.)]

hĕrd[3] *v.i.* & *t.* Go or cause to go in a herd (*together, with* others; esp. fig., persons); tend (sheep, cattle). [ME, f. HERD[1,2]]

Hĕr'dwĭck *n.* (Animal of) hardy breed of mountain sheep from N. England [f. obs. *herdwick* pasture-ground (HERD[2], WICK[2]), perh. because the breed originated in Furness Abbey pastures]

hēre *adv.*, *n.*, & *int.* **1.** *adv.* In or at this place or position (*put it here*; *put it down, in, out, over, under, up, here*; *what is this* or *that dog doing here?*; *has lived here for some years*; (calling attention to person's presence or thing offered) *my son here will show you, here is your coat*); at this point in argument, progress of affairs, situation, etc., (*here I have a question*); ~ (**below**), in this life; ~ **goes!** (colloq., expr. commencement of bold act); *here's* HOW!; **~'s to,** I drink to the health of; ~ **and there,** in various places; **~, there, and everywhere,** in many different places; **neither ~ nor there,** of no importance or relevance; ~ **today, gone tomorrow,** short-lived, merely transient; ~ **we** or **you are,** (colloq.) this is what we or you wanted, the expected place of arrival, etc.; ~ **we go again,** (colloq.) the same undesirable events are recurring. **2.** To this place or position (*comes here every day*; *I don't belong here*); LOOK or *see here!*. **3.** *n.* This place (*get out of here*; *lives somewhere near here*; *fill it up to here*; *shall leave here tomorrow*). **4.** *int.* calling attention or introducing command or remonstration; = I am present (in answer to roll-call). **5.** **~abou't(s),** near this place; **~a'fter,** (*adv.*) in future, later on, in the world to come, (*n.*) the future, the world to come; **~a't,** (arch.) as a result of this; **~by',** by this means, as a result of this; **~i'n,** (formal) in this matter, book, etc.; **~ina'fter,** (formal) below (in this document etc.); **~inbefor'e,** (formal) in a preceeding part (of this document etc.); **~o'f,** (formal) of this; **~to',** (formal) to this matter; **~tofor'e,** (formal) before this time; **~u'nder,** (formal) below (in book etc.); **~un'to,** (arch.) to this; **~upo'n,** after this, in consequence of this; **~wi'th,** with this (esp. of enclosure in letter etc.). [OE *hēr*, = OS, Goth. *hēr*, ON *hér*, OHG *hiar*, app. f. Gmc **hi-* (HE[1])]

hėrĕ'dĭtable *a.* That may be inherited. [f. obs. F *héréditable* or f. med. L *hereditabilis* f. eccl. L *hereditare* f. L *heres -edis* heir; see -ABLE]

hĕrėdĭ'tament (*or* hĭrĕ'd-) *n.* Property that can be inherited; real property; inheritance. [f. med. L *hereditamentum* (as prec.; see -MENT)]

hėrĕ'dĭtar|ȳ *a.* Descending by inheritance; (of disease, instinct, etc.) transmitted from one generation to another; the same as or like what one's parents had (*hereditary creed, hatred*); of, holding position by, inheritance; hence **~ĭLY**[2] *adv.*, **~ĭNESS** *n.* [f. L *hereditarius* (as foll.; see -ARY[1])]

hėrĕ'dĭtȳ *n.* Tendency of like to beget like; property of organic beings by which offspring have nature and characteristics of parents or ancestors; genetic constitution of an individual. [f. F *hérédité* or f. L *hereditas* heirship (as HEIR; see -ITY)]

Hĕ'rėford *n.* (One of a) breed of red and white beef cattle. [~ in England, where it originated]

hĕrē'sĭārch (-k; *or* -z-) *n.* Leader or founder of a heresy. [f. eccl. L f. Gk *hairesiarkhēs* f. as foll. + *-arkhēs* ruler]

hĕ'rės|ȳ *n.* Opinion contrary to the orthodox doctrine of the Christian Church, or to the accepted doctrine on any subject; hence **~iŏ'LOGY** *n.* [ME f. OF (*h*)*eresie*, f. Rom. **heresia* f. eccl. L *haeresis*, in L = school of thought, f. Gk *hairesis* choice, sect (*haireomai* choose)]

hĕ'rėtĭc *n.* Holder of an unorthodox opinion (orig. in the matter of religion); so **hėrĕ'tĭcAL** *a.* [ME, f. OF *heretique* f. eccl. L f. Gk *hairetikos* able to choose (as prec.; see -IC)]

||**hĕ'rĭot** *n.* (Law). Tribute of best live beast or dead chattel, or money payment, or (orig.) return of lent equipment, to lord on decease of tenant. [OE *heregeatwa* (*here* army, *geatwa* trappings)]

hĕ'rĭtab|le *a.* That passes to heirs-at-law (opp. to movable property); transmissible from parent to offspring; capable of inheriting; hence **~LY**[2] *adv.* [ME f. OF (*heriter* f. eccl. L *hereditare*; see HEREDITABLE)]

hĕ'rĭtage *n.* What is or may be inherited; inherited circumstances or benefits; (fig.) portion allotted to anybody; (Bibl.) the ancient Israelites, the Church. [ME f. OF (as prec.; see -AGE)]

hĕ'rĭtor *n.* One who inherits. [ME f. AF *heriter*, OF *heritier* f. as HEREDITARY, assim. to wds in -OR]

hĕrl. Var. of HARL[2].

hĕrm *n.* (Gk Ant.) Squared pillar with head (esp. of Hermes) on top, used as boundary-marker etc. (cf. TERMINUS 4). [f. L *Herma* f. Gk *Hermēs* messenger of the gods]

hĕrmă'phrod|ite *n.* & *a.* **1.** *n.* Human being or animal combining characteristics of both sexes; (Zool.) animal having normally both male and female sexual organs, e.g. earthworm; (Bot.) plant in which same flower has stamens and pistils; (fig.) person or thing combining opposite qualities; ship having characters of two kinds of craft. **2.** *a.* Combining both sexes, or opposite qualities. **3.** Hence **~ĭ'TIC(AL)** *adjs.*, **~ītISM** (2) *n.* [f. L f. Gk *hermaphroditos*, orig. name of son of Hermes and Aphrodite in Gk Myth., who became joined in one body with the nymph Salmacis]

hĕrmėneu't|ĭc *a.* Of interpretation; so **~ICAL** *a.*, **~ICS** *n. pl.*, interpretation, esp. of Scripture. [f. Gk *hermēneutikos* (*hermēneuō* interpret; see -IC)]

hĕrmĕ't|ĭc *a.* **1.** Of alchemy or other occult science (*hermetic art*); esoteric; hence **hĕr'mėtISM** (3) *n.* **2.** **~ic seal,** airtight closure by fusion etc. (orig. as used by alchemists). **3.** With hermetic seal; (fig.) protected from outside agencies; esoteric, recondite; hence **~ICALLY** *adv.* [f. mod. L *hermeticus* irreg. f. *Hermes Trismegistus* thrice-greatest Hermes (as founder of alchemy etc.)]

hĕr'mĭt *n.* Early Christian recluse; person living in solitude; **~-crab,** crab of family Paguridae that lives in mollusc's cast-off shell to protect its shell-less hinder parts; ~ **thrush,** migratory N. Amer. thrush noted for song. [ME f. OF (*h*)*ermite* or f. LL *eremita* f. Gk *erēmitēs* (*erēmia* desert f. *erēmos* solitary; see -ITE[1])]

hĕr'mĭtage *n.* Hermit's abode; solitary abode. [ME, f. OF (*h*)*ermitage* (as prec.; see -AGE)]

hĕrn. See HERON.

hĕr'nĭ|a *n.* (*pl.* **~as** *or* **~ae**). (Path.) Displacement and protrusion of part of organ through aperture in wall of cavity containing it, esp. of abdomen; hence **~AL**, **~ARY**[1], **~ātED**[1], *adjs.* [L]

hĕr'nshaw. See HAWK[1].

hĕr'ō *n.* (*pl.* **~es**). **1.** (Gk Ant.) man of superhuman qualities, favoured by the gods; demigod. **2.** Illustrious warrior; **~'s welcome** (such as is given to hero returning from battle). **3.** Man admired for achievements and noble qualities. **4.** Chief male character in poem, play, or story. **5. ~-worship(per)**, worship(per) of the ancient heroes, of some great man or men, or of a personal hero (sense 3). [ME, f. L f. Gk *hērōs*]

hėrō'ic *a.* & *n.* **1.** *a.* (Of act or quality) of or fit for a hero; (of person) having the qualities of a hero; **the ~ age** (of Greece, before return from Troy). **2.** (Of poetry) dealing with heroes; **~ couplet** (of rhyming iambic pentameters); **~ verse,** that used in heroic poetry (Gk & L hexameter, E iambic pentameter, F alexandrine). **3.** (Of language) grand, high-flown; bold, attempting great things. **4.** Hence **hėrō'**ICALLY *adv.* **5.** *n.* (in *pl.*) Heroic verse; high-flown language or sentiments. [f. F *héroïque* or f. L f. Gk *hērōikos* (as prec.; see -IC)]

hėrōĭ-cŏ'mĭc(al) *adjs.* Combining the heroic with the comic. [f. F *héroï-comique* (as prec., COMIC)]

hĕ'rōĭn *n.* Sedative addictive drug prepared from and acting like morphine, illicitly used to produce intense euphoria. [G, perh. f. as HERO (from its effects on user's opinion of himself) + -IN]

hĕ'rōĭne *n.* Demigoddess; heroic woman; chief female character in poem, play, or story. [f. F *héroïne* or f. L f. Gk *hērōinē*, fem. of *hērōs* HERO; see -INE³]

hĕ'rōĭsm *n.* Heroic conduct or qualities. [f. F *héroïsme* (*héros* HERO; see -ISM)]

hēr'oize, -ise (-īz), *v.* **1.** *v.t.* Make a hero of; make heroic. **2.** *v.i.* Play the hero. [f. HERO + -IZE]

hĕ'ron, hērn (poet. etc.), *n.* Long-legged long-necked wading bird of genus *Ardea*; hence ~RY (3) *n.* [ME, f. OF *hairon* f. Gmc **haigaron*]

hēr'pēs (-z) *n.* Virus disease of skin with outbreaks of blisters; **~ si'mplex** (painless form); **~ zo'ster** (zŏ'-), SHINGLES; hence **hērpĕ'tic** *a.* [ME f. L f. Gk *herpēs -ētos* shingles (*herpō* creep)]

hērpėtŏ'log|ȳ *n.* Study of reptiles; hence ~IST (3) *n.* [f. Gk *herpeton* reptile (*herpō* creep) + -O- + -LOGY]

Herr (hār) *n.* (*pl.* **Herr'en**). Title of German man = Mr.; German man. [G, f. OHG *hērro* compar. of *hēr* exalted]

Herrenvolk (hĕ'renfŏlk; *or* -fōk) *n.* German nation viewed by Nazis as born to mastery; group regarding itself as innately superior. [G, = master-race (as prec., FOLK)]

hĕ'rrĭng *n.* N. Atlantic fish (*Clupea harengus*) much used for food, coming near coast in large shoals to spawn; RED *herring*; **~-bone,** (*n.*) stitch resembling bones of herring, cloth woven in zigzag pattern, (Archit.) zigzag arrangement of stones, bricks, or tiles, (*v.t.*) work with herring-bone stitch, mark with herring-bone pattern, (*v.i.*, Skiing) ascend slope by pointing skis outwards; **~-gull,** large N. Atlantic gull (*Larus argentatus*) with dark wing-tips; **~-pond,** (joc.) sea, esp. North Atlantic. [OE *hǣring*, *hēring*, = OHG *hāring* f. WG **hēringa*; cf. -ING³]

Herr'nhuter (hār'nhōō-) *n.* Member of MORAVIAN sect. [G, f. *Herrnhut* (= the Lord's keeping), name of their first German settlement; see -ER¹]

hērs (-z) *poss. pron. pred.* (& abs.) = HER² (*it is hers*; *hers is best*; *I like hers better*; *don't like that smile* OF *hers*; *my father and hers*; *some friends of hers*); **his and ~**, respectively for husband and wife, or men and women; cf. GET¹ 4. [ME, f. HER² + -S³]

hersĕ'lf *pron.* **1.** Emphat. form corresp. to SHE or HER¹; in her normal state of body or mind (*is quite herself again*); **be ~**, act in her normal or unconstrained manner; **by ~**, without assistance or companions; *a* LAW¹ *unto herself*. **2.** Refl. form corresp. to HER¹ (*has hurt herself*; *seems pleased with herself*; *killed a snake as big as herself*). [OE *hire self* (as HER¹, SELF)]

Herts. *abbr.* Hertfordshire.

hērtz (-ts) *n.* (*pl.* same). Unit of frequency, equal to one cycle per second. [f. H. R. *Hertz*, Ger. physicist d. 1894]

Hēr'tzĭan (-ts-) *a.* **~ wave,** electromagnetic wave of length suitable for use in radio. [f. as prec. + -IAN]

hĕ'sĭt|ant (-z-) *a.* Hesitating; irresolute; so ~ANCE, ~ANCY, *ns.*, **~ant**LY² *adv.* [f. as foll.; see -ANT]

hĕ'sĭt|āte (-z-) *v.i.* Show, speak with, indecision (*about*, *over*); be deterred by scruples, be reluctant *to* (do); hence or cogn. ~A'TION *n.*, **~āt**IVE *a.* [f. L *haesitare* frequent. of *haerēre haes-* stick fast + -ATE³]

Hĕspēr'ĭan *a.* (poet.) Western; (Gk Myth.) of the Hesperides. [f. L f. Gk *Hesperios* (as HESPERUS) + -AN]

hĕsperĭ'dĭ|um *n.* (*pl.* **~a**). Fruit with sectioned pulp inside separable rind, e.g. orange. [f. Gk *Hesperides* nymphs believed to guard golden apples + -IUM]

Hĕ'sperus *n.* Evening star. [ME f. L, f. Gk *hesperos* a. & n., western, evening (star)]

Hĕ'ssĭan *a.* & *n.* **1.** *a.* Of Hesse in Germany; **~ (boot)**, tasselled high boot first worn by Hessian troops; **~ fly,** Amer. midge whose larva destroys wheat [wrongly thought to have been brought to America by Hessian troops]. **2.** *n.* (*h~*). Strong coarse cloth of hemp or jute. [f. *Hesse* + -IAN]

hĕst *n.* (arch.) Behest. [OE *hǣs* f. **haitan* call (see HIGHT), assim. to ME ns. in *-t*]

hĕt *a.* **~ up,** (sl.) excited. [dial. p.p. of HEAT²]

hėtaer'a (-tēr'*a*), **hėtair'a** (-īr'*a*), *n.* (*pl.* **~s** *or* **hetaerae,** *or* **hetairai** *pr.* -ī). Courtesan, mistress, esp. in ancient Greece. [Gk *hetaira*, fem. of *hetairos* companion]

hėtaer'ĭsm (-ēr'-), **hėtair'ĭsm** (-īr'-), *n.* Recognized system of concubinage; communal marriage in a tribe. [f. Gk *hetairismos* prostitution (as HETAERA; see -ISM)]

hĕ'tero- *comb. form.* Other, different, (freq. opp. to HOMO-, occas. to AUTO-, ISO-, ORTHO-, etc.), as: **~chroma'tic,** of several colours; **~cy'clic,** (Chem.) with molecular ring composed of atoms of more than one kind; **~gamous** (-ŏ'g-), (1) irregular as regards stamens and pistils, (2) characterized by **~gamy** (-ŏ'g-) or **~geny** (-ŏ'j-) or **~gony** (-ŏ'g-), alternation of generations; **~graft** (from individual of another species); **~logous** (-ŏ'l-), not homologous; **~merous** (-ŏ'm-), (Bot.) not isomerous; **~mor'phic,** of dissimilar forms; **~mor'phism,** existence in various forms; **~nomous** (-ŏ'n-), subject to different laws (of growth etc.), subject to an external law (cf. *autonomous*); **~nomy** (-ŏ'n-), presence of a different law, subjection to external law; **~pa'thic,** (1) allopathic, (2) differing in effect; **~phony** (-ŏ'f-), (Mus.) performing of same melody differently by different voices etc.; **~phy'llous,** bearing leaves of different forms on same plant; **~pla'stic,** of a heterograft; **~ploid,** not haploid or diploid; **~po'lar,** having dissimilar poles, (Electr.) with armature passing north and south magnet poles alternately; **~se'xual** *a.* & *n.*, (person) characterized by (the normal) attraction to the opposite sex; **~taxy,** abnormal disposition of organs or parts; **~tra'nsplant,** = *heterograft*; **~tro'phic,** deriving its nourishment from outside, not autotrophic. [f. Gk *heteros* other + -O-]

hĕ'teroclite *a.* & *n.* Abnormal (thing or person); (Gram.) irregularly declined (noun). [f. LL f. Gk HETERO(*klitos* f. *klinō* bend, inflect)]

hĕ'terodŏx *a.* (Of person or opinion) not orthodox; so ~Y[1] *n.* [f. LL f. Gk HETERO(*doxos* f. *doxa* opinion)]

hĕ'terodȳne *a.*, & *v.i.* (Radio). Relating to production of, produce, a lower (audible) frequency from the combination of two almost equal high frequencies. [f. as HETERO-, DYNE]

hĕterogĕ'nėous *a.* Diverse in character; composed of diverse elements; (Math.) incommensurable through being of different kinds or degrees; hence or cogn. **hĕterogėnē'-**ITY, ~NESS, *ns.*, ~LY[2] *adv.* [f. med. L *heterogeneus* f. Gk HETERO(*genēs* f. *genos* kind) + -OUS]

hĕterogĕ'nėsĭs *n.* Birth of a living being otherwise than from parent of same kind, esp. spontaneous generation from inorganic matter; hence **hĕterogėnĕ'**TIC *a.* [f. HETERO- + GENESIS]

hĕterō's|ĭs *n.* (*pl.* ~**es** *pr.* -ēz). Tendency of cross-bred individual to show qualities superior to those of both parents. [Gk (*heteros* different)]

hĕterozȳ'g|ōte *n.* Zygote resulting from fusion of unlike gametes; Mendelian hybrid containing dominant and recessive characters and therefore not breeding true; so ~OUS *a.* [f. HETERO- + ZYGOTE]

hĕ'tman *n.* Polish or Cossack military commander. [Pol., prob. f. G *hauptmann* captain]

heu'chera (-k-; *or* hoi'k-) *n.* N. Amer. perennial plant of genus *Heuchera*, of saxifrage family. [mod. L, f. J. H. von *Heucher*, Ger. botanist d. 1747 + -A 1]

heurĭ'st|ĭc (hūr-) *a.* & *n.* **1.** *a.* Serving to discover; (of computer problem-solving) proceeding by trial and error; **~ic method,** system of education under which the pupil is trained to find out things for himself; hence ~ICS *n. pl.* **2.** *n.* (Science of) heuristic procedure. [irreg. f. Gk *heuriskō* find; see -IC]

hē'vėa *n.* S. Amer. tree of genus *Hevea*, whose milky sap yields rubber. [mod. L, f. native name *hevé*; see -A]

hew *v.* (*p.p.* ~**n** *or* ~**ed**). **1.** *v.t.* Chop, cut, (thing *down*, *away*, *off*, etc.) with axe, sword, etc.; cut into shape; ~ one's **way,** make a way for oneself by hewing. **2.** *v.i.* Deal cutting blows *at*, *among*, etc.; *conform *to*. [OE *hēawan*, = OS *hauwan*, OHG *houwan*, ON *höggva* f. Gmc **hauwan*]

***H.E.W.** *abbr.* Department of Health, Education, and Welfare.

hew'er *n.* One who hews; man who cuts coal from seam; **~s of wood and drawers of water,** drudges (Josh. 9:21). [ME, f. HEW + -ER[1]]

***hĕx** *v.* & *n.* **1.** *v.i.* & *t.* Practise witchcraft (on), bewitch. **2.** *n.* Witch; magic spell. [f. Pennsylvanian G *hexe* v., *hex* n., f. G *hexe*(*n*)]

hĕ'xa- *comb. form.* Six, as: **~chord** (-k-), diatonic series of six notes with semitone between third and fourth, used at three different pitches in medieval music; **~de'cimal,** using 16 as basis of counting; **~gon,** plane figure with six sides and angles; so **~gonal** (-ă'g-) *a.*; **~gram,** figure formed by two intersecting equilateral triangles (the angular points coinciding with those of a hexagon), figure of six lines; ~HE'DRAL *a.*, ~HE'DRON *n.*, (solid) with six faces; **~merous** (-ă'm-), having six parts; **~pod** *n.* & *a.*, (insect) with six feet; **~pody** (-ă'p-), line of verse with six feet; **~style** *a.* & *n.*, (portico) of six columns; **~sylla'bic,** of six syllables; **H~teuch** (-k), first six books of O.T.; **~va'lent,** (Chem.) having a valence of six. [Gk (*hex* six)]

hĕ'xăd *n.* Group of six. [f. Gk *hexas* -*ados* (*hex* six); see -AD 1]

hĕxă'mėter *n.* Line of six metrical feet, esp. **dactylic** ~ (five dactyls and trochee or spondee, any of first four feet, and rarely the fifth, being replaceable by spondee); hence **hĕxamĕ'**TRIC *a.*, **hĕxă'mėtr**IST (3) *n.* [ME f. L, f. Gk HEXA(*metros* f. *metron* measure)]

hĕ'xāne *n.* (Chem.) Hydrocarbon of the paraffin series, C_6H_{14}. [f. HEXA- + -ANE]

hĕ'xapla *n.* Sixfold text in parallel columns, esp. of O.T. or N.T. [Gk, neut. pl. of HEXA(*ploos* -fold), orig. of Origen's O.T. text]

hĕ'xōde *n.* Thermionic valve having six electrodes. [G, f. Gk *hex* six + *hodos* way]

hĕ'xōse *n.* (Chem.) Monosaccharide with six carbon atoms in each molecule. [f. HEXA- + -OSE[2]]

hey[1] (hā) *int.* calling attention or expr. joy, surprise, or inquiry, or enthusiastic approval *for*; ~ **presto** (conjuror's phrase of command, hence used to announce surprising transformation etc.). [ME; cf. OF *hay*, Du., G *hei*]

hey[2]. See HAY[2].

hey'-day[1] (hā'-) *int.* (arch.) expr. joy, surprise, etc. [cf. LG *heidi*, *heida*, excl. denoting gaiety]

hey'day[2] (hā'-) *n.* Full bloom, flush, (of youth, vigour, prosperity, etc.). [f. prec.]

H.F. *abbr.* high frequency.

hf. *abbr.* half.

Hf *symb.* hafnium.

H.G. *abbr.* Her or His Grace; Home Guard.

hg *abbr.* hectogram(s).

Hg *symb.* mercury. [f. mod. L *hydrargyrum*]

||**H.G.V.** *abbr.* heavy goods vehicle.

H.H. *abbr.* Her or His Highness; His Holiness.

HH *abbr.* double-hard (pencil-lead).

hh. *abbr.* hands (see HAND[1] 9).

hhd. *abbr.* hogshead(s).

H-hour (ā'chowr) *n.* Hour at which an operation is scheduled to begin. [f. *H* for *hour* + HOUR]

hī *int.* calling attention or *(colloq.) expr. greeting. [parallel form to HEY[1]]

***H.I.** *abbr.* Hawaiian Islands.

hīā'tus *n.* Break or gap, esp. in a series, account, or chain of proof; break between two vowels coming together not in the same syllable, as in *though oft the ear*. [L, = gaping (*hiare* gape)]

hī'bern|āte *v.i.* Spend the winter (of animal) in torpid state, (of person) in mild climate; (fig.) remain inactive; hence ~A'TION *n.* [f. L *hibernare* (*hibernus* wintry) + -ATE[3]]

Hīber'nĭan *a.* & *n.* (Native) of Ireland. [f. L *Hibernia*, *Iverna* f. Gk *Iernē* f. OCelt. **Iveriu* + -AN]

Hīber'nĭcĭsm *n.* Irish idiom, expression, or BULL[4]. [f. as prec. after *Anglicism* etc.]

hĭbĭ'scus *n.* Cultivated herb or shrub of genus *Hibiscus*, rose-mallow. [L, f. Gk *hibiskos* marsh mallow]

hĭc *int.* expr. sound of (esp. drunken) hiccup. [imit.]

hiccough. Var. of foll. (by assim. to COUGH[1,2]).

hĭ'ccup *n.* & *v.* **1.** *n.* Involuntary spasm of respiratory organs, with sudden closure of glottis and characteristic sound; hence ~Y[2] *a.* **2.** *v.i.* Make hiccup. **3.** *v.t.* Say, bring out, with hiccup(s). [imit.]

hĭc jā'cĕt (*or* hĕk yă'kĕt) *n.* Epitaph. [L, = here lies]

***hĭck** *n.* (colloq.) Countryman, farmer, provincial. [familiar form of *Richard*; cf. *Dick*]

***hĭ'ckey** *n.* Gadget. [20th c., of unkn. orig.]

hĭ'ckorȳ *n.* N. Amer. tree of genus *Carya*, allied to walnut, with tough heavy wood; (stick of) its wood. [f. native Virginian *pohickery*]

hĭd, hĭ'dden. See HIDE[2].

hĭdă'lgō *n.* (*pl.* ~**s**). Spanish gentleman. [Sp. (*hijo dalgo* son of something)]

hide[1] *n.*, & *v.t.* **1.** *n.* Animal's skin, raw or dressed; (joc.) human skin (*to save his own hide*; *will tan* *your hide*); **~'bound,** (of cattle) with skin clinging close as result of bad feeding, (fig.) narrow-minded, bigoted; hence (-)**hī'dED**[2] *a.* **2.** *v.t.* (colloq.) Flog. [OE *hȳd*, = OS *hūd*, OHG *hūt*, ON *húth* f. Gmc **hūdhiz* f. IE **kūtis*]

hīde[2] *v.* (*past* **hid,** *p.p.* **hidden** *or* arch. **hid**) & *n.* **1.** *v.t.* Put, keep, out of sight (*hide* one's *light under a* BUSHEL[1]); keep (fact) secret (*from*); keep (thing) from view without intention of secrecy; ~ one's **head,** keep out of sight from shame etc.; **hidden reserves,** extra profits etc. kept concealed in reserve. **2.** *v.i.* Conceal oneself; ~ **out** or **up,** remain in concealment; **~-and--(*go-)seek,** children's game in which players seek one or more hiding from them, (fig.) action involving evasive person or thing; ***~'away, ~-out, hi'd(e)y-hole,** (colloq.) hiding-place. **3.** *n.* ||Place of concealment used in observing or hunting wild animals. [OE *hȳdan*, = MDu. *hüden* f. WG **hūdjan*]

hīde[3] *n.* (Hist.) Measure of land, as much as would support one free family and dependants (from 60 to 120 acres according to locality). [OE *hī(gi)d* (*hīw-*, *hīg-* household)]

hī'dėous *a.* Frightful, repulsive, revolting, to senses or mind (*hideous crime, noise, pattern, scar*); (colloq.) unpleasant; hence ~LY[2] *adv.*, ~NESS *n.* [ME f. AF *hidous*, = OF *hidos*, *-eus*, earlier *hisdos* (*hisde* horror, of unkn. orig.); assim. to -EOUS]

hī'dǐng[1] *n.* (colloq.) Thrashing. [f. HIDE[1] + -ING[1]]

hī'dǐng[2] *n.* In vbl senses; state of remaining hidden (*be in, go into, hiding*); **~-place,** place of concealment. [ME, f. HIDE[2] + -ING[1]]

hīdr|ō'sǐs *n.* (*pl.* **~oses** *pr.* -ō'sēz). (Med.) Perspiration; so ~O'TIC *a.* [mod. L f. Gk (*hidrōs* sweat)]

hīe *v.i.* & *refl.* (*part.* **~'ing** *or* **hy'ing,** *pr.* hī'ĭ-). (arch. or poet.) Go quickly (*to* etc.; *hie to your chamber*; *hied him to the chase*). [OE *hīgian* strive, pant, of unkn. orig.]

hier'ârch (hīr'ârk) *n.* Chief priest; archbishop. [f. med. L f. Gk *hierarkhēs* (*hieros* sacred, *-arkhēs* ruler)]

hier'ârch|y̆ (hīr'ârkĭ) *n.* **1.** Each of three divisions of angels; the angels. **2.** Priestly government; organized priesthood in successive grades. **3.** Organization with grades or classes ranked one above another. **4.** Hence ~IC(AL) (-âr'-) *adjs.*, ~ISM (3) *n.*, ~IZE (3) *v.t.* [ME f. OF *ierarchie* f. med. L (*h*)*ierarchia* f. Gk *hierarkhia* (as prec.; see -Y[1])]

hierā'tǐc (hīr-) *a.* Of the priests (esp. of ancient Egyptian writing of abridged hieroglyphics opp. *demotic*, and of Egyptian and Greek traditional styles of art); priestly. [f. L f. Gk *hieratikos* (*hieraomai* be a priest f. *hiereus* priest; see -IC)]

hier'o- (hīr'*o*) *comb. form.* Sacred, holy, as: **~cracy** (-ŏ'k-), priestly rule; **~gram, ~graph,** sacred inscription or symbol; **~latry** (-ŏ'l-), worship of saints; **~logy** (-ŏ'l-), sacred literature or lore. [f. Gk *hieros* sacred + -O-]

hier'oglȳph (hīr'-) *n.* Figure of an object standing for a word, syllable, or sound, as used in ancient Egyptian and other writing; writing of this kind; secret or enigmatic symbol; (in *pl.*, joc.) writing difficult to make out. [back form. f. foll.]

hieroglȳ'phǐc (hīr-) *a.* & *n.* **1.** *a.* Of or written in hieroglyphs; symbolical. **2.** *n.* (in *pl.*) Hieroglyphs. **3.** Hence ~AL *a.*, **~al**LY[2] *adv.* [f. F *hiéroglyphique* or f. LL f. Gk HIERO(*gluphikos* f. *gluphē* carving; see -IC)]

hier'ophănt (hīr'-) *n.* (Gk Ant.) initiating priest; expounder of sacred mysteries; hence ~IC (-ă'-) *a.* [f. LL f. Gk HIERO(*phantēs* f. *phainō* show)]

hī'-fī *a.* & *n.* (colloq.) **1.** *a.* = HIGH-*fidelity*. **2.** *n.* Equipment for high-fidelity sound-reproduction; use of this as hobby etc. [abbr.]

hǐ'ggle *v.i.* Dispute about terms; haggle. [var. of HAGGLE]

hǐggledy̆-pǐ'ggledy̆ (-geldĭ) *adv.*, *a.*, & *n.* (In) utter confusion and disorder. [rhyming jingle, prob. w. ref. to irregular herding together of pigs]

high (hī) *a.*, *n.*, & *adv.* **1.** *a.* Of great or (*pred.*) specified upward extent (*high heels*; *a high hill*; *one inch high*; *water was waist-high*); situated far above ground, sea level, etc., (*high altitude*); upper, inland, (*High Asia*); coming above the normal or average level (*jersey with high neck*; *high boots*). **2.** Of exalted rank; **the Most H~,** God; **H~ Admiral** etc., chief officer; ~ **card** (that can outrank others, esp. ace or court-card; HOW *is that for high?*; **ace** etc. ~, having this as highest-ranking card); **~er court** (that can overrule decision of another); **~er mammal, plant,** etc., (evolved to a greater degree). **3.** Of exalted quality (*high art*; *high minds*; *high principles*); luxurious (*high living*); (colloq.) intoxicated by or *on* alcohol or drugs; ~ **opinion of** (very favourable). **4.** (Of meat) beginning to go bad; (of game) hung until slightly decomposed and ready to cook. **5.** Great, intense, extreme, powerful, (*high favour, fever, polish, praise, temperature, wind*); extreme in opinion (*a high Tory*). **6.** (Of physical action) extending to or from, or performed at, a considerable distance above ground (*high diving, flying*); (of quantity, value, etc.) greater than what is regarded as normal (*high prices*); (of latitude) near N. or S. pole; (of time) far advanced, fully reached (*high noon, high summer*; *it is high time we left*); (of period) at its peak of development (*High Renaissance*); (of sound) having rapid vibrations, shrill; (of vowel) = CLOSE[1]. **7.** ~ **altar,** chief altar of church; ~ **and dry,** (of ship) out of the water, (fig.) out of the current of events, stranded; ~ **and low,** (people) of all conditions (cf. sense 9); ~ **and mighty,** (colloq.) arrogant, (arch.) of exalted rank; ***~'ball,** (1) drink of spirits and soda etc. served usu. with ice in tall glass, (2) railway signal to proceed; ***~'binder,** ruffian, swindler, assassin; **~-born,** of noble birth; ***~'boy,** tall chest of drawers on legs; **~'brow** *a.* & *n.*, (colloq.) (person) with detached or (consciously) superior intellectual or cultural interests; ~ **camp,** sophisticated CAMP[3]; ~ **chair,** infant's chair with long legs and usu. tray, for use at meals; **H~ Church,** party or principles revering ritual, authority of bishops and priests, saving grace of sacraments, etc.; **H~-Chur'chman,** holder of such principles; **~-class,** of high quality; ~ **colour,** flushed complexion; ~ **command,** army commander--in-chief and staff; **H~ Commission**(**er**), (head of) embassy from one Commonwealth country to another; ||**H~ Court** (**of Justice**), supreme court of justice for civil cases; ~ **day,** festal day; *High* DUTCH[1]; ~ **enema** (delivered into colon); *higher* CRITICISM; **~er education** (at university etc.); **~er mathematics** (beyond what is ordinarily taught in schools); **~'er-ups,** (colloq.) persons of higher rank; *high* EXPLOSIVE; **~-falu'tin(g)** (-ōō'-) *a.* & *n.*, absurdly pompous or pretentious (writing etc.) [perh. f. *fluting*]; ~ **fashion,** *haute couture*; ~ **fidelity,** property of reproducing sound with little distortion of signal, giving result very similar to the original; ~ **finance** (dealing with large sums of money); **~-flown,** extravagant, bombastic; **~-fly'er, -fli'er,** person with ambition or extravagant notions, person or thing with (capacity for) great achievements; **~-fly'ing,** reaching a great height, ambitious; **~ frequency** (esp. in Radio, 3 to 30 megahertz); *high* GEAR; *High* GERMAN²; **~-grade,** of high quality; **~-handed,** overbearing, disregarding the feelings of others; **~ hat,** tall hat, foot-operated cymbals, (fig.) person affecting superiority; **~-hat,** (*a.*) supercilious, *(*v.t.*) treat superciliously, *(*v.i.*) assume superior attitude; **~ holiday,** Jewish New Year or Day of Atonement; *on* one's *high* HORSE¹; *high* JINKS; **~ jump,** athletic contest of jumping as high as possible, (fig.) drastic punishment; **~-key,** (Photog.) consisting of light tones; **~ kick,** dancer's kick high in the air; **~-level,** (of negotiations etc.) conducted by persons of high rank; **~ life,** luxurious existence ascribed to the upper classes; **~'light,** (*n.*) (in painting etc.) any of brightest parts of subject or representation, moment or detail of vivid interest, outstanding feature, (*v.t.*) bring into prominence, draw attention to; **~-lows,** (arch.) boots reaching over ankles; *high* MASS¹; **~-mi'nded,** morally lofty, (arch.) proud; *high*-OCTANE; **~ old,** (colloq.) most enjoyable (time etc.); **~-pitched,** (of sound) high, (of roof) steep, (of style etc.) lofty; **~ places,** upper ranks of an organization; **~ point,** maximum or best state reached; **~ polymer** (of high molecular weight); **~-powered,** having great power or energy, forceful; *high* PRESSURE; **~ priest,** chief priest (esp. of Jews), (fig.) head of any cult; **~-ranking,** of high rank, senior; *high* RELIEF²; ***~-rise,** (of building) having many storeys; **~ road,** main road, (fig.) direct route (*to*); **~ school,** secondary (esp. ‖grammar) school; **~ season,** period of greatest number of visitors at resort etc.; **~ sea(s),** open seas not within any country's jurisdiction; ‖*high* SHERIFF; ***~ sign,** (colloq.) warning or reassuring gesture; **~-speed,** operating at great speed, (of steel) suitable for cutting-tools even when red-hot; *high* SPIRIT¹(*s*); *high*-SPIRITED; **~ spot,** (sl.) important place or feature; **~-ste'pper,** horse that lifts its feet high in walking and trotting, (fig.) stately person; ‖*High* STEWARD; **~ street,** main road, esp. principal street of town with shops etc.; **~-strung,** very sensitive or nervous; **~ table,** elevated table (1) at public dinner, (2) for fellows of college; ***~'tail** *v.i.*, (sl.) move at high speed; ‖*high* TEA; **~-tensile,** (of metal) having great tensile strength; **~ tension,** = *high voltage*; *high* TIDE¹; **~-toned,** stylish, dignified, superior in manner; *high* TREASON; **~-up,** (colloq.) person of high rank; **~ voltage,** electrical potential causing some danger of injury or damage; **~ water,** state of tide when water is highest, time when tide is at the full; **~-wa'ter mark,** level reached at high water, (fig.) maximum recorded value, highest point of excellence etc.; **~, wide, and handsome,** in carefree or stylish manner; **~ wire,** high tight-rope; **~ words,** angry talk; ***~ yellow,** half-caste with light yellow skin. **8.** *n.* A high or the highest level or figure; the highest card dealt or drawn; area of high barometric pressure; = TOP¹ 9 (gear); *(colloq.) high school; (sl.) euphoric state caused by drug; **from on ~,** from heaven or a high place; **on ~,** in or to heaven or a high place; ‖**the H~,** (colloq.) High Street, esp. at Oxford. **9.** *adv.* Far up, aloft; in or to a high degree; at a high price; (of sound) at or to a high pitch; **play ~,** play for high stakes, play card of high value; **run ~,** (of sea) have strong current with high tide, (fig., of feelings) be strong; *search* **~ and low,** everywhere (cf. sense 7). [OE *hēah*, = OS, OHG *hōh*, ON *hár*, Goth. *hauhs* f. Gmc **hauhaz*]

hi'ghland (hī'l-) *n.* & *a.* **1.** *n.* High land (usu. in *pl.*, esp. (*H~s*) of mountainous part of Scotland). **2.** *a.* Of or in highland or the Scottish Highlands; **H~ cattle** (of breed with shaggy hair and long curved widely-spaced horns); **H~ dress,** kilt etc.; *Highland* FLING. **3.** Hence **~ER¹** (4), **~man,** *ns.* [OE *hēahlond* promontory (as prec., LAND¹)]

hī'ghlȳ (hī'lĭ) *adv.* In a high degree (*highly amusing, polished, probable*; *commend, esteem, highly*); honourably, favourably, (*think, speak, highly of*); **~-strung,** = HIGH-*strung*. [OE *hēalīce* (as HIGH, -LY²)]

***hī'gh-mŭck-a-mŭck** (hī'm-) *n.* Person of (esp. conceitedly) great self-importance. [perh. f. Chinook *hiu* plenty + *muckamuck* food]

hī'ghnėss (hī'n-) *n.* **1.** Title of various British and other princes etc. (*His* or *Her Highness* or *Royal*, SERENE, *Imperial*, *Highness*). **2.** State of being figuratively high (*the highness of his character, of taxation*; *fell from sheer highness of ambition*; cf. *the* HEIGHT *of*). [OE *hēanes* (as HIGH, -NESS)]

hīght (hīt) *a.* (arch., poet., or joc.) Called, named. [f. p.p. (from 14th c.) of OE *hātan* command, call, OS *hētan*, OHG *heizzan*, ON *heita*, Goth. *haitan*]

hī'ghway (hī'w-) *n.* Public road (**King's** or **Queen's ~**, regarded as protected by monarch's power); main route; (fig.) ordinary direct course of action; ‖**H~ Code,** official book of guidance for road-users; **~man,** (Hist.) (usu. mounted) man who robs passengers on highway. [f. HIGH + WAY]

H.I.H. *abbr.* Her or His Imperial Highness.

hī'jăck *v.t.*, & *n.* **1.** *v.t.* Seize control of (means of transport, e.g. lorry with goods, aircraft in flight) by (threat of) violence; force (aircraft etc.) *to* new destination thus; steal (contraband etc.) in transit; so **~ER¹** *n.* **2.** *n.* Hijacking. [20th c.; orig. unkn.]

hĭ'jra. Var. of HEGIRA.

hīke *n.* & *v.* (colloq.) **1.** *n.* Long walk in the country undertaken for pleasure or exercise; *increase (of prices etc.). **2.** *v.i.* Walk vigorously or laboriously; go for long walk; HITCH¹-*hike*; be hitched *up*. **3.** *v.t.* Hoist, shove, force to move; *increase. **4.** Hence **hī'kER¹** *n.* [19th c. dial.; orig. unkn.]

hĭlār'ĭous *a.* Mirthful, joyous; boisterously merry; hence or cogn. **~LY²** *adv.*, **~NESS, hĭlă'RITY,** *ns.* [f. L *hilaris* f. Gk *hilaros* cheerful + -OUS]

‖**Hĭ'larȳ** *n.* **~ term,** (in university etc., beginning in Jan.). [f. *Hilarius* bishop of Poitiers d. 367, w. Anglican festival 13 Jan.]

hĭll *n.*, & *v.t.* **1.** *n.* Natural elevation of earth's surface, small mountain; ***over the ~,** (colloq.) past the crisis or acme; UP *hill and down dale*; **the ~s,** (Anglo-Ind.) a hill-station as health-resort etc.; **~ and dale,** (of gramophone record) with groove-undulations in vertical plane; **old as the ~s,** very ancient. **2.** Heap, mound, (*ant-, dung-, mole-, hill*). **3.** ***~-billy,** rustic person from mountains etc., folk music (as) of southern U.S.; **~ climb,** race for vehicles over hilly ground; **~-fort,** fortified place built on hill; **~-man,** inhabitant of hilly country; **~'side,** lateral slope of hill; **~-station,** government settlement in low mountains of N. India; **~'top,** summit of hill. **4.** Hence **~'Y²** *a.* **5.** *v.t.* Form into hill; bank *up* (plants) with soil. [OE *hyll*, = LG *hull*, WG **hulni* f. IE **k(o)l-*]

hĭllō' *int.* (arch.) = HALLO. [var. of HOLLO]

hĭ'llock *n.* Small hill or mound. [ME, f. HILL + -OCK]

hĭlt *n.*, & *v.t.* **1.** *n.* Handle of sword or dagger, or of other weapon or tool; *prove* etc. **up to the ~,** completely. **2.** *v.t.* Furnish with hilt. [OE *hilt(e)*, = OS *hilte*, ON *hjalt*, OHG *helza* f. Gmc **heltaz*]

hī'l|um *n.* (*pl.* ~**a**). (Bot.) point of attachment of seed to seed-vessel; (Anat.) notch etc. where vessel enters organ. [L, = little thing, trifle]

him. See HE¹.

H.I.M. *abbr.* Her or His Imperial Majesty.

Hĭmalay'an *a.* Of the Himalayas. [f. *Himalaya* Mountains in Nepal etc. (Skr., f. *hima* snow + *ālaya* abode) + -AN]

hĭmă'tion *n.* Outer garment of ancient Greeks, worn over the left shoulder and under the right. [Gk]

hĭmsĕ'lf *pron.* Emphat. & refl. form corresp. to HE¹ or HIM (for uses cf. HERSELF). [OE (HIM, SELF)]

Hinaya'na (hēnayah'na) *n.* More conservative form of Buddhism, practised in Burma, Thailand, etc. [Skr. (*hīna* lesser, *yāna* vehicle)]

hīnd¹ *n.* Female of (esp. red) deer, esp. in and after third year. [OE, = OS, ON *hind*, OHG *hinta* f. Gmc **hinthjō* f. IE **kemti-* (**kem-* hornless)]

||**hīnd²** *n.* Farm servant, esp. (Sc. etc.) married and skilled farm-workman, formerly having charge of two horses, and provided with cottage on the farm; steward; rustic, boor. [ME *hine* f. OE *hīne* pl., app. f. *hī(g)na* gen. pl. of *hīgan*, *hīwan* 'members of a family'; cf. HIDE³; for *-d* cf. SOUND²]

hīnd³ *a.* Situated at the back, posterior, (esp. opp. *fore*: *hind leg, wheel*); ~**quar'ters,** hind legs and adjoining parts of quadruped; **on** one's ~ **legs,** (joc.) = *on* one's LEGS (1). [ME, perh. shortened f. OE *bihindan* BEHIND]

hī'nder¹ *a.* Situated at the BACK¹ (sense 5). [ME, perh. f. OE *hinderweard* backward; cf. prec.]

hĭ'nder² *v.t.* Impede, obstruct, prevent, (*you will hinder him, his work, its completion, him from working,* or abs.). [OE *hindrian*, = ON *hindra*, OHG *hintarōn* f. Gmc **hindarōjan* (**hindar* HIND³)]

Hĭ'ndi (-ē) *a.* & *n.* (Of) a group of spoken languages of N. India; (of) a literary form of Hindustani with Sanskrit-based vocabulary and Devanagari script, an official language of India. [f. Urdu *hindī* (*Hind* India)]

hī'ndmōst (*or* -ost) *a.* Furthest behind; most remote. [ME, f. HIND³ + -MOST]

hĭ'ndrance *n.* Obstruction, prevention; obstacle. [ME, f. HINDER² + -ANCE]

hī'ndsīght (-sīt) *n.* Back sight of gun; (colloq.) wisdom after the event (opp. *foresight*). [f. HIND³ + SIGHT¹]

Hĭndu' (-dōō'), (arch.) **Hĭndōō',** (*or* hĭ'-) *n.* & *a.* **1.** Adherent of Hinduism; Indian. **2.** *a.* Of the Hindus; that is a Hindu; Indian. [Urdu, f. Pers. (*Hind* India)]

Hĭ'ndu|ĭsm (-ōō-) *n.* Religious and social system with adherents esp. in India, with belief in reincarnation, worship of several gods, and caste as basis of society; so ~IZE (3) *v.t.* [f. prec. + -ISM]

Hĭndusta'ni (-ah'nē) *a.* & *n.* **1.** *a.* Of Hindustan or its people; of Hindustani. **2.** *n.* Language based on Western Hindi, with admixture of Arabic, Persian, etc., current as standard language and lingua franca in much of N. India and Pakistan; (arch.) Urdu. [Urdu, f. Pers. *hindūstānī* (as HINDU, *-stān* country, *-ī* adj. suf.)]

hĭnge (-nj) *n.* & *v.* **1.** *n.* Movable joint or mechanism like that by which door is hung on side post; natural joint doing similar work, e.g. that of bivalve shell; (**stamp-**)~, small piece of gummed transparent paper for fixing postage stamp in album etc.; (fig.) central principle, critical point, on which all turns; hence **hĭnge**ED² (-njd), ~'LESS (-jl-), *adjs.*, ~'WISE (-jw-) *adv.* **2.** *v.t.* Attach (as) with hinge. **3.** *v.i.* (Of door etc. or fig.) hang and turn *on* (post, principle, etc.). [ME *heng* etc., rel. to HANG¹]

hĭ'nnȳ¹ *n.* Offspring of she-ass and stallion. [f. L *hinnus* f. Gk *hinnos*, *ginnos*]

hĭ'nnȳ², hĭ'nnie, *n.* (Sc. & N. Engl.) = HONEY 2; **singing ~,** currant-cake baked on griddle. [var. of HONEY]

hĭnt *n.* & *v.* **1.** *n.* Slight indication, covert or indirect suggestion (BROAD *hint*; DROP², TAKE¹ 9, *a hint*); small piece of practical information. **2.** *v.t.* Suggest slightly (thing, *that*). **3.** *v.i.* ~ **at,** give a hint of, refer indirectly to. [app. f. obs. *hent* grasp, lay hold of, f. OE *hentan* f. Gmc **hent-*, cogn. w. HUNT¹]

hĭ'nterlănd *n.* District behind coast or river's banks, occas. with suggestion of sparse population or inferior civilization; area served by port or other centre; remote or fringe area. [G (*hinter* behind, *land* LAND¹)]

hĭp¹ *n.* **1.** Projection of pelvis and upper part of thigh-bone on each side of body in men and quadrupeds; *have* (person) **on the ~,** (arch.) at a disadvantage; **smite ~ and thigh** (unsparingly). **2.** (Archit.) Arris of roof from ridge to eaves. **3. ~-bath** (portable, in which one sits immersed to the hips); **~-bone,** bone forming hip, esp. ilium; **~-disease** (of hip-joint, with fungous growth, inflammation, and caries); **~-flask** (for spirits etc., carried in hip-pocket); **~-joint,** articulation of head of thigh-bone with ilium; **~-length** *a.*, (of garment) reaching down to the hips; **~-pocket** (in trousers, just behind hip); **~-roof** (with ends as well as sides inclined). **4.** Hence (-)~PED² (-pt) *a.* (**~ped roof,** = *hip-roof*). [OE *hype*, = OHG *huf*, Goth. *hups* f. Gmc **hupiz*, rel. to HOP²]

hĭp², hĕp¹, *n.* Fruit of (esp. wild) rose. [OE *hēope*, *hīope*, = OS *hiopo*, OHG *hiufa* f. WG **heup-*]

hĭp³, hȳp, *n.* (arch.) Morbid depression of spirits. [abbr. of HYPOCHONDRIA]

hĭp⁴ *v.t.* (**-pp-**). (arch.) Make low-spirited. [f. prec.]

hĭp⁵ *int.* introducing united cheer (*hip, hip, hurrah*). [19th c., of unkn. orig.]

hĭp⁶ *a.* (sl.) = HEP²; **~-cat,** = HEP²-*cat*; hence ~'NESS *n.* [20th c., of unkn. orig.]

hĭppēă'strum *n.* S. Amer. bulbous plant of genus *Hippeastrum* with showy white or red flowers. [mod. L, f. Gk *hippeus* horseman (the leaves appearing to ride on one another) + *astron* star (from the flower-shape)]

hĭ'ppie, hĭ'ppȳ¹, *n.* (sl.) = HIPSTER¹; unconventionally behaving person who is (thought to be) using hallucinogenic drugs and rebelling against organized society. [f. HIP⁶ + -IE, -Y³]

hĭ'ppō *n.* (*pl.* **~s**). (colloq.) Hippopotamus. [abbr.]

hĭ'ppo- *comb. form.* Horse, as: **~cĕ'ntaur,** centaur; **~phagy** (-ŏ'f-), practice of eating horse-flesh; ~PHIL(E) *n.* & *a.*, ~PHO'BIA *n.* [f. Gk *hippos* horse + -o-]

hĭppocă'mp|us *n.* (*pl.* ~**i** *pr.* -ī). Fish of genus *Hippocampus*, sea-horse; ~ **major, minor,** (Anat.) elongated ridges on floor of each lateral ventricle of brain. [L, f. Gk HIPPO(*kampos* sea-monster)]

hĭ'ppocrăs *n.* (Hist.) Wine flavoured with spices. [ME, f. OF *ipocras* Hippocrates (see foll.), prob. because strained through filter called 'Hippocrates' sleeve']

Hĭppocră'tĭc *a.* ~ **oath** (stating obligations and proper conduct of physicians, taken by those beginning medical practice). [f. med. L *Hippocraticus* f. *Hippocrates*, Gk physician of 5th c. B.C. + -IC]

Hĭ′ppocrēne *n.* Poetic or literary inspiration. [name of fountain on Mount Helicon sacred to the Muses, L f. Gk (*hippos* horse, *krēnē* fountain, as having been produced by stroke of Pegasus' hoof)]

hĭ′ppodrōme *n.* (Gk & Rom. Ant.) course for chariot races etc.; circus; (*H*~; used as name of) theatre for various stage entertainments. [F, or f. L f. Gk HIPPO(*dromos* race, course)]

hĭ′ppogriff, -grȳph, *n.* Fabulous griffin-like creature with body of horse. [f. F *hippogriffe* f. It. *ippogrifo* (as HIPPO-, *grifo* GRIFFIN[2])]

hĭppopŏ′tam|us *n.* (*pl.* **~uses,** *or* **~i** *pr.* -ī). Large African pachydermatous tusked hairless short-legged quadruped inhabiting rivers etc. [ME f. L, f. Gk HIPPO(*potamos* river)]

hĭ′ppȳ[1]. See HIPPIE.

hĭ′ppȳ[2] *a.* Having large hips. [f. HIP[1] + -Y[2]]

hĭ′pster[1] *n.* (sl.) One who is hep; hep-cat; hence ~ISM (3) *n.* [f. HIP[6] + -STER]

hĭ′pster[2] *a.* (Of garment) hanging from the hips rather than from the waist. [f. HIP[1] + -STER]

hĭraga′na (-ah′-) *n.* Cursive form of kana. [Jap., = plain kana]

hir′cīne *a.* Goatlike. [f. L *hircinus* (*hircus* he-goat; see -INE[1])]

hīre[1] *n.* Payment under contract for use of thing or for personal service; engagement on these terms; (fig.) reward; **~-car** (available for hire); ||**~-pur′chase** (**system**) (by which hired thing becomes hirer's after certain number of payments); **for** or **on** ~, ready to be hired. [OE *hȳr*, = OS *hūria* f. WG **hūrja*]

hīre[2] *v.t.* Employ (person) for wages or *fee; procure (*from* person), grant (*out*; to person), temporary use of (thing) for stipulated payment; *borrow (money); ***~d girl** or **man,** domestic servant esp. on farm; hence ~ABLE (-*ra*-), ***hīr′**ABLE, *a.* [OE *hȳrian* (as prec.)]

hīr′eling (hīr′l-) *n.* (usu. derog.) One who serves for hire. [OE *hȳrling* (as HIRE[1], -LING[1])]

hir′sūte *a.* Hairy, shaggy; untrimmed; hence ~NESS (-tn-) *n.* [f. L *hirsutus*]

hir′sūtism *n.* Excessive growth of hair. [f. prec. + -ISM]

hĭs (ĭz *or, when stressed,* hĭz) *poss. pron.* Of him(self); (arch.) its; for phrs. see HER[2], HERS. [OE, gen. of HE[1] and IT[1]]

Hĭspă′nĭc *a.* Of Spain (and Portugal); of Spain and other Spanish-speaking countries; hence ~IST (3) *n.*, ~IZE (3) *v.t.* [f. L *Hispanicus* (*Hispania* Spain; see -IC)]

Hĭ′spanĭst *n.* Hispanicist. [f. as prec. + -IST]

Hĭspă′nō- *comb. form.* Spanish (and). [f. L *Hispanus* Spanish + -O-]

hĭ′spĭd *a.* (Bot. & Zool.) Shaggy; bristly. [f. L *hispidus*; see -ID[1]]

hĭss *v.* & *n.* **1.** *v.i.*, & *n.* (Of person, snake, goose, liquid poured on fire, etc.) (make) sharp sibilant sound of *s*, esp. as sign of disapproval or derision. **2.** *v.t.* Express disapproval of (person etc.) thus; ~ **off** (*the stage*), **away, down,** etc., drive off etc. by hisses; utter (words) with angry hiss. [ME; imit.]

hĭst *int.* used to call attention, enjoin silence, or incite dog etc. [16th c.; natural excl.]

hĭ′stamĭne (*or* -ēn) *n.* (Chem.) Simple base present in all body tissues and causing some allergic reactions. [f. as foll. + AMINE]

hĭ′sto- *comb. form.* (Biol.) Tissue, as: **~ge′nesis, ~geny** (-ŏ′j-), production of organic tissues; so **~gene′tic** *a.*; **~logy** (-ŏ′l-), science of organic tissues; **~lysis** (-ŏ′l-), breaking down of organic tissues; **~patho′logy,** (study of) changes in tissues caused by disease. [f. Gk *histos* web + -O-]

hĭ′stogrăm *n.* Diagram in which columns represent frequencies of various ranges of values of a quantity. [f. Gk *histos* mast + -GRAM]

histor′ian *n.* Writer of history (esp. in higher sense, as opp. to mere annalist or compiler); person learned in history; **English, ancient,** ~, writer or student of English, ancient, history. [f. F *historien* f. L (as HISTORY; see -AN)]

hĭstor′iātėd *a.* = STORIATED. [f. med. L *historiare* (as HISTORY); see -ATE[3], -ED[1]]

hĭstŏ′rĭc *a.* Famous in history; (Gram., of tense) normally used of past events (esp. L & Gk imperfect and pluperfect; cf. PRIMARY; ~ **present** (used for past), ~ **infinitive** (used for indicative)); (arch.) = foll. [f. L f. Gk *historikos* (as HISTORY; see -IC)]

hĭstŏ′rĭcal *a.* Of history (*historical evidence, principles*); belonging to history, not to prehistory or legend; (of study of a subject) based on history or an analysis of development in course of time; in connection with history, from the historian's point of view (*of purely historical interest*); belonging to the past, not of the present; (of novel, picture, etc.) dealing with historical events; hence ~LY[2] *adv.* [f. as prec. + -AL]

hĭstŏ′rĭc|ĭsm *n.* Theory that social and cultural phenomena are determined by history; belief that historical events are governed by laws; tendency to regard historical development as most basic aspect of human existence; excessive regard for past styles etc.; hence ~IST (2) *n.* [f. HISTORIC + -ISM, after G *historismus*]

hĭstorĭ′cĭtȳ *n.* Historical genuineness of alleged event etc. [f. HISTORIC + -ITY]

hĭstoriŏ′grapher *n.* Writer of history, esp. official historian of a court etc. [ME, f. F *historiographe* or f. LL f. Gk *historiographos* (as HISTORY; see -GRAPHER)]

hĭstoriŏ′graphȳ *n.* Writing of history; study of history-writing; hence **hĭstoriogră′phĭc**(AL) *adjs.* [f. med. L f. Gk *historiographia* (as foll.; see -GRAPHY)]

hĭ′storȳ *n.* Continuous methodical record of important or public events; study of past events, esp. human affairs; aggregate of past events, course of human affairs; whole train of events connected with nation, person, thing, etc.; eventful past career (*this knife has a history*); systematic account of natural phenomena etc. (NATURAL *history*); historical play; ANCIENT[1] *history*; CASE[1] *history*; **make ~,** influence the course of history, do something memorable. [ME, f. L f. Gk *historia* finding out, narrative, history (*histōr* learned, wise man, cogn. w. WIT[1])]

hĭstriŏ′n|ĭc *a.* & *n.* **1.** *a.* Of actors or acting; stagy, hypocritical, whence **hĭ′striŏn**ISM (2), **~ĭc**ISM (2), *ns.*; hence ~ICALLY *adv.* **2.** *n.* Actor. **3.** (in *pl.*) Theatricals, theatrical art, pretence; insincere actions done merely to impress others. [f. LL *histrionicus* f. L *histrio -onis* actor; see -IC]

hĭt[1] *v.* (**-tt-; hit**). **1.** *v.t.* Strike with blow or missile; (of moving body) strike; knock (part of the body) *against* or *on*; deliver (blow, person etc. a blow). **2.** (fig.) Cause to suffer, wound, (HARD *hit*); have effect on (person); light upon, get at, (thing aimed at); = *hit upon* (see sense 6); ~ **(off)**, represent exactly; fall in with, suit; (colloq.) encounter (*hit a snag*), arrive at (*hit an all-time low*), indulge in (liquor etc.). **3.** (Cricket). Score (runs), strike (ball) or strike ball bowled by (bowler) esp. *for* so many runs, (||~ **for six,** (fig.) defeat in argument etc.); ~ **wicket,** be out by striking wicket with bat etc. **4.** *v.i.* Direct blow (lit. or fig.) *at*; (of moving body) strike *against* or *upon*. **5. ~ and run,** (of attackers, vehicle-driver, etc.) do damage and retreat or make off immediately (cf. TIP²), (Baseball, *a.*) with departure of runner from his base as soon as pitcher begins to throw; ~ **below the belt,** give foul blow (in Boxing, or fig.); ~ **the hay,** (sl.) go to bed; *hit the* HEAD¹-*lines*; **~-or-miss,** (colloq.) casual, careless; ~ **the (right) nail on the head,** guess right, express the exact truth; ***~ the trail,** (sl.) depart. **6.** ~ **back,** retaliate; ~ **it off,** agree or be congenial (*with, together*); ~ **out,** deal vigorous blows (lit. or fig.); ~ **up,** (Cricket) score (runs) energetically; ~ **(up)on,** find (what is sought), esp. by chance. [OE *hittan* f. ON *hitta* meet with, of unkn. orig.]

hĭt² *n.* Blow, stroke; stroke of sarcasm etc. (*at*); stroke of good luck; successful attempt; popular success in public entertainment; **make a ~,** be successful or popular (*with*); ***~ man,** hired assassin; ~ **parade,** programme of popular tunes etc. [ME, f. prec.]

hĭtch¹ *v.* **1.** *v.t.* Move (thing) with jerk; shift slightly; ~ **up,** lift with jerk. **2.** Fasten with loop, hook, etc.; *hitch* one's WAGON *to a star*; **get ~ed,** (sl.) marry. **3.** *v.i.* Become so fastened (*in, on to*, etc.). **4. ~-hike** *v.* & *n.*, ~ *v.i.*, & *n.*, travel, obtain (transport), by begging free rides in passing motor vehicles; **~'ing post,** fixed post for tethering a horse. [ME, of uncert. orig.]

hĭtch² *n.* Jerk, abrupt pull or push; (Naut.) noose or knot of various kinds (**half ~,** formed by passing end of rope round its standing part and then through the bight; CLOVE HITCH); temporary stoppage (TECHNICAL *hitch*); impediment; *(sl.) period of service. [f. prec.]

hĭ'ther (-dh-) *adv.* & *a.* (literary). **1.** To or towards this place; ~ **and thither,** ~ **and yon,** in various directions, here and there. **2.** *a.* Situated on this side; the nearer (of two). **3.** **~to** (*or* -tōō'), up to this time; **~ward,** (arch.) in this direction. [OE *hider*, corresp. to ON *hethra* here, hither, Goth. *hidrē*, f. root **hi*- (HE¹) + suf. *-ther* (as THITHER)]

Hĭ'tler *n.* One who embodies characteristics of Hitler; hence ~ISM, political principles or policy of Nazi party in Germany, ~ITE¹ (1) *n.* [f. A. ~, Ger. dictator d. 1945]

Hĭ'ttīte *n.* & *a.* (Member or language) of a powerful ancient people of Asia Minor and Syria, or their subjects. [f. Heb. *Ḥittīm*]

hive *n.* & *v.* **1.** *n.* **(Bee')~,** artificial habitation for bees; (fig.) busy swarming place; hiveful of bees; swarming multitude; hive-shaped thing. **2.** *v.t.* Place (bees) in hive, house (persons etc.) snugly, hoard *up*. **3.** *v.i.* Enter hive; live together like bees. **4.** ~ **off,** swarm off separately like bees, (fig.) assign (work) to subsidiary department or company. [OE *hȳf* f. Gmc **hūf*-]

hīves (-vz) *n. pl.* Skin eruption; inflammation of larynx etc. [16th c., orig. Sc., of unkn. orig.]

H.K. *abbr.* Hong Kong; House of Keys.

H.L. *abbr.* House of Lords.

hl *abbr.* hectolitre(s).

h'm. Var. of HEM³ 1, 2, HUM².

H.M. *abbr.* headmaster; headmistress; Her or His Majesty('s).

hm *abbr.* hectometre(s).

H.M.A.S. *abbr.* Her Majesty's Australian Ship.

H.M.C.S. *abbr.* Her Majesty's Canadian Ship.

H.M.I. *abbr.* Her Majesty's Inspector (of Schools).

H.M.N.Z.S. *abbr.* Her Majesty's New Zealand Ship.

H.M.S. *abbr.* Her Majesty's Ship.

H.M.S.O. *abbr.* Her Majesty's Stationery Office.

||**H.M.V.** *abbr.* His Master's Voice.

||**H.N.C.** *abbr.* Higher National Certificate.

||**H.N.D.** *abbr.* Higher National Diploma.

hō *int.* expr. surprise, admiration, triumph, derision, or calling attention; added to other *ints.* (HEIGH-*ho*, WHAT *ho*) or (Naut.) to name of destination etc. (*westward ho*). [ME, imit.; cf. ON *hó*]

ho. *abbr.* house.

Ho *symb.* holmium.

hoar *a.* & *n.* **1.** *a.* Grey-haired with age; greyish white; (of thing) grey with age; **~-frost,** frozen water vapour deposited in clear still weather on lawns etc.; ||**~'stone,** ancient boundary stone. **2.** *n.* Hoariness; hoar-frost. [OE *hār*, = OS, OHG *hēr* old, ON *hárr* f. Gmc **hairaz* (**hai*- f. IE **koi*- shine)]

hoard *n.* & *v.* **1.** *n.* Stock, store, (esp. of money) laid by; amassed stock of facts etc.; (Archaeol.) ancient cache of treasure etc. **2.** *v.t.* Amass (money etc., or abs.) and put away, store *up*; store in the mind. **3.** *v.i.* Overstock oneself with food etc. in time of scarcity. [OE *hord*, = OS *hord*, *horth*, OHG *hort*, ON *hodd*, Goth. *huzd* f. Gmc **huzdam*]

hoar'dĭng¹ *n.* In vbl senses. [f. prec. + -ING¹]

hoar'dĭng² *n.* Fence of boards round building during erection or repairs, often used for posting bills; ||structure erected to carry advertisements etc. [f. obs. *hoard* (+ -ING¹) f. AF *h(o)urdis* f. OF *hourd*, *hort*, cogn. w. HURDLE]

hoar'hound. Var. of HOREHOUND.

hoarse *a.* (Of voice) rough and deep-sounding, husky, croaking; having such a voice; hence ~'LY² (-slĭ) *adv.*, **hoar'**SEN⁶ *v.t.* & *i.*, ~'NESS (-sn-) *n.* [ME *hors* f. ON **hars* f. Gmc **hairsaz*; earlier ME *hos*, OE *hās*, OHG *heis(i)* f. Gmc **haisaz*]

hoar'|ȳ *a.* (Of hair) grey, white, with age; having such hair, venerable; old and trite; (Bot. & Entom.) covered with short white hairs; hence ~ĭNESS *n.* [f. HOAR + -Y²]

hoatzin (hwătsē'n) *n.* Tropical Amer. strong--smelling bird whose young climb by means of wing-claws. [native name, imit.]

hoax *v.t.*, & *n.* **1.** *v.t.* Deceive (person) by way of joke. **2.** *n.* Humorous or mischievous deception. [18th c., prob. contr. f. HOCUS]

hŏb¹ *n.* Male ferret; hobgoblin; ***play** or ***raise** ~, cause mischief. [ME, familiar form of *Rob*, short for *Robin* or *Robert*]

hŏb² *n.* Side casing of fireplace, having surface level with top of grate; peg or pin as mark in quoits etc.; = HOBNAIL. [perh. var. of HUB, orig. = lump]

hŏ'bbĭt *n.* One of an imaginary race of half--sized persons in stories by Tolkien; hence ~RY (5) *n.* [invented by J. R. R. Tolkien, Engl. writer d. 1973, and said by him to mean 'hole--builder']

hŏ'bble¹ *v.* **1.** *v.i.* Walk lamely, limp; (fig.) proceed haltingly in action or speech. **2.** *v.t.* Cause to hobble; tie together legs of (horse etc.) to prevent it from straying etc.; tie (legs) thus. [ME, prob. f. LG; cf. HOPPLE, and Du. *hobbelen* rock from side to side]

hŏ'bble² *n.* **1.** Uneven or infirm gait; (arch.) awkward situation. **2.** Rope, clog, etc., for hobbling a horse etc.; ~ **skirt** (so narrow at foot as to impede wearer in walking). [f. prec.]

hŏ'bbledėhoy (-bеld-) *n.* (colloq.) Clumsy or awkward youth between boyhood and manhood; hence ~HOOD *n.*, ~ISH¹ *a.*, (-oi'-). [16th c., of unkn. orig.]

hŏ'bbȳ¹ *n.* Favourite subject or occupation that is not one's main business; (arch.) small horse; (Hist.) early type of velocipede. [ME *hobyn*, *hoby*, f. pet-forms of *Robin*; cf. DOBBIN]

hŏ'bbȳ² *n.* Small species of falcon, *Falco subbuteo*. [ME, f. OF *hobé*, *hobet* dim. of *hobe* small bird of prey]

hŏ'bbȳ-hŏrse *n.* Wicker horse used in morris dance etc.; child's stick with horse's head; rocking-horse; horse on merry-go-round; topic to which one constantly recurs. [f. HOBBY¹ + HORSE¹]

hŏ'bgŏblĭn *n.* Mischievous imp; bogy, bugbear. [f. HOB¹ + GOBLIN]

hŏ'bnail *n.* **1.** Heavy-headed nail for boot-soles; hence ~ED² (-ld) *a.* **2.** ~**(ed) liver** (with many small projections due to cirrhosis). [f. HOB² + NAIL¹]

hŏ'b-nŏb *v.i.* (**-bb-**). Drink together; talk informally (*with*). [f. *hob or nob* = give or take, of alternate drinking; earlier *hab nab*, = have or not have]

***hō'bō** *n.* (*pl.* ~**es**). Wandering workman or tramp. [19th c.; orig. unkn.]

Hŏ'bson *n.* ~**'s choice,** option of taking the one offered or nothing. [f. T. ~, Cambridge carrier d. 1631, who let out horses on this basis]

hŏck¹ *n.* Joint of quadruped's hind leg between true knee and fetlock, pointing backwards; knuckle of pork. [f. obs. *hockshin* f. OE *hōhsinu* (see HOUGH)]

||**hŏck²** *n.* German white wine (prop. that of Hochheim on the river Main). [abbr. of obs. *hockamore* f. G *Hochheimer*]

***hŏck³** *v.t.*, & *n.* (sl.) Pawn, pledge; **in** ~, in pawn, in prison, or in debt. [f. Du. *hok* hutch, prison, debt]

hŏ'ckey *n.* Game played with ball on field (or PUCK² on ICE¹) and curved sticks between goals; (Can.) ice hockey, whence ~IST (3) *n.* [16th c.; orig. unkn.]

Hŏ'cktīde *n.* (Hist.) Old festival kept on second Monday and Tuesday after Easter, orig. with collection of money for church etc. [ME, of unkn. orig.]

hō'cus *v.t.* (||-ss-). Take in, hoax; stupefy (person) with drugs; drug (liquor). [f. obs. n. *hocus* = foll.]

hōcus-pō'cus *n.* & *v.* (**-ss-**). **1.** *n.* Conjuring deception; typical conjuring formula. **2.** *v.i.* & *t.* Play tricks *with* or on. [17th-c. sham L]

hŏd *n.* Builder's light open trough on staff for carrying bricks etc.; receptacle for coal; ~**'man,** labourer who carries hod, (fig.) mechanical worker, literary hack. [prob. = dial. *hot* f. OF *hotte* pannier, of Gmc orig.]

hŏ'dden *n.* (Sc.) Coarse woollen cloth; ~ **grey,** grey hodden, typical rustic garb. [16th c.; orig. unkn.]

||**Hŏdge** *n.* Typical English agricultural labourer. [familiar form of *Roger*]

hŏ'dgepŏdge (-jp-) *n.* = HOTCHPOTCH 1, 3. [ME; assim. to prec.]

Hŏ'dgkĭn (-jk-) *n.* ~**'s disease** (of unknown origin, with progressive anaemia and enlargement of liver etc.). [f. T. ~, Engl. physician d. 1866]

hŏdiĕr'nal *a.* Of the present day. [f. L *hodiernus* (*hodie* today) + -AL]

hŏ'dograph (-ahf) *n.* Curve in which radius vector represents velocity of moving particle. [f. Gk *hodos* way + -GRAPH]

hodŏ'mèter. Var. of ODOMETER.

hōe *n.* & *v.* (*part.* ~**'ing** *pr.* hō'ĭ-). **1.** *n.* Tool for loosening soil, scraping up weeds, etc., with thin metal transverse blade on long handle; DRAW¹-*-hoe*; **Dutch** ~, kind pushed forward by user; *~**-cake,** coarse cake of maize flour orig. baked on blade of hoe; *~**-down,** lively dance(-party). **2.** *v.t.* Weed (crops), loosen (ground), dig up, cut down, with hoe; HARD *row to hoe*. **3.** *v.i.* Use hoe. [ME *howe* f. OF *houe* f. OFrank. **hauwa* f. Gmc **hauwan* HEW]

hŏg¹ *n.* **1.** Domesticated pig, esp. castrated male reared for slaughter; animal of family Suidae (*wart-hog*); ||(dial.) young sheep before first shearing (also **hogg**); (fig.) coarse, gluttonous, inconsiderate, or filthy person; **go the whole** ~, (sl.) do the thing thoroughly; ***live high off** (or **on**) **the** ~ (luxuriously); ~ **in armour,** person ill at ease; *~ **on ice,** (colloq.) insecure person. **2.** ~**('s)-back,** crested hill-ridge; *~ **cholera,** swine-fever; ~**-fish,** fish of genus *Scorpaena* with bristly head; *~**-pen,** pigsty; ~**'s fennel,** weed of genus *Peucedanum* with fennel-like leaves; *~**-tie,** secure by fastening hands and feet or all four feet together, (fig.) restrain, impede; ~**-wash,** kitchen swill etc. for pigs, (fig.) worthless stuff; ~**'weed,** coarse weed of which animals are fond. **3.** Hence ~'GERY (3) (-g-) *n.*, ~'GISH¹ (-g-), ~'LIKE, *adjs.* [OE *hogg*, *hocg*, perh. of Celt. orig.]

hŏg² *v.* (**-gg-**). **1.** *v.t.* & *i.* Raise (back etc.), rise, archwise in the centre. **2.** *v.t.* (colloq.) Appropriate selfishly, take unduly large share of for oneself. [f. prec.]

hō'gan *n.* Amer. Indian hut of logs etc. [Navajo]

||**hŏ'ggėt** (-g-) *n.* Yearling sheep. [f. HOG¹ + -ET¹]

hŏ'ggĭn (-g-) *n.* Mixture of sand and gravel; sifted gravel. [19th c., of unkn. orig.]

hŏ'gmanay *n.* (Sc.) Last day of year; gift of cake etc. demanded by children on that day. [17th c., corresp. in sense and use to OF *aguillanneuf*, of unkn. orig.; the Norman form *hoguinané* may have been the immediate source]

hŏ'gshead (-z-hĕd) *n.* Large cask; liquid or dry measure, usu. about 50 imperial gallons. [ME, f. HOG¹ + -'s 1 + HEAD¹; orig. unexpl.]

hō-hō' *int.* expr. surprise, triumph, or derision. [redupl. of HO]

hō'-hŭm *a.* Dull, uninteresting. [imit. of yawn]

hoick *v.t.* (sl.) Lift or bring (*out* etc.) esp. with jerk. [perh. var. of HIKE]

hoicks. Var. of YOICKS.

hoi polloi (hoi pŏ'loi; *or* -oi') *n.* The majority, the masses, the rabble. [Gk, = the many]

hoist¹ *v.t.*, & *n.* **1.** *v.t.* Raise aloft (esp. flag); raise by means of tackle etc.; ~ one's **flag,** signify that one takes command. **2.** *n.* Hoisting; part of flag nearest staff; group of flags raised as signal; goods elevator, lift. [16th c., alt. of *hoise* f. (15th c.) *hysse*, prob. of LG orig.; cf. LG *hissen*]

hoist² *a.* ~ **with his own petard,** blown up by his own bomb, ruined by his own devices against others. [p.p. of *hoise* (see prec.)]

hoitȳ-toi'tȳ *n.*, *a.*, & *int.* **1.** *n.* (arch.) Riotous or giddy conduct. **2.** *a.* Frolicsome; haughty, petulant. **3.** *int.* expr. surprised protest at undue presumption etc. [f. obs. *hoit* indulge in riotous mirth; orig. unkn.]

***hō'key** *a.* (sl.) Involving hokum. [f. HOKUM + -Y²]

hōkey-pō'key *n.* (colloq.) = HOCUS-POCUS; cheap ice cream sold by street vendors. [f. HOCUS-POCUS; second sense of unkn. orig.]

hŏ'kku (-ōō) *n.* (*pl.* same). = HAIKU. [Jap.]

hō'kum *n.* (sl.) Theatrical plot or business, film scenario, designed to appeal to the uncritical; bunkum. [20th c.; orig. unkn.]

holăr'ctĭc *a.* (Zool.) Pertaining to the whole northern or arctic region. [f. as HOLO- + ARCTIC]

hōld¹ *v.* (**held**; also arch. *p.p.* ~**'en** esp. w. ref. to formal meetings etc.). **1.** *v.t.* Keep fast, grasp; keep (thing) in particular position (*hold it to the light*; ~ thing **over** person, threaten him constantly with it); grasp so as to control (*hold the reins*); keep (*oneself*, one's head, etc.) in particular attitude or condition. **2.** (Of vessel etc.) contain or be able to do so (*jug holds two pints*; *theatre holds 1000 people*); not be unduly intoxicated by (liquor etc.). **3.** Possess, be the owner or holder or tenant of, (property, stocks, land, or abs.: *holds from the king*); have (specified playing-card or cards) in one's hand; have gained (*holds a law degree*; *holds the long-jump record*); (Mil. or fig.) keep possession of (place etc.) against attack; occupy (place, person's thoughts, etc.); engross (person, his attention); dominate (*holds the stage*). **4.** Keep (person etc.) in specified place, condition, etc., (*hold him at bay, prisoner, in suspense*); detain in custody; make (person) adhere *to* (terms, promise; ~ **to bail,** bind by BAIL¹); (Sport) restrict (opponents) *to* (draw etc.). **5.** Observe, celebrate, conduct, (festival, meeting, conversation); use (insolent etc.) language. **6.** Restrain, (*hold your fire, noise,* TONGUE¹); (colloq.) withhold, cease, (~ **everything!,** ~ **it!,** cease action or movement); *hold your* HORSE¹*s!*; **there is no ~ing** *him* etc., he etc. is restive or in high spirits or determined. **7.** Think, believe, (thing, *that,* person etc. *to* be; ~ **it against** person, regard it as to his discredit *that*; ~ **it good,** think it advisable *to* do); (of judge or court) lay down, decide, (*that*); have specified feeling towards (*hold him in esteem, contempt*); ~ thing **cheap,** not value it; ~ **dear,** regard with affection. **8.** *v.i.* Remain unbroken, not give way; (of weather) continue fine; ~ **by, to,** adhere to (choice, purpose, etc.); ~ **with,** (sl., usu. w. neg.) approve of. **9.** ~ (**good, true**), (of law etc.) be valid, apply. **10.** Keep going (*hold on* one's *way*). **11.** (arch.) Restrain oneself; ~ (**hard**)!, stop, wait. **12.** *Hold the* BABY, one's BREATH, COURT¹, *the* FORT, one's GROUND¹, one's or person's HAND¹, HAND¹*s*; ~ one's **head high,** behave proudly and confidently; ~ **the line,** maintain telephone connection; *hold* one's NOSE; *hold to* RANSOM; ~ **water,** (fig.) be sound, bear examination. **13.** ~ **aloof,** avoid communication with persons etc.; ~ **back,** restrain, impede progress of, keep (thing) to or for oneself, hesitate, refrain *from*; *~-back* n., hindrance; ~ **down,** repress, (colloq.) be competent enough to keep (one's job); ~ **forth,** offer (inducement etc.), (usu. derog.) speak at length or publicly; *hold* HARMLESS; ~ **in,** confine, keep in check; ~ **off,** delay, not begin action; ~ **on,** keep one's grasp on something, not ring off, (colloq., in *imper.*) stop; ~ **out,** stretch forth (hand etc.), offer (inducement etc.), maintain resistance, persist, continue to make demand *for*; ~ **out on,** (colloq.) refuse something to (person); ~ **over,** postpone; **~-over* n., relic; ~ **together,** (cause to) cohere; ~ **up,** support, sustain (lit. or fig.), maintain (head etc.) erect (~ *up* one's *head*, (fig.) not be downcast), exhibit, display, (esp. *to* derision etc.), arrest progress of, obstruct, (stop and) rob by (threat of) violence; *~-up* n., robbery of this kind, stoppage or delay by traffic, fog, etc. **14.** **~'all,** portable case for miscellaneous articles; **~'fast,** firm grasp, staple or clamp securing object to wall etc., attachment-organ of alga. [OE *h(e)aldan,* = OS *haldan,* OHG *haltan,* ON *halda,* Goth. *haldan*]

hōld² *n.* Grasp (lit. or fig.; *catch, get, grab, keep,* LAY³, *take, hold of*); manner of holding in wrestling etc.; opportunity of holding, thing to hold by; ~ (**on**), (fig.) influence (over); (arch.) fortress; **get ~ of,** (fig.) acquire, make contact with (person); **with no ~s barred,** all methods being permitted; **take ~,** become established. [OE *heald,* and f. ON *hald* (as prec.)]

hōld³ *n.* Cavity in ship below deck, where cargo is stowed. [f. obs. *holl* f. OE *hol* f. adj. = OS, OHG *hol,* ON *holr* hollow f. Gmc **hulaz* f. IE **kel-* cover; cogn. w. HELL, HELM¹, HOLLOW²; assim. to HOLD¹]

hō'lder *n.* In vbl senses; occupant of office etc.; possessor of title etc.; contrivance for holding something (*cigarette-, pen-, holder*); SMALL*holder.* [ME, f. HOLD¹ + -ER¹]

hō'ldĭng *n.* In vbl senses; tenure of land; land held (‖SMALL *holding*); cards, stocks, etc., held; ~ **company,** one created to hold the shares of other companies; ~ **operation** (to maintain *status quo*). [ME, f. HOLD¹ + -ING¹]

hōle¹ *n.* **1.** Empty place in solid body; deep place in stream etc.; animal's burrow; small mean or dingy abode; (sl.) awkward situation; **~-and-corner,** secret, underhand. **2.** Cavity into which ball etc. must be got in various games; (Golf) point scored by player who gets ball from tee to hole with fewest strokes, terrain or distance from tee to hole. **3.** Aperture through something; **in ~s,** worn so much that holes have formed; ~ **in the heart,** congenital defect in heart membrane; ~ **in the wall,** small dingy place (esp. of business); **pick ~s in,** find fault with; **make a ~ in,** use large amount of; **round** (or **square**) **peg in square** (or **round**) ~, person not fitted for his place. **4.** (Phys.) Position from which electron is absent, esp. acting as mobile positive particle in semi-conductor. **5.** Hence ~-PROOF², **hō'ley²,** *adjs.* [OE *hol,* = ON *hol* f. as HOLD³]

hōle² *v.* **1.** *v.t.* Make holes in; (Naut.) pierce side of (ship); put into hole; ~ (**out**), put (golf-ball, or abs.) into hole. **2.** *v.i.* *~ **up,** (sl.) hide oneself. [OE *holian* (as prec.)]

hŏ'lĭbut. Var. of HALIBUT.

hŏ'lĭday (or -dĭ) *n.,* & *v.i.* **1.** *n.* Day of festivity or recreation, when no work is done; ‖(usu. in *pl.*) period of this, vacation; BANK³, BLIND¹ *man's,* BUS*man's, holiday*; **make ~, take a ~,** have break from work; ‖**on ~, on** one's **~s,** in course of one's vacation; (*attrib.,* of clothes etc.) gay; ~ **camp,** place with organized amusements for people on holiday; **~-maker,** person on holiday. **2.** *v.i.* Spend a holiday. [OE *hāligdæg* (HOLY, DAY)]

hō'lĭlў *adv.* In a holy manner. [OE *hāliglīce* (as HOLY, -LY²)]

hō'lĭnėss *n.* Sanctity; **His H~,** title of pope etc. [OE *hālignes* (as HOLY, -NESS)]

hŏ'l|ĭsm *n.* (Philos.) Tendency in nature to form wholes that are more than the sum of the parts by ordered grouping; so **~ĭ'stIC** *a.* [f. as HOLO- + -ISM]

hŏ'lla¹,² *int., n.,* & *v.* See HOLLO¹,². [f. F *holà* (*ho* HO, *là* there)]

hŏ'lland *n.* Smooth hard-wearing linen fabric; **brown ~,** this unbleached. [f. *H~* = Netherlands (Du., earlier *Holtlant* f. *holt* wood + *-lant* land, describing Dordrecht district)]

hŏ'llandaise (-z) *n.* ~ (**sauce**), creamy sauce of butter, egg-yolks, vinegar, etc., served with fish etc. [F, fem. of *hollandais* Dutch (*Hollande* Holland)]

Hŏ'llander *n.* Dutchman; Dutch ship; engine (invented in Holland) for making paper-pulp from rags. [f. as HOLLAND + -ER¹]

Hŏ'llands (-z) *n.* Gin made in Holland. [f. Du. *hollandsch genever* Dutch gin]

***hŏ'ller** *v.i.* & *t.,* & *n.* (Make, express with) loud cry or noise. [var. of HOLLO²]

hŏ'llō¹, hŏ'lla¹, *int.* & *n.* **1.** *int.* calling attention. **2.** *n.* Cry of 'hollo'. [cogn. w. HOLLA]

hŏ'llō², hŏ'llow¹ (-ō), **hŏ'lla²,** *v.i.* & *t.* Shout; call to (hounds). [as prec.]

hŏ'llow² (-ō) *a., n.,* & *adv.* **1.** *a.* Having a hole, not solid (*hollow* SQUARE¹); having a depression, sunken (*hollow cheeks*); empty, hungry; (of sound) echoing, as if made in or on a hollow container; (fig.) empty (*hollow triumph*), insincere, cynical (*hollow laugh*), false (*hollow promises*). **2.** *n.* Hollow place, hole, valley, basin; **in the ~ of** one's **hand,** entirely subservient to one. **3.** *adv.* Completely (*beaten hollow*). **4.** **~-eyed,** with eyes deep sunk; **~-hearted,** insincere; **~-ware,** hollow articles of metal, china, etc., as pots, kettles, jugs, (opp. *flatware*). **5.** Hence ~LY² *adv.*, ~NESS *n.* [ME *holg, holu hol(e)we* f. OE *holh* cave, cogn. w. HOLE¹]

hŏ'llow³ (-ō) *v.t.* ~ (**out**), excavate; bend into hollow shape. [ME, f. prec.]

hŏ'llȳ *n.* Evergreen shrub of genus *Ilex*, with prickly usu. dark-green leaves, small white flowers, and red berries, used to decorate houses and churches at Christmas; ~ **blue,** azure blue butterfly; ~ **fern** (with glossy fronds reminiscent of holly); ~ **oak,** holm-oak. [OE *hole(g)n*, cogn. w. OS, OHG *hulis*, OFrank. **huls*]

hŏ'llȳhŏck *n.* Tall plant (*Althaea rosa*) with large flowers of many varieties of colour. [ME, orig. = marsh mallow, f. HOLY + obs. *hock* mallow, OE *hoc*, of unkn. orig.]

Hŏ'llȳwood *n.* American cinema industry or its products. [~ in California, principal centre of the industry]

‖**hōlm¹, hōlme,** (hōm) *n.* Islet, esp. in river or near mainland; flat ground by river, submerged in time of flood. [f. ON *holmr*]

hōlm² (hōm) *n.* ~(**-oak**), evergreen oak, *Quercus ilex*. [ME alt. of obs. *holin* f. as HOLLY]

Hō'lmesian (hō'mz-) *a.* Reminiscent of the detective Sherlock Holmes. [f. *Holmes* (cf. SHERLOCK) + -IAN]

hō'lmium *n.* (Chem.) Metallic element of lanthanide series. [mod. L (*Holmia* Stockholm; see -IUM)]

hŏ'lo- *comb. form.* Whole, as: ~**cene,** (Geol.) = RECENT; ~HE'DRAL, (Cryst.) having full number of planes given by complete symmetry; ~**-meta'bolous,** (of insect) undergoing complete metamorphosis; ~**phote,** apparatus for making available nearly all the light of a lamp (in lighthouse etc.). [f. Gk *holos* whole, entire + -o-]

hŏ'locaust *n.* Wholly burnt offering; wholesale sacrifice (fig.) or destruction esp. by fire. [ME, f. OF *holocauste* f. LL f. Gk HOLO(*kauston* burnt f. *kaiō* burn)]

hŏ'lo|grăm *n.* (Phys.) Pattern produced by interference between coherent light-beam and light diffracted etc. from same beam by an object; photograph of such pattern, which when suitably illuminated produces an image of the object in two or three dimensions; hence ~GRA'PHIC *a.*, ~GRAPHY (-ŏ'g-) *n.* [f. HOLO- + -GRAM]

hŏ'lograph¹ (-ahf) *v.t.* Record as hologram. [back form. f. prec., after *telegraph*]

hŏ'lograph² (-ahf) *a.* & *n.* (Document) wholly written by person named as its author. [f. F *holographe* or f. LL f. Gk *holographos* (as HOLO-, -GRAPH)]

hŏlothūr'ian *a.* & *n.* (Animal) of the class Holothurioidea, sea cucumber. [f. mod. L *Holothuria* n. pl. f. Gk *holothourion*, a zoophyte + -AN]

hōlp('en). See HELP¹.

‖**hŏls** (-z) *n.* (colloq.) Holidays. [abbr.]

***Hŏ'lstein** (-tīn) *a.* & *n.* = FRIESIAN. [~ in N.W. Germany]

hō'lster *n.* Leather case for pistol, fixed to saddle or worn on belt or under arm. [17th c.; syn. w. Du. *holster*; orig. unkn.]

hōlt¹ *n.* (arch. or dial.) Wood, copse; wooded hill. [OE, = OS, ON *holt*, OHG *holz* f. Gmc **hultam* f. IE **kldos*]

hōlt² *n.* Animal's (esp. otter's) lair. [var. of HOLD²]

hōlus-bō'lus *adv.* All in a lump, altogether. [app. sham L]

hō'lȳ *a.* & *n.* **1.** *a.* Consecrated, sacred; morally and spiritually perfect; belonging to, empowered by, devoted to, God; of high moral excellence; (in trivial excl.: *holy cow! holy mackerel! holy smoke!*); **holier-than-thou,** (colloq.) having attitude of superior sanctity. **2.** *n.* ~ **of holies,** inner chamber of sanctuary in Jewish temple, separated by veil from outer chamber, (fig.) innermost shrine, thing regarded as most sacred. **3. H~ City,** (1) city held sacred by adherents of a religion, esp. Jerusalem, (2) Heaven; *Holy* COMMUNION; ~ **cross** (of Christ); **H~ Cross Day,** festival of Exaltation of the Cross, 14 Sept.; ~ **day,** religious festival; **H~ Family,** the young Jesus with his mother and St. Joseph (often with St. John Baptist, St. Anne, etc.) as grouped in pictures etc.; *Holy* FATHER¹; **H~ Ghost,** = *Holy Spirit*; *Holy* GRAIL²; *Holy* INNOCENTS' *Day*; ~ **Joe,** (orig. Naut. sl.) clergyman, pious person; **H~ Land,** (1) W. Palestine, esp. Judaea, (2) region similarly revered in non-Christian religions; ~ **name,** (R.C. Ch.) name of Jesus as object of formal devotion; *Holy* OFFICE; *holy* ORDER¹*s*; ~ **place,** outer chamber of sanctuary in Jewish temple, (in *pl.*) places to which religious pilgrimage is made; *Holy* ROMAN² *Empire*; **H~ Rood Day,** (1) festival of Invention of the Cross, (2) = *Holy Cross Day*; *Holy* SACRAMENT; **H~ Saturday,** Saturday in Holy Week; *Holy* SCRIPTURE; **H~ Spirit,** Third Person of the Trinity, God as spiritually acting; *holy* TERROR; **H~ Thursday,** (Anglican Ch.) Ascension Day, (R.C. Ch. & pop.) Thursday in Holy Week; *Holy* TRINITY; *holy* WAR¹; ~ **water,** water dedicated to holy uses, or blessed by a priest; **H~ Week** (before Easter Sunday); ~ **Willie,** hypocritically pious person; **H~ Writ,** holy writings collectively, esp. the Bible; **H~ Year,** (R.C. Ch.) = JUBILEE 1. [OE *hālig*, = OS *hēlag*, OHG *heilag*, ON *heilagr* f. Gmc **hailagaz* (**hailaz* WHOLE)]

hō'lȳstōne *n.*, & *v.t.* (Scour with) soft sandstone used for scouring decks. [18th c., prob. f. prec. + STONE; the stones were called *bibles* etc., perh. because used while kneeling]

hōm, hō'ma, *n.* (Sacred drink of Parsees, juice of) soma plant. [f. Pers. *hōm, hūm*, Avestan *haoma*]

hŏ'mage *n.* Formal public acknowledgement of feudal allegiance; acknowledgement of superiority, dutiful reverence, (*pay* or *do homage to* person or his qualities). [ME f. OF *(h)omage* f. med. L *hominaticum* f. L *homo -minis* man; see -AGE]

****hombre*** (ŏ'mbrā) *n.* Man. [Sp.]

Hŏ'mbûrg *n.* Soft felt hat with narrow curled brim and lengthwise dent in crown. [~ in W. Germany, where first worn]

hōme¹ *n.*, *a.*, & *adv.* **1.** *n.* Dwelling-place; fixed residence of family or household; (U.S., Can., Austral., N.Z.) dwelling-house; **long** or **last ~,** the grave; SECOND *home*. **2.** Native land of oneself or one's ancestors, esp. Britain. **3.** Place where thing is native or most common; ~ **of lost causes,** Oxford University. **4.** Institution of refuge or rest for persons needing care (*children's*, CONVALESCENT, MENTAL¹, *home*; see NURSE²); (colloq.) mental home (*you ought to be in a home*). **5.** (In games) place to be reached by runner etc.; finishing-point in race; (Lacrosse) player in attacking position near opponents' goal. **6.** Home match or win. **7. At ~,** in one's own house or native land, at ease as if in one's own home (*make yourself at home*), familiar or well informed (*in* or *on* or *with* subject etc.), available to callers; **at-ho'me** *n.*, reception of visitors within certain hours during which host or hostess or both have announced that they will be at home; FROM *home*; **a ~ from ~,** place other than one's home where one feels at home, place providing homelike amenities; **near ~,**

(fig.) affecting one closely. **8.** *a.* Of or connected with home; carried on or done at home; proceeding from home; in the neighbourhood of home (‖**H~ Counties,** those nearest to London); played on one's own ground etc. (*home match, win*); carried on or produced in one's own country (*home industries, products*; *the home* TRADE or *market*, opp. *foreign*); treating of domestic affairs of person, country, etc., (‖**H~ Office,** department of **H~ Secretary** or Secretary of State for Home Affairs, dealing with law and order, immigration, etc., in England and Wales; building used for this); that comes home to one (*home question, truth, thrust*). **9.** *adv.* To one's home or country (*come* or *go home*); arrived at home (*he is home*); *at home (*stay home*); to the point aimed at (*the thrust went home*); as far as possible (*drive a nail home*; *press* one's *advantage home*); **come ~ to,** become fully realized by; *come home to* ROOST¹; **~ and dry,** having achieved one's purpose; **nothing to write ~ about,** (colloq.) unexciting, trivial. **10. ~-bird, ~'body,** person who likes to stay at home; **~-born,** native; **~-bred,** bred at home; **~-brewed,** (of beer) brewed at home; **~-coming,** arrival at home; **~ economics,** domestic science; ‖*home* FARM¹; **~-felt,** felt intimately; **~-grown,** grown or produced at home; **H~ Guard,** (member of) British citizen army organized 1940–57 to defend against possible invaders; ‖*home* HELP²; **~'land,** native land, esp. Britain; **~-made,** made at home; **~-making,** creation of a (pleasant) home; **~ movie,** film made at home or of one's own activities; **~ perm,** permanent hair-wave made with equipment for home use; *home* PLATE¹ 12; **~ port** (from which ship originates); **H~ Rule,** government of a country by its own citizens; **~ run,** (Baseball) hit that allows batter to make complete circuit of bases; **~'sick,** depressed by longing for home during absence from it; so **~'sickness** *n.*; **~ signal** (indicating whether or not railway train may proceed into station or to next section of line); **~ straight** or ***stretch,** concluding stretch of racecourse; **~ town** (of one's birth or early life or present fixed residence); **~'work,** work (to be) done at home, esp. lessons to be done by a school-child at home, (fig.) necessary preparation for debate etc. (*do* one's *homework*). **11.** Hence **~'**LESS, **~'**LIKE, (-ml-) *adjs.* [OE *hām*, = OS *hēm*, OHG *heim*, ON *heimr*, Goth. *haims* f. Gmc **haim-*]

hōme² *v.* **1.** *v.i.* (Esp. of trained pigeon) go home; ~ (**in**), (of vessel, missile, etc.) be guided to (or *on*) destination by landmark, radio beam, etc. **2.** *v.t.* Send or guide homewards; furnish (person etc.) with a home. [f. prec.]

hō'mel|ў (-mlĭ) *a.* Simple, plain; primitive; unpretentious; *(of person or features) not attractive in appearance, ugly; hence **~ĭ**NESS *n.* [ME, f. HOME¹ + -LY¹]

***hŏ'mėopăth** etc. See HOMOEOPATH etc.

hō'mer *n.* Homing pigeon; *home run. [f. HOME² + -ER¹]

Homĕ'ric (*or* hō-) *a.* **1.** Of, or in the style of, Homer or the poems ascribed to him; **~ laughter** (like that of Homer's gods as they watched lame Hephaestus hobbling); **~ question** (of authorship of *Iliad* and *Odyssey*). **2.** Large-scale, titanic, (*Homeric conflict*). [f. L f. Gk *Homērikos* (*Homēros* Homer, traditional author of *Iliad* and *Odyssey*; see -IC)]

hō'mespŭn (-ms-) *a.* & *n.* (Cloth made of yarn) spun at home; (anything) plain, homely, unsophisticated, practical. [f. HOME¹ + SPUN]

hō'mestead (-mstĕd) *n.* House with outbuildings; farm; (Austral. & N.Z.) owner's residence on sheep or cattle station; *area of land (usu. 160 acres) granted to settler as home. [OE *hāmstede* (as HOME¹, STEAD)]

hō'meward (-mw-) *adv.* & *a.*, **-wards** (-z) *adv.* (Going, leading) towards home; **~-**BOUND⁵, (esp. of ship) preparing to go, or on the way, home. [OE *hāmweard(es)* (as HOME¹, -WARD(s))]

hō'mey. Var. of HOMY.

hŏ'mĭcīde *n.* **1.** One who kills a human being. **2.** Killing of a human being esp. by another; **justifiable ~** (where no blame attaches to killer, e.g. in executing sentence of death). **3.** Hence **hŏmĭcī'd**AL *a.* [ME f. OF, f. L (1) *homicida*, (2) *homicidium* (HOMO¹ man; see -CIDE)]

hŏmĭlĕ'tic *a.* & *n.* **1.** *a.* Of homilies. **2.** *n.* (usu. in *pl.*) Art of preaching. [f. LL f. Gk *homilētikos* (*homileō* hold converse, consort, f. as foll.; see -ETIC)]

hŏ'mĭlў *n.* Sermon, esp. for spiritual edification of its hearer(s); tedious moralizing discourse; hence **homĭ'lĭ**ARY¹ *n.*, book of homilies. [ME f. OF *omelie*, f. eccl. L f. Gk *homilia* (*homilos* crowd; see -Y¹)]

hō'mĭng *a.* That goes home (cf. HOME²); (of pigeon) trained to fly home, bred for long-distance racing. [f. HOME² + -ING²]

hŏ'mĭnĭd *n.* & *a.* (Member) of the zoological family Hominidae (incl. existing and fossil man). [f. mod. L *Hominidae* f. L HOMO¹ *hominis* man; see -ID¹]

hŏ'mĭnoid *n.* & *a.* Manlike (animal); hominid or pongid. [f. as prec. + -OID]

hŏ'mĭnў *n.* Coarsely ground maize kernels esp. boiled with water or milk. [of Amer. Ind. orig.]

Homo¹ (hŏ'mō) *n.* **1.** (Zool.) (Name of genus including) man. **2. The genus ~,** mankind; **~ *sapiens*** (*pr.* să'pĭĕnz; [L, = wise]), modern man regarded as a species. [L]

hō'mō² *n.* (*pl.* **~s**) & *a.* (colloq.) Homosexual. [abbr.]

hŏ'mō- *comb. form.* Same (freq. opp. to HETERO-), as: **~ce'ntric,** having same centre; **~gamous** (-ŏ'g-), (Bot.) having all florets hermaphrodite or of same sex; **~gene'tic,** having common descent or origin; **~geny** (-ŏ'j-), similarity due to common descent; **~graft** (from another individual of same species); **~graph,** word spelt like another, but of different meaning or origin; **~mor'phic, ~mor'phous,** of same or similar form; **~nomous** (-ŏ'n-), having same law of growth; **~phone,** (1) word having same sound as another, but of different meaning or origin (e.g. *pair, pear*), (2) symbol denoting same sound as another; **~pho'nic,** (Mus.) in unison, characterized by movement of all parts to same melody; **~phonous** (-ŏ'f-), (of music) homophonic, (of word or symbol) being homophone; **~phony** (-ŏ'f-), being homophone or homophonic, homophonic composition; **~-pla'stic,** similar in structure but not in origin; **~tra'nsplant,** = *homograft*; **~zy'gote,** zygote of like gametes, Mendelian hybrid that is not a HETEROZYGOTE and so breeds true; so **~zy'gous** *a.* [f. Gk *homos* same + -O-]

hŏ'moeopăth, *-mėo-, (-mĭ-) *n.* One who practises homoeopathy. [f. G *homöopath* (as foll.; see -PATH)]

hŏmoe|ŏ'pathў, *-mė|ŏ'-, (-mĭ-) *n.* Treatment of disease by drugs (usu. in minute doses) that in healthy person would produce symptoms like those of the disease; so **~opă'th**IC *a.* (often joc., = minute), **~ŏ'path**IST (3) *n.* [f. G *homöopathie* f. Gk *homoios* like; see -PATHY]

hŏmoeostā's|is, *-mėo-, (-mĭ-) *n.* (*pl.* **~es** *pr.* -ēz). Tendency towards relatively stable equilibrium between interdependent elements, esp. as maintained by physiological processes. [mod. L, f. Gk *homoios* like + -STASIS]

hŏmogĕ'nėous *a.* Of the same kind; consisting

of parts all of the same kind, uniform; (Math.) containing terms all of same dimension; hence or cogn. **hŏmogénē'**ITY, ~NESS, *ns.*, ~LY[2] *adv.* [f. med. L *homogeneus* f. Gk HOMO(*genēs* f. *genos* kind) + -OUS]

homŏ'gėnīz|e, -īs|e (-īz), *v.t.* Make homogeneous; treat (milk) so that fat droplets are emulsified and cream does not separate; hence ~A'TION, ~ER[1] (2), *ns.* [f. prec. + -IZE]

hōmoiothėr'mĭc *a.* Warm-blooded. [f. Gk *homoios* like + THERMIC]

hŏmoiou'sĭan *a.* & *n.* (One who held that Father and Son in the Godhead were) of like but not identical substance (cf. HOMOOUSIAN). [f. eccl. L f. Gk *homoiousios* (*homoios* like, *ousia* essence) + -AN]

homŏ'log|āte *v.t.* Acknowledge, admit; confirm; hence ~A'TION *n.* [f. med. L *homologare* agree f. Gk HOMO(*logeō* f. *logos* word) + -ATE[3]]

homŏ'logīze, -īse (-īz), *v.* **1.** *v.i.* Be homologous, correspond. **2.** *v.t.* Make homologous. [f. as foll. + -IZE]

homŏ'logous *a.* Having the same relation, relative position, etc.; corresponding; (Biol.) similar in position and structure but not necessarily in function; (of chromosomes) pairing at meiosis, usu. containing same genes; (of chemical compounds) forming series with constant successive differences of composition. [f. med. L f. Gk HOMO(*logos* ratio, proportion)]

hŏ'molŏgue (-g), ***-lŏg,** *n.* Homologous thing. [F, f. Gk *homologon* neut. a. (as prec.)]

homŏ'logy̆ *n.* Being homologous; correspondence, sameness of relation; hence **hŏmolŏ'g**ICAL *a.* [f. HOMOLOGOUS + -Y[1]]

hŏ'mony̆m *n.* Word of same form as another but different sense (e.g. POLE[1], POLE[2]); homograph or homophone; namesake; so **hŏmony̆'m**IC, **homŏ'ny̆m**OUS, *adjs.* [f. L f. Gk *homōnumon*, neut. a. (as HOMO-, *onoma* name)]

hŏmōou'sian, hŏmou's-, *a.* & *n.* (One who held the persons of the Trinity to be) of the same substance (cf. HOMOIOUSIAN). [f. eccl. L *homoousianus* f. LL f. Gk HOMO(*ousios* f. *ousia* essence) + -AN]

hŏmopō'lar *a.* Having similar poles; (Electr.) generating direct current without use of commutators; (Chem.) covalent. [f. HOMO- + POLAR]

homŏ'pterous *a.* Of the Homoptera, suborder of insects including aphids and cicadas, with wings of uniform texture. [f. HOMO- + *pteron* wing + -OUS]

hŏmosĕ'xūal *a.* & *n.* (Person) being sexually attracted only by persons of one's own sex; relating to same sex; hence ~ITY (-ă'l-) *n.*, ~LY[2] *adv.* [f. HOMO- + SEXUAL]

homŭ'ncūl|e, homŭ'ncūl|us (*pl.* ~*i pr.* -ī), *n.* Little man, manikin. [L *homunculus* (*homo -minis* man; see -CULE)]

hō'my̆ *a.* Suggesting home, homelike. [f. HOME[1] + -Y[2]]

hon (hŭn) *n.* (colloq.) = HONEY 2. [abbr.]

Hon. *abbr.* Honorary; Hono(u)rable.

hōne *n.*, & *v.t.* **1.** *n.* Whetstone, esp. for razors; one of various stones as material for this. **2.** *v.t.* Sharpen on hone. [OE *hān* stone, = ON *hein* f. Gmc **hainō*]

hŏ'nėst (ŏ'-) *a.* **1.** Fair and righteous in speech and act, not lying, cheating, or stealing; sincere; (of act or feeling) showing righteousness; (with patronizing effect; cf. WORTHY) blameless but undistinguished; ~ **broker,** mediator in international, industrial, etc., disputes [orig. of Bismarck]. **2.** (Of gain etc.) got by fair means (**turn** or **earn an ~ penny,** earn money fairly); (of thing) unadulterated, unsophisticated. **3.** (arch., of woman). Chaste, virtuous; **make an ~ woman of,** marry (seduced woman). **4.** (colloq.) ~(**-to-God**), **~-to-goodness,** ~ **Injun,** genuine(ly), real(ly). **5.** Hence ~LY[2] *adv.* [ME, f. OF (*h*)*oneste* f. L *honestus* (*honos* HONOUR[1])]

hŏ'nėsty̆ (ŏ'-) *n.* Being honest; truthfulness; plant of genus *Lunaria* with purple or white flowers, so called from its round translucent pods. [ME, f. OF (*h*)*onesté* f. L *honestas -tatis* (as prec.; see -TY[1])]

ho'ney (hŭ'-) *n.* **1.** Sweet viscid yellow fluid, the nectar of flowers collected and treated by bees and other insects; colour of this; (fig.) sweetness, sweet thing; person or thing excellent of its kind. **2.** (as *voc.*, esp. Ir. & U.S.) Sweetheart, darling. **3.** **~-badger,** ratel; **~-bee,** common hive-bee (*Apis mellifera*); **~-buzzard,** bird of prey of genus *Pernis* feeding on larvae of bees and wasps; **~dew,** (1) sweet sticky substance found on leaves and stems, excreted by aphides, (2) ideally sweet substance, (3) tobacco sweetened with molasses, (4) cultivar of musk-melon with smooth pale skin and sweet green flesh; **~-eater,** Australasian bird of family Meliphagidae with long tongue that can take nectar from flowers; **~-fungus** (with honey-coloured toadstools round trees whose roots it attacks); **~-guide,** (1) small bird of genus *Indicator* etc. showing way to bees' nests, (2) marking on corolla thought to guide bees to nectar; **~-parrot,** lorikeet; **~-pot,** (fig.) posture with hands clasped under hams, ant that can regurgitate food for others; ~ **sac,** enlarged part of bee's gullet where honey is formed; **~suckle,** climbing shrub of genus *Lonicera* with fragrant yellow and pink flowers; **~-sweet,** sweet as honey; **~-tube,** tube on abdomen of aphis once thought to produce honeydew. **4.** Hence ~ED[2] (-nĭd) (lit. or fig.). [OE *hunig*, = OS *honig*, OHG *hona(n)g*, ON *hunang* f. Gmc **huna(n)gam*]

ho'neycōmb (hŭ'nĭkōm) *n.*, & *v.t.* **1.** *n.* Bees' wax structure of hexagonal cells for honey and eggs; second STOMACH of ruminant; cavernous flaw in metal, esp. guns; ornamental or other work hexagonally arranged; fabric made with pattern of raised hexagons etc. **2.** *v.t.* Make full of cavities, undermine; mark with honeycomb pattern. [OE *hunigcamb* (as prec., COMB[1])]

ho'neymōōn (hŭ'nĭm-) *n.*, & *v.i.* **1.** *n.* Holiday spent together by newly married couple; (fig.) initial period of ardour or enthusiasm; **second** ~, honeymoon-like holiday by couple married for some years. **2.** *v.i.* Spend honeymoon (*in* or *at* place). [f. HONEY + MOON[1], orig. w. ref. to waning affection, not to period of a month]

honied. Var. of HONEY*ed.*

Hŏ'nĭton (*or* hŭ'-) *n.* ~ **lace** (with floral sprigs sewn on net or joined by other lace). [~ in Devon]

hŏnk *n.* & *v.* **1.** *n.* Wild goose's cry; harsh sound of (motor) horn. **2.** *v.i.* & *t.* (Cause to) emit or give honk. [imit.]

***hŏ'nky̆** *n.* (Negro sl., derog.) White man or men. [20th c.; orig. unkn.]

hŏ'nky̆-tŏnk *n.* (colloq.) Tawdry drinking-saloon, dance-hall, etc.; ragtime music as played in these. [20th c.; orig. unkn.]

honnête homme (ŏnātŏ'm) *n.* Honest and decent man. [F]

***honor**[1,2]. See HONOUR[1,2].

***honorable.** See HONOURABLE.

hŏnorār'ĭ|um (ŏ-) *n.* (*pl.* **~ums** *or* **~a**). (Voluntary) fee esp. for professional services nominally rendered without payment. [L, neut. (as n.) of *honorarius* (see foll.)]

hŏ'norary̆ (ŏ'-) *a.* **1.** Conferred as an honour (without the usual requirements, functions, etc.; *honorary* DEGREE). **2.** Holding honorary title or position; ~ **secretary, treasurer,** etc., (serving without pay). **3.** (Of obligation) depending on honour, not legally enforceable. [f. L *honorarius* (as HONOUR[1]; see -ARY[1])]

hŏnorĭ'fĭc (ŏ-) *a.* & *n.* (Expression) implying respect (esp. of Oriental forms of speech). [f. L *honorificus* (as HONOUR[1]; see -FIC)]

honoris causa (ŏnôr̄ĭs kow'za) *adv.* As a mark of esteem (esp. of degree awarded without examination). [L, = for the sake of honour]

hŏ'nour[1], *hŏ'nor[1], (ŏ'ner) *n.* **1.** High respect; glory; credit, reputation, good name; nobleness of mind; special right (*have the honour to* do, *of* doing). **2.** Allegiance to what is right or to conventional standard of conduct; (of woman) chastity, reputation for this; ~ **system** (of examinations etc. without supervision, relying on persons' honour). **3.** Exalted position (**your, his, H~,** said to or of County-Court etc. judge, *mayor, and in rustic or Irish speech to or of any person of rank). **4.** Thing conferred as distinction; (Golf) right of driving off first as having won last hole (*it is my honour*); (in *pl.*) civilities rendered to guests etc., esp. *do the honours of* (*the table, a house, the town,* etc.); (in *pl.*) special distinction for proficiency at examination, course of degree studies more specialized than for ordinary pass; ‖BIRTH*day honours*; **last, funeral, ~s,** observances of respect at funeral; **military ~s,** marks of respect paid by troops at burial of soldier, to royalty, etc.; **~s of war,** privileges granted to capitulating force, as that of marching out with colours flying etc.; **~s list** (of persons awarded honours). **5.** Person or thing that brings honour *to* another (*he is an honour to the school, to his profession*). **6.** (In Whist) ace, king, queen, and jack of trumps (in Bridge the ten also, or the four aces at no trumps); **~-trick,** = QUICK trick; **~s are even,** there is equality in the contest (lit. or fig.). **7. In** ~ (celebration) **of; in ~ bound, on** one's ~, under moral obligation (*to* do); **(up)on my ~,** (colloq.) ~ **bright,** (forms of asseveration); **code or law of ~,** rules forming conventional standard of conduct; AFFAIR, ‖COMPANION[1], DEBT, GUARD[1], LEGION, MAID, MATRON, POINT[1], WORD[1], *of honour.* [ME, f. AF *an(o)ur*, OF *(h)onor* f. L *honor -oris* repute, office, beauty]

hŏ'nour[2], *hŏ'nor[2], (ŏ'ner) *v.t.* Respect highly; confer dignity upon; acknowledge; (Commerc.) accept or pay (bill, cheque) when due. [ME, f. OF *onorer* f. L *honorare* (as prec.)]

hŏ'nourable, *hŏ'norable, (ŏ'ner-) *a.* **1.** Worthy of honour; bringing honour to its possessor; consistent with honour; showing honour, not base; man's **intentions** (in courting woman) **are ~,** (colloq.) he has marriage in view; *honourable* MENTION[1]. **2.** (As title indicating eminence or distinction, given to younger sons of Earls, children of Viscounts and Barons, Maids of Honour, Justices of High Court without higher title, Lords of Session, members of Government and judges in Dominions and Colonies, to Members of Parliament by one another, *to members of Congress, cabinet ministers, judges, etc.); ‖**Most H~** (title of Marquises, Privy Council, and Order of Bath); ‖**Right H~** (title of Earls, Viscounts, Barons, Privy Councillors, Lords (Justices) of Appeal, Lord Mayor of London, York, or Belfast, Lord Provost of Edinburgh or Glasgow, etc.). **3.** Hence **hŏ'no(u)rab**LY[2] (ŏ'ner-) *adv.* [ME, f. OF *honorable* f. L *honorabilis* (as prec.; see -ABLE)]

Hon. Sec. *abbr.* Honorary Secretary.

***hōōch** *n.* (colloq.) Alcoholic liquor, esp. inferior or illicit. [abbr. of Alaskan *hoochinoo*, name of a liquor-making tribe]

hŏŏd[1] *n.*, & *v.t.* **1.** *n.* Covering for head and neck, whether part of cloak etc. or separate; separate hoodlike garment worn over university gown etc. to indicate degree; leather covering for hawk's head; *bonnet of motor car; ‖folding waterproof top of motor car, pram, etc.; canopy to protect user of machinery or to remove fumes etc.; hoodlike part of cobra, seal, etc. **2.** *v.t.* Cover with hood. **3.** Hence **~'**ED[1,2] *a.* (**~ed crow,** = HOODIE). [OE *hōd*, = OHG *huot* f. WG **hoda*, cogn. w. HAT]

hŏŏd[2] (*or* hōōd) *n.* (sl.) Gangster, gunman. [abbr. of HOODLUM]

-hŏŏd *suf.* forming *ns.* of condition or quality or grouping f. *ns.* & *adjs.* (*childhood, falsehood, sisterhood*). [OE *-hād*, = OS *-hēd*, OHG *-heit*; orig. an independent n., OE *hād* person, condition, quality, OS *hēd*, OHG *heit*, ON *heithr* honour, Goth. *haidus* manner]

hŏŏ'dĭe *n.* ~ **(crow),** piebald grey and black crow (*Corvus cornix*). [f. HOOD[1] + -IE]

hōō'dlum *n.* Street hooligan, young thug. [19th c.; orig. unkn.]

‖**hŏŏ'dman-blīnd** *n.* (arch.) Blind-man's-buff. [f. *hoodman* hooded man (HOOD[1], MAN[1]) + BLIND[1]]

***hōō'dōō** *n.*, & *v.t.* **1.** *n.* (Thing or person that causes) bad luck. **2.** *v.t.* Make unlucky; bewitch. [alt. of VOODOO]

hŏŏ'dwĭnk *v.t.* Deceive, delude; (arch.) blindfold. [f. HOOD[1] n. + WINK v.]

hōō'ey *n.* & *int.* (sl.) Nonsense, humbug. [20th c.; orig. unkn.]

hōōf *n.* (*pl.* **~s,** *or* **hooves** *pr.* -vz) & *v.* **1.** *n.* Horny casing of foot of horse and other animals; *cloven hoof* (see CLEAVE[1]); **on the ~,** (of cattle) not yet slaughtered; **pad the ~,** (joc.) go on foot; **~-pick** (for removing stones from hoof); hence (-)~ED[2] (-ft) *a.* **2.** *v.t.* Strike with hoof; (sl., of person) kick (another) *out* etc. **3.** *v.i.* Walk or dance; hence **~'**ER[1] *n.*, (sl.) professional dancer. [OE *hōf*, = OS *hōf*, OHG *huof*, ON *hófr* f. Gmc **hōfaz*]

hōō'-ha (-ah) *n.* (colloq.) Uproar, trouble. [20th c.; orig. unkn.]

hŏŏk[1] *n.* **1.** Piece of metal or other material bent back at an angle or with round bend, for catching hold or for hanging things upon; **(fish-)~,** bent piece of wire, usu. barbed, for catching fish; ~ **and eye,** small metal hook and loop as dress-fastener; **~, line, and sinker,** (fig.) entire(ly). **2.** (fig.) Trap, snare; (in *pl.*, sl.) fingers. **3.** Stroke (see foll.) in cricket or golf; (Boxing) short swinging blow with elbow bent and rigid. **4.** Curved cutting intrument, esp. *reaping-hook*. **5.** Sharp bend, e.g. in river; sand-spit with curved end; projecting point of land, esp. *Hook of Holland* [cf. Du. *hoek* corner]; = POT[1]*-hook*; (Mus.) added stroke transverse to stem in symbol for quaver etc. **6. By ~ or by crook,** by one device or another, by fair means or foul; **off the ~,** no longer in difficulty, (of telephone receiver) not on its rest, thus preventing incoming calls; **off the ~s,** (sl.) dead; **on** one's **own ~,** (sl.) on one's own account; **sling** or **take** one's ~, (sl.) = HOOK[2] *it*. **7. ~-nose(d),** (having) aquiline nose; **~'worm,** (disease caused by) kind of nematode worm infesting men and animals, male of which has hooklike spines for attachment. **8.** Hence **~'**LESS *a.*, **~'**LET *n.* [OE *hōc*, = MLG, MDu. *hōk* corner]

hŏŏk[2] *v.* **1.** *v.t.* Grasp with hook; secure with hook(s); ~ **on, up,** etc., attach (as) with hook; **be ~ed (on),** (sl.) be addicted (to) or captivated (by). **2.** Catch (fish or fig. husband etc.) with hook; (sl.) steal. **3.** (Golf) drive (ball, or abs.) slightly to left (of right-handed player); (Cricket) play (ball) round from off to on side with upward stroke; (Rugby Footb.) secure and pass (ball) backward with foot in scrummage; (Boxing) strike (opponent) with elbow bent and rigid. **4.** *v.i.* Be(come) attached (*on, up*, etc.) (as) by hook. **5.** ~ **it,** (sl.) make off, run away; **~-up,** (colloq.) connection, esp. interconnection of broadcasting equipment for special transmissions. [ME, f. prec.]

hoo'kah (-k*a*) *n.* Oriental tobacco-pipe with long flexible or rigid tube, smoke being drawn through water in vase to which tube and bowl are attached. [Urdu, f. Arab. *ḥukkah* casket]

Hooke *n.* ~ **coupling, ~'s joint,** (for transmitting rotary motion between shafts by universal joint); **~'s law** (that strain in elastic body is proportional to applied stress). [f. R. ~, Engl. scientist d. 1703]

hooked (-kt) *a.* **1.** Hook-shaped (*hooked nose*); furnished with hook(s). **2.** In vbl senses; (of rug etc.) made by pulling woollen yarn through canvas with hook. [f. HOOK[1,2] + -ED[2,1]]

hoo'ker[1] *n.* In vbl senses; (Rugby Footb.) player of each team in front row of scrummage who tries to get ball by hooking it; *(sl.) prostitute. [f. HOOK[2] + -ER[1]]

hoo'ker[2] *n.* Small Dutch or Irish fishing-vessel; (derog. or fondly) any ship. [f. Du. *hoeker* (*hoek* HOOK[1]; see -ER[1])]

***hoo'key, *hoo'ky,** *n.* **Play** ~, (sl.) play truant; **blind** ~, gambling guessing-game at cards. [19th c.; orig. unkn.]

hoo'ligan *n.* Young ruffian; one of gang of young street roughs; hence ~ISM (3) *n.* [perh. orig. name of ruffianly Irish family in S.E. London]

hoop[1] *n.*, & *v.t.* **1.** *n.* Circular band of metal, wood, etc., esp. for binding staves of casks etc.; wooden or iron ring trundled along by child; circle of flexible material for expanding a woman's petticoat or skirt; iron arch used in croquet; large ring usu. with paper stretched over it through which circus performer jumps (**go, be put, through the** ~ or **~s,** undergo an ordeal); **~-iron** (in long thin strips for binding casks etc.); **~-la,** game in which rings are thrown in attempt to encircle one of various prizes, (sl.) commotion, pretentious nonsense; ~ **petticoat** (expanded by hoops). **2.** *v.t.* Bind with hoop; surround (as) with hoop. [OE *hōp*, = MDu. *hoop* f. WG **hōpa*]

hoop[2]. Var. of WHOOP.

hoo'poe (-oo) *n.* S. Eur. etc. bird with variegated plumage and large erectile crest. [alt. of ME *hoop* f. OF *huppe* f. L *upupa*, imit. of its cry]

hooray'. Var. of HURRAY.

***hoo'segow** (-sg-) *n.* (sl.) Prison. [f. Amer. Sp. *juzgao*, Sp. *juzgado* tribunal f. L *judicatum* neut. p.p. (as n.) of *judicare* JUDGE[2]]

***Hoo'sier** (-zh*er*) *n.* (Nickname for) native or inhabitant of Indiana. [19th c.; orig. unkn.]

hoot *v.* & *n.* **1.** *v.i.* Make loud sounds, esp. of disapproval or derision or (colloq.) merriment (*at*, or abs.); (of owl) utter cry; (of steam whistle or motor horn) sound. **2.** *v.t.* Assail (person etc.) with derisive shouts; drive (person) *out, away*, etc., by hooting; cause (motor horn etc.) to sound. **3.** *n.* Inarticulate shout, esp. of derision or disapproval; owl's cry; sound of hooter; (colloq.) (cause of) laughter; *do not care, does not matter, is not worth*, **a** ~ or **two ~s,** (sl.) anything at all. [ME *hūten*, perh. imit.]

***hoo'tenanny** *n.* (colloq.) Informal celebratory event. [orig. dial., = 'gadget' etc.]

hoo'ter *n.* In vbl senses; ||siren, steam whistle, esp. as signal for work to begin or cease; ||motor horn; (sl.) nose. [f. HOOT + -ER[1]]

hoots *int.* (Sc. & N. Engl.) expr. dissatisfaction or impatience. [natural excl.; cf. Sw. *hut* begone, W *hwt* away, Ir. *ut* out, all in similar sense]

Hoo'ver *n.*, & *v.t.* **1.** *n.* Vacuum cleaner (prop. one made by the Hoover company). **2.** *v.t.* (colloq.) Clean with Hoover. [P as noun]

hooves. See HOOF.

hop[1] *n.* & *v.* (**-pp-**). **1.** *n.* Climbing perennial plant (*Humulus lupulus*), cultivated for the cones borne by the female; (in *pl.*) ripe cones of this, used for giving bitter flavour to malt liquor etc., (Austral. & N.Z. sl.) beer; *(sl.) opium or other narcotic. **2.** **~-bind, -bine,** climbing stem of hop; **~-fly,** aphis destructive to hops; ||**~-garden, -yard,** field for cultivation of hops; ***~head,** (sl.) drug addict, (Austral. & N.Z. sl.) drunkard; **~-picker,** labourer or machine employed to pick hops; **~-pillow** (stuffed with hops, to produce sleep); **~-pole** (on which hop plant is trained); **~'sack(ing),** (1) (coarse material of hemp etc. for) sack(s) to contain hops, (2) coarse woollen clothing fabric. **3.** *v.t.* Flavour with hops; *~ **up,** (sl., esp. in *p.p.*) stimulate with drug. **4.** *v.i.* Produce or pick hops. [ME *hoppe* f. MLG, MDu. *hoppe* = OS *-hoppo*, OHG *hopfo*]

hop[2] *v.* (**-pp-**). **1.** *v.i.* Spring, (of person) on one foot, (of animal) with all feet at once; (colloq.) make quick change of position or location; ~ **in, out,** (colloq.) get into or out of motor car. **2.** *v.t.* Hop over (ditch etc.); (colloq.) jump on to or into (vehicle), obtain (ride) thus; ~ **the twig** or **stick,** (sl.) depart suddenly, die; ~ **it,** (sl.) go away. **3.** Pass quickly from one (place of specified type) to others, (esp. as *vbl n.* and of aircraft: CLOUD, HEDGE[1], *-hopping*). **4.** **~-o'-my-thumb,** dwarf, pygmy [*o'* = ON[1]]; **~ping mad,** (colloq.) very angry; **~'scotch,** child's game of hopping on one foot and with it pushing (or otherwise moving) flat stone etc., over SCOTCH[2]es marked on ground; ***~-toad,** toad. [OE *hoppian*, = MHG *hopfen*, ON *hoppa*]

hop[3] *n.* **1.** (Action of) hopping; **on the** ~, (colloq.) (1) bustling about, (2) unprepared (*caught on the hop*). **2.** (colloq.) Informal dance. **3.** Distance travelled by air without landing; stage of a flight or journey. **4.** ~, **skip** (or **step**), **and jump,** athletic exercise or contest consisting of these three movements in sequence; LONG[1] *hop*. [f. prec.]

hope[1] *n.* **1.** (in *sing.* or *pl.*) Expectation and desire combined (*of* thing, *of* doing, *that*); (Bibl.) feeling of trust; SET[1] one's *hopes on*. **2.** Ground of hope, promise, probability, (**hoping against** ~, clinging to a mere possibility); person or thing that gives cause for hope; FORLORN *hope*; **not a** ~, (iron.) **some ~(s)!,** (colloq.) no chance at all. **3.** *~ **chest,** = BOTTOM[1] *drawer* (fig.) [OE *hopa, tōhopa*, = OLG *tōhopa*, MLG, MDu. *hope*]

hope[2] *v.* **1.** *v.i.* Look with expectation and desire (*for* thing, or abs.). **2.** *v.t.* Expect and desire (*that, to* do); feel fairly confident *that*. [OE *hopian*, = MDu. *hopen*; cf. prec.]

hō'peful (-pf-) *a.* & *n.* **1.** *a.* Feeling hope; inspiring hope, promising; hence ~NESS *n.* **2.** *n.* (**Young**) ~, young person likely to succeed or (iron.) be disappointed. [f. HOPE[1] + -FUL]

hō'pefully (-pf-) *adv.* In adj. senses; (qualifying whole sentence) it is hoped that (*hopefully, the car will be ready by then*). [f. prec. + -LY[2]]

hō'peless (-pl-) *a.* Feeling no hope; admitting no hope (*a hopeless* CASE[1]); inadequate, incompetent; hence ~LY[2] *adv.*, ~NESS *n.* [f. HOPE[1] + -LESS]

hŏ'plite *n.* Heavy-armed foot-soldier of ancient Greece. [f. Gk *hoplitēs* (*hoplon* weapon; see -ITE[1])]

hŏ'pper[1] *n.* **1.** One who hops; hopping insect, esp. flea or cheese-maggot or young locust. **2.**

Inverted pyramid or cone (orig. with hopping motion) through which grain passes in mill; similar contrivance in various machines. **3.** Barge carrying away mud etc. from dredging-machine and discharging it; railway truck able to discharge coal etc. through floor. [ME, f. HOP² + -ER¹]

hŏ'pper² *n.* Hop-picker. [f. HOP¹ + -ER¹]

hŏ'pple *v.t.*, & *n.* **1.** *v.t.* Fasten together legs of (horse etc.). **2.** *n.* Apparatus for this. [prob. f. LG; cf. early Flem. *hoppelen* = MDu. *hobelen* jump, dance]

‖**Hŏ'ppus** *n.* ~ **(cubic) foot,** unit of timber volume measurement (1·27 cu. ft.) used when calculating from length and girth of tree etc. [f. E. ~, 18th-c. Engl. surveyor]

hōr'arÿ *a.* Of the hours; occurring every hour. [f. med. L *horarius* f. L *hora* HOUR; see -ARY¹]

Horā'tian (-shan) *a.* Of or like (the poems of) Horace. [f. L *Horatianus* (Q. *Horatius* Flaccus, Roman poet d. 8 B.C.; see -AN)]

hōrde *n.* Troop of Tartar or other nomads; (usu. derog.) numerous company, gang, troop. [f. Pol. *horda* f. Turki *ordī, ordū* camp; cf. URDU]

hōr'ehound (hōr'h-) *n.* Herb (*Marrubium vulgare*) with white cottony covering on stem and leaves; its bitter aromatic juice used against coughs etc.; one of various herbs allied to this. [OE *hāre hūne* (*hār* HOAR, *hūne*, a plant)]

hori'zon *n.* **1.** Line at which earth and sky appear to meet; **apparent, sensible, visible,** ~, circle where earth's surface touches a cone whose vertex is at observer's eye; ARTIFICIAL *horizon*; **celestial, rational, true,** ~, great circle of the celestial sphere, plane of which passes through centre of earth and is parallel to that of apparent horizon of a place. **2.** (fig.) Limit of mental perception, experience, interest, etc.; **on the** ~ (fig., of event) just imminent or becoming apparent. **3.** Geological stratum or set of strata, or layer of soil, with particular characteristics; level at which particular group of archaeological remains is found. [ME f. OF *orizon(te)*, f. LL *horizon -ontis* f. Gk *horizōn* (*kuklos*) limiting (circle)]

hŏrĭzŏ'ntal *a.* & *n.* **1.** *a.* Of or at the horizon; parallel to the plane of this, at right angles to the vertical (*horizontal plane*); level, flat; (of machinery etc.) having its parts working in horizontal direction; combining firms engaged in same stage of production (*horizontal* INTEGRATION); involving social groups of equal status etc. **2.** Hence ~ITY (-ă'l-) *n.*, ~LY² *adv.* **3.** *n.* Horizontal line, plane, etc. [F, or mod. L *horizontalis* (as prec.; see -AL)]

hōr'mē *n.* (Psych.) Vital or purposeful energy. [f. Gk *hormē* impulse]

hōr'mōne *n.* (Biol.) Substance, formed by internal secretion, that passes into the blood or sap and stimulates organs to action; synthetic substance with similar effect; hence **hōrmō'nAL** (*or* hōr'mo-) *a.* [f. Gk *hormōn* part. of *hormaō* impel]

hōrn¹ *n.* **1.** Non-deciduous outgrowth, often curved and pointed, on head of cattle, sheep, goats, rhinoceroses, giraffes, and other mammals, found in pairs, single, or one in front of another; *take the* BULL¹ *by the horns*. **2.** Each of two deciduous branched appendages on head of (esp. male) deer. **3.** Projection on head of other animals, as snail's tentacle, insect's antenna, crest of horned owl; emblem of cuckold; **draw in** one's ~**s,** restrain one's ambition or ardour, draw back. **4.** Substance of which horns consist; GATE¹ *of horn*. **5.** Thing made of horn; drinking-vessel, powder-flask, made of horn; SHOE¹*horn*; ~ **of plenty,** cornucopia. **6.** Wind instrument played by lip-vibration (now made not of horn but of brass; *hunting-horn*); **English** ~, cor anglais; **(French)** ~, orchestral instrument with coiled tube, valves, and wide bell; ~('IST), its player. **7.** Instrument for sounding warning signal (FOG²-*horn, motor horn*); cone-shaped part of gramophone etc. **8.** Horn-shaped projection; extremity of moon or other crescent; arm or branch of bay, river, etc.; either alternative of a DILEMMA; (vulg.) erect penis; **the H~,** Cape Horn; GOLDEN *Horn*. **9.** **~'beam,** tree of genus *Carpinus* with hard tough wood; **~'bill,** bird with hornlike excrescence on bill; **~'book,** (Hist.) paper containing alphabet, Lord's Prayer, etc., mounted on wooden tablet with handle, and protected by thin plate of horn; **~-mad,** (arch.) stark mad (orig. of horned beasts); **~-rimmed,** (esp. of spectacles) having rims made of horn; **~'stone,** brittle siliceous rock. **10.** Hence ~ED² (-nd), ~'LESS, *adjs.*; **~ed owl** (with hornlike feathers on head). [OE, = OS, OHG, ON *horn*, Goth. *haurn* f. Gmc **hornaz, -am*, cogn. w. L *cornu*]

hōrn² *v.* **1.** *v.t.* (esp. in *p.p.*) Furnish with horns. **2.** Shorten or cut off (horns of cattle); gore with the horns; adjust (frame of ship) at right angles to line of keel. **3.** *v.i.* ~ **in,** (sl.) intrude (*on*), interfere. [ME, f. prec.]

hōr'nblĕnde *n.* Dark-brown, black, or green mineral, a constituent of granite and many rocks, composed chiefly of silicates of calcium, magnesium, and iron. [G (as HORN¹, BLENDE)]

hōr'ner *n.* Maker of horn spoons, combs, etc.; one who blows a horn. [ME, f. HORN¹ + -ER¹]

hōr'nĕt *n.* Large kind of wasp, inflicting serious sting; **~s' nest,** host of enemies or opponents (*bring a hornets' nest about* one's *ears*). [prob. f. MLG, MDu. *horn(e)te*; OE *hyrnet*, OS *hornut*, OHG *hornuz*, perh. rel. to HORN¹]

hōr'npīpe *n.* (Music for) lively dance, usu. by one person (esp. associated with merry-making of sailors). [name of obs. wind instrument partly of horn, ME, f. HORN¹ + PIPE¹]

hōr'nswŏggle *v.t.* (sl.) Cheat, hoax. [19th c., of unkn. orig.]

hōr'n|ÿ *a.* Of or like horn; hard as horn, callous, (*horny-handed*); (sl.) lecherous; hence ~ĬNESS *n.* [ME, f. HORN¹ + -Y²]

hŏ'rolŏge *n.* (arch.) Timepiece, dial, clock. [ME f. OF *orloge*, f. L f. Gk *hōrologion* (*hōra* time, *-logos* -telling)]

horŏ'log|ÿ *n.* Study of measuring time or making clocks, watches, etc.; so ~ER¹ (3), ~IST (3), *ns.*, **hŏrolŏ'gIC(AL)** *adjs.* [f. Gk *hōra* time + -O- + -LOGY]

hŏ'roscōpe *n.* (Astrol.) Observation of sky and planets at certain moment, esp. at person's birth; diagram showing configuration of planets etc. at particular moment (CAST¹ *a horoscope*); prediction of person's future based on this; hence **hŏroscŏ'pIC(AL)** *adjs.*, **horŏ'scopY¹** *n.* [F, f. L f. Gk *hōroskopos* (*hōra* time, *skopos* observer)]

horrĕ'ndous *a.* (colloq.) Horrifying; hence ~LY² *adv.* [f. L *horrendus* gerundive of *horrēre* bristle, shudder, + -OUS]

hŏ'rrent *a.* (poet.) Bristling; shuddering. [f. L *horrēre* (see prec., -ENT)]

hŏ'rrĭb|le *a.* Exciting, or likely to excite, horror; hideous, shocking; (colloq.) excessive, unpleasant, (*horrible noise, weather*); hence **~le**NESS (-beln-) *n.*, ~LY² *adv.* [ME, f. OF (*h*)*orrible* f. L *horribilis* (*horrēre*; see foll., -IBLE)]

hŏ'rrĭd *a.* Terrible, frightful; (poet.) rough, bristling; (colloq.) disagreeable, objectionable, (*horrid weather, boys*); hence ~LY² *adv.*, ~NESS *n.* [f. L *horridus* (*horrēre* bristle, shudder; see -ID¹)]

horrĭ'f|ĭc *a.* Horrifying; hence ~ICALLY *adv.*

[f. F *horrifique* or f. L *horrificus* (*horrēre*; see prec., -FIC)]

hŏ'rrĭ|fȳ *v.t.* Excite horror in; shock, scandalize; hence ~FICA'TION n. [f. L *horrificare* (as prec.; see -FY)]

hŏrrĭpĭlā'tion *n.* (literary). = GOOSE[1]-*flesh.* [f. LL *horripilatio* f. L *horrēre* to bristle + *pilus* hair; see -ATION]

hŏ'rror *n.* & *a.* **1.** *n.* Painful feeling of loathing and fear; terrified and revolted shuddering; intense dislike (*of*). **2.** Person or thing causing horror; **Chamber of H~s,** place full of horrors (orig. room of criminals etc. in Tussaud's waxworks). **3.** (in *pl.*) **~s!** (excl. of dismay); **the ~s,** fit of horror or depression, esp. as in delirium tremens. **4. ~-struck** or **-stricken,** horrified, shocked. **5.** *a.* (Of literature, film, etc.) designed to attract by arousing pleasurable feelings of horror; **~ comic,** paper like comic but with much violence and sensationalism. [ME, f. OF (*h*)*orrour* f. L *horror -oris* (as prec.; see -OR)]

hors (ōr) *adv.* & *prep.* Outside, as: ***~ concours*** (-kawṅkoor'), (of exhibit or exhibitor) not competing for prize, unrivalled; ***~ de combat*** (-dekaw'ṅbah), out of the fight, disabled. [F]

hors-d'œuvre (ōrdēr'vr; *or* -v) *n.* Extra dish served as appetizer before or (occas.) during meal. [F, = outside the work]

hōrse[1] *n.* **1.** Solid-hoofed herbivorous quadruped (*Equus caballus*) with flowing mane and tail, used as beast of burden and draught, and for riding on; (esp.) adult male horse, stallion or gelding; wooden etc. representation of horse; (collect. *sing.*) cavalry (LIGHT[4] *horse*); SEA-*horse.* **2.** Vaulting-block in gymnasium; frame (often with legs) on which something is supported, as CLOTHES-*horse*; (Naut.) rope or bar in various uses; (Mining) obstruction in vein; (colloq.) (unit of) horsepower; (sl.) heroin. **3.** *Put the* CART *before the horse*; DARK[1] *horse*; FLOG *a dead horse*; *look a* GIFT-*horse in the mouth*; **on** one's **high ~,** behaving with pretentiousness or arrogance; **hold your ~s!,** (colloq.) pause for a moment; **~ of another colour,** thing significantly different; *eat, work,* **like a ~,** with great vigour; **(straight) from the ~'s mouth,** (of information) from person directly concerned or other authoritative source; SWAP *horses*; **to ~,** (as command) mount your horses; WHITE[1] *horses*; WILD *horse*; WILLING[2] *horse*; WOODEN *horse.* **4. *~-and-buggy,** (fig.) out of date; **on ~'back,** mounted on a horse; **~'bean,** broad bean used as fodder; **~-block,** small platform of stone or wood for mounting a horse; **~-box,** closed vehicle for transporting horse, (joc.) large pew; *horse*-BRASS; **~-breaker,** one who breaks in horses; **~-che'stnut,** large ornamental tree with upright conical clusters of white or pink or red flowers, fruit of this (like edible chestnut, but with coarse bitter taste); **~-cloth** (used to cover horse, or as part of trappings); *horse*-COLLAR[1]; *horse*-COPER; **~-doctor,** veterinary surgeon attending horses; **~'flesh,** (1) flesh of horse, esp. as food, (2) horses collectively; **~-fly,** dipterous insect (of various kinds) troublesome to horses; ||**H~ Guards,** (1) cavalry brigade of British Household troops, esp. (*Royal Horse Guards*) second regiment of it, (2) headquarters of such cavalry, esp. a building in Whitehall; **~'hair,** hair from mane or tail of horse; **~ latitudes,** belt of calms at northern edge of N.E. trade winds; **~-laugh,** loud coarse laugh; **~'leech,** large kind of leech, insatiable person, (*daughters of the ~leech*, Prov. 30:15); **~-mackerel,** large fish of the mackerel type, e.g. scad, tunny; **~'man,** (skilled) rider on horseback; **~'manship,** art of riding, skill in riding, on horseback; *horse* MARINES; **~-mushroom** (coarse but edible variety with hollow stem); ***~ opera,** (sl.) western film; **~'play,** boisterous play; **~-pond** (for watering and washing horses, prov. as ducking-place of obnoxious persons); **~'power,** unit of rate of doing work, = 550 foot-pounds per second, about 750 watts; **~-race** (between horses with riders); **~-racing,** sport of conducting horse-races; **~-radish,** plant whose pungent root is scraped or grated as condiment, often made into sauce; **~ sense,** (colloq.) plain rough sagacity; **~-soldier** (mounted on horse); **~-tail,** (1) tail of horse (formerly used in Turkey as standard, or as ensign denoting rank of pasha), (2) cryptogamous plant of genus *Equisetum*, like horse's tail, with hollow jointed stem, (3) = PONY-*tail*; ***~-trading,** dealing in horses, (fig.) shrewd bargaining; **~'whip,** (*n.*) whip for horses, (*v.t.*) chastise (person) with this; **~'woman,** woman who rides on horseback. **5.** Hence ~'LESS (-sl-) *a.*; **~less carriage,** (arch.) motor car. [OE *hors*, = OS, OHG *hros*, ON *hross* f. Gmc **horsam, -az*]

hōrse[2] *v.* **1.** *v.t.* Provide (person, vehicle) with horse(s). **2.** *v.i.* Mount or go on horseback; (colloq.) fool *around.* [f. prec.]

hōr'seshoe (-s-shōō) *n.* Iron shoe for horse shaped like outline of hard part of hoof; thing of this shape, C-shaped object, (e.g. magnet, table, arch in Spanish and Islamic Archit.); ***~ crab,** king-crab. [ME, f. HORSE[1] + SHOE[1]]

hōr'sey. Var. of HORSY.

hōrst *n.* (Geol.) Ridge of land with faults between it and lower regions on each side. [G, = heap]

hōr's|ȳ *a.* Concerned with or devoted to horses or horse-racing; affectedly using dress and language of groom or jockey; hence ~ĭLY[2] *adv.*, ~ĭNESS *n.* [f. HORSE[1] + -Y[2]]

hōr't|ative *a.* Tending or serving to exhort; so ~A'TION *n.*, **~atORY** *a.* [f. L *hortativus* (*hortari* exhort; see -IVE)]

hōrtē'nsĭa *n.* Variety of hydrangea. [mod. L, f. *Hortense* Lepaute, 18th-c. Frenchwoman + -IA[1]]

hōr'tĭcŭlture *n.* Art of garden cultivation; hence **hōrtĭcŭ'lturAL** *a.*, **hōrtĭcŭ'lturIST** (3) *n.*, (-cher-). [f. L *hortus* garden, after *agriculture*]

hortus siccus (hōrtus sĭ'kus) *n.* Arranged collection of dried plants; (fig.) collection of uninteresting facts etc. [L, = dry garden]

Hos. *abbr.* Hosea (O.T.).

hōsă'nna (-z-) *n.* Shout of adoration (Matt. 21:9, 15, etc.). [ME, f. LL f. Gk *hōsanna* f. Heb. *hôšaʿnā* for *hôšîʿa-nnâ* save now!]

hōse (-z) *n.*, & *v.t.* **1.** *n.* (collect. as *pl.*, or arch. *pl.* **ho'sen**). Stockings; **half-~,** socks. **2.** (Hist.) Breeches (DOUBLET *and hose*). **3. ~(-pipe),** flexible tube conveying water for watering plants etc., putting out fires, dispersing rioters, etc. **4.** *v.t.* Provide with hose; drench or spray or water with hose. [OE, = OS, OHG, ON *hosa* f. Gmc **husōn*]

hō'si|er (-zher) *n.* Dealer in hose (||and knitted or woven underclothing); hence ~ERY (1) *n.* [ME, f. HOSE + -IER]

hŏ'spice *n.* House of rest for travellers, esp. one kept by religious order; ||home for the destitute or (esp. terminally) ill. [F, f. L *hospitium* (as HOST[2])]

hŏ'spĭtab|le (*or* -pĭ'-) *a.* Giving, disposed to give, welcome and entertainment to strangers or guests; hence ~LY[2] *adv.* [F (*hospiter* f. med. L *hospitare* entertain; as prec., -ABLE)]

hŏ'spĭtal *n.* Institution for care of the sick or wounded or for giving medical treatment (*go* ||*to hospital*, **to the hospital*; so *in* (*the*) *hospital*); charitable institution (in names, as *Christ's H~*, public school formerly in London); (Hist.) hospice, establishment of Knights Hospitallers; ~ **fever,** kind of typhus formerly prevalent in crowded hospitals; ~ **ship** (to receive sick and wounded seamen, or to convey sick and wounded soldiers home); ~ **train** (taking wounded soldiers from battlefield); hence ~ISM *n.*, adverse effects of prolonged stay in hospital, ~IZE *v.t.*, admit to or treat in hospital, ~IZA'TION *n.* [ME f. OF, f. med. L *hospitale* neut. (as n.) of L *hospitalis* a. (as HOST²; see -AL)]

hŏspĭtă'lĭtў *n.* Friendly and generous reception of guests or strangers or (fig.) of new ideas etc. [ME, f. OF *hospitalité* f. L *hospitalitas -tatis* (as prec.; see -ITY)]

hŏ'spĭtaller, *-aler, *n.* Member of charitable religious order; chaplain (in some London hospitals); **Knight H~,** member of order of military monks founded at Jerusalem *c.* 1048. [ME, f. OF *hospitalier* f. med. L *hospitalarius* (as HOSPITAL; see -ARY¹, -ER² (2))]

hōst¹ *n.* **1.** Large number (*of*; person **is a ~ in himself,** can do as much as a number of ordinary persons); (arch.) army. **2.** (Bibl.) **Lord (God) of ~s** (earthly or heavenly armies); ~**(s) of heaven, heavenly ~,** (1) sun, moon, and stars, (2) the angels. [ME f. OF, f. L *hostis* stranger, enemy, in med. L 'army']

hōst² *n.*, & *v.t.* **1.** *n.* One who receives or entertains another as guest; landlord of inn (*mine host*; **reckon without** one's ~, neglect difficulty, opposition, etc.). **2.** (Biol.) Animal or plant having parasite or commensal; animal that has received transplanted organ etc. **3.** *v.t.* Act as host to (person) or at (event). [ME, f. OF *oste* f. L *hospes -pitis* host, guest]

hōst³ *n.* Bread consecrated in the Eucharist. [ME, f. OF (*h*)*oiste* f. L *hostia* victim]

hŏ'sta *n.* Ornamental perennial of genus *Hosta* (formerly *Funkia*), with clusters of drooping bell-shaped white, blue, or lilac flowers. [mod. L, f. N. T. *Host*, Austrian physician d. 1834 + -A]

hŏ'stage *n.* Person given to or held by another as pledge; pledge, security; ~ **to fortune,** person or thing that one acquires and may then suffer by losing, esp. wife or child; hence ~SHIP (-ĭjsh-) *n.* [ME, f. OF (*h*)*ostage* f. Rom. **obsidaticum* f. LL *obsidatus* hostageship f. L *obses obsidis* hostage; see -AGE]

||**hŏ'stel** *n.* House of residence for students or other special class (YOUTH *hostel*); (arch.) inn. [ME, f. OF (*h*)*ostel* f. med. L (as HOSPITAL)]

hŏ'stelrў *n.* (arch. or literary). Inn. [ME, f. OF (*h*)*ostelerie* f. (*h*)*ostelier* innkeeper (as prec.; see -ERY)]

hō'stĕss *n.* Woman who acts as HOST²; woman employed to welcome and entertain customers at night-club etc.; woman employed as AIR¹ *hostess* or similarly in train etc. [ME, f. OF (*h*)*ostesse* (as HOST², -ESS¹)]

hŏ'stīle *a.* Of an enemy; unfriendly; opposed; ~ **witness** (who gives evidence unfairly and appears hostile to party calling him); hence ~LY² (-l-lĭ) *adv.* [F, or f. L *hostilis* (as HOST¹; see -IL)]

hŏstĭ'lĭtў *n.* Enmity; state of warfare; (in *pl.*) acts of warfare; opposition (in thought etc.). [f. F *hostilité* or f. LL *hostilitas* (as prec.; see -ITY)]

hŏ'stler (ŏ'sler) *n.* **1.** = OSTLER. **2.** *Person in charge of locomotives etc. when not in use. [ME, f. *hosteler* (as OSTLER)]

hŏt¹ *a.* & *adv.* **1.** *a.* Of or at high temperature, very warm (RED, WHITE¹, *-hot*); (of food etc.) prepared by heating and served without cooling; communicating or feeling heat (~ **under the collar,** angry, resentful, or embarrassed). **2.** Producing the sensation of heat (*hot fever, blush*); (of pepper etc.) pungent, biting. **3.** Ardent, passionate; eager (*in hot pursuit*); lustful; angry; excited; exciting; **not so** ~, (colloq.) only mediocre. **4.** (Of scent in hunting, etc.) = WARM¹ 8; (fig., of news etc.) fresh, recent; ||(colloq., of Treasury bills) newly issued. **5.** (Of a hit, return, etc., in ball-games) difficult for opponent to deal with; (of competitor in race or other sporting event) strongly fancied to win (*a hot favourite*); (of player) very skilful. **6.** (Of jazz etc.) strongly rhythmical and emotional. **7.** (sl.) Radioactive; (of goods) stolen, esp. easily identifiable and hence difficult to dispose of; (of person) wanted by police. **8.** BLOW¹ *hot and cold*; **give it him** ~, (colloq.) chastise or reprimand him severely; ~ **and bothered,** exasperated and agitated; ~ **and cold** (of water-supply in hotel etc.); **go ~ and cold,** feel alternately hot and cold owing to fear etc.; ~ **and** ~, (arch., of food) served as soon as cooked; ~ **and strong,** vehement(ly); **make it** or **the place** or **things ~ for, too ~** (uncomfortable, by persecution) **for** or **to hold, him. 9.** *adv.* Hotly, eagerly, angrily. **10.** ~ **air,** (sl.) excited or boastful talk; ~**'bed,** bed of earth heated by fermenting manure, (fig.) place favourable to growth *of* (vice etc.); ~ **blast** (of heated air forced into furnace); ~**-blooded,** ardent, passionate; *sell* etc. *like hot* CAKES; ~ **cathode** (heated to emit electrons); ~ **cockles,** (Hist.) rustic game in which blindfolded person guessed who struck him; *hot cross* BUN; ~ **dog,** (colloq.) hot sausage sandwiched in roll of bread; *hot flash* or FLUSH³ 4; ~**'foot,** in eager haste; *hot* GOSPELLER; ~**'head,** impetuous person; ~**-headed,** impetuous, excitable; ~**'-house,** heated building with glass roof and sides for growing plants out of season or in colder climate; ~ **line,** direct channel of emergency communication, esp. between Washington and Moscow; ~ **money,** capital transferred at frequent intervals; ~**'plate,** heated metal plate etc. for cooking food or keeping it hot; ~**-pot,** mutton, lamb, beef, with potatoes etc. cooked in oven in tight-lidded pot; *hot* POTATO; ~**-press,** (*n.*) press of glazed boards and hot metal plates for smoothing paper or cloth, (*v.t.*) press (paper etc.) in this; ~ **rod,** motor vehicle modified to have extra power and speed; ~ **seat,** (sl.) (1) electric chair, (2) embarrassing or onerous situation; ~**-short,** (of metal) brittle in its hot state [cf. COLD-SHORT]; ~ **spot,** small region that is relatively hot (lit. or fig.); ~ **spring,** = *hot well* (1); ~**'spur,** rash person (sobriquet of Sir H. Percy, d. 1403); ~ **stuff,** (sl.) person of high spirit, vigour, skill, or strong will or passions; ~ **war** (with active hostilities); ~ **water,** (colloq., fig.) trouble, disgrace, (*be in* or *get into hot water*); ~**-wa'ter bottle** or ***bag,** container of rubber, earthenware, etc., filled with hot water as source of warmth; ~ **well,** (1) spring of naturally hot water, (2) reservoir in condensing steam-engine; ~**-wire** *a.*, operated by expansion of heated wire. **11.** Hence ~'TISH¹ 2 *a.*, ~'LY² *adv.*, ~'NESS *n.* [OE *hāt*, = OS *het*, OHG *heiz*, ON *heitr* f. Gmc **haitaz*; cf. HEAT¹]

||**hŏt²** *v.* (-tt-). (colloq.) **1.** *v.t.* Heat, warm *up*, make hot. **2.** *v.i.* Become hot or (fig.) dangerous etc. [f. prec.]

hŏ'tchpŏtch, (esp. Law) **-pŏt,** *n.* **1.** Dish of many mixed ingredients, esp. mutton broth with vegetables. **2.** (Law). Reunion and blending of properties for purpose of securing equal division (esp. of property of intestate parent). **3.** (Confused) mixture, medley. [ME f. AF & OF *hochepot* f. OF (*hocher* shake, POT¹); *-potch* by assim.]

hotĕ'l (*or* hō-, ō-, *o*-) *n.* House for accommodation of travellers etc., (usu. large) inn; (Austral. & N.Z.) public house. [f. F *hôtel*, later form of HOSTEL]

hotĕ'lier *n.* Hotel-keeper. [f. F *hôtelier* f. OF *hostelier*; see HOSTELRY]

Hŏ'ttentŏt *n.* Member of S. Afr. negroid people formerly occupying region near the Cape. [Afrik., perh. = stammerer, w. ref. to their mode of pronunc.]

||**hough** (hŏk) *n.*, & *v.t.* **1.** *n.* = HOCK[1]; cut of beef etc. from this and leg above it. **2.** *v.t.* Hamstring, whence ~'ER[1] *n.* [ME *ho(u)gh* = OE *hōh* (heel) in *hōhsinu* hamstring]

hound[1] *n.* **1.** Dog for hunting, esp. one tracking by scent; ||**the ~s,** pack of foxhounds; **ride to ~s,** be huntsman. **2.** Despicable man; runner who follows scent in HARE and hounds; person keen in pursuit of something (*news-hound*). **3.** Dogfish (NURSE[3]-*hound*). **4.** **~'s-tongue,** cynoglossum; **~'s-tooth,** check pattern with reversed diagonal threads giving notched effect. **5.** Hence ~'ISH[1] *a.* [OE *hund*, = OS *hund*, OHG *hunt*, ON *hundr*, Goth. *hunds* f. Gmc **hundaz* f. IE **kwntós*]

hound[2] *v.t.* Chase or pursue (as) with hound; set (hound, or fig. person) *at* (quarry etc.); urge (person) *on.* [f. prec.]

hour (owr) *n.* **1.** Twenty-fourth part of day and night, 60 minutes, (*1700* etc. **~s,** time of 17 etc. hours after zero on twenty-four-hour clock); **the ~,** each time o'clock of exact number of hours (*bus leaves on the hour, at quarter past the hour*); *the* ELEVENTH *hour*; WATT-*hour*. **2.** Short indefinite period of time; time for or of action etc. (*the hour has come*); *the* present time (*question of the hour*); EVIL *hour*. **3.** The time o'clock (*what is the hour?*); **a late ~,** a time late at night. **4.** (in *pl.*) Fixed time for daily work (*office hours are 9 to 5*; **after ~s,** after closing-time); **till all ~s,** till very late; **small ~s,** 1, 2, etc., a.m.; **good** or **early, bad** or **late, regular, ~s,** (time for getting up or going to bed). **5.** (R.C. Ch.) (Prayers to be said at) one of seven stated times of day appointed for prayer (*book of hours*). **6.** (Astron.) 15° of longitude or R.A. **7.** Distance traversed in one hour by (stated or implied) means of travel (*we are an hour from London*). **8.** **~-circle,** meridian (24 of which are usu. marked on globe); **~'glass,** sand-glass running for an hour; **~-hand** (showing hour on clock etc.); **~-long** *a.* & *adv.*, (lasting) for one hour. [ME *ure* etc. f. AF; OF *ore, eure* f. L f. Gk *hōra* season, hour]

hour'ĭ (hoor'ĭ) *n.* Nymph of Muslim Paradise; voluptuously beautiful woman. [F, f. Pers. *ḥūrī* f. Arab. *ḥūr* pl. of *ḥawra'* gazelle-like (in the eyes)]

hour'lȳ (owr'-) *a.* & *adv.* (Occurring, done, reckoned) every hour; continual(ly), frequent(ly). [f. HOUR + -LY[1,2]]

house[1] *n.* (*pl. pr.* -zĭz). **1.** Building for human habitation or (usu. w. defining pref.) occupation etc. (ALMS*house*, BAKE*house*, LIGHT[1]*house*, SUMMER[1]-*house*, WORK[1]*house*; **~ of God,** church, place of worship; *house of* REFUGE); inn (*a drink* **on the ~,** at innkeeper's expense), place of public refreshment (ALE*house*, COFFEE-*house*, EATING-*house*, PUBLIC *house*); *brothel; (Sc.) dwelling that is one of several in a building. **2.** Building for keeping animals or goods (*hen-house*, STORE*house*, WARE[1]*house*); animal's den, shell, etc. **3.** (Place of abode of) religious fraternity. **4.** (Members of) university college, esp. ||**the H~,** Christ Church, Oxford. **5.** = (boys or girls in) BOARDING-*house* of school; one of divisions of day-school for games etc. **6.** (Building used by) legislative or deliberative assembly (LOWER[3] *House*, UPPER *House*; *House of* COMMONS, LORDS, REPRESENTATIVES; *Houses of* PARLIAMENT; **keep** or **make a H~,** secure presence of enough members for quorum or support in House of Commons); (place of business of) institution or mercantile firm (CLEARING-*-house*, CUSTOM-*house*; also in name of building, as Broadcasting House); ||**the H~,** (colloq.) Stock Exchange, (Polit.) House of Commons or Lords (*a question was asked in the House*), (Hist., euphem.) the workhouse. **7.** (Audience in) theatre (FULL[1] *house*); performance in theatre etc. (*second house starts at 9 o'clock*). **8.** Household, family, dynasty (**the H~ of Windsor,** British Royal Family). **9.** (Astrol.) Twelfth part of heavens. **10.** ||(Army sl.) Gambling form of lotto. **11.** *attrib.* (Of animal) kept in, frequenting, infesting, houses (*house-cat, -cricket, -fly, -sparrow*); living in hospital as member of staff (*house officer, physician, surgeon*). **12.** **~ of call** (where carriers call for commissions, where person may be heard of, etc.); **~ of cards** (built by child out of playing-cards; often fig. of insecure scheme etc.); **~ of ill fame,** (arch.) brothel; **H~ of Keys,** elective branch of Manx legislature; **~ and home,** (emphat.) home; **~-to-~,** carried or performed at each house in turn; BRING *down the house*; **keep ~,** maintain, provide for, a household; **keep open ~,** provide general hospitality; **keep (to) the ~,** not go outdoors; **like a ~ on fire,** vigorously, fast, excellently; MAN[1] *of the house*; ||MOVE[2] *house*; **play ~,** play at being a family in its home; **put** or **set** one's **~ in order,** (fig.) introduce needed reforms; **as safe as ~s,** perfectly safe; **set up ~,** begin to live in a separate dwelling. **13.** ||**~-agent** (for sale and letting of houses); **~ arrest,** detention in one's own house etc., not in prison; **~'boat,** boat fitted up for living in; **~'bote,** (Law) tenant's right to timber for house-repairs [f. as BOOT[2]]; **~-bound,** unable to leave one's house; **~'boy,** boy or man as servant in house; **~'breaker,** (1) = burglar (formerly in daytime only), (2) ||man employed in demolishing old houses; so **~'-breaking** *n.*; **~-broken,** = *house-trained*; **~carl(e),** (Hist.) member of bodyguard of Danish or English king or noble; **~'coat,** woman's usu. long-skirted garment for informal wear in house; ||**~'craft,** skill in household management; **~-dog** (kept to guard house); **~-father, ~-mother, ~-parents,** (in charge of house, esp. of home for children); **~-flag** (flown by a firm's ship); **~ guest,** guest staying for some days in house; **~-hunting,** seeking house to live in; **~'keep,** (colloq.) keep house; **~'keeper,** (1) woman managing affairs of household, (2) person in charge of house, office, etc.; **~'keeping,** management of household affairs, (colloq.) money allowed for this, (fig.) operations of maintenance, record-keeping, etc., in an organization; **~'leek,** plant (*Sempervivum tectorum*) with pink flowers growing on walls and roofs; **~ lights** (in theatre auditorium); **~ magazine** (published by firm and dealing mainly with the firm's activities); **~'maid,** female servant in house, esp. in charge of reception rooms and bedrooms (*~maid's knee*, inflammation of knee-cap due to kneeling); **~'man,** = *houseboy* or ||*house officer* (see sense 11); *house*-MARTIN; **~'master, ~'mistress,** (of school boarding-house); **~-mother, -parents,** (see *house-father*); **~ party** (of guests staying at country house etc.); **~-plant** (grown indoors); **~-proud,** (unduly) preoccupied with the care and beautification of the home; **~-room,** accommodation in house (*would not give it ~-room,* would not take it even as a gift); **~ style,** printer's particular choice between variant spellings etc.; **~-top,** roof of house (*proclaim from the ~-tops*, publicly announce); ||**~-trained,** (of domestic animals or infants) trained to be clean or behave well in the house; **~-warming,** celebration of occupation of new home; **~'work,** cleaning, cooking, etc. **14.** Hence ~'FUL 2 (-sf-) *n.*, ~'LESS (-sl-) *a.* [OE *hūs*, = OS, OHG *hūs*, ON *hús*, Goth. *-hūs* f. Gmc **hūsam*]

house² (-z) *v.t.* Receive (person etc.), store (goods), in house or as house does; provide houses for (population); fix in socket, mortise, etc. [OE *hūsian* (as prec.)]

hou'sehōld (-s-h-) *n.* Occupants of house; domestic establishment; ||*the* royal household; **~ gods,** (Rom. Ant.) lares and penates, (fig.) essentials of home life; **~ management,** art of managing domestic affairs; **~ stuff,** (arch.) furniture etc.; ||**~ troops** (employed nominally to guard sovereign's person); **~ word,** familiar saying or name. [ME, f. HOUSE¹ + HOLD²]

hou'sehōlder (-s-h-) *n.* One who occupies house as his own dwelling (esp. Hist. as entitled to franchise); head of household. [ME, f. HOUSE¹ + HOLDER]

housewife *n.* **1.** (how'swīf). (Usu. married) woman directing household affairs; (*good, bad*) domestic manager; hence **hou'sewife**LY¹ (-swīflĭ) *a.* **2.** (hŭ'zĭf). Case for needles, thread, etc. [ME *hus(e)wif* f. HOUSE¹ + WIFE]

hou'sewiferȳ (-swĭfrĭ) *n.* Housecraft; housekeeping. [ME, f. prec. + -RY]

||**hou'sey(-housey), -ie,** *n.* (Army sl.) = HOUSE¹ 10. [f. HOUSE¹ + -Y³, -IE]

hou'sĭng¹ (-z-) *n.* Horse's cloth covering, for protection or ornament. [ME, = covering, f. obs. *house* f. OF *houce* f. med. L *hultia* f. Gmc **hulfti*]

hou'sĭng² (-z-) *n.* In vbl senses; (provision of) dwelling-houses collectively; shelter, lodging; rigid casing for moving (or sensitive) machinery etc.; **~ estate,** residential district planned as a unit. [f. HOUSE² + -ING¹]

hōve. See HEAVE¹.

hŏ'vel *n.* Open shed, outhouse; miserable dwelling; conical building enclosing kiln. [ME, of unkn. orig.]

hŏ'ver *v.i.*, & *n.* **1.** *v.i.* (Of bird etc., esp. of hawk, or of helicopter etc.) hang in the air (*over* or *about* a spot); linger *about* or *round* (person, place); remain in undecided state *between*. **2.** *n.* Hovering; state of suspense. **3. ~craft,** vehicle or craft supported by air ejected downwards against surface (of land or sea) just beneath it; **~-fly** (of family Syrphidae, hovering with rapidly beating wings); ||**~-plane,** helicopter; **~train** (progressing on air-cushion like hovercraft). [ME, f. obs. *hove* hover, linger + -ER⁵]

how *adv.* & *n.* **1.** *interrog. adv.* By what means? in what way? (*how does he do it?*; *ask him how he does it*; *but how to bridge the gap?*; *how could you do such a vile thing?*); in what condition?; **~ are you?, ~ do you do?, ~ do?,** what is your state of health? (or as merely formal greeting); **~-do--you-do, ~-d'ye-do,** etc., embarrassing situation; **~ is that for high, queer,** etc.? (colloq. invitation to wonder); **~'s that?,** what is your opinion or explanation of that?, (Cricket, to umpire) is batsman out or not?; **~ now?,** (arch.) what is the meaning of this?; ~ (can you show that to be) **so?. 2.** (In indirect statement, rhet. or vulg. =) that (*told us how God was almighty*). **3.** (In question or exclamation) to what extent (*how far is it?*; *how far it is!*; *how many are there?*; *how many there are!*; *how would you like to take my place?*; *how he snores!*). **4.** *rel. adv.* In whatever way, as, (*do it how you can*). **5.** *n.* The way a thing is done (*the how of it*). **6. And ~!,** (sl.) very much so (chiefly used ironically or intensively); **here's ~!,** I drink to your good health; **~ about,** = WHAT *about*; *how* COME 7; **~e'ver,** in whatever way, to whatever extent, nevertheless, (colloq.) = *how* EVER; **~ much?,** what price (*how much is it?*), what amount (*how much do I owe you?*), (joc.) what? (as request for repetition); **~soe'ver, ~soe'er'** (poet.), **~ . . . soever,** in whatsoever way, to whatsoever extent. [OE *hū*, = OS *(h)wō*, OHG *wuo*, f. WG **hwō* (**hwa*-WHO)]

howbē'it *adv.* (arch. or literary). Nevertheless. [f. HOW + BE + IT¹]

how'dah (-*a*) *n.* Seat for two or more, usu. with canopy, on elephant's back. [f. Urdu *hawda* f. Arab. *hawdaj* litter]

***how'dȳ** *int.* = HOW *do you do?* [corrupt.]

how'ĭtzer (-ts-) *n.* Short gun for high-angle firing of shells at low velocities. [f. Du. *houwitser* f. G *haubitze* f. Czech *houfnice* catapult]

howl¹ *v.* **1.** *v.i.* (Of animal) utter long loud doleful cry; (of person) utter long loud cry of pain, derision, merriment, etc., freq. of (esp. child's) loud weeping; (of wind etc.) make prolonged wailing noise. **2.** *v.t.* Utter (words) with howling; **~ down,** reduce to silence by howls of derision. [ME *houle*, = MLG, MDu. *hūlen*, MHG *hiulen* (imit.); cf. OWL]

howl² *n.* Long loud doleful cry of dog, wolf, etc.; loud cry of pain etc.; yell of derision or merriment; (Electr.) howling noise in loudspeaker due to buildup of sound at audio frequencies. [f. prec.]

how'ler *n.* In vbl senses; S. Amer. monkey of genus *Alouatta*; (sl.) glaring blunder. [f. HOWL¹ + -ER¹]

how'lĭng *a.* That howls; *howling* DERVISH; (Bibl.) ~ (dreary) **wilderness;** (sl.) extreme, glaring, (*a howling shame*). [f. HOWL¹ + -ING²]

hoy¹ *n.* Small vessel, usu. rigged as sloop, carrying passengers and goods esp. for short distances. [f. MDu. *hoei, hoede*, of unkn. orig.]

hoy² *int.* used to call attention, drive animals, or (Naut.) hail or call aloft. [ME; natural cry]

hoy'a *n.* Climbing shrub of genus *Hoya*, with pink, white, or yellow waxy flowers. [mod. L, f. T. *Hoy*, Engl. gardener d. 1821 + -A]

hoy'den *n.* Boisterous girl; hence ~ISH¹ *a.* [orig. = rude fellow, prob. f. MDu. *heiden* (= HEATHEN)]

Hoyle *n.* **According to ~,** exact(ly), correct(ly). [f. E. ~, Engl. writer on card-games d. 1769]

h.p. *abbr.* high pressure; hire-purchase; horse-power.

H.Q. *abbr.* headquarters.

***H.R.** *abbr.* House of Representatives.

H.R.H. *abbr.* Her or His Royal Highness.

hr(s). *abbr.* hour(s).

H.S.H. *abbr.* Her or His Serene Highness.

H.T. *abbr.* high tension.

huanaco. Var. of GUANACO.

hŭb *n.* Central part of wheel, rotating on or with axle, and from which spokes radiate; (fig.) central point of interest etc. (esp. *hub of the universe*). [16th c., perh. = HOB²]

hŭ'bble-bŭbble *n.* Rudimentary form of hookah; bubbling sound; confused talk. [redupl. of BUBBLE¹; imit.]

hŭ'bbŭb *n.* Confused din; disturbance, riot; confused yelling of war-cry. [perh. of Ir. orig.; cf. Gael. *ububub* int. of contempt, Ir. *abú*, a war--cry]

hŭ'bbȳ *n.* (colloq.) Husband. [abbr.; see -Y³]

hū'br|is *n.* Insolent pride or presumption; (Gk Tragedy) overweening pride towards the gods, leading to nemesis; so **~ĭ'stIC** *a.* [Gk]

hŭ'ckabăck *n.* Stout linen or cotton fabric with rough surface, for towels etc. [17th c.; orig. unkn.]

hŭ'ckle *n.* Hip; haunch; **~-back(ed)**, hump-back(ed); **~-bone,** hip-bone, knuckle-bone of quadruped. [f. obs. *huck* hip (perh. f. **huk-* be bent) + -LE 1]

hŭ'ckleberrў (-kelb-) *n.* (Blue or black fruit of) low berry-bearing shrub of genus *Gaylussacia* common in N. Amer. [prob. alt. of *hurtleberry*, WHORTLEBERRY]

hŭ'ckst|er[1] *n.* Pedlar, hawker; mercenary person; *publicity agent esp. for broadcast material; hence ~ERY (2) *n.* [ME, prob. f. LG; cf. dial. *huck* to bargain, HAWKER[1], -STER]

hŭ'ckster[2] *v.* **1.** *v.i.* Bargain, haggle. **2.** *v.t.* Carry on petty traffic in (lit. or fig.); adulterate; hence ~ER[1] *n.* [f. prec.]

hŭ'ddle *v.* & *n.* **1.** *v.t.* ||Heap together confusedly; crowd (things etc.) promiscuously *together*, *up*, *into*, etc.; coil one*self up*; put (clothes) *on* hurriedly; hurry *over* or *through*, botch *up*, (work etc.). **2.** *v.i.* Nestle closely *together*, *against*, etc. **3.** *n.* Confused mass; confusion, bustle; (colloq.) close or secret conference. [16th c., perh. f. LG and ult. rel. to **hūd-* HIDE[2]; see -LE 3]

Hūdĭbrā'stĭc *a.* In the metre or manner of S. Butler's *Hudibras*, mock-heroic poem 1663–78, esp. with comical compound rhymes. [after *fantastic* etc.]

hūe[1] *n.* Colour, tint; attribute by virtue of which a colour is red, green, etc.; variety of colour caused by admixture of another; hence **-hūed**[2] (hūd), ~'LESS (hū'l-), *adjs.* [OE *hīew*, *hēw*, form etc., = Goth. *hiwi* f. Gmc **hiujam*; cf. ON *hȳ* down on plant]

hūe[2] *n.* **~ and cry,** loud cry raised for pursuit of wrongdoer, outcry (*against*), clamour, proclamation for capture of criminal. [f. OF *hu* outcry (*huer*, imit.)]

hŭff[1] *v.* **1.** *v.t.* (arch.) Bully, storm at; bully (person *into*, *out of*, thing or do*ing*). **2.** *v.t.* & *i.* (Cause to) take offence. **3.** *v.t.* (Draughts) remove (opponent's man that could have made a capture) from board as forfeit (orig. after blowing on the piece). **4.** *v.i.* Give out puffs of air etc., (fig.) bluster (*huffing and puffing*). [imit. of sound of blowing]

hŭff[2] *n.* Fit of petulance (*in a huff*); (Draughts) act of huffing; hence ~'ISH[1], ~'Y[2], *adjs.* [f. prec.]

hŭg *v.t.* (**-gg-**), & *n.* **1.** *v.t.* Squeeze tightly in one's arms, usu. with affection; (of bear) squeeze (man etc.) between its forelegs; delight in, cling to, (prejudices etc.); (arch.) exhibit fondness for (person); congratulate one*self* (*on* or *for*); keep close to (shore, kerb, etc.); **~-me--tight,** knitted close-fitting usu. sleeveless woollen wrap; hence **~'gABLE** *a.* **2.** *n.* Strong clasp with arms; squeezing grip in wrestling. [16th c., prob. f. Scand.; cf. ON *hugga* console]

hūge *a.* Extremely large, enormous; (of immaterial things) very great; hence ~'NESS (-jn-) *n.* [ME *huge*, *ho*(*w*)*ge* f. OF *ahuge*, *ahoge*, of unkn. orig.]

hū'gelў (-jlĭ) *adv.* Enormously; very much. [ME, f. prec. + -LY[2]]

hū'geous (-jus) *a.* (arch. or joc.) Huge; hence ~LY[2] *adv.*, ~NESS *n.* [f. HUGE + -OUS]

hŭ'gger-mŭgger (-g-; -g-) *n.*, *a.*, *adv.*, & *v.* **1.** *n.* Secrecy; confusion. **2.** *a.* & *adv.* Secret(ly); confused(ly). **3.** *v.t.* Conceal, hush *up*. **4.** *v.i.* Proceed in secret or muddled fashion. [prob. rel. to ME *hoder* huddle, *mokere* conceal; cf. syn. 15th-c. *hoder moder*, 16th-c. *hucker mucker*]

Hū'guenŏt (-ge-; *or* -nō) *n.* (Hist.) French Protestant. [F, assim. of *eiguenot* (f. Du. *eedgenot* f. Swiss G *eidgenoss* confederate) to name of Geneva burgomaster *Hugues*]

***hŭh** (hŭ) *int.* expr. interrogation, contempt, etc. [imit.]

hu'la (hōō'-) *n.*, & *v.i.* ~(-~), (perform) orig. Hawaiian woman's dance; **~ hoop,** large hoop for spinning round body with hula-like movements; **~ skirt,** long grass skirt. [Hawaiian]

hŭlk *n.* Body of dismantled ship, used as store vessel etc. or (in *pl.*, Hist.) as prison; unwieldy vessel; (fig.) big person or mass. [OE *hulc* (= OHG *holko*), & f. MLG, MDu. *hulk*(*e*); cf. Gk *holkas* cargo ship]

hŭ'lkĭng *a.* (colloq.) Bulky; clumsy. [f. prec. + -ING[2]]

hŭll[1] *n.*, & *v.t.* **1.** *n.* Outer covering of fruit, esp. pod of peas and beans, husk of grain, or green calyx of strawberry; (fig.) covering. **2.** *v.t.* Remove hull(s) of. [OE *hulu* (*hul-*, weak grade of *helan* cover; cf. HELE)]

hŭll[2] *n.*, & *v.t.* **1.** *n.* Body or frame of ship, airship, flying boat, etc.; **~ down,** (of ship) so far away that hull is below horizon, (of tank) concealed apart from gun-turret. **2.** *v.t.* Strike (ship) in hull with shot etc. [ME, perh. cogn. w. HOLD[3], or spec. use of prec.]

hŭllabaloō' *n.* Uproar, clamour. [18th c., redupl. of *hallo*, *hullo*, etc.]

hullō'. Var. of HALLO.

hŭm[1] *v.* (**-mm-**). **1.** *v.i.* Make continuous low--pitched sound, as of bee, spinning top, etc.; make slight inarticulate vocal sound, esp. (usu. **~ and haw** or **ha**) of hesitation; (colloq.) be in state of activity (*make things hum*); ||(sl.) smell unpleasantly. **2.** *v.i.* & *t.* Sing (tune etc.) with closed lips. [ME; imit.]

hŭm[2] *n.* Humming sound esp. of hesitation (usu. **~s and haws** or **ha's**), applause, surprise, etc.; (humming sound caused by) unwanted low--frequency variation of electric current etc.; ||(sl.) bad smell. [ME; imit.]

hum[3] *int.* expr. hesitation, dissent, etc. [imit.]

hū'man *a.* & *n.* **1.** *a.* Of or belonging to man (*human* NATURE); that is a man or consists of men (*human creature*, *race*). **2.** Of man as opp. to God (*to err is human, to forgive divine*; *after all, he is only human*). **3.** Having or showing the (esp. better) qualities distinctive of man (*a very human person*); of man as opp. to animals, machines, mere objects, etc. **4.** *Human* ENGINEER[1]; **~ engineering,** (study of) management of industrial labour, esp. as regards man–machine relationships; **~ equation,** = *personal* EQUATION (fig.); **~ interest,** reference to personal emotions (in newspaper story etc.); **~ relations** (concerning people as individuals); **~ rights** (held to be justifiably claimed by any person). **5.** Hence ~NESS (-n-n-) *n.* **6.** *n.* Human being. [ME *humain*(*e*) f. OF, f. L *humanus* (*homo* man; see -AN)]

hūmā'ne *a.* **1.** Benevolent, compassionate; inflicting the minimum of pain (**~ killer,** instrument for painless slaughter of animals). **2.** (Of branch of study) tending to civilize or confer refinement, elegant. **3.** Hence ~LY[2] (-nlĭ) *adv.*, ~NESS (-n-n-) *n.* [different. f. prec. after 1700]

hū'manĭsm *n.* Devotion to human interests; system concerned with human (not divine or supernatural) matters, or with the human race (not the individual), or with man as a responsible and progressive intellectual being; literary culture, esp. that of the Renaissance humanists; doctrine emphasizing importance of common human needs and abstention from profitless theorizing. [f. foll. + -ISM]

hū'manĭst *n.* Adherent of humanism; humanitarian; student (esp. in 14th–16th c.) of Roman and Greek literature and antiquities, whence **hūmanĭ'stĭc** *a.* [f. F *humaniste* f. It. *umanista* (as HUMAN; see -IST)]

hūmănĭtār'ĭan *n.* & *a.* **1.** *n.* One who advocates or practises humane action, philanthropist; one who seeks to promote human welfare. **2.** *a.*

Relating to or holding the views of humanitarians. **3.** Hence ~ISM (3) *n.* [f. foll. + -ARIAN]

hūmă'nĭtў *n.* **1.** Being human; (in *pl.*) human attributes. **2.** The human race; human beings collectively. **3.** Humaneness, benevolence. **4.** (Sc. Univ.) Study of Latin. **5.** (in *pl.*) Learning or literature concerned with human culture, esp. study of Latin and Greek classics. [ME, f. OF *humanité* f. L *humanitas -tatis* (as HUMAN; see -ITY)]

hū'manīz|e, -īs|e (-īz), *v.t.* Make human, give human character to (**~ed milk,** cow's milk prepared to resemble human milk); make humane; hence ~A'TION *n.* [f. F *humaniser* (as HUMAN; see -IZE)]

hū'mankīnd (-n-k-) *n.* Mankind. [f. HUMAN + KIND[1]]

hū'manlў *adv.* In a human manner; by human means; from a human point of view; with human feelings. [f. HUMAN + -LY[2]]

hŭ'mble *a.*, & *v.t.* **1.** *a.* Having or showing low estimate of one's own importance; offered with such estimate (*humble apologies, opinion*); *your humble* SERVANT. **2.** Of lowly rank or condition; (of thing) of modest pretensions, dimensions, etc.; **eat ~ pie,** make humble apology, submit to humiliation [f. UMBLES]. **3.** Hence ~NESS (-beln-) *n.*, **hŭ'mb**LY[2] *adv.* **4.** *v.t.* Make humble, bring low, abase (*oneself* etc.). [ME (*h*)*umble* f. OF, f. L *humilis* lowly (*humus* ground)]

hŭ'mble-bee *n.* Bumble-bee. [ME, prob. f. MLG *hummelbē*, MDu. *hommel*, OHG *humbal*; see BEE]

hŭ'mbŭg *n.* & *v.* (-gg-). **1.** *n.* Fraud, sham; deception; impostor. **2.** ||Kind of hard boiled sweet usu. flavoured with peppermint. **3.** *v.t.* Delude (person *into, out of,* thing or do*ing*). **4.** *v.i.* Be, behave like, impostor. **5.** Hence ~GERY (4) (-g-) *n.* [18th c., of unkn. orig.]

hŭ'mdinger *n.* (sl.) Excellent or remarkable person or thing. [20th c.; orig. unkn.]

hŭ'mdrŭm *a.* & *n.* Commonplace(ness), dull(ness); monotonous (routine etc.). [16th c., prob. f. HUM[1] by redupl.]

hū'meral *a.* & *n.* **1.** *a.* Of the humerus; of the shoulder. **2.** *a.* & *n.* ~ (**veil**), oblong scarf worn on shoulders by officiants at Eucharist. [f. F *huméral* & f. LL *humeralis* (as foll.; see -AL)]

hū'mer|us *n.* (*pl.* ~**i** *pr.* -ī). Bone of the upper arm in man; corresponding bone in other vertebrates. [L, = shoulder]

hū'mic. See HUMUS.

hū'mĭd *a.* Moist, damp; hence **hūmĭ'dĭfīer**[1] *n.* (esp. device for keeping atmosphere moist), **hūmĭ'dĭ**FY *v.t.*, ~LY[2] *adv.* [f. F *humide* or f. L *humidus* (*umēre* be moist; see -ID[1])]

hūmĭ'dĭtў *n.* Humid state; moisture; degree of moisture esp. in atmosphere (**relative ~**, proportion of this quantity to value for saturation at same temperature). [ME, f. OF *humidité* or f. L *humiditas* (as prec.; see -ITY)]

hū'mĭdŏr *n.* Box, room, etc., for keeping cigars or tobacco moist. [f. HUMID after *cuspidor*]

hū'mĭfў. See HUMUS.

hūmĭ'lĭ|āte *v.t.* Make humble, injure the dignity or self-respect of; so ~A'TION *n.* [f. LL *humiliare* (as HUMBLE) + -ATE[3]]

hūmĭ'lĭtў *n.* Humbleness, meekness; humble condition. [ME, f. OF *humilité* f. L *humilitas -tatis* (as HUMBLE; see -ITY)]

hŭ'mmel *a.* (Sc., of cattle or stags) hornless. [ME; cf. LG *hummel* hornless animal]

hŭ'mmĭng *a.* In vbl senses; **~-bird** (of family Trochilidae, making humming sound by vibration of wings); **~-top** (that hums when it spins). [f. HUM[1] + -ING[2]]

hŭ'mmock *n.* Hillock, knoll; *rising ground, esp. in marsh; hump or ridge in ice-field; hence ~Y[2] *a.* [16th c., of unkn. orig.]

hŭ'mmŭm. Var. of HAMMAM.

***hū'mor**[1,2]. See HUMOUR[1,2].

hū'moral *a.* (Med.) Of the bodily humours; relating to body fluids esp. as opp. cells. [F, or f. med. L *humoralis* (as HUMOUR[1]; see -AL)]

hūmorĕ'sque (-k) *n.* (Mus.) Short light capricious composition. [f. G *humoreske* (*humor* f. HUMOUR[1], *-eske* -ESQUE)]

hū'morĭst *n.* Facetious person; humorous talker, actor, or writer; hence **hūmorĭ'st**IC *a.* [f. HUMOUR[1] + -IST]

hū'morous *a.* Showing (sense of) humour; facetious, comic; hence ~LY[2] *adv.*, ~NESS *n.* [f. foll. + -OUS]

hū'mour[1] (-m*er*), ***hū'mor**[1], *n.* **1.** State of mind, mood; inclination, whim, (*in the humour for fighting*). **2.** Facetiousness, comicality (less intellectual and more sympathetic than wit); (**sense of**) ~, faculty of perceiving this and enjoying what is ludicrous or amusing, whence ~LESS *a.* **3. Out of ~,** displeased; **bad, good, ill, ~** (temper), whence -~ED[2] (-*erd*) *a.* **4.** (**Cardinal**) ~, (Hist.) one of four chief fluids of the body (blood, phlegm, choler, melancholy), thought to determine person's physical and mental qualities; AQUEOUS, VITREOUS, *humour.* [ME, f. AF (*h*)*umour*, OF f. L (*h*)*umor* moisture (as HUMID; see -OR)]

hū'mour[2] (-m*er*), ***hū'mor**[2], *v.t.* Gratify, indulge, (person, taste, temper, etc.); adapt oneself to, make concessions to. [f. prec.]

hū'moursome (-m*er*-), ***-mor-,** *a.* Capricious; peevish; hence ~NESS (-mn-) *n.* [f. HUMOUR[1] + -SOME[1]]

hŭmp *n.*, & *v.t.* **1.** *n.* Protuberance, esp. on the back, as deformity or (in camel etc.) as normal feature; **live on** one's ~, be self-sufficient [w. ref. to camel's hump as reserve of nourishment]. **2.** Rounded raised mass of earth etc.; mound over which railway vehicles are pushed so as to run by gravity to desired place. **3.** (fig.) Critical point (of undertaking, ordeal, etc.); **over the ~**, over the worst, well begun. **4.** ||(sl.) Fit of depression or vexation (*it gives me the hump*). **5. ~'back,** (1) (person having) back with a hump, (2) whale with dorsal fin forming hump; **~'backed,** having such a back; **~ bridge** (with steep approach to top). **6.** Hence ~ED[2] (-pt), ~'LESS, *adjs.* **7.** *v.t.* Make hump-shaped; annoy, depress; (||, esp. Austral.) hoist up, shoulder, (one's pack, etc.); (sl.) exert one*self*. [17th c., *hump-backed* replacing *crump-backed*; perh. rel. to LG *humpel* hump, LG *humpe*, Du. *homp* lump, hunk (of bread)]

humph (hmf) *int.*, *n.*, & *v.i.* (Utter) inarticulate sound expr. doubt or dissatisfaction. [imit.]

||**hŭ'mptў** *n.* Low padded cushion seat. [f. *humpty* a. humpbacked, perh. f. foll.]

Hŭmptў-Dŭ'mptў *n.* Short dumpy person; [from nursery rhyme in which name is taken to mean an egg] person or thing that once overthrown cannot be restored; [from Lewis Carroll's *Through the Looking-Glass*] person who makes words mean what he chooses. [perh. f. foll. & DUMPY; *-ty* unexpl.]

hŭ'mpў[1] *a.* Having hump(s); humplike. [f. HUMP + -Y[2]]

hŭ'mpў[2] *n.* (Australian Aboriginal) hut. [f. Aboriginal *oompi*, infl. by HUMP]

hū'm|us *n.* Organic constituent of soil, formed by decomposition of plant materials; hence ~IC *a.*, ~ĬFY *v.t.* & *i.* [L, = soil]

Hŭn *n.* One of an Asiatic warlike nomad race who invaded and ravaged Europe in 4th–5th c.; uncivilized devastator, vandal; (usu. derog.) German (esp. Prussian); hence ~'NISH[1] *a.* [OE *Hūne* pl. f. LL *Hunni* f. Gk *Hounnoi* f. Turki *Hun-yü*]

hŭnch[1] *v.* **1.** *v.t.* Bend or arch convexly; thrust out or up to form a hump. **2.** *v.i.* *Sit thus. [16th c.; orig. unkn.]

hŭnch[2] *n.* **1.** Hump; thick piece; **~'back(ed)**, = *humpback(ed)*. **2.** Hint; premonition, intuitive feeling. [f. *hunch-backed*, 16th c., of unkn. orig.]

hŭ'ndred *a.* & *n.* (*pl.* ~ *or* **~s**). **1.** Ten times ten (*a, one, six, several, hundred men*; *a, one, six hundred of them, of my friends*; *hundreds of men, of them*; *some, several, many,* (arch.) *six, hundreds of*); symbol for this (100, c, C); set of 100, £100, etc.; (**a**) ~ (**and one**), large number of; *1700* etc. HOURS; **not a ~ miles from,** (joc.) in or at or close to; **a ~ to one,** a high probability; **a** or **one ~ per cent,** entire(ly), complete(ly), (usu. *not*) fully recovered; (**a**) **~ and one** etc., one hundred plus one etc., w. corresp. ordinals **~-and-first** etc. **2.** ‖(esp. Hist.) Subdivision of county or shire, having its own court; ‖CHILTERN HUNDREDS. **3.** = foll.; **great** or **long** ~, 120; **~s and thousands,** tiny coloured sweets used chiefly for decorating cakes etc.; **the seventeen-~s,** years 1700–1799. **4.** Hence ~FOLD *a., adv.,* & *n.,* (-)~TH[2] *a.* & *n.* (**Old H~th,** hymn 'All people that . . .', metrical version of Ps. 100 or its tune). [OE, = OS *hunderod*, ON *hundrath* f. Gmc **hundam* hundred + **rath* number]

hŭ'ndredweight (-wăt) *n.* (*pl.* ~ *or* **~s**). (**Long**) ~, ‖112 lb. avoirdupois; (**metric**) ~, 50 kg; (**short**) ~, *100 lb. [f. prec. + WEIGHT[1]]

hŭng. See HANG[1].

Hŭngār'ĭan (-ngg-) *a.* & *n.* **1.** *a.* Of Hungary or its inhabitants. **2.** *n.* Native or inhabitant of Hungary; Magyar language. [f. med. L *Hungaria* f. (*H*)*ungari* Magyar nation; see -AN]

hŭ'nger[1] (-ngg-) *n.* Uneasy or painful sensation, exhausted condition, caused by lack of food; (fig.) strong desire (*for, after,* etc.); **~-march** (undertaken by body of unemployed etc. to call attention to their condition); **~-strike,** refusal of food in order to procure release from prison, improvement of conditions, etc. [OE *hungor*, = OS, OHG *hungar*, ON *hungr* f. Gmc **hungruz*]

hŭ'nger[2] (-ngg-) *v.* **1.** *v.i.* Feel hunger; have craving (*for, after*); (in *p.p.*, arch.) hungry. **2.** *v.t.* Starve (*into* submission, *out of* place etc.). [OE *hyngran*, assim. to prec.]

hŭ'ngr|ȳ (-ngg-) *a.* **1.** Feeling hunger; showing hunger (*a hungry look*); inducing hunger (*a hungry air*); **~y rice,** W. Afr. grain allied to millet. **2.** (fig.) Eager, greedy; (of soil) poor, barren; ‖**H~y Forties,** (Hist.) decade 1840–9 in Britain, a period of great distress among the poor. **3.** Hence **~ĭLY**[2] *adv.*, **~ĭNESS** *n.* [OE *hungrig* (as HUNGER[1]; see -Y[2])]

hŭnk *n.* Large piece cut off; thick or clumsy piece. [19th c., prob. f. LDu.]

hŭ'nkers (-z) *n. pl.* The hams (**on** one's ~, in a squatting position). [orig. Sc., f. *hunker* to squat]

hŭnks *n.* Niggardly man, miser. [17th c.; orig. unkn.]

***hŭ'nkȳ** *n.* (sl., derog.) Person from Central or E. Europe. [prob. f. HUNGARIAN + -Y[3]]

***hŭnkȳ-dōr'ȳ** *a.* (sl.) Excellent. [19th c.; orig. unkn.]

Hŭ'nnĭsh. See HUN.

hŭnt[1] *v.* **1.** *v.i.* & *t.* Pursue wild animals, esp. foxes; chase (these) for food or sport; (of animal) chase (its prey). **2.** *v.i.* Seek *after, for*; oscillate; (of engine etc.) run alternately too fast and too slow. **3.** *v.t.* Drive by pursuit (*away* etc.); scour (district) in pursuit of game; use (horse, hounds) in hunting; *shoot (game); (in *p.p.*, of look etc.) expressing terror as if one were being hunted. **4.** Move place of (bell) in ringing changes (*up* to last place, *down* to first place). **5. ~ down,** bring to bay; **~ out,** track out, find by search; **~ up,** search for and find; **~ the hare, slipper, squirrel, thimble,** games of pursuit or search. [OE *huntian*, weak grade of *hentan* seize]

hŭnt[2] *n.* Hunting (lit. or fig.); association of persons hunting with a pack; hunting district; oscillatory motion; **~ ball** (given by members of hunt). [ME, f. prec.]

hŭ'nter *n.* One who hunts or (fig.) seeks something (FORTUNE[1]-*hunter*); horse for hunting; watch with hinged cover protecting glass or (**half-~**) outer part of it; **~'s moon,** next full moon after harvest moon; hence **hŭ'ntrESS**[1] *n.* [ME, f. HUNT[1] + -ER[1]]

hŭ'ntĭng *n.* In vbl senses; **~-box,** small house for use during hunting-season; **~-cat,** cheetah; *hunting*-CROP[1]; **~-ground,** place where one hunts (lit. or fig.); *happy ~-ground(s)*, life after death (esp. as expected by Amer. Indians), good place for hunting (fig.); **~-horn,** (1) horn used in hunting, (2) second pommel on near side of side-saddle; **~ leopard,** cheetah; **~-lodge,** accommodation for hunters; *hunting* PINK[1]. [OE *huntung* (as HUNT[1], -ING[1])]

Hunts. *abbr.* Huntingdonshire (former county in England).

hŭ'nts|man *n.* (*pl.* **~men**). Hunter; man in charge of (esp. fox)hounds. [f. HUNT[2] + -'S 1 + MAN[1]]

hûr'dle *n.*, & *v.t.* **1.** *n.* Portable rectangular frame strengthened with withes or wooden bars, for temporary fence etc.; wooden frame to be jumped over in race; (in *pl.*) race over such frames; (fig.) obstacle, difficulty; (Hist.) frame on which traitors were dragged to execution. **2.** *v.t.* Fence off etc. with hurdles; leap over (lit. or fig.). [OE *hyrdel* f. Gmc **hurdhilaz* (**hurdhiz* f. IE **krt-*; see -LE 1)]

hûr'dler *n.* One who makes hurdles; one who races over hurdles. [f. prec. + -ER[1]]

hûr'dȳ-gûrdȳ *n.* Musical instrument with droning sound, played by turning handle, esp. one with rosined wheel turned by right hand to sound drone-strings, and keys played by left hand; (colloq.) barrel-organ. [prob. imit.]

hûrl *v.* & *n.* **1.** *v.t.* Throw violently from some position (lit. or fig.); throw (missile etc., or fig.). **2.** *v.i.* Play hurley; hence **~'ING**[1] *n.*, game of hurley. **3.** *n.* Hurling; violent throw. [ME, prob. imit., but corresp. in form and partly sense w. LG *hurreln*]

hûr'ley *n.* (Stick used in) Irish form of hockey. [f. prec.]

hûr'lȳ-bûrlȳ *n.* Commotion, tumult. [redupl. f. HURL V.]

hurrah', hurray', (*or* hŏŏ-) *int., n.,* & *v.i.* **1.** *int.* expr. exultation or approbation. **2.** *n.,* & *v.i.* Cry or shout 'hurrah', 'hurray'. [alt. of HUZZA]

hŭ'rrĭcāne *n.* Storm with violent wind, esp. W. Ind. cyclone; (Meteorol.) wind with velocity of 73 m.p.h. or more; violent commotion; **~-bird,** frigate-bird; **~-deck,** light upper deck; **~-house,** shelter at mast-head or on deck; **~-lamp** (designed to resist high wind). [f. Sp. *huracan*, & Port. *furacão*, of Carib orig.]

hŭ'rrȳ[1] *n.* Great haste; eagerness to get a thing done quickly; eagerness (*to* do, *for* thing); (w. neg. or interrog.) need for haste (*there is no hurry*); (colloq.) *you will not beat that* **in a ~** (easily), *shall not ask again* **in a ~** (willingly); **~-scurry,** (*adv., a.,* & *n.*) (in) disorderly haste, (*v.i.*) proceed thus. [16th c., imit.]

hŭ'rrȳ[2] *v.* **1.** *v.t.* Carry, drive, (person etc. *away, along, into, into* doing, *on,* etc.) with undue haste; (in *p.p.*) hasty, done rapidly owing to lack of time. **2.** *v.i.* Move or act with great or undue haste; **~ along, up,** (colloq.) make haste. [as prec.]

hūrst *n.* Hillock; sandbank in sea or river; wooded eminence; wood. [OE *hyrst*, rel. to OS, OHG *hurst, horst*]

hūrt[1] *n.* Bodily or material injury; harm, wrong; hence ~′FUL, ~′LESS, *adjs.* [ME, f. OF *hurt* (*hurter*; see foll.)]

hūrt[2] *v.* (**hurt**). **1.** *v.t.* Cause bodily injury or pain to; damage; inflict injury upon; distress, wound, (person, his feelings, etc.). **2.** *v.i.* (colloq.) Suffer injury or pain (*does your hand hurt?*). [ME, f. OF *hurter* f. Gallo-Rom. **hurtare*, perh. f. Gmc]

hūr′tle *v.* **1.** *v.i.* Strike *against*; move with clattering or rattling sound; come with a crash; move rapidly. **2.** *v.t.* Hurl swiftly. [f. prec. in obs. sense 'strike forcibly' + -LE 3]

hŭ′sband[1] (-z-) *n.* Married man esp. in relation to his wife (cf. WIFE 2); (arch.) **good, bad,** ~ (manager of his affairs); SHIP[1]'*s husband*; hence ~HOOD, ~SHIP, *ns.*, ~LIKE *a.* [OE *hūsbonda* f. ON *húsbóndi* (as HOUSE[1], BOND[3])]

hŭ′sband[2] (-z-) *v.t.* Manage thriftily, use economically; (arch.) till (ground), cultivate (plants); (arch.) provide with husband, marry, (woman). [ME, f. prec.]

hŭ′sband|man (-z-) *n.* (*pl.* ~**men**). (arch.) Farmer. [ME, f. HUSBAND[1] + MAN[1]]

hŭ′sbandrȳ (-z-) *n.* Farming; (*good, bad*) management of affairs; careful management. [ME, f. HUSBAND[1] + -RY]

hŭsh[1] *n.* Stillness; silence; ~**-money** (paid to prevent disclosure). [f. foll.]

hŭsh[2] *v.* **1.** *v.t.* Silence, quiet; ~ **up,** suppress public mention of (affair). **2.** *v.i.* Be silent (esp. in *imper.* as *int.*). **3.** ~′**aby(e)** *int.* (used to lull child); ~-~, to be kept highly secret; ~ **puppy,** (1) *quickly fried maize bread, (2) light soft shoe (**P**). [back form. f. obs. *husht* a. f. *hust*, WHIST[1], ints.]

hŭsk *n.*, & *v.t.* **1.** *n.* Dry outer covering of some fruits or seeds, esp. of nut or *maize; (fig.) worthless outside part of anything. **2.** *v.t.* Remove husk(s) from. [ME, prob. f. LG *hūske* sheath, dim. of *hūs* HOUSE[1]]

hŭ′sk|ȳ[1] *a.* & *n.* **1.** *a.* Of or full of husks; dry as a husk; (of voice or person) dry in the throat, hoarse, whence ~ĭLY[2] *adv.*, ~ĭNESS *n.* **2.** *a.* & *n.* (colloq.) Tough, strong, hefty, (person). [f. prec. + -Y[2]]

hŭ′skȳ[2] *n.* = ESKIMO *dog.* [perh. contr. f. ESKIMO]

hŭss *n.* Dogfish (esp. nurse-hound) as food. [ME *husk(e)*, of unkn. orig.]

hussār′ (hŏŏz-) *n.* Soldier of light cavalry regiment; (orig.) Hungarian light horseman of 15th c. [f. Magyar *huszár* f. OSerb. *husar* f. It. *corsaro* CORSAIR]

Hŭ′ssīte *n.* Follower of Huss. [f. John *Huss*, Bohemian religious and nationalist reformer d. 1415 + -ITE[1]]

hŭ′ssȳ (*or* -zĭ), **hŭ′zzȳ,** *n.* Woman of light or worthless character; pert girl. [f. HOUSEWIFE]

hŭ′stĭngs (-z) *n.* (Parliamentary) election proceedings; (Hist.) platform from which (before 1872) candidates for Parliament were nominated and addressed electors. [pl. of *husting*, OE, f. ON *hústhing* house of assembly (cf. HOUSE[1], THING)]

hŭ′stle (-sel) *v.* & *n.* **1.** *v.t.* Push roughly, jostle; thrust (person etc. *into, out of*, etc.); impel unceremoniously (*into* thing or do*ing*); (sl.) obtain by forceful action; (sl.) swindle. **2.** *v.i.* Push roughly *against*; push one's way; hurry, bustle. **3.** *n.* Hustling. [f. MDu. *husselen* shake, toss, frequent. of *hutsen*, orig. imit.]

hŭ′stler (-sl-) *n.* In vbl senses; (sl.) prostitute. [f. prec. + -ER[1]]

hŭt *n.* & *v.* (**-tt-**). **1.** *n.* Small mean house of rough construction; (Mil.) temporary wooden etc. house for troops; ~**-circle,** (Archaeol.) ring of stones or earth indicating site of prehistoric hut. **2.** *v.t.* Place (troops etc.) in huts; furnish with huts. **3.** *v.i.* Lodge in hut. **4.** Hence ~′MENT *n.*, hutted encampment. [f. F *hutte* f. MHG *hütte*]

hŭtch *n.* Boxlike pen for rabbits etc.; (derog.) hut, cabin, small house. [ME, = coffer, f. OF *huche* f. med. L *hutica*, of unkn. orig.]

Hŭ′tterīte *n.* Member of (N. Amer. immigrant) sect of anabaptists. [f. J. *Hutter*, Moravian anabaptist d. 1536 + -ITE (1)]

Huzoor′ *n.* (arch.) Title used by Indians in respectful address. [f. Arab. *ḥuḍūr* presence (*ḥaḍara* be present)]

huzza′ (-ah) *int.*, *n.*, & *v.* (arch.) **1.** *int.* expr. exultation, encouragement, or applause. **2.** *n.*, & *v.i.* & *t.* (Make, greet with) the cry 'huzza'. [16th c., perh. orig. sailor's cry when hauling]

hŭ′zzȳ. See HUSSY.

h.w. *abbr.* hit wicket.

H.W.M. *abbr.* high-water mark.

hwȳl *n.* Emotional quality inspiring impassioned eloquence. [W]

Hy. *abbr.* Henry.

hȳ′acĭnth *n.* **1.** Bulbous plant of genus *Hyacinthus* with racemes of bell-shaped (esp. purplish-blue fragrant) flowers; GRAPE *hyacinth*; **wild** or **wood** ~, squill (*Scilla nonscripta*) with drooping bell-shaped flowers; so (esp. as Homeric epithet of doubtful sense for *locks, hair*) ~INE[2] (-sĭ′-) *a.* **2.** Purplish-blue colour of hyacinth. **3.** Precious stone, orange variety of zircon. [f. F *hyacinthe* f. L f. Gk *huakinthos*, flower and gem, also name of youth loved by Apollo]

Hȳ′adēs (-z) *n. pl.* Group of stars in Taurus near Pleiades, whose heliacal rising was thought to foretell rain. [ME, f. Gk *Huades* (acc. to pop. etym., f. *huō* rain, but perh. f. *hus* pig)]

hȳae′na. See HYENA.

hȳ′alĭne (*or* -ēn) *a.* & *n.* **1.** *a.* Glasslike, vitreous; ~ **degeneration** (in which body-tissues become translucent). **2.** *n.* (literary). Smooth sea, clear sky, etc. [f. L f. Gk *hualinos* (*hualos* glass; see -INE[2])]

hȳ′alīte *n.* Colourless variety of opal. [f. Gk *hualos* glass + -ITE[1]]

hȳ′aloid *a.* & *n.* (Anat.) Glassy; ~ (**membrane**), thin transparent membrane enveloping vitreous humour of eye. [f. F *hyaloïde* f. LL f. Gk *hualoeidēs* (as prec.; see -OID)]

hȳ′brĭd *n.* & *a.* **1.** *n.* Offspring of two animals or plants of different species or varieties; person of mixed origins; (fig.) thing composed of incongruous elements, esp. word with parts taken from different languages. **2.** *a.* Cross-bred from different species or varieties; heterogeneous; ~ **vigour,** heterosis; hence ~ISM (1, 2), ~ITY (-ĭ′d-), *ns.* [f. L *hybrida*, (*h*)*ibrida* offspring of tame sow and wild boar, child of freeman and slave, etc.]

hȳ′brĭdīz|e, -is|e (-īz), *v.* **1.** *v.t.* Subject (species etc.) to cross-breeding. **2.** *v.i.* Produce hybrids; (of animal or plant) interbreed. **3.** Hence ~ABLE *a.*, ~A′TION *n.* [f. prec. + -IZE]

hȳ′datĭd *n.* (Path.) Cyst containing watery fluid (esp. one formed by, and containing, a tapeworm larva); tapeworm larva; hence ~ĭFORM (-ĭ′d-) *a.* [f. mod. L f. Gk *hudatis -idos* watery vesicle (*hudōr hudatos* water; see -ID[2])]

hȳ′dra *n.* Thing hard to extirpate; water-snake; freshwater polyp of genus *Hydra* etc., with tubular body and tentacles around mouth. [ME, f. L f. Gk *hudra* water-snake, in Gk Myth. one whose many heads grew again when cut off]

hȳdrā′ngea (-nj*a*) *n.* Shrub of genus *Hydrangea*, with globular clusters of white, blue, or pink flowers. [mod. L, f. Gk *hudōr* water + *aggos* vessel (from cup-shape of seed-capsule)]

hȳ'drant *n.* Pipe (esp. in street) with nozzle to which hose can be attached, for drawing water from main. [irreg. f. HYDRO- + -ANT]

hȳ'drāte[1] *n.* (Chem.) Compound of water with another compound or an element. [F, f. Gk *hudōr* water; see -ATE[1]]

hȳ'dr|āte[2] *v.t.* Combine chemically with water; cause to absorb water; hence ~A'TION *n.* [f. prec.]

hȳdrau'lĭc *a.* & *n.* **1.** *a.* Of water or other liquid conveyed through pipes and channels; operated by movement of liquid (*hydraulic brakes, lift*); concerned with hydraulics (*hydraulic engineer*); ~ **press,** hydrostatic press; ~ **ram,** automatic pump in which kinetic energy of descending column of water raises some of the water above its original level. **2.** Hardening under water (*hydraulic cement*). **3.** Hence **hȳdrau'l**ICALLY *adv.* **4.** *n.* (in *pl.*, usu. treated as *sing.*) Science of conveyance of liquids through pipes etc., esp. as motive power. [f. L f. Gk *hudraulikos* (*hudōr* water, *aulos* pipe; see -IC)]

hȳ'drazine (-ēn) *n.* (Chem.) Colourless alkaline liquid, N_2H_4, used as reducing agent and rocket propellant. [f. HYDROGEN + AZO- + -INE[5]]

hȳ'drĭc *a.* (Chem.) Of or containing hydrogen. [f. HYDROGEN + -IC]

hȳ'drīde *n.* (Chem.) Binary compound of hydrogen esp. with metal. [f. HYDROGEN + -IDE]

hȳdrīŏ'dĭc *n.* (Chem.) Containing hydrogen and iodine (~ **acid,** HI). [f. HYDROGEN + IODINE + -IC]

hȳ'drō *n.* (*pl.* ~**s**). (colloq.) Hotel etc. providing hydropathic treatment; hydroelectric power plant. [abbr.]

hȳ'dro- *comb. form,* w. senses (1) having to do with water, (2, Path.) dropsical, affected with accumulation of serous fluid, (3, Chem.) combined with hydrogen, as: ~**bro'mic,** containing hydrogen and bromine; ~**car'bon,** compound of hydrogen and carbon; ~**cele,** (Path.) accumulation of serous fluid; ~-**ce'phalus,** water on the brain, esp. in young children with resulting mental deficiency; ~**chlor'ic,** containing hydrogen and chlorine (~*chloric acid,* HCl); ~**chlor'ide,** compound of organic base with hydrochloric acid; ~**cya'nic,** containing hydrogen and cyanogen (~*cyanic acid,* HCN, highly poisonous volatile liquid); ~**ele'ctric,** developing electricity by utilization of water-power, (of electricity) produced thus; ~**fluo'ric,** containing hydrogen and fluorine; ~**grapher** (-ŏ'g-) person skilled in, ~**gra'phic(al)** having to do with, ~**graphy** (-ŏ'g-), scientific study of seas, lakes, rivers, etc.; ~**logy** (-ŏ'l-), science of the properties, laws, etc., of water, esp. of its movement on, under, and above land; ~**magne'tic,** involving hydrodynamics and magnetism, magnetohydrodynamic; ~**ma'nia,** craving for water; ~**mecha'nics,** mechanics of liquids; ~**phane,** opal that absorbs water and becomes transparent on immersion [f. Gk *-phanēs* apparent]; ~**phone,** instrument for detection of sound-waves in water; ~**phyte,** aquatic plant (esp. alga), plant needing much moisture; ~**plane,** finlike device enabling submarine to rise or fall, light fast motor boat designed to skim over surface, seaplane; ~**pneuma'tic,** involving combined action of water and air; ~**qui'none,** substance formed by reduction of quinone, used as photographic developer; ~**sphere,** waters of the earth's surface; ~**the'rapy,** hydropathy; ~**ther'mal,** of the action of heated water on earth's crust; ~**thor'ax,** dropsy of the chest; ~**tropism** (-ŏ't-), (of plant-roots etc.) tendency to turn to or from moisture. [f Gk *hudro-* (*hudōr* water; see -o-)]

hȳdrodȳnă'm|ĭc(al) *adjs.* Of forces acting on or exerted by liquids (esp. water); so ~ICS *n.* [f. mod. L *hydrodynamicus* (as HYDRO-, DYNAMIC)]

hȳ'drofoil *n.* (Vessel fitted with) structure designed to generate (esp. lifting) force when moving through liquid, esp. under vessel's hull to lift it out of water at speed. [f. HYDRO-, after AERO*foil*]

hȳ'drogėn *n.* Colourless tasteless odourless gaseous element, the lightest substance known, combining with oxygen to form water;. ~ **bomb,** immensely powerful bomb utilizing explosive fusion of hydrogen nuclei; *hydrogen* PEROXIDE; ~ **sulphide,** colourless poisonous gas, H_2S, with disagreeable smell, formed by rotting animal matter; hence **hȳdrŏ'gėn**OUS *a.* [f. F *hydrogène* (as HYDRO-, -GEN)]

hȳ'drogen|āte (*or* -ŏ'j-) *v.t.* Charge, cause (esp. unsaturated compound) to combine, with hydrogen; hence ~A'TION *n.* [f. prec. + -ATE[3]]

hȳ'droid *a.* & *n.* (Zool.) (Animal) like or allied to the hydra polyp. [f. HYDRA + -OID]

hȳdrŏ'lȳs|ĭs *n.* (*pl.* ~**es** *pr.* -ēz). Decomposition by chemical reaction with water; so **hȳ'drolȳse** (-z), ***-lȳze,** *v.t.*, decompose thus, **hȳdrolȳ't**IC *a.* [f. HYDRO- + -LYSIS]

hȳ'dromĕl *n.* Mixture of honey and water. [ME, f. L f. Gk *hudromeli* (as HYDRO-, *meli* honey)]

hȳdrŏ'|mėter *n.* Instrument for determining density of liquids; so **hȳdromĕ'tr**IC *a.*, ~METRY *n.* [f. HYDRO- + -METER]

hȳdrŏ'path|ȳ *n.* Medical treatment by external and internal application of water; hence **hȳdropă'th**IC *a.*, ~IST (3) *n.* [f. HYDRO-, after *homoeopathy* etc.]

hȳdrophĭ'lĭc *a.* Having affinity for water; wettable by water. [f. HYDRO- + Gk *philos* loving + -IC]

hȳdrophō'bĭa *n.* Aversion to water, esp. as symptom of rabies in man; rabies, esp. in man; morbid dread of water. [LL, f. Gk *hudrophobia* (as HYDRO-, -PHOBIA)]

hȳdrophō'bĭc *a.* **1.** Of or suffering from hydrophobia. **2.** Not readily wettable. [f. prec. + -IC]

hȳdrŏ'pĭc *a.* Dropsical. [ME, f. OE *ydropique* f. L f. Gk *hudrōpikos* (as HYDROPSY; see -IC)]

hȳdropŏ'nĭcs *n.* Soilless culture, art of growing plants without soil, in (sand, etc. containing) water impregnated with nutrients. [f. HYDRO- + Gk *ponos* labour; see -ICS]

hȳ'drŏpsȳ *n.* (arch.) Dropsy. [ME, f. OF *idropesie* f. med. L *(h)ydropisia* f. L *hydropisis* f. Gk *hudrōps* (*hudōr* water)]

hȳdrostă'tĭc *a.* & *n.* **1.** *a.* Of the equilibrium of liquids and the pressure exerted by liquids at rest; ~ **paradox,** principle that any quantity of a perfect liquid, however small, may be made to balance any other quantity; ~ **press,** machine in which pressure of a body of water gives increased force by transmission from small to larger cylinder; hence ~AL *a.*, ~**al**LY[2] *adv.* **2.** *n.* (in *pl.*, usu. treated as *sing.*) Branch of mechanics concerned with the pressure and equilibrium of liquids at rest. [prob. f. Gk *hudrostatēs* hydrostatic balance (as HYDRO-; see STATIC)]

hȳ'drous *a.* (Chem. & Min.) Containing water. [f. Gk *hudōr hudro-* water + -OUS]

hȳdrŏ'xīde *n.* (Chem.) Compound of element or radical with hydroxyl. [f. HYDRO- + OXIDE]

hȳdrŏ'xȳl *n.* (Chem.) Radical containing hydrogen and oxygen, OH; so **hȳdrŏ'xȳ-** *comb. form.* [f. HYDROGEN + OXYGEN + -YL]

hȳdrozō'an *a.* & *n.* (Animal) of class Hydrozoa of mainly marine coelenterates. [f. mod. L

Hydrozoa (as HYDRA, Gk *zōion* animal; see -A) + -AN]

hȳē'na, hȳae'na, *n.* Carnivorous strong-jawed quadruped of order Hyaenidae (**laughing ~,** species whose howl is compared to fiendish laughter); cruel, treacherous, or rapacious person; Tasmanian wolf; **~-dog,** bright-coloured hyena-like S. Afr. canine quadruped. [ME, f. OF *hyene* & f. L f. Gk *huaina* fem. of *hus* pig]

Hȳgei'|a (-jē'*a*) *n.* Personification of health; hence **h~**AN *a.* [f. Gk *Hugeia* goddess of health (*hugiēs* healthy)]

hȳ'gien|e (-jēn) *n.* Principles of maintaining health; practice of these, e.g. by cleanliness; hence ~IC *a.*, ~ICALLY *adv.*, ~ICS *n.*, (-jē'-), ~IST (3) *n.* [f. F *hygiène* f. mod. L f. Gk *hugieinē* (*tekhnē* art) of health (*hugiēs* healthy)]

hȳ'gro- *comb. form.* Moisture, as: **~logy** (-ŏ'l-), study of humidity of atmosphere etc.; **~meter** (-ŏ'm-), instrument for measuring humidity of air or gas; **~me'tric, ~metry** (-ŏ'm-), concerned with, measurement of, humidity; **~philous** (-ŏ'f-), (of plant) growing in moist environment; **~phyte,** = HYDRO*phyte*; **~scope,** instrument indicating but not measuring humidity of air; **~sco'pic,** of the hygroscope, (of substance) tending to absorb moisture from the air. [f. Gk *hugro-* (*hugros* wet, moist; see -O-)]

hȳ'ĭng. See HIE.

Hȳ'ksŏs *n. pl.* Asiatic invaders who ruled Egypt approx. from 17th to 16th c. B.C. [f. Gk *Huksōs*]

hȳ'lĭc *a.* Of matter, material. [f. LL f. Gk *hulikos* (*hulē* matter; see -IC)]

hȳ'lo- *comb. form.* Matter, as: **~mor'phism,** doctrine that primordial matter is first cause of the universe and combines with forms to produce bodies; **~theism,** doctrine that God and matter are identical; **~zo'ism,** doctrine that all matter has life. [f. Gk *hulo-* (*hulē* matter; see -O-)]

Hȳ'mĕn[1] *n.* (Gk & Rom. Myth.) God of marriage; so **hȳmĕnē'**AL *a.* [L, f. Gk *Humēn*]

hȳ'mĕn[2] *n.* (Anat.) Fold of membrane closing part of external orifice of virginal vagina; hence ~AL *a.* [LL, f. Gk *humēn* membrane]

hȳmē'nĭ|um *n.* (*pl.* **~a**). Spore-bearing surface of fungus. [mod. L, f. Gk *humenion* dim. of *humēn* membrane]

hȳmenŏ'pter|an *n.* Insect of order Hymenoptera, e.g. ant, bee, wasp, with four membranous wings; so ~OUS *a.* [f. mod. L *hymenoptera* f. Gk *humenopteros* membrane-winged (as prec., *pteron* wing) + -AN]

hȳmn (hĭm) *n.* & *v.* **1.** *n.* Song of praise to God, esp. metrical composition sung in religious service; song of praise in honour of a god or other exalted being or thing; **~-book** (of hymns); hence **hȳ'mnIC** *a.*, **hȳ'mnIST** *n.*, writer of hymns. **2.** *v.t.* Praise (God etc.) in hymns; express (praise etc.) (as if) in hymns. **3.** *v.i.* Sing hymns. [ME *ymne* etc. f. OF, f. L f. Gk *humnos*]

hȳ'mn|al *a.* & *n.* **1.** *a.* Of hymns. **2.** *n.* Hymn-book; so ~ARY[1] *n.* [n. ME, f. med. L *hymnale* (as prec.; see -AL)]

hȳ'mnod|ȳ *n.* Singing of hymns; composition of hymns, whence ~IST (3) *n.*; hymns collectively. [f. med. L *hymnodia* f. Gk *humnōidia* (*humnos* hymn; cf. PSALMODY)]

hȳmnŏ'grapher *n.* Writer of hymns. [f. Gk *humnographos* (as prec.; see -GRAPHER)]

hȳmnŏ'log|ȳ *n.* Composition or study of hymns; hymns collectively; hence ~IST (3) *n.* [f. HYMN + -O- + -LOGY]

hȳ'oid *a.* & *n.* (Anat.) ~ (**bone**), U-shaped bone between chin and thyroid cartilage; pertaining to this. [f. F *hyoïde* f. mod. L f. Gk *huoeidēs* shaped like letter upsilon (*hu*)]

hȳ'oscine (-ēn) *n.* Poisonous alkaloid used as sedative, got from herbs of genus *Scopolia*, isomeric with hyoscyamine. [f. foll.]

hȳoscȳ'amine (-ēn) *n.* Poisonous alkaloid used as sedative, got from henbane. [f. mod. L f. Gk *huoskuamos* henbane (*hus huos* pig, *kuamos* bean) + -INE[5]]

hȳp. See HIP[3].

hȳp- *pref.* See HYPO-.

hȳpae'thral *a.* Open to the sky, roofless (orig. of Gk temples); open-air. [f. L f. Gk *hupaithros* (as HYPO-, *aithēr* air) + -AL]

hȳpă'llagė *n.* (Rhet.) Transposition of natural relations of two elements in a proposition (e.g. *Melissa shook her doubtful curls*; *apply the wound to water* for *apply water to the wound*). [LL, f. Gk *hupallagē* (as HYPO-, *allassō* exchange)]

hȳpe[1] *v.t.*, & *n.* (sl.) Cheat(ing), trick. [20th c.; orig. unkn.]

hȳpe[2] *n.*, & *v.t.* (sl.) **1.** *n.* Drug addict; hypodermic needle or injection. **2.** *v.t.* **~d up,** stimulated (as if) by hypodermic injection. [abbr. of HYPODERMIC]

hȳ'per- *pref.* w. senses 'over, beyond, above' (*hypergamy*, *hyperphysical*), 'exceeding' (*hyperbola*, *hypersonic*), 'excessive, above normal' (*hyperbole*, *hypersensitive*; opp. HYPO-). [Gk (*huper* over, beyond)]

hȳperae'm|ĭa, *-ē'm|ĭa, *n.* (Path.) Excessive quantity of blood in tissues; hence ~IC *a.* [mod. L (as HYPER-, -AEMIA)]

hȳperaesth|ē'sĭa, *-rės-, (-zĭ*a*) *n.* (Path.) morbid sensitiveness of nerves; excessive sensitiveness; so ~E'TIC *a.* [mod. L (as HYPER-, Gk *-aisthēsia* f. *aisthanomai* perceive)]

hȳpẽr'batŏn *n.* (Rhet.) Inversion of normal order of words, esp. for sake of emphasis (e.g. *this I must see*). [L, f. Gk *huperbaton* (as HYPER-, *bainō* to step)]

hȳpẽr'bola *n.* (*pl.* **~s** *or* **~e**). (Geom.) Plane curve of two equal, infinite branches, formed when double cone is cut by plane making larger angle with base than side of cone makes (cf. ELLIPSE); hence **hȳperbŏ'lIC** *a.* (**~ cosine** etc., function related to rectangular hyperbola as ordinary cosine etc. is related to circle). [mod. L, f. Gk *huperbolē* excess (as HYPER-, *ballō* to throw)]

hȳpẽr'bol|ė *n.* (Rhet.) Exaggerated statement not meant to be taken literally; hence **hȳperbŏ'lICAL** *a.*, ~ISM (4), ~IST (1), *ns.* [L, as prec.]

hȳpẽr'boloid *n.* (Geom.) Solid or surface having plane sections that are hyperbolas or ellipses; hence ~AL *a.* [f. HYPERBOLA + -OID]

hȳperbŏr'ėan (*or* -berē'-) *a.* & *n.* (Inhabitant) of the extreme north of the earth or (colloq.) of a country; (*H~*; Gk Myth.) (one) of a race worshipping Apollo and living in land of sunshine and plenty beyond north wind. [f. LL *hyperboreanus* f. L *hyperboreus* f. Gk *huperboreos* (as HYPER-, *Boreas* god of north wind); see -AN]

hȳpercătalĕ'ctĭc *a.* (Pros.) (Of line) having extra syllable after last foot of normal metre. [f. LL *hypercatalecticus* f. Gk *huperkatalēktos* (as HYPER-, CATALECTIC)]

hȳpercŏ'nscious (-sh*u*s) *a.* Acutely or excessively aware *of*. [f. HYPER- + CONSCIOUS]

hȳpercrĭ'tĭc|al *a.* Too critical, esp. of small faults; hence **~alLY**[2] *adv.*, ~ISM (1) *n.*, ~IZE (1, 2) *v.t.* & *i.* [f. HYPER- + CRITICAL]

hȳperdū'lĭa *n.* (R.C. Ch.) Special veneration offered to Virgin Mary. [med. L (as HYPER-, DULIA)]

hȳperfō'cal *a.* **~ distance** (on which camera lens may be focused to bring maximum range of object-distances into focus). [f. HYPER- + FOCAL]

hȳpẽr'gamȳ *n.* Marriage to person of equal or superior caste or class. [f. HYPER- + Gk *gamos* marriage + -Y[1]]

hȳpergŏ'lĭc *a.* (Of rocket propellant) igniting spontaneously on contact with oxidant etc. [f. G *hypergol* (perh. f. as HYPO-, ERG[1], -OL) + -IC]

hȳpĕ'rĭcum *n.* Herb or shrub of genus *Hypericum*, with pentamerous yellow flowers. [L, f. Gk *hupereikon* (as HYPER-, *ereikē* heath)]

hȳ'permãrkėt *n.* Very large self-service store with wide range of goods, usu. outside town. [f. F *hypermarché* (as HYPER-, MARKET[1])]

hȳpermĕ'trĭc(al) *adjs.* (Of verse) having a redundant syllable; (of syllable) redundant. [f. Gk *hupermetros* (as HYPER-, *metron* measure) + -IC, -ICAL]

hȳpermėtr|ō'pĭa *n.* Condition of having long sight; hence **~ŏ'pic** *a.* [mod. L, f. as prec. + Gk *ōps* eye; see -IA[1]]

hȳ'perŏn *n.* (Phys.) Unstable baryon. [f. HYPER- + -ON]

hȳper|ō'pĭa *n.* = HYPERMETROPIA; hence **~ŏ'pic** *a.* [mod. L, f. HYPER- + Gk *ōps* eye + -IA[1]]

hȳperphȳ'sĭcal (-z-) *a.* Supernatural. [f. HYPER- + PHYSICAL]

hȳpersĕ'nsĭtĭv|e *a.* Abnormally or excessively sensitive; hence **~eNESS** (-vn-), **~ITY** (-ĭ'v-), *ns.* [f. HYPER- + SENSITIVE]

hȳpersŏ'n|ĭc *a.* **1.** Relating to speeds more than about five times that of sound. **2.** Relating to sound-frequencies above about a thousand million hertz. **3.** Hence **~ICALLY** *adv.* [f. HYPER- after *supersonic*, *ultrasonic*]

hȳ'persthēne *n.* Greenish rock-forming mineral, iron magnesium silicate. [f. F HYPER(*stène* f. Gk *sthenos* strength, from its being harder than hornblende)]

hȳpertĕ'ns|ion (-shon) *n.* Abnormally high blood pressure; state of great emotional tension; hence **~IVE** *a.* [f. HYPER- + TENSION]

hȳperthẽr'mĭa *n.* (Med.) Condition of having body-temperature greatly above normal. [f. HYPER- + Gk *thermē* heat + -IA[1]]

hȳpẽr'troph|ȳ *n.* Enlargement (*of* organ etc.) due to excessive nutrition; hence or cogn. **hȳpertrŏ'phIC**, **~ĭED**[2] (-ĭd), *adjs.* [f. mod. L *hypertrophia* (as HYPER-, Gk *-trophia* nourishment)]

hȳpē'thral. Var. of HYPAETHRAL.

hȳ'pha *n.* (*pl.* **~e**). Filament in mycelium of fungus. [mod. L, f. Gk *huphē* web]

hȳ'phen *n.*, & *v.t.* **1.** *n.* Sign (-) used to join two words together, to join separated syllables of word broken at end of line, to divide word into parts, to represent hesitant speech (*b-b-but*), etc. **2.** *v.t.* Join (words) with hyphen; write (compound word) with hyphen. [LL, f. Gk *huphen* together (*hupo* under, *hen* one)]

hȳ'phen|āte *v.t.* = prec. 2 (**~ated Americans**, of mixed nationality: Irish-Americans, etc.); hence **~A'TION** *n.* [f. prec. + -ATE[3]]

hȳ'pno- *comb. form.* Sleep, hypnosis, as: **~ge'nesis,** induction of hypnotic state; **~logy** (-ŏ'l-), science of the phenomena of sleep; **~pae'dia,** learning by hearing while asleep; **~the'rapy,** treatment of disease by hypnosis. [f. Gk *hupnos* sleep + -o-]

hȳpnō's|ĭs *n.* (*pl.* **~es** *pr.* -ēz). Sleep artificially produced; state produced by hypnotism. [mod. L, f. Gk *hupnos* sleep; see -OSIS]

hȳpnŏ't|ĭc *a.* & *n.* **1.** *a.* Of or producing hypnotism; (of drug) soporific; hence **~ICALLY** *adv.* **2.** *n.* Thing that produces sleep; person under (or open to) influence of hypnotism. [f. F *hypnotique* f. LL f. Gk *hupnōtikos* (*hupnoō* put to sleep; see -OTIC)]

hȳ'pnot|ĭsm *n.* (Artificial production of) state resembling deep sleep, in which subject acts only on external suggestion; so **~IST** (1) *n.*, **~IZE** (3) *v.t.* (lit. or fig.) [f. prec. + -ISM]

hȳ'pō[1] *n.* (Photog.) Sodium thiosulphate (incorrectly called HYPO*sulphite*), used in fixing. [abbr.]

hȳ'pō[2] *n.* (*pl.* **~s**). = HYPODERMIC | 3. [abbr.]

hȳpo- *pref.* (usu. **hyp-** bef. vowel or *h*) w. sense 'under' (*hypodermic*), 'below normal' (*hypoxia*; opp. HYPER-), 'slightly' (*hypomania*), (Chem.) containing element combined in low valence (*hypochlorous*, *hypochlorite*), (Mus., of mode) plagal, starting from dominant of, (*hypo-Aeolian* etc.). [Gk (*hupo* under)]

hȳ'poblăst *n.* (Biol.) Innermost layer of gastrula; endoderm. [f. mod. L *hypoblastus* (as HYPO-, -BLAST)]

hȳ'pocaust *n.* (Rom. Ant.) Hollow space under floor in which heat from furnace was accumulated for heating house or bath. [f. L f. Gk *hupokauston* place heated from below (as HYPO-, *kaiō*, *kau-*, burn)]

hȳpochŏ'ndrĭa (-k-) *n.* Morbid depression without real cause; (pop.) (unnecessary) anxiety about one's health. [LL, f. Gk *hupokhondria* soft parts of the body below ribs (whence melancholy was thought to arise; as HYPO-, *khondros* sternal cartilage)]

hȳpochŏ'ndrĭăc (-k-) *a.* & *n.* **1.** *a.* Of or affected by hypochondria. **2.** *n.* Hypochondriac person. [f. F *hypocondriaque* f. Gk *hupokhondriakos* (as prec.; see -AC)]

hȳpocorĭ'stĭc *a.* (Gram.) Of the nature of a pet name. [f. Gk *hupokoristikos* (*hupokorizomai* call by pet names)]

hȳpocŏ'tȳl *n.* (Bot.) Part of embryo or seedling below cotyledon(s). [f. HYPO- + COTYLEDON]

hȳpŏ'crĭsȳ *n.* Simulation of virtue or goodness; dissimulation, pretence. [ME, f. OF *ypocrisie* f. eccl. L f. Gk *hupokrisis* acting of a part, pretence (*hupokrinomai* f. *hupo-* HYPO- + *krinō* decide, judge)]

hȳ'pocrĭt|e *n.* Person guilty of hypocrisy; dissembler, pretender; so **~ICAL** (-ĭ't-) *a.* [ME, f. OF *ypocrite* f. eccl. L f. Gk *hupokritēs* actor (as prec.)]

hȳpocȳ'cloid *n.* (Math.) Curve traced by point on circumference of circle rolling on interior of another circle; hence **~AL** (-oi'd-) *a.* [f. HYPO- + CYCLOID]

hȳpodẽr'm|ĭc *a.* & *n.* **1.** *a.* (Med., of drug etc.) introduced beneath the skin (*hypodermic injection*); (of needle, needle-pointed syringe, etc.) used thus; hence **~ICALLY** *adv.* **2.** (Anat.) Lying under the skin. **3.** *n.* Hypodermic injection or syringe. [f. *hypoderma* subcutaneous tissue (mod. L f. as HYPO- + Gk *derma* skin) + -IC]

hȳpogă'str|ĭum *n.* (*pl.* **~ia**). Lowest (esp. central) region of abdomen; so **~IC** *a.* [mod. L, f. Gk *hupogastrion* (as HYPO-, *gastēr* belly); see -IUM]

hȳpogē'al, hȳpogē'an, *adjs.* (Existing or growing) underground. [f. LL *hypogeus* f. Gk *hupogeios* (as HYPO-, *gē* earth) + -AL, -AN]

hȳ'pogēne *a.* (Geol.) Produced under surface of earth. [f. HYPO- + Gk *gen-* produce]

hȳpogē'|um *n.* (*pl.* **~a**). Underground chamber. [L, f. Gk *hupogeion* neut. (as n.) of *hupogeios* (see HYPOGEAL)]

hȳ'poid *n.* Gear with pinion off centre-line of wheel, to connect non-intersecting shafts. [perh. f. HYPERBOLOID]

hȳpolĭ'mnĭ|on *n.* (*pl.* **~a**). Lower layer of water in stratified lakes. [f. HYPO- + Gk *limnion* dim. of *limnē* lake]

hȳpo|mā'nĭa *n.* Minor form of mania; hence **~mă'nIC** *a.* [mod. L, f. G *hypomanie* (as HYPO-, MANIA)]

hȳ'ponăstȳ *n.* (Bot.) Tendency in plant-organs

to grow more rapidly on underside. [f. HYPO- + Gk *nastos* pressed + -Y^1]

hȳpŏ'phȳs|is *n.* (*pl.* **~es** *pr.* -ēz). (Anat.) = PITUITARY gland; hence **~ėAL**, **~IAL**, (-ofĭ'z-) *adjs.* [mod. L, f. Gk *hupophusis* offshoot (as HYPO-, *phusis* growth)]

hȳpŏ'stas|is *n.* (*pl.* **~es** *pr.* -ēz). **1.** (Med.) Excess of blood in lower parts of organs. **2.** (Metaphys.) Underlying substance, opp. to attributes or to what is unsubstantial; so **~IZE** (3), **hȳpŏ'statIZE** (3), *vbs. t.* **3.** (Theol.) Personality (of Christ), person (of the Godhead); so **hȳpostă'tIC(AL)** *adjs.* [eccl. L, f. Gk *hupostasis* (as HYPO-, STASIS standing, state)]

hȳ'postȳle *a.* (Archit.) Having roof supported on pillars. [f. Gk *hupostulos* (as HYPO-, STYLE)]

hȳpotă'xis *n.* (Gram.) Subordination of one clause to another; so **hȳpotă'ctIC** *a.* [f. Gk *hupotaxis* (as HYPO-, TAXIS arrangement)]

hȳpotĕ'ns|ion (-shon) *n.* Abnormally low blood pressure; hence **~IVE** *a.* [f. HYPO- + TENSION]

hȳpŏ'tėnūse (-z) *n.* Side opposite right angle of right-angled triangle. [f. L f. Gk *hupoteinousa* (*grammē*) subtending (line) fem. part. of *hupoteinō* (as HYPO-, *teinō* stretch)]

hȳpothă'lamus *n.* (Anat.) Organ below brain, controlling body-temperature etc. [mod. L, f. as HYPO-, THALAMUS]

hȳ'pothėc *n.* (Rom. & Sc. Law). Right established by law over thing belonging to debtor; so **hȳpŏ'thėcARY**^{1} *a.* [f. F *hypothèque* f. LL f. Gk *hupothēkē* deposit (as HYPO-, *tithēmi* place)]

hȳpŏ'thėc|āte *v.t.* Pledge, mortgage; hence **~A'TION** *n.* [f. med. L *hypothecare* (as prec.) + -ATE^3]

hȳpothẽr'mĭa *n.* (Med.) Condition of having body-temperature below normal. [f. HYPO- + Gk *thermē* heat + -IA^1]

hȳpŏ'thės|ĭs *n.* (*pl.* **~es** *pr.* -ēz). Supposition made as basis for reasoning, without assumption of its truth, or as starting-point for further investigation from known facts (cf. THEORY); groundless assumption; so **hȳpothĕ'tICAL** *a.* [LL, f. Gk *hupothesis* foundation (as HYPO-, THESIS)]

hȳpŏ'thėsize, -ise (-īz), *v.* **1.** *v.i.* Frame a hypothesis. **2.** *v.t.* Assume as hypothesis. [f. prec. + -IZE]

hȳpŏ'x|ĭa *n.* (Med.) Deficiency of oxygen; hence **~IC** *a.* [f. HYPO- + OX- + -IA^1]

hȳpsŏ'graphȳ *n.* Description or mapping of contours of earth's surface; hence **hȳpsogră'phIC(AL)** *adjs.* [f. Gk *hupsos* height; see -GRAPHY]

hȳpsŏ'mėter *n.* Instrument for estimating altitudes, esp. from boiling-point of water etc.; hence **hȳpsomĕ'trIC** *a.* [f. as prec. + -METER]

hȳr'ăx *n.* Small ungulate mammal of order Hyracoidea, e.g. Syrian rock-rabbit and Afr. rock-badger. [mod. L, f. Gk *hurax* shrew-mouse]

hȳ'son *n.* Kind of green tea from China. [f. Chin. *hsi-ch'un*, lit. bright spring]

hȳ'ssop *n.* Small bushy aromatic herb of genus *Hyssopus*, esp. species used medicinally; (Bibl.) plant whose twigs were used for sprinkling in Jewish rites, bunch of this used in purification. [ME *ysope* f. OE & f. OF f. L f. Gk *hyssōpos*, of Semitic orig.]

hȳsterĕ'ctom|ȳ *n.* (Surg.) Removal of womb; hence **~IZE** (1) *v.t.* [f. Gk *hustera* womb + -ECTOMY]

hȳsterē's|ĭs *n.* (*pl.* **~es** *pr.* -ēz). (Phys.) Lagging of effect when cause varies in amount etc., esp. of magnetic induction behind magnetizing force. [f. Gk *husterēsis* (*hustereō* be behind f. *husteros* coming after)]

hȳstẽr'ĭa *n.* Psychoneurosis with anaesthesia, convulsions, etc., and usu. with disturbance of moral and intellectual faculties; uncontrolled or morbid excitement. [mod. L, f. as foll.; see -IA^1]

hȳstĕ'rĭc *a.* & *n.* **1.** *a.* = foll. **2.** *n.* Hysterical person; (in *pl.*) hysterical fits or convulsions. [f. L f. Gk *husterikos* of the womb (*hustera*; see -IC), hysteria being thought to occur more frequently in women than in men]

hȳstĕ'rĭcal *a.* Of or affected with hysteria; morbidly or uncontrolledly emotional; hence **~LY**^{2} *adv.* [f. as prec. + -AL]

hȳsterŏn prŏ'terŏn *n.* (Rhet.) Figure of speech in which what should come last is put first, inversion of natural order (*I die! I faint! I fail!*). [LL, f. Gk *husteron proteron* latter (put in place of) former]

Hz *abbr.* hertz.

I

I^1, **i**, (ī) *n.* (*pl.* **Is** *or* **I's**). Ninth letter of alphabet; (as Roman numeral) = 1 (**ii** 2, **iii** 3, **iv** (rarely **iiii**) 4, **ix** 9); **I-beam**, girder of I-shaped section.

I^2 (ī) *pron.* (*obj.* **me** *pr.* mĭ *or*, *when stressed*, mē; refl. MYSELF, arch. **me**; *poss.* MY, MINE^3; *pl.* WE etc.). **1.** Sing. *pron.* of 1st pers.; **me**, (colloq.) cf. HER^1 2; (in excl.) *ah me!*, *dear me!*, *silly me!*. **2.** *n.* **The I,** (Metaphys.) the ego, subject or object of self-consciousness. [OE *ic*, = OS *ik*, OHG *ih*, ON *ek*, Goth. *ik* f. Gmc ***eka** f. IE *****egō; *me* f. OE *me*, *mē* acc. & dat., = OS *mī*, OHG *mih*, *mir*, ON, Goth. *mik* f. IE ******me*]

I. *abbr.* Island(s); Isle(s).

I *symb.* iodine.

-i *suf.* **1.** forming *pl.* of *ns.* f. L in *-us* or It. in *-e* or *-o* (*foci*, *dilettanti*, *timpani*). **2.** forming *adjs.* f. names of regions etc. in or near the Middle East (*Israeli*, *Pakistani*). [f. adj. suf. in Semitic & hence in Indo-Iranian languages].

-ĭ- connecting vowel esp. of wds in -ANA, -FEROUS, -FIC, -FORM, -FY, -GEROUS, -VOROUS. [f. or after F f. L]

-ĭa^1 *suf.* forming *ns.* (1) abstract (*hydrophobia*, *mania*, *utopia*), esp. Path. (*anaemia*, *pneumonia*), (2) Bot. classes and genera (*dahlia*, *fuchsia*), (3) names of countries (*Australia*, *India*). [f. or after L & Gk; cf. -A 1]

-ĭa^2 *suf.* forming *pl.* of *ns.* (1) f. Gk in *-ion* or L in *-ium* or *-e* (*paraphernalia*, *atria*, *regalia*), (2) Zool. groups (*Mammalia*); cf. -A 2.

Ia. *abbr.* Iowa.

I.A.E.A. *abbr.* International Atomic Energy Agency.

-ĭal *suf.* forming *adjs.* (*celestial*, *dictatorial*, *terrestrial*, *trivial*, *venial*). [f. or after F *-iel* or f. L *-ialis*; cf. -AL]

ī'ămb *n.* Iambus. [Anglicized f. IAMBUS]

īă'mbĭc *a.* & *n.* (Pros.) **1.** *a.* Of or using iambuses. **2.** *n.* (usu. in *pl.*) Iambic verse. [f. F *iambique* f. LL f. Gk *iambikos* (as foll.; see -IC)]

īă'mb|us *n.* (*pl.* **~uses,** *or* **~i** *pr.* -ī). (Pros.) Foot consisting of one short followed by one long syllable. [L, f. Gk *iambos* iambus, lampoon (*iaptō* **assail** in words, from use by Gk satirists)]

-ĭan *suf.* forming *adjs.* (often used as *ns.*) esp. f. names of persons and places (*Bostonian, Christian, Churchillian, Georgian, Oxonian, Virgilian; theologian*); cf. -AN. [f. or after F *-ien* or f. L *-ianus*]
-ī'asĭs *suf.* See -ASIS.
I.A.T.A. *abbr.* International Air Transport Association.
ĭătrōgĕ'nĭc *a.* (Of disease) caused by process of diagnosis or treatment. [f. Gk *iatros* physician + -O- + -GENIC]
ib. *abbr. ibidem.*
||**I.B.A.** *abbr.* Independent Broadcasting Authority.
Ibēr'ĭan (ī-) *a.* & *n.* (Inhabitant or language) of ancient Iberia, the peninsula now comprising Spain and Portugal; hence **Ibero-** (ī'berō *or* ībēr'ō) *comb. form,* Iberian (and) (*Ibero-American*). [f. L *Iberia* f. Gk *Ibēres* Spaniards, + -AN]
ī'bĕx *n.* Wild goat esp. of Alps and Apennines, with large ridged recurved horns. [L]
ibid. *abbr.* = foll.
ibidem (ĭ'bĭdĕm *or* ĭbī'dĕm) *adv.* In the same book, chapter, passage, etc. [L]
-ĭbĭ'lĭtў *suf.* forming *ns.* f. *adjs.* in -IBLE (*possibility, credibility*). [f. F *-ibilité* or f. L *-ibilitas*; see -ITY]
ī'bĭs *n.* Wading bird of family Threskiornithidae with long curved bill, found in lakes and swamps of warm climates; **sacred ~**, white species venerated by ancient Egyptians. [ME f. L f. Gk]
-ĭble *suf.* forming *adjs.* w. senses as -ABLE (*terrible, defensible, forcible, possible*). [F, or f. L *-ibilis* f. *-i-* of second, third, and fourth conjugations + *-bilis* (see -BLE)]
-ĭblў *suf.* forming *advs.* corresp. to *adjs.* in *-ible.* [f. -IBLE + -LY²]
I.B.M. *abbr.* International Business Machines.
I'bō (ē'-) *n.* (*pl.* same *or* **~s**). (Member or language of) a Negro people of S.E. Nigeria. [native name]
IBRD *abbr.* International Bank for Reconstruction and Development.
I'bsenĭsm (ĭ'-) *n.* Principles and aims of works examining and criticizing social conventions, written by Ibsen and his followers. [f. H. *Ibsen,* Norw. dramatist d. 1906 + -ISM]
-ĭc, (arch.) **-ĭck** *or* **-ĭque** (-k), *suf.* forming *adjs.* & *ns.* (*Arabic, civic, classic, poetic, public, romantic, scenic, tragic; critic, epic, mechanic, music*); (Chem.) in higher valence or degree of oxidation (*ferric, sulphuric*; cf. -OUS); see -ICS, -ITIC. [f. or after F *-ique* or f. L *-icus* or Gk *-ikos*; cf. -ATIC, -ETIC, -FIC, -OTIC]
i/c *abbr.* in charge; internal combustion.
-ĭcal *suf.* forming *adjs.* corresp. to *ns.* or *adjs.* in -IC (*classical, comical, economical, historical, musical*), or to *ns.* in -Y¹ (*pathological, theoretical*). [f. -IC + -AL]
-ĭcallў *suf.* forming *advs.* corresp. to *adjs.* in -IC or -ICAL (*comically, musically, phlegmatically, poetically, tragically*). [f. prec. + -LY²]
I.C.A.O. *abbr.* International Civil Aviation Organization.
I.C.B.M. *abbr.* inter-continental ballistic missile.
***I.C.C.** *abbr.* Indian Claims Commission; Interstate Commerce Commission.
īce¹ *n.* **1.** Frozen water, a brittle transparent crystalline solid; sheet of this on surface of water; **break the ~**, (fig.) make a beginning, break through reserve or stiffness; CUT² *no ice*; **dry ~**, solid carbon dioxide; **on ~**, (of entertainment etc.) performed by skaters, (colloq.) (1) in state of temporary suspension, held in reserve, (2) absolutely certain; **on thin ~**, (fig.) in a risky situation. **2.** (Portion of) frozen confection esp. ||ice cream or water-ice; *(sl.) diamonds. **3.** **~-age**, glacial period (esp. in Pleistocene); **~-axe** (used by mountain-climbers for cutting footholds); **~-bag,** ice-filled rubber bag for medical use; **~'blink,** luminous appearance on horizon, caused by reflection from ice; **~-blue,** very pale blue; **~-boat,** (1) boat mounted on runners for travelling on ice, (2) boat used for breaking ice on river etc.; **~-bound,** confined by ice; ***~'box,** refrigerator; **~-breaker,** = *ice-boat* (2); **~-cap,** permanent covering of ice e.g. in polar lands; **~-cold,** as cold as ice; **~ cream,** frozen flavoured cream or custard; **~-cube,** small block of ice made in refrigerator; **~-fall,** steep part of glacier like frozen waterfall; **~-field,** expanse of ice, esp. in polar regions; **~-fish,** capelin; *ice-*FLOE; **~-foot,** belt of ice along coast in Arctic regions; **~ hockey** (played on skates); **~-house,** building often partly or wholly underground for storing ice; **~ lolly,** water-ice on small stick; **~-machine** (for artificial production of ice); **~'man,** (1) man skilled in traversing ice, (2) maker of ices; (3) dealer in ice; **~-pack,** (1) = PACK¹ 7, (2) quantity of ice applied to body for medical etc. purposes; **~-pick,** needle-like implement with handle for splitting up table ice; **~-plant** (with leaves covered with watery vesicles looking like ice-specks); **~-show,** entertainment by skaters on ice; **~-water** (from or cooled by ice); **~-wool** (glossy kind used in knitting etc.); **~-yacht,** = *ice-boat* (1). [OE *is,* = OS, OHG *is,* ON *íss* f. Gmc **īsam*]
īce² *v.* **1.** *v.t.* Freeze; cover (as) with ice; mix with or cool in ice; cover (cake etc.) with icing; *iced* LOLLY. **2.** *v.i.* Become covered (*over, up*) with ice, freeze *up.* [ME, f. prec.]
-ĭce *suf.* forming (esp. abstract) *ns.* (*avarice, cowardice, jaundice, justice, malice, notice, novice, precipice, service*); cf. -ISE². [f. or after OF, f. L *-itius, -itia, -itium*]
||**I.C.E.** *abbr.* Institution of Civil Engineers; internal combustion engine.
ī'cebĕrg (ī'sb-) *n.* Huge floating mass of ice, detached portion of glacier carried out to sea; (fig.) unemotional or cold-blooded person; **tip of the ~**, part of iceberg (about one-ninth) that projects above surface of sea, (fig.) small evident part of something much larger. [prob. f. Du. *ijsberg* (*ijs* ice, *berg* hill)]
I'celand (ī'sl-) *n.* **~ lichen** or **moss,** edible species of lichen; **~ poppy,** yellow or red orig. Arctic poppy; **~ spar,** transparent variety of calcite with strong double refraction; hence **~ER¹** (4) *n.* [~, island in N. Atlantic]
Icelă'ndĭc (īsl-) *a.* & *n.* (Language) of Iceland. [f. prec. + -IC]
Ichabŏd (ĭ'k-) *n.* (As excl. of regret =) the glory has departed. [Heb.; see 1 Sam. 4:21]
||**I.Chem.E.** *abbr.* Institution of Chemical Engineers.
i' chĭng (ē'ch-) *n.* Ancient Chinese fortune-telling game based on 8 groups of three lines and 64 groups of six lines. [Chin., = book of changes]
ĭchneu'mon (ĭk-) *n.* **1.** Mongoose of N. Africa etc., noted for destroying crocodiles' eggs. **2.** **~(-fly)**, small hymenopterous insect depositing eggs in or on larva of another insect as food for its own larva. [L, f. Gk *ikhneumōn* spider-hunting wasp (*ikhneuō* trace f. *ikhnos* footstep)]
ĭchnŏ'graphў (ĭk-) *n.* (Drawing of) ground-plan of building, map of region, etc. [f. F *ichnographie* or f. L f. Gk *ikhnographia* (*ikhnos* track; see -GRAPHY)]
ī'chŏr (ī'k-) *n.* (Gk Myth.) fluid flowing like blood in veins of gods; (poet.) bloodlike fluid; (Path.) watery fetid discharge from wound etc.; hence **~ous** (ī'ker-) *a.* [f. Gk *ikhōr*]
ĭ'chthўo- (ĭk-) *comb. form.* Fish, as: **~grapher,**

~graphy, (-ŏ'g-), writer on, description of, fishes; ~latry (-ŏ'l-), worship of a fish-god; ~lite, fossil fish; ~logy (-ŏ'l-), study of fishes, whence ~lo'gical, ~logist (-ŏ'l-); ~phagous *a.*, ~phagy *n.*, (-ŏ'f-), fish-eating. [f. Gk *ikhthus* fish + -o-]

ĭ'chthȳoid (ĭ'k-) *a.* & *n.* **1.** *a.* Fishlike. **2.** *n.* Vertebrate of fish type. [f. as prec. + -OID]

ĭchthȳosaur'us, ĭ'chthȳosaur, (ĭk-) *n.* Extinct marine animal of order Ichthyosauria, with large head, tapering body, four paddles, and long tail. [f. ICHTHYO- + Gk *sauros* lizard]

ĭchthȳ|ō'sĭs (ĭk-) *n.* (*pl.* **~oses** *pr.* -ō'sēz). Disease in which epidermis becomes dry and horny; hence ~o'TIC *a.* [f. Gk *ikhthus* fish + -OSIS]

I.C.I. *abbr.* Imperial Chemical Industries.

-ĭ'cian (ĭ'shan) *suf.* forming *ns.* denoting persons skilled in or concerned with subjects having names (usu.) in -IC or -ICS (*logician, magician, physician* f. PHYSIC, *politician, statistician*; *mortician, academician*). [f. or after F *-icien* (as -IC, -IAN)]

ī'cĭcle *n.* Tapering hanging ice-formation, produced by freezing of successive drops trickling from the point of attachment. [ME, f. ICE¹ + (now dial.) *ickle* icicle (= OE *gicel*, ON *jökull* f. Gmc **jakilaz*)]

ī'cĭng *n.* In vbl senses; sugar etc. coating of cake etc.; formation of ice on aircraft; ||~ **sugar** (finely powdered, for icing cakes etc.). [f. ICE² + -ING¹]

-ĭcĭst *suf.* = -ICIAN (*classicist, physicist* f. PHYSICS, *publicist, romanticist*). [f. -IC + -IST]

-ĭ'cĭtȳ *suf.* forming abstract *ns.* esp. f. *adjs.* in -IC (*authenticity, catholicity, electricity, publicity, toxicity*). [f. -IC + -ITY]

-ĭck. See -IC.

-ĭcle. See -CULE.

ī'con, ī'kon, *n.* Image, statue; (Orthodox Ch.) painting, mosaic, etc., of sacred personage, itself regarded as sacred. [L, f. Gk *eikōn* image]

īcŏ'nĭc *a.* Of (the nature of) an image or portrait; (of statue) following a conventional type. [f. L f. Gk *eikonikos* (as prec.; see -IC)]

īcŏ'noclăsm *n.* Breaking of images (lit. or fig.; cf. foll.). [f. foll. after *enthusiasm* etc.]

īcŏ'noclăst *n.* Breaker of images, esp. one who took part in movement in 8th–9th c. against use of images in religious worship in churches of the East, or Puritan of 16th–17th c.; (fig.) one who attacks cherished beliefs; hence ~IC (-ă's-) *a.* [f. med. L f. eccl. Gk *eikonoklastēs* (*eikōn* image, *klaō* break)]

īconŏ'graph|ȳ *n.* Illustration of subject by drawings or figures; book whose essence is pictures; treatise on pictures or statuary; study of portraits esp. of an individual; hence ~ER¹ *n.*, **īconogră'ph**ICAL *adjs.* [f. Gk *eikonographia* sketch (*eikōn* image; see -GRAPHY)]

īconŏ'latrȳ *n.* Worship of images; so **īconŏ'**LATER *n.* [f. eccl. Gk *eikonolatreia* (as ICON, -LATRY)]

īconŏ'logȳ *n.* Study of icons; symbolism. [f. as ICON + -O- + -LOGY]

īconŏ'mėter *n.* (Photog.) direct-vision view-finder (either fixed to camera, or detached and adjustable for various lenses and sizes of plate); (Surv.) optical instrument for ascertaining size or distance of an object; so **īconŏ'**METRY *n.* [f. as ICON + -O- + -METER]

īconŏ'stas|ĭs *n.* (*pl.* **~es** *pr.* -ēz). (Orthodox Ch.) Screen bearing icons and separating the sanctuary from the nave. [f. mod. Gk *eikonostasis* (as ICON, STASIS)]

īcosahĕ'dr|on (-*a*-h-) *n.* Solid figure with twenty faces; hence ~AL *a.* [f. LL *icosahedrum* f. Gk *eikosaedron* (*eikosi* twenty; see -HEDRON)]

īcŏsi- *pref.* Twenty, as: **~dodecahe'dron,** solid figure with twenty triangular and twelve pentagonal faces. [f. Gk *eikosi* twenty]

-ĭcs *suf.* forming *ns.* (treated variously as *pl.* or *sing.*) denoting arts or sciences or branches of study or action (*athletics, mathematics, politics, statics, tactics*), occas. w. corresp. form in *-ic* denoting a particular form or instance (*aesthetic, tactic*). [f. or after F pl. *-iques* or f. L pl. *-ica* or Gk pl. *-ika*]

I.C.S. *abbr.* (Hist.) Indian Civil Service.

ĭ'cterus *n.* (Path.) Jaundice; so **ĭctĕ'r**IC *a.* [L, f. Gk *ikteros*]

ĭ'ctus *n.* (Pros.) Rhythmical or metrical stress. [L, = blow (*icere* strike)]

ī'cȳ *a.* Abounding in or covered with ice; very cold (lit., or fig.: *icy manners*); hence **ī'cĭ**LY² *adv.*, **ī'cĭ**NESS *n.* [f. ICE¹ + -Y²]

ĭd *n.* (Psych.) Inherited instinctive impulses of the individual as part of the unconscious. [L, = that, transl. G *es*]

-ĭd¹ *suf.* forming *adjs.* (*arid, fluid, morbid, rapid, timid, vivid*). [f. F *-ide* f. L *-idus*]

-ĭd² *suf.* forming *ns.* (*pyramid*), esp. (Biol.) of structural constituents (*plastid*), in Bot. of plant belonging to family with name in -aceae (*orchid*). [f. or after F *-ide* f. L *-is -idis* f. Gk *-is -ida* or *-idos*]

-ĭd³ *suf.* forming *ns.* denoting: **1.** (Zool.) Animal belonging to family with name in -idae or class with name in -ida (*canid, arachnid*). **2.** Member of person's family (*Seleucid* f. Seleucus). **3.** (Astron.) Meteor in group radiating from a specified constellation (*Leonid* f. Leo); star of class like one in a specified constellation (*cepheid*). [f. or after L *-ides*, pl. *-idae* or *-ida*]

-ĭd⁴ *suf.* (U.S. or arch.) = -IDE.

***ID** *abbr.* identification.

id. *abbr. idem.*

i.d. *abbr.* inner diameter.

I.D.A. *abbr.* International Development Association.

I.D.B. *abbr.* illicit diamond-buying.

īde *n.* Freshwater fish allied to carp. [f. mod. L *idus* f. Sw. *id*]

-īde *suf.* (Chem.) forming *ns.* denoting (1) binary compounds of an element with another element or radical, the suf. *-ide* being added to the name (usu. abbr.) of the more electronegative element etc. (*sodium chloride, potassium cyanide, calcium carbide*), or various other compounds (*amide, anhydride*, , *peptide, saccharide*), (2) elements of a series (*actinide, lanthanide*). [orig. in OXIDE]

īdė'a *n.* **1.** Archetype, pattern, as distinguished from its realization in individuals; (Platonic Philos.) eternally existing pattern of which individual things in any class are imperfect copies. **2.** Conception, plan, of or *of* thing to be aimed at, created, discovered, etc., (**not my ~ of,** (colloq.) something I regard as the opposite of *fun* etc.; **has no ~,** (colloq.) is utterly incompetent); plan of action; **the big ~,** (usu. iron.) the important intention or scheme. **3.** Notion conceived by the mind (**man of ~s,** resourceful person; **get** or **have ~s,** be ambitious, rebellious, etc.; **put ~s into** person's **head,** suggest ambitions etc. he would not otherwise have imagined); way of thinking (**the young ~,** the child's mind); vague belief, fancy, (*the idea of his doing such a thing*; *I had no, had an, idea* (*that*) *you were there, where you were*); **the very ~!, what an ~!,** etc., (colloq.) that is outrageous, quite impracticable, etc.; **that's an ~,** (colloq.) that proposal etc. is worth considering. **4.** (Descartes, Locke) immediate object of thought or mental perception; (Kant) conception of reason transcending all experience; (Hegel) absolute truth of which all phenomenal existence is the expression. **5.** Hence ~'D², ~ED²,

(-ĭ'ad), ~LESS, *adjs.* [ME f. L, f. Gk, = look, form, kind (*id-* see)]

īdē'al *a.* & *n.* **1.** *a.* Answering to one's highest conception, perfect or supremely excellent; embodying an idea; existing only in idea; visionary; relating to or consisting of (Platonic) ideas; **~ gas** (without attraction between its molecules, and so obeying simple laws); hence ~LY² *adv.* **2.** *n.* Perfect type; actual thing as standard for imitation. [ME, f. F *idéal* f. LL *idealis* (as prec.; see -AL)]

īdē'al|ism (*or* -ē'-) *n.* **1.** Representation of things in ideal or idealized form, imaginative treatment, practice of forming or following after ideals, (cf. REALISM). **2.** (Philos.) System of thought in which the object of external perception is held to consist of ideas (cf. REALISM). **3.** So ~IST (3) *n.*, **~ĭ'stic** *a.* [f. F *idéalisme* or G *idealismus* (as prec.; see -ISM)]

īdēă'lĭtў *n.* Quality of being ideal; ideal thing. [f. IDEAL + -ITY]

īdē'aliz|e (*or* -ē'-), **-is|e** (-īz), *v.t.* Represent (thing, person, or abs.) in ideal form or character; exalt to ideal perfection or excellence; hence ~A'TION, ~ER¹, *ns.* [f. IDEAL + -IZE]

ī'dē|āte *v.* **1.** *v.t.* Imagine, conceive. **2.** *v.i.* Form ideas. **3.** Hence ~A'TION *n.* [f. med. L *ideare* form idea (as IDEA) + -ATE³]

idée fixe (ēdāfē'ks) *n.* (*pl.* ***idées fixes*** *pr.* same). Idea that dominates the mind, obsession. [F, lit. 'fixed idea']

idée reçue (ēdāresü') *n.* (*pl.* ***idées reçues*** *pr.* same). Generally accepted notion or opinion. [F]

idem (ī'dĕm) *n.* or *adv.* (In) the same author; the same word. [ME f. L]

īdĕ'ntĭc *a.* **1.** (Diplom.) **~ note,** simultaneous and uniformly worded expression of opinion from several Powers to another. **2.** = foll. [f. med. L *identicus* (cf. IDENTITY)]

īdĕ'ntĭcal *a.* (Of one thing viewed at different times) the very same; (of different things) agreeing in every detail (*with*); (of twins) developed from a single fertilized ovum, therefore of same sex and usu. very similar in appearance; (Logic & Math.) expressing an identity (**~ proposition,** of the type *Man is man*); hence ~LY² *adv.*, ~NESS *n.* [f. as prec. + -AL]

īdĕ'ntĭ|fў *v.* **1.** *v.t.* Treat (thing) as identical (*with*); associate (person, one*self*) inseparably or very closely *with* (party, policy, etc.); establish identity of, recognize; select by consideration (*identify the best method of solution*). **2.** *v.i.* Associate oneself *with*; regard oneself as sharing characteristics *with* (another person). **3.** Hence **~fīABLE** *a.*, ~FICA'TION *n.* (**~fication card, disc, plate, tag,** etc., object worn or carried and bearing name or an assigned number etc.; **~fication parade,** assembly of persons from whom suspect is to be identified). [f. med. L *identificare* (as IDENTITY; see -FY)]

īdĕ'ntĭkĭt *n.* Reconstructed picture of person (esp. sought by police) assembled from features described by witnesses. [f. IDENTITY + KIT¹]

īdĕ'ntĭtў *n.* Absolute sameness; individuality, personality; condition of being a specified person; (Alg.) equality of two expressions for all values of the literal quantities, expression of this, e.g. $(x+1)^2 =$ (*or* $\equiv$) x^2+2x+1; **~ card, parade,** etc. = *identification card* etc. (cf. IDENTIFY). [f. LL *identitas*, f. L *idem* same (see -ITY)]

ĭ'dēo|grăm, ĭ'dēo|graph (-ahf), *ns.* Character symbolizing idea of a thing without expressing the sequence of sounds in its name (e.g. numeral, many Chinese characters); hence ~GRA'PHIC(AL) *adjs.*, ~GRAPHY (-ŏ'g-) *n.* [f. Gk IDEA + -O- + -GRAM, -GRAPH]

ĭ'dēolŏgue (-g) *n.* Theorist, visionary; adherent of an ideology. [f. F *idéologue* f. Gk IDEA + -LOGUE]

ĭdēŏ'log|ў *n.* **1.** (arch.) Science of ideas; visionary speculation. **2.** Manner of thinking characteristic of a class or individual, ideas at the basis of some economic or political theory or system, (*bourgeois, Marxist, ideology*). **3.** Hence **ĭdēolŏ'gical** *a.*, ~IST (1) *n.* [f. F *idéologie* (as prec.; see -LOGY)]

īdes (īdz) *n. pl.* Eighth day after nones in Roman calendar (15th day of March, May, July, October, 13th of other months). [ME f. OF, f. L *idus* pl., perh. f. Etruscan]

id est (ĭd ĕ'st). That is to say. [L (*id* that, *est* is)]

ĭ'dĭocў *n.* Extreme mental imbecility; utter foolishness, idiotic behaviour or action. [ME, f. IDIOT, prob. after *lunacy*]

ĭ'dĭolĕct *n.* Language as used by an individual person. [f. Gk *idios* own + DIALECT]

ĭ'dĭom *n.* Language of a people or country; specific character of this; form of expression peculiar to a language or person, peculiarity of phraseology approved by usage though having meaning not deducible from those of the separate words; characteristic mode of expression in music, art, etc. [f. F *idiome* or f. LL f. Gk *idiōma -matos* private property (*idioomai* make one's own f. *idios* own, private)]

ĭdĭomă't|ĭc *a.* Characteristic of a particular language; relating to or conforming to idiom; hence ~ICALLY *adv.* [f. Gk *idiōmatikos* peculiar (as prec.; see -IC)]

ĭdĭŏ'pathў *n.* (Path.) Disease not preceded or occasioned by another, or by any known cause; hence **ĭdĭopă'thic** *a.* [f. mod. L f. Gk *idiopatheia* (*idios* own; see -PATHY)]

ĭdĭosў'ncrasў *n.* Mental constitution, view or feeling, mode of behaviour, peculiar to a person; mode of expression peculiar to an author; (Med.) physical constitution peculiar to a person; hence **ĭdĭosўncră'tic** *a.* [f. Gk *idiosugkrasia* (*idios* own, *sun* together, *krasis* mixture)]

ĭ'dĭot *n.* Person so deficient in mind as to be permanently incapable of rational conduct; (colloq.) stupid person, utter fool, whence **ĭdĭŏ'tic** *a.*, **ĭdĭŏ'tically** *adv.* [ME f. OF, f. L *idiota* ignorant person f. Gk *idiōtēs* private person, layman, ignorant person (*idios* own, private)]

ī'dle *a.* & *v.* **1.** *a.* (Of action, thought, word) ineffective, worthless, vain; groundless; having no special purpose (*idle talk, curiosity*); useless; not in use, not working, unemployed; (of time etc.) unoccupied; lazy, indolent; **~ wheel,** intermediate wheel between two geared wheels, esp. to allow them to rotate in same direction; hence ~NESS (ī'deln-) *n.*, **ī'dLY²** *adv.* **2.** *v.i.* Be idle; (of engine) revolve slowly without doing work. **3.** *v.t.* Pass (time etc.) *away* in idleness. [OE *idel*, = OS *idal*, OHG *ītal* empty, useless]

ī'dler *n.* In vbl senses; = IDLE *wheel.* [f. prec. + -ER¹]

ī'dlēsse *n.* Idleness. [pseudo-arch. f. IDLE + -ESS²]

Idō (ē'dō) *n.* Artificial universal language based on Esperanto. [Ido, = offspring]

ī'dol *n.* Image of deity used as object of worship; false god; person or thing that is the object of excessive devotion; (arch.) phantom; (Logic) false mental conception (**~s of the tribe, cave, market, theatre,** four classes of fallacies distinguished by Bacon (1620) referable respectively to limitations of human mind, prejudices of idiosyncrasy, influence of words, philosophical and logical prepossessions). [ME, f. OF *idole* f. L f. Gk *eidōlon* phantom (*eidos* form)]

īdŏ'lat|er *n.* Worshipper of idols; devoted admirer (*of*); hence or cogn. ~RESS¹, ~RY¹ (*honour* person **on this side of ~ry,** short of making a god of him), *ns.*, ~ROUS *a.* [ME *idolatrer* f. OF + -ER¹ or f. *idolatry* + -ER¹, or f. OF *idolâtre* f. Rom. **idolatra* f. LL f. Gk *eidōlolatrēs* (as IDOL; see -LATRY)]

ī'doliz|e, -is|e (-īz), *v.* **1.** *v.t.* Make an idol of; venerate or love to excess. **2.** *v.i.* Practise idolatry. **3.** Hence ~A'TION *n.* [f. IDOL + -IZE]

idō'l|um *n.* (*pl.* **~a**). Mental image, idea; (Logic) fallacy (see IDOL). [L (as IDOL)]

ĭ'dўll, ī'dўl, *n.* Short description in verse or (**prose ~**) in prose of picturesque scene or incident, esp. in rustic life; episode suitable for such treatment, freq. a love-story; hence **ĭdў'llIC** *a.*, ~IST (1) *n.*, ~IZE (1) *v.t.* [f. L f. Gk *eidullion* dim. of *eidos* form]

-ĭe *suf.* **1.** = -Y³ (*bookie, dearie, nightie, oldie*), esp. Sc. & Austral. **2.** (arch.) = -Y¹·² (*litanie, prettie*). [earlier form of -Y]

i.e. *abbr.* that is to say. [f. L ID EST]

||**I.E.E.** *abbr.* Institution of Electrical Engineers.

-ier *suf.* forming personal *ns.* denoting occupation etc., (1) unstressed *pr.* -ĭer etc. (*collier, grazier, hosier*; cf. -YER), (2) stressed *pr.* ēr′ (*bombardier, cavalier*). [(1) ME of various orig.; (2) F, f. L *-arius*]

if *conj.* & *n.* **1.** *conj.* On the condition or supposition that, in the case or circumstances such that, (*if you are* (now) *tired we will sit down*; *if you* (hereafter) *see him give him the message*; *if he has found it he will send it*; *if he had fair warning he has nothing to complain of*; *if he had been warned he has* (or *had*) *nothing to complain of*); (w. past tense implying that condition is not fulfilled: *if I were you*; *if I knew what to do I should do it*; *if he had been warned he would have* (or *would have had*) *nothing to complain of*). **2.** Whenever (*if I feel any doubt I inquire*; *if I felt any doubt I inquired*; *if I had been badly treated I complained*). **3.** Whether (*ask, see, try, if you can turn the handle*). **4.** (In excl. of wish, surprise, etc., without apodosis: *if I only knew!*, *if only I knew!*, I wish I knew; *if I haven't lost my watch!*, I have, to my surprise or disgust; so in polite request: *if you wouldn't mind opening the door?*). **5. As if,** as the case would be if (*it seems as if he meant* (colloq. *means*) *business*; *he talks as* (he would) *if he were drunk*; *nodded, as if to say 'But of course'*; *as if you didn't know*, you know quite well). **6.** (With reduction of protasis to significant word: **if any, if anything, if not, if so,** = if there are any, if it is (not) so, etc.; **if only because, if only to,** even if for no other reason than that, than to). **7.** *n.* Condition, supposition, (*too many ifs about it*); hence **ĭ'ffISH**¹, **ĭ'ffY**², *adjs.*, uncertain. [OE *gif*, = OS *ef* (*of*), OHG *ibu, oba*, ON *ef*, Goth. *ibai*]

I.F. *abbr.* intermediate frequency.

I.F.C. *abbr.* International Finance Corporation.

||**I. Gas E.** *abbr.* Institution of Gas Engineers.

Igbo. Var. of IBO.

ĭ'glōō *n.* Eskimo dome-shaped hut, esp. one built of snow. [Eskimo, = house]

ĭ'gnėous *a.* Of fire, fiery; (Geol.) produced by volcanic or magmatic agency. [f. L *igneus* (*ignis* fire) + -OUS]

ĭgnĭs fă'tūus *n.* (*pl.* **ignes fatui** *pr.* -ēz -ūī). Will-o'-the-wisp. [mod. L, = foolish fire, f. its erratic movement]

ĭgnī't|e *v.* **1.** *v.t.* Set fire to, cause to burn; (Chem.) heat to the point of combustion or chemical change; hence ~ABLE *a.*, ~ER¹ *n.* (esp. for causing electric arc, or combustion in engine cylinder). **2.** *v.i.* Take fire. [f. L *ignire -it-* (*ignis* fire)]

ĭgnĭ'tion *n.* Igniting or being ignited; mechanism for, or act of, starting combustion of mixture in cylinder of internal combustion engine; **~ key** (to operate this mechanism, normally necessary to start engine). [F, or f. med. L *ignitio* (as prec.; see -ION)]

ĭgnī'tron *n.* (Electr.) Mercury-arc rectifier able to carry large currents. [f. IGNITE + -TRON]

ĭgnō'b|le *a.* Of low birth, position, or reputation; mean, base, dishonourable; hence **~le**NESS (-beln-) *n.*, ~LY² *adv.* [F, or f. L *ignobilis* (as IN-², (*g*)*nobilis* noble)]

ĭgnomĭ'nĭous *a.* Causing or deserving ignominy; humiliating; hence ~LY² *adv.* [ME, f. F *ignominieux* or f. L *ignominiosus* (as foll.; see -OUS)]

ĭ'gnomĭnў *n.* Dishonour, infamy; (arch.) infamous conduct. [f. F *ignominie* or L *ignominia* (as IN-², (**g*)*nomen* name); see -Y¹]

ĭgnorā'mus *n.* Ignorant person. [L, = we do not know, (Law, of grand jury) we take no notice of (bill or indictment); mod. sense perh. f. character in Ruggle's 'Ignoramus' (1615) exposing lawyers' ignorance]

ĭ'gnorance *n.* Lack of knowledge (*of* thing, or in general). [ME f. OF, f. L *ignorantia* (as foll.; see -ANCE)]

ĭ'gnorant *a.* Lacking knowledge; behaving in uncouth manner through lack of knowledge; uninformed (*of* or *in* subject, *of* fact); hence ~LY² *adv.* [ME f. OF, f. L (as IGNORE; see -ANT)]

ignoratio elenchi (ĭgnerāshĭō ĭlĕ'ngkī) *n.* (Logic). Argument that appears to refute opponent while actually disproving something not asserted by him. [med. L, transl. Gk *hē tou elegkhou agnoia*, = ignorance of conditions for valid proof]

ĭgnôr'e *v.t.* Refuse to take notice of or accept; intentionally disregard. [f. F *ignorer* or f. L *ignorare* not know, ignore (as IN-², *gno-* know)]

ignotum per ignotius (ĭgnōtum pêr ĭgnō'tĭus) *n.* Explanation obscurer than the thing it is meant to explain. [L, = the unknown by the still less known]

igua'na (ĭgwah'-) *n.* Large W. Ind. and S. Amer. arboreal lizard of family Iguanidae. [Sp., f. Carib *iwana*]

ĭguă'nodŏn (ĭgw-) *n.* Large extinct herbivorous dinosaur. [f. (resemblance to) prec., after *mastodon* etc.]

i.h.p. *abbr.* indicated horsepower.

IHS *abbr.* Jesus. [ME f. LL, repr. Gk *ΙΗΣ* = *Iēs*(*ous*) Jesus; often taken as abbr. of various L wds]

ĭkėba'na (-ah'nah) *n.* Art of Japanese flower arrangement, with formal display acc. to strict rules. [Jap., = living flowers]

ī'kon. See ICON.

ĭl-¹·² *prefs.*, assim. forms of IN-¹·² before *l*.

-ĭl, -ĭle, *suf.* forming *adjs.* or *ns.* denoting relation or capability (*civil, fossil, utensil*; *agile, erectile, fragile, quartile, sessile, versatile*). [OF, f. L *-ilis*]

||**I.L.** *abbr.* Institute of Linguists.

ilang-ilang. Var. of YLANG-YLANG.

||**I.L.E.A.** *abbr.* Inner London Education Authority.

ĭ'lė|um *n.* (*pl.* **~a**). (Anat.) Third and last portion of small intestine; hence ~AL *a.*, ~Ī'TIS *n.* [var. of ILIUM, confused w. foll.]

ĭ'lėus *n.* (Path.) Painful obstruction of intestine, esp. of ileum. [L, f. Gk (*e*)*ileos* colic]

ī'lĕx *n.* Holm-oak; tree or shrub of genus *Ilex*, including common holly. [ME f. L]

ĭ'lĭăc *a.* Of the flank or ilium (*iliac artery*); **~ passion,** (arch.) ileus. [f. LL *iliacus*, in form f. L *ilia* flanks (see -AC), in first sense f. L ILEUS]

I'lĭad (ĭ'-) *n.* Long story esp. *of woes* etc.; story of martial feats. [title of epic poem attributed to Homer and describing climax of siege of Troy, f. L f. Gk *Ilias -ados* (*poiēsis*) (poem) of *Ilion* Ilium = Troy]

ĭ'lĭ|um *n.* (*pl.* **~a**). Bone forming upper part of

each half of human pelvis; corresponding bone in animals. [ME f. L]

ĭlk *a.* **1.** (Sc.) **Of that ~**, of the same (*Guthrie of that ~*, Guthrie of Guthrie). **2.** (colloq.) (*That, his, the same*, etc.) ~, family, class, or set. [OE *ilca* same (**i-* that, the same, **lĭk-* (cf. LIKE[1], -LY[1])]

ĭll *a.*, *n.*, & *adv.*, (WORSE, WORST). **1.** *a.* Out of health, sick, (usu. *pred.*: *he is ill*, *was taken ill*, *fell ill*, *of* or *with* disease, *with anxiety* etc.; *mentally ill people*); (of health) unsound, disordered. **2.** Morally bad (*ill* FAME[1]); hostile, unkind, (**~ blood, ~ feeling, ~ will,** animosity, strife; **~ nature,** churlishness; **~ humour, temper,** moroseness, irritability). **3.** Harmful (*ill effects*); **do an ~ turn to** person, harm him or his interests. **4.** Wretched, disastrous, (*ill fortune*, *ill luck*; **it's an ~ wind that blows nobody good,** most happenings benefit someone). **5.** (arch.) Difficult (*ill to please*). **6.** Faulty, unskilful, (*ill taste, management*); (of manners or conduct) improper; **with an ~ grace,** sullenly; **~ success,** partial or complete failure. **7.** *n.* Evil, the opposite of good; harm, injury; **speak ~** (something unfavourable) **of;** (in *pl.*) misfortunes, causes of harm. **8.** *adv.* Badly, wrongly, (*behaved ill*; TAKE[1] thing *ill*); unfavourably (*it would have gone ill with him*); imperfectly, scarcely, (*ill provided*; *it ill became him to speak*; *can ill afford to do this*); **~ at ease,** embarrassed, uneasy. **9. ~-advi'sed(ly** *pr.* -ĭdlĭ), imprudent(ly); **~-affected,** not well disposed *towards*; *ill*-ASSORTED; **~-behaved,** having bad manners or conduct; **~-bred,** badly brought up, rude; **~ breeding,** bad manners; **~-condi'tioned,** (1) of evil disposition, (2) in bad condition; **~-defined,** not clearly defined; **~-disposed,** (1) disposed to evil, malevolent, (2) unfavourably disposed (*towards*); **~-fa'ted,** destined to, or bringing, bad fortune; **~-favoured,** unattractive, displeasing, objectionable; *ill*-FOUND[1]*ed*; **~-gotten,** gained by evil or unlawful means; **~-hu'moured,** bad-tempered; **~-ju'dged,** unwise; **~-ma'nnered,** having bad manners, rude; **~-na'tured(ly),** churlish(ly); **~-o'mened,** attended by bad omens; **~-starred,** born under an evil star, unlucky; **~-te'mpered,** morose, peevish, irritable; **~-ti'med,** done or occurring at an inappropriate time; **~-trea't, -u'se,** treat badly; so **~-trea'tment, ~-u'se,** *ns.*; **~-wisher,** person who wishes evil to another. [ME, f. ON *illr*, of unkn. orig.]

Ill. *abbr.* Illinois.

ĭllā'tion *n.* Deduction, conclusion; thing deduced. [f. L *illatio* (*illatus* p.p. of *inferre* INFER; see -ATION)]

ĭllā'tĭve (*or* ĭ'la-) *a.* (Of word) stating or introducing an inference; inferential; (Gram., of case) denoting motion into; hence ~LY[2] (-vlĭ) *adv.* [f. L *illativus* (as prec.; see -IVE)]

ĭllē'gal *a.* Not legal; contrary to law; hence or cogn. **ĭllėgă'l**ITY *n.*, ~LY[2] *adv.* [f. F *illégal* or f. med. L IL[2](*legalis* LEGAL)]

ĭllĕ'g|ĭble *a.* Not legible; hence ~IBI'LITY *n.*, **~ĭb**LY[2] *adv.* [f. IL-[2] + LEGIBLE]

ĭllėgĭ'tĭm|ate[1] *a.* & *n.* **1.** *a.* Not authorized by law; improper; not recognized as lawful offspring, bastard; wrongly inferred; naturally abnormal; hence ~ACY *n.*, **~ate**LY[2] (-tlĭ) *adv.* **2.** *n.* One whose position is illegitimate, esp. bastard. [f. LL *illegitimus*, after LEGITIMATE[1]; see IL-[2]]

ĭllėgĭ'tĭm|āte[2] *v.t.* Declare illegitimate; hence ~A'TION *n.* [f. prec.]

ĭllĭ'beral *a.* Without liberal culture, unscholarly; vulgar, sordid; narrow-minded, bigoted; not generous, stingy; hence or cogn. ~ITY (-ă'l-) *n.*, ~LY[2] *adv.* [f. F *illibéral* f. IL[2](*liberalis* LIBERAL) mean, sordid]

ĭllĭ'cĭt *a.* Unlawful, forbidden, (*illicit dealings, intercourse, still*); hence ~LY[2] *adv.* [f. F *illicite* or f. L IL[2](*licitus* LICIT)]

ĭllĭ'mĭt|able *a.* Limitless; hence ~ABI'LITY, **~able**NESS (-beln-), *ns.*, **~ab**LY[2] *adv.* [f. LL *illimitatus* f. as IL-[2] + L *limitatus* p.p. of *limitare* LIMIT[2]; see -ABLE]

ĭllĭ'quĭd *a.* (Of assets) not easily converted into cash; hence ~ITY (-ĭ'd-) *n.* [f. IL-[2] + LIQUID, or f. med. L **illiquidus*]

ĭllĭ'ter|ate *a.* & *n.* **1.** *a.* Uneducated, esp. unable to read; hence ~ACY, **~ate**NESS (-tn-), *ns.*, **~ate**LY[2] (-tlĭ) *adv.* **2.** *n.* Illiterate person. [f. L IL[2](*litteratus* LITERATE)]

ĭ'llnėss *n.* Unhealthy condition of body, state of being ill. [f. ILL + -NESS]

ĭllŏ'gĭcal *a.* Devoid of or contrary to logic; hence ~ITY (-ă'l-) *n.*, ~LY[2] *adv.* [f. IL-[2] + LOGICAL]

ĭllū'de (*or* -ōō'd) *v.t.* (literary). Trick, deceive. [ME, = mock, f. L (as ILLUSION)]

ĭllū'me (*or* -ōō'm) *v.t.* (poet.) Light up, make bright, (lit. or fig.). [shortening of ILLUMINE]

ĭllu'mĭn|āte (-ōō'-) *v.t.* **1.** Light up, make bright; hence ~ANT *a.* & *n.* **2.** Give spiritual or intellectual light to; help to explain (subject); shed lustre upon. **3.** Decorate (buildings etc.) profusely with lights as sign of festivity; decorate (initial letter in manuscript etc.) with gold, silver, and brilliant colours. **4.** So ~A'TION, **~āt**OR, *ns.*, **~at**IVE *a.* [f. L IL[1](*luminare* f. *lumen luminis* light) + -ATE[3]]

ĭllumĭn|a'tĭ (-ōōmĭnah'-) *n. pl.* **1.** (*I~*). Secret society founded by Weishaupt in Bavaria in 1776, holding deistic and republican principles, and organized like Freemasons. **2.** Persons claiming to possess special enlightenment. **3.** So ~ISM (3), ~IST (2), (-ōō'-) *ns.* [pl. of L *illuminatus* or It. *illuminato* p.p. (as prec.)]

ĭllū'mĭne (*or* -ōō'-) *v.t.* (literary). Light up, make bright; enlighten spiritually. [ME, f. OF *illuminer* f. L (as ILLUMINATE)]

ĭllū'sion (-zhon; *or* -lōō'-) *n.* Deception, delusion; (instance of) sense-perception of an external object involving a false belief as to its nature; misapprehension of true state of affairs; transparent kind of tulle; hence ~AL *a.* [ME, f. F f. L *illusio -onis* f. IL[1](*ludere lus-* play) mock; see -ION]

ĭllū'sion|ist (-zhon-; *or* -lōō'-) *n.* **1.** One who disbelieves in objective existence; so ~ISM (3) *n.* **2.** One who produces illusions, esp. conjurer. [f. prec. + -IST]

ĭllū'sĭve (*or* -lōō'-) *a.* = foll. [f. med. L *illusivus* (as ILLUSION; see -IVE)]

ĭllū'sor|ȳ (*or* -lōō'-) *a.* Deceptive (esp. as regards value or content); having the character of an illusion; hence **~ĭ**LY[2] *adv.*, **~ĭ**NESS *n.* [f. eccl. L *illusorius* (as ILLUSION; see -ORY)]

ĭ'llustrāt|e *v.t.* Make clear, explain; make clear by examples; serve as example of; elucidate (description etc.) by drawings or pictures; ornament (book, newspaper, etc.) thus; hence ~OR *n.* [f. L IL[1](*lustrare* light up) + -ATE[3]]

ĭllustrā'tion *n.* Illustrating; example serving to elucidate; drawing or picture illustrating book, article in newspaper, etc. [ME f. OF, f. L *illustratio -onis* (as prec.; see -ATION)]

ĭ'llustratĭve *a.* Serving as explanation or example (*of*); hence ~LY[2] (-vlĭ) *adv.* [f. ILLUSTRATE + -IVE]

ĭllŭ'strĭous *a.* Distinguished, renowned; hence ~LY[2] *adv.*, ~NESS *n.* [f. L IL[1](*lustris*; cf. ILLUSTRATE) + -OUS]

Illȳ'rĭan (ĭ-) *a.* & *n.* (Native, inhabitant, or language) of Illyria; (of) language-group represented by modern Albanian. [f. L *Illyrius* (*Illyria* on Balkan coast of Adriatic) f. Gk *Illurios*, + -AN]

I.L.O. *abbr.* International Labour Organisation.

||**I.L.P.** *abbr.* Independent Labour Party.
-ĭlȳ *suf.* forming *advs.* corresp. to *adjs.* in -Y^2 etc.; cf. -LY^2.
ĭm-^{1,2} *prefs.*, assim. forms of IN-^{1,2} before *b*, *m*, *p*.
I.M. *abbr.* intramuscular.
ĭ'mage^1 *n.* **1.** Artificial imitation of the external form of an object, e.g. statue (esp. of saint etc. as object of veneration). **2.** Optical appearance or counterpart produced by light or other radiation from object reflected in mirror, refracted through lens, etc. **3.** Form, semblance; counterpart as regards appearance (*he is the image of his father*); typical example. **4.** Simile, metaphor; mental representation; idea, conception; character of thing or person as perceived by the public. **5.** Hence ~LESS (-ĭjl-) *a.* [ME f. OF, f. L *imago -ginis*, cogn. w. IMITATE]
ĭ'mage^2 *v.t.* Make an image of, portray; reflect, mirror; picture (thing *to* one*self*); describe vividly; typify; hence ~ABLE (-ja-) *a.* [ME, f. prec.]
ĭ'magerȳ (-ĭj-; *or* -jrĭ) *n.* Images collectively; statuary, carving; mental images collectively; ornate figurative illustration, esp. as used by author for particular effect. [ME, f. OF *imagerie* (as IMAGE^1; see -ERY)]
ĭmă'gĭnab|le *a.* That can be imagined (*the greatest difficulty imaginable*; *took all the trouble imaginable*); hence ~LY^2 *adv.* [ME, f. LL *imaginabilis* (as IMAGINE; see -ABLE)]
ĭmă'gĭnal *a.* Of image(s); (Entom.) of an imago. [f. L (as IMAGE^1) + -AL]
ĭmă'gĭnar|ȳ *a.* Existing only in imagination; (Math.) being the square root of a negative quantity, and plotted graphically in a direction usu. perpendicular to the axis of REAL^2 quantities; hence ~ĭLY^2 *adv.* [ME, f. L *imaginarius* (as prec.; see -ARY^1)]
ĭmăgĭnā'tion *n.* Imagining; mental faculty forming images or concepts of external objects not present to the senses; fancy; creative faculty of the mind. [ME f. OF, f. L *imaginatio -onis* (as IMAGINE; see -ATION)]
ĭmă'gĭnatĭve *a.* Of, given to using, having or showing in a high degree, the faculty of imagination; hence ~LY^2 (-vlĭ) *adv.*, ~NESS (-vn-) *n.* [ME, f. OF *imaginatif -ive* f. med. L *imaginativus* (as foll.; see -ATIVE)]
ĭmă'gĭne *v.t.* Form mental image or concept of, picture to oneself (something non-existent or not present to the senses); think, conceive, (thing, thing or person *to* be or do, *that* it is, *how*, *what*, etc.); guess (*cannot imagine what he is doing all this time*); suppose, be of opinion, (*that*); take into one's head (idea, *that*); (in *imper.* as excl. of surprise) *imagine* (*that*)*!*. [ME, f. OF *imaginer* f. L *imaginari* (as IMAGE^1)]
ĭ'mag|ist *n.* One of a group of early 20th-c. poets who, in revolt against romanticism, sought clarity of expression through the use of precise images; so ~ISM (3) *n.* [f. IMAGE^1 + -IST]
ĭmā'gō *n.* (*pl.* **ima'gines** *pr.* -jĭnēz, *or* ~s). Final and perfect stage of insect after all metamorphoses, e.g. butterfly; (Psych.) idealized mental picture of oneself or another person, esp. parent. [mod. L sense of *imago* IMAGE^1]
ĭma'm (-ah'm) *n.* Leader of prayers in mosque; title of various Muslim leaders, esp. of one succeeding Muhammad as leader of Islam; hence ~ATE^1 *n.* [f. Arab. *'imām* leader (*'amma* precede)]
||**I.Mar.E.** *abbr.* Institute of Marine Engineers.
ĭmbă'lance *n.* Lack of balance; disproportion. [f. IM-^{2} + BALANCE^1]
ĭ'mbècĭle (*or* -ēl) *a.* & *n.* **1.** *a.* Mentally weak, stupid, idiotic; (arch.) physically weak; hence or cogn. ~LY^2 (-l-lĭ) *adv.*, **ĭmbèci'lIC** *a.*, **ĭmbèci'lITY** *n.* **2.** *n.* Person of weak intellect, esp. adult with intelligence equal to that of average child of about 5; stupid person. [f. F *imbécille* f. L *imbecillus* (as IM-^{2}, **becillum* f. *baculum* stick, orig. in sense 'without supporting staff')]
ĭmbĕ'd. See EMBED.
ĭmbī'be *v.t.* Absorb, assimilate, (ideas etc.); drink (liquid, or abs. esp. of drinking alcoholic liquor); inhale (air etc.); absorb (moisture etc.); so **ĭmbĭbĭ'TION** *n.* [ME, f. L IM^1(*bibere* drink)]
ĭ'mbrĭc|āte^1 *v.t.* & *i.* Arrange (leaves, scales of fish, etc.), be arranged, so as to overlap like tiles; hence ~A'TION *n.* [f. L *imbricare* cover with rain-tiles (*imbrex -icis* rain-tile f. *imber* shower) + -ATE^3]
ĭ'mbrĭcate^2 *a.* Having scales etc. arranged to overlap like tiles. [f. L *imbricatus* p.p. (as prec.; see -ATE^2)]
ĭmbrō'gliō (-ō'lyō) *n.* (*pl.* ~s). Confused heap; confused or complicated (esp. political or dramatic) situation. [It. (*imbrogliare* confuse f. as EMBROIL)]
ĭmbrue' (-ōō') *v.t.* Stain (one's hand, sword, etc., *in* or *with* blood, slaughter, etc.). [f. OF *embr(o)uer* bedabble (*em-* IM-^{1}, *breu* f. Rom. **brodum* f. Gmc **brotham*; see BROTH)]
ĭmbru'te (-ōō't) *v.t.* Brutalize. [f. IM-^{1} + BRUTE]
ĭmbūe' *v.t.* Saturate (*with*); dye (*with*); permeate, inspire, (*with* feelings etc.); = IMBRUE. [orig. as p.p., f. F *imbu* or f. L *imbutus* (*imbuere* moisten)]
IMCO *abbr.* Intergovernmental Maritime Consultative Organization.
||**I.Mech.E.** *abbr.* Institution of Mechanical Engineers.
I.M.F. *abbr.* International Monetary Fund.
ĭ'mīde *n.* (Chem.) Compound formed from ammonia by replacing two hydrogen atoms by metal or acid radical. [orig. F; arbitr. alt. of AMIDE]
||**I.Min.E.** *abbr.* Institution of Mining Engineers.
ĭ'mĭt|āte *v.t.* Follow example of, copy action(s) of, mimic; make copy of, reproduce; be (consciously or not) like; so ~ABLE *a.*, ~**āt**OR *n.* [f. L *imitari* (cogn. w. *imago* IMAGE^1) + -ATE^3]
ĭmĭtā'tion *n.* **1.** Imitating (*imitation is the sincerest flattery*) or being imitated. **2.** Copy; counterfeit (often *attrib.*: *imitation gold, leather*). **3.** (Mus.) Repetition of melody etc., usu. at different pitch, in another part or voice. [F, or f. L *imitatio* (as prec.; see -ATION)]
ĭ'mĭtatĭve (*or* -āt-) *a.* Imitating, following model or example (*of*); counterfeit; ~ **arts,** painting and sculpture; ~ **word,** one that reproduces a natural sound (e.g. *fizz*) or whose sound is thought to correspond to appearances etc. of object or action described (e.g. BLOB, JAG^{1,2}, JAM^1, JERK^{1,2}); hence ~LY^2 (-vlĭ) *adv.*, ~NESS (-vn-) *n.* [f. LL *imitativus* (as IMITATE; see -ATIVE)]
||**I.M.M.** *abbr.* Institution of Mining and Metallurgy.
ĭmmă'cūlate *a.* Pure, spotless, perfectly clean; free from fault (usu. neg. or iron.); (Biol.) not spotted; **I~ Conception** (of Virgin Mary, as conceived and remaining free from taint of original sin); hence **ĭmmă'cūl**ACY, ~NESS (-tn-), *ns.*, ~LY^2 (-tlĭ) *adv.* [ME, f. L IM^2(*maculatus* f. *macula* spot); see -ATE^2]
ĭ'mmanent *a.* Indwelling, inherent, (*in*); (of God) permanently pervading the universe (opp. *transcendent*), whence ~ISM (3), ~IST (2), *ns.*; hence **ĭ'mman**ENCE, **ĭ'mman**ENCY, *ns.* [f. LL IM^1(*manēre* remain); see -ENT]
ĭmmatēr'ial *a.* Not material, incorporeal; of no essential consequence, unimportant; hence ~ITY

For other words in *im-* see IM-^{1} or (esp.) IM-^{2}.

(-ă'l-) *n.*, ~IZE (3) *v.t.* [ME, f. LL IM²(*materialis* MATERIAL)]

ĭmmatēr'ĭal|ĭsm *n.* Doctrine that matter does not exist in itself apart from perception; so ~IST (2) *n.* [f. prec. + -ISM]

ĭmmatūr'|e (*or* ĭ'-) *a.* Not mature; unripe; so ~ITY *n.* [f. L IM²(*maturus* MATURE¹)]

ĭmmea'sur|able (-mĕ'zher-) *a.* Not measurable, immense; hence ~ABI'LITY, ~**able**NESS (-beln-), *ns.*, ~**ab**LY² *adv.* [ME, f. IM-² + MEASURABLE]

ĭmmē'dĭate *a.* **1.** (Of person or thing in its relation to another) not separated by any intervening medium; (of relation or action) direct, without intervening medium; ~ **inference** (drawn from single premiss, without intervention of middle term); ~ **knowledge** (gained without reasoning). **2.** Nearest, next, (*the immediate vicinity, future; my immediate family, neighbour, predecessor*); ~ **constituent,** (Ling.) any of the main grammatical or morphological subdivisions of a sentence, phrase, or word. **3.** Occurring at once, without delay, (*an immediate reply*). **4.** Hence **ĭmmē'dĭ**ACY, ~NESS (-tn-), *ns.*, ~LY² (-tlĭ) *adv.* & (colloq.) *conj.* (cf. DIRECTLY). [ME, f. F *immédiat* or f. LL IM²-(*mediatus* MEDIATE¹)]

ĭmmėmōr'ĭal *a.* Ancient beyond memory or record (*from* TIME¹ *immemorial*); very old; hence ~LY² *adv.* [f. med. L IM²(*memorialis* MEMORIAL)]

ĭmmĕ'nse *a.* So great as to be unmeasured, huge; (colloq.) great (*made an immense difference*); (sl.) very good; hence or cogn. ~NESS (-sn-), **ĭmmĕ'ns**ITY, *ns.* [ME f. F, f. L IM²(*mensus* p.p. of *metiri* measure) immeasurable]

ĭmmĕ'nselȳ (-slĭ) *adv.* In an immense degree; (colloq.) very much (*enjoyed myself immensely*). [f. prec. + -LY²]

ĭmmēr'se *v.t.* Dip, plunge, (*in* liquid); cause (person) to be entirely below surface of water, esp. baptize thus; bury, embed, (*in*); involve deeply, absorb, (*in* debt, difficulties, thought, etc.). [f. L IM¹(*mergere mers-* dip)]

ĭmmēr'sion (-shon) *n.* Immersing or being immersed; baptism by plunging whole person in water; (fig.) absorption (*in* thought etc.); (Astron.) disappearance of celestial body behind another or in its shadow; ~ **heater,** electric heater designed for direct immersion in a liquid to be heated, esp. as fixture in hot-water tank. [ME, f. LL *immersio* (as prec.; see -ION)]

ĭ'mmĭgr|āte *v.* **1.** *v.i.* Come as permanent resident (*into* foreign country). **2.** *v.t.* Bring in (person) thus. **3.** Hence or cogn. ~ANT *a.* & *n.*, ~A'TION *n.*, ~**āt**ORY *a.* [f. L IM¹(*migrare* MIGRATE) + -ATE³]

ĭ'mmĭn|ent *a.* (Of event, esp. danger) impending, soon to happen; (arch.) overhanging; hence or cogn. ~ENCE *n.*, ~**ent**LY² *adv.* [f. L IM¹(*minēre*; cf. EMINENT) overhang; see -ENT]

ĭmmĭ'sc|ĭble *a.* That cannot be mixed (*with*); hence ~IBI'LITY *n.*, ~**ĭb**LY² *adv.* [f. LL *immiscibilis* (as IM-², MISCIBLE)]

ĭmmĭ'tĭgab|le *a.* That cannot be mitigated; hence ~LY² *adv.* [f. LL IM²(*mitigabilis*; see MITIGATE, -ABLE)]

ĭmmĭ'xture *n.* Mixing up; being involved (*in*). [f. IM-¹ + MIXTURE]

ĭmmō'bĭle *a.* Immovable; not mobile; motionless; so **ĭmmō'bĭl**ISM *n.*, policy of extreme conservatism, **ĭmmobĭ'l**ITY *n.* [ME f. OF, f. L IM²(*mobilis* MOBILE)]

ĭmmō'bĭlĭz|e, -ĭs|e (-iz), *v.t.* Fix immovably; keep (limb, patient) restricted in movement for healing purposes; restrict free movement of; make (troops, vehicle) incapable of being shifted; withdraw (coins) from circulation to support banknotes; hence ~A'TION *n.* [f. F *immobiliser* (as prec.; see -IZE)]

ĭmmŏ'derate *a.* Excessive, lacking moderation; hence ~LY² (-tlĭ) *adv.* [ME, f. L IM²(*moderatus* MODERATE¹)]

ĭmmŏ'dėst *a.* Having no modesty, forward, impudent; lacking due decency; hence or cogn. ~LY² *adv.*, ~Y¹ *n.* [f. F *immodeste* or f. L IM²-(*modestus* MODEST)]

ĭ'mmol|āte *v.t.* Kill (victim) as sacrifice; (fig.) sacrifice (thing etc. *to* another); so ~A'TION, ~**āt**OR, *ns.* [f. L IM¹*molare* sprinkle with MEAL¹ (*mola*), sacrifice + -ATE³]

ĭmmŏ'ral *a.* Not conforming to, or opposed to, morality; morally evil (esp. in sexual matters); depraved, dissolute; hence or cogn. **ĭmmoră'l**ITY *n.*, ~LY² *adv.* [f. IM-² + MORAL]

ĭmmōr'tal *a.* & *n.* **1.** *a.* Living for ever, not mortal; divine; unfading, incorruptible; that will be famous for all time; *the Immortal* MEMORY; so ~ITY (-ă'l-) *n.*, ~IZE (3) *v.t.*, ~LY² *adv.* **2.** *n.* Immortal being, esp. (in *pl.*) gods of antiquity; person esp. author of enduring fame, (*I*~) member of French Academy; (in *pl.*) royal bodyguard of ancient Persia. [ME, f. L IM²(*mortalis* MORTAL)]

ĭmmōrtĕ'lle *n.* Composite flower of papery texture retaining shape and colour after being dried, esp. helichrysum. [F, fem. of *immortel* = prec.]

ĭmmo'v|able (ĭmōō'-) *a.* & *n.* **1.** *a.* That cannot be moved; motionless; not subject to change (*immovable* FEAST); steadfast, unyielding; emotionless; (Law, of property) consisting of land, houses, etc.; hence ~ABI'LITY, ~**able**NESS (-beln-), *ns.*, ~**ab**LY² *adv.* **2.** *n.* (in *pl.*) Immovable property. [ME, f. IM-² + MOVABLE]

ĭmmū'ne *a.* Having immunity (*from, against, to,* poison, infection, contagion, criticism, etc.); relating to immunity (*immune mechanism*; ~ **body,** antibody). [ME, f. L IM²(*munis* ready for service) exempt from public service or charge; Med. use f. F *immun*]

ĭmmū'nĭtȳ *n.* **1.** (Law). Exemption (*from* taxation, jurisdiction, etc.). **2.** Freedom (*from*); condition of being proof against or exempt from or *from* infection etc.; property by which organisms resist and overcome infection. [ME, f. L *immunitas* (as prec.; see -ITY); Med. use f. F *immunité*]

ĭ'mmūnĭz|e, -ĭs|e (-iz), *v.t.* Render immune (*against* infection etc.); hence ~A'TION *n.* [f. IMMUNE + -IZE]

ĭmmū'nō- *comb. form.* Immunity to infection (*immunochemistry*). [f. IMMUNITY + -O-]

ĭmmūnŏ'log|ȳ *n.* Study of resistance to infection in man and animals; hence **ĭmmūnolŏ'g**IC(AL) *adjs.*, ~IST (3) *n.* [f. as prec. + -LOGY]

ĭmmūr'e *v.t.* Imprison; shut one*self* up; hence ~MENT (-ūr'm-) *n.* [f. F *emmurer* or f. med. L IM¹(*murare* f. *murus* wall)]

ĭmmū't|able *a.* Unchangeable; not subject to variation in different cases; hence ~ABI'LITY *n.*, ~**ab**LY² *adv.* [ME, f. L IM²(*mutabilis* MUTABLE)]

ĭmp¹ *n.* Child of the Devil; little devil; mischievous child; ||(arch.) child. [OE *impa, impe* young shoot, scion, conn. w. foll.]

ĭmp² *v.t.* Add feathers to (wing of falcon) so as to improve its flight; (arch.) enlarge, add by grafting. [OE *impian,* = OHG *impfōn, impitōn* f. Rom. **impotare* f. med. L *impotus* graft f. Gk *emphutos* implanted, p.p. of *emphuō*]

ĭ'mpăct¹ *n.* Striking (*on, against*), collision, (lit. or fig.); (strong) effect, influence; ~ **strength,** ability of a material to resist breaking when struck. [f. L (as IMPINGE)]

ĭmpă'ct² *v.t.* Press or fix firmly (*into, in*); (in *p.p.*, of tooth) wedged between another tooth and jaw, (of fractured bone) with parts pushed together; hence ~ION *n.* [back form. f. *impacted* f. L p.p. (as prec.) + -ED¹]

ĭmpair′ *v.t.* Damage; weaken; so ~MENT *n.* [ME *empeire* f. OF *empeirier* f. Rom. **impejorare* make worse f. as IM-[1] + LL *pejorare* (L *pejor* worse)]

ĭmpă′la (*or* -ah′-) *n.* Small S. Afr. antelope (*Aepyceros melampus*). [Zulu]

ĭmpā′le *v.t.* **1.** Transfix (body etc. *upon* or *with* stake etc., esp. Hist. as form of torture or capital punishment). **2.** (Her.) Combine (two coats of arms) by placing side by side on one shield separated by vertical line down middle. **3.** So ~MENT (-lm-) *n.* [f. F *empaler* or f. med. L IM[1](*palare* f. *palus* stake)]

ĭmpă′lp|able *a.* Imperceptible to the touch; not easily grasped by the mind, intangible; (of powder) very fine, not containing grains that can be felt; hence ~ABI′LITY *n.*, ~**ab**LY[2] *adv.* [F, or f. LL IM[2](*palpabilis* PALPABLE)]

ĭmpă′nel. See EMPANEL.

ĭmpă′radise *v.t.* Bring into state of supreme happiness; enrapture; make a paradise of (place, state). [f. IM-[1] + PARADISE]

ĭmpărisўllă′bĭc *a.* & *n.* (Gram.) (Noun) that has different numbers of syllables in different cases (e.g. L *lapis lapidis*). [f. L *impar* unequal + -I- + SYLLABIC]

ĭmpar′k *v.t.* Enclose (animals) in park; enclose (land) for park. [ME, f. AF *enparker*, OF EM[1](*parquer* f. *parc* PARK[1])]

ĭmpar′t *v.t.* Give share of (thing *to* person etc.); communicate (news etc. *to*); hence ~A′TION, ~MENT, *ns.* [ME, f. OF *impartir* f. L IM[1](*partire* f. *pars* PART[1])]

ĭmpar′tial (-shal) *a.* Not partial, unprejudiced, fair; hence ~ITY (-shĭă′l-) *n.*, ~LY[2] *adv.* [f. IM-[2] + PARTIAL]

ĭmpar′tĭble *a.* (Law, esp. of estate) not divisible. [f. LL IM[2](*partibilis* PARTIBLE)]

ĭmpa′ss|able (-pah′-) *a.* That cannot be traversed; hence ~ABI′LITY, ~**able**NESS (-beln-), *ns.*, ~**ab**LY[2] *adv.* [f. IM-[2] + PASSABLE]

ĭmpa′sse (-ah′s; *or* ă′mpahs) *n.* Blind alley; position from which there is no escape; = DEAD*lock* (2). [F (as IM-[2], *passer* PASS[1])]

ĭmpă′ss|ĭble *a.* Incapable of feeling or emotion; incapable of suffering injury; (Theol.) not subject to suffering; hence ~IBI′LITY, ~**ĭble**NESS (-beln-), *ns.*, ~**ĭb**LY[2] *adv.* [ME f. OF, f. eccl. L IM[2](*passibilis* PASSIBLE)]

ĭmpă′ssion (-shon) *v.t.* (esp. in *p.p.*) Stir the passions of, excite strongly; fill with passion. [f. It. IM[1](*passionare* f. *passione* PASSION[1])]

ĭmpă′ssĭve *a.* **1.** Deficient in or incapable of feeling or emotion; undisturbed by passion, serene. **2.** Without sensation; not subject to suffering. **3.** Hence ~LY[2] (-vlĭ) *adv.*, ~NESS (-vn-), **ĭmpăssĭ′**VITY, *ns.* [f. IM-[2] + PASSIVE]

ĭmpă′stō *n.* (*pl.* ~**s**). Laying on of paint thickly; this style of painting. [It. IM[1](*pastare* f. PASTA)]

ĭmpā′ti|ent (-shent) *a.* Not enduring with composure; (of action) indicating such feeling; intolerant *of*; restlessly desirous (*for* thing, *to* do); hence or cogn. ~ENCE (-shens) *n.*, ~**ent**LY[2] *adv.* [ME f. OF, f. L IM[2](*patiens*; see PATIENT)]

ĭmpaw′n *v.t.* (arch.) Put in pawn; (fig.) pledge, plight. [f. IM-[1] + PAWN[2]]

ĭmpea′ch *v.t.* Call in question, disparage, (character etc.); accuse (person) *of*, charge (*with*); find fault with (thing); accuse of treason or other high crime before competent tribunal; hence or cogn. ~ABLE *a.*, ~MENT *n.* [ME, f. OF *empe(s)cher* impede f. LL IM[1]-(*pedicare* f. *pedica* fetter, f. *pes pedis* foot) entangle]

ĭmpĕ′cc|able *a.* Not liable to sin; (of thing) faultless; hence or cogn. ~ABI′LITY *n.*, ~**ab**LY[2] *adv.*, ~ANCY *n.*, ~ANT *a.* [f. L IM[2](*peccabilis* f. *peccare* sin; see -ABLE)]

ĭmpėcū′nĭ|ous *a.* Having little or no money; hence ~O′SITY *n.* [f. IM-[2] + obs. *pecunious* having money f. L *pecuniosus* (*pecunia* money f. *pecu* cattle; see -OUS)]

ĭmpē′dance *n.* (Electr.) Total effective resistance of electric circuit etc. to alternating current, arising from ohmic resistance and reactance. [f. foll. + -ANCE]

ĭmpē′de *v.t.* Retard by obstructing, hinder. [f. L IM[1](*pedire* f. *pes* foot), lit. shackle the feet of]

ĭmpĕ′dĭment *n.* Hindrance, obstruction; defect in one's speech, e.g. lisp or stammer; hence ~AL (-ĕ′n-) *a.* [ME, f. L *impedimentum* (as prec.; see -MENT)]

ĭmpĕdĭmĕ′nta *n. pl.* Encumbrances; travelling--equipment, esp. of army etc. [L, pl. of *impedimentum* (see prec.)]

ĭmpĕ′l *v.t.* (-ll-). Drive, force, urge by moral action, (person etc. *to* action, *to* do); drive forward, propel; hence ~LENT *a.* & *n.*, ~LER[1] (2) *n.* [ME, f. L IM[1](*pellere puls-* drive)]

ĭmpĕ′nd *v.i.* Hang, be suspended, (*over*); (fig., of danger) hang threateningly (*over*); be about to happen; so ~ENCE, ~ENCY, *ns.*, ~ENT, ~ING[2], *adjs.* [f. L IM[1](*pendēre* hang)]

ĭmpĕ′nėtr|able *a.* That cannot be penetrated; inscrutable, unfathomable; impervious (*to*, *by* ideas etc.); having that property in virtue of which two bodies cannot occupy same place at same time; hence ~ABI′LITY, ~**able**NESS (-beln-), *ns.*, ~**ab**LY[2] *adv.* [ME, f. F *impénétrable* f. L IM[2](*penetrabilis* PENETRABLE)]

ĭmpĕ′nėtrāte *v.t.* Penetrate deeply. [f. IM-[1] + PENETRATE]

ĭmpĕ′nĭt|ent *a.* Not repentant or penitent; hence or cogn. ~ENCE, ~ENCY, *ns.*, ~**ent**LY[2] *adv.* [f. eccl. L IM[2](*paenitens* PENITENT)]

ĭmpĕ′ratĭve *a.* & *n.* **1.** *a.* (Gram., of mood) expressing command (*come here!*); commanding, peremptory; urgent; obligatory; hence ~LY[2] (-vlĭ) *adv.*, ~NESS (-vn-) *n.* **2.** *n.* (Gram.) Imperative mood, whence **ĭmpĕratī′**VAL *a.*; command (CATEGORICAL *imperative*). [f. LL *imperativus* f. IM[1](*perare* = *parare* make ready) command; see -IVE; in Gram. transl. Gk *prostaktikē* (*egklisis* mood)]

ĭmpera′tor (-ah′-) *n.* (Rom. Hist.) Commander (title conferred by salutation of soldiers on victorious general, under the Republic); emperor; so **ĭmpĕrator′**IAL *a.* [L (as prec.; see -OR)]

ĭmpercĕ′pt|ĭble *a.* That cannot be perceived; very slight, gradual, or subtle; hence ~IBI′LITY *n.*, ~**ĭb**LY[2] *adv.* [F, or f. med. L IM[2](*perceptibilis* PERCEPTIBLE)]

ĭmpercĭ′pĭ|ent *a.* Lacking in perception; hence ~ENCE *n.* [f. IM-[2] + PERCIPIENT]

ĭmper′fėct *a.* & *n.* **1.** *a.* Not fully formed or done, incomplete; faulty; (Gram., of tense) denoting (usu. past) action going on but not completed (*he was singing*); *imperfect* RHYME[1]; hence ~LY[2] *adv.* **2.** *n.* Imperfect tense. [ME *imparfit* etc., f. OF *imparfait* f. L *imperfectus* (as IM-[2], PERFECT[1])]

ĭmperfĕ′ction *n.* Incompleteness; faultiness; fault, blemish. [ME f. OF, or f. LL *imperfectio* (as prec.; see -ION)]

ĭmperfĕ′ctĭve *a.* & *n.* (Gram.) **1.** *a.* (Of verb aspect etc.) expressing action without reference to its completion (opp. *perfective*). **2.** *n.* Imperfective aspect or form of verb. [f. IMPERFECT + -IVE]

ĭmper′forate *a.* Not perforated, esp. (Anat.) lacking the normal opening; (of sheet of postage stamps or single stamp) not provided with rows of perforations. [f. IM-[2] + PERFORATE[2]]

ĭmpēr′ĭal *a.* & *n.* **1.** *a.* Of an empire or sovereign state ranking with an empire; (Hist.) of the British Empire (now COMMONWEALTH). **2.** Of an emperor; supreme in authority; majestic, august; magnificent. **3.** (Of weights and measures) used by statute in U.K. (*imperial* GALLON, *acre*, etc.). **4.** Hence ~LY² *adv.* **5.** *n.* Small part of beard left growing beneath lower lip [partly from Napoleon III of France, but found in F 1829, E 1838]; (arch.) trunk for luggage, adapted for roof of coach; size of paper, 762 × 559 or *787 × 584 mm. [ME f. OF, f. L *imperialis* (IMPERIUM; see -AL)]

impēr'ial|ism *n.* Rule of an emperor; (Hist.) extension of British Empire where trade required protection given by imperial rule; (Hist.) union of different parts of British Empire for purposes of warlike defence, internal commerce, etc.; (usu. derog.) (belief in desirability of) acquiring colonies and dependencies; hence **~ĭ'st**IC *a.*, ~IZE (3) *v.t.* [f. prec. + -ISM]

impēr'ialist *n.* Adherent of an emperor, esp. (1600–1800) of German Emperor; advocate of imperial rule; advocate or agent of (esp. British or American) imperialism. [f. IMPERIAL + -IST]

impĕ'rĭl *v.t.* (‖**-ll-**). Bring or put into danger. [f. IM-¹ + PERIL]

impēr'ious *a.* Overbearing, domineering; urgent, imperative; hence ~LY² *adv.*, ~NESS *n.* [f. L *imperiosus* (IMPERIUM; see -OUS)]

impĕ'rĭsh|able *a.* That cannot perish; hence ~ABI'LITY, **~able**NESS (-beln-), *ns.*, **~ab**LY² *adv.* [f. IM-² + PERISHABLE]

imperium (ĭmpēr'ĭum; *or* -ĕ'r-) *n.* Absolute power; empire; ~ ***in imperio,*** supreme authority within jurisdiction of another authority. [L, = command, dominion]

impêr'man|ent *a.* Not permanent; hence ~ENCE, ~ENCY, *ns.* [f. IM-² + PERMANENT]

impêr'mė|able *a.* That cannot be passed through; (Phys.) that does not permit passage of fluids; hence ~ABI'LITY *n.* [f. F *imperméable* or f. LL IM²(*permeabilis* PERMEABLE)]

impermĭ'ssĭble *a.* Not allowable. [f. IM-² + PERMISSIBLE]

imperscrĭ'ptĭble *a.* Not backed by written authority. [f. IM-² + L PER(*scribere script-* write) register; see -IBLE]

impêr'sonal *a.* **1.** (Gram.) ~ **verb** (used only in 3rd person singular without definite subject, e.g. *it rains, methinks*); *impersonal* PRONOUN. **2.** Having no personality; having no personal feeling, reference, or tone. **3.** Hence ~ITY (-ă'l-) *n.*, ~LY² *adv.* [f. LL IM²(*personalis* PERSONAL)]

impêr'son|āte *v.t.* Represent in bodily form, personify; play the part of; pretend to be (another person) for purpose of entertainment or fraud; act (character); hence ~A'TION, **~āt**OR, *ns.* [f. IM-¹ + L *persona* PERSON + -ATE³]

impersŏ'nĭfȳ *v.* (arch.) Personify. [f. IM-¹ + PERSONIFY, after prec.]

impêr'tĭn|ent *a.* **1.** (esp. Law). Irrelevant, intrusive. **2.** Out of place, absurd. **3.** Insolent, saucy, lacking proper respect. **4.** Hence or cogn. ~ENCE *n.*, **~ent**LY² *adv.* [ME f. OF, or f. LL IM²(*pertinens* PERTINENT)]

impertûr'b|able *a.* Not excitable, calm; hence ~ABI'LITY, **~able**NESS (-beln-), *ns.*, **~ab**LY² *adv.* [ME, f. LL IM²(*perturbabilis* f. as PERTURB + -ABLE)]

impêr'vious *a.* Not affording passage (*to* water etc.); (fig.) not responsive *to* (argument etc.); hence ~LY² *adv.*, ~NESS *n.* [f. L IM²(*pervius* PERVIOUS)]

impėtī'gō *n.* (*pl.* **~s**). Contagious acute pustular disease of skin; so **impėtĭ'gĭn**OUS *a.* [ME, f. L *impetigo -ginis* f. IM¹(*petere* seek) assail]

ĭ'mpėtr|āte *v.t.* (Theol.) obtain by request; so ~A'TION *n.*, **~āt**ORY *a.* [f. L IM¹(*petrare* = *patrare* bring to pass) + -ATE³]

impĕ'tūous *a.* Moving violently or rapidly; acting or done with rash or sudden energy; hence or cogn. **impĕtūo'**SITY, ~NESS, *ns.*, ~LY² *adv.* [ME, f. OF *impetueux* f. LL *impetuosus* (as foll.; see -OUS)]

ĭ'mpėtus *n.* Force or energy with which a body moves; (fig.) moving force, impulse. [L, = assault, force, f. IM¹(*petere* seek) assail]

ĭ'mpeyan (-pĭan) *a.* ~ **pheasant,** Indian pheasant of genus *Lophophorus*, with crested head and brilliant plumage. [f. Sir E. *Impey*, Engl. judge d. 1809 and his wife, who sought to naturalize it in England, + -AN]

ĭ'mpĭ *n.* Body of S. Afr. Bantu warriors. [Zulu]

impī'etȳ *n.* Ungodliness; (act etc. showing) lack of dutifulness or reverence. [ME, f. OF *impieté* or f. L IM²(*pietas* f. *pius* PIOUS; see -TY¹)]

impĭ'nge (-nj) *v.i.* & *t.* (Cause to) make impact (*on, upon*); hence ~MENT (-njm-) *n.* [f. L IM¹(*pingere pact-* = *pangere* fix, drive) drive (thing) at]

ĭ'mpious *a.* Not pious; wicked, profane; hence ~LY² *adv.* [f. L IM²(*pius* PIOUS)]

ĭ'mpish *a.* Of or like an imp, mischievous; hence ~LY² *adv.*, ~NESS *n.* [f. IMP¹ + -ISH¹]

implă'c|able *a.* That cannot be appeased, inexorable; hence or cogn. ~ABI'LITY *n.*, **~ab**LY² *adv.* [ME f. F, or f. L IM²(*placabilis* PLACABLE)]

impla'nt¹ (-ah'-) *v.t.* Insert, fix, (*in*); instil (principle, idea, etc., *in* mind etc.); plant; (Biol.) insert (tissue etc.) in a living object; hence ~A'TION *n.* [f. F *implanter* or f. LL IM¹(*plantare* PLANT²) engraft]

ĭ'mplant² (-ah-) *n.* (Biol.) Thing implanted, e.g. piece of tissue or capsule containing radioactive material. [f. prec.]

implau's|ĭble (-z-) *a.* Not plausible; hence or cogn. ~IBI'LITY *n.*, **~ĭb**LY² *adv.* [f. IM-² + PLAUSIBLE]

implea'd *v.t.* (Law). Prosecute or take proceedings against (person); involve in suit. [ME, f. AF *empleder*, OF *empleidier* (as EM-¹, PLEAD)]

implĕ'dge *v.t.* (arch.) Put in pledge, pawn. [f. IM-¹ + PLEDGE¹]

ĭ'mplėment¹ *n.* Tool, instrument, utensil; (in *pl.*) equipment, articles of furniture, dress, etc.; (Sc. Law) full performance. [ME, f. med. L *implementa* pl. f. *implēre* employ f. L IM¹(*plēre plet-* fill); see -MENT]

ĭ'mplėmĕnt² (*or* -mĕ'nt) *v.t.* Complete (contract etc.); fulfil (undertaking); put (decision, plan, etc.) into effect; fill up, supplement; hence ~A'TION *n.* [f. prec.]

implē'tion *n.* (arch.) Filling; fullness. [ME, f. LL *impletio* (as IMPLEMENT¹; see -ION)]

ĭ'mplĭcate¹ *n.* Thing implied. [f. L *implicatus* p.p. of IM¹(*plicare plicat-* or *plicit-* fold); see -ATE¹]

ĭ'mplĭc|āte² *v.t.* Lead to as consequence or inference, whence **~āt**IVE *a.*; show (person) to be concerned (*in* charge, crime, etc.); (in *pass.*) be affected *in* (a thing's operation); (arch.) entwine, entangle. [ME, f. as prec. + -ATE³]

implĭcā'tion *n.* Implicating or implying; what is involved or implied in something else; **by ~**, by what is implied, as a natural inference. [ME, f. L *implicatio* (as IMPLICATE¹; see -ATION)]

implĭ'cĭt *a.* Implied though not plainly expressed; virtually contained (*in*); (Math., of function) not expressed directly in terms of independent variable(s); ~ **faith, obedience,** etc., (not independently reached by the individual, but resting on authority of Church etc., absolute, unquestioning; cf. EXPLICIT); hence ~LY² *adv.*, ~NESS *n.* [f. F *implicite* or f. L *implicitus* (as IMPLICATE¹)]

implō′de *v.i.* & *t.* (Cause to) burst inwards; so **implō′sion** (-zhon) *n.*, **implō′sive** (*or* -z-) *a.* [f. IM-[1] + L *-plodere*, after EXPLODE]

implor′e *v.t.* Beg earnestly for; entreat (person *to* do). [f. F *implorer* or f. L IM[1](*plorare* weep) invoke with tears]

implȳ′ *v.t.* Involve the truth or existence of (thing not expressly asserted; *that*); signify; insinuate, hint; hence **impliėdLY**[2] (*or* -ī′d-) *adv.* [ME, f. OF *emplier* f. L *implicare* (see IMPLICATE[1])]

||**impō′lder** *v.t.* Make a polder of; reclaim from the sea. [f. Du. *inpolderen* (as IN-[1], POLDER)]

impŏ′licy̆ *n.* Bad policy; inexpediency. [f. IM-[2] + POLICY[1], after *impolitic*]

impoli′te *a.* (**-est**). Not courteous; ill-mannered, rude; hence ~LY[2] (-tlĭ) *adv.*, ~NESS (-tn-) *n.* [f. L IM[2](*politus* POLITE)]

impŏ′litic *a.* Not politic; inexpedient; hence ~LY[2] *adv.* [f. IM-[2] + POLITIC]

impŏnderabi′lia *n. pl.* Imponderables. [mod. L, neut. pl. of *imponderabilis* = foll.]

impŏ′nderable *a.* & *n.* **1.** *a.* (Phys.) having no weight; very light; (fig.) that cannot be estimated. **2.** *n.* Imponderable thing (esp. fig., in *pl.*, of qualities, emotions, etc.). [f. IM-[2] + PONDERABLE]

impō′nent *a.* & *n.* (Person) that imposes a duty etc. [f. IMPOSE after *opponent* etc.]

impor′t[1] *v.t.* **1.** Bring, introduce, (thing, esp. goods from another country, *into*); hence ~ABLE *a.*, ~A′TION, ~ER[1], *ns.* **2.** Imply, indicate, signify, (thing, *that*); express, make known, (*that*). **3.** (arch.) Be of consequence to (*it imports us to know*). [ME, f. L IM[1](*portare* carry) bring in, in med. L = imply, be of consequence]

i′mport[2] *n.* **1.** What is implied, meaning; importance. **2.** Importation; (usu. in *pl.*) amount imported; imported article or commodity. [f. prec.]

impor′tance *n.* Being important; weight, significance; personal consequence, dignity. [F, f. med. L *importantia* (as IMPORT[1]; see -ANCE)]

impor′tant *a.* Carrying with it great consequence (*to* person concerned or purpose etc.), weighty, momentous; (of person) having high rank; consequential, pompous; hence ~LY[2] *adv.* [F, f. med. L (as IMPORT[1]; see -ANT)]

impor′tūnate *a.* Persistent, pressing, in solicitation; (of affairs) urgent; hence or cogn. ~LY[2] (-tlĭ) *adv.*, **importū′nity** *n.* [f. L IM[2](*portunus* f. *portus* harbour) inconvenient + -ATE[2]]

importū′ne (*or* -or′-) *v.t.* Solicit pressingly (person, or abs.); solicit for immoral purpose. [f. F *importuner* or f. med. L *importunari* (as prec.)]

impō′s|e (-z) *v.* **1.** *v.t.* (arch.) Place (thing) *upon*. **2.** (Print.) Lay (pages of type) in proper order and secure them in a CHASE[5]. **3.** Lay (tax, duty, charge, obligation, *on* or *upon*); compel compliance with. **4.** Palm off (thing *upon* person); force (one*self*) *on* attention etc. of (person). **5.** *v.i.* Exert influence (*on* person) by impressive character or appearance; hence ~ING[2] *a.* **6.** Practise deception (*on* or *upon*); **~e on** or **upon,** take advantage of (person, esp. willing or good-natured or gullible one). [ME, f. F *imposer* f. L IM[1](*ponere posit-* put) inflict, deceive; see POSE[1]]

imposi′tion (-z-) *n.* Imposing or being imposed; laying on *of hands* (in ordination etc.); impost, tax, duty; piece of deception or imposture or advantage-taking; ||work set as punishment at school. [ME f. OF, or f. L *impositio* (*imponere*; see prec., -ITION)]

impŏ′ss|ible *a.* Not possible, that cannot be done or exist, (*such a thing is impossible*; *it is impossible to alter them*); (loosely) not easy, not convenient, not easily believable; (colloq.) outrageous, intolerable, (*an impossible hat, person*); hence or cogn. ~IBI′LITY *n.*, **~ibLY**[2] *adv.* [ME f. OF, or f. L IM[2](*possibilis* POSSIBLE)]

i′mpōst[1] *n.* Tax, duty, tribute; (sl.) weight carried by racehorse in handicap. [F, f. med. L *impostus, -um* masc. & neut. p.p. (as n.) of *imponere* (see IMPOSE)]

i′mpōst[2] *n.* Upper course of pillar, carrying arch. [f. F *imposte* or f. It. *imposta* fem. p.p. (as n.) of *imporre* f. L *imponere* (see IMPOSE)]

impŏ′st|or *n.* One who assumes a false character or passes himself off as someone else; swindler; hence ~**(o)**ROUS *a.* [f. F *imposteur* f. LL *impos(i)tor* (as IMPOST[1]; see -OR)]

impŏ′st(h)ūme (-tūm) *n.* (arch.) Purulent swelling, abscess, (lit. or fig.). [ME, f. OF *empostume* f. L f. Gk APO(*stēma* f. *sta-* stand) separation into abscess]

impŏ′sture *n.* Fraudulent deception. [F, f. LL *impostura* (as IMPOST[1]; see -URE)]

i′mpot|ent *a.* Powerless; helpless, decrepit; (esp. of male) wholly lacking in sexual power, unable to copulate or reach orgasm or (pop.) to procreate; hence or cogn. ~ENCE, ~ENCY, *ns.*, **~ent**LY[2] *adv.* [ME f. OF, f. L IM[2](*potens* POTENT[1])]

impou′nd *v.t.* Shut up (cattle) in pound; shut up (person, thing) as in pound; take legal possession of; confiscate; (of dam etc.) collect or confine (water). [f. IM-[1] + POUND[2]]

impŏ′verish *v.t.* Make poor; exhaust strength or natural fertility of; hence ~MENT *n.* [ME, f. OF EM[1](*poverir* f. *povre* POOR); see -ISH[2]]

impră′ctic|able *a.* Impossible in practice; (of person or thing) unmanageable; (of road etc.) impassable; hence ~ABI′LITY, **~able**NESS (-beln-), *ns.*, **~ab**LY[2] *adv.* [f. IM-[2] + PRACTICABLE]

***impră′ctical** *a.* Not practical; not practicable; hence ~ITY (-ă′l-) *n.* [f. IM-[2] + PRACTICAL]

i′mprĕc|āte *v.t.* Invoke, call down, (evil *upon* person etc.); so ~A′TION *n.* (esp., spoken curse), **~āt**ORY *a.* [f. L IM[1](*precari* pray) + -ATE[3]]

imprĕci′se *a.* Not precise; hence ~LY[2] (-slĭ) *adv.*, **imprĕci′sion** (-zhon) *n.* [f. IM-[2] + PRECISE]

imprĕ′gn|able[1] *a.* (Of fortress etc.) that cannot be taken by force; (fig.) proof against attack; hence ~ABI′LITY *n.*, **~ab**LY[2] *adv.* [ME f. OF *imprenable* (as IM-[2], *prendre* take, -ABLE)]

imprĕ′gnable[2] *a.* That can be impregnated. [f. IMPREGNATE[2] + -ABLE]

imprĕ′gnate[1] *a.* Pregnant (lit. or fig.); permeated (*with*). [f. LL *impregnatus* p.p. of IM[1](*pregnare* be PREGNANT); see -ATE[2]]

i′mprĕgn|āte[2] (*or* -ĕ′g-) *v.t.* **1.** Make (female) pregnant; (Biol.) fertilize (female reproductive cell or ovum). **2.** Fill, saturate, (*with*); imbue, fill, (*with* feelings, moral qualities, etc.). **3.** Hence or cogn. **~āt**ABLE *a.*, ~A′TION *n.* [f. as prec. + -ATE[3]]

imprĕsar′iō *n.* (*pl.* ~s). Organizer of public entertainments, esp. manager of operatic or concert company. [It. (*impresa* undertaking, as EMPRISE; see -ARY[1])]

imprĕscri′ptible *a.* Not subject to prescription, that cannot be legally taken away, (*imprescriptible right*). [f. med. L *imprescriptibilis* (as IM-[2], PRESCRIBE, -IBLE)]

i′mprĕss[1] *n.* Stamping; mark made by seal, stamp, etc.; (fig.) characteristic mark or quality; = IMPRESSION 3. [f. foll.]

imprĕ′ss[2] *v.t.* Apply (mark etc.) with pressure, imprint, stamp, (*on*); imprint, enforce, (idea etc., *that, what*, etc., *on* person, his mind); mark (thing *with* stamp etc., lit. or fig.); affect or influence deeply, whence ~IBLE *a.*; affect (person) favourably or strongly (*with* idea etc.); (Electr.) apply (voltage etc.) from outside. [ME, f. OF EM¹(*presser* PRESS²)]

ĭmprĕ'ss³ *v.t.* (Hist.) force (men) to serve in army or navy, seize (goods etc.) for public service; (arch.) enlist, make use of, (thing) in argument etc.; hence ~MENT *n.* [f. IM-¹ + PRESS³]

ĭmprĕ'ssion (-shon) *n.* **1.** Impressing (of mark). **2.** Mark impressed; print taken from type or engraving; (printing of) number of copies of book, newspaper, etc., issued at one time; unaltered reprint from standing type or plates (as opp. to *edition*). **3.** Effect produced (esp. on mind or feelings); representation of this by artist, mimic, etc. **4.** Notion, (vague or mistaken) belief, impressed on the mind, (*that is my impression; I was under the impression, had the impression, that*). [ME f. OF f. L *impressio -onis* f. IM¹(*primere press- = premere* PRESS²)]

ĭmprĕ'ssion|able (-shon-) *a.* Susceptible of impressions, easily influenced; hence ~ABI'LITY *n.* [f. F *impressionnable* (*impressionner*, as prec.; see -ABLE)]

ĭmprĕ'ssion|ĭsm (-shon-) *n.* Style of painting, music, or writing, such as to give general tone and effect without elaborate finish or detail; so ~IST (2) *n.*, **~ĭ'stic** *a.* (also = subjective, unsystematic, after IMPRESSION 4). [f. F *impressionnisme* (as IMPRESSION; see -ISM)]

ĭmprĕ'ssĭve *a.* (Of language, scenes, etc.) able to excite deep feeling; deeply impressing mind or senses, esp. so as to cause approval or admiration; hence ~LY² (-vlĭ) *adv.*, ~NESS (-vn-) *n.* [f. IMPRESS² + -IVE]

ĭ'mprĕst *n.* Money advanced to person for use in State business. [f. phr. *in prest* (OF *prest* loan, advance pay; see PRESS³)]

ĭmprĭmā'tur (*or* -ah'-) *n.* Official licence to print (esp. works sanctioned by R.C. Ch.); (fig.) sanction. [L, = let it be printed]

imprimatura (ĭmprēmatoor'*a*) *n.* (Paint.) Coloured transparent glaze as primer. [f. It. *imprimitura* (*imprimere* IMPRESS²; see -URE)]

ĭmprī'mĭs *adv.* (arch.) In the first place. [assim. f. L *in primis* among the first things]

ĭ'mprĭnt¹ *n.* Impression, stamp, (lit. or fig.); **publisher's, printer's,** ~ (name, place etc., on title-page or at end of book). [ME, f. F *empreinte* stamp, fem. p.p. (as n.) of *empreindre* (see foll.)]

ĭmprĭ'nt² *v.t.* Stamp (figure etc. *on*); impress (idea etc. *on* or *in* mind, memory, etc.); impress (quality etc. *on* or *in*); stamp (thing *with* figure); (Psych.) become recognized as object of attachment by (esp. young animal). [ME, f. OF *empreinter* f. *empreindre empreint* f. L *imprimere* (see IMPRESSION)]

ĭmprĭ'son (-z-) *v.t.* Put into prison; (fig.) confine, shut up; so ~MENT *n.* [ME, f. OF EM¹(*prisoner* f. PRISON)]

ĭmprŏ'b|able *a.* Not likely to be true or to happen; existing but not easy to believe true; hence ~ABI'LITY *n.*, **~ab**LY² *adv.* [F, or f. L IM²(*probabilis* PROBABLE)]

ĭmprŏ'bĭtỹ *n.* Wickedness, lack of moral integrity; dishonesty. [f. L *improbitas* (as IM-², PROBITY)]

ĭmprŏ'mptū *adv.*, *n.*, & *a.* Extempore (performance, composition, speech); musical composition having character of improvisation. [F, f. L *in promptu* in readiness (see PROMPT¹)]

ĭmprŏ'per *a.* **1.** Inaccurate, wrong; not properly so called; ~ **fraction** (greater than unity, with numerator greater than denominator). **2.** Unseemly, indecent; not in accordance with rules of conduct. **3.** Hence ~LY² *adv.* [f. F *impropre* or f. L *improprius* (as IM-², PROPER)]

||**ĭmprō'prĭ|āte** *v.t.* Annex (ecclesiastical benefice) to corporation or person as property; place (tithes, ecclesiastical property) in lay hands; so ~A'TION *n.* [f. AL IM¹(*propriare* f. *proprius* own) + -ATE³]

||**ĭmprō'prĭātor** *n.* One to whom benefice is impropriated. [f. prec. + -OR]

ĭmproprī'etỹ *n.* Incorrectness; unfitness; indecency; instance of improper conduct etc. [f. F *impropriété* or f. L IM²(*proprietas* f. *proprius* PROPER; see -TY¹)]

ĭmpro'v|able (-ōō'v-) *a.* That can be improved; suitable for cultivation; hence ~ABI'LITY, **~able**NESS (-beln-), *ns.* [f. foll. + -ABLE]

ĭmpro've (-ōō'v) *v.t.* & *i.* **1.** Make or become better; (in *part.*) giving moral benefit (*an improving book*). **2.** Make good use of (*the occasion, the opportunity*); ~ **on** or **upon,** produce something better than. [orig. *em-*, *improw(e)* f. AF *emprower* f. OF EM-¹ + *prou* profit, infl. by PROVE]

ĭmpro'vement (-ōō'vm-) *n.* Improving or being improved; addition or alteration that adds to value. [ME, f. AF *emprowement* (as prec.; see -MENT)]

ĭmpro'ver (-ōō'v-) *n.* In vbl senses; ||one who works at trade for low wage or none to improve his skill. [f. IMPROVE + -ER¹]

ĭmprŏ'vĭd|ent *a.* Unforeseeing; heedless; thriftless; hence or cogn. ~ENCE *n.*, **~ent**LY² *adv.* [F (as IM-², PROVIDENT)]

ĭmprŏ'vĭsātor (-z-), ***improv(v)isatore*** (ĭmprŏvēzahtôr'ā) (*fem.* ***-satrice*** *pr.* -trē'chā; *pl.* ***-satori*** *pr.* -tôr'ē), *n.* One who improvises or composes extempore. [f. (foll. after) It. *improvvisatore* (*improvvisare*; see foll.; -OR)]

ĭ'mprovĭs|e (-z) *v.t.* Compose, utter, (verse, music, etc., or abs.) extempore; provide or construct (thing, or abs.) extempore; hence or cogn. ~A'TION (*or* -vīz-) *n.*, **ĭmprovĭsatôr'**IAL, ||**ĭmprovī'sat**ORY (*or* -ā'-), (-z-) *adjs.*, ~ER¹ *n.* [f. F *improviser* or f. It. *improvvisare* f. *improvviso* extempore, f. L IM²(*provisus* p.p. as PROVIDE)]

ĭmpru'd|ent (-ōō'-) *a.* Rash, indiscreet; hence or cogn. ~ENCE *n.*, **~ent**LY² *adv.* [ME, f. L IM²(*prudens* PRUDENT)]

ĭ'mpūd|ent *a.* Shamelessly presumptuous; unblushing; insolently disrespectful; hence or cogn. ~ENCE *n.*, **~ent**LY² *adv.* [ME, f. L IM²(*pudens* f. *pudēre* be ashamed; see -ENT)]

ĭmpūdĭ'cĭtỹ *n.* Shamelessness, immodesty. [f. F *impudicité* f. L IM²(*pudicus*, as prec.); see -ITY]

ĭmpū'gn (-ū'n) *v.t.* Assail by words, call in question, (statement, action); hence ~ABLE *a.*, ~MENT *n.* [ME, f. L IM¹(*pugnare* fight) assail]

ĭmpū'ĭss|ant *a.* Impotent, weak; so ~ANCE *n.* [F (as IM-², PUISSANT)]

ĭ'mpŭlse *n.* **1.** Impelling, push; impetus; (Phys.) indefinitely large force acting for very short time but producing finite change of momentum (e.g. blow of hammer), change of momentum caused by such force or by any force; wave of excitation in nerve causing action or inaction of muscle. **2.** Mental incitement; sudden tendency to act without reflection (*did it on (an) impulse*; ~ **buying** of goods because of sudden temptation rather than previous intent). [f. L *impulsus* (as IMPEL)]

ĭmpŭ'lsion (-shon) *n.* Impelling push; mental impulse; impetus. [ME f. OF, f. L *impulsio -onis* (as IMPEL; see -ION)]

ĭmpŭ'lsĭve *a.* Tending to impel; (Phys.) acting as an impulse; (of person, conduct, etc.) apt to be moved, prompted, by sudden impulse; hence ~LY² (-vlĭ) *adv.*, ~NESS (-vn-) *n.* [ME,

f. F *impulsif -ive* or f. LL *impulsivus* (as prec.; see -IVE)]

ĭmpū′nĭtȳ *n.* Being exempt(ed) from punishment, or from injury as consequence of act; **with ~,** in such a way as to be thus exempt(ed). [f. L *impunitas* f. IM^{2}(*punis* f. *poena* penalty); see -ITY]

ĭmpūr′e (*or* ĭ′-) *a.* Dirty; unchaste; mixed with foreign matter, adulterated, (lit. or fig.); (of colour) mixed with another colour; hence or cogn. ~LY^{2} (-ūr′lĭ) *adv.*, **ĭmpūr′**ITY *n.* [ME, f. L IM^{2}(*purus* pure)]

ĭmpū′t|e *v.t.* Attribute, ascribe, (esp. fault etc. *to* person etc.); (Theol.) ascribe (righteousness, guilt, etc., to person) by virtue of similar quality in another; so ~A′TION *n.*, ~ABLE, ~ATIVE, *adjs.* [ME, f. OF *imputer* f. L IM^{1}(*putare* reckon) enter in the account]

I.M.S. *abbr.* Indian Medical Service.

||**I.Mun.E.** *abbr.* Institution of Municipal Engineers.

ĭn^{1} *prep.* **1.** Expr. inclusion or position within limits of space, time, circumstance, etc., (*in Europe, England, London,* or any town, suburb, village, etc., of public or private importance, cf. AT; *in the house, the street, the car, the pond, a box, a crowd, the rain, school,* PRISON, *bed, exile, the 'Mauretania'*; (fig.) *in* CLOVER, *the* DARK^{2}, *haste, health, his sleep, sorrow,* TEAR^{2}*s*); wearing as dress (*in flannels,* SHIRT-*sleeves, gumboots*); with respect to (*blind in one eye*; *in* ITSELF; *weak in Latin*; *lacking in courage*; *a change in the weather*; *seven in number*; *a mile in length*); as a proportionate part of (*one in three failed*; *gradient of one in six*; *she is one in a million*; *40p. in the pound*); as a member of (*serving in the army*; *has shares in the company*); as content of (*there is something in what you say*); (colloq.) as a kind of (*the latest thing in luxury*); that is etc. the person of (*found a friend in Mary*); concerned with or pertaining to (*in politics, fancy, my opinion*); (of animal) pregnant with (*in calf, pig*); under the influence of (*in liquor*); (Mus.) modulated according to (the key of) (*symphony in G*); (Gram.) having as beginning or ending (*words in 'pro-', in '-ation'*); occupied with, with the purpose of, (*in search of*; *in reply to*; *in honour of*); with the form or arrangement or language of (*falling in folds*; *in* ORDER^{1} 7; *packed in tens*; *written in French*); with the instrument or material or means of (*drawn in pencil*; *modelled in bronze*; *coat in green velvet*; *in this way we succeeded*); during the time of (*in the night*; *in May*; *in summer*; *in 1976*; *in his forties*; *finished it in two days*; *drowned in crossing the river*); after the time of (*back in ten minutes*); within the ability of (*as far as in me lies*; **have it in one,** have the capacity *to* do). **2.** Into (w. vbs. of motion or change: *put it in your pocket*; *cut it in two* or *half*; *throw it in the fire*; *slam the door in his face*; *sun was shining in my eyes*). **3.** (Introducing ind. obj.: *believe in, engage in, rejoice in, share in*). **4.** (Forming adv. phr.: *in any case, in common, in fact, in short, in truth, in vain*). **5. In it,** (usu. w. neg.) in the running, a serious competitor; **nothing, little, not much, in it,** no decided advantage to any competitor in race or difference between alternatives etc.; *in so* FAR^{1} *as*; **in that,** since, because, in so far as. [OE, = OS, OHG, Goth. *in*, ON *í* f. IE *(*e*)*n*]

ĭn^{2} *adv.* **1.** Expr. position within certain limits or motion to point at such position (*come in, send him in, walk in,* = into room, house, enclosed ground, etc.); in the house, esp. at home (*will be in tomorrow*); in a publication (*looked for the word, but it was not in*; *is my article in?*); on or to the inward side (*coat with the woolly side in*; *rub, burn, it in*); so as to be enclosed (*hemmed, walled, locked, in*); in fashion, season, office, effective or favourable action, (*short skirts, oysters, the Tories, are in*; *get* one's EYE^{1} *in*; *my luck was in*; TIDE^{1} *is in*; *join in*); functioning as batsman, elected candidate, etc.; (of domestic fire) burning; (of train, boat, season, harvest, request, etc.) having arrived or been received. **2. In at,** present at (the finish etc.); **in between,** in the space(s) or interval(s) between; **in for,** (1) involved in, committed to, about to undergo, (usu. something unpleasant, esp. *it*), (2) engaged in competition for (race, prize, etc.); **have it in for,** seek revenge on (person); *in for a* PENNY; **in and in,** (of breeding) repeated(ly) within same stock; **in on,** (colloq.) sharing in, aware of (secret etc.); **in and out,** sometimes in and sometimes out; **(well) in with,** on friendly terms with. **3. Day, week, year,** etc. **in, day** etc. **out,** throughout a long succession of days etc.; THROW^{1} *in*. **4.** ||**~-off,** (Bill.) losing HAZARD; **~-swinger,** (Cricket) ball that swings towards batsman; **~-tray** (for incoming documents etc.). **5.** (As *suf.* denoting persistent or prolonged action esp. by large numbers: SIT-*in*, TEACH-*in*). [(1) OE *in*(*n*) w. vbs. of motion, = OS, OHG *in*, ON, Goth. *inn*, (2) OE *inne* w. vbs. of position, = OS, OHG, Goth. *inna*, ON *inni*]

ĭn^{3} *a.* **1.** Internal, living etc. inside; **in patient, in-patient,** one who remains as resident in hospital while under treatment. **2.** Fashionable, sophisticated; esoteric; **in-group,** group of persons united by common interests. [f. prec. used attrib.]

ĭn^{4} *n.* **1.** (in *pl.*) Political party in office. **2.** (colloq.) Introduction to or influence with important person. **3. Ins and outs,** turnings to and fro (usu. fig.), details (*of* procedure etc.). [f. IN^{2}]

ĭn-^{1} *pref.* In, on, into, towards, within, (*incoming, induce, influx, ingredient, inlay, insight, intrude, inveterate*). [f. IN^{1,2} or f. or after L (*in* IN^{1})]

ĭn-^{2} *pref.*, = UN-^{2} (*indirect*(*ly*), *indisposition, inedible, inobservance, insane, inseparable, insignificant, insoluble, invaluable, invisible*). [L]

-ĭn *suf.* (Chem.) forming names of neutral substances (*casein, gelatin, papain, protein*) and of antibiotics (*penicillin*). [f. -INE^{5}]

in. *abbr.* inch(es).

In *symb.* indium.

-ina (-ē′na) *suf.* (1) of fem. names and titles (*Georgina, tsarina*), (2) of names of musical instruments (*concertina*), (3) of Zool. groups (*globigerina*). [f. It. or Sp. or f. L]

ĭnabĭ′lĭtȳ *n.* Being unable; lack of power or means. [ME, f. IN-^{2} + ABILITY]

in absentia (ĭn ăbsĕ′ntĭa; *or* -shĭa) *adv.* In (his or her or their) absence. [L]

ĭnaccĕ′ss|ĭble (-ks-) *a.* Not accessible, that cannot be reached; (of person) not open to advances or influence, unapproachable; hence ~IBĬ′LITY *n.*, **~ĭb**LY^{2} *adv.* [ME f. F, or f. LL IN^{2}-(*accessibilis* ACCESSIBLE)]

ĭnă′ccūr|ate *a.* Not accurate; hence ~ACY *n.*, **~ate**LY^{2} (-tlĭ) *adv.* [f. IN-^{2} + ACCURATE]

ĭnă′ct|ion *n.* Absence of action; sluggishness, inertness. [f. IN-^{2} + ACTION]

ĭnă′ctĭv|āte *v.t.* Make inactive or inoperative; hence ~A′TION *n.* [f. IN-^{2} + ACTIVATE]

ĭnă′ctĭve *a.* Not active or inclined to act; indolent; passive; hence or cogn. **ĭnactĭ′v**ITY *n.*, ~LY^{2} (-vlĭ) *adv.* [f. IN-^{2} + ACTIVE]

ĭnă′dėqu|ate *a.* Not adequate (*to* purpose, *to* do); insufficient; incompetent; hence ~ACY *n.*, **~ate**LY^{2} (-tlĭ) *adv.* [f. IN-^{2} + ADEQUATE]

For other words in *im-* see IM-^{1} **or (esp.)** IM-^{2}.

For other words in *in-* see IN-^{1} **or (esp.)** IN-^{2}.

ĭnadmĭ'ss|ĭble *a.* That cannot be admitted or allowed; hence ~IBI'LITY *n.*, ~**ĭb**LY² *adv.* [f. IN-² + ADMISSIBLE]
ĭnadvẽr't|ent *a.* Not properly attentive; negligent; (of action) unintentional; hence or cogn. ~ENCE, ~ENCY, *ns.*, ~**ent**LY² *adv.* [f. IN-² + obs. *advertent* attentive (as ADVERT²; see -ENT)]
ĭnadvī'sable (-z-) *a.* Not advisable. [f. IN-² + ADVISABLE]
ĭnā'lĭen|able *a.* Not alienable; hence ~ABI'LITY *n.*, ~**ab**LY² *adv.* [f. IN-² + ALIENABLE]
ĭna'lter|able (-aw'l- *or* -ŏ'l-) *a.* Unalterable; hence ~ABI'LITY *n.*, ~**ab**LY² *adv.* [f. med. L IN²(*alterabilis* f. as ALTER; see -ABLE)]
ĭnămora't|ō (-rah'-) *n.* (*fem.* ~**a**). Lover. [It., p.p. (as n.) of IN¹(*amorare* f. *amore* f. L *amor* love) enamour]
ĭnā'ne *a.* & *n.* **1.** *a.* Empty, void; silly, senseless; hence or cogn. ~LY² (-nlĭ) *adv.*, **ĭnă'n**ITY *n.* **2.** *n.* (arch.) Empty space. [f. L *inanis* empty, vain]
ī'nănga (ē'-) *n.* (N.Z.) Freshwater fish of family Galaxiidae. [Maori]
ĭnă'nĭmate *a.* Destitute of life; not endowed with animal life (~ **nature,** everything other than the animal world); spiritless, dull; hence or cogn. ~LY² (-tlĭ) *adv.*, **ĭnănĭm**A'TION *n.* [f. LL IN²(*animatus* ANIMATE¹)]
ĭnanĭ'tion *n.* Emptiness, esp. exhaustion from lack of nourishment. [ME, f. LL *inanitio* f. L *inanire* make empty (as INANE); see -ITION]
ĭnappĕ'llable *n.* That cannot be appealed against. [f. obs. F IN²(*appelable* f. *appeler* APPEAL¹; see -ABLE)]
ĭnă'ppėt|ent *a.* Not appetent; so ~ENCE, ~ENCY, *ns.* [f. IN-² + APPETENT]
ĭnă'pplĭc|able *a.* Not applicable, unsuitable, (*to* case, purpose); hence ~ABI'LITY *n.*, ~**ab**LY² *adv.* [f. IN-² + APPLICABLE]
ĭnă'pposĭte (-z-) *a.* Not apposite, out of place; hence ~LY² (-tlĭ) *adv.*, ~NESS (-tn-) *n.* [f. IN-² + APPOSITE]
ĭnapprē'ciab|le (-sh*a*-) *a.* Imperceptible, not worth reckoning; that cannot be appreciated; hence ~LY² *adv.* [f. IN-² + APPRECIABLE]
ĭnapprēcĭā'tion (-shĭ-) *n.* Failure to appreciate; so **ĭnapprē'cĭat**IVE (-shĭ-) *a.* [f. IN-² + APPRECIATION]
ĭnăpprėhĕ'nsĭble *a.* That cannot be grasped (by senses or intellect). [f. IN-² + APPREHENSIBLE]
ĭnapprō'prĭate *a.* Not appropriate; hence ~LY² (-tlĭ) *adv.*, ~NESS (-tn-) *n.* [f. IN-² + APPROPRIATE¹]
ĭnă'pt *a.* Not suitable; unskilful; hence or cogn. ~**ĭ**TUDE, ~NESS, *ns.*, ~LY² *adv.* [f. IN-² + APT]
ĭnar̃'ch *v.t.* Graft by connecting growing branch without separation from parent stock. [f. IN-¹ + ARCH²]
ĭnar̃'m *v.t.* (poet.) Embrace. [f. IN-¹ + ARM¹]
ĭnar̃tĭ'cūlate *a.* Not jointed; (of speech) not articulate, indistinctly pronounced; unable to speak distinctly or express oneself clearly; dumb; hence ~LY² (-tlĭ) *adv.*, ~NESS (-tn-) *n.* [f. LL IN²(*articulatus* ARTICULATE¹)]
ĭnar̃tĭfĭ'cial (-sh*a*l) *a.* (arch.) Lacking in art, inartistic; artless, natural; hence ~LY² *adv.* [f. IN-² + ARTIFICIAL]
ĭnar̃tĭ'st|ĭc *a.* Not following the principles of art; unskilled in or not talented in or not appreciating art; hence ~ICALLY *adv.* [f. IN-² + ARTISTIC]
ĭnasmŭ'ch (-az-) *adv.* **1.** ~ **as,** since, because. **2.** (arch.) In so FAR¹ *as.* [ME, orig. *in as much*]
ĭnattĕ'nt|ĭve *n.* Lacking in attention, heedless; neglecting to show courtesy; hence or cogn. ~ION, ~**ĭve**NESS (-vn-), *ns.*, ~**ĭve**LY² (-vlĭ) *adv.* [f. IN-² + ATTENTIVE]

ĭnau'd|ĭble *a.* That cannot be heard; hence ~IBI'LITY *n.*, ~**ĭb**LY² *adv.* [f. IN-² + AUDIBLE]
ĭnau'gūral *a.* & *n.* **1.** *a.* Of inauguration; (of lecture etc.) given by person being inaugurated. **2.** *n.* Inaugural speech etc. [F (*inaugurer*, f. as foll.)]
ĭnau'gūr|āte *v.t.* Admit (person, *esp. President of U.S.) to office etc. with ceremony; enter with ceremony upon (undertaking etc.); initiate public use of (building etc.); begin, introduce; hence or cogn. ~A'TION, ~**ā**TOR, *ns.*, ~**at**ORY *a.* [f. L IN¹(*augurare* take omens, f. AUGUR¹) + -ATE³]
ĭnauspĭ'cious (-sh*u*s) *a.* Not of good omen; unlucky; hence ~LY² *adv.*, ~NESS *n.* [f. IN-² + AUSPICIOUS]
ĭ'nboard *adv.* & *a.* (Situated) within sides of or towards centre of ship, aircraft, or vehicle. [f. IN¹ + BOARD¹]
ĭ'nbōr̃n *a.* Existing from birth, implanted by nature. [f. IN² + BORN]
ĭnbrea'the (-dh) *v.t.* Breathe (thing) in (lit. or fig.); inspire (person). [ME, f. IN-¹ + BREATHE]
ĭnbree'd *v.t.* (**inbre'd**). Breed within or in and in; (in *p.p.*) innate, inherent by nature. [f. IN-¹, IN² + BREED¹]
ĭ'n-bu͝ilt (-bĭ-) *a.* Built-in. [f. IN² + BUILT]
***Inc.** *abbr.* Incorporated.
I'nca (ĭ'-) *n.* Emperor or king of Peru before Spanish conquest; one of royal race in Peru; member of Amer. Ind. people in Peru etc. before Spanish conquest. [Quechua, = lord, royal person]
ĭncă'lcūl|able (ĭn-k-) *a.* Too great for calculation; that cannot be reckoned beforehand; (of person, character, etc.) uncertain; hence ~ABI'LITY *n.*, ~**ab**LY² *adv.* [f. IN-² + CALCULABLE]
in camera. See CAMERA.
ĭncăndĕ'sce (ĭn-k-) *v.i.* & *t.* (Cause to) glow with heat. [back form. f. foll.; cf. -ESCE]
ĭncăndĕ'sc|ent (ĭn-k-) *a.* Glowing with heat; shining brightly; (of electric or other light) produced by glowing of white-hot filament etc.; hence ~ENCE *n.* [F, f. L IN¹(*candescere* incept. of *candēre* be white); see -ENT]
ĭncăntā'tion (ĭn-k-) *n.* (Use of) magical formula; spell, charm. [ME f. OF, f. LL *incantatio -onis* f. IN¹(*cantare* sing) chant, bewitch; see -ATION]
ĭncā'p|able (ĭn-k-) *a.* Not capable (*of* conduct etc., *of doing*, esp. = too honest etc. to behave thus); not susceptible (*of* improvement etc.); lacking in ordinary powers (*drunk and incapable*); hence ~ABI'LITY *n.*, ~**ab**LY² *adv.* [F, or f. LL IN²(*capabilis* CAPABLE)]
ĭncapă'cĭt|āte (ĭn-k-) *v.t.* Render incapable or unfit (*for* work etc.; *for, from, doing*); disqualify; hence ~ANT, ~A'TION, *ns.* [f. foll. + -ATE³]
ĭncapă'cĭtỹ (ĭn-k-) *n.* Inability (*for doing, for* work etc., *to* do, or abs.); legal disqualification. [f. F *incapacité* or f. LL IN²(*capacitas* CAPACITY)]
ĭncar̃'cer|āte (ĭn-k-) *v.t.* Imprison (lit. or fig.); hence or cogn. ~A'TION, ~**ā**TOR, *ns.* [f. med. L IN¹(*carcerare* f. L *carcer* prison) + -ATE³]
ĭncar̃'nadĭne (ĭn-k-) *a.*, & *v.t.* (poet.) (Dye) flesh-coloured or crimson. [f. F *incarnadin -ine* f. It. *incarnadino* (for *-tino*) f. *incarnato* INCARNATE¹]
ĭncar̃'nate¹ (ĭn-k-) *a.* (Of person, spirit, quality, etc.) embodied in flesh, in human form, (*he is an incarnate fiend, a devil incarnate*); embodied in recognizable or most perfect form. [ME, f. eccl. L *incarnatus* p.p. of IN¹(*carnare* f. L *caro carnis* flesh); see -ATE²]
ĭncar̃'nāte² (ĭn-k-; *or* ĭ'n-k-) *v.t.* Embody in flesh; put (idea etc.) into concrete form, realize; (of person etc.) be living embodiment of (quality). [f. as prec. + -ATE³]
ĭncar̃nā'tion (ĭn-k-) *n.* Embodiment in (esp.

human) flesh, esp. **the I~** (of Christ); impersonation, living type, (*of* quality etc.); (Med.) process of forming new flesh. [ME f. OF, f. eccl. L *incarnatio -onis* (as prec.; see -ATION)]

incase. Var. of ENCASE.

ĭncau'tious (ĭn-kaw'shus) *a.* Heedless, rash; hence ~LY² *adv.*, ~NESS *n.* [f. IN-² + CAUTIOUS]

ĭncĕ'ndiar|y̆ *a.* & *n.* **1.** *a.* Of, guilty of, the malicious setting on fire of property; **~y bomb** (filled with substance(s) for causing fire at point of impact). **2.** (fig.) Tending to stir up strife, inflammatory. **3.** *n.* Incendiary person (lit. or fig.); incendiary bomb. **4.** Hence ~ISM (2) *n.* [ME f. L *incendiarius* f. *incendium* conflagration f. IN¹(*cendere cens-* = **candere* cause to glow) set fire to; see -ARY¹]

ĭ'ncĕnse¹ *n.* Gum or spice producing sweet smell when burned; smoke of this, esp. in religious ceremonial; (fig.) praise, flattery. [ME, f. OF *encens* f. eccl. L *incensum* thing burnt, incense, neut. p.p. (as n.) of L *incendere*; see prec.]

ĭ'ncĕns|e² *v.t.* Fumigate (person, thing) with incense; burn incense to (deity etc.); suffuse with fragrance; hence ~A'TION *n.* [ME, f. OF *encenser* (as prec.)]

ĭncĕ'nse³ *v.t.* Enrage, make angry, (*against, with, at*). [ME, f. OF *incenser* f. L *incendere* (see INCENDIARY)]

ĭ'ncĕnsory̆ *n.* Censer. [f. med. L *incensorium* (as INCENSE¹; see -ORY)]

ĭncĕ'ntĭve *a.* & *n.* **1.** *a.* Tending to incite. **2.** *n.* Incitement (*to* action, *to* do, *to* doing), provocation, motive; payment or concession to stimulate greater output by workers. [ME, f. L *incentivus* setting the tune f. IN¹(*cinere cent-* = *canere* sing) sing to; see -IVE]

ĭncĕ'pt *v.* **1.** *v.i.* (Hist.) Take master's or doctor's degree at university; so ~OR *n.* **2.** *v.t.* (Biol.) Take in (food etc.). [f. L IN¹(*cipere cept-* = *capere* take) begin]

ĭncĕ'ption *n.* Beginning; (Hist.) incepting. [ME f. OF, or f. L *inceptio* (as prec.; see -ION)]

ĭncĕ'ptĭve *a.* & *n.* **1.** *a.* Beginning; initial; (Gram., of verb) that denotes the beginning of an action. **2.** *n.* Inceptive verb. [f. LL *inceptivus* (as INCEPT; see -IVE)]

ĭncĕr'tĭtūde *n.* Uncertainty, doubt. [F, or f. LL *incertitudo* (as IN-², CERTITUDE)]

ĭncĕ'ssant *a.* Unceasing, continual, repeated; hence **ĭncĕ'ss**ANCY, ~NESS, *ns.*, ~LY² *adv.* [F, or f. LL IN²(*cessans* part. of L *cessare* CEASE¹; see -ANT)]

ĭ'ncĕst *n.* Sexual intercourse between persons regarded as too closely related to marry each other. [ME, f. L *incestus* or IN²(*cestum* neut. adj. = *castum* chaste)]

ĭncĕ'stūous *a.* Involving, or guilty of, incest; hence ~LY² *adv.* [f. LL *incestuosus* (as prec.; see -OUS)]

ĭnch¹ *n.* & *v.* **1.** *n.* Twelfth part of FOOT¹ 6, 2·54 cm; (as unit of map-scale) 1 inch representing 1 mile on the ground (*a 2½-inch map*); (as unit of rainfall) quantity that would cover horizontal surface to depth of 1 inch; (of atmospheric or other pressure) amount that balances weight of column of mercury 1 inch high. **2.** Small amount (*would not yield an inch*); **~ by ~, by ~es,** bit by bit, gradually; **every ~,** entirely, the whole distance; *give him an inch and he'll take an* ELL; *flog* person **within an ~ of his life,** almost to death. **3.** (in *pl.*) Stature (*a man of your inches*). **4.** *v.t.* & *i.* Move by inches, edge *in, forward,* etc. [OE *ynce,* = OHG *unza,* Goth. *unkja* f. L *uncia* twelfth part; cf. OUNCE¹]

‖**ĭnch²** *n.* Small (esp. Scottish) island (freq. in place-names). [ME f. Gael. *innis*]

ĭ'nchōate¹ (ĭ'n-k-) *a.* Just begun; undeveloped. [f. L *inchoatus* p.p. of IN¹(*choare, cohare* begin); see -ATE²]

ĭ'nchō|āte² (ĭn-k-) *v.t.* Begin; originate; so ~A'TION *n.*, **~ātĭve** (*or* -kō'*a*-) *a.*, (esp., Gram.) inceptive. [f. as prec. + -ATE³]

ĭ'ncĭdence *n.* Falling on or contact with a thing; manner or range of occurrence or action (*of* disease, taxation, etc.); range, scope, or extent of influence; (Phys.) falling of line, or of thing moving in a line, upon a surface (**angle of ~,** that which incident line, ray, etc., makes with perpendicular to surface at point of incidence). [ME f. OF, or f. med. L *incidentia* (as INCIDENT²; see -ENCE)]

ĭ'ncĭdent¹ *n.* Subordinate or accessory event; event, occurrence; hostile clash of e.g. troops of countries at war (*frontier incident*); public event causing trouble etc.; detached event attracting general attention; distinct piece of action in play or poem; (Law) privilege, burden, etc., attaching to estate etc. [ME f. OF (as foll.)]

ĭ'ncĭdent² *a.* Apt or liable to happen, naturally attaching, (*to*); (Law) attaching *to* (cf. prec.); (of light etc.) falling, striking, (*on, upon*). [ME f. F, or f. L IN¹(*cidere* = *cadere* fall); see -ENT]

ĭncĭdĕ'ntal *a.* Casual, not essential, (*to*); liable to happen *to*; **~ (up)on,** following as subordinate event; **~ music** (introduced during the action of a play). [f. prec. + -AL]

ĭncĭdĕ'ntally̆ *adv.* In adj. senses; by the way, parenthetically. [f. prec. + -LY²]

ĭncĭ'ner|āte *v.t.* Reduce to ashes; consume (body etc.) by fire; hence or cogn. ~A'TION *n.*, **~ātor** *n.* (esp. apparatus for burning refuse etc. to ashes). [f. med. L IN¹(*cinerere* f. *cinis -eris* ashes) + -ATE³]

ĭncĭ'pĭ|ent *a.* Beginning; in an initial stage; hence ~ENCE, ~ENCY, *ns.*, **~ent**LY² *adv.* [f. L (as INCEPT; see -ENT)]

ĭ'ncĭpĭt *n.* First words (of book etc., or fig.). [L = '(here) begins', formerly used by scribes to mark beginning of book or section]

ĭncī'se (-z) *v.t.* Make a cut in; engrave. [f. F *inciser* f. L IN¹(*cidere cis-* = *caedere* cut)]

ĭncĭ'sion (-zhon) *n.* Cutting into a thing; cut, division produced by cutting, notch. [ME f. OF, or f. LL *incisio* (as prec.; see -ION)]

ĭncī'sĭve *a.* Cutting, penetrating; (fig.) mentally sharp, acute; clear and effective; hence ~LY² (-vlĭ) *adv.*, ~NESS (-vn-) *n.* [f. med. L *incisivus* (as INCISE; see -IVE)]

ĭncī'sor (-z-) *n.* Cutting-tooth, any front tooth between the canine teeth in either jaw. [med. L, = cutter (as INCISE; see -OR)]

ĭncī'te *v.t.* Urge, stir up, (person etc. *to* action, *to* do); hence or cogn. **ĭncĭt**A'TION, ~MENT (-tm-), *ns.* [ME, f. F *inciter* f. L IN¹(*citare* rouse; see CITE)]

ĭncĭvĭ'lĭty̆ *n.* (Act of) rudeness or discourtesy. [f. F *incivilité* or f. LL IN²(*civilitas* CIVILITY)]

ĭ'ncĭvĭsm *n.* Lack of loyalty to one's nation (esp. in French Revolution). [f. F IN²(*civisme* f. L *civis* citizen; see -ISM)]

ĭnclĕ'm|ent (ĭn-k-) *a.* (Of weather or climate) severe, esp. cold or stormy; so ~ENCY *n.* [f. F *inclément* or f. L IN²(*clemens* CLEMENT)]

ĭnclī'nable (ĭn-k-) *a.* Inclined, disposed, (*to* thing, *to* do); favourable (*to*). [ME f. OF *enclinable* (as INCLINE¹; see -ABLE)]

ĭnclĭnā'tion (ĭn-k-) *n.* Leaning, slope, slant; dip of magnetic needle; difference of direction of two lines or planes, esp. as measured by angle between them; disposition, propensity, (*to, for, towards,* thing; *to* do) liking, affection, (*for*). [ME f. OF, or f. L *inclinatio* (as foll.; see -ATION)]

For other words in *in-* see IN-¹ or (esp.) IN-².

inclī'ne[1] (ĭn-k-) *v.* **1.** *v.t.* Bend (head, body, one*self*) forward or downward; ~ one's **ear,** listen favourably (*to* person, prayer, etc.). **2.** Dispose (mind, heart, person, thing, *to* do, *to* or *for* thing; *incline our hearts to keep this law*; *I am inclined to think so*; *door is inclined to bang*). **3.** *v.i.* Be disposed (*I incline to think so*); tend (*to* or *towards* fatness etc.). **4.** *v.t.* & *i.* (Cause to) lean or turn away from the vertical etc. direction; **~d plane,** sloping plane (esp. as means of reducing force needed to raise load). [ME *encline* f. OF *encliner* f. L IN[1](*clinare* bend)]

ī'nclīne[2] (ī'n-k-; *or* -ī'n) *n.* Inclined plane; slope. [f. prec.]

inclĭnŏ'mėter (ĭn-k-) *n.* Instrument measuring vertical intensity of earth's magnetic field by dip of magnetic needle; instrument for measuring slope; instrument for measuring inclination of ship or aircraft to horizontal. [f. L *inclinare* INCLINE[1] + -O- + -METER]

inclose. See ENCLOSE.

inclu'de (ĭn-klōō'd) *v.t.* Comprise or embrace (thing etc.) as part of a whole; (in *part.* in abs. constr.) if we include (*six members, including the chairman*); treat or regard as so comprised; (in *p.p.*) shut in, enclosed; ~ **out,** (colloq. or joc.) (specifically) exclude; so **inclu'sION** (ĭn-klōō'zh*o*n) *n.* [ME, f. L IN[1](*cludere clus-* = *claudere* shut)]

inclu'sĭve (ĭn-klōō'-) *a.* Including, comprising, (*of*, or abs.); including the extreme limits stated (*pages 7 to 26 inclusive*); including much or all (*inclusive terms* at hotel etc.); hence ~LY[2] (-vlĭ) *adv.*, ~NESS (-vn-) *n.* [f. med. L *inclusivus* (as prec.; see -IVE)]

incŏ'g (ĭn-k-) *a.*, *adv.*, & *n.* (colloq.) = foll. [abbr.]

incŏ'gnĭtō (ĭn-k-; *or* -ē'tō) *a.*, *adv.*, & *n.* (*pl.* ~**s**). **1.** *a.* & *adv.* With one's name, character, etc., kept secret. **2.** *n.* (Pretended identity, anonymous character, of) person who is incognito. [It., = unknown, f. L IN[2](*cognitus* p.p. of *cognoscere* know)]

incŏ'gnĭz|ant (ĭn-k-; *or* -kŏ'n-) *a.* Unaware, unconscious *of*; so ~ANCE *n.* [f. IN-[2] + COGNIZANT]

incohēr'|ent (ĭn-k-) *a.* Not coherent (lit. or fig.); so ~ENCE, ~ENCY, *ns.*, ~**ent**LY[2] *adv.* [f. IN-[2] + COHERENT]

incombŭ'st|ĭble (ĭn-k-) *a.* That cannot be consumed by fire; hence ~IBI'LITY *n.* [ME, f. med. L IN[2](*combustibilis* COMBUSTIBLE)]

ĭ'ncome (ĭ'n-k-) *n.* Periodical (usu. total annual) receipts from one's business, lands, work, investments, etc.; ~ **group,** section of population graded by income; ~ **tax** (levied on this); **negative ~ tax,** amount deducted from taxable income for certain commitments and paid as supplementary income when exceeding taxable income; NATIONAL *income*. [f. IN[2] + COME]

ĭ'ncomer (ĭ'n-kŭ-) *n.* One who comes in; immigrant; intruder; successor. [f. IN[2] + COMER]

ĭ'ncomĭng[1] (ĭ'n-kŭ-) *n.* Entrance, arrival; (usu. in *pl.*) revenue, income. [ME, f. IN[2] + *coming* (COME, -ING[1])]

ĭ'ncomĭng[2] (ĭ'n-kŭ-) *a.* Coming in (*incoming tide, telephone calls*); succeeding another person; immigrant; (of profit) accruing. [f. IN[2] + *coming* (COME, -ING[2])]

incommĕ'nsur|able (ĭn-k-; -sh*er*- *or* -sy*er*-) *a.* (Of magnitude) having no common measure integral or fractional (*with* another); irrational, surd; not comparable in respect of magnitude; not worthy to be measured *with*; hence ~ABI'LITY *n.*, ~**ab**LY[2] *adv.* [f. LL IN[2](*commensurabilis* COMMENSURABLE)]

incommĕ'nsurate (ĭn-k-; -sh*er*- *or* -sy*er*-) *a.* Out of proportion, inadequate, (*with*, *to*); = prec.; hence ~LY[2] (-tlĭ) *adv.*, ~NESS (-tn-) *n.* [f. IN-[2] + COMMENSURATE]

ĭncommō'de (ĭn-k-) *v.t.* Trouble, annoy; hinder, inconvenience. [f. F *incommoder* or f. L IN[2](*commodare* f. *commodus* convenient; see COMMODE)]

ĭncommō'dĭous (ĭn-k-) *a.* Not affording good accommodation, uncomfortable; hence ~NESS *n.* [f. IN-[2] + COMMODIOUS]

ĭncommū'nĭc|able (ĭn-k-) *a.* That cannot be shared; that cannot be told; that does not communicate; hence ~ABI'LITY, ~**able**NESS (-b*e*ln-), *ns.*, ~**ab**LY[2] *adv.* [f. LL IN[2](*communicabilis* COMMUNICABLE)]

ĭncommūnĭca'dō (ĭn-k-; -ah'-) *a.* Without or deprived of means of communication with others; (of prisoner) in solitary confinement. [f. Sp. *incomunicado* p.p. of *incomunicar* deprive of communication]

ĭncommū'nĭcatĭve (ĭn-k-) *a.* Not communicative, taciturn; hence ~LY[2] (-vlĭ) *adv.*, ~NESS (-vn-) *n.* [f. IN-[2] + COMMUNICATIVE]

ĭncommū'tab|le (ĭn-k-) *a.* Unchangeable; not commutable; hence ~LY[2] *adv.* [ME, f. L IN[2](*commutabilis* COMMUTABLE)]

incŏ'mparab|le (ĭn-k-) *a.* Without an equal, matchless; not to be compared (*with*, *to*); hence ~**le**NESS (-b*e*ln-) *n.*, ~LY[2] *adv.* [ME f. OF, f. L IN[2](*comparabilis* COMPARABLE)]

incompă't|ĭble (ĭn-k-) *a.* Opposed in character, discordant; (of persons) unable to live, work, etc., together in harmony; (of drugs) not suitable for taking at same time; inconsistent (*with*); hence ~IBI'LITY *n.*, ~**ĭb**LY[2] *adv.* [f. med. L IN[2](*compatibilis* COMPATIBLE)]

incŏ'mpėt|ent (ĭn-k-) *a.* & *n.* **1.** *a.* Not qualified or able (*to* do); lacking a desirable ability or qualification; not able to perform its function; not legally qualified; hence or cogn. ~ENCE, ~ENCY, *ns.*, ~**ent**LY[2] *adv.* **2.** *n.* Incompetent person. [f. F *incompétent* or f. LL IN[2](*competens* COMPETENT)]

incomplē'te (ĭn-k-) *a.* Not complete; hence ~LY[2] (-tlĭ) *adv.*, ~NESS (-tn-) *n.* [ME, f. LL IN[2](*completus* COMPLETE[1])]

incŏmprėhĕ'ns|ĭble (ĭn-k-) *a.* That cannot be understood; (arch.) that cannot be contained within limits; hence ~IBI'LITY, ~**ĭble**NESS (-b*e*ln-), *ns.*, ~**ĭb**LY[2] *adv.* [ME, f. L IN[2](*comprehensibilis* COMPREHENSIBLE)]

incŏmprėhĕ'nsion (ĭn-k-; -sh*o*n) *n.* Failure to understand. [f. IN-[2] + COMPREHENSION]

incomprĕ'ss|ĭble (ĭn-k-) *a.* That cannot be compressed; hence ~IBI'LITY *n.* [f. IN-[2] + COMPRESSIBLE]

incomunicado. Var. of INCOMMUNICADO.

inconcei'v|able (ĭn-k*o*nsē'v-) *a.* That cannot be imagined; (colloq.) very remarkable; hence ~ABI'LITY *n.*, ~**ab**LY[2] *adv.* [f. IN-[2] + CONCEIVABLE]

inconclu'sĭve (ĭn-k*o*n-klōō'-) *a.* (Of argument, evidence, action) not decisive or convincing; hence ~LY[2] (-vlĭ) *adv.*, ~NESS (-vn-) *n.* [f. IN-[2] + CONCLUSIVE]

incondĕ'nsable (ĭn-k-) *a.* That cannot be condensed, esp. that cannot be reduced to liquid or solid condition. [f. IN-[2] + CONDENSABLE]

incŏ'ndĭte (ĭn-k-) *a.* (Of literary composition etc.) ill constructed; crude, unpolished. [f. L IN[2](*conditus* p.p. of *condere* put together)]

inconfor'mĭtў (ĭn-k-) *n.* (arch.) Dissimilarity, lack of conformity, (*to*, *with*); nonconformity. [f. IN-[2] + CONFORMITY]

incŏ'ngruous (ĭn-kŏ'nggrōō-) *a.* Disagreeing, out of keeping, (*with*); out of place, absurd; hence or cogn. **incongru'**ITY (ĭn-k*o*nggrōō'-), ~NESS, *ns.*, ~LY[2] *adv.* [f. L IN[2](*congruus* congruous)]

inconsĕ'cūtĭve (ĭn-k-) *a.* Lacking sequence, inconsequent; hence ~LY[2] (-vlĭ) *adv.*, ~NESS (-vn-) *n.* [f. IN-[2] + CONSECUTIVE]

ĭncŏ'nsėqu|ent (ĭn-k-) *a.* Not following naturally, irrelevant; lacking logical sequence; disconnected; hence or cogn. ~ENCE *n.*, ~**ent**LY² *adv.* [f. L IN²(*consequens* CONSEQUENT)]

ĭncŏnsėquě'ntial (ĭn-k-; -shal) *a.* Unimportant; = prec.; hence ~LY² *adv.* [f. IN-² + CONSEQUENTIAL]

ĭnconsĭ'derab|le (ĭn-k-) *a.* Not worth considering; of small size, value, etc.; hence ~**le**NESS (-beln-) *n.*, ~LY² *adv.* [f. obs. F *inconsidérable* or f. LL IN²(*considerabilis* CONSIDERABLE)]

ĭnconsĭ'der|ate (ĭn-k-) *a.* (Of person or action) thoughtless, rash; lacking in regard for feelings etc. of others; hence or cogn. ~**ate**LY² (-tlĭ) *adv.*, ~**ate**NESS (-tn-), ~A'TION, *ns.* [f. L IN²(*consideratus* CONSIDERATE)]

ĭnconsĭ'st|ent (ĭn-k-) *a.* Not in keeping, discordant, incompatible, (*with*); (of single thing) having inconsistent parts; acting at variance with one's own principles or former conduct; hence ~ENCY *n.*, ~**ent**LY² *adv.* [f. IN-² + CONSISTENT]

ĭnconsō'lab|le (ĭn-k-) *a.* (Of person, grief, etc.) that cannot be consoled; hence ~LY² *adv.* [F, or f. L IN²(*consolabilis* f. *consolari* CONSOLE¹; see -ABLE)]

ĭncŏ'nson|ant (ĭn-k-) *a.* Not harmonious (*with, to*); hence ~ANCE *n.* [f. IN-² + CONSONANT¹]

ĭnconspĭ'cūous (ĭn-k-) *a.* Not conspicuous; (Bot., of flowers) small, pale, or green; hence ~LY² *adv.*, ~NESS *n.* [f. L IN²(*conspicuus* CONSPICUOUS) + -OUS]

ĭncŏ'nst|ant (ĭn-k-) *a.* (Of person) fickle, changeable; variable, irregular; hence or cogn. ~ANCY *n.*, ~**ant**LY² *adv.* [ME f. OF, f. L IN²(*constans -antis* CONSTANT)]

ĭncontĕ'stab|le (ĭn-k-) *a.* That cannot be disputed; hence ~LY² *adv.* [F, or f. med. L IN²-(*contestabilis* f. L *contestari* CONTEST²; see -ABLE)]

ĭncŏ'ntĭn|ent (ĭn-k-) *a.* Lacking self-restraint (esp. in regard to sexual desire); unable to control excretions voluntarily; ~ **of,** unable to retain or control (secrets, tongue, excretions etc.); so ~ENCE *n.* [ME f. OF, or f. L IN²(*continens* CONTINENT¹)]

ĭncŏ'ntĭnentlў¹ (ĭn-k-) *adv.* In adj. senses. [f. prec. + -LY²]

ĭncŏ'ntĭnentlў² (ĭn-k-) *adv.* (literary). At once, immediately. [f. arch. *incontinent* adv., ME, f. F *incontenant* f. LL *in continenti* (*tempore*) in continuous (time), + -LY²]

ĭncŏntrovēr'tĭb|le (ĭn-k-) *a.* Indisputable, indubitable; hence ~LY² *adv.* [f. IN-² + CONTROVERTIBLE]

ĭnconvē'nĭence (ĭn-k-) *n.*, & *v.t.* **1.** *n.* Lack of adaptation to personal requirement or ease; instance of this. **2.** *v.t.* Put (person etc.) to inconvenience. [ME f. OF, f. LL *inconvenientia* (as foll.; see -ENCE)]

ĭnconvē'nĭent (ĭn-k-) *a.* Unfavourable to ease or comfort; awkward, troublesome; hence ~LY² *adv.* [ME f. OF f. L IN²(*conveniens -ntis* CONVENIENT)]

ĭnconvēr't|ĭble (ĭn-k-) *a.* Not convertible; (esp. of currency) not convertible into another form on demand; hence ~IBI'LITY *n.*, ~**ĭb**LY² *adv.* [F, or f. LL IN²(*convertibilis* CONVERTIBLE)]

ĭncōōrdĭnā'tion (ĭn-k-) *n.* Lack of co-ordination, esp. of muscular action. [f. IN-² + CO-ORDINATION]

ĭncor'porate¹ (ĭn-k-) *a.* (Of company etc.) formed into a corporation; embodied. [ME, f. as foll.; see -ATE²]

ĭncor'por|āte² (ĭn-k-) *v.* **1.** *v.t.* Unite (*in* one body, *with* another thing); admit as member of company etc., esp. *ad eundem*; combine (ingredients) into one substance; constitute as a legal corporation; (in *p.p.*) forming a legal corporation. **2.** *v.i.* Become incorporated (*with*). **3.** Hence or cogn. ~A'TION, ~**ā**tOR, *ns.* [ME, f. LL IN¹(*corporare* f. L *corpus -oris* body) + -ATE³]

ĭncorpor'ėal (ĭn-k-) *a.* Not composed of matter; of immaterial beings; (Law) having no material existence (*incorporeal hereditament*); hence or cogn. ~ITY (-ă'l-), **ĭncorporē'**ITY (ĭn-k-), *ns.*, ~LY² *adv.* [f. L IN²(*corporeus* f. *corpus -oris* body) + -AL]

ĭncorrĕ'ct (ĭn-k-) *a.* Not in accordance with fact; (of style etc.) improper, faulty; hence ~LY² *adv.*, ~NESS *n.* [ME f. OF, or f. L IN²-(*correctus* CORRECT²)]

ĭncŏ'rrĭg|ĭble (ĭn-k-) *a.* (Of person or habit) incurably bad or depraved; not readily improved; hence ~IBI'LITY *n.*, ~**ĭb**LY² *adv.* [ME f. OF, or f. L IN²(*corrigibilis* CORRIGIBLE)]

ĭncorrŭ'pt|ĭble (ĭn-k-) *a.* **1.** That cannot decay, everlasting; so (Bibl.) ~ION *n.* **2.** That cannot be corrupted, esp. bribed. **3.** Hence ~IBI'LITY *n.*, ~**ĭb**LY² *adv.* [ME f. OF, or f. eccl. L IN²(*corruptibilis* CORRUPTIBLE)]

ĭncră'ssate (ĭn-k-) *a.* (Bot. & Zool.) Of thick or swollen form. [f. LL *incrassatus* p.p. of IN¹(*crassare* f. L *crassus* thick); see -ATE²]

ĭncrea'se¹ (ĭn-k-) *v.* **1.** *v.i.* Become greater in size, amount, etc.; grow in numbers, esp. by propagation; advance (*in* quality, attainment, etc.). **2.** *v.t.* Make greater or more numerous; intensify (quality). [ME, f. OF *encreiss-* st. of *encreistre* f. L IN¹(*crescere* grow)]

ĭ'ncrease² (ĭ'n-k-) *n.* Growth, enlargement; profit, (arch.) crops; growth in numbers, multiplication (of people, animals, or plants); increased amount; **on the** ~, increasing. [ME, f. prec.]

ĭncrĕ'd|ĭble (ĭn-k-) *a.* That cannot be believed; (colloq.) hard to believe, surprising; hence ~IBI'LITY *n.*, ~**ĭb**LY² *adv.* [ME, f. L IN²(*credibilis* CREDIBLE)]

ĭncrĕ'dūlous (ĭn-k-) *a.* ~ (**of,** or abs.), unwilling to believe; hence or cogn. **ĭncrėdū'l**ITY (ĭn-k-) *n.*, ~LY² *adv.* [f. L IN²(*credulus* CREDULOUS)]

ĭ'ncrėment (ĭ'n-k-) *n.* (Amount of) increase; profit (UNEARNED *increment*); (Math.) small amount by which variable quantity increases. [ME, f. L *incrementum* (as INCREASE¹; see -MENT)]

ĭncrĭ'mĭn|āte (ĭn-k-) *v.t.* Charge with crime; involve in accusation; tend to prove guilt of (*incriminating evidence*); hence ~**at**ORY *a.* [f. LL IN¹(*criminare* f. L *crimen*; see CRIME) + -ATE³]

incrust. See ENCRUST.

ĭncrŭstā'tion (ĭn-k-) *n.* Encrusting; crust, hard coating, esp. of fine material; facing of marble etc. on building; (undesired) concretion or deposit on a surface; (fig.) accretion of habit; scab. [F, or f. LL *incrustatio* (as ENCRUST; see -ATION)]

ĭ'ncūbāte (ĭ'n-k-) *v.* **1.** *v.t.* Bring forth young birds etc. from (eggs) by sitting on them or by artificial heat; cause development of (bacteria etc.) by creating suitable conditions. **2.** *v.i.* Sit on eggs, brood. [f. L IN¹(*cubare cubit-* or *cubatlie*) + -ATE³]

ĭncūbā'tion (ĭn-k-) *n.* **1.** Incubating; brooding. **2.** (Path.) Phase through which germs of disease pass before development of first symptoms; period of this. **3.** So **ĭ'ncūbāt**IVE, **ĭ'ncūbāt**ORY, (ĭn-k-) *adjs.* [f. L *incubatio* (as prec.; see -ATION)]

ĭ'ncūbātor (ĭ'n-k-) *n.* Apparatus for hatching eggs or for rearing children born prematurely or for developing micro-organisms. [f. INCUBATE + -OR]

ĭ'ncūb|us *n.* (*pl.* **~uses,** *or* **~i** *pr.* -ī). Evil spirit supposed to descend on sleeping persons; nightmare; person or thing that oppresses like nightmare. [ME f. LL, = L *incubo* nightmare (as INCUBATE)]

ĭ'nculc|āte (ĭ'n-k-) *v.t.* Urge, impress, (fact, habit, idea) persistently (*upon* or *in* person or mind); hence **~A'TION**, **~ātor**, *ns.* [f. L IN[1]-(*culcare* = *calcare* tread f. *calx calcis* heel) + -ATE[3]]

ĭ'nculp|āte (ĭn-k-) *v.t.* Accuse, blame; involve in charge; hence **~A'TION** *n.*, **incŭ'lpatIVE**, **incŭ'lpatORY**, (ĭn-k-) *adjs.* [f. LL IN[1](*culpare* blame f. *culpa* fault) + -ATE[3]]

incŭ'lt (ĭn-k-) *a.* Unpolished, rude; (of person or manners) coarse. [f. L IN[2](*cultus* p.p. of *colere* cultivate)]

incŭ'mbencў (ĭn-k-) *n.* Office, tenure, sphere, of an incumbent. [f. as foll.; see -ENCY]

incŭ'mbent[1] (ĭn-k-) *n.* Holder of ecclesiastical benefice; holder of any office or place. [ME, f. AL *incumbens* part. (as n.) of L *incumbere* (see foll.)]

incŭ'mbent[2] (ĭn-k-) *a.* Lying, pressing, (*on*); resting (*up*)*on* (person) as duty (*it is incumbent on you to warn them*). [f. L IN[1](*cumbere* = *cubare* lie); see -ENT]

incū'nable (ĭn-k-) *n.* = foll. 2. [F, f. as foll.]

incūnā'būl|um (ĭn-k-) *n.* (*pl.* **~a**). **1.** (in *pl.*) Early stages of development of a thing. **2.** Book printed at early date, esp. before 1501. [f. L *incunabula* swaddling-clothes, cradle (as IN-[1], *cunae* cradle)]

incûr' (ĭn-k-) *v.t.* (-rr-). Fall into, bring on oneself, (danger, blame, punishment, displeasure, expense, etc.); hence **~rABLE** *a.* [ME, f. L IN[1](*currere curs-* run)]

incûr'|able (ĭn-k-) *a.* & *n.* (Person) that cannot be cured; hence **~ABI'LITY**, **~ableNESS** (-beln-), *ns.*, **~ablY**[2] *adv.* [ME f. OF, or f. LL IN[2](*curabilis* CURABLE)]

incûr'ĭ|ous (ĭn-k-) *a.* Devoid of curiosity; heedless, careless; hence **~O'SITY** *n.*, **~ousLY**[2] *adv.* [f. L IN[2](*curiosus* careful; see CURIOUS)]

incûr's|ion (ĭn-kěr'shon) *n.* Hostile invasion; sudden attack; raid; so **~IVE** *a.* [ME, f. L *incursio* (as INCUR; see -ION)]

incûr'v|e (ĭn-k-) *v.t.* Bend into a curve; (esp. in *p.p.*) curve inwards; so **~A'TION** *n.* [f. L IN[1](*curvare* CURVE[1])]

ĭ'ncu|s *n.* (*pl.* **~des** *pr.* -kū'dēz). Anvil bone of ear, receiving vibrations from malleus. [L, = anvil]

incū'se[1] (-z) *a.* & *n.* (Impression on coin etc.) hammered or stamped in. [f. L *incusus* p.p. of IN[1](*cudere* forge)]

incū'se[2] (-z) *v.t.* (esp. in *p.p.*) Impress (figure etc.) by stamping; mark (coin etc.) with such figure. [f. as prec.]

Ind (ī-) *n.* (arch. or poet.) India. [ME, f. OF *Inde* f. L INDIA]

Ind. *abbr.* Independent; India(n); Indiana.

inda'ba (-ah'-) *n.* Conference between or with members of S. Afr. native tribes. [Zulu, = business]

indĕ'btėd (-dĕ't-) *a.* Owing money (*to*); owing gratitude (*to* person, or fig. *to* thing, *for* benefit etc.); hence **~NESS** *n.* [ME, f. OF *endetté* p.p. of EN[1](*detter* f. *dette* DEBT) involve in debt + -ED[1]]

indē'cent *a.* Unbecoming, highly unsuitable, (*with indecent haste*); offending against recognized standards of decency (**~ assault**, sexual attack not involving rape; *indecent* EXPOSURE); hence or cogn. **indē'CENCY** *n.*, **~LY**[2] *adv.* [f. F *indécent* or f. L IN[2](*decens* DECENT)]

indėcī'pherable *a.* That cannot be deciphered. [f. IN-[2] + DECIPHERABLE]

indėcĭ'sion (-zhon) *n.* Lack of decision, hesitation. [f. F IN[2](*décision* DECISION)]

indėcī'sĭve *a.* Not decisive; undecided, hesitating; hence **~LY**[2] (-vlĭ) *adv.*, **~NESS** (-vn-) *n.* [f. IN-[2] + DECISIVE]

indėclī'nable *a.* (Gram.) That cannot be declined; having no inflexions. [ME, f. F *indéclinable* f. L IN[2](*declinabilis* DECLINABLE)]

indĕ'corous *a.* Improper; in bad taste; hence **~LY**[2] *adv.*, **~NESS** *n.* [f. L IN[2](*decorus* seemly)]

indėcōr'um *n.* Lack of decorum; improper behaviour. [L, neut. a. (as n.); cf. prec.]

indee'd *adv.* **1.** In truth, really, (*he was, indeed, a remarkable man*; (emphat.) *I shall be very glad indeed*; *this is quick work indeed*; *indeed it is*; *yes, indeed!*); in point of fact (*if indeed such a thing is possible*; *saw her recently, indeed yesterday*). **2.** (As approving or ironic echo: *Who is this Mr. Smith?—Who is he, indeed!* = you may well ask, or, do you really need to ask?). **3.** Admittedly (*there are indeed exceptions*). **4.** (interrog.) Really? is it so? **5.** (As excl. expr. irony, contempt, incredulity, etc.: *He expects to win—Does he, indeed!*). [ME, f. IN[1] + DEED]

indėfă'tĭg|able *a.* (Of persons, qualities, etc.) that cannot be tired out, unwearying, unremitting; hence **~ABI'LITY** *n.*, **~ablY**[2] *adv.* [f. obs. F *indéfatigable* or f. L IN[2](*defatigabilis* f. DE-*fatigare* wear out; see -ABLE)]

indėfea's|ĭble (-z-) *a.* (Esp. of claim, rights, etc.) that cannot be forfeited or annulled; hence **~IBI'LITY** *n.*, **~ĭblY**[2] *adv.* [f. IN-[2] + DEFEASIBLE]

indėfĕ'ctĭble *a.* Unfailing, not liable to defect or decay; faultless. [f. IN-[2] + *defectible* f. LL *defectibilis* (as DEFECT; see -IBLE)]

indėfĕ'ns|ĭble *a.* That cannot be defended (by force of arms or by argument); hence **~IBI'LITY** *n.*, **~ĭblY**[2] *adv.* [f. IN-[2] + DEFENSIBLE]

indėfī'nab|le *a.* That cannot be defined or exactly described; hence **~LY**[2] *adv.* [f. IN-[2] + DEFINABLE]

indĕ'fĭnĭte *a.* **1.** Vague, undefined; unlimited; *indefinite* INTEGRAL. **2.** (Gram.) Not determining the person, thing, time, etc., referred to (*indefinite* ARTICLE[1], PRONOUN); (of tense) denoting an action without specifying whether it is continuous or complete (e.g. Greek aorist, English past). **3.** Hence **~LY**[2] (-tlĭ) *adv.*, **~NESS** (-tn-) *n.* [f. L IN[2](*definitus* DEFINITE)]

indėhĭ'scent *a.* (Bot., of fruit) not splitting open when mature. [f. IN-[2] + DEHISCENT]

indĕ'l|ĭble *a.* (Of mark, stain, ink, etc., and fig. of disgrace, mental feeling, etc.) that cannot be blotted out or removed; (of pencil etc.) that makes such marks; hence **~IBI'LITY** *n.*, **~ĭblY**[2] *adv.* [f. F *indélébile* or f. L IN[2](*delebilis* f. *delere* efface; see -IBLE)]

indĕ'lĭc|ate *a.* Coarse, unrefined; tending to indecency; tactless; hence **~ACY** *n.*, **~ateLY**[2] (-tlĭ) *adv.* [f. IN-[2] + DELICATE]

indĕ'mnĭ|fў *v.t.* Protect or secure (person *from* or *against* harm or loss); secure (person) against legal responsibility (*for* actions); compensate (person *for* loss, expenses incurred, etc.); hence **~FICA'TION** *n.* [f. L IN[2](*demnis* f. *damnum* loss) + -FY]

indĕ'mnĭtў *n.* Security against damage or loss; legal exemption from penalties etc. incurred; compensation for loss incurred; sum paid for this, esp. sum exacted by victorious belligerent as one condition of peace. [ME, f. F *indemnité* f. LL *indemnitas -tatis* (as prec.; see -ITY)]

indĕ'monstrable (*or* -dĭmŏ'n-) *a.* That cannot be proved (esp. of primary or axiomatic truths). [f. IN-[2] + DEMONSTRABLE]

indĕ'nt[1] *v.* **1.** *v.t.* Make toothlike notches in; form deep recesses in (coastline etc.). **2.** Divide (document drawn up in duplicate) into two halves with zigzag line; draw up (document) in exact duplicate. **3.** (Print. etc.) Set back (beginning of line) inwards from margin to mark new paragraph etc. **4.** *v.i.* & *t.* ||Make requisition (orig. written order with duplicate) (*on* or *upon* person *for* thing); order (goods) by an indent; hence ~OR *n.* [ME, f. AF *endenter* f. AL IN¹(*dentare* f. L *dens dentis* tooth)]

ĭndĕ'nt² (*or* ĭ'n-) *n.* Indentation; indenture; ||official requisition for stores; ||order (esp. from abroad) for goods. [f. prec.]

ĭndĕ'nt³ *v.t.* Make a dent in; impress (mark etc.). [ME, f. IN-¹ + DENT 2]

ĭndĕntā'tion *n.* Indenting; cut, notch; zigzag; deep recess in coastline etc. [f. INDENT¹·³ + -ATION]

ĭndĕ'ntion *n.* Indenting of line in printing etc.; = prec. [irreg. f. INDENT¹·³ + -ION]

ĭndĕ'nture *n.*, & *v.t.* **1.** *n.* Indented document (see INDENT¹); any sealed agreement or contract, esp. (usu. in *pl.*) that which binds apprentice to master; formal list, certificate, etc.; indentation. **2.** *v.t.* Bind (person) by indentures, esp. as apprentice. [ME (orig. Sc.), f. AF *endenture* (as INDENT¹; see -URE)]

ĭndėpĕ'ndence *n.* **1.** Being independent (*on*, *of*, *from*, or abs.); independent income. **2. I~ Day,** *4 July (date of declaration of independence of U.S. in 1776), similar festival in other countries. [f. INDEPENDENT + -ENCE]

ĭndėpĕ'ndencў *n.* **1.** (Hist.; *I~*). Congregationalism. **2.** (arch.) = prec. 1. **3.** Independent State. [f. foll. + -ENCY]

ĭndėpĕ'ndent *a.* & *n.* **1.** *a.* Not depending on authority (*of*, or abs.); (Hist.; *I~*) Congregational. **2.** Not depending on something else for its validity, efficiency, (Math.) value, etc., (*independent proof*, *research*, *observer*, *variable*); (of broadcasting) not financed by licence-fees; not needing to earn one's livelihood; **~ income, means,** etc., (making it unnecessary to earn one's livelihood); ||**~ school** (not receiving government grant and not controlled by a local authority). **3.** Not depending on others for one's opinion or conduct; that is an independent in politics etc.; unwilling to be under obligation to others. **4.** Hence ~LY² *adv.* **5.** *n.* Person who acts (in politics etc.) independently of any party; (Hist.; *I~*) Congregationalist. [f. IN-² + DEPENDENT]

ĭndėscrī'b|able *a.* Vague, indefinite; too great, beautiful, bad, etc., to be described; hence ~ABI'LITY *n.*, **~ably**² *adv.* [f. IN-² + DESCRIBABLE]

ĭndėstrŭ'ct|ĭble *a.* That cannot be destroyed; hence ~IBI'LITY *n.*, **~ĭbly**² *adv.* [f. IN-² + DESTRUCTIBLE]

ĭndėtėr'mĭnable *a.* That cannot be ascertained; (of dispute etc.) that cannot be settled. [ME, f. LL IN²(*determinabilis* f. L *determinare*; see DETERMINE, -ABLE)]

ĭndėtėr'mĭnate *a.* **1.** Not fixed in extent, character, etc.; vague; left doubtful; **~ sentence,** one that leaves prisoner's release dependent on his conduct etc.; **~ vowel,** schwa. **2.** (Math., of quantity) not limited to fixed value(s) by the value(s) of another. **3.** Hence **ĭndėtėr'mĭn**ACY, ~NESS (-tn-), *ns.*, ~LY² (-tlĭ) *adv.* [ME, f. LL IN²(*determinatus* DETERMINATE)]

ĭndėtėrmĭnā'tion *n.* Lack of determination; being indeterminate. [f. prec. + -ATION]

ĭndėtėr'mĭn|ism *n.* Doctrine that human action is not wholly determined by motives; so ~IST (2) *n.*, **~ĭ'stic** *a.* [f. IN-² + DETERMINISM]

ĭ'ndĕx *n.* (*pl.* ~es *or*, esp. tech., **ĭ'ndices** *pr.* -ĭsēz), & *v.t.* **1.** *n.* **~ (finger)**, forefinger. **2.** (On instrument) pointer showing value of quantity or position on scale etc. **3. ~ (number)**, quantity indicating relative level of prices or wages at a particular date compared with that at a date taken as standard. **4.** Number expressing physical property etc. in terms of a standard (*refractive index*). **5.** Guiding principle; thing pointing to a conclusion. **6.** Alphabetical list, usu. at end of book, of names, subjects, etc., with references; CARD *index*. **7.** (Hist.; *I~*). List of books forbidden to Roman Catholics, or to be read by them only in expurgated editions [f. L *Index librorum prohibitorum*]. **8.** (Typ.) Hand-shaped symbol used to draw attention to note etc. **9.** (Math.) Exponent. **10.** Hence ~ICAL (-ĕ'-), ~LESS, *adjs.* **11.** *v.t.* Furnish (book) with index; enter (word etc.) in index; (Engin.) move through aliquot part of complete turn or to some other predetermined position; hence ~ER¹ *n.* [ME f. L *index indicis* forefinger, informer, sign, (as IN-¹, **dic-* point out)]

I'ndia (ĭ'-) *n.* ***~ ink,** = INDIAN *ink*; **~man,** (Hist.) ship engaged in trade with India or East Indies; **~ paper,** (1) soft absorbent kind orig. imported from China, used for proofs of engravings, (2) thin tough opaque printing-paper; **~ rubber, i~rubber,** = RUBBER². [~ in Asia, OE f. L, f. Gk (*Indos* river Indus, f. Pers. *hind* = Skr. *sindhu* river; see -IA¹)]

I'ndian (ĭ'-) *a.* & *n.* **1. (East) ~,** (native or inhabitant) of India or E. Indies. **2. (American) ~,** (one) of the aboriginal inhabitants of America or their descendants; ||RED *Indian*. **3. West ~,** (native or inhabitant) of W. Indies. **4.** (Hist.) European, esp. Englishman, formerly resident in India. **5. ~ clubs** (bottle-shaped, for use in gymnastics); **~ cobra,** very venomous species of cobra (*Naja naja*); **~ corn,** maize, N. Amer. cereal (*Zea mays*), or its cobs or grains; **~ cress,** tropaeolum; *Indian* FILE³; *Indian* HEMP; ||**~ ink,** black pigment made orig. in China and Japan, suspension of this in water etc.; **~ meal** (made from Indian corn); **~ millet,** durra; ***~ paintbrush,** plant of genus *Castilleja*; **~ rope-trick,** supposed Indian feat of climbing unsupported rope; **~ shot,** canna; **~ summer,** period of calm dry hazy weather in late autumn in northern U.S. and elsewhere, (fig.) tranquil late period of life etc.; **~ tobacco,** a lobelia; **~ weed,** tobacco. **6.** Hence ~IZE (3) *v.t.* [ME, f. prec. + -AN]

I'ndic (ĭ'-) *a.* Indian; of the group of Indo-European languages comprising Sanskrit and its modern descendants. [f. L f. Gk *Indikos* Indian (see INDIA, -IC)]

ĭ'ndic|āte *v.t.* **1.** Point out, make known, show; suggest, call for; (Med., in *pass.*) be desirable or necessary. **2.** State briefly; be a sign of, express presence of, (thing, *that*, etc.); (in *p.p.*) shown by indicator. **3.** So ~A'TION *n.* [f. L IN¹(*dicare* make known f. as INDEX) + -ATE³]

ĭndĭ'catĭve *a.* & *n.* **1.** *a.* (Gram., of mood) stating a thing as a fact, not as conception, wish, command, etc., of speaker. **2.** (*or* ĭ'ndĭkātĭv). Suggestive, giving indications, *of*. **3.** Hence ~LY² (-vlĭ). **4.** *n.* Indicative mood. [ME, f. F *indicatif -ive* f. LL *indicativus* transl. Gk *horistikē* (*egklisis* mood); see prec., -IVE]

ĭ'ndicātor *n.* Person or thing that points out; recording instrument attached to apparatus etc.; board giving information on current situation; (Chem.) substance changing colour at given stage in chemical reaction; radioactive tracer; device on vehicle to indicate intended change of direction of travel. [f. INDICATE + -OR]

ĭ'ndicatorў (*or* -dĭ'-) *a.* = INDICATIVE 2. [f. INDICATE + -ORY]

indices. See INDEX.

ĭndĭ'cĭ|um (-shĭ-) *n.* (esp. in *pl.* **~a**). Indication, sign; identifying mark; *imprinted mark showing that postage has been paid. [L, f. as INDEX]

indi'ct (-ī't) *v.t.* Accuse (person *for* crime, *as* culprit, *on* charge), esp. by legal process. [ME, f. AF *enditer* indict f. OF *enditier* declare f. Rom. *IN¹(*dictare*; see DICTATE²)]

indi'ctable (-ī't-) *a.* Liable, (of action) rendering one liable, to be indicted. [f. prec. + -ABLE]

indi'ction *n.* **1.** Cycle of 15 years instituted by Constantine as fiscal period in 313; assessment of property-tax by Roman emperors at beginning of each 15 years; this tax. **2.** (arch.) Proclamation. [ME, f. L *indictio* f. IN¹(*dicere dict-* say) proclaim; see -ION]

indi'ctment (-ī't-) *n.* Formal accusation; legal process in which this is made; document containing charge; **bill of ~,** (Hist. & U.S.) written accusation as presented to grand jury. [ME, f. AF *enditement* (as INDICT; see -MENT)]

I'ndies (ĭ'ndĭz) *n. pl.* **1. The ~,** (arch.) India and adjacent regions. **2. East ~,** islands etc. east of India. **3. West ~,** islands of Central America. [pl. of obs. *Indy* INDIA]

indi'fference *n.* Absence of interest or attention (*to, towards,* or abs.); neutrality; unimportance (*a matter of indifference*). [f. L *indifferentia* (as foll.; see -ENCE)]

indi'fferent *a.* **1. ~ to,** having no partiality for or against, having no interest in or sympathy for. **2.** Neither good nor bad; not especially good; fairly bad; **very ~,** definitely bad. **3.** Chemically, magnetically, etc., neutral. **4.** Hence ~LY² *adv.* [ME f. OF, or f. L IN²(*differens* DIFFERENT)]

indi'fferent|ism *n.* Spirit of indifference, professed or practised, esp. in religious matters; so ~IST (2) *n.* [f. prec. + -ISM]

i'ndigēne *n.* (arch.) Indigenous animal, plant, etc. [f. F *indigène* f. L *indigena* (*indi-* = IN-¹, *gen-* be born)]

indi'gėnous *a.* (Esp. of flora and fauna) produced naturally in a region; belonging naturally (*to* soil etc.; or fig.); hence ~LY² *adv.* [f. L *indigena* (see prec.) + -OUS]

i'ndig|ent *a.* Needy, poor; so ~ENCE *n.* [ME f. OF, f. LL *indigēre* (*indi-* = IN-¹, *egēre* need); see -ENT]

indigĕ'stėd *a.* Shapeless; ill-considered; not digested. [f. IN-² + DIGEST² + -ED¹]

indigĕ'st|ible *a.* Difficult or impossible to digest (lit. or fig.); hence ~IBI'LITY *n.* [F, or f. LL IN²(*digestibilis* DIGESTIBLE)]

indigĕ'st|ion (-schon) *n.* (Case of, pain from) difficulty in digesting food; mental state suggestive of this; undigested condition (lit. or fig.); so ~IVE *a.* [ME f. OF, or f. LL IN²(*digestio* DIGESTION)]

indi'gn (-ī'n) *a.* (arch.) Unworthy. [ME, f. OF *indigne* or f. L IN²(*dignus* worthy)]

indi'gnant *a.* Moved by mingled anger and scorn or feeling of injured innocence (*at* thing, *with* person, or abs.); hence ~LY² *adv.* [f. L *indignari* regard as unworthy (as prec.); see -ANT]

indignā'tion *n.* Anger excited by supposed meanness, injustice, wickedness, or misconduct, (*at* thing; *against, with,* person); **~-meeting** (to express public indignation). [ME f. OF, or f. L *indignatio* (as prec.; see -ATION)]

indi'gnitў *n.* Unworthy treatment; slight, insult. [f. F *indignité* or f. L *indignitas* (as INDIGN; see -ITY)]

i'ndigō *n.* (*pl.* ~s). (Blue dye obtained from) plant of genus *Indigofera*; synthetic form of the dye; **~ (blue),** colour between blue and violet in spectrum; **~-bird, ~ bunting,** N. Amer. species of finch with indigo head; **~ snake,** cribo; **~ white,** white crystalline powder formed by reduction of indigo; hence **indigŏ'tic** [-*t*- euphonic] *a.* [16th c. *indico* (f. Sp.), *indigo* (f. Port.), f. L f. Gk *indikon* INDIAN (dye)]

indirĕ'ct *a.* **1.** (Of road etc.) not straight; not going straight to the point. **2.** (Of lighting) from concealed source and diffusely reflected; (Econ., of tax) not direct, paid by consumer in form of increased price for taxed goods; **~ aggression** (by non-military means). **3.** (Gram.) **~ object,** person or thing affected by verbal action but not primarily acted on (e.g. *him* in *give him the book*); **~ passive,** passive having for subject the indirect or prepositional object of the active (e.g. *he* in *he was given the book, he was laughed at*); **~ question,** question in reported speech (*asked who I was*); **~ speech,** = REPORT¹*ed speech.* **4.** Not directly aimed at (*an indirect result*). **5.** Hence ~LY² *adv.*, ~NESS *n.* [ME f. OF, or f. med. L IN²(*directus* DIRECT²)]

indirĕ'ction *n.* Roundabout means (esp. *by indirection,* after Shak. *Hamlet* II. i. 66); deceit, trickery. [f. prec. + -ION]

indiscer'nib|le *a.* & *n.* (Thing) that cannot be discerned or distinguished from another; hence ~LY² *adv.* [f. IN-² + DISCERNIBLE]

indiscer'pt|ible *a.* (literary). Incapable of, not destructible by, separation of parts; hence ~IBI'LITY *n.* [f. IN-² + DISCERPTIBLE]

indi'scipline *n.* Lack of order or control by authority. [f. IN-² + DISCIPLINE¹, or thr. F]

indiscree't *a.* Injudicious, unwary; hence ~LY² *adv.* [ME, f. LL IN²(*discretus*; see DISCREET)]

indiscrē'te *a.* Not divided into distinct parts. [f. L IN²(*discretus* separated; see DISCREET)]

indiscrĕ'tion *n.* Injudicious conduct; accidental or (**calculated ~**) supposedly accidental revelation of official secret etc.; imprudence; imprudent immoral action. [ME f. OF, or f. LL IN²(*discretio* DISCRETION)]

indiscri'min|ate *a.* Confused, promiscuous; making no distinctions; hence **~ate**LY² (-tlĭ) *adv.*, **~ate**NESS (-tn-), ~A'TION, *ns.*, ~ATIVE *a.* [f. IN-² + *discriminate* a. f. L *discriminatus* p.p. (as DISCRIMINATE; see -ATE²)]

indispĕ'ns|able *a.* That cannot be dispensed with, necessary (*to* or *for*); (of law, duty, etc.) that cannot be set aside; hence ~ABI'LITY, **~able**NESS (-beln-), *ns.*, **~ab**LY² *adv.* [f. med. L IN²(*dispensabilis* DISPENSABLE)]

indispō'se (-z) *v.t.* Render unfit or unable (*for* thing; *to* do); make averse (*towards* or *from* thing; *to* do); (esp. in *p.p.*) make (slightly) unwell. [f. IN-² + DISPOSE]

indisposi'tion (-zĭ'-) *n.* Ill health, ailment, (esp. slight or temporary); disinclination (*to* thing; *to* do); aversion (*to, towards*). [F, or f. IN-² + DISPOSITION]

indispū't|able (*or* -dĭ'-) *a.* That cannot be disputed; unquestionable; hence ~ABI'LITY, **~able**NESS (-beln-), *ns.*, **~ab**LY² *adv.* [f. LL IN²(*disputabilis* DISPUTABLE)]

indissŏ'l|ūble *a.* Lasting, stable, (*an indissoluble bond*); that cannot be dissolved or decomposed; hence ~UBI'LITY *n.*, **~ūb**LY² *adv.* [f. L IN²(*dissolubilis* DISSOLUBLE)]

indisti'nct *a.* Not distinct; confused, obscure; hence ~LY² *adv.*, ~NESS *n.* [ME, f. L IN²(*distinctus* DISTINCT)]

indisti'nctive *a.* Not having distinctive features; hence ~LY² (-vlĭ) *adv.* [f. IN-² + DISTINCTIVE]

indisti'nguishab|le (-nggw-) *a.* Not distinguishable (*from*); hence ~LY² *adv.* [f. IN-² + DISTINGUISHABLE]

indi'te *v.t.* Put into words, compose, (poem, speech, etc.); (usu. joc.) write (letter etc.). [ME, f. OF *enditier*; see INDICT]

i'ndium *n.* (Chem.) Rare silver-white soft metallic element occurring with zinc etc. [f. L *indicum* INDIGO w. ref. to its characteristic spectral lines, + -IUM]

ĭndĭvĕr'tĭb|le *a.* That cannot be turned aside; hence ~LY² *adv.* [f. IN-² + DIVERT + -IBLE]

ĭndĭvĭ'dūal *a.* & *n.* **1.** *a.* Single; particular, special, opp. to *general*; having distinct character; characteristic of particular person; designed for use by one person. **2.** *n.* Single member of class; single human being, opp. to *society, family*, etc.; (colloq.) person (*an exceedingly unpleasant individual*). [ME, = 'indivisible', f. med. L *individualis* f. L IN²(*dividuus* f. *dividere* DIVIDE¹)]

ĭndĭvĭ'dūal|ĭsm *n.* Self-centred feeling or conduct, egoism; social theory favouring free action of individuals; so ~IST (2) *n.*, **~ĭ'stic** *a.* [f. prec. + -ISM]

ĭndĭvĭdūă'lĭtў *n.* Separate existence; individual character, esp. when strongly marked; (in *pl.*) individual tastes etc. [f. INDIVIDUAL + -ITY]

ĭndĭvĭ'dūalĭz|e, -ĭs|e (-īz), *v.t.* Give individual character to; specify; hence ~A'TION *n.* [f. INDIVIDUAL + -IZE]

ĭndĭvĭ'dūallў *adv.* Personally, in an individual capacity; in a distinctive manner; one by one, not collectively; ~ **different,** different as individuals though perhaps identical in species. [f. INDIVIDUAL + -LY²]

ĭndĭvĭ'dū|āte *v.t.* Invidualize, form into an individual; so ~A'TION *n.* [f. med. L *individuare* (as INDIVIDUAL) + -ATE³]

ĭndĭvĭ's|ĭble (-z-) *a.* Not divisible; not distributable among a number; hence ~IBI'LITY *n.*, **~ĭb**LY² *adv.* [ME, f. LL IN²(*divisibilis* DIVISIBLE)]

I'ndō- (ĭ'-) *comb. form.* Indian (and); **~-Ar'yan,** (1) Indic (group), (2) Indic-speaking (person); **~-Chine'se,** (native or inhabitant) of Indo-China; **~-Europe'an, ~-Germa'nic,** (speaker of one) of the family of languages spoken over greater part of Europe and Asia as far as N. India; **~-Iranian,** (of) the subfamily of Indo-European languages spoken chiefly in N. India and Iran; **~-Portugue'se,** modified Portuguese as used in India. [f. L f. Gk *Indos* + -O-]

ĭndō'cīle *a.* Not docile; hence **ĭndocĭ'l**ITY *n.* [F, or f. L IN²(*docilis* DOCILE)]

ĭndŏ'ctrĭn|āte *v.t.* Teach, instruct (*in* or *into* subject etc.); imbue with or *with* a doctrine, idea, or opinion; hence ~A'TION *n.* [f. IN-¹ + DOCTRINE + -ATE³]

ĭ'ndōle *n.* (Chem.) Crystalline substance with unpleasant smell, found in faeces etc., and as product of reduction of indigo. [f. INDIGO + L *oleum* oil]

ĭ'ndol|ent *a.* Slothful, lazy; (Med.) causing no pain (*indolent tumour*); hence or cogn. ~ENCE *n.*, **~ent**LY² *adv.* [f. LL IN²(*dolens* f. L *dolēre* suffer pain; see -ENT)]

Indŏ'log|ў (ĭ-) *n.* Study of Indian history, literature, etc.; hence ~IST (3) *n.* [f. INDO- + -LOGY]

ĭndŏ'mĭtab|le *a.* That does not let oneself or itself be subdued, unyielding; stubbornly persistent; hence ~LY² *adv.* [f. LL IN²(*domitabilis* f. L *domitare* tame; see DAUNT, -ABLE)]

Indonē'sian (ĭ'-; -shan) *a.* & *n.* (Native or inhabitant) of Indonesia; (one) of chief pre-Malay population of E. Indies; (language) of language-group spoken in E. Indies, esp. official language of Indonesian Republic. [f. *Indonesia* (f. INDIES after *Polynesia*) + -AN]

ĭ'ndoor (-dōr) *a.* Situated, carried on, used, within a building or under cover (*indoor aerial, games*); (Hist.) within workhouse (*indoor relief*). [earlier *within-door*; cf. foll.]

ĭndoor's (-ōr'z) *adv.* Within a building; under a roof. [earlier *within doors*]

ĭndōr'se. See ENDORSE.

ĭ'ndraught, *ĭ'ndraft, (-ahft) *n.* Drawing in; inward flow or current. [f. IN² + DRAUGHT¹]

ĭ'ndrawn *a.* (Of breath etc.) drawn in; aloof. [f. IN² + DRAWN]

ĭ'ndrĭ *n.* Babacoote. [f. Malagasy *indry* behold, mistaken for its name]

ĭndū'bĭtab|le *a.* That cannot be doubted; hence ~LY² *adv.* [F, or f. L IN²(*dubitabilis* f. *dubitare* to doubt; see -ABLE)]

ĭndū'ce *v.t.* Prevail on, persuade, (*to* do; **nothing will ~ me to,** I will never); bring about, give rise to; (Electr.) produce (current) by induction; (Phys.) cause (radioactivity) by bombardment; (esp. Med.) bring on by artificial means (*induce labour*); infer, derive as an induction. [ME, f. L IN¹(*ducere duct-* lead)]

ĭndū'cement (-sm-) *n.* What induces; attraction that leads one on (*to*). [f. prec. + -MENT]

ĭndŭ'ct *v.t.* Introduce formally into possession (*to* benefice); install (*into* seat, room, status, etc.); introduce, initiate, (*to, into*); *summon to military service, whence ~EE' *n.* [ME, as INDUCE]

ĭndŭ'ctance *n.* (Electr.) Amount of induction or self-induction of a circuit. [f. prec. + -ANCE]

ĭndŭ'ction *n.* **1.** Inducting or inducing; (arch.) preamble, prologue, introduction; (esp. Med.) bringing on by artificial means (*induction of labour*). **2.** Production (*of* facts) to prove general statement; inferring of general law from particular instances (cf. *deduction*); **mathematical ~,** proving truth of theorem by showing (1) that if true of any particular case it is true of the next case in a series, (2) that it is true of one particular case. **3.** Bringing about of electric or magnetic state in a body by proximity (without contact) of electrified or magnetized body; production of electric current in conductor by change of magnetic field; physical quantity measuring amount of such influence; **~-coil** (for generating intermittent high voltage from direct current); ~ **heating** (by induced electric current). **4.** Drawing of fuel mixture into cylinder(s) of internal combustion engine. [ME f. OF, or f. L *inductio* (as INDUCE; see -ION)]

ĭndŭ'ctĭve *a.* (Of reasoning etc.) of, based on, induction; of electric or magnetic induction; hence ~LY² (-vlĭ) *adv.*, ~NESS (-vn-) *n.* [f. LL *inductivus* (as INDUCE; see -IVE)]

ĭndŭ'ctor *n.* One who inducts clergyman; (Electr.) any part of induction apparatus, esp. reactor. [L (as INDUCE; see -OR)]

ĭndūe'. See ENDUE.

ĭndŭ'lge *v.* **1.** *v.t.* Please (person, *oneself*) by compliance with wishes (*in* matter etc.); favour (person *with* thing given); yield freely to (desire etc.). **2.** *v.i.* Take pleasure freely (*in* strong language, cycling, a cigar); (colloq.) partake (too freely) of intoxicants. [f. L *indulgēre indult-* give free rein to]

ĭndŭ'lgence *n.* **1.** Indulging (*in*); self-indulgence. **2.** Privilege granted; **Declaration of I~,** proclamation of religious liberties, esp. under Charles II in 1672 and James II in 1687. **3.** (R.C. Ch.) Remission of temporal punishment still due for sins after sacramental absolution. [ME f. OF, f. L *indulgentia* (as prec.; see -ENCE)]

ĭndŭ'lgenced (-nst) *a.* (R.C. Ch.) (Of prayer, material object, etc.) procuring indulgence to the user. [f. prec. + -ED²]

ĭndŭ'lgent *a.* Indulging or tending to indulge; (too) ready to overlook faults etc.; hence ~LY² *adv.* [F, or f. L (as INDULGE; see -ENT)]

ĭndŭ'lt *n.* (R.C. Ch.) Pope's licence for thing not sanctioned by common law of Church. [F. f. LL *indultum*, neut. p.p. (as n.) f. L (as INDULGE)]
ĭndu'na (-ōō'-) *n.* (S. Afr.) Zulu headman. [Zulu]
ĭ'ndūr|āte *v.t.* & *i.* Make or become hard; make callous or unfeeling; become inveterate; hence or cogn. ~A'TION *n.*, **~ātIVE** *a.* [f. L IN²(*durare* f. *durus* hard) + -ATE³]
ĭndū'sĭ|um (-z-) *n.* (*pl.* ~a). Membranous shield covering fruit-cluster of fern; collection of hairs enclosing stigma of some flowers; case of larva; hence ~AL *a.* [L, = tunic, f. *induere* put on (garment)]
ĭndŭ'strĭal *a.* & *n.* **1.** *a.* Of industry or industries; *industrial* ARCHAEOLOGY; *industrial* ESTATE 5; **the I~ Revolution,** rapid development of British industry by use of machines in the late 18th and early 19th c.; **I~ Workers of the World,** labour organization (1905–) advocating syndicalism and international socialism. **2.** Designed, or only fit, for industrial use (*industrial alcohol*); characterized by highly developed industries (*the industrial nations*). **3.** *n.* (in *pl.*) Shares in industrial companies. **4.** Hence ~ISM (3), ~IST (3), *ns.*, ~IZE (3) *v.t.*, ~LY² *adv.* [f. INDUSTRY + -AL; in 19th c. partly f. F *industriel*]
ĭndŭ'strĭous *a.* Diligent, hard-working; hence ~LY² *adv.* [f. F *industrieux* or f. LL *industriosus* (as foll.; see -OUS)]
ĭ'ndustrў *n.* Diligence; habitual employment in useful work; branch of trade or manufacture, these as a whole (*incentives to industry*); (colloq.) the study of a particular topic. [ME, = skill, f. F *industrie* or f. L *industria* diligence; see -Y¹]
ĭndwĕ'll *v.* (**indwe'lt**). **1.** *v.t.* (Usu. fig., of spirit, principle, etc.) inhabit, occupy. **2.** *v.i.* Be permanently present *in*. **3.** Hence ~ER¹ *n.* [ME, f. IN-¹ + DWELL]
-ine¹ (usu. ĭn) *suf.* forming *adjs.* w. sense 'pertaining to, of the nature of' (*Alpine, asinine, divine, equine, feminine, Florentine, marine, supine*). [f. or after F *-in -ine* or f. L *-inus*]
-ine² (usu. ĭn) *suf.* forming *adjs.* esp. f. names of minerals, plants, etc., (*crystalline, hyacinthine; pristine*). [f. L *-inus* f. or after Gk *-inos*]
-ine³ (*or* ēn) *suf.* forming *fem. ns.* (*heroine, margravine*). [F f. L *-ina* f. Gk *-inē*, or f. G *-in*]
-ine⁴ *suf.* forming (esp. abstract) *ns.* (*discipline, medicine, rapine; concubine, nectarine*). [F, f. L *-ina* fem. = -INE¹]
-ine⁵ (*or* ēn) *suf.* (Chem.) forming *ns.* denoting derived substances, esp. alkaloids, halogens, amines, and amino-acids [f. prec.]
ĭnē'brĭate¹ *a.* & *n.* **1.** *a.* Drunken. **2.** *n.* Drunken person, esp. habitual drunkard. [ME, f. L *inebriatus* p.p. of IN¹(*ebriare* f. *ebrius* drunk); see -ATE²]
ĭnē'brĭ|āte² *v.t.* Make drunk, intoxicate (lit. or fig.); so ~A'TION *n.* [f. as prec. + -ATE³]
ĭnėbrī'etў *n.* (Habit of) drunkenness. [f. IN-¹ + *ebriety* drunkenness f. F *ébriété* or f. L *ebrietas* (*ebrius* drunk; see -TY¹)]
ĭnĕ'd|ĭble *a.* Not edible, esp. from its nature (cf. UNEATABLE); hence ~IBI'LITY *n.* [f. IN-² + EDIBLE]
ĭnĕ'dĭtėd *a.* Not published; published without editorial alterations or additions. [f. IN-² + EDIT*ed*]
ĭnĕ'dūc|able *a.* Incapable of being educated, esp. through mental retardation; hence ~ABI'LITY *n.* [f. IN-² + EDUCABLE]
ĭnĕ'ffab|le *a.* Unutterable, too great for description in words; that must not be uttered; hence ~LY² *adv.* [ME f. OF, or L IN²(*effabilis* f. EF*fari* speak out, utter; see -ABLE)]
ĭnėffā'ce|able (-*sa*-) *a.* That cannot be effaced; hence ~ABI'LITY *n.*, **~ab**LY² *adv.*, (-*sa*-). [f. IN-² + EFFACEABLE]
ĭnėffĕ'ctĭve *a.* Not producing any effect or the desired effect; (of person) inefficient; lacking artistic effect; hence ~LY² (-vlĭ) *adv.*, ~NESS (-vn-) *n.* [f. IN-² + EFFECTIVE]
ĭnėffĕ'ctūal *a.* Without effect; not producing the desired or expected effect; hence ~LY² *adv.*, ~NESS *n.* [ME, f. med. L IN²(*effectualis* EFFECTUAL)]
ĭnĕffĭcā'cious (-sh*us*) *a.* (Of remedy etc.) not efficacious; hence or cogn. ~LY² *adv.*, ~NESS, **ĭnĕ'ffĭc**ACY, *ns.* [f. IN-² + EFFICACIOUS]
ĭnėffĭ'cĭ|ent (-sh*e*nt) *a.* Not efficient; (of person) not fully capable, not well qualified; hence or cogn. ~ENCY *n.*, **~ent**LY² *adv.* [f. IN-² + EFFICIENT]
ĭnėlă'st|ĭc (*or* -ah'-) *a.* Not elastic; unadaptable, inflexible, unyielding; (Phys., of collision) involving a decrease of total kinetic energy; hence ~ICALLY *adv.*, **ĭnėlăstĭ'c**ITY *n.* [f. IN-² + ELASTIC]
ĭnĕ'lėg|ant *a.* Ungraceful; unrefined; (of style) unpolished; hence ~ANCE *n.*, **~ant**LY² *adv.* [f. F *inélégant* f. L IN²(*elegans* ELEGANT)]
ĭnĕ'lĭg|ĭble *a.* Not eligible; undesirable; hence ~IBI'LITY *n.*, **~ĭb**LY² *adv.* [f. IN-² + ELIGIBLE]
ĭnėlŭ'ctab|le *a.* That cannot be escaped from; against which it is useless to strive; hence ~LY² *adv.* [f. L IN²(*eluctabilis* f. E*luctari* struggle out; see -ABLE)]
ĭnĕ'pt *a.* Out of place; absurd, silly; unskilful; hence or cogn. **~ĭ**TUDE, ~NESS, *ns.*, ~LY² *adv.* [f. L IN²(*eptus* = *aptus* APT)]
ĭnĕ'quable *a.* Not uniform; not fairly distributed. [f. L IN²(*aequabilis* EQUABLE) uneven]
ĭnėqua'lĭtў (-ŏ'l-) *n.* Lack of equality in magnitude, quality, rank, circumstances, etc.; variableness; (of surface) irregularity; (Astron.) deviation from uniformity in motion of heavenly body; (Math.) formula affirming that two expressions are not equal. [ME, f. OF *inequalité* or f. L IN²(*aequalitas* EQUALITY)]
ĭnĕ'quĭtab|le *a.* Unfair, unjust; hence ~LY² *adv.* [f. IN-² + EQUITABLE]
ĭnĕ'quĭtў *n.* Unfairness, bias. [f. IN-² + EQUITY]
ĭnėră'dĭcab|le *a.* That cannot be rooted out; hence ~LY² *adv.* [f. IN-² + ERADICABLE]
ĭnĕ'rr|able, ĭnĕ'rr|ant, *adjs.* Not liable to err; hence or cogn. ~ABI'LITY, ~ANCY, *ns.*, **~ab**LY² *adv.* [f. L IN²(*errabilis* & *errans* f. *errare* err; see -ABLE, -ANT)]
ĭnĕ̂r't *a.* Without inherent power of action, motion, or resistance; without active chemical or other properties; sluggish, slow; **~ gas,** = NOBLE *gas*; hence ~LY² *adv.*, ~NESS *n.* [f. L IN²(*ers ertis* f. *ars* ART²)]
ĭnĕ̂r'tia (-sh*a or* -shy*a*) *n.* **1.** (Phys.) Property of matter by which it continues in its existing state of rest or uniform motion in straight line, unless that state is changed by external force; MOMENT *of inertia*; **~ reel** (allowing automatic adjustment of safety-belt rolled round it). **2.** Inertness, sloth; **~ selling,** sending of goods not ordered, in hope that recipients will not take action to refuse them and must later make payment. **3.** Hence ~LESS *a.* [L (as prec.; see -IA¹)]
ĭnĕ̂r'tial (-sh*a*l) *a.* Of inertia; (of navigation etc.) performed automatically in response to forces causing accelerations. [f. prec. + -AL]
ĭnėscā'pable *a.* That cannot be escaped. [f. IN-² + ESCAPABLE]
ĭnėscŭ'tcheon (-ch*o*n) *n.* (Her.) Small escutcheon placed on a larger one. [f. IN² + ESCUTCHEON]
-ĭnėss *suf.* forming *ns.* corresp. to *adjs.* in -Y² etc.; cf. -NESS.
in esse (ĭn ĕ'sĭ) *a.* In actual existence (opp. IN POSSE). [L]

ĭnĕssĕ'ntial (-shal) *a.* & *n.* **1.** *a.* Not necessary; dispensable. **2.** *n.* Inessential thing. [f. IN-[2] + ESSENTIAL]
ĭnĕ'stĭmab|le *a.* Too great, intense, precious, etc., to be estimated; hence ~LY[2] *adv.* [ME f. OF, f. L IN[2](*aestimabilis* ESTIMABLE)]
ĭnĕ'vĭt|able *a.* Unavoidable, sure to happen; that is bound to occur or appear; (colloq.) that is tiresomely familiar; (of character-drawing, development of plot, etc.) so true to nature etc. as to preclude alternative treatment or solution, convincing; hence ~ABI'LITY, **~able**NESS (-beln-), *ns.*, **~ab**LY[2] *adv.* [f. L IN[2](*evitabilis* f. EVitare avoid; see -ABLE)]
ĭnĕxă'ct (-gz-) *a.* Not exact; hence or cogn. ~ĬTUDE, ~NESS, *ns.*, ~LY[2] *adv.* [f. IN-[2] + EXACT[1]]
ĭnĕxcū'sab|le (-z-) *a.* (Of person, action, etc.) that cannot be excused or justified; hence ~LY[2] *adv.* [ME, f. L IN[2](*excusabilis* EXCUSABLE)]
ĭnĕxhau'st|ĭble (-ĭgzaw'-) *a.* That cannot be exhausted; hence ~IBI'LITY *n.*, **~ĭb**LY[2] *adv.* [f. IN-[2] + EXHAUSTIBLE]
ĭnĕ'xor|able *a.* That cannot be persuaded by request or entreaty; relentless; hence ~ABI'LITY *n.*, **~ab**LY[2] *adv.* [F, or f. L IN[2](*exorabilis* f. EX[1]*orare* entreat; see -ABLE)]
ĭnĕxpē'dĭ|ent *a.* Not expedient; hence ~ENCY *n.* [f. IN-[2] + EXPEDIENT]
ĭnĕxpĕ'nsĭve *a.* Not expensive; offering good value for the price; hence ~LY[2] (-vlĭ) *adv.*, ~NESS (-vn-) *n.* [f. IN-[2] + EXPENSIVE]
ĭnĕxpēr'ĭenc|e *n.* Lack of (knowledge or skill gained from) experience; so ~ED[2] (-st) *a.* [f. F *inexpérience* f. LL IN[2](*experientia* EXPERIENCE)]
ĭnĕ'xpērt *a.* Unskilled; hence ~LY[2] *adv.*, ~NESS *n.* [OF, f. L IN[2](*expertus* EXPERT[1])]
ĭnĕ'xpĭab|le *a.* (Of offence) that cannot be expiated; (of resentment etc.) implacable; hence ~LY[2] *adv.* [f. L IN[2](*expiabilis* EXPIABLE)]
ĭnĕ'xplĭc|able *a.* That cannot be explained or accounted for; hence ~ABI'LITY *n.*, **~ab**LY[2] *adv.* [F, or f. L IN[2](*explicabilis* that cannot be unfolded; see EXPLICABLE)]
ĭnĕxplĭ'cĭt *a.* Not definitely or clearly expressed; hence ~LY[2] *adv.*, ~NESS *n.* [f. IN-[2] + EXPLICIT[2]]
ĭnĕxprĕ'ssĭb|le *a.* & *n.* **1.** *a.* That cannot be expressed in words; hence ~LY[2] *adv.* **2.** *n.* (in *pl.*, arch. colloq.) Trousers. [f. IN-[2] + EXPRESSIBLE]
ĭnĕxprĕ'ssĭve *a.* Not expressive; (arch.) inexpressible; hence ~LY[2] (-vlĭ) *adv.*, ~NESS (-vn-) *n.* [f. IN-[2] + EXPRESSIVE]
ĭnĕxpŭ'gnable *a.* Impregnable, invincible, (lit. or fig.). [ME f. F, f. L IN[2](*expugnabilis* f. EX[1]*pugnare* take by storm; see -ABLE)]
ĭnĕxpŭ'ngĭble (-nj-) *a.* That cannot be expunged or obliterated. [f. IN-[2] + EXPUNGE + -IBLE]
in extenso (ĭn ĕkstĕ'nsō) *adv.* In full, at full length. [L]
ĭnĕxtĭ'nguĭshable (-nggw-) *a.* Not quenchable, indestructible, (lit., or fig. of laughter etc.). [f. IN-[2] + EXTINGUISHABLE]
in extremis (ĭn ĕkstrē'mĭs) *a.* At the point of death; (fig.) in great difficulties. [L]
ĭnĕ'xtrĭcab|le *a.* (Of place, state, etc.) that cannot be escaped from; (of knot, problem, etc.) that cannot be unravelled or solved; intricately confused; hence ~LY[2] *adv.* [ME, f. L IN[2](*extricabilis* f. *extricare* EXTRICATE; see -ABLE)]
ĭnfă'llĭbĭl|ĭsm *n.* Principle of papal infallibility; so ~IST (2) *n.* [f. LL *infallibilis* (see foll.) + -ISM]
ĭnfă'll|ĭble *a.* Incapable of erring; (of method, test, proof, etc.) unfailing; hence ~IBI'LITY *n.* (esp. as attribute of the pope speaking *ex cathedra*, defined 1870 by the Vatican Council), **~ĭb**LY[2] *adv.* [ME, f. F *infaillible* or f. LL IN[2](*fallibilis* FALLIBLE)]
ĭ'nfamīze, -īse (-īz), *v.t.* Render infamous. [f. L *infamis* (see foll.) + -IZE]
ĭ'nfamous *a.* Of ill fame, notoriously vile or evil; abominable; (Law) deprived of all or some rights of citizen on account of serious crime; hence or cogn. ~LY[2] *adv.*, **ĭ'nfam**Y[1] *n.* [ME, f. med. L *infamosus* f. L IN[2](*famis* f. *fama* fame) + -OUS]
ĭ'nfancy̆ *n.* Early childhood, babyhood; (Law) being a minor; early state of development. [f. L *infantia* (as foll.; see -ANCY)]
ĭ'nfant *n.* Child during earliest period of life; (Law) minor (under 18); (esp. *attrib.*) thing in early state of development; **~ mortality,** death before age 1; **~ prodigy,** very precocious child; ||**~ school** (for young children, usu. under 7). [ME, f. OF *enfant* f. L IN[2](*fans fantis* part. of *fari* speak) unable to speak]
ĭnfă'nta *n.* (Hist.) Daughter of king and queen of Spain or Portugal (usu. eldest daughter who is not heir to throne); so **ĭnfă'ntė** *n.* (second son). [Sp. & Port., *-a* fem., *-e* masc., f. L (as prec.)]
ĭnfă'ntĭ|cīde *n.* Murder of infant soon after birth, esp. with mother's consent; custom of killing new-born infants; one who kills an infant; hence **~cī'd**AL *a.* [F f. LL *infanticidium, -cida* (as INFANT; see -CIDE)]
ĭ'nfant|īle *a.* Of or as of infants (**~ile paralysis,** poliomyelitis); in its infancy; so ~INE[1] *a.* [F, or f. L *infantilis* (as INFANT; see -IL)]
ĭnfă'ntĭlĭsm *n.* Infantile action etc.; (Path.) state of being mentally or physically undeveloped though of adult age. [f. prec. + -ISM]
ĭ'nfantry̆ *n.* Soldiers marching and fighting on foot; **~man,** soldier of infantry regiment. [f. F *infanterie* f. It. *infanteria* (*infante* youth, infantryman, f. as INFANT; see -RY)]
ĭ'nfārct *n.* (Path.) Region of dead tissue caused by blocking of blood-circulation; so **ĭnfār'ct**ION *n.* [f. mod. L IN[1](*farctus* p.p. of L *farcire* stuff)]
ĭnfă'tū|āte *v.t.* Affect (person) with extreme folly; inspire with extravagant passion; **~ated with,** having an unreasonably strong love for; hence ~A'TION *n.* [f. L IN[1](*fatuare* f. *fatuus* foolish) + -ATE[3]]
ĭ'nfauna *n.* Animals living just below surface of sea-bed. [f. Da. *ifauna* (as IN-[1], FAUNA)]
ĭnfĕ'ct *v.t.* Contaminate (air, water, etc.) with germs or other noxious matter; affect (person, body, mind, *with* disease etc. lit. or fig.); imbue (person *with* pernicious opinion etc.); so ~IVE *a.* [ME, f. L IN[1](*ficere fect-* = *facere* make) taint]
ĭnfĕ'ction *n.* Communication of disease, esp. by agency of air, water, etc.; moral contamination; diffusive influence of example, sympathy, etc. [ME f. OF, or f. LL *infectio* (as prec.; see -ION)]
ĭnfĕ'ctious (-sh*us*) *a.* Infecting with disease, pestilential; (of disease) liable to be transmitted by air, water, etc.; (of emotions etc.) apt to spread, quickly affecting others; hence ~LY[2] *adv.*, ~NESS *n.* [f. prec. + -OUS]
ĭnfėlĭ'cĭtous *a.* Not felicitous; hence ~LY[2] *adv.* [f. IN-[2] + FELICITOUS]
ĭnfėlĭ'cĭty̆ *n.* Unhappiness; a misfortune; inaptness of expression etc. [ME, f. L IN[2](*felicitas* FELICITY)]
ĭnfēr' *v.t.* (**-rr-**). Deduce, conclude, (thing, *that, when,* etc.; *from* fact etc.); (of fact or statement, colloq. of person) suggest truth of, imply; hence **ĭ'nfer**ABLE (*or* -ēr'-) *a.* [f. L IN[1](*ferre* bring)]

For other words in *in-* see IN-[1] or (esp.) IN-[2].

ĭ'nference *n.* Inferring; (Logic) forming of conclusion from premisses; thing inferred; so **ĭnferĕ'nt**IAL (-shal) *a.* [f. med. L *inferentia* (as prec.; see -ENCE)]

ĭnfēr'ior *a.* & *n.* **1.** *a.* Lower, in lower position, of lower rank, quality, etc., (*to*, or abs.); of poor quality; (of planet) having orbit within the earth's; (Bot., of calyx) below ovary, (of ovary) below calyx; (of figures or letters) written or printed below the line; hence ~LY^2 *adv.* **2.** *n.* Person inferior to another esp. in rank (*kind to his inferiors*); inferior letter or figure. [ME f. L, compar. of *inferus* that is below]

ĭnfērĭŏ'rĭtў *n.* State of being inferior; ~ **complex,** unrealistic feeling of general inadequacy caused by actual or supposed inferiority in one sphere, sometimes with aggressive behaviour in compensation, (colloq.) exaggerated feeling of personal inadequacy. [f. prec. + -ITY]

ĭnfēr'nal *a.* Of hell; hellish, fiendish; (colloq.) detestable, tiresome; ~ **machine,** (arch.) apparatus (usu. disguised) for producing explosion destructive of life or property; hence ~LY^2 *adv.* [ME f. OF, f. LL *infernalis* f. L *infernus* situated below; see -AL]

ĭnfēr'nō *n.* (*pl.* ~**s**). Hell (esp. w. ref. to Dante's *Divine Comedy*); scene of horror or distress, esp. conflagration. [It., f. LL *infernus* (see prec.)]

ĭnfēr'rable. Var. of INFERABLE.

ĭnfēr'tīle *a.* Not fertile; hence **ĭnfērtĭ'l**ITY *n.* [F, or f. LL IN^2(*fertilis* FERTILE)]

ĭnfĕ'st *v.t.* (Of vermin, pirates, diseases, etc.) haunt, swarm in or about, (place) esp. with troublesome result or evil intent; so ~A'TION *n.* [ME, f. F *infester* or f. L *infestare* assail (*infestus* hostile)]

||**ĭnfeudā'tion** *n* (Hist.) Enfeoffment; ~ **of tithes,** granting of tithes to laymen. [ME, f. med. L *infeudatio* f. IN^1(*feudare* f. *feudum* FEE); see -ATION]

ĭnfĭbūlā'tion *n.* Fastening with clasp, esp. of genitals to prevent sexual intercourse. [f. L IN^1(*fibulare* f. FIBULA) + -ATION]

ĭ'nfĭdel *n.* & *a.* **1.** *n.* One who does not believe in religion; (Hist.) adherent of religion opposed to Christianity, esp. Muslim; person not an adherent of one's own religion; unbeliever. **2.** *a.* That is an infidel; of unbelievers. [ME, f. F *infidèle* or f. L IN^2(*fidelis* faithful f. *fides* faith)]

ĭnfĭdĕ'lĭtў *n.* Disbelief in Christianity or other religion; disloyalty, unfaithfulness, esp. to husband or wife. [ME, f. F *infidélité* or f. L *infidelitas* (as prec.; see -ITY)]

ĭ'nfield *n.* **1.** Farm land around or near homestead; arable land; land regularly manured and cropped. **2.** (Cricket) part of the ground near the wicket, fieldsmen stationed there; (Baseball) area between the four bases, four fielders stationed on its boundaries hence; ~ER^1, ~**sman** (-z-), *ns.* [f. IN^2 + FIELD]

ĭ'nfighting (-fīt-) *n.* Boxing at closer quarters than arm's length; (fig.) hidden conflict within an organization. [f. IN^2 + FIGHTING]

ĭ'nfill *v.t.* Fill in (cavity etc.); hence ~ING^1 *n.*, (esp.) placing of buildings to occupy gaps between earlier ones. [f. IN^2 + FILL]

ĭ'nfiltr|āte (*or* -fĭ'-) *v.* **1.** *v.t.* Introduce (fluid) by filtration (*into, through*). **2.** *v.t.* & *i.* Permeate by filtration; (cause to) enter gradually and imperceptibly (as settlers, occupying troops, spies, etc.). **3.** Hence ~A'TION, ~**ātor**, *ns.* [f. IN-^{1} + FILTRATE^2]

ĭ'nfĭnĭte *a.* & *n.* **1.** *a.* Boundless, endless; very great; (w. *pl. n.*) innumerable, very many; (Math.) greater than any assignable quantity, (of series) that may be continued indefinitely; (Gram., of verb part) not limited by person or number, e.g. infinitive, gerund, participle; hence ~LY^2 (-tlĭ) *adv.* **2.** *n.* **The I~**, God; **the ~**, infinite space. [ME, f. L IN^2(*finitus* FINITE)]

ĭnfĭnĭtĕ'sĭmal *a.* & *n.* Infinitely or very small (amount); ~ **calculus,** the differential and integral calculuses regarded as one subject; hence ~LY^2 *adv.* [f. mod. L *infinitesimus* f. prec. (cf. CENTESIMAL)]

ĭnfĭ'nĭtĭve *a.* & *n.* (Gram.) (Verb-form) that expresses verbal notion without predicating it of any subject (e.g. *ask, to ask*); so **ĭnfĭnĭtī'v**AL *a.* [f. L IN^2(*finitivus* definite f. *finire -it-* define; see -IVE)]

ĭnfĭ'nĭtūde *n.* Being infinite, boundlessness; boundless number or extent (*of*). [f. L *infinitus*; see INFINITE, -TUDE]

ĭnfĭ'nĭtў *n.* = prec.; infinite distance; (Math.) infinite quantity. [ME, f. OF *infinité* f. L *infinitas* (as INFINITE; see -ITY)]

ĭnfīr'm *a.* Physically weak, esp. through age; (of person, mind, judgement, etc.) weak, irresolute, (*infirm of purpose*); hence or cogn. ~ITY *n.*, ~LY^2 *adv.* [ME, f. L IN^2(*firmus* FIRM^2)]

ĭnfīr'marў *n.* Hospital; sick-quarters in monastery, school, etc.; hence **ĭnfirmār'**IAN *n.*, person in charge of infirmary (esp. in monastery). [f. med. L *infirmaria* (as prec.; see -ARY^1)]

ĭnfĭ'x^1 *v.t.* Fix (thing *in* another); impress (fact etc. *in* mind); (Gram.) insert (formative element) in body of word; hence ~A'TION *n.* [f. IN-^{1} + FIX^1, or f. L IN^1(*figere fix-* fix)]

ĭ'nfix^2 *n.* (Gram.) Formative element infixed in word. [f. IN-^{1}, after *prefix, suffix*]

in flagrante delicto (ĭn flăgrăntĭ dĕlĭ'ktō) *a.* In the very act of committing an offence. [L, = in blazing crime]

ĭnflā'me *v.* **1.** *v.t.* Set ablaze; light up (as) with flame; excite passionately (*inflamed with* or *by*); make hot, esp. cause fever in (body etc.); cause inflammation in; aggravate. **2.** *v.i.* Catch fire; become excited; become morbidly inflamed. [ME, f. OF *enflammer* f. L IN^1(*flammare* f. *flamma* flame)]

ĭnflă'mm|able *a.* & *n.* **1.** *a.* Easily set on fire; easily excited; hence ~ABI'LITY, ~**able**NESS (-beln-), *ns.* **2.** *n.* (usu. in *pl.*) Inflammable substance. [f. prec. + -ABLE, after F *inflammable*]

ĭnflammā'tion *n.* Inflaming (lit. or fig.); (Path.) condition of part of the body with heat, swelling, redness, and usu. pain, esp. as reaction to injury or infection. [f. L *inflammatio* (as INFLAME; see -ATION)]

ĭnflă'mmatorў *a.* Tending to inflame with desire or passion (usu. in bad sense); of, tending to, inflammation of the body. [f. as prec. + -ORY]

ĭnflā't|e *v.t.* Distend with air or gas; puff up (person *with* pride etc.); (Econ.) bring about inflation of (the currency, or abs.), raise (prices) artificially; (in *p.p.*, of language) bombastic; hence ~ABLE *a.*, ~ER^1, ~OR, *ns.* [f. L IN^1(*flare* blow) + -ATE^3]

ĭnflā'tion *n.* Inflating or being inflated; (Econ.) general increase of prices and fall in purchasing value of money, increase in available currency resulting in this; hence ~ARY^1 *a.* [ME, f. L *inflatio* (as prec.; see -ATION)]

ĭnflĕ'ct *v.t.* Bend inwards, curve; (Gram.) vary ending of (word) to express grammatical relation, whence ~IVE *a.*; change pitch of (voice, musical note). [ME, f. L IN^1(*flectere flex-* bend)]

ĭnflĕ'ction. See INFLEXION.

ĭnflĕ'x|ĭble *a.* Unbendable; (fig.) unbending, inexorable; hence ~IBI'LITY *n.*, ~**ĭb**LY^2 *adv.* [f. L IN^2(*flexibilis* FLEXIBLE)]

ĭnflĕ'xion (-kshon), **ĭnflĕ'ction,** *n.* Inflecting;

inflected form of word; suffix etc. used to inflect; modulation of voice; (Geom.) change of curve from convex part to concave; hence ~AL, ~LESS, *adjs.* [F, or f. L *inflexio* (as INFLECT; see -ION)]

ĭnflĭ'ct *v.t.* Lay on (stroke, wound, defeat, *on* or *upon*); impose (suffering, penalty, one*self*, one's company, etc., *on* or *upon*); hence or cogn. ~ABLE *a.*, ~ION *n.* (esp., troublesome or boring experience), ~OR *n.* [f. L IN[1](*fligere flict-* strike)]

ĭnflorĕ'scence *n.* (Bot.) Arrangement of flowers of plant in relation to axis and to each other; collective flower of plant; flowering (lit. or fig.). [f. mod. L *inflorescentia* f. LL IN[1](*florescere*; see FLORESCENCE)]

ĭ'nflow (-ō) *n.* Flowing in; that which flows in; so ~ING[1,2] *n.* & *a.* [f. IN[2] + FLOW 3]

ĭ'nfluence (-lōō-) *n.*, & *v.t.* **1.** *n.* (Astrol.) Supposed flowing from stars of ethereal fluid affecting character and destiny of man. **2.** Action of person or thing *on* or *upon* another, perceptible only in its effects; ascendancy, moral power, (*over, with,* person etc.); thing or person exercising (usu. non-material) power; (colloq., ellipt.) **under the ~** (i.e. of alcohol); UNDUE *influence.* **3.** (Electr., arch.) = INDUCTION. **4.** *v.t.* Exert influence upon, have effect upon. [ME f. OF, or f. med. L *influentia* f. L IN[1](*fluere* flow); see -ENCE]

ĭ'nfluent (-lōō-) *a.* & *n.* **1.** *a.* Flowing in (lit. or fig.). **2.** *n.* Tributary stream. [ME, f. L (as prec.; see -ENT)]

ĭnfluĕ'ntial (-lōōĕ'nshal) *a.* Having great influence; hence ~LY[2] *adv.* [f. med. L *influentia* INFLUENCE + -AL]

ĭnfluĕ'nza (-lōō-) *n.* Acute contagious and infectious febrile disorder caused by virus, usu. with fever, rapid prostration, and severe aching and catarrh, often occurring in epidemics; **gastric ~,** (pop.) intestinal disorder of unknown cause. [It., f. med. L *influentia* INFLUENCE]

ĭ'nflŭx *n.* Flowing in, esp. of stream etc. (*into* river etc.), or of persons or things (*into* place etc.). [f. F, or f. LL IN[1](*fluxus* FLUX)]

ĭ'nfō *n.* (colloq.) Information. [abbr.]

ĭnfō'ld. Var. of ENFOLD.

ĭnfôr'm *v.* **1.** *v.t.* Inspire, imbue, (person, heart, thing, *with* feeling, principle, quality, etc.); impart its quality to, permeate; tell (person *of* or *about* or *on* thing or subject, *that, how,* etc.), whence ~ANT *n.* **2.** *v.i.* Bring charge or complaint (*against* or *on* person). [ME, f. OF *enfo(u)rmer* f. L IN[1](*formare* f. *forma* form) give shape to, fashion, describe]

ĭnfôr'mal *a.* Not according to due form; without ceremony or formality; **~ vote,** (N.Z. & Austral.) invalid vote or voting-paper; hence ~ITY (-ă'l-) *n.*, ~LY[2] *adv.* [f. IN-[2] + FORMAL]

in forma pauperis (ĭn fôrma paw'perĭs) *adv.* (Law). As a poor person not liable for costs of action. [L]

ĭnformā'tion *n.* Informing, telling; thing told, knowledge, (desired) items of knowledge, news, (*on, about*); (Law) charge or complaint lodged with court or magistrate (*against*); **~ retrieval,** tracing of information stored in books, computers, etc.; **~ theory,** quantitative study of transmission of information by signals etc.; hence ~AL *a.* [ME f. OF, f. L *informatio -onis* (as INFORM; see -ATION)]

ĭnfôr'mat|ĭve *a.* Giving information, instructive; so ~ORY *a.* [f. med. L *informativus* (as INFORM; see -ATIVE)]

ĭnfôr'med (-md) *a.* Instructed, knowing the facts, (WELL, *ill, -informed*); educated, intelligent. [p.p. of INFORM]

ĭnfôr'mer *n.* In vbl senses; one who informs against another; (**common**) **~,** one who makes it his business to detect offenders and lay information against them. [ME, f. INFORM + -ER[1]]

infra (ĭ'nfra) *adv.* Below; lower down, further on, (in book or writing). [L, = below]

ĭ'nfra- *pref.* Below (opp. SUPRA-), esp. (Anat.) below or under a part (**~re'nal,** beneath the kidneys). [f. or after L *infra* below, beneath]

ĭnfră'ction *n.* Violation, infringement. [f. L *infractio* (as INFRINGE; see -ION)]

ĭnfra dĭg. *pred. a.* (colloq.) Beneath one's dignity, unbecoming. [abbr. L *infra dignitatem*]

ĭnfralăpsăr'ian *n.* & *a.* (Calvinist) holding doctrine that God's election of some to eternal life was consequent to his prescience of the Fall, or that it contemplated man as already fallen; hence ~ISM (3) *n.* [f. L *infra* beneath + *lapsus* fall + -ARIAN]

ĭnfră'ngĭble (-nj-) *a.* Unbreakable; inviolable. [obs. F, or f. med. L IN[2](*frangibilis* FRANGIBLE)]

ĭnfra-rĕ'd *a.* (Phys.) having wavelength (just) beyond red end of visible spectrum; of or using such radiation. [f. INFRA- + RED]

ĭnfrasŏ'n|ĭc *a.* Of sound waves with pitch below lower limit of human audibility; hence ~ICALLY *adv.* [f. INFRA- + SONIC]

ĭ'nfrastrŭcture *n.* Subordinate parts of an undertaking, esp. permanent installations as basis for military etc. operations. [F (as INFRA-, STRUCTURE)]

ĭnfrē'qu|ent *a.* Not frequent; hence or cogn. ~ENCY *n.*, **~ent**LY[2] *adv.* [f. L IN[2](*frequens* FREQUENT[1])]

ĭnfrĭ'nge (-nj) *v.* **1.** *v.t.* Act contrary to, violate, (law, oath, etc.); act in defiance of (another's rights etc.). **2.** *v.i.* Encroach, trespass, *on* or *upon.* **3.** Hence ~MENT (-jm-) *n.* [f. L IN[1](*fringere fract-* = *frangere* break)]

ĭnfrŭctĕ'scence *n.* (Bot.) Fruit formed from an inflorescence. [F, f. L *fructus* FRUIT, after *inflorescence*]

ĭ'nfŭla *n.* (*pl.* ~e). (Eccl.) Each of two ribbons of bishop's mitre. [L, = woollen fillet worn by priest etc.]

ĭnfŭndĭ'bŭlar *a.* Funnel-shaped. [f. L *infundibulum* funnel f. IN[1](*fundere* pour) + -AR[1]]

ĭnfūr'iate[1] *a.* Excited to fury, frantic. [f. med. L *infuriatus* p.p. (as foll.); see -ATE[2]]

ĭnfūr'iāte[2] *v.t.* Fill with fury, enrage. [f. med. L IN[1](*furiare* f. L *furia* FURY) + -ATE[3]]

ĭnfū's|e (-z) *v.* **1.** *v.t.* Pour (thing *into*); (fig.) instil (grace, spirit, life, etc., *into*); imbue, pervade, (*with* quality etc.). **2.** Steep (herb, tea, etc.) in liquid to extract its soluble constituents, whence ~ER[1] (2) *n.* **3.** *v.i.* Undergo infusion (*let it infuse for five minutes*). **4.** Hence ~ABLE *a.* [ME, f. L IN[1](*fundere fus-* pour)]

ĭnfū's|ĭble (-z-) *a.* That cannot be fused or melted; hence ~IBI'LITY *n.* [f. IN-[2] + FUSIBLE (see FUSE[1])]

ĭnfū'sion (-zhon) *n.* Infusing (lit. or fig.); liquid extract thus obtained; infused element, admixture. [ME f. F, or f. L *infusio* (as INFUSE; see -ION)]

ĭnfūsôr'|ĭa (*or* -z-) *n.pl.* (arch). Class of protozoa found in infusions of decaying animal or vegetable matter; hence ~IAL *a.* (**~ial earth,** kieselguhr), ~IAN *a.* & *n.* [mod. L, neut. pl. (as n.) of *infusorius* (as INFUSE; see -ORY, -IA[2])]

-ĭng[1] *suf.* forming *ns.* f. *vbs.* (occas. f. *ns.*) w. senses (1) vbl action (*asking, driving, fighting, foreboding*), sometimes as occupation (*banking, glass-blowing*) or event (*wedding*) or as inflicted or performed on (*thrashing, the wearing of the green*), (2) thing produced by vbl action (*building, carving, filings, learning*), (3) material for (*clothing, fencing, sacking, scaffolding*), (4) what is used for or affects vbl action (*binding, firm going*), (5) what is to undergo vbl action (*darning, washing*), (6) set or arrangement of (*colouring, feathering*). [OE *-ung, -ing* f. Gmc **-ungā*]

-ĭng[2] *suf.* forming *pres. part.* of *vbs.*, often used as *a.* (*appalling, charming, diverting, heart-breaking, strapping, well-meaning*), sometimes w. sense 'likely to' (*not a marrying man*) or 'suitable to undergo' (*cooking apple*); occas. as *prep.* etc. (*during, notwithstanding*); occas. f. *ns.* (*hulking*). [f. OE *-ende* by confus. w. prec.]

-ĭng[3] *suf.* forming *ns.* w. sense 'one belonging to', 'one having the quality of', or dim., (*farthing, gelding, herring,* RIDING[2]). [OE, f. Gmc **-inga*; cf. -LING[1]]

ĭngăʹther (ĭn-găʹdh-) *v.t.* Gather in, assemble; hence ~ING[1] *n.*, (esp.) harvest. [f. IN[2] + GATHER]

ĭngĕʹmĭnāte (ĭnj-) *v.t.* Repeat, reiterate, (esp. **~ peace,** constantly urge it). [f. L IN[1](*geminare* GEMINATE[2])]

ĭngēʹnĭous (ĭnj-) *a.* Clever at inventing, constructing, organizing, etc.; cleverly contrived (*ingenious machine, explanation, theory*); hence ~LY[2] *adv.* [ME, = 'talented', f. F *ingénieux* or f. L *ingeniosus* (*ingenium* cleverness; cf. ENGINE, -OUS)]

ingénue (ăʹṅzhānōō *or* -ū) *n.* Artless young woman, esp. as a stage type. [F, fem. of *ingénu* INGENUOUS]

ĭngėnūʹĭtў (ĭnj-) *n.* Being ingenious; skill in contriving. [f. L *ingenuitas* ingenuousness (as foll.; see -ITY); E meaning by confus. of INGENIOUS w. foll.]

ĭngĕʹnūous (ĭnj-) *a.* Open, frank; innocent, artless; hence ~LY[2] *adv.*, ~NESS *n.* [f. L IN[1](*genuus* f. **gen-* beget) free-born, frank]

ĭngĕʹst (ĭnj-) *v.t.* Take in (food etc.) by swallowing or absorbing (lit. or fig.); hence or cogn. ~ION (-schon) *n.*, ~IVE *a.* [f. L IN[1](*gerere gest-* carry)]

ĭʹngle (ĭʹnggel) *n.* Fire burning on hearth; **~-nook,** chimney-corner. [orig. Sc., perh. f. Gael. *aingeal* fire, light]

ĭnglôrʹĭous (ĭn-g-) *a.* Shameful, ignominious; obscure; hence ~LY[2] *adv.* [f. L IN[2](*glorius* f. *gloria* glory) + -OUS, or f. IN-[2] + GLORIOUS]

-ĭnglў *suf.* forming *advs.* esp. denoting manner of action or nature of condition (*charmingly, correspondingly, disgustingly, embarrassingly, heart-breakingly, increasingly, inquiringly, irritatingly, mockingly, slantingly, soothingly*). [f. -ING[2] + -LY[2]]

ĭʹngōĭng (ĭn-g-) *a.* Going in, entering; penetrating, thorough. [f. IN[2] + GOING[2]]

ĭʹngot (ĭʹngg-) *n.* Mass (usu. oblong) of cast metal, esp. of gold, silver, or steel. [ME; perh. f. IN[2] + *goten* p.p. of OE *geotan* cast]

ingraft. See ENGRAFT.

ĭʹngrain (ĭʹn-g-) *a.* Dyed in GRAIN; inherent, inveterate, ingrained; **~ carpet** (reversible, with different colours interwoven). [f. *in* GRAIN]

ĭʹngrained (ĭʹn-grānd before *n.*, -āʹnd elsewhere) *a.* Deeply rooted, inveterate; thorough; hence ~LY[2] (-āʹnĭd-) *adv.* [var. of ENGRAIN*ed*]

ĭʹngrāte (ĭʹn-g-; *or* -āʹt) *a.* & *n.* (arch.) Ungrateful (person). [ME, f. L IN[2](*gratus* grateful)]

ĭngrāʹtĭāte (ĭn-grāʹshĭ-) *v.t.* Bring one*self* into favour *with*. [f. L *in gratiam* into favour + -ATE[3]]

ĭngrăʹtĭtūde (ĭn-g-) *n.* Lack of due gratitude. [ME f. OF, or f. LL *ingratitudo* (as INGRATE; see -TUDE)]

ĭngravĕʹsc|ent (ĭn-g-) *a.* (Med.) (Of disease etc.) growing worse; hence ~ENCE *n.* [f. L IN[1](*gravescere* grow heavy f. *gravis* heavy); see -ENT]

ĭngrēʹdĭent (ĭn-g-) *n.* Component part, element, in a mixture or combination. [ME, f. L IN[1](*gredi gress-* = *gradi* step) enter; see -ENT]

ĭʹngrĕss (ĭʹn-g-) *n.* (Right of) going in; (Astron.) start of eclipse or transit. [ME, f. L *ingressus* (as prec.)]

ĭʹngrowĭng (ĭʹn-grōĭ-) *a.* Growing inwards, esp. (of nail) growing into the flesh; so **ĭʹn**GROWN *a.*, **ĭʹn**GROWTH *n.*, (ĭʹn-grō-). [f. IN[2] + GROW + -ING[2]]

ĭʹnguĭnal (ĭʹnggw-) *a.* Of the groin. [f. L *inguinalis* (*inguen -inis* groin; see -AL)]

ingulf. Var. of ENGULF.

ĭngûrʹgĭt|āte (ĭn-g-) *v.t.* Swallow greedily; (fig.) engulf; so ~AʹTION *n.* [f. L IN[1](*gurgitare* f. *gurges gurgitis* whirlpool) + -ATE[3]]

ĭnhăʹbĭt *v.t.* (Of person or animal) dwell in, occupy, (region, town, house, or fig.); hence or cogn. ~ABLE *a.*, ~ANT, ~AʹTION, *ns.* [ME *inhabite, enhabite* f. OF *enhabiter* or f. L IN[1](*habitare* dwell; see HABIT[2])]

ĭnhăʹbĭtancў *n.* Residence as inhabitant, esp. during specified period so as to acquire rights etc. [f. as prec. + -ANCY]

ĭnhāʹl|e *v.t.* Breathe in (air, gas, etc., or abs.; lit. or fig.); take (esp. tobacco-smoke or abs. of this) into the lungs; hence or cogn. ~ANT, ~ER[1] (2), *ns.* (esp. Med. = agent, device, for inhaling), **ĭnhal**AʹTION *n.* [f. L IN[1](*halare* breathe)]

ĭnhârmŏʹnĭc *a.* (esp. Mus.) Not harmonic. [f. IN-[2] + HARMONIC]

ĭnhârmōʹnĭous *a.* Not harmonious; hence ~LY[2] *adv.* [f. IN-[2] + HARMONIOUS]

ĭnhērʹe *v.i.* (Of qualities etc.) exist, abide, essentially or permanently *in*; (of rights etc.) be vested *in* (person etc.). [f. L IN[1](*haerēre haes-* to stick)]

ĭnhērʹ|ent *a.* Existing in or *in* something esp. as permanent or characteristic attribute; vested *in* (person etc.) as right or privilege; hence or cogn. ~ENCE *n.*, **~ent**LY[2] *adv.* [f. L (as prec.; see -ENT)]

ĭnhĕʹrĭt *v.t.* Receive (property, rank, title) by legal descent or succession; derive (quality, character) from one's progenitors or predecessors; (abs.) succeed as heir; hence ~OR, ~RESS[1], **ĭnhĕʹrĭ**TRIX, *ns.* [ME, f. OF *enheriter* f. LL IN[1](*hereditare* f. L *heres heredis* heir)]

ĭnhĕʹrĭt|able *a.* Capable of inheriting or of being inherited (lit. or fig.); hence ~ABIʹLITY *n.* [ME f. AF (as prec.; see -ABLE)]

ĭnhĕʹrĭtance *n.* Inheriting; what is inherited (lit. or fig.). [ME, f. AF *inheritaunce* (OF *enheriter*; see INHERIT, -ANCE)]

ĭnhēʹsion (-zhon) *n.* Inhering. [f. LL *inhaesio* (as INHERE; see -ION)]

ĭnhĭʹbĭt *v.t.* **1.** Forbid, prohibit, (person etc. *from* doing; esp. in Eccl. Law); forbid (ecclesiastic) to exercise clerical functions. **2.** Hinder, restrain, or prevent, (action, process); (in *p.p.*) subject to inhibition. **3.** Hence or cogn. ~OR *n.*, ~ORY *a.* [f. L IN[1](*hibēre hibit-* = *habēre* hold)]

ĭnhĭbĭʹtion *n.* Inhibiting or being inhibited; (Psych.) restraint of direct expression of an instinct; (colloq.) emotional resistance to thought or action. [ME f. OF, or f. L *inhibitio* (as prec.; see -ITION)]

ĭnhŏmogĕʹnėous *a.* Not homogeneous; hence **ĭnhŏmogėnēʹ**ITY *n.* [f. IN-[2] + HOMOGENEOUS]

ĭnhŏʹspĭtab|le (*or* -pĭʹ-) *a.* Not hospitable; (of region, coast, etc.) not affording shelter etc.; hence **~le**NESS (-beln-) *n.*, ~LY[2] *adv.* [obs. F (as IN-[2], HOSPITABLE)]

ĭnhŏspĭtăʹlĭtў *n.* Being inhospitable. [f. L *inhospitalitas* (as IN-[2], HOSPITALITY)]

ĭnhūʹman *a.* **1.** (Of person or conduct) brutal, unfeeling, barbarous; hence or cogn. ~ITY (-ăʹn-) *n.*, ~LY[2] *adv.* **2.** Not of the ordinary human type. [f. L IN[2](*humanus* HUMAN)]

inhūmā'ne *a.* Not humane; hence ~LY² (-nlĭ) *adv.* [f. L *inhumanus* (see prec.), & f. IN-² + HUMANE; orig. = prec.]

inhū'm|e *v.t.* (literary). Bury; hence ~A'TION *n.* [f. L IN¹(*humare* f. *humus* ground)]

ĭnĭ'mĭcal *a.* Hostile (*to*); harmful (*to*); hence ~LY² *adv.* [f. LL *inimicalis* f. L IN²(*imicus* = *amicus* friend); see -AL]

ĭnĭ'mĭtab|le *a.* That defies imitation; hence ~leNESS (-beln-) *n.*, ~LY² *adv.* [F, or f. L IN²(*imitabilis* IMITABLE)]

ĭnĭ'quĭt|ў *n.* Unrighteousness, wickedness; gross injustice; hence ~OUS *a.* [ME, f. OF *iniquité* f. L *iniquitas -tatis* f. IN²(*iquus* = *aequus* just); see -ITY]

ĭnĭ'tial (-shal) *a., n.,* & *v.t.* (**-ll-** *or* **-l-**). **1.** *a.* Of, existing or occurring at, the beginning, (*initial stage, expenses, difficulties*); ~ **letter, consonant,** etc., (standing at beginning of word); ~ **teaching alphabet,** 44-letter phonetic alphabet devised to help those learning to read and write English; hence ~LY² *adv.* **2.** *n.* Initial letter, esp. (in *pl.*) first letters of words of (esp. person's) name(s). **3.** *v.t.* Mark or sign with initials. [f. L *initialis* f. *initium* beginning f. IN¹(*ire it-* go); see -AL]

ĭnĭ'tĭ|āte¹ (-shĭ-) *v.t.* Begin, set going, originate; admit (person), esp. with introductory rites or forms, (*into* society, office, secret; *in* or *into* mysteries, science, etc.); hence or cogn. ~A'TION, ~**ātOR**, *ns.*, ~**atORY** (-shya- *or* -sha-) a. [f. L *initiare* (*initium*; see prec.) + -ATE³]

ĭnĭ'tĭ|ate² (-shĭ-) *a.* & *n.* (Person) who has been initiated. [f. as prec.; see -ATE²]

ĭnĭ'tiatĭve (-shya- *or* -sha-) *n.* & *a.* **1.** *n.* First step, origination; **take the** ~, be the first to take action (*in doing*); **on** one's **own** ~, without being prompted by others. **2.** Power or right to begin something; **have the** ~, (esp., Mil.) be able to make enemy conform to one's movements. **3.** Ability to initiate things, enterprise, (esp. w. neg., expressed or implied: *he lacks, has little* or *no, initiative*). **4.** Right of citizen(s) outside legislature to originate legislation (as in Switzerland). **5.** *a.* Beginning, originating. [F (as INITIATE¹; see -IVE)]

ĭnjĕ'ct *v.t.* Drive, force, (fluid, medicine, *into* cavity etc.) by or as by syringe; fill (cavity etc. *with*) by injecting; administer medicine etc. to (person) by injecting; place (object, quality, etc.) where needed in, or as part of, something; hence ~OR *n.* [f. L IN¹(*jicere ject-* = *jacĕre* throw)]

ĭnjĕ'ction *n.* Injecting; liquid or solution injected; FUEL *injection*; ~ **moulding,** shaping of rubber or plastic articles by injecting heated material into mould. [F, or f. L *injectio* (as prec.; see -ION)]

ĭnjudĭ'cious (-jōōdĭ'shus) *a.* Unwise, ill-judged; hence ~LY² *adv.*, ~NESS *n.* [f. IN-² + JUDICIOUS]

I'njun (ĭ'-) *n.* (colloq. or *dial.) American Indian (HONEST *Injun*). [corrupt.]

ĭnjŭ'nction *n.* Authoritative admonition or order; judicial process restraining person from wrongful act or compelling restitution etc. to injured party, whence **ĭnjŭ'nct** *v.t.* (colloq.). [f. LL *injunctio* f. L *injungere* ENJOIN; see -ION]

ĭ'njure *v.t.* Do wrong to; hurt (lit. or fig.), harm, impair. [back form. f. INJURY]

ĭ'njured (-jerd) *a.* In vbl senses; wronged; showing sense of wrong, offended, (*in an injured voice*). [p.p. of prec.]

injur'ĭa (-oor'-) *n.* (Law). Infringement of another's rights. [L; see INJURY]

injur'ĭous (-oor'-) Wrongful; (of language) insulting, calumnious; hurtful; hence ~LY² *adv.*, ~NESS *n.* [ME, f. F *injurieux* or f. L *injuriosus* (as foll.; see -OUS)]

ĭ'njurў *n.* Wrongful action or treatment; harm, damage; ||~ **time,** (Footb.) extra playing-time allowed by referee to compensate for that lost when players have been hurt. [ME, f. AF *injurie* f. L IN²(*juria* f. *jus juris* right) wrong; see -Y¹]

ĭnjŭ'stĭce *n.* Lack of equity, unfairness; unjust act; **do** person **an** ~, judge him unfairly. [ME f. OF, f. L IN²(*justitia* JUSTICE)]

ĭnk *n.*, & *v.t.* **1.** *n.* Fluid (black, red, etc.) for writing with pen or marking with rubber stamp etc.; MARKING-*ink*. **2.** Viscous paste used to mark paper etc. in printing, duplicating, writing with ball-pen, etc. **3.** Black liquid ejected by cuttlefish etc. to darken water and assist its escape. **4.** ~**-blot test,** Rorschach test; ~**-horn,** small vessel of horn formerly used for holding ink (~*-horn term*, literary word); ~**-pad** (for inking rubber stamp etc.); ~**-slinger,** (derog.) professional writer; ~**'stand,** stand for one or more bottles to hold ink, often with pen-tray etc.; ~**-well** (pot fitted into hole in desk). **5.** Hence ~'Y² *a.* **6.** *v.t.* Mark (*in, over,* etc.) with ink; cover (printing types etc.) with ink so as to print from them; apply ink to; ~ **out,** obliterate with ink; hence ~'ER¹ (1, 2) *n.* [ME *enke, inke* f. OF *enque* f. LL *encau(s)tum* f. Gk *egkauston* (as EN-², CAUSTIC) purple ink used by Roman emperors for signature]

ĭ'nklĭng *n.* Hint, slight knowledge or suspicion, (*of*). [f. ME *inkle* utter in an undertone + -ING¹; orig. unkn.]

ĭnlai'd. See INLAY¹.

ĭ'nland (*or* -ănd) *n., a.,* & *adv.* **1.** *n.* Interior of country, parts remote from sea or frontiers. **2.** *a.* Placed in interior of country; carried on within limits of a country (*inland trade*); ~ **duty** (on inland trade); *inland* NAVIGATION; ||~ **revenue** (consisting of taxes and inland duties); ||**I~ Revenue,** government department responsible for assessing and collecting these; *inland* SEA. **3.** *adv.* In or towards interior of country. **4.** Hence ~ER¹ (4) *n.*, ~ISH¹ *a.* [f. IN² + LAND¹]

ĭ'n-law *n.* (colloq., usu. in *pl.*) Relative by marriage. [f. IN¹ + LAW¹]

ĭnlay'¹ *v.t.* (**inlai'd**). Embed (thing *in* another) so that their surfaces are even; ornament (thing *with* another inlaid); insert (page, illustration, etc.) in space cut in larger stouter page. [f. IN-¹ + LAY³]

ĭ'nlay² (*or* -ā') *n.* Inlaid work; filling shaped to fit tooth-cavity. [f. prec.]

ĭ'nlĕt (*or* -ĕt) *n.* Small arm of sea, creek; piece inserted; way of entry. [ME, f. IN² + LET² v.]

ĭ'nlĭer *n.* (Geol.) Space occupied by one formation and completely surrounded by later formation. [f. IN², after *outlier*]

in loco parentis (ĭn lŏkō perĕ'ntĭs) *adv.* In place of a parent. [L]

ĭ'nlў *adv.* (poet.) Inwardly, in the heart; intimately; thoroughly. [OE *innlice* (as IN², -LY²)]

ĭ'nlўĭng *a.* Situated within, or near a centre. [f. IN² + LYING²]

ĭ'nmāte *n.* Occupant (*of* house etc.), esp. one of several; occupant of hospital, prison, or other institution. [prob. orig. f. INN + MATE², assoc. w. IN²]

in medias res (ĭn mĕdĭahs rĕ'z) *adv.* Into the midst of things; into the middle of a narrative, without preamble. [L]

in memoriam (ĭn mĭmŏr'ĭăm) *prep.* & *n.* **1.** *prep.* In memory of. **2.** *n.* Writing, notice, etc., in memory of a deceased person. [L]

ĭ'nmōst (*or* -ost) *a.* Most inward; (fig.) deepest, most intimate. [f. OE *innemest* (as IN²; see -MOST)]

For other words in *in-* see IN-¹ or (esp.) IN-².

inn *n.* **1.** House providing lodging etc. for payment, esp. for travellers; house providing alcoholic liquor for consumption on the premises; **~'keeper,** one who keeps an inn. **2.** ||**Inns of Court,** (buildings in London belonging to) four legal societies having exclusive right of admitting persons to practise at the English bar; ||**Inns of Chancery,** (Hist.) buildings in London formerly used as hostels for law students. [OE *inn* (as IN²)]

ĭ'nnards (-z) *n. pl.* (colloq.) Entrails. [f. dial. etc. pronunc. of *inwards* (see INWARD 2)]

ĭnnā'te (*or* ĭ'n-) *a.* Inborn, natural; (Philos.) originating in the mind; hence ~LY² (-tlĭ) *adv.*, ~NESS (-tn-) *n.* [ME, f. L IN¹(*natus* p.p. of *nasci* be born)]

ĭ'nner *a.* & *n.* **1.** *a.* Interior, internal, inward; ||**~ bar,** Queen's or King's COUNSEL¹ collectively; **~-directed,** governed by standards formed early in one's life; **~ man** or **woman,** soul or mind, (joc.) stomach; **~ space,** (1) region between earth and outer space, or below surface of sea, (2) part of mind not normally perceived consciously; ***~-spring,** = INTERIOR-*-sprung*; *Inner* TEMPLE¹; **~ tube,** separate inflatable tube inside cover of pneumatic tyre; hence ~MOST *a.* **2.** *n.* Division of target next outside bull's-eye; shot that strikes this. [OE *innera* a., compar. of IN²]

ĭnnėr'v|āte (*or* ĭ'-) *v.t.* Supply (organ etc.) with nerves; hence ~A'TION *n.* [f. IN-¹ + L *nervus* nerve + -ATE³]

***ĭ'nnĭng** *n.* Innings at baseball etc. [f. *in* v. go in (f. IN²) + -ING¹]

ĭ'nnĭngs (-z) *n.* (*pl.* same, *or* colloq. **~es**). **1.** (Cricket etc.) Portion of game during which a side is in or batting; play of one batsman during his turn. **2.** (fig.) Tenure of office, dominance, of political party, cause, etc.; period during which person has opportunity to achieve something. [pl. of prec.]

ĭ'nnocent *a.* & *n.* **1.** *a.* Free from moral wrong, sinless; unacquainted with evil. **2.** Not guilty (*of* crime etc.); **~ of,** (colloq.) without. **3.** Simple, guileless; harmless; naïve; pretending to be guileless. **4.** Hence or cogn. **ĭ'nnoc**ENCE, **ĭ'nnoc**ENCY, *ns.*, ~LY² *adv.* **5.** *n.* Innocent person, esp. young child; (in *pl.*) young children killed by Herod after birth of Jesus (Matt. 2:16); (**Holy**) **I~s' Day,** 28 Dec. [ME f. OF, or f. L IN²(*nocens -ent-* part. of *nocēre* hurt); see -ENT]

ĭnnŏ'cūous *a.* Not injurious, harmless (esp. of snakes); inoffensive; hence or cogn. **ĭnnocū'**ITY, ~NESS *ns.*, ~LY² *adv.* [f. L IN²(*nocuus* f. as prec.) + -OUS]

ĭnnŏ'mĭnate *a.* Unnamed; **~ bone,** (Anat.) bone formed from three original bones: ilium, ischium, and pubis. [f. LL IN²(*nominatus* p.p. of *nominare*; see NOMINATE, -ATE²)]

ĭ'nnov|āte *v.i.* Bring in novelties; make changes *in*; hence or cogn. ~A'TION, **~āt**OR, *ns.*, **~āt**IVE, **~āt**ORY, *adjs.* [f. L IN¹(*novare* make new, alter, f. *novus* new) + -ATE³]

ĭnnŏ'xious (-kshŭs) *a.* Harmless; hence ~LY² *adv.*, ~NESS *n.* [f. L IN²(*noxius* NOXIOUS)]

ĭnnūĕ'ndō *n.* (*pl.* **~es** *or* **~s**), & *v.i.* **1.** *n.* Oblique hint, allusive remark (usu. depreciatory). **2.** *v.i.* Make innuendoes. [L, abl. gerund of IN¹(*nuere* nod), = by nodding at, pointing to]

ĭnnū'merab|le *a.* Too many to count; hence ~LY² *adv.* [ME, f. L IN²(*numerabilis* NUMERABLE)]

ĭnnū'mer|ate *a.* Not numerate; unacquainted with basic principles of mathematics and science; so ~ACY *n.* [f. IN-² + NUMERATE]

ĭnnūtr|ĭ'tion *n.* Lack of nutrition; so ~I'TIOUS² *a.* [f. IN-² + NUTRITION]

ĭnobsėr'vance (-z-) *n.* Inattention; non-observance (*of* law etc.). [F, or f. L IN²(*observantia* OBSERVANCE)]

ĭnŏ'cūl|āte *v.t.* Treat (person or animal) *with* agent of disease by injection etc. to induce milder form of it and so safeguard against its attacks; implant (disease etc.) thus (*on* or *into* person etc.); (fig.) imbue (person etc.) *with* opinions etc.; (arch.) insert (bud, scion) in plant, treat (plant) thus; hence or cogn. ~ABLE, ~ATIVE, *adjs.*, ~A'TION, **~āt**OR, *ns.* [ME in last sense, f. L IN¹(*oculare* f. *oculus* eye, bud) engraft + -ATE³]

ĭnŏ'cūl|um *n.* (*pl.* **~a**). Substance used for inoculation. [mod. L, f. as prec.]

ĭnō'dorous *a.* Having no odour. [f. L IN²(*odorus* ODOROUS), or f. IN-² + ODOROUS]

ĭnoffĕ'nsĭve *a.* Unoffending; not objectionable; hence ~LY² (-vlĭ) *adv.*, ~NESS (-vn-) *n.* [f. IN-² + OFFENSIVE]

ĭnoffĭ'cious (-shŭs) *a.* (Law). Not in accordance with moral duty. [f. L IN²(*officiosus* dutiful; see OFFICIOUS), or f. IN-² + OFFICIOUS]

ĭnŏ'perable *a.* (Surg.) That cannot suitably be operated on (*inoperable cancer*). [f. F *inopérable* (as IN-², OPERABLE)]

ĭnŏ'peratĭve *a.* Not working or taking effect. [f. IN-² + OPERATIVE]

ĭnŏ'pportūne *a.* Not appropriate, esp. as regards time; unseasonable; hence ~LY² (-nlĭ) *adv.*, ~NESS (-n-n-) *n.* [f. L IN²(*opportunus* OPPORTUNE)]

ĭnor'dĭnate *a.* Immoderate, excessive; intemperate; disorderly; hence ~LY² (-tlĭ) *adv.* [ME, f. L IN²(*ordinatus* p.p. of *ordinare* ORDAIN)]

ĭnorgă'nĭc *a.* **1.** Having no organized physical structure. **2.** (Chem., of compound etc.) of mineral origin, not organic; **~ chemistry,** that of inorganic substances. **3.** Not arising by natural growth, extraneous; (Philol.) not explainable by normal etymology. [f. IN-² + ORGANIC]

ĭnŏ'scūl|āte *v.i.* & *t.* Join by running together; join closely; hence ~A'TION *n.* [f. IN-¹ + L *osculare* furnish with mouth (*osculum* dim. of *os* mouth) + -ATE³]

in partibus (ĭn par'tĭbŭs) *adv.* (Of R.C. titular bishop, or fig.) in heretical territory. [orig. *in partibus infidelium*, L = in the regions of the unbelievers]

in petto (ĭn pĕ'tō) *adv.* Secretly (esp. of cardinals appointed but not named as such). [It., = in the breast]

in posse (ĭn pŏ'sĭ) *a.* In the condition of being possible (opp. IN ESSE). [L]

in propria persona (ĭn prōprĭa persō'na) *adv.* In his or her own person. [L]

in puris naturalibus (ĭn pūrĭs nătūrā'lĭbŭs) *a.* Stark naked. [L]

ĭ'nput (-ŏŏt) *n.*, & *v.t.* (**-tt-**; **input** *or* **inputted**). **1.** *n.* What is put in; place where energy, information, etc., enters a system. **2.** *v.t.* Put in or *into*; supply (data, programs, etc., *to* computer). [f. IN² + PUT¹]

ĭ'nquĕst (*or* ĭn-kw-) *n.* **1.** Legal or judicial inquiry to ascertain matter of fact; inquisition; inquiry by coroner's court into cause of death; **great** or **last ~**, Last JUDGEMENT. **2.** Coroner's jury; **grand** or **great ~**, (Hist.) grand jury (||*grand ~ of the nation*, House of Commons). [ME f. OF *enqueste* f. Rom. **inquesta* fem. p.p. (as n.) of **inquaerere* (see INQUIRE)]

ĭnquī'ėtūde (*or* ĭn-kw-) *n.* Uneasiness of mind or body. [ME f. OF, or f. LL *inquietudo* f. L IN²(*quietus* QUIET²); see -TUDE]

ĭ'nquĭlīne (*or* ĭn-kw-) *n.* Animal living in the home of another, commensal. [f. L *inquilinus* sojourner (IN-¹, *colere* dwell)]

ĭnquīr'|e, ||**ėnquīr'|e,** (*or* ĭn-kw-) *v.* **1.** *v.i.* Make search (*into* matter); seek information (*of* = from person; *about*, *after*, thing etc.); **~e after** or **for** person, ask how he is; ask *for* (goods in shop etc.). **2.** *v.t.* Ask to be told (person's name, business, etc., *whether*, *how*, etc.). **3.** Hence ~ER[1] *n.* [ME *enquere* f. OF *enquerre* f. Rom. **inquaerere* f. L IN[1](*quirere quisit-* = *quaerere* seek)]

ĭnquīr'ȳ, ||**ėnquīr'ȳ,** (*or* ĭn-kw-) *n.* Asking; question; (official) investigation; **court of ~** (Mil., investigating circumstances of mishap etc.); ||**~ agent,** private detective; **~ office** (answering questions from callers etc.). [f. prec. + -Y[1]]

ĭnquĭsĭ'tion (-z-; *or* ĭn-kw-) *n.* Search, investigation; judicial or official inquiry; **the I~,** (Hist.) R.C. ecclesiastical tribunal for suppression of heresy, esp. very severe one in Spain; hence ~AL *a.* [ME f. OF, f. L *inquisitio -onis* examination (as INQUIRE; see -ION)]

ĭnquĭ'sĭtive (-z-; *or* ĭn-kw-) *a.* Inquiring, seeking knowledge; unduly inquiring, prying; hence ~LY[2] (-vlĭ) *adv.*, ~NESS (-vn-) *n.* [ME, f. OF *inquisitif -ive* f. LL *inquisitivus* (as prec.; see -IVE)]

ĭnquĭ'sĭtor (-z-; *or* ĭn-kw-) *n.* Official investigator; (Hist.) officer of the Inquisition (**Grand I~,** director of court of Inquisition in some countries; **I~-General,** head of this in Spain). [f. F *inquisiteur* f. L *inquisitor -oris* (as INQUIRE; see -OR)]

ĭnquĭsĭtōr'ĭal (-z-; *or* ĭn-kw-) *a.* Of or like an inquisitor; offensively prying; (Law, of criminal procedure) in which proceedings are secret or prosecutor is judge, opp. *accusatorial*; hence ~LY[2] *adv.* [f. med. L *inquisitorius* (as prec.; see -ORY) + -AL]

in re (ĭn rē') *prep.* = RE[2] 1. [L, = in the matter (of)]

I.N.R.I. *abbr.* Jesus of Nazareth, King of the Jews. [f. L *Iesus Nazarenus Rex Iudaeorum*]

ĭ'nroad *n.* Hostile incursion, raid; (fig.) intrusion *on* or *into*, esp. so as to consume (*makes inroads on my time*). [f. IN[2] + ROAD[1] in sense 'riding']

ĭ'nrŭsh *n.* Rushing in, influx. [f. IN[2] + RUSH[2]]

ins. *abbr.* inches; insurance.

ĭnsalū'br|ĭous (*or* -lōō'-) *a.* (Of climate or place) unhealthy; so ~ITY *n.* [f. L IN[2](*salubris* SALUBRIOUS)]

ĭnsā'ne *a.* Not of sound mind, mentally deranged; extremely foolish, irrational; (of asylum etc.) for insane persons; hence or cogn. ~LY[2] (-nlĭ) *adv.*, **ĭnsă'n**ITY *n.* [f. L IN[2](*sanus* healthy)]

ĭnsă'nĭtarȳ *a.* Not sanitary; harmful to health. [f. IN-[2] + SANITARY]

ĭnsā'ti|able (-sha-) *a.* That cannot be satisfied; inordinately greedy (*of*); hence ~ABI'LITY *n.*, **~ab**LY[2] *adv.* [ME f. OF *insaciable*, or f. L IN[2](*satiabilis* SATIABLE)]

ĭnsā'tiate (-shyat) *a.* Never satisfied. [f. L IN[2](*satiatus*; see SATIATE[1])]

ĭ'nscāpe *n.* Inward essential quality of observed objects as embodied in literary, artistic, etc., expression. [perh. f. IN-[1] + -SCAPE]

ĭnscrī'b|e *v.t.* Write (words etc. *in* or *on* stone, metal, paper, book, etc.); enter name of (person) on list or in book; ||(esp. in *p.p.*) issue (stock etc.) in form of shares with registered holders; mark (sheet, tablet, etc., *with* characters); place informal dedication (*to* person) in or on (book etc.); (Geom.) describe (figure) within another so that some particular points (or all angular points) of it lie on the boundary of that other (cf. CIRCUMSCRIBE), whence ~ABLE *a.* [f. L IN[1](*scribere script-* write)]

ĭnscrĭ'ption *n.* **1.** Words inscribed, esp. on monument, coin, stone, etc.; informal dedication of book etc. (see prec.); hence or cogn. ~AL, **ĭnscrĭ'pt**IVE, *adjs.* **2.** ||Inscribing (*of* loan). [ME, f. L *inscriptio* (as prec.; see -ION)]

ĭnscru't|able (-rōō'-) *a.* That cannot be understood by investigation; wholly mysterious; hence ~ABI'LITY, **~able**NESS (-beln-), *ns.*, **~ab**LY[2] *adv.* [ME, f. eccl. L IN[2](*scrutabilis* f. *scrutari* search; see SCRUTINY, -ABLE)]

ĭ'nsĕct *n.* Small invertebrate segmented animal; arthropod of class Insecta, having head, thorax, abdomen, two antennae, three pairs of thoracic legs, and usu. one or two pairs of thoracic wings; (fig.) insignificant or contemptible person or creature; **~-powder** (for killing or driving away insects). [f. L *insectum* (*animal*) notched (animal) f. IN[1](*secare sect-* cut)]

ĭnsĕctār'ĭum, ĭnsĕ'ctarȳ, *n.* Place for keeping insects. [f. as prec. + -ARIUM, -ARY]

ĭnsĕ'ctĭ|cīde *n.* Insect-killer, esp. preparation used for killing insects; hence **~cī'd**AL *a.* [f. INSECT + -I- + -CIDE]

ĭnsĕ'ctĭ|vōre *n.* Mammal of order Insectivora feeding on insects etc., e.g. hedgehog and mole; so ~VOROUS (-ĭ'v-) *a.* (also of plants that capture and absorb insects). [F, f. mod. L *insectivorus* (as INSECT; see -VORE)]

ĭnsĕctŏ'logȳ *n.* Science of insects, esp. in their economic relations to man. [f. F *insectologie* (as INSECT; see -LOGY)]

ĭnsėcūr'|e *a.* Unsafe; not firm; (of ice, ground, etc.) liable to give way; hence or cogn. **~e**LY[2] (-ūr'lĭ) *adv.*, ~ITY *n.* [f. med. L IN[2](*securus* SECURE), or f. IN-[2] + SECURE]

ĭnsĕ'mĭn|āte *v.t.* Sow (seed etc., lit. or fig., *in*); introduce semen into; hence ~A'TION *n.* (ARTIFICIAL *insemination*). [f. L IN[1](*seminare* f. SEMEN) + -ATE[3]]

ĭnsĕ'nsāte *a.* Without sensibility, unfeeling; stupid; without physical sensation; hence ~LY[2] (-tlĭ) *adv.* [f. eccl. L IN[2](*sensatus* f. *sensus* SENSE; see -ATE[2])]

ĭnsĕnsĭbĭ'lĭtȳ *n.* Lack of mental feeling or emotion; indifference (*to*); unconsciousness. [f. F *insensibilité* or f. LL *insensibilitas* (as foll.; see -ITY)]

ĭnsĕ'nsĭb|le *a.* **1.** Too small or gradual to be perceived, inappreciable; hence ~LY[2] *adv.* **2.** Without one's mental faculties, unconscious; deprived of sensation. **3.** Unaware (*of*, *to*, *how*, etc.); emotionless, callous. [ME f. OF, or f. L IN[2](*sensibilis* SENSIBLE)]

ĭnsĕ'nsĭtĭve *a.* Not sensitive (*to* touch, sight, light, mental or moral impressions); hence ~LY[2] (-vlĭ) *adv.*, ~NESS (-vn-), **ĭnsĕnsĭtĭ'v**ITY, *ns.* [f. IN-[2] + SENSITIVE]

ĭnsĕ'ntient (-shĭ-; *or* -shent) Not sentient; inanimate. [f. IN-[2] + SENTIENT]

ĭnsĕ'par|able *a.* & *n.* **1.** *a.* That cannot be separated; (Gram., of prefix, or verb in respect of it) that cannot be used as separate word (e.g. *dis-*, *mis-*, *un-*); hence ~ABI'LITY *n.*, **~ab**LY[2] *adv.* **2.** *n.* (usu. in *pl.*) Inseparable person or thing, esp. friend. [ME, f. L IN[2](*separabilis* SEPARABLE)]

ĭnsĕr't[1] *v.t.* Place, fit, thrust, in (thing *in*, *into*, another, *between* edges etc.); introduce (letter, word, article, advertisement, *in* or *into* written matter, newspaper, etc.); (Anat. etc., in *p.p.*) attached (at specific point). [f. L IN[1](*serere sert-* join)]

ĭ'nsĕrt[2] *n.* Thing inserted. [f. prec. or foll.]

ĭnsĕr'tion *n.* Inserting; thing inserted, esp. in writing or print; each appearance of an advertisement in newspaper etc.; ornamental needlework etc. inserted into plain material (*lace insertions*); (Anat. etc.) mode or place of attachment of muscle, organ, etc.; placing of spacecraft in desired orbit. [f. LL *insertio* (as INSERT¹; see -ION)]

ĭ'nsĕt¹ *n.* Extra page(s) inserted in folded sheet or in book; small map, photograph, etc., inserted within border of larger; piece let into dress. [f. IN² + SET²]

ĭnsĕ't² *v.t.* (**-tt-;** ~ *or* **~ted**). Put in as an inset. [f. IN² + SET¹]

ĭnshă'llah (*-a*) *int.* If Allah wills it. [f. Arab. *in šā' Allah*]

ĭnshôr'e *adv.* & *a.* Close to shore; ~ **of,** nearer to shore than. [f. IN² + SHORE¹]

ĭnsīde *n., a., adv.,* & *prep.* **1.** *n.* (-ī'd). Inner side or surface, (of path) side next to wall or away from road; inner part, interior; (colloq., in *sing.* or *pl.*) stomach and bowels; position affording inside information; (Hist.) passenger travelling inside coach etc.; ||**the** ~ (middle part) *of a week* etc.; *turned* **i'nside ou't,** so that inner side becomes outer, (fig.) in utter confusion; *know* **i'nside ou't** (thoroughly). **2.** *a.* (ĭ'-). Situated on or in, derived from, the inside; (Footb. & Hockey) nearer to centre of field (*inside forward*; ~ **left, right,** inside forward on left, right, side); ~ **information** (not accessible to outsiders); ~ **job,** (colloq.) burglary etc. of premises by person living or working there; ~ **track** (shorter because of curve). **3.** *adv.* (-ī'd). On or in or to the inside; (sl.) in prison; (colloq.) ~ **of** (in less than) *a week* etc. **4.** *prep.* (-ī'd). On the inner side of, within; in less than (*inside an hour*). [f. IN³ + SIDE¹]

ĭnsī'der *n.* One who is within some society, organization, etc. (cf. OUTSIDER); one who is in the secret. [f. prec. + -ER¹]

ĭnsĭ'dĭous *a.* Treacherous, crafty; proceeding or progressing secretly or subtly (*insidious disease*); hence ~LY² *adv.,* ~NESS *n.* [f. L *insidiosus* cunning f. IN¹(*sidiae* f. *sedēre* sit) ambush; see -OUS]

ĭ'nsīght (-īt) *n.* Penetration (*into* character, circumstances, etc.) with the understanding; instance of this; hence ~FUL *a.* [ME, = 'discernment', prob. of Scand. & LG orig. (as IN-¹, SIGHT¹)]

ĭnsĭ'gn|ĕ *n.* (*pl.* ~**ia**). Badge. [L (see foll.)]

ĭnsĭ'gnĭa *n.* (as *sing.* or *pl.*) Badges, distinguishing marks, (*of* office, honour, etc.). [L, pl. of *insigne* neut. (as n.) of IN¹(*signis* f. *signum* SIGN¹) distinguished; see -IA²]

ĭnsĭgnĭ'fĭc|ant *a.* Unimportant, trifling; contemptible; meaningless; hence ~ANCE, ~ANCY, *ns.,* ~**ant**LY² *adv.* [f. IN-² + SIGNIFICANT]

ĭnsĭncēr'e *a.* Not sincere; not candid; hence or cogn. ~LY² (-ēr'lĭ) *adv.,* **ĭnsĭncĕ'r**ITY *n.* [f. L IN²(*sincerus* SINCERE)]

ĭnsĭ'nū|āte *v.t.* Introduce (thing, one*self, into* place; one*self,* person, *into* favour, office, etc.) gradually or subtly; convey indirectly, hint obliquely, (idea, *that*); hence or cogn. ~A'TION, ~**āt**OR, *ns.,* ~**āt**IVE *a.* [f. L IN¹(*sinuare* curve) + -ATE³]

ĭnsĭ'pĭd *a.* Tasteless; lacking flavour; lacking liveliness, dull, uninteresting; hence ~ITY (-ĭ'd-), ~NESS, *ns.,* ~LY² *adv.* [f. F *insipide* or f. LL IN²(*sipidus* = L *sapidus* SAPID)]

ĭnsĭ'st *v.* **1.** *v.i.* Dwell long or emphatically (*on*). **2.** *v.i.* & *t.* ~ (**on**), maintain positively, (*insist on his innocence*; *insist* (*on it*) *that he is innocent*). **3.** *v.i.* Make a stand *on* as essential (*I insist on being present, on your being present, on your presence, on it that you shall be present*). [f. L IN¹(*sistere* stand) stand on, persist]

ĭnsĭ'st|ent *a.* Insisting (*on,* or abs.); obtruding itself on one's attention; so ~ENCE, ~ENCY, *ns.,* ~**ent**LY² *adv.* [f. prec. + -ENT]

in situ (ĭn sī'tū) *adv.* In its (original) place. [L]

ĭnsobrī'etў *n.* Intemperance, esp. in drinking. [f. IN-² + SOBRIETY]

ĭnsōfâr' *adv.* = *in so* FAR¹.

ĭnsolā'tion *n.* Exposure to the sun's rays, for purposes of bleaching etc., as medical treatment, or as cause of disease. [f. L *insolatio* f. IN¹(*solare* f. *sol* sun); see -ATION]

ĭ'nsōle *n.* = SOCK¹ 2; fixed inner sole of boot or shoe. [f. IN³ + SOLE¹]

ĭ'nsol|ent *a.* Offensively contemptuous; insulting; hence or cogn. ~ENCE *n.,* ~**ent**LY² *adv.* [ME, = 'arrogant', f. L IN²(*solens* part. of *solēre* be accustomed); see -ENT]

ĭnsŏ'l|ūble *a.* That cannot be solved; that cannot be dissolved; hence ~UBI'LITY, ~**ūble**NESS (-beln-), *ns.,* ~**ūb**LY² *adv.* [ME f. OF, or f. L IN²(*solubilis* SOLUBLE)]

ĭnsŏ'lv|ent *a.* & *n.* (Debtor) unable to pay debts; relating to insolvency (*insolvent laws*); hence ~ENCY *n.* [f. IN-² + SOLVENT]

ĭnsŏ'mnĭ|a *n.* Habitual sleeplessness; hence ~AC *n.* & *a.* [L, f. IN²(*somnis* f. *somnus* sleep) sleepless; see -IA¹]

ĭnsomŭ'ch *adv.* To such an extent *that*; inasmuch *as*. [ME, orig. *in so much*]

ĭnsou'cĭ|ant (-ōō'-; *or* ăṅsōō'syahṅ) *a.* Carefree, unconcerned; so ~ANCE (*or* -ṅs) *n.* [F (as IN-², *souciant* part. of *soucier* care)]

ĭnspă'n *v.t.* (**-nn-**). (S. Afr.) Yoke (oxen etc.) in team to vehicle; harness animal(s) to (wagon). [f. Du. IN¹(*spannen* stretch f. as SPAN²)]

ĭnspĕ'ct *v.t.* Look closely into; examine officially (*inspect passports*); so ~ION *n.* [f. L IN¹(*spicere spect-* = *specere* look at), or its frequent. *inspectare*]

ĭnspĕ'ctor *n.* One who inspects; official employed to supervise a service and make reports; ||police officer below superintendent and above sergeant; ~ **general,** chief inspector; ||~ **of taxes,** official assessing income tax payable; hence ~ATE¹, ~SHIP, *ns.,* ~IAL (-ôr'-) *a.* [L (as prec.; see -OR)]

ĭnspirā'tion *n.* **1.** Drawing in of breath. **2.** Inspiring; divine influence, esp. that which is thought to prompt poets etc. and that under which books of Scripture are held to have been written, whether **verbal** ~ (dictating every word), **plenary** ~ (covering all subjects treated), or **moral** ~ (confined to moral and religious teaching), whence ~ISM (3), ~IST (2), *ns.* **3.** Thought etc. that is inspired, prompting; sudden brilliant or timely idea. **4.** Inspiring principle. **5.** Hence ~AL *a.* [ME f. OF, f. LL *inspiratio -onis* (as INSPIRE; see -ATION)]

ĭ'nspirātor *n.* Apparatus for drawing-in air or vapour. [LL (as foll.; see -OR)]

ĭnspīr'e *v.t.* **1.** Breathe in, inhale, (air etc., or abs.); hence **ĭnspī'rat**ORY *a.* **2.** Infuse thought or feeling into (person; esp. of divine or supernatural agency); animate (person etc. *with* feeling); infuse (feeling *into* person etc.), create (feeling *in* person); (in *p.p.*) secretly suggested by or emanating from influential person etc., (of guess) intuitive but accurate. [ME, f. OF *inspirer* f. L IN¹(*spirare,* breathe)]

ĭnspĭ'rĭt *v.t.* Put life into, animate; encourage (person *to* action, *to* do); hence ~ING² *a.* [f. IN-¹ + SPIRIT¹]

ĭnspĭ'ss|āte (*or* ĭ'-) *v.t.* (literary). Thicken, condense; hence ~A'TION *n.* [f. LL IN¹(*spissare* f. L *spissus* thick) + -ATE³]

inst. *abbr.* instant (*the 6th inst.*); institute; institution.

ĭnstabĭ'lĭtў *n.* Lack of stability, being unstable. [ME, f. F *instabilité* f. L *instabilitas -tatis* f. IN²(*stabilis* STABLE¹); see -ITY]

ĭnsta'll (-aw'l) *v.t.* **1.** Place (person *in* office or rank) with ceremonies, whence ~ANT *a.* & *n.* **2.** Establish (person, one*self, in* place, condition, etc.); place (heating or lighting apparatus etc.) in position for use. [f. med. L IN[1](*stallare* f. *stallum* STALL[1])]

installā'tion *n.* Installing or being installed; apparatus etc. installed. [f. med. L *installatio* (as prec.; see -ATION)]

insta'lment, *insta'llment, (-aw'l-) *n.* Each of several parts, successively falling due, of sum payable; each of several parts (esp. of serial story etc.) supplied, published, etc. at different times; ***~ plan,** payment by instalments, esp. hire-purchase. [alt. f. obs. *estallment* f. AF *estalement* (*estaler* fix; see -MENT), prob. assoc. w. prec.]

i'nstance[1] *n.* **1.** Fact illustrating a general truth, person or thing for which an assertion is valid, example; particular case (*in your, this, instance*); **for ~**, as an example. **2. At the ~** (request, suggestion) **of. 3.** (Law). Process, suit; **court of first ~** (primary jurisdiction). **4. In the first ~**, in the first place, at the first stage of a proceeding. [ME f. OF, f. L *instantia* (as INSTANT[1]; see -ANCE)]

i'nstance[2] *v.t.* Cite (fact, case) as an instance; (usu. in *pass.*) exemplify. [f. prec.]

i'nstancy *n.* Urgency; pressing nature. [f. L *instantia* (see INSTANCE[1], -ANCY)]

i'nstant[1] *a.* Occurring immediately; (of food) that can be prepared easily for immediate use; (fig.) hurriedly produced; urgent, pressing; (Commerc.) of the current month (*the 6th instant*); (arch.) of the present moment. [ME f. F, f. L IN[1](*stare* stand) be present, press upon; see -ANT]

i'nstant[2] *n.* **1.** Precise (esp. the present) point of time, = MOMENT 1, (*come this instant; I went that instant* or *on the instant*); *I told you* **the ~** (as soon as) *I knew.* **2.** Short space of time, = MOMENT 1, (*in an instant; not an instant too soon*). [after med. L *instans* (*tempus*) present (time); see prec.]

instantā'nėous *a.* Occurring or done in an instant or instantly; (Phys.) existing at a particular instant; hence ~LY[2] *adv.*, ~NESS *n.* [f. med. L *instantaneus* f. L *instans* (see INSTANT[1]) after eccl. L *momentaneus*, + -OUS]

instă'nter *adv.* (arch. or joc.) Immediately, at once. [L (*instans*; see INSTANT[1])]

instă'nti|āte (-shĭ-) *v.t.* Represent by an instance; so ~A'TION *n.* [f. L *instantia* (see INSTANCE[1]) + -ATE[3]]

i'nstantly *adv.* Immediately, at once; (arch.) urgently, pressingly. [ME, f. INSTANT[1] + -LY[2]]

i'nstar *n.* Stage in life of insect etc. between two ecdyses. [L, = form]

instā'te *v.t.* Install, establish, *in* office etc. [f. IN-[1] + STATE[1]]

in statu pupillari (ĭn stătū pūpĭllar'ĭ) *a.* Under guardianship; in junior status at university, not having master's degree. [L]

in statu quo (ĭn stătū kwō') *a.* In the same state as formerly. [L; cf. STATUS]

instaurā'tion *n.* (Act of) restoration, renewal; so **i'nstaurāt**OR *n.* [f. L *instauratio* f. IN[1](*staurare*; cf. RESTORE, -ATION)]

instea'd (-ĕ'd) *adv.* As a substitute or alternative; in place *of* (*instead of this; instead of going*); cf. STEAD. [ME, f. IN[1] + STEAD]

i'nstėp *n.* Upper surface of foot between toes and ankle; part of shoe etc. fitting over or under this; instep-shaped thing. [16th c., ult. f. as IN-[1] + STEP[1], but immed. orig. uncert.]

i'nstĭg|āte *v.t.* Urge on, incite, (person *to* action, *to* do esp. something evil); bring about (revolt, murder, etc.) thus; hence or cogn. ~A'TION, ~**āt**OR, *ns.* [f. L IN[1](*stigare* prick) + -ATE[3]]

instĭ'l, *instĭ'll, *v.t.* (**-ll-**). Put in (liquid *into* thing) by drops; infuse (feeling, ideas, etc., *into* person, mind, etc.) gradually; hence or cogn. **instill**A'TION, ~MENT, *ns.* [f. L IN[1](*stillare* drop); cf. DISTIL]

i'nstinct[1] *n.* **1.** Innate propensity to certain seemingly rational acts performed without conscious intention; innate usu. fixed pattern of behaviour esp. in response to certain simple stimuli; HERD[1] *instinct.* **2.** Innate impulse; intuition, unconscious skill, (*for*). **3.** Hence **instĭ'nct**IVE, **instĭ'nctū**AL, *adjs.*, **instĭ'nctive**LY[2] (-vlĭ) *adv.* [ME, = 'impulse', f. L *instinctus* f. IN[1](*stinguere stinct-* prick) incite]

instĭ'nct[2] *pred. a.* Imbued, charged, (*with* life, beauty, force, etc.). [f. L p.p. (as prec.)]

i'nstitūte[1] *n.* **1.** Society or organization for promotion of scientific, educational, or other public object; building used by this; *brief instruction-course for teachers etc. **2.** Principle of instruction; (in *pl.*) digest of elements of a subject, esp. of jurisprudence, (*Institutes of Justinian*). [f. L *institutum* design, precept, neut. p.p. (as n.) of *instituere* (see foll.)]

i'nstitūte[2] *v.t.* Establish, found; initiate (inquiry etc.); appoint (person *to* or *into* cure of souls). [ME, f. L IN[1](*stituere -tut-* = *statuere* set up) establish, arrange, teach]

institū'tion *n.* **1.** Instituting; establishment (of person) in cure of souls. **2.** Established law, custom, or practice; (colloq., of person etc.) familiar object. **3.** = INSTITUTE[1] 1, esp. for charitable or social purpose. [ME f. OF, f. L *institutio -onis* (as prec.; see -ION)]

institū'tional *a.* Of or like institution(s); (of religion) expressed or organized through institutions (churches etc.); suggestive of typical charitable institutions; *(of advertising) intended to create prestige rather than immediate sales; hence ~ISM (2) *n.* [f. prec. + -AL]

institū'tionalize, -ise (-īz), *v.t.* Make institutional; place or keep (person needing care) in an institution. [f. prec. + -IZE]

instrŭ'ct *v.t.* Teach (person etc. *in* subject); inform (person *that, when,* etc.); (of client, solicitor) give information to (solicitor, counsel); direct, command, (person *to* do); so ~OR (esp. *teacher ranking below professors), ~**r**ESS[1], *ns.* [ME, f. L IN[1](*struere struct-* pile up) build, teach]

instrŭ'ction *n.* Teaching; (esp. in *pl.*) making known to person what he is required to do, direction, order; (in *pl.*) directions to solicitor or counsel; expression in computer program defining and effecting an operation; hence ~AL *a.* [ME f. OF, f. LL *instructio -onis* (as prec.; see -ION)]

instrŭ'ctive *a.* Tending to instruct, conveying a lesson; hence ~LY[2] (-vlĭ) *adv.*, ~NESS (-vn-) *n.* [f. INSTRUCT + -IVE]

i'nstrument (-rōō-) *n.*, & *v.t.* **1.** *n.* Thing used in performing an action; person so made use of; tool, implement, esp. for delicate or scientific work; measuring-device, esp. in aeroplane and serving to determine position etc. when visibility is bad; (**musical**) **~**, contrivance for producing musical sounds by vibration of strings, membranes, etc., or of body of air in pipe etc.; formal, esp. legal, document. **2.** *v.t.* Arrange (music) for instruments; equip with (measuring-)instruments. [ME f. OF, or f. L *instrumentum* (as INSTRUCT; see -MENT)]

instrumĕ'ntal (-rōō-) *a.* Serving as instrument or means (*to* purpose, *in* work, *in doing*), whence

~ITY (-ă'l-) *n.*; of, or arising from, an instrument (*instrumental error*); (of music) performed on instruments (opp. *vocal*), whence ~IST (3) *n.*; (Gram., of case) denoting the means or instrument; hence ~LY² *adv.* [ME f. F, f. med. L *instrumentalis* (as INSTRUMENT; see -AL)]

ĭnstrumĕntā'tion (-ro͞o-) *n.* Arrangement or composition of music for instruments; provision or use of mechanical instruments in industry; operation with scientific, surgical, or other instrument; instrumentality. [F (*instrumenter* f. as INSTRUMENT; see -ATION)]

ĭnsubôr'dĭn|ate *a.* Disobedient, rebellious; so ~A'TION *n.* [f. IN-² + SUBORDINATE¹]

ĭnsubstă'ntial (-shal) *a.* Not real; lacking solidity or substance; hence ~ITY (-shĭă'l-) *n.* [f. LL IN²(*substantialis* SUBSTANTIAL)]

ĭnsŭ'fferab|le *a.* Intolerable; unbearably arrogant, conceited, etc.; hence ~LY² *adv.* [f. IN-² + SUFFERABLE]

ĭnsuffĭ'ciencў (-shen-) *n.* Being insufficient; (Med.) inability of an organ to perform its normal function (*renal insufficiency*). [ME, f. LL *insufficientia* (as foll.; see -ENCY)]

ĭnsuffĭ'cient (-shent) *a.* Not sufficient, inadequate; hence ~LY² *adv.* [ME f. OF, f. LL IN²-(*sufficiens* SUFFICIENT)]

ĭ'nsŭffl|āte *v.t.* Blow, breathe, (air, gas, powder, etc.) into cavity of the body etc.; treat (nose etc.) thus; (Eccl.) blow or breathe on (person) to symbolize spiritual influence; hence or cogn. ~A'TION *n.*, ~**ā**TOR *n.*, (esp.) device for blowing powder on surface of object in order to make latent fingerprints visible. [f. LL IN¹(*sufflare* blow upon f. as SUB- + L *flare* blow) + -ATE³]

ĭ'nsūlar *a.* **1.** Of (the nature of) an island or (Physiol.) islet; of Britain (esp. w. ref. to a development of Latin handwriting current in the British Isles in the early Middle Ages). **2.** Of or like islanders, esp. ignorant of or indifferent to other countries and their culture, narrow-minded; hence ~ISM (2) *n.* **3.** Hence ~ITY (-ă'r-) *n.*, ~LY² *adv.* [f. LL *insularis* (as foll.; see -AR¹)]

ĭ'nsūl|āte *v.t.* **1.** (arch.) Make (land) into an island. **2.** Detach (person, thing) from surroundings, isolate. **3.** Isolate (thing) by interposition of non-conductors, to prevent passage of electricity or heat or sound. **4.** Hence ~A'TION *n.* [f. L *insula* island + -ATE³]

ĭ'nsūlātor *n.* Thing or substance used for insulation against electricity etc.; device to support telegraph-wires etc. or prevent contact between electrical conductors. [f. prec. + -OR]

ĭ'nsūlĭn *n.* Hormone secreted by islets of Langerhans in vertebrates and controlling passage of sugar from blood to tissues. [f. L *insula* island + -IN]

ĭ'nsŭlt¹ *n.* Insulting speech or action; (Med.) (agent causing) damage to the body. [f. F *insulte*, or f. eccl. L IN¹(*sultus* = *saltus* leap, as foll.)]

ĭnsŭ'lt² *v.t.* Treat with scornful abuse, subject to indignity; (of person or thing) offend modesty or self-respect of. [f. L IN¹(*sultare* = *saltare*, frequent. of *salire salt-* leap)]

ĭnsū'per|able (*or* -o͞o'-) *a.* (Of barrier etc. and fig. of difficulty etc.) that cannot be surmounted or overcome; hence ~ABI'LITY *n.*, ~**ab**LY² *adv.* [ME f. OF, or f. L IN²(*superabilis* SUPERABLE])

ĭnsuppôr'tab|le *a.* That cannot be endured; unjustifiable; hence ~LY² *adv.* [F (as IN-², SUPPORT, -ABLE)]

ĭnsur'ance (-shoor'-) *n.* Insuring; sum paid for this, premium; ‖NATIONAL *Insurance*; ~ **agent, company,** etc., (undertaking insurance dealings for or as insurer); *insurance* POLICY²; ‖~ **stamp** (certifying payment of regular amount for National Insurance). [earlier *ensurance* f. OF *enseürance* (as ENSURE; see -ANCE)]

ĭnsur'ant (-shoor'-) *n.* Person to whom insurance policy is issued. [f. foll. + -ANT]

ĭnsur'|e (-shoor') *v.t.* **1.** Secure payment of sum of money in event of or *against* loss of or damage or injury to (property, life, person, etc., or abs.; cf. ASSURANCE) by payment of premium; (of owner of property etc. or of insurance company etc.) secure payment of (sum of money) thus; **the ~ed,** the person in respect of whom such payment is secured. **2.** *Ensure. **3.** Hence ~ABLE *a.* [ME, var. of ENSURE]

ĭnsur'er (-shoor'-) *n.* One who insures property in consideration of premium, underwriter. [f. prec. + -ER¹]

ĭnsûr'g|ent *a.* & *n.* **1.** *a.* Rising in active revolt; (of sea etc.) rushing in; hence ~ENCY *n.* **2.** *n.* Rebel. [F, f. L IN¹(*surgere surrect-* rise); see -ENT]

ĭnsurmou'ntab|le *a.* That cannot be surmounted or overcome; hence ~LY² *adv.* [f. IN-² + SURMOUNTABLE]

ĭnsurrĕ'ction *n.* Rising in open resistance to established authority; incipient rebellion; hence ~AL, ~ARY¹, *adjs.*, ~IST (3) *n.* [ME f. OF, f. LL *insurrectio -onis* (as INSURGENT; see -ION)]

ĭnsuscĕ'pt|ĭble *a.* Not susceptible (*of* treatment, *to* agency, etc.); hence ~IBI'LITY *n.* [f. IN-² + SUSCEPTIBLE]

int. *abbr.* interior; internal; international.

ĭntă'ct *a.* Untouched; entire; unimpaired. [ME, f. L IN²(*tactus* p.p. of *tangere* touch)]

ĭntă'gliātėd (-tă'l-) *a.* Decorated with surface carving. [f. It. *intagliato* p.p. of IN¹(*tagliare* cut)]

ĭntă'gliō (-tă'l- *or* -tah'l-) *n.* (*pl.* ~**s**), & *v.t.* **1.** *n.* Engraved design; (esp. incised) carving in hard material; gem with incised design; process of printing from engraved design. **2.** *v.t.* Engrave (material, design) in intaglio. [It. (as prec.)]

ĭ'ntāke *n.* Action of taking in; place where water is taken into channel or pipe from river, where fuel or air enters engine, etc.; airway into mine; person(s) or thing(s) or quantity taken in or received; (N. Engl.) land reclaimed from moor etc. [f. IN² + TAKE¹]

ĭntă'ng|ĭble (-nj-) *a.* That cannot be touched; that cannot be grasped mentally; hence ~IBI'LITY *n.*, ~**ĭb**LY² *adv.* [F, or f. med. L IN²(*tangibilis* TANGIBLE)]

ĭntâr'sia *n.* Mosaic woodwork made esp. in 15th-c. Italy. [f. It. *intarsio*]

ĭ'ntėger *n.* Whole number; thing complete in itself. [L, adj. = untouched, whole; see ENTIRE]

ĭ'ntėgral *a.* & *n.* **1.** *a.* Of, or necessary to the completeness of, a whole; whole, complete; forming a whole (*integral design*). **2.** (Math.) Of, or denoted by, an integer; involving only integers (e.g. as coefficients in a function); ~ **calculus** (dealing with finding and properties of integrals of functions; cf. DIFFERENTIAL). **3.** Hence or cogn. ~ITY (-ă'l-) *n.*, ~LY² *adv.* **4.** *n.* (Math.) Quantity of which given function is derivative, containing indeterminate additive constant (**indefinite** ~), or calculated as difference between its values at specified limits (**definite** ~); function satisfying given differential equation. [f. LL *integralis* (as prec.; see -AL)]

ĭ'ntėgrănd *n.* (Math.) Function that is to be integrated. [f. L *integrandus* gerundive of *integrare*; see INTEGRATE², -ND¹]

ĭ'ntėgrant *a.* (Of parts) component, making up a whole. [f. F *intégrant* (*intégrer* f. as INTEGRATE²; see -ANT)]

ĭ'ntėgrate¹ *a.* Made up of parts; whole, complete. [f. L *integratus* (as foll.; see -ATE²)]

ĭ'ntėgr|āte² *v.* **1.** *v.t.* Complete (imperfect thing) by addition of parts; combine (parts) into a whole. **2.** (Math.) find the integral of; (esp. in *part.*) indicate mean value or total sum of (temperature, area, etc.), whence **~ātor** *n.* **3.** *v.t.* & *i.* Bring or come into equal membership of society, esp. without regard to race or religion; end (racial) segregation (of or at). **4. ~ated circuit,** small chip etc. of material designed to replace conventional electrical circuit of many components. **5.** Hence **~ātive** *a.* [f. L *integrare* make whole (as INTEGER) + -ATE[3]]

ĭntĕgrā'tion *n.* Integrating; ending of racial segregation; (Psych.) combination of diverse elements of perception etc.; **horizontal ~** (of firms engaged in same stages or types of manufacture); **vertical ~** (of firms engaged in successive stages in production of goods). [f. L *integratio* (as prec.; see -ATION)]

ĭntĕgrā'tionist *n.* Advocate of racial integration. [f. prec. + -IST]

ĭntĕ'grĭtȳ *n.* Wholeness, entirety; soundness; uprightness, honesty. [ME, f. F *intégrité* or f. L *integritas* (as INTEGER; see -ITY)]

ĭntĕ'gūment *n.* Skin, husk, rind, or other (usu. natural) covering; hence **~al, ~ary[1]**, (-ĕ'n-) *adjs.* [f. L *integumentum* f. IN[1](*tegere* cover); see -MENT]

ĭ'ntĕllĕct *n.* Faculty of knowing and reasoning; understanding; person, persons collectively, of good understanding. [ME f. OF, or f. L *intellectus* perception (as INTELLIGENT)]

ĭntĕllĕ'ct|ion *n.* Action or process of understanding, esp. as opp. to imagination; so **~ive** *a.* [ME, f. med. L *intellectio* (as INTELLIGENT; see -ION)]

ĭntĕllĕ'ctūal *a.* & *n.* **1.** *a.* Of, appealing to, requiring or given to the exercise of, intellect. **2.** *a.* & *n.* (Person) possessing a good understanding, enlightened (person). **3.** Hence or cogn. **~ity** (-ă'l-) *n.*, **~ize** (2, 3) *v.t.* & *i.*, **~ly[2]** *adv.* [ME, f. L *intellectualis* (as INTELLECT; see -AL)]

ĭntĕllĕ'ctūal|ĭsm *n.* Doctrine that knowledge is wholly or mainly derived from pure reason; (excessive) exercise of intellect only; so **~ist** (2) *n.* [f. prec. + -ISM]

ĭntĕ'llĭgence *n.* **1.** Intellect, understanding; hence **ĭntĕllĭgĕ'ntial** (-shal) *a.* **2.** Quickness of understanding, sagacity, (of person or animal); **~ quotient,** number denoting ratio of given person's intelligence to the normal or average; **~ test** (designed to measure intelligence rather that acquired knowledge). **3.** Intelligent or rational being. **4.** Information, news; (persons employed in) collecting information, esp. that of military value; **~ department** (engaged in collecting information esp. secretly). [ME f. OF, f. L *intelligentia* (as INTELLIGENT; see -ENCE)]

ĭntĕ'llĭgencer *n.* Bringer of news, informant; secret agent, spy. [f. prec. + -ER[1]]

ĭntĕ'llĭgent *a.* Having or showing (usu. a high degree of) understanding; clever, quick of mind; hence **~ly[2]** *adv.* [f. L *intelligere -lect-* understand (as INTER-, *legere* gather, pick out, read); see -ENT]

ĭntĕllĭgĕ'ntsĭa *n.* Class of intellectuals regarded as possessing culture and political initiative; class of persons doing intellectual work. [Russ., f. Pol. *inteligencja* f. L (as INTELLIGENCE)]

ĭntĕ'llĭg|ĭble *a.* That can be understood, comprehensible *to*; (Philos.) that can be apprehended only by the intellect, not by the senses; hence **~ibi'lity** *n.*, **~ĭbly[2]** *adv.* [f. L *intelligibilis* (as INTELLIGENT; see -IBLE)]

ĭntĕ'mper|ate *a.* (Of person or conduct or speech) immoderate, unbridled, violent; excessive in the indulgence of an appetite; addicted to drinking; hence or cogn. **~ance** *n.*, **~ately[2]** (-tlĭ) *adv.* [ME, f. L IN[2](*temperatus* TEMPERATE)]

ĭntĕ'nd *v.t.* **1.** Have as one's purpose (*we intend to go*; *we intend going*; *we intended no harm*; *we intend that it shall be done today*); (in *p.p.*) done on purpose; (in *part.*) who intends to be (*intending visitor*). **2.** Design, destine, (person, thing; *for* a purpose or *as* something: *we intend our son for the Bar*; *intend him to go*; *intend it as a stopgap*); *this bun* **is ~ed for you** (to eat), *this daub* **is ~ed for** (meant to represent) **me. 3.** Mean (*what exactly do you intend by the word?*). [ME *entende, intende* f. OF *entendre, intendre* f. L IN[1](*tendere tent-* or *tens-* stretch, tend) strain, direct, purpose]

ĭntĕ'nd|ant *n.* (Esp. as title of foreign officials) superintendent or manager of public business etc.; hence **~ancy** *n.* [F, f. L (as prec.; see -ANT)]

ĭntĕ'ndĕd *n.* (colloq.) Person one intends to marry, esp. fiancé(e) (*your, his, her, intended*). [f. p.p. of INTEND]

ĭntĕ'ndment *n.* Intention, meaning; true meaning as fixed by law. [ME, f. OF *entendement* meaning (as INTEND; see -MENT)]

ĭntĕ'nse *a.* (**~r, ~st**). (Of quality etc.) existing in a high degree, violent, vehement; having some quality in high degree; (of feeling or action) eager, ardent; (of person) feeling, apt to feel, strong emotion; hence **~ly[2]** (-slĭ) *adv.*, **~ness** (-sn-) *n.* [ME f. OF *intens*, or f. L *intensus* (as INTEND)]

ĭntĕ'nsĭ|fȳ *v.t.* & *i.* Make or become (more) intense; (Photog.) increase opacity of (negative); hence **~fica'tion, ~fīer[1]**, *ns.* [f. prec. + -I- + -FY]

ĭntĕ'nsion (-shon) *n.* Intensity, high degree, of a quality; strenuous exertion of mind or will; (Logic) internal content of a concept, whence **~al** *a.* [f. L *intensio* (as INTEND; see -ION)]

ĭntĕ'nsĭtȳ *n.* Quality of being intense; (measurable) amount of some quality, e.g. force, brightness, magnetic field. [f. INTENSE + -ITY]

ĭntĕ'nsive *a.* & *n.* **1.** *a.* Of or relating to intensity as opp. to extent; producing intensity; (Gram.) expressing intensity, giving force; vigorous, thorough; concentrated, directed to a single point or area or subject, (*intensive bombardment, study*); (Econ.) serving to increase production from given area (*intensive methods, agriculture*); (as *suf.*) making much use of (*capital-intensive, labour-intensive*); **~ care,** medical treatment with constant observation of patient; hence **~ly[2]** (-vlĭ) *adv.* **2.** *n.* (Gram.) Intensive word etc. [F *intensif -ive* or f. med. L *intensivus* (as INTEND; see -IVE)]

ĭntĕ'nt[1] *n.* Intention, purpose, (*with intent to defraud* etc.; *with malicious, good,* etc., *intent*); **to all ~s and purposes,** practically, virtually. [ME f. OF (1) *entent* f. L *intentus* n., (2) *entente* f. Rom. **intenta* fem. p.p., both as INTEND]

ĭntĕ'nt[2] *a.* Resolved, bent, (*on* doing, *on* object); attentively occupied (*on*); (of faculties, looks, etc.) earnest, eager; hence **~ly[2]** *adv.*, **~ness** *n.* [f. L *intentus* a. (as INTEND)]

ĭntĕ'ntion *n.* **1.** Intending, one's purpose *of* doing or *to* do; thing intended, object, purpose, whence (-)**~ed[2]** (-nd) *a.*; ultimate aim; (in *pl.*, colloq.) purposes in respect of proposal of marriage (cf. HONOURABLE). **2.** (Med.) **Second ~,** healing of wound by granulation, **first ~,** healing without this by immediate reunion of parts; *intention* TREMOR. **3.** (Logic). Conception; **first ~s,** primary conceptions of things (e.g. a tree, an oak), **second ~s,** secondary conceptions (e.g. difference, identity, species). **4.** (Theol.) **Special, particular, ~,** special object for which mass is celebrated etc. [ME f. OF *entencion* f. L *intentio* stretching, purpose (as INTEND; see -ION)]

intĕ'ntional *a.* Done on purpose; hence ~LY² *adv.* [f. F *intentionnel* or f. med. L *intentionalis* (as prec.; see -AL)]

intẽr' *v.t.* (-rr-). Deposit (corpse etc.) in earth, tomb, etc.; bury. [ME, f. OF *enterrer* f. Rom. *IN¹(*terrare* f. *terra* earth)]

i'nter- *pref.* w. sense 'between', forming: **1.** *vbs.*, *ns.*, & *adjs.*, expr. mutual or reciprocal action or relation, or with sense 'among', 'between', as: **~-a'llied,** pertaining to two or more allies (in war etc.); **~be'd,** embed (thing) between others; **~ce'nsal,** between two censuses; **~-city,** existing or travelling between cities; **~colle'giate,** carried on etc. between colleges or *universities; **~colo'nial,** carried on etc. between colonies; **~colu'mnar,** placed or existing between two columns; **~columnia'tion,** placing of columns at intervals, such interval; **~-contine'ntal,** connecting, situated or travelling or existing between, different continents; **~conver'tible,** interchangeable; **~cro'ss** *v.t.* & *i.*, lay or lie across each other, (cause to) breed with each other; **~denomina'tional,** relating to more than one (religious) denomination; **~-departme'ntal,** pertaining to more than one department; **~di'gitate,** interlock like clasped fingers; **~discipli'nary** (*or* -dĭ'-), of or between different branches of learning; **~flow** *n.*, & *v.i.*, flow into each other; **~gala'ctic,** situated between galaxies; **~-governme'ntal,** pertaining to more than one government; **~grada'tion,** gradual approximation; **~grade,** (*v.i.*) pass into another form by intervening grades, (*n.*) such grade; **~-grow'th,** growing of things into each other; **~ja'cent,** lying between; **~kni't,** intertwine; **~la'p** *v.i.*, overlap; **~li'nk,** link together (things, one *with* another, or abs.); **~migra'tion,** reciprocal migration; **~ocea'nic,** between or connecting two oceans; **~per'sonal,** (of relations) between persons; **~plai't,** plait together; **~pla'netary,** (pertaining to travel) between planets; **~provi'ncial,** situated or carried on between provinces; **~pu'nction,** (arch.) punctuation; **~ra'cial,** existing between different races; **~ste'llar,** between stars; **~ta'ngle,** tangle together; **~te'xture,** interweaving; **~tri'bal,** existing between different tribes; **~twi'st,** twist together; **~vei'n,** intersect (as) with veins; **~-war,** existing in the period between two wars; **~wor'k,** (*v.t.*) interweave (lit. or fig.), (*v.i.*) work upon each other; **~wrea'the,** wreathe together. **2.** scientific terms, esp. *adjs.*, w. sense 'between', as: **~arti'cular,** between contiguous surfaces of a joint; **~ato'mic,** between atoms; **~co'stal,** between the ribs (of body or ship), between veins of leaf; **~crur'al,** between the legs; **~di'gital,** between fingers or toes; **~fa'cial,** included between two faces of crystal or other solid; **~fe'moral,** between the thighs; **~fi'brillar,** between fibrils; **~gla'cial,** between glacial periods; **~lo'bular,** situated between lobes; **~mole'cular,** between molecules; **~node,** (Bot.) part of stem between two of the knots from which leaves arise, (Anat.) slender part between two joints, esp. bone of finger or toe; **~nu'clear,** between nuclei; **~o'sculate,** inosculate; **~-o'sseous,** between bones; **~pari'etal,** between right and left parietal bones of skull; **~se'ptal,** between septa or partitions; **~speci'fic,** formed from different species; **~spi'nal,** **~spi'nous,** between spines or spinous processes; **~stratifica'tion,** **~stra'tified,** interspersion, interspersed, (*with* strata); **~ver'tebral,** between vertebrae. [f. OF *entre-* or f. L *inter* between, among]

inter. *abbr.* intermediate.

i'nterăct¹ *n.* Interval between two acts of play; interlude. [f. INTER- + ACT¹, after F *entr'acte*]

interă'ct² *v.t.* Act reciprocally, act on each other; hence ~ANT *a.* & *n.*, ~ION *n.*, ~IVE *a.* [f. INTER- + ACT²]

inter alia (ĭnter ā'lĭa) *adv.* Amongst other things. [L]

interblĕ'nd *v.* **1.** *v.t.* Mingle (things, one *with* another). **2.** *v.i.* Blend with each other. [f. INTER- + BLEND¹]

interbree'd *v.t.* & *i.* (-bre'd). (Cause to) produce hybrid person or animal or plant. [f. INTER- + BREED¹]

intẽr'calarў (*or* -erkă'-) *a.* (Of day or month) inserted in calendar to harmonize calendar with solar year, e.g. 29 Feb. in leap years; (of year) having such addition; interpolated, intervening. [f. L *intercalari(u)s* (as foll.; see -ARY¹)]

intẽr'cal|āte *v.t.* Insert (intercalary day etc., or abs.); interpose (anything out of ordinary course, esp. in *p.p.* of strata); so ~A'TION *n.* [f. L INTER(*calare* proclaim) + -ATE³]

intercē'de *v.i.* Interpose on behalf of another, plead (*with* one person *for* another). [f. F *intercéder* or f. L INTER(*cedere cess-* go) intervene]

intercĕ'pt¹ *v.t.* Seize, catch, stop, (person, message, vehicle, etc.) on the way from place to place; cut off (light etc. *from*); check, stop, (motion etc.); (Math.) mark off (space) between two points etc.; hence ~ION *n.*, ~IVE *a.*, ~OR *n.* (esp. aircraft seeking to intercept enemy raiders). [f. L INTER(*cipere cept-* = *capere* take)]

i'ntercĕpt² *n.* (Math.) Part of line between two points of intersection with other lines. [f. prec.]

inter|cĕ'ssion (-shon) *n.* Interceding, esp. by prayer; so **~cĕ'ssOR** *n.*, **~cĕssŏr'**IAL, **~cĕ'ssORY**, *adjs.* [F, or f. L *intercessio* (as INTERCEDE; see -ION)]

i'nterchānge¹ (-nj) *n.* Reciprocal exchange (*of* things) between two persons etc.; alternation; road junction designed so that traffic streams do not intersect. [f. foll.]

interchā'nge² (-nj) *v.t.* (Of two persons) exchange (things) with each other; put each of (two things) in the other's place; alternate; hence or cogn. ~ABI'LITY, **~able**NESS (-beln-), *ns.*, ~ABLE *a.*, **~ab**LY² *adv.*, (-ja-). [ME, f. OF *entrechangier* (*entre-* INTER-, *changer* CHANGE²)]

i'ntercŏm *n.* (colloq.) System of intercommunication by radio or telephone, esp. in aircraft. [abbr.]

intercommū'nĭc|āte *v.i.* Communicate mutually; (of rooms etc.) have free passage into each other; so ~A'TION *n.* [f. AL INTER(*communicare*; see COMMUNICATE) + -ATE³]

intercommū'nion (-yon) *n.* Mutual communion; mutual action or relation, esp. between religious bodies. [f. INTER- + COMMUNION]

intercommū'nĭtў *n.* Quality of being common to various groups etc.; having things in common. [f. INTER- + COMMUNITY]

interconnĕ'ct *v.t.* & *i.* Connect with each other; so ~ION *n.* [f. INTER- + CONNECT]

i'ntercourse (-ōrs) *n.* Social communication, dealings, between individuals; communion between man and God; communication for trade purposes etc. between different countries etc.; =SEXUAL *intercourse*. [ME, f. OF *entrecours* exchange, commerce, f. L INTER(*cursus* f. *currere curs-* run)]

intercŭ'rr|ent *a.* (Of time or event) inter-

For other words in *inter-* see INTER-.

vening; (of disease) (1) occurring during progress of another, (2) recurring at intervals; hence ~ENCE *n.* [f. L (as prec.; see -ENT)]

ĭ'ntercŭt *v.t.* (-tt-; -cut). (Cinemat.) Alternate (shots) with contrast of distance etc. by cutting. [f. INTER- + CUT²]

ĭnterdėpĕ'nd *v.i.* Depend on each other; so ~ENCE, ~ENCY, *ns.*, ~ENT *a.* [f. INTER- + DEPEND]

ĭ'nterdĭct¹ *n.* Authoritative prohibition; (Sc. Law) injunction; (R.C. Ch.) sentence debarring person or (esp.) place from ecclesiastical functions and privileges. [ME f. OF *entredit* f. L *interdictum* p.p. (as n.) of INTER(*dicere dict-* say) interpose, forbid by decree]

ĭnterdĭ'ct² *v.t.* Prohibit (action); forbid use of; restrain (person *from* doing); forbid (thing *to* person); so ~ION *n.*, ~ORY *a.* [ME, f. prec.]

ĭ'nterėst¹ (*or* -tr-) *n.* **1.** Legal concern, title, right, (*in* property); pecuniary stake (*in* commercial undertaking etc.); **declare an** or one's ~ (in an undertaking, before discussion of it); VEST²*ed interests.* **2.** Advantage, profit, (*it is* (*in* or *to*) *your interest to go*; *I do it in your interest*(*s*); *in the interest*(*s*) *of truth*; *look after* one's *own interests*). **3.** Thing in which one is concerned; principle in which a party is concerned; party having a common interest (*the brewing interest*). **4.** Selfish pursuit of one's own welfare; self-interest. **5.** Concern, curiosity, (*take an interest, no interest, in*); quality exciting these or holding one's attention (*this has no great interest for me, is of no interest to me*); LOSE *interest.* **6.** Money paid for use of money lent or for not exacting repayment of debt; **with** ~, (fig.) with increased force etc. (*returned the blow, his kindness, with interest*); **simple** ~ (reckoned on principal only, and paid at fixed intervals); **compound** ~ (reckoned on principal and on accumulations of interest). [ME, earlier *interesse* f. AF f. med. L, alt. app. after OF *interest*, both f. L *interest*, 3rd sing. pres. of INTER(*esse* be) matter, make a difference]

ĭ'nterėst² (*or* -tr-) *v.t.* Cause (person) to take personal interest or share (*in*); (in *p.p.*) having a private interest, not impartial or disinterested, (*interested parties, motives*); excite curiosity or attention of. [alt. (after prec.) f. earlier *interess*, f. F *intéresse* f. L *interesse* (see prec.)]

ĭ'nterėstĭng (*or* -tr-) *a.* Causing curiosity, holding the attention; **in an ~ condition,** (arch.) pregnant; hence ~LY² *adv.* [f. prec. + -ING²]

ĭ'nterfāce *n.* **1.** Surface forming common boundary between two regions. **2.** Place, or piece of equipment, where interaction occurs between two systems, processes, etc. [f. INTER- + FACE¹]

ĭ'nterfācing *n.* Stiffish material between two layers of fabric in garment etc. [f. INTER- + FACING]

ĭnterfēr'|e *v.i.* (Of thing) come into collision or opposition or incompatibility (*with*); (of person) meddle (*with*, or abs.), whence ~ING² *a.*; intervene, take part, (*in*); (Phys., of light-waves etc.) combine in different phases so as to cause partial or complete neutralization; (of horse) knock one leg against another; **~e with,** (euphem.) molest or assault sexually. [f. OF *s'entreferir* strike each other (*entre-* INTER-, *ferir* f. L *ferire* strike)]

ĭnterfēr'ence *n.* Interfering (*with*); (Radio) fading of received signals by interference of waves from different sources or paths, or (esp.) by (intrusion of) atmospherics or unwanted signals; hence **ĭnterferĕ'nt**IAL (-shal) *a.* [irreg. f. prec. + -ENCE, after *difference* etc.]

ĭnterferŏ'mėter *n.* Instrument for measuring wavelengths etc. by means of interference phenomena; hence **ĭnterfĕromĕ'tr**IC *a.*, **ĭnterferŏ'**METRY *n.* [f. INTERFERE + -O- + -METER]

ĭnterfēr'ŏn *n.* Protein inhibiting development of virus in cell. [f. INTERFERE + -ON]

ĭntēr'fluent (-ōō-) *a.* Flowing into each other. [f. L INTER(*fluere* flow); see -ENT]

ĭnterfū'se (-z) *v.* **1.** *v.t.* Intersperse, mix, (thing *with*); blend (things) together. **2.** *v.i.* (Of two things) blend with each other. **3.** So **ĭnterfū'**SION (-zhon) *n.* [f. L INTER(*fundere fus-* pour)]

ĭ'nterĭm *adv.*, *n.*, & *a.* **1.** *adv.* (arch.) Meanwhile. **2.** *n.* Intervening time (*in the interim*); **the I~,** (Eccl.) truce, pending a General Council, between German Protestants and the Papacy in 16th c. **3.** *a.* Intervening; provisional, temporary; **~ dividend** (paid between two annual etc. balances and not in pursuance of a published balance-sheet). [L (INTER + adv. suf. *-im*)]

ĭntēr'ior *a.* & *n.* **1.** *a.* Inner (opp. *exterior*); situated within (relative *to*); remote from coast or frontier, inland; internal, domestic, (opp. *foreign*); existing in mind or soul, inward; coming from inside; drawn, photographed, etc., within a building; **~ angle** (between adjacent sides of rectilinear figure); **~ decoration** (of interior of building or room); **~ monologue,** form of writing representing character's inner thoughts; **~-sprung,** (of mattress etc.) with springs inside; hence ~IZE (3) *v.t.*, ~LY² *adv.* **2.** *n.* Interior part, inside; (picture of) inside of building or room; inner nature, soul; (department dealing with) home affairs of a country (*Minister of the Interior*). [L, compar. of *inter* among]

ĭnterjĕ'ct *v.t.* Throw in, interpose (remark etc.) abruptly; remark parenthetically. [f. L INTER-(*jicere ject-* = *jacĕre* throw)]

ĭnterjĕ'ction *n.* Ejaculation, exclamation; natural ejaculation viewed as part of speech (e.g. *ah!*, *whew!*, *dear me!*); interposed remark; hence ~AL, ~ARY¹, **ĭnterjĕ'ct**ORY, *adjs.* [ME f. OF, f. L *interjectio -onis* (as prec.; see -ION)]

ĭnterlā'ce *v.* **1.** *v.t.* Bind together intricately, entangle; interweave (often fig.); mingle (two things, one *with* another); present (lines forming television picture) in two sequences each containing alternate lines. **2.** *v.i.* Cross each other intricately. **3.** Hence ~MENT (-sm-) *n.* [ME, f. OF *entrelacier* (*entre-* INTER-, *lacier* LACE²)]

ĭnterlar'd *v.t.* Mix (writing, speech, *with* foreign words etc.). [f. F *entrelarder* (*entre-* INTER-, *larder* LARD²)]

ĭ'nterlea|f *n.* (*pl.* ~ves). Extra leaf (usu. blank) between leaves of book. [f. foll.]

ĭnterlea've *v.t.* Insert (usu. blank) leaves between leaves of (book etc.; lit. or fig.). [f. INTER- + LEAF, *leaves*]

ĭnterlī'ne¹ *v.t.* Insert words between lines of (document etc.); insert (words) thus; so **ĭnterlĭnė**A'TION *n.* [ME, f. med. L INTER-(*lineare* f. L *linea* LINE²)]

ĭnterlī'n|e² *v.t.* Put extra lining between ordinary lining and material of (garment); hence ~ING¹ (2, 4) *n.* [f. INTER- + LINE⁴]

ĭnterlĭ'nėar *a.* Written or printed between the lines of a text. [ME, f. med. L INTER(*linearis* LINEAR)]

ĭnterlŏ'ck *v.* & *a.* **1.** *v.i.* Engage with each other by overlapping etc. **2.** *v.t.* (usu. in *pass.*) Lock or clasp within each other. **3.** Connect (switches etc.) so that they cannot be operated independently or unsafely. **4.** *a.* (Of fabric) knitted with closely interlocking stitches. [f. INTER- + LOCK³]

ĭnterlŏ'cū|tor *n.* One who takes part in dialogue

or conversation (**my ~tor,** the person in conversation with me); centre man of Negro minstrel troupe; hence or cogn. **interlocū'tion**, **~tress**¹, ~TRIX, *ns.* [mod. L, f. L INTER(*loqui locut-* speak); see -OR]

interlŏ'cūtorў *a.* Of dialogue or conversation; (of decree etc.) given in the course of a legal action. [f. med. L *interlocutorius* (as prec.; see -ORY)]

ĭ'nterlōper *n.* Intruder, one who (esp. for profit) thrusts himself into others' affairs; (Hist.) unauthorized trader; so **ĭ'nterlōpe** *v.i.* [f. INTER- (as in *intermeddle*) + *loper* (as in *landloper*)]

ĭ'nterlūde (*or* -ōōd) *n.* **1.** Pause between acts of play; what fills this up; (Mus.) instrumental piece played between verses of psalm or hymn etc. **2.** Intervening time or space of different character. **3.** Event, amusing incident, etc., interposed. **4.** (Hist.) Dramatic or mimic representation between acts of miracle plays or moralities. [ME, = light dramatic item between acts of morality play, f. med. L INTER(*ludium* f. *ludus* play)]

ĭntermă'rriage (-rĭj) *n.* Marriage between members of different families, castes, tribes, etc., or (loosely) between near relations. [f. INTER- + MARRIAGE]

ĭntermă'rrў *v.i.* (Of tribes, nations, families, etc.) become connected by marriage (*with* other tribes etc.). [f. INTER- + MARRY¹]

ĭntermĕ'ddle *v.i.* Concern oneself (*with, in*, esp. what is not one's business). [ME, f. AF *entremedler* (*entre-* INTER-; see MEDDLE)]

ĭntermē'dĭarў *a.* & *n.* **1.** *a.* Acting between parties, mediatory; intermediate. **2.** *n.* Intermediary person or thing, esp. mediator. [f. F *intermédiaire* f. It. *intermediario* f. L *intermedius* (see foll., -ARY¹)]

ĭntermē'dĭate¹ *a.* & *n.* **1.** *a.* Coming between two things in time, place, or order; (of missile's range) less than inter-continental; ~ **frequency** (to which radio signal is converted during heterodyne reception); hence ~LY² (-tlĭ) *adv.* **2.** *n.* Intermediate thing; (Chem.) compound formed by one reaction and then taking part in another, esp. during synthesis of commercial products. [f. med. L *intermediatus* (as INTERMEDIUM; see -ATE²)]

ĭntermē'dĭ|āte² *v.i.* Act as intermediary, mediate, (*between*); hence ~A'TION, **~ātor**, *ns.* [f. INTER- + MEDIATE²]

ĭntermē'dĭ|um *n.* (*pl.* **~a** *or* **~ums**). Intermediate thing, medium. [LL, neut. (as n.) of L INTER(*medius* middle)]

intẽr'ment *n.* Burial. [ME, f. INTER + -MENT]

ĭntermĕ'zz|ō (-tsō) *n.* (*pl.* **~i** *pr.* -ē, *or* **~os**). Short light dramatic or other performance between acts of drama or opera; short movement connecting main divisions of large musical work, or independent piece of this type. [It., f. L INTERMEDIUM]

intẽr'mĭnab|le *a.* Endless; tediously long; hence **~leness** (-bеln-) *n.*, ~LY² *adv.* [ME f. OF, or f. LL IN²(*terminabilis* f. L *terminare*; *see* TERMINATE, -ABLE)]

ĭntermĭ'ngle (-nggel) *v.* **1.** *v.t.* Mix together (two things, one *with* another). **2.** *v.i.* Mingle (*with*). [f. INTER- + MINGLE]

ĭntermĭ'ssion (-shon) *n.* Pause, cessation; period of inactivity; *(musical selection during) interval in theatre performance etc. [F, or f. L *intermissio* (as foll.; see -ION)]

ĭntermĭ't *v.t.* & *i.* (-tt-). Suspend, discontinue; stop for a time (esp. of fever, pain, etc., or of pulse). [f. L INTER(*mittere miss-* let go)]

ĭntermĭ'tt|ent *a.* Ceasing for a time; occurring at intervals, not continuous or steady; hence or cogn. ~ENCE *n.*, **~ent**LY² *adv.* [f. L (as prec.; see -ENT)]

ĭntermĭ'x *v.t.* & *i.* Mix together, intermingle; so ~TURE *n.* [back form. f. *intermixed, intermixt* f. L *intermixtus* p.p. of INTER(*miscēre* mix)]

intẽ'rn¹ *v.t.* Oblige to reside within limits of country etc.; confine (esp. enemy alien or prisoner of war) within prescribed limits; hence ~EE', ~MENT, *ns.* [f. F *interner* (*interne* f. L *internus* internal)]

***ĭ'ntẽrn**² *n.*, & *v.i.* **1.** *n.* Advanced student or recent graduate residing in hospital and acting as assistant physician or surgeon; teacher undergoing practical training; hence ~SHIP *n.* **2.** *v.i.* Serve as intern. [after F *interne* (see prec.)]

intẽr'nal *a.* & *n.* **1.** *a.* Of, or situated in, the inside or invisible part (opp. *external*); of the inner nature of a thing, intrinsic; (of remedy etc.) applied within the body; relating to the interior of the body (*internal injuries, organs*); of the domestic affairs of a State; pertaining to students attending a university as well as being examined there; of the mind or soul, inward, subjective; ~ **combustion engine** (in which motive power is derived from explosion of mixture of gas, or vaporized oil or petrol, and air in the cylinder); ~ **evidence** (derived from what is contained in thing discussed); *~ (inland) **revenue**; *internal* RHYME¹; *internal* WORK¹; hence ~ITY (-ă'l-) *n.*, ~IZE (3) *v.t.*, ~LY² *adv.* **2.** *n.* (in *pl.*) Intrinsic qualities. [f. mod. L *internalis* (as INTERN¹; see -AL)]

internat. *abbr.* = foll.

ĭnternă'tional *a.* & *n.* **1.** *a.* Existing, or carried on, between different nations; agreed on by all or many nations (*international candle, date-line, driving licence*; ~ **system of units,** system of physical units based on the metre, kilogram, second, ampere, kelvin, candela, and mole, with prefixes to indicate multiplication or division by a power of ten; ~ **unit,** standard quantity of vitamin etc.); ~ **law,** body of rules regarded by nations as governing their mutual behaviour in peace and war; hence ~ITY (-ă'l-) *n.*, ~LY² *adv.* **2.** *n.* Contest (usu. in sports) between representatives of different nations; such representative. **3.** (*I~*). One of four associations founded to promote socialist or communist action (1864–1876, 1889– , 1919–1943, 1936–). **4.** Member of any of these associations. [f. INTER- + NATION + -AL]

Internătiona'le (ĭ-; -ah'l) *n.* **1. The** ~, (orig. French) revolutionary song adopted by socialists. **2.** = prec. 3. [F, fem. of *international* adj. f. prec.]

ĭnternă'tional|ĭst *n.* **1.** One who advocates community of interests and friendly co-operation between nations; supporter of INTERNATIONAL 3; so ~ISM (3) *n.* **2.** One versed in international law. [f. INTERNATIONAL + -IST]

ĭnternă'tionalīz|e, -īs|e (-īz), *v.t.* Make international, esp. bring (territory etc.) under combined protection etc. of different nations; hence ~A'TION *n.* [f. INTERNATIONAL + -IZE]

***ĭ'ntẽrne.** Var. of INTERN².

ĭnternē'cīne *a.* Mutually destructive. [orig. = deadly, f. L *internecinus* f. *internecio* massacre f. INTER(*necare* kill) slaughter; see -INE¹]

ĭntẽrnee'. See INTERN¹.

intẽr'nĭst *n.* Specialist in internal diseases. [f. INTERNAL + -IST]

intẽr'nment. See INTERN¹.

ĭnternŭ'ncial (-shal) *a.* Of an internuncio; (of nerves) communicating between different parts of the system. [f. foll. + -AL]

ĭnternŭ'ncĭō (-shĭō) *n.* (*pl.* **~s**). Pope's am-

For other words in *inter-* see INTER-.

bassador when or where no nuncio is employed; (Hist.) minister representing (esp. Austrian) government at Constantinople. [f. It. *internunzio* f. L INTER(*nuntius* messenger)]

ĭnterōcĕ'ptĭve *a.* (Biol.) Relating to stimuli produced within an organism, esp. in the viscera. [irreg. f. L *internus* interior + -O- + RECEPTIVE]

ĭnterpā'ge *v.t.* Print or insert on intermediate pages. [f. INTER- + PAGE³]

ĭntėr'pĕll|āte *v.t.* (In European etc. parliaments) interrupt order of the day by demanding explanation from (Minister concerned); so ~A'TION, ~ātOR, *ns.* [f. L INTER(*pellare* thrust f. *pellere* drive) + -ATE³]

ĭnterpĕ'nĕtr|āte *v.t.* & *i.* Penetrate thoroughly, pervade; penetrate reciprocally; so ~A'TION *n.*, ~ātIVE *a.* [f. INTER- + PENETRATE]

ĭ'nterplay *n.* Reciprocal action; operation of two things on each other. [f. INTER- + PLAY²]

ĭnterplea'd *v.i.* & *t.* (Cause to) litigate with each other in order to settle a point in which a third party is concerned. [ME, f. AF *enterpleder* (as INTER-, PLEAD)]

I'nterpŏl (ĭ'-) *n.* International Criminal Police Commission. [abbr.]

ĭntėr'pol|āte *v.t.* Make insertions in (book etc.), esp. so as to give false impressions as to date etc.; introduce (words) thus; interpose orally; (Math. etc.) insert (intermediate terms) in series, estimate from known values etc. others lying in the same range; so ~A'TION, ~ātOR, *ns.* [f. L INTER(*polare* cogn. w. *polire* POLISH¹) furbish up + -ATE³]

ĭnterpō's|e (-z) *v.* **1.** *v.t.* Insert, make intervene, (*between*); put forth, introduce, (veto, objection, authority, etc.) by way of interference; say (quoted words) as an interruption. **2.** *v.i.* Intervene (*between* disputants etc.); make an interruption. **3.** Hence ~AL *n.* [f. F *interposer* f. L INTER(*ponere* put); see POSE¹]

ĭntėrposĭ'tion (-z-) *n.* Interposing; thing interposed; interference. [ME f. OF, or f. L *interpositio* f. INTER(*ponere posit-* place); see -ITION]

ĭntėr'prĕt *v.* **1.** *v.t.* Expound the meaning of (abstruse or foreign words, writings, dreams, etc.); make out the meaning of; bring out the meaning of, render, by artistic representation or performance; explain, understand, in specified manner (*we interpret this as a threat*). **2.** *v.i.* Act as interpreter. **3.** Hence or cogn. ~ABLE, ~ātIVE, ~IVE, *adjs.*, ~A'TION *n.* [ME, f. OF *interpreter* or f. L *interpretari* explain, translate (INTER*pres -pretis* explainer)]

ĭntėr'prĕt|er *n.* One who interprets; one whose office it is to translate the words of persons speaking different languages, esp. orally in their presence; hence ~**er**SHIP, ~RESS¹, *ns.* [ME f. AF *interpretour*, OF *interpreteur* f. LL *interpretator -oris* (as prec.; see -OR)]

ĭnterrĕ'gn|um *n.* (*pl.* ~**ums** *or* ~**a**). Period during which State has no normal ruler, esp. between end of king's reign and accession of successor; interval, pause. [L INTER(*regnum* REIGN¹)]

ĭnterrėlā't|ėd *a.* Mutually related or connected; so ~ION, ~**ion**SHIP, *ns.* [f. INTER- + p.p. of RELATE]

ĭntĕ'rrogāt|e *v.t.* Ask questions of (person etc.), esp. closely or formally; obtain information-signal from (automatic device); so ~OR *n.* [ME, f. L INTER(*rogare* ask) + -ATE³]

ĭntĕrrogā'tion *n.* Interrogating; question; ~ **point** etc., QUESTION¹-mark. [ME f. F, or f. L *interrogatio* (as prec.; see -ATION)]

ĭnterrŏ'gatĭve *a.* & *n.* **1.** *a.* Of, or having the form or force of, a question; of inquiry (*an interrogative tone*); (Gram.) used in questions (*interrogative* PRONOUN); hence ~LY² (-vlĭ) *adv.* **2.** *n.* Interrogative word, esp. pronoun. [f. LL *interrogativus* (as INTERROGATE; see -IVE)]

ĭnterrŏ'gatorў *a.* & *n.* **1.** *a.* Of inquiry (*an interrogatory tone*). **2.** *n.* Question, set of questions, esp. (Law) one formally put to accused person etc. [f. LL *interrogatorius* (as INTERROGATE; see -ORY)]

ĭnterrŭ'pt *v.t.* Act so as to prevent from proceeding continuously (action, process, speech, person speaking, etc., or abs.); obstruct (view etc.); break the continuity of; ~**ed screw** (with part of thread cut away); hence or cogn. ~ION *n.*, ~IVE, ~ORY, *adjs.* [ME, f. L INTER(*rumpere rupt-* break)]

ĭnterrŭ'pter, -or, *ns.* One who interrupts; device for interrupting esp. electric current. [f. prec. + -ER¹, -OR]

inter se (ĭnter sē') *adv.* Between or among themselves. [L]

ĭntersĕ'ct *v.* **1.** *v.t.* Divide (thing) by passing or lying across it. **2.** *v.i.* (Of lines etc.) cross or cut each other. [f. L INTER(*secare sect-* cut)]

ĭntersĕ'ction *n.* Intersecting; point, line, elements, common to intersecting lines, surfaces, sets; place where two roads intersect; hence ~AL *a.* [f. L *intersectio* (as prec.; see -ION)]

ĭ'ntersĕx *n.* Condition of being abnormally intermediate between male and female; individual in this condition. [f. INTER- + SEX]

ĭntersĕ'xūal *a.* Existing between the sexes; of intersex. [f. INTER- + SEXUAL]

ĭ'nterspāce *n.*, & *v.t.* **1.** *n.* Interval of space or time. **2.** *v.t.* Put interspace(s) between. [ME, f. INTER- + SPACE¹]

ĭntersper's|e *v.t.* Scatter, place here and there (*between, among*); diversify (thing) *with* (others so scattered); hence ~ION (-shon) *n.* [f. L INTER(*spergere spers-* = *spargere* scatter)]

***ĭ'nterstāte** *a.* Existing, carried on, between states esp. of the U.S. [f. INTER- + STATE¹]

ĭntėr'stĭce *n.* Intervening space; chink, crevice. [f. L *interstitium* f. INTER(*sistere stit-* stand)]

ĭnterstĭ'tial (-shal) *a.* Of, forming, occupying, interstice(s). [f. as prec. + -AL]

ĭntertrĭ'gō *n.* (*pl.* ~**s**). (Path.) Inflammation by rubbing of one area of skin on another. [L, f. INTER(*terere trit-* rub)]

ĭntertwi'ne *v.* **1.** *v.t.* Entwine (things, one *with* another). **2.** *v.i.* Become entwined. **3.** Hence ~MENT (-nm-) *n.* [f. INTER- + TWINE]

ĭ'nterval *n.* **1.** Intervening time or space; pause; break, gap, esp. in theatre etc. performance; ~ **signal** (indicating continuity of radio transmission during short interval in broadcast programme); **at ~s,** here and there, now and then. **2.** (Mus.) Difference of pitch between two sounds, in melody or harmony. **3.** Distance between persons or things in respect of qualities. **4.** Hence **ĭntervă'll**IC *a.* [ME, ult. f. L INTER(*vallum* rampart) space between ramparts, interval]

ĭntervē'n|e *v.i.* Come in as something extraneous; occur in the mean time; (of person or thing) come between so as to prevent or modify result etc. (*between* persons, *in* affair); (Law) interpose in lawsuit to which one was not an original party (‖esp. of Queen's Proctor in divorce cases), whence ~ER¹,⁴ *n.*; lie, be situated, *between*; so ~**ĭ**ENT *a.*, **ĭntervĕ'nt**ION *n.* [f. L INTER(*venire vent-* come)]

ĭ'nterview (-vū) *n.*, & *v.t.* **1.** *n.* Meeting of persons face to face, esp. for purpose of consultation; oral examination of candidate for employment etc.; meeting between journalist and person whose views are sought for publication; similar meeting as part of radio or television programme. **2.** *v.t.* Have interview with (person); hence ~EE′, ~ER^1, *ns.* [f. F *entrevue* f. *s'entrevoir* see each other (*entre-* INTER-, *voir* f. L *vidēre* see); cf. VIEW]

inter vivos (ĭnter vī′vōs) *adv.* Between living persons (esp. of gift as opp. legacy). [L]

ĭntervŏ′lve *v.t.* (arch.) Wind, roll up, (things) within each other. [f. INTER- + L *volvere* roll]

ĭnterwea′ve *v.t.* (**-wo′ve; -wo′ven**). Weave together, interlace, (things, one *with* another); blend (things) intimately. [f. INTER- + WEAVE^1]

ĭnterwī′nd *v.t.* & *i.* (**-wou′nd**). Wind together. [f. INTER- + WIND^3]

ĭntĕ′st|ate *a.* & *n.* **1.** *a.* (Of person) not having made a will (*he died intestate*); hence ~ACY *n.* **2.** *n.* Intestate person. [ME, f. L IN^2(*testatus* p.p. of *testari* make will f. *testis* witness); see -ATE^2]

ĭntĕ′stĭn|e^1 *n.* (in *sing.* or *pl.*) Lower part of alimentary canal from pyloric end of stomach to anus; **large ~e,** caecum, colon, and rectum; **small ~e,** duodenum, jejunum, and ileum; so ~AL *a.* [f. L *intestinum* neut. adj. (as n.); see foll.]

ĭntĕ′stĭne^2 *a.* (Of war etc.) internal, domestic, civil. [f. L *intestinus* internal (*intus* within)]

***inthrall.** Var. of ENTHRAL.

ĭnthrōnīzā′tion. See ENTHRONIZATION.

ĭ′ntĭmacy̆ *n.* State of being intimate; (euphem.) sexual intercourse. [f. foll. + -ACY]

ĭ′ntĭmate^1 *a.* & *n.* **1.** *a.* Close in acquaintance, familiar, (*intimate friend, friendship*); (euphem.) having sexual intercourse *with*; (of connection etc.) close; (of knowledge etc.) resulting from close familiarity; (of mixing etc.) thorough; essential, intrinsic; closely personal; (of diary) recording emotions etc. frankly; promoting close personal relationships; hence ~LY^2 (-tlĭ) *adv.* **2.** *n.* Intimate friend. [f. as foll.; see -ATE^2]

ĭ′ntĭm|āte^2 *v.t.* Make known, state, announce, (fact, wish, *that*); imply, hint; so ~A′TION *n.* [f. LL *intimare* announce f. L *intimus* inmost + -ATE^3]

ĭntĭ′mĭd|āte *v.t.* Overawe with fear, esp. in order to influence conduct; hence ~A′TION, ~**ātOR**, *ns.* [f. med. L IN^1(*timidare* f. *timidus* TIMID) + -ATE^3]

ĭntĭ′nction *n.* Dipping of the Eucharistic bread in the wine, to enable the communicant to receive both elements together. [f. LL *intinctio* f. L IN^1(*tingere tinct-* TINGE)]

||**ĭntĭ′tūle** *v.t.* Entitle (Act of Parliament etc.; usu. in *p.p.*). [f. OF *intituler* f. LL IN^1(*titulare* f. L *titulus* title)]

ĭ′nto (*or* -tŏŏ) *prep.* **1.** Expr. motion or direction to a point within a thing, lit. or fig., (*come into the garden*; *throw it into the fire*; *look into the box, the matter, the future*; *inquire into it*; *get into trouble*; COME *into property*; *ran into a pillar*; *4* (*divided*) *into 20 = 5*; *watching far into the night*). **2.** Expr. change, condition, result, (*turn stones into gold*; *translate into English*; *grow into an adult*; *collect them into heaps*; *divide them into three classes*; *flogged into submission*). **3.** (colloq.) Interested in; knowledgeable about. [OE *in*(*n*)*tō* (as IN^2, TO^1)]

ĭntŏ′lerab|le *a.* That cannot be endured; hence ~**le**NESS (-bln-) *n.*, ~LY^2 *adv.* [ME f. OF, or f. L IN^2(*tolerabilis* TOLERABLE)]

ĭntŏ′ler|ant *a.* Not tolerant (*of*, esp. religious opinions differing from one's own); hence or cogn. ~ANCE *n.*, ~**ant**LY^2 *adv.* [f. L IN^2(*tolerans* TOLERANT)]

ĭ′ntonāte *v.t.* Intone. [f. med. L *intonare* (see INTONE) + -ATE^3]

ĭntonā′tion *n.* Reciting in intoning voice; (Church Mus.) opening phrase of plainsong melody; utterance or production of musical tones; modulation of voice, accent. [f. med. L *intonatio* (as foll.; see -ATION)]

ĭntō′ne *v.t.* Recite (psalm, prayer, etc., or abs.) with prolonged sounds, esp. in monotone; utter with particular tone. [f. med. L IN^1(*tonare* f. L *tonus* TONE^1)]

in toto (ĭn tō′tō) *adv.* Completely. [L]

ĭntŏ′xĭcant *a.* & *n.* Intoxicating (liquor). [f. foll. + -ANT]

ĭntŏ′xĭc|āte *v.t.* Make drunk; excite, exhilarate, beyond self-control (*intoxicated with* or *by*); hence ~**ātING**^{2} *a.*, ~A′TION *n.* [f. med. L IN^1(*toxicare* poison f. L *toxicum*; see TOXIC) + -ATE^3]

ĭntra- *pref.* forming *adjs.* usu. f. *adjs.*, w. senses 'on the inside, within', as: **~cra′nial,** within the skull; **~mur′al,** existing or done within walls, forming part of ordinary university teaching or studies; **~mu′scular,** in(to) muscle(s); **~na′tional,** (not inter)national; **~-uterine,** within the womb; **~ve′nous,** in(to) vein(s). [f. L *intra* inside]

ĭntră′ct|able *a.* Not docile, refractory; (of thing) not easily dealt with; hence ~ABI′LITY, ~**able**NESS (-bеln-), *ns.*, ~**ab**LY^2 *adv.* [f. L IN^2(*tractabilis* TRACTABLE)]

ĭntrā′dŏs *n.* Lower or inner curve or arch. [F INTRA(*dos* back f. L *dorsum*)]

ĭntră′nsĭg|ent (*or* -z-) *a.* & *n.* **1.** *a.* Uncompromising, esp. in politics; so ~ENCE *n.* **2.** *n.* Intransigent person. [f. F *intransigeant* f. Sp. *los intransigentes* extreme republicans in Cortes, ult. f. as IN-^{2} + L TRANS(*igere* = *agere* act) come to an understanding; see -ENT]

ĭntră′nsĭtĭve (*or* -z-; *or* -ah′-) *a.* (Gram.) That does not take a direct object (cf. TRANSITIVE); hence ~LY^2 (-vlĭ) *adv.* [f. LL IN^2(*transitivus* TRANSITIVE)]

ĭ′ntrant *n.* (arch.) One who enters a college, association, religious order, etc. [f. L *intrare* enter; see -ANT]

ĭntrĕ′pĭd *a.* Fearless, brave; hence **ĭntrĕpĭ′d**ITY *n.*, ~LY^2 *adv.* [f. F *intrépide* or f. L IN^2(*trepidus* alarmed)]

ĭ′ntrĭc|ate *a.* Perplexingly entangled or complicated; involved; obscure; hence ~ACY *n.*, ~**ate**LY^2 (-tlĭ) *adv.* [ME, f. L IN^1(*tricare* f. *tricae* tricks); see -ATE^2]

ĭ′ntrĭgant *n.* (*fem.* ~e). Intriguer. [f. F *intriguant* (*intriguer*; see INTRIGUE^1, -ANT)]

intriguant(e). Var. of prec.

intrī′gu|e^1 (-ē′g) *v.* **1.** *v.i.* Carry on underhand plot; employ secret influence (*with*); (arch.) have secret amour (*with*); hence ~ER^1 (-ē′ger) *n.* **2.** *v.t.* Puzzle, rouse the interest or curiosity of. [f. F *intriguer* f. It. *intrigare* f. L (as INTRICATE)]

intrī′gue^2 (-ē′g) *n.* Underhand plotting or plot; (arch.) secret amour. [F, f. It. *intrigo* (*intrigare*; see prec.)]

ĭntrĭ′ns|ĭc *a.* Belonging naturally, inherent, essential, (*intrinsic value*); hence ~ICALLY *adv.* [ME, = interior, f. F *intrinsèque* f. LL *intrinsecus* f. L *intrinsecus* adv. inwardly]

ĭ′ntrō *n.* (*pl.* ~s). (colloq.) Introduction. [abbr.]

ĭntro- *pref.* w. sense 'into', as: **~fle′xion,** inward bending; **~gre′ssion,** going or coming in; **~susce′ption,** intussusception. [f. L *intro* to the inside]

ĭntrodū′ce *v.t.* **1.** Bring in; place in, insert; bring into use (custom, idea, improvement, etc., *into* place, system, etc.). **2.** Usher in, bring forward, (matter etc.); begin, come immediately before the start of. **3.** Make known, esp. in formal manner (person, one*self*, *to* another); present (broadcast programme etc.) to audience. **4.** Draw attention or extend understanding of (person *to* subject etc.) for first time; bring (bill etc.) before Parliament etc. **5.** So **ĭntrodŭ'ct**ORY *a.* [ME, f. L INTRO(*ducere duct-* lead)]

ĭntrodŭ'ction *n.* Introducing; thing introduced; preliminary explanatory matter prefixed to book, lecture, etc.; introductory treatise; formal presentation of one person to another; **letter of ~** (given by one person to another and introducing him to a third). [ME f. OF, or f. L *introductio* (as prec.; see -ION)]

ĭntrō'ĭt (*or* ĭ'-) *n.* (Eccl.) Psalm or antiphon sung while priest approaches altar to celebrate Mass or Holy Communion. [ME f. OF, f. L *introitus* f. INTRO(*ire it-* go)]

ĭntrojĕ'ction *n.* (Psych.) Unconscious incorporation of external ideas into one's own mind. [f. INTRO- after *projection*]

ĭntromĭ't *v.t.* (**-tt-**). (arch.) Let in, admit, (*into*); insert; so **ĭntromĭ'ss**ION (-shon) *n.*, (esp. Sc. Law) intermeddling with the property of another, **~t**ENT *a.*, (esp., Biol., of male organ) copulatory. [f. L INTRO(*mittere miss-* send) introduce]

ĭntrospĕ'ct *v.i.* Examine one's own thoughts and feelings; hence ~ION *n.*, examination or observation of one's own mental processes, ~IVE *a.* [f. L INTRO(*spicere spect-* = *specere* look)]

ĭntrovēr'sion *n.* Introverting (esp. Psych., opp. EXTROVERSION); so **ĭ'ntrovērt**[1] *n.* & *a.*, **ĭ'ntrovērt**ED[1] *a.*, (person) characterized by introversion, unsociable or reserved (person). [f. foll. after *eversion* etc.]

ĭntro|vēr't[2] *v.t.* Turn (mind, thought) inwards upon itself; (esp. Zool.) withdraw (organ etc.) within its own tube or base, like finger of glove, so **~vēr'**SIBLE *a.*; hence **~vēr'**SIVE, **~vēr't**IVE, *adjs.* [f. mod. L INTRO(*vertere* turn)]

ĭntru'd|e (-rōō'd) *v.* **1.** *v.t.* Thrust, force, (thing *into*); force (thing, one*self*, *on* or *upon* person). **2.** *v.i.* Come uninvited, thrust oneself in, (*into* place, company, etc., *on* or *upon* person, his privacy, etc.). **3.** Hence ~ER[1] *n.* (e.g. burglar, raiding aircraft). [f. L IN[1](*trudere trus-* thrust)]

ĭntru'sion (-rōō'zhon) *n.* Intruding; forcing in; forcing oneself in (*into, on, upon*); (Geol.) body of rock forced between strata etc. while molten; (Law) occupation of vacant estate etc. to which one has no claim; (Hist.) settlement of minister of Church of Scotland without consent of congregation, whence ~IST (2) *n.*; so **ĭntru'**SIVE (-rōō's-) *a.* [ME f. OF, or f. med. L *intrusio* (as prec.; see -ION)]

ĭntrŭ'st. See ENTRUST.

ĭ'ntūb|āte *v.t.* (Med.) Insert tube into (larynx etc.) to keep it open; hence ~A'TION *n.* [f. IN-[1] + L *tuba* tube + -ATE[3]]

ĭntū'ĭt *v.t.* & *i.* Know by intuition; receive knowledge by direct perception. [f. L IN[1](*tuēri tuit-* look) consider]

ĭntūĭ'tion *n.* Immediate apprehension by the mind without reasoning; immediate apprehension by sense; immediate insight; hence ~AL *a.* [f. LL *intuitio* (as prec.; see -ION)]

ĭntūĭ'tion(al)|ĭsm *n.* (Philos.) Doctrine that the perception of truth is by intuition; doctrine that in perception external objects are known immediately by intuition; intuitivism; so ~IST (2) *n.* [f. INTUITION(AL) + -ISM]

ĭntū'ĭtĭve *a.* Of, possessing, perceived by, intuition; hence ~LY[2] (-vlĭ) *adv.*, ~NESS (-vn-) *n.* [f. med. L *intuitivus* (as INTUIT; see -IVE)]

ĭntū'ĭtĭv|ĭsm *n.* Doctrine that ethical principles are matters of intuition; so ~IST (2) *n.* [f. prec. + -ISM]

ĭntūmĕ'sc|e *v.i.* Swell up; so ~ENCE *n.*, ~ENT *a.* [f. L IN[1](*tumescere* incept. of *tumēre* swell)]

ĭntussuscĕ'ption *n.* **1.** (Biol.) Taking in of foreign matter by living organism, and its conversion into organic tissue. **2.** (Path.) Inversion of one portion of intestine within another. [F, or mod. L *intussusceptio*, f. L *intus* within + *susceptio* f. SUS(*cipere cept-* = *capere* take) take up; see -ION]

ĭntwī'ne. Var. of ENTWINE.

ĭnŭ'nction *n.* Smearing or rubbing with oil. [ME, f. L IN[1](*unctio* UNCTION)]

ĭ'nund|āte *v.t.* Overflow, flood, (land etc. *with* water, or fig.: *inundated with inquiries*); so ~A'TION *n.* [f. L IN[1](*undare* flow f. *unda* wave) + -ATE[3]]

ĭnūr'e *v.* **1.** *v.t.* Accustom, habituate, (person etc. *to* thing, *to* do), whence ~MENT (-ūr'm-) *n.* **2.** *v.i.* (esp. Law). Come into operation, take effect. [ME, f. AF **eneurer* (**en eure* in use f. *en* in + **eure* f. OF *e(u)vre* work f. L OPERA[1])]

ĭnūr'n *v.t.* (arch.) Put (ashes of cremated body) in an urn. [f. IN-[1] + URN]

in utero (ĭn ū'terō) *adv.* In the womb, before birth. [L]

ĭnū'tĭle *a.* Useless; so **ĭnūtĭ'l**ITY *n.* [ME f. F, f. L IN[2](*utilis* useful f. *uti* use; see -IL)]

in vacuo (ĭn vă'kūō) *adv.* In a vacuum (lit. or fig.). [L]

ĭnvā'd|e *v.t.* Make hostile inroad into (country etc.); swarm into; (fig., of sound, disease, feeling, etc.) assail; encroach upon (rights etc.); hence ~ER[1] *n.* [f. L IN[1](*vadere vas-* go)]

ĭnvă'gĭn|āte *v.t.* Put in a sheath; turn (tube etc.) inside out; so ~A'TION *n.* [f. IN-[1] + L *vagina* sheath + -ATE[3]]

ĭ'nvalĭd[1] (*or* -ēd) *a.* & *n.* (Person) enfeebled or disabled by illness or injury; ~ **carriage, chair, diet,** etc., (for use by invalids); hence ~ISM (2) *n.* [f. L IN[2](*validus*; see VALID); pronunc. (-ēd) after F *invalide*]

ĭnvali'd[2] (-ē'd; *or* ĭ'n-) *v.* **1.** *v.t.* Disable (person) by illness (usu. in *pass.*); treat as an invalid; remove from active service, send *home* etc., as an invalid. **2.** *v.i.* Become an invalid, go on the sick-list. [f. prec.]

ĭnvă'lĭd[3] *a.* Not valid, esp. having no legal force; hence ~LY[2] *adv.* [f. as INVALID[1]]

ĭnvă'lĭd|āte *v.t.* Make (esp. argument etc.) INVALID[3]; hence ~A'TION *n.* [f. med. L IN[2](*validare* f. *validus* VALID) + -ATE[3]]

ĭnvalĭ'dĭtў *n.* Lack of validity; bodily infirmity. [f. F *invalidité* or f. med. L *invaliditas* (as INVALID[1]; see -ITY)]

ĭnvă'lūab|le *a.* Above valuation, inestimable; hence ~LY[2] *adv.* [f. IN-[2] + VALUABLE]

ĭ'nvār, Ĭ'-, *n.* Iron-nickel alloy with negligible coefficient of expansion, used in manufacture of clocks and scientific instruments. [abbr. of foll.; P]

ĭnvār'ĭ|able *a.* Unchangeable; always the same; (Math.) constant, fixed; hence ~ABI'LITY, **~able**NESS (-beln-), *ns.*, **~ab**LY[2] *adv.* [F, or f. LL IN[2](*variabilis* VARIABLE)]

ĭnvār'ĭ|ant *a.* & *n.* **1.** *a.* Invariable; hence ~ANCE *n.* **2.** *n.* (Math.) Function remaining unchanged when specified transformation is applied. [f. IN-[2] + VARIANT]

ĭnvā'sion (-zhon) *n.* Invading; encroachment; so **ĭnvā'**SIVE *a.* [F, or f. LL *invasio* (as INVADE; see -ION)]

ĭnvĕ'ctĕd *a.* (Her.) Bordered by or consisting of a series of small convex lobes. [f. as INVEIGH + -ED[1]]

For other words in *in-* see IN-[1] or (esp.) IN-[2].

invĕ'ctive *n.* Violent attack in words; abusive oratory. [ME f. OF, f. LL *invectivus* a., *invectiva (oratio)* as n. (as foll.; see -IVE)]

invei'gh (-vā') *v.i.* Speak violently, rail loudly, *against*. [f. L IN[1](*vehi* pass. of *vehere vect-* carry) go into, assail]

invei'gle (-vē'- *or* -vā'-) *v.t.* Entice, tempt, guilefully persuade, (*into* place, conduct, etc.; *into* doing); cajole; hence ~MENT (-gelm-) *n.* [earlier *enve(u)gle* f. AF *envegler*, OF *aveugler* to blind (*aveugle* blind prob. f. Rom. **ab oculis* without eyes)]

invĕ'nt *v.t.* Create by thought, originate, (new method, instrument, etc.); concoct (false story etc.); so ~OR *n.* (esp. in Law, patentee of invention), ~RESS[1] *n.* [ME, = discover, f. L IN[1](*venire vent-* come) find, contrive]

invĕ'ntion *n.* Inventing; thing invented, contrivance, esp. one for which patent is granted; fictitious story; (Mus.) short piece developing simple idea; inventiveness; **I~ of the Cross,** (festival on 3 May commemorating) reputed finding of the Cross by Helena mother of Constantine, A.D. 326. [ME, f. L *inventio* (as prec.; see -ION)]

invĕ'ntive *a.* Able to invent, original in devising; showing originality in devising; hence ~LY[2] (-vlĭ) *adv.*, ~NESS (-vn-) *n.* [ME f. F *inventif -ive* or f. med. L *inventivus* (as INVENT; see -IVE)]

ĭ'nventorў *n.*, & *v.t.* **1.** *n.* Detailed list (of goods, furniture, etc.); stock of goods in this; *trader's stock. **2.** *v.t.* Enter (goods etc.) in inventory; make inventory of. [ME, f. med. L *inventorium* f. LL *-arium* (as INVENT; see -ORY)]

Invernĕ'ss (ĭ-) *n.* ~ **cloak** or **coat, i~**, man's sleeveless cloak with removable cape. [~ in Highland, Scotland]

invẽr'se (*or* ĭ'n-) *a.* & *n.* **1.** *a.* Inverted in position, order, or relation; ~ **ratio, proportion,** (between two quantities one of which increases in proportion as the other decreases); ~ **square law** (by which intensity of gravitational force, illumination, etc., decreases in inverse proportion to square of distance); hence ~LY[2] (-slĭ) *adv.* **2.** *n.* Inverted state; thing that is the direct opposite (*of* another). [f. L *inversus* p.p. of *invertere* (see INVERT)]

invẽr'sion (-shon) *n.* Turning upside down; reversal of normal position, order, or relation, e.g. (Gram.) of order of words, (Meteorol.) of variation of air temperature with altitude; reversal of a ratio; (Mus.) process or result of inverting; (Chem.) reversal of direction of rotation of plane of polarized light; **(sexual)** ~, homosexuality; so **invẽr'**SIVE *a.* [f. L *inversio* (as foll.; see -ION)]

invẽr't[1] *v.t.* **1.** Turn upside down; turn (foot) inwards; **~ed comma,** comma placed upside down (single or paired) above the line before quotation, ||(in *pl.*) quotation-marks. **2.** Reverse position, order, or relation, of; (Mus.) change relative position of notes of (chord, interval) by placing lowest note higher, usu. by an octave; subject to inversion; *inverted* PLEAT. [f. L IN[1](*vertere vers-* turn)]

ĭ'nvẽrt[2] *n.* Inverted arch, as at bottom of sewer; homosexual; ~ **sugar,** mixture of dextrose and laevulose. [f. prec.]

invẽr'tėbrate (*or* -āt) *a.* & *n.* **1.** *a.* Not having backbone or spinal column or (usu.) notochord; (fig.) lacking firmness of character. **2.** *n.* Invertebrate animal or (fig.) person. [f. mod. L IN[2](*vertebrata* pl. f. as VERTEBRA; see -ATE[2])]

invĕ'st *v.* **1.** *v.t.* Clothe (person etc. *in* or *with*); cover as garment; clothe, endue, (person etc. *with* qualities, insignia of office, rank, etc.). **2.** Lay siege to. **3.** Employ (money *in* stocks etc.) esp. for profit. **4.** *v.i.* ~ **in,** put money into (stocks), (colloq.) expend money on (*invest in a car*). **5.** Hence ~OR *n.* [ME, f. F *investir* or f. L IN[1](*vestire vestit-* clothe f. *vestis* clothing); sense 3 f. It. *investire*]

invĕ'stig|āte *v.t.* Examine, inquire into, study carefully; make official inquiry into; hence or cogn. ~A'TION, ~**āt**OR, *ns.*, ~**āt**IVE, ~**āt**ORY, *adjs.* [f. L IN[1](*vestigare* track) + -ATE[3]]

invĕ'stiture *n.* Formal investing of person (*with* office), esp. ceremony at which sovereign confers honours; enduing (*with* attributes). [ME, f. med. L *investitura* (as INVEST; see -URE)]

invĕ'stment *n.* Investing of money; money invested; property in which money is invested; investiture; (arch.) clothing; (Mil.) act of besieging, blockade; ~ **trust** (that buys and sells shares in selected companies to make profit for its members). [f. INVEST + -MENT]

invĕ'ter|ate *a.* Long-established; (of disease, habit, prejudice, etc.) deep-rooted, obstinate; (of person) habitual (*an inveterate smoker*); hence ~ACY *n.*, ~**ate**LY[2] (-tlĭ) *adv.* [ME, f. L IN[1](*veterare* make old f. *vetus veteris* old); see -ATE[2]]

invĭ'dious *a.* (Of conduct etc.) giving or likely to give offence, esp. by real or seeming injustice etc.; (of thing) likely to excite ill feeling against the possessor; hence ~LY[2] *adv.*, ~NESS *n.* [f. L *invidiosus* (*invidia* ENVY[1]; see -IOUS)]

invĭ'gil|āte *v.i.* Keep watch; ||supervise candidates at examination; hence ~A'TION, ~**āt**OR, *ns.* [f. L IN[1](*vigilare* watch f. *vigil* watchful) + -ATE[3]]

invĭ'gor|āte *v.t.* Make vigorous; animate; hence ~**āt**IVE *a.*, ~A'TION, ~**āt**OR, *ns.* [f. med. L *IN[1](*vigorare* make strong) + -ATE[3]]

invĭ'nc|ible *a.* Unconquerable (lit. or fig.); **~ible ignorance** (that cannot be overcome by the ignorant person himself); hence ~IBI'LITY *n.*, ~**ib**LY[2] *adv.* [ME f. OF, f. L IN[2](*vincibilis* VINCIBLE)]

invi'ol|able *a.* Not to be violated; (of law, person, place, etc.) to be kept sacred from infraction, profanation, etc.; hence ~ABI'LITY *n.*, ~**ab**LY[2] *adv.* [F, or f. L IN[2](*violabilis* VIOLABLE)]

invi'olate *a.* (Of law, place, etc.) not violated; unbroken; unprofaned; hence **invi'ol**ACY, ~NESS (-tn-), *ns.*, ~LY[2] (-tlĭ) *adv.* [ME, f. L IN[2](*violatus* p.p. of *violare* treat violently); see -ATE[2]]

invĭ'sĭb|le (-z-) *a.* That cannot be seen by the eye, either by nature or because hidden; too small to be seen; (arch.) not prepared to receive callers; **~le exports, imports,** items not appearing in lists of exported or imported goods but for which payment is made by or to another country, e.g. shipping and insurance services; **~le ink** (for writing words etc. that cannot be seen until the paper is heated or otherwise treated); **~le mending** (of clothing etc., so carefully done as to be undetectable); hence **invĭs**IBI'LITY (-z-), ~**le**NESS (-beln-), *ns.*, ~LY[2] *adv.* [ME f. OF, or f. L IN[2](*visibilis* VISIBLE)]

invī't|e *v.t.*, & *n.* **1.** *v.t.* Request courteously to come (*to* dinner, *to* one's house, *in*, etc.); request courteously (*to* do what is presumably agreeable); solicit courteously (suggestions, opinions, confidences); bring on, tend to bring on, (thing) unintentionally; (of thing) present inducements, attract, whence ~ING[2] *a.*; so **invĭt**A'TION, ~EE', *ns.*, ~**at**ORY *a.* **2.** *n.* (*or* ĭ'-). (vulg.) Invitation. [f. F *inviter* or f. L *invitare*]

in vitro (ĭn vĭ'trō; *or* vē'-) *adv.* (Biol.) In a test-tube or other laboratory environment (opp. foll.). [L, = in glass]

in vivo (ĭn vē'vō) *adv.* (Biol.) In the living body. [L]

invocā'tion *n.* **1.** Invoking, calling upon God etc. in prayer; **the** ~, (esp.) the words 'In the name of the Father' etc. as used by preacher before sermon. **2.** Appeal to one's muse for inspiration or assistance in poem. **3.** Hence **invŏ'cat**ORY (*or* ĭ'nvokā-) *a.* [ME f. OF, f. L *invocatio -onis* (as INVOKE; see -ATION)]

ĭ'nvoice *n.*, & *v.t.* **1.** *n.* List of goods shipped or sent, or services performed, with prices and charges. **2.** *v.t.* Make invoice of (goods); send invoice to (person). [app. orig. *invoyes* pl. of *invoy* = ENVOY[1]; *-ce* as in *dice, truce*]

invō'ke *v.t.* Call on (deity etc.) in prayer or as witness; appeal to (person's authority etc.); summon (spirit) by charms; ask earnestly for (vengeance, help, etc.). [f. F *invoquer* f. L IN[1](*vocare* call)]

ĭ'nvolūcr|e (-*ker*; *or* -lōō-) *n.* Covering, envelope; (Anat.) membranous envelope; (Bot.) whorl of bracts surrounding inflorescence; hence ~AL *a.* [F, or f. L *involucrum* (as INVOLVE)]

invŏ'luntar|y̆ *a.* Done without exercise of the will, unintentional; (of limb, muscle, movement) not controlled by the will; hence ~**ĭ**LY[2] *adv.*, ~**ĭ**NESS *n.* [f. LL IN[2](*voluntarius* VOLUNTARY)]

ĭ'nvolūte (*or* -ōōt) *a.* & *n.* **1.** *a.* Involved, intricate. **2.** Curled spirally; (Bot.) rolled inwards at edges. **3.** *n.* (Geom.) Locus of point fixed on straight line that rolls without sliding on a curve and is in the plane of that curve (cf. EVOLUTE). [f. L *involutus* p.p. of *involvere* (see INVOLVE)]

ĭ'nvolūtėd (*or* -ōōt-) *a.* Complicated, abstruse; = prec. 2. [f. prec. + -ED[1]]

involu'tion (-lōō'-) *n.* Involving; entanglement; intricacy; curling inwards; part so curled; (Math.) raising of quantity to any power. [f. L *involutio* (as foll.; see -ION)]

invŏ'lve *v.t.* **1.** Wrap (thing *in* another); wind spirally. **2.** Entangle (person, thing, *in* difficulties, mystery, etc.); implicate (person *in* charge, crime, etc.); include (*in*); imply, entail. **3.** (in *p.p.*) Concerned (*in*), in question; complicated in thought or form (*an involved sentence*). [ME, f. L IN[1](*volvere volut-* roll)]

invŏ'lvement (-vm-) *n.* Involving or being involved (*in, with*); financial embarrassment; complicated affair. [f. prec. + -MENT]

invŭ'lner|able *a.* That cannot be wounded or hurt (esp. fig.); hence ~ABI'LITY *n.*, ~**ab**LY[2] *adv.* [f. L IN[2](*vulnerabilis* VULNERABLE)]

ĭ'nward *a.*, *n.*, & *adv.* **1.** *a.* Situated within; mental, spiritual; directed towards the inside, coming in; fully acquainted *with*. **2.** *n.* (in *pl.*) Entrails. **3.** *adv.* Inwards. [OE *innanweard* (*innan* IN[2]; see -WARD)]

ĭ'nwardly̆ *adv.* On the inside; (of speaking) inaudibly, not aloud; in mind or spirit. [OE *inweardlīce* (as prec., -LY[2])]

ĭ'nwardnėss *n.* Inner nature, essence; quality of being inward; spirituality; close familiarity. [f. INWARD + -NESS]

ĭ'nwards (-z) *adv.* (Of motion or position) towards the inside; within the mind or soul. [ME, f. INWARD adv.; see -WARDS]

inwea've, ėnwea've, *v.t.* (**-wo've; -wo'ven**). Weave in (thing *with* another, lit. or fig.). [f. IN-[1], EN-[1] + WEAVE[1]]

inwrap. Var. of ENWRAP.

inwrou'ght (ĭnraw't, before *n.* ĭ'n-) *a.* (Of fabric) decorated (*with* pattern); (of pattern) wrought (*in* or *on* fabric); (fig.) intimately blended (*with*). [f. IN[2] + WROUGHT]

inya'la (-ah'-) *n.* (*pl.* same). Large S. Afr. antelope (*Tragelaphus angasi*). [f. Zulu *inxala*]

iod-. See IODO-.

iŏ'dĭc *a.* Containing iodine in chem. combination, esp. ~ **acid** (HIO_3); hence **ī'od**ATE[1] (3) *n.* [f. IODINE + -IC]

ī'odide *n.* (Chem.) Binary compound of iodine. [f. foll. + -IDE]

iŏ'dĭn|āte (*or* ī'o-) *v.t.* Treat or impregnate with iodine; so ~A'TION *n.* [f. foll. + -ATE[3]]

ī'odĭn|e (*or* -ēn) *n.* Non-metallic element forming black crystals and violet vapour, resembling chlorine and bromine in chemical properties, used in medicine and photography; alcoholic solution of this as antiseptic; hence ~ISM (5) *n.*, ~IZE (5) *v.t.* [f. F *iode* f. Gk *iōdēs* violet-like (*ion* violet; see -OID) + -INE[5]]

iōdo-, (esp. bef. vowel) **iod-,** *comb. form.* (Chem.) Iodine. [f. prec. + -O-]

iŏ'dofôrm *n.* Compound of iodine chemically analogous to chloroform, a pale yellow solid with antiseptic properties. [f. prec. after *chloroform*]

I.O.M. *abbr.* Isle of Man.

ī'on *n.* One of the electrically charged particles into which the atoms or molecules of certain substances (esp. salts, acids, and bases) are dissociated by solution in water, and which make such a solution a conductor of electricity; similar particle formed when neutral atom etc. loses or gains electron(s); similarly charged molecule of gas occurring e.g. in air exposed to X-rays; ~ **exchange,** reaction of interchange between ions of like charge, used in water-softening etc.; ~ **exchanger,** substance or equipment for this process. [Gk, neut. part. of *eimi* go]

-ion *suf.* forming *ns.* of action, condition, etc., usu. f. *vbs.* (*destruction, legion, objection*; cf. -SION, -TION, -XION), occas. corresp. to *adjs.* etc. (*communion, union*). [f. or after F, or f. L *-io -ionis*]

Iō'nĭan (ī-) *a.* & *n.* **1.** *a.* Of Ionia. **2.** ~ **mode,** (Mus.) (1) ancient Greek MODE, reputedly soft and effeminate in character, (2) eleventh of church modes (with C as final and G as dominant), corresp. to modern major key of C. **3.** *n.* Native or inhabitant of Ionia, esp. member of part of the Hellenic people which occupied Attica, western Asia Minor, Ionian Islands, etc. [f. L f. Gk *Iōnios* + -AN]

Iŏ'nĭc[1] (ī-) *a.* Of Ionia; ~ **dialect** (of Greek, from which Attic developed); ~ **order,** (Archit.) Greek ORDER[1] characterized by two lateral volutes of the capital. [f. L f. Gk *Iōnikos*; see -IC]

iŏ'nĭc[2] *a.* Of ions; using ions (*ionic propulsion*). [f. ION + -IC]

iō'nĭum *n.* Naturally occurring radioactive thorium isotope, of mass 230. [f. ION + -IUM]

ī'oniz|e, -ĭs|e (-iz), *v.t.* & *i.* Convert or be converted into ion(s); hence ~ABLE *a.*, ~A'TION *n.* [f. ION + -IZE]

iŏ'nosph|ēre *n.* Ionized region of upper atmosphere, able to reflect radio waves for transmission round the earth; hence ~**ĕ'r**IC *a.* [f. ION + -O- + SPHERE]

-ior[1] *suf.*, later or U.S. spelling of -IOUR.

-ior[2] *suf.* forming *adjs.* of comparison (*senior, ulterior*). [L]

iō'ta *n.* Ninth Greek letter (Ι, ι) = i (*iota* SUBSCRIPT); smallest amount, JOT[1]. [Gk *iōta*]

IOU (īōū') *n.* Signed document bearing these letters followed by specified sum, constituting formal acknowledgement of debt. [= *I owe you*]

-iour, *-ior, *suf.* forming *ns.*, = -I- representing some formative or stem element + *-our* -OR (*paviour, saviour*).

-ious *suf.* forming *adjs.* w. sense 'characterized by, full of', esp. corresp. to *ns.* in *-ion* (*cautious, contagious, curious, invidious, religious, spacious, specious, various*). [f. or after F *-ieux* f. L *-iosus* (as -I-, -OUS)]

For other words in *in-* see IN-[1] or (esp.) IN-[2].

I.O.W. *abbr.* Isle of Wight.

I.P.A. *abbr.* International Phonetic Alphabet (or Association).

ĭ'pĕcăc *n.* (colloq.) = foll. [abbr.]

ĭpĕcăcūă'nha (-*na*) *n.* Root of a S. Amer. shrub, used as emetic, diaphoretic, and purgative. [Port., f. Tupi-Guarani *ipekaaguéne* emetic creeper]

ĭpomoe'a (-ē'*a*) *n.* Twining tropical plant of genus *Ipomoea*, with trumpet-shaped flower, esp. sweet potato. [mod. L, f. Gk *ips ipos* worm + *homoios* like; see -A]

i.p.s. *abbr.* inches per second.

ipse dixit (ĭpsĭ dĭ'ksĭt) *n.* Dogmatic statement resting merely on speaker's authority. [L, = he himself (the master) said it, transl. Gk *autos epha* used of Pythagoras]

ĭpsĭlă'teral *a.* Belonging to or occurring on same side of body. [irreg. f. L *ipse* self + -I- + LATERAL]

ipsissima verba (ĭpsĭsĭm*a* vėr'b*a*) *n. pl.* The precise words. [L]

ipso facto (ĭpsō fă'ktō) *adv.* By that very fact or act; thereby. [L]

I.Q. *abbr.* intelligence quotient.

-ique. See -IC.

ĭr-[1,2] *prefs.*, assim. forms of IN-[1,2] before *r*.

I.R. *abbr.* infra-red.

Ir *symb.* iridium.

I.R.A. *abbr.* Irish Republican Army.

ĭra'dė (-ah'dĭ) *n.* (Hist.) Written decree of Sultan of Turkey. [Turk., f. Arab. *'irāda* will]

Irā'nĭan (ĭ-) *a.* & *n.* **1.** *a.* Of Iran (Persia); (of languages) of the group of Indo-European languages including Persian, Pushtu, Avestan, and Kurdish. **2.** *n.* Iranian person or language-group. [f. *irān* native name of Persia + -IAN]

Ira'qi (ĭrah'kĭ) *a.* & *n.* (Native, inhabitant, or modern Arabic dialect) of Iraq. [f. *Iraq* in S.W. Asia + -I]

ĭră'sc|ible (*or* īr-) *a.* Irritable, hot-tempered; hence ~IBI'LITY *n.*, ~**ĭb**LY[2] *adv.* [ME f. F, f. LL *irascibilis* f. L *irasci* grow angry (*ira* anger; see -IBLE)]

īrā'te (*or* īr-) *a.* Angry, enraged; hence ~LY[2] (-tlĭ) *adv.* [f. L *iratus* (*ira* anger); see -ATE[2]]

I.R.B.M. *abbr.* intermediate-range ballistic missile.

īre *n.* (rhet. or poet.) Anger; hence ~'FUL (īr'f-) *a.* [ME f. OF, f. L *ira*]

īrĕ'nic(al) (*or* īr-) *adjs.* Aiming or aimed at peace. [f. Gk *eirēnikos* (see EIRENICON, -IC, -ICAL)]

īrē'nĭcŏn. Var. of EIRENICON.

īrĭdā'ceous (-sh*us*; *or* ĭ'r-) *a.* (Bot.) Of the iris family (Iridaceae). [f. mod. L *iridaceus* (as IRIS; see -ACEOUS)]

ĭrĭdĕ'sc|ent *a.* Showing colours like those of rainbow; changing colour with position; hence ~ENCE *n.* [f. L IRIS + -ESCENT]

īrĭ'dĭum (*or* ĭr-) *n.* White metallic element of the platinum group used esp. in hard alloys. [mod. L, f. L IRIS + -IUM]

īr'ĭs *n.* **1.** Flat circular coloured membrane behind cornea of eye, with circular opening (PUPIL) in centre. **2.** Perennial herbaceous plant of genus *Iris* chiefly with tuberous roots, sword-shaped leaves, and showy flowers. **3.** ~ (**diaphragm**), adjustable diaphragm of thin overlapping plates for regulating size of central hole, e.g. for admission of light to lens or lens system. [ME f. L *iris iridis* f. Gk *iris iridos* (goddess of) rainbow, iris]

Ir'ĭsh (īr'-) *a.* & *n.* **1.** *a.* Of or from Ireland or its inhabitants; ||~ **bridge,** open stone drain carrying water across road; *Irish* BULL[4]; ~ **deer** or **elk,** large extinct deer of Ireland and England; ~ **Gaelic,** Irish (language); ~**man,** (1) man of Irish birth or descent, (2) prickly N.Z. shrub; ~ **moss,** dried carrageen; ~ **Sea** (between England & Wales and Ireland); *Irish* STEW[2]; ~ **terrier** (rough-haired reddish-brown kind); ~ **whisk(e)y,** kind distilled in Ireland esp. from malted barley; ~**woman,** woman of Irish birth or descent. **2.** Resembling the Irish, esp. w. ref. to their reputation for illogicality (cf. BULL[4]). **3.** Hence ~ISM (2, 4) *n.*, ~IZE (3) *v.t.*, ~RY (5) *n.* **4.** *n.* Celtic language of Ireland; (colloq.) bad temper; **the** ~, (pl.) persons of Irish birth or descent. [ME, f. OE *Iras* the Irish + -ISH[1]]

īrī'tĭs *n.* Inflammation of the iris. [G, irreg. f. as IRIS + -ITIS]

īrk *v.t.* Disgust, tire, bore, esp. *it irks me, him*, etc. [ME, of unkn. orig.]

īr'ksome *a.* Tedious, tiresome; hence ~LY[2] (-mlĭ) *adv.*, ~NESS (-mn-) *n.* [ME, = tired etc., f. prec. + -SOME[1]]

I.R.O. *abbr.* ||Inland Revenue Office; International Refugee Organization.

ĭrō'kō *n.* (*pl.* ~s). (Wood of) Afr. tree of genus *Chlorophora.* [Ibo]

iron[1] (ī'*ern*) *n.* & *a.* **1.** *n.* Silver-white widely distributed metal of great strength, much used for tools etc.; (fig., as type of unyieldingness: *a man of, a will of, iron*). **2.** Preparation of iron as tonic. **3.** Tool or implement made of iron (*branding, curling, grappling, -iron*); golf-club with iron or steel head and sloping face for lofting ball; implement (orig. of iron) with smooth flat base and means of heating used to smooth clothes etc.; (usu. in *pl.*) fetter (esp. **in** ~**s,** fettered at ankles or handcuffed); (esp. in *pl.*) stirrup; (usu. in *pl.*) leg-support to rectify malformations etc. **4. The** ~ **entered into his soul** [Ps. 105:18, L mistranslation of Heb. 'his person entered into the iron', i.e. fetters], he became permanently affected by ill-treatment etc.; **strike while the** ~ **is hot,** act promptly at a good opportunity; **have (too) many** ~**s in the fire** (undertakings or resources). **5.** *a.* Of iron; very robust (*iron constitution*); firm, unyielding, merciless, (*iron will, rule*). **6. I**~ **Age,** era of iron implements and weapons; ~**-bark,** species of eucalyptus with thick solid bark and hard wood; ~**-bound,** bound with iron, (of coast) rock-bound, (fig.) rigorous, hard and fast; **I**~ **Chancellor,** Bismarck; ~**clad,** (*a.*) clad in, protected with, iron, (*n.*, Hist.) ship cased with plates of iron; **I**~ **Cross,** German military decoration; **I**~ **Curtain,** (fig.) barrier to passage of persons and information at (esp. Western) limit of Soviet sphere of influence; **I**~ **Duke,** 1st Duke of Wellington; ~**-grey** *a.* & *n.*, (of) the colour of freshly broken iron; ~ **horse,** (arch.) locomotive engine; ~ **lung,** rigid case fitted over patient's body, used for administering prolonged artificial respiration by means of mechanical pumps; ~**master,** manufacturer of iron; ~**-mould,** *~**-mold,** spot caused by iron-rust or ink-stain; *iron* PYRITES; ~ **ration,** (soldier's) modicum of tinned etc. food to be used only in emergency; **I**~**sides,** man of great bravery, esp. (as *pl.*) Cromwell's troopers in Civil War; ~**stone,** (1) hard iron-ore, (2) kind of hard white pottery; ~**ware,** (esp. domestic) articles made of iron; ~**work,** work in iron, things made of iron; ~**works** (as *sing.* or *pl.*), place where iron is smelted or iron goods are made. [OE *iren, īsern*, = OS, OHG *īsarn*, ON *ísarn*, Goth. *eisarn* f. Gmc **īsarnam*, prob. f. Celt.]

iron[2] (ī'*ern*) *v.t.* Furnish or cover with iron; shackle with irons; smooth (clothes etc.) with flat-iron etc. (see prec., sense 3), whence ~ING[1] (1, 5) *n.* (~**ing-board,** flat surface usu. on legs of adjustable height, to support clothes etc. being ironed); ~ **out,** (fig.) remove (difficulties etc.); hence ~ER^1 (1, 2) *n.* [ME, f. prec.]

īrŏ'n|ic(al) *adjs.* Of (the nature of), using, said in, addicted to, irony; hence ~ICALLY *adv.* [f. F *ironique* or f. LL f. Gk *eirōnikos* dissembling (as IRONY^1; see -IC)]

īr'on|ist *n.* One who uses irony; so ~IZE (2) *v.i.* [f. Gk *eirōn* dissembler + -IST]

||**i'ronmong|er** (ī'ernmŭngg-) *n.* Dealer in hardware etc.; hence ~ERY (1, 2, 3) *n.*, (also, sl., firearms). [f. IRON^1 + MONGER]

īr'ony̆^{1} *n.* Expression of one's meaning by language of opposite or different tendency, esp. simulated adoption of another's point of view or laudatory tone for purpose of ridicule; ill-timed or perverse arrival of event or circumstance in itself desirable, as if in mockery of the fitness of things; use of language that has an inner meaning for a privileged audience and an outer meaning for the persons addressed or concerned (occas. including speaker; cf. TRAGIC *irony*); SOCRATIC *irony*. [f. L f. Gk *eirōneia* simulated ignorance (*eirōn* dissembler; see -Y^1)]

i'rony̆^{2} (ī'ernĭ) *a.* Of or like iron. [ME, f. IRON^1 + -Y^2]

I'roquoi|s (ĭ'rokwoi) *n.* (*pl.* same). Amer. Indian of powerful confederacy of five tribes formerly inhabiting New York State; hence ~AN (-oi'*a*n) *a.* & *n.*, (member or language-group) of Iroquois Indians. [F, f. Algonquin]

ĭrrā'dĭ|ant *a.* (rhet.) Shining brightly; hence ~ANCE *n.* [f. as foll.; see -ANT]

ĭrrā'dĭāt|e *v.t.* Shine upon; (fig.) throw light on (subject); light up (face etc. *with* joy etc.); subject to action of radiation (e.g. sunlight, ultraviolet rays, X-rays, or neutrons); hence ~IVE *a.* [f. L IR^1(*radiare* f. *radius* RAY^1) + -ATE^3]

ĭrrădĭā'tion *n.* Irradiating; shining, illumination, (lit. or fig.); apparent extension of edges of illuminated object seen against dark background. [F, or f. LL *irradiatio* (as prec.; see -ATION)]

ĭrră'tional *a.* & *n.* **1.** *a.* Unreasonable, illogical, absurd; not endowed with reason; (Math., of root etc.) not rational, not commensurable with the natural numbers (e.g. non-terminating decimal); hence ~ITY (-ă'l-) *n.*, ~IZE (3) *v.t.*, ~LY^2 *adv.* **2.** *n.* Irrational number, surd. [f. L IR^2(*rationalis* RATIONAL)]

ĭrrėclai'mab|le *a.* That cannot be reclaimed or reformed; hence ~LY^2 *adv.* [f. IR-^{2} + RECLAIMABLE]

ĭrrĕ'concīl|able *a.* & *n.* **1.** *a.* Implacably hostile; (of ideas etc.) incompatible; hence ~ABI'LITY, **~able**NESS (-beln-), *ns.*, **~ab**LY^2 *adv.* **2.** *n.* Uncompromising opponent of political measure etc. [f. IR-^{2} + RECONCILABLE]

ĭrrėco'verab|le (-kŭ'-) *a.* That cannot be recovered or remedied; hence ~LY^2 *adv.* [f. IR-^{2} + RECOVERABLE]

ĭrrėcū'sable (-z-) *a.* That must be accepted. [f. F *irrécusable* or f. LL IR^2(*recusabilis* f. L *recusare* refuse; see RECUSANT, -ABLE)]

ĭrrėdee'mab|le *a.* That cannot be redeemed; (of government annuity) not terminable by repayment; (of paper currency) for which issuing authority does not undertake ever to pay coin; irreclaimable, hopeless, absolute, whence ~LY^2 *adv.* [f. IR-^{2} + REDEEMABLE]

ĭrrėdĕ'nt|ist *n.* **1.** (*I*~). Advocate of return to Italy of all Italian-speaking districts. **2.** Greek, Pole, etc., of similar views. **3.** So ~ISM (3) *n.* [f. It. *irredentista* f. (*Italia*) *irredenta* unredeemed (Italy)]

ĭrrėdū'c|ĭble *a.* That cannot be brought (*to* desired condition); that cannot be reduced (*irreducible minimum*); that cannot be simplified; hence ~IBI'LITY *n.*, **~ĭb**LY^2 *adv.* [f. IR-^{2} + REDUCIBLE]

ĭrrĕ'fragab|le *a.* (Of statement, argument, person) indisputable, unanswerable; (of rules etc.) inviolable; hence ~LY^2 *adv.* [f. LL IR^2(*refragabilis* f. RE*fragari* oppose); see -ABLE]

ĭrrėfră'ngĭble (-nj-) *a.* Inviolable; (Opt.) incapable of being refracted. [f. IR-^{2} + REFRANGIBLE]

ĭrrĕ'fūt|able (*or* -rĭfū'-) *a.* That cannot be refuted; hence ~ABI'LITY *n.*, **~ab**LY^2 *adv.* [f. LL IR^2(*refutabilis* REFUTABLE)]

ĭrrĕ'gūlar *a.* & *n.* **1.** *a.* Not regular, contrary to rule or moral principle; abnormal; not of symmetrical form; (of surface) uneven; disorderly; uneven in duration, order, etc.; (of flower) having unequal petals etc.; (Gram., of verb, noun, etc.) not inflected normally; (of troops etc.) not pertaining to regular army; hence or cogn. ~ITY (-ă'r-) *n.*, ~LY^2 *adv.* **2.** *n.* (in *pl.*) Irregular troops. [ME, f. OF *irreguler* f. LL IR^2(*regularis* REGULAR)]

ĭrrĕ'latĭve *a.* Unconnected, unrelated, (*to*); having no relations, absolute; irrelevant; hence ~LY^2 (-vlĭ) *adv.* [f. IR-^{2} + RELATIVE]

ĭrrĕ'lėv|ant *a.* Not relevant; that does not apply (*to* matter in hand); hence ~ANCE, ~ANCY, *ns.*, **~ant**LY^2 *adv.* [f. IR-^{2} + RELEVANT]

ĭrrėlĭ'g|ion (-jon) *n.* Hostility to, or disregard of, religion; hence or cogn. **~ion**IST (2) *n.*, ~IOUS (-j*u*s) *a.* [f. F *irréligion* or f. L IR^2(*religio* RELIGION)]

ĭrrėmē'dĭab|le *a.* That cannot be remedied; hence ~LY^2 *adv.* [f. L IR^2(*remediabilis* REMEDIABLE)]

ĭrrėmĭ'ssĭb|le *a.* Unpardonable; unalterably obligatory; hence ~LY^2 *adv.* [ME f. OF, or f. eccl. L IR^2(*remissibilis* REMISSIBLE)]

ĭrrėmo'v|able (-mōō'-) *a.* That cannot be removed, esp. from office; hence ~ABI'LITY *n.*, **~ab**LY^2 *adv.* [f. IR-^{2} + REMOVABLE]

ĭrrĕ'parab|le *a.* (Of injury, loss, etc.) that cannot be rectified or made good; hence **~le**NESS (-beln-) *n.*, ~LY^2 *adv.* [ME f. OF, f. L IR^2-(*reparabilis* REPARABLE)]

ĭrrėplā'ceable (-sa-) *a.* Not replaceable; of which the loss cannot be made good. [f. IR-^{2} + REPLACEABLE]

ĭrrėprĕ'ssĭb|le *a.* & *n.* **1.** *a.* That cannot be repressed or restrained; hence ~LY^2 *adv.* **2.** *n.* (colloq.) Irrepressible person. [f. IR-^{2} + REPRESS + -IBLE]

ĭrrėproa'ch|able *a.* Free from blame, faultless; hence ~ABI'LITY *n.*, **~ab**LY^2 *adv.* [f. F IR^2-(*réprochable*, as REPROACH; see -ABLE)]

ĭrrėsĭ'st|ĭble (-zĭ'-) *a.* Too strong, convincing, delightful, etc., to be resisted; hence ~IBI'LITY *n.*, **~ĭb**LY^2 *adv.* [f. med. L IR^2(*resistibilis*, as RESIST; see -IBLE), or f. IR-^{2} + RESISTIBLE]

ĭrrĕ'solūte (-z-; *or* -ōōt) *a.* Undecided, hesitating; lacking in resoluteness; hence or cogn. ~LY^2 (-tlĭ) *adv.*, ~NESS (-tn-), **ĭrrĕsol**U'TION (-z-; -ū'- *or* -ōō'-), *ns.* [f. IR-^{2} + RESOLUTE]

ĭrrėsŏ'lvable (-z-) *a.* That cannot be resolved into parts; (of problem) that cannot be solved. [f. IR-^{2} + RESOLVABLE]

ĭrrėspĕ'ctĭve *a.* ~ **of,** not taking into account, without reference to, (*the posts were filled irrespective of nationality*); hence ~LY^2 (-vlĭ) *adv.* [f. IR-^{2} + RESPECTIVE]

ĭrrėspŏ'ns|ĭble *a.* Not responsible for (esp. one's own) conduct; acting or done without due sense of responsibility; hence ~IBI'LITY *n.*, **~ĭb**LY^2 *adv.* [f. IR-^{2} + RESPONSIBLE]

ĭrrėspŏ'nsĭve *a.* Not responsive (*to*); hence ~NESS (-vn-) *n.* [f. IR-^{2} + RESPONSIVE]

ĭrrėtĕ'ntĭve *a.* (Esp. of memory) not retentive; hence ~NESS (-vn-) *n.* [f. IR-^{2} + RETENTIVE]

ĭrrėtrie'v|able *a.* That cannot be retrieved;

hence ~ABI'LITY *n.*, ~**ab**LY² *adv.* [f. IR-² + RETRIEVABLE]

ĭrrĕ'ver|ent *a.* Lacking reverence; hence or cogn. ~ENCE *n.*, ~**ĕ'nt**IAL (-shal) *a.*, ~**ent**LY² *adv.* [f. L IR²(*reverens* REVERENT)]

ĭrrĕvẽr'sĭble *a.* Unalterable; not reversible; hence ~IBI'LITY *n.*, ~**ĭb**LY² *adv.* [f. IR-² + REVERSIBLE]

ĭrrĕ'voc|able *a.* Unalterable; gone beyond recall; hence ~ABI'LITY *n.*, ~**ab**LY² *adv.* [ME, f. L IR²(*revocabilis* REVOCABLE)]

ĭ'rrĭg|āte *v.t.* (Of stream etc.) supply (land) with water; water (land) with channels etc.; (Med.) supply (wound, etc.) with constant flow of liquid; (fig.) refresh as with moisture; hence or cogn. ~ABLE, ~**āt**IVE, *adjs.*, ~A'TION, ~**āt**OR, *ns.* [f. L IR¹(*rigare* moisten) + -ATE³]

ĭ'rrĭt|able *a.* **1.** Quick to anger, touchy; hence ~**ab**LY² *adv.* **2.** (Of organ etc.) very sensitive to contact etc.; (Biol.) responding actively to physical stimulus. **3.** So ~ABI'LITY *n.* [f. L *irritabilis* (as IRRITATE¹; see -ABLE)]

ĭ'rrĭt|ant *a.* & *n.* **1.** *a.* Irritating (esp. physically); hence ~ANCY *n.* **2.** *n.* Irritant substance or agent (lit. or fig.). [f. IRRITATE¹ or f. as IRRITATE², + -ANT]

ĭ'rrĭtāt|e¹ *v.t.* **1.** Excite to anger, annoy, vex, (*irritated at, by, with, against*). **2.** Excite, produce uneasy sensation in, (bodily organ etc.); (Biol.) stimulate (organ etc.) to action. **3.** Hence or cogn. **ĭrrĭt**A'TION *n.*, ~IVE *a.* [f. L *irritare* + -ATE³]

ĭ'rrĭtāte² *v.t.* (Sc. etc. Law). Make null and void, defeat. [f. LL *irritare* f. L IR²(*ritus* = *ratus* established) invalid + -ATE³]

ĭrrŭ'pt *v.i.* Invade; enter forcibly or violently (*into*); so ~ION *n.* [f. L IR¹(*rumpere rupt-* break)]

***I.R.S.** *abbr.* Internal Revenue Service.

Ir'vĭngīte (ẽr'v-) *n.* Member of a religious body called by its members the Catholic (and) Apostolic Church. [f. E. *Irving*, minister of Ch. of Scotland d. 1834, on whose principles it was founded, + -ITE¹ (1)]

is. See BE.

Is. *abbr.* Island(s); Isle(s).

Is(a). *abbr.* Isaiah (O.T.).

Īsabĕ'lla, I'sabĕl, (ĭz-) *a.* & *n.* Greyish yellow; hence **ĭsabĕ'll**INE¹ (ĭz-) *a.* [f. name *Isabella*, F *Isabelle*; immed. ref. unkn.]

īsagŏ'g|ic *a.* Introductory; hence ~ICS *n. pl.*, study of literary and external history of Bible. [f. L f. Gk *eisagōgikos* f. *eisagōgē* introduction (*eis* into, *agōgē* leading f. *agō* to lead); see -IC]

ī'satĭn *n.* (Chem.) Crystalline reddish-yellow substance got from indigo by oxidation. [f. L f. Gk *isatis* woad + -IN]

I.S.B.N. *abbr.* international standard book number.

ĭschae'm|ĭa, *ĭschē'm|ĭa, (-k-) *n.* (Med.) Reduction of blood supply to part of body; hence ~IC *a.* [mod. L, f. Gk *iskhaimos* (*iskhō* keep back); see -AEMIA]

ĭ'schĭ|um (-k-) *n.* (*pl.* ~a). Curved bone forming base of each half of pelvis; hence or cogn. ~**ă'd**IC, ~AL, ~A'TIC, *adjs.* [L, f. Gk *iskhion* hip-joint; cf. SCIATIC]

-ise¹. See -IZE.

-ise² *suf.* forming *ns.* of quality, state, or function, (*exercise, expertise, franchise, merchandise*); cf. -ICE. [f. or after F or OF *-ise* f. L *-itia* etc.]

-ise³. See -ISH².

īsentrŏ'pĭc *a.* Having equal entropy. [f. ISO- + ENTROPY + -IC]

-ĭsh¹ *suf.* forming *adjs.* (& *advs.*) f. *ns.* etc. **1.** Of nationality (*British, Danish*); w. sense 'belonging to, of the nature of' (*boyish, heathenish*), esp. derog. (*bookish, foppish, stand-offish, uppish*). **2.** W. sense 'somewhat' (*reddish, roughish, soonish*). **3.** (colloq.) Denoting approximate time of day or age (*eightish, fortyish*). [OE *-isc*, = OS, OHG *-isc*, ON *-iskr*, Goth. *-isks*]

-ĭsh², -ise³, *suf.* forming *vbs.* (*advertise, blemish, chastise, finish, perish, relish, vanish*). [f. or after F *-iss-* (in extended stem of vbs. in *-ir*) f. L *-isc-* incept. suf.]

I'shmāel (ĭ'-) *n.* Outcast, one at war with society; hence ~ITE¹ (1) *n.* [name of son of Abraham and Hagar, Gen. 16:12]

ī'sĭnglass (ī'zĭngglahs) *n.* **1.** Whitish semitransparent substance, a form of gelatin, got from viscera of some fish, esp. sturgeon, and used in making jellies, glue, etc. **2.** Mica. [corrupt. of obs. Du *huisenblas* sturgeon's bladder, assim. to GLASS¹]

I'slăm (ĭ'z-; *or* -ahm; *or* -ah'm) *n.* Religion of Muslims, revealed through Muhammad as Prophet of Allah; the Muslim world; hence ~IC (-ă'm-), ~**ĭ't**IC, *adjs.*, ~ISM (3), ~ITE¹ (1), *ns.* [f. Arab. *islām* submission (to God) (*aslama* resign oneself)]

ī'sland (ī'l-) *n.*, & *v.t.* **1.** *n.* Piece of land surrounded by water; (fig.) anything detached or isolated, esp. woodland surrounded by prairie, TRAFFIC *island*; (Naut.) ship's superstructure, bridge, etc.; (Physiol.) detached portion of tissue or group of cells (cf. ISLET); hence ~ER¹ (4) *n.* **2.** *v.t.* Make into an island, isolate; dot (as) with islands. [OE *īgland* (*ī(e)g* island, LAND¹); *-s-* by assoc. w. ISLE]

īsle (il) *n.*, & *v.t.* **1.** *n.* Island (poet., or with proper name; *Isle of Wight, British Isles*; usu. of small islands). **2.** *v.t.* (poet.) Make into an isle; place (as) on isle. [ME f. OF *ile* f. L *insula*; later ME & OF *isle* after L]

ī'slĕt (ī'l-) *n.* Little island; isolated tract or spot; detached portion of tissue (**~s of Langerhans,** groups of pancreatic cells secreting insulin). [OF, dim. of *isle*; see prec., -ET¹]

ĭsm *n.* (often derog.) Any distinctive doctrine or practice (*isms and ologies*). [foll. used as n.]

-ĭsm *suf.* forming abstract *ns.*: (1) of action or its result f. *vbs.* in -IZE (*baptism, organism*); (2) of typical conduct or condition f. *ns.* denoting classes or *adjs.* denoting qualities (*heroism, barbarism, diamagnetism*); (3) of system or principle f. name of subject or founder or connected catchword (*Conservatism, Arianism, jingoism*); (4) of peculiarity in language (*Americanism, Gallicism, archaism*); (5) of pathological condition, esp. induced by excessive use of drug etc., (*alcoholism, dwarfism, Parkinsonism*). [f. or after F *-isme* f. L f. Gk *-ismos* or *-isma* f. *-izō* -IZE]

Ismai'lĭ (ĭzmī'-) *n.* Member of Muslim sect that seceded from Shiah in 9th c., now regarding Aga Khan as their imam. [f. *Isma'il* descendant of Muhammad's son-in-law d. 760 + -I]

isn't. See BE.

ī'so- *comb. form.* **1.** Equal, as: **~cheim** (-kīm), line on map connecting places with same average temperature in winter [f. Gk *kheima* winter weather]; **~chroma'tic,** of same colour; **~chronous** (-ŏ'k-), occupying equal time, occurring at same time; **~cli'nal** (-ī'-), **~cli'nic** (-ĭ'-), corresponding to equal values of magnetic dip; **~dyna'mic,** corresponding to equal values of (magnetic) force; **~ge'otherm,** line or surface connecting points in interior of earth having same temperature; **~gloss,** line between areas that differ in one linguistic feature; **~go'nic,** corresponding to equal values of magnetic declination; **~hel,** line on map connecting places with same duration of sunshine [f. Gk *hēlios* sun]; **~hy'et** (-hī'et), line on map connecting places with same amount of rainfall [f. Gk *huetos* rain]; **~nomy** (-ŏ'n-), equality before the law; **~phote,** line of equal brightness or illumination; ~**pleth,** line on map connecting places with equal incidence of a meteorological etc. feature [f. Gk *plēthos* fullness]; ~**sei'smal** (-ī'z-) *n.* & *a.*, (line on map) connecting places with equal strength of earthquake shock; ~**there** (-ēr), line on map connecting places with same average temperature in summer [f. Gk *theros* summer]. **2.** (Chem.) Isomeric (esp. of hydrocarbon with branched chain of carbon atoms: *isobutane*). [f. Gk *isos* equal]

I.S.O. *abbr.* ||Imperial Service Order; International Organization for Standardization.

ī'sob|ār *n.* Line on map connecting places with same atmospheric pressure at a given time or on average over a given period; curve or formula for physical system at constant pressure; one of two or more isotopes of different elements, with same atomic weight; hence ~**ă'ric** *a.* [f. Gk *isobarēs* of equal weight (as ISO-, *baros* weight)]

isŏ'cracy̆ *n.* (System of government in which all have) equal political power; so **īsocră'tic** *a.* [f. Gk *isokratia* (as ISO-, -CRACY)]

īsocȳ'clĭc *a.* (Chem.) Having molecular ring composed of atoms of one kind. [f. ISO- + CYCLIC]

ī'solāt|e *v.t.* Place apart or alone; (Chem.) free (substance) from combination with all others; (Electr.) insulate; subject (person etc.) to quarantine; hence ~ABLE *a.*, ~OR *n.* [orig. in p.p., f. F *isolé* f. It. *isolato* f. LL *insulatus* f. L *insula* island; see -ATE[3], -ED[1]]

ī'solātĭng *a.* In vbl senses; (of language) having each element as an independent word without inflexions. [f. prec. + -ING[2]]

īsolā'tion *n.* Isolating or being isolated; **in** ~, considered without regard to relationships; ~ **hospital, ward,** (for patients with contagious or infectious diseases); hence ~ISM (3) *n.*, policy of holding aloof from affairs of other countries or political groups, ~IST (2) *n.*, advocate of this policy. [f. ISOLATE + -ATION]

ī'solātĭve *a.* (Philol., of sound-change) occurring independently of neighbouring sounds. [f. ISOLATE + -IVE]

ī'som|ēr *n.* (Chem.) One of two or more substances composed of molecules having the same atoms differently arranged and therefore different properties; hence or cogn. ~**ĕ'ric** *a.*, **isŏ'merism** (2) *n.*, **isŏ'merize** (3) *v.t.* [G, f. Gk *isomerēs* sharing equally (as ISO-, *meros* share)]

isŏ'merous *a.* (Bot., of flower) having same number of petals in each whorl. [f. Gk *isomerēs* (see prec.) + -OUS]

isomĕ'tr|ic *a.* Of equal measure; (of drawing etc.) with plane of projection at equal angles to three principal axes of object depicted; (Physiol., of muscle action) developing tension while muscle is prevented from contracting, whence ~ICS *n. pl.*, system of physical exercises in which muscles are caused to act against each other or against a fixed object. [f. Gk *isometria* (as ISO-, -METRY) + -IC]

ī'somŏrph *n.* Substance or organism isomorphic with another; hence or cogn. ~IC, ~OUS, (-ŏr'-) *adjs.*, having same (esp. crystal) form, exactly corresponding in form and relations, ~ISM (2) (-ŏr'-) *n.* [f. ISO- + Gk *morphē* form]

-ĭson *suf.* forming *ns.*, w. senses of -ATION, (*comparison, garrison, jettison, venison*). [f. OF -*aison* etc. f. L -*atio* etc. (see -ATION)]

ī'sopŏd *n.* Crustacean of order Isopoda, incl. wood-lice and allied marine and freshwater species, often parasitic, with seven equal pairs of legs. [f. F *isopode* f. mod. L *Isopoda* (as ISO-, Gk *pous podos* foot)]

isŏ'scelēs (-z) *a.* (Of triangle) having two sides equal. [LL, f. Gk ISO(*skelēs* f. *skelos* leg)]

isŏ'stasy̆ *n.* (Geol.) General state of equilibrium of earth's crust, with rise and fall of land relative to sea; hence **īsostă'tic** *a.* [f. ISO- + Gk *stasis* station + -Y[1]]

ī'sothĕrm *n.* Line on map connecting places with same temperature at a given time or on average over a given period; curve or formula for changes in physical system at constant temperature; so ~AL (-ĕr'-) *a.* [f. F *isotherme* f. as ISO- + Gk *thermē* heat]

īsotŏ'nĭc *a.* Having same osmotic pressure; (Physiol., of muscle action) taking place with normal contraction. [f. Gk *isotonos* (as ISO-, TONE[1]) + -IC]

ī'sotōpe *n.* One of two or more forms of an element differing from each other in atomic weight, and in nuclear but not chemical properties; hence **īsotŏ'pic** *a.*, **isŏ'topy**[1] *n.* [f. ISO- + Gk *topos* place (i.e. in periodic table of elements)]

īsotrŏ'p|ĭc *a.* Having the same physical properties in all directions; hence ~ICALLY *adv.*, **isŏ'tropy**[1] *n.* [f. ISO- + Gk *tropos* turn + -IC]

I'srāel (ĭ'z-; *or* -āl *or* -ĭel) *n.* **1.** **(Children of)** ~, Jewish or Hebrew nation or people; so ~ITE[1] (1) *n.* **2.** (fig.) God's elect. [later name of Jacob, their traditional ancestor, eccl. L f. Gk *Israēl* f. Heb. *yisrā'ēl* he that strives with God (Gen. 32:28)]

Israe'lĭ (ĭzrā'-) *a.* & *n.* (Inhabitant) of State of Israel. [f. as prec. + -I]

ĭ'ssūant *a.* (Her., esp. of beast with only upper part shown) rising from bottom or top of a bearing. [f. ISSUE[2] + -ANT]

ĭ'ssūe[1] (*or* ĭ'shōō) *n.* **1.** Outgoing, outflow; termination (*of* action etc.); (arch.) discharge of blood etc., incision to procure this. **2.** Way out, outlet; place of emergence of stream etc. **3.** (Law). Progeny, children, (*without male issue*). **4.** Result, outcome; **force the** ~, compel decision; **in the** ~, as things turn(ed) out. **5.** Point in question, important topic for discussion (*make an issue of it; what are the real issues?*), esp. (Law) between contending parties in action; ~ **of fact** (when fact is denied), ~ **of law** (when application of the law is contested). **6. At** ~, (of persons) at variance, (of things) in dispute; **join** or **take** ~, proceed to argue (*with* person *on* point agreed upon as basis of dispute). **7.** Giving out, issuing, (*of* bills of exchange, shares, notes, stamps, etc.); number or quantity of coins, notes, copies of newspaper, supplies, etc., issued at one time; whole number of copies of book etc. put on sale at one time; one of regular series of magazine etc. (*in the May issue*). **8.** Hence ~LESS *a.* [ME f. OF, f. Rom. **exuta* fem. (as n.) of **exutus* for L *exitus* p.p. of *exire* (see EXIT[2])]

ĭ'ssū|e[2] (*or* ĭ'shōō) *v.* **1.** *v.i.* Go or come out (often *out, forth*); emerge from a condition; be derived, spring, (*from*); result (*from*); end, result, (*in*); come out, be published. **2.** *v.t.* Send forth; publish, put into circulation, (notes, newspaper, etc.), whence ~ABLE *a.*, ~ANCE *n.*; give out (book *from* library, orders *to* subordinate, etc.); supply (thing *to* person, person *with* thing) esp. for official use. [ME, f. prec.]

-ĭst *suf.* forming personal *ns.*: (1) of agent, corresp. to Gk vbs. in -*izō* or (possible) E vbs. in -IZE, (*antagonist, circumlocutionist, plagiarist*); (2) of adherent of creed etc. in -ISM (*atheist, Darwinist, fatalist, nonconformist*); (3) of one concerned with any subject (*copyist, cyclist, dentist, parodist, pathologist, tobacconist*), e.g. as player of musical instrument (*violinist*). [=F -*iste*, L -*ista* f. Gk -*istēs* (-*izō* -IZE, -*tēs* agent-suf.)]

ĭ'sthm|us (*or* ĭ'smus) *n.* Narrow piece of land connecting two larger bodies of land; (Anat. & Bot.) narrow part connecting two larger parts;

so ~IAN *a.* (esp. of Isthmus of Corinth; **I~ian Games,** biennial national festival in ancient Greece). [L, f. Gk *isthmos*]

ĭ'stlė *n.* Fibre used for cord, nets, etc., got from species of agave etc. [f. Mex. *ixtli*]

ĭt[1] *pron.* (*obj.* **it;** *refl.* ITSELF *or* arch. **it,** *poss.* ITS, *pl.* THEY etc.). **1.** The thing previously mentioned or implied or easily identified; the person in question: **who is it** (that knocks etc.)?, **it** (the person that knocks etc.) **is I;** the animal or young child of unknown or immaterial sex. **2.** (As subj. of impers. v.) *it rains, it is cold; so it seems; it* (the season) *is winter; it* (the day) *is Ash Wednesday, it is Ash Wednesday today; it* (the time) *is 6 o'clock; it* (the distance) *is 6 miles to Oxford; it says in the Bible* (the Bible says) *that all men are liars; I would go if it were not* (would go but) *for the expense.* **3.** (As subj. anticipating deferred virtual subj. in more or less conscious apposition) *it is absurd talking* (or *to talk*) *like that; it is incredible that he should refuse; it is a dirty business, this meat-canning; is it difficult to learn Greek?.* **4.** (Anticipating deferred subj. introduced by THAT[2], separated from it by adv. predicate) *it is seldom that he fails; it is in vain that you quibble; it is to him that you must apply;* (anticipating deferred obj. introduced by THAT[2]) *saw to it that they obeyed; I take it that you agree.* **5.** (As antecedent to relative of either number and any gender, separated by predicate) *it was a purse that he dropped; it was the Russians that began it.* **6.** (As indef. obj. w. *v.t.* or *i.*, or *prep.*) *face it out; carry it off successfully; confound it!; run for it; lord it over him; watch it!; give it him (hot); have done it* (blundered); AT *it; be* FOR *it;* WITH *it;* see HAVE[1] 12. **7.** Exactly what is needed; the extreme limit of achievement etc.; (colloq.) sexual intercourse, sex appeal; **that's it,** (colloq.) that is (1) the problem, (2) what is wanted, (3) the end; **this is it,** (colloq.) the expected event is at hand. **8.** (In children's games) player who has to catch others. [OE *hit* neut. nom. & acc. of HE[1]]

||**it**[2] *n.* (colloq.) Italian vermouth (*gin and it*). [abbr.]

||**I.T.A.** *abbr.* Independent Television Authority.

i.t.a. *abbr.* initial teaching alphabet.

ital. *abbr.* italic (type).

Ită'lian (ĭtă'lyan) *a.* & *n.* **1.** *a.* Of Italy; ~ **handwriting** (developed in Italy and now current in almost all countries using Roman alphabet); ~ **millet,** foxtail millet; ~ **vermouth** (sweet); ||~ **warehouse**(**man**) (for supply of Italian groceries, fruits, olive oil, etc.). **2.** *n.* Language or native or inhabitant of Italy. **3.** Hence or cogn. ~ATE[2] (*or* -āt) *a.*, having Italian style or appearance, ~ISM (2, 4) *n.*, ~IZE (3) *v.t.* & *i.* [ME, f. It. *Italiano* (*Italia* Italy); see -AN]

ĭtă'lĭc *a.* & *n.* **1.** *a.* (*I~*). Of ancient Italy (**I~ languages,** Latin, Oscan, and Umbrian). **2.** ~ **hand**(**writing**), (simulation of) original form of Italian handwriting; ~ **type,** (Print.) sloping type introduced by Aldus Manutius of Venice (*c.* 1500), as *Italia* at end of this entry. **3.** *n.* Italic type, letter in this (now used esp. for emphasis or distinction, e.g. to indicate foreign word). [f. L f. Gk *Italikos* (*Italia* Italy; see -IC)]

ĭtă'lĭcize, -ise (-īz), *v.t.* Print (words) in italics, usu. for emphasis or distinction. [f. prec. + -IZE]

Ită'lĭot, -ōte, (ĭ-) *n.* & *a.* (Inhabitant) of Greek colonies in ancient Italy. [f. Gk *Italiōtēs* (*Italia* Italy; see -OT[2])]

Ită'lō- (ĭ-) *comb. form.* Italian (and), as *Italo-German*, ~PHIL(E) *n.* & *a.* [f. ITALIAN + -O-]

ĭtch[1] *n.* Irritation in the skin; contagious disease accompanied by this and caused by the **~-mite,** which burrows in the skin; restless desire, hankering, (*for* thing, *to* do; SEVEN-*year itch*); hence ~'Y[2] *a.* [OE *gycce* (as foll.)]

ĭtch[2] *v.i.* **1.** Feel irritation of skin, causing desire to scratch it; **it ~es,** there is an itching. **2.** (Of person or his fingers) crave uneasily (*for* thing, *to* do); **~ing palm** etc., avariciousness. [OE *giccan, gyccan,* = OS *jukkian,* OHG *jucchen* f. WG **juk-*]

-īte[1] *suf.* forming *ns.* w. sense 'person or thing belonging to or connected with': (1) in names of persons (*Israelite, Stagirite, Luddite, Pre-Raphaelite*); (2) in names of fossil organisms (*ammonite, belemnite*), of minerals (*anthracite, calcite, graphite*), of constituent parts of body or organ (*somite*), of explosives (*cordite, dynamite*), of commercial products (*ebonite, vulcanite*), of salts of acids having names in *-ous* (*nitrite, sulphite*). [f. or after F *-ite* f. L f. Gk *-itēs*]

-ĭte[2] *suf.* forming *adjs.* (*erudite, favourite, composite*), *ns.* (*appetite*), & *vbs.* (*expedite, unite*). [f. or after L *-itus* p.p. of vbs. in *-ēre, -ere, -ire*]

ī'tem *n.* & *adv.* **1.** *n.* Article or unit included in enumeration (prop. not the first); entry of this in account etc.; short piece of news etc. in newspaper etc.; hence ~IZE (3) *v.t.*, state by items. **2.** *adv.* Likewise, also, (introducing mention of item). [n. f. adv., L, = in like manner, also]

ĭ'ter|āte *v.t.* Repeat (quoted words etc.); make (charge, assertion, objection, etc.) repeatedly; hence or cogn. ~ANCE, ~ANCY, ~A'TION, *ns.*, ~ATIVE *a.* (esp. Gram., = frequentative). [f. L *iterare* (*iterum* again) + -ATE[3]]

ĭthȳphă'llĭc *a.* & *n.* **1.** *a.* Of the phallus carried in Bacchic festivals; (of statue etc.) having erect penis; lewd; in the metre used for Bacchic hymns. **2.** *n.* Poem in this metre; licentious poem. [f. LL f. Gk *ithuphallikos* (*ithus* straight, *phallos* PHALLUS; see -IC)]

-ĭ'tĭc *suf.* forming *adjs.* & *ns.* corresp. to *ns.* in -ITE[1], -ITIS, etc., (*Semitic, arthritic, syphilitic*). [f. or after F *-itique* f. L f. Gk *-itikos*; see -IC]

ītĭ'ner|ant *a.* Travelling from place to place; (of justices) travelling on circuit; (of Methodist ministry) moving from circuit to circuit; hence ~ACY, ~ANCY, *ns.* [f. as ITINERATE; see -ANT]

ītĭ'nerarȳ *n.* & *a.* **1.** *n.* Route; record of travel; guidebook. **2.** *a.* Of travelling; of roads. [f. LL *itinerarius* a., *-um* n. f. L *iter itineris* journey; see -ARY[1]]

ītĭ'ner|āte *v.i.* Travel from place to place; (of Methodist minister) move from circuit to circuit; hence ~A'TION *n.* [f. LL *itinerari* (as prec.) + -ATE[3]]

-ĭ'tion *suf.* forming *ns.* w. senses as -ATION (*admonition, perdition, position*). [f. or after F, or f. L *-itio -itionis* f. p.p. stems in *-it-* (cf. -ITE[2]); see -ION]

-ĭ'tious[1] (-ĭ'shus) *suf.* forming *adjs.* w. sense 'related to, having the nature of' (*excrementitious, supposititious*). [f. L *-icius* + -OUS, by confus. of *c* and *t* in LL and med. L MSS.]

-ĭ'tious[2] (-ĭ'shus) *suf.* forming *adjs.* corresp. to *ns.* in *-ition* (*ambitious, nutritious, suppositious*). [f. L *-itio* etc. (cf. -ITION) + -OUS]

-ī'tĭs *suf.* forming *ns.*, esp. names of inflammatory diseases (*appendicitis, bronchitis*) or (colloq.) of states of mind etc. fancifully regarded as diseases (*electionitis*). [Gk *-itis*, forming fem. of adjs. in *-itēs* (*nosos* disease)]

-ĭtive *suf.* forming *adjs.* w. senses as -ATIVE (*positive, transitive*). [f. or after F *-itif -itive* or f. L *-itivus* f. p.p. stems in *-it-* (cf. -ITE[2]); see -IVE]

I.T.O. *abbr.* International Trade Organization.

-ĭtor *suf.* See -OR.

-ĭtorȳ *suf.* See -ORY.

-ĭtous *suf.* forming *adjs.* corresp. to *ns.* in -ITY

(*calamitous, felicitous*). [f. or after F *-iteux* f. L *-itosus*]
its *poss. pron.* Of it(self). [f. IT¹ + -S³]
it's = *it is*. [f. IT¹ + 's 3]
ĭtsĕ'lf *pron.* Emphat. and refl. form corresp. to IT¹; *a* LAW¹ *unto itself*; **by ~**, automatically, apart from its surroundings; **in ~**, apart from its surroundings, viewed in its essential qualities etc. (*not in itself a bad thing*). [OE, f. IT¹ + SELF, but often treated as ITS + SELF; cf. *its own self*]
ĭtsȳ-bĭ'tsȳ, ĭttȳ-bĭ'ttȳ, *adjs.* (colloq., usu. derog.) Tiny, insubstantial. [childish redupl. of LITTLE, infl.by BIT²]
I.T.U. *abbr.* International Telecommunication Union.
||**ITV** *abbr.* independent television.
-ĭtȳ *suf.* forming *ns.* denoting quality or condition (*authority, humility, purity, suavity*), or instance or degree of this (*a monstrosity, a profanity*; *humidity, porosity*). [f. or after F *-ité* f. L *-itas -itatis*; cf. -TY¹]
I.U. *abbr.* international unit.
I.U.(C.)D. *abbr.* intra-uterine (contraceptive) device.
-ĭum *suf.* forming *ns.*: names of metallic elements (*sodium, uranium*; also **-um,** as *tantalum*), region of body (*pericardium, hypogastrium*), biological structure (*mycelium, prothallium*), and miscellaneous wds (*pandemonium, symposium*). [f. or after L *-ium* f. Gk *-ion*]
I.V. *abbr.* intravenous.
-ĭve *suf.* forming *adjs.* w. sense 'tending to, having the nature of' (*active, descriptive, evasive, reflexive*) & *ns.* (*adjective, captive*); see -ATIVE, -ITIVE; hence **-ĭve**LY² (-vlĭ) *adv. suf.*, **-ĭve**NESS (-vn-) *n. suf.* [f. or after F *-if -ive* f. L *-ivus*]
ī'vorȳ *n.* **1.** Hard creamy-white substance composing main part of tusks of elephant, hippopotamus, walrus, narwhal, and (**fossil ~**) mammoth; **vegetable ~**, hard endosperm of seed of a COROZO palm (**~-nut**); **black ~**, (Hist.) African Negro slaves; GATE¹ *of ivory*. **2.** Colour of ivory. **3.** (sl., in *pl.*) Dice, billiard-balls, piano-keys, teeth. **4.** (in *pl.*) Articles made of ivory. **5. ~ black,** black pigment from calcined ivory; **~ gull** (*Pagophila eburnea*, flying very far north); **~ tower,** seclusion or withdrawal from (harsh realities of) the world. [ME, f. OF *yvoire* f. Rom. **eboreum* f. L *ebur -oris*]
ī'vȳ *n.* Climbing evergreen shrub (*Hedera helix*) with usu. dark-green shining five-angled leaves; GROUND¹ *ivy*; **~ geranium,** pelargonium with leaves like ivy; ***Ivy League,** group of famous colleges in eastern U.S.; *ivy-leaved* TOAD*flax*. [OE *īfig*, rel. to MLG *if(lōf)*, OHG *ebah*]
I.W.W. *abbr.* Industrial Workers of the World.
ĭ'xĭa *n.* S. Afr. iridaceous plant of genus *Ixia*, with large showy flowers. [L f. Gk, a kind of thistle]
Ixīō'nĭan (ĭ-) *a.* Of *Ixion*, king of Thessaly in Gk myth, punished by being bound to eternally revolving wheel in Hades. [f. Gk *Ixiōn* + -IAN]
ĭ'zard *n.* Goatlike antelope of Pyrenees, allied to chamois. [f. F *isard*; orig. unkn.]
-īze, -īse¹ (-īz), *suf.* forming vbs. w. senses (1) *v.t.* treat in specified way (*catechize, monopolize*), (2) *v.i.* follow specified practice (*philosophize*), have specified feeling (*sympathize*), (3) *v.t.* & *i.* bring or come into specified state (*Anglicize, pulverize, volatilize*), (4) *v.t.* & *i.* treat or act according to method of (*bowdlerize, pasteurize*), (5) *v.t.* impregnate with or affect with or provide with (*oxidize, syphilize, accessorize*); so **-īza'**TION, **-īz**ER¹, *n. sufs.* [f. or after F *-iser* f. LL *-izare* f. Gk *-izō*]
ĭ'zzard *n.* (arch.) The letter Z (*from A to Izzard*). [var. of ZED]
ĭ'zzat *n.* (Ind. etc.) Honour, reputation, self-respect. [Arab. *'izzah* glory]

J

J, j, (jā) *n.* (*pl.* **Js** *or* **J's**). Tenth letter of alphabet; (as Roman numeral in prescriptions etc.) = *i* in final position (*ij, vj*).
J. *abbr.* jack; joule(s); Judge; Justice.
jăb *v.t.* (**-bb-**), & *n.* **1.** *v.t.* Poke roughly; stab; thrust (thing) abruptly (*into*). **2.** *n.* Abrupt blow with pointed thing or fist; (colloq.) hypodermic injection. [var. (orig. Sc.) of JOB³]
jă'bber *v.* & *n.* **1.** *v.i.* Speak volubly and with little sense; chatter like monkeys etc. **2.** *v.t.* Utter (words) rapidly and indistinctly. **3.** *n.* Jabbering; gabble, gibberish. [imit.; see -ER⁵]
jă'bberwŏckȳ *n.* Nonsensical writing for comic effect. [f. title of poem in Lewis Carroll's *Through the Looking-Glass* (1871)]
jă'bĭru (-ōō) *n.* Large tropical Amer. stork; similar bird of Old World. [f. Tupi-Guarani *jabirú*]
jăboră'ndĭ *n.* Dried leaflets of S. Amer. shrub of genus *Pilocarpus*, with diuretic and sudorific properties. [f. Tupi-Guarani *jaburandi*]
jă'bŏt (zhă'bō) *n.* Ornamental frill of lace etc. on front of woman's bodice; (Hist.) frill on man's shirt-front. [F, orig. = crop of bird, prob. f. **gab-* crop, maw]
jă'cana *n.* Small tropical wading bird of family Jacanidae, with disproportionately large straight claws (enabling it to walk on floating leaves). [f. Port. *jaçaná* f. Tupi-Guarani *jasaná*]
jăcară'nda *n.* **1.** Tropical Amer. tree of genus *Dalbergia* etc. with hard scented wood. **2.** Tropical Amer. etc. tree of genus *Jacaranda*, with trumpet-shaped blue flowers. [Tupi-Guarani]
jă'cĭnth *n.* Reddish-orange gem, variety of zircon. [ME *iacynt* etc. f. OF *iacinte* or f. med. L *jacint(h)us* f. L *hyacinthus* HYACINTH]
jăck¹ *n.* **1.** (*J~*). Familiar form of name *John*, esp. as type of common man; **J~ and Jill,** lad and lass, man and woman; **every man ~**, every individual man. **2.** = *Jack tar*; ||labourer, man who does odd jobs, etc.; CHEAP*jack*; LUMBER²*jack*; STEEPLE*jack*. **3.** Court-card usu. ranking below king and queen. **4.** Machine for turning spit in roasting meat; machine for lifting heavy weights; machine for lifting wheel of vehicle off ground while changing or cleaning it; BOOT¹*jack*; figure of man striking bell on clock; device with quill to pluck string of harpsichord etc.; device using single plug to connect telephone circuits etc. **5.** (Bowls). Small white ball for players to aim at. **6.** Male of various animals; = PIKE³, esp. young or small one. **7.** (in *pl.*, treated as *sing.*) Game played with jackstones. **8.** *(sl.) Detective; money. **9. J~-a-dandy,** dandy; **~'ass,** male ass, stupid person (*~'assery*, stupid behaviour; *laughing ~ass*, giant kingfisher of Australia, with loud discordant cry); **~'boot,** large boot coming above knee, worn esp. by 17th–18th-c. cavalry, (fig.) oppressive behaviour; **~'daw,** thievish small

crow haunting church towers [cf. DAW]; J~ **Frost,** frost personified; ***~'hammer,** pneumatic hammer; **~-in-office,** self-important official; **~-in-the-box,** toy figure that springs out of box when it is opened; **J~-in-the-green,** man or boy enclosed in framework covered with leaves in May-Day sports; ||**J~ Ketch,** common hangman [f. name of executioner 1663–86]; **~-knife,** (*n.*) large clasp-knife for the pocket, dive in which body is first doubled up and then straightened, accidental folding of articulated vehicle (also as *v.i.* & *t.*); **~ of all trades,** one who can turn his hand to anything; **~-o'-lantern,** (1) will-o'-the-wisp (lit. or fig.), (2) lantern of pumpkin or turnip rind with holes cut to represent facial features; **~-plane** (medium-sized, for coarse joinery); **~'pot,** (Poker) accumulating pool that can only be opened by player holding two jacks or better, large esp. accumulating prize in lottery etc. (*hit the ~pot*, be remarkably lucky); **~ pudding,** buffoon, clown; ***~-rabbit,** large prairie hare with very long ears and hind legs; **~-rafter,** short rafter in hip-roof; **before you can** or **could say J~ Robinson,** very quickly or suddenly; **~-snipe,** small species of snipe; **~'stone,** small round pebble or metal object used with others in tossing-games; **~'straw,** spillikin; **J~ tar,** sailor; **~-towel,** roller towel. [ME *Iakke*, by-name for *John* (erron. assoc. w. F *Jacques* James)]

jăck² *v.t.* ~ **(up),** raise (as) with JACK¹ (sense 4); ~ **in** or ~ **up,** abandon (attempt etc.). [f. prec.]

jăck³ *n.* Ship's flag, smaller than ensign, esp. one flown at bow, indicating nationality; UNION *Jack*; **~-staff,** (1) staff at bow for jack, (2) staff carrying flag that is to show above mast-head. [prob. = JACK¹]

jăck⁴ *n.* (arch. or Hist.) Foot-soldier's sleeveless padded tunic; = BLACK¹*jack* (1). [ME, f. OF *jaque*, of uncert. orig.]

jăck⁵ *n.* E. Ind. fruit, like bread-fruit but coarser. [f. Port. *jaca* f. Malayalam *chakka*]

jă'ckal (-awl) *n.* Wild animal related to dog, esp. *Canis aureus*, of size of fox, formerly supposed to hunt up lion's prey for him; (fig.) person who does preparatory drudgery etc. or who assists another's immoral behaviour. [f. Turk. *çakal* f. Pers. *šagāl*]

jă'ckanāpes (-ps) *n.* Pert fellow; coxcomb; pert child; (arch.) tame monkey. [earliest form *Jack Napes* (1450), supposed to refer to Duke of Suffolk, whose badge was an ape's clog and chain]

jă'ckaroo, jă'ckeroo, *n.* (Austral. colloq.) Inexperienced newcomer to Australia; trainee on sheep-station etc. [f. JACK¹ + KANGAROO]

jă'ckėt *n.*, & *v.t.* **1.** *n.* Sleeved short outer garment for man or woman (**dust his ~,** thrash him); thing similarly worn (*life-jacket, strait jacket*). **2.** Outer covering round boiler etc. for protection, to maintain desired temperature, etc. **3.** Paper wrapper, freq. coloured and artistically designed, in which bound book is issued. **4.** Animal's coat; *potatoes cooked* **in their ~s** (skins). **5.** *v.t.* Cover with jacket. [ME, f. OF *ja(c)quet* dim. of *jaque* JACK⁴; see -ET¹]

Jā'cob *n.* **~'s ladder,** (1) plant with corymbs of blue or white flowers, and leaves suggesting ladder, (2, Naut.) rope ladder with wooden rungs, (3) endless chain of buckets; **~'s staff,** (1) surveyor's iron-shod rod used instead of tripod, (2) instrument for measuring distances and heights. [f. ~ in Genesis (w. ref. to 28:12), f. Heb. *ya'ăkōb* supplanter]

Jăcobē'an *a.* & *n.* **1.** *a.* Of the reign of James I (esp. Archit.); of St. James the Less or his Epistle; (of furniture) of the colour of dark oak. **2.** *n.* Jacobean person; = JACOBITE 2. [f. mod. L *Jacobaeus* f. eccl. L *Jacobus* James f. Gk *Iakōbos* = prec.; see -EAN]

Jă'cobĭn¹ *n.* **1.** Dominican friar [from convent near to church of S. Jacques in Paris]. **2.** Member of extreme democratic club established in Paris in old Jacobin convent (1789); sympathizer with its principles; extreme radical; hence ~IC(AL) (-ĭ'n-) *adjs.*, ~ISM (3) *n.*, ~IZE (3) *v.t.* [ME f. F, f. med. L *Jacobinus* f. eccl. L *Jacobus* (see prec., -INE¹)]

jă'cobĭn² *n.* Pigeon with reversed feathers on back of neck, suggesting cowl. [f. F *jacobine*, fem. (as prec.)]

Jă'cob|īte *n.* **1.** Adherent of James II after his abdication, or of his descendants or of the Stuarts; hence **~ĭ'tICAL** *a.*, **~ītISM** (3) *n.* **2.** Admirer of Henry James (Amer. novelist and critic d. 1916). **3.** Follower of Jacobus Baradaeus (6th-c. Syrian Monophysite monk). [f. L *Jacobus* James (see JACOBEAN) + -ITE¹]

jă'conėt *n.* Cotton cloth like cambric, esp. dyed waterproof kind for poulticing etc. [f. Urdu *jagannāthi* f. *Jagannath* (now Puri) in India, place of origin (see JUGGERNAUT)]

Jă'cquârd (-kârd) *n.* Apparatus with perforated cards, invented by J. M. *Jacquard* of Lyons (d. 1834) to facilitate weaving of figured fabrics; ~ **(loom),** loom fitted with this; fabric thus made, with intricate variegated pattern.

jacquerie (zhăkerē') *n.* (Revolt of) peasantry. [F, f. OF *jaquerie* (esp. of peasants' rising in N. France against nobles in 1357–8) f. *Jacques* James (see -ERY)]

jăctā'tion *n.* **1.** (literary). Boasting. **2.** = foll. 2. [f. L *jactatio* (*jactare* frequent. of *jacĕre* throw; see -ATION)]

jăctĭtā'tion *n.* **1.** (Law). ~ **of marriage,** offence of falsely claiming to be a person's wife or husband. **2.** (Med.) Restless tossing of body in illness; twitching of limb or muscle. [sense 1 f. med. L *jactitatio* false declaration f. L *jactitare* boast, frequent. of *jactare* (see prec., -ATION); sense 2 f. prec.]

jāde¹ *n.*, & *v.t.* **1.** *n.* Inferior, wearied, or worn-out horse. **2.** (In reprobation, usu. playful) a woman. **3.** *v.t.* (esp. in *p.p.*) Wear out with hard work or surfeit. [ME; orig. unkn.]

jāde² *n.* **1.** Silicate of calcium and magnesium, a hard green, blue, or white stone, used as ornament or for implements. **2.** Silicate of sodium and aluminium like this in appearance. **3.** Green colour of jade. [F; *le jade* for *l'ejade* f. Sp. (*piedra de*) *ijada* (stone of) the colic, f. Rom. **iliata* f. L *ilia* flanks]

jā'deīte (-dīt) *n.* = prec. 2. [f. prec. + -ITE¹ (2)]

j'adoube (zhahdōō'b) *int.* (Chess) expr. intention not to move man that one is about to touch. [F, = I adjust]

jae'ger¹ (yā'ger) *n.* German or Austrian rifleman; skua. [f. G *jäger* hunter (*jagen* to hunt)]

Jae'ger² (yā'ger) *n.* Kind of woollen clothing-material excluding all vegetable fibres as unwholesome; garment of this. [19th c., **P**; f. G. ~, inventor]

Jă'ffa *n.* ~ **(orange),** large oval thick-skinned variety of orange. [~ in Israel, near where it was first grown]

jăg¹ *n.* Sharp projection, e.g. point of rock; hence **~'GY²** (-gĭ) *a.* [f. foll.]

jăg² *v.t.* **(-gg-).** Cut or tear in uneven manner; make indentations in; hence **~'GER¹** (2) (-g-) *n.* [ME; prob. imit.]

jăg³ *n.* (sl.) Drinking bout; spree; (colloq.) period of indulgence in activity, emotion, etc. [16th c., = load for one horse; orig. unkn.]

||**Jăg⁴** *n.* (colloq.) Jaguar (car). [abbr. of proprietary name]

jäger. Var. of JAEGER¹.

jă'ggėd[1] (-g-) *a.* With irregularly cut or torn edge; deeply indented; hence ~LY[2] *adv.*, ~NESS *n.* [ME, f. JAG[1,2] + -ED[2,1]]
***jăgged**[2] (-gd) *a.* (sl.) Drunk. [f. JAG[3] + -ED[2]]
jă'ggerỹ (-g-) *n.* Coarse brown Indian sugar made from palm-sap; other crude sugar. [f. Indo-Port. *jag(a)ra* f. Kanarese *sharkare* f. Skr. *śarkarā* sugar]
jă'gūar (*or* -gwer) *n.* Large carnivorous spotted feline (*Panthera onca*) inhabiting some wooded parts of America. [f. Tupi-Guarani *yaguara*]
jăguarŭ'ndĭ (-gw-) *n.* Grey long-tailed feline (*Felis jaguarondi*) of S. & Central America. [Tupi-Guarani]
Jah, Jah'veh (yah'vā), *n.* = JEHOVAH 1; hence **Jah'**VIST (2) *n.* = JEHOVIST. [Heb.]
jai alai (hī'alī) *n.* Game like pelota played with large curved wicker baskets. [Sp. f. Basque]
jail etc. See GAOL etc.
Jain (jīn) *n.* & *a.* (Member) of a non-Brahminical Indian sect, with doctrines like those of Buddhism; hence ~'ISM (3), ~'IST (2), *ns.* [Hindi, f. Skr. *jainas* of a Buddha or saint (*jinas* f. root *ji* conquer)]
jāke *a.* (sl.) All right, satisfactory. [prob. f. *Jake* abbr. of *Jacob*]
jă'lap *n.* Purgative drug got esp. from tuberous roots of a Mex. climbing plant (*Exogonium purga*). [F, f. Sp. *jalapa* f. *Jalapa*, *Xalapa*, Mex. city, f. Aztec *Xalapan* sand by the water (*xalli* sand, *atl* water, *pan* upon)]
jalŏ'pỹ *n.* Dilapidated old motor vehicle or aircraft. [20th c.; orig. unkn.]
jă'lousie (zhă'lo͞ozē) *n.* Slatted shutter or blind to admit air and light but not rain etc. [F (as JEALOUSY)]
jăm[1] *v.* (**-mm-**) & *n.* **1.** *v.t.* Squeeze (thing) into space between two surfaces; cause (part of machine) to be no longer movable so that it cannot work, make (machine) unworkable in this way; squeeze (things) together in compact mass; thrust (thing) violently (*into* confined space); block, fill up, (passage etc.) by crowding into it; ~ **on,** apply (brakes) forcibly. **2.** *v.i.* Become tightly wedged; (of machine) become unworkable by jamming of part. **3.** *v.t.* (Radio) Make (message, transmitter) unintelligible by causing interference. **4.** *n.* Crush, squeeze, stoppage (of machine etc.) due to jamming; crowded mass (LOG[1]-*jam*, TRAFFIC *jam*); (colloq.) dilemma, awkward position. **5.** ~**-packed,** (colloq.) very full; ~ **session,** (Jazz) improvised playing by group. [imit.]
jăm[2] *n.*, & *v.t.* (**-mm-**). **1.** *n.* Conserve of fruit, made by boiling it with sugar to a thick consistency (~ **tomorrow,** pleasant thing continually promised but usu. never produced); ‖(colloq.) something easy or pleasant (MONEY *for jam*); hence ~**'mỹ**[2] *a.* **2.** *v.t.* Spread with jam; make into jam. [perh. = prec.]
Jam. *abbr.* Jamaica; James (N.T.).
jămb (-m) *n.* Side post of doorway, window, etc.; (in *pl.*) stone sides of fireplace. [ME, f. OF *jambe* f. Rom. **gamba* leg f. LL *gamba* hoof]
jămboree' *n.* Celebration, merry-making; large rally of Scouts. [19th c., of unkn. orig.]
ja'mmỹ. See JAM[2].
Jan. *abbr.* January.
jāne *n.* (sl.) Woman. [f. name *Jane*]
Jā'neite (-nī-) *n.* Admirer of Jane Austen's novels. [f. *Jane* Austen, Engl. novelist d. 1817 + -ITE[1] (1)]
jă'ngle (-nggel) *v.i.* & *t.*, & *n.* **1.** (Make) harsh or discordant sound; cause (bell etc.) to do this; cause irritation to (nerves etc.) by discord; speak or utter in discordant or noisy way. **2.** (arch.) Dispute, wrangle. [ME, f. OF *jangler*, of uncert. orig.]
jă'nĭtor *n.* Door-keeper; caretaker of building; hence ~IAL (-ôr'-) *a.* [L (*janua* door; see -OR)]
jă'nĭzarỹ, jă'nĭssarỹ, *n.* (Hist.) one of body of Turkish infantry forming Sultan's guard and chief part of army (14th–19th c.); Turkish soldier; (fig.) devoted follower or supporter. [ult. f. Turk. *yeniçeri* (*yeni* new, *çeri* troops)]
‖**jă'nnock** *a.* (dial.) Straightforward, honest, genuine. [19th c.; orig. unkn.]
Jă'nsen|ĭst *n.* (Hist.) Member of party in R.C. Ch. esp. in France holding with Jansen the perverseness and inability for good of the natural human will; so ~ISM (3) *n.*, ~**ĭ'st**IC *a.* [f. C. *Jansen*, Du. theologian d. 1638 + -IST]
Jă'nūarỹ *n.* First month of year. [ME f. AF *Jenever*, f. L *Januarius* (*mensis* month) of Janus; see foll., -ARY[1]]
Jā'nus-fāced (-st) *a.* Facing both ways at once; (fig.) hypocritical, insincere. [f. *Janus*, Rom. god of gates and beginnings, shown with faces on front and back of head, + FACE[1] + -ED[2]]
Jăp *a.* & *n.* (colloq., often derog.) Japanese. [abbr.]
japă'n[1] *n.* Hard varnish, esp. kind brought orig. from Japan; work in Japanese style. [f. *Japan* in Asia, app. f. Malay *Japang*, *Japung* f. Chin. *Jih-pun* (*jih* sun, *pun* origin)]
japă'n[2] *v.t.* (**-nn-**). Varnish with japan; make black and glossy as with japan. [f. prec.]
Jăpanē'se (-z) *a.* & *n.* (*pl.* same). (Native or inhabitant or language) of Japan; ~ **cedar,** cryptomeria; ~ (**flowering**) **cherry** (hybrid kind with pink or white usu. double flowers); ~ **maple,** ornamental purple-flowered maple (*Acer palmatus*); ~ **medlar,** loquat; ~ **print** (in water-colour from wood-blocks); ~ **quince,** japonica; ~ **silk,** lightweight silk fabric with gum removed after weaving. [f. *Japan* (see JAPAN[1]) + -ESE]
jāpe *v.i.*, & *n.* (literary). Jest. [ME, of uncert. orig.]
Japhĕ'tĭc *a.* Of, (supposedly) descended from, Japheth, third son of Noah (Gen. 10:2 ff.); (arch.) Indo-European. [f. mod. L *Japheti* descendants of *Japheth* + -IC]
Jă'plish *n.* Language blending Japanese and English, used in Japan. [f. JAPANESE + ENGLISH[1]]
japŏ'nĭca *n.* Ornamental red-flowered variety of quince. [mod. L, fem. of *japonicus* Japanese]
jar̂[1] *n.* Harsh or grating sound; thrill of nerves or feelings, shock; lack of harmony, disagreement; quarrel. [as foll.]
jar̂[2] *v.* (**-rr-**). **1.** *v.i.* Sound discordantly; have discordant or painful effect (*on* or *upon* person, his ear, nerves, etc.); strike with grating sound (*on*, *upon*, *against*, object); (of body affected) vibrate or resound discordantly; (of opinion, statement, action) be out of harmony, disagree, (*with*); dispute, wrangle. **2.** *v.t.* Cause (thing) to jar; send shock through (nerves). [16th c.; prob. imit.]
jar̂[3] *n.* Spoutless earthenware, stoneware, or glass vessel with or without handle(s), usu. cylindrical (LEYDEN *jar*); contents of this; ‖(colloq.) glass of beer etc.; hence ~'FUL 2 *n.* [f. F *jarre* f. Arab. *jarra*]
jar̂[4] *n.* (arch. or colloq.) **On the** ~, ajar. [late form of obs. *char*; see AJAR[1]]
jardinière (zhar̂dĭnyar̂') *n.* Ornamental pot or stand for display of growing flowers in room, on window-sill, etc.; dish of mixed vegetables. [F]
jar̂'gon[1] *n.* Unintelligible words, gibberish; barbarous or debased language; mode of speech familiar only to a group or profession (*critics' jargon*; *scientific, law, jargon*); (arch.) twittering of birds; hence ~IC (-ŏ'n-), ~**ĭ'st**IC, *adjs.*, ~IZE (2, 3) *v.t.* & *i.* [ME, f. OF, of unkn. orig.]

jar'gon², **jargoo'n**, *n.* Translucent, colourless, or smoky variety of zircon. [F, f. It. *giargone*, prob. ult. f. as ZIRCON]

jargone'lle *n.* Early-ripening variety of pear. [F, dim. of prec.]

jarl (y-) *n.* (Hist.) Old Norse or Danish chief. [ON, orig. man of noble birth; = EARL]

jă'rrah (-*a*) *n.* (Durable timber of) Austral. mahogany gum-tree (*Eucalyptus marginata*). [f. Aboriginal *djarryl*]

Jas. *abbr.* James (also in N.T.).

jă'smĭn(e) (*or* -z-), **jĕ'ssamĭn(e)**, *n.* Shrub of genus *Jasminum* with white or yellow flowers, esp. **common** or **white ~**, climbing shrub (*J. officinale*) with fragrant flowers; **red ~**, a red-flowered frangipani (*Plumeria rubra*); **winter ~** (*J. nudiflorum*, with yellow flowers). [16th c., f. F *jasmin*, *jessemin* f. Arab. *yās(a)mīn* f. Pers. *yāsamīn*]

jă'spé (-ā) *a.* Like jasper, randomly coloured (esp. of cotton fabric). [F, p.p. of *jasper* marble (*jaspe* JASPER)]

jă'sper *n.* Opaque variety of quartz, usu. red, yellow, or brown. [ME, f. OF *jasp(r)e* f. L f. Gk *iaspis*, of oriental orig.]

Jat (jaht) *n.* Member of Indo-Aryan people widely distributed in N.W. India. [f. Hindi *jāt*]

jā'tō *n.* (*pl.* **~s**). (Aeron.) Jet-assisted take-off; auxiliary jet engine(s) to provide temporary extra thrust at take-off. [abbr.]

jau'ndĭce *n.*, & *v.t.* **1.** *n.* (Path.) Condition often caused by obstruction of bile and marked by yellowness of skin, fluids, and tissues, and occas. by disordered vision; (fig.) envy or jealousy. **2.** *v.t.* Affect with jaundice; (fig., esp. in *p.p.*) affect (person, his judgement etc.) with envy or resentment or jealousy. [ME *iaunes* f. OF *jaunice* yellowness (*jaune* yellow; see -ICE)]

jaunt *v.i.*, & *n.* (Take) excursion or journey, esp. for pleasure; **~'ing-car,** light two-wheeled horse-drawn vehicle used in Ireland. [16th c.; orig. unkn.]

jau'nt|ȳ *a.* & *n.* **1.** *a.* Having or affecting easy sprightliness or airy self-satisfaction; hence **~ĭLY²** *adv.*, **~ĭNESS** *n.* **2.** *n.* ||(colloq.) Master-at-arms. [17th c. *jentee* repr. F *gentil* (see GENTLE); assim. to -Y²]

***ja'va¹** (jah'-) *n.* (sl.) Coffee. [f. *Java coffee* (as foll.)]

Ja'va² (jah'-) *n.* *Java* MAN¹ 3; **~ sparrow,** a weaver-bird (*Padda oryzivora*). [name of island in Indonesia]

Ja'van (jah'-) *a.* & *n.* (Native) of Java. [f. prec. + -AN]

Javanē'se (jah'-; -z) *a.* & *n.* (*pl.* same). = prec.; (of) the Malayan language of Java. [f. prec. + -ESE]

jă'velĭn (*or* -vl-) *n.* Light spear thrown by hand as weapon or in athletic sport. [f. F *javeline*, *javelot*, f. Gallo-Rom. *gabalottus*]

Javĕ'lle (zh-) *n.* **~ water,** solution of sodium hypochlorite for bleaching, disinfecting, etc. [~ in France]

jaw *n.* & *v.* **1.** *n.* Upper or (usu.) lower jaw; **upper ~, lower ~,** one of the bones (or sets of bones) forming framework of mouth and biting and masticating apparatus in vertebrates; **~-bone,** (1) each of the two bones forming lower jaw in most mammals, (2) these two combined into one in others, (3, *sl.) = CREDIT¹ 3. **2.** (in *pl.*) Bones of mouth including teeth, mouth; narrow mouth of valley, channel, etc.; gripping-members of machine, e.g. vice; (fig.) gripping-power (*of death* etc.). **3.** (colloq.) Loquacity (**hold your ~**, stop talking); sermonizing talk, lecture (esp. ||PI² *jaw*); **~-breaker,** word that is very long, or hard to pronounce. **4.** *v.i.* (sl.) Speak esp. at tedious length. **5.** *v.t.* (sl.) Persuade by talking; admonish, lecture, (person). [ME, f. OF *joe* cheek, jaw, of uncert. orig.]

jay *n.* Noisy chattering arboreal European bird (*Garrulus glandarius*) with vivid blue, black, and white feathers; related bird of subfamily Garrulinae; (fig.) impertinent chatterer, simpleton; **~-walker,** pedestrian who crosses, or walks in, street or road without regard for traffic; **~-walk** *v.i.*, behave thus. [ME f. OF, f. LL *gaius*, *gaia*, perh. f. L name *Gaius* (cf. *jackdaw*, *robin*)]

jăzz *n.*, *a.*, & *v.* **1.** *n.* Music and dance of U.S. Negro origin with characteristic harmony and strong ragtime rhythm, often improvised; (sl.) deceptive talk, nonsense, matter (*all that jazz*); **~ band** (suitable for playing jazz, e.g. piano, trumpet, saxophone, banjo, bass, and drums); **~'man,** man who plays jazz; hence **~'Y²** *a.*, of or like jazz, unrestrained, vivid. **2.** *v.i.* Play, dance, indulge in, jazz. **3.** *v.t.* Arrange (music) as jazz; make (pattern etc.) vivid or grotesque; brighten or liven *up*. [20th c.; perh. orig. = copulation]

||**J.C.R.** *abbr.* Junior Combination Room; Junior Common Room.

jea'lous (jĕ'l-) *a.* Solicitous *for* or for preservation *of* (rights etc.); feeling resentment or envy (*of* person, his advantages, etc.) on account of known or suspected rivalry esp. in sexual love; (Bibl., of God) intolerant of disloyalty; (of inquiry, supervision, etc.) vigilant; hence **~LY²** *adv.* [ME, f. OF *gelos* f. med. L *zelosus* (as ZEAL; see -OUS)]

jea'lousȳ (jĕ'lu-) *n.* Quality or state of being jealous. [ME, f. OF *gelosie* (as prec.; see -Y¹)]

jean (*or* jān) *n.* Twilled cotton cloth; (in *pl.*) trousers of jean or denim, esp. tight-fitting informal trousers. [ME, attrib. use of *Jene* f. OF *Janne* f. med. L *Janua* Genoa]

jeep *n.* Small sturdy motor vehicle with four-wheel drive. [P; orig. U.S., f. *G.P.* = *g*eneral *p*urposes, infl. by 'Eugene the *Jeep*', animal in comic strip]

jeer¹ *n.* (Naut., usu. in *pl.*) Tackle for hoisting and lowering lower yards. [ME; orig. unkn.]

jeer² *v.* & *n.* **1.** *v.i.* & *t.* Scoff derisively (*at* or at); deride. **2.** *n.* Gibe, taunt. [16th c.; orig. unkn.]

jehad. See JIHAD.

Jėhō'vah (-*a*), **Yah'veh** (-ā), **Yah'weh** (-ā), *ns.* **1.** Name of God in O.T. **2. Jehovah's Witness,** member of fundamentalist millenary sect rejecting supremacy of State over religious principles. [repr. Heb. *YHVH* (given the vowels of *adonai* 'my lord' to indicate substitution of latter word in reading, hence erron. med. L *Iehoua(h)*), perh. = he that is]

Jėhō'vĭst, Yah'vĭst, *ns.* Author(s) of parts of Hexateuch where God is called 'Jehovah' (cf. ELOHIST); hence **Jēhōvĭ'stIC, Yahvĭ'stIC,** *adjs.* [f. prec. + -IST]

Jē'hū *n.* (joc.) Driver, esp. reckless one. [2 Kgs. 9:20]

jėju'ne (-ōō'n) *a.* Meagre, scanty; (of land) barren; unsatisfying to the mind; puerile; hence **~LY²** (-nlĭ) *adv.*, **~NESS** (-n-n-) *n.* [orig. = fasting, f. L *jejunus*]

jėju'num (-jōō'-) *n.* (Anat.) Portion of small intestine between duodenum and ileum. [L, neut. of *jejunus* fasting]

Jĕkȳll and Hȳ'de *n.* Single person in whom two personalities alternate. [f. R. L. Stevenson's story *The Strange Case of Dr. Jekyll and Mr. Hyde*]

jĕll *v.i.* (colloq.) Set as jelly; (fig.) take definite form. [back form. f. JELLY]

jĕ'llaba *n.* Loose hooded cloak worn by Arab men. [f. Arab. *jallaba*, *jallābīya*]

jĕ′llȳ *n.* & *v.* **1.** *n.* Soft stiffish semitransparent food, consisting chiefly of gelatin, got from skin, bones, etc., by boiling and cooling; similar preparation of juice of fruit etc.; substance of similar consistency; (sl.) gelignite; **~ baby,** soft gelatinous sweetmeat moulded in shape of baby; **~-bag** (for straining juice for jelly); **~fish,** usu. marine coelenterate with stinging tentacles and saucer-shaped gelatinous body, (fig.) spineless person; ***~ roll,** Swiss roll made with jelly instead of jam. **2.** *v.t.* & *i.* (Cause to) set as jelly, congeal; set (cooked eels etc.) in jelly. [ME, f. OF *gelee* frost, jelly, f. Rom. *gelata* (L *gelare* freeze f. *gelu* frost; see -Y[4])]

‖**jĕ′mmȳ** *n.* **1.** Crowbar used by burglars, usu. made in sections. **2.** Sheep's head as food. [pet-form of name *James*; see -Y[3]]

je ne sais quoi (zhenesākwah′) *n.* An indefinable something. [F, = I do not know what]

jĕ′nnėt *n.* Small Spanish horse. [f. F *genet* f. Sp. *jinete* light horseman f. Arab. *zenāta* Berber tribe famous as horsemen]

jĕ′nnȳ *n.* **1.** Locomotive crane; = SPINNING-*jenny*; (Bill.) losing hazard down side of table into middle pocket (**short ~**) or far corner pocket (**long ~**); CREEPING *Jenny*. **2.** She-ass; **~ wren,** (esp. pop. and childish name for) wren. [pet-form of name *Janet*; see -Y[3]]

jeo′pardīze (jĕ′p-), **-ise** (-īz), *v.t.* Put into jeopardy, endanger. [f. foll. + -IZE]

jeo′pardȳ (jĕ′p-) *n.* Danger, esp. of severe loss or harm; danger resulting from being on trial for criminal offence. [ME *iuparti* f. OF *iu* (*ieu*) *parti* divided (i.e. even) game, f. L *jocus* game + *partitus* p.p. of *partiri* divide f. *pars partis* part]

jėquĭ′rĭtȳ *n.* Twining shrub (*Abrus precatorius*) with particoloured red and black seeds used for ornament and in medicine. [f. F *jéquirity* f. Tupi-Guarani *jekiriti*]

Jer. *abbr.* Jeremiah (O.T.).

jẽr′bĭl. See GERBIL.

jẽrbō′a *n.* Small Afr. desert rodent of family Dipodidae, with long hind legs and great jumping powers. [med. L, f. Arab. *yarbū*ʻ flesh of loins, jerboa]

jĕrėmī′ad *n.* Lamentation, doleful complaint. [f. F *jérémiade* f. *Jérémie* Jeremiah f. eccl. L *Jeremias*, w. ref. to Lamentations of Jeremiah in O.T.; see -AD]

Jĕrėmī′ah (-*a*) *n.* Doleful prophet or denouncer of the times. [w. ref. as prec.]

jerfalcon. Var. of GYRFALCON.

Jĕ′rĭchō (-kō) *n.* **Go to ~**, (colloq., esp. in *imper.*) go to a distant place, go away. [~ in Israel]

jẽrk[1] *n.* Sharp sudden pull, twist, etc.; involuntary spasmodic contraction of muscle; (in *pl.*) spasmodic movements of limbs or face, esp. in religious excitement; PHYSICAL *jerks*; (sl.) stupid, foolish, or insignificant person. [16th c.; perh. imit.]

jẽrk[2] *v.* **1.** *v.t.* Pull, thrust, twist, etc., with a jerk; throw with suddenly arrested motion; (of weight-lifter) raise (weight) from shoulder-level to above head; ***~′water** *n.* & *a.*, (colloq.) rustic (town), slow (train), unimportant (person etc.). **2.** *v.i.* Move with a jerk. [as prec.]

jẽrk[3] *v.t.* Cure (esp. beef) by cutting in long slices and drying in sun. [f. Amer. Sp. *charquear* (*charqui* f. Quechua *echarqui* dried flesh)]

jẽr′kĭn *n.* Sleeveless jacket; (Hist.) man's close-fitting jacket, often of leather. [16th c.; of unkn. orig.]

jẽr′k|ȳ *a.* Having sudden abrupt movements; spasmodic; hence **~ĭLY**[2] *adv.*, **~ĭNESS** *n.* [f. JERK[1] + -Y[2]]

jĕrobō′ăm *n.* Winebottle of 8–12 times ordinary size. [f. name of 'a mighty man of valour' 'who made Israel to sin', 1 Kgs. 11:28, 14:16]

jĕ′rrȳ *n.* **1.** ‖(sl.) Chamber-pot; (*J~*) German (soldier), Germans collectively. **2. ~ -builder, -building,** builder, building, of unsubstantial houses with bad materials; **~-built,** so built; **~can, je′rrican,** kind of (orig. German) 5-gallon can for petrol or water. [variously f. prec., *Jeremy*, *German*, etc.; see -Y[3]]

jĕrrȳmă′nder. Var. of GERRYMANDER.

jẽr′sey (-zĭ) *n.* **1.** (*J~*). (Animal of) breed of dairy cattle from Jersey. **2.** Plain knitted fabric. **3.** Close-fitting woollen knitted pullover, esp. as worn by sailor etc.; similar garment worn as undervest. [f. *Jersey*, largest of Channel Islands]

Jeru′salem (-rōō′-) *n.* **The New ~**, heavenly abode of the blessed; *Jerusalem* ARTICHOKE. [~, holy city in Israel]

jĕss *n.*, & *v.t.* **1.** *n.* Short strap of leather, silk, etc., round legs of hawk used in falconry. **2.** *v.t.* Put jesses on (hawk). [ME *ges* f. OF *ges* nom. sing. & acc. pl. of *get* f. Rom. **jectus* for L *jactus* throw (*jacĕre jact-* to throw)]

jĕ′ssamĭn(e). See JASMINE.

Jĕ′ssė *n.* **~ window** (showing Christ's descent from Jesse, usu. in form of tree). [name of David's father (1 Sam. 16:12); see Is. 11:1, Matt. 1:6, 16]

jĕst[1] *n.* Piece of raillery, taunt; joke (**break a ~**, utter it); fun (**in ~**, not seriously); object of derision (*a standing jest*); **~-book,** book of jests. [orig. = exploit, f. OF *geste* f. L *gesta*, neut. pl. p.p. of *gerere* do]

jĕst[2] *v.i.* Joke; jeer; speak or act in trifling manner. [f. prec.]

jĕ′ster *n.* One who jests, esp. (Hist.) professional maker of amusement maintained in court or noble household. [f. prec. + -ER[1]]

Jē′sū (-zū) *n.* (arch.) (Voc. form of name of) JESUS. [ME, f. OF obl. case *Iesu*]

Jĕ′sūĭt (-z-) *n.* Member of Society of Jesus, R.C. order founded by Ignatius Loyola and others (1534); (derog., arch.) dissembling person, equivocator; **~s′** (cinchona) **bark**; hence **Jĕsūĭ′tICAL** (-z-) *a.* (lit. or derog.), **~ISM** (2), **~RY** (4), *ns.*, **~IZE** (3) *v.t.* & *i.* [f. F *jésuite* or f. mod. L *Jesuita* (*Jesus*; see foll., -ITE[1])]

Jē′sus (-z-) *n.* **Society of ~** (see prec.); **~ (Christ)!,** (vulg.) excl. expr. surprise, impatience, etc. [name of founder of Christian religion d. *c.* A.D. 30]

jĕt[1] *n.* & *a.* (Made of) hard black lignite taking brilliant polish; **~(-black)**, (of) colour of this, deep glossy black. [ME, f. AF *geet*, **jeet*, OF *jaiet* f. L f. Gk *gagatēs* (*Gagai* in Asia Minor)]

jĕt[2] *n.* **1.** Stream of water, steam, gas, flame, etc., shot forward or upwards esp. from small opening; spout, nozzle, for emitting water etc. thus; (colloq.) jet engine or plane. **2. ~ engine** (using jet propulsion for forward thrust, esp. of aircraft); **~ lag,** delayed bodily effects felt after long flight by jet aircraft (esp. owing to difference of local time); **~ plane** (with jet engine); **~-propelled,** having jet propulsion, (fig.) very fast; **~ propulsion** (by backward ejection of high-speed jet of gas etc.); **~ set,** wealthy élite making frequent air journeys between social or business events; **~ stream,** jet from jet engine, (Meteorol.) strong wind blowing in narrow range of altitudes in the atmosphere. [f. foll. & F f. *jeter* (as foll.)]

jĕt[3] *v.* (**-tt-**). **1.** *v.t.* & *i.* Spurt forth in jets; (cause to) project forward; ‖(in *p.p.*, of pocket) with edges of aperture bound, to prevent ravelling. **2.** *v.i.* (colloq.) Travel by jet plane. [f. F *jeter* throw f. Rom. **jectare* = L *jactare* frequent. of *jacĕre jact-* throw; sense 2 f. prec.]

jeté (zhetā′) *n.* (Ballet). Hop accompanied by kick with other leg. [F, p.p. of *jeter* throw (see prec.)]

jĕ′tsam *n.* Goods thrown overboard from ship to lighten it, esp. such as are washed ashore (cf. FLOTSAM). [contr. of foll.]

jĕ′ttison *n.*, & *v.t.* **1.** *n.* Throwing of goods overboard, esp. to lighten ship in distress; (fig.) abandonment. **2.** Throw (goods) overboard thus; (fig.) abandon. [ME, f. AF *getteson*, OF *getaison* f. L *jactatio -onis* (*jactare* throw; see JET³, -ISON)]

jĕ′tton *n.* Counter with stamped or engraved device. [f. F *jeton* (*jeter* throw, add up accounts; see JET³)]

jĕ′ttў¹ *n.* Pier or mole running out to protect harbour or coast; landing-pier. [ME, f. OF *jetee*, fem. p.p. (as n.) of *jeter*; see JET³, -Y⁴]

jĕ′ttў² *a.* Jet-black. [f. JET¹ + -Y²]

jeu (zhēr) *n.* (*pl.* ~*x pr.* same), ~ ***de mots*** (dəmō′), play on words, pun; ~ ***d'esprit*** (dĕsprē′), witty or humorous (usu. literary) trifle. [F, = play, game, f. L *jocus* jest]

jeune premier (zhērn prəmyā′) *n.* (Theatr.) Actor playing part of youthful hero. [F, lit. 'first young man']

jeunesse dorée (zhērnĕs dōr′ā) *n.* = GILD¹*ed youth.* [F]

Jew¹ (jōō) *n.* **1.** Person of Hebrew descent; person whose religion is Judaism; WANDER*ing Jew.* **2.** (derog., colloq.) Person who drives hard bargains, usurer. **3.** **~-baiting,** systematic persecution of Jews; **jew-fish,** large Austral. food-fish of various species, esp. mulloway; **~'s-ear,** edible cup-shaped fungus; **~'s harp,** small lyre-shaped musical instrument played by holding metal frame between teeth and striking metal tongue with finger. **4.** Hence ~′ESS¹ *n.*, ~′ISH¹ *a.* [ME, f. OF *giu* f. L *judaeus* f. Gk *ioudaios* f. Aram. *yehûdāi* = Heb. *yehûdî* (*yehûdâh* Judah)]

jew² (jōō) *v.t.* ~ **(down)**, (derog., colloq.) cheat, bargain with (person) to lower his price. [f. prec. 2]

jew′el (jōō′-) *n.*, & *v.t.* (‖-ll-). **1.** *n.* Ornament containing precious stone(s), worn for personal adornment; precious stone (used also in watches because of hardness); highly prized person or thing; **~-fish,** scarlet and green tropical fish; hence ~LY² *a.* **2.** *v.t.* (esp. in *p.p.*) Adorn or furnish with jewels; fit (watch) with jewels for the pivot-holes. [ME, f. AF *j(e)uel*, OF *joel*; orig. uncert.]

jew′eller, *-eler, (jōō′-) *n.* Maker of or dealer in jewels or jewellery; **~'s rouge,** finely divided rouge for polishing. [ME, f. AF *jueler*, OF *juelier* (as prec.; see -ER²)]

jew′ellerў, jew′elrў, (jōō′-) *n.* Jewels collectively or as adornment; gems or ornaments worn for personal adornment. [ME f. OF *juelerie* (as prec.; see -ERY), & f. JEWEL, JEWELLER + -ERY, -RY]

Jewrў (joor′ĭ) *n.* Jews collectively; (Hist.) Jews' quarter in town etc. [ME, f. AF *juerie*, OF *juierie* (as JEW¹; see -RY)]

jėzai′l (-zī′l) *n.* Long Afghan musket. [f. Urdu *jazā'il*]

Jĕ′zėbel (*or* -bĕl) *n.* Shameless or profligate woman; woman who puts garish colour on her face. [~, wife of Ahab (1 Kgs. 16, 19, 21)]

***J.G.** *abbr.* junior grade (esp. of rank in Navy).

jĭb¹ *n.* **1.** Triangular staysail from outer end of jib-boom to fore-topmast-head in large ships, from bowsprit to mast-head in smaller ones; **cut of his ~,** his personal appearance; **~-boom,** spar run out from end of bowsprit. **2.** Projecting arm of crane. [17th c., of unkn. orig.]

jĭb² *v.* (**-bb-**). **1.** *v.t.* Pull (sail, yard) round from one side of ship to the other. **2.** *v.i.* (Of sail etc.) swing round thus. [17th c., of unkn. orig.]

jĭb³ *v.i.* (**-bb-**). **1.** (Of horse etc.) stop and refuse to go on, move backwards or sideways instead of going on; hence **~′BER¹** *n.* **2.** (fig.) Refuse to proceed in some action; **~ at,** show repugnance to (course of action, person). [19th c., of unkn. orig.]

jĭ′bba(h) (-b*a*) *n.* Long cloth coat (as) worn by Muslim men. [Egypt. var. of Arab. *jubba*]

***jībe¹** *v.i.* (colloq.) Fit or agree (*with*). [19th c., of unkn. orig.]

jībe². See GIBE, GYBE.

jĭ′ff(ў) *n.* (colloq.) Very short time (*in a jiffy*; (*wait*) *half a jiff*). [18th c., of unkn. orig.]

jĭg¹ *n.* **1.** Lively jumping dance; music for this, usu. in triple time. **2.** Appliance that holds a piece of work and guides the tools operating upon it. **3.** (sl.) Joke, trick; **the ~ is up,** success is now impossible. [16th c., of unkn. orig.]

jĭg² *v.* (**-gg-**). **1.** *v.i.* Dance a jig. **2.** *v.t.* & *i.* Move up and down rapidly and jerkily. **3.** *v.t.* Separate coarser and finer portions of (ore) by shaking it under water in box with perforated bottom. **4.** Work upon with a jig; equip with jigs; **~′saw,** machine fretsaw; **~saw (puzzle),** picture pasted on board and cut in irregular pieces with jigsaw to form puzzle of reassembling them. [prob. f. prec.]

jĭ′gger¹ (-g-) *n.* **1.** (Naut.) Small tackle consisting of a double and single block with rope; small sail at stern; small smack having this. **2.** (Bill. sl.) device forming rest for cue; (Golf) iron club with narrow face. **3.** One who jigs ore. **4.** (sl.) Contrivance, gadget. **5.** (Small glass holding) measure of spirits etc. **6.** Woman's short loose jacket. **7.** **~-mast,** (1) small mast at stern, (2) aftermost mast in four-master. [partly f. prec. + -ER¹]

jĭ′gger² (-g-) *n.* = CHIGOE or *CHIGGER 2. [corrupt.]

jĭ′ggered (-g*e*rd) *a.* (colloq.) (As mild oath) confounded (*I'll be jiggered*). [euphem.]

‖**jĭggerў-pō′kerў** (-g-) *n.* (colloq.) Underhand scheming; hocus-pocus, nonsense. [cf. Sc. *joukery-pawkery* (*jouk* dodge, skulk)]

jĭ′ggle *v.t.* Rock or jerk lightly. [f. JIG² + -LE 3, or f. JOGGLE¹]

jĭha′d, jėha′d, (-ah′d) *n.* Religious war of Muslims against unbelievers; (fig.) campaign for or against a doctrine etc. [f. Arab. *jihād*]

Jĭll. Var. of GILL⁴ (JACK¹ *and Jill*).

jĭlt *n.*, & *v.t.* **1.** *n.* Person (esp. woman) who capriciously casts off lover after encouraging him. **2.** *v.t.* Act as jilt towards, be faithless to. [17th c., of unkn. orig.]

***Jĭm Crow′** (-ō′) *n.* **1.** (derog.) Negro; racial segregation esp. of Negroes; hence ~ISM (3) *n.* **2.** Implement for straightening iron bars or rails by screw pressure. [nickname]

jĭ′m-jăms (-z) *n. pl.* (sl.) Delirium tremens; fit of depression or nervousness. [fanciful redupl.]

***jĭ′mmў.** Var. of JEMMY 1.

***jĭ′mson** *n.* ~ **(weed)**, highly poisonous tall weed (*Datura stramonium*) with large trumpet-shaped flowers. [f. *Jamestown* in Virginia]

jĭ′ngle (-ngg*e*l) *n.* & *v.* **1.** *n.* Mingled noise like that of small bells, links of chain, etc.; thing designed to make this; repetition of same or similar sounds in words, esp. if designed to catch the attention; words intended to attract by sound rather than sense; Irish and Australian covered two-wheeled vehicle. **2.** *v.i.* & *t.* Make, cause (keys etc.) to make, a jingle; (of writing) be full of alliterations, rhymes, etc. [ME; imit.]

jĭ′ngō (-nggō) *n.* (*pl.* **~es**). **1.** (In asseverations) by (the living) ~! 2. Supporter of bellicose policy, blustering patriot (orig. supporter of Disraeli's policy in 1878, f. use of *by jingo* in popular song); hence ~ISM (2), ~IST (2), *ns.*, ~ĭ'STIC *a.* [17th c.; orig. conjurer's gibberish]

jĭnk *v.* & *n.* **1.** *v.i.* Move elusively, dodge; make tricky turn in Rugby football; (sl.) manœuvre aircraft, be manœuvred, jerkily to avoid anti-aircraft fire etc. **2.** *v.t.* Elude by dodging. **3.** *n.* Act of jinking; **high ~s,** boisterous sport, merry-making. [orig. Sc.; prob. imit. of nimble motion]

jĭnnee' (*pl.* **jinn**), **jĭnn,** *ns.* (Muslim Myth.) Spirit lower than angels, able to appear in human and animal forms, and having supernatural power over men. [f. Arab. *jinnī*, pl. *jinn*; cf. GENIE]

jĭnrĭ'ckshа, jĭnrĭ'kĭsha, *n.* (arch.) = RICKSHAW. [Jap. *jinrikisha* (see RICKSHAW)]

jĭnx *n.* (colloq.) Person or thing that brings bad luck. [perh. var. of *jynx* wryneck, charm]

jĭpĭja'pa (hĭpĭhah'pa) *n.* = TOQUILLA. [Sp., f. *Jipijapa* in Ecuador]

***jĭ'tney** *n.* (sl.) Five cents; motor bus carrying passengers at low rates; thing of poor quality. [20th c., of unkn. orig.]

jĭ'tter *v.i.*, & *n.* (colloq.) **1.** *v.i.* Be nervous, act nervously; **~bug,** (1) person addicted to dancing to hot music, (2) nervous person. **2.** *n.* (in *pl.*) Extreme nervousness; hence ~Y[2] *a.*, nervy, jumpy. [20th c., of unkn. orig.]

jiu-jitsu. Var. of JU-JITSU.

jīve *n.*, & *v.i.* **1.** *n.* Fast, lively jazz music; lively dancing esp. to jazz. **2.** *v.i.* Play jive; dance (to) jive. [20th c.; orig. uncert.]

Jno. *abbr.* John.

Jnr. *abbr.* Junior.

jō *n.* (*pl.* **joes**). (Sc.) Sweetheart, beloved. [var. of JOY[1]]

jŏb[1] *n.* **1.** Piece of work, esp. one done for hire or profit; (sl.) a crime, esp. a robbery; product of work, esp. if well done. **2.** Transaction in which private advantage prevails over duty or public interest. **3.** Paid position of employment; anything one has to do; (colloq.) difficult task. **4. Bad ~,** unsatisfactory state of affairs (*make the best of a bad job*), thing on which labour or concern is wasted; **good ~,** satisfactory or fortunate state of affairs; **~s for the boys,** (colloq.) profitable situations etc. to reward one's supporters; **just the ~,** (sl.) precisely what is wanted; **make a (good) ~ of,** do thoroughly or successfully; **on the ~,** at work, in the course of doing a piece of work; **out of a ~,** unemployed. **5. ~ lot,** lot of goods bought as speculation, miscellaneous group of articles; ||**~'master,** one who lets out horses and carriages for limited periods; **~-sheet** (for recording details of jobs done); **~-work** (done and paid for by the job). **6.** Hence ~'LESS *a.*, unemployed. [16th c., of unkn. orig.]

jŏb[2] *v.* **(-bb-). 1.** *v.i.* Do jobs. **2.** *v.t.* ||Hire (horse, carriage) for definite time or job; let out on hire thus. **3.** *v.t.* & *i.* Buy and sell (stock, goods) as middleman; deal in stocks; **~ backwards,** (fig.) use hindsight. **4.** Turn position of trust to private advantage; deal corruptly with (matter), whence ~'BERY (4) *n.*; *(sl.) swindle. **5.** Hence **~'ber**[1] *n.* (esp. = STOCK*jobber* or *wholesaler), **~'bing**[2] *a.* (esp. of carpenter, gardener, printer, etc.). [f. prec.]

jŏb[3] *v.* **(-bb-)** & *n.* **1.** *v.t.* Prod, stab slightly. **2.** *v.i.* Thrust *at* (thing). **3.** *n.* Prod. thrust, jerk at horse's bit. [ME, app. imit.; cf. JAB]

Jōb[4] *n.* Patriarch, story of whose patience in adversity forms Book of Job in O.T. (**would try the patience of ~,** is vexatious); **~'s comforter,** one who under guise of comforting aggravates distress; **~'s tears,** seeds of a grass (*Coix lacryma-jobi*) used as beads.

||**jōbā'tion** *n.* (colloq.) (Esp. lengthy) reprimand. [f. obs. *jobe* reprove (f. JOB[4]) + -ATION]

jŏ'bber. See JOB[2].

||**jŏ'bbernowl** (-ōl) *n.* (colloq.) Stupid head; stupid person. [f. obs. *jobard* (F, f. OF *jobe* silly) + (now dial.) *noll* head]

||**Jŏck**[1] *n.* (Army sl.) Scottish (esp. Highland) soldier. [Sc. form of JACK[1]]

jŏck[2] *n.* (colloq.) Jockey. [abbr.]

jŏ'ckey[1] *n.* (Esp. professional) rider in horse-races; **~ cap** (with long peak, as worn by jockeys); ||**J~ Club,** club established at Newmarket, the body controlling horse-racing; hence ~DOM, ~SHIP (3), *ns.* [dim. of JOCK[1]; see -Y[3]]

jŏ'ckey[2] *v.* **1.** *v.t.* Outwit, cheat; get (person etc.) *away*, *out*, *in*, etc., by trickery; manœuvre or cheat (person *into*, *out of*, doing). **2.** *v.i.* Cheat; **~ for position,** try to gain an advantageous position esp. by skilful manœuvring or unfair action. [f. prec.]

jŏ'ck-străp *n.* Support or protection for male genitals, worn esp. by sportsmen. [f. vulg. *jock* genitals + STRAP]

jocō'se *a.* Playful; fond of joking; waggish; hence ~LY[2] (-slĭ) *adv.*, ~NESS (-sn-), **jocŏ'sity,** *ns.* [f. L *jocosus* (*jocus* jest; see -OSE[1])]

jŏ'cūlar *a.* Merry, fond of joking; of the nature of a joke, humorous; hence ~ITY (-ă'r-) *n.*, ~LY[2] *adv.* [f. L *jocularis* (*joculus* dim. of *jocus* jest; see -AR[1])]

jŏ'cund *a.* Merry, cheerful, sprightly; pleasant; hence or cogn. **jocŭ'nd**ITY *n.*, ~LY[2] *adv.* [ME f. OF, f. L *jocundus*, *jucundus* (*juvare* delight)]

jŏ'dhpurs (-dperz) *n. pl.* Long breeches for riding etc., close-fitting from knee to ankle. [f. *Jodhpur* in India]

jŏ'ey *n.* (Austral.) Young kangaroo; young animal. [f. Aboriginal *joè*]

jŏg *v.* **(-gg-)** & *n.* **1.** *v.t.* Shake with push or jerk; nudge (person), esp. to arouse attention; stimulate (person's, or one's own, memory). **2.** *v.i.* Move up and down with unsteady motion; (of horse) move at jogtrot; proceed laboriously, trudge, (*on*, *along*); go on one's way; proceed, get through the time, (*we must jog on somehow*; *matters jog along*); *run at slow pace esp. as physical exercise, whence **~'g**ER[1] (-g-) *n.* **3. ~'trot,** slow regular trot, (fig.) monotonous progression. **4.** *n.* Shake, push, nudge; slow walk or trot. [ME; app. imit.]

jŏ'ggle[1] *v.* & *n.* **1.** *v.t.* & *i.* Shake, move, (as) by repeated jerks. **2.** *n.* Slight shake; act or action of joggling. [f. prec. + -LE 3]

jŏ'ggle[2] *n.*, & *v.t.* **1.** *n.* Joint of two pieces of stone or timber, contrived to prevent their sliding on one another; notch in one of two pieces, projection in the other, or small piece let in between the two, for this purpose. **2.** *v.t.* Join with joggle. [perh. f. *jog* = JAG[1]]

Jōhă'nnīne *a.* Of the apostle John. [f. L (as JOHN; see -INE[1])]

Jōhă'nnĭsbĕrger (-g-) *n.* Fine white wine from *Johannisberg* in the Rheingau. [G]

Jŏhn (jŏn) *n.* **1.** *(*j~*). Lavatory. **2.** *John* BARLEY*corn*; **~ Bull,** English nation, typical Englishman; **~ Chinaman,** (derog.) typical Chinese; **~ Citizen,** average man; **~ Collins,** Collins made with gin; **~ Doe,** fictitious character in law (cf. RICHARD *Roe*), *average man; *John* DORY[1]; **~-o'-Groat's(-House),** extreme north of Scotland (*from ~-o'-Groat's to Land's End*, through Great Britain); ***~ Hancock, Henry,** person's signature. [man's Christian name; ME, f. LL *Jo(h)annes* f. Gk *Iōannēs* f. Heb. *yôḥānān*]

jŏ'hnnȳ (jŏ'nĭ) *n.* ||Fellow, man; ||**J~ Armstrong,** (Naut. sl.) hand-power; **J~ Raw,** novice; **~-cake,** cake of (U.S.) maize-meal or (Austral.) wheat-meal; **~-come-lately,** (colloq.) recently arrived person; ***~-jump-up,** violet or pansy. [f. JOHN + -Y³]

John|sō'nĭan (jŏn-) *a.* Of or like S. Johnson, esp. in using many long words of Latin derivation; so **~sonE'SE** *n.* [f. S. *Johnson*, Engl. man of letters and lexicographer d. 1784 + -IAN]

joie de vivre (zhwahdevē'vr) *n.* Feeling of healthy and exuberant enjoyment of life. [F, = joy of living]

join *v.* & *n.* **1.** *v.t.* Put together, fasten, unite, (things, one *to* another, *together*); connect (two points) by (esp. straight) line; unite (persons, one *with* or *to* another) in marriage, friendship, alliance, etc. (*join* FORCE¹*s*). **2.** *v.i.* Come together, be united, (*with, to,* or abs.); take part with others (*in* doing or action; **~ in,** take part); **~ up,** enlist in army etc. **3.** *v.t.* Come into the company of (person); associate oneself with (person) *in* action etc.; become member of (club, army, etc.); take or resume one's place in (regiment, ship, company, etc.); be or become connected or continuous with (*the Cherwell joins the Thames at Oxford*). **4. ~ battle,** begin fighting; **~ hands,** clasp one's hands together, clasp each other's hands, (fig.) combine in action or enterprise; *join* ISSUE¹. **5.** *n.* Point, line, or surface of junction. [ME, f. OF *joindre* (st. *joign-*) f. L *jungere junct-* join f. IE **jug-*; cf. YOKE]

joi'nder *n.* (Law). Joining, union. [AF, f. OF *joindre* to join; see prec., -ER⁴]

joi'n|er *n.* In vbl senses; one who makes furniture, house fittings, and other woodwork that is lighter than carpenter's, whence **~ERY** (1, 2) *n.*; (colloq.) person who readily joins societies etc. [ME, f. AF *joignour*, OF *joigneor* (as JOIN; see -OR, -ER²)]

joint¹ *n.* **1.** Place at which two things are joined together. **2.** Structure in animal body by which two bones are fitted together; **out of ~,** (of bone) dislocated, (fig.) out of order; *put* person's NOSE *out of joint*. **3.** Part of stem from which leaf or branch grows. **4.** Point at which, contrivance by which, two parts of artificial structure are joined, rigidly or so as to allow of movement; piece of flexible material as hinge of book-cover; (Geol.) fissure in mass of rock. **5.** One of the parts of which a body is made up; one of the parts into which butcher divides carcass, esp. as roasted and served at table. **6.** (sl.) Place of meeting or resort; marijuana cigarette. **7. ~-stool** [orig. *joined-*], (Hist.) one made of parts fitted by a joiner, night-stool, commode. **8.** Hence **~'LESS** *a.* [ME, f. OF, p.p. (as n.) of *joindre* JOIN]

joint² *a.* Held or done by, belonging to, two or more persons etc. in conjunction (*joint account, action, opinion, estate*); (esp. of person) sharing (*with* others in possession, action, state, etc.; *joint author, favourite, heir, owner*); *joint and* SEVERAL; **during their ~ lives,** while they are both or all alive; **~ stock,** capital held jointly, common fund, (*attrib.*) holding, formed on basis of, a joint stock (*joint-stock bank, company*); hence **~'LY²** *adv.* [ME f. OF p.p. (as prec.)]

joint³ *v.t.* Connect by joints; fill up joints of (masonry etc.) with mortar etc., point; prepare (board etc.) for being joined to another by planing its edge; divide (body, member) at a joint or into joints. [f. JOINT¹]

joi'nter *n.* In vbl senses; plane for jointing; tool for jointing masonry; workman employed in jointing wires, pipes, etc. [f. prec. + -ER¹]

joi'ntrĕss *n.* Widow who holds a jointure. [f. obs. *jointer* joint possessor + -ESS¹]

joi'nture *n.*, & *v.t.* **1.** *n.* Estate settled on wife for period during which she survives husband. **2.** *v.t.* Provide (wife) with jointure. [ME f. OF, f. L *junctura* (as JOIN; see -URE)]

joist *n.* One of parallel timbers stretched on edge from wall to wall for ceiling laths or floor boards to be nailed to; hence **~'ED²** *a.* [ME f. OF *giste* f. Rom. **jacitum* neut. p.p. of L *jacēre* lie]

jōke¹ *n.* Thing said or done to excite laughter; witticism, jest; ridiculous thing, person, or circumstance; **no ~,** a serious matter; **practical ~,** trick played on person in order to have laugh at his expense; **standing ~,** what is regarded as irremediably ridiculous; hence **jō'k(e)Y²** *a.* [orig. sl., perh. f. L *jocus* jest]

jōk|e² *v.* **1.** *v.i.* Make jokes; **~ing apart,** seriously (after there has been joking). **2.** *v.t.* Poke fun at, banter. [f. prec. or f. L *jocari* to jest (as prec.)]

jō'ker *n.* One who jokes; (sl.) fellow, man; (Cards) odd (often blank) card in some games, counting as (highest) trump or as WILD card; *clause unobtrusively inserted in bill or document and affecting its operation in way not immediately apparent; unexpected factor or resource. [f. prec. + -ER¹]

jokul, *jökull,* (yō'kōōl; *or* yẽr'-) *n.* Snow-mountain in Iceland. [Icel. *jökull* ICICLE]

jolie laide (zhŏlē lā'd) *n.* (*pl.* ***jolies laides*** *pr.* same). = BELLE LAIDE. [F (*jolie* pretty, *laide* ugly, fem. adjs.)]

jŏ'llĭ|fȳ *v.i.* Make merry, esp. in drinking; hence **~FICA'TION** *n.* [f. JOLLY¹ + -FY]

jŏ'llĭtȳ *n.* Merry-making, festivity. [ME, f. OF *joliveté* (as foll.; see -TY¹)]

jŏ'llȳ¹ *a., adv., n.,* & *v.t.* **1.** *a.* Joyful; slightly drunk; festive, jovial, (**the ~ god,** Bacchus; **~ Roger,** pirates' black flag). **2.** (colloq., of person or thing). Very pleasant, delightful, (often iron.: *he must be a jolly fool to do it*). **3.** *adv.* (colloq.) Very (*he was jolly miserable*; *for he's a jolly good fellow*; *you will jolly well have to*). **4.** *n.* ||(sl.) Royal Marine. **5.** *v.t.* (colloq.) Flatter, cajole, (usu. *jolly along*); chaff, banter. [ME f. OF *jolif* gay, pretty, perh. f. ON *jól* YULE]

jŏ'llȳ² *n.* **~(-boat)**, clinker-built ship's-boat, smaller than cutter. [18th c., of unkn. orig.; cf. 16th–17th c. *jolywat, gellywatte* and YAWL]

jōlt *v.* & *n.* **1.** *v.t.* Shake (person etc.) with jerk from seat etc., esp. in locomotion; give mental shock to, perturb. **2.** *v.i.* (Of vehicle) move along with jerks, as on rough road. **3.** *n.* Such jerk; surprise, shock; hence **~'Y²** *a.* [16th c., of unkn. orig.]

Jon. *abbr.* Jonah; Jonathan.

Jō'nah (*-a*) *n.* Person who brings, or is believed to bring, bad luck. [~ in O.T.]

Jŏ'nathan *n.* **1.** ||(**Brother**) **~,** personified people of, typical citizen of, United States. **2.** Kind of red-skinned Amer. dessert apple. [perh. f. ~ Trumbull, 18th-c. governor of Connecticut]

Jōnes (-nz) *n.* KEEP¹ *up with the Joneses.* [common surname]

jongleur (zhaw'ṅglẽr) *n.* (Hist.) Itinerant minstrel. [F, var. of *jougleur* JUGGLER]

jŏ'nquĭl *n.* Species of narcissus with rushlike leaves and clusters of fragrant white and yellow flowers. [f. mod. L *jonquilla* or F *jonquille* f. Sp. *junquillo* dim. of JUNCO]

Jŏr'dan *n.* **~ almond,** fine almond esp. from Malaga. [ME, prob. f. OF or Sp. *jardin* GARDEN, assim. to name of river (see foll.)]

Jŏrdā'nĭan *a.* & *n.* (Native or inhabitant) of kingdom of the Jordan. [f. *Jordan*, river of Palestine flowing into Dead Sea, + -IAN]

jŏr'um *n.* Large drinking-bowl; its contents, esp. punch. [perh. f. *Joram* (2 Sam. 8:10)]

Jos. *abbr.* Joseph.
***jŏsh** *n.* & *v.* (sl.) **1.** *n.* Good-natured joke, leg-pull. **2.** *v.t.* Hoax, banter. **3.** *v.i.* Indulge in ridicule. **4.** Hence ~'ER¹ *n.* [19th c.; orig. unkn.]
Josh. *abbr.* Joshua (O.T.).
jŏss *n.* Chinese idol; **~-house,** Chinese temple; **~-stick** (of fragrant tinder mixed with clay, as incense). [perh. ult. f. Port. *deos* f. L *deus* god]
||**jŏ'sser** *n.* (sl.) Fool; fellow. [f. prec. + -ER¹; cf. Austral. sense 'clergyman']
jŏ'stle (-*sel*) *v.* & *n.* **1.** *v.i.* Knock or push *against*; struggle *with* (person *for* thing). **2.** *v.t.* Push against, elbow; push (person *away*, *from*, etc.). **3.** *n.* Jostling; collision (lit. or fig.). [ME; earlier *justle*, f. JUST³, JOUST + -LE 3]
jŏt¹ *n.* (Usu. w. neg. expressed or implied) small amount, whit (*not one jot or tittle*). [f. L f. Gk IOTA; cf. Matt. 5:18]
jŏt² *v.t.* (-tt-). Write (usu. *down*) briefly or hastily; hence **~'TER¹** *n.*, (esp.) small pad or notebook for memoranda etc., **~'TING¹** (2) *n.* [f. prec.]
joule (jōōl) *n.* Unit of work or energy, work done by force of one newton when its point of application moves one metre in the direction of action of the force, work done or heat generated by a current of one ampere flowing for one second against a resistance of one ohm. [f. J. P. *Joule*, Engl. physicist d. 1889]
jounce *v.t.* & *i.* Bump, bounce, jolt. [ME, of unkn. orig.]
jour'nal (jẽr'-) *n.* **1.** (In bookkeeping by double entry) book in which each transaction is entered, with statement of accounts to which it is to be debited and credited. **2.** Daily record of events; (Naut.) log-book; **the J~s,** (Parl.) record of daily proceedings. **3.** Daily or other newspaper; other periodical, esp. one dealing with current events or learned topics. **4.** Part of shaft or axle that rests on bearings [hist. unexpl.]; **~-bearing** (supporting this); **~-box** (enclosing journal and bearings). [ME, f. OF *jurnal* f. LL *diurnalis* DIURNAL]
jour'nal|ĭst (jẽr'-) *n.* One whose business it is to edit, or write for, a journal (sense 3), esp. a newspaper; hence or cogn. ~E'SE *n.*, style of language said to be characteristic of (hasty or inferior) newspaper writing, ~ISM (2) *n.*, **~ĭ'stic** *a.* [f. prec. + -IST]
jour'nalize (jẽr'-), **-ise** (-īz), *v.t.* & *i.* Record in, or keep, private journal. [f. JOURNAL + -IZE]
jour'ney (jẽr'-) *n.*, & *v.i.* **1.** *n.* Distance travelled in specified time (*a day's, 4 days', journey*); expedition to some distance, round of travel (usu. by land; cf. VOYAGE; *take, undertake, perform, a journey*); travelling of vehicle along route at stated time; **~man,** qualified mechanic or artisan who works for another, reliable but not outstanding worker, (fig.) mere hireling; *~man clock*, secondary clock adjusted or controlled by another; **~-work,** work of a journeyman (esp. fig.). **2.** *v.i.* Make a journey. [ME; (v. f. AF *journeyer*) f. OF *jornee* day, day's work or travel, f. Rom. **diurnata* day (LL *diurnum* day f. L *diurnus* daily); see -Y⁴]
joust (*or* jōōst), **jŭst³**, *v.i.*, & *n.* (Engage in) combat between two knights etc. on horseback with lances. [ME, (n. f. OF *juste*) f. OF *juster* bring together f. Rom. **juxtare* approach f. L *juxta* near]
Jōve *n.* Jupiter; **by ~!** (excl. of surprise or approval). [ME, f. L *Jovis* gen. of OL *Jovis* used as gen. of JUPITER]
jō'vĭal *a.* Merry; convivial; hearty and good-humoured; hence ~ITY (-ă'l-) *n.*, ~LY² *adv.* [F, f. LL *jovialis* of Jupiter (as prec.; see -AL), w. ref. to supposed influence of planet Jupiter on those born under it]
Jō'vĭan *a.* Of or like Jupiter; of the planet Jupiter. [f. as JOVE + -IAN]
jowâr' *n.* Durra. [f. Hindi *jawār*]
jowl *n.* **1.** Jawbone; jaw; cheek, esp. CHEEK *by jowl*. **2.** External throat or neck when prominent, dewlap of cattle, crop of bird. **3.** Head and shoulders of salmon and other fish. [(1) ME *chavel* jaw (f. OE *ceafl*); (2) ME *cholle* neck (f. OE *ceole*); (3) ME *cholle* head of man, beast, or fish]
joy¹ *n.* **1.** Vivid emotion of pleasure, gladness, (*at, in, of*); **no ~,** (colloq.) no satisfaction or success; WISH person *joy of it*. **2.** Thing that causes delight. **3. ~-bells** (rung on festive occasions); **~-ride,** (colloq.) pleasure-ride in motor car etc., usu. without its owner's permission; **~'stick,** (sl.) control-lever of aeroplane. **4.** Hence or cogn. ~'LESS, ~'OUS, *adjs*. [ME, f. OF *joie* f. Rom. **gaudia* fem. f. L *gaudia* pl. of *gaudium* (*gaudēre* rejoice)]
joy² *v.i.* & *t.* (chiefly poet.) Rejoice; gladden. [ME, f. OF *joïr* rejoice f. Rom. **gaudire* for L *gaudēre* rejoice]
joy'ance *n.* (chiefly poet.) Rejoicing; festivity; delight. [f. prec. + -ANCE]
Joy'cėan *a.* & *n.* **1.** *a.* Of or characteristic of (the writings of) Joyce. **2.** *n.* Specialist in or admirer of Joyce's works. [f. J. *Joyce*, Ir. poet and novelist d. 1941 + -EAN]
joy'ful *a.* Full of, showing, or causing, joy; hence ~LY² *adv.*, ~NESS *n.* [ME, f. JOY¹ + -FUL]
J.P. *abbr.* Justice of the Peace.
Jr. *abbr.* Junior.
jt. *abbr.* joint.
ju'bĭl|āte (jōō'-) *v.i.* Exult, make demonstrations of joy; hence or cogn. ~ANCE, ~A'TION, *ns.*, ~ANT *a.* [f. L *jubilare* shout esp. for joy + -ATE³]
Jubĭlatė De'ō (jōōbĭlahtĭ dā'ō) *n.* Canticle consisting of Ps. 100. [L, = shout ye to God, its first words]
ju'bĭlee (jōō'-) *n.* **1.** (Jewish Hist.) year of emancipation and restoration, kept every 50 years, (see Lev. 25); (R.C. Ch.) period of remission from penal consequences of sin, granted under certain conditions for a year usu. at intervals of 25 years. **2.** Anniversary (esp. fiftieth, **golden ~**); DIAMOND *jubilee*; SILVER¹ *jubilee*. **3.** Season of rejoicing; exultant joy. [ME, f. OF *jubilé* f. LL *jubilaeus* (*annus* year) of jubilee f. Gk *iōbēlaios* (*iōbēlos* f. Heb. *yōbēl* ram, ram's-horn trumpet, jubilee) by assoc. w. L *jubilare* (see JUBILATE)]
Jud. *abbr.* Judith (Apocr.).
Judae'an, *Judē'an, (jōō-) *a.* & *n.* (Inhabitant) of Judaea in ancient Palestine. [f. *Judaea* + -AN]
Judae'ō-, *Judē'ō-, (jōō-) *comb. form.* Jew(ish), as **~-German,** Yiddish; ~PHOBE *n.* & *a.* [f. L *judaeus* Jewish + -O-]
Judā'ĭc (jōō-) *a.* Of or characteristic of Jews. [f. L f. Gk *Ioudaïkos* (*Ioudaios* JEW¹; see -IC)]
Ju'dā|ĭsm (jōō'-) *n.* Religion of the Jews, with belief in one God and based on Mosaic and rabbinical teachings; Jews collectively; hence ~IST (2) *n.* [ME, f. LL *Judaismus* f. Gk *Ioudaïsmos* (as prec.; see -ISM)]
Ju'dāize (jōō'-), **-ise** (-īz), *v.* **1.** *v.i.* Follow Jewish customs or rites. **2.** *v.t.* Make Jewish; convert to Judaism. [f. LL *judaizare* f. Gk *ioudaïzō* (as JUDAIC; see -IZE)]
Ju'das (jōō'-) *n.* Infamous traitor; (*j~*) peep-hole in door; **~-colour(ed),** (of beard etc.) red; **~ kiss,** act of betrayal (Matt. 26:48); **~-tree** (with purple flowers usu. appearing before the leaves). [name of apostle who betrayed Christ]
jŭ'dder *v.i.*, & *n.* **1.** *v.i.* (Esp. of mechanism) shake noisily or violently; (of singer's voice) oscillate in intensity. **2.** *n.* Instance of juddering. [imit.; cf. SHUDDER]

Judg. *abbr.* Judges (O.T.).

jŭdge[1] *n.* **1.** Public officer appointed to hear and try causes in court of justice (SOBER *as a judge*); (of God) supreme arbiter (*as God is my judge*). **2.** (Jewish Hist.) Officer having temporary authority in Israel in period between Joshua and the kings; (in *pl.*) seventh book of O.T., containing history of this period. **3.** Person appointed to decide dispute or contest; person who decides a question; person who is qualified to decide on merits of thing or question (*am no judge of that*; *good judge of claret*). **4. J~ Advocate General,** civil officer in supreme control of courts martial in army or air force; **~-made law,** principles based on judges' decisions; ||*judge's* MARSHAL[1]; ||**J~s' Rules** (regarding admissibility of accused's statements as evidence). **5.** Hence **~'SHIP** (1, 2) (-jsh-) *n.* [ME f. OF *juge* f. L *judex judicis* (*jus* right, *-dicus* speaking)]

jŭdge[2] *v.* **1.** *v.t.* Pronounce sentence on (person) in court of justice; try (cause); decide (question); have authority over as JUDGE[1] (esp. sense 2); act as JUDGE[1] (sense 3) of; form opinion about, estimate, appraise, (person etc. *by* his deeds etc.); (arch.) criticize, censure, (*judge not that ye be not judged*); conclude, consider, suppose, (thing *to be*, *that*, etc., *from* or *by* data). **2.** *v.i.* Act as judge; form a judgement (*of* thing etc.). [ME, f. OF *jug(i)er* f. L *judicare* (*judex*; see prec.)]

jŭdgemă'tĭc|(al) (-jm-) *adjs.* (colloq.) Judicious, discerning; hence **~alLY**[2] *adv.* [f. JUDGE[1] after *dogmatic*]

jŭ'dgement, jŭ'dgment, (-jm-) *n.* **1.** Sentence of court of justice, decision by judge; **J~ of Paris,** (Gk. Myth.) award of golden apple by Paris to Aphrodite, leading to abduction of Helen and to Trojan War; **the Last J~** (of mankind by God at end of world); SIT *in judgement*. **2.** Misfortune viewed as sign of divine displeasure (often joc.: *it is a judgement on you for getting up late*). **3.** Criticism; opinion, estimate, (*in my judgement*; **against** one's **better ~**, contrary to what one really feels to be advisable); critical faculty, discernment, (*error of judgement*); good sense. **4. J~ Day, day of ~,** (of God's final judgement); **~ debt** (for whose payment a judgement has been given); **~ creditor, debtor,** (for, against, whom judgement has been given); **~-seat,** judge's seat, tribunal; ||**~ summons** (for failure to pay judgement debt). [ME, f. OF *jugement* (as JUDGE[2]; see -MENT)]

ju'dĭcature (jōō'-) *n.* **1.** Administration of justice; **Supreme Court of J~** in England (consisting of Court of Appeal and High Court of Justice; the latter is composed of the Queen's Bench, the Chancery, and the Family divisions, and the Court of Criminal Appeal). **2.** Judge's (term of) office; body of judges; court of justice. [f. med. L *judicatura* f. L *judicare*; see JUDGE[2], -URE]

judĭ'cial (jōōdĭ'shal) *a.* **1.** Of, done by, proper to, a court of law; **~ factor,** (Sc.) official RECEIVER; **~ murder,** legal but unjust death sentence; *judicial* SEPARATION. **2.** Inflicted as a divine judgement. **3.** Having the function of judgement (*a judicial assembly*). **4.** Of, or proper to, a judge; expressing a judgement, critical; impartial. **5.** Hence **~LY**[2] *adv.* [ME, f. L *judicialis* (as foll.; see -AL)]

judĭ'ciarў (jōōdĭ'sherĭ) *n.* The judges of a State collectively. [f. L *judiciarius* (*judicium* judgement f. *judex* JUDGE[1]; see -ARY[1])]

judĭ'cious (jōōdĭ'shus) *a.* Sensible, prudent; sound in discernment and judgement; hence **~LY**[2] *adv.*, **~NESS** *n.* [f. F *judicieux* f. L *judicium* (as prec.); see -OUS]

ju'dō (jōō'-) *n.* (*pl.* **~s**). Modern refined form of ju-jitsu; hence **~ka** (*pl.* same), **~IST**, student of or expert in judo. [Jap. (*jū* gentle, *dō* way)]

Ju'dў (jōō'-) *n.* See PUNCH[4]; *(colloq.) woman. [pet-form of name *Judith*; see -Y[3]]

jŭg[1] *n.* **1.** Deep vessel for holding liquids, with handle and often with spout or lip shaped for pouring; *large jar with narrow mouth; hence **~'FUL** 2 *n.* **2. (Stone) ~,** (sl.) prison. [perh. f. *Jug*, pet-form of *Joan* etc.]

jŭg[2] *v.t.* (**-gg-**). Stew, boil, (hare, rabbit) in jug or jar (usu. in *p.p.*); (sl.) imprison. [f. prec.]

jŭg[3] *v.i.* (**-gg-**). (Of nightingale or other bird) utter sound *jug*; so **jug, jug-jug,** *ns.* [imit.]

Jŭ'ggernaut (-g-) *n.* **1.** (Hind. Myth.) Krishna, eighth avatar of Vishnu; his idol at Puri in Orissa, annually dragged in procession on huge car, under wheels of which devotees are said to have formerly thrown themselves. **2.** (fig.) Institution or notion to which persons blindly sacrifice themselves or others; (*j~*) large overpowering force or object, very large and heavy motor vehicle. [f. Hindi *Jagannath* f. Skr. *Jagannātha* (*jagat-* world, *nāthás* lord)]

jŭ'ggins (-gĭnz) *n.* (sl.) Simpleton. [perh. f. proper name *Juggins* (as JUG[1]); cf. MUGGINS]

jŭ'ggle *v.* & *n.* **1.** *v.i.* Perform conjuring tricks; perform feats of dexterity (*with* objects tossed up and caught); **~ with,** deceive (person), misrepresent (facts), rearrange adroitly. **2.** *v.t.* Perform juggling feats with; cheat (person etc. *out of* thing); bring, get, change, (*away*, *into*, etc.) by trickery. **3.** *n.* Piece of juggling, fraud. [ME, back form. f. foll., or f. OF *jogler*, *jugler* f. L *joculari* jest (*joculus* dim. of *jocus* jest)]

jŭ'ggl|er *n.* One who juggles; conjurer; trickster, impostor; so **~ERY** (2, 4) *n.* [ME, f. OF *jo(u)glere -eor* f. L *joculator -oris* (as prec.; see -ER[2])]

Jugoslav. See YUGOSLAV.

jŭ'gūlar *a.* & *n.* **1.** *a.* Of the neck or throat; **~ veins,** great veins of neck, conveying blood from head. **2.** (Of fish) having ventral fins in front of pectoral. **3.** *n.* Jugular vein. [f. LL *jugularis* f. L *jugulum* collar-bone, throat, dim. of *jugum* YOKE; see -AR[1]]

jŭ'gūlāte *v.t.* Kill by cutting throat; (fig.) arrest course of (disease etc.) by powerful remedy etc. [f. L *jugulare* (*jugulum*; see prec.) + -ATE[3]]

juice (jōōs) *n.* Liquid part of vegetables or fruits; fluid part of animal body or substance, esp. secretion (*gastric*, *pancreatic*, *juice*; STEW[2] *in* one's *own juice*); (fig.) essence or spirit of anything; (sl.) petrol or electricity used in engine etc.; hence **~'LESS** (-sl-) *a.* [ME, f. OF *jus* f. L *jus* broth, juice]

jui'c|ў (jōō'-) *a.* Full of juice, succulent; (colloq., of weather) wet; (colloq.) of rich intellectual quality, interesting, racy, scandalous; hence **~ĬLY**[2] *adv.*, **~ĬNESS** *n.* [ME, f. prec. + -Y[2]]

ju-jĭ'tsu (jōōjĭ'tsōō) *n.* Japanese system of unarmed combat seeking to utilize opponent's strength and weight to his disadvantage. [f. Jap. *jūjutsu* (*jū* gentle, *jutsu* science)]

ju-ju (jōō'jōō) *n.* (W. Afr.) Charm or fetish; supernatural power attributed to this. [perh. f. F *joujou* toy]

ju'jube (jōō'jōōb) *n.* (Edible acid berry-like drupe of) plant of genus *Zizyphus*; lozenge of gelatin etc. flavoured with or imitating this. [F, or f. med. L *jujuba* ult. f. Gk *zizuphon*]

ju-jutsu. Var. of JU-JITSU.

juke-bŏx (jōō'k-) *n.* Machine that automatically plays selected gramophone record when coin is inserted. [f. Gullah *juke* disorderly + BOX[2]]

Jul. *abbr.* July.

ju'lĕp (jōō'-) *n.* Sweet drink, esp. as vehicle for medicine; medicated drink as mild stimulant etc.; *iced and flavoured spirit and water, esp.

K·

mint julep. [ME f. OF, f. Arab. *julāb* f. Pers. *gulāb* (*gul* rose, *āb* water)]

Ju'lian (jōō'-) *a*. Of Julius Caesar; ~ **calendar** (introduced by him, in which the year consisted of 365 days, every fourth year having 366; cf. GREGORIAN); ~ **day,** (Astron.) day as numbered in one sequence from 4713 B.C. (*Julian day 2442779 begins at noon on 1 Jan. 1976*); ~ **year,** (average length of) year of Julian calendar, (Astron.) year of Julian days. [f. L *Julianus* (*Julius*; see -AN)]

juliĕ'nne (zhōō- *or* jōō-) *n*. Clear soup of vegetables cut in thin strips and cooked in meat broth. [F, f. name *Jules* or *Julien*]

Ju'liet (jōō'-) *n*. ~ **cap,** small network ornamental cap worn by brides etc. [f. heroine of Shakespeare's *Romeo & Juliet*]

Julȳ' (jōō-) *n*. (*pl*. ~**s**). Seventh month of year. [ME, f. AF *julie* f. L *Julius* (*mensis* month), named after Julius Caesar]

***jŭ'mbal, *jŭ'mble**[1], *n*. Thin crisp sweet cake, usu. ring-shaped. [perh. var. of *gimmal* (see GIMBALS)]

jŭ'mble[2] *v.i.* & *t*. Move about in disorder; mix *up*, confuse. [prob. imit.]

jŭ'mble[3] *n*. Confused assemblage; ‖articles for jumble sale; muddle; jolting; ‖~ **sale** (of miscellaneous cheap usu. second-hand articles at bazaar etc.); hence **jŭ'mbly**[2] *a*. [f. prec.]

jŭ'mbō *n*. (*pl*. ~**s**) & *a*. **1.** *n*. Big clumsy person, animal, or thing; very large specimen; =*jumbo jet*. **2.** *a*. Very large of its kind; ~ **jet,** large jet plane able to carry several hundred passengers. [prob. f. second element in MUMBO-JUMBO]

jŭ'mbŭck *n*. (Austral.) Sheep. [Aboriginal]

jŭmp[1] *n*. **1.** Act of jumping; **broad* or ‖LONG[1] *jump*; HIGH *jump*; **get the ~ on,** (sl.) get an advantage over by anticipation; **on the ~,** (colloq.) bustling about; **one ~ ahead,** having progressed one stage farther (than rival in plans etc.). **2.** Sudden movement caused by shock or excitement; **the ~s,** (sl.) nervousness, the fidgets, delirium tremens. **3.** Abrupt rise in amount, price, value, etc.; ~ (**bid**), (Bridge) bid higher than is necessary to overcall in the relevant suit. **4.** Sudden transition; gap in series, argument, etc. **5.** Obstacle to be jumped by horse etc.; SKI-*jump*. **6.** **~-cut,** (Cinemat.) removal of middle part of shot to give discontinuity of action; **~-jet,** V.T.O.L. jet plane; ***~-rope,** skipping-rope; ***~ seat,** folding seat in motor car; ~ **suit,** one-piece garment for whole body, orig. worn by paratroops. [f. foll.]

jŭmp[2] *v*. **1.** *v.i.* Move up off ground etc. by bending and sudden muscular extension of legs or (of fish) tail; move suddenly with jump or bound (*up* from seat etc., *from* high place, *out*, etc.; ~ **in,** get quickly into vehicle etc.); give sudden movement from excitement, shock, etc., esp. *jump for joy*. **2.** Rise suddenly in price etc. **3.** Come *to*, arrive *at*, (conclusion) over-hastily; come suddenly *into* prominence etc. **4.** Agree, coincide, (*together*, one *with* another). **5.** ~ **at,** (fig.) accept (offer, bargain) eagerly; ~ **down** person's **throat,** reprimand or contradict him fiercely; ~ **in the lake,** (colloq.) go away and cease being a nuisance; **~-off,** deciding round in horse-jumping contest; **~ing-o'ff** *a*., starting (*place*, *point*; lit. or fig.); ~ **on,** attack crushingly (lit. or fig.); *jump out of* one's SKIN[1]; *jump over the* BROOM*stick*; ~ **to it,** make an energetic start; **~ed-up** (-pt-) *a*., upstart. **6.** *v.t.* Pass over (gate etc.) by jumping; (of train, tram, etc.) leave (the rails); move or pass over (intervening thing) to point beyond; *get on or off (train etc.) quickly, esp. in illegal manner; abandon contrary to one's undertaking (*jump bail*); ~ **ship,** (of seaman) be deserter before end of his contract. **7.** Help (child etc.) to jump *down* etc.; cause (thing) to jump; use (horse) for jumping. **8.** (esp. in *p.p.*) Cook (potatoes etc.) in frying-pan, occasionally shaking them. **9.** Pounce upon (thing); act before time prescribed by (*jump the* GUN; ‖~ **the queue,** push forward out of one's turn, take precedence of others waiting). **10.** Take summary possession of (claim allegedly abandoned or forfeited by former occupant). **11.** Skip over (subject, part of book, etc.). **12.** Drill (rock, hole in rock) with jumper. **13.** Hence **~'ABLE** *a*. [16th c.; prob. imit.]

jŭ'mper[1] *n*. In vbl senses; member of Welsh Methodist body (or later sects) who jump(ed) as part of worship; jumping insect, e.g. flea; (Electr.) short wire used to make or break circuit; rope made fast to keep yard, mast, etc., from jumping; heavy chisel-ended iron bar for drilling blasting-holes. [f. prec. + -ER[1]]

jŭ'mper[2] *n*. Loose outer jacket of canvas etc. worn by sailors etc.; ‖woman's knitted pullover; *pinafore dress. [prob. f. (17th c., now dial.) *jump* short coat perh. f. F *jupe* f. Arab. *jubba*; cf. JIBBAH]

jŭ'mpĭng *a*. In vbl senses; ~ **bean,** seed of Mexican plant that jumps owing to movement of enclosed larva; ~ **deer,** N. Amer. black-tailed deer. [f. JUMP[2] + -ING[2]]

jŭ'mp|ȳ *a*. Characterized by sudden movements esp. of nervous excitement; hence **~ĭNESS** *n*. [f. JUMP[1] + -Y[2]]

Jun. *abbr*. June; Junior.

jŭ'ncō *n*. (*pl*. ~**s** *or* ~**es**). Small Amer. finch of genus *Junco*. [Sp., f. L *juncus* rush plant]

jŭ'nction *n*. Joining; joint, meeting-place; place where railway lines or roads meet and unite; (Electronics) region of transition in semiconductor between regions where conduction is mainly by electrons and mainly by holes; ~ **box** (containing junction of electric cables etc.). [f. L *junctio* (as JOIN; see -ION)]

jŭ'ncture *n*. Joining; place where things join; concurrence of events, state of affairs, (*at this juncture*). [ME, f. L *junctura* (as JOIN; see -URE)]

June (jōōn) *n*. Sixth month of year; **~'berry,** = SERVICE[2]-*berry* (2). [ME, f. OF *juin* & f. L *Junius* var. of *Junonius* sacred to JUNO]

Ju'ngian (yŏŏ'-) *a*. & *n*. (Disciple) of Jung or his system of analytical psychology with complex classification of personality types. [f. C. G. *Jung*, Swiss psychologist d. 1961 + -IAN]

jŭ'ngle (-nggel) *n*. (Area of) land overgrown with underwood or tangled vegetation, esp. in tropics, (**law of the ~,** state of ruthless competition); scene of ruthless struggle for survival (*blackboard jungle* in schools, *concrete jungle* in cities); wild tangled mass; ~ **fever,** severe form of malaria; ~ **gym,** structure of bars for children to climb on in playing; hence **jŭ'ngl**ED[2] (-eld), **jŭ'ng**LY[2], (-ngg-) *adjs*. [f. Hindi *jangal* f. Skr. *jangala* desert, forest]

ju'nior (jōō'-) *a*. & *n*. **1.** *a*. Less advanced in age; inferior in age or standing *to*; of less or least standing, of lower or lowest position, (*junior partner*); (of school) having pupils in a younger age-range; *of year before final year at university, high school, etc.; ***~ college** (offering two-year course esp. in preparation for completion at senior college); ‖~ **combination** or **common room** (for use by junior members of college); hence **~ITY** (-ŏ'r-) *n*. **2.** (Appended to name for distinction, esp. of son from father) junior to another of same name. **3.** *n*. Junior person; one's inferior in length of service etc. (*is my junior*); junior student; *(colloq.) the son in a family. [L, compar. of *juvenis* young]

ju'niorate (jōō'-) *n*. (In Society of Jesus etc.)

two-years' course attended by those intending to enter priesthood. [f. prec. + -ATE[1]]

ju'nĭper (jōō'-) *n.* Evergreen shrub of genus *Juniperus*, esp. one with prickly leaves and dark purple berry-like cones yielding **oil of ~** (used in medicine and in flavouring gin etc.). [ME, f. L *juniperus*]

jŭnk[1] *n.*, & *v.t.* **1.** *n.* Old cables or ropes cut up for oakum etc.; discarded material, rubbish; ||lump, chunk; (Naut.) hard salt meat; lump of tissue in sperm whale, containing spermaceti; (sl.) narcotic drug, esp. heroin, whence ~'IE *n.*, drug addict; ***~ mail,** unsolicited advertising matter sent by post; **~-shop** (selling cheap second-hand goods or (derog.) antiques). **2.** *v.t.* *Discard as junk. [ME, of unkn. orig.]

jŭnk[2] *n.* Flat-bottomed sailing vessel used in China seas, with prominent stem and lugsails. [f. obs. F *juncque*, Port. *junco*, or Du. *jonk*, f. Jav. *djong*]

junker (yŏŏ'ngker) *n.* (Hist.) Young German nobleman; member of exclusive (Prussian) aristocratic party. [G, earlier *junkher* (f. OHG as YOUNG, HERR); cf. YOUNKER]

jŭ'nkėt *n.*, & *v.i.* **1.** *n.* Dish of sweetened and flavoured curds, often with fruit or cream; feast; *pleasure outing; *official's tour at public expense. **2.** *v.i.* Feast, picnic; hence ~ING[1] *n.* [ME *jonket*, f. OF *jonquette* rush-basket (*jonc* rush f. L *juncus*)]

Ju'nō (jōō'-) *n.* (*pl.* ~s). Woman of stately beauty; hence ~E'SQUE *a.* [L, goddess of marriage, wife of Jupiter]

Junr. *abbr.* Junior.

jŭ'nta *n.* **1.** Body of persons acting towards common aim, esp. political clique or faction after revolution or *coup d'état*. **2.** Deliberative or administrative council in Spain or Italy. [Sp. & Port., f. L *juncta*, fem. p.p. (as JOIN)]

jŭ'ntō *n.* (*pl.* ~s). = prec. 1. [erron. f. prec.]

Ju'pĭter (jōō'-) *n.* Largest planet of solar system. [ME, f. L *Jup(p)iter* king of the gods (OL *Jovis pater*; cf. JOVE, PATER)]

jur'al (joor'-) *a.* Of law, of (moral) rights and obligations. [f. L *jus juris* law, right + -AL]

Jură'ssic (joor-) *a.* & *n.* (Geol.) (Of the) middle mesozoic period or system, with prevalence of oolitic limestone as in Jura Mountains. [f. F *jurassique* (*Jura*); cf. *liassic*, *Triassic*]

||**jur'at[1]** (joor'-) *n.* Municipal officer (esp. of Cinque Ports) like alderman; honorary judge or magistrate in Channel Is. [ME, f. med. L *juratus* p.p. (as n.) of L *jurare* swear]

jur'at[2] (joor'-) *n.* Statement of circumstances in which affidavit was made. [f. L *juratum* neut. p.p. (as n.); see prec.]

jurĭ'dĭcal (joor-) *a.* Of judicial proceedings; relating to the law. [f. L *juridicus* (*jus juris* law, *-dicus* saying f. *dicere* say) + -AL]

jurĭsconsŭ'lt (joor-) *n.* One learned in law, jurist. [f. L *jurisconsultus* (*jus juris* law, *consultus* skilled; see CONSULT)]

jurĭsdĭ'ction (joor-) *n.* Administration of justice (*over* or *of*); legal or other authority; extent of this, territory it extends over; hence ~AL *a.* [ME *jure-*, *juri-*, *jurisdiccioun* f. OF *jure-*, *juridiction* & f. L *jurisdictio* (as prec.; see DICTION)]

jurĭspru'd|ence (joorĭsprōō'-) *n.* **1.** Science or philosophy of human law; hence **~ĕ'ntIAL** (-ōōdĕ'nshal) *a.* **2.** Skill in law; so ~ENT *a.* & *n.* [f. LL *jurisprudentia* (as prec., L *prudentia* knowledge; see PRUDENCE)]

jur'ist (joor'-) *n.* One versed in law; legal writer; student of or graduate in law; *lawyer; hence ~IC(AL) (-ĭ's-) *adjs.* [f. F *juriste* or f. med. L *jurista* (*jus juris* law; see -IST)]

jur'or (joor-) *n.* Member of jury; one who takes an oath (cf. NON*juror*). [ME, f. AF *jurour*, OF *jureor* f. L *jurator -oris* (*jurare -at-* swear; see -OR)]

jur'ȳ (joor'ĭ) *n.* **1.** Body of persons sworn to render verdict on question submitted to them in court of justice or coroner's court; GRAND *jury*; **petty** or **trial ~** (of 12 persons who try final issue of fact in civil or criminal cases and pronounce verdict); **special ~** (of persons of certain station in society, opp. **common ~**); **~ of matrons** (Hist., in cases where pregnancy was pleaded to obtain stay of execution). **2.** Body of persons selected to award prizes in competition. **3.** **~-box,** enclosure for jury in court; **~man, ~woman,** member of jury. [ME, f. AF & OF *juree* oath, inquiry, f. *jurata* fem. p.p. (as n.) of L *jurare* swear; cf. -Y[4]]

jur'ȳ-|mast (joor'ĭmahst) *n.* (Naut.) Temporary mast in place of broken or lost one; so **~-rigged** etc. of other makeshifts. [perh. f. **iuerie* f. OF *ajurie* aid]

jŭ'ssive *a.* (Gram.) Expressing a command. [f. L *jubēre juss-* command + -IVE]

jŭst[1] *a.* (Of person or conduct) equitable, fair, (*to* person etc.; *the* SLEEP[1] *of the just*); (of treatment etc.) deserved (*a just reward*); (of feelings, opinions, etc.) well-grounded (*just resentment, fear*); right in amount etc., proper; hence ~'LY[2] *adv.*, ~'NESS *n.* [ME, f. OF *juste* f. L *justus* (*jus* right)]

jŭst[2] *adv.* **1.** Exactly (*just at that spot*; *just there*; *just three o'clock*; *just then*; *come just as you are*; *just as I opened the door*; *it is just as you say, just what I want*); (w. interrog. wds asking for precise information: *just how did you do it?*; *I wonder just how good he is*); **~ about,** (colloq.) almost (exactly), almost completely; **that is ~ it** (precisely the point in question); **~ so,** (1) exactly arranged (*she likes everything just so*), (2) it is exactly as you say. **2.** Barely, no more than, (*I just managed it*; ||*I just saw him*; (*wait*) *just a minute, please*). **3.** Exactly or nearly at that or this moment (||*I have just seen him*; **I just saw him*); **~ now,** (1) at this moment, (2) a little time ago. **4.** (colloq.) Simply, merely, (*it's just that I don't like him*; *just* (*you*) *wait till I catch you!*; *we are just good friends*; *it just doesn't make sense*; *just listen to that cheering!*); **~ in case,** as a precaution. **5.** (colloq.) Positively (*it is just splendid*); quite (*not just yet*; *it is just as well that I checked*); (sl.) really, indeed, (*won't I just give him a pasting!*). [ME, f. prec.]

jŭst[3]. See JOUST.

jŭ'stice *n.* **1.** Just conduct; fairness; exercise of authority in maintenance of right; **poetic(al) ~,** due allocation of reward of virtue and punishment of vice; ROUGH *justice*. **2.** Judicial proceedings (*was duly brought to justice*; *Court of Justice*); ***Department of J~** (headed by Attorney-General). **3.** Magistrate; judge, esp. (in England) of Supreme Court of Judicature, whence ~SHIP (-s-sh-) *n.*; LORD *Justice* (*of Appeal, Clerk, General*); ||**Mr. J~,** form of address or reference to judge; **J~ of the Peace,** lay magistrate appointed to preserve peace in county, town, etc. **4.** **Do ~ to,** treat fairly, show due appreciation of; **do oneself ~,** perform in manner worthy of one's abilities; **in ~ to,** out of fairness to; **with ~,** reasonably. [ME f. OF, f. L *justitia* (as JUST[1]; see -ICE)]

jŭstĭ'ciable (-shya-) *a.* Subject to jurisdiction. [OF, f. *justicier* bring to trial f. med. L *justitiare* (as prec.); see -ABLE]

jŭstĭ'ciar (-shyer) *n.* Chief political and judicial officer under Norman and early Plantagenet kings. [as foll.; see -AR[2]]

jŭstĭ'ciarȳ (-shyerĭ) *n.* & *a.* **1.** *n.* Administrator of justice; = prec.; **Court of J~,** supreme criminal court in Scotland. **2.** *a.* Of the administration of justice. [f. med. L *justitiarius* f. L *justitia*; see JUSTICE, -ARY[1]]

jŭ'stĭfi|able *a.* That can be legally or morally justified (*justifiable* HOMICIDE); hence ~ABI'LITY *n.*, ~**ab**LY[2] *adv.* [F (*justifier*; see foll., -ABLE)]

jŭ'stĭ|fȳ *v.t.* Show the justice or rightness of (person, act, etc.); vindicate, (of circumstances, esp. in *pass.*) be such as to justify; (Theol.) declare (person) free from penalty of sin on ground of Christ's righteousness or (R.C.) of the infusion of grace; (Print.) adjust (line of type) to fill a space neatly; demonstrate correctness of (assertion etc.); adduce adequate grounds for (conduct, claim, etc.); **~fy bail,** show by oath of person furnishing bail that he has sufficient funds to do so; so ~FICA'TION *n.*, **~fĭcāt**ORY *a.* [ME, f. F *justifier* f. LL *justificare* do justice to f. L *justus* JUST[1]; see -FY]

jŭt *n.*, & *v.i.* (**-tt-**). **1.** *n.* Projection, protruding point. **2.** *v.i.* Protrude, project (often *out, forth*). [var. of JET[2,3]]

jute[1] (jōōt) *n.* Fibre from bark of E. Ind. plants of genus *Corchorus*, used for sacking, mats, cords, etc. [f. Bengali *jhōṭo* f. Skr. *jūṭa* = *jaṭā* braid of hair]

Jut|e[2] (jōōt) *n.* Member of Low German tribe that settled in Britain in 5th–6th c.; hence ~'ISH[1] *a.* [repr. med. L *Jutae, Juti,* in OE *Eotas, Iotas* = Icel. *Iótar* people of Jutland in Denmark]

juvenĕ'sc|ence (jōō-) *n.* (Transition from infancy to) youth; so ~ENT *a.* [f. L *juvenescere* reach age of youth (*juvenis* young); see -ENCE]

ju'venīle (jōō'-) *a.* & *n.* **1.** *a.* Young, youthful; suited to or characteristic of youth; ~ **court** (for trial of persons below specified age); ~ **delinquent,** offender below age of legal responsibility; ~ **delinquency,** offences by such; hence or cogn. ~LY[2] (-l-lĭ) *adv.*, **juvenĭ'l**ITY (jōō-) *n.* **2.** *n.* Young person; (Commerc.) book intended for young people; actor playing part of youthful person. [f. L *juvenilis* (as prec.; see -IL)]

juvenĭ'lĭa (jōō-) *n. pl.* Works produced by author or artist in youth. [L, neut. pl. of *juvenilis* (see prec.)]

jŭxtapō'se (-z) *v.t.* Place (things) side by side; place (thing) thus *to* or *with* another; so **jŭxta**POSI'TION (-z-) *n.* [f. F *juxtaposer* f. L *juxta* next; see POSE[1]]

K

K, k, (kā) *n.* (*pl.* **Ks** *or* **K's**). Eleventh letter of alphabet.

K. *abbr.* kelvin(s); King('s); Köchel.

k *abbr.* kilo-.

K *symb.* potassium. [f. mod. L *kalium* (as KALI; see -IUM)]

Ka'aba (kah'*aba*) *n.* Sacred building at Mecca, Muslim Holy of Holies containing sacred black stone. [f. Arab. *ka'ba*]

kă'bbala. Var. of CABBALA.

kabŏ'b. Var. of KEBAB.

kabu'kĭ (-ōō'-) *n.* Traditional popular Japanese drama with highly stylized song etc., acted by males only. [Jap. (*ka* song, *bu* dance, *ki* art)]

Kabȳ'le *n.* Member or language of Berber tribe of Algeria, Morocco, and Tunis. [f. Arab. *ḳabā'il* tribes]

kachi'na (-ē'-) *n.* Amer. Ind. ancestral spirit; ~ (**dancer**), one who represents kachina in ceremonial dances; ~ **doll,** wooden doll representing kachina. [Hopi, = supernatural]

Kă'ddĭsh *n.* Jewish mourner's prayer; doxology in the synagogue service. [f. Aram. *ḳaddîš* holy]

kadi. Var. of CADI.

***kă'ffeeklătsch** (-fāklăch) *n.* Meeting for informal conversation and drinking of coffee. [G (*kaffee* coffee, *klatsch* gossip)]

Kă'ffir, (arch.) **Că'ffre** (-*fer*), *n.* Member or language of a S. Afr. people of Bantu family; (derog.) Bantu inhabitant of S. Africa; **k~ (corn)**, E. Afr. variety of sorghum, grown also in other dry regions; ~ **lily,** S. Afr. herbaceous plant (*Clivia miniata*) with showy flowers. [f. Arab. *kāfir* infidel (*kafara* not believe)]

kaffiyeh. Var. of KEFFIYEH.

Kă'fir *n.* Native of Kafiristan in central Asia. [f. as KAFFIR]

Kăfkaĕ'sque (-sk) *a.* Resembling the writings of Kafka, esp. in nightmare quality. [f. F. *Kafka*, Austrian novelist d. 1924 + -ESQUE]

kă'ftan. See CAFTAN.

ka'gō (kah'-) *n.* (*pl.* ~s). Japanese basket-work palanquin slung on pole. [f. Jap. *kango*, of Chin. orig.]

kai'l(yard). See KALE.

kai'nĭt(e) (kī'n-) *n.* Hydrated magnesium and potassium chloride and sulphate, used as fertilizer. [G *kainit* f. Gk *kainos* new; see -ITE[1]]

kai'ser (kī'z-) *n.* (Hist.) Emperor, esp. German Emperor, Emperor of Austria, or head of Holy Roman Empire; hence ~SHIP *n.* [in mod. E f. G *kaiser* and Du. *keizer*; in ME f. OE *cāsere* f. Gmc adoption (thr. Gk *kaisar*) of L CAESAR]

ka'ka (kah'-) *n.* Large olive-brown New Zealand parrot; so **~pō** *n.* (*pl.* ~s), New Zealand owl-like nocturnal parrot. [Maori (*po* = night)]

kăkėmō'nō *n.* (*pl.* ~s). Japanese wall-picture (usu. painted or inscribed on silk or paper and mounted on rollers). [Jap. (*kake-* hang, *mono* thing)]

kala-azâr' (kah-) *n.* Infectious disease of oriental tropics, caused by protozoan parasite *Leishmania donovani* and transmitted by bite of fly. [Assamese (*kālā* black, *āzār* disease)]

kāle, kail, *n.* **1.** Variety of cabbage, esp. one (**curly** ~) with wrinkled leaves and no compact head; **Scotch** ~, kind with purplish leaves; SEA-*-kale*. **2.** Broth made of this or other vegetables; *(sl.) money. **3.** **~'yard,** (Sc.) kitchen-garden; **~yard school,** writers of fiction describing, with much use of the vernacular, everyday life in Scotland. [ME; northern form of COLE]

kalei'do|scōpe (-lī'd-) *n.* Tube through which are seen symmetrical figures, produced by reflections of pieces of coloured glass etc., and varied by rotation of the tube; (fig.) constantly changing group of bright or interesting objects; hence **~scŏ'p**IC(AL) *adjs.* [f. Gk *kalos* beautiful + *eidos* form + -SCOPE]

kalends. Var. of CALENDS.

kă'lĭ *n.* Glasswort (*Salsola kali*), from which potash was obtained. [f. Arab. *ḳali* ALKALI]

kă'lmĭa *n.* Evergreen showy-flowered N. Amer. shrub of genus *Kalmia*. [mod. L, f. P. *Kalm*, Sw. botanist d. 1779 + -IA[1]]

Kă'lmŭck *a.* & *n.* (Member or language) of a Buddhist Mongol people living in western U.S.S.R. [f. Russ. *kalmyk*]

ka'lŏng (kah'-) *n.* Indonesian frugivorous fox-bat, largest known bat. [Malay]

kă'lpa *n.* (Hinduism). Great age of the world; day of Brahma (4,320,000,000 years), after which world is destroyed. [Skr.]

Ka'ma (kah'-) *n.* Hindu god of love. [Skr.]

kāme *n.* Short ridge of sand and gravel deposited from water of melted glacier. [Sc. form of COMB[1]]

kămikā'zė *n.* Japanese aircraft laden with explosives and deliberately crashed by its pilot on its target; its pilot. [Jap. (*kami* divinity, *kaze* wind)]

kă'mpŏng *n.* Malayan enclosure or village. [Malay; cf. COMPOUND[3]]

ka'na (kah'-) *n.* One of various Japanese syllabaries. [Jap.]

kană'ka (*or* -ah'-) *n.* South Sea Islander, esp. one formerly employed on forced labour in Australia. [Hawaiian, = man]

Kănarē'se (-z) *n.* (*pl.* same). (Member of) Dravidian people living in western India; their language. [f. *Kanara* in India + -ESE]

kăngaroō' (-ngg-) *n.* **1.** Marsupial mammal of genus *Macropus* with strongly developed hindquarters and great leaping-power, found in Australia, Tasmania, etc.; ||Australian; ~ **dog** (for hunting kangaroos); ~ **hare,** ~ **mouse,** small marsupials like hare and mouse; ~ **paw,** Austral. herb with green and red woolly flowers; **~-rat,** (1) = RAT[1] *kangaroo,* (2) pouched nocturnal rodent of S.W. United States. **2.** ||~ **closure** (when chairman in committee selects some amendments for discussion and excludes others); ~ **court,** improperly constituted illegal court held by strikers etc. [perh. f. Aboriginal name]

kă'njĭ *n.* Japanese writing using Chinese characters. [Jap.]

Kă'nnada *n.* Kanarese language. [f. Kanarese *kannada*]

kanoō'n *n.* Instrument like zither, with fifty to sixty strings. [f. Pers. or Arab. *ḳānūn*]

Kans. *abbr.* Kansas.

Kă'ntĭan *a.* Of Kant or his philosophy esp. of a priori categories of thought whereby sense-impressions are co-ordinated; hence ~ISM (3) *n.* [f. I. *Kant,* Ger. philosopher d. 1804 + -IAN]

KANU (kah'noō) *n.* Kenya African National Union. [abbr.]

kā'olĭn *n.* Fine white clay produced by decomposition of felspar, used in making porcelain; hence ~IZE (3) *v.t.* [F, f. Chin. *kao-ling,* name of mountain (*kao* high, *ling* hill)]

kā'ŏn *n.* (Phys.) One of several mesons having mass several times that of pions. [f. K (letter used as symbol for the particle) + -ON]

kăpě'llmeister (-mī-) *n.* (*pl.* same). Conductor of orchestra, opera, choir, etc.; ~ **music,** uninspired music in routine style. [G (*kapelle* court orchestra f. It. *cappella* CHAPEL, *meister* master)]

kā'pŏk *n.* Fine cotton-like material surrounding seeds of a tropical tree (*Ceiba pentandra*), used for stuffing cushions etc. [ult. f. Malay *kāpoq*]

kă'ppa *n.* Tenth Greek letter (Κ, κ) = k. [Gk]

kăpu't (-oŏ't) *pred. a.* (sl.) Done for, smashed, ruined, out of order. [f. G *kaputt*]

kărabi'ner (-ē'-) *n.* Coupling link with safety closure, used by mountaineers. [G, lit. 'carbine']

Kār'aīte *n.* Member of Jewish sect in Crimea etc. that rejects rabbinical tradition and interprets scriptures literally. [f. Heb. *ḳᵉrā'îm* scripturalists (*ḳārā* read) + -ITE[1]]

karakul. See CARACUL.

***kă'rat.** Var. of CARAT (esp. of gold quality).

kara'tė (-ah'-) *n.* Japanese system of unarmed combat using hands, feet, etc., as weapons. [Jap. (*kara* empty, *te* hand)]

kār'm|a *n.* (Buddhism & Hinduism). Sum of person's actions in one of his successive states of existence, viewed as deciding his fate for the next; destiny; hence ~IC *a.* [Skr., = action, fate]

karŏ'ss *n.* Mantle of animals' skins with the hair on, used by S. Afr. tribesmen. [f. Afrik. *karos,* of uncert. orig.]

kă'rrĭ *n.* (Hard dark-red timber) of tall W. Austral. tree (*Eucalyptus diversicolor*). [Aboriginal]

kar(r)oō' *n.* Elevated plateau of clayey soil in S. Africa, waterless in dry season. [Hottentot]

kārst *n.* Region with underground drainage and many cavities etc. caused by dissolution of rock. [name of such region in Yugoslavia]

kārt *n.* = GO[1]-*kart.* [abbr.]

kārtě'll. Var. of CARTEL.

kă'ryo- *comb. form.* (Biol.) Nucleus of cell, as: **~plasm,** protoplasm of cell nucleus; **~type,** character of cell nucleus as determined by nature of all chromosomes, systematized diagram of chromosomes. [f. Gk *karuon* kernel + -O-]

kasbah. See CASBAH.

kătabă'tĭc *a.* (Meteorol.) (Of wind) caused by air flowing downwards; cf. ANABATIC. [f. Gk *katabatikos* (*katabainō* go down; see -IC)]

kată'bolĭsm. Var. of CATABOLISM.

kătaka'na (-ah'-) *n.* Angular form of kana. [Jap., = side kana]

kătathermŏ'mėter *n.* Instrument to determine cooling of air or rate of air-flow past evaporating liquid etc. [f. as CATA- + THERMOMETER]

kă'thōde. Var. of CATHODE.

kā'tўdĭd *n.* Large green grasshopper common in U.S. [imit. of sound it makes]

kaur'ĭ (kowr'ĭ) *n.* Coniferous tree (*Agathis australis*) of New Zealand, yielding valuable timber and a resin, **~-gum.** [Maori]

ka'va (kah'-) *n.* (Intoxicating beverage from crushed roots of) a Polynesian shrub, *Piper methysticum.* [Polynesian]

ka'wa-kawa (kah'wakah-) *n.* Ornamental N.Z. shrub (*Piper excelsum*) with aromatic leaves. [Maori]

kay'ăk (kī'-) *n.* Eskimo one-man canoe of light wooden framework covered with sealskins; small covered canoe resembling this. [Eskimo]

kay'ō *v.t.,* & *n.* (*pl.* **~s**). (colloq.) **1.** *v.t.* Knock out, stun by blow. **2.** *n.* Knock-out. [repr. pr. of *K.O.*]

kazoō' *n.* Toy musical instrument into which player sings or hums. [19th c., app. w. ref. to sound produced]

K.B. *abbr.* King's Bench.

||**K.B.E.** *abbr.* Knight Commander (of the Order) of the British Empire.

K.C. *abbr.* King's College; King's Counsel.

kc(/s) *abbr.* kilocycles (per second).

||**K.C.B.** *abbr.* Knight Commander (of the Order) of the Bath.

||**K.C.I.E.** *abbr.* Knight Commander (of the Order) of the Indian Empire.

||**K.C.M.G.** *abbr.* Knight Commander (of the Order) of St. Michael & St. George.

||**K.C.S.I.** *abbr.* Knight Commander (of the Order) of the Star of India.

||**K.C.V.O.** *abbr.* Knight Commander of the Royal Victorian Order.

K.D. *abbr.* knocked down.

K.E. *abbr.* kinetic energy.

ke'a (kā'a) *n.* Green parrot (*Nestor notabilis*) of New Zealand said to attack sheep for their kidney-fat. [Maori, imit.]

kėbă'b (*or* -ah'b) *n.* (usu. in *pl.*) Meat cooked in small pieces with ginger, garlic, etc., usu. on skewer. [f. Urdu f. Arab. *kabāb*]

kěck *v.i.* Make sound as if about to vomit; ~ **at,** reject (food etc.) with loathing. [imit.]

kědge *v.* & *n.* **1.** *v.i.* Move ship by means of hawser attached to small anchor; (of ship) move thus. **2.** *v.t.* Move (ship) thus. **3.** *n.* ~(**-anchor**), small anchor for this purpose. [perh. spec. use of obs. *cagge*, dial. *cadge* bind, tie]

kĕ'dgeree (*or* -ē') *n.* Indian dish of rice, split pulse, onions, eggs, etc.; European dish of fish, rice, eggs, etc. [f. Hindi *khichṛī*, Skr. *k'rsara* dish of rice and sesame]

keek *v.i.*, & *n.* (Sc.) Peep. [ME *kike*; cf. MDu., MLG *kiken*]

keel[1] *n.* & *v.* **1.** *n.* Lowest longitudinal timber of vessel, on which framework of the whole is built up; combination of iron plates serving same purpose in iron vessel; (poet.) ship; EVEN[2] *keel*; **false** ~ (attached to bottom of true keel to protect it); ~**-blocks** (on which keel rests during building etc.); ~**-haul,** haul (person) under keel as punishment, (fig.) rebuke severely. **2.** Ridge along breastbone of many birds; (Bot.) prow-shaped pair of petals in corolla, etc. **3.** Hence ~'LESS (-l-l-) *a.* **4.** *v.t.* & *i.* ~ (**over**), (cause to) turn over or fall down. **5.** *v.t.* Turn (ship) keel upwards. [ME *kele*, f. ON *kjölr* f. Gmc **keluz*]

||**keel**[2] *n.* Flat-bottomed vessel, esp. of kind used on Tyne etc. for loading colliers; amount carried by this. [ME *kele* f. MLG *kēl*, MDu. *kiel*, ship, boat, = OE *cēol* etc. f. Gmc **keulaz*]

kee'lĭvīne *n.* (Sc.) Lead pencil. [18th c., of unkn. orig.]

kee'lson. See KELSON.

keen[1] *n.* Irish funeral song accompanied with wailing. [f. Ir. *caoine* (as foll.)]

keen[2] *v.* **1.** *v.i.* Utter the keen. **2.** *v.t.* Bewail (person) thus; utter in wailing tone. **3.** Hence ~'ER[1] *n.*, (esp.) professional mourner at Irish funerals. [f. Ir. *caoinim* wail]

keen[3] *a.* **1.** Having sharp edge or point; (of edge etc.) sharp. **2.** (Of sound, light, etc.) penetrating, vivid, strong; (of wind, frost, etc.) piercingly cold; (of pain etc.) acute, bitter; ||(of price) exceptionally low because of competition; *(colloq.) excellent. **3.** (Of person, desire, interest) eager, ardent, (*keen sportsman*; ~ **as mustard,** enthusiastic [w. later pun on *Keen's mustard*]; ~ **on,** (colloq.) much attracted by (person, thing, do*ing*). **4.** (Of eyes, sight, smell) sharp, highly sensitive; intellectually acute. **5.** Hence ~'LY[2] *adv.*, ~'NESS (-n-n-) *n.* [OE *cēne*, = OHG *kuoni*, ON *kœnn* f. Gmc **kōnjaz*]

keep[1] *v.* (**kept**). **1.** *v.t.* Pay due regard to, observe, stand by, (law, promise, faith, treaty, appointment; *keep the* PEACE, one's WORD[1] 5). **2.** Celebrate (feast, ceremony, etc.). **3.** Guard, protect, (person, as *God keep you!*; fortress, town, etc., goal at football etc.; *keep* WICKET); (abs.) act as wicket-keeper. **4.** Have charge of; retain possession of (*you may keep the change*), not lose or destroy; **you can** ~ **it,** (colloq.) I do not want what is being offered. **5.** Maintain (place etc.) in proper order (*keep* HOUSE[1]; *keep open* HOUSE[1]); carry on, manage, (shop etc.); maintain (diary, accounts, books) by making requisite entries. **6.** Provide for sustenance of (family, one*self*, etc.); own and manage (cows, bees, etc.); maintain (woman) as mistress. **7.** Have (commodity) habitually on sale. **8.** Preserve in being, continue to have or do, (*keep* COMPANY, PACE[1], STEP[2], TIME[1], GUARD[1], *a* LOOK-*out*, WATCH[1], ORDER[1] 12). **9.** Maintain in proper or specified condition (often in spec. senses: *keep the* BALL[1] *rolling*, POT[1] *boiling*, one's COUNTENANCE[1], one's HAIR *on*, one's HEAD[1]); ~ one's **balance,** not lose it (lit. or fig.); *keep in* MIND[1]. **10.** Detain (person *in prison*, *in custody*, etc.; *what kept you so long?*); restrain (person, thing, one*self*, *from* do*ing*, *from* thing). **11.** Reserve (thing *for* future time etc.). **12.** Conceal (*keep* one's COUNSEL[1], *a secret*). **13.** Continue to follow (way, course); ~ **track of,** follow the course or development of. **14.** Remain in (one's *bed* or *room*, *the* HOUSE[1], one's *seat*); retain one's place in (the saddle, field, the stage, one's ground, etc.) against opposition; ~ one's **feet,** not fall. **15.** *v.i.* Remain (indoors etc.); ||(colloq., esp. Camb. Univ.) reside (*where do you keep?*). **16.** Remain in specified condition (*keep fit*, *in good health*, *in* TOUCH[2] *with*, *cool*, (colloq.) *friends*; *I hope it keeps fine*; **how are you** ~**ing?,** what is your state of health?); continue in specified direction, course, or action, (*keep straight on for two miles*; *keep* (*to the*) *left*; *she keeps giggling*). **17.** (Of food, etc.) remain in good condition, not decay; (fig., of news etc.) admit of being reserved for later occasion. **18.** (w. *preps.*): ~ (work, cause to work, persistently) **at**; ~ (abstain or refrain) **from**; ~ **off,** avoid (subject etc.), not go on (*the grass* etc.), not (allow to) come close to or touch; ~ **to,** adhere to (course, promise), confine oneself to; ~ (thing etc.) *to* one*self*, (1) refuse to share it with others, (2) not allow others to know of it; ~ one*self to* one*self*, avoid society. **19.** (w. *advs.*): ~ **away,** avoid coming, prevent from coming; ~ **back,** hold back, retard progress of, conceal, stay at a distance (*from*); ~ **down,** hold in subjection, keep low in amount, not vomit (food eaten), (Mil.) lie low in skirmishing; ~ **in,** confine, restrain, (feelings etc.), confine (schoolchild) after hours, keep (fire) burning, remain indoors, remain on good terms *with*; ~ one's HAND[1] *in*; ~ **off,** ward off, avert, not (allow to) come close or touch; ~ **on,** continue to hold, use, show, employ, etc., continue (do*ing*), ||nag (*at*); ~ **out,** not let enter, stay outside; ~ **together,** remain, cause to remain, together; ~ **under,** hold in subjection; ~ **up,** prevent (one's spirits, prices, etc.) from sinking, maintain (*keep* one's END[1] *up*; ~ *it up*, not relax or slacken), keep in repair, in efficient or proper state, etc., (*keep up appearances*; *keep up your Greek*), carry on (correspondence etc.), cause (person) to remain out of bed at night, not give way, proceed at equal pace *with* (~ **up with the Joneses,** strive to remain on terms of obvious social equality with one's neighbours). [OE *cēpan*, of unkn. orig.]

keep[2] *n.* **1.** (Hist.) Tower, stronghold, donjon. **2.** Maintenance, food required for this, (*you don't earn your keep*); pasture. **3. For** ~**s,** (colloq.) permanently. [f. prec.]

kee'per *n.* In vbl senses; = GAME[1]*keeper*, WICKET-*keeper*; custodian of museum, art gallery, forest, etc.; (arch.) lunatic's attendant; ring that keeps another, esp. wedding-ring, on the finger; bar of soft iron across poles of horse-shoe magnet to maintain its strength; fruit etc. that keeps (sense 17) well. [ME, f. KEEP[1] + -ER[1]]

kee'pĭng *n.* In vbl senses; custody, charge, (*in safe keeping*; *in his keeping*); agreement, harmony, (orig. esp. of painting; *in*, *out of*, ~ (*with*)). [ME, f. KEEP[1] + -ING[1]]

kee'psāke *n.* Thing kept for sake, or in remembrance, of giver. [f. KEEP[1] + SAKE[1]]

kee'shŏnd (kā's-h-) *n.* (Breed of) Dutch dog with thick curly hair like large Pomeranian. [Du.]

kĕf *n.* Drowsy state produced by bhang etc.; enjoyment of idleness; substance smoked to produce kef. [f. Arab. *kayf* enjoyment, well-being]

kĕffi'yeh (-fē'yā) *n.* Bedouin Arab's kerchief worn as head-dress. [f. Arab. *keffiya*, *kūfiyya*, perh. f. LL *cofea* COIF]

kĕg *n.* Small barrel, usu. of less than ||10 or *30 gal. [f. ME *cag*, f. ON *kaggi*, of unkn. orig.]

*kĕ'gler *n.* Player at skittles or similar game. [G (*kegel* skittle)]
kĕlp *n.* **1.** Large brown seaweed burnt for ash. **2.** Calcined ashes of seaweed used because of the sodium carbonate, iodine, etc., they contain, formerly in making soap and glass. [ME *cūlp(e)*, of unkn. orig.]
kĕ'lpĭe *n.* **1.** (Sc.) Water-spirit, usu. in form of horse, reputed to delight in the drowning of travellers etc. **2.** Austral. sheep-dog orig. bred from Scottish collie. [18th c., of unkn. orig.]
kĕ'lson, kee'lson, *n.* Line of timber fastening ship's floor-timbers to keel. [ME *kelswayn*, *-sweyn*, *-syng*, perh. f. LG *kielswīn* (*kiel* KEEL[1], prob. *swīn* SWINE used as name of a timber)]
Kĕlt[1]. Var. of CELT[1].
kĕlt[2] *n.* (Sc.) Salmon or sea trout after spawning. [ME; orig. unkn.]
kĕ'lter. See KILTER.
kĕ'lvĭn *n.* Degree (equal to Celsius degree) of **K~ scale** of temperature (with zero at absolute zero). [f. Lord *Kelvin*, Brit. physicist d. 1907]
kĕmp *n.* Coarse hair in wool; hence ~'Y[2] *a.* [ME, f. ON *kampr* beard, whisker]
kĕmpt *a.* Combed, neatly kept. [p.p. of (now dial.) *kemb* COMB[2], f. OE *cemban* f. Gmc **kambjan* (as COMB[1])]
kĕn[1] *n.* Range of sight or knowledge (*in*, *out of*, *beyond*, one's *ken*). [f. foll.]
kĕn[2] *v.t.* (**-nn-**; **kent**). (Sc. & N. Engl.) Recognize at sight; know (person, thing, fact, *that* etc.). [OE *cennan*, = OS *kennian*, OHG *kennen*, ON *kenna*, Goth. *kannjan* f. Gmc. **kann-* know, CAN[2]]
kenă'f *n.* (Fibre, used like jute, of) Asian plant (*Hibiscus cannabinus*). [Pers.]
kĕ'nnel[1] *n.* & *v.* (||**-ll-**). **1.** *n.* Small structure for shelter of house-dog or hounds; (in *pl.*) boarding establishment for dogs; pack of dogs; mean dwelling. **2.** *v.i.* Live in, go to, kennel. **3.** *v.t.* Put into, keep in, kennel. [ME, f. AF **kenil*, OF *chenil* f. med. L **canile* f. L *canis* dog]
kĕ'nnel[2] *n.* Gutter in street etc. [earlier *cannel* f. ONF *canel* CHANNEL[1]]
kĕ'nnĭng *n.* Periphrastic expression in OE and ON poetry, e.g. 'oar-steed' = ship. [ME, = 'teaching' etc., f. KEN[2] + -ING[1]]
***kē'nō** *n.* (*pl.* ~**s**). Game of chance resembling bingo. [19th c.; orig. unkn.]
kėnō'sĭs *n.* (Theol.) Renunciation of divine nature, at least in part, by Christ in the Incarnation; hence **kėnŏ'tɪc** *a.* [Gk *kenōsis* (*kenoō* to empty f. *kenos* empty; see -OSIS)]
kĕ'notrŏn *n.* (Electr.) Type of high-vacuum diode rectifier. [f. Gk *kenos* empty + -o- + -TRON]
kĕ'nspĕckle *a.* (Sc.) Conspicuous. [f. *kenspeck*, of Scand. orig. (cogn. w. KEN[2]) + -LE 1]
kĕnt. See KEN[2].
Kĕ'ntĭsh *a.* Of Kent, England; ||~ **fire,** prolonged volley of rhythmic applause or demonstration of dissent; ~ **man** (esp. born W. of Medway, opp. *man of Kent* born E.); ~ **rag,** hard compact limestone found in Kent. [OE *Centisc* (*Cent* f. L *Cantium*; see -ISH[1])]
kĕ'ntlėdge *n.* (Naut.) Pig-iron etc. used as permanent ballast. [f. F *quintelage* ballast, w. assim. to *kentle* obs. var. of QUINTAL; see -AGE]
Kĕntŭ'ckȳ *n.* ~ **Derby,** annual race for 3-year-old horses at Louisville, Kentucky. [~ in U.S., prob. f. Iroquois]
Kĕ'nyan *a.* & *n.* (Native or inhabitant) of Kenya. [f. *Kenya* in E. Africa + -AN]
kĕ'pĭ (*or* kā'-) *n.* French military cap with horizontal peak. [f. F *képi* f. Swiss G *käppi* dim. of *kappe* cap]
Kĕ'pler *n.* ~'**s laws,** three theorems about the nature of planetary motion; hence ~IAN (-ēr'-) *a.* [f. J. ~, Ger. astronomer d. 1630]
kĕpt. See KEEP[1].
kėră'mĭc. Var. of CERAMIC.
kĕ'ratĭn *n.* Protein forming the basis of horns, claws, nails, feathers, hair, etc. [f. Gk *keras keratos* horn + -IN]
kĕ'ratō-. See CERATO-.
kĕ'ratōse *a.* (Of sponge) composed of horny substance. [f. Gk *keras keratos* horn + -OSE[1]]
||**kẽrb** *n.* Stone edging to pavement or raised path; ~ **drill,** simple procedure to promote safety of pedestrian about to cross road; ~'**stone,** one of stones forming kerb; ~(*stone*) *market*, (place for) sale of securities after hours or of shares not dealt with on the Stock Exchange; ~ **weight** (of motor car without occupants or luggage). [var. of CURB]
kẽr'chief (*or* -ĭf) *n.* Cloth used to cover head; (poet.) handkerchief; hence ~ED[2] (-ft) *a.* [ME *c(o)urchef* f. AF *courchef*, OF *couvrechief* (*couvrir* COVER[1], CHIEF[1] head)]
kẽrf *n.* Slit made by cutting, esp. with saw; cut end of felled tree. [OE *cyrf* f. Gmc **kurbhiz* (as CARVE)]
kerfŭ'ffle *n.* (colloq.) Fuss, commotion. [orig. Sc.]
kẽr'mės (-z) *n.* Female of an insect, *Kermes ilicis*, formerly taken to be a berry, feeding on ~(**oak**), an evergreen oak (*Quercus coccinea*) of S. Europe and N. Africa; red dyestuff consisting of dried bodies of these; ~ (**mineral**), bright red amorphous trisulphide of antimony. [f. F *kermès* f. Arab. & Pers. *ḳirmiz*; cogn. with CRIMSON]
kẽr'mĭs *n.* Periodical fair in Holland etc., with much noisy merry-making; *charity bazaar. [Du. orig. = mass on anniversary of dedication of church, when yearly fair was held (*kerk* f. as CHURCH[1], *mis*, *misse* MASS[1])]
kẽrn[1] *n.* (Print.) Part of metal type projecting beyond body or shank; hence ~ED[2] (-nd) *a.* [perh. f. F *carne* corner f. OF *charne* f. L *cardo cardinis* hinge]
kẽrn[2], **kẽrne,** *n.* (Hist.) Light-armed Irish foot-soldier; peasant, boor. [ME, f. Ir. *ceithern*]
kẽr'nel *n.* Softer (usu. edible) part within hard shell of nut or stone-fruit; body of seed within husk etc., e.g. grain of wheat; (esp. fig.) nucleus, centre of formation, essential part. [OE *cyrnel*, dim. of CORN[1]; see -LE 1]
kĕ'rosēne, -ine (-ēn), *n.* (U.S., Austral., N.Z., or tech.) Fuel-oil obtained by distillation of petroleum or from coal or bituminous shale, paraffin oil. [irreg. f. Gk *kēros* wax + -ENE]
Kĕ'rrȳ *n.* (One of) breed of very small black dairy cattle; ~ **blue,** (breed of) terrier with silky blue-grey coat. [~ in Ireland]
kẽr'sey (-zĭ) *n.* Kind of coarse narrow cloth woven from long wool, usu. ribbed. [ME, prob. f. *K~* in Suffolk]
kẽr'seymēre (-zĭ-) *n.* Twilled fine woollen cloth. [alt. of *cassimere*, var. of CASHMERE, assim. to prec.]
kerȳ'gma *n.* (*pl.* ~**ta**). Proclamation of religious truth, esp. of the Christian gospel, opp. *didache*; hence **kĕrȳgmă'tɪc** *a.* [Gk *kērugma -matos* proclamation (*kērussō* proclaim)]
kĕ'strel *n.* Small falcon (esp. *Falco tinnunculus*) often hovering in the air with head to wind. [ME *castrell*, perh. f. F dial. *casserelle*, F *créc(er)elle*, perh. imit. of its cry]
kĕtch *n.* Two-masted fore-and-aft rigged sailing-boat with mizen-mast stepped forward of rudder. [ME *catche*, prob. f. CATCH[1,2]]
kĕ'tchup *n.* Sauce made from tomatoes, mushrooms, etc., with vinegar and other flavouring, used as condiment. [f. Chin. dial. *kōechiap* pickled-fish brine]

kē'tōne *n.* One of a class of organic compounds containing the group CO with double bond to carbon, of which acetone is the simplest. [f. G *keton* alt. of *aketon* ACETONE]

kĕ'ttle *n.* **1.** Vessel, usu. of metal with spout and handle, for boiling water in; FISH¹-*kettle*; **a (pretty) ~ of fish,** (awkward) state of affairs. **2. ~drum(mer),** (player of) hollow brass or copper hemisphere, over edge of which parchment is stretched and tuned to definite note; **~-holder,** piece of cloth etc. to protect hand from heat of kettle-handle. **3.** Hence ~FUL 2 (-telf-) *n.* [ME, f. ON *ketill* = OE *cetel, cietel,* OS *ketel,* OHG *kezzil,* Goth. *katils* f. Gmc **katilaz* f. L *catillus* dim. of *catinus* deep food-vessel]

keV *abbr.* kilo-electron-volt.

kew'pie *n.* Small chubby doll with wings and curl or topknot. [f. CUPID + -IE; ***P**]

key¹ (kē) *n.* **1.** Instrument, usu. of metal, for moving bolt of lock forwards or backwards to lock or unlock; **get** or **have the ~ of the street,** be shut out for the night, homeless; GREEK, MASTER¹, SKELETON, *key.* **2.** HOUSE¹ *of Keys*; **St. Peter's ~s,** two keys crosswise as borne in papal arms. **3.** What gives or precludes opportunity for or access to something. **4.** (in *pl.*) Ecclesiastical authority as transmitted to pope as successor of St. Peter (cf. sense 2). **5.** Place that by its position gives control of sea, territory, etc. **6.** Solution, explanation; literal translation of foreign book; first move in chess-problem solution; book of solutions of mathematical problems etc.; word or system for solving cipher or code. **7.** (Mus.) system of notes definitely related to each other, based on particular note, and predominating in a piece of music (*a study in the key of C major*); (fig.) tone, style, of thought or expression (**high ~, low ~,** with mainly bright, dark, tones, lit. or fig.). **8.** Piece of wood or metal inserted between others to secure them. **9.** Part of first coat of wall plaster passing between laths and so securing the rest; roughness of surface helping adhesion of plaster etc. **10.** Lever pressed by finger in playing organ, piano, flute, concertina, etc.; similar lever in typewriter, in punch for cards or tape, etc.; mechanical device for making or breaking electric circuit, e.g. in telegraphy. **11.** Instrument for grasping screws, pegs, nuts, etc., esp. one for winding clock etc. **12.** Samara of sycamore etc. **13. ~'bar,** rod carrying type in typewriter and moved by striking corresponding key; **~'board,** set of keys on typewriter, piano, etc.; **~-bugle** (fitted with keys to increase number of different sounds); **~'hole** (by which key is put into lock); **~ industry,** one essential to the carrying on of others, e.g. coal-mining, dyeing; **~ man** (occupying vital position in an organization); **~ map** (in bare outline, to simplify use of full map); ||**~ money,** payment demanded from incoming tenant for provision of key to premises; **~ move,** (Chess) = sense 6; **~'note,** (Mus.) note on which key is based, (fig.) prevailing tone or idea (*~note speech,* designed to set prevailing tone at conference, rally, etc.); **~-ring** (for keeping keys on); *key* SIGNATURE; **~'stone,** voussoir at summit of arch locking the whole together, (fig.) central principle etc. on which all depends; **~'way,** groove to receive key; **~'word,** (1) key to cipher etc. (see sense 6), (2) significant word used in indexing (*~word in context,* listed with words next to it in source document). **14.** Hence ~'LESS *a.* [OE *cæg(e),* = OFris. *kei, kay,* of unkn. orig.]

key² (kē) *v.t.* Fasten (*in, on,* etc.) with pin, wedge, bolt, etc.; regulate pitch of strings of (piano etc.); roughen (surface) to help adhesion of plaster etc.; identify by means of key; word (advertisement in particular periodical) so that answers to it can be identified (usu. by varying the form of address given); (fig.) **~ up,** stimulate (person *to* do, *to* condition etc.), raise, tone or standard of, brace up, raise (offer, demand, endeavour). [ME, f. prec.]

key³ (kē) *n.* Low island or reef, esp. in W. Indies. [f. Sp. *cayo* shoal, reef, infl. by QUAY]

Key'nesĭan (kā'nz-) *a.* & *n.* (Adherent) of the economic theories of Keynes, esp. regarding State control of the economy through money and taxes; hence ~ISM (3) *n.* [f. Lord *Keynes,* Brit. economist d. 1946 + -IAN]

||**K.G.** *abbr.* Knight (of the Order) of the Garter.

kg *abbr.* kilogram(s).

K.G.B. (kājēbē') *n.* U.S.S.R. secret police since 1960. [Russ., abbr. of *Komitet Gosudarstvennoĭ Bezopasnosti* State security committee]

Kgs. *abbr.* Kings (O.T.).

khă'ddar (kă'-) *n.* Indian homespun cloth. [Hindi]

kha'kĭ (kah'-) *a.* & *n.* **1.** *a.* Dust-coloured, dull brownish-yellow. **2.** *n.* Khaki fabric of twilled cotton or wool, used esp. in military dress. [f. Urdu *k̲ākī* dust-coloured (*k̲āk* dust)]

khă'msĭn (kă'-) *n.* Oppressive hot S. or S.E. wind in Egypt for about 50 days in March, April, and May. [Arab. *k̲amsīn* (*k̲amsūn* fifty)]

khan¹ (kăn *or* kahn) *n.* Title of rulers and officials in Central Asia,. Afghanistan, etc.; (Hist.) supreme ruler of Turkish, Tartar, and Mongol tribes, and emperor of China, in Middle Ages; hence ~'ATE¹ (1) *n.* [f. Turki *k̲ān* lord]

khan² (kăn *or* kahn) *n.* Caravanserai. [f. Arab. *k̲ān* inn]

Khėdī'v|e (kĭdē'v) *n.* (Hist.) Title of viceroy of Egypt under Turkish Government 1867–1914; hence ~(I)AL *adjs.* [f. F *khédive* ult. f. Pers. *k̲adīv* prince]

Khmer (kmār) *a.* & *n.* (Native or language) of ancient Khmer kingdom in S.E. Asia or of modern Cambodia. [native name]

khuskhus. Var. of CUSCUS¹.

kHz *abbr.* kilohertz.

kĭă'ng *n.* Tibetan ass with thick furry coat. [f. Tibetan *kyang*]

||**kĭ'bble¹** *n.* Iron hoisting-bucket used in mines. [f. G *kübel,* = OE *cyfel* f. med. L *cupellus* corn-measure, dim. of *cuppa* cup]

kĭ'bble² *v.t.* Grind coarsely. [18th c.; orig. unkn.]

kĭbbu'tz (-ōō'ts) *n.* (*pl.* **~im** *pr.* -ē'm). Communal esp. farming settlement in Israel; so **~nĭk** *n.,* member of kibbutz. [f. mod. Heb. *ḳibbūṣ* gathering]

kībe *n.* Ulcerated chilblain, esp. on heel. [ME, prob. f. W *cibi*]

kĭ'bĭtz (-ts; *or* -bĭ'-) *v.i.* (colloq.) Act as kibitzer. [back form. f. foll.]

kĭ'bĭtzer (-ts-; *or* -bĭ'-) *n.* (colloq.) Meddlesome person, one who gives advice gratuitously; one who watches a game of cards from behind the players; meddlesome looker-on. [f. Yiddish *kibitser* f. G *kiebitz* lapwing, busybody]

kĭ'blah (-*a*) *n.* Point to which Muslims turn at prayer, i.e. (direction of) temple at Mecca; mihrab. [f. Arab. *ḳibla* that which is opposite]

kĭ'bŏsh *n.* (sl.) Nonsense; **put the ~ on,** put an end to, finally dispose of. [19th c.; orig. unkn.]

kĭck¹ *n.* **1.** Act of kicking; **more ~s** (harshness) **than halfpence** (kindness). **2.** (colloq.) Resilience (*has no kick left*); sharp stimulant effect, pleasurable thrill, (*has some kick in it*; *get a kick out of this*; *did it for kicks*). **3.** Recoil of gun when discharged. **4.** (Footb.) ||**good, bad,** etc.,

~ (kicker); ~-**pleat** (in narrow skirt, to allow free movement); ~'**sorter,** (colloq.) device for selecting and counting electrical pulses of specified amplitudes; ~-**start(er),** lever on motor cycle etc. for starting engine by downward push with foot; ~-**turn,** form of standing turn in skiing. [f. foll.]

kĭck[2] *v.* **1.** *v.i.* Strike out with the foot (esp. *at* object etc. to be moved); *kick against the* PRICK[1]*s*; *kick over the* TRACE[2]*s*; **alive and** ~'**ing,** (colloq.) fully active. **2.** Show annoyance, dislike, etc., (*against, at,* proposal, treatment). **3.** *v.t.* Strike with foot to propel or as sign of annoyance etc.; (sl.) abandon (habit); *kick the* BUCKET[1]; *kick* one's HEEL[1]*s*. **4.** Drive, move, (thing) by kicking. **5.** (Footb.) Score (goal) by a kick. **6.** Drive forcibly and contemptuously (*out, downstairs,* etc.; ~ person **upstairs,** fig., shelve him by giving him peerage or titular promotion). **7.** ~ **about** or **around,** treat (person) roughly or scornfully, discuss (idea) unsystematically, move idly from place to place, be unused or unwanted; ~'**back,** (1) recoil, (2) payment for help in making profit or for showing favour etc.; ~-**down,** device for gear-changing in motor vehicle by full depression of accelerator; ~ **off,** remove (shoes) by kicking, (Footb.) begin game, (colloq.) start; ~-*off* n., start of game by kicking ball; ~ **up,** raise (dust), create (fuss, noise), ~ *up its heels* (of playful horse). [ME *kike,* of unkn. orig.]

kĭck[3] *n.* Indentation in bottom of glass bottle. [19th c.; orig. unkn.]

kĭ'cker *n.* In vbl senses; horse given to kicking. [f. KICK[2] + -ER[1]]

kĭ'ckshaw *n.* (arch.) Fancy dish in cookery (usu. derog.); toy, trifle. [f. F *quelque chose* something]

kĭd[1] *n.,* & *v.i.* (**-dd-**). **1.** *n.* Young of goat; leather from skin of this, used for gloves, shoes, handbags, etc.; (sl.) child, *young person, whence ~'DIE, ~'DY[3], *n.*; ~ **brother, sister,** (sl.) younger brother, sister; ~-**glove** *a.,* (1) over-dainty, avoiding everyday work etc., (2) using great tact, avoiding unnecessary violence; ~**(s') stuff,** (sl.) something very simple or easy. **2.** *v.i.* (Of goat) give birth to kid. [ME *kide* f. ON *kith* f. Gmc **kidhjam*]

kĭd[2] *v.t.* (**-dd-**), & *n.* (sl.) Hoax, humbug, deceive (*don't kid yourself*), tease. [perh. f. prec.]

kĭd[3] *n.* Small wooden tub esp. (formerly) sailor's mess-tub. [perh. var. of KIT[1]]

Kĭ'dderminster *n.* ~ **carpet** (ingrain, with pattern formed by intersection of two cloths of different colours). [~ in Hereford & Worcester]

kĭ'ddie, kĭ'ddy. See KID[1].

kĭ'ddle *n.* Barrier in river with opening fitted with nets etc. to catch fish; arrangement of stake-nets on sea-beach. [ME, f. AF *kidel,* OF *quidel, guidel*]

kĭ'dnăp *v.t.* (**-pp-** *or* ***-p-**). Steal (child); carry off (person etc.) by illegal force or fraud esp. to obtain ransom; so ~PER[1], *~ER[1], *n.* [back form. f. *kidnapper* (KID[1], *nap* = NAB, -ER[1])]

kĭ'dney *n.* **1.** One of pair of glandular organs in abdominal cavity of mammals, birds, and reptiles, serving to excrete urine and so remove nitrogenous matter from blood; **artificial** ~, apparatus performing functions of human kidneys in place of damaged organ. **2.** Kidney of sheep, ox, or pig, as food. **3.** Temperament, nature, kind, (*a man of that kidney, of the right kidney*). **4.** ~ **(potato),** oval potato. **5.** ~ **bean,** (1) dwarf French bean, (2) scarlet runner bean; ~ **machine,** = *artificial kidney* (see sense 1); ~-**shaped,** oval but with one side concave and the other convex; *kidney*-VETCH. [ME *kidnei,* pl. *kidneiren,* app. partly f. *ei* EGG[1]]

kie-kie (kē'kē) *n.* N.Z. climbing plant with edible bracts, and leaves used for baskets etc. [Maori]

kier *n.* Vat in which cloth is boiled for bleaching etc. [f. ON *ker* tub, = OHG *kar,* Goth. *kas*]

kie'selguhr (-zelgoor) *n.* Diatomaceous earth used for polishing and as absorbent of nitro-glycerine in manufacture of dynamite. [G (*kiesel* gravel, dial. *guhr* earthy deposit)]

kif. Var of KEF.

***kike** *n.* (sl., derog.) Jew. [20th c.; orig. uncert.]

kĭ'lderkĭn *n.* Cask for liquids etc., containing 16 or 18 gal.; this as measure. [ME, alt. of *kinderkin* f MDu. *kinde(r)kin, kinneken,* dim. of *kintal* QUINTAL; see -KIN]

Kĭlkĕ'nnў *n.* ~ **cats,** two cats said to have fought until only tails remained, (fig.) two combatants who annihilate each other. [~ in Ireland]

kĭll[1] *v.t.* **1.** Deprive of life, put to death, slay, (~ **two birds with one stone,** effect two purposes at once); (of disease, grief, shock, drink, poison, etc.) cause the death of; (colloq.) cause severe pain to (*my feet are killing me*); ~ **off,** get rid of (number of persons etc.) by killing; ~ one**self,** (colloq.) exert oneself unduly. **2.** (abs.) Perform act of killing, do execution; **shoot to** ~ (not only to warn or wound). **3.** Obtain (meat) by killing animals. **4.** Represent in fiction etc. as dead (*kill your villain in the last chapter*). **5.** Destroy vitality of (plant, disease, etc.); destroy, put an end to, (feelings etc.); switch off (spotlight, engine, etc.); (colloq.) eat or drink, esp. consume whole contents of (bottle). **6.** Neutralize (colour etc.) by contrast. **7.** Spend (time) unprofitably while awaiting future event. **8.** Overwhelm (person) with admiration, amusement, etc.; *dressed* etc. **to** ~, showily or fascinatingly. **9.** (Lawn Tennis) strike (ball) so that it cannot be returned; (Footb.) stop (ball) dead. **10.** Totally defeat (bill in Parliament). **11.** ~ (fatally harm) **with kindness** (that is mistaken or excessive); ~ **or cure** (of remedies that either cure completely or prove fatal; or fig.); ~'**joy,** one who throws gloom over social enjoyment; ~-**time** *n.* & *a.* (occupation) intended to kill time. [ME *cŭlle, kille,* perh. ult. cogn. w. QUELL]

kĭll[2] *n.* Act of killing; animal(s) killed, esp. by sportsman; destruction or disablement of submarine, aircraft, etc.; **in at the** ~, (fig.) present at the time of victory. [f. prec.]

kĭ'lldeer *n.* Large Amer. ring-plover (*Charadrius vociferus*) with plaintive note. [imit.]

kĭ'ller *n.* One who or that which kills; murderous ruffian; HUMANE *killer*; ~ **whale,** voracious cetacean (esp. *Orcina orca*). [f. KILL[1] + -ER[1]]

kĭ'llĭck *n.* Heavy stone used by small craft as anchor; small anchor; ‖(Navy sl.) leading seaman. [17th c., of unkn. orig.]

kĭ'llĭfĭsh *n.* Small fish of family Cyprinodontidae used as bait; tropical fish of family Poeciliidae. [perh. f. *kill* stream (f. Du. *kil*) + FISH[1]]

kĭ'llĭng[1] *n.* In vbl senses; (fig.) great (esp. financial) success (*make a killing*); ~-**bottle** (containing poisonous vapour to kill insects collected as specimens). [ME, f. KILL[1] + -ING[1]]

kĭ'llĭng[2] *a.* In vbl senses; (colloq.) overwhelmingly attractive, amusing, etc.; hence ~LY[2] *adv.* [ME, f. KILL[1] + -ING[2]]

kĭln *n.* Furnace or oven for burning, baking, or drying, esp. (**lime-**~) for calcining lime, or (**brick-**~) for baking bricks; ~-**dry** *v.t.,* dry in kiln. [OE *cylene* f. L *culina* kitchen]

kĭ'lō (*or* kē'-) *n.* (*pl.* ~**s**). Kilogram; kilometre. [F, abbr.]

kĭ'lo- *pref.* denoting factor of 1,000, as: ~**cycle**

(*per second*), **~hertz,** unit of vibration frequency = 1,000 cycles per second; **~litre,** measure of 1,000 litres, approx. 35·31 cu. ft. or ‖3·44 quarters; **~ton(ne),** (esp.) unit of explosive power equivalent to 1,000 tons of T.N.T.; *kilovolt*; **~watt,** power of 1,000 watts, approx. 1·34 h.p.; **~watt-hour,** amount of energy equal to one kilowatt operating for one hour. [F, f. Gk *khilioi* thousand]

kĭ'logrăm, -grămme, *n.* Unit of mass in the metric system, equal to the mass of the international prototype kept at Sèvres near Paris, approx. 2·205 lb.; **~-metre,** quantity of energy that will raise one kilogram to height of one metre. [F *kilogramme* (as prec., GRAM²)]

kĭ'lomētre, *kĭ'lomēter, (*or* -ŏ'mĭ-) *n.* Distance of 1,000 metres, approx. 0·62 mile; hence **kĭlomĕ'tr**IC *a.* [f. F *kilomètre* (as KILO-, METRE²)]

kĭlt¹ *v.t.* Tuck up (skirts) round body; (esp. in *p.p.*) gather in vertical pleats. [ME, of Scand. orig.; cf. Da. *kilte* (*op*) tuck (up), Sw. dial. *kilta* swathe, OIcel. *kilting*, *kjalta* skirt, lap]

kĭlt² *n.* Skirt, usu. of tartan cloth, reaching from waist to knee, with many pleats at back and sides, part of Highland man's dress; similar garment worn by children and women; hence ~'ED² *a.*, ~'IE *n.*, wearer of a kilt, esp. kilted Highland soldier. [f. prec.]

***kĭ'lter, kĕ'lter,** *n.* Good working order (**out of ~,** not working properly). [17th c., of unkn. orig.]

kĭ'mberlīte *n.* = BLUE¹ *ground*. [f. *Kimberley* in S. Afr. + -ITE¹ (2)]

kĭmō'nō *n.* (*pl.* **~s**). Long loose Japanese robe with wide short sleeves, held together by a sash; woman's dressing-gown or wrap modelled on this. [Jap.]

kĭn *n.* & *a.* **1.** *n.* Ancestral stock, family, (*comes of good kin*); one's relative(s); KITH *and kin*. **2.** *a.* Related (*we are kin*; *he is kin to me*). **3. Of ~,** akin, related by blood ties or (fig.) in character; **near of ~,** closely related; NEXT *of kin*. **4.** Hence ~'LESS *a.* [OE *cynn*, = OS, OHG *kunni*, ON *kyn*, Goth. *kuni* f. Gmc **kunjam* f. weak grade of **kin-*, **kan-*, **kun-* f. IE **gen-* etc. produce]

-kin *suf.* forming dim. *ns.* (*catkin*, *lambkin*, *manikin*, *napkin*; also in names, as *Peterkin* or *Perkin*). [f. or after MDu. *-kijn*, *-ken*, OHG *-chīn* (G *-chen*)]

kĭnaesth|ē'sĭa, *kĭnesth|ē'sĭa, (-ĭsthē'z-) *n.* Sense of muscular effort in voluntary movement of body; hence **~ĕ'**TIC *a.* [f. Gk *kineō* move + *aisthēsis* sensation + -IA¹]

kĭ'ncōb *n.* Rich Indian fabric embroidered with gold or silver. [f. Urdu f. Pers. *kamkāb* (*kamkā* damask f. Chin. *kin* gold)]

kīnd¹ *n.* **1.** Race, natural group, of animals, plants, etc., (*human kind*; *the rabbit kind*). **2.** Class, SORT¹, variety, (*what kind, of what kind, is it?*; *of a different kind*); **something of the ~,** something like the thing in question; **nothing of the ~,** not at all like it; **of a ~,** (derog.) scarcely deserving the name (*we had coffee of a kind*); **two of a ~,** two that are similar in some important respect. **3.** (Eccl.) Each of the two elements in the Eucharist. **4.** (In transposed constr.) **what ~ of** *tree is this?*, of what kind is this tree?, *this is* **the ~ of** *thing I meant* (a thing of the kind I meant); **this** or (colloq.) **these ~ of** *men* (men of this kind) *annoy me*. **5.** (Implying looseness, vagueness, exaggeration, etc., in the term used) *he is a kind of stockbroker*, *of millionaire*; *felt a kind of compunction*; (colloq.) *I* **~ of** (to some extent) *expected it*, *felt kind of sorry for him*. **6.** (arch.) Nature in general (*the law of kind*); way, fashion, natural to person etc. (*they act after their kind*). **7.** Character, quality; *they differ* **in ~** (not merely in degree). **8. In ~,** (of payment) in goods or natural produce, not in money, (of repayment, esp. fig.) in the same form (*repay his insolence in kind* = with insolence). [OE *cynd*(*e*), *gecynd*(*e*) f. Gmc **gakundiz* (as Y-, KIN, *-*diz* abstract suf.)]

kīnd² *a.* Of gentle or benevolent nature; friendly in one's conduct *to* (person etc.); showing friendliness; affectionate; **~-hearted,** having a kind heart; hence ~'NESS *n.* [OE *gecynde* (as prec.); orig. = 'natural, native']

kĭ'nda (colloq.) = *kind of*. [f. KIND¹ 5 + -A]

kĭ'ndergarten *n.* School for young children, esp. teaching by object-lessons, toys, games, etc. [G, = children's garden]

kĭ'ndle *v.* **1.** *v.t.* Set on fire, light, (flame, fire, substance); (fig.) inflame, inspire, (passion etc.), stir up (person *to* emotion etc., *to* do). **2.** *v.i.* Catch fire, burst into flame; (fig.) become animated, glow with passion etc. **3.** *v.t.* & *i.* Make or become bright; **~ (up),** (cause to) glow. **4.** Hence **kĭ'ndl**ING¹ *n.*, (esp., in *sing.* or *pl.*) small wood for lighting fires. [ME, f. ON *kynda* kindle + -LE 3; cf. ON *kindill* candle, torch]

kĭ'ndlȳ¹ *adv.* In adj. senses; (in polite request or iron. command: *kindly acknowledge this letter*; *will you kindly shut the door behind you*); **take ~,** accept with pleasure; **take ~ to,** be pleased by; **thank ~** (with hearty appreciation). [OE *gecyndelice* (as KIND², -LY²)]

kĭ'ndl|ȳ² *a.* Kind, kind-hearted; (of climate etc.) pleasant, genial; (arch.) native-born (*a kindly Scot*); hence **~ĭ**LY² *adv.*, **~ĭ**NESS *n.* [OE *gecyndelic* (as KIND¹, -LY¹)]

kĭ'ndrėd *n.* & *a.* **1.** *n.* Blood relationship; (fig.) resemblance in character; one's relative(s). **2.** *a.* Related by blood; (fig.) allied, connected, similar, (*frost and kindred phenomena*; **~ spirit,** person felt to be congenial). [ME, f. KIN + *-red* f. OE *rǣden* condition]

kīne. See COW¹.

kīnėmă't|ĭc *a.* Of motion considered abstractly without reference to force or mass; *kinematic* VISCOSITY; hence ~ICAL *a.*, ~ICALLY *adv.*, ~ICS *n.*, science of pure motion. [f. Gk *kinēma -matos* motion (*kineō* move) + -IC]

kinematograph. Var. of CINEMATOGRAPH.

kĭnē'sĭ|cs *n. pl.* (often treated as *sing.*) (Study of) body movements etc. contributing to communication, e.g. shrug of shoulders; so **~ŏ'**LOGY *n.*, study of mechanics of body movements. [f. Gk *kinēsis* motion (as foll.) + -ICS]

kĭnĕ'tĭc *a.* Of or due to motion; **~ art** (depending on movement for its effect); *kinetic* ENERGY; **~ theory of heat, of gases,** (that heat, the gaseous state, is due to motion of particles); hence **kĭnĕ'**TICS *n.*, science of the relations between the motions of bodies and the forces acting upon them. [f. Gk *kinētikos* (*kineō* move; see -ETIC)]

kĭng¹ *n.* **1.** Male sovereign (esp. hereditary) ruler of independent state; **Kings,** two books of O.T. dealing with history esp. of kingdom of Judah. **2. K~ Emperor** (Hist., of U.K. and India, or of Austria-Hungary); **K~ Log, K~ Stork,** rulers going to extremes of *laissez-faire*, active oppression (w. ref. to fable of Jupiter and the frogs); **K~ of ~s,** (1) God, (2) title assumed by many Eastern kings; **~ of terrors,** Death; **K~ Charles spaniel** (small black-and-tan kind); **K~ Charles's Head,** *idée fixe* [f. Dickens's *David Copperfield*, ch. xiv]; ‖*King's* BENCH, BOUNTY, COLOUR¹, COUNSEL¹, ENGLISH¹, EVIDENCE, GUIDE¹, HIGHWAY, MESSENGER, PROCTOR SCOUT¹, SHILLING, SPEECH; **K~ of the Castle,** children's game of seeking to displace rival from mound. **3.** Great merchant etc. (*fur, railway, king*; cf. LORD 1). **4.** ~ **of beasts,** lion; ~ **of birds,** eagle. **5.** Best kind (*of* fruits, plants, etc.). **6.** Piece in chess that has to be protected from checkmate (**~'s bishop, knight, pawn, rook,** those placed nearest king at start); piece in draughts made by crowning a man that has traversed the board and reached opponent's base-line; court-card bearing representation of king and usu. ranking next below ace. **7.** **~'bird,** (1) kind of bird of paradise, (2) Amer. tyrant fly-catcher; **~'bolt,** main or large bolt; ~ **cobra,** large very venomous hooded Indian snake (*Naja hannah*); **~-crab,** (1) large marine arthropod esp. of genus *Limulus* having horse-shoe-shaped carapace, (2) *large edible spider-crab; **~'craft,** skilful exercise of royalty; **~'cup,** (1) buttercup, (2) ||marsh marigold; **~-fish,** fish of remarkable size etc., esp. opah or mulloway; **~'fisher,** small bird of family Alcedinidae with dagger-shaped bill and brilliant plumage, feeding on fish it captures by diving; ***K~ James('s) Bible** or **Version,** = AUTHORIZED *Version*; **~'maker,** one who sets up kings by his power, esp. Earl of Warwick in reign of Henry VI; ||**K~ of Arms,** chief herald (at College of Arms; Garter, Clarenceux, and Norroy & Ulster; in Scotland: Lyon); ~ **penguin** (large species *Aptenodytes patagonica*); **~'pin,** = *kingbolt*, (fig.) essential or leading person or thing; **~-post,** upright post from tie-beam to rafter-top; **~'s evil,** scrofula, formerly held to be curable by royal touch; **~-size(d)** *a.*, larger than normal, very large; ||**K~'s Scholar** (holding scholarship on royal foundation). **8.** Hence ~'HOOD, ~'LING[1], ~'SHIP (1), *ns.*, ~'LESS *a.*, ~'LET *n.*, (1) petty king, (2) small bird of family Regulidae, e.g. firecrest and goldcrest, ~'LIKE *a.* & *adv.*, ~'LY[1] *a.* [OE *cyning, cyng*, = OS, OHG *kuning* f. Gmc **kuningaz* (as KIN, -ING[3])]

kĭng[2] *v.t.* Make (person) king; ~ **it,** act the king, govern. [ME, f. prec.]

kĭ'ngdom *n.* **1.** Organized community headed by king or queen; MIDDLE[1] *Kingdom*; UNITED *Kingdom*. **2.** Territory subject to king; spiritual reign of God, sphere of this, (*the kingdom of heaven; thy kingdom come*); **~-come,** (sl.) the next world. **3.** Domain; province of nature, esp. *animal, vegetable, mineral, kingdom*. **4.** Hence ~ED[2] (-md) *a.* [OE *cyningdōm* (as KING[1], -DOM)]

kī'nĭn *n.* Peptide formed in blood after injury and causing sensation of pain; compound promoting cell division and inhibiting ageing in higher plants. [f. Gk *kineō* move + -IN]

kĭnk *n.* & *v.* **1.** *n.* Short backward twist in wire or chain or rope or tube or hair such as may cause obstruction or a break; (fig.) mental twist, crotchet. **2.** *v.i.* & *t.* (Cause to) form a kink. [f. MLG *kinke* f. **ki(n)k-* bend; vb. prob. f. Du. *kinken*]

kĭ'nkajou (-ōō) *n.* Carnivorous nocturnal arboreal animal of central & S. America, with prehensile tail, allied to racoon. [f. F *quincajou* f. N. Amer. Ind.; cf. Algonquin *kwingwaage* wolverine]

kĭ'nkȳ *a.* Having (many) kinks; bizarre, perverted (esp. sexually). [f. KINK + -Y[2]]

kĭ'nnĭkĭnĭc *n.* Mixture of dried sumac-leaves, bark of willow, etc., as substitute for tobacco, or mixed with it; any plant used for this. [Algonquin, lit. 'mixture']

kī'nō (kē'-) *n.* (*pl.* **~s**). Gum of various trees, resembling catechu, and used in medicine and tanning as astringent. [W. Afr.]

-kĭns (-z) *suf.* = -KIN (w. suggestion of endearment, as *babykins*); cf. -S[4].

kĭ'ns|folk (-zfōk) *n. pl.* Relations by blood; so ~'MAN[1], ~'WOMAN, *ns.* [ME, f. KIN + 's 1 + FOLK]

kĭ'nshĭp *n.* Blood relationship; similarity or alliance in character. [f. KIN + -SHIP]

kī'ŏsk (kē'-) *n.* Light out-of-door or ||indoor structure for sale of newspapers, food, etc.; bandstand etc.; structure in street etc. for public telephone; light open pavilion in Turkey and Iran. [f. F *kiosque* f. Turk. *kiūshk* pavilion f. Pers. *guš*]

kĭp[1] *n.* Hide of young or small animal as used for leather. [ME, of unkn. orig.]

kĭp[2] *n.*, & *v.i.* (**-pp-**). (sl.) **1.** Common lodging-house; bed. **2.** *n.*, & *v.i.* Sleep; (place to) lie down for sleep. [cf. Da. *kippe* mean hut]

kĭ'pper[1] *n.* **1.** Male salmon in spawning season. **2.** Kippered fish, esp. herring. [ME, of uncert. orig.]

kĭ'pper[2] *v.t.* Cure (salmon, herring, etc.) by splitting open, cleaning, rubbing with salt, pepper, etc., and drying in open air or smoke. [f. prec.]

Kirghi'z (kẽrgē'z) *a.* & *n.* (Member or language) of a Mongol people living in central Asia between Volga and Irtysh rivers. [Kirghiz]

kĭ'rĭ *n.* Japanese paulownia(-wood). [Jap.]

||**kĩrk** *n.* **1.** (Sc. & N. Engl.) Church. **2. The K~ (of Scotland),** Church of Scotland as opp. to Church of England or to Episcopal Church in Scotland; **~'man,** member of Kirk of Scotland; **~-session,** lowest court in Kirk of Scotland and (Hist.) other Presbyterian Churches, composed of ministers and elders. [ME, f. ON *kirkja* f. OE *cir(i)ce* CHURCH[1]]

kĩr'sch(wasser) (kẽr'shvahs*er*) *n.* Spirit distilled from fermented liquor of wild cherries. [G (*kirsche* cherry, *wasser* water)]

kĩr'tle *n.* (arch.) Woman's gown or outer petticoat; man's tunic or coat. [OE *cyrtel*, = ON *kyrtill* tunic f. Gmc **kurtilaz*, ult. perh. f. L *curtus* short; see -LE 1]

kĭ'smĕt (*or* -z-) *n.* Destiny, fate. [Turk., f. Arab. *ḳisma(t)* (*ḳasama* divide)]

kĭss[1] *n.* Touch given with lips (see foll.; BLOW[1] *a kiss*); (Bill.) impact between moving balls; small sweetmeat or piece of confectionery; **~-curl,** small curl of hair on forehead, in front of ear, or at nape; ~ **of death,** apparently friendly act causing ruin; ~ **of life,** artificial respiration in which air is breathed from mouth through patient's mouth into his lungs; ~ **of peace,** ceremonial kiss in Eucharist as sign of unity. [ME, f. foll.]

kĭss[2] *v.t.* **1.** Touch with the lips, esp. as sign of love, affection, greeting, or reverence; express thus (*kiss me good night*); (abs., of two persons) touch each other's lips thus; (Bill., of ball) touch (ball) with KISS[1] (also abs. of two balls). **2.** ~ **away,** remove (tears etc.) with kisses; ~ **the book** (Bible, in taking oath); ~ **the dust,** yield abject submission, be overthrown; ~ **goodbye to,** (fig.) accept loss of; ~ **the ground,** prostrate oneself in token of homage, (fig.) be brought low; ~ one's **hand to,** BLOW[1] a kiss to; ~ **hands** or **the hand** (of sovereign etc. as ceremonial salutation or on appointment to office); ~ **the rod,** accept chastisement submissively; **~-in-the-ring,** game for young people in which one pursues and kisses another of opposite sex; **~-me-quick,** (1) small bonnet standing far back on head, (2) = KISS[1]-*curl*. **3.** Hence ~'ABLE *a.* [OE *cyssan*, = OS *cussian*, OHG *kussen*, ON *kyssa* f. Gmc **kussjan* (**kussaz* a kiss)]

kĭ'sser *n.* In vbl senses; (sl.) face, mouth. [f. prec. + -ER[1]]

kĭ'ssĭng[1] *a.* In vbl senses; ~ **cousin,** ~ **kin(d),** distant relative(s) given formal kiss at occasional meeting; **~-crust,** soft crust where loaf has touched another in baking. [ME, f. KISS[2] + -ING[2]]

ki'ssing[2] *n.* In vbl senses; ||~**-gate** (hung in U- or V-shaped enclosure). [f. KISS[2] + -ING[1]]
kist. Var. of CIST[1].
Kiswahi'li (-swahhē'-) *n.* Swahili language. [Swahili (*ki-* pref. for abstract or inanimate object)]
kit[1] *n.* & *v.* (**-tt-**). **1.** *n.* ||Wooden tub for various purposes, e.g. to hold fish. **2.** (Articles carried in) soldier's etc. pack etc.; personal equipment, esp. as packed for travelling; workman's outfit of tools etc.; set of parts sold together from which thing may be made; clothing etc. for a particular activity or situation (*riding-kit*; *tropical kit*); ~**'bag** (for carrying soldier's or traveller's kit). **3.** *v.t.* & *i.* Fit out, be fitted out, with kit (often *out* or *up*). [ME, f. MDu. *kitte* wooden vessel; orig. unkn.]
kit[2] *n.* Kitten; young fox etc. [abbr.]
kit[3] *n.* (Hist.) Small fiddle used esp. by dancing-master. [perh. f. L *cithara* (see CITHERN)]
ki't-căt *n.* ~ (**portrait**), portrait of less than half-length, but including hands. [f. *K~ Club*, club of Whig politicians founded under James II, f. Christopher (or *Kit*) *Cat*, keeper of pie-house where club met]
ki'tchen *n.* Part of house, hotel, etc., where food is cooked; SOUP-*kitchen*; (Mus. sl.) percussion department of orchestra; ~ **garden** (for growing one's own fruit and vegetables); ~**-maid,** maidservant employed in kitchen, usu. under cook; *kitchen* MIDDEN; *~ **police,** (Mil.) enlisted men instructed to help cooks; ~ **sink,** (fig.) extreme realism in painting, drama, etc., (*everything but the ~ sink*, everything imaginable); ~**-stuff,** kitchen requisites, esp. vegetables; ~**-ware,** hardware used in kitchen. [OE *cycene*, = OS **kukina*, OHG *chuhhina* f. WG **kocina*, **cocina* var. of LL *coquina* f. L *coquere* cook]
ki'tchener *n.* ||Cooking-range; person in charge of monastery kitchen. [ME, f. prec. + -ER[1]]
kitchene'tte *n.* Small room, alcove, etc., used as kitchen (and pantry). [f. KITCHEN + -ETTE]
kite *n.* & *v.* **1.** *n.* Large bird of prey, of hawk family, with long wings, usu. forked tail, and no tooth in bill. **2.** Rapacious person, sharper. **3.** Toy consisting of light wooden etc. frame, usu. in form of symmetrical quadrilateral or of triangle with segment of circle on base, with paper etc. stretched over it and usu. with long tail, flown in strong wind by string; BOX[2]-*kite*; **fly a ~,** (fig.) make experiment to gauge public opinion etc. **4.** (Commerc. sl.) accommodation bill (**fly a ~,** raise money by this); ||(sl.) aeroplane. **5.** (in *pl.*) Highest sails of ship, set only in light wind. **6.** ~ **balloon,** sausage-shaped captive balloon for military observations; ||**K~'mark,** official mark (representing a stylized kite) on goods approved by the British Standards Institution. **7.** *v.i.* Soar or move like kite; *(colloq.) move quickly. **8.** *v.t.* Cause to do this; (Commerc. sl.) convert into kite. [OE *cȳta*, of unkn. orig.]
kith *n.* ~ **and kin,** friends and relations. [OE *cȳthth* f. Gmc **kunthithō* f. **kunth-* known; cf. UNCOUTH, -TH[1]]
kitōō'l. See KITTUL.
kitsch (kich) *n.* Worthless pretentiousness in art; art of this type; hence ~'Y[2] *a.* [G]
ki'tten *n.* & *v.* **1.** *n.* Young of cat; young ferret etc.; skittish young girl; **have ~s,** (colloq.) be very nervous or upset; hence ~ISH[1] *a.* **2.** *v.t.* & *i.* Give birth to (kittens). [ME *kito(u)n*, *ketoun* f. AF **kitoun*, **ketoun*, OF *chitoun*, *chetoun* dim. of *chat* CAT[1], assim. to -EN[2]]
ki'ttiwāke *n.* Small sea-gull of genus *Rissa*. [imit. of its cry]
ki'ttle *a.* Ticklish, difficult to deal with, esp. ~ **cattle** (usu. fig. of persons or things). [f. ME (now Sc. & dial.) *kittle* tickle, prob. f. ON *kitla* = OS *kitilon*, OHG *kizzilōn*]
kittu'l (-ōō'l), **kitōō'l,** *n.* E. Ind. palm-tree (*Caryota urens*); strong black fibre from leaf-stalks of this. [f. Sinh. *kitūl*]
ki'tty[1] *n.* (Pet-name for) kitten. [f. KIT[2] + -Y[3]]
ki'tty[2] *n.* Pool in some card games; joint fund (*how much is there left in the kitty?*); (Bowls) jack. [19th c.; orig. unkn,]
ki'wi (kē'wē) *n.* **1.** Apteryx, flightless N.Z. bird. **2.** (*K~*; colloq.) New Zealander. [Maori]
***K.K.K.** *abbr.* Ku-Klux-Klan.
kl *abbr.* kilolitre(s).
klă'xon *n.* Powerful electric (motor-)horn. [**P**]
Klein (klīn) *n.* ~ **bottle,** (Math.) closed surface with only one side, formed by passing neck of bottle through side of bottle to join hole in base. [f. F. ~, Ger. mathematician d. 1925]
klĕpht *n.* One of the Greeks who after Turkish conquest of Greece in 15th c. maintained independence in mountains; brigand. [f. mod. Gk *klephtēs* f. Gk *kleptēs* thief]
klĕpto|mā'nia *n.* Irresistible tendency to steal what one could afford to buy; hence ~MA'NIAC *n.* & *a.* [f. Gk *kleptēs* thief + -O- + -MANIA]
klieg *n.* ~ (**light**), powerful lamp in film studio etc. [f. A. T. & J. H. *Kliegl*, Amer. inventors d. 1927, 1959]
kli'pdas (-ahs) *n.* S. Afr. hyrax (*Procavia capensis*). [Afrik. (*klip* rock, *das* badger)]
kli'pspringer *n.* Small S. Afr. antelope like chamois. [Afrik. (*klip* rock, *springer* jumper)]
Klŏ'ndike *n.* Source of valuable material. [f. ~ in Yukon, Canada, where gold was found in 1896]
klōōf *n.* Ravine or valley in S. Africa. [Du.,=cleft]
klȳ'strŏn *n.* (Electr.) Device for amplifying or generating microwaves by forming electrons into bunches as they cross a gap. [f. Gk *kluzō klus-* wash over + -TRON]
km *abbr.* kilometre(s).
K-mĕ'sŏn (kāmē'z-) *n.* = KAON. [f. K + MESON]
kn. *abbr.* knot(s) (see KNOT[1] 2).
knăck *n.* Acquired or intuitive faculty of doing a thing adroitly; trick or habit of action, speech, etc.; (arch.) ingenious device. [ME, prob. = ME *knack* sharp blow or sound, of LG orig., ult. imit.]
||**knă'ck|er** *n.* One who buys and slaughters useless horses, whence ~ERY (3) *n.*; one who buys old houses, ships, etc., for the materials. [19th c.; orig. unkn.]
knăg *n.* Knot in wood, base of a branch; short dead branch, peg for hanging things on; hence ~'GY[2] (-gĭ) *a.* [ME, perh. f. LG *knagge*]
knăp[1] *n.* (chiefly dial.) Crest of hill, rising ground. [OE *cnæp(p)*, perh. cogn. w. ON *knappr* knob]
knăp[2] *v.t.* (**-pp-**). Break (flints for roads or building) with hammer, whence ~'PER[1] (1, 2) *n.*; (arch.) knock, rap, snap asunder. [ME, imit.]
knă'psăck *n.* Soldier's or traveller's canvas or leather bag, strapped to back and used for carrying necessaries. [MLG, prob. f. *knappen* bite + SACK[1]]
knă'pweed *n.* Common weed of genus *Centaurea*, esp. *C. nigra*, with hard stem and light purple flowers on dark globular head. [ME, orig. *knopweed* f. KNOP + WEED]
knar *n.* Knot in wood, esp. protuberance covered with bark on trunk or at root of tree. [ME *knarre*, rel. to MLG, MDu., MHG *knorre* knobbed protuberance]
knāv|e *n.* **1.** Unprincipled or dishonest man, rogue; hence ~'ERY (4) *n.*, ~'ISH[1] *a.* **2.** (Cards) = JACK[1] 3. [OE *cnafa* boy, servant, = OHG *knabo* f. WG **knabho*]

knead *v.t.* Work up (moist flour or clay) into dough or paste; make (bread, pottery) thus; (fig.) blend, weld together; operate on (muscles etc.) as if kneading, massage; hence ~′ABLE *a.*, ~′ER¹ (1, 2) *n.* [OE *cnedan*, = OS *knedan*, OHG *knetan*, ON *knotha* f. Gmc **kned-*, **knad-*]

knee¹ *n.* **1.** Joint between thigh and lower leg in man; corresponding joint in animal; upper surface of thigh of sitting person (*hold child* etc. *on* one's *knee*); **bend** or **bow the** ~, kneel esp. in submission; **on** one's **~s, on bended** ~(**s**), kneeling in worship, supplication, or submission; **give a ~ to,** support (pugilist) on one's knee between rounds, act as second to; *on the knees of the* GODS; **bring** person **to his ~s,** reduce him to submission. **2.** Part of garment covering knee. **3.** Thing like knee in shape or position, esp. piece of wood or iron with angular bend; sharp turn in graph. **4. ~-breeches** (reaching down to or just below knee); **~′cap,** (1) convex bone in front of knee-joint, (2) protective covering for knee; **~-deep,** immersed up to the knees, (fig.) deeply involved *in*; **~-deep, ~-high,** so deep or high as to reach the knees; **~-hole,** space for knees, esp. between columns of drawers at each side of desk etc.; **~ holly,** butcher's broom; **~-jerk,** sudden involuntary kick caused by blow on tendon below knee; **~-joint,** (1) joint of knee, (2) joint of two pieces hinged together; **~-length,** so long as to reach the knees; **~-pan,** kneecap. [OE *cnēo*(*w*), = OS *knio*, OHG *kneo*, ON *knē*, Goth. *kniu* f. Gmc **knewam* f. IE **gneuom*]

knee² *v.t.* Touch or strike with the knee; (colloq.) cause (trousers) to bulge at knees. [f. prec.]

kneel *v.i.* (**knelt** *or* ***~ed**). Fall or rest on the knee(s) esp. in prayer or reverence (*to* person); hence ~′ER¹ *n.*, (esp.) hassock etc. to kneel on. [OE *cnēowlian* (as KNEE¹)]

knĕll¹ *n.* Sound of bell, esp. of one rung solemnly after death or at funeral; (fig.) announcement, event, etc., regarded as an omen of death or extinction; **ring the** ~, announce or herald abolition etc. *of*. [OE *cnyll* (as foll.)]

knĕll² *v.* (arch.) **1.** *v.i.* (Of bell) ring, esp. at death or funeral; give forth doleful sound; (fig.) sound ominously. **2.** *v.t.* Proclaim as by a knell. [OE *cyllan*; perh. infl. by *bell*]

knĕlt. See KNEEL.

knew. See KNOW¹.

knĭ′ckerbŏcker *n.* **1.** (*K~*). New Yorker; descendant of original Dutch settlers in New York. **2.** (in *pl.*) Loose-fitting breeches gathered in at knee. [f. Diedrich *K~*, pretended author of W. Irving's *History of New York* (1809)]

knĭ′ckers (-z) *n. pl.* ‖Woman's or girl's undergarment covering lower part of body and having separate legs or leg-holes; *knickerbockers; *boy's short trousers. [abbr. of prec.]

knĭ′ck-knăck (nĭ′knăk) *n.* Light dainty article of furniture, dress, or food; trinket, toy, useless ornament; hence ~ERY (2, 5) *n.*, ~ISH¹ *a.* [redupl. of *knack* in obs. sense 'trinket']

knīfe *n.* (*pl.* **knives** *pr.* nīvz), & *v.t.* **1.** *n.* Metal blade with sharpened longitudinal edge fixed in handle either rigidly or with hinge, used as cutting instrument or as weapon; **the** ~, surgical operation(s); WAR¹ *to the knife*; **get** one's **~ into,** show malicious or vindictive spirit towards (person); **that one could cut with a** ~, (colloq., fig.) very obvious or oppressive; **before you can say** ~, (colloq.) very quickly or suddenly. **2.** Cutting-blade forming part of machine. **3. ~-board,** board on which knives are cleaned, ‖(Hist.) double bench placed lengthways on top of omnibus; ‖**~-boy** (Hist., employed to clean table-knives); **~-edge,** (1) edge of knife, (2) steel wedge on which pendulum etc. oscillates, (3) arête, (4) position of extreme uncertainty; **~-grinder,** (1) itinerant sharpener of knives etc., (2) one who grinds knives etc. in process of making; **~-machine** (for cleaning knives); **~-pleat** (narrow and flat, usu. overlapping another); **at ~-point,** under threat of injury by knife; **~-rest,** metal or glass support for carving-knife or -fork at table. **4.** *v.t.* Cut or stab with knife; *(sl.) seek to defeat by underhand means. [OE *cnif* f. ON *knífr*, = MLG *knif*, MDu. *cnijf*, f. Gmc **knībhaz*]

knight (nīt) *n.*, & *v.t.* **1.** *n.* Military follower, esp. one devoted to service of lady as her attendant or champion in war or tournament; **~-service,** (Hist.) tenure of land by military service. **2.** (Hist.) Man, usu. one of noble birth who had served as page and squire, raised to honourable military rank by king or other qualified person. **3.** Man on whom corresponding rank is conferred as reward for personal merit or services to Crown or country. **4.** (Hist.) ~ (**of the shire**), gentleman representing shire or county in parliament. **5.** (Rom. Ant.) one of the class of *equites*, orig. cavalry of Roman army; (Gk Ant.) citizen of second class at Athens. **6.** Chess piece, usu. with shape of horse's head. **7.** (w. following n. in apposition, etc.; *pl.* usu. **~s** —): *knight* BACHELOR, COMMANDER, ‖COMPANION¹, HOSPITALLER, TEMPLAR; ~ **errant,** medieval knight wandering in search of chivalrous adventures, (fig.) person of chivalrous or of quixotic spirit; **~-e′rrantry,** practice or conduct of a knight errant; *knight* MARSHAL¹; ~ **of the road,** (1) highwayman, (2) commercial traveller, (3) tramp. **8.** Hence ~′HOOD (-t-h-) *n.*, ~′LIKE, ~′LY¹, *adjs.*, ~′LY² *adv.* (poet.). **9.** *v.t.* Confer knighthood on. [OE *cniht* boy, youth, hero, = OS, OHG *kneht* f. WG **knehta*]

knī′ghtage (nī′t-) *n.* Whole body of knights; list and account of knights. [f. prec. + -AGE]

knish (k-n-) *n.* Dumpling of flaky dough filled with cheese etc. and baked or fried. [Yiddish f. Russ.]

knĭt *v.* (**-tt-; ~′ted** *or*, esp. fig., **knit**). **1.** *v.t.* Form (close texture, garments etc. of this, or abs.) of interlocking loops of yarn or thread; make (a plain stitch) in knitting; contract (brow) in vertical wrinkles. **2.** *v.t.* & *i.* Make or become close or compact (esp. in *p.p.*; *a well-knit frame*); (fig.) unite (*together*) intimately by means of common interests, marriage, etc.; (of parts of broken bone) become joined (*together*) again as one. **3.** ~ **up,** repair by knitting, (fig.) close up, conclude, (argument etc.); **~′wear,** knitted garments. [OE *cnyttan*, = MDu., MLG *knutten* f. WG **knuttjan* (**knutto* KNOT¹)]

knĭ′tting *n.* In vbl senses; work in process of being knitted; **~-machine** (for mechanical knitting of garments etc.); **~-needle,** slender rod of steel, wood, plastic, etc., two or more of which are used together in knitting. [ME, f. prec. + -ING¹]

knŏb *n.* & *v.* (**-bb-**). **1.** *n.* Rounded protuberance, esp. at end or on surface of thing; such handle of door or drawer, attachment of this shape for pulling, turning, etc.; small lump (of butter, sugar, coal, etc.); **~′kerrie** [after Afrik. *knopkierie*], short stick with knobbed head as weapon of S. Afr. tribes; **~′stick,** knobbed stick used esp. as weapon, ‖(arch.) = SCAB 3; **with ~s on,** (sl.) = that and more (phr. indicating ironic or emphatic agreement, or in retort to insult etc.); hence **~′BY²** *a.* **2.** *v.t.* Furnish with knob(s). **3.** *v.i.* Bulge *out*. [ME f. MLG *knobbe* knot, knob, bud; cf. KNOP, NOB¹, NUB]

knŏ'bbl|e *n.* Small knob; hence ~Y² *a.* [ME, dim. of prec.; cf. Du. & LG *knobbel*]

knŏck¹ *v.* **1.** *v.t.* & *i.* Strike with audible sharp blow; strike door, strike *at the door* etc. to seek admittance; make by knocking (*knock a hole in*); **knock* (*on*) WOOD. **2.** *v.i.* (Of motor or other engine) make thumping or rattling noise as result of loose bearing or other mechanical defect; = PINK⁶. **3.** *v.t.* (sl.) Criticize; ||make strong impression on, astonish; ||**~'ing-shop,** (sl.) brothel. **4.** ~ **on the head,** stun or kill (person etc.) by blow on head, (fig.) put an end to (scheme etc.); ~ one's **head against,** (fig.) come into unpleasant collision with (unfavourable facts or conditions). **5.** Drive (thing) *in, out, off,* etc., by striking (cf. sense 6); *knock into a* COCK²*ed hat*; ~ person **into the middle of next week,** (colloq.) send him flying; *knock* SPOT¹*s off*; ~ **the bottom out of,** render (argument etc.) invalid. **6.** ~ **about,** strike repeatedly, treat roughly, be casually present, wander, lead irregular life; *~'about* a., boisterous, wandering irregularly, (of clothes) suitable for rough use; ~ **against,** collide with, come across casually; ||~ **back,** (sl.) eat or drink, disconcert; ~ **down,** strike (person etc.) to ground with blow, demolish, (fig.) cause to succumb, (at auction) dispose of (article *to* bidder) by knock with hammer, (colloq.) lower (prices), *(sl.) steal, (Commerc.) take (machinery, furniture, etc.) to pieces to save space in transport; *~-down* a., (of blow, lit. or fig.) overwhelming, (of price) very low, (of price at auction) reserve, (of furniture etc.) easily dismantled; ~ **off,** strike off with blow, leave off work, leave off (work), (colloq.) dispatch (business) or rapidly compose (verses etc.), deduct (sum *from* price, bill, etc.), (sl.) steal, *(sl.) kill; ~ **on,** (Rugby Footb.) propel (ball) with hand or arm towards opponents' goal-line; ~ **out,** empty (one's tobacco-pipe) by tapping, make unconscious by hitting on head, disable (boxer) so that he cannot rise within usu. ten seconds, (fig.) defeat esp. in knock-out competition, (colloq.) make (plan etc.) hastily; *~-out* n. & a., (blow) that knocks boxer etc. out, (competition) in which loser of each match is eliminated, ||one of gang who join auction to buy goods at low price and afterwards resell among themselves, this practice, such sale, (sl.) outstanding or irresistible person or thing; *~-out drops* (added to drink in order to make drinker unconscious); ~ **sideways,** (colloq.) discomfit; ~ **together,** put together hastily or roughly; ~ **under,** submit, knuckle under; ~ **up,** drive upwards with blow, make or arrange hastily, score (runs) rapidly at cricket, ||arouse (person) by knocking at door, exhaust, make ill, become exhausted or suffer breakdown, *(sl.) make pregnant; *~-up* n., practice or casual game at tennis etc. **7.** ~ **knees,** abnormal condition with leg(s) curved inward at the knee; so **~-knee**D² *a.* [OE *cnocian,* = ON *knoka,* prob. imit.]

knŏck² *n.* Act of knocking; sharp or audible blow; rap esp. at door; sound of knocking in motor etc. engine (see prec.); (colloq.) innings at cricket; ~ **for** ~ **agreement** (between insurers, whereby each pays his own policy-holders regardless of liability); **take the** ~, (sl.) be hard hit financially. [ME, f. prec.]

knŏ'cker *n.* In vbl senses; appendage, usu. of iron or brass, so hinged to door that it may be struck against metal plate to call attention (||**up to the** ~, sl., in good condition, to perfection); ||**~-u'p,** person who goes from house to house awakening others at required time. [ME, f. KNOCK¹ + -ER¹]

knōll¹ *n.* Small hill, mound. [OE *cnoll* hilltop, rel. to MDu., MHG *knolle* clod, ON *knollr* hilltop]

knōll² *v.t.* & *i.*, & *n.* (arch.) = KNELL¹˒²; summon by sound of bell. [ME, var. of KNELL¹˒², perh. imit.]

knŏp *n.* (Ornamental) knob; ornamental loop or tuft in yarn; (arch.) flower-bud. [ME, f. MLG, MDu. *knoppe,* = OHG *knoph*]

knŏ'pkierie (k-n-) *n.* (S. Afr.) = KNOB*kerrie.* [Afrik.]

knŏt¹ *n.* **1.** Intertwining or tangling of parts of one or more ropes, strings, tresses, etc., to fasten them together; ribbon etc. so tied as ornament or adjunct to dress; **tie in ~s,** (colloq.) render (person) completely baffled or confused. **2.** (Naut.) Division marked by knots on log-line, as measure of speed; unit of ship's or aircraft's speed equivalent to one nautical MILE per hour; (pop.) one nautical mile; **at the rate of ~s,** (colloq.) very fast. **3.** Difficulty, problem, (GORDIAN *knot*); central point in problem or plot of story etc. **4.** That which forms or maintains a union (esp. of wedlock). **5.** Hard lump in animal body; excrescence in stem, branch, or root, of plant; (hard mass formed in trunk at insertion of branch, causing) round cross-grained piece in board; node on stem of plant. **6.** Group or cluster *of* persons or things. **7.** ||(**Porter's**) ~, double shoulder-pad and forehead-loop used for carrying loads. **8.** **~-garden,** intricately designed formal garden; **~-grass,** common weed (*Polygonium aviculare*) with intricate creeping stems and small pale pink flowers; **~-hole** (in board, where knot (sense 5) has fallen out); **~'work,** ornamental work representing or consisting of intertwined cords. **9.** Hence **~'**LESS *a.* [OE *cnotta,* = Du. *knot,* MHG *knotze* f. WG **knutto*]

knŏt² *v.* (**-tt-**). **1.** *v.t.* Tie (string etc.) in knot; knit (one's brows); unite closely or intricately; entangle; **get ~ted!**, (sl.) stop annoying me. **2.** *v.i.* & *t.* Make knots for fringes, make (fringe) thus; hence **~'**TING¹ *n.* [f. prec.]

knŏt³ *n.* Small wading bird (esp. *Calidris canutus*) of sandpiper family. [ME; orig. unkn.]

knŏ'tt|ȳ *a.* Full of knots; (fig.) puzzling, hard to explain, (*knotty subject, question, point*); hence **~ĭ**LY² *adv.*, **~ĭ**NESS *n.* [ME, f. KNOT¹ + -Y²]

knout (*or* nōōt) *n.*, & *v.t.* (Flog with) scourge formerly used in Russia, often fatal in its effects. [F, f. Russ. *knut* f. Icel. *knútr,* cogn. w. KNOT¹]

know¹ (nō) *v.* (**knew** *pr.* nū; **~n** *pr.* nōn). **1.** Recognize, identify, (*I knew him at once*; *knew him for an American*; *would you know him again?*); be able to distinguish (one *from* another, *a* HAWK¹ *from a handsaw*; *not know* person *from* ADAM¹). **2.** Be acquainted with (thing, place, person) *by* SIGHT¹, *to speak to,* etc. (~ **by name,** (1) have heard the name of, (2) be able to give the name of); (Math., in *pass.*, of quantity etc.) have known value; have personal experience of (fear etc.), be subject to (*her joy knew no bounds*); be on intimate terms with; (arch.) have sexual intercourse with. **3.** Have in the mind, be able to recall, be aware of (fact), be aware, have learnt, (*that, how, what,* etc.); ~ (person or thing) **to be** or **do** (that he etc. is or does); *let me know, let it be known,* (see LET² 5); (in *p.p.*) of which there is knowledge as a fact (*a known thief*). **4.** Be able to use (a language etc.), have theoretical or practical understanding of (subject). **5.** **All** one **~s** (**how**), all one can, (*adv.*) to the utmost of one's power; **before** one **~s where** one **is,** with baffling rapidity; **don't I ~ it,** (colloq., expr. rueful assent); **I don't ~ that** *I like this,* (colloq.) I am fairly sure that . . . not; **don't you ~**

(colloq. parenthetic expletive: *it's such a bore, don't you know*); **for all** or **aught I ~**, so far as my knowledge is concerned; GOD or HEAVEN or *the* LORD (*only*) *knows*; **has been ~n to** do, is known to have done; **I ~ what,** I have a new idea or suggestion to propose; *I wouldn't know* (see WILL[1] 7); **I knew it,** I was sure that that would happen; **not if I ~ it,** only against my will; **not ~ what hit** one, be suddenly killed or utterly disconcerted; **not want to ~**, refuse to take notice (of); **what do you ~ (about that)?** (colloq. excl. of surprise); **you ~**, (colloq., reminding hearer that he knows or should know a thing, or as mere gap-filler in conversation); **you ~ something?** or **what?**, I am going to tell you something; **you ~ what he** or **it is,** you are familiar with his or its characteristics, difficult nature, etc.; YOU-*know-what* or *-who*; **you never ~**, nothing future is completely certain; **that's all you' ~ (about it)**, you are more ignorant than you think. **6. ~ about,** have information about; **~-all,** (would-be) omniscient person; **~ better (than that, than to** do), be too wise or well-informed of the facts to believe that, too well-mannered to behave thus, etc.; **~ how,** know the way to do something; **~-*how*** n., faculty of knowing how, practical knowledge, technical expertness; **~-it-all,** (colloq.) = *know-all*; **~-nothing,** (1) ignorant person, (2) agnostic; **~ of,** be aware of, have heard of, (*not that I ~ of*, not so far as I know); **~** one's **own mind,** not vacillate; *know the* ROPES, one's STUFF; **~ a thing or two,** be experienced or shrewd; **~ what's what,** have proper knowledge of the world and of things in general; *know* WHO'*s who*. **7.** Hence **~'ABLE** *a*. [OE (*ge*)*cnāwan*, = OHG *-cnā(h)en*, ON *knā*, f. IE **gn-* etc., cogn. w. CAN[2], KEN[2]]

know[2] (nō) *n*. (colloq.) **In the ~**, knowing (about) the thing in question or what is not generally known. [f. prec.]

knowe. Sc. & N. Engl. var. of KNOLL[1].

know'ing[1] (nō'ĭ-) *n*. In vbl senses; **there is no ~**, no one can tell. [ME, f. KNOW[1] + -ING[1]]

know'ing[2] (nō'ĭ-) *a*. In vbl senses; showing knowledge, shrewd; (usu. derog.) cunning, wary; hence **~NESS** *n*. [ME, f. KNOW[1] + -ING[2]]

know'ingly̆ (nō'ĭ-) *adv*. In a knowing manner; consciously, intentionally, (*I have never knowingly injured him*). [ME, f. prec. + -LY[2]]

know'lĕdge (nŏ'l-) *n*. **1.** Knowing, familiarity gained by experience, (*of* person, thing, fact); CARNAL *knowledge*. **2.** Person's range of information; *it* **came to my ~**, became known to me; **to my ~**, (1) so far as I know, (2) as I know for certain. **3.** Theoretical or practical understanding (*of* subject, language, etc.); the sum of what is known (*every branch of knowledge*); (Philos.) certain understanding, opp. to opinion. **4.** Hence **~ABLE** (nŏ'lĭja-) *a*., (colloq.) well-informed, intelligent. [ME *knaulege*, w. earlier v. *knawlechen*, f. as KNOW[1] + OE *-lǣcan* (*lāc* as in WEDLOCK)]

known. See KNOW[1].

Knt. *abbr*. Knight.

knŭ'ckle *n*. & *v*. **1.** *n*. Bone at finger-joint, esp. at root of finger; projection of carpal or tarsal joint of quadruped; joint of meat consisting of this with parts above and below it; RAP[1] *on* or *over the knuckles*; **near the ~**, (colloq.) verging on the indecent; **~-bone,** bone forming knuckle, animal's limb-bone with ball-like end, knuckle of meat, sheep's metacarpal or metatarsal bone, (in *pl*.) these bones used in game of JACK[1]s; **~duster,** metal instrument protecting knuckles from injury in striking, and increasing force of blow. **2.** *v.t.* Strike, press, rub, with knuckles. **3.** *v.i.* **~ (down)**, place knuckles on ground in playing at marbles; **~ down,** apply oneself earnestly (*to* work etc.); **~ down** or **under,** give in, submit (*to*). [ME *knokel* f. MLG, MDu. *knökel*, dim. of *knoke* bone]

knûr, ||**knûrr,** *n*. Hard excrescence on trunk of tree; hard concretion; hard ball used in game of *knur and* SPELL[4]. [ME *knorre*, var. of KNAR]

knûrl *n*. Small projecting knob, ridge, etc.; hence **~ED**[2] (-ld) *a*. [f. prec.]

knŭt (*or* k-n-). Joc. var. of NUT 2.

K.O. *abbr*. knock-out; **~('d)**, knocked out.

kō'a *n*. (Dark red wood of) Hawaiian tree (*Acacia koa*). [Hawaiian]

kōa'la (-ah'-) *n*. **~ (bear)**, tailless arboreal Australian marsupial (*Phascolarctos cinereus*) with thick grey fur and large ears. [f. Aboriginal *kūl(l)a*]

kō'ăn *n*. Riddle used in Zen to teach inadequacy of logical reasoning. [Jap., = public plan]

kō'bŏld *n*. (Gmc Myth.) Familiar spirit, brownie; underground spirit in mines etc. [G; cf. COBALT]

Kö'chel (kẽr'χel) *n*. **~ number** etc. (of a composition by Mozart as listed in Köchel's complete catalogue of his works). [f. L. von ~, Austrian scientist d. 1877]

kō'dăk *n*. (Make of) small camera held in hand. [*P]

Kō'dĭăk *n*. **~ bear** (large brown Alaska species). [f. ~ Island, Alaska]

koedoe. S. Afr. var. of KOODOO.

kō'el *n*. Indian or Australasian cuckoo of genus *Eudynamys*. [f. Hindi *kóil* f. Skr. *kokila*]

koh'-ĭ-noor (kō'ĭ-) *n*. Large diamond; anything superb (*of* its class). [name of famous Indian diamond, property of British Crown since 1849, f. Pers. (*kūh* mountain, *i* of, *nūr* light)]

kohl (kōl) *n*. Powder, usu. antimony sulphide or lead sulphide, used in East to darken eyelids etc. [f. Arab. *kuḥl*]

kohlra'bĭ (kōlrah'-) *n*. Cabbage with turnip-shaped edible stem. [G, f. It. *cavoli rape* pl. f. med. L *caulorapa* (see COLE, RAPE[3])]

Koi'nē (*or* -ā) *n*. The common language of the Greeks from the close of classical period to the Byzantine era; (*k~*) common language shared by various peoples, lingua franca. [f. Gk *koinē* (*dialektos*) common (language)]

kōla. See COLA.

kolĭ'nsky̆ *n*. (Fur of) Siberian mink. [f. Russ. *kolinskiĭ* (*Kola* in N.W. Russia)]

kŏ'lkhŏz (-kŏz) *n*. Collective farm in U.S.S.R. [Russ., f. *kollektivnoe khozyaĭstvo* collective farm]

kŏ'llergăng *n*. Mill with vertical rollers for crushing paper-pulp. [G]

kŏmĭtă'(d)jĭ. Var. of COMITADJI.

komō'dō *n*. **~ dragon** or **lizard,** very large monitor lizard (*Varanus komodoensis*). [f. *K~* Island in Indonesia]

Kŏ'msomŏl *n*. (Member of) U.S.S.R. organization for young people. [Russ., f. *Kommunisticheskiĭ Soyuz Molodezhi* Communist League of Youth]

kōō'dōō, kudu (kōō'dōō), *n*. Large white-striped spiral-horned Afr. antelope of genus *Strepsiceros*. [f. Xhosa-Kaffir *iqudu*]

***kōōk** *n*. & *a*. (sl.) Crazy or eccentric (person); hence **~'Y**[2] *a*. [20th c.; prob. f. CUCKOO]

kōō'kabŭrra (*or* kŏŏ'-) *n*. (Austral.) Laughing JACK[1]ass. [Aboriginal]

kō'pĕ(c)k. Var. of COPECK.

kŏ'pje (-pĭ), **kŏ'ppĭe,** *n*. (S. Afr.) Small hill. [Du. *kopje*, Afrik. *koppie*, dim. of *kop* head]

Kōra'n (-ah'n; *or* kor-) *n*. Sacred book of the Muslims, collection of Muhammad's oral revelations, written in Arabic; hence **~IC** (*or* -ă'-) *a*. [f. Arab. *ḳur'ān* recitation (*ḳara'a* read)]

Korē'an *a.* & *n.* (Native or language) of Korea. [f. *Korea* in E. Asia + -AN]
kŏr'fball (-awl) *n.* Game like basketball played by teams of 12 men and women. [f. Du. *korfbal* (*korf* basket, *bal* ball)]
kō'sher *a.* & *n.* **1.** *a.* (Of food or shop where food is sold or used) fulfilling requirements of Jewish law; (colloq.) correct, genuine, legitimate. **2.** *n.* Kosher food or shop. [f. Heb. *kāšēr* proper]
kō'tō *n.* (*pl.* ~s). Japanese musical instrument with 13 long silk strings. [Jap.]
kōtow', kowtow', *n.*, & *v.i.* **1.** *n.* Chinese custom of touching ground with forehead as sign of worship or absolute submission. **2.** *v.i.* Perform the kotow; act obsequiously (*to* person etc.). [f. Chin. *k'o-t'ou* (*k'o* knock, *t'ou* head)]
kou'mĭss (kōō'-) *n.* Fermented liquor prepared from mare's or other milk, used by Asian nomads or medicinally. [f. Tartar *kumiz*]
kour'băsh (koor'-) *n.* Whip of (esp. hippopotamus) hide as instrument of punishment in Turkey and Egypt. [f. Arab. *kurbāj* f. Turk. *kırbāç* whip]
kowhai (kō'ī *or* kō'wī) *n.* Golden-flowered N.Z. tree or shrub of genus *Sophora*. [Maori]
kowtow'. See KOTOW.
||**K.P.** *abbr.* Knight (of the Order) of St. Patrick.
k.p.h. *abbr.* kilometres per hour.
Kr *symb.* krypton.
kraal (-ahl) *n.* S. Afr. village of huts enclosed by fence; enclosure for cattle or sheep. [Afrik., f. Port. *curral*, of Hottentot orig.]
kraft (-ahft) *n.* ~ (**paper**), strong smooth brown wrapping-paper. [G, = strength]
krait (-īt) *n.* Highly venomous E. Asian snake of genus *Bungarus*. [f. Hindi *karait*]
kra'ken (-ah'-) *n.* Mythical sea-monster said to appear off coast of Norway. [Norw.]
krans (-ah-) *n.* (S. Afr.) Precipitous or overhanging wall of rocks. [Afrik., f. Du. *krans* coronet]
Kraut (-owt) *n.* (derog.) German. [f. SAUERKRAUT]
krĕ'mlĭn *n.* Citadel within Russian town, esp. that of Moscow; **the K~**, the U.S.S.R. Government; hence **K~ŏ'**LOGY *n.*, study and analysis of Soviet policies. [F, f. Russ. *kreml'*, of Tartar origin]
krie'gspiel *n.* War-game in which blocks representing troops etc. are moved about on maps; form of chess with umpire, in which each player has only limited information about opponent's moves. [G (*krieg* war, *spiel* game)]
krĭll *n.* Tiny planktonic crustaceans eaten by whales etc. [f. Norw. *kril* tiny fish]
krĭ'mmer *n.* Grey or black fur from wool of young Crimean lambs. [G (*Krim* Crimea)]
kris, crease[2]**, creese,** (krēs) *n.* Malay dagger with wavy blade. [ult. f. Malay *k(i)ris*]
Krĭ'shnaĭsm *n.* Worship of Krishna, great deity of later Hinduism, worshipped as incarnation of Vishnu. [f. *Krishna* + -ISM]
kromĕ'skȳ *n.* Minced meat or fish rolled in bacon and fried. [app. f. Russ. *kromochka*, dim. of *kroma* slice of bread]
krō'n|a *n.* Monetary unit of Sweden (*pl.* ~*or*) and of Iceland (*pl.* ~*ur*). [Sw. & Icel., = CROWN[1]]
krō'ne (-*e*) *n.* (*pl.* ~**r**). Monetary unit of Denmark and of Norway. [Da. & Norw., = CROWN[1]]
Krōō, Kru (-ōō), *n.* & *a.* (Member) of Negro race on coast of Liberia, skilful as seamen. [W. Afr.]
krŭ'mmhŏrn *n.* Medieval wind instrument with double reed and curved end. [G (*krumm* crooked, *horn* HORN[1])]
krȳ'ptŏn *n.* (Chem.) Rare inert gaseous element. [f. Gk *krupton* hidden, neut. adj. f. *kruptō* hide]
||**K.S.** *abbr.* King's Scholar.
Ksha'trĭya (-ah'-) *n.* Member of second of four great Hindu castes, the military caste. [Skr. (*kshatra* rule)]
K.St.J. *abbr.* Knight (of the Order) of St. John.
K.T. *abbr.* Knight Templar; ||Knight (of the Order) of the Thistle.
Kt. *abbr.* Knight.
kū'dŏs *n.* (colloq.) Glory, renown. [Gk]
kudu. See KOODOO.
Kū'fĭc. See CUFIC.
***Kū'-Klŭx(-Klă'n)** *n.* Secret society hostile to Negroes, orig. formed in southern States after Civil War. [perh. f. Gk *kuklos* circle, + CLAN]
ku'krĭ (kōō'-) *n.* Curved knife broadening towards point, used by Gurkhas. [f. Hindi *kukrī*]
ku'lăk (kōō'-) *n.* Well-to-do Russian peasant; peasant working for his own profit in Soviet Russia. [Russ., = fist, tight-fisted person]
ku'lan (kōō'-) *n.* Wild ass of S.W. Asia, closely related to kiang. [Tartar]
kultur (kooltoor') *n.* (esp. derog.) Civilization as conceived by the Germans (with implication of racial arrogance and militarism); ***~kampf,*** conflict between civil and ecclesiastical authorities esp. as regards control of schools. [G, f. L *cultura* CULTURE]
kumis(s). Var. of KOUMISS.
kümmel (kōō'mel) *n.* Sweet liqueur flavoured with caraway seeds. [G, f. as CUMIN]
kumquat. See CUMQUAT.
kung fu (kōōngfōō') *n.* Chinese form of karate. [Chin.]
kurbash. Var. of KOURBASH.
kŭrchatō'vĭum *n.* (Chem.) Artificially produced transuranic metallic element. [f. I. V. *Kurchatov*, Russ. physicist d. 1960 + -IUM]
Kûrd (*or* koord) *n.* One of a tall pastoral people in Kurdistan etc.; hence ~'ISH[1] *a.* & *n.*, (Iranian language) of the Kurds. [Kurdish]
kŭ'rrajŏng *n.* Austral. tree yielding tough bast fibre. [Aboriginal]
kursaal (koor'zahl) *n.* Building for use of visitors at (esp. German) health resort; casino. [G (*kur* CURE[1], *saal* room)]
kûrtō'sĭs *n.* (Statistics). Sharpness of peak of frequency-distribution curve. [mod. L, f. Gk *kurtōsis* bulging (*kurtos* convex f. *kurtos, kurtē* lobster-pot)]
kV *abbr.* kilovolt(s).
kvăss *n.* Russian rye-beer. [f. Russ. *kvas*]
kW *abbr.* kilowatt(s).
kwashiŏr'kŏr (kwŏ-) *n.* (Path.) Tropical disease of children, caused by insufficiency of protein in diet. [native name in Ghana]
KWIC *abbr.* keyword in context.
KWOC *abbr.* keyword out of context.
Ky. *abbr.* Kentucky.
kȳ'anīte *n.* Aluminium silicate as blue crystalline mineral. [f. Gk *kuanos* dark blue + -ITE[1]]
kȳ'anīze, -ise (-īz), *v.t.* Treat (wood) with solution of corrosive sublimate to prevent decay. [f. J. H. *Kyan*, Engl. inventor d. 1850 + -IZE]
kȳ'bŏsh. Var. of KIBOSH.
kȳle *n.* Narrow channel between island and island or mainland in W. Scotland. [f. Gael. *caol* strait]
ky'lĭn (kē'-) *n.* Fabulous composite animal figured on Chinese and Japanese pottery. [f. Chin. *ch'i-lin* (*ch'i* male, *lin* female)]
||**kȳ'lōe** *n.* One of breed of small long-horned Scottish cattle. [f. *K~* in Northumberland]
kȳ'mograph (-ahf) *n.* Instrument recording

variations in pressure, e.g. in sound-waves, or successive positions of moving object, e.g. heart. [f. Gk *kuma* wave + -O- + -GRAPH]

kȳph|ō'sĭs *n.* (*pl.* **~oses** *pr.* -ō'sēz). (Med.) Curvature of spine, convex backwards (opp. *lordosis*); hence **~O'TIC** *a.* [mod. L, f. Gk *kuphōsis* (*kuphos* bent; see -OSIS)]

***kyrie* (*eleison*)** (kēr'ĭĭ ĭlā'ĭson; *or* -ĭā -ŏn; *or* kĭ'rĭē) *n.* **1.** (First word(s) of) short petition used in Roman and Orthodox Churches, esp. at beginning of Mass; musical setting of these. **2.** Response to commandments in Communion Service in Anglican Church. [ME f. med. L, f. Gk *Kurie eleēson* Lord, have mercy]

L

L, l, (ĕl) *n.* (*pl.* **Ls** *or* **L's**). Twelfth letter of alphabet; right-angled joint of pipes etc.; (as Roman numeral) 50 (**li** 51, **lv** 55, **lx** 60); *(colloq.) elevated railway (cf. EL).

L. *abbr.* Lake; ||learner-driver; Liberal; Licentiate; (Biol.) Linnaeus.

£ *abbr.* = POUND[1] 2, pounds (*£5*; *£E* = Egyptian pound(s), etc.). [f. L *libra*]

l. *abbr.* left; line; lire; litre(s); (arch.) POUND[1] 2.

la. See LAH.

L.A. *abbr.* Library Association; Los Angeles.

La. *abbr.* Louisiana.

La *symb.* lanthanum.

laa'ger (lah'g-) *n.* & *v.* **1.** *n.* Camp, encampment, esp. in circle of wagons; (Mil.) park for armoured vehicles. **2.** *v.t.* Form (vehicles) into laager; encamp (persons) in laager. **3.** *v.i.* Encamp. [Afrik., f. Du. *leger*; see LEAGUER[1]]

lăb *n.* (colloq.) Laboratory. [abbr.]

Lab. *abbr.* Labour; Labrador.

lă'barum *n.* Constantine the Great's imperial standard, with Christian symbols added to Roman military symbols; symbolic banner. [LL, of unkn. orig.]

lă'bdanum. Var. of LADANUM.

lăbėfă'ction *n.* (literary). Shaking, weakening, downfall. [f. L *labefacere* weaken (*labi* fall, *facere* make); see -FACTION]

lā'bel *n.*, & *v.t.* (||-ll-). **1.** *n.* Slip of paper, card, linen, metal, etc., for attaching to object and indicating its nature, owner, name, destination, etc.; piece of paper on centre of gramophone record describing its contents, company manufacturing gramophone records with distinctive label; (fig.) short classifying phrase or name applied to persons etc. (freq. derog. in literary or artistic criticism); adhesive stamp; (Archit.) dripstone; (Her.) mark of eldest son, consisting of superimposed horizontal bar with (usu. 3) downward projections. **2.** *v.t.* Attach label to; assign to a category (*as*, or abs.); replace (atom) by atom of a (usu. radioactive) isotope as means of identification; replace atom in (molecule) or atoms in molecules of (substance) thus; (in *p.p.*) made identifiable thus. [ME f. OF, = ribbon, prob. f. Gmc (as LAP[1]) + dim. -EL]

lā'bĭa. See LABIUM.

lā'bĭal *a.* & *n.* **1.** *a.* Of the lips; (Anat. & Zool.) of, like, serving as, a lip, liplike part, or labium. **2.** (Mus.) **~ pipe** in organ, one furnished with lips, flue-pipe. **3.** *a.* & *n.* (Phonet.) (Sound) requiring partial or complete closure of lips (*p, b, f, v, m, w*, and vowels in which lips are rounded, as ōō); hence **~ISM** (1) *n.*, **~IZE** (3) *v.t.* [f. med. L *labialis* f. L *labia* lips; see -AL]

lā'bĭate *a.* & *n.* **1.** (Bot.) (Plant) with corolla or calyx divided into two parts suggesting lips. **2.** *a.* (Bot. & Zool.) Like lip or labium. [f. mod. L *labiatus* (as LABIUM; see -ATE[2])]

lā'bĭle *a.* (Phys. & Chem.) Unstable, liable to displacement or change; hence **labĭ'lITY** *n.* [ME, f. LL *labilis* (*labi* fall; see -IL)]

lā'bĭō- *comb. form.* Of the lip(s) (and), as: **~de'ntal,** (sound) made with lip and teeth, e.g. *f, v*; **~-ve'lar,** (sound) made with lips and soft palate, e.g. *w*. [f. as foll. + -O-]

lā'bĭ|um *n.* (*pl.* **~a**). **1.** (Anat., usu. in *pl.*) Lip of female pudendum; **~a major'a, minor'a,** outer, inner, folds of labia. **2.** Lower part of mouth of insect, crustacean, etc.; inner lip of univalve shell. **3.** Lip, esp. the lower one, of labiate plant's corolla. [L, = lip]

***lā'bor** etc. See LABOUR[1,2] etc.

labŏ'ratorў (*or* lă'ber-) *n.* Room or building used for experiments in natural science, esp. chemistry, or for research (lit., or fig.: *laboratory of the mind* etc.); LANGUAGE *laboratory*; **~ animal** (of species commonly used for laboratory experiments). [f. med. L *laboratorium* (L *laborare* LABOUR[2]; see -ORY)]

labôr'ĭous *a.* Hard-working; toilsome; (of style etc.) showing signs of toil, not facile or fluent; hence **~LY**[2] *adv.*, **~NESS** *n.* [ME, f. OF *laborieus* f. L *laboriosus* (as foll.; see -IOUS)]

lā'bour[1] (-ber), ***lā'bor**[1], *n.* **1.** Bodily or mental work, exertion, (HARD *labour*; **~ in vain, lost ~,** fruitless efforts; **~ of love,** task one delights in or does for love of someone). **2.** Toil tending to supply wants of the community; body of those who contribute by toil to production, labourers; the labouring classes as a political force; (*L~*) the Labour Party. **3.** Task (**~ of Hercules,** one needing enormous strength etc.). **4.** Pains of childbirth, (uterine contractions in) process of giving birth, (*in labour*). **5. L~ Day** (celebrated in honour of workers, esp. 1 May or *first Monday in Sept.); **L~ Exchange,** (colloq. or Hist.) employment exchange; **~ force,** body of workers employed; *labour*-INTENSIVE; **~-market,** supply of labour with reference to demand on it; **L~ Party,** (Polit.) party representing interests esp. of workers; **~-saving,** designed to reduce or eliminate work; ***~ union,** trade union. [ME, f. OF *labo(u)r* f. L *labor -oris*]

lā'bour[2] (-ber), ***lā'bor**[2], *v.* **1.** *v.i.* Use labour, exert oneself, work hard (**~ing man,** labourer); strive *for* purpose *to* do; advance with difficulty (*wheels labour in the sand*); be troubled (*her labouring heart*) or impeded; suffer *under* (delusion etc.); (of ship) roll or pitch heavily. **2.** *v.t.* (arch. or poet.) Till (ground). **3.** Elaborate, work out in (excessive) detail, treat at (great) length, (*I will not labour the point*); (in *p.p.*) much elaborated, showing signs of labour, done with great effort, not spontaneous. [ME, f. OF *labourer* f. L *laborare* (*labor* LABOUR[1])]

lā'bourer (-ber-), ***lā'borer,** *n.* One who labours, (esp.) man doing for wages work that requires strength or patience rather than skill or training, or assisting skilled workman. [ME, f. OF *laboureur* (as prec.; see -ER[2])]

lā'bourite (-ber-), ***lā'borite,** *n.* Member or adherent of Labour Party. [f. LABOUR[1] + -ITE[1] (1)]

K L

Lă′bradŏr *n.* ~ **(dog, retriever)**, breed of retriever with black or golden coat. [~ in Canada]

lā′bret *n.* Piece of shell, bone, etc., inserted in lip as ornament. [f. foll. + -ET¹]

lā′br|um *n.* (*pl.* ~**a**). Upper lip of insect. [L, = lip, cogn. w. LABIUM]

labûr′num *n.* Small leguminous tree of genus *Laburnum*, with poisonous seeds, esp. an ornamental species (*L. anagyroides*) with racemes of bright yellow flowers. [L]

lă′byrĭnth *n.* Complicated irregular structure with many passages hard to find way through or about without guidance, maze; intricate or tortuous arrangement; (Anat.) complex cavity of internal ear, with membranous structure within bony case; entangled state of affairs; hence ~INE² (-ĭ′nthīn) *a.* [f. F *labyrinthe* or f. L f. Gk *laburinthos*]

lăc¹ *n.* Resinous substance secreted on trees by ~ **insect** of S.E. Asia as protective covering, used as varnish etc. [ult. f. Hind. *lākh* f. Prakrit *lakkha* f. Skr. *lākṣā*]

lăc². See LAKH.

‖**L.A.C.** *abbr.* Leading Aircraftman.

lă′ccolĭth *n.* (Geol.) Dome-shaped intrusion of igneous rock from beneath sedimentary rocks. [f. Gk *lakkos* reservoir + -LITH]

lāce¹ *n.* **1.** Cord or leather strip for fastening or tightening opposite edges of shoes, corsets, etc., by help of eyelets or hooks; braid for trimming men's coats etc. (usu. *gold* or *silver lace*). **2.** Fine open fabric of linen, cotton, silk, woollen, or metal threads usu. with inwrought or applied patterns; hence **lā′cy²** *a.* **3.** ~**-glass** (Venetian, with lacelike designs); ~**-pillow,** pad laid on lap of person making lace; ~**′wing,** neuropterous fly; ~**′wood,** timber of plane tree. [ME, f. OF *laz, las*, f. Rom. **lacium* f. L *laqueus* noose]

lāce² *v.* **1.** *v.t.* ~ **(up)**, fasten or tighten (shoe, corsets, etc.) with lace(s); compress waist of (person) thus with corset-laces; ~**-up** *a.* & *n.*, (shoe) provided with lace. **2.** Interlace or embroider (fabric) *with* thread etc.; pass (cord etc.) *through*. **3.** Trim with lace; diversify *with* streaks of colour. **4.** Lash, beat, defeat. **5.** Flavour, fortify, (coffee, beer, etc.) with dash of spirits. **6.** *v.i.* ~ **into,** = sense 4. **7.** Hence **lā′**CING¹ (1, 3, 6) *n.* [ME, f. OF *lacier* f. Rom. **laciare* (as prec.)]

lă′cer|āte *v.t.* Mangle, tear, (esp. flesh or tissues); (fig.) afflict, distress, (heart, feelings); hence or cogn. ~ABLE *a.*, ~A′TION *n.* [f. L *lacerare* (*lacer* torn) + -ATE³]

lacĕr′tian, -tīne, *adjs.* Of lizards; lizard-like. [f. L *lacerta* lizard + -IAN, -INE¹]

lă′chĕs (-z) *n.* (Law) negligence in performing a legal duty, delay in asserting right, claiming privilege, etc.; culpable negligence. [ME, f. AF *laches(se)*, OF *laschesse* (*lasche* f. Rom. **lascus* for L *laxus* loose)]

lăchrўma Chrĭ′stĭ (lăk-; krĭ′-) *n.* Strong sweet red wine of S. Italy. [L, = Christ's tear]

lă′chrўmal (-k-) *a.* & *n.* **1.** *a.* Of or for tears; ~ **vase** (to hold tears of mourners etc.). **2.** (Anat.) concerned in secretion of tears (*lachrymal canal, duct, gland, sac*). **3.** *n.* Lachrymal vase; (in *pl.*) lachrymal organs. [ME, f. med. L *lachrymalis* f. L *lacrima* tear]

lăchrўmā′tion (-k-) *n.* Flow of tears. [f. L *lacrimatio* (*lacrimare* weep, as prec.; see -ATION)]

lă′chrўmātor (-k-) *n.* Tear-gas. [f. as foll. + -OR]

lă′chrўmatorў (-k-) *a.* & *n.* **1.** Of or causing tears. **2.** *n.* Phial of kind found in ancient Roman tombs and conjectured to be lachrymal vases. [f. L *lacrima* tear + -ORY]

lă′chrўmōse (-k-) *a.* Tearful, given to weeping; hence ~LY² (-slĭ) *adv.* [f. L *lacrimosus* (*lacrima* tear; see -OSE¹)]

lacĭ′nĭate, lacĭ′nĭātėd, *adjs.* (Bot. & Zool.) Cut into deep narrow irregular segments. [f. L *lacinia* flap of garment; see -ATE², -ED¹]

lăck *n.* & *v.* **1.** *n.* Not having; want, need, *of* **(no** ~, plenty *of*; **for** ~, owing to want or absence *of*). **2.** *v.t.* Be without, not have when needed, be deficient in, (*lacks money, courage*). **3.** *v.i.* ~ **for,** have none or insufficient of; ~′ING² *a.*, undesirably absent or deficient (*money was lacking; is lacking in courage*). **4.** ~**′land,** (person) having no land, (*L-*) nickname of King John; ~**-lustre,** (of eye etc.) dull. [ME *lac, lacen*, corresp. to MDu., MLG *lak* deficiency, MDu. *laken* to lack]

lăckadai′sĭcal (-z-) *a.* Languishing, affected, given to airs and graces, feebly sentimental; unenthusiastic, listless; hence ~LY² *adv.*, ~NESS *n.* [f. arch. *lackaday, -daisy*, int. (ALACK) + -ICAL]

lă′cker. Var. of LACQUER.

lă′ckey *n.*, & *v.t.* **1.** *n.* Footman, manservant (usu. liveried); servant; obsequious person, parasite; servile political follower; ~ **moth** (whose striped caterpillars resemble footman's livery). **2.** *v.t.* Dance attendance on, behave servilely to. [f. F *laquais*, obs. *alaquais* f. Cat. *alacay* = Sp. ALCALDE]

Lacō′nĭan *a.* & *n.* (Inhabitant or dialect) of Laconia, Spartan. [f. L *Laconia* Sparta f. Gk *Lakōn* Spartan, + -AN]

lacŏ′n|ĭc *a.* Brief, concise, sententious; given to such speech or style; hence ~ICALLY *adv.*, ~ĭCISM (2) *n.* [f. L f. Gk *Lakōnikos* (*Lakōn* Spartan; see -IC), the Spartans being known for their terse speech]

lă′conism *n.* Brevity of speech; short pithy saying. [f. Gk *lakōnismos* (*lakōnizō* behave like Spartan; see prec., -ISM)]

lă′cquer (-k*er*) *n.*, & *v.t.* **1.** *n.* Coloured varnish of shellac dissolved in alcohol used esp. as coating for brass; sap of ~**-tree** (*Rhus vernicifera*) taking hard polish and used to varnish wood etc.; synthetic liquid that dries to form protective film; substance sprayed on hair to keep it in place. **2.** *v.t.* Coat with lacquer. [f. obs. F *lacre* sealing-wax, f. unexpl. var. of Port. *laca* LAC¹]

lacquey. Var. of LACKEY.

lacrim-, lacrym-. Vars. of LACHRYM-.

lacrŏ′sse (*or* -aw′s) *n.* Game like hockey, but with ball driven by and caught and carried in crosse. [F (*la* the, CROSSE)]

lă′ctāte¹ *n.* (Chem.) Salt or ester of lactic acid. [f. LACTIC + -ATE¹ (3)]

lăctā′te² *v.i.* Secrete milk. [f. as foll. + -ATE³]

lăctā′tion *n.* Suckling; secreting of milk. [f. L *lactare* suckle (*lac lactis* milk) + -ATION]

lă′ctėal *a.* & *n.* **1.** *a.* Of milk; conveying chyle or other milky fluid. **2.** *n.* (in *pl.*) Lymphatic vessels of mesentery conveying chyle. [f. L *lacteus* (*lac*; see prec.) + -AL]

lăctĕ′scence *n.*, **lăctĕ′scent** *a.* Milky (appearance); (yielding) milky juice. [f. L *lactescere* (*lactēre* be milky f. as foll.); see -ESCENCE, -ESCENT]

lă′ctĭc *a.* (Chem.) Of milk; ~ **acid** (formed in sour milk). [f. L *lac lactis* milk + -IC]

lăctĭ′ferous *a.* Yielding milk or milky fluid. [f. LL *lactifer* (as prec.; see -FEROUS)]

lă′ctō- *comb. form.* Milk, as: ~METER (-ŏ′m-), instrument for testing density of milk; ~**pro′tein,** albuminous constituent of milk. [f. L *lac lactis* milk + -O-]

lă′ctōse *n.* Sugar present in milk, less sweet than sucrose. [f. as prec. + -OSE²]

lacū′n|a *n.* (*pl.* ~**ae** *or* ~**as**). Hiatus, blank, missing portion (esp. in ancient MS., book, etc.), empty part; cavity in bone, tissue, etc.; hence ~AL, ~AR¹, ~ARY¹, ~OSE¹, *adjs.* [L, = pool (*lacus* LAKE¹)]

lacŭ'strīne *a.* Of, dwelling or growing in, lake(s); ~ **age** (of LAKE[1]-dwellings). [f. L *lacus* LAKE[1] (after *palustris* marshy) + -INE[1]]

||**L.A.C.W.** *abbr.* Leading Aircraftwoman.

lā'cȳ. See LACE[1].

lăd *n.* Boy, youth, young fellow, young son; man, fellow; stable-man or -woman (of any age); **my ~, the ~s,** (cf. BOY); **~'s love,** southernwood; hence **~'DIE** *n.* [ME *ladde,* of unkn. orig.]

lă'danum *n.* Gum resin from plants of genus *Cistus,* used in perfumery etc. [L, f. Gk *ladanon* (*lēdon* mastic)]

lă'dder *n.* & *v.* **1.** *n.* Set of steps (called *rungs*) inserted usu. in two uprights of wood or metal or in two cords to serve as (usu. portable) means of ascending building etc.; SALMON-*ladder*; SNAKES *and ladders*; STEP[2]-*ladder.* **2.** ||Vertical flaw in stocking etc. caused by stitch(es) becoming undone through several rows; hence ~PROOF[2] *a.* **3.** (fig.) Means of rising in the world or attaining object (**kick down the ~,** abandon friends or occupation that have helped one to rise); see RUNG[1]. **4. ~-back,** (chair) with back made of horizontal bars between uprights; **~-dredge** (with buckets carried round on ladder-like chain); **~-stitch,** transverse bars in embroidery; **~ tournament** (with contestants listed and each entitled to gain higher place if he can defeat one just above him). **5.** *v.i.* ||Develop ladder (sense 2). **6.** *v.t.* ||Cause ladder (sense 2) in. [OE *hlǣd(d)er,* = MDu. *lēdere,* OHG *leitara* f. WG **hlaidr-* f. Gmc **hli-, *hlai-* (LEAN[2])]

lāde *v.t.* (*p.p.* **la'den**). **1.** Put cargo on board (ship); ship (goods) as cargo (BILL[4] *of lading*), whence **lā'DING**[1] (3) *n.* **2.** (in *p.p.*) (Of vehicle, beast of burden, person, tree, branch, table, etc.) loaded (*with*); painfully burdened *with* sin, sorrow, etc. [OE *hladan,* = OS, OHG *hladan,* ON *hlatha,* Goth. *-hlathan;* cf. LAST[2]]

la-dĭ-da' (lahdĭdah') *n.* & *a.* **1.** *n.* (Person given to) swagger or pretension in manners and pronunciation. **2.** *a.* Pretentious in this way. [imit. of pronunc. used]

ladies. See LADY.

lā'dĭfȳ. See LADYFY.

Ladi'n (-ē'n) *n.* Rhaeto-Romanic of the Engadine. [Romansh, f. L *latinus* LATIN]

Ladi'nō (-ē'-) *n.* (*pl.* **~s**). **1.** Spanish dialect of Sephardic Jews. **2.** Mestizo or white person in Central America. [Sp., orig. = Latin, f. L (as prec.)]

lā'dle *n.,* & *v.t.* **1.** *n.* Large spoon, with cup-shaped bowl and long handle, for transferring liquids; vessel for transporting molten metal in foundry; hence **~FUL** 2 (-delf-) *n.* **2.** *v.t.* Transfer (liquid) with ladle from one receptacle to another; **~ out,** (fig.) distribute, esp. lavishly. [OE *hlædel* (*hladan* LADE, -LE 1)]

lā'dȳ *n.* **1.** Ruling woman (*lady of the house* or *manor; Lady* SUPERIOR; *our sovereign lady*); **find the ~,** = THREE-*card trick.* **2.** Woman to whom man is chivalrously devoted; mistress. **3. Our L~,** Virgin Mary; hence *Lady's bed-straw, finger,* etc. (see sense 13). **4.** Woman belonging to the upper class, or fitted for it by manners, habits, and sentiments, (corresp. to *gentleman*; ||**~ of the bedchamber, ~-in-waiting,** lady attending queen or princess). **5.** (Courteous or formal synonym for) woman (when used as *voc.,* only poet. or vulg. in *sing.,* but usu. form of address in *pl.*); **ladies and gentlemen** (in addressing company of both sexes); YOUNG *lady.* **6.** ||(*L~,* title used as less formal prefix for) Marchioness (of), Countess (of), Viscountess, Baroness, (also prefixed to Christian name of) daughter of duke, marquis, or earl, (or to husband's Christian name of) wife or widow of holder of courtesy title *Lord* William etc., (or to surname of) wife or widow of baronet or knight; **L~ Mayoress,** wife of Lord Mayor. **7. My ~,** form of address used chiefly by servants etc. to holders of title *Lady*; **my dear** or **good ~** (as *voc.* in gen. use); OLD *lady.* **8.** Wife (arch. or vulg., exc. of those who hold title *Lady* or in respectful ref.; *my* or *your lady wife*); **your good ~,** your wife. **9.** (*attrib.,* usu. courteous or formal) Female (*lady clerk, doctor, friend, president, dog,* etc.). **10.** ||**The ladies** or **ladies',** (as *sing. n.*) women's public lavatory. **11. Ladies' chain,** figure in quadrille etc.; **Ladies' Gallery** (in House of Commons, reserved for ladies). **12.** *Lady of* EASY *virtue*; PAINT[2]*ed lady.* **13. L~-altar** (in Lady chapel); **~bird, *~bug,** coleopterous insect of family Coccinellidae, usu. reddish-brown with black spots; **L~ Bountiful,** beneficent lady in village etc. [character in Farquhar's *Beaux' Stratagem*]; **~-chair,** seat made by two persons' interlaced hands to carry wounded man etc.; **L~ chapel** (in large church, often E. of high altar, dedicated to Virgin Mary); **~-clock, -cow,** ladybird; **L~ Day,** Feast of the Annunciation, 25 Mar.; **~-fern** (slender kind); ***~finger,** finger-shaped sponge-cake; ||*lady* HELP[2]; **~-killer,** man devoting himself to making conquests of women; **~-love,** man's sweetheart; *Lady's* BED[1]*straw*; **~'s companion,** roll containing cottons etc.; **L~'s finger,** kidney-VETCH; **L~'s laces,** kind of striped grass; **~'s-maid,** personal maid-servant of lady; **ladies' man, ~'s man,** (fond of female society); **L~'s mantle,** rosaceous plant of genus *Alchemilla* with yellowish-green clustered flowers; **~-smock,** = cuckoo flower (1); **~'s slipper,** orchidaceous wild and garden plant with usu. yellow bag- or slipper-shaped flowers; **L~'s tresses,** white-flowered orchis of genus *Spiranthes.* **14.** Hence **~HOOD** *n.* [OE *hlǣfdige* (*hlāf* LOAF[1], **dig-* knead; cf. DOUGH); in *Lady Day* etc. f. OE gen. *hlæfdigan* (Our) Lady's]

lā'dȳfȳ, lā'dĭfȳ, *v.t.* Make lady of; call 'lady'; (in *p.p.*) having the airs of a FINE[2] lady. [f. prec. + -FY]

lā'dylike *a.* With manners etc. of a lady; (of man) effeminate; befitting a lady. [f. LADY + -LIKE]

lā'dȳshĭp *n.* Being a lady; **her, your, ~, their ~s,** she, you, they, (in respectful mention of or address to holder(s) of title *Lady*; also iron.). [ME, f. LADY + -SHIP)]

l(a)e'vō- (lē'-) *comb. form.* Left, esp. (Chem.) w. ref. to property of causing plane of polarized light ray to rotate to left (opp. DEXTRO-); **~ro'tatory,** (of substance) having this property; **~tartaric acid** etc. (form having this property). [f. L *laevus* left + -O-]

l(a)e'vūlōse (lē'v-) *n.* (Chem.) Laevorotatory fructose in fruit and honey. [f. as prec. + -ULE + -OSE[2]]

lăg[1] *v.i.* (**-gg-**), & *n.* **1.** *v.i.* Go too slow, not keep pace, fall behind or *behind* (adv. or prep.); * = STRING 15. **2.** *n.* Lagging, delay; (Phys.) (amount of) retardation in current or movement (**~ of tide,** interval by which it falls behind mean time at 1st and 3rd quarters of moon; cf. PRIMING[2]); TIME[1]-*lag.* **3.** Hence **~'GARD** *n.* & *a.,* **~'GER**[1] *n.,* **~'GING**[2] *a.,* (-g-). [orig. 'hindmost person', 'hang back'; perh. f. a fanciful distortion of LAST[3] in children's game (*fog, seg, lag,* = 1st, 2nd, last, in dial.)]

lăg[2] *v.t.* (**-gg-**), & *n.* (sl.) **1.** *v.t.* Send to prison; ||apprehend, arrest; hence **~'GING**[1] (-g-) *n.,* term of imprisonment. **2.** *n.* Convict, esp. *old lag.* [19th c.; orig. unkn.]

lăg[3] *n.,* & *v.t.* (**-gg-**). **1.** *n.* (Piece of) non-heat-conducting cover of boiler etc. **2.** *v.t.* Enclose in lags; hence **~'GING**[1] (1, 3) (-g-) *n.* [prob. f.

Scand.; cf. ON *lögg* barrel-rim, cogn. w. LAY³]

lă'gan *n.* (Law). Goods or wreckage lying on bed of sea, sometimes with buoy etc. for later retrieval of them. [OF, perh. of Scand. orig., f. root of LIE³, LAY³]

la'ger (lah'g-) *n.* Light kind of (orig. German or Bohemian) beer. [f. G *lager-bier* beer brewed for keeping (*lager* store)]

***lagniăppe** (lă'nyăp *or* lahnyă'p) *n.* Thing given as bonus or gratuity. [Louisiana F, f. Sp. *la ñapa*]

lă'gomorph *n.* (Zool.) Animal of order Lagomorpha, e.g. hare or rabbit. [f. Gk *lagōs* hare + *morphē* form]

lagoo'n *n.* Stretch of salt water separated from sea by low sandbank; enclosed water of atoll; *small freshwater lake near larger lake or river. [f. F *lagune* or f. It. & Sp. *laguna* f. L LACUNA]

lah, la, (lah) *n.* (Mus.) Sixth note of scale in movable-doh system; the note A in fixed-doh system. [ME, f. L *labii*; see GAMUT]

la'har (lah'-h-) *n.* Flow of volcanic mud. [Jav.]

lā'ic *a.* & *n.* Non-cleric(al), lay(man), secular, temporal; so ~AL *a.*, **~al**LY² *adv.* [f. LL f. Gk *laïkos* (*laos* people; see -IC)]

lā'iciz|e, -is|e (-iz), *v.t.* Make LAY²; subject (school etc.) to control, make (office) tenable, by laymen; hence ~A'TION *n.* [f. prec. + -IZE]

laid. See LAY³.

lain. See LIE³.

lair *n.* & *v.* **1.** *n.* Place where domestic animals lie down; ‖shed or enclosure for cattle on way to market, whence ~'AGE (1, 3) *n.*; wild animal's lying-place, (fig.) person's hiding-place. **2.** *v.i.* & *t.* Go to, rest or place in, lair. [OE *leger*, = OS *legar*, OHG *leger* bed, camp, Goth. *ligrs* bed f. Gmc **leg-* LIE³]

laird *n.* (Sc.) Landed proprietor; hence ~'SHIP *n.* [Sc. form of LORD]

laissez-aller, laisser-, (lāsā ă'lā) *n.* Unconstrained freedom, absence of constraint. [F, = let go]

laissez-faire, laisser-, (lāsāfar') *n.* Government abstention from interference with individual action esp. in commerce. [F, = let act]

laissez-passer, laisser-, (lāsāpă'sā) *n.* Permit, document allowing holder to pass. [F, = let pass]

lā'itў *n.* Body of those who are laymen in respect of religion or a profession. [ME, f. LAY² + -ITY]

lāke¹ *n.* Large body of water entirely surrounded by land; **the Great L~s,** Superior, Huron, Michigan, Erie, and Ontario, along boundary of U.S. and Canada; **~-country, L~ District, L~'land, the L~s,** region of English lakes in Cumbria; **~-dweller,** prehistoric inhabitant of **~-dwellings,** built on piles driven into bed or shore of lake; **L~ Poets,** Coleridge, Southey, and Wordsworth, who lived in Lake District; **L~land terrier,** breed of small stocky terrier originating in Lakeland; hence ~'LESS *a.*, ~'LET *n.*, (-kl-). [ME f. OF *lac* f. L *lacus* basin, pool, lake]

lāke² *n.* Reddish pigment, orig. made from lac; pigment made from dye on inert base of metal oxide; any insoluble product of soluble dye and mordant. [var. of LAC¹]

lăkh (-k), **lăc²,** *n.* (Ind.) A hundred thousand (*of* rupees etc.). [f. Hind. *lākh* f. Skr. *lakṣa*]

Lă'llan *a.* & *n.* (Sc.) **1.** *a.* Of the Lowlands of Scotland. **2.** *n.* ~(s), Lowland Scots dialect, esp. as literary language. [var. of LOWLAND]

lăllā'tion *n.* Pronunciation of *r* as *l*; imperfect speech (as) of young children. [f. L *lallare* sing lullaby + -ATION]

***lă'llўgăg** *v.i.* (-gg-). (sl.) Loiter; cuddle amorously. [20th c.; orig. unkn.]

lăm¹ *v.* (-mm-). (sl.) Thrash, hit (*into*) hard with stick etc. [perh. f. Scand.; cf. ON *lemja* beat so as to LAME]

***lăm²** *n.* (sl.) **On the ~,** fleeing. [20th c.; orig. unkn.]

Lam. *abbr.* Lamentations (O.T.).

la'ma (lah'-) *n.* Tibetan or Mongolian Buddhist priest; **Dalai L~** (dă'lī), chief lama of Tibet; **Pa'nchen** or **Ta'shi L~,** lama ranking next after Dalai Lama; hence ~ISM (3) *n.*, ~IST (2) *n.* & *a.*, (-*a*-ĭ-). [f. Tibetan *blama* (w. silent *b*)]

Lamar'ck|ĭan *a.* & *n.* (Follower) of Lamarck or his theory of organic evolution by the inheritance of acquired characters; so ~ISM (3) *n.* [f. J.-B. *Lamarck*, Fr. botanist and zoologist d. 1829 + -IAN]

lama'serў (-mah'-) *n.* Monastery of lamas. [f. F *lamaserie* irreg. f. *lama* LAMA]

lămb (-m) *n.* & *v.* **1.** *n.* Young of sheep; **as well be hanged** or **hung for a sheep as (for) a ~,** sin boldly, go the whole hog; **like a ~ (to the slaughter),** unresistingly. **2.** Flesh of lamb as food. **3.** Young member of church flock; innocent, weak, or dear person; **The L~ (of God),** Christ. **4. ~'s fry,** lamb's testicles or other offal as food; **~'skin** (with wool on, or as leather); **~'s lettuce,** salad-plant of genus *Valerianella*; **‖~'s-tails,** hazel catkins; **~'s--wool,** soft fine wool used in knitted garments. **5.** Hence ~'HOOD (-mh-), ~'KIN (-mk-), *ns.*, ~'LIKE (-ml-) *a.* **6.** *v.t.* (In pass., of lamb) be brought forth; tend (lambing ewes), whence ~'ER¹ (-m*er*) *n.* **7.** *v.i.* Give birth to lamb. [OE, = OS, OHG, ON, Goth. *lamb* f. Gmc **lambaz*]

lămbā'ste, -bă'st, *v.t.* (colloq.) Thrash, beat; criticize severely. [f. LAM¹ + BASTE³]

lă'mbda (-md*a*) *n.* Eleventh Greek letter (Λ, λ) = l; **~ moth** (with Λ-shaped mark on wings). [ME, f. Gk *la(m)bda*]

lă'mb|ent *a.* (Of flame or light) playing on surface without burning it, with soft radiance; (of eyes, sky, etc.) softly radiant; (of wit etc.) lightly brilliant; hence ~ENCY *n.*, **~ent**LY² *adv.* [f. L *lambere* lick; see -ENT]

lă'mbert *n.* Unit of surface brightness, corresponding to emission of one lumen per square centimetre. [f. J. H. *Lambert*, Ger. physicist d. 1777]

Lă'mbeth *n.* **~ Conference,** regular assembly of all bishops of Anglican Communion; **~ degree,** honorary degree conferred by Archbishop of Canterbury. [f. Archbishop of Canterbury's palace at ~ in London]

lă'mbrequin (-kĭn) *n.* *Short piece of drapery over top of door or window, or hung from mantelpiece; (Her.) mantling. [F, f. Du. **lamperkin*, dim. of *lamper* veil; see -KIN]

lāme *a.*, & *v.t.* **1.** *a.* Disabled by injury or defect in a limb, esp. foot or leg, limping or unable to walk normally, (of person, animal, limb, one's steps, etc.; *lame of*, or *in, a leg* etc.). **2.** (Of argument, story, excuse) imperfect, unsatisfactory, unconvincing; (of metre) halting; ***~-brain,** stupid person; **~ duck,** disabled person, defaulter on Stock Exchange, firm etc. unable to meet its financial obligations, *official about to retire after not being re-elected. **3.** Hence **lā'**MISH¹ 2 *a.*, ~'LY² (-mlĭ) *adv.*, ~'NESS (-mn-) *n.* **4.** *v.t.* Make lame, disable, (lit. or fig.). [OE *lama*, = OS *lamo*, OHG *lam*, ON *lami* f. Gmc **lamaz*]

lamé (lah'mā) *a.* & *n.* (Material) with gold or silver thread inwoven. [F]

lamĕ'll|a *n.* (*pl.* ~ae). Thin plate, scale, layer, or film, esp. of bone or tissue; hence ~AR¹, **lă'mell**ATE², **~ĭ**FORM, ~OSE¹, *adjs.* [L, dim. of LAMINA]

lamĕ'llĭbrănch (-ngk) *n.* Bivalve mollusc of

class Lamellibranchia, e.g. oyster. [f. as prec. + -I- + Gk *bragkhia* gills]

lamĕ'llĭcōrn *n.* & *a.* (Beetle) having lamelliform antennae, e.g. stag-beetle. [f. mod. L *lamellicornis* f. L LAMELLA + *cornu* horn]

lamĕ'nt *n.* & *v.* **1.** *n.* Passionate expression of grief; elegy, dirge. **2.** *v.t.* Express or feel grief for or about, be distressed at, regret; (in *p.p.*) mourned for (esp. conventionally of the dead: *your late lamented father*). **3.** *v.i.* ~ **for** or **over,** or abs., = sense 2. [n. f. L *lamentum*, or f. v. f. F *lamenter* or f. L *lamentari*]

lă'mentab|le *a.* (Of event, fate, condition, character, etc.) deplorable, regrettable; (arch.) mournful; hence ~LY² *adv.* [ME f. OF, or f. L *lamentabilis* (as prec.; see -ABLE)]

lămentā'tion *n.* Lamenting, lament; **L~s (of Jeremiah),** O.T. book on destruction of Jerusalem in 6th c. B.C. [ME f. OF, or f. L *lamentatio* (as LAMENT; see -ATION)]

lă'mĭn|a *n.* (*pl.* ~**ae**). Thin plate, scale, layer, or flake, of metal, bone, membrane, stratified rock, vegetable tissue, etc.; hence ~OSE¹ *a.* [L]

lă'mĭnar *a.* Consisting of laminae; (Phys., of flow) taking place along fixed streamlines, not turbulent. [f. prec. + -AR¹]

lă'mĭn|āte¹ *v.* **1.** *v.t.* Beat or roll (metal) into thin plates; overlay with metal plates; manufacture by placing layer on layer. **2.** *v.t.* & *i.* Split into layers or leaves. **3.** Hence ~A'TION *n.* [f. LAMINA + -ATE³]

lă'mĭnate² *a.* & *n.* **1.** *a.* In form of lamina(e). **2.** *n.* Laminated structure or material, esp. of layers fixed together to form rigid or flexible material. [f. LAMINA + -ATE²]

Lă'mmas *n.* First day of August, formerly observed as harvest festival (**latter ~,** non-existent date, day that will never come). [OE *hlāfmæsse* (as LOAF¹, MASS¹)]

lă'mmergeyer (-gīer) *n.* Bearded vulture, largest European bird of prey. [f. G *lämmergeier* (*lämmer* lambs, *geier* vulture)]

lămp *n.* & *v.* **1.** *n.* Vessel with oil and wick for giving light; transparent vessel enclosing candle, gas-jet, wire made incandescent by electricity when required, or other illuminant, (**smell of the ~,** betray nocturnal study, be laborious in style etc.); SAFETY, SPIRIT¹-, SUN-, *lamp.* **2.** (fig.) Sun, moon, star; source of spiritual or intellectual light, hope, etc. **3.** **~'black,** pigment made from soot; **~-chimney,** glass cylinder making draught for lamp-flame; **~-holder,** device for supporting (esp. electric) lamp; **~'light** (given by lamp(s)); **~'lighter,** man who lights street lamps (usu. Hist.; *like a ~-lighter*, with great speed), *spill for lighting lamps; **~'post, ~-standard,** (supporting street lamp); **~'shade** (placed over lamp to soften or intercept its light). **4.** Hence ~'LESS *a.* **5.** *v.i.* Shine. **6.** *v.t.* Supply with lamps; illuminate; *(sl.) look at. [ME, f. OF *lampe* f. LL *lampada* f. acc. of L f. Gk *lampas* torch]

lămpōō'n *n.*, & *v.t.* **1.** *n.* Virulent or scurrilous piece of satire; hence ~IST (1) *n.* **2.** *v.t.* Write lampoon(s) against; hence ~ER¹ *n.* [f. F *lampon*, conjectured to be f. *lampons* let us drink (*lamper* gulp down f. *laper* LAP⁵)]

lă'mprey *n.* Eel-like aquatic vertebrate with sucker mouth, gill-pouches, and opening on top of head. [ME, f. OF *lampreie* f. med. L *lampreda*; cf. LL *lampetra*, perh. f. L *lambere* lick + *petra* stone]

Lăncă'strĭan *a.* & *n.* **1.** (Inhabitant or native) of Lancashire or Lancaster. **2.** (Adherent) of family descended from John of Gaunt Duke of Lancaster (4th son of Edward III), or of the Red Rose party supporting it in the Wars of the Roses; cf. YORK¹. [f. *Lancaster* + -IAN]

lance¹ (lah-) *n.* **1.** Weapon with long wooden shaft and pointed steel head used by horseman in charging; similar implement for spearing fish or killing harpooned whale; FREE¹ *lance*; **break a ~,** argue *for* or *with*. **2.** Lancer. **3.** **~-corporal,** (sl.) **~-jack,** N.C.O. below corporal; **~-sergeant,** corporal acting as sergeant. **4.** **~-fish,** sand-eel; **~-snake,** venomous Amer. snake of genus *Bothrops*, fer de lance; **~'wood,** tough elastic W. Ind. wood used for carriage-shafts, fishing-rods, etc. [ME f. OF, f. L *lancea*; *lance-corporal* on anal. of obs. *lancepesade* lowest grade of N.C.O. ult. f. It. *lancia spezzata* broken lance]

lance² (lah-) *v.t.* **1.** (poet.) Fling, launch. **2.** (Surg.) Prick or cut open with lancet. **3.** Pierce with lance. [ME, f. OF *lancier* (*lance*; see prec.)]

la'ncelėt (lah'nsl-) *n.* Small marine animal of genus *Branchiostoma* etc. burrowing in sand. [f. LANCE¹ + -LET]

lă'ncėolate *a.* Shaped like lance-head, tapering to each end. [f. LL *lanceolatus* (*lanceola* dim. of *lancea* lance; see -ATE²)]

la'ncer (lah'-) *n.* Soldier of cavalry regiment orig. armed with lances; (in *pl.*) quadrille for 8 or 16 pairs, music for it. [f. F *lancier* (as LANCE¹; see -ER²)]

la'ncėt (lah'-) *n.* **1.** Surgical instrument usu. with two edges and point for small incisions. **2.** ~ **(arch, light, window,** etc.), narrow arch or window with pointed head; hence ~ED² *a.* [ME, f. OF *lancette* (as LANCE¹; see -ET¹)]

la'ncĭnātĭng (lah'-) *a.* (Of pain) acute, shooting. [f. *lancinate* pierce f. L *lancinare* to tear; see -ATE³, -ING²]

Lancs. *abbr.* Lancashire.

lănd¹ *n.* **1.** Solid part of earth's surface (opp. *sea, water, air*; *travel by land*); **how the ~ lies,** (fig.) what is the state of affairs. **2.** Ground, soil, expanse of country (||LIE⁴, *LAY³, *of the land*); this as basis for agriculture, building, etc. **3.** Country, nation, State, (*land of hope and glory*); *land of* CAKES; ~ **of the leal,** heaven; *in the land of the* LIVING²; *land of* PROMISE¹. **4.** Landed property, (in *pl.*) estates. **5.** (S. Afr.) Ground fenced off for tillage. **6.** Strip of plough or pasture land parted from others by drain-furrows. **7.** Space between rifling-grooves in gun. **8.** **~-agent, -agency,** (1) ||steward(ship) of estate, (2) agent, agency, for sale etc. of estates; **~-bank** (issuing banknotes on securities of landed property); **~-breeze** (blowing seaward from land); **~-bridge,** neck of land between two land masses; **~-crab,** crab that lives on land but breeds in sea; **~'fall,** approach to land esp. for first time on sea or air voyage; ~ **force(s)** (military, not naval or air); **~-form,** natural feature of earth's surface; ||**~-girl** (doing farmwork, esp. in wartime); **~-grabber,** illegal seizer of land, (esp.) man who took Irish farm after eviction of tenant; *~ **grant,** grant of public land (*~*-grant college*, state college granted such land under acts of 1862 and 1890); **~'holder,** proprietor or (usu.) tenant of land; **~-hunger, -hungry,** eager(ness) to acquire land; **~'lady,** (1) woman keeping inn, boarding-house, or lodgings, (2) woman having tenants; **~-law,** (usu. in *pl.*) law of landed property; **~-line,** means of telegraphic communication over land; **~-locked,** almost or quite enclosed by land; **~'lubber,** (Naut.) person unfamiliar with the sea and ships; **~'mark,** (1) object marking boundary of country, estate, etc., (2) conspicuous object in district etc., (3) object or event or change marking stage in process or turning-point in history; ~ **mass,** large area of land; **~-mine,** (1) explosive mine laid in or on ground, (2) parachute mine; *~ **office** (recording dealings in public land); ***~-office business,** enormous trade; **~-owner,** owner of land; **~'rail,** corncrake; **L~'s End,** western point of Cornwall; **~-shark,** (1) one who lives by swindling seamen ashore, (2) = *land-grabber*; **~-slater,** wood-louse; **~'slide,** = *landslip*, (fig.) overwhelming majority of votes for one side, esp. in an election; **~'slip,** sliding down of mass of land on cliff or mountain; **~'sman** (-z-), non-sailor; **~-tax** (assessed on landed property); **~-tie,** rod, beam, or piece of masonry, securing or supporting wall etc. by connecting some part of it with the ground; **~-wind** (blowing seaward from land). **9.** Hence ~'LESS *a.*, ~'WARD *a.*, *adv.*, & *n.*, ~'WARDS *adv.* [OE, = OS *land*, OHG *lant*, ON, Goth. *land* f. Gmc **landam*]

lănd[2] *v.* **1.** *v.t.* & *i.* Set or go ashore (in *p.p.* = having come ashore; see -ED[1] (2)), disembark (*at*). **2.** Bring (aircraft, its passengers etc.), (of aircraft etc.) come down, to ground or surface of water. **3.** Bring to, (also ~ **up**) reach or find oneself in, a certain place, stage, or position. **4.** *v.t.* Deal (person blow etc.; *landed him one in the eye*); present (*with* problem etc.). **5.** Set down from vehicle; bring (fish) to land, (fig.) win (prize etc.), obtain (appointment etc.), esp. against strong competition. **6.** *v.i.* Alight after jump etc. (lit. or fig.); ~ **on** one's **feet,** get well out of difficulty by luck. [ME, f. prec.]

Land[3] (lahnt) *n.* (*pl.* **Länder** *pr.* lĕ'n-). Province of (Federal Republic of) Germany; province of Austria. [G (as LAND[1])]

lă'ndau *n.* Four-wheeled carriage with top, such that the back half of the top can be raised and lowered and the front half removed. [*L~* near Karlsruhe, where first made]

lăndaulĕ't *n.* Small landau; motor car with folding hood over rear seats. [f. prec. + -LET]

lă'nddrŏst (-d-d-) *n.* (Hist.) Rural magistrate in S. Africa. [Afrik. (*land* LAND[1], *drost* bailiff)]

lă'ndėd *a.* Possessed of land (**the ~ interest,** owners and holders of land); consisting of land (*landed estate, property*). [ME, f. LAND[1] + -ED[2]]

lă'ndgrāve *n.* (*fem.* **-gravine** *pr.* -avēn). (Hist.) German title of nobility. [MLG; MHG *lantgrāve* (as LAND[1], G *graf* COUNT[3])]

lă'ndĭng *n.* In vbl senses; ~**(-place)**, place for disembarking; platform between two flights of stairs; HARD, SOFT, *landing*; **~-craft,** any of numerous types of naval craft esp. designed for putting ashore troops and equipment; **~-gear,** undercarriage; **~-net** (for landing large fish that has been hooked); **~-stage,** platform, often floating, on which passengers and goods are disembarked; **~-strip,** airstrip. [ME, f. LAND[2] + -ING[1]]

lä'ndler (lĕ'ndl*er*) *n.* (Music for) Austrian dance in triple time, precursor of waltz. [G (*Landl* Upper Austria; see -ER[1])]

lă'ndlōper *n.* (esp. Sc.) Vagabond. [f. MDu. *landlooper* (as LAND[1], *loopen* run f. as LEAP[1], -ER[1])]

lă'ndlôrd *n.* Person who lets land or (part of) building to tenant; keeper of inn, boarding-house, or lodgings; hence ~ISM *n.*, system by which land is owned by landlords receiving fixed rents from tenants (esp. derog. of former Irish system), advocacy of this. [ME, f. LAND[1] + LORD]

lăndŏ'cracy̆ *n.* (joc.) The landed class; so **lă'ndo**CRAT *n.* [f. LAND[1] + -O- + -CRACY]

lă'ndscāpe (*or* -ns-) *n.* & *v.* **1.** *n.* (Picture representing, art reproducing, or actual piece of) inland scenery; ~ **architecture** or ~ **gardening, architect** or **gardener,** laying-out of, one who lays out, grounds in imitation of natural scenery; **~-marble** (with treelike markings); **~-painter** (who paints landscapes), so **lă'ndscāp**IST (1) *n.* **2.** *v.t.* & *i.* Improve by, engage in, landscape gardening. [f. MDu. *landscap* (as LAND[1], -SHIP)]

lāne *n.* **1.** Narrow road usu. between hedges (**it is a long ~ that has no turning,** change is sure to come); narrow street. **2.** Passage made or left between rows of persons. **3.** Strip of road for single line of traffic; strip of track or water for runner, rower, or swimmer in race. **4.** Course prescribed for or regularly followed by ships (**ocean ~**) or aircraft. [OE, = OFris. *lana*, *laen*, MDu. *lāne*, of unkn. orig.]

lăng sy̆ne *adv.* & *n.* (Sc.) (In) the old days; cf. AULD. [= *long since*]

lă'nguage (-nggwĭj) *n.* **1.** A vocabulary and way of using it prevalent in one or more countries; ARTIFICIAL, DEAD, *language*. **2.** Method of expression (**finger ~**, talk by conventional signs with fingers; ~ **of flowers,** symbolic meanings attached to various kinds); system of symbols and rules for writing computer programs. **3.** Words and their use; faculty of speech; person's style of expressing himself; (**bad**) ~, oaths and abusive talk; STRONG *language*; **speak the same ~**, have similar outlook and way of expressing oneself. **4.** Professional or sectional vocabulary. **5.** Literary style, wording. **6.** ~ **laboratory,** room equipped with tape-recorders etc. for learning foreign languages by repeated practice; **~-master,** teacher of (usu. mod. foreign) language(s). [ME f. OF *langage* f. Gallo-Rom. **linguaticum* f. L *lingua* tongue; see -AGE]

langue de chat (lahṅdeshah') *n.* Very thin finger-shaped piece of chocolate or crisp biscuit. [F, = cat's tongue]

langue d'oc (lahṅgedŏ'k), ***langue d'oïl*** (lahṅgedoi'l), *ns.* Medieval French as spoken south, north, of the Loire, the basis of modern Provençal and modern French respectively. [f. OF *langue* language f. L *lingua* tongue, *de* of, *oc* (f. L *hoc*), *oïl* (f. L *hoc ille*), these being the respective forms for *yes*]

lă'nguĭd (-nggwĭd) *a.* Inert, lacking vigour; indisposed to exertion; spiritless, apathetic; (of ideas etc.) not vivid, uninteresting; (of trade etc.) sluggish, slow-moving; faint, weak; hence ~LY[2] *adv.*, ~NESS *n.* [f. F *languide* or f. L *languidus* (as foll.; see -ID[1])]

lă'nguĭsh (-nggw-) *v.i.* Grow or be feeble, lose or lack vitality; live *under* enfeebling or depressing conditions; grow slack, lose intensity; droop, pine (*for*); put on languid look, affect sentimental tenderness, whence **~ĭng**LY[2] *adv.*; hence ~MENT *n.* [ME, f. OF *languir* (-ISH[2]) f. Rom. **languire* for L *languēre*, rel. to LAX[1]]

lă'nguor (-ngg*er*) *n.* Faintness, fatigue; inertia, lack of alertness; soft or tender mood or effect; slackness, dullness, drooping state; (of air etc.) oppressive stillness; so ~OUS *a.* [ME f. OF, f. L *languor -oris* (as prec.; see -OR)]

langur' (langgoor') *n.* Asian long-tailed monkey esp. of genus *Presbytis*. [Hindi]

lă'nĭary̆ *a.* & *n.* (Tooth) adapted for tearing, canine. [f. L *laniarius* (*lanius* butcher f. *laniare* to tear; see -ARY[1])]

lanĭ'ferous, lanĭ'gerous, *adjs.* Wool-bearing. [f. L *lanifer*, *-ger* (*lana* wool; see -FEROUS, -GEROUS)]

lănk *a.* Shrunken, spare; tall and lean; (of grass etc.) long and flaccid; (of hair) straight and limp, not wavy or curly. [OE *hlanc* f. Gmc **hlank-*; cf. FLANK, LINK[1]]

lă'nk|y̆ *a.* (Of person or limbs) ungracefully lean and long or tall; hence **~ĬLY**[2] *adv.*, **~ĬNESS** *n.* [f. prec. + -Y[2]]

lă'nner *n.* (Female) S. Eur. falcon of species *Falco biarmicus*. [ME, f. OF *lanier* perh. f. OF *lanier* cowardly, orig. = weaver f. L *lanarius* wool-merchant (*lana* wool; see -ER[2])]

lă'nnerėt *n.* Male lanner (smaller than female). [ME, f. OF *laneret* (as prec.; see -ET[1])]

lă'nolĭn *n.* Fat which permeates sheep's wool, extracted as basis for ointments etc. [G, f. L *lana* wool + *oleum* oil + -IN]

lă'nsquėnĕt (-kĭ-) *n.* Card-game of German origin; German mercenary soldier in 16th–17th c. [F, f. G *landsknecht* (as LAND[1], *knecht* soldier f. OHG *kneht*; see KNIGHT)]

lă'ntern *n.* **1.** (Lamp with) transparent case protecting flame of candle etc.; = MAGIC *lantern*, whence ~IST (3) *n.*; ‖**parish ~**, the moon. **2.** Light-chamber of lighthouse; structure on top of dome or room with glazed sides to admit light, similar structure for ventilation etc.; proboscis of lantern-fly. **3.** **~-fly,** insect of family Fulgoridae, formerly thought to be luminous; **~ jaws** (long and thin, giving hollow look to face); **~-slide** (for projection by magic lantern etc.); **~-wheel,** lantern-shaped gear-wheel, trundle. [ME, f. OF *lanterne* f. L *lanterna* f. Gk *lamptēr* torch, lamp]

lă'nthanīde *n.* (Chem.) Element of the **~ series** from lanthanum or cerium to lutetium (atomic numbers 57–71), all being metals with similar chemical properties. [f. G *lanthanid* (as foll.; see -IDE)]

lă'nthanum *n.* (Chem.) Metallic element, first of lanthanide series. [f. Gk *lanthanō* escape notice + -UM, from having remained undetected in cerium oxide]

‖**lă'nthorn** (-*tern*) *n.* Lantern. [pop. assim. of *lantern* to *horn*, common former material]

lanū'gō *n.* (*pl.* **~s**). Fine soft hair esp. on human foetus. [L, = down (*lana* wool)]

lă'nyard *n.* (Naut.) short rope or line attached to something to secure it; cord attached to breech mechanism for firing gun; cord hanging round neck or looped round shoulder, to which knife, whistle, etc., may be attached. [ME, f. OF *laniere, lasniere*; assim. to YARD[1]]

Lāodĭcē'an *a.* & *n.* (Person who is) lukewarm, esp. in religion or politics. [f. L *Laodicea* in Asia Minor + -AN; see Rev. 3:16]

Lao'tian (low'sh*a*n *or* lahō'sh*a*n) *a.* & *n.* (Native, inhabitant, or language) of Laos. [f. *Laos* in S.E. Asia + -IAN]

lăp[1] *n.* **1.** Hanging part or flap of garment, saddle, etc.; lobe of ear. **2.** Front part of skirt held up to contain something; front of body from waist to knees of sitting person, with dress, as place on which child is nursed or object held (lit., or fig. *in the lap of luxury* etc.); **in** or **on** person's ~, (fig.) as his responsibility (*in the lap of the* GODS); hence ~'FUL 2 *n.* **3.** Hollow among hills. **4.** **~-dog,** small pet dog; ***~'robe,** travelling-rug; **~'stone,** shoemaker's stone held in lap to beat leather on. [OE *læppa*, = OS *lappo*, OHG *lappa*; cf. ON *leppr* rag]

lăp[2] *v.* (**-pp-**). **1.** *v.t.* Coil, fold, wrap, (garment etc. *about, round*, as advs. or preps.); enfold, swathe, *in* wraps etc.; (of influence etc.) surround, encircle; (esp. in *pass.*) enfold caressingly. **2.** Cause to overlap; lead (competitor in race) by one or more laps. **3.** *v.i.* Project *over* (thing, or abs.). [ME, prob. f. prec.]

lăp[3] *n.* **1.** Amount of overlapping, overlapping part, (**half-~**, joining of rails, shafts, etc., by halving thickness of each at end and fitting together). **2.** Layer or sheet (of cotton etc. being made) wound on roller; single turn of rope, silk, thread, etc., round drum or reel; one circuit of race-track etc. (**~ of honour,** ceremonial circuit of football pitch etc. by winners), (fig.) section of journey etc., esp. *last lap*. **3.** **~-joint,** = *half-lap* (see above); **~-strake,** clinker-built (boat); **~-weld** *n.*, & *v.t.*, (with overlapping edges). [ME, f. prec.]

lăp[4] *n.*, & *v.t.* (**-pp-**). **1.** *n.* Rotating disc for polishing gem or metal. **2.** *v.t.* Polish with lap. [perh. f. prec.]

lăp[5] *v.* (**-pp-**) & *n.* **1.** *v.i.* & *t.* Take up liquid, drink (*up* liquid), with tongue as cat does; consume (liquid, or fig.) greedily (usu. *up* or *down*); (of water) move, beat upon (shore), with rippling sound of lapping. **2.** *n.* Liquid food for dogs, (sl.) weak beverage, any liquor; single act of lapping, amount taken up by it; sound of wavelets on beach etc. [OE *lapian*, = MLG, MDu. *lapen*, OHG *laffan* f. Gmc **lap-*]

lă'paro- *comb. form.* (Anat. & Surg.) Flank, as ~TOMY (-ŏ't-) *n.*, cutting of abdominal walls for access to cavity of abdomen. [f. Gk *lapara* flank (*laparos* soft)]

lapĕ'l *n.* Part of front of coat etc. folded back; hence ~LED[2] (-ld) *a.* [f. LAP[1] + -EL]

lă'pĭcīde *n.* Cutter of stones or inscriptions on stone. [f. L *lapicida* irreg. f. *lapis -idis* stone; see -CIDE]

lă'pĭdarў *a.* & *n.* **1.** *a.* Concerned with stones; engraved on stone, (of style) suitable for inscriptions, dignified and concise. **2.** *n.* Cutter, polisher, or engraver, of gems. [ME, f. L *lapidarius* (*lapis -idis* stone; see -ARY[1])]

lă'pĭd|āte *v.t.* (literary). Throw stones at; stone to death; so ~A'TION *n.* [f. L *lapidare* (as prec.) + -ATE[3]]

lapĭ'llī *n. pl.* Stone fragments ejected from volcanoes. [It. f. L, pl. dim. of *lapis* stone]

lăpĭs lă'zūlī *n.* Sodium aluminium silicate-sulphate used as gem; bright blue pigment from it; its colour. [ME, f. L *lapis* stone + med. L *lazuli* gen. of *lazulum* f. Pers. (as AZURE)]

Lă'plănder *n.* Inhabitant of Lapland. [f. *Lapland* f. Sw. *Lappland* (as LAPP, LAND[1]), + -ER[1]]

Lăpp *n.* & *a.* **1.** *n.* One of nomadic race of northern Scandinavia; their language. **2.** *a.* Of the Lapps or their language. [f. Sw. *Lapp*, perh. orig. term of contempt; cf. MHG *lappe* simpleton]

lă'ppėt *n.* Flap, fold; loose or overlapping piece of garment, flesh, membrane, etc.; lobe of ear etc.; streamer of woman's head-dress; **~-(-moth)**, kind of large moth, whose caterpillars have side-lobes; hence ~ED[2] *a.* [f. LAP[1] + -ET[1]]

Lă'ppĭsh *a.* & *n.* **1.** *a.* Lapp. **2.** *n.* Lapp language. [f. LAPP + -ISH[1]]

lăpse[1] *n.* Slip of memory, tongue, or pen, slight mistake; weak or careless deviation from what is right, moral slip; falling away *from* faith or *into* heresy; decline to lower state; passage or interval *of* time; (Law) termination of right or privilege through disuse; (arch., of water) gentle flow; **~ rate,** (Meteorol.) rate of fall of temperature with increasing height. [f. L *lapsus* (*labi laps-* glide, slip, fall)]

lăpse[2] *v.i.* Fail to maintain position or state for want of effort or vigour; fall *back* or *away* (*into* inferior or previous or ordinary state); (of benefice, estate, right, etc.) become void, revert *to* someone, by non-fulfilment of conditions, absence of heirs, etc.; glide, flow, subside, pass *away*; (in *p.p.*) that has lapsed (see -ED[1] (2)). [partly f. L *lapsare* (as prec.), partly f. prec.]

lapsus (lă'ps*u*s) *n.* (*pl.* same). Slip (usu. in **~ *linguae*** *pr.* lĭ'nggwē, slip of the tongue, **~ *calami*** *pr.* kă'lamī, slip of the pen). [L; see LAPSE[1]]

Lapū'tan *a.* Chimerical, visionary, absurd. [f. *Laputa* in Swift's 'Gulliver's Travels', whose inhabitants engaged in visionary projects, + -AN]

lă'pwĭng *n.* Bird of plover family (*Vanellus vanellus*), with crested head and shrill cry, pewit.

[OE *hlēapewince* (*hlēapan* LEAP¹, as WINK, w. ref. to manner of flight), assim. to LAP², WING]

lar *n.* **1.** (*pl.* **lar'es** *pr.* lar'ēz *or* lar'āz). Ancient-Roman household deity; **lares (and penates)**, the home. **2.** (*pl.* ~s *pr.* -z). White-handed gibbon (*Hylobates lar*) of S.E. Asia. [L]

lar'board (-berd) *n.* & *a.* (Naut.; arch. or U.S.) = PORT⁵. [ME *lad*(*d*)*e*-, *lathe*- (perh. = LADE + BOARD¹), later assim. to *starboard*]

lar'cen|ȳ *n.* (Law) felonious taking away of another's personal goods with intent to convert them to one's own use (**grand, petty,** ~**y,** of property above, below, value of 12d. (5p.), or of $200); theft; hence ~ER¹, ~IST (1), *ns.*, ~OUS *a.* [f. AF **larcenie*, f. OF *larcin* f. L *latrocinium* (*latro* robber, mercenary f. Gk *latreus*); see -Y¹]

larch *n.* Bright-foliaged deciduous coniferous tree of genus *Larix*, yielding Venice turpentine, tough timber, and bark used in tanning; ~**('wood)**, its wood. [f. MHG *larche*, f. OHG **larihha* f. L *larix -icis*]

lard¹ *n.* Internal fat of abdomen of pigs esp. when rendered and clarified for use in cooking and pharmacy; hence ~'Y² *a.* (~**y-cake,** cake made with lard, currants, etc.). [ME, f. OF *lard* bacon, f. L *lar*(*i*)*dum* cogn. w. Gk *larinos* fat]

lard² *v.t.* **1.** Insert strips of bacon in (meat etc.) before cooking (~**'ing-needle, -pin,** instrument for doing this). **2.** Garnish (talk, writing) *with* metaphors, technical terms, foreign words, etc. [ME, f. OF *larder* (as prec.)]

lar'der *n.* Room or cupboard for storing meat and other provisions. [ME f. AF; OF *lardier* f. med. L *lardarium* (as LARD¹, -ER² (2))]

lar'don, lardōō'n, *n.* Strip of bacon or pork used to lard meat. [ME f. F *lardon* (as LARD¹; see -OON)]

lardȳ-dar'dȳ *a.* (sl.) Affected and languidly dandified. [cf. LA-DI-DA]

lares. See LAR.

large *a.*, *n.*, & *adv.* **1.** *a.* Of wide range, comprehensive, (*large powers, discretion*); (of artistic treatment) free, sweeping, broad. **2.** Of considerable or relatively great magnitude (more formal than *big*, and without emotional implications of *great*); *as large as, larger than,* LIFE; ~ **of limb,** with large limbs. **3.** (Of agent) doing thing on a large scale (*large and small farmers*); (as distinctive epithet) of the larger kind (*large intestine*). **4.** ~**-handed,** generous; ~**-hearted,** ~**-souled,** kindly; ~**-minded,** liberal, not narrow-minded; ~**-scale,** made or occurring on a large SCALE³ or in large amounts. **5.** Hence **lar'**GISH¹ 2 *a.*, ~'NESS (-jn-) *n.*, **lar'**GEN⁶ *v.i.* & *t.* (poet.). **6.** *n.* **At** ~, at liberty, free, (of narration etc.) at full length with details, as a body or whole (*popular with the people at large*), *representing a whole State etc. and not merely a part of it, without particularizing, without specific aim (*scatters imputations at large*); ***ambassador at** ~ (appointed for special duties, not to any one country); **gentleman at** ~, gentleman attached to the court without special duties, person who has no occupation; STATUTES *at large*; **in** ~, on a large scale (opp. *in little*). **7.** *adv.* BY¹ *and large*; BULK², LOOM², *large*; WRIT² *large.* [ME f. OF, f. fem. of L *largus* copious]

lar'gelȳ (-jlĭ) *adv.* In adj. senses; to a great or preponderating extent (*is largely due to*). [f. prec. + -LY²]

largĕ'ss, -ĕ'sse, (*or* lar'jĭs; *or* -zh-) *n.* Money or gifts freely bestowed esp. by great person on occasion of rejoicing; generous or plentiful bestowal. [ME, f. OF *largesse* f. Rom. **largitia* f. L *largus* copious; see -ESS²]

larghĕ'ttō (-gĕ'-) *adv.*, *a.*, & *n.* (*pl.* ~s). (Mus.) (Movement) in fairly slow time. [It., dim. of foll.]

lar'gō *adv.*, *a.*, & *n.* (*pl.* ~s). (Mus.) (Movement) in slow time with broad dignified treatment. [It., = broad]

lă'rĭat *n.* Rope for tethering horse etc.; lasso. [f. Sp. *la reata* (*reatar* tie again f. as RE- + L *aptare* adjust f. *aptus* APT, fit)]

lark¹ *n.* **1.** Small bird of family Alaudidae, with sandy-brown plumage and long hind-claws, esp. the skylark; **rise with the** ~, get up early; ~**-heel,** ~**'spur,** plant of genus *Delphinium* with spur-shaped calyx. **2.** Bird of some other families (*meadow-lark, titlark*). [OE *lāferce*, *læwerce*, = MLG, MDu. *lēwer*(*i*)*ke*, OHG *lērihha*, ON *lævirki*, of unkn. orig.]

lark² *n.*, & *v.t.* (colloq.) **1.** *n.* Frolic, spree, amusing incident (**what a** ~**!,** how amusing!), whence ~'Y² *a.*; ||type of activity etc. **2.** *v.i.* Play tricks, frolic (*about*). [19th c.; orig. uncert.]

larn *v.t.* & *i.* **1.** (joc. or vulg.) = LEARN. **2.** *v.t.* (colloq.) Teach, instruct, (*that'll larn you*). [dial. form of LEARN]

lă'rrĭkĭn *n.* (Austral.) Young street rowdy, hooligan. [perh. f. name *Larry* (pet-form of *Lawrence*) + -KIN]

lă'rrup *v.t.* (colloq.) Thrash. [dial., perh. f. LATHER]

Lă'rrȳ *n.* (As) **happy as** ~, extremely happy. [20th c., of uncert orig.; cf. LARRIKIN]

lă'rum. Var. (arch.) of ALARM¹; cf. ALARUM.

lar'v|a *n.* (*pl.* ~**ae**). Insect from time of leaving egg till transformation into pupa, grub; immature form of other animals that undergo some metamorphosis; hence ~AL *a.*, ~ĬCIDE (1) *n.* [L, = ghost, mask]

laryng-. See LARYNX.

larȳ'ngoscōpe (-ngg-) *n.* Mirror apparatus for examining larynx. [f. LARYNX + -O- + -SCOPE]

lărȳngŏ'tomȳ (-ngg-) *n.* Cutting into larynx from without, esp. to provide breathing-channel. [f. as prec. + -TOMY]

lă'rȳn|x *n.* (*pl.* ~**ges** *pr.* -ĭ'njēz). Cavity in throat containing vocal cords; hence ~**gē**AL (-ĭ'nj-) *a.*, & *n.*, hypothetical phonetic element of laryngeal quality supposed to have existed in Proto-Indo-European, ~**g**IC (-ĭ'nj-) *a.*, ~**gi'**TIS (-nj-), ~**gŏ'**LOGY (-ngg-), *ns.* [mod. L, f. Gk *larugx -ggos*]

lasă'gnĕ (-ă'nyĕ; *or* -ah'-) *n. pl.* Pasta in wide ribbon form, esp. as served with minced meat and sauce. [It., pl. of *lasagna* f. L *lasanum* cooking-pot]

Lă'scar *n.* E. Indian sailor. [ult. f. Urdu & Pers. *laškar* = 'army', misapplied; cf. LASHKAR]

lascĭ'vĭous *a.* Lustful, wanton; inciting to lust; hence ~LY² *adv.*, ~NESS *n.* [ME, f. LL *lasciviosus* f. L *lascivia* lustfulness (*lascivus* sportive, wanton; see -OUS)]

lāse (-z) *v.i.* Function as or in laser; (of substance etc.) undergo physical processes employed in laser. [back form. f. foll.]

lā'ser (-z-) *n.* Device generating intense beam of highly coherent monochromatic radiation in one direction, by stimulation of emission from excited atoms etc., optical MASER. [f. *l*ight *a*mplification by *s*timulated *e*mission of *r*adiation; cf. MASER]

lăsh¹ *v.* **1.** *v.i.* Make sudden movement of limb, tail, etc.; pour or rush vehemently; strike violently *at* or *against*; hit or (of horse) kick *out*; break *out* into excess, strong language, etc. **2.** *v.t.* Beat with lash, flog; move suddenly and forcefully (*lashed its tail*); (of waves or rain) beat upon; castigate in words, rebuke, satirize; urge as with lashes (~ **oneself into a fury,** work up a rage). **3.** Fasten (*down, on, together, to* something) with cord, twine, etc.; ~**-up** *a.* & *n.*, makeshift, improvised (structure), (sl.) muddle(d), failure. [sense 1 ME, prob. imit.; sense 2 f. foll.; sense 3 ME, perh. of LG orig.]

lăsh² *n.* Stroke with thong, whip, etc.; flexible part of whip (**the ~**, punishment of flogging); eyelash, whence ~'LESS *a.*; goading influence. [f. prec. 1]

lă'sher *n.* In vbl senses; ||esp. (water rushing over) weir, pool below weir. [f. LASH¹ + -ER¹]

lă'shĭng *n.* In vbl senses; cord used for lashing; (in *pl.*, sl.) plenty, abundance, (*of*). [f. LASH¹ + -ING¹]

lă'shkar *n.* Body of armed Indian tribesmen. [f. Urdu (as LASCAR)]

lasque (lahsk) *n.* Flat, ill-formed, or veiny diamond. [perh. f. Pers. *lašk* piece]

lăss *n.* Girl (esp. Sc., N. Engl., or poet.); man's sweetheart; hence ~'IE *n.* [ME *lasce* f. **lask* f. ON *laskwa* unmarried (fem.)]

lă'ssĭtūde *n.* Weariness, languor, disinclination to exert or interest oneself. [F, or f. L *lassitudo* (*lassus* tired; see -TUDE)]

lă'ssō (*or* lasōō') *n.* (*pl.* ~**s** *or* ~**es**), & *v.t.* **1.** *n.* Sp. Amer. noosed rope of untanned hide etc. for catching cattle etc. **2.** *v.t.* Catch with lasso. [f. Sp. *lazo* LACE¹]

last¹ (lah-) *n.* Shoemaker's wooden or metal model for shaping shoe etc. on; **stick to** one's ~, not meddle with things one does not understand (w. ref. to L prov. *ne sutor ultra crepidam*). [OE *lǣste* last, *lǣst* boot, *lāst* footprint; cf. OHG *leist* last, Goth. *laists-* track, ON *leistr* foot f. Gmc **laist-*; cf. LAST⁴]

last² (lah-) *n.* Commercial measure of weight, capacity, or quantity, varying with place and goods (~ **of wool,** 12 sacks or 4,368 lb.; ~ **of herrings,** 12 barrels; ~ **of malt,** 10 qr. or 80 bushels). [OE *hlæst* load, = MLG, MDu. *last*, OHG *hlast* f. WG **hlatsta* f. Gmc **hlath-* LADE]

last³ (lah-) *a.*, *n.*, & *adv.* **1.** *a.* After all others, coming at the end, (**the ~ two** etc., the last and the last but one etc.; **second ~, ~ but one,** next to the last; ~ **but not least,** last in order of mention or occurrence but not of importance); **~-across,** children's game of being last to cross road in front of approaching vehicle; *last* DITCH; ~ **minute** or **moment,** time immediately before a decisive event; ~ **name,** surname; *last* POST⁴, QUARTER¹ 9, STRAW¹; ~ **thing** (*adv.*, colloq.), as final act (esp. before going to bed); ~ **word,** conclusive or definitive statement, final contribution to dispute, latest fashion. **2.** Belonging to the end, esp. of life or the world; **L~ Day,** Judgement Day; *last* HOME¹, HONOUR¹*s*, INQUEST; *Last* JUDGEMENT; *on* one's *last* LEGS; *last* RESPECT¹*s*; ~ **rites,** religious ceremony for person near death; ~ **sleep,** death; **L~ Supper** (of Christ and his disciples on eve of Crucifixion); **the four ~ things,** death, judgement, heaven, and hell; ~ **trump,** trumpet to wake the dead on Judgement Day; ~ **words,** person's dying words. **3.** Next before expressed or implied point of time, latest up to now or then, most recent, (*in the last fortnight*; *last Christmas*; *last Tuesday* or *Tuesday last*); ~ **evening, night, week, month, year,** *ns.* & *advs.*, (during) the evening etc. most recently past. **4.** Lowest, of least rank or estimation. **5.** Only remaining (*last crust, resource*). **6.** Least likely, willing, suitable, etc., *to* (*should be the last to do it*; *is the last thing to try*). **7.** Utmost, extreme, (*is of the last importance*). **8.** *n.* Last-mentioned person or thing (*the, this, which, last*); most recent letter etc.; last day or moments, death, (*the* or *his* etc. *last*); last day of month; last performance of certain acts (*breathe, look*, one's *last*); last mention or sight (*shall never hear the last of it, see the last of him*); **at (long) ~,** in the end, after much delay; **to** or **till the ~,** to the end, esp. till death. **9.** *adv.* After all others (esp. in comb., as *last-mentioned*); on the last occasion before the present (*when did you see him last?* or *last see him?*); (in enumerations) in the last place, finally. [OE *latost* superl. of *læt* a., *late* adv.; see LATE¹, -EST¹; loss of *-t-* as in BEST¹]

last⁴ (lah-) *v.* **1.** *v.i.* Go on, remain unexhausted or adequate or alive for specified or long time; suffice (*will last me eight months*; *will last my time*). **2.** *v.t.* ~ **out,** continue esp. in vigour or use at least as long as. [OE *lǣstan*, = OS *lēstian* execute, OHG *leisten* afford, Goth. *laistjan* follow f. Gmc **laist-* LAST¹]

la'stĭng (lah'-) *a.* & *n.* **1.** *a.* Enduring, permanent, (*no lasting benefit*); durable; hence ~LY² *adv.*, ~NESS *n.* **2.** *n.* Kind of durable cloth. [ME, f. prec. + -ING²]

la'stlў (lah'-) *adv.* In the last place, finally. [ME, f. LAST³ + -LY²]

lat. *abbr.* latitude.

Lătaki'a (-ē'*a*) *n.* Kind of Turkish tobacco chiefly used in mixtures. [~ (ancient *Laodicea*) in Syria]

lătch *n.* & *v.* **1.** *n.* Small bar falling into catch and lifted by lever etc. from outside, as fastening for door or gate; small spring-lock of outer door catching when door is closed and worked from outside by key; **~'key,** any outer-door key, (fig.) symbol of emancipation, (*~key child*, child given key to enter home on return from school etc., when mother is absent); **on the ~,** fastened by latch only, not locked. **2.** *v.t.* Fasten with latch. **3.** *v.i.* (colloq.) ~ **on to,** (1) attach oneself to, (2) understand. [prob. f. (now dial.) *latch* v. seize f. OE *læccan* f. Gmc **lakk-*]

lă'tchĕt *n.* (arch.) Thong for fastening shoe. [ME, f. OF *lachet*, var. of *lacet* dim. of *laz* LACE¹]

lāte¹ *a.* (*compar.* **la'ter** *or* LATTER; *superl.* **la'test** *or* LAST³) & *n.* **1.** *a.* After the due or usual time (*was late for dinner*; *it is too late to go*); (of agent or action) doing or done after proper time (*late comer*; *late rising*). **2.** Backward in flowering, ripening, etc. **3.** Far on in day or night (~ **dinner,** in evening; ~ **hours,** after usual time for rising or going to bed); far on in time (*on Wednesday* **at ~st,** then if not before); far on in a period, development, etc., (*late stained glass*; *in the late 19th century*; *late* LATIN). **4.** No longer alive, no longer having specified status etc., that was recently so-and-so, (**the ~** *prime minister*, dead or resigned; *my late husband, residence*). **5.** Of recent date (*the late floods, war*; **of ~ years,** in the last few years); **~st,** most recent (news etc., or abs.). **6.** ||~ **fee** (on letter posted after ordinary collection time). **7.** Hence **lā'tEN**⁶ *v.t.* & *i.*, ~'NESS (-tn-) *n.*, **lā'tISH**¹ 2 *a.* & *adv.* **8.** *n.* **Of ~,** recently. [OE *læt*, = OS *lat*, OHG *laz*, ON *latr*, Goth. *lats* f. Gmc **lataz* slow (**lat-* f. IE **lad-*, cogn. w. LET¹)]

lāte² *adv.* (**la'ter; la'test,** LAST³). After proper time (*better late than never*); far on in time (*this happened later on*; **sooner or ~r, early or ~, soon or ~,** at some future time, eventually); at or till late hour (*we sat late*); (poet.) recently, lately, (*I sent thee late a rosy wreath*); formerly but not now (*late of Oxford*); at late stage of development etc. (*traces remained as late as Stuart times*); ~ **in the day,** (colloq.) at a late stage, esp. unreasonably late in the proceedings etc. [OE *late*, adv. form of prec.]

latee'n *a.* ~ **sail** (triangular on long yard at angle of 45° to mast); (of ship etc.) so rigged. [f. F (*voile*) *latine* Latin (sail), named as common in Mediterranean]

lā'telў (-tlĭ) *adv.* Not long ago, recently, in recent times. [OE *lætlīce* (as LATE¹, -LY²)]

La Tène (lah tĕn) *a.* Relating to the second Iron-Age culture of central & W. Europe. [~

in Switzerland, where remains of it were first identified]

lā'tent *a.* Hidden, concealed; existing but not developed or manifest; dormant; *latent* HEAT¹; ~ **image,** (Photog.) invisible image that may be developed; hence **lā'tENCY** *n.*, ~LY² *adv.* [f. L *latēre* be hidden; see -ENT]

-later *suf.* See -LATRY.

lă'teral *a.* & *n.* **1.** *a.* Of, at, towards, from, the side, side-; ~ **branch** of family (descended from brother or sister of person in direct line); ~ **thinking,** seeking to solve problems by unorthodox or apparently illogical methods; hence ~LY² *adv.* **2.** *n.* Side part, member, or object, esp. lateral shoot or branch. [f. L *lateralis* (*latus lateris* side; see -AL)]

Lă'teran *a.* ~ **Council,** one of five general councils of Western Church held in cathedral of St. John Lateran, Rome. [f. L *Laterana, -num,* district of Rome where family of Plautii *Laterani* resided]

lă'terīte *n.* Red or yellow friable ferruginous surface clay hardening in air, much used for road-making in tropics. [f. L *later* brick + -ITE¹ (2)]

lā'tĕx *n.* (*pl.* **~es,** *or* **la'tices** *pr.* -ĭsēz). Milky fluid of (esp. rubber) plant; synthetic product resembling this. [L, = liquid]

lath (lah-) *n.* (*pl. pr.* -ths *or* -dhz), & *v.t.* **1.** *n.* Piece of sawn or split timber in form of thin strip about an inch wide esp. for use as support for slates or plaster or as material for trellis or Venetian blind (**as thin as a** ~, of persons, whence ~'Y² *a.*); ~ **and plaster,** material for interior wall-facings, ceilings, partitions, etc. **2.** *v.t.* Provide (wall, ceiling) with laths; hence ~'ING¹ (3) *n.* [OE *lætt,* **læthth-,* = OS, OHG *latta*]

‖**lāthe¹** (-dh) *n.* (Hist.) Administrative district of Kent. [OE *lǣth* estate, = ON *láth*]

lāthe² (-dh) *n.* Machine for shaping wood, metal, ivory, etc., by rotating article against tools used; **~-bed,** lower framework of lathe with slot from end to end for adjustment; **~-head,** headstock of lathe. [prob. rel. to ODa. *lad* structure, frame, f. ON *hlath,* rel. to *hlatha* LADE]

lă'ther (-dh-; *or* lah'-) *n.* & *v.* **1.** *n.* Froth of soap etc. and water; frothy sweat esp. of horse; (fig.) state of agitation; hence ~Y² *a.* **2.** *v.t.* Cover (esp. chin etc. for shaving) with lather; beat, thrash, whence ~ING¹ (1) *n.* **3.** *v.i.* (Of horse) become covered with lather; (of soap etc.) form lather. [OE *lēathor* n., *lēthran* v., = ON *lauthr* washing-soda, *leythra* to lather f. Gmc (**lauthrian* v. f.) **lauthram* f. IE **loutrom*]

la'thĭ (lah'tĭ) *n.* (Ind.) Long heavy iron-bound bamboo stick used as weapon esp. by police. [f. Hindi *lāṭhī*]

lătĭfŭ'ndĭa *n. pl.* Large estates, esp. as characterizing a country's social system. [L (*latus* broad, *fundus* estate)]

Lă'tĭn *a.* & *n.* **1.** *a.* Of Latium or its ancient inhabitants; of ancient Romans; of, like, in, the Indo-European language of the ancient Romans. **2.** Of the Roman Catholic Church; ~ (= WESTERN) **Church;** ~ **rite,** religious ceremonial using Latin, esp. in Western Church. **3.** (Of peoples) inheriting Roman customs etc., speaking one of the languages descended from Latin; ~ **America,** parts of Central & S. America where Spanish or Portuguese is main language, whence *L~-Ame'rican* a. & n.; ~ **cross,** plain cross with lowest arm longer than the other three; **the ~ peoples,** inhabitants of France, Spain, Portugal, Italy, etc.; ~ **Quarter** [F *Quartier Latin*], educational centre of Paris, where Latin was spoken in the Middle Ages, noted for its unconventional mode of life; ~ **square,** arrangement of *n* letters etc. each occurring *n* times, in a square array of n^2 compartments so that no letter appears twice in same row or column. **4.** *n.* The Latin language; **old** ~ (before about 75 B.C., pre-classical); **classical** ~, that of leading writers of late republican and early imperial Rome, about 75 B.C. to A.D. 200; **late** ~ (about A.D. 200 to 600); **medieval** ~ (about A.D. 600 to 1500); **modern** ~ (since A.D. 1500, used esp. in scientific classifications); DOG¹ *Latin;* LAW¹ *Latin;* **low** ~, medieval, or late and medieval, Latin; PIG *Latin;* **popular** ~ (informal, of classical times); **silver** ~ (literary language of 1st c. A.D.); **thieves'** ~, secret cant of thieves etc.; **vulgar** ~ (informal, of classical times); hence or cogn. ~ISM (4), ~IST (3), *ns.*, ~LESS *a.* **5.** Inhabitant of Latium; (Rom. Ant.) Italian with special rights of citizenship. [ME f. OF, or f. L *Latinus* (*Latium* district of Italy including Rome)]

Lă'tĭnāte *a.* Having the character of Latin. [f. prec. + -ATE²]

lă'tĭnė *adv.* In Latin (giving Latin equivalent of word etc.). [L]

Latĭ'nĭtȳ *n.* Way a person speaks or writes Latin; quality of Latin style or grammar. [f. L *latinitas* (as LATIN; see -ITY)]

Lă'tĭniz|e, -īs|e (-īz), *v.* **1.** *v.t.* Give Latin form to (word), put into Latin; make conformable to ideas, customs, etc., of the ancient Romans, Latin peoples, or Latin Church. **2.** *v.i.* Use Latin forms, idioms, etc. **3.** Hence ~A'TION, ~ER¹, *ns.* [f. LL *latinizare* (as LATIN; see -IZE)]

***Lati'nō** (-ē'-) *n.* (*pl.* ~s). Latin-American inhabitant of U.S. [Amer. Sp.]

lā'tĭsh. See LATE¹.

lă'tĭtūde *n.* **1.** Freedom from narrowness, liberality of interpretation, tolerated variety of action or opinion. **2.** (Geog.) Angular distance on a meridian (*degree, minute,* etc., *of latitude*); place's angular distance on its meridian N. or S. of equator (*latitude 40° N.* etc.); (usu. in *pl.*) regions, climes, esp. w. ref. to temperature, (**high ~s,** near N. or S. pole; **low ~s,** near equator); hence **lătĭtū'dĭnAL** *a.* **3.** (Astron.) Angular distance of heavenly body or point esp. from ecliptic. **4.** (arch.) Breadth, scope. [ME, = breadth, f. L *latitudo -dinis* (*latus* broad; see -TUDE)]

lătĭtūdĭnār'ĭan *a.* & *n.* (Person) allowing latitude esp. in religion, (one who is) indifferent as to particular creeds and forms of worship; hence ~ISM (3) *n.* [f. L (as prec.) + -ARIAN]

lă'trĭa *n.* (R.C. Ch.) Supreme worship due to God alone. [LL, f. Gk *latreia* worship (*latreuō* serve)]

latri'ne (-ē'n) *n.* Place for urination and defecation, esp. in camp, barracks, hospital, etc.; ~ **rumour,** (sl.) wild rumour arising from gossip in latrines. [F, f. L *latrina* for *lavatrina* (*lavare* wash)]

-latrȳ *suf.* forming *ns.* denoting worship (*idolatry, Mariolatry,* & joc. *Bardolatry* etc.), w. corresp. *ns.* in *-later* denoting worshipper. [f. Gk (as LATRIA, and *-latrēs* -worshipper)]

lă'tten *n.* Alloy of copper, zinc, lead, and tin, formerly used for monumental brasses and church articles. [ME *latoun,* f. OF *laton, leiton*]

lă'tter *attrib. a.* **1.** (arch.) Later, second, (~ **grass, ~math,** aftermath). **2.** Belonging to end of period, world, etc., (**in these ~ days,** at this late period of the world's history; ~ **end,** conclusion of a period, esp. death). **3.** Following another (*the latter part of the year*); second-mentioned of two (opp. FORMER¹); last-mentioned of three or more; **the ~,** second- or last-mentioned thing or person. **4.** ~ **day,** Judgement Day; **~-day,** modern (*L~-day*

Saints, Mormons' name for themselves); ***~-wit,** thinking of rejoinder etc. after opportunity of making it is lost. [OE *lætra*, compar. of *læt* LATE[1]]

lă'tterlў *adv.* Towards the end of life or some period; nowadays, of late. [f. prec. + -LY[2]]

lă'ttice *n.* **1.** Structure of cross laths with interstices, serving as screen, door, etc.; ~(**-work**), laths so arranged. **2.** Regular arrangement of atoms or molecules in a crystal. **3.** ~ **frame** or **girder,** girder made of two flanges connected by iron lattice-work; ~ **window,** one having lattice, or small panes set in diagonally crossing strips of lead. **4.** Hence **lă'ttice**D[2] (-st) *a.*, **lă'tti**CING[1] (6) *n.* [ME, f. OF *lattis* (*latte* lath f. WG ***latta**, *-is* -ICE)]

Lă'tvĭan *a.* & *n.* (Native or inhabitant) of Latvia; Lettish. [f. *Latvia*, republic of U.S.S.R. + -AN]

laud *n.*, & *v.t.* **1.** *n.* (Esp. in hymns) praise; hymn of praise. **2.** (Eccl., in *pl.*) (Office of) first of the canonical hours of prayer, often said together with matins. **3.** *v.t.* Praise, celebrate; so ~A'TION, **~ā'**TOR, *ns.*, ~'ATIVE, **~'a**TORY, *adjs.* [ME, n. f. OF *laude*, v. f. L *laudare*, f. L *laus laudis* praise]

lau'd|able *a.* Commendable, praiseworthy; (Med., of secretion) healthy, sound; hence ~ABI'LITY *n.*, **~ab**LY[2] *adv.* [ME, f. L *laudabilis* (as prec.; see -ABLE)]

lau'danum (-dn-; *or* lŏ'-) *n.* Tincture of opium. [mod. L, name given by Paracelsus to a costly medicament, later applied to preparations containing opium; perh. var. of LADANUM]

laugh (lahf) *v.* & *n.* **1.** *v.i.* Make the sounds and movements of face and body by which lively amusement, sense of the ludicrous, exultation, and scorn, are instinctively expressed; have these emotions; ~ **in** person's **face,** show open contempt for him; ~ **in** or **up** one's **sleeve,** be secretly amused; **don't make me** ~, (colloq., iron.) that is ridiculous; ~ **on the other** or **wrong side of** one's **face** or **mouth,** change from joy or amusement to sorrow or vexation; **he ~s best who ~s last** (warning against premature exultation). **2.** (poet. or rhet.) (Of water, landscape, corn, etc.) be lively with play of movement or light. **3.** *v.t.* Utter laughingly; hold up *to scorn*; get (person) *out of* habit, belief, etc., by ridicule (~ person, opinion, etc., **out of court,** deprive of a hearing by ridicule). **4.** ~ **at,** (1) make fun of, ridicule, (2) look pleasantly or smile at; ~ **away,** dismiss (subject) with a laugh, while away (time) with jests; ~ **down,** silence with laughter; ~ **off,** get rid of (embarrassment etc.) with a jest; ~ **over,** discuss with laughter. **5.** Hence ~'ER[1] *n.* **6.** *n.* Sound made in, act of, laughing (**join in the ~,** esp. of person taking banter good-humouredly; **have** or **get the ~ of** or **on** person, **have the ~ on** one's **side,** turn the tables on opponent); (colloq.) comical thing (*that's a laugh*); person's manner of laughing. [OE *hlæhhan, hliehhan,* = OS ***hlahhian**, OHG *hlahhan*, ON *hlæja*, Goth. *hlahjan* f. Gmc ***hlah-** f. IE ***klak-**, imit.]

lau'ghab|le (lah'f-) *a.* Exciting laughter, amusing; hence ~LY[2] *adv.* [f. prec. (n. or v.) + -ABLE]

lau'ghĭng[1] (lah'f-) *n.* **1.** In vbl senses; **no ~ matter,** serious thing, not a fit subject for laughter. **2.** **~-gas,** nitrous oxide (with exhilarating effect when inhaled) used as anaesthetic; **~-stock,** person or thing generally ridiculed. [ME, f. LAUGH + -ING[1]]

lau'ghĭng[2] (lah'f-) *a.* In vbl senses; *laughing* HYENA; *laughing* JACK[1]*ass*; (sl.) satisfactorily placed; hence ~LY[2] *adv.* [ME, f. LAUGH + -ING[2]]

lau'ghter (lah'f-) *n.* Laughing; HOMERIC *laughter.* [OE *hleahtor*, = OHG *hlahtar*, ON *hlátr* f. Gmc ***hlahtraz** (as LAUGH)]

launce (lahns *or* lăns) *n.* Sand-eel. [perh. f. LANCE[1]; cf. *garfish*]

launch[1] (*or* lah-) *v.* & *n.* **1.** *v.t.* Hurl, discharge, send forth, (missile, blow, censure, threat, decree). **2.** Set (vessel) afloat; send off, start, (person, enterprise, rocket, etc.) on a course. **3.** *v.i.* Burst (usu. **out**) *into* expense, strong language, etc.; ~ **out,** spend money freely, expatiate in words. **4.** Go *forth, out,* on an enterprise. **5.** Hence ~'ER[1] *n.*, (esp.) structure to hold rocket etc. during launching, rocket releasing satellite into orbit; **~'ing pad, site,** etc., (from which rockets are launched). **6.** *n.* Process of launching ship, rocket, etc.; ~ **pad** etc. = *launching pad* etc. [ME, f. AF *launcher*, ONF *lanchier*, OF *lancier* LANCE[2]]

launch[2] (*or* lah-) *n.* Man-of-war's largest boat, used for shore-going, visiting other ships, etc.; motor-driven pleasure-boat on rivers etc. [f. Sp. *lancha* pinnace perh. f. Malay *lancharan* (*lanchār* swift)]

lau'nder *v.t.* Wash, starch, iron, etc., (linen etc.); wash (clothes etc.); hence ~E'TTE, **laundre'tte, *lau'ndromat** [P], establishment with automatic washing-machines available for public use. [f. ME *launder* n., washer of linen, contr. of *lavander* f. OF *lavandier* f. Rom. ****lavandarius*** f. L *lavanda* things to be washed, neut. pl. gerundive of *lavare* wash]

lau'ndrėss *n.* Woman who launders linen etc. as occupation. [f. *launder* n. (see prec.) + -ESS[1]]

lau'ndrў *n.* Establishment for laundering linen etc.; batch of clothes sent to or from laundry. [contr. f. *lavendry* (f. OF *lavanderie*) after LAUNDER; see -RY]

laur'a *n.* (Hist.) Group of hermits' cells in Egypt etc. [Gk, = alley]

laur'ėate (*or* lŏ'r-) *a.* & *n.* **1.** *a.* Wreathed with, (of wreath) consisting of, laurel; worthy of laurels as poet. **2.** *a.* & *n.* (**Poet**) **L~,** poet receiving stipend as member of British Royal Household writing poems for State occasions; hence ~SHIP (-tsh-) *n.* [f. L *laureatus* (*laurea* laurel-wreath f. *laurus* laurel; see -ATE[2])]

lau'rel (lŏ'-) *n.*, & *v.t.* (||-ll-). **1.** *n.* (arch.) Bay-tree. **2.** Foliage of bay-tree as emblem of victory or distinction in poetry (collect. *sing.*, or *pl.*; *reap, win, laurels*; **look to** one's **~s,** beware of losing pre-eminence; **rest on** one's **~s,** cease to strive for further glory). **3.** Plant with dark-green glossy leaves like bay-tree, e.g. (CHERRY-) *laurel*, MOUNTAIN *laurel*, SPURGE *laurel*. **4.** *v.t.* Wreathe with laurel. [ME *lorer* f. OF *lorier* f. Prov. *laurier* (*laur* f. L *laurus*); *-l* by dissim.]

laurustī'nus (lŏ-) *n.* Evergreen winter-flowering shrub (*Viburnum tinus*). [mod. L f. L *laurus* laurel + *tinus* wild laurel]

lăv *n.* (colloq.) Lavatory. [abbr.]

la'va (lah'-) *n.* Matter flowing from volcano; solid substance it cools into; kind or bed of lava. [It. (*lavare* wash f. L)]

lavā'bō (*or* -vah'-) *n.* (*pl.* **~s**). Ritual washing of celebrant's hands at offertory; towel or basin used for this; monastery washing-trough; wash-basin. [L, = I will wash, first wd of Ps. 26:6]

lă'vage *n.* (Med.) Washing-out of an organ. [F (*laver* wash, f. as LAVE; see -AGE)]

lavā'tion *n.* Washing. [f. L *lavatio* (*lavare* wash; see -ATION)]

lă'vatorў *n.* **1.** (Room or building or compartment with) receptacle for urine and (usu.) faeces, usu. with means of disposing of them; ~ **paper,** = TOILET-*paper*. **2.** *(Room or compartment with) equipment for washing face and hands. **3.** (arch.) Vessel for washing hands etc. [ME, in sense 3, f. LL *lavatorium* f. L *lavare -at-* wash; see -ORY]

lāve[1] *v.t.* (poet. or literary). Wash, bathe; (of

stream etc.) wash against, flow along. [ME, f. OF *laver* f. L *lavare* wash, perh. coalescing w. OE *lafian* wash by pouring water on, rel. to MDu. *laven*, OHG *labōn* refresh f. L *lavare*]

lāve² *n.* (Sc.) Remainder. [OE *lāf*, = OHG *leiba*, ON *leif*, Goth. *laiba* f. Gmc **laibhō* (as LEAVE²)]

lă'vėnder *n.*, & *v.t.* **1.** *n.* Small shrub of genus *Lavandula*, with narrow leaves and lilac or purple flowers, cultivated for perfume; its flowers and stalks laid among linen etc.; **lay up in ~**, (fig.) preserve piously for future use. **2.** Pale blue colour with trace of red. **3. ~ cotton,** shrub with strongly scented leaves; **~-water,** perfume of distilled lavender, alcohol, and ambergris. **4.** *v.t.* Put lavender among (linen). [ME, f. AF *lavendre*, ult. dissim. f. med. L *lavandula* etc.]

lā'ver¹ *n.* Edible seaweed of various species. [L]

lā'ver² *n.* **1.** (Bibl.) Large brazen vessel for Jewish priests' ablutions. **2.** (arch.) Washing or fountain basin; font. [ME *lavo(u)r* f. OF *laveo(i)r* f. LL (as LAVATORY)]

lă'verock. Sc. var. of LARK¹.

lă'vĭsh *a.*, & *v.t.* **1.** *a.* Giving or producing without stint, profuse, prodigal, (*of* money etc., *in* giving); very or over abundant; hence ~LY² *adv.*, ~NESS *n.* **2.** *v.t.* Bestow or spend (money, effort, blood, admiration, etc.) profusely. [ME, f. obs. *lavish*, *lavas* n. profusion, f. OF *lavasse* deluge of rain (*laver* wash; see -ISH²)]

law¹ *n.* **1.** Body of enacted or customary rules recognized by a community as binding, this personified, (*forbidden by* or *under British law*; *the law forbids, allows*; *the law of the land*); **the ~ of the Medes and Persians,** unalterablė law [Dan. 6:12]; **lay down the ~**, talk authoritatively, hector. **2.** One of these rules. **3.** Their controlling influence, law-abiding state of society, (*law and order*); **necessity knows no ~** (takes precedence over the laws); **be a ~ unto oneself,** do what one feels is right, take one's own line, disregard convention; **a ~ unto itself,** thing that does not behave in customary manner. **4.** The laws as a social system (‖BARRISTER-*at-law*; COURT¹ *of law*) or subject of study (*read law*, ‖*study the law*, **study law*); **at** or **in ~**, according to the laws, whence SON-*in-law* etc. (orig. w. ref. to lawful wedlock); MATTER¹ *of law*. **5.** Binding injunctions (**give the ~ to,** impose one's will upon; *his word is law*). **6.** (With defining word) one of the branches of the study of law, the laws concerning specified subject (*commercial law*; *the law of contract, of evidence*; CANON, CIVIL, COMMON¹, MARTIAL, STATUTE, *law*); INTERNATIONAL *law* or **~ of nations; bachelor, doctor,** etc., **of ~s** (= in jurisprudence, orig. w. ref. to canon and civil law). **7.** The statute and common law (opp. *equity*). **8.** (In pred. use, of decisions, opinions, etc.; also **good, bad,** etc., ~) borne out, or not, by the relevant laws (*it may be common sense, but it is not law*). **9.** *The* legal profession; legal knowledge. **10.** Judicial remedy, lawcourts as providing it, litigation, (*go to law*; **have** or **take the ~ of** or **on** person, sue him; **take the ~ into** one's **own hands,** redress one's grievance by force); **the Law Courts,** ‖(esp.) London building where the higher courts are held. **11.** God's commandments as expressed in the Bible or implanted by nature in the human mind; **~ (of Moses)**, (precepts of) Pentateuch, Mosaic dispensation. **12.** Rule of action or procedure, esp. in an art, department of life, or game; *law of* HONOUR¹; *laws of* WAR¹. **13. ~ (of nature), natural ~**, correct statement of invariable sequence between specified conditions and specified phenomenon (cf. GRESHAM, GRIMM, KEPLER, NEWTON, PARKINSON², etc.); laws of nature, regularity in nature (*where they saw chance, we see law*). **14.** Allowance or start given to hunted animal or competitor in race; time of grace, respite. **15. ~-abiding(ness)**, obedient, obedience, to law; *law* AGENT; **~-breaker,** one who violates the law; **~ calf,** unstained calf-leather used for binding law-books; *law*COURT¹; **~ French,** the Anglo-Norman terms used in English law(-books); **~'giver,** one who makes (esp. code of) laws; ‖**~-hand,** handwriting used in legal documents; **~ Latin,** barbarous Latin of early English statutes; ‖**Law Lord,** Lord of Appeal in Ordinary or other member of House of Lords qualified to perform its legal work; **~'maker,** legislator; ***~'man,** police officer, sheriff, etc.; **~ merchant,** mercantile law; **~ officer,** legal functionary, ‖esp. Attorney-General or Solicitor-General or Lord Advocate; **~-stationer** (selling stationery needed by lawyers ‖and undertaking engrossing of documents); **~'suit,** prosecution of claim in lawcourt; **~-term,** (1) word or expression used in law, (2) period appointed for sitting of lawcourts. [OE *lagu* f. ON **lagu* pl. of *lag* something 'laid down' or fixed, cogn. w. LAY³]

law². Var. of LAWK.

law'ful *a.* Permitted, appointed, qualified, or recognized, by law, not illegal or (of child) illegitimate; *lawful* WIFE; hence ~LY² *adv.*, ~NESS *n.* [ME, f. LAW¹ + -FUL]

lawk(s) *int.* (vulg.) expr. astonishment; **lawk-a-mussy,** (vulg.) = Lord have mercy. [corrupt. of LORD, perh. after ALACK]

law'lėss *a.* (Of country etc.) where law is non-existent or inoperative; regardless of, disobedient to, uncontrolled by, law; unbridled, licentious; hence ~LY² *adv.*, ~NESS *n.* [ME, f. LAW¹ + -LESS]

lawn¹ *n.* Fine woven linen or cotton, used e.g. for bishop's sleeves; hence ~'Y² *a.* [ME, prob. f. *Laon* in France]

lawn² *n.* **1.** (Expanse of) grass-covered land; close-mown turf-covered piece of pleasure-ground or garden; (arch.) glade. **2.** ***~ bowling,** the game of BOWL²s; **~-mower,** machine with revolving cutters for mowing lawns; ‖**~ sand,** mixture of sand with weed-killers and fertilizers for use on lawns; **~-sprinkler,** machine for watering lawns etc.; **~ tennis,** modification of tennis played by two persons (*singles*) or four (*doubles*) on usu. outdoor court ('grass' or 'hard') without walls. [f. ME *laund(e)* = glade, f. OF *launde* f. OCelt. **landā* LAND¹]

lawrĕ'ncĭum (*ler-*) *n.* (Chem.) Artificially produced transuranic metallic element. [f. E. O. *Lawrence*, Amer. physicist d. 1958 + -IUM]

Lawrĕ'ntian (*lerĕ'nshan*) *a.* Of or pertaining to (the work of) T. E. or D. H. Lawrence. [f. T. E. *Lawrence*, Engl. military leader and author d. 1935, or D. H. *Lawrence*, Engl. author d. 1930, + -IAN, after L *Laurentius* Laurence]

law'yer (*or loi'er*) *n.* Member of legal profession, esp. attorney or ‖solicitor; person versed in law (*good, no,* etc., *lawyer*); **Penang ~**, walking-stick of Penang palm [perh. f. native tree-name]; SEA *lawyer*. [ME *law(i)er* f. LAW¹; see -ER¹, -YER]

lăx¹ *a.* Loose, relaxed, not compact; negligent, careless, not strict, vague; (Phonet.) pronounced with vocal muscles relaxed; hence or cogn. ~'ITY *n.*, ~'LY² *adv.* [ME, f. L *laxus*, cogn. w. SLACK]

lăx² *n.* (Swedish or Norwegian) salmon. [OE *leax*, *læx*, = OHG *lahs*, ON *lax* f. Gmc **lahs-*]

lă'xatĭve *a.* & *n.* (Medicine) tending to cause evacuation of the bowels. [ME, f. OF *laxatif -ive* or f. LL *laxativus* f. L *laxare* loosen (as LAX¹; see -ATIVE)]

lay¹ *n.* Short lyric or narrative poem meant to

be sung; narrative poem; song; (poet.) song of birds. [ME, f. OF *lai*, Prov. *lais*, of unkn. orig.]

lay² *a.* **1.** Non-clerical, not in orders; of or done by layman or laity; non-professional, not expert, (esp. w. ref. to law or medicine). **2.** ~ **brother,** ~ **sister,** person who has taken habit and vows of religious order but is employed in manual labour and excused other duties; ~ **clerk,** singing man in cathedral or collegiate church, parish clerk; ~ **communion,** (1) membership of church as layman, (2) communicating of laity in Eucharist; ~ **deacon,** man in deacon's order but also following secular employment; ||~ **lord,** peer who is not a LAW¹ Lord; **~'man,** one of the laity, non-expert in regard to some profession, art, or science, (esp. law or medicine); ~ **reader,** layman licensed to conduct religious services; ~ **rector,** layman receiving rectorial tithes; ~ **sister** (see *lay brother*); *lay* VICAR. [ME, f. F *lai* f. eccl. L f. Gk *laïkos* LAIC]

lay³ *v.* (**laid**) & *n.* **1.** *v.t.* Prostrate (*lay* LOW¹); (of wind or rain) beat down (crops); cause (sea, wind, dust, misgivings, ghost) to subside, (Naut.) sail so far as to bring (land etc.) below horizon, (opp. RAISE). **2.** Deposit; place in recumbent posture (~ **to sleep** or **rest,** lit., or fig. = bury; ~ one's **bones,** be buried *in* specified place); (of hen bird) produce (egg, or abs.); put down (amount, one's head or life, etc.) as wager, stake, (abs.) announce readiness to bet (*that*); (sl.) copulate with. **3.** Place, set, apply, put, (~ **heads together,** consult one another; *lay to* HEART; *lay hounds on scent*; ~ **hold on** or **of,** seize, grasp, (fig.) benefit from (opponent's weak point etc.); *lay* one's *hopes on*; *lay* SIEGE *to*; *lay snare, trap, ambush*; *lay great* STORE *by* or *on*; *lay* WAIT²); locate (scene; *scene of tale is laid in London*); put (limb etc.) in specified position (*horse laid his ears back*; *lay* one's HAND¹ *on*; ~ **hands on,** (1) seize, appropriate, (2) do violence to, esp. one*self* = commit suicide, (3) find: *cannot lay my hands on it,* (4) confirm or ordain by imposition of hands); aim (large gun); (w. compl.) bring into specified state (*lay land fallow, under water*); ~ person **under obligation,** oblige him, **under necessity,** compel him, **under contribution,** make him contribute; *lay by the* HEEL¹*s*; ~ **bare,** denude, reveal; ~ **open,** (1) reveal, explain, (2) break skin of (part of body); ~ **waste,** ravage. **4.** Present, put forward, (*lay claim to*; ~ **a charge,** make accusation; ~ **an information,** bring indictment in legal form); place (facts, question) for consideration *before* person; ||(Parl.) = *lay on the* TABLE 10 (to give information to the House of Commons); (of plaintiff) fix claim for (damages) *at* certain sum; impute (fault) *to* person's *charge*, *at* or *to* his *door*, (arch.) *to* him; represent (evil) as consequent *on* some cause. **5.** Impose (penalty, command, obligation, burden, tax), cast (blame), (*up*)*on* (~ **emphasis,** STRESS, **weight, on,** emphasize, treat as important); bring (stick etc.) down *on*; (abs.) ~ **into,** (sl.) belabour, ~ **about one,** hit out on all sides. **6.** Dispose, arrange, esp. horizontally (foundation, floor, bricks, submarine cable; ~ **table, cloth,** or **breakfast** etc., prepare table for meal; ~ **the fire,** put fuel ready for lighting); make (strand, rope) by twisting yarn or strands; fix outlines of, devise (plan, plot); put (colour etc.) on a surface in layers; cover, coat, strew, (surface) *with* carpet, metal, straw, etc.; **laid paper** (with ribbed surface owing to wires used in making); **laid work,** embroidery with sewed-down thread along lines. **7.** *v.i.* (Naut. or vulg.) = LIE³; ~ **on your oars,** stop rowing but keep oars out; ||**~'about,** habitual loafer or tramp. **8.** ~ **aside,** put away, cease to use or practise or think of, abandon, save (money etc.) for future needs; ~ **back,** cause to slope back from vertical; ~ **by,** = *lay aside*; ~*-by* n. (pl. ~*-bys*), ||extra strip alongside road to provide place for vehicles to stop without obstructing other traffic, similar arrangement on canal or railway, (Austral. & N.Z.) system of reserving article by deposit for later purchase; ~ **down,** put on the ground etc. (~ *down* one's *arms*, surrender), relinquish (office, hopes), pay or wager (money), sacrifice (one's life), (begin to) construct (ship, railway), formulate (rule, principle, course; *lay down the* LAW¹), set down (chart etc.) on paper, convert (land) into pasture (*in, to, under, with,* grass, clover, etc.), store (wine) in cellar; ~ **in,** provide oneself with stock of; ~ **off,** discharge (temporarily) owing to shortage of work, (colloq.) desist; ~*-off* n., (period of) such temporary discharge, time of reduced activity; ~ **on,** impose (tax, command, penalty), deal blows, inflict (blows, or *it*), ply (lash etc.), apply coat of (paint etc.; *lay it on* THICK or *with a* TROWEL), provide pipes etc. supplying (gas, water, electricity), provide (refreshments, entertainment, means of transport, etc.); ~ **out,** spread, expose to view etc., prepare (body) for burial, (sl.) kill, (colloq.) put (person) out of action temporarily at football etc., expend (money), dispose (grounds, garden) according to a plan, (*refl.*) take pains *to* do; ~*'out* n., disposing or arrangement of ground etc., (in plans etc.) drawing showing arrangement, make-up of book, newspaper, advertisement, etc.; ~ **up,** store, put by, save (money, or abs.), lay (rope; see sense 6), (in *pass.*) be confined to bed or house. **9.** *n.* Direction or amount of twist in rope-strands; way, position, or direction, in which something (esp. country) lies, lie (**lay of the land*); (sl.) line of business, job; (sl.) (partner in) copulation; **in** ~, (of hen) in condition to lay eggs; **~-day** (allowed for loading or unloading cargo); **~'shaft,** secondary or intermediate shaft for transmission of power in machine. [OE *lecgan*, = OS *leggian*, OHG *legen, lecken*, ON *legja*, Goth. *lagjan* f. Gmc **leg-*, **lag-* LIE³]

lay⁴. See LIE³.

lay'er *n.* & *v.* **1.** *n.* In vbl senses. **2.** Thickness of matter (esp. one of several) spread over surface; ~ **cake** (made in layers with filling between). **3.** (Hort.) Shoot fastened into earth to strike root while attached to parent plant; **~-stool,** root from which layers are produced. **4.** Hence ~ED² (*-erd*) *a.* **5.** *v.t.* (Hort.) Propagate as layer. **6.** *v.i.* (Of crops) be laid by wind or rain. [ME, f. LAY³ + -ER¹]

layĕtte *n.* Clothes, toilet articles, and bedding, needed for new-born child. [F, dim. of OF *laie* drawer f. MDu. *laege*; see -ETTE]

lay' fĭgure (*-ger*) *n.* Jointed wooden figure of human body used by artists for arranging drapery on etc.; unimportant person, nonentity; unreal character in novel etc. [*lay* f. obs. *layman* lay figure f. Du. *leeman* (obs. *led* joint)]

||**lay'stall** (-awl) *n.* Refuse heap. [f. LAY³ + STALL¹]

lă'zar *n.* (arch.) Poor and diseased person, esp. leper; **~-house,** = foll. [ME, f. med. L *lazarus* f. proper name (Luke 16:20)]

lăzarĕ't, -ĕ'ttō (*pl.* **-os**), *n.* Hospital for diseased poor, esp. lepers; building or ship for quarantine; after part of ship's hold, used for stores. [(F *lazaret*) f. It. *lazzaretto* (*lazzaro* LAZAR)]

lāze *v.* & *n.* (colloq.) **1.** *v.i.* Be lazy. **2.** *v.t.* Pass (time) *away* in laziness. **3.** *n.* Time spent in lazing. [back form. f. LAZY]

lă'zūlĭ *n.* = LAPIS LAZULI. [abbr.]

lā'zy̆ *a.* & *v.* **1.** *a.* Averse to labour, indolent, slothful; appropriate to or inducing indolence; (of river etc.) slow-moving. **2.** **~-bones,** lazy person; **~ Susan,** revolving food-stand for table; **~-tongs,** arrangement of zigzag levers for picking up distant objects. **3.** Hence **lā'zĭ**LY[2] *adv.*, **lā'zĭ**NESS *n.* **4.** *v.i.* & *t.* Laze. [earlier *laysie, lasie, laesy,* perh. of LG orig.; cf. LG *lasich* idle]

lb. *abbr.* POUND[1] 1, pounds. [f. L *libra*]

l.b. *abbr.* leg-bye(s).

l.b.w. *abbr.* leg before wicket.

l.c. *abbr.* letter of credit; *loco citato*; lower case.

||**L.C.C.** *abbr.* (Hist.) London County Council.

||**L.C.J.** *abbr.* Lord Chief Justice.

L.C.M. *abbr.* least (or lowest) common MULTIPLE.

L/Cpl. *abbr.* Lance-Corporal.

Ld. *abbr.* Lord.

Ldg. *abbr.* Leading (Seaman etc.).

L.D.S. *abbr.* Licentiate in Dental Surgery.

-le, -el, *suf.* **1.** Forming *ns.* w. dim. sense (*bramble*) or denoting appliance (*thimble, handle, bridle, girdle*), agent (*beadle*), etc., and *adjs.* f. *vbs.*, w. sense 'apt or liable to' (*brittle, fickle, nimble*) [ME f. OE *-el(a), -(e)le* n., *-ol, -ul, -el* a.]. **2.** Forming *ns.* mainly w. (orig.) dim. sense (*angle, castle, mantle, novel, tunnel*) or sense as -AL (*battle, cattle*) [ME *-el(le)* f. OF *-el* f. L *-ellus, -ellum* or OF *-ele* f. L *-ella*, or f. L *-ale*, or f. F *-aille* f. L *-alia* (as -AL), or f. F *-eille* f. L *-icula*, or f. L *-ulus* etc.]. **3.** Forming *vbs.* w. frequent. or dim. sense (*crumple, dazzle, nestle, snarl, twinkle, wriggle*) [ME *-(e)len* f. OE *-lian* f. Gmc *-ilōjan*].

lea[1] *n.* (poet.) Tract of open ground, esp. grassland. [OE *lēa(h)*, cogn. w. OHG *lōh* grove, f. Gmc **lauh-* f. IE **louq-*]

lea[2] *n.* Measure of yarn (300, 200, 120, or 80 yards, according to type and place). [ME *lee*, perh. f. F *lier* f. L *ligare* to bind]

L.E.A. *abbr.* Local Education Authority.

leach *v.t.* Make (liquid) percolate through some material; subject (bark, ore, ash, soil) to action of percolating fluid; remove (soluble matter *away* or *out*) by such means. [prob. repr. OE *leccan* to water, f. WG **lakkjan*]

lead[1] (lĕd) *n.*, & *v.t.* **1.** *n.* Heavy easily fusible soft malleable base metal of dull pale bluish-grey colour (RED *lead*; **white ~,** mixture of lead carbonate and hydrated lead oxide used as pigment); = BLACK[1]*lead*, (hence) thin stick of graphite in or for pencil; bullet(s). **2.** Lump of lead used in SOUND[3]ing water (**cast** or **heave the ~,** lower it from ship; ||SWING *the lead*). **3.** ||(in *pl.*) Strips of lead used to cover roof, piece of (esp. horizontal) lead-covered roof; lead frames or cames holding glass of lattice or stained-glass window. **4.** (Print.) Metal strip to give space between lines. **5.** **~ pencil** (of graphite usu. enclosed in cedar); **~-poisoning,** acute or chronic poisoning by taking of lead into the body; **~'sman** (-z-), sailor who heaves the lead; **~ tetraethyl,** = TETRA*ethyl lead*; **~ wool,** lead in a fibrous state, used for jointing water-pipes; **~-work,** plumber's or glazier's work; **~-works,** place where lead ore is smelted; **~'wort,** = PLUMBAGO 2. **6.** Hence **~'**LESS *a.* **7.** *v.t.* (esp. in *p.p.*) Cover, weight, frame (panes), with lead; (Print.) separate lines of (printed matter) with leads; add lead (compound) to (petrol etc.). [OE *lēad*, = MLG *lōd*, MHG *lōt* plummet f. WG **lauda*]

lead[2] *v.* (**led**). **1.** *v.t.* Cause to go with one (**~ captive,** take away as prisoner). **2.** (Of person, or fig. of motive, circumstance, etc.) conduct, guide, esp. by going in front (*led me to the house I was looking for*; *curiosity, chance, led him to Rome*); *lead* person *a* DANCE[2]; **~** person **a (dog's) life,** harass him constantly; *lead the* WAY 2. **3.** (Of commander) direct movements of. **4.** Guide (person) by the hand or by contact, (animal) by halter etc., (**led horse,** spare horse led by groom etc.; **led captain,** hanger-on, toady, parasite; **~** woman **to altar,** marry her); guide by persuasion (*is easier led than driven*; **~ astray,** esp. tempt to sin etc.; **~ by the nose,** induce to do submissively all one wishes). **5.** Guide actions or opinions of, bring by argument etc. *to* conclusions, induce *to* do (**~** person **to suppose** etc., deceive him into thinking *that*); ply (witness) with leading questions. **6.** (Of road etc.) be route for (person, or usu. abs.) *to* or *into* place (*all roads lead to Rome*); **~ to,** (fig.) have as result (*this led to confusion*). **7.** Make (rope, water, etc.) go *through* pulley, channel, etc. **8.** Pass, go through, spend, (life etc., esp. w. epithet: *lead a miserable existence, a double life*). **9.** Have first place in (*lead the dance, the van, the world in sugar production*); (abs.) go first, be first at some point in race, be ahead in game (*Kent led on the first innings*), make one's start *with*. **10.** Direct by example (*lead orchestra, band, chorus,* etc.), set (fashion); be official director or spokesman of (party), ||act as leading counsel in (case, or usu. abs.). **11.** *v.t.* & *i.* (Cards). Play as first card, be first player, in trick; play one of (suit) when leading; **~ away from,** lead card of suit-holding including (ace etc., usu. to one's disadvantage); **~ through,** cause holder of (ace etc.) to play to trick before another player (usu. to one's advantage); **~ up to,** allow holder of (ace etc.) to play to trick after another player (usu. to one's disadvantage). **12.** **~ away,** (usu. in *pass.*) induce to follow unthinkingly; **~-in** *n.*, introductory matter, (Electr.) wire connecting radio receiver to external aerial; **~ off,** begin (dance, conversation, or abs.); **~-off** *n.*, commencement; **~ on,** entice into going farther than was intended; *lead up the* GARDEN (*path*); **~ up to,** form preparation for, serve to introduce, direct conversation towards, (subject). **13.** Hence **~'**ABLE *a.* [OE *lǣdan*, = OHG *leiten*, OS *lēdjan*, ON *leitha* f. Gmc **laidhjan* (**laidhō* LOAD[1])]

lead[3] *n.* **1.** Guidance given by going in front, example, (*follow the lead of*; **give** person **a ~,** encourage him by doing thing, e.g. leaping fence in hunting, first, (fig.) provide him with clue). **2.** Leading place, leadership, (*is in the lead*; *take the lead*); amount by which competitor is ahead of others (*a lead of five minutes, five miles*). **3.** Artificial watercourse, esp. one leading to mill; (Electr.) conductor conveying current from source to place of use; pitch of screw; channel in ice-field; string, strap, etc., for leading or controlling a dog; (Cards) act or right of playing first in game or to trick (**return ~,** lead suit already led by partner), card led; (Theatr.) (player of) chief part. **4.** **~ screw** (moving the carriage of a lathe); **~ story,** item of news given greatest prominence in newspaper etc.; **~ time** (between initiation and completion of production process). [ME, f. prec.]

lea'den (lĕ'd-) *a.* (As) of lead; heavy, slow, burdensome, (*leaden limbs*); inert, depressing, (*leaden rule*); lead-coloured (*leaden skies*); *leaden* SEAL[2]. [OE *lēaden* (as LEAD[1], -EN[5])]

lea'der *n.* In vbl senses (FOLLOW-*my-leader*); **L~ of House** (**of Commons** or **of Lords**), member of Government with official initiative in business; ||counsel who leads in case, Q.C., or senior counsel of circuit; front horse in team or tandem (cf. WHEELER); *conductor of orchestra; leading performer in orchestra, quartet, choir, etc., ||esp. leading first-violin player; shoot growing at apex of stem or principal branch; ||= LEADING[2] *article*; tab to assist threading of film, tape, etc., on reel; (Print., in *pl.*) line of dots or dashes to guide eye; hence ~LESS *a.*, ~SHIP (1, 3, 4) *n.* [OE *lǣdere* (as LEAD², -ER¹)]

lea'dĭng¹ *n.* In vbl senses; *men* **of light and ~,** deservedly influential; **~-rein** (to lead horse with); **~-staff** (attached to ring in bull's nose); **~-strings,** strings with which children were formerly taught to walk (*in ~-strings*, in state of pupillage). [ME, f. LEAD² + -ING¹]

lea'dĭng² *a.* In vbl senses; ‖ranking just below N.C.O. (*leading aircraftman, seaman*); ‖**~ article,** editorial expression of opinion at full length in newspaper; **~ case,** (Law) case serving as precedent for deciding others; **~ edge,** foremost edge of aircraft's wing, etc., forward edge of propeller-blade, (Electr.) part of pulse in which amplitude increases, (opp. *trailing edge*); **~ lady, man,** (taking chief part in play); **~ light,** prominent influential person; **~ motive,** *leitmotiv*; **~ note** or ***tone,** seventh note of diatonic scale of any key, semitone below key-note; **~ question** (prompting desired answer). [f. LEAD² + -ING²]

lea'dĭng³ (lĕ'-) *n.* In vbl senses (esp. Print.). [f. LEAD¹ + -ING¹]

leaf *n.* (*pl.* **leaves** *pr.* -vz) & *v.* **1.** *n.* Relatively broad flat organ (usu. green) of plant springing from side of stem or branch or direct from root; (pop.) petal (esp. *rose-leaf*); (collect.) foliage (**fall of the ~,** autumn); state of having leaves out (*is in, comes into, leaf*); (collect.) leaves of tobacco or tea. **2.** Single thickness of folded paper, esp. (= 2 pages) in book (*take a leaf out of* person's BOOK¹; **turn over a new ~,** improve one's conduct). **3.** Very thin sheet of metal, esp. gold or silver, or of horn, marble, talc, etc. **4.** Hinged part or flap of door, shutter, table (also used of extra section inserted in expansible table), bridge (= bascule), or rifle-sight. **5.** *Layer of fat around pig's kidneys. **6.** **~-green,** (of) the colour of green leaves; **~-insect** (having wings resembling leaf of plant); ***~-lard** (made from leaf, sense 5); **~-miner,** caterpillar eating through leaves; **~-monkey,** langur; **~-mould,** soil composed chiefly of decaying leaves; **~ spring** (made of strips of metal); **~-stalk,** petiole. **7.** Hence ~'AGE (1) *n.*, (-)~ED² (-ft), ~'LESS, ~'Y², *adjs.* **8.** *v.i.* Put forth leaves; **~ through,** = sense 9. **9.** *v.t.* *Turn over leaves or pages of (book etc.). [OE *lēaf*, = OS *lōf*, OHG *loup*, ON *lauf*, Goth. *laufs* f. Gmc **laubhaz-, -am*]

lea'flėt *n.* **1.** (Bot.) one division of compound leaf; young leaf. **2.** Small leaf of paper, or sheet or leaves folded but not stitched, with printed matter, esp. for distribution free of charge. [f. prec. + -LET]

league¹ (-g) *n.* Varying measure of travelling-distance, usu. about three miles. [ME, ult. f. LL *leuga, leuca*, of Gaulish orig.]

league² (-g) *n.* & *v.* **1.** *n.* Agreement made for mutual protection and assistance or prosecution of common interests, parties (whether States or individuals) to such compact, (*Solemn League and* COVENANT; ‖PRIMROSE *League*; **in ~ with,** allied with). **2.** Group of sports clubs who play each other for championship; class of contestants (in sports, or fig.: *in the big league*); **~ table,** list of these in order of rank; ‖RUGBY *League*. **3. L~ of Nations** (established by the treaty of peace 1919 to try to prevent war, now replaced by UNITED *Nations*). **4.** *v.t.* & *i.* Join in league (*with*). [f. F *ligue* or f. It. *liga*, var. of *lega* f. *legare* bind f. L *ligare*]

lea'guer¹ (-ger) *n.* & *v.* = LAAGER. [f. Du. *leger* camp, cogn. w. LAIR]

lea'guer² (-ger) *n.* Member of league. [f. LEAGUE² + -ER¹]

leak *n.* & *v.* **1.** *n.* Hole caused by injury, wear, etc., through which fluid makes way into or out of vessel that is immersed in or contains it or through a dike (SPRING¹ *a leak*); fluid thus passing through; (escape of) electric charge from imperfectly insulated conductor; disclosure of secret information. **2.** *v.t.* & *i.* Let fluid, (of fluid) pass, out or in through leak; disclose (secret etc.); **~ (out),** (of secret etc.) become known. **3.** Hence ~'AGE *n.*, action of leaking, what leaks out or in, disclosure of secrets. [ME, prob. of LG orig.; cf. MDu. *lek* n. (cogn. w. ON *leki*), *lēken* v. (ON *leka*), f. Gmc **lek-*, **lak-* LACK]

lea'k|ў *a.* Having leak(s); given to letting out secrets; hence ~INESS *n.* [f. prec. + -Y²]

leal *a.* (Sc.) Loyal, honest, (LAND¹ *of the leal*). [ME f. AF; OF *leel, loial*, as LOYAL]

lean¹ *a.* & *n.* **1.** *a.* (Of person) thin, not plump; meagre, of poor quality, not nourishing, (*lean crops, diet*; **~ years,** years of scarcity); unremunerative; (of meat) consisting chiefly of muscular tissue, not of fat; hence ~'NESS (-n-n-) *n.* **2.** *n.* Lean part of meat. [OE *hlǣne* f. Gmc **hlainjaz*]

lean² *v.* (**~ed** *pr.* lēnd *or* lĕnt, *or* ‖**~t** *pr.* lĕnt) & *n.* **1.** *v.i.* Incline one's body against something for support, support oneself, (of thing) be supported in sloping position, *against* or *on*; **~ upon,** (Mil.) have as protection on flank. **2.** Rely or depend (*up*)*on* (*lean on a* REED¹). **3.** Incline body *back, forward, over, towards*, etc., (*lean over* BACKWARDS). **4.** Stand obliquely, out of the perpendicular, (*leaning tower*). **5.** Have tendency (*to* mercy etc.), be partial *to* or *towards* cause, opinion, or person, whence ~'ING¹ (1) *n.* **6.** *v.t.* Place (thing) in leaning position. **7.** **~-to,** building with roof resting against side of larger building or wall. **8.** *n.* Inclination, slope, (*has a decided lean to the right*). [OE *hleonian, hlinian*, = OS *hlinon*, OHG (*h*)*linēn* f. Gmc **hli-*]

leap¹ *v.* (**~ed** *pr.* lēpt *or* lĕpt, *or* **~t** *pr.* lĕpt). **1.** *v.i.* & *t.* Jump (*leapt at the offer, into prominence*; *heart leaps up*; **~ to the eye,** be very obvious; LOOK¹ *before you leap*). **2.** **~-frog,** (*n.*) game in which player vaults with parted legs over another bending down, (*v.t.* & *i.*; **-gg-**) perform such vault (over), (fig.) overtake alternately. **3.** Hence ~'ER¹ *n.* [OE *hlēapan*, = OS *-hlōpan*, OHG *loufan*, ON *hlaupa*, Goth. *-hlaupan* f. Gmc **hlaupan*]

leap² *n.* Jump (*leap in the* DARK²; **by ~s and bounds,** with startlingly rapid progress); thing to be jumped; (Geol.) fault; **~-day,** 29 Feb.; **~ year,** (1) year with extra day, now 29 Feb. [perh. because fixed festivals after February in leap year fall two days of the week, instead of as usual one, later than in the preceding year], (2) intercalary year; *~-year proposal*, (joc.) proposal of marriage by woman to man, traditionally allowable only in leap year. [OE *hlȳp*, **hliep*, = OHG *hlouf*, ON *hlaup* f. Gmc **hlaupiz* (as prec.)]

learn (lẽrn) *v.* (**~ed** *pr.* -nd *or* -nt, *or* **~t**). **1.** *v.t.* Get knowledge of (subject) or skill in (art etc.) by study, experience, or being taught, (*from* study etc., *from* or *of* teacher). **2.** Commit to memory (esp. **~ by heart** or **rote**). **3.** Become aware by information or from observation *that, how*, etc. (**I am** or **have yet to ~,** I do not know, usu. w. implication of disbelief); be informed of, ascertain. **4.** (arch., joc., or vulg.) Teach. **5.** *v.i.* Receive instruction, get knowledge or skill; become informed *of*. **6.** Hence ~'ABLE *a.*, ~'ER¹ *n.*; **~er(-driver),** one who has begun to drive a motor vehicle but has not yet passed the driving test. [OE *leornian*, = OS *linōn*, OHG *lirnēn, lernēn* f. Gmc **lis-*, **lais-*; cf. LORE¹]

lear'nėd (lẽr'-) *a.* Deeply read, erudite; showing profound knowledge; ‖(in conventionally courteous mention of lawyer in House of Commons, lawcourts, etc.) learned in the law (esp. *my learned* FRIEND or *brother*); (of language, PROFESSION, etc.) pursued or studied by, (of words in a language) introduced by, (of publication or society) concerned with interests of, learned persons; hence ~LY[2] *adv.* [ME, f. prec. in sense 'teach' + -ED[1]]

lear'ning (lẽr'-) *n.* In vbl senses; (possession of) knowledge got by study, esp. of language or literature or history as subjects of systematic investigation (**the new ~,** studies, esp. of Greek, introduced into England in 16th c., the Renaissance). [OE *leornung* (as LEARN, -ING[1])]

lease *n.*, & *v.t.* **1.** *n.* Contract by which one party (*lessor*), usu. in consideration of rent, conveys land or tenement to another (*lessee*) for specified time (*put out to, take a, lease*; *by* or *on lease*); **a new ~ of** or ***on life,** prospect of continued (vigorous) living due to recovered health or removal of anxiety etc., or of further use (of thing) after repair etc.; **~'hold(er),** (person having) tenure, property held, by lease; **L~-Lend,** = LEND-*Lease*. **2.** *v.t.* Grant or take lease of; **~'back,** sale of property followed by lease of it back to vendor so that rent to buyer compensates cost of purchase. [ME, f. AF *les*, OF *lais, leis*, (*lesser, laissier* leave, f. L *laxare* make loose (*laxus*))]

leash *n.*, & *v.t.* **1.** *n.* Thong by which hounds or coursing-dogs are held (**hold in ~,** control; **straining at the ~,** eager to begin); group of three hounds, hares, etc.; *dog*-LEAD[3] 3; (Weaving) cord with eye to receive warp-thread extending between parallel laths of loom-heddle. **2.** *v.t.* Connect, hold in, with leash. [ME, f. OF *lesse, laisse* f. spec. use of *laisser* let run on slack lead; see LEASE]

least *a.*, *n.*, & *adv.* **1.** *a.* Smallest, slightest, (**the ~,** esp. after neg., any however small; *least common* MULTIPLE; *line of least* RESISTANCE); very small (species or variety, e.g. *least tern*). **2.** *n.* Least amount (**to say the ~ of it,** to put the case moderately; **~ said soonest mended,** discussion will only make things worse); **at ~,** at all events, even if a wider statement is disputable; **at (the) ~,** at the lowest computation; **(in) the ~,** in the smallest degree, at all. **3.** *adv.* In the least degree. [OE *lǣst, lǣsest* f. Gmc **laisistaz*, superl. of **laisiz* (LESS; see -EST[1])]

lea'stways (-z; dial. or vulg.), **lea'stwise** (-z), *advs.* Or at least, or rather. [f. prec. + -WAYS, -WISE]

||**leat** *n.* Open watercourse conducting water to mill etc. [OE *-gelǣt* (as Y- + root of LET[2])]

lea'ther (lĕ'dh-) *n.*, & *v.t.* **1.** *n.* Skin of animal prepared for use by tanning or similar process; **patent ~** (with fine black varnished surface); **~ and** (prop. **or**) **prunella,** a matter of indifference, a difference in clothes only [see Pope *Essay on Man* iv. 204]; **nothing like ~,** one's own goods will serve all purposes. **2.** Article, or part of one, made of leather; piece of leather for polishing with; thong (esp. *stirrup-leather*); (sl.) cricket-ball or football; (in *pl.*) leggings or breeches. **3. ~-back,** largest existing turtle, with flexible shell; **~ carp** (scaleless variety); **~-cloth,** strong fabric coated to resemble leather; **~-head,** (sl.) stupid person; **~-jacket,** ||crane-fly grub with tough skin; **~-neck,** (Naut.) soldier or marine [w. ref. to leather stock formerly worn]. **4.** Hence ~E'TTE (2) *n.*, **~n** (arch.) [-EN[5]], ~Y[2] (esp. of meat etc., tough), *adjs.* **5.** *v.t.* Cover with leather; wipe or polish with leather; beat, thrash, (orig. w. leather thong). [OE *lether*, = OS *lethar*, OHG *ledar*, ON *lethr* f. Gmc **lethram* f. IE **letrom*]

lea'theroid (lĕ'dh-) *n.* Cotton paper chemically treated and resembling rawhide. [f. prec. + -OID]

leave[1] *n.* **1.** Permission (*to* do); **by your ~** (apology, often iron., for taking liberty, making unwelcome statement, etc.; *without a 'with your ~' or a 'by your ~'*, (colloq.) without even asking permission); **take ~ to,** venture or presume to. **2.** (In Services, offices, schools) **~ (of absence),** permission to be absent from duty, period for which this lasts (**on ~,** absent thus; SICK[1]*-leave*; ||TICKET *of leave*). **3. Take** (one's) **~ (of),** bid farewell (to); **take ~ of** one's **senses,** go mad; hence **~-tāk**ING[1] (1) *n.* **4.** FRENCH *leave*; WAY-*-leave*. [OE *lēaf*, = OHG **louba* f. WG **laubha*; cf. LIEF, LOVE[1]]

leave[2] *v.t.* (**left**), & *n.* **1.** *v.t.* Cause to or let remain, depart without taking, have at time of one's death, (*leaves a wife and three sons*; *has left his gloves, a slimy trail, a permanent scar, a bad impression on us*; *six from seven leaves one*; **~ much** etc. **to be desired,** be unsatisfactory); bequeath; **be left with,** retain (feeling etc.), be burdened with (responsibility etc.). **2.** Abstain from consuming or dealing with; (in *pass.*) remain over or *over*; **left-overs,** (esp.) food not consumed at earlier meal. **3.** Let remain in specified state; *this* **~s me cool** or **cold,** does not excite me; **~ it at that,** (colloq.) abstain from comment or further action; **be well** etc. **left** (provided for by legacy etc.); **~ undone, unsaid,** etc., not do (up), refrain from saying, etc. **4.** Commit or refer *to* another agent etc. than oneself (*nothing was left to chance*); **~ him to himself,** do not try to control him; **~ it to me,** let me deal with it. **5.** Allow (person or thing) *to* do something without interference or assistance (*leave the future to take care of itself*); **~ be,** (colloq.) not interfere with. **6.** Deposit, entrust, (thing, instructions, message), station (person), to be seen to, delivered, etc., or to discharge function, in one's absence; ||**left luggage** (deposited at railway office etc. for later retrieval); **~ card on** person (arch., as equivalent of formal call). **7.** Go away from, cease to remain in or on, (*left him quite well an hour ago*; *leave this* or *here*; *leave the track, the* ROOM); (abs.) depart (*we leave tomorrow*; often *for* destination). **8.** Pass (object) so that it is in specified relative direction (*leave the church on the left*). **9.** Cease to reside at (place), attend (school), belong to (society), or serve (employer); also abs. (*I am leaving at Christmas*). **10.** Abandon, forsake, desert, (esp. *leave in the* LURCH[1]); **get left,** (colloq.) be deserted or worsted; **left at the post,** beaten from start of race; **left for dead** etc., abandoned as being beyond rescue. **11. ~ alone,** not have dealings with, not interfere with (*leave* WELL[3] *alone*); **~ behind,** go away without, leave as consequence or visible sign of passage, pass; **~ go,** (vulg.) relax one's hold; **~ hold of,** cease holding; **~ off,** cease to wear, discontinue (habit, doing, *work*), (abs.) come to or make an end; **~ out,** omit, not include; ||**~ over,** let stand over for the time being. **12.** Hence **lea'**VER[1] *n.*, **lea'**VING[1] (2) *n.* (usu. in *pl.*) **13.** *n.* (Bill.) Position in which player leaves the balls. [OE *lǣfan*, = OS *-lēbian*, OHG *leiban*, ON *leifa*, Goth. *-laibjan* f. Gmc **laibhjan* remain (**laibhō* remainder)]

leaved (-vd) *a.* Having leaves; (in *comb.*) having leaf or leaves of specified kind or number (*four-leaved clover*). [ME, f. LEAF + -ED[2]]

lea'ven (lĕ'-) *n.*, & *v.t.* **1.** *n.* Substance added to dough to produce fermentation, esp. yeast, or fermenting dough reserved for purpose; (fig.) spreading and transforming influence (Matt.

13:33), tinge or admixture *of* some quality; **the old ~**, traces of unregenerate state (1 Cor. 5:6, 7). **2.** *v.t.* Ferment (dough) with leaven; permeate and transform, modify *with* tempering element. [ME f. OF *levain* f. Gallo-Rom. spec. use of L *levamen* relief (*levare* lift)]

leaves. See LEAF.

Lĕbanē'se (-z) *a.* & *n.* (*pl.* same). (Native or inhabitant) of Lebanon. [f. *Lebanon* in S.W. Asia + -ESE]

lebensraum (lā'benzrowm) *n.* (Hist. or fig.) Territory which the Germans believed was needed for their natural development. [G, = living-space]

lĕ'cher *n.* Lewd or unchaste man, fornicator, debauchee; so ~OUS *a.*, **lĕ'ch**ERY (4) *n.* [ME, f. OF *lecheor* etc. (*lechier* live in debauchery or gluttony, f. Frank. **likkōn* f. Gmc **likkōjan* lick)]

lĕ'cĭthĭn *n.* Complex fatty substance containing phosphorus and found in egg-yolk etc.; preparation of this, used to emulsify foods etc. [f. Gk *lekithos* egg-yolk + -IN]

lĕ'ctern *n.* Reading-desk or singing-desk in church, esp. that for the lessons; *similar desk for lecturer etc. [ME *lettorne* f. OF *let(t)run*, med. L *lectrum* (*legere lect-* read)]

lĕ'ction *n.* Text-reading found in particular copy or edition. [f. L *lectio* reading (as prec.; see -ION)]

lĕ'ctionarў *n.* Book containing, list of, portions of Scripture appointed to be read at divine service. [ME, f. med. L *lectionarium* (as prec.; see -ARY[1])]

lĕ'ctor *n.* Reader (esp. of lessons in church service, or in university). [L (*legere lect-* read; see -OR)]

lĕ'cture *n.* & *v.* **1.** *n.* Discourse before audience or class on given subject, usu. by way of instruction; admonition, reproof, (**read** person **a ~**, reprove him). **2.** *v.i.* Deliver lecture(s) (*on* subject). **3.** *v.t.* Instruct or entertain (class, audience, etc.) by lecture; admonish, reprimand. **4.** Hence **lĕ'ctur**ER[1] (-kch*er*-) *n.* [ME f. OF, or f. med. L *lectura* f. L (as prec.; see -URE)]

lĕ'ctureshĭp (-kch*er*sh-) *n.* Office of lecturer. [f. prec. + -SHIP (irreg. formation)]

lĕ'cўth|us *n.* (*pl.* ~i *pr.* -ī). (Gk Ant.) Narrow-necked vase or flask. [f. Gk *lēkuthos*]

lĕd. See LEAD[2].

le'derhōsen (lā-; -z-) *n.* Leather shorts as worn by men in Bavaria etc. [G, = leather trousers]

lĕdge *n.* Narrow horizontal surface projecting from wall etc.; shelflike projection on side of rock or mountain; ridge of rocks, esp. below water; (Mining) stratum of metal-bearing rock; hence **lĕ'dg**Y[2], **lĕdg**ED[2] (-jd), *adjs.* [perh. f. ME *legge* LAY[3]]

lĕ'dger *n.* & *a.* **1.** *n.* Principal book of the set used for recording trade transactions, containing debtor-and-creditor accounts; horizontal timber in scaffolding, parallel to face of building; flat gravestone; **~-tackle,** kind of fishing-tackle in which lead weight keeps bait on bottom. **2.** *a.* (Mus.) = LEGER. [ME, f. senses of Du. *ligger* and *legger* (*liggen* LIE[3], *leggen* LAY[3]; see -ER[1]), & pronunc. of ME *ligge*, *legge*, (-je)]

lee *n.* Shelter given by neighbouring object (*under the lee of*); ~ (**side**), sheltered side, side away from wind, (opp. *windward*, *weather side*); **~-board,** plank frame fixed to side of flat-bottomed vessel and let down into water to diminish leeway; *lee gage* or GAUGE[1] 2; *lee* HELM[2]; **~ shore,** shore to leeward of ship; **~'way,** lateral drift of ship to leeward of desired course, (fig.) allowable deviation, *margin of safety; *make up ~way*, (fig.) struggle out of bad position, recover lost time etc. [OE *hlēo*, = OS *hleo*, *hlea*, ON *hlé* f. Gmc **hlēw-*]

leech[1] *n.* (arch., poet., or joc.) Physician, healer; **~'craft,** art of healing. [OE *lǣce*, = OS *lāki*, OHG *lāhhi*, Goth. *lēkeis* f. Gmc **lǣkjaz* f. IE **lēgios*]

leech[2] *n.* **1.** Aquatic blood-sucking worm of class Hirudinea, esp. *Hirudo medicinalis* formerly much used medicinally for bleeding; **stick like a ~** (persistently). **2.** Person who extorts profit from others. [OE *lǣce*, = MDu. *lake*, assim. to prec.]

leech[3] *n.* Perpendicular or sloping side of square sail; side of fore-and-aft sail away from mast or stay. [ME, perh. rel. to ON *lik*, a nautical term of uncert. meaning]

Lee-E'nfield (-ĕ'-) *n.* Type of rifle in use by British and other armies since 1900. [f. J. P. *Lee*, Amer. designer of bolt action d. 1904, + *Enfield* near London, where form of rifling was designed]

leek *n.* Vegetable (*Allium porrum*) related to onion, but with lower leaves and bulb in cylindrical white form; this as Welsh national emblem; **eat the ~**, pocket affront (see Shak. *Henry V* v. i. 10). [OE *lēac*, = OHG *louh*, ON *laukr* f. Gmc **laukaz*, *-am*]

leer[1] *v.i.*, & *n.* Glance (esp. sideways) with sly, lascivious, or malign expression. [perh. f. obs. *leer* cheek f. OE *hlēor*, as though 'to glance over one's cheek']

leer[2]. Var. of LEHR.

leer'ў *a.* (sl.) Knowing, sly; wary *of*. [perh. f. obs. *leer* looking askance f. LEER[1], + -Y[2]]

lees (-z) *n. pl.* Sediment of wine etc. (**drink, drain, to the ~**, lit. or fig.); dregs, refuse. [pl. of ME f. OF *lie*, f. med. L *lia* f. Gaulish **lig(j)a*]

leet[1] *n.* (esp. Hist.) (**Court**) ~, yearly or half-yearly court of record that lords of certain manors might hold; its jurisdiction or district. [ME, f. AF *lete* (= AL *leta*), of unkn. orig.]

leet[2] *n.* (Sc.) Selected list of candidates for some office; **short ~**, = SHORT *list*. [ME *lite* etc., prob. f. AF & OF *lit(t)e*, var. of *liste* LIST[1]]

lee'ward (*or*, esp. Naut., lōō'erd) *a.*, *adv.*, & *n.* **1.** *a.* & *adv.* On or towards the sheltered side (opp. *windward*). **2.** *n.* This direction (*to leeward*; *on the leeward of*); hence ~LY[1] *a.*, (of ship) apt to fall to leeward. [f. LEE + -WARD]

lĕft[1] *a.*, *adv.*, & *n.* **1.** *a.* (opp. RIGHT[1]). On or towards that side of human body which has normally the less-used hand, on or towards that part of an object which is analogous to person's left side or (with opposite sense) which is nearer to spectator's left hand (*left side*, *eye*, etc.; *left flank* of army etc.); *left* BANK[1]; *left* BOWER[3]; (Polit., often *L*~) of the left (see sense 4); **have two ~ feet,** be clumsy; **~ field,** (Baseball) part of field on third-base side, to catcher's left; **~ hand,** hand of left side, region or direction on left side of person (*at*, *on*, *to*, one's *left hand*); *marry* **with the ~ hand,** morganatically (see LEFT-HANDED); **~-hand,** placed on the left hand (*left-hand* DRIVE[2]), done with the left hand (*left-hand blow*), (of rope) twisted counter-clockwise; **~-hand screw,** LEFT-HANDED screw; **over the ~ (shoulder,** now rare), sl. phr. denoting that what is said is to be taken with a negative; **~ turn** (that brings one's front to face as one's left side did before); **~ wing** (of army, football etc. team, or political party, cf. sense 4), whence **~-wi'nger,** member of this; hence ~'MOST *a.*, ~'WARD *a.* & *adv.*, ~'WARDS *adv.* **2.** *adv.* On or to the left side; **~ and right,** = RIGHT[4] *and left*. **3.** *n.* Left-hand part or region or direction; left-hand side of stage when facing audience; (Boxing) (blow with) left hand; (in marching etc.) left foot; left wing of army. **4.** (Polit., often *L*~). (In continental legislatures) more radical section of legislative chamber seated on president's left; radicals collectively; more advanced or innovative section of any group; hence (colloq.) ~'ISH[1] *a.*, ~'ISM (3) *n.*, principles or policy of the political left, ~'IST (2) *n.* [ME *lüft, lift, left*, f. OE **lyft*, orig. sense 'weak, worthless' in OE *lyft-ādl* paralysis]

lĕft[2]. See LEAVE[2].

lĕft-hă'ndėd *a.* **1.** Having left hand more serviceable than right, using it by preference; awkward, clumsy; ambiguous, double-edged, of doubtful sincerity or validity, (esp. of compliment, also occas. of marriage); (of marriage) morganatic [from German custom by which bridegroom gave bride his left hand in such marriages]. **2.** (Of tool etc.) made to suit use of, (of blow) struck with, left hand; towards the left, turning to left; (of screw) advanced by turning to left. **3.** Hence ~LY[2] *adv.*, ~NESS *n.* [f. LEFT[1] *hand* + -ED[2]]

lĕft-hă'nder *n.* Left-handed person (esp. in games) or blow. [f. LEFT[1] *hand* + -ER[1]]

lĕ'ftў *n.* (colloq.) Left-handed person; left-winger in politics. [f. LEFT[1] + -Y[3]]

lĕg *n.*, & *v.t.* (-gg-). **1.** *n.* Organ of support and locomotion in animal, esp. lower limb of human body; part of this from hip to ankle; SEA-*legs*. **2.** *The* BOOT[1] *is on the other leg*; **feel** or **find** one's **~s,** become able to stand or walk; **give** person **a ~ up,** help him to mount or to get over obstacle (lit. or fig.); **have no ~s,** (of golf-ball etc., colloq.) have not enough momentum to reach desired point; **have the ~s of,** be able to go faster than; **keep** one's **~s,** not fall; **on** one's or **its last ~s,** near death or end of usefulness etc.; **on** one's **~s,** (1) standing esp. to make speech, (2) well enough to walk about; **pull** person's **~**, deceive him jokingly; **shake a ~,** (sl.) (1) dance, (2) make a start; **show a ~,** (sl.) get out of bed; **stand on** one's **own ~s,** be self-reliant or independent; **has not a ~ to stand on,** cannot support argument by facts or sound reasons; **stretch** one's **~s,** take walking exercise; **take to** one's **~s,** run away. **3.** (Esp. hind) leg of animal as food; leg of bird as food; **~-of-mutton sail, sleeve,** (so shaped). **4.** (arch.) Obeisance made by drawing back one leg and bending other. **5.** (Cricket). Part of field on playing batsman's side and behind his wicket (opp. OFF; *hit to leg*; **~ stump,** stump nearest this; **~ break,** etc., deviation of ball from leg side; LONG[1], SHORT, SQUARE[2], ~, fieldsmen at various positions there). **6.** Artificial leg (*cork, wooden*, etc., *leg*). **7.** Part of garment covering (part of) leg. **8.** More or less leg-shaped support, pole, prop, of machine etc., or support of chair, table, bed, etc.; one branch of forked object; side of triangle other than base or hypotenuse. **9.** (Naut.) Run made on single tack (usu. *long, short, leg*). **10.** (colloq.) One of two or three games constituting a round; section of relay race; hop or stage of long-distance flight or journey. **11. Give ~-bail,** decamp; **~ before wicket,** (of batsman) out because of illegally obstructing ball with part of body other than hand; *leg*-BYE[1]; **~-guard,** pad in cricket; *leg*-IRON[1]; **~'man,** person employed to go about gathering news etc.; **~-pull,** (colloq.) joking attempt to deceive person; **~-rest,** support for seated invalid's leg; **~-room,** space to extend legs of seated person; **~-show,** theatrical performance by scantily dressed women; **~ theory,** (Cricket) bowling to leg with fieldsmen massed on that side; **~ trap,** (Cricket) group of fieldsmen near wicket on leg side. **12.** Hence (-)~GED[2] (-gd), ~'LESS, *adjs.* **13.** *v.t.* **~ it,** walk or run hard; propel (boat) through canal-tunnel by pushing with legs against tunnel-sides, whence ~ **gER**[1] (-g-) *n.* [ME, f. ON *leggr* f. Gmc **lagjaz*]

lĕ'gacў *n.* Sum of money or article bequeathed; material or immaterial thing handed down by predecessor; **~-hunter,** person who pays court to another to secure legacy. [ME, f. OF *legacie* legateship, f. med. L *legatia* (as LEGATE[2]; see -ACY)]

lē'gal *a.* **1.** Of, based on, falling within province of, occupied with, law; **~ aid,** payment from public funds allowed, in cases of need, to help pay for legal advice or proceedings; **~ fiction,** assertion accepted as true (though probably fictitious) to achieve useful purpose esp. in legal matters; *legal* PROCEEDINGS; *legal* SEPARATION. **2.** Required or appointed by law; ***~ holiday,** = ||BANK[3] *holiday*; *legal* TENDER[2]. **3.** Recognized by law, as distinguished from equity. **4.** Lawful; hence ~IZE (3) *v.t.* **5.** (Theol.) Of the Mosaic law; of salvation by works not faith. **6.** Hence ~LY[2] *adv.* [f. F *légal* or f. L *legalis* (*lex legis* law; see -AL), cf. LEAL, LOYAL]

lē'gal|ism *n.* Exaltation of law or formula, red tape; (Theol.) preference of the Law to the Gospel, doctrine of justification by works; so ~IST (2) *n.*, **~ĭ'stIC** *a.* [f. prec. + -ISM]

lėgă'lĭtў *n.* Lawfulness; = prec. [f. F *légalité* or f. med. L *legalitas* (as LEGAL; see -ITY)]

lĕ'gate[1] *n.* **1.** Ecclesiastic deputed to represent pope; **~ a latere** (ah lă'terā), one of highest class and full powers; hence **lĕ'gatINE**[1] (-ĭn) *a.* **2.** (Rom. Hist.) deputy of general, (deputy of) governor of province; (arch.) ambassador, delegate. **3.** Hence ~SHIP (-tsh-) *n.* [OE, f. OF *legat* f. L *legatus* p.p. (as n.) of *legare* commission]

lėgā't|e[2] *v.t.* Bequeath (often *give and legate*); so ~OR *n.* [f. L *legare* bequeath + -ATE[3]]

lĕgatee' *n.* Recipient of legacy. [f. prec. + -EE]

lėgā'tion *n.* Sending of legate or deputy; body of deputies; diplomatic minister and his suite (esp. when he does not rank as ambassador), his official residence; legateship. [ME f. OF, or f. L *legatio* (as LEGATE[1]; see -ION)]

lėga'tō (-ah'-) *a.*, *adv.*, & *n.* (*pl.* ~s). (Passage to be performed) in smooth connected manner, without breaks. [It., = bound, p.p. of *legare* f. L *ligare* bind]

lĕ'gend *n.* **1.** (Hist.) Collection of lives of saints or similar stories, esp. **the** (**Golden**) **L~**, a particular 13th-c. collection. **2.** Traditional story popularly regarded as historical, myth, such literature or tradition; hence ~RY (5) *n.* **3.** Inscription or motto, esp. on coin or medal; (Print.) caption; wording on map etc. explaining symbols used. [ME, f. OF *legende* f. med. L *legenda* what is to be read, neut. pl. gerundive of L *legere* read]

lĕ'gendarў *a.* Of or connected with legends; described in legend; (colloq.) remarkable enough to be a subject of legend. [f. med. L *legendarius* (as prec.; see -ARY[1])]

lĕ'ger *a.* (Mus.) **~ line,** short line added for notes above or below range of staff. [var. of LEDGER]

lĕ'gerdemain *n.* Sleight of hand, conjuring tricks, juggling; trickery, sophistry. [ME, f. F *léger de main* light of hand, dextrous]

lĕ'ggĭng (-g-) *n.* (usu. in *pl.*). Outer covering of leather etc. for leg from knee to ankle. [f. LEG + -ING[1]]

lĕ'gg|ў (-gĭ) *a.* Lanky-legged (esp. of boy, colt, puppy); (of woman) having attractively long legs; hence ~ĭNESS *n.* [f. LEG + -Y[2]]

lĕ'ghorn (*or* lĭgor'n) *n.* (Hat of) fine plaited straw; small hardy breed of domestic fowl. [imported f. *L~* (*Livorno*) in Italy]

lĕ'g|ĭble *a.* (Of handwriting or print) clear,

capable of being read; hence ~IBI'LITY *n.*, ~ĭbLY² *adv.* [ME, f. LL *legibilis* (*legere* read; see -IBLE)]

lē'gion (-jon) *n.* **1.** Division of 3,000–6,000 men, including complement of cavalry, in ancient Roman army; ‖**Royal British L~,** national association of ex-service men (and now women) formed 1921; ***American L~,** similar association formed 1919; **foreign ~,** body of foreign volunteers in modern, esp. French, army. **2.** Vast host, multitude, or number (**their name is L~, they are ~,** they are numberless; cf. Mark 5:9). **3. L~ of Honour,** French order of distinction founded 1802. **4.** Hence ~ED² (-nd) *a.*, (poet.) arrayed in legions. [ME f. OF, f. L *legio -onis* (*legere* choose; see -ION)]

lē'gionarў (-jo-) *a.* & *n.* **1.** *a.* Of legion(s). **2.** *n.* Member of a legion. [f. L *legionarius* (as prec.; see -ARY¹)]

lēgionnair'e (-jo-) *n.* Member of foreign legion; member of American or Royal British Legion. [f. F *légionnaire* (as LEGION)]

lĕ'gĭslāte *v.i.* Enact laws; make provision by laws *for*. [back form. f. foll.]

lĕgĭslā'tion *n.* (Enacting of) laws; hence **lĕ'gĭsl**ATIVE *a.* [f. LL *legis latio* (*lex legis* law, *latio* proposing f. *lat-* p.p. st. of *ferre* bring; see -ION)]

lĕ'gĭslātor *n.* Lawgiver; member of legislative body. [L (as LEGISLATION; see -OR)]

lĕ'gĭslāture *n.* Legislative body of a State. [f. prec. + -URE]

lē'gĭst *n.* Person versed in law. [ME, f. F *légiste* or f. med. L *legista* f. L *lex legis* law; see -IST]

lėgĭ't *a.* & *n.* (colloq.) Legitimate (drama or theatre). [abbr.]

lėgĭ'tĭm|ate¹ *a.* **1.** (Of child) lawfully begotten and born, esp. by persons lawfully married to each other; (of parent, birth, descent, etc.) with, of, through, etc., legitimate children. **2.** Lawful, proper, regular, conforming to standard type; **the ~ate drama** or **theatre,** body of plays of recognized merit, normal comedy and tragedy as dist. from musical comedy, farce, revue, etc. **3.** (Of sovereign's title) based on strict hereditary right; (of sovereign etc.) having legitimate title. **4.** Logically admissible. **5.** Hence ~ACY *n.*, **~ate**LY² (-tlĭ) *adv.*, **~at**IZE (3) *v.t.* [f. med. L *legitimatus*, p.p. of *legitimare* (see foll., -ATE²)]

lėgĭ'tĭm|āte² *v.t.* Make legitimate by decree, enactment, or proof; justify, serve as justification for; hence ~A'TION *n.* [f. med. L *legitimare* f. L *legitimus* lawful (*lex legis* law) + -ATE³]

lėgĭ'tĭm|ĭsm *n.* Adherence to sovereign or pretender whose claim is based on direct descent (esp. in Spanish and French politics); so ~IST (2) *n.* & *a.* [f. F *légitimisme* (*légitime* f. L; see prec., -ISM)]

lėgĭ'tĭmīz|e, -īs|e (-iz), *v.t.* Legitimatize, make legitimate; hence ~A'TION *n.* [f. as LEGITIMATE², + -IZE]

lĕ'gūme *n.* Edible pod of leguminous plant; vegetable used for food. [f. F *légume* f. L *legumen -minis* (*legere* pick), because pickable by hand]

lėgū'mĭnous *a.* Of or like the botanical family Leguminosae (e.g. pea and bean), having seeds in pods and usu. root-nodules able to fix nitrogen. [f. mod. L *leguminosus* (as prec.; see -OUS)]

lehr (lēr) *n.* Annealing-furnace for glass. [17th c.; orig. unkn.]

lei (lā *or* lā'ē) *n.* Polynesian garland of flowers. [Hawaiian]

Leibnĭ'tzĭan (lībnĭ'ts-) *a.* & *n.* (Follower) of the philosophy of Leibnitz (regarding matter as a multitude of monads and assuming pre-established harmony between spirit and matter). [f. G. W. *Leibnitz*, Ger. philosopher d. 1716 + -IAN]

Leics. *abbr.* Leicestershire.

leishmanī'as|ĭs (lē-) *n.* (*pl.* **~es** *pr.* -ēz). Disease due to parasitic protozoan of genus *Leishmania*. [f. W. B. *Leishman*, Brit. physician d. 1926 + -I- + -ASIS]

lei'ster (lē'-) *n.*, & *v.t.* (Pierce with) pronged salmon-spear. [f. ON *ljóstr* (*ljósta* to strike)]

lei'sure (lĕ'zher) *n.* (Opportunity *to* do, *for*, afforded by) free time, time at one's own disposal; **wait** etc. person's ~, wait till he has leisure; **at ~,** (1) not occupied, (2) deliberately, without hurry; **at** one's **~,** when one has time; hence ~LESS (-erl-) *a.* [ME f. AF *leisour*, OF *leisir* f. n. use of L *licēre* be allowed; see -URE]

lei'sured (lĕ'zherd) *a.* Having (ample) leisure. [f. prec. + -ED²]

lei'surel|ў (lĕ'zher-) *a.* & *adv.* **1.** *a.* Having, acting or done at, leisure, deliberate; hence ~ĭNESS *n.* **2.** *adv.* Deliberately, without haste. [f. LEISURE + -LY¹,²]

leitmotiv, -if, (lī'tmōtēf) *n.* (Mus. etc.) Theme associated throughout piece or work with some person, situation, or sentiment. [G (as LEAD², MOTIVE¹)]

L.E.M. *abbr.* lunar excursion module.

lĕ'man *n.* (arch.) Lover, sweetheart; unlawful lover or (now usu.) mistress. [ME *leofman* (as LIEF, MAN¹)]

lĕ'mma *n.* (*pl.* **~ta** *or* **~s**). Assumed or demonstrated proposition used in argument or proof; argument or subject of literary composition, dictionary entry, annotation, etc., prefixed as heading; motto appended to picture etc. [L, f. Gk *lēmma -matos* thing assumed, f. root of *lambanō* take]

lĕ'mmė *v.* (colloq.) = *let me*. [contr.]

lĕ'mmĭng *n.* Small arctic rodent of genus *Lemmus* etc., of which one species migrates in large numbers and has been reputed to continue headlong into the sea and drown. [Norw.]

lĕ'mon¹ *n.* **1.** Pale-yellow oval acid-juiced fruit used for flavouring and for making the beverage ~ADE 1 (-ā'd) *n.*; **salt(s) of ~,** potassium oxalate used in removing ink-stains or rust. **2.** Tree (*Citrus limon*) bearing lemons. **3.** Pale-yellow colour. **4.** (sl.) Unattractive girl; unsatisfactory person or thing, failure. **5.** ~ **balm,** mint plant (*Melissa officinalis*) with leaves smelling and tasting of lemon; *lemon* CHEESE¹ or *curd*; **~-drop,** boiled sweet flavoured with lemon; **~ grass,** fragrant tropical grass of genus *Cymbopogon* yielding oil smelling of lemon; **~-plant,** lemon VERBENA; **~ pudding** (flavoured with lemon); ‖**~ squash,** drink of lemon-juice, crushed lemons, and other ingredients, often sold in concentrated form; **~-squeezer,** instrument for pressing juice out of lemon; *lemon* THYME; *lemon* VERBENA. **6.** Hence ~Y² *a.* [ME, f. OF *limon* f. Arab. *līma*; cf. LIME²]

lĕ'mon² *n.* ~ **(sole),** kind of plaice resembling sole. [f. F *limande*]

lē'mur *n.* Nocturnal mammal of Madagascar, of genus *Lemur*, allied to monkeys but with pointed muzzle; hence **lĕ'mūr**INE¹, **lĕ'mūr**OID, *adjs.* & *ns.* [mod. L, f. L *lemures* pl. spirits of the dead, from its spectre-like face]

lĕnd *v.t.* **(lent).** **1.** Grant (*to* person) use of (thing) on understanding that it or its equivalent shall be returned; allow use of (money) at interest, or of (books etc.) for hire; *lending* LIBRARY. **2.** Bestow, contribute, (something of temporary service or effect, as enchantment, aid, dignity); **~ an ear** or one's **ears,** listen; **~ a (helping) hand,** help. **3.** Accommodate one*self* *to* some policy or purpose; (of thing) ~ **itself to,** be serviceable for. **4. L~-Lease,** arrangement (1941) whereby U.S. supplied equipment etc. to U.K. and allies, orig. as loan in return for use of British-owned military bases. **5.** Hence ~'ABLE *a.*, ~'ER¹, ~'ING¹ (1, 4), *ns.* [ME, earlier *lēne(n)* f. OE *lǣnan* (*lǣn* LOAN¹)]

lĕngth (*or* -ngkth) *n.* **1.** Measurement from end to end; greater of two or greatest of three dimensions of a body; extent of a garment in vertical direction when worn; MEASURE² one's *length.* **2.** Extent in, of, or with regard to, time (*a stay of some length*; *the length of a speech*). **3.** Distance thing extends (*at* ARM¹*'s length*; *ships a cable's length apart*); length of horse, boat, etc., as measure of lead in race. **4.** Degree of thoroughness in action (usu. w. *go*: *prepared to go* (*to*) *all lengths* or *any length*; *went to great lengths*; *will not go the length of asserting*). **5.** (Pros.) Vowel's or syllable's quantity. **6.** (Cricket). Distance from batsman at which ball pitches (*bowler keeps a good length*); proper amount of this (~ or **good--~ ball,** that pitches at right length). **7.** Long stretch or extent; piece of material of certain length; full extent of one's body. **8. At ~,** at last or after a long time; **at** (FULL¹, **great, some**) ~, in detail, without curtailment. **9.** ‖**~'man,** employee with duty of maintaining section of railway or road. **10.** Hence ~'WAYS *adv.*, ~'WISE *adv.* & *a.* [OE *lengthu*, = Du. *lengte*, ON *lengd* f. Gmc **langithō* (as LONG¹, -TH¹)]

lĕ'ngthen (*or* -ngkth-) *v.t.* & *i.* Make or become longer; (Pros.) make (vowel) long. [ME, f. prec. + -EN⁶]

lĕ'ngth|ȳ (*or* -ngkthĭ) *a.* (Of speech, writing, style, speaker, etc.) of unusual length, prolix, tedious; hence **~ĭLY²** *adv.*, **~ĭNESS** *n.* [f. LENGTH + -Y²; 18th c., orig. U.S.]

lē'ni|ent *a.* Tolerant, gentle, not disposed to severity; (of punishment etc.) mild; (arch.) emollient; hence ~ENCE, ~ENCY, *ns.*, ~**ent**LY² *adv.* [f. L *lenire lenit-* soothe (*lenis* gentle); see -ENT]

Lĕ'nĭn|ĭsm *n.* Policy and (esp. communistic) economic principles of Lenin; so ~IST (2), ~ITE¹(1), *ns.* [f. N. *Lenin* (name assumed by V. I. Ulyanov), Russ. statesman d. 1924 + -ISM]

lĕ'nĭtĭve *a.* & *n.* Soothing (drug, appliance), palliative. [ME, f. med. L *lenitivus* (as LENIENT; see -IVE)]

lĕ'nĭtȳ *n.* Mercifulness; act of mercy. [f. F *lénité* or f. L *lenitas* (*lenis* gentle; see -ITY)]

lĕ'nō *n.* (*pl.* ~**s**). Open-work fabric with warp threads twisted in pairs before weaving. [f. F *linon* (*lin* flax f. L *linum*)]

lĕns (-z) *n.* Piece of glass or other transparent substance with both sides (or one only) curved for concentrating or dispersing light-rays in telescope, spectacles, etc.; combination of lenses in photography; (Anat.) = CRYSTALLINE *lens*; (Zool.) one facet of compound eye; (Phys.) device for focusing or otherwise modifying direction of movement of sound, electrons, etc.; hence ~ED² (-zd), ~'LESS, *adjs.* [L *lens lentis* lentil (from similarity of shape)]

Lĕnt¹ *n.* Period from Ash Wednesday to Easter Eve of which the 40 weekdays are devoted to fasting and penitence in commemoration of Christ's fasting in the wilderness; ‖(in *pl.*) Lent--term boat-races at Cambridge; ‖~ **lily,** (esp. wild) daffodil; ‖~ **term,** university etc. term in which Lent falls. [ME, f. LENTEN]

lĕnt². See LEND.

-lent *suf.* forming *adjs.* (*pestilent, violent*; cf. -ULENT). [f. L *-lentus* -ful]

Lĕ'nten *a.* Of, in, or appropriate to, Lent; ~ **face,** dismal look; ~ **fare** (without meat). [orig. n. = 'spring', f. OE *lencten*, prob. f. WG **lang-* LONG¹, perh. w. ref. to lengthening of day in spring; now regarded as a. f. LENT¹ + -EN⁵]

lĕ'ntĭcĕl *n.* (Bot.) Aeration-pore in stems and some roots. [f. mod. L *lenticella* dim. of L LENS]

lĕntĭ'cūlar *a.* **1.** Shaped like lentil or lens, biconvex. **2.** Of the lens of the eye. [f. L *lenticularis* (as foll.; see -AR¹)]

lĕ'ntĭl *n.* (Biconvex seed of) leguminous plant (*Lens esculenta*) grown for food. [ME f. OF *lentille* f. L *lenticula* (as LENS; see -CULE)]

lĕ'ntĭsk *n.* Mastic tree. [ME, f. L *lentiscus*]

lĕ'ntō *a.* & *adv.* (Mus.) Slow(ly). [It.]

lĕ'ntoid *a.* = LENTICULAR 1. [f. L LENS + -OID]

Lē'ō *n.* Sign of the ZODIAC, the Lion. [OE f. L, = LION]

Lē'onĭd *n.* One of the meteors that seem to radiate from the constellation Leo. [f. L LEO *leonis* + -ID³]

lē'onīne¹ *a.* Lionlike; of lions. [ME, f. OF *leonin -ine* or f. L *leoninus* (as prec.; see -INE¹)]

Lē'onīne² *a.* & *n.* **1.** *a.* Of, made or invented by, Leo; ~ **City,** part of Rome round Vatican fortified by Leo IV; ~ **verse,** (1) medieval Latin verse in hexameter or elegiac metre with internal rhyme (e.g. *Daemon languebat, monachus tunc esse volebat*), (2) English verse with internal rhymes (e.g. *The fair breeze blew, the white foam flew*). **2.** *n.* (in *pl.*) Leonine verse. [f. *Leo*, man's Christian name, as prec.]

leo'pard (lĕ'p-) *n.* **1.** Large African and S. Asian carnivorous quadruped (*Felis pardus*) with dark--spotted yellowish-fawn or (**black** ~) black coat, panther; **hunting** ~, cheetah; **snow-~,** OUNCE²; **can the ~ change his spots?,** innate character persists [Jer. 13:23]. **2.** (Her.) Lion passant guardant as in arms of England. **3.** (*attrib.*, in names of animals etc.) Spotted like leopard. **4. ~'s bane,** (1) yellow-flowered plant of genus *Doronicum*, (2) herb Paris. **5.** Hence ~ESS¹ *n.* [ME f. OF, f. LL f. late Gk *leopardos* (as LION, PARD¹)]

lē'otârd *n.* Close-fitting one-piece garment worn by acrobats, ballet-dancers, etc. [f. J. *Léotard*, Fr. trapeze performer d. 1870]

lĕ'per *n.* Person suffering from leprosy; (fig.) person shunned on moral grounds. [ME, prob. attrib. use of *leper* leprosy f. OF *lepre* f. L f. Gk *lepra* fem. (as n.) of *lepros* scaly (*lepos* scale)]

lĕpĭdŏ'pter|ous *a.* Of the Lepidoptera, order of insects with four membranous scale-covered wings, including butterflies and moths; hence ~AN *a.* & *n.*, ~IST (3) *n.* [f. Gk *lepis -idos* scale + *pteron* wing + -OUS]

lĕ'porine *a.* Of or like hares. [f. L *leporinus* (*lepus -oris* hare; see -INE¹)]

lĕ'prechaun (-k-) *n.* (Ir.) Diminutive sprite. [f. OIr. *luchorpán* (*lu* small, *corp* body)]

lĕ'prosȳ *n.* Chronic infectious bacterial disease affecting skin and nerves, resulting in mutilations and deformities; (fig.) moral corruption or contagion. [f. foll. + -Y¹]

lĕ'prous *a.* Having, like, (as) of, leprosy. [ME f. OF, f. LL *leprosus* (*lepra*; see LEPER, -OSE¹)]

lĕ'pto- *comb. form.* Small, narrow, as: **~cepha'lic, ~ce'phalous,** narrow-skulled; **~da'ctyl** *n.* & *a.*, (bird) with long slender toes; **~spiro'sis,** infectious disease caused by spirochaete of genus *Leptospira*. [f. Gk *leptos* fine, small, thin, delicate + -O-]

lĕ'pt|on¹ *n.* (*pl.* ~**a**). Greek coin worth $\frac{1}{100}$ of a drachma. [f. Gk *lepton* (*nomisma* coin) neut. of *leptos* small]

lĕ'ptŏn² *n.* (Phys.) Elementary particle without strong interaction. [f. as LEPTO- + -ON]

Lĕ'sbian (-z-) *a.* & *n.* **1.** *a.* Of Lesbos. **2.** Of homosexuality in women. **3.** *n.* (or *l*~). Homosexual woman; hence ~ISM (2) *n.* [f. L f. Gk

Lesbios f. *Lesbos*, island in Aegean Sea, home of Sappho (see SAPPHISM), + -IAN]

lèse-majesté (lāzmă'zhĕstā), **lēse-mă'jėstў** (-zm-), *n.* Treason; affront to sovereign or ruler; (joc.) presumptuous conduct. [(f.) F *lèse-majesté* f. L *laesa majestas* injured sovereignty (*laedere laes-* injure, *majestas* MAJESTY)]

lē'sion (-zhon) *n.* Damage, injury; (Path.) morbid change in functioning or texture of organ etc. [ME f. OF, f. L *laesio -onis* (*laedere laes-* injure; see -ION)]

lĕss *a.*, *prep.*, *n.*, & *adv.* **1.** *a.* (Of size, degree, duration, number, etc.) smaller (opp. *greater*; *in a less degree*, *of less magnitude* or *importance*; *of two evils choose the less*; *may your* SHADOW[1] *never grow less*). **2.** Of smaller quantity, not so much, not so much of, (opp. *more*; *find less difficulty*; *eat less meat*). **3.** Of lower rank etc. (*no less a person than*; *James*, *Ajax*, *the Less*). **4.** *prep.* Minus, deducting, (*a year less three days*; *dividend paid less tax*). **5.** *n.* Smaller amount, quantity, or number (*cannot take* (*much*) *less*; *for* (*far* or *much*) *less than £100*; *is little less than disgraceful*); NOTHING *less than*; **in ~ than no time,** (joc.) very quickly or soon; **~ of,** (colloq.) reduce or eliminate (imper.; *less of your impudence!*). **6.** *adv.* To smaller extent, in lower degree, (NO[3] *less*; NONE *the less*); **much** or **still ~,** with even greater force of denial (*do not suspect him of negligence*, *still* or *much less of dishonesty*). [OE *lǣssa* a., *lǣs* adv., f. Gmc **laisizō*, **laisiz* compar. f. **laisa-* f. IE **loiso-*]

-lėss *suf.* forming *adjs.* & *advs.* f. *ns.*, w. sense 'not having, without, free from', and f. *vbs.*, w. sense 'unable to be —ed', (*doubtless*, *guileless*, *homeless*, *numberless*, *powerless*, *shell-less*; *fathomless*, *relentless*, *tireless*); hence **-lėss**LY[2] *adv. suf.*, **-lėss**NESS *n. suf.* [OE *-lēas* (*lēas* devoid of)]

lĕssee' *n.* Holder of, tenant (*of* house, theatre, etc.) under, lease; hence ~SHIP *n.* [ME f. AF p.p., OF *lessé* (as LEASE; see -EE)]

lĕ'ssen *v.i.* & *t.* Decrease, diminish. [ME, f. LESS + -EN[6]]

lĕ'sser *attrib. a.* Not so great as the other or the rest, minor, (*the lesser evils of life*). [double compar., f. LESS + -ER[3]]

lĕ'sson *n.*, & *v.t.* **1.** *n.* Portion of Scripture etc. read at divine service, esp. one of two readings from O.T. (**first ~**) and N.T. (**second ~**) at morning and evening prayer in Church of England. **2.** Thing to be learnt by pupil; amount of teaching given at one time, time assigned to it, (in *pl.*) systematic instruction *in* subject (*give* or *take lessons in*). **3.** Occurrence, example, rebuke, or punishment, that serves or should serve as encouragement or warning; thing inculcated by experience or study. **4.** *v.t.* (arch.) Instruct; admonish, rebuke. [ME, f. OF *leçon* f. L *lectio -onis* (see LECTION)]

lĕ'ssor̂ *n.* Person who lets on lease. [AF (*lesser*; see LEASE, -OR)]

lĕst *conj.* In order that not, for fear that, (*lest we forget*); (*fear* etc.) ~, that. [OE *thȳ lǣs the* whereby less that, later *the læste*, ME *lest*(*e*)]

lĕt[1] *v.t.* (**-tt-; ~'ted** *or* **~**), & *n.* **1.** *v.t.* (arch.) Hinder, obstruct. **2.** *n.* Stoppage, hindrance, (arch. exc. in *without let or hindrance*). **3.** (Rackets, Lawn Tennis, etc.) Obstruction of ball or player in certain ways, requiring ball to be served again. [OE *lettan*, = OS *lettian*, OHG *lezzen*, ON *letja*, Goth. *latjan* hinder, f. Gmc **lata-* LATE[1]]

lĕt[2] *v.t.* & *aux.* (**-tt-; let**), & *n.* **1.** *v.t.* Allow or cause (liquid, air) to escape (*let blood*). **2.** ||Grant use of (rooms, land, etc.) for rent or hire (*to* person *for* period; **to ~,** offered for rent). **3.** Award (contract for work). **4.** Allow to, not prevent or forbid, (*we let them go*; *will go if you will let me*; LIVE[2] *and let live*). **5.** Cause to *know* or *be known*. **6. ~ alone,** not interfere with, attend to, or do (*let* WELL[3] *alone*), (in *imper.*) not to mention, far less or more (*hasn't got a radio, let alone television*); **~ be,** not interfere with, attend to, or do; **~ down,** lower, fail to support (another, or user) at need, disappoint (*~ him down gently*, avoid humiliating him abruptly), lengthen (garment); *~-down* n., disappointment; **~ drop** or **fall,** drop (lit., or fig. hint, significant word) intentionally or by accident, (Geom.) draw (perpendicular) from outside point (*up*)*on* or *to* line; *let* FLY[2]; **~ go,** release, set at liberty, lose hold of, lose or relinquish hold *of*, dismiss from thought, cease discussion of, cease to restrain (*~ oneself go*, (1) relax, cease to take trouble, (2) give way to enthusiasm, impulse, etc.); **~ in,** admit or open door to (lit., or fig.: *let in a flood of light*; *this would let in all sorts of evils*; *~ oneself in*, with latchkey) etc., involve in loss etc., insert into surface of something; *~ in for*, involve in (loss or difficulty); *~ in on*, allow to share; **~ into,** allow to enter, insert into surface of, make acquainted with (secret etc.); **~ loose,** release or unchain (dog, fury, maniac, etc.); **~ off** (*adv.*), discharge (gun, firework, or fig. joke etc.), not punish or compel, punish *with* light penalty, allow or cause (liquid, steam, etc.) to escape, ||let (part of house etc.); *~-off* n., being allowed to escape something (esp. in cricket, not being caught etc. when there is a chance); **~ off** (*prep.*), excuse (person penalty); **~ on,** (sl.) reveal secret, pretend (*let on that he had succeeded*); **~ out,** open door for exit of, exculpate, allow (person etc., secret or *that*) to depart or escape (*let the* CAT[1] *out of the bag*), release from restraint, make (garment) looser esp. by adjustment at seams, put out to rent esp. to several tenants, or to contract; *~-out* n., opportunity to escape; *let* RIP[2]; *let me* SEE[1] 13; *let* SLIP[1] 3; **~ through,** allow to pass; **~ up,** (colloq.) become less severe, diminish, relax one's efforts; *~-up* n., cessation, diminution. **7.** *v. aux.* supplying 1st and 3rd persons of imper. in exhortations (*let us pray*; *let you and me*, *let us*, colloq. *let's*, *try now*; *let us not*, colloq. *let's not* or *don't let's*, *be greedy*), commands (*let it be done*, *let him do it, at once*; *let there be light*); assumptions (*let AB be equal to CD*), and permission or challenge (*let him do his worst*). **8.** *n.* ||Act of letting (sense 2). [OE *lǣtan*, = OS *lātan*, OHG *lāzan*, ON *láta*, Goth. *lētan* f. Gmc **lǣt-* rel. to **lat-* LATE[1]]

-lėt *suf.* forming *ns.* usu. dim. (*leaflet*, *ringlet*, *tartlet*) or denoting articles of attire etc. (*armlet*). [orig. f. OF *-elet* (as -LE 2, -ET[1]) wrongly understood in wds such as *crosslet*, *hamlet*]

lē'thal *a.* Causing, sufficient or designed to cause, death; **~ chamber** (for killing animals painlessly); hence **lėthă'l**ITY *n.*, ~LY[2] *adv.* [f. L *let*(*h*)*alis* (*letum* death; see -AL)]

lĕ'thargў *n.* Morbid drowsiness, prolonged and unnatural sleep; torpid, inert, or apathetic state, lack of interest and energy; so **lėthar̂'g**IC *a.* [ME f. OF *litargie*, f. LL f. Gk *lēthargia* (*lēthargos* forgetful f. *lēth-*, *lanthanomai* forget); see -Y[1]]

Lē'thē *n.* (River in Hades in Gk Myth. producing) forgetfulness of the past; hence **Lēthē'**AN *a.* [L, use of Gk *lēthē* forgetfulness (as prec.)]

Lĕtt *n.* Member of a people living near the Baltic, mainly in Latvia; Lettish language. [f. G *Lette* f. Lettish *Latvi*]

lĕ'tter *n.*, & *v.t.* **1.** *n.* Character representing one or more of the simple or compound sounds used in speech, one of the alphabetic symbols; *school or college initial as mark of proficiency in games etc.; (Print.) type(s), fount of type, (BLACK[1] *letter*); PROOF[1] *before letters*. **2.** Written or printed message addressed to person(s), usu. sent by post or messenger and fairly long; *letter of* CREDIT¹; *letter of* INTRODUCTION OR CREDENCE; (in *pl.*) addressed document of legal or formal kind for various purposes (*letters* MISSIVE, ||PATENT¹, *of* ADMINISTRATION, *of* MARQUE¹, etc.). **3.** Precise terms of statement (**to the ~,** with adherence to every detail), strict verbal interpretation (opp. *spirit*; esp. **in ~ and in spirit,** in form and substance; *according to the letter of the law*). **4.** (in *pl.*) Literature, acquaintance with books, erudition, (**man of ~s,** scholar, author; **the commonwealth** or **republic of ~s,** authors as a body, literature; **the profession of ~s,** authorship); hence ~ED² (-*erd*) *a.* **5.** **~-balance** (for ascertaining postage from weight of letters); **~-bomb,** terrorist explosive device sent by post; **~-book** (in which copies of correspondence are kept); **~-box** (into which letters are delivered or posted); **~-card,** folded card with gummed edge for posting as letter; **~-case,** pocket-book for holding letters; **~-head**(**ing**), printed (heading on) stationery; **~-lock,** kind of lock opened by choosing out of certain letters on it a word or other combination that has been previously made when closing it; **~-paper,** paper for letters; **~-perfect,** (Theatr.) knowing one's part perfectly; **~press,** (1) contents of illustrated book other than the illustrations, (2) printed matter relating to illustrations, (3) printing from raised type, not from plates, blocks, etc.; **~-scale**(**s**), = *letter-balance*; **~-writer,** (1) person who writes letters, (2) book giving guidance on writing letters. **6.** Hence ~LESS *a.* **7.** *v.t.* Impress title etc. on (book-cover); inscribe letters on; classify with letters of the alphabet; hence ~ING¹ (1, 6) *n.* [ME, f. OF *lettre* f. L *litera, littera* letter of alphabet, (in pl.) epistle, literature]

Lĕ'ttic *a.* & *n.* = foll.; (of) the group of languages comprising Lettish, Lithuanian, and Old Prussian. [f. LETT + -IC]

Lĕ'ttish *a.* & *n.* (Language) of the Letts. [f. LETT + -ISH¹]

lettre de cachet (lĕtr de kă'shā) *n.* Official order (orig. from French king) for imprisonment, exile, etc. [F, = sealed letter]

lĕ'ttuce (-tĭs) *n.* Garden herb of genus *Lactuca* with crisp leaves much used as salad; plant of similar type eaten by animals (LAMB'*s lettuce*). [ME *letus*(*e*), rel. to OF *laituē* f. L *lactuca* (*lac lactis* milk, w. ref. to its milky juice)]

leu'co- *comb. form.* White, as: **~blast,** immature leucocyte; **~cyte,** white or colourless corpuscle of blood or found in lymph etc.; **~rrhoe'a** (-rē'*a*), mucous discharge from female genitals; **~tome,** instrument for **~tomy** (-ŏ't-), incision into white tissue of frontal lobe of brain to relieve some cases of mental disorder. [f. Gk *leukos* white + -O-]

leucō'ma *n.* (Path.) White opacity of cornea. [f. as prec. + -OMA]

leukae'm|ĭa, *leukē'm|ĭa, *n.* (Med.) Disease in which there is an excess of white corpuscles in tissues and usu. in the blood; hence ~IC *a.* [mod. L, f. Gk *leukos* white + *haima* blood; see -IA¹]

Lev. *abbr.* Leviticus (O.T.).

Lėvă'nt¹ *n.* Eastern part of Mediterranean with its islands and neighbouring countries; *Levant* MOROCCO. [F, part. of *lever* rise, used as n. = point of sunrise, east]

||**lėvă'nt²** *v.i.* Abscond, bolt, esp. with betting or gaming losses unpaid; hence **lėvă'nter¹** [-ER¹] *n.* [f. prec.]

lėvă'nter² *n.* (*L~*) inhabitant of Levant; strong easterly Mediterranean wind. [f. LEVANT¹+-ER¹]

Lėvă'ntīne (*or* lĕ'van-) *a.* & *n.* Of, trading to, inhabitant of, the Levant. [f. LEVANT¹ + -INE¹]

lėvā'tor *n.* (Anat.) Muscle that raises structure or organ. [mod. L, f. L = one who lifts (*levare* raise)]

lĕ'vee¹ (-vĭ) *n.* (Hist.) reception of visitors on rising from bed; ||assembly held by sovereign or his representative at which men only are received; assembly of visitors or guests esp. at formal reception. [f. F *levé* var. of *lever* rising (*lever* to rise; see LEVY, -EE)]

***levee²** (lĭvē' *or* lĕ'vĭ) *n.* Embankment against river floods; natural embankment built up by river; landing-place. [f. F *levée* fem. p.p. of *lever* raise (see LEVY, -EE)]

lĕ'vel *n.*, *a.*, & *v.* (||-ll-). **1.** *n.* Instrument giving line parallel to plane of horizon for testing whether things are horizontal; surveyor's instrument for giving horizontal line of sight. **2.** Horizontal line or plane (**on a ~ with,** in same horizontal plane as, (fig.) equal with; **on the ~,** (colloq.) truthful(ly), honest(ly); **find** one's **~,** reach right place with regard to others; **water finds its ~,** its surface in communicating receptacles or regions will be at same height unless they have no common level). **3.** Plane or standard in social, moral, or intellectual matters; plane of rank or authority (*consultations at Cabinet level*); height or value reached (*eye level,* SEA-*level*; *sugar level in blood*). **4.** More or less level surface; flat country. **5.** *a.* Horizontal, perpendicular to the plumb-line; on a level or equality (*with,* or abs.); ||**~ crossing** (of railway and road, or two railways, at same level); *level* PEG²*ging*; **~ race** (in which leading competitors are close together). **6.** Even, equable, uniform, well-balanced, in quality, style, temper, judgement, etc.; **~-headed,** mentally well-balanced, cool; **do** one's **~ best,** (colloq.) not be remiss, make all possible efforts. **7.** Hence ~LY² *adv.*, ~NESS *n.* **8.** *v.t.* Make level, even, or uniform; place on same level, bring *up* or *down* to a standard; raze, lay low, (*to* or *with the ground, in the dust,* or abs.); knock (person) down; abolish (distinctions); aim (missile, gun, or abs.), lay (gun), direct (satire, criticism, accusation, or abs.), (*at* or *against*); (Surv.) ascertain differences of height of (land, or abs.). **9.** *v.t.* & *i.* **~ off,** make or become level or smooth; **~ out,** make or become level, remove differences from. **10.** **~ling-screw** (for adjusting parts of machine etc. to exact level). [ME, f. OF *livel* f. Rom. **libellum* for L *libella* dim. of *libra* scales, balance]

lĕ'veller, *lĕ'veler, *n.* In vbl senses; person who would abolish social distinctions, advocate of equality; (*L~*) extreme radical dissenter in 17th-c. England. [f. prec. + -ER¹]

lē'ver *n.* & *v.* **1.** *n.* Bar used to prize up heavy or fixed object; (Mech.) device consisting of straight bar or other rigid structure of which one point (*fulcrum*) is fixed, another is connected with the force (*weight*) to be resisted or acted upon, and a third is connected with the force (*power*) applied (**~ of first order** with fulcrum, **of second order** with weight, **of third order** with power, between the other two); (fig.) means of exerting moral force; **~ escapement** (with connection between escape wheel and balance made by two levers); **~ watch** (with lever escapement). **2.** *v.i.* Use lever. **3.** *v.t.* Lift, move, act on, with lever (*along, away, out, over, up,* etc.). [ME f. AF; OF *levier, leveor* (*lever* raise; see LEVY)]

lē'verage *n.* Action of, way of applying, lever; set or system of levers; power, mechanical advantage gained by use, of lever; means of accomplishing a purpose, power, influence; *(Finance) gearing. [f. prec. + -AGE]

lĕ'verėt *n.* Young (esp. first-year) hare. [ME f. AF, dim. of *levre*, OF *lievre* f. L *lepus leporis* hare; see -ET[1]]

lĕ'vĭable. See LEVY.

lėvī'athan *n.* **1.** (Bibl.) Sea-monster. **2.** Huge ship; anything very large of its kind; (in allusion to book by Hobbes, 1651) autocratic monarch or State. [ME f. LL, f. Heb. *liwyātān*]

lĕ'vĭg|āte *v.t.* Reduce to fine smooth powder; make smooth paste of; hence ~A'TION *n.* [f. L *levigare* (*levis* smooth) + -ATE[3]]

lĕ'vĭn *n.* (arch. or poet.) (Flash of) lightning. [ME *leven*(*e*), prob. f. ON]

lĕ'vĭr|ate *n.* Ancient-Jewish etc. custom by which dead man's brother or next of kin had to marry the widow; hence ~**ă'tic**(AL) *adjs.* [f. L *levir* brother-in-law + -ATE[1]]

lē'vĭs (-z) *n. pl.* Type of (orig. blue) denim jeans or overalls reinforced with rivets. [f. *Levi* Strauss, orig. U.S. manufacturer in 1860s]

lĕ'vĭt|āte *v.i.* & *t.* (Cause to) rise and float in air (esp. w. ref. to spiritualism); hence ~A'TION *n.* [f. L *levis* light, after *gravitate*]

Lē'vīte *n.* One of tribe of Levi, esp. of that part of it which provided assistants to priests in worship in Jewish temple. [ME, f. LL *levita* f. Gk *leuitēs* (*Leui* f. Heb. *lēwî* Levi)]

Lėvĭ'tic|al *a.* Of Levites or the tribe of Levi; of Levites' ritual; of Leviticus. [f. LL *leviticus* f. Gk *leuitikos* (as prec.; see -IC) + -AL]

Lėvĭ'tĭcus *n.* Third book of Pentateuch, with Levitical law and ritual. [ME f. LL *Leviticus* (sc. *liber* book); see prec.]

lĕ'vĭtỹ *n.* Lack of serious thought, frivolity, unbecoming jocularity; inconstancy; undignified behaviour; (arch.) lightness of weight. [f. L *levitas* (*levis* light; see -ITY)]

lē'vo-, lē'vūlōse. See LAEVO-, LAEVULOSE.

lĕ'vỹ *n.*, & *v.t.* **1.** *n.* Collecting of contribution, tax, etc., (**capital** ~, appropriation by the State of a fixed proportion of all or some of the wealth in the country), or of property to satisfy legal judgement. **2.** Enrolling of men for war etc.; amount or number thus enrolled, body of men enrolled, (in *pl.*) men enrolled. **3.** *v.t.* Raise (contribution, taxes), impose (rate, toll), whence **lĕ'vĭ**ABLE *a.*; raise (sum, or abs.) by legal execution or process *on* person's goods; extort (*levy blackmail*). **4.** Enlist, enrol, (soldiers, army); collect men and munitions for, proceed to make, (war; usu. *upon* or *against*). [ME, f. OF *levee* fem. p.p. (as n.) of *lever* f. L *levare* raise (*levis* light); see -Y[4]]

lewd *a.* Lascivious, unchaste, indecent, obscene; hence ~'LY[2] *adv.*, ~'NESS *n.* [OE *lǣwede* LAY[2]; orig. unkn.]

lew'ĭs[1] (lōō'-) *n.* Iron contrivance for gripping heavy blocks of stone for lifting. [18th c.; orig. unkn.]

Lew'ĭs[2] (lōō'-) *n.* ~ **gun,** light machine-gun with magazine, air cooling, and operation by gas from its own firing. [f. I. N. ~, Amer. soldier d. 1931, its inventor]

lew'ĭsīte (lōō'-) *n.* Irritant and vesicant poison gas developed for use in chemical warfare. [f. W. L. *Lewis*, Amer. chemist d. 1943 + -ITE[1] (2)]

lĕ'xĭcal *a.* Of the words of a language (opp. *grammatical*); (as) of a lexicon; hence ~LY[2] *adv.* [f. Gk *lexikos* & as LEXICON + -AL]

lĕxĭcŏ'|graphỹ *n.* Dictionary-making; so ~GRAPHER *n.*, **lĕxĭco**GRA'PHICAL *a.* [f. foll. + -GRAPHY]

lĕ'xĭcon *n.* Dictionary, esp. of Greek, Hebrew, Syriac, or Arabic; (fig.) vocabulary of a person, of a language, of a branch of knowledge, etc. [mod. L, f. Gk *lexikon* (*biblion* book), neut. of *lexikos* (*lexis* word f. *legō* speak; see -IC)]

lĕxĭ'graphỹ *n.* System of writing in which each character represents a word. [f. Gk *lexis* (see prec.) + -GRAPHY]

lĕ'xĭs *n.* Words, vocabulary; total stock of words in a language. [Gk; see LEXICON]

lex talionis (lĕks tălĭō'nĭs) *n.* Law of retaliation (whereby punishment resembles offence committed, in kind and degree). [L]

ley (lā) *n.* Land temporarily under grass; ~ **farming,** alternate growing of crops and grass. [ME, orig. adj., perh. f. OE **lǣge*, cogn. w. LAY[3], LIE[3]]

Ley'den (lī'-) *n.* ~ **jar,** kind of electrical condenser with glass jar as dielectric between sheets of tin foil. [f. ~ (now *Leiden*) in Holland, where it was invented (1745)]

L.F. *abbr.* low frequency.

l.h. *abbr.* left hand.

li (lē) *n.* Chinese unit of distance, about ⅜ mile. [Chin.]

L.I. *abbr.* Light Infantry; *Long Island.

Li *symb.* lithium.

līabĭ'lĭtỹ *n.* Being liable (‖**limited** ~, being legally responsible only to limited amount for debts of trading company to which one belongs); what one is liable for, (in *pl.*) debts or pecuniary obligations; person or thing that causes disadvantage through one's responsibility therefor. [f. foll. + -ITY]

lī'able *a.* Legally bound, answerable *for*, subject or amenable *to* tax or penalty, under obligation *to* do; exposed or open *to*, apt *to* do or suffer, something undesirable (*difficulties are liable to occur*). [ME, perh. f. AF **liable* that may be bound, f. OF *lier* f. L *ligare* bind; see -ABLE]

lĭai'se (-z) *v.i.* (colloq.) Make liaison (sense 3) *with* or *between*. [back form. f. foll.]

lĭai'son (-z-) *n.* **1.** Illicit sexual association between a man and a woman. **2.** Sounding of ordinarily silent final consonant before vowel beginning following word (or mute *h* in French). **3.** (Mil. etc.) Connection, co-operation; ~ **officer** (acting as go-between for allied forces or units of the same force). **4.** Egg-yolk thickening for sauces. [F (*lier* bind f. L *ligare*; see -ISON)]

lĭa'na (-ah'-), **lĭa'ne** (-ah'n), *n.* Climbing and twining plant of tropical forest etc. [F *liane*, *lierne* clematis, of uncert. orig.]

lī'ar *n.* Teller (esp. habitual) of lie(s); ~ **dice,** game with poker dice in which false result of throw may be announced. [OE *lēogere* (as LIE[2], -AR[3])]

lī'as *n.* Blue limestone rock in S.W. England; (Geol., *L*~) lower strata of Jurassic series, blue argillaceous limestone rich in fossils; hence **līă'ssic** *a.* [ME, f. OF *liois* hard limestone, prob. of Gmc orig.]

Lĭb. *abbr.* Liberal; (colloq.) Liberation (cf. WOMAN).

lĭbā'tion *n.* (Pouring of) drink-offering to god; (joc.) potation. [ME, f. L *libatio* (*libare* pour as offering; see -ATION)]

lī'bel *n.*, & *v.t.* (‖-ll-). **1.** (Civil & Eccl. Law) plaintiff's written declaration; (Sc. Law) statement of grounds of charge. **2.** (Law). Published false statement damaging to person's reputation; act of publishing it; **criminal** ~, deliberate defamatory statement in permanent form; (**public**) ~, publication of what is blasphemous, obscene, seditious, or treasonable; cf. SLANDER. **3.** (pop.) False and defamatory oral or written statement; thing that brings discredit *on* by misrepresentation etc. (*the portrait is a libel on him*; *the book, play, is a libel on human nature*). **4.** Hence ~LIST (1) *n.*, ~LOUS *a.* **5.** *v.t.* Defame by libellous statements; accuse falsely and maliciously; (Law) publish libel against, whence ~LER[1] *n.*; (Eccl. etc. Law) bring suit against, whence ~LANT (1), ~LEE', *ns.* [ME f. OF, f. L *libellus* dim. of *liber* book; see -EL, -LE 2]

lī'ber *n.* Bast. [L, = bark]

lĭ'beral *a.* & *n.* **1.** *a.* Directed to general broadening of mind, not professional or technical (*liberal culture, education, studies*); ~ **arts,** medieval trivium and quadrivium, *arts as dist. from science and technology. **2.** Generous, open-handed, not sparing *of*; ample, abundant; not rigorous or literal; open-minded, candid, unprejudiced. **3.** (Polit.) Favourable to democratic reform and individual liberty, (moderately) progressive (*the Liberal Party*); hence ~ISM (3), ~IST (2), *ns.*, ~**ĭ'stic** *a.*, ~IZE (3) *v.t.* & *i.* **4.** Hence ~LY² *adv.* **5.** *n.* (*L~*). Member of (esp. the British) Liberal Party. [ME, orig. 'befitting a free man', f. OF f. L *liberalis* (*liber* free (man); see -AL)]

lĭberă'lĭtў *n.* Free giving, munificence; freedom from prejudice, breadth of mind. [ME, f. OF *liberalité* or f. L *liberalitas* (as prec.; see -ITY)]

lĭ'ber|āte *v.t.* Set at liberty, set free *from*; (Chem.) release from state of combination; free (country) from enemy occupation; (sl.) steal; so ~A'TION, ~**āt**OR, *ns.* [f. L *liberare* (*liber* free) + -ATE³]

lĭbertār'ian *n.* & *a.* Believer, believing, in free will (opp. *necessitarian*); advocate of liberty; hence ~ISM (3) *n.* [f. LIBERTY + -ARIAN]

lĭber'ticide *n.* & *a.* (literary). Destroyer, destructive, of liberty. [F (as LIBERTY; see -CIDE)]

lĭ'bertīn|e (*or* -ēn) *n.* & *a.* Free thinker, free-thinking, on religion; (one) who follows his own inclinations; dissolute, licentious, (man); CHARTER²*ed libertine*; hence ~AGE (2), ~ISM (2), *ns.* [f. L *libertinus* freedman (*libertus* made free, f. *liber* free; see -INE¹)]

lĭ'bertў *n.* **1.** Being free from captivity, imprisonment, slavery, or despotic control; personification of this; CAP¹ *of liberty*; **civil ~,** being subject only to laws established on behalf of community; *liberty of* CONSCIENCE, *of the* PRESS¹ 5; ~ **of the subject,** rights of subject under constitutional rule. **2.** Right or power to do as one pleases or *to* do something; (Philos.) freedom from control of fate or necessity. **3.** Setting aside of rules, licence; **take the ~ to** do, **of doing,** presume or venture to do; **take liberties,** behave in improperly familiar manner (*with* person, or abs.), deal (unduly) freely *with* rules or facts. **4.** (in *pl.*) Privileges, immunities, or rights, enjoyed by prescription or grant; (Hist., in *sing.*, or *pl.*) area having such privileges etc., district controlled by city though outside its boundary, area outside prison where some prisoners might reside. **5. At ~,** free (*set at liberty*), having the right *to* do, disengaged. **6.** ***L~ Bell** (in Philadelphia, rung at adoption of Declaration of Independence); ||~ **boat** (Naut., carrying liberty men); **L~ Hall,** place where one may do as one likes; ~ **horse** (performing in circus without rider); ~ **man,** sailor with leave to go ashore; **L~ ship,** prefabricated U.S.-built freighter of 1939–45 war. [ME, f. OF *liberté* f. L *libertas -tatis* (*liber* free; see -TY¹)]

lĭbĭ'dĭnous *a.* Lustful; hence ~LY² *adv.* [ME, f. L *libidinosus* (*libido -dinis* lust; see -OUS)]

lĭbĭ'dō (*or* -ē'-) *n.* (*pl.* ~s). Psychic drive or energy, esp. that associated with sex instinct; hence **lĭbĭ'dĭn**AL *a.* [L; see prec.]

Lĭ'bra *n.* Sign of the ZODIAC, the Balance or Scales. [ME, f. L, orig. = pound weight]

lībrār'ian *n.* Custodian of or assistant in library; hence ~SHIP (1, 3) *n.* [f. L *librarius* (see foll.) + -AN]

lī'brarў *n.* **1.** Room or building containing books for reading or reference; room in large house devoted to books. **2.** A collection of books for use by the public or by some class of persons; similar collection of films, records, computer routines, etc.; public institution charged with care of such collection; **lending ~** (from which books may be temporarily taken away with or ||without payment); **reference ~** (in which books may be consulted but not taken away); ||**free ~, public ~,** (used by public without payment and usu. supported by local rates); *circulating library* (see CIRCULATE); *RENTAL *library*. **3.** Person's book-collection; series of books issued by publisher in similar bindings etc. as being connected in some way. **4. ~ edition** (of good size and print and strongly bound); ***~ science,** study of librarianship; ~ **school** (teaching librarianship). [ME, f. OF *librairie* f. L *libraria* (*taberna* shop), fem. of *librarius* bookseller's, of books (*liber libri* book; see -ARY¹, -Y¹)]

lībrā'te *v.i.* Oscillate like balance-beam; be poised, balance; sway, quiver; hence **lī'bra**TORY *a.* [f. L *librare* (*libra* balance) + -ATE³]

lībrā'tion *n.* Librating; ~ **of moon,** apparent oscillation by which parts near edge of disc are alternately visible and invisible. [f. L *libratio* (as prec.; see -ATION)]

lĭbrĕ'tt|ō *n.* (*pl.* ~*i pr.* -ē, *or* ~*os*). Text of opera or other long musical vocal work; hence ~IST (1) *n.* [It., dim. of *libro* book f. L *liber libri*]

Lĭ'bўan (*or* -yan) *a.* & *n.* (Inhabitant or native) of ancient N. Africa W. of Egypt, or of modern Libya; (poet.) N. African; (of) the Berber language or the group of Hamitic languages to which it belongs. [f. L *Libya* f. Gk *Libuē* + -AN]

līce. See LOUSE.

lī'cence¹, *lī'cense¹, *n.* **1.** Leave, permission, (*have I your licence to remove the fence?*). **2.** Permit from government etc. to marry, print something, preach, be driver or owner of vehicle on public road, own a dog, gun, or television set, carry on some trade (esp. that in alcoholic liquor), etc.; university certificate of competence in some faculty; ***~ plate,** number plate of licensed vehicle. **3.** Liberty of action esp. when excessive, abuse of freedom, disregard of law or propriety; licentiousness. **4.** Writer's or artist's irregularity in grammar, metre, perspective, etc., esp. for sake of effect (*poetic licence*). [ME f. OF, f. L *licentia* (*licēre* be lawful; see -ENCE); *-se* by confus. w. foll.]

lī'cense², -ce², *v.t.* **1.** (arch.) Allow (person *to* do, thing to be done); (in *p.p.*) allow complete freedom to (*a licensed libertine*). **2.** Grant permit (see prec. 2) to (person; ||*licensed* VICTUALLER); authorize use of (premises) for certain purpose, esp. sale and consumption of alcoholic liquor; authorize publication of (book etc.) or performance of (play). **3.** Hence **līcens**EE' *n.*, (esp.) one who holds a licence to sell alcoholic liquor, **lī'cens**ER¹ *n.*, (esp.) official licensing publication of books or performance of plays. [ME, f. prec.; *-se* on anal. of *practise, prophesy*, vbs., cf. *practice, prophecy*, ns.; perh. after *advise, advice*, where the sound differs]

līcĕ'ntiate (-shĭat) *n.* Holder of university licence or attestation of competence from collegiate or examining body; licensed preacher not yet having appointment, esp. in Presbyterian Church. [ME, f. med. L *licentiatus* p.p. (as n.) of *licentiare* f. L *licentia* (see LICENCE¹) + -ATE¹]

līcĕ'ntious (-shus) *a.* Lascivious, lewd; (arch.) disregarding accepted rules or conventions; hence ~LY² *adv.*, ~NESS *n.* [f. L *licentiosus* (*licentia*; see LICENCE¹, -OUS)]

lĭch, lўch, *n.* **~-gate,** roofed gateway of churchyard where coffin awaits clergyman's arrival; **~-house,** mortuary; ||**~-owl,** screech-owl (boding death); ~**-stone** (to place coffin on at lich-gate). [OE *līc* corpse, = OS *līc*, OHG *līh*, ON *lík*, Goth. *leik* f. Gmc **līkam* body, form, appearance]

lichee, lichi. Vars. of LITCHI.

lī'chen (-k-; *or* lĭ'ch-) *n.* **1.** Plant organism of group Lichenes, composed of fungus and alga in association, usu. of green, grey, or yellow tint growing on and colouring rocks, tree-trunks, roofs, walls, etc.; hence ~ED[2] (-nd) *a.*, ~**ŏ'**LOGY *n.* **2.** Skin-disease with reddish eruption. **3.** Hence ~OUS *a.* [L, f. Gk *leikhēn*]

lĭ'cĭt *a.* Lawful, not forbidden; hence ~LY[2] *adv.* [f. L *licitus* p.p. of *licēre* be lawful]

lĭck *v.t.*, & *n.* **1.** *v.t.* Pass tongue over to taste, moisten, clean, etc.; ~ one's **chops** or **lips** (in relish or anticipation of food); ~ **into shape,** give proper form to, make presentable or efficient [f. bears' supposed treatment of their cubs]; ~ person's **boots** or **shoes,** show servility to him; ~ one's **wounds,** (fig.) remain in retirement after defeat. **2.** Take *up* or *off*, make *clean*, by licking; (of waves, flame, etc.) play lightly over, (of flame) swallow *up* in passing. **3.** (sl.) Thrash (person, fault *out of* person), beat in fight or competition, excel, whence ~'ING[1] (1) *n.*; surpass comprehension of (*this licks me, has got me licked*). **4.** ~**'spittle,** toady. **5.** *n.* Act of licking with tongue (**a ~ and a promise,** (colloq.) hasty performance of task, esp. of washing oneself); = SALT-*lick*; smart blow with stick etc.; (sl.) pace (*at a great lick*; *full* or *at full lick*). [OE *liccian*, = OS *liccon*, *leccon*, OHG *leckōn* f. WG **likkōjan* ult. f. IE **ligh-*]

lĭ'ckerĭsh, lĭ'quorĭsh, (-ker-) *a.* Fond of dainty fare; greedy, longing; lecherous. [alt. f. ME *lickerous* f. AF **likerous*, OF *lecheros*; see LECHER, -OUS]

lĭcketȳ-splĭ't *adv.* (colloq.) At full speed, headlong. [prob. f. LICK (cf. *at full lick*) + SPLIT[1]]

lĭ'corice. See LIQUORICE.

lĭ'ctor *n.* (Rom. Hist.; usu. in pl.) Officer attending consul or other magistrate, bearing fasces, and executing sentence on offenders. [ME f. L, perh. rel. to *ligare* bind]

lĭd *n.* **1.** Hinged or detached part to cover opening or close aperture, esp. for opening at top of vessel; **with the ~ off,** with all horrors etc. exposed to view; ||**put the** (**tin**) **~ on,** (sl.) (1) be the culmination (of), surpass all, (2) put a stop to. **2.** Operculum of shell or plant; = EYE[1]*lid*; (sl.) hat. **3.** Hence (**-**)**~'**D**ED**[2], ~'LESS, *adjs.* [OE *hlid*, = OHG (*h*)*lit*, ON *hlith* f. Gmc **hlidham* (**hlidh-* cover)]

lī'dō (*or* lē'-) *n.* (*pl.* **~s**). Public open-air swimming-pool or pleasure-beach. [It., name of bathing-beach near Venice, f. L *litus* shore]

līe[1] *n.* **1.** Intentional false statement; **tell a ~,** utter this; **act a ~,** deceive without verbal lying; **white ~** (excused or justified by its motive); **give person the ~** (**in his throat**), accuse him of lying (grossly); **give the ~ to** supposition etc., serve to show its falsity. **2.** Imposture, thing that deceives. **3.** ~**-detector,** instrument for measuring pulse-rate, respiration, etc., so as to detect physiological changes accompanying tension due to telling of lies. [OE *lyge* f. Gmc **leug-* etc., assim. to foll.]

līe[2] *v.* (*part.* LYING[2]). **1.** *v.i.* Speak falsely, tell lie(s) (*to* person); ~ **in** one's **teeth** or **throat,** (arch. or joc.) lie outrageously or infamously. **2.** (Of thing) be deceptive (*the camera cannot lie*). **3.** *v.t.* Get (oneself, person) *into* or *out of* by lying. [OE *lēogan*, = OS, OHG *liogan*, ON *ljúga*, Goth. *liugan* f. Gmc **l*(*e*)*ug-*]

līe[3] *v.i.* (*part.* LYING[2]; *past* **lay**; *p.p.* **lain,** Bibl. **lī'en**). **1.** (Of person or animal) have one's body in more or less horizontal position along ground or surface (*lie asleep*, *sick*, *dying*, *dead*, etc.; *lie* DOGGO; *let* SLEEP[2]*ing dogs lie*; **~ on the bed one has made,** endure consequences of past acts). **2.** (arch.) Have sexual intercourse *with*. **3.** (Of the dead) be buried *at* or *in*; *lie in* STATE[1]. **4.** Take lying position (*down*, *back*, etc.); be kept or remain in specified state (*lie in prison*, *at the mercy of*, *helpless*, *fallow*, *idle*, CLOSE[1], LOW[1], PERDU, *in ambush*, *in* WAIT[2]); (of game-bird) not rise; (of troops) be encamped *at*, *in*, *near*, a place. **5.** (Of thing) be at rest, usu. more or less horizontally, on surface (*lie at the* DOOR *of*; **~ in ruins** or **in the dust,** be overthrown or fallen; **~ on the table,** be laid on the TABLE 10; **~ heavy,** be a weight on one's stomach or conscience); be stored up in specified place (*money lying at the bank*); be situated (*land lying high*, *to the east*, *round*; *how the* LAND[1] *lies*); be spread out to view (*lie on the surface*, *before us*, *open*); (of road, course of travel, etc.) lead *through*, *by*, *along*, *among*, etc.; (of ship) float in berth or at anchor; (of abstract thing) exist, be found, reside, be arranged or related, in some position or manner (*the choice lies between these three*; *my sympathy lies with Mary*; *knows where his interest lies*; *how do these facts lie to each other?*; *the remedy lies in education*; *her strength lay in her weakness*; **as far as in me ~s,** to the best of my power; **~s with you,** is your business or right *to* do); (Law) be admissible or sustainable (*action*, *appeal*, *objection*, *will not lie*). **6. ~ about,** be left carelessly out of place; **~ by,** be unused, keep quiet or retired; **~ down,** have brief rest in or on bed etc., whence ~*-down* n.; **~ down under,** accept without protest; **lying down,** in abject manner, not standing up to opponent etc., (*take defeat* etc., esp. *it*, *lying down*); **~ in,** (1) be brought to bed in childbirth (*lying-in hospital*), (2) ||(colloq.) lie idly in bed late in the morning, whence ~*-in* n.; **~ off,** (Naut.) stand some distance from shore or other ship; **~ over,** be deferred; **~ to,** (Naut.) come almost to a stop with head near wind by backing or shortening sail; **~ up,** go into or be in retirement, take to one's bed or room, (of ship) go into dock or be out of commission. **7.** ~**-abed,** late riser. [OE *licgan*, = OS *liggian*, OHG *liggen*, ON *liggja* f. Gmc **ligjan* (**leg-*, **lag-*, **lǣg-*, f. IE **legh-*, **logh-*)]

lie[4] *n.* Way, direction, or position, in which thing lies (||~ **of the land,** (fig.) state of affairs); position of golf-ball to be struck (*recovered well from a bad lie*); place where animal or bird is accustomed to lie. [f. prec.]

Liebfraumilch (lē'pfrowmĭlχ) *n.* Mild white Rhine wine. [G (*Liebfrau* Virgin Mary, patroness of convent where it was first made, *milch* milk)]

lied (lēt) *n.* (*pl.* **~'er** pr. lē'*der*). German song or poem of ballad kind. [G]

lief *adv.* Gladly, willingly, (usu. I *had* or *would as lief* do one thing *as* another). [orig. adj., f. OE *lēof* dear, pleasant, = OS *liof*, OHG *liub*, ON *ljúfr*, Goth. *liufs* f. Gmc **leubhaz*; cf. LEAVE[1], LOVE[1]]

liege *a.* & *n.* **1.** *a.* (Of superior) entitled to receive, (of vassal) bound to give, feudal service or allegiance; **~ lord,** feudal superior, sovereign; **~'man,** sworn vassal, faithful follower. **2.** *n.* Liege lord (esp. *my liege* in voc.); (usu. in *pl.*) vassal, subject. [ME, f. OF *li*(*e*)*ge* f. med. L *laeticus* (*letus*, *litus*, prob. f. Gmc)]

lī'en[1] (lē'en) *n.* Right *on* property to keep possession of it till debt due in respect of it is discharged. [F, f. OF *loien* f. L *ligamen* bond (*ligare* bind)]

lī'en[2]. See LIE[3].

liĕr'ne *n.* Short rib connecting bosses and intersections of vaulting-ribs. [ME f. F; cf. LIANA]

lieu (lū) *n.* **In ~**, in the place, instead, (*of*). [ME f. F, f. L *locus* place]

Lieut. *abbr.* Lieutenant.

lieutĕ'n|ant (lĕft-, lẹft-, in Navy lĕt- *or* lẹt-) *n.* **1.** Deputy, substitute, vicegerent, acting for a superior (**L~ant of the Tower,** acting commandant of Tower of London; ||LORD *Lieutenant*, ||DEPUTY *lieutenant*); (***first**) **~ant,** army officer next below captain; navy officer next below lieutenant-commander; ||FLIGHT¹ *lieutenant*; SECOND *lieutenant*; **~ant-colonel, -commander, -general,** officers ranking just below colonel etc.; **~ant-governor,** acting or deputy governor of state, province, etc., under governor(-general). **2.** Hence **~ANCY** *n.* [ME f. OF (LIEU place, TENANT holder)]

life *n.* (*pl.* **lives** *pr.* -vz). **1.** State of functional activity and continual change peculiar to organized matter, and esp. to the portion of it constituting an animal or plant before death, animate existence, being alive; **a matter of ~ and death,** something on which it depends whether one shall live or die, (fig.) something of vital importance; *life and* LIMB¹; **come to ~,** emerge from unconsciousness or inactivity; **for** one's **~, for dear ~,** (as if) to escape death; **cannot for the ~ of me,** could not even if my life depended on it; **lay down** one's **~,** accept being killed; **lose** one's **~,** be killed (*many lives were lost*, many were killed); *a new* LEASE *of life*; **not on your ~,** (colloq.) most certainly not; *a* PRICE *on his life*; **save** one's **~,** avoid death; **save** person's **~,** prevent his dying; SELL one's *life dear(ly)*; STAFF¹ *of life*; **take ~,** kill person(s) or animal(s); **take** one's **(own) ~,** kill oneself; **take** one's **~ in** one's **hands,** risk it; **upon my ~** (form of asseveration). **2.** Energy, liveliness, vivacity, animation; vivifying influence (*was the life*, or *life and soul, of the party*); **put some ~ into it,** (colloq.) act more energetically. **3.** Living things and their activity (*very little life to be seen*); the living form or (esp. nude) model, life-size figure etc., (*taken from the life*); **as large as ~,** (1) life-size, (2) in person (*here he is, as large as life*); **larger than ~,** exaggerated; *portray* etc. **to the ~,** with fidelity to the original; **true to ~,** with accurate representation of persons' behaviour etc.; hence **~'LIKE** (-fl-) *a.* **4.** Period from birth to death, birth to present time (*have done it all my life*), or present time to death; **get the fright, have the** TIME¹, etc., **of** one's **~,** (colloq.) be frightened, enjoy oneself, as never before; **~ (sentence), ~ annuity, ~ membership,** etc., (to continue for rest of person's life); **for ~,** for the rest of one's life. **5.** INSURE one's *life*; **expectation of ~,** average period that person at specified age may expect to live; **a good, bad, ~,** person likely to pass, fall short of, this average. **6.** Fresh start after narrowly escaped death (lit. or fig.); **cat has nine lives** (is hard to kill); *batsman* etc. *is* **given a ~,** not put out when he gives a chance; *player in game has three* **lives,** successive chances before being put out. **7.** Individual's actions and fortunes, manner of existence; particular aspect or type of this (*his* SEX *life, private life*; *village life*); **make ~ easy,** not create problems; **in ~,** to be experienced anywhere (*nothing in life surpasses that*); **this ~** (on earth); **the other, the future, eternal, everlasting, ~,** state of existence after death; *the* SIMPLE *life*; **this is the ~** (expr. contentment); **what a ~!** (expr. discontent). **8.** Written story of person's life, biography. **9.** Active part of existence, business and pleasures of the world; HIGH, LOW¹, *life*; SEE¹ *life*. **10.** (Theol.) Salvation, regenerate condition; WATER¹ *of life*. **11.** Time for which an inanimate thing exists or continues to function (*battery has a life of two years*). **12. ~-and-death,** vitally important; **~'belt** (of buoyant material to support body in water); **~-blood,** blood necessary to life, vitalizing influence; **~'boat** (of special construction for saving life in storms); **~-breath,** inspiring influence, sustaining principle; *life*BUOY¹; **~ cycle,** series of forms of an organism between successive occurrences of a given form; **~ estate,** property that one holds for life but cannot dispose of further; **~ expectancy,** expectation of life (see sense 5); **~-giving,** that gives, sustains, or restores, physical or spiritual life; **~-guard,** (1) bodyguard of soldiers, (2) *expert swimmer to rescue bathers from drowning; ||**L~ Guards,** regiment of household cavalry (now armoured corps); **~ history,** (1) history of person's life, (2) series of developments of organism from egg etc. to death; **~ insurance** (for payment on death of insured person); **~ interest,** right to life estate; **~-jacket** (as *lifebelt*); **~'line,** (1) rope used for life-saving, e.g. that attached to lifebuoy, diver's signalling line, (fig.) sole means of communication, (2) (Palmistry) = LINE² *of life*; **~'long,** continued throughout a life; **~-office** (dealing in life insurance); **~ peer(age)** (with title lapsing at death); **~-preserver,** (1) short stick with heavily loaded end, (2) life-jacket etc.; **~-saver,** person or thing that saves from death or from serious difficulty, esp. (Austral. & N.Z.) = *life-guard* (2); **~ sciences,** biology and kindred subjects; **~-size(d),** of the same size as the living person etc.; **~-style,** individual's way of life; **~-table,** statistics of expectation of life; **~'time,** duration of person's life (*chance* etc. *of a ~time*, such as occurs only once in a person's life), duration of existence (= sense 11); **~-work,** task pursued throughout life. [OE *līf*, = OS *līf*, ON *líf*, OHG *līb* life, body, f. Gmc **lībham* (**lībh-*; cf. LIVE²)]

lī'felėss (-fl-) *a.* No longer living; unconscious; not having life, inanimate; lacking animation or vigour; hence **~LY²** *adv.*, **~NESS** *n.* [OE *līflēas* (as LIFE, -LESS)]

lī'fer *n.* (sl.) Person sentenced to, sentence of, imprisonment for life. [f. LIFE + -ER¹]

lĭft *v.* & *n.* **1.** *v.t.* Raise to higher position, take up, hoist, (*up, off, out*); elevate to higher plane of thought or feeling; give upward direction to (eyes, face); **~ (up)** one's **hands** or **heart** (in prayer etc.); **~** one's **hand** (to take oath); **~ a hand,** make the slightest effort, usu. *to* do; **~ a hand against,** strike (person); **~ up** one's **head,** recover vigour after prostration; **~ down,** pick up and bring to lower position; **~-off,** (*a.*) removable simply by lifting, (*n.*) vertical take-off of spacecraft or rocket; **~ up** one's **voice,** (1) sing or speak, (2) cry out. **2.** Hold or have on high (*church lifts its spire*); steal (esp. cattle), take (passage, information) as plagiarist; strike (tent etc.); dig up (potatoes etc. at harvest); hit (cricket-ball) into air; remove (barrier, restriction); carry as passenger in vehicle; **have** one's **face ~ed,** undergo face-lifting. **3.** *v.i.* Yield to upward force (*window will not lift*); (of cloud, fog, darkness) rise, disperse; (of floor) swell upwards, bulge. **4.** *n.* Lifting; carrying of person as passenger in vehicle; transport by air, quantity thus transported; one layer of leather in heel of boot or shoe; ||apparatus for raising and lowering persons or things to other floor of building; apparatus for carrying persons up or down mountain etc.; supporting or elevating influence; amount of rise of water in canal lock; rise in level of ground; upward pressure which the air exerts on an aircraft, counteracting the force of gravity. [ME, f. ON *lypta* f. Gmc **luftjan* (**luftuz* air)]

li'gament *n.* **1.** (Anat.) Short band of tough flexible fibrous tissue binding bones together; any membranous fold keeping organ in position. **2.** Similar structure in oyster etc. **3.** (arch.) Bond of union. **4.** Hence ~AL, ~ARY[1], ~OUS, (-mĕ'n-) *adjs.* [ME, f. L *ligamentum* bond (*ligare* bind; see -MENT)]

lig|ā'te *v.t.* (Surg.) Tie up (bleeding artery etc.); hence ~A'TION *n.* [f. L *ligare* + -ATE[3]]

li'gature *n.*, & *v.t.* **1.** *n.* Thing used in tying, esp. band or cord used to tie up bleeding artery, strangulate tumour, etc.; thing that unites, bond; tying, ligation; (Mus.) slur, tie; (Print.) two or more letters joined (*fi* etc.). **2.** *v.t.* Bind with ligature. [ME, f. LL *ligatura* (as prec.; see -URE)]

li'ger (-g-) *n.* Offspring of lion and tigress. [f. LION + TIGER]

light[1] *n.* **1.** The natural agent that stimulates the sense of sight; visible electromagnetic radiation from sun, fire, lamp, etc. **2.** Medium or condition of space in which this is present and therefore sight is possible (opp. *darkness*). **3.** Appearance of brightness (*saw a distant light*; NORTHERN, SOUTHERN, *lights*; ZODIACAL *light*). **4.** Amount of illumination in place (**in a good ~**, easily visible; *bad light stopped play*); one's fair or ordinary share of this (**stand in** person's **~**, deprive him of this, (fig.) prejudice his chances). **5.** Vivacity, enthusiasm, or inspiration in person's eyes; **~ of** person's **countenance,** his favour, approving presence, or sanction (often iron.). **6.** Sun's direct or diffused or reflected rays, daylight; SEE[1] *the light* (*of day*). **7.** Being visible or exposed; **come, bring, to ~,** be revealed, reveal; **come to ~ with,** (Austral. & N.Z. colloq.) produce (money etc.). **8.** Object from which brightness emanates (**~ of** one's **eyes** or **life,** beloved person), sun or other heavenly body, ignited candle or lamp or the like (GREEN[1], RED, *light*); (collect.) lamps etc. illuminating place; beacon lamp esp. of ship or lighthouse; lighthouse; traffic-light; (fig.) eminent person, luminary; *light under* BUSHEL[1]; **festival of ~s,** Hanukkah; **out like a ~,** deeply asleep (or otherwise unconscious); **~s out,** bedtime in school etc., (Mil.) last bugle-call of day. **9.** Mental illumination, elucidation (**throw** or **shed ~ upon** or **on,** help to explain), enlightenment (**by the ~ of nature,** without aid of revelation or teaching; *light and* LEADING[1]; SEE[1] *the light*); (in *pl.*) facts or discoveries serving to explain subject (*we have many new lights upon it since then*); (in *pl.*) one's natural or acquired mental powers (usu. *do* one's *best* etc. *according to* one's *lights*). **10.** Aspect in which thing is viewed (**in the ~ of** *these facts*, with the help given by; **appeared in the ~ of** *a scoundrel*, seemed to be; **place in a good ~,** represent favourably). **11.** (In crossword etc.) one of the words to be deduced from clues. **12.** (Theol.) Brightness of heaven, illumination of soul by divine truth. **13.** Window or opening in wall for admission of light; perpendicular division of mullioned window; window of vehicle (‖QUARTER[1]-*light*); glazed compartment of side or roof in greenhouse. **14.** (Paint.) Illuminated surface; part of picture represented as lighted up. **15.** (Law). Light falling on windows, the obstruction of which by neighbour is illegal (ANCIENT[1] *lights*). **16.** Flame or spark serving to ignite (**strike a ~,** produce this with match etc., also ‖as *int.* of surprise etc.); thing used for igniting, spill, taper, match. **17. ~ due, duty,** toll on ships for maintenance of lighthouses and lightships; **~'house,** tower or other structure containing beacon light to warn or guide ships at sea; **~ meter,** instrument for measuring intensity of light, esp. exposure meter; **~ pen,** photoelectric device for communicating with computer by movement esp. over screen of cathode-ray tube; *light*-PROOF[2]; **~'ship,** moored or anchored ship with beacon light; **~ show,** display of changing coloured lights for entertainment; *light*-TIGHT; **~-year,** (Astron.) distance light travels in one year, about 6 million million miles. **18.** Hence ~'LESS *a.* [OE *lēoht*, *līht*, = OS, OHG *lioht* f. WG **leuhta* f. IE **leuktom* (**leuk-* white)]

light[2] (līt) *a.* Well provided with light, not dark; pale (often prefixed to *adjs.* & *ns.* of colour: *light-blue ribbon*; *I prefer light blue*; *light* BLUE[2]). [f. as prec.]

light[3] (līt) *v.* (**lit** *or* **~'ed;** as *attrib. a.* usu. *~ed*). **1.** *v.t.* Set (lamp etc., fire, fuel, tobacco, etc.) burning. **2.** Give light to (room, street, etc.); cause (eyes, face, etc.) to light (sense 5). **3.** Show (person his) way or surroundings with a light. **4.** *v.i.* (Of fuel, lamp, etc.) take fire, begin to burn or be bright. **5.** (Of eyes, face, etc.) brighten with animation. **6. ~ up,** (1) = sense 1, (abs.) begin to smoke cigarette, pipe, etc., kindle lights in street or room at dusk, (2) light (room etc.) brightly, make conspicuous by light, (3) = sense 5; **~ing-u'p time** (after which vehicles on road must show prescribed lights); **lit up,** (sl.) drunk. **7.** Hence ~'ING (1, 2, 6) *n.* [OE *līhtan*, = OS *liuhtian*, Goth. *liuhtjan* f. Gmc (**leuht-* LIGHT[1])]

light[4] (līt) *a.* & *adv.* **1.** *a.* Of little weight, not heavy; (Phys., of isotope etc.) having not more than the usual mass; deficient in weight (*light coin* etc.); not abundant (*light traffic*). **2.** Of low density (*light metal*). **3.** Having, or intended for, a small load; (of ship) unladen; (of guns, battleship, etc.) of the smaller or light-armed kind; (of locomotive) with no train attached; (of railway) for transport of light loads only; (Mil.) carrying only light arms (*light brigade*); (of ship, cart, etc.) made lightly for small loads and quick movement. **4.** (Of building) not looking heavy, graceful, elegant; (Print., of type) not heavy or bold. **5.** Acting gently, applied delicately, not violent, (*light touch, blow, rain, wind, step*, etc.); **~ hand,** lit., or fig. = tactful management. **6.** Not dense or tenacious; porous, friable, (*light soil, pastry*). **7.** Easy to digest (*light meal*); (of wine or beer) not strong. **8.** Not important (**make ~ of,** treat as of no consequence); slight, not severe. **9.** Trivial, venial, not grave; jesting, thoughtless, frivolous. **10.** Wanton, unchaste, (esp. of woman or her conduct). **11.** Nimble, quick-moving, (*light of foot*; *light heels, movements, rhythm*); **~ fingers** (good at stealing). **12.** Easily borne (*light punishment, taxation, rule, expense*) or done (*light work, task*). **13.** Aimed or aiming merely at entertainment (*light literature, writer, comedy, comedian, programme*). **14.** (Of sleep) easily disturbed, not profound, (so *light sleeper*). **15.** Free from sorrow, cheerful, hopeful, (*light heart*). **16.** Giddy (*light in the head*). **17. ~-armed,** with light weapons or armour; **~er-than-air',** (of aircraft) weighing less than the air it displaces; **~-fingered,** apt to steal; **~'foot,** nimble; **~-hea'ded,** giddy, delirious, frivolous; **~-hear'ted,** (1) cheerful, gay, (2) (unduly) optimistic or casual; **~ horse**(**man**), (member of) light-armed cavalry; **~ industry** (producing small or light articles); **~ infantry** (with light weapons); **~-mi'nded,** frivolous; **~ oil,** a lighter-than-water oil obtained from coal tar by distillation at low temperature; **~-o'-love,** fickle woman, prostitute; *light* OPERA[1]; **~'-weight** *a.* & *n.*, (man or animal or garment) below average weight (see BOX[5]), (fig.) (person) of little ability or importance. **18.** Hence ~'LY[2] *adv.* **19.** *adv.* In light manner (*tread, sleep, light*); with minimum load (*travel light*); **~ come ~ go,** what is easily gained is soon lost. [OE *lēoht, līht,* = OS *-līht,* OHG *līht(i),* ON *léttr,* Goth. *leihts* f. Gmc **linhtaz* (**lingw-* f. IE **leňghʷ-*)]

līght[5] (līt) *v.i.* (**lit** *or* **~'ed**). **1.** (arch.) Alight, descend, come down. **2.** Chance, come by chance, (*up*)*on.* **3.** (sl.) **~ into,** attack; **~ out,** depart. [OE *līhtan,* = OHG *līhten,* ON *létta* f. Gmc **līhtjan* (**linht-* LIGHT[4]; sense f. idea of relieving horse etc. of weight)]

lī'ghten[1] (lī't-) *v.* **1.** *v.t.* Reduce load of (ship etc.); bring relief to (mind, heart, etc.); reduce weight of, (fig.) mitigate. **2.** *v.i.* Grow lighter in weight etc. [ME, f. LIGHT[4] + -EN[6]]

lī'ghten[2] (lī't-) *v.* **1.** *v.t.* Shed light upon, make bright (lit., or fig., *lighten our darkness*). **2.** *v.i.* (Of face, eyes, sky, etc.) grow bright, shine, flash; (of sky, clouds, or *it*) emit lightning. [ME, f. LIGHT[2] + -EN[6]]

lī'ghter[1] (lī't-) *n.* In vbl senses; device for lighting cigarettes etc. e.g. with flint, steel, and fuel, or electrically. [f. LIGHT[3] + -ER[1]]

lī'ghter[2] (lī't-) *n.*, & *v.t.* **1.** *n.* Boat, usu. flat-bottomed, for unloading and loading ships not brought to wharf and for transporting goods in harbour; **~'man,** worker on lighter; hence ~AGE (4) *n.* **2.** *v.t.* Remove (goods) in lighter. [ME, f. MDu. *lichter* (as LIGHT[5] in sense 'unload'; see -ER[1])]

lī'ghtish[1,2] *adjs.*, **lī'ghtness**[1,2] *ns.*, (lī't-). In adj. senses. [f. LIGHT[2,4] + -ISH[1] 2, -NESS]

lī'ghtning (lī't-) *n.* & *a.* **1.** *n.* Visible electric discharge between clouds or cloud and ground (BALL[1] *lightning*; **forked ~,** lightning-flash in form of zigzag or branching line; **sheet ~,** lightning-flash of diffused brightness; **summer ~,** sheet lightning without audible thunder, result of distant storm); **like** (**greased** colloq.) **~,** with greatest conceivable speed; ***~-bug,** firefly; **~-conductor, *~-rod,** metal rod or wire fixed to exposed part of building or to mast to divert lightning into earth or sea. **2.** *a.* Very quick (*with lightning speed*); **~ chess** (in which moves must be made at very short intervals); **~ strike,** (1) being struck by lightning, (2) labour strike at short notice by way of surprise. [ME, different. f. *lightening* vbl n. of LIGHTEN[2]]

līghts (līts) *n. pl.* Lungs of sheep, pigs, bullocks, etc., used as a food esp. for cats and dogs. [ME, n. use of LIGHT[4]; cf. LUNG]

lī'ghtsome[1] (lī't-) *a.* Light, graceful, elegant, in appearance; light-hearted, merry; nimble; hence ~LY[2] (-mlĭ) *adv.*, ~NESS (-mn-) *n.* [ME, f. LIGHT[4] + -SOME[1]]

lī'ghtsome[2] (lī't-) *a.* Light-giving, luminous; well lighted, bright. [ME, f. LIGHT[1] + -SOME[1]]

lī'ghtwood (lī't-) *n.* Tree with light wood; *(tree with) wood that burns with bright flame. [f. LIGHT[4,1] + WOOD]

lign-ă'lōes (lină'lōz) *n.* The drug aloes; aromatic E. Ind. wood from tree of genus *Aquilaria*; aromatic Mexican wood from tree of genus *Bursera.* [ME, f. LL *lignum aloes* wood of the ALOE]

lĭ'gnėous *a.* (Of plant) woody (opp. *herbaceous*). [f. L *ligneus* (as foll.) + -OUS]

lĭ'gnĭ- *comb. form.* Wood, as: ~FEROUS (-ĭ'f-), ~FORM, *adjs.*, ~FY *v.t.* & *i.* [f. L *lignum* wood + -I-]

lĭ'gnĭn *n.* (Bot.) Stiffening material in cell-walls of woody tissue. [f. as prec. + -IN]

lĭ'gnīte *n.* Brown coal showing traces of plant structure, intermediate between bituminous coal and peat. [F, f. as LIGNI- + -ITE[1] (2)]

lĭgnum vī'tae (*or* -vē'tī) *n.* = GUAIACUM 2. [L, = wood of life]

lĭ'grōĭn *n.* Solvent derived from petroleum. [20th c., of unkn. orig.]

lĭ'gūlate *a.* (Bot.) With strap-shaped florets. [f. as foll. + -ATE[2]]

lĭ'gūle *n.* (Bot.) Narrow projection from top of leaf-sheath of grass. [f. L *ligula* strap, spoon (*lingere* lick; see -ULE)]

lī'kable. Var. of LIKE[2]*able.*

līke[1] *a.*, *prep.*, *adv.*, *conj.*, & *n.* **1.** *a.* (often governing *n.* like trans. part.; **more, most, ~,** occas., esp. poet., **lī'ker, lī'kest**). Similar, resembling something or each other or the original, (*in like manner*; *on this and the like subjects*; *the two letters are very like*; *as like as two peas*; *the picture is not like*); **~ father ~ son, ~ master ~ man,** etc., as the one is so will the other be. **2.** (Alg. etc.) **~ charges, signs** (both positive or both negative); **~ quantities** (expressed by same letters). **3.** (arch.) **~ with** or **to,** similar to (*beings of like passions with us*; *like to the lark at break of day arising*). **4.** Resembling, such as, as good as; **what is he, it, ~?,** what sort of person is he, thing is it?; LOOK *like*; *like* THAT[1]; **more ~ it,** nearer what is required; *a critic* **~ you,** of the class that you exemplify; **nothing ~'** (*as* or *so good, as* or *so many,* etc., or abs.) not nearly; SOMETHING *like.* **5.** Characteristic of (*that is like your impudence*; *it was like him to think of himself last*). **6.** In suitable state or right mood for doing (LOOK *like*; *feel like working* or *stopping work*), or for having (*feel like a rest, a cup of tea*). **7.** (arch. or colloq.) Likely (*as like as not*; *like enough*; **had ~ to have done,** narrowly escaped doing). **8.** **~-minded,** having same tastes, views, etc. **9.** *prep.* In the manner of, to the same degree as, (*cannot do it like you*; *do not talk like* THAT[1]; *like a* SHOT[1]; *like* MAD[1]; *like* HELL; **~ so,** (colloq.) in this manner; **~ fun, anything,** etc., vigorously, intensely). **10.** (In proverbial or joc. pseudo-proverbial phrs., emphasizing vbs.) *blush like a peony, drink like a fish, fit like a glove, get on like a house on fire, smoke* (i.e. tobacco) *like a chimney, spread like wildfire, swear like a trooper, swim like a duck*; *hate* person etc. *like poison, scatter them like chaff.* **11.** *adv.* (arch. or colloq.) Likely (cf. sense 7). **12.** (arch.) **~ as,** in the same manner as. **13.** (vulg.) So to speak (*by way of argument, like*). **14.** *conj.* (colloq.) As (*cannot do it like you do*; *the snow is falling like in January*); *as if (*ate like he had starved for days*); **tell it ~ it is,** give the facts. **15.** *n.* Counterpart, equal, like thing or person, (*mix with your likes*; *shall not see his like again*; *did you ever see the like of it?*; *compare like with like*); **the ~s of me,** (colloq.) persons so humble as I; **the ~s of you,** (colloq.) persons so distinguished as you. **16.** (Golf). *The* stroke that equalizes number of strokes played by each side. **17.** (ellipt. use of *a.*; *pl.* same). Thing(s) of the same kind (*will never do the like again*); **and the ~,** and similar things, et cetera, (*music, painting, and the like*); **or the ~,** or other thing(s) of the same kind. [ME *līc, līk,* shortened form (= ON *líkr*) of OE *gelīc* = OS *gelīc,* OHG *gilīh,* ON *glíkr,* Goth. *galeiks* f. Gmc **galīkaz*; see Y-, LICH]

līke[2] *v.t.*, & *n.* **1.** *v.t.* (arch. or joc.) Be pleasing to (usu. impers.: *it likes me not, well,* etc.). **2.** Find agreeable, congenial, or satisfactory, feel attracted by, wish for, (*I like you, the offer, his visits,* (iron.) *his impudence* or *that, her to be within reach, to see* or *seeing them now and then*; *do not like such subjects discussed*; *should* (*very*) *much like to come, like you to come*; *should like time to consider it*); **should ~ to know** or **see,** (iron.) think you will find it hard to tell me, am not likely to see; **how do you ~ it?**, do you like it much or little or dislike it?; hence ~'ABLE (-ka-) *a.* **3. If you ~** (expr. consent to request: *I will come if you like, you may come if you like*, or limited assent: *I am* shy *if you like*, i.e. but not misanthropic, or emphatic selection: I *am shy if you like*, i.e. but someone else is not). **4.** *n.* (usu. in *pl.*) Liking(s), predilection(s) (esp. *likes and dislikes*). [OE *līcian*, = OS *līkon*, OHG *līhhēn*, ON *líka*, Goth. *leikan* f. Gmc ***līkōjan* (**līkam*; see LICH)]

-līke *suf.* forming *adjs.* f. *ns.*, w. sense 'similar to' (*godlike, ladylike, plumbago-like, shell-like*). [f. LIKE[1]]

lī'kelihood (-kl-) *n.* Being likely (**in all ~**, very probably). [ME, f. foll. + -HOOD]

lī'kelȳ (-klĭ) *a.* & *adv.* **1.** *a.* Such as might well happen, or be or prove true, or turn out to be the thing specified, probable, (*a likely story*, often iron.; *it is not likely* (*that*) *he will come*; *his most likely destination is London*). **2.** To be reasonably expected *to* (*he* or *this is* or *was not likely to come* or *happen*); promising, apparently suitable for purpose or *to* do or be, capable-looking, (*called at every likely house*; *six likely young fellows*; *the likeliest place for smugglers* or *to find him*). **3.** *adv.* Probably (*more* or *most* or *quite* or *very likely*). **4. As ~ as not,** with equal chances of happening etc. or not; **not ~!**, (colloq.) that is quite impossible. **5.** Hence **lī'kelĭ**NESS (-kl-) *n.* [ME, f. ON *líkligr* (as LIKE[1], -LY[1])]

lī'ken *v.t.* Find or point out resemblance in (thing or person) *to*. [ME, f. LIKE[1] + -EN[6]]

lī'kenėss (-kn-) *n.* Being like, resemblance (*between, to*); semblance, guise, form (*in the likeness of*); representation, copy, portrait (**take** person's **~**, portray him). [OE *gelīknes* (as LIKE[1], -NESS)]

lī'kewise (-kwīz) *adv.* Also, moreover, too; **do ~**, act similarly. [for *in like wise*]

lī'kĭng *n.* What one likes, one's taste (*is it to your liking?*); regard, fondness, taste, fancy, *for* (*have a liking for him, for precise statements*; *no liking for flattery*). [OE *līcung* (as LIKE[2], -ING[1])]

lī'lac *n.* & *a.* **1.** *n.* Shrub of genus *Syringa*, esp. *S. vulgaris* with fragrant pale pinkish-violet, or white, blossoms. **2.** *a.* & *n.* (Of) pale pinkish-violet colour. [obs. F f. Sp., f. Arab. *līlāk* f. Pers. *līlak* var. of *nīlak* bluish (*nīl* blue)]

lĭlĭā'ceous (-shus) *a.* Of the lily family Liliaceae; lily-like. [f. LL *liliaceus* f. L *lilium* lily; see -ACEOUS]

lĭllĭpū'tian (-shan) *a.* & *n.* Diminutive (person or thing). [f. *Lilliput* in Swift's 'Gulliver's Travels' + -IAN]

lĭlt *v.* & *n.* (Sc. or literary). **1.** *v.t.* & *i.* Sing or speak merrily or rhythmically. **2.** *n.* (Song with) marked rhythmical cadence or swing; light springing gait. [ME *lilte, lülte*, of unkn. orig.]

lĭ'lȳ *n.* **1.** (Flower of) bulbous herb of genus *Lilium* bearing large showy white or reddish or purplish often spotted flowers on tall slender stem, esp. *L. candidum*, the white or madonna lily; plant of family Liliaceae with similar flowers; **gild the ~**, try to improve what is already quite satisfactory; **~ of the valley,** spring herb with two large leaves and racemes of white bell-shaped fragrant flowers; WATER[1]-*-lily*. **2.** Person or thing of special whiteness or purity (**lilies and roses,** fair complexion); heraldic fleur-de-lis (**the lilies,** arms of old French monarchy, Bourbon dynasty). **3.** (*attrib.*) Delicately white (*lily maid, hand*, etc.); pallid. **4. ~-iron,** harpoon with detachable head for killing swordfish; **~-livered,** cowardly; **~-pad,** floating leaf of water-lily; **~-white** (as a lily). **5.** Hence **lĭ'lĭ**ED[2] (-lĭd) *a.* [OE *lilie* f. L *lilium* prob. f. Gk *leirion*]

lī'ma (lē'-) *n.* **~ (bean)**, (flat white seed of) *Phaseolus limensis* of tropical America. [f. *L~* in Peru]

lĭmb[1] (-m) *n.*, & *v.t.* **1.** *n.* Leg, arm, or wing; *escape* **with life and ~**, without grave injury; **tear ~ from ~**, completely dismember with violence. **2.** (Orig. **~ of the devil** or **Satan**) mischievous child; **~ of the law,** lawyer, policeman, etc. **3.** Main branch of tree (**out on a ~**, (fig.) isolated, stranded, at a disadvantage); one of four branches of cross; clause of sentence; spur of mountain. **4.** Hence (-)~ED[2] (-md), ~'LESS, *adjs.* **5.** *v.t.* Dismember (body). [OE *lim*, = ON *limr*, prob. f. Gmc ***li-* as in dial. *lith*]

lĭmb[2] (-m) *n.* Graduated edge of quadrant etc.; edge (*eastern, lower*, etc., *limb*) of sun, moon, etc.; broad part of petal, sepal, or leaf. [f. F *limbe* or f. L *limbus* hem, border]

lĭ'mbĕck. Var. (arch.) of ALEMBIC.

lĭ'mber[1] *n.*, & *v.t.* **1.** *n.* Detachable front of gun-carriage (two wheels, axle, pole, and ammunition-box as seat). **2.** *v.t.* **~ (up)**, attach limber to (gun), fasten together two parts of (gun-carriage, or abs.). [ME *limo(u)r*, app. rel. to med. L *limonarius* (*limo -onis* shaft); for *-b-* cf. *slumber*]

lĭ'mber[2] *n.* (Naut.) Gutter on either side of keelson for drainage to pump-well. [f. F *lumière* light, hole, limber, f. Rom. ***luminaria* f. pl. of L *luminare* lamp (LUMEN)]

lĭ'mber[3] *a.*, & *v.t.* **1.** *a.* Flexible; lithe, nimble. **2.** *v.t.* **~ (up)**, make limber (person, body etc., or abs.). [perh. f. LIMBER[1], w. ref. to movement of shafts]

lĭ'mbō *n.* (*pl.* **~s**). Region on border of hell, supposed abode of pre-Christian righteous persons and unbaptized infants; prison, confinement; condition of neglect or oblivion. [ME, f. med. L phr. *in limbo*, f. *limbus* (see LIMB[2])]

Lĭ'mbûrger (-g-) *n.* Soft white cheese with characteristic strong smell, orig. made in Limburg. [Du., f. *Limburg* in Belgium; see -ER[1]]

līme[1] *n.*, & *v.t.* **1.** *n.* **Bir'd~**, (arch.) **~**, sticky substance made from holly bark and spread on twigs to catch small birds. **2. (Qui'ck)~**, white caustic alkaline earth (calcium oxide) got by heating limestone etc. and used for making mortar, as fertilizer, etc.; **slaked ~**, this after combination with water, calcium hydroxide; hence ~'LESS (-ml-), **lī'm**Y[2], *adjs.* **3. ~-burner,** maker of lime; **~-kiln** (for heating limestone); **~'light,** intense white light got by heating cylinder of lime in oxyhydrogen flame; *the ~light*, (fig., w. ref. to use in theatre) full glare of publicity; **~-pit** (for steeping hides to remove hair); **~'stone,** rock composed mainly of calcium carbonate; **~-twig** (smeared with birdlime); **~-wash,** mixture of lime and water for coating walls; **~ water,** solution of calcium hydroxide as antacid or to detect carbon dioxide by white precipitate of calcium carbonate. **4.** *v.t.* Smear (twigs), catch (bird), with birdlime; trap as if with birdlime; treat, dress (land), with lime; steep (skins) in lime and water; bleach (wood) by treating with lime. [OE *līm*, = MDu., OHG *līm*, ON *lím* f. Gmc ***līm-* cogn. w. **laim-* LOAM]

līme[2] *n.* Round fruit of tree *Citrus medica*, like lemon but smaller and more acid; **~-juice** (used as drink and esp. as antiscorbutic); ***~-juicer,** (sl.) British person esp. sailor (also ***lī'mey**) or ship [because use of lime-juice was enforced in British Navy]. [F, f. mod. Prov. *limo*, Sp. *lima* f. Arab. *līma*; cf. LEMON[1]]

līme[3] *n.* **~(-tree)**, ornamental tree of genus *Tilia* esp. *T. europaea* with heart-shaped leaves and small fragrant yellowish blossom. [alt. of *line* = *lind*; see LINDEN]

lī'mĕn *n.* (Psych.) = THRESHOLD; hence **lī'mĭn-**

AL *a.* [L *limen liminis* = threshold, representing G *schwelle*]

lĭ'merĭck *n.* Kind of humorous verse, esp. five--line form often epigrammatic or indecent, with rhymes *aabba* (popularized by Edward Lear's nursery rhymes). [said to be f. chorus 'Will you come up to Limerick?' sung after extempore verses contributed by each member of party, f. *L*~ in Ireland]

‖**lī'me-wort,** ‖**lĭ'mpwort,** (-ĕrt) *n.* = BROOK¹-*lime*. [f. **lime*, **lempe*, OE *hleomece*, + WORT]

***lī'mey** *n.* See LIME².

lĭ'mĭt¹ *n.* Bounding line, terminal point (**upper, lower,** ~, largest and smallest possible or permissible amount); line or point that may not or cannot be passed (**within ~s,** to some extent but not unrestrictedly; **without** ~, unlimited(ly); **is the** ~, (sl.) is the last straw, intolerable, etc.; ***off ~s,** out of bounds); (Math.) quantity which function or sum of series can be made to approach as closely as desired; ~ **man** (receiving longest start allowed in handicap, opp. *scratch*); hence ~LESS *a.* [ME, f. L *limes limitis* frontier]

lĭ'mĭt² *v.t.* Confine within limits, set (usu. non--material) bounds to, restrict *to*; serve as limit to; (in *p.p.*) few or scanty; ‖*limited* (LIABILITY) *company*; **~ed edition** (with limited number of copies); **~ed monarchy** etc. (subject to constitutional restrictions, opp. *absolute*); ***~ed (train)**, fast train with limited accommodation and stops; so ~ATIVE *a.* [ME, f. OF *limiter*, or f. L *limitare* (as prec.)]

lĭ'mĭtarȳ *a.* Subject to restriction; of, on, serving as limit. [f., or f. L *limitaris* as, LIMIT¹ + -ARY²]

lĭ'mĭtā'tion *n.* Limiting; limited condition, disability or inability, (**has his ~s,** is untalented in some directions); limiting rule or circumstance; legally specified period beyond which action cannot be brought, estate or law is not to continue, etc., (**statute of ~s,** any statute that fixes such period). [ME, f. L *limitatio* (as LIMIT²; see -ATION)]

lĭ'mĭtrōphe *a.* (Of district etc.) on frontier, adjacent *to*. [F, f. LL *limitrophus* f. L *limes* limit + Gk *-trophos* -feeding, orig. of lands set apart for support of frontier troops]

lĭmn (-m) *v.t.* (arch. or literary). Paint (picture); depict, portray; hence **lĭ'mn**ER¹ *n.* [f. obs. *lumine* illuminate (MSS.), f. OF *luminer* f. L *luminare* (LUMEN)]

lĭmnŏ'log|ȳ *n.* Study of physical phenomena of lakes and other fresh waters; hence **lĭmnolŏ'-**GICAL *a.*, ~IST (3) *n.* [f. Gk *limnē* lake + -o- + -LOGY]

lĭ'mousine (-ōōzēn) *n.* Motor car with enclosed body and partition behind driver; luxurious motor car. [F, orig. caped cloak worn in former French province of *Limousin*]

lĭmp¹ *v.i.*, & *n.* **1.** *v.i.* Walk lamely, (of verse) halt; (of damaged ship, aircraft, etc.) proceed slowly or with difficulty. **2.** *n.* Lame walk. [cogn. w. OE *lemp-healt* lame, MHG *limpfen* limp, f. WG **lamp-* f. IE **lomb-*]

lĭmp² *a.* Not stiff, flexible, (of bookbinding) not stiffened with millboard; (fig.) lacking energy; hence ~'LY² *adv.*, ~'NESS *n.* [18th c., of unkn. orig., perh. rel. to prec., w. sense 'hanging loose']

lĭ'mpėt *n.* Marine gastropod mollusc with shallow conical shell sticking tightly to rocks; (fig.) person, esp. State employee, who clings to office; ~ **mine** (attached to ship's hull and exploding after set time). [OE *lempedu* f. med. L *lampreda* limpet, LAMPREY]

lĭ'mpĭd *a.* (Of liquid, atmosphere, eyes, literary style) pellucid, clear, not turbid; hence or cogn. ~LY² *adv.*, ~ITY (-ĭ'd-), ~NESS, *ns.* [f. F *limpide* or f. L *limpidus*, perh. cogn. w. LYMPH]

lĭ'mpkĭn *n.* Wading-bird of genus *Aramus*, intermediate between crane and rail. [f. LIMP¹ + -KIN, from its movements]

‖**limpwort.** See LIME-WORT.

lĭ'mūl|us *n.* (*pl.* ~**i** *pr.* -ī). = KING¹-*crab* (1). [mod. L, f. L *limulus* dim. of *limus* askew]

lī'mȳ. See LIME¹.

lī'nage *n.* Number of lines in printed matter; payment according to this. [f. LINE² + -AGE]

lĭ'nchpĭn *n.* Pin passed through axle-end to keep wheel in place; (fig.) element or person vital to an organization etc. [f. ME *linch* f. OE *lynis*, = OS *lunisa*, + PIN¹]

Lĭ'ncoln (-ngkon) *n.* ~ **green,** bright green cloth made at Lincoln, formerly worn by outlaws etc. in Sherwood Forest. [~ in England]

lĭncrŭ'sta (-n-k-) *n.* Wallpaper covered with embossed linoleum. [f. L *linum* flax + *crusta* rind]

Lincs. *abbr.* Lincolnshire.

lĭ'nctus *n.* Medicine to be licked up; soothing syrupy cough-mixture. [L (*lingere* lick)]

lĭ'ndāne *n.* Colourless crystalline isomer of benzene hexachloride used as insecticide. [f. T. van der *Linden*, Du. chemist b. 1884 + -ANE]

lĭ'nden *n.* Lime-tree. [orig. a., f. OE *lind* lime-tree (= OHG *linta*, ON *lind*), + -EN⁵; cf. LIME³]

līne¹ *n.* Fine long flax separated from the tow by hackling. [OE *līn*, = OS, OHG, ON *līn*, Goth. *lein* f. Gmc **līnam*, cogn. w. or f. L *linum* flax]

līne² *n.* **1.** Piece of rope (esp. Naut., e.g. for sounding; so prob. **hard ~s,** bad luck, hardship); = CLOTHES-*line*. **2.** Wire or cable for telegraph or telephone, connection by this (HOLD¹ *the line*; *the line is bad*; PARTY¹ *line*); **~'man** (employed to keep such wire etc. in repair). **3.** Cord bearing fish-hook(s); **~-fishing** (opp. *net-fishing*); HOOK¹, *line, and sinker*; **give** person ~ **enough,** let him go his own way for a time in order to secure or detect him later. **4.** Cord for measuring, levelling, etc. (PLUMB¹-*line*); **by rule and** ~, with precision. **5.** (in *pl.*) One's lot in life [Ps. 16:6, w. ref. to marking out land]; *reins for horse etc. **6.** Long narrow mark traced on surface; use of these in draughtsmanship (*boldness, purity, of line*; *translate life* etc. *into line and colour*); **~-drawing** (done with pen or pencil); **~-engraving** (done with incised lines, opp. *etching* and *mezzotint*); **~-work** (with pen or pencil, not wash etc.); ~ **of beauty,** line with two opposite curves like elongated S. **7.** One of the very narrow horizontal sections in which televised scenes are photographed and reproduced. **8.** Narrow range of spectrum that is noticeably brighter or darker than adjacent parts. **9.** (Games). Mark limiting court or ground or special parts of them. **10.** Thing resembling traced mark, band of colour, seam, furrow, wrinkle (~ **of life, fortune,** etc., folds in palm of hand regarded as significant in palmistry). **11.** (Math.) Straight or curved continuous extent of length without breadth; track of moving point. **12.** Curve connecting all points having specified common property; **the L~**, the equator; *line* SQUALL; ~ **of force,** (Phys.) curve whose direction at each point is that of electric etc. force there. **13.** Straight line; *line of* FIRE¹; **in** ~, so as to form a straight line (*with*); *picture* **hung on the** ~, exhibited with its centre about level with spectator's eye; ~ **of sight** or **vision** (along which observer looks). **14.** Contour, outline, lineament (*the savage lines of his mouth*); shape to which garment is designed; (in *pl.*) plan or draft (esp. of ship in horizontal, vertical, and oblique sections) or manner of procedure (*on conservative, political, the same*, etc., *lines*; *on the lines laid down by* person). **15.** (As measure) $\frac{1}{12}$ inch. **16.**

Limit, boundary, (*dividing line*); **above the ~,** (Bridge) not scoring towards game, (Econ.) relating to current expenditure; DRAW[1] *the line*; **on the ~,** (1) not clearly one thing or the other, (2) offered without reserve (*put* or *lay on the line*). **17.** Row of persons or things; **come, bring, into ~,** agree or conform or co-operate, induce to do so; **in ~ for,** likely to get; **in ~ with,** in accordance with; **out of ~,** discordant; ***stand in ~,** form queue; TOE *the line*. **18.** (Mil.) Connected series of field-works (esp. in *pl.*, of defences facing enemy); ||row of tents or huts in camp; **up the ~,** to the battle-front. **19.** (Naut.) **~ abreast,** number of parallel ships ranged on line crossing keels at right angles; **~ ahead,** ships following in a string; **~ (of battle),** ships drawn up in battle array. **20.** (Mil.) Double row (front and rear ranks) of men ranged side by side, arrangement of companies side by side (opp. *column*; *drawn up in, form, wheel into, line*); **all along the ~,** at every point, (lit., or fig. of success etc.). **21. The ~,** regular and numbered army regiments (not auxiliary forces or ||Guards). **22.** *Group of football players forming line before scrimmage (**~'man,** member of this). **23.** Row of words in page or newspaper column (READ *between the lines*); ||(in *pl.*) = MARRIAGE *lines*; **~-filling,** flourish or ornament in blank space at end of line in MS.; **~-printer,** machine for printing results from computer etc. a line at a time. **24.** Short letter (*just a line to tell you the news*). **25.** Single verse of poetry; (in *pl.*) piece of poetry (often *upon* subject or *to* person); ||(in *pl.*) specified amount (*100* etc. *lines*) of verse, repeated admonition, etc., to be written out as school punishment; (in *pl.*) words of actor's part. **26.** Series or regular succession of steamers, buses, aircraft, etc., plying between certain places; company conducting this (*shipping line*; *airline*). **27.** Connected series of persons or things following one another in time (*can show a long line of heroes*), esp. several generations of family (*male, female, direct,* etc., *line*); family, lineage, stock (*comes of a good line*). **28.** Direction, course, track, (*line of* MARCH[4], *communication,* etc.; ASSEMBLY *line*). **29.** (Railways). Single track of rails (**up, down, ~,** for UP, DOWN[5], trains); one branch of system (*main, branch, loop, line*) or whole system under one management; **the end of the ~,** (fig.) point at which further effort becomes fruitless. **30.** Course followed esp. in riding to hounds (*take, keep to,* one's *own line*; often also fig.; **get a ~ on,** (colloq.) learn something about; *line of least* RESISTANCE). **31.** Course of procedure, conduct, thought, etc., (HARD *line*; PARTY[1] *line*). **32.** Department of activity, province, branch of business, (**in the ~ of** *duty* etc., as a proper part of; *something* **in, out of,** one's **~,** that interests or concerns one, or not; SHOOT[1] *a line*). **33.** (Commerce.) Class of goods; order for or stock of this. [ME *li(g)ne* f. OF *ligne* f. Rom. **linja* f. L *linea* (*linum* flax), & f. OE *līne* rope, series, = OHG, ON *līna*, f. Gmc f. L *linea*]

line[3] *v.* **1.** *v.t.* Mark *in, off, out,* with lines on paper etc.; cover with lines (*a face lined with pain*). **2.** Draw (persons or things) *up* in line (*with*). **3.** *v.t.* & *i.* Spread *out* in line, come *up* to line. **4.** *v.t.* Post troops etc. along (road, hedge, etc.), (of troops) form open or close line along (pass etc.), (of persons or things) stand at fairly short intervals along (street, wall, etc.). **5. ~-out,** (Rugby Footb.) parallel lines of opposing forwards at right angles to touch-line when ball is thrown in; **~-up,** line of persons for inspection, arrangement of persons in team etc. [ME, f. prec.]

līne[4] *v.t.* Apply layer of (usu. different) material to inside of (garment, box, vessel, bag, etc.); fill (purse, pocket, stomach, etc.); serve as lining for; hence **lī'ning**[1] (2, 4) *n.* (*every cloud has a* SILVER[1] *lining*). [ME, f. LINE[1], w. ref. to use of linen for linings]

line[5] *v.t.* (Of dog, wolf, etc.) copulate with (bitch). [ME, f. OF *ligner*]

lĭ'nėage *n.* Lineal descent, ancestry, pedigree. [ME f. OF *li(g)nage* f. Rom. **lineaticum* f. L *linea* LINE[2]; see -AGE]

lĭ'nėal *a.* In the direct line of descent or ancestry (opp. *collateral*); of or in line(s), linear; hence **~LY**[2] *adv.* [ME f. OF, f. LL *linealis* (as LINE[2]; see -AL)]

lĭ'nėament *n.* (usu. in *pl.*) Distinctive feature or characteristic, esp. feature of face. [ME, f. L *lineamentum* (*lineare* make straight f. *linea* LINE[2]); see -MENT]

lĭ'nėar *a.* **1.** Of or in line(s) (*linear perspective*); of length (*linear extent*). **2.** (Math. & Phys.) Involving one dimension only; **~ accelerator** (in which particles travel in straight lines, not in closed orbits); **~ equation** (of first degree); hence **~IZE** (3) *v.t.* **3.** Long, narrow, and of uniform breadth. **4.** (Paint.) Using clear outlines, expressed in lines rather than masses. **5. L~ A, B,** two related forms of ancient writing discovered in Crete and Greece. **6.** Hence **~ITY** (-ă'r-) *n.*, **~LY**[2] *adv.* [f. L *linearis* (*linea* LINE[2]; see -AR[2])]

lĭnėā'tion *n.* Drawing of, marking with, arrangement of, lines. [ME, f. L *lineatio* (*lineare*; see LINEAMENT, -ATION)]

lĭ'nėn *a.* & *n.* **1.** *a.* Made of flax (*linen cloth*). **2.** *n.* Cloth woven from flax; particular kind of this; (collect.) shirts, sheets, cloths, etc., of linen, calico, etc., (**wash** one's **dirty ~ at home, in public,** keep, not keep, quiet about domestic quarrels etc.); undergarments; sheets and pillowcases; table-linen. **3.** ||**~-draper,** dealer in linen, calico, etc.; **~fold,** carved or moulded ornament representing a fold or scroll of linen. [OE *linen*, = OS, OHG *linin* f. WG (as LINE[1]; see -EN[5])]

lī'ner[1] *n.* In vbl senses; removable metal lining to avoid wear and tear in machinery etc. [f. LINE[4] + -ER[1]]

lī'ner[2] *n.* Ship, usu. steamer, belonging to line of passenger ships; aircraft belonging to a regular line, used esp. for passenger transport, air liner; train belonging to regular line. [f. LINE[2] 26 + -ER[1]]

lī'nes|man (-nz-) *n.* (*pl.* **~men**). ||Soldier of line regiment; (Lawn Tennis, Footb.) official assisting umpire or referee esp. by deciding whether or where ball touches or crosses line; ||man employed to test safety of railway lines; = *lineman* (LINE[2] 2). [f. LINE[2] + 's 1 + MAN[1]]

lĭng[1] *n.* Long slender N. Eur. sea-fish (*Molva molva*) used (usu. cured) for food. [ME *leng(e)*, prob. f. MDu.; cogn. w. LONG[1]]

lĭng[2] *n.* Heather of various species, esp. *Calluna vulgaris*; hence **~'Y**[2] *a.* [ME f. ON *lyng*]

-lĭng[1] *suf.* forming *ns.* **1.** Denoting person or thing connected with (*hireling, nursling, sapling*) or having the property of being (*grayling, underling*) or undergoing (*starveling*). **2.** Denoting diminutive (*codling, duckling*), often derog. (*lordling*). [OE, f. as -LE 1 + -ING[3]; sense 2 f. ON]

-lĭng[2] *suf.* forming *advs.* & *adjs.* (*darkling, grovelling*); cf. -LONG. [OE, f. Gmc **ling-* extend]

lĭ'nga(m) (-ngg-) *n.* Phallus (esp. as symbol of Siva). [Skr. *lingam*, lit. 'mark']

lĭ'nger (-ngg-) *v.* **1.** *v.i.* Put off departure esp. because of reluctance to go; stay about, not depart or arrive at expected or right time; dally *round* place or *over* or (*up*)*on* subject; (of invalid or moribund custom) drag *on* a feeble existence; be protracted (*lingering disease, agonies*); be tardy, delay. **2.** *v.t.* ~ (**out**), pass (time) slowly; throw (time) *away* in delays. **3.** Hence ~ER[1] *n.* [ME *lenger*, frequent. of *leng* f. OE *lengan*, = OHG *lengen* f. Gmc **langjan* lengthen (**lang*- LONG[1]); see -ER[5]]

li'ngerie (lă'ṅzherē) *n.* Women's underwear. [F (*linge* linen; see -ERY)]

li'ngō (-nggō) *n.* (*pl.* ~**es**). (derog. or joc.) Foreign language; vocabulary of special subject or class of people. [prob. f. Port. *lingoa* f. L *lingua* tongue]

lĭngua fră'nca (-nggwa) *n.* Mixture of Italian with French, Greek, Arabic, and Spanish, used in the Levant; any language serving as medium between different nations whose own languages are not the same; system providing mutual understanding. [It., = Frankish tongue]

li'ngual (-nggwal) *a.* **1.** (Anat.) Of the tongue. **2.** (Phonet.) Formed by the tongue; hence ~IZE (3) *v.t.* **3.** Of speech or languages. [f. med. L *lingualis* f. L *lingua* tongue; see -AL]

li'nguifŏrm (-nggw-) *a.* (Bot., Anat., & Zool.) Tongue-shaped. [f. L *lingua* tongue + -I- + -FORM]

li'nguĭst (-nggwĭst) *n.* Person skilled in foreign languages (*good, bad, no, linguist*) or in linguistics. [f. L *lingua* language + -IST]

lĭngui'st|ic (-nggwĭ'-) *a.* Of the study of languages; of language; hence ~ICALLY *adv.* [f. prec. + -IC]

lĭngui'stics (-nggwĭ'-) *n.* Science of language(s), esp. as regards nature and structure. [f. F *linguistique* or G *linguistik* (as prec.; see -ICS)]

li'nguo- (-nggwo) *comb. form.* Tongue, as: ~**de'ntal,** (of sound) made with tongue and teeth. [f. L *lingua* tongue + -O-]

||**li'nhay** (lĭ'nĭ) *n.* (dial.) Farm-shed or outbuilding open along front. [17th c., orig. unkn.; first element perh. f. LEAN[2]]

li'niment *n.* Embrocation, usu. made with oil. [f. LL *linimentum* f. L *linire* smear; see -MENT]

li'ning. See LINE[4].

lĭnk[1] *n.* & *v.* **1.** *n.* One ring or loop of chain; measure equal to 1/100 of surveying chain or 7·92 in.; = CUFF[1]-*link*; loop in knitting etc.; connecting part, thing or person that unites others, filler of gap, member of series (MISSING *link*); ~(**'man**), player between forwards and half-backs or strikers and backs in football etc., person providing continuity in broadcast programme. **2.** *v.t.* Connect, join, (things, persons) *together* or (thing, person) *to*; clasp (hands); hook (arm *in* or *through* another's, or arms). **3.** *v.i.* Attach oneself *on* or *in* to system, company, etc. **4.** ~ **up,** connect, combine; ~-*up* n., act or result of linking up. **5.** Hence ~'AGE (1, 3) *n.* [ME, f. ON **hlenkr* f. Gmc **hlankjaz*, cogn. w. LANK]

lĭnk[2] *n.* Torch of pitch and tow formerly used for lighting people along streets; ~**'boy,** ~**'man,** (employed to carry links). [16th c., perh. f. med. L *li(n)chinus* wick f. Gk *lukhnos* light]

lĭnks *n. pl.* **1.** (Sc.) Level or undulating sandy ground near sea-shore, with turf and coarse grass. **2.** (as *sing.* or *pl.*) Golf-course, esp. one resembling sense 1. [pl. of *link* 'rising ground' f. OE *hlinc* perh. cogn. w. LEAN[2]]

lĭnn *n.* (Sc.) Waterfall; pool below this; precipice, ravine. [f. Gael. *linne*]

Linn. *abbr.* (Biol.) Linnaeus.

Lĭnnae'an *a.* & *n.* (Follower) of Linnaeus or his system of classifying plants; **Linne'an Society,** English society publishing journals etc. on natural history. [f. *Linnaeus* latinized name of C. von *Linné*, Sw. naturalist d. 1778 + -AN]

li'nnĕt *n.* Common brown or grey finch (*Carduelis cannabina*); **green** ~, greenfinch. [f. OF *linette* (*lin* flax, f. its food)]

linn(e)y. Var. of LINHAY.

li'nō *n.* (*pl.* ~**s**). Linoleum; ~**cut,** (print made from) design cut in relief on block of linoleum. [abbr.]

lĭnō'lèum *n.* Floor-cloth of canvas with thick coat of oxidized linseed oil etc.; hence ~ED[2] (-md) *a.* [f. L *linum* flax + *oleum* oil]

li'notȳpe *n.* Machine for producing lines of words at one casting as substitute for type-setting with single types, used in printing newspapers. [= *line o' type*; P]

li'nsăng *n.* Civet-cat of genus *Linsang* in E. Indies or *Poiana* in Africa. [Jav.]

li'nseed *n.* Seed of flax; ~ **cake,** linseed (with the ~ **oil** pressed out for use in paint etc.) as cattle-food; ~ **meal,** ground linseed. [OE *līnsǣd* (as LINE[1], SEED)]

lĭnsey-wŏŏ'lsey (-z-; -zĭ) *n.* Dress material of coarse inferior wool woven on cotton warp (orig. of wool and flax); (fig.) strange medley, nonsense. [ME, f. *linsey* coarse linen, prob. f. *Lindsey* in Suffolk, + WOOL, w. jingling termination]

li'nstŏck *n.* (Hist.) Match-holder used to fire cannon. [earlier *lintstock* f. Du. *lontstok* (*lont* match, *stok* stick), w. assim. to LINT]

lĭnt *n.* Soft material for dressing wounds, made by ravelling or scraping linen cloth; fluff; (Sc.) flax; ~**-white,** flaxen in colour. [ME *lyn(n)et*, perh. f. OF *linette* linseed (*lin* flax; see LINE[1], -ET[1])]

li'ntel *n.* Horizontal timber or stone over door or other aperture; hence ~LED[2], *~ED[2], (-ld) *a.* [ME f. OF *lintel* threshold, f. Rom. **limitale* (cf. var. OF *lintier* f. **limitare*) by confus. w. LL *liminare* f. L *limen* threshold; see LIMIT[1], -LE 2]

***li'nter** *n.* Machine for removing short fibres from cotton seeds after ginning; (in *pl.*) these fibres. [f. LINT + -ER[1]]

li'nȳ *a.* Marked with lines; wrinkled; (Art) using line too much. [f. LINE[2] + -Y[2]]

li'on *n.* **1.** Large powerful tawny African and S. Asian (formerly also European) carnivorous mammal (*Felis leo*) with tufted tail and (in the male) flowing shaggy mane; ~ **in the way** or **path,** obstacle, esp. imaginary [Prov. 26:13]; ~**'s mouth,** perilous position; ~**'s provider,** (arch.) jackal (lit. or fig.); ~**'s share,** largest or best part. **2.** ~(**-heart**), courageous person (esp. as nickname of Richard I); ~**-hearted,** brave (and generous). **3.** (in *pl.*) Sights worth seeing in town etc. [from custom of showing country visitors the lions formerly kept in Tower of London]. **4.** Person of literary or other celebrity sought after to be shown off at social gatherings; ~**-hunter,** host or hostess depending much on such persons; hence ~'HOOD, ~'SHIP, *ns.* **5.** National emblem of Great Britain (**the British L**~, the nation personified; ~ **and unicorn,** supporters of British royal coat of arms; **twist the** ~**'s tail,** defy or insult Britain); representation of lion (esp. Her.). **6.** (*L*~). *The* zodiacal sign Leo. **7.** Hence ~ESS[1], ~ET[1], *ns.*, ~-LIKE *a.* [ME, f. AF *liun* f. L *leo -onis* f. Gk *leōn leontos*]

li'onize, -ise (-īz), *v.t.* **1.** (arch.) See or show the sights (see prec. 3) of (place). **2.** Treat (person) as celebrity, make a lion (see prec. 4) of. [f. LION + -IZE]

lĭp *n.*, & *v.t.* (**-pp-**). **1.** *n.* One of the fleshy parts forming edges of opening of mouth (*upper, lower* or *under, lip*); pink portion of this (*redden* one's *lips*); **bite** one's ~ (in vexation or to repress emotion, stifle laugh, etc.); **curl** one's ~ (in scorn); **escape** one's ~**s,** be uttered thoughtlessly; **hang** one's ~ (in humiliation); **hang on**

person's ~**s,** listen with rapt attention to all he says; **lick** or **smack** one's ~**s** (in enjoyment or anticipation of food, or fig.); **pass** one's ~**s,** be eaten, spoken, etc.; **stiff upper** ~, firmness or fortitude. **2.** (sl.) Saucy talk, impudence, (*none of your lip!*). **3.** Edge of cup, vessel, cavity, wound, etc., esp. part that is shaped for pouring from. **4.** (In *comb.*) From the lips only, professed, not heartfelt or sincere, (*lip-Christian, -worship*). **5.** ~**-deep,** superficial, insincere; ~**-language, -reading, -speaking,** use and interpretation of motions of lips to and by the deaf or when hearing is prevented by noise etc.; ~**-read** *v.t.* & *i.*, understand by, use, lip-reading; ~**'salve,** ointment for sore lips, (fig.) flattery; ~**-service** (proffered but not performed); ~**'stick,** (*n.*) stick of cosmetic for colouring lips, (*v.t.*) apply lipstick to. **6.** Hence (-)~PED[2] (-pt), ~'LESS, *adjs.* **7.** *v.t.* Touch with lips, apply lips to; (of water) just touch, lap; (Golf) hit ball just to edge of (hole), (of ball) reach edge of (hole) but fail to drop in. [OE *lippa*, = MLG, MDu. *lippe* f. Gmc **lipjon*, rel. to **lep*- f. IE **leb*-]

lī'pāse *n.* (Chem.) Enzyme able to decompose fats. [f. Gk *lipos* fat + -ASE]

lĭ'pĭd, lĭ'pīde, *n.* (Chem.) Fat or fatlike substance, e.g. ester of a higher aliphatic acid. [F *lipide* (as prec.; see -IDE)]

lĭpŏ'graphȳ *n.* Omission of letter(s) or word(s) in writing. [f. Gk *lip*- st. of *leipō* omit + -O- + -GRAPHY]

Lĭppĭza'ner (-tsah'-) *n.* Horse of fine white breed used esp. in displays of dressage. [G (*Lippiza* in Yugoslavia)]

lĭqu|ā'te *v.t.* Separate or purify (metals) by liquefying; hence ~A'TION *n.* [f. L *liquare* melt (cogn. w. LIQUOR) + -ATE[3]]

lĭ'quė|fȳ *v.t.* & *i.* Bring (solid or gas) or come into liquid condition; hence or cogn. ~FA'CIENT *a.* & *n.*, ~FA'CTION *n.*, ~**fă'ct**IVE, ~**fī**ABLE, *adjs.*, ~**fī**ER[1] (1, 2) *n.* [f. F *liquéfier* f. L *liquefacere* (*liquēre* be liquid; see -FY)]

lĭquĕ'scent *a.* Becoming, or apt to become, liquid. [f. L *liquescere* (as prec.; see -ESCENT)]

lĭqueur' (-kūr') *n.* Strong spirituous liquor sweetened and flavoured with aromatic substances and usu. drunk in small quantities after meals; mixture of sugar and alcohol or wines used to flavour champagne; ~ **brandy** (of special quality for drinking as liqueur); ~**-glass,** very small glass for liqueurs. [F, = LIQUOR]

lĭ'quid *a.* & *n.* **1.** (Substance that is) incompressible but offering no resistance to change of shape, neither solid nor gaseous, resembling water or oil in normal state; ~ **air, oxygen,** etc., (reduced to liquid state by intense cold); ~ **fire,** burning oil etc. projected from flame-thrower; ~ **measure,** (unit for) measurement of volume of liquids. **2.** *a.* Watery; having the transparency, translucence, or brightness, of pure water (*liquid lustre, eyes, sky, air, blue*). **3.** (Of sounds) flowing clear, fluent, pure, not grating or discordant, not guttural, vowel-like, (*blackbird's liquid notes; in his liquid Italian*). **4.** Not fixed, unstable, (*has very liquid convictions* or *principles*). **5.** (Of assets) easily converted into cash. **6.** Hence ~IZE (3) *v.t.*, ~LY[2] *adv.*, ~NESS *n.*; ~**īz**ER[1] *n.* machine used to make food into purée etc. **7.** *n.* (Phonet.) Sound denoted by one of the letters *l*, *r*, and occas. *m*, *n*. [ME, f. L *liquidus* (*liquēre* be liquid; see -ID[1])]

lĭquĭdă'mbar *n.* (Tree of genus *Liquidambar* yielding) resinous gum. [mod. L, app. f. L *liquidus* (see prec.) + med. L *ambar* amber]

lĭ'quĭd|āte *v.* **1.** *v.t.* Pay, clear off, (debt). **2.** Put an end to, suppress, get rid of (often by violent means). **3.** Wind up, ascertain liabilities and apportion assets of, (company, firm); hence ~**āt**OR *n.* **4.** *v.i.* (Of company) be liquidated. **5.** Hence ~A'TION *n.*; **go into** ~**ation,** (of company) have its affairs wound up, become bankrupt. [f. med. L *liquidare* make clear (as LIQUID) + -ATE[3]]

lĭquĭ'dĭtȳ *n.* State of being liquid; state of having liquid assets. [f. F *liquidité* or f. med. L *liquiditas* (as LIQUID, -ITY)]

lĭ'quĭdus *n.* ~ (**curve**), curve in graph of temperature and composition of a mixture, above which the substance is entirely liquid. [L (see LIQUID)]

lĭ'quor (-*ker*) *n.* & *v.* **1.** *n.* Liquid part of secretion or product of operation; liquid used as wash etc. **2.** Water used in brewing; liquid (usu. fermented or distilled) for drinking (MALT[1] *liquor*; SPIRITUOUS *liquor*; **in** ~, **the worse for** ~, more or less drunk). **3.** Water in which food has been boiled; (Pharm., *pr.* lī'kwôr) solution of specified drug in water (*liquor ammoniae* etc.). **4.** *v.t.* Dress (leather, shoes) with grease or oil; steep (malt etc.) in water. **5.** *v.t.* & *i.* (sl.) ~ (**up**), (cause to) drink large amount of alcoholic liquor. [ME f. OF *lic(o)ur*, f. L *liquor -oris* (*liquēre*; see LIQUID, -OR)]

lĭ'quorĭce (-*ker*-), **lĭ'corĭce,** *n.* (Black substance used in medicine and as sweetmeat made from) root of leguminous plant *Glycyrrhiza glabra*; the plant. [ME, f. AF *lycorys*, OF *licoresse* f. LL *liquiritia* f. Gk *glukurrhiza* (*glukus* sweet, *rhiza* root)]

lĭ'quorĭsh (-*ker*-) *a.* = LICKERISH; fond of, indicating fondness for, liquor; hence ~LY[2] *adv.*, ~NESS *n.* [var. of LICKERISH, misapplied]

lir'a (lēr'*a*) *n.* Italian monetary unit (*pl.* usu. **lire** *pr.* -ā); Turkish monetary unit. [It., f. Prov. *liura* f. L *libra* POUND[1] 2]

lisle (līl) *n.* ~ (**thread**), fine smooth cotton thread made orig. at Lille. [f. *L*~, former sp. of *Lille* in N.E. France]

lĭsp *v.* & *n.* **1.** *v.i.* Substitute sound like (th) or (dh) for sibilants in speaking; (of child) speak with imperfect pronunciation. **2.** *v.t.* ~ (**out**), say with a lisp. **3.** *n.* Lisping pronunciation; rippling of waters, rustling of leaves. [OE **wlispian* (*wlisp* a. lisping, = OHG *lisp* stammering, *lispen* to lisp; imit.)]

lĭ'ssom, lĭ'ssome, *a.* Lithe, supple, agile; hence ~NESS (-mn-) *n.* [contr. of **lithsom* (as LITHE, -SOME[1])]

lĭst[1] *n.*, & *v.t.* **1.** *n.* ||Selvage or edge of cloth, usu. of different material; such edges used as a material (*list slippers*). **2.** (in *pl.*) Palisades enclosing tilt-yard; (fig.) scene of contest (**enter the** ~**s against,** challenge or accept challenge of, usu. to controversy). **3.** Roll or catalogue of names, of persons or things belonging to a class, of articles with prices, of things to be done, etc.; **active** ~ (of officers in army or navy or air force liable to be called on for service); ||CIVIL, FREE[1], SICK[1]-, *list*; ~ **price** (as shown in published list). **4.** *v.t.* Enter in list; (in *p.p.*, of securities) approved for dealings on stock exchange; ||~**ed building** (included in official list of buildings with architectural or historical importance, and thus protected from demolition etc.). **5.** *v.t.* & *i.* (arch.) Enlist. [OE *līsta*, = OHG *līsta* f. Gmc **līstōn*; in sense 2 thr. OF *lisse*, in sense 3 thr. F *liste* w. sense 'strip of paper']

lĭst[2] *v.t.* (3 *sing. pres.* ~ *or* ~**'eth**; *past* ~ *or* ~**'ed**). (arch.) **1.** (*impers.*) Be pleasing to (*shall do what him listeth; did as him list*). **2.** Desire, choose, (*to* do, or abs.; *ye who list to hear; wind bloweth where it listeth*). [OE *lystan*, = OS *lustian*, OHG *lusten*, ON *lysta* f. Gmc **lustjan* (**lust*-; cf. LUST)]

lĭst[3] *n.*, & *v.i.* Lean(ing) over to one side (of ship, owing to leak, shifting cargo, subsidence, etc.; cf. HEEL³; also of building, fence, etc.). [17th c., of unkn. orig.]

list⁴ *v.i.* & *t.* (arch.) Listen (to), hear. [OE *hlystan* (*hlyst* sense of hearing, = OS, ON *hlust* f. Gmc **hlustiz* f. IE **klustis* f. **klu-* hear)]

lĭ'sten (-sn) *v.i.* Make effort to hear something, hear with attention person speaking; give attention with ear *to* (person or sound or story); yield *to* (person furnishing) temptation or request; ~ **for,** seek to hear (sound etc.) by waiting alertly for it; ~ **in,** tap telephonic communication, use radio receiving set (*to* transmitter); **~ing-post,** point near enemy's lines for detecting his movements by sound, (fig.) place for gathering of information from reports etc.; hence ~ER¹ (-sn-) *n.*, (1) one who listens (**good ~er,** one who habitually listens with interest or sympathy), (2) person receiving broadcast radio programmes. [OE *hlysnan*, = MHG *lüsenen* f. WG **hlusinōjan* (**hlus-*; see prec.)]

***lĭ'ster** *n.* Plough with double mould-board. [f. *list* prepare land for crop + -ER¹]

lĭ'sting *n.* (Drawing up of) LIST¹ 3; ‖selvage (see LIST¹ 1). [f. LIST¹ + -ING¹]

lĭ'stlėss *a.* Languid, indifferent, uninterested, (such that one is) disinclined for exertion; hence ~LY² *adv.*, ~NESS *n.* [ME, f. obs. *list* inclination f. LIST², + -LESS]

lĭt. See LIGHT³,⁵.

lĭ'tanў *n.* Series of petitions for use in church services or processions recited by clergy and responded to usu. in recurring formula(s) by people; **the L~**, that contained in the Book of Common Prayer; **~-desk, -stool,** (at which reciter of litany kneels). [ME f. OF *letanie*, f. eccl. L f. Gk *litaneia* prayer (*litē* supplication)]

litchi' (lēchē') *n.* (Sweetish pulpy shelled fruit of) tree *Litchi chinensis*, orig. from China. [f. Chin. *li-chi*]

-līte *suf.* forming names of minerals (*rhyolite, zeolite*). [F, f. Gk *lithos* stone]

***liter.** See LITRE.

lĭ'teracў *n.* Ability to read and write. [f. LITERATE + -CY, after *illiteracy*]

‖lĭterae hūmānĭōr'ēs (-z) *n.* = POLITE letters (esp. as name of school of classics and philosophy at Oxford). [L, = the more humane studies]

lĭ'teral *a.* & *n.* **1.** *a.* Of, in, expressed by, letter(s) of alphabet; (Alg.) not numerical; ~ **error,** misprint of a letter. **2.** Following the letter, text, or exact or original words (*literal translation, transcript*, etc.); hence ~ISM (4) *n.* **3.** Taking words in their usual or primary sense and applying the ordinary rules of grammar, without mysticism or allegory or metaphor, (*literal interpretation*; **I hear nothing in the ~ sense of the word,** with the ears as opp. other means of getting news); hence ~ISM (3), ~IST (2), *ns.*, ~IZE (3) *v.t.* **4.** ~(**-minded**), (of person) prosaic, matter-of-fact. **5.** So called without exaggeration (*literal extermination*); (colloq.) so called with some exaggeration (*a literal flood of pamphlets*). **6.** Hence ~ITY (-ă'l-), ~NESS, *ns.*, ~LY² *adv.* **7.** *n.* Literal error. [ME f. OF, or f. LL *litteralis* f. L (as LETTER; see -AL)]

lĭ'terar|ў *a.* **1.** Of, constituting, occupied with, literature or books and written composition esp. of the kind valued for quality of form; *literary* EXECUTOR; **~y history** of a thing, history of its treatment in literature; **~y man,** author, scholar; **~y property,** exclusive right of publication, books etc. subject to this. **2.** (Of word or idiom) uncolloquial, used chiefly by writers. **3.** Hence ~ĭLY² *adv.*, ~ĭNESS *n.* [f. L *litterarius* (as LETTER; see -ARY¹)]

lĭ'terate *a.* & *n.* **1.** (Person) able to read and write. **2.** *n.* ‖Man admitted to Anglican orders without university degree. [ME, f. L *litteratus* (as LETTER; see -ATE²]

lĭtera'tĭ (-ah'-) *n. pl.* Men of letters, the learned class. [L, pl. of *lit(t)eratus* (see prec.)]

literatim (lĭterā'tĭm; *or* -ah'-) *adv.* Letter for letter, textually, literally. [med. L]

lĭterā'tion *n.* Representation of sounds etc. by letter(s) of alphabet. [f. L (as LETTER) + -ATION]

lĭ'terātor *n.* = LITTÉRATEUR. [L, = teacher of ABC, grammarian (as LITERATE; see -OR)]

lĭ'terature (*or* -trĭcher) *n.* Literary production (*engaged in literature*); realm of letters, writings of country or period; writings whose value lies in beauty of form or emotional effect; *the* books etc. treating *of* a subject; (colloq.) printed matter; (arch.) acquaintance with books. [ME, = literary culture, f. L *litteratura* (as LITERATE; see -URE)]

-lĭth *suf.* denoting types of stone (*laccolith, monolith*). [f. Gk *lithos* stone]

lĭ'tharge *n.* Lead monoxide esp. in red form. [ME f. OF *litarge*, f. L f. Gk *litharguros* (*lithos* stone, *arguros* silver)]

līthe (-dh) *a.* Flexible, supple; hence ~'NESS (-dhn-) *n.*, ~'SOME¹ (-dhs-) *a.* [OE *līthe*, = OS *līthi*, OHG *lindi* soft, f. WG **linthja-* f. Gmc & IE **len-*]

lĭ'thĭa *n.* Lithium oxide; ~ **water** (containing lithium salts and used against gout). [mod. L, alt. of earlier *lithion* f. Gk neut. of *litheios* (*lithos* stone), after *soda* etc.]

lĭ'thĭc¹ *a.* Of stone; (Path.) of the STONE (sense 5). [f. Gk *lithikos* (as prec.; see -IC)]

lĭ'thĭc² *a.* (Chem.) Of lithium. [f. foll. + -IC]

lĭ'thĭum *n.* (Chem.) Soft silver-white metallic element, the lightest alkali metal. [f. LITHIA + -IUM]

lĭ'thō *n.* (*pl.* ~**s**), *a.*, & *v.t.* (colloq.) (Produce by) lithographic (process). [abbr.]

lĭ'tho- *comb. form.* Stone, esp. (1) Path. w. ref. to the STONE (sense 5), (2) Print. w. ref. to use of STONE (sense 4). [f. Gk *lithos* stone + -O-]

lĭ'thograph (-ahf) *n.*, & *v.t.* **1.** *n.* Lithographic print. **2.** *v.t.* Print by lithography; write or engrave on stone. [back form. f. foll.; see -GRAPH]

lĭthŏ'graphў *n.* Process of obtaining prints from stone or metal surface so treated that what is to be printed can be inked but the remaining area rejects ink; hence **lĭthŏ'**GRAPHER *n.*, **lĭtho**GRA'PHIC *a.* [f. G *lithographie* (as LITHO-, -GRAPHY)]

lĭthŏ'logў *n.* Science of the nature and composition of stones and rocks; hence **lĭtholŏ'g**ICAL *a.* [f. LITHO- + -LOGY]

lĭ'thophўte *n.* (Bot.) Plant that grows on stone. [f. LITHO- + -PHYTE]

lĭ'thopōne *n.* White pigment of zinc sulphide and barium sulphate. [f. LITHO- + Gk *ponos* work]

lĭ'tho|sphēre *n.* Earth's crust; solid earth (opp. hydrosphere and atmosphere); hence **~sphĕ'**RIC *a.* [f. LITHO- + SPHERE]

lĭthŏ'tom|ў *n.* Operation of cutting into bladder to remove stone; hence ~IST (1) *n.*, ~IZE (1) *v.t.* [f. LL f. Gk *lithotomia* (as LITHO-, -TOMY)]

lĭthŏ'trĭt|ў *n.* Operation of crushing stone in bladder into small particles that can be passed through urethra; hence ~IST (1) *n.*, ~IZE (1) *v.t.* [f. LITHO- + L *terere trit-* rub + -Y¹]

Lĭthūā'nĭan *a.* & *n.* (Native, inhabitant, or language) of Lithuania. [f. *Lithuania*, republic of U.S.S.R. + -AN]

lĭ'tĭg|āte *v.* **1.** *v.i.* Go to law, be party to lawsuit. **2.** *v.t.* Contest (point) at law; hence ~ABLE *a.* **3.** Hence ~ANT (1) *n.* & *a.*, ~A'TION *n.* [f. L *litigare* (*lis litis* lawsuit) + -ATE³]

lĭtĭ′gious (-jus) *a.* Given to litigation, fond of going to law; disputable at law, offering matter for lawsuit; of lawsuits; hence ~LY² *adv.*, ~NESS *n.* [ME, f. OF *litigieux* or f. L *litigiosus* (*litigium* litigation; cf. prec., -OUS)]

lĭ′tmus *n.* Blue colouring-matter got from lichens that is turned red by acid and restored to blue by alkali; **~-paper** (unsized and stained with litmus as test for acids or alkalis). [ME, f. ONorw. *litmosi* f. ON *litr* dye + *mosi* moss]

lĭ′totēs (-z) *n.* Ironical understatement, esp. expressing of an affirmative by the negative of its contrary (*no small* for *great*). [LL, f. Gk *litotēs* (*litos* plain, meagre)]

lĭ′tre, *li′ter, (lē′ter) *n.* Unit of capacity in metric system, volume of one kilogram of water under standard conditions, 1 cubic decimetre or about $1\frac{3}{4}$ pints. [F (*litron*, an obs. measure of capacity, f. med. L f. Gk *litra* Sicilian monetary unit)]

Litt. D. *abbr.* Doctor of Letters. [f. L *Litterarum Doctor*]

lĭ′tter *n.*, & *v.t.* **1.** *n.* Vehicle containing couch shut in by curtains and carried on men's shoulders or by beasts of burden; framework with couch for transporting sick and wounded. **2.** Straw, rushes, etc., as bedding esp. for animals; straw and dung of farmyard. **3.** Odds and ends, leavings, state of untidiness, disorderly accumulation of papers etc.; hence ~Y² *a.* **4.** The young animals brought forth at a birth. **5. ~-basket, -bin,** (for deposit of waste paper, etc.); ***~bug, ~-lout,** person who carelessly leaves refuse in street etc. **6.** *v.t.* **~ (down)**, provide (horse etc.) with litter as bed, spread litter or straw on (floor) or in (stable). **7.** (Of objects lying about, or of person *with* these) make (place) untidy; scatter and leave lying. **8.** Give birth to (whelps etc., or abs.). [ME, f. AF *litere*, OF *litiere* f. med. L *lectaria* f. L *lectus* bed; see -ER² (2)]

littérateur (lētĕrahtêr′) *n.* Literary man. [F]

lĭ′ttle *a.* (LESS, LESSER, **li′ttler**; LEAST, **li′ttlest**; *also* **smaller, smallest**), *n.*, & *adv.* (LESS, LEAST). **1.** *a.* Small (often with emotional implications not given by *small*; cf. GREAT), not great or big; working etc. on only a small scale (*the little shopkeeper is being put out of business by the supermarkets*); (as distinctive epithet) of smaller or smallest size etc. (*little* AUK, BEAR¹, FINGER, SLAM, *toe*); **~ Switzerland** etc. (small area reminiscent of). **2.** Young (*a little boy, girl, child*; **the ~ Joneses,** the Jones children; **~ man** or **woman,** boy or girl (esp. as joc. or affectionate *voc.*); **his, her, its, our, ~ ones,** children, cubs, etc.); younger (*little brother, sister*). **3.** As of a child, evoking tenderness, condescension, amusement, etc., (*her poor little efforts to please*; *we know his little ways*); *so that is* **your ~ game,** what you are hoping to do undetected; **the ~ woman,** (colloq.) one's wife. **4.** Short in stature, distance, or time, (*a little man*; *will go a little way with you*; *wait a little while*). **5.** Trivial, unimportant, (*exaggerates every little difficulty*); mean, paltry, contemptible, (*with the little cunning of little minds*; *you little sneak*). **6.** Not much (*gained little advantage from it*; *very little butter left*; *did little or no damage*; *has but little faith in it*). **7. A ~,** some though not much, even a small amount of, [prob. f. sense 10 w. ellipsis of *of*] (*give me a little butter*; *a little care would have prevented it*); **in ~,** on a small scale; **no ~,** considerable, a good deal of, (*took no little trouble over it*). **8. *~ dipper,** = *Little* BEAR¹; **~-ease,** (Hist.) prison-cell too small to stand or lie full-length in; **~ end,** smaller end of connecting-rod, attached to piston; *Little* ENGLANDER; **||~-go,** (arch.) first examination for B.A. degree at Cambridge or Oxford; ***L~ League,** baseball league for boys of 8–12; **~ magazine** (literary, usu. with experimental writing and in small format); **~ Mary,** (colloq.) the stomach; **L~ Masters,** group of 16th-c. German engravers, followers of Dürer, named from size of their prints; ******little* OLD 5; **the ~ people,** fairies; *Little* RUSSIAN. **9.** Hence ~NESS (-teln-) *n.* **10.** *n.* Not much, only a small amount, a mere trifle, (*got but, very, rather, little out of it*; *the little of his work that remains*; *did what little I could*; **~ or nothing,** hardly anything; *did* **not a ~** *for the cause*, much; THINK *little of*); *a* certain but no great amount (*knows a little of everything*; **a ~,** rather, somewhat; **not a ~,** extremely); (for a) short time or distance (*after, for, a little*; **~ by ~, by ~ and ~,** by degrees). **11.** *adv.* To a small extent only (*little-known authors*; *is little more than speculation*); not at all (*he little knows, thought*, etc.). [OE *lȳtel*, = OS *luttil*, OHG *luzzil* f. WG **luttila* f. Gmc **lut-*]

lĭ′ttoral *a.* & *n.* **1.** *a.* Of or on the shore. **2.** *n.* Region lying along the shore. [a. f. L *lit(t)oralis* (*litus -oris* shore; see -AL); n. thr. F, or It. *littorale*]

lĭtûr′g|ĭcal *a.* Of or related to liturgies or public worship; hence or cogn. **~ĭcal**LY² *adv.*, **~**ICS, **~ĭŏ′**LOGY, **lĭ′turg**IST (3), *ns.* [f. med. L f. Gk *leitourgikos* (as foll.; see -ICAL)]

lĭ′turgȳ *n.* **1.** Communion office of Orthodox Church. **2.** Form of public worship; set of formularies for this; *the* Book of Common Prayer. **3.** (Gk Ant.) Public office or duty performed gratuitously by rich Athenian. [f. F *liturgie* or f. LL f. Gk *leitourgia* public worship (*leitourgos* minister f. **leitos* public + *-ergos* performing)]

lĭ′vable. Var. of LIVEABLE.

līve¹ *attrib. a.* **1.** That is alive, living; (joc.) actual, not pretended or pictured or toy (*a real live burglar, steam-engine, mountain*); (of broadcast; also *pred.*) heard or seen during the occurrence of an event, not recorded or edited. **2.** Full of power, energy, or importance, not obsolete or exhausted, (*make the question a live issue*); glowing (*live coals*); (of shell, match, wire, etc.) unexploded, unkindled, charged with or carrying electricity; (of rock) not detached, seeming to form part of the earth's frame; (of wheel etc. in machinery) moving or imparting motion. **3.** *Live* BAIT²; **~ birth** (of living child, opp. *still birth*); **~ load,** weight of persons or goods in building or vehicle; **~-oak,** Amer. evergreen tree (*Quercus virginiana*); **~ steam** (direct from boiler); **~′stock,** animals kept or dealt in for use or profit; **~ weight** (of animal before being killed); **~ wire,** (fig.) highly energetic forceful person. [f. ALIVE]

lĭve² *v.* **1.** *v.i.* Be alive, have animal or vegetable life. **2.** Subsist (*up*)*on* (*lives on fruit*); depend for subsistence (*lives on his wife, on* or *off his wife's earnings*, etc.); (fig.) sustain one's position or repute (*up*)*on* (*lives on his reputation*), get livelihood *by* one's wits etc. or *by* doing; **~ on air,** (appear to) take no food; **~ and let ~,** condone others' failings so as to secure same treatment for oneself; *live from* HAND¹ *to mouth.* **3.** Conduct oneself (honestly, viciously, like a saint, etc.; **~ up to** one's **principles, faith,** etc., put them into practice; **~ up to** one's **promise, reputation,** etc., not fall short of it; **~ up to** one's **income** etc., spend it all). **4.** Arrange one's habits, expenditure, feeding, etc.; **~ in a small way** (cheaply and quietly); **~ out of a suitcase** etc. (keeping all one's belongings in it during temporary residence); **~ to oneself** (in isolation); **~ well** (on luxurious food). **5.** *v.t.* (w. cogn. obj.) Spend, pass, experience, (*live a virtuous*, DOUBLE^1, *life*; *he lived what he narrated*); **~ it up,** live gaily and extravagantly; **~ out,** survive. **6.** Wear *down* (scandal, prejudice, effect of past guilt) by blameless course of life. **7.** Express in one's life (*live a lie*). **8.** *v.i.* Enjoy life intensely or to the full (*you haven't lived till you've drunk champagne*). **9.** Continue alive, have one's life prolonged, (*patient cannot live*; *lived to regret his decision, to see his children's children*); **~ and learn,** continually discover new facts as one lives; **~ through,** survive, remain alive at the end of; **~ to,** survive and reach (*lived to a great age*); **long ~ the Queen!** (excl. of loyalty). **10.** (Of thing) survive (*his memory lives*); (of ship) escape destruction. **11.** Make one's permanent abode (||**~ in, out,** of shop-assistant or domestic servant residing on premises or not); spend daytime *in* room (*room does not seem to be lived in*); **~ together,** (esp. of man and woman not his wife) share dwelling-place; **~ with,** (1) share dwelling-place with (esp. as *live together*), (2) tolerate, find congenial. [OE *libban*, *lifian*, = OS *libbian*, OHG *lebēn*, ON *lifa*, Goth. *liban* f. Gmc **libh-* remain]

lĭ'veable (-va-) *a.* (Of house, room, climate, etc.) fit to live in; (of life) worth living; **~ (with)**, companionable, easy to live with. [f. prec. + -ABLE]

lĭ'velĭhood (-vl-) *n.* Means of living, sustenance. [OE *līflād* (*līf* LIFE, *lād* course; see LOAD^1), assim. to obs. *livelihood* liveliness]

lĭ'velŏng^1 (-vl-) *a.* (poet. or rhet.) Whole length of (**the ~ day, night, summer,** with implication of weariness or delight). [ME *lefe longe* (as LIEF, LONG^1), assim. to LIVE^2]

lĭ'velŏng^2 (-vl-) *n.* Orpine. [f. LIVE^2 + LONG^2]

lĭ'vel|y̆ (-vlĭ) *a.* Lifelike, realistic, (*a lively description*); full of life, vigorous, energetic, brisk, vivid, interesting, (*lively horse, dance, recollection, discussion*; **look ~,** move more quickly or energetically); (joc.) exciting, dangerous, difficult, (*police had a lively time*; *press is making it* or *things lively for them*); (of colour) bright; gay, vivacious; (of boat etc.) rising lightly to waves; hence **~ĭLY^2** *adv.*, **~ĭNESS** *n.* [OE *līflic* (as LIFE, -LY^1)]

lĭ'ven *v.t.* & *i.* (colloq.) **~ (up)**, brighten, cheer. [f. LIFE + -EN^6]

lĭ'ver^1 *n.* **1.** Large glandular organ in abdomen of vertebrates, secreting bile. **2.** Disordered state of liver; biliousness. **3.** **~(-colour)**, dark reddish brown. **4.** Flesh of some animals' liver used as food. **5.** (arch.) Liver as seat of emotion (**white** or **lily ~**, cowardice). **6.** *Liver* CHESTNUT; ||**~ salts** (to cure dyspepsia or biliousness); **~ sausage** (filled with cooked liver etc.); **~ of sulphur,** liver-coloured mixture of potassium sulphides etc., used as lotion in skin disease; **~wort,** lichen-like plant with liver-shaped leaves. **7.** Hence **~LESS** *a.* [OE *lifer*, = MDu. *lever*, OHG *libara*, ON *lifr* f. Gmc **librō*]

lĭ'ver^2 *n.* One who lives in specified way (*clean, loose, liver*); **good ~,** (1) virtuous person, (2) person given to good LIVING^1. [ME, f. LIVE^2 + -ER^1]

lĭ'verĭsh *a.* Suffering from disorder of liver; peevish, glum; hence **~NESS** *n.* [f. LIVER^1 + -ISH]

Lĭverpŭ'dlĭan *a.* & *n.* (Native or inhabitant) of Liverpool. [joc. f. *Liverpool* in Merseyside + PUDDLE^1 + -IAN]

lĭ'verȳ^1 *n.* **1.** (Hist.) provision of food or clothing for retainers etc.; allowance of provender for horses; *place where horses can be hired; **at ~,** (of horse) kept for owner and fed and groomed for fixed charge. **2.** Distinctive clothes worn by member of City Company or person's servant (**in, out of, ~,** of servant, so attired or in plain clothes), (fig.) distinctive guise or marking (*birds in their winter livery*; *the livery of grief*); hence **lĭ'verĭED^2** (-ĭd) *a.* **3.** Membership of City livery company (**take up** one's **~,** become liveryman). **4.** (Law). Legal delivery of property; writ allowing this. **5.** ||**~ company,** one of London City companies that formerly had distinctive costume; **~ cupboard,** small cupboard for keeping food etc. overnight; ||**~ fine,** payment for becoming member of livery company; **~man,** (1) ||member of livery company, (2) keeper of or attendant in livery stable; **~ servant** (wearing livery); **~ stable** (where horses are kept at livery or let out for hire). [ME, f. AF *liveré*, OF *livrée* fem. p.p. (as n.) of *livrer* DELIVER; see -Y^4]

lĭ'verȳ^2 *a.* Of the consistency or colour of liver; ||(of soil) tenacious; (colloq.) liverish. [f. LIVER^1 + -Y^2]

lĭ'vĭd *a.* Of bluish leaden colour; discoloured as by bruise; ||(colloq.) furiously angry; hence or cogn. **~ITY** (-ĭ'd-), **~NESS**, *ns.*, **~LY^2** *adv.* [f. F *livide* or f. L *lividus* (*livēre* be bluish; see -ID^1)]

lĭ'vĭng^1 *n.* **1.** In vbl senses; **cost of ~** (of basic necessities of life); STANDARD *of living*. **2.** Livelihood, maintenance, (*make* one's *living as* teacher etc., *out of* or *by* begging etc.); **it's a ~,** (joc.) the work provides subsistence though not inspiration. **3.** ||(Eccl.) Position as vicar or rector with income and/or property. **4.** **Good ~,** luxurious feeding; **plain ~ and high thinking,** frugal and philosophic life. **5.** **~-room** (for general day use); **~-space,** = LEBENSRAUM; *living* WAGE^1. [ME, f. LIVE^2 + -ING^1]

lĭ'vĭng^2 *a.* In vbl senses; contemporary, now existent, (*no man living could do better*; *the greatest living master of irony*; **the ~,** those now alive; **in the land of the ~,** alive); (of likeness or image of person) exact; (of water) perennially flowing; (of rock etc.) = LIVE^1 2; (of language) still in vernacular use; **~ death,** state of hopeless misery; **within ~ memory** (that of persons still living); **~ theatre** (opp. cinema). [OE *lifende* (as LIVE^2, -ING^2)]

lĭxĭ'vĭ|āte *v.t.* Separate (substance) into soluble and insoluble constituents by percolation of liquid; hence **~A'TION** *n.* [f. L *lixivius* made into lye (*lix*) + -ATE^3]

lĭ'zard *n.* Reptile of suborder Lacertilia having usu. long body and tail, four legs, movable eyelids, and scaly or granulated hide. [ME f. OF *lesard(e)* f. L *lacertus*; assim. to -ARD]

||**L.J.** *abbr.* (*pl.* **L.JJ.**) Lord Justice.

'll *v.* (chiefly after pronouns) = SHALL or WILL^1 (*I'll, he'll, that'll*). [abbr.]

L.L. *abbr.* Lord Lieutenant.

ll. *abbr.* lines.

lla'ma (lah'- *or* lyah'-) *n.* S. Amer. ruminant allied to camel but smaller, humpless, and woolly-haired, used as beast of burden, esp. variety of guanaco; (material made of) its wool. [Sp., prob. f. Quechua]

lla'nō (lah'- *or* lyah'-) *n.* (*pl.* **~s**). S. Amer. treeless grassy plain or steppe; hence **llaner'ō** (lyahnār'ō) *n.* (*pl.* **~s**), inhabitant of the llanos. [Sp., f. L *planum* PLAIN^1 7]

LL.B., LL.D., LL.M., *abbrs.* Bachelor, Doctor, Master, of Laws. [f. L *legum baccalaureus, doctor, magister*; cf. LAW^1 6]

Lloyd's (loidz) *n.* Incorporated society of underwriters in London; **~ List,** daily publication devoted to shipping news; **~ Register,** (society producing) annual alphabetical list of ships assigned to various classes. [orig. meeting in coffee-house established (1688) by Edward *Lloyd*]

L.M. *abbr.* long metre; lunar module.

lm *abbr.* lumen(s).

||**L.M.B.C.** *abbr.* Lady Margaret Boat Club (St. John's College, Cambridge).

L.M.H. *abbr.* Lady Margaret Hall.

||**L.M.S.** *abbr.* London Mathematical Society; (Hist.) London, Midland, & Scottish, London Missionary Society.

ln *abbr.* natural logarithm.

lō *int.* **1.** (arch.) Look!, see!, behold!. **2. Lo and behold!,** (joc.) here is a surprising fact. [OE *lā* int. of surprise etc., & ME *lō* = *lōke* LOOK]

loach *n.* Small edible freshwater fish of family Cobitidae. [ME, f. OF *loche*, of unkn. orig.]

load[1] *n.* **1.** What is (to be) carried, burden; amount usu. or actually carried (*cart-load of bricks*; *plane-load of people were killed*); unit of measure or weight of certain substances; **get a ~ of,** (sl.) notice, listen attentively to. **2.** Material object or force acting as weight or clog; resistance of machinery to motive power; pressure of superstructure on arch etc.; (Electr.) amount of power supplied by dynamo or generating station at any given time. **3.** Burden of responsibility, care, grief, etc., (**take a ~ off** person's **mind,** relieve him of anxiety). **4.** (in *pl.*, colloq.) Plenty, superabundance, heaps, a lot, *of*. **5. ~-displacement, -draught,** (of ship when laden); **~ line,** Plimsoll line; **~-shedding,** temporary curtailment of supply of electricity to a specific area to prevent excessive load on generating plant; **~'star,** = LODE*star*; **~'stone, lo'destone,** magnetic oxide of iron, piece of it used as magnet, thing that attracts, [= *way stone*; see etym.]. [OE *lād* way, journey, conveyance, = OHG *leita*, ON *leith* way, course, f. Gmc **laidhō* (cf. LEAD[2], LODE)]

load[2] *v.* **1.** *v.t.* Put load on or aboard (person, vehicle, ship, etc.); place (load, cargo) aboard ship, on vehicle, etc. **2.** Add weight to, be burden upon, oppress *with* (*stomach loaded with food*); weight with lead (*a loaded cane*); (in *p.p.*, of dice etc.) so weighted as to fall more often than usual with a certain face up, (fig.) not giving one a fair chance. **3.** Strain bearing-capacity of (*table loaded with food*). **4.** Supply or assail overwhelmingly *with* (*loaded her with gifts, praise, work, abuse*; *air loaded with soot*); (in *p.p.*, sl.) rich or drunk or *drugged. **5.** Charge (firearm; **am ~ed,** have my gun etc. charged); insert film in (camera). **6.** Charge with some hidden implication (esp. in *p.p.*; *a loaded question*). **7.** Add extra charge to (insurance premium) for special reason(s). **8.** *v.i.* **~ (up)**, (of ship, vehicle, or person) take load aboard. [ME, f. prec.]

loa'der *n.* In vbl senses; attendant loading sportsman's guns; loading-machine; (in *comb.*) gun, machine, etc., loaded in specified way (*breech, muzzle, front, top, -loader*), so **-loa'd**ING[2] *a.* [f. prec. + -ER[1]]

loa'dĭng *n.* In vbl senses; (Electr.) maximum current or power taken by an appliance. [ME, f. LOAD[2] + -ING[1]]

loaf[1] *n.* (*pl.* **loaves** *pr.* lōvz). **1.** Quantity of bread baked alone or as separate or separable part of batch, usu. of some standard weight; **brown, white, ~** (of brown, white, bread); **loaves and fishes,** personal profit as inducement to religious profession or public service [see John 6:26]; **half a ~ is better than no bread** (motto of compromise, opp. *all or nothing*). **2.** (sl.) Head (**use** one's **~,** use one's common sense). **3. (Sugar-)~,** conical moulded mass of sugar (**~ sugar,** this as whole or cut into lumps). **4. (Meat** etc.) **~,** minced or chopped meat moulded into loaflike shape and cooked, usu. to be eaten cold. [OE *hlāf*, = OHG *leip*, ON *hleifr*, Goth. *hlaifs* f. Gmc **hlaibhaz*]

loaf[2] *v.* & *n.* **1.** *v.i.* Spend time idly; saunter. **2.** *v.t.* **~ away,** spend (time) in loafing. **3.** *n.* Act or spell of loafing. [prob. back form. f. foll.]

loa'fer *n.* Person who loafs; *leather shoe shaped like moccasin with flat heel. [perh. f. G *landläufer* vagabond]

loam *n.* Paste of clay and water, composition of moistened clay and sand with chopped straw etc. used in making bricks, plastering, etc.; fertile soil of clay and sand with admixture of decayed vegetable matter, whence **~'**Y[2] *a.* [OE *lām*, = MDu. *leem*, OHG *leimo* f. WG **laima* (**lai-* be sticky; cf. LIME[1])]

loan[1] *n.*, & *v.t.* **1.** *n.* Thing, esp. sum of money, lent to be returned with or without interest; word, custom, etc., adopted by one people from another. **2.** Lending or being lent (*on loan*; **may I have the ~ of,** may I borrow). **3.** Money contribution from individuals or public bodies to State expenses that is acknowledged as debt; arrangement or contract by which a government receives advances of money usu. for stipulated interest. **4. ~ collection** (of pictures etc. lent by owners for exhibition); **~-holder,** person holding debentures or other acknowledgements of loan, mortgagee; ***~ shark,** (colloq.) one who lends money at usurious interest; **~-translation,** expression adopted by one language from another in more or less literally translated form (e.g. *reason of State* f. F *raison d'état*, F *gratte-ciel* f. *skyscraper*); **~-word,** word adopted by one language from another in more or less modified form (e.g. *morale, naïve*). **5.** *v.t.* Grant loan of; hence **~'**ABLE *a.*, **~**EE', **~'**ER[1], *ns.* [ME *lan(e)* f. ON *lán*, = OE *lǣn* (cf. LEND), MDu. *lēne*, OHG *lēhan* f. Gmc **laihwn-*]

loan[2], **loa'nĭng,** *ns.* (Sc.) Lane; open place where cows are milked. [ME var. of LANE, + -ING[1]]

loath, lōth, *pred. a.* Disinclined, reluctant, unwilling, (usu. *to* do, or abs.; *for* person *to* do, or *that*); **nothing ~,** quite willing(ly); **~-to-depart,** (arch.) tune played as farewell. [OE *lāth*, = OS *lēth*, OHG *leid*, ON *leithr* f. Gmc **laithaz*]

loath|e (-dh) *v.t.* Regard with disgust, abominate, detest; hence **~'**ING[1] (1) *n.* [OE *lāthian* f. Gmc **laithōjan* (as prec.)]

loa'thl|ȳ (-dh-) (arch. or literary) = foll.; hence **~**ĬNESS *n.* [OE *lāthlic* (as LOATH, -LY[1])]

loa'thsome (-dh-) *a.* Causing nausea or disgust, offensive to the senses, sickening, repulsive, odious; hence **~**LY[2] (-mlĭ) *adv.*, **~**NESS (-mn-) *n.* [ME, f. *loath* n. disgust (f. LOATHE) + -SOME[1]]

loaves. See LOAF[1].

lŏb *v.* (**-bb-**) & *n.* **1.** *v.i.* (arch.) Walk, run, or move, heavily or clumsily or slowly. **2.** *v.t.* Toss, bowl, or send, (ball) with slow or high-pitched motion. **3.** *n.* Ball high in air at lawn tennis, table-tennis, etc.; (Cricket) slow underhand ball. [v. f. n., prob. f. LDu.]

lō'b|āte *a.* (Biol.) Having lobe(s); hence **~**A'TION *n.* [f. LOBE + -ATE[2]]

lŏ'bbȳ *n.* & *v.* **1.** *n.* Porch, ante-room, entrance-hall, corridor; (in House of Commons etc.) large hall open to public used esp. for interviews between M.P.s and others, (also **division ~**) one of two corridors to which members retire to vote; body of those who lobby. **2.** *v.t.* Seek to influence (members of legislature), get (bill etc.) *through*, by interviews etc. in lobby; solicit support of (influential person). **3.** *v.i.* Frequent lobby of legislature, solicit members' votes; hence **~**IST (1) *n.* [f. med. L *lobia*, *lobium* LODGE[1]]

lōbe *n.* Roundish and flattish projecting or pendulous part, often one of two or more such parts divided by fissure (*lobe of liver* or *lungs*; *lobes* *of brain*); lower soft pendulous external part of ear; hence **lō'b**AR¹ *a.* (esp. of the lungs, as *lobar pneumonia*), **lōb**ED² (-bd), ~'LESS (-bl-), *adjs.* [f. LL f. Gk *lobos* lobe, pod]

lobĕ'ctomў *n.* (Med.) Excision of lobe of an organ, as of a lung, thyroid gland, etc. [f. prec. + -ECTOMY]

lobē'lĭa *n.* Herbaceous plant of genus *Lobelia* with blue, scarlet, white, or purple flowers having deeply cleft corolla. [f. M. de *Lobel*, Flemish botanist in England d. 1616 + -IA¹]

lŏ'blŏllў *n.* **1.** ~ **boy, man,** (Naut.) surgeon's attendant, surgeon's mate. **2.** ~ **pine,** *Pinus taeda*, growing in swamps of southern U.S. [perh. f. dial. *lob* eat up noisily + dial. *lolly* soup]

lōbŏ'tom|ў *n.* (Med.) = LEUCO*tomy*. [f. LOBE + -O- + -TOMY]

lŏ'bscouse *n.* Sailor's dish of meat stewed with vegetables and ship's biscuit. [18th c., of unkn. orig.; cf. Du. *lapskous*, Da., Norw., G *lapskaus*]

lŏ'bster *n.*, & *v.i.* **1.** *n.* Large marine stalk-eyed ten-footed long-tailed edible crustacean of family Homaridae, with large claws formed by first pair of feet, bluish black before and scarlet after boiling; its flesh as food (*lobster* THERMIDOR); **~-pot,** basket in which lobsters are trapped. **2.** *v.i.* Catch lobsters. [OE *lopustre*, corrupt. of L *locusta* crustacean, LOCUST, assim. to -STER]

lŏ'būl|e *n.* Small lobe; hence ~AR¹ *a.* [f. LOBE + -ULE]

lŏ'bworm (-wẽrm) *n.* Large earthworm used as fishing-bait; LUG¹worm. [f. LOB in obs. sense 'pendulous object']

local¹. Var. of LOCALE.

lō'cal² *a.* & *n.* **1.** *a.* In regard to place; ~ **habitation,** position in space as test of thing's material existence; ~ **surname** (derived from name of place). **2.** Belonging to, existing in, or peculiar to certain place(s); of one's own neighbourhood (*the local lawyer*); of or affecting a part and not the whole (*local pain*); ||(on envelope) for delivery in this town or district; not widely distributed (*the globe-flower is very local*); ~ **action,** (Law) one that must relate to a specific place, e.g. trespass; ~ **anaesthetic** (acting on only a small area of the body); ||~ **authority,** body charged with administration of local government; ~ **call,** telephone call to nearby place, charged at low rate; ~ **colour,** details characteristic of scene or time of novel etc. and added to give realism, (Paint.) colouring of separate objects in picture; *local* DERBY; ||**L~ Examinations** (set by university board and held in various places); ||~ **government,** system of administration of county, district, parish, etc., by elected representatives of those who live there; ~ **option** or **veto,** system whereby inhabitants of a district may prohibit sale of alcoholic liquor there; ~ **preacher,** Methodist layman authorized to preach in his own circuit; ~ **time** (measured from sun's transit over meridian of place). **3.** Hence ~LY² *adv.* **4.** *n.* Inhabitant of, professional man practising in, particular district; local preacher; (item of) local news in newspaper; postage stamp current only in limited district; train serving all stations of district; ||(colloq.) *the* local public house; ||(in *pl.*) Local Examination(s); *local branch of trade union. [ME f. OF, f. LL *localis* f. L *locus* place; see -AL]

loca'le (-ah'l) *n.* Scene or locality of operations or events. [f. F *local* n. f. as foll., respelt to indicate stress; cf. MORALE]

lō'calĭsm *n.* Attachment to a place; limitation of ideas etc. resulting from this; favouring of what is local; a local idiom, custom, etc. [f. LOCAL² + -ISM]

locă'lĭtў *n.* Position of a thing, place where it is; site or scene of something; faculty of remembering and recognizing district or places, finding one's way, etc., (BUMP² *of locality*). [f. F *localité* or f. LL *localitas* (as LOCAL²; see -ITY)]

lō'calīz|e, -īs|e (-īz), *v.t.* Invest with the characteristics of a particular place; restrict or assign to particular place; attach to districts, decentralize; hence ~ABLE *a.*, ~A'TION *n.* [f. LOCAL² + -IZE]

locā'te *v.* **1.** *v.t.* Establish in (proper) place, (in *pass.*) be situated. **2.** State locality of; discover exact place of (*locate the enemy's camp*). **3.** *v.i.* *Take up residence or business (*in* place). [f. L *locare* (*locus* place) + -ATE³]

locā'tion *n.* Locating or being located; (position in) a particular place; (S. Afr.) area where African natives are obliged to live; (Cinemat.) place, other than studio, where (part of) film is made (*on location*). [f. L *locatio* (as prec.; see -ATION)]

lŏ'catĭve *a.* & *n.* (Gram.) (Case of nouns etc.) denoting place where. [f. as LOCATE + -IVE, after *vocative*]

loc. cit. *abbr.* in the passage already quoted. [f. LOCO CITATO]

lŏch (lŏχ *or* lŏk) *n.* (Sc.) **1.** Lake. **2.** Arm of the sea, esp. when narrow or partially land-locked. [ME f. Gael.]

lŏ'chĭ|a (-k-) *n.* Discharge from uterus after childbirth; hence ~AL *a.* [mod. L, f. Gk *lokhia* neut. pl. (as n.) of *lokhios* of childbirth]

lō'cī. See LOCUS.

lŏck¹ *n.* Portion of fairly long hair that hangs together; (in *pl.*) hair of head; tuft of wool or cotton; hence -~ED² (-kt) *a.* [OE *locc*, = OS *lok*, OHG *loc*, ON *lokkr* f. Gmc **lokkaz*]

lŏck² *n.* **1.** Appliance for fastening door, lid, etc., with bolt that requires key of particular shape to work it (**under ~ and key,** locked up); appliance to keep wheel from revolving or slewing; wrestling-hold that keeps opponent's arm etc. fixed; ~ (**forward**), (Rugby Footb.) player in second row of scrum. **2.** Mechanism for exploding charge of gun (**~, stock, and barrel,** whole of thing, completely). **3.** Confined section of canal or river where level can be changed for raising and lowering boats between adjacent sections by use of gates and sluices. **4.** = AIR¹*lock* (2). **5.** Interlocking, e.g. block or jam of vehicles in street. **6.** Turning of front wheels of vehicle to change its direction of motion (**full ~,** maximum extent of this). **7.** ||~ (**hospital**), hospital for venereal disease. **8.** **~'fast,** (Sc.) secured with lock; **~-keeper, ~'s-man,** keeper of canal etc. lock; **~-knit,** (fabric) knitted with interlocking stitch; **~-nut,** (Mech.) nut screwed down on another to keep it tight; **~'smith,** maker and mender of locks; **~-step,** marching with each man as close as possible to the one in front; **~-stitch** (made by sewing-machine by firmly locking together two threads or stitches). **9.** Hence ~'LESS *a.* [OE *loc*, = OS *lok*, OHG *loh* hole, ON *lok* lid, end, f. Gmc **lokam*]

lŏck³ *v.* **1.** *v.t.* Fasten (door, box, etc.) with lock, shut *up* (house etc.) by fastening doors thus; ~ **the stable door after the horse has bolted** or **been stolen,** take precautions too late. **2.** Shut (person, thing) *up*, *in*, or *into*; (of land, hills, etc., usu. in *pass.*) enclose; (fig.) store (*up* or *away*) inaccessibly (*facts locked up in hieroglyphics*; *capital locked up in land*); hold fast *in* sleep, enchantment, etc.; keep (person) *out* by locking door (esp. of employer coercing workmen by refusing them work until they accept his conditions; **~-out** *n.*, this procedure, cf. STRIKE 12). **3.** *v.t.* & *i.* Bring or come into rigidly fixed position, stop moving or revolving, engage, (cause to) catch, fasten by interlacing or fitting of corresponding parts, entangle; (in *p.p.*) joined *in* hostile or other embrace. **4.** *v.t.* Provide (canal etc.) with locks; convey (boat) *up* or *down* through lock. **5.** *v.i.* (Of door, box, etc.) have means of being fastened with lock; go through canal etc. lock. **6.** **~'jaw,** (pop. name for) trismus, variety of tetanus, tonic spasm of muscles of mastication causing jaws to remain rigidly closed; **~-up,** (time of) locking up school etc. for night, unrealizable state of invested capital or amount of capital locked up, house or room for temporary detention of prisoners, ||(premises etc.) that can be locked up. [ME, f. prec.]

lŏ'ckage *n.* Amount of rise or fall effected by canal locks; toll for use of lock; use or number of locks. [f. LOCK² + -AGE]

lŏ'cker *n.* In vbl senses; small cupboard, esp. one of many reserved or reservable each for individual's use in public place, e.g. in **~-room** of cricket pavilion or in schoolroom; (Naut.) chest or compartment for clothes, stores, ammunition, etc., (**not a shot in** one's or **the ~**, no money in one's pocket, no chance left; DAVY JONES's *locker*). [ME, f. LOCK³ + -ER¹]

lŏ'ckėt *n.* Metal plate or band on scabbard; small ornamental case holding portrait, lock of hair, etc., and usu. hung from neck. [f. OF *locquet* dim. of *loc* latch, lock, f. WG (as LOCK²); see -ET¹]

lō'cō¹ *n.* (*pl.* **~s**). (colloq.) Locomotive engine. [abbr.]

lō'cō² *n.* (*pl.* **~es** *or* **~s**) & *a.* **1.** *n.* **~(-weed)**, poisonous leguminous plant of U.S. causing brain disease in cattle eating it. **2.** *a.* (sl.) Crazy. [Sp., = insane]

loco citato (lŏkō sĭtā'tō; *or* -ah'-) *adv.* In the passage already quoted. [L, = in the place cited]

lōcomō't|ion *n.* (Power of) motion from place to place; travel, way (esp. artificial) of travelling; so **~**ORY *a.* [f. L *loco* abl. of *locus* place + *motio* MOTION¹; suggested by the scholastic phr. *in loco movēri* move in space]

lō'comōtĭve (*or* -mō'-) *a.* & *n.* **1.** *a.* Of locomotion (*locomotive power*), (joc.) of travel (*in these locomotive days*). **2.** Having power of or given to locomotion, not stationary, (*locomotive bivalves, crane*); **~ engine** (that goes from place to place by its own power, esp. for drawing train along rails). **3.** *n.* Locomotive engine. [f. as prec.; see -IVE]

lō'comōtor *n.* & *a.* **1.** *n.* (arch.) Locomotive person or thing. **2.** *a.* Of locomotion (*locomotor* ATAXY). [f. as prec. + MOTOR]

lŏ'cūl|us *n.* (*pl.* **~i** *pr.* -ī). (Zool., Anat., & Bot.) One of a number of small separate cavities; hence **~**AR¹ *a.* [L, dim. of LOCUS]

lō'cum *n.* (colloq.) = foll. [abbr.]

lōcum tĕ'nĕn|s (-z) *n.* (*pl.* **~tes** *pr.* -ĕ'ntēz). Deputy acting esp. for clergyman or doctor; hence **lōcum-tĕ'nen**CY *n.* [med. L, (one) holding place; cf. foll. & TENANT]

lō'cus *n.* (*pl.* **lo'ci** *pr.* -sī). **1.** (Math.) Curve etc. formed by all points satisfying particular equation of relation between co-ordinates, or by point, line, or surface, moving according to mathematically defined conditions. **2.** (Biol.) Normal position of gene on chromosome. **3.** **~ *classicus,*** best-known or most authoritative passage on a subject; **~ *in quo,*** scene of event; **~ *standi,*** recognized position, right to intervene, appear in court, etc. [L, = place]

lō'cust *n.* **1.** Any of various African and Asian short-horned edible grasshoppers of family Acrididae, migrating in swarms and consuming all vegetation of districts; (fig.) person of devouring or destructive propensities; *cicada. **2.** **~ (bean)**, carob; **~ (tree)**, (1) carob tree, (2) false acacia, (3) kowhai. **3.** **~-bird, -eater,** any of various birds feeding on locusts. [ME, f. OF *locuste* f. L *locusta* lobster, locust]

locū'tion *n.* Style of speech; word or phrase considered in regard to style, idiom. [ME f. OF, or f. L *locutio* (*loqui locut-* speak; see -ION)]

lŏ'cūtorў *n.* Parlour or conversation-room in monastery; grille for interviews between inmates of monastery and outsiders. [f. med. L *locutorium* (as prec.; see -ORY)]

lōde *n.* Vein of metal ore; **~'star, loa'dstar,** star that is steered by, esp. the pole-star, (fig.) guiding principle, object of pursuit; **~'stone,** = LOAD¹*stone*. [var. of LOAD¹]

lō'den *n.* Thick waterproof woollen cloth; dark green colour in which this is often made. [G]

lŏdge¹ *n.* **1.** (arch.) Small esp. temporary dwelling. **2.** Cottage at gates of park or in grounds of large house, occupied by gardener or other servant; house (e.g. in Scottish Highlands) occupied in the hunting or shooting season; large house; hotel esp. at resort. **3.** Porter's room at gate of college, factory, or house of chambers or flats. **4.** (Freemasonry, Friendly Societies, etc.) (Place of meeting for) members of branch; **grand ~**, governing body of Freemasons and similar societies. **5.** Residence of head of college at Cambridge (cf. LODGINGS). **6.** Beaver's or otter's lair. **7.** N. Amer. Indian's tent or wigwam. **8.** Local branch of trade union. [ME *log(g)e* f. OF *loge* arbour, hut, f. med. L *laubia, lobia* (cf. LOBBY), f. Gmc **laubja* (**laubham* LEAF)]

lŏdg|e² *v.* **1.** *v.t.* Provide with sleeping-quarters; receive as guest or inmate; establish as resident in house or room(s). **2.** Serve as habitation for, contain; (in *pass.*) be contained *in*. **3.** Leave *in* place or *with* person for safety. **4.** Deposit in court or with official a formal statement of (complaint, information); bring forward (objection etc.). **5.** Place (power etc.) *in, with, in the hands of*, (person). **6.** (Of wind or rain) lay (crops) flat. **7.** *v.t.* & *i.* (Make, let) stick or remain in place without falling or going further (*lodged a bullet, bullet lodged, in his brain; tide lodges mud in the cavities*). **8.** *v.i.* Reside, be situated; ||be inmate paying for accommodation in another's house, whence **~'**ER¹ *n.* **9.** (Of crops) be laid flat by wind or rain. [ME, f. OF *logier* (as prec.)]

lŏ'dgement, lŏ'dgment, (-jm-) *n.* (Mil.) temporary defensive work on captured part of enemy's works; establishing oneself on enemy's ground; stable position gained, foothold, (*make, effect, a lodgement*); (Law) deposit(ing) of money; accumulation of matter intercepted in fall or transit. [f. F *logement* (as prec.; see -MENT)]

lŏ'dgĭng *n.* In vbl senses; accommodation in hired rooms; dwelling-place, abode, (in *pl.*) room(s) hired elsewhere than in hotel for residing in, (in *pl.*) residence of head of college at Oxford (cf. LODGE¹); **~-house** (in which lodgings are let); ||*common ~-house* (usu. one with dormitory in which bed can be had for the night); **~ turn,** spell of duty in railway service or vehicle-driving during which employee sleeps away from home for a night. [ME, f. LODGE² + -ING¹]

lō'ĕss *n.* Deposit of fine light-coloured wind-blown dust in Rhine, Mississippi, and other river valleys, very fertile when irrigated. [f. G *löss* f. Swiss G. *lösch* loose (*lösen* loosen)]

lŏft (*or* lawft) *n.*, & *v.t.* **1.** *n.* Attic; *upstairs room; room over stable esp. for hay and straw;

pigeon-house; gallery in church or hall (*organ--loft, rood-loft*). **2.** (Golf). Backward slope in club-head; lofting stroke. **3.** *v.t.* Hit, throw, kick, etc., (ball) high up, clear (obstacle) thus; (esp. in *p.p.*) give loft to (golf-club). [OE f. ON *lopt* (pr. lawft) air, sky, upper room, f. Gmc (as LIFT)]

lŏ'fter (*or* law'-) *n.* Golf-club for lofting the ball. [f. prec. + -ER¹]

lŏ'ft|ȳ (*or* law'-) *a.* Of imposing height, towering, soaring, (*lofty mountain, flight, stature*; not used of persons); consciously superior or dignified (*lofty contempt, good humour*); exalted, distinguished, high-flying, high-flown; elevated, sublime, grandiose; hence **~ĭLY²** *adv.*, **~ĭNESS** *n.* [ME, f. LOFT (as in *aloft*) + -Y²]

lŏg¹ *n.*, & *v.t.* (**-gg-**). **1.** *n.* Unhewn piece of felled tree, or similar rough mass of wood esp. cut for firewood; **in the ~**, unhewn; KING¹ *Log*; *float, lie, fall*, **like a ~**, in helpless or stunned state; **sleep like a ~** (soundly). **2.** Float attached to line wound on reel for gauging speed of ship, other apparatus for same purpose, (**heave, throw, the ~**, use this; **sail by the ~**, calculate ship's position by it); PATENT¹ *log*. **3. ~(-book)**, (1) book with permanent record made of all events occurring during ship's or aircraft's voyage(s) (including rate of ship's progress shown by log), (2) traveller's diary etc., (3) regularly maintained record of progress or performance; **~-book,** ‖book showing registration details of motor vehicle; **~ cabin,** hut built of logs; **~-jam,** crowded mass of logs in river, (fig.) deadlock; **~-line** (to which float of ship's log is attached); **~-rolling,** (1) mutual help, esp. to assist each other's political projects [f. phr. *you roll my log and I'll roll yours*], (2) sport of trying to knock opponent off floating log on which both stand; **~'wood,** (wood, used in dyeing, of) W. Ind. tree (*Haematoxylon campechianum*). **4.** *v.t.* Cut into logs; enter (distance made etc.) in ship's log-book, (of ship) make (distance); enter (seaman's name with offence committed) in log-book, fine (offender); enter (data etc.) in regular record; attain (cumulative total of time etc. thus recorded). [ME, of unkn. orig.]

lŏg² *n.* Logarithm (esp. prefixed to number or algebraic symbol whose logarithm is to be indicated). [abbr.]

***-lŏg.** See -LOGUE.

lō'ganbĕrrȳ *n.* Fruit got by cross between raspberry and dewberry. [f. J. H. *Logan*, Amer. horticulturist d. 1928 + BERRY¹]

lŏ'gan(-stōne) *n.* Poised heavy stone rocking at a touch. [= *logging* (*log* to rock) + STONE]

lŏgaoe'dĭc (-*aē'*-) *a.* & *n.* (Line of verse) composed of mixed dactyls and trochees, or anapaests and iambuses. [f. LL f. Gk *logaoidikos* (*logos* speech, *aoidē* song; see -IC)]

lŏ'garĭthm (-dhem *or* -them) *n.* One of a class of arithmetical functions tabulated to assist calculation by substituting addition and subtraction for multiplication and division, and the latter two for involution and evolution; power to which fixed number (the *base*) must be raised to produce given number (*the logarithm of 1000 to base 10 is 3*); **common ~** (to base 10); **Napierian** or **natural ~** (to base denoted by *e*, about 2·72); hence **lŏgarĭ'thmic** (*or* -dh-) *a.* [f. mod. L *logarithmus* f. Gk *logos* reckoning, ratio + *arithmos* number]

loge (lōzh *or* lōj) *n.* Box in theatre etc. [F]

-loger *suf.* forming *ns.* = -LOGIST (*astrologer, campanologer*). [after ASTROLOGER]

***lŏ'gger** (-g-) *n.* Lumberjack. [f. LOG¹ + -ER¹]

lŏ'ggerhead (-gerhĕd) *n.* **1.** (arch.) Blockhead, fool. **2.** Iron instrument with ball at end heated for melting pitch etc. **3.** Large-headed turtle (esp. *Caretta caretta*). **4. At ~s,** disagreeing or disputing (*with*). [prob. f. dial. *logger* block of wood for hobbling a horse, + HEAD¹]

lŏ'ggia (-jy*a*) *n.* Open-sided gallery or arcade; open-sided extension of house. [It., = LODGE¹]

lŏ'gĭc *n.* Science of reasoning, proof, thinking, or inference; particular scheme of or treatise on this; chain of reasoning, correct or incorrect use of argument, ability in argument, arguments (CHOP⁴ *logic*; *argues with great learning and logic*; *is not governed by logic*); inexorable force, converting-power, compulsion, (*the logic of events, facts, necessity, war*, etc.); arrangement of elements in computer to perform specified task; so **logĭ'**CIAN *n.* [ME, f. OF *logique* f. LL *logica* f. Gk *logikē* (*tekhnē* art) of reason (LOGOS; see -IC)]

-lŏ'gĭc, -lŏ'gĭcal, *sufs.* forming *adjs.* corresp. esp. to *ns.* in -LOGY: *pathological, physiologic(al), theological, zoological*. [f. or after Gk *-logikos* f. adjs. & ns. in *-logos, -logia* -LOGY; see -IC, -ICAL]

lŏ'gĭcal *a.* Of logic or formal argument; not contravening the laws of thought, correctly reasoned; deducible, defensible on ground of consistency, reasonably to be believed or done; capable of correct reasoning; **~ atomism,** (Philos.) theory that all propositions can be analysed into simple independent elements; *logical* NECESSITY; *logical* POSITIVISM; hence **~ITY** (-ă'l-) *n.*, **~LY²** *adv.* [f. med. L *logicalis* f. LL *logica* (see LOGIC, -AL)]

lō'gĭ|on (*or* lŏ'g-) *n.* (*pl.* **~a**). Saying of Christ not recorded in canonical Gospels but preserved elsewhere. [Gk, = oracle (LOGOS)]

-logĭst *suf.* forming *ns.* meaning 'person skilled in *-logy*' (*etymologist, geologist, zoologist*). [f. (or f. as) -LOGY + -IST]

logĭ'stĭcs *n. pl.* Art of moving, lodging, and supplying troops and equipment; so **logĭ'stic** *a.* [f. F *logistique* (*loger* LODGE²; see -ICS)]

lŏ'gō *n.* (*pl.* **~s**). (colloq.) = LOGOTYPE 2. [abbr.]

lŏ'gogrăm *n.* Sign or character representing a word, esp. in shorthand. [f. Gk *logos* word + -GRAM]

logŏ'grapher *n.* (Gk Ant.) One of the Greek prose historians before Herodotus; ancient--Greek professional speech-writer for lawcourts. [f. LL *logographus* accountant or f. Gk *logographos* prose-writer (see LOGOS, -GRAPHER)]

logŏ'machȳ (-kĭ) *n.* (literary). Dispute about words, controversy turning on merely verbal points. [f. Gk *logomakhia* (LOGOS, *-makhia* -fighting)]

lŏgorrhoe'a, *-rhē'a, (-rē'*a*) *n.* Excessive flow of words esp. in mental illness. [f. as foll. + Gk *rhoia* flow]

Lŏ'gŏs *n.* The Word of God, or Second Person of the Trinity. [Gk, = word, reason, account, cogn. w. *legō* speak, choose, used in mystic sense by Hellenistic and Neo-Platonist philosophers and by St. John]

lŏ'gotȳpe *n.* **1.** Word, or more letters than one, cast in one piece but not as ligature, for use in printing. **2.** (Single piece of type bearing) non--heraldic device chosen as badge of organization and used in advertisements, on notepaper, etc. [f. Gk *logos* word + TYPE¹]

-lŏgue (-g), ***-lŏg,** *suf.* forming *ns.* denoting talk (*dialogue, monologue*), compilation (*catalogue*), or occas. = -LOGIST (*ideologue, sinologue*). [f. or after F *-logue* f. Gk *-logos, -logon*]

***lō'g|ȳ** (-gĭ) *a.* Lethargic, sluggish; dull, inert; hence **~ĭLY²** *adv.*, **~ĭNESS** *n.* [19th c., of unkn. orig.]

-logȳ *suf.* forming *ns.* denoting (1) character of speech or language (*tautology*), (2) subject of study (*mineralogy, sociology, theology, zoology*), (3) discourse (*trilogy*). [f. F *-logie* or f. med. L or f. Gk *-logia* (as LOGOS; see -Y¹)]

loin *n.* **1.** (in *pl.*) Part of body on both sides of spine between false ribs and hip-bones (**gird up** one's **~s,** prepare for journey or effort; **fruit, child,** etc., **of, sprung from,** etc., one's **~s,** one's begotten offspring). **2.** Joint of meat that includes the loin vertebrae. **3. ~'cloth,** cloth worn round loins esp. as sole garment. **4.** Hence ~ED² (-nd) *a.* [ME, f. OF *loigne* f. Rom. **lumbea* fem. of **lumbeus* a. f. L *lumbus*]

loir (loi'*er*) *n.* Large species of dormouse. [F, f. pop. L **lēre*, f. L *glis gliris*]

loi'ter *v.* **1.** *v.i.* Linger on the way, hang about; travel indolently and with frequent pauses. **2.** *v.t.* Pass (time etc.) *away* in loitering. **3.** Hence ~ER¹ *n.* [ME, f. MDu. *loteren* wag about]

lŏll *v.* **1.** *v.t.* Hang (one's tongue) out; let (one's head or limbs) rest lazily on something. **2.** *v.i.* (Of tongue) hang (*out*); stand, sit, or recline, in lazy attitude. [ME; prob. imit.]

Lŏ'llard *n.* One of the 14th-c. heretics who followed Wyclif or held opinions like his; hence ~ISM (3) *n.* [f. MDu. *lollaerd* (*lollen* mumble; see -ARD)]

lŏ'llĭpŏp *n.* Large usu. flat rounded boiled sweet on small stick; ||~ **man** etc., (colloq.) official using circular sign on stick to stop traffic so that children may cross road. [perh. f. dial. *lolly* tongue + POP²]

lŏ'llop *v.i.* (colloq.) Flop about; move or proceed in a lounging or ungainly way. [prob. f. LOLL, assoc. w. TROLLOP]

lŏ'llȳ *n.* **1.** (colloq.) Lollipop; (Austral.) a sweet; **ice(d)** ~, water-ice on small stick. **2.** (sl.) Money. [abbr. of LOLLIPOP]

Lŏ'mbard *n.* & *a.* **1.** *n.* One of the Germanic 6th-c. conquerors of Italy; native of Lombardy. **2.** *a.* Of the Lombards or Lombardy, Lombardic; ~ **Street,** a London street formerly occupied by Lombard bankers, and still containing many of chief London banks, (transf.) the money market, financiers as a body, (~ **Street to a China orange,** great wealth against one ordinary object, virtual certainty, long odds). [ME, f. OF *lombard* or MDu. *lombaerd*, f. It. *lombardo* f. med. L *Longobardus*, L *Lango-*, f. Gmc **Langobardhaz* (LONG¹, L *Bardi* name of the people)]

Lŏmbar̄'dĭc *a.* Of the Lombards or Lombardy (esp. of N. Ital. 7th–13th-c. architecture and 15th–16th-c. painting). [f. prec. + -IC]

Lŏ'mbardȳ *n.* ~ **poplar** (variety with especially tall slender form). [~ in N. Italy]

lō'mĕnt *n.* (Bot.) Kind of pod that breaks up when mature into one-seeded joints; hence ~A'CEOUS *a.* [f. L *lomentum* bean-meal (orig. cosmetic) f. *lavare* wash]

Lo'ndon (lŭ'-) *n.* ~ **clay,** geological formation in lower division of Eocene in S.E. England; ~ **ivy,** (arch.) clinging fog or smoke of London; ~ **particular,** (arch.) kind of thick fog peculiar to London; ~ **plane,** hybrid plane-tree resistant to smoke and often planted in streets; ~ **pride,** a pink-flowered saxifrage; ~ **smoke,** dull grey colour; hence ~ER¹ (4), ~ISM (4), *ns.*, ~IZE (3) *v.t.* [~, capital of U.K.]

lōne *attrib. a.* **1.** (poet. or rhet.) Solitary, companionless, unfrequented, uninhabited, lonely. **2.** ~ **hand,** hand played or player playing against the rest at quadrille and euchre, (fig.) person or action without allies; ~ **scout,** Scout who does not have regular access to a Scout troop; ***L~ Star (State),** Texas; *lone* WOLF. **3.** Feeling or making feel lonely. **4.** (Of woman) single or widowed. [ME, f. ALONE]

lō'nel|ȳ (-nlĭ) *a.* Solitary, companionless, isolated; unfrequented; sad because without friends or company (**~y heart,** such person); hence ~ĬNESS *n.* [f. prec. + -LY¹]

lō'ner *n.* Person or animal that prefers not to associate with others. [f. LONE + -ER¹]

lō'nesome (-ns-) *a.* Solitary, lonely; feeling lonely or forlorn; causing such feeling; **by** or **on** one's ~, all alone; hence ~LY² (-mlĭ) *adv.*, ~NESS (-mn-) *n.* [f. LONE + -SOME¹]

lŏng¹ *a.* (**~'er, ~'est,** *pr.* -ngg-) & *n.* **1.** *a.* Measuring much from end to end in space or time, not soon traversed or finished, (*a long line, journey, way off*; *a long life, time ago*); (seemingly) more than the stated amount (*ten long miles*); *long in the* TOOTH; (colloq., of person) tall. **2.** Far-reaching, acting at a distance, involving great interval or difference, (*little* PITCHER¹*s have long ears*); (of a chance) involving much risk; (of odds in betting) very uneven; (of bill of exchange) maturing at distant date; (of person's memory) retaining things for a long time. **3.** (Usu. appended to measurement) having specified length or duration (*tail 6 in. long*; *vacation is two months long*; *as* BROAD *as it is long*). **4.** Of elongated shape; remarkable for or distinguished by or concerned with length or duration. **5.** Expressed by many digits or consisting of many individuals (~ **figure** or **price,** heavy cost); (of family) having many children; (of bill) containing many or exorbitant items. **6.** Lengthy, prolix, tedious. **7.** Of more than the usual numerical amount (*long* DOZEN, HUNDRED-(WEIGHT), TON¹). **8.** Lasting, going far back or forward in time, (*a long friendship, farewell*). **9.** (Phonet. & Pros.) (Of vowel or syllable) having the greater of the two recognized durations, stressed; (of Engl. vowel) having the pronunciation shown in its name (e.g. *pile* and *cute* have long, *pill* and *cut* short, *i* and *u*). **10.** (St. Exch. etc.; of stocks, stockbroker, etc.) bought, buying, etc., in large quantities in advance, with expectation of rise in price. **11.** **~-and-short work,** (Archit.) alternation of tall quoins with flat slabs; ~ **arm,** (1) far-reaching power, (2) pole with hook etc. for use at height beyond ordinary reach; *make a ~ arm,* reach out for something; **~-bill,** bird with long bill, esp. snipe; **~'boat,** sailing-ship's largest boat; **~'bow** (drawn by hand and shooting long feathered arrow; *draw the ~bow,* tell exaggerated or invented stories); **~-chain,** (of molecule) containing chain of many carbon atoms; ||*by a long* CHALK¹; ~ **clay,** churchwarden pipe; **~-clothes,** (arch.) **~-coats,** clothes of baby in arms; ~ **date,** distant date for maturing of bill etc.; **~-dated,** not due for early payment or redemption; **~-day,** (of plant) needing long daily period of light to cause flowering; **~-distance,** (of weather forecast) long-range, (of telephone call, public transport, etc.) between distant places; *long* DIVISION; ~ **drink** (served in tall glass); **~-eared,** stupid (like an ass), (of owl) having long ear-tufts; ~ **face,** dismal expression; ~ **field,** (1) = *long off* or *long on,* (2) part of field behind bowler; ~ **finger,** middle finger; ||~ **firm,** swindlers who obtain goods but do not pay; ~ **game,** (Golf) driving and play before approaching the green; **~-hair(ed),** (person) with hair longer than usual, esp. intellectual or hippie; **~'hand,** ordinary writing (opp. shorthand or typing or printing); ~ **handle,** (Cricket) hitting freely; ~ **haul,** transport of goods, or other effort made, over a long distance; **~-hea'ded,** shrewd, far-seeing, sagacious; *long* HOME¹; ~ **hop,** short-pitched ball in cricket, easily hit; **~'horn,** one of a breed of cattle with long horns, beetle of family Cerambycidae with very long antennae; ~ **johns,** (colloq.) underpants with full-length legs; ||~ **jump,** athletic contest of jumping as far as possible along the ground in one leap; *at long* LAST[3] 8; ~ **leg,** (position of) cricket fieldsman far behind batsman on leg side; **~-legged,** (fig.) speedy; **~-lived** (-ĭvd), having a long life, durable; ~ **mark,** macron; ~ **measure,** measure of length (metres, miles, etc.); ~ **metre,** (1) hymn stanza of four lines with 8 syllables each, (2) quatrain of iambic tetrameters with alternate lines rhyming; **make a ~ nose,** cock a SNOOK[2]; ~ **off,** ~ **on,** (position of) cricket fieldsman far behind bowler and towards off, on, side; ~ **on,** (colloq.) well supplied with; **L~ Parliament,** English parliament elected 1640 and dissolved 1660; ~ **pig,** (transl. of cannibals' name for) human flesh as food; ~ **purse,** plenty of money; **~-range,** having a long range, relating to a long period of future time; ~ **robe,** legal profession; **in the ~ run,** in the end, as the ultimate outcome (after all vicissitudes); *long* SEA; ~ **service,** prolonged service in one post, esp. (Mil.) enlistment for many years; **~'shanks,** (1) = STILT 3, (2, *L-*) nickname of Edward I; ~ **ship,** (Hist.) warship with many rowers; **~-short story,** short story longer than the average; ~ **shot,** wild guess or venture, bet at long odds, (Cinemat.) shot including objects at a distance; *not by a ~ shot,* far from, by no means; ~ **sight,** ability to see clearly only what is comparatively distant; **~-sighted,** having long sight, (fig.) having imagination or foresight; **~-sleeved,** with sleeves reaching below elbow; *of long* STANDING[1]; **~'stop,** (position of) cricket fieldsman directly behind wicket-keeper; ~ **suit,** many cards of one suit in a hand (esp. more than 3 or 4 in hand of 13), (fig.) thing at which one excels; *long* TERM; **~-term,** occurring in or relating to a long period of time; ~ **time** *adv.*, (arch.) for a long time; **~-time,** that has been such for a long time; ~ **tongue,** loquacity; ~ **trousers** (opp. *shorts*); ||~ **vacation,** summer vacation of lawcourts and universities; ~ **view(s),** consideration of remote effects; ~ **waist,** low or deep waist of dress; ~ **wave,** radio wave of more than 1,000 metres wavelength; *long* WHIST[3]; ~ **wind,** ability to run a long distance without rest or (fig.) to talk or write at tedious length; **~-winded,** having such ability. **12.** Hence ~'ISH[1] 2 *a.*, ~'WAYS, ~'WISE, *advs.* **13.** *n.* A long interval or period (*shall see you before long*; *shall not be away for long*; *will not take long*; *it is long since I saw him*); **at (the) ~est,** to mention the most distant date possible. **14.** Recital at length (**the ~ and the short of it,** all that can or need be said, the total upshot). **15.** Long syllable or vowel; mark indicating that vowel is long; (St. Exch.) long-dated stock, person who buys long; || = *long vacation*; **~s and shorts,** quantitative verse, (Archit.) = *long-and-short work.* [OE *long, lang,* = OS, OHG *lang,* ON *langr,* Goth. *laggs* f. Gmc **langaz*]

lŏng[2] *adv.* (**~'er, ~'est,** *pr.* -ngg-). **1.** For a long time (*have long thought so*); *long* LIVE[2] . . . *!*; **so** or **as ~ as,** during the whole time that, provided that, if only; so[1] *long!*. **2. Be ~ doing,** (prob. by confus. of *adv.* & *a.*) **be ~ in doing,** (ellipt.) **be ~,** take a long time, be slow, to do, (*he was long finding it out*; *the chance was long in coming*; *wait here, for I shall not be long*); **not be ~ for this world,** have only short time to live. **3.** By a long time (*long before, after, since, ago*); (appended to *ns.* of duration) throughout specified time (*all day long, his life long*). **4.** (in *compar.*, with *no, any, much,* etc.) After implied point of time (*shall not wait any longer*); **no ~er,** not now or henceforth as formerly. **5. ~-ago** *a.* & *n.*, (belonging to) the distant past; **~-drawn(-out),** (unduly) prolonged; **~-playing,** (of gramophone record) playing for about 10 to 30 minutes on each side; *long-*STANDING[2]; **~-suffering** *n.* & *a.*, bearing provocation patiently. [OE *lange* (as prec.)]

lŏng[3] *v.i.* Wish earnestly or vehemently *for* thing or *to* do; hence ~'ING[1] (1) *n.*, ~'ING[2] *a.* [OE *langian* seem LONG[1] to]

-lŏng *suf.* forming *adjs.* & *advs.* (1) w. sense as LONG[2] 3 (*day-long, lifelong*), (2) = -LING[2] (*headlong, sidelong*). [f. LONG[1]]

long. *abbr.* longitude.

longaeval. Var. of LONGEVAL.

lŏnganĭ'mĭtȳ (-ngg-) *n.* (arch.) Long-suffering, forbearance. [ME, f. LL *longanimitas* (LL (*longanimis* f. L *longus* long + *animus* spirit, after Gk *makrothumia*; see -ITY)]

longe. See LUNGE[1].

lŏ'ngeron (-nj-) *n.* (usu. in *pl.*) Longitudinal member of aeroplane's fuselage. [F, = girder]

lŏngē'val (-nj-) *a.* (arch.) Long-lived, long-lasting. [f. L *longaevus* (*longus* long, *aevum* age) + -AL]

lŏngĕ'vĭtȳ (-nj-) *n.* Long life. [f. LL *longaevitas* (as prec.; see -ITY)]

lŏ'ngĭcorn (-nj-) *n.* Longhorn beetle. [f. mod. L *longicornis* f. L *longus* long + -I- + *cornu* horn]

lŏ'ngĭtūde (-nj- *or* -ngg-) *n.* **1.** (Geog.) Angular distance east or west from a standard meridian, e.g. that of Greenwich, to the meridian of any place, reckoned up to 180° E. or W. **2.** (Astron.) Angular distance eastward on ecliptic from vernal equinoctial point to point within 90° of any body or point and on great circle through it perpendicular to ecliptic; similar distance in other reference systems. **3.** (arch. or joc.) Length. [ME, f. L *longitudo -dinis* (*longus* long; see -TUDE)]

lŏngĭtū'dĭnal (-nj-) *a.* Of or in length; running lengthwise; of longitude; ~ **wave** (vibrating in direction of propagation); hence ~LY[2] *adv.* [f. as prec. + -AL]

Lŏ'ngobard *n.* = LOMBARD 1. [f. med. L *Longobardi* (see LOMBARD)]

lŏ'ng-shore *a.* Existing or found or employed on, frequenting, the shore; **~man,** landsman employed in loading and unloading ships, shore-fishing, etc. [f. *along shore*]

longueur (lawnger') *n.* Tedious passage in book etc.; tedious stretch of time. [F, = length]

lonī'cera *n.* Shrub of genus *Lonicera*, honeysuckle. [f. A. *Lonicerus*, Ger. botanist d. 1586 + -A]

lōō[1] *n.* Round card-game with penalties paid to the pool; (having to pay) this penalty. [abbr. of obs. *lanterloo* f. F *lantur(e)lu*, refrain of a song]

||**lōō**[2] *n.* (colloq.) Lavatory. [20th c.; orig. uncert.]

lōō'bȳ *n.* Lazy or stupid person [ME, of unkn. orig.]

lōōf. Var. of LUFF.

lōō'fah (-*a*) *n.* Pod of the plant *Luffa aegyptiaca* used as flesh-brush or sponge. [f. Egypt. Arab. *lūfa*, the plant]

lŏŏk *v.* & *n.* **1.** *v.i.* Use one's sight, turn eyes in some direction; ~ **before you leap,** avoid precipitate action. **2.** *v.t.* Contemplate, examine; ~ person **through and through,** observe him searchingly; look (person, *death,* etc.) *in the* EYE[1](*s*) or *in the* FACE[1]; *look a* GIFT*-horse in the mouth*; **~'ing-glass,** glass mirror. **3.** Express, threaten, show, by one's looks (*look compassion, death,* DAGGERS, etc.). **4.** Ascertain or observe by sight *what, who, how, whether,* etc.; ~ **what you've done!, who's here!,** etc., (excl. of rebuke or surprise). **5.** *v.i.* Make visual or (fig.) mental search (*I'll look in the morning*; *instead of reforming others let him look at home*); inquire (*when one looks deeper*); take care or make sure *that,* expect *to* do; ~ **(here)!** (demanding attention or expostulating); ~**-see,** (sl.) survey, inspection; ~ **sharp,** [orig. = keep strict watch] lose no time, bestir oneself; ~ **you!**, observe this fact. **6.** (Of thing) face, be turned, have or afford outlook, in some direction (*towards, onto, into, over, down,* etc.). **7.** Have specified appearance, seem, (*look a fool, foolish, to be real, every inch a king,* one's BEST[1]); ~ **alive!**, make haste; ~ **small,** be exposed as mean etc.; ~ **well** or **ill,** (1) seem in good or bad health, (2, of thing; *also ~ **good** or **bad**) seem to be going well or ill; ~ **as if,** suggest by appearance the belief that; ~ **like,** have appearance of being, ||seem to be, threaten or promise, indicate presence of, (*it looks like this, like rain, like rats; he looks like an angel, a policeman, biting, winning*); hence ~'ING[2] *a.* (*good-looking, grave-looking,* etc.). **8.** Seem to be (~ one's **age,** seem as old as one really is; ~ **oneself again,** seem recovered). **9.** (w. *preps.*): ~ **about** one, examine one's surroundings, take time to form plans; ~ **after,** follow with the eye, seek for, attend to, take care of; ~ **at,** direct one's eyes or attention at, examine or consider thus; *to ~ at,* in outward appearance; *to ~ at him* etc., judging by his etc. appearance; *will not ~ at,* refuses to take, rejects, scorns; ~ *down* one's *nose at,* (colloq.) regard with contempt or with covert displeasure; ~ **for,** expect, hope or be on the watch for, search for (*look for* TROUBLE); ~ **into,** examine the inside of (box etc.), dip into (book), investigate; ~ **on,** regard *as,* regard (coldly, *with* distrust etc.); ~ **over,** inspect, (arch.) overlook or pardon; ~ **through,** direct one's sight through (window etc.), penetrate (veil etc.) with sight or (pretence or pretender) with insight, inspect exhaustively or successively, ignore by pretending not to see, glance through (book etc.); ~ **to,** consider, take care of, be careful about (*look to your manners; look to it that*), keep watch over, rely on (person or thing) *for,* expect, count upon, aim at; ~ **upon,** = *look on* (see above). **10.** (w. *advs.*): ~ **about** or **around,** be on the watch, make search *for,* let one's eyes rove; ~ **back,** be half-hearted about enterprise one has begun (usu. w. neg.), turn one's thoughts (*up*)*on* or *to* something past, cease to progress (usu. w. neg.), ||make a second call later; ~ **down (up)on,** consider oneself superior to; ~ **forward to,** anticipate (usu. with pleasure, also *with apprehension* etc.); ~ **in,** make short visit or call, (colloq.) watch television; ~*-in* n., informal call or visit, chance of participation or success; ~ **on,** be (mere) spectator; ~ **out,** direct one's sight or put one's head out of window etc., be vigilant, keep one's eyes open *for* expected person, be prepared *for* squalls etc., have or afford outlook *on, over,* etc., ||select or find by inspection; ~*-out* n., watch, looking out, (*keep a good look-out; on the look-out for* or *to* do), post of observation, man or party or boat stationed to look out, view over landscape, prospect of luck (*it's a bad* or *poor look-out for him*), person's own concern (*that is his ~-out,* he must deal with that himself); ~ **over,** inspect one by one or part by part (*must look them over soon*); ~ **round,** look in every or another direction, examine objects of interest in a place, or possibilities etc. with a view to deciding on a course of action; ~ **through,** survey with searching glance (*looked him through*), inspect exhaustively or successively; ~ **up,** improve in price or prosperity, search for (esp. word in dictionary or facts in book of reference), (colloq.) go to visit (person), raise eyes; ~ *up to,* respect, venerate; ~ person *up and down,* scrutinize him keenly or contemptuously. **11.** *n.* Act of looking, directing of eyes to look at thing or person, glance, (*a kind, scornful, look*); (in *sing.* or *pl.*) appearance of face, expression, personal aspect, (**good ~s,** beauty); (of thing) appearance (*the place has a European look; the peasant look in knitwear;* **don't like the ~ of this,** find it alarming). [OE *lōcian,* = OS *lōkon* f. WG **lōk-, *lōg-*]

loo'ker *n.* In vbl senses; person having specified appearance (*good-looker*); (colloq.) attractive woman; ~**-o'n,** one who is a mere spectator. [ME, f. prec. + -ER[1]]

lōōm[1] *n.* Apparatus for weaving yarn or thread crosswise into fabric. [ME *lōme* f. OE *gelōma* tool (as Y-, **lōma* apparatus)]

lōōm[2] *v.i.,* & *n.* **1.** *v.i.* Appear indistinctly, be seen in vague and often magnified or threatening shape, (lit. or fig.; often *loom large* etc.). **2.** *n.* Vague often exaggerated first appearance of land at sea etc. [prob. f. LDu.; cf. EFris. *lōmen* move slowly, MHG *lüemen* be weary]

lōōm[3]. Var. of LOON[2].

lōōm[4] *n.* (Inboard part of) shaft of oar. [f. Scand.; cf. Norw. *lumm*]

lōōn[1] *n.* (Sc. or arch.) Scamp, idler; lad. [ME, of unkn. orig.]

lōōn[2] *n.* Diving bird, esp. grebe or large diver; crazy person (cf. foll.). [alt. f. *loom* f. ON *lómr*]

lōō'nȳ *n.* (sl.) Lunatic; ~**-bin,** mental home or hospital. [abbr.; see -Y[2]]

lōōp[1] *n.* & *v.* **1.** *n.* Figure produced by a curve, or doubled string etc., that crosses itself; attachment or ornament formed of cord, thread, etc., so crossed and fastened at crossing; ring or curved piece of metal as handle etc.; contraceptive coil; ~(**-line**), railway or telegraph line that diverges from main line and joins it again; manœuvre in which aeroplane is flown upside down between climb and dive; (Skating) curve crossing itself made on single edge; (Electr.) complete circuit for current; endless strip of tape or film allowing continuous repetition; hence ~'Y[2] *a.,* (sl.) crazy. **2.** *v.t.* Form (string etc.) into loop(s); enclose (as) with loop; fasten (*up, back*) or join (*together*) with loop(s); ~ **the** ~, (Aeron.) perform loop. **3.** *v.i.* (Esp. of looper larvae) form loop. [ME, of unkn. orig.]

lōōp[2] *n.* = LOOPHOLE. [ME, of unkn. orig.]

lōō'per *n.* Caterpillar of geometer moth, progressing by arching itself into loops; contrivance in sewing-machine etc. for making loops. [f. LOOP[1] + -ER[1]]

lōō'phōle (-p-h-) *n.,* & *v.t.* **1.** *n.* Narrow vertical slit in wall for shooting or looking through or to admit light or air; outlet, means of evading rule etc. **2.** *v.t.* Make loopholes in (wall etc.). [f. LOOP[2] + HOLE[1]]

lōōse[1] *a.* **1.** Released from bonds or restraint; (of animal) not confined or tethered etc.; LET[2] *loose.* **2.** Detached or detachable from its place (*come, get, work, loose*); **cut** ~, begin to act freely; *play* FAST[3] *and loose.* **3.** Hanging partly free (esp. *loose end;* **at a ~ end, *at ~ ends,** without definite occupation); not rigidly fixed, apt to shift, (*have a* SCREW *loose*); not fastened together or held in container etc. (*loose papers, hair, tea*). **4.** Slack, relaxed, not tense or tight, (**with a ~ rein,** lit. of riding, fig. indulgently); (of tongue) likely to speak indiscreetly; (of bowels) tending to diarrhoea; ~ **build** or **make,** ungainly figure; ~**-limbed,** having supple limbs. **5.** Not compact, dense, or serried (*loose soil, fabric;* ~ **order,** arrangement of soldiers etc. with wide intervals); (Footb., of ball) not in any player's possession, (of play etc.) with players not close together. **6.** (Of statement, idea, etc.) inexact, indefinite, vague, incorrect; (of translation) not close or faithful; (of style) ungrammatical; (of agent) doing the act loosely (*loose thinker*); (Cricket, of bowling) inaccurately pitched, (of fielding) careless or bungling. **7.** Morally lax, dissolute, promiscuous, wanton in speech or act. **8.** *Loose* BOX²; **~ change,** money as coins in pocket etc. for casual use; ||**~ cover,** removable cover for chair etc.; **~-leaf** *a.*, (of ledger, notebook, etc.) with each leaf separate and removable; (in *comb.*) loosely (*loose-flowing, -fitting*). **9.** Hence **~'**LY² (-slĭ) *adv.*, **~'**NESS (-sn-) *n.*, **loo'**SISH¹ 2 *a.* [ME *lōs* f. ON *lauss* (= OE *lēas* untrue, OS, OHG *lōs*, Goth. *laus*), f. Gmc **lausaz*]

loose² *v.t.* Release, set free, free from constraint; untie, undo, (knot, fetters, seal, hair of head); detach from moorings; **~** (**off**), discharge (arrow), (abs.) discharge gun (*at*); relax (*loose hold*). [ME, f. prec.]

loose³ *n.* **1.** Loose play in football (*in the loose*); state of freedom or unrestrainedness (**on the ~,** having a spree). **2.** Free expression (*give a loose to* one's *feelings*). [f. LOOSE¹,²]

loo'sen *v.t.* & *i.* Make or become less tight or compact or firm; relieve (bowels) from constipation or (cough) from dryness; relax (discipline etc.); **~** person's **tongue,** make him speak freely. [ME, f. LOOSE¹ + -EN⁶]

loo'sestrife (-s-s-) *n.* Marsh plant of genus *Lysimachia*, esp. *L. vulgaris* (**golden** or **yellow ~**); marsh plant of genus *Lythrum*, esp. *L. salicaria* (**purple** or **red** or **spiked ~**). [f. LOOSE² + STRIFE, mistransl. of L f. Gk *lusimakhion* (Gk pers. name of discoverer *Lusimakhos*), as if directly f. *luō* undo, *makhē* battle]

loot *n.*, & *v.t.* **1.** *n.* Goods taken from enemy, spoil; booty, illicit gains made by official; *(sl.) money. **2.** *v.t.* Plunder, sack, (city, building, etc., or abs.); carry off as booty; hence **~'**ER¹ *n.* [f. Hindi *lūṭ*]

lŏp¹ *n.* & *v.* (**-pp-**). **1.** *n.* Smaller branches and twigs of trees (**~ and top, ~ and crop,** trimmings of tree). **2.** *v.t.* Cut off branches and twigs and rarely top of (tree); strip tree of (branches etc. *off, away*); cut *off* or off (person's limb or head). **3.** *v.i.* Make lopping strokes *at*. [n. f. v., ME f. OE **loppian*; cf. obs. *lip* to prune]

lŏp² *v.* (**-pp-**) & *n.* **1.** *v.i.* & *t.* Hang limply; (of animal) let (ears) hang. **2.** *v.i.* Slouch, dawdle, hang about; move with short bounds. **3. ~-ears,** drooping ears; so **~-eared** *a.*; **~-ear,** = sense 5. **4.** Hence **~'**PY² *a.* **5.** *n.* Lop-eared rabbit. [cogn. w. LOB]

lōpe *v.i.*, & *n.* (Run with) long bounding stride (esp. of animals). [ME, var. of Sc. *loup* f. ON *hlaupa* LEAP¹]

lŏ'pho- *comb. form.* Crested, as: **~branch** (-ăngk), (fish) with gills arranged in tufts; **~dont,** (animal) with transverse ridges on crowns of molars; **~phore,** tentacled disc at mouth of bryozoan. [f. Gk *lophos* crest + -O-]

lŏpsī'dĕd *a.* With one side lower or smaller than the other, unevenly balanced; hence **~**LY² *adv.*, **~**NESS *n.* [f. LOP² + SIDE¹ + -ED²]

loq. *abbr. loquitur.*

loquā'cious (-shus) *a.* Talkative; (of birds, water) chattering, babbling; hence or cogn. **~**LY² *adv.*, **~**NESS, **loquă'**CITY, *ns.* [L *loquax -acis* (*loqui* talk); see -ACIOUS]

lō'quat (-ŏt) *n.* (Small reddish fruit of) orig. Chinese and Japanese tree, *Eriobotrya japonica*. [f. Chin. *luh kwat* rush orange]

loquitur (lŏ'kwĭtėr) *v.i.* 3 *sing. pres.* Speaks (with speaker's name added, as stage-direction or to inform reader). [L]

||**lor** *int.* (vulg.) = LORD 6. [abbr.]

lor'al *a.* Of the LORE². [f. LORE² + -AL]

lor'an *n.* System of navigation using signal pulses from four radio transmitters. [f. *long-range navigation*]

lor'cha *n.* Ship with hull of European shape but Chinese rig. [Port.]

lord *n.*, *int.*, & *v.t.* **1.** *n.* Master, ruler, chief, prince, sovereign, (*our sovereign lord the King*; *Lord of* MISRULE; **~s of creation,** (1) mankind, (2, joc.) men as opp. women); (poet. or rhet.) owner (*lord of a few acres*; cf. LANDLORD); magnate in some trade (*the cotton lords*; cf. KING¹ 3). **2.** Feudal superior (MESNE *lord*; *lord of the* MANOR). **3. ~** (**and master**), (poet. or joc.) husband. **4.** (Astrol.) Dominant planet. **5. L~** (**God**), (usu. with *the*, exc. in *voc.*) God (*the Lord gave, and the Lord hath taken away; blessed be the name of the Lord*); **L~** (**only**) **knows,** (colloq.) I cannot guess (*who, how*, etc.). **6.** *int.* (colloq.) **L~!, oh L~(y)!, good L~!,** (expr. surprise or consternation); **L~ have mercy, L~ bless me** or **my soul** or **you** or **us,** *Lord* LOVE² *you*, (expr. surprise). **7.** *n.* **Our L~, the L~,** Christ; **in the year of our L~** (of the Christian era); **L~'s day,** Sunday; **the L~'s Prayer,** the Our Father, prayer taught by Christ to his disciples (Matt. 6:9–13); **the L~'s Supper,** the Eucharist; **the L~'s table,** (1) Christian altar, (2) Eucharist. **8.** Nobleman, peer of the realm or person entitled by courtesy to the title *Lord* (see below) as part of his ordinary style (**live, treat, like a ~,** fare, entertain, sumptuously; *drunk* **as,** *swear* **like, a ~,** excessively; ||**~-in-waiting, ~ of the bedchamber,** nobleman attending queen, king); **the L~s,** the TEMPORAL and SPIRITUAL peers of Parliament; **House of L~s,** (1) upper legislative chamber of United Kingdom, (2) committee of specially qualified members of this appointed as ultimate judicial appeal court, (3) building where these bodies meet. **9.** ||**L~s** (**Commissioners**), members of board performing duties of high State office put in commission; **First L~,** president of such board; **Sea L~,** naval member of Admiralty Board; **L~s of Session,** judges of Scottish Court of Session. **10.** *Lord* ADVOCATE¹; **L~ of Appeal** (**in Ordinary**), member of House of Lords (2) (see sense 8); **L~ Bishop** (ceremonious title of any bishop); *Lord* CHAMBERLAIN, (*High*) CHANCELLOR; ||**L~ Chief Justice,** president of Queen's Bench Division; *Lord* (*High*) COMMISSIONER; ||**L~ Justice** (**of Appeal**), judge in Court of Appeal; **L~ Justice Clerk,** vice-president of Scottish Court of Session; **L~ Justice General,** Lord President as head of Scottish Court of Justiciary; ||**L~ Lieutenant,** (1) viceroy of Ireland till 1922, (2) chief executive authority and head of magistrates in each county; *Lord* ||LYON, MAYOR, ||PRESIDENT, ||PRIVY *Seal*, ||PROVOST, ||RECTOR, ||(*High*) STEWARD. **11.** ||(Prefixed as part of less formal personal designation of) marquis, earl, viscount, or baron, (whether peer, or peer's eldest son holding his father's second title by courtesy; never with *of*: *the Earl of Derby* or (*the*) *Lord Derby*; always used in place of *Baron* except very formally). **12.** (Prefixed to Christian name, with or without surname, of) younger son of duke or marquis. **13. My ~,** respectful or polite form of address or (arch.) reference to nobleman (below duke), bishop, lord mayor, lord provost, or judge of supreme court. **14. ~s and ladies,** wild arum. **15.** Hence **~'**LESS *a.*, **~'**LING¹ 2 *n.* **16.** *v.t.* Rule *over* like a lord (usu. in *pass.*: *will not be lorded over*, or with *it*: *lording it over his household*); ennoble, confer title of *Lord* upon. [OE *hlāford* f. *hlāfweard* = bread-keeper (as LOAF¹, WARD¹)]

lor'dl|ȳ *a.* Haughty, imperious, lofty, disdainful; grand, magnificent, fit for or belonging to a lord; hence **~ĭ**NESS *n.* [OE *hlāfordlic* (as prec., -LY¹)]

lord|ō'sĭs *n.* (*pl.* **~oses** *pr.* -ō'sēz). (Med.) Curvature of spine, convex forwards (opp. *kyphosis*); hence **~o'tic** *a.* [mod. L, f. Gk *lordōsis* (*lordos* bent backwards; see -OSIS)]

Lord's (-z) *n.* Cricket ground in London, headquarters of the M.C.C. and English cricket. [f. T. *Lord* d. 1832, maker of successive grounds named after him, + 's 1]

lor'dship *n.* Dominion, rule, ownership *of* or *over*; domain, estate, manor; being a lord; **his, your, ~, their ~s,** he, you, they, (in respectful mention of or address to holder(s) of title *Lord*; also iron.). [OE *hlāfordscipe* (as LORD, -SHIP)]

lor'dy̆ *int.* See LORD 6. [f. LORD + -Y[3]]

lore[1] *n.* **1.** (arch.) Doctrine; erudition, scholarship. **2.** Body of traditions and knowledge on a subject (*ghost, bird, sacred*, etc., *lore*). [OE *lār*, = OS, OHG *lēra* f. WG **laiza* f. Gmc **laizō* (**lais-* LEARN)]

lore[2] *n.* (Zool.) Straplike surface, in birds between eye and upper mandible, in snakes between eye and nostril. [f. L *lorum* strap]

lorgnĕ'tte (-nyĕ't), **lor'gnon** (-nyawṅ), *ns.* (in *sing.* or *pl.*) Pair of eyeglasses or opera-glasses held by long handle. [F (*lorgner* to squint; see -ETTE)]

lŏ'rĭcate *a.* (Zool.) Having defensive armour of bone, plates, scales, etc. [f. L *loricatus* (*lorica* breastplate f. *lorum* strap; see -ATE[2])]

lŏ'rĭkeet (*or* -ē't) *n.* Small brightly-coloured Polynesian parrot allied to the lory. [dim. of LORY, after *parakeet*]

lŏ'rĭmer, lŏ'rĭner, *n.* (Hist.) Bit-maker, spurrier, (now only in title of a livery company). [ME, f. OF *loremier, -nier* (*lorain* harness-strap f. Rom. **loranum* f. L *lorum* thong); see -ER[2] (2)]

lor'ĭs *n.* Small slender tailless nocturnal arboreal lemur (**slender ~,** *Loris gracilis* of S. India etc.; **slow ~,** *Bradicebus tardigradus* of E. Indies etc.). [F, perh. f. obs. Du. *loeris* clown]

lorn *a.* (arch. or joc.) Desolate, forlorn. [p.p. of obs. *leese* f. OE *-lēosan* lose]

||**lŏ'rry̆** *n.* Motor truck for transporting goods, troops, etc.; long flat low wagon; truck used on railways and tramways. [19th c., orig. N. Engl., perh. f. name *Laurie*]

lor'y̆ *n.* Bright-plumaged parrot-like Asian bird. [f. Malay *lūri*]

lose (lōōz) *v.* (**lost** *pr.* lŏst *or* lawst). **1.** *v.t.* Be deprived of, cease by negligence, misadventure, separation, death, etc., to possess or have, (*property, honour*, person's *confidence, limb, father, friend*, etc.); get rid of (a cold etc.); *lose* FACE[1], GROUND[1] 7, one's HEAD[1] 22, (one's) HEART; **~ interest,** (of person) cease to be interested, (of thing) cease to interest; *lost* LABOUR[1]; *lose* one's LIFE, one's MIND[1]; **lost motion,** imperfect transmission of mechanical motion owing to looseness etc.; **~** (one's) **patience,** become impatient (*with*); **~** one's **patient,** (of doctor) (1) fail to keep him alive, (2) be left by him for another doctor; **~** one's **temper,** become angry; **lost wax,** *cire perdue*; **~ way,** (of ship or boat) begin to move less quickly. **2.** (in *pass.*) Disappear, perish, die or be dead, (*letter-writing is a lost art*; *the ship and all hands were lost*); **lost to** person, taken from his possession; **lost to** *sense of duty, shame*, etc., no longer affected by them; **lost soul** (damned). **3.** *v.i.* Suffer loss or detriment, incur disadvantage, be the worse off in money or otherwise *by* transaction etc., (*the publisher lost by it*; *I lost on the deal*); (of clock etc.) become slow, indicate time earlier than correct time; *story* **does not ~ in the telling,** is, if anything, exaggerated; **~ in,** suffer loss as regards (*the work loses in freshness*); **~ out,** (colloq.) be unsuccessful, suffer loss; **you can't ~,** (colloq.) you must inevitably profit. **4.** *v.t.* Become unable to find, fail to keep in sight or follow or mentally grasp, (*lose a document*, one's *way, the thread of a discourse, a person* etc. under observation); (in *p.p.*) having strayed or become separated from owner etc. (*lost dog*); **get lost,** (sl., usu. in *imper.*) cease to be annoying; **lost generation,** culturally and emotionally unstable generation reaching maturity *c.* 1915–25; **~** one**self in, be lost in,** be engrossed in (book etc.); **~ itself in, be lost in,** be obscured or merged in; *lose* SIGHT[1] *of*; *Lost* TRIBES. **5.** Spend (time, opportunities, efforts) to no purpose, waste; **be lost** (**up**)**on,** fail to influence or draw the attention of. **6.** Fail to obtain, catch, see, or hear, (*lose* one's *train, a legacy, a word* or *remark, a fox*); fail to carry (motion); forfeit (stake, right to thing); be defeated in (game, race, battle, bet, lawsuit, or abs.); *lost* CAUSE[1]; **losing battle, game,** (in which defeat seems inevitable); **losing game,** test of skill in forcing opponent to win; *losing* HAZARD; *lose the* TOSS. **7.** Cause person the loss of, cost, (*will lose you your place*). **8.** Hence **lo'sable** (lōō'z-) *a.* [OE *losian* perish, destroy (*los* loss); later sense-development infl. by obs. (cogn.) *leese*, and pronunc. prob. by LOOSE[1]]

lō'sel (-z-) *n.* (arch.) Profligate, rake; ne'er-do-well. [ME, app. f. *los-*, stem of *leese*; see LORN]

lo'ser (lōō'z-) *n.* In vbl senses (**be a ~ by,** suffer loss by; **good ~,** person not dejected or angered by losing game etc.); person, horse, etc., that loses race etc.; ||(Bill.) losing HAZARD; (Bridge) card that will not take a trick. [ME, f. LOSE + -ER[1]]

lŏss (*or* laws) *n.* **1.** Losing or being lost (see LOSE). **2.** Person, thing, or amount lost (CUT[2] one's *losses*; *loss in weight on heating*; *suffered heavy losses*). **3.** Detriment, disadvantage, resulting from loss (person etc. **is a great, no,** etc., **~,** the loss of him is a serious blow, a matter of indifference, etc.). **4. At a ~** (*for, to discover*, etc.), puzzled, not knowing what to do; **at a ~,** (*sold* etc.) for less than was paid for it; DEAD *loss*; PROFIT[1] *and loss*; **~-leader,** article sold at a loss to attract customers for other articles. [ME *los, loss(e)*, prob. back form. f. *lost*, p.p. of LOSE]

löss (lērs). Var. of LOESS.

lost. See LOSE.

lŏt *n.*, & *v.t.* (**-tt-**). **1.** *n.* One of a set of objects used to secure a chance decision in dividing goods, selecting officials, etc., (*draw* or *cast* or *throw lots* usu. *between, for, who*, etc.; THROW[1] or CAST[1] *in* one's *lot with*). **2.** This method of deciding (*chosen by lot*); choice resulting from it (*the lot fell upon me*). **3.** What falls to person by lot, share (*have neither* PART[1] *nor lot in*); person's destiny, fortune, condition, (*the lot falls to me, it falls to my lot, it falls to me as my lot, to* do). **4.** ||Tax, due, (SCOT[1] *and lot*). **5.** Plot or allotment of land, *esp. for a specific purpose (*film lot*; *parking lot*); ***across ~s,** over fields etc. as short cut. **6.** Article or set of articles offered separately at sale, item at auction; **bad ~,** disreputable or vicious person. **7.** Number or quantity of persons or things of same kind or associated in some way; **the** (**whole**) **~,** the total number or quantity; **that's the ~,** (colloq.) there is no more to come. **8.** (colloq.) Considerable number or amount, *a* good or great deal (*saw a lot of accidents*; *goes to the theatre a lot*); (in *pl.*) a great quantity or number (*there is lots of soup left*; *has lots of friends*). **9.** *v.t.* Divide (land, usu. *out*, or goods for sale) into lots. [OE *hlot* portion, choice, f. Gmc **hleut-*, **hlaut-*, **hlut-*]

lōth. See LOATH.

Lothār'īō (*or* -ar'-) *n.* (*pl.* **~s**). Libertine, rake. [character in Rowe's *Fair Penitent* (1703)]

lō'tion *n.* Liquid preparation used externally to heal wound, beautify skin, etc. [ME f. OF, or f. L *lotio* (*lavare lot-* wash; see -ION)]

lŏ'ttery̆ *n.* Arrangement for distributing prizes by chance among purchasers of tickets (**~-wheel,** wheel with box used for shuffling numbers corresponding to those on tickets); (fig.) thing that defies calculation (*life, marriage, is a lottery*). [prob. f. Du. *loterij* (as LOT, -ERY)]

lŏ'ttō *n.* Game of chance with drawing of numbers, as in lottery, and cards bearing various rows of numbers, winner being first to have card with a row of numbers all of which have been drawn. [It.]

lō'tus *n.* **1.** Plant represented in ancient Greek legend as inducing luxurious dreaminess and distaste for active life; **~-eater, ~-land,** person given to, place of, indolent enjoyment. **2.** Egyptian water-lily of genus *Nymphaea*; Indian water-plant with large pink flowers, of genus *Nelumbo*; this as used symbolically in Hinduism and Buddhism (**~ position,** cross-legged position of meditation); bird's-foot trefoil or other plant of genus *Lotus*. [L, f. Gk *lōtos*, of Semitic origin]

louche (lo͞osh) *a.* Oblique; disreputable, shifty. [F, = squinting]

loud *a.* & *adv.* **1.** *a.* Strongly audible; *loud* PEDAL[1]; **~spea'ker,** (esp. Naut.) **~ hailer,** apparatus that converts (sound through) electrical impulses into sound loud enough to be heard at some distance. **2.** Clamorous, noisy; (of colour, dress, pattern, manners) obtrusive, conspicuous, flashy. **3.** Hence ~'EN[6] *v.i.*, ~'ISH 2 *a.*, ~'LY[2] *adv.*, ~'NESS *n.* **4.** *adv.* Loudly (*don't talk so loud; laughed loud and long*); **out ~,** aloud (*laughed out loud when I read it*); *loud-spoken* (see SPEAK 10). [OE *hlūd*, = OS *hlūd*, OHG *hlūt* f. WG **hludha* f. IE **klutos* (**klu-* hear)]

lough (lŏχ) *n.* (Ir.) Lake, arm of sea. [f. Ir. *loch* LOCH, w. spelling of obs. *lough* lake, ME f. same source]

louis (lo͞o'ĭ) *n.* (*pl.* same *pr.* -z). **1.** **~(-d'or)** (-dôr), (Hist.) French gold coin of (about) 20 francs. **2.** **L~ Treize** (trāz), **Quatorze** (kătôr'z), **Quinze** (kănz), **Seize** (sāz), styles of furniture etc. prevalent in reigns of kings Louis XIII, XIV, XV, XVI, of France. [f. *Louis*, Christian name of many kings of France]

loung|e (-nj) *v.i.*, & *n.* **1.** *v.i.* Go lazily, saunter; loll, recline; idle; hence ~'ER[1] *n.* **2.** *n.* Spell of lounging, saunter, stroll. **3.** Place where one can lounge, esp. entrance-hall or gallery furnished for the purpose; place at airport etc. with seats for waiting passengers; sitting-room in house. **4.** Sofa or deep chair. **5.** **~e chair,** comfortable easy chair; **~e lizard,** (sl.) idler in fashionable society; ||**~e suit,** man's ordinary suit for day wear in offices etc., with tailless jacket. [perh. f. obs. *lungis* lout]

loupe (lo͞op) *n.* Magnifying instrument of lens(es) mounted on frame. [F]

lour, lower[2], (lowr) *v.i.*, & *n.* **1.** *v.i.* Frown, scowl, look sullen, (*on, upon, at*); (of clouds, sky, storm) look dark and threatening. **2.** *n.* Scowl; gloominess of sky etc., whence ~'Y[2] *a.* [ME *loure*, of unkn. orig.]

louse *n.*, & *v.t.* **1.** *n.* (*pl.* **lice**). Parasitic insect (*Pediculus humanus*) infesting human hair and skin and transmitting many diseases; other insect of order Anoplura or Mallophaga parasitic on mammals, birds, fish, or plants; **~'wort,** plant of genus *Pedicularis* with purple-pink flowers found in marshes and wet fields. **2.** (sl., *pl.* **~s**). Contemptible person. **3.** *v.t.* Remove lice from; **~ up,** (sl.) make a mess of. [OE *lūs*, pl. *lȳs*, = OHG *lūs*, ON *lús*]

lou's|y̆ (-zĭ) *a.* **1.** Infested with lice. **2.** (sl.) Disgusting; disgustingly bad or ill (*I feel lousy today*); abundantly supplied *with* (money etc.), swarming *with*. **3.** Hence ~ĭLY[2] *adv.*, ~ĭNESS *n.* [ME, f. prec. + -Y[2]]

lout[1] *n.* Awkward fellow, bumpkin; rough-mannered or unpleasantly aggressive man; hence ~'ISH[1] *a.* [perh. f. foll.]

lout[2] *v.i.* (arch.) Bow, make obeisance. [OE *lūtan*, = ON *lúta* f. Gmc **leut-*]

lou'ver, lou'vre, (lo͞o'*ver*) *n.* Domed turret-like erection on hall-roof etc. with side openings to let smoke out or air in; **~s, ~-boards,** arrangement of overlapping boards (or strips of glass etc.) to admit air but exclude light or rain; arrangement of overlapping strips of metal to admit cooling air to engine; hence **lou'v(e)**RED[2] (lo͞o'verd) *a.* [ME, f. OF *lov(i)er* skylight, prob. f. Gmc & cogn. w. LODGE[1]]

lo'vab|le (lŭ'-) *a.* Deserving love, amiable; hence ~**le**NESS (-beln-) *n.*, ~LY[2] *adv.* [f. LOVE[2] + -ABLE]

lo'vage (lŭ'-) *n.* S. European herb (*Levisticum officinale*) grown for use in flavouring etc.; white-flowered herb of genus *Ligustrum*. [ME *loveache* alt. f. OF *levesche* f. LL *levisticum* f. L *ligusticum* neut. of *ligusticus* Ligurian]

love[1] (lŭv) *n.* **1.** Warm affection, attachment, liking, or fondness, paternal benevolence (esp. of God), affectionate devotion, (*of, for, to,* or *towards* person; *for* or *to* thing); **give** person's **~ to,** convey affectionate message from him to (another); **send** one's **~,** send such message (*to*); **for the ~ of,** for the sake or in the name of (*God, Heaven,* (sl.) *Mike,* etc.), esp. in adjurations; *play* **for ~,** for the pleasure of it, not for stakes; **for ~ or money,** by any means, esp. *cannot get it* etc. *for love or money*; LABOUR[1] *of love*; **there's no ~ lost between them,** they dislike each other. **2.** Sexual affection or passion or desire, relation between sweethearts; this feeling as a literary subject, a personified influence, or a god; representation of Cupid, or of naked winged child, symbolizing love; **in ~,** inspired by sexual love; **in ~ with,** feeling such love for, (fig.) fond of (a pursuit, thing, etc.); **fall in ~,** enter state of being in love; **out of ~,** no longer in love (*with*); *all's* FAIR[2] *in love and war*; **~ in a cottage,** marriage on insufficient means; **make ~,** (1) pay amorous attentions *to*, (2) have or seek sexual intercourse. **3.** Beloved one, sweetheart, (esp. of woman); (as colloq. form of address by or to woman or to child); **my ~** (as form of address between husband and wife, sweethearts, etc.). **4.** (colloq.) Delightful person or pretty thing (*he is an old love; what loves of teacups!*). **5.** (In games) no score, nothing, nil; **~ all,** neither side has yet scored; **~ game, set,** (in which loser has not scored). **6.** **~ affair,** (usu. temporary) relationship between two people in love; **~-apple,** (arch.) tomato; **~-begotten,** illegitimate; **~-bird,** parakeet esp. of genus *Agapornis* said to pine away at death of its mate; **~-child** (illegitimate); **~-feast,** (1) meal in token of brotherly love among early Christians, (2) religious service among Methodists etc. imitating this; **~-hate** (**relationship**), intense emotional response involving both love and hate; **~-in-a-mist,** garden plant (*Nigella damascena*) with blue flowers amid green bracts; **~-in-idleness,** wild pansy; **~-knot,** = TRUE-*love knot*; **~-letter** (between sweethearts and concerned with love); **~-lies-bleeding,** garden plant of genus *Amaranthus* with long drooping spike of purple-red bloom; **~'lock,** tress or curl worn on temple or forehead; **~'lorn,** pining with love, deserted by one's lover; **~-making,** (1) courtship, (2) sexual intercourse; **~-match,**

marriage made for love's sake; **~-nest,** place of intimate love-making; **~-philtre,** philtre; **~-seat,** armchair or sofa for two persons; **~'sick,** languishing with love; **~-song** (about or expressing love); **~-story,** novel etc. of which main theme is love, facts of a wooing etc.; **~-token,** thing given as sign of love. **7.** Hence ~'SOME^1 (-vs-) *a.* (literary), lovable, lovely, loving, ~'WORTHY (-vw-) *a.* [OE *lufu*, = OHG *luba*, Goth. *-lubō* f. Gmc **leubh-*, **laubh-*, **lubh-*; cf. LIEF, LEAVE^1, BELIEVE]

love^2 (lŭv) *v.* **1.** *v.t.* Hold dear, bear or make love to, be in love with, be fond of; *love me, love my* DOG^1; **Lord ~ you!** (excl. of surprise at person's mistake etc.); **I ~ my love with an A, a B,** etc., formula in game of forfeits. **2.** *v.i.* Be in love. **3.** *v.t.* Cling to, delight in, enjoy having, be addicted to, admire or be glad of the existence of, (life, honour, comfort, golf, do*ing*, virtue, man who knows his own mind, etc.). **4.** (w. inf. or gerund) Be (habitually) inclined (*children love to ape their elders*); (colloq.) like, be delighted, (*he simply loves to find* or *finding mistakes*; *Will you come?—I should love to*). [OE *lufian* (as prec.)]

lo'velėss (lŭ'vl-) *a.* Unloving; unloved; hence ~LY^2 *adv.*, ~NESS *n.* [ME, f. LOVE^1 + -LESS]

lo'vel|y̆ (lŭ'vlĭ) *a.* & *n.* **1.** *a.* Attractively or admirably beautiful; *beautiful in moral quality; (colloq.) delightful, very pleasing to any of the senses, intensely amusing; **~y and,** (colloq.) delightfully (*lovely and warm*); hence ~ĬLY^2 *adv.*, ~ĬNESS *n.* **2.** *n.* Glamorously beautiful woman or girl, esp. showgirl. [OE *luflic* (as LOVE^1, -LY^1)]

lo'ver (lŭ'-) *n.* **1.** Person (esp. man) in love with another (*it was a lover and his lass*), (in *pl.*) pair in love; **~'s knot,** = LOVE^1-*knot.* **2.** Person (esp. man) having illicit love affair. **3.** Admirer, devotee, *of* thing, action, or idea, (*lover of music, cleanliness*; *music-lover*). **4.** Hence ~LESS *a.*, ~LIKE, ~LY^{1,2}, *adjs.* & *advs.* [ME, f. LOVE^2 + -ER^1]

lo'vey (lŭ'-) *n.* (colloq.) = LOVE^1 3; **~-dovey,** (*n.*) = *lovey*, (*a.*) fondly affectionate, esp. unduly sentimental. [f. LOVE^1 + -Y^3]

lo'vĭng (lŭ'-) *a.* That loves, affectionate; manifesting or proceeding from love; **~-cup,** large drinking-vessel with two or more handles, passed round at banquet; **~-kindness,** tenderness and consideration; hence ~LY^2 *adv.*, ~NESS *n.* [OE *lufiende*; see LOVE^2, -ING^2]

low^1 (lō) *a.*, *n.*, & *adv.* **1.** *a.* (Of thing) not reaching far up, not reaching the normal or average level, not high or tall, (*low hills, house, shoe, forehead, flying, stature*); (of dress, neckline, etc.) leaving wearer's neck and part of shoulders and breast exposed. **2.** Not elevated in geographical etc. position; (of sun, moon, etc.) near horizon; (of person's BOW^4) with head close to ground. **3.** Of or in humble rank or position (*of low birth*; HIGH *and low*). **4.** Not exalted or sublime, commonplace, undignified, uncivilized, not highly organized; abject, mean, degraded, coarse, vulgar, (*low cunning*; *low slang*); (of playing-card) that outranks few or no others. **5.** Poorly nourished, not nourishing, indicative of poor nutrition, lacking vigour, dejected, (*low condition, diet*; *low* SPIRIT^1*s*; *low*-SPIRITED). **6.** Not intense (*low fever*); of small or less than normal amount as measured by a scale or degrees (*low attendances, prices, wages, rates, temperature*); (of latitude) near equator; **~ opinion of** (very unfavourable); **at ~est,** to mention the least possible amount etc.; *lowest common* DENOMINATOR, MULTIPLE. **7.** (Of sound) not shrill or high up, having slow vibrations; not loud (*a low whisper*); (of vowel) = OPEN^1. **8.** (Of liquid, receptacle, supply of anything, esp. fig. of purse or money) nearly exhausted or empty. **9. ~-born,** of humble birth; ***~'boy,** table with drawers and fairly short legs; **~-bred,** having vulgar manners; **~'brow** *a.* & *n.*, (colloq.) (one who is) not highly intellectual or cultured (opp. *highbrow*); **~-browed,** lit., also (of rocks) beetling, (of building etc.) with low entrance, gloomy; **Low Church,** party or principles giving only low place to ritual, authority of bishops and priests, saving grace of sacraments, etc., approximating to protestant nonconformity; **Low-Chur'chman,** holder of such principles; **~-class,** of low quality or social class; **~ comedian,** actor in **~ comedy** (in which subject and treatment border on farce); **Low Countries,** Netherlands (Holland), Belgium, and Luxembourg; **~-cut,** (of neckline etc.) = sense 1; **~-down,** (*a.*) abject, mean, dishonourable, (*n.*, sl.) true facts, inside information; *Low* DUTCH^1; **~ frequency** (esp. in Radio, 30 to 300 kilohertz); *low* GEAR; *Low* GERMAN^2; **~-grade,** of low quality; **~-key,** restrained, (Photog.) consisting of dark tones; *low* LATIN; **~ life,** that of the lower classes; **~-lying,** at low altitude (above sea-level etc.); *low* MASS^1; **~-pitched,** (of sound) low, (of roof) not very steep; **~ point,** minimum or worst state reached; **~-powered,** having little power or energy; *low* PRESSURE, PROFILE, RELIEF^2; ***~-rise,** (of building) having few storeys; **~ season,** period of relatively few visitors at resort etc.; **Low Sunday** (next after Easter); **~ tension,** = *low voltage*; *low* TIDE^1; **~ voltage,** electric potential safe for general use; **~ water,** state of tide when water is lowest, time of extreme ebb (*in ~ water*, short of money or other assets); *~-wa'ter mark*, level reached at low water, (fig.) minimum recorded value, point of least excellence, etc.; **Low Week** (beginning with Low Sunday). **10.** Hence ~'ISH^1 2 *a.*, ~'NESS *n.* **11.** *n.* A low or the lowest level or figure; area of low barometric pressure. **12.** *adv.* In or to a low position (lit. or fig.; *hangs low*; *aim low*; *bowed low*; *never fell so low as that*); in low tone (*talk low*); (of sound) at or to a low pitch. **13. Bring ~,** depress or reduce, in health, wealth, or position; **lay ~,** overthrow, bring down, humble; **lie ~,** crouch, be prostrate or dead or abased, keep quiet or out of the way, say nothing, bide one's time; **play ~,** (1) gamble for small stakes, (2) play low-ranking card; RUN^1 *low*; **tackle ~** (Rugby Footb., at or below waist). [ME *lāh*, f. ON *lágr*, = MDu. *lage*, MHG *læge* f. Gmc **lǣg-* (LIE^3)]

low^2 (lō) *v.* & *n.* **1.** *v.i.* Utter cry (as) of cattle, moo. **2.** *v.t.* Say with lowing sound. **3.** *n.* Cry of cattle. [OE *hlōwan*, = OS *hlōian*, OHG *hluoen*, f. Gmc **hlō-* f. IE **klā-*]

low'er^1 (lō'er) *v.* **1.** *v.t.* Let or haul down; cause to descend; (colloq.) drink; **~ (away),** (Naut. abs.) let down boat, haul down sail, etc. **2.** Diminish height or elevation of (*lower* one's *eyes*, one's *gun*); reduce strength of; diminish (price etc.); degrade, disgrace. **3.** *v.t.* & *i.* Diminish in intensity or pitch (*lower your voice*). **4.** *v.i.* Sink, descend, slope downwards; (of price etc.) come down. [ME, f. LOWER^3]

lower^2. See LOUR.

low'er^3 (lō'er) *a.* & *adv.* **1.** *a.* Less high in place, situated below another part, (*lower lip, atmosphere, Jurassic*, etc.), situated on less high land (*Lower Egypt*) or to the south (*Lower California*); *lower* CASE^2; **~ deck,** deck immediately over hold, ‖petty officers and men of Navy or of ship; *lower* JAW; **~ regions,** hell, realm of the dead; **~ world,** (1) the earth, (2) hell. **2.** Less high in rank, dignity, etc., (*the lower classes*); **L~ Chamber,** = *Lower House*; ~

court (subject to overruling by another on appeal etc.); *lower* CRITICISM; **L~ Empire,** Roman Empire from reign of Constantine onwards; **the L~ House** (in legislature, esp.) House of Commons; **~ mammal, plant,** etc., (evolved to only slight degree, e.g. platypus, fungus). **3.** Hence ~MOST *a.* **4.** *adv.* In or to lower position etc. (cf. LOW¹ 12). [ME, compar. of LOW¹]

low'land (lō'l-) *n.* & *a.* **1.** *n.* Low land (usu. in *pl.*, esp. of part of Scotland lying S. and E. of Highlands). **2.** *a.* Of or in lowland or the Scottish Lowlands. **3.** Hence ~ER¹ (4) *n.* [f. LOW¹ + LAND¹]

low'l|ȳ (lō'-) *a.* & *adv.* **1.** *a.* Humble in feeling, behaviour, rank, or condition, modest, unpretending; (of organism etc.) evolved to only slight degree; hence ~ĭLY² *adv.*, ~ĭNESS *n.* **2.** *adv.* In lowly manner. [ME, f. LOW¹ + -LY¹,²]

lŏx¹ *n.* Liquid oxygen. [abbr.]

***lŏx**² *n.* Smoked salmon. [f. Yiddish *laks*, cogn. w. LAX²]

lŏ'xodr|ōme *n.* Rhumb-line; so **~ŏ'mic** *a.*, of (sailing by) rhumb-lines. [f. Gk *loxos* oblique + *dromos* course]

loy'al *a.* True, faithful, to duty, love, or obligation (*to* person etc.); faithful in allegiance to sovereign, government, or mother country, (**~ toast,** toast drunk as evidence of allegiance to sovereign etc.); exhibiting loyalty; hence or cogn. ~ISM (3), ~IST (2), ~TY¹, *ns.*, ~IZE (3) *v.t.*, ~LY² *adv.* [F, f. OF *loial* etc. f. L *legalis* LEGAL]

lŏ'zėnge (-nj) *n.* **1.** Rhombus, diamond figure, esp. as bearing in heraldry; lozenge-shaped shield for spinster's or widow's arms; lozenge-shaped facet of cut gem; lozenge-shaped pane in casement. **2.** Small tablet (orig. lozenge-shaped) of flavoured sugar, medicine, meat essence, etc., to be dissolved in mouth. [ME, f. OF *losenge*, perh. deriv. of Rom. **lausa* (cf. Prov. *lausa* tombstone), of Gaulish or Iberian origin]

lŏ'zėnged (-njd) *a.* With lozenges of alternate colours; with lozenge panes. [f. prec. + -ED²]

lŏ'zėngȳ (-njĭ) *a.* (Her.) Divided into lozenges. [f. OF *losengié* (as LOZENGE; see -Y⁴)]

L.P. *abbr.* long-playing (record); low pressure.

L.P.G. *abbr.* liquefied petroleum gas.

‖**L-plāte** (ĕ'lp-) *n.* Sign bearing letter L, affixed to front and rear of motor vehicle to indicate that it is being driven by learner. [f. L + PLATE¹]

‖**L'pool** *abbr.* Liverpool.

Lr *symb.* lawrencium.

l.s. *abbr.* place of the seal (on document). [f. L *locus sigilli*]

L.S.D. *abbr.* lysergic acid diethylamide.

£.s.d. (ĕlĕsdē') *n.* Pounds, shillings, and pence (in former British currency); money, riches. [f. L *librae, solidi, denarii* pounds, shillings, pence]

L.S.E. *abbr.* London School of Economics.

'lt *v.* (arch.) = *wilt* (*thou'lt*). [abbr.]

L.T. *abbr.* low tension.

Lt. *abbr.* Lieutenant(-); light.

Ltd. *abbr.* Limited.

Lu *symb.* lutetium.

***luau** (lōō-ow') *n.* Hawaiian-style party. [f. Hawaiian *lu'au*]

lŭ'bber *n.* Big clumsy fellow, lout; clumsy seaman; **~'s hole,** (Naut.) hole in platform of ship's TOP¹ (sense 7), used to avoid climbing by futtock shrouds; **~('s) line,** (Naut.) line marked on compass showing direction of ship's head; hence ~LIKE *a.*, ~LY¹,² *a.* & *adv.* [ME, perh. f. OF *lobeor* swindler, parasite (*lober* deceive)]

lū'brĭc|āte (*or* lōō'-) *v.t.* Make slippery or smooth by applying fluid or unguent; minimize friction of (machinery) with grease etc. (lit. or fig.); hence ~ANT *a.* & *n.*, **~ātor**, ~A'TION, *ns.* [f. L *lubricare* (*lubricus* slippery) + -ATE³]

lūbrĭ'cious (-shus), **lū'brĭcous,** (*or* lōō-), *adjs.* Slippery, smooth, oily, (lit. or fig.); lewd, wanton. [f. L *lubricus* slippery + -IOUS, -OUS]

lūbrĭ'cĭtȳ (*or* lōō-) *n.* Slipperiness, smoothness, oiliness, (lit. or fig.); lewdness, wantonness. [ME, f. F *lubricité* or f. LL *lubricitas* (as prec.; see -ITY)]

***lubrĭtôr'ium** (lōō-) *n.* Place where motor vehicles are lubricated. [f. LUBRICATE after *sanatorium*]

Lū'can (*or* lōō'-) *a.* Of St. Luke. [f. eccl. L *Lucas* f. Gk *Loukas* Luke, + -AN]

lūcar'ne *n.* Dormer window. [F, f. Prov. *lucana*]

lūce (*or* lōōs) *n.* = PIKE³ (esp. when full-grown). [ME, f. OF *lu(i)s* f. LL *lucius*]

lū'c|ent (*or* lōō'-) *a.* Shining, luminous; translucent; hence ~ENCY *n.* [f. L *lucēre* shine (as LUX); see -ENT]

‖**lūcer'ne,** ‖**lūcer'n,** *n.* Leguminous European plant (*Medicago sativa*) with clover-like leaves and flowers, used for fodder, alfalfa. [f. F *luzerne*, f. mod. Prov. *luzerno* glow-worm, w. ref. to the shiny seeds]

Luciă'nĭc (lōō-) *a.* After the manner of Lucian, witty and scoffing. [f. Gk *Loukianos* Lucian, Gk writer d. *c.* A.D. 190, + -IC]

lū'cĭd (*or* lōō'-) *a.* **1.** Clear, pellucid, (usu. fig. of reasoning, literary style, etc.); **~ interval,** period of sanity between attacks of madness, or of quiet between disturbances. **2.** (poet.) Bright. **3.** (Entom. & Bot.) With smooth shining surface. **4.** Hence or cogn. ~ITY (-ĭ'd-) *n.*, ~LY² *adv.* [f. F *lucide* or It. *lucido* or f. L *lucidus* bright (*lucēre* shine f. as LUX; see -ID¹)]

Lu'cĭfer (lōō'-) *n.* **1.** (Planet Venus as) morning star. **2.** The chief rebel angel, Satan, before his fall (*as proud as Lucifer*) [f. misunderstanding of Is. 14:12]. **3.** (arch.) **l~ (match),** friction MATCH³. [OE f. L, = light-bringing, morning-star, (as LUX, *-fer* f. *ferre* bring)]

lucĭ'fūgous (lōō-) *a.* (literary or tech.) Avoiding the light. [f. L *lucifugus* (as LUX, *fugere* flee) + -OUS]

***lu'cīte** (lōō'-) *n.* = PERSPEX. [f. as prec. + -ITE¹ (2)]

lŭck *n.* **1.** (Chance as bestower of) good or ill fortune, fortuitous events affecting one's interests, person's apparent tendency to be (un)fortunate, supposed tendency of chance to bring a succession of (un)favourable events; **as ~ would have it,** (un)fortunately; **bad ~,** (omen of) ill fortune (*bad ~ to him!*, as imprecation); **down on** one's **~,** dispirited by misfortune, temporarily unfortunate; **good ~,** (omen of) good fortune; *good ~ to you*, (1) I wish you well, (2) you are being rash; HARD *luck*; **just my ~,** I am unlucky as usual; PUSH¹ one's *luck*; **try** one's **~,** make a venture; **with ~,** if all goes well; WORSE *luck!*; **you never know your ~,** you may be lucky. **2.** Good fortune, success due to chance: **for ~,** to bring good fortune; **have the ~,** be fortunate enough *to*; **in ~('s way),** having good fortune; **no ~,** lack of success; **no such ~,** unfortunately not; **out of ~,** unsuccessful; hence ~'LESS *a.* **3.** ‖**~-money,** ‖**-penny,** (1) piece of money kept for luck, (2) sum returned by seller to buyer. [ME, f. LG *luk*, f. MLG *geluke*, = MDu. *ghelucke*, MHG *gelücke*]

lŭ'ckĭlȳ *adv.* **1.** By luck; in a fortunate manner. **2.** (Qualifying whole sentence or clause) which is etc. a fortunate thing, thank goodness, (*luckily for me I was wrong*; *needed a book which was luckily still available*). [ME, f. foll. + -LY²]

lŭ'ckȳ¹ *a.* Constantly attended by good luck, enjoying it on a particular occasion, having as much success or happiness as one deserves and more; right by luck, of the nature of a fluke, (*lucky guess, hit, shot*); coming in the nick of time; presaging, bringing, worn etc. for, good luck, well-omened, (*lucky charm, penny, stone, day*); **~-bag,** ||**~ dip, -tub,** (at bazaars etc. containing articles of more or less value for one of which payer of small sum may dip; fig. of miscellany or medley from which one obtains something by chance); *lucky* STAR[1] 4; hence **lŭ'ckĭ**NESS *n.* [f. LUCK + -Y[2]]

||**lŭ'ckȳ**[2] *n.* (sl.) **Cut** one's **~**, escape, make off. [19th c.; orig. unkn.]

lŭ'ckȳ[3] *n.* (Sc.) Elderly woman. [f. LUCKY[1] as term of endearment]

lu'crative (lōō'-) *a.* Yielding gain, profitable; hence **~**LY[2] (-vlĭ) *adv.*, **~**NESS (-vn-) *n.* [ME, f. L *lucrativus* (*lucrari* to gain; see foll., -ATIVE)]

lu'cre (lōō'ker) *n.* (derog.) Pecuniary profit or gain (FILTHY *lucre*). [ME f. F, or f. L *lucrum*]

lu'cūbrāt|e (lōō'-) *v.i.* Express one's meditations in writing; produce lucubrations; hence **~**OR *n.* [f. L *lucubrare* work by lamplight (as LUX) + -ATE[3]]

lucūbrā'tion (lōō-) *n.* Nocturnal study or meditation; literary work esp. of pedantic or elaborate character. [f. L *lucubratio* (as prec.; see -ATION)]

lu'cūlent (lōō'-) *a.* (arch.) Clear, convincing, lucid, (*luculent proof, instance, explanation*); hence **~**LY[2] *adv.* [ME, = 'shining', f. L *luculentus* (as LUX; cf. -ULENT)]

Lūcŭ'llan *a.* Profusely luxurious. [f. L. L. *Lucullus*, Roman general of 1st C. B.C. famous for his lavish banquets, + -AN]

lucus a non lucendo (lōōkus ah nŏn lōōsĕ'ndō; *or* lū-, ā, -kĕ'-) *n.* Paradoxical derivation; reference of effect to paradoxical cause, explanation by contraries. [L, = *lucus* (grove) is derived from *lucēre* (shine) because there is no light there]

||**lŭd** *n.* = LORD (in **my ~, m'~**, repr. counsel's pronunc. in addressing judge).

Lŭ'ddite *n.* & *a.* (Member) of bands of English artisans (1811–16) who raised riots for destruction of machinery; (person) similarly engaged in seeking to obstruct progress. [perh. f. Ned *Lud*, insane person who destroyed two stocking-frames about 1779; see -ITE[1]]

lū'dĭcrous (*or* lōō'-) *a.* Absurd, ridiculous; exciting or deserving derision; hence **~**LY[2] *adv.*, **~**NESS *n.* [f. L *ludicrus* prob. f. *ludicrum* stage-play (*ludere* play; see -OUS)]

||**lu'dō** (lōō'-) *n.* Simple game played with dice and counters on special board. [L, = I play]

lues (lōō'ēz) *n.* Plague; **~** (**venerea** *pr.* vĭnēr'ĭa), syphilis; hence (irreg.) **lue**'TIC (lōōĕ't-) *a.* [L]

lŭff *n.* & *v.* (Naut.) **1.** *n.* Side of fore-and-aft sail next to mast or stay; ||broadest part of ship's bow where sides begin to curve in. **2.** *v.t.* & *i.* Bring ship's head, bring head of (ship), nearer wind; turn (helm) so as to secure this; (yacht-racing) get windward side of (opponent); raise or lower (jib of crane). [ME *lo(o)f* f. OF *lof*, prob. f. LG]

lŭ'ffa. Var. of LOOFAH.

Luftwaffe (lōō'ftvahfe) *n.* (Hist.) German Air Force. [G]

lŭg[1] *n.* **~('worm)**, large marine worm used as bait. [17th c.; orig. unkn.]

lŭg[2] *n.* = LUGSAIL. [abbr.]

lŭg[3] *v.* (-gg-) & *n.* **1.** *v.t.* Drag or tug (heavy object) with effort or violence; bring (subject etc.) irrelevantly *in* or *into*; force (person) *along*, *to* place, etc. **2.** *v.i.* Pull hard *at*. **3.** *n.* Hard or rough pull; *(in *pl.*) affectation. [ME, prob. f. Scand.; cf. Sw. *lugga* pull person's hair (*lugg* forelock)]

lŭg[4] *n.* **1.** (Sc. & N. Engl.) Ear. **2.** Projection on an object by which it may be carried, fixed in place, etc. **3.** *(sl.) Stupid or commonplace person. [prob. of Scand. orig.; cf. prec.]

L

luge (lōōzh) *n.*, & *v.i.* **1.** *n.* Short raised toboggan for one person seated. **2.** *v.i.* Ride on luge. [F]

lŭ'ggage *n.* Suitcases, bags, etc., (for) containing traveller's belongings; **~-van,** railway carriage for passengers' luggage. [f. LUG[3] + -AGE]

lŭ'gger (-g-) *n.* Small ship with four-cornered sails set fore and aft. [f. foll. + -ER[1]]

lŭ'gsail (*or* -sal) *n.* Four-cornered sail bent on yard slung at a third or quarter of its length from one end. [prob. f. LUG[4] + SAIL[1]]

lugū'brious (lōō- *or* lo͝o-; *or* -gōō'-) *a.* Doleful, dismal, mournful; hence **~**LY[2] *adv.*, **~**NESS *n.* [f. L *lugubris* (*lugēre* mourn) + -OUS]

lu'kewarm (lōō'kwôrm; *or* -ôr'm) *a.* Moderately warm, tepid; not zealous, indifferent; hence **~**LY[2] *adv.*, **~**NESS *n.* [ME, f. (now dial.) *luke*, *lew*, f. OE **hlēow*, = ON *hlýr* warm, + WARM[1]]

lŭll *v.* & *n.* **1.** *v.t.* Soothe or send to sleep by sounds or caresses, quiet (suspicion etc.) usu. by deception; (in *pass.*) be deluded *into* (undue confidence), (of sea, storm) be made quiescent. **2.** *v.i.* (Of storm or noise) lessen, fall quiet. **3.** *n.* Intermission in storm (lit. or fig.) or in any activity. [ME, imit. of sounds used in lulling child]

lŭ'llabȳ *n.*, & *v.t.* **1.** *n.* Soothing refrain or song to put child to sleep. **2.** *v.t.* Sing to sleep. [f. as prec. + *-by* as in BYE-BYE[1]]

***lu'lu** (lōō'lōō) *n.* (sl.) Remarkable or excellent person or thing. [19th c., perh. f. *Lulu*, pet-form of *Louise*]

lŭmbā'gō *n.* (*pl.* **~**s). Rheumatic affection in muscles of loins. [L (*lumbus* loin)]

lŭ'mbar *a.* (Of artery, vein, nerve, vertebra, etc.) of or in loin(s); **~ puncture,** spinal puncture in this area. [f. med. L *lumbaris* f. L *lumbus* loin; see -AR[1]]

lŭ'mber[1] *v.i.* Move in clumsy blundering noisy way (*along, past, by*, etc.); hence **~**ING[2] *a.* (esp., ponderous), **~**SOME[1] *a.* [ME *lomere*, perh. imit.]

lŭ'mber[2] *n.* & *v.* **1.** *n.* Disused articles of furniture etc. taking up room (**~-room,** in which such things are kept); useless or cumbrous material. **2.** *Partly prepared timber; **~jack, ~man,** feller, dresser, or conveyer of lumber. **3. ~-jacket,** hip-length stout jacket fastening up to neck. **4.** *v.t.* Fill *up* inconveniently, obstruct, (room, place); encumber *with*; heap together, treat, as lumber. **5.** *v.i.* Cut and prepare forest timber; hence **~**ER[1], **~**ING[1], *ns.* [perh. f. prec.; later assoc. w. obs. *lumber* pawnbroker's shop]

lŭ'mbrĭcal *a.* & *n.* **~** (**muscle**), one of the muscles flexing fingers or toes. [f. mod. L *lumbricalis* f. L *lumbricus* earthworm, w. ref. to the shape]

lū'mĕn (*or* lōō'-) *n.* **1.** (Phys.) Unit of light flux, flux per unit solid angle from uniform source of one candela. **2.** (*pl.* **lu'mina**). (Anat., Bot., etc.) Cavity within tube, cell, etc. [L *lumen luminis* a light, an opening]

lū'mĭnal (*or* lōō'-) *n.* Phenobarbitone. [P.]

lū'mĭnance (*or* lōō'-) *n.* Amount of light emitted from surface in given direction. [f. L *luminare* illuminate (as LUMEN) + -ANCE]

lū'mĭnarȳ (*or* lōō'-) *n.* Natural light-giving body, esp. sun or moon; person having much intellectual, moral, or spiritual influence. [ME, f. OF *luminarie* or f. LL *luminarium* f. L LUMEN; see -ARY[1]]

lūmĭnĕ'sc|ent (*or* lōō-) *a.* Emitting light without being hot; hence **~**ENCE *n.* [f. as LUMEN + -ESCENT]

lūmĭnĭ'ferous (*or* lōō-) *a.* Producing or transmitting light. [f. as LUMEN + -I- + -FEROUS]

lū'mĭnous (*or* lōō'-) *a.* **1.** Emitting or full of light, bright, shining, (**~ paint,** phosphorescent kind making thing visible in darkness); hence **lūmĭno′sɪᴛʏ** *n.* (*or* lōō-). **2.** Of light (*luminous intensity*). **3.** (Of writer etc.) throwing light upon subject. **4.** Hence ~ʟʏ² *adv.*, ~ɴᴇss *n.* [ME f. OF *lumineux* or f. L *luminosus* (as ʟᴜᴍᴇɴ; see -ᴏᴜs)]

||**lŭ′mmė** *int.* (vulg.) of surprise or emphasis. [= (*Lord*) *love me*]

***lŭ′mmox** *n.* (colloq.) Clumsy or stupid person. [19th c. in U.S. & dial.; orig. unkn.]

lŭmp¹ *n.* & *v.* **1.** *n.* Compact shapeless or unshapely mass (~ **in throat,** feeling of pressure there caused by emotion); (sl.) great quantity, lot, heap; mass of clay or dough ready for moulding or baking; protuberance, excrescence, swelling, bruise; heavy dull or ungainly person; ||**the** ~, casual workers in building and other trades; **in the** ~, taking things as a whole, in a general manner; ~ **sugar** (broken or cut or shaped into lumps or cubes); ~ **sum,** (1) sum covering number of items, (2) money paid down at once (opp. *instalments*). **2.** *v.t.* Put together in one lump, mass together, treat as all alike, disregard differences between or among, (*together*, *with*, *in with*, *under* title etc.). **3.** *v.i.* Rise or collect into lumps; go heavily *along*, sit heavily *down*. [ME, perh. of Scand. orig.]

lŭmp² *n.* ~(**′fish**), ugly spiny-finned leaden-blue fish (*Cyclopterus lumpus*) clinging tightly to objects by sucking-disc on belly; ~**-sucker,** this or a related fish. [f. MLG *lumpen*, MDu. *lumpe*, perh. = prec.]

lŭmp³ *v.t.* (colloq.) Be displeased at, put up with ungraciously, (used in antithesis with *like*: *if you don't like it you can lump it*, I don't care whether you like it or not). [imit.; cf. *dump*, *grump*, etc.]

lu′mpenprōlėtārĭat (lōō′-) *n.* (derog.) Ignorantly contented lower orders of society uninterested in revolutionary advancement. [G (*lumpen* rag, rogue; see ᴘʀᴏʟᴇᴛᴀʀɪᴀᴛ)]

lŭ′mpĭsh *a.* Heavy and clumsy; stupid, lethargic; hence ~ʟʏ² *adv.*, ~ɴᴇss *n.* [f. ʟᴜᴍᴘ¹ + -ɪsʜ¹]

lŭ′mp|ў *a.* Full of or covered with lumps; (of water) cut up by wind into small waves; hence ~ɪʟʏ² *adv.*, ~ɪɴᴇss *n.* [f. ʟᴜᴍᴘ¹ + -ʏ²]

lu′na (lōō′-) *n.* ~ (**moth**), N. Amer. moth (*Actias luna*) with crescent-shaped spots on wings. [L, = moon]

lu′nacў (lōō′-) *n.* Being a lunatic, insanity [orig. of the intermittent kind attributed to changes of moon]; (Law) such mental unsoundness as interferes with civil rights or transactions (||**Master in L**~, (Hist.) officer investigating cases of alleged lunacy); great folly. [f. ʟᴜɴᴀᴛɪᴄ + -ᴀᴄʏ]

lū′nar (*or* lōō′-) *a.* **1.** Of, in, as of, concerned with, determined by, the moon; ~ **cycle,** Metonic cycle; ~ **distance,** angular distance of moon from sun, planet, or star, used in finding longitude at sea; ~ (**excursion**) **module,** module for journey from spacecraft in orbit round moon to moon's surface and back; ~ **month,** period of moon's revolution, esp. interval between new moons of about 29½ days, (pop.) period of four weeks; ~ **nodes,** points at which moon's orbit cuts ecliptic; ~ **observation,** finding of longitude by lunar distance; ~ **rainbow** (made by moon's rays); *lunar* ʏᴇᴀʀ. **2.** (Of light, glory, etc.) pale, feeble; crescent-shaped, lunate, (esp. ~ **bone** in wrist); of or containing silver (from alchemists' use of *luna* 'moon' for silver; ~ **caustic,** silver nitrate esp. in stick form). [f. L *lunaris* (as ʟᴜɴᴀ; see -ᴀʀ¹)]

lū′nāte (*or* lōō′-) *a.* & *n.* **1.** *a.* Crescent-shaped (~ **bone** in wrist). **2.** *n.* Crescent-shaped prehistoric implement etc. [f. L *lunatus* (as ʟᴜɴᴀ; see -ᴀᴛᴇ²)]

lu′natĭc (lōō′-) *a.* & *n.* Insane (person; see ʟᴜɴᴀᴄʏ), mad(man); (of action etc.) outrageously foolish; eccentric, foolish, (person); ~ **asylum,** (Hist.) mental home or hospital; *lunatic* ғʀɪɴɢᴇ. [ME, f. OF *lunatique* f. LL *lunaticus* f. L ʟᴜɴᴀ; see -ᴀᴛɪᴄ]

lūnā′tion (*or* lōō-) *n.* Interval between new moons, about 29½ days. [ME, f. med. L *lunatio* (as prec.; see -ᴀᴛɪᴏɴ)]

lŭnch *n.* & *v.* **1.** *n.* Midday meal; light refreshment taken between breakfast and dinner (where latter is taken at midday); ~**-hour,** ~**-time,** (when lunch is taken); ~**-room,** restaurant with quick service of lunches. **2.** *v.t.* Provide lunch for. **3.** *v.i.* Take lunch. [f. foll.]

lŭ′ncheon (-nchon) *n.* **1.** (formal). = prec. 1; *light meal taken at any time of day. **2.** ~ **meat,** meat in loaf form ready to cut and eat; ||~ **voucher** (given to employee as part of pay and exchangeable for food at many restaurants). **3.** Hence *~ᴇ′ᴛᴛᴇ *n.*, establishment serving light lunches. [17th c., of uncert. orig.]

lūne (*or* lōōn) *n.* (Geom.) Crescent-shaped figure formed on sphere or plane by two arcs intersecting at two points. [F, f. L ʟᴜɴᴀ]

lūnĕ′tte (*or* lōō-) *n.* Arched aperture in concave ceiling to admit light; crescent-shaped or semicircular space in dome or ceiling decorated with painting etc.; (Fortif.) work larger than redan, with two faces and two flanks; watch-glass of flattened shape. [F, dim. of *lune* (see prec., -ᴇᴛᴛᴇ)]

lŭng *n.* Either of the pair of organs used to draw in air and bring it into contact with the blood in man and most vertebrates (**good** ~**s,** ability to use exhaled air to produce strong voice); ɪʀᴏɴ¹ *lung*; ~**s of London** etc., parks and open spaces in or close to great city; ~**-fish** (having lungs as well as gills); ~**-power,** power of voice; ~**′wort,** (1) herb *Pulmonaria officinalis,* with white-spotted leaves likened to diseased lung, (2) lichen (*Lobaria pulmonaria*) once supposed to be good for lung-disease; hence -~ᴇᴅ² (-ngd), ~′ʟᴇss, *adjs.*, ~′ғᴜʟ 2 *n.* [OE *lungen,* = MLG *lunge*, OHG *lungun*, ON *lunga* f. Gmc **lung-* f. IE **lngh-*, cogn. w. ʟɪɢʜᴛ⁴]

lŭnge¹, longe, (lŭnj) *n.*, & *v.t.* **1.** *n.* Long rope with which horse-breaker holds horse while he makes it canter in circle; circular exercise-ground for training horses. **2.** *v.t.* Exercise (horse) with or in lunge. [F *longe*, *allonge* (as foll.)]

lŭnge² (-nj) *n.* & *v.* **1.** *n.* Thrust with sword etc. esp. in fencing; sudden forward movement, plunge, rush; gymnastic movement of foot with knee bent while other foot remains fixed. **2.** *v.i.* Make lunge in fencing etc., deliver blow from shoulder in boxing, (*at*, *out*). **3.** *v.t.* Drive (weapon, sting, etc.) violently in some direction. [f. earlier *allonge,* F, f. *allonger* lengthen (*à* to, *long* ʟᴏɴɢ¹)]

lu′ngi (lōō′nggē) *n.* (Ind.) (Cotton material for) man's loincloth. [Urdu]

lūnĭsō′lar (*or* lōō-) *a.* Of sun and moon; ~ **period** (of 532 years between repetitions of both solar and lunar cycles); ~ **precession** (due to joint action of sun and moon); ~ **year** (with divisions regulated by changes of moon, and average length made to agree with solar year). [f. L *luna* moon + -ɪ- + L *sol* sun + -ᴀʀ¹]

lū′nūla (*or* lōō′-) *n.* (*pl.* ~e). Crescent-shaped mark, esp. white mark at base of finger-nail; crescent-shaped Bronze Age ornament. [L, dim. of ʟᴜɴᴀ]

lu′pĭn, lu′pĭne¹, (lōō′-) *n.* Garden or fodder plant of genus *Lupinus*, with long tapering spikes of blue, purple, pink, white, or yellow flowers; (in *pl.*) seeds of lupin. [ME, f. L *lupinus*]

lū′pīne² (*or* lōō′-) *a.* Of wolf or wolves; wolflike. [f. L *lupinus* (*lupus* wolf; see -ɪɴᴇ¹)]

lu′p|us (lōō′-) *n.* Ulcerous disease of skin, esp.

tuberculosis of skin; hence ~ĭFORM, ~OID, ~OUS, *adjs.* [L, = wolf]

lur (loor) *n.* Bronze S-shaped trumpet of prehistoric times, still used in Scandinavia to call cattle. [Da. & Norw.]

lûrch^1 *n.* **Leave in the ~,** desert (friend, ally) in difficulties. [orig. = state of score in some games in which winner was far ahead of loser, f. F *lourche* game like backgammon, also bad defeat in this]

lûrch^2 *n.*, & *v.i.* **1.** *n.* Sudden lean or deviation to one side, stagger. **2.** *v.i.* Make lurch(es), stagger. [orig. Naut., *lee-lurch* alt. of *lee-latch* drifting to leeward]

lûr'cher *n.* **1.** (arch.) Petty thief, swindler; spy. **2.** ||Cross-bred dog between collie or sheep-dog and greyhound, used esp. by poachers. [f. obs. *lurch* v. var. of LURK, + -ER^1]

lûre^1 (*or* loor) *n.*, & *v.t.* **1.** *n.* Falconer's apparatus for recalling hawk (bunch of feathers, within which it finds its food while being trained, attached to thong); thing used to entice, decoy; enticing quality *of* a pursuit etc. **2.** *v.t.* Recall (hawk) with lure; entice (person, animal; usu. *away* or *into*). [ME, f. OF *luere* f. Gmc **lōthr-* (cf. **lathōn* invite)]

lure^2. Var. of LUR.

lûr'ĭd (*or* loor'-) *a.* **1.** Ghastly, wan, glaring, unnatural, stormy, terrible, in colour or combination of colours or lights (of complexion, landscape, sky, lightning, thunder-clouds, smoky flame, glance, etc.); **cast a ~ light on,** explain or reveal (facts or character) in tragic or terrible way. **2.** Sensational, horrifying, (*lurid details*); showy, gaudy, (*paperbacks with lurid covers*). **3.** (Bot. etc.) Of dingy yellowish brown. **4.** Hence ~LY^2 *adv.*, ~NESS *n.* [f. L *luridus* (*luror* wan or yellow colour; see -ID^1)]

lûrk *v.i.* Be hidden *in, under, about,* etc.; escape notice, exist unobserved, be latent, (*have a lurking sympathy for*); **~'ing-place,** hiding-place. [ME, perh. f. LOUR w. frequent. *-k* as in *talk*]

lŭ'scious (-sh*u*s) *a.* Richly sweet in taste or smell; excessively sweet, cloying; (of language or literary style) over-rich in sound, imagery, or voluptuous suggestion; appealing to the senses, voluptuously attractive; hence ~LY^2 *adv.*, ~NESS *n.* [ME, perh. alt. of obs. *licious* f. DELICIOUS]

lŭsh^1 *a.* (Of vegetation, esp. grass) luxuriant and succulent. [ME, perh. var. of obs. *lash* soft, f. OF *lasche* lax (see LACHES); assoc. w. prec.]

lŭsh^2 *n.* & *v.* (sl.) **1.** *n.* Liquor, drink; *alcoholic, drunkard. **2.** *v.t.* & *i.* Ply with, or drink, alcoholic liquor. [18th c., perh. joc. use of prec.]

Lusĭtā'nĭan (lōō-) *a.* & *n.* (Inhabitant) of ancient Lusitania or modern Portugal. [f. *Lusitania,* ancient province mainly corresponding to Portugal]

lŭst *n.*, & *v.i.* **1.** *n.* Animal desire for sexual indulgence, lascivious passion, whence ~'FUL *a.*; passionate enjoyment *of* or desire *of* or *for* (*lust of battle, for power*); (Bibl. & Theol.) sensuous appetite regarded as sinful (*lusts of the flesh*). **2.** *v.i.* Have strong or excessive (esp. sexual) desire (usu. *after* or *for*). [OE, = OHG *lust,* ON *losti,* Goth. *lustus* f. Gmc **lust-*; cf. LIST^2]

***lŭ'ster^{1,2}.** See LUSTRE^{1,2}.

lŭ'stral *a.* Of, or used in, ceremonial purification. [f. L *lustralis* (as LUSTRUM; see -AL)]

lŭ'str|āte *v.t.* Purify by expiatory sacrifice, ceremonial washing, or other such rite; so ~A'TION *n.* [f. L *lustrare* (as LUSTRUM) + -ATE^3]

lŭ'stre^1 (-t*er*), ***lŭ'ster^1,** *n.*, & *v.t.* **1.** *n.* Gloss, refulgence; shining surface, brilliance, bright light, radiant beauty; hence ~LESS, **lŭ'str**OUS, *adjs.* **2.** Splendour, glory, distinction, (*add lustre to*; *throw* or *shed lustre on*). **3.** (Prismatic glass pendant of) chandelier. **4.** ||Thin dress-material with cotton warp, woollen weft, and lustrous surface. **5.** Iridescent glaze on pottery and porcelain; ~(**ware**) (provided with this). **6.** *v.t.* Put lustre on (cloth, pottery, etc.). [F, f. It. *lustro* (*lustrare* f. L *lustrare* illuminate)]

lŭ'stre^2 (-t*er*), ***lŭ'ster^2,** *n.* = LUSTRUM. [ME, Anglicized f. foll.]

lŭ'str|um *n.* (*pl.* ~**a** *or* ~**ums**). Period of five years. [L, orig. purificatory sacrifice after quinquennial census]

lŭ'st|ȳ *a.* Healthy and strong; vigorous, lively; hence ~ĭHOOD (arch.), ~ĭNESS, *ns.*, ~ĭLY^2 *adv.* [ME, f. LUST + -Y^2]

lusus (***naturae***) (lōō'sus natūr'ē; *or* lū'-; *or* -toor'ī) *n.* Sport or freak of nature, strikingly abnormal natural production. [L]

lū'tanĭst, lū'tenĭst, (*or* lōō'-) *n.* Lute-player. [f. med. L *lutanista* (*lutana* LUTE^1; see -IST)]

lūte^1 (*or* lōōt) *n.* Guitar-like instrument much used in 14th–17th c., with pear-shaped body. [ME, f. F *lut, leüt,* prob. f. Prov. *laüt* f. Arab. *al-'ūd*]

lūt|e^2 (*or* lōōt) *n.*, & *v.t.* **1.** *n.* Clay or cement used to stop hole, make joint airtight, coat crucible, protect graft, etc.; rubber seal for jar etc. **2.** *v.t.* Apply lute to. **3.** Hence ~'ING^1 (3) *n.* [ME; n. f. OF *lut* f. L *lutum* mud, clay; v. f. L *lutare*]

lutecium. Var. of LUTETIUM.

lūtėo- (*or* lōō-) *comb. form.* Orange-coloured, as: **~fu'lvous,** orange-tawny. [f. as foll. + -o-]

lū'tėous (*or* lōō'-) *a.* Of deep orange yellow or greenish yellow. [f. L *luteus* (*lutum* WELD^1) + -OUS]

lū'testrĭng (-ts-; *or* lōō'-) *n.* (arch.) Glossy silk fabric. [app. f. *lustring* f. F *lustrine* or f. It. *lustrino* (*lustro* LUSTRE^1), assim. to LUTE^1, STRING]

Lūtē'tian (-sh*a*n; *or* lōō-) *a.* (arch.) Parisian. [f. L *Lutetia* ancient name of Paris + -AN]

lūtē'tium (-sh*u*m; *or* lōō-) *n.* (Chem.) Heaviest element of lanthanide series. [f. F *lutécium* f. as prec. + -IUM]

Lū'theran (*or* lōō'-) *a.* & *n.* (Follower) of Martin Luther; (member) of Church accepting the Augsburg confession of 1530, with justification by faith alone as cardinal doctrine; hence ~ISM (3) *n.*, ~IZE (2, 3) *v.i.* & *t.* [f. M. *Luther,* Ger. religious leader d. 1546 + -AN]

Lu'tine (lōō'tēn) *a.* **~ bell** (at Lloyd's, rung to announce loss of a ship or arrival of overdue ship). [name of ship wrecked 1799]

lŭx *n.* (*pl.* same). (Phys.) Unit of illumination, one lumen per square metre. [L *lux lucis* light]

lŭ'x|āte *v.t.* Dislocate (joint etc.); so ~A'TION *n.* [f. L *luxare* + -ATE^3]

lŭxe (*or* lŏŏks) *n.* Luxury; cf. DE LUXE. [F, f. L *luxus*]

lŭxūr'ĭ|ant (*or* -gz- *or* -gzhoor'-) *a.* Prolific (lit., or fig. of imagination etc.); profuse in growth, exuberant, rank; (of literary or artistic style) florid, richly ornamented; hence ~ANCE *n.*, **~ant**LY^2 *adv.* [f. L *luxuriare* grow rank (*luxuria* LUXURY); see -ANT]

lŭxūr'ĭāte (*or* -gz- *or* -gzhoor-) *v.i.* Revel, enjoy oneself, *in* or *on*; take one's ease, be luxurious. [f. as prec. + -ATE^3]

lŭxūr'ĭous (*or* -gz- *or* -gzhoor'-) *a.* Fond of or contributing to luxury; self-indulgent, voluptuous; very comfortable; hence ~LY^2 *adv.*, ~NESS *n.* [ME, f. OF *luxurios* f. L *luxuriosus* (as foll.; see -OUS)]

lŭ'xurȳ (-ksh*e*rĭ) *n.* (Habitual use of) choice or costly food, dress, furniture, etc.; thing that one enjoys; thing desirable for comfort or enjoyment but not indispensable; luxuriousness; (*attrib.*) relating to luxuries, comfortable and expensive (*a luxury flat*). [ME, f. OF *luxurie, luxure* f. L *luxuria* (*luxus* abundance); see -Y^1]

||**L.V.** *abbr.* luncheon voucher.

Lw *symb.* lawrencium.

L.W.M. *abbr.* low-water mark.
lx *abbr.* lux(es).
LXX *abbr.* Septuagint; seventy.
-lȳ¹ *suf.* forming *adjs.* esp. f. *ns.*, w. sense 'having the qualities of' (*kingly, lovely, motherly, rascally*), or 'recurring at intervals of' (*daily, hourly*). [f. or after OE *-lic*, = OS *-lik*, OHG *-lih*, ON *-ligr*, *-legr*, Goth. *-leiks* f. Gmc *likam* form]
-lȳ² *suf.* forming *advs.* f. *adjs.* (orig. corresp. to those in -LY¹, now f. those of almost any kind; *beastly cold, ghastly pale, hourly, purposely; boldly, feebly, nastily, pathetically, volubly*); often as part of compd. suf., e.g. *-ably, -edly, -fully, -ically, -ily, -ingly, -ously*. [f. or after OE *-līce*, = OS *-līko*, OHG *-līhho*, ON *-liga*, Goth. *-leikō* f. as prec.]
lȳcă'nthropȳ *n.* Mythical transformation of person into wolf (cf. WEREWOLF); form of madness in which patient imagines himself an animal and exhibits depraved appetites, change of voice, etc.; hence **lȳ'canthrōpe** *n.*, person exhibiting lycanthropy. [f. mod. L f. Gk *lukanthrōpia* (*lukos* wolf, *anthrōpos* man; see -Y¹)]
lycée (lē'sā) *n.* State secondary school in France. [F, f. L (as foll.)]
Lȳcē'um *n.* Garden at Athens in which Aristotle taught, his philosophy and followers (cf. ACADEMY, GARDEN, PORCH); (U.S. or Hist.) literary institution, lecture-hall, teaching-place. [L, f. Gk *Lukeion* neut. of *Lukeios* epithet of Apollo (from whose neighbouring temple the Lyceum was named)]
lȳch. See LICH.
lychee. Var. of LITCHI.
lȳ'chnĭs (-k-) *n.* Perennial herb of genus *Lychnis*, e.g. ragged robin. [L, f. Gk *lukhnis* a red flower (*lukhnos* lamp)]
lȳ'copŏd *n.* Club-moss, esp. of genus *Lycopodium*. [Anglicized f. foll.]
lȳcopō'dĭum *n.* = prec.; fine powder from spores of this, used as absorbent in surgery, and in making fireworks etc. [mod. L f. Gk *lukos* wolf + *pous podos* foot; see -IUM]
lȳ'ddīte *n.* High explosive chiefly of picric acid. [f. *Lydd* in Kent, where first tested, + -ITE¹]
Lȳ'dĭan *a.* & *n.* (Language or inhabitant) of ancient Lydia; ~ **mode,** (1) ancient Greek MODE, reputedly effeminate in character, (2) fifth of church modes (with F as final and C as dominant). [f. L f. Gk *Ludios* of Lydia in Asia Minor + -AN]
lȳe *n.* Water made alkaline by lixiviation of vegetable ashes; any strong alkaline solution esp. for washing; any cleansing substance. [OE *lēag*, = MDu. *lōghe*, OHG *louga*, ON *laug* hot bath f. Gmc **laugō* (**lau-* f. IE **lou-* wash; cf. LATHER)]
lȳ'ĭng¹ *n.* In vbl senses; place to lie (*dry lying*); *lying in* (see LIE³ 6); *lying in* STATE¹. [ME, f. LIE²,³ + -ING¹]
lȳ'ĭng² *a.* In vbl senses; deceitful, false, whence ~LY² *adv.*; *lying down* (see LIE³ 6); LOW¹-*lying*. [f. LIE²,³ + -ING²]
‖**lȳ'ke-wāke** *n.* Watch kept at night over dead body. [perh. f. ON **líkavaka*; cf. LICH, WAKE²]
lȳ'me-grass (-ahs) *n.* Blue-green grass of genus *Elymus*, planted on sand to keep it from shifting. [perh. f. LIME¹, w. ref. to its binding effect, + GRASS]
lȳmph *n.* **1.** (poet.) Pure water. **2.** (Physiol.) Colourless alkaline fluid from tissues or organs of body, like blood but without red corpuscles; ~ **gland** or **node,** small mass of tissue where lymph is purified and lymphocytes are formed. **3.** Exudation from sore etc.; (**calf** or **vaccine**) ~, = VACCINE 2. **4.** Hence ~'OID, ~'OUS, *adjs.* [f. F *lymphe* or f. L *lympha*, *limpa* water]
lȳmphă'tĭc *a.* & *n.* **1.** *a.* Of, secreting, conveying, lymph (*lymphatic gland, system*). **2.** (Of person or TEMPERAMENT) flabby, pale, sluggish, (qualities formerly attributed to excess of lymph). **3.** *n.* Veinlike vessel conveying lymph. [orig. = 'frenzied', f. L *lymphaticus* mad f. Gk *numpholēptos* seized by nymphs, now assoc. w. LYMPH (on anal. of *spermatic* etc.)]
lȳ'mphocȳte *n.* Form of leucocyte occurring in lymph. [f. LYMPH + -O- + -CYTE]
lȳncē'an *a.* Lynx-eyed, keen-sighted. [f. L f. Gk *lugkeios* (*lugx* lynx) + -AN]
lȳnch *n.*, & *v.t.* **1.** ~ **law,** procedure of self--constituted illegal court that summarily executes or otherwise punishes person charged with offence. **2.** *v.t.* Execute (person) thus. [orig. U.S., earlier *Lynch's law*, named after Capt. W. Lynch of Virginia *c.* 1780]
‖**lȳ'nchėt** *n.* Ridge or ledge formed by prehistoric ploughing on slope. [f. *linch* f. OE *hlinc*; cf. LINKS]
lȳ'nchpĭn. Var of LINCHPIN.
lȳnx *n.* Animal of subgenus *Lynx* of cat genus, with tufted ear-tips, short tail, spotted fur, and proverbially keen sight; its fur; ~**-eyed,** keen--sighted. [ME f. L, f. Gk *lugx*]
Lȳ'on *n.* (**Lord**) ~, ~ **King of Arms,** chief herald of Scotland, presiding over ~ **Court** (cf. KING¹ 7). [arch. form. of LION; named f. lion on royal shield]
lȳophĭ'lĭc *a.* (Of colloid) readily dispersed by solvent; hence **lȳŏ'phĭl**IZE *v.t.*, freeze-dry. [f. Gk *luō* loosen, dissolve + Gk *philos* loving + -IC]
lȳophō'bĭc *a.* (Of colloid) not lyophilic. [f. as prec. + -PHOBE + -IC]
lȳr'ate *a.* (Biol.) Lyre-shaped. [f. as foll. + -ATE²]
lȳre *n.* (Gk Ant.) Instrument like harp but of size to be held up in left hand and played with plectrum, and with strings supported by two symmetrically curved and yoked horns, chiefly used for accompanying voice; ~**-bird,** Australian bird of genus *Menura*, the male with lyre-shaped tail display; ~**-flower,** bleeding heart. [ME, f. OF *lire* f. L f. Gk *lura*]
lȳ'rĭc *a.* & *n.* **1.** *a.* Of or for the lyre, meant to be sung; of the nature of, expressed or fit to be expressed in, song (*lyric drama, opera*); (of poem) expressing writer's own thoughts and sentiments usu. briefly and in stanzas or strophes; (of poet) writing in this manner. **2.** *n.* Lyric poem; (in *pl.*) lyric verses; (Theatr.) words of song. [f. F *lyrique* or f. L f. Gk *lurikos* (as prec.; see -IC)]
lȳ'rĭcal *a.* = prec.; resembling, couched in or using language appropriate to, lyric poetry; (colloq.) highly enthusiastic; hence ~LY² *adv.* [f. as prec. + -AL]
lȳ'rĭcĭsm *n.* Lyric character; a lyrical expression; high-flown sentiments. [f. LYRIC + -ISM]
lyr'ĭst *n.* **1.** (līr'-). Player on lyre. **2.** (lĭ'r-). Lyric poet. [f. L f. Gk *luristēs* (*lura* lyre)]
lȳsēr'gĭc *a.* ~ **acid,** crystalline acid got from ergot or synthetically; ~ **acid diethylamide,** a powerful hallucinogenic drug. [f. hydro*lys*is + *erg*ot + -IC]
lȳ's|ĭs *n.* (*pl.* ~**es** *pr.* -ēz). (Physiol.) Disintegration of bacterial or other cells. [L, f. Gk *lusis* loosening (*luō* loosen)]
-lȳs|ĭs *suf.* (*pl.* ~**es** *pr.* -ēz) forming *ns.* denoting disintegration or decomposition (*electrolysis, haemolysis*). [f. as prec.]
lȳ'sŏl *n.* Mixture of cresols and soft soap, used as disinfectant. [***P**; f. Gk *lusis* (see LYSIS) + -OL]
lȳthe (-dh) *n.* (Sc.) Pollack. [18th c., of unkn. orig.]
-lȳ'tĭc *suf.* forming *adjs.* corresp. to *ns.* in -LYSIS. [f. Gk *lutikos* (as LYSIS; see -IC)]
lȳ'tta *n.* (*pl.* ~**e**). = WORM¹ 4. [L, f. Gk, orig. = rabies]

M

M, m, (ĕm) *n.* (*pl.* **Ms** *or* **M's**). Thirteenth letter of alphabet; (as Roman numeral) 1,000 (**mi** 1,001; **mm** 2,000; **mcmlxxvi** 1,976); (Print.) em.

M. *abbr.* Master; mega-; Member of; *Monsieur*; ||motorway.

m. *abbr.* maiden (over); male; mare; mark(s) (as monetary unit); married; masculine; metre(s); mile(s); milli-; million(s); minute(s).

m' *a.* = *my* in *m'lud*, *m'tutor*, etc.

'm *v.* & *n.* (colloq.) = *am* in *I'm*; = *madam* in *yes'm* etc. [abbr.]

ma (mah) *n.* (vulg.) Mother. [abbr. of MAMMA[1]]

M.A. *abbr.* Master of Arts; Military Academy.

ma'am (mahm, măm, *or* mum) *n.* Madam (esp. used by servants or in addressing Queen or royal princess). [abbr.]

maar (mâr) *n.* Volcanic crater formed by explosion. [G]

măc[1]. See MACK[1].

Măc[2] *n.* (colloq.) Scotsman; *man (esp. as *voc.*). [f. *Mac-* as patronymic prefix in many Scottish & Irish surnames]

maca'bre (-ah'br) *a.* Grim, gruesome. [ME, f. OF *macabré*, perh. f. *Macabé* Maccabee, w. ref. to miracle play containing slaughter of the Maccabees]

macā'cō[1] *n.* (*pl.* ~**s**). Macaque or similar monkey. [Port., = monkey, f. Fiot *makaku* some monkeys (*kaku* monkey)]

macā'cō[2] *n.* (*pl.* ~**s**). Lemur, esp. of genus *Lemur*. [f. F *mococo*, of unkn. orig.; cf. F *maki* lemur f. Malagasy *maka*]

macă'dam *n.* Material for road-making with successive layers of broken stone of nearly uniform size, each subjected to pressure before next is laid; TAR[1] *macadam*; hence ~IZE (1) *v.t.* [f. J. L. *McAdam*, Brit. surveyor d. 1836, who advocated this method]

maca'que (-ah'k) *n.* Monkey of genus *Macacus*. [F, f. as MACACO[1]]

măcarō'nĭ *n.* **1.** Pasta formed into long tubes, used as food; ~ **cheese,** savoury dish of macaroni and cheese baked. **2.** (*pl.* ~**es**). (Hist.) 18th-c. dandy imitating continental fashions. [f. It. *maccaroni*, f. late Gk *makaria* barley food]

măcarŏ'nĭc *a.*, & *n.* in *pl.* (Verses) of burlesque form containing Latin (or other foreign) words and vernacular words with Latin etc. terminations. [f. mod. L *macaronicus* f. obs. It. *macaronico*, joc. f. as prec.; cf. -IC]

măcarōō'n *n.* Small cake or biscuit of ground almonds, white of egg, sugar, etc. [f. F *macaron* f. It. (as MACARONI)]

Macă'ssar *a.* & *n.* ~ **(oil)**, (Hist.) kind of oil for the hair. [f. *Macassar*, district in Celebes, whence its ingredients were said to come]

macaw'[1] *n.* Long-tailed brightly coloured Amer. parrot of genus *Ara* etc. [f. Port. *macao*, of unkn. orig.]

macaw'[2] *n.* Palm-tree of genus *Acrocomia*, with nuts yielding fragrant oil. [Carib]

Macc. *abbr.* Maccabees (Apocrypha).

Mă'ccabees (-z) *n. pl.* (**Books of the**) ~, four books of Jewish history and theology, of which first and second are in Apocrypha; so **Măccabē'**AN *a.* [name of Jewish family that led revolt *c.* 170 B.C. under Judas *Maccabaeus*]

***McCâr'thy̆ism** (makâr'-) *n.* Policy of hunting out (suspected) Communists and removing them esp. from Government departments. [f. J. R. *McCarthy*, U.S. senator d. 1957 + -ISM]

McCoy' (makoi') *n.* (colloq.) **The real** ~, the real thing, the genuine article. [19th c., of uncert. orig.]

māce[1] *n.* **1.** (Hist.) heavy usu. metal-headed and spiked club; heavy club used by policeman etc. **2.** Staff of office resembling this; ||symbol of Speaker's authority in House of Commons; ~**(-bearer)**, official carrying mace. **3.** Stick used in game of bagatelle. [ME, f. OF *mace*, *masse* f. Rom. **mattea* club]

māce[2] *n.* Dried outer covering of nutmeg, used as spice. [ME *macis* (taken as pl.) f. OF *macis*, f. L *macir* a red spicy bark]

mă'cédoine (-ĭdwahn) *n.* Mixed fruit or vegetables esp. cut up small or in jelly. [F]

mā'cer *n.* Mace-bearer, esp. (Sc.) lawcourt official keeping order. [ME, f. OF *massier* (*masse*; see MACE[1], -ER[2])]

mă'cer|āte *v.t.* & *i.* Soften by soaking; waste away by fasting; hence ~A'TION, ~**ātor**, *ns.* [f. L *macerare* + -ATE[3]]

Mach (mahχ *or* măk *or* mahk) *n.* ~ **(number)**, ratio of the speed of a body to the speed of sound in the surrounding medium; ~**'meter,** indicator of air speed as Mach number; ~ **one, two,** etc., speed corresponding to Mach number of one, two, etc. [f. E. ~, Austrian physicist d. 1916]

macha'n (-ah'n) *n.* (Anglo-Ind.) Elevated platform used in tiger-shooting etc. [Hindi]

machĕ'tė (*or* -ā'-), **mă'tchėt,** *n.* Broad heavy knife used in Central America and W. Indies as implement and weapon. [Sp. (*macho* hammer f. LL *marcus*)]

măchĭavĕ'llĭan (-k-) *a.* Deceitful, perfidious, cunning; hence ~ISM (1) *n.* [f. N. dei *Machiavelli*, Florentine philosopher d. 1527, author of *Il Principe*, a treatise on statecraft advocating use of even unscrupulous means to strengthen the State]

machĭ'col|āte *v.t.* (usu. in *p.p.*) Furnish (parapet etc.) with openings between supporting corbels for dropping stones etc. on assailants; hence ~A'TION *n.* [f. OF *machicoler*, ult. f. Prov. *machacol* (*macar* crush, *col* neck)]

machicoulis (mahshĭkōō'lĭ) *n.* Machicolation. [f. F *machicoulis* (as prec.)]

mă'chĭn|āte (-k-) *v.i.* Lay plots, intrigue; so ~A'TION, ~**ātor**, *ns.* [f. L *machinari* contrive (as foll.) + -ATE[3]]

machi'ne (-shē'n) *n.*, & *v.t.* **1.** *n.* Apparatus for applying mechanical power, having several parts each with definite function; bicycle, motor cycle, etc.; aircraft; computer; *bathing-machine* (see BATHE[1]). **2.** Person who acts mechanically and without intelligence, or with unfailing regularity. **3.** (Mech.) Instrument that transmits force or directs its application; **simple** ~, one without combination of parts, e.g. lever. **4.** Controlling system of an organization (*party*, *political*, *propaganda*, *war*, *machine*). **5.** ~ **age,** era of many mechanical devices; ~**-gun,** (*n.*) mounted gun mechanically loaded and fired, delivering continuous fire, (*v.t.*) shoot at with machine-gun; ~**-made,** (1) made by machine, (2) stereotyped, monotonously regular; **~-readable,** in form that computer can respond to; **~ tool,** mechanically operated tool for working on metal, wood, or plastics. **6.** *v.t.* Make or operate on with machine (esp. of sewing and printing). [F, f. L *machina* f. Gk *makhana* (Doric), *mēkhanē* (*mēkhos* contrivance, cogn. w. MAY[1])]

machi'nerў (-shē'-) *n.* Machines; works of a machine, mechanism; organized system, means arranged *for* doing; group of contrivances, esp. supernatural persons and incidents, used in literary work. [f. prec. + -ERY]

machi'nĭst (-shē'-) *n.* One who makes or controls machinery; one who works (esp. sewing-)machine. [f. F *machiniste* & f. MACHINE + -IST]

machĭ'smō (*or* -ĕ'z-) *n.* Need to prove one's virility or courage by daring action. [Sp. (*macho* MALE f. L *masculus*; see -ISM)]

machtpolitik (mahχtpŏlĭtē'k) *n.* = POWER *politics.* [G]

macintosh. Var. of MACKINTOSH.

măck[1], măc[1], *n.* (colloq.) ||Mackintosh (coat); *mackinaw. [abbr.]

măck[2] *n.* (sl.) Pimp, procurer. [abbr. of obs. *mackerel* f. OF *maquerel*, **makeler* f. MDu. *makelaer* broker]

mă'ckerel *n.* (*pl.* ~ *or* ~**s**). N. Atlantic sea-fish (*Scomber scombrus*) used as food and approaching shore in shoals in summer to spawn; **~ breeze** or **gale** (strong, and thus favourable to mackerel-catching); **~ shark,** porbeagle; **~ sky** (dappled with rows of small white fleecy clouds, like pattern on mackerel's back). [ME, f. AF *makerel*, OF *maquerel*]

***mă'ckĭnaw** *n.* Heavy woollen cloth; warm belted coat of this. [f. *M~* City, Michigan]

mă'ckĭntŏsh *n.* Waterproof material of rubber and cloth for garments, esp. that patented by C. *Macintosh*, Sc. inventor d. 1843; ||cloak or coat of this, or of any waterproof material.

mă'ckle *n.* Blurred impression in printing. [f. F *macule* f. L MACULA]

mă'cle *n.* Twin crystal; dark spot in mineral. [F, f. L MACULA]

||**M'Naghten** (maknaw'ten) *n.* **~ rules** (governing decision as to criminal responsibility of insane person). [f. name of 19th-c. accused]

Mâcon (mahkaw'ṅ) *n.* White or red burgundy produced in the neighbourhood of *Mâcon* in France.

macra'mé (-rah'mĭ) *n.* Fringe or trimming of knotted thread or cord; art of making this. [f. Turk. *makrama* bedspread f. Arab. *mikrama*]

mă'cro- *comb. form.* Long, large, large-scale, as: **~bio'tic,** relating to a diet of pure vegetable foods etc. intended to prolong life; **~cepha'lic, ~ce'phalous,** having a long or large head; **~cosm,** the great world, the universe, any great whole; **~-economics,** study of general economics of large units; **~molecule,** (Chem.) molecule containing very large number of atoms; **~photography** (at fairly low magnification); **~sco'pic,** (1) visible to the naked eye, (2) regarded in terms of large units. [f. Gk *makro-* (*makros* long, large; see -o-)]

mă'crŏn *n.* Written or printed mark (¯) of long or stressed vowel. [f. Gk *makron* neut. a. (as prec.)]

mă'cūl|a *n.* (*pl.* ~**ae**). Dark spot; spot, esp. permanent one, in skin, whence ~AR[1] *a.*, ~A'TION *n.*; **~a (lutea** *pr.* lōō'tĭa), region of greatest visual acuity in retina. [ME f. L, = spot, mesh]

măd[1] *a.* **1.** With disordered mind, insane; frenzied; extravagantly gay; (of person or conduct or idea) wildly foolish; **like ~,** furiously, violently, (*I ran like mad*). **2.** Wildly excited, infatuated, (*after, about, for, on,* thing, subject, etc.; *cricket-mad*); (colloq.) annoyed (*I was mad at missing my train*). **3.** (Of animal) rabid (*mad bull, dog*). **4. ~'cap** *n.* & *a.*, wildly impulsive (person); **~-doctor,** (arch.) physician treating the insane; **~'house,** mental home or hospital, (fig.) confused uproar; **~'man, ~'woman,** mad person. **5.** Hence ~'LY[2] *adv.* (also, colloq., passionately or extremely), ~'NESS *n.* [OE *gemǣd(e)d*, p.p. of **gemǣden* f. *gemād* mad, = OS *gimēd*, OHG *gameit* foolish, boastful, Goth. *gamaiths* crippled, f. Gmc **gamaidhaz*]

măd[2] *v.* (**-dd-**) **1.** *v.t.* *Make angry. **2.** *v.i.* (arch.) Be mad, act madly; **the ~ding crowd** (frenzied, in Gray's *Elegy*; now often taken as = maddening). [ME, f. prec.]

mă'dam *n.* **1.** Polite or respectful formal address or mode of reference to woman. **2.** (euphem.) Woman brothel-keeper. **3.** (derog.) Conceited, pert, etc., young woman. [ME, f. OF *ma dame* my lady]

Madame (madah'm *or* mă'dam) *n.* (*pl.* ***Mesdames*** *pr.* mādă'm *or* mādah'm). Title used of or to French-speaking woman, corresponding to Mrs. or madam; (*m~*) = prec. 1. [F, as prec.]

mă'dden *v.t.* & *i.* Make or become mad; irritate. [ME, f. MAD[1] + -EN[6]]

mă'dder *n.* Herbaceous plant (*Rubia tinctorum*) with yellowish flowers; red dye got from its root; synthetic substitute for this dye. [OE *mædere*, = ON *mathra*, OHG *matara*]

māde. See MAKE[1].

Madeir'a (-ēr'*a*) *n.* Fortified white wine produced in Madeira; **~ cake,** kind of rich sweet sponge-cake. [~, island in Atlantic; Port., = timber, f. L *materia* MATTER[1], from its thick woods]

mă'deleine (-dlān) *n.* Small rich cake. [F]

Mademoiselle (mădam(w)azĕ'l) *n.* (*pl.* ***Mesdemoiselles*** *pr.* mādmwazĕ'l). Title used of or to unmarried French-speaking woman, corresponding to Miss or madam; (*m~*) young Frenchwoman, French governess. [F (*ma* my, *demoiselle* DAMSEL)]

Mădĭson A'vėnūe (-ă'-) *n.* American publicity and advertising industry. [street in New York City]

madŏ'nna *n.* (Picture or statue of) Virgin Mary; **~ lily** (white *Lilium candidum*, as in pictures of the Virgin Mary). [It. (*ma* = *mia* my, *donna* lady f. L *domina*)]

madră's *n.* Cotton fabric with coloured or white stripes etc. [f. *M~* in India]

mă'drė|pôre *n.* Perforated coral of genus *Madrepora*; animal producing this; hence **~pŏ'ric** *a.* [f. F *madrépore* or mod. L *madrepora* f. It. *madrepora* (*madre* mother, *poro* PORE[1])]

mă'drĭg|al *n.* Short amatory poem; part-song for several voices, prop. with elaborate contrapuntal imitation and without instrumental accompaniment; hence **~ā'lIAN, ~alE'SQUE,** *adjs.* [f. It. *madrigale* f. med. L *matricalis* mother-f. as MATRIX, -AL (cf. *mother church*)]

Mădurē'se (-z) *a.* & *n.* (*pl.* same). (Language or member) of an Indonesian people in Java etc. [f. *Madura* province + -ESE]

maduro (mahdoor'ō) *a.* & *n.* (*pl.* ~**s**). Full-flavoured (cigar). [Sp., = matured f. L (as MATURE[1])]

Maecē'nas *n.* Generous patron of literature or art. [f. G. ~, Roman statesman d. 8 B.C., patron of Horace and Virgil]

mae'lstrom (mā'l-) *n.* Whirlpool on W. coast of Norway; great whirlpool (lit. or fig.). [early mod. Du., f. *malen* grind, whirl + *stroom* STREAM]

mae'năd *n.* Bacchante (lit. or fig.). [f. L f. Gk *Mainas -ados* (*mainomai* rave)]

maestoso (mīstō'sō; *or* mahĕs-) *adv.* (Mus.) Majestically. [It.]

maĕ'str|ō (mah-; *or* mī's-) *n.* (*pl.* **~os,** *or* **~i** *pr.* -ē). Great musical composer, teacher, or conductor; masterly performer in any sphere. [It., = master]

Mae Wĕ'st (mā-) *n.* (sl.) Inflatable life-jacket. [professional name of Amer. film actress b. 1892, noted for her large bust]

mă'ffĭck *v.i.* Exult riotously. [back form. f. *Mafeking* (pr. mă'fĭking) in S. Africa (relief of which in 1900 was celebrated extravagantly in London etc.), treated as gerund]

mă'fĭa (*or* mah'-) *n.* **1.** Hostility to law and its ministers among Sicilian population, often shown in crimes; those who share in this. **2.** (*M~*). Organized international body of criminals esp. in U.S. and orig. among Italian immigrants. [It. dial. (Sicilian), = bragging]

mafĭō's|ō (mah-) *n.* (*pl.* **~i** *pr.* -ē). Member of the mafia. [It. (as prec.)]

măg *n.* (colloq.) Magazine (sense 2); magnesium; magneto. [abbr.]

măgazi'ne (-zē'n) *n.* **1.** Store for arms, ammunition, and provisions, for use in war; store for gunpowder or other explosives; chamber containing supply of cartridges fed automatically to breech of gun; similar device in camera, slide-projector, etc. **2.** Periodical publication (now usu. illustrated) containing contributions by various writers. [f. F *magasin* f. It. *magazzino* f. Arab. *makzin* pl. of *makzan* storehouse (*kazana* store up)]

mă'gdalėn *n.* Reformed prostitute; home for magdalens. [f. Mary *Magdalen(e)* of Magdala in Galilee (Luke 8:2), identified with the sinner of Luke 7:37; f. eccl. L *Magdalena* f. Gk *Magdalēnē*]

Măgdalē'nĭan *a.* & *n.* (Archaeol.) (Culture) of the (latest) palaeolithic period in Europe, with horn and bone tools. [f. F *Magdalénien* of La *Madeleine*, Dordogne, France, where remains were found, + -IAN]

Mă'gdėbûrg. See HEMISPHERE. [~ in E. Germany]

māge *n.* (arch.) Magician; learned person. [ME, Anglicized f. MAGUS]

Măgėllă'nĭc *a.* Of Magellan; ~ **clouds,** two galaxies visible in the southern sky that are the nearest to the Galaxy. [f. F. *Magellan*, Port. explorer d. 1521, + -IC]

magĕ'nta *n.* & *a.* **1.** *n.* Brilliant crimson aniline dye, fuchsine; colour of this. **2.** *a.* Coloured with or like magenta. [f. *M~* in N. Italy, site of battle (1859) shortly before the dye was discovered]

mă'ggot *n.* **1.** Larva, esp. of cheese-fly or bluebottle; **red ~,** larva of wheat-midge. **2.** Whimsical fancy. **3.** Hence **~Y**² *a.* [ME, perh. alt. f. *maddock*, earlier *mathek* f. ON *mathkr*; cf. MAWKISH]

Magi. See MAGUS.

Mā'gĭan *a.* & *n.* (One) of the Magi or magi; magician; hence **~ISM** (3) *n.* [f. L MAGUS + -IAN]

mă'gĭc *n.*, *a.*, & *v.t.* (**-ck-**). **1.** *n.* Supposed art of influencing course of events by occult control of nature or of spirits, witchcraft, (**black, white, natural,** ~, involving invocation of devils, angels, no personal spirit; SYMPATHETIC *magic*); inexplicable or remarkable influence producing surprising results (**like** ~, very rapidly). **2.** *a.* Of magic; used or usable in magic; producing surprising results; ~ **carpet,** mythical carpet able to transport person on it to any place; ~ **eye,** (1) small cathode-ray tube used to indicate correct tuning of radio receiver, (2) photoelectric device used for automatic control; ~ **lantern,** simple form of image-projector using slides; ~ **square,** one divided into smaller squares each containing a (usu. different) number, so arranged that sum of vertical, horizontal, or diagonal row is always same. **3.** *v.t.* (**-ck-**) Change or make (as if) by magic; ~ **away,** cause to disappear thus. [ME, f. OF *magique* a. & n. f. L *magicus* a., LL *magica* n., f. Gk *magikos* (as MAGUS; see -IC)]

mă'gĭcal *a.* Of magic; resembling, or produced as if by, magic; hence **~LY**² *adv.* [f. prec. + -AL]

magĭ'cian (-shan) *n.* One skilled in magic, wizard, conjurer. [ME, f. OF *magicien* f. LL *magica* as prec.; see -ICIAN]

magilp. Var. of MEGILP.

Mă'gĭnōt (-nō) *n.* ~ **Line,** line of fortifications on N.E. border of France before 1940, (fig.) line of defence on which one blindly relies; **~-minded,** obsessed with defence of *status quo*. [f. A. ~, Fr. minister of war d. 1932]

măgĭstēr'ĭal *a.* Of, or conducted by, a magistrate; invested with authority; dictatorial; (of opinion, writings, etc.) authoritative; hence **~LY**² *adv.* [f. med. L *magisterialis* f. LL *magisterius* f. L *magister* MASTER¹]

magĭ'stral *a.* Of a master or masters; (Pharm., of remedy etc.) devised by physician for particular case, not included in the pharmacopoeia (cf. OFFICINAL). [F, or f. L *magistralis* (*magister* MASTER¹; see -AL)]

mă'gĭstr|āte *n.* Civil officer administering law; person conducting court of summary jurisdiction (||STIPENDIARY or JUSTICE of the Peace); **~ates' court** (for minor cases and preliminary hearings); hence or cogn. **~ACY, ~āteSHIP** (-tsh-), **~atURE,** *ns.* [ME, f. L *magistratus* (orig. office of) magistrate (as prec.; see -ATE¹)]

Măglemō'sĭan (-z-) *a.* & *n.* (Of) a N. European mesolithic culture, with bone and stone implements. [f. *Maglemose* in Denmark, where articles from it were found, + -IAN]

mă'gma *n.* (*pl.* **~ta** *or* **~s**). Crude pasty mixture of mineral or organic matter; (semi-)molten stratum under solid crust of earth, from which igneous rock is formed by cooling; hence **măgmă'tIC** *a.* [ME, = solid residue; L f. Gk *magma -atos* f. root of *massō* knead]

Măgna Chār'ta (k-) *or* **Cār'ta** *n.* Great charter of English personal and political liberty obtained from King John in 1215; any similar document establishing rights. [med. L, = great charter]

măgnā'lĭum *n.* Light rigid alloy of aluminium and magnesium. [f. *magnesium* + *aluminium* + -IUM]

măgnă'nĭmous *a.* Noble, generous, not petty, in feelings or conduct; showing magnanimity; hence or cogn. **măgnanĭ'mITY** *n.*, **~LY**² *adv.* [f. L *magnanimus* (*magnus* great, *animus* mind) + -OUS]

mă'gnāte *n.* Wealthy or eminent man (*cotton, financial, magnate*). [ME, f. LL *magnas -atis* f. L *magnus* great]

măgnē'si|a (-sha) *n.* **1.** Magnesium oxide. **2.** (pop.) Hydrated magnesium carbonate, white powder used as antacid and cathartic; MILK¹ *of magnesia*. **3.** Hence **~AN** (-shan) *a.* [ME f. med. L, f. Gk *Magnēsia* (*lithos* stone) of Magnesia in Asia Minor, orig. ref. to loadstone]

măgnē'sĭum (*or* -z-; *or* -shyum) *n.* Silver-white metallic element present in magnesia; ~ **flare, light,** blinding light got by burning magnesium wire. [f. prec.; see -IUM]

mă'gnėt *n.* **1.** Piece of iron, steel, alloy, ore, etc., having the properties of attracting iron and of pointing approximately north and south when suspended, natural (as in loadstone) or induced by contact with a magnet, by magnetic induction, or by electric current; **bar ~** (in form of straight bar); **horseshoe ~** (in shape of bar bent till ends nearly meet); PERMANENT *magnet*.

2. = LOAD[1]*stone*. **3.** (fig.) Thing that attracts. [ME, f. L *magnes magnetis* f. Gk *magnēs* = *Magnēs -ētos* (*lithos* stone) of Magnesia (cf. MAGNESIA)]

măgnĕ'tic *a.* **1.** Having properties of magnet; producing, produced by, acting by, magnetism; ~ **compass,** = COMPASS[1] 3; ~ **equator,** aclinic line; *magnetic* FIELD 6; ~ **inclination,** = *magnetic* DIP[2]; ~ **mine,** submarine mine detonated by approach of large mass of metal, e.g. ship; *magnetic* MOMENT, NEEDLE, NORTH, POLE[2]; ~ **storm,** disturbance of earth's magnetic field by charged particles from sun etc.; *magnetic* TAPE. **2.** Capable of acquiring properties of, or being attracted by, a magnet. **3.** (fig.) Very attractive; (arch.) mesmeric. **4.** Hence **măgnĕ'tICALLY** *adv.* [f. LL *magneticus* (as prec.; see -IC)]

mă'gnĕtism *n.* **1.** (Science of) magnetic phenomena; natural agency producing these; ANIMAL *magnetism*; **terrestrial** ~, magnetic properties of the earth as a whole. **2.** (fig.) Attraction, personal charm. **3.** So **mă'gnĕtIST** (3) *n.* [f. mod. L *magnetismus* (as MAGNET; see -ISM)]

mă'gnĕtīte *n.* Magnetic iron oxide. [f. G *magnetit* (as MAGNET, -ITE[1] (2))]

mă'gnĕtīz|e, -is|e (-īz), *v.t.* Give magnetic properties to; make into a magnet; attract (lit. or fig.) as magnet does; hence ~ABLE *a.*, ~A'TION *n.* [f. MAGNET + -IZE]

măgnē'tō *n.* (*pl.* ~**s**). Electric generator using permanent magnets (esp. for ignition in internal combustion engines, producing the required intermittent high-tension current independently of a battery). [abbr. of MAGNETO-*electric*]

măgnē'tō- *comb. form.* Magnet, magnetic, magnetism, as: ~**-ele'ctric,** (of electric generator) using permanent magnets, so ~**-electri'city;** ~**graph,** instrument recording variation of magnetic quantities; ~**hydrodyna'mic,** relating to movement of electrically conducting fluid in magnetic field; ~**meter** (-ŏ'm-), instrument measuring magnetic forces, esp. terrestrial magnetism; ~**-mo'tive force,** sum of magnetizing forces along circuit; ~**sphere,** region in which earth's magnetic field is effective; ~**stri'ction,** change in size caused by magnetization. [f. Gk *magnēs* (see MAGNET) + -O-]

mă'gnĕtŏn *n.* (Phys.) Unit of magnetic MOMENT of atom etc. [f. F *magnéton* (as MAGNETIC; see -ON)]

mă'gnĕtrŏn *n.* Electron tube for amplifying or generating microwaves, with flow of electrons controlled by external magnetic field. [f. MAGNET + -TRON]

măgnĭ'fĭc(al) *adjs.* (arch.) Magnificent, sublime. [ME, f. F *magnifique* or f. L *magnificus* (*magnus* great; see -FIC), + -AL]

măgnĭ'fĭcăt *n.* Song of praise; (*M*~) a canticle (see etym.). [f. hymn of Virgin Mary in Luke 1:46–55, used as canticle, and beginning thus in Vulgate; L, 3rd sing. of *magnificare* MAGNIFY]

măgnĭfĭcā'tion *n.* Magnifying or being magnified; amount of this, apparent enlargement of object by lens. [f. MAGNIFY + -FICATION]

măgnĭ'fĭc|ent *a.* Splendid, stately; sumptuously constructed or adorned; splendidly lavish; (colloq.) fine, excellent; hence or cogn. ~ENCE *n.*, ~**ent**LY[2] *adv.* [F, or f. L *magnificent-* stem seen in compar. and superl. of *magnificus* MAGNIFIC]

măgnĭ'fĭcō *n.* (*pl.* ~**es**). Venetian magnate; grandee. [It., = MAGNIFIC]

mă'gnĭ|fȳ *v.t.* Increase apparent size of (thing), as with lens (~**fying glass**) or microscope; exaggerate; intensify; (arch.) extol; hence ~**fīer**[1] (2) *n.* [ME, f. OF *magnifier* or f. L *magnificare* (*magnificus*; see MAGNIFIC, -FY)]

măgnĭ'loqu|ent *a.* Lofty in expression; boastful; hence ~ENCE *n.*, ~**ent**LY[2] *adv.* [f. L *magniloquus* (*magnus* great, *-loquus* -speaking) + -ENT]

mă'gnĭtūde *n.* Largeness; size; importance; (Astron.) (class of fixed stars arranged according to) degree of brightness (*first*, *seventh*, etc., *magnitude*; **apparent** ~, as seen from the earth; **absolute** ~, as seen at standard distance of ten parsecs, giving a measure of intrinsic luminosity); (fig.) **of the first** ~ (importance). [ME, f. L *magnitudo* (*magnus* great; see -TUDE)]

măgnō'lia *n.* Tree of genus *Magnolia*, cultivated for its dark-green foliage and waxlike flowers; ***M~ State,** Mississippi. [mod. L, f. P. *Magnol*, Fr. botanist d. 1715 + -IA[1]]

mă'gnum *n.* (Bottle containing) two quarts ($\frac{1}{2}$ gal. or *$\frac{2}{5}$ U.S. gal.) of wine or spirits. [L, neut. (as n.) of *magnus* great]

magnum opus. See OPUS.

mă'gpīe *n.* **1.** European & Amer. crow (*Pica pica*) with long pointed tail and black-and-white plumage; idle chatterer; random collector. **2.** Bird with plumage like magpie (e.g. Austral. bird of genus *Gymnorhina*); (rifle shot that strikes) outermost division but one of target. [f. *Mag* abbr. of woman's name *Margaret* + PIE[1]]

mă'guey (-gwā) *n.* Agave plant, esp. that which yields pulque. [Sp., f. Haitian]

mā'g|us *n.* (*pl.* ~**i** *pr.* -jī). Member of ancient Persian priestly caste; sorcerer; **the** (**three**) **Magi,** the 'wise men' from the East who brought offerings to the infant Christ (Matt. 2:1). [ME f. L, f. Gk *magos* f. OPers. *magus*]

Mă'gyar *n.* & *a.* **1.** (*or* mŏ'dyer). (Member or language) of the people now predominant in Hungary; Hungarian. **2.** ~ (**blouse**), blouse with ~ **sleeves** (cut in one piece with main part of garment). [native name]

ma'halĕb (mah'-h-) *n.* Small cherry (*Prunus mahaleb*) with kernels yielding oil for perfume. [earlier *macaleb* f. F, f. Arab. *maḥlab*]

mahara'ja, -jah, (mah-h*a*rah'j*a*) *n.* (Hist.) Title of some Indian princes. [f. Hindi *mahārājā* (*mahā* great; see RAJA)]

mahara'nee, -ra'nĭ, (mah-h*a*rah'nĭ) *n.* (Hist.) Maharaja's wife or widow. [f. Hindi *mahārānī* (*mahā* great; see RANEE)]

mahari'shĭ (mah-h*a*-) *n.* Great Hindu sage. [f. Hindi (as prec., RISHI)]

mahă'tma (m*a*-h-) *n.* (Buddhism) one of a class of persons with preternatural powers, supposed to exist in India and Tibet; (Theosophy) sage or adept; person regarded with reverence. [f. Skr. *mahātman* (*mahā* great, *ātmán* soul)]

Mahaya'na (mah-h*a*yah'n*a*) *n.* School of Buddhism with syncretistic features and worship of gods, practised in China, Japan, and Tibet. [Skr. (*mahā* great, *yāna* vehicle)]

Mah'dĭ *n.* Spiritual and temporal leader expected by Muslims; claimant of this title, esp. one of several leaders of insurrection in Sudan; hence **Mah'd**ISM (3), **Mah'd**IST (2), *ns.* [f. Arab. *mahdīy* he who is guided right, p.p. of *hadā* guide]

mah-jŏ'ng, -ngg (-ng), *n.* Game (orig. Chinese) for four played with 136 or 144 pieces called tiles. [Chin., = sparrows]

mah'lstĭck. See MAULSTICK.

mahŏ'ganȳ (m*a*-h-) *n.* Reddish-brown wood from tropical tree (esp. W. Ind. tree of genus *Swietenia*), much used for furniture, and taking high polish; tree yielding mahogany; (arch.) dining-table (**have** one's **knees under** person's ~, be dining with him); colour of mahogany, reddish-brown. [17th c.; orig. unkn.]

Mahometan. Var. of MUHAMMADAN.

Mahou'nd (m*a*-hōō'nd) *n.* (arch.) Muhammad (regarded mistakenly as a god). [ME f. OF *Mahun* (*Mahomet* Muhammad)]

mahou't (m*a*-how't) *n.* Elephant-driver. [f. Hindi *mahāut* f. Skr. *mahāmātra* high official, lit. 'great in measure']

Mahratta. See MARATHA.
mah'seer *n.* Large Indian freshwater game-fish (*Barbus mosal*). [f. Hindi *mahāsir*]
maid *n.* **1.** (arch. or poet.) Girl; young (unmarried) woman, virgin; spinster. **2.** (rhet.) Young woman; **the M~ (of Orleans)**, Joan of Arc. **3.** ~**('servant)**, female servant esp. for indoor work (HOUSE¹*maid*, NURSE¹*maid*). **4.** ~ **of all work,** female servant doing general housework, (fig.) person doing many jobs; ~ **of honour,** (1) unmarried lady attending queen or princess, (2) kind of custard tartlet, (3) *principal bridesmaid; OLD *maid.* **5.** Hence ~'ISH¹ *a.*, ~'Y³ *n.* [ME, abbr. of MAIDEN]
maidan (mīdah'n) *n.* (Anglo-Ind.) Open space in or near town; parade-ground. [f. Urdu f. Arab. *maydān*]
mai'den *n.* & *a.* **1.** *n.* (arch. or poet.) = MAID 1. **2.** (Hist.) Kind of guillotine used at Edinburgh. **3.** = *maiden over*; maiden horse. **4.** *a.* Unmarried (*maiden aunt, lady*); ~ **name** (before marriage). **5.** (Of female animal) unmated; (of horse) that has never won prize, (of race) open to such horse; (of plant) grown from seed; (of speech by M.P., voyage, etc.) first; (of fortress etc.) never captured; (of soldier, sword, etc.) untried. **6.** ||~ **assize,** one with no cases for trial; ~ **over,** (Cricket) over in which no runs are scored. **7.** ~**hair,** fern of genus *Adiantum* with fine hair-like stalks and delicate fronds; ~**hair tree,** ginkgo; ~**head** [see -HEAD], (1) virginity, (2) = HYMEN². **8.** Hence ~HOOD *n.*, ~ISH¹, ~LIKE, ~LY¹, *adjs.* [OE *mægden*, dim. (-EN²) f. *mægeth* = OS *magath*, OHG *magad*, Goth. *magaths* f. Gmc **magadiz* maid]
maieu'tic (māū'-) *a.* (Of Socratic mode of inquiry) serving to bring out a person's latent ideas into clear consciousness. [f. Gk *maieutikos* (*maieuomai* act as midwife (*maia*); see -IC)]
mai'gre¹ (-*ger*) *a.* (R.C. Ch.) (Of day) on which abstinence from meat is ordered; (of food) suitable for eating on maigre days. [F, lit. lean; cf. MEAGRE]
mai'gre², ***mai'ger,** (-*ger*) *n.* Large Mediterranean food-fish, *Sciaena aquila*, = BAR³; fish of family Sciaenidae. [F]
mail¹ *n.* **1.** Armour composed of rings or chains, defensive armour for the body; **coat of** ~, jacket covered with this. **2.** Protective shell or scales of animals. **3.** Hence ~ED² (-ld) *a.* (~**ed fist,** physical force). [ME, f. OF *maille* f. L *macula* spot, mesh]
mail² *v.t.* Clothe (as) with mail. [f. prec.]
mail³ *n.*, & *v.t.* **1.** *n.* Bag of letters for conveyance by post; this system of conveyance, the POST²; matter so conveyed; all that is so conveyed on one occasion; ~ **(coach, train,** etc.), vehicle carrying this; letters etc. delivered at one place on one occasion; (as newspaper name: *Daily Mail, Oxford Mail*). **2.** ~**-bag,** large bag for carrying mail; ~**-boat** (carrying mail); *~**'-box,** letter-box; *~ **carrier,** postman; ||~**-cart,** (1) cart for carrying mail by road, (2) light vehicle for carrying children; *~ **drop,** receptacle for mail; *~**'man,** postman; ~ **order,** order for goods to be sent by post (~*-order firm*, firm doing business mainly on this system). **3.** *v.t.* Send (letters etc.) by post; hence *~'ABLE *a.*, acceptable for conveyance by post. **4.** ~**'ing list** (of persons to whom advertising matter etc. is to be posted). [ME f. OF *male* wallet f. WG (= OHG) **malha*]
maillot (mǎyō') *n.* Dancer's or gymnast's tights; woman's one-piece bathing-suit; = JERSEY 3. [F]
maim *v.t.* Mutilate, cripple, (lit. or fig.). [ME *maynhe* etc. f. OF *mahaignier* etc., of unkn. orig.]
main¹ *n.* (In game of hazard) number (5, 6, 7, 8, or 9) called by player before dice are thrown; match between fighting-cocks. [16th c.; prob. f. MAIN³ *chance*]
main² *n.* **1.** Principal channel, duct, etc., for water, sewage, etc., or (usu. in *pl.*) for supply of electricity. **2.** (arch. or poet.) Mainland; high seas; SPANISH *Main.* **3. In the** ~, for the most part. **4. With might and** ~, with all one's force. [f. foll.; orig. = physical force (as in sense 4); OE *mægen*, = OS *megin*, OHG *magan*, ON *magn* f. Gmc **mag-*; cf. MAY¹]
main³ *attrib. a.* **1.** Exerted to the full (*by main force*); chief in size or extent (*the main body of an army* etc.); principal, most important, as *the main point* (in argument), *the main road* (in district), *the main clause* (in sentence), whence ~'LY² *adv.* **2.** *Have an eye to* **the ~ chance,** one's own interests; ~**'land,** large continuous extent of land, excluding neighbouring islands etc., largest island in Orkneys and Shetlands; ~ **line,** (1) chief railway line, (2) *chief road or street, (3, sl.) principal vein esp. as site of drug injection; ~**'line** *v.i.*, (sl.) take drugs thus; ~**'spring,** principal spring of watch, clock, etc., (fig.) chief motive power or incentive; *~ **stem,** (colloq.) main street; ~**'stream,** principal current of river etc., (fig.) prevailing trend of opinion, fashion, etc., (of jazz) neither traditional nor modern; ~ **street,** principal street of town, (fig., after S. Lewis's novel *Main Street*, 1920) materialistic ideals. **3.** (Naut.) ~ **brace** (attached to main yard; *splice the ~ brace*, (Hist.) serve extra rum ration); *main* COURSE¹; ~ **deck,** (in man-of-war) deck next below spar-deck, (in merchantman) upper deck between poop and forecastle; ~**'mast,** principal mast; ~**'sail** (*or* -*sal*), (in square-rigged vessel) lowest sail on mainmast, (in fore-and-aft rigged vessel) sail set on after part of mainmast; ~**'stay,** stay from maintop to foot of foremast, (fig.) chief support; ~**'top,** platform above, ~**-to'pmast,** mast above, head of lower mainmast; ~ **yard,** yard on which mainsail is extended. [ME, partly f. ON *megenn, megn* a., partly f. OE *mægen-* (as prec.)]
maintai'n *v.t.* Cause to continue, continue one's action in, retain in being, (war, contest, lawsuit, condition, position, attitude, relations, correspondence); cause (person etc.) to continue *in* (condition, possession of thing, etc.); support (life, one's state in life) by nourishment, expenditure, etc.; furnish (one*self*, one's family, etc.) with means of subsistence; provide means for (garrison etc. to be equipped, building or road to be repaired, etc.; ||~**ed school,** one supported from public funds); take action to preserve (machine etc.) in good order; give aid to (cause, party); assert as true (opinion, statement, *that*); hence ~ABLE *a.*, ~ER¹, ~OR, *ns.*, (esp. Law, one guilty of MAINTENANCE). [ME, f. OF *maintenir* f. Rom. **manutenēre* f. L *manu tenēre* hold in the hand]
mai'ntėnance *n.* Maintaining or being maintained; (provision of) enough to support life (SEPARATE¹ *maintenance*); = ALIMONY 2; (Law) former offence of aiding a party in litigation without lawful cause; **cap of** ~, cap or hat worn as symbol of official dignity or carried before a sovereign etc.; ~ **man** (employed to keep equipment etc. in repair). [ME f. OF (*maintenir*; see prec., -ANCE)]
maisonĕ'tte, -nn-, (-z-) *n.* Small house; part of a house let separately (usu. not all on one floor). [F *maisonnette*, dim. of *maison* house; see -ETTE]
maître d'hôtel (mātr dōtĕ'l) *n.* Major-domo; head waiter; ~ **butter, sauce,** (containing lemon-juice and chopped parsley). [F, = master of house]

maize *n.* Indian corn, N. Amer. cereal *Zea mays*; its grain; yellow colour of maize cobs. [f. F *maïs* or f. Sp. *maiz*, of Carib orig.]

Maj. *abbr.* Major(-).

majĕ'st|ic *a.* Possessing stateliness or grandeur, imposing; hence ~ICALLY *adv.* [f. foll. + -IC]

mă'jĕstȳ *n.* **1.** Impressive stateliness of aspect, bearing, language, etc. **2.** Sovereign power; **Your, His, Her, M~** (forms used in speaking to or of sovereign or sovereign's wife or widow: *Her Majesty the Queen*; *Her Majesty the Queen Mother*; *Her Majesty's Stationery Office*; *Her Britannic Majesty*). **3.** Representation of God or Christ enthroned within aureole. [ME, f. OF *majesté* f. L *majestas -tatis* (as MAJOR^{2}; see -TY^{1})]

Măjlĭ's *n.* Parliament of various N. Afr. or Middle Eastern countries, esp. Iran. [Pers., = assembly]

majŏ'lĭca, maiŏ'- (mayŏ'-) *n.* Renaissance Italian earthenware with coloured ornamentation on opaque white enamel; modern imitation of this. [f. It. *majolica*, f. former name of island of Majorca]

mā'jor^{1} *n.* Officer next below lieutenant-colonel and above captain; **~-general,** officer next below lieutenant-general; hence ~E'TTE *n.* (see DRUM^{1}), ~SHIP *n.* [F, short for *sergent-major* SERGEANT-major, orig. a high rank (f. as foll.)]

mā'jor^{2} *a.*, *n.*, & *v.i.* **1.** *a.* Greater (not foll. by *than*) of two things, classes, etc.; of full age; ||(in schools) *Smith* etc. **~**, the elder of the two Smiths or the first to enter the school; **~ axis** (of conic, passing through its foci); ***~ league,** highest-ranking baseball etc. league (or fig.); **~ part,** majority (*of*); *major* PLANET^{1}, PROPHET; **~ suit,** (Bridge) spades or hearts; FRIARS *Major*. **2.** Unusually important or serious or significant (*major road, war*); (of operation) presenting possible danger to patient's life. **3.** (Logic). (Of term) occurring in predicate of conclusion of syllogism; (of premiss) containing major term. **4.** (Mus.) (Of interval) normal or perfect (cf. MINOR), as in major scale, (*major third*); (of key) in which scale has major third; (of scale) with semitones above third and seventh notes. **5.** *n.* (Mil.) Officer in charge of section of band instruments (DRUM^{1} *major*, PIPE^{1} *major*, TRUMPET-*major*); SERGEANT-*major*. **6.** *n.* Person of full age; (Logic) major term or premiss; *student's special subject or course; *student specializing in a subject (*is a philosophy major*). **7.** *v.i.* *(Of student) undertake study or qualify *in* as special subject. [ME f. L, compar. of *magnus* great]

mājor-dō'mō *n.* (*pl.* **~s**). Chief official of Italian or Spanish princely household; house-steward, butler. [orig. *mayordome* f. Sp. *mayordomo*, It. *maggiordomo* f. med. L *major domus* highest official of the household (as prec., DOME)]

majŏ'rĭtȳ *n.* **1.** Greater number or part (*of*); **the (great) ~**, the dead (esp. *join the (great) ~*, die); ABSOLUTE or *overall majority*; **~ verdict** (given by more than half of jury, but not unanimous). **2.** Number by which votes cast on one side exceed those on other; party etc. receiving greater number of votes (**in the ~**, belonging to or constituting this). **3.** Full age (*attained his majority*). **4.** Rank of MAJOR^{1}. [f. F *majorité* f. med. L *majoritas -tatis* (as MAJOR^{2}; see -ITY)]

mă'juscūl|e *a.* & *n.* (Palaeogr.) Large (letter), whether capital or uncial; (written in) large lettering; hence ~AR^{1} (-ŭ's-) *a.* [F, f. L *majuscula* (*littera* letter), dim. of MAJOR^{2}; see -CULE]

māke^{1} *v.* (**made**). **1.** *v.t.* Construct, frame, create, from parts or other substances, (*God made man (a rational creature)*; *bees make cells of wax*; *made in England*; *can make almost anything out of bamboo*; *hydrogen and nitrogen make ammonia*); **made,** (of person) built, formed, (*well-made, loosely-made*); **made dish,** food prepared from several separate foods; **made road** (artificially prepared, with surfacing-materials added); **be made for,** be ideally suited to; **be made of,** consist of (*pipes are made of clay*); **have it made,** (sl.) be sure of success; *made to* MEASURE^{1}; *made to* ORDER^{1} 17. **2.** Compose, write, (book etc.); prepare (will etc.). **3.** Prepare (tea, coffee, etc.) for use; shuffle (pack of cards) for dealing; arrange and light materials for (a fire); arrange bedclothes on (bed) for further use; *make* HAY^{1}. **4.** Cause to exist, bring about, (disturbance, difficulties, trouble, an enemy, sport, noise, one's mark in the world, a corner in wheat); *make no* BONE^{1}*s*; *make* FRIENDS; *make* FUN OR GAME^{1} *of*; *make a* NAME^{1} *for oneself*; *make* PEACE; *make place* or ROOM (*for*); *make a point of* (see POINT^{1} 11); **~ time,** find an occasion when time is available (*for doing* or *to* do), *make sexual advances; *make* (one's or *its*) WAY. **5.** (Electr.) Complete, close, (circuit; opp. *break*). **6.** Result in (*it makes a difference*; *'find' makes in the past tense 'found'*); amount to (*2 and 2 make 4*); constitute (*one* SWALLOW^{2} *does not make a summer*). **7.** Establish, enact, (distinctions, rules, laws). **8.** Collect, get together, (a HOUSE^{1}, a quorum); **~ a bag,** kill number of game; **~ a book,** arrange series of bets on an event; **~ sail,** spread (additional) sail(s), start on voyage; *make* WATER^{1}. **9.** Cause (obj. of prep. *of*) to become (*make an* EXAMPLE^{1}, *an* EXHIBITION, *a* FOOL^{1}, *of* person or *oneself*); *make a* HABIT^{1}, *a* PRACTICE^{1}, *of*; **~ a day,** NIGHT, **week,** etc., **of it,** carry activity etc. on through the day etc. **10.** Frame in the mind (*make a judgement of*); feel (doubt, scruples, *of* or *about*). **11.** (Naut.) Discern, come in sight of. **12.** Arrive at; achieve place in (team, prize-list, etc.); (sl.) catch (a train etc.), win affections of, esp. seduce (person); **~ it,** succeed in traversing a certain distance, (fig.) be successful, (sl.) achieve copulation (*with*). **13.** Form, be counted as, (*this makes the tenth time*; *will you make one of the party?*); serve for (*this makes pleasant reading*); become, turn out to be, (*she will make a good wife*; *he would make a good preacher*). **14.** Gain, acquire, procure, (*money, a living, a profit*, one's *fortune*); (Cards) win (trick), play (card) to advantage, win number of tricks that fulfils (contract); obtain as result (*made a loss on the transaction*); (Cricket) score (runs). **15.** Secure the advancement of; **made man,** one who has attained success in life; SELF-*made*; **~ or break, ~ or mar,** cause success or ruin of; **~** one's **day** etc., be essential factor in success of it. **16.** Cause to be (*make it hot, known, plain*; *make oneself a martyr*; *make oneself* SCARCE; *make him a duke*); convert *into*; choose as (*shall we make it Tuesday then?*); bring to (chosen value etc.; *add one and make it a round dozen*). **17.** Consider to be (*what do you make the time?*; *I make it 5 miles*); consider (*what bird do you make that to be?*). **18.** Cause, compel, (to) (*make him repeat it*; *he was made to repeat it*); *make* BELIEVE (and see 28); **~ do,** use (with) temporary expedients, manage *with* (something) as an inferior or temporary substitute. **19.** Represent as, cause to appear to do or be, (*he makes Richard the king's son*). **20.** Execute (bodily movement, *a* BACK^{1}, BOW^{4}, FACE^{1}, LEG); perform (journey etc., and with many ns. expr. vbl action, as *an acquisition, attempt, blunder, effort, mistake, purchase, speech, start, venture*); wage (war *on, against, with*); travel along (*make a bee-line for*); accomplish (distance, speed, etc.); **~** (eat) **a good breakfast** etc.; *make* HEAD^{1} 22, LOVE^{1}, SHIFT^{2}. **21. ~ of,** construct from, (fig.) conclude to be the meaning or character of (*can you make* *anything of it?*; *what am I to make of your behaviour?*); **made of money,** (colloq.) very rich; **~ much, little, the best,** etc., **of,** (1) derive much etc. advantage from, (2) give much etc. attention to, attach much etc. importance to; *make* LIGHT⁴ *of*; *make a* HASH² *of*; *make* HEAD¹ *or tail of*; *make a* MEAL² *of*, *make the* MOST *of*; *make* NOTHING *of*. **22.** *v.i.* Proceed (*towards* etc.); **~ after,** (arch.) pursue; **~ away** or **off,** depart hastily; **~ off with,** carry away, steal. **23.** Act as if with intention *to* do (*he made to go*); **~ as if** or **though,** act as if one were about *to* do or as one would if one *had* etc.; *make* BOLD, CERTAIN, FREE¹, GOOD, MERRY², SURE. **24.** (Of tide) begin to flow or ebb. **25. ~ against,** be unfavourable to; **~ away with,** get rid of, kill, squander; **~ for,** conduce to (happiness etc.), confirm (view), proceed towards (place), assail; **~ over,** transfer possession of (thing *to* person), refashion (garment etc.); ***~ with,** (sl.) (exert oneself to) supply. **26. ~ out,** draw up, write out, (list, document, cheque *to*, or *in favour of*, person), get together with difficulty (*articles put in to make out a volume*), (try to) prove (*how do you make that out?*, *you make me out* (*to be*) *a hypocrite*), understand (*I can't make him out, can't make out what he wants*), decipher (handwriting etc.), distinguish by sight or hearing (*I made out a figure in the distance*), (colloq.) make progress, fare, (*how did you make out?*), pretend (*he made out that he liked it*). **27. ~ up,** serve or act to overcome (deficiency), complete (amount, party), compensate (*make up lost ground*; *make up for lost time*; *we must* **~ it up to** (compensate) *him somehow*), compound, put together, prepare, (medicine, hay *into* bundles, butter, beds for use, etc.), sew together (parts of garment etc.), get together (company, sum of money), arrange (type) in pages, compile (list, account, document), concoct (story), (of parts) compose (whole), prepare (actor) for his part by dressing, false hair, etc., apply cosmetics (to), arrange (marriage etc.), settle (dispute); **~ (it) up,** be reconciled; *make up* one's MIND¹; **~ up to,** court, curry favour with; **~-up** *n.*, disguise of actor, cosmetics etc. used for this, making up of type, type made up, (cosmetics for) woman's facial adornment, composition or constitution, person's character and temperament. **28. ~'bate,** (arch.) one who foments strife; **~-believe** *a.* & *n.*, pretended, pretence; **~'ready,** (Print.) final preparation for printing; **~'shift** *a.* & *n.*, (serving as) temporary substitute or device; **~'weight,** small quantity added to make full weight (lit., or fig. of extra person), (fig.) unimportant point added to make argument seem stronger. [OE *macian*, = OS *makon*, OHG *mahhōn* f. WG ***makōjan** (***mak-** fit, suitable, cogn. w. MATCH¹)]

māke² *n.* **1.** (Of natural or manufactured thing) kind of structure or composition; build of body; mental or moral disposition; origin of manufacture (*British make*; *our own make of shoes*); shuffling of cards; **on the ~,** (sl.) intent on gain, *(sl.) looking for sexual partners. **2.** (Electr.) Making of contact, position in which this is made. [ME, f. prec.]

mā'ker *n.* In vbl senses; **the, our,** etc., **M~,** God; (arch.) poet. [ME, f. MAKE¹ + -ER¹]

mā'king *n.* **1.** In vbl senses; **be the ~ of,** ensure success or favourable development of; **in the ~,** in course of being made or formed. **2.** (in *pl.*) Earnings, profits; essential qualities for becoming (*he has the makings of a general*); (U.S. & Austral.) paper and tobacco for rolling a cigarette. [OE *macung* (as MAKE¹, -ING¹)]

ma'kō¹ (mah'-) *n.* (*pl.* **~s**). Blue Pacific shark (*Isurus glaucus*). [Maori]

ma'kō² (mah'-) *n.* (*pl.* **~s**). Small handsome N.Z. tree with large racemes of reddish flowers [Maori]

măl- *pref.* **1.** Bad(ly) (*malpractice, maltreat*), faulty (*malfunction*). **2.** Not (*maladroit, malcontent*). [f. F *mal* badly f. L *male*]

Mal. *abbr.* Malachi (O.T.).

Mală'cca *n.* **~ cane,** rich-brown cane from stem of palm-tree *Calamus rotang*, used for walking-sticks etc. [~ in Malaysia]

mă'lachite (-kit) *n.* Hydrated copper carbonate as bright-green mineral taking high polish and used for ornament. [f. OF *melochite* f. L *molochites* f. Gk *molokhitis* (*molokhē* = *malakhē* mallow; see -ITE¹)]

mă'laco- *comb. form.* Soft, as: **~derm,** soft-skinned reptile etc.; **~logy** (-ŏ'l-), science of molluscs; **~ptery'gian** *a.* & *n.*, soft-finned (fish). [f. Gk *malakos* soft + -o-]

mălacŏ'stracan *a.* & *n.* (Member) of the crustacean order Malacostraca, e.g. crab, lobster, shrimp. [f. as prec. + Gk *ostrakon* shell + -AN]

măladjŭ'st|ėd *a.* Not correctly adjusted; (of person) not satisfactorily adjusted to one's environment and conditions of life; so **~**MENT *n.* [f. MAL- + p.p. of ADJUST]

măladmĭ'nĭst|er *v.t.* Administer or manage inefficiently or badly or improperly; so **~r**A'TION *n.* [f. MAL- + ADMINISTER]

mă'ladroit (*or* -oi't) *a.* Clumsy, bungling; hence **~**LY² *adv.*, **~**NESS *n.* [F (as MAL-, ADROIT)]

mă'ladў *n.* Ailment, disease, (lit. or fig.). [ME, f. OF *maladie* (*malade* sick f. Rom. ***male habitus** f. L *male* ill, *habitus* p.p. of *habēre* have)]

māla fī'dė *adv.* & *a.* (Acting, done) in bad faith. [L]

Mă'laga *n.* White or red fortified wine from Málaga. [*Málaga* in S. Spain]

Mălagă'sў *a.* & *n.* (Language or native or inhabitant) of Madagascar. [orig. *Malegass*, *Madegass* f. *Madagascar*]

malai'se (-z) *n.* Bodily discomfort, esp. without development of specific disease; feeling of uneasiness. [F, f. OF *mal* bad + *aise* EASE¹]

mă'lamūte, mă'lemūte, *n.* Eskimo dog. [name of Alaskan Eskimo tribe]

malanders. Var. of MALLENDERS.

mă'lapert *a.* & *n.* (arch.) Impudent, saucy, (person). [ME f. OF (as MAL-, *apert* = *espert* EXPERT¹)]

mă'laprŏp(ĭsm) *n.* Ludicrous misuse of word, esp. in mistake for one resembling it (e.g. *derangement of epitaphs* for *arrangement of epithets*). [f. Mrs. *Malaprop* (f. foll.) in Sheridan's 'The Rivals']

mălăpropō's (-pō') *adv.*, *a.*, & *n.* (Thing) inopportunely (said, done, or happening). [f. F *mal à propos* (*mal* ill; see APROPOS)]

mā'lar *a.* & *n.* (Bone) of the cheek. [f. mod. L *malaris* f. L *mala* jaw; see -AR¹]

malar'|ĭa *n.* Intermittent and remittent fever caused by bite of mosquito, which conveys protozoan parasite of genus *Plasmodium*; unwholesome atmosphere caused by exhalations of marshes, to which these fevers were formerly attributed; hence **~**IAL, **~**IAN, **~**IOUS, *adjs.* [f. It. *mal'aria* bad air]

malar'key *n.* (sl.) Humbug, nonsense. [20th c.; orig. unkn.]

mălathi'on *n.* Insecticide containing phosphorus, with low toxicity to plants and mammals. [f. diethyl *male*ate + *thio*-acid + -ON]

Malay' *a.* & *n.* (Language or member) of a people predominating in Malaysia and Indonesia; hence **~**AN *a.* & *n.*, **~**O- *comb. form.* [f. Malay *malāyu*]

Mălaya'lam (-yah'-) *n.* Dravidian language of Malabar district of S. India. [native]

mă'lcontĕnt *a.* & *n.* Discontented (person), (one) inclined to rebellion. [F (as MAL-, CONTENT[3])]

mal de mer (măldemār') *n.* Seasickness. [F, = sickness of sea]

māle *a.* & *n.* **1.** *a.* Of the sex that can beget offspring by performing the fertilizing function (*male child, slave, dog; male nurse*); (of plants) whose flowers contain only fecundating organs, or thought of as male because of colour etc. (~ **fern,** *Dryopteris filixmas*, commonest lowland fern in U.K.); of men or male animals or plants (*the male sex; male (voice) choir*); (of parts of machinery etc.) designed to enter or fill the corresponding female part (*male screw*); *male* RHYME[1]; hence ~'NESS (-ln-) *n.* **2.** *n.* Male person or animal. [ME f. OF *ma(s)le*, f. L *masculus* (*mas* a male; see -CULE)]

mălėdi'ct|ion *n.* (Utterance of) curse; so ~IVE, ~ORY, *adjs.* [ME, f. L *maledictio* f. *maledicere* speak evil of (*male* ill, *dicere dict-* speak); see -ION]

mă'lėfăctor *n.* Criminal; evil-doer; so **mălėfă'ct**ION *n.* [ME f. L, f. *malefacere* (*male* ill, *facere fact-* do); see -OR]

malĕ'fĭc *a.* (Of magical arts etc.) harmful, baleful. [f. L *maleficus* (*male* ill; see -FIC)]

malĕ'fĭc|ent *a.* Hurtful (*to*); criminal; so ~ENCE *n.* [f. *maleficence* f. as prec. after *malevolence*]

mă'lemūte. See MALAMUTE.

malĕ'vol|ent *a.* Desirous of evil to others; hence or cogn. ~ENCE *n.*, ~**ent**LY[2] *adv.* [f. OF *malivolent* or f. L *malevolens* (*male* ill, *volens* willing, part. of *velle*)]

mălfea'(s|ance (-ē'z-) *n.* (Law). Evil-doing, esp. official misconduct; so ~ANT *a.* & *n.* [f. AF *malfaisance* f. OF MAL(*faisant* part. of *faire* do f. L *facere*); see -ANCE; cf. MISFEASANCE]

mălfŏrmā'tion *n.* Faulty formation; so **mălfŏr'm**ED[1] (-md) *a.* [f. MAL- + FORMATION]

mălfŭ'nction *n.*, & *v.i.* Fail(ure) to function in normal or satisfactory manner. [f. MAL- + FUNCTION]

mā'lĭc *a.* (Chem.) ~ **acid** (derived from unripe apples and other fruits). [f. F *malique* f. L *malum* apple; see -IC]

mă'lĭce *n.* **1.** Active ill-will; desire to tease; **bear** ~ (**to** or **towards** or **against**), cherish vindictive feelings (against). **2.** (Law). Wrongful intention, esp. as increasing guilt of certain offences, esp. murder; *malice* AFORE*thought* or PREPENSE. **3.** So **malĭ'c**IOUS (-sh*us*) *a.*, given to or arising from malice. [ME f. OF, f. L *malitia* (*malus* bad; see -ICE)]

malī'gn[1] (-ī'n) *a.* (Of thing) injurious; (of disease) malignant; malevolent; hence or cogn. **malĭ'gn**ITY *n.*, ~LY[2] *adv.* [ME, f. OF *malin maligne* or f. L *malignus* (*malus* bad; cf. BENIGN)]

malī'gn[2] (-ī'n) *v.t.* Speak ill of, slander. [ME, f. OF *malignier* f. LL *malignare* contrive maliciously f. L *malignus* (see prec.)]

malĭ'gn|ant *a.* & *n.* **1.** *a.* (Of disease) very virulent or infectious (*malignant cholera*); (of tumour) tending to spread and to recur after removal, cancerous; *malignant* PUSTULE. **2.** Harmful; feeling or showing intense ill will. **3.** *n.* & *a.* (Hist.) Supporter of, supporting, Charles I against Parliament. **4.** Hence ~ANCY *n.*, ~**ant**LY[2] *adv.* [f. LL *malignare* (as prec.; see -ANT)]

malĭ'nger (-ngg-) *v.i.* Pretend, produce, or protract, illness in order to escape duty (esp. of soldiers, sailors, etc.); so ~ER[1] *n.* [back form. f. *malingerer* app. f. F *malingre*, perh. f. as MAL- + *haingre* weak]

mā'lĭsm *n.* Doctrine that the world is a bad one. [f. L *malus* bad + -ISM]

mă'lĭson (-z-) *n.* (arch.) Curse. [ME, f. OF *mal(e)ison* f. L (as MALEDICTION)]

măll (*or* mawl) *n.* **1.** Sheltered walk as promenade; *shopping precinct. **2.** (Hist.) Game of pall-mall; alley for it; mallet for it. [var. of MAUL[1]; applied to *The Mall* in London (orig. a pall-mall alley), whence sense 1]

mă'llard *n.* Wild drake or duck (*Anas boscas*); its flesh. [ME f. OF, prob. f. **maslart* (as MALE; see -ARD)]

mă'llėable *a.* (Of metal etc.) that can be hammered or pressed out of shape without tendency to return to it or to fracture; (fig.) adaptable, pliable; hence **măllė**ABI'LITY *n.* [ME f. OF, f. med. L *malleabilis* f. L *malleare* to hammer (MALLEUS); see -ABLE]

mă'llee *n.* (Austral.) (Scrub formed by) one of various eucalyptuses flourishing in arid areas; ~**-bird, -fowl, -hen,** megapode (*Leipoa ocellata*) like small turkey. [Aboriginal]

mă'llėmŭck, mŏ'llȳmawk, *n.* Fulmar, petrel, or similar bird. [f. Du. *mallemok* (*mal* foolish, *mok* gull)]

mă'llenders (-z) *n. pl.* Dry scabby eruption behind horse's knee. [ME, f. OF *malandre* sing. f. L *malandria* pl. neck-pustules]

măllē'ol|us *n.* (*pl.* ~**i** *pr.* -ī). (Anat.) Bone of hammer-head shape, esp. one forming projection on either side of ankle. [L, dim. of MALLEUS]

mă'llėt *n.* Hammer, usu. of wood; implement for striking croquet or polo ball. [ME, f. OF *maillet* (*mailler* to hammer f. *mail* hammer f. L *malleus*)]

mă'llė|us *n.* (*pl.* ~**i** *pr.* -ī). Bone of middle ear transmitting vibrations of tympanum to incus. [L, = hammer]

mă'llow (-ō) *n.* Plant of genus *Malva*, esp. species with hairy stems and leaves and purple flowers. [OE *meal(u)we* f. L *malva*]

malm (mahm) *n.* Soft chalky rock; loamy soil from disintegration of this; fine-quality brick made originally from malm, marl, or similar chalky clay. [OE **mealm*, = ON *malmr* ore, Goth. *malma* sand f. Gmc **mel-* grind (cf. MEAL[1])]

mălmai'son *n.* Large usu. pink variety of carnation. [f. F *Souvenirs de Malmaison* memories of Malmaison (château of Empress Josephine near Paris)]

ma'lmsey (mah'mzĭ) *n.* Strong sweet wine from Greece, Spain, Madeira, etc. [ME, f. MDu., MLG *malmesie, -eye*, f. *Monemvasia* in the Morea, Greece; cf. MALVOISIE]

mălnūtrĭ'tion *n.* Insufficient nutrition; condition where diet omits some foods necessary for health. [f. MAL- + NUTRITION]

mălō'dorous *a.* Evil-smelling. [f. MAL- + ODOROUS]

mălpră'ctĭce *n.* Wrongdoing; (Law) physician's improper or negligent treatment of patient; (Law) illegal action for one's own benefit while in (esp. official) position of trust. [f. MAL- + PRACTICE[1]]

malt[1] (mawlt *or* mŏlt) *n.* Barley or other grain prepared by steeping, germination, and drying for brewing or distilling or vinegar-making; (colloq.) malt liquor; ~**-house** (for preparing and storing malt); ~ **liquor** (made from malt by fermentation, not distillation, e.g. beer, stout). [OE *m(e)alt*, = OS *malt*, OHG *malz*, ON *malt* f. Gmc **maltaz*, cogn. w. MELT[2]]

malt[2] (mawlt *or* mŏlt) *v.* **1.** *v.t.* Convert (grain) into malt; ~**ed milk** (made from dried milk and preparation of malt). **2.** *v.i.* (Of seeds) become malt when germination is checked by drought. [ME, f. prec.]

Ma'lta (maw'- *or* mŏ'-) *n.* ~ **fever,** undulant fever. [~, island in Mediterranean, where it was common]

Maltē'se (mawltē'z; *or* mŏ-) *a.* & *n.* (*pl.* same).

(Language, native, or inhabitant) of Malta; ~ **cat** (bluish-grey short-haired breed); ~ **cross** (with arms broadened outwards, often indented at ends); ~ **dog, terrier,** small breed of spaniel, of terrier. [f. prec. + -ESE]

mă'ltha *n.* Cement of pitch and wax or other ingredients. [L f. Gk]

Mălthū'sian (-z-) *a.* & *n.* (Follower) of Malthus; hence ~ISM (3) *n.* [f. T. R. *Malthus*, Engl. clergyman d. 1834, who advocated sexual restraint as means of preventing increase of population beyond means of subsistence, + -IAN]

ma'ltĭng (maw'- *or* mŏ'-) *n.* In vbl senses; malt-house. [ME, f. MALT² + -ING¹]

ma'ltōse (maw'- *or* mŏ'-) *n.* (Chem.) Sugar produced by hydrolysis of starch under action of malt, saliva, etc. [F (as MALT¹, -OSE²)]

măltrea't *v.t.* Ill-treat; hence ~MENT *n.* [f. F MAL(*traiter* TREAT)]

ma'ltster (maw'l(t)ster; *or* mŏ'-) *n.* One who makes malt. [ME, f. MALT¹ + -STER]

mălvā'ceous (-shus) *a.* (Bot.) Of the genus *Malva*; of the family Malvaceae. [f. L *malvaceus* (as MALLOW; see -ACEOUS)]

mălversā'tion *n.* Corrupt behaviour in position of trust; corrupt administration (*of* public money etc.). [F (*malverser* f. L *male* badly + *versari* behave; see -ATION)]

mălvoisie' (-vwazē') *n.* Malmsey. [ME f. OF *malvesie* f. F form of *Monemvasia*; see MALMSEY]

măm *n.* (colloq. or childish). Mother. [f. as MAMMA¹]

mama. See MAMMA¹.

mă'mba *n.* Venomous S. African snake of genus *Dendroaspis*. [f. Zulu *m'namba*]

mă'mbō *n.* (*pl.* ~s). Latin-Amer. dance like rumba; music for it. [Amer. Sp., prob. f. Haitian]

mă'melon *n.* Small rounded hillock. [F, = nipple (*mamelle* breast f. L MAMILLA)]

Mă'mėluke (-ōōk) *n.* (Hist.) Member of military body (orig. Circassian slaves) that ruled Egypt 1254–1811. [f. F *mameluk*, ult. f. Arab. *mamlūk* slave (*malaka* possess)]

mamĭ'll|a, *mamm-, *n.* (*pl.* ~**ae**). Nipple of woman's breast; nipple-shaped organ etc.; hence ~ARY¹, ~ATE², *adjs.* [L, dim. of MAMMA²]

mamma'¹, mama', (-ah') *n.* (Child's name for) mother; ***~'s boy,** boy or man who has been unduly cosseted by his mother. [imit. of child's *ma, ma*]

mă'mm|a² *n.* (*pl.* ~**ae**). Milk-secreting organ of female in mammals; corresponding non-secreting structure in males; hence ~ARY¹, ~ĬFORM, *adjs.* [OE f. L]

mă'mmal *n.* Animal of class Mammalia, having mammae for nourishment of young, and usu. quadruped with hair or fur, e.g. man, dog, rabbit, whale; hence **mammā'lIAN** *a.* & *n.*, **mammă'LOGY** *n.* [Anglicized f. mod. L *mammalia* neut. pl. of L *mammalis* (as MAMMA²; see -AL)]

mămmalĭ'ferous *a.* (Geol.) Containing mammalian remains. [f. prec. + -I- + -FEROUS]

mă'mmarў. See MAMMA².

mămmee' *n.* Tropical American tree with large red-rinded yellow-pulped fruit. [f. Sp. *mamei* f. Haitian]

***mammĭ'lla.** See MAMILLA.

Mă'mmon *n.* Wealth regarded as idol or evil influence; the worldly rich; **the ~ of unrighteousness,** wealth ill used or ill gotten; hence ~ISH¹ *a.*, ~ISM (3), ~IST (2), ~ITE¹, *ns.* [ME, f. LL *Mam(m)ona* f. Gk *mamōnas* f. Aram. *māmōn* riches; see Matt. 6:24, Luke 16:9–13]

mă'mmoth *n.* & *a.* **1.** *n.* Large extinct elephant, with hairy coat and curved tusks. **2.** *a.* Huge. [f. Russ. *mamo(n)t*, prob. of Siberian orig.]

mă'mmў *n.* (Child's word for) mother; *Negro woman in charge of white children. [f. as MAMMA¹ + -Y³]

măn¹ *n.* (*pl.* **men**). **1.** Human being, individual of genus *Homo*, distinguished from other animals by superior mental development, power of articulate speech, and upright posture, (**a ~ and a brother,** a fellow human being); (in indefinite or general application) person (*any, no, man; some, few, men*); (**all**) **to a ~,** all without exception. **2.** The human race (*man is born unto trouble; man is a political animal*); **rights of ~,** = HUMAN *rights*. **3.** Human being of specified historical period (*Renaissance man*), esp. prehistoric type named from place where remains were found (*Heidelberg, Java, Peking, Piltdown, Man*); INNER, NEW¹, OLD, OUTER, *man*. **4.** Adult human male, opp. to woman, boy, or both; ~ **and boy,** (*adv.*) from boyhood upwards; **be a ~, play the ~,** be manly, not show fear; **~ to ~,** (*adv.*) with candour; **separate** or **sort out the men from the boys,** (colloq.) find those who are truly virile or competent; LITTLE *man*. **5.** (As *voc.*, expr. impatience) *nonsense, man!*; (as general mode of address among hippies etc.) *dig that, man*; **my** (**good**) ~ (patronizing); *man* ALIVE!. **6. A ~,** one (*what can a man do in such a case?*). **7.** Individual (male) person; one's opponent, allocated assistant, etc.; **as one ~,** in unison; **as a ~,** viewed simply in regard to his personal character; **the** (**very**) ~, the most suitable man *for*; *if you want noise*, **he is your ~** (can supply you); **I'm your ~** (accept your offer etc.); **be** one's **own ~,** (1) be free to act, be independent, (2) be in full possession of one's faculties, senses, etc.; *man* FRIDAY; *every man* JACK¹; **~ of God,** saint or clergyman; *man of* HONOUR¹ 1; **~ of the house,** householder; **~ of Kent** (see KENTISH); *man of* LETTERS; *man of the* MOMENT; **~ in the moon,** semblance of man seen in full moon; *man of* SIN¹; **~ in** or ***on the street,** ordinary average man (esp. as opp. expert); *man of* STRAW¹; *man about* TOWN; **~-of-war,** armed ship of country's navy (PORTUGUESE *man-of-war*); *man of the* WORLD; BEST¹ *man*; HANDY*man*. **8.** *suf.* Man concerned or dealing or skilful with or describable as (*clergyman, countryman, Dutchman,* GENTLEMAN, HORSE¹*man, oarsman,* POST²*man*); ship of specified type (INDIA*man*, MERCHANT*man*). **9. *The Man,** (sl.) the police, (Negro sl.) white men. **10.** Husband (*man and wife*). **11.** (Hist.) vassal; manservant, valet; workman (*the employers locked out the men*). **12.** (usu. in *pl.*) Soldiers, sailors, etc., esp. those not officers. **13.** One of a set of objects of same or different forms used in playing chess, draughts, etc. **14. ~-at-arms,** (arch.) soldier, esp. heavy-armed and mounted; **~-child,** (arch.) male child; **~-day** (as *man-hour*); **~-eater, ~-eating** *a.*, (cannibal, shark or tiger) eating human flesh, (colloq.) biting horse; **me'nfolk,** men in general, the men of one's family; **~'handle,** move by human effort alone, (sl.) handle roughly; **~-hater,** one who hates mankind or the male sex; **~'hole,** opening in floor, sewer, etc., for man to pass through; **~-hour,** work done by one man in one hour; **~-hunt,** organized search for person (esp. criminal); **~-made,** (of textile etc.) artificially made, synthetic; *man*-MILLINER; **~'power,** (1) power of man in work, (2) amount of men available for military or other service; **men's** (**room**), lavatory for men; **~'servant** (pl. *me'nservants*), male servant; **~-size(d),** of size of or adequate to a man; **~'slaughter,** killing of human being, (Law) unlawful killing of human being without malice aforethought; **~-tailored,** (of women's clothes) tailored in style of men's clothes; **~'trap** (for catching men, esp. trespassers); **me'nswear** (-z-), clothes for men; **~-week, -year,** (as *man-hour*). **15.** Hence ~'LESS *a.* [OE *man(n)*, pl. *menn*, = OS, OHG *man*, ON *mathr*, Goth. *manna* f. Gmc **mann-*, **mannon-*]

măn² *v.t.* (**-nn-**). Furnish (fort, ship, industrial undertaking, etc.) with man or men for service or defence; act thus in respect of (*man the pumps*); (Naut.) place men at (part of ship); fill (post); fortify spirits or courage of (esp. one*self*). [OE *mannian* (as prec.)]

Man. *abbr.* Manitoba.

ma'na (mah'-) *n.* Power, authority, prestige; supernatural or magical power. [Maori]

mă'nacle *n.*, & *v.t.* **1.** *n.* (usu. in *pl.*) Fetter for the hand, handcuff, (fig.) restraint. **2.** *v.t.* Fetter with manacles. [ME f. OF *manicle* handcuff f. L *manicula* dim. of *manus* hand]

mă'nage¹ *n.* (arch.) Training of horse; trained movements of horse; riding-school. [f. It. *maneggio* (as foll.); cf. MANÈGE]

mă'nage² *v.* **1.** *v.t.* Handle, wield, (tool etc.); conduct (undertaking etc.); control (household, institution, State); be manager of (team etc.); take charge of (cattle etc.); take control of (person, animal); gain one's ends with (person etc.) by tact, flattery, dictation, etc.; succeed in achieving (*she managed a smile*); contrive (*to* do; often iron.: *he managed to muddle it*). **2.** *v.i.* Succeed in one's aim (often *with* inadequate material etc.). **3.** *v.t.* (With *can* or *be able to*) cope with, make proper use of, do what is suggested or appropriate regarding, (*can you manage this matter, another slice, lunch next Saturday?*, or abs., *can you manage by yourself?*). [f. It. *maneggiare* f. Rom. **manidiare* f. L *manus* hand]

mă'nage|able (-nĭja-) *a.* That can be managed; easily controlled, wielded, accomplished, etc.; hence ~ABI'LITY, **~able**NESS (-beln-), *ns.*, **~ab**LY² *adv.* [f. prec. + -ABLE]

mă'nagement (-nĭjm-) *n.* In vbl senses; trickery, deceit; persons managing a business (**the ~**, governing body, board of directors, etc.); administration of business concerns or public undertakings; (Med.) technique of treatment *of* disease etc. [f. MANAGE² + -MENT]

mă'nager (-nĭj-) *n.* **1.** Person conducting a business, institution, etc.; person controlling activities of person or team in sports, entertainment, etc. **2.** ||Member of either House of Parliament appointed with others for some duty in which both Houses are concerned. **3. Good, bad,** etc., ~ (of money, household affairs, etc.). **4.** ||(Law). Person appointed, usu. by Court of Chancery, to manage a business for benefit of creditors etc. **5.** Hence ~ESS¹ (*or* ~ĕ's), ~SHIP, *ns.*, **mănagēr'**IAL *a.* [f. MANAGE² + -ER¹]

mă'naging (-nĭj-) *a.* In vbl senses; having executive control or authority (*managing director*); fond of being in control of affairs; (arch.) economical. [f. MANAGE² + -ING²]

mă'nakin *n.* Brightly-coloured small tropical Amer. bird of family Pipridae. [var. of MANIKIN]

mañana (manyah'na) *adv.* & *n.* Tomorrow (as symbol of easy-going procrastination in Spanish-speaking countries); the indefinite future. [Sp.]

mănatee' *n.* Large aquatic herbivorous mammal of genus *Trichechus*, sea-cow. [f. Sp. *manati* f. Carib *manattouï*]

Mă'nchĕster *n.* ||**~ goods,** cotton textiles; **~ School,** (Hist.) adherents of doctrines of free trade and *laissez-faire*. [~ in N.W. England]

mănchĭnee'l *n.* W. Ind. tree (*Hippomane mancinella*) with poisonous and caustic milky sap and acrid apple-like fruit. [f. F *mancenille* f. Sp. *manzanilla* dim. of *manzana* apple]

Mănchu' (-ōō') *a.* & *n.* (Member) of Tartar people forming last Chinese imperial dynasty (1644–1912); (of) their language, now spoken in part of N.E. China. [Manchu, = pure]

mă'nciple *n.* Officer who buys provisions for college, one of the Inns of Court, etc. [ME f. AF & OF, f. L *mancipium* purchase (*manceps* buyer f. *manus* hand + *capere* take)]

Măncū'nian *a.* & *n.* (Inhabitant) of Manchester; (past or present member) of Manchester Grammar School. [f. L *Mancunium* name of settlement on site of MANCHESTER + -AN]

-măncy̆ *suf.* forming *ns.* w. sense 'divination by' (GEO*mancy*, NECROMANCY). [f. OF *-mancie* f. LL *-mantia* f. Gk *manteia* divination; see -CY]

Măndae'an *a.* & *n.* (Member or language) of a Gnostic sect hostile to Christianity, surviving in Iraq. [f. Aram. *mandaiia* Gnostics (*manda* knowledge) + -AN]

mă'ndala *n.* Symbolic circular figure as religious symbol of universe; (Psych.) such symbol in dream, representing dreamer's search for completeness and self-unity. [f. Skr. *máṇḍala* disc]

măndā'mus *n.* Judicial writ issued as command to inferior court, or ordering person to perform public or statutory duty. [L, = we command]

mă'ndarĭn¹ *n.* **1.** (Hist.) Chinese official in any of 9 grades. **2.** Standard spoken Chinese language. **3.** Party leader; bureaucrat; respected (esp. reactionary) person. **4.** Nodding toy figure in Chinese costume. **5. ~ collar,** high upright collar not quite meeting in front; **~ duck,** small Chinese duck (*Aix galericulata*) noted for its bright plumage; **~ sleeve** (loose and open below elbow). **6.** Hence ~ATE¹ (1, 4) *n.* [f. Port. *mandarim* f. Malay f. Hind. *mantrī* f. Skr. *mantrin* counsellor]

mă'ndarĭn², **-ine** (-ēn), *n.* **~ (orange)**, small flat loose-skinned deep-coloured orange. [F *mandarine* perh. f. as prec. 1, w. ref. to yellow robes]

mă'ndatary̆ *n.* (Law). One to whom a MANDATE¹ is given; (Hist.) State receiving mandate. [f. LL *mandatarius* (as foll.; see -ARY¹)]

mă'ndāte¹ *n.* Judicial or legal command from superior; commission to act for another, esp. (Hist.) one from League of Nations to a State (the mandatary) to govern former German etc. colony; papal rescript; (poet.) command; (Law) commission by which mandatary undertakes to perform gratuitously some service, with indemnity against loss by him; [after F *mandat*] political authority supposed to be given by electors to (party in) parliament. [f. L *mandatum*, neut. p.p. (as n.) of *mandare* command (*manus* hand, *dare* give); see -ATE¹]

măndā'te² *v.t.* Commit (territory etc. *to* mandatary). [f. as prec. + -ATE³]

mă'ndatory̆ *a.* & *n.* **1.** *a.* Of or conveying a command; compulsory. **2.** *n.* = MANDATARY. [f. LL *mandatorius* f. L (as MANDATE¹; see -ORY)]

mă'ndĭble *n.* Jaw, esp. lower jaw in mammals and fishes; upper or lower part of bird's beak; either half of crushing organ in arthropod's mouth-parts; so **măndĭ'bū**LAR¹, **măndĭ'bū**LATE², *adjs.* [ME f. OF, or f. LL *mandibula* (*mandere* chew)]

măndō'la *n.* Large early form of mandolin. [It.]

mă'ndolĭn, -ĭne, *n.* Musical instrument of lute kind with paired metal strings, played with plectrum. [F *mandoline* f. It. *mandolino* dim. (as prec.)]

măndôr'la *n.* = VESICA 2. [It., = almond]

măndră'gora *n.* = foll., esp. as type of narcotic (Shak. *Othello* III. iii. 330). [OE f. med. L, f. L f. Gk *mandragoras*]

mă'ndrāke *n.* Poisonous plant with white or purple flowers and large yellow fruit, and having emetic and narcotic properties, with root once thought to resemble human form and to shriek when plucked. [ME *mandrag(g)e*, prob. f. MDu. *mandrag(r)e* f. med. L as prec., assoc. w. MAN[1], *drake* dragon; cf. DRAKE[1]]

mă'ndrel *n.* (In lathe) shaft to which work is fixed while being turned; cylindrical rod round which metal or other material is forged or shaped; ||miner's pick. [16th c.; orig. unkn.]

mă'ndrĭll *n.* Large fierce W. Afr. baboon (*Mandrillus sphinx*). [prob. f. MAN[1] + DRILL[3]]

mă'ndūc|āte *v.t.* (literary). Chew, eat; so ~A'TION *n.*, **~ātory** *a.* [f. L *manducare* chew (*manduco* guzzler f. *mandere* chew) + -ATE[3]]

māne *n.* Long hair on neck of horse, lion, etc., (fig.) long hair of person; hence (-)**māned**[2] (-nd), ~'LESS (-nl-), *adjs.* [OE *manu*, = OHG *mana*, ON *mén* f. Gmc **manō*]

manège, manege, (manā'zh) *n.* Riding-school; movements of trained horse; horsemanship. [F *manège* f. It. (as MANAGE[1])]

mā'nēs (-z; *or* mah'nāz) *n. pl.* Deified souls of departed ancestors; (as *sing.*) shade of departed person, as object of reverence. [ME f. L]

***maneuver**[1,2]. See MANŒUVRE[1,2].

mă'nful *a.* Brave, resolute; hence ~LY[2] *adv.*, ~NESS *n.* [ME, f. MAN[1] + -FUL]

mă'ngabey (-nggabā) *n.* Small long-tailed W. Afr. monkey of genus *Cercocebus*. [f. *M*~, region of Madagascar]

mă'nganēse (-ngganēz; *or* -ē'z) *n.* **1.** Black mineral used in glass-making etc. **2.** (Chem.) Metallic element of which this is the oxide. **3.** Hence **măngă'nic**, **mă'nganous**, (-ngg-) *adjs.* [f. F *manganèse*, f. It. *manganese*, alt. f. MAGNESIA]

mānge (-nj) *n.* Skin disease in hairy and woolly animals, caused by an arachnid parasite and occas. communicated to man. [ME *mangie*, *maniewe* f. OF *manjue*, *mangeue* itch f. *mangier manju-* eat f. L (as MANDUCATE)]

mă'ngel(-wûrzel), mă'ngold(-wûrzel), (-ngg-) *n.* Large kind of beet, used as cattle food. [G *mangoldwurzel* (*mangold* beet, *wurzel* root)]

mā'nger (-nj-) *n.* Long open box or trough in stable etc. for horses or cattle to eat from; DOG[1] *in the manger*. [ME, f. OF *mangeoire*, *mangeure* f. Rom. **manducatoria* f. L (as MANDUCATE; see -ORY)]

mă'ngle[1] (-nggel) *n.*, & *v.t.* **1.** *n.* Machine of two or more cylinders for squeezing water from and pressing washed clothes. **2.** *v.t.* Press (clothes) in mangle. [f. Du. *mangel(stok)* (*mangelen* to mangle ult. f. Gk *magganon*; *stok* staff, STOCK)]

mă'ngle[2] (-nggel) *v.t.* Hack, cut about, mutilate, by blows; cut roughly so as to disfigure; spoil (quotation, text, etc.) by gross blunders, make (words) unrecognizable by mispronouncing. [f. AF *ma(ha)ngler*, app. frequent. of *mahaignier* MAIM]

mă'ngō (-nggō) *n.* (*pl.* **~es** *or* **~s**). (Indian tree *Mangifera indica*, bearing) fleshy fruit yellowish-red in colour, eaten ripe or used green for pickles etc. [f. Port. *manga* f. Malay *mangā* f. Tamil *mānkāy* (*mān* mango-tree, *kāy* fruit)]

mangold(-wurzel). See MANGEL.

mă'ngonel (-ngg-) *n.* (Hist.) Military engine for throwing stones etc. [ME, f. OF *mangonel(le)*, f. med. L *manganellus* dim. of LL *manganum* f. Gk *magganon*]

mă'ngosteen (-ngg-) *n.* (E. Ind. tree, *Garcinia mangostana*, bearing) fruit with thick reddish-brown rind and white juicy pulp. [f. obs. Malay *manggustan*]

mă'ngrōve (-ngg-) *n.* Tropical tree or shrub of genus *Rhizophora* growing in shore-mud with many tangled roots above ground. [17th c., of uncert. orig.; assim. to GROVE]

mā'ng|ȳ (-njĭ) *a.* Having the mange; squalid, shabby; hence **~ĭLY**[2] *adv.*, **~ĭNESS** *n.* [f. MANGE + -Y[2]]

mănhă'ttan *n.* Cocktail made of vermouth, whisky, etc. [f. *M*~, borough of New York City]

mă'nhŏŏd *n.* State of being a man (in any sense; *manhood* SUFFRAGE); manliness, courage; the men of a country. [ME, f. MAN[1] + -HOOD]

mā'nĭa *n.* Mental derangement marked by excitement, hallucination, and violence; excessive enthusiasm (*for* thing, *for* doing). [ME f. LL f. Gk, = madness (*mainomai* be mad, cogn. w. MIND[1]; see -IA[1])]

-mā'nĭa *suf.* denoting (scientifically) a special type of madness (*kleptomania*, *megalomania*, *nymphomania*), (pop.) eager pursuit (*bibliomania*) or admiration (*Anglomania*). [f. as prec.]

mā'nĭăc *a.* & *n.* (Person) affected with mania; raving mad(man); hence **manī'acal** *a.*, **manī'acally**[2] *adv.* [f. LL f. late Gk *maniakos* (as MANIA; see -AC)]

-mā'nĭăc *suf.* forming *adjs.* & *ns.* w. sense '(person) affected with -MANIA' (*nymphomaniac*). [f. as prec.]

mă'nĭc *a.* Of or affected by mania; **~-depressive,** (*a.*) relating to mental disorder with alternating periods of elation and depression, (*n.*) person having such disorder. [f. MANIA + -IC]

Mănĭchee' (-kē'; *or* mă'-) *n.* Adherent of religious system (3rd–5th c.) that represented Satan as coeternal with God; (Philos.) dualist; hence **Mănĭch(a)e'an** *a.* & *n.*, **Mănĭch(a)e'ism** (3) *n.*, (-kē'-). [f. LL f. late Gk *Manikhaios*, f. *Manes* or *Manichaeus* Persian founder of sect]

mă'nĭcūr|e *n.*, & *v.t.* **1.** *n.* (One who undertakes professional) cosmetic treatment of hands and finger-nails. **2.** *v.t.* Apply manicure treatment to (hands, person). **3.** Hence ~IST (3) *n.* [F, f. L *manus* hand + *cura* care]

mă'nĭfĕst[1] *n.* Cargo-list for use of Customs officers; list of passengers in aircraft or of trucks etc. in goods train. [f. It. MANIFESTO]

mă'nĭfĕst[2] *a.* Clear, obvious, to eye or mind; hence ~LY[2] *adv.* [ME, f. OF *manifeste* or f. L *manifestus* (*manus* hand, **festus* struck)]

mă'nĭfĕst[3] *v.* **1.** *v.t.* Show plainly to eye or mind; be evidence of, prove; display, evince, (quality, feeling) by one's acts etc.; (of thing) reveal *itself*; record in a manifest. **2.** *v.i.* (Of ghost) appear. **3.** So ~A'TION *n.*, ~ATIVE (-ĕ's-) *a.* [ME, f. OF *manifester* or f. L *manifestare* (as prec.)]

mănĭfĕ'stō *n.* (*pl.* **~s**). Public declaration of policy by sovereign, State, political party, or other body. [It. (*manifestare* f. L, as MANIFEST[2])]

mă'nĭfōld *a.* & *n.* **1.** *a.* (literary). Having various forms, applications, component parts, etc.; performing several functions at once; many and various (*manifold vexations*); hence ~LY[2] *adv.*, ~NESS *n.* **2.** *n.* Manifold thing; (Mech.) pipe or chamber with several openings. [OE *manigfeald*, = OHG *managfalt*, Goth. *managfalths* (as MANY, -FOLD)]

mă'nĭkĭn *n.* Little man, dwarf; artist's lay figure; anatomical model of the body; = MANAKIN. [f. Du. *manneken*, dim. of *man* MAN[1]; see -KIN]

Manĭ'la *n.* Cigar or cheroot as made in Manila; ~ (**hemp**), strong fibre of a Philippine tree (*Musa textilis*); **m**~ (**paper**), brown wrapping-paper made from Manila hemp. [~ in Philippines]

manĭ'lla[1] *n.* Metal bracelet used by Afr. tribes as medium of exchange. [Sp., prob. dim. of *mano* hand f. L *manus*]

Manĭ'lla[2]. Var. of MANILA.

manĭ′lle *n.* Second best trump or honour in ombre and quadrille. [F, f. Sp. *malilla* dim. of *mala* bad f. L *malus*]

mă′nĭŏc *n.* Cassava; flour made from it. [f. Tupi *mandioca*]

mă′nĭple *n.* **1.** (Rom. Ant.) Subdivision of legion, containing 120 or 60 men. **2.** Eucharistic vestment, strip hanging from left arm. [OF, or f. L *manipulus* handful, troop, (*manus* hand)]

manĭ′pūl|āte *v.t.* Handle, treat, esp. with skill (material, thing, question); manage (person, property, etc.) by dextrous (esp. unfair) use of influence etc.; (Surg.) manually examine and treat part of body for fracture etc.; hence or cogn. ~A′TION, ~**āt**OR, *ns.*, ~**āt**IVE, ~**āt**ORY, *adjs.* [back form. f. *manipulation* f. F f. mod. L *manipulatio* (**manipulare* f. as prec.), after F *manipuler*; see -ATE³]

Manit. *abbr.* Manitoba.

mă′nĭtou (-ōō) *n.* (Amer. Ind.) Good or evil spirit as object of reverence; thing having supernatural power. [f. Algonquin *manito*, *-tu* he has surpassed]

mănkīnd (-n-k-) *n.* **1.** (-ī′-). Human species. **2.** (mă′-). Men in general. [ME, f. MAN¹ + KIND¹]

mă′nlīke *a.* Having (good or bad) qualities of a man; (of woman) mannish; (of animal) resembling a human being. [ME, f. MAN¹ + -LIKE]

mă′nl|ÿ *a.* Having a man's virtues, courage, frankness, etc.; (of woman) having a man's qualities; (of things, quality, etc.) befitting a man; hence ~**ĭ**NESS *n.* [ME, f. MAN¹ + -LY¹]

mă′nna *n.* Substance miraculously supplied as food to Israelites in the wilderness (Exod. 16); spiritual nourishment, esp. the Eucharist; sweet dried juice from **~-ash** (*Fraxinus ornus*) and other plants, used as mild laxative; unexpected benefit. [OE f. LL f. Gk, f. Aram. *mannā* f. Heb. *mān*, explained as = *mān hū?* what is it?, but prob. = Arab. *mann* exudation of common tamarisk (*Tamarix gallica*)]

mănned (-nd) *a.* (Of aircraft, spacecraft, etc.) containing human crew. [p.p. of MAN²]

mă′nnėquin (-kĭn) *n.* Person, usu. woman, employed by dressmaker etc. to display clothes by wearing them; dummy for display of clothes in shop. [F, = MANIKIN]

mă′nner *n.* **1.** Way a thing is done or happens (*in* or *after this manner*); **adverb of ~**, one that asks or tells how; **to the ~ born,** (Shak. *Hamlet* I. iv. 15) destined by birth to be subject to the custom, (colloq.) naturally fitted for the position etc. **2.** (in *pl.*) Modes of life, conditions of society; **comedy of ~s** (with satirical portrayal of these in a society). **3.** Outward bearing, style of utterance etc. **4.** (in *pl.*) Behaviour in social intercourse (*good*, *bad*, etc., *manners*); polite social behaviour, habits indicating good breeding (*he has no manners*); hence ~LESS *a.* **5.** Style in literature or art (*sketch in the manner of Rembrandt*); mannerism. **6.** (arch.) Kind, sort, (*what manner of man is he?*). **7. All ~ of,** (see ALL 1); **no ~ of,** no . . . at all; **in a ~ (of speaking)**, in some sense, to some extent, so¹ to speak; *manner of means* (see MEAN¹ 5). [ME f. AF *manere*, OF *maniere* f. Rom. **manuaria* mode of handling, fem. (as n.) of L *manuarius* of the hand (*manus*); see -ARY¹]

mă′nnered (-erd) *a.* Behaving (in specified way: *ill*, *well*, *rough*, *-mannered*); (of style, artist, writer) showing mannerism. [ME, f. prec. + -ED²]

mă′nner|ĭsm *n.* Excessive addiction to a distinctive manner in art or literature; trick of style; trick or gesture of speech (esp. of an actor); style of Italian art preceding Baroque, with contorted figures; hence ~IST (2) *n.*, ~**ĭ′s**TIC(AL) *adjs.* [f. MANNER + -ISM]

mă′nnerl|ÿ *a.* & *adv.* **1.** *a.* Well-mannered, polite; hence ~**ĭ**NESS *n.* **2.** *adv.* Politely. [f. MANNER + -LY¹˒²]

mă′nnĭkĭn. Var. of MANIKIN.

mă′nnĭsh *a.* (Of woman, usu. derog.) masculine; characteristic of man as opp. to woman (*his mannish air of superiority*); hence ~NESS *n.* [OE *mennisc* f. (& assim. to) MAN¹ + -ISH¹]

manœu′vre¹, ***maneu′ver¹,** (-nōō′ver) *n.* Planned movement, (in *pl.*) large-scale exercise, of troops, warships, etc.; deceptive or elusive movement; skilful plan; MASS² *of manœuvre*. [F *manœuvre* (as foll.)]

manœu′vr|e², ***maneu′ver²,** (-nōō′ver) *v.i.* & *t.* Perform, cause (troops etc.) to perform, manœuvres; employ artifice; force, drive, manipulate, (person, thing, *into*, *out*, *away*, etc.) by scheming or adroitness; hence ~ABLE *a.*, ~ER¹ *n.* [f. F *manœuvrer* f. med. L *man(u)operare* f. L *manus* hand + *operari* to work]

manŏ′mėter *n.* Pressure-gauge for gases and vapours; hence **mănomĕ′tr**IC *a.* [f. F *manomètre* f. Gk *manos* thin; see -METER]

mă′nor *n.* **1.** English territorial unit, orig. of nature of feudal lordship, now consisting of lord's demesne and of lands from whose holders he may exact certain fees etc.; **lord of the ~**, person or corporation having rights of this; **~-house,** his mansion; hence **manôr′**IAL *a.* **2.** (sl.) Unit area of police administration. [ME, f. AF *maner*, OF *maneir*, f. L *manēre* remain]

manqué (mah′ṅkā) *a.* (placed after *n.*) That might have been but is not, that has missed being, (*a Napoleon*, *comic actor*, *manqué*). [F, p.p. of *manquer* lack]

mă′nsard *n.* ~ **(roof)**, roof of which each face has two slopes, the lower one steeper. [f. F *mansarde* f. F. *Mansard*, Fr. architect d. 1666]

mănse *n.* Ecclesiastical residence, esp. Scottish Presbyterian minister's house; **son** or **daughter of the ~**, child of Presbyterian etc. minister. [ME, f. med. L *mansus*, *-sa*, *-sum*, house (*manēre mans-* remain)]

-manshĭp *suf.* forming *ns.* denoting skill in subject or activity, esp. when used to disconcert another person. [orig. in GAMESMANSHIP after *craftsmanship*, *sportsmanship*, etc.]

mă′nsion (-shon) *n.* Large residence (‖in *pl.* often of large buildings divided into flats); ‖**~-house,** house of lord of manor or landed proprietor, official residence, esp. (**the M~ House**) of Lord Mayor of London. [ME f. OF f. L *mansio -onis* a staying (as MANSE; see -ION)]

mă′nsuėtūde (-swĭ-) *n.* (arch.) Meekness, docility, gentleness. [ME f. OF, or f. L *mansuetudo* (*mansuetus* gentle, tame f. *manus* hand + *suetus* accustomed; see -TUDE)]

mă′ntel *n.* ~**(piece)**, (1) structure of wood, marble, etc., above and around fireplace, (2) = *mantelshelf*; ~**(shelf)**, shelf projecting from wall above fireplace. [var. of MANTLE¹]

ma′ntelėt *n.* (Hist.) Short loose sleeveless mantle etc.; bullet-proof screen for gunners. [ME f. OF, dim. of *mantel* MANTLE¹; see -ET¹]

mă′ntĭc *a.* Of divination. [f. Gk *mantikos* (*mantis* prophet; see -IC)]

-mă′ntĭc *suf.* forming *adjs.* corresp. to *ns.* in -MANCY (*necromantic*). [f. as prec.]

măntĭ′lla *n.* Lace scarf worn by Spanish woman over hair and shoulders. [Sp., dim. of *manta* MANTLE¹]

mă′ntĭs *n.* Orthopterous insect of genus *Mantis*; **praying ~**, species that holds forelegs in position suggesting hands folded in prayer. [Gk, = prophet]

măntĭ′ssa *n.* Fractional part of logarithm. [L, = makeweight]

mă′ntle¹ *n.* **1.** Loose sleeveless cloak esp. of

woman; (fig.) covering. **2.** Fragile lacelike tube fixed round gas-jet to give incandescent light. **3.** Outer fold of skin enclosing mollusc's viscera. **4.** Bird's back, scapulars, and wing-coverts esp. if of distinctive colour. **5.** (Geol.) Region between crust and core of earth. [ME f. OF, f. L *mantellum* cloak]

mă'ntle² *v.* **1.** *v.t.* Clothe (as) in mantle; cover, conceal, envelop. **2.** *v.i.* (Of liquid) become covered with coating or scum; (of blood) suffuse cheeks, (of face) glow, with blush. [ME, f. prec.]

mă'ntlėt. Var. of MANTELET.

mă'ntlĭng *n.* (Her.) Ornamental (representation of) drapery etc. behind and around shield. [f. MANTLE¹,² + -ING¹]

mă'ntra *n.* Vedic hymn; Hindu or Buddhist devotional incantation. [Skr., = instrument of thought (*man* think)]

mă'ntūa *n.* (Hist.) Woman's loose gown in 17th–18th c.; **~-maker,** dressmaker. [corrupt. of *manteau* (F, as MANTLE¹), after *M~* in Italy]

mă'nūal *a.* & *n.* **1.** *a.* Of, done with, the hands (*manual labour*); worked by hand, not by automatic equipment, (*manual fire-engine, gear-change, telephone exchange*); **~ alphabet,** deaf-and-dumb alphabet; SIGN¹ *manual*; hence **~**LY² *adv.* **2.** *n.* Small book for handy use; reference book, handbook; organ keyboard played with hands not feet; (Mil.) exercise in handling rifle etc.; (Hist.) book of the forms to be used by priests in the administration of the Sacraments. [ME f. OF *manuel*, f. (& later assim. to) L *manualis* (*manus* hand; see -AL)]

mănūfă'ctorў *n.* Place where product is manufactured; factory, workshop. [f. foll., after *factory*]

mănūfă'cture¹ *n.* Making of articles by physical labour or machinery, esp. on large scale; branch of such industry (*woollen manufacture*; **of home, English,** etc., **~**, made at home etc.); (derog.) merely mechanical production (*of* literature etc.). [F, f. It. *manifattura*, & L *manufactum* made by hand; see -URE]

mănūfă'ctur|e² *v.t.* Bring (material) into form fit for use; produce (articles) by labour, esp. by machinery on large scale, (derog. of literary work etc.); invent, fabricate, (evidence, story); hence **~**ER¹ *n.* [f. prec.]

manu'ka (-ōō'-; *or* mah'nu-) *n.* (Austral. & N.Z.) Tree or shrub of genus *Leptospermum*, with aromatic leaves and hard timber. [Maori]

mănūmĭ't *v.t.* (**-tt-**). (Hist.) Set (slave) free; so **mănūmĭ'ss**ION *n.* [ME, f. L *manumittere* (*manus* hand, *emittere emiss-* send forth)]

manūr'e¹ *n.* Any substance, e.g. dung or compost or artificial material, (to be) spread over or mixed with soil to fertilize it; hence **manūr'**IAL *a.* [f. foll.]

manūr'e² *v.t.* Apply manure to (land etc., or abs.; lit. or fig.). [ME, f. AF *mainoverer* = OF *manouvrer* MANŒUVRE²]

mă'nūscrĭpt *a.* & *n.* (Book, document) written by hand or typed, not printed; author's copy in this form, submitted for publication. [f. med. L *manuscriptus* (*manu* by hand, *scriptus* p.p. of *scribere* write)]

mă'nward *a.* (arch.) Tending or directed towards man. [ME, f. MAN¹ + -WARD]

Mănx *a.* & *n.* **1.** *a.* Of the Isle of Man; **~ cat,** tailless variety; **~'man,** native or inhabitant of Isle of Man. **2.** *n.* Celtic language of Isle of Man; (as *pl.*) *the* Manx people. [f. ON **Manskr* (*Mōn Man-* f. OIr. *Manu* Isle of Man, *-skr* -ISH¹)]

ma'nў (mě'-) *a.* & *n.* Great in number, numerous, (*many times*; (poet. or rhet.) *many a time* (*and oft*), *many and many a time*; *many people wish, many wish, many of us wish, many a man wishes*; *how many* (*of them*) *can I have?*; *as many* (*of them*) *as you like*; *his reasons were many and good*); **as ~**, that number of (*six mistakes in as many lines*); **as ~ again,** the same number additionally (*sixty here and as many again in London*); **~'s the,** there are many —s that (*many's the tale he has told us*); **~'s the time,** often (*many's the time I have seen you do it*); **the ~**, the multitude of people; **the one and the ~**, (Philos.) unity and plurality; **one too ~**, not wanted, in the way; **be (one) too ~ for,** outwit, baffle; **a good, a great, ~**, a fair, a large, number; **~-headed beast, monster,** the populace; **~plies,** third STOMACH of ruminant; **~-sided,** having many sides, aspects, capabilities, interests, etc. [OE *manig*, = OS, OHG *manag*, Goth. *manags* f. Gmc **managaz*]

mănzanĭ'lla *n.* Pale very dry Spanish sherry. [Sp., lit. 'camomile']

mănzanĭ'ta (-ē'-) *n.* Californian shrub of genus *Arctostaphylos*. [Sp., dim. of *manzana* apple]

Mao (mow) *a.* Of style worn in Communist China (*Mao cap, jacket*, etc.). [f. *Mao* Tse-tung, Chinese Communist statesman d. 1976]

Mao'|ism (mow'-) *n.* Communist doctrines of Mao Tse-tung; hence **~**IST (2) *n.* [f. as prec. + -ISM]

Maor'i (mowr'ĭ) *n.* & *a.* (Member or language) of brown Polynesian aboriginal race in New Zealand; **~land,** New Zealand. [native name]

măp¹ *n.* Representation (usu. on plane surface, cf. *globe*) of (part of) earth's surface, showing physical and political features etc., or of the heavens, showing positions of stars etc.; (sl.) face; **(wipe) off the ~**, (colloq.) (render) of no account, obsolete, in(to) oblivion, very distant; **on the ~**, (colloq.) to be reckoned with, prominent, important (*put on the ~*, make prominent etc.); hence **~'**LESS *a.* [f. L *mappa* napkin; in med. L *mappa* (*mundi*) map of world]

măp² *v.t.* (**-pp-**). Represent on map; (Math.) associate each element of (set) with one element of another set; **~ out,** plan out, arrange in detail (course of conduct, one's time, etc.). [f. prec.]

mā'ple *n.* Tree or shrub of genus *Acer* grown for shade, ornament, wood, or sugar; its wood; **~-leaf,** emblem of Canada; **~ sugar** (got by evaporating sap of sugar maple etc.); *maple* SYRUP. [ME *mapul* etc., f. OE *mapeltrēow*, *mapulder*]

măquě'tte (-k-) *n.* Sculptor's small preliminary model in wax, clay, etc.; preliminary sketch. [F, f. It. *machietta* dim. of *macchia* spot]

maquillage (mahkĭyah'zh) *n.* (Applying of) make-up or cosmetics. [F (*maquiller* make up f. OF *masquiller* stain; see -AGE)]

Ma'quis (mah'kē) *n.* Secret army of patriots in France during German occupation (1940–45); member of this. [F, = brushwood, f. Corsican It. *macchia* thicket]

mar *v.t.* (**-rr-**). Impair fatally, ruin, esp. *make* (*or mend*) *or mar*; spoil, disfigure, impair perfection of; **~'plot,** one who hinders undertaking by officiousness. [OE *merran*, = OS *merrian* hinder, OHG *merren*, ON *merja* bruise, Goth. *marzjan* cause to stumble]

Mar. *abbr.* March.

mă'rabou (-bōō) *n.* Large W. Afr. stork; = ADJUTANT 2; tuft of down from wing or tail of marabou as trimming for hat etc. [F, f. Arab. (as foll.), the stork being regarded as holy]

mă'rabout¹ (-bōōt) *n.* Muslim hermit or monk, esp. in N. Africa; shrine marking marabout's burial-place. [F, f. Port. *marabuto* f. Arab. *murābiṭ* holy man (*ribāṭ* frontier station, where he acquired merit by combat against the infidel)]

marabout². Var. of MARABOU.

mară'ca *n.* Hand-held clublike gourd containing beans, beads, etc., shaken (usu. in pairs) as percussion instrument. [f. Port. *maracá*, prob. f. Tupi]

măraschi'nō (-kē'-) *n.* (*pl.* **~s**). Strong sweet liqueur from a small black Dalmatian cherry; **~ cherry** (preserved in this). [It. (*marasca* small black cherry, for *amarasca* f. *amaro* bitter f. L *amarus*)]

mară'sm|us (-z-) *n.* Wasting away of body; hence ~IC *a.* [mod. L, f. Gk *marasmos* (*marainō* wither)]

Mară'tha, Mahra'tta, (mară'-; *or* -rah'-) *n.* Member of a warlike Indian race; so **Mara'thĭ, Mahra'ttĭ,** (mară'tĭ; *or* -rah'-) *n.*, their language. [f. Hindi *Marhaṭṭa* f. Skr. *Māhārāshṭra* great kingdom]

mă'rathon *n.* Long-distance road race, esp. of 26 miles 385 yards as a principal event of modern Olympic Games; feat of endurance, undertaking of long duration. [f. *M~* in Greece, scene of decisive battle in 490 B.C., whence messenger ran with news to Athens]

marau'd *v.i.* & *t.* Make plundering raid (on); go about pilfering; plunder; hence ~ER[1] *n.* [f. F *marauder* (*maraud* rogue)]

mărave'dĭ (-vā'-) *n.* (Hist.) Gold or copper Spanish coin. [ME f. Sp., f. Arab. *Murābiṭīn* MARABOUT[1]s, Moorish dynasty at Cordova 1087–1147]

mar'ble *n.*, & *v.t.* **1.** *n.* Limestone in metamorphic crystalline (or granular) state and capable of taking polish, used in sculpture and architecture; this as type of hardness or durability or smoothness (often *attrib.*); (in *pl.*) collection of sculptures (*Elgin Marbles*); **~ cake** (with mottled appearance, made of light and dark sponge). **2.** Small ball of marble, clay, glass, etc., as toy; (in *pl.*) game using these. **3.** Hence **mar'bly**[2] *a.* **4.** *v.t.* (esp. in *p.p.*) Stain, colour, (paper, edges of book, soap) to look like variegated marble; (in *p.p.*, of meat) streaked with alternating layers of lean and fat. [ME, f. OF *marbre*, *marble*, f. L *marmor* f. Gk *marmaros* shining stone]

marc *n.* Refuse of pressed grapes etc.; brandy made from this. [F (*marcher* tread, MARCH[5])]

Mar'can *a.* Of St. Mark. [f. L *Marcus* Mark + -AN]

mar'casite *n.* Crystallized iron pyrites; piece of this as adornment. [ME, f. med. L *marcasita*, f. Arab. *markašīṭā* f. Pers.; assoc. w. -ITE[1] (2)]

marcĕ'l *n.*, & *v.t.* (**-ll-**). **1.** *n.* **~ (wave)**, kind of deep wave in hair. **2.** *v.t.* Wave (hair) thus. [f. *Marcel* Grateau, Paris hairdresser d. 1936, who invented the method]

marcĕ'sc|ent *a.* (Of part of plant) withering but not falling; hence ~ENCE *n.* [f. L *marcescere* incept. of *marcēre* wither; see -ESCENT]

March[1] *n.* Third month of year; *March* HARE. [ME, f. OF *march(e)*, dial. var. of *marz*, *mars*, f. L *Martius* (*mensis* month) of Mars]

march[2] *n.* (Hist.) Boundary, frontiers, (often in *pl.*, esp. of borderland between England and Scotland or Wales); tract of (often disputed) land between two countries. [ME, f. OF *marche* f. Rom. *marca* f. OFrank. **marka* f. Gmc **markō* MARK[1]]

march[3] *v.i.* (Of countries, estates, etc.) border *upon*, have common frontier *with*. [ME, f. OF *marchir* (*marche*; see prec.)]

march[4] *n.* **1.** (Mil.) Marching of troops; **line** (route) **of ~**. **2.** Long toilsome walk; progress (*of* events, time, intellect, mind). **3.** Distance covered by troops in a day; FORCE[2]*d march*; STEAL *a march on*. **4.** Uniform step of troops etc. (*quick*, *slow*, *march*); **~ past,** marching of troops in line past saluting-point at review. **5.** (Mus.) Composition meant to accompany march (DEAD *march*). [f. foll. or F *marche* (*marcher*; see foll.)]

march[5] *v.* **1.** *v.i.* Walk *away*, *forth*, *past* (reviewing officer or sovereign), *out*, etc., in military manner with regular and measured tread; advance thus *on* (place to be attacked). **2.** Walk or proceed steadily. **3.** ‖**~'ing order,** equipment or formation for marching; **~'ing orders,** direction for troops to depart for war etc., (fig.) dismissal. **4.** *v.t.* Cause to march or go *away*, *on*, *off*, etc. [f. F *marcher*, f. Gallo-Rom. **marcare* f. LL *marcus* hammer]

mar'chioness (-sho-) *n.* Marquis's wife or widow; woman holding rank of marquis in her own right. [f. med. L *marchionissa* (*marchio -onis* captain of the marches f. as MARCH[2]; see -ESS[1])]

mar'chpāne. Var. (arch.) of MARZIPAN.

marcō'nĭ *n.* & *v.* (arch.) **1.** *n.* = foll. **2.** *v.t.* & *i.* Send (message) thus. [f. G. *Marconi*, It. inventor of system of wireless telegraphy d. 1937]

marcō'nĭgrăm *n.* (arch.) Message sent by Marconi's system of wireless telegraphy. [f. as prec. + -GRAM]

Mardi Gra's (mardēgrah') *n.* (Merry-making on) Shrove Tuesday; last day of carnival. [F, = fat Tuesday]

mar'ē[1] *n.* (*pl.* **maria** *pr.* mar'ĭa). **1. ~ clau'sum,** sea under jurisdiction of particular country; **~ li'berum,** sea open to all nations. **2.** (Astron.) Large dark flat area on moon, once thought to be sea; similar area on Mars. [L, = sea]

māre[2] *n.* Female of equine animal, esp. horse; GREY[1] *mare*; SHANKS's *mare*; **~'s nest,** illusory discovery; **~'s-tail,** (1) tall slender marsh plant (*Hippuris vulgaris*), (2, in *pl.*) long straight streaks of cirrus cloud. [OE **mēre* etc., = MDu., MLG *mer(r)ie*, OHG *mar(i)ha*, ON *merr* f. Gmc **marhjōn* (**marhaz* horse f. IE **markos*; cf. MARSHAL[1])]

marĕ'mma *n.* Low marshy unhealthy country by seashore. [It., f. L *maritima* (as MARITIME)]

mar'garine (-ēn; *or* -j-; *or* -ē'n) *n.* Butter--substitute made from edible oils and animal fats with milk etc. [F, misapplication of a chem. term, f. *margarique* f. Gk *margaron* pearl; see -IC, -IN[1], -INE[5]]

mar'gay *n.* Small S. Amer. tiger-cat (*Felis tigrina*). [F, f. Tupi *mbaracaīa*]

marge[1] *n.* (poet.) Margin. [F, f. L (as MARGIN)]

marge[2] *n.* (colloq.) Margarine. [abbr.]

mar'gent *n.* (arch. or poet.) = foll. [alt. as in *ancient*, *pageant*, etc.]

mar'gin *n.*, & *v.t.* **1.** *n.* Edge or border of surface; hence ~ATE[2], ~ātED[1], *adjs.* **2.** Condition near the limit below or beyond which a thing ceases to be possible etc.; extra amount (of time, money, etc.) over and above the necessary or minimum (*by a narrow margin*; *margin of profit*, *of safety*); sum deposited with stockbroker to cover risk of loss on transaction on account. **3.** Plain space beside main body of print etc. on page; **~ release,** device on typewriter to continue word etc. into margin normally imposed by adjustable stop. **4.** *v.t.* Furnish with margin or marginal notes. [ME, f. L *margo -ginis*]

mar'gĭnal *a.* Of, written in, the margin; having marginal notes; of, at, the edge; (of sea) adjacent to shore of a State; (of land) difficult to cultivate and yielding little profit; close to the limit (esp. of no further profit etc.); barely adequate or provided for (‖**~ seat,** one where M.P. has only small majority and is likely to be unseated at next election); **~ cost** (added by making one extra copy, etc.); hence ~ITY (-ă'l-) *n.*, ~LY[2] *adv.* [f. med. L *marginalis* (as prec.; see -AL)]

margĭnā'lĭa *n. pl.* Marginal notes. [med. L, neut. pl. of *marginalis*; see prec., -IA[2]]

mar'grāve *n.* (Hist.) Hereditary title of some princes of Holy Roman Empire (orig. of military governor of border province). [f. MDu. *markgrave* border count (as MARK¹, *grave* COUNT³ f. OLG *grēve*)]

mar'gravine (-ēn) *n.* Margrave's wife. [f. Du. *markgravin* (as prec.; see -INE³)]

mar'guerite (-gerēt; *or* -ē't) *n.* Chrysanthemum like ox-eye daisy. [F, f. L *margarita* f. Gk *margaritēs* (*margaron* pearl; see -ITE¹)]

mar'ia. See MARE¹.

mariage de convenance (măriahzh de kaw'n-venahns) *n.* = *marriage of* CONVENIENCE. [F]

Mar'ian *a.* & *n.* (Person devoted to) the Virgin Mary, Mary I Queen of England, or Mary Queen of Scots; English Catholic of 1553–58. [f. L *Maria* Mary + -AN]

mă'rigōld *n.* Plant of genus *Calendula* or *Tagetes*, with golden or bright yellow flowers; CORN¹ *marigold*; MARSH *marigold*. [ME, f. *Mary* (prob. the Virgin) + dial. *gold* marigold]

mărijua'na, -hua'na, (mărihwah'na) *n.* Dried leaves, flowering tops, and stems of HEMP (sense 1), used to make a hallucinogenic drug esp. for cigarettes (*reefers*). [Amer. Sp.]

mari'mba *n.* Xylophone of Afr. & Central--Amer. natives; modern orchestral instrument evolved from this. [Congo]

mari'na (-ē'-) *n.* Place with moorings for pleasure-yachts etc. [It. & Sp. fem. a., f. *marino* f. L (as MARINE)]

mărinā'de *n.*, & *v.t.* **1.** *n.* Pickle etc. of wine, vinegar, oil, herbs, spices, etc.; fish or meat treated with this. **2.** *v.t.* Pickle with, steep in, marinade. [F, f. Sp. *marinada* (*marinar* pickle in brine, f. *marino*, as MARINE; see -ADE)]

mă'rināte *v.t.* = prec. 2. [f. It. *marinare* or F *mariner* (as foll.) + -ATE³]

mari'ne (-ē'n) *a.* & *n.* **1.** *a.* Of, found in, produced by, the sea; of shipping or naval matters (*marine insurance*; ~ **stores,** new or old ships' material and similar odds and ends as merchandise); for use at sea; *marine* TRUMPET. **2.** *n.* Country's shipping, fleet, or navy, (esp. *mercantile* or *merchant marine*). **3.** Sea picture. **4.** Member of body of troops trained to serve on land or sea (‖ROYAL *Marines*); **tell that to the (horse) ~s,** (colloq.) you will not deceive me with that. [ME, f. OF *marin marine* f. L *marinus* (*mare* sea; see -INE¹)]

mă'riner *n.* Sailor, seaman; **master ~,** captain of merchant ship; **~'s compass,** = COMPASS 3. [ME f. AF; OF *marinier* f. med. L *marinarius* f. L (as prec.; see -ER²)]

Mariŏ'latrў *n.* (derog.) Worship of the Virgin Mary. [f. L *Maria* Mary + -LATRY, after *idolatry*]

mărionĕ'tte *n.* Puppet worked by strings. [f. F *marionnette* (*Marion* dim. of *Marie* Mary; see -ETTE)]

mă'rish *n.* & *a.* (arch.) Marsh(y). [ME & OF *mareis* f. med. L *mariscus* f. WG (as MARSH)]

Mar'ist *n.* Member of R.C. Society of Mary. [f. F *Mariste* (*Marie* Mary; see -IST)]

mă'rital (*or* meri't-) *a.* Of a husband; of or between husband and wife; of marriage; hence ~LY² *adv.* [f. L *maritalis* (*maritus* husband; see -AL)]

mă'ritime *a.* Living or found near the sea; connected with the sea or seafaring (*maritime insurance*). [f. L *maritimus* (*mare* sea)]

mar'joram *n.* Aromatic herb of genus *Origanum* or *Majorana*, used in cookery. [ME & OF *majorane*, f. med. L *majorana*, of unkn. orig.]

mark¹ *n.* **1.** Target or other object to be aimed at; (sl.) intended victim of swindler etc.; (Boxing) pit of stomach; **beside, off, wide of, the ~,** not hitting it, (fig.) not to the point, irrelevant; EASY *mark*. **2.** Desired object (*hit, miss*, OVERSHOOT¹, *the mark*); one's ~, (sl.) what one prefers. **3.** Sign, indication, (*of* quality, character, feeling, etc.); **~ of mouth,** depression in horse's incisor tooth indicating age. **4.** Affixed or impressed sign, seal, etc.; (followed by numeral) particular design of piece of equipment etc. **5.** Cross etc. made in place of signature by illiterate person. **6.** Written or printed symbol; this as sign of good or bad conduct, or as characterizing quality of work; EXCLAMATION, PUNCTUATION, QUESTION¹, *mark*; BLACK¹ *mark*. **7.** Unit of numerical award of merit in examination (*he gained 46 marks*, FULL¹ *marks*). **8.** Line etc. serving to indicate position; piece of material used to indicate position on SOUND³ing-line; runner's starting-point in race (*get on your marks*); **off the ~,** having made a start; **on the ~,** (smartly) ready to start; **below, up to,** etc., **the ~** (the usual standard, esp. of person's health). **9.** (Rugby & Austral. Footb.) Heel-mark on ground made by player who has caught the ball direct from kick or knock-on or throw-forward by opponent. **10.** Trace, visible sign, left by person or thing; stain, scar, etc.; BIRTH*mark*; **make** one's **~,** attain distinction; **of ~,** noteworthy; (as apology for mentioning anything horrible etc.) **(God) save the ~** (freq. sarcastic or impatiently scornful). **11.** (Hist.) Tract of land held in common by Teutonic or medieval German village community. [OE *me(a)rc*, = OS *marka*, OHG *marcha*, ON *mörk*, Goth. *marka* f. Gmc **markō* boundary]

mark² *v.t.* **1.** Make a mark on (thing or person) by stamping, cutting, writing, hitting, etc.; put distinguishing or identifying mark or name to or on (clothes etc.); give distinctive character to (*to mark the occasion*); attach figures indicating prices to (goods); (in *pass.*) have natural marks (*is marked with silver spots*). **2. ~ out,** trace out boundaries for (ground), plan (course), destine (*marked out for slaughter*). **3. ~ off,** separate (thing *from* another, lit. or fig.) by boundary. **4.** Name or indicate (place on map, length of syllable) by signs or marks. **5.** Record (points gained in games); allot marks to (student's work etc.); = READ 10. **6.** Manifest (one's displeasure etc. *by*). **7.** Accompany, be a feature of, (*no triumph marks her manner*; *day was marked by severe storms*). **8. ~ time,** move feet as in marching, but without advancing, (fig.) act routinely or unprogressively, await opportunity to advance. **9.** See, notice; observe mentally (*mark my words*; *without any obligation, mark you*); ~ **(down)**, note and remember spot to which (grouse etc.) has retired, choose as one's victim etc. **10.** ‖(Footb. etc.) Keep close to (opponent) so as to hamper him if he receives ball. **11. ~ down,** mark at a lower price; **~ up,** mark at a higher price; ~*-up* n., amount added by shopkeeper to cost-price of goods to cover overhead charges and profit. [OE *mearcian*, = OS *markon*, OHG *marchōn*, ON *marka* observe, f. WG **markōjan* (as prec.)]

mark³ *n.* **1.** (Hist.) Denomination of weight for gold and silver; English money of account. **2.** Monetary unit in Germany, Finland, etc. [OE *marc*, = MDu. *marc*, MHG *marke*, ON *mörk*, prob. rel. to med. L *marca*, *marcus*]

mark|ed (-kt) *a.* In vbl senses; (clearly) noticeable or evident (*a marked difference*), whence **~'ėd**LY² *adv.*, **~'ėd**NESS *n.*; (of playing--cards) given distinctive marks on their backs to assist cheating; **~ed man,** (1) one whose conduct is watched with suspicion or hostility, (2) one expected to reach eminence. [OE (p.p. of MARK²)]

mar'ker *n.* In vbl senses; one who marks down

game; one who records score, esp. in billiards; flare etc. to direct aircraft pilot to target; bookmark; memorial stone etc.; thing to mark place reached. [ME, f. MARK² + -ER¹]

mâr'kėt¹ *n.* **1.** Gathering of people for purchase and sale of provisions, livestock, etc.; time of this; **bring** one's **eggs** or **hogs to a bad ~**, fail in one's schemes. **2.** Open space or covered building in which provisions, cattle, etc., are exposed for sale. **3. Make a ~ of,** (fig.) barter away. **4.** Demand (*for* commodity or service; *goods find a ready market*); place where there is such demand; conditions as regards, opportunity for, buying or selling; *the* trade in (corn etc.); **be in the ~ for,** wish to buy; **be on the ~, come into the ~**, be offered for sale; **put on the ~**, offer for sale; BUY*er's*, SELL*er's, market*. **5.** BLACK¹ *market*; (**European**) **Common M~**, ||**the M~**, the European Economic Community, an economic and political association of certain (European) countries as a unit with internal free trade and common external tariffs; MONEY-*-market*; STOCK-*market*. **6.** Rate of purchase and sale, market value, (*the market fell*); PLAY¹ *the market*; **up-~**, in the direction of higher-priced goods. **7. ~ cross** (erected in market-place); **~-day** (on which market is held, usu. weekly); ||**~ garden** (in which vegetables are grown for market); **~ overt,** open market; **~-place,** open space in town, where market is held, (fig.) scene of actual dealings; **~ research,** study of possible buyers for one's goods; **~ town** (where market is held); **~ value,** value as saleable thing (dist. from cost and from BOOK¹ value). [ME f. OS *-market*, OHG *-marchāt* f. L *mercatus* (*mercari* buy; see MERCHANT)]

mâr'kėt² *v.* **1.** *v.i.* Buy or sell in market. **2.** *v.t.* Sell (goods) in market or elsewhere; hence ~ABLE *a.*, ~ING¹ (1) *n.* [ME, f. prec.]

mâr'khôr (-kôr) *n.* Large spiral-horned wild goat of N. India. [f. Pers. *mār-kẖwār* (*mār* serpent, *kẖwār* -eating)]

mâr'kĭng *n.* In vbl senses; colouring of feathers, skin, etc.; identification symbol on aircraft etc.; **~-ink** (indelible, for marking linen etc.). [ME, f. MARK² + -ING¹]

mâr'ksman *n.* (*pl.* **-men**). One skilled or practised in aiming at mark, esp. one who attains certain standard of proficiency in rifle practice; hence ~SHIP (1, 3) *n.* [f. MARK¹ + 's 1 + MAN¹]

mârl *n.*, & *v.t.* **1.** *n.* Soil consisting of clay and lime, a valuable fertilizer; hence ~'Y² *a.* **2.** *v.t.* Apply marl to (ground). [ME, f. OF *marle* f. med. L *margila* f. L *marga*]

Mârlbūr'ĭan *a.* & *n.* (Past or present member) of Marlborough College. [f. *Marlborough* (as if **Marlbury*) + -IAN]

***mâr'lĭn** *n.* Large sea-fish of genus *Makaira*. [f. MARLINSPIKE, w. ref. to its pointed snout]

mâr'lĭne *n.* (Naut.) Small line of two strands; **~-spike,** = foll. [ME, f. Du. *marlijn* (*marren* bind, *lijn* LINE²)]

mâr'lĭnspike *n.* (Naut.) Pointed iron tool used to separate strands of rope or wire. [orig. app. *marling-spike* f. *marl* fasten with marline (f. Du. *marlen* frequent. of MDu. *marren* bind) + -ING¹ + SPIKE¹]

mâr'līte *n.* Kind of marl that is not reduced to powder by action of air. [f. MARL + -ITE¹]

mâr'malāde *n.* Conserve of oranges or other citrus fruit, made like jam; **~ cat** (with orange fur). [f. F *marmelade* f. Port. *marmelada* (*marmelo* quince f. L f. Gk *melimēlon* f. *meli* honey + *mēlon* apple; see -ADE)]

mâr'mīte *n.* **1.** Flavouring extract made from fresh brewer's yeast. **2.** (*or* mârmē't). Earthenware cooking-vessel. [**P**; F, = cooking-pot]

mâr'molīte *n.* Laminated pale-green serpentine. [irreg. f. Gk *marmairō* shine; see -LITE]

mârmôr'ėal *a.* (poet.) Of or like marble. [f. L *marmoreus* (as MARBLE) + -AL]

mâr'mosĕt (-z-) *n.* Small tropical Amer. monkey of family Callithricidae, with bushy tail. [f. OF *marmouset* grotesque image, of unkn. orig.]

mâr'mot *n.* Burrowing rodent of genus *Arctomys*. [f. F *marmotte* prob. f. Romansch *murmont* f. L *murem* (nom. *mus*) *montis* mountain mouse]

mă'rocain *n.* Dress-fabric of crêpe type made in silk (or other materials). [F, = Moroccan (*Maroc* Morocco)]

Mă'ronīte *n.* One of a sect of Syrian Christians dwelling chiefly in Lebanon. [f. med. L *Maronita* (*Maro* 5th-c. Syrian founder; see -ITE¹)]

maroo͞'n¹ *a.* & *n.* **1.** (Of) brownish-crimson colour. **2.** *n.* Explosive device giving loud report. [f. F *marron* chestnut f. It. *marrone* f. med. Gk *maraon*]

maroo͞'n² *n.* One of class of Negroes, orig. fugitive slaves, in mountains and forests of Surinam and W. Indies; marooned person. [f. F *marron*, f. Sp. *cimarrón* wild (*cima* peak; see -OON)]

maroo͞'n³ *v.* **1.** *v.t.* Put (person) ashore and leave him on desolate island or coast as punishment; (of floods etc.) make (person) unable to leave place safely. **2.** *v.i.* Idle, hang about. [f. prec.]

mârque¹ (-k) *n.* (Hist.) **Letter(s) of ~ (and reprisal)**, licence to fit out armed vessel and employ it in capture of enemy's merchant shipping, (in *sing.*) ship carrying such licence. [ME f. F, f. Prov. *marca* (*marcar* seize as a pledge)]

mârque² (-k) *n.* Make of motor car, as opp. to specific type (*the Jaguar marque*). [F, = MARK¹]

mârquee' (-kē') *n.* Large tent; *canopy over entrance to large building. [f. MARQUISE 3, taken as pl. & assim. to -EE]

mâr'quėtrў, -terĭe, (-kĭ-) *n.* Inlaid work in wood, ivory, etc. [F *marqueterie* (*marqueter* variegate f. MARQUE²; see -RY)]

mâr'quĭs, mâr'quėss, *n.* Nobleman ranking between duke and (in U.K.) earl or (elsewhere) count; hence ~ATE¹ (1) *n.* [ME, f. OF *marchis* f. Rom. **marchensis* (as MARCH², -ESE)]

mârquī'se (-kē'z) *n.* **1.** (In foreign nobility) marchioness. **2.** Finger-ring set with oval pointed cluster of gems. **3.** (arch.) Tent, marquee. [F, fem. of *marquis* (as prec.)]

mârquĭsĕ'tte (-kĭz-) *n.* Fine light cotton, rayon, or silk fabric for net curtains etc. [F, dim. of *marquise*; see prec., -ETTE]

mă'rram *n.* Shore grass (*Ammophila arenaria*) that binds sand with its tough rhizome. [f. ON *marálmr* (*marr* sea, *hálmr* HAULM)]

Marra'nō (-ah'-) *n.* (*pl.* **~s**). (Hist.) Jew or Moor in medieval Spain accepting, or simulating acceptance of, Christianity, esp. to avoid persecution. [Sp.]

mă'rriage (-rĭj) *n.* **1.** Condition of man and woman legally united for purpose of living together and usu. procreating lawful offspring; act or ceremony or procedure establishing this condition; **by ~**, as result of this (*related by marriage*); *give* or *take* **in ~**, as husband or wife; *marriage of* CONVENIENCE; CIVIL *marriage*. **2.** (fig.) Intimate union (*the marriage of true minds*); (Cards) union of king and queen of same suit. **3. ~ articles,** antenuptial agreement respecting rights of property and succession; **~-bed,** (fig.) marital intercourse; **~-broker,** one who arranges marriages for payment; **~ bureau,** establishment arranging introductions between persons wishing to marry; **~ certificate** (stating that marriage ceremony has taken place, with names, date, etc.); ~ **guidance,** assistance to married couples who have problems in living together harmoniously; ~ **licence,** LICENCE[1] to marry; ||~ **lines,** marriage certificate; ~ **market,** supply and demand of eligible partners for marriage; ~ **portion,** dowry; *marriage* SETTLEMENT. [ME f. OF *mariage* (*marier* MARRY[1]; see -AGE)]

mă'rriageable (-rĭj*a*-) *a.* Old enough to marry; (of age) fit for marriage. [f. prec. + -ABLE]

mă'rrĭed (-ĭd) *a.* & *n.* **1.** *a.* United in marriage; of person(s) so united (*married life, love, name*). **2.** *n.* Married person (*young marrieds*). [ME, p.p. of MARRY[1]]

mărrŏn glacé (glah'sā) *n.* Chestnut preserved in and coated with sugar as sweetmeat. [F, = iced chestnut; cf. GLACÉ]

mă'rrow (-ō) *n.* **1.** Soft fatty substance in cavities of bones, often taken as typifying rich food or vitality, (*chilled* **to the** ~, right through); **spinal** ~, substance forming spinal cord. **2.** Essential part (*pith and marrow*). **3.** (**Vegetable**) ~, white-fleshed edible gourd, the fruit of *Cucurbita pepo.* **4.** ~**bone,** bone containing edible marrow, (in *pl.*, joc.) knees; ~(**fat**), kind of large pea; *~ **squash,** vegetable marrow. **5.** Hence ~LESS, ~Y[2], *adjs.* [OE *mearg, mærg,* = OS, OHG *marg,* ON *mergr* f. Gmc **mazg-*]

mă'rrў[1] *v.* **1.** *v.t.* (Of priest etc. or in *p.p.*) join (persons, one *to* another) in marriage; (of parent or guardian) give (son, daughter, etc.) in marriage; (of person) take as wife or husband in marriage; ~ **off,** find wife or husband for (one's son or daughter). **2.** (fig.) Unite intimately; correlate (things) as pair; (Naut.) splice (rope-ends) together without increasing girth. **3.** *v.i.* Take husband or wife; ~ **into,** become member of (family) by marriage; hence ~ING[2] *a.*, (esp.) likely to marry (*not a marrying man*). [ME, f. OF *marier* f. L *maritare* (*maritus* husband)]

mă'rrў[2] *int.* (arch.) expr. surprise, asseveration, indignation, etc.; ~ **come up** (expr. indignant or contemptuous surprise). [ME, = (the Virgin) *Mary*]

Mârs (-z) *n.* Planet fourth in order of distance from sun, next beyond earth. [L *Mars Martis,* name of Roman god of war]

Mârsa'la (-sah'-) *n.* Dark sweet fortified wine like light sherry. [~ in Sicily, where orig. made]

Mârseillai'se (-s*e*lā'z) *n.* National anthem of France, first sung in Paris by Marseilles patriots. [F, fem. adj. f. *Marseille* Marseilles; cf. -ESE]

mârsh *n.* **1.** Low land flooded in winter and usu. watery at all times; (*attrib.*, in many names of plants and animals found in marshes). **2.** ~ **fever,** malaria; ~ **gas,** methane; ~**-harrier,** species of HARRIER[3]; ~**'land,** land consisting of marshes; ~ **mallow,** (confection made from root of) shrubby herb (*Althaea officinalis*) growing near salt marshes; ~*'mallow,* soft sweet made from sugar, albumen, gelatin, etc.; ~ **marigold,** golden-flowered ranunculaceous plant (*Caltha palustris*) growing in moist meadows etc.; ~ **tit,** grey tit (*Parus palustris*) inhabiting marshland; ~ **trefoil,** buckbean. **3.** Hence ~'Y[2] *a.* [OE *mer(i)sc,* = MLG, MDu. *mersch* f. WG **marisk-*]

mâr'shal[1] *n.* **1.** High officer of state (||EARL *Marshal*); officer of highest rank in some armies; ||AIR[1] *Marshal*; ||FIELD *Marshal*; ||**M~ of the Royal Air Force** (officer of highest rank); **knight** ~, (Hist.) officer of royal household with judicial functions; ||(**judge's**) ~, official accompanying judge on circuit, with secretarial duties. **2.** Officer arranging ceremonies, controlling procedure at races, etc.; *head of police or fire department; PROVOST *marshal*; hence ~SHIP *n.* [ME f. OF *mareschal,* f. LL *mariscalcus* f. Gmc **marhaskalkaz* (**marhaz* horse; see MARE[2]; **skalkaz* servant)]

mâr'shal[2] *v.* (||-ll-). **1.** *v.t.* Arrange in due order (persons at table etc., soldiers, facts, one's thoughts, etc.); (Her.) combine (coats of arms); conduct (person) ceremoniously (*into* etc.). **2.** *v.i.* Take up positions in due arrangement; ~**ling yard,** = RAILWAY-yard (in which goods trains etc. are assembled). [ME. f. prec.]

mâr'shalsea *n.* (Hist.) Court held, prison in Southwark (London) controlled, by knight marshal. [alt. f. *marshalcy* f. MARSHAL[1] + -CY]

mârsū'pĭal *a.* & *n.* **1.** *a.* (Anat.) Of or like a pouch (*marsupial muscle*). **2.** *a.* & *n.* (Animal) of the class of mammals characterized by having a pouch in which to carry their young, which are born incompletely developed. [f. mod. L *marsupialis* f. L f. Gk *marsupion* pouch dim. of *marsipos* purse; see -AL]

mârt *n.* Market-place; auction room; trade centre. [ME, f. obs. Du. *mart,* var. of *markt* MARKET]

mâr'tagon *n.* Lily (*Lilium martagon*) with small purple turban-like flowers. [F, f. Turk. *martagān* a form of turban]

Mârtĕ'llō *n.* (*pl.* ~s). ~ (**tower**), small circular fort, usu. on coast to prevent hostile landing. [alt. f. Cape *Mortella* in Corsica, where such a tower proved difficult to capture in 1794]

mâr'tėn *n.* Animal of genus *Martes,* like weasel, with valuable fur. [ME, f. MDu. *martren* f. OF (*peau* skin) *martrine,* fem. adj. f. *martre* f. WG **marthr-* f. Gmc **marthuz*]

mâr'tĕnsīte (-z-) *n.* Chief constituent of hardened steel. [f. A. *Martens,* Ger. metallurgist d. 1914 + -ITE[1]]

mâr'tial (-sh*a*l) *a.* **1.** Of, suitable for, appropriate to, warfare; hence ~IZE (3) *v.t.* **2.** ~ **law,** military government, by which ordinary law is suspended. **3.** Warlike, brave; fond of fighting. **4.** (*M~*). Martian. **5.** Hence ~LY[2] *adv.* [ME f. OF, or f. L *martialis* of MARS; see -IAL]

Mâr'tian (-sh*a*n) *a.* & *n.* (Hypothetical inhabitant) of Mars. [ME, f. OF *martien* or f. L *Martianus* (MARS; see -IAN)]

mâr'tĭn *n.* Bird of swallow family, esp. **house-~** (*Delichon urbica*), which builds mud nest on house walls etc., and ||SAND-*martin.* [prob. f. St. *Martin* (see MARTINMAS)]

mârtĭnĕ't *n.* Strict (esp. military or naval) disciplinarian; hence ~(**t**)ISH[1] *a.* [f. J. *Martinet,* 17th-c. French drill-master]

mâr'tĭngāle (-ngg-) *n.* **1.** Strap, or set of straps, fastened at one end to nose-band, at other end to girth, of horse to prevent rearing etc.; (Naut.) rope for holding down jib-boom. **2.** Gambling system of continually doubling stakes in hope of eventual win that must yield net profit. [F, of uncert. orig.]

mârti'nĭ (-ē'nĭ) *n.* Cocktail of gin, French vermouth, orange bitters, etc. [perh. f. *Martini* & Rossi, It. firm selling vermouth]

Mâr'tĭnmas *n.* St. Martin's day, 11 Nov.; ~ **summer,** St. Martin's SUMMER[1]. [ME, f. St. *Martin,* bishop of Tours in 4th c., + MASS[1]]

mâr'tlėt *n.* **1.** (arch.) Swift or house-MARTIN. **2.** (Her.) Imaginary footless bird as charge. [f. F *martelet* alt. f. *martinet* dim. f. MARTIN]

mâr'tyr *n.*, & *v.t.* **1.** *n.* One who undergoes penalty of death for persistence in Christian faith or obedience to law of Church, or undergoes death or suffering for any great cause; ~ **to,** constant sufferer from (ailment); **make a ~ of oneself,** (pretend to) accept discomfort etc., in order to be more highly thought of. **2.** *v.t.* Put to death as martyr; torment. [OE *martir* f. eccl. L f. Gk *martur, martus -uros* witness]

mar'tyrdom *n.* Sufferings and death of martyr; torment. [OE *martyrdōm* (as prec., -DOM)]
mar'tyriz|e, -is|e (-īz), *v.t.* Make a martyr of (*oneself*, person); hence **~A'TION** *n.* [ME, f. LL *martyrizare* (as MARTYR; see -IZE)]
martyr|ŏ'logy̆ *n.* List or register, history, of martyrs; hence **~OLO'GICAL** *a.*, **~ŏ'LOGIST** *n.* [f. med. L f. eccl. Gk *marturologion* (as MARTYR, *logos* account; see -LOGY)]
mar'tyry̆ *n.* Shrine or church erected in honour of martyr. [ME, f. med. L f. Gk *marturion* martyrdom (as MARTYR)]
mar'vel[1] *n.* Wonderful thing; wonderful example *of* (quality); (arch.) astonishment; **~ of Peru,** showy garden plant (*Mirabilis jalapa*) with flowers opening in afternoon. [ME, f. OF *merveille* f. LL *mirabilia* neut. pl. of L *mirabilis* (*mirari* wonder at; see MIRACLE, -ABLE)]
mar'vel[2] *v.i.* (||**-ll-**). (literary). Be surprised (*at, that*); wonder (*how, why*, etc.). [ME, f. OF *merveiller* (*merveille*; see prec.)]
mar'vellous, *mar'velous, *a.* Astonishing; extremely improbable; excellent; hence **~LY**[2] *adv.*, **~NESS** *n.* [ME, f. OF *merveillos* (*merveille*; see MARVEL[1], -OUS)]
Mar'xian *a.* & *n.* (Adherent) of the doctrines of Marx. [f. K. *Marx*, Ger. socialist d. 1883 + -IAN]
Mar'x|ism *n.* Political and economic theory of Marx, advocating abolition of private property, and State provision of work and subsistence for all; **~ism-Le'ninism,** this as developed by Lenin (cf. LENINISM); so **~IST** (2) *n.* & *a.* [f. as prec. + -ISM]
mar'zipăn *n.* Paste of ground almonds, sugar, etc., made up into small cakes, etc. or used on top of large cakes; piece of marzipan. [G, f. It. *marzapane*]
măscar'a *n.* Cosmetic for darkening the eyelashes, eyebrows, etc. [It. *mascara, maschera* MASK[1]]
mă'scle (-skel) *n.* (Her.) Lozenge voided, with central lozenge-shaped aperture. [ME f. AF, f. AL *ma(s)cula* f. L MACULA]
mă'scŏn *n.* (Astron.) Concentration of dense matter with strong gravitational pull below moon's surface. [f. *mass concentration*]
mă'scŏt *n.* Person or animal or thing that is supposed to bring luck. [f. F *mascotte* f. mod. Prov. *mascotto* fem. dim. of *masco* witch]
mă'scŭline (*or* mah'-) *a.* & *n.* **1.** *a.* Of men; manly, vigorous; (of woman) having qualities appropriate to a man. **2.** (Gram.) Having gender proper to men's names. **3.** (Pros.) **~ rhyme** (between words ending in stressed syllables); **~ ending,** ending of line with stressed syllable. **4.** Hence **~LY**[2] (-nlĭ) *adv.*, **~NESS** (-n-n-), **măscŭlĭ'nITY** (*or* mah-), *ns.* **5.** *n.* Masculine gender or word. [ME, f. OF *masculin -ine* f. L *masculinus* (as MALE; see -INE[1])]
mā'ser (-z-) *n.* Device using stimulated emission of radiation by excited atoms etc. to amplify or generate highly monochromatic electromagnetic radiation, esp. microwaves; cf. LASER. [f. *m*icrowave *a*mplification by *s*timulated *e*mission of *r*adiation]
măsh[1] *n.* Malt mixed with hot water to form wort for brewing; mixture of boiled grain, bran, etc., given warm to horses etc.; soft pulp made by crushing, mixing with water, etc.; ||(sl.) mashed potatoes (*sausage and mash*); confused mixture; **~-tub** (in which malt is mashed). [OE *māsc* = MLG *mēsch*, MHG *meisch* crushed grapes, f. WG **maisk-*, perh. cogn. w. MIX]
măsh[2] *v.t.* Mix (malt) with hot water to form wort; crush or pound to a pulp; reduce (potatoes etc.) to uniform mass by crushing. [ME, f. prec.]
măsh[3] *v.t.*, & *n.* (arch. sl.) **1.** *v.t.* Excite sentimental admiration in (person of opposite sex); **be ~ed on,** have such admiration for; so **~'ER**[1] *n.*, man who poses as dashing beau. **2.** *n.* Person thus admired; such admiration. [back form. f. *masher*, prob. f. prec.]
mă'shie *n.* (Golf). Iron used for lofting or for medium distances; **~ niblick,** club intermediate between mashie and niblick. [perh. f. F *massue* club]
mask[1] (mah-) *n.* Covering, usu. of velvet or silk, for concealing face at balls etc., or of wire, gauze, etc., for protection e.g. of fencer, or worn by surgeon to prevent infection of patient, etc., or of any material as disguise; respirator used to filter inhaled air or to supply gas for inhalation; hollow figure of human head worn by ancient Greek and Roman actors; likeness of person's face, esp. one made by taking mould from face (DEATH-*mask*); (fig.) disguise (*throw off the mask*); (arch.) masked person; (Photog.) screen used to exclude part of image; face or head of fox; = PACK[1] 10 for face. [f. F *masque* f. It. *maschera* f. Arab. *maskara* buffoon (*sakira* to ridicule)]
mask[2] (mah-) *v.t.* **1.** Cover (face etc.) with mask; (in *pass.*) be disguised with mask. **2.** (Mil.) Conceal (battery etc.) from enemy's view, hinder (army etc.) from action by watching with adequate force, hinder (friendly force) by standing in its line of fire. **3.** Disguise, conceal, (taste, one's feelings, etc.); protect from some process. **4. ~ed ball** (at which masks are worn). [f. prec.]
ma'sker, ma'squer, (mah'sk-) *n.* One who takes part in masquerade or masque. [f. prec. + -ER[1]]
măskĭnŏ'nge (-nj *or* -njĭ) *n.* Large N. Amer. pike esp. in Great Lakes. [ult. f. Ojibwa, = great fish]
mă'soch|ism (-k-; *or* -zo-) *n.* Form of (esp. sexual) perversion in which person derives pleasure from his own pain or humiliation (opp. SADISM); (colloq.) enjoyment of what appears to be painful or tiresome; so **~IST** (2) *n.*, **~ĭ'stIC** *a.* [f. L. von Sacher-*Masoch*, Austrian novelist d. 1895, who described a case of it, + -ISM]
mā'son *n.*, & *v.t.* **1.** *n.* One who builds with stone; **~'s mark,** device carved on stone by mason who dressed it. **2.** (*M~*). Freemason; hence **Masŏ'nIC** *a.* **3.** *v.t.* Build or strengthen with masonry. [ME, f. OF (*maçonner* v. f.) *masson*, ONF *machun*, f. Rom. **matio*, **macio, -onis*, prob. f. Gmc **mattjon*]
Māson-Dĭ'xon *a.* **~ line,** boundary between Maryland and Pennsylvania, taken as northern limit of slave-owning states before abolition of slavery in U.S. [f. C. *Mason* & J. *Dixon*, 18th-c. Engl. astronomers who partly surveyed it]
mā'sonry̆ *n.* **1.** Mason's work, stonework. **2.** (*M~*). Freemasonry. [ME, f. OF *maçonerie* (as MASON; see -ERY)]
Mă'sorah (-*a*) *n.* Body of traditional information and comment on text of Hebrew Bible. [f. Heb. *māsōreṯ*, perh. = bond]
Mă'sor|ēte *n.* Jewish scholar contributing to the Masorah; hence **~E'TIC** *a.* [f. F *Massoret* & mod. L *Massoreta*, orig. misuse of Heb. (see prec.), assim. to -ETE]
masque (mahsk) *n.* Amateur dramatic and musical entertainment esp. in 16th–17th c., orig. in dumb show, later with metrical dialogue; dramatic composition for this. [var. of MASK[1]]
masquer. See MASKER.
măsquerā'de[1] (-sk-; *or* mah-) *n.* Masked ball; false show, pretence. [f. Sp. *mascarada* (*máscara* mask; see -ADE)]

măsquerā'de² (-sk-; *or* mah-) *v.i.* Appear in disguise, assume false appearance, (*as*). [f. prec.]

măss¹ (*or* mahs) *n.* (A) celebration (usu. R.C.) of the Eucharist (*mass was said*; *we attend, go to, hear, mass*; *masses were said for his soul*); liturgy used in this; musical setting of parts of this; **high ~** (with incense, music, and assistance of deacon and subdeacon); **low ~** (with no music and minimum of ceremony). [OE *mæsse* f. eccl. L *missa*, f. L *mittere miss-* dismiss, perh. f. concluding dimissory words *Ite, missa est*]

măss² *n.* & *v.* **1.** *n.* Coherent body of matter of indefinite shape; dense aggregation of objects (*a mass of fibres*); (in *sing.* or *pl.*) large number or amount (*of*); a main portion (of a painting etc.) as perceived by the eye; unbroken expanse (*of* colour etc.); **a ~ of,** full of or covered with (mistakes, bruises, etc.); **the (great) ~,** the majority (*of*); **the ~es,** the ordinary people; **in the ~,** in the aggregate. **2.** (Phys.) quantity of matter a body contains, as measured by its acceleration under a given force, or by the changes in velocity when it strikes a given body; **centre of ~,** point representing mean position of matter in a body or system. **3.** (*attrib.*) Relating to large numbers of persons or things, large-scale, (*mass audience, murder, -produced*); **~ action,** action by large numbers (*law of ~ action*, Chem. law that reaction rate is proportional to concentration of reacting substances); **~ defect,** (Phys.) difference between mass and mass number of isotope; *mass* ENERGY; **~ grave** (in which many persons are buried at same time); **~ hysteria** (affecting many persons at same time); **~ of manœuvre,** body of troops kept free to meet strategic needs; **~ media,** means of communication (e.g. newspapers or broadcasting) to large numbers of people; **~ medication,** administration of medicinal substance to many persons at once, e.g. through water supply; **~ meeting,** large assembly of people to express political etc. views; **~ number,** (Phys.) total number of protons and neutrons in atomic nucleus; ‖**~ observation,** study and recording of social habits and opinions of ordinary people; **~ production** (of large quantities of a standardized article by standardized mechanical processes); **~ radiography,** quick routine radiographic examination of the chests of large numbers of people; **~ spectrograph,** apparatus separating isotopes according to mass by passage in ionic form through electric and magnetic fields, and detecting them photographically; **~ spectrometer,** similar device with electrical detection; **~ spectrum,** distribution of isotopes shown by these instruments; **~ transport,** public transport as opp. private cars etc. **4.** Hence **~'**LESS *a.* **5.** *v.t.* & *i.* Gather into mass; (Mil.) concentrate (troops). [ME; (v. f. OF *masser*) f. OF *masse* f. L *massa* f. Gk *maza* barley-cake (perh. rel. to *massō* knead)]

Mass. *abbr.* Massachusetts.

mă'ssacre (-ker) *n.*, & *v.t.* **1.** *n.* General slaughter, carnage, (of persons, occas. of animals); utter defeat or destruction. **2.** *v.t.* Make a massacre of; murder cruelly or violently (a number of persons). [(v. f. F *massacrer* f.) F *massacre*; in OF *maçacre*, shambles, butchery; orig. unkn.]

mă'ssage (-ahzh) *n.*, & *v.t.* **1.** *n.* Rubbing, kneading, etc., of muscles and joints of the body with the hands, to stimulate their action, cure strains, etc. **2.** *v.t.* Treat (part, person) thus. [F (*masser* treat with massage, perh. f. Port. *amassar* knead, f. *massa* dough; see MASS², -AGE)]

mă'ssé (mă'sā) *n.* (Bill.) Stroke made with cue held vertical. [F, p.p. of *masser* make such stroke (as MACE¹)]

măssē'ter *n.* One of two chewing-muscles from temporal bone to lower jaw. [f. Gk *masētēr* (*masaomai* chew)]

măsseu|r' (-ēr') *n.* (*fem.* **~se** *pr.* -ēr'z). One who provides massage professionally. [F (*masser*; see MASSAGE)]

mă'ssĭcŏt *n.* Yellow lead monoxide, used as pigment. [F, perh. rel. to It. *marzacotto* unguent prob. f. Arab. *mashaḳūnyā*]

mă'ssif (-ēf; *or* -ē'f) *n.* Mountain heights forming a compact group. [F adj. (see foll.) as n.]

mă'ssĭve *a.* **1.** Large and heavy or solid; (of features, head, etc.) relatively large, of solid build; (Min.) not definitely crystalline; (Geol.) without structural divisions. **2.** (fig.) Solid, substantial; impressive, imposing; unusually large. **3.** Hence **~**LY² (-vlĭ) *adv.*, **~**NESS (-vn-) *n.* [ME f. F *massif -ive* f. OF *massiz* (see MASSY, -IVE)]

Massorah, Massorete, etc. Vars. of MASORAH etc.

mă'ss|y̆ *a.* (arch. or rhet.) Solid; weighty; hence **~ĭness** *n.* [ME, perh. f. OF *massiz* f. pop. L **massiceus* f. L *massa* MASS²; see -Y²]

mast¹ (mah-) *n.*, & *v.t.* **1.** *n.* Long pole of timber, iron, etc., set up on ship's keel to support sails; flag-pole; **before the ~,** serving as ordinary seaman (quartered in forecastle); HALF-*mast* (*high*); hence (of ship) **-~'**ED² *a.*, **-~'**ER¹ *n.* **2. ~-head,** (1) highest part of mast, esp. of lower mast as place of observation or punishment, (2) title etc. of newspaper etc. at head of front or editorial page, (3, *v.t.*) send (sailor) to mast-head, raise (sail) to position on mast. **3.** Post, or lattice-work upright, for supporting a radio or television aerial; **(mooring-)~,** strong steel tower to top of which an airship can be moored. **4.** *v.t.* Furnish with masts. [OE *mæst*, = OHG *mast* f. WG **masta* f. IE **mazdos*]

mast² (mah-) *n.* Fruit of beech, oak, chestnut, and other forest-trees, esp. as food for pigs. [OE *mæst*, = MDu., OHG *mast*, WG **masta* f. IE **mazdos*, prob. cogn. w. MEAT]

mă'staba *n.* **1.** (Archaeol.) Ancient Egyptian tomb with sloping sides and flat roof. **2.** Stone etc. bench attached to house in Islamic countries. [f. Arab. *masṭabah*]

măstĕ'ctomy̆ *n.* (Surg.) Excision or amputation of a breast. [f. Gk *mastos* breast + -ECTOMY]

ma'ster¹ (mah'-) *n.* & *a.* **1.** *n.* Person having control; (Naut.) captain of merchant vessel (*master* MARINER); employer; owner of dog, horse, etc.; owner of slave; person in control of pack (*of foxhounds* etc.); male head of household (*master of the house*); (*M~*) courtesy title of eldest son of Sc. viscount or baron (*the Master of Falkland*); **be ~ of,** have at one's disposal, know how to control; **be** one's **own ~,** be independent or free to do as one wishes; **make oneself ~ of,** acquire thorough knowledge of or facility in using. **2.** One who has or gets the upper hand (*we will see which of us is master*). **3.** Male teacher or tutor, esp. SCHOOL¹*master*; revered teacher in philosophy etc.; holder of university degree orig. giving him authority to teach in university (*Master of Arts* etc.); **the M~,** Christ. **4.** Skilled workman, or one in business on his own account, (*master carpenter, mason*). **5.** Great artist (LITTLE *Masters*; OLD *master*); picture etc. by a master; (Chess etc.) player of proved ability at international level. **6.** Head of college, school, etc.; presiding officer of livery company, Masonic lodge, etc. **7.** Thing from which series of copies (of film, gramophone record, etc.) is made. **8.** Part of machine directly controlling another (cf. SLAVE). **9.** (As title of functionaries) *Master of Ceremonies* (see CEREMONY); **M~ in Chancery,** chief clerk of Chancery Division; **M~ of the Horse,** third official in English royal household; ||*Master in* LUNACY; *Master of* MISRULE; **M~** (organizer, leader, esp. in Royal Household and Inns of Court) **of the Revels**; ||*Master of the* ROLL[1]*s*. **10.** (Prefixed, esp. by servants and in address of letter, to name of boy or young man not old enough for *Mr.*) *Master Tom, Master* (*Tom or T.*) *Jones*; (arch. as title of man of high rank, learning, etc.). **11. ~-at-arms,** chief police officer on man-of-war or merchant ship; *Master* GUNNER; **~-hand,** (action of) person having commanding power or great skill; **~-key** (opening many locks, each also opened by separate key); **~ mason,** (1) (see sense 4), (2) fully qualified Freemason, who has passed third degree; **~-mind,** (*n.*) (possessor of) outstanding intellect, person directing an enterprise, (*v.t.*) plan and direct (an enterprise); **~piece,** consummate piece of workmanship, one's best work; **~singer,** = MEISTERSINGER; **~-stroke,** surpassingly skilful act (of policy etc.); **~-switch,** switch controlling electricity etc. supply to an entire system; **~ touch,** masterly manner of dealing with something. **12.** Hence ~DOM, ~HOOD, *ns.*, ~LESS *a.* **13.** *a.* Commanding, superior, (*a master spirit*); main, principal, (*master bedroom*); controlling others (*master plan*). [OE *mægester* (later also f. OF *maistre*) f. L *magister*, prob. cogn. w. *magis* more]

ma'ster² (mah'-) *v.t.* Overcome, defeat; reduce to subjection; acquire complete knowledge of (subject) or facility in using (instrument etc.); rule as a master. [ME, f. prec.]

ma'sterful (mah'-) *a.* Self-willed, imperious; masterly; hence ~LY² *adv.*, ~NESS *n.* [ME, f. MASTER¹ + -FUL]

ma'sterl|ў (mah'-) *a.* Worthy of a master, very skilful; hence ~ĭNESS *n.* [f. MASTER¹ + -LY¹]

ma'stershĭp (mah'-) *n.* Dominion, control; office or function of (esp. school)master. [ME, f. MASTER¹ + -SHIP]

ma'sterў (mah'-) *n.* Sway, dominion; *the* upper hand; masterly skill; masterly use or knowledge (*of* instrument, subject). [ME, f. OF *maistrie* (as MASTER¹; see -Y¹)]

mă'stĭc *n.* Gum or resin exuding from bark of certain trees (esp. *Pistacia lentiscus*), used in making varnish; ~ **(tree)**, tree yielding this; type of cement esp. made with asphalt; liquor flavoured with mastic gum, made in Turkey and Greece. [ME f. OF, f. LL *mastichum* f. L f. Gk *mastikhē*, perh. f. *mastikhaō* (w. ref. to its use as chewing-gum; see foll.)]

mă'stĭc|āte *v.t.* Grind (food) with teeth, chew; hence or cogn. ~A'TION, ~ātOR, *ns.* ~ātORY *a.* [f. LL *masticare* f. Gk *mastikhaō* gnash the teeth + -ATE³]

ma'stiff (mah'-) *n.* Large strong dog with drooping ears and pendulous lips. [ME, ult. f. OF *mastin* f. Rom. **mansuetinus* f. L *mansuetus* tame; see MANSUETUDE]

măsti'tĭs *n.* Inflammation of mammary gland (breast or udder). [f. Gk *mastos* breast + -ITIS]

mă'stodŏn *n.* Large extinct mammal of genus *Mammut*, like elephant, with nipple-shaped tubercles on crowns of molar teeth; hence **măstodŏ'ntIC** *a.* [mod. L, f. Gk *mastos* breast + *odous odontos* tooth]

mă'stoid *a.* & *n.* (Anat.) **1.** *a.* Shaped like woman's breast; **~ process,** conical prominence on temporal bone behind ear, to which muscles are attached. **2.** *n.* Mastoid process; (colloq.) mastoiditis; hence ~I'TIS *n.*, inflammation of mastoid process. [f. F *mastoïde* or mod. L *mastoides* f. Gk *mastoeidēs* (*mastos* breast; see -OID)]

mă'sturb|āte *v.i.* & *t.* Produce sexual orgasm (of) by manual stimulation of genitals etc., not by sexual intercourse; so ~A'TION *n.*, ~ātORY *a.* [f. L *masturbari* + -ATE³]

măt¹ *n.* Piece of coarse fabric of plaited rushes, straw, etc., for lying upon, packing furniture, etc.; piece of this or other material for wiping shoes upon, esp. door-mat; piece of cork, rubber, plastic, etc., to protect surface from heat or moisture of object placed on it; small rug; piece of resilient material to protect falling jumper, wrestler, etc.; **on the ~,** (sl.) in trouble (orig. in army, on the orderly-room mat before the C.O.). [OE *m(e)att(e)*, = OHG *matta* f. WG f. LL *matta*]

măt² *v.* (**-tt-**). **1.** *v.t.* Cover or furnish with mats; entangle (*together*) in thick mass (esp. in *p.p.*; *matted hair*). **2.** *v.i.* Become matted. [f. prec.]

măt³. See MATT.

mă'tadōr *n.* Man appointed to kill bull in bullfight; a principal card in ombre, quadrille, etc.; domino game in which piece played must make total of seven. [Sp. (*matar* kill f. Pers. *māt* dead)]

mătch¹ *n.* **1.** Person able to contend with another as an equal (*find, meet,* one's *match*; *be* (*more than*) *a match for*); person equal to another in some quality (*we shall never see his match*); person or thing exactly like or corresponding to another. **2.** Contest of skill etc. in which persons or teams strive against each other. **3.** Matrimonial alliance; **make a ~,** bring this about. **4.** Person viewed in regard to his or her eligibility for marriage, esp. as to rank or fortune, (*he is an excellent match*). **5. ~'board,** one with tongue cut along one edge and groove along another, so as to fit with similar boards; **~'maker,** person fond of scheming to bring about marriages; **~ play,** (Golf) play in which the score is reckoned by counting the holes won by each side, opp. *medal play*; **~ point,** state of a game when one side needs only one more point to win the match, this point, (Bridge) unit of scoring in matches and tournaments. [OE *gemæcca* mate, companion, f. Gmc **gamakjon* fit, suitable; cf. MAKE¹]

mătch² *v.* **1.** *v.t.* (arch.) Join (person *with* another) in marriage. **2.** Prove to be a match for; place (person etc.) in conflict or contest *against* another (**well ~ed,** fit to contend with each other, live together, etc., on equal terms); place (person, thing) in competition *with*. **3.** *v.t.* & *i.* Be equal, correspond in quantity, quality, colour, etc., to or *with* (thing etc., or abs.; *the carpets match the wallpaper*; *these ribbons do not match, do not match* (*with*) *your hat*; *trimmed with velvet to match*); find material etc. that matches with (another; *can you match this silk?*); find person or thing suitable for another (*matching unemployed workers with vacant posts*); **to ~,** (fig.) corresponding in quality, number, etc., with what has been mentioned. **4.** (Electr.) Produce or have adjustment of (circuits) such that maximum power is transmitted between them. **5.** Hence ~'ABLE *a.* [ME, f. prec.]

mă'tch³ *n.* Short piece of wood (**~'stick**), wax, etc., tipped with composition that bursts into flame when rubbed on rough or **(safety ~)** specially prepared surface; piece of wick, cord, etc., designed to burn at uniform rate, for firing cannon etc.; **~'box** (for holding matches); **~'lock,** (gun with) lock in which match is placed for igniting powder; **~'wood,** wood suitable for matches, minute splinters, (*make*

~*wood of*, utterly smash). [ME, f. OF *mesche, meiche*, perh. f. L *myxa* lamp-nozzle]

mă'tchĕt. See MACHETE.

mă'tchlĕss *a.* Without an equal, peerless; hence ~LY² *adv.* [f. MATCH¹ + -LESS]

māte¹ *n.*, & *v.t.* (Chess) = CHECKMATE; **fool's ~** (in which first player is mated at opponent's second move); **scholar's ~** (in which second player is mated at opponent's fourth move); **self-~, sui-~,** (in which player forces opponent to mate him); SMOTHER*ed mate*; STALEMATE. [ME, f. F *mat(er)*; see CHECKMATE]

māte² *n.* **1.** Companion, fellow worker; (as general colloq. form of address among equals, esp. sailors or labourers). **2.** One of a pair, esp. of birds; fitting partner in marriage; (in *comb.*) fellow member or joint occupant of (*team-mate, room-mate*). **3.** (Naut.) Officer on merchant ship who sees to execution of master's commands and takes command in his absence. **4.** Assistant to a worker (*cook's, plumber's, surgeon's, mate*). **5.** Hence ~'LESS (-tl-) *a.* [ME, f. MLG *mate* (*gemate* f. WG **gamato* messmate f. **ga-* Y-, **mat* MEAT)]

māte³ *v.t.* & *i.* Join (two persons, one *with* another) in marriage; marry (*with*, or abs.); come or bring together for breeding (of animals); pair (birds), (of birds) pair; keep company, (Mech.) fit well, (*with*). [f. prec.]

mă'té (-ā) *n.* (Vessel for) infusion of leaves of a S. Amer. shrub (*Ilex paraguayensis*); the shrub, or its leaves. [f. Sp. *mate* f. Quechua *mati*]

‖**mă'telōt,** ‖**mă'tlo(w),** (mă'tlō) *n.* (sl.) Sailor. [F *matelot*]

matelote (mă'telōt) *n.* Dish of fish etc. with sauce of wine, onions, etc. [F, f. as prec.]

mā'ter *n.* ‖(sl.) Mother; DURA MATER, PIA MATER; **~fami'lias,** woman head of family or household (cf. PATERFAMILIAS). [L]

matēr'ĭal *a.* & *n.* **1.** *a.* Concerned with the matter, not the form, of reasoning; of matter, corporeal; **~ theory of heat** (that it is a material substance). **2.** (Of conduct, point of view, etc.) not spiritual; concerned with bodily comfort etc. (*material well-being*). **3.** Important, essential, (*to*, or abs.; *at the material time*). **4.** Hence ~ITY (-ă'l-) *n.*, ~LY² *adv.* **5.** *n.* Matter from which thing is made (RAW *material*); (in *sing.* or *pl.*) elements, constituent parts, (*of* substance, *for* historical composition etc.); cloth, fabric; (in *pl.*) things needed for an activity (*building, cleaning, writing, materials*); person(s) or thing(s) suitable to receive a given training, got from a specified source, etc. (*academic, experimental, material*). [ME, f. OF *materiel, -al*, f. LL *materialis* f. L (as MATTER¹; see -AL)]

matēr'ĭal|ĭsm *n.* Opinion that nothing exists but matter and its movements and modifications; doctrine that consciousness and will are wholly due to material agency; (Art) tendency to lay stress on material aspect of objects; tendency to prefer material possessions and physical comfort to spiritual values; so ~IST (2) *n.*, **~ĭ'stIC** *a.* [f. prec. + -ISM]

matēr'ĭalīz|e, -īs|e (-īz), *v.* **1.** *v.t.* Make, or represent as, material; make materialistic. **2.** *v.t.* & *i.* Cause (spirit) to appear, (of spirit) appear, in bodily form; make or become actual fact. **3.** Hence ~A'TION *n.* [f. MATERIAL + -IZE]

matēr'ĭa mĕ'dĭca *n.* (Science of origin and properties of) remedial substances used in practice of medicine. [mod. L, transl. Gk *hulē iatrikē* healing material]

matériel (matērĭĕ'l) *n.* Stock-in-trade, available means, esp. materials and equipment in warfare (opp. *personnel*). [F, adj. as n. (as MATERIAL)]

matēr'nal *a.* Of or like a mother; motherly; related through the mother (**~ uncle,** mother's brother); of the mother in pregnancy and childbirth; hence ~LY² *adv.* [ME, f. OF *maternel* or f. L *maternus* (*mater* mother); see -AL]

matēr'nĭtў *n.* Motherhood; motherliness; **~ home, hospital, nurse, ward,** (for women during and just after childbirth); **~ dress, wear,** (suitable for pregnant woman). [f. F *maternité* f. med. L *maternitas -tatis* f. L *maternus* (see prec., -ITY)]

mā't|ey, mā't|ў, *a.* (**~ier, ~iest**) & *n.* **1.** *a.* Sociable, familiar and friendly (*with*); hence ~eyNESS, ~ĭNESS, (-ĭn-) *n.* **2.** *n.* (esp. as colloq. *voc.*) ‖Mate, companion. [f. MATE² + -Y²˒³]

***măth** *n.* (colloq.) Mathematics. [abbr.]

măthėmă'tĭcal *a.* Of mathematics; (of proof etc.) rigorously precise; *mathematical* INDUCTION, TABLE*s*; hence ~LY² *adv.* [f. F *mathématique* or f. L f. Gk *mathēmatikos* (*mathēma -matos* science f. *manthanō*, root **math-*, learn; see -ICAL)]

măthėmă'tĭcs *n. pl.* (also treated as *sing.*) **(Pure) ~,** abstract science of space, number, and quantity; **(applied) ~,** this applied to branches of physics, astronomy, etc.; (as *pl.*) use of mathematics in calculation etc.; so **măthėmatĭ'**CIAN *n.* [prob. f. F *mathématiques* pl. f. L f. Gk *mathēmatika* (as prec.; see -ICS)]

‖**măths** *n.* (colloq.) Mathematics. [abbr.]

matĭ'cō (-tē'-) *n.* (*pl.* **~s**). Tropical Amer. wild pepper; its leaves used as styptic. [Sp., dim. of *Mateo* Matthew, said to be f. name of a soldier who discovered its properties]

Matĭ'lda *n.* (Austral.) Bushman's bundle, swag; **walk** or **waltz ~,** carry this. [f. woman's Christian name]

mă'tĭn *n.* **1.** (in *pl.*) Office of one of the canonical hours of prayer, prop. a night office, but also recited with lauds at daybreak or on previous evening. **2.** (in *pl.*) Morning prayer in Church of England. **3.** (poet.; in *sing.* or *pl.*) Morning song of birds. [ME f. OF *matines* f. eccl. L *matutinas*, acc. fem. pl. a. (as n.) f. L *matutinus* of the morning (*Matuta* dawn-goddess; see -INE¹)]

mă'tĭnée, *-nee, (-nā) *n.* Afternoon theatrical or musical performance; **~ coat,** baby's short coat; **~ idol,** handsome actor appealing to feminine playgoers etc. [F, = what occupies a morning (MATIN morning)]

‖**matlo(w).** See MATELOT.

mă'trass *n.* Long-necked glass vessel with round or oval body, used for distilling etc. [f. F *matras*, of uncert. orig.]

mā'trĭarch (-k) *n.* Woman corresponding in status to patriarch (usu. joc.); hence **mātrĭar'ch**AL (-k-) *a.* [f. L *mater* mother on false anal. of PATRIARCH]

mā'trĭarchў (-kĭ) *n.* Social organization in which mother is head of family and descent is reckoned through female line. [f. prec. after PATRIARCHY]

‖**matrĭ'c** *n.* (colloq.) Matriculation. [abbr.]

mā'trĭcīd|e *n.* One who kills his, killing of one's, mother; hence ~AL *a.* [f. L *matricida, matricidium* (*mater* mother; see -CIDE)]

matrĭ'cūl|āte *v.t.* & *i.* Admit (student) to membership of university; be thus admitted; hence ~A'TION *n.* (also as name of examination to qualify for this), **~ātORY** *a.* [f. med. L *matricculare* enrol f. LL *matricula* register, dim. of L MATRIX, + -ATE³]

mătrĭlĭ'nėal *a.* Of or based on (kinship with) the mother or the female line. [f. L *mater matris* mother + LINEAL]

mătrĭlō'cal *a.* Of system of marriage where husband goes to live with wife's group. [f. as prec. + LOCAL²]

mă'trĭmonў *n.* **1.** Rite of marriage; state of being married. **2.** A card-game; combination of king and queen of trumps in some card-games. **3.** So **mătrĭmō'ni**AL *a.* [ME, f. AF *matrimonie*, OF *matremoi(g)ne* f. L *matrimonium* (*mater matris* mother; see -MONY)]

mā'tr|ix *n.* (*pl.* **~ices** *pr.* -ĭsēz, *or* **~ixes**). **1.** Womb; place in which thing is developed; formative part of animal organ. **2.** Mass of rock etc. enclosing gems etc. **3.** (Biol.) Substance between cells. **4.** Mould in which printer's types, gramophone records, etc., are cast or shaped. **5.** (Math.) Rectangular array of quantities in rows and columns that is treated as a single quantity. [L, = breeding-female, womb, register (*mater matris* mother; cf. -TRIX)]

mā'tron *n.* **1.** Married woman, esp. one of dignity and sobriety; **~ of honour,** married woman attending bride at wedding; JURY *of matrons*. **2.** Woman managing domestic arrangements of school etc.; woman in charge of nurses in hospital. **3.** Hence ~AGE (1, 2), ~HOOD, ~SHIP, *ns.*, ~AL, ~LY[1] (esp. w. ref. to staidness or portliness), *adjs.* [ME, f. OF *matrone* f. L *matrona* (*mater matris* mother)]

mătt, măt[3]**,** *a.*, *n.*, & *v.t.* (**-tt-**). **1.** *a.* (Of colour, surface, etc.) dull, without lustre. **2.** *n.* Border of dull gold round framed picture; appearance of unburnished gold. **3.** *v.t.* Make (gilding etc.) dull; frost (glass). [(v. f. F *mater*) f. F *mat* n. & a., identical w. *mat* MATE[1]; see CHECKMATE]

Matt. *abbr.* Matthew (also in N.T.).

mă'ttamōre *n.* Subterranean dwelling or storehouse. [f. F *matamore* f. Arab. *maṭmūra* (*ṭamara* bury)]

mătte *n.* Impure product of smelting of sulphide ores, esp. those of copper or nickel. [F]

mă'tter[1] *n.* **1.** That which has mass and occupies space; physical substance in general, as opp. to *spirit, mind*, etc. **2.** (Physiol.) Substance in or from the body (*faecal matter*; GREY, WHITE[1], *matter*); purulent discharge. **3.** (Logic). Particular content of proposition, distinguished from its form. **4.** Material for thought or expression; substance of book, speech, etc., (often opp. to *manner* or *form*). **5.** What is or may be a good reason (*of* or *for* complaint, regret, etc.). **6.** Thing(s) esp. of specified kind (*postal, printed, reading, matter*); (Print.) body of a printed work, as type or as printed sheets; **no ~**, it is of no importance (*when, how*, etc., or abs.; *will do it no matter what the consequences*); **what ~?,** that need not disquiet us. **7.** Affair, thing to be done or considered, esp. of specified kind (*a* HANGING[1] *matter*; *no* LAUGHING[1] *matter*; *money matters*); **a ~ of,** thing that pertains to or depends (solely) on (*a matter of common knowledge*; *it is only a matter of time before he gives in*; *that is a matter of habit*), approximately (*for a matter of 40 years*); *a matter of* COURSE[1]; **a ~ of fact,** what pertains to the sphere of fact (opp. to *opinion* etc.), esp. *as a matter of fact* (often in correcting another's misunderstanding), (Law) part of judicial inquiry concerned with truth of alleged facts (opp. to **~ of law**); *~-of-fact* a., unimaginative, prosaic; *a matter of* FORM[1], *of* RECORD[2]; **the ~,** thing that is amiss (*with*; *something is the matter, there is something the matter, with him* etc.); **what is the ~ with,** surely there is no objection to; **for that ~, for the ~ of that,** (1) so far as that is concerned, (2) and indeed also (something further); **in the ~ of,** as regards. [ME f. AF *mater(i)e*, OF *matiere* f. L *materia* timber, substance, subject of discourse]

mă'tter[2] *v.i.* **1.** Be of importance, signify, (*to* person etc.; *it matters how, when*, etc.; esp. w. neg.). **2.** Secrete or discharge pus. [f. prec.]

mă'tterÿ *a.* Purulent, festering. [ME, f. MATTER[1] + -Y[2]]

Mă'tthew (-thū) *n.* **~ principle,** 'unto every one that hath shall be given' (Matt. 25:29). [f. St. ~, traditional author of 1st Gospel]

mă'ttĭng *n.* In vbl senses; fabric of hemp, bast, grass, etc., for mats (*coconut matting*). [f. MAT[1,2] + -ING[1]]

||**mattins.** Var. of MATIN (sense 2).

mă'ttock *n.* Agricultural tool of PICK[1] shape, with an adze and a chisel edge as ends of head. [OE *mattuc*, of unkn. orig.]

mă'ttoid *n.* Person of erratic mind, mixture of genius and fool. [f. It. *mattoide* (*matto* insane; see -OID)]

mă'ttrĕss *n.* Canvas case stuffed with hair, straw, feathers, foam rubber, etc., as bed or support for bed; SPRING[2], WIRE, *mattress*. [ME f. OF *materas* f. It. *materasso* f. Arab. *almaṭraḥ* the place, the cushion (*ṭaraḥa* throw)]

mă'tūrāte *v.i.* (Med.) (Of boil etc.) come to maturation. [f. L (as MATURE[2]) + -ATE[3]]

mătūrā'tion *n.* **1.** (Med.) Formation of purulent matter; causing of this, whence **matūr'at**IVE *a.* **2.** Ripening of fruit; maturing, development. [ME f. F, or f. med. L *maturatio* f. L (as MATURE[2]; see -ATION)]

matūr'e[1] *a.* (**~r, ~st**). Complete in natural development, ripe; with fully developed powers of body and mind, adult; (of thought, intentions, etc.) duly careful and adequate; (of bill etc.) due for payment; hence or cogn. ~LY[2] (-ūr'lĭ) *adv.*, ~NESS (-ūr'n-), **matūr'**ITY, *ns.* [ME, f. L *maturus* timely, early]

matūr'e[2] *v.t.* & *i.* Develop fully; ripen; perfect (plan etc.); come to maturity; (of bill etc.) become due for payment. [ME, f. L *maturare* (as prec.)]

mătūtī'nal (*or* matū'tĭnal) *a.* Of, or occurring in, the morning; early. [f. LL *matutinalis* f. L *matutinus* (see MATIN)]

mā'tÿ. See MATEY.

ma'tzō (mah'tsō) *n.* (*pl.* **~s,** *or* **~th** *pr.* -t). Unleavened bread for Passover. [Yiddish, f. Heb. *maṣṣāh*]

maud *n.* Scots shepherd's grey striped plaid; travelling-rug like this. [18th c.; orig. unkn.]

mau'dlĭn *a.* & *n.* **1.** *a.* Weakly or tearfully sentimental, esp. of tearful and effusive stage of drunkenness. **2.** *n.* Weak or mawkish sentiment. [a. f. n. (w. ref. to pictures of weeping Mary Magdalen), ME f. OF *Madeleine* f. eccl. L *Magdalena* MAGDALEN]

mau'gre (-ger) *prep.* (arch.) In spite of. [ME, = ill will, f. OF *maugré* (*mal* bad f. L *malus*, *gré* pleasure f. L *gratus* pleasing)]

maul[1] *n.* Special heavy hammer, commonly of wood, esp. for driving piles. [ME, f. OF *mail* f. L *malleus* hammer]

maul[2] *v.t.*, & *n.* **1.** *v.t.* Beat and bruise; handle (thing, subject, quotation) roughly or carelessly; damage by criticism. **2.** *n.* Brawl; (Rugby Footb.) loose scrum. [ME, f. prec.]

mau'lstĭck, mah'lstĭck, *n.* Light stick held by (right-handed) painter in left hand as support for right, with padded leather ball at one end. [f. Du. *maalstok* (*malen* to paint, *stok* stick)]

mau'nder *v.i.* Move or act listlessly or idly; talk in dreamy or rambling manner. [perh. f. obs. *maunder* beggar, to beg]

Mau'ndÿ *n.* **1.** ||Distribution of **~ money** (specially minted silver coins) by the Queen to the poor on **~ Thursday** (next before Easter). **2.** (R.C. Ch.) Ceremony of washing the feet of poor people (John 13:14). [ME, f. OF *mandé* f. L *mandatum* MANDATE[1], commandment (John 13:34)]

Mau'rĭst (mō'-) *n.* Member of congregation of French Benedictine monks founded 1618 famous for scholarship and literary industry.

[f. St. *Maur*, disciple of St. Benedict d. 584 + -IST]

Maurĭ'tian (merĭ'shan) *a.* & *n.* (Native or inhabitant) of Mauritius. [f. *Mauritius*, island in Ind. Ocean + -AN]

mausolē'um *n.* Magnificent tomb, orig. that of *Mausolus* king of Caria erected at his order by his queen Artemisia in 4th c. B.C. [L, f. Gk *Mausōleion* (*Mausōlos* Mausolus)]

mauvaise honte (mōvāzaw'ṅt) *n.* Unjustified shame; painful diffidence. [F, = ill shame]

mauvais quart d'heure (mōvā kārdẽr') *n.* Short but unpleasant experience, interview, etc. [F, = bad quarter of an hour]

mauve (mōv) *n.* & *a.* **1.** *n.* Bright but delicate pale purple dye from coal-tar aniline. **2.** *a.* Of the colour of this. [F, lit. = mallow, f. L *malva*]

mă'verĭck *n.* Unbranded calf or yearling; unorthodox or undisciplined person. [f. S. A. *Maverick*, Texas engineer who owned but did not brand cattle *c.* 1850]

mā'vĭs *n.* (poet. or dial.) Song-THRUSH[1]. [ME, f. OF *mauvis*, of uncert. orig.]

mavour'neen (-oor'-) *n.* & *int.* My darling. [f. Ir. *mo mhuirnín* (*mo* my, *muirnín* dim. of *muirn* love; see -EEN)]

maw *n.* Stomach of animal or (joc.) person, esp. last of ruminant's four stomachs; **~'worm,** intestinal worm. [OE *maga*, = MDu. *maghe*, OHG *mago*, ON *magi* f. Gmc **magon*]

maw'kĭsh *a.* Of faint sickly flavour; feebly or falsely sentimental; hence ~LY[2] *adv.*, ~NESS *n.* [f. obs. *mawk* maggot f. ON *mathkr* f. Gmc **mathon*, + -ISH[1]]

mawl. Var. of MAUL[1].

max. *abbr.* maximum.

mă'xĭ *n.* (colloq.) Maxi-coat, -skirt, etc. [abbr.]

mă'xĭ- *comb. form.* Very large or long (*maxi-coat*). [abbr. of MAXIMUM; cf. MINI-]

măxĭ'll|a *n.* (*pl.* **~ae**). Jaw(bone), esp. upper jaw in most vertebrates; masticatory mouth-part of many arthropods; hence ~ARY[1] (*or* mă'-) *a.* [L, = jaw]

mă'xĭm[1] *n.* A general truth drawn from science or experience; principle, rule of conduct. [ME, f. F. *maxime* or f. med. L *maxima* (*propositio*), fem. a. (as MAXIMUM)]

Mă'xĭm[2] *n.* Single-barrelled quick-firing machine-gun, with water round barrel to keep parts cool. [f. Sir H. S. ~, its Amer.-born inventor d. 1916]

mă'xĭmal *a.* Being or relating to a maximum; greatest possible in size, duration, etc.; hence ~LY[2] *adv.* [f. MAXIMUM + -AL]

mă'xĭmalist *n.* Person who holds out for the maximum of his demands and rejects compromises. [f. as prec. + -IST, orig. as transl. of Russ. (see BOLSHEVIK)]

mă'xĭmiz|e, -is|e (-iz), *v.t.* Increase or enhance to the utmost; hence ~A'TION *n.* [f. L *maximus* (see foll.) + -IZE]

mă'xĭmum *n.* (*pl.* **ma'xima**) & *a.* Highest (amount) possible, attained or attainable, usual, etc., (*reaches a, its, the maximum at noon*); **~ price** (that may not by law etc. be exceeded); **~ thermometer** (automatically recording highest temperature within given period); **~ and minimum thermometer** (combining this and MINIMUM thermometer). [mod. L, neut. (as n.) of L *maximus* superl. of *magnus* great]

mă'xwĕll *n.* Unit of magnetic flux, corresponding to field of one gauss. [f. J. C. *Maxwell*, Brit. physicist d. 1879]

may[1] *v. aux.* (*pres.* **may** exc. 2 *sing.* (arch.) **mayst** or **may'est,** *neg.* **may not,** (colloq.) **mayn't**; *past* **might** *pr.* mīt exc. 2 *sing.* (arch.) **mi'ghtest,** *neg.* **might not,** (colloq.) **mightn't** *pr.* mī'tent; no other parts used). **1.** Expr. possibility (*it may be true*, opp. *it cannot be true*; *it may not be true*, opp. *it must be true*; *it may or may not be true*; *you may* (WELL[3]) *walk ten miles without seeing one*); *he* ~ or **might** (= will perhaps) *lose his way*; *I* ~ **have** *been* (= was perhaps) *wrong*; *I was afraid he* **might** (= would perhaps) *lose his way*; *afraid he* **might have** (= had perhaps) *lost it*; *we* ~ or **might as well** *go* (as not); **that is as ~ be,** the truth of that is not yet determined; **be that as it ~,** irrespective of the situation regarding that. **2.** Expr. permission (*you may go*, opp. *you may not* or *must not* or *cannot go*; *I wish I might*); **you might** (= I request you to) *call at the baker's*; **you** etc. **might** (= you etc. ought to, yet do not) *offer to help*; **you** etc. **might** (= you etc. ought to) *have offered*; (iron.) *who are you, may* or *might I ask?* **3.** (In purpose-clauses, and after *wish*, *fear*, etc.) *take, took, such a course as may, might, avert the danger*; *I hope he may, hoped he might, succeed.* **4.** (Expr. wish) *may you live to repent it!*; *may the best man win!*; *may it please your ladyship.* **5.** (In questions, emphasizing uncertainty) *who may* or *might you be?*. **6. Might-have-been,** a past possibility, a person who might have been more eminent. [OE (1 sing.) *mæg*, of preterite-present form; OS, OHG, Goth. *mag*, ON *má*, f. Gmc **mag-* be strong f. IE **mogh-*, **megh-*; cf. MAIN[2], MIGHT[1]]

may[2] *n.* (poet.) Maiden. [ME, perh. f. ON *mær*, Goth. *mawi* f. Gmc **maujō*]

May[3] *n.* **1.** Fifth month of year; (poet.) bloom, prime; **Queen of the ~,** girl chosen to be queen of games on May Day. **2.** (*may*). Hawthorn (blossom). **3.** ||(Camb. Univ.; in *pl.*) Examinations held in May; boat-races held during ~ **Week** (late in May or early in June). **4. ~-apple,** Amer. herb bearing yellow egg-shaped fruit in May; **~-bug,** cockchafer; ~ **Day,** 1 May esp. as festival with dancing, or as international holiday in honour of workers; **~'day,** international radio distress-signal [repr. pr. of F *m'aider* help me]; ||**~'fair,** opulent district in West End of London [named from fair formerly held there in May]; **~'flower,** any flower that blooms in May; **may'fly,** insect of order Ephemeroptera, living briefly in spring; **may'pole,** pole painted and decked with flowers and ribbons, for dancing round on May Day; ~ **queen,** Queen of the May. [ME, f. OF *mai* f. L *Maius* (*mensis* month) of the goddess *Maia*]

ma'ya[1] (mah'-) *n.* (Hindu Philos.) Illusion, esp. the material world regarded as unreal. [f. Skr. *māyā*]

Ma'y|a[2] (mah'-) *n.* Member or language of an Amer. Ind. people of Guatemala and Mexico until 15th c.; hence ~AN *a.* [native name]

may'bē (*or* -bĭ), (arch.) **mayhă'p,** *advs.* Perhaps, possibly. [ME, f. *it may be, it may hap*]

may'hĕm *n.* **1.** (Hist.) Crime of maiming person so as to render him partly or wholly defenceless. **2.** (fig.) Violent and damaging action. [f. AF *mahem*, OF *mayhem* (as MAIM)]

may'ing *n.* & *a.* Participating in May Day festivities. [ME, f. MAY[3] + -ING[1]]

mayonnai'se (-ā'z) *n.* (Dish of salmon, chicken, etc., with) dressing of egg-yolks, oil, vinegar, etc. [F, perh. f. *mahonnais -aise* of Port *Mahon* in Minorca]

mayor (mār) *n.* Head of municipal corporation of city or borough (||in some large cities **Lord M~**; *Lord Mayor's* SHOW[2]); ||head of district council with status of borough; **~ of the palace,** (orig. under Merovingian kings) nominal subordinate to whom the power of his titular superior has passed; hence **may′or**AL *a.* [ME, f. OF *maire* f. L (as MAJOR²)]

mayor′altў (mār′-) *n.* Mayor's (period of) office. [ME, f. OF *mairalté* (as prec.; see -AL, -TY¹)]

mayor′ėss (mār′-) *n.* Mayor's wife (LADY *Mayoress*); female mayor; lady fulfilling ceremonial duties of mayor's wife. [f. MAYOR + -ESS¹]

may′weed *n.* Stinking camomile, *Anthemis cotula.* [earlier *maidwede* f. obs. *maithe(n)* f. OE *magothe, mægtha* + WEED]

mă′zard, mă′zzard, *n.* **1.** (arch.) Head, face. **2.** Wild sweet cherry (*Prunus avium*) of Europe. [alt. of MAZER; cf. -ARD]

măzari′ne (-ē′n) *n.* & *a.* Deep rich blue. [17th c., perh. f. name of Cardinal *Mazarin*, Fr. statesman d. 1661, or Duchesse de *Mazarin*, Fr. noblewoman d. 1699]

Mă′zdaïsm *n.* Zoroastrianism. [f. Avestan *mazda*, the good principle in ancient-Persian theology]

māze *n.*, & *v.t.* **1.** *n.* Complex network of paths, labyrinth; network of paths and hedges designed as puzzle for those who try to penetrate it; (fig.) confusion, confused mass, etc. **2.** *v.t.* (esp. in *p.p.*) Bewilder, confuse. [ME, n. f. v., orig. in p.p.; cogn. w. AMAZE]

mā′zer *n.* (Hist.) Hardwood drinking-bowl, usu. silver-mounted. [ME, f. OF *masere*, of Gmc orig.; cf. OHG *masar* maple, excrescence on tree f. **mas-* spot (cf. MEASLES)]

***mazu′ma** (-ōō′-) *n.* (sl.) Money. [Yiddish]

mazûr′ka *n.* Lively Polish dance in triple time; music for this. [F, or f. G *masurka*, f. Pol. *mazurka* woman of province *Mazovia*]

mā′z|ў *a.* Resembling a maze; full of turnings; hence ~ĭLY² *adv.*, ~ĭNESS *n.* [f. MAZE + -Y²]

mă′zzard. See MAZARD.

M.B. *abbr.* Bachelor of Medicine. [f. L *Medicinae Baccalaureus*]

M.B.A. *abbr.* Master of Business Administration.

||**M.B.E.** *abbr.* Member (of the Order) of the British Empire.

M.C. *abbr.* Master of Ceremonies; *Member of Congress; ||Military Cross.

Mc(/s) *abbr.* megacycles (per second).

M.C.C. *abbr.* Marylebone Cricket Club.

McCarthyism, McCoy. See **MacC-.**

M.Ch(ir). *abbr.* Master of Surgery. [f. L *Magister Chirurgiae*]

M.Com. *abbr.* Master of Commerce.

M.D. *abbr.* Doctor of Medicine. [f. L *Medicinae Doctor*]; Managing Director; mentally deficient.

Md. *abbr.* Maryland.

Md *symb.* mendelevium.

***MDT** *abbr.* Mountain Daylight Time.

me¹. See I².

mē², mi (mē), *n.* (Mus.) Third note of scale in movable-doh system; the note E in fixed-doh system. [ME, f. L *mira*; see GAMUT]

Me. *abbr.* Maine; *Maître* (title of Fr. advocate).

mea culpa (mēa kŭ′lpa *or* māa kōō′lpa) *n.* & *int.* (expr.) acknowledgement of one's fault or error. [L, = by my fault]

mead¹ *n.* Alcoholic liquor of fermented honey and water. [OE *me(o)du*, = MLG *mede*, OHG *metu, mitu*, ON *mjöthr* f. Gmc **meduz* f. IE **medhu-*]

mead² *n.* (poet. or arch.) = foll. [OE *mǣd* f. Gmc **mǣdwō* (**mētwā* mowed land, cogn. w. MOW³)]

mea′dow (mĕ′dō) *n.* Piece of grassland, esp. one used for hay; low well-watered ground, esp. near river; ~ **brown,** common brown butterfly; **~-grass** (of genus *Poa*); ***~ lark,** bird of genus *Sturnella*, akin to bobolink; ~ **pipit,** brown and white Old World pipit (*Anthus pratensis*); ~ **saffron,** perennial plant (*Crocus sativus*) abundant in meadows, with lilac flowers; **~sweet,** rosaceous plant of genus *Filipendula* or *Spiraea*, common in meadows, with creamy-white fragrant flowers; hence ~Y² *a.* [OE *mǣdwe*, obl. case of *mǣd* (see prec.)]

mea′gre, *mea′ger, (-*ger*) *a.* (Of person etc.) lean, thin; (esp. of meals) poor, scanty; (of literary composition, ideas, etc.) lacking fullness, unsatisfying; hence ~LY² *adv.*, ~NESS *n.* [ME f. AF *megre*, OF *maigre* f. L *macer*]

meal¹ *n.* Edible part of any grain or pulse (usu. exc. wheat) ground to powder; (Sc.) oatmeal; *maize flour; powdery substance made by grinding; **~-beetle,** insect (*Tenebrio molitor*) infesting granaries etc.; **~-worm,** its larva. [OE *melu*, = OS, OHG *melo*, ON *mjöl* f. Gmc **melwam* (**mel-* etc. f. IE)]

meal² *n.* Customary (or any) occasion of taking food; food so taken; **make a ~ of,** (1) consume as meal, (2) make (task etc.) seem unduly laborious; **~-ticket,** ticket entitling one to meal, esp. at specified place with reduced cost, (fig.) thing or person that provides for one; **~′time,** usual time of eating. [OE *mǣl* mark, fixed time, meal, = OS, OHG, ON *māl*, Goth. *mēl* f. Gmc **mǣlam* f. IE **mē-* to measure]

mea′lĭe *n.* (usu. in *pl.*) (S. Afr.) Maize; corn--cob. [f. Afrik. *milie* f. Port. *milho* maize, millet f. L *milium*]

mea′lў *a.* **1.** Of, like, containing, meal; (of boiled potatoes) dry and powdery; **~-bug,** insect infesting vines etc., whose body is covered with white powder. **2.** (Of horse) spotty; (of complexion) pale; ~(**-mouthed**), not outspoken, afraid to use plain expressions. **3.** Hence **mea′lĭ**NESS *n.* [f. MEAL¹ + -Y²]

mean¹ *n.* **1.** Condition, quality, virtue, course of action, equally removed from two opposite (usu. blameworthy) extremes; GOLDEN *mean.* **2.** (Math.) Term, or one of terms, between first and last terms of arithmetical, geometrical, etc., progression (*2 and 8 have arithmetic mean 5, geometric mean 4*). **3.** (in *pl.*, often treated as *sing.*) That by which a result is brought about (*it has been a means of extending our trade*; *by fair means or foul*); WAYS *and means*; **~s of grace,** sacraments etc. **4.** (in *pl.*) Money resources (*he lives beyond his, on his own, means*; **~s test,** official inquiry as to proof of need before financial assistance is given); wealth (*a man of means*). **5. By all** (**manner of**) **~s,** in every possible way, at any cost, certainly; **by no** (**manner of**) **~s, not by any** (**manner of**) **~s,** not at all, certainly not; **by ~s** (the agency, instrumentality) **of** (person, thing, doing). [ME, f. foll., partly thr. F]

mean² *a.* (Of quantity) equally far from two extremes; ~ **free path,** average distance travelled by gas molecule etc. between collisions; ~ **proportional,** geometric MEAN¹ of two quantities; ~ **sea level** (half-way between mean levels of high and low water); ~ **sun,** fictitious sun moving in celestial equator at mean rate of real sun; ~ **time** (based on mean sun); **in the ~** (intervening) **time** or **while**; **~′time, ~′while,** *advs.*, in the mean time. [ME, f. AF *me(e)n*, f. OF *meien, moien* f. L *medianus* MEDIAN]

mean³ *a.* **1.** (Of capacity, understanding, etc.) inferior, poor; ~ **white,** = POOR *white.* **2.** Not imposing in appearance, shabby; **no ~,** a very good (*he is no mean scholar*). **3.** Ignoble, small--minded, (*a mean trick*); malicious, ill-tempered; *vicious, nastily behaved; *(colloq.) (1) unwell, (2) secretly ashamed, (*feel mean*); *(sl.) skilful. **4.** Niggardly, not generous or liberal. **5.** Hence ~′LY² *adv.*, ~′NESS (-n-n-) *n.* [OE (*ge*)*mǣne*, = OS *gimēni*, OHG *gimeini*, Goth.

gamains f. Gmc **gamainiz* (**ga-* Y-, **mainiz* f. **moinis* f. **moi-*, **mei-* exchange)]

mean[4] *v.t.* (~t *pr.* mĕnt). **1.** Have as one's purpose, have in mind, (*mischief*, BUSINESS, *to* do). **2.** Design, destine, for a purpose etc. (*mean it to be used*; *mean it for a stopgap*); *he* **was ~t** (by parents etc., or by Providence) *for a soldier*; *it is* **~t for** *you*, you are to receive it or take note of it; *I* ~ *you* **to** (am determined that you shall) *go*; **~ well** (**to, towards, by**), be kindly disposed (towards). **3.** Intend to convey (specified sense) or indicate (object) or refer to (thing) (*I mean that it is impossible*; *I mean his father, his own hat, Richmond in Surrey*). **4.** Be of some (specified) importance *to* (person), esp. as source of benefit or object of affection etc. **5.** (Of words or event or person) signify, import, (thing, *that*); have as equivalent in another language (*'mensa' means 'table'*); entail, involve, (*it means catching the early train*); portend (*this means war*); **what do you ~ by it?** can you justify such behaviour etc.?. [OE *mǣnan*, = OS *mēnian*, OHG *meinen* f. WG **mainjan* f. IE **mēn-*; cf. MIND[1]]

meă'nder *n.*, & *v.i.* **1.** *n.* (in *pl.*) Sinuous windings of river; winding paths. **2.** Circuitous journey; ornamental pattern of lines winding in and out, fret. **3.** *v.i.* Wander at random; (of stream) wind about. [f. L *maeander* f. Gk *Maiandros*, winding river in Phrygia]

meă'ndrīne *a.* Full of windings (esp. of corals of genus *Maeandra*, with surface like human brain). [f. prec. + -INE[1]]

mea'nĭe, mea'nȳ, *n.* (colloq.) Niggardly or small-minded person. [f. MEAN[3] + -IE, -Y[3]]

mea'nĭng[1] *n.* What is meant; significance; importance; **with ~**, significantly; hence **~**FUL, **~**LESS, *adjs.* [ME, f. MEAN[4] + -ING[1]]

mea'nĭng[2] *a.* Expressive, significant, whence ~LY[2] *adv.*; WELL-*meaning.* [f. MEAN[4] + -ING[2]]

means. See MEAN[1].

meant. See MEAN[4].

mea'nȳ. See MEANIE.

mea'sles (-zelz) *n.* (as *pl.* or *sing.*) Acute infectious virus disease marked by red spots on skin; such spots; tapeworm disease of pigs; GERMAN[2] *measles.* [ME *masele(s)* f. MLG *masele*, MDu. *masel* pustule, OHG *masala*, cogn. w. MAZER]

mea'slȳ (-z-) *a.* Of or affected with measles; (of pork) infested with tapeworms; (sl.) inferior, contemptible, worthless. [f. prec. + -Y[2]]

mea'surab|le (mĕ'zher-) *a.* That can be measured; **within a ~le distance of,** getting near (something undesirable); hence ~LY[2] *adv.*; [ME, f. OF *mesurable* f. LL *mensurabilis* f. L *mensurare* (as foll.; see -ABLE)]

mea'sure[1] (mĕ'zher) *n.* **1.** Size or quantity found by measuring; **for good ~**, as something beyond the minimum, as a finishing touch; **short, full,** ~, less, not less, than professed amount; ||*clothes* **made to ~** (in accordance with measurements taken); **take** person's **~**, measure him for clothes etc., (fig.) gauge his character, abilities, etc. **2.** Degree, extent, amount, (esp. **in a** or **in some ~**, partly); **a ~ of,** some degree of. **3.** Vessel of standard capacity for transferring fixed quantities of liquids etc. (*pint measure*). **4.** Rod, tape, etc., for measuring (TAPE-*measure*; *yard-measure*). **5.** Unit of capacity, e.g. bushel (*20 measures of wheat*). **6.** System of measuring (*liquid, linear,* LONG[1], *measure*). **7.** That by which a thing is computed (*a chain's weakest link is the measure of its strength*). **8.** Quantity contained in another an exact number of times; **greatest common ~**, greatest number that is a factor of each of given numbers. **9.** Prescribed extent or quantity (**set ~s to,** limit; **beyond ~**, excessively); (Print.) width of page or column of type. **10.** Poetical rhythm, metre; metrical group of dactyl or two iambuses, trochees, spondees, etc.; time of piece of music; (Mus.) bar; (arch.) dance (*tread a measure*). **11.** Suitable action (*take measures to ensure that*). **12.** Legislative enactment. **13.** Mineral stratum (COAL *measures*). [ME f. OF *mesure* f. L *mensura* (*metiri mens-* measure; see -URE)]

mea'sure[2] (mĕ'zher) *v.* **1.** *v.t.* Ascertain extent or quantity of (thing) by comparison with fixed unit or with object of known size; ascertain size and proportions of (person) for clothes. **2.** Look (person) up and down (*with* one's *eye*). **3.** Mark off or *off* (line etc. of given length). **4. ~** one's **length,** accidentally fall flat on the ground; **~ swords,** (of duellists) see that swords are of equal length, (fig.) try one's strength *with* (person). **5.** Estimate (quality, person's character, etc.) by some standard or rule. **6.** Deal *out* (thing *to* person). **7.** Bring (one*self*, one's strength etc.) into competition *with.* **8.** (poet.) Traverse (distance). **9.** *v.i.* Take measurements; be of specified size (*it measures six inches*); **~ up (to),** have necessary qualifications (for); **mea'suring-jug, -tape,** etc., (marked at various points to assist measurement); **mea'suring-worm,** caterpillar of geometer moth. [ME, f. OF *mesurer* f. L *mensurare* (as prec.)]

mea'sured (mĕ'zherd) *a.* In vbl senses; rhythmical, regular in movement, (*measured tread*); (of language) carefully weighed; hence ~LY[2] *adv.* [p.p. of prec.]

mea'surelėss (mĕ'zherl-) *a.* Not measurable, infinite. [ME, f. MEASURE[1] + -LESS]

mea'surement (mĕ'zherm-) *n.* Act or result of measuring; (in *pl.*) detailed dimensions. [f. MEASURE[2] + -MENT]

meat *n.* **1.** Animal flesh as food, usu. (cf. BUTCHER[1]'*s meat*) excluding fish and poultry; *edible part of fruits, nuts, eggs, shellfish, etc.; **green ~**, grass, green vegetables, as food; WHITE[1] *meat.* **2.** (arch.) Food of any kind. **3.** **One man's ~ is another man's poison,** not everybody likes the same things; *this was* **~ and drink** (a source of great pleasure) *to him.* **4.** (arch.) A meal (*before, at, after, meat*). **5.** (fig.) Principal or most useful part *of.* **6. ~-axe,** butcher's cleaver; *meat* BALL[1] 5; **~-fly** (whose larvae feed on meat); *meat* LOAF[1]; **~-man,** butcher; **~-safe,** cupboard for storing meat, usu. of wire gauze etc.; ||**~ tea,** tea at which meat is served, high TEA. **7.** Hence ~'LESS *a.* [OE *mete* food, = OS *meti*, *mat*, OHG *maz*, ON *matr*, Goth. *mats* f. Gmc **matiz*, **matam*, (**mat-* measure; cf. METE[2])]

mēā'tus *n.* (*pl.* ~ *or* ~*es*). (Anat.) (Orifice of) channel or passage in the body; **auditory ~**, channel of the ear. [L, = passage (*meare* flow, run)]

mea't|ȳ *a.* Full of meat, fleshy; (fig.) full of substance; of or like meat; hence **~ĭ**LY[2] *adv.*, ~ĬNESS *n.* [f. MEAT + -Y[2]]

Mĕ'cca *n.* Place one aspires to visit; birthplace of a faith, policy, pursuit, etc. [~ in Arabia, birthplace of Muhammad and chief place of Muslim pilgrimage]

mėcca'nō (-ah'-) *n.* Set of miniature usu. metal parts from which engineering models can be constructed. [P]

mėchă'nĭc (-k-) *n.* **1.** Handicraftsman; skilled workman, esp. one who makes or uses machinery. **2.** (in *pl.*) Branch of applied mathematics dealing with motion and tendencies to motion; science of machinery; method of construction or routine operation. [orig. a., ME, f. OF *mecanique* or f. L f. Gk *mēkhanikos* (as MACHINE; see -IC)]

mĕchă′nĭcal (-kă′-) *a.* **1.** Of machines or mechanism. **2.** Of the nature of handicraft. **3.** Working or produced by machinery. **4.** ~ **advantage,** ratio of exerted to applied force in machine; ~ **drawing** (done with compasses etc.); *mechanical* ENGINEER[1] 4; ~ **equivalent,** value of unit (*of heat*) in terms of mechanical work; *mechanical* POWERS; ~ **transport,** motor branch of R.C.T. **5.** (Of person or action) like a machine, automatic, lacking originality. **6.** (Of agency, principle, etc.) belonging to mechanics; (of theory etc.) explaining phenomena by assumption of mechanical action, whence ~ISM (3) *n.* **7.** Of mechanics as a science. **8.** Hence ~LY[2] *adv.*, ~NESS *n.*, **mĕchă′nĭco-** (-kă′-) *comb. form.* [ME, f. L (as prec.; see -AL)]

mĕchanĭ′cian (-kanĭ′shan) *n.* One skilled in constructing machinery. [f. MECHANIC + -IAN]

mĕ′chanĭsm (-k-) *n.* Structure, adaptation of parts, of machine (lit. or fig.); system of mutually adapted parts working together (as) in machine; mode of operation of a process; (Art) mechanical execution, technique; (Philos.) doctrine that all natural phenomena, including life, allow mechanical explanation by physics and chemistry. [f. mod. L *mechanismus* f. Gk (as MACHINE; see -ISM)]

mĕ′chan|ĭst (-k-) *n.* Mechanician; expert in mechanics; (Philos.) one who holds the doctrine of mechanism (see prec.), whence **~ĭ′st**IC *a.* [f. MECHANIC + -IST]

mĕ′chanīz|e (-k-), **-īs|e** (-īz), *v.t.* Give mechanical character to; introduce machines in; (Mil.) re-equip by substituting motor transport for horse-drawn vehicles, replacing cavalry by tanks and armoured cars, etc. [f. MECHANIC + -IZE]

Mĕ′chlĭn (-k-) *n.* ~ **(lace)**, lace made at *Mechlin* (now *Mechelen* or *Malines*) in Belgium.

M.Econ. *abbr.* Master of Economics.

mècō′nĭum *n.* (Med.) Dark substance forming first faeces of new-born infant. [L, lit. poppy--juice, f. Gk *mēkōnion* (*mēkōn* poppy)]

Mĕd *n.* (colloq.) Mediterranean Sea. [abbr.]

M.Ed. *abbr.* Master of Education.

med. *abbr.* medium.

mĕ′dal *n.* Piece of metal, usu. in form of coin, struck or cast with inscription and device to commemorate event etc., or awarded as distinction to soldier, scholar, athlete, etc., for services rendered, proficiency, etc.; **the reverse of the** ~, the other side of a question; ~ **play,** (Golf) play in which the score is reckoned by counting the number of strokes taken for the round, opp. *match play*; hence ~**l**ED[2] (-ld), **mėdă′ll**IC, *adjs.* [f. F *médaille* f. It. *medaglia* f. Rom. **medallia* f. pop. L **metallea* n. pl. f. L *metallum* METAL]

mėdă′llion (-yon) *n.* Large medal; thing so shaped, e.g. decorative panel or tablet, portrait, etc. [f. F *médaillon* f. It. *medaglione* augment. of *medaglia* (see prec.)]

mĕ′dallĭst, *mĕ′dalĭst, *n.* Engraver or designer of medals; recipient of (specified) medal (*gold medallist*). [f. MEDAL + -IST]

mĕ′ddl|e *v.i.* Busy oneself unduly *with*, interfere *in*; hence ~ER[1] *n.*, ~**e**SOME[1] (-dels-) *a.* [ME, f. OF *medler*, var. of *mesler* f. Rom. **misculare* f. L *miscēre* mix]

Mēde *n.* One of the earliest Iranian inhabitants of Media in Persia; **law of the ~s and Persians,** immutable law (Dan. 6:8). [ME, f. L *Medi* pl. f. Gk *Mēdoi*]

mē′dĭa[1] *n.* (*pl.* ~e). **1.** (Phonet.) Voiced stop, e.g. *g, b, d.* **2.** (Biol.) Middle membrane enclosing artery or other vessel. [L, fem. of *medius* middle]

mē′dĭa[2] *n.* Pl. of MEDIUM (esp. sense 6).

mēdĭae′val. See MEDIEVAL.

mē′dĭal *a.* Situated in the middle; of average size; hence ~LY[2] *adv.* [f. LL *medialis* f. L *medius* middle; see -AL]

mē′dĭan[1] *a.* & *n.* **1.** *a.* Situated in the middle. **2.** *n.* (Anat.) median artery, vein, nerve, etc.; (Geom.) straight line drawn from any vertex of triangle to middle of opposite side; (Statistics) value of a quantity such that exactly half of a given population have greater values of that quantity. [f. F *médiane* or f. L *medianus* (as prec.; see -AN)]

Mē′dĭan[2] *a.* & *n.* (One) of the Medes; (inhabitant) of ancient Media. [f. MEDE + -IAN]

mē′dĭant *n.* (Mus.) Third note of diatonic scale of any key. [f. F *médiante* f. It. *mediante* part. (as n.) of obs. *mediare* come between, f. L (as MEDIATE[2]; see -ANT)]

mēdĭăstī′n|um *n.* (*pl.* ~**a**). (Anat.) Membranous middle septum, esp. between lungs; hence ~AL *a.* [mod. L, f. med. L *mediastinus* medial, after L *mediastinus* drudge (*medius* middle)]

mē′dĭate[1] *a.* Connected not directly but through some other person or thing; involving intermediate agency; hence ~LY[2] (-tlĭ) *adv.* [ME, f. L *mediatus* p.p. of *mediare* (see foll., -ATE[2])]

mē′dĭ|āte[2] *v.* **1.** *v.t.* Form connecting link between; be the medium for bringing about (result) or conveying (gift etc.). **2.** *v.i.* Intervene (*between* two persons) for purpose of reconciling them. **3.** So ~A′TION *n.* [f. LL *mediare* f. L *medius* middle, + -ATE[3]]

mē′dĭatīz|e, -īs|e (-īz), *v.t.* Annex (State) to another State, leaving former sovereign his title and some rights of government; hence ~A′TION *n.* [f. F *médiatiser* (*médiat* f. as MEDIATE[1]; see -IZE)]

mē′dĭātor *n.* One who mediates, esp. Christ as mediating between God and man; hence or cogn. **mēdĭatōr′**IAL, **mē′dĭat**ORY, *adjs.*, **mē′dĭā**TRIX *n.* (esp. Virgin Mary). [ME, f. OF *mediatour* f. LL *mediator -oris* (as MEDIATE[2]; see -OR)]

mĕ′dĭc[1] *n.* (sl.) Doctor; medical student. [f. L *medicus* physician (*medēri* heal)]

mĕ′dĭc[2]. Var. of MEDICK.

mĕ′dĭcable *a.* Admitting of remedial treatment. [f. L *medicabilis* (as MEDICATE; see -ABLE)]

mĕ′dĭcal *a.* & *n.* **1.** *a.* Of the art of medicine in general or as opp. to surgery, obstetrics, etc.; ~ **attendant,** one's physician; ~ **certificate** (of fitness or unfitness to work etc.); ~ **examination** (to determine person's physical fitness); ~ **examiner,** physician making medical examinations or *acting like coroner; ~ **jurisprudence,** forensic medicine; ~ **man,** ~ **practitioner,** physician or surgeon; ‖~ **officer,** person in charge of health services of local authority or other organization; ~ **school** (in which physicians etc. are trained); ~ **student,** person studying for qualification in medicine. **2.** (Of disease) requiring medical, not surgical, treatment; (of hospital ward etc.) used for patients receiving such treatment. **3.** Hence ~LY[2] *adv.* **4.** *n.* (colloq.) Medical examination; medical student. [f. F *médical* or f. med. L *medicalis* f. L *medicus*; see MEDIC[1], -AL]

mėdĭ′cament (*or* mĕ′d-) *n.* Substance used in curative treatment. [f. F *médicament* or f. L *medicamentum* (as MEDICATE; see -MENT)]

***Mĕ′dĭcāre** *n.* Federal system of health insurance for those over 65. [f. MEDICAL + CARE[1]]

mĕ′dĭc|āte *v.t.* Treat medically; impregnate with medicinal substance; hence or cogn. ~A′TION *n.*, ~**āt**IVE *a.* [f. L *medicari* administer remedies to (*medicus*; see MEDIC[1], -ATE[3])]

Mĕdĭcē′an *a.* Of the Medici family, rulers of Florence in 15th c. [f. mod. L *Mediceus* f. It. *Medici*, + -AN]

mĕdĭ'cĭnal *a.* & *n.* Of medicine; (substance) having healing properties; hence ~LY² *adv.* [ME f. OF, f. L *medicinalis* (as foll.; see -AL)]
mĕ'dĭcine (mĕ'dsĭn *or* mĕ'dĭsĭn) *n.*, & *v.t.* **1.** *n.* Art of restoring and preserving health, esp. by means of remedial substances and regulation of diet etc., as opp. to surgery and obstetrics. **2.** Substance, esp. one taken internally, used in this; (among primitive peoples) spell, charm, fetish, (~**-man,** magician). **3. A dose** etc. **of** one's **own** ~, treatment such as one is accustomed to giving others; **take** one's ~, submit to disagreeable thing; ~ **ball,** stuffed leather ball thrown and caught as means of exercise; ~ **chest,** box containing remedies. **4.** *v.t.* (arch.) Give medicine to; cure with medicine. [ME, (v. f. OF *medeciner*) f. OF *medecine* f. L *medicina* (*medicus*; see MEDIC¹, -INE⁴)]
mē'dĭck *n.* Leguminous plant of genus *Medicago*, esp. lucerne. [ME, f. L *medica* f. Gk *Mēdikē poa* Median grass]
mĕ'dĭcō *n.* (*pl.* ~s). (colloq.) Medical practitioner or student. [It., f. L (as MEDIC¹)]
mĕ'dĭcō- *comb. form.* Medical (and) (*medico-legal*). [f. L *medicus* (see MEDIC¹) + -O-]
mĕdĭē'val *a.* Of or imitating the Middle Ages; (fig.) old-fashioned; ~ **history** (of 5th–15th c.); *medieval* LATIN; hence ~ISM (2), ~IST (3), *ns.*, ~IZE (2, 3) *v.t.* & *i.*, ~LY² *adv.* [f. mod. L *medium aevum* f. L *medius* middle + *aevum* age, + -AL]
mēdĭō'cre (-ker; *or* mē'-) *a.* Of middling quality, neither good nor bad; fairly bad. [f. F *médiocre* or f. L *mediocris* of middle height or degree (*medius* middle, *ocris* rugged mountain)]
mēdĭŏ'crĭtў *n.* In adj. senses; mediocre person. [ME, f. F *médiocrité* f. L *mediocritas* (as prec.; see -ITY)]
mĕ'dĭtāt|e *v.* **1.** *v.t.* Plan mentally, design. **2.** *v.i.* Exercise the mind in (esp. religious) contemplation (*on* or *upon* subject). **3.** Hence or cogn. **mĕdĭt**A'TION, ~OR, *ns.* [f. L *meditari*, frequent. f. IE **med-* measure, + -ATE³]
mĕ'dĭtatĭve *a.* Inclined to meditate; indicative of meditation; hence ~LY² (-vlĭ) *adv.*, ~NESS (-vn-) *n.* [f. prec. + -IVE]
mĕdĭterrā'nean *a.* & *n.* **1.** *a.* (arch.) (Of land) remote from coast. **2.** (Of water area) land-locked; **M**~ (**Sea**), that which separates Europe from Africa. **3.** Of the region of the Mediterranean Sea; (of person) dark-complexioned and not tall. [f. L *mediterraneus* inland (*medius* middle, *terra* land) + -AN]
mē'dĭum *n.* (*pl.* **me'dia** *or* ~s) & *a.* **1.** *n.* Middle quality, degree, etc., (*between* extremes, or abs.); HAPPY *medium.* **2.** Intervening substance through which impressions are conveyed to senses etc., e.g. air; (fig.) environment, conditions of life. **3.** Agency, means, (*by* or *through the medium of*); ~ **of circulation,** what serves as instrument of commercial transactions, e.g. coin. **4.** Liquid, e.g. oil, water, with which pigments are mixed for use in painting. **5.** (*pl.* ~s). Person claiming to have communication with the spirits of the dead etc. and reveal its results to others; hence ~ISM (3) *n.*, ~**ĭ'stIC** *a.* **6.** Means by which something is communicated; material or form used by artist, musical composer, etc.; (in *pl.*) = MASS² *media.* **7.** *a.* Intermediate between two degrees or amounts, average, moderate; ~ **bowler,** ~ **pace,** (Cricket, neither fast nor slow); *medium* TERM¹; ~ **wave,** radio wave having wavelength between 100 and 1,000 metres. [L, = middle, neut. (as n.) of *medius* middle]
mĕ'dlar *n.* (Tree, *Mespilus germanica*, with) fruit like small brown apple, eaten when decayed; **Japan**(**ese**) ~, loquat. [ME, f. OF *medler* (**medle*, **mesdle* f. *mesle* f. L f. Gk *mespilē*, *-on*)]
mĕ'dley *n.*, *a.*, & *v.t.* **1.** *n.* Heterogeneous mixture; mixed company; literary miscellany; musical composition made from various previous ones; ~ **relay,** relay race between teams in which each member runs a different distance or uses a different swimming-stroke. **2.** *a.* (arch.) Mixed, motley. **3.** *v.t.* (arch.) Make a medley of, intermix. [ME, f. OF *medlee* var. of *meslee* f. Rom. **misculata* (as MEDDLE)]
Médŏ'c (mā-) *n.* Red Bordeaux wine from *Médoc* district in S.W. France.
mĕdŭ'lla *n.* Marrow of bone; spinal marrow; ~ (**oblongata** *pr.* ŏblŏnggah'ta; L, = prolonged), hindmost segment of brain; central part of some organs, esp. hair or kidney; soft internal tissue of plants; hence **mĕdŭ'llARY²** *a.* [L, = pith, marrow, prob. cogn. w. *medius* middle]
mĕdū'sa *n.* (*pl.* ~e *or* ~s). (Zool.) Jellyfish; sexually reproductive form of hydrozoan or scyphozoan, with jelly-like body and stinging tentacles; hence **mĕdū'sAN** *a.* [L, f. Gk *Medousa*, name of a Gorgon with snakes for hair]
meed *n.* (literary or arch.) Reward; merited portion (*of* praise etc.). [OE *mēd*, = OS *mēda*, OHG *mēta* f. WG **mēda* cogn. w. Goth. *mizdō*, Gk *misthos* reward]
meek *a.* Piously humble and submissive; submitting tamely to injury etc.; hence ~'LY² *adv.*, ~'NESS *n.* [ME *me*(*o*)*c* f. ON **miúkr*, *mjúkr* soft, gentle]
meer'kăt *n.* Suricate. [Du., = sea-cat]
meer'schaum (-sham) *n.* Hydrated magnesium silicate, found in soft white masses chiefly in Turkey; tobacco-pipe with bowl made from this. [G, = sea-foam (*meer* sea, *schaum* foam), transl. Pers. *kef-i-daryā*, w. ref. to its frothiness]
meet¹ *n.* Meeting of hounds and men for hunt, or of cyclists, athletes, etc., for competition; *meeting-place of railway trains. [f. foll.]
meet² *v.* (**met**). **1.** *v.t.* Come face to face with (person coming from opposite direction); go to place to be present at arrival of (person, train, etc.); make the acquaintance of (*pleased to meet you*; **John, meet Mary*); ~ (person) **half-way,** (fig.) respond to friendly advances of, make a compromise with; WELL³ *met!*. **2.** (Of line, road, river, moving object, etc.) reach point of contact with (another line etc.); ~ **the eye, ear,** be visible, audible; ~ person's **eye,** see he is looking at one, look at him in one's turn; **more in it than** ~**s the eye,** hidden qualities or complications. **3.** Oppose in battle or duel or contest; grapple with (evils etc.). **4.** Come by accident or design into the company of. **5.** Experience, receive, suffer, (one's death, fate, etc.). **6.** Come into conformity with (person, his wishes). **7.** Satisfy (demand; ~ **the case,** be adequate); give valid answer to (objection etc.); pay (cost); pay (bill) at maturity. **8.** *v.i.* (Of two or more persons) come face to face; be in opposition in contest etc.; come *together* (*they had* or *were met together*); assemble for purpose of conference, business, etc. **9.** Come into contact (*waistcoat* **won't** ~, is too small in girth to be fastened); (of qualities) unite in same person; *make* END¹*s meet.* **10.** ~ **with,** happen to meet (person, obstacle, etc.), = sense 5, * = sense 4; ~ **up with,** (colloq.) happen to meet (person). [OE *mētan*, = OS *mōtian*, ON *mœta*, Goth. *gamotjan* f. Gmc **gamōtjan* (**mōtam* meeting; cf. MOOT)]
meet³ *a.* (arch.) Suitable, fit, proper, (*for* thing, *to* do, *to* be done); *it is* ~ (proper) *that*; hence ~'LY² *adv.*, ~'NESS *n.* [ME (*i*)*mete* repr. OE *gemǣte* f. Gmc **gamǣtja-* (**ga-* Y-, **mǣt-* METE²)]

mee'ting *n.* In vbl senses; (arch.) duel; race-meeting; assembly of people for entertainment, discussion, etc.; assembly (esp. of Quakers) for worship; persons assembled (*address the meeting*); **~-house,** place of worship (U.S., or derog. exc. of Quakers); **~-place** (appointed for meeting). [ME, f. MEET[2] + -ING[1]]

M.E.F. *abbr.* Middle East Forces.

mĕ'ga- *comb. form.* **1.** Large, as: **~cepha'lic,** large-headed; **~lith,** (Archaeol.) large stone, esp. as monument; **~li'thic,** made of, marked by use of, large stones; **~sco'pic,** visible to naked eye; **~ther'ium,** huge extinct herbivorous slothlike animal. **2.** Denoting factor of one million (10^6), as: **~death,** death of one million persons (esp. as unit of results of war); *megahertz*; **~ton(ne)**, one million tons, esp. = this quantity of T.N.T. as unit of equivalent explosive power; *megavolt*; *megawatt*. [Gk (*megas* great)]

mĕgalo- *comb. form.* Great, as: **~ma'nia,** insanity of self-exaltation, passion for grandiose things; **~saur'us,** huge extinct carnivorous lizard. [Gk (*megas megal-* great; see -O-)]

mĕgalŏ'polĭs *n.* A great city or its way of life; populous area surrounding one or more cities. [f. prec. + Gk *polis* city]

mĕ'gaphōne *n.* Large speaking-trumpet for carrying sound of voice to a distance. [f. MEGA- + -PHONE]

mĕ'gapōde, mĕ'gapŏd, *n.* Bird of mainly Australasian family Megapodidae, building mound of debris in which eggs are laid and hatched. [f. mod. L *Megapodius* (genus-name) f. as MEGA- + Gk *pous podos* foot]

||**mĕ'gger** (-g-) *n.* (Electr.) Apparatus for measuring insulation resistance. [**P**; cf. MEGOHM]

mėgĭ'lp (-g-) *n.* Vehicle (usu. linseed oil and varnish) for oil colours. [18th c.; orig. unkn.]

mĕ'gohm (-ōm) *n.* (Electr.) Unit of resistance, one million ohms. [f. MEGA- 2 + OHM]

mē'grĭm[1] *n.* Migraine; whim, fancy; (in *pl.*) depression, low spirits; (in *pl.*) staggers, vertigo, in horses etc. [ME *mygrane* f. OF MIGRAINE]

mē'grĭm[2] *n.* Small flounder or similar flat-fish. [19th c.; orig. unkn.]

mei'nĭe (mā'-) *n.* (arch.) Family; retinue; multitude of persons. [ME, f. OF *meinee*, *mesnee* f. Rom. **mansionata* f. L (as MANSION)]

mei|ō'sĭs (mī-) *n.* (*pl.* **~o'ses** *pr.* -ō'sēz). **1.** = LITOTES. **2.** (Biol.) Process of division of cell nuclei whereby diploid number of chromosomes is halved, to be combined with another half-set at fertilization; cf. MITOSIS. **3.** Hence **~o'**TIC *a.* [mod. L, f. Gk *meiōsis* (*meioō* lessen, f. *meiōn* less; see -OSIS)]

Mei'stersinger (mī's-; *or* -zĭ-) *n.* (*pl.* same). One of the German lyric poets and musicians of 14th–16th c. organized in guilds and having elaborate technique. [G (*meister* MASTER[1], *singer* SINGER)]

mĕ'lamine (-ēn) *n.* White crystalline organic base, a polymer of cyanamide; **~ (resin)**, plastic made from melamine and an aldehyde. [f. *melam* (arbitrary) + AMINE]

mĕlanchō'lĭa (-n-k-) *n.* Mental illness marked by depression and ill-grounded fears. [LL; see MELANCHOLY]

mĕlanchŏ'lĭc (-n-k-) *a.* Melancholy; liable to melancholy; *melancholic* TEMPERAMENT. [ME, f. OF *melancolique* f. L f. Gk *melagkholikos* (as foll.; see -IC)]

mĕ'lancholȳ (-n-k-) *n.* & *a.* **1.** *n.* (Habitual or constitutional tendency to) sadness and depression; pensive sadness; (Hist.) one of the four HUMOUR[1]s, black bile. **2.** *a.* (Of person) sad, gloomy; (of thing) saddening, depressing; (of words etc.) expressing sadness. [ME, f. OF *melancolie* f. LL f. Gk *melagkholia* (*melas melanos* black, *kholē* bile); see -Y[1]]

Mĕlanē'sian (-shan) *a.* & *n.* (Member or language) of dark-skinned and frizzy-haired dominant race in Melanesia. [f. *Melanesia*, island-group in W. Pacific (f. Gk *melas* black + *nēsos* island + -IA[1]) + -AN]

mélange (mālah'ṅzh) *n.* Mixture, medley. [F (*mêler* mix, as MEDDLE)]

mĕ'lanĭn *n.* Dark-brown or black pigment in hair, skin, etc., of coloured races or melanotic patient or in melanism. [f. Gk *melas melanos* black + -IN]

mĕ'lanĭsm *n.* Darkness of colour (esp. of animals) resulting from abnormal development of black pigment in skin, hair, etc. [f. as prec. + -ISM]

mĕlan|ō'sĭs *n.* (*pl.* **~oses** *pr.* -ō'sēz). Morbid deposit, abnormal development, of black pigment in tissue; hence **~o'**TIC *a.* [mod. L, f. Gk (as MELANIN) + -OSIS]

Mĕ'lba *n.* **~ toast,** thin crisp toast; PEACH[1] *Melba*. [f. Dame N. ~, Australian soprano d. 1931]

***mĕld**[1] *v.t.* & *i.* Merge, blend, combine. [perh. f. MELT[2] + WELD[2]]

mĕld[2] *v.* & *n.* **1.** *v.t.* & *i.* (In some card-games) declare for a score. **2.** *n.* Act of melding; group of cards (to be) melded. [f. G *melden* announce]

mêlée, *mĕ'lee, (mĕ'lā) *n.* Confused fight, skirmish, scuffle; muddle. [F (as MEDLEY)]

mĕ'lĭc *a.* (Of poem, esp. Gk lyric) meant to be sung. [f. L f. Gk *melikos* (*melos* song; see -IC)]

mĕ'lĭnīte *n.* French explosive like lyddite. [f. F *mélinite* f. Gk *mēlinos* quince-yellow (*mēlon* apple); see -ITE[1]]

mē'lĭor|āte *v.t.* & *i.* Improve; hence **~a'**TION *n.*, **~ā**TIVE *a.* [f. LL *meliorare* (as foll.) + -ATE[3]]

mē'lĭor|ĭsm *n.* Doctrine that the world may be made better by human effort; so **~**IST (2) *n.* [f. L *melior* better + -ISM]

mĕlĭ'sma (-z-) *n.* (*pl.* **~ta**). (Mus.) Melodic music or tune; hence **mĕlĭsmă'**TIC (-z-) *a.* [Gk]

mĕllĭ'ferous *a.* Yielding or producing honey. [f. L *mellifer* (*mel* honey; see -FEROUS)]

mĕllĭ'flu|ous (-lōō-) *a.* (Of voice, words) sweet as honey; so **~**ENCE *n.*, **~**ENT *a.*, **~ous**LY[2] *adv.*, **~ous**NESS *n.* [ME, f. OF *melliflue* or f. LL *mellifluus* (*mel* honey, *fluere* flow) + -OUS]

mĕ'llow (-ō) *a.* & *v.* **1.** *a.* (Of fruit) soft, sweet, and juicy; (of wine) well-matured; (of earth) rich, loamy; (of character) softened by age or experience; (of sound, colour, light) full and pure without harshness; genial, jovial; partly intoxicated; hence **~**LY[2] *adv.*, **~**NESS *n.* **2.** *v.t.* & *i.* Make or become mellow. [ME, perh. f. attrib. use of OE *melu melw-* MEAL[1]]

mėlō'dėon, -dĭon, *n.* American organ. [f. MELODY + HARMONIUM, w. Graecized ending]

mėlŏ'dĭc *a.* Of or relating to melody; **~ minor,** (Mus.) scale with major 6th and 7th ascending, minor 6th and 7th descending. [f. F *mélodique* f. LL *melodicus* f. Gk *melōidikos* (as MELODY; see -IC)]

mėlō'dĭous *a.* Of or producing melody; sweet-sounding; hence **~**LY[2] *adv.*, **~**NESS *n.* [ME, f. OF *melodieus* (as MELODY; see -OUS)]

mĕ'lodĭst *n.* Singer; composer of melodies. [f. MELODY + -IST]

mĕ'lodīze, -īse (-īz), *v.* **1.** *v.i.* Make melody. **2.** *v.t.* Make melodious. [f. MELODY + -IZE]

mĕ'lodrama (-rah-) *n.* Sensational dramatic piece with crude appeals to emotions and usu. happy ending; language or behaviour or occurrence suggestive of this; (Hist.) play with songs interspersed and with orchestral music accompanying the action; hence **mĕlo-**

dramă'tic *a.*, **mĕlodramă'tically** *adv.*, **mĕlodră'matist** (1) *n.*, **mĕlodră'matize** (1, 3) *v.t.* [earlier *-drame* f. F *mélodrame* f. Gk *melos* music + F *drame* DRAMA]

mĕ'lodÿ *n.* Sweet music; musical arrangement of words; arrangement of single notes in musically expressive succession; principal part in harmonized music, air. [ME, f. OF *melodie* f. LL *melodia* f. Gk *melōidia* (*melos* song; see ODE, -Y¹)]

mĕ'lon *n.* (Sweet fruit of) gourd, esp. MUSK-*-melon* or WATER¹*-melon*; (sl.) spoils or profits to be shared. [ME f. OF, f. LL *melo -onis*, abbr. of L *melopepo* f. Gk *mēlopepōn* (*mēlon* apple, *pepōn* gourd f. *pepōn* ripe)]

mĕlt¹ *n.* Melted metal etc.; amount melted at a time; process of melting; **~-water** (formed by melting of snow and ice, esp. from glacier). [f. foll.]

mĕlt² *v.* (*p.p.* **~'ed** or, as *a.* of substances not easily melted, **mo'lten** *pr.* mō'-). **1.** *v.i.* Become liquefied by heat; (colloq., of person) suffer extreme heat; (of food) be easily dissolved *in the mouth*; (of clouds) break *into rain*; (of person, heart, feelings) be softened by or *with* pity or love, dissolve *into tears*, (*the melting mood*); (of sound) be soft and liquid; pass by imperceptible degrees *into* (another form); **~ away,** disappear by liquefaction, dwindle away, (colloq., of person) depart unobtrusively. **2.** *v.t.* Change to liquid condition by heat; soften (person, feelings); **~ down** (coin, plate, etc., to use the metal as raw material). **3.** **~'ing-point,** temperature at which solid melts; **~'ing-pot,** (fig.) place of reconstruction or vigorous mixing. [OE *meltan, mieltan,* = ON *melta* digest f. Gmc **maltjan* dissolve (**melt-* f. IE **meld-*; cogn. w. MALT¹)]

mĕ'lton *n.* Cloth with close-cut nap, for overcoats etc.; ||**M~ Mow'bray** (mō'b-) **pie,** kind of meat pasty. [f. *M~ Mowbray* in Leics.]

mĕ'mber *n.* **1.** Part or organ of body, esp. limb; **unruly ~,** (arch.) the tongue [Jas. 3:5–8]; **~ of Christ,** (fig.) Christian. **2.** Constituent portion of complex structure; person belonging to a society etc.; **M~** (one formally elected to take part in proceedings) **of Parliament, *of Congress**; person admitted to lowest grade of order, e.g. to Order of the British Empire, 5th class (M.B.E.), or to Royal Victorian Order, 4th or 5th class (M.V.O.). **3.** Part or branch of political body. **4.** Division or clause of sentence; group of figures, part of numerical expression; one side of equation. **5.** Hence (-)~ED² (*-erd*), ~LESS, *adjs.* [ME f. OF *membre* f. L *membrum* limb]

mĕ'mbership *n.* Being a member; number of members; body of members. [f. prec. + -SHIP]

mĕ'mbrāne *n.* Pliable sheetlike connective tissue or lining in animal or vegetable body; similar structure formed in some diseases; skin of parchment, forming part of a roll; so **mĕmbrana**'CEOUS, **mĕmbrā'neous**, **mĕ'mbranous**, *adjs.* [f. L *membrana* skin of body, parchment, (as MEMBER)]

membrum virile (mĕmbrum vĭrī'lĭ) *n.* Penis. [L, = male member]

mĕmĕ'ntō *n.* (*pl.* **~es** *or* **~s**). Object serving as reminder or warning, or kept as memorial of person or event; **~ *mori*** (mŏr'ī; L, = remember you must die), warning or reminder of death (e.g. skull). [L, imper. of *meminisse* remember]

mĕ'mō *n.* (*pl.* **~s**). (colloq.) Memorandum. [abbr.]

mĕ'moir (-wâr) *n.* Record of events; history written from personal knowledge or special sources of information; (esp. in *pl.*) (auto)-biography; essay on learned subject specially studied by the writer; hence ~IST (1) *n.* [f. F *mémoire* masc., spec. use of *mémoire* fem. MEMORY]

mĕmorabĭ'lia *n. pl.* Memorable things. [L, neut. pl. (as foll.)]

mĕ'mor|able *a.* Worth remembering, not to be forgotten, easily remembered; hence ~ABI'LITY *n.*, **~ably**² *adv.* [ME, f. *mémorable* or f. L *memorabilis* (*memorare* bring to mind f. *memor* mindful; see -ABLE)]

mĕmoră'nd|um *n.* (*pl.* **~a** *or* **~ums**). Note to help the memory; record of events etc. for future use; (Law) document recording terms of contract, agreement, establishment of company, etc.; informal letter without signature; informal diplomatic message. [ME, f. L, neut. sing. gerundive of *memorare* (see prec.)]

mėmŏr'ĭal *a.* & *n.* **1.** *a.* (Of statue, festival, building, religious service, etc.) serving to commemorate; of memory; ***M~ Day,** day (usu. 30 May) commemorating those who died on active service. **2.** *n.* Memorial object, custom, etc.; (usu. in *pl.*) record, chronicle; informal diplomatic paper; statement of facts as basis of petition etc. **3.** Hence ~IST (1) *n.* [ME f. OF, or f. L *memorialis* (as MEMORY; see -AL)]

mėmŏr'ĭalīze, -īse (-iz), *v.t.* Commemorate; address memorial to (person or body). [f. prec. + -IZE]

mėmŏria tĕ'chnica (tĕ'k-) *n.* System or contrivance used to assist memory. [mod. L, = artificial memory]

mĕ'morīze, -īse (-iz), *v.t.* Commit to memory. [f. foll. + -IZE]

mĕ'morÿ *n.* **1.** Faculty by which things are recalled to or kept in the mind; this in an individual (**a good ~,** ability to retain and recall much); **commit to ~,** learn so as to be able to recall. **2.** Recovery of one's knowledge by mental effort; recollection, remembrance; **from ~,** without verification in books etc.; **in ~ of,** as a record of, to keep alive the remembrance of. **3.** (In computer) = STORE 3. **4.** Act of remembering; person or thing remembered. **5.** Posthumous repute (*his memory has been censured*; *of happy memory*); **the Immortal M~** (toast to Sc. poet Robert Burns d. 1796). **6.** Length of time over which memory extends (*beyond, within, the memory of men*; *within* LIVING² *memory*). [ME, f. OF *memorie, memoire* f. L *memoria* (*memor* mindful, remembering, cogn. w. MOURN; see -Y¹)]

mĕ'msahĭb *n.* (Anglo-Ind., Hist.) European married lady as spoken of or to by Indians. [f. MA'AM + SAHIB]

mĕn. See MAN¹.

mĕ'nace¹ *n.* **1.** (literary). Threat. **2.** Dangerous or obnoxious thing or person. [ME, f. Rom. **minacia* = L *minaciae* pl. (*minax* threatening f. *minari* threaten)]

mĕ'nace² *v.t* & *i.* Threaten, esp. in malignant or hostile manner. [ME, f. AF *manasser*, OF *menacier* f. Rom. **minaciare* (as prec.)]

ménage (mānah'zh) *n.* Domestic establishment; **~ *à trois*** (ah trwah), household consisting of husband, wife, and lover of one of these. [f. OF *manaige* f. Rom. **mansionaticum* f. L (as MANSION; see -AGE)]

mėnă'gerĭe *n.* Collection of wild animals in captivity for exhibition etc. [f. F *ménagerie* (as prec.; see -ERY)]

mĕnâr'chė (-kĭ) *n.* Onset of first menstruation. [mod. L, f. as MENO- + Gk *arkhē* beginning]

mĕnd¹ *n.* Repaired hole in material etc.; **on the ~,** improving in health or (of affairs etc.) condition. [f. foll.]

mĕnd² *v.* **1.** *v.t.* Restore to sound condition, repair, (broken article, torn clothes, damaged road, etc.); add fuel to (fire); cut (worn quill pen) to required shape; ~ **or end,** improve or abolish; LEAST *said soonest mended*; *mend* one's FENCE¹*s*; ~ one's **manners** or **ways,** improve them; ~ **matters,** rectify or improve state of affairs; ~ one's **pace,** walk more quickly; hence ~'ABLE *a.* **2.** *v.i.* Regain health. [ME, f. AF *mender* (*amender* AMEND)]

mĕndā'cious (-sh*u*s) *a.* Lying, untruthful; hence or cogn. ~LY² *adv.*, **mĕndă'**CITY *n.* [f. L *mendax -dacis* perh. f. *mendum* fault; see -ACIOUS]

mĕndelē'vium *n.* (Chem.) Artificially produced transuranic element. [f. D. I. *Mendeleev*, Russ. chemist d. 1907 + -IUM]

Mĕ'ndelism *n.* Theory of heredity showing that recurrence of certain inherited characters depends on presence of genes; so **Mĕndē'l**IAN *a.* & *n.* [f. G. J. *Mendel*, Austrian botanist d. 1884 + -ISM]

mĕ'ndic|ant *a.* & *n.* **1.** *a.* Begging; ~**ant friar** (living solely on alms); hence or cogn. ~ANCY, **mĕndĭ'**CITY, *ns.* **2.** *n.* Beggar; mendicant friar. [f. L *mendicare* beg (*mendicus* beggar f. *mendum* fault); see -ANT]

menfolk. See MAN¹.

mĕnhā'den *n.* Large herring of genus *Brevoortia* on E. coast of N. America, used for manure, and yielding valuable oil. [Algonquian; cf. Narragansett *munnawhatteaûg*]

mĕ'nhir (-ēr) *n.* (Archaeol.) Tall upright usu. prehistoric monumental stone. [f. Breton *men hir* (*men* stone, *hir* long)]

mē'nĭal *a.* & *n.* **1.** *a.* (Of service) degrading, servile; (of servant, usu. derog.) domestic; hence ~LY² *adv.* **2.** *n.* Menial servant. [ME f. AF (MEINIE; see -AL)]

mē'nĭnx *n.* (usu. in *pl.* **meni'nges** *pr.* mĭnĭ'njēz). Any of three membranes enveloping brain and spinal cord (dura mater, arachnoid, pia mater); hence **mėnĭ'ngė**AL *a.*, **mĕnĭngi**'TIS *n.*, (-nj-), **mėnĭ'ngo**CELE (-ngg-) *n.*, hernia of meninges. [mod. L, f. Gk *mēnigx -iggos* membrane]

mėnĭ'sc|us *n.* (*pl.* ~**i** *pr.* -sī). Lens convex on one side, concave on the other; (Math.) figure of crescent form; (Phys.) curved upper surface of liquid in tube. [mod. L, f. Gk *mēniskos* crescent dim. of *mēnē* moon]

Mĕ'nnonite *n.* Member of a Protestant sect that arose in Friesland in 16th c. with tenets resembling those of Quakers and Baptists. [f. *Menno* Simons, founder d. 1559]

mĕ'no- *comb. form.* Menstruation, as: ~**rrha'gia** (-rā'-) excessive flow, ~**rrhoe'a** (-rē'*a*) ordinary flow, of the menses. [f. Gk *mēn mēnos* month]

mēnŏ'logy̆ *n.* Calendar, esp. that of Greek Church, with biographies of saints. [f. mod. L *menologium* f. eccl. Gk *mēnologion* (*mēn* month, *logos* account); see -Y¹]

mĕ'nopaus|e (-z) *n.* Final cessation of menses; period of woman's life (usu. between 40 and 50) when this occurs; hence ~AL *a.* [f. mod. L *menopausis* (as MENO-, PAUSE)]

mėnôr'ah (-*a*) *n.* Seven-branched candelabrum used in Jewish worship. [Heb., = candlestick]

mĕ'nsēs (-z) *n. pl.* Flow of blood etc. from mucous lining of human or primate womb, occurring in women at intervals of about one lunar month. [L, pl. of *mensis* month]

Mĕ'nshėvĭk *n.* (Hist.) Russian socialist of the more moderate party (cf. BOLSHEVIK). [f. Russ. *Men'shevik* member of minority (*men'she* less)]

mens rea (mĕnz rē'*a*) *n.* Criminal intent of an action. [L, = guilty mind]

mĕ'nstrual (-ōō-) *a.* Of the menses. [ME, f. L *menstrualis* (as MENSTRUUM; see -AL)]

mĕ'nstru|āte (-ōō-) *v.i.* Discharge the menses; hence ~A'TION *n.* [f. LL *menstruare* (as foll.) + -ATE³]

mĕ'nstruous (-ōō-) *a.* Of the menses; menstruating. [ME, f. OF *menstrueus* or f. LL *menstruosus* (as foll.; see -OUS)]

mĕ'nstru|um (-ōō-) *n.* (*pl.* ~**a**). Solvent (lit. or fig.). [ME f. L, neut. (as n.) of *menstruus* monthly (*mensis* month) f. alchemical parallel between transmutation into gold and supposed action of menses on ovum]

mĕ'nsūrable *a.* Measurable, having fixed limits; (Mus.) having fixed rhythm and notes of definite duration. [F, or f. LL *mensurabilis* (*mensurare* to measure f. L *mensura* MEASURE¹; see -ABLE)]

mĕ'nsūral *a.* Of measure; (Mus.) = prec. [f. L *mensuralis* (*mensura* MEASURE¹; see -AL)]

mĕnsūrā'tion *n.* Measuring; (Math.) rules for finding lengths, areas, and volumes. [f. LL *mensuratio* (as MENSURABLE; see -ATION)]

-ment *suf.* forming *ns.* expr. result or means of vbl action (*fragment, implement, ligament, ornament; abridgement, amazement, embankment, treatment*); also f. *adjs.* (*merriment, oddment*). [f. or after F f. L *-mentum*]

mĕ'ntal¹ *a.* & *n.* **1.** *a.* Of the mind; done by the mind; ‖(colloq.) affected with mental disorder. **2.** ~ **age,** degree of person's mental development expressed as age at which same degree is attained by average child; ~ **arithmetic** (performed without use of written figures); ~ **asylum, home, hospital,** establishment for care of mental patients; *mental* BLOCK¹; ~ **cruelty,** infliction of suffering on another's mind, esp. as grounds for divorce; ~ **defective, deficiency,** (condition of) person unable to deal with his ordinary affairs; ~ **illness,** disorder of the mind; ~ **patient,** sufferer from mental illness; *mental* RESERVATION. **3.** Hence ~LY² *adv.* **4.** *n.* (colloq.) Mental patient. [ME f. OF, or f. LL *mentalis* f. L *mens -ntis* mind; see -AL]

mĕ'ntal² *a.* Of the chin. [F, f. L *mentum* chin; see -AL]

mĕ'ntal|ism *n.* (Philos.) doctrine that mind, and not the material world, is real; (Psych.) doctrine that the mind may be studied by introspection; so ~IST (2) *n.* [f. MENTAL¹ + -ISM]

mĕntă'lĭty̆ *n.* What is mental or in or of the mind; (degree of) intellectual power; mental character or outlook. [f. MENTAL¹ + -ITY]

mĕntā'tion *n.* Mental action; state of mind. [f. L *mens -ntis* mind + -ATION]

mĕ'nthŏl *n.* Camphor-like substance got from oil of peppermint etc., used to relieve local pain etc. [G, f. L *mentha* MINT³; see -OL 2]

mĕ'ntion¹ *n.* Mentioning, naming, (*of* thing); formal reference to meritorious person (in mil. dispatches etc.; **honourable** ~, award of merit to candidate in examination, work of art, etc., not entitled to prize); **make** (**no**) ~ **of,** (not) refer to. [ME f. OF, f. L *mentio -onis* (**men-* root of *mens* mind; see -ION)]

mĕ'ntion² *v.t.* Refer to, remark upon, specify by name (esp. thing not obviously essential to context; *this was expressly mentioned*); (in deprecation of apology or thanks) **don't** ~ **it;** (introducing fact or thing of secondary or, as rhet. artifice, of primary importance) **not to** ~; hence ~ABLE *a.* [f. F *mentionner* (*mention*; see prec.)]

mĕ'ntôr *n.* Experienced and trusted adviser. [F, f. L f. Gk *Mentōr* adviser of the young Telemachus in Homer's *Odyssey* and Fénelon's *Télémaque* (root **men-* think)]

mĕ'nū *n.* List of dishes to be served or available in restaurant etc. [F adj. (as n., = detailed list) f. L *minutus* MINUTE³]

mėow'. Var. of MIAOW.

‖**mĕ'pacrine** (-ēn) *n.* Quinacrine. [f. *m*ethyl + *p*aludism (=malaria) + *acridine*]

Mĕphĭst|ŏ'phėlēs (-z) *n.* Evil spirit to whom Faust, in German legend, sold his soul; fiendish person; hence **~ŏphėl**E'AN, **~ophē'l**IAN, *adjs.* [G, 16th c., of unkn. orig.]

mėphī'tĭs *n.* Noxious emanation, esp. from the earth; noisome or poisonous stench; so **mėphĭ'-**TIC *a.* [L]

-mėr *suf.* (Chem.) forming *ns.* denoting substance of a specified class, esp. polymer, (*dimer, isomer, tautomer*). [f. Gk *meros* part, share]

mėr'cantīle *a.* Of trade, commercial; trading; mercenary, fond of bargaining; ~ **marine,** shipping employed in commerce. [F, f. It. (*mercante* MERCHANT; see -IL)]

mėr'cantĭl||ĭsm *n.* Old economic theory that money is the only form of wealth; so ~IST (2) *n.* [f. prec. + -ISM]

mercă'ptan *n.* (Chem.) Substance like an alcohol but with sulphur in place of oxygen. [f. mod. L *mercurium captans* capturing mercury]

Mėrcā'tor *n.* **~'s projection,** map projection of globe on cylinder, with straight lines of latitude and longitude at right angles. [f. G. ~ (Latinized f. Kremer), Flemish-born geographer d. 1594]

mėr'cėnar|ў *a.* & *n.* **1.** *a.* Working merely for money or other reward; hired; hence ~ĭNESS *n.* **2.** *n.* Hired soldier in foreign service. [ME, f. L *mercenarius* (*merces -edis* reward; see -ARY[1])]

||**mėr'c|er** *n.* Dealer in textile fabrics, esp. silks and other costly materials; hence ~ERY (1) *n.* [ME f. AF; OF *mercier* f. Rom. **merciarius* f. L *merx mercis* goods; see -ER[2] (2)]

mėr'cerīze, -īse (-īz), *v.t.* Treat (cotton fabric or thread) under tension with caustic alkali to give greater strength and impart lustre. [f. J. *Mercer*, alleged inventor of the process d. 1866 + -IZE]

mėr'chandīse (-z) *n.* & *v.* **1.** *n.* Commodities of commerce, goods for sale. **2.** *v.i.* & *t.* Trade (in). [ME, f. OF *marchandise* (*marchand*; see foll., -ISE[2])]

mėr'chant *n.* **1.** Wholesale trader, esp. with foreign countries; (U.S. & Sc.) retail trader. **2.** ~ **bank** (dealing in commercial loans and financing); ~ **fleet, *marine, ||navy, service,** mercantile marine; **~man,** ~ **ship,** ship conveying merchandise; ~ **prince,** wealthy merchant; LAW[1] *merchant.* **3.** (sl.) Person fond of an activity etc. (SPEED-*merchant*). [ME, f. OF *marchand, marchant* f. Rom. **mercatare* frequent. of L *mercari* trade (*merx mercis* merchandise); see -ANT]

mėr'chantable *a.* Saleable, marketable. [ME, f. *merchant* v. f. OF *march(ĕ)ander* (*marchand*; see prec.) + -ABLE]

mėr'cĭful *a.* Having, showing, or feeling mercy; hence ~LY[2] *adv.*, ~NESS *n.* [ME, f. MERCY + -FUL]

mėr'cĭlėss *a.* Pitiless; showing no mercy; hence ~LY[2] *adv.*, ~NESS *n.* [ME, f. MERCY + -LESS]

mercūr'ĭal *a.* & *n.* **1.** *a.* (Of person) sprightly, ready-witted, volatile; hence ~ITY (-ă'l-) *n.* **2.** Of or containing mercury; (*M*~) of the planet Mercury; hence ~LY[2] *adv.* **3.** *n.* Mercurial drug; hence ~ISM (5) *n.*, ~IZE (5) *v.t.* [ME, f. OF *mercuriel* or f. L *mercurialis* (as foll.; see -AL)]

mėr'cūrў *n.* **1.** (*M*~). Roman god of eloquence, skill, thieving, etc., and messenger of gods; guide, messenger, (arch., exc. in newspaper titles). **2.** (*M*~). Planet nearest to sun. **3.** White normally liquid metal usu. got from cinnabar and used in barometers, thermometers, amalgams, and mirrors, (**the ~ is rising,** weather is improving), quicksilver; hence **mercūr'**IC, **mercūr'**OUS (*or* mėr'-), *adjs.* (Chem.). **4.** Plant of genus *Mercurialis.* [ME, f. L *Mercurius* (*merx mercis* merchandise)]

mėr'cў *n.* & *a.* **1.** *n.* Compassion, forbearance, shown by one to another (esp. offender) who is in his power and has no claim to kindness; God's forbearance and forgiveness of sins; **have ~ on** or **upon,** show mercy to; ~ (**me**)!, ~ **on** or **upon us,** (excl. of terror or surprise). **2.** Compassionateness; **at the ~ of,** wholly in the power of, liable to danger or harm from. **3.** Act of mercy; ERRAND *of mercy*; **that is a** ~ (blessing, thing to be thankful for); **left to the tender mercies of,** at the mercy of, (usu., iron.) exposed to probable rough handling by. **4. ~-seat,** golden covering of Ark of Covenant, throne of God, Christ as propitiation. **5.** *a.* Administered or performed out of mercy or pity for suffering person (*mercy killing*). [ME f. OF *merci* f. L *merces -edis* reward, in LL pity, thanks]

mēre[1] *n.* Lake, pond, (arch. or poet., exc. in place names). [OE, = OS, OHG *meri*, ON *marr* sea, Goth. *mari-* f. Gmc **mari* f. IE **mori-*]

mēre[2] *attrib. a.* That is solely or no more or better than (what the noun implies) (*a mere swindler; the merest buffoonery*); **no** ~, by no means only a; (Law) ~ **right** (without possession); hence ~'LY[2] (mēr'lĭ) *adv.* [ME, f. AF *meer*, OF *mier* f. L *merus* unmixed]

mĕ'rė[3] *n.* Maori war-club, esp. one made of greenstone. [Maori]

mĕrėtrĭ'cious (-sh*us*) *a.* Of or befitting a prostitute; (of ornament, literary style, etc.) showily but falsely attractive; hence ~LY[2] *adv.*, ~NESS *n.* [f. L *meretricius* f. *meretrix -tricis* harlot (*merēri* be hired; see -TRIX) + -OUS]

mėrgă'nser *n.* Diving fish-eating northern duck of genus *Mergus* etc., with long narrow serrated hooked bill. [mod. L, f. L *mergus* diver (*mergere* dive) + *anser* goose]

mėrg|e *v.i.* & *t.* Lose, cause (thing) to lose, character or identity *in* (another); embody (title, estate, *in* greater one); join or blend gradually; hence ~'ENCE *n.* [f. L *mergere mers-* dip, plunge, partly thr. legal AF *merger*]

mėr'ger *n.* Merging, esp. of estate in another; combining of two commercial companies etc. into one; absorbing of minor offence in a greater one. [f. AF (as prec.; see -ER[4])]

merĭ'dĭan *n.* & *a.* **1.** *n.* Circle passing through celestial poles and zenith of any place on earth's surface; circle of constant longitude, passing through given place and the terrestrial poles (**prime** ~, that from which longitude is reckoned, esp. Greenwich meridian); corresponding line on map; (arch.) point at which sun or star attains highest altitude; (fig.) prime, full splendour. **2.** *a.* Of noon; (fig.) of the period of greatest splendour, vigour, etc. [ME, f. OF *meridien* or f. L *meridianus* a. (*meridies* midday f. *medius* middle + *dies* day; see -AN)]

merĭ'dĭonal *a.* & *n.* **1.** *a.* Of (the inhabitants of) the south (esp. of Europe); of a meridian. **2.** *n.* Inhabitant of the south (esp. of France). [ME f. OF, f. LL *meridionalis* (irreg. f. L *meridies*; see prec., -AL)]

merĭ'ngue (-ă'ng) *n.* Confection of sugar, white of eggs, etc., baked crisp; small cake or shell of this, usu. decorated or filled with whipped cream etc. [F, of unkn. orig.]

merĭ'nō (-rē'-) *n.* (*pl.* **~s**). ~ (**sheep**), variety of sheep with fine wool; soft woollen or wool-and-cotton material like cashmere, orig. of merino wool; fine woollen yarn. [Sp., of uncert. orig.]

mĕ'rĭstĕm *n.* (Bot.) Growing tissue of small cells in plants; hence ~A'TIC *a.* [f. Gk *meristos* divisible (*merizō* divide f. *meros* part), after *xylem*]

mĕ'rĭt *n.*, & *v.t.* **1.** *n.* Quality of deserving well; excellence, worth; (Theol.) good deeds as entitling to future reward; (usu. in *pl.*) thing that entitles to reward or gratitude; **make a ~ of,** view, represent, (one's own conduct) as meritorious; **the ~s,** the intrinsic rights and wrongs (*of* case etc., esp. Law); *judge* (proposal etc.) **on its ~s,** with regard only to its intrinsic excellences etc.; ||**Order of M~** (founded 1902, for distinguished achievement); *~ **system,** practice of giving public office to those most competent for it. **2.** *v.t.* Deserve, be worthy of, (reward, punishment, consideration, etc.). [ME; (v. f. F *mériter*) f. OF *merite* f. L *meritum* price, value, neut. p.p. (as n.) of *merēri* earn, deserve]

mĕrĭtŏ'cracy̆ *n.* Government by persons selected according to merit in competition; group of persons thus selected; society thus governed. [f. prec. + -O- + -CRACY]

mĕrĭtôr'ious *a.* (Of person or act) having merit, deserving reward, praise, or gratitude; deserving commendation for thoroughness etc.; hence ~LY² *adv.*, ~NESS *n.* [ME, f. L *meritorius* (*merēri merit-* earn; see -ORY) + -OUS]

mêrle *n.* (arch. or Sc.) Blackbird. [ME f. F, f. L *merulus, -la*]

mêr'lĭn *n.* Small Eur. or N. Amer. falcon (*Falco columbarius*). [ME, f. AF *merilun* f. OF *esmerillon* augment. f. *esmeril* f. Frank. **smeril*]

mêr'lon *n.* Solid part of embattled parapet, between two embrasures. [F, f. It. *merlone* (*merlo* battlement)]

mêr'maid *n.* Imaginary half-human sea creature, with head and trunk of woman and tail of fish; **~'s purse,** = SEA-*purse*; so **mêr'**MAN¹ *n.* [ME, f. MERE¹ in obs. sense 'sea' + MAID]

mĕ'ro- *comb. form.* Partly, partial, as: **~blast,** ovum that is partly germinal, partly nutritive; ~HE'DRAL, (of crystal) having less than full number of faces corresponding to its symmetry. [f. Gk *meros* part + -O-]

-merous *suf.* (esp. Bot. & Entom.) Having so many parts (*dimerous, 5-merous*). [f. Gk (as prec.) + -OUS]

Mĕrovĭ'ngĭan (-nj-) *a.* & *n.* (Member) of the Frankish dynasty founded by Clovis and reigning in Gaul and Germany *c.* 500–750. [f. F *mérovingien* f. med. L *Merovingi* f. L *Meroveus* name of reputed founder; see -ING³, -IAN]

mĕ'rrĭment *n.* Hilarious enjoyment; mirth, fun. [f. MERRY² + -MENT]

mĕ'rrў̆¹ *n.* Gean. [f. F *merise,* taken as pl. (cf. CHERRY)]

mĕ'rrў̆² *a.* Joyous; full of laughter or gaiety; (colloq.) slightly tipsy; **make ~,** be festive; **make ~ over,** make fun of; **~ andrew,** mountebank's assistant, clown, buffoon, (lit. or fig.); **~ Christmas!** (as salutation); ||*merry* DANCERS; **~** or **merrie** (pleasant) **England; ~-go-round,** revolving machine with wooden horses or cars for riding on at fair etc.; **~ hell,** (sl.) great disturbance (*play merry hell with*); **~-making,** festivity; **~ men,** companions of outlaw etc., (joc.) person's assistants; **the M~ Monarch,** Charles II; **~thought,** wishbone of bird; hence **mĕ'rrĭ**LY² *adv.* [OE *myr(i)ge* f. Gmc **murgjaz* (cf. MIRTH); perh. = Gmc **murgjaz* short]

***me'sa** (mā'-) *n.* High rocky tableland with precipitous sides. [Sp., lit. 'table', f. L *mensa*]

mésalliance (māză'lĭahṅs) *n.* Marriage with person of inferior social position. [F (*més-* MIS-; see ALLIANCE)]

mĕ'scăl *n.* **1.** (Liquor got from) maguey plant. **2.** Peyote cactus; **~ buttons,** its disc-shaped dried tops. [f. Sp. *mezcal* f. Nahuatl *mexcalli*]

mĕ'scaline (-ēn), **-in,** *n.* Hallucinogenic alkaloid present in mescal buttons. [f. prec. + -INE⁵]

Mesdames, Mesdemoiselles. See MADAME, MRS.; MADEMOISELLE.

mèsee'ms (-z) *v.i. impers.* (arch.) It seems to me. [ME, f. *me* dat. + SEEMS]

mèsĕmbrўă'nthèmum (-z-) *n.* S. Afr. plant of genus *Mesembryanthemum,* with bright pink or white flowers opening at about noon. [mod. L, f. Gk *mesēmbria* noon + *anthemon* flower]

mĕsĕncĕ'phalŏn *n.* Midbrain. [f. Gk *mesos* middle + *encephalon* (see ENCEPHALIC)]

mĕ'senterў̆ *n.* Fold of peritoneum attaching some part of intestinal canal to posterior wall of abdomen; hence **mĕsĕntĕ'r**IC *a.*, **mĕsĕnterĭ'**TIS *n.* [f. med. L f. Gk *mesenterion* (as MESO-, *enteron* intestine)]

mĕsh¹ *n.* Open space, interstice, of net, sieve, etc.; (in *pl.*) network, (fig.) snare; network fabric; (Physiol., in *pl.*) interlaced structure; **in ~,** (of teeth of wheels) engaged. [earlier *meish, meash, mash* f. MDu. *maesche, masche* f. Gmc **mǣsk-*, **mask-*]

mĕsh² *v.* **1.** *v.t.* Catch in net (lit. or fig.). **2.** *v.i.* (Of teeth of wheel) be engaged (*with* others), (fig.) be harmonious. [f. prec.]

mē'sĭal (-z-) *a.* Of, in, directed towards, middle line of a body; hence ~LY² *adv.* [irreg. f. Gk *mesos* middle + -IAL]

mesic. See MESON.

mĕ'smer|ĭsm (mĕ'z-) *n.* (arch. or fig.) Hypnotic state produced in patient by operator's influence over will and nervous system; doctrine concerning, influence producing, this; hence **mĕsmĕ'r**IC *a.*, ~IST (1) *n.*, ~IZE (4) *v.t.*, (mĕz-). [f. F. A. *Mesmer,* Austrian physician d. 1815 + -ISM]

mēsne (mēn) *a.* (Law). Intermediate; **~ lord** (holding estate from superior feudal lord); **~ process,** proceedings in suit intervening between primary and final process; **~ profits** (received from estate by tenant between two dates). [ME f. law F, var. of AF *meen,* MEAN²; cf. DEMESNE]

mĕ'so- (*or* -z-) *comb. form.* Middle, intermediate, as: **~blast,** middle germ-layer of embryo; **~carp,** middle layer of pericarp; **~cepha'lic,** (of skull) intermediate between brachycephalic and dolichocephalic; **~derm,** = *mesoblast*; **~ga'ster,** membrane attaching stomach to dorsal wall of abdomen; **~li'thic,** of Stone Age between palaeolithic and neolithic; **~morph,** person with innate muscular body-build; **~phyll,** inner tissue of leaf; **~phyte,** plant needing moderate amount of moisture; **~sphere,** region of atmosphere from top of stratosphere to altitude about 50 miles; **~tron,** orig. name of MESON; **~zo'ic,** of second geological period (cf. CAINOZOIC, PALAEOZOIC). [f. Gk *mesos* middle + -O-]

mĕ'sŏn (-z-) *n.* (Phys.) Elementary unstable particle intermediate in mass between proton and electron, found in cosmic rays and atomic nuclei; hence **mĕ'sIC**, **mèsŏ'n**IC, (-z-) *adjs.* [f. MESO*tron*; see -ON]

mĕ'squite, -quit, (-kēt) *n.* N. Amer. leguminous tree of genus *Prosopis,* with pods (**~ beans**) used as fodder; **~ grass,** (of genus *Bouteloua,* found near mesquite tree). [f. Mex. Sp. *mezquite*]

mĕss¹ *n.* **1.** Portion of liquid or pulpy food (freq. *savoury mess*); **~ of pottage,** material comfort etc. for which something higher is sacrificed (Gen. 25:29–34). **2.** Liquid or mixed food for hounds etc.; (derog.) disagreeable concoction or medley. **3.** Dirty or untidy state of things; spilt liquid etc.; domestic animal's excreta; state of confusion, embarrassment, or trouble; **make a ~ of,** bungle (undertaking). **4.** Company of persons who take meals together, esp. in the fighting services; meal so taken; place where such meals are taken; **~-jacket,** short close-fitting coat worn at mess;

~-**kit,** soldier's cooking and eating utensils; ~'**mate,** one of the same (usu. ship's) mess; ~ **tin,** small oval bucket as part of mess-kit. [ME, f. OF *mes* portion of food f. LL *missus* course at dinner, p.p. of *mittere* send]

mĕss[2] *v.* **1.** *v.t.* ~ (**up**), make a mess of, dirty, interfere with, muddle (business). **2.** *v.i.* Potter *about* or *around*; take one's meals (*with*, or abs.). [f. prec.]

mĕ'ssage[1] *n.* Oral or written communication sent or transmitted by one person to another; mission, errand; prophet's, writer's, or preacher's, inspired or significant communication; **get the** ~, (collóq.) understand what is meant. [ME f. OF, f. Rom. **missaticum* f. L *mittere miss-* send; see -AGE]

mĕ'ssage[2] *v.t.* Send as a message; transmit (plan etc.) by signalling etc. [f. prec.]

Messeigneurs. See MONSEIGNEUR.

mĕ'ssėnger (-nj-) *n.* One who carries a message; person employed to carry messages; **King's** or **Queen's M**~, courier in diplomatic service; ~ **RNA** (carrying genetic information from gene to ribosome). [ME & OF *messager* (as MESSAGE[1]; see -ER[2]); *-n-* as in *harbinger, passenger, porringer, scavenger, wharfinger*]

Mėssī'ah (-*a*) *n.* Promised deliverer of Jews; Christ regarded as this; (would-be) liberator of oppressed people or country; hence ~SHIP *n.* [ME f. OF *Messie* f. LL f. Gk *Messias* f. Aram. *m'shīḥā*, Heb. *māšīaḥ* anointed (*māšaḥ* anoint); *Messiah* alt. sp. to give the wd a more Hebraic appearance]

Mĕssĭă'nĭc *a.* Of the, inspired by hope or belief in a, Messiah; so **Mėssī'an**ISM (3) *n.* [f. F *messianique* (as prec., after *rabbinique* rabbinical)]

Messieurs. See MONSIEUR.

Mĕ'ssrs. (-*serz*) *n.* (used as *pl.* of MR., esp. as prefix to name of firm or to list of men's names). [abbr. of prec.]

mĕ'ssuage (-swĭj) *n.* (Law). Dwelling-house with outbuildings and land assigned to its use. [ME, f. AF *mes(s)uage*, perh. alt. sp. f. *mesnage* dwelling f. OF *manaige*; see MÉNAGE]

mĕ'ss|y̆ *a.* That is, or is accompanied by, a mess (sense 3); untidy, slovenly, difficult to deal with; hence ~ĬLY[2] *adv.*, ~ĬNESS *n.* [f. MESS[1] + -Y[2]]

mĕsti'zō (-tē'-) *n.* (*pl.* ~s). Spanish or Portuguese half-caste, esp. offspring of Spaniard and Amer. Indian. [Sp., f. Rom. **mixticius* f. L *mixtus* p.p. of *miscēre* mix]

mĕt[1]. See MEET[2].

mĕt[2] *a.* (colloq.) Meteorological, metropolitan, etc.; **the Met,** ||the Meteorological Office, *the Metropolitan Opera House (New York). [abbr.]

mĕ'ta- *pref.* (usu. **met-** bef. vowel or *h*), w. sense of change of position or condition (*metabolism*), behind, after (*metaphysics*), beyond (*metacarpus*), of a higher or second-order kind (*metalanguage*); (Chem.) (1) relating to two carbon atoms separated by one other in a benzene ring, (2) relating to a compound formed by dehydration (*metaphosphate*). [Gk *meta-, met-, meth-* (*meta* with, after)]

mėtă'bolĭsm *n.* Process, in organism or single cell, by which nutritive material is built up into living matter (**constructive** ~) or protoplasm is broken down into simpler substances for special functions (**destructive** ~); **basal** ~, this process as occurring in organism completely at rest; so **mĕtabŏ'l**IC *a.*, **mėtă'bol**IZE (3) *v.t.* [f. Gk *metabolē* change f. META(*ballō* throw) change + -ISM]

mĕtacar̄'p|us *n.* (*pl.* ~**i** *pr.* -ī). Part of hand between wrist and fingers; set of bones in this; hence ~AL *a.* [mod. L, f. Gk *metakarpon* (as META-, CARPUS)]

mĕ'tacĕntre, ***-ter,** *n.* Point of intersection between line (vertical in equilibrium) through centre of gravity of floating body and vertical line through centre of pressure after slight angular displacement, which must be above the centre of gravity to ensure stability; hence **mĕtacĕ'ntr**IC *a.* [f. F *métacentre* (as META-, CENTRE[1])]

mē'tage *n.* Official measuring of load of coal etc.; duty paid for this. [f. METE[2] + -AGE]

mĕtagĕ'nėsĭs *n.* Alternation of generations between sexual and asexual reproduction; so **mĕtagėn**E'TIC *a.* [mod. L (as META-, GENESIS)]

mĕ'tal *n.*, *a.*, & *v.t.* (||-**ll**-). **1.** *n.* Any of a class of substances such as gold, silver, copper, iron, lead, tin, aluminium, uranium, etc., all of which are crystalline when solid and many of which are opaque, ductile, malleable, dense, good conductors of heat and electricity, and characterized by a peculiar lustre; alloy of these; BELL[1]-, BRITANNIA, GUN-, TYPE[1]-, WHITE[1], YELLOW, *metal*; HEAVY *metal*. **2.** (Mil.) Tanks, armoured vehicles, etc. **3.** Material used for making glass, in molten state; ROAD[1]-*metal*; ||(in *pl.*) rails of a railway line (*train* **leaves the** ~**s,** is derailed). **4.** (Her.) Gold or silver as tincture. **5.** ~**work,** (product of) shaping objects from metal. **6.** *a.* Made of metal. **7.** *v.t.* Furnish or fit with metal; ||make or mend (road) with road-metal. [ME f. OF, or L f. Gk *metallon* mine]

mĕ'talănguage (-nggwĭj) *n.* Language used to discuss a language; system of propositions about propositions. [f. META- + LANGUAGE]

mėtă'llĭc *a.* **1.** Of metal(s); ~ **currency,** gold, silver, copper, etc., cf. PAPER[1]. **2.** Characteristic of metals; ~ **lustre,** peculiar sheen of metals; ~ **sound** (like struck metal, sharp and ringing); ~ **voice** (harsh and unmusical). **3.** Hence or cogn. **mėtă'll**ICALLY *adv.*, **mĕ'tall**INE[1] *a.* [f. F *métallique* f. L f. Gk *metallikos* (as METAL; see -IC)]

mĕ'tallīz|e, -īs|e (-īz), ***-alīz|e,** *v.t.* Render metallic; coat with thin layer of metal; hence ~A'TION *n.* [f. METAL + -IZE]

mĕtallŏ'graphy̆ *n.* Descriptive science of structure and properties of metals. [f. as METAL + -O- + -GRAPHY]

mĕ'talloid *a.* & *n.* **1.** *a.* Having form or appearance of metal. **2.** *n.* Element with characteristics both of metals and of non-metals. [f. METAL + -OID]

mėtă'llophōne *n.* (Mus.) Instrument like xylophone but with metal bars. [f. METAL + -O- + -PHONE]

mėtă'llurgy̆ (*or* mĕ'*talēr*-) *n.* Art of working metals, esp. of extracting metals from their ores; hence **mĕtallûr'g**IC(AL) *adjs.*, **mėtă'llurg**IST (3) (*or* mĕ'*tal*-) *n.* [f. Gk *metallon* metal + *-ourgia* working; see -Y[1]]

mĕ'tamēre *n.* (Zool.) One of several similar segments of animal body. [f. META- + Gk *meros* part]

mĕtamĕ'rĭc *a.* (Chem.) having same proportional composition and molecular weight, but different chemical properties; (Zool.) of metameres; so **mĕ'ta**MER, **mĕtă'mer**ISM (2), *ns.* [f. as prec. + -IC]

mĕtamôr'ph|ĭc *a.* Of, or marked by, metamorphosis; (Geol., of rock) that has undergone transformation by natural agencies, whence ~ISM (1) *n.* [f. META- + Gk *morphē* form + -IC]

mĕtamôr'phōse (-z) *v.t.* Change in form, turn (*to* or *into* new form); change nature of. [f. F *métamorphoser* (*métamorphose* = foll.)]

mĕtamôr'phos|ĭs (*or* -fō'-) *n.* (*pl.* ~**es** *pr.* ~ēz). Change of form (by magic or by natural development etc.); changed form; change of character, conditions, etc.; (Zool.) change (usu. rapid) between immature form and adult, e.g.

of insect. [L, f. Gk *metamorphōsis* f. META- (*morphoō* f. *morphē* form) transform; see -OSIS]

mě'taph|or *n.* Application of name or descriptive term or phrase to an object or action to which it is not literally applicable (e.g. *a glaring error, food for thought, leave no stone unturned*); instance of this; **mixed ~or,** combination of inconsistent metaphors (*this tower of strength will forge ahead*); hence **~ŏ'ric**(AL) *adjs.*, **~ŏ'ricalLY**[2] *adv.* [f. F *métaphore* or f. L f. Gk *metaphora* f. META(*pherō* bear) transfer]

mě'taphr|āse (-z) *n.*, & *v.t.* **1.** *n.* Translation, esp. word-for-word, opp. *paraphrase.* **2.** *v.t.* Put into other words. **3.** So **~ă'stic** *a.* [f. mod. L f. Gk *metaphrasis* (*metaphrazō* translate; see META-, PHRASE)]

mětaphy̆'sic (-z-) *n.* (System of) metaphysics. [ME; see METAPHYSICS]

mětaphy̆'sical (-z-) *a.* & *n.* **1.** *a.* Of metaphysics; based on abstract general reasoning; over-subtle; incorporeal; supernatural; visionary; (of some 17th-c. poets, esp. Cowley and Donne) addicted to fanciful conceits and far-fetched imagery; hence **~LY**[2] *adv.* **2.** *n.* (esp. in *pl.*) **The M~s,** the metaphysical poets. [f. as foll. + -AL]

mětaphy̆'s|ics (-z-) *n. pl.* (often treated as *sing.*) Theoretical philosophy of being and knowing; philosophy of mind; (pop.) abstract or subtle talk, mere theory; so **~i'cian** *n.*, **~icize** (2) *v.i.* [ME *metaphysic*, later -ICS, f. OF *métaphysique* f. med. L *metaphysica* fem. sing. & neut. pl., f. med. Gk *metaphusika* f. Gk *ta meta ta phusika* the works (of Aristotle) placed after (META-) the *Physics*]

mětapl|ā'sia (-z-) *n.* (Physiol.) Transformation of one form of tissue into another; so **~ă'stic** *a.* [mod. L, f. G *metaplase* f. Gk META(*plasis* f. *plassō* mould); see -IA[1]]

mě'taplăsm *n.* (Biol.) Non-living part of protoplasm. [f. META- after PROTOPLASM]

mětapŏ'litics *n. pl.* (often derog.) Abstract political science. [f. META- after METAPHYSICS]

měta|stā'ble *a.* (Of state of equilibrium) stable only under small disturbances; passing to another state so slowly as to seem stable; hence **~stabi'lity** *n.* [f. META- + STABLE[1]]

mětă'stas|is *n.* (*pl.* **-es** *pr.* -ēz). (Physiol.) Transference of bodily function, disease, etc., from one part or organ to another; transformation of chemical compounds into others in process of assimilation by an organism; hence **~ize** (3) *v.i.*, **mětastă'tic** *a.* [LL f. Gk (*methistēmi* change; see META-, STASIS)]

mětatar̆'s|us *n.* (*pl.* **~i** *pr.* -ī). Part of foot between ankle and toes; set of bones in this; hence **~al** *a.* [mod. L (as META-, TARSUS)]

mėtă'thės|is *n.* (*pl.* **~es** *pr.* -ēz). (Gram.) transposition of sounds or letters in word; (Chem.) interchange of (groups of) atoms between two molecules; so **mětathě'tic**(AL) *adjs.* [LL, f. Gk, f. META(*tithēmi* place) transpose; see THESIS]

métayage (mě'tāyahzh) *n.* Land tenure in which farmer pays part (usu. half) of produce as rent to owner, who furnishes stock and seed. [F (as foll.; see -AGE)]

métayer (mě'tāyā) *n.* Tenant of land on *métayage* system. [F, f. med. L *medietarius* f. L *medietas* half; see MOIETY, -ARY[1]]

mětazō'an *a.* & *n.* (Zool.) (Member) of the subkingdom Metazoa, comprising multicellular animals with differentiated tissues. [f. *Metazoa* f. Gk META- + *zōia* pl. of *zōion* animal, + -AN]

mēte[1] *n.* Boundary, boundary stone, esp. (Law) *metes and bounds.* [ME f. OF, f. L *meta* boundary, goal]

mēte[2] *v.t.* (literary) Apportion, allot, (punishment, reward); (poet. or Bibl.) measure; **~-wand, -yard,** (fig.) standard of estimation. [OE *metan*, = OS *metan*, OHG *mezzan*, ON *meta*, Goth. *mitan* f. Gmc **met-*, **mæt-* MEET[3] f. IE **med-*, **mod-*]

mětěmpsy̆chō's|is (-k-) *n.* (*pl.* **~es** *pr.* -ēz). Supposed transmigration of soul of human being or animal at death into new body of same or different species; hence **~ist** (2) *n.* [LL, f. Gk *metempsukhōsis* (as META-, EN-[2], *psukhē* soul, -OSIS)]

mē'tėor *n.* (Any atmospheric phenomenon, esp.) bright moving body formed by small mass of matter from outer space rendered luminous by compression of air on entering earth's atmosphere; (*attrib.*) = foll. 2; **~ shower,** group of meteors appearing to come from one point in sky. [ME, f. mod. L *meteorum* f. Gk *meteōron* neut. (as n.) of *meteōros* lofty (as META-, *aeirō* raise)]

mētėŏ'ric *a.* **1.** Of the atmosphere; dependent on atmospheric conditions. **2.** Of meteors; (fig.) like a meteor, dazzling, rapid, transient. **3. ~ stone,** meteorite. [partly f. prec. + -IC; partly f. med. L *meteoricus* f. as prec.]

mē'tėorīte *n.* Fallen meteor, fragment of rock or metal reaching earth's surface from outer space. [f. METEOR + -ITE[1]]

mē'tėorograph (-ahf) *n.* Apparatus recording several meteorological phenomena at same time. [f. F *météorographe* (as METEOR, -GRAPH)]

mē'tėor|oid *n.* Body moving through space, of same nature as those which by passing through earth's atmosphere become visible as meteors; hence **~oi'dal** *a.* [f. METEOR + -OID]

mētėorolŏ'gical *a.* Of meteorology; ||**M~ Office,** government department providing weather forecasts etc.; *meteorological* TIDE[1]; hence **~LY**[2] *adv.* [f. foll. + -ICAL]

mētėorŏ'log|y̆ *n.* Study of motions and phenomena of atmosphere, esp. for weather forecasting; atmospheric character (*of* region); so **~ist** (3) *n.* [f. Gk *meteōrologia* (as METEOR; see -LOGY)]

mē'ter[1] *n.*, & *v.t.* **1.** *n.* Person or thing that measures esp. instrument for recording quantity of substance supplied (GAS[1], WATER[1], etc., *meter*); = PARK[2]*ing-meter*, TAXIMETER; **~ maid,** woman employed to report offences against parking-meter regulations. **2.** *v.t.* Measure by meter. [ME, f. METE[2] + -ER[1]]

***mē'ter**[2,3]. See METRE[1,2].

-mėter (*or* -mē-) *suf.* **1.** Forming names of automatic measuring instruments (*barometer, calorimeter, galvanometer, thermometer, voltmeter*). **2.** (Pros.) Forming names of lines with specified number of measures (*dimeter, pentameter*). [f. Gk *metron* measure]

mě'thadōne *n.* Powerful synthetic analgesic drug used as substitute for morphine or heroin. [f. 6-di*methy*lamino-4,4-*d*iphenyl-3-heptan*one*]

měthămphě'tamīne (*or* -ēn) *n.* Amphetamine derivative with quicker and longer action, used as stimulant. [f. METHYL + AMPHETAMINE]

mě'thāne *n.* (Chem.) Odourless colourless inflammable gaseous hydrocarbon, CH_4, simplest member of paraffin series. [f. METHYL + -ANE]

mě'thanŏl *n.* (Chem.) Methyl alcohol. [f. prec. + ALCOHOL]

Mě'thedrīne (*or* -ēn) *n.* Methamphetamine in hydrochloride form. [**P,** f. METHYL + BENZEDRINE]

mėthě'glin *n.* (Hist. or dial.) Spiced or medicated kind of mead. [f. W *meddyglyn* (*meddyg* healing f. L *medicus*, *llyn* liquor)]

mėthi̇'nks *v.i.* *impers.* (*past* **methou'ght** *pr.* -aw't). (arch.) It seems to me. [OE *mē thyncth* (*mē* dat. ME[1], *thyncth* 3rd sing. of *thyncan* seem, THINK)]

mě'thod *n.* Special form of procedure esp. in any branch of mental activity; (Theatr.)

technique of acting based on actor's thorough emotional identification with character; orderly arrangement of ideas; scheme of classification; orderliness, regular habits; **there's ~ in his** etc. **madness,** (joc.) his etc. conduct or proposal is not so mad as it seems. [f. F *méthode* or f. L f. Gk *methodos* pursuit of knowledge (as META-, *hodos* way)]

***mėthŏ'dĭc** *a.* Methodical; methodological. [f. LL f. Gk *methodikos* (*methodos* METHOD; see -IC)]

mėthŏ'dĭcal *a.* Characterized by method or order; hence ~LY^2 *adv.* [f. as prec.; see -ICAL]

Mĕ'thodĭst *n.* **1.** Member of any of several Protestant religious bodies (now united) originating in the 18th-c. evangelistic movement of Charles and John Wesley and George Whitefield; hence **Mĕ'thod**ISM (3) *n.*, **Mĕthodĭ'st**IC(AL) *adjs.* **2.** (*m*~). One who follows or advocates a method or system of procedure. [f. mod. L *methodista* (as METHOD; see -IST); sense 1 prob. f. following a specified 'method' of devotional study]

mĕ'thodīze, -īse (-īz), *v.t.* Reduce to order; arrange in orderly manner. [f. METHOD + -IZE]

mĕthodŏ'logy̆ *n.* Science of method; body of methods used in a particular branch of activity; so **mĕthodo**LO'GICAL *a.* [f. mod. L *methodologia* or F *méthodologie* (as METHOD, -O-, -LOGY)]

methought. See METHINKS.

‖**mĕths** *n.* (colloq.) Methylated spirit. [abbr.]

Mėthū'selah (-zela; *or* -ōō'-) *n.* Pre-Noachian patriarch stated (Gen. 5:27) to have lived 969 years (hence as type of longevity). [ME, f. Bibl. Heb. *m^{e}tûšelaḥ*]

mĕ'thy̆l (*or* mē'thīl) *n.* (Chem.) Hydrocarbon radical CH_3, present in methane and many organic compounds; **~ alcohol,** colourless volatile inflammable liquid CH_3OH, the simplest alcohol; hence **mėthy̆'l**IC *a.* [G, or F *méthyle*, back form. f. G *methylen*, F *méthylène* (see METHYLENE)]

mĕ'thy̆lāte *v.t.* Mix, impregnate, (esp. alcohol to make it unfit for drinking and so exempt it from duty) with methyl alcohol (*methylated spirit(s)*). [f. prec. + -ATE^3]

mĕ'thy̆lēne *n.* (Chem.) Hydrocarbon radical CH_2, present in many polymers. [f. F *méthylène* f. Gk *methu* wine + *hulē* wood; see -ENE]

mĕ'tĭc *n.* (Gk Ant.) Alien living in Greek city with some privileges of citizenship. [irreg. f. Gk *metoikos* (as META-, -*oikos* dwelling)]

mėtĭ'cūlous *a.* (Over-)scrupulous about minute details; (colloq.) very careful, accurate; hence ~LY^2 *adv.*, ~NESS *n.* [f. L *meticulosus* (*metus* fear); see -OUS]

métier (mĕ'tyā) *n.* One's trade, profession, or department of activity; one's forte. [F, f. Rom. **misterium* for L *ministerium* service (MINISTER^1)]

me'tĭf (mā'-) *n.* Offspring of white person and quadroon; =foll. [f. F *métif*, alt. of *métis* (see foll.)]

me'tĭs (mā'-) *n.* Offspring of white person and Amer. Indian, esp. in Canada. [f. F *métis*, OF *mestis* f. Rom. **mixticius* (see MESTIZO)]

mĕ'tŏl *n.* White soluble powder used as photographic developer. [G, an arbitr. name]

Mėtŏ'nĭc *a.* **~ cycle,** period of 19 years (235 lunar months) covering all the changes of the moon's position relative to the sun and the earth. [f. Gk *Metōn*, Athenian astronomer of 5th c. B.C. + -IC]

mĕ'tony̆m *n.* Word used in metonymy. [back form. f. foll., after *synonym*]

mėtŏ'ny̆my̆ *n.* Substitution of the name of an attribute or adjunct for that of the thing meant (e.g. *crown* for *king*, *the turf* for *horse-racing*); hence **mĕtony̆'m**ICAL *a.* [f. LL f. Gk *metōnumia* (as META-, *onoma*, *onuma* name)]

mĕ'tōpe *n.* (Archit.) Square space between triglyphs in Doric frieze. [f. L f. Gk *metopē* (as META-, *opē* hole for beam-end)]

mē'tre^1 (-ter), ***mē'ter**^{2}, *n.* Any form of poetic rhythm, determined by character and number of feet; metrical group, measure; hence **mėtrɪ'**CIAN, **mĕ'tr**ICS, **mĕ'tr**IST (3), *ns.* [OE f. OF, & f. L f. Gk *metron* measure f. IE **me-*]

mē'tre^2 (-ter), ***mē'ter**^{3}, *n.* Unit of length in metric system (about 39·4 in.); CUBIC *metre*, SQUARE^2 *metre*; **~-candle,** unit of illumination equal to that at one metre from a source of one candela. [f. F *mètre* (as prec.)]

mĕ'trĭc *a.* Of the METRE^2; **~ system,** decimal measuring-system with the metre, and the litre and (kilo)gram determined by it, as units of length, capacity, and weight or mass; **go ~,** (colloq.) adopt the metric system; *metric* HUNDREDWEIGHT; *metric* TON^1. [f. F *métrique* (as prec.; see -IC)]

-mĕ'trĭc(al) *sufs.* forming *adjs.* corresp. to *ns.* in -METER, -METRY, (*geometric, geometrical, thermometric*); hence **-mĕ'trĭcal**LY^2 *adv. suf.* [f. or after F *-métrique* f. L (as foll.)]

mĕ'trĭcal *a.* Of, or composed in, metre (*metrical psalms*); of, or involving, measurement (*metrical geometry*); hence ~LY^2 *adv.* [ME, f. L f. Gk *metrikos* (as METRE^1; see -ICAL)]

mĕ'trĭc|āte *v.i.* & *t.* Change or adapt to metric system of measurement; so ~A'TION *n.*, ~IZE (3) *v.t.* [f. METRIC + -ATE^3]

metrician, metrics, metrist. See METRE^1.

Mĕ'trō, *Métro*, *n.* (*pl.* ~*s*). (colloq.) Underground railway (esp. in Paris). [abbr. of F *métropolitain* METROPOLITAN]

mėtrŏ'logy̆ *n.* Science or system of weights and measures; hence **mĕtrolŏ'g**IC(AL) *adjs.* [f. Gk (as METRE^1) + -LOGY]

mĕ'tronōme *n.* (Mus.) Instrument marking time at selected rate by means of pendulum etc.; hence **mĕtronŏ'm**IC *a.* [f. Gk *metron* measure + *nomos* law]

mētrony̆'mĭc *a.* & *n.* (Name) derived from name of a mother or female ancestor. [f. Gk *mētēr mētros* mother, after *patronymic*]

mėtrŏ'polĭs *n.* Chief city of a country, capital, (‖**the ~,** London); metropolitan bishop's see; centre of activity. [LL, f. Gk *mētropolis* parent State (*mētēr mētros* mother, *polis* city)]

mĕtropŏ'lĭtan *a.* & *n.* **1.** *a.* Of a or the metropolis; belonging to, forming (part of), mother country as dist. from its colonies etc.; of an ecclesiastical metropolis. **2.** *a.* & *n.* **~ (bishop),** bishop having authority over bishops of a province, in the Western Church equivalent to archbishop, in the Orthodox Church ranking above archbishop and below patriarch, whence ~ATE^1 *n.*; ‖**~ magistrate,** paid professional magistrate in London (cf. STIPENDIARY). **3.** *n.* Inhabitant of a metropolis. [ME, f. LL *metropolitanus* f. Gk *mētropolitēs* (as prec.; see -ITE^1, -AN)]

mētrŏrrhā'gĭa (-ōrā'-) *n.* Bleeding from the womb. [mod. L, f. Gk *mētra* womb + as HAEMORRHAGE]

-mėtry̆ *suf.* forming names of procedures and systems corresp. to instruments in -METER (*calorimetry, thermometry*). [after *geometry* etc. f. Gk *-metria* (*-metrēs* measurer, as METRE^1); see -Y^1]

mĕ'ttl|e *n.* Quality of person's disposition or temperament; natural ardour; spirit, courage; **on** one's **~e,** incited to do one's best; hence (-)~ED^2 (-teld), ~ESOME^1 (-tels-), *adjs.* [var. of METAL n.]

meu *n.* Baldmoney. [irreg. f. L *meum* f. Gk *mēon*]

mē'um *n.* **~ and *tuum*** (tū'um), mine and thine (used to express rights of property). [L, neut. of *meus* mine]

MeV *abbr.* mega-electron-volt(s).
mew[1] *n.* Gull, esp. common gull (*Larus canus*). [OE *mǣw*, = OS *mēu*, MDu., MLG *mēwe* f. Gmc **mai*(*g*)*wiz*]
mew[2] *n.*, & *v.t.* **1.** *n.* Cage for hawks, esp. while moulting. **2.** *v.t.* Put (hawk) in mew; (fig.) shut *up*, confine. [ME, f. OF *mue* (*muer*; see foll.)]
mew[3] *v.t.* (arch.) (Of hawk) moult, shed, (feathers). [ME, f. OF *muer* f. L *mutare* change]
mew[4] *v.i.*, & *n.* **1.** *v.i.* (Of cat or sea-bird) utter sound *mew*. **2.** *n.* This sound, esp. of cat. [ME; imit.]
mew[5]. Var. of MEU.
mewl *v.i.* Cry feebly, whimper; mew like cat. [imit.; cf. MIAUL]
||**mews** (-z) *n.* Set of stabling round open yard, now often converted into dwellings. [pl. (now used as sing.) of MEW[2], orig. of royal stables on site of hawks' mews at Charing Cross]
Mĕ'xĭcan *a.* & *n.* (Native or inhabitant) of Mexico; (person) of Mexican descent; (language) spoken in Mexico, esp. Nahuatl. [f. Sp. *mexicano* (*Mexico* f. *Mexitli* Aztec war-god; see -AN)]
mėzēr'ėon *n.* Small Eur. & Asian shrub (*Daphne mezereum*) with fragrant purple or pink flowers and red berries. [med. L, f. Arab. *māzaryūn*]
mĕzu'z|ah (-ōō'za) *n.* (*pl.* ~**oth**). Parchment inscribed with religious texts and attached in case to door-post of Jewish house. [f. Heb. *mᵉzûzāh* door-post]
mĕ'zzanine (-ēn; *or* mĕ'tsa-) *n.* Low storey between two others (usu. between ground and first floors); (Theatr.) floor beneath stage, *dress circle. [F, f. It. *mezzanino* dim. of *mezzano* middle f. L *medianus* MEDIAN[1]]
mezza voce (mĕdza vō'chā; *or* -tsa) *adv.* (Mus.) With less than full strength of voice or sound. [It., = half voice]
mezzo (mĕ'dzō; *or* -tsō) *adv.* (esp. Mus.) Half, moderately; ~ ***forte***, fairly loud; ~ ***piano***, fairly soft; ~***-rilievo*** (-rĭlyā'vō), half-relief, in which figures project half their true proportions; ~**-soprano**, (person with, part for) voice between soprano and contralto. [It., f. L *medius* middle]
mĕ'zzōtĭnt (-dzō-; *or* -tsō-) *n.*, & *v.t.* **1.** *n.* Method of engraving in which plate is roughened uniformly, lights and half-lights being given by scraping away the roughness thus produced, deep shadows by leaving it; print produced by this. **2.** *v.t.* Engrave in mezzotint; hence ~ER[1] *n.* [f. It. *mezzotinto* f. *mezzo* half (see prec.) + *tinto* TINT]
M.F. *abbr.* medium frequency.
mf *abbr. mezzo forte.*
||**M.F.H.** *abbr.* Master of Foxhounds.
M.G. *abbr.* machine-gun; Morris Garages.
mg *abbr.* milligram(s).
Mg *symb.* magnesium.
M.G.B. *abbr.* motor gun-boat.
Mgr. *abbr. Monseigneur*; *Monsignor.*
***M.H.** *abbr.* Medal of Honor.
MHD *abbr.* magnetohydrodynamics.
mhō (mō) *n.* (*pl.* ~**s**). (Electr.) Unit of conductance, reciprocal of ohm. [OHM reversed]
M.H.R. *abbr.* Member of the House of Representatives.
MHz *abbr.* megahertz.
mi. See ME[2].
||**M.I.** *abbr.* Military Intelligence (**M.I.5**, security service; **M.I.6**, espionage department); Mounted Infantry.
***mi.** *abbr.* mile(s).
mĭaow' (mĭow') *n.*, & *v.i.* (Make) cry of cat, mew. [imit.]
mĭă'sm|a (-z-) *n.* (*pl.* ~**ata** *or* ~**as**). Infectious or noxious emanation; hence ~AL, ~A'TIC *adjs.* [Gk, = defilement (*miainō* pollute)]
mĭau'l *v.i.* Cry like cat, mew. [f. F *miauler*; imit.]
Mic. *abbr.* Micah (O.T.).
mī'ca *n.* One of several minerals composed of aluminium silicate with other silicates, found as small glittering scales in granite etc., or in crystals that can be separated into thin transparent plates; ~**-schist, -slate,** slaty rock of quartz and mica; hence **mĭcA'CEOUS** *a.* [L, = crumb]
Mĭcaw'ber *n.* Person perpetually idling and trusting that something good will turn up; hence ~ISH[1] *a.*, ~ISM (3) *n.* [character in Dickens's *David Copperfield*]
mīce. See MOUSE[1].
M.I.C.E. *abbr.* Member of the Institution of Civil Engineers.
mīcĕ'lle *n.* (Chem.) Minute aggregation of molecules in some colloidal solutions. [f. mod. L *micella* dim. of L *mica* crumb]
Mich. *abbr.* Michaelmas; Michigan.
Mĭ'chaelmas (-kel-) *n.* Feast of St. Michael, 29 Sept.; ~ **daisy,** aster flowering at Michaelmas; ||~ **term** (in university etc., beginning at or near Michaelmas). [f. St. *Michael* (OE, f. Heb. *mîkā'ēl* who is like God?) + MASS[1]]
M.I.Chem.E. *abbr.* Member of the Institution of Chemical Engineers.
***Mĭ'chĭgan** (-shĭ-) *n.* = NEWMARKET 2. [~ in U.S.]
mĭck *n.* (sl., derog.) Irishman; Roman Catholic. [f. man's Christian name *Michael*)
mĭ'ckey[1], **mĭ'ckў**, *n.* (sl.) **Take the ~ (out of)**, act disrespectfully or teasingly (towards). [20th c.; orig. uncert.]
Mĭ'ckey[2] (**Fĭ'nn**) *n.* (sl.) Strong alcoholic drink, esp. containing narcotic or laxative. [20th c.; orig. uncert.]
Mĭckey Mou'se *n.* (sl.) Electrical distributor releasing bombs from aircraft. [f. mouselike character in Disney's cartoons]
mĭ'ckle, mŭ'ckle, *a.* & *n.* (arch. or Sc.) **1.** *a.* Much, great. **2.** *n.* Large amount (in prov. *many a little*, or *pickle*, *makes a mickle*, erron. *many a mickle makes a muckle*). [ME, f. ON *mikell*, = OE *micel*, OS *mikil*, OHG *michil*, Goth. *mikils* f. Gmc **mikilaz* f. IE **meg*-]
mī'cro- *comb. form.* **1.** Small, as: ~**bio'logy,** study of micro-organisms; ~**card,** opaque card bearing microphotograph of document etc. [P]; ~**cepha'lic** *a.* & *n.*, ~**ce'phalous** *a.*, (person) with abnormally small head; ~**circuit,** integrated circuit or other very small circuit; ~**climate,** climate of small area; ~**cline,** green and blue felspar [from its cleavage planes' being at not quite 90°]; ~**cry'stalline,** having crystalline structure visible only under the microscope; ~**dot,** photograph of document etc. reduced to size of dot; ~**-electro'nics,** design, manufacture, and use of microcircuits; ~**fiche** (*pl.* same), piece of film bearing microphotograph of document etc.; ~**film,** (*n.*, & *v.t.*) (photograph on) length of film bearing microphotograph of document etc.; ~**graph,** photograph taken with microscope; ~**groove,** (gramophone record having) very narrow groove; ~**lith,** (Archaeol.) minute worked flint usu. as part of composite tool; ~**meter** (-ŏ'm-), instrument for measuring small objects or angular distances; ~**miniaturiza'tion,** making of electronic devices with greatly reduced size; ~**-organism,** organism not visible to naked eye, e.g. bacterium or virus; ~**pho'tograph,** photograph reduced to very small size; ~**phyte,** microscopic plant; ~**seism,** very slight earthquake tremor; ~**some,** minute granule in protoplasm;

~**spore,** (parasitic fungus with) small spore; ~**structure,** arrangement of metal etc. crystals visible under microscope; ~**technique,** skill in use of microscope; ~**tome,** instrument for cutting thin sections for microscope; ~**tone,** (Mus.) interval smaller than semitone; ~**wave,** electromagnetic wave of length between about 50 cm and 1 mm. **2.** Denoting factor of one millionth (10^{-6}: *microgram, microsecond, microwatt*). [f. Gk *mikro-* (*mikros* small)]

mī'crōbe *n.* Minute living being, micro-organism (esp. of bacteria causing diseases and fermentation); hence **micrō'bIAL, micrŏ'bIC,** *adjs.* [F, f. Gk *mikros* small + *bios* life]

mī'crocŏsm *n.* Man viewed as epitome of the universe; any community or complex unity so viewed; miniature representation (*of*); hence **microcŏ'smIC** (-z-) *a.* [ME, f. F *microcosme* or f. med. L *micro(s)cosmus* f. Gk *mikros kosmos* little world]

mī'crŏn *n.* One millionth of a metre. [f. Gk *mikron* neut. of *mikros* small; cf. MICRO- 2]

Micronē'sian (-sh*a*n) *a.* & *n.* (Inhabitant or language) of Micronesia. [f. *Micronesia,* island-group in W. Pacific (f. as MICRO- + Gk *nēsos* island + -IA[1]) + -AN]

mī'crophōne *n.* Instrument for intensifying small sounds or converting sound waves into electrical energy variations which may be reconverted into sound after transmission by wire or radio. [f. MICRO- + -PHONE]

mī'croscōpe *n.* Instrument magnifying objects by means of lens(es) so as to reveal details invisible to naked eye. [f. mod. L *microscopium* (as MICRO-, -SCOPE)]

microscŏ'p|ic *a.* **1.** Of the microscope; so ~ICAL *a.* **2.** Too small to be visible (in detail) without microscope; regarded in terms of small units. **3.** Hence ~ICALLY *adv.* [f. prec. + -IC]

micrŏ'scopy̆ *n.* Use of the microscope; so ~IST (3) *n.* [f. MICROSCOPE + -Y[1]]

mī'crūrgy̆ *n.* Manipulation of individual cells etc. under microscope. [f. MICRO- + Gk *-ourgia* work]

mictūrĭ'tion *n.* Urination; (arch.) unduly frequent desire to urinate. [f. L *micturire -it-,* desiderative f. *mingere mict-* urinate; see -ION]

mĭd[1] *a.* (*superl.* ~**most**). **1.** That is the middle of (usu. as comb. after *in*: *in mid-air, career, Channel, course, ocean, stream, week; from mid-June to mid-August; the mid-term examinations*). **2.** That is in the middle, medium, half; (Phonet., of vowel) pronounced with tongue neither high nor low. **3.** ~**'brain,** part of brain developing from middle of primitive or embryonic brain; ***Mideast,** Middle East; ~**'field,** (Footb.) part of field away from goals; ~**-iron,** (Golf) iron with medium loft; ~**-line,** median line; ~**-o'ff, -o'n,** (Cricket) (position of) fieldsman near bowler on off, on, side; ~**'rib,** central rib of leaf; ***~'town,** region between downtown and uptown; ~**'way** (*or* -ā') *adv.*, in middle of distance between places; ***Midwest,** Middle West; ~**wi'cket,** (Cricket) (position of) fieldsman near leg boundary and opposite middle of pitch. [OE **midd,* = OS *middi,* OHG *mitti,* ON *mithr,* Goth. *midjis* f. Gmc **midhja-,* **medhja-* f. IE **medhjo-*]

mĭd[2]. Var. (poet.) of AMID.

Mī'das *n.* ~ **touch,** ability to make money in all one's activities. [f. ~, fabled king of Phrygia, whose touch turned all things to gold]

mĭ'dday (-d-d-) *n.* Noon; time near noon. [OE *middæg* (as MID[1], DAY)]

mĭ'dden *n.* Dunghill; refuse heap near dwelling; **kitchen** ~, prehistoric refuse-heap, chiefly of shells and bones. [ME *myddyng,* of Scand. orig.; cf. Da. *mødding* (*møg* MUCK[1], *dynge* heap)]

mĭ'ddle[1] *attrib. a.,* & *n.* **1.** *a.* (Of member of group) so placed as to have same number of members on each side; equidistant from extremities; intermediate in rank, quality, etc.; average (*a man of middle height*); (of language) pertaining to period between old and modern forms (*Middle* ENGLISH[1]). **2.** ~ **age,** (between youth and old age); ~**-aged,** of such age; *middle-age(d)* SPREAD[2]; **the M~ Ages** (about 1000–1400, or in a wider sense 600–1500); **M~ America,** (1) Mexico and Central America, (2) the American middle class; ‖~ **article,** brief essay of literary kind in weekly or other journal, often placed between leading articles and book-reviews; ~**-brow** *a.* & *n.,* (colloq.) (person) claiming to be or regarded as only moderately intellectual; ~ **C,** (Mus.) C near middle of piano keyboard, note between treble and bass staves, at about 260 hertz frequency; ~ **class,** class of society between upper and lower, incl. professional and business workers and their families; ‖~ **common room** (for use by graduate members of college who are not fellows); ~ **course,** a compromise between two extremes; *middle* DISTANCE; ~ **ear,** cavity of central part of ear behind drum; ~ **earth,** world as between heaven and hell; *Middle* EAST; *middle* FINGER; ~ **game,** central phase of chess game; **M~ Kingdom,** China (orig. of Honan as central and sovereign State), or Egypt *c.* 2000–1800 B.C.; ~ **life,** the middle part of life, middle age; ~**man,** any of the traders who handle a commodity between its producer and consumer; ~ **name,** name between first name and surname, (fig.) person's most characteristic quality (*sobriety is his middle name*); ~**-of-the-road,** (of person or course of action) moderate, avoiding extremes; ~ **passage,** sea journey between W. Africa and W. Indies (w. ref. to the slave trade); ~**-sized,** of medium size; *Middle* TEMPLE[1]; ~ **term,** (Logic) term common to both premisses (*principle of excluded* ~, that anything must be included either under a given term or under its negative); ~ **voice,** (Gram.) voice of (esp. Gk) verbs expr. reciprocal or reflexive action; ~ **watch** (from midnight to 4 a.m.); ~ **way,** (1) = *middle course,* (2) eightfold path of Buddhism between indulgence and asceticism; ~**weight** (see BOX[5]*ing weights*); **Middle* WEST. **3.** *n.* Middle point or position or part (of); waist; middle voice; middle term; ‖middle article; KNOCK[1] *into the middle of next week*; **in the** ~ **of,** while (do*ing*), during (process). [OE *middel,* = OS *middil,* OHG *mittil* f. WG **middila* f. Gmc **midjha-* MID[1]; see -LE 1]

mĭ'ddle[2] *v.t.* Place in the middle; (Footb.) return (ball, or abs.) from wing to midfield in front of goal; (Cricket) strike (ball) with middle of bat; (Naut.) fold in the middle. [f. prec.]

mĭ'ddling *a., n.,* & *adv.* **1.** *a.* (Commerc., of goods) of the second of three grades; (**fair to**) ~, moderately good; second-rate; (colloq.) fairly well (in health); hence ~LY[2] *adv.* **2.** *n.* (in *pl.*) Middling goods, esp. flour of medium fineness. **3.** *adv.* Fairly or moderately (*middling good, fast*). [ME, of Sc. orig., prob. f. MID[1] + -LING[2]]

Middx. *abbr.* Middlesex.

mĭ'ddy̆[1] *n.* (colloq.) Midshipman; ~ (**blouse**), woman's or child's loose blouse with collar as worn by sailors. [abbr.; see -Y[3]]

mĭ'ddy̆[2] *n.* (Austral.) Measure of beer. [20th c.; orig. unkn.]

mĭdge *n.* Gnatlike insect; small person; (Zool.) dipterous insect of family Chironomidae. [OE *mycg(e),* = OS *muggia,* OHG *mucca,* ON *mý* f. Gmc **mugjaz, *mugjōn*]

mĭ'dgėt *n.* & *a.* Extremely small person, esp.

when exhibited as curiosity; very small (thing). [f. prec. + -ET¹]

mĭ'dĭ *n.* Garment of medium length, between maxi and mini. [f. MID¹ after MINI]

mĭdĭnĕ'tte *n.* Parisian shop-girl (esp. milliner's assistant). [F (*midi* midday, *dînette* light dinner)]

mĭ'dland *n.* & *a.* **1.** *n.* Middle part of country; **the M~s,** the inland counties of central England. **2.** *a.* Of or in the midland or Midlands; Mediterranean. **3.** Hence ~ER¹ (4) *n.* [f. MID¹ + LAND¹]

mĭ'dmōst. See MID¹.

mĭ'dnight (-nīt) *n.* The middle of the night, (time near) 12 o'clock at night; intense darkness; **~ blue,** very dark blue; *midnight* OIL¹; **~ sun,** sun visible at midnight during summer in polar regions. [OE *midniht* (as MID¹, NIGHT)]

Mĭ'drăsh *n.* (*pl.* **~im** *pr.* -ă'shēm). Ancient Jewish commentary on part of Hebrew scriptures. [f. Bibl. Heb. *midrāš* commentary (*dāraš* study)]

mĭ'drĭff *n.* Diaphragm between thorax and abdomen; region of front of body over this; (part of) garment fitted to this region. [OE *midhrif* (as MID¹, *hrif* belly)]

mĭ'dship *n.* Middle part of ship or boat; **~man,** rank between naval cadet and sub-lieutenant; **~s,** = AMIDSHIPS. [f. MID¹ + SHIP¹]

mĭdst *n., adv.,* & *prep.* **1.** *n.* **In the ~ of,** among, in the MIDDLE¹ of; **in our, their, your, ~,** among us, them, you. **2.** *adv.* (arch.) **First, ~, and last,** throughout. **3.** *prep.* (poet.) Amidst. [ME *middest, middes* f. *in middes, in middan* (IN¹, MID¹ as n.)]

mĭ'dsŭmmer (*or* -ŭ'-) *n.* Period of or near summer solstice, about 21 June; **M~('s) Day,** 24 June; **~ madness,** extreme folly. [OE *midsumor* (as MID¹, SUMMER¹)]

mĭ'dwĭ|fe *n.* (*pl.* **~ves** *pr.* -vz). Person (usu. woman) trained to assist others in giving birth; hence **mĭ'dwĭf**ERY (2) (-frĭ) *n.* [ME, prob. f. obs. prep. *mid* with (OE; cf. G *mit*) + WIFE woman, in sense 'one who is with the mother']

mĭdwĭ'nter *n.* Period of or near winter solstice, about 22 Dec. [OE (as MID¹, WINTER)]

M.I.E.E. *abbr.* Member of the Institution of Electrical Engineers.

mien *n.* (literary). Look or bearing of person, as showing character or mood. [prob. f. obs. *demean* n. f. DEMEAN¹, assim. to F *mine* expression]

mĭff *n.,* & *v.t.* (colloq.) **1.** *n.* Petty quarrel; huff. **2.** *v.t.* Put out of humour, offend. [perh. imit.; cf. G *muff*, excl. of disgust]

might¹ (mīt) *n.* Great (bodily or mental) strength; power to enforce one's will (usu. in contrast with *right*); **with all** one's **~,** to the utmost of one's power; *with might and* MAIN². [OE *miht, mieht,* = OS, OHG *maht,* Goth. *mahts* f. Gmc **mahtiz* (**mag-* MAY¹, be able)]

might². See MAY¹.

mī'ght|ȳ (mī'tĭ) *a.* & *adv.* **1.** *a.* Powerful, strong, in body or mind; **~y works,** (Bibl.) miracles. **2.** Massive, bulky; (colloq.) great, considerable; HIGH *and mighty.* **3.** Hence ~ILY² *adv.,* ~INESS *n.* **4.** *adv.* (colloq.) Very (*that is mighty easy*). [OE *mihtig* (as MIGHT¹, -Y²)]

mĭgnonĕ'tte (mĭnyo-) *n.* **1.** Annual plant of genus *Reseda,* esp. a species (*R. odorata*) with fragrant grey-green flowers; colour of these. **2.** Light fine narrow pillow-lace. [f. F *mignonnette* dim. of *mignon* small; see -ETTE]

mī'grain|e (*or* mē'-) *n.* Recurrent paroxysmal headache often with nausea and disturbance of vision; hence ~OUS *a.* [F, f. LL f. Gk *hēmicrania* (as HEMI-, CRANIUM, -IA¹); orig. of headache confined to one side of head]

mīgrā'te (*or* mī'-) *v.i.* Move from one place (country, town, college, house) to another; (of bird or fish) come and go with the seasons; move under natural forces; hence or cogn. **mī'gr**ANT *a.* & *n.,* **migr**A'TION, **mīgrā'**TOR, *ns.,* **mī'grat**ORY *a.* [f. L *migrare* + -ATE³]

mih'rab (mē'rahb) *n.* Niche etc. in mosque used to show direction of Mecca. [f. Arab. *miḥrāb*]

mĭka'dō (-kah'-) *n.* (*pl.* **~s**). Emperor of Japan. [Jap. (*mi* august, *kado* door)]

||**mike¹** *v.i.,* & *n.* (sl.) **1.** *v.i.* Shirk work, idle. **2.** *n.* Idling (*on the mike*). [19th c.; orig. unkn.]

mike² *n.* (colloq.) Microphone. [abbr.]

mike³ *n.* (sl.) = MICK; **for the love of Mike,** for Heaven's SAKE¹. [abbr. of man's Christian name *Michael*]

mĭl *n.* One-thousandth of an inch, as unit measure for diameter of wire etc. [f. L *millesimum* thousandth (*mille* thousand)]

mĭlā'dȳ *n.* (Form used in speaking of or to) English noblewoman or great lady. [F, f. E *my lady*; cf. MILORD]

mī'lage. Var. of MILEAGE.

Mĭlanē'se (-z) *a.* & *n.* (*pl.* same). (Native or inhabitant) of Milan; **~ silk,** finely woven silk or rayon. [It. (*Milano* Milan in Lombardy; see -ESE)]

mĭlch *a.* (Of domestic mammal) giving, or kept for, milk; **~ cow,** (fig.) source of regular (and easy) profit, esp. person from whom money is easily obtained. [ME *m(i)elche,* OE **mielce* f. Gmc **melukjaz* (as MILK¹)]

mīld *a.* **1.** Gentle and conciliatory; (of rule, punishment, illness, etc.) not severe. **2.** (Of weather, esp. in winter) moderately warm; (of medicine) operating gently; (of food, tobacco, etc.) not sharp or strong in taste etc.; (of beer) not strongly flavoured with hops, opp. to *bitter* (||**~ and bitter,** mixture of mild and bitter beer; DRAW¹ *it mild*). **3.** Tame, feeble, lacking energy or vivacity. **4.** **~ steel** (containing small percentage of carbon, strong and tough, but not readily tempered). **5.** Hence ~'EN⁶ *v.t.* & *i.,* ~'LY² *adv.* (**to put it ~ly,** without any exaggeration), ~'NESS *n.* [OE *milde,* = OS *mildi,* OHG *milti,* ON *mildr,* Goth. *-milds* f. Gmc **mildh-* f. IE **meldh-,* **moldh-*]

mĭ'ldew *n.* & *v.* **1.** *n.* Destructive growth of minute fungi on plants; similar growth on paper, leather, etc., exposed to damp; hence ~Y² *a.* **2.** *v.t.* & *i.* Taint, be tainted, with mildew. [OE *mildēaw, meledēaw,* = OHG *militou* f. Gmc **melith* honey + **dawwaz* DEW¹]

mīle *n.* **1.** Unit of linear measure, now (**statute ~**) 1,760 yards, about 1·609 kilometre, (orig.) Roman measure of 1,000 paces, about 1,620 yards; ||**Admiralty, air, geographical, nautical, sea, ~,** unit of approx. 2,025 yards or one minute of great circle of earth; SQUARE² *mile*; **not a hundred** or **a million ~s from,** (joc.) in or at or close to. **2.** (colloq.) Great distance (STICK¹ *out a mile*; *miles apart, away, better, too big*; *beat him by miles*). **3.** Race extending over a mile. **4.** **~-post** (placed at distance of one mile from finishing-point of race etc.); **~'stone,** stone set up on road to mark distance in miles, (fig.) stage, event, in life, progress, etc. [OE *mīl,* = OHG *mīl(l)a,* ON *míla* f. WG **milja* f. L *mil(l)ia* pl. of *mille* thousand]

mī'leage (mī'lĭj) *n.* Number of miles travelled, used, etc.; number of miles travelled by vehicle per gallon etc. of fuel; travelling expenses (per mile); (fig.) benefit, profit. [f. prec. + -AGE]

mī'ler *n.* (colloq.) Man or horse qualified or trained specially to run a mile; HALF-*miler,* QUARTER¹-*miler.* [f. MILE + -ER¹]

Mīlē'sian¹ (-zyan) *a.* & *n.* (Inhabitant or native) of Miletus; **~ tale,** one of a set of short erotic stories in ancient times. [f. L f. Gk *Milēsios* (*Milētos* Miletus, city of Asia Minor) + -AN]

Mīlē′sian[2] (-shăn) *a.* & *n.* (joc.) Irish(man). [f. *Milesius*, fabulous Sp. king whose sons are said to have conquered Ireland *c.* 1300 B.C., + -AN]

mĭ′lfoil *n.* Common yarrow, *Achillea millefolium*, with small white flowers and finely divided leaves. [ME f. OF, f. L *millefolium* (*mille* thousand, *folium* leaf), after Gk *muriophullon*]

mĭ′lĭarў *a.* (Path.) Like millet-seed in size or form; ~ **fever** (marked by rash like measles, with vesicles of form of millet-seed); ~ **tuberculosis** (with small tubercular nodules throughout body). [f. L *miliarius* (*milium* millet; see -ARY[1])]

milieu (mē′lyẽr) *n.* (*pl.* **~x** *or* **~s,** *pr.* -z). Environment, state of life, social surroundings. [F (*mi* MID[1], LIEU place)]

mĭ′lĭtant *a.* & *n.* **1.** *a.* Engaged in warfare (CHURCH *militant*); combative, aggressively active; hence **mĭ′lĭt**ANCY *n.*, ~LY[2] *adv.* **2.** *n.* Militant person. [ME f. OF, f. L (as MILITATE; see -ANT)]

mĭ′lĭtar|ĭsm *n.* Spirit or tendencies of the professional soldier; undue prevalence of military spirit or ideals; hence **~ĭ′st**IC *a.* [f. F *militarisme* (as MILITARY; see -ISM)]

mĭ′lĭtarĭst *n.* Student of military science; one dominated by military ideas. [f. MILITARY + -IST]

mĭ′lĭtarīz|e, -īs|e (-īz), *v.t.* Make military or warlike; equip with military resources; imbue with militarism; hence ~A′TION *n.* [f. foll. + -IZE]

mĭ′lĭtarў *a.* & *n.* **1.** *a.* Of, done by, befitting, soldiers, the army, or all armed forces (*military service*); ~ **academy** (for training army officers); ~ **band,** wood-wind, brass, and percussion combination; ~ **chest,** treasury of army; ~ **fever,** enteric; *military* HONOUR[1]*s*; ~ **orchis** (having fancied resemblance to soldier); ~ **police** (fulfilling functions of police among soldiers); ~ **tenure,** feudal holding of land in return for service as soldier; ~ **testament,** soldier's will made orally; hence **mĭ′lĭtarĭ**LY[2] *adv.* **2.** *n.* (as *sing.* or *pl.*) Soldiers, *the* army, (opp. police or civilians). [f. F *militaire* or f. L *militaris* (*miles militis* soldier; see -ARY[2])]

mĭ′lĭtāte *v.i.* (Of facts, evidence) have force, tell, (*against*, rarely *in favour of*, conclusion etc.). [f. L *militare* (*miles militis* soldier) + -ATE[3]]

milĭ′tia (-shȧ) *n.* Military force, esp. one raised from among civil population and supplementing regular army in emergency; **~man,** member of the militia. [L, = military service (*miles*; see prec., -IA[1])]

mĭlk[1] *n.* **1.** Opaque white fluid secreted by female mammals for nourishment of their young; milk of cow etc. as food; ~ **for babes,** simple forms of literature, doctrine, etc., opp. to *strong meat*; CONDENSED *milk*; *dried* or *powdered milk* (cf. DRY[2]); ~ **and honey,** abundant means of prosperity; ~ **of human kindness,** kindness natural to humanity; **no use crying over spilt** ~ (irremediable loss or error); ~ **and water,** feeble or insipid or mawkish discourse or sentiment. **2.** Milklike juice of plants, e.g. in coconut; milklike preparation of herbs, drugs, etc.; ~ **of magnesia,** white suspension of magnesium hydroxide in water as antacid or laxative [P]; ~ **of sulphur,** amorphous powder of sulphur formed by precipitation. **3.** ~ **bar** (for sale of beverages made from milk, other non-alcoholic drinks, ice cream, etc.); ~ **chocolate** (for eating, made with milk); ~ **fever,** mild fever shortly after parturition; ‖**~-float,** light low vehicle used in delivering milk; **~-leg,** painful swelling, esp. of legs, after childbirth; **~′maid,** woman who milks or works in dairy; **~′man,** man who sells or delivers milk; **~-powder,** milk dehydrated by evaporation; ~ **pudding** (of rice, sago, tapioca, etc., baked with milk in dish); ~ **punch,** drink made of spirits and milk; ~ **run,** (fig.) routine expedition or service journey; ~ **shake,** drink of milk, flavouring, etc., mixed by shaking; **~′sop,** spiritless man or youth; ~ **sugar,** lactose; ~ **thistle,** sow[2]*thistle*; **~-tooth,** temporary tooth in young mammals; **~-walk,** milkman's round; **~′weed,** one of various wild plants with milky juice; **~-white,** white like milk; **~′wort,** plant of genus *Polygala* formerly supposed to increase women's milk. [OE *milc*, *meol(o)c*, = OS *miluk*, OHG *miluh*, ON *mjólk*, Goth. *miluks* f. Gmc **meluks* (**melk-* to milk f. IE **melg-*)]

mĭlk[2] *v.t.* Draw milk from (cow, ewe, goat, etc.); get money out of, exploit, (person); (sl.) tap (telegraph or telephone wires etc.); extract juice, venom, etc., from (tree, snake, etc.); **~′ing-machine,** device for milking cows mechanically. [OE *milcian* (as prec.)]

mĭ′lk|ў *a.* Of, like, mixed with, milk; (of gem or liquid) cloudy, not clear; effeminate, weakly amiable; **M~y Way,** faintly luminous band of countless stars encircling the heavens, the Galaxy; hence **~ĭ**NESS *n.* [ME, f. MILK[1] + -Y[2]]

mĭll[1] *n.* **1.** Building fitted with machinery for grinding corn (WATER[1]*-mill*; WINDMILL); **put, go, through the ~,** subject to, undergo, training or experience or suffering; **the ~s of God grind slowly,** retribution is often delayed. **2.** Any mechanical apparatus for grinding corn; apparatus for grinding any solid substance to powder or pulp (COFFEE, PEPPER[1], *powder, -mill*). **3.** Any machine, or building fitted with machinery, for manufacturing-processes etc., (*cotton*, PAPER[1], *silk, -mill*; ROLL[2]*ing, saw, -mill*). **4.** Boxing-match; fist fight. **5. ~′board,** stout pasteboard for bookbinding etc.; **~-dam,** dam put across stream to make it usable by mill; **~-hand,** worker in mill or factory; **~-pond,** water retained by mill-dam (*like a ~-pond*, said of calm sea); **~-race,** current of water that drives mill-wheel; **~-rind,** iron support of upper millstone; **~′stone,** one of pair of circular stones for grinding corn, (fig.) heavy burden (cf. Matt. 18:6); *see far into a ~stone*, (usu. iron.) be extraordinarily acute; *between upper and* NETHER *~stone*, subject to irresistible pressure; *~stone grit*, a hard siliceous Carboniferous rock just below coal strata; **~-wheel,** wheel used to drive water-mill; **~′wright,** one who designs or erects mills. [OE *mylen* f. Gmc **mulino, -na* f. LL *molinum, -na* f. L *mola* grindstone, mill (*molere* grind)]

mĭll[2] *v.* **1.** *v.t.* Thicken (cloth etc.) by fulling; grind (corn), produce (flour), in mill; (esp. in *p.p.*) produce regular markings on edge of (coin); cut or shape (metal) with rotating tool; beat (chocolate etc.) to froth; (sl.) beat, strike, fight, (person). **2.** *v.i.* (Of cattle or persons) move round and round in a confused mass. [f. prec.]

***mĭll**[3] *n.* One-thousandth of a dollar as money of account. [f. L *millesimum* thousandth (see MIL), on anal. of CENT]

mille-feuille (mēlfŭ′ĭ) *n.* Rich confection of puff pastry split and filled with jam, cream, etc. [F, = thousand-leaf]

millėnār′ian *a.* & *n.* Of the millennium; (person) believing in this; hence ~ISM (3) *n.* [f. as foll. + -AN]

mĭ′llėnarў (*or* -ĕ′-) *a.* & *n.* (Period) of 1,000 years; (festival) of the thousandth anniversary; of, (person) believing in, the millennium. [f. LL *millenarius* consisting of a thousand (*milleni* distrib. of *mille* thousand; see -ARY[1])]

millĕ′nni|um *n.* (*pl.* **~ums** *or* **~a**). Period of a thousand years, esp. that of Christ's prophesied reign in person on earth (Rev. 20:1–5); (fig.)

period of good government, great happiness, and prosperity; hence ~AL *a.* [mod. L, f. L *mille* thousand after BIENNIUM]

mĭ'llėpēde, mĭ'llĭpēde, *n.* Myriapod of class Diplopoda with numerous legs usu. placed on each segment in double pairs; terrestrial isopod crustacean, esp. common wood-louse. [f. L *millepeda* wood-louse (*mille* thousand, *pes pedis* foot)]

mĭ'llėpōre *n.* Reef-building coral of genus *Millepora.* [f. F *millépore* or mod. L *millepora* (L *mille* thousand, *porus* PORE¹)]

mĭ'ller *n.* Proprietor or tenant of corn-mill; one who works or owns any mill; **~'s thumb,** small freshwater fish of genus *Cottus*, a bullhead. [ME *mylnere*, prob. f. MLG, MDu. *molner, mulner*, OS *mulineri* f. LL *molinarius* (*molina* MILL¹); assim. to MILL¹]

mĭllĕ'sĭmal *a.* & *n.* Thousandth (part); consisting of thousandths; hence ~LY² *adv.* [f. L *millesimus* (*mille* thousand) + -AL]

mĭ'llėt *n.* Cereal plant, esp. *Panicum miliaceum*, bearing large crop of small nutritious seeds; its seed; **~-grass,** tall woodland grass, *Milium effusum.* [ME f. F, dim. of *mil* f. L *milium*]

mĭ'llĭ- *comb. form.* Thousand, esp. denoting factor of one thousandth, as: **~a'mmeter** (for measuring current in **milliamperes**); *milli*BAR⁴; **~gram** (about ·015 of English grain); **~litre** (about ·061 cu. in.); **~metre** (about ·039 in.); *millisecond*; *millivolt*; *milliwatt.* [f. L *mille* thousand + -I-]

‖**mĭ'llĭard** (-yerd) *n.* One thousand millions. [F (*mille* thousand)]

mĭ'llĭn|er *n.* Person (usu. woman) who makes or sells women's hats; **man-~er,** (fig.) man busied in trifling occupations; hence ~ERY (1) *n.* [f. *Milan* + -ER¹; orig. = vendor of goods from Milan]

mĭ'llĭon (-yon) *a.* & *n.* (for *pl.* usage see HUNDRED). One thousand thousand (things, *of* things, or abs.); a million ‖pounds or *dollars; enormous number (*not a million* MILES *from*; cf. HUNDRED, THOUSAND); **the ~,** the bulk of the population; hence ~FOLD *a.* & *adv.*, (-)~TH² *a.* & *n.* [ME f. OF, prob. f. It. *millione* (*mille* thousand, *-one* augment. suf.; see -OON)]

mĭllionair'e (-yon-) *n.* Person possessing a million pounds, dollars, francs, etc.; person of great wealth. [f. F *millionnaire* (as prec.; see -ARY¹)]

mĭ'llĭpēde. See MILLEPEDE.

Mĭlls (-z) *n.* **~ bomb,** oval hand-grenade. [f. Sir W. ~, its inventor (d. 1932)]

mīlŏ'mėter *n.* Instrument for measuring number of miles travelled by a vehicle. [f. MILE + -O- + -METER]

mĭlōr'd *n.* (Esp. French word for) English lord or wealthy Englishman. [F, f. E *my lord*; cf. MILADY]

mĭlt *n.* Spleen in mammals; analogous organ in other vertebrates; seed-filled reproductive gland of male fish. [OE *milt(e)* = MDu. *milte*, OHG *milzi*, ON *milti* f. Gmc **miltjaz*, **miltjōn*, perh. cogn. w. MELT²]

mĭ'lter *n.* Male fish in spawning-time. [f. prec. + -ER¹]

Mĭltō'nĭan, Mĭltŏ'nĭc, *adjs.* Of, or in the manner of, Milton. [f. J. *Milton*, Engl. poet. d. 1674 + -IAN, -IC]

mīme *n.* & *v.* **1.** *n.* (Gk & Rom. Ant.) simple farcical drama marked by mimicry; similar modern performance with gestures and usu. without words. **2.** Performer in this; pantomimist, buffoon. **3.** *v.i.* & *t.* Act with mimic gestures, usu. without words. [f. L f. Gk *mimos*]

M.I.Mech.E. *abbr.* Member of the Institution of Mechanical Engineers.

mĭ'mėograph (-ahf) *n.*, & *v.t.* (Reproduce by) apparatus for holding stencils of written pages, from which many copies may be taken. [irreg. f. Gk *mimeomai* imitate; see -GRAPH]

mĭmē'sĭs *n.* (Biol.) Close external resemblance of an animal to another that is distasteful or harmful to predators of the first. [f. Gk *mimēsis* imitation (as prec.)]

mĭmĕ't|ic *a.* Of, or addicted to, imitation, mimicry, or mimesis; hence ~ICALLY *adv.* [f. Gk *mimētikos* (as prec.; see -ETIC)]

mĭ'mĭc¹ *a.* & *n.* **1.** *a.* Having aptitude for mimicry; imitating; imitative, esp. for amusement, **2.** *n.* Person skilled in ludicrous imitation. [f. L f. Gk *mimikos* (as MIME; see -IC)]

mĭ'mĭc² *v.t.* (**-ck-**). Ridicule by imitating (person, manner, etc.); copy minutely or servilely; (of thing) resemble closely. [f. prec.]

mĭ'mĭcrў *n.* Mimicking; thing that mimics another; (Zool.) mimesis. [f. MIMIC¹ + -RY]

M.I.Min.E. *abbr.* Member of the Institution of Mining Engineers.

mĭmĭnў-pĭ'mĭnў *a.* Over-refined, finical. [imit.]

mĭmō'sa (*or* -*za*) *n.* Leguminous shrub of genus *Mimosa* with globular flower-heads, incl. common sensitive plant (*M. pudica*); acacia. [mod. L, app. f. L (as MIME, from being as sensitive as animals) + *-osa* fem. suf.; see -OSE¹]

mĭ'mūlus *n.* Flowering plants of genus *Mimulus*, incl. musk and monkey-flower. [mod. L, app. dim. of L (as MIME, perh. w. ref. to masklike flowers)]

M.I.Mun.E. *abbr.* Member of the Institution of Municipal Engineers.

Mĭn *n.* Chinese dialect of Fukien province in S.E. China. [Chin.]

min. *abbr.* minim; minimum; minute(s).

Min. *abbr.* Minister; Ministry.

mī'na¹ *n.* (*pl.* ~e). Ancient monetary unit in Greek-speaking countries; ancient unit of weight in Greece, Egypt, etc., about 1 lb. [L, f. Gk *mna*]

mī'na², mȳ'na, mȳ'nah (-*a*), *n.* Bird of starling family in S.E. Asia, esp. talking species *Gracula religiosa.* [f. Hindi *mainā*]

mĭnā'cious (-sh*us*) *a.* Threatening, menacing; hence ~LY² *adv.*, **mĭn**A'CITY *n.* [f. L *minax minacis* (*minari* threaten); see -ACIOUS]

mĭ'narĕt (*or* -ĕ't) *n.* Slender turret connected with mosque and having balcony from which muezzin calls at hours of prayer. [F, or Sp. *minarete* f. Turk. *minare* f. Arab. *manār(a)* lighthouse, minaret (*nār* fire, light)]

mĭ'natorў *a.* Threatening, menacing; expressing threat. [f. LL *minatorius* (*minari* -*at*- threaten; see -ORY)]

mĭnce¹ *n.* Minced meat; **~'meat,** mixture of currants, raisins, sugar, apples, candied peel, spices, etc., for **~ pie** (usu. small round pie, containing this); *make ~meat of*, utterly defeat (person, argument, etc.). [f. foll.]

mĭnce² *v.* **1.** *v.t.* Cut (meat etc.) very small; (usu. w. neg.) **~ matters,** use polite expressions in condemnation. **2.** Restrain (one's words) within bounds of politeness. **3.** *v.t.* & *i.* Utter (words), walk, with affected delicacy; hence **mĭ'ncĭng**LY² *adv.* **4.** Hence **mĭ'nc**ER¹ (1, 2) *n.* [ME, f. OF *mincier* f. Rom. **minutiare* f. L (as MINUTIA)]

mīnd¹ *n.* **1.** Remembrance (*bear, have, keep, in mind*); **bring** or **call to ~,** remember, cause to be remembered; **come to ~, come into** one's **~,** be remembered; MONTH'*s mind*; **put** person **in ~ of,** make him remember; **put out of** one's **~,** deliberately forget about; *out of* SIGHT¹ *out of mind*; TIME¹ *out of mind.* **2.** Candid opinion; SPEAK one's *mind*; **give** person **a piece of** one's **~,** scold or reproach him. **3.** Opinion (*in* or *to* *my mind he is a genius*); **be in** (or **of**) **a** or **one** or **the same** ~, agree in opinion; **be in two ~s,** be undecided (*about*); **change** one's ~, adopt new plan or opinion; **have a ~ of** one's **own,** be capable of forming opinions independently of others; **have a good** or **great,** (**half**) **a, ~ to,** feel much, somewhat, tempted or inclined to; **know** one's **own** ~, not vacillate; **make up** one's ~, decide, resolve, (*to* do, *to* course of action etc., or abs.), reconcile oneself *to* inevitable fact; **read** person's ~, know what he is thinking, without being told. **4.** Direction of thoughts or desires; ABSENCE *of mind*; **cast** one's **~ back,** recall an earlier time; **give** or **put** or **set** or **turn** one's **~ to,** direct one's attention to; **have it in** ~, intend; **have on** one's ~, be troubled by thought of; **keep** one's **~ on,** continue to think about; **open** or **close** one's **~ to,** be willing, unwilling, to consider; PRESENCE *of mind*; **set** one's **~ on,** desire to attain; **to** one's ~, as one would like it. **5.** Way of thinking and feeling (*frame, state, of mind*; *the Victorian mind*). **6.** Seat of consciousness, thought, volition and feeling. **7.** Soul, opp. to body or material things (*mind may triumph over matter*); **~'s eye,** mental view. **8.** Person, as embodying mental qualities. **9.** Intellectual powers, opp. to will and emotions; hence ~'LESS *a.*, (esp.) stupidly ill-behaved. **10.** Normal condition of mental faculties; **lose** one's ~, become insane; **out of** one's ~, insane; **in** one's **right** ~, sane. **11.** **~-reader,** = THOUGHT^{1}-*reader*; **~-set,** (fixed) direction of thought; **~-stuff,** (Philos.) supposed rudimentary form of psychical existence regarded as the reality of which matter is an aspect. [ME *mynd* f. OE *gemynd*, = OHG *gimunt*, Goth. *gamunds* f. Gmc **gamundhiz* (as Y-, **mun-* weak grade of **men-* etc. f. IE **men-*, **mon-*, **mn-* think)]

mind^{2} *v.t.* & *i.* **1.** Bear in mind (chiefly in *imper.*); ~ (**you**), (parenth.) please take note; give heed to (*never mind the expense*); *be obedient to. **2.** Concern oneself about; **never** ~, (*imper.*), (1) do not be troubled, take comfort, (2) I refuse to answer your question; ~ one's **P's and Q's,** be careful as to speech or behaviour. **3.** Apply oneself to (business etc.; *mind your own* BUSINESS). **4.** (usu. w. neg. or interrog.) Object to (thing, person, *that*, doing; *would you mind ringing?*); **I should not ~, don't ~ if I have,** (should like) *a cup of tea*; **if you don't ~** (have no objection); **do you ~?**, (iron.) please stop that. **5.** Remember and take care (*mind* (*that*) thing is done). **6.** ~ (**out for**), be on one's guard against or about, remember existence of (*mind the step*); ~ **away** or **out, ~ your back,** (colloq.) let me pass. **7.** Have charge of; **~ the shop** or ***store,** (fig.) have charge of affairs. **8.** Hence ~'ER^{1} *n.*, one whose business it is to attend to something, esp. child or machinery. [ME, f. prec.]

mi'ndėd *a.* Disposed (*to* do); inclined to think (in specified way: *mechanically, politically, minded*); (in *comb.*) having (specified kind of) mind (*high-minded*; *small-minded*), inclined to concern oneself with (*car-minded*). [f. MIND^{1} + -ED^{2}]

mi'ndful *a.* Taking thought or care (*of*, or abs.); hence ~LY^{2} *adv.*, ~NESS *n.* [ME, f. MIND^{1} + -FUL]

mine^{1} *n.* **1.** Excavation in earth for extracting metal, coal, salt, etc., (**~'worker,** one who works in this); (fig.) abundant source (*of* information etc.); ||iron ore. **2.** (Mil. etc.) Subterranean gallery in which explosive is placed to blow up fortifications, (formerly) subterranean passage under wall of besieged fortress. **3.** Receptacle filled with explosive placed in or on ground for destroying enemy personnel or material, or moored beneath or floating on or near surface of water for destroying or impeding enemy ships; **~-detector,** instrument indicating presence of mines; **~'field,** area of land or sea in which mines have been laid, (fig.) area presenting many unseen hazards; **~'layer,** ship or aircraft for laying mines; **~'sweeper,** ship for clearing away floating or submarine mines. [ME, f. OF *mine*, (perh. f. *miner*; see foll.), or f. foll.]

mine^{2} *v.t.* & *i.* **1.** Burrow in (earth); make (hole) underground; make subterranean passages under; (fig.) undermine. **2.** (Mil. etc.) Lay mines under or in. **3.** Obtain (metal, coal, etc.) from mine; dig in (earth etc., or abs.) for or *for* ore etc. **4.** Hence **mi'**NING^{1} (1) *n.* [ME, f. OF *miner*, perh. f. Celt.]

mine^{3} *poss. pron.* See MY. [OE *min*, = OS, OHG *min*, ON *minn*, Goth. *meins* f. Gmc **minaz* f. IE **mei* locative of **me* ME^{1} (cf. I^{2}) + adj. suf. **-no-*]

mi'ner *n.* One who works in a mine; soldier whose duty it is to lay mines; burrowing insect or grub. [ME, f. OF *minëor*, *minour* (as MINE^{2}; see -OR)]

mi'neral *a.* & *n.* **1.** *a.* Obtained by mining; belonging to any of the species into which inorganic substances are classified; *mineral* KINGDOM; ~ **oil,** petroleum; ~ **water,** (1) water found in nature impregnated with mineral substance, (2) artificial imitation of this, esp. soda-water, (3) other effervescent drink, e.g. ginger-beer; *mineral* WAX^{1}; *mineral* WOOL. **2.** *n.* Mineral substance or object; ||(esp. in *pl.*) = *mineral water* (2, 3). **3.** Hence ~IZE (3) *v.t.* & *i.*, change (partly) into mineral. [ME f. OF, or f. med. L *mineralis* (*minera* ore f. OF *miniere* mine f. Rom. **minaria* f. **mina*(*re*) MINE^{1,2})]

minėr|ă'logy̆ *n.* Science of minerals; hence **~alŏ'g**ICAL *a.*, **~ă'log**IST (3) *n.* [irreg. f. prec. + -LOGY]

minėstrō'nė *n.* Thick soup containing vegetables and pasta or rice. [It.]

mi'nėver. Var. of MINIVER.

Ming *n.* (Porcelain contemporary with) Chinese ruling dynasty 1368–1644. [Chin.]

mi'ngle (-nggel) *v.t.* & *i.* Mix, blend; ~ **their** etc. **tears,** weep together; ~ **with,** go about among. [ME *mengel* f. obs. *meng* f. OE *mengan*, cogn. w. AMONG, + -LE 3]

||**mi'ngy̆** (-njĭ) *a.* (colloq.) Mean, stingy. [perh. f. MEAN^{3} and STINGY]

mi'nĭ *n.* (colloq.) Minicar, miniskirt, etc. [abbr.]

mi'nĭ- *comb. form.* Miniature, very small of its kind, (*minibus, minicab, minicar*); **~skirt** (ending well above the knees). [abbr.]

mi'nĭāte *v.t.* Paint with vermilion; illuminate (manuscript). [f. L *miniare* (MINIUM) + -ATE^{3}]

mi'nĭatur|e (*or* -nĭcher) *n.*, *a.*, & *v.t.* **1.** *n.* Picture in illuminated manuscript; small-scale minutely finished portrait, usu. on ivory or vellum; this branch of painting (*portrait in miniature*), whence ~IST (3) *n.*; reduced image; **in ~e,** on a small scale. **2.** *a.* Represented on small scale; small-scale; smaller than normal; **~e camera** (producing small negatives). **3.** *v.t.* Represent in miniature. [f. It. f. med. L *miniatura* f. L *miniare* (as prec.; see -URE)]

mi'nĭatūrĭz|e (*or* -nĭcher-), **-is|e** (-īz), *v.t.* Make miniature; produce in smaller version. [f. prec. + -IZE]

mi'nĭfy̆ *v.t.* Represent as smaller or less important than it is; lessen in size or importance. [irreg. f. L *minor* less, *minimus* least, after MAGNIFY]

mi'nĭkĭn *n.* & *a.* Diminutive (creature); affected, mincing. [f. obs. Du. *minneken* (*minne* love, *-ken*, *-kijn* -KIN)]

mi'nĭm *n.* ||(Mus.) note half as long as semibreve; single down-stroke of pen; object or portion of the smallest size or importance; sixtieth part of fluid drachm, about a drop. [ME, f. L *minimus* smallest]

mĭ'nĭmal *a.* Very minute or slight; being or relating to a minimum; least possible in size, duration, etc.; hence ~LY^2 *adv.* [f. as prec. + -AL]

mĭ'nĭmalĭst *n.* Person ready to accept a minimum provisionally (opp. MAXIMALIST). [f. prec. + -IST, orig. as transl. of Russ. (see MENSHEVIK)]

mĭ'nĭmīz|e, -īs|e (-īz), *v.t.* Reduce to, or estimate at, smallest possible amount or degree; estimate or represent at less than the true value or importance; hence ~A'TION *n.* [f. as MINIM + -IZE]

mĭ'nĭm|um *n.* (*pl.* **~a**) & *a.* Least (amount) possible, attained or attainable, usual, etc., (*reaches a, its, the minimum at midnight*); **~um thermometer** (automatically recording lowest temperature within given period); **~um wage** (than which, by law or agreement, less is not to be offered). [L, neut. (as n.) of *minimus* least]

mī'nĭng. See MINE^2.

mĭ'nion (-yon) *n.* (derog.) Favourite child, servant, animal, etc.; favourite of king etc.; servile agent, slave; **~s of the law,** gaolers, police, etc. [f. F *mignon*, OF *mignot*, of Gaulish orig.]

mĭ'nĭsh *v.t.* & *i.* (arch.) Diminish; reduce in power etc. [ME, f. OF *menu(i)sier* f. Rom. **minutiare* (see MINCE^2); assim. to -ISH^2]

mĭ'nĭster^1 *n.* **1.** Person employed in execution *of* (purpose, will, etc.). **2.** Person at head of (main branch of) government department. **3.** Diplomatic agent accredited by one State to another, usu. ranking below ambassador. **4.** ~ (**of religion**), clergyman ‖esp. in Presbyterian and Nonconformist Churches; ~ (**general**), superior of some religious orders. **5.** PRIME^2 *minister*; ‖**M~ of the Crown,** member of the Cabinet; ‖**M~ of State,** departmental senior minister intermediate between head of department and junior minister. [ME, f. OF *ministre* f. L *minister* servant (*minus* less); cf. MASTER^1]

mĭ'nĭster^2 *v.* **1.** *v.i.* Render aid or service (*to* person, cause, etc.; **~ing angel,** w. ref. to Mark 1:13, esp. of sick-nurse etc.); (arch.) be helpful, contribute, (*to* result). **2.** *v.t.* (arch.) Furnish, supply, (help etc.). [ME, f. OF *ministrer* f. L *ministrare* (as prec.)]

mĭnĭstēr'ĭal *a.* **1.** Of a minister of religion or his office. **2.** Of a governmental minister; siding with the Ministry against the Opposition, whence ~IST (2) *n.* **3.** (arch.) Concerned with the execution of orders or law; subsidiary, instrumental. **4.** Hence ~LY^2 *adv.* [f. F *ministériel* or f. LL *ministerialis* f. L (as MINISTRY; see -AL)]

mĭnĭstrā'tion *n.* Giving aid or service; ministering, esp. in religious matters; supplying (*of*); so **mĭ'nĭstr**ANT *a.* & *n.*, **mĭ'nĭstr**ATIVE *a.* [ME f. OF, or f. L *ministratio* (as MINISTER^2; see -ATION)]

mĭ'nĭstrȳ *n.* **1.** Ministering, ministration. **2.** *The* body of ministers of the government or of religion; *the* clerical profession. **3.** Government department headed by minister (*Ministry of Defence*); building occupied by it. **4.** Office as religious minister, priest, etc.; period of tenure of this. [ME, f. L *ministerium* (MINISTER^1)]

mĭ'nĭum *n.* (Hist.) Red lead; vermilion. [ME f. L]

mĭ'nĭver *n.* Plain white fur used in ceremonial costume. [ME, f. AF *menuver*, OF *menu vair* (as MENU, VAIR)]

mĭnk *n.* Small semi-aquatic stoatlike animal of family Mustelidae, esp. *Mustela vison*; its thick brown fur; coat made of this. [cf. Sw. *mänk*, *menk*]

Minn. *abbr.* Minnesota.

mĭ'nnėsĭnger *n.* German lyric poet and singer in 12th–14th c. [G (*minne* love, obs. *singer* singer), f. love's being their chief theme]

mĭ'nnow (-ō) *n.* Small freshwater fish (esp. ‖*Phoxinus phoxinus*); **Triton among the ~s,** one who seems great from insignificance of others. [late ME *menow*, perh. repr. OE **mynwe*, *myne*, OHG *muniwa*; infl. by ME *menuse* f. OF *menuise* f. Rom. **minutia* pl. small objects (as MINUTIA)]

Mĭnō'an *a.* & *n.* (Archaeol.) (Person) of the Cretan Bronze-Age civilization (*c.* 3000–1000 B.C.) named from excavations at palace of (legendary king) Minos at Knossos. [f. Gk *Minōs* + -AN]

mī'nor *a.*, *n.*, & *v.i.* **1.** *a.* Lesser (not followed by *than*) of two things, classes, etc.; not yet of full age; ‖(in schools) *Smith* etc. ~, the younger of the two Smiths or the second to enter the school; FRIARS *Minor*; ~ **axis** (of conic, perpendicular to major axis); ~ **canon,** clergyman not member of chapter, assisting in daily cathedral service; ***~ league** (in baseball, or fig.; opp. MAJOR^2 *league*); *minor* ORDER^1*s*; ~ **piece,** (Chess) bishop or knight; ~ **planet,** asteroid; *minor* PROPHET; ~ **suit,** (Bridge) diamonds or clubs. **2.** Comparatively unimportant (*minor poet*); (of operation) presenting no danger to patient's life. **3.** (Logic). (Of term) occurring as subject of conclusion of syllogism; (of premiss) containing minor term. **4.** (Mus.) (Of interval) less by a semitone than major interval; (of key) in which scale has minor third (**in a ~ key,** (fig.) doleful(ly)); HARMONIC, MELODIC, *minor scale*. **5.** *n.* = MINORITE; (Logic) minor term or premiss; minor key etc.; person under full age; *student's subsidiary subject or course. **6.** *v.i.* *(Of student) undertake study *in* as minor subject etc. [L, = less, cogn. w. *minuere* lessen]

Mĭnŏr'ca *n.* ~ (**fowl**), black variety of domestic fowl brought from Spain. [f. Sp. *Menorca* Minorca, second largest of the Balearic Islands]

Mī'norėss *n.* (Hist.) Nun of order founded by St. Clare and St. Francis. [f. OF *menouresse* (*menour* f. L MINOR; see -ESS^1)]

Mī'norite *n.* Franciscan friar. [f. MINOR (because regarding themselves as a humble order) + -ITE^1]

mĭnŏ'rĭtȳ *n.* **1.** State of being under full age, period of this. **2.** Smaller number or part (*of*), esp. smaller party voting together against majority; number of votes cast for this; state of having less than half the votes. **3.** Small group of persons differing from others in race, religion, language, opinion on a topic, etc. **4.** (*attrib.*) Relating to or done by a minority. [f. F *minorité* or f. med. L *minoritas* f. L MINOR; see -ITY]

Mī'notaur *n.* (Gk Myth.) Bull-headed man kept in Cretan labyrinth and fed with human flesh. [ME f. OF, f. L f. Gk *Minōtauros* (*Minōs*, legendary king of Crete, husband of Minotaur's mother, + *tauros* bull)]

mĭ'nster *n.* Church of a monastery; name given to some large or important churches. [OE *mynster* = OHG *munistri*, ON *mustari* f. pop. L **monisterium* f. eccl. L f. Gk *monastērion* MONASTERY]

mĭ'nstrel *n.* **1.** Medieval singer or musician, who sang or recited (often his own) poetry; (Hist.) person who entertained his patrons with singing, buffoonery, etc. **2.** (usu. in *pl.*) One of a band of public entertainers, with blackened faces etc., performing songs and music ostensibly of Negro origin. [ME, f. OF *menestral* entertainer, servant, f. Prov. *menest(ai)ral* officer, employee, musician, f. LL *ministerialis* official, officer (see MINISTERIAL)]

mĭ'nstrelsy̆ *n.* Minstrel's art; body of minstrels; minstrel poetry. [ME, f. OF *menestralsie* (as prec.)]

mĭnt¹ *n.* Place where money is coined, usu. under State authority; vast sum *of money*; (fig.) source of invention etc.; **in ~ condition, state,** (as if) fresh from the mint, (of book, print, postage stamp, etc.) fresh, unsoiled, perfect; **~-mark,** mark placed on coin to show at what mint it was struck (also fig.); **~-master,** superintendent of coinage at mint. [OE *mynet*, = OS *munita*, OHG *muniz(za)* f. WG **munita* f. L *moneta* MONEY]

mĭnt² *v.t.* Make (coin) by stamping metal; invent, coin, (word, phrase, etc.); hence **~'AGE** (3, 4) *n.* [ME, f. prec.]

mĭnt³ *n.* Aromatic plant of genus *Mentha*, esp. spearmint; peppermint (lozenge); *mint* JULEP; **~ sauce** (of finely chopped spearmint leaves with vinegar and sugar, eaten esp. with roast lamb). [OE *minte*, = OHG *minza* f. WG **minta* f. L *ment(h)a* f. Gk *minthē*]

mĭ'nūĕnd *n.* (Math.) Quantity or number from which another is to be subtracted. [f. L *minuendus* gerundive of *minuere* diminish]

mĭnūĕ't *n.* Slow stately dance for two in triple measure; music for this, or in same rhythm and style (often as movement in suite, sonata, or symphony). [f. F *menuet* (*menuet* a. = fine, delicate, dim. of MENU; see -ET¹)]

mī'nus *prep.*, *a.*, & *n.* **1.** *prep.* With the subtraction of (symbol −); below zero (*temperature of minus ten degrees*); (colloq.) lacking, deprived of, (*returned minus shoes and stockings*). **2.** *a.* (Math.) negative; (Electr.) having negative charge; *minus* SIGN¹. **3.** *n.* The symbol (−); negative quantity; disadvantage. [L, neut. of MINOR]

mĭ'nuscūl|e *a.* & *n.* **1.** (Palaeogr., of kind of cursive script developed in 7th c.) small (letter). **2.** Lower-case (letter); extremely small. **3.** Hence **~AR**¹ (-ŭ's-) *a.* [F, f. L *minuscula* (*littera* letter), dim. of MINOR; see -CULE]

mĭ'nute¹ (-ĭt) *n.* **1.** Sixtieth part of an hour; distance traversed in one minute (cf. HOUR; *twenty minutes from the station*); = MOMENT; short time, instant; exact point of time; **the ~,** (colloq.) the present time (cf. MOMENT); **up to the ~,** having latest information, in the latest fashion; **the ~ (that),** as soon as; **just a ~, wait a ~,** (colloq.) (1) I shall not keep you waiting for long, (2) I wish to comment or object; LAST³ *minute*. **2.** Sixtieth part of angular degree. **3.** Rough draft, memorandum; (in *pl.*) brief summary of proceedings of assembly, committee, etc.; official memorandum authorizing or recommending a course of action. **4. ~-book** (for writing minutes in); **~-gun** (fired at intervals of a minute at funeral etc.); **~-hand** (indicating minutes on watch or clock); ***~-man,** (Hist.) American militiaman of revolutionary period (because ready to march at a minute's notice); **~-mark** (′, also denoting linear feet; cf. SECOND-*mark*); **~ steak** (thin slice, that can be cooked quickly). [ME f. OF, f. LL *minuta* n., f. fem. of *minutus* MINUTE³; senses 1 & 2 f. med. L *pars minuta prima* first minute part, cf. SECOND; sense 3 perh. f. med. L *minuta scriptura* draft in small writing]

mĭ'nute² (-ĭt) *v.t.* **1.** (arch.) Find the exact time of. **2.** Record in minutes; send minute to (person); **~ (down),** make a note of. [f. prec.]

mīnū'te³ *a.* Very small; trifling, petty; (of inquiry, inquirer, etc.) accurate, detailed, precise; hence **~LY**² (-tlĭ) *adv.*, **~NESS** (-tn-) *n.* [ME, f. L *minutus*, p.p. of *minuere* lessen]

mĭnū'tĭa (-shĭa) *n.* (usu. in *pl.* ~e). Precise or trivial or minor detail. [L, = smallness, in pl. trifles (*minutus*; see prec.)]

mĭnx *n.* Pert or sly girl. [16th c., of unkn. orig.]

Mī'ocēne *a.* & *n.* (Geol.) (Of the) division of the Tertiary preceding the Pliocene. [irreg. f. Gk *meiōn* less + *kainos* new]

mī|ō'sĭs, my̆|ō'sĭs, *n.* (*pl.* ~oses *pr.* -ō'sēz). Excessive contraction of eye-pupil; hence **~O'TIC** *a.* [f. Gk *muō* shut the eyes + -OSIS]

M.I.Prod.E. *abbr.* Member of the Institution of Production Engineers.

mir (mēr) *n.* Russian pre-Communist village community. [Russ.]

mĭrabĕ'lle *n.* (Small round yellow fruit of) a Eur. species of plum-tree similar to bullace and damson; liqueur distilled from it. [F]

mirabile dictu (mĭrahbĭlā dĭ'ktōō) *adv.* Wonderful to relate. [L]

mĭ'racle *n.* **1.** Marvellous event due to some supposed supernatural agency; remarkable occurrence; remarkable specimen (*of* ingenuity, impudence, etc.); **to a ~,** (arch.) surprisingly well. **2. ~ (play),** dramatic representation in Middle Ages, based on life of Christ or saints. [ME f. OF, f. L *miraculum* object of wonder (*mirari* wonder f. *mirus* wonderful)]

mĭră'cūlous *a.* Of the nature of a miracle; supernatural; surprising; hence **~LY**² *adv.*, **~NESS** *n.* [f. F *miraculeux* or f. med. L *miraculosus* f. L (as prec.; see -OUS)]

mĭradŏr' *n.* Belvedere on Spanish house. [Sp. (*mirar* to look)]

mĭ'rage (-ahzh; *or* -ah'-) *n.* Optical illusion caused by atmospheric conditions, esp. appearance of sheet of water in desert or on hot road; illusory thing. [F (*se mirer* be reflected, f. L *mirare* look at; see -AGE)]

mīre¹ *n.* **1.** Swampy ground, bog; *stick, find oneself*, **in the ~,** (fig.) in difficulties. **2.** Mud, dirt. [ME, f. ON *mýrr* f. Gmc **meus-*, **mus-*, cogn. w. MOSS]

mīre² *v.t.* **1.** Plunge in mire; (fig.) involve in difficulties. **2.** Defile, bespatter, (lit. or fig.). [ME, f. prec.]

mirepoix (mēr'pwah) *n.* Sautéd chopped vegetables used in sauces etc. [F, f. Duc de *Mirepoix*, Fr. general d. 1757]

mĭrk. Var. of MURK.

mĭ'rror *n.*, & *v.t.* **1.** *n.* Polished surface (usu. of amalgam-coated glass, or metal) reflecting image, looking-glass; (fig.) what gives faithful reflection or true description of thing (*hold the mirror up to*); **~ carp** (with large shiny scales); **~ image** (with structure reversed, or occas. identical); **~ symmetry** (as of object and its image in mirror); **~ writing** (backwards, with result like mirror reflection of ordinary writing). **2.** *v.t.* Reflect as in mirror (lit. or fig.). [ME f. OF *mirour*, f. Rom. **miratorium* f. L *mirare* look at]

mĭrth *n.* Merriment, laughter; hence **~'FUL, ~'LESS,** *adjs.* [OE *myrgth* (as MERRY², -TH¹)]

MIRV *abbr.* multiple independently targeted re-entry vehicle (type of missile).

mīr'y̆ *a.* Muddy; vile. [ME, f. MIRE¹ + -Y²]

mĭs-¹ *pref.* to *vbs.* and vbl derivs., w. sense 'amiss', 'badly', 'wrongly', 'unfavourably', (*mislead, misshapen, mistrust*), or intensifying unfavourable meaning contained in *v.* (*misdoubt*). [OE, = OS, ON *mis-*, OHG, Goth. *missa-* f. Gmc **missa-* (1) divergent (2) mutual]

mĭs-² *pref.* to *vbs., adjs.,* & *ns.*, w. sense 'amiss', 'badly', 'wrongly', or negative, (*misadventure, mischief*). [f. OF *mes-* f. Rom. **minus-* f. L MINUS]

mĭsadvĕ'nture *n.* (Piece of) bad luck; (Law) death due to accident without crime or negligence. [ME, f. OF *mesaventure* (*mesavenir* turn out badly f. as MIS-[2] + ADVENT; cf. ADVENTURE[1])]
mĭsalī'gn (-ī'n) *v.t.* Give wrong alignment to; so ~MENT *n.* [f. MIS-[1] + ALIGN]
mĭsallī'ance *n.* Unsuitable alliance, esp. unsuitable marriage. [f. MIS-[1] + ALLIANCE, after MÉSALLIANCE]
mĭ'santhrōpe (*or* -z-) *n.* Hater of mankind; one who avoids human society; hence or cogn. **mĭsanthrŏ'pic**(AL) *adjs.*, **mĭsă'nthrop**IST (1), **mĭsă'nthropy**[1], *ns.*, **mĭsă'nthrop**IZE (2) *v.i.*, (*or* -z-). [F, f. Gk *misanthrōpos* (*misos* hatred, *anthrōpos* man)]
mĭsapplȳ' *v.t.* Apply (esp. funds) wrongly; so **mĭs**APPLICA'TION *n.* [f. MIS-[1] + APPLY]
mĭsăpprĕhĕ'n|d *v.t.* Misunderstand (words, person); so ~SION (-shon) *n.*, ~SIVE *a.* [f. MIS-[1] + APPREHEND]
mĭsapprō'prĭ|āte *v.t.* Apply (usu. another's money) to wrong (esp. one's own) use; so ~A'TION *n.* [f. MIS-[1] + APPROPRIATE[2]]
mĭsbĕc|o'me (-ŭ'm) *v.t.* (**~a'me; ~o'me**). Be unsuitable or unbecoming to. [f. MIS-[1] + BECOME]
mĭsbĕgŏ'tten *a.* Illegitimate, bastard; contemptible, disreputable. [f. MIS-[1] + *begotten* p.p. of BEGET]
mĭsbĕhā've *v.t.* Behave (one*self*, or abs.) improperly; so **mĭs**BEHA'VIOUR *n.* [ME, f. MIS-[1] + BEHAVE]
mĭsbĕlie'f *n.* Wrong religious belief; false opinion. [ME, f. MIS-[1] + BELIEF]
mĭsbĕsee'm *v.t.* (arch.) Misbecome. [f. MIS-[1] + BESEEM]
misc. *abbr.* miscellaneous.
mĭscă'lcūl|āte *v.t.* Calculate (amount, results, etc., or abs.) wrongly; so ~A'TION *n.* [f. MIS-[1] + CALCULATE]
mĭsca'll (-aw'l) *v.t.* Call by wrong or inappropriate name; (arch. or dial.) call (person) names. [ME, f. MIS-[1] + CALL[1]]
mĭscă'rriage (-rĭj; *or* mĭ'-) *n.* **1.** Miscarrying (of letter, scheme, etc.); ~ (failure of court to attain the ends) **of justice. 2.** Untimely delivery (of pregnant woman), abortion (esp. if spontaneous); (Med.) delivery of (prob. non-viable) foetus in 12th–28th week of pregnancy. [f. foll., after CARRIAGE]
mĭscă'rrȳ *v.i.* (Of person or business or scheme) fail, be unsuccessful; (of woman) have miscarriage, be delivered prematurely (*of* child); (of letter) fail to reach destination. [ME, f. MIS-[1] + CARRY[1]]
mĭsca'st (-kah'-) *v.t.* (**misca'st**). Add (accounts etc.) wrongly; allot unsuitable part to (actor). [f. MIS[1]- + CAST[1]]
mĭscĕgĕnā'tion *n.* Interbreeding of races, esp. of whites with non-whites. [irreg. f. L *miscēre* mix + *genus* race + -ATION]
mĭscellā'nĕa *n.* Literary miscellany; collection of miscellaneous items. [L, neut. pl. (as foll.)]
mĭscellā'nĕous *a.* Of mixed composition or character; (w. *pl. n.*) of various kinds; (of persons) many-sided; hence ~LY[2] *adv.*, ~NESS *n.* [f. L *miscellaneus* (*miscellus* mixed f. *miscēre* mix; see -ANEOUS)]
mĭscĕ'llanȳ (*or* mĭ'sel-) *n.* Mixture, medley; book containing collection of studies etc. or various literary compositions; hence **mĭscĕ'llan**IST (3) *n.* [f. F *miscellanées* fem. pl., or f. L MISCELLANEA, assim. to -Y[1]]
mĭscha'nce (-ah'ns) *n.* (Piece of) bad luck. [ME, f. OF *mesch(e)ance* (*mescheoir*; see MIS-[2], CHANCE[1])]
mĭ'schief (-chĭf) *n.* **1.** Harm or injury caused by person or other agent (**do** person **a ~**, wound or kill him); **make ~**, create discord; **the ~** (annoying part) *of it is that* etc. **2.** Causer or cause of harm or annoyance. **3.** Vexatious but not malicious conduct, esp. of children; pranks, scrapes, (*get into, keep out of, mischief*). **4.** Playful malice, archness, satire, (*eyes full of mischief*). **5. The ~**, (colloq.) the Devil (*where the mischief have you been?*). [ME, f. OF *meschief* (*meschever* f. as MIS-[2], *chever* come to end f. *chef* head; see CHIEF[1])]
mĭ'schievous (-chĭv-) *a.* (Of thing) having harmful effects; (of person, conduct, etc.) disposed to acts of playful malice or mild vexatiousness; hence ~LY[2] *adv.*, ~NESS *n.* [ME, f. AF *meschevous* f. OF *meschever* (see prec., -OUS)]
mĭ'schmĕtall (-shm-) *n.* Alloy of lanthanide metals that ignites on exposure to air. [G (*mischen* mix, *metall* metal)]
mĭ'sc|ĭble *a.* That can be mixed (*with*); hence ~IBI'LITY *n.* [f. med. L *miscibilis* f. L *miscēre* mix; see -IBLE]
mĭsconcei've (-sē'v) *v.* **1.** *v.i.* Have a wrong idea or conception (*of*, or abs.). **2.** *v.t.* Misunderstand (word, person). **3.** So **mĭs**CONCE'PTION *n.* [ME, f. MIS-[1] + CONCEIVE]
mĭscŏ'nduct *n.* Improper conduct, esp. adultery; bad management; so **mĭs**CONDU'CT[2] *v.t.* & *refl.* [f. MIS-[1] + CONDUCT[1]]
mĭsconstrue' (-ōō') *v.t.* Put wrong construction on (word, action); mistake meaning of (person); so **mĭs**CONSTRU'CTION *n.* [ME, f. MIS-[1] + CONSTRUE]
mĭscŏ'pȳ *v.t.* Copy incorrectly. [f. MIS-[1] + COPY[2]]
mĭscou'nt *n.*, & *v.t.* & *i.* (Make) wrong count, esp. of votes; count (things) wrongly. [ME, f. MIS-[1] + COUNT[1,2]]
mĭ'screant *a.* & *n.* **1.** *a.* Depraved; (arch.) heretical. **2.** *n.* Vile wretch, villain; (arch.) heretic. [ME, f. OF *mescreant* (as MIS-[2], *creant* part. of *croire* f. L *credere* believe; see -ANT)]
mĭscūe' *n.*, & *v.i.* (Bill.) **1.** *n.* Failure to strike ball properly with cue. **2.** *v.i.* Make a miscue. [f. MIS-[1] or MISS[2] + CUE[2]]
mĭsdā'te *v.t.* Date (event, letter, etc.) wrongly. [f. MIS-[1] + DATE[3]]
mĭsdea'l *v.* (**misdea'lt** *pr.* -dĕ'-) & *n.* **1.** *v.i.* & *t.* Make mistake in dealing (cards). **2.** *n.* Mistake in dealing cards; misdealt hand. [f. MIS-[1] + DEAL[2]]
mĭsdee'd *n.* Evil deed; crime. [OE *misdǣd* (as MIS-[1], DEED)]
mĭsdee'm *v.* (arch. or poet.) **1.** *v.t.* Have wrong opinion of; mistake (person, thing *for* another). **2.** *v.i.* Form wrong judgement (*of*). [ME; cf. ON *misdœma* (see MIS-[1], DEEM)]
mĭsdĕmea'nant *n.* Person convicted of misdemeanour or guilty of misconduct. [f. arch. *misdemean* misbehave (MIS-[1], DEMEAN[1]) + -ANT]
mĭsdĕmea'nour (-ner), ***-or,** *n.* (Law) indictable offence, (in U.K. formerly) less heinous than felony; offence, misdeed. [ME, f. MIS-[1] + DEMEANOUR]
mĭsdĭrĕ'ct *v.t.* Direct (person, letter, blow, etc.) wrongly; (of judge) instruct (jury) wrongly; so **mĭs**DIRE'CTION *n.* [f. MIS-[1] + DIRECT[1]]
mĭsdo'ĭng (-dōō'-) *n.* Misdeed. [ME, f. MIS-[1] + DOING]
mĭsdou'bt (-ow't) *v.t.* Have doubts as to the truth or existence of; have misgivings, be suspicious, about; suspect (*that*). [f. MIS-[1] + DOUBT[2]]
mise (mēz *or* mīz) *n.* **1.** (Hist.) Settlement by agreement, as **M~ of Lewes** (between Henry III and barons, 1264). **2. *~ en scène*** (mēzahṅsā'n), scenery and properties of acted play,

(fig.) surroundings of an event. [ME f. OF, fem. p.p. (as n.) of *mettre* put f. L *mittere miss-* send, put]

mī'ser (-z-) *n.* One who hoards wealth and lives miserably; avaricious person. [L, = wretched]

mĭ'serab|le (-z-) *a.* Wretchedly unhappy or uncomfortable; (of event etc.) causing wretchedness; contemptible, mean, (*a miserable hovel*); hence ~LY² *adv.* [ME, f. F *misérable* f. L *miserabilis* pitiable (*miserari* to pity f. *miser* wretched; see -ABLE)]

misère (mĭzār') *n.* (Cards). Declaration undertaking to win no tricks. [F, = poverty, MISERY]

mĭserēr'ė (-z-; *or* -ār'ĭ) *n.* Cry for mercy; = foll. 3. [ME, f. L, imper. of *miserēri* have mercy (as MISER); first word of Ps. 51 in L]

mĭsĕ'ricŏrd (-z-) *n.* **1.** Apartment in monastery in which some relaxations of rule were permitted. **2.** Dagger for giving the *coup de grâce*. **3.** Shelving projection on under side of hinged seat in choir stall, serving (when seat was turned up) to support person standing. [ME, f. OF *misericorde* f. L *misericordia* (*misericors* compassionate f. stem of *miserēri* pity + *cor cordis* heart)]

mī'serl|ȳ (-z-) *a.* Like a miser, niggardly; hence ~ĬNESS *a.* [f. MISER + -LY¹]

mĭ'serȳ (-z-) *n.* Wretched state of mind or of outward circumstances; thing causing this; *misère*; wretched or (colloq.) discontented or grumpy person; **out of its ~**, (of animal) released from suffering, esp. by being killed. [ME, f. AF **miserie*, OF *misere*, or f. L *miseria* (as MISER; see -Y¹)]

mĭsfea'sance (-za-) *n.* (Law). Transgression, esp. wrongful exercise of lawful authority. [ME, f. OF *mesfaisance* (*mesfaire* misdo f. as MIS-² + *faire* do f. L *facere*); see -ANCE; cf. MALFEASANCE]

mĭsfīr'e *v.i.*, & *n.* (Of gun, motor engine, etc.) fail(ing) to go off or start action or function regularly; fail(ing) to have intended effect. [f. MIS-¹ + FIRE²·¹; cf. MISS² *fire*]

mĭ'sfĭt *n.* Garment etc. that does not fit the person it is meant for; person unsuited to his environment, his work, etc. [f. MIS-¹ + FIT⁴]

mĭsfŏr'tune (-chun *or* -choon) *n.* Bad luck (*more his misfortune than his fault*); instance of this. [f. MIS-¹ + FORTUNE¹]

mĭsgĭ've (-g-) *v.t.* (**misga've**; **misgi'ven**). (Of person's mind, heart, etc.) fill (him) with suspicion or foreboding (*about* thing, *that*). [f. MIS-¹ + GIVE¹]

mĭsgĭ'vĭng (-g-) *n.* Feeling of mistrust or apprehension. [f. prec. + -ING¹]

mĭsgo'vern (-gŭ'-) *v.t.* Govern (State etc.) badly; so ~MENT *n.* [ME, f. MIS-¹ + GOVERN]

mĭsguī'd|e (-gī'd) *v.t.* (chiefly in *p.p.*) Mislead, cause to err in thought or action; hence ~ĖDLY² *adv.* [ME, f. MIS-¹ + GUIDE²]

mĭshă'ndle (-s-h-) *v.t.* Handle (person, thing) roughly or rudely, ill-treat; deal with incorrectly or ineffectively. [f. MIS-¹ + HANDLE²]

mĭ'shăp (-s-h-; *or* -ă'p) *n.* Unlucky accident. [ME, f. MIS-¹ + HAP¹]

mĭshear' (-s-h-) *v.t.* (**mishear'd** *pr.* -hēr'd). Hear incorrectly or imperfectly. [ME, f. MIS-¹ + HEAR]

mĭshĭt (-s-h-) *n.*, & *v.t.* (**-tt-**; **mishit**). **1.** *n.* (mĭ'-). Faulty or bad hit. **2.** *v.t.* (-ĭ't). Hit (a ball) faultily. [f. MIS-¹ + HIT²·¹]

mĭ'shmăsh *n.* Confused mixture. [ME; redupl. of MASH¹]

Mĭ'shnah (-*a*) *n.* Collection of precepts forming basis of Talmud, and embodying Jewish oral law; hence **Mĭshnā'**IC *a.* [f. Heb. *mišnāh* (teaching by) repetition]

mĭsĭnfŏr'm *v.t.* Give wrong information to, mislead; so **mis**INFORMA'TION *n.* [ME, f. MIS-¹ + INFORM]

mĭsĭntĕr'prĕt *v.t.* Give wrong interpretation to; make wrong inference from; so ~A'TION *n.* [f. MIS-¹ + INTERPRET]

mĭsjŭ'dge *v.t.* & *i.* Judge wrongly; have wrong opinion of or *of*. [f. MIS-¹ + JUDGE²]

mĭslay' *v.t.* (**mislai'd**). Put (thing) by accident where it cannot readily be found; (euphem.) lose. [ME, f. MIS-¹ + LAY³]

mĭslea'd *v.t.* (**misle'd**). Lead astray, cause to go wrong, in conduct or belief. [OE *mislǣdan* (as MIS-¹, LEAD²)]

mĭslī'ke *v.t.* (arch.) Dislike. [OE *mislīcian* (as MIS-¹, LIKE²)]

mĭsmă'nage *v.t.* Manage badly or wrongly; so ~MENT (-ĭjm-) *n.* [f. MIS-¹ + MANAGE²]

mĭsmătch *v.t.*, & *n.* **1.** *v.t.* (-ă'ch). Match unsuitably or incorrectly. **2.** *n.* (mĭ'-). Bad match. [f. MIS-¹ + MATCH²·¹]

mĭsnā'me *v.t.* = MISCALL. [f. MIS-¹ + NAME²]

mĭsnō'mer *n.* Use of wrong name; wrong (use of) name or term. [ME f. AF, f. OF *mesnom(m)er* (as MIS-², *nommer* name f. L *nominare* f. as NOMINATE; see -ER⁴)]

mĭsŏ'gam|ȳ *n.* Hatred of marriage; hence ~IST (2) *n.* [f. Gk *misos* hatred + *gamos* marriage + -Y¹]

mĭsŏ'gȳn|ĭst (*or* -g-) *n.* One who hates all women; so ~Y¹ *n.* [f. as prec. + Gk *gunē* woman + -IST]

mĭsŏ'log|ȳ *n.* Hatred of reason, discussion, or knowledge; hence ~IST (2) *n.* [f. Gk *misos* hatred + -LOGY]

mĭsonē'|ĭsm *n.* Hatred of what is new; hence ~IST (2) *n.* [f. as prec. + Gk *neos* new + -ISM]

mĭ'spĭckel *n.* (Min.) Arsenical pyrites. [G]

mĭsplā'ce *v.t.* Put in wrong place or hands; bestow (affections) on wrong object; place (confidence) amiss; time (words, action) badly; so ~MENT (-sm-) *n.* [f. MIS-¹ + PLACE²]

mĭsplay' *n.*, & *v.t.* Play(ing) in wrong or ineffective manner [f. MIS-¹ + PLAY²·¹]

mĭsprĭnt *n.*, & *v.t.* **1.** *n.* (mĭ'-). Mistake in printing. **2.** *v.t.* (-ĭ'nt). Print wrongly. [n. f. v., f. MIS-¹ + PRINT²]

mĭsprĭ'sion¹ (-zhon) *n.* (Law). Wrong action or omission, esp. **~ of treason** or **felony**, (orig.) minor form of these, (now) concealment of one's knowledge of treasonable intent etc. [ME, f. AF *mesprisioun* f. OF *mesprison* error (*mesprendre* to mistake f. as MIS-², *prendre* take)]

mĭsprĭ'sion² (-zhon) *n.* (arch.) Contempt; failure to appreciate the value (*of*). [f. foll., after prec.]

mĭsprī'ze *v.t.* Despise; fail to appreciate. [ME, f. OF *mesprisier* (as MIS-², PRIZE¹)]

mĭspronou'nce *v.t.* Pronounce (word etc.) wrongly; so **mis**PRONUNCIA'TION *n.* [f. MIS-¹ + PRONOUNCE]

mĭsquō'te *v.t.* Quote wrongly; so **mis**QUOTA'TION *n.* [f. MIS-¹ + QUOTE]

mĭsrea'd *v.t.* (**misrea'd** *pr.* -rĕ'd). Read or interpret wrongly. [f. MIS-¹ + READ]

mĭsrėmĕ'mber *v.t.* Remember imperfectly or incorrectly. [f. MIS-¹ + REMEMBER]

mĭsrėpŏr't *n.*, & *v.t.* (Give) false or incorrect report (of). [ME, f. MIS-¹ + REPORT²·¹]

mĭsrĕprėsĕ'nt (-zĕ'-) *v.t.* Represent wrongly, give false account of; so ~A'TION *n.* [f. MIS-¹ + REPRESENT]

mĭsru'le (-ōō'l) *n.*, & *v.t.* **1.** *n.* Bad government; disorder; **Lord, Master, of M~**, (Hist.) person presiding over Christmas revels in nobleman's house, Inn of Court, etc. **2.** *v.t.* Govern badly. [ME, f. MIS-¹ + RULE]

mĭss¹ *n.* **1.** Failure to hit or attain; **a ~ is as good as a mile**, failure or escape is what it is, however narrow the margin; NEAR² *miss*. **2.** (Bill.) failure to hit object-ball (**give a ~**, avoid hitting object-ball so as to leave one's own in safe position); **give** (thing) **a ~**, avoid, leave alone, (*shall give the party, the prunes, a miss*). **3.** (colloq.) = MISCARRIAGE 2. [OE, = loss, cogn. w. foll.]

miss[2] *v.* **1.** *v.t.* (Of person or missile) fail to hit (mark etc., or abs.); fail to reach, find, get, or meet; let slip (opportunity); fail to catch (train etc.; **~ the boat** or **the bus,** lose an opportunity). **2.** Fail to see (event) or hear or understand (remark, joke, etc.); **not ~ much,** be alert. **3. ~ (out)**, leave out (words etc. in reading, writing, etc.); fail to keep (appointment) or perform. **4.** Notice esp. with regret the absence of, feel the want of; **be ~'ing,** not have. **5.** *v.i.* (Of internal combustion engine) misfire. **6. ~ fire,** (of gun) fail to go off, (fig.) fail in one's object; ***~ out (on)**, fail to get (something), be unsuccessful; *miss* STAY[2]*s*. **7.** Hence **~'**ABLE *a.* [OE *missan*, = OHG *missen*, ON *missa* f. Gmc **missjan* (**missa-* MIS-[1])]

mĭss[3] *n.* **1.** (*M~*). (As title of unmarried woman or girl without higher title, or retained by married woman for professional etc. reasons) *Miss Smith* (pl. *the Miss Smiths, the Misses Smith*); (as title of beauty queen from specified region) *Miss France, Miss World*; (as *voc.* without name, to teacher or shop assistant, or from servant etc.) young woman. **2.** (usu. derog. or playful). Girl, esp. schoolgirl, often w. implication of silliness or sentimentality, whence **~'**ISH[1] *a.* **3.** (Commerc.) Garment size suitable for young women. [abbr. of MISTRESS]

Miss. *abbr.* Mississippi.

mĭ'ssal *n.* (R.C.) Book containing service of Mass for whole year; book of prayers, esp. illuminated one. [ME, f. med. L *missale* neut. (as n.) of eccl. L *missalis* of the mass (*missa* MASS[1]; see -AL)]

mĭ'ssel *n.* **~(-thrush)**, large thrush (*Turdus viscivorus*) that feeds on mistletoe etc. berries. [OE *mistel* basil, mistletoe, = OHG, ON *mistil*; orig. unkn.]

mĭsshāpe (-s-sh-) *v.t.* Give bad shape or form to (lit. or fig.). [ME, f. MIS-[1] + SHAPE[1]]

mĭsshā'pen (-s-sh-) *a.* Ill-shaped, deformed, distorted. [ME, f. MIS-[1] + *shapen* arch. p.p. of SHAPE[1]]

mĭ'ssile *a.* & *n.* (Object or weapon) suitable for throwing at a target or for discharge from machine or engine; self-propelling weapon directed by remote control (GUIDE[2]*d missile*) or automatically; hence **~**RY (1, 5) (-lrĭ) *n.* [f. L *missilis* (*mittere miss-* send; see -IL)]

mĭ'ssing *a.* In vbl senses; not found, not in its place, (*there is a page missing*; *a page is missing*; *here is the missing page*; cf. MISS[2] 4); (of soldier etc.) neither present after battle etc. nor known to have been killed or wounded; **~ link,** thing lacking to complete a series, hypothetical intermediate type, esp. between man and anthropoid apes. [f. MISS[2] + -ING[2]]

mĭ'ssion (-shon) *n.* **1.** Body of persons sent to foreign country to conduct negotiations etc. **2.** Body sent by religious community to propagate its faith; field of missionary activity; missionary post; organization in a district for conversion of the people; course of religious services etc. for this purpose. **3.** Task of political or other mission; operational sortie, esp. dispatch of aircraft or spacecraft. **4.** Person's vocation or divinely appointed work in life. [F, or f. L *missio* (*mittere miss-* send; see -ION)]

mĭ'ssionarў (-sho-) *a.* & *n.* **1.** *a.* Of, concerned with, characteristic of, religious or similar missions. **2.** *n.* Person who goes on missionary work. [f. mod. L *missionarius* f. L (as prec.; see -ARY[1])]

mĭ'ssioner (-sho-) *n.* Missionary; person in charge of parochial mission. [f. MISSION + -ER[1]]

mĭ'ssĭs, mĭ'ssus, (*or* -sĭz) *n.* **1. The ~**, (vulg. or joc.) my or your wife. **2.** (vulg., as *voc.*) Form of address to woman. [corrupt. of MISTRESS; cf. MRS.]

mĭ'ssĭve *a.* & *n.* **1.** *a.* **Letter(s) ~**, letter from sovereign to dean and chapter nominating person to be elected bishop. **2.** *n.* = LETTER 2, esp. official one or (joc.) long or serious one. [ME, f. med. L *missivus* f. L (as MISSION; see -IVE)]

mĭsspĕ'll (-s-s-) *v.t.* (for forms see SPELL[2]). Spell wrongly; hence **~**ING[1] *n.* [f. MIS-[1] + SPELL[2]]

mĭsspĕ'nd (-s-s-) *v.t.* (**misspe'nt**). Spend amiss or wastefully (esp. in *p.p.*). [ME, f. MIS-[1] + SPEND]

mĭsstā'te (-s-s-) *v.t.* State wrongly; so **~**MENT (-tm-) *n.* [f. MIS-[1] + STATE[2]]

mĭsstĕ'p (-s-s-) *n.* Wrong step or action; *faux pas.* [f. MIS- + STEP[2]]

missus. See MISSIS.

mĭ'ssў *n.* Affectionate, playful, or derog., form of address to young girl. [f. MISS[3] + -Y[3]]

mĭst *n.* & *v.* **1.** *n.* Water vapour near ground in droplets smaller than raindrops and causing obscuration of the atmosphere; **Scotch ~**, thick mist and drizzle (frequent on Scottish hills). **2.** Dimness or blurring of sight caused by bodily disorder or by tears; condensed vapour obscuring windscreen etc.; cloud of particles resembling mist. **3.** Hence **~'**FUL *a.*, **~'**LIKE *a.* & *adv.* **4.** *v.t.* & *i.* Cover, be covered, (as) with mist. [OE *mist*, = MLG, MDu. *mist*, Icel. *mistur* f. Gmc **mihstaz*]

mĭstā'ke[1] *n.* Misunderstanding of a thing's meaning; thing incorrectly done or thought through ignorance or inadvertence; **and,** or **make, no ~**, undoubtedly (emphasizing statement). [f. foll.]

mĭstā'ke[2] *v.* (**mistoo'k; ~n**). **1.** *v.t.* Misunderstand meaning or intention of (person, statement, purpose); choose wrongly (*mistake* one's *vocation*); wrongly take (one *for* another); **there is no mista'king,** one is sure to recognize (person or thing). **2.** *v.i.* Err in opinion. **3.** (in *p.p.*) Wrong in opinion, (of action etc.) ill-judged, (*you are mistaken*; *mistaken kindness*); hence **~n**LY[2] *adv.*, **~n**NESS (-n-n-) *n.* **4.** Hence **mĭstā'k**ABLE *a.* [ME, f. ON *mistaka* (as MIS-[1], *taka* TAKE[1])]

mĭ'ster *n.*, & *v.t.* **1.** *n.* (vulg., as *voc.*) Form of address to man. **2.** Person without title of nobility etc. (*a mere mister*). **3.** *v.t.* Address or speak of as *Mr.* [weakened form of MASTER[1] in unstressed use before name; cf. MR.]

mĭ'stĭgrĭs *n.* (Cards). (Blank card in) a variety of poker. [f. F *mistigri* jack of clubs]

mistī'me *v.t.* Say, do, (thing) at wrong time. [OE *mistimian* (as MIS-[1], TIME[2])]

mistle. Var. of MISSEL.

mĭ'stletōe (-seltō) *n.* Parasitic plant (*Viscum album*) growing on apple and other trees, and bearing white glutinous berries used in making birdlime; **kiss under the ~** (w. ref. to custom permitting kissing of girl standing below mistletoe hung as Christmas decoration). [OE *misteltān* (= ON *mistiltienn*; as MISSEL, *tān* twig)]

mistoo'k. See MISTAKE[2].

mĭ'stral (*or* -trah'l) *n.* Cold N. or N.W. wind in Mediterranean provinces of France etc. [F & Prov., f. L (as MAGISTRAL)]

mĭstrăns|lā'te (*or* -z-; *or* -trah-) *v.t.* Translate incorrectly; so **~la'**TION *n.* [f. MIS-[1] + TRANSLATE]

For other words in *mis-* see MIS-[1,2].

mĭstrea't *v.t.* Treat badly; hence ~MENT *n.* [ME, f. MIS-[1] + TREAT]

mĭ'strĕss *n.* **1.** Woman in authority over servants; female head of household. **2.** Woman who has power to control or dispose *of* (*you are mistress of the situation, of yourself; you are your own, the dog's, mistress*; cf. MASTER[1]); woman head of college, school, etc.; (fig.) ~ **of the seas,** chief naval power. **3.** Woman who has thorough knowledge (*of* subject). **4.** Woman loved and courted by a man; woman illicitly occupying place of wife or having permanent illicit sexual relationship with man. **5.** ||Female teacher in school or of special subject (*music mistress*). **6.** ||**M~ of the Robes,** lady charged with care of Queen's wardrobe; WARDROBE *mistress.* **7.** (arch. or dial., as title) = MRS. **8.** Hence ~-SHIP *n.* [ME f. OF *maistresse* (*maistre* MASTER[1]; see -ESS[1])]

mĭstrī'al *n.* Trial vitiated by error; *inconclusive trial. [f. MIS-[1] + TRIAL]

mĭstrŭ'st *v.t.*, & *n.* **1.** *v.t.* Feel no confidence in (person, one*self*, one's powers, etc.); be suspicious of. **2.** *n.* Lack of confidence; suspicion. [ME, f. MIS-[1] + TRUST]

mĭstrŭ'stful *a.* Lacking confidence or trust; suspicious *of*; hence ~LY[2] *adv.*, ~NESS *n.* [f. prec. 2 + -FUL]

mĭ'st|ў *a.* Of, or covered with, mist; indistinct in form; (fig.) obscure, vague, (*a misty idea*); hence ~ĭLY[2] *adv.*, ~ĭNESS *n.* [OE *mistig* (as MIST, -Y[2])]

mĭsŭnderstă'nd *v.t.* (**-stoo'd**). Take (words etc., or abs.) in wrong sense; (esp. in *p.p.*) misinterpret words or actions of (person); so ~ING[1] *n.* [ME, f. MIS-[1] + UNDERSTAND]

mĭsū'sage (-zĭj) *n.* Wrong or improper usage; ill-treatment. [f. MIS-[1] + USAGE]

mĭsū's|e[1] (-z) *v.t.* Use wrongly, apply to wrong purpose; ill-treat; hence ~ER[1] *n.* [ME, f. MIS-[1] + USE[2]]

mĭsū'se[2] *n.* Wrong or improper use or application. [ME, f. MIS-[1] + USE[1]]

M.I.T. *abbr.* Massachusetts Institute of Technology.

mite *n.* **1.** Small arachnid of order Acari, esp. **cheese-~** (found in cheese), ITCH[1]-*mite*; hence **mī'tY**[2] *a.* **2.** (Hist.) Flemish copper coin of small value; (pop.) half a farthing (as in Mark 12:42); modest contribution, the best one can do, (*let me offer my mite of comfort*); **a ~,** (*adv.*, colloq.) somewhat (**not a ~,** not at all). **3.** Small object, esp. child; **a ~ of a** (a tiny) *child* etc. [sense 1 f. OE *mīte*, = MLG, MDu. *mīte*, OHG *mīza* gnat f. Gmc **mītōn*; sense 2 ME, f. MLG, MDu. *mīte*, prob. of same orig.]

***mī'ter**[1,2]. See MITRE[1,2].

Mĭ'th|ras *n.* Persian god identified with sun, worshipped in Europe during first three centuries A.D.; hence **~rā'**IC *a.*, **~rā**ISM (3), **~rā**IST (2), *ns.* [L f. Gk, f. OPers. *Mithra* f. Skr. *Mitra* a Vedic god]

mĭthrĭ'dat|ize, -ī|se (-īz), *v.t.* Render proof against poison by gradually increasing doses of it; so **mĭthrĭdă'**TIC *a.*, ~ISM (1) *n.* [f. *mithridate* supposed universal antidote (*Mithridates* VI, king of Pontus d. 63 B.C., supposed to have used this method) + -IZE]

mĭ'tĭg|āte *v.t.* Appease (anger etc.); alleviate (pain, grief); reduce severity of (punishment); moderate (heat, cold, severity, guilt, etc.); so ~ABLE *a.*, ~A'TION *n.*, **~ā**TORY *a.* [ME, f. L *mitigare* (*mitis* mild) + -ATE[3]]

mitōchŏ'ndrĭ|on (-k-) *n.* (*pl.* ~**a**). (Biol.) Organelle in most cells, containing enzymes needed for metabolic processes. [mod. L, f. Gk *mitos* thread + *khondrion* dim. of *khondros* granule]

mĭt|ō'sĭs *n.* (*pl.* **~oses** *pr.* -ō'sēz). (Biol.) Division of a cell or nucleus with longitudinal splitting of all chromosomes into pairs distributed equally between resulting two cells or nuclei; hence ~O'TIC *a.* [mod. L, f. Gk *mitos* thread; see -OSIS]

mĭtrailleu'se (-trahyėr'z) *n.* Many-barrelled breech-loading machine-gun discharging small missiles simultaneously or in rapid succession. [F, fem. agent-n. f. *mitrailler* (*mitraille* small missiles f. OF *mi(s)traille* small money, f. *mite* MITE)]

mī'tral *a.* Of or like a mitre; ~ **valve,** two-cusped valve between left atrium and left ventricle of heart. [f. mod. L *mitralis* f. L (as foll.; see -AL)]

mī'tre[1] (-ter), ***mī'ter**[1], *n.* **1.** Bishop's and abbot's tall cap, deeply cleft at top, esp. as symbol of episcopal office; hence **mī't(e)**RED[2] (-terd) *a.* **2.** [perh. diff. wd]. Joint of two pieces of wood etc. at angle of 90°, such that line of junction bisects this angle (**~-block, -board, -box,** guide for saw in cutting mitre-joints; **~-wheels,** pair of bevelled cog-wheels with teeth set at 45° and axes at right angles); similar joint of pieces of cloth etc. [ME f. OF, f. L f. Gk *mitra* girdle, turban]

mī'tre[2] (-ter), ***mī'ter**[2], *v.* **1.** *v.t.* Bestow mitre on. **2.** *v.t.* & *i.* Join with mitre. [ME, f. prec.]

mitt *n.* Lace or knitted glove not covering fingers; mitten; baseball glove for catching ball; *(sl.) hand (**frozen ~,** chilly reception). [abbr. of foll.]

mĭ'tten *n.* Kind of glove with thumb but no (or no separate) fingers, for warmth or protection in hedgers' work etc.; (in *pl.*, sl.) boxing-gloves; **give, get, the (frozen) mitten,** (sl.) dismiss (person), be dismissed; hence ~ED[2] (-nd) *a.* [ME, f. OF *mitaine*, f. Rom. **medietana* (sc. *muffula* MUFFLE[2]) f. L *medietas* half (see MOIETY)]

mĭ'ttĭmus *n.* Warrant committing person to prison or (Hist.) ordering documents to be sent to another court; (arch. colloq.) dismissal from office. [ME f. L, = we send]

Mĭ'ttў *n.* (**Walter**) ~, person given to extravagant day-dreams of his own triumphs. [hero of story by J. Thurber]

mĭx *v.* & *n.* **1.** *v.t.* Put together, combine (two or more substances or groups or qualities etc., one *with* another) so that the particles or members or constituent parts of each are diffused among those of the others; prepare (compound, cocktail, etc.) by mixing ingredients; ~ **one's drinks,** drink different alcoholic liquors in succession. **2.** *v.i.* Join, be mixed (*oil will not mix with water*); (of persons) be harmonious or sociable (*with*), have dealings *with*, participate *in*; (of things) be compatible. **3. ~ in, ~ it,** (colloq.) start fighting; **~ up,** (1) mix thoroughly, (2) confuse esp. in thought, so ~*-up* n.; **be ~ed up,** be involved (*in* or *with* shady dealings etc.). **4.** *n.* (colloq.) Mixture; proportion of materials in a mixture; merging of film pictures or sounds; ingredients prepared commercially for making cake etc. or for a process such as concrete-making. [back form. f. foll. taken as p.p.]

mĭxed (-kst) *a.* In vbl senses (see prec.); of diverse qualities or elements; (of group of persons) containing persons from various classes, esp. of doubtful status; tangled; **~(-up),** (colloq.) mentally confused, muddled, ill-adjusted; for persons of both sexes (*mixed school, bathing*); ~ **bag,** assortment of diverse things or persons; ~ **blessing,** thing having advantages but also disadvantages; **~ chalice,** sacramental wine with ceremonial addition of water; ~ **crystal** (formed from more than one substance); ~ **doubles,** (Tennis etc.) doubles game with man and woman as partners on each side; ~ **farming** (with both crops and livestock); ~ **feelings** (e.g. some pleasure and some dismay at same event); ~ **grill,** dish of various grilled meats and vegetables; ~ **marriage** (between persons of different race or religion); *mixed* METAPHOR; ~ **number** (containing integer and fraction); ||~ **tithe** (from animals fed on the land); hence **mĭ'xĕd**NESS *n.* [ME *mixt* f. OF *mixte* f. L *mixtus* p.p. of *miscēre* mix]

||**mĭ'xen** *n.* (arch. or dial.) Dunghill. [OE, f. Gmc **mihsa*; see -EN[3]]

mĭ'xer *n.* In vbl senses; apparatus for mixing foods etc.; apparatus for merging pictures in television or cinematography; apparatus controlling combination of various sounds in preparation of sound films or in broadcasting; **good, bad,** ~, (colloq.) one who gets on well, badly, with other people (esp. those of a different social class). [f. MIX + -ER[1]]

Mĭxolȳ'dĭan *a.* ~ **mode,** (1) ancient Greek MODE, (2) seventh of church modes (with G as final and D as dominant). [f. Gk *mixoludios* half--Lydian (*mixos* mixed; see LYDIAN)]

mĭ'xture *n.* **1.** Mixing or being mixed. **2.** Thing or (fig.) person that is the result of mixing; medical preparation of this kind (*cough mixture*; **the ~ as before,** (fig.) the same treatment repeated); mechanical mixing of two substances, involving no change in their character, opp. to chemical combination; gas or vaporized petrol or oil mixed with air, forming explosive charge in internal combustion engine; HEATHER *mixture*. [ME f. F, or f. L *mixtura* (as MIXED; see -URE)]

mĭ'zen, mĭ'zzen, *n.* (Naut.) ~**(-sail)**, lowest fore-and-aft sail of full-rigged ship's ~**-mast** (next aft of main-mast); ~ **yard** (on which mizen is extended). [ME, f. F *misaine* f. It. *mezzana* mizen-sail, fem. of *mezzano* middle; see MEZZANINE]

mĭ'zzle[1] *v.i. impers.*, & *n.* Drizzle; hence **mĭ'zzly**[2] *a.* [ME, prob. f. LG *miseln*; cf. MDu. *miezelen*]

||**mĭ'zzle**[2] *v.i.* (sl.) Run away, decamp. [18th c.; orig. unkn.]

Mk. *abbr.* mark.

M.K.S.(A.) *abbrs.* metre-kilogram-second(-ampere) system of measurement.

Mkt. *abbr.* Market.

ml. *abbr.* mile(s); millilitre(s).

M.L.A. *abbr.* Member of Legislative Assembly; Modern Language Association (of America).

M.L.C. *abbr.* Member of Legislative Council.

MLF *abbr.* multilateral (nuclear) force.

M.Litt. *abbr.* Master of Letters. [f. L *Magister Litterarum*]

Mlle *abbr. Mademoiselle.*

Mlles *abbr. Mesdemoiselles.*

MM. *abbr. Messieurs.*

M.M. *abbr.* Maelzel's metronome; ||Military Medal.

mm *abbr.* millimetre(s).

Mme *abbr. Madame.*

Mmes *abbr. Mesdames.*

m.m.f. *abbr.* magnetomotive force.

M.Mus. *abbr.* Master of Music.

||**M.N.** *abbr.* Merchant Navy.

Mn *symb.* manganese.

||**M'Naghten.** See **MacN-.**

mnėmŏ'nĭc (n-) *a.* & *n.* **1.** *a.* Of, or designed to aid, the memory. **2.** *n.* Mnemonic device; (in *pl.*) art of, system for, improving memory. **3.** Hence **mnē'mon**IST (3) (n-) *n.* [f. med. L f. Gk *mnēmonikos* (*mnēmōn* mindful f. *mna-* remember; see -IC)]

mō *n.* (*pl.* **mos**). (sl.) Moment (*wait a mo*). [abbr.]

M.O. *abbr.* Medical Officer; money order.

Mo. *abbr.* Missouri.

***mo.** *abbr.* month.

Mo *symb.* molybdenum.

mō'a *n.* Extinct flightless N.Z. bird of family Dinornithidae, more or less resembling ostrich; cf. DINORNIS. [Maori]

moan[1] *n.* **1.** Long murmur of physical or mental suffering; low plaintive sound of wind etc. **2.** Complaint, grievance; suffering; **make** (one's) ~, (arch.) complain. **3.** Hence ~'FUL *a.* [ME, f. OE **mān* f. Gmc **main-*]

moan[2] *v.* **1.** *v.i.* Make moan(s). **2.** *v.t.* Utter (words) with moans; lament (misfortune etc.); lament for (dead person etc.). [f. prec.]

moat *n.*, & *v.t.* **1.** *n.* Deep wide ditch surrounding house, castle, etc., usu. filled with water. **2.** *v.t.* Surround (as) with moat. [ME *mot(e)* f. OF *mot(t)e* mound]

mŏb[1] *n.* **1.** The populace; rabble, tumultuous crowd; promiscuous assemblage of persons; (Austral.) flock or herd; (sl.) associated group of persons. **2.** ~ **law,** ~ **rule,** (imposed and enforced by mob); ||~**'sman** (-z-), (arch.) well--dressed pickpocket; ~**'ster,** (sl.) gangster; ||SWELL *mob.* **3.** Hence ~**'bish**[1] *a.*, ~**ŏ'**CRACY *n.* [abbr. of *mobile* n. (17th c.) short for *mobile vulgus*, L, = excitable crowd (MOBILE)]

mŏb[2] *v.* (-bb-). **1.** *v.t.* (Of mob) attack; crowd round and molest or acclaim. **2.** *v.i.* Assemble in a mob. [f. prec.]

mŏ'b-căp *n.* Woman's large indoor cap covering whole of hair, worn in 18th and early 19th c. [f. obs. (18th c.) *mob*, orig. = slut, + CAP[1]]

mō'bile *a.* & *n.* **1.** *a.* Movable, not fixed, free to move; (of face etc.) readily changing its expression; (of person or mind) changing (too) easily; (of troops) that may be easily moved from place to place; (of shop etc.) accommodated in vehicle so as to serve various places; (of person) able to change one's social status; so **mobĭ'l**ITY *n.* **2.** *n.* Structure of metal, plastic, cardboard, etc., that may be hung so as to turn freely. [ME f. F, f. L *mobilis* (*movēre* move; see -IL)]

mobĭ'lĭarȳ *a.* (Law). Relating to movable property. [f. F *mobiliaire* f. L (as prec.; see -ARY[1])]

mō'biliz|e, -is|e (-īz), *v.t.* Render movable, bring into circulation; prepare (forces, or abs.) for active service; hence or cogn. ~ABLE *a.*, ~A'TION *n.* [f. F *mobiliser* (as MOBILE; see -IZE)]

Mö'bĭus (mẽr'-) *n.* ~ **strip** etc., (Math.) surface with only one side and edge formed by joining ends of rectangle after twisting one end through 180°. [f. A. F. ~, Ger. mathematician d. 1868]

mobsman, mobster. See MOB[1].

mŏ'ccasĭn *n.* Footwear of soft deerskin etc. worn by N. Amer. Indians, trappers, etc., with sole joined to U-shaped flat vamp and no heel; similar shoe in ordinary wear; Amer. viper of genus *Agkistrodon*. [f. Powhatan *mockasin*, Ojibwa *makisin*]

Mŏ'cha[1] (-ka) *n.* Moss agate. [prob. f. as foll.]

mŏ'cha[2] (-ka) *n.* Fine quality of coffee; coffee (and chocolate) flavouring; soft kind of sheepskin. [f. *M*~, Arabian port at entrance of Red Sea, whence the coffee orig. came]

mŏck[1] *n.* (arch.) Derision; thing deserving scorn; imitation, counterfeit. [ME, f. MOCK[3]]

mŏck[2] *attrib. a.* Sham, imitation (esp. without intent to deceive), pretended; ~ **duck** or **goose,** pork with sage-and-onion stuffing; ~**-heroic** *a.* & *n.*, burlesquing (of) heroic style; ~ **moon,** paraselene; *mock* ORANGE[1]; ~ **sun,** parhelion; ~ **turtle soup** (made from calf's head etc.). [f. prec. & foll.]

mŏck[3] *v.* **1.** *v.t.* Subject to ridicule; defy contemptuously; delude; ridicule by imitation; mimic, counterfeit. **2.** *v.i.* Scoff *at.* **3.** **~'ing-bird,** bird that mimics notes of other birds, esp. Amer. song-bird (*Mimus polyglottos*); **~-up,** experimental model showing appearance of (part of) proposed book, ship, etc. **4.** Hence ~'ER[1] *n.* [ME *mokke, mocque,* f. OF *mo(c)quer* deride f. Rom. **moccare*]

mŏ'ckerў *n.* Derision; subject or occasion of this; counterfeit or absurdly inadequate representation (*of*); ludicrously or insultingly futile action etc. [ME, f. OF *moquerie* (as prec.; see -ERY)]

mŏd[1] *n.* Gaelic congress for music and poetry. [f. Gael. *mōd*]

mŏd[2] *n.* & *a.* (colloq.) **1.** *n.* Modification; ||(*Mod*) 1960s teenager of group notable for sophistication and tidiness [f. MODERN]. **2.** *a.* Modern; ~ **cons,** modern conveniences. [abbr.]

mō'dal *a.* Of mode or form as opp. to substance; (of legacy etc.) having directions as to mode in which it is to be applied; (Gram.) of the mood of a verb, (of verb, e.g. *would*) used to express mood of another verb, (of particle) denoting manner; (Logic, of proposition) in which predicate is affirmed of subject with some qualification, or which involves affirmation of possibility, impossibility, necessity, or contingency; (Statistics & Mus.) of mode(s); hence ~LY[2] *adv.* [f. med. L *modalis* f. L (as MODE; see -AL)]

modă'lĭtў *n.* Being modal; (in *sing.* or *pl.*) (prescribed) method of procedure. [f. med. L *modalitas* (as prec.; see -ITY)]

mōde *n.* **1.** Way, manner, in which thing is done; method of procedure; prevailing fashion or custom; **the ~,** (arch.) the fashion in dress etc. **2.** (Mus.) Ancient Greek scale system used in diatonic composition (DORIAN, LYDIAN, etc., *mode*); medieval scale for composition of church plainsong; each of the two chief scale systems in more modern music (MAJOR[2], MINOR, *mode*). **3.** (Logic). Character of modal proposition; = MOOD[2]. **4.** *(Gram.) = MOOD[2]. **5.** (Statistics). Value of variable corresponding to its greatest frequency of occurrence. [F, & f. L *modus* measure f. IE **mod-*, **med-*]

mŏ'del[1] *n.* & *a.* **1.** *n.* Representation in three dimensions of proposed structure etc. esp. on smaller scale (WORKING[2] *model*); simplified description of system etc. to assist calculations and predictions. **2.** Figure in clay, wax, etc., to be reproduced in other material; (copy of) garment etc. by well-known designer. **3.** Design, style of structure, esp. of motor vehicle. **4.** Person or thing proposed for imitation; person employed to pose for artist; mannequin, person employed to display clothes etc. by wearing them. **5. The New M~,** plan for reorganization of Parliamentary army in England 1644–5. **6.** *a.* Exemplary, ideally perfect. [f. F *modelle* f. It. *modello* f. Rom. **modellus* f. L MODULUS]

mŏ'del[2] *v.* (||-ll-). **1.** *v.t.* Fashion, shape, (figure) in clay, wax, etc.; give shape to, frame, (document, argument, etc.); (Art) cause to appear three-dimensional; form (thing) *after, on, upon,* a model; (of person acting as model) display (garment) by wearing it. **2.** *v.i.* Act or pose as model (see prec. 4). [f. prec.]

mŏ'derat|e[1] *a.* & *n.* **1.** *a.* Avoiding extremes, temperate in conduct or expression; (of wind) of medium strength; fairly or tolerably large or good; (of prices) low; hence **~ELY**[2] (-tlĭ) *adv.*, **~ENESS** (-tn-) *n.* **2.** *n.* One who holds moderate opinions in politics etc.; hence ~ISM (3) *n.* [ME, f. L *moderatus* p.p. of *moderare* reduce, control, cogn. w. MODEST; see -ATE[2]]

mŏ'derāte[2] *v.* **1.** *v.t.* Render less violent, intense, rigorous, etc. **2.** *v.i.* (Of fury, scorn, storm, etc.) become less vehement. **3.** *v.t.* & *i.* Act as moderator (of or to). [f. as prec. + -ATE[3]]

mŏderā'tion *n.* **1.** Moderating; moderateness; **in ~,** in a moderate manner or degree. **2.** (*M~*; in *pl.*) First public examination in some faculties for Oxford B.A. degree. **3.** Retardation of neutrons by MODERATOR 2. [ME f. OF, f. L *moderatio -onis* (as MODERATE[1]; see -ATION)]

moderato (mŏderah'tō) *adv.* (Mus.) At moderate pace. [It. (as MODERATE[1])]

mŏ'derātor *n.* **1.** Arbitrator; mediator; presiding officer; examiner for Moderations; Presbyterian minister presiding over any ecclesiastical body; hence ~SHIP *n.* **2.** Substance used in nuclear reactor to retard neutrons. [ME f. L (as MODERATE[1]; see -OR)]

mŏ'dern *a.* & *n.* **1.** *a.* Of the present and recent times; ~ **English** (from 1500 onwards); ~ **history** (subsequent to Middle Ages); ~ **languages** (as subject of study, those spoken at present time, esp. in Europe); *modern* LATIN; ||~ **school** (in which modern arts, not classical or technical, subjects are chiefly or exclusively taught). **2.** In current fashion, not antiquated. **3.** Hence or cogn. **moder'nITY**, **~IZA'TION**, ~NESS (-n-n-), *ns.*, ~IZE (3) *v.t.* & *i.*, ~LY[2] *adv.* **4.** *n.* Person living in modern times. [f. F *moderne* or f. LL *modernus* f. L *modo* just now]

mŏ'dern|ism *n.* **1.** Modern view(s) or method(s), esp. tendency in matters of religious belief to subordinate tradition to harmony with modern thought; so ~IST (2) *n.*, **~ĭ'stIC** *a.* **2.** Modern term or expression. [f. prec. + -ISM]

mŏ'dėst *a.* Having a humble or moderate estimate of one's own merits; diffident, retiring, bashful; (esp. of woman) decorous in manner and conduct, scrupulously chaste; (of demand, statement, etc.) not excessive or exaggerated (freq. iron.); (of thing) unpretentious in appearance, amount, etc.; hence or cogn. ~LY[2] *adv.*, ~Y[1] *n.*; **~y (vest)**, garment or piece of lace etc. to show at woman's neck and conceal bosom. [f. F *modeste* f. L *modestus* keeping due measure]

mŏ'dĭcum *n.* Small quantity (*of* food, truth, etc.). [L, = short distance or time, neut. (as n.) of *modicus* moderate (*modus* measure)]

mŏdĭfĭcā'tion *n.* Modifying or being modified; change made. [F, or f. L *modificatio* (as foll.; see -FICATION)]

mŏ'dĭ|fȳ *v.t.* Make less severe or decided, tone down; make partial changes in; (Gram.) qualify sense of (word etc.); change (vowel) by umlaut; hence or cogn. **~fīABLE**, **~fĭcātORY**, *adjs.*, **~fīER**[1] *n.* [ME, f. OF *modifier* f. L *modificare* (as MODE; see -FY)]

modĭ'llion (-yon) *n.* (Archit.) Projecting bracket under corona of cornice in Corinthian and other orders. [f. F *modillon* f. It. *modiglione* f. Rom. **mutellio -onis* (**mutellus* for L *mutulus* mutule)]

mō'dĭsh *a.* (Usu. derog. of person) fashionable; hence ~LY[2] *adv.*, ~NESS *n.* [f. MODE + -ISH[1]]

mŏdi'ste (-ē'st) *n.* Milliner, dressmaker. [F (as MODE; see -IST)]

Mŏds (-z) *n.* (colloq.) = MODERATIONS. [abbr.]

mŏ'dūlar *a.* Of, or consisting of, modules or moduli. [f. mod. L *modularis* f. L MODULUS; see -AR[1]]

mŏ'dūl|āte *v.* **1.** *v.t.* Regulate, adjust; moderate. **2.** Adjust or vary tone or pitch of (speaking voice); alter amplitude or frequency or phase of (wave) by wave of a lower frequency to convey a signal. **3.** *v.i.* (Mus.) Pass (*from* one key *to* another). **4.** Hence or cogn. ~A'TION, **~ātOR**, *ns.* [f. L *modulari* measure, adjust to rhythm (MODULUS) + -ATE[3]]

mŏ'dūle *n.* Standard or unit for measuring; (Archit.) unit of length for expressing proportions, e.g. semidiameter of column at base; standardized part or independent unit in construction esp. of furniture, building, spacecraft, or electronic system. [F, or f. L (as foll.); see -ULE]

mŏ'dūl|us *n.* (*pl.* **~i** *pr.* -ī). (Math. & Phys.) Constant multiplier or coefficient; constant that gives ratio between amount of physical effect and that of force producing it; number used as divisor for considering numbers in sets giving same remainder when divided by it; magnitude of vector or of complex number treated as such. [L, = measure, dim. of foll.]

modus (mō'dus) *n.* ~ ***operandi*** (-ă'ndī), way a person goes about a task, way a thing operates; ~ ***vivendi*** (-ĕ'ndī), arrangement between disputants pending settlement of debate, arrangement between people(s) who agree to differ. [L (see MODE; *operandi* of operating, *vivendi* of living)]

Moebius. Var. of MÖBIUS.

mofĕ'tte *n.* (Fissure in earth from which issues) exhalation of mephitic or volcanic gas. [F, or f. It. (Naples) *mofetta*]

mŏg, mŏ'ggie (-gĭ), *ns.* (sl.) Cat. [20th c., of dial. orig.]

Mogŭ'l (*or* mō'-) *n.* & *a.* Mongolian; ~ **empire,** empire established in India by Mongolians under **the** (**Great** or **Grand**) ~, emperor of Delhi in 16th–19th c.; (colloq.; *m~*) important or influential person. [f. Pers. & Arab. *muġūl* f. as MONGOL]

M.O.H. *abbr.* ||Master of Otter-hounds; Medical Officer of Health.

mō'hair *n.* (Yarn or fabric from) hair of angora goat; mixture of this with wool or cotton. [ult. f. Arab. *mukayyar*, lit. choice, select (*kayyara* choose)]

Mohă'mmėdan. See MUHAMMADAN.

Mō'hawk *n.* Member or language of a tribe of N. Amer. Indians; (Skating) step from either edge of skate to same edge on other foot in opposite direction (cf. CHOCTAW). [native name]

mō'hō *n.* (*pl.* **~s**). Discontinuity between earth's crust and mantle. [f. A. *Mohorovičić*, Yugoslav seismologist d. 1936]

Mō'hŏck *n.* (Hist.) One of a class of aristocratic ruffians infesting London streets at night in 18th c. [f. MOHAWK]

mō'hōle *n.* Proposed hole to be drilled through sea-bed to earth's mantle. [f. MOHO + HOLE[1]]

||**moi'der,** ||**moi'ther** (-dh-), *v.t.* (dial.) Perplex, confuse, worry, (esp. in *p.p.*). [17th c.; orig. unkn.]

moi'dōre *n.* Former Portuguese gold coin, current in England in 18th c. [f. Port. *moeda d'ouro* (*moeda* money, *de* of, *ouro* gold)]

moi'etȳ *n.* (Law or literary) half; (loosely) one of two parts into which thing is divided. [ME, f. OF *moit(i)é* f. L *medietas -tatis* middle (*medius* a. middle; see -TY[1])]

moil *v.i.*, & *n.* Drudge(ry), esp. *toil and moil*. [ME, f. OF *moillier* moisten, paddle in mud, f. Rom. **molliare* f. L *mollis* soft]

moire (mwâr) *n.* ~ (**antique**), watered fabric, usu. silk, orig. mohair. [F, earlier *mouaire*, f. MOHAIR]

moiré (mwâr'ā) *a.* & *n.* **1.** *a.* (Of silk) watered; (of metal) having clouded appearance like watered silk. **2.** *n.* This appearance; = prec. [F, p.p. of *moirer*, f. as prec.]

moist *a.* Slightly wet, damp; (of season etc.) rainy; (of disease) marked by discharge of matter etc.; hence **~'LY**[2] *adv.*, **~'NESS** *n.* [ME, f. OF *moiste*, perh. f. Rom. **muscidus* mouldy, wet, f. L *mucidus* (cf. MUCUS) and *musteus* fresh (as MUST[1])]

moi'sten (-sen) *v.t.* & *i.* Make or become moist. [f. prec. + -EN[6]]

moi'sture *n.* Water or other liquid diffused in small quantity as vapour, within solid, condensed on surface, etc.; hence **~LESS** (-cherl-) *a.* [ME, f. OF *moistour* (as MOIST; see -URE)]

moi'stūrīz|e, -īs|e (-īz), (*or* -scher-) *v.t.* Make less dry (esp. skin by use of cosmetic); hence **~ER**[1] (2) *n.* [f. prec. + -IZE]

moither. See MOIDER.

mōke *n.* (sl.) ||Donkey; (Austral.) very poor horse; *(derog.) Negro. [19th c., perh. f. a proper name]

mō'kō *n.* (*pl.* **~s**). Maori system of tattooing. [Maori]

mō'ksa *n.* (Hinduism etc.) Release from cycle of existences. [f. Skr. *mokṣa*]

mōl *abbr.* MOLE[4](s).

mō'lal *a.* (Chem., of solution) containing one mole of solute per kilogram of solvent. [f. MOLE[4] + -AL]

mō'lar[1] *a.* & *n.* **1.** *a.* (Usu. of mammal's back teeth) serving to grind. **2.** *n.* Molar tooth. [f. L *molaris* (*mola* millstone; see -AR[1])]

mō'lar[2] *a.* Of mass; acting on or by means of large masses or units. [f. L *moles* mass + -AR[1]]

mō'lar[3] *a.* (Chem.) Of MOLE[4](s); (of solution) containing one mole of solute per litre; hence **molă'rITY** *n.* [f. MOLE[4] + -AR[1]]

molă'ssės (-z) *n. pl.* (treated as *sing.*) Uncrystallized syrup drained from raw sugar; *syrup got from sugar in process of refining, treacle. [f. Port. *melaço* f. LL *mellaceum* MUST[1] (*mel* honey; see -ACEOUS)]

***mōld**[1–4], ***mō'lder**[1,2], etc. See MOULD[1–4], MOULDER[1,2], etc.

mōle[1] *n.* Abnormal pigmented prominence on human skin. [OE *māl*, = OHG *meil(a)*, Goth. **mail* f. Gmc **mail-*]

mōle[2] *n.* Small burrowing insectivore of genus *Talpa* with (usu. blackish) velvety fur and very small eyes, formerly thought to be blind; any mammal of family Talpidae; **~-cricket,** nocturnal burrowing insect; ~ **drain,** hollow drainage channel like mole's burrow; **~'hill,** small mound thrown up by mole in burrowing (*make a mountain out of a ~hill*, exaggerate obstacle etc.); **~'skin,** (1) skin of mole as fur, (2) kind of cotton fustian with surface shaved before dyeing, (3, in *pl.*) clothes, esp. trousers, of this. [ME *molle*, prob. f. MDu. *moll(e)*, *mol*, MLG *mol*, *mul*]

mōle[3] *n.* Massive structure, usu. of stone, as pier, breakwater, or junction between places separated by water; artificial harbour. [f. F *môle* f. L *moles* mass]

mōle[4] *n.* (Chem.) = GRAM[2]-*molecule*, quantity containing as many molecules as there are atoms in 0·012 kg of the isotope carbon-12. [f. G *mol* (*molekül* MOLECULE)]

mōle[5] *n.* (Med.) Abnormal mass of tissue in uterus. [f. F *môle* f. L *mola* millstone]

molĕ'cūlar *a.* Of, relating to, consisting of, molecules; ~ **weight,** ratio between mass of one molecule of a substance and one-twelfth of mass of an atom of the isotope carbon-12; hence **~ITY** (-ă'r-) *n.*, **~LY**[2] *adv.* [f. foll. + -AR[1]]

mŏ'lėcūle *n.* (Phys. & Chem.) one of the minute groups of atoms (in some elements, esp. the noble gases, one of the single atoms) of which material substances consist, the smallest portion to which a substance can be reduced by subdivision without losing its chemical identity; (loosely) small particle. [f. F *molécule* f. mod. L *molecula* dim. of L *moles* mass; see -CULE]

molĕ'st *v.t.* Meddle hostilely or injuriously with (person); so **mŏlėstA'TION** *n.* [f. OF *molester* or f. L *molestare* annoy (*molestus* troublesome)]

molĭ'ne *a.* (Her., of cross) having each extremity broadened and curved back like ends of mill-rind. [prob. f. AF *moliné* (*molin* MILL[1])]

Mō'lĭn|ĭsm *n.* **1.** Doctrine of Luis *Molina*, Sp. Jesuit d. 1600, that efficacy of grace depends on the will that freely accepts it. **2.** Doctrine of Miguel de *Molinos*, Sp. priest d. 1696; quietism. **3.** Hence ~IST (2) *n.* [f. *Molina, Molinos*, + -ISM]

mŏll *n.* (colloq.) Prostitute; gangster's female companion. [pet-form of woman's Christian name *Mary*]

mŏ'llĭ|fȳ *v.t.* Appease, soften; so ~FICA'TION *n.* [ME, f. F *mollifier* or f. L *mollificare* (*mollis* soft; see -FY)]

mŏ'llusc, *-sk, *n.* Animal belonging to the phylum Mollusca of soft-bodied and usu. hard-shelled animals, including limpets, snails, cuttlefish, oysters, mussels, etc.; hence **mollŭ'scAN, mollŭ'scOUS**, *adjs.*, **mollŭ'scOID** *a.* & *n.* [f. mod. L *mollusca*, neut. pl. (as n.) of L *molluscus* (*mollis* soft)]

mŏ'llȳ *n.* Effeminate man or boy, milksop; ~**-coddle,** (*n.*) milksop, (*v.t.*) coddle, pamper. [f. as MOLL + -Y[3]]

mŏ'llȳmawk. See MALLEMUCK.

Mō'lŏch (-k) *n.* Canaanite idol to whom children were sacrificed; (fig.) tyrannical object of sacrifices; (*m*~) spiny slow-moving grotesque-looking Austral. reptile of genus *Moloch*. [LL, f. Gk *Molokh* f. Heb. *mōlek*]

molŏ'ss|us *n.* (*pl.* ~**i** *pr.* -ī). (Pros.) Foot consisting of three long syllables. [L, f. Gk *Molossos* of Molossia in Epirus]

Mŏ'lotŏv (-f) *n.* ~ **bread-basket,** explosive container scattering incendiary bombs; ~ **cocktail,** anti-tank incendiary hand-grenade. [f. V. M. ~, Russ. statesman b. 1890]

***mōlt.** See MOULT.

mō'lten. See MELT[2].

molto (mŏ'ltō) *adv.* (Mus.) Very (preceding or following direction: *molto sostenuto*; *allegro molto*). [It., f. L *multus* much]

mō'lȳ *n.* Fabulous herb with white flower and black root, endowed with magic properties; a yellow-flowered wild garlic (*Allium moly*). [L, f. Gk *mōlu*]

molȳ'bdenīte *n.* Molybdenum disulphide as ore. [f. as foll. + -ITE[1]]

molȳ'bdėnum *n.* Silver-white brittle metallic element used in steel for making high-speed tools etc. [mod. L, earlier *-dena*, orig. molybdenite, lead ore, L f. Gk *molubdaina* plummet (*molubdos* lead); see -UM]

***mŏm** *n.* (colloq.) = MUMMY[2]; hence ~'ISM *n.*, excessive reverence for one's mother. [abbr. of MOMMA]

mō'ment *n.* **1.** Very brief portion of time, instant; short period of time (*wait a moment*); exact point of time; **one** ~, **half a** ~, **just a** ~, (ellipt.) wait a MINUTE[1]; **in a** ~, (1) instantly, (2) very soon; **not for a** ~, never; *came* **the (very)** ~ (as soon as) *I heard of it*; *timed* **to the** ~ (with absolute accuracy); **the** ~ (time that affords an opportunity); *am, was, busy* **at the** ~ (just now, then); *man* **of the** ~ (important at the time in question); LAST[3] *moment*; PSYCHOLOGICAL *moment*; **this** ~, immediately (*come here this moment*); ~ **of truth,** time of final sword-thrust in bullfight, (fig.) time of crisis or test. **2.** (Phys.) Product of force and distance from its line of action to a point, expressing its power of causing rotation about that point; product of charge etc. and length of dipole; property of magnet that interacts with applied field to give mechanical moment; ~ **of inertia,** quantity by which angular acceleration of a body must be multiplied to give corresponding torque; ~ **of momentum,** ANGULAR momentum. **3.** Importance (*of great, little, moment*). [ME f. OF, f. L MOMENTUM]

mō'mentar|ȳ *a.* Lasting only a moment; short-lived, transitory; hence ~**ĭLY**[2] *adv.* (* = foll.), ~**ĭNESS** *n.* [f. L *momentarius* (as prec.; see -ARY[1])]

mō'mentlȳ *adv.* From moment to moment; every moment; for a moment. [f. MOMENT + -LY[2]]

momĕ'ntous *a.* Having great importance; hence ~LY[2] *adv.*, ~NESS *n.* [f. MOMENT + -OUS]

momĕ'nt|um *n.* (*pl.* ~**a**). **1.** (Mech.) Quantity of motion of moving body, product of its mass and its velocity; ANGULAR *momentum*; CONSERVATION *of momentum*. **2.** Impetus gained by movement (lit. or fig.). [L (*movimentum* f. *movēre* move; see -MENT)]

***mŏ'mma, *mŏ'mmȳ,** *ns.* (colloq. or childish). Mother. [var. of MAMMA[1], MUMMY[2]]

Mō'mus *n.* Fault-finder, captious critic. [f. Gk *Mōmos* god of ridicule]

Mon. *abbr.* Monday; Monmouthshire (former county in England).

mŏ'nachal (-k-), **mŏ'nacal,** *a.* Monastic; monkish; so **mŏ'nach**ISM (3) (-k-) *n.* [f. F *monacal* or eccl. L *monachalis* f. LL (as MONK; see -AL)]

mŏ'nad *n.* The number one, unit; ultimate unit of being (e.g. a soul, an atom, a person, God), esp. in philosophy of Leibniz, whence ~ISM (3) *n.*; (Biol.) simple organism, e.g. one assumed as first term in genealogy of living beings; so **monă'd**IC *a.* [f. F *monade* or f. LL f. Gk *monas -ados* unit (*monos* alone; see -AD)]

mŏnadĕ'lphous *a.* (Bot.) (Of stamens) having filaments united into one bundle; (of plant) with such stamens. [f. Gk *monos* one + *adelphos* brother + -OUS]

monă'ndrous *a.* (Bot.) Having (flowers with) a single stamen. [f. Gk *monandros* (*monos* one, *anēr andros* male) + -OUS]

monă'ndrȳ *n.* Custom of having only one husband at a time. [f. MONO- after *polyandry*]

mŏ'narch (-k) *n.* **1.** Sovereign with title of king, queen, emperor, empress, or equivalent; supreme ruler (lit. or fig.). **2.** Large orange and black butterfly (*Danaus plexippus*). **3.** Hence **monar̂'ch**AL, **monar̂'ch**IC(AL), (-k-) *adjs.* [ME, f. F *monarque* or f. LL *monarcha* f. Gk *monarkhēs, -os*, (*monos* alone, *arkhō* to rule)]

mŏ'narch|ĭsm (-k-) *n.* Principles of, attachment to, monarchy; so ~IST (2) *n.* [f. F *monarchisme* (as foll.; see -ISM)]

mŏ'narchȳ (-kĭ) *n.* (State under) monarchical government; *constitutional* or LIMIT[2]*ed monarchy*. [ME, f. OF *monarchie* f. LL f. Gk *monarkhia* rule of one (as MONARCH; see -Y[1])]

mŏ'nasterȳ *n.* Residence of community (usu. of monks) living secluded under religious vows. [ME, f. eccl. L f. eccl. Gk *monastērion* (*monazō* live alone f. *monos* alone)]

monă'st|ĭc *a.* Of or like monks, nuns, friars, etc.; of monasteries; *monastic* vow; hence ~ICALLY *adv.*, ~**ĭc**ISM (3) *n.*, ~**ĭc**IZE (3) *v.t.* [f. F *monastique* or f. LL f. Gk *monastikos* (*monazō*; see prec., -IC)]

mŏnatŏ'mĭc *a.* (Chem.) Consisting of (molecules each containing) one atom; having one replaceable atom or radical. [f. MONO- + ATOM + -IC]

monaur'al *a.* = MONO*phonic*. [f. MONO- + AURAL[2]]

mŏ'nazīte *n.* Phosphate mineral from India, Brazil, etc., containing rare-earth elements and thorium. [f. G *monazit* f. Gk *monazō* (see MONASTERY), f. its rarity; see -ITE[1]]

mondaine (mawṅdā'n) *n.* & *a.* (Woman) of the fashionable world; worldly (woman). [F, fem. of *mondain* (see MUNDANE)]

Mo'nday (mŭ'-; *or* -dĭ) *n.* & *adv.* **1.** *n.* Day of week, following Sunday; **St. ~**, Monday on which little work is done, as if regarded as saint's day. **2.** *adv.* (cf. FRIDAY 2). [OE *mōnandæg* day of the moon, transl. LL *lunae dies* after Gk *hēmera Selēnēs*]

Mo'ndayish (mŭ'ndĭish) *a.* (Of clergy) indisposed as result of Sunday work; (of others) slack as result of Sunday holiday. [f. prec. + -ISH[1]]

monde (mawnd) *n.* The fashionable world, society; the set in which one moves. [F, = world, f. L (as foll.)]

mŏ'ndĭal *a.* World-wide. [F, f. eccl. L *mundialis* f. L *mundus* world; see -IAL]

mo'nètar|ȳ (mŭ'-) *a.* Of the currency in use; (consisting) of money; hence **~IST** *n.*, one who advocates control of money as chief method of stabilizing the economy. [f. F *monétaire* or f. LL *monetarius* f. L (as MONEY; see -ARY[1])]

mo'nètiz|e (mŭ'-), **-īs|e** (-īz), *v.t.* Put (a metal) into circulation as money; give fixed value as currency; hence **~A'TION** *n.* [f. F *monétiser* f. L (as foll.; see -IZE)]

mo'ney (mŭ'-) *n.* **1.** Current medium of exchange in form of portable pieces of stamped metal; this and promissory documents representing it (**paper ~**), esp. government and bank notes; particular form of money; (in *pl.*; also **monies**) sums of money; property viewed as convertible into money; rich person(s) (*marry money*); purchasing power of money. **2.** *Money of* ACCOUNT[2]; BIG *money*; COIN[2] *money*; CONSCIENCE *money*; **in the ~**, (1) winning money prizes, (2) having plenty of money; **there is ~ in,** profit can be had from; ‖**~ for jam** or **old rope,** (sl.) profit for little or no trouble; *for* LOVE[1] *or money*; **make ~**, acquire wealth; **~ makes the mare (to) go** (provides a motive for action); **the one for my ~** (that I prefer); **put ~ into,** make investment in; *a* RUN[2] *for* one's *money*; **time is ~**, waste of time means loss of profit. **3. ~-bag,** bag for money, (in *pl.*) wealth; **~-bags,** (as *sing.*) wealthy or avaricious person; **~-bill,** proposed legislation for grant of funds; **~-box,** closed box into which savings or contributions are dropped through slit; **~-changer,** one whose business it is to change money at stated rate; **~-grubber,** person sordidly intent on amassing money; **~-grubbing** *a.* & *n.*, (given to) this practice; **~-lender,** one whose business it is to lend money at interest; **~-making** *a.* & *n.*, (allowing) acquisition of wealth; **~-market,** sphere of operation of dealers in short-dated loans, stocks, etc.; *money* ORDER[1] 16; ‖**~-spinner,** small red spider thought to bring good luck, (fig.) something that brings in much money, e.g. successful book, film, play, etc.; **~'s-worth,** anything recognized as equivalent to money, good value for one's money; **~wort,** plant with round glossy leaves. **4.** Hence **~LESS** (mŭ'nĭl-) *a.* [ME, f. OF *moneie* f. L *moneta* mint, money, orig. title of Juno, in whose temple at Rome money was minted]

mo'neyed (mŭ'nĭd) *a.* Rich; consisting of money, (*moneyed resources, assistance*); **~ interest,** the class concerned in money as a possession. [ME, f. prec. + -ED[2]]

mo'neyer (mŭ'nĭer) *n.* (Hist.) One who makes metal into coins. [ME, f. OF *mon(n)ier* f. LL *monetarius* f. L (as MONEY; see -ER[2])]

'mong. Var. (poet.) of AMONG.

mo'nger (mŭ'ngg-) *n.* Dealer, trader, (chiefly in *comb.*; lit., as *fishmonger, ironmonger*, or fig., usu. derog., as *scandalmonger, verse-monger*). [OE *mangere* (*mangian* to traffic f. Gmc **mangōjan* f. L *mango* dealer; see -ER[1])]

Mŏ'ngol (-ngg-) *n.* & *a.* **1.** (Member) of Asian people now inhabiting Mongolia, formerly extending to E. Europe. **2.** (Person) with Mongoloid characteristics. **3.** (*m~*). (Person) suffering from mongolism. [native name, perh. f. *mong* brave]

Mŏngō'lĭan (-ngg-) *a.* & *n.* (Native or language) of Mongolia; Mongol; Mongoloid. [f. prec. + -IAN]

mŏ'ngolĭsm *n.* Congenital mental deficiency with Mongoloid appearance. [f. MONGOL + -ISM]

Mŏ'ngoloid (-ngg-) *a.* & *n.* (Person) resembling Mongolians in racial origin or in having broad flat (yellowish) face; = MONGOL 3. [f. MONGOL + -OID]

mŏ'ngōōse (-ngg-) *n.* (*pl.* **~s**). Small carnivorous tropical mammal of genus *Herpestes*, esp. a species common in India, able to kill venomous snakes unharmed; species of lemur (*Lemur mongoz*). [f. Marathi *mangūs*]

mo'ngrel (mŭ'ngg-) *n.* & *a.* **1.** *n.* Dog of no definable type or breed, other animal or plant resulting from crossing of different breeds or types; (derog.) person not of pure race. **2.** *a.* Of mixed origin, nature, or character. **3.** Hence **~ISM** (2) *n.*, **~IZE** (3) *v.t.*, **~LY**[1] *a.* [app. f. root **mang-*, **meng-*, **mong-*, mix; cf. MINGLE, -REL]

'mongst. Var. (poet.) of AMONGST.

mō'nĭal *n.* Mullion. [ME, f. OF *moinel* middle (*moien* MEAN[2]; see -AL)]

mŏ'nĭcker, mŏ'nĭker, *n.* (sl.) Name. [19th c.; orig. unkn.]

monies. See MONEY 1.

monĭ'lĭform *a.* With form suggesting necklace or string of beads. [f. F *moniliforme* or mod. L *moniliformis* f. L *monile* necklace; see -FORM]

mŏ'n|ĭsm *n.* Doctrine that only one ultimate principle or being exists; any of the theories that deny the duality of matter and mind; hence **~IST** (2) *n.*, **monĭ'stIC** *a.* [f. mod. L *monismus* f. Gk *monos* single; see -ISM]

monĭ'tion *n.* Warning (*of* danger); formal notice from bishop or ecclesiastical court admonishing person to refrain from some offence. [ME f. OF, f. L *monitio -onis* (*monēre monit-* warn; see -ITION)]

mŏ'nĭtor *n.* & *v.* **1.** *n.* (arch.) One who admonishes. **2.** Senior pupil in school with duties of keeping order etc., = PREFECT 3; pupil given specified duties in class etc.; hence **mŏnĭtōr'IAL** *a.*, **~SHIP** *n.* **3.** Tropical lizard of genus *Varanus*, supposed to give warning of approach of crocodiles. **4.** Shallow-draught warship of heavy gunpower. **5.** One who listens to and reports on foreign broadcasts, misuse of official telephones, etc. **6.** Detector of radioactive contamination, esp. in workers in an atomic plant. **7.** Television receiver used in selecting or verifying the broadcast picture. **8.** Hence **mŏ'nĭtrESS**[1] *n.* **9.** *v.t.* & *i.* Act as monitor (of); regulate strength of (recorded or transmitted signal); maintain regular surveillance (over). [L (as prec.; see -OR)]

mŏ'nĭtorȳ *a.* & *n.* **1.** *a.* Warning, admonitory. **2.** *n.* Bishop's or pope's letter of admonition. [f. L *monitorius* (as MONITION; see -ORY)]

monk (mŭ-) *n.* Member of community of men living apart from the world under vows of poverty, chastity, and obedience; **~'fish,** angler-fish; **~'s cloth,** rough cotton cloth in basket weave; **~ shoe** (with strap over instep); **~'shood** (-s-h-), poisonous plant (*Aconitum napellus*) with hood-shaped flowers; hence **~'HOOD, ~'SHIP,** *ns.* [OE *munuc*, = OS *munik*, OHG *munih*, ON *múnkr*, f. pop. L **monicus* var. of LL f. Gk *monakhos* solitary (*monos* alone)]

mo'nkerȳ (mŭ'-) *n.* (derog.) Monastic life; monastery; monks; monkish practices. [f. prec. + -ERY]

mo'nkey (mŭ'-) *n.* & *v.* **1.** *n.* Mammal of a group closely allied to and resembling man, ranging from anthropoid apes to marmosets; (esp.) small long-tailed member of order Primates; (as term of playful contempt, to or of person) *young monkey* etc.; POWDER-*monkey*. **2.** ~ (**engine**), machine hammer for pile-driving etc.; globular earthenware water-vessel with straight upright neck. **3.** (sl.) **Have a ~ on** one's **back,** be a drug addict; **make a ~ of,** humiliate by making appear ridiculous; ‖**get** one's **~ up,** become angry. **4.** (sl.) ‖£500; *$500. **5.** **~-bread,** (fruit of) baobab tree; **~ business,** (sl.) mischief; **~-cup,** pitcher-plant; **~-flower,** kind of mimulus with bright yellow flowers; **~-jacket,** short close-fitting one worn by sailors etc.; **~-nut,** peanut; **~-puzzle,** Chile pine, prickly tree of genus *Araucaria* with interlaced branches; ***~shines,** ‖**~-tricks,** (sl.) mischief; **~-wrench,** one with adjustable jaw. **6.** Hence ~ISH[1] (-kĭĭ-) *a.* **7.** *v.t.* Mimic, mock. **8.** *v.i.* Play mischievous tricks (*with*), fool *about* or *around* (*with*). [16th c., of unkn. (perh. LG) orig.]

mo'nkĭsh (mŭ'-) *a.* Of monks, monastic; (usu. derog.) characteristic of monks. [f. MONK + -ISH[1]]

mŏ'nnĭker. Var. of MONICKER.

mŏ'nō *a.* & *n.* (*pl.* **~s**). (colloq.) Monophonic (reproduction, record, etc.). [abbr.]

mŏ'no- *comb. form.* (bef. vowel usu. **mon-**). One, alone, single, (Chem., forming names of compounds) containing one atom or group of a specified kind, as: **~ba'sic,** (Chem.) having one replaceable hydrogen atom; **~car'pic, ~car'pous,** bearing fruit only once; **~ce'phalous,** (Bot.) having only one head; **~cli'nal** (-ī'-), (of strata) dipping in one and the same direction; **~cli'nic** (-ĭ'-), (of crystal) having one axial intersection oblique; **~cot, ~cotyle'don(ous),** (flowering plant) with single cotyledon; **~cracy** (-ŏ'k-), government by one person only; **~cro'tic,** (of pulse) with single beat; **mono'cular** (-ŏ'k-), with, adapted to, one eye; **~culture,** cultivation of only one crop; **~cycle,** unicycle; **~cyte,** large type of leucocyte; **~da'ctylous,** having one finger, toe, or claw; **~drama,** dramatic piece for one performer; **~ge'nesis,** development of all beings from single cell; so **~gene'tic** *a.*; **~geny** (-ŏ'j-), theoretical descent of mankind from one pair of ancestors; **~glot** *a.* & *n.*, (person) using only one language; **~gynous** (-ŏ'j-), having only one pistil; **~gyny** (-ŏ'j-), custom of having only one wife at a time; **~hull,** boat with single hull, opp. *catamaran* etc.; **~hy'dric,** (Chem.) containing one hydroxyl group; **~latry** (-ŏ'l-), worship of one god without denying that others may exist; **~layer,** monomolecular layer; **~li'ngual,** = *monoglot* a.; **~me'tallism,** standard of currency based on one metal; **~mole'cular,** (of layer) only one molecule in thickness; **~mor'phic, ~mor'phous,** not changing form during development; **~nucleo'sis,** glandular fever; **~pe'talous,** having corolla in one piece, or petals united into tube; **~pho'nic,** (of sound-reproduction) using only one channel of transmission (cf. STEREOPHONIC), (Mus.) homophonic; **~phthong,** single vowel sound, whence **~phtho'ngal** (-ngg-) *a.*; **~-plane,** aeroplane with one set of wings (cf. BIPLANE); **~psy'chism** (-*o*sī'k-), theory that all souls are one; **~rhyme,** poem in which all lines have same rhyme; **~sa'ccharide,** (Chem.) sugar with one carbonyl group in each molecule; **~sper'mous,** (Bot.) having one seed; **~stichous** (-ŏ'stĭk-), (Bot. & Zool.) arranged in, or consisting of, one layer or row; **~stro'phic,** consisting of repetitions of one strophic arrangement; **~tint,** monochrome; **~ty'pic,** having only one type or representative; **~va'lent,** (Chem.) univalent. [Gk (*monos* alone; see -o-)]

mŏ'nochōrd (-k-) *n.* (Mus.) Instrument with single string, esp. for determination of musical intervals. [ME, f. OF *monocorde* f. LL f. Gk MONO(*khordon* f. *chordē* CHORD[1])]

mŏnochromă'tĭc (-k-) *a.* (Of light or other radiation) containing only one colour or wavelength or energy; executed in monochrome. [f. MONO- + CHROMATIC]

mŏ'nochrōme (-k-) *n.* & *a.* **1.** *n.* Picture done in (different tints of) one colour, or in black and white only; representation in one colour. **2.** *a.* Having or using only one colour, (esp.) in black and white only. [ult. f. Gk MONO(*khrōmatos* f. *khrōma* colour)]

mŏ'nocle *n.* Single eye-glass. [F, orig. a. f. LL *monoculus* one-eyed (as MONO-, *oculus* eye)]

mŏ'nocŏque (-k) *n.* Aircraft or vehicle structure without chassis separate from body. [F (as MONO-, *coque* shell)]

mŏ'nod|y̆ *n.* Ode sung by single actor in Greek tragedy; poem in which mourner bewails someone's death; hence or cogn. **monŏ'dic** *a.*, ~IST (1) *n.* [f. LL *monodia* f. Gk *monōidia* f. *monōidos* singing alone (as MONO-, ODE); see -Y[1]]

monoe'cious (-ē'shus) *a.* (Bot.) with unisexual male and female organs on same plant; (Zool.) hermaphrodite. [f. mod. L *Monoecia* class of such plants (Linnaeus) f. Gk *monos* single + *oikos* house; see -IA[2]]

monŏ'gam|y̆ *n.* Practice or state of being married to one person at a time; (Zool.) habit of having only one mate at a time; hence or cogn. ~IST (2) *n.*, ~OUS *a.* [f. F *monogamie* f. eccl. L f. Gk MONO(*gamia* f. *gamos* marriage); see -Y[1]]

mŏ'nogrăm *n.* Two or more letters, esp. person's initials, interwoven as device; hence **mŏnogrammă'tic**, **~med**[2] (-md), *adjs.* [f. F *monogramme* f. LL *monogramma* f. Gk **monogrammos* (as MONO-, -GRAM)]

mŏ'nograph (-ahf) *n.*, & *v.t.* **1.** *n.* Separate treatise on single object or class of objects. **2.** *v.t.* Write monograph on. **3.** Hence **monŏ'grapher**[1], **monŏ'graphist** (1), *ns.*, **mŏnogră'phic** *a.* [earlier *monography* f. mod. L *monographia* (*monographus* writer on single genus or species); see MONO-, -GRAPH, -GRAPHY]

mŏ'nolĭth *n.* Single block of stone, esp. shaped into pillar or monument; large block of concrete; person or thing like monolith in being massive, immovable, or solidly uniform; hence **mŏnolĭ'thic** *a.* [f. F *monolithe* f. Gk MONO(*lithos* stone)]

mŏ'nologu|e (-ŏg) *n.* Scene in drama in which a person speaks alone; dramatic composition for one performer; long speech by one person in a company; hence **mŏnolŏ'gic(al)** *adjs.*, **monŏ'logist** (1), ~IST (1) (-gĭ-), *ns.*, **monŏ'logize** (2) *v.i.* [F, = one who likes to hear himself talk, f. Gk MONO*logos* speaking alone; see -LOGUE]

mŏnomā'nĭ|a *n.* Obsession of mind by one idea or interest; hence ~AC *n.*, ~ACAL (-manī'-) *a.* [f. F *monomanie* (as MONO-, -MANIA)]

‖**mŏ'nomârk** *n.* Combination of letters and/or figures registered as identification mark for goods, articles, addresses, etc. [f. MONO- + MARK[1]]

mŏ'nomer *n.* (Chem.) Unit in polymer molecule; compound that can be polymerized; hence **mŏnomĕ'ric** *a.* [f. MONO- + -MER]

monō'mĭal *n.* & *a.* (Alg.) (Expression) consisting of one term. [f. MONO- after *binomial*]

For other words in *mono-* **see** MONO-.

Monŏ'phȳsīte *n.* One who holds there is only one nature (partly divine, partly and subordinately human) in the person of Christ. [f. eccl. L f. eccl. Gk MONO(*phusitēs* f. *phusis* nature; see -ITE¹)]
monŏ'pol|ĭst *n.* One who favours monopoly; one who has monopoly (*of*); so **~ĭ'stɪc** *a.* [f. MONOPOLY + -IST]
monŏ'polīz|e, -īs|e (-īz), *v.t.* Obtain exclusive possession or control of (trade, commodity, the conversation, person's attention, etc.); hence ~A'TION *n.* [f. foll. + -IZE]
monŏ'polȳ *n.* Exclusive possession of the trade in some commodity; this conferred as privilege by State; exclusive possession, control, or exercise (*of* or **on*); thing that is monopolized. [f. L f. Gk MONO(*pōlion* f. *pōleō* sell)]
mŏ'norail *n.* Railway in which track consists of a single rail. [f. MONO- + RAIL¹]
mŏ'nosȳll|able *n.* Word of one syllable; **speak in ~ables,** answer little but *Yes* or *No*, with intentional curtness; so **~ă'bɪc** *a.* [f. MONO- + SYLLABLE]
mŏ'nothē|ĭsm *n.* Doctrine that there is only one God; hence ~IST (2) *n.*, **~ĭ'stɪc** *a.* [f. MONO- + Gk *theos* god + -ISM]
Monŏ'thèlīte *n.* One who holds that Christ had only one will but two natures (cf. MONOPHYSITE). [ME, f. med. L *monothelita* f. late Gk MONO-(*thelētēs* f. Gk *thelō* to will)]
mŏ'notōne *a.* & *n.*, & *v.t.* **1.** *a.* & *n.* (Utterance of successive syllables) without change of pitch. **2.** *a.* (Math.) = foll. **3.** *n.* Sameness of style in writing. **4.** *v.t.* Recite, speak, sing, in unvaried tone. [f. mod. L f. late Gk MONO(*tonos* TONE¹)]
mŏnotŏ'n|ĭc *a.* Uttered in monotone; (Math.) either never decreasing or never increasing; hence ~ICALLY *adv.* [f. prec. + -IC]
monŏ'ton|ous *a.* (Of sound or utterance) without variation in tone or cadence; lacking in variety, wearisome through sameness; hence or cogn. ~IZE (3) *v.t.*, **~ous**LY² *adv.*, **~ous**NESS, ~Y¹, *ns.* [f. prec. + -OUS]
mŏ'notrēme *n.* (Zool.) Mammal of subclass Monotremata of primitive egg-laying Australasian animals with single vent. [f. MONO- + Gk *trēma -matos* hole]
mŏ'notȳpe *n.* Impression on paper from inked design on glass etc.; (*M*~; P) composing-machine that casts and sets up single types. [f. MONO- + TYPE¹]
monŏ'xīde *n.* (Chem.) Oxide containing one oxygen atom combined with one atom of metal or non-metal (*carbon monoxide* etc.). [f. MONO- + OXIDE]
Monrōe' *n.* **~ doctrine, ~ism** (-ō'ĭ-), U.S. policy of objecting to interference by European powers in Latin America and to further colonization in America, similar policy elsewhere; hence ~IST (2) (-ō'ĭ-) *n.* [f. J. ~, U.S. President d. 1831, who formulated the policy (1823)]
Monseigneur (mawṅsĕnyẽr') *n.* (*pl.* ***Messeigneurs*** *pr.* mĕsĕnyẽr'). Title given to eminent French person, esp. prince, cardinal, archbishop, or bishop. [F (*mon* my, *seigneur* lord)]
Monsieur (mosyẽr') *n.* (*pl.* ***Messieurs*** *pr.* mĕsyẽr'). Title used of or to French-speaking man, corresponding to Mr. or sir; Frenchman; (Hist.) title of second son or next younger brother of French king. [F (*mon* my, *sieur* lord)]
Monsignor (mŏnsēnyŏr') *n.* (*pl.* ~*i*). Title of some R.C. prelates, officers of papal court, and others. [It., after MONSEIGNEUR; see SIGNOR]
mŏnsōō'n *n.* Wind in S. Asia, esp. in Indian Ocean, blowing from S.W. in summer (**wet ~**) and N.E. in winter (**dry ~**); rainy season accompanying wet monsoon; other wind with periodic alternations; hence ~AL *a.* [f. obs. Du. *monssoen* f. Port. *monção* f. Arab. *mawsim* fixed season (*wasama* to mark)]
mŏ'nster *n.* & *a.* **1.** *n.* Misshapen animal or plant; grossly malformed foetus etc. **2.** Imaginary animal compounded of incongruous elements, e.g. centaur, sphinx, griffin. **3.** Inhumanly cruel or wicked person, inhuman example *of* (cruelty etc.). **4.** Animal or thing of huge size. **5.** *a.* Huge. [ME, f. OF *monstre* f. L *monstrum* portent, monster (*monēre* warn)]
mŏ'nstrance *n.* (R.C. Ch.) Open or transparent vessel with gold or silver frame, in which the Host is exposed for veneration. [ME, = demonstration, f. med. L *monstrantia* f. L *monstrare* show; see -ANCE]
mŏnstrŏ'sĭtȳ *n.* Monstrousness; = MONSTER 1, 2; outrageous thing. [f. LL *monstrositas* (as foll.; see -ITY)]
mŏ'nstrous *a.* & *adv.* **1.** *a.* Abnormally formed, of the nature of a monster; huge; outrageously wrong or absurd; atrocious; hence ~LY² *adv.*, ~NESS *n.* **2.** *adv.* (arch.) Extremely. [ME, f. OF *monstreux* or f. L *monstrosus* (as MONSTER; see -OUS)]
mŏns Vĕ'nerĭs (-nz-) *n.* Rounded mass of fat on woman's abdomen above vulva. [L, = mount of Venus]
Mont. *abbr.* Montana.
mŏ'ntage (-ahzh) *n.* Selection, cutting, and piecing together as a consecutive whole of separate sections of cinema or television film; (production of) composite picture made from various elements; (production of) composite whole from juxtaposed pieces of music, painting, photographs, etc. [F (*monter* MOUNT²; see -AGE)]
mŏ'ntāne *a.* Of or inhabiting mountainous country. [f. L *montanus* (as MOUNT¹; see -ANE)]
mŏntbrē'tia (-sha) *n.* Iridaceous hybrid plant of genus *Crocosmia*, with bright orange-coloured flowers. [mod. L, f. A. F. E. Coquebert de *Montbret*, Fr. botanist d. 1801 + -IA¹]
mŏ'ntė *n.* Spanish game of chance, played with 45 cards; **three-card ~**, game of Mexican origin played with 3 cards, similar to THREE-CARD trick. [Sp., = mountain, heap of cards]
Mŏntėnē'grĭn *n.* & *a.* (Inhabitant) of Montenegro in S.W. Yugoslavia. [f. *Montenegro* (Venetian It., = black mountain); cf. -INE¹]
Mŏntėssŏr'ĭ *n.* **~ system** (of educating very young children by direction of their natural activities rather than strict control). [f. M. ~, It. educationalist d. 1952, who initiated it *c.* 1900]
month (mŭ-) *n.* (**Calendar**) ~, any of usu. twelve portions into which year is divided or any period between same dates in successive such portions; period of 28 days; LUNAR *month*; *month of* SUNDAYS; THIS *day month*; **~'s mind,** mass etc. in commemoration of deceased person a month after death, ‖(arch.) strong inclination, liking. [OE *mōnath*, = OS *mānoth*, OHG *mānōd*, ON *mánuthr*, Goth. *mēnōths* f. Gmc **mǣnōth*-, cogn. w. MOON¹]
mo'nthlȳ (mŭ'n-) *a.*, *adv.*, & *n.* **1.** *a.* & *adv.* (Occurring, published, done, etc.) once a month; **~ nurse** (attending woman during first month after childbirth); **~ rose,** China rose supposed to flower monthly. **2.** *n.* Monthly periodical; (in *pl.*, arch.) menses. [f. prec. + -LY¹,²]
mŏ'ntĭcūle *n.* Small hill; small mound caused by volcanic eruption; slight protuberance on surface of animal etc. [F, f. LL *monticulus* dim. of *mons* MOUNT¹; see -CULE]
mŏ'nūment *n.* Written record; anything en-

For other words in *mono-* see MONO-.

during that serves to commemorate or make celebrated, esp. structure or building (||**the M~,** column in London commemorating fire of 1666); stone or other structure placed over grave or in church etc. in memory of the dead; ||ANCIENT[1] *monument.* [ME f. F f. L, *monu-, monimentum* (*monēre* remind; see -MENT)]

mŏnūmĕ'ntal *a.* **1.** Of, or serving as, a monument; ~ **mason,** maker of tombstones etc. **2.** (Of literary work) massive and permanent; extremely great, stupendous, (*monumental achievement, blunder, ignorance*). **3.** Hence ~LY[2] *adv.* [f. prec. + -AL]

mŏnūmĕ'ntalize, -ise (-īz), *v.t.* Record or commemorate (as) by monument. [f. prec. + -IZE]

-mony̆ *suf.* forming *ns.* esp. denoting abstract state or quality (*acrimony, matrimony, testimony*). [f. L *-monia, -monium,* cogn. w. -MENT]

moo *v.i.,* & *n.* (Make) characteristic vocal sound of cattle, = LOW[2]; **~-cow,** (childish name for) cow. [imit.]

mooch *v.* (sl.) **1.** *v.i.* Loiter *about,* walk slowly *along.* **2.** *v.t.* Steal; *beg. [ME, prob. f. OF *muchier* hide, skulk]

mood[1] *n.* State of mind or feeling; (in *pl.*) fits of melancholy or bad temper; **in the ~, in no ~,** inclined, disinclined, (*for* thing, *to* do). [OE *mōd* mind, thought, = OS *mōd,* OHG *muot,* ON *móthr* anger, grief, Goth. *mōths* f. Gmc **mōdhaz, -am*]

mood[2] *n.* **1.** (Gram.) Form(s) of verb serving to indicate whether it is to express fact, command, wish, etc., (*indicative, imperative, subjunctive, mood*); (distinction of meaning expressed by) group of such forms. **2.** (Logic). Any of the classes into which each of the figures of valid categorical syllogism is subdivided. [var. of MODE, assoc. w. prec.]

moo'd|y̆ *a.* Gloomy, sullen; hence **~ĭLY**[2] *adv.,* **~ĭNESS** *n.* [OE *mōdig* brave (as MOOD[1], -Y[2])]

moo'lah (*-a*) *n.* (sl.) Money. [20th c.; orig. unkn.]

moo'lvĭ(e) *n.* Muslim doctor of the law; learned person, teacher, (esp. as term of respect among Muslims in India). [f. Urdu *mulvī* f. Arab. *mawlawīy* judicial; cf. MULLAH]

moon[1] *n.* **1.** Satellite of the earth, revolving round it monthly, illuminated by sun and reflecting some light to earth; this in particular month, regarded as a distinct object from that visible in other months (*age of the moon;* FULL[1] *moon;* NEW[1] *moon;* HARVEST, HUNTER'*s, moon*), or when visible (*there is no moon tonight*); (poet.) month (*in the moon when nights are brightest*); satellite of any planet; **the ~,** thing unlikely to be attained (*cry for the moon*), anything no matter how unattainable (*promised her the moon*); *once in a* BLUE[1] *moon;* MAN[1] *in the moon;* **old ~ in new ~'s arms** (during first quarter, when dark part is faintly seen by earth-light); **over the ~,** in raptures, highly excited; ||SHOOT[1] *the moon.* **2. ~'beam,** ray of moonlight; **~'calf,** born fool; **~-face** (round like full moon); **~-fish,** opah; **~'-flower,** ox-eye daisy; **~'light,** (*n.*) light of moon, (*a.*) lighted by the moon (*~light flit(ting),* removal of household goods by night to avoid paying rent), (*v.i.,* colloq.) have two paid occupations, esp. one by day and one by night; **~'lit,** lighted by the moon; **~'quake,** tremor of moon's surface; **~'rise, ~'set,** (moment of) moon's rising, setting; **~'shine,** (1) visionary talk or ideas, (2) illicitly distilled or smuggled alcoholic liquor; ***~'shiner,** (sl.) illicit distiller, liquor-smuggler; **~-shot,** (launching of) spacecraft travelling to moon; **~'stone,** felspar of pearly appearance; **~'struck,** deranged in mind. **3.** Hence ~'LESS *a.* [OE *mōna,* = OS, OHG *māno,* ON *máni,* Goth. *mēna* f. Gmc **mǣnon,* cogn. w. MONTH]

moon[2] *v.* **1.** *v.i.* Move or look listlessly (*about, around,* etc.); **~ over,** be inactive or inattentive because infatuated by. **2.** *v.t.* Pass *away* (time) in listless manner. [f. prec.]

Moon[3] *n.* **~ type,** system of writing and printing for the blind, in which the characters are represented by large raised lines. [f. W. ~, Engl. inventor d. 1894]

moo'nshee *n.* Secretary or language-teacher in India. [f. Urdu *munshī* f. Arab. *munši'* writer]

moo'ny̆ *a.* Of or like the moon; listless, stupidly dreamy. [f. MOON[1,2] + -Y[2]]

moor[1] (*or* mor̂) *n.* Tract of open waste ground, esp. if covered with heather; tract of ground preserved for shooting; *fen; **~'fowl, ~ game,** red grouse; **~'cock,** male of this; **~'hen,** (1) female of this, (2) water-hen; **~'land,** country abounding in heather; hence ~'ISH[1], ~'Y[2], *adjs* [OE *mōr* waste land, marsh, mountain, = OS *mōr* marsh, OHG *muor* f. Gmc **mōraz,* **mōram*]

Moor[2] (*or* mor̂) *n.* One of a Muslim people of mixed Berber and Arab descent, inhabiting N.W. Africa; **~('man),** Indian Muslim; hence ~'ISH[1] *a.* (**~ish idol,** brightly-coloured Pacific fish of genus *Zanclus*). [ME f. OF *More* f. L f. Gk *Mauros* inhabitant of Mauretania, region of N. Africa]

moor[3] (*or* mor̂) *v.t.* Attach (boat or other floating thing) to fixed object; hence ~'AGE (3, 4) *n.* [ME *more,* prob. f. (M)LG *mōren*]

moor'ĭng (*or* mor̂'-) *n.* **1.** In vbl senses; *mooring*-MAST[1]. **2.** (usu. in *pl.*) Permanent anchors and chains laid down for ships to be moored to; what a floating object is moored to. **3.** (in *pl.*) Place where vessel is moored. [ME, f. prec. + -ING[1]]

moose *n.* (*pl.* same). N. Amer. animal closely allied to or same as European elk. [f. Narragansett *moos*]

moot *n., a.,* & *v.t.* **1.** *n.* (Hist.) assembly; (Law) students' discussion of hypothetical case for practice. **2.** *a.* Debatable, undecided, (*that is a moot point*); *(Law) having no practical significance. **3.** *v.t.* Raise (question) for discussion. [(v. f. OE *mōtian* converse) f. OE (*ge*)*mōt* f. Gmc *(*ga*)*mōtam,* cogn. w. MEET[1]]

mŏp[1] *n.* Bundle of coarse yarn or cloth fastened at end of stick, for cleaning floors etc.; similarly-shaped instrument for various purposes; thick mass of hair like mop; **~('head),** (person with) this; ||**Mrs. Mop(p),** (joc.) charwoman; hence ~'PY[2] *a.* [ME *mappe,* perh. ult. conn. w. L *mappa* napkin]

mŏp[2] *v.t.* (**-pp-**). Wipe or clean (as) with mop; wipe tears, sweat, etc., from (face, brow, etc.); wipe (tears etc.) thus; **~ the floor with,** (sl.) = WIPE *the floor with;* **~ up,** wipe up (as) with mop, (sl.) absorb (profits etc.), dispatch, make an end of, (Mil.) complete the occupation of (district etc.) by capturing or killing troops left there, capture or kill (stragglers). [f. prec.]

mŏp[3] *v.i.* (**-pp-**), & *n.* (arch. or literary). **~ and mow,** make grimaces; **~s and mows,** grimaces. [perh. imit. of pout; see MOW[2]]

||**mŏp**[4] *n.* (Hist.) A fair or gathering in the autumn at which farm-hands and servants were hired. [perh. = *mop-fair* (at which MOP[1] was carried by maidservant seeking employment)]

mō'pe *v.* & *n.* **1.** *v.i.* Abandon oneself to listless condition; (arch., *refl.* or *pass.*) make one*self,* be, the victim of ennui. **2.** *n.* One who mopes; **the ~s,** depression of spirits. **3.** Hence **mō'**PISH[1] *a.* [16th c.; orig. unkn.]

mō'pĕd *n.* Motorized bicycle. [Sw. (*mo*tor, *ped*aler pedals)]

mō'pōke, mor̂'epor̂k (mor̂'p-) *n.* **1.** (N.Z.)

Spotted brown owl. **2.** (Austral.) Small brown owl of genus *Ninox*; Tasmanian nightjar. [imit. of bird's note]

||**Mŏpp.** See MOP[1].

mŏ'ppėt *n.* (Endearing term for) baby, little girl, etc.; (colloq.) child. [f. obs. *moppe* baby, doll, + -ET[1]]

moquĕ'tte (-kĕ't) *n.* Material of wool on cotton, with pile or loops, used for carpets and upholstery. [F, perh. f. obs. It. *mocaiardo* mohair]

mōr *n.* Humus formed under acid conditions. [Da.]

mōr'a, mōr'ra, *n.* Italian game in which player guesses number of fingers held up at that moment by another. [It. *mora*]

morai'ne *n.* Debris carried down and deposited by glacier. [F, f. It. dial. *morena* f. F dial. *mor(re)* snout f. Rom. **murrum* round object]

mŏ'ral *a.* & *n.* **1.** *a.* Concerned with goodness or badness of character or disposition, or with the distinction between right and wrong; (of literary work etc.) dealing with regulation of conduct; concerned with rules of morality; virtuous in general conduct; (of rights etc.) founded on moral law; capable of moral action (*man is a moral agent*). **2.** ~ **certainty,** probability so great as to allow no reasonable doubt; ~ **courage** (to meet contempt etc. rather than abandon right course of action); ~ **cowardice,** fear of others' disapproval; *moral* INSPIRATION; ~ **law,** conditions to be satisfied by any right course of action; ~ **philosophy,** ethics; ~ **pressure,** persuasion through moral sense; **M~ Re-Armament,** (beliefs of) Oxford Group, Buchmanism, esp. as applied to international relations; *moral* SCIENCE; ~ **sense,** ability to distinguish right and wrong; ~ **support** (giving psychological rather than physical help); ~ **theology,** ethics as branch of theology; ~ **victory,** defeat that has some of the satisfactory elements of victory. **3.** Hence ~LY[2] *adv.* **4.** *n.* Moral lesson (esp. at end) of fable, story, event, etc. (**draw the** ~, show what it is); moral maxim or principle (**point a** ~, illustrate or apply it); (in *pl.*) moral habits, esp. sexual conduct. [ME, f. L *moralis* (*mos moris* custom, pl. *mores* morals; see -AL)]

mora'le (-ah'l) *n.* Moral condition, esp. (of troops or workers) as regards discipline and confidence. [f. F *moral* respelt to preserve pronunc.; cf. LOCALE]

mŏ'ralism *n.* Natural system of morality, religion reduced to moral practice. [f. MORAL + -ISM]

mŏ'ral|ĭst *n.* One who practises or teaches morality; one who follows a natural system of ethics; hence **~ĭ'stic** *a.* [f. MORAL + -IST]

moră'lĭtў *n.* Moral science; (in *pl.*) moral principles, points of ethics; particular system of morals (*commercial morality*); degree of conformity to moral principles; (esp. good) moral conduct; moralizing; ~ **(play)**, (Hist.) kind of drama with abstract qualities as main characters and inculcating moral lesson, popular in 16th c. [ME, f. OF *moralité* or f. LL *moralitas* f. L (as MORAL; see -ITY)]

mŏ'ralīz|e, -īs|e (-īz), *v.* **1.** *v.i.* Indulge in moral reflection or talk (*on* subject). **2.** *v.t.* Interpret morally, point the moral of; make (more) moral. **3.** Hence ~A'TION *n.* [f. F *moraliser* or f. med. L *moralizare* f. L (as MORAL; see -IZE)]

moră'ss *n.* (literary). Bog, marsh; (fig.) entanglement (*morass of vice*). [f. Du. *moeras* (assim. to *moer* MOOR[1]) f. MDu. *marasch* f. OF (as MARISH)]

mŏratōr'ĭ|um *n.* (*pl.* **~ums** *or* **~a**). (Period of) legal authorization to debtors to postpone payment; temporary prohibition or suspension (*on* activity). [mod. L, neut. (as n.) of LL *moratorius* delaying f. L *morari -at-* to delay (*mora* delay); see -ORY]

Morā'vian *a.* & *n.* (Native or inhabitant) of Moravia; (one) of Protestant sect holding Hussite doctrines and accepting Bible as only source of faith, founded in Saxony by emigrants from Moravia. [f. *Moravia*, now part of Czechoslovakia + -AN]

mōr'bid *a.* (Of mind, ideas, etc.) unwholesome, sickly; given to morbid feelings; (colloq.) melancholy; (Med.) of the nature, or indicative, of disease; ~ **anatomy** (of diseased organs etc.); hence ~LY[2] *adv.*, ~ITY (-ĭ'd-), ~NESS, *ns.* [f. L *morbidus* (*morbus* disease; see -ID[1])]

morbidezza (mōrbĭdĕ'tsa) *n.* Extreme delicacy in art; (Paint.) lifelike delicacy in flesh-tints. [It. (*morbido* tender, f. as prec.)]

mōrbĭ'fĭc *a.* Causing disease. [f. F *morbifique* or mod. L *morbificus* f. L *morbus* disease; see -FIC]

mōrbĭ'llī *n. pl.* (Spots characteristic of) measles. [L, pl. of *morbillus* pustule (*morbus* disease)]

morceau (mōrsō') *n.* (*pl.* **~x** *pr.* -z). Short literary or musical composition. [F (as MORSEL)]

mōrd|ā'cious (-shus) *a.* = foll.; so ~A'CITY *n.* [f. L *mordax -acis* (*mordēre* bite; see -ACIOUS)]

mōr'd|ant *a.* & *n.* **1.** *a.* (Of sarcasm etc.) caustic, biting; hence ~ANCY *n.* **2.** Pungent, smarting. **3.** *a.* & *n.* Corrosive or cleansing (acid). **4.** (Substance) serving to fix colouring-matter or gold-leaf on another substance. [ME f. F, part. of *mordre* bite f. L *mordēre*; see -ANT]

mōr'dent *n.* (Mus.) Grace consisting of one rapid alternation of written note with note immediately below it; pralltriller. [G, f. It. *mordente* part. of *mordere* bite (as prec.; see -ENT)]

mōre *a.*, *n.*, & *adv.* **1.** *a.* Existing in greater or additional quantity, amount, or degree, (*there is more truth in it than you think*; *10 is 2 more than 8*; *added one more line*; *bring some more water*); greater in degree (*more's the pity*; *the more fool you*). **2.** *n.* Greater quantity or number (*more in it than* MEET[2]*s the eye*; *hope to see more of you* (see you more often); *more than one person has found it so*). **3.** *adv.* In greater degree (*you must attend more to details*; *more in sorrow than in anger*; *more frightened than hurt*); moreover; again (*once*, *twice*, etc., *never*, *more*). **4.** (Forming compar. of *adjs.* & *advs.*, esp. those of more than one syllable) *more absurd(ly)*, *more curious*, *more easily*, *more truly*. **5.** ~ **and** ~, in an increasing degree; *more* LIKE[1] *it*; ~ **of,** to a greater extent (*more of a poet than a musician*); ~ **or less,** (1) in greater or less degree, (2) or thereabouts; ~ **so,** (the same) to a greater degree; ~ **than,** (colloq.) (1) exceedingly (*happy* etc.), (2) thing that . . . not (*you remembered to thank her, which is more than I did*); **any** ~, (to) any greater or further quantity or extent; **neither ~ nor less than,** simply, literally, (*absurd*, *cheating*, etc.); NO[3] *more*; THE *more*; WHAT *is more*. [OE *māra*, = OS, OHG *mēro*, ON *meiri*, Goth. *maiza* f. Gmc **maizon* (**maiz* adv. f. IE **meis*)]

moree'n *n.* Strong ribbed woollen or (woollen and) cotton material for curtains etc. [perh. fanciful f. MOIRE]

mōr'eish (mōr'ĭ-) *a.* (colloq.) Pleasant to eat, causing desire for more. [f. MORE + -ISH[1]]

morĕ'l[1] *n.* (Esp. black) nightshade. [ME, f. OF *morele*, fem. (as n.) of *morel* dark brown f. Rom. **maurellus* f. L *Maurus* MOOR[2]]

morĕ'l[2] *n.* Edible fungus of genus *Morchella*. [f. F *morille* f. Du. *morilje*]

morĕ'llō *n.* (*pl.* **~s**). Bitter kind of dark cherry. [f. It. *morello* blackish f. med. L *morellus* f. L (as MOREL[1])]

mōreō'ver (mōrō'v-) *adv.* (literary). Further, besides, (introducing or accompanying new statement). [ME, f. MORE + OVER]

morepork. See MOPOKE.

mo͡r'ēs (-z; *or* -āz) *n. pl.* Customs or conventions regarded as essential to or characteristic of a community. [L, pl. of *mos* custom]

Morĕ'scō. Var. of MORISCO.

Morĕ'sque (-k) *a.* Moorish in style or design. [F, f. It. *moresco* (*Moro* MOOR²; see -ESQUE)]

mo͡rgană't|ĭc *a.* (Of marriage) between man of high rank and woman of lower rank, who remains in her former station, their issue having no claim to succeed to possessions or title of father; (of wife) so married; hence ~ICALLY *adv.* [f. F *morganatique* or G *morganatisch* f. med. L *morganaticus* (*matrimonium ad morganaticam*, prob. f. Gmc **morgangeba* morning gift from husband to wife on morning after consummation of marriage, this being such wife's only claim on husband's possessions)]

mo͡r'gen (-g-) *n.* (S. Afr.) Area of land, about two acres. [Du., = morning, app. as being area ploughed in a morning]

mo͡rgue¹ (-g) *n.* Mortuary; (Journ.) repository where miscellaneous material for reference is kept. [F, orig. name of Paris building in which bodies of persons found dead were exposed for identification, perh. = foll.]

morgue² (mo͡rg) *n.* Haughty demeanour, esp. as English characteristic. [F, of unkn. orig.]

mŏ'rĭbŭnd *a.* At the point of death (lit. or fig.). [f. L *moribundus* (*mori* die)]

mŏ'rĭon *n.* (Hist.) Helmet without beaver or visor. [F, f. Sp. *morrion* (*morro* f. Rom. **murrum* round object)]

Morĭ'scō *a.* & *n.* (*pl.* ~*s or* ~*es*). **1.** *a.* Moorish. **2.** *n.* MOOR², esp. in Spain; morris dance. [Sp. (*Moro* MOOR²)]

mo͡r'ĭsh. Var. of MOREISH.

Mo͡r'mon *n.* (Nickname for) member of millenary religious body (Church of Jesus Christ of Latter-day Saints) founded 1830 by Joseph Smith on basis of revelations in **Book of ~** (named from its supposed author); hence ~ISM (3) *n.*

mo͡rn *n.* **1.** (poet.) Morning; dawn. **2.** (Sc.) Morrow (**the ~**, tomorrow; **the ~'s ~**, tomorrow morning). [OE *morgen*, = OS, OHG *morgan* f. Gmc **murganaz*]

mo͡r'nay *n.* Cheese-flavoured white sauce. [20th c.; orig. uncert.]

mo͡r'nĭng *n.* Early part of day, ending at noon, or at hour of midday meal (*in* or *during the morning*; **in the ~**, (also, colloq.) tomorrow; *on Monday morning*); this time spent in a particular way; (colloq.) = GOOD *morning*; (fig.) early part (of life etc.); (poet.) dawn; (*attrib.*) occurring or done in the morning, (of clothes) conventionally worn in the morning; **~ after,** (colloq.) hangover; **~ coat** (with front cut away to form tails); **~ dress,** (1) daytime wear, (2) man's morning coat and striped trousers; **~ gift** (see MORGANATIC, etym.); **~ glory,** twining plant of genus *Ipomoea*, with trumpet-shaped flowers; **~ paper,** newspaper published in the morning; *morning* PRAYER¹; **~-room,** sitting-room for the morning; **~ sickness,** nausea in morning in early pregnancy; **~ star,** Venus (or other planet or bright star) seen in east before sunrise; **~ watch,** (Naut.) 4–8 a.m. watch. [ME *mor(we)ning* f. *morwen* MORN + -ING¹, after *evening*]

Mo͡r'ō *n.* (*pl.* ~*s*). Muslim of the Philippines. [Sp., = MOOR²]

Morŏ'ccan *a.* & *n.* (Native or inhabitant) of Morocco. [f. as foll. + -AN]

morŏ'ccō *n.* (*pl.* ~*s*). Fine flexible leather made (orig. in Morocco) from goatskins tanned with sumac (**French ~**, inferior small-grained kind; **Levant ~**, high-grade large-grained kind); imitation of this in grained calf etc. [~ in N.W. Africa, f. It. *Marocco* f. name of chief city *Marrakesh*]

mo͡r'ŏn *n.* Adult with intelligence equal to that of average child of 8–12; (colloq.) very stupid or degenerate person; hence **morŏ'nic** *a.* [f. Gk *mōron*, neut. of *mōros* foolish]

morō'se *a.* Sullen, gloomy, and unsocial; hence ~LY² (-slĭ) *adv.*, ~NESS (-sn-) *n.* [f. L *morosus* peevish etc. (*mos moris* manner; see -OSE¹)]

mo͡rph *n.* Allomorph. [back form.]

mo͡r'phēme *n.* (Ling.) Morphological element considered in respect of its functional relations in a linguistic system; smallest meaningful morphological unit of a language (e.g. *in*, *come*, *-ing*, opp. *income*, *incoming*, etc.); hence **mo͡rphē'mic** *a.*, **mo͡rphē'mics** *n.*, study of word-structure. [f. F *morphème* (as PHONEME, f. Gk *morphē* form)]

Mo͡r'pheus *n.* Roman god of dreams or sleep; **in the arms of ~**, asleep. [ME f. L]

mo͡r'phĭne (*or* -ēn), (pop.) **mo͡r'phĭa,** *ns.* Alkaloid narcotic principle of opium, used to alleviate pain; hence **mo͡r'phĭnism** (5) *n.* [f. G *morphin* & mod. L *morphia*, f. prec.; see -INE⁵, -IA¹]

mo͡rphogĕ'nĕsĭs *n.* (Biol.) Development of form in organisms. [mod. L, f. as foll. + GENESIS]

mo͡rphŏ'log|ȳ *n.* (Biol.) study of the form of animals and plants; (Philol.) study of the form of words, system of forms in a language; hence **mo͡rpholŏ'gical** *a.*, ~IST (3) *n.* [f. Gk *morphē* form + -O- + -LOGY]

mo͡r'ra. See MORA.

mŏ'rrĭs¹ *a.* & *n.* ‖~ (**dance**), traditional dance by persons in fancy costume, usu. as characters in legend, with ribbons and bells; **~ dancer, ~ man,** performer in this; **~-pike,** (Hist.) form of pike supposed to be of Moorish origin. [f. *morys*, var. of MOORISH]

Mŏ'rrĭs² *n.* **~ chair,** type of plain easy chair with adjustable back. [f. William ~, Engl. poet and craftsman d. 1896]

mŏ'rrow (-ō) *n.* (literary). **The ~**, the following day; ‖GOOD *morrow*; **on the ~ of,** (fig.) in the time following. [ME *morwe*, *moru*, f. as MORN; cf. SORROW]

mo͡rse¹ *n.* Walrus. [ult. f. Lappish *moršša*]

Mo͡rse² *n.*, *a.*, & *v.* **1.** *n.* & *a.* (Of) the alphabet or code invented by S. F. B. *Morse*, Amer. electrician d. 1872, in which letters are represented by various combinations of two signs, e.g. dot and dash, long and short flash, etc. **2.** *v.t.* & *i.* Signal by Morse code.

mo͡rse³ *n.* Clasp, often jewelled etc., of cope. [ME, f. OF *mors* f. L *morsus* bite, catch (*mordēre mors-* to bite)]

mo͡r'sel *n.* Mouthful, small piece (*of* food etc.); fragment. [ME f. OF, dim. of *mors* a bite (as prec.; see -LE 2)]

mo͡rt¹ *n.* Note sounded on hunting-horn at death of deer etc. [ME f. OF, f. L *mors mortis* death]

mo͡rt² *n.* Salmon in third year. [16th c.; orig. unkn.]

mo͡rt³ *n.* (dial.) *A* great amount or number *of*. [perh. f. N. Engl. *murth* f. ON *mergth* multitude, assoc. w. foll.]

mo͡r'tal *a.* & *n.* **1.** *a.* Subject to death; causing death, fatal, (*to*, lit. or fig.; *mortal* SIN¹); (of battle) fought to the death; (of enemy) implacable; (of pain, fear, affront, etc.) intense, very serious; accompanying death (*mortal agony*); (sl.) very great (*in a mortal hurry*); (sl.) long and tedious (*for two mortal hours*); (sl.) whatsoever (*every mortal thing*; **no ~** *use* etc., no use etc. at all). **2.** Hence ~LY² *adv.* **3.** *n.* Mortal (esp. human) being; (joc.) person (*a thirsty mortal*). [ME, f. OF *mortal*, *mortel* or f. L *mortalis* (*mors mortis* death; see -AL)]

mŏrtă'lĭtȳ *n.* Mortal nature; loss of life on large scale; number of deaths in given period etc.; ~ (**rate**), death rate; ~ **tables** (showing expectation of life at various ages etc.). [ME, f. OF *mortalité* f. L *mortalitas -tatis* (as prec.; see -ITY)]

mŏr'tar *n.*, & *v.t.* **1.** *n.* Vessel of hard material, e.g. marble, in which ingredients are pounded with pestle. **2.** Short large-bore cannon for throwing shells at high angles; contrivance for firing lifeline or firework. **3.** Mixture of lime or cement, sand, and water, (orig. made in a mortar) for joining stones or bricks; **bricks and** ~, buildings; hence ~LESS, ~Y[2], *adjs.* **4.** ~**-board,** board for holding mortar, stiff square academic cap. **5.** *v.t.* Plaster or join with mortar; attack or bombard with mortars. [ME, f. AF *morter*, OF *mortier* f. L *mortarium*; partly f. LG]

mŏr'tgage[1] (mŏr'gĭj) *n.* Conveyance of property by debtor to creditor as security for debt (esp. incurred by purchase of the property), with proviso that it shall be returned on payment of debt within certain period; deed effecting this; (loan resulting in) such debt. [ME f. OF, = dead pledge (*mort* f. L *mortuus* dead, *gage* GAGE[1])]

mŏr'tgag|e[2] (mŏr'gĭj) *v.t.* Convey (property) by mortgage; pledge (one*self*, one's powers etc., *to* object etc.); hence ~EE' (-jē') *n.*, creditor in mortgage, ~ER[1] (-jer), ~OR (-jŏr'), *ns.*, debtor in mortgage. [f. prec.]

mŏr'tice. See MORTISE.

***mŏrtĭ'cian** (-shan) *n.* Undertaker, manager of funerals. [f. L *mors mortis* death + -ICIAN]

mŏr'tĭ|fȳ *v.* **1.** *v.t.* Bring (body, the flesh, passions, etc.) into subjection by self-denial or discipline; cause (person) to feel humiliated, wound (feelings). **2.** *v.i.* (Of flesh) be affected by gangrene or necrosis. **3.** So ~FICA'TION *n.* [ME, f. OF *mortifier* f. eccl. L *mortificare* kill, subdue (*mors mortis* death; see -FY)]

mŏr'tĭse, -ĭce, *n.*, & *v.t.* **1.** *n.* Hole in a framework designed to receive the end of some other part, esp. a TENON; ~ **chisel** (with stout blade, for cutting mortises); ~ **lock** (recessed in frame of door etc.). **2.** *v.t.* Join (things *together*, one *to* or *into* another) securely, esp. by mortise and tenon; cut mortise in. [ME, f. OF *mortoise* f. Arab. *murtazz* fixed in]

mŏr'tmain *n.* (Law). (Condition of) lands or tenements held inalienably by ecclesiastical or other corporation; **in** ~, (fig.) as if under posthumous control. [ME, f. AF, OF *mortemain* f. med. L *mortua manus* dead hand, prob. in allusion to impersonal ownership]

mŏr'tūarȳ *a.* & *n.* **1.** *a.* Of death or burial. **2.** *n.* Building in which dead bodies may be kept for a time. [ME; (n. f. AF *mortuarie* f. med. L *mortuarium*) f. L *mortuarius* (*mortuus* dead; see -ARY[1])]

mŏr'ula *n.* (*pl.* ~**e**). (Zool.) Fully segmented ovum from which blastula is formed. [mod. L, dim. of L *morum* mulberry]

mŏr'wŏng *n.* Australasian food-fish of genus *Cheilodactylus.* [Aboriginal]

mosā'ĭc[1] (-z-) *a.*, *n.*, & *v.t.* (**-ck-**). **1.** *a.* & *n.* (Form or work of art) in which pictures etc. are produced by joining together minute pieces of glass, stone, etc., of different colours; arrangement of photosensitive elements in television camera; (Biol.) chimera; (fig.) diversified (thing). **2.** ~ (**disease**), virus disease causing leaf-mottling in plants, esp. tobacco, maize, and sugar-cane; ~ **gold,** (1) tin disulphide, (2) alloy of copper and zinc used in cheap jewellery etc. **3.** Hence ~IST (3) *n.* **4.** *v.t.* Adorn with mosaics; combine (as) into mosaic. [ME, f. F *mosaïque* f. It. *mosaico* f. med. L *mosaicus, musaicus* f. Gk *mous(e)ion* mosaic work (*mousa* MUSE[1])]

Mosā'ĭc[2] (-z-) *a.* Of Moses, esp. ~ **Law** (in Pentateuch). [f. F *mosaïque* or mod. L *Mosaicus* (*Moses, Moyses* f. Heb. *Mōšeh*)]

mōsasaur'us *n.* Large extinct marine reptile. [mod. L, f. *Mosa* river Meuse (near which it was first discovered) + Gk *sauros* lizard]

mŏschatĕ'l (-k-) *n.* Small plant (*Adoxa moschatellina*) with pale-green flowers and musky smell. [f. F *moscatelle* f. It. *moscatella* (*moscato* musk)]

mōsĕ'lle (-z-) *n.* Dry white wine produced near the river *Moselle* in Germany.

mō'sey (-zĭ) *v.i.* (sl.) Walk (*along*) in leisurely or aimless manner. [19th c.; orig. unkn.]

mōsha'v (-ah'v) *n.* (*pl.* ~**im**). Co-operative association of Israeli smallholders. [f. Heb. *mošāb*, lit. 'dwelling']

Moslem. See MUSLIM.

mŏsque (-k) *n.* Muslim place of worship. [f. F *mosquée* f. It. *moschea* f. Arab. *masjid*]

mŏsqui'tō (-kē'-) *n.* (*pl.* ~**es**). **1.** Gnat esp. of genus *Culex* or *Anopheles*, female of which punctures skins of man and animals with long proboscis and sucks their blood; ~**-net** (to keep off mosquitoes). **2.** *~ **boat,** motor torpedo-boat; ~ **craft,** small light nimble naval vessels. [Sp. & Port., dim. of *mosca* f. L *musca* fly]

mŏss *n.*, & *v.t.* **1.** *n.* Small herbaceous cryptogam of class Musci, some growing in bogs, others on surface of ground, trees, stones, etc., in crowded masses; **rolling stone gathers no** ~, one who constantly changes his place or employment will not grow rich; hence ~'Y[2] *a.* **2.** (Sc. & N. Engl.) (Peat-)bog. **3.** ~ **agate,** agate with mosslike dendritic markings; ~**-grown,** overgrown with moss; ~**-hag,** (Sc.) broken ground from which peat has been taken; ~**-rose,** garden variety of cabbage rose, with mosslike growth on calyx and stalk; ~**-stitch,** alternate plain and purl in knitting; ~**'trooper,** freebooter of Scottish Border in 17th c. **4.** *v.t.* Cover with moss. [OE *mos* bog, moss, = OHG *mos* f. Gmc **musam*]

***mŏ'ssbŭnker** *n.* Menhaden. [f. Du. *marsbanker*, of unkn. orig.]

mosso (mŏ'sō) *adv.* (Mus.) With animation or speed. [It., p.p. of *muovere* move]

mōst *a.*, *n.*, & *adv.* **1.** *a.* Existing in greatest quantity or degree (*you have made most mistakes*; *see who can make the most noise*). **2.** *n.* Greatest quantity or number (*this is the most I can do*); **make the** ~ **of,** (1) employ to the best advantage, (2) represent at its best or worst. **3.** *a.* & *n.* The majority (of) (*most people think so*; *most of it is*, *of them are, missing*; *his singing is better than most*); **for the** ~ **part,** in the main, usually; hence ~'LY[2] *adv.* **4.** *adv.* In the highest degree (*this is most interesting*; *what most annoys me*). **5.** (Forming superl. of *adjs.* & *advs.*, esp. those of more than one syllable) *most ludicrous(ly)*, *most certain(ly)*; *most favoured* NATION; ||*Most* HONOURABLE; *Most* REVEREND. **6. At** (**the**) ~, as the greatest amount; **ten at** (**the**) ~, not more than ten; *this is* **at** ~ (no better than) *a makeshift.* **7.** *(colloq.) Almost. [OE *māst*, = OS *mēst*, OHG *meist*, ON *mestr*, Goth. *maists* f. Gmc **maistaz* (**mais* more; see -EST[1])]

-most (*or* mōst) *suf.* forming *adjs.* w. superl. sense f. *preps.* & other wds indicating relative position (*foremost, inmost, topmost, uttermost*). [OE *-mest* f. Gmc *-*mo-* + *-*isto* -EST[1]]

mot (mō) *n.* (*pl. pr.* mōz). Witty saying; BON MOT; ~ ***juste*** (zhōō'st), the expression that conveys a desired shade of meaning with more precision than any other. [F, = word, f. Gallo-Rom. **mottum* for L *muttum* uttered sound (*muttire* murmur)]

||**M.O.T.** *abbr.* Ministry of Transport; ~ **test,** (colloq.) compulsory annual test of motor vehicles of more than a specified age.

mōte *n.* Particle of dust; ~ **in** person's **eye,** fault that is trifling compared to one's own (see Matt. 7:3). [OE *mot*, corresp. to Du. *mot* dust, sawdust, of unkn. orig.]

mōtĕ'l *n.* Hotel or group of furnished cabins by the roadside, where motorists and their vehicles may be accommodated. [portmanteau wd f. MOTOR + HOTEL]

mōtĕ't *n.* (Mus.) Anthem (usu. unaccompanied) in R.C. or Lutheran Church. [ME f. OF, dim. of MOT; see -ET[1]]

mŏth *n.* **1.** Small nocturnal lepidopterous insect of family Tineidae breeding in cloth etc., on which its larva feeds; (**the**) ~, (ravages of) such insects; hence ~'Y[2] *a.* **2.** Insect of order Lepidoptera excluding butterflies, without clubbed antennae and mainly nocturnal, apt to scorch itself by fluttering about light; (fig.) person hovering around temptation. **3.** **~-ball,** (*n.*) ball of naphthalene etc. for keeping moths away from clothes (*in ~-balls*, (fig.) stored out of use for considerable time), (*v.t.*) place in moth-balls; **~-eaten,** destroyed by moths, (fig.) antiquated, time-worn; *moth*-PROOF[2] *a.*, & *v.t.* [OE *moththe*; cf. MDu., MLG, MHG *motte*, ON *motti*]

mo'ther[1] (mŭ'dh-) *n.* **1.** Female parent; (**adoptive**) ~, woman who has adopted a child; EXPECTANT or *pregnant mother*. **2.** Quality, condition, etc., that gives rise to another (*necessity is the mother of invention*). **3.** Head of female religious community (often *Mother* SUPERIOR). **4.** (Title used of or to) elderly woman of lower class. **5.** (**Artificial**) ~, apparatus for rearing chickens without hen. **6.** **M~ Carey's chicken,** stormy PETREL; **M~ Carey's goose,** largest species of petrel; **M~ Church** (as of maternal authority); **M~-Church** (whence others have sprung); **~ country,** country in relation to its colonies; **~craft,** skill in looking after one's children as a mother; **~ earth,** earth as mother of its inhabitants etc., (joc.) the ground; **~(-fucker)**, (vulg.) despicable or unpleasant person; ***M~ Goose rhyme,** nursery rhyme; **M~ Hubbard,** loose cloak or overall [f. nursery-rhyme character]; **~-in-law,** mother of one's wife or husband; **~land,** native country; **~-naked,** stark naked; **M~ of God,** Virgin Mary; **~-of-pearl,** smooth shining iridescent substance forming inner layer of oyster etc. shell; **~-of-thousands** or **-millions,** ivy-leaved toadflax; **M~'s Day,** ‖= MOTHER[2]*ing Sunday*, *similar festival on second Sunday in May; ‖*mother's* HELP[2]; ‖**~ ship** (in charge of torpedo-boats, submarines, etc.); ‖**~s' meeting** (in parish etc. for pastoral instruction, or fig. for agitated discussion); **~'s son,** man, esp. *every mother's son of* (*you* etc.); **~ tongue,** (1) one's native language, (2) language from which others spring; **~ wit,** native wit, common sense. **7.** Hence ~HOOD *n.*, ~LESS, ~LIKE, *adjs.* [OE *mōdor*, = OS *mōdar*, OHG *muotar*, ON *móthir* f. Gmc **mōthar-* f. IE **māter-*]

mo'ther[2] (mŭ'dh-) *v.t.* Give birth to (usu. fig.); protect as a mother; acknowledge or profess oneself the mother of (child, lit. or fig.); ‖**M~ing Sunday,** 4th Sunday in Lent, with old custom of visiting parents with gifts. [f. prec.]

mo'ther[3] (mŭ'dh-) *n.* ~ (**of vinegar**), mucilaginous substance produced in vinegar during fermentation by mould-fungus; hence ~Y[2] *a.* [prob. = MOTHER[1]; cf. MDu. *moeder*, G *mutter* in same sense]

mo'therl|y̆ (mŭ'dh-) *a.* Having or showing the good (esp. tender or kind) qualities of a mother; hence ~ĭNESS *n.* [OE *mōdorlic* (as MOTHER[1], -LY[1])]

mōti'f (-ē'f) *n.* Distinctive feature, dominant idea, in artistic or literary composition; (Mus.) = FIGURE[1] 8; ornament of lace etc. sewn separately on dress; ornament on vehicle identifying maker etc. [F (as MOTIVE)]

mō'tile *a.* (Zool. & Bot.) Capable of motion; hence **motĭ'lITY** *n.* [f. L *motus* motion (as MOVE[2]); see -IL]

mō'tion[1] *n.* **1.** Moving, change of place; manner of moving the body in walking etc.; change of posture; gesture; **go through the ~s,** simulate an action by gestures, (fig.) make pretence, do something only superficially; **in ~,** moving, not at rest; **put** or **set in ~,** set going or working; **~ picture,** = FILM 3; TIME[1]-*and-motion*. **2.** Formal proposal in deliberative assembly; (Law) application by party etc. for rule or order of court. **3.** Evacuation of bowels; (in *sing.* or *pl.*) faeces. **4.** Piece of moving mechanism; **~-work,** mechanism of hands of clock or watch. **5.** Hence ~AL, ~LESS, *adjs.* [ME f. OF, f. L *motio -onis* (as MOVE[2]; see -ION)]

mō'tion[2] *v.* **1.** *v.t.* Direct (person *to*, *towards*, *away*, etc.; *to* do) by sign or gesture. **2.** *v.i.* Make gesture (*to* person) directing him (*to* do). [f. prec.]

mō'tĭv|āte *v.t.* Supply a motive to, be the motive of; cause (person) to act in a particular way; stimulate interest of (person in studying etc.); hence ~A'TION *n.* [f. foll. 3 + -ATE[3]]

mō'tĭve[1] *a.* & *n.* **1.** *a.* Tending to initiate movement, whence **mōtĭ'vITY** *n.*; **~ power,** moving or impelling power, esp. form of mechanical energy used to drive machinery, e.g. steam, electricity. **2.** Concerned with movement. **3.** *n.* What induces a person to act, e.g. desire, fear, circumstance; hence ~LESS (-vl-) *a.* **4.** = MOTIF. [ME, f. OF *motif* a. & n. f. LL *motivus* a. (as MOVE[2]; see -IVE)]

mō'tĭve[2] *v.t.* = MOTIVATE. [f. prec. 3]

mŏ'tley *a.* & *n.* **1.** *a.* Diversified in colour; of varied character (*a motley crew*). **2.** *n.* Incongruous mixture; (Hist.) jester's particoloured dress; **wear ~,** play the fool. [ME *mottelay*, perh. f. AF **motelé*, f. MOTE]

mō'tor *n.*, *a.*, & *v.* **1.** *n.* What imparts motion; machine supplying motive power for carriage or vessel, esp. internal combustion engine, or for other device with moving parts; ‖= *motor car*; **~'man,** driver of tram, underground train, etc. **2.** *a.* Giving, imparting, or producing motion; **~ area,** part of frontal lobe of brain associated with initiation of muscular action; **~ nerve** (carrying impulses from brain or spinal cord to muscle); hence **motôr'IAL,** **mō'tORY,** *adjs.* **3.** Driven by motor (*motor boat*, *mower*, *ship*); **~ bicycle,** motor cycle or moped; **~ bike,** (colloq.) = *motor cycle*; **~ bus,** bus with motor engine; ‖**~ car,** car with motor engine for use on ordinary roads; **~ coach,** long-distance motor bus; **~ cycle,** two-wheeled motor-driven road vehicle without pedal propulsion; hence **~-cyclist;** *motor* SCOOTER; **~ vehicle,** vehicle with motor engine for use on ordinary roads. **4.** Of or for motor vehicles; ‖**~ spirit,** petrol or other fuel for internal combustion engines. **5.** *v.i.* & *t.* ‖Go or convey in motor car; hence ~ABLE *a.*, (of road) that can be traversed by motor vehicles. [L, = mover (as MOVE[2]; see -OR)]

***mō'torcāde** *n.* Procession or parade of motor cars. [f. prec., after *cavalcade*]

mō'torĭst *n.* Driver of motor car. [f. MOTOR + -IST]

mō'torīz|e, -īs|e (-īz), *v.t.* Equip (troops etc.) with motor transport; furnish with motor for propulsion etc. hence ~A'TION *n.* [f. MOTOR + -IZE]

||**mō'torway** *n.* Road specially constructed and controlled for fast motor traffic. [f. MOTOR + WAY]
mŏtte *n.* Mound forming site of castle, camp, etc. [ME f. OF *mote* (as MOAT)]
mŏ'ttle *n.*, & *v.t.* **1.** *n.* Irregular arrangement of spots or confluent blotches of colour; such spot. **2.** *v.t.* (esp. in *p.p.*) Mark (soap etc.) with mottle. [prob. back form. f. MOTLEY]
mŏ'ttō *n.* (*pl.* ~**es**). Sentence inscribed on some object and expressing appropriate sentiment; word or sentence accompanying coat of arms or crest; maxim adopted as rule of conduct; verses etc. in paper cracker; quotation prefixed to book or chapter; (Mus.) recurrent phrase having some symbolical significance. [It., as MOT]
motu proprio (mōtū prō'priō) *n.* (*pl.* ~*s*). Administrative papal bull without seal. [L, = of our own accord]
||**mouch.** Var. of MOOCH.
mouchoir (mōō'shwâr) *n.* Handkerchief. [F]
moue (mōō) *n.* = POUT². [F; see MOW²]
mou'fflon (mōō'-) *n.* Wild mountain sheep (*Ovis musimon*) of S. Europe. [f. F *mouflon* f. It. *muflone* f. Rom. **mufro -onis*]
mouillé (mōō'yā) *a.* (Phonet., of consonant) palatalized. [F, = wetted]
mou'jĭk, mu'zhĭk, (mōō'zhĭk) *n.* (Hist.) Russian peasant. [Russ. *muzhik*]
mould¹ (mōld), ***mōld¹,** *n.* Loose earth; upper soil of cultivated land, esp. if rich in organic matter; **man of ~,** mere mortal; **~-board,** board in plough that turns over the furrow-slice. [OE *molde*, = MDu. *moude*, OHG *molta*, ON *mold*, Goth. *mulda* f. Gmc **moldō* (**mul-*, **mel-* grind; cf. MEAL¹)]
mould² (mōld), ***mōld²,** *n.* **1.** Pattern or template used by mason, bricklayer, etc., as guide in shaping mouldings; hollow form into which molten metal etc. is cast to cool into required shape; metal or earthenware vessel used to give shape to puddings etc., pudding etc. so shaped; (fig.) **cast in** *heroic* etc. **~,** of such character. **2.** Form, shape, esp. of animal body; (Archit.) moulding, group of mouldings. [ME *mold(e)*, app. f. OF *modle* f. L MODULUS]
mould³ (mōld), ***mōld³,** *v.t.* Produce (object) in certain shape, *out of* (elements), *on* or *upon* (pattern), lit. or fig.; bring into certain shape; shape (bread) into loaves. [ME, f. prec.]
mould⁴ (mōld), ***mōld⁴,** *n.* Woolly or furry growth of minute fungi on things of animal or vegetable origin that lie for some time in moist warm air. [ME prob. f. obs. *mould* a., p.p. of *moul* grow mouldy f. ON **mugla, mygla*]
mou'lder¹ (mō'l-), ***mō'lder¹,** *n.* One who moulds, esp. workman making moulds for casting. [ME, f. MOULD³ + -ER¹]
mou'lder² (mō'l-), ***mō'lder²,** *v.i.* Decay to dust, rot *away*, (lit. or fig.). [perh. f. MOULD¹ + -ER⁵, but cf. Norw. dial. *muldra* crumble]
mou'ldĭng (mō'l-), ***mō'ldĭng,** *n.* In vbl senses; moulded object, esp. ornamental variety of outline in cornices etc. of building, or similar shape of woodwork, etc.; strip of wood thus shaped for attachment; **~-board** (on which dough is kneaded); **~-plane** (for shaping mouldings); **picture-~** (for framing pictures, or along wall for hanging framed pictures from). [ME, f. MOULD³ + -ING¹]
mou'ld|ў (mō'l-), ***mō'ld|ў,** *a.* Overgrown with mould; (fig.) stale, out-of-date; (sl.) dull, miserable, boring; hence **~ĭNESS** *n.* [ME, f. MOULD⁴ + -Y²]
moulin (mōōlă'ṅ) *n.* Nearly vertical shaft in glacier, formed by surface water falling through crack in ice. [F, lit. = mill]
moult (mōlt), ***mōlt,** *v.* & *n.* **1.** *v.t.* & *i.* (Of bird) shed (feathers), shed feathers, in changing plumage (lit. or fig.); (of animal) shed hair, shell, etc. **2.** *n.* Moulting. [ME *moute* f. OE **mutian*, = OHG *mūzzōn*, WG f. L *mutare* change; *-l-* after *fault* etc.]
mound¹ *n.* Ball of gold etc. representing earth, surmounting crown etc., and used in heraldry. [ME, f. OF *monde* f. L *mundus* world]
mound² *n.*, & *v.t.* **1.** *n.* Elevation of earth or stones, esp. of earth heaped on grave; hillock; heap, pile; (Baseball) slight elevation on which pitcher stands; **~-builder,** (1) one of prehistoric N. Amer. Indian race who erected mounds, (2) megapode bird. **2.** *v.t.* Enclose with, heap up in, mounds. [orig. = hedge or fence; 16th c., of unkn. orig.]
mount¹ *n.* **1.** Mountain, hill, (arch. exc. before name, as *Mount Everest, Mount of Olives*); SERMON *on the Mount.* **2.** (Palmistry). Fleshy prominence on palm of hand. [ME, f. OE *munt* & OF *mont* f. L *mons montis* mountain]
mount² *v.* **1.** *v.t.* Ascend (hill, stairs, etc., or abs.). **2.** Get on (horse etc. or abs.) for purpose of riding; put (person) on horse etc.; furnish (person) with horse; (in *p.p.*) serving on horseback or bicycle (*mounted police, infantry*). **3.** (Of animal) get upon for copulation. **4.** Raise (guns) into position on a fixed mounting; place (object) *on* elevated support; bring into readiness for operation; put (picture etc.) in a MOUNT³; fit (gem etc.) in gold etc.; fix (object) on microscope slide. **5.** Put (play) on stage; display (article of costume); prepare (specimens etc.) for display or preservation. **6.** Take action to effect (effort, programme, etc.; orig. Mil. of offensive); **~ guard,** perform duty of guarding (*over* thing etc.). **7.** *v.i.* Move upwards; (of blood) rise into cheeks; **~** (**up**), (fig.) increase in amount or intensity. **8.** Rise to higher level of rank, power, etc. **9.** Hence **~'ING¹** (1, 4) *n.* (**~ing-block,** block of stone provided to help in mounting one's horse). [ME, f. OF *munter, monter* f. Rom. **montare* f. L (as prec.)]
mount³ *n.* Margin surrounding picture or photograph; card on which drawing is mounted; setting for gem etc.; ornamental metal parts of thing; stamp-HINGE; horse for person's riding; chance of riding, esp. as jockey. [f. prec.]
mou'ntain (-tĭn) *n.* **1.** Large natural elevation of earth's surface, large or high and steep hill, esp. one over 1,000 ft. high; *waves ran* **~s** (very) **high, ~-high. 2.** Large heap or pile, huge quantity *of.* **3. The M~,** extreme party in French Revolution (1792) occupying elevated position in chamber of assembly. **4.** *Make a mountain out of a* MOLE²*hill*; **move ~s,** make every possible effort. **5. ~ ash,** (1) tree of genus *Sorbus* with delicate pinnate leaves and scarlet berries, rowan, (2) eucalyptus like old ash-tree; **~ chain,** connected series of mountains; **~ cock,** capercaillie; **~ devil,** moloch; **~ dew,** (colloq.) Scotch whisky esp. illicitly distilled; **~ goat,** white goatlike animal (*Oreamnos montanus*) of Rocky Mountains etc.; **~ laurel,** N. Amer. shrub *Kalmia latifolia*; **~ linnet,** twite; **~ lion,** puma; **~ panther,** ounce; **~ range,** line of mountains connected by high ground; **~ sickness,** malady caused by rarefied air at great heights; **~side,** slope of mountain below summit; ***M~ Time,** standard time of parts of Canada and U.S. in or near Rocky Mountains; **~ tobacco,** a species of arnica; **~ trout,** (Austral.) small minnow popular in aquaria. [ME, f. OF *montaigne* f. Rom. **montania* fem. (or neut. pl.) of **montanius* a. f. L (as MOUNT¹)]
mountaineer' (-tĭn-) *n.* Dweller amongst mountains; one skilled in mountain climbing, whence **~ING¹** *n.* [f. prec. + -EER]

mou'ntainous (-tĭn-) *a.* Abounding in mountains; huge. [f. MOUNTAIN + -OUS]

mou'ntėbănk *n.* Itinerant quack appealing to audience from platform; clown; charlatan; hence ~ERY (4) *n.* [f. It. *montambanco* = *monta in banco* MOUNT^{2} on bench]

Mou'ntĭe *n.* (colloq.) Member of Royal Canadian Mounted Police. [f. MOUNT^{2}*ed* + -IE]

mourn (mōrn) *v.* **1.** *v.i.* Feel sorrow or regret (*for* or *over* dead person, lost thing, loss, misfortune, etc.); show conventional signs of grief for period after person's death. **2.** *v.t.* Sorrow for (dead person, regretted or past thing). [OE *murnan*, = OS *mornon*, OHG *mornēn* be anxious, ON *morna*, Goth. *maurnan*]

mour'ner (mōr'-) *n.* One who mourns, esp. who attends funeral of friend or relation; person hired to attend funeral. [ME, f. prec. + -ER^{1}]

mour'nful (mōr'-) *a.* Expressing mourning; doleful, sad, sorrowful; hence ~LY^{2} *adv.*, ~NESS *n.* [f. MOURN + -FUL]

mour'nĭng (mōr'-) *n.* In vbl senses; (wearing of) black clothes as sign of mourning; DEEP^{1}, HALF, *mourning*; **in** ~, wearing such garments, (sl., of eye) blacked in fighting, (sl., of finger-nails) dirty; **~-band** (of black crape etc. round sleeve or hat as token of mourning); **~-coach** (attending funeral); **~ dove,** Amer. dove with plaintive note; **~-paper,** notepaper with black edge; **~-ring** (worn as memorial of deceased person). [ME, f. MOURN + -ING^{1}]

mousa'ka (mōōsah'-) *n.* Greek dish of minced meat, aubergine, eggs, etc. [Gk or Turk.]

mouse^{1} (mows) *n.* (*pl.* **mice**). Small rodent esp. of genus *Mus*, or small shrew or vole; timid, shy, or retiring person; (sl.) black eye; **~-colour(ed),** dark grey with yellow tinge; **~ deer,** chevrotain; **~-ear,** (1) a hawkweed, (2) forget-me-not; **~ hare,** pika; **~'trap** (for catching mice; *~trap cheese*, of poor quality); hence **mou'sy**^{2} *a.* [OE *mūs*, pl. *mȳs*, = OS, OHG *mūs*, ON *mús* f. Gmc f. IE **mūs-*]

mouse^{2} (*or* -z) *v.i.* (Of cat or owl) hunt for or catch mice, whence **mou'ser**^{1} (*or* -z-) *n.*; search industriously, prowl *about* (as if) in search of something. [ME, f. prec.]

moussaka. Var. of MOUSAKA.

mousse (mōōs) *n.* Dish of cold whipped cream or eggs or creamlike substance flavoured with fruit, chocolate, etc.; meat or fish purée with whipped cream etc. incorporated. [F, = moss, froth]

mousseli'ne (mōōslē'n) *n.* Muslin-like fabric of silk etc.; **~-de-laine,** dress material of wool and cotton; **~-de-soie** (-swah), thin silk fabric of muslin-like texture. [F; see MUSLIN, DELAINE]

mousta'ch|e, *mus-, (mustah'sh) *n.* Hair on either side (usu. in *pl.*) or both sides of (usu. man's) upper lip; similar hair round mouths of some animals; **~e-cup** (with partial cover to protect moustache when drinking); hence ~ED^{2} (-sht) *a.* [F, f. It. *mostaccio* f. Gk *mustax -akos*]

Moustēr'ĭan (mōō-) *a.* (Archaeol.) Of a middle palaeolithic epoch with flints worked on one side only. [f. F *moustérien* (*Le Moustier* in S.W. France, where remains of it were found) + -IAN]

mou'sȳ. See MOUSE^{1}.

mouth^{1} (mowth) *n.* (*pl. pr.* -dhz). **1.** External orifice in head, with cavity behind it containing apparatus of biting and mastication and vocal organs; this cavity. **2.** (sl.) Talkativeness; impudent talk, cheek. **3.** (Of horse, with reference to his readiness to feel and obey pressure of bit) *good, bad, hard, mouth.* **4.** **~ to feed,** person who consumes food but does no useful work; *mouth* WATER^{2}*s*; DOWN^{3} *in the mouth*; **give** ~, (of dog) bark, bay; **in** person's ~, when said by him (*that sounds strange in your mouth*); **keep** one's ~ **shut,** (sl.) not reveal secret; LAUGH *on the other* or *wrong side of* one's *mouth*; **make a wry** ~, grimace in disgust; **put** one's **money where** one's ~ **is,** (sl.) be ready to support one's opinions by action; *not* OPEN^{2} one's *mouth*; **out of** person's **own** ~, using his actual words; **put words into** person's ~, (1) tell him what to say, (2) represent him as having said them; **shut** person's ~, (sl.) prevent him from revealing something; **take words out of** person's ~, say what he was about to say; WORD^{1} *of mouth*. **5.** Opening of bag, sack, cave, furnace, cannon, trumpet, volcano, etc.; place where river enters sea. **6.** **~-breeder,** fish carrying eggs and young in mouth; **~-filling,** bombastic; **~-organ,** thin rectangular box containing metal reeds, each tuned to a note, moved before mouth while air is blown or sucked through it to play tunes; **~'piece,** (1) part of pipe, musical instrument, telephone, etc., placed between or near lips, (2) one who speaks for another or others (sl., lawyer); **~'wash,** liquid antiseptic etc. for use in mouth. **7.** Hence (-)~ED^{2} (-dhd), ~'LESS, *adjs.* [OE *mūth*, = OS *mūth*, OS, OHG *mund*, ON *munnr*, *muthr*, Goth. *munths* f. Gmc **munthaz* f. IE **mntos*]

mouth^{2} (mowdh) *v.* **1.** *v.t.* Utter (words or abs.) esp. pompously or very distinctly, rant, declaim; take (food) in, touch with, the mouth; train mouth of (horse). **2.** *v.i.* Grimace; move lips silently. [ME, f. prec.]

mou'thful (-ōōl) *n.* Quantity that fills the mouth; small quantity (*of* food etc.); something difficult to say; *(sl.) something important said. [f. MOUTH^{1} + -FUL]

mou'thȳ (-dhĭ) *a.* Railing, ranting; bombastic. [f. MOUTH^{1} + -Y^{2}]

mo'v|able (mōō'-) *a.* & *n.* **1.** *a.* That can be moved; (Law, of property) that can be removed, personal as opp. to REAL^{2}; *movable* DOH; *movable* FEAST; hence ~ABI'LITY, **~able**NESS (-beln-), *ns.* **2.** *n.* Article of furniture that may be removed from the house, opp. to *fixture*; (in *pl.*) personal property. [ME, f. OF (as MOVE^{2}; see -ABLE)]

move^{1} (mōōv) *n.* Moving of a man in chess or other game; player's turn to do this; change of residence, business premises, etc.; device, step taken to secure object; **on the** ~, (1) progressing, (2) moving about; **make a** ~, initiate action, e.g. rise and go from dinner-table etc.; **get a ~ on,** (sl.) hurry up, bestir oneself. [ME, f. foll.]

move^{2} (mōōv) *v.* **1.** *v.t.* Change position of; change position of (man) in chess etc.; put or keep in motion, shake, stir; *move* HEAVEN *and earth*; ||**~ house,** change one's place of residence. **2.** Change posture of (one's body, limbs, etc.); cause (bowels) to be evacuated. **3.** Provoke (laughter, anger, etc., *in* person, person *to* these); affect (person) with (usu. tender or sympathetic) emotion. **4.** Prompt, incline, (person *to* action, *to* do); **the spirit** (orig. in Quaker use, = Holy Spirit) **~s** person, he feels inclined (*to* do). **5.** Make formal application to (court etc. *for*); propose (question, resolution, *that* thing be done) in deliberative assembly. **6.** *v.i.* Go or pass (*about, away*, etc.) from place to place; make progress (*the work moves slowly*); (of merchandise) be sold; make a move at chess etc.; (fig.) initiate action (*moved to halt inflation*); live, be socially active, *in* specified group etc. (*moves in the best circles*). **7.** Change one's place of residence; **~ about,** do this often; **~ in,** take possession of new abode, begin new job, etc.; so **~ out.** **8.** **~ along** or **on,** go to new place (e.g. as policeman's order to person who stands too long in one place); **~ over** or **up,** adjust one's position to make room for another. **9.** (Of person or part of body) change posture; (of inanimate thing) undergo change of position. **10.** (Of bowels) be moved. **11.** Make request or application (*for*). **12.** Hence ~′LESS (-vl-) *a.*, (literary) motionless. [ME, f. AF *mover*, OF *moveir* f. L *movēre mot-*]

moveable. Var. (esp. Law) of MOVABLE.

mo′vement (mōō′vm-) *n.* Moving; military evolution; moving parts of mechanism (esp. of clock or watch), particular group of these; mental impulse; progressive development of poem, story, etc.; (Mus.) principal division of a musical work (e.g. suite, sonata, symphony), having a distinctive structure of its own; (series of combined actions and endeavours of) body of persons for special object (*the* OXFORD *Movement*; *the Labour movement*); activity in market for some commodity, rise or fall in price; = MOTION[1] 3. [ME f. OF, f. med. L *movimentum* (as MOVE[2]; see -MENT)]

mo′ver (mōō′-) *n.* In vbl senses; one who moves proposal; **prime ~,** initial source (natural or mechanical) of motive power, (fig.) author of fruitful idea. [ME, f. MOVE[2] + -ER[1]]

***mo′vĭe** (mōō′-) *n.* (colloq.) = FILM 3; ~**(-house)**, cinema. [f. MOVING *picture* + -IE]

mo′vĭng (mōō′-) *a.* In vbl senses; affecting with emotion (cf. MOVE[2] 3), whence ~LY[2] *adv.*; ~ ||**pavement** or ***sidewalk,** structure like conveyer belt for pedestrians; ~ **picture,** continuous picture of events (e.g. FILM 3) obtained by projecting on screen etc. a sequence of photographs taken at very short intervals; ~ **staircase,** escalator. [ME, f. MOVE[2] + -ING[2]]

mow[1] (mō) *n.* (U.S. or dial.) Stack of hay, corn, etc.; place in barn where hay etc. is heaped; **~′burnt,** spoilt by becoming overheated in the mow. [OE *mūga*, = ON *múgi* swath, crowd]

mow[2] (*or* mō) *n.*, & *v.i.* See MOP[3]. [ME, prob. f. OF *mo(u)e* mouth, lip, pout, or f. MDu. *mouwe*, in same senses]

mow[3] (mō) *v.t.* (*p.p.* also ~**n**). Cut down (grass etc. or abs.) with scythe or machine; cut down produce of (field) or grass etc. of (lawn) thus; destroy sweepingly; ~ **down,** kill or destroy randomly or in great numbers; hence ~′ER[1] (1, 2) (mō′*er*) *n.* [OE *māwan*, = OHG *māen* f. Gmc **mǣ-*; cf. MEAD[2]]

mŏ′xa *n.* Down from dried leaves of *Artemisia moxa*, etc., burnt on skin as counter-irritant. [f. Jap. *mokusa* (*moe kusa* burning herb)]

***mŏ′xĭe** *n.* (sl.) Energy, courage, daring. [f. trade name of a drink]

moy′a *n.* Volcanic mud. [former name of mountain in Ecuador]

Mōză′rab *n.* (Hist.) Christian owning allegiance to Moorish king but allowed his own religion; hence ~IC *a.* [f. Sp. *Mozarabe* f. Arab. *musta'rib* would-be Arab]

M.P. *abbr.* Member of Parliament; military police(man).

mp *abbr. mezzo piano.*

m.p. *abbr.* melting-point.

m.p.g. *abbr.* miles per gallon.

m.p.h. *abbr.* miles per hour.

M.Phil. *abbr.* Master of Philosophy.

M.P.S. *abbr.* Member of the Pharmaceutical, Philological, or Physical Society.

Mr. (mĭ′ster) *n.* (*pl.* MESSRS.) Title of man without higher title, or prefixed to designation of office etc., (*Mr. Jones, Mr. Secretary, Mr. Speaker*); **Mr. Right,** (joc.) destined husband. [abbr. of MISTER]

M.R. *abbr.* Master of the Rolls.

M.R.A. *abbr.* Moral Re-Armament.

M.R.B.M. *abbr.* medium-range ballistic missile.

||**M.R.C.** *abbr.* Medical Research Council.

M.R.C.A. *abbr.* multi-role combat aircraft.

Mrs. (mĭ′sĭz) *n.* (*pl.* same or MESDAMES). Title of married woman without higher title; *Mrs.* GRUNDY; ||*Mrs.* MOP[1](P). [abbr. of MISTRESS; cf. MISSIS]

MS. (ĕmĕ′s) *abbr.* manuscript.

Ms. (mĭz) *n.* Title of woman without higher title, used as fem. of MR. without distinction between married and unmarried (cf. MRS., MISS[3]). [by comb. of these earlier forms]

M.S. *abbr.* Master of Science or Surgery; *motor ship; multiple sclerosis.

M.Sc. *abbr.* Master of Science.

***Msgr.** *abbr. Monseigneur*; *Monsignor.*

MSS. (ĕmĕ′sĭz) *abbr.* manuscripts.

***MST** *abbr.* Mountain Standard Time.

M.T. *abbr.* mechanical transport.

Mt. *abbr.* Mount.

M.T.B. *abbr.* motor torpedo-boat.

M.Tech. *abbr.* Master of Technology.

mū *n.* Twelfth Greek letter (M, μ) = m; μ (as symbol) = MICRO- 2; **mu-meson,** = MUON. [Gk]

mŭch *a.*, *n.*, & *adv.*, (MORE, MOST). **1.** *a.* Existing in great quantity (*much trouble*; *too much noise*; *not much rain*); **a bit ~,** (colloq.) somewhat excessive or immoderate; HOW *much*; SO[1] *much*; THIS *much*; THAT[1] *much*; **too ~ for,** (1) more than a match for, (2) beyond what is endurable by; hence ~′LY[2] *adv.* (joc.). **2.** *n.* Great quantity (*I have put up with much*; *much of what you say is true*); MAKE[1], THINK, *much of*; *not much* IN[1] *it*; **not ~ of a,** (colloq.) not a great, a somewhat poor, (*am not much of a scholar*; *it was not much of a party*); **not ~ to look at,** insignificant or unpleasing in appearance; **not come to ~,** have little success. **3.** *adv.* In a great degree (*much to my surprise*; qualifying *v.* or *p.p.*, cf. VERY[1]: (*I much regret the mistake*; *was much annoyed*; qualifying compar. or superl. adj.: *much better*; *much the most likely*); approximately (*much the same*; **~ of a size,** about the same size); for a large part of one's time (*is much in society*); **~ as,** though . . . much (*cannot come, much as I should like to*); *much* LESS; *much* OBLIGED; **as ~,** that (quantity etc.; *I thought as ~,* I thought so; *as ~ again,* such as will double the amount). [ME, f. *muchel* MICKLE; for shortening cf. BAD, WENCH]

mŭ′chnėss *n.* Greatness in quantity or degree; **much of a ~,** very nearly the same or alike. [ME, f. prec. + -NESS]

mū′cĭlage *n.* Viscous substance obtained from plant seeds etc. by maceration; *solution of gum; so **mūcĭlă′gĭnous** *a.* [ME f. F, f. LL *mucilago -ginis* musty juice (MUCUS)]

mŭck[1] *n.* Farmyard manure; (colloq.) dirt, filth, anything disgusting; (colloq.) untidy state, mess, (**make a ~ of,** bungle); **~-rake** (for collecting muck, usu. fig. of predilection for worthless or unsavoury matters, whence **~-raking** *a.* & *n.*); ||**~ sweat** (profuse); **~′worm,** worm that lives in muck, (fig.) miser; hence ~′Y[2] *a.* [ME *muk*, prob. f. Scand.; cf. ON *myki* dung, cogn. w. MEEK]

mŭck[2] *v.* **1.** *v.t.* Make dirty; remove muck (*out*) from; manure with muck; ||**~ (up)**, (sl.) bungle (job). **2.** *v.i.* (sl.) ||Go aimlessly *about*; ||fool *about with*; **~ in,** share tasks etc. equally (*with* another). [ME, f. prec.]

mŭ′cker *n.* (sl.) ||Heavy fall (lit. or fig.; **come a ~,** experience this); *rough or coarse person. [f. MUCK[1] + -ER[1]]

mŭ′ckle. See MICKLE.

mūcō′sa *n.* Mucous membrane. [mod. L, fem. of *mucosus* (see foll.)]

mū′cous *a.* Of or covered with mucus; **~ membrane,** internal prolongation of the skin so covered; so **mūco′**SITY *n.* [f. L *mucosus* (as MUCUS; see -OUS)]

mū'crō *n.* (*pl.* **~nes** *pr.* -ō'nēz). (Bot. & Zool.) Sharp-pointed part or organ; so **mū'cronATE²** *a.* [L *mucro -onis* sharp point]

mū'cus *n.* Slimy substance secreted by mucous membrane; gummy substance found in all plants; slimy substance exuded by some animals, esp. fishes. [L]

mŭd *n.* **1.** Wet soft earthy matter; hard ground from drying of area of this; (fig.) what is worthless or polluting (**his name is ~**, his reputation is at present impaired); **as clear as ~**, (joc.) not at all clear; **fling, sling, throw, ~,** make disgraceful imputations; **here's ~ in your eye!** (sl. drinking toast); STICK¹ *in the mud.* **2. ~-bath** (in mud of mineral springs, for rheumatism etc., or gen. of game etc. taking place amid much mud); **~'fish** (burrowing in mud, esp. N.Z. *Neochanna apoda*); **~-flap** (behind wheel of vehicle, to catch mud etc. thrown up); **~-flat,** stretch of muddy land left uncovered at low tide; **~'guard,** (metal) hood covering wheel of cycle, car, etc., to protect rider, pedestrians, etc., from mud; **~'lark,** one who dabbles, works, or (of bird) lives, in mud, esp. street urchin; **~ pack,** cosmetic paste applied thickly to face; **~ pie,** mud made into pie shape by child; ***~ puppy,** large salamander; **~ skipper,** fish able to leave water and leap on mud; **~ volcano** (discharging mud). [ME *mode, mudde,* prob. f. MLG *mudde,* MHG *mot* bog]

mŭ'ddle¹ *n.* Disorder; muddled condition; **make a ~ of,** bungle; **~-headed(ness),** stupid(ity), confused (state). [f. foll.]

mŭ'ddle² *v.* **1.** *v.t.* Bewilder, esp. with drink; mix (things *up, together*) blunderingly; mismanage (affair); *crush and mix (ingredients for drink), whence **mŭ'ddlER¹** (2) *n.* **2.** *v.i.* Busy oneself (*with*) in confused and ineffective way; **~ along** or **on,** progress in haphazard way; **~ through,** attain one's end by tenacity not skill or efficiency. [perh. f. MDu. *moddelen,* frequent. of *modden* dabble in mud (as MUD; see -LE 3)]

mŭ'dd|ȳ *a.*, & *v.t.* **1.** *a.* Like, abounding in, covered with, mud; (of liquid) turbid; (of light) dull; (of colour) impure; mentally confused; obscure; hence **~ĭLY²** *adv.*, **~ĭNESS** *n.* **2.** *v.t.* Make muddy. [ME, f. MUD + -Y²]

mudéjar (mōōdhā'hār) *n.* & *a.* **1.** *n.* Christianized Moor in medieval Spain. **2.** *a.* Of style of architecture originated by these. [Sp., f. Arab. *mudajjan* allowed to remain]

mue'slĭ (mōō'zlĭ) *n.* Food of chopped cereals, dried fruit, nuts, honey, etc. [Swiss G]

muĕ'zzĭn (mōō-) *n.* Muslim crier who proclaims hours of prayer usu. from minaret. [f. Arab. *mu'addin* part. of *'addana* proclaim (*'udn* ear)]

mŭff¹ *n.* Woman's fur or other covering (usu. cylindrical) into which both hands are thrust from opposite ends to keep them warm; EAR¹-*muff*; FOOT¹-*muff.* [f. Du. *mof,* MDu. *moffel, muffel* f. med. L *muff(u)la,* of unkn. orig.]

mŭff² *n.*, & *v.t.* **1.** *n.* Person who is awkward or stupid, orig. in some athletic sport; failure, esp. to catch ball at cricket etc.; hence **~'ISH¹** *a.* **2.** *v.t.* Bungle, miss (catch, ball, etc.); blunder in (theatrical part etc.). [19th c., of unkn. orig.]

||**mŭffėtee'** *n.* Worsted cuff worn on wrist. [app. irreg. f. MUFF¹]

mŭ'ffĭn *n.* (***English**) **~**, light flat round spongy cake, eaten toasted and buttered; ||**~-bell** (Hist., rung by **~-man,** seller of muffins in street). [18th c.; orig. unkn.]

mŭffĭneer' *n.* Small castor for sprinkling salt or sugar on muffins. [f. prec. + -EER]

mŭ'ffle¹ *n.* Thick part of upper lip and nose of ruminants and rodents. [f. F *mufle,* of unkn. orig.]

mŭ'ffle² *n.* Receptacle in furnace where substances may be heated without contact with combustion products; similar chamber in kiln for baking painted pottery. [f. F *moufle* mitten; cf. MUFF¹]

mŭ'ffle³ *v.t.* Wrap, cover *up,* (one*self,* one's throat etc., or abs.) for warmth; prevent from speaking; wrap up (oars at rowlocks, bell, drum, horse's hoofs) to deaden sound for secrecy or solemnity; (usu. in *p.p.*) repress, deaden, sound of (curse etc.). [ME, perh. f. OF *enmoufler* (*moufle* thick glove, as MUFF¹)]

mŭ'ffler *n.* Wrap or scarf worn for warmth; thing used to deaden sound, esp. felt pad between hammer and string of piano; *silencer of motor vehicle. [f. prec. + -ER¹]

mŭ'ftĭ *n.* **1.** Muslim priest or expounder of law. **2.** Plain clothes worn by one who has right to wear uniform (esp. *in mufti*). [f. Arab. *muftī,* part. of *'aftā* decide point of law]

mŭg¹ *n.* **1.** Drinking-vessel, usu. cylindrical, with or without handle; its contents; hence **~'FUL** 2 *n.* **2.** (sl.) Face, mouth; *hoodlum. [prob. f. Scand.; sense 2 prob. f. grotesque faces on mugs]

||**mŭg²** *n.* (sl.) Simpleton; gullible person; **a ~'s game,** senseless or unprofitable activity. [perh. f. prec. w. ref. to look of stupidity]

||**mŭg³** *v.* (**-gg-**) & *n.* (sl.) **1.** *v.i.* Study hard (*at* subject, or abs.). **2.** *v.t.* **~ (up),** learn (subject) by hard study. **3.** *n.* One who studies hard. [19th c.; orig. unkn.]

mŭg⁴ *v.t.* (**-gg-**). Thrash; strangle; rob with violence esp. in public place; hence **~'gING¹** (-g-) *n.* [prob. f. MUG¹ 2]

mŭg⁵ *v.i.* (**-gg-**). (sl.) Make faces, esp. before audience, camera, etc. [f. MUG¹ 2]

mŭ'gger¹ (-g-) *n.* In vbl senses. [f. MUG³⁻⁵ + -ER¹]

mŭ'gger² (-g-) *n.* Broad-nosed Indian crocodile (*Crocodylus palustris*) venerated by many Hindus. [f. Hindi *magar*]

mŭ'ggĭns (-gĭnz) *n.* (*pl.* **~es** *or* same). (colloq.) Simpleton; person who allows himself to be outwitted; card-game like snap. [perh. the surname *M~*, w. allus. to MUG²]

Mŭggletō'nian (-gelt-) *a.* & *n.* (Member) of sect founded by, and believing in personal inspiration of, L. Muggleton and John Reeve, *c.* 1650. [f. Lodowick *Muggleton,* Engl. preacher d. 1698 + -IAN]

mŭ'gg|ȳ (-gĭ) *a.* (Of weather, day, etc.) oppressively damp and warm; hence **~ĭNESS** *n.* [f. dial. *mug* mist, drizzle f. ON *mugga,* + -Y²]

mŭ'gwort (-ērt) *n.* Wormwood plant, esp. *Artemisia vulgaris.* [OE *mucgwyrt* (as MIDGE, WORT)]

***mŭ'gwŭmp** *n.* Great man, boss; one who holds aloof from party politics; one who sits on the fence. [f. Algonquin *mugquomp* great chief]

Muhă'mmadan, Mohă'mmėdan, *n.* & *a.* (Person believing in Allah as God according to revelation) of Muhammad; Muslim; hence **~ISM** (3) *n.*, **~IZE** (3) *v.t.* [f. *Muhammad,* Arabian prophet d. 632 + -AN]

mūlă'ttō *n.* (*pl.* **~s** *or* ***~es**) & *a.* **1.** *n.* Offspring of White person and Negro. **2.** *a.* Of colour of mulattos, tawny. [f. Sp. *mulato* young mule, mulatto, irreg. f. *mulo* MULE¹]

mŭ'lberrȳ *n.* Tree of genus *Morus,* leaves of which are much used for feeding silkworms; its purple or white fruit; **paper ~**, small Asiatic tree (*Broussonetia papyrifera*) of same family, whose bark is used for paper-making. [ME *mol-, mool-, mulberry,* dissim. f. *murberie* f. OE **murberie, mōrberie,* = OHG *mōrberi, murberi* f. L *morum*; see BERRY¹]

mŭ'lch (*or* -lsh) *n.*, & *v.t.* **1.** *n.* Mixture of wet straw, leaves, etc., spread to protect roots of newly planted trees etc. **2.** *v.t.* Treat with mulch. [prob. use as n. of *mulsh* soft; cf. dial. *melsh* mild f. OE *melsc*]

mŭlct *n.*, & *v.t.* **1.** *n.* Fine imposed for offence. **2.** *v.t.* Punish (person) by fine (*in* amount), fine (person amount); deprive (person etc. *of*); swindle (person), obtain by swindling. [earlier *mult(e)* f. L *mul(c)ta*; v. thr. F *mul(c)ter* & L *mulctare*]

mūle[1] *n.* **1.** Offspring (usu. sterile) of he-ass and mare, or (pop.) of she-ass and stallion (prop. *hinny*), used as beast of draught and burden and undeservedly noted for obstinacy; stupid or obstinate person; hybrid plant or animal; ~ **canary,** cross between canary and other finch. **2.** Kind of spinning-machine invented by Crompton, intermediate between earlier types. [ME f. OF *mul(e)* f. L *mulus mula*]

mūle[2]. Var. of MEWL.

mūle[3] *n.* Backless slipper. [F]

mūlėteer′ *n.* Mule-driver. [f. F *muletier* (*mulet* dim. of OF *mul* MULE[1]; see -ET[1], -EER)]

mŭ′lga *n.* (Austral.) Widely distributed shrubby acacia (*Acacia aneura*); its wood; scrub, bush. [Aboriginal]

mūliĕ′brĭtў *n.* Womanhood; normal characteristics of a woman (opp. *virility*); softness, effeminacy. [f. LL *muliebritas* f. L *mulier* woman; see -ITY]

mū′lĭsh *a.* Like a mule; stubborn; hence ~LY[2] *adv.*, ~NESS *n.* [f. MULE[1] + -ISH[1]]

mŭll[1] *n.* Thin soft plain muslin. [abbr. of *mulmull* f. Hindi *malmal*]

mŭll[2] *n.*, & *v.t.* (colloq.) **1.** *n.* ||Muddle, mess, (*make a mull of*). **2.** *v.t.* ||Make a mull of (catch at cricket etc.); *ponder (*over*). [perh. f. *mull* grind to powder, ME *mul* dust f. MDu.]

mŭll[3] *v.t.* Make (wine, beer) into hot drink with sugar, spices, egg-yolk, etc. [17th c.; orig. unkn.]

mŭll[4] *n.* (Sc.) Promontory (*Mull of Kintyre*). [ME; cf. Gael. *maol*, Icel. *múli*]

mŭll[5] *n.* (Sc.) Snuff-box. [var. of MILL[1], box orig. having a grinder]

mŭll[6] *n.* Humus formed under non-acid conditions. [G, f. Da. *muld*]

mŭ′llah (-*a*) *n.* Muslim learned in Islamic theology and sacred law. [f. Pers., Turk., Urdu *mullā* f. Arab. *mawlā*]

mŭ′llein (-lĭn) *n.* Herbaceous plant of genus *Verbascum*, with woolly leaves and yellow flowers. [ME, f. OF *moleine* f. Gaulish **melena*]

mŭ′ller *n.* Stone etc. used for grinding powders etc. on slab. [ME, perh. f. AF **moloir* (*moldre* grind; see -ER[2])]

mŭ′llėt *n.* Fish of family Mullidae (**red** ~) or Mugilidae (**grey** ~), valued for food. [ME, f. OF *mulet* dim. f. L *mullus* red mullet f. Gk *mollos*]

***mŭ′llĭgan** *n.* (colloq.) Stew of odds and ends of food. [perh. f. name *Mulligan*]

mŭllĭgataw′nў *n.* Highly seasoned soup orig. from India; ~ **paste,** curry paste used for this. [f. Tamil *milagutannīr* pepper-water]

mŭ′llĭgrŭbs (-z) *n. pl.* Depression of spirits; stomach-ache. [16th c. *mulliegrums*, of unkn. orig.]

mŭ′llion (-yon) *n.* Vertical bar dividing lights in window (cf. TRANSOM); hence ~ED[2] (-yond) *a.* [prob. metathetic f. MONIAL]

mŭ′llock *n.* **1.** (Austral. & dial.) Refuse, rubbish. **2.** (Austral.) Rock containing no gold; refuse from which gold has been extracted; ridicule. [ME dim. of *mul* dust, rubbish, f. MDu.; see -OCK]

mŭ′lloway (-owā) *n.* (Austral.) Large marine food-fish (*Sciaena antarctica*). [19th c.; orig. unkn.]

mŭltă′ngūlar (-ngg-) *a.* Many-angled. [f. med. L *multangularis* (as MULTI-, ANGULAR)]

mŭltē′ĭtў *n.* (arch.) Manifoldness. [f. L *multus* many; cf. HAECCEITY]

mŭ′lti- *pref.* Many; as: ~**colour**(**ed**), of many colours; ~**fid,** (Bot. & Zool.) cleft into many parts; ~**foil,** (Archit.) ornament consisting of more than 5 foils; ~**form,** having many forms, of many kinds; so ~**for′mity** *n.*; ~**la′teral,** having many sides, (of agreement, treaty, etc.) in which three or more parties participate; ~**li′ngual,** in or using many languages; ~**millionair′e,** person with fortune of several millions; ~**na′tional,** operating in several countries; ~**no′mial** *a.* & *n.*, = POLYNOMIAL [after *binomial*]; ~**parous** (-ĭ′p-), (1) bringing forth many young at a birth, (2) having borne more than one child; ~**par′tite,** divided into many parts; ~**phase,** (Electr.) = POLYPHASE; ~**po′lar,** having many POLE[2]s; ~**-purpose,** serving more than one purpose; ~**ra′cial,** (composed) of many races of men; ~**-role,** having more than one role or function; ~**-stage,** (of rocket etc.) having several stages of operation; ~**-storey,** having several (esp. similarly designed) storeys; ~**va′lent,** (Chem.) having a valence of more than two, or a variable valence; ~**valve,** (of shell etc.) having several valves; ~ **vocal** (-ĭ′v-), having many meanings; ~**-way,** having several paths of communication etc. [L (*multus* much, many; see -I-)]

mŭltĭfār′ĭous *a.* Having great variety; (w. *pl. n.*) many and various; hence ~LY[2] *adv.*, ~NESS *n.* [f. L *multifarius* + -OUS]

mŭ′ltĭple *a.* & *n.* **1.** *a.* Having several or many parts, elements, or individual components; (Bot., of fruit) collective; (w. *pl. n.*) many and various. **2.** ~**-choice,** (of question in examination) accompanied by several possible answers from which what is incorrect is to be deleted; *multiple* PERSONALITY; ~**poi′nding,** (Sc. Law) action by holder of goods etc. claimed by more than one other person, causing them to interplead; *multiple* SCLEROSIS; ||~ **shop** or **store** (with branches in various places); *multiple* STANDARD; ~ **star,** several stars so close as to seem one, esp. when forming a connected system. **3.** *n.* Quantity that contains another some number of times without remainder (*56 is a multiple of 7*; **least** or **lowest common** ~, least quantity that is a multiple of two or more given quantities); multiple shop or store. [F, f. LL *multiplus* f. L (as foll.)]

mŭ′ltĭplĕx *a.*, & *v.t.* **1.** *a.* Manifold, of many elements; involving simultaneous transmission of several messages along a channel of communication. **2.** *v.t.* Transmit thus. [L (as MULTI-, -*plex* -*plicis* -fold)]

mŭ′ltĭplĭcable *a.* Multipliable. [OF, or f. med. L *multiplicabilis* f. L (as MULTIPLY[1]; see -ABLE)]

mŭltĭplĭcă′nd *n.* Quantity to be multiplied by MULTIPLIER. [f. med. L *multiplicandus* gerundive of L *multiplicare* (as MULTIPLY[1]; see -ND[1])]

mŭltĭplĭcā′tion *n.* Multiplying, esp. the arithmetical process; ~ **sign,** ×, as in 2×3; ~ **table,** table of products of factors (esp. from 1 to 12) taken in pairs; so **mŭltĭplĭ′c**ATIVE *a.* [ME f. OF, or f. L *multiplicatio* (as MULTIPLY[1]; see -ATION)]

mŭltĭplĭ′cĭtў *n.* Manifold variety; **a, the,** ~ (great number) **of.** [f. LL *multiplicitas* (as MULTIPLEX; see -ITY)]

mŭ′ltĭplĭer *n.* In vbl senses; quantity by which MULTIPLICAND is multiplied; (Econ.) factor by which an increment of income exceeds the resulting increment of saving or investment; (Electr.) instrument for increasing a small current etc. so as to make it more easily used or measured. [ME, f. foll. + -ER[1]]

mŭ′ltĭpl|ў[1] *v.* **1.** *v.t.* Produce large number of (instances etc.); breed (animals), propagate (plants). **2.** *v.i.* Increase in number esp. by procreation. **3.** *v.t.* Obtain from (number, or abs.) another that is a specified number of times its value (*multiply 6 by 4* or *4 by 6* or arch. *6 into 4 and get 24*; *multiplying by ⅓ is the same as dividing by 3*). **4.** Hence ~**IABLE** *a.* [ME, f. OF *multiplier* f. L *multiplicare* (as MULTIPLEX)]

mŭ'ltiplȳ[2] *adv.* In adj. senses. [f. MULTIPLE + -LY[2]]

mŭ'ltitūde *n.* Numerousness; great number (*of*); large gathering of people, crowd; **the ~**, the common people; **noun of ~**, collective noun. [ME f. OF, f. L *multitudo -dinis* (*multus* many; see -TUDE)]

mŭltitū'dinous *a.* Very numerous; consisting of many individuals or elements; (of ocean etc.) vast; hence ~LY[2] *adv.*, ~NESS *n.* [f. L (as prec.) + -OUS]

mŭltivẽr'sitȳ *n.* Large university with many different departments. [f. MULTI- + UNIVERSITY]

multum in parvo (mŏoltum ĭn pâr'vō; *or* mŭ-) *n.* Much in small compass. [L = much in little]

||**mŭ'lture** *n.* Toll of grain or flour paid to miller. [ME, f. OF *mo(u)lture* f. med. L *molitura* (*molere molit-* grind; see -URE)]

mŭm[1] *int.* & *a.* (colloq.) **1.** *int.* Silence! (esp. *mum's the word*). **2.** *a.* Silent (*keep mum*). [ME, imit. of closed lips]

mŭm[2] *v.i.* (**-mm-**). Act in dumb show. [cf. prec., and MLG *mummen*]

mŭm[3] *n.* (Hist.) Kind of beer orig. brewed in Brunswick. [f. G *mumme*]

||**mŭm**[4] *n.* (colloq.) = MUMMY[2]. [abbr.]

mŭ'mble *v.* & *n.* **1.** *v.i.* Speak indistinctly. **2.** *v.t.* Utter indistinctly; bite, chew, (as) with toothless gums. **3.** *n.* Indistinct utterance. [ME *momele*, as MUM[1], -LE 3; cf. LG *mummelen*]

mŭmbō-jŭ'mbō *n.* (*pl.* ~**s**). Meaningless ritual; language or action intended to mystify or confuse; object of senseless veneration. [f. *Mumbo Jumbo*, grotesque idol said to have been worshipped by some Negro tribes]

mŭ'mchance (-ahns) *a.* & *adv.* (arch. or dial.) Silent(ly), saying nothing. [orig. n., = dumb show, f. MLG *mummenschanze* masked serenade (*mummen* f. OF as foll.; *schanz* f. OF CHANCE[1])]

mŭ'mmer *n.* Actor in traditional dumb show or (arch. sl.) in theatre. [ME, f. OF *momeur* (*momer* MUM[2]; see -ER[2])]

mŭ'mmerȳ *n.* Performance by mummers; ridiculous (esp. religious) ceremonial. [f. OF *momerie* (as prec.; see -ERY)]

mŭ'mmi|fȳ *v.t.* Preserve (body) as mummy; shrivel, dry up, (tissues etc., esp. in *p.p.*); hence ~FICA'TION *n.* [f. foll. + -FY]

mŭ'mmȳ[1] *n.* **1.** Body of human being or animal embalmed for burial esp. in ancient Egypt; dried-up body. **2.** Pulpy substance or mass, esp. *beat* (thing) *to a mummy*. **3.** Rich brown pigment. [f. F *momie* f. med. L *mumia* f. Arab. *mūmiyā* f. Pers. *mūm* wax]

||**mŭ'mmȳ**[2] *n.* (colloq.) Mother. [imit. of child's pronunc.; cf. MAMMA[1], -Y[3]]

mŭmp[1] *v.i.* (arch. or dial.) Be silent and sullen; assume demure expression, whence ~'ING[2] *a.* [imit. of mouth-shape]

||**mŭmp**[2] *v.i.* (arch. or dial.) Beg, go about begging. [prob. f. obs. Du. *mompen* cheat]

mŭmps *n. pl.* (treated as *sing.*) Contagious and infectious virus disease with swelling of parotid glands; sulks, whence **mŭ'mp**ISH[1] *a.* [16th c., f. MUMP[1]]

mŭnch *v.t.* Eat (food, or abs.) with much action of jaws, as cattle chew fodder, and usu. with evident enjoyment. [ME, imit.; cf. CRUNCH]

Mŭnchau'sen (-z-) *n.* Extravagantly mendacious story(-teller). [f. Baron ~, hero of book of fantastic adventures written in English by R. E. Raspe, a German (1785), perh. based on life of Baron K. F. von *Münchhausen*, Ger. soldier d. 1797]

mŭ'ndāne *a.* Of this world, worldly; of the universe, cosmic; dull, routine; hence ~LY[2] (-nlĭ) *adv.*, ~NESS (-n-n-) *n.* [ME, f. OF *mondain* f. LL *mundanus* f. L *mundus* world; see -ANE]

mŭ'ngō (-nggō) *n.* (*pl.* ~**s**). Wool from heavily felted substance, used in making cloth of poorer quality than shoddy. [poss. f. dial. *mong* mixture & Sc. man's Christian name *Mungo* applied to Yorks. dogs]

Mū'nĭch (-k) *n.* Act of appeasement between nations or other groups. [f. the agreement to dismember Czechoslovakia made in 1938 at ~ in S. Germany]

mūnĭ'cĭpal *a.* **1.** Of or under local self-government or corporate government of city or town; hence ~ISM (2), ~IST (2, 3), *ns.*, ~IZE (3) *v.t.* **2.** Carried on etc. by a municipality (*municipal debt, restaurant, trading, undertaking*); *municipal* CORPORATION. **3.** Of particular State, opp. to international. **4.** Hence ~LY[2] *adv.* [f. L *municipalis* (*municipium* f. *municeps -cipis* citizen who had privileges of Roman citizens f. *munia* civic offices + root of *capere* take); see -AL]

mūnĭcĭpă'lĭtȳ *n.* Town or district, having local self-government; governing body of this. [f. F *municipalité* (*municipal*, as prec.; see -ITY)]

mūnĭ'fĭc|ent *a.* Splendidly generous, bountiful; hence or cogn. ~ENCE *n.*, ~**ent**LY[2] *adv.* [f. L *munificent-*, var. stem of *munificus* (*munus* gift; see -FIC, -ENT)]

mū'nĭment *n.* (usu. in *pl.*) Document kept as evidence of rights or privileges; archives. [ME f. OF, f. L *munimentum* defence, in med. L title-deed (*munire -it-* fortify; see -MENT)]

mūnĭ'tion *n.*, & *v.t.* **1.** *n.* (in *pl.*) Military weapons, ammunition, equipment, and stores; hence ~ER[1] *n.*, person who makes or supplies munitions. **2.** *v.t.* Supply with munitions. [F, f. L *munitio -onis* fortification (as prec.; see -ITION)]

munnion. Var. of MULLION.

munshi. Var. of MOONSHEE.

mŭ'ntjăk, -ăc, *n.* Small deer of S.E. Asia, of genus *Muntiacus*, the male with tusks and small antlers. [f. Sundanese *minchek*]

Mŭntz (-ts) *n.* ~ (**metal**), alloy (60% copper, 40% zinc) used for sheathing ships etc. [f. G. F. ~, Engl. manufacturer d. 1857]

mū'ŏn *n.* (Phys.) Unstable elementary particle like electron but with mass about 200 times greater. [f. μ (MU) as symbol for it + -ON]

mūr'age *n.* (Hist.) Tax levied for building or repairing walls of town. [ME f. OF, in med. L *muragium* f. OF *mur* f. L *murus* wall; see -AGE]

mūr'al *a.* & *n.* **1.** *a.* Of or like a wall; on a wall (*mural paintings*); ~ **crown,** (Rom. Ant.) crown or garland given to soldier who first scaled wall of besieged town. **2.** *n.* Mural painting etc. [F, f. L *muralis* (*murus* wall; see -AL)]

mûr'der[1] *n.* Unlawful killing of human being with malice aforethought; (fig.) highly dangerous or troublesome state of affairs; exclamation of alarm (also as *int.*); **cry blue ~**, (sl.) make extravagant outcry; **get away with ~**, (sl.) do whatever one wishes; JUDICIAL *murder*; (prov.) ~ **will out** (cannot be hidden). [OE *morthor*, = Goth. *maurthr* f. Gmc **murthram* f. IE **mrt-*, & OF *murdre* f. Gmc]

mûr'der[2] *v.t.* Kill (human being) unlawfully with malice aforethought; kill wickedly or inhumanly; (colloq.) utterly defeat, spoil by bad execution, mispronunciation, etc.; hence ~ER[1], ~ESS[1], *ns.* [ME, f. prec.]

mûr'derous *a.* (Of person, weapon, action, etc.) capable of, bent on, involving, murder; hence ~LY[2] *adv.* [f. MURDER[1] + -OUS]

mūre *v.t.* Immure; wall or shut *up*. [ME, f. OF *murer* (*mur*; see MURAGE)]

mūr'|ĕx *n.* (*pl.* ~**ices** *pr.* -ĭsēz, *or* ~**exes**). Mollusc of genus *Murex*, yielding purple dye. [L]

mūrĭă'tĭc *a.* (arch.) Hydrochloric *acid*; so **mūr'ĭATE**[1] (3) *n.*, chloride. [f. L *muriaticus* pickled in brine (*muria*; see -ATIC)]

mūr'ĭne *a.* Of or like mice. [f. L *murinus* (*mus muris* mouse; see -INE[1])]

mûrk *n.* & *a.* **1.** *n.* Darkness; air obscured by fog etc. **2.** *a.* (arch.) (Of night, day, place, etc.) dark; misty, dense. [prob. f. Scand.; cf. ON *myrkr*]

mûr'k|ȳ *a.* Dark, gloomy; (of darkness) thick; dirty; hence ~**ĭLY**[2] *adv.*, ~**ĭNESS** *n.* [ME, f. prec. + -Y[2]]

mûr'mur[1] *n.* Subdued continuous sound, as of waves, brook, etc.; (Med.) such sound heard in auscultation of heart and indicating abnormality; subdued expression of discontent; softly spoken or nearly inarticulate word or speech; hence ~OUS *a.* [ME, f. OF *murmure* or f. L *murmur*; cf. foll.]

mûr'mur[2] *v.* **1.** *v.i.* Make subdued continuous sound; complain in low tones, grumble, (*at, against*). **2.** *v.t.* Utter (words) in low voice. [ME, f. OF *murmurer* f. L *murmurare*; cf. Gk *mormurō* (of water) roar, Skr. *marmaras* noisy]

mûr'phȳ *n.* (sl.) Potato. [Ir. surname]

mŭ'rra. See MURRHINE.

mŭ'rrain (-rĭn) *n.* Infectious disease in cattle; (arch.) **a** ~ (plague) **on you!** [ME, f. AF *moryn*, OF *morine* (*morir* f. Rom. **morire* for L *mori* die)]

mŭ'rrey *a.* & *n.* (arch.) (Of) the colour of a mulberry, purple-red; (Her.) sanguine. [ME, f. OF *moré* f. med. L *moratus* (*morum* mulberry; see -Y[4])]

mŭ'rrhĭne (-rĭn) *a.* Of a precious substance called **murra,** used in ancient Rome; ~ **glass,** modern delicate glassware from the East, with coloured metal particles embedded in it. [f. L *murr(h)inus* (*murra* f. late Gk *morria*; see -INE[1])]

murther. Var. (arch.) of MURDER[1,2].

Mus. B(ac). *abbrs.* Bachelor of Music. [f. L *Musicae Baccalaureus*]

mŭ'scadĭne *n.* Musk-flavoured kind of grape. [perh. Engl. form. f. Prov. MUSCAT; see -INE[4]]

mŭ'scarĭne *n.* Poisonous alkaloid from fungus *Amanita muscaria.* [f. L *muscarius* (*musca* fly; see -ARY[1], -INE[5])]

mŭ'scat *n.* Muscadine; strong sweet white wine from muscadines. [F, f. Prov. *muscat muscade* a. (*musc* MUSK; see -ATE[1])]

mŭscatĕ'l, -dĕ'l, *ns.* = prec.; raisin from muscadine. [ME f. OF, f. Prov. **muscadel* dim. of *muscat* (see prec.)]

mŭ'scle (-sel) *n.*, & *v.i.* **1.** *n.* Any of the contractile fibrous bands or bundles that produce movement in animal body; **not move a** ~, be perfectly motionless. **2.** That part of the animal body which is composed of muscles, chief constituent of flesh; (muscular) power. **3.** ~**-bound,** with muscles stiff and inelastic through excessive exercise or training; ~**man** (with highly developed muscles, esp. as intimidator). **4.** Hence ~LESS (-l-l-) *a.* **5.** *v.i.* (sl.) ~ **in,** intrude by violent means. [F, f. L *musculus* dim. of *mus* mouse, f. fancied mouselike form of some muscles]

mŭscŏ'log|ȳ *n.* Bryology, study of mosses; so ~IST (3) *n.* [f. mod. L *muscologia* f. L *muscus* moss; see -LOGY]

mŭscova'dō (-vah'-) *n.* (*pl.* ~**s**). Unrefined sugar got from juice of sugar-cane by evaporation and draining off molasses. [f. Sp. *mascabado* (sugar) of lowest quality]

mŭ'scovīte[1] *n.* Common mica. [f. obs. syn. MUSCOVY *glass* + -ITE[1]]

Mŭ'scovīte[2] *n.* & *a.* (arch.) Russian; (citizen) of Moscow. [f. mod. L *Muscovita* (*Muscovia* = foll.; see -ITE[1])]

Mŭ'scovȳ *n.* **1.** (arch.) Russia. **2.** ~ **duck,** tropical Amer. duck (*Cairina moschata*) with slight smell of musk. [f. obs. F *Muscovie* f. mod. L *Moscovia* f. Russ. *Moskva* Moscow]

mŭ'scūlar *a.* Of or affecting the muscles; having well-developed muscles; ~ **Christianity,** Christian life of cheerful physical activity as described in writings of C. Kingsley; *muscular* DYSTROPHY; *muscular* STOMACH; hence **mŭscūlă'rITY** *n.* [f. earlier *musculous* (as MUSCLE; see -AR[1])]

mŭ'scūlature *n.* Muscular system of body or organ. [F, f. L (as MUSCLE; see -URE)]

Mus. D(oc). *abbrs.* Doctor of Music. [f. L *Musicae Doctor*]

mūse[1] (-z) *n.* **1. The Muses,** (Gk & Rom. Myth.) nine goddesses, daughters of Zeus and Mnemosyne, inspirers of poetry, music, drama, etc. **2.** (**The**) ~, poet's inspiring goddess, poet's genius. [ME f. OF, or f. L f. Gk *mousa*]

mūse[2] (-z) *v.* & *n.* (literary). **1.** *v.i.* Ponder, reflect, (*on, upon*); gaze meditatively (*on* scene etc.). **2.** *v.t.* Say meditatively. **3.** *n.* (arch.) Fit of abstraction. [ME, f. OF *muser* to waste time f. Rom. **musare*, perh. f. med. L *musum* muzzle]

mūsĕ'tte (-z-) *n.* Kind of small bagpipe; soft pastoral tune imitating bagpipe's sound; dance for which this served; reed stop on organ; *small knapsack. [ME f. OF, dim. of *muse* bagpipe; see -ETTE]

mūsē'um (-z-) *n.* Building used for storing and exhibition of objects illustrating antiquities, natural history, arts, etc.; ~ **piece,** specimen of art, manufacture, etc., fit for a museum, (derog.) old-fashioned or quaint person, machine, etc.; hence **mūsėŏ'LOGY** (-z-) *n.* [L, f. Gk *mouseion* seat of the Muses (*mousa*)]

mŭsh[1] *n.* Soft pulp; *maize porridge; feeble sentimentality; hence ~'Y[2] *a.* [app. var. of MASH[1]]

mŭsh[2] *v.i.*, & *n.* (N. Amer.) (Go on) journey across snow with dog-sledge; (in *imper.*, as command to dogs pulling sledge) get moving. [prob. corrupt. f. F *marchons* imper. of *marcher* advance]

mŭ'shrōōm (*or* -ōōm) *n.*, & *v.i.* **1.** *n.* Edible fungus, esp. *Agaricus campestris*, with stem and domed cap, proverbial for rapid growth (~ **growth** etc., sudden development or thing suddenly developed); (fig.) upstart; ~ (**cloud**), cloud of mushroom shape esp. from nuclear explosion; ~**-colour(ed)**, pale yellowish-brown. **2.** *v.i.* Gather mushrooms; spring up rapidly; expand and flatten like mushroom cap. [ME, f. OF *mousseron* f. LL *mussirio -onis*]

mū'sĭc (-z-) *n.* **1.** Art of combining sounds of voice(s) or instrument(s) to achieve beauty of form and expression of emotion; sounds so produced; pleasant sound, e.g. song of bird, murmur of brook, cry of hounds; **set** (poem etc.) **to** ~, provide it with music to which it may be sung; ~ **to** one's **ears,** something very pleasant to hear; *music of the* SPHERES. **2.** Musical compositions; written or printed score of musical composition. **3. Face the** ~, face one's critics etc., not shirk consequences; **rough** ~, noisy uproar, esp. with vexatious intention. **4.** *~ **box,** = MUSICAL *box*; ~ **drama,** opera without formal arias etc. and governed by dramatic considerations; ‖~**-hall,** (place for) singing, dancing, variety, and other entertainments; ~**-paper** (with printed staves etc. for writing music score); ~**-stool** (with adjustable height of seat, for pianist). [ME, f. OF *musique* f. L f.

Gk *mousikē* (*tekhnē* art) of the Muses (*mousa* MUSE¹; see -IC)]

mū'sĭcal (-z-) *a.* & *n.* **1.** *a.* Of music; (of sounds, voice, etc.) melodious, harmonious; fond of or skilled in music; set to or accompanied by music. **2.** ||~ **box,** mechanical musical instrument played by causing toothed cylinder to strike comblike metal plate within box; ~ **chairs,** parlour game in which players circulate round chairs one fewer than they till music ceases, when the one who finds no seat is eliminated, and a chair is removed before the next round; ~ **comedy,** light dramatic entertainment of songs, dialogue, and dancing connected by a slender plot; ~ **film** (in which music is an important feature); ~ **glasses,** instrument in which notes are produced by rubbing graduated glass bowls or tubes; *musical* INSTRUMENT; ~ **saw,** bent saw played with violin-bow; *musical* SOUND². **3.** Hence ~ITY (-ă'l-), ~NESS, *ns.*, ~LY² *adv.* **4.** *n.* Musical film or comedy. [ME f. OF, f. med. L *musicalis* f. L *musica*; see prec., -AL]

***mūsĭca'le** (-zĭkah'l) *n.* Musical party. [F, fem. a. (as prec.)]

mūsĭ'cian (-zĭ'shan) *n.* Person skilled in science or practice of music. [ME, f. OF *musicien* (*musique*; see MUSIC, -ICIAN)]

mūsĭcŏ'log|ў (-z-) *n.* Study of music other than that directed to proficiency in performance or composition; hence ~IST (3) *n.*, **mūsĭcolŏ'g**ICAL (-z-) *a.* [f. F *musicologie* or MUSIC + -O- + -LOGY]

musique concrète (mūzēk kawṅkrĕ't) *n.* = CONCRETE¹ *music.* [F]

mŭsk *n.* **1.** Odoriferous reddish-brown substance secreted in gland by male musk-deer, used as basis of perfumes and as stimulant etc.; plant with musky smell, or *Mimulus moschatus* (which formerly smelt of musk). **2.** **~-deer,** small hornless ruminant of Central Asia, of genus *Moschus*; **~-duck,** (1) = MUSCOVY *duck*, (2) Australian duck (*Biziura lobata*) with musky smell; **~-melon,** common melon (*Cucumis melo*); **~-ox,** shaggy ruminant with curved horns (*Ovibos moschatus*) found in Arctic America; **~-rat,** (fur of) large N. Amer. aquatic rodent with musky smell (*Ondatra zibethica*); **~-rose,** rambling rose (*Rosa moschata* etc.) with large white flowers having musky fragrance; **~--thistle,** nodding thistle (*Carduus nutans*), whose flowers have musky fragrance; **~-tree, -wood,** Australian tree esp. of genus *Olearia*, with musky smell. **3.** Hence ~'Y² *a.* [ME, f. LL *muscus* f. Pers. *mušk*, perh. f. Skr. *muska* scrotum (from shape of musk-deer's gland)]

mŭ'skĕg *n.* Level swamp or bog in Canada. [Cree]

***mŭ'skellŭnge** (-nj) *n.* = MASKINONGE. [Algonquian]

mŭ'skėt *n.* (Hist.) Infantry soldier's (esp. smooth-bored) light gun; **~-shot,** (range of) shot fired from musket; hence or cogn. ~EER' *n.*, soldier armed with musket, ~RY (1, 5) *n.* [f. F *mousquet* f. It. *moschetto* crossbow bolt (*mosca* fly)]

Mŭ'slĭm (*or* mŏŏ'-), **Mŏ'slem,** (*or* -z-) *a.* & *n.* Believer in Islam; Muhammadan. [f. Arab. *muslim*, part. of *aslama*; see ISLAM]

mŭ'slĭn (-z-) *n.* Fine delicately woven cotton fabric; *cotton cloth in plain weave; hence ~ED² (-nd) *a.* [f. F *mousseline* f. It. *mussolina* (*Mussolo* Mosul in Iraq, where it was made; see -INE¹)]

mŭ'smon *n.* Moufflon. [f. L *musimo* f. Gk *mousmōn*]

mŭ'squash (-ŏsh) *n.* (Fur of) MUSK-rat. [Algonquian]

***mŭss** *v.t.*, & *n.* (colloq.) **1.** *v.t.* ~ **(up)**, disarrange, throw into disorder. **2.** *n.* State of confusion, untidiness, mess; hence ~'Y² *a.* [app. var. of MESS¹]

mŭ'ssel *n.* Bivalve mollusc of genus *Mytilus* (marine, edible), *Unio* (freshwater, pearl--forming), etc.; ~ **plum,** (arch.) dark purple plum. [ME, f. OE *mus(c)le*, = OS, OHG *muscula*, & f. MLG *mussel*, f. Rom. **muscula* bivalve, fem. corresp. to L *musculus* (as MUSCLE)]

Mŭ'ssulman *n.* (*pl.* **~mans** *or* **~men**) & *a.* (arch.) Muslim. [f. Pers. *musulmān*, orig. a. f. *muslim* (as MUSLIM)]

mŭst¹ *n.* New wine; grape-juice before fermentation is complete. [OE, f. L *mustum* neut. (as n.) of *mustus* new]

mŭst² *n.* Mustiness, mould. [back form. f. MUSTY]

mŭst³, mŭsth (-t), *a.* & *n.* **1.** *a.* (Of male elephant or camel) in state of frenzy. **2.** *n.* This state. [f. Urdu f. Pers. *mast* intoxicated]

mŭst⁴ (*or, when unstressed,* must) *v. aux.* (*pres.* and *past* **must,** *neg.* **must not,** (colloq.) **mustn't** *pr.* mŭ'sent; no other parts used) & *n.* **1.** *v.* Be obliged to (do) (*you must find it*, opp. *you do not have to* or *need not find it*, past *you had to find it*; *you knew you must find it*; *it must be found*; *you must not do it*, opp. *you may do it*; *it must not be done*); (interrog., iron.) *must you slam the door?*; (ellipt.) *I must* (go) *away*; *if I must, I will*; *I must down to the seas again.* **2.** Ought to (do) (w. necessity less emphasized: *we must see what can be done*; *I must ask you to retract that*); **you ~ know,** I now tell you; **I ~ say** (cannot refrain from saying). **3.** Be certain to (do) (*you must lose whichever happens*, opp. *you cannot lose*); *you* ~ **be** (surely are) *aware of this, joking, the secretary*; *he* ~ **be** (clearly is) *mad*; (as past tense, reporting reflection made at the time) *it was too late now to retreat, he must make good his word or incur lasting disgrace*; (as past or historic present, w. reference to perverse destiny) *just as I was getting better, what must I do but break my leg?, just as I was busiest, he must come worrying.* **4.** ~ **have** done, (1) surely did or has done (*you must have known quite well what I meant*; *it must have stopped raining by now*), (2) necessarily would have done (*you must have caught it if you had run*); *must* NEEDS. **5.** (w. neg. belonging in sense to dependent vb.; cf. MAY¹) *you must not infer* (must avoid the inference), *you must never contradict.* **6.** *n.* (colloq.) Thing that cannot or should not be overlooked or missed. [OE *mōste* past of *mōt* may, pret.-pres. = OS *mōt*, *muot*, OHG *muoz*, Goth. *gamōtan* find room]

***mustache.** See MOUSTACHE.

musta'chiō (-ah'shō) *n.* (*pl.* ~s). (arch.) Moustache; hence ~ED² (-ōd) *a.* [f. Sp. *mostacho* & f. It. (as MOUSTACHE)]

mŭ'stăng *n.* Wild horse of Mexico and California; ~ (small red Texas) **grape.** [f. Sp. *mestengo* f. *mesta* company of graziers, & Sp. *mostrenco*]

mŭ'stard *n.* Plant of genus *Brassica* with pods and yellow flowers, esp. **black** and **white** ~, seeds of which are ground, made into paste, and used as condiment (||**English** ~) or for poultice or ~ **plaster**; *(sl.) thing that provides zest; ***cut the** ~, (sl.) reach requisite standard; **grain of ~ seed,** small thing capable of vast development (Matt. 13:31); KEEN³ *as mustard*; ||~ **and cress,** white mustard with cress used in seed-leaf for salad; **field** ~, charlock; ||**French** ~ (mixed with vinegar); ~ **gas,** colourless oily liquid, whose vapour is a powerful irritant and vesicant; **~-pot** (for table mustard). [ME, f. OF *mo(u)starde*, f. Rom. **mosto* MUST¹; orig. the condiment as prepared w. must]

mŭ'ster¹ *n.* Assembling of men for inspection

etc. (**pass ~**, be accepted as adequate); assembly, collection; **~-book** (for registering military forces); **~-roll,** official list of officers and men in army or ship's company (lit. or fig.). [ME f. OF *mo(u)stre* f. Rom. n. (**mostrare* v. f. L *monstrare* show)]

mŭ'ster² *v.* **1.** *v.t.* Collect (orig. soldiers) for inspection, to check numbers, etc.; ***~ in,** enrol (recruits); ***~ out,** discharge (soldiers). **2.** *v.t.* & *i.* Collect, get together. **3.** *v.t.* ~ (**up**), summon (courage, strength, etc.). [ME, f. OF *mo(u)strer* f. L (as prec.)]

musth. See MUST³.

mŭ'st|ȳ *a.* Mouldy; of mouldy or stale smell or taste; (fig.) stale, antiquated; hence **~ĭ**NESS *n.* [perh. alt. f. *moisty* (MOIST) by assoc. w. MUST¹]

mū'table *a.* Liable to change; fickle; hence **mūt**ABI'LITY *n.* [f. L *mutabilis* (*mutare* change; see -ABLE)]

mū'tagen *n.* (Biol.) Agent causing mutation; hence ~IC (-ĕ'n-) *a.* [f. MUTATION + -GEN]

mū'tant *a.* & *n.* (Biol.) (Form) resulting from mutation. [f. L *mutare* change; see -ANT]

mūtā'te *v.t.* & *i.* (Cause to) undergo mutation. [back form. f. foll.]

mūtā'tion *n.* **1.** Change, alteration; (Biol.) genetic change which when transmitted to offspring gives rise to heritable variation; **~ stop,** (Mus.) organ stop in which notes produced are not at normal pitch but at that of some harmonic (other than mere octaves). **2.** (Gram., of vowel) = UMLAUT, (of consonant in Celtic language) change determined by preceding word. [ME, f. L *mutatio* (*mūtare* change; see -ATION)]

mutatis mutandis (mōōtahtĭs mōōtă'ndĭs) *adv.* With due alteration of details (in comparing cases). [L]

mŭtch *n.* (Sc.) Woman's or child's linen cap. [ME, f. MDu. *mutse*, MHG *mütze* f. med. L *almucia* AMICE²]

mūte¹ *a.* & *n.* **1.** *a.* Silent; not emitting articulate sound; (of hounds) not giving tongue; (Law) **stand ~ of malice,** deliberately refuse to plead. **2.** (Of person or animal) dumb; not expressed in speech (*mute appeal, adoration*); temporarily bereft of speech; **~ swan,** common white swan. **3.** (Of consonant) plosive; (of letter) silent. **4.** Hence ~'LY² (-tlĭ) *adv.*, ~'NESS (-tn-) *n.* **5.** *n.* Mute consonant; dumb person (DEAF *mute*); actor whose part is in dumb show; dumb servant in Oriental countries; hired mourner; clamp on bridge for deadening resonance of strings of violin etc., pad or cone for deadening sound of wind instrument. [ME f. OF *muet*, dim. of *mu* f. L *mutus*; assim. to L]

mūte² *v.t.* Deaden, muffle, the sound of (esp. musical instrument); tone down. [f. prec.]

mūte³ *v.i.* & *t.* (arch.) (Of birds) void faeces, discharge thus. [ME, f. OF *meutir*, *esmeutir*, *esmeltir* f. Frank. **smeltjan* SMELT¹]

mū'tĭl|āte *v.t.* Deprive (person etc.) of limb or organ; cut off, destroy the use of, (limb etc.); render (book etc.) imperfect by excision etc.; hence or cogn. ~A'TION, **~āt**OR, *ns.* [f. L *mutilare* (*mutilus* maimed) + -ATE³]

mūtineer' *n.* One who mutinies. [f. F *mutinier* (*mutin* rebellious f. *muete* movement f. Rom. **movita* f. L *movēre* move)]

mū'tĭnous *a.* Rebellious; tending to mutiny; hence ~LY² *adv.* [f. obs. *mutine* rebellion f. F *mutin* (see prec.) + -OUS]

mū'tĭnȳ *n.*, & *v.i.* **1.** *n.* Open revolt against constituted authority, esp. by soldiers etc. against officers; **the** (**Indian** or **Sepoy**) **M~,** revolt of Bengal native troops, 1857–8; ‖**M~ Act,** (Hist.) annual ordinance dealing with offences against military and naval discipline. **2.** *v.i.* Revolt, engage in mutiny, (*against*, or abs.). [f. obs. *mutine* v. or n. f. as prec., + -Y¹]

mū'tĭsm *n.* Muteness; silence; dumbness. [f. F *mutisme* f. L (as MUTE¹); see -ISM]

mŭtt *n.* (sl.) Ignorant, stupid, or blundering person; (derog.) dog. [abbr. of *mutton-head*]

mŭ'tter *v.* & *n.* **1.** *v.i.* Speak low in barely audible manner; murmur, grumble, (*against*, *at*). **2.** *v.t.* Utter (words etc.) in low tone; (fig.) say in secret. **3.** *n.* Muttering; muttered words. [ME, f. as MUTE¹ + -ER⁵]

mŭ'tton *n.* Flesh of sheep as food; (joc.) sheep (**return to** one's **~s,** [after F phr.] come back to one's main topic); **dead as ~,** quite dead; **eat** person's **~,** (arch.) dine with him; LEG *of mutton*; **~-bird,** (Austral.) sooty shearwater; **~ chop,** (1) piece of mutton (usu. rib and half vertebra to which it is attached) for frying etc., (2) side-whiskers shaped like this; **~ dressed as lamb,** (colloq.) elderly woman got up to look young; **~-head,** (colloq.) dull, stupid person; hence ~Y² *a.* [ME f. OF *moton*, f. med. L *multo -onis* prob. f. Gaulish]

mū'tūal *a.* **1.** (Of feeling, action, etc.) felt, done, by each to(wards) the other (*mutual affection, benefit, suspicion*); standing in (specified) relation to each other (*mutual well-wishers*); **~ admiration society,** set of persons who overestimate each other's merits; ***~ fund,** unit trust; **~ induction** (Electr., between adjacent circuits); **~ insurance company** (in which some or all of the profits are divided among the policy-holders). **2.** (colloq.) Common to two or more persons (*our mutual friend, interest*). **3.** Hence ~ITY (-ă'l-) *n.*, ~LY² *adv.* [ME, f. OF *mutuel* f. L *mutuus* mutual, borrowed, cogn. w. *mutare* change; see -AL]

mū'tūal|ĭsm *n.* Doctrine that mutual dependence is necessary to social well-being; so ~IST (2) *n.* [f. prec. + -ISM]

***mū'tūel** *n.* Totalizator. [abbr. of PARI-MUTUEL]

mū'tūle *n.* (Archit.) Block projecting under cornice in Doric order. [F, f. L *mutulus*]

muu-muu (mōō'mōō) *n.* Woman's loose brightly-coloured dress. [Hawaiian]

mu'zhik. See MOUJIK.

‖**mŭzz** *v.t.* (sl.) Make muzzy. [18th c., of unkn. orig.]

mŭ'zzle¹ *n.* Projecting part of animal's head including nose and mouth; open end of firearm; contrivance of strap or wire put over animal's head to prevent its biting, eating, etc.; **~-loader,** gun that is loaded through the muzzle; **~ velocity** (with which projectile leaves muzzle of gun). [ME, f. OF *musel* f. Gallo-Rom. **musellum* dim. of med. L *musum*; cf. MUSE²]

mŭ'zzle² *v.t.* Put muzzle on (animal, its mouth, or fig. a person); impose silence upon; (Naut.) take in (sail). [ME, f. prec.]

mŭ'zz|ȳ *a.* Dull, spiritless; mentally hazy; stupid from liquor-drinking; hence **~ĭ**LY² *adv.*, **~ĭ**NESS *n.* [18th c., of unkn. orig.; cf. MUZZ]

M.V. *abbr.* motor vessel; muzzle velocity.

Mv *symb.* (arch.) mendelevium.

‖**M.V.O.** *abbr.* Member of the Royal Victorian Order.

MW *abbr.* megawatt(s).

mW *abbr.* milliwatt(s).

Mx. *abbr.* maxwell(s); Middlesex (former county in England).

mȳ (*or* mĭ) *poss. pron. attrib.* Of me (in *pred.* & abs. use, & arch. before vowel, **mine**: *my house*; *mine eyes have seen*; *this one is mine*; for phrs. see HER², HERS); *my* LADY, LORD; **me and mine** (my relatives); (in affectionate, sympathetic, jocular, or patronizing use, prefixed to some wds in voc.) *my boy, child, dear* (*fellow*), *friend*, *man*; (in excl. of surprise) *my!*, *oh my!*, *my* GOD!, *my* WORD[1]!, etc. [ME *mi*, reduced f. *min* MINE[3]]

M.Y. *abbr.* motor yacht.

myă'lgia (-*ja*) *n.* (Path.) Pain in muscle(s). [mod. L, f. Gk *mus* muscle; see -ALGIA]

mȳ'alism *n.* Sorcery akin to obeah, practised esp. in W. Indies. [f. *myal*, prob. of W. Afr. orig., + -ISM]

mȳ'all *n.* Austral. acacia, with hard scented wood used for fences and pipes. [f. Aboriginal *maiāl*]

myasthē'nia *n.* Weakness of muscles. [mod. L, f. Gk *mus* muscle; cf. ASTHENIA]

mycē'li|um *n.* (*pl.* **~a**). (Bot.) Vegetative part of fungus, consisting of microscopic threadlike hyphae; hence **~AL** *a.* [mod. L, f. Gk *mukēs* mushroom, after EPITHELIUM]

Mycēnae'an *a.* (Archaeol.) Of the late Helladic culture illustrated by remains at Mycenae in Greece, and by Homer. [f. L *Mycenaeus* + -AN]

mycŏ'log|y *n.* Study of fungi; hence **~IST** (3) *n.* [f. Gk *mukēs* mushroom + -O- + -LOGY]

mycorrhi'z|a (-orī'-) *n.* (*pl.* **~ae**). Symbiotic fungus in plant roots; hence **~AL** *a.* [mod. L, f. as prec. + Gk *rhiza* root]

mycō's|is *n.* (*pl.* **~es** *pr.* -ēz). Presence of, disease caused by, parasitic fungi. [f. as MYCOLOGY + -OSIS]

mycŏ'trophy *n.* Condition of plant having mycorrhizae in its roots and perhaps thus being helped to assimilate nutrients. [f. G *mykotrophie* f. as MYCOLOGY + Gk *trophē* nourishment]

mydrī'asis *n.* Excessive dilatation of eye-pupil. [L, f. Gk *mudriasis*]

mȳ'ėlin *n.* White substance forming sheath of nerve-fibres. [f. as foll. + -IN]

myėlī'tis *n.* Inflammation of spinal cord. [mod. L, f. Gk *muelos* marrow; see -ITIS]

myėlō'ma *n.* (*pl.* **~s** *or* **~ta**). Tumour of bone-marrow. [f. as prec. + -OMA]

mȳ'lodŏn *n.* Extinct gigantic sloth of genus *Mylodon*, with cylindrical teeth. [mod. L, f. Gk *mulē* mill, molar, + *odous odontos* tooth]

myna(h). See MINA[2].

mynheer' *n.* Title used of or to Dutch-speaking man, corresponding to Mr. or Sir; Dutchman. [f. Du. *mijnheer* (*mijn* my, *heer* master)]

myo- *comb. form.* Muscle, as: **~car'dium,** muscular substance of heart; **~logy** (-ŏ'l-), science of muscles. [f. Gk *mus muos* muscle + -O-]

mȳ'ōpe *n.* Short-sighted person. [F, f. LL f. Gk *muōps* (*muō* shut, *ōps* eye)]

myō'pia *n.* Short-sightedness, in which light from distant objects is focused before reaching retina and so forms blurred image; hence **myŏ'pIC** *a.* [mod. L, f. as prec.; see -IA[1]]

myō'sis. See MIOSIS.

myosō'tis, mȳ'osōte, *n.* Small plant of genus *Myosotis* with blue, pink, or white flowers, esp. forget-me-not. [f. L f. Gk *muosōtis* (*mus muos* mouse, *ous ōtos* ear)]

mȳ'riad *a.* & *n.* (poet. or rhet.) Ten thousand; (of) indefinitely great number. [f. LL f. Gk *murias -ados* (*murioi* 10,000)]

mȳ'riapŏd, mȳ'riopŏd, *a.* & *n.* (Arthropod) with many legs, of the group Myriapoda comprising centipedes and millepedes. [f. mod. L *Myriapoda* f. as prec. + Gk *pous podos* foot]

myr'midon (mẽr'-) *n.* Hired ruffian; base servant (**~ of the law,** policeman, bailiff, etc.). [f. L f. Gk *Murmidones* pl., warlike Thessalian people who followed Achilles to Troy]

myrŏ'balan *n.* Astringent plumlike fruit of E. Ind. tree of genus *Terminalia*, used in ink and in dyeing, tanning, etc. [F, or f. L *myrobalanum* f. Gk *murobalanos* (*muron* unguent, *balanos* acorn)]

myrrh[1] (mẽr) *n.* Gum resin from trees of genus *Commiphora*, used in perfumery and medicine, and in incense; hence **~'IC, ~'Y**[2], *adjs.* [OE *myrra, myrre*, = OS, OHG *myrra* f. L *myrr(h)a* f. Gk *murra*, of Semitic orig.]

myrrh[2] (mẽr) *n.* SWEET cicely. [f. L f. Gk *murris*]

myr'tle (mẽr'-) *n.* Plant of genus *Myrtus*, esp. **common ~,** shrub with dark shiny evergreen leaves, white scented flowers, and black berries, sacred to Venus; *periwinkle plant; BOG[1] *myrtle*; so **myrtA'CEOUS** (mẽrtā'shus) *a.*, of family Myrtaceae including myrtles. [ME, f. med. L *myrtilla, -us*, dim. of L f. Gk *murtos*]

myse'lf *pron.* **1.** Emphat. form corresp. to I[2] or ME[1] (*I saw it myself*); **I ~** (for my part) *am doubtful*; for phrs. see HERSELF 1. **2.** Refl. form corresp. to ME[1] (cf. HERSELF 2). **3.** (poet.) = I[2] (*myself am blind*). [f. ME[1] + SELF; *my-* partly after *herself* regarded as f. HER[2]]

mȳ'stagŏgue (-ŏg) *n.* Teacher of mystical doctrines, esp. (Gk Ant.) to candidates for initiation in Eleusinian and other mysteries; hence **mystagŏ'gIC(AL)** *adjs.* [F, or f. L f. Gk *mustagōgos* (*mustēs*, see MYSTIC; *-agōgos* -leading)]

mystēr'ious *a.* Full of, or wrapped in, mystery; (of person) delighting in mystery; hence **~LY**[2] *adv.*, **~NESS** *n.* [f. F *mystérieux* (*mystère* f. OF as foll.; see -OUS)]

mȳ'stery[1] *n.* **1.** Hidden or inexplicable matter; **make a ~ of,** treat as impressive secret. **2.** Secrecy, obscurity, (*is wrapped in mystery*); (practice of) making a secret of (unimportant) things. **3.** Religious truth divinely revealed, esp. one beyond human reason; religious rite, esp. (in *pl.*) Eucharist. **4.** (in *pl.*) Secret religious rites of Greeks, Romans, etc. **5.** Miracle play. **6. ~ (novel, play,** etc.), fictional work in which reader etc. is invited to try to identify murderer etc.; **~ ship,** warship disguised as tramp steamer etc. to decoy submarines in 1914–18 war; **~ tour** or **trip,** pleasure excursion to unspecified destination. [ME, f. AF **misterie*, OF *mistere* or f. L f. Gk *mustērion*, cogn. w. MYSTIC]

mȳ'stery[2] *n.* (arch.) Handicraft, trade, esp. (in indentures) *art and mystery*. [ME, f. med. L *mi(ni)sterium* (MINISTRY), assoc. w. prec.]

mȳ'stic *a.* & *n.* **1.** *a.* Spiritually allegorical or symbolic; occult, esoteric; of hidden meaning, mysterious; mysterious and awe-inspiring. **2.** *n.* One who seeks by contemplation and self-surrender to obtain union with or absorption into the Deity, or who believes in spiritual apprehension of truths beyond the understanding. **3.** Hence **~ISM** (3) *n.* (often derog.). [ME, f. OF *mystique* or f. L f. Gk *mustikos* (*mustēs* initiated person f. *muō* close eyes or lips, initiate; see -IC)]

mȳ'stical *a.* Of mystics or mysticism; having direct spiritual significance; hence **~LY**[2] *adv.* [ME, f. as prec. + -ICAL]

mȳ'sti|fy *v.t.* Hoax, make use of credulity of; bewilder; wrap up in mystery; so **~FICA'TION** *n.* [f. F *mystifier* (irreg. f. as MYSTIC OR MYSTERY[1]; see -FY)]

mysti'que (-tē'k) *n.* Atmosphere of mystery and veneration investing some creeds, doctrines, arts, professions, etc., or personages; any professional skill or technique which mystifies and impresses the layman. [F, f. OF as MYSTIC]

myth *n.* Traditional narrative usu. involving supernatural or fancied persons etc. and embodying popular ideas on natural or social phenomena etc.; allegory (*Platonic myth*); fictitious person or thing or idea; so **~'IC(AL)** *adjs.*, **mȳ'thicalLY**[2] *adv.* [f. mod. L *mythus* f. LL *mythos* f. Gk *muthos*]

mȳ'thic|ize, -|ise (-īz), *v.t.* Treat (story etc.) as a myth, interpret mythically; so **~ISM** (1), **~IST** (1), *ns.* [f. MYTHIC + -IZE]

mytho- *comb. form.* Myth, as: **~ge'nesis,** production of myths; **~grapher** (-ŏ'g-), compiler of myths; **~graphy** (-ŏ'g-), representation of myths in plastic art; **~ma'nia,** excessive tendency to tell lies; **~poe'ia** (-pē'*a*), construction of myths; **~poe'ic** (-pē'ĭk), making, or productive of, myths. [f. Gk *muthos* myth + -o-]

mȳthŏ'log|ȳ *n.* Body of myths, esp. relating to particular person or subject; study of myths; hence or cogn. ~ER[1], ~IST (3), *ns.*, **mȳtholŏ'gɪc**(AL) *adjs.*, ~IZE (2, 3) *v.t.* & *i.* [ME, f. F *mythologie* or f. LL f. Gk *muthologia* (as prec.; see -LOGY)]

mȳ'th|us *n.* (*pl.* **~i** *pr.* -ī). (arch.) Myth. [mod. L (see MYTH)]

mȳxoedē'ma, *mȳxed-, (-*e*d-) *n.* Metabolic disease caused by deficient action of thyroid gland, with thickening of subcutaneous tissues and loss of physical and mental energy. [f. Gk *muxa* mucus + OEDEMA]

mȳxō'ma *n.* (*pl.* **~s** *or* **~ta**). Tumour of mucous or gelatinous tissue; hence **~to'**SIS (*or* -*om*-) *n.*, virus disease causing myxomas in rabbits. [mod. L, f. Gk *muxa* mucus; see -OMA]

N

N, n, (ĕn) *n.* (*pl.* **Ns** *or* **N's**). Fourteenth letter of alphabet; (Print.) en; (Math.) indefinite number; **to the nth,** to any required power, (fig.) to any extent, to the utmost.

-n[1,2]. See -EN[1,5].

N. *abbr.* (Chess) knight; New; newton(s); North(ern).

n. *abbr.* name; nano-; neuter; nominative; noon; note; noun.

N *symb.* nitrogen.

na *adv.* (Sc.) **1.** (nah). = NO[4]. **2.** (n*a*, after *v. aux.*). = NOT (*canna, didna*).

Na *symb.* sodium.

***N.A.A.C.P.** *abbr.* National Association for the Advancement of Colored People.

||N.A.A.F.I. (nă'fĭ) *abbr.* Navy, Army, and Air Force Institutes (canteen for servicemen).

năb *v.t.* (**-bb-**). (sl.) Apprehend, arrest; catch in wrongdoing. [17th c., also *napp*, as in KIDNAP; orig. unkn.]

nā'bŏb *n.* **1.** (Hist.) Muslim official or governor under Mogul empire. **2.** (arch.) Wealthy luxury-loving person, esp. one who has returned from India with fortune. [f. Port. *nababo* or Sp. *nabab*, f. Urdu (as NAWAB)]

nă'carăt *n.* Bright orange-red colour. [F, perh. f. Sp. & Port. *nacardo* (*nacar* NACRE)]

nacĕ'lle *n.* Outer casing of aeroplane's engine; car of airship. [F, f. LL *navicella* dim. of L *navis* ship]

nā'cre (-k*er*) *n.* (Shellfish yielding) mother-of-pearl; hence **nā'creo**US, **nā'cro**US, *adjs.* [F]

nā'dir (*or* -ēr) *n.* Point of heavens directly under observer (opp. ZENITH); (transf.) lowest point, place or time of greatest depression etc. [ME f. OF, f. Arab. *nazir* (*as-samt*) opposite (to zenith)]

nae'v|us, *nē'v|us, *n.* (*pl.* **~i** *pr.* -ī). Birthmark in form of sharply defined red patch in skin; = MOLE[1]. [L]

Nă'ffȳ *n.* (sl.) = N.A.A.F.I. [phonet. sp.]

năg[1] *n.* Small riding-horse or pony; (colloq.) horse. [ME, of unkn. orig.]

năg[2] *v.* (**-gg-**). **1.** *v.i.* Find fault or scold persistently (*at* person); (of pain etc.) be persistently felt. **2.** *v.t.* Annoy by nagging. [of dial., perh. Scand. or LG, orig.; cf. Norw. & Sw. *nagga* gnaw, irritate, LG (*g*)*naggen* provoke]

Na'ga (nah'-) *n.* **1.** (Hindu Myth.) One of a race of semi-human serpents, genii of rain, rivers, etc. **2.** Member of group of tribes in or near Naga Hills of Burma. [f. Skr. *nāga* serpent]

naga'na (-ah'n*a*) *n.* Disease of livestock in Africa, caused by a trypanosome and transmitted by tsetse fly. [f. Zulu *nakane*]

nā'gôr *n.* Senegal antelope (*Redunca redunca*). [F, arbitr. form. by Buffon f. earlier *nanguer*]

Nah. *abbr.* Nahum (O.T.).

Nahua'tl (n*a*wah'-) *a.* & *n.* (Member or language) of group of peoples in S. Mexico and Central America, incl. Aztecs; hence ~AN *a.* [Sp. f. Nahuatl]

nai'ad (nī'-) *n.* (*pl.* **~s,** *or* **~es** *pr.* -ēz). Water-nymph; nymph of dragonfly etc. [f. L f. Gk *Naias -ados* (*naō* flow; see -AD 1)]

naïf (nahē'f) *a.* = NAÏVE. [F masc. a.]

nail[1] *n.* **1.** Horny covering of upper surface of tip of finger or toe; **bite** one's **~s** (as habit, or in impatience or frustration); TOOTH *and nail*; **~-biting,** (fig.) causing helpless anxiety; **~-brush** (for cleaning nails); ***~ enamel, ~ polish, ||~ varnish,** (for making nails lustrous); **~-file, ~-scissors,** (for trimming nails); hence -~ED[2] (-ld) *a.* **2.** Claw, talon; hard excrescence on upper mandible of some soft-billed birds. **3.** Small metal spike usu. with point and broadened head driven in, with hammer to hold things together or as peg or protection (cf. HOBNAIL) or ornament; **hard as ~s,** (1) in good physical condition, (2) callous; **hit the (right) ~ on the head,** give true explanation, propose or do right thing, hit the mark; *nail in* one's COFFIN; **on the ~,** without delay, esp. of payment; **~-head,** architectural ornament like head of nail. **4.** Old measure of cloth length ($2\frac{1}{4}$ in.). **5.** Hence ~'LESS (-l-l-) *a.* [OE *nægel*, = OS, OHG *nagal*, ON *nagl* f. Gmc **naglaz* f. IE **nogh-*]

nail[2] *v.t.* **1.** Fasten with nail(s) (*on, to, together, down, in,* etc.); *nail* COLOUR[1]*s to mast*; **~ (to counter** or **to barn door**), expose as spurious or vile; **~ up,** close, or affix at height, with nail(s). **2.** Fix or keep fixed (person, attention, etc.); secure, catch, engage, succeed in getting hold of, (person or thing); **~ down,** define precisely, bind (person *to* promise etc.). [OE *næglan* (as prec.)]

nai'ler *n.* Nail-maker; hence **nai'l**ERY (3) *n.* [f. NAIL[2] + -ER[1]]

nai'nsoōk *n.* Fine soft cotton fabric, orig. Indian. [f. Hindi *nainsukh* (*nain* eye, *sukh* pleasure)]

naï've (nahē'v), **naive** (nāv), *a.* Artless, innocent, unaffected; unconsciously and amusingly simple; hence ~LY[2] (-vlĭ) *adv.* [F, fem. of *naïf* f. L *nativus* NATIVE[2]]

naï'vetȳ (nahē'vtĭ), **nai'vetȳ** (nā'vetĭ), ***naïveté*** (nahē'vtā), *n.* State or quality of being naïve; naïve action. [F *naïveté* (as prec.; see -TY[1])]

nā'kėd *a.* **1.** Without clothes, nude, (*as naked as my mother bore me*). **2.** Defenceless; (of sword etc.) unsheathed; plain, undisguised, (*the naked truth*; *naked facts*; *in its naked absurdity*); exposed for examination (*his naked soul*). **3.** Devoid *of*; treeless, leafless, barren; (of rock) exposed, without soil or vegetation; (of room) without furnishings; without ornament. **4.** (Of light, flame, etc.) exposed to air, not protected from wind etc. or from contact with inflammable vapour etc., unshaded. **5.** Without leaves, hairs, scales, shell, etc.; without addition, comment, support, evidence, etc., (*naked faith, quotations, word, assertion*); unassisted; ~ **eye** (without telescope, microscope, etc.). **6.** ~ **boys,** ~ **lady,** ~ **ladies,** meadow saffron, flowering while leafless. **7.** Hence ~LY² *adv.*, ~NESS *n.* [OE *nacod*, = OHG *nackut*, ON *nökkvithr*, Goth. *naqad-* f. Gmc **naquadhaz*]

nā'ker *n.* (Hist.) Kettledrum. [ME, f. OF *nacre*, *nacaire* f. Arab. *nakkāra* drum]

||**N.A.L.G.O.** (nă'lgō) *abbr.* National and Local Government Officers' Association.

***N.A.M.** *abbr.* National Association of Manufacturers.

nămbў-pă'mbў *a.* & *n.* **1.** *a.* Insipidly pretty, weakly sentimental, lacking vigour. **2.** *n.* Talk or person of this kind. [fanciful form. on name of *Ambrose* Philips, Engl. pastoral writer d. 1749]

nāme¹ *n.* **1.** Word by which individual person, animal, place, or thing, is spoken of or to (*mention person by name*); **by** ~, called (*Tom by name*); KNOW¹ *by name*; **of** (or **by**) **the** ~ **of,** called; **the** ~ **of the game,** (colloq.) purpose or essence of action etc.; **put** one's ~ **down for,** apply as candidate etc., promise to subscribe; **keep** one's ~ **on, take** one's ~ **off, the books,** remain, cease to be, member of college, club, etc.; **have to** one's ~, possess; TAKE¹ person's *name in vain*; USE² person's *name*; **what's in a** ~?, names are arbitrary labels; WHAT'*s-its*(or *his*)-*-name*. **2.** Word denoting any object of thought, esp. one applicable to many individuals; CALL¹ person *names*; PROPER *name*. **3.** Person as known, famed, or spoken of, (*adore the name of God*; *Nelson himself and many great names were there*). **4.** All who go under one name; family, clan, people. **5.** Reputation (*has an ill, a good, name*; *give a dog a bad name*; *has a name for honesty, the name of being honest*; *bequeath a great name*; *persons of name*; one's *good name*); (*attrib.*) widely known and esteemed (*a name brand*); **make a** ~ **for oneself, win oneself a** ~, become famous. **6.** Merely nominal existence, practically non-existent thing, (opp. *fact, reality, deed*; *virtuous in name* (*only*); *honour had become a name*). **7. In** person's ~, **in the** ~ **of,** invoking, relying upon, calling to witness, (*in God's* or *Heaven's name*; *in the name of goodness, common sense*), acting as deputy for or in the interest of (*open in the name of the law*; *did it in the name of friendship*); **in** one's **own** ~, independently, without authority. **8.** ~**-calling,** (merely) abusive language; ~**-child,** one named after (*of*) another person; ~**-day,** (1) day of saint after whom person is named, (2)|| = TICKET-*day*; ~**-dropping,** familiar mention of names of the famous as form of boasting; ~**-part,** title-role; ~**-plate** (affixed with name of occupant etc.); ~**'sake** (-ms-), person or thing with same name as another (*his namesake*) [prob. f. phr. *for the name's sake*]; ~**-tape** (for garment etc., with name of owner). [OE *nama, noma*, = OS, OHG *namo*, ON *nafn, namn*, Goth. *namo* f. Gmc **namon* f. IE; cogn. w. L *nomen*, Gk *onoma*]

nāme² *v.t.* **1.** Give name to (*after*, **for*, *from*), call by (specified name); call (person or thing) by right name. **2.** Nominate, appoint (*to* office etc.). **3.** Mention, specify; cite as instance; **not to be** ~**d on** or **in the same day with,** quite inferior to; **you** ~ **it,** (colloq.) no matter what; ~ **names,** mention specific persons' names (esp. in accusation). **4.** ||(Of Speaker) mention (M.P.) as disobedient to the chair. **5.** Specify as something desired; ~ **the day,** arrange date (esp. of woman fixing date for her wedding). **6.** Hence **nā'me**ABLE (-ma-) *a.* [OE (*ge*)*namian* (as prec.)]

nā'melėss (-ml-) *a.* Having no name, bearing no name-inscription; obscure, inglorious; not mentioned by name, left unnamed on purpose (esp. *who shall be nameless*); anonymous, unknown; inexpressible, indefinable; too bad to be named, abominable, loathsome, (esp. *nameless vices*); hence ~LY² *adv.*, ~NESS *n.* [ME, = undistinguished, f. NAME¹ + -LESS]

nā'melў (-mlĭ) *adv.* That is to say, in other words. [ME, f. NAME¹ + -LY²]

nă'ncў *n.* & *a.* (sl.) Effeminate (man or boy); homosexual. [woman's name, pet-form of *Ann*]

nănkee'n (*or* -n-k-) *n.* Yellow cotton cloth; colour or (in *pl.*) trousers of this. [f. *Nankin*(*g*) in China, where orig. made]

nă'nnў *n.* **1.** ~**(-goat)**, female goat. **2.** Child's nurse. [f. as NANCY]

nă'nō- *pref.* denoting factor of 10^{-9} (*nanosecond*). [f. L f. Gk *nanos* dwarf + -o-]

nā'ŏs *n.* (*pl.* **na'oi**). (Gk Ant. etc.) Inner part of temple. [Gk, = temple]

năp¹ *v.i.* (**-pp-**), & *n.* **1.** *v.i.* Sleep lightly or briefly; **catch** ~**'ping,** find asleep, take unawares or off guard, detect in negligence or error. **2.** *n.* Short sleep, doze, esp. by day (often *take a nap*). [OE *hnappian*, rel. to OHG (*h*)*naffezan* to slumber]

năp² *n.*, & *v.t.* (**-pp-**). **1.** *n.* Surface given to cloth by raising and then cutting and smoothing the short fibres, pile, whence ~'LESS *a.*; soft or downy surface. **2.** *v.t.* Raise nap on (cloth). [ME *noppe* f. MDu., MLG *noppe* nap, *noppen* trim nap from]

năp³ *n.*, & *v.t.* (**-pp-**). **1.** *n.* Card-game in which players declare numbers of tricks they expect to take, up to maximum of five; call of five in this game; ~ **hand,** (fig.) position that justifies confident expectation of winning if one takes a risk; **go** ~, risk attempting to take all five tricks in nap, (fig.) risk everything, win all matches etc. in a series. **2.** Betting of all one's money on one chance; tipster's choice for this. **3.** *v.t.* Name (horse) as probable winner. [abbr. of orig. name of game NAPOLEON]

nă'pa. See NAPPA.

nă'palm (-ahm) *n.*, & *v.t.* **1.** *n.* Thickening agent made from naphthalene and coconut oil; jellied petrol made from this, used in bombs. **2.** *v.t.* Attack with napalm bombs. [f. NAPHTHENIC + *palmitic acid* in coconut oil]

nāpe *n.* Back of or usu. *of* neck. [ME, of unkn. orig.]

nā'perў *n.* (Sc. or arch.) Household, esp. table, linen. [ME, f. OF *naperie* (*nape* as NAPKIN; see -ERY)]

nă'phtha *n.* Inflammable oil got by dry distillation of organic substances, as coal, shale, or petroleum. [L, f. Gk, = inflammable volatile liquid issuing from earth, of Oriental orig.]

nă'phthalēne *n.* White crystalline substance got in distilling coal-tar and used in manufacture of dyes etc. and in moth-balls; hence **năphthă'l**IC *a.* [f. prec. + *-l-* + -ENE]

nă'phthēn|**e** *n.* (Chem.) Saturated cyclic hydrocarbon; hence ~IC (-ē'n-) *a.* (~**ic acid,** any carboxylic acid from refining of petroleum). [f. NAPHTHA + -ENE]

Nā'pĭer *n.* ~**'s bones,** slips of bone etc. marked for use in arithmetical calculations; hence ~IAN (-pēr'ĭan) *a.* (see LOGARITHM). [f. J. ~, Sc. mathematician d. 1617]

nă'pkĭn *n.* (**Table-**)~, square piece of linen, paper, etc., for wiping lips or fingers at meals, or serving fish etc. on; small towel; ||piece of towelling etc. worn by baby to absorb or retain excreta; *SANITARY *napkin*; **lay up** etc. **in a** ~, make no use of (Luke 19:20); ~**-ring,** ring to hold (and distinguish) person's table-napkin when not in use. [ME, f. OF *nappe* f. L *mappa* (MAP¹), + -KIN]

napŏ'lèon *n.* French gold twenty-franc piece of Napoleon I (**double ~**, forty-franc piece); 19th-c. form of high boot; the game NAP³; **mille-feuille*. [f. F *napoléon* (*Napoléon*, name of 19th-c. French emperors)]

Napōlèŏ'n|ĭc *a.* Of, like, etc., Napoleon I or the Napoleon family; hence or cogn. ~ICALLY² *adv.*, **Napō'lèon**ISM (3), **Napō'lèon**IST (2), *ns.* [f. as prec. + -IC]

nă'p(p)a *n.* Leather made by special process from skin of sheep or goat. [f. *Napa* in California]

nă'ppy̆¹ *a.* & *n.* (arch.) Foaming (ale etc.); heady, strong. [app. f. NAP² + -Y²]

||**nă'ppy̆²** *n.* (colloq.) Baby's napkin. [abbr.; see -Y³]

na'pu (nah'pōō) *n.* Chevrotain of Malaya. [f. Malay *nāpu*]

nar'cèine *n.* Narcotic alkaloid got from opium. [f. F *narcéine* f. Gk *narkē* numbness + -INE⁵]

narcĭ'ss|ĭsm *n.* (Psych.) Tendency to self--worship, excessive or erotic interest in one's own personal features; hence **~ĭ'st**IC *a.* [f. *Narcissus* (Gk *Narkissos*) youth who fell in love with his reflection in water, + -ISM]

narcĭ'ss|us *n.* (*pl.* **~i** *pr.* -ī, *or* **~uses**). Bulbous plant of genus *Narcissus*, esp. *N. poeticus* bearing heavily scented single white spring flower with undivided corona edged with crimson and yellow. [L, f. Gk *narkissos*, perh. f. *narkē* numbness, w. ref. to its narcotic effects]

nar'colĕpsy̆ *n.* Disease with fits of somnolence; hence **narcolĕ'pt**IC *a.* & *n.*, (patient) having this disease. [f. as foll., after EPILEPSY]

narcō's|ĭs *n.* (*pl.* **~es** *pr.* -ēz). Operation or effects of narcotics; state of insensibility. [f. Gk *narkōsis* (*narkoō* benumb); see -OSIS]

narcŏ't|ĭc *a.* & *n.* (Substance) inducing drowsiness, sleep, stupor, or insensibility; (fig.) soporific; of narcosis; hence ~ICALLY *adv.*, **nar'cot**ISM (5) *n.*, **nar'cot**IZE (3, 5) *v.t.* [ME, f. OF *narcotique* or f. med. L f. Gk *narkōtikos* (as prec.; see -OTIC)]

nard *n.* (Plant yielding) aromatic balsam of ancients; spikenard. [ME, f. L f. Gk *nardos* f. Semitic wd]

nardōō' *n.* (Aboriginal food of spores of) Austral. clover-like plant (*Marsilea drummondii*). [Aboriginal]

nar'ghĭlè (-gĭ-) *n.* Oriental tobacco-pipe with smoke drawn through water, HOOKAH. [f. Pers. *nārgīleh* (*nārgīl* coconut)]

||**nark** *n.*, & *v.t.* (sl.) **1.** *n.* Police decoy or spy; (Austral.) annoying person or thing. **2.** *v.t.* Annoy, infuriate; **~ it,** (*imper.*) stop that. [f. Romany *nāk* nose]

narr|ā'te *v.t.* Give continuous story or account of; (abs.) utter or write narrative; so ~A'TION *n.* [f. L *narrare* + -ATE³]

nă'rratĭve *n.* & *a.* **1.** *n.* Tale, story, recital of facts, esp. story told in first person; kind of composition or talk that confines itself to these. **2.** *a.* In the form of, or concerned with, narration; hence ~LY² (-vlĭ) *adv.* [f. F *narratif -ive* f. LL *narrativus* (as prec.; see -IVE)]

narrā'tor *n.* Person who narrates, e.g. by describing events between speeches in broadcast play or by commentary during film. [L (as NARRATE; see -OR)]

nă'rrow (-ō) *a.*, *n.*, & *v.* **1.** *a.* Of small width in proportion to length, lacking breadth, constricted; (of vowel) tense; of small size, confined or confining, (*within narrow bounds* etc.). **2.** Of limited scope, restricted, (*in the narrowest sense*); with little margin (*a narrow majority, escape*). **3.** Lacking in breadth of view or sympathy, illiberal, prejudiced, exclusive, self-centred. **4.** Searching, precise, exact, (*after a narrow examination*). **5. ~ bed, cell, house,** the grave; ||**~ boat,** canal boat (esp. less than 7 ft. wide); **~ circumstances,** poverty; **~ cloth** (less than 52 in. wide); **~-mi'nded,** = sense 3; ||**~ seas,** English Channel and Irish Sea; *narrow* SQUEAK; **~ way,** righteousness (Matt. 7:14). **6.** Hence ~ISH¹ 2 *a.*, ~LY² *adv.*, ~NESS *n.* **7.** *n.* (usu. in *pl.*) Narrow part of a sound, strait, river, pass, or street. **8.** *v.t.* & *i.* Make or become narrower, diminish, lessen, contract, restrict. [OE *nearu nearw-*, = OS *naru* f. Gmc **narwaz*]

nar'thĕx *n.* Railed-off western porch etc. in early Christian church, used by women, penitents, catechumens, etc. [L, f. Gk *narthēx* giant fennel, stick, casket, narthex]

nar'whal (-wal) *n.* Arctic delphinoid cetacean (*Monodon monoceros*), the male with long straight horn(s) developed from one or both of its two teeth. [f. Du. *narwal* f. Da. *narhval* (*hval* whale); cf. ON *náhvalr* (perh. f. *nár* corpse, w. ref. to skin-colour)]

***nar'y̆** *a.* (colloq.) Not a, no; **~ a,** not one. [f. *ne'er a*]

||**N.A.S.** *abbr.* National Association of Schoolmasters; Noise Abatement Society.

***N.A.S.A.** (nă'sa) *abbr.* National Aeronautics and Space Administration.

nā'sal (-z-) *a.* & *n.* **1.** *a.* Of the nose; **~ organ,** (joc.) nose. **2.** (Of letter or sound) pronounced with nose passage open, e.g. *m*, *n*, *ng*, or Fr. *en*, *un*, etc.; (of voice or speech) having the twang described as speaking through the nose; hence ~IZE (2, 3) *v.i.* & *t.* **3.** Hence **nasă'l**ITY (-z-) *n.*, ~LY² *adv.* **4.** *n.* Nasal letter or sound; nose--piece on helmet. [F, or f. med. L *nasalis* f. L *nasus* nose; see -AL]

nă'sc|ent *a.* In the act of being born, just beginning to be, not yet mature; (Chem.) just being formed and therefore unusually reactive (*nascent hydrogen*); so ~ENCY *n.* [f. L *nasci* be born; see -ENT]

nā'seberry̆ (-zb-) *n.* Sapodilla. [f. Sp. & Port. *néspera* medlar f. L (see MEDLAR); assim. to BERRY¹]

nā'sō- (-z-) *comb. form.* Nose, as: **~-frontal,** of nose and forehead. [f. L *nasus* nose + -O-]

nă'stĭc *a.* (Bot.) Of movement not determined by external stimulus. [f. Gk *nastos* squeezed together (*nassō* to press); see -IC]

nastur'tium (-shum) *n.* **1.** (Bot.) Pungent--tasting cruciferous plant of genus *Nasturtium*, e.g. watercress. **2.** (pop.) Trailing garden plant of genus *Tropaeolum*, with bright orange, yellow, or red flowers and pungent-tasting leaves. [L]

na'st|y̆ (nah'-) *a.* Disgustingly dirty, filthy; obscene, delighting in obscenity; disagreeable to smell or taste, unpalatable (lit. or fig.); annoying, objectionable (**~y bit** or **piece of work,** (colloq.) unpleasant or contemptible person); (of weather etc.) foul, wet, stormy; hard to deal with or get rid of, serious (*a nasty sea, fence, blow, illness*; **a ~y one,** rebuff, snub, awkward question, disabling blow, etc.); ill--natured, ill-tempered, spiteful *to*; hence **~ĭ**LY² *adv.*, **~ĭ**NESS *n.* [ME, of unkn. orig.]

Nat. *abbr.* National; Nationalist; Natural.

nā'tal *a.* Of or from one's birth. [ME, f. L *natalis* (as NATION; see -AL)]

nată'lĭty̆ *n.* Birth rate. [f. F *natalité* (as prec.; see -ITY)]

natā'tion *n.* (literary). Act or art of swimming. [f. L *natatio* (*natare* swim; see -ATION)]

nātator'ial, nā'tatory̆, *adjs.* Swimming; of swimming. [f. LL *natatorius* f. L *natator* swimmer (as prec.; see -ORY, -AL)]

***nātator'ium** *n.* (Esp. indoor) swimming-pool. [LL, neut. (as n.) of *natatorius* (see prec.)]

nătch *adv.* (colloq.) = NATURALLY 2. [abbr.]
nā'tēs (-z) *n. pl.* (Anat.) Buttocks; anterior pair of optic lobes in brain. [L]
nā'th(e)lėss (-thl-) *adv.* (arch.) Nevertheless. [ME, f. OE *nā* not (*ne* not, *ā* ever) + THE 2 + *lǣs* LESS 6]
nā'tion *n.* **1.** Large number of people of mainly common descent, language, history, etc., usu. inhabiting a territory bounded by defined limits and forming a society under one government; **most favoured** ~ (to which State accords lowest scale of import duties). **2.** Tribe of N. Amer. Indians; ||(in medieval and some Sc. universities) body of students from particular country or district. **3. Law of ~s,** international law; LEAGUE² *of Nations*; UNITED *Nations*. **4.** Hence ~HOOD *n.*; **~-wide** *a.*, extending over whole nation. [ME f. OF, f. L *natio -onis* (*nasci nat-* be born; see -ION)]
nă'tional *a.* & *n.* **1.** *a.* Of a or the nation, common to the whole nation; peculiar to or characteristic of a particular nation. **2.** ~ **anthem,** song adopted by nation to express patriotism or loyalty, e.g. 'God save the Queen'; **N~ Assembly,** elected house of legislature in various countries, esp. (Hist.) in France 1789–91; ||**N~ Assistance,** (former official name for) supplementary benefits under National Insurance; *~ **bank** (chartered under federal government); *~ **convention** (of major political party, nominating candidates for presidency etc.); *National* DEBT; ||**N~ Government,** coalition government under MacDonald 1931–5; ||~ **grid,** (1) network of high-voltage electric power lines between major power-stations, (2) metric system of geographical co-ordinates used in maps of British Isles; ***N~ Guard,** primary reserve force partly maintained by the states but available for federal use; ||**N~ Health Service,** system of national medical service paid for mainly by taxation (1948–); ~ **holiday** (observed throughout a country); ~ **income,** total money earned within a nation; ||**N~ Insurance,** system of compulsory contribution from all adults below pension age and from employers to provide State assistance in sickness, unemployment, retirement, etc.; ~ **newspaper** (circulating throughout the country); ~ **park,** area of countryside subject to strict control of building etc. and under State supervision to maintain its value to the public; ||~ **service,** service in armed forces under conscription; **N~ Socialist,** member of highly nationalistic totalitarian party in power in Germany 1933–45; ||**N~ Trust,** private body for preserving historic or beautiful places. **3.** Hence ~LY² *adv.* **4.** *n.* ||(*N~*) = GRAND *National*. **5.** One's fellow countryman (*consul's powers over his own nationals*); citizen of a specified country. [F (as prec.; see -AL)]
nă'tional|ĭsm *n.* Patriotic feeling, principles, or efforts; policy of national independence; so ~IST (2) *n.*, **~ĭ'st**IC *a.* [f. prec. + -ISM]
nătionă'lĭtȳ *n.* Being national, national quality; patriotic sentiment; one's nation of origin (*what is his nationality?*); a nation (*men of all nationalities*); existence as a nation; race forming part of one or more political nations. [f. NATIONAL + -ITY]
nă'tionalīz|e, -īs|e (-iz), *v.t.* Make national; make into a nation; naturalize (foreigner); convert (land, railways, coal-mines, steel industry, firm etc.) into national property or undertakings; hence ~A'TION *n.* [f. F *nationaliser* (as NATIONAL; see -IZE)]
nā'tĭve¹ *n.* **1.** ~ **of,** person born, or whose parents are domiciled at his birth, in (place). **2.** Local inhabitant; (Austral.) white person born in Australia. **3.** Member of non-European or less civilized people; (S. Afr.) Negro. **4.** Indigenous animal or plant; oyster reared wholly or partly in British waters, esp. in artificial beds. [ME, orig. = person born as slave, f. AL *nativus* n. f. L *nativus* a. (see foll.)]
nā'tĭve² *a.* **1.** Belonging to a person or thing by nature, innate, inherent, natural *to*; hence ~LY² (-vlĭ) *adv.* **2.** Unadorned, simple, artless. **3.** Of one's birth, where one was born; belonging to one by right of birth. **4.** (Of metal etc.) found in pure or uncombined state; ~ **rock** (in its original place). **5.** Born in a place (esp. of non-Europeans), indigenous, not exotic; of the natives of a place; (Austral. & N.Z.) resembling an animal or plant familiar elsewhere (~ **bear,** = KOALA); **go** ~, (of white person) adopt (less civilized) mode of life of natives where one lives. [ME, f. OF *natif -ive* or f. L *nativus* (as NATION; see -IVE)]
nā'tĭv|ĭsm *n.* (Philos.) Doctrine of innate ideas; so ~IST (2) *n.* [f. prec. + -ISM]
natĭ'vĭtȳ *n.* Birth of Christ, the Virgin Mary, or St. John the Baptist; picture of the Nativity of Christ; festival of Christ's Nativity, Christmas, or of birth of Virgin (8 Sept.) or St. John (24 June); birth; (Astrol.) horoscope; ~ **play** (dealing with birth of Christ). [ME, f. OF *nativité* f. LL *nativitas -tatis* f. L (as NATIVE²; see -ITY)]
N.A.T.O., Nato, (nā'tō) *abbr.* North Atlantic Treaty Organization.
nā'tron *n.* Native hydrated sodium carbonate. [F, f. Sp. *natrón* f. Arab. *naṭrūn* f. Gk *nitron* NITRE]
||**NATSOPA** (nătsō'pa) *abbr.* National Society of Operative Printers, Graphical & Media Personnel.
nă'tter *v.i.*, & *n.* (colloq.) **1.** *v.i.* Chatter idly; grumble, talk fretfully. **2.** *n.* Aimless chatter; grumbling talk. [orig. Sc., imit.]
nă'tterjăck *n.* Species of small toad (*Bufo calamita*) with yellow stripe down back and running instead of hopping. [perh. f. prec., from its loud croak, + JACK¹]
nă'ttĭer blue (-ōō) *n.* Soft shade of blue. [much used by J. M. *Nattier*, Fr. painter d. 1766]
nă'tt|ȳ *a.* Spruce, trim, daintily tidy; deft-handed; showing deftness; hence ~ĬLY² *adv.*, ~ĬNESS *n.* [orig. sl., perh. rel. to NEAT²; see -Y²]
nă'tural (-cher-) *a.* & *n.* **1.** *a.* Based on the innate moral sense, instinctive, (*natural law, justice,* VIRTUE*s*). **2.** Established by nature (*natural resources*; *natural* YEAR); ~ **numbers,** 1, 2, 3, etc.; *natural* LOGARITHM; ~ **selection,** process favouring survival of organisms best adapted to their environment. **3.** (Mus.) ~ **note,** not sharp or flat, so *B natural, F natural,* etc.; ~ **key** or **scale** (having no sharps or flats, i.e. C major or A minor). **4.** ~ **classification,** scientific arrangement according to natural features, esp. (Bot.) Jussieu's arrangement of species in ~ **orders** according to likeness as opp. Linnaeus's sexual system. **5.** Normal, conformable to the ordinary course of nature, not exceptional or miraculous or irregular; ~ **death** (by age or disease, not accident, poison, or violence); *natural* MAGIC. **6.** Not enlightened or communicated by revelation (*the natural man*); ~ **religion,** deism (opp. *revealed religion*); ~ **theology,** knowledge of God as gained by reason and light of nature. **7.** Physically existing, not spiritual or intellectual or fictitious, concerned with physical things, (*the natural world*); one's ~ **life,** duration of one's life on earth; *natural* LAW¹. **8.** Existing in or by nature, not artificial, innate, inherent, self-sown, uncultivated, (*in its natural state*); ~ **childbirth** (with mother taught to relax and so not needing

anaesthesia etc.); ~ **food** (without preservatives etc.); *natural* GAS[1]; ~ **language** (opp. artificial language or code); ~ **uranium** (not enriched). **9.** Lifelike; unaffected, easy-mannered, not disfigured or disguised. **10.** Not surprising, to be expected. **11.** Spontaneous or easy *to* (*comes natural to him*). **12.** Destined to be such by nature (*natural enemies*, *antithesis*; *is a natural linguist*). **13.** So related by nature only, illegitimate, (*natural son*, *child*, *brother*, etc.). **14.** Dealing with nature as a study; ~ **history,** (1) study of natural objects, esp. of animal or vegetable life, and esp. as set forth for popular use, (2) aggregate of facts about the natural objects or the characteristics of a place or class; ~ **historian,** writer on natural history; ~ **philosophy,** physics; ~ **philosopher,** physicist; *natural* SCIENCE. **15.** ~**-born,** having the character or position by birth; ~**-coloured,** not given any artificial colouring. **16.** Hence ~NESS *n.* **17.** *n.* Person mentally deficient from birth; person who is naturally expert in some respect or endowed *for* a role or activity; thing that is by nature suitable *for* or successful, a certainty. **18.** (Mus.) Sign denoting return to natural pitch after sharp or flat; natural note, white key on piano. **19.** Hand making 21 as first dealt in *vingt-et-un*; throw of 7 or 11 at craps. **20.** Pale fawn colour. [ME f. OF *naturel* f. L *naturalis* (as NATURE; see -AL)]

nă'turalĭsm (-cher-) *n.* Action based on natural instincts; moral or religious system on purely natural basis; (Philos.) view of the world that excludes the supernatural or spiritual; realistic method, adherence to nature, in literature and art; indifference to conventions. [f. prec. + -ISM, in Philos. after F *naturalisme*]

nă'turalĭst (-cher-) *n.* & *a.* **1.** *n.* One who believes in or practises naturalism; student of animals or plants. **2.** *a.* = foll. [f. F *naturaliste*, & NATURAL + -IST]

năturalĭ'st|ĭc (-cher-) *a.* Of, or according to, naturalism; of natural history; hence ~ICALLY *adv.* [f. prec. + -IC]

nă'turaliz|e (-cher-), **-is|e** (-iz), *v.* **1.** *v.t.* Admit (alien) to citizenship; adopt (foreign word, custom, etc.); introduce (animal, plant) into another country. **2.** *v.i.* Become naturalized. **3.** *v.t.* Free from conventions, make natural; exclude from the miraculous, place on naturalistic basis; cause to appear natural. **4.** *v.i.* Study natural history. **5.** Hence ~A'TION *n.* [f. F *naturaliser* (as NATURAL; see -IZE)]

nă'turallȳ (-cher-) *adv.* **1.** In adj. senses. **2.** As a natural result; as might be expected, of course. [f. NATURAL + -LY[2]]

nā'ture *n.* **1.** Thing's essential qualities (**in** or **by** or **from the** (**very**) ~ **of the case** or **of things,** inevitably if one considers these qualities); person's or animal's innate qualities or character (*it is not* (*in*) *her nature to act like that*; **by** ~, innately; GOOD, ILL, SECOND, *nature*; hence **-nā'tur**ED[2] (-cherd) *a.*); (**human**) ~, general characteristics and feelings of mankind (TOUCH[2] *of nature*); specified element of human character (*the rational*, *animal*, *moral*, *nature*); person of specified character (*sanguine natures do not feel this*). **2.** Kind, sort, class, (*things of this nature*; *is in* or *of the nature of a command*). **3.** Inherent impulses determining character or action (**against** ~, unnatural, immoral; see also sense 5). **4.** Vital force or functions or needs (*nature is exhausted*; *such a diet will not support nature*; CALL[2] *of nature*, EASE[2] or RELIEVE *nature*). **5.** Physical power causing phenomena of material world, these phenomena as a whole, (**N**~, these personified; *all nature looks gay*; *Nature is the best physician*); **against** or **contrary to** ~, miraculous(ly); **back to** ~, returning to what are regarded as natural conditions of living; *in the* COURSE[1] *of nature*; **debt of** ~, death; **from** ~, using natural objects as models (*paint from nature*); **in** ~, (1) actually existing, (2) anywhere, at all; LAW[1] *of nature*; **one of N**~**'s,** a natural member of the class of (*gentlemen* etc.); **state of** ~, (1) unregenerate condition (opp. *state of* GRACE), (2) condition of man before society is organized, (3) uncultivated or undomesticated state of plants or animals, natural occurrence of minerals, (3) bodily nakedness. **6.** ~ **cure,** naturopathy; ~**-printing,** method of producing print of leaves etc. by pressing them on prepared plate; ~ **study** (as school subject), practical study of plant and animal life, physical phenomena, etc.; ~ **trail,** path through woods etc. designed to draw attention to interesting natural objects. [ME f. OF, f. L *natura* (*nasci nat-* be born; see -URE)]

nā'tur|ĭsm (-cher-) *n.* Naturalism; worship of natural objects; nudism; so ~IST (2) *n.* [f. prec. + -ISM]

nāturŏ'pathȳ (-cher-) *n.* Treatment of disease by seeking to assist natural recovery; so **nā'turo**PATH 1 *n.*, **nāturopă'th**IC *a.*, (-cher-). [f. NATURE + -O- + -PATHY]

naught (nawt) *n.* & *pred. a.* (arch.) **1.** *n.* Nothing, NOUGHT; **bring to** ~, ruin, baffle; **come to** ~, be ruined or baffled; **set at** ~, disregard, despise. **2.** *a.* Worthless, useless. [OE *nāwiht*, *-wuht* (*nā*, see NO[2]; *wiht* WIGHT)]

nau'ght|ȳ (naw'tĭ) *a.* (used of, to, or by children, or in imit. of childish speech). Wayward, disobedient, badly behaved; wicked, blameworthy, unbecoming, indecent; hence ~ĬLY[2] *adv.*, ~ĬNESS *n.* [ME, f. prec. + -Y[2]]

nau'plĭ|us *n.* (*pl.* ~**i** *pr.* -ī). Larva of some crustaceans. [L, a kind of shellfish, or (*N*~) f. Gk *Nauplios* son of Poseidon]

nau'sėa (*or* -z- *or* -sha) *n.* Feeling of sickness with inclination to vomit; sea-sickness; loathing. [L, f. Gk *nausia* (*naus* ship)]

nau'sėāt|e (*or* -z- *or* -shāt) *v.* **1.** *v.t.* Reject (food; usu. fig.) with loathing; affect with nausea, whence ~ING[2] *a.* **2.** *v.i.* Feel sick (*at*), loathe food, occupation, etc. [f. L *nauseare* (as prec.) + -ATE[3]]

nau'sėous (*or* -z- *or* -shus) *a.* Causing nausea; offensive to taste or smell, nasty; disgusting, loathsome; hence ~LY[2] *adv.*, ~NESS *n.* [f. L *nauseosus* (as NAUSEA; see -OUS)]

nautch *n.* Indian exhibition of professional dancing-girls (~**-girl,** one of these). [f. Urdu (Hindi) *nāch* f. Prakrit *nachcha* f. Skr. *nṛitja* dancing]

nau'tĭcal *a.* Of sailors or navigation, naval, maritime; ~ **almanac,** year-book containing astronomical and tidal information for navigators etc.; *nautical* MILE; hence ~LY[2] *adv.* [f. F *nautique* or f. L f. Gk *nautikos* (*nautēs* sailor f. *naus* ship); see -ICAL]

nau'tĭlus *n.* (*pl.* ~**es,** *or* **nau'tili** *pr.* -ī). **Paper** ~, small cephalopod of genus *Argonauta*, of which the female has very thin shell and webbed sail-like arms; **pearly** ~, cephalopod of genus *Nautilus*, with chambered shell having nacreous septa. [L, f. Gk *nautilos*, lit. sailor (as prec.)]

Nă'vajō, Nă'vahō, (-ahō) *n.* (*pl.* ~**s**). (Member or language of) Amer. Ind. people in New Mexico and Arizona. [Sp., = pueblo]

nā'val *a.* Of, in, for, etc., ships or (usu.) the or a navy (~ **academy** (for training naval officers); ~ **architect,** designer of ships; ~ **officer,** officer in navy; ~ **stores,** all materials used in shipping); fought, won, etc., by or consisting of or based on ships of war; hence ~LY[2] *adv.* [f. L *navalis* (*navis* ship; see -AL)]

nă'varin (-ăṅ) *n.* Casserole of lamb or mutton with vegetables. [F]

nāve[1] *n.* Hub of wheel. [OE *nafu, nafa,* = OHG *naba,* ON *nöf* f. Gmc **nabō* f. IE **nobhā*; cf. NAVEL]

nāve[2] *n.* Body of church esp. from west door to chancel, usu. separated by pillars from aisles. [f. med. L *navis* f. L *navis* ship]

nā'vel *n.* Depression in front of belly left by detachment of umbilical cord (**contemplate** one's ~, indulge in philosophical quietism); central point of anything; ~ **orange,** large orange with navel-like formation at top; ~**-string,** umbilical cord; ~**wort,** pennywort or other plant with round centrally-depressed leaves. [OE *nafela,* = OHG *nabalo,* ON *nafli* f. Gmc **nabhalon* f. IE *(*o*)*nobh-*; cf. NAVE[1]]

navĭ'cūlar *a.* & *n.* **1.** *a.* Boat-shaped (of shrines, and of parts of plants or body); ~ **bone** in hand or usu. foot; ~ **disease** (in horse's navicular bone). **2.** *n.* Navicular bone or disease. [f. F *naviculaire* or f. LL *navicularis* f. L *navicula* dim. of *navis* ship; see -AR[1]]

nă'vĭg|able *a.* (Of river, sea, etc.) affording passage for ships; seaworthy (*in navigable condition*); (of balloon) steerable, dirigible; hence ~ABI'LITY *n.* [F, or f. L *navigabilis* (as foll.; see -ABLE)]

nă'vĭgāte *v.* **1.** *v.i.* Sail (in) ship; (of passenger in vehicle) assist driver by indicating correct route. **2.** *v.t.* Sail over or up or down (sea, river); manage, direct course of, (ship or aircraft). [f. L *navigare* (*navis* ship, *agere* drive) + -ATE[3]]

năvĭgā'tion *n.* Navigating (**inland** ~, communication by canals and rivers); methods of determining ship's or aircraft's position and course by geometry and astronomy; voyage; ~**-coal,** steam-coal; ~ **lights** (on aircraft, indicating its position and direction of flight). [F, or f. L *navigatio* (as prec.; see -ATION)]

nă'vĭgātor *n.* One charged with or skilled in navigation; sea explorer; ||(arch.) navvy. [L (as NAVIGATE; see -OR)]

||**nă'vvȳ** *n.*, & *v.i.* **1.** *n.* Labourer employed in excavating etc. for canals, railways, roads, etc.; = STEAM *navvy.* **2.** *v.i.* Work as navvy. [abbr. of prec.]

nā'vȳ *n.* **1.** Whole body of State's ships of war with their crews and all the organization for their maintenance; officers and men of this; (poet.) fleet; ||MERCHANT *navy.* **2.** ~ (**blue**), dark blue used in naval uniform; ||~ **cut,** cake tobacco finely sliced; ***N**~ **Department,** government department in charge of navy; ||**N**~ **List,** official book with all naval officers' names and other information; *~ **yard,** government shipyard with civilian labour. [ME, = fleet, f. OF *navie* ship, fleet f. Rom. & pop. L *navia* ship, f. L *navis*]

nawa'b (nawah'b *or* -aw'b) *n.* **1.** (Hist.) Title of governor or nobleman in India. **2.** Title of distinguished Muslim in Pakistan. [f. Urdu *nawwāb* pl. f. Arab. *nā'ib* deputy; cf. NABOB]

nay *adv.* & *n.* **1.** *adv.* (arch.) = NO[4]; why, well, (vaguely introducing comment on another's statement etc.). **2.** Or rather, and even, and more than that, (*weighty, nay, unanswerable*). **3.** *n.* The word 'nay'; negative vote; **will not take** ~, disregards refusals; **say** ~, ~**'say,** utter denial or usu. refusal, refuse or contradict (*cannot say him nay*); cf. YEA. [ME, f. ON *nei* (*ne* not, *ei* AYE[2])]

Nă'zarēne *n.* & *a.* (Native or inhabitant) of Nazareth, esp. Christ; (in Jewish or Muslim use) Christian; (member) of an early Jewish-Christian sect. [ME, f. LL f. Gk *Nazarēnos* (*Nazaret* Nazareth; see -ENE 2)]

Nă'zarīte[1] *n.* Native or inhabitant of Nazareth. [f. LL *Nazaraeus* f. Gk *Nazaraios* + -ITE[1] (1)]

Nă'zarīte[2], **Nă'zirīte,** *n.* Hebrew who had taken certain vows of abstinence (Num. 6). [f. LL *Nazaraeus* f. Heb. *nāzīr* (*nāzar* separate or consecrate oneself) + -ITE[1] (1)]

nāze *n.* Promontory, headland. [f. place-names; cf. NESS]

Na'z|ĭ (nah'tsĭ *or* nah'zĭ) *n.* & *a.* (Member) of the German National Socialist party; hence ~IDOM, ~(ĭ)ISM (3), *ns.*, ~IFY *v.t.* [repr. pronunc. of *Nati-* in G *Nationalsozialist*]

N.B. *abbr.* New Brunswick; no ball; Scotland (North Britain); *nota bene.*

Nb *symb:* niobium.

***N.B.C.** *abbr.* National Broadcasting Company.

||**N.B.G.** *abbr.* (colloq.) no bloody good.

N. by E., N. by W., *abbrs.* North by East, West.

N.C. *abbr.* North Carolina.

||**N.C.B.** *abbr.* National Coal Board.

N.C.O. *abbr.* non-commissioned officer.

N.C.R. *abbr.* no carbon required.

||**N.C.U.** *abbr.* National Cyclists' Union.

-nd[1] *suf.* forming *ns.* & *adjs.* w. sense '(person or thing) to be treated in specified way' (*dividend, ordinand, reverend*). [f. or after L *-andus, -endus* of gerundives]

-nd[2] *suf.* forming *ns.* (*fiend, friend*). [OE *-ond,* orig. part. ending]

N.D(ak). *abbr.* North Dakota.

n.d. *abbr.* no date.

Nd *symb.* neodymium.

né (nā) *a.* Born (used in adding man's former name after his present name: *Lord Beaconsfield, né Benjamin Disraeli*). [F, p.p. of *naître* be born; cf. NÉE]

N.E. *abbr.* North-East(ern).

Ne *symb.* neon.

***N.E.A.** *abbr.* National Education Association.

Nēă'nderthal (-tahl) *a.* Of or belonging to the type of man widely distributed in palaeolithic Europe, with retreating forehead and massive brow-ridges. [f. ~, valley in the Rhineland, Germany, where parts of a skeleton were found in 1857]

neap *a.*, *n.*, & *v.* **1.** *a.* & *n.* ~(**-tide**): see TIDE[1]. **2.** *v.i.* (Of tide) tend towards neap, reach highest point of neap tide. **3.** *v.t.* (In *pass.*, of ship) be kept aground, in harbour, etc., by neaping of tides. [OE *nēpflōd* (cf. FLOOD), of unkn. orig.]

Nēapŏ'lĭtan *a.* & *n.* (Native or inhabitant) of Naples; ~ **ice,** ice cream made in layers of different colours and flavours, sweetmeat of similar appearance; ~ **violet,** double sweet-scented kind of viola. [ME, f. L *Neapolitanus* (*Neapolites* n. f. L f. Gk *Neapolis* Naples f. *neos* new + *polis* city; see -AN)]

near[1] *adv.* & *prep.* (compar. & superl. also used as *preps.*). **1.** *adv.* To or at a short distance, in(to) proximity in space or time; **far and** ~, everywhere; ~ **at hand,** within easy reach, not far in the future; ~ **by,** not far off; ~ **upon,** (arch.) not far in time from. **2.** (arch.) Almost, nearly, *not* nearly or anything like. **3.** Closely (*as near as one can guess; the nearer it resembles him the less I like it*); (arch.) parsimoniously (*lives very near*); **go** ~ **to** do, **come** or **go** ~ **doing,** nearly do. **4.** *prep.* Near to, to or at a short distance (in space, time, condition, or resemblance) from (*occurs near the end; comes no nearer the end; near* one's HEART; *the time draws near Christmas; sun is near setting; hope came near fulfilment; who comes nearest him in wit?*); *near the* KNUCKLE, *the* WIND[1]; NOWHERE *near.* **5.** (in *comb.*) Resembling, intended as a substitute for (*near-beer*); that is almost (*near-hysterical; a near-Communist*). [ME, f. ON *nær,* orig. compar. of *ná* = OE *nēah* NIGH]

near^2 *a.* (often governing *n.* in *pred.* use; so also in compar. & superl.). **1.** Closely related (*near relation*; *near and dear*), intimate (*a near friend*). **2.** (Of part of animal or vehicle ‖or road, or horse etc. in team) left [orig. of side from which one mounted, opp. OFF] (*the near fore leg*, ‖*near side front wheel*). **3.** Close at hand, close to, in place or time (*the nearest man*; *in the near future*; *the man near* or *nearest you*; *is nearer* (*to*) *us*); **~'by** *a.*, close in position; *Near* EAST; **~ work** (that must be done with the eye close to it). **4.** (Of road or way) direct. **5.** Close, narrow, (*a near guess*, *resemblance*, *translation*, *race*, GO^2, *escape*); niggardly. **6. ~ miss,** (lit. or fig.) not a hit, but near enough to have effect (e.g. to damage target in bombing); **~-sighted,** short-sighted; **~ thing,** narrow escape. **7.** Hence **~'ISH**^{1} 2 *a.*, **~'NESS** *n.* [ME, f. prec.]

near^3 *v.i.* & *t.* Draw near (to), approach. [f. NEAR^{1,2}]

Nēâr'ctĭc *a.* (Zool.) Of arctic and temperate parts of N. America. [f. NEO- + ARCTIC]

near'lȳ *adv.* **1.** Closely (*nearly related*; *concerns me nearly*; *correspond*, *resemble*, *nearly*). **2.** Within a (very) little, almost; **not ~,** nothing like, far from (*not nearly enough*). [f. NEAR^2 + -LY^2]

neat^1 *n.* (*sing.*, or collect. as *pl.*; arch.) Any bovine animal; (collect.) cattle; **~'herd,** cowherd; **~-house,** shed for cattle; **~'s-foot, ~'s-tongue,** (used as food); **~'s-leather** (made from hide of ox). [OE *nēat*, = OS *nōt*, OHG *nōz*, ON *naut* f. Gmc **nautam* (**naut-* make use of)]

neat^2 *a.* (Of liquor, esp. alcoholic) undiluted; of elegant simplicity in form or arrangement, nicely made or proportioned; (of language, style, sayings) brief, clear, and pointed, cleverly phrased, epigrammatic; deft, dextrous, cleverly done; tidy, methodical; *(sl.) excellent; **~-handed,** dextrous; hence **~'EN**^{6} *v.t.*, **~'LY**^{2} *adv.*, **~'NESS** *n.* [f. F *net* f. L *nitidus* shining (*nitēre* shine)]

neath *prep.* (poet.) Beneath. [f. BENEATH]

nĕb *n.* (Sc. & N. Engl.) Beak or bill; nose; snout; tip, spout, point. [OE *nebb* = ON *nef*, rel. to MDu., MLG *nebbe* f. Gmc **nabhja-*; cf. NIB]

N.E.B. *abbr.* New English Bible.

Neb(r). *abbr.* Nebraska.

nĕ'bbĭsh *n.* & *a.* (colloq.) Submissive, timid, (person). [f. Yiddish *nebach* poor thing!]

nĕ'būla *n.* (*pl.* *~e or ~s*). **1.** (Astron.) Bright or dark area due to reflection or absorption of light by cloud of dust or gas; bright area due to galaxy or large cloud of distant stars. **2.** (Med.) Clouded spot on cornea causing defective vision. [L, = mist]

nĕ'būlar *a.* Of nebula(e); **~ theory** or **hypothesis** (that solar and stellar systems were developed from nebulae); so **nĕbū'lIUM** *n.*, hypothetical element causing observed bright lines in spectrum of nebulae, now known to be due to oxygen etc. in highly ionized state. [f. prec. + -AR^1]

nĕ'būlous *a.* **1.** (Astron.) Of or like nebula(e); **~ star,** small cluster of indistinct stars, or star in luminous haze. **2.** Cloudlike; hazy, vague, indistinct, formless; clouded, turbid. **3.** So **nĕbūlo'SITY** *n.* [ME, f. F *nébuleux* or f. L *nebulosus* (as NEBULA; see -OUS)]

nĕ'būlȳ *a.* (Her.) Of wavy form, represented as cloud. [f. F *nébulé* f. med. L *nebulatus* f. L NEBULA; see -Y^4]

nĕcĕssâr'ĭan *n.* & *a.* = NECESSITARIAN; hence **~ISM** (3) *n.* [f. NECESSARY + -ARIAN]

nĕ'cĕssarĭlȳ (*or* -sĕ'r-) *adv.* As a necessary result, inevitably. [f. foll. + -LY^2]

nĕ'cĕssarȳ *a.* & *n.* **1.** *a.* Indispensable, requisite, (*to* or *for* person etc.; *it is necessary that*, *to* do); requiring to, that must, be done. **2.** Determined by predestination or natural laws, not by free will; happening or existing by necessity (*necessary evil*); (of concept or mental process) inevitably resulting from nature of things or the mind, inevitably produced by previous state of things; (of agent) having no independent volition. **3.** *n.* Thing without which life cannot be maintained (*the necessaries of life*) or is unduly harsh; **the ~,** (sl.) money or action needed for a purpose (*provide*, *find*, *do*, *the necessary*). [ME, f. AF **necessarie*, OF *necessaire* f. L *necessarius* (*necesse* needful; see -ARY^1)]

nĕcĕssĭtâr'ĭan *n.* & *a.* (Person) denying free will and maintaining that all action is determined by antecedent causes (opp. *libertarian*); hence **~ISM** (3) *n.* [f. NECESSITY + -ARIAN]

nĕcĕ'ssĭtāte *v.t.* **1.** *Force, compel, (person) *to* do. **2.** Render necessary, involve as condition or accompaniment or result. [f. med. L *necessitare* compel (as NECESSITY) + -ATE^3]

nĕcĕ'ssĭtous *a.* Poor, needy. [f. F *nécessiteux* or foll. + -OUS]

nĕcĕ'ssĭtȳ *n.* **1.** Constraint or compulsion regarded as a law prevailing through the material universe and governing all human action; **logical ~,** compulsion to believe that of which the opposite is inconceivable. **2.** Constraining power of circumstances, state of things compelling to certain course; LAY^3 *under necessity*; **of ~,** unavoidably; **make a virtue of ~,** claim credit for alacrity or sense of duty when doing what one cannot avoid doing, do thing with a good grace; **~ knows no law** (absolves from any offence). **3.** Imperative need (*for*; *necessity is the mother of invention*); indispensability (*of*; *the necessity of protecting life and property*); indispensable thing, necessary; (in *sing.* or *pl.*) want, poverty, hardship, pressing need. [ME, f. OF *necessité* f. L *necessitas -tatis* (*necesse* needful; see -ITY)]

nĕck^1 *n.* & *v.* **1.** *n.* Part of body that connects head with shoulders; BREAK^1 one's *neck*, *neck of* task etc.; **dead from the ~ up,** (sl.) without any sign of intelligence; **get it in the ~,** suffer fatal or severe blow; **pain in the ~,** (colloq.) annoying or tiresome person or thing; **risk** one's **~,** take chance of being killed by falling etc.; **save** one's **~,** escape hanging; STICK^1 one's *neck out*; **talk through** (**the back of**) one's **~,** (sl.) talk foolishly or wildly; **up to** one's **~,** (colloq.) very deeply involved *in*; **~ and crop,** headlong, bodily; **~ and ~,** running level in race; **~ or nothing,** desperately, staking all on success. **2.** Length of horse's head and neck as measure of its lead in race; flesh of animal's neck as food (esp. *neck of lamb* or *mutton*); part of shirt etc. around neck; (sl.) impudence (*you've got a neck asking that*). **3.** Narrow part of cavity or vessel, esp. of bottle near mouth, or of passage, pass, or channel; pass, narrow channel, isthmus; part of violin etc. bearing finger-board; narrow connecting part between two parts of thing; (Geol.) solidified lava or igneous rock in old volcano crater or pipe; (Archit.) lower part of capital; ***~ of the woods,** (colloq.) locality. **4. ~'band,** part of garment around neck; **~'cloth,** cravat; **~'erchief** (-chĭf), square of cloth worn round neck [f. KERCHIEF]; **~'lace** (-lĭs), ornament of precious stones or metal, or beads etc., worn round neck; **~'line,** outline of opening of garment at neck; **~'tie,** band of silk etc. (giving appearance of) securing shirt-collar; **~-verse,** (Hist.) Latin words (usu. beginning of Ps. 51) printed in black letter, by reading which person claiming benefit of clergy might save his neck; **~'wear,** (Commerc.) collars and ties. **5.** Hence (-)**~ED**^{2} (-kt) *a.* **6.** *v.i.* (sl.) (Of couples) clasp one another round the neck, engage in amorous fondling. **7.** *v.t.* (sl.) Hug, embrace, (person). **8.** *v.t.* & *i.* Form narrowed part (in). [OE *hnecca*, = MDu. *nac*, *necke*, OHG (*h*)*nac*, ON *hnakki* nape f. Gmc **hnak*(*j*)- f. IE **knok*-]

‖**nĕck²** *n.* (dial.) Last sheaf of corn cut. [ME; orig. unkn.]

nĕ'cking *n.* (Archit.) = NECK¹ 3. [f. NECK¹ + -ING¹]

nĕ'cklet *n.* Ornament or fur garment for neck. [f. NECK¹ + -LET]

nĕ'cro- *comb. form.* Corpse, as: **~bio'sis,** decay in tissues of body; **~ge'nic,** produced by contact with dead bodies; ~LATRY (-ŏ'l-); ~LOGY (-ŏ'l-), death-roll or obituary notice; **~phagous** (-ŏ'f-) that feeds on carrion; **~polis** (-ŏ'p-), (esp. ancient) cemetery; **ne'cropsy** or **~scopy** (-ŏ's-), post-mortem examination. [f. or after Gk *nekro-* (*nekros* corpse; see -O-)]

nĕ'cromănc|y̆ *n.* Art of predicting by means of communicating with the dead; magic, enchantment; so ~ER¹ *n.*, **nĕcromă'nt**IC *a.* [ME, f. OF *nigromancie* f. med. L *nigromantia* changed (by assoc. w. L *niger nigri* black) f. LL f. Gk *nekromanteia* (as prec.; see -MANCY)]

nĕcrŏ'phĭl|y̆ *n.* Morbid (esp. erotic) attraction to corpses; so **nĕ'cro**PHIL(E), **nĕcrophĭ'l**IA¹, ~ISM (1), *ns.* [f. as NECRO- + Gk *-philia* loving; see -Y¹]

nĕcr|ō'sĭs *n.* (*pl.* **~o'ses** *pr.* -ō'sēz). (Path.) Death of circumscribed piece of tissue, esp. of bones; hence or cogn. ~O'TIC *a.*, **~ō'se, nĕ'crot**IZE (3), *vbs. i.* [mod. L, f. Gk *nekrōsis* (*nekroō* kill; see NECRO-, -OSIS)]

nĕ'ctar *n.* **1.** (Gk & Rom. Myth.) drink of the gods; any delicious drink. **2.** Sweet fluid produced by plants and made into honey by bees. **3.** Hence or cogn. **nĕctār'**EAN, **nĕctār'**EOUS, ~ED² (-*erd*), **~ĭ'**FEROUS, ~OUS, *adjs.* [f. L f. Gk *nektar*]

nĕ'ctarĭne (*or* -ēn) *n.* Kind of peach with thin downless skin and firm flesh. [n. use of arch. adj. f. NECTAR + -INE¹]

nĕ'ctary̆ *n.* Flower's or plant's nectar-secreting organ. [f. mod. L *nectarium* (as NECTAR; see -ARY¹)]

N.E.D. *abbr.* (arch.) Oxford English Dictionary (orig. New English Dictionary).

‖**N.E.D.C.** *abbr.* National Economic Development Council.

Nĕ'ddy̆ *n.* (colloq.) Donkey; ‖ = prec. [dim. of *Ned*, pet-form of man's name *Edward*; see -Y³]

***née*, *nee,** (nā) *a.* Born (used in adding married woman's maiden name after her surname: *Mrs. Smith, née Jones*). [F, fem. p.p. of *naître* be born]

need¹ *n.* **1.** Circumstances requiring some course of action (*if need arise* or *be* or *were*; *there is no* etc. *need, feel the need, have no need, to* do or *of* doing or abs.); **have ~,** require *to*; **had ~,** ought to (*had need remember*). **2.** Necessity for presence or possession *of* (*the need of further securities*); **have ~ of,** require, want. **3.** Emergency, crisis, time of difficulty, (*a friend in need is a friend indeed*; *failed him in his need*; **at ~,** in time of need); destitution, lack of necessaries, poverty. **4.** Thing wanted, respect in which want is felt, requirement, (*my needs are few*). **5. ~'fire,** (1) fire got from dry wood by friction, and thought to have magical properties, (2) beacon, bonfire. [OE *nēd*, = OS *nōd*, OHG *nōt*, ON *nauth*, *neyth*, Goth. *nauths* f. Gmc **naudhiz*, **nauthiz*]

need² *v.* **1.** *v.i.* (arch.) Be necessary; **it ~s not,** it is needless; *more* **than ~s,** than is necessary. **2.** *v.t.* Stand in need of, require. **3.** Be under necessity or obligation to or *to* do (*it needs to be done with care*; *need you ask?*; (ellipt.) *don't be away longer than you need*); (in 3 *sing. pres. neg.* or *interrog.* **need** without *to*: *he need not trouble himself*; *need she have come at all?*; (colloq.) *it needn't*, or *doesn't need to, be finished*; **~ not have done,** did not need to do). [OE *nēodian* (*nēod* desire, var. of prec.)]

nee'dful *a.* Requisite, necessary, indispensable, (*to, for*, or abs.; *it is needful to* do, or *that*); **the ~,** what is necessary, (sl.) money or action needed for a purpose; hence ~NESS *n.* [ME, f. NEED¹ + -FUL]

nee'dle *n.*, & *v.t.* **1.** *n.* Thin round long piece of steel etc. pointed at one end and with eye for thread at other used in sewing; similar instrument without eye, used in KNITTING, crocheting, etc.; PIN¹*s and needles*; **sharp as a ~,** lit., or fig. acute, observant; **~ in a haystack,** thing so buried among or concealed by many others as to make search for it hopeless; **~'s eye,** least possible aperture, esp. w. ref. to Matt. 19:24. **2. (Magnetic) ~,** piece of magnetized steel used as indicator on dial of compass and in magnetic and electric apparatus, esp. in telegraphy. **3.** Pointed etching instrument; pointed surgical instrument; pointed end of hypodermic syringe; thin pointed piece of metal, wood, etc., that receives and transmits the vibrations set up by a revolving gramophone record; similar device used in making the record; steel pin exploding cartridge of breech-loader. **4.** Obelisk (*Cleopatra's Needle*); sharp rock, peak. **5.** Beam used as temporary support during underpinning. **6.** Needle-shaped crystal. **7.** Leaf of fir or pine. **8.** ‖(sl.) Fit of nervousness (*got the needle while waiting*). **9. ~-bath,** shower-bath with fine strong spray; **~-book,** book-shaped case for sewing-needles; **~cord,** fine corduroy fabric; **~craft,** skill in needlework; **~-fish,** garfish (*Belone belone*) or other long fish with slender jaws; **~ful,** length of thread etc. put into needle at one time; ‖**~ game, match,** etc., one closely contested and arousing exceptional personal feeling; **~-lace** (made with needles not bobbins); **~-point,** (1) fine sharp point, (2) = *needle-lace*, (3) gros point; **~ valve** (closed by thin tapering part); **~woman,** (1) seamstress, (2) *good* or *bad* user of sewing-needle; **~work,** sewing or embroidery. **10.** *v.t.* Sew, pierce, or operate on, with needle; thread (one's *way*) between or through things; underpin with needle-beams; incite, irritate, prod into action. [OE *nǣdl*, = OS *nādla*, OHG *nādala*, ON *nál*, Goth. *nēthla* f. Gmc **nēthlō*, **nētlā* (**nē-* sew)]

nee'dlĕss *a.* Unnecessary, uncalled for; **~ to say,** (parenth.) which I need not tell you; hence ~LY² *adv.*, ~NESS *n.* [ME, f. NEED¹ + -LESS]

nee'dments *n. pl.* Things needed, esp. personal necessaries carried on journey. [f. NEED¹,² + -MENT + -S¹]

needs (-z) *adv.* **1.** (arch.) Of necessity. **2. ~ must** (do, or ellipt.) cannot help or avoid or get out of doing; **must ~** do, (1) foolishly insists or insisted on doing, (2) = *needs must* do. [OE *nēdes* (as NEED¹, -S³)]

nee'd|y̆ *a.* (Of person) poor, destitute, without necessaries; (of circumstances) characterized by poverty; hence **~ĭ**NESS *a.* [ME, f. NEED¹ + -Y²]

ne'er (nār) *adv.* **1.** (poet.) = NEVER 1. **2. ~ a,** = NEVER a; **~-do-well,** (orig. Sc.) **~-do-weel,** good-for-nothing (person). [ME contr. of NEVER]

nĕfār'ious *a.* Wicked, iniquitous; hence ~LY² *adv.*, ~NESS *n.* [f. L *nefarius* (*nefas* wrong f. *ne-* not + *fas* divine law) + -OUS]

neg. *abbr.* negative.

nĕgā'te *v.t.* Nullify; deny existence of; imply or involve non-existence of; be the negation of. [f. L *negare* deny (*neg-* not) + -ATE³]

nėgā′tion *n.* Denying; negative statement or doctrine; refusal, contradiction, denial *of*; (Logic) assertion that a certain proposition is false; absence or opposite of something actual or positive; negative or unreal thing, nonentity; so **nĕ′gat**ORY *a.* [F, or f. L *negatio* (as prec.; see -ATION)]

nėgā′tionist *n.* One who denies accepted beliefs without proposing substitutes. [f. prec. + -IST]

nĕ′gative[1] *a.* **1.** Expressing or implying denial, prohibition, or refusal, (*negative statute, vote, answer*); **~ proposition,** (Logic) negation. **2.** Lacking, or consisting in the lack of, positive attributes (**~ virtue,** abstention from vice); marked by absence of qualities (*negative reaction; test gave a negative result*); **~ evidence, instance,** (of non-occurrence of something). **3.** (Alg., of quantity) less than zero, to be subtracted from others or from zero (**~ sign,** —); in direction opposite that regarded as POSITIVE; *negative* FEEDBACK; **~ quantity,** (joc.) nothing. **4.** (Electr.) Of the kind of charge carried by electrons (opp. POSITIVE); containing or producing such charge; **~ pole,** (of magnet) south-seeking pole. **5.** Of opposite nature to thing regarded as positive (*debt is negative capital*); *negative* INCOME *tax*. **6.** (Photog.) Having lights and shades of the actual object or scene reversed, or colours replaced by complementary ones. **7.** Hence **~**LY[2] (-vli) *adv.*, **~**NESS (-vn-), **nĕgati′**VITY, *ns.* [ME, f. OF *negatif -ive* or f. LL *negativus* (as NEGATE; see -IVE)]

nĕ′gative[2] *n.* **1.** Negative statement, reply, or word (*it is hard to prove a negative; two negatives make an affirmative*); **the ~**, position opposing the affirmative; **in the ~**, negative(ly) (*the answer is in the ~*, no), so as to reject proposal etc. **2.** Negative quality, absence of something, (*his character is made up of negatives*). **3.** (Photog.) Negative image on developed film etc., from which positive pictures are obtained. [ME, = prohibition, f. F *negative* or LL *negativa* (*sententia* opinion, etc.) f. *negativus* (as prec.)]

nĕ′gative[3] *v.t.* Veto, reject, refuse to accept or countenance; disprove (inference, hypothesis); contradict (statement); neutralize (effect). [f. NEGATIVE[1]]

nĕ′gativ|ism *n.* Attitude of negationist; so **~**IST (2) *n.*, **~ĭ′st**IC *a.* [f. NEGATIVE[1] + -ISM]

nėglĕ′ct *v.t.*, & *n.* **1.** *v.t.* Slight, disregard, not pay attention(s) to; leave uncared-for; leave undone, be remiss about; omit *to* do or do*ing*. **2.** *n.* Neglecting or being neglected; disregard *of*; negligence; hence **~**FUL *a.* [f. L *neglegere -lect-* (*neg-* not, *legere* choose, pick up)]

néglĭgé, nĕ′glĭgee, (nĕ′glĭzhā) *n.* Free-and-easy or unceremonious attire; woman's loose informal garment(s). [F, p.p. of *négliger* = prec.]

nĕ′glĭg|ence *n.* Lack of proper care or attention, (piece of) carelessness, (CONTRIBUTORY *negligence*); freedom from restraint or artificiality in literature or art; so **~**ENT *a.* (*of* duty etc.), **~ent**LY[2] *adv.* [ME f. OF, or f. L *negligentia* (*negligere*, = *neglegere*; see NEGLECT, -ENCE)]

nĕ′glĭgĭble *a.* That need not be considered (*negligible* QUANTITY). [obs. F (*négliger* NEGLECT; see -IBLE)]

nėgō′tiable (-sha-) *a.* That can be negotiated; open to discussion or modification. [f. foll. + -ABLE]

nėgō′ti|āte (-shĭ-) *v.* **1.** *v.i.* Confer (*with* another) with view to compromise or agreement. **2.** *v.t.* Arrange (affair), bring about (desired result), by negotiating. **3.** Transfer (cheque etc.) to another for a consideration, convert into cash or notes, get or give value for (cheque etc.) in money. **4.** Clear, get over or through, dispose of, (fence, obstacle, difficulty). **5.** Hence or cogn. **~**ANT, **~**A′TION (-sĭ- *or* -shĭ-), **~āt**OR, *ns.* [f. L *negotiari* (*negotium* business f. *neg-* not + *otium* leisure) + -ATE[3]]

Nē′grĕss. See NEGRO.

Nėgrĭ′llō *n.* (*pl.* **~**s). One of dwarf Negro people in Central and S. Africa. [Sp., dim. of NEGRO]

Nėgrī′tō (-rē′-) *n.* (*pl.* **~s**). One of small Negroid people in the Malayo-Polynesian region. [as prec.]

Nē′grĭtūde *n.* Quality of being a Negro; affirmation of the value of Negro culture. [f. F *négritude* NIGRITUDE]

Nē′grō *n.* (*pl.* **~es;** *fem.* **Ne′gress**) & *a.* **1.** *n.* Member of black-skinned (orig.) African race of mankind. **2.** *a.* Of this race, black-skinned, (*Negro* MINSTREL 2); occupied by or connected with Negroes (*Negro* SPIRITUAL); (of animals, *n~*) black or dark (*negro ant, bat, monkey*). **3. n~-head,** (1) strong black plug tobacco, (2) inferior indiarubber. **4.** Hence **~**HOOD *n.*, **~**PHIL(E) *a.* & *n.*, **~**PHO′BIA *n.* [Sp. & Port., f. L *niger nigri* black]

Nē′groid *a.* & *n.* (Member) of division of mankind having characteristics typical of Negro race (esp. black skin, woolly hair, and flat nose); hence **~**AL (-oi′-) *a.* [f. prec. + -OID]

Nē′grōĭsm *n.* Advancement of Negro interests and rights; idiom etc. used mainly by Negroes. [f. NEGRO + -ISM]

Nē′gus[1] *n.* Ruler of Ethiopia. [f. Amh. *n'gus* king]

nē′gus[2] *n.* Hot sweetened wine and water. [f. Col. F. *Negus* d. 1732, its inventor]

Neh. *abbr.* Nehemiah (O.T.).

neigh (nā) *v.i.*, & *n.* (Utter) cry (as) of horse. [OE *hnægan*, = MDu. *neyen*, MHG *nēgen*, of imit. orig.]

nei′ghbour, *-bor, (nā′ber) *n.* & *v.* **1.** *n.* Dweller next door, near, in same street or village or district, or in adjacent country, (*my neighbour Jones; are next-door neighbours; his nearest neighbour is 12 miles away; our neighbours across the Channel*), esp. regarded as one who should be friendly (*good, bad, neighbours*) or as having claim on others' friendliness; **duty to** one's **~** (to any fellow man). **2.** Person or thing near or next to another (*my neighbour at dinner; falling tree brought down its neighbour*). **3.** (*attrib.*) Neighbouring. **4.** Hence **~**LESS *a.*, **~**SHIP *n.* **5.** *v.t.* & *i.* Adjoin, border on or (*up*)*on*; hence **~**ING[2] *a.* [OE *nēahgebūr* (as NIGH; *gebūr*, cf. BOOR)]

nei′ghbourhood, *-bor-, (nā′ber-) *n.* **1.** Neighbourly feeling or conduct. **2.** Nearness, vicinity *of* (**in the ~ of** *£100*, about). **3.** Neighbours, people of a district; district, esp. one forming a community within a town or city. [ME, f. prec. + -HOOD]

nei′ghbourl|y̆, *-bor-, (nā′ber-) *a.* Characteristic of or befitting neighbour(s); friendly, kindly; hence **~ĭ**NESS *n.* [f. NEIGHBOUR + -LY[1]]

nei′ther (nī′dh-; *or* nē′dh-) *adv., conj., a.,* & *pron.* **1.** *adv.* (Introducing word, clause, etc., that is to be negatived equally with a following one(s) attached to it by *nor*) not either, not on the one hand, (*neither knowing nor caring; would neither come in nor go out; neither fish nor flesh nor fowl*; (arch.) *neither does cowardice ensure nor courage preclude defeat; neither* HERE *nor there*); (vulg., w. neg.) either (*I don't know that neither*); not either, also not, (*if you do not go, neither shall I; he did not go and neither did I; he should not have gone, (and) neither did he*). **2.** *conj.* (arch.) Nor, nor yet, (*I know not, neither can I guess*). **3.** *a.* & *pron.* Not either, not the one nor the other, (*neither accusation, neither of the accusations, is true; neither of them knows*, often also irreg. *know*); (loosely) none of any number of specified things. [ME *naither*, *neither*, f. OE *nowther* contr. of *nōhwæther* (as NO², WHETHER); assim. to EITHER]

nĕk *n.* (S. Afr.) = COL 1. [Du., = NECK¹]

nĕ'kton *n.* Group of forms of free-swimming organic life found at various depths in the ocean and in lakes, taken collectively. [G, f. Gk *nēkton* neut. of *nēktos* swimming (*nēkhō* swim)]

nĕ'llў *n.* **1.** Largest species of petrel. **2.** ||**Not on your ~,** (sl.) certainly not. [perh. f. the woman's name *Nelly*]

nĕ'lson *n.* Wrestling-hold in which arm is passed under opponent's arm from behind and hand is applied to his neck. [app. f. name *Nelson*]

nėlŭ'mbō *n.* (*pl.* **~s**). Plant of genus *Nelumbo*, Indian LOTUS. [mod. L, f. Sinh. *neḷum*(*bu*)]

nĕ'matocўst *n.* Cell in jellyfish etc. containing coiled thread that can be projected as sting. [f. as foll. + CYST]

nĕ'matōde *a.* & *n.* (Worm) of slender unsegmented cylindrical shape. [f. Gk *nēma* -*matos* thread + -ODE]

nĕ'mbūtal *n.* Sodium salt of pentobarbitone, used as sedative and anticonvulsant. [**P**; f. *Na* (=sodium) + 5-*e*thyl-5-(1-*m*ethyl*but*yl) barbiturate + -AL; cf. BARBITAL]

nem. con. *abbr. nemine contradicente.*

Nėmē'an *a.* (Gk. Ant.) ~ **games** (held at Nemea in alternate years); ~ **lion** (said to have been killed by Hercules). [f. L *Nem*(*a*)*eus* f. Gk *Nemeaios* (*Nemea* near Argos); see -AN]

nėmẽr'tine *a.* & *n.* (Worm) of class Nemertea of marine flatworms, often brightly coloured. [f. mod. L *Nemertes* f. Gk *Nēmertēs* name of a sea nymph + -INE¹]

nėmē'sia (-zh*a*) *n.* S. Afr. plant of genus *Nemesia*, cultivated for its variously coloured irregular flowers. [mod. L, f. Gk *nemesion*, name of a similar plant; see -IA¹]

nĕ'mės|ĭs *n.* (*pl.* **~es** *pr.* -ēz). Retributive justice; downfall caused by, agent of, this. [Gk, = righteous indignation, personified as goddess of retribution (*nemō* give what is due)]

nemine (nĕ'mĭnĭ; *or* nā'-) *pron.* ~ ***contradicente*** or ***dissentiente*** (kŏntrădĭsĕ'ntĭ *or* -kĕ'-; dĭsĕntĭĕ'ntĭ), unanimously (or with no dissenting vote). [abl. of L *nemo* nobody]

ne'ne (nā'nā) *n.* Hawaiian species of goose. [f. Hawaiian *nēnē*]

nĕ'nūphãr *n.* Water-lily. [med. L, f. Arab. & Pers. *nīnūfar*, *nīlūfar* [f. Skr. *nīlōtpala* blue lotus (*nīla* blue, *utpala* lotus)]

nēō- *comb. form.* New, modern, later, revived, as: **~-Ca'mbrian,** (Geol.) of the later Cambrian period or system; **~cla'ssic**(**al**), of a revival of classical style or treatment in art, literature, music, etc.; **~-colo'nialism,** use of economic, political, or other means of obtaining or retaining influence over former colonies; **~-He'llenism,** revival of Greek ideals; **~my'cin,** antibiotic related to streptomycin; **~pe'ntane,** isomer of pentane, the last to be discovered; **~-Pla'tonism,** 3rd-c. mixture of Platonic ideas with Oriental mysticism, similar doctrine in medieval and later times; **~-schola'sticism,** revival and restatement of teachings of medieval schoolmen; **~tro'pical,** of tropical and S. America; **~zo'ic,** (Geol.) of later period of geological history, post-palaeozoic or post-mesozoic. [Gk (*neos* new; see -O-)]

nēodў'mĭum *n.* (Chem.) Metallic element of lanthanide series. [f. NEO- + DIDYMIUM]

nēolĭ'thĭc *a.* Of the later Stone Age, when ground or polished stone weapons and implements prevailed. [f. NEO- + Gk *lithos* stone + -IC]

nēolō'gĭan *a.* & *n.* **1.** *a.* Of, inclined to, marked by, neologism in theology. **2.** *n.* Neologist in theology. [f. NEOLOGY + -AN]

nėŏ'log|ĭsm, nėŏ'log|ў, *ns.* Coining or using of new words, new-coined word; tendency to or adoption of novel or rationalistic religious views; so **~IST** (1) *n.*, **~IZE** (2) *v.i.* [f. F *néologisme*, *néologie*, f. as NEO-, -LOGY, -ISM]

nē'ŏn *n.* (Chem.) Inert gaseous element occurring in traces in the atmosphere and giving orange-red glow when electricity is passed through it in a sealed low-pressure tube, whence its use in lights and illuminated advertisements (*neon lamp, light, sign*). [Gk, neut. of *neos* new]

nē'onāte *n.* New-born child; so **nēonā'tal** *a.* [f. mod. L *neonatus* (as NEO-, NATION)]

nēŏntŏ'log|ў *n.* Study of organisms not yet extinct; hence **~IST** (3) *n.* [f. NEO- + ONTOLOGY]

nē'ophrŏn *n.* White Egyptian vulture or other bird of genus *Neophron*. [name of man turned into vulture in *Metamorphoses* of Antoninus Liberalis (2nd c.)]

nē'ophўte *n.* New convert esp. among primitive Christians or Roman Catholics; newly ordained R.C. priest; novice of religious order; beginner, novice, tiro. [f. eccl. L f. N.T. Gk *neophutos* newly planted (as NEO-, *phuton* plant)]

nē'oplăsm *n.* (Path.) New growth of tissue in some part of body, esp. tumour; so **nēoplă'stic** *a.* [f. NEO- + Gk PLASMA formation]

nē'oprēne *n.* Synthetic rubberlike polymer. [f. NEO- + *chloroprene* etc. (perh. f. PROPYL + -ENE)]

nėŏ'tėnў *n.* (Zool.) Retention of juvenile features in adult animal; sexual maturity in larval form. [f. G *neotenie* f. as NEO- + Gk *teinō* extend]

nēotĕ'rĭc *a.* Recent, newfangled, modern. [f. LL Gk *neōterikos* (*neōteros* compar. of *neos* new; see -IC)]

Nĕpalē'se (-z) *a.* & *n.* (*pl.* same). = foll. [f. *Nepal* (see foll.) + -ESE]

Nėpa'lĭ (-aw'-) *a.* & *n.* (Native, inhabitant, or language) of Nepal. [f. *Nepal*, country N.E. of India, + -I]

nėpĕ'nthė *n.* = foll. 1. [var. of foll., after It. *nepente*]

nėpĕ'nthēs (-z) *n.* **1.** (poet.) Drug causing forgetfulness of grief. **2.** Pitcher-plant of genus *Nepenthes*. [L, f. Gk *nēpenthes* (*pharmakon* drug), neut. of *nēpenthēs* (*nē-* not, *penthos* grief)]

nĕphelŏ'|mėter *n.* Instrument for measuring turbidity of liquid; so **nĕphelomĕ'tric** *a.*, **~METRY** *n.* [f. Gk *nephelē* cloud + -O- + -METER]

nĕ'phew (*or* -v-) *n.* Brother's or sister's son. [ME f. OF *neveu* f. L *nepos nepotis* grandson, nephew]

nėphŏ'logў *n.* Study of the clouds. [f. Gk *nephos* cloud + -O- + -LOGY]

nĕ'phrīte *n.* = JADE² 1. [f. G *nephrit* f. Gk *nephros* kidney, w. ref. to its supposed efficacy in kidney disease; see -ITE¹ (2)]

nėphrĭ'tĭc *a.* Of or in the kidneys, renal; of nephritis. [f. LL f. Gk *nephritikos* (as foll.; see -IC)]

nėphrī'tĭs *n.* Inflammation of the kidneys. [LL, f. Gk (*nephros* kidney; see -ITIS)]

nĕphr|(o)- *comb. form.* Kidney, as: **~E'CTOMY** *n.*, excision of kidney; **~ŏ'LOGY, ~ŏ'TOMY,** *ns.* [f. Gk (as prec.) + -O-]

ne plus ultra (nē plŭs ŭ'ltr*a* *or* nā plo͞os o͞o'ltrah) *n.* Prohibition of advance, impassable obstacle; furthest point attained or attainable; highest pitch or form *of*, acme, culmination. [L, = not further beyond, supposed inscription on Pillars of Hercules (Strait of Gibraltar) prohibiting passage by ships]

nĕ'pot|ĭsm *n.* Undue favour in appointing one's relatives to office (orig. by popes for illegitimate sons called nephews); so **~IST** (1) *n.* [f. F *népotisme* f. It. *nepotismo* (*nepote* NEPHEW; see -ISM)]

Nĕ'ptūne *n.* **1.** (Roman god of) the sea (**~'s cup,** sponge of genus *Poterion*). **2.** One of the farthest planets of the solar system, discovered in 1846 from mathematical computations. [ME f. F, or f. L *Neptunus*]

Nĕptū′nĭan *a.* & *n.* (Geol.) produced by water action; (person) maintaining aqueous origin of certain rocks, so **Nĕ′ptūn**IST (2) *n.* (opp. *Plutonist* or *Vulcanist*); of planet Neptune. [f. L *Neptunius* (as prec.) + -AN]

nĕptū′nĭum *n.* (Chem.) Transuranic element produced when uranium atoms absorb bombarding neutrons. [f. NEPTUNE, planet next beyond Uranus, + -IUM]

||**N.E.R.C.** *abbr.* Natural Environment Research Council.

nēr′ėĭd *n.* Sea-nymph; (Zool.) long sea-worm or centipede. [f. L f. Gk *Nērēis -idos* daughter of sea-god Nereus; see -ID[3] 2]

nėrī′nė *n.* Bulbous S. Afr. plant of genus *Nerine* with showy red or pink flowers, e.g. Guernsey lily. [mod. L, f. L name of water-nymph]

nẽr′ka *n.* Sockeye salmon. [native name]

nero antico (nārō ahntē′kō) *n.* Kind of black marble found in Roman ruins. [It.]

nẽr′olĭ *n.* Essential oil from flowers of bitter orange, used in perfumery. [f. F *néroli* f. It. *neroli*, perh. f. name of Italian princess]

Nėrō′nĭan *a.* (As) of Nero or his times; cruel, licentious, tyrannical. [f. L *Neronianus* f. C. C. *Nero -onis*, Rom. emperor d. A.D. 68; see -IAN]

nẽrts. See NUT 1.

nẽr′v|āte *a.* (Bot.) (Of leaf) having ribs; so ~A′TION *n.* [f. foll. + -ATE[2]]

nẽrve *n.*, & *v.t.* **1.** *n.* Fibre or bundle of fibres connecting and conveying impulses of sensation and motion between brain or spinal cord or ganglionic organ and some part of the body; material constituting these. **2.** (in *pl.*) Bodily state in regard to physical sensitiveness and interaction between brain and other parts, disordered state in these respects, exaggerated sensitiveness, nervousness; **does not know what ~s are,** has equable and confident temperament; **bundle of ~s,** very nervous person; **a fit of ~s,** nervous state; **get on** person's **~s,** be a source of worry or irritation or annoyance to him; **has iron ~s, ~s of steel,** etc., is not easily upset or frightened; **~ war,** = WAR[1] *of nerves*. **3.** (poet. or arch.) Sinew, tendon. **4. Strain every ~,** make all possible efforts. **5.** Vigour, energy. **6.** (Bot.) Rib, esp. midrib, of leaf. **7.** Coolness in danger, boldness, assurance, (**lose** one's **~,** become timid or irresolute); (colloq.) audacity, impudence, (*had the nerve, has a nerve, to ask for more*). **8. ~-cell,** cell transmitting impulses in nerve tissue; **~-centre,** group of closely connected ganglion-cells, (fig.) centre of control; **~ gas,** poison gas that affects the nervous system; **~-knot,** (arch.) ganglion; **~-racking,** greatly straining the nerves. **9.** Hence **(-)nẽrv**ED[2] (-vd) *a.*, **nẽr′v**O- *comb. form.* **10.** *v.t.* Give strength, vigour, or courage, to; brace one*self* to face danger or suffering. [ME, = sinew, f. L *nervus*, rel. to Gk *neuron*]

nẽr′velėss (-vl-) *a.* Inert, lacking vigour or spirit, listless; (of style) flabby, diffuse; (Bot. & Entom.) without nervures; (Anat. & Zool.) without nerves; confident, not nervous; hence ~LY[2] *adv.*, ~NESS *n.* [f. prec. + -LESS]

nẽr′vine *a.* & *n.* (Med.) (Medicine) relieving nerve-disorders. [f. F *nervin* (as NERVE; see -INE[1])]

nẽr′vous *a.* **1.** (arch.) Sinewy, muscular. **2.** (Of literary style) vigorous, terse. **3.** Full of nerves; of the nerves (**~ system,** nerves and nerve-centres as a whole, allowing organism to co-ordinate its response to environment; **central ~ system,** brain and spinal cord); affecting, or acting on, the nerves (**~ breakdown,** severe weakness or disorder of nerves). **4.** Having disordered or delicate nerves, excitable, highly strung, easily agitated, timid; ||**~ of doing,** afraid to do. **5.** Hence ~LY[2] *adv.*, ~NESS *n.* [ME, f. L *nervosus* (as NERVE; see -OUS)]

nẽr′vure (-yer) *n.* One of the tubes forming framework of insect's wing, vein; principal vein of leaf. [F (*nerf* NERVE; see -URE)]

nẽr′vy̆ *a.* **1.** (poet.) Sinewy, strong. **2.** Jerky, nervous. **3.** (sl.) Cool, confident, impudent; trying to the nerves. [f. NERVE + -Y[2]]

nĕ′science (nĕ′shyens) *n.* Not knowing, absence of knowledge *of*. [f. LL *nescientia* f. L *nescire* not know (*ne-* not, *scire* know); see -ENCE]

nĕ′scient (nĕ′shyent) *a.* & *n.* Ignorant (*of*); agnostic. [f. as prec.; see -ENT]

nĕss *n.* Promontory, headland, cape. [OE *næs*, = ON *nes*, LG *nesse*, rel. to OE *nasu* NOSE]

-nėss *suf.* forming *ns.* from *adjs.*, expr. state or condition (*bitterness, clearness, conceitedness, happiness, lovingness, up-to-date-ness*), instance of this (*a kindness*), or material in a state (*foulness*). [OE *-nes(s), -nis(s)*, = OS, OHG *-nessi, -nissi*, Goth. *-nassus* f. Gmc **n* in p.p. of strong vbs. + **-assus* (**-atjan* vbl suf.)]

nĕst *n.* & *v.* **1.** *n.* Structure or place made or chosen by bird for laying eggs and sheltering young (**it's an ill bird that fouls its own ~,** one should not speak ill of home etc.; FEATHER[2] one's *nest*); animal's or insect's abode or spawning or breeding place. **2.** Snug or secluded retreat, lodging, shelter, bed, receptacle; haunt *of* robbers etc.; fostering-place *of* vice etc. **3.** Brood or swarm in same nest etc.; collection or series of similar objects; **~ of tables** (fitting one under another when not in use). **4. ~-egg,** (1) real or imitation egg left in nest to induce hen to go on laying there, (2) sum of money kept as reserve or nucleus. **5.** Hence ~′FUL 2 *n.*, ~′LIKE *a.* **6.** *v.i.* Make or have nest in specified place, take to nest-building; take wild birds' nests or eggs; fit together like nest of tables. **7.** *v.t.* (in *p.p.*) Established (as) in nest; (of boxes etc.) packed one inside another. [OE, = OHG *nest* f. IE **nizdo-* (**ni* down, **sed-* sit)]

nĕ′stle (-sel) *v.* **1.** *v.i.* Settle oneself, be settled, comfortably *down*, or *in, into, among*, etc., leaves, wraps, chair, etc.; press oneself affectionately (*close*) *to* or *up to* person; lie half-hidden or embedded. **2.** *v.t.* Push (head, face, shoulder, etc.) affectionately or snugly *in* or *into*; (usu. in *p.p.*) hold as if in nest. [OE *nestlian*, = MDu., MLG *nestelen* (as prec.; see -LE 3)]

nĕ′stlĭng (-sl-) *n.* Bird too young to leave nest. [ME, f. NEST + -LING[1], or f. prec. + -ING[3]]

Nĕ′stŏr (*or -er*) *n.* Wise old man, senior of company etc. [name of character in Homer's *Iliad*]

Nĕstŏr′ĭan *a.* & *n.* (Adherent) of doctrine of Nestorius, asserting that Christ embodied distinct divine and human persons; hence ~ISM (3) *n.* [f. LL *Nestorianus* (*Nestorius*, patriarch of Constantinople 428–31); see -IAN]

nĕt[1] *n.* & *v.* (-tt-). **1.** *n.* Fabric of twine, cord, hair, etc., joined at intervals to form a set of meshes; piece of this used for catching fish, birds, etc., or for protecting fruit, confining hair, holding cargo, keeping away mosquitoes, dividing tennis-court, enclosing practice-ground for cricket batsmen, etc.; football or hockey or lacrosse goal-space enclosed by net. **2.** Moral or mental snare; means of catching or entrapping a person; spider's web; reticulation, network. **3. ~′ball,** game in which ball has to be thrown so as to fall through an elevated horizontal ring from which net hangs; **~ curtain** (of fine-meshed material); **~′work,** (*n.*) arrangement with intersecting lines and interstices recalling those of net, complex system of railways, rivers, canals, etc., chain of interconnected persons or operations or electrical conductors, group of broadcasting stations connected for simultaneous broadcast of same programme, (*v.t.*) broadcast thus. **4.** Hence ~'FUL 2 *n.* **5.** *v.t.* Cover, confine, catch, with net(s); put (ball) in net or goal; fish (river etc.) with nets, set nets in (river); make (purse, hammock, etc.) by netting; (usu. in *p.p.*) mark with netlike pattern, reticulate. **6.** *v.i.* Make netting. [OE *net(t)*, = OS *net(ti)*, OHG *nezzi*, ON *net*, Goth. *nati*]

nĕt², **nĕtt**, *a.*, & *v.t.* (**-tt-**). **1.** *a.* Free from deduction, remaining after necessary deductions (*of*), (~ **profit,** true profit, actual gain after working expenses have been paid, opp. *gross profit*); (of price) off which discount is not allowed; (of weight) excluding that of container etc.; (of effect, result, etc.) ultimate, effective; *net* TON¹. **2.** *v.t.* Gain or yield (sum) as net profit. [F; see NEAT²]

nĕ'ther (-dh-) *a.* (arch. or joc.) = LOWER³ 1 (*nether lip, jaw*); ~ **garments** etc., trousers; ~ **man** or **person,** legs etc.; ~ **millstone,** (fig.) hard heart etc.; ~ **regions,** ~ **world,** hell, underworld; hence ~MOST *a.* [OE *nithera* etc., = OS *nithiri*, OHG *nidari*, ON *nethri* f. Gmc **nithar* down(wards)]

Nĕ'therlander *n.*, **Nĕ'therlandĭsh** *a.*, (-dh-). (Native or inhabitant) of the Netherlands. [f. Du. *Nederlander*, *Nederlands(ch)* (*Nederland*; see foll.)]

Nĕ'therlands (-dh-; -z) *n.* **1.** Kingdom of Holland in N. Europe. **2.** (Hist.) Low Countries. [f. Du. *Nederland* (as NETHER, LAND¹)]

nĕ'tsuke (-sŏŏkā) *n.* (*pl.* ~**s,** *or* same). Carved button-like ornament worn by Japanese to suspend articles from girdle. [Jap.]

nĕtt. See NET².

nĕ'ttĭng *n.* In vbl senses; netted string, thread, or wire; piece of this used for various purposes. [f. NET¹ + -ING¹]

nĕ'ttle *n.*, & *v.t.* **1.** *n.* Plant of genus *Urtica*, including two common species growing profusely on waste land and covered with stinging hairs; other plant resembling these, esp. DEAD *nettle*; GRASP *the nettle*; ~**-rash,** eruption on skin in patches like those made by nettle stings. **2.** *v.t.* Sting with nettles; irritate, provoke, annoy. [OE *net(e)le*, = OS *netila*, OHG *nezzila*, OSw. *netla* f. Gmc **natilōn*; see -LE 1]

neume, neum, *n.* (Mus.) Sign in plainsong indicating note or group of notes to be sung to a syllable. [ME f. OF *neume*, f. med. L *neu(p)ma* f. Gk *pneuma* breath]

neur'al (nūr'-) *a.* (Anat.) Of the nerves; of the central nervous system; situated on same side of body as the central nervous system, dorsal. [f. Gk *neuron* nerve + -AL]

neură'lg|ia (nūră'lj*a*) *n.* Intense intermittent pain due to affection of nerve(s) esp. of head or face; hence ~IC *a.* [mod. L, f. as prec.; see -ALGIA]

neurăsth|ē'nĭa (nūr-) *n.* Debility of nerves causing fatigue, listlessness, etc.; so ~**ĕ'n**IC *a.* & *n.* [f. Gk *neuron* nerve + ASTHENIA]

neurā'tion (nūr-) *n.* Distribution of nervures, venation. [irreg. f. Gk *neuron* nerve + -ATION]

neur|ī'tĭs (nūr-) *n.* Inflammation of nerve(s); hence ~**ĭ't**IC *a.* [f. as foll. + -ITIS]

neur'ō- (nūr'ō) *comb. form.* Nerve(s), as: ~**gli'a** (*or* -ŏ'glĭa), non-nervous supporting tissue in nervous system; ~**-mu'scular,** of nerves and muscles; ~**path,** person of abnormal nervous sensibility or affected by nervous disease; so ~**pa'thic** *a.*, ~**pathy** (-ŏ'p-) *n.*; ~**patho'logy,** pathology of nervous system; ~**physio'logy,** physiology of nervous system; ~**pterous** (-ŏ'p-), of the Neuroptera, order of insects having four membranous transparent wings with reticulate neuration, e.g. lacewing; ~**-sur'gery** (performed on nervous system); ~**tomy** (-ŏ't-), cutting of nerve esp. to produce sensory paralysis. [f. Gk *neuron* nerve + -o-]

neurŏ'log|ȳ (nūr-) *n.* Scientific study of nerve systems; hence **neurolŏ'g**ICAL (nūr-) *a.*, ~IST (3) *n.* [f. mod. L f. mod. Gk *neurologia* (as prec.; see -LOGY)]

neurō'ma (nūr-) *n.* (*pl.* ~**s** *or* ~**ta**). Tumour on nerve or in nerve-tissue. [f. as foll. + -OMA]

neur'ŏn, neur'ōne, (nūr'-) *n.* Nerve-cell and its appendages; hence **neurŏ'n**IC (nūr-) *a.* [Gk *neuron* nerve]

neurō's|ĭs (nūr-) *n.* (*pl.* ~**es** *pr.* -ēz). Functional derangement due to disorders of nervous system, esp. without organic change; behaviour showing inability to take rationally objective view of life. [mod. L (as NEURO-; see -OSIS)]

neurŏ't|ĭc (nūr-) *a.* & *n.* **1.** (Person) suffering from neurosis. **2.** Of neurosis; (colloq.) showing undue adherence to unrealistic idea of things. **3.** Hence ~ICALLY *adv.*, ~**ĭc**ISM (2) *n.* [f. prec.; see -OTIC]

neu'ter *a.*, *n.*, & *v.t.* **1.** *a.* (Gram.) (of noun etc.) neither masculine nor feminine; (of verb) intransitive. **2.** Neutral in war, argument, opinion, etc.; **stand** ~, remain neutral, declare neutrality. **3.** (Bot.) without pistils and stamens, asexual; (Entom.) sexually undeveloped, sterile. **4.** *n.* Neuter noun, adjective, pronoun, verb, or gender; sexually undeveloped female insect, esp. bee or ant; castrated animal; neutral person. **5.** *v.t.* Castrate. [ME, f. OF *neutre* or f. L *neuter* neither (*ne-* not, *uter* either)]

neu'tral *a.* & *n.* **1.** *a.* Not assisting either of two belligerent States, belonging to a State that thus stands aloof, exempted or excluded from active or passive hostilities; taking neither side in dispute or difference of opinions; indifferent, impartial. **2.** Not distinctly marked or coloured, indefinite, vague, indeterminate; ~ **tint,** grey or slate-colour; *neutral* VOWEL. **3.** (Chem.) neither acid nor alkaline; (Electr.) neither positive nor negative; (Entom. & Bot.) sexually undeveloped, asexual; *neutral* EQUILIBRIUM; ~ **gear,** condition in which engine is disconnected from driven parts. **4.** Hence or cogn. ~ITY (-ă'l-) *n.*, ~LY² *adv.* **5.** *n.* Neutral State or person; subject of neutral State; neutral gear. [ME f. obs. F, or f. L *neutralis* of neuter gender (as prec.; see -AL)]

neu'traliz|e, -is|e (-īz), *v.t.* Make neutral; counterbalance, render ineffective by opposite force or effect; exempt or exclude (place) from sphere of hostilities; hence ~A'TION *n.* [f. F *neutraliser* f. med. L *neutralizare* (as prec.; see -IZE)]

neutri'nō (-ē'-) *n.* (*pl.* ~**s**). (Phys.) Either of two stable elementary particles with zero electric charge and probably zero mass, interacting only very slightly with matter. [It., dim. of *neutro* neutral (as NEUTER)]

neu'trŏn *n.* Elementary particle of about same mass as proton but without electric charge, present in all atomic nuclei except those of ordinary hydrogen; ~ **star,** hypothetical very dense star composed mainly of neutrons. [f. NEUTRAL + -ON]

Nev. *abbr.* Nevada.

névé (nĕ'vā) *n.* Expanse of granular snow not yet compressed into ice at head of glacier. [Swiss F, = glacier, f. Rom. **nivatum* f. L *nix nivis* snow]

nĕ'ver *adv.* **1.** At no time or moment, on no occasion, not ever, (*have never been there*; *never even looked*; *never before, since, yet*). **2.** ~ **is a long time** or **word** or **day** (comment on rash renunciation or despair or negative prophecy); ~, ~ (emphat.); **it is ~ too late to mend,** reformation is always possible; NOW *or never*; ~ **say die,** do not despair. **3.** Not . . . at any time, not . . . ever, (*is never likely to succeed*; *I never remember her winning*); not at all (*never fear*; *never* MIND[2]). **4.** (colloq., expr. surprise or incredulity, in sentence or ellipt.) Surely not, you do not mean it, (*you never left the key in the lock!*; '*He ate the whole turkey.*'—'*Never!*'; **I ~ did!, Well, I ~!,** i.e. heard of such a thing etc.). **5.** ~ **a,** not a, no . . . at all; ~ **a one,** none; ~ **so,** (in concessive clause) to unlimited extent (*task was beyond him, though he work never so hard*); ~ **the,** (w. compar.) = NONE *the*. **6.** (in *comb.* w. participles etc.) *never-to-be-forgotten, -ending, -failing,* etc. **7. ~mor'e,** at no future time; **N~ N~ (Land),** northern Queensland; ||**never--ne'ver,** (colloq.) hire-purchase; **~thele'ss** *adv.* & *conj.*, despite that, but despite that, notwithstanding, all the same. [OE *nǣfre* (*ne* not, *ǣfre* EVER)]

***nē'vus.** See NAEVUS.

new[1] *a.* **1.** Not existing before, now first made, brought into existence, invented, introduced, known or heard of, experienced, or discovered, (*New* TESTAMENT); unfamiliar or unaccustomed *to*. **2.** Renewed, fresh, further, additional, different, changed, (*a new morality*; *the new chairman*; *my new tailor*); (in place-names) discovered or founded later than and named after (*New Orleans*; *New Zealand*); *new* BIRTH; *new* BROOM; *new* DEAL[2]; *turn over a new* LEAF; **a ~ life,** living in conditions very different from previous ones; **~ man,** (Theol.) one converted to Christianity (*put on the ~ man*, show conversion by reforming oneself); *New* MODEL[1]; *new* STYLE. **3. The ~** (as distinctive epithet implying difference of character) later, modern, (derog.) newfangled, advanced in method or doctrine; **the ~ mathematics** (using SET[2] theory etc. in elementary teaching); **the ~ poor, rich,** classes recently impoverished, enriched, by social changes etc.; **the ~ woman,** (derog.) woman who aspires to freedom and independence and rejects convention; *the New* WORLD. **4.** Of recent origin, growth, arrival, or manufacture, now first used, not worn or exhausted, (*new potatoes, bread, wine, cheese*; *new furniture, clothes*; *new countries, soil*; *a heart, pleasures, ever new*; *fifteen new members*); (of a language) modern, in use since medieval times; **as good as ~,** not having been impaired (as) by wear and tear; **New Christian,** Marrano; *new* CHUM; **~ foundation,** cathedral etc. founded after Reformation; **~ look,** fashion in women's dress *c.* 1947 marked esp. by longer and fuller skirt, (colloq.) up-to-date appearance. **5.** (Of family or person) lately risen to position. **6. ~'comer,** person lately arrived; **New Englander,** inhabitant of **New England,** six N.E. states of U.S.A.; **~-fa'shioned,** made in or following a new fashion; ***New Left,** extremist radical movement among students etc.; **~ light,** person accepting modern or liberal views on religious matters; **~ moon,** moon when first seen as crescent after conjunction with sun, time of such appearance; **New'speak,** artificial official language in Orwell's *1984*; **~ star,** nova; ||**~ town** (established as completely new settlement with government sponsorship); **~ year,** coming or lately begun year, first few days of year, esp. in civil calendar (**New Year's Day, *New Year's,** 1 Jan.; **New Year's Eve,** 31 Dec.); **New Yorker,** native or inhabitant of New York; **New Zealander,** (1, Hist.) Maori, (2) inhabitant of New Zealand of European descent. **7.** Hence ~'ISH[1] 2 *a.*, ~'NESS *n.* [OE *nīwe*, OS, OHG *niuwi*, ON *nýr*, Goth. *niujis* f. Gmc **neujaz* f. IE **newjos*]

new[2] *adv.* (preceding, and now usu. hyphened with, word it qualifies). **1.** Newly, recently, just; **~-blown,** having just come into bloom (lit. or fig.); **~-born,** recently born (and see 2); **~-come,** lately arrived; **~-found,** recently discovered or disclosed; **~-laid,** (of egg) freshly laid; **~-mown,** (of hay etc.) freshly cut. **2.** Anew, afresh, re-; **~-born,** regenerated (and see 1); **~-model,** rearrange, recast. [OE *nīwe* (as prec.)]

New'castle (-ahsel) *n.* **~ disease,** serious respiratory disease of fowls, caused by virus; COALS *to Newcastle*. [f. ~ upon Tyne, in N.E. England]

new'el *n.* Centre pillar of winding stair (**open** or **hollow ~,** central well of winding stair); post supporting stair-handrail at top or bottom. [ME, f. OF *no(u)el* knob f. med. L *nodellus* dim. of L *nodus* knot; see -LE 2]

newfă'ngled (-nggeld) *a.* (derog.) Different from the good old fashion, objectionably novel. [f. (now dial.) *newfangle* ME f. *newe* NEW[2] + *-fangel* f. OE **fangol* inclined to take, + -ED[1]]

Newfou'ndland *n.* **~ (dog),** (dog of) large breed with thick coarse coat, noted for sagacity and swimming powers. [name of Canadian province, an island at mouth of St. Lawrence river]

new'lў *adv.* **1.** Recently (usu. with *p.p.* = NEW[2] 1; *the newly-discovered country*; *a guest newly arrived*); **~-wed,** (person) recently married. **2.** In new manner. [OE *nīwlīce* (as NEW[1], -LY[2])]

New'mar̂kėt *n.* **1. ~ (coat),** close-fitting overcoat for man or woman. **2.** Card-game in which players seek to play cards corresponding to duplicates on table and thus win stakes on these. [~ in Cambridgeshire, noted for horse-races]

news (-z) *n. pl.* (usu. treated as *sing.*) **1.** Tidings, new or interesting information, fresh events reported, (*have you heard the* or *this news?*; *was in the news last year*; *that is news to me*); **bad, good, ~,** report of unwelcome, welcome, events etc.; *that is* **no ~,** already well known; **no ~ is good ~,** absence of information justifies continued optimism. **2.** Medium for transmitting news; (regular) broadcast report of fresh events; (*N~*) part of newspaper title (*Evening News*, *Wallasey News*). **3. ~'agent, *~ dealer,** dealer in newspapers, etc.; **~-boy, ~-girl,** (who delivers or sells newspapers); **~ bulletin,** collection of items of news, esp. for broadcasting; **~'cast(er),** radio or television broadcast(er) of news reports; ||**~ cinema,** = *news theatre*; **~ conference,** press conference; ***~'hawk, *~'hound,** reporter; **~-letter,** printed informal bulletin of club etc., (Hist.) letter sent out periodically to convey news to country towns etc.; **~'monger,** a gossip; **~'paper** (-s-), printed publication usu. daily or weekly containing news, advertisements, literary matter, correspondence, etc.; **~'paperman** (-s-), journalist; **~'print,** paper for printing newspapers on; **~-reader,** = *newscaster*; **~-reel,** cinema film giving the news of the day; **~-room,** (1) room reserved for newspaper-reading, (2) room where news is prepared for broadcasting etc.; **~-sheet,** simple form of newspaper, news-letter; **~-stand,** stall for sale of newspapers; **~ theatre,** cinema showing mainly news-reels; **~-vendor,** newspaper-seller; **~'-worthy,** important or interesting enough to be mentioned as news. **4.** Hence ~'LESS, ~'Y[2], *adjs.* [ME, pl. of NEW[1] after OF *noveles* or med. L *nova* neut. pl. of L *novus* new]

newt *n.* Small tailed amphibian esp. of genus

Triturus, eft. [ME, for *ewt* (*a newt = an ewt*; cf. NICKNAME) var. of *evet* EFT]

new'ton *n.* **1.** (Phys.) Unit of force, force that, acting for one second on a mass of one kilogram, gives it a velocity of one metre per second. **2. N~'s laws of motion,** three propositions about the relations between forces acting and motions occurring. [f. Sir I. *Newton*, Engl. scientist d. 1727]

Newtō'nĭan *a.* Of Newton or his theory of the universe; devised etc. by Newton; classical (*Newtonian mechanics*); (of telescope) with oblique mirror to reflect image to side of tube. [f. as prec. + -IAN]

nĕxt *a., adv., prep.,* & *n.* **1.** *a.* Lying, living, being, nearest or nearest *to* (*in the next house*; *my next neighbour*; *the shop next to the corner*; *the chair next to the fire*); *next* DOOR[1]; **~ friend,** (Law) person acting on behalf of a minor or other person legally incompetent; **~ but one,** with one other intervening; **~ to,** (fig.) almost (*next to nothing*; *next to impossible*), *(sl.) very friendly with. **2.** Soonest come to, first ensuing, immediately following, coming nearest in order etc. *to*, immediately before, (*will ask the next man I see, the next policeman*; *shall return next year, next Friday, on Friday next*; *she arrived* (*the*) *next day*; *the Sunday next before Easter*; *the next two letters are from the same person*; *the next town to London in size*); **~-best,** second-best; *next* WORLD. **3.** *adv.* In the next place or degree, on the next occasion, (*in the week next ensuing*; *placed his chair next to hers*; *next came a strange figure*; *when I next saw him he was lame*); WHAT *next?*. **4.** *prep.* (arch.) In or into the next place to, on the next occasion to, in the next degree to, (*I was standing next him*; *placed his chair next hers*; *loves him next her own child*). **5.** *n.* Next person or thing (**~ of kin,** person most closely related by kin to someone); next letter, issue, etc., (*will tell you in my next*; *to be continued in our next*); next week etc. (*the Friday, week, year,* etc., *after next*); **~ please,** ask your next question, let the next person come, etc. [OE *nēhsta*, = OS *na(h)isto*, OHG *nāhisto*, ON *næstr*, superl. (as NIGH; see -EST[1])]

nĕ'xus *n.* Bond, link, connection, (usu. fig.); **the cash ~** (consisting in money payments). [L (*nectere nex-* bind)]

NF., Nfld., *abbrs.* Newfoundland.

||**N.F.U.** *abbr.* National Farmers' Union.

n.g. *abbr.* no good.

||**N.G.A.** *abbr.* National Graphical Association.

ngai'ō (nī'ō) *n.* (pl. **~s**). Small N.Z. tree (*Myoporum laetum*) with edible fruit and light white timber. [Maori]

N.H. *abbr.* New Hampshire.

||**N.H.S.** *abbr.* National Health Service.

||**N.I.** *abbr.* National Insurance; Northern Ireland.

Ni *symb.* nickel.

nī'acĭn *n.* Nicotinic acid. [f. NICOTINIC + ACID + -IN]

Nīă'gara *n.* Cataract, torrent, deluge. [f. ~ Falls, famous N. Amer. waterfall]

nĭb *n.,* & *v.t.* (**-bb-**). **1.** *n.* Point of quill pen; metal or quill pen-point; point of tool etc. **2.** (in *pl.*) Coffee-beans or cocoa-beans removed from their shells. **3.** *v.t.* Make, mend, insert nib of, (pen). [prob. f. MDu. *nib* or MLG *nibbe*, var. of *nebbe* NEB]

nĭ'bble *v.* & *n.* **1.** *v.t.* Take small bites at; **~ off,** remove thus. **2.** *v.t.* & *i.* Bite gently or cautiously or playfully (esp. of fish with bait, or rabbit); **~ at,** lit., and fig. of dallying with temptation, bargain, etc. **3.** *v.i.* Carp *at*, make trifling criticisms. **4.** *n.* Act of nibbling, esp. of fish at bait; enough (grass etc.) to nibble at. [prob. of LDu. orig.; cf. LG *nibbeln* gnaw]

nĭ'blĭck *n.* (Golf). Iron with large round heavy head, used esp. for playing out of bunkers. [19th c.; orig. unkn.]

nĭbs (-z) *n.* (sl.) **His** etc. **~**, burlesque title after *His Grace* etc. [19th c.; cf. earlier (cant) *nabs*]

nīce *a.* **1.** Fastidious, dainty, hard to please, of refined or critical tastes; precise, punctilious, scrupulous, particular, (*must not be too nice about the means*). **2.** Requiring precision, care, tact, or discrimination, (*a nice experiment, question, problem, point, negotiation*). **3.** Minute, subtle, (*a nice distinction, shade of meaning*). **4.** Attentive, close, (*a nice inquiry, observer*). **5.** Delicately sensitive, discriminative, or deft, (*a nice ear, judgement, hand*). **6.** (colloq.) Agreeable, attractive, delightful, well-flavoured, satisfactory, kind, friendly, considerate, generally commendable, (iron.) disgraceful (*made a nice mess of it*); **~ work,** task well performed. **7. ~ (and),** (colloq.) satisfactor(il)y in respect of specified quality (*house stands nice and high*; *car is going nice and fast*; *this is a nice long one*); **~-looking,** (colloq.) pretty or of engaging appearance; **not very ~,** (colloq.) unpleasant. **8.** Hence **~**'LY[2] (-slĭ) *adv.,* **~**'NESS (-sn-) *n.,* **nī'**CISH[1] 2 *a.* [ME, = stupid, wanton; OF, = silly, simple, f. L *nescius* ignorant (as NESCIENCE)]

niceish. Var. of NICISH (see NICE 8).

Nīcē'ne (*or* nī'-) *a.* Of Nicaea in Bithynia; **first** and **second ~ Councils,** held A.D. 325, 787, to settle the Arian controversy and the question of images; **~ Creed,** formal statement of Christian belief based on that adopted at first Nicene Council. [ME, f. LL *Nic(a)enus* (L f. Gk *Nikaia* Nicaea)]

nī'cėtȳ *n.* Punctiliousness; precision, accuracy, (**to a ~**, exactly); intricate or subtle quality (*a point of great nicety*); minute distinction, subtle or unimportant detail, (in *pl.*) minutiae. [ME, f. OF *niceté* (as NICE; see -TY[1])]

nĭche (*or* nēsh) *n.,* & *v.t.* **1.** *n.* Shallow recess in wall to contain statue, vase, etc.; (fig.) place destined or suitable for person's occupation (**~ in the temple of fame,** right to be remembered for one's achievements); (Ecol.) appropriate combination of conditions for a species to thrive. **2.** *v.t.* Place (statue etc.) in niche (usu. in *p.p.*); ensconce, settle, (esp. one*self*, or in *p.p.*) in a recess or corner. [F (*nicher* make a nest, OF *nichier* f. Rom. **nidicare* f. L *nidus* nest)]

nī'chrōme (-k-) *n.* Alloy of nickel and chromium used for electrical resistors. [f. NICKEL + CHROME]

nī'cĭsh. See NICE 8.

nĭck[1] *n.* Notch serving as catch, guide, mark, etc.; (Print.) groove on side of piece of type to ensure correct placing; (sl.) prison, police station; **in good ~,** (colloq.) in good condition; **in the ~ of time,** only just in time, just at the right moment. [ME, perh. f. foll.]

nĭck[2] *v.* **1.** *v.t.* Make nick(s) in, indent; make incision at root of (horse's tail), cut (horse) thus, to make him carry tail higher; just catch (the right time, a train, etc.); ||(sl.) catch, arrest, (criminal etc.); ||(sl.) steal. **2.** *v.i.* Cut *in* by short cut, at corner, etc., in hunting or racing; (of breeding stock) mingle *well* etc. with others. [16th c.; orig. unkn.]

Nĭck[3] *n.* **Old ~,** the Devil. [prob. f. familiar form of man's name *Nicholas*]

nĭ'ckel *n.,* & *v.t.* (||**-ll-**). **1.** *n.* Hard silver-white lustrous ductile metallic element much used esp. in alloys; U.S. five-cent piece; **~ brass,** alloy of copper, nickel, and zinc; **~-plate** *v.t.,* coat with nickel by plating; **~ silver,** (alloy like) German silver; **~ steel,** alloy of steel with nickel; hence **~**IC, **~**OUS, *adjs.* **2.** *v.t.* Coat with nickel. [abbr. of G *kupfernickel* copper-coloured ore f. which nickel was first got (*kupfer* copper, *nickel* demon, w. ref. to disappointing nature of ore, which yielded no copper)]

***nĭckelō′dėon** *n.* (colloq.) Juke-box. [f. prec. + MELODEON]

||**nĭ′cker** *n.* (sl.) One pound sterling. [20th c.; orig. unkn.]

nĭ′ck-năck. Var. of KNICK-KNACK.

nĭ′cknāme *n.*, & *v.t.* **1.** *n.* Name jokingly or contemptuously added to or substituted for person's, place's, or thing's proper name; abbreviation or familiar form of (esp. Christian) name. **2.** *v.t.* Call (person or thing) by a nick-name; give nickname to. [ME, f. *eke-name*, with *n* from *an* (cf. NEWT); *eke* = addition, f. OE *ēaca* (as EKE¹), NAME¹]

nĭ′col *n.* ~ **(prism)**, device formed of two pieces of calcite cemented together so as to polarize transmitted and reflected light. [f. W. *Nicol*, Sc. physicist d. 1851, its inventor]

nĭcō′tian (-sh*a*n) *a.* & *n.* (arch.) **1.** *a.* Of tobacco. **2.** *n.* Tobacco-smoker. [f. as foll. + -IAN]

nĭ′cotin|e (-tēn) *n.* Poisonous alkaloid extracted as oily liquid from tobacco; hence ~ISM (5) *n.*, ~IZE (5) *v.t.* [F, f. mod. L *nicotiana* (*herba*) tobacco-plant, f. J. *Nicot*, Fr. diplomat & introducer of tobacco into France 1560; see -INE⁵]

nĭcotĭ′nĭc *a.* ~ **acid,** vitamin of B group, white crystalline derivative of pyridine, formed by oxidation of nicotine and acting to prevent pellagra. [f. prec. + -IC]

nĭ′ctĭt|āte *v.i.* Close and open the eyes, wink; **~ating membrane,** third or inner eyelid of many animals; hence ~A′TION *n.* [f. med. L *nictitare* frequent. of L *nictare* blink + -ATE³]

nīdamĕ′ntal *a.* (Of gland etc.) serving as receptacle for ova in molluscs etc. [f. L *nidamentum* (as NIDUS; see -MENT) + -AL]

nĭ′d(d)ering *n.* & *a.* (pseudo-arch.) Base or cowardly (person). [misreading of obs. *nithing* f. ON *nithingr*; given currency by Sir W. Scott]

nĭ′ddle-nŏddle *a.* & *v.* **1.** *a.* Nodding, quivering, unsteady. **2.** *v.t.* & *i.* Keep nodding, sway. [redupl. f. NOD; see -LE 3]

||**nide** *n.* Brood of pheasants. [f. F *nid* or f. L NIDUS]

nĭ′dĭf|ĭcāte, nĭ′dĭf|ȳ, *vbs. i.* Build nest(s); so **~ĭca′tion** *n.* [f. L *nidificare* (NIDUS; see -FY, -ATE³)]

nĭ′d-nŏd *v.i.* & *t.* (**-dd-**). Keep nodding. [redupl. f. NOD]

nī′d|us *n.* (*pl.* **~i** *pr.* -ī, *or* **~uses**). Place in which insect etc. deposits eggs; place in which spores or seeds develop; place of origin or development *of* disease, or *for* quality, doctrine, etc.; natural receptacle; collection of eggs, tubercles, etc. [L, f. IE (as NEST)]

niece *n.* Brother's or sister's daughter. [ME f. OF, f. pop. L **neptia* f. L *neptis* granddaughter]

nĭĕ′ll|ō *n.* (*pl.* **~i** *pr.* -ē, *or* **~os**). Black composition of sulphur with silver, lead, or copper, for filling engraved lines in silver or other metal; (specimen of) such ornamental work; hence **~ōED²** (-ōd) *a.* [It., f. L *nigellus* dim. of *niger* black]

Nier′steiner (-tīn-) *n.* Rhenish wine from Nierstein. [G]

Nie′tzschė|an (nē′ch-) *a.* & *n.* (Follower) of Nietzsche; (supporter) of his principles, esp. w. ref. to the possibility of a superman able to overcome unworthy desires and thus dominate other persons; hence **~an**ISM (3), ~ISM (3), *ns.* [f. F. W. *Nietzsche*, Ger. philosopher d. 1900 + -AN]

||**nĭff** *n.* & *v.* (sl.) Smell, stink; hence ~′Y² *a.* [orig. dial.]

***nĭ′ftȳ** *a.* (sl.) Spruce, smart, stylish; excellent; clever. [19th c.; orig. uncert.]

nĭ′ggard *n.* & *a.* **1.** *n.* Parsimonious person, grudging giver *of*. **2.** *a.* (rhet. or poet.) = foll. [ME, alt. f. earlier (obs.) *nigon*, prob. of Scand. orig.; cf. NIGGLE, -ARD]

nĭ′ggardl|ȳ *a.* & *adv.* **1.** *a.* Parsimonious, miserly; sparing, scanty; giving or given grudgingly or in small amounts; hence **~ĭ**NESS *n.* **2.** *adv.* In niggardly manner. [f. prec. + -LY¹,²]

nĭ′gger (-g-) *n.* **1.** (derog.) Negro; dark-skinned person. **2.** ~ **in the woodpile** or ***fence,** (sl.) suspicious circumstance, something that spoils a good thing; **work like a ~,** toil very hard. **3. ~(-brown),** (arch.) dark shade of brown; **~head,** (1) = NEGRO-*head* (1), (2) bollard; *nigger* MINSTREL 2. [18th c. alt. f. *neger* (16th c.) f. F *nègre* f. Sp. *negro* NEGRO]

nĭ′ggle *v.* **1.** *v.i.* Spend time, be over-elaborate, on petty details; find fault in petty manner. **2.** *v.t.* Cause minor irritation to. [app. of Scand. orig.; cf. Norw. *nigla*]

nĭ′ggling *a.* Trifling, petty; lacking in breadth of view or boldness of effect; (of handwriting) cramped. [f. prec. + -ING²]

nigh (nī) *adv.*, *prep.*, & *a.* (arch., literary, or dial.) = NEAR¹,² (w. same usage of compar. & superl.); WELL*nigh*. [OE *nē(a)h*, = OS, OHG *nāh*, ON *ná-*, Goth. *nēhwa*]

night (nīt) *n.* **1.** Dark period between day and day, time from sunset to sunrise; darkness prevailing in the night (*black* or *dark as night*; *went forth into the night*); period of figurative darkness (*the night of ignorance* or *barbarism*); nightfall (*shall not reach home before night*); weather or experiences or occupation of a night (**have a good** or **bad ~,** sleep well or not, be comfortable during the night or not); evening on which performance etc. occurs (FIRST *night*); **all ~ (long),** throughout the night; **at ~,** during the night, at nightfall, in the evening, in the period 6 p.m. to midnight (*ten o'clock at night*); **by ~,** during the night, under cover of darkness; GOOD *night*; LAST³ *night*; **make a ~ of it,** spend night in festivity; **~ and day,** at all times, without ceasing; **~ out,** (1) festive evening, (2) evening of the week on which servant is free to go out; OVERNIGHT¹,²; **spend the ~ with,** (esp.) be provided with sleeping-place by (often implying sexual intimacy); **stay the ~,** remain until next day; **turn ~ into day,** work etc. by night as if it were day (with necessary bright lights); **work ~s,** be on night-shift. **2.** (in *comb.*) By, like, during, appropriate to, employed for, active in, the night (*night-veiled*, *-black*, *-flying*, *-attire*, *-porter*, *-moth*); ||**~-bell** (to summon person at night, esp. on street-door of doctor's house); **~-bird,** (esp.) owl or nightingale; **~-blindness,** nyctalopia; **~-boat,** passenger-boat crossing in a night; **~′cap,** (1) cap worn in bed, (2) drink (esp. alcoholic) taken before going to bed; **~-chair,** = *night-stool*; **~-clothes** (worn in bed); **~-club,** establishment open at night for dancing, supper, etc.; *night*-COMMODE; **~-dress,** woman's or child's loose garment worn in bed; **~′fall,** end of daylight; **~ fighter,** aeroplane used for interception at night; **~-glass,** short telescope for use at night; **~-gown,** = *night-dress*, (Hist.) dressing-gown; **~-hag,** female demon supposedly riding in the air at night, nightmare; **~-hawk,** (1) nightjar or mopoke, (2) thieving or other nocturnal prowler; **~′jar,** harsh-voiced nocturnal bird of family Caprimulgidae; ***~ letter,** telegram sent cheaply at night; **~-life,** urban entertainment open at night; **~-light,** short thick candle, or electric bulb, giving dim light through night for child, invalid, etc.; **~-line** (left with baited hooks to catch fish by night); **~-long** *a.* & *adv.*, (lasting) for whole night; **~'man** (employed to remove night-soil); **~'mare,** (1) female monster supposedly sitting upon and seeming to suffocate sleeper, incubus, (2) oppressive or paralysing or terrifying or fantastically horrible dream or (colloq.) experience (whence **~'marish** *a.*), (3) haunting fear or thing vaguely dreaded; **~-ni'ght,** (colloq.) good night; **~ nurse** (employed to attend patient(s) during night); **~-owl,** owl flying by night, (colloq.) person active at night; **~-piece,** (painting of) night scene or landscape; **~-rail,** (Hist.) woman's loose dressing-gown etc.; ***~-robe,** = *night-dress*; **~ safe,** receptacle for money etc. deposited at bank when it is closed; **~-school** (providing evening instruction for those working by day); **~-season,** (arch.) night-time; **~-shift,** shift of workmen employed during night; **~-shirt,** boy's or man's long shirt for sleeping in; **~-soil,** contents of cesspools etc. removed at night, esp. for use as manure; **~-spot,** (colloq.) night-club; ***~'stick,** policeman's truncheon; **~-stool,** close-stool for use at night; **~-time,** night as a state of things or opportunity (*in the ~-time*, by night); **~-watch,** (person or party keeping) watch by night, Hebrew or Roman division (one of three or four) of the night (*in the ~-watches*, during the anxious, wearisome, wakeful, etc., night); **~-watchman,** person keeping watch by night, (Cricket) inferior batsman sent in near close of day to avoid dismissal of better one in adverse conditions; **~-work** (that is, or must be, done by night). **3.** Hence ~'LESS *a.* [OE *neaht*, *niht*, = OS, OHG *naht*, ON *nátt*, Goth. *nahts* f. Gmc ***naht-** f. IE ***nokt-**]

nī'ghtĭe (nī'tĭ) *n.* (colloq.) Night-dress. [abbr.; see -IE]

nī'ghtĭngāle (nī'tĭngg-) *n.* Small reddish-brown migratory thrush of genus *Luscinia*, the male singing melodiously and powerfully both by night and in the day. [OE *nihtegala* (whence obs. *nightgale*), OS, OHG *nahta-*, *nahtigala*, ON *nætrgali* f. Gmc (as NIGHT, ***galan** sing); for *-n-* cf. FARTHINGALE]

nī'ghtlў[1] (nī't-) *a.* Happening, done, existing, etc., in the night; happening every night; (literary) of or suiting night. [OE *nihtlic* (as NIGHT, -LY[1])]

nī'ghtlў[2] (nī't-) *adv.* Every night. [ME, f. NIGHT + -LY[2]]

nī'ghtshāde (nī't-) *n.* **1.** Plant of genus *Solanum*; **black ~,** *S. nigrum*, with white flowers and black poisonous berries; **woody ~,** *S. dulcamara*, with purple flowers and bright red berries. **2.** **Deadly ~,** belladonna plant; **enchanter's ~,** white-flowered plant of genus *Circaea*. [OE *nihtscada*, = OHG *nahtscato*, app. f. as NIGHT + SHADE[1], prob. w. ref. to poisonous properties]

nighty. Var. of NIGHTIE.

nĭgrĕ'sc|ent *a.* Blackish; so ~ENCE *n.* [f. L *nigrescere* grow black (*niger nigri* black); see -ENT]

nĭ'grĭtūde *n.* Blackness (lit. or fig.). [f. L *nigritudo* (as prec.; see -TUDE)]

nihil ad rem (nīhĭl ăd rĕ'm) *pred. a.* Irrelevant. [L, = nothing to the matter]

nī'hĭl|ĭsm (*or* nī'ĭl-) *n.* Negative doctrines, total rejection of current beliefs, in religion or morals; (Philos.) scepticism that denies all existence; doctrine of Russian extreme-revolutionary party in 19th–20th c. finding nothing to approve of in the established order; hence ~IST (2) *n.*, **~ĭ'stic** *a.* [f. L *nihil* nothing + -ISM]

nīhĭ'lĭtў *n.* Non-existence, nothingness; mere nothing, trifle, nullity. [f. med. L *nihilitas* (as prec.; see -ITY)]

nihil obstat (nīhĭl ŏ'bstăt) *n.* (R.C. Ch.) certificate that book is not open to objection on religious grounds; (fig.) authorization, official approval. [L, = nothing hinders]

-nĭk *suf.* forming *ns.* denoting person associated with specified thing or quality (*beatnik*, *nogoodnik*). [f. Russ. (as SPUTNIK) & Yiddish]

nĭl *n.* Nothing, no number or amount, (esp. in scoring at games etc.; *three goals to nil*). [L, = *nihil* nothing]

nĭ'lgai (-gī) *n.* Large short-horned Indian antelope (*Boselaphus tragocamelus*). [f. Hindi *nīlgāī* (*nīl* blue, *gāī* cow)]

nĭll *v.t.* & *aux.* (arch.) = WILL[1] not; **will he ~ he,** = WILLY-NILLY. [OE *nyle* (*ne* not, *wile* WILL[1])]

Nīlŏ'mėter *n.* Graduated pillar etc. showing height to which Nile rises during annual floods. [f. Gk *Neilometrion* (see foll., -METER)]

Nīlŏ'tĭc *a.* Of the Nile or Nile region or its inhabitants or languages. [f. L f. Gk *Neilōtikos* (*Neilos* Nile; see -OTIC)]

nĭm *n.* Game in which two players must alternately take one or more objects from one of several heaps and seek to avoid taking (or to take) the last remaining object. [20th c., perh. f. arch. *nim* to take (as foll.), or G *nimm* imper. of *nehmen* take]

nĭ'mble *a.* Quick in movement, agile, swift; (of mind etc.) versatile, clever, quick to apprehend; dextrous; hence ~NESS (-beln-) *n.*, **nĭ'mb**LY[2] *adv.* [OE *næmel* quick to seize (*niman* take f. Gmc ***neman**; see -LE 1), with *-b-* as in THIMBLE]

nĭmbō-strā't|us *n.* (*pl.* **~i** *pr.* -ī). (Meteorol.) Low dark-grey layer of cloud. [f. foll. + -o- + STRATUS]

nĭ'mb|us *n.* (*pl.* **~i** *pr.* -ī, *or* **~uses**). Bright cloud or halo investing deity or person or thing; bright disc or aureole round or over head of saint etc. in picture; (Meteorol.) rain-cloud; hence **~us**ED[2] (-st) *a.* [L, = cloud, aureole]

nĭmī'etў *n.* (literary). Excess, too much. [f. L *nimietas* (*nimis* too much; see -TY[1])]

nĭmĭnў-pĭ'mĭnў *a.* Affected, mincing; spiritless. [cf. MIMINY-PIMINY and NAMBY-PAMBY]

Nĭ'mrŏd *n.* Great hunter or sportsman. [f. Heb. *Nimrōd* valiant; see Gen. 10:8, 9]

nĭ'ncompōōp *n.* Simpleton, foolish person. [17th c. *nicompoop*, of uncert. orig.; perh. f. man's name *Nicholas* + obs. *poop* to cheat]

nīne *a.* & *n.* One more than eight; symbol for this (9, ix, IX); card with nine pips; time of nine o'clock; (in *pl.*) gloves, shoes, etc., of ninth size; **the N~,** the Muses; *baseball team; **dressed to the ~s** (very elaborately); **~ days' wonder,** novelty that attracts much attention but is soon forgotten; **~-tenths,** (fig.) nearly all; **~ times out of ten,** nearly always; **~ to five,** ordinary office hours; *possession is nine* POINT[1]*s of the law*; *cat has nine lives* (see LIFE); ||**~'pins,** skittles with nine objects to be knocked down by throwing a ball; ||**999,** telephone number for emergency services; hence ~'FOLD (-nf-) *a.* & *adv.* [OE *nigon*, = OS *nigun*, *nigon* f. Gmc ***nigun**, var. of ***niwun** f. IE *(*e*)*newn*]

nīnetee'n (-nt-; *or* nī'-) *a.* & *n.* One more than eighteen; symbol for this (19, xix, XIX); **1984** (w. ref. to totalitarian State described in Orwell's novel so titled); ||*nineteen to the* DOZEN; so ~TH[2] *a.* (**~th hole,** (joc.) golf-club's bar) & *n.* [OE *nigontȳne*, OS *nigentein*, OHG *niunzehan*, ON *nitján*; see prec., -TEEN]

nī'net|ў (-ntĭ) *a.* & *n.* **1.** Nine times ten; symbol for this (90, xc, XC); (in *pl.*) numbers etc., esp. years of a life or a century, from 90 to 99; hence **~ĭ**ETH[1] *a.* & *n.* **2.** **~y-one,** (arch.) **one and ~y,**

etc., ninety plus one etc., with corresp. ordinals **~y-first** etc.; **~y-nine out of a hundred,** (fig.) nearly all. [OE *nigontig* (as NINE, -TY²)]
Nĭ'nėvīte *n.* Inhabitant of Nineveh. [f. eccl. L *Ninivitae* pl. (*Ninive* Nineveh, ancient capital of Assyria; see -ITE¹ (1))]
nĭ'nnȳ *n.* Simpleton, foolish person. [perh. for *innocent*; see -Y³]
ni'non (nē'nawṅ) *n.* Lightweight silk dress fabric. [F]
nīnth *a.* & *n.* **1.** *a.* Next after eighth; **~ part,** one of nine equal parts into which thing is or may be divided. **2.** *n.* Ninth part; ninth day of month; (Mus.) interval of octave and second. [f. NINE + -TH²]
nī'nthlȳ *adv.* In the ninth place (in enumerations). [f. prec. + -LY²]
Nī'obė *n.* Inconsolable bereaved woman; hence **Nīobē'**AN *a.* [f. Gk *Niobē*, legendary daughter of Tantalus turned to stone while weeping for her slain children]
nīō'b|ĭum *n.* (Chem.) Rare metallic element usu. found associated with tantalum; hence ~IC, ~OUS, *adjs.* [f. prec. + -IUM]
nĭp¹ *v.* (**-pp-**) & *n.* **1.** *v.t.* Pinch, squeeze sharply, bite; pinch *off* (bud etc.); check growth of (esp. *nip in the* BUD¹; lit. or fig.); (of cold) affect injuriously, pain, whence **~'PING**² *a.*; take *up*, *out*, etc., hurriedly or unobserved. **2.** *v.i.* ||(sl.) Step etc. nimbly *in*(*to*), *out*, *up*. **3.** *n.* Pinch, sharp squeeze, bite; (arch.) sharp saying, sarcasm; (check to vegetation caused by) coldness of air; ***~ and tuck,** neck and neck. [ME, prob. of LDu. orig.]
nĭp² *n.* & *v.* (**-pp-**). **1.** *n.* Small quantity of spirits etc. as pick-me-up. **2.** *v.i.* & *t.* Take nips (of). [prob. abbr. of *nipperkin* small measure, of LDu. orig.; cf. LG, Du. *nippen* to sip]
Nĭp³ *n.* & *a.* (sl., derog.) Japanese. [f. NIPPONESE]
nī'pa (*or* nē'-) *n.* E. Ind. palm-tree (*Nipa fruticans*) with creeping trunk and large feathery leaves; alcoholic drink from its sap. [Sp. & Port., f. Malay *nipah*]
nĭ'pper *n.* In vbl senses; *fish that nips bait or other fishes; ||(sl.) young boy or girl; (in *pl.*) implement with jaws for gripping or cutting, forceps, pincers, pliers; (in *pl.*, arch.) pince-nez; horse's incisor tooth; crustacean's claw. [f. NIP¹,² + -ER¹]
nĭ'pple *n.* **1.** Small projection in which mammary ducts terminate in mammal of either sex; teat, esp. of woman's breast; teat of feeding-bottle. **2.** Nipple-like protuberance on skin, glass, metal, etc.; small rounded elevation on mountain; (Hist.) perforated projection of musket-lock on which percussion-cap was placed; *short section of pipe with screw-thread at each end for coupling. **3. ~-wort,** yellow-flowered weed (*Lapsana communis*). [16th c. also *neble, nible*, perh. dim. f. *neb* + -LE 1]
Nĭ'ppon *n.* Japan; hence **~E'SE** *n.* & *a.*, **Nĭppō'n**IAN *a.* [f. Jap. *Dai Nippon* Japan (lit. 'great land of the rising sun'; cf. JAPAN¹)]
nĭ'pp|ȳ *a.* (colloq.) Active, nimble; chillingly cold; hence **~ĭLY**² *adv.* [f. NIP¹ + -Y²]
nĭrva'na (-vah'-; *or* nēr-) *n.* (Buddhism & Hinduism). Beatitude attained by extinction of individuality and desires, with release from effects of karma. [f. Skr. *nirvāṇa* (*nirvā* be extinguished f. *nis* out + *vā-* to blow)]
***nisei'** (nēsā') *n.* Person whose parents were immigrants from Japan. [Jap., lit. 'second generation']
nī'si *a.* (Law). Subject to conditions as regards taking effect (DECREE *nisi*; *rule nisi*). [L, = 'unless']
nisi prius (nisī pri'us) *n.* (Law). Hearing of civil cases by judges in Crown Court or (Hist.) assize court. [L, = 'unless before', in writ directing sheriff to provide jury unless judges came before specified date]
Nĭ'ssen *n.* **~ hut,** tunnel-shaped hut of corrugated iron with cement floor. [f. P. N. ~, Brit. engineer d. 1930, its inventor]
nĭt *n.* Egg of louse or other parasitic insect; (sl.) stupid person; **~-picking** *n.* & *a.*, (colloq.) fault-finding in petty manner. [OE *hnitu*, = MDu., MLG *nēte*, OHG (*h*)*niz* f. WG **hnito* f. IE **knidā*]
***nī'ter.** See NITRE.
***nī'terȳ** *n.* (colloq.) Night-club. [f. *nite* (phonet. sp. of NIGHT) + -ERY]
nĭ'tĭd *a.* (literary). Bright, shining, (lit. or fig.). [f. L *nitidus* (*nitēre* shine; see -ID¹)]
nī'trāte¹ *n.* Salt or ester of nitric acid; potassium or sodium nitrate as fertilizer. [F (as NITRE; see -ATE¹ (3))]
nītr|ā'te² *v.t.* Treat, combine, or impregnate, with nitric acid; hence **~A'TION** *n.* [f. foll. + -ATE³]
nī'tre (*-er*), ***nī'ter,** *n.* Saltpetre, potassium nitrate; **Chile ~,** sodium nitrate. [ME f. OF, f. L f. Gk *nitron*, of Semitic orig.]
nī'trĭc *a.* Of or containing nitrogen; **~ acid,** clear colourless pungent highly corrosive and caustic liquid, HNO_3; **~ oxide,** colourless gas (NO). [f. F *nitrique* (as prec.; see -IC)]
nī'trīde *n.* (Chem.) Binary compound of nitrogen. [f. NITRE + -IDE]
nī'trĭ|fȳ *v.t.* Impregnate with nitrogen; turn into nitrous or nitric acid; hence **~FICA'TION** *n.* [f. F *nitrifier* (as NITRE; see -FY)]
nī'trīle *n.* (Chem.) Compound of alkyl radical with cyanogen. [f. NITRE; see -IL]
nī'trīte *n.* Salt or ester of nitrous acid. [f. NITRE + -ITE¹ (2)]
nī'trō- *comb. form.* Of, containing, made with or by use of, nitric acid or nitre or nitrogen, as: **~-acid,** compound of nitric acid with organic acid; **~be'nzene,** poisonous yellow oil used to make aniline etc.; **~-ce'llulose,** cellulose nitrate used in lacquers etc.; **~-chalk,** fertilizer made of calcium carbonate and ammonium nitrate; **~-compound** (made by action of nitric acid and containing a nitro-group); **~-explosive** (prepared by means of nitric acid); **~-gly'cerine,** yellowish oily violently explosive liquid made by adding glycerine to mixture of nitric and sulphuric acids; **~-group,** NO_2; **~-lime,** calcium cyanamide, used as fertilizer; **~-powder,** gunpowder made with nitric acid. [Gk (as NITRE; see -O-)]
nī'trogėn *n.* Colourless tasteless odourless gaseous element forming four-fifths of atmosphere, and present in composition in nitrates, proteins, etc.; **~ cycle,** continuous transfer of nitrogen in various forms from soil to plants to animals, and back by decay; **~ fixation,** formation of compounds from atmospheric nitrogen; hence **nītrŏ'gėn**OUS *a.* [f. F *nitrogène* (as NITRO-, -GEN)]
nī'trous *a.* Of, like, impregnated with, nitre; **~ acid** (HNO_2, containing less oxygen than nitric acid); **~ oxide,** colourless sweetish-smelling gas (N_2O) used as anaesthetic, laughing-gas. [f. L *nitrosus* (as NITRE; see -OUS), partly thr. F *nitreux*]
nĭttȳ-grĭ'ttȳ *n.* (sl.) Realities or basic facts of a matter. [20th c.; orig. uncert.]
nĭ'twĭt *n.* (colloq.) Stupid person; hence **~TED**² *a.*, stupid. [perh. f. NIT + WIT²]
||**nĭx**¹ *int.* (sl.) giving warning to confederates etc. that person in authority is approaching. [19th c., perh. = NIX³]
nĭx² *n.* (*fem.* **~'ie**). Water-elf. [G (fem. *nixe*)]
nĭx³ *n.* (sl.) Nothing; * = NO⁴. [f. G *nichts* nothing (dial. & colloq. *nix*)]

N.J. *abbr.* New Jersey.
||**N.L.C.** *abbr.* National Liberal Club.
***N.L.R.B.** *abbr.* National Labor Relations Board.
N. M(ex). *abbr.* New Mexico.
N.N.E., N.N.W., *abbrs.* north-north-east, -west.
nō[1] *a.* **1.** Not any (*no circumstances could justify it; no two of them are alike*); *no* NEWS (*is good news*); (if) *no bishop,* (then) *no king; king* **or no** *king,* regardless of the king, his kingship, etc. **2.** Not a, quite other than, (*service of no honourable kind; is no part of my plan; is no genius; no* LITTLE; *no* SMALL); hardly any (*is no distance; did it in no time*); **there is** etc. **no —ing,** none is etc. possible (*there's no accounting for tastes; there was no mistaking what he meant*). **3.** (ellipt. as slogan, notice, etc.) We will not have any, let there not be any, there is not any, no . . . is allowed, (*no Popery, no surrender, no parking,* etc.). **4.** ***No-account,** unimportant, worthless; **no-ball,** (*n.*) unlawfully delivered ball in cricket (counting one to batting side if not otherwise scored from), umpire's announcement of this, (*v.t.*) pronounce (bowler) to have bowled no-ball; **no-being,** (arch.) non-existence; **no-clai'm(s) bonus,** reduction of insurance premium charged to one who has not claimed payment under the insurance in preceding period; **no date,** (of book etc.) not bearing a date of publication etc.; *no dice* (see DIE[1]), DOUBT[1], END[1]; **no entry** (notice prohibiting vehicles or persons from entering a road or place); ***no-fault,** (of insurance) valid regardless of allocation of blame for accident etc.; *no* FEAR[1], FLOWERS, GO[2], GOOD; ***no-hi'tter,** baseball game in which team does not get a man to first base; **no-ho'per,** (Austral. sl.) useless person; *no* JOKE[1], JOY[1]; **no man,** no person; **no man's land,** piece of waste, unowned, or debatable ground, (Mil.) space between opposed trenches, (fig.) area not clearly belonging to any one subject etc.; **no-meaning,** (arch.) nonsense; *by no* MEAN[1]*s*; *no* MISTAKE[1]; **no one,** (pron.) no person, (*a.*) no single (*no one man could lift it*); ***no place,** nowhere; **no side,** (Rugby Footb.) (referee's announcement of the) end of the game; **no thoroughfare** (notice that path, street, etc. is closed at other end, or that passage is not permitted); **no trump(s),** (Bridge) declaration or bid involving playing without a trump suit; **no-tru'mper,** hand on which a no-trump bid can be, or has been, made; **no'way(s), no'wise,** in no manner, not at all; **no'whence, no'whither,** from, to, no place; NOWHERE; *no* WHIT[1]; *no* WONDER[1]. [ME, f. *nān, nōn* NONE, orig. only bef. consonants]
nō[2] *adv.* **1. Or no,** or not (*pleasant or no, it is true*); **whether or no,** (1) in either case, (2) which of a case and its negative (*tell me whether or no*). **2.** (Sc.) Not (*will ye no come back again?*). [OE *nō, nā* (*ne* not, *ō, ā,* ever)]
nō[3] *adv.* **1.** (w. *compar.*) By no amount, not at all, (*no better than before*); **is no better than she should be,** is morally suspect; *no* LONG[2]*er*; **no sooner had he said it than,** as soon as he had said it; **no sooner said than done,** done immediately after being mentioned. **2. No less (than),** as much (*n., a.,* or *adv.*) or many or important (as) (*gave me £50, no less,* or *no less than £50; no less than ten people have told me; is no less than a scandal, a no less fatal victory; no less a person than Gladstone*). **3. No more,** (*n.*) nothing further (*have no more to say; want no more of it*), (*a.*) not any more (*no more wine?*), (*adv.*) no longer (**is no more,** is dead or passed away), never again, to no greater extent (*is no more a lord than I am; could no more do it than fly in the air*), just as little, neither, (*you did not come, and no more did he*). [OE *nā*; see prec.]
nō[4] *adv.* equivalent to negative sentence, & *n.* (*pl.* **noes**). **1.** *adv.* The answer to your question is negative, your request or command will not be complied with, the statement made or course of action intended or conclusion arrived at is not correct or satisfactory, the negative statement made is correct; **say no,** refuse request, deny statement made; **no, no** (emphat.); **no, nor,** or **no, not,** (substituting stronger phrase: *a man could not lift it, no, nor half a dozen; have not found so great faith, no, not in Israel*). **2.** *n.* The word or answer *no,* a denial or refusal, negative vote, (*two noes make a yes*; **will not take no for an answer,** persists in spite of refusals); **the noes have it,** negative voters are in majority. [ME, = prec.]
nō[5], **noh** (nō), *n.* Traditional Japanese drama with dance and song, evolved from Shinto rites. [Jap.]
No. *abbr.* *North; number [f. L *numero,* abl. of *numerus* number].
n.o. *abbr.* (Cricket) not out.
No *symb.* nobelium.
Nōā'chĭan, Nōā'chĭc, (-k-) *adjs.* Of the patriarch Noah or his time. [f. *Noach* = NOAH + -IAN]
Nō'ah (-*a*) *n.* **~'s ark,** (1) ark in which Noah, his family, and animals were saved, (2) imitation of it as child's plaything, (3) large or cumbrous or old-fashioned trunk or vehicle, (4) small bivalve (*Arca noae*) with boat-shaped shell. [name of Heb. patriarch in Gen. 6]
nŏb[1] *n.,* & *v.t.* (**-bb-**). **1.** *n.* (sl.) Head; **his ~,** (Cribbage) score of one point for holding jack of same suit as card turned up by dealer. **2.** *v.t.* (Boxing). Hit on the head. [perh. var. of KNOB]
||**nŏb**[2] *n.* (sl.) Person of wealth or high social position. [orig. Sc. *knabb, nab*; 18th c., orig. unkn.]
||**nŏ'bble** *v.t.* (sl.) Tamper with (racehorse) to prevent its winning; secure support of (person) by underhand means; get hold of (money etc.) dishonestly; catch (criminal). [prob. = dial. *knobble, knubble* knock, beat, f. KNOB + -LE 1]
nŏ'bbut *adv.* (dial.) Only, no more than. [f. NO[2] + BUT[1]]
nŏ'bbў *a.* (sl.) Suitable for a NOB[2]; smart, elegant. [f. NOB[2] + -Y[2]]
Nō'bĕl (*or* -ĕ'l) *n.* **~ prize,** one of the annual prizes (for physics, chemistry, physiology or medicine, literature, economic sciences, and the promotion of peace) awarded from the bequest of Alfred *Nobel* (d. 1896), Sw. inventor of dynamite.
nōbē'lĭum *n.* (Chem.) Artificially produced transuranic element. [f. as prec. + -IUM]
nobĭ'liarў (-lyerĭ) *a.* Of (the) nobility; **~ particle,** preposition, as French *de,* German *von,* prefixed to title of nobility. [f. F *nobiliaire* (as NOBLE; see -ARY[1])]
nobĭ'lĭtў *n.* Noble character, mind, birth, or rank; *the* or *a* class of nobles. [ME, f. OF *nobilité* or f. L *nobilitas* (as foll.; see -ITY)]
nō'ble *a.* & *n.* **1.** *a.* Illustrious by rank, title, or birth, belonging to the nobility; of lofty character or ideals; showing greatness of character, magnanimous, morally elevated; splendid, magnificent, stately, imposing, impressive, in appearance; excellent, admirable, (*a noble horse, cellar,* etc.); **~ gas,** gaseous element of group that almost never combine with other elements; **~man, ~woman,** member of the nobility, person of noble rank or birth, peer(ess); **~ metal,** gold, silver, platinum, etc. (resisting chemical action, not corroding or tarnishing in air or water, not easily attacked by acids); **~-mi'nded,** honourable, magnanimous; **~ savage,** idealized primitive man in Romantic literature; **~ science,** boxing; hence **~**NESS

(-beln-) *n.*, **nō'b**LY² *adv.* **2.** *n.* Nobleman, noblewoman; former English gold coin usu. worth 6s. 8d. [ME f. OF, f. L (*g*)*nobilis* (*gnō- KNOW)]

noblesse (noblĕ's) *n.* The class of nobles (esp. of a foreign country); ~ ***oblige*** (ŏblē'zh), privilege entails responsibility. [ME = nobility, f. OF (as prec.; see -ESS²)]

nō'bodў *pron.* & *n.* **1.** *pron.* No person; *nobody's* BUSINESS. **2.** *n.* Person of no importance, authority, or position. [ME, f. NO¹ + BODY¹ (= person)]

nŏck *n.*, & *v.t.* **1.** *n.* Notch at either end of bow for holding string; notch(ed horn piece in butt) of arrow for receiving bowstring. **2.** *v.t.* Set (arrow) on string. [ME, perh. = *nock* forward upper corner of some sails, f. MDu. *nocke*]

nŏctā'mbūl|ant, -l|ous, *adjs.* Walking by night; so ~IST *n.*, sleep-walker. [f. L *nox noctis* night + *ambulare* walk; see -ANT, -OUS]

nŏctĭ'vagant, -vagous, *adjs.* Wandering by night. [f. L *noctivagus* (as prec., *vagari* wander) + -ANT, -OUS]

nŏ'ctūle *n.* Largest British species of bat, *Nyctalus noctula.* [F, f. It. *nottola* bat]

nŏ'cturn *n.* (R.C. Ch.) Part of matins orig. said at night. [ME, f. OF *nocturne* or f. eccl. L *nocturnum* neut. (as n.) of L *nocturnus* (see foll.)]

nŏctur'nal *a.* Of, in, done by, active in, the night; ~ **emission,** involuntary emission of semen during sleep. [f. LL *nocturnalis* f. L *nocturnus* of the night (*nox noctis* night)]

nŏ'cturne *n.* Dreamy musical piece; (Paint.) night-piece. [F (as NOCTURN)]

nŏ'cūous *a.* Noxious, harmful. [f. L *nocuus* (*nocēre* hurt) + -OUS]

nŏd *v.* (-dd-) & *n.* **1.** *v.i.* Incline head slightly and briefly in salutation (~**ding acquaintance,** very slight one *with* person or subject), assent, or command; let head fall forward in drowsiness, be drowsy, make mistake due to drowsiness or momentary lack of attention (**Homer sometimes ~s,** the best of us may be dull or make a slip); (of building etc., or fig.) incline from perpendicular (*nodding to its fall*); (of plumes) dance up and down as a result of motion. **2.** *v.t.* Incline (head); signify (assent etc.) by nod. **3.** *n.* Nodding of the head; this as sign of absolute power (*the empire was at, was dependent on, his nod*); **land of Nod,** sleep (w. pun on phr. in Gen. 4:16); **on the** ~, (colloq.) (1) on credit, (2) with merely formal assent and no discussion. [ME *nodde*; orig. unkn.]

nŏ'ddle¹ *n.* (colloq.) Head. [ME *nodle*; orig. unkn.]

nŏ'ddle² *v.t.* Nod or wag (head). [f. NOD + -LE 3]

nŏ'ddў *n.* Simpleton; tropical sea-bird of genus *Anous,* resembling tern. [prob. f. obs. *noddy* foolish, which is perh. f. NOD + -Y²]

nōde *n.* **1.** Knob on root or branch; point at which leaves spring from stem; hard swelling esp. on gouty or rheumatic joint. **2.** (Astron.) intersection point of planet's orbit and ecliptic or of two great circles of celestial sphere; hence **nō'd**ICAL *a.* **3.** (Phys.) Point or line of rest in vibrating body. **4.** (Math.) Point at which curve crosses itself. **5.** Hence **nō'd**AL *a.* [f. L *nodus* knot]

nod|ō'se *a.* Knotty, knotted; so ~ō'SITY *n.* [f. L *nodosus* (as prec.; see -OSE¹)]

nŏ'dūl|e *n.* Small rounded lump of anything (e.g. carbon in cast iron, mineral on sea-bed); small node in plant, swelling on root of legume, containing bacteria; small knotty tumour, node, ganglion; hence ~AR¹, **~ātėd** [-ATE², -ED¹], ~OSE¹, ~OUS, *adjs.*, ~A'TION *n.* [f. L *nodulus* dim. of *nodus* (see foll., -ULE)]

nō'd|us *n.* (*pl.* **~i** *pr.* -ī). Knotty point, difficulty, complication in plot of story etc. [L, = knot]

Nōĕ'l *n.* Christmas (esp. as int. in carols). [F, f. L (as NATAL)]

nōĕ'tĭc *a.* & *n.* **1.** *a.* Of the intellect; purely intellectual or abstract; given to intellectual speculation. **2.** *n.* (in *sing.* or *pl.*) Science of the intellect. [f. Gk *noētikos* (*noētos* intellectual f. *noeō* apprehend; see -IC)]

nŏg¹ *n.*, & *v.t.* (-gg-). **1.** *n.* Pin, peg, small block, of wood; snag or stump on tree; nogging. **2.** *v.t.* Secure with nogs; build in form of (*brick-* etc.) ~'**g**ING¹ (-g-) *n.*, i.e. brickwork etc. in timber frame. [17th c.; orig. unkn.]

nŏg² *n.* ‖Strong beer brewed in East Anglia; = EGG¹-*nog.* [17th c.; orig. unkn.]

nŏ'ggin (-g-) *n.* Small mug; small measure, usu. ¼ pint, of liquor; (sl.) head. [17th c.; orig. unkn.]

noh. See NO⁵.

nō'how *adv.* In no way, by no means; (dial.) out of order, out of sorts. [f. NO¹ + HOW]

noil *n.* (in *sing.* or *pl.*) Short wool-combings. [prob. f. OF *noel* f. med. L *nodellus* dim. of L *nodus* knot]

noise (-z) *n.* & *v.* **1.** *n.* Loud outcry, clamour, shouting, din of voices and movements; any sound, esp. loud or harsh or undesired one; irregular fluctuations accompanying but not relevant to a transmitted signal; (in *pl.*) conventional remarks, or speechlike sounds without actual words, (*made sympathetic noises*); **~s off,** sounds made off stage but heard by audience of play; BIG *noise*; **make a** ~, lit., or fig. talk or complain much *about*, be much talked of, attain notoriety *in the world*; **~-maker,** device for making loud noise at festivity etc. **2.** *v.t.* Make public, spread abroad, (person's fame, fact; *it was noised abroad that*). **3.** *v.i.* (arch.) Make (much) noise. [ME f. OF, = outcry, disturbance, f. L NAUSEA]

noi'selėss (-zl-) *a.* Silent; making no avoidable noise; hence ~LY² *adv.*, ~NESS *n.* [f. prec. + -LESS]

noisĕ'tte¹ (nwahzĕ't) *n.* Kind of rose, cross between China and musk roses. [f. P. *Noisette,* Fr. rose-grower, 1817]

noisĕ'tte² (nwahzĕ't) *n.* Small round piece of meat etc. [F, dim. of *noix* nut; see -ETTE]

noi'some *a.* (literary). Harmful, noxious; evil-smelling; objectionable, offensive; hence ~NESS (-mn-) *n.* [ME, f. obs. *noy* (f. ANNOY) + -SOME¹]

noi's|ў (-zĭ) *a.* Clamorous, turbulent; full of, making much, noise; (of colour, garment, etc.) loud, conspicuous; hence ~**ĭ**LY² *adv.*, ~**ĭ**NESS *n.* [f. NOISE + -Y²]

nolens volens (nōlĕnz vō'lĕnz) *adv.* (literary). Willy-nilly, perforce. [L participles, = unwilling, willing]

noli me tangere (nōlĭ mē tă'njerĭ; *or* mā tă'nggerĭ) *n.* Warning against meddling or approach; person or thing that must not be touched; picture of Christ as he appeared to Mary Magdalen at sepulchre (John 20:17); (arch.) lupus. [L, = do not touch me]

***nŏ'llė(-prŏs)** *v.t.* = NOL-PROS.

nolle prosequi (nŏlĭ prŏ'sĭkwī) *n.* (Law). Relinquishment by plaintiff or prosecutor of (part of) his suit, stay of proceedings, entry of it on record. [L, = to refuse to pursue]

****nolo contendere*** (nōlō kontĕ'nderĭ) *n.* (Law). Plea acknowledging validity of conviction but not guilt. [L, = I do not wish to contend]

nolo episcopari (nōlō ĕpĭskopar'ī) *n.* (Formula expressing) avoidance of responsible office. [LL, = I do not wish to be a bishop]

***nŏl-prŏ's** *v.t.* (-ss-). (Law). Relinquish by *nolle prosequi.* [abbr.]

nom. *abbr.* nominal.

nō'mad *n.* & *a.* (Member of tribe) roaming from place to place for pasture; wanderer, wandering; hence or cogn. **nomă'dic** *a.*, **nomă'dically** *adv.*, ~ISM (2) *n.*, ~IZE (2) *v.i.* [f. F *nomade* f. L f. Gk *nomas -ados* (*nemō* to pasture)]

nom de guerre (nŏmdegâr') *n.* (*pl.* **-ms** *pr.* same). Pseudonym, sobriquet, assumed name under which person fights, plays, writes, etc. [F, = war-name]

nom de plume (nŏmdeplōō'm) *n.* (*pl.* **-ms** *pr.* same). Writer's pseudonym, title or initials or borrowed name under which he writes. [formed in E of F words = pen-name, after prec.]

nō'mĕn *n.* (Rom. Ant.) Second or gentilitial name, e.g. Marcus *Tullius* Cicero. [L, = name]

nō'menclātor *n.* Slave etc. orig. in ancient Rome with duty of announcing names of persons met, usher assigning places at banquet; giver or inventor of names, esp. in scientific classification. [L (*nomen* name, *calare* call; see -OR)]

nomĕ'ncl|ature (*or* nŏ'menklā-) *n.* Person's or community's system of names for things; terminology of a science etc.; systematic naming; catalogue, register; so ~ATIVE *a.* [F, f. L *nomenclatura* (as prec.; see -URE)]

nŏ'mĭnal *a.* **1.** Of, as, like, a noun (*nominal and verbal roots*). **2.** Of or in names (*nominal and essential distinctions*); ~ **definition,** statement of all that is connoted in name of concept. **3.** Existing in name only, not real or actual, (*nominal and real prices, rulers*); (of sum of money, rent, etc.) virtually nothing, much below actual value of thing; ~ **value,** face value (of coin, shares, etc.); hence ~LY² *adv.* **4.** Consisting of, giving, the names (*nominal list of officers* etc.; *nominal roll*). [ME f. F, or f. L *nominalis* (*nomen -inis* name; see -AL)]

nŏ'mĭnal|ĭsm *n.* (Philos.) Doctrine that universals or general ideas are mere names (opp. *realism*); so ~IST (2) *n.*, **~ĭ'stic** *a.* [f. F *nominalisme* (as prec.; see -ISM)]

nŏ'mĭnāt|e *v.t.* **1.** Call by name of, mention by name, name or appoint (date, place). **2.** Appoint, or propose for election, to office (*a board of six nominated and six elected members*; *the candidates were nominated today*); hence or cogn. ~OR, **nŏmĭnee'**, *ns.* [f. L *nominare* (as NOMINAL) + -ATE³]

nŏmĭnā'tion *n.* In vbl senses; right of nominating for appointment (*have a nomination at your disposal*). [ME f. OF, or f. L *nominatio* (as prec.; see -ATION)]

nŏ'mĭnatĭve *a.* & *n.* **1.** (Gram.) (Case) used as, or in agreement with, subject of verb (*nominative* ABSOLUTE); word in this case; hence **nŏmĭnatī'val** *a.* **2.** *a.* (*pr.* -ātĭv). Of, or appointed by, nomination (*the nominative and the elective principles*). [ME, f. OF *nominatif -ive* or f. L *nominativus* (as NOMINATE; see -IVE), transl. Gk *onomastikē* (*ptōsis* case)]

nŏ'mo|grăm *n.* Graphical presentation of relations between quantities whereby value of one may be found by simple geometrical construction (e.g. drawing a straight line) from those of others; hence ~GRA'PHIC *a.*, **nomŏ'graphy** *n.* [f. Gk *nomo-* (*nomos* law; see -O-) + -GRAM]

nŏmothĕ'tic *a.* Legislative; stating laws. [f. obs. *nomothete* legislator f. Gk *nomothetēs*, + -IC]

nŏn- *pref.* freely usable to give negative sense: (1) with *vbl n.* = not doing, failure to do, abstention from doing, (*non-acceptance, non-attendance, non-compliance, non-delivery, non-existence, non-fulfilment, non-observance, non-payment, non-smoking compartment*), (2) with *n.* formed from *adj.* = failure to be, not being, (*non-belligerency, non-violence*), (3) with *n.* of designation = person, thing, or all, that is not of the kind designated (*non-ego, non-member, non-starter*); occas. w. implication of pretence: *non-event*), (4) with *n.* to form *attrib. a.* = not connected with or not involving the thing (*non-party, non-union*), (5) with *adj.* = failing to be, not being, one who is not, thing that is not, (*non-alcoholic, non-communicant* a. & n., *non-essential* a. & n., *non-existent, non-operational, non-productive, non-professional, non-uniform, non-verbal*), (6) with *adj.* = neither such nor its (usu. blameworthy) opposite (dist. from IN-², UN-²; *non-moral*), (7) with *adv.* = not thus (*non-sexually, non-contentiously*), (8) with *v.* to form *adj.* = not doing, not behaving in specified way, not to be treated in specified way, (*non-skid, non-stick, non-iron*), as: **~-abstai'ner** (3), one who does not abstain (esp. from liquor); **~-a'ccess** (1), impossibility of access for sexual intercourse (in questions of paternity etc.); **~-aggre'ssion** (1), refraining from aggression; **~-ali'gnment** (1), (esp. Polit., of State) not being aligned with others; **~-appear'ance** (1) (esp. in lawcourt as party or witness); **~-belli'gerent** (5) *a.* & *n.*, (State) taking no active or declared part in war; **~-claim** (1), failure to make claim within legal time; **~-colle'giate** (5), not attached to a college, not having colleges; **~-co'mbatant** (5) *a.* & *n.*, (person) not fighting (esp. in war as being civilian, army chaplain, etc.); **~-commi'ssioned** (5), (esp. of officer) not holding commission; **~-commi'ttal** (1) *a.* & *n.*, avoiding committing oneself to definite course of action or side of question; **~-condu'cting** (5), **-condu'ctor** (3), (substance) that does not conduct heat or electricity; **~-content** (5), negative voter in House of Lords; **~-contri'butory** (5), not involving contributions (e.g. to pension scheme); **~-co-opera'tion** (1) (esp. of civil disobedience under Gandhi in India); **~-denomina'tional** (5), not restricted as regards religious denomination; **~-dri'ver** (3), one who does not drive a vehicle; **~-effe'ctive** (6) *a.* & *n.*, (soldier etc.) not available for active service; **~-e'go** (3), (Philos.) all that is not the conscious self; **~-Eucli'dean** (5), denying or dispensing with assumption(s) of Euclidean geometry; **~-event** (3), occurrence that has no special significance (despite possible attempt to give it this); **~-fea'sance** (1) (-z-), (Law) omission of necessary action; **~-fe'rrous** (5), (of metal) other than iron or steel; **~-fi'ction** (3), literary matter based directly on fact (opp. novels etc.); **~-fla'm(mable)** (5), not inflammable; **~-hu'man** (6), not of the human race; **~-interfer'ence, ~-interve'ntion,** (1), principle or practice of keeping aloof from others' disputes (esp. Polit.); **~-i'ron** (8), (of fabric) that needs no ironing; **~-joi'nder** (1), (Law) omission of partner etc. to become party to suit; **~-jur'ing** (5), **~jur'or** (3), (Hist.) (beneficed clergyman) refusing oath of allegiance in 1689; **~-jur'y** (4), tried without jury; **~-li'near** (5) (esp. Math.); **~-lo'gical** (6), proceeding by means other than logic; **~-metal** (3), **-meta'llic** (5), (esp., Chem.) (element) that is not a metal; **~-mo'ral** (6), unconcerned with morality (cf. *amoral, immoral*); **~-na'tural** (6), not belonging to the natural order of things; **~-nu'clear** (5), not involving nuclei or nuclear energy; **~-par'ty** (4), independent of political parties; **~-playing** (5) (esp. of captain of sports team who does not himself take part); **~-pro'fit(-making)** (4, 5), (of enterprise) not conducted primarily with a view to gain; **~-prolifera'tion** (1) (esp. of nuclear weapons); **~-retur'nable** (5) (esp. of container to seller); **~-ri'gid**

(6) (esp. of airship kept inflated by pressure of gas within); **~-ski'd** (8), (of tyres) safe against skidding; **~-sli'p** (8), designed to avoid slipping; **~-smo'ker** (3), person who does not smoke, train-compartment etc. where smoking is forbidden; **~-star'ter** (3), (fig., colloq.) idea not worth considering further; **~-stick** (8), (esp.) that food will not adhere to during cooking; **~-u'nion** (4), not belonging to trade union, not made by members of a trade union; **~-vi'olence** (2), **~-vi'olent** (5), abstaining from use of violence to gain one's ends; **~-vo'ting** (5), (of shares) not entitling holder to vote; **~-whi'te** (5) *a.* & *n.*, (person) belonging to other than white race. [f. or after ME *no(u)n-* f. AF *noun-*, OF *non-*, *nom-* f. L *non* not]

nŏ'na- *pref.* Nine, as: **~gon,** plane figure with nine sides and angles. [L (*nonus* ninth)]

nŏ'nage *n.* Being under age, minority; immaturity, early stage. [ME, f. AF *nounage*, OF *nonage* (as NON-, AGE¹)]

nŏnagėnār'ian *a.* & *n.* (Person) from 90 to 99 years old. [f. L *nonagenarius* (*nonageni* 90 each; see -ARY¹) + -AN]

nō'narў *a.* & *n.* **1.** *a.* (Arith., of SCALE³ of notation) having nine as basis. **2.** *n.* Group of nine. [f. L *nonus* ninth + -ARY¹]

nŏnce *n.* **For the ~,** for the time being or present occasion; **~-word** (coined for one occasion). [ME **for than anes* = for the one (occasion), alt. by wrong division (cf. NEWT)]

nŏ'nchal|ant (-sh-) *a.* Unexcited, unmoved, cool, indifferent; hence **~**ANCE *n.*, **~ant**LY² *adv.* [F, part. of *nonchaloir* (as NON-, *chaloir* be concerned)]

non-com. *abbr.* non-commissioned (officer).

non compos (mentis) (nŏn kŏ'mpŏs mĕ'ntĭs) *a.* Not in one's right mind. [L, = not having control of one's mind]

nŏnconfôr'mĭst (-n-k-) *n.* One who does not conform to doctrine or discipline of an established Church, esp. (*N~*) member of (usu. Protestant) sect dissenting from Anglican Church; one who does not conform to a prevailing principle; so **nŏnconfôr'm**ISM (3) *n.* [f. NON- (3) + CONFORMIST]

nŏnconfôr'mĭtў (-n-k-) *n.* Principles, practice, the body, of nonconformists, Protestant dissent; failure to conform (*to* rule etc.); lack of correspondence between things. [f. NON- (1) + CONFORMITY]

nŏ'nda *n.* (Edible fruit of) rosaceous Queensland tree (*Parinarium nonda*). [Aboriginal]

nŏ'ndėscrĭpt *a.* & *n.* (Person or thing) not easily classified, neither one thing nor another, hybrid. [f. NON- (5) + *descript* described f. L *descriptus* (as DESCRIBE)]

none (nŭn) *pron.*, *a.*, & *adv.* **1.** *pron.* Not any (one) *of* (*none of them came*; *none of them is* (or *are*, acc. to sense) *required*; *none of this concerns me*; *none of your impudence!*); no person, no one, (*none can tell*); no persons (*none but fools have ever believed it*); **~ other,** no other person (*than*). **2.** *a.* (usu. ellipt. = *no* with reference defined by noun previously used or shortly to follow). No, not any, not to be counted in specified class, (*you have money and I have none*; *he is none of your canting hypocrites*; *his understanding is none of the clearest*; *this is none other, but the house of God*; *seeking rest and finding none*; *if a linguist is wanted, I am none*; *would rather have a bad reputation than none at all*; *poetry we have almost none*); **~-so-pretty,** LONDON pride. **3.** *adv.* By no amount, not at all, (w. *the* and compar., *so*, or *too*: *am none the wiser*, *none the better for it*; **~ the less,** nevertheless; *are none so fond of him*; *the pay is none too high*). [OE *nān* (*ne* not, *ān* ONE)]

nŏnĕ'ntĭtў *n.* **1.** Non-existence, non-existent thing, figment. **2.** Person or thing of no importance. [f. med. L *nonentitas* non-existence (as NON- (1), ENTITY)]

nōnes (-nz) *n. pl.* **1.** Ninth day by inclusive reckoning before ides in Roman calendar (7th day of March, May, July, October, 5th of other months). **2.** (Eccl.) (Office of) fifth of the canonical hours of prayer, orig. said at ninth hour (3 p.m.). [sense 1 f. OF *nones* f. L *nonae* fem. pl., sense 2 pl. of *none* f. F f. L *nona* fem. sing. (*nonus* ninth); cf. NOON]

nŏn ĕ'st *a.* (colloq.) Non-existent, absent. [f. foll.]

non est inventus (nŏn ĕst ĭnvĕ'ntus) *n.* Sheriff's statement, in returning writ, that defendant is not to be found within his jurisdiction. [L, = he was not found]

nonesuch. See NONSUCH.

nŏnĕ't *n.* (Mus.) (Composition for) group of nine instruments or voices. [f. It. *nonetto* (*nono* ninth f. L *nonus*); see -ET¹]

nonetheless. Var. of NONE *the less*.

nonĭ'llion (-yon) *n.* ||Ninth power of a million; *tenth power of a thousand. [obs. F, f. L *nonus* ninth, after *billion*]

nō'nĭus *n.* Contrivance for graduating mathematical instruments, of which the vernier is an improved form. [mod. L, f. P. *Nuñes*, Port. mathematician d. 1577]

nŏ'npareil (-el) *a.* & *n.* Unrivalled or unique (person or thing). [F (as NON-, *pareil* equal f. pop. L *pariculus* dim. of L *par*)]

non placet (nŏn plā'sĕt) *n.* Negative vote in church or university assembly. [L, = it does not please]

nŏnplŭ's *n.*, & *v.t.* (-ss-). **1.** *n.* State of perplexity, standstill, (usu. **at a ~,** perplexed; *reduce* etc. *to a nonplus*). **2.** *v.t.* Reduce to hopeless perplexity. [f. L *non plus* not more]

non possumus (nŏn pŏ'sūmus) *n.* Statement of inability to act in a matter. [L, = we cannot]

nŏn-rĕ'sĭd|ent (-z-) *a.* & *n.* (Person) sojourning in place only for short time or residing elsewhere; (clergyman) not residing where his duties require him; (of post) not requiring holder to reside; so **~**ENCE *n.* [f. NON- (3, 5) + RESIDENT]

nŏ'nsense *n.* & *int.* **1.** *n.* Absurd or meaningless words or ideas, foolish or extravagant conduct; instance of this; arrangement etc. that one disapproves of; **no-~** *a.*, serious, without flippancy. **2.** *int.* You are talking or proposing nonsense, it surely cannot be true, etc. **3. ~-book** (meant to amuse by absurdity); **~ verses** (having no sense or only an absurd one). **4.** Hence **nŏnsĕ'nsi**CAL *a.*, **nŏnsĕ'nsical**LY² *adv.* [f. NON- (3) + SENSE]

non sequitur (nŏn sĕ'kwĭter) *n.* Conclusion that does not logically follow from the premisses. [L, = it does not follow]

nŏ'n-stŏp *a.*, *n.*, & *adv.* **1.** *a.* & *n.* (Train etc.) not stopping at intermediate places; (of journey, performance, etc.) done without stop or intermission. **2.** *adv.* Without stopping or pausing. [f. NON- (8) + STOP¹]

no'n(e)sŭch (nŭ'ns-) *n.* Person or thing that is unrivalled, paragon; plant (*Medicago lupulina*) like lucerne with black pods. [f. NONE + SUCH, usu. now assim. to NON-]

nŏ'nsuit (-ūt *or* -ōōt) *n.*, & *v.t.* (Law). **1.** *n.* Stoppage of suit by judge when plaintiff fails to make out legal case or bring sufficient evidence. **2.** *v.t.* Subject (plaintiff) to nonsuit. [ME, f. AF *no(u)nsuit* (as NON- (1), SUIT)]

nŏn-U' (-ū') *a.* (colloq.) Not characteristic of the upper class. [f. NON- (5) + U³]

nŏn-ū'sage (-z-), **nŏn-ū'se,** *ns.* Failure to use. [f. NON- (1) + USAGE, USE¹]

nŏn-ū'ser (-z-) *n.* (Law). Neglect to use a right,

whereby it may be lost. [f. AF **nounuser* (as NON- (1), USE², -ER⁴)]

nōō'dle¹ *n.* Simpleton; hence ~DOM (-deld-) *n.* [18th c.; orig. unkn.]

nōō'dle² *n.* Strip of dough made of flour and eggs, dried and used in soups. [f. G *nudel*]

nōōk *n.* Secluded corner or place, recess. [ME *nok(e)* corner, of unkn. orig.]

nōōn *n.* **1.** Twelve o'clock in the day, midday; **~'day, ~'tide, *~'time,** midday. **2.** Culminating point; ~ **of night,** (poet.) midnight. [OE *nōn*, = OS *nōn(e)*, OHG *nona*, ON *nón* f. L *nona* (*hora*) ninth hour; orig. = 3 p.m. (cf. NONES)]

no one. See NO¹.

nōōse *n.*, & *v.t.* **1.** *n.* Loop with running knot, tightening as rope or wire is pulled, esp. in snare, lasso, or hangman's halter; the marriage tie; snare or bond; **put** one's **head in a** ~, bring about one's own downfall. **2.** *v.t.* Capture with noose, ensnare; make noose on (cord); arrange (cord) in noose *round* neck etc. [ME *nose*, perh. f. OF *no(u)s* f. L *nodus* knot]

nō'pal *n.* Amer. cactus of genus *Nopalea*, esp. a species grown in plantations for breeding cochineal; hence ~RY (3) *n.* [F & Sp., f. Nahuatl *nopalli* cactus]

***nōpe.** Var. (colloq.) of NO⁴.

nor (*or, when stressed,* nŏr) *conj.* & *adv.* **1.** *conj.* And not, and no more, neither, and not either, (*had neither arms nor provisons; not a man nor a child was to be seen; I said I had not seen it, nor had I; 'I cannot go'—'Nor can I'; all that is true, nor must we forget . . .*); (poet. or arch. w. omission of preceding *neither*: *thou nor I have made the world*). **2.** *adv.* (poet. or arch.) **Nor . . . nor . . .**, neither . . . nor . . . . [ME, contr. f. obs. *nother* f. OE *nawther, nāhwæther* (as NO², WHETHER)]

nŏr' = NORTH, esp. in compds. (*nor'ward, nor'wester*). [abbr.]

Nŏr'dĭc *a.* & *n.* (Person) of the tall blond dolichocephalic Germanic people found in N. Europe esp. in Scandinavia; (native or inhabitant) of Scandinavia, Finland, or Iceland. [f. F *nordique* (*nord* north; see -IC)]

Nŏr'folk (-ok) *n.* ~ **jacket,** man's loose belted jacket, with box pleats. [~ in England]

||**nŏr'land** *n.* Northern region. [contr. of NORTH*land*]

nŏrm *n.* Standard, pattern, type; standard quantity to be produced or amount of work to be done; customary behaviour etc. [f. L *norma* carpenter's square]

nŏr'mal *a.* & *n.* **1.** *a.* (Geom.) Standing at right angles, perpendicular. **2.** Conforming to standard, regular, usual, typical; free from mental or emotional disorder; (Chem., of solution) containing one gram-equivalent of solute per litre; ~ **school** (in France etc., for training teachers); hence ~CY, ~ITY (-ă'l-), *ns.*, ~IZE (3) *v.t.*, ~LY² *adv.* **3.** *n.* (Geom.) normal line; normal value of temperature etc., esp. = BLOOD-*heat*; usual state, level, etc. [F, or f. L *normalis* (as prec.; see -AL)]

Nŏr'man *n.* & *a.* **1.** *n.* Inhabitant or native of Normandy, descendant of mixed Scandinavian and Frankish race there established; Norman French; Norman style. **2.** *a.* Of the Normans; *Norman* CONQUEST; ~ **English,** English as spoken or influenced by Normans; ~ **French,** French as spoken by Normans or later in English lawcourts; ~ **style** (Archit., with round arches and heavy pillars, whence ~E'SQUE *a.*). **3.** Hence ~ISM (2, 4) *n.*, ~IZE (3, 4) *v.t.* & *i.* [f. OF *Normans* pl. of *Normant* f. ON *Northmathr* (as NORTH, MAN¹)]

nŏr'matĭve *a.* Of or establishing a norm. [f. F *normatif -ive* f. L NORMA; see -ATIVE]

Nŏrn *n.* One of the female Fates of Scandinavian mythology. [ON; orig. unkn.]

||**Nŏ'rroy** *n.* ~ **(and Ulster),** third KING¹ of Arms, with jurisdiction north of the Trent (and in N. Ireland). [ME, f. AF **norroi* (*nor-* north, *roi* king)]

Nŏrse *n.* & *a.* **1.** *n.* The Norwegian language; the Scandinavian language-group; **Old** ~, Germanic language of Norway and its colonies, or of Scandinavia, down to 14th c. **2.** (as *pl.*) *The* Norwegians. **3.** *a.* Of ancient Scandinavia, esp. of Norway; so **~'land, ~'man.** [f. Du. *noor(d)sch* (*noord* north; see -ISH¹)]

nŏrth *adv.*, *n.*, & *a.* **1.** (Towards, at, near) point of horizon to left of person facing east; **(to the)** ~ **(of),** in a northward direction (from); ~ **wind,** wind blowing from the north; *north* BY¹ *east* or *west*; *lies* ~ **and south,** lengthwise along a line running from north to south. **2.** (w. uses and derivs. like those of *north*) **~-east, ~-west,** compass point midway between north and east or west; **~-~-east, ~-~-west,** compass point midway between north and north-east or north-west; **~-east, ~-west, passage,** passage for ships along northern coast of Europe and Asia, northern coast of America, formerly thought of as possible routes to the East and from Atlantic to Pacific; **the N~-West,** north-western part of country (esp. of Canada). **3.** *n.* Compass point lying north (**magnetic** ~, point indicated by north end of compass-needle). **4.** (usu. *N~*). Part of country or town lying to the north, esp. ||~ **(country),** northern part of England (north of Humber; so *~-cou'ntryman*); *the* Arctic; *the Northern STATE¹s; card-player occupying position designated 'north'. **5. N~ American,** (native or inhabitant) of North America, esp. of U.S. or Canada; **~'bound,** travelling northwards; **N~ Briton,** Scot; **N~'land,** (poet.) northern lands, northern part of a country; ~ **light** (from the north, esp. as desired by painters and in factory design); **N~'man,** native of Scandinavia, esp. of Norway; *North* POLE²; **N~ Sea** (between Britain, Netherlands, Germany, and Scandinavia); **N~ star,** = POLE²-*star*. **6.** Hence ~'WARD *a.* & *n.*, ~'WARD(s) *adv.* [OE, = OS *north*, OHG *nord*, ON *northr*, of unkn. orig.]

Nŏrthă'nts. *abbr.* Northamptonshire.

nŏrthea'ster *n.* N.E. wind. [f. NORTH-*east* + -ER¹]

***nŏr'ther** *n.* Strong cold north wind blowing in autumn and winter over Texas, Florida, and Gulf of Mexico. [f. NORTH + -ER¹]

nŏr'therlў (-dh-) *a.*, *adv.*, & *n.* In a northern position or direction; (wind) blowing (nearly) from the north. [f. NORTH, as *easterly* etc.]

nŏr'thern (-dh-) *a.* & *n.* **1.** Of or (dwelling) in the north; lying or directed towards the north; *Northern* HEMISPHERE; ~ **lights,** aurora borealis; *Northern* STATE¹*s*; hence ~ER¹ (4) *n.*, ~MOST *a.* **2.** *n.* Inhabitant of the north, esp. of the Northern States. [OE *northerne* (as NORTH, -ERN)]

nŏr'thĭng *n.* (Naut. etc.) Distance travelled or measured northward; northerly direction. [f. NORTH + -ING¹]

Northumb. *abbr.* Northumberland.

Nŏrthŭ'mbrĭan *a.* & *n.* (Native or dialect) of ancient Northumbria (England N. of Humber) or modern Northumberland. [f. obs. *Northumber*, persons living beyond Humber, f. OE *Northhymbre*, + -IAN]

nŏrthwĕ'ster *n.* N.W. wind. [f. NORTH-*west* + -ER¹]

Nŏr'way *n.* ~ **lobster,** slender Eur. lobster (*Nephrops norvegicus*); ~ **rat,** common brown rat (*Rattus norvegicus*). [~ in N. Europe, OE *Norweg* f. ON *Norvegr* (as NORTH, WAY)]

Nŏrwē′gian (-jan) *a.* & *n.* (Native, inhabitant, or language) of Norway. [f. med. L *Norvegia* + -AN, w. assim. to prec.]

nŏr′-wĕ′ster *n.* Northwester; glass of strong liquor; oilskin hat, sou'wester. [f. NORTH-WESTER]

Nos. *abbr.* numbers. [cf. No.]

nōse (-z) *n.* & *v.* **1.** *n.* Organ of face or head of man or animal, placed above mouth, containing nostrils, and serving for breathing and smelling; **as plain as the ~ in** or **on your face,** easily seen; **by a ~,** (win in race etc.) by very narrow margin; **count ~s,** count those present, one's supporters, etc., decide question by mere numbers; *cut off* one's *nose to* SPITE one's *face*; **follow** one's **~,** go straight forward, be guided by instinct; **hold** one's **~,** compress nostrils between fingers to avoid bad smell; **keep** one's **~ clean,** behave properly, avoid trouble; *keep* one's *nose to the* GRIND*stone*; LEAD[2] *by the nose*; LOOK *down* one's *nose at*; *make a* LONG[1] *nose*; **~ of wax,** (arch.) person or thing easily influenced or moulded; ***on the ~,** (sl.) precisely; **parson's** or **pope's ~,** rump of (cooked) fowl; **pay through the ~,** be overcharged, have to pay exorbitant price; **poke, thrust,** etc., one's **~,** pry or intrude *into* something or *in*; **put** person's **~ out of joint,** supplant or disconcert or frustrate him; **rub** person's **~ in it,** remind him humiliatingly of his error; **see no further than** one's **~,** be short-sighted (lit. or fig.); *bite* or SNAP person's *nose off*; **speak through** one's **~,** pronounce words with nasal twang; THUMB one's *nose*; **turn up** one's **~ at,** show disdain for; **under** person's **~,** straight before him, regardless of his displeasure; **with** one's **~ in the air,** haughtily. **2.** Sense of smell; **has a good ~** (esp. of dog, and fig. of detective etc.). **3.** Odour or perfume of hay, tea, wine, tobacco, etc. **4.** Open end of nozzle of pipe, tube, bellows, retort, etc. **5.** Prow, projecting part; = NOSING; front end of motor car, aircraft, etc. **6.** (sl.) Informer of police. **7.** **~-ape,** proboscis monkey; **~′bag** (containing fodder, for hanging on horse's head); **~′band,** lower band of bridle passing over nose and attached to cheek-straps; **~′bleed,** instance of bleeding from the nose; **~-cone,** cone-shaped nose of rocket etc.; **~′dive,** (*n.*) aeroplane's downward plunge, (*v.i.*) make this; **~-flute,** musical instrument blown with nose in Fiji etc.; **~′gay** [*gay* in obs. n. use = ornament], bunch of (esp. sweet-scented) flowers; **~-monkey,** proboscis monkey; **~-piece,** (1) = *noseband*, (2) part of helmet etc. protecting nose, (3) part of microscope to which object-glass is attached; **~′pipe,** piece of piping used as nozzle; **~-rag,** (sl.) pocket handkerchief; **~′ring** (fixed in nose of bull etc. for leading, or of person for ornament); **~-wheel,** landing-wheel under nose of aircraft. **8.** Hence **(-)nōsED**[2] (-zd), **~′LESS** (-zl-), *adjs.* **9.** *v.t.* Perceive smell of, discover by smell, (fig.) detect, smell *out*; smell at, rub with the nose, thrust nose against or into. **10.** *v.i.* Sniff (*at, about* adv. or prep.), pry or search (*after, for*). **11.** *v.i.* & *t.* Push one's way, push (one's *way*), with the nose (esp. of ship). [OE *nosu*, = MDu. *nōse*, rel. to OE *nasu*, OHG *nasa*, ON *nös*; cf. NAZE, NESS]

nō′ser (-z-) *n.* Strong head wind. [f. prec. + -ER[1]]

nosey. See NOSY.

nŏsh *v.* & *n.* (sl.) **1.** *v.t.* & *i.* Eat or drink, esp. between meals; **~-up,** (large) meal. **2.** *n.* Food or drink, esp. snack. [Yiddish]

nō′sing (-z-) *n.* Rounded edge of step, moulding, etc., or metal shield for it. [f. NOSE + -ING[1]]

nosŏ′graphy̆ *n.* Systematic description of diseases; so **nosŏ′LOGY** *n.*, (branch of medical science dealing with) classification of diseases. [f. Gk *nosos* disease + -O- + -GRAPHY]

nŏstă′lg|ia (-j*a*) *n.* Homesickness as a disease; regretful or wistful memory of an earlier time; sentimental yearning *for* (some period of) the past; hence **~IC** *a.* [mod. L, f. Gk *nostos* return home; see -ALGIA]

nŏ′stŏc *n.* Gelatinous blue-green unicellular alga of genus *Nostoc*. [name invented by Paracelsus]

Nŏstradā′mus *n.* Prediction-monger, professed seer. [Latinized f. M. de *Nostredame*, Fr. astrologer and physician d. 1566]

nŏ′strĭl *n.* Either opening in nose admitting air to lungs and smells to olfactory nerves; **stink in the ~s of,** be offensive to; hence **(-)~lED**[2] (-ld) *a.* [OE *nosthyrl, nosterl* (*nosu* NOSE, *thȳr(e)l* hole; cf. THRILL)]

nŏ′strum *n.* Medicine prepared by person recommending it, quack remedy, patent medicine; pet scheme for political or social reform, panacea. [L, neut. of *noster* our, used in sense 'of our own make']

nō′sy̆, nō′sey, (-zĭ) *a.* & *n.* Large-nosed (person); having distinctive (good or bad) smell; (sl.) inquisitive (**N~ Parker,** busybody); hence **nō′sILY**[2] *adv.*, **nō′sINESS** *n.*, (-z-). [f. NOSE + -Y[2]]

nŏt *adv.* **1.** (arch.) Negativing and following ordinary verbs (*I know not*, I do not know; *I doubt not*; *say not so*; *fear not*; *know ye not me?*). **2.** (Often **n't** joined to word) negativing auxiliaries or BE and following them or (in questions having *not* in full) their subjects (*I cannot* or *can't say*; *he will not, he won't*, (arch.) *he'll not, come*; *she is not, isn't*, (vulg.) *ain't, here*; (*you*) *do not* or *don't worry*; *didn't you*, (formal) *did you not, tell me?*; *am I not, ain't I, aren't we, smart?*). **3.** Negativing and preceding participles and infinitives (*not knowing, I cannot say*; *asked him not to come*: *that is how not to do it*). **4.** Used elliptically for negative sentence or verb or phrase (*Are you ill? Not at all. Not so. If it clears we will go out*; *if not, not. Popular or not, it is right. I hope not. I would as soon do it as not*); *as* LIKELY *as not*; **~ at all,** (in polite reply to thanks) there is no need to thank me; **~ that,** it is not to be inferred, however, (*if he said so—not that he ever did—he lied*); **~ but what,** (formal) **~ but that,** (arch.) **~ but,** (1) all the same or nevertheless (*I cannot do it*; *not but what* etc. *a stronger man might*), (2) not (*such* etc. . . .) that . . . not (*not such a fool but what* etc. *he can see it*). **5.** Preceding word etc. that is to be rejected for one that follows with *but* or to emphasize by contrast one already used (*He is not my son, but yours*, or *but my nephew. He is your son,* (*and*) *not mine*). **6.** Preceding emphatic appended pronoun after negative statement etc. (*they will not be* '*had*', *not they*). **7.** Preceding *a* with sense 'not even one' (*not a hair of your head shall be touched*); **~ a thing,** nothing at all. **8.** Preceding in litotes or periphrasis a word of opposite sense to that which is to be conveyed (*not a few*; *not unconnected with*; *not seldom*); **~ once or** (or **nor**) **twice,** many times; **~ so** (or **too**) **well,** somewhat badly or ill; **~ least,** with considerable importance; *not* VERY[1]; **~ quite,** (1) almost, (2) noticeably not (*not quite proper*), (3) ||(ellipt., colloq.) socially unacceptable; *not* HALF. **9.** **~-being,** non-existence; **~-self,** = NON-*ego*; **~ sufficient** (written by banker on dishonoured cheque). [ME contr. of NOUGHT]

nota bene (nōta bĕ′nā) *v. imper.* Observe what follows, take notice, (usu. drawing attention to a following qualification of what has preceded). [L, = note well]

nōtabĭ'lĭtў̆ *n.* Prominent person; being notable (*names of no historical notability*); ||(arch.) housewifely skill. [ME, f. OF *notabilité* or f. LL & med. L *notabilitas* (as foll.; see -ITY)]

nō'table *a.* & *n.* **1.** *a.* Worthy of note, remarkable, striking, eminent; (arch., of woman; occas. pr. nŏ't-) capable, bustling, housewifely; hence **nō'tab**LY[2] *adv.* **2.** *n.* Eminent person; **Assembly of N~s,** (Fr. Hist.) irregular council serving as temporary parliament in emergencies. [ME f. OF, f. L *notabilis* (as NOTE[2]; see -ABLE)]

***nō'tarīz|e, -īse** (-īz), *v.t.* Attest as notary. [f. foll. + -IZE]

nō'tarў *n.* ~ (**public**), person publicly authorized to draw up or attest contracts etc., protest bills of exchange, etc., and perform other formalities; hence **notār'ĭal** *a.*, **notār'ĭal**LY[2] *adv.* [ME, f. L *notarius* secretary (as NOTE[1]; see -ARY[1])]

notā'te *v.t.* Write in notation. [back form. f. foll.]

notā'tion *n.* Representing of numbers, quantities, pitch and duration of sound, etc., by symbols; any set of symbols used for this, esp. in Arith., Alg., and Mus.; set of symbols used to represent chess moves, dance steps, etc.; *note, annotation; SCALE[3] *of notation.* [F, or f. L *notatio* (as NOTE[2]; see -ATION)]

nŏtch *n.*, & *v.t.* **1.** *n.* V-shaped indentation in edge or on convex surface; nick made on stick etc. in order to keep count; *defile, pass; hence ~ED[2] (-cht), ~'Y[2], *adjs.* **2.** *v.t.* Make notches in; make *into* saw etc. by notching; score (items etc.; often *up*, *down*) by notches (lit. or fig.); secure or insert (steps in staircase etc.) by notches. [f. AF (*noche* n. perh. f.) **nocher* v., of uncert. orig.]

nōte[1] *n.* **1.** Written sign representing pitch and duration of a musical sound; key of pianoforte etc.; single tone of definite pitch made by musical instrument, voice, engine, etc.; (single tone in) bird's song or call; significant sound or way of expressing oneself (*must sound a note of warning*; *there is a note of optimism in his report*); **strike a false, the right,** ~, act inappropriately, suitably. **2.** Sign, token, characteristic, distinguishing feature, proof of genuineness, guarantee consisting *of*, (*these are the notes of Neo-paganism*; *catholicity is one note of the true Church*; *has the note of catholicity*); (arch.) stigma, mark of censure, (*on which the law has set a note of infamy*); (arch.) = MARK[1] 6 (*of exclamation* or *interrogation*). **3.** Brief record of facts, impressions, or topics for speech or lecture or article (usu. in *pl.*: *make* or *take a note of* or *notes*; COMPARE[1] *notes*; *preaches from notes*; *spoke for an hour without a note*); annotation appended to passage in book etc., footnote; short or informal letter; formal diplomatic communication; ~ (**of hand**), written promise to pay sum by certain time; ||= BANK[3]*note* (*five-pound note*); DEMAND[1], PROMISSORY, *note.* **4.** Eminence (*critic*, *philosopher*, *person*, **of** ~, distinguished); notice, attention, (*worthy of note*; **take ~ of,** observe; hence ~'WORTHY (-twěrdhĭ) *a.*). **5.** **~'book** (for entering memoranda in); **~'case,** pocket wallet for holding banknotes; **~'paper** (of kind used for (esp. private) correspondence); **~-row,** = SERIES 8. **6.** Hence ~'LESS *a.*, ~'LET *n.*, (-tl-). [ME f. OF, f. L *nota* mark]

nōte[2] *v.t.* Observe, notice, give or draw attention to; set down or *down* as thing to be remembered or observed; annotate (book etc.); (in *p.p.*) celebrated, well known *for.* [ME, f. OF *noter* f. L *notare* (as prec.)]

no'thĭng (nŭ'-) *n.*, *a.*, & *adv.* **1.** *n.* No thing (with *adj.* following; *nothing great is easy*). **2.** Not anything (*nothing has been done*; *have nothing to do today*); ~ **doing** (sl., announcing failure or refusal); ~ **else than,** ~ (**else**) **but,** merely, only, unmistakably (*force* etc.; *did nothing but grumble*); ~ **for it,** no alternative *but to*; ~ **if not,** primarily (*critical*, *thorough*, etc.); **has ~ in him,** is insignificant or lacks individuality; **there is ~ in it** or **to it,** it is untrue or unimportant or straightforward (cf. also IN[1] 5); ~ **less than,** (1) at least, not a matter less important than, (*expected nothing less than a riot*; *is nothing less than scandalous*), (2, occas.) the very opposite of, not . . . at all; *nothing like* LEATHER; **is ~ to,** (1) does not concern or influence, (2) cannot compare with; **~ venture ~ win** or **have** (excuse for or encouragement to bold action); *be* or *have nothing to* DO[1] *with*; **come to ~,** turn out useless, fail; **feel like ~ on earth,** (colloq.) suffer severe indisposition or embarrassment; **for ~,** without payment, to no purpose; **count** or **go for ~,** be unappreciated or profitless; **have ~ on,** (1) possess no advantage over, know of nothing discreditable about, (iron.) be much inferior to, (2) be naked, (3) be free of engagements; **like ~ on earth,** (colloq.) (ugly etc.) to an extreme degree; **look like ~ on earth,** (colloq.) be very ugly, garish, etc.; **make ~ of,** do without hesitation, treat as a trifle, be unable to understand or use or deal with; **mean ~ to,** not be understood, admired, desired, etc., by; NECK[1] *or nothing*; **no ~** (as colloq. conclusion of list of negatives: *no bread, no butter, no cheese, no nothing*); **to say ~ of,** = *not to* MENTION[2]; STOP[1] *at nothing*; THINK *nothing of*; **to ~,** to complete disappearance; **with ~ on,** naked or otherwise inadequately clothed. **3.** (Arith.) No amount, nought, (*multiply 6 by nothing, and the result is nothing*). **4.** Non-existence, what does not exist. **5.** Trifling thing, event, remark, or person, (*he is nothing without his money*; *the little nothings of life*; *whisper soft nothings*; *the new commander-in-chief was a nothing*). **6. Be ~,** belong to no religious denomination, be an atheist or agnostic. **7.** *a.* (colloq.) Unimportant, trivial. **8.** *adv.* Not at all, in no way, (*differs nothing from*; *helps us, avails, nothing*; *is nothing* LIKE[1] *as* or *so good* etc.; *is nothing near so extensive*; *nothing daunted*; *nothing* LOATH); *(as *int.*, colloq.) not at all (*Is it gold? Gold nothing; it's pinchbeck*). [OE *nān thing* (as NO[1], THING)]

no'thĭngnėss (nŭ'-) *n.* Non-existence, the non-existent; worthlessness, triviality, unimportance, insignificance, trifles. [f. prec. + -NESS]

nō'tĭce *n.*, & *v.t.* **1.** *n.* Intimation, intelligence, warning, (*give, have, notice*; **at short, a moment's, ten minutes',** etc., ~, with such time for preparation); information or directions posted on notice-board. **2.** Formal intimation of something or instructions *to* do something (*notice to* QUIT[2]; *till* FURTHER *notice*); announcement by party to agreement that it is to terminate at specified time (esp. between landlord and tenant or employer and employed; *give a week's* etc. *notice*; *she is under notice*). **3.** Heed, attention, cognizance, observation, (*brought it to his notice*); **come into** or **to** or **under ~,** attract attention; **take no ~ of,** (1) not observe, (2) take no action in consequence of; **take ~ that,** I warn you that; **take ~,** show signs of intelligence or interest (cf. SIT 7 *up*). **4.** Paragraph or article upon something (esp. review of book, play, etc.) in newspaper or magazine. **5.** ||**~-board** (bearing notice, or provided for notices to be posted on). **6.** *v.t.* Remark upon, speak of. **7.** Perceive (*that*, *how*), take notice of; treat with politeness or condescension. **8.** Serve with notice, give notice to. **9.** Hence **~**ABLE *a.*, **~ab**LY[2] *adv.*, (-sa-).

[ME f. OF, f. L *notitia* being known (*notus* p.p. of *noscere* know; see -ICE)]

nō'tifiable *a.* (Of disease) that must be notified to public-health authorities. [f. foll. + -ABLE]

nō'ti|fȳ *v.t.* Make known, announce, report; inform, give notice to, (person *of, that*, or abs.); so ~FICA'TION *n.* [ME, f. OF *notifier* f. L *notificare* (*notus* known; see NOTICE, -FY)]

nō'tion *n.* **1.** General concept under which particular thing may be classed; **first, second, ~s,** (Philos.) = *first, second,* INTENTIONS. **2.** Idea, conception, (*the notion of my doing it is absurd; I have not the faintest notion what he means*); view, opinion, theory, vaguely held or insecurely based (*has a notion that; such is the common notion*). **3.** Faculty, capability, or intention *of* (*has no notion of obeying, obedience, discipline, letting himself be made a fool of*). **4.** (in *pl.*) *Miscellaneous small wares, esp. cheap useful ingenious articles or haberdashery. [f. L *notio* idea (*notus*; see NOTICE, -ION)]

nō'tional *a.* **1.** (Of knowledge etc.) speculative, not based on experiment or demonstration; hence ~IST (2) *n.* **2.** (Of thing, relation, etc.) existing only in thought, imaginary. **3.** (Gram., of verb) conveying its own meaning, principal, not auxiliary. **4.** Hence ~LY² *adv.* [obs. F, or f. med. L *notionalis* (as prec.; see -AL)]

nō'tochōrd (-k-) *n.* Rudimentary or embryonic spinal cord or column. [f. Gk *nōton* back + -O- + CHORD¹]

notŏr'ious *a.* (Of fact) well or commonly known (*it is notorious that*); (with designations of persons, conduct, etc., that imply condemnation) undisguised, widely talked of, generally known to deserve the name, (*notorious smuggler, offender, vice*); unfavourably known (*for* some quality or conduct, or abs.; *a ship notorious for ill-luck; the notorious Titus Oates*); hence or cogn. **nōtorī'e**TY¹ *n.*, ~LY² *adv.* [f. med. L *notorius* f. L *notus* known (see NOTICE, -ORY) + -OUS]

notŏr'nĭs *n.* Rare flightless N.Z. bird of genus *Notornis*. [f. Gk *notos* south + *ornis* bird]

Nŏtts. *abbr.* Nottinghamshire.

nŏtwĭthstă'ndĭng (*or* -dh-) *prep., adv., & conj.* **1.** *prep.* Without regard to or prevention by, not the less for, (*notwithstanding his objections; this notwithstanding*). **2.** *adv.* Nevertheless, all the same. **3.** *conj.* (arch.) Although, in spite of the fact that or *that*. [ME, orig. abs. part. f. NOT + WITHSTAND + -ING²]

nou'gat (nōō'gah) *n.* Sweetmeat of sugar, honey, nuts, and egg-white. [F, f. Prov. *nogat* (*noga* nut; see -ATE¹)]

nought (nawt) *n.* **1.** (poet. or arch.) Nothing (for phrs. cf. NAUGHT). **2.** Figure 0, cipher; ||**~s and crosses,** game in which usu. nine spaces in square array are filled alternately with noughts and crosses by two players seeking to complete a row of three of either kind. [OE *nōwiht* (*ne* not, *ōwiht*, var. of *āwiht* AUGHT¹)]

nou'mĕn|on *n.* (*pl.* ~**a**). Object of intellectual intuition devoid of all phenomenal attributes; hence ~AL *a.*, ~**al**LY² *adv.* [G, f. Gk *nooumenon* neut. pres. part. pass. of *noeō* apprehend, taken by Kant as antithesis to PHENOMENON]

noun *n.* (Gram.) **1.** Word or phrase used as name of person, place, or thing, substantive. **2.** (arch.) Substantive (~ **substantive**) or adjective (~ **adjective**). **3.** Hence ~'AL *a.* [ME f. AF, = OF *nun, num*, f. L *nomen* name]

nou'rĭsh (nŭ'-) *v.t.* **1.** Sustain with food (lit. or fig.); hence ~ING² *a.* **2.** Foster, cherish, nurse, (feeling, hope, etc.) in one's heart. [ME, f. OF *norir* (-ISH²) f. L *nutrire*]

nou'rĭshment (nŭ'-) *n.* Sustenance, food; nourishing. [ME, f. prec. + -MENT]

nous (nows) *n.* (Gk Philos.) mind, intellect; (colloq.) common sense, gumption. [Gk]

nouveau riche (nōōvō rē'sh) *n.* (*pl.* **-ux -es** *pr.* same). One who has recently acquired (usu. ostentatious) wealth. [F, = new rich]

nouvelle (nōō'vĕl) *n.* Short novel; ~ ***vague*** (vahg), new trend (esp. in Fr. film-making of early 1960s). [F, fem. of *nouveau* new; *vague* wave]

Nov. *abbr.* November.

nō'va *n.* (*pl.* ~**e** *or* ~**s**). Star showing sudden large increase of brightness and then subsiding. [L, fem. of *novus* new, since orig. thought to be new star]

novā'tion *n.* (Law). Substitution of new debtor, contract, etc., for former one. [f. LL *novatio* f. L *novare* make new (*novus* new); see -ATION]

nŏ'vel¹ *n.* Fictitious prose narrative of book length portraying characters and actions credibly representative of real life in continuous plot; **the** ~, this type of literature; hence ~E'SE *n.*, style characteristic of inferior novels, ~E'SQUE *a.* [f. It. *novella* (*storia* story) fem. of *novello* new f. L *novellus* (*novus*); see -LE 2]

nŏ'vel² *a.* Of new kind or nature, strange, hitherto unknown. [ME f. OF, f. L *novellus* (see prec.)]

nŏvelĕ'tt|e *n.* Short novel, story of moderate length, (||freq. derog. of light romance, whence ~ISH¹ *a.*); (Mus.) piano piece of free form with several themes. [f. NOVEL¹ + -ETTE]

nŏ'vel|ĭst *n.* Novel-writer; hence ~**ĭ'st**IC *a.* [f. NOVEL¹ + -IST]

nŏ'velīz|e, -is|e (-īz), *v.t.* Convert (drama, facts) into a novel; hence ~A'TION *n.* [f. NOVEL¹ + -IZE]

novĕ'lla *n.* Short novel or narrative; tale such as those in Boccaccio's *Decameron*. [It. (see NOVEL¹)]

nŏ'veltȳ *n.* New or unusual thing or occurrence; novel character of something; small decoration or toy of novel design. [ME, f. OF *novelté* (as NOVEL²; see -TY¹)]

Novĕ'mber *n.* Eleventh month of year. [ME f. OF *novembre* f. L *November* (*novem* nine; cf. DECEMBER, SEPTEMBER)]

novē'na *n.* (R.C. Ch.) Devotion consisting of special prayers or service on nine successive days. [med. L, f. L *novem* nine]

novêr'cal *a.* (arch.) Stepmotherly. [f. L *novercalis* (*noverca* stepmother; see -AL)]

nŏ'vĭce *n.* Person received in religious house on probation before taking the vows; new convert; inexperienced person, beginner, tiro. [ME f. OF, L *novicius* (*novus* new; see -ICE)]

novĭ'cĭate, -tĭate, (-shĭ-) *n.* Novice's probationary period or initiation or apprenticeship; novice (esp. in religion); quarters assigned to novices. [f. F *noviciat* or f. med. L *noviciatus* (as prec.; see -ATE¹)]

nō'vocaine *n.* Local anaesthetic derived from benzoic acid. [f. L *novus* new + COCAINE]

now *adv., conj., & n.* **1.** *adv.* At the time when, or of which, one is writing or speaking; by this time; under the present circumstances (*I cannot now ever believe you again*); immediately (*must go now*); in the immediate past (*just now*; (arch.) *even now, but now*); on this further occasion (*well, what do you want now?*); (in narrative or discourse) then, next, by that time, (*Caesar now marched east; now let us consider the second point; now to put the cap back on; it was now clear*); HOW *now?*; **(every) ~ and then, (every) ~ and again,** from time to time, intermittently; **~ . . . ~ . . ., ~ . . . then . . ., ~ . . . and again . . .,** at one moment . . . at another moment . . .; **~ for it!, ~ or never!,** this is the moment to act; **~ that,** = sense 3. **2.** (Without temporal force, giving sentence various tones: soothing, exclaiming, reproving, explanatory, threatening, etc.) pray, I beg, I insist, I warn you, and yet, you must know, it must be admitted, surely, (*Now what do you mean by it?. Now why didn't I think of that?. Oh, come now!. No nonsense, now!. You have revealed the secret; now you were paid to keep it. Now Barabbas was a robber. Now this was bad enough, but—. Now then, what mischief are you up to?. Now, now, behave yourself!. You don't mean it, now*). **3.** *conj.* ~ (**that**), consequently upon or simultaneously with the fact that (*Now I am a man I think otherwise. Now* (*that*) *you mention it, I do remember. You ought to write, now that you know the address*). **4.** *n.* This time, the present (chiefly after *preps.*: *is there by, before, till, now*); **as of** ~, at this time; **for** ~, until a later time (*goodbye for now*). [OE *nū*, = OS, OHG, ON, Goth. *nū*, corresp. to L *nunc*, Gk *nun*, Skr. *nū*]

now'aday *a.* Of nowadays. [f. foll.]

now'adays (-z) *adv.* & *n.* (At) the present day, (in) these (advanced or newfangled) times. [ME, f. NOW *adv.* + A³ + DAY + -S³]

Nowel(l). Vars. of NOEL.

nowhence, nowhither. See NO¹.

nō'where (nō'wār) *adv.* & *pron.* (In or to) no place; ~ **near,** not nearly; **be, come in,** ~, not be placed in race or competition; **come from** ~, be suddenly evident or successful; **get** ~, make no progress, give (person) no success; **in the middle of** ~, (colloq.) far from towns etc. [OE *nāhwǣr* (as NO¹, WHERE)]

nowt *n.* (colloq. or dial.) Nothing. [var. of NOUGHT]

nŏ'xious (-kshus) *a.* Harmful, unwholesome; hence ~LY² *adv.*, ~NESS *n.* [f. L *noxius* (*noxa* harm) + -OUS]

noyade (nwahyah'd) *n.* Execution by drowning, esp. wholesale as in France in 1794. [F (*noyer* drown f. L *necare* f. *nex* slaughter; see -ADE)]

noyau (nwah'yō) *n.* (*pl.* ~**x** *pr.* -z). Liqueur of brandy flavoured with fruit-kernels. [F, = kernel, f. Rom. **nucale* neut. (as n.) of LL *nucalis* f. L *nux nucis* nut]

nŏ'zzle *n.* Spout, mouthpiece, end fitted to hose etc. to form jet. [f. NOSE + -LE 1]

N.P. *abbr.* Notary Public.

n.p. *abbr.* new paragraph; no place of publication.

Np *symb.* neptunium.

||**N.P.A.** *abbr.* Newspaper Publishers' Association.

||**N.P.L.** *abbr.* National Physical Laboratory.

N.R. *abbr.* North RIDING².

nr. *abbr.* near.

N.R.A. *abbr.* *National Recovery Administration; ||National Rifle Association.

N.S. *abbr.* new series; new style; Nova Scotia.

||**N.S.B.** *abbr.* National Savings Bank.

***N.S.C.** *abbr.* National Security Council.

***N.S.F.** *abbr.* National Science Foundation.

||**N.S.P.C.C.** *abbr.* National Society for the Prevention of Cruelty to Children.

N.S.W. *abbr.* New South Wales.

N.T. *abbr.* New Testament; (Austral.) Northern Territory; no trumps.

n't *adv.* = NOT 2 (*isn't, mustn't*). [abbr.]

nth. See N.

Nth. *abbr.* North.

N.T.P. *abbr.* normal temperature and pressure.

nū *n.* Thirteenth Greek letter (Ν, ν) = n. [Gk]

nū'ance (*or* -ah'ns) *n.* Delicate difference in or shade of meaning, feeling, opinion, colour, etc. [F (*nuer* to shade, ult. f. L *nubes* cloud; see -ANCE)]

nŭb *n.* Small knob or lump, esp. of coal; small residue, stub; point or gist (*of* matter or story). [app. var. of *knub*, f. MLG *knubbe, knobbe* KNOB]

***nŭ'bbĭn** *n.* Dwarfed or imperfect maize ear or other vegetable; = NUB. [f. prec.]

nŭ'bbl|e *n.* Small knob or lump; hence ~Y² *a.* [dim. of NUB; see -LE 1]

nū'bile *a.* Marriageable (esp. of woman); hence **nūbĭ'l**ITY *n.* [f. L *nubilis* (*nubere* become wife of; see -IL)]

nū'chal (-k-) *a.* Of nape of neck. [f. *nucha* nape, f. med. L *nucha* medulla oblongata f. Arab. *nukā'* spinal marrow]

nūcĭ- *comb. form.* Nut, as **nūcĭ'**FEROUS, **nūcĭ'**VOROUS, *adjs.* [f. L *nux nucis* nut]

nū'clėar *a.* Of, relating to, constituting, a nucleus; using nuclear energy (*nuclear weapon*); ~ **bomb,** = ATOMIC *bomb*; ~ **disarmament,** renunciation of nuclear weapons; ~ **energy** (released or absorbed during reactions taking place in atomic nuclei); ~ **family,** father, mother, and child(ren); ~ **fission,** = FISSION 2; ~ **fuel,** source of nuclear energy; *nuclear* FUSION; ~ **physics** (dealing with the atomic nucleus); ~ **power,** (1) power derived from nuclear energy, (2) country possessing nuclear weapons; ~(**-powered**) *a.*, (of ship) using nuclear power; *nuclear* REACTOR; ~ **warfare,** = ATOMIC *warfare*. [f. NUCLEUS + -AR¹]

nū'clėāse *n.* (Chem.) Enzyme causing hydrolysis of nucleic acids. [f. NUCLEIC + -ASE]

nū'clėāte *v.t.* & *i.* Form (into) a nucleus. [f. LL *nucleare* form kernel (NUCLEUS) + -ATE³]

nūclē'ĭc *a.* ~ **acid,** one of two acids (DNA and RNA) present in all cells and having many nucleotide molecules linked in long chain. [f. NUCLEUS + -IC]

nū'clėō-. See NUCLEUS.

nūclē'ol|us *n.* (*pl.* ~**i** *pr.* -ī). Spherical body in nucleus of living cell in resting state; hence ~AR¹ *a.* [LL, dim. of L NUCLEUS]

nū'clėŏn *n.* (Phys.) Proton or neutron; particle of which these are regarded as different states. [f. NUCLEUS + -ON]

nūclėŏ'n|ĭc *a.* Of nucleons or nucleonics; so ~ICS *n. pl.* (treated as *sing.*), branch of science and technology concerned with atomic nuclei and nucleons, esp. practical use of nuclear phenomena. [f. NUCLEAR after *electronics*, & f. prec. + -IC]

nū'clėoside *n.* (Chem.) Compound of a sugar with a heterocyclic base. [f. NUCLEO- + -OSE² + -IDE]

nū'clėotide *n.* (Chem.) Compound of phosphate group linked to sugar of nucleoside. [f. NUCLEO- + *t* + -IDE]

nū'clė|us *n.* (*pl.* ~**i** *pr.* -ī). **1.** (Astron.) Condensed part of comet's head. **2.** (Phys.) Positively charged central portion constituting main mass of atom. **3.** Central part or thing round which others are collected; kernel of aggregate or mass; beginning meant to receive additions. **4.** (Biol.) Dense central part of plant or animal cell, containing genetic material; central part of ovule or seed; group of nerve-cells. **5.** Hence ~O- *comb. form*; ~**o-pro'tein,** compound of protein with nucleic acid. [L, = kernel, inner part, dim. of *nux nucis* nut]

nū'clide *n.* (Phys.) Particular kind of atom defined by composition of its nucleus; hence **nūclĭ'd**IC *a.* [f. NUCLEUS + Gk *eidos* form; cf. -IDE]

nūde *a.* & *n.* **1.** *a.* Naked, bare, unclothed, undraped; ~ **contract,** (Law) contract lacking a consideration and therefore void unless under seal; so **nū'dĭ-** *comb. form* (Zool.), **nū'd**ITY *n.* **2.** Flesh-coloured. **3.** *n.* Nude human figure in painting, sculpture, photography, etc.; nude person; **the** ~, the undraped figure, unclothed state. **4.** Hence **nū'd**IST *n.*, one who lives unclothed as much as possible (on grounds of health) or advocates doing so; so **nū'd**ISM (3) *n.* [f. L *nudus*]

nŭdge *v.t.*, & *n.* **1.** *v.t.* Push slightly with elbow to draw attention privately, (fig.) draw attention of; push gradually. **2.** *n.* Such push. [17th c.;

orig. unkn.; cf. Norw. dial. *nugga, nyggja* to push, rub]

nŭff *n.* (colloq.) = ENOUGH (esp. ~ **said,** that is agreed or fully explained). [abbr.]

nū'gatorў *a.* Trifling, worthless, futile; inoperative, not valid. [f. L *nugatorius* (*nugari* trifle f. *nugae* jests; see -ORY)]

nŭ'ggar *n.* Large broad-beamed boat used on upper Nile. [f. Arab. *nukkār*]

nŭ'ggėt (-g-) *n.* Rough lump of native gold, platinum, or (fig.) something valuable. [app. f. dial. *nug* lump etc. + -ET[1]]

nui'sance (nū's-) *n.* **1.** Anything injurious or obnoxious to the community or member of it and for which legal remedy exists. **2.** Obnoxious person, offensive object, annoying action, anything disagreeable or inconvenient (*what a nuisance!*); ~ **value** (resulting from capacity to harass or frustrate). [ME f. OF, = hurt (*nuire nuis-* f. L *nocēre* to hurt; see -ANCE)]

||**N.U.J.** *abbr.* National Union of Journalists.

***nūke** *n.* (sl.) Nuclear bomb. [abbr.]

nŭll *a.* & *n.* **1.** *a.* ~ (**and void**), not binding, invalid. **2.** Without character or expression. **3.** Non-existent, amounting to nothing; of zero (~ **instrument,** used by adjustment to give reading of zero). **4.** *n.* Dummy letter in a cipher. [f. F *nul nulle* or f. L *nullus* none (*ne* not, *ullus* any)]

nŭ'lla(-nŭlla) *n.* (Austral.) Hardwood club used by Aborigines. [Aboriginal]

nulla bona (nŭla bō'na) *n.* Sheriff's return stating that party has no goods to be distrained upon. [L, = no goods]

nŭ'llah (-*a*) (Anglo-Ind.) Stream, watercourse, ravine. [f. Hindi *nālā*]

nŭllĭfĭ'dĭan *n.* & *a.* (Person) having no religious faith or belief. [f. med. L *nullifidius* f. L *nullus* none + *fides* faith; see -IAN]

nŭ'llĭ|fў *v.t.* Cancel, neutralize; hence ~FICA'TION *n.* [f. NULL + -I- + -FY]

nŭllĭ'par|a *n.* Woman who has never borne a child; hence ~OUS *a.* [mod. L, f. L *nullus* none + -I- + *-para* fem. of *-parus* (*parere* bear)]

nŭ'llĭpōre *n.* Form of marine vegetation able to secrete lime, like coral. [f. L *nullus* none + PORE[1]]

nŭ'llĭtў *n.* Being null, invalidity, (esp. of marriage; ~ **suit,** to establish this); act, document, etc., that is null; nothingness; a mere nothing; a nonentity. [f. F *nullité* or f. med. L *nullitas* f. L *nullus* none; see -ITY]

||**N.U.M.** *abbr.* National Union of Mineworkers.

Num. *abbr.* Numbers (O.T.).

nŭmb (-m) *a.*, & *v.t.* **1.** *a.* Deprived of feeling or power of motion (*numb with cold, shock,* etc.); **~-fish,** the electric ray or torpedo; **~'skull,** numskull; hence ~'LY[2] *adv.*, ~'NESS *n.* **2.** *v.t.* Make numb; (fig.) stupefy, paralyse. [ME *nome(n)* p.p. of NIM take; for *-b* cf. THUMB]

nŭ'mbat *n.* Small Austral. marsupial of genus *Myrmecobius.* [Aboriginal]

nŭ'mber[1] *n.* **1.** Count, sum, or aggregate, of or *of* persons or things or abstract units; count of things etc. up to a certain one, showing latter's position in series; symbol or figure representing such count, esp. as identifying one member of a series (e.g. registered vehicle, telephone); person or thing (esp. single issue of magazine, single song etc. in opera, concert, etc.) whose place in series is indicated by such figure; (colloq.) person, garment, job, etc.; (in *pl.*; *N~s*) O.T. book containing census; BACK[1] *number*; **by ~s,** following simple instructions identified by numbers; GOLDEN *number*; **have** person's ~, (sl.) understand his motives etc.; **in ~s,** (of publication) in successive numbered parts; **make** one's ~ **with,** (sl.) contact (a person); ROUND[1] *numbers*; **to the ~ of,** amounting to as many as (*80* etc.); one's ~ **is up,** (colloq.) one dies; ~ **one,** (*n.*) oneself (*always takes care of number one*), (*a.*) first in rank or importance, first-rate; **~-plate** (bearing number, esp. of registered vehicle); **~s game,** action involving only arithmetical work, *lottery based on occurrence of unpredictable numbers in results of races etc.; ||**N~ Ten (Downing Street),** official London house of Prime Minister. **2.** Company (**is of our ~,** is included among us); (in *sing.* or *pl.*) *large, small,* etc., or (fairly) large, collection or group *of* or abs. (*were present in* (*great*) *numbers, only in small numbers; saw a* (*great*) *number of birds; a small number came; there are numbers who live by begging*). **3.** (in *pl.*) Numerical preponderance (*won by* (*force of*) *numbers*). **4.** Numerical reckoning (*the laws of number and proportion pervade Nature*); **without ~, out of ~,** ~LESS *a.*, innumerable; **in ~,** when counted or estimated, numerically, (*one people exceeds another in number*). **5.** (Gram.) Class of word-forms including all singular, all plural, or all dual etc. words (*Greek has three numbers; 'things' is of the plural number*). **6.** (arch.) Rhythm; (in *pl.*) groups of musical notes, metrical feet, verses. [ME f. AF *numbre,* OF *nombre* f. L *numerus*]

nŭ'mber[2] *v.t.* **1.** Count, ascertain number of; (in *pass.*) be restricted in number (**his days** or **years are ~ed,** he has not long to live). **2.** Include, regard as, *among, in,* or *with* some class. **3.** ~ (**off**), assign number(s) to, distinguish with number(s). **4.** Have lived, live, (so many years); be able to show (so many inhabitants etc.); amount to (specified number). [ME, f. OF *nombrer* f. L *numerare* (as prec.)]

||**nŭ'mbles** (-belz) *n. pl.* (arch.) Deer's entrails. [ME, f. OF *numbles, nombles* loin etc., f. L *lumbulus* dim. of *lumbus* loin; cf. UMBLES]

nŭ'mdah *n.* Embroidered felt rug from India etc. [f. Urdu *namdā*; see NUMNAH]

nū'm|ĕn *n.* (*pl.* ~**ina**). Local or presiding deity. [L *numen -minis*]

nū'merable *a.* That can be numbered. [f. L *numerabilis* (as NUMBER[2]; see -ABLE)]

nū'meral *a.* & *n.* **1.** (Word, figure, group of figures) denoting a number. **2.** *a.* Of number. [f. LL *numeralis* f. L (as NUMBER[1]; see -AL)]

nū'mer|ate *a.* Acquainted with basic principles of mathematics and science; hence ~ACY *n.* [f. L *numerus* number + -ATE[2], after *literate*]

nūmerā'tion *n.* Method or process of numbering or computing; calculation; assigning of numbers; (Arith.) expression in words of number written in figures; ~ **table** (showing value of figures according to their place in system of notation). [ME, f. L *numeratio* payment, in LL numbering (as NUMBER[2]; see -ATION)]

nū'merātor *n.* Number above line in vulgar fraction showing how many of the parts indicated by the denominator are taken (e.g. 2 in $\frac{2}{3}$); person who numbers. [f. F *numérateur* or f. LL *numerator* (as NUMBER[2]; see -OR)]

nūmĕ'rĭcal *a.* Of, in, denoting, etc., number(s); hence ~LY[2] *adv.* [f. med. L *numericus* (as NUMBER[1]; see -IC) + -AL]

nūmerŏ'log|ў *n.* Divination by numbers; study of occult meaning of numbers; hence **nūmerolŏ'g**ICAL *a.*, ~IST (3) *n.* [f. L *numerus* number + -O- + -LOGY]

nū'merous *a.* Comprising many units (*a numerous clientele, library, family, army, class*); (with *pl. n.*) many (*received numerous gifts*); (arch.) coming from or containing many individuals (*the numerous voice of the people; the university is numerous*), (of verse or prose) rhythmic, harmonious; hence ~LY[2] *adv.* [f. L *numerosus* (as prec.; see -OUS)]

nū'mĭnous *a.* Of a numen; spiritual; indicating presence of divinity; awe-inspiring. [f. L NUMEN + -OUS]

nūmĭsmă't|ĭc (-z-) *a.* Of coins or coinage; of coins and related things (e.g. medals); hence ~ICALLY *adv.*, ~ICS, **nūmĭ'smat**IST (3), **nūmĭsmatŏ'**LOGY, (-z-) *ns.* [f. F *numismatique* f. L *numisma* f. Gk *nomisma -atos* current coin (*nomizō* use currently; see -ISM, -ATIC)]

nŭ'mmarў *a.* Of or in coin(s). [f. L *nummarius* (*nummus* coin; see -ARY[1])]

nŭ'mmūlīte *n.* Disc-shaped fossil shell of foraminiferous protozoan in Tertiary strata. [f. L *nummulus* dim. of *nummus* coin, + -ITE[1] (2)]

nŭ'mnah (-*a*) *n.* Saddle-cloth, pad placed under saddle. [f. Urdu *namdā* f. Pers. *namad* carpet]

nŭ'mskŭll *n.* Stupid person; head (esp. of stupid person). [f. NUMB + SKULL]

nŭn *n.* Woman living in convent usu. under vows of poverty, chastity, and obedience; ||blue tit; ||smew; **~'s cloth, ~'s veiling,** thin woollen material; hence ~'HOOD, ~'SHIP, *ns.*, ~'LIKE, **~'n**ISH[1], *adjs.* [ME, partly f. OE *nunne*, = OHG, ON *nunna*, f. eccl. L *nonna* fem. of *nonnus* monk, orig. title given to elderly person, partly f. OF *nonne*]

nŭ'natăk *n.* Isolated peak of rock projecting above surface of land ice or snow e.g. in Greenland. [Eskimo]

nŭ'n-buoy (-boi) *n.* Buoy circular in middle and tapering to each end. [f. obs. *nun* child's top + BUOY[1]]

nunc dimittis (nŭngk dĭ'mĭtĭs) *n.* **1.** Canticle beginning *Nunc dimittis* from Luke 2:29. **2.** Permission to depart; **sing ~,** be willing to depart from life etc. [L, = now lettest thou depart]

nŭ'nciatūre (-sh*a*t-) *n.* (Tenure of) office of nuncio. [f. It. *nunziatura* (as foll.); see -URE]

nŭ'nciō (-shĭō) *n.* (*pl.* **~s**). Pope's permanent diplomatic representative in another country. [It., f. L *nuntius* messenger]

nŭ'ncūp|āte *v.t.* Declare (will, testament) orally, not in writing; so ~A'TION *n.*, ~ATIVE *a.* [f. L *nuncupare* name + -ATE[3]]

nŭ'nnerў *n.* Religious house for nuns, convent. [ME, f. AF **nonnerie* (*nonne* NUN; see -ERY)]

||**N.U.P.E.** *abbr.* National Union of Public Employees.

nŭ'ptial (-sh*a*l) *a.* & *n.* **1.** *a.* Of marriage or wedding; ~ **flight** (of ants etc., with mating). **2.** *n.* (usu. in *pl.*) Wedding. [F, or f. L *nuptialis* (*nuptiae* wedding f. *nubere nupt-* become wife)]

||**N.U.R.** *abbr.* National Union of Railwaymen.

nûrse[1] *n.* **1.** **(Dry-)~,** woman employed to take charge of young children; WET-*nurse*. **2.** Country etc. that fosters some quality etc. (*the nurse of liberty*). **3.** Nursing or being nursed; **at ~, put out to ~,** (of child, or fig. of estate). **4.** **(Sick-)~,** person, usu. woman, employed in & usu. trained for care of the sick or infirm. **5.** (Forestry) tree planted as shelter to others; (Entom.) sexually imperfect bee, ant, etc., caring for young brood, worker. **6.** **~-child,** foster-child; **~-frog** (of which male carries eggs till hatched); **~'maid,** young woman employed to take charge of child(ren), (fig.) one who takes solicitous care of another. [reduced f. ME and OF *norice*, *nurice* f. LL *nutricia* fem. of L *nutricius* (*nutrix -icis* f. *nutrire* nourish)]

nûrse[2] *v.t.* & *i.* **1.** Suckle (child), give suck, act as wet-nurse; act as nurse(maid) to, have charge of; (in *pass.*) be brought up (*in* luxury, certain place, etc.). **2.** Foster, tend, promote development of, (the arts, hatred, etc.); manage (plants, estate) with solicitude; cherish (grievance etc.). **3.** Tend (sick person); try to cure (sickness, injured part); be sick-nurse. **4.** Hold or clasp (baby, one's knees or foot) carefully or caressingly; sit close over (fire); treat carefully. **5.** ||Keep favour of (electoral constituency) by continued attentions. **6.** (Bill.) Keep (balls) together for series of cannons. **7.** ||**Nur'sing home,** private hospital, house for surgical operations, reception of invalids, etc.; **nursing father,** foster-father; **nursing mother,** (1) suckling woman, (2) foster-mother. [later form of ME *nur(i)sh* f. NOURISH, assim. to prec.]

nûrse[3] *n.* One of several large sharks; **~-hound,** a dogfish (*Scyliorhinus stellaris*). [ME, perh. var. of HUSS, w. *n-* as in NEWT, assim. to NURSE[1]]

nûr'serў *n.* **1.** Room or place for children and their nurses; DAY *nursery*. **2.** Practice, institution, sphere, place, in or by which qualities or classes of people are fostered or bred. **3.** Plot of ground in which young plants are reared for transplantation, esp. trees etc. for sale; fish-rearing pond; place where animal life is developed. **4.** (Bill.) Grouped balls (see NURSE[2]; esp. *nursery cannon*). **5.** **~man,** owner of or worker in plant nursery; ~ **rhyme,** simple traditional song or story in rhyme for children; ~ **school** (for young children esp. under 5); ~ **slopes,** part of skiing-resort slopes suitable for beginners; ~ **stakes,** race for two-year-old horses. [ME, prob. f. AF **noricerie* (as NURSE[1]; see -ERY)]

nûr's(e)lĭng (-sl-) *n.* Infant, esp. in relation to its nurse; ~ **of,** person or thing bred in or fostered by. [f. NURSE[2] + -LING[1]]

nûr'ture *n.*, & *v.t.* **1.** *n.* Bringing up, training, fostering care; nourishment. **2.** *v.t.* Nourish, rear, foster, train, educate. [ME, f. OF *nour(e)ture* (as NOURISH; see -URE)]

||**N.U.S.** *abbr.* National Union of Students.

nŭt *n.*, & *v.i.* (**-tt-**). **1.** *n.* Fruit consisting of hard or leathery shell enclosing edible kernel; pod containing hard seeds (EARTH[1]-*nut*, PEA*nut*); ||*can't shoot* etc. **for ~s,** (sl.) even tolerably well; HARD or *tough nut to crack*; **~s (to you)** (sl. excl. of derision; also **nerts**). **2.** (arch. sl.) Showy young man. **3.** (sl.) Head (**off** one's ~, crazy; **do** one's ~, go crazy); crazy or cranky person; (in *pl.*, as *a.*) crazy; **~s about** or **on,** enthusiastic about, skilful at. **4.** Small usu. hexagonal metal block pierced with female screw-thread to adjust or fasten bolt etc. and operated by spanner; **~s and bolts,** (fig.) practical details. **5.** Holder that tightens or relaxes horse-hair of violin-bow etc.; fixed bridge at upper end of strings of violin etc. **6.** Small lump of coal, butter, etc. **7.** **~-brown,** coloured like ripe hazel-nut (esp. of girl's complexion, or of ale); **~-butter,** food like butter made from nuts; **~-case,** (sl.) crazy person; **~'cracker,** (usu. in *pl.*) instrument for cracking nuts, prominent chin and nose with points naturally, or by loss of teeth, near each other; **~-gall,** gall found on dyer's oak used as dyestuff; **~'hatch** (-t-h-), small climbing bird feeding on nuts, insects, etc. [rel. to HATCH[2]]; **~-house,** (sl.) mental home or hospital; ***~-meat,** kernel of nut; **~-oil** (got from hazel-nuts and walnuts, and used in paints and varnishes); **~-palm,** Australian cycad bearing edible nuts; **~-pine,** N. Amer. pine with edible nutlike seeds; **~'shell,** hard exterior covering of nut, tiny receptacle or dwelling, brief(est possible) way of expressing (*can give it to you in a nutshell*); **~-tree,** tree bearing nuts, esp. hazel; **~-weevil,** beetle laying eggs in green hazel and filbert nuts. **8.** *v.i.* Seek or gather nuts (*go nutting*). [OE *hnutu*, = MLG, MDu. *note*, OHG *(h)nuz*, ON *hnot* f. Gmc **hnut-*]

||**N.U.T.** *abbr.* National Union of Teachers.

nū'tant *a.* (Bot.) Nodding, drooping. [f. L *nutare* frequent. of *-nuere* nod + -ATE[3]]

nūtā'tion *n.* Nodding; (Astron.) oscillation of earth's axis making motion of pole of equator round pole of ecliptic wavy; oscillation of spinning top; curvature in stem of growing plant. [f. L *nutatio* (as prec.; see -ION)]

nŭ'tmĕg *n.* Hard aromatic spheroidal seed got from fruit of evergreen E. Ind. tree (*Myristica fragrans*) used as spice and in medicine; **~-apple,** fruit of nutmeg-tree yielding mace and nutmeg. [ME; partial transl. of AF **nois mugue*, OF *nois mug(u)ede* f. Rom. **nuce muscata* f. L *nux* nut + LL *muscus* MUSK]

nū'trĭa *n.* Skin or fur of coypu. [Sp., = otter]

nū'trĭent *a.* & *n.* (Substance) serving as or providing nourishment. [f. L *nutrire* nourish; see -ENT]

nū'trĭment *n.* Nourishing food (lit. or fig.); hence ~AL (-ĕ'n-) *a.* [f. L *nutrimentum* (as prec.; see -MENT)]

nūtrĭ'tion *n.* (Supplying or receiving of) nourishment, food; hence ~AL *a.*, of or relating to nutrition, ~IST (3) *n.*, one who studies human nourishment. [F, or f. LL *nutritio* (as NUTRIENT; see -ITION)]

nūtrĭ'tious (-sh*us*) *a.* Nourishing, efficient as food; hence ~LY[2] *adv.*, ~NESS *n.* [f. L *nutritius* (as NURSE[1]; see -ITIOUS[2])]

nū'trĭtĭve *a.* & *n.* **1.** *a.* Serving as nutritious food; concerned in nutrition. **2.** *n.* Nutritious article of food. [ME, f. F *nutritif -ive* f. med. L *nutritivus* (as NUTRIENT; see -IVE)]

nŭ'ttȳ *a.* Abounding in nuts; tasting like nuts, of rich mellow flavour; (sl.) crazy; ~ **about** or **on,** (sl.) = NUTS *about*. [f. NUT + -Y[2]]

nŭx vŏ'mĭca *n.* Seed of E. Ind. tree (*Strychnos nux-vomica*) yielding strychnine. [med. L, f. L *nux* nut + *vomicus* (*vomere* vomit; see -IC)]

nŭ'zzle *v.i.* & *t.* Burrow or press or rub or sniff with the nose, press nose or press (nose) *into* or *against*; nestle, lie snug, (also *refl.*). [ME, f. NOSE[1] + -LE 3]

N.W. *abbr.* North-West(ern).

N.Y. *abbr.* New York.

nyala. Var. of INYALA.

N.Y.C. *abbr.* New York City.

nȳctalō'pĭa *n.* **1.** Night-blindness, recurrent loss of vision in twilight and dark. **2.** Inability to see clearly except at night. [LL, f. Gk *nuktalōps* (*nux nuktos* night, *alaos* blind, *ōps* eye; see -IA[1]); incorrect second sense due to overlooking of *-al-*]

nȳctĭtrŏ'pĭc *a.* (Bot.) Turning in certain direction at night. [f. Gk *nukti-* comb. form of *nux nuktos* night + *tropos* turn; see -IC]

||**nȳe.** Var. of NIDE.

nȳ'lghau (-gaw) *n.* = NILGAI. [f. Hind. f. Pers. *nīlgāw* (*nīl* blue, *gāw* cow)]

nȳ'lŏn *n.* Synthetic polymer of great toughness, lightness, and elasticity, widely used in industry and in textile fabrics; nylon fabric; (in *pl.*) stockings made of nylon. [invented wd, after *cotton, rayon*]

nȳmph *n.* **1.** One of class of mythological semi-divine maidens inhabiting sea, rivers, fountains, hills, woods, or trees, or attending superior deities; hence or cogn. ~Ē'AN, ~'LIKE, *adjs.* **2.** (poet.) Young and beautiful woman. **3.** Immature form of insect which resembles adult; young dragonfly or damselfly. **4.** So ~'AL *a.* [ME, f. OF *nimphe* f. L f. Gk *numphē*]

nȳ'mphae *n. pl.* (Anat.) Labia minora. [L, pl. of *nympha* (see prec.)]

nȳ'mphĕt (*or* -ĕ't) *n.* Young nymph; nymphlike or sexually attractive young girl. [f. NYMPH + -ET[1]]

nȳ'mphō *n.* (*pl.* **~s**). (colloq.) Nymphomaniac. [abbr.]

nȳ'mpholĕpsȳ *n.* Ecstasy or frenzy caused by desire of the unattainable. [f. foll., after *epilepsy*]

nȳ'mphol|ĕpt *n.* Person inspired by violent enthusiasm esp. for an ideal; hence **~ĕ'pt**IC *a.* [f. Gk *numpholēptos* caught by nymphs (as NYMPH, *lambanō* take)]

nȳmpho|mā'nĭa *n.* (Path.) Morbid and uncontrollable sexual desire in women; hence ~MA'NIAC *n.* [mod. L (as NYMPH, -O-, -MANIA)]

nȳstă'gm|us *n.* (Eye-disease common among miners, with) continual rapid oscillation of eyeballs; hence ~IC *a.* [f. Gk *nustagmos* nodding (*nustazō* nod)]

N.Z. *abbr.* New Zealand.

O

O[1], **o,** (ō) *n.* (*pl.* **Os** *or* **O's**). **1.** Fifteenth letter of alphabet. **2.** (*O*). (As numeral in telephone numbers etc.) nought, zero.

O[2] (ō) *int.* (arch., poet., or rhet.) prefixed to name in vocative (*O God our help*) or expr. wish, entreaty, etc., (*O for the touch of a vanish'd hand*; *O come, all ye faithful*; *O* THAT[2]). [ME; natural excl. of sudden feeling]

O'[1] (ō or *o*) *pref.* of Irish patronymic names (*O'Connor*). [Ir. *ó, ua*, descendant]

o'[2] (*o*) *prep.* Of, on, (arch., poet., or dial., exc. in some phrs.): (= OF) *o'clock, Jack-o'-lantern, will-o'-the-wisp*, (colloq.) *cup o' tea*, (= ON[1]) *cannot sleep o' nights*. [abbr.]

-ō *suf.* forming usu. sl. or colloq. variants or derivatives (*beano, smoko, wino*). [perh. f. OH as joc. suf.]

-o-, terminal vowel of combining forms of wds; prop. used in Gk compounds (-I- being usu. in L), but now extended to many scientific and other terms made wholly or partly f. non-Gk wds (*occipito-frontal, spectroscope, serio-comic*) and, in meaning, expressing not merely modification of second element by first (*Franco-German* = essentially German with some French characteristics), but equal or any other relations (*Franco-German war*); available as general formative of combining forms (*socio-*), esp. for wds in *-ic(al)* (*chemico-, politico-*); often elided before vowel (*neuralgia*).

O. *abbr.* Ohio; Old.

O *symb.* oxygen.

oaf *n.* (*pl.* **~s,** *or* **oaves** *pr.* -vz). Stupid person; awkward lout; hence ~'ISH[1] *a.* [orig. = elf's child, var. of obs. *auf* f. ON *álfr* elf]

oak *n.* **1.** Tree and shrub of genus *Quercus*, of which the best known species is a forest tree yielding hard timber and acorns and having irregularly lobed leaves; BUR, **dyer's,** HOLM[2], **scarlet, white,** etc., ~, other species of *Quercus*; **dwarf, ground,** SHE-, etc., ~, plants named from some resemblance to oak esp. in leaves. **2.** Wood of the oak (HEART *of oak*); (poet.) wooden ships; ||outer door of university college rooms (**sport** one's ~, shut this to exclude visitors); leaves of oak esp. as formerly worn on 29 May (see sense 5); ‖**the Oaks,** annual race at Epsom for three-year-old fillies [f. name of estate]. **3.** (*attrib.*, =, but now more usual than) oaken. **4.** **~-apple, -fig,** -GALL⁴, **-plum, -potato, -spangle, -wart,** kinds of excrescence produced on oaks by gall-flies. **5.** ‖**~-apple day,** 29 May (Charles II restored 1660), on which oak-apples or oak-leaves were worn in memory of the ROYAL-oak incident; **~-beauty, -egger, -hook-tip, -lappet,** kinds of moth bred on or resembling leaf etc. of oak; **~-fern,** a polypody (*Gymnocarpium dryopteris*) with tripartite fronds having subdivisions shaped like oak leaves; **~-tree,** = sense 1; **~-wood,** (1) forest, copse, etc., of oaks, (2) wood of the oak. **6.** Hence ~'EN⁵ *a.*, ~'LET, ~'LING¹ 2, *ns.* [OE *āc*, = OHG *eih*, ON *eik* f. Gmc **aiks*]

oa'kum *n.* Loose fibre got by picking old rope to pieces and used esp. in caulking (**pick** ~, make this, esp. as formerly common task of convicts and paupers). [OE *ǣ-*, *ācumbe*, lit. 'off-combings']

O. & M. *abbr.* organization and methods.

‖**O.A.P.** *abbr.* old-age pension(er).

oar *n.* & *v.* **1.** *n.* Pole with blade used (usu. in even numbers) to propel boat by leverage against water, esp. one worked by single rower (cf. SWEEP² 4) with both hands (cf. SCULL), or to steer; **chained to the ~,** constrained to work hard and long [w. allus. to galley-slaves]; **have an ~ in,** be (meddlesomely) concerned with; **pulls a good ~,** is good at rowing; **put in** one's ~ or **put** one's ~ **in,** interfere; **rest on** one's **~s,** lie or ***lay on** one's **~s,** relax one's efforts. **2.** Oarsman, rower, (*good, bad, young, practised*, etc., *oar*); (fig.) wing, fin, arm used in swimming, etc.; stirring implement used in brewing. **3.** **~-fish,** ribbon-fish of genus *Regalecus*; ***~'lock,** rowlock; **~'sman, ~'swoman,** (-z-) rower; **~'smanship** (-z-), art of rowing; **~'weed,** large littoral alga esp. of genus *Laminaria*. **4.** Hence ~'AGE (1) *n.* (poet.), (-)~ED² (ŏrd), ~'LESS, ~'Y² (poet.), *adjs.* **5.** *v.t.* & *i.* (poet.) Row (*boat, water*, one's *way*). [OE *ār*, = ON *ár* f. Gmc **airō*, perh. cogn. w. Gk *eretmos* oar]

O.A.S. *abbr.* on active service; Organization of American States.

ōā's|ĭs *n.* (*pl.* **~es** *pr.* -ēz). Fertile spot in desert (lit. or fig.). [LL f. Gk, app. of Egypt. orig.]

oast *n.* Hop-drying kiln; **~-house,** building containing this. [OE *āst*, = MLG *eist* f. Gmc **aistaz*, **aithtaz* f. IE **aidh-* burn]

oat *n.* **1.** (in *pl.*) (Grain yielded by) hardy cereal (*Avena sativa*) grown in cool climates as food for humans and horses; **feel** one's **~s,** (colloq.) be lively or *self-important; **off** one's **~s,** (colloq.) lacking appetite for food. **2.** Oat-plant; variety of oats; **wild ~,** tall grass (*Avena fatua*) resembling oats (**sow** one's **wild ~s,** indulge in youthful follies before becoming steady). **3.** (poet.) Oat-stem used as musical pipe by shepherds etc.; pastoral or bucolic poetry. **4.** **~'cake,** thin unleavened cake made of oatmeal, esp. in Scotland and N. England; **~-grass,** = wild oat (see sense 2); **~'meal,** meal from oats used esp. in oatcakes and porridge, greyish-fawn colour. **5.** Hence ~'EN⁵ *a.* [OE *āte*, pl. *ātan*, of unkn. orig.]

oath *n.* (*pl. pr.* ōdhz). **1.** Solemn appeal to God or revered or dreaded person or object, in witness that statement is true or promise shall be kept; **take an, make, swear an, ~,** bind oneself thus; **on** or **under ~,** having thus sworn, made or stated or given by sworn person; **on** one's **~,** with solemn assertion of truth. **2.** (Form of words containing) statement or promise so corroborated (*oath of allegiance, office, supremacy*, etc.). **3.** Name of God etc. used as expletive to give emphasis or express anger etc., piece of profanity in speech, curse. [OE *āth*, = OS *ēth*, OHG *eid*, ON *eithr*, Goth. *aiths* f. Gmc **aithaz*]

O.A.U. *abbr.* Organization of African Unity.

ob- *pref.* (usu. assim. to **oc-, of-, op-,** before *c, f, p* respectively) occurring mainly in wds derived from L wds already containing it, w. senses: **1.** Exposure, openness, (*object, obnoxious, obtrude, obverse*). **2.** Meeting (*occasion, occur, offend*), facing (*observe, obstetric, obviate, obvious, opportune*), direction (*oblation, oblong, offer*), spontaneity or compliance (*obey, obsequious*). **3.** Opposition or hostility (*objurgate, obloquy, obstreperous, opponent, oppress, opprobrium*), resistance (*obdurate, obstinate*). **4.** Hindrance, blocking, concealment, (*obese, obfuscate, oblige, obliterate, obsess, obstacle, obstruct, occlude, occult*). **5.** Finality or completeness (*obsolete, obtain, occident, occupy*). **6.** (In mod. sci. wds, perh. f. as OBVERSE) inversely, in direction or manner contrary to the usual, (*obconical, obcordate, oblanceolate, obovate*). [L (*ob* towards, against, in the way of)]

‖**O.B.** *abbr.* Old Boy; outside broadcast.

ob. *abbr.* obiit.

Obad. *abbr.* Obadiah (O.T.).

ŏbblĭga'tō (-ah'-) *a.* & *n.* (*pl.* **~s**). (Mus.) **1.** *a.* (Of accompaniment or part) inseparable, forming integral part of the composition, (opp. *ad libitum*). **2.** *n.* Such part or accompaniment. [It., = obligatory, f. L *obligatus* p.p. (as OBLIGE)]

ŏbcŏ'nĭcal *a.* (Biol.) In form of inverted cone. [f. OB- 6 + CONICAL]

ŏbcor'dāte *a.* (Biol.) In heart shape attached at apex. [f. OB- 6 + CORDATE]

ŏ'bdūrate (*or* -ūr'-) *a.* Hardened against moral influence or persuasion; impenitent, stubborn; hence **ŏ'bdūr**ACY *n.*, ~LY² (-tlĭ) *adv.* [ME, f. L *obduratus* p.p. of OB(*durare* harden f. *durus* hard); see -ATE²]

‖**O.B.E.** *abbr.* Officer (of the Order) of the British Empire.

ō'bėah (-*a*), **ō'bĭ¹,** *n.* Kind of sorcery practised by Negroes esp. in W. Indies. [W. Afr.]

ōbē'chė *n.* (Light-coloured timber of) W. Afr. tree (*Triplochiton scleroxylon*). [Nigerian name]

obē'dĭence *n.* **1.** Obeying as act or practice or quality; submission to another's rule; compliance with law or command; task or duty in monastery or convent; compliance with monastic rule; **in ~ to,** actuated by or in accordance with; **passive ~,** (1) surrender to another's will without co-operation, (2) compliance with commands irrespective of their nature. **2.** (Eccl., esp. R.C.) Being obeyed, (sphere of) authority, district or body of persons bound to obedience, (*return to the obedience of Rome; not belonging to either the Roman or the Byzantine obedience*). [ME f. OF, f. L *obedientia* (as OBEY; see -ENCE)]

obē'dĭent *a.* Submissive to or complying with superior's will, dutiful; acting in obedience *to*; ‖*your obedient* SERVANT; hence ~LY² *adv.* [ME f. OF, f. L *obediens -entis* (as OBEY; see -ENT)]

obēdĭĕ'ntiarў (-sherĭ) *n.* Holder of any office under superior in monastery or convent. [f. med. L *obedientiarius* (as OBEDIENCE; see -ARY¹)]

obei's|ance (obā's-) *n.* Gesture, esp. bow or curtsy, expressing submission, respect, or salutation, (*make an, do, pay, obeisance*); deference, homage, submission, (*do, make, pay, obeisance*); so ~ANT *a.*, showing deference, obsequious. [ME, f. OF *obeissance* (as OBEY; see -ANCE)]

ŏ'belĭsk (*or* -ĭl-) *n.* **1.** Tapering usu. monolithic shaft of stone square or rectangular in section with pyramidal apex; mountain, tree, etc., of similar shape. **2.** Mark (— or ÷) used in ancient MSS. to indicate that word or passage is spurious etc.; reference mark (†; **double ~**, ‡). [f. L f. Gk *obeliskos* dim. of *obelos* SPIT¹]

ŏ'belīze (*or* -ĭl-), **-īse** (-īz), *v.t.* Mark with obelisk as spurious etc. [f. Gk *obelizō* (*obelos*; see prec., -IZE)]

ŏ'bel|us *n.* (*pl.* **~i** *pr.* -ī). = OBELISK 2. [L, f. Gk *obelos* SPIT¹]

obē's|e (*or* ō-) *a.* Very fat, corpulent; so **~ITY** *n.* [f. L OB(*esus* p.p. of *edere* eat) having eaten oneself fat]

obey' (obā') *v.* **1.** *v.t.* Comply with bidding of, be obedient to; execute (command); be actuated by (force, impulse). **2.** *v.i.* Do what one is told to do. [ME, f. OF *obeir* f. L OB(*edire* = *audire* hear)]

ŏ'bfusc|āte *v.t.* Darken, obscure, confuse, (mind, judgement, topic, etc.); stupefy, bewilder; hence **~A'TION** *n.*, **~ātory** *a.* [f. LL OB(*fuscare* f. *fuscus* dark) + -ATE³]

ō'bĭ¹. See OBEAH.

ō'bĭ² *n.* Bright broad sash worn by Japanese women and children. [f. Jap. *ōbi* belt]

obiit (ŏ'bĭĭt) *v.i.* 3 *sing. past.* Died (with date of death). [L, f. OB(*ire it-* go) die]

ŏ'bĭt *n.* (Hist.) memorial service esp. in institution on anniversary of founder's or benefactor's death; (record of) date of person's death; (colloq.) obituary. [ME f. OF, f. L *obitus* death (as prec.)]

obiter dict|um (ŏbĭter dĭ'ktum) *n.* (*pl.* **~a**). Judge's expression of opinion uttered in arguing point or giving judgement but not essential to his decision and therefore without binding authority; incidental remark. [L (*ob iter* by the way, *dictum* thing said)]

obĭ'tūar|ȳ *n.* & *a.* **1.** *n.* Notice of death(s) esp. in newspaper, brief biography of deceased person; hence **~IST** (1) *n.* **2.** *a.* Recording a death; concerning decease of a person. [f. med. L *obituarius* f. L *obitus* death (as OBIIT; see -ARY¹)]

ŏ'bjėct¹ *n.* **1.** Thing placed before eyes or presented to one of the senses; material thing; thing observed with optical instrument or represented in picture. **2.** Person or thing of affecting, esp. pitiable or ridiculous, appearance. **3.** Person or thing to which action or feeling is directed, subject *of* or *for*, (*the Bible had been the object of his study*; *he is a proper object of* or *for charity*). **4.** Thing aimed at, end, purpose; **no ~**, not an important matter (esp. implying that the other party may make his own terms in the specified respect: *money, time, distance*, etc. (*is*) *no object*). **5.** (Philos.) Thing thought of or apprehended as correlative to the thinking mind or subject, external thing, *the* non-ego. **6.** (Gram.) Noun or noun-equivalent governed by active transitive verb or by preposition; DIRECT², INDIRECT, *object*. **7. ~-ball** (at which player aims his own ball in billiards etc.); **~-finder,** contrivance for registering position of object on mounted microscope-slide so as to find it again; **~-glass,** lens in telescope etc. nearest the object; **~ language** (that is discussed by a metalanguage); **~-lesson,** instruction about a material object that is present for inspection, (fig.) striking practical illustration of some principle; **~-object,** object of sense or thought as it is in fact. **8.** Hence **~LESS** *a.* [ME, f. med. L *objectum* thing presented to the mind, p.p. of L OB(*jicere ject-* throw)]

objĕ'ct² *v.* **1.** *v.t.* Adduce (quality, fact, *that*) as objection (*to* or *against* theory etc.); state (usu. *that*) as damaging fact *to* or *against* person etc. **2.** *v.i.* State objection, feel or express disapproval, have objection or dislike *to* (*I object to being treated like this*). **3.** Hence **~OR** *n.* (CONSCIENTIOUS *objector*). [ME, f. L *object-* (see prec.)]

objĕ'ctĭ|fȳ *v.t.* Present as object of perception; make objective, express in concrete form, embody; hence **~FICA'TION** *n.* [f. OBJECT¹ + -I- + -FY]

objĕ'ction *n.* Objecting; thing objected; adverse reason or statement; expression or feeling of disapproval or dislike. [ME f. OF, or f. LL *objectio* (as OBJECT¹; see -ION)]

objĕ'ctionab|le *a.* Open to objection; undesirable, unpleasant, offensive, disapproved of; hence **~LY²** *adv.* [f. prec. + -ABLE]

objĕ'ctīve *a.* & *n.* **1.** *a.* (Philos.) Belonging not to the consciousness or the perceiving or thinking SUBJECT², but to what is presented to this, external to the mind, real. **2.** (Of person, writing, picture, discussion, etc.) dealing with outward things, exhibiting actual facts uncoloured by exhibitor's feelings or opinions; (Med., of symptoms) observed by another and not only felt by patient; hence **~NESS** (-vn-), **ŏbjėctĭ'vITY**, *ns.* **3.** (Gram.) Constructed as, appropriate to, the object (**~ case** in English, that governed by transitive verb or preposition, distinguished in form from the subjective only in some personal pronouns, as *him*, cf. *he*; **~ genitive,** as in 'the fear *of God*', 'timor *Dei*', cf. SUBJECTIVE); hence **ŏbjėctī'vAL** *a.* **4. ~ point,** (Mil.) point towards which the advance of troops is directed, (transf.) point or thing aimed at, = OBJECT¹ 4. **5.** Hence **~LY²** (-vlĭ) *adv.* **6.** *n.* = OBJECT¹*-glass*; objective case; objective point. [f. med. L *objectivus* (as OBJECT¹; see -IVE)]

objĕ'ctĭv|ĭsm *n.* Tendency to lay stress on what is objective; doctrine that knowledge of non-ego is prior and superior to that of ego; so **~IST** (2) *n.* [f. prec. + -ISM]

objet d'art (ŏbzhādâr') *n.* (*pl.* **-ets** *pr.* same). Small artistic object. [F, lit. 'object of art']

objet trouvé (ŏbzhā trōō'vā) *n.* (*pl.* **-ts -és** *pr.* same). Object found or picked up at random and presented as rarity or work of art. [F, lit. 'found object']

ŏ'bjûrg|āte *v.t.* (literary). Chide, scold; hence **~A'TION** *n.*, **~ātory** (*or* objẽr'ga-) *a.* [f. L OB(*jurgare* quarrel f. *jurgium* strife) + -ATE³]

ŏblā'ncėolate *a.* (Bot.) Lanceolate with more pointed end at base. [f. OB- 6 + LANCEOLATE]

ŏ'blāte¹ *n.* Person dedicated to monastic or religious life or work. [F, f. med. L n. sense of L *oblatus* p.p. of OF(*ferre* bring) offer]

ŏ'blāte² (*or* oblā't) *a.* (Geom., of spheroid) flattened at poles (cf. PROLATE). [f. mod. L *oblatus* (as prec; cf. PROLATE)]

oblā'tion *n.* (Presenting of bread and wine to God in) Eucharist; thing offered to God, sacrifice, victim; donation for pious uses; hence **~AL**, **ŏ'blatORY**, *adjs.* [ME f. OF, or f. LL *oblatio* (as OBLATE¹; see -ION)]

ŏ'blĭgāte¹ *v.t.* (usu. in *p.p.*) Bind (person, legally or morally) *to* do. [f. L (as OBLIGE) + -ATE³]

ŏ'blĭgate² *a.* (Biol.) That has to be such (*obligate parasite* etc.; opp. *facultative*). [ME, f. L *obligatus* p.p. (as OBLIGE; see -ATE²)]

ŏblĭgā'tion *n.* **1.** Binding agreement, esp. one enforceable under legal penalty, written contract or bond; constraining power of a law, precept, duty, contract, etc.; **of ~**, obligatory; **day of ~** (on which all are required to attend Mass or Communion). **2.** One's bounden duty, a duty, burdensome task; (indebtedness for) service or benefit (*be*, LAY³, *put, under an obligation*; *repay an obligation*). [ME f. OF, f. L *obligatio -onis* (as OBLIGE; see -ATION)]

oblĭ'gatorȳ (*or* ŏ'blĭgā-) *a.* Legally or morally binding, compulsory and not merely permissive; constituting an obligation. [ME, f. LL *obligatorius* (as foll.; see -ORY)]

oblī'ge *v.* **1.** *v.t.* (arch. or Law). Bind (person, one*self*) by oath, promise, contract, etc., *to* person or *to* do. **2.** Be binding on; constrain, compel, *to* do; make indebted by conferring favour, gratify *by* doing or *with*, perform a service for (person requesting it, or abs.). **3.** *v.i.* (colloq.) Make contribution to entertainment (*with* song etc., or abs.). **4.** *v.t.* (in *pass.*) Be bound (*to* person) by gratitude (*for* small service); **much ~d,** thank you. [ME, f. OF *obliger* f. L OB(*ligare* bind)]

ŏblĭgee' *n.* (Law). Person to whom another is bound by contract or to whom bond is given (cf. OBLIGOR). [f. prec. + -EE]

oblī'ging *a.* Courteous, accommodating, ready to do service or kindness; hence ~LY^2 *adv.*, ~NESS *n.* [f. OBLIGE + -ING^2]

ŏ'blĭgor *n.* (Law). One who binds himself to another by contract or gives bond. [f. OBLIGE + -OR]

oblī'que (-ēk) *a.*, *n.*, & *v.i.* **1.** *a.* Slanting, declining from the vertical or horizontal, diverging from straight line or course; *oblique* SPHERE. **2.** (Geom.) (of line, plane figure, surface) inclined at other than right angle, (of angle) acute or obtuse, (of cone, cylinder, etc.) with axis not perpendicular to plane of base; (Anat.) neither parallel nor perpendicular to body's or limb's long axis; (Bot., of leaf) with unequal sides. **3.** Not going straight to the point, roundabout, indirect. **4.** (Gram.) **~ case** (other than nominative or vocative); **~ oration** or **speech,** = REPORT^1*ed speech*. **5.** Hence or cogn. ~LY^2 *adv.*, ~NESS, **oblī'quITY,** *ns.* **6.** *n.* Oblique muscle, stroke (/), etc. **7.** *v.i.* (esp. Mil.) Advance obliquely. [ME f. F, f. L *obliquus*]

oblĭ'ter|āte *v.t.* Blot out, efface, erase, destroy, leave no clear traces of; deface (postage stamp etc.) to prevent further use; hence ~A'TION *n.* [f. L OB(*li*(*t*)*terare* f. *li*(*t*)*tera* LETTER) + -ATE^3]

oblĭ'vĭon *n.* Having or being forgotten, disregard, unregarded state; amnesty (*Act* or *Bill of Oblivion*); **fall into ~,** be forgotten or disused. [ME f. OF, f. L *oblivio -onis* (*oblivisci* forget; see -ION)]

oblĭ'vĭous *a.* Forgetful, unmindful, (*of*); **~ to** or **of,** unaware or unconscious of; hence ~LY^2 *adv.*, ~NESS *n.* [ME, f. L *obliviosus* (as prec.; see -OUS)]

ŏ'blŏng *a.* & *n.* **1.** *a.* Deviating from square form by having one long axis, rectangular with adjacent sides unequal; (of paper, book, rectangular postage stamp or panel, etc.) greater in breadth than height. **2.** *n.* Oblong figure or object. [ME, f. L OB(*longus* long) longish]

ŏ'bloquy̆ *n.* Abuse, detraction; being generally ill spoken of. [ME, f. LL *obloquium* contradiction f. L OB(*loqui* speak) deny]

ŏbmūtĕ'sc|ence *n.* (arch.) Obstinate silence; so ~ENT *a.* [f. L OB(*mutescere* f. *mutus* dumb; see -ESCENCE)]

obnŏ'xious (-kshus) *a.* **1.** (arch.) Liable *to* harm or evil or attack. **2.** Offensive, objectionable, disliked; hence ~LY^2 *adv.* **3.** Hence ~NESS *n.* [f. L *obnoxiosus* or OB(*noxius* f. *noxa* harm); assoc. w. NOXIOUS; see -OUS]

ŏbnū'bĭl|āte *v.t.* (literary). Darken (as) with cloud, obscure (lit. or fig.); hence ~A'TION *n.* [f. L OB(*nubilare* f. *nubes* cloud) + -ATE^3]

ō'bōe, (arch.) **hautboy** (hō'boi), *n.* Wood-wind double-reed instrument of treble pitch and plaintive incisive tone; its player; organ reed-stop imitating it; hence **ō'bōIST** (3) *n.* [(It. *oboe*) f. F *hautbois* (*haut* high, *bois* wood)]

ŏ'bol *n.* Ancient-Greek coin, one-sixth of drachma. [f. L *obolus* f. Gk *obolos*, var. of *obelos* OBELISK]

ŏbō'vāte *a.* (Biol.) Ovate with narrower end at base. [f. OB- 6 + OVATE^1]

obscē'ne *a.* Indecent, esp. grossly or repulsively so; lewd; ‖(Law, of publication) tending to deprave or corrupt; (colloq.) highly offensive, morally repugnant; (arch.) repulsive, loathsome; hence ~LY^2 (-nlĭ) *adv.*, ~NESS (-n-n-) *n.* [f. F *obscène* or f. L *obsc*(*a*)*enus* ill-omened, abominable]

obscĕ'nĭty̆ *n.* Being obscene; instance of this in action, speech, etc. [f. L *obscaenitas* (as prec.; see -ITY)]

obscūr'ant *n.* Opponent of inquiry, enlightenment, and reform; one who deliberately avoids clarity or withholds explanation; hence ~ISM (3), ~IST (2), *ns.*, (*or* ŏbskūră'-). [G, f. L *obscurans* (*obscurare*; see OBSCURE, -ANT)]

obscūr'e *a.*, & *v.t.* **1.** *a.* Dark, dim; (of colour) dingy, dull, indefinite; indistinct, not clear; *obscure* (=neutral) VOWEL. **2.** Hidden, remote from observation; unnoticed; unknown to fame, humble. **3.** Unexplained, doubtful; not easily understood or clearly expressed. **4.** Hence or cogn. ~LY^2 (-ūr'lĭ) *adv.*, **obscūr'ITY** *n.* **5.** *v.t.* Make obscure, dark, indistinct, or unintelligible; dim glory of, outshine; conceal from sight; so **ŏbscūrA'TION** *n.* [ME; a. f. OF *obscur* f. L *obscurus* dark; v. f. a. or f. L *obscurare* (*obscurus*)]

obscurum per obscurius (ŏbskūrum pĕr ŏbskūr'ĭus) *n.* = IGNOTUM PER IGNOTIUS. [L, = the obscure by the still more obscure]

ŏbsėcrā'tion *n.* Earnest entreaty. [ME, f. L *obsecratio* f. OB(*secrare* = *sacrare* f. *sacer sacri* sacred) entreat]

ŏ'bsėquies (-ĭz) *n. pl.* Funeral rites; a funeral; hence **obsē'quĭAL** *a.* [ME, pl. of obs. *obsequy* f. AF *obsequie*, OF *obseque* f. med. L *obsequiae* f. L *exsequiae* funeral rites (see EXEQUIES), assoc. w. *obsequium* (see foll.)]

obsē'quĭous *a.* Servile, fawning; (arch.) obedient, dutiful; hence ~LY^2 *adv.*, ~NESS *n.* [ME, f. L *obsequiosus* f. OB(*sequium* f. *sequi* follow) compliance]

obsėr'vance (-z-) *n.* Keeping or performance of or *of* law, duty, custom, ritual, etc.; act of religious or ceremonial character, customary rite; the rule of a religious order; (arch.) respect, deference. [ME f. OF, f. L *observantia* (as OBSERVE; see -ANCE)]

obsėr'vant (-z-) *a.* & *n.* **1.** *a.* Attentive in observance; acute or diligent in taking notice; hence ~LY^2 *adv.* **2.** *n.* (*O*~). Member of branch of Franciscan order that observes the strict rule. [F (as OBSERVE; see -ANT)]

ŏbservā'tion (-z-) *n.* **1.** Noticing or being noticed, perception, faculty of taking notice; *post, attitude,* **of ~,** favourable for watching from or in; **~ car** (in train esp. in U.S., so built as to afford good views). **2.** (Mil.) Watching of fortress or hostile position or movements; **~ post** (esp. for watching effect of artillery fire). **3.** Accurate watching and noting of phenomena as they occur in nature (cf. *experiment*) with regard to cause and effect or mutual relations; noting of symptoms of patient, behaviour of suspect, etc., (**under ~,** being watched thus). **4.** Taking of sun's or other heavenly body's altitude to find latitude or longitude. **5.** Remark or statement, esp. one that is of the nature of comment. **6.** Hence ~AL *a.*, **~al**LY^2 *adv.* [ME, f. L *observatio* (as OBSERVE; see -ATION)]

obsėr'vatory̆ (-z-) *n.* Building etc. whence natural, esp. astronomical or meteorological, phenomena may be observed. [f. mod. L *observatorium* f. L *observare*; see foll., -ORY]

obsėr'v|e (-z-) *v.* **1.** *v.t.* Keep, follow, adhere to, perform duly, (law, command, appointed time, method, principle, silence, rite, anniversary, etc.). **2.** Perceive, mark, watch, take notice of, become conscious of, (person, thing, *that*, *how*); **the ~ed of all ~ers,** person etc. on whom etc. attention is concentrated. **3.** Examine and note (phenomena) without aid of experiment. **4.** Say, esp. by way of comment. **5.** *v.i.* Make remark(s) *on*. **6.** Hence ~ABLE *a.* [ME, f. OF *observer* f. L OB(*servare* keep) watch, attend to]

obsẽr'ver (-z-) *n.* In vbl senses; interested spectator; person who attends conference etc. to note proceedings but does not participate; person trained to notice and identify aircraft, or carried in aeroplane to note enemy's position etc.; (in newspaper titles, as *The Observer, Rochdale Observer*). [f. prec. + -ER[1]]

obsĕ'ss *v.t.* (Of evil spirit, delusion, or fixed idea) haunt, harass, preoccupy, fill mind of, (*obsessed by* or *with*); hence ~IVE *a.* [f. L OB-(*sidēre sess-* = *sedēre* sit) besiege]

obsĕ'ssion *n.* Obsessing or being obsessed; unreasonably persistent idea in the mind; condition in which such ideas are present; hence ~AL *a.* [f. L *obsessio* (as prec.; see -ION)]

obsĭ'dĭan *n.* Dark vitreous lava or volcanic rock like bottle-glass. [f. L *obsidianus*, error for *obsianus* (*Obsius* name of finder of a similar stone, mentioned by Pliny; see -IAN)]

ŏbsolĕ'sc|ent *a.* Becoming obsolete, going out of use or date; (Biol., of organ once developed more fully) gradually disappearing; so ~ENCE *n.* [f. L OB(*solescere* f. *solēre* be accustomed; see -ESCENT)]

ŏ'bsolēte *a.* Disused, discarded, antiquated; (Biol.) less developed than formerly or in cognate species, rudimentary; hence ~NESS (-tn-), **ŏ'bsolēt**ISM (3, 4), *ns.* [f. L *obsoletus* p.p. (as prec.)]

ŏ'bstacle *n.* Thing that obstructs progress; **~-race** (in which artificial or natural obstacles have to be passed). [ME f. OF, f. L *obstaculum* f. OB(*stare* stand) impede]

obstĕ'tr|ĭc(al) *adjs.* Of midwifery, of childbirth and the processes immediately preceding and following it, as branch of medicine and surgery; hence ~ICS, **ŏbstĕtrĭ**'CIAN, *ns.* [f. mod. L *obstetricus* for L *obstetricius* f. *obstetrix* midwife f. OB(*stare* stand) be present; see -TRIX]

ŏ'bstĭn|ate *a.* Firmly adhering to one's chosen course of action or opinion, not easily persuaded; inflexible, self-willed; unyielding, not readily responding to treatment etc.; hence or cogn. ~ACY *n.*, **~ate**LY[2] (-tlĭ) *adv.* [ME, f. L *obstinatus* p.p. of OB(*stinare* deriv. of *stare* stand) persist]

obstrĕ'perous *a.* Noisy, vociferous; turbulent, unruly, noisily resisting control; hence ~LY[2] *adv.*, ~NESS *n.* [f. L *obstreperus* f. OB(*strepere* make noise) + -OUS]

obstrŭ'ct *v.t.* Close up, fill with impediments, make impassable or difficult of passage; prevent or retard progress of, impede. [f. L OB(*struere struct-* build)]

obstrŭ'ction *n.* Blocking or being blocked, making or becoming more or less impassable; hindering, esp. of Parliamentary business by deliberate delays, whence ~ISM (3), ~IST (2), *ns.*; obstacle; (Path.) blockage in bodily passage, esp. in intestine. [f. L *obstructio* (as prec.; see -ION)]

obstrŭ'ctĭve *a.* & *n.* **1.** *a.* Causing, intended to produce, obstruction; hence ~LY[2] (-vlĭ) *adv.*, ~NESS (-vn-) *n.* **2.** *n.* Obstructive person or thing. [f. OBSTRUCT + -IVE]

obstū'pĕfȳ *v.t.* Stupefy, esp. mentally. [f. L OB(*stupefacere*; see STUPEFY)]

obtai'n *v.* **1.** *v.t.* Acquire, have granted to one, get; hence or cogn. ~ABLE *a.*, ~MENT, **obtĕ'n**TION, *ns.* **2.** *v.i.* Be prevalent or established or in vogue. [ME, f. OF *obtenir* f. L OB(*tinēre tent-* = *tenēre* hold) keep]

obtĕ'st *v.* (arch.) **1.** *v.t.* Adjure, supplicate, call to witness. **2.** *v.i.* Protest. **3.** So **ŏbtĕst**A'TION *n.* [f. L OB(*testari* f. *testis* witness)]

obtru'de (-ōō'd) *v.* **1.** *v.t.* Thrust forward (*upon* or *on* person or his attention) importunately. **2.** *v.i.* Be or become obtrusive. **3.** So **obtru'**SION (-ōō'zhon) *n.* [f. L OB(*trudere trus-* push)]

obtrŭ'ncāte *v.t.* (literary). Cut off top of. [f. L OB(*truncare* f. *truncus* maimed) + -ATE[3]]

obtru'sĭve (-ōō'-) *a.* Obtruding oneself; unduly noticeable; hence ~LY[2] (-vlĭ) *adv.*, ~NESS (-vn-) *n.* [f. as OBTRUDE + -IVE]

obtŭ'nd *v.t.* (Med.) Blunt, deaden, (sense or faculty). [ME, f. L OB(*tundere tus-* beat)]

ŏ'btūr|āte *v.t.* Stop up, close, seal, (orifice in body, breech of gun, etc.); hence or cogn. ~A'TION, **~ātor**, *ns.* [f. L *obturare* + -ATE[3]]

obtū'se *a.* Of blunt form, not sharp-pointed or sharp-edged; (of angle) greater than one and less than two right angles; (of pain, the senses) dull, not acute; stupid, slow of perception; hence ~LY[2] (-slĭ) *adv.*, ~NESS (-sn-), **obtū'**SITY, *ns.* [f. L *obtusus* p.p. (as OBTUND)]

ŏ'bvẽrse *a.* & *n.* **1.** *a.* Narrower at base or point of attachment than at apex or top (esp. as general term for wds in OB- 6: *obovate, oblanceolate*, etc.); answering as counterpart to something else; hence ~LY[2] (-slĭ) *adv.* **2.** *n.* Side of coin or medal bearing the head or principal design (cf. REVERSE[3]); face of anything meant to be presented to view, front; counterpart of a fact or truth. [f. L *obversus* p.p. (as foll.)]

obvẽr't *v.t.* (Logic). Infer another proposition with contradictory predicate by changing quality of (proposition), e.g. from *no men are immortal* to *all men are mortal*; so **obvẽr'**SION (-shon) *n.* [f. L OB(*vertere vers-* turn)]

ŏ'bvĭāte *v.t.* Clear away, get rid of, get round, neutralize, (danger, inconvenience, etc.). [f. LL OB(*viare* f. *via* way) withstand + -ATE[3]]

ŏ'bvĭous *a.* Open to eye or mind, clearly perceptible, palpable, indubitable; hence ~LY[2] *adv.*, ~NESS *n.* [f. L *obvius* (*ob viam* in the way) + -OUS]

oc- *pref.*, assim. form of OB- before *c*.

O.C. *abbr.* Officer Commanding.

ŏcari'na (-rē'-) *n.* Small egg-shaped terracotta or metal wind instrument. [It. (*oca* goose, from its shape; see -INA[1])]

O'ccam (ŏ'-) *n.* **~'s razor,** principle that the fewest possible assumptions are to be made in explaining a thing. [f. William of ~, Engl. philosopher d. *c.* 1350]

occā'sion (-zhon) *n.*, & *v.t.* **1.** *n.* Juncture suitable for doing something, opportunity, (**take ~**, avail oneself of opportunity *to* do). **2.** Reason, ground, justification, incitement, need, (*there is no occasion to be angry*). **3.** Subsidiary, incidental, or immediate cause (*the cause of a revolution may be obscure while its occasion is obvious*). **4.** (in *pl.*) Affairs, business, (esp. *go about* one's *lawful occasions*). **5.** (Particular time marked by) special occurrence (*on this festive occasion*; *on the occasion of his marriage*; *celebrate the occasion*; *dressed, dismantled, for the occasion*); **rise to the ~**, show requisite ability, energy, etc.; **(up)on ~**, whenever need arises, now and then. **6.** *v.t.* Be the occasion or cause of, bring about esp. incidentally, cause (action etc., or person or thing *to* do). [ME f. OF, or f. L *occasio* juncture, reason, f. OC(*cidere cas-* = *cadere* fall) go down; see -ION]

occā'sional (-zho-) *a.* Arising out of, made or meant for, adapted for use on, acting on, special occasion(s); happening irregularly; as occasion presents itself; coming now and then, not regular or frequent; ~ **cause,** secondary cause, occasion; ||~ **licence** (to sell liquor only at specified times and places); ~ **table,** small table for use as required; hence ~ITY (-ă'l-) *n.*, ~LY² *adv.* [f. prec. + -AL]

occā'sional|ĭsm (-zho-) *n.* Doctrine of some Cartesians that volition and sensation are connected with the following and preceding material phenomena not causally but as separately produced by God on the same occasion; so ~IST (2) *n.* [f. prec. + -ISM]

O'ccĭdent (ŏ'ks-) *n.* (poet. or rhet.) **1.** *The* west; western Europe; Europe, America, or both, as opp. countries east of them. **2.** European in contrast to Oriental civilization. [ME f. OF, f. L *occidens -entis* setting, sunset, west (as OCCASION; see -ENT)]

ŏccĭdĕ'ntal (ŏks-) *a.* & *n.* **1.** *a.* Of the Occident; western; of Western nations, whence ~ISM (2), ~IST (2, 3), *ns.*, ~IZE (3) *v.t.*; hence ~LY² *adv.* **2.** *n.* (*O*~). Native or inhabitant of the Occident. [ME f. OF, or f. L *occidentalis* (as prec.; see -AL)]

ŏ'ccĭpŭt (ŏ'ks-) *n.* (Anat.) Back of head; so **ŏccĭ'pĭt**AL *a.*, **ŏccĭ'pĭto-** *comb. form,* (ŏks-). [ME f. L oc(*ciput -pitis = caput* head)]

occlu'de (-lōō'd) *v.t.* Stop up, close, obstruct, (pores, orifice); (Chem.) absorb and retain (gases); **~d front** (Meteorol., resulting from occlusion). [f. L oc(*cludere clus- = claudere* shut)]

occlu's|ion (-lōō'zhon) *n.* Occluding; (Meteorol.) overtaking of warm front of depression by cold front, with upward displacement of warm air between them; (Dent.) position of teeth when jaws are brought together; (Phonet.) momentary closure of vocal passage; so ~IVE *a.* [f. as prec. + -ION]

ŏccŭ'lt¹ (*or o-*) *a.* Kept secret, esoteric; recondite, mysterious, beyond the range of ordinary knowledge; involving the supernatural, mystical, magical, whence ~ISM (3), ~IST (2, 3), *ns.*; (Med.) not obvious on inspection; hence ~LY² *adv.*, ~NESS *n.* [f. L oc(*culere -cult-*; cf. *celare* hide)]

ŏccŭ'lt² (*or o-*) *v.* **1.** *v.t.* Conceal, cut off from view by passing in front, (usu. Astron., of concealing body much greater in apparent size than concealed body). **2.** *v.i.* **~ing light** in lighthouses, one that is cut off at regular intervals. **3.** So **ŏccult**A'TION *n.* [f. L *occultare* frequent. of *occulere* (see prec.)]

ŏ'ccŭp|ant *n.* Person holding property, esp. land, in actual possession; one who occupies, or resides or is in, a place; one who establishes title to ownerless thing by taking possession; hence ~ANCY *n.* [F, or f. L *occupans -antis* (as OCCUPY; see -ANT)]

ŏccŭpā'tion *n.* Occupying or being occupied; taking or holding possession, esp. of country or district by military force (**army of** ~, left to hold occupied region till regular government is set up); tenure, occupancy; what occupies one, means of passing one's time, temporary or regular employment, business, calling, pursuit; ~ **bridge, road,** etc., (private for use of occupiers of land); ||~ **franchise,** right to vote as tenant. [ME f. AF *ocupacioun*, OF *occupation* f. L *occupatio -onis* (as OCCUPY; see -ATION)]

ŏccŭpā'tional *a.* Of occupation(s); ~ **disease, hazard,** (to which a particular occupation renders one especially liable); ~ **therapy,** mental or physical activity to assist recovery from disease or injury. [f. prec. + -AL]

||**ŏ'ccŭpīer** *n.* Person in (esp. temporary or subordinate) possession esp. of land or house, holder, occupant. [ME, f. foll. + -ER¹, or f. AF *occupiour*]

ŏ'ccŭpȳ *v.t.* Take possession of (country, region, town, strategic position) by military force or settlement; hold (office), reside in, be tenant of; take up or fill (space, time), reside or be in (place, position); place oneself in (building etc.) esp. as political demonstration; (esp. in *pass.* or *refl.*) keep busy or engaged (*with* or *in* thing or do*ing*). [ME, f. AF **occupier*, OF *occuper* f. L oc(*cupare = capere* take) seize]

occŭr' *v.i.* (-rr-). Be met with, be found, exist, in some place or conditions; come into one's mind (esp. *it occurs to me that*); come into being as event or process at or during some time. [f. L oc(*currere* run) go to meet, present itself]

occŭ'rrence *n.* Occurring (**is of frequent** ~, often occurs); incident, event. [f. *occurrent* that occurs (F, f. L *occurrens -entis* f. as prec.; see -ENT) + -ENCE]

ō'cean (ō'shan) *n.* **1.** Great body of water surrounding the land of the globe; one of the main areas into which geographers divide this (usu. reckoned as five, the *Atlantic, Pacific, Indian, Arctic,* and *Antarctic, Oceans*). **2.** *The* sea; (poet.) the sea (*the dark unfathom'd caves of ocean*); immense expanse or quantity of anything (*oceans of time*). **3.** **~-going,** (of ship) able to cross the oceans; ~ **greyhound,** swift ship, esp. passenger liner; *ocean* LANE; *ocean* TRAMP. **4.** Hence ~WARD(s) *adv.* [ME f. OF *occean(e)*, f. L f. Gk *ōkeanos* stream encircling earth's disc, Atlantic]

Oceā'nĭ|a (ōshĭ-) *n.* Islands of Pacific and adjacent seas; hence ~AN *a.* & *n.* [mod. L, f. F *Océanie* f. L (as prec.; see -IA¹)]

ōceă'nĭc (*or* ōshĭ-) *a.* Of, like, etc., the ocean; of the part of the ocean distant from the continents; (of climate) governed by the ocean; (*O*~) of Oceania. [f. OCEAN + -IC]

Ocē'anĭd (os-) *n.* (*pl.* **~s,** *or* **~es** *pr.* -ă'nĭdēz). (Gk Myth.) Ocean nymph. [f. Gk *ōkeanis -idos* daughter of Ocean; see -ID³ 2]

ōcean|ŏ'graphȳ (ōsha-) *n.* Study of the oceans; hence ~**ŏ**'GRAPHER *n.*, ~**o**GRA'PHIC(AL) *adjs.* [f. OCEAN + -O- + -GRAPHY]

ocĕ'll|us *n.* (*pl.* ~**i** *pr.* -ī). One of simple as opposed to compound eyes of insects etc.; facet of compound eye; spot of colour surrounded by ring of other colour, whence **ŏ'cĕll**ATE² **ŏ'cĕllāt**ED¹, *adjs.* [L, dim. of *oculus* eye]

ō'cĕlot *n.* Leopard-like feline (*Felis pardalis*) of S. and Central America; its fur. [F, abridged by Buffon f. Nahuatl *tlal(ocelotl* jaguar) of the field, and applied to different animal]

ŏch (ŏχ) *int.* (Sc. & Ir.) expr. surprise or regret, = *oh, ah.* [Gael. & Ir.]

***ocher.** See OCHRE.

ŏchlŏ'cracȳ (ŏkl-) *n.* Mob rule; hence **ŏ'chlo**CRAT *n.*, **ŏchlo**CRA'TIC *a.*, (ŏkl-). [f. F *ochlocratie* f. Gk *okhlokratia* (*okhlos* mob; see -CRACY)]

ŏchō'ne (ŏχ-) *int.* (Sc. & Ir.) expr. regret or lament, = *oh, alas.* [f. Gael. & Ir. *ochóin*]

ō'chre, *ō'cher, (ō'ker) *n.* Mineral of clay and hydrated ferric oxide, used as pigment varying from light yellow to brown; pale brownish yellow; hence ~ISH¹, ***ō'cher**OUS, **ō'chrĕ**OUS, **ō'chr**OUS, **ō'chr**Y², (ōk-) *adjs.* [ME, f. OF *ocre* f. L f. Gk *ōkhra* yellow ochre (*ōkhros* pale yellow)]

-ock *suf.* forming *ns.* orig. w. dim. sense (*hillock, bullock*). [f. or after OE *-uc, -oc*]

o'clŏ'ck. See O'², CLOCK¹.

O.C.R. *abbr.* optical character recognition.

Oct. *abbr.* October.

oct. *abbr.* octavo.

ŏct- *comb. form.* = OCTA-, OCTO-, before vowel.

ŏcta- *comb. form.* Eight, as **ŏctă'**MEROUS *a.*; **~va'lent,** (Chem.) having a valence of eight. [f. Gk *okta-* (*oktō* eight)]

ŏ'ctachōrd (-k-) *a.* & *n.* Eight-stringed (musical instrument); series of eight notes, e.g. the diatonic scale; hence ~AL (-kor′d-) *a.* [f. L f. Gk *oktakhordos* (as prec.; see CHORD[1])]

ŏ′ctăd *n.* Group of eight. [f. LL f. Gk *oktas -ados* (*oktō* eight; see -AD 1)]

ŏ′ctagon *n.* Plane figure with eight sides and angles; object or building with this cross-section; so **ŏctă′gonAL** *a.* [f. L f. Gk OCTA-(*gōnos* f. *gōnia* angle)]

ŏctahĕ′dr|on *n.* (*pl.* ~ons *or* ~a). Solid figure contained by eight plane faces, and usu. eight triangles (**regular ~on,** by equal and equilateral triangles); body, esp. crystal, in form of regular octahedron; hence ~AL *a.* [f. Gk *oktaedron* (see OCTA-, -HEDRON)]

ŏctă′mėter *n.* (Pros.) Verse of eight measures. [f. OCTA- after *hexameter*]

ŏ′ctāne *n.* Hydrocarbon of paraffin series, C_8H_{18}; **high-~,** (of fuel used in internal combustion engines) having good antiknock properties, not detonating readily during the power stroke; **~ number** or **rating** (indicating antiknock properties of fuel, and equal to 100 for one type of octane). [f. OCT- + -ANE 2]

ŏ′ctant *n.* **1.** Arc of circle = $\frac{1}{8}$ of circumference; $\frac{1}{8}$ of area of circle, contained within two radii and such arc; one of eight parts into which three planes intersecting (esp. at right angles) at point divide space or solid body round it. **2.** (Astron.) Point in body's apparent course 45° distant from given point, esp. point at which moon is 45° from conjunction or opposition with sun. **3.** Instrument in form of graduated eighth of circle used in astronomy and navigation. [f. L *octans -antis* half-quadrant (*octo* eight)]

ŏ′ctarchy̆ (-kĭ) *n.* Government by eight rulers; eight kingdoms reckoned by some historians as established by Angles and Saxons in Britain (cf. HEPTARCHY). [f. OCT- after *heptarchy*]

ŏctaroo̅′n. See OCTOROON.

ŏ′ctastȳle *a.* & *n.* (Portico or building) with eight columns at end or in front. [f. L f. Gk OCTA(*stulos* pillar)]

O′ctateuch (ŏ′-; -k) *n.* First eight books of Bible. [f. LL f. Gk OCTA*teukhos*; cf. PENTATEUCH]

ŏ′ctave (-ĭv) *n.* **1.** Seventh day after a festival; period of eight days including festival and its octave. **2.** Group or stanza of eight lines, octet. **3.** (Mus.) Note having twice or half the frequency of vibration of given note and lying eight diatonic degrees (alphabetical notes, both extreme notes being counted) above or below it (**second ~,** having four times or a quarter the frequency, sixteen degrees above or below; so **third** etc. ~); interval between note and its octave; series of notes filling this; note and its octave sounding together. **4.** Group of eight. **5.** Last of eight parrying positions in fencing. **6.** ||Wine-cask holding $\frac{1}{8}$ pipe. **7. ~-coupler,** device connecting organ keys or pedals an octave apart so that both notes are sounded by one key; **~-flute,** (1) piccolo, (2) organ flute-stop sounding an octave higher than the ordinary. [ME f. OF, f. L *octava* (*dies* day, reckoned inclusively) fem. of *octavus* eighth (*octo* eight)]

ŏctā′vō *n.* (*abbr.* **8vo**; *pl.* ~s). (Size of) book or page given by folding sheet three times to form quire of eight leaves. [L, abl. of *octavus* (see prec.), in phr. *in octavo* in an eighth (of a sheet)]

ŏctĕ′nnĭal *a.* Lasting, or occurring every, eight years. [f. LL OCT(*ennium* f. *annus* year) period of eight years + -AL]

ŏctĕ′t, ŏctĕ′tte, *n.* **1.** (Mus.) (Composition for) group of eight instruments or voices. **2.** Group of eight; first eight lines of sonnet; (Chem.) stable group of eight electrons. [f. It. *ottetto* or G *oktett*, assim. to OCT-, DUET, QUARTET(TE)]

ŏctĭ′llion (-lyon) *n.* ||Eighth power of a million; *ninth power of a thousand; hence ~TH[2] *a.* & *n.* [F, f. L *octo* eight, after *billion*]

ŏcto- *comb. form.* Eight. [f. L *octo* or Gk *oktō* eight]

Octō′ber (ŏ-) *n.* Tenth month of year; ||(arch.) beer brewed in October. [OE f. L (as prec.; cf. DECEMBER, SEPTEMBER)]

Octō′brĭst (ŏ-) *n.* Member of moderate party in Russian Duma. [f. prec. + -IST, because supporter of Imperial Constitutional Manifesto of 30 Oct. 1905]

ŏctōcĕntē′nary̆ (*or* -sĕ′ntĭn-), **ŏctōcĕntĕ′nnĭal,** *ns.* (Festival of the) 800th anniversary. [f. OCTO- + CENTENARY, CENTENNIAL]

ŏctōdĕ′cĭmō *n.* (*pl.* ~s). (Size of) book or page given by folding sheet into eighteen leaves. [f. *in octodecimo* f. L OCTO(*decimus* tenth) eighteenth; cf. OCTAVO]

ŏctogėnār′ĭan *a.* & *n.* (Person) from 80 to 89 years old. [f. L *octogenarius* (*octogeni* 80 each; see -ARY[1]) + -AN]

ŏctonār′ĭ|us *n.* (*pl.* ~i *pr.* -ī). (Pros.) Verse of eight feet; hence ~AN *a.* & *n.* [L (see foll.)]

ŏ′ctonary̆ *a.* & *n.* **1.** *a.* Based on the number eight. **2.** *n.* Group of eight; eight-line stanza (esp. of divisions of Ps. 119). [f. L *octonarius* containing eight (*octoni* eight each f. *octo* eight); see -ARY[1]]

ŏ′ctopŏd *n.* Eight-armed cephalopod of order Octopoda, e.g. octopus or argonaut. [f. Gk *oktōpous -podos* (*oktō* eight, *pous* foot)]

ŏ′ctopus *n.* (*pl.* **~es,** *or* **octo′podes** *pr.* -ŏ′podēz). Cephalopod mollusc of family Octopodidae, with eight suckered arms round mouth; (fig.) organized and usu. harmful ramified power or influence. [f. Gk *oktōpous* (see prec.)]

ŏctoroo̅′n, -tar-, *n.* Offspring of quadroon and white, person of one-eighth Negro blood. [f. OCTO- after QUADROON]

ŏctosy̆llă′bĭc *a.* & *n.* Eight-syllabled (verse). [f. LL OCTO(*syllabus* f. L *syllaba* SYLLABLE) + -IC]

ŏctosy̆′llable *n.* & *a.* = prec.; word of eight syllables. [f. LL *octosyllabus* (see prec.), after *syllable*]

ŏ′ctroi (-rwah) *n.* Duty levied in some European countries on goods entering town; place where, officials by whom, it is levied. [F (*octroyer* grant, f. Gallo-Rom. **auctoricare*, med. L *auctorizare*; see AUTHORIZE)]

||O.C.T.U. (ŏ′ktū) *abbr.* Officer Cadets Training Unit.

ŏ′ctūple *a.*, *n.*, & *v.* **1.** *a.* & *n.* Eightfold (amount). **2.** *v.t.* & *i.* Multiply by eight. [F, or f. L *octuplus* a. (*octo* eight; cf. DOUBLE[1])]

ŏ′cūlar *a.* & *n.* **1.** *a.* Of, for, by, with, etc., the eye(s) or sight, visual; **~ demonstration** or **proof** (perceived by the eyes); *ocular* SPECTRUM; hence ~LY[2] *adv.* **2.** *n.* Eyepiece of optical instrument. [f. F *oculaire* f. LL *ocularis* (*oculus* eye; see -AR[1])]

ŏ′cūlarĭst *n.* Maker of artificial eyes. [f. F *oculariste* (as prec.; see -IST)]

ŏ′cūlate *a.* = OCELLATE. [f. L *oculatus* (*oculus* eye; see -ATE[2])]

ŏ′cūl|ĭst *n.* One who specializes in treatment of eye disorders or defects; hence **~ĭ′stIC** *a.* [f. F *oculiste* f. L *oculus* eye; see -IST]

ŏcūlō- *comb. form.* Eye, as: **~na′sal,** of eye and nose. [f. L *oculus* eye + -O-]

ŏd[1] *n.* Hypothetical power once thought to pervade nature and account for various scientific phenomena; hence **ŏ′dIC** *a.* [arbitrary term coined in G by Baron von Reichenbach, Ger. scientist d. 1869]

ŏd[2] *n.* (arch.) = GOD (as *int.* or in oaths: *od rot it*, *od(d)s bodikins*, etc.). [corrupt.]

O.D. *abbr.* ordnance datum.

o.d. *abbr.* outer diameter.

ō′dal. Var. of UDAL.

ō'dalĭsque (-k) *n.* (Hist.) Eastern female slave or concubine, esp. in Turkish Sultan's seraglio. [F, f. Turk. *odalık* (*oda* chamber, *lık* function)]

ŏdd *a.* & *n.* **1.** *a.* Left over when the rest have been distributed or divided into pairs. **2.** (Of number) not divisible by two (**~ and even,** a game of chance); (of things or persons numbered consecutively) bearing such number (*no parking on odd dates*). **3.** (Appended to number, sum, weight, etc.) with something over of lower denomination etc. (**forty ~**, between 40 and 50; **sixty thousand ~**, with some extra hundreds, tens, or units; **sixty ~ thousand,** between 60 and 70 thousand; **twelve pounds ~**, between £12 and £13). **4.** By which round number, given sum, etc., is exceeded (*Here is a pound note; pay the bill and keep the odd money. There are 1006; what shall we do with the odd six?*). **5.** Additional, casual, beside the reckoning, unconnected, unoccupied, incalculable, unpredictable, (*picks up odd bargains; do it at odd moments; in some odd corner*); **~ numbers, volumes,** (belonging to incomplete sets of magazines, books). **6.** Extraordinary, strange, queer, remarkable, eccentric; hence ~'ISH[1] 2 *a.*, ~'LY[2] *adv.* **7. ~'ball, ~ fish,** (colloq.) eccentric person; **O'ddfellow,** member of a fraternity similar to Freemasons; **~ job,** casual isolated piece of work; **~ man,** (1) person who has deciding vote in committee etc. with evenly divided members, (2) ‖man who does odd jobs; **~ man out,** (1) method of selecting one of three or more persons e.g. by tossing coins, (2) person or thing differing from all others of a group in some respect; **~ trick,** (1) thirteenth trick at whist when each side has won six, (2) trick at bridge won by a side that already has six or more. **8.** Hence ~'NESS *n.* **9.** *n.* (Golf). *The* stroke which one side plays after the LIKE[1] 16; handicap of one stroke at each hole. **10.** See ODDS. [ME, f. ON *odda-* in *odda-mathr* third man, odd man, f. *oddi* angle, triangle]

ŏ'ddĭtў *n.* Strangeness; peculiar trait; queer person; fantastic object, strange event. [f. prec. + -ITY]

ŏ'ddment *n.* Odd article, something left over; (in *pl.*) odds and ends, ‖(Print.) matter other than text. [f. ODD + -MENT]

ŏdds (-z) *n. pl.* (sometimes treated as *sing.*). **1.** (arch.) Inequalities (**make ~ even,** do away with these). **2.** Difference giving advantage (*it makes no odds*; **what's the ~?**, what does it matter?). **3.** Variance, strife, (*are at odds with fate, with their neighbours*). **4.** Balance of advantage (*the odds are in your favour; won against* (*all*) *the odds; have fought against longer odds*). **5.** Equalizing allowance to weaker competitor (*give, receive, odds*). **6.** Ratio between amounts staked by parties to bet; **lay, give, ~** *of three to one*, (said of party offering the higher amount); **take ~**, offer the lower amount; **~-on,** state when (betting odds indicate that) success is more likely than failure; **over the ~**, above generally agreed price etc. **7.** Chances or balance of probability in favour of or against some result (*it is odds* or *long odds that* or *but, the odds are that, he will do it; long odds against his doing it*); **by all ~**, certainly. **8. ~ and ends,** (vulg.) **~ and sods,** remnants, stray articles. [app. pl. of ODD n.; cf. NEWS]

ōde *n.* **1.** (Hist.) Poem meant to be sung (**choral ~**, song of chorus in Greek play etc.). **2.** Lyric. usu. rhymed, often in form of address, usu. of exalted style, often in varied or irregular metre, and usu. between about 50 and 200 lines in length. [f. F, f. LL *oda* f. Gk *ōidē* Attic form of *aoidē* song (*aeidō* sing)]

-ōde *suf.* **1.** forming *ns.* w. sense 'thing of the nature of' (*geode, phyllode, trematode*). **2.** (Electr.) forming names of electrodes (*cathode, diode*). [sense 1 f. Gk *-ōdēs* adj. ending (see -o-, *-eidēs* -like); sense 2 f. Gk *hodos* way]

ōdē'um *n.* (*pl.* **~s** *or* **ode'a**). Building for musical performances, esp. among ancient Greeks and Romans. [f. F *odéum* or f. L *odeum* f. Gk *ōideion* (as ODE)]

ŏ'dĭc. See OD[1].

ō'dĭous *a.* Hateful, repulsive; hence ~LY[2] *adv.*, ~NESS *n.* [ME, f. OF *odieus* f. L *odiosus* (as foll.; see -OUS)]

ō'dĭum *n.* General or widespread dislike or reprobation incurred by person or attaching to action (*exposed me to odium; the odium of the transaction*); **~ *theologicum*** (thēolŏ'jĭkum), bitterness proverbially characterizing theologians who disagree. [L, = hatred (*odi* to hate)]

odŏ'mėter *n.* Instrument for measuring distance travelled by wheeled vehicle. [f. F *odomètre* f. Gk *hodos* way; see -METER]

ōdŏ'nto- *comb. form.* Tooth, as: **~glo'ssum,** orchid with large handsome flowers having toothlike process on lip; ~LOGY (-ŏ'l-), scientific study of the teeth; **~rhy'nchous** (-rĭ'ngkus), (of bird) having toothlike serrations in the bill. [f. Gk *odous odont-* tooth + -o-]

ōdŏ'ntoid *a.* Toothlike; **~ process** (projection from second cervical vertebra). [f. Gk *odontoeidēs* (as prec.; see -OID)]

***ō'dor.** See ODOUR.

ōdorĭ'ferous *a.* Diffusing (usu. agreeable) scent, fragrant; hence ~LY[2] *adv.* [ME, f. L *odorifer* (as ODOUR; see -FEROUS)]

ō'dorous *a.* Having scent; = prec.; hence ~LY[2] *adv.* [f. L *odorus* fragrant (as foll.) + -OUS]

ō'dour, *ō'dor, (ō'der) *n.* **1.** Property of a substance that has pleasant or unpleasant or any effect on the nasal sense of smell; hence ~LESS *a.* **2.** Fragrance; (arch., usu. in *pl.*) substance(s) emitting sweet scent, perfume(s). **3.** (fig.) Savour, trace, (*no odour of intolerance attaches to it*); *good* or *bad* or *ill* repute or favour (*is in bad odour with the authorities*); **~ of sanctity,** reputation for holiness (orig. lit., sweet odour exhaled by dying or exhumed saint). [ME f. AF *odour*, OF *odor* f. L *odor -oris* smell, scent]

O'dўssey (ŏ'-) *n.* **1.** Epic poem attributed to Homer and describing adventures of Odysseus (Ulysses) returning to Ithaca from siege of Troy; any of the 24 books of this. **2.** (*o~*). Series of wanderings, long adventurous journey. [f. L f. Gk *Odusseia* (*Odusseus* Odysseus; see -Y[1])]

O.E.C.D. *abbr.* Organization for Economic Co-operation and Development.

oe'cĭst (ē's-) *n.* Founder of (esp. ancient-Greek) colony. [f. Gk *oikistēs* (*oikizō* settle f. *oikos* house; see -IST)]

oecology. Var. of ECOLOGY.

oecumenical etc. Var. of ECUMENICAL etc.

O.E.D. *abbr.* Oxford English Dictionary.

oedē'ma, *edē'ma, (ēd- *or* ĭd-) *n.* (Path.) Swollen state of tissue etc. with serous fluid, local dropsy; hence ~TOSE[1], ~TOUS, *adjs.* [LL, f. Gk *oidēma -atos* (*oideō* swell)]

Oe'dĭpus (ē'd-) *n.* Solver of riddles; **~ complex,** (Psych.) manifestation of infantile sexuality towards parents, with attraction to parent of opposite sex (esp. mother) and jealousy of other parent; hence **Oe'dĭp**AL (ē'd-) *a.* [f. Gk *Oidipous*, who solved the Sphinx's riddle, and in ignorance married his mother]

O.E.E.C. *abbr.* (Hist.) Organization for European Economic Co-operation.

œillade (ẽryah'd) *n.* (Esp. amorous) glance of eye. [F (*œil* eye; see -ADE)]

oenŏ'log|ў, *ēn-, (ēn-) *n.* Knowledge or study

of wines; hence ~ICAL (ēnolŏ'j-) *a.*, ~IST (3) *n.* [f. Gk *oinos* wine + -O- + -LOGY]

oe'nophil|e (ē'-) *n.* Connoisseur of wines; so ~IST (1) (ēnŏ'fĭl-) *n.* [f. as prec. + -PHIL(E)]

***O.E.O.** *abbr.* Office of Economic Opportunity.

***O.E.P.** *abbr.* Office of Emergency Preparedness.

o'er (ōr) *adv.* & *prep.* (poet.) = OVER; so **o'er-** (ōr) *pref.* [contr.]

oer'stĕd (ĕr'-) *n.* Unit of magnetic field strength. [f. H. C. *Oersted*, Da. physicist d. 1851]

oesŏ'phag|us, *ēs-, (ēs-) *n.* (*pl.* **~i** *pr.* -jī, *or* **~uses**). Canal from mouth to stomach, gullet; hence **~eal** (ēsofă'jĭal *or* ēsŏfajē'al) *a.* [ME, f. Gk *oisophagos*]

oe'strogĕn, *ē's-, (ē's-) *n.* Sex hormone or other substance capable of developing and maintaining female characteristics of body; hence ~IC (-jĕ'n-) *a.* [f. foll. + -O- + -GEN]

oe'str|um, oe'str|us, *ē's-, (ē's-) *n.* Sexual HEAT of animals, rut; (arch.) stimulus; hence ~OUS *a.* [f. Gk *oistros* gadfly, frenzy]

œuvre (ĕrvr) *n.* (Totality of) works of an author, painter, composer, etc. [F, = work, f. L OPERA¹]

of (ov *or, when stressed*, ŏv) *prep.* connecting its *n.* or *pron.* w. preceding *n.*, *a.*, *adv.*, or *v.*, and indicating relations roughly classified as follows: **1.** Removal, separation, point of departure, privation, (*north, within a mile, in front, upwards, have the advantage, of*; *wide of the mark*; *heal, rid, ease, deliver, rob, of*; *destitute, empty, free, bare, of*; *take* LEAVE¹ *of*; *balk, cheat, defraud, deprive, disappoint, of*; *independently, guiltless, irrespective, of*); OUT *of*; *(of time) = to (*a quarter of six* = 5.45). **2.** Origin, derivation, cause, agency, authorship, (*be, come, descend, spring, born, of*; *borrow, buy, win, receive, hire,* thing *of*; *have comfort, wish* person *joy, of*; *ask, demand, learn, expect, of*; *of* one's *own* ACCORD²; *of* COURSE¹, *of* RIGHT³, *of* NECESSITY; **of itself,** = *by* or *in* ITSELF; *die of*; *smell, taste, of*; *tired, ashamed, afraid,* SICK¹, *glad, proud, of*; *it was kind, foolish, naughty, clever, cruel, well done, of you to say so*; *has the approval of his master*; *the works of Shakespeare, the 'Iliad' of Homer*); (arch., w. *pass.*) by (*warned of God*; *rejected of men*). **3.** Material, substance, closer definition, identity, (*house of cards*; *built of brick*; *an inch of rain*; *make a* FOOL¹, *the* BEST¹, *of*; MAKE¹ *much of*; *a family of eight*; *the name of Jones*; *the class of idiots*; *city of Rome, Isle of Man, University of Oxford, Battle of Waterloo, vice of drunkenness*; *a fool of a man, her scamp of a husband, the worst liar of any man I know*; *your letter of 1 May*; *had a bad time, troublesome journey, of it*); **be of,** possess (*importance, interest, value, etc.*). **4.** Concern, reference, direction, respect, (*think well of him*; *never heard of it*; *was informed of the fact*; *is true of every case*; *what of it?*; *repent, beware, of*; *cannot conceive, approve, think, of*; *does not admit* or *allow of*; *accuse, convict, suspect, of*; *avail, bethink,* oneself *of*; *short, guilty, certain, sure, confident, fond, of*; *swift of foot, blind of an eye, hard of heart, hard of hearing*; *on behalf of, in respect of*; *at 30 years of age*). **5.** Objective relation (*the levying of taxes*; *love of virtue*; *for* FEAR¹ *of*; *in* SPITE *of*; *in search of knowledge*; *great eaters of pork*; *redolent, productive, fruitful, lavish, prodigal, sparing, capable, sensible, careful, observant, desirous, impatient, characteristic, destructive, indicative, of*); (arch. or vulg.) *what are you a-doing of?* what are you doing?. **6.** Description, quality, condition, (*man of tact, person of consequence, case of measles, farm of 100 acres, the hour of prayer, coat of many colours*; *potatoes of our own growing*; *in the act of, on the point of, departing*; *girl of ten years*, or, with mixed construction, *of ten years old*). **7.** Partition, classification, inclusion, selection, (*no more of that*; **some,** or **five, of us,** (1) a portion, or five, of us (who are more numerous), (2) we, being several or five persons; *any part, the whole, of it*; *too much of a gentleman to do that*; *the most dangerous of enemies*; **he of all men,** he most or least of all; *this of all times, here of all places*; **is the one thing of all others that,** (illogically, = out of all things that); **of all the impudence!** (that can be imagined); **song of songs, holy of holies,** (those best deserving the name); **a friend of mine, of the vicar's,** i.e. (orig.) in the number of my, the vicar's, friends, but illogically extended, as *that long nose of his, this only son of the vicar's*; *drink deep of flattery, partake of food*; *was* **sworn of the Council,** admitted as member; *his temper is* **of the quickest,** belongs to the quickest class; *a sort of thud*; *comes in* **of an evening,** (colloq.) at some time in the evenings; **of old, yore, late years,** LATE¹ 8, somewhere in the specified periods). **8.** Belonging, connection, possession, (*we of the middle class*; *companions of his exile*; *articles of clothing*; *the manners of today*; *a thing of the past*; *the tip of the iceberg*; *the master of the house*; *the widow of the man who was killed*; *a topic of conversation*; *the cause, result, counterpart, opposite, image, of*; *for the sake of*). [OE, unaccented form of *æf*, = OS, ON, Goth. *af*, OHG *ab*(*a*) f. Gmc **abh*(*a*) f. IE **ap*(*o*)]

of- *pref.*, assim. form of OB- before *f*.

***ō'fay** *n.* (esp. Negro sl.) White person. [20th c.; orig. unkn.]

ŏff (*or* awf) *adv.*, *prep.*, *a.*, *n.*, & *v.t.* **1.** *adv.* Away, at or to a distance, (*rode off*; *is far, three miles, two years, off*; *went off on a new line of thought*; *beat off the attack*; *keep assailant off*; *ward off disaster*); **take** oneself, **be,** MAKE¹, **~,** depart (*to*); **~ with you!,** go; **~ with his head!,** behead him; FALL¹ *off*; GO¹ *off*; PUT¹ *off*; **~ we go!,** (1) we are starting, (2) let us start; **they're ~!,** horse-race has started; RIGHT⁴ *off*; STRAIGHT *off*. **2.** (So as to be) out of position, not on or touching or dependent or attached, loose, separate, gone, got rid of, incorrect or insufficient, (*my hat is off*; *take his clothes off*; *cut, break, shake, throw,* etc., *off*; DOZE, DROP², *off*); = *off colour*; (Theatr.), not on the stage (NOISES *off*); LAUGH, SLEEP², **walk,** etc. **~,** get rid of by such action; **be ~** *with the old love*, have severed connection; **get** one's *daughters, stock*, **~,** dispose of by marriage, sale; **the gilt is ~,** disillusionment has come; **the meat** etc. **is ~** (has begun to decay); ǁ**a bit ~,** (sl.) somewhat annoying or unfair. **3.** So as to break continuity or continuance or cease or not begin operation, discontinued, stopped, not obtainable, (**broke ~,** ceased to speak; *turn off the gas, the light, the radio*; *cut off supplies*; *fence off the paddock*; *leave off work*; *the engagement, bargain, strike, is off*); (of employee) not at work (*is off sick*); (of item on menu etc.) no longer available; **~ and on,** intermittently, waveringly, now and again. **4.** To the end, entirely, so as to be clear, (*clear, drink, kill, pay, polish, sell,* TELL¹, *work, off*); to decide a tie etc. (*play-off,* JUMP²-*off*, etc.). **5.** Situated as regards money, supplies, etc., (*well, better, badly, comfortably,* etc., *off*; *how are you off for sugar?*). **6.** *prep.* From, away or down or up from, disengaged or distant from, (so as to be) no longer on or not yet on, (*chased them off the grass*; *is off the beaten track*; *fell off a ladder*; *caught me off balance*; *take cover off dish*; *eats off silver plate*; (colloq.) *won a lot of money off him*; *lay some distance off shore*; *took something off the price*; *is off duty* or *work*; *cut a slice off, dine off, the joint*; *was only a yard off me*; *keep ship two points off the wind*); not quite (**~ white,** with grey or yellow tinge); (of garment) designed so as not to cover (*off the shoulders*); not attracted by for the time being (*off* one's *food, off smoking*); no longer obliged to use (*am off my diet*); leading from or not far from (*in a street off the Strand*); (Golf) with an official handicap of (*plays off three*); at sea opposite (*sank off Cape Horn*); *off* BEAM[1]; ~ **colour,** not in good health, *somewhat indecent; *off the* CUFF[1]; ~ one's **feet,** (colloq.) to a condition of no longer being able to stand (*I was run off my feet with jobs to do*; *carry* or *sweep* person *off his feet*, make him enthusiastic or excited); *off* FORM[1]; *off* one's GAME[1]; *off* one's HAND[1]*s*, one's HEAD[1], *LIMIT[1]*s*, *the* MAP[1]; ~ **the peg,** (of clothes) ready-made; ~ **the point,** irrelevant(ly); *off the* RECORD[2], *the* REEL[1]. **7. ~-beat,** (*n.*, Mus.) unaccented part of bar, (*a.*) not coinciding with the beat, (fig.) unusual or eccentric or unconventional; **~-ce′ntre,** not quite coinciding with central position; **~-cut,** remnant of paper, timber, etc., after cutting, usu. sold more cheaply; **~-glide,** (Phonet.) glide made in leaving a sound; **~-key,** out of tune (lit. or fig.); **~-line** *a.* & *adv.*, (Computers) not directly connected or on-line, operating non-simultaneously with the process for which the computation is done; **~-load,** unload; **~-peak,** (for use) away from the peak of electricity consumption, traffic, etc.; ‖**~-putting,** (colloq.) repellent, disconcerting; **~′scourings,** refuse, dregs, (*of*; lit. or fig.); **~′shore,** situated at sea some distance from the shore, (of purchases etc.) made or registered abroad, (of wind) blowing seawards; **~si′de,** (Footb. etc.) between ball and opponents' goal, esp. in situation where player may not play the ball; **~si′der,** (Austral. colloq.) assistant, partner, deputy; **~-sta′ge** *a.* & *adv.*, not on the stage, not visible to audience; **~-street,** (esp. of parking of vehicles) not on the street. **8.** *a.* Farther, far, (*on the off side of the wall*); (of part of animal or vehicle ‖or road, or horse etc. in team) right [opp. NEAR[2], orig. w. ref. to side from which one mounted] (*the off leader, front wheel, hind leg, side*); (Cricket) towards, in, or coming from, that half of the field (as divided by line through two middle stumps) in which playing batsman does not stand (opp. ON[2], LEG; *an off drive*, whence **~dri′ve** *v.t.*; *off stump*; LONG[1] *off*; MID[1]-*off*; *an off break*); subordinate, divergent, (*in an off street*; fig. of argument etc., *that is an off issue*); contingent, improbable, (*there is an off chance that*); disengaged (*will do it when I have an off moment*); **~-day** (when one is not at one's best); ‖**~-licence,** (place with) licence to sell beer etc. for consumption off the premises; **~′print,** printed copy of article etc. that was orig. part of larger publication; **~-season, ~-time,** (when business etc. is fairly slack); ***~-year** (when no national elections take place). **9.** *n.* (Cricket) the off side; start of horse-race. **10.** *v.t.* (colloq.) Announce intention of abandoning or annulling (negotiation, agreement, undertaking); withdraw from negotiation or engagement with (person). [different. sp. of OF, since 15/16th c.]

Off. *abbr.* Office; Officer.

ŏ′ffal *n.* Refuse, waste stuff, scraps, garbage; parts cut off as waste from carcass meant for food, esp. entrails, also head, tail, kidneys, heart, tongue, liver, etc.; carrion, putrid flesh; low-priced fish (e.g. cod as opp. to sole or other prime fish); bran or other by-product of grain (often in *pl.*); offscourings, dregs. [ME, f. MDu. *afval* (*af* OFF, *vallen* FALL[1])]

‖**offĕ′nce, *offĕ′nse,** *n.* Attacking, aggressive action, taking the offensive, (*the best* DEFENCE *is offence*); wounding of the feelings, wounded feeling, annoyance, umbrage, (*no offence was meant*; *is quick to take offence*; *give offence to*; *cannot be done without offence*); transgression, misdemeanour, illegal act, (esp. *commit an offence against*); **no ~,** (colloq.) I did not intend to offend you; hence **~**LESS (-sl-) *a.* [orig. = stumbling (-block), ME & OF *offens* f. L *offensus* annoyance, and ME & F *offense* f. L *offensa* a striking against, hurt, displeasure, both f. OF(*fendere fens-* strike)]

offĕ′nd *v.* **1.** *v.i.* Stumble morally, do wrong, transgress, (*against* law, decency, person, etc.), whence **~**ER[1] *n.* (FIRST *offender*), **~**ING[2] *a.* **2.** *v.t.* Wound feelings of, anger, cause resentment or disgust in or through outrage, (*am sorry you are offended*; *offended at* or *by* thing, *with* or *by* person; *offends the eye, the taste, her delicacy, my sense of justice*, or abs.); hence **~ĕd**LY[2] *adv.* [ME, f. OF *offendre* f. L (as prec.)]

***offĕ′nse.** See OFFENCE.

offĕ′nsĭve *a.* & *n.* **1.** *a.* Aggressive, intended for or used in attack, (*offensive weapon, movement*; opp. DEFENSIVE); giving or meant to give offence, insulting, (*offensive language*); disgusting, ill-smelling, nauseous, repulsive; hence **~**LY[2] (-vlĭ) *adv.*, **~**NESS (-vn-) *n.* **2.** *n.* Attitude of assailant, aggressive action, (*take, act* or *be on, abandon, the offensive*); an attack, offensive campaign or stroke, (*the long-expected German offensive*); aggressive action for any purpose (*peace offensive*). [f. F *offensif -ive* or f. med. L *offensivus* (as OFFENCE; see -IVE)]

ŏ′ffer[1] *v.* **1.** *v.t.* Present (victim, first-fruits, prayer) *to* deity, revered person, etc., by way of sacrifice, give in worship or devotion; hence **~**ING[1] (4) *n.* **2.** Hold out in hand, or tender in words or otherwise, for acceptance or refusal or consideration (*offered me his flask to drink from*; *was offered £5, a lift, good prospects, a free pardon*; *offer* oneself, one's *services, an opinion, a few remarks*, etc.; *offer no apology*); hence **~**ING[1] (2) *n.* **3.** (arch., abs.) Make proposal of marriage. **4.** Show for sale. **5.** Give opportunity to enemy for *battle*. **6.** Express readiness *to* do or provide if desired; attempt, try to show, (violence, resistance, etc., often *to*); show an intention *to* do (*offered to strike me*). **7.** (Of thing) present to sight or notice (*each age offers its characteristic riddles*). **8.** *v.i.* Present itself, occur, (*as opportunity offers*; *the first path that offered*). [OE *offrian* in religious sense, = OS *offron*, ON *offra*, f. L OF(*ferre* bring); other senses f. OF *offrir*, of same orig.]

ŏ′ffer[2] *n.* Expression of readiness to give or do or pay or provide if desired, or to sell on terms (**on ~,** for sale at certain, e.g. reduced, price), proposal esp. of marriage; bid. [ME, f. prec.]

ŏ′ffertorÿ *n.* (Eccl.) Part of mass or communion service preceding canon, at which alms of congregation are usu. collected; (by confus. w. OFFER[1]*ing*) the alms collected; collection of money at religious service. [ME, f. eccl. L *offertorium* (LL *offert-* for L *oblat-* p.p. st. of *offerre* OFFER[1]; see -ORY) offering]

ŏffhă′nd (*or* awf-) *adv.* & *a.* **1.** Without preparation or premeditation. **2.** Unceremonious(ly), informal(ly), curt(ly); so **~**ED[2] *a.* **~ĕd**LY[2] *adv.* [f. OFF 6 + HAND[1]]

ŏ′ffĭce *n.* **1.** Piece of kindness, attention, service, (**ill** etc. **~**) disservice, (*owing to, by, through, the good* or *ill offices of*). **2.** Duty attaching to one's position, task, function, (*it is my office, the office of the arteries, to*). **3.** Position with duties attached to it, place of authority or trust or service, esp. of public kind (*was given an office under the Government*), tenure of official position esp. that of minister of State (*take, enter upon, hold, leave, resign, office*; JACK[1]-*in-office*) or party forming Government (*out of office for 13 years*). **4.** Ceremonial duty (esp. *perform* **the last ~s** *to*, rites due to the dead). **5.** (Eccl.) Authorized form of worship, daily service of R.C. breviary (also **divine ~**; **say ~,** recite this), Anglican morning and evening prayer, (introit at beginning of) mass or communion service, any occasional service such as the **O~ for the Dead. 6.** Place for transacting business (*goes down to the office at 9 a.m.*); room etc. in which the clerks of an establishment work, counting-house; room in which any kind of administrative or clerical work is done; (with qualification) room etc. set apart for business of particular department of large concern (‖*booking, inquiry, goods, lost-property, -office* in railway station) or local branch of dispersed organization (*our Manchester office*; *a* POST² *office*) or company for specified purpose (*insurance, fire* or *fire-insurance, -office*); *consulting-room of doctor etc. **7.** (*O~*). Quarters or staff or collective authority of a Government department etc. (*the* ‖FOREIGN, ‖HOME¹, POST², *Office*) or part thereof (*Passport Office*). **8.** ‖(in *pl.*) Parts of house devoted to household work, storage, etc. **9.** (sl.) Hint, signal, (*give, take, the office*). **10. Holy O~**, the Inquisition; **~-bearer,** official or officer; **~-block,** large building designed to contain business offices; **~-boy** (employed to do minor jobs in business office); **~ hours** (during which business is regularly conducted); **~-worker,** employee in business office. [ME f. OF, f. L *officium* performance of a task (in med. L also office, divine service), for **opificium* (*opus* work, *facere -fic-* do)]

ŏ'ffĭcer *n.*, & *v.t.* **1.** *n.* Holder of public, civil, or ecclesiastical office, sovereign's servant or minister, appointed or elected functionary, (usu. w. qualifying word(s): *Officer of the Household*; *medical officer* (*of health*); *probation officer*; *returning officer*; *scientific officer*). **2.** President, treasurer, secretary, etc., of society. **3.** Bailiff (*sheriff's officer*); constable (*police officer*). **4.** Person holding authority in navy, army, air force, or mercantile marine, esp. with commission in army or navy (GENERAL, STAFF¹, COMMISSION¹*ed*, FIELD, COMPANY¹, WARRANT¹-, NON-*commissioned*, FLAG⁴-, PETTY, *officer*); **~ of arms,** herald or pursuivant; **~ of the day** (responsible for guard and inspection on a particular day). **5.** Member of grade below commander in Order of the British Empire etc. **6.** *v.t.* (usu. in *p.p.*). Provide with officers; act as commander of. [ME, f. AF *officer*, OF *officier* f. med. L *officiarius* f. L *officium* (see prec., -ARY¹, -ER²)]

offĭ'cial (-shal) *a.* & *n.* **1.** *a.* Of an office, the discharge of duties, or the tenure of an office; holding office, employed in public capacity (‖*Official* REFEREE); derived from or vouched for by person(s) in office, properly authorized; (Med.) according to the pharmacopoeia, officinal; usual with persons in office (*official solemnity, red tape*, etc.); hence **~**LY² *adv.* **2.** *n.* **~ (principal)**, presiding officer or judge of archbishop's, bishop's, or esp. archdeacon's court. **3.** Person holding public office or engaged in official duties; hence **~**DOM, **~**E'SE (= officials' jargon), **~**ISM (2), *ns.* [a. 16th c. f. L *officialis* (as OFFICE; see -AL); n. ME orig. f. OF f. L *officialis*]

offĭ'cĭ|āte (-shĭ-) *v.i.* **1.** Discharge priestly office, perform divine service; so **~**ANT (1) *n.* **2.** Act in some official capacity, esp. on particular occasion (usu. *as* host, best man, etc.). [f. med. L *officiare* perform divine service (*officium*; see OFFICE) + -ATE³]

ŏffĭcī'nal (*or* ofĭ'sĭ-) *a.* (Of herb or drug) used in medicine or the arts; (of medical preparation) kept ready at druggists', made from pharmacopoeia recipe (cf. MAGISTRAL), (of name) adopted in pharmacopoeia; hence **~**LY² *adv.* [f. med. L *officinalis* f. L *officina* workshop; see -AL]

offĭ'cious (-shus) *a.* **1.** (Given to) offering service that is not wanted, doing or undertaking more than is required, intrusive, meddlesome, whence **~**NESS *n.* **2.** (Diplom., opp. *official*) informal, unofficially friendly or candid, not binding. **3.** Hence **~**LY² *adv.* [f. L *officiosus* obliging (*officium*; see OFFICE, -OUS)]

ŏ'ffĭng (*or* aw'-) *n.* Part of visible sea distant from shore or beyond anchoring-ground (*was seen in the offing*); position at distance from shore (*gain, keep*, etc., *an offing*); **in the ~**, (fig.) not far away, likely to appear. [perh. f. OFF + -ING¹]

ŏ'ffĭsh (*or* aw'-) *a.* (colloq.) Inclined to aloofness; hence **~**NESS *n.* [f. OFF + -ISH¹; cf. *uppish*]

ŏ'ffsĕt (*or* aw'-) *n.*, & *v.t.* (**-tt-; offset**). **1.** *n.* (arch.) Start, set-off, outset. **2.** Short side-shoot from stem or root serving for propagation; offshoot, scion, mountain-spur. **3.** Compensation, set-off, consideration or amount diminishing or neutralizing effect of contrary one. **4.** (Surv.) Short distance measured perpendicularly from main line of measurement. **5.** (Archit.) Sloping ledge in wall etc. where thickness of part above is diminished. **6.** Bend made in pipe etc. to carry it past obstacle. **7.** (Print.) Transfer of ink to clean sheet laid on freshly-printed surface; **~ (process)**, method of printing in which ink is transferred from plate or stone to uniform rubber surface and thence to paper etc. **8.** *v.t.* (*or* -ĕ't). Counterbalance, compensate; (esp. in *p.p.*) place out of line; print by offset process. [f. OFF + SET¹]

ŏ'ffshōōt (*or* aw'-) *n.* Side-shoot or branch (lit. or fig.), derivative. [f. OFF + SHOOT¹]

ŏ'ffsprĭng (*or* aw'-) *n.* Person's child(ren) or descendant(s); animal's young or descendant(s); (fig.) result. [OE *ofspring* (OF from, *springan* SPRING¹)]

O.F.M. *abbr.* Order of Friars Minor.

O.F.S. *abbr.* Orange Free State.

ŏft (*or* aw-) *adv.* (arch.) Often (*oft-told, oft-recurring*; *many a time and oft*); **~-times,** often. [OE, = OS *oft*(*o*), OHG *ofto*, ON *oft*, Goth. *ufta*]

ŏ'ften (*or* ŏ'fen *or* aw'-) *adv.* & *a.* (**~er, ~est**). **1.** *adv.* Frequently, many times, at short intervals, (with sing. generalized or pl. subj.) in a considerable proportion of the instances (*the victim often dies, the victims often die, of it*); **as ~ as not,** in (about) half the instances; **every so ~**, from time to time; **more ~ than not,** in more than (about) half the instances; **once too ~** (w. ref. to discomfiture after several successes); **~ and ~** (emphatic form); **~times,** (arch.) often. **2.** *a.* (arch.) Frequent. [ME; extended f. prec., prob. after *selden* = SELDOM]

ŏ'gam. See OGHAM.

ŏ'gdōăd *n.* Group of eight. [f. LL f. Gk *ogdoas -ados* (*ogdoos* eighth f. *oktō* eight; see -AD)]

ō'gee (*or* -ē') *n.* & *a.* (Moulding) showing in section a double continuous curve, concave below passing into convex above; S-shaped (line); **~ arch** etc. (with two ogee curves meeting at apex); hence **~'d** [-ED²] *a.* [app. f. OGIVE, as being the usu. moulding in groin-ribs]

ŏ'g(h)am (ŏ'gam) *n.* Ancient British and Irish alphabet of twenty characters formed by parallel strokes on either side of or across a continuous line; inscription in this; one of the characters. [OIr. *ogam*, referred to *Ogma*, supposed inventor]

ogī'val *a.* Of ogive arch; ogee-shaped. [F, or f. foll. + -AL]

ō'gīve (*or* ojī'v) *n.* Diagonal groin or rib of vault; pointed or Gothic arch, whence **ogī'**VAL *a.* [ME f. F, of unkn. orig.]

ō'gle *v.* & *n.* **1.** *v.i.* Cast amorous glances. **2.** *v.t.* Eye amorously. **3.** Hence **ō'gl**ER¹ *n.* **4.** *n.* Amorous glance. [prob. f. LDu.; cf. LG *oegeln*, frequent. of *oegen* look at (-LE 3)]

O'gpu (ŏ'gpōō) *n.* Former (1922–35) organization for combating counter-revolutionary activities in Soviet Russia. [initial letters of *Obedinennoe Gosudarstvennoe Politicheskoe Upravlenie*, United State Political Administration]

ō'gre (-*ger*) *n.* Man-eating giant in folklore etc.; terrifying person; hence ~ISH[1], **ō'grISH**[1], *adjs.*, **ō'grESS**[1] *n.* [F, first used by Perrault 1697, of unkn. orig.]

Ogy'gian (*o*-) *a.* Of obscure antiquity, prehistoric. [f. L f. Gk *Ōgugios* of Ogyges mythical king of Attica or Boeotia]

oh[1] (ō) *int.* expr. surprise, pain, entreaty, etc., (*oh, what a lie!*; *oh, how horrible!*; *oh, do come*; *oh for wings!*; *oh dear me!*; *oh yes you wi'll*); *oh* BOY; **oh' no,** certainly not; **oh no'** (expr. horror); **oh-oh** (expr. disappointment); **oh well** (expr. resignation to thing); **oh' yes** (expr. firm assertion); **oh ye's?** (expr. scepticism). [var. of O[2]]

oh[2] (ō) *n.* = O[1] 2.

o.h.c. *abbr.* overhead camshaft.

ohm (ōm) *n.* (Electr.) **1.** Unit of resistance, transmitting current of 1 ampere when subjected to potential difference of 1 volt; hence ~'AGE *n.*, electrical resistance measured in ohms, ~'IC *a.*, ~'METER *n.* **2. Ohm's law** (stating that current is proportional to voltage and inversely proportional to resistance). [f. G. S. *Ohm*, Ger. physicist d. 1854]

O.H.M.S. *abbr.* On Her (or His) Majesty's Service.

ōhō' *int.* expr. surprise or exultation. [ME, f. O[2] + HO]

ōhō'ne. Var. of OCHONE.

o.h.v. *abbr.* overhead valve.

-oid *suf.* forming *adjs.* & *ns.* w. sense '(something) having the form of or resembling' (*asteroid*, *rhomboid*, *thyroid*); hence ~'AL *adj. suf.*, **~'alLY**[2] *adv. suf.* [f. mod. L *-oides* f. Gk *-oeidēs* (as -o-, *-eidēs* having the form of, f. *eidos* form)]

ōĭ'dĭ|um *n.* (*pl.* **~a**). (Fungus of genus *Oidium* bearing) conidium forming part of a chain; plant-mildew caused by this fungus. [mod. L, f. Gk *ōion* egg + *-idion* dim. suf.]

oil[1] *n.* **1.** One of various liquid viscid unctuous usu. inflammable chemically neutral substances lighter than and insoluble in water but soluble in alcohol and ether, classified as non-volatile **fatty** or **fixed ~s** of animal or vegetable origin, used as varnishes, lubricants, illuminants, soap constituents, etc., ESSENTIAL or **volatile ~s** chiefly of vegetable origin, giving plants etc. their scent, used in medicine and perfumery, and MINERAL *oils* used as fuels and illuminants. **2.** *Petroleum; (Austral. & N.Z. sl.) news, facts; *oil of* VITRIOL; STRAP-*oil*; POUR *oil on the flames*, *on the waters* or *on troubled waters*; **burn the midnight ~**, read or work far into the night; **strike ~**, (lit.) find petroleum by sinking shaft, (fig.) attain prosperity or success; **~ and vinegar** or **water,** type of dissimilar or irreconcilable things. **3.** (often in *pl.*) = *oil-colour*, (colloq.) picture painted in oil-colours; (colloq., usu. in *pl.*) = *oilskin*. **4. ~-bird, -nut, -palm, -plant, -seed, -tree,** species of bird etc. from which oil is got; **~-heater, -lamp, -stove,** (using oil as fuel etc.). **5. ~-bomb,** incendiary bomb containing oil; **~'cake,** mass of compressed linseed etc. left when oil has been expressed, used as cattle food or manure; **~'can** (containing oil, esp. long-nozzled to oil machinery); **~'cloth,** (1) fabric waterproofed with oil, (2) oilskin, (3) canvas coated with linseed etc. oil and used to cover table or floor; **~-colour,** (usu. in *pl.*) paint made by grinding pigment in oil; **~ drum,** metal drum used for transporting oil; **~ engine** (driven by explosion of vaporized oil mixed with air); **~'field,** district yielding mineral oil; **~-fired,** using oil as fuel; **~-gauge,** (1) hydrometer measuring specific gravity of oils, (2) device for testing level of lubricant oil in engine etc.; **~-gland** (secreting oil); **~-hole** (in machinery to receive lubricating oil); **~'man,** maker or seller of oils, *operator of oil-well; **~-meal,** ground oilcake; **~-paint,** = *oil-colour*; **~-painting,** art of painting, picture painted, in oil-colours, (*she is no oil-painting*, (colloq.) she is ugly); **~-pan,** engine sump; **~-paper** (made transparent or waterproof by soaking in oil); **~-press,** apparatus for pressing oil from seeds etc.; *oil* RIG[1]; **~-shale** (yielding oil by distillation); **~'skin,** cloth waterproofed with oil, garment or (in *pl.*) suit of this; *oil*-SLICK; **~-spring** (yielding mineral oil); **~'stone,** (fine-grained stone used with oil as) whetstone; *oil*-TANKER; **~-well** (from which mineral oil is drawn). **6.** Hence ~'LESS (-l-l-) *a.* [ME *oli*, *oile* f. AF, ONF *olie* = OF *oile* etc. f. L *oleum* (olive) oil (*olea* OLIVE)]

oil[2] *v.* **1.** *v.t.* Apply oil to, lubricate; **~ the wheels,** lit., or fig. make things go smoothly by courtesy, bribery, etc.; *go on oiled* WHEEL[1]*s*; ~ person('s **hand** or **palm**), bribe him; ~ one's **tongue,** say smooth things, flatter. **2.** *v.i.* & *t.* (with *butter*, *grease*, etc., as subj. or obj.) Turn into oily liquid. **3.** *v.t.* Impregnate or treat with oil; **~ed silk** (waterproofed with oil); (in *p.p.*, sl.) drunk (**well ~ed,** very drunk). **4.** *v.t.* & *i.* Supply with oil; (of ship etc.) take oil on board as fuel. [ME, f. prec.]

oi'ler *n.* In vbl senses; oilcan for oiling machine; oil-tanker; *oil-well; *(in *pl.*) oilskins. [f. prec. + -ER[1]]

oi'l|ÿ *a.* Of, like, containing much, covered or soaked with, oil; (of manner etc.) fawning, insinuating, unctuous; hence **~ĭLY**[2] *adv.*, **~ĭNESS** *n.* [f. OIL[1] + -Y[2]]

oi'ntment *n.* Unctuous preparation applied to skin to heal or beautify, unguent; FLY[1] *in the ointment*. [ME *oignement*, *ointment* f. OF *oignement* f. pop. L **unguimentum* f. L (as UNGUENT); forms *oint-* after obs. *oint* anoint (OF, p.p. of *oindre* ANOINT)]

Oir'eachtas (ĕr'*a*χthăs) *n.* Legislature of Irish Republic: the President, Dáil, and Seanad. [Ir.]

O.K. (ōkā'), **ōkay',** *a.* & *adv.*, *n.*, & *v.t.* (colloq.) **1.** *a.* & *adv.* All right, satisfactor(il)y; (as int.) I agree. **2.** *n.* Approval, sanction. **3.** *v.t.* Mark 'O.K.'; approve, sanction. [orig. U.S., initials of Old Kinderhook, N.Y., birthplace of President Van Buren, used as election slogan]

oka'pĭ (-ah'-) *n.* Bright-coloured partially striped Central-Afr. ruminant (*Okapia johnstoni*) discovered 1900, with likeness to giraffe, deer, and zebra. [Mbuba]

ōkay'. See O.K.

ōkey-dō'ke(y) *a.* & *adv.* (sl.) = O.K. [redupl.]

Okla. *abbr.* Oklahoma.

ŏ'kra *n.* Tall malvaceous orig. Afr. plant (*Hibiscus esculentus*) with mucilaginous seed-pods used as a vegetable and for thickening soups. [W. Afr. native name]

-ŏl *suf.* (Chem.) **1.** Termination of ALCOHOL, used in names of alcohols in the wider sense or analogous compounds (*methanol*, *phenol*). **2.** = L *oleum* oil (*benzol*, *menthol*).

ōld *a.* (cf. ELDER[1], ELDEST) & *n.* **1.** *a.* Advanced in age, far on in natural period of existence, not young or near its beginning, (**the ~,** old people; **young and ~,** everyone); made long ago, long in use, worn or damaged in the passage of time, (*an old book, suit, teapot*). **2.** Having characteristics, experience, feebleness, etc., of age (*old head on young* SHOULDERS; *child has an old face*; *old* BUFFER[2], *fogy*, etc.; *a man is as old* *as he feels*); worn, dilapidated, shabby. **3.** (Appended to period of time) of age (*is ten years old*; *could read Greek at ten years old*; cf. OF 6); *four* etc. **-year-~** (*pl.* **-~s**), person or animal, esp. racehorse, of that age. **4.** Practised or inveterate *in* action or quality or as agent etc. (*old in crime, folly, cunning, diplomacy*; *an old trooper*, CAMPAIGNer, *offender*). **5.** Dating from far back, made long ago, long established or known or familiar or dear, ancient, not new or recent, primeval, (**of ~ standing,** long established; *old as the hills*; *Old England*; *Old Night*; *old friends*; *the old* STORY[1]; *an old debt, grudge, old* SCORES; *an old name, family*); (of wine) matured with keeping; (w. description or name of person as playful or friendly mention): *you old rascal!, there's old George!*; (colloq.) **~ chap, fellow,** etc., (sl.) **~ bean, egg, fruit, stick, thing,** TOP[3], etc., = *old man* (6); **the ~ one** or **gentleman, Old Harry, Nick,** SCRATCH[2], etc., the Devil; **good ~** (with name, sl. exclamation in real or iron. commendation of person's or thing's performance); **have a fine, good,** HIGH, etc., **~ time** etc., (sl.) be well amused or entertained; ***little ~** (in affectionate or playful ref. to person or thing); **any ~ thing,** (sl.) anything no matter what (so **any ~ how** etc.). **6.** Belonging only or chiefly to the past, obsolete or obsolescent, out of date, antiquated, antique, concerned with antiquity, not modern, bygone, only lingering on, former, quondam; **the good ~ days** or **times,** customs etc. of earlier generations, regarded as better; **~ fashions** (that have gone or are going out); **~ London, Paris, England,** etc., London etc. as it once was, or the extant relics of its former state; (of language) as used in former or earliest times (*Old* ENGLISH[1], LATIN, NORSE, SAXON, SLAVONIC). **7.** *Old* ADAM[1]; **~ age,** period of life from about 65 or 70 onwards; *old-age* PENSION(ER); **~ bachelor,** man confirmed in bachelorhood; *Old* BAILEY[1]; **Old Believer,** member of Russian sect, orig. protesting against 17th-c. liturgical reforms; **~ bird,** wary person; *my* etc. **~ bones,** I etc. who am old; **~ boy,** (1) former member of school (so *Old Etonian* etc.; *~-boy network*, supposed system of favouritism among those associated since school-days), (2, colloq.) elderly man, (as *voc.*) = *old man* (6); **~ clothes,** (1) worn or shabby clothes, (2) discarded clothes; **~-clo'thes-man,** dealer in discarded clothes; *Old* CONTEMPTIBLES; **~ country,** (1) country long inhabited or civilized, (2) *the* mother country of colonists etc.; ***Old Dominion,** Virginia; **~-established,** long established; ||**~ face,** style of type imitating 18th-c. designs; **~-fa'shioned,** (*a.*) in or according to old fashion(s), conservative, antiquated, (*~-fashioned look*, of dignified reproof), (*n.*) *cocktail of whisky, bitters, etc.; **~ foundation,** cathedral etc. founded before Reformation; **Old French** (esp. of period before 1400); **~ girl,** fem. of *old boy*; ***Old Glory,** U.S. national flag; **~ gold,** colour of tarnished gold, dull brownish-golden colour; **~ guard,** original or past or conservative member(s) of party etc.; **~ hand,** practised workman, person with much experience (*at doing*), (Austral. Hist.) former convict; *old* HAT; *Old* HUNDREDTH; **~ lady** (lit., or colloq. to or of mother or elderly wife); ||*Old Lady of Threadneedle Street*, Bank of England; *old* LAG[2]; ***~-line,** established, conservative; **~ maid,** (1) elderly spinster, (2) precise tidy fidgety man, (3) round game at cards in which players try not to be left with unpaired queen; **~-mai'dish,** fussy and prim; **~ man,** (1) lit., (2) southernwood, (3, sl.) employer, manager, headmaster, (Naut. sl.) ship's captain, (4, colloq.) husband, (5, colloq.) father, (6, colloq., as *voc.*) male person or animal regarded with affection or intimacy, (7, Theol.) *the* unregenerate self, (8, Austral.) adult male kangaroo; **~** *man of the sea*, person who cannot be shaken off [f. Arabian-Nights tale of Sindbad]; **~** *man's beard*, (1) clematis, esp. traveller's joy, (2) *kind of moss (*Tillandsia usneoides*); **~ master,** (painting by) great painter of former times, esp. of 13th–17th c. in Europe; *old* MOON[1]; **~ one,** (1) *the* Devil, (2) familiar joke; ||**Old Pals Act,** (joc.) doctrine that friends should help each other to the maximum extent; *Old* PRETENDER; *old* RETAINER; *old* SALT; **~ school,** one's former school; *of the old* SCHOOL[1]; ||**~ school tie,** necktie of characteristic pattern worn by former members of a particular (public) school, (fig.) mark of sentimental or excessive loyalty to traditional values and ideas; **~ soldier,** former or long-serving soldier, (fig.) experienced person; *come the ~ soldier over*, seek to impose on esp. on grounds of greater experience; *old* STAGER; *old* STYLE; ||*old* SWEAT; *Old* TESTAMENT; **~-time,** belonging to old times, (of dancing) comprising kinds of dance known for many years; ***~-ti'mer,** person with long experience or standing; *old wives' tale* (see WIFE); **~ woman,** (1) fem. of *old man* (1, 4, 5), (2) fussy or timid man; **~-wo'manish,** fussy and timid; *Old* WORLD; **~-world,** belonging to old times (also joc. *~e-worlde* pr. -dĭ; -dĭ); **~ year,** year just ended or about to end. **8.** Hence **~'**ISH[1] 2 *a.*, **~'**NESS *n.* **9.** *n.* **Of ~** *a.* & *adv.*, (living) in the old time (*the men of old*; *of old there were giants*); *have heard it* **of ~**, since long ago. [OE *ald*, = OS *ald*, OHG *alt* f. WG **aldha* (**al-* grow, nourish)]

ō'lden[1] *a.* (literary). Old-time, of a former age, (esp. *the olden time*). [ME, f. OLD + -EN[5]]

ō'lden[2] *v.t.* & *i.* Make or grow feeble etc. as with age. [f. OLD + -EN[6]]

ō'ldĭe *n.* (colloq.) Old person or thing. [f. OLD + -IE]

ō'ldster *n.* Old person. [f. OLD + -STER, after *youngster*]

-ōle *suf.* (Chem.) forming names of compounds esp. heterocyclic (*indole*). [f. L *oleum* oil; cf. -OL 2]

ōlėā'ceous (-shus) *a.* (Bot.) Of the family Oleaceae, incl. olive and jasmine. [f. mod. L *Oleaceae* f. L *olea* olive-tree; see -ACEOUS]

ōlėă'gĭnous *a.* Having properties of or producing oil; oily, greasy, (lit. or fig.). [f. F *oléagineux* f. L *oleaginus* (*oleum* oil)]

ōlėă'nder *n.* Evergreen poisonous Mediterranean shrub (*Nerium oleander*) with leathery lanceolate leaves and fine red, white, or pink flowers. [med. L]

ōlėă'ster *n.* The wild olive (*Olea oleaster*); small yellow-flowered tree like it, of genus *Elaeagnus.* [ME f. L (*olea* olive-tree; see -ASTER)]

ōlėcrā'non *n.* (Anat.) Bony prominence on upper end of ulna at elbow. [f. Gk *ōle*(*no*)*kranon* (*ōlenē* elbow, *kranion* head)]

ō'lėfĭn, -ĭne, *n.* (Chem.) Hydrocarbon of series C_nH_{2n}. [f. F *oléfiant* oil-forming (w. ref. to oily ethylene dichloride) + -IN, -INE[5]]

ōlē'ĭc *a.* (Chem.) **~ acid,** unsaturated fatty acid present in many fats and soaps; hence **ō'lė**ATE[1] (3) *n.* [f. as foll. + -IC]

ōlėĭ'ferous *a.* Yielding oil. [f. L *oleum* oil + -I- + -FEROUS]

***ō'lėō** *n.* (*pl.* **~s**). Oleomargarine. [abbr.]

ō'lėo- *comb. form.* Oil, as: **~graph,** picture printed in oil-colours; **~mar'garine** (*or* -ē'n), fatty substance extracted from beef fat and serving as constituent of margarine, *margarine made from vegetable oils; **~meter** (-ŏ'm-), instrument for determining density and purity of oils; **~-re'sin,** natural or artificial mixture of essential oil and resin, e.g. BALSAM 1. [f. L *oleum* oil + -O-]

ō'lèum *n.* Concentrated sulphuric acid containing excess sulphur trioxide in solution as oily corrosive liquid. [L, = oil]

||**O lěvel** (ō'-) *n.* = ORDINARY *level* (in G.C.E.). [abbr.]

ŏlfă'ct|ion *n.* (Med.) Smelling, sense of smell; so ~IVE *a.* [f. L *olfactus* a smell (*olēre* to smell, *facere fact-* make); see -ION]

ŏlfă'ctorў *a.* Concerned with smelling (*olfactory nerves*). [f. L **olfactorius* (*olfactare* frequent. of *olfacere*, as prec.)]

olĭ'banum *n.* Aromatic gum resin from tree of genus *Boswellia*, used as incense. [ME, f. med. L, f. LL f. Gk *libanos* frankincense, of Semitic orig.]

ŏ'lĭd *a.* (arch.) Rank-smelling, fetid. [f. L *olidus* (*olēre* smell; see -ID¹)]

ŏ'lĭgarch (-k) *n.* Member of oligarchy. [f. Gk *oligarkhēs* (*oligoi* few, *arkhō* to rule)]

ŏ'lĭgarchў (-kĭ) *n.* Government, State governed, by small group of persons; members of such government; so **ŏlĭgar'ch**IC(AL) (-kĭ-) *adjs.* [f. F *oligarchie* or med. L f. Gk *oligarkhia* (as prec.; see -Y¹)]

ŏ'lĭgo- *comb. form.* Few, slight, as: **~car'pous,** having few fruits; **O~cene,** (Geol.) between Miocene and Eocene; **~mer,** (Chem.) polymer with up to 5 monomer units; **~poly** (-ŏ'p-), state of limited competition between few producers or sellers (cf. MONOPOLY). [f. Gk *oligos* small, *oligoi* few + -O-]

ō'lĭō *n.* (*pl.* **~s**). Mixed dish, hotchpotch, stew of various meats and vegetables; medley, farrago, miscellany. [f. Sp. *olla* stew f. L *olla* jar]

ŏlĭvā'ceous (-sh*u*s) *a.* (Biol. etc.) Olive-green, of dusky yellowish green. [f. OLIVE + -ACEOUS]

ŏ'lĭvarў *a.* (Anat.) Olive-shaped, oval. [f. L *olivarius* (as foll.; see -ARY¹)]

ŏ'lĭve *n.* & *a.* **1.** ~**(-tree)**, evergreen tree (*Olea europaea*) with narrow leaves hoary below and axillary clusters of small white flowers, bearing olives (sense 2). **2.** Small oval drupe with hard stone and bitter pulp, of dusky yellowish green when unripe and bluish black when ripe, yielding oil, and pickled unripe for eating as relish. **3.** Leaf, branch, or wreath of olive-tree as emblem of peace; **~-branch,** (fig.) something done to show disposition for reconciliation. **4.** ~**(-wood)**, wood of the olive-tree. **5.** (Shell of) olive-shaped gastropod of genus *Oliva*; olivary body in brain. **6.** (in *pl.*) Slices of beef or veal rolled up with onions and herbs and stewed. **7.** Olive-shaped bar or button for fastening garment by insertion in corresponding loop. **8.** Olive colour (see sense 10). **9. ~-branch,** (1) see sense 3, (2, joc.) child (w. ref. to Ps. 128:3); **~ crown,** garland of olive as sign of victory; **~ drab,** greyish olive colour of U.S. army uniforms; **~ oil** (extracted from olives). **10.** *a.* ~**(-green)**, coloured like the unripe olive. **11.** (Of complexion) yellowish-brown. [ME f. OF, f. L *oliva* f. Gk *elaia* (*elaion* oil)]

ŏ'lĭvĭne (*or* -ēn) *n.* Magnesium iron silicate mineral, usu. olive-green. [f. L *oliva* OLIVE + -INE⁵]

ŏlla podri'da (-rē'-) *n.* = OLIO. [Sp., lit. 'rotten pot' (as OLIO, L *putridus*; cf. PUTRID)]

ŏlm *n.* Cave-dwelling salamander of genus *Proteus*. [G]

ŏ'logў *n.* (joc.) Any science or theory. [f. foll.]

-ŏ'logў *suf.* See -LOGY.

ōlorō'sō *n.* (*pl.* **~s**). Heavy medium-sweet sherry. [Sp., lit. 'fragrant']

Olў'mpĭăd (*o*-) *n.* Period of four years between celebrations of Olympic games, used by ancient Greeks in dating events (776 B.C. being first year of first Olympiad); celebration of modern Olympic games; regular international contest in chess etc. [ME, f. F *Olympiade*, or f. L f. Gk *Olumpias -ad-* (*Olumpios*; see foll., -AD)]

Olў'mpĭan (*o*-) *a.* & *n.* **1.** *a.* Of Olympus, celestial; (of manners etc.) magnificent, condescending, superior; = foll. **2.** *n.* Dweller in Olympus, one of the greater ancient-Greek gods; person of great attainments; person of superhuman calmness and detachment. [f. L *Olympus* or foll. + -IAN]

Olў'mpĭc (*o*-) *a.* & *n.* **1.** *a.* Of or at Olympia in Elis in the Peloponnese. **2.** Of the **~ games,** (1) games held at Olympia every four years by ancient Greeks with athletic, literary, and musical competitions, (2) modern international athletic and sports meeting at various places, held every four years since 1896, except in 1916, 1940, and 1944. **3.** *n.* (in *pl.*) Olympic games; **Winter ~s,** similar contest in winter sports etc. in same years. [f. L f. Gk *Olumpikos* of Olympus or Olympia (the latter being named from the games in honour of Zeus of *Olympus*)]

Olў'mpus (*o*-) *n.* Mountain in N. Thessaly on which chief Greek gods were thought to dwell; divine abode, heaven. [L, f. Gk *Olumpos*]

||**O.M.** *abbr.* (Member of the) Order of Merit.

-ō'ma *suf.* forming *ns.* denoting tumours and other abnormal growths (*carcinoma*). [mod. L, f. Gk *-ōma* suf. denoting result of vbl action]

ŏ'madhaun (-dawn) *n.* (Ir.) Foolish person. [f. Ir. *amadán* fool]

omā's|um *n.* (*pl.* **~a**). Third STOMACH of ruminant. [L, = bullock's tripe]

ŏ'mbre (-b*er*) *n.* Card-game for three, popular in Europe in 17th–18th c. [f. Sp. *hombre* man, w. ref. to one player who seeks to win the pool]

ombré (aw'ṅbrā) *a.* (Of fabric etc.) having gradual shading of colour from light to dark. [F, p.p. of *ombrer* shadow (as UMBER)]

ŏ'mbro- *comb. form.* Rain, as ~LOGY (-ŏ'l-), ~METER (-ŏ'm-), *ns.* [f. Gk *ombros* rain-shower + -O-]

ŏ'mbuds|măn (-bo͝odzm-) *n.* (*pl.* **~men**). Official appointed to investigate individuals' complaints against public authorities. [Sw., = legal representative]

-ome *suf.* forming *ns.* denoting objects or parts of a specified nature (*rhizome, trichome*). [var. of -OMA]

ō'mĕga *n.* Last letter (Ω, ω) of Greek alphabet, = ō (cf. OMICRON); last of series, final development etc., (ALPHA *and Omega*). [Gk, *ō mega* = great O]

ŏ'melĕtte, ŏ'melĕt, (ŏ'ml-) *n.* Beaten eggs cooked in melted butter and folded and often flavoured with or containing herbs, cheese, chopped ham, jam, etc. (**savoury ~,** with herbs etc.; **sweet ~,** with sugar or jam; **one cannot make an ~ without breaking eggs,** something must be sacrificed in order to achieve one's purpose). [F *omelette*, obs. *amelette* by metath. f. *alumette* var. of *alumelle* (*lemele* knife-blade f. L LAMELLA)]

ō'mĕn *n.*, & *v.t.* **1.** *n.* Occurrence or object (supposedly) portending good or evil, prognostic, presage; prophetic signification (*is of good* etc. *omen*). **2.** *v.t.* Foreshow, give presage of; ILL-*omened*. [L *omen ominis*]

omĕ'nt|um *n.* (*pl.* **~a**). Fold of peritoneum connecting stomach with other viscera; hence ~AL *a.* [L]

omī'cron *n.* Fifteenth Greek letter (O, o) = ŏ (cf. OMEGA). [Gk, *o micron* = small O]

ŏ'mĭnous *a.* Giving or being an omen (*of* good or evil, or abs.), portentous; of evil omen, inauspicious, foreshowing disaster, threatening; hence ~LY² *adv.* [f. L *ominosus* (OMEN; see -OUS)]

omĭ'ssion (-shon) *n.* Omitting, non-inclusion; non-performance, neglect, duty not done; **sins of ~ and commission,** leaving undone those things which ought to be done, and doing those things which ought not to be done; so **omĭ's-**SIVE *a.* [ME f. OF, or f. LL *omissio* (as foll.; see -ION)]

omĭ't *v.t.* (**-tt-**). Leave out, not insert or include; leave undone, neglect do*ing*, fail *to* do; so **omĭ'ss**IBLE *a.* [ME, f. L *omittere -iss-* (*o-* for OB-, *mittere* send)]

ŏmnĭ- *comb. form.* All-, of all things, in all ways or places, (cf. PAN-), as: **~co'mpetent,** having jurisdiction in all cases, able to deal with all matters; **~dire'ctional,** (of aerial etc.) receiving or transmitting in all directions; **~far'ious,** of all sorts; **omni'fic,** all-creating; **omni'genous,** of all kinds. [L (*omnis* all)]

ŏ'mnĭbus *n.* & *a.* **1.** *n.* Bus; omnibus book. **2.** *a.* Serving several objects at once, comprising several items, (*an omnibus bill, resolution, clause,* etc.); **~ book** or **volume,** low-priced volume containing several stories, plays, etc. (freq. by one author); **~ box** (in theatre, holding a number of subscribers). [F, f. L dat. pl. of *omnis,* = for all]

ŏmnĭ'pot|ent *a.* Having infinite power (**the O~ent,** God); having full or absolute power; having very great influence; hence or cogn. ~ENCE *n.*, **~ent**LY² *adv.* [ME f. OF, f. L *omnipotens* (as OMNI-, POTENT)]

ŏmnĭprĕ's|ent (-z-) *a.* Present everywhere at same time; widely or constantly met with; so ~ENCE *n.* [f. med. L OMNI(*presens* PRESENT¹)]

ŏmnĭ'scĭ|ent (*or* -shye-) *a.* Having infinite or very extensive knowledge; hence or cogn. ~ENCE *n.*, **~ent**LY² *adv.* [f. med. L *omnisciens -entis* (as OMNI-, *scire* know; see -ENT)]

ŏmnĭum gă'therum (-dh-) *n.* (colloq.) Miscellaneous assemblage of persons or things, strange mixture. [mock L (L *omnium* of all, GATHER)]

ŏmnĭ'vorous *a.* Feeding on many kinds of food, esp. on both plants and flesh; (fig.) reading, observing, etc., whatever comes one's way; hence ~LY² *adv.*, ~NESS *n.* [f. L *omnivorus* (as OMNI-, -VOROUS)]

ō'moplāte *n.* (arch.) Shoulder-blade, scapula. [f. Gk *ōmoplatē* (*ōmos* shoulder, *platē* blade)]

ŏ'mphalo- *comb. form.* Navel, as: **~tomy** (-ŏ't-), dividing of umbilical cord. [f. Gk (as foll.) + -o-]

ŏ'mphalŏs *n.* (Gk Ant.) boss on shield, conical stone at Delphi supposed to be central point of earth; centre, hub, (*the centre and omphalos of a world-wide empire*). [Gk, = navel, boss, hub]

ŏn¹ *prep.* (see UPON for idiomatic preference). **1.** (So as to be) supported by or attached to or covering or enclosing (*sat on the table; floats on the water; is on the horns of a dilemma; everywhere on earth; lives on the Continent, on an annuity; a scholar on the foundation; a colonel on half-pay; is, gets, falls, on his knees* etc.; *travels on foot, wheels, the wing, the wings of the wind; tread on air,* person's *toes; dropped it, threw him, on the floor; came on deck; standing on a ladder; put a notice on the board; hangs on the wall; walks on the ceiling; has a blister on his heel; went on board; is on the jury, committee, general staff, *team; a writer on the press, the 'Mail'; dog is on the chain*); **on** one, carried with one, about one's person, (*have you a match on you?; rings on her fingers*); *on* one's HAND¹*s*, one's HEAD¹. **2.** With axis, pivot, basis, motive, standard, conformation, or guarantee, consisting in (*turn on* one's *heel; works on a ratchet; based on fact; imprisonment on suspicion; swear on my conscience, on the Bible; had it on good authority; decided on this evidence; did it on purpose; can be explained on your theory; heard it on the radio; spoke on the telephone; got it on good terms; on account of; on the average; on penalty of death; *ten cents on the dollar; a tax on petrol; borrowed money on* (*the security of*) *his house; interest on* one's *capital; profit on sales*). **3.** (So as to be) close to, in the direction of, touching, arrived at, against, just at, (*house is on the shore, road; *on Fifth Avenue; on the right, North, far side, both sides, of; Clacton-on-Sea; Abingdon-on-Thames; marched on London; hit him on the head; a box on the ear; serve a notice, writ, on; lay hold on; seize on; bowling is on the wicket* (is straight); *drew his knife on me; smile, frown, turn* one's *back, on; make an attack on; a curse, plague,* etc., *on him, it!; rose on their oppressors; ship is driving on the rocks, on shore*); *on* FORM¹; *on* one's GAME¹. **4.** (Of time) during, exactly at, contemporaneously with, immediately after or before, as a result of, (*happened on the morning* etc. *of 29 May, on Christmas Eve, on the next day; does not run on Sundays* or *on a Sunday; on the* HOUR; *on the* INSTANT²; *on the stroke of midnight;* CASH¹ *on delivery;* **on time, schedule, the minute,** etc., punctual(ly); *on arriving, my return, analysis, examination, I found; the time is just on nine o'clock*). **5.** In manner specified by adj. (*on the cheap, sly,* SQUARE¹); in state or action specified by noun (*on fire,* TAP¹, *loan, lease, sale, strike, guard; on the look-out, move, run, wane, watch; on* one's *best behaviour*). **6.** Concerning, about, (while) engaged with, so as to affect, (*keen, mad, bent, determined, set, on;* GONE *on; die, rat, walk out, on; court martial was held on him; my opinion on free trade; writes, speaks, lectures, on finance; a book, an essay, on grammar; killed on active service; is here on business, duty, holiday, leave; is on antibiotics, heroin, the Pill; Armstrong on trumpet; meditating on vanity; take vengeance on* person; *have* NOTHING *on* person; *the laugh was, the drinks are, on* (colloq., = at the expense of) *me; did it on my way there; went on an errand; is not binding on us; work tells severely on him; title was conferred on him; draw cheque on bank; condoled with him on his loss*). **7.** Added to (*ruin on ruin; put twopence on the price*). **8. on-line** *a.* & *adv.*, (Computers) (carried out while) directly connected to the central processing unit, directly controlled by the computer; **o'nshore,** (of wind) blowing landwards; **onsi'de,** (Footb. etc.) not OFFside; **on-stage** *a.* & *adv.*, on the stage, visible to audience; **on-street** (esp. of parking of vehicles, opp. *off-street*). [OE *on, an,* = OS, OHG *an*(*a*), ON *á*, Goth. *ana* f. Gmc, cogn. w. Gk *ana*]

ŏn² *adv., a.,* & *n.* **1.** *adv.* (So as to be) supported by, attached to, covering, enclosing, or touching, something (*has, put, his hat on; put the table-cloth on; keep your* HAIR *on*). **2.** In some direction, towards something, farther forward, towards point of contact, in advanced position or state, with continued movement or action, in operation or activity, (LOOK, MOVE², *on; from that day on; was well on in the day; getting on for two o'clock*); **broadside, end,** etc., **on** (with that part forward); (ellipt., = imper. of *go* or *come on*) *on, Stanley, on!; happened earlier, early, late*(*r*), *on* (see EARLY, LATE²); **on and on,** continually on(wards); *and* SO¹ *on;* **speak, wait, work,** etc., **on,** continue to do so; (Cricket, of bowler) bowling; (of play, film, broadcast programme, etc.) being performed; (of actor etc.) on the stage; (of gas, water, etc.) running or available; (of electric current etc.) in or into state of flowing or activation of equipment etc.; (of proposed event, strike, etc.) to take place, not cancelled; (of employee) on duty. **3.** CARRY¹, CATCH¹,

COME, GET[1], GO[1], HOLD[1], KEEP[1], PUT[1], TAKE[1], TRY, *on*. **4. Be on,** (colloq.) be willing to participate or approve, make bet, be practicable or acceptable; **be on at,** (colloq.) nag or grumble at (person); **be on to** (person), be aware of his intentions etc., find fault with, nag (*he's always on to me*); **be on to** (thing), notice it, be able to make use of it, realize its importance; **what are you on about?,** (sl.) what is your cause of complaint?; HAVE[1] *on*; **on and off,** = OFF *and on*; **on to, onto,** *compd. prep.* (corresponding to *on* as *into* to *in*, but usu. written as two words) to a position on (*ran on to the track*; cf. *ran on to the end*, = sense 2). **5. O'ncoming** *a.* & *n.*, approach(ing) from the front; ‖**o'n-cost,** overhead expense; **o'nfall** *n.*, assault; **o'nflow,** onward flow; **o'ngoing** (ŏ'n-gōĭng) *a.*, continuing to exist etc.; **on-glide,** (Phonet.) glide made in beginning a sound; **o'nlooker,** = LOOKER-*on*; **on-o'ff** *a.*, (of switch etc.) having two positions, 'on' and 'off'; **o'nrush,** onward rush. **6.** *a.* (Cricket). Towards or in part of field on playing batsman's side and in front of his wicket (opp. OFF; *an on drive*, whence **on-dri've** *v.t.*; LONG[1] *on*; MID[1]-*on*). **7.** ‖**On-licence,** (place with) licence to sell beer etc. for consumption on the premises. **8.** *n.* The on side in cricket (*a fine drive to the on*). [OE, f. prec.]

-ŏn *suf.* (Phys. etc.) forming *ns.* denoting elementary particles (*meson, neutron*), quanta (*photon*), molecular units (*codon*), or substances (*interferon, parathion*). [f. ION, orig. in *electron*]

ŏ'nager *n.* Wild ass, esp. *Equus onager* of Central Asia; ancient military engine for throwing rocks. [ME f. L, f. Gk *onagros* (*onos* ass, *agrios* wild)]

ō'nan|ĭsm *n.* Masturbation; coitus interruptus; hence **~i'stic** *a.* [f. F *onanisme* or mod. L *onanismus*, f. *Onan* (Gen. 38:9); see -ISM]

‖**O.N.C.,** ‖**O.N.D.,** *abbrs.* Ordinary National Certificate, Diploma.

once (wŭns) *adv., conj.,* & *n.* **1.** *adv.* For one time or on one occasion only, multiplied by one, by one degree, (*have read it more than once*; *not once in a hundred times*; *shall die once*); **~ or twice, ~ and again,** a few times; **~ again, ~ more,** an additional time; **~ (and) for all,** in final manner, definitively; **(every) ~ in a while,** from time to time; **(for) ~ in a while** or ‖**way,** very rarely; **~ and away,** (1) = *once for all*, (2) = *once in a way*; **~ bitten twice shy,** pain, loss, etc., teaches caution; **for (this, that) ~,** on this or that one occasion, even if on no other. **2.** (In negative or conditional or indefinite clause etc.) ever, at all, even for one or the first time, (*if we once lose sight of him*; *when once he understands*; *have not seen him here once*; *once past the fence we are safe*). **3.** On a certain but unspecified past occasion (also **~ upon a time**), at some period in the past, former(ly), (*once there was a giant*; *a once-famous doctrine*). **4. At ~,** immediately, without delay, at the same time, (*do it at once, please*; *don't all crowd in at once*; *at once stern and tender*); **all at ~,** (1) all together, (2) without warning. **5. ~-over,** (colloq.) (preliminary) inspection (often with additional sense of cursoriness). **6.** *conj.* As soon as, if once, when once, (*once he hesitates, we have him*; *once I can get this job done*). **7.** *n.* One time, performance, etc., (*once is enough for me*; *happened only that once*; cf. sense 1). [ME *ānes, ōnes*, f. ONE + -s[3]]

‖**o'ncer** (wŭ'nser) *n.* (sl.) £1 note. [f. ONCE + -ER[1]]

ŏnco- *comb. form.* (Med.) Tumour, as: **~ge'nic, ~genous** (-ŏ'j-), *adjs.*, tumour-producing. [f. Gk *ogkos* mass + -O-]

on dit (awn dē') *n.* (*pl. pr.* same). Piece of gossip or hearsay. [F, = they say]

one (wŭn) *a., n.,* & *pron.* **1.** *a.* Single and integral in number, neither none nor fractional nor plural, numbered by the first or lowest integer, half of two, a; **~ man, ~ vote,** opp. PLURAL *vote*; **~-third** etc., part that is of size such that three etc. make whole; **~-and-twenty** etc., = twenty etc. plus one, twenty etc. -one; **~-and-twentieth** etc., twenty etc. -first; **~ dozen, hundred,** etc., (precise or formal for *a*); **~ man in ten, a thousand,** etc., relatively few; **for ~ thing** (not to mention others); **~ or two,** lit., or = a few. **2.** *The* only, single, forming a unity, united, identical, the same, unchanging, a particular but undefined, to be contrasted with another, (*the one way to succeed*; *no one man is equal to it*; *is one and undivided*; *all in one direction*; *cried out with one voice*); **be made ~,** be married; **become ~,** coalesce; *one* WITH; **neither ~ thing nor the other,** of (undesirably) mixed nature; **~ day,** (1) on a day unspecified, (2) at some unspecified future date. **3.** *n.* (often used as substitute for repetition of previously expressed or implied noun). The number one, thing numbered with it, written symbol (1, i, I) for it, a unit, unity, a single thing or person or example, (*one is half of two*; *write down a one, three ones*; *came in ones and twos*; *sell scores where they sold ones*; *this is the only one*; *I lose a neighbour and you gain one*; *the big book and the little one*; *pick me out a good one, some good ones*; *which one* or *ones, what kind of a one, do you like?*; *that one, the one in the window, will do*); (colloq.) story, joke, (*have you heard the one about the dog that could play poker?*), drink (QUICK *one*; *one for the* ROAD[1]); (colloq.) ‖pound note, *dollar bill; **(all) in ~,** combined; **at ~,** reconciled, in agreement; **book, part, volume,** etc., **~** (first in series); **make ~,** (arch.) be member of a group; **never a ~,** none; NUMBER[1] *one*; TEN *to one*; ‖*in the* YEAR *one*. **4.** *a.* (used ellipt. for *a*, or for sense 1, with noun often merely implied). Single person or thing of the kind expressed or implied (*one of them lost his* or *her hat*; *just one of those* THINGS; *one of the richest men in England*; *shall see you again one of these fine days*); *at ~ o'clock, at ~,* (i.e. hour); *like ~ o'clock*, (colloq.) vigorously; *~ and sixpence* (Hist.; i.e. shilling); *gave him ~ in the eye, that was a nasty ~, ~ in the eye for the Liberals*, (i.e. blow, lit. or fig.); **for ~,** being one, even if alone (*I for one do not believe it*); *go one* BETTER[1]; *is one too* MANY (*for*); ALL *one*; *one and* ALL; **~ by ~, ~ after another,** singly, successively; **~ with another,** on the average; **(the) ~ . . . the other** (formula distinguishing two things: *one is good, the other bad*; *took (the) one and left the other*); **~ another** (formula of reciprocity with *one* orig. subjective and *another* objective or possessive: *struck one another, write to one another, buy one another's goods*). **5.** *pron.* A person of specified kind (*little, dear, loved, ones*; *behaved like one frenzied*; (colloq.) *what a one he is to make excuses* or *for making excuses!*; *he was one who had an eye for such mysteries*; *bought it from one Stephens*); ANYONE, NO[1] *one*, etc.; **many a ~,** many people; **the Holy One, One above,** God; **the Evil One,** the Devil. **6.** (arch.) A particular but unspecified person (*one came running*). **7.** Any person, esp. the speaker or writer, as representing people in general (poss. *one's*, obj. *one*, reference-form *one*, refl. *oneself*; (arch. or U.S.) *his, him, he* and *him, himself*, (colloq.) *their, them, they* and *them, themselves*: *if one cuts off one's nose, one hurts only oneself*; *it offends one to be told one is not wanted*); (colloq.) I (*one let it pass, for one did not want to seem mean*). **8. ~-armed bandit,** (sl.) fruit-machine etc. operated by pulling down armlike handle; **~-eyed,** having only, or blind in, one eye, (fig., sl.) petty; **~-handed,** having, done or used etc. with one hand only; **~-horse,** drawn or worked by single horse, (fig., sl.) petty, poorly equipped; **~-idea'd, ~-ideaed,** possessed by single idea, narrow-minded; **~-legged,** having only one leg, (fig.) one-sided, unequal; **~-man,** requiring, consisting of, done or managed by, one man (*one-man band, bus, exhibition of paintings*); **~-night stand,** (colloq.) single performance of play, concert, etc., in a place; **~-off,** made as one (article etc.) only, not repeated; **~-piece,** (of bathing-suit etc.) made as a single connected garment, not two-piece; **~se'lf,** reflexive, and emphatic appositional, form of *one* (sense 7) (*to starve oneself is suicide*; *to do right oneself is the great thing*; cf. HERSELF); **~-shot,** (colloq.) involving a single action or effort; **~-sided,** having, occurring on, one side only (*a ~-sided street,* with houses on one side only; *a ~-sided plant,* with leaves or flowers all on one side of stem), larger etc. on one side, partial, unfair, prejudiced; **~'step,** vigorous kind of foxtrot in duple time; **~-time,** former; *~-time pad,* pad of ciphers each for use once only; **~-(to-)one,** with correspondence of one member of one group to one of another; **~-track,** (of mind etc.) able to think of only one topic; **~-two,** (colloq.) delivery of two punches in quick succession; **~-up,** scoring one point more than opponent, (fig.) maintaining a psychological advantage, whence *~-u'pmanship* (colloq.); **~-way,** operating or moving in only one direction, *(of ticket) single not return; *~-way street* (where traffic may move in one direction only). **9.** Hence ~'FOLD *a.* [OE *ān,* = OS *ēn,* OHG *ein,* ON *einn,* Goth. *ains* f. Gmc **ainaz* f. IE **oinos*]

-ōne *suf.* forming *ns.* (Chem.) denoting various compounds, esp. ketones (*acetone*). [f. Gk *-ōnē* fem. patronymic]

oneir'ĭc (-īr'-) *a.* Of dreams. [f. Gk *oneiros* dream + -IC]

oneir'o- (onīr'-) *comb. form.* Dream, as: **~cri'tic,** interpreter of dreams; **~logy** (ŏnīrŏ'-), study and interpretation of dreams; ~MANCY *n.* [f. as prec. + -O-]

o'nenėss (wŭ'n-n-) *n.* Being one, singleness; singularity, uniqueness; wholeness, unity, union, agreement, concord; identity, sameness, changelessness. [f. ONE + -NESS]

||**o'ner** (wŭ'-) *n.* (sl.) Remarkable or pre-eminent person or thing; severe blow. [f. ONE + -ER¹]

ŏ'nerous *a.* Burdensome, causing or requiring trouble; (Law) accompanied by obligations; hence ~LY² *adv.*, ~NESS *n.* [ME, f. OF *onereus* f. L *onerosus* (*onus oneris* burden; see -OUS)]

oneself. See ONE 7, 8.

o'nion (ŭ'nyon) *n.* (Plant *Allium cepa* with) edible rounded bulb of many concentric coats and pungent smell and flavour, much used in cooking or eaten pickled or in salad; **know** one's **~s,** (sl.) be good at one's job; **off** one's ~, (sl.) crazy; **~ dome,** bulbous cupola as often found on churches in Russia etc.; **~-skin,** (1) outermost or any outer coat of onion, (2) thin smooth translucent paper; hence ~Y² *a.* [ME, f. AF *union,* OF *oignon* f. Gallo-Rom. **unione* f. L *unio -onis*]

ō'nlȳ¹ *attrib. a.* That is (or are) the one (or all the) specimen(s) of the class, sole, (*the only way is to die*; *the only child of his parents*; *the only instances known*; *was an only son*; *only you can help me*; *my one and only hope*); best or alone worth considering (*gliding is the only sport*); ~ (or **onlie**) **begetter,** person solely responsible for originating something [w. allus. to dedication of Shak. *Sonnets* 1609]; **~-begotten,** begotten as the only child. [OE *ānlic, ǣnlic* (as ONE, -LY¹)]

ō'nlȳ² *adv.* & *conj.* **1.** *adv.* Solely, merely, exclusively, and no one or nothing more or besides or else, and that is all, (*is right only because it is customary*; *one and one only*; *it will only make matters worse*; *I can only guess what happened*; *has only just succeeded* or *arrived*; *I not only heard it, but saw it*); IF *only*. **2.** No longer ago than (*came only yesterday*); with no better result than (*picked it up, only to drop it again*). **3.** ~ **too** *glad, true,* etc., glad etc. and not, as might be expected or desired, the opposite. **4.** *conj.* It must however be added that, but then, (*he makes good resolutions, only he never keeps them*); with the exception, were it not, that (*he does well, only that he is nervous at the start*; *I would describe it, only* (*that*) *you would be bored*). [ME *onliche,* partly f. prec., partly f. OE *ǣnlīce* after prec.; cf. ONE, -LY²]

||**o.n.o.** *abbr.* or near offer.

ŏnomă'stĭc *a.* Relating to name(s). [f. Gk *onomastikos* (*onoma* name)]

onŏmato|poe'ia (-pē'*a*; *or* ŏnomă-) *n.* Formation of names or words from sounds that resemble those associated with the object or action to be named, or that seem naturally suggestive of its qualities; word so formed (e.g. *cuckoo, sizzle*); hence or cogn. **~poe'**IC (-pē'-), **~pōĕ't**IC, *adjs.* [LL, f. Gk *onomatopoiïa* word-making (*onoma -matos* name, *poieō* make)]

ŏ'nsĕt *n.* Attack, assault, impetuous beginning, (esp. *at the first onset*). [f. ON¹ + SET² (cf. SET¹ *on*)]

ŏ'nslaught (-awt) *n.* Onset, fierce attack. [earlier *anslaight* f. MDu. *aenslag* (*aen* on, *slag* blow) w. assim. to obs. *slaught* slaughter]

-ŏnt *suf.* (Biol.) denoting an individual of a specified type (*symbiont*). [f. Gk *ōn ont-* being]

Ont. *abbr.* Ontario.

onto *prep.* See ON² 4.

ŏnto|gĕ'nėsĭs *n.* (Biol.) Origin and development of an individual (cf. PHYLO*genesis*); hence **~gėnĕ't**IC *a.* [f. as foll. + Gk *genesis* birth]

ŏntŏ'gėnȳ *n.* = prec. [f. Gk *ōn ont-* being, part. of *eimi* be, + -O- + -GENY]

ŏntŏ'log|ȳ *n.* Branch of metaphysics dealing with the nature of being; so **ŏntolŏ'g**ICAL *a.*, ~IST (3) *n.* [f. mod. L *ontologia* (as prec.; see -LOGY)]

ō'nus *n.* Burden, duty, responsibility; ~ ***probandi*** (*pr.* -ă'ndī), = BURDEN¹ *of proof.* [L]

ŏ'nward *adv.* & *a.*, **ŏ'nwards** (-z) *adv.* **1.** *adv.* Further on, towards the front, with advancing motion. **2.** *a.* Directed onward. [f. ON² + -WARD(S)]

ŏ'nȳmous *a.* Not anonymous. [back form. f. ANONYMOUS; see AN- 4]

ŏ'nȳx *n.* Kind of chalcedony with different colours in layers; ~ **marble** (with banded onyx-like structure). [ME f. OF *oniche, onix,* f. L f. Gk *onux* finger-nail, onyx]

ōo-, *ōō-, *comb. form.* (Biol.) Egg, ovum, as: **o'ocyte,** female gametocyte; **oo'gamous** (ōŏ'g-), reproducing by union of mobile male and immobile female cells; **ooge'nesis,** production or development of ovum; **oo'logy** (ōŏ'l-), study or collecting of birds' eggs; **oophore'ctomy,** ovariectomy; **o'osperm,** fertilized ovum. [f. Gk *ōion* egg + -O-]

ōō'dles (-delz) *n.* (colloq.) Great quantity, superabundance, (*oodles of money*). [19th c. U.S.; orig. unkn.]

ōōf *n.* (sl.) Money, cash; hence ~'Y² *a.*, rich. [f. Yiddish *ooftisch,* G *auf dem tische* on the table (of money in gambling)]

ooh (ōō) *int.* expr. surprised pleasure, excitement, pain, etc. [imit.]

ō'olīte *n.* Rock, esp. limestone, made up of rounded grains; (Geol.) series of fossiliferous Jurassic rocks of this type; hence **ōolĭ't**IC *a.* [f. F *oölithe* (as OO-; see -LITE)]

oo'long *n.* Dark kind of cured China tea. [f. Chin. *wulung*, = black dragon]
oomiak. Var. of UMIAK.
oo'mpah *n.* Rhythmical sound of deep-toned brass instruments in military band etc. [imit.]
oomph *n.* (sl.) Attractiveness, esp. sex appeal; energy, enthusiasm. [20th c.; orig. uncert.]
-oon *suf.* forming *ns.*, orig. f. F wds in stressed *-on* (*dragoon*), esp. f. It. *-one* f. L *-o -onis* (*balloon, buffoon*); replaced by *-on* in recent borrowings and those with unstressed *-on* (*baron*).
oont *n.* (Anglo-Ind.) Camel. [f. Hindi *ūnt*]
oops *int.* on making obvious mistake (cf. WHOOPS). [natural excl.]
ooze[1] *n.* **1.** Wet mud, slime, esp. in river-bed or estuary or on ocean bottom. **2.** Tanning liquor, infusion of oak-bark etc. **3.** Exudation, sluggish flow, something that oozes. **4.** Hence **oo'zy**[2] *a.* [sense 1 f. OE *wāse*, = ON *veisa* puddle; sense 2 f. OE *wōs* juice, sap, = ON *vás*; sense 3 f. foll.]
ooze[2] *v.* **1.** *v.i.* (Of moisture) pass slowly through the pores of a body, exude, percolate; (of substance) exude moisture; (fig.) leak *out* or *away* (*the secret oozed out; my courage is oozing away*). **2.** *v.t.* Emit steadily (lit. or fig.; moisture, information, confidence, encouragement). [ME *wōsen*, f. prec. 2]
op- *pref.*, assim. form of OB- before *p*.
O.P. *abbr.* Dominican [f. *Order of Preachers*, L *Ordo Praedicatorum*]; observation post; opposite prompt.
o.p. *abbr.* out of print; overproof.
op. *abbr.* & (colloq.) *n.* or *a.* = OPERATION 2, 3; operator; optical (*op art*); opus.
opă'citȳ *n.* Being opaque; obscurity of meaning, obtuseness of understanding. [f. F *opacité* f. L *opacitas -tatis* (as OPAQUE; see -ITY)]
ō'pah (*-a*) *n.* Rare brilliant-coloured large N. Atlantic fish (*Lampris regius*) of mackerel family. [W. Afr. name]
ō'pal *n.* Amorphous quartzlike form of hydrated silica, some kinds of which show changing colours (e.g. **common ~**, milk-white or bluish with green, yellow, and red reflections); **~ glass,** semi-translucent white glass. [f. F *opale* or f. L *opalus*, prob. ult. f. Skr. *upalas* precious stone]
ōpalĕ'sc|ent *a.* Showing changing colours like opal; so ~ENCE *n.* [f. prec. + -ESCENT]
ō'paline *a.* & *n.* **1.** *a.* Opal-like, opalescent, iridescent. **2.** *n.* Opal glass. [f. OPAL + -INE[1]]
opā'que (-k) *a.* (**~r, ~st**) & *n.* **1.** *a.* Not transmitting light, not transparent; impenetrable to sight; not lucid, obscure; obtuse, dull-witted; hence ~LY[2] *adv.*, ~NESS *n.* **2.** *n.* Opaque thing or substance. [ME *opak*, f. L *opacus*; sp. now assim. to F]
op. cit. *abbr.* in the work already quoted. [f. L *opere citato*]
ōpe *a.*, & *v.t.* & *i.* (poet.) = OPEN[1,2]. [ME, v. f. a., reduced f. OPEN[1] on anal. of *p.p.* (cf. *awake, wove*, f. *awaken, woven*)]
O.P.E.C. *abbr.* Organization of Petroleum Exporting Countries.
ō'pen[1] *a.* (**~er, ~est**) & *n.* **1.** *a.* Not closed or blocked up, allowing entrance or passage or access, having gate or door or lid or part of boundary withdrawn, unenclosed, with ends not joined, unconfined, unobstructed, uncovered, bare, exposed, undisguised, public, manifest, not exclusive or limited, (*open gate, passage, church, drawer, box, bottle, field, grave, drain, sore, road, sea, carriage, hostilities, scandal, contempt*; LAY[3] *open*; *door flew open*); (of boat) undecked; (of ears) eagerly attentive; (of mouth) with lips apart in voracity, frankness, etc., or esp. in gaping stupidity or surprise; (of mind) accessible to new ideas, unprejudiced or undecided; (of meeting) admitting all persons, not only members etc.; (of exhibition, building, shop, etc.) accessible to visitors or customers; (of race, championship, scholarship, etc.) unrestricted as to competitors, (of champion etc.) having won such a contest; (of electrical circuit) not continuous; (of river, harbour) free of ice; (of weather, winter) not frosty; (of bowels) not constipated; (of return ticket) without specified date of travel; ||(of cheque) not crossed; **~ to,** willing to receive (*offers, persuasion*, etc.), liable to (*attack, misinterpretation, question*, etc.), available to (*there are three courses open to us*); **throw ~,** cause to be suddenly or widely open, make accessible *to*. **2.** Expanded, unfolded, outspread, spread out, not close, with (wide) intervals, porous, communicative, frank, (*open book* lit. or fig.; *open flower*); (of eyes) watchful (**with ~ eyes,** (1) consciously, under no misapprehension, (2) in eager attention or surprise); (of face) ingenuous-looking; **be ~ with,** speak frankly to. **3.** (Mus.) (Of note) (1) produced from unstopped pipe or string or without slide, key, or piston, (2) written with head as outline, e.g. minim. **4.** (Phonet.) (Of vowel) produced with relatively wide opening of mouth (cf. CLOSE[1]); (of syllable) ending in vowel. **5.** ||**~ access,** (in library) system whereby users themselves can take books from shelves; **in the ~ air,** not in building etc.; *with open* ARM[1]*s*, whence **~-ar'med** *a.*; **O~ Brethren,** less exclusive section of Plymouth Brethren; **~cast,** (of mine or mining) with removal of surface layers and working from above, not from shafts; **~ city** (that is not defended even if attacked); **~ country,** (1) land affording wide views, (2) land free from houses or fences; **~ court** (not *in camera*, or to which public are admitted); **the ~ door,** free admission of immigration or foreign trade; *force an ~ door*, demand from willing giver; **~-ended,** having no predetermined limit or boundary; **~-field system** (of medieval agriculture, with arable land of village apportioned in unenclosed strips to villagers); **~ hand,** generosity, whence **~-ha'nded** *a.*; **~ harmony** (of chord with wide intervals); **~ heart,** frankness, unsuspiciousness, kindliness, cordiality, whence **~-hear'ted** *a.*; **~-heart,** (of surgery) with heart exposed and no blood circulating through it; **~-hearth process** (for making steel, in shallow reverberatory furnace); *keep open* HOUSE[1]; **~ ice** (through which navigation is possible); **~ letter** (esp. of protest, printed in newspaper etc. but addressed to a person); **~ market** (with free competition of buyers and of sellers); **~-mi'nded,** with open mind, unprejudiced; **~-mouthed** (-dhd), with mouth open esp. in surprise; **~ order,** (Mil. etc.) formation with wide spaces between men, units, or ships; **~-plan,** (of house, office, estate, etc.) with few interior walls; **~ prison,** = PRISON *without bars*; **~ question,** matter on which differences of opinion are legitimate; **~ sandwich** (without bread on top); **~ score** (Mus., with different staff for each part); ||**~ season** (opp. CLOSE[1] *season*); *open* SECRET; ***~ shelf,** = *open access*; so **~ shelves**; **~ shop** (opp. CLOSED *shop*); **~-and-shut case,** (colloq.) perfectly straightforward matter; **~ society** (without rigid structure or beliefs); **~ town** (as *open city*); ||**O~ University** (teaching mainly by broadcasting and correspondence, and open even to those without scholastic qualifications); *open* VERDICT; **~ weave** (of fabric with noticeable space between threads etc.); **~-work,** pattern with interstices in metal, lace, etc. **6.** Hence

~NESS (-n-n-) *n.* **7.** *n.* **The ~,** open space or country or air, public notice or view. **8.** Open championship etc. [OE, = OS *opan*, OHG *offan*, ON *opinn* f. Gmc **upanaz* (as UP)]

ō'pen² *v.* **1.** *v.t.* Make open or more open; remove cork or cap of (bottle); start or establish or set going (business, shop, account, innings, bidding, debate, campaign, etc.); (abs.) = open a book (*I opened at p. 12*); ceremonially declare (building etc.) to be completed and in use; break up (ground) with plough etc.; cause evacuation of (bowels); bring (prospect, lit. or fig.) to view; reveal or communicate (intentions etc.); make (mind, heart, etc.) more sympathetic or enlightened; (of counsel in lawcourt) make preliminary statement in (case) before calling witnesses. **2.** *v.i.* Become open or more open; (of door, room, etc.) give or have access *into* (passage), *on to* (lawn), etc.; (of prospect, lit. or fig.) be revealed; begin speaking, writing, etc., (*by mentioning, with compliment*, etc.); make a start (*session opened yesterday; story opens with a murder*); (of hounds, and derog. of men) begin to give tongue; *the* HEAVENS *opened.* **3.** *v.t.* & *i.* (Naut.) Get view of by change of position, come into full view, (*take care not to open the obelisk; the harbour light opened*). **4. ~ out,** unfold, develop, expand, accelerate, become communicative; **~ up,** make accessible, bring to notice, reveal, accelerate, begin shooting or sounding. **5.** *Open the* BALL²; *open the* DOOR *to*; **~** one's **eyes,** show surprise; **~** person's **eyes,** undeceive or enlighten him; **~ fire,** begin shooting; **not ~** one's **lips** or **mouth,** remain silent; *open* PARLIAMENT; *open* SESAME; **~** one's **shoulders,** (of batsman) hit freely. **6.** Hence **~**ABLE *a.* [OE *openian*, = OS *opanon*, OHG *offanōn* (as prec.)]

ō'pener (ō'pn-) *n.* In vbl senses; device for opening bottles, tins, etc.; first item on programme etc.; opening batsman; (in *pl.*) cards entitling holder to open betting in poker etc. [f. prec. + -ER¹]

ō'pening¹ (ō'pn-) *n.* In vbl senses; pair of facing pages in book; gap, passage, aperture; commencement, initial part; counsel's preliminary statement of case; (Chess) recognized sequence of moves for beginning of game; opportunity, favourable situation *for* (employment, transaction, etc.); **~ time,** hour at which business begins, esp. in sale of alcoholic drinks. [ME, f. OPEN² + -ING¹]

ō'pening² (ō'pn-) *a.* In vbl senses; initial, first, (*his opening remarks*); **~ batsman,** one of two who begin the innings. [ME, f. OPEN² + -ING²]

ō'penly̆ *adv.* Without concealment, publicly, frankly. [OE *openlice* (as OPEN¹, -LY²)]

ŏ'pera¹ *n.* **1.** Dramatic performance or composition of which music is an essential part, branch of art concerned with this, place where it is performed; performance humorously compared to opera (*SOAP *opera*); GRAND *opera*; **comic ~** (with much spoken dialogue, usu. with humorous treatment); **light ~** (not on serious theme); ***opéra comique*** (ŏpāra kŏmē'k; with spoken dialogue, not necessarily humorous); ***opéra bouffe, ~ buffa,*** (bōōf, bōō'fa; of farcical character); **~ *seria*** (sēr'ĭa *or* sār'-), 18th-c. opera on heroic theme with arias. **2. ~-cloak, -hood,** (lady's, for wearing at opera or to evening parties); **~-glass(es),** small binoculars for use at opera or theatre; **~-hat,** man's tall collapsible hat; **~-house,** theatre for performance of opera; ‖**~ top** (of petticoat etc., cut low with narrow straps orig. for wearing with evening dress). [It. f. L, = labour, work]

ŏ'pera². See OPUS.

ŏ'perable *a.* That can be operated; (Surg.) that can be treated by operation. [f. LL *operabilis* f. L (as OPERATE; see -ABLE)]

ŏ'perănd *n.* (Math.) Quantity etc. to which an operation is applied. [f. L *operandum*, neut. gerundive of *operari*; see foll., -ND¹]

ŏ'perāt|e *v.* **1.** *v.i.* Be in action, produce an effect, exercise influence, (*the tax operates to our disadvantage*); play (*up*)*on* person's fears etc., try to act (*up*)*on*; (of medicines etc.) have desired effect, act. **2.** Perform surgical or other operation (*on*); (try to) execute purpose; (Mil.) carry on strategic movements; (of stockbroker etc.) buy and sell esp. with view to influencing prices. **3.** *v.t.* Bring about, accomplish; manage, work, conduct. **4. ~ing-room, -table,** (for use in surgery); ‖**~ing-theatre,** room for surgical operations (orig. when done before students). [f. L *operari* work (*opus operis* work) + -ATE³]

ŏperă't|ic *a.* Of or like OPERA¹; hence **~**ICALLY *adv.* [irreg. f. OPERA¹, after *dramatic*]

ŏperā'tion *n.* **1.** Operating or being operated; working, action, way thing works, (time or range of) efficacy or validity, scope, (*is in, comes into, operation; its operation is easily explained*); active process, activity, performance, discharge of function, (*the operation of breathing, thinking, pruning*, etc.); financial transaction; **~(s) research,** = OPERATIONAL *research.* **2.** (Surg.) Act done with hand or instrument to some part of body to remedy deformity, injury, disease, pain, etc. **3.** Strategic movement of troops, ships, etc. (COMBINED *operation*); (as part of code-name for military or civil campaign: *Operation Overlord, Plowshare*); **~s room** (from which operations are controlled). **4.** (Math.) Subjection of number or quantity or function to process affecting its value or form, e.g. multiplication, differentiation. [ME f. OF, f. L *operatio -onis* (as OPERATE; see -ATION)]

ŏperā'tional *a.* Engaged in or on operation(s); used for operation(s); able to operate or function; ‖**~ research,** scientific study of business and other operations, providing quantitative basis for management decisions. [f. prec. + -AL]

ŏ'perative *a.* & *n.* **1.** *a.* Having effect, in operation, efficacious; (Law) expressing intent to perform a transaction; practical, not theoretical or contemplative; having principal relevance (*'may' is the operative word*); of surgical operations; hence **~**LY² (-vlĭ) *adv.* **2.** *n.* Worker, artisan, mechanic, mill-hand; *private detective. [f. LL *operativus* f. L (as OPERATE; see -IVE)]

ŏ'peratize, -ise (-īz), *v.t.* Put (drama etc.) into operatic form. [irreg. after *dramatize*; cf. OPERATIC]

ŏ'perātor *n.* One who operates; one who makes connections of lines in telephone exchange; person who engages in business, esp. speculatively or shrewdly; (Math.) symbol or function denoting an operation. [LL, f. L (as OPERATE; see -OR)]

opėr'cūl|um *n.* (*pl.* **~a**). Fish's gill-cover; plate or flap closing aperture of mollusc's shell when animal is retracted; similar lidlike structure in plants, eggs of some insects, etc.; hence **~**AR¹, **~**ATE², *adjs.*, **~**I- *comb. form.* [L (*operire* cover; see -CULE)]

ŏperĕ'tta *n.* One-act or short opera; light opera; musical comedy. [It. (dim. of OPERA; cf. -ETTE)]

ŏ'perōse *a.* (arch.) Requiring or showing or taking great pains, laborious; hence **~**LY² (-slĭ) *adv.*, **~**NESS (-sn-) *n.* [f. L *operosus* (*opus operis* work; see -OSE¹)]

ŏ'phĭcleide (-līd) *n.* Obsolete wind instrument consisting of tapering brass tube bent double serving as bass or alto to key-bugle; powerful organ reed-stop. [f. F *ophicléide* f. Gk *ophis* serpent + *kleis kleidos* key]

ophĭ'dĭan *a.* & *n.* (Member) of the Ophidia or Serpentes, suborder of reptiles including the snakes; snake(like). [f. mod. L *Ophidia* f. Gk *ophis* snake + -IA²; see -AN]

ŏphĭo- *comb. form.* Snake, as ~LATRY (-ŏ'l-), serpent-worship, ~LOGY (-ŏ'l-), *ns.* [f. Gk *ophis* snake + -O-]

ŏ'phīte *n.* (Min.) Serpentine, serpentine marble; hence **ophĭ'tic** *a.* [f. L f. Gk *ophitēs* (as prec.; see -ITE¹ (2))]

ŏphthă'lmĭa, ŏphthălmī'tĭs, *ns.* Inflammation of the eye, esp. conjunctivitis. [LL, mod. L, f. Gk (*ophthalmos* eye); see -IA¹, -ITIS]

ŏphthă'lmĭc *a.* Of the eye; affected with ophthalmia; good for eye-disease; ||~ **optician** (qualified to prescribe as well as dispense spectacles etc.). [f. L f. Gk *ophthalmikos* (as prec.; see -IC)]

ŏphthă'lmo- *comb. form.* Eye, as ~LOGY (-ŏ'l-), scientific study of the eye; ~SCOPE, instrument for inspecting retina etc. [f. Gk *ophthalmos* eye + -O-]

ō'pĭate¹ *a.* & *n.* **1.** *a.* Containing opium; narcotic, soporific. **2.** *n.* Drug containing opium and easing pain or inducing sleep; (fig.) thing that causes inaction or soothes the feelings. [f. med. L *opiatus, -um* (as foll.; see -ATE²)]

ō'pĭāte² *v.t.* Mix with opium; stupefy. [f. med. L *opiare* f. L OPIUM, + -ATE³]

opī'ne *v.t.* Express or hold the opinion (*that*). [f. L *opinari* think, believe]

opĭ'nion (-yon) *n.* **1.** Judgement or belief based on grounds short of proof, provisional conviction, view held as probable, (**in my** ~, as it seems to me; **be of** ~ **that,** believe; **a matter of** ~, disputable point); (**public**) ~, views or sentiments, esp. on moral questions, prevalent among people in general; ~ **poll,** = GALLUP *poll.* **2.** What one thinks on or *on* a particular question, a belief, a conviction, (*the courage of, act up to,* one's *opinions*). **3.** Formal statement by expert when consulted of what he holds to be the fact or the right course, professional advice, (*you had better have another, a second, opinion*); *(Law) formal statement of reasons for judgement given. **4.** Estimate (*have, formed, a very high, good, poor, low, favourable, opinion of him*); favourable estimate (*has a great opinion of himself; have no opinion of Frenchmen*). [ME f. OF, f. L *opinio -onis* (as OPINE; see -ION)]

opĭ'nionātėd (-nyo-) *a.* Obstinate in opinion, dogmatic; self-willed; hence ~NESS *n.* [f. obs. *opinionate* in same sense, f. prec. + -ATE²]

opĭ'nionātĭve (-nyo-) *a.* = prec. [f. OPINION + -ATIVE]

ŏpĭsŏ'mėter *n.* Instrument for measuring curved lines as on map, made of wheel running on screw and afterwards returned to original position by rolling along straight scale. [f. Gk *opisō* backwards + -METER]

opĭ'stho- *comb. form.* Behind, as: ~GRAPH, (Gk & Rom. Ant.) parchment or slab with writing on both sides. [f. Gk *opisthen* behind + -O-]

ō'pĭum *n.* Reddish-brown heavy-scented bitter drug prepared from juice of the opium POPPY (*Papaver somniferum*), smoked or eaten as stimulant, intoxicant, or narcotic, and used as sedative (LAUDANUM) in medicine; ~ **den,** haunt of opium-smokers; ~ **habit** (of taking opium); hence ~ISM (5) *n.*, ~IZE (5) *v.t.* [ME, f. L f. Gk *opion* poppy-juice (*opos* juice)]

ŏpodĕ'ldŏc *n.* Liniment made with soap. [wd used and prob. made by Paracelsus (*c.* 1540) for kinds of mėdical plaster]

opŏ'panăx *n.* Fetid gum resin formerly used in medicine, from root of *Opopanax chironium*; gum resin like myrrh, used in perfumery; ~ **tree,** sponge-tree. [ME f. L f. Gk (*opos* juice, *panax* f. as PANACEA)]

opŏ'ssum *n.* **1.** American small arboreal or aquatic nocturnal marsupial of family Didelphidae, with thumbed hind-foot (see also POSSUM). **2.** (Austral.) Phalanger resembling Amer. opossum. [f. Virginian Ind. *āpassūm*]

opp. *abbr.* opposite.

ŏ'ppĭdan *a.* & *n.* **1.** (Inhabitant) of a town. **2.** *n.* ||Non-colleger at Eton, living in boarding-house in town. [f. L *oppidanus* of town other than Rome (*oppidum* town; see -AN)]

ŏ'ppĭl|āte *v.t.* (arch. Med.) Block up, obstruct; so ~A'TION *n.* [f. L OP(*pilare* ram down)]

||**ŏ'ppō** *n.* (*pl.* ~**s**) (sl.) Colleague, friend. [f. OPPOSITE *number*]

oppō'nencȳ *n.* Antagonism, opposition. [f. foll. + -ENCY]

oppō'nent *a.* & *n.* **1.** *a.* Opposing, contrary, opposed; ~ **muscle** (opposing thumb or lateral digit to other digit). **2.** *n.* Person opposed or on opposing side in contest etc. [f. L OP(*ponere* place); see -ENT]

ŏ'pportūne (*or* -ū'n) *a.* (Of time) suitable, well--selected or as favourable as if chosen; (of action or event) well-timed, done or occurring by design or chance at favourable time; hence ~LY² (-nlĭ) *adv.*, ~NESS (-n-n-) *n.* [ME, f. OF *opportun -une* f. L OP(*portunus* f. *portus* harbour), orig. of wind driving towards harbour]

ŏpportū'n|ĭsm (*or* ŏ'-) *n.* Allowing of due or undue weight to circumstances of the time in determining policy; grasping of opportunities when they occur; preference of what can to what should be done, compromise, practical politics, adaptation to circumstances; putting of expediency before principle; so ~IST (2) *n.* [f. prec. + -ISM, after It. (*-ismo*) and F (*-isme*), Polit. terms]

ŏpportū'nĭtȳ *n.* Favourable situation, good chance, (*of* doing, *to* do, *for* action, or abs.; *find, make, get, seize, give, afford, an opportunity; take the* (*first*) *opportunity of*). [ME, f. OF *opportunité* f. L *opportunitas -tatis* (as OPPORTUNE; see -ITY)]

oppō's|e (-z) *v.t.* **1.** Place or produce or cite (thing, person) as obstacle, antagonist, counterpoise, or contrast, *to*, represent (things) as antithetical, (*to fury let us oppose patience; you are opposing things that are practically identical; to Plato I oppose Aristotle; opposed himself to it with all his power*); place (thumb or big toe) against finger(s) or other toe(s) front to front, whence ~ABLE (-z-) *a.* **2.** Set oneself against (person, thing); withstand, resist, obstruct, propose the rejection of (resolution, motion, application, etc.); (abs.) act as opponent(s) or as check (*the duty of an Opposition is to oppose; the opposing team*). **3.** (in *p.p.*) Contrary, opposite, contrasted, (*characters strongly opposed; black is opposed to white; a proper meal as opposed to just a snack; theories as opposed to facts*); (of person) hostile, adverse, (*is firmly opposed to the merger*). **4.** Hence ~LESS (-zl-) *a.*, (poet. or rhet.) irresistible. [ME, f. OF *opposer* f. L *opponere* (see OPPONENT, POSE¹)]

ŏ'pposĭte (-z-) *a.*, *n.*, *adv.*, & *prep.* **1.** *a.* Having position on the other or farther side, facing, front to front or back to back, (*on opposite sides of the square; came from, went in, opposite directions; the tree opposite to the house*); (of angles) between opposite directions of two intersecting lines; (of leaves etc.) placed at same height on opposite sides of stem, or placed straight in front of other organ, opp. ALTERNATE¹; ~ **number,** person or thing similarly placed in another set etc. to the given one. **2.** Of contrary kind, diametrically different *to* or *from*, being the other of a contrasted pair, (*of an opposite kind to, from, what I expected*); **the ~ sex,** men in relation to women or vice versa. **3.** Hence ~LY² (-tlĭ) *adv.*, ~NESS (-tn-) *n.* **4.** *n.* Opposite thing or term (*you are cold-blooded, she is the opposite*; *black is the opposite of white*; *the most extreme opposites have some qualities in common*). **5.** *adv.* & *prep.* In opposite place, position, or direction (to) (*tree stands opposite, opposite the house*); across the street (*there was an explosion opposite*); **~ prompt,** side of theatre stage usu. to actor's right; **play ~,** (of lead in stage-play or film) have (specified actor or actress) as one's leading man or lady. [ME f. OF, f. L *oppositus* p.p. of *opponere*; see OPPONENT, -ITE¹]

ŏpposĭ'tion (-z-) *n.* **1.** Placing opposite; opposing (of thumb); contrast, antithesis; diametrically opposite position (esp. Astrol. & Astron., of two heavenly bodies when their longitude differs by 180°, opp. *conjunction*); **in ~,** (of planet) opposite sun. **2.** (Logic). Relation between two propositions with same subject and predicate but differing in quantity or quality or both. **3.** Antagonism, resistance, being hostile, (*offer, meet with, determined opposition*; *did it in opposition to public opinion*). **4.** ‖**The O~, Her Majesty's O~,** chief parliamentary party opposed to that in office (*the Leader of the Opposition*; *from the Opposition benches*); **in ~,** occupying this position, esp. opp. *in office*. **5.** Any party opposed to some proposal; one's competitors or rivals. **6.** Hence ~AL *a.* [ME f. OF, f. L OP-(*positio* POSITION)]

oppŏ'sĭtĭve (-z-) *a.* Adversative, antithetic; fond of opposing. [f. med. L *oppositivus* (as prec.; see -IVE)]

opprĕ'ss *v.t.* Overwhelm with superior weight or numbers or irresistible power; lie heavy on, weigh down, (spirits, imagination, etc.); govern tyrannically, keep under by coercion, subject to continual cruelty or injustice; so ~ION (-shon), ~OR, *ns.* [ME, f. OF *oppresser* f. med. L OP-(*pressare* f. L *premere* PRESS²)]

opprĕ'ssĭve *a.* Oppressing; tyrannical; difficult to endure; (of weather etc., esp.) hot and close; hence ~LY² (-vlĭ) *adv.*, ~NESS (-vn-) *n.* [f. F *oppressif -ive* f. med. L *oppressivus* (as prec.; see -IVE)]

opprō'brĭous *a.* Conveying reproach; abusive, vituperative; hence ~LY² *adv.* [ME, f. LL *opprobriosus* (as foll.; see -OUS)]

opprō'brĭum *n.* Disgrace attaching to some act or conduct, infamy; cause of this. [L, f. OP(*probrum* disgraceful act)]

oppū'gn (-ū'n) *v.t.* Controvert, call in question; hence ~ER¹ *n.* [ME, f. L OP(*pugnare* fight) attack, besiege]

oppŭ'gn|ant *a.* Attacking, opposing; so ~ANCE, ~ANCY, **ŏppŭgn**A'TION, *ns.* [f. as prec.; see -ANT]

ŏ'psĭmăth *n.* (literary). One who learns only late in life; so **ŏpsĭ'math**Y¹ *n.* [f. Gk *opsimathēs* (*opse* late, *math-* learn)]

ŏ'psonĭn *n.* Substance in blood serum assisting action of phagocytes; hence **ŏpsŏ'n**IC *a.* [f. Gk *opsōnion* victuals + -IN]

ŏpt *v.i.* Exercise an option, make choice, (*between* alternatives or *for* alternative); **~ out (of),** choose not to participate (in); hence ~'ANT *n.* (esp. person who may choose one of two nationalities). [f. F *opter* f. L *optare* choose, wish]

ŏ'ptatĭve (*or* ŏptā'-) *a.* & *n.* (Gram.) **1.** *a.* Expressing wish; **~ mood,** set of verb-forms of this kind, distinct chiefly in Sanskrit and Greek; hence ~LY² (-vlĭ) *adv.* **2.** *n.* Optative mood. [f. F *optatif -ive* f. LL *optativus* (as prec.; see -ATIVE)]

ŏ'ptĭc *a.* & *n.* **1.** *a.* (Anat.) Of the eye or sense of sight (*optic nerve, neuritis,* etc.); **~ angle** (between lines from extremities of object to eye, or from two eyes to one point); **~ axis,** (1) axis of eye, (2) direction in doubly refracting crystal for which no double refraction occurs; **~ lobe,** dorsal lobe of midbrain, from which optic nerves arise. **2.** *n.* Lens etc. in optical instrument; (arch. or joc.) eye. **3.** ‖Device fastened to neck of bottle for measuring out spirits [P]. **4.** (in *pl.*, treated as *sing.*) Science of sight and esp. of the laws of light as its medium; science of similar behaviour of other radiation or particles (*electron optics*); components of optical instrument. [f. F *optique* or f. med. L f. Gk *optikos* (*optos* seen f. *op-* see); sense 4 renders med. L f. Gk *optika* n. pl.; see -IC]

ŏ'ptĭcal *a.* **1.** Visual, ocular; **~ art** (giving illusions of movement by use of contrasting colours); **~ illusion,** (instance of) involuntary mental misinterpretation of thing seen, due to its deceptive appearance. **2.** Of sight or light in relation to each other; belonging to optics; constructed to assist sight or on the principles of optics; **~ activity,** (Chem.) property of rotating plane of polarization of light; **~ glass** (very pure, for lenses etc.); **~ microscope** (using direct perception of light, opp. electron microscope etc.). **3.** Hence ~LY² *adv.* [f. prec. + -AL; see -ICAL]

ŏptĭ'cian (-shan) *n.* Maker or seller of optical instruments, esp. spectacles. [f. F *opticien* f. med. L *optica* (see OPTIC, -ICIAN)]

ŏ'ptĭmal *a.* = OPTIMUM. [f. L *optimus* best + -AL]

ŏ'ptĭm|ĭsm *n.* Doctrine, esp. as set forth by Leibniz, that the actual world is the best of all possible worlds; view that good must ultimately prevail over evil in the universe; hopeful disposition, inclination to take favourable views (cf. PESSIMISM); so ~IST (2) *n.*, **~ĭ'st**IC *a.*, **~ĭ'st**ICALLY *adv.* [f. F *optimisme* f. L OPTIMUM; see -ISM]

ŏ'ptĭmīze, -īse (-īz), *v.* **1.** *v.t.* Make optimum; make the most of. **2.** *v.i.* Be optimist. [f. L *optimus* best + -IZE]

ŏ'ptĭm|um *n.* (*pl.* **~a**) & *a.* **1.** *n.* Most favourable (natural) conditions (for growth, reproduction, etc.); best compromise between opposing tendencies. **2.** *a.* Best or most favourable (*optimum temperature*). [L, neut. (as n.) of *optimus* best]

ŏ'ption *n.* Choice, choosing, thing that is or may be chosen, (*make* one's *option*; SOFT *option*; *none of the options is satisfactory*); liberty of choosing, freedom of choice, (LOCAL² *option*; *imprisonment without the option* (*of a fine*); **have no ~ but to,** must; **keep** or **leave** one's **~s open,** not commit oneself); (St. Exch. etc.) purchased right to call for, or make delivery, or either, within specified time of specified stocks etc. at specified rate. [F, or f. L *optio* (st. of *optare* choose; see -ION)]

ŏ'ptional *a.* Not obligatory; hence ~LY² *adv.* [f. prec. + -AL]

ŏptŏ'|mēter *n.* Instrument for testing the refractive power and visual range of the eye; hence **~mĕtr**IST (3) *n.*, sight-tester, ~METRY *n.* [f. Gk *optos* seen + -METER]

ŏ'ptophōne *n.* Instrument converting light into sound, and so enabling the blind to read print etc. by ear. [f. as prec. + -PHONE]

ŏ'pūl|ent *a.* Rich, wealthy; abounding, abundant, profuse; hence or cogn. ~ENCE *n.*, **~ent**LY² *adv.* [f. L *opulens, opulentus* (*opes* wealth; see -ULENT)]

ōpŭ'ntia (-sha) *n.* Cactus of genus *Opuntia*; prickly pear. [L, name of a plant, f. *Opus -untis* in Locris in ancient Greece]

ŏ'pus *n.* (*pl.* **o'pera**). **1.** Musician's separate composition or set of compositions of any kind (used esp. in citing it from among his works by number usu. indicating order of publication; abbr. *op.*: *Beethoven op. 15*). **2.** ~ (***magnum***), ***magnum opus,*** great literary undertaking, writer's or other artist's chief production. [L, = work]

opŭ'scūl|e, opŭ'scūl|um (*pl.* **~a**), *ns.* Minor musical or literary composition. [(*-ule* F) f. L *opusculum* dim. of prec.; see -CULE]

ōr¹ *n.* & *a.* (Her.) Gold or yellow (colour). [F, f. L *aurum* gold]

ōr² *prep.* & *conj.* (arch.) Before (in time), esp. (poet.) *or ever, or e'er.* [OE *ār* f. ON *ár*, = OE *ǣr* ERE]

or³ (*when stressed,* ōr) *conj.* introducing second of two alternatives (*white or black*), all but the first of any number (*white or grey or black*), only the last of any number (*white, grey, or black*), the second of each of several pairs (*white or black, red or yellow, blue or green*), (poet.) each of two (*or in the heart or in the head*); *or* ELSE; *or* SO¹ 11; **not A or B,** not A, and also not B. An alternative introduced by *or* may be (1) on equal footing with preceding (*will you be there or not?*; *any Tom, Dick, or Harry*); (2) as true as the preceding (*ripe tomatoes are red or yellow*); (3) mere synonym (*common or garden heliotrope*); (4) indication that preceding is doubtfully accurate (**one or two, five or six,** etc., a few); (5) explanation of preceding (*saw a dug-out or hollowed-tree boat*); (6) statement of only remaining possibility or choice given (often after *either*; *a thing must surely be or not be*; *for goodness' sake either take it or leave it*); (7) statement of result of rejection etc. of preceding (often with *else*; *she must weep or she must die*; *run, or else you will be late*); (8) second etc. member of indirect question or conditional protasis after *whether* (*ask him whether he was there or not*; *must do it whether I like or dislike it*); (9) significant afterthought (*he obviously knows the reason—or is he bluffing?*). [reduced form of obs. *other* conj. (which superseded OE *oththe* or), of uncert. orig.]

-or *suf.* **1.** Forming *ns.* (1) denoting condition, f. or after OF *-or, -ur* or f. L *-or -oris* (*error, horror, tremor*), (2) denoting agent, f. or after AF *-eour*, OF *-ĕor, -ĕur* or f. L *-ator, -etor, -itor* (*donor, emperor, tailor, vendor*), (3) denoting agent, f. L *-or* (*actor, doctor, inventor*; *creator, creditor, equator, escalator*), (4) f. other *sufs.* (*bachelor, mirror, sailor*), (5) *=-OUR (*color*); in Law opp. -EE (*mortgagor, obligor*); of inanimate opp. personal agents (*conveyor, resistor, sensor*; cf. -ER¹). **2.** Forming *adjs.* f. AF *-our* f. L *-or*, w. comparative sense (*major, senior*).

O.R. *abbr.* operational research; other ranks.

ŏ'rache, ŏ'rach, *n.* Wild or kitchen-garden plant of genus *Atriplex*, esp. species used instead of spinach. [ME *arage* f. AF *arasche* f. L *atriplex* f. Gk *atraphaxus*]

ŏ'racle *n.* **1.** Place at which ancient Greeks etc. were accustomed to consult their deities for advice or prophecy; ‖**work the ~,** secure desired answer by secretly influencing priests etc., (fig.) bring secret influence to bear in one's favour. **2.** Response, often ambiguous or obscure, given at such place. **3.** (Personal or other means of conveying) divine inspiration or revelation. **4.** Person or thing (regarded as) serving as infallible though mysterious guide, test, or indicator; authoritative, profoundly wise, or mysterious adviser or advice, judge or judgement, prophet or prophecy. [ME f. OF, f. L *oraculum* (*orare* speak)]

oră'cūlar *a.* Of oracle(s); mysterious or ambiguous like the ancient oracles; hence **~ITY** (-ăr-) *n.*, **~LY**² *adv.* [f. L (as prec.) + -AR¹]

ōr'acy̆ *n.* Ability to express oneself fluently in speech. [f. L *os oris* mouth + -ACY, after *literacy*]

ōr'al *a.* & *n.* **1.** *a.* Spoken, verbal, by word of mouth, not written, (*oral examination, tradition*); done or taken by the mouth (*oral contraceptive*); (Anat.) of the mouth; **~ sex,** fellatio, cunnilingus, etc.; **~ society** (that has not reached the stage of literacy); hence **~LY**² *adv.* **2.** *n.* (colloq.) Oral examination etc. [f. LL *oralis* f. L *os oris* mouth; see -AL]

ŏ'range¹ (-ĭnj) *n.* & *a.* **1.** *n.* (Evergreen tree, *Citrus aurantium* or *C. sinensis*, bearing fragrant white flowers and) large roundish many-celled juicy acid or sweet fruit enclosed in bright reddish-yellow tough rind; fruit or plant resembling this; *bitter* or SEVILLE *orange*; BLENHEIM *Orange*; BLOOD¹ *orange*; CHINA¹ *orange*; MANDARIN² *orange*; **mock ~,** the shrub *Philadelphus coronarius*, with strong-scented white usu. clustered flowers; TANGERINE *orange*; hence **ŏ'rang**ERY (3) (-ĭnj-) *n.* **2. ~(-colour),** reddish yellow like colour of orange, between red and yellow in spectrum; orange pigment. **3. ~-blossom,** flowers of orange, often worn by bride at wedding; **~-flower water,** solution of neroli in water; *orange* MARMALADE; **~-peel,** (rough surface resembling) skin of orange; *orange* SQUASH¹; **~-stick,** thin pointed stick usu. of orange-wood for manicuring finger-nails; **~-tip,** butterfly having wings tipped with orange; **~-wood** (of orange tree). **4.** *a.* Orange-coloured, reddish-yellow. [ME f. OF *orenge*, ult. f. Arab. *nāranj* f. Pers. *nārang*]

O'range² (ŏ'rĭnj) *a.* Of the extreme Protestants in Ireland, esp. in Ulster, whence **~ISM** (3) *n.*; **~man,** member of political society formed 1795 to support Protestantism in Ireland; **~man's Day,** 12 July in N. Ireland as holiday on anniversary of battles of 1690 and 1691. [prob. f. ~ Lodge of Belfast Freemasons, named after William of ~ (William III), member of princely house from ~ in S. France]

ŏrangeā'de (-ĭnjā'd) *n.* Effervescent or still drink of orange juice etc.; synthetic substitute for this. [f. ORANGE¹ + -ADE 1]

Orangism. Var. of ORANGE²*ism.*

ōrăng-u'tăn, -ou'tăng, (-ōō't-) *n.* Large long-armed arboreal anthropoid ape (*Pongo pygmaeus*) of Borneo and Sumatra. [Malay *ōrang ūtan* wild man]

orā'te *v.i.* (joc. or derog.) Make speech, hold forth, play the orator. [back form. f. foll.]

orā'tion *n.* **1.** Formal address or harangue or discourse esp. of ceremonial kind. **2.** (Gram.) Language, way of speaking; **direct ~,** ***oratio recta,*** person's words as actually spoken; **indirect** or **oblique ~,** ***oratio obliqua,*** = REPORT¹*ed speech.* [ME, f. L *oratio* discourse, prayer (*orare* speak, pray; see -ATION)]

ŏ'rator *n.* **1.** Maker of a speech; eloquent public speaker; ‖**public ~,** official at Oxford or Cambridge speaking for university on ceremonial occasions. **2.** *Plaintiff in chancery. [ME, f. AF *oratour*, OF *orateur* f. L *orator -oris* speaker, pleader, (as prec.; see -OR)]

ŏratōr'iō *n.* (*pl.* **~s**). Semi-dramatic musical composition usu. on sacred theme performed by soloists, chorus, and orchestra, without action, scenery, or costume. [It., f. eccl. L *oratorium*, orig. of musical services at church of ORATORY¹ of St. Philip Neri in Rome]

ŏ'ratory̆¹ *n.* **1.** Small chapel, place for private worship. **2.** (*O~*). R.C. religious society of simple priests without vows founded in Rome 1564 to give plain preaching and popular services; branch of this in England etc.; hence **ŏratōr'**IAN *a.* & *n.* [ME, f. AF *oratorie*, OF *oratoire* f. eccl. L *oratorium* neut. (as n.) of L *oratorius* (*orare* pray, speak; see -ORY)]

ŏ'ratorў[2] *n.* (Art of making) speeches, rhetoric; highly coloured presentation of facts; eloquent or exaggerating language; hence **ŏratŏ'r**ICAL *a.* [f. L *oratoria* (*ars* art) of speaking, fem. of *oratorius* (see prec.)]

ôrb *n.* & *v.* **1.** *n.* Sphere, globe; heavenly body; (poet.) eyeball, eye. **2.** Globe surmounted by cross as part of regalia. **3.** *v.t.* & *i.* Enclose in, form or gather into, orb. [f. L *orbis* ring]

ôrbĭ'cūl|ar *a.* Circular, disc-shaped, ring-shaped (**~ar muscle,** sphincter); spherical, globular, rounded, (fig.) forming complete whole; hence or cogn. **~ă'r**ITY *n.*, **~ar**LY[2] *adv.*, ~ATE[2] *a.* (of leaf etc.). [ME, f. LL *orbicularis* f. L *orbiculus* dim. of *orbis* ring; see -CULE, -AR[1]]

ôr'bĭt *n.* & *v.* **1.** *n.* Eye-socket; border round eye of bird or insect. **2.** Curved usu. closed course of planet, comet, satellite, spacecraft, etc.; path of electron round atomic nucleus; state of motion in an orbit (*in, into, orbit*); (fig.) range, sphere of action. **3.** *v.i.* (Of satellite etc.) move in an orbit; fly in a circle. **4.** *v.t.* Move in orbit round (body etc.); put into orbit. **5.** Hence ~ER[1], spacecraft (planned to be) in orbit. [f. L *orbita* track of wheel or moon, in med. L eye-cavity, fem. (as n.) of *orbitus* circular (*orbis* ring)]

ôr'bĭtal *a.* & *n.* **1.** *a.* (Anat., Astron., & Phys.) Of orbit(s). **2.** (Of road) passing round the outside of a city. **3.** *n.* (Phys.) State or function representing possible motion of electron round atomic nucleus. [f. prec. + -AL]

ôrc, ôr'ca, *n.* Cetacean of genus *Orca*, esp. killer whale; sea or other monster. [f. F *orque* or f. L *orca* kind of whale]

Orcā'dĭan (ôr-) *a.* & *n.* (Native or inhabitant) of Orkney. [f. L *Orcades* Orkney Islands + -IAN]

orch. *abbr.* orchestra; orchestrated by.

ôr'chard *n.* Enclosure with fruit-trees; ~IST, **~man,** fruit-grower; hence ~ING[1] *n.*, cultivation of fruit-trees. [OE *ortgeard* f. L *hortus* garden + YARD[2]]

ôrchĕ'st|ic (-k-) *a.* Of dancing; hence ~ICS *n.* [f. Gk *orkhēstikos* (*orkhēstēs* dancer; see foll.)]

ôr'chĕstra (-k-) *n.* **1.** Semicircular space in front of ancient-Greek theatre-stage where chorus danced and sang. **2.** Part of modern theatre or concert-room assigned to band or chorus; *theatre stalls; ~ **stalls,** front rows of stalls. **3.** (Mus.) Body of instrumental performers, usu. large combination of string, wood-wind, brass, and percussion instruments, esp. in theatre or concert-room; hence **ôrchĕ'str**AL (-k-) *a.* [L, f. Gk *orkhēstra* (*orkheomai* to dance)]

ôr'chĕstr|āte (-k-) *v.t.* Compose, arrange, or score, for orchestral performance; (fig.) combine (elements of) harmoniously; hence ~A'TION, **~āt**OR, *ns.* [f. prec. + -ATE[3]]

ôrchĕstri'na (-kĭstrē'-), ***ôrchĕ'strĭon** (-k-), *ns.* Mechanical instrument meant to give orchestra-like effect. [f. ORCHESTRA + -INA[1]; cf. *accordion*]

ôr'chĭd (-k-) *n.* Member of large family Orchidaceae of monocotyledonous plants, often epiphytic, usu. with one petal much larger than the other two and in exotic kinds having fantastic shapes and brilliant colours; hence ~A'CEOUS *a.*, ~IST (3), **~ŏ'**LOGY, *ns.* [f. mod. L *Orchid-(ac)eae*, irreg. f. L ORCHIS; see -ID[2]]

ôr'chĭl, ôrchĭ'lla, *n.* Red or violet dye from lichen, esp. *Roccella tinctoria*; lichen yielding it. [ME, f. OF *orcheil* etc., perh. ult. f. L *herba urceolaris* plant for polishing glass pitchers (*urceolus* pitcher); cf. ARCHIL]

ôr'chĭs (-k-) *n.* Orchid, esp. wild kind, or of genus *Orchis* with tuberous root and erect fleshy stem having spike of usu. purple or red flowers. [L f. Gk *orkhis*, orig. = testicle (w. ref. to shape of tuber)]

ôrchī'tĭs (-k-) *n.* Inflammation of the testicles. [mod. L, f. Gk *orkhis* testicle; see -ITIS]

ôr'cĭn(ŏl) *n.* (Chem.) Colourless crystalline substance extracted from lichens and yielding various dyes by chemical treatment. [f. mod. L *orcina* f. It. *orcello* orchil + -IN; see -OL]

ord. *abbr.* ordinary.

ôrdai'n *v.t.* **1.** (Eccl.) appoint ceremonially to Christian ministry, confer holy orders (esp. those of deacon or priest) on, (*was ordained priest, elder*, etc., or abs.). **2.** (Of God, fate, etc.) destine, appoint, (*has ordained the time, death as our lot, us mortal, us to die, that we should live*). **3.** Appoint authoritatively, decree, enact, (thing, *that*; *what the laws ordain*). **4.** So ~MENT *n.* [ME, f. AF *ordeiner*, OF *ordein-* stressed stem of *ordener* f. L *ordinare* (*ordo -inis* order)]

ôrdea'l (*or* -ē'al *or* ôr'dēl) *n.* **1.** Ancient Gmc mode of deciding suspected person's guilt or innocence by subjecting him to physical test such as plunging hand in boiling water, safe endurance of which was taken as divine acquittal. **2.** Experience that tests character or endurance, severe trial. **3.** ~ **bean,** Calabar bean; ~ **tree,** tanghin. [OE *ordāl, ordēl*, = OS *urdēli*, OHG *urteili* judgement f. Gmc **uzdailjam* (**uz-* out, **dailjan* DEAL[2])]

ôr'der[1] *n.* **1.** Social class or rank, set of persons separate and homogeneous as regards social level, (*the higher, lower, orders; all orders and degrees of men; the order of baronets; the clerical, military, order*); kind, sort, (*talents of a high, considerations of quite another, order*). **2.** Any of the nine grades of angelic beings (seraphim, cherubim, thrones, dominations, principalities, powers, virtues, archangels, angels); grade of Christian ministry (**holy ~s,** those of bishop, priest, and deacon; **minor ~s,** (R.C. Hist.) those of acolyte, exorcist, reader, and door-keeper); (**holy**) **~s,** status of clergyman; **take** (**holy**) **~s,** be ordained; **in** (**holy**) **~s,** ordained. **3.** Fraternity of monks and friars, or formerly of knights, bound by common rule of life (*the Franciscan order; the order of Templars*); company usu. instituted by sovereign to which distinguished persons are admitted by way of honour or reward (*Order of the* GARTER, *the* BATH[1], MERIT; *Royal* VICTORIAN *Order*), insignia worn by members of this (*sent him, wears, the order of the Golden Fleece*). **4.** (Archit.) Mode of treatment with established proportions between parts, esp. one of the **five** (**classical**) **~s,** Doric, Ionic, Corinthian, Tuscan, and Composite, of column and entablature, the first three being Greek in origin, the others Roman. **5.** (Math.) degree of complexity (*equation* **of the first ~**, involving only first derivative etc.); ~ (**of magnitude**), class in a system of classification determined by size, usu. by powers of 10; **of, in, on, the ~ of,** having the order of magnitude specified by (*errors of the order of one in a million*), approximately (*of the order of 7%*). **6.** (Biol.) Classification-group below class and above family; NATURAL *order*. **7.** Sequence, succession, manner of following, (*in alphabetical, chronological*, etc., *order*; *in order of merit; follow the order of events; inverts the natural order*; **in ~**, one after another according to some principle; **out of ~**, not systematically arranged); regular array, condition in which every part or unit is in its right place, tidiness, normal or healthy or efficient state, (*drew them up in order; are scattered without any order; love of order*; **in bad ~, out of ~, not in ~,** not working rightly; **in ~, in good ~, in working** etc. **~**, ready or fit for use; OPEN[1] *order*); (Mil.) style of dress and equipment (REVIEW[1] *order*). **8.**

(arch.) Suitable action, measures, (*take order to do*; **take ~ with,** arrange, dispose of). **9.** Constitution of the world, way things normally happen, collective manifestations of natural forces or laws, natural or moral or spiritual system with definite tendencies, (esp. *the order of nature* or *things* or *the world*; *the old order changeth*; *whether there is a moral order or not*). **10.** Stated form of divine service (*the order of confirmation*). **11.** Principles of decorum and rules of procedure accepted by legislative assembly or public meeting, or enforced by its president (*Speaker called him to order*); **O~! O~!**, protest against infringement of it; **call to ~**, (of chairman) declare (meeting) open; **point of ~**, (interruption of debate etc. with) inquiry whether something being said or done is **in** or **out of ~**, i.e. according or not according to rules etc.; **~ of the day,** programme, business set down for treatment, (fig.) prevailing state of things, principal topic of action, procedure decided upon; **~-paper,** written or printed order of the day. **12.** Prevalence of constituted authority, law-abiding state, absence of riot, turbulence, and violent crime, (LAW[1] *and order*; *order was restored*; **keep ~**, enforce it). **13.** (Mil.) **The ~**, position of company etc. with arms ordered (see ORDER[2]). **14. In ~ to** do, with a view to, for the purpose of, doing; **in ~ that,** with the intention or to the end that. **15.** (in *sing.* or *pl.*) Command, injunction, authoritative direction or instruction, (*gave orders, an order, the order, for* thing *to be* done, *that* it *should be* done, etc.; *judge gave, made, refused, an order*; *is obedient to orders*); ||**O~ in Council,** sovereign's order on some administrative matter given by advice of Privy Council; **by ~**, according to direction of the proper authority; *till* FURTHER *orders*; STANDING[2] *orders*. **16.** (Banking etc.) Instruction to pay money or deliver property, signed by owner or responsible agent; **money ~** (for payment of specified sum, esp. issued by Post Office for payment at another branch); ||**postal ~**, ||**post-office ~**, kinds of Post-Office money order, the latter payable only to a specified person; STANDING[2] *order*. **17.** (Commerc. etc.) direction to manufacturer, tradesman, waiter, etc., to supply something; quantity of goods thus supplied; **made to ~**, made according to special directions, to suit individual measurements, etc., (opp. *ready-made*), (fig.) exactly what is wanted; **is on ~**, has been ordered but not yet received; *a large* or TALL *order*; **~-book** (in which tradesman enters orders); **~-clerk** (with duty of entering orders); **~-form,** outline of order, in which details are to be filled in by customer. **18.** Pass admitting bearer gratis, cheap, or as privilege, to theatre, museum, private house, etc.; **~ to view,** house-agent's request for client to be allowed to inspect premises. [ME f. OF *ordre* f. L *ordo ordinis* row, array, degree, command, etc.]

ŏr'der[2] *v.t.* **1.** Put in order, array, regulate, (*order* one's *affairs*; *they order this matter better in France*); **~ arms,** (Mil.) stand rifle with butt on ground and hold it close to right side. **2.** (Of God, fate, etc.) ordain (*so we hoped, but it was otherwise ordered*); command, bid, prescribe, (*order a retreat*, thing *to be* done, *thing done, person *to* do, *that* person or thing *should*); command or direct (person etc.) to go *to, away, home,* etc., (**~ about,** send hither and thither, domineer over); direct manufacturer, tradesman, waiter, etc., to supply; tell waiter etc. what is to be served at (meal). [ME, f. prec.]

ŏr'derlў *a.* & *n.* **1.** *a.* Methodically arranged or inclined, regular, obedient to discipline, not unruly, well-behaved; hence **ŏr'derlĭ**NESS *n.* **2.** (Mil.) Of orders, charged with conveyance or execution of orders; ||**~ book,** regimental or company book for entry of orders; ||**~ officer,** officer of the day; **~ room** (in barracks, for company's business). **3.** *n.* Soldier in attendance on officer to carry orders etc.; attendant in (esp. military) hospital for cleaning etc. work; ||street cleaner. [f. ORDER[1] + -LY[1]]

ŏr'dĭnal *a.* & *n.* **1.** (Number) defining thing's position in series, (*'first'*, *'twentieth'*, etc., *are ordinals* or *ordinal numbers*; cf. CARDINAL). **2.** *a.* (Biol.) Of an ORDER[1] (sense 6). **3.** *n.* (Eccl.) Service-book, esp. one with forms of service used at ordinations. [ME, f. LL *ordinalis* & med. L *ordinale* neut. (as n.), f. L (as ORDER[1]; see -AL)]

ŏr'dĭnance *n.* Authoritative direction, decree; enactment by local authority; religious rite; (arch.) ordonnance. [ME, f. OF *ordenance* f. med. L *ordinantia* f. L *ordinare* (see ORDAIN, -ANCE)]

ŏr'dĭnănd *n.* Candidate for ordination. [f. L *ordinandus*, gerundive of *ordinare* ORDAIN; see -ND[1]]

ŏr'dinarў *a.* & *n.* **1.** *a.* Regular, normal, customary, usual, not exceptional, not above the usual, commonplace; ||(of shares, stock, etc.) not preference or deferred; ||**in ~** appended to *physician* etc., by permanent appointment, not temporary or extraordinary; **in the ~ way** *I should refuse*, if the circumstances were not exceptional; **out of the ~**, unusual; ||**~ level,** G.C.E. examination of basic standard; **~ seaman** (of lower rating than able seaman); hence **ŏr'dinarĭ**LY[2] *adv.*, **ŏr'dinarĭ**NESS *n.* **2.** *a.* & *n.* ||(Person) having immediate or *ex officio* and not deputed jurisdiction; **the O~**, archbishop in province, bishop in diocese; **(Lord) O~** in Scotland, one of judges of Court of Session constituting Outer House. **3.** *n.* Rule or book laying down order of divine service. **4.** ||Public meal provided at fixed time and price in inn etc.; ||establishment providing this; *tavern. **5.** (Her.) Charge of earliest, simplest, and commonest kind (esp. chief, pale, bend, fesse, bar, chevron, cross, saltire). **6.** Early type of bicycle, with one large and one very small wheel. [ME, f. L *ordinarius* orderly (as ORDER[1]; see -ARY[1]); n. thr. AF & OF *ordinarie*]

ŏr'dĭnate *n.* (Math.) Straight line from any point drawn parallel to one co-ordinate axis and meeting the other, (usu.) co-ordinate parallel to *y*-axis; any of series of parallel chords of conic section in relation to bisecting diameter (esp. used of half the chord, from curve to diameter). [f. L (*linea*) *ordinate* (*applicata*) line applied parallel (*ordinare*; see ORDAIN)]

ŏrdĭnā'tion *n.* Arrangement in ranks, classification; conferring of holy orders esp. as priest or deacon, admission to church ministry; decreeing, ordainment. [ME f. OF, or f. L *ordinatio* (as ORDAIN; see -ATION)]

ŏr'dnance *n.* Mounted guns, cannon; branch of government service dealing esp. with military stores and materials; ||**~ datum,** mean sea level as defined for ||**~ survey** (Government survey of Great Britain and (formerly) Ireland, preparing accurate and detailed maps of the whole country). [ME, var. of ORDINANCE]

ŏr'donnance *n.* Systematic arrangement esp. of literary or architectural work. [F, f. OF *ordenance* (see ORDINANCE)]

Ordovĭ'cian (ŏr-; -shan) *a.* & *n.* (Geol.) (Of) the second palaeozoic period or system, below Silurian and above Cambrian. [f. L *Ordovices* ancient British tribe in N. Wales + -IAN]

ŏr'dūre *n.* Excrement, dung; obscenity, foul language. [ME f. OF (*ord* foul f. L *horridus*; see HORRID, -URE)]

ōre *n.* Solid naturally-occurring mineral

aggregate from which metal or other valuable constituent(s) may be usefully extracted; (poet.) metal, esp. gold. [in form repr. OE *ār* brass (= OS, OHG *ēr*, ON *eir*, Goth. *aiz* f. Gmc **aiz* f. IE **ajiz*); in sense repr. OE *ōra* unwrought metal = Du. *oer*, LG *ūr*, of unkn. orig.]
Ore. *abbr.* Oregon.
ŏr'ėad *n.* (Gk & Rom. Myth.) Mountain nymph. [ME, f. L *oreas -ados* f. Gk *oreias* (*oros* mountain; see -AD 1)]
orĕ'ctĭc *a.* (Philos. & Med.) Of desire or appetite. [f. Gk *orektikos* (*oregō* stretch out; see -IC)]
Oreg. *abbr.* Oregon.
ŏrėga'nō (-ah'-) *n.* Dried wild marjoram (*Origanum vulgare*), used as seasoning. [Sp., = ORIGANUM]
O'rėgon (ŏ'-) *n.* ~ **pine,** Douglas fir. [~ in U.S.]
ŏr'ėide. See OROIDE (etym.).
ŏrėŏ'graphy̆, ŏrėŏ'logy̆, etc. Vars. of OROGRAPHY, OROLOGY, etc.
ŏr'e-weed. Var. of OAR*weed*.
ŏrfe *n.* Golden-coloured IDE. [G & F; cf. L f. Gk *orphos* sea-perch]
ŏr'fray. See ORPHREY.
ŏr'gan *n.* **1.** Musical instrument of pipes supplied with wind by bellows, sounded by keys, and distributed into sets or stops having special tone, which in turn form groups or partial organs (*great, choir, swell, solo, pedal, organ*) each with separate keyboard; hence ~IST (3) *n.* **2.** = BARREL[1]-*organ*; **~-grinder,** player of this. **3.** Keyboard wind-instrument with metal reeds, harmonium; AMERICAN *organ*; MOUTH[1]-*organ*. **4.** Part of animal or vegetable body adapted for special vital function (*organs of speech, perception, digestion*, etc., *vocal, reproductive, organs*; *nasal organ*; *organ of* CORTI); (arch.) person's voice with reference to its quality or power; (Phren.) region of brain held to be seat of particular faculty. **5.** Medium of communication, mouthpiece of opinion, esp. newspaper or magazine or review representing a party, cause, sect, pursuit, etc. **6. ~-bird,** Tasmanian bird of shrike family with discordant note; **~-blower,** person or mechanism working bellows of musical organ; **~-builder** (of musical organs); **~-loft,** gallery in church or concert-room for organ; **~-pipe,** pipe of musical organ, natural formation (e.g. cactus or coral) with vertical parts like grouped pipes of organ; **~-screen,** ornamental screen often between choir and nave on which organ is placed in cathedral etc.; **~-stop,** set of pipes of similar tone in musical organ, handle of mechanism that brings it into action. [ME, f. OE *organa* & OF *organe*, f. L f. Gk *organon* tool, f. IE **worg-* WORK[1]]
ŏrgă'ndie, *-dy̆, (*or* ŏr'ga-) *n.* Fine translucent cotton etc. muslin, usu. stiffened. [f. F *organdi*, of unkn. orig.]
ŏrganĕ'lle *n.* (Biol.) Organized or specialized structure within a cell. [f. mod. L *organella* dim.; see ORGAN, -LE 2]
ŏrgă'nĭc *a.* **1.** (Physiol.) of the bodily organs, vital; (Path., of disease) affecting structure of an organ (opp. *functional*). **2.** Having organs or organized physical structure, of animals or plants, (opp. *inorganic*); (of food etc.) produced without artificial fertilizers or pesticides. **3.** (Chem.) (Of compound etc.) existing as constituent of organized bodies or formed from bodies so existing, containing carbon in its molecule; ~ **chemistry,** that of carbon compounds. **4.** Constitutional, inherent, fundamental, structural; ~ **law** (stating formal constitution of a country). **5.** Organized or systematic or co-ordinated (*organic unity*; *an organic whole*). **6.** Hence **ŏrgă'n**ICALLY *adv.* [f. F *organique* f. L f. Gk *organikos* (as ORGAN; see -IC)]
ŏr'ganĭsm *n.* Organized body with connected interdependent parts sharing common life; (material structure of) individual living animal or plant; whole with interdependent parts compared to living being. [f. F *organisme* (as ORGANIZE; see -ISM)]
ŏr'ganĭst. See ORGAN 1.
ŏrganīzā'tion, -īs- (-īz-), *n.* Organizing or being organized; organized body or system or society (~ **man,** one who regards these as taking priority over individuals' needs); hence ~AL *a.* [ME, f. med. L *organizatio*, or f. foll. + -ATION]
ŏr'ganīz|e, -īs|e (-īz), *v.t.* **1.** (usu. in *p.p.*) Furnish with organs, make organic, make into living being or tissue. **2.** Form into an organic whole, form (an organic whole); enrol as members of formal body, e.g. trade union; give orderly structure to, frame and put into working order, make arrangements for or initiate (undertaking involving co-operation). **3.** Hence ~ABLE *a.*, ~ER[1] *n.* [ME, f. OF *organiser* f. med. L *organizare* f. L (as ORGAN; see -IZE)]
ŏr'ganō- *comb. form.* **1.** (esp. Biol.) Organ, as: **~le'ptic,** affecting the organs of sense; **~the'rapy,** treatment of disease with extracts of organs. **2.** (Chem.) Organic, as: **~meta'llic,** (of compound) organic and containing a metal. [f. Gk (as ORGAN) + -O-]
ŏr'ganŏn, ŏr'ganum, *n.* Instrument of thought, means of reasoning, system of logic. [Gk (*-on*) & L (*-um*), see ORGAN; *Organon* was title of Aristotle's logical writings, and *Novum* (new) *Organum* that of Bacon's]
ŏrgă'nza *n.* Thin stiff transparent dress-fabric of silk or synthetic fibre. [prob. f. *Lorganza* **P**]
ŏr'ganzine (-ēn) *n.* Silk thread in which the main twist is in contrary direction to that of the strands. [f. F *organsin* f. It. *organzino*, of unkn. orig.]
ŏr'găsm *n.* Violent excitement, rage, paroxysm; climax of sexual excitement esp. in coition; hence **ŏrgă'sm**IC (-z-), **ŏrgă'st**IC, *adjs.* [f. F *orgasme* or mod. L f. Gk *orgasmos* (*orgaō* swell, be excited)]
ŏr'gėăt (*or* -zhah) *n.* Cooling drink made from barley or almonds and orange-flower water. [F, f. Prov. *orjat* (*ordi* barley f. L *hordeum*)]
ŏrgiă'stĭc *a.* Of the nature of an orgy. [f. Gk *orgiastikos* (*orgiastēs* agent-n. f. *orgiazō* celebrate orgy)]
ŏr'gūlous *a.* (arch.) Haughty; splendid. [ME, f. OF *orguillus* (*orguill* pride f. Frank. **urgōli*)]
ŏr'gy̆ *n.* **1.** (Gk & Rom. Ant.; usu. in *pl.*) Secret rites in worship of various gods, esp. in that of Bacchus celebrated with wild dancing, drinking, and singing. **2.** Drunken or licentious revel, (in *pl.*) revelry or debauchery; excessive indulgence in an activity. [orig. pl., f. F *orgies* f. L f. Gk *orgia* pl. f. IE **worg-* WORK[1]]
-ŏr'ial. See -ORY.
ŏ'rĭbĭ *n.* Small S. Afr. antelope of genus *Ourebia*. [Afrik., app. f. Hottentot]
ŏr'iel *n.* Large windowed polygonal recess built out usu. from upper storey and supported from ground or on corbels; ~ (**window**), window of oriel, projecting window of upper storey. [ME, f. OF *oriol* gallery, of unkn. orig.]
ŏr'ĭent[1] *n.* & *a.* **1.** *n.* (*O*~). (poet. or rhet.) *The* east. **2.** (*O*~). *The* East, *the* countries E. of Mediterranean, esp. E. Asia. **3.** Orient pearl. **4.** *a.* (poet.) Oriental. **5.** (Of precious stones and pearls of finest kinds, as coming anciently from the East) lustrous, sparkling, precious; (arch.) radiant, (of sun, daylight, etc., or fig.) rising, nascent. [ME f. OF, f. L *oriens -entis* rising, sunrise, east, (*oriri* rise; see -ENT)]
ŏr'ĭĕnt[2] (*or* ŏ'r-) *v.* **1.** *v.t.* Place (building etc.) so as to face E., build (church) with chancel end

due E., bury with feet eastward; place or exactly determine position of with regard to points of compass, settle or find bearings of, (fig.) bring into clearly understood relations, direct *towards*; ~ one**self,** determine how one stands in relation to one's surroundings. **2.** *v.i.* Turn eastward or in specified direction. [f. F *orienter* (*orient*: see prec.)]

ōriĕ'ntal (*or* ŏr-) *a.* & *n.* **1.** *a.* Of the Orient, of the East or countries E. of Mediterranean, esp. E. Asian; occurring in or coming from or characteristic of the civilization etc. of the East; hence ~ISM (2, 4), ~IST (3), *ns.*, ~IZE (2, 3) *v.i.*, & *t.* **2.** (arch.) Easterly. **3.** (Of pearl etc.) orient. **4.** Hence ~LY² *adv.* **5.** *n.* (*O*~). Native or inhabitant of the Orient. [ME f. OF, or f. L *orientalis* (as ORIENT¹; see -AL)]

ŏ'rientāte (*or* ōr'-) *v.t.* & *i.* = ORIENT². [prob. back form. f. foll.]

ōrientā'tion (*or* ōr-) *n.* Orienting (oneself) or being oriented; relative position; faculty by which birds etc. find their way home from a distance; ~ **course** (for information of newcomers to university etc.). [app. f. ORIENT² + -ATION]

ōrienteer'ing *n.* Competitive sport of finding one's way on foot across rough country with map and compass. [f. Sw. *orientering*]

ŏ'rifice *n.* Aperture, mouth of cavity, perforation, vent. [F, f. LL *orificium* (*os oris* mouth, *-ficere* = *facere* make)]

ŏ'riflămme *n.* Sacred banner of St. Denis, banderole of red silk on lance received by early French kings from abbot of St. Denis on starting for war; (fig.) anything material or ideal serving as rallying-point in struggle; bright conspicuous object, blaze of colour, etc. [ME f. OF, f. L *aurum* gold + *flamma* flame]

ŏriga'mi (-ah'-) *n.* Japanese art of folding paper into intricate designs. [Jap.]

ŏ'rigan, ori'ganum, *n.* Wild marjoram or other plant of genus *Origanum.* [(ME f. OF *origan*) f. L f. Gk *origanon*]

ŏ'rigin *n.* Derivation, beginning or rising or coming from something, person's ancestry, source, starting-point, (*a word of Latin origin*; *country of origin*; *a man of humble origin*); (Anat.) place at which muscle is more firmly attached or nerve begins in brain etc.; (Math.) fixed point from which co-ordinates are measured. [f. F *origine* or f. L *origo -ginis* (*oriri* rise)]

ori'ginal *a.* & *n.* **1.** *a.* Existing from the first, primitive, innate, initial, earliest; ~ **sin,** innate depravity held to be common to all human beings in consequence of the Fall. **2.** That has served as pattern, of which copy or translation has been made, not derivative or dependent, first-hand, not imitative, novel in character or style, inventive, creative, thinking or acting for oneself, (*where is the original picture?*; *what does the original Greek say?*; *is it an original drawing or a woodcut?*; *made a very original remark*; *has an original mind*); ~ **print** (made directly from artist's own work on wood, stone, etc., and printed by him or under his supervision). **3.** Hence or cogn. **originā'l**ITY *n.*, ~LY² *adv.* **4.** *n.* Pattern, original model, thing from which another is copied or translated, (*several transcripts from the same original*; *the original is in the National Gallery*; *reads 'Don Quixote' in the original*); eccentric person. [ME f. OF, or f. L *originalis* (as prec.; see -AL)]

ori'gin|āte *v.* **1.** *v.t.* Give origin to, initiate, cause to begin; hence ~ATIVE *a.* **2.** *v.i.* Have origin, begin, (usu. *from* or *in* thing or place, *with* or *from* person). **3.** So ~A'TION, ~**ā**TOR, *ns.* [f. med. L *originare* (as ORIGIN) + -ATE³]

ōrinā'sal (-z-) *a.* Of, sounded with, both mouth and nose (esp. of French nasalized vowels). [f. L *os oris* mouth + -I- + NASAL]

ōr'iōle *n.* Bird of genus *Oriolus*, esp. **golden** ~ with black and yellow plumage in male; Amer. bird of family Icteridae with similar coloration. [f. med. L *oriolus* f. OF *oriol* f. L *aureolus* dim. of *aureus* golden (*aurum* gold)]

Orī'on (*o*-) *n.* (Astron.) Brilliant constellation on equator, figured as hunter with belt and sword; ~**'s belt,** three bright stars in short line across middle of the constellation; ~**'s hound,** Sirius. [ME f. L, f. Gk *Ōriōn*, name of legendary hunter]

-ōr'ious. See -ORY.

ŏ'rison (-z-) *n.* (arch., usu. in *pl.*) A prayer. [ME, f. AF *ureison*, OF *oreison*, f. L (as ORATION); see -ISON]

-ōr'ium *suf.* forming *ns.* denoting place (*auditorium*, *crematorium*). [L, neut. of adjs. in *-orius* (see -ORY)]

Ori'ya (ōrē'*a*) *n.* (Member or language of) Hindu people of Orissa. [Hindi]

ōrle *n.* (Her.) Narrow band, or border of charges, near edge of shield. [F *o*(*u*)*rle* (*ourler* to hem f. Rom. **orulare* f. **orula* dim. of L *ora* edge)]

ōr'lop *n.* Lowest deck of ship with three or more decks. [ME, f. MDu. *overloop* covering (*overloopen* run over; see OVER-, LEAP¹)]

ōr'mer *n.* Edible univalve mollusc of genus *Haliotis*, sea-ear. [Channel-Is. F, f. F *ormier* f. L *auris maris* ear of sea]

ōr'molu (-lōō) *n.* Gilded bronze used in decorating furniture; gold-coloured alloy of copper, zinc, and tin; articles made of or decorated with these; (fig.) showy trash. [f. F *or moulu* powdered gold (for use in gilding)]

ōr'nament¹ *n.* **1.** (Eccl., usu. in *pl.*) Accessories of worship (e.g. altar, chalice, sacred vessels, service-books); ~(**s**) **rubric,** that immediately before Order for Morning and Evening Prayer in Book of Common Prayer. **2.** Thing used or serving to adorn, quality or person whose existence or presence confers grace or honour, (*mantelpiece crowded with ornaments*; *was an ornament to his country* or *age*). **3.** (Mus., in *pl.*) Grace-notes. **4.** Adorning, being adorned, embellishment, features or work added for decorative purposes, (*a tower rich in ornament*; *more for ornament than for use*). [ME f. AF *urnement*, OF *o*(*u*)*rnement* f. L *ornamentum* equipment (*ornare* adorn; see -MENT)]

ōr'namĕnt² *v.t.* Adorn, beautify; hence ~A'TION *n.* [f. prec.]

ōrnamĕ'ntal *a.* & *n.* **1.** *a.* Serving as or constituting ornament(s); hence ~ISM (3), ~IST (2, 3), *ns.*, ~LY² *adv.* **2.** *n.* Ornamental thing, esp. plant grown for its beauty. [f. ORNAMENT¹ + -AL]

ōrnā'te *a.* Elaborately adorned; (of literary style) embellished with flowery language etc.; hence ~LY² (-tlĭ) *adv.*, ~NESS (-tn-) *n.* [ME, f. L *ornatus* p.p. of *ornare* adorn; see -ATE²]

***ōr'ner|y̆** *a.* (colloq.) Of poor quality; coarse, unpleasant, cantankerous; hence ~**ĭ**NESS *n.* [var. of ORDINARY]

ōrni'thic *a.* Of or pertaining to birds. [f. Gk *ornithikos* birdlike (as foll.; see -IC)]

ōr'nitho- *comb. form.* Bird, as: ~**mancy,** divination by the flight and cries of birds; ~**rhy'nchus** (-rĭngk-), platypus [Gk *rhugkhos* bill]; ~**scopy** (-ŏ's-), observation of birds esp. by augurs. [Gk (*ornis ornithos* bird)]

ōrnĭthŏ'log|y̆ *n.* Study of birds; so **ōrnĭtholŏ'g**ICAL *a.*, ~IST (3) *n.* [f. mod. L *ornithologia* f. Gk *ornithologos* treating of birds (as prec.; see -LOGY)]

ōrogĕ'nĕsĭs, ōrŏ'genȳ, *ns.* (Geol.) Process of

formation of mountains; so **ōrogène'tic, ōrogĕ'nic,** *adjs.* [f. Gk *oros* mountain + GENESIS, -GENY]

ŏrŏ'graphy̆ (*or* ōr-) *n.* Branch of physical geography dealing with mountains; hence **ŏrogra'phic(al)** (*or* ōr-) *adjs.* [f. Gk *oros oreos* mountain + -O- + -GRAPHY]

ōr'ōide *n.* Gold-coloured alloy of copper and zinc. [f. *oreide* a similar or identical alloy, f. F *oréide* (OR[1] gold); assim. to -OID]

ŏrŏ'log|y̆ (*or* ōr-) *n.* Study of mountains; hence **ŏrolŏ'gical** *a.*, ~IST (3) *n.* [f. Gk *oros oreos* mountain + -O- + -LOGY]

ŏ'rotŭnd (*or* ōr'-) *a.* (Of utterance or phrasing) with full voice, imposing, dignified; pompous, magniloquent, pretentious. [f. L *ore rotundo* with well-turned speech, lit. with round mouth (Horace *Ars Poetica* 323)]

ōr'phan *n.* & *a.*, & *v.t.* **1.** *n.* & *a.* (Child) bereaved of parent(s); (fig.) (person) bereft of previous protection or advantages; hence ~HOOD *n.*, ~IZE (3) *v.t.* **2.** *v.t.* Bereave of parent(s). [ME, f. LL f. Gk *orphanos* bereaved]

ōr'phanage *n.* Orphanhood; institution for orphans' education etc. [f. prec. + -AGE]

Orphē'an (ōr-; *or* ōr'fĭ-) *a.* Like the music of Orpheus, melodious, entrancing. [f. L *Orpheus a.* f. Gk *Orpheios* (*Orpheus*; see foll.) + -AN]

Or'ph|ic (ōr'-) *a.* Of Orpheus or the mysteries or doctrines associated with his name, oracular, mysterious; Orphean; so ~ISM (3) *n.* [f. L f. Gk *Orphikos* (*Orpheus*, legendary Gk poet and lyre-player; see -IC)]

ōr'phrey, ōr'fray, *n.* Ornamental often richly embroidered stripes and borders of ecclesiastical vestment. [ME *orfreis* (taken as pl.) (gold) embroidery f. OF, f. med. L *aurifrisium* etc. f. L *aurum* gold + *Phrygius* Phrygian, also 'embroidered']

ōr'pĭment *n.* Arsenic trisulphide as mineral, formerly used as yellow dye and as artists' pigment; RED *orpiment*. [ME f. OF, f. L *auripigmentum* (*aurum* gold, *pigmentum* PIGMENT)]

ōr'pĭne, ōr'pĭn, *n.* Succulent herbaceous purple-flowered plant (*Sedum telephium*). [ME, f. OF *orpine*, prob. alt. of prec., orig. of yellow-flowered species of same genus]

Or'pĭngton (ōr'-) *n.* (Bird of) large breed of usu. buff white-legged poultry. [~ in Kent]

ŏ'rra *a.* (Sc.) Odd, not matched, occasional, extra. [18th c.; orig. unkn.]

ŏ'rrery̆ *n.* Clockwork model of the planetary system. [named after 4th Earl of *Orrery*, for whom one was made]

ŏ'rrĭs[1] *n.* Iris plant, esp. *Iris florentina*; ~**(-root)**, fragrant root of this or other iris used in perfumery and medicine; **~-powder,** powdered orris-root. [16th c., app. an unexpl. alt. of IRIS]

ŏ'rrĭs[2] *n.* Gold or silver lace or embroidery. [*c.* 1700, perh. alt. of *orfreis* ORPHREY]

ōrt *n.* (arch.; usu. in *pl.*) Refuse scrap(s), leavings. [ME, pl. f. MLG *orte*, perh. f. *o(o)r*-out (cf. ORDEAL) + *eten* EAT]

ōr'tho- *comb. form.* **1.** Straight, rectangular, upright, right, correct, as: **~cepha'lic,** with breadth of skull from ¾ to ⅘ of length, between mesocephalic and dolichocephalic; **~chroma'tic,** giving fairly correct relative intensity to colours in photography by being sensitive to all except red; **~clase,** common felspar in crystals with two cleavages at right angles [Gk *klasis* breaking]; **~do'ntia, ~do'ntics,** correction of irregularities in teeth and jaws; so **~do'ntic** *a.*, **~do'ntist** *n.*; **~ge'nesis,** view of evolution according to which variations follow a defined direction and are not merely sporadic and fortuitous; **~gnathous** (-ŏ'g-), upright-jawed, not prognathous; **~gonal** (-ŏ'g-), of or involving right angles; **~pterous** (-ŏ'p-), of the insect order Orthoptera with straight narrow forewings, including cockroaches, crickets, grasshoppers, etc.; **~rho'mbic,** (Cryst.) having three unequal axes at right angles to each other; **~tone,** (word) having independent accent, not enclitic or proclitic. **2.** (Chem.) (1) relating to two adjacent carbon atoms in benzene ring, (2) relating to acids and salts (e.g. *orthophosphates*) giving *meta-* compounds on removal of water; **~-hydrogen,** form of hydrogen molecule with nuclear spins in same direction. [f. Gk *orthos* straight + -O-]

ōr'thodŏx *a.* Holding correct or currently accepted opinions esp. on religious doctrine, not heretical or independent-minded or original; generally accepted as right or true esp. in theology, in harmony with what is authoritatively established, approved, conventional; (of Judaism) with strict retention of traditional observances; **O~ Church,** the Eastern or Greek Church separated from Western Church in 9th c., recognizing Patriarch of Constantinople as head, and the national Churches of Russia, Romania, Greece, etc., in communion with it; hence ~LY[2] *adv.* [f. eccl. L f. Gk ORTHO(*doxos* f. *doxa* opinion) right in opinion]

ōr'thodŏxy̆ *n.* Being orthodox. [f. LL f. late Gk *orthodoxia* sound doctrine (as prec.; see -Y[1])]

ōr'thōĕp|y̆ (*or* ōrthō'ĭpĭ) *n.* Science of (correct) pronunciation of words; hence ~IC (-ĕ'p-) *a.*, ~IST (3) *n.* [f. Gk ORTHO(*epeia* f. *epos* word) correct speech; see -Y[1]]

ōrthŏ'graphy̆ *n.* **1.** Correct or conventional spelling; spelling with reference to its correctness (*his orthography is shocking*). **2.** Perspective projection used in maps and elevations in which the observer is supposed infinitely distant so that the projection lines are parallel; map etc. so projected. **3.** So **ōrthogră'phic(al)** *adjs.*, **ōrthogră'phĭcally**[2] *adv.* [ME, f. OF *ortografie* f. L f. Gk ORTHO(*graphia* -GRAPHY)]

ōrthopae'd|ics, *-pē'-, *n.* Branch of surgery dealing with correction of deformities of bones or muscles, esp. in children; so ~IC *a.*, ~IST (3) *n.* [f. F ORTHO(*pédie* f. Gk *paideia* rearing of children) + -ICS]

ōrthŏ'pt|ic *a.* (Med.) Relating to correct or normal use of eyes; hence ~ICS *n.* (esp. of remedial treatment of eye-muscles), ~IST (3) *n.* [f. ORTHO- + Gk *optikos* of sight (see OPTIC)]

ōr'tolan *n.* Small Eur. bird (*Emberiza hortulana*) frequenting gardens, esteemed as table delicacy. [F f. Prov., lit. gardener f. L *hortulanus* (*hortulus* dim. of *hortus* garden; see -AN)]

Orvĭe'tō (ōrvĭā'tō) *n.* (*pl.* ~s). White wine made near *Orvieto* in central Italy.

Orwĕ'llĭan (ōr-) *a.* Of or characteristic of the writings of Orwell. [f. G. *Orwell*, pseudonym of E. A. Blair, Engl. writer of political satires (e.g. *1984*) d. 1950]

-ory̆ *suf.* forming: **1.** *ns.* usu. denoting place (*dormitory, glory, laboratory, oratory, refectory*) [f. ONF & AF *-orie*, OF *-oire* or f. L *-oria*, -ORIUM]. **2.** *adjs.* (& *ns.*) usu. w. sense of (person or thing) relating to or involving vbl action (*accessory, amatory, compulsory, inhibitory, perfunctory, predatory, promissory*). [f. AF *-ori(e)*, OF *-oir(e)* or f. L *-orius*]

ŏ'ry̆x *n.* Large straight-horned African antelope of genus *Oryx*. [ME f. L f. Gk *orux* stonemason's pickaxe, f. its pointed horns]

O.S. *abbr.* old style; ordinary seaman; ordnance survey; outsize; out of stock.

Os *symb.* osmium.

O.S.A. *abbr.* Order of St. Augustine.

O'sāge (ō'-) *n.* ~ **orange,** N. Amer. thorny tree (*Maclura pomifera*) with hard orange-coloured wood. [name of N. Amer. Indian tribe]

O.S.B. *abbr.* Order of St. Benedict.

O'scan (ŏ'-) *a.* & *n.* (Of or in) the ancient language of Campania, allied to Latin, surviving only in inscriptions. [f. L *Oscus* + -AN]

O'scar (ŏ'-) *n.* One of the statuettes awarded by the Academy of Motion Picture Arts & Sciences for excellence in film acting, directing, etc. [man's Christian name]

ŏ'scill|āte *v.* **1.** *v.i.* & *t.* (Cause to) swing like pendulum; move to and fro between two points. **2.** *v.i.* Vacillate, vary between extremes of opinion, action, condition, etc. **3.** (Electr., of current) undergo high-frequency alternations as across spark-gap or in valve-transmitter circuit; (of radio receiver) radiate electromagnetic waves owing to faulty operation. **4.** Hence or cogn. ~A'TION, ~**ātor**, *ns.*, ~**ātory** (*or* osĭ'la-) *a.* [f. L *oscillare* swing + -ATE[3]]

oscĭ'llo- *comb. form.* Oscillation esp. of electric current, as: ~**graph,** device for recording oscillations; ~**scope,** device for viewing oscillations, usu. by display on screen of cathode-ray tube. [f. as prec. + -O-]

ŏ'scine, ŏ'scinine, *adjs.* (Of bird) passerine. [f. L *oscen -cinis* song-bird (as OB-, *canere* sing) + -INE[1]]

ŏscĭtā'tion *n.* Yawning, drowsiness; inattention, negligence. [f. L *oscitatio* (*oscitare* gape f. *os* mouth, *citare* move; see -ATION)]

ŏ'scūlar *a.* Of the mouth; (joc.) of kissing. [f. L *osculum* mouth, kiss, (dim. of *os* mouth; see -CULE) + -AR[1]]

ŏ'scūl|āte *v.* **1.** *v.i.* & *t.* (arch. or joc.) Kiss. **2.** *v.i.* (Biol., of species etc.) be related through intermediate species etc., have common characters *with* another or with each other. **3.** *v.t.* (Math., of curve or surface) have contact of higher than first order with, meet at three or more coincident points. **4.** Hence or cogn. ~ANT *a.*, ~A'TION *n.* [f. L *osculari* kiss (as prec.) + -ATE[3]]

ŏ'scūlātorў *a.* & *n.* **1.** *a.* Of kissing or osculation. **2.** *n.* = PAX 1. [f. as prec. + -ORY]

ŏ'scūl|um *n.* (*pl.* ~**a**). Mouthlike aperture, esp. of sponge. [L; see OSCULAR]

-ōse[1] *suf.* forming *adjs.* denoting possession of a quality (*bellicose, grandiose, jocose, morose, verbose*); hence **-ōse**LY[2] (-slĭ) *adv. suf.*, **-ōse**NESS (-sn-) *n. suf.* (cf. -OSITY). [f. or after L *-osus*]

-ōse[2] *suf.* (Chem.) forming names of carbohydrates (*cellulose, sucrose*). [after GLUCOSE]

O.S.F. *abbr.* Order of St. Francis.

ō'sĭer (-z-; *or* ō'zher) *n.* (Shoot of) species of willow, esp. *Salix viminalis*, used in basketwork; ~**-bed,** place where these are grown. [ME f. OF; cf. med. L *auseria* osier-bed]

-ō'sĭs *suf.* forming *ns.* (*pl.* ~**o'ses** *pr.* -ō'sēz) denoting process or condition (*apotheosis, metamorphosis*), esp. pathological state (*acidosis, neurosis, thrombosis*). [f. L or f. Gk *-ōsis* suf. of vbl ns. (*-oō* vbl ending)]

-ŏ'sĭtў *suf.* forming *ns.* f. *adjs.* in -OSE[1] and -OUS (*verbosity, curiosity*). [f. F *-osité* or f. L *-ositas -ositatis*; see -ITY]

Osmă'nlĭ (ŏs-; *or* ŏz-) *a.* & *n.* = OTTOMAN[1]. [Turk. (*Osman* f. Arab. *'uṯmān* (see OTTOMAN[1]), *-lı* adj. suf.)]

ŏ'smĭum (ŏ'z-) *n.* Hard bluish-white metal of the platinum group, the heaviest known metal. [f. Gk *osmē* smell (from the pungent smell of its tetroxide) + -IUM]

ŏsmō's|ĭs (ŏz-) *n.* (*pl.* ~**es** *pr.* -ēz). Tendency of solvent to diffuse through porous partition into more concentrated solution; hence **ŏsmo**'TIC *a.*, **ŏsmŏ't**ICALLY *adv.*, (ŏz-). [orig. *osmose,* after F f. Gk *ōsmos* push; see -OSIS]

ŏ'smund (*or* ŏz-) *n.* Fern of genus *Osmunda*, esp. *O. regalis* with very large fronds. [ME, f. AF *osmunde*]

ŏ'sprey (*or* -ā) *n.* **1.** Large bird (*Pandion haliaetus*) preying on fish of inland waters. **2.** Egret-plume on woman's hat or bonnet. [ME, f. OF *ospres*, app. ult. repr. L *ossifraga* osprey (*os* bone, *frangere* break)]

ŏ'ssėĭn *n.* Organic substance of bones. [f. L (as foll.) + -IN]

ŏ'ssėous *a.* Consisting of bone, ossified; having bony skeleton (*osseous and cartilaginous fishes*). [f. L *osseus* (*os ossis* bone) + -OUS]

ŏ'ssĭa *conj.* (Mus.) Or (indicating an alternative and usu. easier passage to be played). [It.]

Ossĭă'nĭc (ŏ-) *a.* Of the (bombastic) style used in Macpherson's 18th-c. purported translations of Ossian's poems. [f. *Ossian*, legendary Gaelic bard + -IC]

ŏ'ssĭcle *n.* (Anat.) small bone, e.g. of middle ear; (Zool.) small piece of bony or chitinous or calcareous substance in animal framework. [f. L *ossiculum* dim. (as OSSEOUS; see -CULE)]

O'ssĭe (ŏ'zĭ) *n.* & *a.* (sl.) Australian. [abbr.; see -IE]

ŏ'ssĭfrage *n.* Osprey. [f. L *ossifrage*; see OSPREY]

ŏ'ssĭ|fў *v.i.* & *t.* Turn into bone, harden; make or become rigid or callous or unprogressive; so **ŏssĭ'**FIC *a.*, ~FICA'TION *n.* [f. F *ossifier* f. L *os ossis* bone; see -FY]

ŏ'ssūarў *n.* Receptacle for bones of dead, charnel-house, bone-urn; cave in which ancient bones are found. [f. LL *ossuarium* (irreg. f. *os*; see prec., -ARY[1])]

***O.S.T.** *abbr.* Office of Science and Technology.

ŏstėĭ'tĭs *n.* (Path.) Inflammation of bone substance. [f. Gk *osteon* bone + -ITIS]

ŏstĕ'nsĭb|le *a.* Professed, for show, put forward to conceal the real, (*his ostensible function was as interpreter*); hence ~LY[2] *adv.* [F, f. med. L *ostensibilis* f. L *ostendere -ens-* stretch out to view (as OB-, *tendere* stretch); see -IBLE]

ŏstĕ'nsĭve *a.* Directly demonstrative; (of definition) indicating by direct demonstration that which is signified by a term. [f. LL *ostensivus* (as prec.; see -IVE)]

ŏstĕ'nsorў *n.* Receptacle for displaying Host to congregation, monstrance. [f. med. L *ostensorium* (as OSTENSIBLE; see -ORY)]

ŏstĕntā't|ion *n.* Pretentious display esp. of wealth or luxury, showing off, attempt or intention to attract notice; hence ~IOUS *a.*, ~**ious**LY[2] *adv.*, (-shus). [ME f. OF, f. L *ostentatio -onis* (*ostentare* frequent. of *ostendere*; see OSTENSIBLE, -ATION)]

ŏ'stėō- *comb. form.* Bone, as: ~**-arthri'tis,** degenerative arthritis esp. in elderly persons; ~**ge'nesis,** formation of bone; ~**graphy** (-ŏ'g-), scientific description of the bones; ~**logy** (-ŏ'l-), anatomy dealing with skeleton and bones, animal's bony structure; ~**mala'cia,** softening of bone by loss of mineral substance; ~**myeli'tis,** inflammation of (esp. the marrow) of a bone; ~**phyte,** small outgrowth from bone; ~**poro'sis,** brittleness of bones due to porosity from loss of mineral substance. [f. Gk *osteon* bone + -O-]

ŏstėŏ'pathў *n.* Curative treatment aiming at correcting supposed deformation of spine etc. as cause of many diseases; hence **ŏ'stėo**PATH 1 *n.*, **ŏstėopă'th**IC *a.* [f. prec. + -PATHY]

ŏstĭna'tō (-ah'-) *n.* (*pl.* ~**s**) & *a.* (Mus.) (Melodic figure) repeated through all or part of a piece. [It., = OBSTINATE]

||**ŏ'stler** (ŏ'sl-) *n.* Stableman at inn. [f. earlier HOSTLER, *hosteler* f. AF; OF (*h*)*ostelier* f. as HOSTEL; see -ER[2]]

ŏ'strac|ize, -|ise (-īz), *v.t.* **1.** (In ancient Athens etc.) banish (dangerously powerful or unpopular citizen) for ten or five years by voting-system in which name of person to be ostracized was written on potsherd. **2.** Exclude from society, favour, or common privileges, refuse to associate with. **3.** So ~ISM (1) *n.* [f. Gk *ostrakizō* (*ostrakon* shell, potsherd)]

ŏ'strac|ŏn *n.* (*pl.* ~**a**). Potsherd used in ostracizing or for inscribing. [f. Gk *ostrakon* (see prec.)]

ŏ'strich *n.* Swift-running flightless African and formerly Arabian bird *Struthio camelus*, largest living bird, with wing and tail feathers valued as ornaments, swallowing hard substances to assist working of gizzard, and reputed to bury its head in sand when pursued, in the belief that it cannot be seen (*has the digestion of an ostrich*; *is following an ostrich policy*); (fig.) person who refuses to accept facts; **~-farm** (breeding ostriches for feathers); **~-plume,** feather or bunched feathers of ostrich. [ME, f. OF *ostric(h)e* f. Rom. **avistruthius* f. L *avis* bird, LL f. Gk *strouthiōn* ostrich (*strouthos* sparrow, ostrich)]

O'strogŏth (ŏ'-) *n.* Member of Eastern branch of Goths, who conquered Italy in 5th–6th c.; hence ~IC (-ŏ'th-) *a.* [f. LL *Ostrogothi* pl. f. Gmc **austro-* EAST + LL *Gothi* GOTHS]

-ot[1] *suf.* forming *ns.* (orig. dim.; *ballot, chariot, parrot*). [F]

-ot[2], **-ote,** *suf.* forming *ns.* denoting persons (*idiot, patriot, zealot*), e.g. natives etc. of a place (*Cypriot*). [f. F *-ote*, L *-ota* Gk *-ōtēs*]

O.T. *abbr.* Old Testament.

ō'tarỹ *n.* Eared SEAL[1]. [f. mod. L *otaria* f. Gk *ous ōtos* ear]

||**O.T.C.** *abbr.* Officers' Training Corps.

-ote. See -OT[2].

o'ther (ŭ'dh-) *a., n.* or *pron.,* & *adv.* **1.** *a.* Not the same as one or more or some already mentioned or implied, separate in identity, distinct in kind, alternative or further or additional, *the* etc. only remaining, (*we have other evidence*; *other people think otherwise*; *have no other place to go to*; *must leave it till some other time*; *on the other side of the river, of the road*; *a few other examples would be useful*; *give me some other ones*; *now open the, your, other eye*); **the ~ day, night, week,** etc., (*adv.*) a few days etc. ago; *on the other* HAND[1]; *other* RANK[1]*s*; **~ than** or (arch.) **from,** different from (*any person other than yourself*; *do not wish her other than she is*); ||*the other* PLACE[1]; **the ~ thing,** an unexpressed alternative; **~ things being equal,** if conditions are or were alike in everything but the point in question; *the other* WORLD; ANOTHER (||*A. N. Other*); EVERY *other*; NONE *other*; **someone, something, some time, some way,** etc., **or ~,** some unspecified or unknown person, thing, (at) some unspecified time, (in) some unspecified way, etc. **2.** (Often ellipt. with numerals, as) ANOTHER; **the ~ two,** etc., the other two etc. persons or things, of kind not needing specification. **3. ~-directed,** governed by external circumstances and trends; **~guess** *a.* [corrupt. of ~*gates* adv. & a. (GATE[2], -s[3]) in another way], (arch.) of very different kind; **~where(s),** (arch. or poet.) elsewhere; **~-wor'ldly,** concerned with the future life or some imagined world to the neglect of the present or real one. **4.** *n.* or *pron.* (orig. ellipt. use of *a.*, but now w. pl. usu. ~**s**). Other person, thing, specimen, etc. (*give me one other*, ANOTHER, *some others, the two others*; *do good to others*; *if this soap is, these pillows are, too soft, have you any other, others?*; *one or other of us will be there*; *he acts while others talk*; *where have the others got to?*; (arch.) *in other of his sermons*; *one* or *each neutralizes the other*); *they neutralize* EACH *other* or ONE *another*; *I can do* **no ~,** (arch.) nothing else; **of all ~s** (see OF 7). **5.** *adv.* Otherwise (*other than cursorily, than by repeating it*). [OE *ōther*, = OS *ōthar, andar*, OHG *andar*, ON *annarr*, Goth. *anthar* f. Gmc **antheraz.* f. IE **ánteros*]

o'thernĕss (ŭ'dh-) *n.* Being other, diversity, difference; thing or existence that is not the thing mentioned or the thinking subject. [f. prec. + -NESS]

o'therwīse (ŭ'dherwīz) *adv.* & *a.* **1.** *adv.* In a different way (*could not have acted otherwise*; *am otherwise engaged that day*; *Judas, otherwise* (*called* or *known as*) *Iscariot*; occas. preceded by *any* or *no* with reminiscence of its etym.: *could do it no otherwise*; *does not influence him any otherwise than by example*); if circumstances are or were or had been different, else, or else, (*seize the chance, otherwise you will regret it*); in other respects (*he is unruly, but not otherwise blameworthy*); **and ~, or ~,** = *and* or *or* followed by the negation or opposite of a preceding *n.* or *a.* (*the merits or otherwise of the Bill*, i.e. or demerits; *additions automatic and otherwise*, i.e. and not automatic); **~-minded,** having different, or jarring, inclinations or views, averse to current opinions. **2.** *a.* In a different state (*the matter is quite otherwise*; *a sentence I could wish otherwise*; *how can it be otherwise than useless?*); that would otherwise exist (*their otherwise dullness*). [OE *on ōthre wisan* (as OTHER, WISE[2])]

ō'tĭc *a.* Of or relating to the ear. [f. Gk *ōtikos* (*ous ōtos* ear; see -IC)]

-ŏ'tĭc *suf.* forming *adjs.* (& *ns.*) corresp. to *ns.* in -OSIS, in sense 'affected with or producing or resembling -osis' (*hypnotic, narcotic, neurotic, osmotic*); hence **-ŏ'tICALLY** *adv. suf.* [f. or after F *-otique* f. L f. Gk *-ōtikos* (*-ōtēs* n. suf., *-ōtos* a. suf.; see -IC)]

ō'tiōse (*or* ō'shĭ-) *a.* Not required, serving no practical purpose, functionless; (arch.) indolent or futile; hence ~LY[2] (-slĭ) *adv.*, ~NESS (-sn-) *n.* [f. L *otiosus* (*otium* leisure; see -OSE[1])]

otī'tĭs *n.* Inflammation of the ear; **~ media** (of the middle ear). [mod. L (as OTO-, -ITIS)]

ō'to- *comb. form.* Ear, as: **~lith,** particle or larger body of calcareous matter in ear; **~logy** (-ŏ'l-), science of ear diseases, anatomy of the ear, etc.; **~(rhino)laryngo'logy,** study of the ears, (nose,) and larynx; **~scope,** instrument for examining cavity of ear, or for auscultation of sounds in it. [Gk *ōto-* (*ous ōtos* ear; see -O-)]

ottava rima (otahva rē'ma) *n.* Stanza of eight lines, 11-syllabled in Italian, 10-syllabled in English, with rhymes *abababcc* (as in Byron's *Don Juan*). [It., lit. eighth rhyme]

ŏ'tter *n.* **1.** Furred aquatic fish-eating mammal of genus *Lutra* etc. with short legs, round feet, and webbed toes; its fur; SEA *otter*. **2.** Piece of board used to carry fishing-bait in water; type of paravane esp. as used on non-naval craft. **3. ~-board,** device for keeping mouth of trawl open; **~-dog, -hound,** (of breed used in otter-hunting); **~-spear** (used in otter-hunting). [OE *otr, ot(t)or*, = MDu., MLG *otter*, OHG *ottar*, ON *otr* f. Gmc **otraz* f. IE **udros*]

ŏ'ttō[1]. See ATTAR.

O'ttō[2] (ŏ'-) *n.* **~ engine,** type of internal combustion engine with four piston-strokes in cycle, as in most motor vehicles. [f. N. A. ~, Ger. engineer d. 1891]

O'ttoman[1] (ŏ'-) *a.* & *n.* **1.** *a.* Of the dynasty of Osman or Othman I, his branch of the Turks, or the empire ruled by his descendants; Turkish; *Ottoman* PORTE. **2.** *n.* Ottoman person, Turk. [F, f. Arab. *'uṯmānī* adj. of Othman (*'uṯmān*)]

ŏ'ttoman[2] *n.* Cushioned seat like sofa or chair without back or arms, often a box with cushioned top; footstool of similar design; heavy fabric of silk with cotton or wool. [f. F *ottomane* fem. (as prec.)]

O.U. *abbr.* ‖Open University; Oxford University.

oubliĕ'tte (ōō-) *n.* Secret dungeon with entrance only by trapdoor. [F (*oublier* forget); see -ETTE]

ouch[1] *n.* (arch.) Clasp or buckle, often jewelled; setting of precious stone. [ME *ouche* f. *nouche*, OF *nouche*, *nosche*, f. OFrank. *nuskja* buckle, clasp; for loss of *n-* cf. ADDER]

ouch[2] *int.* of pain or annoyance. [imit.; cf. G *autsch*]

O.U.D.S. *abbr.* Oxford University Dramatic Society.

ought[1], **aught**[2], (awt) *n.* (colloq.) Figure denoting nothing, nought. [perh. f. *an ought* for *a* NOUGHT; cf. ADDER]

ought[2] (awt) *v. aux.* (the only form in use, except arch. **~'est** or **~st**, is **ought** serving as present or past finite) expr. duty, rightness, shortcoming, advisability, or strong probability; *neg.* **~ not,** (colloq.) **~n't** *pr.* aw'tent, (vulg.) **didn't** or **hadn't ~**; the past sense (except when merely due to sequence of tenses in reporting etc.) is indicated by a following perf. inf.: *we ought to love our neighbours*; *it ought not to be allowed*; *you ought to know, to have known, better*; *you ought to have seen his face when he realized*; *he ought to be there by now*; *Cambridge ought to win*; *it ought to be done at once, to have been done long ago*; *I told you it ought to be, to have been, done*; *ought you to have done that?*; *I said it, and still think I ought to have said it*; *he ought to have been a lawyer, not a don.* [OE *āhte*, past of *āgan* OWE]

ought[3]. Var. of AUGHT[1].

ouija (wē'jah; *or* -yah; *or* -*a*) *n.* **~(-board)**, board lettered with alphabet and other signs, used with planchette or movable pointer to obtain messages in spiritualistic seances. [**P**; f. F *oui* yes and G *ja* yes]

ounce[1] *n.* Unit of weight, 1/16 lb. avoirdupois, 1/12 lb. (480 grains) in troy and apothecaries' weight; (fig.) small quantity (*an ounce of practice is worth a pound of theory*); ‖**fluid ~**, 8 drachms, 1/20 pint, 1·734 cu. in.; ***fluid ~**, 1/16 pint, 1·804 cu. in. [ME & OF *unce*, f. L *uncia* twelfth part of pound or foot (cf. INCH[1])]

ounce[2] *n.* Asian feline (*Uncia uncia*), the mountain panther or snow-leopard, smaller than leopard but marked like it. [ME, f. AF **unce*, OF *once* for earlier *lonce* (*l* mistaken for def. art.), = It. *lonza* f. Rom. **luncia* f. L LYNX]

O.U.P. *abbr.* Oxford University Press.

our *a.* **1.** Of or belonging to us (see WE), that we are concerned with or speaking or thinking of, (*is in our midst*; *our friend will have to watch his step*; *for all our sakes*; *acting on our behalf*; *have done our share*). **2.** Of all people; **Our Father,** (1) the creator of us human beings, (2) the LORD's Prayer; *Our* LADY, LORD, SAVIOUR. **3.** Of Us the king or queen, emperor or empress (*given under Our seal*); of us the present spokesman of a newspaper etc. (*a worthless book in our opinion*). [OE *ūre* orig. gen. pl. of 1st pers. pron. = of us (thus OS *ūser*, OHG *unsēr*, ON *vár*, Goth. *unsara*), later treated as possessive adj. (= OS *unsa*, OHG *unsēr*, ON *várr*, Goth. *unsar*)]

-our (*er*) *suf.*, = -OR in sense (1) (*colour*) or (arch.) other senses (*tenour*).

ours (-z) *pron.* & *pred. a.* **1.** The one(s) belonging to us (*ours is a large family*; *I like ours better*; *let me give you one of ours*; *look at* **this garden of ~**, this our garden). **2.** *pred. a.* Belonging to us (*became ours by purchase*). [ME, f. OUR + -S[3]]

oursĕ'lf *pron.* replacing MYSELF when used by sovereign, newspaper-writer, etc., who uses *we* instead of *I* (cf. OUR 3); = ONE*self* after *we* = ONE (*can we imagine a world in which ourself does not exist?*). [ME, f. as foll. + SELF]

oursĕ'lves (-vz) *pron.* **1.** (emphat.) We or us in person, in particular, in our normal condition, and not others, or alone, (usu. in apposition with *we*, and either next after it or later, rarely substituted for it; usu. substituted for *us*, rarely after it in apposition: *we ourselves will see to it*; *we will see to it ourselves*; *ourselves are first to be thought of*; *it was good for the others, if not for ourselves*; *let us do it ourselves*). **2.** (refl.) The person(s) previously described as *we* or *us* (*we shall only harm, do harm to, ourselves*; *we cannot persuade ourselves that the Government is in earnest*; *to see ourselves as others see us*). [ME *our*(*e*) *selfs*; cf. OUR, YOURSELVES]

-ous *suf.* forming *adjs.* meaning 'abounding in, characterized by, of the nature of' (*envious*, *fabulous*, *glorious*, *grievous*, *hazardous*, *mountainous*, *murderous*, *poisonous*); cf. -ACIOUS, -EOUS, -FEROUS, -IOUS, -VOROUS, etc.; (Chem.) denoting state of lower valence than -IC (*ferrous*); hence **-ous**LY[2] *adv. suf.*, **-ous**NESS *n. suf.* (cf. -OSITY). [f. or after AF *-ous*, OF *-eus*, f. L *-osus*; cf. -OSE[1]]

ousel. See OUZEL.

oust *v.t.* Put out of possession, eject, deprive *of*, expel *from*, drive out, force oneself or be put into the place of; so **~'**ER[4] *n.*, (Law & U.S.) ejection. [f. AF *ouster*, OF *oster* take away, f. L OB(*stare* stand) oppose, hinder]

out *adv.*, *prep.*, *n.*, *a.*, *int.*, & *v.t.* **1.** *adv.* Away from or not in or at a place, the right or normal state, the fashion, etc., (*keep him out*; *get out* (*of here*)!; TIDE[1] *is out*; *her son is out in Canada*; *anchored some way out*; *on the voyage out*; *crinolines are out*); not in one's house, office, etc., (*an evening* or *night out*; *go out for a walk, for a meal*); (of tooth) extracted; (of joint etc.) dislocated (*put his shoulder out*); (Polit., of party etc.) not in office; (of batsman, batter, etc.) no longer taking part as such because of having been caught etc. (*side was all out for 51*; **not ~**, not having been dismissed thus); away from centre of operations (*boarded out, contracted out*); (of time) not spent in working; (of workers) on strike; (of jury) considering verdict in private; (of fire, candle, etc.) no longer burning; no longer visible (*inscription has been painted out*); in error (*was 3% out in my calculations*; *your guess was not far out*); not worth considering (*that idea is out*); no longer on friendly terms (*with*); unconscious, (Boxing) unable to defend oneself (*out for the* COUNT[1]). **2.** In(to) the open, publicity, existence, notice, hearing, view, or clearness; (of book etc.) published; (of star etc.) visible at nightfall; (of flowers etc.) no longer in bud, open; (of chicken etc.) hatched; (of rash etc.) visible; (of secret) revealed; (of young woman, arch.) introduced to society; (w. superl.) known to exist (*is the best game out*); *out and* ABOUT; *out at* ELBOW[1]*s*; **~ for,** having one's interest or effort directed to, intent on; **~ to,** keenly striving to (do); ALL *out*; STRAIGHT *out*; WAY *out*; *murder*, *truth*, etc., **will ~**, is sure to be discovered; WRONG *side out*. **3.** To or at an end, completely, (*she had her cry* or *sleep out*; *tired out*; *sold out*; *storm blew itself out*; *hear me out*; *die out*; FIGHT[1] *it out*; *before the week is out*); in finished form (*have not typed it out yet*); (in radio conversation etc.) transmission ends; **~ and away,** by far; **~ and ~**, thorough(ly), surpassing(ly). **4. ~ of** *prep.*, from within, not within, from among, beyond range of, (so as to be) without, from, owing to, by use of (material), at specified distance from (town, port, etc.), beyond, transgressing rules of, (*come out of the house*; *I was never out of England*; *nine people out of ten know that*; *must choose out of these*; *is out of sight*; *was swindled out of his money*; *is out of breath, his mind, work, spades and hearts, sugar,* etc.; *get* *money out of him; got value out of the treatment; asked out of curiosity; what did you make it out of?; is seven miles out of Liverpool*), (of animal) having as dam (*filly out of Lutetia*); *out of* DATE[2]; *out of* DOORS; ~ **of drawing,** incorrectly drawn; *out of* HAND[1]; ~ **of it,** not included, forlorn; *out of* KEEPING; *out of* NUMBER[1], ORDER[1], POCKET[1], *the* QUESTION[1]; *out of* SORT[1]*s*; *out of the* WAY; *out of this* WORLD. **5.** *prep.* Out of (FROM 13 *out*); *out at (*looked out the window*). **6.** *n.* Way of escape; **at ~s,** at variance or enmity; **the ~s,** the party out of office; *the* IN[4]*s and outs.* **7.** *a.* (Of match) played away; (of island) away from the mainland; ~ **size** (beyond the ordinary; see OUTSIZE); **~-tray** (for documents etc. dealt with and to be taken elsewhere). **8.** *int.* = *get* etc. *out!*; (arch.) expr. abhorrence, reproach, etc., (*Out upon you!*). **9.** ~ **with,** let us eject, dismiss, etc., (unwanted person); ~ **with it,** say what you are thinking. **10.** *v.t.* Put out; (sl. or colloq.) eject forcibly; (Boxing) knock out. [OE (= OS, ON, Goth.) *ūt*, OHG *ūz*, cogn. w. Skr. *ud-*]

out- *pref.* = prec. *adv.* or *a.* or *prep.*, to *vbs.* or *ns.* **1.** To *vbs.*, w. sense of outward action, manifestation, completion, etc., (OUTBLAZE, OUTSPREAD). **2.** To participles and gerunds as in 1, but often with specialized sense (OUTCAST, OUTSTANDING). **3.** To *ns.* as in 1, giving sense of (a) vbl action (OUTBREAK, OUTBURST), (b) that which acts (OUTCROP, OUTGROWTH), (c) that which is acted upon, made, done, etc., (OUTCRY, OUTLOOK), (d) place or time of action (OUTLET, OUTSET). **4.** To *ns.*, w. sense (a) external (OUTLINE, OUTSIDE), (b) separate, away from the centre or main body, (OUTHOUSE, OUTPOST). **5.** To *ns.*, forming *adjs.* & *advs.* w. sense '(that is) out of' (OUTDOORS, OUTLAW). **6.** With general sense of excess, (a) to *vbs.*, w. idea of acting successfully or to a greater extent (OUTFACE), (b) to *vbs.* or *ns.*, forming *v.t.* whose obj. is a person or thing surpassed or defeated by more, better, or longer action (or action as) (OUTVOTE, OUTRUN, OUTGENERAL), (c) to *vbs.*, forming *v.t.* whose obj. is person or thing exceeded by continued action (OUTGROW, OUTLIVE, OUTSTAY), (d) to *ns.* or *adjs.*, forming *v.t.* whose obj. is person or thing surpassed in some respect (OUTCLASS, OUTNUMBER, OUTWIT), (e) to name of person noted for some quality, forming *v.t.* (usu. w. name repeated as obj.) indicating that even he is surpassed in that quality (OUT-HEROD).

out-ă'ct *v.t.* Surpass in acting or performing. [f. OUT- 6(b) + ACT[2]]

ou'tage *n.* Period of non-operation of power-supply etc. [f. OUT + -AGE]

out-and-ou'ter *n.* (sl.) Thorough or supreme person or thing; extremist. [f. OUT *and out* + -ER[1]]

ou'tbăck *n.* (esp. Austral.) Remote inland districts; hence **~ER[1]** *n.* [f. OUT + BACK[3]]

outbă'lance *v.t.* Outweigh (lit. or fig.). [f. OUT- 6(a) + BALANCE[2]]

outbĭ'd *v.t.* (**-dd-; outbi'd**). Bid higher than (other person) at auction; offer more than; surpass in exaggeration etc. [f. OUT- 6 (b) + BID[1]]

outblā'ze *v.* **1.** *v.i.* Blaze out(wards). **2.** *v.t.* Blaze more brightly than. [f. OUT- 1, 6(b) + BLAZE[2]]

ou'tboard *a.* & *adv.* On or towards, or nearer than something else to, outside of ship, aircraft, or vehicle; (of motor) attached externally to stern of boat. [f. OUT- 5 + BOARD[1]]

ou'tbound *a.* Outward bound. [f. OUT- 2 + BOUND[5]]

outbrā've *v.t.* Face defiantly; outdo in bravery. [f. OUT- 6(a, b) + BRAVE[2]]

ou'tbreak (-āk) *n.* Breaking out (esp. fig. of anger, war, disease, volcano, etc.); outcrop; insurrection. [f. OUT- 3 (a) + BREAK[2]]

ou'tbreedĭng *n.* Breeding from animals not closely related. [f. OUT- 2 + BREEDING]

ou'tbuĭldĭng (-bĭ-) *n.* Detached subordinate building, outhouse. [f. OUT- 4(b) + BUILDING]

ou'tbûrst *n.* Bursting out; explosion of feeling esp. in angry words; outcrop. [f. OUT- 3(a) + BURST[2]]

ou'tcast (-kah-) *a.* & *n.* (Person) cast out from home and friends; homeless and friendless (vagabond). [ME, f. OUT- 2 + p.p. of CAST[1]]

ou'tcaste[1] (-kah-) *n.* & *a.* (Ind.) (Person) who has lost his caste or has no caste. [f. OUT- 5 + CASTE]

outca'ste[2] (-kah'-) *v.t.* (Ind.) Cause (person) to lose his caste. [f. prec.]

outcla'ss (-ah's) *v.t.* Belong to higher class than; defeat easily. [f. OUT- 6(d) + CLASS]

||**ou't-cŏllėge** *a.* Belonging to college but not residing there. [f. OUT- 5 + COLLEGE]

ou'tcome (-ŭm) *n.* Result, visible effect. [f. OUT- 3(b) + obs. *come* n. (as COME)]

ou'tcrŏp *n.*, & *v.i.* (**-pp-**). **1.** *n.* Emergence of stratum, vein, or rock, at surface; stratum etc. thus emerging; (fig.) manifestation. **2.** *v.i.* Crop out, appear as outcrop. [f. OUT- 3(a, b) + CROP[1]]

ou'tcrȳ *n.* Crying out; clamour, uproar. [ME, f. OUT- 3(a, c) + CRY[1]]

outda'nce (-ah'ns) *v.t.* Surpass in dancing. [f. OUT- 6(b) + DANCE[1]]

outdār'e *v.t.* Overcome by daring; outdo in daring. [f. OUT- 6(a, b) + DARE]

outdā'tėd *a.* Out of date; obsolete. [p.p. of *outdate* v. f. OUT- 1 + DATE[3]]

outdĭ'stance *v.t.* Get far ahead of, leave (competitor) behind completely. [f. OUT- 6(d) + DISTANCE]

outdo' (-ōō') *v.t.* (**outdi'd; outdo'ne** *pr.* -dŭ'n; cf. DO[1]). Exceed or excel in doing or performance, be superior to, surpass. [f. OUT- 6(b) + DO[1]]

ou'tdoor (-ōr) *a.* Done or existing or used out of DOORS; ||**~ relief,** (Hist.) = OUT-RELIEF. [f. OUT- 5 + DOOR]

outdoor's (-ōr'z) *adv.* & *n.* **1.** *adv.* Outside buildings, out of doors, in or into the open air. **2.** *n.* The world outside buildings, the open air. [f. as prec. + -S[1]]

ou'ter *a.* & *n.* **1.** *a.* Farther from centre or inside, relatively far out, external, of the outside; objective, physical, not subjective or psychical; *outer* BAR[1]; ~ **garments, ~wear,** (worn over other clothes); **O~ House** (of Sc. Court of Session, where judges sit singly); ~ **man** or **woman,** personal appearance, dress; ~ **space,** universe beyond earth's atmosphere; **the ~ world,** people outside one's own circle; hence **~MOST** *a.* **2.** *n.* Division of target farthest from bull's-eye; shot that strikes this. [ME, f. OUT, replacing UTTER[1]]

outfā'ce *v.t.* Abash by staring or by confident demeanour; defy. [f. OUT- 6(a) + FACE[2]]

ou'tfall (-awl) *n.* Mouth of river, drain, etc., where it empties into sea etc. [f. OUT- 3(d) + FALL[2]]

ou'tfield *n.* **1.** Outer part of cricket or baseball field; hence **~ER[1]** *n.* **2.** Outlying land. [f. OUT- 4(b) + FIELD]

ou'tfightĭng (-fīt-) *n.* Fighting other than at close range. [f. OUT- 4(b) + FIGHT[1] + -ING[1]]

ou'tfĭt *n.* Complete equipment or set of things for a purpose; set of clothes to be worn together; (colloq.) group of persons regarded as a unit, organization. [f. OUT- 3(b) + FIT[4]]

For other words in *out-* see OUT-.

ou'tfĭtter *n.* Supplier of equipment, esp. men's clothing. [f. prec. + -ER[1]]

outflă'nk *v.t.* Have flank extending beyond that of (enemy); outmanœuvre (thus, or fig.). [f. OUT- 6(d) + FLANK]

ou'tflow (-ō) *n.* Outward flow; amount that flows out. [f. OUT- 3(a, b) + FLOW]

outflȳ' *v.t.* (**-flew'; -flow'n**). Surpass in flying; fly farther or faster than. [f. OUT- 6(b) + FLY[2]]

outfŏ'x *v.t.* (colloq.) Outwit. [f. OUT- 6(b) + FOX[2]]

outgĕ'neral *v.t.* (‖**-ll-**). Outdo in generalship; get the better of by superior strategy or tactics. [f. OUT- 6(b) + GENERAL]

outgō'[1] *v.t.* (**outwe'nt; outgo'ne** *pr.* -gŏ'n *or* -gaw'n; cf. GO[1]). (arch.) Go faster than; surpass. [f. OUT- 6(b) + GO[1]]

ou'tgō[2] *n.* (*pl.* **~es** *pr.* -ōz). Expenditure. [f. OUT- 3(b) + GO[2]]

ou'tgōing *a.* & *n.* **1.** *a.* Going out; retiring from office; friendly, sociable. **2.** *n.* Going out; (in *pl.*) expenditure. [f. OUT- 2, 3(a, b) + GOING[1,2]]

outgrow' (-ō') *v.t.* (**-grew'; -grow'n**). Grow faster than; become taller than (person) or too big for (clothes, one's strength); leave behind (childish ailment or habit or taste) as one grows or develops. [f. OUT- 6(b, c) + GROW]

ou'tgrowth (-ōth) *n.* Process of growing out; that which grows out; offshoot, natural product. [f. OUT- 3(a, b) + GROWTH]

outguĕ'ss (-gĕ's) *v.t.* Guess correctly what is intended by (another). [f. OUT- 6(a) + GUESS]

outgŭ'n *v.t.* (**-nn-**). Surpass in power of guns (lit. or fig.). [f. OUT- 6(d) + GUN]

out-hĕ'rod *v.t.* Exceed in evil or extravagance (usu. *out-herod Herod*). [f. OUT- 6(e) + *Herod*, blustering tyrant in miracle-plays, representing Herod (ruler of Judaea in time of Christ)]

ou'thouse (-t-h-) *n.* (*pl. pr.* -zĭz). House or building or shed belonging to main house and built near or against it; *outdoor lavatory. [ME, f. OUT- 4(b) + HOUSE[1]]

ou'tĭng *n.* Pleasure-trip, holiday away from home; appearance in outdoor contest etc. [f. OUT *v.* = put out, go out + -ING[1]]

outjŏ'ckey *v.t.* Outwit by adroitness or trickery. [f. OUT- 6(b) + JOCKEY[2]]

outjŭ'mp *v.t.* Surpass in jumping. [f. OUT- 6(b) + JUMP[2]]

outlă'ndĭsh *a.* Looking or sounding foreign; unfamiliar, bizarre, uncouth. [OE *ūtlendisc* (*ūtland* foreign country f. OUT + LAND[1]; see -ISH[1])]

outla'st (-lah'-) *v.t.* Last longer than (person, thing, or duration). [f. OUT- 6(a, b) + LAST[4]]

ou'tlaw *n.*, & *v.t.* **1.** *n.* Person deprived of protection of law; banished or exiled person. **2.** *v.t.* Declare (person) outlaw, make illegal, proscribe. **3.** So **~RY** *n.*, condition of or condemnation as outlaw. [OE (*ūtlagian* v. f.) *ūtlaga* f. ON *útlagi* (*útlagr* outlawed f. *út* OUT + **lagu* LAW[1])]

ou'tlay *n.* What is spent on something. [f. OUT- 3(c) + LAY[3]]

ou'tlĕt *n.* Means of exit or escape; market for goods; *(Electr.) power point. [ME, f. OUT- 3(d) + LET[2]]

ou'tlīer *n.* Outlying part or member; (Geol.) minor part of formation separated from main body by denudation. [f. OUT- 3(b) + LIE[3] + -ER[1]]

ou'tlīne *n.*, & *v.t.* **1.** *n.* (in *sing.* or *pl.*) Line(s) enclosing the apparently plane figure presented by any object to sight, contour, external boundary; sketch containing only contour lines and no shading (**in ~**, so sketched); rough draft, verbal description of essential parts only, summary; (in *pl.*) main features, general principles. **2.** *v.t.* Draw or describe in outline; mark outline of in decorating etc. [f. OUT- 4(a) + LINE[2]]

outlĭ've *v.t.* Live longer than; live beyond (specified period or date); live through (an experience); = LIVE[2] *down*. [ME, f. OUT- 6(b, c) + LIVE[2]]

ou'tlo͝ok *n.* Looking out; what is seen on looking out, view, prospect (esp. fig.); mental attitude. [f. OUT- 3(a, c) + LOOK]

ou'tlȳing *a.* Situated far from a centre, remote. [f. OUT- 2 + LYING[2]]

outmanœu'vre, *-maneu'ver, (-no͞o'ver) *v.t.* Outdo in manœuvring; outgeneral. [f. OUT- 6(b) + MANŒUVRE]

outmă'tch *v.t.* Be more than a match for, surpass. [f. OUT- 6(a) + MATCH[2]]

outmea'sure (-ĕ'zh*er*) *v.t.* Exceed in quantity or extent. [f. OUT- 6(a) + MEASURE[2]]

outmō'dėd *a.* No longer in fashion; obsolete. [f. OUT + MODE + -ED[1]]

ou'tmōst *a.* Outermost; uttermost. [ME, var. of *utmest* UTMOST]

ou'tnėss *n.* Externality, objectivity. [f. OUT + -NESS]

outnŭ'mber *v.t.* Exceed in number. [f. OUT- 6(d) + NUMBER[1]]

outpā'ce *v.t.* Go faster than, outdo in contest. [f. OUT- 6(d) + PACE[1]]

ou't-pātient (-shent) *n.* Hospital patient who is not in the hospital except briefly from time to time when receiving treatment. [f. OUT 7 + PATIENT]

ou't-pĕnsioner (-sho-) *n.* One who receives a pension from an institution without having to live there. [f. OUT 7 + PENSIONER]

outplay' *v.t.* Surpass in playing; play better than. [f. OUT- 6(b) + PLAY[1]]

outpoi'nt *v.t.* Score more points than. [f. OUT- 6(d) + POINT[1]]

ou'tpōst *n.* Post or detachment set at a distance from main body of army esp. to prevent surprise; distant branch or settlement. [f. OUT- 4(b) + POST[2]]

ou'tpourĭng (-pôr-) *n.* What is poured out; (usu. in *pl.*) spoken or written expression of emotion. [f. OUT- 3(c) + POUR + -ING[1]]

ou'tput (-o͝ot) *n.*, & *v.t.* (**-tt-; ou'tput** *or* **ou't-putted**). **1.** *n.* (Quantity or amount of) product of a process, esp. of manufacture, or of mental or artistic work; (Electr.) power etc. delivered by an apparatus; place where energy, information, etc., leaves a system. **2.** *v.t.* Put or send out; (of computer) supply (results etc.). [f. OUT- 3(c) + PUT[2]]

ou'trāge *n.*, & *v.t.* **1.** *n.* Forcible violation of others' rights, sentiments, etc. (*never safe from outrage*); deed of violence, gross or wanton offence or indignity (*an outrage upon decency, justice*, etc.); strong resentment (*at*). **2.** *v.t.* Do violence to, subject to outrage, injure, insult, violate, ravish; infringe (law, morality, etc.) flagrantly; cause to feel strong resentment. [ME, f. OF *outrage* (*outrer* exceed f. *outre* f. L *ultra* beyond; see -AGE)]

outrā'geous (-j*us*) *a.* Immoderate, extravagant, extraordinary; violent, furious; grossly cruel, immoral, offensive, or abusive; hence **~LY**[2] *adv.*, **~NESS** *n.* [ME, f. OF *outrageus* (as prec.; see -OUS)]

outrā'nge (-nj) *v.t.* (Of gun or its user) have longer range than. [f. OUT- 6(d) + RANGE[2]]

outră'nk *v.t.* Be superior in rank to. [f. OUT- 6(d) + RANK[1]]

outré (o͞o'trā) *a.* Outside the bounds of what is usual or proper; eccentric or indecorous. [F, p.p. of *outrer* (see OUTRAGE)]

outrea'ch *v.t.* Reach farther than; surpass; (poet.) stretch out (arm etc.). [f. OUT- 1, 6(b) + REACH[1]]

‖**ou't-rėlief** *n.* (Hist.) Assistance given to poor

persons not living in workhouse etc. [f. OUT 7 + RELIEF¹]

outrī'de *v.t.* (**-ro'de; -ri'dden**). Ride better, faster, or farther than; (of ship) come safely through (storm etc.). [f. OUT- 6(b, c) + RIDE]

ou'trīder *n.* Mounted attendant riding ahead of or with carriage; motor-cyclist acting as guard in similar manner; *herdsman keeping cattle within bounds. [f. OUT- 4(b) + RIDER]

ou'trĭgged (-gd) *a.* (Of boat etc.) having outriggers. [f. OUT- 2 + RIG¹ + -ED¹, after foll.]

ou'trĭgger (-g-) *n.* Beam, spar, or framework, rigged out and projecting from or over ship's side for various purposes; similar projecting beam etc. in building; log etc. fixed parallel to canoe to stabilize it; extension of splinter-bar enabling extra horse to be harnessed outside shafts, such horse; iron bracket bearing rowlock attached horizontally to boat's side to increase leverage of oar, boat with these. [f. OUT- 4(b) + RIG¹ + -ER¹; perh. partly after obs. (Naut.) *outligger*]

outright (-rīt) *adv.* & *a.* **1.** *adv.* (-ī't). Altogether, entirely, once for all, not by degrees or instalments or half and half, (*kill, buy, outright*); without reservation, openly. **2.** *a.* (ow'-). Downright, direct, thorough; hence ~NESS *n.* [ME, f. OUT + RIGHT⁴]

outrī'val *v.t.* (‖-ll-). Outdo as rival. [f. OUT- 6(a) + RIVAL]

outrŭ'n *v.t.* (**-nn-; -ra'n; -ru'n**). Run faster or farther than; escape; go beyond (specified point or limit). [f. OUT- 6(b, c) + RUN¹]

ou'trŭsh *n.* Rushing out; violent overflow. [f. OUT- 3(a, b) + RUSH²]

outsĕ'll *v.t.* (**-so'ld**). Sell more than; be sold in greater quantities than. [f. OUT- 6(b) + SELL]

ou'tsĕt *n.* Start, commencement, (*at* or *from the outset*). [f. OUT- 3(d) + SET²]

outshī'ne *v.t.* (**-sho'ne**). Shine brighter than; (fig.) surpass in splendour or excellence. [f. OUT- 6(b) + SHINE¹]

outside *n.*, *a.*, *adv.*, & *prep.* **1.** *n.* (-ī'd; *or* ow'-). External side or surface, outer parts, (*knows only the outsides of books*); (of path) side away from wall or next to road; external appearance, outward aspect; all that is without, the world as distinguished from the thinking subject, (*impressions from the outside*); position on outer side (*open the door from the outside; on the outside looking in*); (colloq.) highest computation (*there were a hundred, it is a mile, at the outside*); (in *pl.*) outer sheets of ream of paper; ‖(Hist.) passenger travelling on outside of coach etc.; outside player in football etc.; ~ **in,** = INSIDE *out.* **2.** *a.* (ow'-). Of, on, nearer, the outside, outer; ‖~ **broadcast** (not made from studio); ~ **edge,** progression on outer edge of one skate, (Cricket) edge of bat away from batsman; ~ **seat** (nearer the end); ~ **track** (longer because of curve); ~**work** (done off the premises). **3.** (Of a chance) remote, very unlikely; (of player in football etc.) positioned nearest to edge of field (*outside forward, left, three-quarter*, etc.); not belonging to some circle or institution; (of broker) not member of Stock Exchange; greatest existent or possible or probable (*quote the outside prices*). **4.** *adv.* (-ī'd). On or to the outside, the open air, open sea, etc., not within or enclosed or included; (sl.) not in prison; **come** ~, come out from room or house (esp. said as challenge to fight). **5.** ~ **and in,** outside and inside; ~ **of,** = sense 6; **get** ~ **of,** (sl.) eat or drink. **6.** *prep.* (-ī'd). External to, not included in, beyond the limits of, other than, not in, to or at the outside of, at or to the exterior of, (*natural forces are outside morality; cannot go outside the evidence; has few interests outside his work; met her outside the post office*). [f. OUT- 4(a) + SIDE¹]

outsī'der *n.* Non-member of some circle, party, profession, etc., uninitiated person, layman; person without special knowledge, breeding, etc., or not fit to mix with good society (RANK³ *outsider*); competitor thought to have no chance in race or competition. [f. prec. + -ER¹]

ou'tsīght (-īt) *n.* Sight of what is external (opp. *insight*). [f. OUT- 3(a) + SIGHT¹]

outsĭ't *v.t.* (**-tt-; -sa't**). Sit beyond duration of; sit longer than (another). [f. OUT- 6(b) + SIT]

ou'tsīze *a.* & *n.* (Of) exceptionally large size (in garments, measurements, etc.) or (fig.) exceptionally great development; outsize person or thing. [f. OUT 7 + SIZE¹]

ou'tskîrts *n. pl.* Outer border or fringe of town, district, subject, etc. [f. OUT- 4(b) + SKIRT + -S¹]

outsmâ'rt *v.t.* (colloq.) Outwit, be cleverer than. [f. OUT- 6(d) + SMART²]

outspă'n *v.* (**-nn-**) & *n.* (S. Afr.) **1.** *v.i.* & *t.* Unyoke, unharness. **2.** *n.* Act, time, or place of outspanning. [f. Du. *uitspannen* (as OUT, SPAN²); cf. INSPAN]

outspĕ'nd *v.t.* (**-spe'nt**). Spend more than (resources etc., or another). [f. OUT- 6(b) + SPEND]

outspō'ken *a.* Given to or involving plain speaking, frank; hence ~LY² *adv.*, ~NESS (-n-n-) *n.* [f. OUT- 2 + SPOKEN]

outsprea'd (-ĕ'd) *v.t.* (**outsprea'd**), & *a.* **1.** *v.t.* Spread out, expand. **2.** *a.* Spread out, fully extended or expanded. [ME, f. OUT- 1, 2 + SPREAD¹]

outstă'ndĭng *a.* Conspicuous, eminent, esp. by excellence, whence ~LY² *adv.*; that is not yet determined or settled. [f. OUT- 2 + STANDING²]

outstâr'e *v.t.* Outdo in staring; abash by staring. [f. OUT- 6(b) + STARE]

ou'tstātion *n.* Station at a distance from headquarters or from populous areas. [f. OUT- 4(b) + STATION]

outstay' *v.t.* Stay longer than (another); stay beyond the limit of (one's invitation etc.; *outstay* one's WELCOME). [f. OUT- 6(b, c) + STAY¹]

outstĕ'p *v.t.* (**-pp-**). Step outside or beyond. [f. OUT- 6(c) + STEP¹]

ou'tstrĕtched (-cht) *a.* Stretched out or forth (esp. of person's arms). [f. OUT- 2 + STRETCH + -ED¹]

outstrĭ'p *v.t.* (**-pp-**). Pass in running etc.; surpass in competition or relative progress or ability. [f. OUT- 6(b) + obs. *strip* run fast]

ou't-swinger *n.* (Cricket). Ball that swings away from batsman. [f. OUT- 3(b) + SWING*er*]

out-ta'lk (-aw'k) *v.t.* Outdo or overcome in talking. [f. OUT- 6(b) + TALK]

out-tŏ'p *v.t.* (**-pp-**). Surmount, surpass in height (lit. or fig.). [f. OUT- 6(d) + TOP¹]

ou't-tûrn *n.* Quantity produced; result of a process or sequence of events. [f. OUT- 3(c) + TURN²]

outvă'lūe *v.t.* Be of greater value than. [f. OUT- 6(d) + VALUE]

outvie' *v.t.* (**-vy'ing**). Outdo in contest or rivalry. [f. OUT- 6(b) + VIE]

outvō'te *v.t.* Defeat by majority of votes. [f. OUT- 6(b) + VOTE]

outwa'lk (-aw'k) *v.t.* Outdo in walking; walk beyond. [f. OUT- 6(b) + WALK¹]

ou'tward *a.*, *adv.*, & *n.* **1.** *a.* (arch.) Outer. **2.** Directed towards the outside; going out; bodily, external, material, visible, apparent, superficial; **the** ~ **eye** (opp. *mind's eye*); ~ **form,** appearance; ~ **man,** (Theol.) body as opp. soul, (joc.) clothing etc. (cf. OUTER *man*);

For other words in *out-* see OUT-.

to ~ seeming, apparently; ~ **things,** the world around us; hence ~LY² *adv.* **3.** *adv.* Outwards; ~ **bound,** (of ship or passenger) going away from home. **4.** *n.* Outward appearance. [OE *ūtweard* (as OUT, -WARD)]

ou'twardness *n.* External existence, objectivity; interest or belief in outward things, objective-mindedness. [f. prec. + -NESS]

ou'twards (-z) *adv.* In an outward direction; towards what is outside. [OE *ūtweardes* (as OUTWARD, -S³)]

outwa'tch (-ŏ'ch) *v.t.* Keep awake longer than; keep awake beyond end of (night etc.). [f. OUT- 6(b, c) + WATCH²]

outwear' (-ār') *v.t.* **(-wor'e; -wor'n).** Wear out or away; pass (time) by endurance; live beyond duration of (undesirable state). [f. OUT- 1, 6(c) + WEAR¹]

outwei'gh (-wā') *v.t.* Exceed in weight, value, importance, or influence. [f. OUT- 6(b) + WEIGH]

outwi't *v.t.* **(-tt-).** Be too clever or crafty for, deceive by greater ingenuity. [f. OUT- 6(d) + WIT²]

ou'twith (-dh) *prep.* (Sc.) Outside. [ME, f. OUT adv. + WITH]

ou'twork (-ĕrk) *n.* **1.** Advanced or detached part of fortification. **2.** Work done outside shop or factory that arranges it; hence ~ER¹ *n.* [f. OUT- 4(b) + WORK¹]

outwor'n *a.* Out of date, obsolete; worn out, exhausted. [f. OUT- 2 + WORN]

ou'zel, ou'sel, (ōō'zel) *n.* = RING¹ *ouzel*; **water ~**, diving bird of genus *Cinclus*. [OE *ōsle* blackbird, = OHG *amsala*; orig. unkn.]

ou'zō (ōō'-) *n.* (*pl.* **~s**). Greek spirituous drink flavoured with aniseed. [mod. Gk]

ō'va. See OVUM.

ō'val *a.* & *n.* **1.** *a.* Egg-shaped or ellipsoidal; having the outline of an egg, or elliptical; hence ~ITY (-ă'l-) *n.*, ~LY² *adv.*, ~NESS *n.* **2.** *n.* Closed curve with one axis considerably longer than the other, like ellipse or outline of egg; thing with oval outline; ||**the O~**, the Surrey County cricket ground at Kennington Oval in S. London. [f. med. L *ovalis* (as OVUM; see -AL)]

ō'var|y̆ *n.* **1.** Either of two reproductive organs in which ova are produced in female animals; hence **~ĭE'CTOMY, ~ĭŏ'TOMY, ~I'TIS,** *ns.* **2.** Lower part of pistil, consisting of one or more carpels, from which fruit is formed. **3.** Hence **ovār'IAN** *a.* [f. mod. L *ovarium* (as OVUM; see -ARY¹)]

ō'vāte¹ *a.* (Biol.) Egg-shaped as solid or in outline, oval. [f. L *ovatus* (as OVUM; see -ATE²)]

ō'vate² *n.* Member of third class of Welsh bards. [f. assumed L **Ovates* pl., Gk *Ouateis*]

ovā'tion *n.* Enthusiastic reception, spontaneous applause; (Rom. Ant.) lesser form of TRIUMPH. [f. L *ovatio* (*ovare* exult; see -ATION)]

o'ven (ŭ'-) *n.* **1.** Brick or stone or iron receptacle for baking bread or other food in; **Dutch ~**, (1) metal box of which open side is turned towards ordinary fire, (2) covered cooking-pot for braising etc. **2.** Chamber for heating or drying; small furnace or kiln used in chemistry, metallurgy, etc. **3. ~-bird,** S. Amer. bird of genus *Furnarius* making domed nests; **~-ready,** (of food) prepared before sale so as to be ready for immediate cooking in oven; **~ware,** dishes that can be used for cooking food in oven. [OE *ofen*, = OHG *ovan*, ON *ofn*, Goth. **auhns* f. Gmc **ohwnaz* f. IE **ukw(h)nos*]

ō'ver *adv.*, *n.*, *a.*, & *prep.* **1.** *adv.* Outward and downward from brink or from erect position (*lean, fall, jump, knock,* etc., *over*). **2.** So as to cover or touch whole surface (*brush, paint, it over*); ONCE-*over*. **3.** With motion above something, so as to pass across something, (*climb look, boil, over*). **4.** So as to produce fold or reverse position, upside down, (*bend it over*; TURN¹ *over*); overleaf (*see over*); (Cricket, as umpire's call) change to bowling from opposite end; *roll* ~ **and** ~, so that same point comes uppermost repeatedly. **5.** Across a street or other space or distance (*take this over to the post office*; *is over in, am going over to, has come over here from, America*); ~ **against,** in opposite situation to, adjacent to, in contrast with; **asked him ~** (to come as visitor from place not far off). **6.** With transference or change from one hand, party, etc., to another (*went over to the enemy*; *handed over the tickets*; GIVE¹ *over*); ~ **(to you),** (in radio conversation etc.) I await your reply, action, etc. **7.** Too, in excess, in addition, besides, more, apart, till later time, more (*anxious* etc.) than is right (see OVER- 6), (*shall have something over*; *£20 and over*); HOLD¹, STAND¹, *over*; **not ~ well** etc., fairly badly etc.; ~ **and above,** moreover, into the bargain. **8.** From beginning to end, with repetition, with detailed consideration, (*read, count, over*; *did it six times over*; *talk* or *think the matter over*); **(all) ~ again,** ***~,** (*begin* etc.) a second time (from the beginning); ~ **and** ~, many times. **9.** At an end, settled, (*the struggle is over*; *get it over* (*and done*) *with*). **10. All ~,** (1) completely finished, (2) in or on one's whole body etc. (*went hot and cold all over*; *is all over mud*), (3) in characteristic attitude, behaviour, etc. (*that is Jones all* ~, that is what one would expect of Jones). **11.** *n.* (Cricket). Number of balls (orig. 4 or 5, later 6 or 8) bowled between two calls of 'over' (sense 4); the play that results; MAIDEN *over*. **12.** *a.* Upper, outer, superior, extra, (usu. as pref.; see OVER- 1). **13.** *prep.* Above, in or to position higher than, on, at all or various points upon, to and fro upon, all through, round about, concerning, engaged with, (*an umbrella over his head*; *bridge over the Thames*; *projects over the street*; *doubt hangs over the question*; *writing over the signature 'Disgusted'*; *with his hat over his eyes*; *draw a veil over it*; *a change came over him*; *blush spread over his face*; *rice is grown all over India*; *you may travel over Europe* or *Europe over and not find it*; *the* WORLD *over*; *sitting over the fire, lunch, a glass of wine,* etc.; *heard it over the radio*; *spoke over the telephone*; *pause over the details*; *laugh over the absurdity of it*; *go to sleep over* one's *work*); (Math.) divided by (*a over b* = *a/b*); ~ **all,** from end to end (see OVERALL); **all ~,** in or on all parts of, (sl.) very attentive or effusive to (person); HAND¹ *over hand*; *over* one's HEAD¹; *over head and* EAR¹*s*. **14.** With or so as to get or give superiority or preference to, beyond, more than, in comparison with, (*is king, reigns, has jurisdiction, over*; *was victor, won the victory, was victorious, over*; *set him over the rest*; *has no control over herself*; *give me the preference over him*; *cost over £50*; *decrease of 25 over last year*); ~ **and above,** besides, not to mention. **15.** Out and down from, down from edge of, so as to clear, across, on or to the other side of, throughout, through duration of, till end of, (*fell over the edge, the precipice*; *stumbled over a tree-root*; *jumped over the brook*; *looking over the hedge*; *spoke over her shoulder*; *running over the meadow*; *if we can tide over the next month*; *has deteriorated over the years*; *will not live over today*; *can you stay over Wednesday?*); ~ **the way,** facing on opposite side of street. **16.** Hence ~LY² *adv.* (chiefly U.S. & Sc.), excessively, too. [OE *ofer*, = OS *obar*, OHG *ubar*, *ubiri*, ON *yfir*, Goth. *ufar*, f. Gmc **ubheri* f. IE **uperi* compar. of **upó* from under towards]

ō'ver- *pref.* = prec. *a.* or *prep.* or *adv.* **1.** To *ns.*, w. sense 'upper, outer, of higher kind, upside down, extra, to or in higher position', (OVERCOAT, OVERLORD, OVERTIME). **2.** As *prep.* to *ns.*, forming *n.*, *a.*, or *adv.*, (OVERALL, OVERBOARD, OVERTIME). **3.** As *prep.* to *vbs.*, forming *v.t.* whose obj. is that of *over* following the original *v.* in an equivalent phrase, & similarly to vbl derivs., (OVERHANG[1] a thing = *hang over* it; OVERCOME, OVERRIDE, OVERSIGHT). **4.** As *adv.* in local senses (above, by way of cover, down from above or from erectness, past, beyond, in addition) to *vbs.* or vbl derivs. (OVERSHADOW, OVERBALANCE[1], OVERWHELM, OVERTAKE, OVERHEAR). **5.** As *adv.* in sense of completely, effectually, into submission, to *vbs.* or vbl derivs. (OVERAWE, OVERJOYED). **6.** As *adv.* or *a.* to *vbs.*, *adjs.*, *advs.*, or *ns.*, with sense of excess over what is desirable or suitable or true, or over a definite limit, (OVERDO, OVERPAY, OVERWORK). **7.** As *adv.* to *vbs.*, with sense of harming oneself by doing action to excess (OVEREAT, OVERSLEEP). **8.** As *adv.* to *vbs.* or vbl derivs. or *adjs.*, with sense of 'more than' (OVERDUE, OVERFILL). **9.** As *prep.* to *n.*, *v.i.*, etc. forming *v.t.* usu. with sense of 'exceeding' (OVERPOWER, OVERTOP).

ōver-abou'nd *v.i.*, **-abŭ'ndance** *n.*, **-abŭ'ndant** *a.*, **-abŭ'ndantlў** *adv.* See OVER- 6.

ōvera'ct *v.t.* & *i.* Act (part, emotion, etc.), act part, with exaggeration. [f. OVER- 6 + ACT[2]]

ōver-ă'ctive *a.*, **-ăctĭ'vĭtў** *n.* See OVER- 6.

ō'verall (-awl) *n.*, *a.*, & *adv.* **1.** *n.* ||Garment worn over others as protection from wet, dirt, etc. while working; (in *pl.*) outer trousers or leggings or combination suit as protection from dirt in work or (child's) playing, ||close-fitting cavalry trousers. **2.** *a.* From end to end (*overall length*); total, inclusive of all; taking into account all aspects. **3.** *adv.* (*or* -aw'l). In all parts; taken as a whole. [f. OVER- 2 + ALL]

ōver-ănxī'etў (-ngz-) *n.*, **-ă'nxious** *a.*, **-ă'nxiouslў** *adv.*, (-ngkshŭ-). See OVER- 6.

ōverar'ch *v.t.* Form arch over; hence ~ING[2] *a.* [f. OVER- 4 + ARCH[2]]

ō'verarm *a.* & *adv.* (Cricket & Swimming) = OVERHAND. [f. OVER- 1 + ARM[1]]

ōverawe' *v.t.* Restrain by awe; keep in awe. [f. OVER- 5 + AWE]

ōverbă'lance[1] *v.* **1.** *v.t.* & *i.* (Cause to) lose balance and fall; capsize. **2.** *v.t.* Outweigh (lit. or fig.). [f. OVER- 4, 8 + BALANCE[2]]

ō'verbălance[2] *n.* (Amount of) excess. [f. prec.]

ōverbear' (-ār') *v.t.* (**-bor'e; -bor'ne**). Bear down or upset by weight or force; put down or repress by power or authority; surpass in importance etc., outweigh; hence ~ING[2] *a.*, domineering, masterful. [f. OVER- 4 + BEAR[3]]

ōverbĭ'd[1] *v.t.* (**-dd-; overbi'd**). Make higher bid than; (Bridge) (1) bid more on (one's hand, or abs.) than its strength warrants, (2) overcall. [f. OVER- 9, 6 + BID[1]]

ō'verbĭd[2] *n.* Bid that is higher than another or higher than is justified. [f. as prec. + BID[2]]

ō'verblouse (-z) *n.* Garment like BLOUSE 2 but worn without tucking into skirt or trousers. [f. OVER- 1 + BLOUSE]

ōverblow' (-ō') *v.t.* (**-blew'; -blow'n**). (Mus.) Blow (pipe etc.) so strongly as to produce harmonic instead of fundamental note. [f. OVER- 6 + BLOW[1]]

ōverblow'n (-ō'n) *a.* **1.** (Of storm etc.) passed over; excessively inflated or pretentious. **2.** (Of flower, or fig. of woman's beauty) too fully open, past its prime. [sense 1 p.p. of *overblow* f. OVER- 4, 6 + BLOW[1]; sense 2 f. OVER- 6 + p.p. of BLOW[3]]

ō'verboard *adv.* From within ship into water (*fall overboard*); **go ~**, (colloq.) be highly enthusiastic; **throw ~**, lit., or fig. = abandon, discard. [f. OVER- 2 + BOARD[1]]

ōverbō'ld *a.* See OVER- 6.

ōverbŏŏ'k *v.t.* Make too many bookings for (aircraft flight etc., or abs.). [f. OVER- 8 + BOOK[2]]

ō'verbōōt *n.* Boot worn over other boot or shoe. [f. OVER- 1 + BOOT[1]]

ōverbrĭ'm *v.* (**-mm-**). **1.** *v.t.* Flow over brim of (*the liquor that o'erbrims the cup*). **2.** *v.i.* (Of vessel or liquid) overflow at the brim. [f. OVER- 3 + BRIM[2]]

ōverbuĭ'ld (-bĭ'-) *v.t.* (**-bui'lt**). Build over or upon; place too many buildings on (land). [f. OVER- 3, 9 + BUILD[1]]

ōverbûr'den[1] *v.t.*, **-bûr'densome** *a.* See OVER- 6.

ō'verbûrden[2] *n.* Excessive burden; (Mining etc.) rock etc. that is to be removed in order to expose the deposit sought. [f. OVER- 4, 1 + BURDEN[1]]

ōverbu'sў (-bĭ'zĭ) *a.*, **-buy'** (-bī') *v.t.* & *i.* See OVER- 6.

ōverca'll[1] (-aw'l) *v.t.* (Bridge). Make higher bid than (previous bid, opponent, or abs.); || = OVERBID[1] (1). [f. OVER- 9, 6 + CALL[1]]

ō'vercall[2] (-awl) *n.* (Bridge). Act or instance of overcalling. [f. as prec. + CALL[2]]

ōvercă'nopў *v.t.* (literary). Form canopy over. [f. OVER- 4 + CANOPY]

ōvercă'pĭtalize, -ise (-īz), *v.t.* Fix or estimate capital of (company etc.) too high. [f. OVER- 6 + CAPITALIZE]

ōver-car'eful (-ār'f-) *a.* See OVER- 6.

ōverca'st[1] (-ah'-) *v.t.* (**overca'st**). **1.** (esp. in *p.p.*) Cover (sky etc.) with clouds or darkness. **2.** Stitch over (edge) to prevent unravelling. [ME, f. OVER- 9 + CAST[1]]

ō'vercast[2] (-ah-) *n.* Cloud covering (part of) sky. [f. prec.]

ōver-cau'tion *n.*, **-cau'tious** (-shŭs) *a.* See OVER- 6.

ōverchar'ge[1] *v.t.* Put too much (explosive, electric, etc.) charge into; put exaggerated or excessive detail into (description, picture, etc.); charge too high a price for (thing) or to (person); charge (specified sum) beyond right price. [ME, f. OVER- 6 + CHARGE[2]]

ō'vercharge[2] *n.* Excessive charge (of explosive etc. or of money; see prec.). [f. OVER- 6 + CHARGE[1]]

ō'verchĕck *n.* (Cloth with) combination of two different-sized check patterns. [f. OVER- 1 + CHECK[3]]

ōverclou'd *v.t.* Cover (as) with cloud(s); make obscure. [f. OVER- 4 + CLOUD]

ō'vercoat *n.* Coat worn outside another, esp. over indoor clothes for warmth in cold weather; protective coat of paint etc. [f. OVER- 1 + COAT]

ōverco'me (-ŭ'm) *v.* (**-ca'me; -co'me**). **1.** *v.t.* Prevail over, master; (in *p.p.*) exhausted, made helpless, affected with great emotion (*with* or *by*); **~ with liquor**, drunk. **2.** *v.i.* Be victorious. [OE *ofercuman* (as OVER- 3, COME)]

ōver-cŏmpĕnsā'tion *n.* (Psych.) Exaggerated correction of real or fancied defect of character. [f. OVER- 6 + COMPENSATION]

ōver-cŏ'nfĭdence *n.*, **-cŏ'nfĭdent** *a.*, **-cŏ'nfĭdentlў** *adv.*, **-cōō'ked** (-kt) *a.*, **-crēdū'lĭtў** *n.*, **-crĕ'dūlous** *a.* See OVER- 6.

ōvercrŏ'p *v.t.* (**-pp-**). Exhaust (land) by continuous cropping. [f. OVER- 6 + CROP[2]]

ōvercrow' (-ō) *v.t.* Exult or triumph over. [f. OVER- 3 + CROW[3]]

ōvercrow'd *v.t.*, **-cūrĭŏ'sĭtў** *n.*, **-cūr'ĭous** *a.*, **-cūr'ĭouslў** *adv.*, **-dĕ'lĭcacў** *n.*, **-dĕ'lĭcate** *a.* See OVER- 6.

For other words in *over-* see OVER-.

ōverdėvě'lop *v.t.* Develop too greatly; (Photog.) treat with developer for too long or otherwise excessively. [f. OVER- 6 + DEVELOP]

ōverdo' (-o͞o') *v.t.* (**overdi'd; overdo'ne** *pr.* -dŭ'n; cf. DO[1]). Carry to excess, go too far in; (esp. in *p.p.*) cook too much; fatigue, exhaust; ~ **it** or **things,** (1) work too hard, (2) exaggerate, carry an action too far. [OE *oferdōn* (as OVER- 6, DO[1])]

ō'verdōse[1] *n.* Excessive dose (of drug etc.). [f. OVER- 6 + DOSE]

ōverdō'se[2] *v.t.* Give excessive dose of or to. [f. OVER- 6 + DOSE]

ō'verdraft (-ahft) *n.* Overdrawing of bank account; amount by which sums drawn exceed credit balance. [f. OVER- 6 + DRAFT[1]]

ōverdraw' *v.* (**-drew'; -draw'n**). **1.** *v.t.* Draw cheque in excess of the amount credited to (one's account); (in *p.p.*) having overdrawn one's account; exaggerate in describing or depicting. **2.** *v.i.* Overdraw one's account. [f. OVER- 6 + DRAW[1]]

ōverdrě'ss[1] *v.* **1.** *v.t.* Dress with too much display or formality. **2.** *v.i.* Overdress oneself. [f. OVER- 6 + DRESS[1]]

ō'verdrěss[2] *n.* Dress worn over another dress or a blouse etc. [f. OVER- 1 + DRESS[2]]

ōverdrǐ'nk *v.i.* & *refl.* (**-dra'nk; -dru'nk**). Drink too much. [f. OVER- 7 + DRINK[1]]

ōverdrī've[1] *v.t.* (**-dro've; -dri'ven**). Drive (horse etc.), work (person), to exhaustion. [f. OVER- 6 + DRIVE[1]]

ō'verdrīve[2] *n.* Mechanism in motor vehicle providing gear ratio higher than that of usual top gear. [f. OVER- 1 + DRIVE[2]]

ōverdūe' *a.* Past the time when due or ready; not yet paid, arrived, born, etc., though after the expected time. [f. OVER- 8 + DUE[1]]

ōver-ea'ger *a.*, **-ea'gerlỹ** *adv.*, **-ea'gernėss** *n.*, (-g-), **-ear'nėst** (-ẽr'-) *a.* See OVER- 6.

ōverea't *v.i.* & *refl.* (**-a'te; -ea'ten**). Eat too much. [f. OVER- 7 + EAT]

ōver-ě'mphasǐs *n.*, **-ě'mphasīze** *v.t.* See OVER- 6.

ōverě'stǐm|āte[1] *v.t.* Form too high an estimate of; hence ~A'TION *n.* [f. OVER- 6 + ESTIMATE[2]]

ōverě'stǐmate[2] *n.* Too high an estimate. [f. OVER- 6 + ESTIMATE[1]]

ōver-ėxci'te *v.t.*, **-ėxẽr'tion** (-gz-) *n.*, **-ėxpō'se** (-z) *v.t.*, **-ėxpō'sure** (-zh*er*) *n.* See OVER- 6.

ō'verfall (-awl) *n.* Turbulent stretch of sea etc. caused by strong current or tide over submarine ridge, or by meeting of currents; structure for overflow of water from canal or lock. [f. OVER- 4 + FALL[2]]

ōver-fati'gue (-ē'g) *v.t.*, & *n.* See OVER- 6.

ōverfee'd *v.i.* & *t.* (**-fe'd**). Feed too much. [f. OVER- 7 + FEED[1]]

ōverfǐ'll *v.t.* & *i.* Fill to overflowing. [OE *oferfyllan* (as OVER- 8, FILL)]

ōverfǐ'sh *v.t.* Fish (stream etc.) too much and thus deplete it. [f. OVER- 6 + FISH[2]]

ōverflow'[1] (-ō') *v.* **1.** *v.t.* Flow over (brim etc.); flow over brim of; flood (surface); (of crowd etc.) extend beyond limits of (room etc.). **2.** *v.i.* (Of receptacle) be so full that contents overflow it, (of contents) overflow container; (of kindness, harvest, etc.) be very abundant. [f. OE *oferflōwan* (as OVER- 3, FLOW)]

ō'verflow[2] (-ō) *n.* What overflows or is superfluous; outlet for excess liquid; ~ **meeting** (for those who cannot find room at principal meeting, and therefore meet elsewhere). [f. (as) prec.]

ōverflȳ' *v.t.* (**-flew'; -flow'n**). Fly over or beyond (place or territory); so **ō'ver**FLIGHT[1] *n.* [f. OVER- 3 + FLY[2]]

ō'verfōld *n.* (Geol.) Fold of strata such that middle part is upside down. [f. OVER- 4 + FOLD[2]]

ōverfŏ'nd *a.* ~ **of,** having too great an affection or liking for; hence ~LY[2] *adv.*, ~NESS *n.* [f. OVER- 6 + FOND]

ōverfulfǐ'l, *-ll, (-fo͝ol-) *v.t.* (**-ll-**). Fulfil (plan etc.) before appointed time; hence ~MENT *n.* [f. OVER- 6 + FULFIL]

ōverfu'll (-o͝o'l) *a.* Filled to overflowing or excessively. [f. OVER- 8 + FULL[1]]

ō'verglāze *n.* & *a.* **1.** *n.* Second glaze applied to pottery. **2.** *a.* (Of painting etc.) done on glazed surface. [f. OVER- 1, 2 + GLAZE]

ō'verground *a.* Raised above the ground; not underground. [f. OVER- 2 + GROUND[1]]

ōvergrow' (-ō') *v.t.* (**-grew'; -grow'n;** esp. in *p.p.*, of plants, lit. or fig.). Grow over, overspread; grow over so as to choke; grow too big for (one's strength etc.); so **ō'ver**GROWTH *n.* [ME, f. OVER- 3, 6, 7 + GROW]

ō'verhănd *a.* & *adv.* With hand above object held; with hand above shoulder (*overhand bowling*); with palm of hand downward or inward; (Swimming) with one or both arms lifted out of water during stroke; ~ **knot,** simple knot made by forming loop and passing free end through it. [f. OVER- 1 + HAND[1]]

ōverhă'ng[1] *v.t.* & *i.* (**-hu'ng**). Jut out (over); (fig.) impend (over). [f. OVER- 3 + HANG[1]]

ō'verhăng[2] *n.* Fact or amount of overhanging; overhanging part. [f. prec.]

ōver-hā'ste *n.*, **-hā'stǐlȳ** *adv.*, **-hā'stȳ** *a.* See OVER- 6.

ōverhau'l[1] *v.t.* Take to pieces in order to examine; examine condition of (and repair if necessary); overtake. [orig. Naut., = release (rope-tackle) by slackening, f. OVER- 4 + HAUL]

ō'verhaul[2] *n.* Thorough examination (with repairs if necessary). [f. prec.]

ōverhea'd[1] (-ě'd) *adv.* Above one's head; in the sky or in the storey above. [f. OVER- 2 + HEAD[1]]

ō'verhead[2] (-ěd) *a.* & *n.* **1.** *a.* Placed overhead (*overhead wires*); (of driving mechanism) above the object driven; (of expenses) arising from management, office supplies, interest on borrowed capital, etc., as distinct from business transactions. **2.** *n.* (in *pl.* or **sing.*) Overhead expenses. [f. prec.]

ōverhear' *v.t.* (**-hear'd**). Hear as eavesdropper or as unperceived or unintentional listener. [f. OVER- 4 + HEAR]

ōverhea't *v.t.* Heat to excess, make too hot (lit. or fig.); (in *p.p.*) too passionate about a matter. [ME, f. OVER- 6 + HEAT[2]]

ōver-ǐndŭ'lge *v.t.* & *i.*, **-ǐndŭ'lgence** *n.*, **-ǐndŭ'lgent** *a.* See OVER- 6.

ōver-ǐ'ssūe (*or* -ǐ'sho͞o) *v.t.*, & *n.* **1.** *v.t.* Issue notes, shares, etc.) beyond authorized amount or ability to pay. **2.** *n.* Things or amount so issued. [f. OVER- 6 + ISSUE[2]]

ōverjoy'ed (-oi'd) *a.* Filled with extreme joy (*at*). [p.p. of *overjoy*, f. OVER- 5 + JOY[2]]

ō'verkǐll *n.* Amount by which (capacity for) destruction (lit. or fig.) exceeds what is necessary for victory over or annihilation of enemy. [f. OVER- 6 + KILL[2]]

ōver-lā'bour (-*er*), ***-lā'bor,** *v.t.*, **-lā'den** *a.* See OVER- 6.

ōverlă'nd[1] *adv.* By land, not by sea. [f. OVER- 2 + LAND[1]]

ō'verlănd[2] *a.* & *v.* **1.** *a.* (Proceeding) entirely or partly by land. **2.** *v.t.* & *i.* (Austral.) Drive (livestock) or go long distance overland; hence ~ER[1] *n.* [f. prec.]

ōverlă'p[1] *v.* (**-pp-**). **1.** *v.t.* Partly cover; cover and extend beyond. **2.** *v.i.* (Of two or more things) partly coincide, not be completely separate. [f. OVER- 3 + LAP[2]]

ō'verlăp[2] *n.* Fact or process or amount of overlapping; overlapping part. [f. prec.]

ōver-lar'ge *a.* See OVER- 6.

ōverlay'[1] *v.t.* (**-lai'd**). **1.** Cover surface of *with* coating etc. **2.** Overlie. [ME, f. OVER- 4 + LAY[3]]

ō'verlay[2] *n.* Thing laid over another; coverlet, small tablecloth, etc.; transparent sheet to be superimposed on another sheet. [f. prec.]

ōverlay'[3]. See OVERLIE.

ōverlea'f *adv.* On other side of leaf (of book). [f. OVER- 2 + LEAF]

ōverlea'p *v.t.* (for forms see LEAP[1]). Leap over, surmount; omit, ignore. [OE *oferhlēapan* (as OVER- 3, LEAP[1])]

ōverlie' *v.t.* (**-ly'ing; -lay'; -lai'n**). Lie on top of; smother (child) thus. [ME, f. OVER- 3 + LIE[3]]

ōverlĭ've *v.t.* Live beyond (specified age, another, or abs.). [OE *oferlibban* (as OVER- 9, LIVE[2])]

ōverloa'd[1] *v.t.*, **ō'verload**[2] *n.*, **ōver-lŏ'ng** *a.* See OVER- 6.

ōverloo'k *v.t.* **1.** Have prospect of or over from above; be higher than. **2.** Fail to observe; take no notice of, allow (offence) to go unpunished. **3.** Superintend, oversee; hence ~ER[1] (ō'-) *n.* **4.** Bewitch with the evil eye. [ME, f. OVER- 3 + LOOK]

ō'verlord *n.* Supreme lord, suzerain; hence ~SHIP *n.* [ME, f. OVER- 1 + LORD]

ō'verlў. See OVER 16.

ō'ver|măn[1] *n.* (*pl.* **~men**). Overseer in colliery; (Philos.) = SUPERMAN. [f. OVER- 1 + MAN[1]]

ōvermă'n[2] *v.t.* (**-nn-**). Provide with too many men as crew, staff, etc. [f. OVER- 6 + MAN[2]]

ō'vermăntel *n.* Ornamental shelves etc. over mantelpiece. [f. OVER- 2 + MANTEL]

ōver-ma'nў (-ĕ'-) *a.* See OVER- 6.

ōverma'ster (-ah'-) *v.t.* (usu. fig.) Master completely, conquer; hence ~ING[2] *a.* [ME, f. OVER- 5 + MASTER[2]]

ōvermă'tch *v.t.* Be more than a match for, defeat by superior strength etc. [f. OVER- 8 + MATCH[2]]

ō'ver-measure (-ĕ'zh*er*) *n.* Amount beyond what is proper or sufficient. [f. OVER- 6 + MEASURE[1]]

ōver-mŏ'dėst *a.*, **-mŏ'dėstlў** *adv.*, **-mŭ'ch** *a.*, *n.*, & *adv.*, **-nī'ce** *a.*, **-nī'cenėss** (-sn-), **-nī'cėtў,** *ns.* See OVER- 6.

ōvernī'ght[1] (-ī't) *adv.* On the preceding evening with a view to, or as regarded from, the next day; from one day to the next (*stayed overnight*; *cannot change* one's *habits overnight*). [ME, f. OVER- 2 + NIGHT]

ō'vernīght[2] (-īt) *a.* Done etc. overnight; for use etc. overnight. [f. prec.]

ōverpa'ss[1] (-ah's) *v.t.* Pass over or across or beyond; get to the end of, surmount. [ME, f. OVER- 3 + PASS[1]]

ō'verpass[2] (-ahs) *n.* Road that crosses another by means of bridge. [f. OVER- 4 + PASS[2]]

ōverpa'ssed, ōverpa'st, (-ah'st) *a.* That has gone by, past. [p.p. of OVERPASS[1]; cf. PAST[1]]

ōverpay' *v.t.* (**-pai'd**). Recompense (person, service) too highly; hence ~MENT *n.* [f. OVER- 6 + PAY[2]]

ōver-peo'pled (-ē'peld) *a.* Containing too many people. [f. OVER- 6 + PEOPLE + -ED[1]]

ōverpersuā'de (-sw-) *v.t.* Persuade (person) in spite of his contrary judgement or inclination. [f. OVER- 5 + PERSUADE]

ōverpĭ'tch *v.t.* (Cricket) bowl (ball) so that it pitches or would pitch too near the stumps; (fig.) exaggerate. [f. OVER- 6 + PITCH[2]]

ōverplay' *v.t.* Play (part) to excess; give undue importance to; ~ one's **hand,** (Cards, or fig.) be unduly optimistic as to one's capabilities. [f. OVER- 6 + PLAY[1]]

ō'verplŭs *n.* Surplus, superabundance. [ME, partial transl. of AF SURPLUS or med. L *su(pe)rplus*]

ōverpoi'se (-z) *v.t.* (arch.) Outweigh. [f. OVER- 8 + POISE[1]]

ōver-pŏ'pūl|ātėd *a.* Over-peopled; hence ~A'TION *n.* [f. OVER- 6 + POPULATE + -ED[1]]

ōverpow'er *v.t.* Reduce to submission, subdue; make (thing) ineffective or imperceptible by greater intensity; (of heat, emotion, etc.) be too intense for, overwhelm; hence ~ING[2] *a.* [f. OVER- 9 + POWER]

ōverprai'se (-z) *v.t.*, & *n.*, **-prĕ'ssure** (-sh*er*) *n.* See OVER- 6.

ōverprĭ'nt[1] *v.t.* **1.** (Photog.) Print (positive) darker than was intended. **2.** Print too many copies of (work, or abs.). **3.** Print further matter on (already printed surface, esp. postage stamp). [f. OVER- 6, 3 + PRINT[2]]

ō'verprĭnt[2] *n.* Words etc. overprinted; postage stamp having these. [f. prec.]

ōver-prodū'ce *v.t.* Produce more of (commodity; usu. abs.) than is wanted; so **ōver--produ'ction** *n.* [f. OVER- 6 + PRODUCE[2]]

ō'verproof *a.* Containing more alcohol than proof spirit does. [f. OVER- 2 + PROOF[1]]

ōverrā'te *v.t.* Have too high an opinion of; ‖give too high assessment for rates. [f. OVER- 6 + RATE[2]]

ōverrea'ch *v.t.* Circumvent, outwit, get the better of by cunning or artifice; ~ **oneself,** strain oneself by reaching too far, defeat one's object by going too far. [f. OVER- 9, 7 + REACH[1]]

ōver-rėă'ct *v.i.* Respond more violently etc. than is justified. [f. OVER- 6 + REACT]

ōver-rėfī'ne *v.t.* Refine too much, make too subtle distinctions in (matter, or abs.). [f. OVER- 6 + REFINE]

ōverrī'de *v.t.* (**-ro'de; -ri'dden**). **1.** Ride over (enemy country) with armed force; trample (person) under one's horse's hoofs; (fig.) trample underfoot, supersede arrogantly, refuse to comply with, have or claim superior authority or precedence over, make ineffective; move so as to extend over; (of part of fractured bone) overlap another part. **2.** Exhaust (horse etc.) by riding. [f. OVER- 3, 6 + RIDE]

‖**ō'verrīder** *n.* Vertical attachment on motor--car bumper to prevent another bumper from becoming locked behind it. [f. prec. + -ER[1]]

ōverrī'pe *a.* See OVER- 6.

ōverrŭ'ff *v.t.* Overtrump. [f. OVER- 9 + RUFF[4]]

ōverru'le (-ōō'l) *v.t.* Set aside (decision, argument, proposal) by virtue of superior authority; annul decision by or reject proposal of (person) thus. [f. OVER- 9 + RULE]

ōverrŭ'n[1] *v.t.* (**-nn-; -ra'n; -ru'n**). Flood (land); ravage (country) with hostile force; (of vermin, weeds, etc.) swarm or spread over; exceed (limit, due time, etc.); (Print.) carry over (word etc.) to next line or page. [OE *oferyrnan* (as OVER- 3, RUN[1])]

ō'verrŭn[2] *n.* (Amount of) overrunning; slowing of vehicle engine by friction of road on wheels, transmitted through gearbox. [f. prec.]

ōversai'ling *a.* (Of part of building) projecting beyond what is below. [f. OVER- 3 + SALLY[1] + -ING[2]]

ōver-scru'pūlous (-ōō'-) *a.* See OVER- 6.

ōversea'[1]**, ōversea's**[1] (-z), *advs.* Across or beyond the sea. [ME, f. OVER- 2 + SEA (+ -S[1])]

ō'versea[2]**, ō'verseas**[2] (-z), *adjs.* Lying beyond the sea, foreign; pertaining to transport, countries, etc., across the sea. [f. prec.]

ōversee' *v.t.* (**-saw'; -see'n**). Superintend

For other words in *over-* see OVER-.

(workers, doing of work, etc.); hence **ō'verseer**[1] (-sēr) *n.* (‖*overseer of the poor,* (Hist.) parish officer with duty of assisting the poor from public funds). [OE *oferséon* look at from above (as OVER- 3, SEE[1])]

ōversĕ'll *v.t.* (**-so'ld**). Sell more of (commodity etc., or abs.) than one can deliver; (fig.) exaggerate merits of. [f. OVER- 6 + SELL]

ōver-sĕ'nsĭtĭve *a.*, **-sĕ'nsĭtĭvenėss** (-vn-) *n.* See OVER- 6.

ōversĕ't *v.t.* (**-tt-; overse't**). Overturn, upset; set up (type) in excess. [f. OVER- 4, 6 + SET[1]]

ō'versew (-sō) *v.t.* (*p.p.* **~n** *or* **~ed**). Sew (two edges) with every stitch in same direction through both edges and thread between stitches passing across and outside the join; join sections of (book) by stitch of this type. [f. OVER- 4 + SEW]

ōver-sĕ'xed (-kst) *a.* Having unusually great sexual desires. [f. OVER- 6 + SEX + -ED[2]]

ōvershă'dow (-dō) *v.t.* Shelter from sun; cast into the shade; make apparently less important by one's own brilliance. [OE *ofersceadwian* (as OVER- 4, SHADOW[2])]

ō'vershoe (-ōō) *n.* Shoe of rubber, felt, etc., worn over another as protection from wet, cold, etc. [f. OVER- 1 + SHOE[1]]

ōvershōō't[1] *v.t.* (**-sho't**). Send missile, travel, beyond (*mark* etc.; lit., or fig. of exaggeration, excess, etc.); (of aircraft) pass beyond limit of (runway etc.) when landing; **o'vershot wheel** (turned by water flowing above it). [ME, f. OVER- 3 + SHOOT[1]]

ō'vershōōt[2] *n.* Act or amount of overshooting. [f. prec.]

ōversī'de *adv.* Over side of ship (into smaller boat, or into sea). [f. OVER- 2 + SIDE[1]]

ō'versight (-īt) *n.* Supervision; omission to notice, mistake due to inadvertence. [ME, f. OVER- 3 + SIGHT[1]]

ōver-sĭ'mplĭfȳ *v.t.* Distort (problem, or abs.) by stating it in too simple terms; so **ōver-simplifica'tion** *n.* [f. OVER- 6 + SIMPLIFY]

ō'versize, -zed (-zd), *adjs.* Of more than the usual size. [f. OVER- 6 + SIZE[1] (+ -ED[2])]

ō'verskĭrt *n.* Outer or second skirt. [f. OVER- 1 + SKIRT]

ō'verslaugh (-aw) *n.*, & *v.t.* **1.** ‖(Mil.) Passing over of one's turn of duty, pass over (duty), in consideration of another duty that takes precedence of it. **2.** *v.t.* *Pass over in favour of another; *omit to consider. [f. Du. (*overslag* n. f.) *overslaan* omit (as OVER, *slaan* strike)]

ōverslee'p *v.i.* & *refl.* (**-sle'pt**). Sleep too long; continue sleeping after intended time of waking. [ME, f. OVER- 7 + SLEEP[2]]

ō'versleeve *n.* Separate sleeve covering ordinary sleeve to protect it etc. [f. OVER- 1 + SLEEVE]

ōver-solĭ'cĭtous *a.*, **-solĭ'cĭtūde** *n.* See OVER- 6.

ō'versoul (-ōl) *n.* God as spirit animating the universe and including all human souls. [f. OVER- 1 + SOUL]

ōverspĕ'nd *v.* (**-spe'nt**). **1.** *v.t.* Spend more than (specified amount). **2.** *v.i.* & *refl.* Spend too much. [f. OVER- 6, 7 + SPEND]

ō'verspĭll *n.* What is spilt over or overflows; (fig.) surplus population leaving a country or city to live elsewhere. [f. OVER- 4 + SPILL[1]]

ōverspreа'd (-ĕ'd) *v.t.* (**-sprea'd**). Become spread or diffused over; cover or occupy surface of; (esp. in *pass.*) cover *with* (*high mountains overspread with trees*). [OE *ofersprǣdan* (as OVER- 3, 4, SPREAD[1])]

ōversta'ff (-ah'f) *v.t.* Provide too many persons as staff for. [f. OVER- 6 + STAFF[1]]

ōverstā'te *v.t.* State too strongly; exaggerate; hence **~ment** (-tm-) *n.* [f. OVER- 6 + STATE[2]]

ōverstay' *v.t.* Stay longer than (time, one's welcome, etc.). [f. OVER- 9 + STAY[1]]

ō'versteer *v.i.*, & *n.* (Of motor vehicle) (have) tendency to turn more sharply than was intended. [f. OVER- 6 + STEER[1]]

ōverstĕ'p *v.t.* (**-pp-**). Pass beyond (boundary, lit. or fig.). [f. OVER- 3 + STEP[1]]

ōverstŏ'ck *v.t.*, **-strai'n** *v.t.*, & *n.*, **-strĕ'ss** *v.t.*, & *n.*, **-stre'tch** *v.t.* See OVER- 6.

ōverstrŭng *a.* **1.** (ō'-). (Of piano) with strings in sets crossing each other obliquely. **2.** (-ŭ'ng). (Of person, his nerves, etc.) (too) highly strung or intensely strained. [f. OVER- 4, 6 + STRUNG]

ōverstŭ'dȳ *v.t.*, & *n.* See OVER- 6.

ōverstŭ'ff *v.t.* Stuff more than is necessary; (in *p.p.*, of furniture) made soft and comfortable by thick upholstery. [f. OVER- 6 + STUFF]

ōver-subscrī'be *v.t.* (usu. in *p.p.*) Subscribe more than amount of (shares offered for sale, etc.). [f. OVER- 8 + SUBSCRIBE]

ōversŭ'btle (-ŭ'tel) *a.*, **-supplȳ'** *v.t.*, & *n.*, **-swĕ'll** *v.t.* See OVER- 6.

ō'vert (*or* ōvẽr't) *a.* Openly done, unconcealed, patent; **market ~**, OPEN[1] market; hence **~ly**[2] *adv.* [ME f. OF, p.p. of *ovrir* open f. L *aperire*]

ōvertā'ke *v.t.* (**-too'k; -ta'ken**). Come abreast with, by faster movement reach same point at same time as, (person or thing moving ahead of one in same direction); pass (such person or thing, or abs.) by faster movement; (of storm, misfortune, etc.) come suddenly or unexpectedly upon (person etc.); become level with or exceed (compared value etc.). [ME, f. OVER- 4 + TAKE[1]]

ōverta'sk (-ah'-) *v.t.* Give or be too heavy a task to or for. [f. OVER- 6 + TASK]

ōvertă'x *v.t.* Make excessive demand on (person for tax, or as regards his strength etc.). [f. OVER- 6 + TAX[1]]

ōverthrow'[1] (-ō') *v.t.* (**-threw'; -throw'n**). Upset, knock down; cast out from power, vanquish; subvert, put an end to, (institution etc.). [ME, f. OVER- 4 + THROW[1]]

ō'verthrow[2] (-ō) *n.* **1.** Defeat, subversion. **2.** (Cricket). Fielder's return of ball, not stopped near wicket and thus allowing further run(s). [sense 1 f. prec.; sense 2 f. OVER- 6 + THROW[2]]

ō'verthrŭst *n.* (Geol.) Thrust of (esp. lower) strata on one side of fault over those on other side. [f. OVER- 3 + THRUST]

ō'vertīme *n.* & *adv.* (Time during which person works) in addition to regular hours; payment for this. [f. OVER- 1, 2 + TIME[1]]

ōvertīr'e *v.t.* See OVER- 6, TIRE[1].

ō'vertōne *n.* (Mus.) = *upper* PARTIAL; (fig.) (subtle or elusive) secondary quality or implication. [f. OVER- 1 + TONE[1], after G *oberton*]

ōvertŏ'p *v.t.* (**-pp-**). Be or become higher than; surpass. [f. OVER- 9 + TOP[1]]

ōvertrai'n *v.t.* & *i.* Subject to or undergo too much (esp. athletic) training, with consequent loss of proficiency. [f. OVER- 6, 7 + TRAIN]

ō'vertrĭck *n.* (Bridge). Trick taken in excess of one's contract. [f. OVER- 6 + TRICK]

ōvertrŭ'mp *v.t.* Play higher trump than (another player, or abs.). [f. OVER- 9 + TRUMP[2]]

ō'verture *n.* **1.** Opening of negotiations with another, formal proposal or offer, (usu. in *pl.*, esp. *make overtures to*). **2.** (Mus.) Orchestral piece opening opera, oratorio, etc. (**concert ~**, one-movement composition in same style). **3.** Beginning of poem etc. [ME f. OF, f. L *apertura* APERTURE]

ōvertûr'n[1] *v.t.* & *i.* (Cause to) fall down or over, upset; overthrow, subvert, abolish, invalidate. [ME, f. OVER- 4 + TURN[1]]

ō'vertûrn[2] *n.* Upsetting, subversion. [f. OVER- 4 + TURN[2]]

ōver-ū'se[1] (-z) *v.t.*, **ōver-ū'se**[2] *n.*, **-vă'lūe** *v.t.* See OVER- 6.

ō'verview (-vū) *n.* General survey. [f. OVER- 3 + VIEW]

ōverwee'ning *a.* Arrogant, presumptuous, conceited, self-confident. [ME, f. OVER- 6 + WEEN + -ING²]

ō'verweight¹ (-wāt) *n.* & *a.* **1.** *n.* Preponderance; excessive or extra weight. **2.** *a.* (-wā't). Beyond allowed or suitable weight (*luggage, person, is overweight*). [f. OVER- 1, 2 + WEIGHT¹]

ōverwei'ght² (-wā't) *v.t.* Load unduly (*with*). [f. OVER- 6 + WEIGHT²]

ōverwhĕ'lm *v.t.* Bury or drown beneath superincumbent mass, submerge utterly; crush; bring to sudden ruin or destruction; overpower with emotion or *with* excess of business etc.; hence ~ING² *a.*, irresistible by force of numbers, influence, amount, etc. [f. OVER- 4 + WHELM]

ōverwī'nd *v.t.* (**-wou'nd**). Wind (watch etc.) beyond proper stopping-point. [f. OVER- 6 + WIND³]

ōverwĭ'nter *v.* Spend the winter (*at, in,* etc.). [f. OVER- 3 + WINTER]

ōverwor'k (-ẽr'k) *v.* & *n.* **1.** *v.t.* & *i.* (Cause to) work too hard. **2.** *v.t.* Weary or exhaust with too much work; (fig.) make excessive use of. **3.** *n.* Excessive work. [f. OVER- 6 + WORK¹,²]

overwrī'te (ōverī't) *v.* (**-wrō'te; -wrĭ'tten**). **1.** *v.t.* Write on top of (other writing); write too much about. **2.** *v.i.* & *refl.* Write too much or too elaborately. [f. OVER- 3, 7 + WRITE]

ōverwrou'ght (ōveraw't) *a.* Over-excited; suffering reaction from over-excitement. [f. OVER- 6 + WROUGHT]

ōver-zea'l *n.*, **-zea'lous** (-ĕ'-) *a.* See OVER- 6.

ō'vĭ-¹ *comb. form.* Egg, ovum, as: **~duct,** canal through which ova pass from ovary esp. in oviparous animals; **~form,** egg-shaped; **~parous** (-ĭ'-), (Zool.) producing young by means of eggs expelled from body before being hatched (cf. VIVIPAROUS), whence **~pa'rity** *n.*; **~po'sit** (-ŏ'z-), lay egg(s), esp. with **~po'sitor,** pointed tubular organ with which female insect deposits eggs, whence **~posi'tion** *n.* [f. L OVUM + -I-]

ō'vĭ-² *comb. form.* Sheep, as: **~bo'vine** *a.* & *n.*, (animal) having character intermediate between sheep and ox, musk-ox; ~CIDE *n.*, (joc.) sheep-killing. [f. L *ovis* sheep + -I-]

Ovĭ'dĭan (*o*-) *a.* Of or like (the poems of) Ovid. [f. P. *Ovidius* Naso (Ovid), Roman poet d. A.D. 17 + -IAN]

ō'vīne *a.* Of or like sheep. [f. LL *ovinus* f. L *ovis* sheep; see -INE¹]

ō'void *a.* & *n.* **1.** *a.* Egg-shaped as solid or as surface; oval with one end more pointed than the other. **2.** *n.* Ovoid body or surface. [f. F *ovoïde* f. mod. L *ovoides* (as OVUM; see -OID)]

ō'vol|ō *n.* (*pl.* **~i** *pr.* ~ē). (Archit.) Convex moulding of quarter-circle or quarter-ellipse section, receding downwards. [It., dim. of *ovo* egg f. L OVUM]

ōvotĕ'st|ĭs *n.* (*pl.* **~es** *pr.* -ēz). (Zool.) Organ producing both ova and spermatozoa. [f. as foll. + TESTIS]

ōvōvĭvĭ'parous *a.* (Zool.) Producing young by means of eggs hatched within the body. [f. OVUM + -O- + VIVIPAROUS]

ŏ'vūl|āte *v.i.* Produce ovules or ova; discharge ova from ovary; so ~A'TION *n.*, **~āt**ORY *a.* [f. mod. L *ovulum* (as foll.) + -ATE³]

ō'vūl|e *n.* Rudimentary seed, female germ-cell of seed-plants; unfertilized ovum; hence ~AR¹ *a.* [F, f. med. L *ovulum*, dim. of foll.]

ō'vum *n.* (*pl.* **o'va**). Female germ-cell in animals, capable of developing into new individual when fertilized by male sperm; egg esp. of mammal, fish, or insect. [L, = egg]

ow *int.* expr. sudden pain. [imit.]

owe (ō) *v.t.* (OWING). **1.** Be under obligation to (re)pay (person money, money *to* person, money) or render (person honour etc., gratitude etc. *to* person; **~ it to oneself to** do, need to do in order to avoid unfairness to oneself); (abs.) be in debt (*for* thing, with creditor in dat.: *he owes not any man; I owe you for your services, owed for all my clothes*); ~ person **a grudge,** cherish resentment against him. **2.** Be indebted for *to* person or thing (*we owe to Newton the principle of gravitation; he owes his success to good luck; I owe him much*). [a pret.-pres. v. like CAN², DARE, MAY¹: OE *āgan* (see OUGHT²), = OS *ēgan*, OHG *eigan*, ON *eiga*, Goth. *aigan* f. Gmc **aig-* f. IE *(*o*)*ik-*]

Ow'ĕn|ĭsm (ō'ĭ-) *n.* Communistic co-operation advocated by Robert Owen; so ~ITE¹ (1) *n.* [f. R. *Owen*, Welsh social reformer d. 1858 + -ISM]

ow'ĭng (ō'ĭ-) *pred. a.* Yet to be paid, owed, due, (*paid all that was owing*); **~ to,** attributable to, caused by, (*all this was owing merely to ill luck*), (as *prep.*) on account of (*owing to the drought, crops are short*). [ME, f. OWE + -ING²]

owl *n.* **1.** Large-headed hook-beaked large-eyed soft-plumaged usu. nocturnal bird of prey of order Strigiformes (BARN¹-*owl*, HORN¹*ed* or LONG¹-*-eared owl, tawny owl,* etc.); **~s to Athens,** = COAL¹*s to Newcastle* [the owl being an emblem on Athenian coins]. **2.** Solemn person, wise-looking dullard; hence ~'ISH¹ *a.* **3.** ~ (**pigeon**), variety of pigeon with owl-like head. **4.** **~-light,** dusk, twilight; **~-monkey,** douroucouli; **~-parrot,** (arch.) kakapo. **5.** Hence ~'ERY (3) *n.* [OE *ūle*, = OLG **ūla*, ON *ugla* f. Gmc **uwwalōn*]

ow'lĕt *n.* Small or young owl. [earlier *howlet*, dim. of OWL, assim. to HOWL]

own¹ (ōn) *a.* **1.** (Appended to possessive adj. or case) in full ownership, proper, peculiar, individual, and not another's, (*saw it with my own eyes; has a value all its own; let person* STEW² *in his own juice; loves truth for its own sake; be* one's *own* MAN¹; *may I have it for my* (*very*) *own?*); **my** ~ (*sweetheart* etc.) (expr. affection, esp. in voc.); (often also used to emphasize not the ownership, but the identity of the subject etc.): *cooks her own meals, every man his own lawyer, am my own master*; (abs.) private property, kindred, etc., (*may I not do what I will with my own?; came unto his own, and his own received him not*); **of** one's ~, belonging to one (exclusively) (*I have nothing of my own; will give you one of my own; has a way of her own in such matters*); **come into** one's ~, get possession of one's rightful property, be properly esteemed etc.; **get** one's ~ **back,** (colloq.) get even, revenge oneself (*on*); **hold** one's ~, maintain position, not be defeated or lose strength; **on** one's ~, independent(ly), on one's own account or responsibility or resources, alone, unrivalled; *in a* CLASS *of* or *on* one's or *its own.* **2.** (Without preceding possessive) ~ **brother, sister,** (with both parents the same); ~ **cousin,** first cousin. [OE *ǣgen*, *āgen*, = OS *ēgan*, OHG *eigan*, ON *eiginn* f. Gmc **aiganaz* f. p.p. of **aigan* possess; see OWE]

own² (ōn) *v.* **1.** *v.t.* Have as property, possess; (in *p.p.*, in *comb.*) held as property by (*State-owned*); acknowledge authorship, paternity, or possession, of (*child, pamphlet, hat, that nobody will own*); admit as existent, valid, true, etc., (*owns his deficiencies, himself indebted,* (*that*) *he did not know*); submit to (person's dominance etc.) without protest. **2.** *v.i.* Confess *to* (*owns to a sense of shame, to having* done); ~ **up,** (colloq.) make frank confession. [OE *āgnian* (*āgen* OWN¹)]

ow'ner (ō'-) *n.* One who owns as property;

For other words in *over-* **see** OVER-.

(sl.) captain of ship; ~**-driver, -occupier,** etc., one who both owns and drives vehicle, occupies house, etc.; hence ~LESS *a.*, ~SHIP (1) *n.* [ME, f. OWN[2] + -ER[1]]

ŏx (*pl.* **o'xen**). **1.** Any bovine animal, individual of kinds of large usu. horned cloven-footed ruminant used when domesticated for draught, for supplying milk, and for eating as meat. **2.** Castrated male of domestic species (*Bos taurus*) of this; **the black ox has trod on** one's **foot,** misfortune or old age has come upon one; *play the* GIDDY *ox.* **3. Ox-bird,** dunlin; **ox-bow,** (1) U-shaped collar of ox-yoke, (2) horseshoe bend in river, (3) lake formed from this when river cuts across narrow end; **ox-fence,** strong cattle-fence or jumping-obstacle of railing(s), hedge, and often ditch; **ox-gall** (used for cleansing, and in painting and pharmacy); **o'xherd,** cowherd; **o'xhide,** (leather from) hide of ox; **o'xlip,** primula, (pop.) hybrid of primrose and cowslip [f. as COWSLIP]; **ox-pecker,** Afr. bird feeding on ticks on animals; **o'xtail,** tail of ox, much used for soup-making; **ox-tongue,** (1) tongue of ox, esp. for cooking, (2) bugloss. [OE *oxa*, = OS, OHG *ohso*, ON *uxi*, *oxi*, Goth *auhsa* f. Gmc **ohson* f. IE **uksin-*]

ŏx- *comb. form.* (Chem.) = OXY- (2) (*oxazole*) or OXALIC (*oxamide*). [abbr.]

ŏxă'lĭc *a.* (Chem.) ~ **acid,** highly poisonous and sour acid, $(COOH)_2$, found in wood sorrel and other plants; so **ŏ'xal**ATE[1] (3) *n.* [f. F *oxalique* f. L f. Gk *oxalis* wood sorrel; see -IC]

||**O'xbrĭdge** (ŏ'-) *n.* (Characteristics of) Oxford and Cambridge universities, esp. as being of ancient foundation. [portmanteau wd f. *Ox*(*ford*) + (*Cam*)*bridge*]

ŏ'xer *n.* Ox-fence. [f. OX + -ER[1]]

ŏ'x-eye (-ī) *n.* **1.** Eye of ox; large human eye, whence **ŏ'x-eye**ED[2] (-īd) *a.* **2.** Plant with flower like eye of ox; **white** ~, ~ **daisy,** *Chrysanthemum leucanthemum*; **yellow** ~, corn marigold. [ME, f. OX + EYE[1]]

Oxf. *abbr.* Oxford.

O'xfăm (ŏ'-) *abbr.* Oxford Committee for Famine Relief.

O'xford (ŏ'-) *n.* ~ **accent,** style of pronouncing English in manner supposed affected and characteristic of members of Oxford University; ||~ **bags,** very wide trousers; ~ **blue** (dark, sometimes with purple tinge); ~ **clay,** deposit of stiff blue clay underlying coral rag in English Midland counties; ~ **frame,** picture-frame of which sides cross each other at corners and project; ~ **Group** (**Movement**), religious movement founded at Oxford 1921, with discussion of personal problems by groups; ~ **Movement,** Tractarianism; ~ **shoe,** ***o'xford,** low shoe lacing over instep; ~ **Tracts,** the 'TRACT[2]s for the Times'. [~ in England]

ŏ'xĭd|ant *n.* Oxidizing agent; so ~ATE[3] *v.t.* (arch.), ~A'TION *n.*, ~ATIVE *a.* [F, part. of *oxider* (as foll.); see -ANT]

ŏ'xīde *n.* Binary compound of oxygen. [F (*oxygène* OXYGEN, *-ide* after *acide* ACID[1])]

ŏ'xĭdīz|e, -īs|e (-īz), *v.* **1.** *v.t.* Cause to combine with oxygen; cover (metal) with coating of oxide, make rusty. **2.** *v.i.* Take up, or enter into combination with, oxygen; rust. **3.** ~**ed silver,** (incorrect name for) silver with dark coat of silver sulphide. **4.** Hence ~ABLE *a.*, ~A'TION, ~ER[1] (2), *ns.* [f. prec. + -IZE]

O'xon. (ŏ'-) *abbr.* Oxfordshire; of Oxford (University or diocese). [f. L *Oxoniensis*; see foll.]

Oxō'nĭan (ŏ-) *a.* & *n.* (Member) of Oxford University; (native or citizen) of Oxford. [f. *Oxonia* Latinized name of *Ox*(*en*)*ford* + -AN]

ŏ'xter *n.*, & *v.t.* (Sc. & N. Engl.) **1.** *n.* Armpit; inner side of upper arm. **2.** *v.t.* Support with or by taking the arm, put under the arm; hug. [f. OE *ōhsta*, *ōxta*]

ŏ'xў- *comb. form.* (1) Sharp, as: ~**car'pous,** with pointed fruit; ~**o'pia,** abnormal keenness of vision. (2, Chem.) Oxygen, as: ~**-ace'tylene,** consisting of, involving use of, a mixture of oxygen and acetylene (~*-acetylene blowpipe*, for producing intensely hot flame for welding etc.); so ~**-hy'drogen** *blowpipe*, *flame*, *light*, etc.; ~**acid,** ~**salt,** (containing oxygen); ~**haemoglo'bin,** bright red compound of oxygen and haemoglobin in arteries etc. [f. Gk *oxu-* (*oxus* sharp, acid)]

ŏ'xўgėn *n.* Colourless tasteless odourless gas, most abundant of all elements, existing in air and combined in water and most minerals and organic substances, and essential to animal and vegetable life; ~ **mask** (placed over nose and mouth to supply oxygen for breathing); ~ **tent,** enclosure to allow patient to breathe air with increased oxygen content; hence **ŏxў'gėn**OUS *a.* [f. F *oxygène* acidifying principle (as OXY- (2), -GEN); it was at first held to be the essential principle in formation of acids]

ŏ'xўgėn|āte (*or* ŏksĭ'-) *v.t.* Supply, treat, or mix, with oxygen, oxidize; charge (blood) with oxygen by respiration; so ~A'TION *n.* [f. F *oxygéner* (as prec.) + -ATE[3]]

ŏ'xўgėnīze (*or* ŏksĭ'-), **-īse** (-īz), *v.t.* = prec. [f. OXYGEN + -IZE]

ŏxўmŏr'on *n.* (Rhet.) Figure of speech with pointed conjunction of seemingly contradictory expressions (e.g. *faith unfaithful kept him falsely true*). [f. Gk *oxumōron* neut. (as n.) of *oxumōros* pointedly foolish (*oxus* sharp, *mōros* foolish)]

ŏxўtō'cĭn *n.* Pituitary hormone controlling uterine contraction and release of milk, used in synthetic form to induce labour etc. [f. *oxytocic* accelerating parturition f. Gk *oxutokia* sudden delivery (as OXY- (1), *tokos* childbirth), + -IN]

ŏ'xўtōne *a.* & *n.* (Gk Gram.) (Word) with acute accent on last syllable. [f. Gk *oxutonos* (as OXY- (1), *tonos* tone)]

oy'er *n.* Criminal trial under the writ of ~ **and terminer** or commission to judges on circuit to hold courts. [ME, f. AF *oyer et terminer* f. L *audire* hear, *et* and, *terminare* determine; see -ER[4]]

ōyĕ'z, ōyĕ's, *int.* uttered, usu. thrice, by public crier or court officer to command silence and attention. [ME, f. AF, OF *oiez*, *oyez* imper. pl. of *oïr* hear f. L *audire*]

oy'ster *n.* Edible bivalve mollusc of genus *Ostrea* or family Ostreidae, usu. eaten alive; oyster-shaped morsel of meat in fowl's back; something regarded as containing all that one desires (*the world's my oyster*); (sl.) taciturn person; **vegetable** ~, salsify; ~**-bank, -bed,** part of sea-bottom where oysters breed or are bred; ~**-catcher,** coastal wading bird of genus *Haematopus*; ~**-farm,** sea-bottom used for breeding oysters; ~**-knife** (of shape adapted for opening oysters); ~**-park,** oyster-bed or -farm; ~**-plant,** salsify; ~(**-white**), white with pale grey tinge. [ME & OF *oistre* f. L *ostrea*, *ostreum* f. Gk *ostreon*]

oz. *abbr.* ounce(s). [It. (*onza* ounce)]

ōzŏ'cerīte, -ker-, *n.* Waxlike fossil paraffin used for candles, insulating, etc. [f. G *ozokerit* f. Gk *ozō* smell + *kēros* wax; see -ITE[1]]

ō'zōn|e (*or* -ō'n) *n.* Form of oxygen with three atoms in molecule, having pungent refreshing odour; (pop.) invigorating air at seaside etc.; (fig.) exhilarating influence; hence **ozŏ'n**IC *a.*, ~IZE (3, 5) *v.t.* [f. G *ozon* f. Gk, neut. part. of *ozō* smell; see -ONE]

***ozt.,** ||**oztr.,** *abbrs.* troy ounce(s).

P

P, p, (pē) *n.* (*pl.* **Ps** *or* **P's**). Sixteenth letter of alphabet; MIND[2] one's *P's and Q's*.
P *abbr.* (Chess) pawn; POISE[2].
p. *abbr.* page; (decimal) pence or penny; PIANO[1]; pico-.
P *symb.* phosphorus.
pa[1] (pah) *n.* (vulg.) Father. [abbr. of PAPA]
pa[2] (pah), **pah**[2], *n.* Maori camp or village (formerly fortified). [Maori *pà* (*pà* block up)]
P.A. *abbr.* personal assistant; Press Association; public address.
p.a. *abbr.* per annum.
Pa. *abbr.* pascal; Pennsylvania.
Pa *symb.* protactinium.
pă'būlum *n.* Food (esp. fig., *mental pabulum*). [L (*pascere* feed)]
||**P.A.B.X.** *abbr.* private automatic branch (telephone) exchange.
pă'ca *n.* Rodent of genus *Cuniculus*, esp. spotted cavy of S. & Central America. [Sp. & Port., f. Tupi]
pāce[1] *n.* **1.** Single step in walking or running; space traversed in this (about 30 in.); space between successive stationary positions of same foot in walking (about 60 in.). **2.** Mode of walking or running, gait; any of various (esp. ambling or racking) gaits of (esp. trained) horse etc.; (fig.) **put** person **through his ~s,** test his qualities in action etc. **3.** Speed in walking or running; rate of progression (lit. or fig.); **go the ~,** go at great speed, (fig.) indulge in dissipation; **keep ~,** advance at equal rate (*with*); **set the ~,** regulate the speed or rate of progress; **stand** or **stay the ~,** be able to keep up with others. **4. ~-maker,** (1) rider, runner, etc., who sets pace for another in race etc., (2) region of vertebrate heart initiating contraction in each beat, or electrical device performing same function; **~-setter,** = *pace-maker* (1). **5.** Hence **-pāc**ED[2] (-st) *a.* [ME, f. OF *pas* f. L *passus* (*pandere pass-* stretch)]
pāce[2] *v.* **1.** *v.i.* Walk with slow or regular pace; (of horse) = AMBLE; hence **pā'c**ING[1] *n.*, harness-racing for pacing horses. **2.** *v.t.* Traverse by pacing; measure (distance *out*) by pacing; set pace for (rider, runner, etc.). **3.** Hence **pā'c**ER[1] *n.* [f. prec.]
pace[3] (pā'sĭ *or* pah'chā) *prep.* (In announcing contrary opinion) with all due respect or deference to (person named). [L, abl. of *pax* peace]
pacha etc. See PASHA etc.
pachĭ'nkō *n.* Japanese form of pin-ball. [Jap.]
pachi'sĭ (-chē'-) *n.* Four-handed Indian game with six cowries used like dice. [Hindi, = of 25, the highest throw]
pă'chўdĕrm (-k-) *n.* Thick-skinned mammal, esp. elephant or rhinoceros; (fig.) thick-skinned person; so **păchўdĕr'mat**OUS (-k-) *a.* [f. F *pachyderme* f. Gk *pakhudermos* (*pakhus* thick, *derma -matos* skin)]
paci'fĭc *a.* & *n.* **1.** *a.* Tending to peace; of peaceful disposition; characterized by peace, tranquil; hence **paci'f**ICALLY *adv.* **2.** *a.* & *n.* (*P~*). (Of or adjoining) the ocean between America eastward and Asia westward; **P~ Time,** standard time used in Pacific region of Canada and U.S. [f. F *pacifique* or f. L *pacificus* (*pax pacis* peace; see -FIC)]
păcĭfĭcā'tion *n.* Pacifying; being pacified; treaty of peace; so **paci'fĭcat**ORY *a.* [F, f. L *pacificatio -onis* (as PACIFY; see -FICATION)]
pă'cĭf|ism *n.* Doctrine that the abolition of war is both desirable and possible; (support of) policy of arbitration in international disputes; so ~IST (2) *n.* [f. F *pacifisme* (*pacifier*; see foll.)]
pă'cĭf|ў *v.t.* Appease (person, anger, excitement, etc.); bring (country etc.) to state of peace; hence ~IER[1] *n.*, (*esp.) baby's dummy. [ME, f. OF *pacifier* or f. L *pacificare* (as PACIFIC; see -FY)]
păck[1] *n.* **1.** Bundle of things wrapped up or tied together for carrying, esp. on shoulder or back, e.g. pedlar's bundle, soldier's or walker's knapsack. **2.** A measure of various goods, e.g. 500 sheets of gold leaf. **3.** (usu. derog.) Lot or set (*pack of fools, lies, nonsense, thieves*, etc.). **4.** Number of hounds kept together for hunting, or of animals (esp. wolves) or birds (esp. grouse) naturally associating; organized group of Cub Scouts or Brownies, or of submarines etc. **5.** (Rugby Footb.) Team's forwards. **6.** ||Set of playing-cards. **7.** Large area of large crowded pieces of floating ice in sea. **8.** Quantity of fish, fruit, etc., packed in a season etc.; method of packing, or set of things packed, for selling (**pack of cigarettes*). **9.** (Med.) Wrapping of (part of) body in wet sheet etc.; sheet etc. so used. **10.** Application of medicinal or cosmetic substance to skin etc.; substance so applied; MUD *pack*. **11. ~-drill,** military punishment of walking up and down in full marching equipment (*no names no ~-drill*, discretion will prevent punishment); **~-horse** (for carrying packs); **~-ice,** = sense 7; **~'man,** (arch.) pedlar; ***~-rat,** large hoarding rodent; **~-saddle** (adapted for supporting packs); **~'thread,** stout thread for sewing or tying up packs. [ME f. MDu., MLG *pak*, of unkn. orig.]
păck[2] *v.* **1.** *v.t.* Put (things) together into bundle, box, bag, etc., for transport or storing (often **~ up,** esp. abs.); **~ed meal** etc. (prepared beforehand and put in container for carrying to place of eating). **2.** Put closely together; crowd together; (Naut.) **~ on** (hoist) **all sail;** form (hounds etc.) into pack; place (cards) together in pack. **3.** Cover (thing) with something pressed tightly round; (Med.) wrap (body or part of it) in wet sheet etc. **4.** (sl.) Carry or possess (gun etc.); be capable of delivering (a punch) with skill or force. **5.** Fill (bag, box, case, etc.) with clothes etc. (~ one's **bags,** prepare to depart); cram (space etc. *with*); load (animal) with pack; fill (theatre etc.) with spectators. **6. ~ off,** send or drive (person) away, esp. summarily; **~ed out,** (colloq.) crowded. **7.** (sl.) **~ it in,** end it, finish; **~ it up,** desist. **8.** *v.i.* Crowd together; (of animals) form pack. **9.** Depart with one's belongings; **send ~ing,** dismiss (person) abruptly. **10.** (sl.) **~ up,** retire from contest, activity, etc.; (of machine etc.) cease to function, break down. **11.** Hence ~'ER[1] *n.* [ME, f. MDu., MLG *pakken*; cf. prec.]
păck[3] *v.t.* Select (jury etc.) so as to secure biased decision in one's favour. [prob. f. obs. v. *pact*, f. PACT]
pă'ckage *n.*, & *v.t.* **1.** *n.* Bundle of things packed, parcel; box etc. in which goods are packed; **~ (deal),** transaction agreed to as a whole, the less favourable items as well as the more

favourable; ~ **holiday, tour,** etc., (with fixed route etc. at fixed inclusive price). **2.** *v.t.* Make up into or enclose in a package; hence **pă'ckaging**[1] (-kĭj-) *n.*, (making of) wrapper(s) or container(s) for goods. [f. PACK[2] + -AGE]

pă'ckėt *n.* **1.** Small package; (colloq.) considerable sum of money won or lost; ||**catch, cop, stop, a** ~, (sl.) be (severely) injured etc.; ||PAY[1]-*packet*. **2.** ~(**-boat**), mail-boat. [f. PACK[1] + -ET[1]]

pă'cking *n.* In vbl senses; (oil-absorbing) material closing a joint or assisting in lubrication of an axle; substance used to fill gaps in order to protect fragile objects, etc.; **~-box, ~-gland,** = STUFFING-*box*; **~-case,** (usu. wooden) case or framework for packing goods in; **~-needle,** large needle for sewing up packages; **~-sheet,** sheet for packing goods in, (Med.) wet sheet used in hydropathy. [ME, f. PACK[2] + -ING[1]]

păct *n.* Agreement, treaty. [ME, f. OF *pact(e)* f. L *pactum*, neut. p.p. (as n.) of *pacisci* agree]

păd[1] *n.* (arch.) **1.** (sl.) Road (**gentleman, knight, squire, of the** ~, highwayman); = FOOT[1]*pad*. **2.** ~(**-nag**), easy-paced horse. [16th c. cant, f. Du., LG *pad* PATH]

păd[2] *v.* (**-dd-**). **1.** *v.t.* Tramp along (road etc.) on foot; ||~ **it,** ||~ **the hoof,** (sl.) go on foot. **2.** *v.i.* Travel on foot; walk with soft dull steady sound of steps. [f. prec., or LG *padden* tread]

păd[3] *n.* **1.** Soft stuffed saddle without frame. **2.** Cushion or soft stuffing used to diminish jarring, fill out hollows, absorb fluid, etc.; guard for leg and ankle in cricket etc. (SHIN-*pad*); ink-soaked block, usu. in box, for inking rubber stamp. **3.** Number of sheets of blotting-, writing-, or drawing-paper fastened together at one edge. **4.** Fleshy cushion forming sole of foot in some quadrupeds; paw of fox, hare, etc. **5.** *Floating leaf of water-lily. **6.** (sl.) Bed, lodging; house. **7.** Flat surface for helicopter take-off, rocket launching, etc. **8.** Handle to which various tools can be fitted (**~-saw,** small compass-saw). [prob. of Du. or LG orig.]

păd[4] *v.t.* (**-dd-**). Furnish with a pad, stuff; fill out or *out* (sentence, publication, etc.) with superfluous matter; **~ded cell,** room with padded walls in mental hospital; hence **~'ding**[1] (4) *n.* [f. prec.]

pă'ddle[1] *n.* **1.** Small spadelike implement with long handle; short broad-bladed oar used without rowlock; **double** ~ (with blade at each end); ***~-ball,** game like squash played with wooden paddle. **2.** One of the boards fitted round circumference of paddle-wheel or mill-wheel; paddle-shaped instrument; (Zool.) fin or flipper. **3. ~-wheel,** wheel for propelling ship (**~-boat, ~-steamer,** etc.), with boards round circumference so as to press backward against water. [15th c., of unkn. orig.; cf. syn. (Sc. & N. Engl.) *pattle*]

pă'ddle[2] *v.* & *n.* **1.** *v.i.* & *t.* Move on water, propel canoe, by means of paddles (~ one's **own canoe,** (fig.) depend on oneself alone); row gently. **2.** *v.t.* *Spank, thrash. **3.** *n.* Action or spell of paddling. [f. prec.]

pă'ddle[3] *v.i.* Dabble with the feet or wade about in shallow water; (arch.) toy with the fingers (*in, on, about,* thing); (of child) toddle. [prob. of LDu. orig.; cf. LG *paddeln* tramp about]

pă'ddock[1] *n.* Small field, esp. near stable or as part of stud farm; turf enclosure adjoining racecourse, where horses or cars are brought together before race; (Austral. & N.Z.) field, plot of land. [app. var. of (now dial.) *parrock* (OE *pearruc*; see PARK[1])]

||**pă'ddock**[2] *n.* (arch. or dial.) Frog or toad. [f. ME *padde* (= ON *padda*, MDu., MLG *padde*) toad, + -OCK]

Pă'ddy̆[1] *n.* (Nickname for) Irishman. [pet-form of *Padraig* = *Patrick*; see -Y[3]]

pă'ddy̆[2] *n.* Rice before threshing or in the husk; ~(**-field**), field where rice is grown. [f. Malay *pādi*]

||**pă'ddy̆**[3], ||**pă'ddy̆whăck,** *ns.* (colloq.) Rage, fit of temper. [f. PADDY[1]]

pă'ddy̆mĕlon. Var. of foll.

pă'dėmĕlon *n.* Small wallaby of coastal scrub. [corrupt. of Aboriginal name]

Pa'dĭshah (pah'-) *n.* Shah of Iran; (Hist.) Sultan of Turkey; *(colloq.; *p*~) important or influential person. [f. Pers. *pād(i)šāh* (*pati* lord; see SHAH)]

pă'dlŏck *n.*, & *v.t.* **1.** *n.* Detachable lock hanging by pivoted hook on object fastened. **2.** *v.t.* Secure with padlock. [ME, f. LOCK[2]; first elem. unexpl.]

padou'k *n.* Timber-tree of genus *Pterocarpus*; its wood, resembling rosewood. [Burm.]

pa'drė (pah'-; *or* -drā) *n.* (colloq.) Chaplain in army etc. [It., Sp., & Port., = father, priest, f. L *pater patris* father]

pă'dūasoy *n.* Strong corded silk fabric much worn in 18th c. (cf. POULT-DE-SOIE). [earlier *poudesoy* f. F *pou-de-soie*, of unkn. orig.; assoc. w. *Padua* in Italy]

pae'an *n.* Chant of thanksgiving for deliverance (orig. addressed to Apollo or Artemis); song of praise or triumph. [L, f. Doric Gk *paian* hymn to Apollo under name of *Paian*, orig. physician of the gods]

pae'derăst etc. See PEDERAST etc.

paediă'tr|ĭc, *pēdiă'tr|ĭc, *a.* Relating to children and their diseases; hence ~I'CIAN, ~ICS, ~IST (3), *ns.* [f. foll. + Gk *iatros* physician + -IC]

pae'dō-, *pē'dō-, *comb. form.* Child, as: **~-baptism,** infant baptism; **~phi'lia,** sexual love directed towards children. [f. Gk *pais paidos* boy, child + -O-]

paĕ'lla (pah-) *n.* Spanish dish of rice, chicken, seafood, etc., cooked and served in large shallow pan. [Cat., f. OF *paele* f. L *patella* pan]

pae'on *n.* Metrical foot of one long syllable placed first, second, third, or fourth (**first** etc. ~) and three short; hence **paeŏ'nic** *a.* [L, f. Gk *paiōn*, Attic form of *paian* PAEAN]

pae'ony̆. See PEONY.

pā'gan *n.* & *a.* Heathen; unenlightened or irreligious (person); hence ~DOM, ~ISM (2), *ns.*, ~ISH[1] *a.*, ~IZE (3) *v.t.* & *i.* [ME, f. L *paganus* civilian (*pagus* country district; see -AN); sense 'heathen' in Christian L (Tertullian, Augustine)]

pāge[1] *n.*, & *v.t.* **1.** *n.* Boy or man, usu. in livery, employed to attend to door, go on errands, etc.; boy employed as personal attendant of person of rank, bride, etc.; (Hist.) boy in training for knighthood and attached to knight's service; **~-boy,** (1) = *page*, (2) woman's hair-style with hair long and rolled under at the ends; hence ~'HOOD (-jh-), ~'SHIP (-jsh-), *ns.* **2.** *v.t.* Summon by means of or as by a page, calling out name of wanted person until he is found. [ME f. OF, perh. f. It. *paggio* f. Gk *paidion*, dim. of *pais paidos* boy]

pāge[2] *n.* (One side of) leaf of book, periodical, etc.; what is printed etc. on this; (fig.) episode that might fill page in written history etc.; (in *pl.*) passage in book etc. (*his finest pages*). [F, f. L *pagina* (*pangere* fasten)]

pāge[3] *v.t.* Put consecutive numbers on pages of (book etc.) for use in reference. [f. prec.]

pă'geant (-jant) *n.* Brilliant spectacle, esp. procession, arranged for effect; spectacular procession, or play performed in the open, illustrating history of a place; tableau, allegorical device, etc., on fixed stage or moving vehicle;

(fig.) empty or specious show; hence ~RY (5) *n.* [ME *pagyn*, of unkn. orig.]

pă'gĭnal *a.* Of pages; corresponding page for page; so **pă'gĭn**ARY¹ *a.* [f. LL *paginalis* (as PAGE²; see -AL)]

pă'gĭn|āte *v.t.* Page (book etc.); hence ~A'TION *n.* [f. F *paginer* f. L *pagina* PAGE² + -ATE³]

pagō'da *n.* **1.** Sacred building, esp. tower usu. of pyramidal form, in India, China, etc.; ornamental imitation of this. **2. ~-tree,** tree of various species resembling pagoda in shape; *shake the ~-tree,* (Hist.) make one's fortune quickly in India (w. ref. to ~ as name of gold coin). [f. Port. *pagode*, prob. ult. f. Pers. *butkada* idol temple]

pagūr'ĭan *a.* & *n.* (Of) the hermit-crab. [f. L f. Gk *pagouros* kind of crab + -IAN]

pah¹ *int.* expr. disgust or contempt. [natural utterance]

pah². See PA².

Pah'lavĭ *n.* Language of Persia under Sassanian kings. [f. Pers. *pahlawī* (*pahlav* f. *parthava* Parthia)]

paid. See PAY².

pail *n.* Vessel, usu. round, of wood or metal for carrying liquids etc.; amount contained in this (*half a pail of milk*); hence ~'FUL *n.* [OE *pægel* gill; cf. MDu. *pegel* gauge; assoc. w. OF *paelle* (see PAELLA)]

paillasse. Var. of PALLIASSE.

paillĕ'tte (pīyĕ't *or* pălyĕ't) *n.* Piece of bright metal used in enamel painting; spangle. [F, dim. of *paille* f. L *palea* straw, chaff]

pain¹ *n.* **1.** Suffering or distress of body (from injury or disease) or mind; *pain in the* NECK¹; **in ~,** undergoing this. **2.** (in *pl.*) Throes of childbirth; trouble taken (*take pains*; *be at pains to* do; *get* a thrashing etc. *for* one's *pains*). **3.** Punishment (*pains and penalties*); **on** or **under ~ of** (death or other punishment that would be incurred). **4. ~-killer,** medicine for alleviating pain; **~'staking** (-z-), careful, industrious. [ME, f. OF *peine* f. L *poena* penalty]

pain² *v.t.* & *i.* **1.** *v.t.* Inflict pain upon; (in *p.p.*) expressing pain (*pained look*). **2.** *v.i.* Give rise to pain, ache (*my arm is paining*). [ME, f. OF *pener* f. LL *poenare* (as prec.)]

pai'nful *a.* **1.** Causing pain; grievous, vexatious; (esp. of part of body) suffering pain. **2.** Causing trouble or difficulty; laborious. **3.** Hence ~LY² *adv.*, ~NESS *n.* [ME, f. PAIN¹ + -FUL]

pai'nlĕss *a.* Not suffering or causing pain; hence ~LY² *adv.*, ~NESS *n.* [f. PAIN¹ + -LESS]

paint¹ *n.* Colouring-matter, esp. when suspended in liquid in order to impart colour to a surface; LUMINOUS *paint*; colouring-matter to adorn face etc., rouge etc.; **as pretty** etc. **as ~,** very pretty etc.; **~'box,** box containing dry paints before use; **~'brush,** house-painter's or artist's brush. [f. foll.]

paint² *v.t.* **1.** Portray, represent, (object, or abs.) in colours; adorn (wall etc.) with painting; (fig.) represent (incident etc.) in words vividly as by painting; **not so black as he is ~ed,** better than he is asserted to be. **2.** Cover surface of (object) with paint; apply paint of specified colour to (*paint the door green*); *paint* (=*gild*) *the* LILY; **~ out,** efface with paint; **~ the town red,** (sl.) cause commotion by riotous spree etc.; **~ed lady,** orange-red butterfly with black and white spots. **3.** Apply liquid or cosmetic to (face etc., or abs.); apply (liquid to skin etc.; *paint iodine on the cut*). [ME, f. *peint* p.p. of OF *peindre* f. L *pingere pict-* paint]

pai'nter¹ *n.* One who paints pictures; workman who colours woodwork etc. with paint; **~'s colic,** form of colic to which painters who work with lead are liable; so **pai'ntr**ESS¹ *n.* [ME, f. OF *peintour* f. Rom. **pinctor -oris* f. L *pictor* (as prec.; see -ER²)]

pai'nter² *n.* Rope attached to bow of boat for making it fast to ship, stake, etc.; **cut the ~,** (fig.) effect a separation. [ME, prob. f. OF *penteur* rope from mast-head; cf. G *pentertakel* (*pentern* fish the anchor)]

pai'nterlў *a.* Characteristic of a painter, artistic; characteristic of paintings; (of a painting) not using clearly defined outlines. [f. PAINTER¹ + -LY¹]

pai'ntĭng *n.* In vbl senses; art of representing or depicting by colours on surface; product of this. [ME, f. PAINT² + -ING¹]

pai'ntў *a.* Of paint; (of picture etc.) overcharged with paint. [f. PAINT¹ + -Y²]

pair¹ *n.* **1.** Set of two persons or things, couple, (esp. of things that usu. exist or are used in couples, as gloves, SHOE¹s, sculls, heels, eyes); two playing-cards of same denomination; (Cricket) =*pair of* SPECTACLES. **2.** Article consisting of two corresponding parts not used separately (*pair of scissors*, *tongs*, *trousers*). **3.** Engaged or married couple; mated couple of animals; ~ (**of horses**), two horses harnessed side by side; (Parl. etc.) two voters on opposite sides absenting themselves from division by mutual arrangement, person willing to act thus (*cannot find a pair*). **4.** The other member of a pair (*where is the pair to this sock?*). **5.** Flight *of stairs* or (fixed or portable) *steps*. **6. ~-horse** *a.*, for a pair of horses; **~-oar,** boat rowed by two oarsmen; **~ production,** (Phys.) conversion of radiation quantum into electron and positron; **~ royal,** set of three cards of same denomination. [ME, f. OF *paire* f. L *paria* neut. pl. of *par* equal]

pair² *v.t.* & *i.* Arrange (persons, things), be arranged, in couples; unite in love or marriage; (of animals) mate; unite (*with* one of opposite sex); **~ off,** arrange or go off in pairs, (Parl. etc.) make a pair, (colloq.) marry (*with*). [f. prec.]

pai's|a (pī'-) *n.* (*pl.* **~e** *pr.* -ā). Coin of India, Pakistan, and Bangladesh, one-hundredth of rupee or taka. [Hindi]

Pai'sley (-z-) *a.* (Of garment) made of soft wool woven or printed with bright coloured design of usu. curved abstract figures. [~ in Strathclyde, Scotland]

***pajamas.** See PYJAMAS.

||**Păk, Pă'kĭ,** *ns.* (sl.) Pakistani. [abbr.]

pa'kėha (pah'kĭhah) *n.* (N.Z.) White man; **~ Maori,** white man living as Maori. [Maori]

Pakĭsta'nĭ (pah-; -ah'-) *a.* & *n.* (Native) of Pakistan. [Hind.; see -I]

păl *n.*, & *v.i.* (-ll-). **1.** *n.* Comrade, mate; ||OLD *Pals Act*. **2.** *v.i.* (sl.) ~ (**up**), associate (*with*). [E Gipsy, = brother, mate, ult. f. Skr. *bhrātr* BROTHER]

pă'lace *n.* Official residence of sovereign, president, archbishop, or bishop; stately mansion; spacious building for entertainment, refreshment, etc.; ||GIN²-*palace*; **~ revolution,** overthrow of sovereign etc. without civil war. [ME, f. OF *palais* f. L *Palatium*, hill in Rome, house of emperor Augustus built on this]

pă'ladĭn *n.* Any of the Twelve Peers of Charlemagne's court, of whom the Count Palatine was the chief; knight errant, champion. [f. F *paladin* f. It. *paladino* f. L *palatinus* (see PALATINE¹)]

Pălaeâr'ctĭc *a.* (Zool.) Of the arctic and temperate regions of the Old World. [f. foll. + ARCTIC]

pă'laeō-, *pă'lēō-, *comb. form.* Ancient, old, (esp.) of ancient times, as : **~anthropo'logy,** study of fossil man; **~bo'tany,** study of fossil plants; **~climato'logy,** study of climate in past times; **~ma'gnetism,** (study of) magnetism remaining in rocks from past times. [f. Gk *palaios* ancient]

Pă'laeocēne, *Pă'lēocēne, *a.* & *n.* (Geol.) (Of) lowest division of tertiary period or system. [f. prec. + Gk *kainos* new]

pălaeŏ'|graphy̆, *pălēŏ'|graphy̆, *n.* Study of ancient writing and inscriptions; hence ~GRAPHER *n.*, **pălaeo**GRA'PHIC(AL) *adjs.* [f. F *paléographie* f. mod. L *palaeographia* (as PALAEO-, -GRAPHY)]

pălaeolĭ'thĭc, *pălēolĭ'thĭc, *a.* (Archaeol.) Of a period in which primitive stone implements were used. [f. PALAEO- + Gk *lithos* stone + -IC]

pălaeŏntŏ'|logy̆, *pălēŏntŏ'|logy̆, *n.* Study of life in the geological past; hence **pălaeŏnto**LO'GICAL *a.*, ~LOGIST *n.* [f. PALAEO- + Gk *onta* neut. pl. of *ōn* being, part. of *eimi* be, + -O- + -LOGY]

pălaeozō'ĭc, *pălēozō'ĭc, *a.* & *n.* (Geol.) (Of the) geological era containing the oldest forms of highly organized life (reptiles, seed-bearing plants, etc.). [f. PALAEO- + Gk *zōē* life, *zōos* living + -IC]

palae'stra, palĕ'stra, *n.* (esp. Gk & Rom. Ant.) Wrestling-school, gymnasium. [ME f. L *palaestra*, f. Gk *palaistra* (*palaiō* wrestle)]

pă'lafĭtte *n.* Prehistoric hut on piles over lake in Switzerland or N. Italy. [F, f. It. *palafitta* pile-fence (*palo* stake, *fitto* fixed)]

pă'lais (-lā) *n.* **~ (de danse)** (-dedah'ńs), public hall for dancing. [F, = (dancing) hall]

pălanqui'n, pălankee'n, (-n-kē'n) *n.* Covered litter for one, in India and the East, carried usu. by four or six men. [f. Port. *palanquim*; cf. Hindi *pālkī*, f. Skr. *palyanka*, *paryanka* bed, couch (*pari* around)]

pă'lat|able *a.* Pleasant to the taste; (fig.) agreeable to the mind; hence ~ABI'LITY *n.*, **~ab**LY² *adv.* [f. PALATE + -ABLE]

pă'latal *a.* & *n.* **1.** *a.* Of the palate; (Phonet., of sound) made by placing tongue against (usu. hard) palate, e.g. *y* in *yes*, whence ~IZE (3) *v.t.* **2.** *n.* Palatal sound. [F (as foll.; see -AL)]

pă'late *n.* **1.** Structure closing upper part of mouth cavity in vertebrates; **hard, soft, ~**, its front, back, part; *cleft palate* (see CLEAVE¹). **2.** Sense of taste; mental taste, liking. [ME, f. L *palatum*]

palā'tial (-shal) *a.* Like a palace; splendid; hence ~LY² *adv.* [f. L (as PALACE) + -AL]

pală'tĭnate *n.* **1.** Territory under a Count Palatine. **2.** ||(Durham Univ.) Light shade of purple or lavender; blazer of this colour as sports distinction. [f. foll. + -ATE¹]

Pă'latīne¹ *a.* **(Count) ~**, count having within his territory jurisdiction such as elsewhere belongs only to sovereign (in Engl. Hist. also **Earl ~**); **County ~**, his territory (still in England of Lancashire and Cheshire). [ME, f. F *palatin -ine* f. L *palatinus* of the PALACE; see -INE¹]

pă'latīne² *a.* & *n.* **1.** *a.* Of the palate; **~ bones,** two bones forming hard palate. **2.** *n.* Palatine bone. [f. F *palatin -ine* (as PALATE; see -INE¹)]

pă'latogrăm *n.* Record of areas of contact between tongue and palate in producing a sound. [f. L *palatum* PALATE + -O- + -GRAM]

pala'ver (-lah'-) *n.* & *v.* **1.** *n.* Conference, (prolonged) discussion, esp. (Hist.) between African or other natives and traders etc.; profuse or idle talk; cajolery; (sl.) affair, business. **2.** *v.i.* Talk profusely. **3.** *v.t.* Flatter, wheedle. [f. Port. *palavra* word f. L (as PARABLE)]

pāle¹ *n.* **1.** Pointed piece of wood for fence etc., stake; boundary (esp. fig.; **beyond the ~**, outside bounds of civilized behaviour etc.). **2.** (Hist.) **The (English) P~**, part of Ireland under English rule; **the P~**, part of Russia to which Jews were confined. **3.** (Her.) Vertical stripe in middle of shield; **in ~**, arranged vertically. [ME, f. OF *pal* f. L *palus* stake]

pāle² *a.* (Of person or complexion) of whitish or ashen appearance; (of colour) faint, not dark or deep; faintly coloured; of faint lustre, dim; **~-face,** supposed N. Amer. Ind. name for white man; hence ~'LY² (-l-lĭ) *adv.*, ~'NESS (-ln-) *n.* [ME, f. OF *pal(l)e* f. L *pallidus* (*pallēre* be pale)]

pāle³ *v.* **1.** *v.i.* Grow pale; (fig.) become pale in comparison (*before* or *beside*). **2.** *v.t.* Make pale. [ME, f. OF *palir* (as prec.)]

pā'lėa *n.* (*pl.* **~e**). (Bot.) Chafflike bract, esp. in flower of grasses. [L, = chaff]

pāled (-ld) *a.* Having palings. [f. PALE¹ + -ED²]

***pā'lēo-.** See PALAEO-.

Pălėstĭ'nĭan *n.* & *a.* **1.** *n.* Native or inhabitant of Palestine. **2.** *a.* Of, pertaining to, or connected with, Palestine. [f. *Palestine* in S.W. Asia + -IAN]

palĕ'stra. See PALAESTRA.

pă'letōt (-etō) *n.* Loose cloak for man or woman; 19th-c. woman's fitted jacket. [F]

pă'lėtte *n.* Artist's thin wooden slab held in hand and used for holding and mixing colours when painting; colours used by particular artist or on particular occasion; **~-knife,** thin steel blade with handle for mixing colours or for use in kitchen etc. [F, dim. of *pale* shovel f. L *pala* spade]

pă'lfrey (*or* paw'-) *n.* (arch. or poet.) Saddle-horse for ordinary riding, esp. for ladies. [ME, f. OF *palefrei* f. med. L *palefredus*, LL *paraveredus* f. Gk *para* beside, extra, + L *veredus* light horse, of Gaulish orig.]

Pa'lĭ (pah'-) *n.* Language used in canonical books of Buddhists. [f. Skr. *pāli-bhāsā* (*pāli* canon, *bhāsā* language)]

pă'lĭmpsēst *n.* & *a.* **1.** *n.* Writing-material or manuscript on which the original writing has been effaced to make room for a second writing; monumental brass turned and re-engraved on reverse side. **2.** *a.* (Of document or brass) so treated. [f. L f. Gk *palimpsēstos* (*palin* again, *psaō* rub smooth)]

pă'lĭndrōme *n.* & *a.* (Word, verse, etc.) that reads the same backwards as forwards (e.g. *rotator*); hence **pălĭndrŏ'mic** *a.* [f. Gk *palindromos* running back again (*palin* again, *drom-* run)]

pā'lĭng *n.* (in *sing.* or *pl.*) (Fence of) pales. [f. PALE¹ + -ING¹]

pălĭn|gĕ'nėsĭs (-nj-) *n.* Regeneration (lit. or fig.); revival; (Biol.) exact reproduction of ancestral character in ontogenesis, whence **~gėnĕ'**TIC *a.* [f. Gk *palin* again + *genesis* birth, GENESIS]

pă'lĭnōde *n.* Poem in which author retracts thing said in former poem; recantation. [F, or f. LL *palinodia* f. Gk *palinōidia* (*palin* again, *ōidē* song)]

pălĭsā'de *n.*, & *v.t.* **1.** *n.* Fence of pales or of iron railings; (Mil.) strong pointed wooden stake used in close defensive row; *(in *pl.*) line of high cliffs. **2.** *v.t.* Furnish or enclose with palisade. [f. F *palissade* f. Prov. *palissada* (*palissa* paling f. Gallo-Rom. **palicea* f. L *palus* stake)]

pā'lĭsh *a.* Somewhat pale. [ME, f. PALE² + -ISH¹]

pall¹ (pawl) *n.* Cloth, usu. of black or purple or white velvet, spread over coffin, hearse, or tomb; woollen shoulder-band with front and back pendants, worn by pope and some metropolitans and archbishops; (Her.) Y-shaped charge representing front of this; (fig.) mantle, cloak, (*pall of darkness*, *of smoke*); **~'bearer,** person helping to carry or accompany coffin at funeral. [OE *pæll*, f. L *pallium* cloak]

pall² (pawl) *v.* **1.** *v.i.* Become uninteresting; **~ on,** cease to interest or attract (person, mind, taste). **2.** *v.t.* Satiate, cloy. [ME, f. APPAL]

Pallā'dĭan *a.* (Archit.) In the neoclassical style of Palladio; ~ **window,** = VENETIAN *window.* [f. A. *Palladio*, It. architect d. 1580 + -AN]
pallā'dĭ|um¹ *n.* (*pl.* ~**a**). Image of Pallas on which safety of Troy was held to depend; safeguard. [ME, f. L f. Gk *palladion* (*Pallas Pallados* epithet of Athene)]
pallā'dĭum² *n.* Rare hard white metallic element of platinum group. [mod. L, f. *Pallas*, an asteroid discovered (1803) just previously, + -IUM; cf. CERIUM]
pă'llėt¹ *n.* Straw bed; mattress. [ME *pail(l)et* f. AF *paillete* straw, f. OF *paille* f. L *palea*]
pă'llėt² *n.* Flat wooden blade with handle, used by potters etc.; artist's palette; projection on part of machine, serving to change mode of motion of wheel; projection transmitting motion from escapement to pendulum etc.; valve under each pipe in wind-chest of organ; portable platform for transporting and storing loads. [f. F PALETTE]
pă'lliăsse (-lyăs; *or* -lyă's) *n.* Straw mattress. [f. F *paillasse* f. It. *pagliaccio* f. Rom. **paleaceum* f. L *palea* straw]
pă'llĭ|āte *v.t.* Alleviate (disease) without curing; extenuate, excuse; so ~A'TION *n.* [f. LL *palliare* cloak (*pallium*) + -ATE³]
pă'llĭative *a.* & *n.* (Thing) that serves to palliate. [f. F *palliatif -ive* or f. med. L *palliativus* (as prec.; see -IVE)]
pă'llĭd *a.* Pale, esp. from sickness etc.; hence ~LY² *adv.*, ~ITY (-ĭ'd-), ~NESS, *ns.* [f. L *pallidus* (as PALE²)]
pă'llĭ|um *n.* (*pl.* ~**a** *or* ~**ums**). Man's large rectangular cloak esp. as worn by ancient Greeks; pope's etc. PALL¹; mantle of mollusc, whence ~AL *a.* [L]
păll-mă'll (*or* pĕlmĕ'l) *n.* (Hist.) Game in which ball was driven through iron ring suspended in long alley. [f. obs. F *pallemaille* f. It. *pallamaglio* (*palla* ball, *maglio* mallet)]
pă'llor *n.* Pallidness, paleness. [L (*pallēre* be pale; see -OR)]
pă'llȳ *a.* (colloq.) Friendly. [f. PAL + -Y²]
palm¹ (pahm) *n.* **1.** Tree of family Palmae (chiefly tropical, usu. with upright unbranched stem and head of large pinnate or fan-shaped leaves); branch of palm-tree as symbol of victory; supreme excellence, prize for this, (esp. *bear* or *yield the palm*); branch of various trees substituted for palm in northern countries, esp. in celebrating Palm Sunday. **2.** ~ **civet,** paradoxure; ~**-honey,** refined sap of coquito palm; ~**-oil,** (1) oil got from various palms, (2) (with pun on PALM²) bribe-money; **P~ Sunday,** Sunday before Easter, on which Christ's entry into Jerusalem is celebrated by processions in which branches of palm are carried; ~ **wine,** alcoholic drink from fermented palm-sap. **3.** So **pălm**A'CEOUS *a.* [OE *palm(a)*, = OS, OHG *palma*, ON *pálmr*, Gmc f. L *palma* PALM², its leaf being likened to a spread hand]
palm² (pahm) *n.* Part of hand between wrist and fingers, esp. its inner surface; part of glove that covers this; breadth (about 4 in.) or length (about 8 in.) of hand as measure; palmate part of antler; GREASE² person's *palm*; **in the** ~ (= HOLLOW²) **of** one's **hand;** ~**-oil** (see prec.); hence (-)'ED² (pahmd) *a.*, ~'FUL 2 *n.* [ME f. OF *paume*, f. L *palma*; later assim. to L]
palm³ (pahm) *v.t.* Impose or thrust fraudulently (thing *on* person); conceal (cards, dice, etc.) in hand; touch or strike with palm; bribe. [f. prec.]
pă'lmar *a.* Of or in the palm of the hand. [f. L *palmaris* (as PALM²; see -AR¹)]
pă'lmarȳ *a.* Bearing the palm, pre-eminent. [f. L *palmarius* (as PALM¹; see -ARY¹)]
pă'lmāte *a.* PALM²-shaped; having lobes etc. like spread fingers. [f. L *palmatus* (as PALM²; see -ATE²)]
pa'lmer (pah'm-) *n.* **1.** (Hist.) Pilgrim returning from Holy Land with palm branch or leaf; itinerant monk under vow of poverty. **2.** ~(**-worm**), destructive hairy caterpillar. **3.** Hairy artificial fly in angling. [ME f. AF, = OF *palmier* f. med. L *palmarius* pilgrim (as PALMARY); cf. -ER²]
pălmĕ'tte *n.* (Archaeol.) Ornament of radiating petals like palm-leaf. [F, dim. of *palme* PALM¹; see -ETTE]
pălmĕ'ttō *n.* (*pl.* ~**s**). Palm-tree esp. of small size, e.g. dwarf fan-palm (*Chamaerops humilis*). [f. Sp. *palmito*, dim. of *palma* PALM¹, assim. to It. wds in *-etto*]
pă'lmĭpĕd, -pēde, *a.* & *n.* Web-footed (bird). [f. L *palmipes -pedis* (as PALM², *pes pedis* foot)]
pa'lmĭstrȳ (pah'm-) *n.* Divination from lines etc. in palm of hand; so [as back form.] **pa'lm**IST (3) (pah'm-) *n.* [ME, f. PALM² + second element (orig. *-estry*) unexpl.]
pa'lmȳ (pah'mĭ) *a.* Of, like, abounding in, palms; triumphant, flourishing, (*palmy days*). [f. PALM¹ + -Y²]
pălmȳr'a *n.* Palm (*Borassus flabellifer*) grown in India and Sri Lanka, with fan-shaped leaves used for matting etc. [f. Port. *palmeira* palm-tree, assim. to *Palmyra* in Syria]
palō'lō *n.* (*pl.* ~**s**). Worm living in Pacific reefs and caught as delicacy on coming to sea-surface for breeding. [native name in Samoa and Tonga]
pălomi'nō (-mē'-) *n.* (*pl.* ~**s**). Golden or cream-coloured horse with light-coloured mane and tail, orig. bred in S.W. of U.S. [Amer. Sp., f. Sp. *palomino* young pigeon (*paloma* dove f. L *palumba*)]
***palōō'ka** *n.* (sl.) Poor performer at sport; lout. [20th c.; orig. unkn.]
pălōvĕr'dė *n.* Yellow-flowered thorny tree of genus *Cercidium* in Arizona etc. [Amer. Sp., = green tree]
pălp¹. Var. of PALPUS.
pălp² *v.t.* Feel, handle. [f. L *palpare*]
pă'lp|able *a.* That can be touched or felt; readily perceived by senses or mind; hence ~ABI'LITY *n.*, ~**ab**LY² *adv.* [ME, f. LL *palpabilis* (as PALPATE; see -ABLE)]
pă'lpal *a.* Of palpus or palpi. [f. mod. L *palpalis* (PALPUS; see -AL)]
pălp|ā'te *v.t.* Examine by touch (esp. in medical examination); so ~A'TION *n.* [f. L *palpare* feel + -ATE³]
pă'lpėbral *a.* Of the eyelids. [f. LL *palpebralis* (*palpebra* eyelid; see -AL)]
pă'lpĭtāte *v.i.* Pulsate, throb; tremble (*with* fear, pleasure, etc.). [f. L *palpitare* frequent. of *palpare* touch gently + -ATE³]
pălpĭtā'tion *n.* Throbbing, trembling; increased activity of heart due to exertion, agitation, or disease. [f. L *palpitatio* (as prec.; see -ATION)]
pă'lp|us *n.* (*pl.* ~**i** *pr.* -ī). Segmented sense-organ at mouth of insect, feeler. [L (*palpare* feel)]
pa'lsgrāve (paw'lz-) *n.* Count PALATINE¹. [f. Du. *paltsgrave* (*palts* palatinate, *grave* count)]
pa'lstāve (paw'l-) *n.* Celt of bronze etc. shaped to fit into split handle. [f. Da. *paalstav* f. ON *pálstavr* (*páll* hoe f. L *palus* stake, *stafr* STAFF¹)]
pa'lsȳ (paw'lzĭ *or* pŏ'lzĭ) *n.*, & *v.t.* **1.** *n.* Paralysis, esp. with involuntary tremors; (fig.) cause or condition of utter helplessness. **2.** *v.t.* Affect with palsy, paralyse (usu. fig.). [ME *pa(r)lesi* f. OF *paralisie* f. Rom. **paralisia* f. L (PARALYSIS)]

pa'lter (paw'l- *or* pŏ'l-) *v.i.* Shuffle, equivocate, (*with* person); haggle (*with* person *about* thing); trifle (*with* subject). [16th c.; orig. unkn.]

pa'ltr|y̆ (paw'l- *or* pŏ'l-) *a.* Worthless, petty, contemptible; hence ~INESS *n.* [16th c., f. *paltry* trash, app. f. *palt, pelt,* rubbish + -RY (cf. *trumpery*); cf. LG *paltrig* ragged]

palū'dal (*or* pă'l-) *a.* Of a marsh; malarial. [f. L *palus -udis* marsh + -AL]

pā'ly̆[1] *a.* (poet.) Somewhat pale. [f. PALE[2] + -Y[2]]

pā'ly̆[2] *a.* (Her.) Divided into equal vertical stripes. [f. OF *palé* (*pal* PALE[1]; see -Y[4])]

păly̆nŏ'|logy̆ *n.* Study of pollen in connection with plant geography, dating of fossils, allergies, etc.; hence **păly̆no**LO'GICAL *a.*, ~LOGIST *n.* [f. Gk *palunō* sprinkle + -O- + -LOGY]

pă'mpa *n.* (usu. in *pl.*, *pr. -az or -as*). Large treeless plain in S. America south of the Amazon, esp. in Argentina; **~s-grass,** large ornamental grass orig. from S. America. [Sp., f. Quechua *pampa* plain]

pă'mper *v.t.* Over-indulge (person, tastes, etc.), spoil (person) with luxury. [ME, frequent. of obs. *pamp* cram; cf. -ER[3]]

pămper'ō (-ār'ō) *n.* (*pl.* **~s**). Strong cold S.W. wind blowing from Andes to Atlantic. [Sp., f. as PAMPA]

pă'mphlėt *n.* Small usu. unbound treatise, esp. in prose on subject of current interest. [ME, f. *Pamphilet*, familiar name of 12th-c. L amatory poem *Pamphilus seu de Amore*; see -ET[1]]

pămphlėteer' *n.*, & *v.i.* **1.** *n.* Writer of pamphlets. **2.** *v.i.* Write pamphlets. [f. prec. + -EER]

păn[1] *n.* **1.** Metal or earthenware or plastic vessel, usu. shallow, for domestic purposes, (BED[1]*pan*, FRY[2]*ing-pan*, SAUCE*pan*, WARM[2]*ing-pan*). **2.** Pan-like vessel in which substances are heated etc.; bowl of pair of scales; bowl of water-closet; part of lock that held the priming in obsolete types of gun; hollow in ground (SALT-*pan*); hard substratum of soil; *(sl.) face. **3.** Contents of pan. **4.** Hence ~'FUL 2 *n.* [OE *panne*, = OS *panna*, OHG *phanna*, f. WG **panna*, perh. ult. f. L *patina* dish]

păn[2] *v.* (**-nn-**). **1.** *v.t.* (colloq.) Criticize severely. **2.** ~ **off, out,** wash (gold-bearing gravel) in pan. **3.** *v.i.* ~ **out,** yield gold, (fig., of actions etc.) succeed, work, (*well* etc.). [f. prec.]

păn[3] *v.* (**-nn-**) & *n.* **1.** *v.t.* Swing (camera) horizontally to give panoramic effect or follow moving object. **2.** *v.i.* (Of camera) be moved thus. **3.** *n.* Panning movement. [f. PANORAMA]

pan[4] (pahn) *n.* Leaf of the betel; this enclosing lime and areca-nut parings, chewed by Asians. [Hindi, f. Skr. *parṇa* feather, leaf]

păn- *comb. form.* All, as: (1) relating to the whole universe (**panco'smism,** doctrine that material universe is all that exists); (2) relating to the whole of a continent, racial group, religion, etc., (*pan-American, pan-Hellenism, pan-Anglican*). [Gk (*pan*, neut. of *pas* all)]

pănacē'a *n.* Universal remedy. [L, f. Gk *panakeia* f. PAN(*akēs* remedy) all-healing]

pana'che (-ah'sh *or* -ă'sh) *n.* Tuft or plume of feathers, esp. as head-dress or on helmet; (fig.) display, swagger, verve. [F, f. It. *pennacchio* f. LL *pinnaculum* dim. of *pinna* feather]

pana'da (-nah'-) *n.* Bread boiled to pulp and flavoured; thick paste of flour etc. [Sp., f. Rom. **panata* f. L *panis* bread; see -ADE]

pănama' (-ah') *n.* ~ (**hat**), hat of fine pliant strawlike material made (orig. in Ecuador) from leaves of the screw-pine. [f. *P~* in Central America]

Pănamā'nĭan *a.* & *n.* (Native or inhabitant) of Panama. [f. as prec. + euphonic *-n-* + -IAN]

pănatĕ'lla *n.* Long thin cigar. [f. Sp. *panatela* long thin biscuit f. It. *panatella* dim. of *panata* (as PANADA)]

pă'ncāke (-n-k-) *n.*, & *v.i.* **1.** *n.* Thin flat batter-cake fried in pan (**flat as a** ~, quite flat), sometimes rolled up with filling; flat cake (e.g. of make-up); **P~ Day,** Shrove Tuesday (on which pancakes are traditionally eaten); ~ **landing** (of aircraft descending vertically in level position). **2.** *v.i.* Make pancake landing. [ME, f. PAN[1] + CAKE]

panchay'at (pŭnchī'at) *n.* (Ind.) Village council. [Hindi, f. Skr. *pancha* five]

pănchromă'tĭc (-n-kr-) *a.* (Photog.) (Of film etc.) sensitive to all visible spectrum colours. [f. PAN- + CHROMATIC]

păncrā'tĭum (-n-k-) *n.* (Gk Ant.) Athletic contest in wrestling and boxing; hence **păncră'**TIC (-n-k-) *a.* [L, f. Gk *pagkration* (as PAN-, *kratos* bodily strength)]

pă'ncrė|as *n.* **1.** Gland near stomach discharging a digestive secretion (*pancreatic juice*) into duodenum and insulin into blood. **2.** Hence **~ă'**TIC *a.*, **~atī'**TIS *n.* [mod. L, f. Gk *pagkreas* (as PAN-, *kreas -atos* flesh)]

pă'ncrėatĭn *n.* Enzyme(s) present in pancreatic juice; digestive extract prepared from animal pancreases. [f. as prec. + -IN]

pă'nda *n.* **1.** Indian racoon-like animal, with reddish-brown fur and long bushy tail. **2.** (**Giant**) ~, large rare bearlike black-and-white mammal of E. Tibet and W. China. **3.** ||~ **car,** police patrol car with broad white stripe over body. [Nepali name]

Păndē'an *a.* Of the god Pan; ~ **pipe,** = PAN-PIPE. [irreg. f. Gk *Pan* (cf. PANIC[2]) + -EAN]

pă'ndĕct *n.* (usu. in *pl.*) Compendium in 50 books of Roman civil law made by order of Justinian in 6th c.; complete body of laws. [f. F *pandecte*, or f. L f. Gk PAN(*dektēs* f. *dekhomai* receive) all-receiver]

păndĕ'mĭc *a.* & *n.* (Disease) prevalent over the whole of a country or over the whole world. [f. Gk PAN(*dēmos* people) + -IC]

păndėmō'nĭum *n.* Abode of all demons; (place of) lawless violence or uproar; utter confusion. [mod. L (Milton) f. PAN- + Gk *daimōn* DEMON; see -IUM]

pă'nder *n.*, & *v.i.* **1.** *n.* Go-between in clandestine amours, procurer; one who ministers to evil designs. **2.** *v.i.* Minister (*to* base passions or evil designs). [f. *Pandare*, character in Boccaccio and in Chaucer's *Troilus and Criseyde*, f. L f. Gk *Pandaros*]

pă'ndĭt (*or* pŭ'-) *n.* = PUNDIT 1. [Hindi, as PUNDIT]

P. & O. *abbr.* Peninsular and Oriental Steamship Company.

Păndōr'a[1] *n.* **~'s box,** (Gk Myth.) box in which Hope alone remained when by its rash opening all other blessings were lost to (or all ills were let loose upon) mankind. [f. Gk *Pandōra* all-gifted (as PAN-, *dōron* gift)]

păndōr'a[2], **păndōr'e,** *n.* Stringed instrument like cithern. [f. It. *pandora* etc. f. LL f. Gk *pandoura* three-stringed lute]

||**p. & p.** *abbr.* postage and packing.

pāne[1] *n.* Single sheet of glass in compartment of window; rectangular division of chequered pattern etc. [ME, f. OF *pan* f. L *pannus* piece of cloth]

pāne[2]. Var. of PEEN.

pănėgy̆'rĭc *n.* & *a.* Laudatory (discourse); so ~AL *a.* [f. F *panégyrique* f. L f. Gk *panēgurikos* of public assembly, f. PAN(*ēguris* = *agora* assembly); see -IC]

For other words in *pan-* see PAN-.

pă'nėgўrize, -īse (-iz), *v.t.* Speak or write in praise of, eulogize; so **pănėgў'rist** (1) *n.* [f. Gk *panēgurizō* (as prec.; see -IZE)]

pă'nel^{1} *n.* **1.** Slip of parchment; list of jury; jury; ||(Sc. Law) person(s) on trial, the accused. **2.** ||(Hist.) List of doctors registered in a district as accepting patients under National Insurance Act. **3.** Team in broadcast or public quiz programme etc.; body of experts assembled for discussion or consultation; hence **~list**, *~IST, *n.*, member of this. **4.** Distinct compartment of surface, esp. of wainscot, door, etc., often sunk below or raised above general level. **5.** Piece of material esp. of different kind or colour inserted in woman's dress etc. **6.** **~-beater,** workman who beats out metal panels of motor vehicles; ~ **game,** quiz etc. played by panel (sense 3); ~ **heating** (of rooms by panels in wall etc. containing sources of heat); **~-pin,** thin nail with very small head; **~-saw** (with small teeth for cutting thin wood for panels). [ME & OF, = piece of cloth, saddle-cushion, f. Rom. **pannellus* dim. of L *pannus*; cf. PANE^{1}]

pă'nel^{2} *v.t.* (||-ll-). Fit (wall, door, etc.) with panels; ornament (dress etc.) with panel(s); hence **~ling**^{1} (2), *~ING^{1} (2), *n.* [f. prec.]

păng *n.* Shooting pain; sudden sharp mental pain. [16th c.; var. of earlier *pronge, prange,* MLG *prange* pinching, Goth. *anapraggan* oppress]

pă'nga (-ngg*a*) *n.* African machete. [native name in E. Africa]

Pănglŏ'ssian (-ngg-) *a.* Excessively optimistic. [f. *Pangloss*, character in Voltaire's 'Candide' + -IAN]

păngō'lĭn (-ngg-) *n.* Scaly ant-eater of Asia and Africa. [f. Malay *peng-gōling* roller (from habit of rolling itself up)]

***pă'nhăndle** *n.* & *v.* **1.** *n.* Narrow strip of one political division of a country extending between two others. **2.** *v.t.* & *i.* (sl.) Beg (from) in street. [f. PAN^{1} + HANDLE^{1}]

pă'nĭc^{1} *n.* Grass of genus *Panicum*, e.g. Italian millet and other cereals. [OE, f. L *panicum* (*panus* thread on bobbin, millet-ear f. Gk *pēnos* web)]

pă'nĭc^{2} *a.*, *n.*, & *v.* (**-ck-**). **1.** *a.* (Of terror) unreasoning, excessive; excessively hasty through fear; for use in emergency (*panic bolt, button, stations*). **2.** *n.* Infectious fright, sudden alarm (e.g., in commerce) leading to hasty measures; **~-monger,** one who fosters a panic; **~-stricken, ~-struck,** affected with panic; hence **~ky**^{2} *a.* **3.** *v.t.* & *i.* Affect or be affected with panic; *amuse (audience etc.) greatly. [f. F *panique* f. mod. L f. Gk *panikos* (*Pan* rural god causing terror)]

pă'nĭcle *n.* (Bot.) Loose irregular type of compound inflorescence, as in oats. [f. L *paniculum* dim. of *panus* thread]

pănjă'ndrum *n.* Mock title of exalted personage; pompous official or pretender. [app. invented in nonsense verse by S. Foote 1755]

||**pă'nnage** *n.* (Right of or payment for) pasturage of pigs; acorns, beech-mast, etc., as food for pigs. [ME, f. OF *pasnage, pannage* f. med. L *pastionaticum* (L *pastio* pasture f. *pascere past-* feed; see -AGE)]

pănne *n.* ~ (**velvet**), velvet-like fabric of silk or rayon with flattened pile. [F]

pă'nnier (-ny*er*) *n.* **1.** Basket, esp. one carried, usu. in pairs, by beast of burden or on bicycle or on the shoulders; bag similarly carried on bicycle or motor cycle; covered basket for surgical instruments and medicines for ambulance. **2.** (Hist.) (Frame supporting) part of skirt looped up round hips. [ME, f. OF *panier* f. L *panarium* bread-basket (*panis* bread; see -ARY^{1})]

pă'nnĭkĭn *n.* Small metal drinking-vessel; its contents. [f. PAN^{1} + -KIN, after *cannikin*]

pă'nopl|ў *n.* Complete suit of armour; (fig.) complete or splendid array; hence **~ĭed**^{2} (-lĭd) *a.* [f. F *panoplie* or f. mod. L f. Gk PAN(*oplia* f. *hopla* arms) full armour of hoplite]

pănŏ'ptĭc *a.* Showing or seeing the whole at one view. [f. Gk *panoptos* seen by all, *panoptēs* all-seeing + -IC]

***pănŏ'ptĭcon** *n.* Circular prison with cells round warders' well in centre. [f. PAN- + Gk *optikos* of sight, OPTIC]

pănora'ma (-rah'-) *n.* Picture of landscape etc. arranged on inside of cylindrical surface or successively rolled out before spectator; photograph containing wide view, esp. one made with rotating camera; continuous passing scene; unbroken view of surrounding region (lit. or fig.); hence **pănoră'mic** *a.* [f. PAN- + Gk *horama* view (*horaō* see)]

pă'n-pīpe(**s**) *n.* Musical instrument made of series of reeds or pipes fixed together with mouthpieces in line. [f. *Pan*, Greek rural god, + PIPE^{1}]

pă'nsў (-zĭ) *n.* **1.** Garden plant (*Viola tricolor*) with flowers of various rich colours. **2.** (colloq.) ~ (**boy**), effeminate man, male homosexual. [f. F *pensée* thought, pansy (*penser* think f. L *pensare* frequent. of *pendere pens-* weigh)]

pănt^{1} *v.* & *n.* **1.** *v.i.* Gasp for breath; (fig.) yearn (*for* or *after* thing; *to* do); (of heart etc.) throb violently. **2.** *v.t.* Utter gaspingly (*out*). **3.** *n.* Gasp; throb. [ME, f. AF **panter* f. OF *pantaisier* pant, f. Rom. **pantasiare* for **phantasiare* f. Gk *phantasioō* cause to imagine (as FANTASY)]

pănt^{2}**.** See PANTS.

păntagru'el|ĭsm (-ōō'-) *n.* Extravagant coarse satirical humour; so **păntagruĕ'lian** (-ōō-) *a.*, ~IST (1) *n.* [f. *Pantagruel*, character in Rabelais + -ISM]

păntalĕ't(**te**)**s** (-ts) *n. pl.* (Hist.) Woman's long drawers with frill at ankle; woman's cycling trousers etc. [dim. of foll.; see -ET^{1}, -ETTE]

păntalōō'n *n.* **1.** Character in Italian comedy wearing pantaloons (sense 2); clown's butt and abettor in pantomime. **2.** (Hist.; usu. in *pl.*) Garment of breeches and stockings in one piece, close-fitting breeches down to ankle as transition from knee-breeches to trousers. **3.** *(in *pl.*, arch.) Trousers. [f. F *pantalon* f. It. *pantalone,* Venetian character in Italian comedy, perh. f. *San Pantaleone*, favourite Venetian saint in former times]

||**păntĕ'chnĭcon** (-kn-) *n.* **1.** (arch.) Furniture warehouse (orig. name of a bazaar). **2.** ~ (**van**), large van for removing furniture. [f. PAN- + Gk *tekhnikon* (neut.) of art (*tekhnē*; see -IC)]

pă'nthė|ĭsm *n.* Doctrine that God is everything and everything God; worship of all gods; so ~IST (2) *n.*, **~ĭ'stic**(AL) *adjs.* [f. PAN- + Gk *theos* god + -ISM]

pă'nthėon (*or* -ē'on) *n.* Temple dedicated to all the gods, esp. circular one at Rome; deities of a people collectively; building in which illustrious dead are buried or have memorials. [ME, f. L f. Gk PAN(*theion* holy f. *theos* god)]

pă'nther *n.* Leopard; *puma; hence ~ESS^{1} *n.* [ME f. OF *pantere* f. L *panthera* f. Gk *panthēr*]

pă'ntĭe|s (-tĭz) *n. pl.* (colloq.) Short trousers worn by children; short-legged or legless knickers worn by women and girls; **~-belt,** ***~-girdle,** woman's very light corset made in this shape. [dim. of PANTS; see -IE]

pă'ntĭhōse (-z) *n.* = *tights* (TIGHT 9). [f. PANTIES + HOSE]

pă'ntīle *n.* Roof tile transversely curved to ogee shape, one curve being much larger than the other. [f. PAN^{1} + TILE]

păntĭsŏ'cracў *n.* (Hist.) Utopian community in which all are equal and all rule. [f. Gk *pas pantos* all + *isokratia* ISOCRACY]

||**pă'ntō** *n.* (*pl.* **~s**). (colloq.) = PANTOMIME 1. [abbr.]

pănto- *comb. form.* All, as: **~lo'gic, panto'logy** (-ŏ'l-), (of) universal knowledge; **~mor'phic,** taking all shapes; **~sco'pic,** having wide range of vision. [f. Gk *pas pantos* all + -O-]

pă'nto|graph (-ahf) *n.* **1.** Instrument with jointed rods for copying plan etc. on any scale; hence ~GRA'PHIC *a.* **2.** Jointed framework conveying current to electric vehicle from overhead wires. [f. prec. + Gk *-graphos* writing]

pă'ntomīm|e *n.* & *v.* **1.** ||Dramatic entertainment usu. produced about Christmas and based on fairy-tale, with singing, dancing, clowning, topical jokes, transformation scene, and stock roles. **2.** Dumb show. **3.** (Rom. Hist.) Actor performing in dumb show. **4.** Hence or cogn. **păntomĭ'm**IC *a.*, ~IST (3) *n.* **5.** *v.t.* & *i.* Express (thing), express oneself, by dumb show. [F, or f. L f. Gk PANTO(*mimos* MIME)]

păntothĕ'nĭc *a.* **~ acid,** vitamin of B group essential to growth, found in liver etc. [f. Gk *pantothen* from all sides (as PANTO-) + -IC]

pă'ntrў *n.* Room in which bread and other provisions or (*butler's, housemaid's, pantry*) plate, table-linen, etc., are kept; **~man,** butler or his assistant. [ME, f. AF *panetrie,* OF *paneterie* (*panetier* baker f. Rom. **panatarius* f. LL *panarius* bread-seller f. L *panis* bread); see -ERY]

pănts *n. pl.* (colloq.) **1.** Trousers or slacks; **pant(s) suit,** trouser suit; (*bore, scare, talk,* etc.) **the ~ off,** (sl.) to a state of extremity; **with** one's **~ down,** (sl.) in state of embarrassing unpreparedness etc. **2.** ||Underpants. **3.** Panties. [abbr. of PANTALOONS]

panty-hose. Var. of PANTIHOSE.

***pă'ntўwaist** *n.* & *a.* **1.** *n.* Child's garment of short trousers buttoned to bodice. **2.** *n.* & *a.* Effeminate (person). [f. PANTIES + WAIST]

pă'nzer (-tser) *a.* & *n.* **1.** *a.* Armoured (*panzer division, troops*). **2.** *n.* (in *pl.*) Armoured troops. [G, = coat of mail]

păp¹ *n.* (arch. or dial.) Nipple esp. of woman; (in *pl.*) conical hilltops side by side. [ME, of Scand. orig., ult. imit. of sucking]

păp² *n.* Soft or semi-liquid food for infants or invalids; mash, pulp; undemanding reading-matter; hence **~'py**² *a.* [ME, prob. f. MLG, MDu. *pappe*, prob. f. med. L **pappa* f. L *pappare* eat]

papa' (-ah') *n.* (arch., esp. childish). Father. [F f. LL, f. Gk *pap(p)as*]

pā'pacў *n.* Pope's (tenure of) office; papal system. [ME, f. med. L *papatia* (*papa* pope; see -ACY)]

papā'ĭn *n.* Enzyme got from unripe papaws, used to tenderize meat. [f. PAPAYA + -IN]

pā'pal *a.* Of the pope or his office; **P~ States,** (Hist.) pope's temporal dominions esp. in central Italy; hence ~ISM (3), ~IST (2), *ns.*, ~IZE (3) *v.t.* & *i.*, ~LY² *adv.* [ME f. OF, f. med. L *papalis* f. eccl. L *papa* POPE¹; see -AL]

papā'verous *a.* Like or allied to the poppy; so **papāver**A'CEOUS *a.* [f. L *papaver* poppy + -OUS]

papaw', pawpaw', *n.* **1.** (Oblong orange edible fruit of) palmlike tropical Amer. tree of which stem, leaves, and fruit contain a milky juice that makes meat tender. **2.** *N. Amer. tree with purple flowers and oblong edible fruit. [earlier *papay(a)* f. Sp. & Port. *papaya*, of Carib orig.]

papay'a (-pī'*a*) *n.* = PAPAW 1. [var. of PAPAW]

pā'per¹ *n.* & *a.* **1.** *n.* Substance used for writing, printing, drawing, wrapping up parcels, etc., made of compactly interlaced fibres of rags, straw, wood, etc., in thin sheet; **commit to ~,** write down; **on ~,** in theory, judging from statistics, etc., (*on paper he is the better man*), in writing; **put pen to ~,** begin writing. **2.** Negotiable documents, e.g. bills of exchange; = *paper money*; (sl.) free passes to theatre etc. **3.** (in *pl.*) Documents proving person's or ship's identity, standing, etc.; documents belonging to or relating to a person or matter. **4.** Set of questions to be answered at one session in examination; written answers to these. **5.** = NEWS*paper*. **6.** Piece of paper, esp. as wrapper etc. **7.** Document printed on paper (||GREEN *Paper,* ||WHITE¹ *Paper*); essay or dissertation, esp. one read to learned society. **8.** *a.* Made of paper; flimsy like paper; conducted by means of writings (*paper warfare*); written on paper but not really existing (*paper profits*). **9. ~back** *n.* & *a.*, (book) bound in paper (often as cheap version or reprint); **~-boy, -girl,** (who delivers or sells newspapers); **~-chase,** cross-country run in which a trail of torn-up paper is laid by one or more runners to set a course for the rest; **~-clip,** piece of bent wire by which a few sheets of paper may be held together; **~-hanger,** one whose business is to cover walls with wallpaper; **~-knife,** blunt knife of ivory, wood, etc., for opening sealed envelopes, leaves of book, etc.; **~-mill** (in which paper is made); **~ money,** banknotes etc. used as currency; *paper* MULBERRY; *paper* NAUTILUS; *paper* TIGER; **~weight,** small heavy object for preventing loose papers from being displaced; **~work,** office administration and record-keeping. **10.** Hence ~Y² *a.* [ME f. AF *papir,* = OF *papier* f. L PAPYRUS]

pā'per² *v.t.* Enclose in paper; decorate (wall etc.) with paper (**~ over the cracks,** seek to disguise flaws or dissension); furnish with paper; (sl.) fill (theatre etc.) by giving free passes. [f. prec.]

Pā'phĭan *a.* Of (esp. illicit) sexual love. [f. L *Paphius* (*Paphos*, city in Cyprus sacred to Aphrodite or Venus) + -AN]

papier mâché (păpyā mă'shā; *or* mah'-) *n.* Moulded paper pulp used for boxes, trays, etc. [F, = chewed paper]

papĭlionā'ceous (-yonā'sh*u*s) *a.* (Bot.) With corolla like a butterfly. [f. mod. L *papilionaceus* f. L *papilio -onis* butterfly; see -ACEOUS]

papĭ'lla *n.* (*pl.* **~e**). Small nipple-like protuberance in a part or organ of the body, e.g. from dermis into epidermis; (Bot.) small fleshy projection on plant; hence or cogn. **pă'pĭll**ARY¹, **pă'pĭll**ATE² (2), **pă'pĭll**OSE¹, *adjs.* [L, = nipple, dim. of PAPULA]

păpĭllō'ma *n.* Wartlike tumour, often arising from papilla(e). [f. prec. + -OMA]

papĭ'llon (-ly*o*n) *n.* (Breed of) toy dog with ears suggesting form of butterfly. [F, = butterfly, f. as PAPILIONACEOUS]

pā'pĭst *n.* Advocate of papal supremacy; (usu. derog.) Roman Catholic; hence **papĭ'st**IC(AL) *adjs.*, ~RY (5) *n.* [f. F *papiste* or mod. L *papista* f. eccl. L *papa* POPE¹; see -IST]

papōō'se *n.* N. Amer. Indian young child. [Algonquin]

pă'pp|us *n.* (*pl.* **~i** *pr.* -ī). (Bot.) Downy appendage on fruit of thistles, dandelions, etc.; hence ~OSE¹ *a.* [L, f. Gk *pappos*]

pă'prĭka (*or* paprē'-) *n.* Ripe (red) PEPPER¹; red condiment made from it. [Magyar]

pă'pūl|a *n.* (*pl.* **~ae**). Pimple; small fleshy projection on plant; hence ~AR¹, ~OSE¹, ~OUS, *adjs.* [L]

pă'pūle *n.* = prec. [f. L *papula*; see -ULE]

păpўrā'ceous (-sh*u*s) *a.* (Biol.) Of the nature of, or as thin as, paper. [f. L PAPYRUS + -ACEOUS]

păpўrŏ'|logў *n.* Study of ancient papyri; hence

For other words in *pan-* see PAN-.

păpўroLO'GICAL *a.*, ~LOGIST *n.* [f. as foll. + -o- + -LOGY]

papȳr'|us *n.* (*pl.* **~i** *pr.* -ī). Aquatic plant of sedge family, paper reed; ancient writing--material prepared by Egyptians etc. from stem of this; MS. written on this. [ME f. L, f. Gk *papuros*]

pār¹ *n.* **1.** Equality, equal footing, esp. *on a par* (*with*); **~ of exchange,** recognized value of one country's currency in terms of another's; (of stocks, shares, etc.) **at ~**, at face value, **above ~**, at a premium, **below ~**, at a discount. **2.** Average or normal amount, degree, health, or condition, (*above, below, up to, par*). **3.** (Golf). Number of strokes a first-class player should normally require for a hole or course (calculated according to a formula and usu. less than the BOGEY¹ figures). [L, *a.* & *n.*, = equal, equality]

||**pār²** *n.* (colloq.) Paragraph. [abbr.]

par- *pref.* See PARA-¹.

pă'ra *n.* (colloq.) Parachutist; paragraph. [abbr.]

păra-¹ *pref.* (usu. **par-** bef. vowel or *h*) meaning: **1.** Beside (*parabola, paramilitary, parathyroid*). **2.** Beyond (*paradox, paranormal*). **3.** (Chem.) modification of (*paraldehyde*). **4.** (Chem.) Relating to diametrically opposite carbon atoms in a benzene ring (*paradichlorobenzene*). [f. or after Gk *para-* (*para* beside, past, beyond)]

păra-² *comb. form.* Protect, ward off, (*parachute, parasol*). [F f. It. (*para* imper. of *parare* defend)]

pară'bas|is *n.* (*pl.* **~es** *pr.* -ēz). Chorus's address to audience in ancient Greek comedy. [Gk, f. PARA¹(*bainō* go) step forward]

părabī|ō'sĭs *n.* (*pl.* **~oses** *pr.* -ō'sēz). (Biol.) Natural or artificial joining of two individuals; hence **~**O'TIC *a.* [mod. L, f. as PARA-¹ + Gk *biōsis* mode of life (*bios* life; see -OSIS)]

pă'rable *n.* Narrative of imagined events used to typify moral or spiritual relations (*the parables of Christ in the Gospels*); allegory. [ME, f. OF *parabole*, f. LL sense 'allegory, discourse' of L *parabola* comparison (as foll.)]

pară'bola *n.* Open plane curve formed by intersection of cone with plane parallel to its side, resembling path of projectile under action of gravity. [mod. L, f. Gk PARA¹(*bolē* a throw f. *ballō*) placing side by side, comparison]

părabŏ'l|ĭc *a.* **1.** Of or expressed in a parable. **2.** Of or like a parabola. **3.** Hence **~**ICALLY *adv.* [f. LL f. Gk *parabolikos* (as prec.; see -IC)]

părabŏ'lĭcal *a.* = prec. 1. [f. as prec. + -AL]

pară'boloid *n.* **~ (of revolution)**, solid generated by rotation of parabola about its axis of symmetry; solid having two or more non--parallel parabolic cross-sections; hence **~**AL *a.* [f. PARABOLA + -OID]

părace̅'tamŏl *n.* (Tablet of) compound forming white crystalline powder, a mild analgesic and antipyretic. [f. *para-acetylaminophenol*]

pară'chronĭsm (-k-) *n.* Error in chronology, esp. assignment of too late date. [f. PARA-¹ + Gk *khronos* time + -ISM, perh. after *anachronism*]

pă'rachut|e (-shōōt) *n.*, *a.*, & *v.* **1.** *n.* Umbrella--shaped apparatus of silk etc. allowing person or heavy object to descend safely from a height, esp. from aircraft; similar natural or artificial device, e.g. one that opens behind aircraft to retard its motion when landing. **2.** *a.* (To be) dropped by parachute (*parachute flare, troops*). **3.** *v.t.* & *i.* Convey or descend (as if) by means of parachute. **4.** Hence **~**IST *n.*, user of parachute, (in *pl.*) parachute troops. [F (as PARA-², CHUTE)]

pă'raclēte *n.* Advocate; (*P~*) the Holy Spirit as advocate or counsellor (John 14:16, 26, etc.). [ME, f. OF *paraclet* f. LL f. Gk PARA¹(*klētos* f. *kaleō* call) call in aid]

parā'de¹ *n.* **1.** Display, ostentation, esp. *make a parade of* (one's virtue etc.). **2.** Muster of troops for inspection, esp. one held regularly at set hours; **~(-ground)** (used for this); **on ~**, mustering thus, (fig.) displaying oneself in a formal or purposeful manner. **3.** Public square or promenade. **4.** Public procession; group of persons or things passed in review. [F, = show, f. Sp. *parada* and It. *parata* f. Rom. **parata* f. L *parare* prepare, furnish; see -ADE]

parā'de² *v.* **1.** *v.t.* Assemble (troops) for review or other purpose; display ostentatiously; march through (streets etc.) with display. **2.** *v.i.* March in procession with display. [f. prec.]

părădīchlōrobĕ'nzēne (-k-) *n.* White crystalline readily subliming compound used esp. against moths. [f. PARA¹- + DI-² + CHLORO-² + BENZENE]

părădĭ'ddle *n.* Drum roll with alternate beating of sticks. [imit.]

pă'radigm (-īm) *n.* Example or pattern, esp. of inflexion of noun, verb, etc.; hence **părădĭgmă'tic** *a.* [f. LL f. Gk *paradeigma* f. PARA¹-(*deiknumi* show) show side by side]

pă'radīse *n.* **1.** (**Earthly**) **~**, garden of Eden. **2.** Abode of God and of the righteous after death, heaven; region or state of supreme bliss; BIRD *of paradise*; FOOL¹'*s paradise*. **3.** Park in which animals are kept. **4.** Hence or cogn. **pă'radīsAL**, **părădĭsā'IC(AL)** [irreg. after *Mosaic* etc.], **părădĭ'sėAN**, **părădĭ'sĭAC(AL)**, **părădĭ'sĭAL**, **părădĭ'sĭAN**, **părădĭ'sIC(AL)**, *adjs.* [ME, f. OF *paradis* f. LL f. Gk *paradeisos* f. Avestan *pairidaēza* park (*pairi* around, *diz* shape); cf. PARVIS]

pă'radōs (*or* -dō) *n.* Elevation of earth behind fortified place to secure from rearward attack, esp. mound along back of trench. [F (PARA-², *dos* back f. L *dorsum*)]

pă'radŏx *n.* Statement contrary to accepted opinion; seemingly absurd though perhaps actually well-founded statement (HYDROSTATIC *paradox*); self-contradictory or essentially absurd statement; person or thing conflicting with preconceived notions of what is reasonable or possible; paradoxical quality or character; hence or cogn. **~**ER¹ (3), **~**IST (3), **~ĭcă'lITY**, **~**Y¹, *ns.*, **părădŏ'xICAL** *a.* [f. LL f. Gk *paradoxon* neut. adj. (PARA-¹, *doxa* opinion)]

părădŏ'xūre *n.* Palm civet, animal of genus *Paradoxurus* with remarkably long curving tail. [f. mod. L *paradoxurus* f. Gk *paradoxos* (see prec.) + *oura* tail]

pă'raffĭn *n.*, & *v.t.* **1.** *n.* Colourless tasteless odourless inflammable oily or waxy substance got by distillation from petroleum or shale and used for making candles etc. (**~ wax,** solid paraffin obtained by distillation from shale or petroleum; ||**liquid ~**, odourless tasteless mild laxative); ||**~ (oil)**, oil so obtained and used as fuel or illuminant or lubricant; (Chem.) hydrocarbon belonging to methane series, with general formula C_nH_{2n+2}. **2.** *v.t.* Treat with paraffin. [G (1830), f. L *parum* little + *affinis* related, from small affinity it has for other substances]

pă'ragōgė *n.* (Gram. & Philol.) Addition of letter or syllable to a word in some contexts or as a language develops; hence **părăgŏ'gIC** *a.* (*the t in 'peasant' is paragogic*). [LL, f. Gk *paragōgē* derivation (as PARA-¹, *agōgē* f. *agō* lead)]

pă'ragon *n.*, & *v.t.* **1.** *n.* Model of excellence; supremely excellent person or thing, model (*of* virtue etc.); perfect diamond of 100 carats or more. **2.** *v.t.* (poet.) Compare (thing *with*). [obs. F, f. It. *paragone* touchstone, f. med. Gk *parakonē* whetstone]

pă'ragraph (-ahf) *n.*, & *v.t.* **1.** *n.* Distinct passage or section in book etc., usu. marked by indentation of first line; symbol (usu. ¶) formerly used to mark new paragraph, now as reference mark; detached item of news etc. in newspaper, freq. without heading, whence ~ER[1] (3), ~IST (3), *ns*. **2.** Hence **părágrá'phic** *a*. **3.** *v.t.* Write paragraph about (person, thing); arrange (article etc.) in paragraphs. [f. F *paragraphe* or f. med. L f. Gk PARA[1](*graphos* f. *graphō* write) short stroke marking break in sense]

pă'ra-hўdrogėn *n*. Form of hydrogen molecule with spins of nuclei in opposite directions. [f. PARA-[1] + HYDROGEN]

pă'rakeet, *pă'rrakeet, pă'roquĕt (-kĕt), *n*. Small (esp. long-tailed) parrot. [f. OF *paroquet*, It. *parrocchetto*, *perrochetto*, Sp. *periquito*, perh. ult. f. dims. of *Pierre* etc. Peter; cf. PARROT]

pără'ldėhўde *n*. Polymer of ALDEHYDE 1, used as narcotic and sedative. [f. PARA-[1] + ALDEHYDE]

păralīpŏ'mėna, -leip- (-līp-), *n. pl.* Books of Chronicles in O.T., containing particulars omitted from Kings. [ME, f. eccl. L f. Gk *paraleipomena* f. PARA[1](*leipō* leave) omit]

părali'ps|is, păralei'ps|is (-lī'-), *n*. (*pl*. ~**es** *pr*. -ēz). Trick of securing emphasis by professing to say little or nothing of subject, e.g. *I say nothing of his antecedents, how from youth upwards* etc. [f. LL f. Gk PARA[1](*leipsis* f. *leipō* leave) passing over]

pă'rall|ăx *n*. (Angular amount of) apparent displacement of object, caused by actual change of point of observation; hence **~ă'ctic** *a*. [f. F *parallaxe* f. mod. L f. Gk *parallaxis* change (*parallassō* to alternate f. as PARA-[1], *allassō* exchange f. *allos* other)]

pă'rallĕl[1] *a*. & *n*. **1.** *a*. (Of lines etc.) continuously equidistant, (of line) having this relation *to*; ~ **bars,** pair of parallel rails supported on posts for gymnastic exercises; ~ **ruler,** two rulers connected by pivoted cross-pieces, for drawing parallel lines; *parallel* SPHERE. **2.** (fig.) Precisely similar, analogous, or corresponding. **3.** *n*. ~ (**of latitude**), each of the parallel circles of constant latitude on earth's surface (*the 49th parallel*), or corresponding line on map; similar circle on celestial sphere; person or thing precisely analogous to another; comparison (*draw a parallel between two things*); two parallel lines (||) as reference mark; **in** ~, (Electr., of conductors etc.) arranged so as to join at common points at each end. [f. F *parallèle* f. L f. Gk *parallēlos* (PARA-[1], *allēlos* one another)]

pă'rallĕl[2] *v.t.* Represent as similar, compare, (things, one *with* another); find or mention something parallel or corresponding to; be parallel to, correspond to. [f. prec.]

părallĕlĕ'pĭpĕd (*or* -epĭ'pĭd) *n*. (Geom.) Solid bounded by parallelograms. [f. Gk *parallēlepipedon* (as PARALLEL[1], EPI(*pedon* ground) plane surface)]

pă'rallĕlĭsm *n*. Being parallel (lit. or fig.); comparison or correspondence of successive passages, esp. in Hebrew poetry. [f. Gk *parallēlismos* f. *parallēlizō* place side by side (as PARALLEL[1]; see -IZE, -ISM)]

părallĕ'logrăm *n*. Four-sided plane rectilinear figure whose opposite sides are parallel; ~ **of forces,** (parallelogram illustrating) theorem that if two forces acting at a point be represented in magnitude and direction by two sides of a parallelogram meeting at that point, their resultant is represented by the diagonal drawn from that point. [f. F *parallélogramme* f. LL f. Gk *parallēlogrammon* (as PARALLEL[1], *grammē* line)]

pară'log|ĭsm *n*. Illogical reasoning (esp. of which reasoner is unconscious, cf. SOPHISM); fallacy; so ~**IST** (1) *n*., ~**IZE** (2) *v.i.* [f. F *paralogisme* f. LL f. Gk *paralogismos* f. *paralogizomai* reason falsely f. PARA[1](*logos* reason) contrary to reason]

pă'ralўs|e (-z), ***pă'ralўz|e,** *v.t.* Affect with paralysis; (fig.) render powerless, cripple; hence ~**A'TION** *n*. [f. F *paralyser* (*paralysie*; cf. PALSY)]

pară'lўs|ĭs *n*. (*pl*. ~**es** *pr*. -ēz). Nervous disease with impairment or loss of motor or sensory function of nerves; (fig.) state of utter powerlessness. [L, f. Gk *paralusis* f. PARA[1](*luō* loosen) disable]

păralў't|ĭc *a*. & *n*. (Person) affected with paralysis (lit. or fig.); ||(sl.) very drunk; hence ~**ICALLY** *adv*. [ME, f. OF *paralytique* f. L f. Gk *paralutikos* (as prec.; see -IC)]

păramăgnĕ'tĭc *a*. & *n*. (Body or substance) tending to become weakly magnetized so as to lie parallel to a magnetic field force; hence **păramă'gnėtISM** (3) *n*. [f. PARA-[1] + MAGNETIC]

păramă'tta. Var. of PARRAMATTA.

paramē'cĭum. See PARAMOECIUM.

paramĕ'dĭcal *a*. (Of services etc.) supplementing and supporting medical work. [f. PARA-[1] + MEDICAL]

pară'mėter *n*. (Math.) quantity constant in case considered, but varying in different cases; (esp. measurable or quantifiable) characteristic or feature; hence **păramĕ'trIC** *a*., **pară'mėtrIZE** (3) *v.t.* [mod. L, f. Gk *para* beside + *metron* measure]

părami'lĭtarў *a*. Ancillary to and similarly organized to military forces. [f. PARA-[1] + MILITARY]

pă'ramō *n*. (*pl*. ~**s**). High treeless plateau in tropical S. America. [Sp. & Port., f. L *paramus*]

păramoe'cĭum (-mē'-), **-mē'cĭum,** *n*. Ciliated slipper-shaped protozoan of genus *Paramecium*. [mod. L, f. Gk PARA[1](*mēkēs* f. *mēkos* length) oval]

pă'ramount *a*. Supreme; in supreme authority; pre-eminent (*of paramount importance*); hence ~**CY** *n*., ~**LY**[2] *adv*. [f. AF *paramont* f. OF *par* by + *amont* above (cf. AMOUNT[1])]

pă'ramour (-oor) *n*. (arch. or rhet.) Illicit lover of married man or woman. [ME, f. OF *par amour* by love]

par̂'ăng *n*. Malay heavy sheath-knife. [Malay]

păranoi'a *n*. Mental derangement with delusions of grandeur, persecution, etc.; abnormal tendency to suspect and mistrust others; hence **păranoi'AC, pă'ranOID,** *adjs*. & *ns*. [mod. L f. Gk, f. PARA[1](*noos* mind) distracted]

păranor̂'mal *a*. Lying outside the range of normal scientific investigations etc.; hence ~**LY**[2] *adv*. [f. PARA-[1] + NORMAL]

pă'rapėt (*or* -ĕt) *n*. Low wall at edge of balcony, roof, etc., or along sides of bridge etc.; (Mil.) defence of earth or stone to conceal and protect troops, esp. mound along front of trench; hence ~**ED**[2] *a*. [F, or f. It. PARA[2](*petto* breast f. L *pectus*) breast-high wall]

pă'raph *n*. Flourish after signature, orig. as precaution against forgery. [ME, f. F *paraphe* f. med. L *paraphus* for *paragraphus* PARAGRAPH]

păraphernā'lĭa *n. pl.* (sometimes treated as *sing.*) Personal belongings; equipment, accessories, appurtenances, etc.; (Hist.) articles of personal property that law allowed married woman to keep and treat as her own. [med. L, n. f. neut. pl. a. f. LL f. Gk PARA[1](*pherna* f. *phernē* dower); cf. -AL, -IA[2]]

pă'raphrāse (-z) *n*., & *v.t.* **1.** *n*. Free rendering or amplification of a passage, expression of its sense in other words; one of a collection of metrical paraphrases of passages of Scripture used in Church of Scotland etc.; so **păraphră'stIC** *a*. **2.** *v.t.* Express meaning of (passage) in other words. [F, or f. L f. Gk *paraphrasis* f. PARA[1](*phrazō* tell)]

păraplē'g|ia *n.* (Path.) Paralysis of legs and part or whole of trunk; so ~IC *a.* & *n.* [mod. L, f. Gk *paraplēgia* f. PARA[1](*plēssō* strike)]

părapsȳchŏ'log|ȳ (-*ra*sīk-) *n.* Study of mental phenomena outside sphere of ordinary psychology (hypnosis, telepathy, etc.); so **părapsȳcho**LO'GICAL (-*ra*sīk-) *a.*, ~IST (3) *n.* [f. PARA-[1] + PSYCHOLOGY]

pă'raquat (-ŏt) *n.* Quick-acting herbicide, becoming inactive on contact with soil. [f. PARA-[1] + QUATERNARY (f. position of bond between two parts of molecule rel. to quaternary nitrogen atom)]

pă'rasăng *n.* Ancient-Persian measure of length, about 3¼ miles. [f. L f. Gk *parasaggēs*, of Pers. orig.]

părasėlē'n|ė *n.* (*pl.* ~**ae**). Bright spot on lunar halo, mock moon. [mod. L, f. as PARA-[1] + Gk *selēnē* moon]

pă'rasīt|e *n.* Self-seeking hanger-on, toady; animal or plant living in or on another and drawing nutriment directly from it; plant that climbs about another plant, wall, etc.; unprofitable dependent person or thing; (Philol.) inorganic sound or letter developing from an adjacent one; hence or cogn. **părasĭ'tĭ**C(AL) *adjs.*, **părasĭ'tĭ**CIDE (1), ~ISM (2), ~**ŏ'**LOGY; *ns.* [f. L f. Gk PARA[1](*sitos* food) one who eats at another's table]

pă'rasĭtize, -ise (-iz), *v.t.* (usu. in *p.p.*) Infest as a parasite. [f. prec. + -IZE]

pă'rasŏl (*or* -ŏ'l) *n.* Light umbrella used to give protection from sunlight. [F, f. It. PARA[2](*sole* sun f. L *sol*)]

părasȳmpathĕ'tĭc *a.* (Anat.) Relating to the part of the nervous system that connects with nerve cells in or near viscera. [f. PARA-[1] + SYMPATHETIC, because some of these nerves run alongside sympathetic nerves]

părasȳ'nthėsĭs *n.* (Philol.) Derivation from a compound, as *black-eyed* from *black eye*(*s*) + *-ed*; so **părasȳnthĕ'tĭ**C *a.* [f. Gk *parasunthesis* (as PARA-[1], SYNTHESIS)]

părată'xĭs *n.* (Gram.) Placing of clauses etc. one after another, without words to indicate co-ordination or subordination, as *Tell me, how are you?*; so **părată'ctĭ**C *a.* [f. Gk PARA[1](*taxis* arrangement f. *tassō* arrange)]

părathī'on *n.* Agricultural insecticide of high toxicity. [f. PARA-[1] + THIO- + -ON]

părathȳr'oid *a.* & *n.* (Anat.) (Gland) adjacent to thyroid, secreting hormone that regulates calcium levels in body. [f. PARA-[1] + THYROID]

pă'ratrōōp|s *n. pl.* Parachute troops; hence ~ER[1] *n.*, member of these. [f. PARACHUTE + TROOP + -S[1]]

paratȳ'phoid *n.* & *a.* (One of numerous kinds) of fever resembling typhoid, but caused by different bacteria. [f. PARA-[1] + TYPHOID]

pă'ravāne *n.* Torpedo-shaped device towed at a depth regulated by its vanes or planes to cut the moorings of submerged mines. [f. PARA-[1] + VANE]

par'boil *v.t.* Boil incompletely in cooking; (fig.) overheat (person). [ME, f. OF *parbo*(*u*)*illir* f. LL PER(*bullire* boil) boil thoroughly, confus. w. PART[1]]

par'bŭckle *n.*, & *v.t.* **1.** *n.* Rope for raising or lowering casks and cylindrical objects, the middle being secured at the upper level, and both ends passed under and round the object and then hauled or let slowly out. **2.** *v.t.* Raise (*up*) or lower (*down*) thus. [earlier *parbunkle*, of unkn. orig.; assoc. w. BUCKLE[1]]

par'cel[1] *n.* & *adv.* **1.** *n.* Part (arch.); PART[1] *and parcel*. **2.** Piece of land, esp. as part of estate. **3.** Goods etc. wrapped up in single package; bundle of thing(s) so wrapped, usu. in paper; ~ **post**, branch of postal service concerned with parcels. **4.** (Commerc.) Quantity dealt with in one transaction. **5.** *adv.* (arch.) Partly (*parcel blind, drunk*). **6.** ~ **gilt**, partly gilded, esp. (of cup etc.) with inner surface gilt. [ME f. OF *parcelle* f. Rom. **particella* f. L *particula* (as PART[1]; see -CULE)]

par'cel[2] *v.t.* (‖-**ll**-). Divide (*out*) into portions; wrap (*up*) as parcel; (Naut.) cover (caulked seam) with canvas strips and pitch, wrap (rope) with canvas strips, whence ~**L**ING[1] (4) *n.* [f. prec.]

par'cėnarȳ *n.* Joint heirship. [f. AF *parcenarie* = OF *parçonerie* (as foll.; see -ERY)]

par'cėner *n.* Joint heir. [ME f. AF, = OF *parçonier* f. Rom. **parti*(*ti*)*onarius* (as PARTITION; see -ER[2])]

parch *v.* **1.** *v.t.* (Of sun, thirst, etc.) make (earth, person, etc.) hot and dry; roast (corn, peas etc.) slightly. **2.** *v.i.* Become hot and dry. [ME *perch, parche*, of unkn. orig.]

par'chment *n.* Skin, esp. of sheep or goat, prepared for writing, painting, etc.; manuscript written on this; (**vegetable**) ~, high-grade paper made to resemble parchment; parchment-like skin, esp. husk of coffee-bean; hence ~Y[2] *a.* [ME f. OF *parchemin* f. Rom. **particaminum*, blending LL *pergamina* of Pergamum (Bergama in Turkey) w. *Parthica pellis* Parthian skin, scarlet-dyed leather]

par'clōse (-z) *n.* Screen or railing in church to separate chapel etc. [ME, f. OF *parclos -ose* p.p. (as n.) of *parclore* (*par-* PER-; see CLOSE[3])]

pard[1] *n.* (arch.) Leopard. [ME f. OF, f. L f. Gk *pardos, pardalis*]

***pard**[2], ***par'dner,** *ns.* (sl.) Partner, comrade. [corrupt.]

par'dalōte *n.* Small brightly-coloured Austral. bird of genus *Pardalotus*, with spotted plumage. [f. mod. L f. Gk *pardalōtos* spotted like a leopard (as PARD[1])]

par'don[1] *n.* **1.** Forgiveness; (R.C. Ch.) = INDULGENCE, festival at which this is granted; (**free**) ~, (Law) remission of legal consequences of crime or conviction; **general** ~ (for offences generally, or to number of persons not named individually). **2.** Courteous forebearance; (**I beg your**) ~, **beg** ~, (formula of apology for thing done, for dissent or contradiction, or for not hearing or understanding what was said). [ME f. OF *perdun, pardun* f. *pardoner* (see foll.)]

par'don[2] *v.t.* Forgive (person, offence, person his offence); make (esp. courteous) allowances for, excuse, (person, fault, person *for* doing; ~ **me,** = *I beg your* PARDON[1]); so ~ABLE *a.*, ~**ab**LY[2] *adv.* [ME, f. OF *pardoner, perduner* f. med. L PER(*donare* give) concede, remit]

par'doner *n.* (Hist.) Person licensed to sell papal pardons or indulgences. [ME f. AF (as PARDON[1]; see -ER[2])]

pare *v.t.* Trim (thing) by cutting away irregular parts etc.; cut away skin, rind, etc., of (fruit etc.); (fig.) diminish little by little (*away, down*); shave, cut, (edges etc.) *off, away*; hence **par'**ER[1] (2), **par'**ING[1] (1, 2), *ns.* [ME, f. OF *parer* adorn, peel (fruit), f. L *parare* prepare]

părėgŏ'rĭc *a.* & *n.* ~ (**elixir**), camphorated tincture of opium used as analgesic. [f. LL f. Gk *parēgorikos* soothing (as PARA-[1], *-agoros* speaking f. *agora* assembly)]

pareir'a (-ār'*a*) *n.* Drug from root of Brazilian shrub, used as diuretic etc. [f. Port. *parreira* vine trained against wall]

parĕ'nchȳm|a (-ngk-) *n.* (Anat.) essential substance of gland, organ, etc., as distinguished from flesh and connective tissue; (Bot.) cellular material, usu. soft and succulent, found esp. in softer parts of leaves, pulp of fruits, bark and pith of stems, etc.; hence ~AL, **părĕnchy̆'matous** (-ngk-), *adjs.* [f. Gk *paregkhuma* something poured in besides (as PARA-¹, *egkhuma* infusion f. *egkheō* pour in f. *en* in + *kheō* pour)]

pā̆r'ent *n.* One who has begotten or borne offspring, father or mother; forefather (**our first ~s,** Adam and Eve); one who has adopted a child; animal or plant from which others are derived; (fig.) source, origin, (*of* evils etc.); initiating organization etc.; **~-tea'cher association,** organization consisting of, and promoting good relations between, teachers and their pupils' parents; hence or cogn. **parĕ'ntAL** *a.*, ~HOOD (-t-h-) *n.* [ME f. OF, f. L *parens parentis* (*parere* bring forth; see -ENT)]

pā̆r'entage *n.* Descent from parents, lineage, (*his parentage is unknown*). [ME f. OF (as prec.; see -AGE)]

parĕ'nteral *a.* (Med.) Administered or occurring elsewhere than in the alimentary canal. [f. PARA-¹ + Gk *enteron* intestine + -AL]

parĕ'nthės|ĭs *n.* (*pl.* ~es *pr.* -ēz). Word, clause, or sentence, inserted into a passage to which it is not grammatically essential, and usu. marked off by brackets, dashes, or commas (**in ~,** thus inserted, lit. or fig.); (pair of) round bracket(s) ( ) used for this; (fig.) interlude, interval. [LL, f. Gk *parenthesĭs* f. *parentithēmi* put in beside (as PARA-¹, EN-², *tithēmi* place)]

parĕ'nthėsīze, -īse (-īz), *v.t.* Insert (words etc., or abs.) as parenthesis; put between marks of parenthesis. [f. prec. + -IZE]

părenthĕ'tĭc *a.* Of, or inserted as a, parenthesis; (fig.) interposed; so ~AL *a.*, **~allY²** *adv.* [f. PARENTHESIS, after *synthesis, synthetic*, etc.]

parẽr'g|on *n.* (*pl.* ~a). Subsidiary work, work apart from one's main employment; ornamental accessory. [L, f. Gk *parergon* (as PARA-¹, *ergon* work)]

pă'rės|ĭs *n.* (*pl.* ~es *pr.* -ēz). (Med.) Partial paralysis, affecting muscular motion but not sensation; so **parE'TIC** *a.* [mod. L, f. Gk, f. *pariēmi* let go (as PARA-¹, *hiēmi* let go)]

par excellence (pār ĕ'kselahṅs) *adv.* By virtue of special excellence, above all others that may be so called, (*Mayfair was the fashionable quarter par excellence*). [F, f. L *per excellentiam*]

pār'fait (-fā) *n.* Rich iced pudding of whipped cream, eggs, etc.; layers of ice cream, fruit, etc., served in tall glass. [F (*parfait* PERFECT¹)]

pargana. Var. of PERGUNNAH.

pār'gėt *v.t.*, & *n.* **1.** *v.t.* Plaster (wall etc.), esp. with ornamental pattern. **2.** *n.* Plaster thus applied. [ME, f. OF *pargeter, parjeter* (*par* all over, *jeter* throw; cf. JET³)]

pārhē'l|ĭon (*or* -lyon) *n.* (*pl.* ~ia). Bright spot on solar halo, mock sun; hence **~ī'ACAL,** ~IC, *adjs.* [f. L f. Gk *parēlion* (as PARA-¹, *hēlios* sun)]

pă'rĭah (-*a*; *or* parī'*a*) *n.* Member of a low caste in S. India; member of low or no caste; (fig.) social outcast; **~-dog,** = PYE-DOG. [f. Tamil *paraiyar* pl. of *paraiyan* hereditary drummer (*parai* drum)]

Pār'ĭan *a.* & *n.* **1.** *a.* Of the island of Paros in the Aegean, famed for white marble. **2.** *n.* Fine white kind of porcelain. [f. L *Parius* of Paros + -AN]

parī'etal *a.* **1.** (Anat.) Of the wall of the body or of any of its cavities; **~ bone,** one of pair forming part of sides and top of skull. **2.** (Bot.) Of the wall of a hollow structure etc. **3.** *Pertaining to residence within a college. [f. F *pariétal* or f. LL *parietalis* (*paries -etis* wall; see -AL)]

pari mutuel (pahrē mū'tūĕl) *n.* Form of betting in which winners divide losers' stakes (less a percentage for management); totalizator. [F, = mutual stake]

pari passu (pārī pă'sōō; *or* părĭ) *adv.* With equal pace; simultaneously and equally. [L]

Pă'rĭs *n.* **~ green,** poisonous chemical used as pigment and insecticide; **~ white,** fine WHITING¹ used in polishing; PLASTER¹ *of Paris.* [~ in France]

pă'rĭsh *n.* **1.** (**Ecclesiastical**) ~, area having its own church and clergyman. **2.** ‖(**Civil**) ~, district constituted for purposes of civil government, orig. (Hist.) for poor-law administration; **go on the ~,** (Hist.) receive parochial relief. **3.** Inhabitants of a parish. **4.** *County in Louisiana. **5. ~ clerk,** official performing various duties connected with the church, esp. (formerly) leading the responses; ‖**~ council,** administrative body in civil parish; ‖*parish* LANTERN; **~ pump** (fig., w. ref. to purely parochial or restricted outlook); **~ register,** book recording christenings, marriages, and burials, at parish church. [ME *paroche, parosse* f. OF *paroche, paroisse* f. eccl. L *parochia, paroechia* f. Gk *paroikia* sojourning f. *paroikos* (PARA-¹, *-oikos* -dwelling f. *oikeō* dwell)]

parĭ'shioner (-sho-) *n.* Inhabitant of parish. [f. obs. *parishen* (ME f. OF *parossien*; as prec., -IAN) + -ER¹]

Parĭ'sĭan (-z-) *a.* & *n.* (Native or inhabitant) of Paris in France. [f. F *parisien* (*Paris*; see -IAN)]

pă'rĭson *n.* Rounded mass of glass formed by rolling immediately after taking from furnace. [f. F *paraison* (*parer* prepare f. L *parare*; see -ISON)]

părĭsy̆llă'bĭc *a.* & *n.* (Gram.) (Noun) that has same number of syllables in all cases (e.g. L *aedes aedis*). [f. L *par* equal + -I- + SYLLABIC]

pă'rĭty̆¹ *n.* Equality, esp. among members or ministers of church, or among occupational groups as regards pay etc.; parallelism, analogy, (*parity of reasoning*); (Commerc.) equivalence in another currency, being at PAR¹; (of number) fact of being even or odd; (Phys., of quantity) fact of changing its sign or remaining unaltered under a given transformation of co-ordinates etc. [f. F *parité* or f. LL *paritas* (as PAR¹, -ITY)]

pă'rĭty̆² *n.* (Med.) Fact of having borne children; number of children previously borne. [f. as -PAROUS + -ITY]

pārk¹ *n.* **1.** Large enclosed piece of ground, usu. with woodland and pasture, attached to country house etc.; enclosure in town ornamentally laid out for public recreation; *sports ground; large tract of land kept in natural state for public benefit (*national park*). **2.** (Space occupied by) artillery, stores, etc., in encampment; area assigned for motor cars etc. to be left in; = OYSTER-*park*. **3. ~'land,** open grassland with tree-clumps etc.; ***~'way,** highway in park etc. prohibited to heavy vehicles. **4.** Hence ~'ISH¹ *a.* [ME, f. OF *parc* f. med. L *parricus*, of Gmc orig., cogn. w. OE *pearruc* (see PADDOCK¹)]

pārk² *v.t.* **1.** Enclose (ground) in or as park; (Mil.) arrange (artillery etc.) compactly in a park; place or leave (vehicle, or abs.), usu. temporarily, in park or elsewhere; (colloq.) deposit and leave, usu. temporarily; **~ oneself,** (sl.) sit down. **2.** ***~'ing-lot,** outdoor area for parking vehicles; **~'ing-meter,** coin-operated meter receiving fees for parking vehicle in street and indicating time allowed; **~'ing-ticket,** notice of fine etc. imposed for parking vehicle illegally. [f. prec.]

pār'ka *n.* Skin jacket with hood attached, worn by Eskimos; similar garment worn by mountaineers etc. [Aleutian]

‖**pār'kĭn** *n.* (dial.) Gingerbread made with oatmeal and treacle. [perh. f. name *Parkin*, dim. of *Peter*]

Pār'kĭnson¹ *n.* **~'s disease,** progressive disease

of nervous system, with tremor, muscular rigidity, and emaciation; hence ~ISM (5) *n.* [f. J. ~, Engl. surgeon d. 1824]

Pâr'kĭnson² *n.* **~'s law,** (joc.) fact that work will always last as long as the time available for it. [f. C. N. ~, Engl. writer b. 1909]

||**pâr'kȳ** *a.* (sl. or dial.) (Of air, morning, etc.) chilly. [19th c.; orig. unkn.]

||**Parl.** *abbr.* Parliament(ary).

pâr'lance *n.* (Particular) way of speaking as regards choice of words (*in common, legal*, etc., *parlance*). [OF (*parler* speak f. Rom. **paraulare* f. **paraula* f. L *parabola* (see PARABLE), in LL 'speech'; see -ANCE)]

***pâr'lay** *v.t.*, & *n.* **1.** *v.t.* Use (money won on bet) as further stake; increase in value (as if) by parlaying. **2.** *n.* Act of parlaying; bet so made. [f. *paroli* such action in faro (F f. It., f. *paro* like f. L *par* equal)]

pâr'ley¹ *n.* Conference for debating of points in dispute, esp. (Mil.) discussion of terms for armistice etc.; **beat** or **sound a ~**, call for it by drum or trumpet. [perh. f. OF *parlee*, fem. p.p. (as n.) of *parler* speak; see PARLANCE]

pâr'ley² *v.* **1.** *v.i.* Discuss terms (of armistice *with* enemy etc.). **2.** *v.t.* Speak (esp. foreign language). [f. prec.]

pârleyvōō' (-lĭv-) *n.*, & *v.i.* (joc.) **1.** *n.* French language; Frenchman. **2.** *v.i.* Speak French. [f. F *parlez-vous* (*français*)? do you speak (French)?]

pâr'liament (-lam-) *n.* **1.** (*P~*). Council forming with the Sovereign the supreme legislature of United Kingdom, consisting of House of Lords (Spiritual and Temporal) and House of Commons (representatives of counties, towns, etc.); **Houses of P~**, these jointly or the buildings where they meet; MEMBER *of Parliament*; **open P~**, (of Sovereign) declare it open with ceremonial. **2.** Body of persons belonging to Parliament for period between successive dissolutions. **3.** Corresponding legislative assembly in other countries. [ME f. OF *parlement* speaking (as PARLANCE; see -MENT)]

pârliamentâr'ĭan (-lam-) *n.* & *a.* **1.** *n.* Skilled debater in parliament; adherent of Parliament in Civil War of 17th c. **2.** *a.* = foll. [f. prec. + -ARIAN]

pârliamĕ'ntarȳ (-lam-) *a.* **1.** Of parliament; ||**~ agent** (charged with interests of party concerned in private legislation of Parliament). **2.** ||(*P~*). Enacted or established by Parliament; **P~ Commissioner for Administration,** ombudsman in United Kingdom; *Parliamentary* (*Private* or *Under-*)SECRETARY. **3.** (Of language) admissible in Parliament, (colloq.) civil. [f. PARLIAMENT + -ARY¹]

pâr'lour (-ler), ***pâr'lor,** *n.* Ordinary sitting-room of family in private house; room in mansion, convent, inn, etc., for private conversation; * shop etc. providing specified goods or services (*beauty parlour, ice cream parlour*); place for milking cows; ***~ car,** luxuriously fitted railway coach; **~ game,** indoor game, esp. word-game; **~maid,** maid who waits at table; **~ socialist** etc., one who advocates doctrines without trying to put them into effect; **~ tricks,** (usu. derog.) social accomplishments. [ME f. AF *parlur*, OF *parleor, parleur* f. Rom. **paraulare* (see PARLANCE)]

pâr'lous *a.* & *adv.* (arch. or joc.) **1.** *a.* Perilous; hard to deal with; surprisingly clever etc. **2.** *adv.* Extremely. [ME, = PERILOUS]

Pâr'ma *n.* **~ violet,** sweet-scented violet with lavender-coloured flowers. [~ in Italy]

Pârmēsă'n (-z-; *or* pâr'-) *a.* & *n.* **~ (cheese),** kind of hard cheese made at Parma and elsewhere, used esp. in grated form. [F, f. It. *parmegiano* of Parma in Italy]

Pârnă'ssĭan *a.* & *n.* **1.** *a.* Of Parnassus; poetic. **2.** *a.* & *n.* (Member) of group of French poets in late 19th c., emphasizing strictness of form, named from anthology *Le Parnasse contemporain* (1866). [f. Mount *Parnassus* in Greece, anciently sacred to Muses + -IAN]

parō'chĭal (-k-) *a.* Of a parish; *(of school) denominational; (fig., of affairs, opinions, etc.) confined to narrow area; hence ~ISM (2), **parōchĭă'l**ITY (-k-), *ns.*, ~IZE (3) *v.t.*, ~LY² *adv.* [ME, f. AF *parochiel*, OF *parochial* f. eccl. L *parochialis* (as PARISH; see -AL)]

pă'rod|ȳ *n.*, & *v.t.* **1.** *n.* Composition in which an author's characteristics are humorously imitated; feeble imitation, travesty. **2.** *v.t.* Compose parody of (literary work, manner, etc.). **3.** So **parŏ'dĭ**C *a.*, ~IST (3) *n.* [f. LL *parodia* or f. Gk *parōidia* burlesque poem (as PARA-¹, *ōidē* ode)]

parō'l *a.* & *n.* (Law). Oral (declaration); (of document) not given under seal. [f. OF *parole* (as foll.)]

parō'le *n.*, & *v.t.* **1.** *n.* Word of honour; prisoner's promise that he will not attempt escape if conditionally liberated; liberation on these terms; **on ~**, liberated on this understanding. **2.** (Mil.) Password used only by officers of guard (cf. COUNTERSIGN¹). **3.** *v.t.* Put (prisoner) on parole; hence **parōl**EE' *n.* [F, = word, f. Rom. **paraula*; see PARLANCE]

păronomā'sĭa (-z-) *n.* Word-play, pun. [L, f. Gk *paronomasia* (as PARA-¹, *onomasia* naming f. *onomazō* to name f. *onoma* name)]

pă'ronȳm *n.* Word cognate with another; word formed from a foreign word; so **parŏ'nȳm**OUS *a.* [f. Gk *parōnumon*, neut. (as n.) of *parōnumos* (as PARA-¹, *onuma* name)]

paroquet. See PARAKEET.

parŏ'tĭd *a.* & *n.* **1.** *a.* Situated near the ear; **~ gland** (salivary, in front of ear, with **~ duct,** opening into mouth). **2.** *n.* Parotid gland. [f. F *parotide* or f. L f. Gk *parōtis -idos* (as PARA-¹, *ous ōtos* ear)]

părotī'tĭs *n.* Inflammation of parotid gland; mumps. [f. prec. + -ITIS]

-parous *suf.* Bearing offspring of specified number or kind (*multiparous, viviparous*). [f. L *-parus* -bearing (*parere* bring forth) + -OUS]

pă'roxȳsm *n.* Fit of disease; fit (*of* rage, laughter, etc.); hence **păroxȳ'sm**AL (-zm-) *a.* [f. F *paroxysme* f. med. L f. Gk *paroxusmos* f. *paroxunō* exasperate (as PARA-¹, *oxunō* sharpen f. *oxus* sharp)]

parŏ'xȳtōne *a.* & *n.* (Gk Gram.) (Word) with acute accent on last syllable but one. [f. mod. L f. Gk *paroxutonos* (as PARA-¹, OXYTONE)]

pâr'pen *n.* Stone passing through wall from side to side, with two smooth vertical faces. [ME, f. OF *parpain*, prob. f. Rom. **perpannius* f. L *per* through, *pannus* piece of cloth, in Rom. 'piece of wall']

pâr'quet (-kĭ *or* -kā) *n.*, & *v.t.* **1.** *n.* Wooden flooring of pieces of wood, often of different kinds, arranged in pattern; *theatre stalls; so ~RY (1) (-kĭt-) *n.* **2.** *v.t.* Floor (room) thus. [F, = small compartment, floor, dim. of *parc* PARK¹; see -ET¹]

pârr *n.* Salmon in banded form, younger than smolt. [18th c., of unkn. orig.]

părramă'tta *n.* Light dress fabric of wool and silk or cotton. [f. *P~* in New South Wales]

pă'rrĭ|cide *n.* **1.** One who murders his father or near relative; one who murders person regarded as sacred; person guilty of treason against his country. **2.** Any of these crimes. **3.** So **~cī'd**AL *a.* [F, or f. L (1) *par(r)icida* (2) *-cidium*, of uncert. orig., assoc. in L w. *pater* father and *parens* parent; see -CIDE]

pă'rrot *n.*, & *v.t.* **1.** *n.* Bird with short hooked bill, of order Psittaciformes, mainly tropical, of which many species have beautiful plumage, and some can be taught to repeat words; person who repeats another's words or imitates his actions unintelligently, whence ~RY (4) *n.*; **~-fashion,** repeating or imitating thus; **~-fish,** scarus, with mouth like parrot's bill; hence ~LET *n.*, small S. Amer. parrot of genus *Forpus*. **2.** *v.t.* Repeat (words, or abs.) mechanically, drill (person etc.) to do this. [prob. f. obs. or dial. F *perrot* parrot, dim. of *Pierre* Peter; cf. PARAKEET]

pă'rrȳ *v.t.*, & *n.* **1.** *v.t.* Turn aside, ward off, avert, (weapon, blow, awkward question), esp. with one's own weapon etc. **2.** *n.* Act of parrying. [prob. repr. F *parez* imper. of *parer* f. It. *parare* ward off]

pârse (-z) *v.t.* Describe (word in context) grammatically, stating inflexion, relation to sentence, etc.; resolve (sentence) into its component parts and describe them grammatically. [perh. f. ME *pars* parts of speech f. OF *pars*, pl. of *part* PART[1], infl. by L *pars* part]

pâr'sĕc *n.* Unit of stellar distance, about 3¼ light-years, the distance at which a star would have a parallax of one second of arc, i.e. at which the mean radius of the earth's orbit subtends this angle. [f. PARALLAX + SECOND]

Pârsee' *n.* **1.** Adherent of Zoroastrianism, descendant of Persians who fled to India from Muslim persecution in 7th–8th c.; hence ~ISM (3) *n.* **2.** = PAHLAVI. [f. Pers. *pārsī* Persian (*pārs* Persia)]

pâr'sĭm|onȳ *n.* Carefulness in employment of money etc. or (fig.) of immaterial things; excessive carefulness with money, meanness; **law of ~ony** (that no more causes or forces should be assumed than are necessary to account for the facts); hence **~ō'nĭ**OUS *a.* [ME, f. L *parsimonia, parcimonia* (*parcere pars-* spare; see -MONY)]

pâr'sley *n.* Biennial umbelliferous plant (*Petroselinum crispum*) with white flowers and aromatic leaves, used for seasoning and garnishing dishes; ~ **fern** (with leaves like parsley); *parsley* SAUCE. [ME *persil* etc. f. OF *peresil* f. Rom. **petrosilium* f. L f. Gk *petroselinon* (*petra* rock, *selinon* parsley), & ME *petrosilye* f. OE *petersilie*, f. Rom. as above]

pâr'snĭp *n.* (Biennial umbelliferous plant, *Pastinaca sativa*, with yellow flowers and) large pale yellow tapering root used as culinary vegetable; *fine words* BUTTER[2] *no parsnips*. [ME *pas(se)nep* (w. assim. to *nep* turnip) f. OF *pasnaie* f. L *pastinaca*]

pâr'son *n.* Rector; vicar or any beneficed clergyman; (colloq.) any (esp. Protestant) clergyman; **~-bird,** (N.Z.) = TUI; *parson's* NOSE; hence or cogn. ~AGE (5) *n.*, **pârsŏ'nic**(AL) *adjs.* [ME *person(e)*, *parson* f. OF *persone* f. L *persona* PERSON (in med. L rector)]

pârt[1] *n.* & *adv.* **1.** *n.* Some but not all of a thing or number of things; (*a*) *part of it was spoilt, parts of it are excellent,* (*a*) *part of them have arrived,* (*a*) *great part of this is true, the most* or *greater part* (the majority) *of them failed.* **2.** Division of book, broadcast serial, etc., esp. as much as is issued etc. at one time. **3.** Portion of human or animal body (**the ~s,** genitals); component of machine etc. **4.** Each of several equal portions of a whole; **three ~s** (quarters); *gold content is five parts per million*; *take 3 parts of sugar, 5 of flour,* etc. **5.** Portion allotted, share; **have neither ~ nor lot in,** (arch.) not be concerned in; ART[2] *and part*; person's share in action, his duty, (*I have done my part*; *it was not my part to interfere*). **6.** Character assigned to actor on stage; words spoken by actor on stage; copy of these; (fig.) **play** *a noble, an unworthy,* **~,** behave nobly etc.; **play a ~,** (1) contribute by action etc., (2) act deceitfully. **7.** (Mus.) Melody or other constituent of harmony assigned to particular voice or instrument. **8.** (in *pl.*) Abilities; *a man of* (*good, many*) *parts*. **9.** (in *pl.*) Region (*a stranger in these parts*; *from foreign parts*). **10.** Side in agreement or dispute. **11.** *Parting of hair. **12.** **For the most ~,** in most cases, mostly; **for my ~,** so far as I am concerned; **in ~(s),** partly; **on the ~ of,** proceeding from (*there was no objection on my part*), done etc. by; **~ and parcel,** essential part *of*; **~ of speech,** each of the grammatical classes of words (in English usu. noun, adjective, pronoun, verb, adverb, preposition, conjunction, interjection); **take ~,** assist (*in* doing, *in* discussion etc.); **take the ~ of,** support, back up; **take** (words, action) **in good ~,** not be offended at. **13.** **~-exchange,** transaction in which article is given as part of payment for more expensive one; **~-owner,** one who owns in common with others; **~-song,** song with three or more voice-parts, freq. without accompaniment, and harmonic rather than contrapuntal in character; **~ time,** less than FULL[1] *time* (so *~-time* a., occupying or using only part of one's working time, *~-timer* n.); **~-work,** publication appearing in several parts at different times. **14.** *adv.* In part, partly (*made part of iron and part of wood*; *is part iron part wood*; *a lie that is part truth*). [ME f. OF, f. L *pars partis*]

pârt[2] *v.* **1.** *v.t.* & *i.* Divide into parts (*the crowd parted and let him through*; *the cord parted* (broke)). **2.** *v.t.* Separate (hair of head on either side of parting) with comb; separate (combatants, friends, fool and his money, etc.; *till death us do part*); *part* BRASS *rags with*; *part* COMPANY. **3.** *v.i.* Quit one another's company (*let us part friends*; *the best of friends must part*); (arch.) depart (*the curfew tolls the knell of parting day*); **~ from,** say goodbye to; **~ with,** give up, surrender, (property etc.). **4.** (colloq.) Part with one's money, pay, (*if I know him, he won't part*). **5.** (arch.) Distribute in shares. [ME, f. OF *partir* f. L *partire, partiri* (as prec.)]

pârtā'k|e *v.* (**partoo'k; parta'ken**). **1.** *v.i.* Take a share or part (*in* or *of* thing, *with* person); take, esp. eat or drink some or (colloq.) all *of* (*he partook of our lowly fare, partook of a bun*); have some (*of* quality etc.; *his manner partakes of insolence*). **2.** *v.t.* (arch.) Take a share in. **3.** Hence ~ABLE *a.* [16th c., back form. f. *partaker, partaking* = *part-taker* etc.]

pâr'tan *n.* (Sc.) Crab. [ME, app. f. Celt.]

pârter're (-tār') *n.* Level space in garden occupied by flower-beds; part of ground-floor of auditorium of theatre, behind orchestra. [F, = *par terre* on the ground]

pârthĕno|gĕ'nĕsĭs *n.* (Biol.) Reproduction from gametes but without fertilization, esp. as normal process in invertebrates and lower plants; so **~gĕnĕ'tic** *a.* [mod. L, f. Gk *parthenos* virgin + as GENESIS]

Pâr'thian *a.* Of Parthia, ancient kingdom of W. Asia; **~ shot** etc., remark, glance, etc., reserved for moment of departure, like missile shot backwards by retreating Parthian horseman. [f. *Parthia* + -AN]

parti (pârtē') *n.* Person regarded as eligible etc. in the marriage market (*is quite a parti*); ***~ pris*** (-prē'), preconceived view, bias. [F, = party, side]

pâr'tial (-shal) *a.* & *n.* **1.** *a.* Biased, unfair; **~ to,** having a liking for (person or thing). **2.** Forming only a part, not complete, (*a partial success*); **~ eclipse** (in which part only of the luminary is covered or darkened); **~ tone,** (Mus.) any constituent of a complex tone; *partial* VERDICT. **3.** Hence ~LY² *adv.* **4.** *n.* (Mus.) Partial tone; **upper ~s,** those higher than main note produced from string, pipe, etc., harmonics, overtones. [ME, f. OF *parcial* f. LL *partialis* (as PART¹; see -AL)]

pārtĭă'lĭtȳ (-shĭ-) *n.* Bias, favouritism; fondness (*for*). [ME, f. OF *parcial(i)té* f. med. L *partialitas* (as prec.; see -ITY)]

par'tĭble *a.* That can or must be divided (*among*; esp. of heritable property). [f. LL *partibilis* f. L (as PART²; see -IBLE)]

pārtĭ'cĭp|āte *v.i.* Have share, take part, (*in* thing, *with* person); have something *of* (*his poems participate of the nature of satire*); so ~ANT, ~A'TION, ~ātOR, *ns.*, ~ātORY *a.*; ~ātING² *a.*, *(of insurance etc.) entitling to share of company's additional profits. [f. L *participare* (*particeps -cipis* taking part f. as PART¹ + *-cip-* = *cap-* st. of *capere* take) + -ATE³]

par'tĭcĭple *n.* Verbal adjective qualifying noun but retaining some properties of verb, e.g. tense and government of object, as *qualifying* here (also used in compound verb-forms; *is going, has gone*); so **pārtĭcĭ'pĭAL** *a.* [ME f. OF, by-form of *participe* f. L *participium* (as prec.)]

par'tĭcle *n.* Minute portion of matter (ELEMENTARY *particle*); smallest possible amount (*has not a particle of sense*); minor part of speech, esp. short indeclinable one; common prefix or suffix such as *un-, out-, -ness, -ship*. [ME, f. L *particula* (as PART¹; see -CULE)]

par'tĭcoloured (-ŭlerd) *a.* Partly of one colour, partly of another or others. [f. PARTY² + COLOURED]

partĭ'cūlar *a.* & *n.* **1.** *a.* Relating to one as distinguished from others, special; ||**P~ Baptists,** (Hist.) body holding doctrines of *particular election* and *particular redemption* (i.e. of only some of the human race); *particular* INTENTION. **2.** (Logic). (Of proposition) in which something is predicated of some, not all, of a class (opp. *universal*). **3.** One considered apart from others, individual, (*this particular tax is no worse than others*; *particular* AVERAGE¹). **4.** Worth notice, special, (*took particular trouble*; *for no particular reason*). **5.** Minute (*full and particular account*); scrupulously exact, fastidious (*about, what* or *as to what* one eats etc.). **6.** Hence or cogn. ~ITY (-ă'r-) *n.*, ~LY² *adv.* **7.** *n.* Detail, item; **in ~,** especially (*mentioned one case in particular*), specifically (*did nothing in particular*); (in *pl.*) detailed account or information. [ME f. OF *particuler* f. L *particularis* (as PARTICLE; see -AR¹)]

partĭ'cūlar|ĭsm *n.* Doctrine of particular election or redemption; exclusive devotion to a party, sect, etc.; principle of leaving political independence to each State in an empire etc.; so ~IST (2) *n.* [f. F (*-isme*), mod. L (*-ismus*), & G *partikularismus* (as prec.; see -ISM)]

partĭ'cūlarīz|e, -īs|e (-īz), *v.t.* Name specially or one by one, specify, (items, or abs.); hence ~A'TION *n.* [f. F *particulariser* (as PARTICULAR; see -IZE)]

partĭ'cūlāte (*or* -*at*) *a.* & *n.* (Matter) in the form of separate particles. [f. L *particula* PARTICLE + -ATE²]

partie carrée (pārtē kărā') *n.* Party of four persons, esp. two men and two women. [F, = square party]

par'tĭng *n.* In vbl senses; leave-taking (often attrib.: *parting injunctions*; **~ shot,** = PARTHIAN *shot*); dividing line of combed hair; **~ of the ways,** point at which road divides into two or more, (fig.) point at which choice must be made between courses of action. [f. PART² + -ING¹]

pārtĭsă'n¹ (-z-), **-ză'n¹,** (*or* par't-) *n.* **1.** Adherent of party, cause, etc., esp. unreasoning one (often *attrib.*: *in a partisan spirit*). **2.** (Mil.) Guerrilla; (Hist.) member of light irregular troops employed in special enterprises. **3.** Hence ~SHIP *n.* [F, f. It. dial. *partigiano* etc. (*parte* PART¹; see -AN)]

par'tĭsan² (-z-), **-zan²,** *n.* (Hist.) Long-handled spear like halberd. [f. obs. F *partizane* f. obs. It. *partesana, partigiana* (as prec.)]

pārtī't|a (-ē'-) *n.* (*pl.* **~e** *pr.* -ā). (Mus.) Suite; air and set of variations on it. [It., fem. p.p. of *partire* divide f. as PART²]

par'tīte *a.* Divided (esp. in *comb.*, as *tripartite*); (Bot. & Entom.) divided (nearly) to the base. [f. L *partitus* p.p. of *partiri* PART²]

pārtĭ'tion *n.*, & *v.t.* **1.** *n.* Division into parts; such part; structure separating two such parts, esp. slight wall, whence ~ED² (-shond) *a.*; (Law) division of real property between joint tenants etc. **2.** *v.t.* Divide into parts; **~ off,** separate (part of room etc.) by a partition. [ME f. OF, f. L *partitio -onis* (as prec.; see -ION)]

par'tĭtĭve *a.* & *n.* (Gram.) (Word) denoting part of a collective whole (e.g. *some, any*); **~ genitive,** that used to indicate a whole divided into parts, expressed in English by *of*, as in *most of us*; hence ~LY² (-vlĭ) *adv.* [f. F *partitif -ive* or f. med. L *partitivus* (as PARTITE; see -IVE)]

partizan¹,². See PARTISAN¹,².

Par'tlėt *n.* (arch.) (Personal name for) hen. [f. OF *Pertelote*, proper name, of unkn. orig.]

par'tlȳ *adv.* With respect to a part; in some degree. [f. PART¹ + -LY²]

par'tner *n.*, & *v.t.* **1.** *n.* Sharer (*with* person, *in* or *of* thing). **2.** Person associated with others in business of which he shares risks and profits; **~** (one who engages jointly) **in crime** (lit. or fig.); SLEEP²*ing partner*. **3.** Wife or husband. **4.** Companion in dance (esp. *dancing partner*); player associated with another in game and scoring jointly with him. **5.** (Naut., in *pl.*) Timber framework round hole in deck through which mast, pump, etc., passes. **6.** Hence ~LESS *a.*, ~SHIP *n.*, state of being a partner, joint business. **7.** *v.t.* Associate (persons, one *with* another) as partners; be partner of. [ME, alt. of PARCENER, after PART¹]

par'trĭdge *n.* (*pl.* **~** *or* **~s**). Game-bird of genus *Perdix* etc., esp. **common** or **grey ~** (*Perdix perdix*); **~-berry,** N. Amer. trailing evergreen (*Mitchella repens*) with edible but insipid scarlet berries; **~-wood,** (1) dark-striped hard red wood used for cabinet work etc., (2) speckled effect produced on wood by a certain fungus. [ME *partrich* etc. f. OF *perdriz* etc. f. L f. Gk *perdix -dicis*; for *-dge* cf. CABBAGE]

pārtūr'ĭent *a.* About to give birth (lit., or fig. of the mind etc.). [f. L *parturire* be in labour (incept. f. *parere part-* bring forth); see -ENT]

pārtūrĭ'tion *n.* Act of bringing forth young, childbirth, (lit. or fig.). [f. LL *parturitio*, f. as prec.; see -ION]

par'tȳ¹ *n.* **1.** Body of persons united in a cause, opinion, etc.; attachment to such body, taking of sides on public questions; **the P~,** (esp.) the Communist party; **~ line,** policy adopted by a party (and see sense 4); **~ politics** (governed by rivalry between parties); **~ spirit,** (usu. derog.) zeal for a party (and see sense 2). **2.** Body of persons travelling or working together (*fishing, reading, -party*); social gathering, esp. of invited guests at private house, (*birthday, dinner, tea, -party*); **~ spirit,** enthusiasm for taking part in such gatherings (and see sense 1). **3.** Each of two or more persons making the two sides in legal action, contract, marriage, etc., (THIRD *party*); accessary (*to* action); (vulg. or joc.) person (*an old party with spectacles*).

4. ~-coloured, = PARTICOLOURED; **~ line,** telephone line shared by two or more subscribers (and see sense 1); **~-wall,** wall shared by each of the occupiers of the two buildings etc. that it separates. [ME, f. OF *partie*, f. Rom. **partita* fem. p.p. (as n.) of L *partire* (see PART²)]

par'tў² *a.* (Her.) Divided into parts of different tinctures. [ME, f. OF *parti*, f. L (as prec.)]

par'venu (-ōō) *n.* & *a.* (Person) of obscure origin but having gained wealth or position, upstart. [F, p.p. of *parvenir* arrive f. L PER(*venire* come)]

par'vĭs, par'vīse, *n.* Enclosed area in front of cathedral, church, etc.; room over church-porch. [ME, f. OF *parvis*, *pare(v)is*, f. Rom. **paravisus* f. LL *paradisus* PARADISE, court in front of St. Peter's, Rome]

pas (pah) *n.* (*pl.* same). **1.** Precedence (*dispute, give, take, the pas*). **2.** Step in dancing; **~ *de chat*** (pahdeshah'), leap in which each foot in turn is raised to opposite knee; **~ *de deux*** (pahdedér'), dance for two persons; *pas* GLISSÉ; **~ *seul*** (pahsér'l), solo dance. [F, = step]

pă'scal *n.* Unit of pressure, one newton per square metre. [f. B. *Pascal*, Fr. scientist d. 1662]

pă'schal (-k-) *a.* **1.** Of the Jewish Passover; **~ lamb,** lamb sacrificed at Passover, (fig.) Christ. **2.** Of Easter. [ME, f. OF *pascal* f. eccl. L *paschalis* (*pascha* f. Gk *paskha* f. Aram. *pasḥa*, rel. to Heb. *pesaḥ* PASSOVER; see **-AL**)]

păsh *n.* (sl.) Passion (*for*). [abbr.]

pa'sha, pa'cha, (pah'sha) *n.* (Hist.) Title (placed after name) of Turkish officer of high rank, e.g. military commander, governor of province, etc.; **~lĭc** *n.*, pasha's province or jurisdiction. [f. Turk. *paşa*, prob. = *başa* (*baş* head, chief)]

păshm *n.* Under-fur of hairy quadrupeds in Tibet etc., esp. that of goats as used for Cashmere shawls. [f. Pers. *pašm* wool]

Pa'shtō (pŭ'-) *n.* & *a.* = PUSHTU.

paso doble (pahsō dō'blā) *n.* (Ballroom dance based on) Latin-American style of marching. [Sp., = double step]

pă'sque-flower (-skf-) *n.* Anemone with bell-shaped purple flowers. [earlier *passe-flower*, f. F *passe-fleur*; assim. to *pasque* = obs. *pasch* (as PASCHAL), Easter]

păsquĭnā'de *n.* Lampoon, satire, orig. one exhibited in public place. [f. It. *pasquinata* (*Pasquino*, statue at Rome on which Latin verses were annually posted; see -ADE)]

pass¹ (pahs) *v.* (*p.p.* **~ed** *or as adj.* PAST¹, *both pr.* pahst). **1.** *v.i.* Move onward, proceed, (*along, down, over, on*, etc.); circulate, be current; be accepted *as*; be currently known *by* or *under the name of*; *(of person with some Negro ancestry) be accepted as White. **2.** Be transported *from* place *to* place; change (*into* something, *from* one state *to* another); die (usu. *pass hence, pass from among us*, etc., and see sense 15); go by (*saw the procession pass*; *time passes rapidly*; *remarks pass unnoticed*); come to an end (*kingdoms and nations pass*; *paroxysm has passed*). **3.** Get through, effect a passage (**~ed pawn,** chess pawn with no opposing pawn ahead on its own or adjacent files); go uncensured, be accepted as adequate, (*let the matter pass*); (of bill in Parliament, proposal, etc.) be sanctioned; (of candidate) satisfy examiner. **4.** Happen, be done or said, (*I saw* or *heard what passed* or *was passing*). **5.** Adjudicate (*upon*); (of judgement) be given (*for* plaintiff etc.). **6.** (Cards). Forgo one's opportunity, e.g. of making a bid; throw up one's hand. **7.** *v.t.* Leave (thing etc.) on one side or behind, as one goes (**has ~ed the chair,** has been chairman, president, mayor, etc.); overtake; not declare or pay (dividend); go across (sea, frontier, mountain range). **8.** (Of bill) be examined and approved by (House of Commons etc.); reach standard required by (examiner, examination); *pass* MUSTER¹. **9.** Outstrip; surpass; be too great for (*it passes my comprehension*). **10.** Transport (usu. w. *prep.* or *adv.*; cf. sense 15); move, cause to go, (*passed his hand across his forehead*; *pass flour through a sieve*; *pass a rope round it*; *pass in* one's CHECK¹*s*; **~** one's **eye over,** read (document) cursorily); (Footb., Hockey, etc.) kick or throw or hit (ball, or abs.) to or *to* another player of one's own side. **11.** Cause to go by (*pass troops* etc. *in review*); cause or allow (bill in Parliament, candidate for examination, etc.) to proceed as being found satisfactory after scrutiny; **~ed master,** = PAST¹ *master* (2). **12.** Spend (*time, the winter*, etc.). **13.** Hand, transfer, (*read this and pass it round, to Bob*; *please pass the salt*); cause (coin, esp. base coin) to circulate; (arch.) pledge (one's *word, oath*, etc.). **14.** Utter (criticism, judicial sentence, *on* or *upon*); *pass the* TIME¹ *of day*; discharge from body as or with excreta (**~ water,** urinate). **15.** (w. *advs.*): **~ away,** (fig.) die, cease to exist, come to an end; **~ by,** walk etc. past; **~ off,** (of feelings etc.) disappear gradually, (of proceedings) be carried through (*smoothly* etc.), palm off (thing or person *on* person *for* or *as* what it etc. is not), evade or lightly dismiss (awkward remark etc.); **~ on,** proceed on one's way, (fig.) die, transmit to next person in series; **~ out,** depart, complete military training, (fig.) die, (colloq.) become unconscious; **~ over,** (fig.) die, or as in sense 16 (*pass it over in silence*); **~ up,** (colloq.) refuse or neglect (opportunity etc.). **16.** (w. *preps.*): **~ by,** omit, disregard, walk etc. past; **~ for,** be accepted as; **~ over,** omit, disregard, ignore claims of (person) to promotion etc., make no remark on (*pass over his subsequent conduct*); **~ through,** experience. [ME, f. OF *passer* f. Rom. **passare* f. L *passus* PACE¹]

pass² (pahs) *n.* **1.** Passing, esp. of examination or at cards; ||attainment of standard that satisfies university examiners and entitles to **~ degree** but not to honours degree. **2.** BRING *to pass*; *come to pass* (COME 8). **3.** Critical position (*things have come to a* (*strange, pretty*) *pass*). **4.** Written permission to pass into or out of a place, or to be absent from quarters; = FREE¹ *pass*. **5.** Thrust in fencing; juggling trick; passing of hands over anything, as in conjuring or mesmerism; **make a ~ at,** (colloq.) make amorous advances to. **6.** (Footb. etc.) Transference of ball to another player of one's own side. **7. ~'book,** (1) book supplied by bank to person having current or deposit account, showing all sums deposited and drawn, (2) (S. Afr.) document to be carried by non-white persons; **~'key,** (1) private key to gate etc. for special purposes, (2) master-key; ||**~'man,** one who takes pass degree at university; **~-mark,** minimum mark needed to pass examination; **~'word,** selected word or phrase known only to one's own side and used to distinguish friend from enemy. [partly f. prec., partly f. F *passe* (*passer*, as prec.)]

pass³ (pahs) *n.* **1.** Narrow passage through mountains; this as commanding access to a country; **sell the ~,** (fig.) betray a cause. **2.** Navigable channel, esp. at river's mouth; passage for fish over weir. [ME, var. of PACE¹, infl. by F *pas* and by PASS¹]

pa'ssab|le (pah'-) *a.* In vbl senses; that can pass muster, fairly good, whence **~LY²** *adv.* [ME f. OF (as PASS¹; see -ABLE)]

păssaca'glia (-ah'lya) *n.* (Mus.) Instrumental piece usu. with ground bass, derived from old dance. [It., f. Sp. *pasacalle* (*pasar* pass, *calle* street; because often played in streets)]

pă'ssage[1] *n.* **1.** Passing, transit (BIRD *of passage*); transition from one state to another; voyage or crossing from port to port. **2.** Liberty or right to pass through; right of conveyance as passenger by sea or air; **work** one's ~, earn this right by labour (lit. or fig.). **3.** Passing of a bill etc. into law. **4.** ~(**way**), way by which one passes, corridor etc. giving communication between different rooms in house. **5.** Duct etc. in the body; **back** ~, (colloq.) rectum; **front** ~, (colloq.) vagina. **6.** (in *pl.*) What passes between two persons mutually, interchange of confidences etc. **7.** ~ **of** or **at arms,** fight (lit. or fig.). **8.** Short part of book etc. (*famous, difficult, corrupt,* PURPLE, *passage*); particular phrase or short section in a piece of music. [ME f. OF (as PASS[1]; see -AGE)]

pă'ssage[2] *v.* **1.** *v.i.* (Of horse or rider) move sideways, by pressure of rein on horse's neck and of rider's leg on opposite side. **2.** *v.t.* Make (horse) do this. [f. F *passager*, earlier *passéger* f. It. *passeggiare* to walk, pace (*passeggio* walk f. L *passus* PACE[1])]

pă'ssant *a.* (Her.) (Of animal) walking and looking to dexter side, with three paws on ground and right fore-paw raised. [ME f. OF, part. of *passer* PASS[1]; see -ANT]

passé (pă'sā) *a.* (*fem.* ***~e*** *pr.* same). Past the prime, esp. (of woman) past the period of greatest beauty; behind the times, out of date. [F, p.p. of *passer* PASS[1]]

***pă'ssel** *n.* (Large) group *of* (persons etc.). [alt. of PARCEL[1]]

passementerie (pă'smentrĭ) *n.* Trimming of gold or silver lace, braid, beads, etc. [F (*passement* gold lace etc. f. *passer* PASS[1]; see -MENT, -ERY)]

pă'ssėnger (-nj-) *n.* Traveller in public conveyance by land or water or air; traveller in or on private conveyance (other than driver, pilot, etc.); FOOT[1]-*passenger*; (colloq.) member of team, crew, etc., who does, or can do, no effective work; **~-mile,** one mile travelled by one passenger, as unit of traffic; **~-pigeon,** extinct wild pigeon of N. America, capable of long flight; ~ **seat** (esp. in motor vehicle next to driver's seat); ~ **train** (opp. goods train). [ME f. OF *passager* n., f. OF adj. *passager* passing (as PASSAGE[1], -ER[2]); *-n-* as in *messenger* etc.]

pȧsse-partou't (păspȧrtōō'; *or* pah-) *n.* Master-key; picture-frame (esp. for mounted photographs) consisting of two pieces of glass fastened together at edges with adhesive tape; adhesive tape or paper used thus. [F, = passes everywhere]

pa'sser (pah'-) *n.* In vbl senses; **~-by,** one who goes past, esp. casually. [ME, f. PASS[1] + -ER[1]]

pă'sserīne *a.* & *n.* **1.** (Bird) of the order Passeriformes, perching (esp. song-)bird. **2.** *a.* Of the size of a sparrow. [f. L *passer* sparrow + -INE[1]]

pă'ss|ĭble *a.* (Theol.) Capable of feeling or suffering; so ~IBI'LITY *n.* [ME f. OF, or f. LL *passibilis* f. L *pati pass-* suffer; see -IBLE]

passim (pă'sĭm) *adv.* (Of allusions, phrases, etc., to be found in specified author or book) in many places, here and there throughout (*this occurs in Milton passim*). [L (*passus* scattered f. *pandere* spread)]

pa'ssĭng[1] (pah'-) *n.* In vbl senses; **in** ~, by the way, in the course of a speech etc.; **~-bell** (rung to announce person's death); **~-note, *~-tone,** (Mus., not belonging to the harmony but interposed to secure smooth transition). [ME, f. PASS[1] + -ING[1]]

pa'ssĭng[2] (pah'-) *a.* & *adv.* **1.** *a.* In vbl senses; transient, fleeting; cursory, incidental; ~ **shot,** (Tennis) stroke intended to place ball beyond and out of reach of opponent. **2.** *adv.* (arch.) Very (*passing strange, rich*). [ME, f. PASS[1] + -ING[2]]

pă'ssion[1] (-shon) *n.* **1.** Strong emotion; outburst of anger (*flew into a passion*); sexual love; strong enthusiasm (*for* thing, *for* doing), object arousing this. **2.** (*P~*). *The* sufferings of Christ on the Cross, (musical setting of) narrative of this from Gospels. **3. ~-flower,** plant of genus *Passiflora* [flower of which was supposed to suggest instruments of the Crucifixion]; **~-fruit,** edible fruit of some species of passion-flower, granadilla; **~-play,** miracle play representing Christ's Passion; **P~ Sunday,** fifth Sunday in Lent; **P~tide,** last two weeks of Lent; **P~ Week,** (1) week between Passion Sunday and Palm Sunday, (2) = HOLY *Week*. **4.** Hence ~LESS *a.* [ME f. OF, f. LL *passio -onis* f. L *pati pass-* suffer; see -ION]

pă'ssion[2] (-shon) *v.i.* (poet.) Feel or express passion. [f. OF *passionner* (as prec.)]

pă'ssional[1] (-sho-) *n.* Book of the sufferings of saints and martyrs. [f. med. L *passionale* neut. adj. (as n.) f. L *passio* PASSION[1]]

pă'ssional[2] (-sho-) *a.* Of, or marked by, passion. [f. PASSION[1] + -AL]

pă'ssionate (-sho-) *a.* Dominated by or easily moved to strong feeling, esp. love or anger; due to passion; (of language etc.) showing passion; hence ~LY[2] (-tlĭ) *adv.*, ~NESS (-tn-) *n.* [ME, f. med. L *passionatus* (as PASSION[1]; see -ATE[2])]

Pă'ssionĭst (-sho-) *n.* Member of a R.C. order pledged to do their utmost to keep alive the memory of Christ's Passion. [f. PASSION[1] + -IST]

pă'ssĭv|āte *v.t.* Make passive; hence ~A'TION *n.* [f. foll. + -ATE[3]]

pă'ssĭve *a.* & *n.* **1.** *a.* Suffering action, acted upon. **2.** (Gram.) ~ **voice,** that comprising those forms of transitive verbs that attribute the verbal action to the person etc. to whom it is directed (the logical object), as *He was seen by us*; (of verb etc.) in passive voice; INDIRECT *passive*; cf. ACTIVE, MIDDLE[1]. **3.** Offering no opposition, submissive; *passive* OBEDIENCE; ~ **resistance,** non-violent refusal to co-operate. **4.** Not active, inert; (of debt) incurring no interest-payment; (of metal etc.) abnormally unreactive. **5.** Hence ~LY[2] (-vlĭ) *adv.*, ~NESS (-vn-), **păssĭ'v**ITY, *ns.* **6.** *n.* (Gram.) Passive voice or form of verb. [ME, f. OF *passif -ive*, or f. L *passivus* (as PASSION[1]; see -IVE)]

Pa'ssōver (pah'-) *n.* Jewish spring festival commemorating liberation of Israelites from Egyptian bondage, held from 14th to 21st day of seventh month of Jewish year; = PASCHAL *lamb*. [f. *pass over*, pass without touching, w. ref. to exemption of Israelites from death of first-born (Exod. 12)]

pa'sspōrt (pah'-) *n.* Official document certifying identity and citizenship, permitting person(s) specified in it to travel to and from foreign country, establishing his identity and nationality, and entitling him to protection; (fig.) thing that ensures admission to or attainment of (*flattery is the sole passport to his favour*). [f. F *passeport* (*passer* PASS[1], PORT[1])]

past[1] (pah-) *a.* & *n.* **1.** *a.* Having passed (PASS[1]); gone by in time (*his prime is past*; *our past years*; *in times past*); just gone by (*the past month*; *for some time past*); (Gram.) expressing past action or state (*past tense, participle*); relating to a former time (*past president*); ~ **definite,** ~ **historic,** (Gram.) tense expressing completed action in the past; ~ **master,** (1) one who has been master in guild, Freemasons' lodge, etc., (2, fig.) thorough master (*in* or *of* a subject); *past* PERFECT[1]. **2.** *n.* Past time, esp. *the past*; what has happened in past time (*cannot undo the* *past*); person's past life or career, esp. one that is not creditable (*a woman with a past*); past tense. [p.p. of PASS[1]]

past[2] (pah-) *prep.* & *adv.* **1.** *prep.* Beyond in time or place (*stayed till past two o'clock*; *half past three*; *old man past seventy*; *ran past the house*); beyond the range or duration or compass of (*past belief, endurance, bearing, caring,* PRAYING *for*); ~ **it,** (sl.) incompetent through senility etc., ineffective after long use; **not put it** ~ person (*to* do), (colloq.) regard him as (esp. morally) capable (of doing). **2.** *adv.* So as to pass by (*hasten past*). [ME, f. prec. as in *is past* = 'has passed' w. obj.]

pă'sta (*or* pah'-) *n.* (Dish made from cooked) dried flour paste used in Italian cooking in various shapes (macaroni, spaghetti, vermicelli, etc.). [It., = PASTE[1]]

pāste[1] *n.* **1.** Flour moistened and kneaded, with butter, suet, lard, etc., as cooking material. **2.** Sweet doughy confection (*almond paste*). **3.** Easily spread preparation of ground meat, fish, etc., (*anchovy paste*). **4.** Cement of flour or starch and water. **5.** Soft plastic mixture for any purpose (*toothpaste*). **6.** Hard vitreous composition used in making imitation gems. **7.** Mixture of clay, water, etc., used in making pottery. **8.** ~**'board,** stiff substance made by pasting together sheets of paper, (*attrib.*, fig.) unsubstantial, flimsy. [ME f. OF, f. LL *pasta* small square medicinal lozenge f. Gk *pastē* (*pastos* sprinkled)]

pāste[2] *v.t.* Fasten with paste; stick *up* (playbill etc.) on wall with paste; cover (thing *with* paper etc.) by pasting; (sl.) beat, thrash, bomb etc. heavily; ~**'down,** outer blank leaf of book pasted on inside of cover; ~**-up,** document prepared for copying etc. by pasting various materials on a backing. [f. prec.]

pă'stel (*or* -ĕ'l) *n.* Artists' crayon made of dried paste compounded of pigments with gum solution; drawing in pastel, whence ~(**l**)IST (3) *n.*; ~ **colour** etc. (light and subdued). [F, or f. It. *pastello*, dim. of *pasta* PASTE[1]]

pă'stern *n.* Part of horse's foot between fetlock and hoof; corresponding part in other animals. [ME *pastron* f. OF *pasturon* (*pasture* hobble f. **pastoire* f. med. L *pastoria* f. L *pastorius* of a shepherd; see PASTOR)]

pă'steurīz|e (-*ter*-; *or* -sch*er*- *or* pah'-), **-īs|e** (-īz), *v.t.* Subject (milk etc.) to Pasteur's method of partial sterilization by heating; hence ~A'TION *n.* [f. L. *Pasteur*, Fr. chemist d. 1895 + -IZE]

păstĭ'cciō (-ĭ'chō) *n.* (*pl.* ~**s**). = foll. [It. (see foll.)]

păsti'che (-ē'sh) *n.* Medley, esp. musical composition, or picture, made up from various sources; literary or other work of art composed in the style of a well-known author. [F, f. It. *pasticcio* f. Rom. **pasticius* f. LL *pasta* PASTE[1]]

pă'stille (*or* -tēl) *n.* Small roll of aromatic paste burnt as fumigator etc.; = LOZENGE 2. [F, f. L *pastillus* little loaf, lozenge (*panis* loaf)]

pa'stīme (pah'-) *n.* Recreation; game, sport. [f. PASS[1] + TIME[1]]

pa'stor (pah'-) *n.* **1.** Minister in charge of church or congregation, whence ~SHIP *n.*; person exercising spiritual guidance. **2.** Pink species of starling. [ME f. AF & OF *pastour* f. L *pastor -oris* shepherd (*pascere past-* feed, graze; see -OR)]

pa'storal (pah'-) *a.* & *n.* **1.** *a.* Of shepherds; relating to flocks and herds; (of land) used for pasture; (of poem, picture, etc.) portraying country life, whence ~ISM (2) *n.* **2.** Of a pastor; concerned with spiritual guidance of a body of Christians; ~ **epistles** (of Paul to Timothy and Titus, dealing with pastor's work); ~ **staff,** crosier; ~ **theology** (considering religious truth in relation to spiritual needs). **3.** Hence ~ITY (-ă'l-) *n.*, ~LY[2] *adv.* **4.** *n.* Pastoral play, poem, poetry, or picture; letter from pastor, esp. bishop, to clergy or people. [ME, f. L *pastoralis* (as prec.; see -AL)]

păstora'l|ė (-ah'-) *n.* (*pl.* ~**i** *pr.* -ē, *or* ~**es**). Simple opera etc. with rural subject; slow quiet instrumental composition with notes flowing in groups of three and usu. with drone notes in bass suggesting bagpipes. [It., f. as prec.]

pa'storalĭst (pah'-) *n.* (Austral.) Sheep- or cattle-farmer. [f. PASTORAL + -IST]

pa'storate (pah'-) *n.* Pastor's (tenure of) office; body of pastors; *parsonage. [f. PASTOR + -ATE[1]]

pā'strў *n.* (Baked) flour-paste; article(s) of food made wholly or partly of this; ~**-cook,** one who makes pastry, esp. for public sale. [f. PASTE[1] after OF *pastaierie*; see -ERY]

pa'sturage (pah'sch*er*-; *or* -tūr-) *n.* Pasturing; herbage for cattle etc.; pasture-land. [OF (as foll.; see -AGE)]

pa'sture (pah'-) *n.* & *v.* **1.** *n.* Herbage for cattle, sheep, etc.; (piece of) land covered with this; **common** ~, use of herbage by cattle of several owners. **2.** *v.t.* Lead or put (cattle) to pasture; (of sheep etc.) eat down (grassland); put sheep etc. on (land) to graze. **3.** *v.i.* Graze. [ME f. OF, f. LL *pastura* (as PASTOR; see -URE)]

pă'stў[1] (*or* pah'-) *n.* Pie of meat, fruit, jam, etc., enclosed in paste and baked without dish. [ME, f. OF *pasté(e)* f. med. L **pastata* f. LL *pasta* PASTE[1]; see -Y[4]]

pā'stў[2] *a.* Of or like paste; ~(**-faced**), of pale complexion. [f. PASTE[1] + -Y[2]]

păt[1] *n.* **1.** Light stroke or tap, esp. with hand as caress etc.; ~ **on the back** (fig., as token of approbation). **2.** Small mass (esp. of butter) formed by patting. **3.** Sound made by striking lightly with something flat. [ME; prob. imit.]

păt[2] *v.* (**-tt-**). **1.** *v.t.* Strike (thing) gently with flat surface (~**'ball,** poor or feeble cricket or lawn tennis); flatten thus (~**-a-cake** [first words of a nursery rhyme] child's game with patting of hands); strike gently with inner surface of hand or fingers, esp. to mark sympathy, approbation, etc.; ~ (person, one**self**) **on the back,** (fig.) express approbation of, congratulate. **2.** *v.i.* Beat lightly *upon*. [16th c., f. (or rel. to) prec.]

păt[3] *adv.* & *a.* Apposite(ly), opportune(ly), (*story came pat to his purpose*); (known thoroughly and) ready for any occasion (*has the story* (*off*) *pat*); **stand** ~, (Poker) retain hand dealt to one, not draw other cards, (fig.) refuse to change, stick to one's decision etc. [16th c., rel. to PAT[1,2]]

Păt[4] *n.* (Nickname for) Irishman. [abbr. of *Patrick*]

Pat. *abbr.* Patent.

pătagī'|um *n.* (*pl.* ~**a**). (Zool.) Wing-membrane of bat or similar animal; scale covering wing-joint in Lepidoptera. [med. L use of L f. Gk *patageion* gold edging on tunic]

pătavĭ'nĭtў *n.* Dialectal characteristics of Patavium (Padua) as seen in Livy's Latin; provincialism. [f. L *patavinitas* (*Patavinus* of Padua; see -INE[1], -ITY)]

pătch[1] *n.* **1.** Piece of cloth, metal, etc., put on to mend hole or rent; piece of plaster etc. put over wound; pad worn to protect injured eye; (Mil.) piece of cloth on uniform as badge of unit; **not a** ~ **on,** (colloq.) not comparable to, very much inferior to. **2.** (Hist.) Small disc etc. of black silk stuck on either side of face, worn esp. by women in 17th–18th c. for adornment. **3.** Large or irregular distinguishable area on surface; **in** ~**es,** in isolated areas or periods of time; ||**strike a bad** ~, go through a period of bad luck or difficulty. **4.** Piece of ground; number of plants growing in one place (*brier-patch*); area patrolled by police etc. **5.** Scrap, remnant. **6.** **~-pocket** (consisting of piece of cloth sewn on garment); **~ test,** test for allergy by applying to the skin patches containing allergenic substances; **~'work,** work made up of fragments of different kinds and colours (lit. or fig.; often *attrib.*). **7.** Hence ~'ERY (1) *n.* [ME *pacche, patche,* perh. var. of *peche* f. AF **peche,* OF *pieche* dial. var. of *piece* PIECE¹]

pătch² *v.t.* Put patch(es) on; ~ **(up)**, repair with patches; (of material) serve as patch to; ~ **(up)**, (fig.) repair, set to rights (matter, trouble, quarrel), esp. hastily or temporarily; ~ **(up)**, put together hastily; piece (things) together (lit. or fig.); appear as patches on (surface). [f. prec.]

pă'tchoulĭ (-o͝olĭ; *or* pacho͞o'-) *n.* Odoriferous E. Ind. plant; perfume got from it. [native name in Madras]

pă'tch|ȳ *a.* Having patches; irregular, uneven in quality; hence ~**ĭLY**² *adv.*, ~**ĭNESS** *n.* [f. PATCH¹ + -Y²]

pāte *n.* (arch. or colloq.) Head, often as representing seat of intellect; hence **-pā'tED**² *a.* [ME, of unkn. orig.]

pâté (pă'tā; *or* pah'-) *n.* Pie, patty; paste of meat etc.; ~ **de foie gras** (de fwah grah), paste or pie of fatted goose liver. [F, f. OF *pasté* (as PASTY¹)]

patĕ'lla *n.* (*pl.* ~**e**). Kneecap, whence **patĕ'llAR**¹, **patĕ'llATE**², *adjs.*; (Rom. Ant.) small pan. [L, dim. of *patina* (see foll.)]

pă'ten *n.* Shallow dish used for bread at Eucharist; thin circular plate of metal. [ME, f. AF **pateine,* OF *patene* or f. L *patena, -ina* shallow dish f. Gk *patanē* plate]

pă'tent¹ *a.* **1.** ||**Letters ~** [OF *lettres patentes,* med. L *litterae patentes*], = PATENT² 1. **2.** Conferred or protected by PATENT²; (of food, medicine, etc.) proprietary; *patent* LEATHER; ~ **log,** elaborated rotary form of ship's log, recording speed on dial fixed on taffrail; ~ **still** (allowing continuous distillation). **3.** (fig.) To which one has proprietary claim; (colloq.) such as might be patented, ingenious, well-contrived. **4.** (Of door etc.) open; (fig.) plain, obvious; hence **pă'tENCY** *n.*, ~LY² *adv.* [ME f. OF, and f. L *patēre* lie open; see -ENT]

pă'tent² *n.* **1.** Open letter from sovereign etc. conferring right, title, etc., esp. sole right for a period to make, use, or sell, some invention. **2.** Government grant of exclusive privilege of making or selling new invention; invention or process so protected; (fig.) sign that one is entitled to something, possesses a quality, etc., (*a patent of gentility*). **3.** ~ **agent, *attorney,** (specializing in procurement of patents); ~ **office** (from which patents are issued); ||~**-roll** (recording patents issued in U.K. in a year). [abbr. of *letters* PATENT¹]

pă'tent³ *v.t.* Obtain patent for (invention); hence ~ABLE *a.* [f. prec.]

pătentee' *n.* Taker-out or holder of a patent; person for the time being entitled to the benefit of a patent. [f. PATENT² + -EE]

||**pā'ter** *n.* (sl.) Father. [L]

păterfamĭ'lĭăs *n.* (Rom. Law, or joc.) Head of family or household. [L]

patẽr'nal *a.* **1.** Of or like a father; fatherly; related through the father (~ **grandmother,** father's mother). **2.** (Of government, legislation, etc.) limiting the freedom of the subject by well-meant regulations, whence ~ISM (3), ~IST (2), *ns.*, ~**ĭ'stIC** *a.* **3.** Hence ~LY² *adv.* [f. LL *paternalis* f. L *paternus* (*pater* father); see -AL]

patẽr'nĭtȳ *n.* Fatherhood (~ **test,** test to determine from blood samples whether a man may be or cannot be father of a particular child); one's paternal origin; (fig.) authorship, source. [ME, f. OF *paternité* or f. LL *paternitas* (as prec.; see -ITY)]

păternŏ'ster *n.* **1.** The Lord's Prayer, esp. in Latin; **devil's ~,** (1) this said backwards, (2) muttered imprecation. **2.** Bead in rosary indicating that paternoster is to be said; series of like things, e.g. moving compartments serving as lift; ~ **(line)**, weighted fishing-tackle with hooks at intervals. [OE, f. L *pater noster* our father]

path *n.* (pahth; *pl. pr.* pahdhz). **1.** Footway, esp. one merely made by walking, not specially constructed. **2.** Track laid for foot or cycle racing. **3.** Line along which person or thing moves; (fig.) course of action, line of conduct. **4.** **~'finder,** explorer, aircraft (or its pilot) sent ahead of bombers to guide them to their objective and mark out their targets; **~'way,** = sense 1, (Biochem. etc.) sequence of reactions by which energy is made available. **5.** Hence ~'LESS *a.* [OE *pæth,* = OLG *pad,* OHG *pfad* f. WG **path-*]

-păth *suf.* forming *ns.* denoting: **1.** Practitioner of curative treatment (*homoeopath, osteopath*). **2.** Sufferer from a disease (*psychopath*). [sense 1 back form. f. -PATHY; sense 2 f. Gk *-pathēs* -sufferer (as PATHOS)]

Patha'n (-tah'n) *n.* Member of a people inhabiting N.W. Pakistan and S.E. Afghanistan. [Hindi]

pathĕ't|ĭc *a.* **1.** Exciting pity or sadness or contempt; of the emotions; **~ic fallacy,** crediting inanimate things with human emotions. **2.** Hence ~ICS *n. pl.*, study of, indulgence in, or demonstration of, emotions; ~ICALLY *adv.* [f. F *pathétique,* f. LL f. Gk *pathētikos* (as PATHOS; see -ETIC)]

pă'thĭc *n.* Victim; catamite. [f. L f. Gk *pathikos* passive (as PATHOS; see -IC)]

pătho- *comb. form.* Disease, as: **~gnomo'nic,** characteristic of a particular disease; **~gnomy** (-ŏ'g-), study of the emotions. [f. Gk *pathos* suffering (see PATHOS)]

pă'thogėn *n.* Agent causing disease; so **pāthogE'NIC**, **pathŏ'GENOUS**, *adjs.* [f. prec. + -GEN]

păthogĕ'nėsĭs, pathŏ'gėnȳ, *ns.* Mode of development of a disease; so **păthogėnĕ'tIC** *a.* [f. PATHO- + GENESIS, -GENY]

pătholŏ'gĭcal *a.* Of pathology; (apparently) morbid (*a pathological dislike of dogs*); hence ~LY² *adv.* [f. foll. + -ICAL]

pathŏ'log|ȳ *n.* Science of bodily diseases; symptoms of a disease; hence ~IST (3) *n.* [f. F *pathologie* or mod. L *pathologia* (as PATHO-, -LOGY)]

pā'thŏs *n.* Quality in speech, writing, events, etc., that excites pity or sadness. [f. Gk *pathos* suffering, rel. to *paskhō* suffer, *penthos* grief]

-pathȳ *suf.* forming *ns.* denoting curative treatment (*allopathy, homoeopathy, hydropathy*), or feeling (*telepathy*). [f. Gk *patheia* suffering; see -Y¹]

pā'tience (-shens) *n.* **1.** Calm endurance of pain or of any provocation; perseverance; forbearance; quiet and self-possessed waiting for something; **have no ~ with,** be irritated by, be unable to bear patiently (person, his conduct, etc.); **lose** (one's) ~, become impatient (*with*); **out of ~ with,** no longer able to endure; *the patience of* JOB⁴. **2.** ||Game of cards, usu. for one player, in which cards are to be brought into specified arrangement. [ME f. OF, f. L *patientia* (as foll.; see -ENCE)]

pā'tient (-shent) *a.* & *n.* **1.** *a.* Having or showing patience; ~ **of,** (arch.) (1) enduring with patience, (2) admitting of or compatible with (*the facts are patient of two interpretations*); hence

~LY^2 *adv.* **2.** *n.* Person under medical or dental or psychiatric treatment; person accepted by doctor etc. for treatment if this is needed in future. **3.** Person undergoing action (opp. *agent*). [ME f. OF, f. L *patiens -entis* (*pati* suffer; see -ENT)]

pă'tĭn|a *n.* Incrustation, usu. green, on surface of old bronze, esteemed as ornament; similar alteration on other surfaces; gloss produced by age on woodwork; hence **~ātėd** [-ATE^2], ~OUS, *adjs.*, ~A'TION *n.* [It., f. L *patina* dish]

pă'tĭō *n.* (*pl.* **~s**). Inner court open to sky in Spanish or Sp.-Amer. house; paved usu. roofless area adjoining and belonging to house. [Sp.]

pătĭ'ssĕrĭe *n.* Pastry-cook's shop or wares. [f. F *pâtisserie* f. med. L *pasticium* pastry (*pasta* PASTE^1); see -ERY]

Pă'tna *n.* **~ rice,** variety of rice with long firm grains. [~ in India, where orig. grown]

pă'tois (-twah) *n.* (*pl.* same *pr.* -z). Dialect of common people in a region, differing materially from the literary language; jargon. [F, = rough speech, perh. f. OF *patoier* treat roughly (*patte* paw)]

||**pā'trĭal** *a.* & *n.* (Person) having right of abode in U.K. through British birth of parent; hence **pātrĭă'l**ITY *n.* [obs. F, or f. med. L *patrialis* f. L *patria* fatherland (*pater* father); see -AL]

pā'trĭarch (-k) *n.* **1.** Father and ruler of family or tribe; (Bibl., in *pl.*) (1) sons of Jacob, (2) Abraham, Isaac, and Jacob, and their forefathers. **2.** (In early and Orthodox Churches) bishop, esp. of Antioch, Alexandria, Constantinople, Jerusalem, or Rome; (R.C. Ch.) bishop ranking next above primates and metropolitans, and immediately below the pope; head of a Uniat community. **3.** Founder of an order, science, etc.; venerable old man; oldest member of a group. **4.** So **pātrĭar'ch**AL (-k-) *a.* [ME, f. OF *patriarche* f. eccl. L f. Gk *patriarkhēs* (*patria* family f. *patēr* father, *-arkhēs* -ruler)]

pā'trĭarchate (-k-) *n.* Office, see, or residence, of ecclesiastical patriarch; rank of tribal patriarch. [f. med. L *patriarchatus* (as prec.; see -ATE^1)]

pā'trĭarch|ȳ (-kĭ) *n.* Patriarchal system of society, government, etc.; so ~ISM (3) *n.* [f. med. L f. Gk *patriarkhia* (as PATRIARCH; see -Y^1)]

patrĭ'cian (-shan) *n.* & *a.* **1.** *n.* (Hist.) Ancient Roman noble (cf. PLEBEIAN); member of a noble order in later Roman Empire; officer representing Roman emperor in provinces of Italy and Africa; nobleman in some Italian republics. **2.** *a.* Noble, aristocratic; of the ancient Roman nobility. [ME, f. OF *patricien* f. L *patricius* having noble father (*pater patris* father; see -ICIAN)]

patrĭ'cĭate (-shĭ-) *n.* Patrician order, aristocracy; rank of patrician. [f. L *patriciatus* (as prec.; see -ATE^1)]

pă'trĭcīde *n.* = PARRICIDE (esp. w. ref. to murder of one's father); hence **pătrĭcī'd**AL *a.* [f. LL *patricida, patricidium,* alt. of L *parricida, parricidium,* (see PARRICIDE), after *pater* father]

pătrĭlĭ'nėal *a.* Of or based on (kinship with) father or descent through male line. [f. L *pater patris* father + LINEAL]

pătrĭlō'cal *a.* Of system of marriage where wife goes to live with husband's group. [f. as prec. + LOCAL^2]

pă'trĭmonȳ *n.* Property inherited from one's father or ancestors, heritage (lit. or fig.); endowment of church etc.; hence **pătrĭmō'nĭ**AL *a.* [ME *patrimoigne* f. OF *patrimoine* f. L *patrimonium* (*pater patris* father; see -MONY)]

pă'trĭot *n.* One who defends or is zealous for his country's prosperity, freedom, or rights; hence or cogn. **pătrĭŏ'tĭ**C *a.*, ~ISM (3) *n.* [f. F *patriote* f. LL f. Gk *patriōtēs* (*patrios* of one's fathers f. *patēr patros* father; see -OT^2)]

patrĭ'st|ĭc *a.* Of (the study of the writings of) the Fathers of the Church; hence ~ICS *n.*, such study. [f. G *patristisch* f. L *pater patris* father; see -IST, -IC]

patrō'l *n.* & *v.* (**-ll-**). **1.** *n.* Going the ROUND^{2}s of garrison, camp, etc.; perambulation of town etc. by police (**~ car,** car used for this; ***~ wagon,** police van for prisoners); routine operational voyage of ship or of aircraft; routine monitoring of astronomical etc. phenomena. **2.** Detachment of guard, police constable(s), etc., assigned for patrol (**~man,** *police constable); detachment of troops sent out to reconnoitre; unit of usu. six in Scout troop or Guide company. **3.** *v.i.* Act as patrol. **4.** *v.t.* Go round (camp, town, etc.) as patrol. [(f. G *patrolle* f. F *patrouille*) f. F *patrouiller* paddle in mud (*patte* paw)]

patrŏ'log|ȳ *n.* Study, or a collection, of writings of the Fathers of the Church; hence **pătrolo'gical** *a.*, ~IST (3) *n.* [f. Gk *patēr patros* father + -O- + -LOGY]

pā'tron *n.* One who countenances, protects, or gives influential support to (person, cause, art, etc.); (esp. regular) customer of shop etc.; ~ (**saint**), tutelary saint of person, place, etc.; (Rom. Ant.) (1) former owner of manumitted slave, (2) protector of a CLIENT; ||one who has right of presenting to benefice; so **pā'tron**ESS^1 *n.* [ME f. OF, f. L *patronus* protector of clients, defender (*pater patris* father)]

pă'tronage *n.* Support or encouragement given by patron; ||right of presenting to benefice or office; patronizing airs; customer's support. [ME f. OF (as prec.; see -AGE)]

pă'tronal (*or* patrō'-) *a.* Of a patron saint (*the patronal festival* etc.). [F, or f. LL *patronalis* (as PATRON; see -AL)]

pă'troniz|e, -is|e (-īz), *v.t.* Act as patron towards, support, encourage, (person, practice, shop, etc.); treat condescendingly, whence **~ing**LY^2 *adv.* [f. obs. F *patroniser* or f. med. L *patronizare* (as PATRON; see -IZE)]

pătronȳ'mĭc *a.* & *n.* (Name) derived from name of a father or ancestor. [f. LL f. Gk *patrōnumikos* f. *patrōnumos* (*patēr patros* father, *onuma, onoma* name); see -IC]

***patrōō'n** *n.* (Hist.) Possessor of landed estate with manorial privileges (finally abolished *c.* 1850) under Dutch governments of New York and New Jersey. [Du., = PATRON]

***pă'tsȳ** *n.* (sl.) Person who is ridiculed, deceived, or victimized. [20th c.; orig. unkn.]

pă'ttée (-tā *or* -tĭ) *a.* (Of cross) having almost triangular arms becoming very broad towards their ends. [F (*patte* paw; see -Y^4)]

pă'tten *n.* Shoe with sole made thick or set on iron ring etc., for raising wearer's foot out of mud etc. [ME, f. OF *patin* (*patte* paw, *-in* -INE^1)]

pă'tter^1 *n.* Language of a profession or class; deceptive speech of conjurer etc.; rapid speech introduced into song; words of comic song. [f. foll.]

pă'tter^2 *v.t.* & *i.* Repeat (prayers etc.) in rapid mechanical way; talk glibly. [ME, f. *pater* = PATERNOSTER]

pă'tter^3 *v.* & *n.* **1.** *v.i.* Make rapid succession of taps, as rain on window-pane; run with short quick steps. **2.** *v.t.* Cause (water etc.) to patter. **3.** *n.* Rapid succession of taps or short light steps. [f. PAT^2 + -ER^5]

pă'ttern *n.*, & *v.t.* **1.** *n.* Excellent or ideal example (*she is a pattern of domestic virtues*). **2.** Model or design or working instructions from which thing is to be made; sample (of tailor's cloth, wallpaper, etc.). **3.** Decorative design as executed on carpet, wallpaper, cloth, etc.; regular form or order (*behaviour pattern*; *pattern* *of* one's *daily life*); marks made by shots, bombs, etc., on area of target; ~ **bombing** (on large area, not single target); **~-room, -shop,** part of foundry etc. in which patterns are prepared. **4.** *v.t.* Model (thing *after* or *on* design etc.). **5.** Decorate with pattern. [ME *patron* (see PATRON); different. in sense and sp. since 16th–17th c.]

pă'ttȳ *n.* **1.** Little pie or pastry; **~pan** (for baking patty in). **2.** *Small flat cake of minced meat etc. [f. F *pâté* PASTY[1]]

pă'tūlous *a.* Open, expanded; (of boughs etc.) spreading; hence ~LY[2] *adv.*, ~NESS *n.* [f. L *patulus* (*patēre* be open) + -OUS]

pau'a (pow'*a*) *n.* Large edible N.Z. shellfish of genus *Haliotis*; its ornamental shell; fish-hook made from this. [Maori]

pau'cĭtȳ *n.* Smallness of number or quantity. [ME, f. OF *paucité* or f. L *paucitas* (*paucus* few; see -ITY)]

Paul *n.* *Rob* PETER[1] *to pay Paul*; ~ **Jones,** (dance in which there is) exchange of dance-partners according to prescribed movement [Amer. naval officer d. 1792]; ~ **Pry,** inquisitive person [character in comedy by J. Poole 1825]. [man's Christian name; ME, f. OF *Pol* f. L *Paulus*]

Pau'līne *a.* & *n.* **1.** *a.* Of St. Paul (*the Pauline epistles*). **2.** *n.* Past or present member of St. Paul's School in London. [ME, f. med. L *Paulinus* (as prec.; see -INE[1])]

paulow'nĭa (-ō'-) *n.* Chinese tree of genus *Paulownia*, with fragrant purple flowers. [f. Anna *Paulovna*, Russ. princess d. 1865 + -IA[1]]

paunch *n.*, & *v.t.* **1.** *n.* Belly, stomach; protruding abdomen, whence ~'Y[2] *a.*; ruminant's first STOMACH, rumen; (Naut.) thick strong mat, (**rubbing** ~) wooden shield on mast, to prevent chafing. **2.** *v.t.* Disembowel (animal). [ME, f. AF *pa(u)nche*, ONF *panche* f. Rom. **pantice* f. L *pantex panticis* bowels]

pau'per *n.* Person without means of livelihood, beggar; (Hist.) recipient of poor-law relief; person who may sue *in forma pauperis*; hence ~DOM, ~ISM (2), *ns.*, ~IZE (3) *v.t.* [L, = poor]

pause (-z) *n.*, & *v.i.* **1.** *n.* Interval of inaction or silence, esp. due to hesitation; temporary stop; **give ~ to,** cause (person) to hesitate. **2.** Break made in speaking or reading; (Mus.) mark (𝄐) over note or rest that is to be lengthened by some unspecified amount. **3.** *v.i.* Make a pause, wait; linger *upon* (word etc.). [ME f. OF, or f. L *pausa* f. Gk *pausis* (*pauō* stop); v. f. n. or f. F *pauser* or f. L *pausare*]

pā'vage *n.* Paving; tax or toll towards paving of streets. [ME f. OF (*paver* PAVE; see -AGE)]

pă'van, pava'ne (-ah'n), *n.* Stately dance in which dancers were elaborately dressed; music for this. [f. F *pavane* f. Sp. *pavana*, poss. f. *pavon* peacock]

pāve *v.t.* Cover (street, floor, etc.) with or (fig.) as with pavement (***paved with stone, with flowers, with good intentions***); (fig.) prepare ***the way*** (*for* or *to* changes, reform, etc.); hence **pā'VER**[1], **pā'vior** or **pā'VIOUR** (-vy*er*), *ns.* [ME, f. OF *paver*, back form. f. as PAVEMENT]

pavé (pă'vā) *n.* Pavement; setting of jewels placed close together. [F, p.p. of *paver* (see prec.)]

pā'vement (-vm-) *n.* **1.** Covering of street, floor, etc., made of stones, tiles, wooden blocks, asphalt, etc., ||esp. paved footway at side of road, *esp. roadway; ~ **artist,** ||one who draws with chalks on pavement to get money from passers-by, *one who displays paintings etc. on pavement. **2.** (Zool.) Pavement-like formation of close-set teeth etc. [ME f. OF, f. L *pavimentum* (*pavire* beat, ram; see -MENT)]

pavĭ'lion (-lyon) *n.*, & *v.t.* **1.** *n.* Tent, esp. large peaked one; light ornamental building; building used for entertainments; ||building adjacent to cricket or other ground for players and spectators; detached building at hospital; projecting (usu. highly decorated) subdivision of building; temporary stand at exhibition; part of cut gem-stone below girdle. **2.** *v.t.* Enclose in or furnish with pavilion. [ME, f. OF *pavillon* f. L *papilio -onis* butterfly, tent]

pavio(u)r. See PAVE.

pă'vĭs(e) *n.* (Hist.) Convex shield covering whole body used in sieges etc. [ME, f. OF **paveis*, *pavais* f. It. *pavese* f. med. L *pavense* (*scutum* shield) of *Pavia* in Italy, where orig. made]

pavlō'va *n.* (Austral. & N.Z.) Meringue cake, usu. served with cream etc. [f. A. *Pavlova*, Russ. ballerina d. 1931]

pă'vonīne *a.* Of or like a peacock. [f. L *pavoninus* (*pavo -onis* peacock; see -INE[1])]

paw[1] *n.* Foot of animal having claws or nails, opp. *hoof*; (colloq.) person's hand. [ME *pawe*, *powe* f. OF *poue* etc. f. Rom. f. Frank. **pauta*]

paw[2] *v.t.* & *i.* Strike with paw: (of horse) strike (ground), strike ground, with hoofs; (colloq.) handle awkwardly or rudely or indecently. [f. prec.]

||**paw'k|ȳ** *a.* (Sc. & dial.) Drily humorous; shrewd; hence ~ĬLY[2] *adv.*, ~ĬNESS *n.* [f. Sc. & N. Engl. dial. *pawk* trick, of unkn. orig., + -Y[2]]

pawl *n.*, & *v.t.* **1.** *n.* Lever with catch for teeth of wheel or bar; (Naut.) short bar used to lock capstan, windlass, etc., and prevent it from recoiling. **2.** *v.t.* Secure (capstan etc.) with pawl. [perh. f. LG & Du. *pal*, rel. to *pal* fixed]

pawn[1] *n.* Chess-man of smallest size and value; (fig.) unimportant person subservient to others' plans. [ME, f. AF *poun*, OF *peon* f. med. L *pedo -onis* foot-soldier f. L *pes pedis* foot; cf. PEON]

pawn[2] *n.* **1.** (usu. fig.) Thing left in another's keeping as security, pledge. **2.** State of being pledged (*in* or *at pawn*); **~'broker,** one who lends money at interest on security of personal property pawned; **~'broking,** his occupation; **~'shop,** his place of business; **~-ticket,** his receipt for thing pledged. [ME, f. OF *pan*, *pand*, *pant* pledge, security f. WG **panda*]

pawn[3] *v.t.* Deposit (thing) as security for payment of money or performance of action; (fig.) pledge (one's life, honour, word). [f. prec.]

pawpaw'. See PAPAW.

păx *n.* **1.** Tablet with representation of Crucifixion etc. formerly kissed at Mass by priest and people. **2.** Kiss of peace as liturgical or ceremonial form. **3.** ||(school sl., as *int.*). Peace!, truce!. [ME f. L, = peace]

||**P.A.X.** *abbr.* private automatic (telephone) exchange.

pay[1] *n.* **1.** Payment; wages; **in the** ~ (employment) **of. 2. ~-bed,** hospital bed whose use is paid for by user; **~-claim,** demand for increase of pay; **~-day,** day on which payment is (to be) made, ||(Stock Exch.) day on which transfer of stock has to be paid for; *~ **dirt,** ~ **gravel,** ground worth working for ore (lit. or fig.); *~ **envelope,** = *pay-packet*; **~'load,** productive or useful part of load of aircraft, rocket, etc.; **~'master,** official who pays troops, workmen, etc. (often fig.); ||**Paymaster General,** minister at head of department of Treasury through which payments are made; ||**~-packet** (containing employee's wages); ~ **phone,** *~ **station,** coin-box telephone; **~-roll,** list of employees receiving regular pay. [ME, f. OF *paie* (*payer*; see foll.)]

pay[2] *v.* (**paid**). **1.** *v.t.* Give (person) what is due in discharge of debt or for services done or goods received; (fig.) reward, recompense; *pay him in his own* COIN[1]; *the* DEUCE[2] or *devil to pay*; ~ **off,** pay in full and discharge or be quit of (ship's crew, creditor, debt, etc.); ~ (person) **out** or **back,** punish him or be revenged on him; *pay the* PIPER; **put paid to,** (colloq.) deal effectually with (person), terminate (hopes etc.). **2.** Recompense (work); **paid holidays** (during which normal wages continue to be paid). **3.** Hand over (money owed *to* person; *paid the fee to the clerk, paid him his fee*); hand over the amount of (debt, wages, ransom); (esp. Naut.) let rope *out* or *away* by slackening it. **4.** ~ **in,** pay to one's own or another's banking account; ~ one's **way,** not get into debt; ~ **its way,** be profitable; ~ **up,** pay full amount of (arrears, or abs.); **paid-up member** (who has made all necessary payments for membership). **5.** Render, bestow, (attention, respect, court, compliment, visit, *to*; CALL[2] *on*). **6.** (Of business etc.) yield adequate return to (person). **7.** *v.i.* Hand over money to discharge debt etc.; (of business etc.) yield adequate return, be profitable or advantageous; **~ing guest,** boarder. **8.** ~ **for,** hand over the price of, bear the cost of, (fig.) be punished for (fault etc.); *pay through the* NOSE; ~ **off,** yield good results, succeed, (of ship) turn to leeward through movement of helm; *~-off* n., (sl.) act of payment, climax, final reckoning. **9.** ||**~-as-you-earn,** method of collecting income tax by deducting at source as income is earned. **10.** Hence ~EE', ~'ER[1], *ns.* [ME, f. OF *payer* f. L *pacare* appease (*pax pacis* peace)]

pay[3] *v.t.* (Naut.) Smear with pitch, tar, etc., as defence against wet. [f. OF *peier* f. L *picare* (*pix picis* PITCH[1])]

pay'able *a.* That must be paid, due; that may be paid; (of mine etc.) profitable. [ME, f. PAY[2] + -ABLE]

||**P.A.Y.E.** *abbr.* pay-as-you-earn.

pay'ment *n.* Paying; amount paid; (fig.) recompense. [ME, f. OF *paiement* (as PAY[2]; see -MENT)]

pay'nĭm *n.* (arch.) Pagan; non-Christian, esp. Muslim. [ME, f. OF *pai(e)nime* f. eccl. L *paganismus* heathenism (as PAGAN; see -ISM)]

payō'la *n.* Bribe(ry) offered in return for deliberate help in promoting a commercial product by unsanctioned means. [f. PAY[1] + *-ola* as in *Victrola*, make of gramophone]

paysage (pāzah'zh) *n.* Rural scene, landscape; landscape painting, whence **pay'sag**IST (3) *n.* [F (*pays* country; see PEASANT, -AGE)]

Pb *symb.* lead. [f. L *plumbum*]

||**P.B.I.** *abbr.* (colloq.) poor bloody infantry.

P.B.X. *abbr.* private branch exchange (private telephone switchboard).

P.C. *abbr.* police constable; Privy Councillor.

p.c. *abbr.* per cent; postcard.

***pct.** *abbr.* per cent.

***P.D.** *abbr.* Police Department.

pd. *abbr.* paid.

Pd *symb.* palladium.

p.d.q. *abbr.* (sl.) pretty damn quick.

***P.D.T.** *abbr.* Pacific Daylight Time.

P.E. *abbr.* physical education.

p/e *abbr.* price/earnings (ratio).

pea *n.* **1.** Hardy climbing leguminous plant (*Pisum sativum*) whose seeds grow in pods and are used for food; its seed (**green ~s,** the seeds gathered unripe for food); SPLIT[1] *peas*; **as like as two ~s,** indistinguishable. **2.** Similar plant (CHICK-PEA, EVERLASTING *pea*, SWEET *pea*). **3.** **~-green,** colour of green peas; **~'nut,** (plant *Arachis hypogaea*, whose fruit is a pod containing) seed used as food and yielding oil (*~nut butter*, paste of ground roasted peanuts; *~nuts*, (sl.) paltry thing, esp. small amount of money); **~-shooter,** toy tube from which dried peas are shot by blowing; ~ **soup** (made from esp. dried peas); **~-sou'per,** (colloq.), thick yellow fog; **~-stick** (on which pea-plant is trained in garden). [back form. f. PEASE taken as *pl.*; cf. CHERRY]

peace *n.* **1.** Freedom from or cessation of war (*peace with honour*; *peace at any price*; **make** (bring about) ~); *a* treaty of peace between two powers at war. **2.** Freedom from civil disorder; **the (queen's)** ~, general peace of the realm as secured by law; BREACH[1] *of the peace*; JUSTICE *of the Peace*. **3.** Quiet, tranquillity; (in and after Bibl. use) *peace be with you, peace to his ashes!*; mental calm (*peace of mind*). **4. At** ~, in state of friendliness or quietness, not at strife (*with*); **hold** one's ~, keep silence; **keep the** ~, prevent, or refrain from, strife; **make** one's ~, bring oneself back into friendly relations (*with*). **5.** ***P~ Corps,** organization of young people to work in developing countries; **~'maker,** one who brings about peace; **~-offering,** propitiatory or conciliatory gift, (Bibl.) offering presented as thanksgiving to God; **~-pipe,** calumet, tobacco-pipe as token of peace among N. Amer. Indians; **~-time,** period when a country is not at war. [ME f. AF *pes*, OF *pais* f. L *pax pacis*]

pea'ceab|le (-sa-) *a.* Disposed or tending to peace; free from disturbance, peaceful; hence ~**le**NESS (-beln-) *n.*, ~LY[2] *adv.* [ME f. OF *peisible, plaisible* f. LL *placibilis* pleasing f. L *placēre* please; see -IBLE]

pea'ceful (-sf-) *a.* Characterized by peace; belonging to a state of peace; not violating or infringing peace (*peaceful* COEXISTENCE); hence ~LY[2] *adv.*, ~NESS *n.* [ME, f. PEACE + -FUL]

peach[1] *n.* **1.** Large fruit, usu. round, with downy white or yellow skin flushed with red, highly flavoured sweet pulp, and rough stone; ~(**-tree**), tree (*Prunus persica*) bearing this; (sl.) person or thing of superlative merit, attractive young woman. **2.** **~-blow,** (Oriental porcelain-glaze of) delicate purplish-pink colour; ~ **brandy,** spirituous liquor from peach juice; **~-colour(ed),** (of) yellowish pink; ~ **Melba,** confection of ice cream and peaches with liqueur etc. [f. Dame N. *Melba*, Austral. soprano d. 1931]; **~es and cream,** (fig. of complexion) creamy skin with downy pink cheeks. **3.** Hence ~'Y[2] *a.* [ME, f. OF *peche, pesche*, f. med. L *persica* f. L *persicum* (*malum*), lit. Persian apple]

peach[2] *v.* (colloq. or arch.) **1.** *v.i.* Turn informer; inform (*against* or *on* accomplice). **2.** *v.t.* Inform against. [ME, f. *appeach* f. AF *enpecher*, OF *empechier* IMPEACH]

pea'-chĭck *n.* Young peafowl. [f. as PEACOCK + CHICK[1]]

pea'cŏck *n.* & *v.* **1.** *n.* Male peafowl, bird with splendid plumage and tail-coverts that can be expanded erect like fan (often as the type of ostentatious display; *proud as a peacock*). **2.** ~ (**blue**), lustrous blue of peacock's neck; ~ **butterfly** (with ocellated wings); ~ **coal** (iridescent). **3.** *v.t.* Plume one*self*. **4.** *v.i.* Make display; strut about ostentatiously, whence ~ERY (4) *n.*; (Austral. sl.) acquire best land in a district. **5.** Hence ~ISH[1], ~-LIKE, *adjs.* [ME *pecock* f. OE *pēa* f. L *pavo*, + COCK[1]]

pea'fowl *n.* Peacock or peahen, pheasant of genus *Pavo*. [f. as prec. + FOWL]

pea'hĕn *n.* Female peafowl. [ME, f. as PEACOCK + HEN]

pea'-jăckėt *n.* Sailor's short double-breasted overcoat of coarse woollen cloth. [prob. f. Du. *pijjakker* (*pij* coat of coarse cloth, *jekker* jacket), assim. to JACKET]

peak[1] *n.*, & *v.i.* **1.** *n.* Projecting part of brim of cap. **2.** (Naut.) Narrow part of ship's hold esp. at bow (*forepeak*) or stern (*after-peak*); upper outer corner of sail extended by gaff. **3.** Pointed top, esp. of mountain; point e.g. of beard or hair (WIDOW'S *peak*). **4.** Highest point in curve or record of fluctuations or in career etc.; **~ hour,** time of most intense traffic etc.; **~-load,** maximum of electric power demand etc. **5.** Hence ~ED^{2} (-kt), ~'Y^{2}, *adjs.* **6.** *v.i.* Reach highest value, quality, etc. [prob. back form f. *peaked* var. of dial. *picked* pointed (PICK^{1}, -ED^{2})]

peak^{2} *v.i.* Waste away, esp. *peak and pine*; (in *p.p.*) sharp-featured, pinched; so ~'Y^{2} *a.*, sickly, puny. [16th c.; of unkn. orig.]

peak^{3} *v.t.* & *i.* (Naut.) Tilt (yard) vertically; place (oars) apeak; (of whale) raise (tail, flukes), raise tail or flukes, straight up in diving vertically. [prob. f. APEAK]

pea'kȳ^{1,2}. See PEAK^{1}, PEAK^{2}.

peal^{1} *n.* & *v.* **1.** *n.* Loud ringing of bell(s), esp. series of changes on set of bells; set of bells; loud volley of sound, esp. of thunder or laughter. **2.** *v.i.* Sound forth in a peal. **3.** *v.t.* Utter sonorously; ring (bells) in peals. [ME *pele* f. *apele* APPEAL^{2}]

peal^{2} *n.* Salmon grilse. [16th c.; orig. unkn.]

pean^{1} *n.* (Her.) Fur represented as sable spotted with or. [16th c.; orig. unkn.]

***pē'an^{2}.** Var. of PAEAN.

pear (pār) *n.* Fleshy fruit usu. with brown or yellow skin, tapering towards stalk; ~**(-tree)**, tree (*Pyrus communis*) bearing this; *alligator* or AVOCADO *pear*; ANCHOVY *pear*; PRICKLY *pear*. [OE *pere*, *peru*, = MDu., MLG *pere* f. pop. L **pira* f. L *pirum*]

pearl^{1} (pe͞rl) *n.* **1.** Concretion, usu. white or bluish-grey, formed within shell of **~-oyster** or other bivalve mollusc, having beautiful lustre and highly prized as gem; imitation of this; (in *pl.*) necklace of pearls; MOTHER^{1}-*of-pearl*; SEED-*pearl*. **2.** Precious thing, finest example (*of* its kind); **cast ~s before swine,** offer good thing to one incapable of appreciating it. **3.** Pearl-like thing, e.g. dew-drop, tear, tooth. **4. ~ ash,** commercial potassium carbonate; **~ barley** (reduced by attrition to small rounded grains); **~-diver,** one who dives for pearl-oysters; **~-fisher,** one who fishes for pearl-oysters; **~ lamp,** frosted-glass electric-light bulb; **~ millet,** tall cereal (*Pennisetum glaucum*); **~ onion,** very small onion used in pickles; **~'wort,** weed of genus *Sagina*. **5.** Hence ~ED^{2} (-ld) *a.*, adorned with pearls, formed into pearl-like drops or grains, like pearl in colour etc. [ME f. OF *perle*, f. Rom. **perla*, prob. f. **pernula* dim. of L *perna* leg (applied to leg-of-mutton-shaped bivalve)]

pearl^{2} (pe͞rl) *v.* **1.** *v.t.* Sprinkle with pearly drops; make pearly in colour etc.; reduce (barley etc.) to small rounded grains. **2.** *v.i.* Form pearl-like drops; fish for pearl-oysters, whence ~'ER^{1} *n.* [ME, f. prec.]

‖**pearl^{3}** (pe͞rl) *n.* Picot. [var. of PURL^{1}]

pear'lȳ (pe͞r-) *a.* & *n.* **1.** *a.* Resembling a pearl; containing pearls or mother-of-pearl; adorned with pearls; **P~ Gates** (of Heaven); ‖**~ king, queen,** costermonger, his wife, wearing pearlies; *pearly* NAUTILUS. **2.** *n.* (in *pl.*) ‖Costermongers' clothes decorated with mother-of-pearl buttons; pearly kings and queens. [ME, f. PEARL^{1} + -Y^{2}]

‖**pear'main** (pār'- *or* pe͞r'-) *n.* Variety of apple with firm white flesh. [ME, = warden pear, f. OF *parmain*, *permain*, prob. f. Rom. **Parmanus* of *Parma* in Italy]

***peart** (pe͞rt) *a.* Lively; cheerful. [var. of PERT]

pea'sant (pĕ'z-) *n.* Countryman, rustic; worker on the land, esp. labourer or small farmer; hence ~RY (1) *n.* [ME, f. AF *paisant*, OF *paisent*, earlier *paisenc* (*pais* country f. Rom. **pagensis* f. L *pagus* canton; see -ING^{3})]

pea'scŏd (-z-). Var. of PEASE*cod*.

pease (-z) *n.* Peas (esp. **~-pudding,** pudding of boiled peas, eggs, etc.); **~'cod,** (arch.) pea-pod. [OE *pise* pea, pl. *pisan*, f. LL *pisa* f. L *pisum* f. Gk *pison*; cf. PEA]

peat^{1} *n.* **1.** (Cut piece of) vegetable matter decomposed in water and partly carbonized, used for fuel etc.; **~'bog, ~'moss,** bog composed of peat; **~'reek,** smoke of, or whisky distilled over, peat-fire. **2.** Hence ~'ERY (3) *n.*, ~'Y^{2} *a.* [ME, f. AL *peta*, perh. f. Celt. **pett-*; cf. PIECE^{1}]

peat^{2} *n.* (arch., derog.) Person, esp. woman, (*proud peat*). [16th c.; orig. unkn.]

peau-de-soie (pōd*e*swah') *n.* Smooth finely-ribbed satiny fabric of silk or rayon. [F, = skin of silk]

***pea'vey** *n.* Lumberjack's cant-hook with projecting spike near end. [f. *Peavey*, surname of inventor]

pĕ'bble *n.* Small stone worn and rounded by action of water (**not the only ~ on the beach,** not without competitors to be reckoned with); colourless transparent rock-crystal used for spectacles, lens of this, (colloq.) thick spectacle-lens; agate or other gem, esp. found as pebble in streams; **~-dash,** mortar with pebbles in it as coating for wall; hence **pĕ'bbly**^{2} *a.* [OE *papel-stān* pebble-stone, *pyppelripig* pebble-stream; orig. unkn.]

pébrine (pābrē'n) *n.* Epidemic disease of silkworms, characterized by black spots. [F, f. Prov. *pebrino* (*pebre* PEPPER^{1})]

p.e.c. *abbr.* photoelectric cell.

pėcă'n *n.* (Pinkish-brown smooth nut of) a hickory (*Carya illinoensis*) of the Mississippi region. [f. earlier *paccan*, of Algonquian orig.]

pĕ'cc|able *a.* Liable to sin; hence ~ABI'LITY *n.* [F, f. med. L *peccabilis* (*peccare* sin; see -ABLE)]

pĕccadĭ'llō *n.* (*pl.* **~es** *or* **~s**). Trifling offence, venial sin. [f. Sp. *pecadillo*, dim. of *pecado* sin, f. L (as foll.)]

pĕ'cc|ant *a.* Sinning; morbid, inducing disease; so ~ANCY *n.* [F, or f. L *peccare* sin; see -ANT]

pĕ'ccarȳ *n.* American gregarious wild pig of genus *Tayassu*. [f. Carib *pakira*]

pĕcca'vĭ (-ah'-) *int.* & *n.* (expr.) confession of guilt. [L, = I have sinned]

pêche Mĕ'lba (pāsh- *or* pĕsh-) *n.* = PEACH^{1} *Melba*. [F]

pĕck^{1} *n.* Measure of capacity for dry goods, = 2 gallons or 8 quarts; vessel used for this; **a ~** (large number, amount) *of troubles*, *of dirt*. [ME f. AF *pek*, of unkn. orig.]

pĕck^{2} *v.* & *n.* **1.** *v.t.* Strike (thing) with beak (**~'ing order,** social hierarchy, orig. as observed among domestic fowls; **~ out,** pluck out thus); make (hole etc.) thus; kiss (person's cheek etc.) hastily or perfunctorily; (colloq.) eat (food, or abs.), esp. in nibbling or listless fashion; mark with short strokes; break (*up*, *down*, etc.) with pick etc. **2.** *v.i.* Strike *at* (thing) with beak, (fig.) carp *at*. **3.** *n.* Stroke with beak, mark made with this; hasty or perfunctory kiss; **~ order,** = *pecking order*. **4.** (sl.) Food. [ME, prob. f. MLG *pekken*, of unkn. orig.]

pĕ'cker *n.* Bird that pecks (*flower-pecker*, *woodpecker*); *(sl.) penis; ‖**keep your ~ up,** (sl.) maintain your courage. [f. prec. + -ER^{1}]

pĕ'ckĭsh *a.* (colloq.) Hungry; *irritable. [f. PECK^{2} + -ISH^{1}]

Pĕ'cksnĭff *n.* Unctuous hypocrite talking much of benevolence etc.; hence **Pĕcksnĭ'ff**IAN *a.* [character in Dickens's *Martin Chuzzlewit*]

pĕcori'nō (-ē'-) *n.* (*pl.* **~s**). Italian ewe-milk cheese. [It. (*pecorino* a. of ewes f. *pecora* sheep)]

pĕ′ct|ĕn *n.* (*pl.* **~ens,** *or* **~ines** *pr.* -ĭnēz). **1.** (Zool.) Comblike structure of various kinds in animal bodies; so **~ĭn**ATE², **~ĭnāt**ED¹, *adjs.*, **~ĭn**A′TION *n.*, (Zool. & Bot.). **2.** Scallop of genus *Pecten.* [f. L *pecten pectinis* comb]

pĕ′ct|ĭn *n.* (Chem.) Soluble gelatinous carbohydrate derivative acting as setting agent in jams and jellies; so ~IC *a.* [f. Gk *pēktos* congealed (*pēgnumi* make solid) + -IN]

pĕ′ctoral *n.* & *a.* **1.** *n.* Ornamental breastplate esp. of Jewish high priest; pectoral fin, medicine, etc. **2.** *a.* Of or for the breast or chest; good for chest disease; worn on the breast; **~ cross,** cross so worn by bishops etc.; **~ fin** (on side of fish). [ME f. OF, f. L *pectorale* n., *pectoralis* a. (*pectus pectoris* breast, chest; see -AL)]

pĕ′ctōse *n.* (Chem.) Insoluble carbohydrate derivative found in unripe fruits etc. and converted into pectin by ripening, heating, etc. [f. PECTIC + -OSE²]

pĕ′cūl|āte *v.t.* & *i.* Embezzle (money); so ~A′TION, **~āt**OR, *ns.* [f. L *peculari* rel. to *peculium* (see foll.) + -ATE³]

pėcū′lĭar *a.* & *n.* **1.** *a.* Belonging exclusively *to*; belonging to the individual, esp. one's *own peculiar* (character etc.); particular, special, (*a point of peculiar interest*). **2.** Strange, odd, (*a peculiar flavour*; *he has always been a little peculiar*). **3. ~ people,** (1) the Jews, (2) God's elect, (3) (**P~ People**) evangelical fundamentalist Christian denomination founded 1838 relying on divine healing for cure of disease. **4.** *n.* Peculiar property, privilege, etc.; parish or church exempt from jurisdiction of diocese in which it lies; (*P~*) one of the *Peculiar People* (3). [ME, f. L *peculiaris* of private property (*peculium* f. *pecu* cattle; see -AR¹)]

pėcūlĭă′rĭtў *n.* Being peculiar; characteristic; (instance of) unusualness. [f. prec. + -ITY]

pėcū′lĭarlў *adv.* As regards oneself alone, individually, (*does not affect him peculiarly*); especially, more than usually, (*peculiarly annoying*); oddly (*they dress peculiarly*). [f. PECULIAR + -LY²]

pėcū′nĭar|ў *a.* (Consisting) of money (*pecuniary aid, considerations*); (of offence) having money penalty; hence **~ĭ**LY² *adv.* [f. L *pecuniarius* (*pecunia* money f. *pecu* cattle; see -ARY¹)]

pĕ′dagŏgue (-g) *n.* (arch. or derog.) Schoolmaster, teacher; hence or cogn. **pĕdagŏ′g**IC(AL) (-ŏ′g- *or* -ŏ′j-) *adjs.*, **pĕ′dagŏg(u)**ISM (1) (-gĭ-) *n.* [ME, f. L f. Gk *paidagōgos* (*pais paidos* boy, *agōgos* guide)]

pĕ′dagŏg|ў (*or* -gĭ) *n.* Science of teaching; so ~ICS (*or* -gŏg-) *n.* [f. F *pédagogie* f. Gk *paidagōgia* (as prec.; see -Y¹)]

pĕ′dal¹ *n.* & *v.* (‖-ll-). **1.** *n.* (Mus., in organ) (1) any of wooden keys played upon by the feet, (2) foot-lever for drawing out several stops at once or other purposes; (in piano) foot-lever for making the tone more sustained and fuller (**loud ~**) or softer (**soft ~**); (in harp) foot--lever for altering pitch of strings; foot-lever in various machines, esp. for transmitting power to wheel of bicycle (**~ cycle**) or tricycle; (Mus.) note sustained in one part, usu. bass, through successive harmonies some of which are independent of it; **~-pushers,** women's sports trousers reaching to calf. **2.** *v.i.* Play on organ pedals; work cycle pedals; ride bicycle. **3.** *v.t.* Work (bicycle) by pedals. [f. F *pédale* f. It. *pedale* f. L (as foll.)]

pĕ′dal² *a.* **1.** (Zool.) Of the feet or foot (esp. of mollusc). **2.** (Math.) **~ triangle** (formed by feet of perpendiculars or other concurrent lines from vertices of a triangle). [f. L *pedalis* (*pes pedis* foot; see -AL)]

pĕ′dalō *n.* (*pl.* **~s**). Pedal-operated pleasure--boat. [f. PEDAL¹]

pĕ′dant *n.* One who overrates or parades book--learning or technical knowledge or insists on strict adherence to formal rules; one who is obsessed by a theory; doctrinaire; hence or cogn. **pėdă′nt**IC *a.*, ~IZE (2, 3) *v.t.* & *i.*, ~RY (1, 4, 5) *n.* [f. F *pédant* f. It. *pedante*; app. f. as PEDAGOGUE + -ANT]

pĕ′date *a.* (Zool.) footed; (Bot., of leaf) having divisions like toes or bird's claws. [f. L *pedatus* (*pes pedis* foot; see -ATE²)]

pĕ′ddle *v.* **1.** *v.i.* Follow occupation of pedlar; busy oneself with trifles. **2.** *v.t.* Sell as pedlar; (fig.) deal out in small quantities, retail. [back form. f. PEDLAR; in sense 'trifle' orig. var. of PIDDLE]

***pĕ′ddler.** Var. of PEDLAR.

pĕ′deră′stў, pae′d-, *n.* Sodomy with a boy; so **pĕ′derăst** *n.*, one who commits pederasty. [f. mod. L f. Gk *paiderastia* (*pais paidos* boy, *erastēs* lover); see -Y¹]

pĕ′dėstal *n.*, & *v.t.* (‖-ll-). **1.** *n.* Base supporting column or pillar; base of statue etc. (**put** or **set on a ~,** (fig.) regard as highly admirable or important); each of two supports of knee-hole table; foundation (lit. or fig.). **2.** *v.t.* Set or support on pedestal. [f. F *piédestal* f. It. *piedestallo* (*piè* foot f. L *pes pedis, di* of, *stallo* STALL¹)]

pėdĕ′strĭan *a.* & *n.* **1.** *a.* Going or performed on foot; of walking; for walkers (**~ crossing,** part of road where pedestrians going across have priority over traffic; *pedestrian* PRECINCT); prosaic, dull, uninspired. **2.** *n.* One who walks in street etc.; one who walks as athletic performance, whence ~ISM (2) *n.*; hence ~IZE (2, 3) *v.i.* & *t.* [f. F *pédestre* or f. L *pedester -tris* + -IAN]

***pēdĭă′trĭc** etc. See PAEDIATRIC etc.

pĕ′dĭcăb *n.* Rickshaw pulled by cyclist. [f. PEDAL¹ + -I- + CAB]

pĕ′dĭcel, pĕ′dĭcle, *ns.* Small (esp. subordinate, cf. PEDUNCLE) stalklike structure in plant or animal; (Surg.) part of graft left temporarily attached to original site; hence **pĕ′dĭcell**ATE², **pėdĭ′cūl**ATE², *adjs.* [f. mod. L *pedicellus* & L *pediculus* dim. of *pes pedis* foot; see -CULE]

pėdĭ′cūlar, pėdĭ′cūlous, *adjs.* Louse-infested; so **pĕdĭcūl**O′SIS *n.* [f. L *pedicularis, -losus* (*pediculus* louse; see -AR¹, -OUS)]

pĕ′dĭcūre *n.*, & *v.t.* **1.** *n.* Care or treatment of feet, esp. of toe-nails; person who practises this. **2.** *v.t.* Treat (feet) by removing corns etc. [f. F *pédicure* f. L *pes pedis* foot + *curare* (see CURE²)]

pĕ′dĭgree *n.* & *a.* **1.** *n.* Genealogical table; ancestral line (of man or animal); derivation (of word); ancient descent; hence **pĕ′dĭgre**ED² *a.* **2.** *a.* Having a recorded line of descent, esp. one showing pure breeding (*pedigree cattle*). [ME *pedegru* etc., f. AF **pe de gru,* OF **pie de grue* crane's foot, mark denoting succession in pedigrees]

pĕ′dĭment *n.* Triangular part crowning front of building in Grecian style, esp. over portico; similarly placed member of same or other form in Roman and Renaissance styles; hence **pĕdĭmĕ′nt**AL, ~ED², *adjs.* [earlier *pedament, periment*, perh. corrupt. of PYRAMID]

pĕ′dlar *n.* Travelling vendor of small wares usu. carried in pack; (fig.) retailer (*of* gossip etc.); **~'s French,** (arch.) thieves' cant, gibberish; hence **pĕ′dla**RY (5) *n.* [ME *pedlere* alt. of *pedder* f. *ped* pannier, of unkn. orig.]

***pēdō-.** See PAEDO-.

pėdŏ′|logў *n.* Science of natural soils; hence **pĕdo**LO′GICAL *a.*, ~LOGIST *n.* [f. Russ. *pedologiya*, f. Gk *pedon* ground; see -LOGY]

pėdŏ′mėter *n.* Instrument for estimating distance travelled on foot by recording number of steps taken. [f. F *pédomètre* f. L *pes pedis* foot; see -O-, -METER]

pėdŭ'nc|le (-ŭ'ngkel) *n.* (Bot.) stalk of flower, fruit, or cluster, esp. main stalk bearing solitary flower or subordinate stalks (*pedicels*); (Zool.) stalklike process in animal body; hence **~ūl**AR[1], **~ūl**ATE[2], *adjs.* [f. mod. L *pedunculus* f. L *pes pedis* foot; see -UNCLE]

pee *v.i.*, & *n.* (colloq.) **1.** *v.i.* Urinate. **2.** *n.* Urination; urine. [f. *piss*]

peek *v.i.*, & *n.* Peep (*in, out*, etc.); (take) quick or sly look. [ME *pike, pyke*, of unkn. orig.]

pee'kabōō *n.* & *a.* **1.** *n.* * = BO-PEEP. **2.** *a.* (Of garment etc.) transparent or with pattern of small holes. [f. prec. + BOO]

peel[1] *n.* (Hist.) Small square tower built in 16th c. in border counties of England and Scotland for defence against forays. [ME *pel* stake, palisade, f. AF & OF *pel* f. L *palus* stake; cf. PALE[1]]

peel[2] *n.* Shovel, esp. baker's shovel for bringing loaves etc. into or out of oven. [ME & OF *pele* f. L *pala*, rel. to *pangere* fix]

peel[3] *v.* & *n.* **1.** *v.t.* Strip the peel (sense 4), rind, bark, etc., from (orange, potato, tree, etc.); take *off* (skin, peel, etc.); (Croquet) send (another player's ball) through hoop; **keep** one's **eyes ~ed,** (sl.) watch carefully (*for*). **2.** *v.i.* (Of tree, animal body, etc.) become bare of bark, skin, etc.; (of bark, surface, skin, etc.) come off or *off* like peel; (sl., of person) strip for exercise etc.; **~ off,** veer away and detach oneself from group of marchers etc. **3.** Hence **~'er**[1] [-ER[1] (1, 2)] *n.*, ~'ING[1] (2) *n.* (*potato peelings*). **4.** *n.* Rind, outer coating, of fruit, potato, prawn, etc.; **candied ~** (usu. of citrus fruits, used in cookery etc.). [in 17th c. different. f. PILL[2]]

pee'ler[2] *n.* **1.** ||(arch. sl.) Policeman. **2.** (*P~*; Hist.) Member of Irish constabulary, founded under Peel's secretaryship. [f. Sir Robert *Peel*, Engl. statesman d. 1850 + -ER[1]]

Pee'līte *n.* (Polit. Hist.) Conservative supporting Peel, esp. w. ref. to repeal of corn-laws (1846). [f. as prec. + -ITE[1]]

peen *n.*, & *v.t.* **1.** *n.* Wedge-shaped or thin end of a hammer-head (opp. *face*). **2.** *v.t.* Hammer with peen; treat with stream of metal shot. [17th c.; also *pane*, app. f. F *panne* f. Du. *pen* f. L *pinna* point]

peep[1] *v.i.*, & *n.* (Make) feeble shrill sound (as) of young birds, mice, etc., chirp, squeak. [imit.; cf. CHEEP]

peep[2] *v.i.* Look through narrow aperture (*at, into*, etc.); look furtively (**~ing Tom,** voyeur [f. name of Coventry tailor in story of Lady Godiva]); (of daylight, flower, distant object) come (*out*) slowly or partly into view, emerge, (fig., of quality etc.) show itself unconsciously; **~-bo,** = BO-PEEP; **~-toe**(**d**) *a.*, (of shoe) leaving toes partly bare. [ME; cf. PEEK, PEER[3]]

peep[3] *n.* Furtive or peering glance; first appearance, esp. *of dawn, of day* (**~-of-day boys,** Protestant organization in Ireland (1784–95) searching opponents' houses at daybreak for arms); **~-hole,** small hole to peep through; **~-show,** small exhibition of pictures etc. viewed through lens in small orifice; **~-sight,** aperture backsight of some rifles. [f. prec.]

pee'per *n.* One who peeps; (sl.) eye. [f. PEEP[2] + -ER[1]]

pee'pul. Var. of PIPAL.

peer[1] *n.* **1.** Equal in civil standing or rank (*jury of his peers*); equal in any respect (*you will not easily find his peer*), whence ~'LESS *a.*; **~ group,** those of the same status as, and associated with, a person. **2.** Member of one of the degrees (duke, marquis, earl, viscount, baron) of nobility in United Kingdom, whence ~'ESS[1] *n.*; LIFE *peer*; **~ of the realm,** one of class of peers whose adult members may all sit in House of Lords. **3.** Noble of any country. [ME, f. AF & OF *pe(e)r* f. L *par* equal]

peer[2] *v.t.* & *i.* (Cause to) rank equally *with*. [ME, f. OF *perer* f. LL *pariare* f. L *par* equal]

peer[3] *v.i.* Look searchingly (*into, at*, etc.); appear, peep out; (arch.) come into view. [var. of *pire*, LG *pīren*; perh. partly f. APPEAR]

peer'age *n.* The peers (PEER[1] 2); nobility, aristocracy; rank of peer or peeress (LIFE *peerage*); book containing list of peers with genealogy etc. [ME, f. PEER[1] + -AGE]

peeve *n.* (sl.) Cause of annoyance; mood of vexation. [back form. f. PEEVISH]

peeved (-vd) *a.* (sl.) Irritated, annoyed. [f. foll. + -ED[1]]

pee'vĭsh *a.* Querulous, irritable; hence ~LY[2] *adv.*, ~NESS *n.* [ME, = foolish, mad, spiteful, etc., of unkn. orig.]

pee'wĭt. See PEWIT.

pĕg[1] *n.* **1.** Pin or bolt of wood, metal, etc., usu. round and slightly tapering, for holding together parts of framework etc., stopping up vent of cask, hanging hats etc. on, holding ropes of tent, tightening or loosening strings of violin etc., marking cribbage scores, etc.; ||CLOTHES-*peg*. **2. A ~ to hang** (discourse etc.) **on,** suitable occasion, pretext, or theme, for; **off the ~,** (of clothes) ready-made; *square peg in round* HOLE[1]; **take** person **down a ~** (**or two**), humble him. **3.** ||A drink, esp. of spirits. **4. ~-board,** board with holes and pegs, esp. for game, as toy, or for commercial displays; **~-leg,** (wearer of) artificial leg; **~'top,** pear-shaped spinning-top with metal peg; ~*top skirt* or *trousers* (wide at hips, narrow below). [ME, prob. of LDu. orig.; cf. MDu. *pegge*, Du. dial. *peg*, LG *pigge*]

pĕg[2] *v.* (**-gg-**). **1.** *v.t.* Fix (thing *down, in, out*, etc.) with peg; **~ down,** restrict (*to* rules etc.). **2.** (Stock Exch.) prevent price of (stock etc.) from falling (or rising) by freely buying (or selling) at given price; stabilize (prices, wages, exchange rates, etc.). **3.** Mark (score) with pegs on cribbage-board (**level ~ging,** even scores, lit. or fig.); mark *out* boundaries of (mining claim etc.). **4.** *v.i.* **~** (**away**), work persistently (*at*); **~ out,** (Croquet) hit peg with ball as final stroke in game, (Cribbage) score winning point, (sl.) die, be ruined. [f. prec.]

Pĕ'gasus *n.* (Gk Myth.) winged horse that with stroke of hoof caused fountain Hippocrene to flow on Mt. Helicon; (fig.) poetic genius; hence **Pĕgasē'**AN (*or* pĭgā'sĭan) *a.* [L, f. Gk *Pēgasos* (*pēgē* spring)]

pĕ'gmatīte *n.* Coarsely crystalline type of granite. [f. Gk *pēgma -atos* thing joined together (*pēgnuō* fasten) + -ITE[1]]

Peh'levĭ (pā'-). Var. of PAHLAVI.

P.E.I. *abbr.* Prince Edward Island.

pei'gnoir (pā'nwâr) *n.* Woman's loose dressing-gown. [F (*peigner* to comb)]

peine forte et dure (pān fort ā dūr') *n.* (Hist.) Pressing to death, inflicted on person charged with felony who refused to plead. [F, = severe and hard punishment]

pē'jorative (*or* pĭjŏ'r-) *a.* & *n.* Depreciatory (word) (*the pejorative suffix -aster*). [f. F *péjoratif -ive* f. LL *pejorare* make worse (*pejor*); see -ATIVE]

pĕ'kan *n.* N. Amer. carnivorous mammal of weasel family, valued for fur. [Can. F, f. Abnaki *pékané*]

pēke *n.* (colloq.) Pekingese dog. [abbr.]

Pēkĭngē'se, Pēkĭnē'se, (-z) *n.* (*pl.* same) & *a.* (Inhabitant) of Pekin(g) in China; small short-legged snub-nosed dog with long silky hair. [f. *Pekin(g)* + -ESE]

pĕ'kōe *n.* Superior kind of black tea. [f. Chin. dial. *pek-ho* (*pek* white, *ho* down), leaves being picked young with down on them]

pĕ′lage *n.* Fur, hair, wool, etc., of quadruped. [F (*poil* hair; see -AGE)]

Pėlā′gĭan[1] *a.* & *n.* (Follower) of the monk Pelagius (4th–5th c.), who denied doctrine of original sin; hence ~ISM (3) *n.* [f. eccl. L *Pelagianus* (*Pelagius*; see -AN)]

pėlā′gĭan[2] *a.* & *n.* Of, inhabiting, inhabitant of, the open sea. [f. L f. Gk *pelagios* of the sea (*pelagos*) + -AN]

pėlă′gĭc *a.* Of, or performed on, the open sea (*pelagic sealing, whaling*); (of marine life) belonging to the upper layers of the open sea. [f. L f. Gk *pelagikos* (as prec.; see -IC)]

pĕlar̄gō′nĭum *n.* Plant of genus *Pelargonium*, with showy flowers and usu. fragrant leaves (in cultivation pop. called *geranium*). [mod. L, f. Gk *pelargos* stork; cf. GERANIUM]

Pėlă′sgĭc (-zj- *or* -zg-) *a.* Of the Pelasgians, an ancient people inhabiting coasts and islands of E. Mediterranean and Aegean. [f. Gk *Pelasgikos* (*Pelasgoi* Pelasgians; see -IC)]

pēle. Var. of PEEL[1].

pĕ′lerĭne (*or* -ē′n) *n.* Woman's long narrow cape or tippet. [f. F *pèlerine*, fem. of *pèlerin* PILGRIM]

pĕlf *n.* (usu. derog. or joc.) Money, wealth. [ME, f. ONF **pelfe*, var. of OF *pelfre, peufre* spoils, of unkn. orig.; cf. PILFER]

pĕ′lham (-lam) *n.* Bridle combining curb and snaffle. [f. surname *Pelham*]

pĕ′lĭcan *n.* Large gregarious water-fowl of genus *Pelecanus*, with pouch in bill for storing fish, fabled to feed its young with its own blood; ‖**~ crossing,** pedestrian crossing with traffic lights operated by pedestrians; ***P~ State,** Louisiana. [OE *pellican* & OF *pelican*, f. LL *pelicanus* f. Gk *pelekan* prob. f. *pelekus* axe w. ref. to its bill]

pėlĭ′sse (-ē′s) *n.* Woman's mantle with armholes or sleeves, reaching to ankles; fur-lined mantle or cloak, esp. as part of hussar's uniform. [F, f. med. L *pellicia* (*vestis* garment) of fur (*pellis* skin)]

pėllă′gr|a *n.* Deficiency disease characterized by cracking of skin and often ending in insanity; hence ~OUS *a.* [It., f. *pelle* skin, after *podagra*]

pĕ′llėt *n.*, & *v.t.* **1.** *n.* Small ball of paper, bread, etc.; pill; small mass of material regurgitated by bird of prey or excreted by rodent etc.; small shot; hence ~IZE (3) *v.t.* **2.** *v.t.* Make into pellet(s); hit with (esp. paper) pellets. [ME f. OF *pelote*, f. Rom. **pilotta* dim. of L *pila* ball]

pĕ′llĭcle *n.* Thin skin; membrane; film; so **pĕllĭ′cūlAR**[1] *a.* [f. F *pellicule* f. L *pellicula*, dim. of *pellis* skin]

pĕ′llĭtorȳ *n.* **1. ~ of Spain,** plant with pungent-flavoured root, used as local irritant etc. **2. ~ of the wall,** low bushy plant with greenish flowers growing on or at foot of walls. [sense 1 alt. f. ME f. OF *peletre, peretre*, f. L f. Gk *purethron* feverfew; sense 2 f. earlier *peritorie, paretorie* f. AF *paritarie*, OF *paritaire* f. LL *parietaria* (*paries -etis* wall)]

pĕll-mĕ′ll *adv.*, *a.*, & *n.* **1.** *adv.* In disorder, promiscuously; headlong, recklessly. **2.** *a.* Confused, tumultuous. **3.** *n.* Confusion, medley, mêlée. [f. F *pêle-mêle*, OF *pesle mesle, mesle pesle*, etc., redupl. of *mesle* (*mesler* mix)]

pėllū′cĭd (*or* -ōō′-) *a.* Transparent, clear, not distorting images or diffusing light; clear in style or expression; mentally clear; hence **pĕllūcĭ′dITY** (*or* -ōō-) *n.*, ~LY[2] *adv.* [f. L *pellucidus* f. PER (*lucēre* shine); see -ID[1]]

Pĕ′lman|ĭsm *n.* System of memory-training, orig. that devised by the *Pelman* Institute; card-game based on this; hence ~IZE *v.t.*, learn or memorize by Pelmanism. [P]

pĕ′lmėt *n.* Valance or narrow pendent border (esp. over window or door to conceal curtain rods). [prob. f. F PALMETTE]

pėlor′us *n.* Sighting device like ship's compass for taking bearings. [perh. f. *Pelorus*, reputed name of Hannibal's pilot]

pėlō′ta *n.* Basque game played in walled court with ball and wicker racket. [Sp., = ball, augment. of *pella* f. L *pila*]

pĕlt[1] *n.* **1.** Skin of sheep or goat with short wool on; undressed skin of fur-bearing animal; raw skin of sheep etc. stripped of wool or fur; so **pĕ′ltRY** (1) *n.* **2.** (joc.) Human skin. [ME, f. obs. *pellet* skin dim. of *pel* f. AF *pell*, OF *pel*, or back form. f. *peltry*, AF *pelterie*, OF *peleterie* (*pėletier* furrier), ult. f. L *pellis* skin]

pĕlt[2] *v.* & *n.* **1.** *v.t.* Assail with missiles (lit. or fig.); strike repeatedly with missiles. **2.** *v.i.* (Of rain etc.) beat with violence; fire repeatedly *at*; run fast. **3.** *n.* Pelting; **(at) full ~,** as fast as possible. [16th c., of unkn. orig.]

pĕ′lt|a *n.* (*pl.* **~ae**). Small light shield of ancient Greeks, Romans, etc.; (Bot.) shieldlike structure, whence ~ATE[2] *a.* [L, f. Gk *peltē*]

pĕ′lv|ĭs *n.* (*pl.* **~es** *pr.* -ēz, *or* **~ises**). (Anat.) Basin-shaped cavity formed in most vertebrates by haunch-bones with sacrum and other vertebrae, whence ~IC *a.*; basin-like cavity of kidney. [L, = basin]

Pĕ′mbrōke (*or* -ŏŏk) *n.* Variety of Welsh corgi with short tail; **~ (table),** table on four fixed legs with hinged flaps that can be raised and supported. [~ in Dyfed, Wales]

Pembs. *abbr.* Pembrokeshire (former county in Wales).

pĕ′mmĭcan *n.* N. Amer. Ind. cake of dried and pounded meat mixed with melted fat; beef so treated and flavoured with currants etc. for travellers in Arctic etc. [f. Cree *pimecan* (*pime* fat)]

pĕ′mphĭg|us *n.* (Path.) Formation of watery vesicles or eruptions on skin of body; hence ~OID, ~OUS, *adjs.* [mod. L, f. Gk *pemphix -igos* bubble]

pĕn[1] *n.* Small enclosure for cows, sheep, poultry, etc., or for other purposes; (Jamaica) farm, plantation; enclosure (often with concrete roof) for sheltering submarines. [OE *penn*, of unkn. orig.]

pĕn[2] *v.t.* (**-nn-**). Enclose, shut *up*, shut *in*; shut up (cattle etc.) in pen. [ME *pennen*, app. f. OE **pennian* (as prec.)]

pĕn[3] *n.*, & *v.t.* (**-nn-**). **1.** *n.* Quill-feather with quill pointed and split in two, for writing with ink; similar instrument of steel, gold, etc., fitted into rod of wood, plastic, etc. (**~′holder**); FOUNTAIN-*-pen*; *put pen to* PAPER[1]. **2.** Writing, style of writing, (*made a living with his pen*; *wields a formidable pen*; *the pen is mightier than the sword*). **3. ~ and ink,** instruments of writing, writing; **~-and-ink** *a.*, drawn or written with these; **~-feather,** quill-feather of bird's wing; **~-friend,** friend with whom one corresponds without meeting; **~′knife,** small knife usu. carried in pocket; **~-light,** small electric torch shaped like fountain-pen; **~′man,** (1) one who writes a (*good, bad*, etc.) hand, (2) author; **~′manship,** skill in writing, style of handwriting, action or style of literary composition; **~-name,** literary pseudonym; **~-pal,** (colloq.) = *pen-friend*; **~-pusher, ~-pushing,** (colloq.) clerical work(er); **~′wiper,** appliance usu. of small pieces of cloth for wiping pen after use. **4.** *v.t.* Write, compose and write, (letter etc.). [ME f. OF *penne*, f. L *penna* feather]

pĕn[4] *n.* Female swan. [16th c.; orig. unkn.]

***pĕn**[5] *n.* (sl.) Penitentiary. [abbr.]

P.E.N. *abbr.* International Association of Poets, Playwrights, Editors, Essayists, and Novelists.

Pen. *abbr.* Peninsula.

pē′nal *a.* Of punishment; concerned with

inflicting this (*penal laws*); (of offence) punishable, esp. by law; inflicted as punishment (~ **servitude,** (Hist.) imprisonment with compulsory labour); inflicted as if by way of punishment (*penal taxation*); used as place of punishment (*a penal colony*); hence ~LY² *adv.* [ME f. OF, or f. L *poenalis* (*poena* PAIN¹); see -AL]

pē'nalize, -ise (-īz), *v.t.* Make or declare (action) penal; subject to penalty or comparative disadvantage. [f. prec. + -IZE]

pě'naltў *n.* **1.** Punishment, esp. payment of sum of money, for breach of law, rule, or contract, (*on* or *under penalty of* dismissal etc.); money thus paid; **the ~ of,** disadvantage resulting from (quality etc.). **2.** Disadvantage imposed on competitor in sports etc. who has broken rule or won previous contest; (Bridge etc.) points gained by opponents when contract is not fulfilled; ~ (**bully, corner, kick, shot,** etc.), action in various games allowed as redress to side against which foul has been committed; ~ **area,** (Assoc. Footb.) part of ground in front of goal in which foul by defenders involves award of penalty kick; ~ **box,** (Ice Hockey) place for penalized players and some officials. [f. AF **penalte*, F *pénalité* f. med. L *penalitas* (as PENAL; see -ITY)]

pě'nance *n.*, & *v.t.* **1.** *n.* (R.C. & Orthodox Ch.) Sacrament including contrition, confession, satisfaction, and absolution. **2.** Act of self-mortification as expression of penitence, esp. one imposed by priest; **do ~,** perform such act. **3.** *v.t.* Impose penance on. [ME f. OF, f. L *poenitentia* (as PENITENT; see -ANCE)]

pĕnă'nnūlar *a.* Almost ringlike. [f. L *paene* almost + ANNULAR]

pėna'tēs (-ah'tēz; *or* -āz) *n. pl.* (Rom. Myth.) Household gods, esp. of the store-room; see LAR. [L (*penus* provision of food)]

pĕnce. See PENNY.

pe'nchant (pah'ṅshahṅ) *n.* Inclination, liking, (*for*). [F, part. of *pencher* incline]

pě'ncil¹ *n.* **1.** Instrument for drawing or writing, esp. of graphite, chalk, etc., enclosed in cylinder of wood or in metal case with tapering end; similarly shaped device used as cosmetic etc. **2.** (Optics) set of rays meeting at a point; (Geom.) figure formed by set of straight lines meeting at a point. **3.** (fig.) Draughtsman's art or style. **4.** (arch. or tech.) Artist's paint-brush. **5.** **~-case,** holder for pencil(s) etc.; **~-sharpener,** device with cutting edge for sharpening pencil by rotation. [ME, f. OF *pincel* f. Gallo-Rom. **penicellum* f. L *penicillum* paintbrush dim. of *peniculus* brush dim. of *penis* tail]

pě'ncil² *v.t.* (‖-ll-). Tint or mark (as) with lead pencil; write with pencil; write tentatively; (esp. in *p.p.*) mark delicately with thin parallel or concentric lines of colour or shading; hence ~LER¹ *n.*, (‖esp., sl.) bookmaker. [f. prec.]

pě'ndant¹, pě'ndent¹, *n.* **1.** Hanging ornament, esp. one attached to necklace, bracelet, etc. **2.** (Naut.) Short rope hanging from head of mast etc. with eye at lower end for receiving hooks of tackles. **3.** = PENNANT 1. **4.** Shank and ring of pocket-watch by which it is suspended. **5.** (*or pr.* pah'ṅdahṅ). Match, parallel, companion, complement, (*to*). [ME, f. OF (*-ant*), f. *pendre* hang f. L *pendere*; see -ANT]

pě'ndent², pě'ndant², *a.* Hanging; overhanging; undecided, pending, whence **pě'nd**ENCY *n.*; (Gram.) of which the construction is incomplete, esp. ~ **nominative** (with no verb). [ME, f. as prec.]

pendente lite (pĕndĕ'ntĭ lī'tĭ) *adv.* (Law). During the progress of a suit. [L]

pĕndĕ'ntīve *n.* (Archit.) Spherical triangle formed by intersection of dome with two adjacent arches springing from supporting columns. [f. F *pendentif -ive* adj. (as PENDANT¹; see -IVE)]

pě'nding *a.* & *prep.* **1.** *a.* Undecided, awaiting decision or settlement, (*a suit, a treaty, was then pending*); about to come into existence (*patent pending*); **~-tray** (to contain documents awaiting decision). **2.** *prep.* During (*pending these negotiations*, orig. = while these negotiations are pending); until (*pending his return*). [after F *pendant* (see PENDANT², -ING²)]

pĕndră'gon *n.* Title of ancient British or Welsh prince. [W, = chief war-leader (*pen* head, *dragon* standard)]

pě'ndūlāte *v.i.* Swing like pendulum; (fig.) be undecided. [f. PENDULUM + -ATE³]

pě'ndūline *a.* (Of nest) suspended; (of bird) building such nest. [F (as foll.; see -INE¹)]

pě'ndūlous *a.* (Of ears, breasts, bird's nest, flower etc.) suspended, drooping, hanging down; oscillating; hence ~LY² *adv.* [f. L *pendulus* (*pendēre* hang) + -OUS]

pě'ndūlum *n.* Body suspended so as to be free to swing, esp. rod with weighted end regulating movement of clock's works; **swing of the ~,** tendency to alternation of power between political parties, or to oscillation of public opinion between extremes; COMPENSATION *pendulum*. [f. L neut. adj. (as prec.)]

pē'nėplain *n.* (Geol.) Region that is almost a plain, in consequence of erosion. [f. L *paene* almost + PLAIN¹]

pě'nėtrā'lĭa *n. pl.* Innermost shrine or recesses. [L, neut. pl. of *penetralis* interior (as foll.; see -AL)]

pě'nėtr|āte *v.* **1.** *v.t.* Find access into or through, pass through; (of man) bring penis into vagina of (woman); permeate; imbue (person, thing, *with*); (fig.) see into, find out, discern (person's mind, meaning, design, the truth); (of sight) pierce through (darkness, thicket, etc.). **2.** *v.i.* Make a way (*into, through, to*); be absorbed by the mind (*my hint did not penetrate*); (in *part.*) gifted with or suggestive of insight, (of voice etc.) easily heard through or above other sounds. **3.** Hence or cogn. ~ABI'LITY, ~A'TION, **~āt**OR, *ns.*, ~ABLE, **~āt**IVE, *adjs.* [f. L *penetrare* place or enter within (*penitus* interior) + -ATE³]

pě'nguĭn (-nggwĭn) *n.* Sea-fowl of southern hemisphere with wings developed into scaly flippers with which it swims under water. [16th c., orig. = great auk; of uncert. orig.]

pē'nĭal *a.* Of the penis. [f. PENIS + -AL]

pě'nĭcĭllate *a.* (Biol.) Having or forming small tuft(s); marked with streaks as of pencil or brush. [f. L *penicillum* (PENCIL¹) + -ATE²]

pĕnĭcĭ'llĭn *n.* Antibiotic of group produced naturally on moulds, able to prevent growth of certain disease-causing bacteria. [f. mod. L *Penicillium* genus of moulds f. L *penicillum* (PENCIL¹), + -IN]

pē'nīle *a.* Of the penis. [f. mod. L *penilis* (PENIS); see -IL]

pėnĭ'nsūla *n.* Piece of land almost surrounded by water or projecting far into the sea. [f. L *paeninsula* (*paene* almost, *insula* island)]

pėnĭ'nsūlar *a.* & *n.* **1.** *a.* Of (the nature of) a peninsula; (Hist.) of Spain and Portugal, or of the war there in 1808–14. **2.** *n.* Inhabitant of a peninsula. [f. prec. + -AR¹]

pėnĭ'nsūlāte *v.t.* Make (land) into a peninsula. [f. PENINSULA + -ATE³]

pē'nĭs *n.* (*pl.* **~es** *or* **pe'nes** *pr.* -ēz). Copulatory and (in mammals) urinatory organ of male animal; ~ **envy,** (Psych.) woman's or girl's subconscious desire to be male. [L, = tail, penis]

pě'nĭt|ent *a.* & *n.* **1.** That repents; hence or cogn. ~ENCE *n.*, **~ent**LY² *adv.* **2.** *n.* Repentant sinner, person doing penance under direction of confessor; (in *pl.*) various R.C. orders associated for mutual discipline etc. [ME f. OF, f. L *paenitens* (*paenitēre* repent; see -ENT)]

pĕnĭtĕ'ntial (-nsh*a*l) *a.* Of penitence or penance; **~ psalms,** seven psalms (6, 32, 38, 51, 102, 130, 143) with especial expression of penitence; hence ~LY² *adv.* [f. OF *penitencial* f. LL *paenitentialis* (*paenitentia* penitence f. as prec.; see -ENCE, -AL)]

pĕnĭtĕ'ntiarў (-sh*e*rĭ) *n.* & *a.* **1.** *n.* Office in papal court deciding questions of penance, dispensations, etc., (**Grand P~**, cardinal presiding over this); *reformatory prison. **2.** *a.* Of penance; of reformatory treatment; *(of offence) making culprit liable to prison sentence. [ME f. med. L *paenitentiarius* a. & n. (as PENITENCE; see -ARY¹)]

Penn(a). *abbr.* Pennsylvania.

pĕ'nnant *n.* **1.** (Naut.) Tapering flag, esp. that flown at mast-head of vessel in commission; **broad ~**, short swallow-tailed pennant distinguishing commodore's ship in squadron. **2.** = PENDANT¹ 2. **3.** = PENNON. **4.** *Flag denoting sports championship etc. [blend of PENDANT¹ and PENNON]

pĕ'nnilĕss *a.* Having no money; poor, destitute. [ME, f. PENNY + -LESS]

pĕ'nnill *n.* (*pl.* **~ion** *pr.* -ĭ'lyon). (Stanza of) improvised verse sung to harp at eisteddfod etc. [W (*penn* head)]

pĕ'nnon *n.* Long narrow flag, triangular or swallow-tailed, esp. as military ensign of lancer regiments; long pointed streamer of ship; flag; hence ~ED² (-nd) *a.* [ME f. OF, f. L *penna* feather; see -OON]

pĕ'nn'orth. See PENNY*worth.*

Pĕnnsўlvā'nĭ|a *n.* **~a Dutch,** (dialect of High German spoken by) descendants of 17th–18th c. German and Swiss immigrants to Pennsylvania etc.; hence ~AN *a.*, (*esp., Geol.) upper Carboniferous period or system. [~ in U.S.]

pĕ'nnў *n.* (*pl.* usu. **pe'nnies** for separate coins, **pence** for sum of money). **1.** British bronze coin worth 1/100 of pound; monetary unit represented by this, abbr. *p.* **2.** (Hist.) British bronze coin worth 1/240 of pound; monetary unit represented by this, abbr. *d.* **3.** *(colloq.) Cent. **4.** (Bibl.) Denarius. **5. Like a bad ~**, repeatedly present when not desired; **the ~ drops,** understanding dawns; **pennies from heaven,** unexpected benefits; *an* HONEST *penny*; **in for a ~, in for a pound,** thing once begun must be concluded at all costs; **in ~ numbers,** in small quantities at a time; PETER'*s pence*; **~ plain, twopence coloured** (mocking cheap showiness); **a pretty ~**, a large sum of money; SPEND *a penny*; **take care of the pence,** be economical in small outlays; **a ~ for your thoughts** (said to person deep in thought); **two a ~**, almost worthless though readily obtainable. **6. ~-a-line** *a.*, (of writing) cheap and superficial; **~-a-li'ner,** hack writer; **~ black,** first adhesive postage stamp (U.K., 1840, value one penny, printed in black); ||**~ blood,** (sl.) = *penny* DREADFUL; ||**~ farthing,** (colloq.) old type of high bicycle; ||*penny* GAFF³; *penny-in-the-*SLOT¹; **~-pinching,** (*n.*) niggardliness, (*a.*) niggardly; ||**~ post** (for conveyance of letters at former ordinary charge of 1d. irrespective of distance); **~weight,** measure of weight, 24 grains, 1/20 of an ounce troy; *penny* WHISTLE; **~ wise,** (over-)careful in small expenditures, esp. *penny wise and pound foolish,* careful in small but wasteful in large matters; **~worth, penn'orth,** (pĕ'nĭwĕrth, pĕ'n*e*rth), as much as can be bought for a penny (*not a pennyworth,* not the least bit), a bargain (*a good* or *bad pennyworth*). [OE *penig, penning,* = OS *penning,* OHG *pfenning,* ON *penningr,* f. Gmc **panningaz, *pandingaz,* perh. rel. to PAWN²]

-pennў *suf.* forming *adjs.* w. sense 'costing . . . pence' (*fivepenny, twopenny-halfpenny*). [f. prec.]

pĕ'nnўroyal *n.* Creeping species of mint (*Mentha pulegium*) cultivated for supposed medicinal virtues; *aromatic herb of genus *Hedeoma* or *Monardella.* [app. f. earlier *puliol*(*e*) *ryall* f. AF *puliol,* OF *pouliol* f. Rom. **pulegeolum* f. L *pulegium* + as ROYAL]

pĕ'nnўwort (-ĕrt) *n.* Plant with rounded leaves (**wall ~**, *Umbilicus rupestris,* growing in crevices; **marsh** or **water ~**, *Hydrocotyle vulgaris,* growing in marshy places). [ME, f. PENNY + WORT]

pēnŏ'log|ў *n.* Study of punishment of crime and of prison management; hence **pēnolŏ'g**ICAL *a.*, ~IST (3) *n.* [f. L *poena* penalty + -O- + -LOGY]

pensée (pahṅsā') *n.* A thought or reflection put into literary form. [F]

pĕ'nsīle *a.* Hanging down, pendulous; (of bird etc.) building pensile nest. [f. L *pensilis* (*pendēre pens-* hang; see -IL)]

pĕ'nsion (-sh*o*n) *n.*, & *v.t.* **1.** *n.* Periodic payment made esp. by government, company, or employer, in consideration of past service or on retirement etc.; similar payment to person who is not a professed servant for good will, secret service, etc., or to artist, scientist, etc., to enable him to carry on work of public interest; periodic payment by government to persons above specified age (*old-age pension*), widows, etc.; hence ~LESS *a.* **2.** (*pr.* pah'ṅsyawṅ). European boarding-house providing all or some meals at fixed rate; *live* **en ~**, as boarder. **3.** *v.t.* Grant pension to; bribe with pension; **~ off,** dismiss with pension, cease to employ (lit. or fig.). [ME f. OF, f. L *pensio -onis* payment (*pendere pens-* pay; see -ION)]

pĕ'nsionable (-sh*o*-) *a.* Entitled, (of services etc.) entitling person, to pension. [f. prec. + -ABLE]

pĕ'nsionarў (-sh*o*-) *a.* & *n.* (Recipient) of a pension; creature, hireling; **Grand P~**, (Hist.) first minister of Holland and Zealand (1619–1794). [f. med. L *pensionarius* (as PENSION; see -ARY¹)]

pĕ'nsioner (-sh*o*-) *n.* Recipient of pension, esp. old-age pension; ||(Camb. Univ.) undergraduate without financial support from college. [ME f. AF; OF *pensionier,* f. as prec.]

pĕ'nsĭve *a.* Plunged in thought; sorrowfully thoughtful; hence ~LY² (-vlĭ) *adv.*, ~NESS (-vn-) *n.* [ME, f. OF *pensif -ive* (*penser* think f. L *pensare* frequent. of *pendere pens-* weigh)]

pĕnstē'mon. Var. of PENTSTEMON.

pĕ'nstŏck *n.* Sluice, flood-gate; *channel for conveyance of water to water-wheel. [f. PEN¹ in sense 'mill-dam' + STOCK]

pĕnt *a.* Closely confined, shut *in* or *up.* [p.p. of *pend* var. of PEN²]

pĕ'nta- *comb. form.* **1.** Five, as: **~chord** (-k-), musical instrument with five strings, series of five musical notes; **~gynous** (-tă'jĭ-), having five pistils; ~HE'DRON, solid figure with five faces; **~merous** (-tă'm-), (Bot.) having five parts in flower-whorl, (Zool.) having five joints; **penta'ndrous,** having five stamens; **~prism,** pentagonal prism used in viewfinder to get constant deviation of all rays of light through 90°; **pentato'mic,** (Chem.) having five atoms (of a specified kind) in the molecule; **~va'lent,** (Chem.) having a valence of five. **2.** (Chem., forming names of compounds) containing five atoms or groups of a specified kind (*pentachloride, pentoxide*). [Gk (*pente* five)]

pĕ'ntacle *n.* Figure used as symbol, esp. in magic, e.g. pentagram. [f. med. L *pentaculum* (as PENTA-; see -CULE)]

pĕ'ntăd *n.* The number five; group of five. [f. Gk *pentas -ados* (*pente* five; see -AD 1)]

pĕ′ntagon *n.* Plane figure with five sides and angles; ***the P~**, (pentagonal Washington headquarters of) leaders of U.S. defence forces; so **pĕntă′gon**AL *a.* [f. F *pentagone* or f. LL f. Gk *pentagōnon* (as PENTA-, -GON)]

pĕ′ntagrăm *n.* Five-pointed star formed by producing sides of pentagon both ways till they intersect, formerly used as mystic symbol. [f. Gk *pentagrammon* (as PENTA-, -GRAM)]

pĕntă′mĕter *n.* **1.** (Gk & L Pros.) Form of dactylic verse composed of two halves each of two feet (dactyls in second half, dactyls or spondees in first) and long syllable, chiefly used alternately with hexameters to form elegiac verse. **2.** Verse of five feet, e.g. English iambic verse of ten syllables. [L, f. Gk *pentametros* (as PENTA-, -METER)]

pĕ′ntāne *n.* (Chem.) Hydrocarbon of the paraffin series, C_5H_{12}. [f. Gk *pente* five + -ANE (2)]

pĕ′ntăngle (-nggel) *n.* Pentagram. [ME, perh. f. med. L **pentangulum*, *pentaculum* PENTACLE, assim. to L *angulus* ANGLE[1]]

Pĕ′ntateuch (-k) *n.* First five books of O.T., traditionally ascribed to Moses; hence **pĕntateu′ch**AL (-kal) *a.* [f. eccl. L f. eccl. Gk PENTA- (*teukhos* implement, book) of five books]

pĕntă′thlon *n.* Athletic contest comprising five different events for competitor. [Gk (*pente* five, *athlon* contest)]

pĕntatŏ′nĭc *a.* (Mus.) Consisting of five notes; relating to such a scale. [f. PENTA- + TONE[1] + -IC]

Pĕ′ntėcŏst *n.* **1.** Jewish harvest festival, on fiftieth day after the second day of Passover (Lev. 23:15, 16); synagogue ceremony on anniversary of giving of Law on Mount Sinai. **2.** Whit Sunday. **3.** Hence **pĕntėcŏ′st**AL *a.* [OE *pentecosten* & OF *pentecoste*, f. eccl. L f. Gk *pentēkostē* (*hēmera*) fiftieth (day)]

pĕ′nthouse (-t-h-) *n.* (*pl. pr.* -zĭz). Sloping roof, esp. as subsidiary structure attached to wall of main building; house or flat on roof of tall building; awning, canopy, etc. [ME *pentis*, AF **pentis* f. OF *apentis*, *-dis*, f. med. L *appendicium*, in LL = appendage, f. L (as APPEND)]

pĕntĭmĕ′nt|ō *n.* (*pl.* ~i). Reappearance of earlier underlying painting when layer added later becomes transparent, revealing artist's change of mind etc. [It., = repentance]

***pĕntobar′bĭtăl**, ‖**pĕntobar′bĭtōne**, *ns.* Narcotic and sedative barbiturate drug. [f. PENTA- + -O- + BARBITAL, BARBITONE]

pĕ′ntōde *n.* Thermionic valve having five electrodes. [f. Gk *pente* five + *hodos* way]

pĕ′nt-rōōf *n.* Roof sloping in one direction only. [f. PENTHOUSE + ROOF]

pĕntstē′mon (*or* pĕ′ntstēmon) *n.* Amer. herbaceous plant of genus *Penstemon*, with showy flowers and five stamens, one sterile. [mod. L, irreg. f. PENTA- + Gk *stēmōn* warp, used for 'stamen']

pĕ′ntўl *n.* = AMYL. [f. PENTANE + -YL]

pėnŭ′lt (*or* pē′-) *a.* & *n.* Last but one (esp. of syllable). [abbr. of L *paenultimus* (see foll.) or of foll.]

pėnŭ′ltĭmate *a.* & *n.* **1.** *a.* Last but one. **2.** *n.* Last syllable but one. [f. L *paenultimus* (*paene* almost, *ultimus* last), after *ultimate*]

pėnŭ′mbr|a *n.* (*pl.* ~*ae or* ~*as*). Partly shaded region around shadow of opaque body, esp. around total shadow of moon or earth in eclipse; less dark outer part of sunspot; partial shadow; hence ~AL *a.* [mod. L, f. L *paene* almost + UMBRA shadow]

pėnūr′ĭous *a.* Poor, scanty; stingy, grudging, whence ~LY[2] *adv.*, ~NESS *n.* [f. med. L *penuriosus* (as foll.; see -OUS)]

pĕ′nūrў *n.* Destitution, poverty; lack, scarcity, (*of*). [ME, f. L *penuria*, perh. rel. to *paene* almost; see -Y[1]]

pē′on (*or* pūn) *n.* (Ind. etc.) office-messenger, attendant, orderly; (Sp. Amer.) day-labourer; bullfighter's assistant; (Hist.) worker held in servitude in southern U.S. [f. Port. *pedo* & Sp. *peon*, f. med. L *pedo -onis* walker f. L *pes pedis* foot; cf. PAWN[1]]

pē′onage *n.* Employment or service of peons. [f. prec. + -AGE]

pē′onў, pae′onў, *n.* Plant with large globular red, pink, or white flowers, in cultivation often double. [OE *peonie* f. L f. Gk *paiōnia* (*Paiōn*, physician of the gods; cf. PAEAN)]

peo′ple (pē′pel) *n.*, & *v.t.* **1.** *n.* Persons composing community, tribe, race, or nation, (*the English people*; *English-speaking peoples*; *a warlike people*). **2.** (as *pl.*) Persons belonging to a place or forming a company or class etc. (*chosen people* (see CHOOSE); PECULIAR *people*; *the people of the western counties were in revolt*; *the people here are furious*); subjects of king etc.; congregation of parish priest etc.; armed followers, retinue, workpeople, etc.; parents or other relatives (*his people are sure to hear of it*); *the* persons not having special rank or position in a country etc.; persons in general (*people don't like to be kept waiting*). **3.** (as *sing.* or *pl.*) *The* body of enfranchised or qualified citizens. **4.** *v.t.* Fill with people, populate, fill (place *with* animals etc.); (of persons, animals, etc.) inhabit, occupy, fill, (esp. in *p.p.*; *a thickly peopled country*). [ME, f. AF *poeple*, *people*, OF *pople*, *peuple*, f. L *populus*]

pĕp *n.*, & *v.t.* (**-pp-**). (sl.) **1.** *n.* Vigour, go, spirit; **~ pill** (containing stimulant drug); **~ talk,** exhortation to activity or courage; hence **~′p**Y[2] *a.*, (sl.) full of pep. **2.** *v.t.* Fill with vigour, ginger *up*. [abbr. of PEPPER[1]]

‖**P.E.P.** *abbr.* Political and Economic Planning.

pĕperi′nō (-rē′-) *n.* Light porous (usu. brown) volcanic rock formed of small grains of sand, cinders, etc. [It. (*pepere* pepper)]

pĕ′plum *n.* Short flounce of blouse etc. worn over skirt; (Gk Ant.) woman's outer garment. [L, f. Gk *peplos*]

pē′pō *n.* (*pl.* ~s). Fleshy fruit of melon or cucumber type, with numerous seeds. [L, = pumpkin, f. Gk *pepōn* abbr. of *pepōn sikuos* ripe gourd]

pĕ′pper[1] *n.* **1.** Pungent aromatic condiment got from dried berries of certain plants (esp. *Piper nigrum*) used whole or ground into powder when unripe (**black ~**) or when either ripe or husked (**white ~**); (fig.) anything pungent. **2.** Plant of genus *Capsicum*; its fruit, used unripe (**green ~**) or ripe (**red** or **yellow ~**) as vegetable or source of condiment; CAYENNE *pepper*; **sweet ~**, pepper with relatively mild taste. **3. ~-and-salt,** cloth of dark and light threads woven together, showing small dots of dark and light intermingled; **~box,** (1) small usu. round box with perforated lid for sprinkling pepper, (2) ‖irregular buttress in Eton fives-court; **~corn,** dried berry of *Piper nigrum*, esp. as nominal rent; **~-mill** (for grinding peppercorns by hand); **~-pot,** (1) = *pepperbox* (1), (2) W. Ind. dish of meat etc. stewed with cayenne pepper etc., (3, colloq.) Jamaican. [OE *piper*, *pipor*, = OS *pipari*, *pepar*, OHG *pfeffar*, f. L *piper* f. Gk *peperi* f. Skr. *pippali-* berry, peppercorn]

pĕ′pper[2] *v.t.* Sprinkle or treat with pepper; besprinkle as with pepper; pelt with missiles (lit. or fig.); punish severely. [f. prec.]

pĕ′ppermĭnt *n.* Species of mint (*Mentha piperita*) grown for its essential oil; (Austral.) eucalyptus yielding similar oil; oil of peppermint; lozenge or sweetmeat flavoured with this. [f. PEPPER[1] + MINT[3]]

pĕ′pperў *a.* Of, like, abounding in, pepper;

(fig.) pungent, stinging, hot-tempered. [f. PEPPER[1] + -Y[2]]

pĕ′ppў. See PEP.

pĕ′psin *n.* Enzyme contained in gastric juice, converting proteins into peptones in presence of weak acid. [G, f. Gk *pepsis* digestion (**pep-* cook) + -IN]

pĕ′ptĭc *a.* & *n.* Digestive; ~ **glands** (secreting gastric juice); ~ **ulcer** (in stomach or duodenum). [f. Gk *peptikos* able to digest (as PEPTONE; see -IC)]

pĕ′ptīde *n.* (Chem.) Compound with two or more amino-acids linked in linear sequence with elimination of water molecules. [f. G *peptid*, back form. f. as POLYPEPTIDE]

pĕ′pt|ōne *n.* Protein derivative soluble in water and non-coagulable by heat, formed from protein by action of pepsin in the process of digestion; hence ~**on**IZE (3) *v.t.* [f. G *pepton* f. Gk *peptos*, neut. *pepton* cooked]

pẽr *prep.* **1.** Through, by, by means or instrumentality of, (*per post, rail, steamer, bearer*); **as per,** in accordance with (*as per instructions*); **as ~ usual,** (joc.) as usual. **2.** For each (*two pounds per man*; *five miles per hour*). **3.** (Her.) In the direction of (*party per pale*, divided in a vertical direction). [L]

per- *pref.* **1.** Through, all over, (*perforate, pervade*); completely, very, (*perfervid, perturb*); to destruction, to the bad, (*pervert, perdition*). **2.** (Chem.) Having maximum of some element in combination: (1) in names of binary compounds in *-ide* (*peroxide*), (2) in names of oxides, acids, etc., in *-ic* (*perchloric, permanganic*); (3) in names of salts of these acids (*perchlorate, permanganate*). [f. L *per-* (as prec.)]

peradvĕ′nture *adv.* & *n.* (arch. or joc.) **1.** *adv.* Perhaps; **if, lest, ~,** if, lest, it chance that. **2.** *n.* Uncertainty, chance, conjecture; doubt (*beyond* or *without* (*all* or *a*) *peradventure*). [ME, f. OF *per* or *par auenture* by chance (as PER, ADVENTURE[1])]

perai. See PIRANHA.

perăʹmbūl|āte *v.* **1.** *v.t.* Walk through, over, or about, (streets, country, etc.); travel through and inspect (territory); formally establish boundaries of (parish etc.) by walking round them. **2.** *v.i.* Walk from place to place. **3.** Hence or cogn. ~A′TION *n.*, ~**āt**ORY *a.* [f. L PER(*ambulare* walk) + -ATE[3]]

||**perăʹmbūlātor** *n.* = PRAM[2]. [f. prec. + -OR]

pẽr ă′nnum *adv.* For each year. [L]

percā′le *n.* Closely woven cotton fabric like calico. [F, of uncert. orig.]

pẽr că′put, pẽr că′pĭta, *adv.* & *a.* For each person. [L, = by head(s)]

percei′v|e (-sē′v) *v.t.* Apprehend with the mind, observe, understand, (circumstance, *that, how*, etc.); apprehend through one of the senses, esp. sight; hence ~ABLE *a.* [ME, f. AF **perceiver*, OF **perceivre, perçoivre*, f. L PER(*cipere cept-* = *capere* take)]

pẽr cĕ′nt(.), *percĕ′nt, *adv.* & *n.* **1.** *adv.* In every hundred; **cent ~,** (arch.) interest equal to principal; ||**three** etc. **~s,** public securities yielding interest of 3 etc. per cent. **2.** *n.* Percentage; one part in every hundred (*half a per cent*). [f. PER + CENT]

percĕ′ntage *n.* Rate or proportion per cent; proportion (*only a small percentage of books are worth reading*). [f. prec. + -AGE]

percĕ′ntīle *n.* (Statistics). One of 99 values of a variable dividing a population into 100 equal groups as regards the value of that variable. [f. PER CENT; see -IL]

pẽr′cĕpt *n.* (Philos.) Object of perception; mental product, as opp. to action, of perceiving. [f. L *perceptum* perceived (thing), neut. p.p. of *percipere* PERCEIVE, after *concept*]

percĕ′pt|ĭble *a.* That can be perceived by senses or intellect; hence ~IBI′LITY *n.*, ~**ĭb**LY[2] *adv.* [OF, or f. LL *perceptibilis* f. L (as PERCEIVE; see -IBLE)]

percĕ′pt|ion *n.* Act or faculty of perceiving; intuitive recognition (*of* truth, aesthetic quality, etc.); (Philos.) action by which the mind refers its sensations to external object as cause; hence ~**ion**AL *a.* [ME, f. L *perceptio* (as PERCEIVE; see -ION)]

percĕ′ptĭve *a.* Having perception; discerning, sensitive; hence ~LY[2] (-vlĭ) *adv.*, ~NESS (-vn-), **pẽrcĕptĭ′v**ITY, *ns.* [f. med. L *perceptivus* (as PERCEIVE; see -IVE)]

pẽrch[1] *n.* (*pl.* ~ *or* ~**′es**). Spiny-finned freshwater food-fish of genus *Perca*. [ME, f. OF *perche* f. L f. Gk *perkē*]

pẽrch[2] *n.* **1.** Horizontal bar for bird to rest upon; anything serving for bird etc. to rest upon; (fig.) elevated or secure position; **knock** (person) **off his ~,** vanquish, destroy, make less confident or condescending. **2.** Measure of length esp. for land, 5½ yds.; (**square**) ~, 30¼ sq. yds. [ME, f. OF *perche* f. L *pertica* pole]

pẽrch[3] *v.* **1.** *v.i.* Alight or rest as or like bird (*on* bough etc.); (of person or thing) settle, alight, rest, (*on*); hence ~′ER[1] *n.*, one of large class of passerine birds with feet adapted for perching. **2.** *v.t.* (esp. in *p.p.*) Place (as) on perch (*town perched on a hill*). [ME, f. OF *percher* (as prec.)]

percha′nce (-ah′-) *adv.* (arch.) By chance; possibly, maybe. [ME, f. AF *par chance* (*par* by, CHANCE[1])]

percheron (pār′sherawṅ) *n.* Strong and swift horse orig. bred in le *Perche*, district of N. France. [F]

perchlõr′|ĭc (-k-) *a.* (Chem.) Containing chlorine in maximum valence (*perchloric acid*); hence ~ATE[1] (3) *n.* [f. PER- 2 + CHLORIC]

percĭ′pĭ|ent *a.* & *n.* **1.** *a.* Perceiving, conscious; discerning; hence ~ENCE *n.* **2.** *n.* One who perceives esp. something outside range of senses. [f. L (as PERCEIVE; see -ENT)]

pẽr′col|āte *v.* **1.** *v.i.* (Of liquid, or fig.) filter, ooze, *through*. **2.** *v.t.* Ooze through, permeate; (of person or strainer) strain (liquid, powder) through pores etc.; prepare (coffee) by repeated downward passage of boiling water through ground beans. **3.** Hence or cogn. ~A′TION, ~**āt**OR, *ns.* [f. L PER(*colare* strain f. *colum* strainer) + -ATE[3]]

pẽr cŏ′ntra *adv.* On the opposite side (of account, assessment, etc.). [It.]

percŭ′ss *v.t.* (Med.) Tap gently with finger or instrument for purposes of diagnosis etc. [f. L PER(*cutere cuss-* = *quatere* shake) strike]

percŭ′ssion (-shon) *n.* Forcible striking of one (usu. solid) body against another; (Med.) percussing; (Mus.) playing by striking (*percussion band, instrument*), group of such instruments in orchestra; ~ **cap,** small metal or paper device in (real or toy) firearm, containing explosive powder and exploded by fall of a hammer; hence or cogn. **percŭ′ss**IVE *a.* [F, or f. L *percussio* (as prec.; see -ION)]

percūtā′nėous *a.* Made or done through the skin. [f. L *per cutem* through the skin + -ANEOUS, after *cutaneous*]

pẽr dī′ĕm (*or* -dē′-) *adv.*, *a.*, & *n.* **1.** *adv.* & *a.* For each day. **2.** *n.* Allowance or payment for each day. [L]

perdĭ′tion *n.* Eternal death, damnation. [ME, f. OF *perdiciun* or f. eccl. L *perditio* f. L PER(*dere dit-* = *dare* give) destroy; see -ITION]

pẽrdū(e)′ *a.* **1.** (Mil.) Placed as an outpost in hiding (*lie perdu*). **2.** (**perdue** esp. *fem.*) Hidden (*information, spy, had remained perdu*). [F, p.p. of *perdre* lose (as prec.)]

perdūr′|able *a.* Permanent; eternal; durable; hence ~ABI′LITY *n.*, **~ably**^{2} *adv.* [ME f. OF, f. LL PER(*durabilis* DURABLE)]

père (pār) *n.* The father, senior, (appended to name to distinguish between father and son of same names; cf. FILS); **Père David deer,** large grey slender-antlered deer named after Father A. David, Fr. missionary d. 1900. [F, = father]

pĕ′rĕgrĭn|āte *v.i.* (arch. or joc.) Travel, journey; so ~A′TION, **~āt**OR, *ns.* [f. L *peregrinari* (as foll.) + -ATE^3]

pĕ′rĕgrĭne *a.* & *n.* **1.** *a.* (arch.) Foreign, imported from abroad, outlandish. **2.** ~ **(falcon)**, kind of falcon much used for hawking. [f. L *peregrinus* (*peregre* abroad, f. *per* through + *ager* field; see -INE^1)]

perĕ′mptor|ȳ (*or* pĕ′rĭm-) *a.* (Law) final, not open to appeal or challenge (**~y challenge,** prisoner's objection to proposed juror by right without need to give reason); (of statement or command) admitting no denial or refusal; absolutely fixed, essential; (of person etc.) dogmatic, imperious, dictatorial; hence **~ĭ**LY^2 *adv.*, **~ĭ**NESS *n.* [f. AF *peremptorie*, OF *peremptoire* f. L *peremptorius* deadly, decisive, f. PER(*imere empt-* = *emere* take, buy) destroy, cut off; see -ORY]

perĕ′nnial (-nyal) *a.* & *n.* **1.** *a.* Lasting through, (of stream) flowing through all seasons of, the year; lasting long or for ever; (of plant) living several years (cf. ANNUAL); hence **perĕnniă′l**ITY *n.*, ~LY^2 *adv.* **2.** *n.* Perennial plant; HERBACEOUS *perennial*. [f. L PER(*ennis* f. *annus* year) + -AL]

pĕr′fĕct^1 *a.* & *n.* **1.** *a.* Complete, not deficient; faultless; (Mus., of pitch) absolute; thoroughly trained or skilled (*in* duties etc.); (colloq.) exceedingly satisfactory. **2.** Exact, precise, (*a perfect square, circle*; see SQUARE^1 6); entire, unqualified, (*a perfect stranger*; *perfect nonsense*). **3.** (Math., of number) equal to sum of its divisors; (Gram., of tense) denoting completed event or action viewed in relation to the present (**future** ~, tense giving sense *will have done*; **past** ~, pluperfect); (Bot.) having all four whorls of the flower, (of fungus) in stage where sexual spores are formed; ~ **interval,** (Mus.) fourth or fifth as it would occur in major or minor scale starting on the lower note of the interval, or octave. **4.** Hence ~LY^2 *adv.*, (esp.) quite, quite well, completely, ~NESS *n.* **5.** *n.* Perfect tense. [ME and OF *parfit*, *perfet* f. L *perfectus* p.p. of PER(*ficere fect-* = *facere* do) complete]

perfĕ′ct^2 (*or* pĕr′fĭkt) *v.t.* Complete, carry through; make perfect; improve; complete printing of (sheet) by printing second side; so ~IBI′LITY *n.*, **perfĕ′ct**IBLE *a.* [f. prec.]

perfĕ′ction *n.* Completion; making perfect; full development; faultlessness (**to** ~, exactly, completely); comparative excellence; perfect person or thing; highest pitch, extreme, perfect specimen or manifestation, (*of* quality etc.); an accomplishment. [ME f. OF, f. L *perfectio -onis* (as PERFECT^1; see -ION)]

perfĕ′ction|ĭst *n.* One who holds that religious or moral perfection may be attained; (usu. derog.) one who aims at perfection in his work; (*P~ist*; Hist.) member of communistic community of Oneida Creek, N.Y.; hence ~ISM (3) *n.* [f. prec. + -IST]

perfĕ′ctĭve *a.* & *n.* (Gram.) **1.** *a.* (Of verb aspect etc.) expressing completion of action (opp. *imperfective*). **2.** *n.* Perfective aspect or form of verb. [f. med. L *perfectivus* (as PERFECT^1; see -IVE)]

***perfĕ′ctō** *n.* (*pl.* **~s**). Large thick cigar pointed at each end. [Sp., = perfect]

perfĕr′vĭd *a.* Very fervid. [f. mod. L *perfervidus* (as PER-, *fervidus* FERVID)]

pĕr′fĭdȳ *n.* Breach of faith, treachery; so **perfĭ′dĭ**OUS *a.* (*perfidious* ALBION). [f. L *perfidia* f. PER(*fidus* f. *fides* faith) treacherous]

perfō′lĭate *a.* (Bot.) Having the stalk apparently passing through the leaf. [f. mod. L *perfoliatus* (as PER-, FOLIATE^1)]

pĕr′for|āte^1 *v.* **1.** *v.t.* Make hole(s) through, pierce, esp. make rows of holes in (sheet) to assist in separating stamps, coupons, etc.; make an opening into; pass or extend through. **2.** *v.i.* Penetrate (*into*, *through*, etc.). **3.** Hence or cogn. ~A′TION, **~āt**OR, *ns.*, **~āt**IVE *a.* [f. L PER (*forare* pierce) + -ATE^3]

pĕr′forate^2 *a.* Perforated. [f. L *perforatus* p.p. of *perforare* (see prec.)]

perfor′ce *adv.* Unavoidably, necessarily. [ME, f. OF *par force* by FORCE^1]

perfor′m *v.* **1.** *v.t.* Carry into effect, be agent of, (command, promise, task, operation, etc.); go through, execute, (public function, play, piece of music, etc.). **2.** *v.i.* Act in play; play, sing, etc.; (of trained animal) execute tricks etc. at public show etc.; hence ~ING^2 *a.* (**~ing arts,** those, such as drama, that require public performance). **3.** Hence ~ABLE, ~ATIVE, *adjs.*, ~ER^1 *n.* [ME, f. AF *parfourmer*, f. OF *parfournir* (assim. to *forme* FORM^1), f. *par* PER- + *fournir* FURNISH]

perfor′mance *n.* Execution (*of* command etc.); carrying out, doing; notable feat; performing of play, piece of music, or public exhibition (*there are two performances a day*; *the afternoon performance*); achievement under test; (colloq.) action resembling a public exhibition, ridiculous or contemptible behaviour. [f. prec. + -ANCE, perh. thr. AF]

pĕr′fūme^1 *n.* Sweet smell; smell; fluid containing essence of flowers etc., scent. [f. F *parfum* (as foll.)]

perfū′me^2 (*or* pĕr′fūm) *v.t.* (esp. in *p.p.*) Impart sweet scent to; impregnate with sweet smell. [f. F *parfumer* f. obs. It. *parfumare*, *perfumare* (as PER-, *fumare* smoke, FUME); orig. of smoke from burning substance]

perfū′m|er *n.* Maker or seller of perfumes; hence ~ERY (1, 2, 3) *n.* [f. prec. + -ER^1]

perfŭ′nctor|ȳ *a.* Done merely for sake of getting through a duty, acting thus, superficial, mechanical, (*a perfunctory inspection*, *inquirer*); hence **~ĭ**LY^2 *adv.*, **~ĭ**NESS *n.* [f. LL *perfunctorius* careless f. L PER(*fungi funct-* perform); see -ORY]

perfū′s|e (-z) *v.t.* Besprinkle (*with* water etc.); cover, suffuse, (*with* radiance etc.); pour or diffuse (water etc.) through or over; (Med.) cause a fluid to pass through (organ etc.); so ~ION (-zhon) *n.*, ~IVE (-s-) *a.* [f. L PER(*fundere fus-* pour)]

pĕr′gola *n.* Arbour or covered walk, formed of growing plants trained over trellis-work. [It., f. L *pergula* projecting roof (*pergere* proceed)]

pergŭ′nnah (-*a*), **perga′na** (-gŭ′-), *n.* Division of territory in India, group of villages. [f. Urdu *pargana* district]

perhă′ps (*or* prăps) *adv.* It may be, possibly, (*perhaps he has lost it*; *he has perhaps lost it*; *perhaps you would like to see it?*). [f. PER + HAP^1 + -S^1]

pĕr′ĭ *n.* (Pers. Myth.) fairy, good (orig. evil) genius; beautiful or graceful being. [f. Pers. *pārī*]

pĕ′rĭ- *pref.* **1.** Round, about, as: **~chon′drium** (-k-), membrane enveloping cartilages (except at joints); **~clī′nal,** (Geol.) sloping down in all directions from central point; **~gynous** (perĭ′jĭ-), (of stamens) situated around pistil or ovary; **~pteral** (perĭ′p-), (of temple) surrounded by single row of pillars; **~stome,** (Bot.) fringe of small teeth around mouth of capsule in mosses, (Zool.) parts around mouth in various invertebrates. **2.** (Astron. etc.) Point nearest to (*perigee, perihelion*). [f. Gk *peri* around, about]

pĕ'rĭanth *n.* (Bot.) Outer part of flower. [f. F *périanthe* f. mod. L *perianthium* f. as prec. + Gk *anthos* flower]

pĕ'rĭapt *n.* Thing worn about the person as charm, amulet. [f. F *périapte* f. Gk PERI(*apton* f. *haptō* fasten)]

pĕrĭcar'd|ĭum *n.* (*pl.* **~ia**). Membranous sac enclosing the heart; hence **~ĭAC**, **~ĭAL**, *adjs.*, **~ī'TIS** *n.* [mod. L, f. Gk *perikardion* (as PERI-, *kardia* heart; see -IUM)]

pĕ'rĭcarp *n.* (Bot.) Vessel containing seed, with pulp if present, formed from wall of ripened ovary. [f. F *péricarpe* or f. mod. L f. Gk PERI-(*karpion* f. *karpos* fruit) pod, shell]

pĕ'rĭclāse *n.* Mineral consisting mainly of magnesia. [f. mod. L *periclasia*, erron. f. Gk *peri* exceedingly + *klasis* breaking, from its perfect cleavage]

perĭ'copė *n.* Short passage, paragraph; portion of Scripture read in public worship. [f. LL f. Gk PERI(*kopē* cutting f. *koptō* cut)]

pĕrĭcrā'nĭum *n.* Membrane enveloping skull; (arch., joc.) skull, brain, intellect. [mod. L, f. Gk PERI(*kranion* skull)]

pĕ'rĭdŏt *n.* Green variety of olivine, esp. as precious stone. [ME f. OF *peritot*, of unkn. orig.]

pĕ'rĭgee *n.* Point (in orbit of moon, planet, or artificial satellite) nearest to earth; hence **pĕrĭgē'AN** *a.* [f. F *périgée* f. mod. L f. Gk PERI(*geion* f. *gē* earth)]

pĕrĭglā'cĭal (*or* -shal) *a.* Of a region adjoining a glacier. [f. PERI- + GLACIAL]

pĕrĭhē'lĭ|on (*or* -lyon) *n.* (*pl.* **~a**). Point (of planet's or comet's orbit) nearest to sun. [Graecized f. mod. L *perihelium* f. as PERI- + Gk *hēlios* sun]

pĕ'ril *n.*, & *v.t.* (‖-ll-). **1.** *n.* Danger; **in ~ of** (in danger of losing) one's *life* etc.; **you do it at your ~**, if you do it you take the risk; *keep off* **at your ~** (take the risk if you do not). **2.** *v.t.* Expose to danger, imperil. [ME f. OF, f. L *peric(u)lum* (**per-* try; see -CULE)]

pĕ'rilous *a.* Full of risk, dangerous, hazardous; exposed to imminent risk of destruction etc.; hence **~LY²** *adv.*, **~NESS** *n.* [ME, f. OF *perillous* f. L *periculosus* (*periculum*; see prec.)]

pĕ'rilūne *n.* Point in body's orbit about moon where it is closest to moon's centre. [f. PERI- + L *luna* moon, after *perigee*]

perĭ'mėter *n.* Circumference or outline of closed figure; length of this; outer boundary of camp, fortification, airfield, etc.; instrument for measuring field of vision. [f. F *périmètre* or f. L f. Gk PERI(*metros* f. *metron* measure)]

per impossibile (pẽr ĭmpŏsĭ'bĭlā) *adv.* By means of something that is in fact impossible. [L]

pĕrĭnā'tal *a.* Of the time immediately before and after birth. [f. PERI- + NATAL]

per incuriam (pẽr ĭnkūr'ĭam) *adv.* (Law). By oversight (of judge etc.). [L]

pĕrĭnē'|um *n.* (Anat.) Region of the body between anus and scrotum or vulva; hence **~AL** *a.* [f. LL f. Gk *perinaion*]

pēr'ĭod *n.* & *a.* **1.** *n.* Amount of time between recurrences of astronomical or other phenomena; time of planet's revolution. **2.** Time during which disease runs its course; (time of) occurrence of menstruation. **3.** Distinct portion of history, life, etc.; any portion of time (*showers and bright periods*; *spread the work over a period*); time allocated for lesson in school; (Geol.) time forming part of era; **the ~**, the part of history under discussion, esp. the present day (*the girl, costume, catchwords*, etc., *of the period*). **4.** Complete sentence, esp. one consisting of several clauses; (in *pl.*) rhetorical language. **5.** Full pause at end of sentence; = FULL¹ *stop* (**put a ~ to,** bring to an end); (appended to statement, stressing its completeness; *we want the best, period*). **6.** Set of figures marked off in large number to assist in reading; set of figures repeated in recurring decimal; (Chem.) sequence of elements between two noble gases in periodic table. **7.** *a.* (Esp. of furniture, dress, and architecture) belonging to or characteristic of a particular (past) period. [ME, f. OF *periode* f. L f. Gk PERI(*odos* = *hodos* way)]

pērĭŏ'dĭc¹ *a.* **1.** Of revolution of heavenly body, (*periodic motion*; *periodic* VARIATION); recurring at regular intervals, so **pērĭodĭ'CITY** *n.*; recurring at intervals; **~ function,** (Math.) function returning to same value at regular intervals; **~ table,** (Chem.) arrangement of elements in order of atomic numbers and in which elements of similar chemical properties appear at regular intervals. **2.** (Of diction etc.) expressed in PERIODS (sense 4). [f. F *périodique* or f. L f. Gk *periodikos* (as prec.; see -IC)]

pērĭŏ'dĭc² *a.* (Chem.) Containing maximum proportion of iodine (*periodic acid*); hence **pērī'odATE¹** (3) *n.* [f. PER- 2 + IODIC]

pērĭŏ'dĭcal *a.* & *n.* **1.** *a.* = PERIODIC¹ 1; hence **~LY²** *adv.* **2.** *a.* & *n.* (Magazine etc.) published at regular intervals, e.g. monthly. [f. PERIODIC¹ + -AL]

pērĭodizā'tion *n.* Dividing of history into periods. [f. PERIOD + -IZE + -ATION]

pĕrĭodŏ'nt|al *a.* (Med.) Of the tissues surrounding the teeth; hence **~ICS**, **~IST** (3), *ns.* [f. PERI- + Gk *odous odontos* tooth + -AL]

pĕrĭodŏntŏ'logy̆ *n.* Study of structures surrounding and supporting teeth. [f. PERI- + Gk *odous odontos* tooth + -O- + -LOGY]

pĕrĭŏ'stė|um *n.* (*pl.* **~a**). Membrane enveloping the bones where no cartilage is present; hence **~AL** *a.*, **pĕrĭŏstī'TIS** *n.* [mod. L f. Gk PERI(*osteon* bone)]

pĕrĭpatĕ't|ĭc *a.* & *n.* **1.** (*P~ic*). Aristotelian [from Aristotle's custom of walking in Lyceum while teaching]. **2.** *a.* Going from place to place on one's business, itinerant; hence **~ICALLY** *adv.* **3.** Hence **~ĭCISM** (2, 3) *n.* **4.** *n.* (usu. joc.) Traveller; itinerant dealer; (in *pl.*) journeyings to and fro. [ME, f. OF *peripatetique* or f. L f. Gk *peripatētikos* f. PERI(*pateō* walk); see -IC]

pĕrĭpėtei'a (-ī'a *or* -ē'a) *n.* Sudden change of fortune in drama or in life. [Gk (as PERI-, *pet-* f. *piptō* fall)]

perĭ'pheral *a.* & *n.* **1.** *a.* Of the periphery; (Anat.) near the surface of the body; of minor importance; (of equipment etc.) used with a computer but not an integral part of it; hence **~LY²** *adv.* **2.** *n.* Piece of peripheral equipment etc. [f. foll. + -AL]

perĭ'phery̆ *n.* Bounding line esp. of round surface; external boundary or surface; outer or surrounding region. [f. LL f. Gk PERI(*phereia* f. *pherō* bear) circumference; see -Y¹]

perĭ'phras|ĭs *n.* (*pl.* **~es** *pr.* -ēz). Roundabout way of speaking, circumlocution; roundabout phrase; so **pĕrĭphră'stIC** *a.* (*~tic conjugation, genitive*, one formed analytically w. aux. v., w. prep., instead of by inflexion; *did go* = *went*, *of Caesar* = *Caesar's*). [L f. Gk, f. PERI(*phrazō* declare)]

perĭ'que (-ē'k) *n.* Dark strong-flavoured Louisiana tobacco. [Louisiana F]

pĕ'rĭscōpe *n.* Apparatus with tube and mirror by which observer in trench, submerged submarine, rear of crowd, etc., can see things otherwise out of sight. [f. PERI- + -SCOPE]

pěriscŏ'pic *a.* Of periscope(s); (of lens) allowing distinct vision over wide angle. [f. prec. + -IC]

pě'rish *v.* **1.** *v.i.* Suffer destruction, lose life or normal qualities, come to untimely end (*by the sword* etc.); ~ **the thought!**, I sincerely hope it will not be so. **2.** *v.t.* (Of cold or exposure) reduce to distress or inefficiency or moribund state (*we were perished with cold*; *in perishing cold*; *the heat had perished all vegetation*), whence ~**ingLY**² *adv.* **3.** Hence ||~ER¹ *n.*, (sl.) annoying person, ||~ING² *a.* & *adv.*, (sl.) confounded(ly). [ME, f. OF *perir* (see -ISH²) f. L PER(*ire* go) pass away]

pě'rishable *a.* & *n.* **1.** *a.* Liable to perish; subject to speedy decay; hence ~NESS (-beln-) *n.* **2.** *n.* (in *pl.*) Things (esp. foodstuffs in transit) subject to this. [f. prec. + -ABLE]

pě'rispěrm *n.* Mass of albumen outside embryo-sac in some seeds. [f. PERI- + Gk *sperma* seed]

pěrispō'mėn|on *a.* & *n.* (*pl.* ~**a**). (Gk Gram.) (Word) with circumflex accent on last syllable. [Gk, neut. part.; cf. CIRCUMFLEX]

perĭ'ssō- *comb. form.* Uneven, odd, redundant, as: ~**da'ctylate,** (Zool. of ungulate) having an odd number of toes on each foot. [f. Gk *perissos*]

perĭ'stalĭth *n.* (Archaeol.) Ring of standing stones round burial-mound etc. [irreg. f. Gk PERI(*statos* standing) + -LITH]

pěrĭstă'l|tic *a.* (Physiol.) of the automatic muscular movement consisting of successive wavelike contractions and relaxations, by which contents of alimentary canal etc. are propelled along it; of a pump operating by similar action; so ~**sĭs** *n.*, peristaltic movement, ~TICALLY *adv.* [f. Gk *peristaltikos* (as PERI-, *stellō* place); see -IC]

pě'rĭstȳle *n.* Row of columns surrounding temple, court, cloister, etc.; space so surrounded. [f. F *péristyle* f. L f. Gk PERI(*stulon* f. *stulos* pillar)]

pěrĭton|ē'um *n.* (*pl.* ~**e'ums** *or* ~**e'a**). (Anat.) Double serous membrane lining cavity of abdomen; hence ~**ē'**AL *a.*, ~I'TIS *n.* [LL, f. Gk PERI(*tonaion* f. *-tonos* stretched)]

pě'rĭwĭg *n.* (esp. Hist.) Wig; hence ~**GED**² (-gd) *a.* [alt. of PERUKE, w. *-wi-* for F *-u-* sound]

pě'rĭwĭnkle¹ *n.* Plant of genus *Vinca*, esp. evergreen trailing plant with blue or white flowers; ~ (**blue**), colour of blue periwinkles. [ME f. AF *pervenke*, OF *pervenche* f. LL *pervinca*, w. assim. to foll.]

pě'rĭwĭnkle² *n.* Winkle. [16th c., of unkn. orig.]

pěr'jur|e *v. refl.* ~**e oneself,** swear falsely; (in *p.p.*) guilty of or involving perjury; so ~ER¹ *n.* [ME, f. OF *parjurer* f. L PER(*jurare* swear)]

pěr'jurȳ *n.* Swearing to statement that one knows to be false; wilful utterance of false evidence while on oath; breach of oath; hence **perjur'ĭous** (-joor'-) *a.* [ME, f. AF *perjurie*, f. OF *parjurie* f. L *perjurium* (as prec.)]

pěrk¹ *v.* & *a.* (colloq.) **1.** *v.i.* ~ (**up**), recover confidence or courage. **2.** *v.t.* Raise (head etc.) briskly; smarten *up*; ~ (**up**), restore confidence or courage of. **3.** *a.* Perky. [ME, perh. f. var. of PERCH²]

||**pěrk**² *n.* (colloq., usu. in *pl.*) Perquisite. [abbr.]

pěrk³ *v.* (colloq.) **1.** *v.i.* (Of coffee) make bubbling sound in percolator. **2.** *v.t.* Percolate (coffee). [abbr. of PERCOLATE]

pěr'k|ȳ *a.* Self-assertive, saucy, pert; lively, cheerful; hence ~ĬLY² *adv.*, ~ĬNESS *n.* [f. PERK¹ + -Y²]

pěr'līte *n.* Obsidian or other vitreous rock with concentric structure, expandable by heating. [F (*perle* PEARL¹; see -ITE¹)]

pěrm¹ *n.*, & *v.t.* (colloq.) (Give) permanent wave (to). [abbr.]

pěrm² *n.*, & *v.t.* (colloq.) (Make) permutation (of). [abbr.]

pěr'mafrŏst (*or* -awst) *n.* Subsoil remaining below freezing-point throughout the year in polar regions. [f. PERMANENT + FROST]

pěr'malloy *n.* Alloy of nickel and iron that is easily magnetized and demagnetized. [f. PERMEABLE + ALLOY¹]

pěr'manent *a.* Lasting, or intended to last or function, indefinitely (opp. *temporary*); ~ **gas,** substance remaining gaseous under all normal conditions; ~ **magnet** (retaining its power without continued excitation); ~ **set,** (amount of) irreversible deformation of substance after being subjected to stress; ||*Permanent* (*Under-*) SECRETARY; ~ **tooth** (following milk-tooth in mammal and lasting most of life); ~ **wave,** artificial wave in the hair intended to last for some time, produced by one of several processes; ||~ **way,** finished road-bed of railway; hence or cogn. **pěr'man**ENCE, **pěr'man**ENCY (esp. = permanent thing or arrangement), *ns.*, ~LY² *adv.* [ME f. OF, or f. L PER(*manēre* remain); see -ENT]

permă'nganāte (-ngg-; *or* -*at*) *n.* (Chem.) Salt of permanganic acid, esp. **potassium** ~ (used in solution as disinfectant and oxidizer). [f. foll. + -ATE¹ (3)]

pěrmăngă'nĭc (-ngg-) *a.* (Chem.) Containing manganese in maximum valence (*permanganic acid*). [f. PER- 2 + MANGANIC]

pěrmėabĭ'lĭtȳ *n.* Ability to be permeated; (Phys.) quantity measuring substance's influence on magnetic flux in region it occupies. [f. PERMEABLE + -ITY]

pěr'mė|āte *v.* **1.** *v.t.* Penetrate throughout, pervade, saturate. **2.** *v.i.* Diffuse itself *through*, *among*, etc. **3.** Hence or cogn. ~ANCE, ~A'TION, *ns.*, ~ABLE, ~ANT, *adjs.* [f. L PER(*meare* pass, go) + -ATE³]

pěr mě'nsěm *adv.* For each month. [L]

Pěr'mĭan *a.* & *n.* (Geol.) (Of) latest palaeozoic period or system, above Carboniferous. [f. *Perm* in Russia + -IAN]

permĭ'ssĭb|le *a.* Allowable; hence ~LY² *adv.* [ME f. F, or f. med. L *permissibilis* (as PERMIT¹; see -IBLE)]

permĭ'ssion (-shon) *n.* Consent or liberty (*to* do). [ME f. OF, or f. L *permissio* (as PERMIT¹; see -ION)]

permĭ'ssive *a.* **1.** Giving permission; ~ **legislation** (giving powers, but not enjoining their use). **2.** Tolerant, liberal, esp. in sexual matters, (*the permissive society*). **3.** Hence ~LY² (-vlĭ) *adv.*, ~NESS (-vn-) *n.* [ME, f. OF (*-if -ive*), or f. med. L *permissivus* (as foll.; see -IVE)]

permĭ't¹ *v.* (-tt-). **1.** *v.t.* Give consent or opportunity (for) (*permit me to say*; *appeals are permitted*; *permit him access to it*; *will not permit it to be altered*; *hole to permit escape of steam*). **2.** *v.i.* Give opportunity (*weather permitting*); admit *of* (alteration, delay, etc.). [f. L PER(*mittere miss-* let go)]

pěr'mĭt² *n.* Written order giving permission to act, esp. for entry into a place, landing or removal of dutiable goods, etc.; permission. [f. prec.]

***pěr'mĭt**³ *n.* Large W. Ind. sea game-fish of genus *Trachinotus*. [f. Sp. *palometa*]

pěrmĭttĭ'vĭtȳ *n.* (Electr.) Quantity measuring substance's ability to store electrical energy in electric field. [f. PERMIT¹ + -IVE + -ITY]

pěrmūtā'tion *n.* **1.** Variation of the order of a set of things; any one such arrangement. **2.** (pop.) Combination or selection of specified number of items from larger group (esp. of matches in football pool). [ME f. OF, or f. L *permutatio* (as foll.; see -ATION)]

permū'te *v.t.* Alter the sequence or arrangement of. [ME, f. L PER(*mutare* change)]
pērn *n.* Honey-buzzard. [f. mod. L *pernis*, erron. f. Gk *pternis* a kind of hawk]
pernĭ'cious (-shus) *a.* Destructive, ruinous, fatal; ~ **anaemia,** severe progressive freq. fatal form of anaemia; hence ~LY² *adv.*, ~NESS *n.* [f. L *perniciosus* (*pernicies* ruin f. *nex necis* death; see -OUS)]
pernĭ'ckėtў *a.* (colloq.) Fastidious; (over-) precise; ticklish, requiring tact or careful handling. [19th c. Sc., of unkn. orig.]
pērnŏctā'tion *n.* Passing the night; (Eccl.) all-night vigil. [f. LL *pernoctatio* f. L PER(*noctare* f. *nox noctis* night); see -ATION]
pĕronē'al *a.* (Anat.) Of or near the fibula. [f. mod. L *peronaeus* peroneal muscle (*perone* fibula f. Gk *peronē* pin, fibula)]
pĕ'ror|āte *v.i.* Sum up and conclude speech, so ~A'TION *n.*; speak at length. [f. L PER(*orare* speak)]
perŏ'xīde *n.*, & *v.t.* **1.** *n.* (Chem.) compound of oxygen with another element containing the greatest possible proportion of oxygen; (**hydrogen**) ~, (1) colourless viscid liquid, H_2O_2, (2) aqueous solution of this, used as antiseptic and (esp.) to bleach hair; ~ **blonde,** (usu. derog.) woman with hair bleached thus. **2.** *v.t.* Bleach (hair) with peroxide. [f. PER- 2 + OXIDE]
perpĕ'nd¹ *v.t.* (arch.) Ponder, consider, (matter, or abs.). [f. L PER(*pendere* weigh)]
pēr'pend². Var. of PARPEN.
pērpendĭ'cūlar *a.* & *n.* **1.** *a.* At right angles to plane of horizon; (of ascent, cliff, etc.) very steep; erect, upright; (joc.) in standing position; (Geom.) at right angles (*to* given line, plane, or surface); **P~ style,** (Archit.) third stage of English Gothic (15th–16th c.), with vertical tracery in large windows; hence ~ITY (-ă'r-) *n.*, ~LY² *adv.* **2.** *n.* Perpendicular line; plumb-rule or other instrument for showing perpendicular line; **the** ~, perpendicular line or direction; *is out of* (*the*) ~, is not straight up and down. [ME, f. L *perpendicularis* (*perpendiculum* plumb-line f. PER- + *pendĕre* hang); see -AR¹]
pēr'pėtr|āte *v.t.* Perform, commit, (crime, blunder, pun or other thing viewed as outrageous); hence ~A'TION, ~**āt**OR, *ns.* [f. L PER(*petrare* = *patrare* effect) + -ATE³]
perpĕ'tūal *a.* **1.** Eternal; permanent during life; applicable or valid for ever or for indefinite time; continuous; (colloq.) frequent, repeated (*this perpetual nagging*). **2.** ~ **calendar** (that can be used for any year or over a long period of time); ~ **check,** (Chess) position where draw is obtained by repeated checking of king; ~ **curate,** (Hist.) clergyman of new church, or appointed at instance of lay rector of benefice to execute spiritual duties of benefice (now called *vicar*); ~ **motion** (of hypothetical machine running for ever unless subject to external forces or wear); ~ **screw,** ENDLESS screw. **3.** Hence ~LY² *adv.* [ME f. OF *perpetuel* f. L *perpetualis* (*perpetuus* f. *perpes -etis* continuous; see -AL)]
perpĕ'tū|āte *v.t.* Make perpetual; preserve from oblivion; hence or cogn. ~ANCE, ~A'TION, ~**āt**OR, *ns.* [f. L *perpetuare* (as prec.) + -ATE³]
pērpėtū'ĭtў *n.* Quality of being perpetual (**in, to, for,** ~, for ever); perpetual possession or position; perpetual annuity. [ME, f. OF *perpetuité* f. L *perpetuitas -tatis* (as PERPETUAL; see -ITY)]
perplĕ'x *v.t.* Bewilder, puzzle, (person, his mind); complicate, confuse, (matter); (arch., esp. in *p.p.*) entangle, intertwine; hence ~**ėd**LY², ~**ing**LY², *advs.* [back form. f. *perplexed* f. obs. *perplex* a. f. OF *perplexe* or f. L PER(*plexus* p.p. of *plectere* plait) + -ED¹]
perplĕ'xĭtў *n.* Bewilderment; thing that bewilders; (arch.) entangled state. [ME, f. OF *perplexité* or f. LL *perplexitas* (as prec.; see -ITY)]
per pro(c). *abbr.* = foll.
per procurationem (pēr prŏkūrātiō'nĕm) *adv.* By proxy; through an agent. [L]
pēr'quĭsĭte (-z-) *n.* Casual profit additional to normal revenue or emolument; thing that has served its primary use and to which subordinate or servant has then a customary right; incidental benefit attaching to employment etc.; customary gratuity; (fig.) thing to which person has sole right. [ME, f. med. L *perquisitum* f. L PER(*quirere quisit-* = *quaerere* seek) search diligently for]
pĕ'rron *n.* (Steps leading up to) platform in front of door of church or other large building. [ME f. OF, f. Rom. **petro petron-* augment. of L *petra* stone; see -OON]
||**pĕ'rrў** *n.* Drink like cider, made from juice of pears fermented. [ME *pereye* etc. f. OF *peré* f. Rom. **piratum* f. L *pirum* pear; see -Y⁴]
pērse *a.* & *n.* (arch.) Bluish-grey (colour). [ME, f. OF *pers*, f. med. L *persus*, of unkn. orig.]
per se (pērsē' *or* -sā') *adv.* By or in itself, intrinsically. [L]
pēr'sėc|ūte *v.t.* Pursue with enmity and ill-treatment; subject to penalties on grounds of religious or political beliefs; harass, worry; importune (person *with* questions etc.); so ~**ū'**TION *n.* (~**ution complex** or **mania,** insane delusion that one is persecuted), ~**ūt**OR *n.* [ME, f. OF *persecuter* back form. f. *persecuteur* persecutor f. LL *persecutor* f. L PER(*sequi secut-* follow) pursue]
pērsėvēr'|ance *n.* Steadfast pursuit of an aim, constant persistence; (Theol.) continuance in state of grace. [ME f. OF, f. L *perseverantia* (as PERSEVERE; see -ANCE)]
persĕ'ver|āte *v.i.* Continue action etc. for unusually or excessively long time; (Psych., of action or mental state) tend to be spontaneously repeated; so ~A'TION *n.* [f. L *perseverare* (see foll.) + -ATE³]
pērsėvēr'e *v.i.* Continue steadfastly, persist, (*in* course of action, *in* doing, *at* or *with* task etc., or abs.). [ME, f. OF *perseverer* f. L *perseverare* persist f. PER(*severus* severe) very strict]
Pēr'sian (-shan) *a.* & *n.* (Native or language) of Persia (Iran); ~ **carpet** or **rug** (made in Persia with fine skilful weave and traditional patterns); ~ (**cat**), cat of breed with long silky hair and thick tail; ~ **lamb,** silky tightly-curled fur of young caracul. [ME f. OF *persien* f. med. L **Persianus* (*Persia*; see -AN)]
pērsiĕ'nnes (-nz) *n. pl.* Window shutters, or outside blinds, with louvers. [F, fem. pl. (as n.) of obs. *persien* Persian (see prec.)]
pēr'sĭflage (-ahzh) *n.* Light raillery, banter. [F (*persifler* banter f. as PER- + *siffler* whistle; see -AGE)]
persĭ'mmon *n.* (Edible fruit of) American or E. Asian tree of genus *Diospyros*. [corrupt. of Algonquian wd]
persĭ'st *v.i.* Continue firmly or obstinately (*in* opinion, course of action, do*ing*) esp. against obstacles, remonstrance, etc.; (of institution, custom, phenomenon, etc.) continue in existence, survive. [f. L PER(*sistere* stand)]
persĭ'st|ent *a.* Persisting; enduring; constantly repeated; (Biol., of horns, leaves, etc.) remaining, instead of falling off in the normal manner; hence or cogn. ~ENCE, ~ENCY, *ns.*, ~**ent**LY² *adv.* [f. prec., or back form. f. *persistence*, after *insistent*]
pēr'son *n.* **1.** Individual human being (*a cheerful and forthright person*; *found a friend in the person of his landlord*). **2.** Living body of human being

(*he had a fine person; attracted by her fortune, not her person*); *acting, appearing,* **in his own (proper)** ~ or **in** ~ (himself, personally); (euphem.) genitals (*expose* one's *person*). **3.** (Law). Human being (**natural** ~) or body corporate (**artificial** ~) with recognized rights and duties. **4.** Character in play or story. **5.** One of three modes of being of the Godhead: Father (**First P**~), Son (**Second P**~), and Holy Spirit (**Third P**~). **6.** (Gram.) One of three classes of personal pronouns, verb-forms, etc., denoting respectively the person etc. speaking (**first** ~), spoken to (**second** ~), or spoken of (**third** ~). [ME, f. OF *persone* f. L *persona* actor's mask, character in play, human being]

persō'na *n.* (*pl.* ~**e**). Aspect of personality as shown to or perceived by others (opp. *anima*); ~ ***grata*** (grah'ta), person (esp. diplomat) acceptable to certain others; ~ ***non grata*** (nŏn), person not acceptable. [L, as prec.]

pe͡r'sonable *a.* Handsome, comely; pleasing by one's appearance and demeanour. [ME, f. PERSON + -ABLE]

pe͡r'sonage *n.* Person of rank or importance; person; character in play etc. [ME, f. PERSON + -AGE, infl. by med. L *personagium* effigy & F *personnage*]

pe͡r'sonal *a.* **1.** One's own, individual, private, (*to suit his personal convenience; personal* EQUATION; *personal* TOUCH²; *this is personal to myself*); of the body and clothing (one's *personal appearance; personal hygiene*). **2.** Done, made, etc., in person (*personal* SERVICE¹ 7, *acquaintance, interview; made a personal appearance at the meeting*). **3.** Directed or referring to an individual (*personal call, letter*); directed hostilely to an individual (*personal abuse, remarks*); (given to) making personal remarks (*do not let us become personal*); ~ **column,** part of newspaper devoted to short advertisements of personal or semi-personal nature. **4.** Of, or existing as, a person, not an abstraction or a thing (*a personal God*). **5.** (Law). ~ **property** or **estate,** chattels or chattel interests in land, all property except land and those interests in land that pass to one's heir; cf. REAL². **6.** (Gram.) Of or denoting one of the three persons, esp. *personal* PRONOUN. [ME f. OF, f. L *personalis* (as PERSON; see -AL)]

pe͡rsonă'lĭtȳ *n.* **1.** Being a person; personal existence or identity; ~ **cult,** extreme adulation of an individual; **multiple** ~, (Psych.) the apparent existence of two or more distinct personalities alternating in one individual; SPLIT¹ *personality.* **2.** Distinctive personal character. **3.** Person, esp. a celebrity (*television personality*). **4.** (Of remarks) fact of being aimed at an individual, (usu. in *pl.*) such remark. [ME, f. OF *personalité* f. LL *personalitas -tatis* (as prec.; see -ITY)]

pe͡r'sonalīz|e, -īs|e (-īz), *v.t.* Personify; make personal, esp. by marking with owner's name etc.; hence ~A'TION *n.* [f. PERSONAL + -IZE]

pe͡r'sonallȳ *adv.* In person, in one's own person, (*he conducted them personally; writ was served on them personally*); as a person (*a God existing personally*); for one's own part (*personally, I see no objection*). [f. PERSONAL + -LY²]

pe͡r'sonaltȳ *n.* Personal estate (opp. *realty*). [f. AF *personalté* (as PERSONAL; see -TY¹)]

pe͡r'sonate¹ *a.* (Bot., of corolla) having the opening of the lips closed by upward projection of the lower, as in snapdragon. [f. L *personatus* masked (as foll.; see -ATE²)]

pe͡r'son|āte² *v.t.* Play the part of (character in drama, also fig.); pretend to be (person) esp. for fraudulent purpose, impersonate; hence ~A'TION, ~**āt**OR, *ns.* [f. LL *personare* (as PERSON) + -ATE³]

persŏnĭfĭcā'tion *n.* Personifying; person or thing viewed as striking example or embodiment *of* (quality etc.). [f. foll.; see -FICATION]

persŏ'nĭfȳ *v.t.* Attribute personal nature to (abstraction or thing); symbolize (quality) by figure in human form; (esp. in *p.p.*) embody (quality) in one's own person, exemplify typically. [f. F *personnifier* (as PERSON; see -FY)]

pe͡rsonnĕ'l *n.* Body of persons employed in public undertaking, armed forces, factory, office, etc.; ~ **carrier,** armoured vehicle for transporting troops; ~ **department, manager,** etc., (concerned with appointment, advising, training, etc., of employees). [F, = personal, *a.* as *n.*]

perspĕ'ctive *n.* & *a.* **1.** *n.* Art of delineating solid objects on plane surface so as to give same impression of relative positions, magnitudes, etc., as the actual objects do when viewed from particular point; picture so drawn; apparent relation between visible objects as to position, distance, etc.; (fig.) relation in which parts of subject are viewed by the mind; view, prospect, (lit. or fig.); **in** ~, drawn or viewed (lit. or fig.) according to rules of perspective; hence **pe͡rspĕctī'**VAL *a.* **2.** *a.* Of or in perspective; hence ~LY² (-vlĭ) *adv.* [ME, f. med. L *perspectiva* (*ars* art) f. PER(*spicere spect-* look); see -IVE]

Pe͡r'spĕx, p-, *n.* Tough unsplinterable transparent acrylic thermoplastic, much lighter than glass. [**P**; f. L PER(*spicere spect-* look)]

pe͡rspĭcā'cious (-shus) *a.* Having mental penetration or discernment; hence or cogn. ~LY² *adv.*, ~NESS, **pe͡rspĭcă'**CITY, *ns.* [f. L *perspicax -acis* (as prec.; see -ACIOUS)]

perspĭ'cūous *a.* Easily understood, clearly expressed; (of person) expressing things clearly; hence or cogn. **pe͡rspĭcū'**ITY, ~NESS, *ns.*, ~LY² *adv.* [ME, = transparent, f. L *perspicuus* (as PERSPECTIVE) + -OUS]

pe͡rspĭrā'tion *n.* Perspiring; = SWEAT 1, 2; hence **perspī'rat**ORY *a.* [F (as foll.; see -ATION)]

perspīr'e *v.i.* & *t.* = SWEAT 7, 8. [f. F *perspirer* f. L PER(*spirare* breathe)]

persuā'd|e (-sw-) *v.t.* Cause (person, one*self*) to have belief (*of* fact, *that* thing is so); induce (person *to* do, *into* action); (in *p.p.*) convinced (*of* thing, *that*); hence or cogn. ~ABLE *a.*, ~ER¹˒² *n.*, (esp., sl.) gun etc., **persuā'**SIBLE (-sw-) *a.* [f. L PER(*suadēre suas-* advise)]

persuā'sion (-swā'zhon) *n.* **1.** Persuading; persuasiveness. **2.** Belief, conviction, (*it is my private persuasion that he is mad*); religious belief, sect holding this, (*he is of the Roman Catholic persuasion*); (joc.) kind, sort, (*no one of the male persuasion was present*). [ME, f. L *persuasio* (as prec.; see -ION)]

persuā'sive (-sw-) *a.* & *n.* **1.** *a.* Able to persuade; hence ~LY² (-vlĭ) *adv.*, ~NESS (-vn-) *n.* **2.** *n.* Motive, inducement. [f. F *persuasif -ive* or f. med. L *persuasivus* (as PERSUADE; see -IVE)]

pe͡rt *a.* Saucy or impudent in speech or conduct; (of clothes etc.) neat and suggestive of jauntiness; = PEART; hence ~'LY² *adv.*, ~'NESS *n.* [ME, f. OF *apert* f. L *apertus* p.p. of *aperire* open, & f. OF *aspert* f. L *expertus* EXPERT¹]

P.E.R.T. *abbr.* programme evaluation and review technique.

pertai'n *v.i.* Belong as part, appendage, or accessory, *to*; be appropriate (*to*); have reference or relate *to*. [ME, f. OF *partenir* f. L PER(*tinēre* = *tenēre* hold)]

pe͡rtĭnā'cious (-shus) *a.* Stubborn, persistent, obstinate, (in a course of action etc.); hence or cogn. ~LY² *adv.*, ~NESS, **pe͡rtĭnă'**CITY, *ns.* [f. L PER(*tinax* = *tenax* TENACIOUS)]

pe͡r'tĭn|ent *a.* Pertaining, relevant, apposite, (*to* matter being considered etc.); to the point;

hence or cogn. ~ENCE, ~ENCY, *ns.*, ~entLY[2] *adv.* [ME f. OF, or f. L (as PERTAIN; see -ENT)]

pertŭr'b *v.t.* Throw into confusion or disorder; disturb mentally, agitate; (Phys. etc.) cause deviation of motion or of other behaviour of (body etc.); so **pĕrturb**A'TION *n.*, ~ATIVE (*or* pĕr'terbāt-) *a.* [ME, f. OF *pertourber* f. L PER(*turbare* disturb)]

pertŭ'ssĭs *n.* (Path.) Whooping cough. [mod. L, f. PER- + L *tussis* cough]

peru'ke (-ōō'k) *n.* (esp. Hist.) Wig. [f. F *perruque* f. It. *perrucca, parrucca*, of unkn. orig.]

peru'se (-ōō'z) *v.t.* Read, esp. thoroughly or carefully; (fig.) examine (person's face etc.) carefully; hence **peru'sAL** 2 (-ōō'zal) *n.* [ME, prob. f. AL *PER(*usare* f. Rom. **usare* USE[2]) use up]

Peru'vĭan (-ōō'-) *a.* & *n.* **1.** *a.* Of Peru; ~ **bark** (of cinchona tree). **2.** *n.* Native or inhabitant of Peru. [f. mod. L *Peruvia* Peru + -AN]

pervā'de *v.t.* Spread throughout, permeate, saturate, (lit., or fig. of influences etc.); be rife among or through; hence **pervā'sION** (-zhon), **pervā'sĭveNESS** (-vn-), *ns.*, **pervā'sIVE** *a.*, **pervā'sĭveLY**[2] (-vlĭ) *adv.* [f. L PER(*vadere vas-go*)]

pervĕr'se *a.* Persistent in error; different from what is reasonable or required; wayward; peevish; perverted, wicked; (of verdict) against weight of evidence or judge's direction; hence or cogn. ~LY[2] (-slĭ) *adv.*, ~NESS (-sn-), **pervĕr'sITY**, *ns.* [ME, f. OF *pervers perverse*, f. L *perversus* (as PERVERT[1])]

pervĕr'sion (-shon) *n.* Perverting, being perverted; perverted form of a thing; preference for a form of sexual activity other than normal intercourse. [ME, f. L *perversio* (as foll.; see -ION)]

pervĕr't[1] *v.t.* Turn aside (thing) from its proper use or nature; misconstrue, misapply, (words etc.); lead astray (person, mind) from right opinion or conduct or esp. religious belief; (in *p.p.*) showing perversion; hence **pervĕr'sIVE** *a.* [ME, f. OF *pervertir* or f. L PER(*vertere vers-* turn)]

pĕr'vĕrt[2] *n.* Perverted person, apostate; person showing perversion of sexual instincts. [f. prec.; cf. CONVERT[2]]

pĕr'vious *a.* Affording passage (*to*); permeable; (fig.) accessible (*to* reason etc.); hence ~NESS *n.* [f. L PER(*vius* f. *via* way) + -OUS]

Pe'sach (pā'sahχ) *n.* Passover festival. [f. Heb. *Pesaḥ*]

pese'ta (-sā'-) *n.* Spanish orig. silver coin and monetary unit. [Sp., dim. of *pesa* weight f. L *pensa* pl. of *pensum* (see POISE[1])]

Peshi'tō, Peshi'tta, (-shē'-) *n.* Principal ancient Syriac version of O.T. and N.T. [f. Syriac *p'šīṭṭâ* simple, plain]

***pĕ'skȳ** *a.* (colloq.) Troublesome, confounded, annoying. [18th c., perh. f. **pesty* (PEST, -Y[2])]

pe'sō (pā'-) *n.* (*pl.* ~**s**). Silver coin and monetary unit in several Latin-American countries and in Philippines. [Sp., = weight, f. L *pensum* (see POISE[1])]

pĕ'ssarȳ *n.* (Med.) Instrument worn in vagina to prevent uterine displacements or as contraceptive; vaginal suppository. [ME, f. LL *pessarium, pessulum* (*pessum, pessus* f. Gk *pessos* oval stone)]

pĕ'ssĭm|ĭsm *n.* Tendency to look at the worst aspect of things or expect bad results (cf. OPTIMISM); doctrine that this world is the worst possible, or that all things tend to evil; so ~IST (2) *n.*, ~**ĭ'stIC** *a.*, ~**ĭ'stICALLY** *adv.* [f. L *pessimus* worst + -ISM, after *optimism*]

pĕst *n.* Troublesome, annoying, or destructive person, animal, or thing; (arch.) pestilence, plague; ~**-house,** hospital for sufferers from plague etc. [f. F *peste* or f. L *pestis* plague]

pĕ'ster *v.t.* Trouble, annoy; importune (*kept pestering me for an interview*). [prob. f. *impester* f. F *empestrer* encumber; infl. by PEST]

pĕ'stĭcīde *n.* Substance for destroying pests, esp. insects. [f. PEST + -I- + -CIDE (1)]

pĕstĭ'ferous *a.* Noxious, pestilential; (fig.) bearing moral contagion, pernicious. [f. L *pestifer, -ferus* (as PEST; see -FEROUS)]

pĕ'stĭlence *n.* Fatal epidemic disease, esp. bubonic plague. [ME f. OF, f. L *pestilentia* (as foll.; see -ENCE)]

pĕ'stĭlent *a.* Destructive to life, deadly; (fig.) injurious to morals etc.; (colloq.) troublesome, annoying; hence ~LY[2] *adv.* [f. L *pestilens, pestilentus* (*pestis* plague; see -LENT)]

pĕstĭlĕ'ntial (-shal) *a.* Of pestilence; pestilent; hence ~LY[2] *adv.* [ME, f. med. L *pestilentialis* f. L *pestilentia* (as prec.); see -IAL]

pĕ'stle (-sel) *n.* & *v.* **1.** *n.* Club-shaped instrument for pounding substances in a mortar; appliance for pounding etc. **2.** *v.t.* Pound (as) with pestle. **3.** *v.i.* Use pestle. [ME, f. OF *pestel* f. L *pistillum* dim. of **pistrum* (*pinsare pist-* pound)]

pĕstŏ'log|ȳ *n.* Scientific study of pests (esp. harmful insects) and of methods of dealing with them; hence **pĕstolŏ'gICAL** *a.*, ~IST (3) *n.* [f. PEST + -O- + -LOGY]

pĕt[1] *n., a.,* & *v.t.* (**-tt-**). **1.** *n.* Animal tamed and kept as favourite or treated with fondness; darling, favourite; ~**-cock,** small stop-cock for draining, letting out steam, etc. **2.** *a.* Kept as pet (*pet lamb*); of or for pet animals (*pet food, shop*); favourite (~ **aversion** etc., (joc.) thing or person particularly disliked); expressing fondness or familiarity (*pet-form* of name etc., *pet name*). **3.** *v.t.* Treat as a pet; fondle (esp. person of opposite sex erotically; or abs.). [16th c. Sc. & N. Engl. dial.; orig. unkn.]

pĕt[2] *n.* Offence at being slighted, ill-humour, (*be in a pet*). [16th c., of unkn. orig.]

Pet. *abbr.* Peter (N.T.).

pĕ'tal *n.* Each of the divisions of the corolla of a flower; hence ~INE (-ĭn), (-)~(**l**)ED[2] (-ld), ~OID, *adjs.* [f. mod. L *petalum*, in LL metal plate f. Gk *petalon* leaf (*petalos* outspread)]

pĕ'talŏn *n.* Gold plate on mitre of Jewish high priest. [Gk; see prec.]

pètar'd *n.* (Hist.) small engine of war used to break down door etc. by explosion (HOIST[2] *with his own petard*); kind of firework, cracker. [f. F *pétard* (*péter* break wind; see -ARD)]

pĕ'tasus *n.* Ancient Greek low-crowned broad-brimmed hat, esp. as worn by Hermes; winged hat of Hermes. [L, f. Gk *petasos*]

pètaur'ĭst *n.* Marsupial of genus *Petaurista*, with patagium enabling it to take flying leaps. [f. Gk *petauristēs* performer on springboard (*petauron*); see -IST]

Pēte *n. For Pete's* SAKE[1]. [abbr. of foll.]

Pē'ter[1] *n.* **1.** BLUE[1] *Peter*; ~ **Pan,** person who retains youthful features etc. and seems not to age; ~ *Pan collar* (flat, with rounded ends); **rob ~ to pay Paul,** take away from one to give to another, discharge one debt by incurring another. **2.** ~**'s fish,** haddock or other fish with marks supposed to have been made by St. Peter's thumb and finger; ~**-penny,** ~**'s penny** or **pence,** (Hist.) annual tax of penny paid to papal see, (since 1860) voluntary payments to papal treasury. [man's Christian name, f. eccl. L f. eccl. Gk *Petros*, lit. 'stone', transl. Aram. *kēpâ* surname given to St. Peter by Jesus (Matt. 16:17); ~ *Pan* hero of play by Barrie (1904)]

pē'ter[2] *v.i.*, & *n.* **1.** *v.i.* ~ **out,** (of stream, vein of ore, or fig.) give out, come to an end. **2.** (Bridge). Play an echo. **3.** *n.* (Bridge). = ECHO[1]. [19th c.; orig. unkn.]

pē'ter[3] *n.* (sl.) Prison cell; safe; **~'man,** safe-breaker. [perh. f. PETER[1]]

pē'tersham *n.* Thick ribbed or corded silk ribbon. [f. Lord *Petersham*, Engl. army officer d. 1851]

pě'thĭdine (-ēn) *n.* Synthetic soluble analgesic derived from piperidine. [perh. f. PIPERIDINE + ETHYL]

pě'tiōl|e *n.* (Bot.) Slender stalk joining leaf-blade to stem; hence ~AR[1], ~ATE[2], *adjs.* [f. F *pétiole* f. L *petiolus* little foot, stalk]

pě'tĭt[1] (-tĭ) *a.* (Law). = PETTY. [ME f. OF, = small, f. Rom. ****pittittus***, perh. imit. of child's speech]

petit[2] (petē') *a.* ~ ***bourgeois*** (boor'zhwah), member of lower middle classes; ~ ***four*** (foor), very small fancy cake etc.; ~***-maître*** (-mā'tr), dandy, coxcomb; ~ ***mal,*** mild form of epilepsy without loss of consciousness; ~ ***point*** (pwăn), (1) embroidery on canvas using small stitches, (2) tent-stitch; ~***s pois*** (pwah), small green peas; ~ ***verre*** (vār), glass of liqueur. [F, = small (as prec.)]

petite (petē't) *a.* (Of woman) of small dainty build; ~ ***bourgeoisie*** (boorzhwahzē'), lower middle classes. [F, fem. of prec.]

pėtĭ'tion *n.* & *v.* **1.** *n.* Asking, supplication, request; formal written supplication from one or more persons to sovereign etc.; (Law) formal written application to court for writ, order, etc.; **P~ of Right,** (Hist.) parliamentary declaration of rights and liberties of the people assented to by Charles I in 1628, (Law) common-law remedy against Crown for recovery of property. **2.** *v.t.* Make petition to (sovereign etc. *for* thing, *to* do). **3.** *v.i.* Ask humbly (*for* thing, *to* be allowed to do etc.). **4.** Hence ~ARY[1] *a.*, ~ER[1] *n.* [ME f. OF, f. L *petitio -onis* (*petere petit-* seek; see -ION)]

petitio principii (pĭtĭshĭō prĭnsĭ'pĭī) *n.* Begging the question (see BEG 4). [L, = assuming a principle (see prec.)]

pě'trel *n.* Sea-bird of family Procellariidae or Hydrobatidae, usu. flying far from land; **storm(y)** ~, small petrel of N. Atlantic with black and white plumage and long wings, (fig.) person causing unrest. [17th c., also *pitteral*, of uncert. orig.; later assoc. w. St. Peter (Matt. 14:30; see -REL)]

Pē'trĭ *n.* ~ **dish,** shallow covered dish for culture of bacteria etc. [f. J. R. ~, Ger. bacteriologist d. 1921]

pětrĭfă'ction *n.* Petrifying; petrified substance or mass. [f. foll. after *stupefaction*; see -FACTION]

pě'trĭfȳ *v.* **1.** *v.t.* Change into stone; (fig.) paralyse or stupefy with astonishment, terror, etc., (*petrified with fear* etc.); deprive (mind, doctrine, etc.) of vitality. **2.** *v.i.* Turn into stone (lit. or fig.). [f. F *pétrifier* f. med. L *petrificare* f. L f. Gk *petra* rock; see -FY]

Pē'trine *a.* Of St. Peter. [f. eccl. L *Petrus* PETER[1] + -INE[1]]

pě'tro- *comb. form.* **1.** Rock, as: *petro*GE'NESIS; **~glyph,** (esp. prehistoric) rock-carving. **2.** Petroleum, as PETROCHEMISTRY; **~dollar,** dollar available in petroleum-exporting country. [f. Gk *petros* stone or *petra* rock + -O-]

pětrōchě'mĭcal (-k-) *a.* & *n.* **1.** *a.* Of petrochemistry or petrochemicals. **2.** *n.* Substance industrially obtained from petroleum or natural gas. [f. foll. + CHEMICAL]

pětrōchě'mĭstrȳ (-k-) *n.* Chemistry of rocks; chemistry of petroleum. [f. PETRO- + CHEMISTRY]

pėtrŏ'|graphȳ *n.* Scientific description of composition and formation of rocks; hence ~GRAPHER *n.*, **pětro**GRA'PHIC(AL) *adjs.* [f. PETRO- + -GRAPHY]

‖**pě'trol** *n.* Refined petroleum used as fuel in motor vehicles, aircraft, etc.; **~-pump,** machine for transferring this esp. from underground reservoir to tank in motor vehicle. [f. F *pétrole* f. med. L PETROLEUM]

***pětrolā'tum** *n.* Petroleum jelly. [mod. L, f. prec. + *-atum*; see -ATE[1]]

pėtrō'lėum *n.* Hydrocarbon oil found in upper strata of earth, refined for use as fuel for heating and in internal-combustion engines, as illuminant, as dry-cleaning agent, etc.; ~ **ether,** volatile liquid distilled from petroleum; ~ **jelly,** translucent solid mixture of hydrocarbons got from petroleum and used as lubricant etc. [med. L, f. L f. Gk *petra* rock + L *oleum* oil]

pėtrŏ'lĭc *a.* Of petrol or petroleum. [f. PETROL + -IC]

pėtrŏ'log|ȳ *n.* Study of origin, structure, etc., of rocks; so **pětrolŏ'g**IC(AL) *adjs.*, ~IST (3) *n.* [f. PETRO- + -LOGY]

pě'tronel *n.* (Hist.) Large pistol used esp. by horse-soldiers in 16th–17th c. [f. F *petrinal*, var. of *poitrinal* n. f. a. (*poitrine* chest f. Rom. **pectorina* f. L *pectus -oris*; see -AL); the butt end rested against the chest in firing]

pē'trous *a.* Of or like rock; (Anat.) hard (part of the temporal bone, protecting the inner ear). [f. L *petrosus* (L f. Gk *petra* rock; see -OUS)]

pě'ttĭcoat *n.* **1.** Woman's or child's undergarment hanging from waist or shoulders, or (Hist.) outer skirt, (*have known him since he was* **in ~s,** a young child; *a Cromwell* **in ~s,** in all but her sex). **2.** Woman or girl; (in *pl.*) the female sex; (*attrib.*) feminine; ~ **government,** dominance of women in the home or in politics. **3.** Hence ~ED[2], ~LESS, *adjs.* [ME, f. *petty coat*]

pě'ttĭfŏg *v.i.* (**-gg-**). Practise legal chicanery; quibble or wrangle about petty points. [back form. f. foll.]

pě'ttĭfŏgg|er (-g-) *n.* Inferior legal practitioner; rascally lawyer; petty practitioner in any activity; hence ~ERY (4) *n.*, ~ING[2] *a.* (-g-). [f. PETTY + *fogger* underhand dealer, prob. f. *Fugger* family of merchants in Augsburg (15th–16th c.)]

pě'ttĭsh *a.* Peevish, petulant, easily put out; hence ~LY[2] *adv.*, ~NESS *n.* [f. PET[2] + -ISH[1]]

pě'ttĭtōes (-ōz) *n. pl.* Pig's trotters, esp. as food. [orig. = offal, f. F *petite oie* giblets of a goose, w. assim. to PETTY, TOE*s*]

pě'tt|ȳ *a.* Unimportant, trivial; contemptible; minor, inferior, on a small scale, (*petty princes, farmers*); (Law) of lesser importance (cf. GRAND; *petty* JURY, *petty* LARCENY, *petty* SESSIONS, *petty* TREASON); **~y bourgeois,** = PETIT[2] *bourgeois*; **~y cash,** (money from or for) small cash items of receipt or expenditure; **~y officer,** naval N.C.O.; hence **~ĭ**LY[2] *adv.*, **~ĭ**NESS *n.* [ME *pety*, var. of PETIT[1]]

pě'tūl|ant *a.* Peevishly impatient or irritable; hence or cogn. ~ANCE *n.*, **~ant**LY[2] *adv.* [f. F *pétulant* f. L *petulans -antis* (**petulare* f. *petere* seek; see -ANT)]

pėtū'nĭa *n.* Plant of genus *Petunia* with white, purple, red, etc., funnel-shaped flowers; dark violet or purple colour. [mod. L, f. F *petun* f. Guarani *petȳ* tobacco; see -IA[1]]

pėtū'ntsė (*or* -ōō'n-) *n.* White powdered granite used in China for making porcelain. [f. Chin. *pai-tun-tze* (*pai* white, *tun* stone + suf. *-tze*)]

pew *n.*, & *v.t.* **1.** *n.* (In church) enclosed compartment or fixed bench with back; (colloq.) seat (*find, take, a pew*); **~-rent** (for pew or seats in church); hence ~'AGE (4) *n.*, ~'LESS *a.* **2.** *v.t.* Furnish with pews; enclose in pew. [ME *pywe*, *puwe* f. OF *puye* balcony f. L *podia* pl. of PODIUM]

pē'wĭt, pee'wĭt, *n.* Lapwing; its cry; ~ (**gull**), black-headed gull. [imit.]

pew'ter *n.* Grey alloy of tin with lead or other

metal; utensil(s) of this; ||(sl.) tankard etc. as prize; hence ~ER[1] *n.*, worker in pewter. [ME f. OF *peutre*, *peualtre* f. Rom. **peltrum*, of unkn. orig.]

peyō′t|ė (pāō′-) *n.* **1.** Mexican cactus of genus *Lophophora*. **2.** Hallucinogenic drug prepared from this plant. **3.** Hence ~ISM (3) *n.*, Amer. Ind. religion using peyote sacramentally. [Amer. Sp., f. Nahuatl *peyotl*]

Pf. *abbr.* pfennig.

***Pfc** *abbr.* Private First Class.

pfĕ′nnĭg *n.* Small German copper coin, worth $\frac{1}{100}$ of a mark. [G, cogn. w. PENNY]

P.G. *abbr.* paying guest.

pH (pēā′ch) *n.* (Chem.) Negative decimal logarithm of hydrogen-ion concentration in moles per litre, giving measure of acidity or alkalinity of a solution. [G, f. *potenz* power + *H* symbol for hydrogen]

phae′ton (fā′-) *n.* Light open four-wheeled carriage usu. drawn by pair of horses; *touring-car. [f. F *phaéton* f. L f. Gk *Phaethōn*, son of Helios the sun god and famous for bad driving of sun-chariot (*phaethōn* shining)]

phāge (*or* fahzh) *n.* = BACTERIOPHAGE. [abbr.]

phăgėd|ae′na, *-d|ē′na, *n.* Spreading ulcer; so **~ae′n**IC, *~**ē′n**IC, *a.* [L, f. Gk *phagedaina* (*phag-* eat)]

phă′go|cȳte *n.* Leucocyte etc. capable of absorbing foreign matter, esp. bacteria, in the body; hence **~cȳ′t**IC *a.* [f. Gk *phag-* eat + -o- + -CYTE]

phă′gocȳtīze, -ise (-īz), **-ōse,** *v.t.* Consume by phagocytosis. [f. prec. + -IZE, & back form. f. foll.]

phăgocȳtō′s|ĭs *n.* (*pl.* **~es** *pr.* ~ēz). Consumption of bacteria etc. by phagocytes. [f. PHAGOCYTE + -OSIS]

-phagous *comb. form.* Eating (*ichthyophagous*). [f. L f. Gk *-phagos* + -OUS]

-phagȳ *comb. form.* Eating of (*ichthyophagy*). [f. Gk *-phagia* + -Y[1]]

phă′lănge (-nj) *n.* = PHALANX 3. [F, f. L PHALANX]

phală′ngėal (-nj-) *a.* (Anat.) Of a phalanx. [f. prec. + -AL]

phală′nger (-nj-) *n.* Australian arboreal thick-furred marsupial, e.g. flying squirrel or opossum. [F, f. Gk *phalaggion* spider's web, f. webbed toes of its hind feet]

phă′lanst|erȳ *n.* (Buildings of) socialistic PHALANX; so **~ēr′**IAN *a.* & *n.* [f. F *phalanstère* (f. foll. after *monastère* monastery)]

phă′lăn|x *n.* (*pl.* **~xes,** *or* **~ges** *pr.* -njēz). **1.** (Gk Ant.) Line of battle, esp. body of Macedonian infantry drawn up in close order. **2.** Set of persons etc. forming compact mass, or banded together for common purpose; (Hist.) socialistic community of about 1800 persons as proposed by Fourier. **3.** (Anat.) bone of finger or toe; (Bot.) bundle of stamens united by filaments. [L, f. Gk *phalagx -ggos*]

phă′larōpe *n.* Small wading and swimming bird of family Phalaropodidae, noted for tameness. [F, f. mod. L *Phalaropus*, irreg. f. Gk *phalaris* coot + *pous podos* foot]

phă′ll|us *n.* (*pl.* **~i** *pr.* -ī, *or* **~uses**). Image of the (usu. erect) penis, venerated in some religious systems as symbolizing generative power in nature; penis or clitoris; so ~IC *a.*, ~(**ĭc**)ISM (3) *ns.* [LL, f. Gk *phallos*]

phană′rĭot *n.* Member of class of Greek officials in Constantinople under Ottoman Empire. [f. mod. Gk *phanariōtēs* f. *Phanar* part of city where they lived, f. Gk *phanarion* lighthouse (on the Golden Horn); see -OT[2]]

phă′nerogăm *n.* (Bot.) Plant that has stamens and pistils, flowering plant, (cf. CRYPTOGAM); so ~IC (-ă′m-), **phănerŏ′gam**OUS, *adjs.* [f. F *phanérogame* f. Gk *phaneros* visible + *gamos* marriage]

phă′ntasīze, phă′ntast. Vars. of FANTASIZE, FANTAST.

phă′ntăsm *n.* Illusion, phantom; illusive likeness (*of*); supposed vision of absent (living or dead) person; hence **phăntă′sm**AL, **phăntă′sm**IC, (-z-) *adjs.* [ME, f. OF *fantasme* f. L f. Gk *phantasma* (*phantazō* make visible f. *phainō* show)]

phăntăsmag|ŏr′ĭa (-z-) *n.* Optical device for rapidly varying size of images on screen; shifting scene of real or imagined figures; hence **~ŏ′r**IC *a.* [prob. f. F *fantasmagorie* (as prec. + fanciful ending)]

phă′ntasȳ. See FANTASY.

phă′ntom *n.* & *a.* **1.** *n.* (Mere) apparition, spectre; image (*of*); vain show, form without substance or reality; mental illusion. **2.** *a.* Merely apparent, illusive; ~ **circuit,** arrangement of telegraph etc. wires equivalent to an extra circuit; ~ **limb,** sensation apparently coming from limb previously removed by amputation. [ME f. OF *fantosme* f. pop. L **fantauma* f. Gk (as PHANTASM)]

Phār′aoh (fār′ō) *n.* Title of ruler of ancient Egypt; **~'s serpent,** chemical toy burning and uncoiling in serpentine form; hence **Phāraō′n**IC *a.* [OE, f. eccl. L f. Gk *Pharaō* f. Heb. *par'ōh* f. Egypt. *pr-'o* great house]

Phă′rĭsee *n.* One of ancient Jewish sect (cf. SADDUCEE, ESSENE) distinguished by strict observance of traditional and written law, held to have pretensions to superior sanctity; self-righteous person, formalist, hypocrite; so **Phărĭsā′**IC(AL) *adjs.*, **Phă′rĭsā**ISM (3) *n.* [OE *fariseus* & OF *pharise* f. eccl. L *pharisaeus* f. Gk *Pharisaios* f. Aram. *p'rīšayyâ* pl. f. Heb. *pārûš* separated]

phārmaceu′t|ĭcal (*or* -kū′-) *a.* Of or engaged in pharmacy; of the use or sale of medicinal drugs; hence or cogn. **~ĭcal**LY[2] *adv.*, ~ICS *n.* [f. LL f. Gk *pharmakeutikos* (*pharmakeutēs* druggist f. *pharmakon* drug) + -AL]

phār′macĭst *n.* Person skilled in or practising pharmacy; pharmaceutical chemist. [f. PHARMACY + -IST]

phārmacŏ′log|ȳ *n.* Science of action of drugs on the body; hence **phārmaco**LO′GICAL *a.*, ~IST (3) *n.* [f. mod. L *pharmacologia* f. Gk *pharmakon* drug; see -LOGY]

phārmacopoe′i|a (-pē′*a*) *n.* Book (esp. one officially published) containing list of drugs with directions for use; stock of drugs; hence ~AL (-pē′*al*) *a.* [mod. L, f. Gk *pharmakopoiia* (*pharmakopoios* drug-maker f. as prec. + *-poios* making)]

phār′macȳ *n.* Preparation and (esp. medicinal) dispensing of drugs; pharmacist's shop, dispensary. [ME, f. OF *farmacie* f. med. L f. Gk *pharmakeia* practice of the druggist (*pharmakeus* f. *pharmakon* drug)]

phār′ōs *n.* Lighthouse or beacon to guide mariners. [L, f. Gk *Pharos* island off Alexandria, lighthouse on this]

pharȳ′ngo- (-ngg-) *comb. form.* Pharynx, as: **~cele,** abnormal enlargement at base of pharynx; **~scope,** instrument for inspecting pharynx; **~tomy** (-ŏ′t-), incision into pharynx. [f. as foll. + -o-]

phă′rȳnx *n.* Cavity, with enclosing muscles and mucous membrane, behind nose and mouth, and connecting them to oesophagus; hence **pharȳ′ng**AL (-ngg-), **phărȳngē′**AL (-nj-), *adjs.*, **phărȳng**ī′TIS (-nj-) *n.* [mod. L, f. Gk *pharugx -ggos*]

phāse (-z) *n.*, & *v.t.* **1.** *n.* Stage of change or development; aspect of moon or planet, according to amount of illumination (esp. applied to new moon, first quarter, full moon, last quarter); aspect (of situation or question); genetic or seasonal variety of animal's coloration etc. **2.** (Phys.) Particular stage in periodically recurring sequence of movements or changes (esp. of alternating electric currents); **in ~,** having the same phase at the same time; **out of ~,** not in phase; **three-~,** (of electric generator, motor, etc.) designed to supply or use simultaneously three separate alternating currents of the same voltage, but with phases differing by ⅓ of a period. **3.** (Chem.) Physically distinct form of matter that can be present in a system; **~ rule** (relating numbers of phases, constituents, and degrees of freedom). **4.** Hence **phā'**SIC (-z-) *a.* **5.** *v.t.* Carry out (programme etc.) in phases or stages; **~ in** or **out,** bring gradually into or out of use. [f. F *phase* & f. earlier *phasis*, f. Gk *phasis* appearance (*phan-* show)]

phă'tĭc *a.* (Of speech etc.) used to convey general sociability rather than to communicate specific meaning, e.g. *nice morning, isn't it?* [f. Gk *phatos* spoken (*phan-* speak) + -IC]

Ph.D. *abbr.* Doctor of Philosophy. [f. L *philosophiae doctor*]

phea'sant (fĕ'z-) *n.* Long-tailed game-bird of genus *Phasianus* etc., orig. Asian; **~-eyed,** (of flower) marked like eye of pheasant; **~'s-eye,** (1) plant of genus *Adonis*, with dark centre, (2) common narcissus; hence **~**RY (3) *n.* [ME, f. AF *fesaunt* f. OF *faisan* f. L f. Gk *phasianos* (bird) of river *Phasis* in Asia Minor]

phėnă'cėtĭn *n.* Antipyretic acetyl derivative of phenol. [f. foll. + ACETYL + -IN]

phēno- *comb. form.* **1.** (Chem.) Derived from benzene (*phenol, phenyl*). **2.** Showing (*phenocryst*). [f. Gk *phainō* shine (w. ref. to substances used for illumination), show + -O-]

***phēnobar'bĭtăl,** ||**phēnobar'bĭtōne,** *ns.* Narcotic and sedative barbiturate drug used esp. in epilepsy. [f. prec. 1 + BARBITAL, BARBITONE]

phē'nocrȳst *n.* Large or conspicuous crystal in porphyritic rock. [f. F *phénocryste* (as PHENO- 2, CRYSTAL)]

phē'nŏl *n.* (Chem.) Hydroxyl derivative of aromatic hydrocarbon, esp. monohydroxybenzene (C_6H_5OH), used in dilute form as antiseptic and disinfectant. [f. F *phénole* (*phène* benzene f. as PHENO-; see -OL)]

phėnŏ'log|ȳ *n.* Study of the times of recurring natural phenomena esp. in relation to climatic conditions; so **phēnolŏ'g**ICAL *a.*, **~**IST (3) *n.* [f. PHENOMENON + -LOGY]

phėnŏ'mėnal *a.* Of the nature of a phenomenon; perceptible by, or evidenced only by, the senses; concerned with phenomena; remarkable, prodigious; hence **~**LY^{2} *adv.*, **~**IZE *v.t.*, make, or represent as, phenomenal. [f. PHENOMENON + -AL]

phėnŏ'mėnal|ĭsm *n.* Doctrine that phenomena are the only objects of knowledge; so **~**IST (2) *n.*, **~ĭ'st**IC *a.* [f. prec. + -ISM]

phėnŏmėn|ŏ'logȳ *n.* Science of phenomena; description and classification of phenomena; hence **~olo'**GICAL *a.* [f. foll. + -O- + -LOGY]

phėnŏ'mėn|on *n.* (*pl.* **~a**). Thing that appears or is perceived, esp. thing the cause of which is in question; (Philos.) that of which a sense or the mind directly takes note, immediate object of perception; remarkable person, thing, occurrence, etc. [f. LL f. Gk *phainomenon* neut. part. (as n.) of *phainomai* appear (*phainō* show)]

phē'no|tȳpe *n.* (Biol.) Set of observable characteristics of individual or group as determined by genotype and environment; hence **~tȳ'p**IC *a.* [f. G *phaenotypus* (as PHENO- 2, TYPE^{1})]

phē'nȳl *n.* (Chem.) Radical formed from benzene by removal of hydrogen atom. [f. PHENO- + -YL]

phĕ'ro|mōne *n.* (Biol.) Substance secreted and released by animal for detection and response by another of same species; hence **~mō'n**AL *a.* [f. Gk *pherō* convey + -O- + HORMONE]

phew *int.* expr. impatience, discomfort, relief, astonishment, or disgust. [imit. of puffing]

phī *n.* Twenty-first Greek letter (Φ, φ) = ph; ***Phi Beta Kappa,** (member of) oldest Amer. college fraternity, named from initial letters of its Gk motto, = 'philosophy the guide to life'. [Gk]

phī'al *n.* Small glass bottle, esp. for liquid medicine. [ME, f. OF *fiole* f. L *phiola, phiala* f. Gk *phialē* broad flat vessel; cf. VIAL]

phĭl-. See PHILO-.

-phĭl, -phīle, *suf.* forming *ns.* & *adjs.* w. sense '(one who is) fond of', as *bibliophil(e), Russophil(e)*. [f. Gk *philos* dear, loving]

Phil. *abbr.* Philadelphia; Philharmonic; Philippians (N.T.); Philosophy.

phĭ'labĕg. Var. of FILIBEG.

phĭladĕ'lphus *n.* Deciduous shrub of genus *Philadelphus*, esp. mock orange. [mod. L, f. Gk *philadelphon*]

phĭlă'nder *v.i.* Flirt with or *with* woman; be one who flirts habitually; hence **~**ER^{1} *n.* [f. *philander* n. f. Gk PHIL(*andros* f. *anēr* male person) fond of men, taken as name of lover]

phĭ'lanthrōpe *n.* = PHILANTHROPIST. [f. Gk PHIL(*anthrōpos* human being)]

phĭlanthrŏ'p|ĭc *a.* Loving one's fellow men, benevolent, humane; hence **~**ICALLY *adv.* [f. F *philanthropique* (as prec.; see -IC)]

phĭlă'nthrop|ȳ *n.* Love of mankind; practical benevolence; hence **~**ISM (3), **~**IST (2), *ns.*, **~**IZE (1, 2) *v.t.* & *i.* [f. LL f. Gk *philanthrōpia* (as PHILANTHROPE; see -Y^{1})]

phĭlă'tel|ȳ *n.* Collection and study of postage stamps; hence **phĭlatĕ'l**IC *a.*, **~**IST (3) *n.* [f. F PHIL(*atélie* f. Gk *ateleia* exemption from payment f. *a-* not + *telos* toll, tax)]

-phīle. See -PHIL.

Philem. *abbr.* Philemon (N.T.).

phĭlharmŏ'nĭc (*or* -lar-) *a.* Fond of music (*philharmonic society*). [f. F *philharmonique* f. It. *filarmonico* (as PHIL-, HARMONIC)]

phĭ'lhĕllēne (*or* -hĕ'-) *a.* & *n.* (Person) friendly to the Greeks or (Hist.) supporting the cause of Greek independence; hence **phĭlhĕllē'n**IC *a.*, **phĭlhĕ'llėn**ISM (3), **phĭlhĕ'llėn**IST (2), *ns.* [f. Gk PHIL(*ellēn* HELLENE)]

-phĭ'lĭa *suf.* forming *ns.* w. sense 'love of, fondness for' (*coprophilia*); hence **~phĭ'l**IC *adj. suf.* (*bibliophilic*). [Gk (*philos* loving; see -IA^{1})]

Phĭlĭ'ppĭc *n.* **1.** (in *pl.*) Orations of Demosthenes against Philip of Macedon; Cicero's orations against Antony. **2.** (*p~*). Bitter invective. [f. L f. Gk *philippikos* (*Philippos* Philip; see -IC)]

phĭlĭppi'na (-pē'-), **phĭlĭppi'ne**^{1} (-ē'n), **phĭlopoe'na** (-pē'-), ***-opē'na,** *n.* Almond or other nut with double kernel, the finding of which at dessert etc. and sharing it with person of the opposite sex involves giving or receiving of a present at next meeting; the present; the custom. [f. G *Philippchen* little Philip alt. of *vielliebchen* darling dim. of *viellieb* very dear]

Phĭ'lĭppine^{2} (-ēn) *a.* Of the Philippine Islands; Filipino. [f. *Philip* II of Spain + -INE^{1}]

Phĭ'lĭstīne *n.* & *a.* **1.** *n.* Member of warlike people in ancient Palestine; uncultured person, one whose interests are material and commonplace, whence **phĭ'lĭstĭn**ISM (2) *n.* **2.** *a.* Uncultured, commonplace, prosaic. [ME, f. F *Philistin* or LL f. Gk *Philistinos* = *Palaistinos* f. Heb. *pᵉlištī*]

phĭllū'men|ist (*or* -lōō'-) *n.* Collector of matchbox labels; so ~Y[1] *n.* [f. PHIL- + L *lumen* light + -IST]

phĭlo- *comb. form.* (**phil-** bef. vowel or *h*). Liking, fond of, as: **~bib'lic,** fond of books; **~de'ndron,** tropical Amer. climbing plant; **~gynist** (-ŏ'j-), lover of women; **~proge'nitive,** prolific, loving one's offspring; **~te'chnic** (-tĕ'k-), fond of (esp. the industrial) arts. [f. or after Gk *philo-* (*phileō* to love, *philos* friend)]

phĭlŏ'log|ȳ *n.* Science (esp. historical and comparative) of language(s); *study of literature; (arch.) love of learning and literature; hence ~ER[1], **phĭlolō'g**IAN, ~IST (3), *ns.*, **phĭlolŏ'g**ICAL *a.*, ~IZE (2) *v.i.* [f. F *philologie* f. L f. Gk PHILO- (*logia* = -LOGY) love of learning]

Phĭ'lomĕl, Phĭlomē'la, *ns.* (poet.) The nightingale. [earlier *philomene* f. med. L *philomena* f. L f. Gk *philomēla* nightingale; cap. w. ref. to myth of Philomela]

philop(o)ena. See PHILIPPINA.

phĭlŏ'sopher *n.* Seeker after wisdom; person skilled in philosophy or in one of its branches; one who regulates his life by the light of philosophy; one who shows philosophic calmness in trying circumstances; **~s'** (or **~'s**) **stone,** supreme object of alchemy, substance supposed to change other metals into gold or silver. [ME, f. AF *philosofre* var. of OF *philosophe* f. L f. Gk *philosophos* (as PHILO-, SOPHIST)]

phĭlosŏ'ph|ĭc(al) *adjs.* Of, or consonant with, philosophy; skilled in or devoted to philosophy (*philosophical society*); wise; calm under adverse but irremediable circumstances; temperate; hence ~ICALLY *adv.* [f. LL *philosophicus* f. L *philosophia* (see PHILOSOPHY, -IC, -ICAL)]

phĭlŏ'sophīze, -īse (-īz), *v.* **1.** *v.i.* Play the philosopher; speculate, theorize; moralize. **2.** *v.t.* Render philosophic. [app. f. F *philosopher* + -IZE]

phĭlŏ'sophȳ *n.* Seeking after wisdom or knowledge, esp. that which deals with ultimate reality, or with the most general causes and principles of things and ideas and human perception and knowledge of them, physical phenomena (*natural philosophy*), and ethics (*moral philosophy*); advanced learning in general (*doctor of philosophy*); philosophical system; system of principles for conduct of life; serenity, calmness. [ME f. OF *filosofie* f. L f. Gk PHILO(*sophia* wisdom f. *sophos* wise)]

-phĭlous *suf.* = -PHILIC. [f. med. L f. Gk *-philos* + -OUS]

phĭ'ltre (-*ter*), ***phĭ'lter,** *n.* Drink supposed to be able to excite sexual love in drinker. [f. F *philtre* f. L f. Gk *philtron* (*phileō* to love)]

-phĭlȳ *suf.* = -PHILIA. [f. as -PHILIA + -Y[1]]

phīm|ō'sĭs *n.* (*pl.* **~oses** *pr.* -ō'sēz). Constriction and non-retractability of foreskin; hence ~O'TIC *a.* [mod. L, f. Gk, = muzzling]

phĭz *n.* (arch., colloq.) Face; expression of face. [abbr. of *phiznomy* = PHYSIOGNOMY]

phlėb|ī'tĭs *n.* Inflammation of walls of vein; hence **~ĭ't**IC *a.* [mod. L, f. Gk (as foll.) + -ITIS]

phlėbŏ'tom|īze, -īse (-īz), *v.* **1.** *v.i.* Practise phlebotomy. **2.** *v.t.* Bleed (person, part of body). **3.** So ~IST (3) *n.* [f. F *phlébotomiser* (*phlébotomie*, as foll.; see -IZE)]

phlėbŏ'tomȳ *n.* (esp. Hist.) Blood-letting as medical operation. [ME, f. OF *flebothomi* f. LL f. Gk *phlebotomia* (*phleps phlebos* vein; see -TOMY)]

phlĕgm (flĕm) *n.* **1.** Thick viscous (semi-)fluid substance secreted by mucous membranes of respiratory passages, esp. when morbid or excessive and discharged by cough etc., whence ~'Y[2] (flĕ'mĭ) *a.* **2.** (Hist.) this substance regarded as a HUMOUR[1]; coolness, calmness, sluggishness, apathy, (supposed to result from predominance of phlegm in constitution); hence **phlĕgmă't**IC *a.*, **phlĕgmă't**ICALLY *adv.* [ME & OF *fleume* f. LL f. Gk *phlegma -atos* inflammation (*phlegō* burn)]

phlō'ĕm *n.* (Bot.) Soft tissue of stems (opp. XYLEM). [f. Gk *phloos* bark]

phlogĭ'stĭc (*or* -g-) *a.* Of phlogiston; (Med.) inflammatory. [f. as foll. or f. Gk *phlogistos* inflammable + -IC]

phlogĭ'ston (*or* -g-) *n.* Substance formerly supposed to exist in all combustible bodies, and to be released in combustion. [mod. L, f. Gk (*phlogizō* set on fire f. *phlox phlogos* flame; see -IZE)]

phlŏx *n.* Plant of genus *Phlox*, with clusters of flowers of various colours. [L f. Gk name of a plant (lit. flame)]

-phōbe *suf.* forming *ns.* & *adjs.* w. sense '(one who is) not fond of, (person) disliking or fearing' (*Gallophobe, Russophobe, xenophobe*). [F, f. L f. Gk *-phobos*, adj. suf. f. *phobos* fear]

phō'b|ia *n.* (Morbid) fear or aversion; hence ~IC *a.* & *n.* [foll. used as separate wd]

-phō'bĭa *suf.* forming abstract *ns.* corresp. to *adjs.* in -PHOBE (*Gallophobia, Russophobia, xenophobia*); hence **-phō'b**IC *suf.* forming *adjs.* [L f. Gk]

phoe'bė (fē'-) *n.* Amer. flycatcher of genus *Sayornis*. [imit.; infl. by name *Phoebe*]

Phoe'bus (fē'b-) *n.* (poet.) The sun. [L, f. Gk *Phoibos* sun-god]

Phoenĭ'cian (fĭnĭ'shan; *or* -nē'-) *a.* & *n.* (Inhabitant) of Phoenicia (ancient name for part of coast of Syria) or its colonies. [ME, f. OF *phenicien* f. L *Phoenicia* f. L f. Gk *Phoinikē* Phoenicia (*Phoinix -ikos* Phoenician); see -AN]

phoe'nix (fē'-) *n.* (Myth.) bird, the only one of its kind, that after living five or six centuries in Arabian desert burnt itself on funeral pile and rose from the ashes with renewed youth to live through another cycle; unique person or thing. [OE & OF *fenix* f. L f. Gk *phoinix* Phoenician, purple, phoenix]

phō'las *n.* = PIDDOCK. [mod. L, f. Gk *phōlas* that lurks in a hole (*phōleos*)]

phŏn *n.* (Phys.) Unit of loudness of sounds. [f. Gk *phōnē* sound]

phō'n|āte *v.i.* Utter vocal sound; hence **phon**A'TION *n.*, **~at**ORY *a.* [f. Gk *phōnē* voice + -ATE[3]]

phonau'tograph (-ahf) *n.* Apparatus for automatic visible recording of vibrations of sound. [f. F *phonautographe* (as prec., AUTO-, -GRAPH)]

phōne[1] *n.* & *v.* (colloq.) Telephone; **~-in** *n.*, broadcast programme during which listeners or viewers telephone to the studio etc. and participate. [abbr.]

phōne[2] *n.* (Phonet.) Simple vowel or consonant sound. [f. as foll.]

-phōne *suf.* forming *ns.* & *adjs.* meaning (1) instrument using sound (*dictaphone, xylophone*), (2) that uses a specified language (*anglophone*). [f. Gk *phōnē* voice, sound]

phō'nēme *n.* (Phonet.) Unit of significant sound in a specified language; hence **phōnē'm**IC *a.*, **phōnē'm**ICS *n.* [f. F *phonème* f. Gk *phōnēma* sound, speech (*phōneō* speak)]

phonĕ'ndoscōpe *n.* Apparatus for making small sounds (esp. in human body) distinctly audible. [f. as -PHONE + Gk *endon* within + -O- + -SCOPE]

phonĕ'tĭc *a.* Representing vocal sounds (*phonetic* ALPHABET), esp. (of system of spelling) using always same symbol for same sound, whence ~ISM (3), ~IST (2), *ns.*, ~IZE (3) *v.t.*; of vocal sounds; hence **phonĕ't**ICALLY *adv.* [f. mod. L f. Gk *phōnētikos* (*phōneō* speak; see -ETIC)]

phonĕ'tĭcs *n. pl.* (usu. treated as *sing.*) (Study of) phonetic phenomena; hence **phōnĕtĭ'**CIAN *n.* [f. prec. + -ICS]
phō'nĕtĭst *n.* Person skilled in phonetics; advocate of phonetic spelling. [f. PHONETICIST]
phō'n|ey, phō'n|ȳ, *a.* (~ier, ~iest) & *n.* (sl.) **1.** *a.* Sham, counterfeit; fictitious; fraudulent; hence ~**ĭ**LY[2] *adv.*, ~**ĭ**NESS *n.* **2.** *n.* Phoney person or thing. [20th c.; orig. unkn.]
phŏ'nĭc *a.* Of sound, acoustic; of vocal sounds. [f. Gk *phōnē* voice + -IC]
phō'no- *comb. form.* Sound, as: ~**lite,** clinkstone; ~**meter** (-ŏ'm-), instrument recording number or force of sound-waves; ~**scope,** (1) apparatus for testing musical strings, (2) instrument for representing sound-vibrations in visible form. [f. Gk *phōnē* voice, sound + -o-]
phō'nogrăm *n.* Symbol representing spoken sound; sound-record made by phonograph. [f. PHONO- + -GRAM]
phō'nograph (-ahf) *n.*, & *v.t.* **1.** *n.* ||Earlier form of gramophone using cylinders and able to record as well as reproduce sound; *gramophone. **2.** *v.t.* Record or reproduce by phonograph. [f. as PHONO- + -GRAPH]
phonŏ'graphȳ *n.* Writing in (esp. shorthand) symbols corresponding to sounds of speech; recording of sounds by phonograph; hence **phōnogră'phi**C *a.* [f. as PHONO- + -GRAPHY]
phonŏ'log|ȳ *n.* Study of sounds in a language; hence **phōnolŏ'gi**CAL *a.*, ~IST (3) *n.* [f. PHONO- + -LOGY]
phō'nŏn *n.* (Phys.) Quantum of sound or elastic vibrations. [f. Gk *phōnē* sound + -ON]
phō'nȳ. See PHONEY.
phoo'ey *int.* expr. disgust. [imit.]
-phōre *suf.* forming *ns.* w. sense 'bearer' (*ctenophore, semaphore*); so **-phor**OUS *adj. suf.* [f. mod. L f. Gk *-phoros -phoron* bearing, bearer (*pherō* bear)]
phōr'mĭum *n.* Liliaceous plant of genus *Phormium* whose fibre is used commercially; New Zealand flax. [mod. L, f. Gk *phormion* a species of plant]
phŏ'sgēne *n.* Colourless poisonous gas, carbon oxychloride. [f. Gk *phōs* light + -GEN (1), w. ref. to its orig. production by action of sunlight on chlorine and carbon monoxide]
phŏ'sphāte *n.* Salt or ester of phosphoric acid, esp. used as fertilizer; effervescent drink containing small amount of phosphate; hence **phŏsphă'ti**C *a.* [F (*phosphore* PHOSPHORUS; see -ATE[1] (3))]
phŏ'sphēne *n.* Appearance of rings of light produced by pressure on eyeball, due to irritation of retina. [irreg. f. Gk *phōs* light + *phainō* show]
phŏ'sphīde *n.* (Chem.) Binary compound of phosphorus with other element or radical. [f. PHOSPHO- + -IDE]
phŏ'sphine (-ēn) *n.* (Chem.) Colourless ill-smelling gas, phosphorus trihydride; hence **phŏsphĭ'ni**C *a.* [f. PHOSPHO- + -INE[5], after *amine*]
phŏ'sphīte *n.* (Chem.) Salt or ester of phosphorous acid. [F (as PHOSPHO-, -ITE[1])]
phŏspho- *comb. form.* Phosphorus. [abbr.]
phŏ'sphor[1] *n.* Synthetic fluorescent or phosphorescent substance. [G, f. L PHOSPHORUS]
phŏ'sphor[2] *n.* = PHOSPHORUS; ~ **bronze,** tough hard bronze alloy containing a small proportion of phosphorus, used (esp.) for bearings. [abbr.]
phŏ'sphorāte *v.t.* Combine or impregnate with phosphorus. [f. PHOSPHORUS + -ATE[3]]
phŏsphor|ĕ'scence *n.* Radiation similar to fluorescence but detectable after excitation ceases; emission of light without combustion or perceptible heat; so ~E'SCE *v.i.*, ~E'SCENT *a.* [f. PHOSPHORUS + -ESCENCE]
phŏsphŏ'rĭc. See PHOSPHORUS.
phŏ'sphorīte *n.* Non-crystalline form of apatite. [f. PHOSPHORUS + -ITE[1]]
phŏ'sphor|us *n.* Non-metallic element existing in allotropic forms, incl. a yellowish waxlike substance undergoing slow combustion at ordinary temperatures and hence appearing luminous in the dark; hence or cogn. **phŏsphŏ'ri**C, ~OUS, *adjs.*, ~ISM (5) *n.* [L, = morning star, f. Gk *phōsphoros* (*phōs* light, *-phoros* -bringing)]
phŏ'ssȳ *a.* ~ **jaw,** (colloq.) gangrene of jawbone caused by phosphorus poisoning. [abbr.; see -Y[3]]
phŏt *n.* (Phys.) Unit of illumination, one lumen per square centimetre. [f. Gk *phōs phōtos* light]
phō'tĭc *a.* Of light; (of ocean layers) reached by sunlight. [f. as prec. + -IC]
phō'tĭsm *n.* Hallucinatory sensation or vision of light. [f. Gk *phōtismos* (*phōtizō* shine f. *phōs phōtos* light; see -ISM)]
phō'tō *n.* (*pl.* ~s), & *v.t.* = PHOTOGRAPH; ~ **finish,** close finish of race (photographed to enable judge to decide winner etc.), or of any contest. [abbr.]
phō'to- (*or* -ō) *comb. form.* **1.** Light, as: ~**cell,** photoelectric cell; ~**che'mistry,** study of chemical effects of light; ~*che'mical* a.; ~**conducti'vity,** conductivity due to action of light; ~**ele'ctric,** marked by or utilizing emission of electrons from substances exposed to light (~*electric cell*, device using this effect to generate current; ~*electri'city* n.); ~**meter** (-ŏ'm-), instrument for measuring light; ~*me'tric* a., ~*metry* (-ŏ'm-) n.; ~**phobia,** (Path.) dread of light; ~**se'nsitive,** reacting chemically etc. to light; ~**sphere,** luminous envelope of sun or star from which its light and heat radiate; ~*sphe'ric* a.; ~**sy'nthesis,** process in which energy of sunlight is used by green plants to build up complex substances from carbon dioxide and water; ~*synthe'tic* a.; ~**tropism** (-ŏ'tr-), tendency of plant etc. to bend or turn towards or away from source of light; ~*tro'pic* a.; ~**volta'ic,** relating to production of electric current at junction of two substances exposed to light. **2.** Photography, as: ~**composi'tion,** filmsetting; ~**copier,** machine for photocopying documents; ~**copy** *n.*, & *v.t.*, (make) photograph of document for use as copy of that document; ~**ge'nic** (-jĕ'-), (1) producing or emitting light, (2) apt to be a good subject for photographs; ~**gram,** photograph; ~**gra'mmetry,** use of photography for surveying; ~**li'tho** (colloq.), ~**litho'graphy,** lithography with plates made photographically; ~**mi'crograph,** photograph of object enlarged by microscope; ~*micro'graphy* n.; ~**-o'ffset,** offset printing with plates made photographically; ~**setting,** filmsetting; ~**stat** (*P; *n.*, & *v.t.*) = *photocopy*. [f. Gk *phōs phōtos* light, or f. as prec.]
phō'tograph (-ahf) *n.*, & *v.t.* **1.** *n.* Picture taken by means of chemical action of light or other radiation on sensitive film. **2.** *v.t.* Take photograph of (person etc., or abs.). **3.** Hence **photŏ'graph**ER[1], **photŏ'graph**Y[1], *ns.*, **phōto**GRA'PHIC *a.* [f. PHOTO- + -GRAPH]
phōtogravūr'e *n.* Picture produced from photographic negative transferred to metal plate and etched in; this process. [F (as PHOTO-, *gravure* engraving)]
phō'tŏn *n.* Quantum of electromagnetic radiation energy, proportional to frequency of radiation. [f. Gk *phōs phōtos* light, after *electron*; see -ON]
phrā'sal (-z-) *a.* (Gram.) Consisting of a phrase; ~ **verb,** idiomatic phrase of verb and adverb (and preposition) (*break down, look forward to*). [f. foll. + -AL]

phrāse (-z) *n.*, & *v.t.* **1.** *n.* Mode of expression, diction, (*felicity of phrase*; *in Eliot's phrase, 'not with a bang but a whimper'*); an idiomatic expression; small group of words usu. without predicate, esp. preposition with the word(s) it governs, equivalent to adjective, adverb, or noun (e.g. the house *on the hill*, I refuse *to do it*); short pithy expression; (Mus.) short and more or less distinct passage of about four bars ending in cadence, forming part of longer passage or of whole piece; **~-book** (listing frequent expressions with equivalents in foreign language, for use by tourists etc.). **2.** *v.t.* Express in words; divide (music) into phrases, esp. in performance, whence **phrā'sING**[1] (-z-) *n.* [f. earlier *phrasis*, f. L f. Gk (*phrazō* declare, tell)]

phrā'sėogrăm (-z-) *n.* Written symbol representing a phrase, esp. in shorthand. [f. as prec. + -O- + -GRAM]

phrā'sė|ŏlogy̆ (-z-) *n.* Choice or arrangement of words; mode of expression; hence **~olŏ'gICAL** *a.* [f. mod. L *phraseologia* f. Gk *phraseōn* gen. pl. of *phrasis* PHRASE; see -LOGY]

phrā'try̆ *n.* Unit of kinship in ancient Greece; tribal division among primitive peoples. [f. Gk *phratria* (*phratēr* clansman, cogn. w. BROTHER)]

phrėă'tĭc *a.* (Geol., of water) situated underground but reachable by wells. [f. Gk *phrear phreatos* well + -IC]

phrėnĕ't|ĭc *a.* Frantic; fanatic; hence **~ICALLY** *adv.* [ME, var. of FRENETIC]

phrĕ'nĭc *a.* (Anat.) Of the diaphragm. [f. F *phrénique* f. Gk *phrēn phrenos* diaphragm, mind; see -IC]

phrėnŏ'log|y̆ *n.* Study of external conformation of cranium as supposed index to development and position of organs belonging to the various mental faculties; hence **phrĕnolŏ'gICAL** *a.*, ~IST (3) *n.* [f. as prec. + -O- + -LOGY]

Phry̆'gĭan *a.* & *n.* **1.** *a.* Of Phrygia, ancient country in Asia Minor, or its people or language; **~ bonnet** or **cap,** ancient conical cap with top bent forwards, now identified with cap of liberty; **~ mode,** (Mus.) (1) ancient Greek MODE, reputedly warlike in character, (2) third of church modes (with E as final and C as dominant). **2.** *n.* Phrygian person or language. [f. L *Phrygianus* (*Phrygia*; see -AN)]

phthă'l|ĭc *a.* (Chem.) Derived from naphthalene; **~ic acid,** one of three isomeric dicarboxylic acids derived from benzene; hence ~ATE[1] (3) *n.* [abbr. of NAPHTHALIC]

phthĭ'sĭcal (-z-; *or* thĭ'- *or* tĭ'-) *a.* Of or having phthisis. [f. *phthisic* phthisis f. OF *tisike* f. Rom. *(*ph*)*thisica* f. L *phthisicus* a. (as foll.); see -ICAL]

phthī'sĭs (*or* thī'- *or* tī'-) *n.* Progressive wasting disease, now esp. pulmonary tuberculosis. [L f. Gk (*phthinō* to decay)]

phŭt *n.* & *adv.* **1.** *n.* Dull sound of impact, or of collapse of inflated object, etc. **2.** *adv.* **Go ~,** (colloq.) collapse (lit. or fig.). [f. Hindi *phaṭnā* to burst]

phy̆lă'ctery̆ *n.* Small leather box containing Hebrew texts on vellum, worn by Jews at morning weekday prayer to remind them to keep the law (**make broad the ~**, make a display of righteousness); (usu. ostentatious) religious observance; amulet, charm; fringe, border. [ME, f. OF **filaterie* f. LL f. Gk *phulaktērion* amulet (*phulassō* guard)]

phy̆lĕ'tĭc *a.* (Biol.) Of a phylum; racial. [f. Gk *phuletikos* (*phuletēs* tribesman f. *phulē* tribe; see -IC)]

phy̆'llo- *comb. form.* Leaf, as: **~phagous** (-ŏ'f-), feeding on leaves; **~pod** *a.* & *n.*, leaf-footed (crustacean); **~stome,** leaf-nosed bat; **~taxis, ~taxy,** arrangement of leaves on axis or stem. [f. Gk *phullo-* (*phullon* leaf)]

phy̆'llōde *n.* Flattened petiole resembling a leaf. [f. mod. L *phyllodium* f. Gk *phullōdēs* leaflike (as prec.)]

phy̆lloxēr'a *n.* Plant-louse of genus *Phylloxera*, esp. of species attacking vines. [mod. L, f. Gk *phullon* leaf + *xēros* dry]

phy̆lo- *comb. form.* (Biol.) Race, tribe, as: **~ge'nesis, ~geny** (-ŏ'j-), (history of) evolution of animal or plant type; *~gene'tic, ~ge'nic*, adjs. [f. Gk *phulon, phulē*]

phȳ'l|um *n.* (*pl.* **~a**). (Biol.) Major division of animal or plant kingdom, containing species having same general form. [mod. L, f. Gk *phulon* race]

phy̆'sĭc (-z-) *n.*, & *v.t.* (**-ck-**). **1.** *n.* Art of healing; medical profession; (colloq.) medicine (*a dose of physic*); **~ garden** (for cultivation of medicinal plants). **2.** *v.t.* Dose with physic (lit. or fig.). [ME, f. OF *fisique* medicine f. L f. Gk *phusikē* (*epistēmē* knowledge) of nature (*phusis*; see -IC)]

phy̆'sĭcal (-z-) *a.* **1.** Of matter, material, (*physical force*, opp. to *moral*); of, or according to the laws of, nature (*physical explanations of miracles*; *a physical impossibility*); belonging to physics; bodily (*physical examination, exercise, strength, love, beauty, education, training*). **2. ~ chemistry** (applying physics to study chemical behaviour); **~ geography** (dealing with natural features); **~ jerks,** (sl.) physical exercises; **~ science,** study of inanimate natural objects. **3.** Hence ~LY[2] *adv.* [ME, f. med. L *physicalis* f. L *physica* (as prec.; see -AL)]

phy̆sĭ'cian (-zĭ'shan) *n.* One who practises the healing art including medicine and surgery; one legally qualified in both medicine and surgery; (esp.) specialist in medical diagnosis and treatment; (fig.) healer. [ME f. OF *fisicien* (as PHYSIC; see -ICIAN)]

phy̆'sĭcĭst (-ĭ'z-) *n.* Person skilled in physics. [f. PHYSICS + -IST]

phy̆'sĭcky̆ (-z-) *a.* Suggestive of physic. [f. PHYSIC + -Y[2]]

phy̆'sĭcō- (-z-) *comb. form.* Physical, of physics, (and), as: **~-chemical,** pertaining to physics and chemistry or to physical chemistry. [f. Gk *phusikos* (see PHYSIC) + -O-]

phy̆'sĭcs (-z-) *n.* Science dealing with properties and interactions of matter and energy. [f. pl. of *physic* a. (as n.) physical, after L *physica*, Gk *phusika* natural things]

phy̆sĭŏ'cracy̆ (-z-) *n.* Government according to natural order esp. as advocated by 18th-c. economists; so **phy̆'sĭoCRAT** (-z-) *n.* [f. F *physiocratie* f. Gk *phusio-* (*phusis* nature; see -O-, -CRACY)]

phy̆sĭŏ'gnom|y̆ (-zĭŏ'n-) *n.* Art of judging character from features of face or form of body, whence ~IST (3) *n.*; cast of features, type of face; external features of country etc.; characteristic (moral or other) aspect; hence **phy̆sĭognŏ'mIC(AL)** (-zĭon-) *adjs.* [ME *fisnomie* etc. f. OF *phisonomie* f. med. L *phisonomia* f. Gk *phusiognōmonia* judging of a man's nature (by his features) (*phusis* nature, *gnōmōn* judge f. **gnō-* know)]

phy̆sĭŏ'graph|y̆ (-z-) *n.* Description of nature, of natural phenomena, or of a class of objects; physical geography; hence ~ER[1] *n.*, **phy̆sĭo-gră'phIC(AL)** (-z-) *adjs.* [f. F *physiographie* (as foll; see -GRAPHY)]

phy̆sĭolŏ'gĭc|(al) (-z-) *a.* Pertaining to physiology; **~al salt solution** (with concentration about equal to that of body fluids); hence **~alLY**[2] *adv.* [f. foll. + -IC, -ICAL]

phy̆sĭŏ'log|y̆ (-z-) *n.* Science of functions and phenomena of living organisms and their parts; these functions; hence ~IST (3) *n.* [f. F *physiologie* or f. L f. Gk *phusiologia* (*phusis* nature; see -LOGY)]

phȳsĭothĕ'rap|ȳ (-z-) *n.* Treatment of disease or injury or deformity by massage, heat, exercises, etc., not by drugs; hence ~IST (3) *n.* [f. Gk *phusio-* (as prec.) + THERAPY]

phȳsi'que (-zē'k) *n.* Bodily structure, organization, and development. [F, *n.* f. *a.* (as PHYSIC)]

-phȳte *suf.* forming *ns.* denoting a vegetable or plantlike organism (*saprophyte*, *zoophyte*); hence **-phȳ'tIC** *adj. suf.* [f. Gk *phuton* plant (*phuō* come into being)]

phȳto- *comb. form.* Plant, as: **~ge'nesis, ~geny** (-ŏ'j-), generation or evolution of plants; **~graphy** (-ŏ'g-), descriptive botany; **~mer,** structural unit in plant; **~patho'logy,** pathology of plants; **~phagous** (-ŏ'f-), feeding on plants; **~plan'kton,** plankton consisting of plants; **~tomy** (-ŏ't-), dissection of plants; **~to'xic,** poisonous to plants; **~zo'on,** zoophyte. [f. as prec. + -o-]

pī^1 *n.* Sixteenth Greek letter (Π, π) = p; (Math., π) symbol of ratio of circumference (Gk *periphereia*) of circle to diameter (approx. 3·14159); **pi-meson,** = PION. [Gk]

||**pī^2** *a.* (school etc. sl.) Pious; **pi jaw,** sermonizing, long dull moral lecture. [abbr.]

***pī^3.** See PIE^3.

pīă'cūlar *a.* Expiatory; needing expiation. [f. L *piacularis* (*piaculum* expiation f. *piare* appease; see -AR^1)]

pĭă'ffe *v.i.* (Of horse etc.) move as in trot, but slower. [f. F *piaffer* to strut]

pĭă'ffer *n.* Movement of piaffing. [f. as prec.]

pīa mā'ter *n.* (Anat.) Delicate inner membrane enveloping brain and spinal cord. [med. L, = tender mother, transl. of Arab. *al-'umm al-raḳiḳa*; cf. DURA MATER]

pi'anĭsm (pē'*a*-) *n.* Art or technique of piano-playing. [f. PIANO^2 + -ISM]

pĭanĭ'ssĭm|ō *a., adv.,* & *n.* (*pl.* **~os,** *or* **~i** *pr.* -ē). (Mus.) (Passage to be) performed very softly. [It., superl. of PIANO^1]

pi'anĭst (pē'*a*-) *n.* Player of piano; hence **pĭanĭ'stIC** *a.* [f. F *pianiste* (as PIANO^2; see -IST)]

pĭa'n|ō^1 (-ah'-) *a., adv.,* & *n.* (*pl.* **~os,** *or* **~i** *pr.* -ē). (Mus.) (passage to be) performed softly; (fig.) subdued(ly). [It., f. L *planus* flat, (of sound) soft]

pĭă'nō^2 *n.* (*pl.* **~s**). Musical instrument with metal strings struck by hammers worked by levers from a keyboard (vibration being stopped by dampers when keys are released), and with PEDAL^{1}s regulating character of tone; GRAND, UPRIGHT, *piano*; PLAYER-*piano*; **~-accordion,** accordion with melody played from small piano-like keyboard; **~ organ,** mechanical piano constructed like barrel-organ; **~-player,** (1) pianist, (2) contrivance for playing piano automatically; **~-stool** (to provide seat for player and hold esp. sheet music). [It., abbr. of foll.]

pĭănofŏr'tė *n.* (Formal name for) PIANO^2. [It., earlier *piano e forte* soft and loud, expressing its gradation of tone]

pianō'la (pē*a*-) *n.* (*P~*) make of automatic piano-player; easy task, esp. bridge hand needing no skill. [P]

piassa'va (pē*a*sah'v*a*) *n.* Stout fibre from leaf-stalks of various Amer. and Afr. palm-trees. [Port., f. Tupi *piaçába*]

pĭă'stre (-t*er*), ***pĭă'ster,** *n.* Small coin of Middle Eastern countries. [f. F *piastre* f. It. *piastra* (*d'argento*) plate (of silver), f. as PLASTER^1]

pĭă'zza (-ts*a*) *n.* Public square or market-place esp. in Italian town; *veranda of house. [It., f. as PLACE^1]

pi'brŏch (pē'brŏk; *or* -χ) *n.* Series of variations on a theme for bagpipe, esp. martial or funerary. [f. Gael. *piobaireachd* art of piping (*piobair* piper f. *piob* f. E PIPE^1)]

pī'ca^1 *n.* Unit of type-size ($\frac{1}{6}$ inch); size of letters in typewriting (10 per inch). [f. AL *pica* 15th-c. book of rules about church feasts, perh. f. as PIE^1]

pī'ca^2 *n.* (Path.) Eating of substances other than normal food. [mod. or med. L, = magpie]

pĭ'cadŏr *n.* Mounted man with lance in bull-fight. [Sp. (*picar* prick)]

pĭcarĕ'sque (-k) *a.* (Of a style of fiction) dealing with adventures of rogues. [F, f. Sp. *picaresco* (*pícaro* rogue; see -ESQUE)]

pĭcarōō'n *n.* Rogue; thief; pirate; pirate ship. [f. Sp. *picarón* (as prec.; see -OON)]

***pĭcayu'ne** (-yōō'n) *n.* & *a.* **1.** *n.* Small coin, esp. 5-cent piece; (colloq.) insignificant person or thing. **2.** *a.* (colloq.) Mean, contemptible; trifling, petty. [f. F *picaillon* Piedmontese coin, cash, f. Prov. *picaioun*, of unkn. orig.]

pĭccalĭ'llĭ *n.* Pickle of chopped vegetables, mustard, and hot spices. [18th c., perh. f. PICKLE + CHILLI]

||**pĭ'ccanĭnnȳ,** ***pĭ'ck-,** *n.* & *a.* **1.** *n.* Small Negro or Australian Aboriginal child. **2.** *a.* (arch.) Very small; baby. [W. Ind. Negro, f. Sp. *pequeño* or Port. *pequeno* little]

pĭ'ccolō *n.* (*pl.* **~s**). Small flute, sounding an octave higher than the ordinary; its player. [It., = small (flute)]

pĭchĭcĭă'gō *n.* (*pl.* **~s**). Small S. Amer. burrowing animal allied to armadillos. [f. Sp. *pichiciego* perh. f. Guarani *pichey* armadillo + Sp. *ciego* blind f. L *caecus*]

pĭck^1 *n.* **1.** Tool consisting of iron bar usu. curved with point at one end and point or chisel-edge at other, with wooden handle passing through middle perpendicularly, used for breaking up hard ground, masonry, etc., and in quarries etc. **2.** Instrument for picking; plectrum. [ME, app. var. of PIKE^1]

pĭck^2 *v.* **1.** *v.t.* Break surface of (ground etc.) with or as with pick; make (HOLE^1*s* etc.) thus. **2.** Probe (teeth with toothpick, nostril with finger, etc.) to remove extraneous or unwanted matter; *pluck strings of (banjo etc.). **3.** Clear (BONE^1, carcass) of adherent flesh; detach (flower, fruit, etc.) from place where it grew. **4.** (Of bird) take up (grains etc.) in bill; (of person) eat (food, or meal, or abs.) in small bits. **5.** Select carefully (*pick* one's *words, way, steps*; *picked men*). **6.** Pull apart (*pick oakum*); **~ to pieces,** (fig.) criticize hostilely. **7.** *v.t.* & *i.* **~ and choose,** select carefully or fastidiously; ~ person's **brains,** extract his ideas or information for one's own use; **~ a lock,** open it (esp. with intent to rob) with pointed instrument, skeleton key, etc.; ~ person's **pocket,** steal its contents from him while he is wearing the garment etc.; *pick a* QUARREL^2; **~ and steal,** pilfer. **8. ~ at,** (1) = *pick on* (1), (2) eat without interest; **~ off,** pluck off, shoot (persons etc.) deliberately one by one; **~ on,** (1) nag at, find fault with, (2) select; **~ out,** take from among larger number, distinguish from surrounding objects, relieve (ground colour *in* or *with* another), make out (meaning of passage etc.), play (tune) by ear on piano etc.; **~ over,** select best from; **~ up,** lay hold of and take up from ground etc., accept responsibility for paying (bill etc.), raise (feet) clear of ground, (Golf, ellipt.) pick up one's ball esp. when conceding hole, raise one*self* after a fall etc., gain, acquire (livelihood, germ, knowledge of language, profit, tricks, information), succeed in seeing with telescope or searchlight, hearing with radio, etc., take (person, or thing overtaken) along with one, make acquaintance of (person) casually, (of police etc.) find and take into custody, regain (lost path etc., flesh, spirit), recover health, (of weather, share-prices, etc.) improve, make acquaintance *with*, (of motor engine) recover speed or accelerate quickly etc., (in games) select sides by alternate choosing; **~-up** *n.*, picking up, person met casually, small open motor truck, part of record-player carrying stylus, detector of vibrations etc. **9. ~'lock,** person who picks locks, instrument used for this; **~-me-up,** tonic (lit. or fig.) to relieve depression; **~'pocket,** one who steals from pockets (see sense 7); ||**~'thank,** (arch.) sycophant. **10.** Hence ~'ABLE *a.* [ME, earlier *pike*, of unkn. orig.]

pĭck³ *n.* Picking; selection; right to select (*he had first pick of their father's collection*); *the* best part *of* (**the ~ of the bunch,** the best of the lot). [f. prec.]

pĭ'ck-a-băck, *pĭ'ggy̆băck (-g-), *adv.* (Of way person or thing is carried) on shoulders or back like a bundle; on the back or top of a larger object. [16th c.; orig. unkn.]

***pĭ'ckanĭnny̆.** See PICCANINNY.

pĭ'ckăxe, *pĭ'ckăx, *n.* & *v.* **1.** *n.* = PICK¹ 1. **2.** *v.t.* Break (ground etc.) with pickaxe. **3.** *v.i.* Work with pickaxe. [ME *pikois* f. OF *picois*, rel. to PIKE¹; assim. to AXE]

pĭ'ckelhaube (-howb*e*) *n.* (Hist.) German soldier's spiked helmet. [G]

pĭ'cker *n.* In vbl senses; one who gathers or collects (*hop-picker, rag-picker*). [f. PICK² + -ER¹]

pĭ'ckerel *n.* (*pl.* ~ *or* **~s**). Young pike. [ME, dim. of PIKE³; see -REL]

pĭ'ckėt *n.* & *v.* **1.** *n.* Pointed stake or peg driven into ground to form palisade, tether horse, etc.; (Hist.) (stake with pointed top on which person stood on one foot as) form of military punishment. **2.** (Mil.) Small body of troops sent out to watch for enemy etc., or held ready in quarters, party of sentries, outpost; camp-guard doing police duty in garrison town etc. **3.** (usu. in *pl.*, or *attrib.* in ~ **line** etc.) Person stationed by trade union etc. to dissuade men from work during strike etc. **4.** *v.t.* Secure (place) with stakes; tether (animal); post (men) as pickets; beset (factory, workmen) with pickets. **5.** *v.i.* Act as picket. [f. F *piquet* pointed stake (*piquer* prick, f. *pic* PICK¹; see -ET¹)]

pĭ'ckĭng *n.* In vbl senses; (in *pl.*) gleanings, remaining scraps; (in *pl.*) perquisites, pilferings. [ME, f. PICK² + -ING¹]

pĭ'ckle *n.*, & *v.t.* **1.** *n.* Brine, vinegar, or similar liquor in which meat, fish, vegetables, etc., are preserved (ROD *in pickle*); food, esp. (in *pl.*) vegetables, preserved in pickle; acid solution for cleaning metal etc.; (colloq.) plight (*sad, sorry*, iron. *nice*, etc., *pickle*); (colloq.) mischievous child. **2.** *v.t.* Preserve in pickle; treat with pickle; (in *p.p.*, sl.) drunk. [ME *pekille, pykyl*, f. MDu., MLG *pekel*, of unkn. orig.]

Pĭckwĭ'ckĭan *a.* (joc.) (Of words or their sense) not in accordance with the usual meaning, conveniently understood so as to avoid offence etc. [f. *Pickwick* (character in Dickens's *Pickwick Papers*) + -IAN]

***pĭ'cky̆** *a.* (colloq.) Excessively fastidious. [f. PICK² + -Y²]

pĭ'cnĭc *n.*, & *v.i.* (**-ck-**). **1.** *n.* Pleasure outing including meal out of doors; (colloq.) something especially agreeable or easily accomplished (**no ~**, not an easy job). **2.** *v.i.* Take part in picnic. **3.** Hence **~ker**¹ *n.*, **~ky**² *a.* (colloq.). [f. F *pique-nique*, of unkn. orig.]

pī'cō- (*or* pē'-) *pref.* denoting factor of 10^{-12}, as ~METRE². [f. Sp. *pico* beak, peak, little bit]

pī'cot (pē'kō) *n.* Small loop of twisted thread in edging to lace etc. [F, dim. of *pic* peak, point]

pĭcotee' *n.* Carnation of which flowers have light ground with darker edging to petals. [f. F *picoté -ée* p.p. of *picoter* prick (as prec.)]

pĭ'cquėt (pĭ'kĭt). Var. of PICKET 2.

pĭ'cr|ĭc *a.* ~ **acid,** yellow very bitter substance used in dyeing and surgery, and in explosives; hence ~ATE¹ (3) *n.* [f. Gk *pikros* bitter + -IC]

Pĭct *n.* One of an ancient people in N. Britain; hence ~'ISH¹ *a.* [ME, f. LL *Picti* perh. f. *pingere pict-* paint, tattoo]

pĭ'ctograph (-ahf), **pĭ'ctogrăm,** *ns.* Pictorial symbol; primitive record consisting of these; hence **pĭctogră'phic** *a.*, **pĭctŏ'graphy**¹ *n.* [f. L *pingere pict-* paint + -O- + -GRAPH, -GRAM]

pĭctōr'ĭal *a.* & *n.* **1.** *a.* Of, or expressed in, picture(s); illustrated; picturesque; hence ~LY² *adv.* **2.** *n.* Journal, postage stamp, etc., with picture(s) as main feature. [f. LL *pictorius* f. L *pictor* painter (as foll.) + -AL]

pĭ'cture *n.*, & *v.t.* **1.** *n.* Painting or drawing of person(s) or object(s) esp. as work of art; portrait; beautiful object (*her hat is a picture*). **2.** Scene, total visual or mental impression produced, (fig.) conjuncture or affair (**in the ~,** fully informed or noticed; **out of the ~,** irrelevant); *she looks* **the very picture** (a perfect example) *of health, of misery*. **3.** = FILM 3; visible presentation of this; image on television screen; ||(in *pl.*) cinema (performance). **4. ~-book** (consisting chiefly or wholly of pictures); **~-card,** court-card; **~-gallery,** (hall etc. containing) collection of pictures; **~-goer,** one who frequents the cinema; ~ **hat,** lady's wide-brimmed and highly decorated hat as in pictures by Reynolds and Gainsborough; *picture*-MOULDING; ||**~-palace,** cinema; ~ **postcard** (with picture on one side); ||**~-theatre,** cinema; ~ **window,** large window facing attractive view; **~-writing,** mode of recording events etc. by pictures as in early hieroglyphs etc. **5.** *v.t.* Represent in picture; describe graphically; imagine (*to oneself*). [ME, f. L *pictura* (*pingere pict-* paint; see -URE)]

pĭcturĕ'sque (-kch*e*rĕ'sk) *a.* Like, or fit to be the subject of, a striking picture; (of language etc.) strikingly graphic, vivid; hence ~LY² *adv.*, ~NESS *n.* [f. F *pittoresque* f. It. *pittoresco* (*pittore* painter f. L as PICTORIAL; see -ESQUE); assim. to prec.]

pĭ'cturize, -ise, (pĭ'kch*e*rīz) *v.t.* Make into picture, esp. into cinema film. [f. PICTURE + -IZE]

pĭ'cul *n.* Chinese weight (133⅓ lb.). [f. Malay *pikul* man's load]

pĭ'ddl|e *v.i.* **1.** Work or act in trifling way; hence ~ING² *a.*, (colloq.) trifling, trivial. **2.** (colloq. or childish). Urinate. [in sense 1 perh. f. PEDDLE, in sense 2 prob. f. PISS + PUDDLE¹]

pĭ'ddock *n.* Bivalve mollusc of genus *Pholas* used for bait. [18th c.; orig. unkn.]

pĭ'dgĭn, pĭ'geon² (-jĭn *or* -jon), *a.* & *n.* **1.** *a.* ~ **English,** jargon chiefly of English words used between Chinese and Europeans. **2.** *n.* Simplified English or other language used for communication between persons of different nationality etc.; (colloq.) (a person's) business, job, or particular concern. [corrupt. of *business*]

pī'-dŏg. See PYE-DOG.

pīe¹ *n.* Magpie; other bird (||RAIN¹-*pie*, SEA *pie*); pied animal. [ME f. OF, f. L *pica*]

pīe² *n.* **1.** Dish of meat, fish, fruit, etc., enclosed in or covered with paste etc. and baked (*easy, nice*, etc., **as ~,** very easy etc.; **have a finger in the ~,** be (esp. officiously) concerned in the matter; **~ in the sky,** prospect of future happiness after present suffering); similar object (MUD *pie*). **2.** ~ **chart** (representing relative quantities by areas of sectors of circle); **~'crust,** baked paste of pie; (*promises are*) *like* **~***crust*, made to be broken; ~*crust table* (with ornamental edge like piecrust); **~-eyed,** (sl.) drunk; **~'man,** vendor of pies. [ME, perh. = prec., f. miscellaneous contents compared to objects collected by magpie]

pie[3], ***pī**[3], *n.*, & *v.t.* **1.** *n.* Confused mass of printers' type; (fig.) chaos. **2.** *v.t.* Mix (type). [perh. transl. F PÂTÉ = prec.]

pīe'bald (pī'bawld) *a.* & *n.* **1.** *a.* (Usu. of animal, esp. horse) of two colours irregularly arranged, esp. black and white; (fig.) motley, mongrel. **2.** *n.* Piebald animal. [f. PIE[1] + BALD]

piece[1] *n.* **1.** One of the distinct portions of which thing is composed or into which it is divided or broken (**in one ~**, unbroken, (fig.) unharmed; **in ~s,** broken; **break to ~s,** break into fragments; **go to ~s,** (fig.) collapse; PICK[2], PULL[1], etc., *to pieces*); one of the things of which a set is composed (*piece of furniture*; *21-piece tea-set*; *five-piece band*). **2.** Enclosed portion *of* (land); **~ of water,** small lake etc. **3.** Detached portion (*of* a substance); *a piece of* one's MIND[1]. **4.** Definite quantity (e.g. of wallpaper = 12 yds.) in which thing is made up for sale etc. **5. ~ of work,** thing made by working (lit. or fig.; NASTY *piece of work*). **6.** Example, specimen, (*a piece of impudence*; *fine piece of painting, cricket*, etc.); item (*piece of news*); (derog.) person, esp. woman; *piece of* GOODS. **7.** Firearm; artillery weapon. **8.** Man (esp. other than pawn) at chess; man at draughts etc. **9.** Coin (*penny, ten-cent, piece*); **~ of eight** (i.e. REAL[1]s), Spanish dollar. **10.** Picture; literary or musical composition, usu. short; drama. **11.** *Paid* **by the ~** (according to amount done); **of a ~,** uniform, consistent, in keeping (*with*); **say** one's ~, (fig.) give one's opinion, make prepared statement. **12. ~-goods,** textile fabrics (esp. Lancashire cotton goods) woven in standard lengths; **~-rates, ~-work,** (paid by the piece). [ME f. AF *pece*, OF *piece* f. Rom. **pettia*, prob. of Gaulish orig.; cf. PEAT[1]]

piece[2] *v.t.* Put together, form into a whole; join threads in spinning, whence **pie'**CER[1] *n.*; eke *out*; make *out* (story, theory, chain of evidence) by combination of parts; join *together*; patch *up*. [ME, f. prec.]

pièce de résistance (pēās de rāzē'stahṅs) *n.* (*pl.* ***pièces pr.*** same). Most substantial dish at meal; most important or remarkable item. [F]

pie'cemeal (-sm-) *adv.* & *a.* **1.** *adv.* Piece by piece, part at a time. **2.** *a.* Done etc. piecemeal. [ME, f. PIECE[1] + *-meal* f. OE *mǣlum* (instr. dat. pl. of *mǣl* MEAL[2])]

pīed (pīd) *a.* Particoloured: **Pied Piper,** delusive enticer [f. Browning's poem]. [ME, f. PIE[1] + -ED[2], orig. of friars]

pied-à-terre (pyādahtār') *n.* (*pl.* ***pieds-à-terre pr.*** same). Place kept available as temporary quarters when needed. [F, lit. 'foot to earth']

pie'dmŏnt *n.* Region at foot of mountains. [f. *P~* in Italy, region at foot of Alps]

pie-dog. See PYE-DOG.

pier *n.* Breakwater, mole; structure of iron or wood open below running out into sea and used as promenade and landing-stage; support of arch or of span of bridge, pillar; solid masonry between windows etc.; **~-glass,** large mirror (orig. used to fill up this). [ME *per*, f. AL *pera*, of unkn. orig.]

pierce *v.* **1.** *v.t.* (Of sharp instrument etc., or fig. of cold, pain, grief, glance, discernment, discerning person, shriek, etc.) penetrate; prick (substance *with* pin etc.); make hole in (cask, ear-lobe for ear-ring, etc.); force one's way through or into. **2.** *v.i.* Penetrate *through, into*, etc. [ME, f. OF *percer*, f. Rom. **pertusiare* f. L PER(*tundere tus-* thrust) bore through]

Pīēr'ian (*or* -ĕ'rĭ-) *a.* (Of Pieria in N. Thessaly, reputed home) of the Muses. [f. L *Pierius* + -AN]

pier'rōt (pēr'ō) *n.* (*fem.* **pierre'tte**). French pantomime character; itinerant minstrel with whitened face and loose white dress. [F, dim. of *Pierre* PETER[1]]

pietà (pyātah') *n.* Picture or sculpture of Virgin Mary holding dead body of Christ on her lap. [It., f. L (as PIETY)]

pietas (pī'etahs) *n.* Respect due to ancestor, forerunner, etc. [L; see PIETY]

pī'et|ism *n.* Spener's movement for revival of piety in Lutheran Church in 17th c.; pious sentiment; exaggeration or affectation of this; so ~IST (2) *n.*, **~ĭ'stic**(AL) *adjs.* [f. G *pietismus* (as PIETY; see -ISM)]

pī'etў *n.* Quality of being pious; act etc. showing this. [ME, f. OF *pieté* f. L *pietas -tatis* dutifulness (as PIOUS; see -TY[1]); cf. PITY]

pīēzō|-ėlĕ'ctrĭc *a.* Becoming electrically polarized under pressure; so ~-ELECTRI'CITY *n.* [f. Gk *piezō* press + -O- + ELECTRIC]

pīėzŏ'mėter *n.* Instrument for measuring magnitude or direction of pressure. [f. as prec. + -METER]

pĭ'ffl|e *v.i.*, & *n.* (sl.) **1.** *v.i.* Talk or act feebly, trifle; hence ~ER[1] *n.*, ~ING[2] *a.*, trivial, worthless. **2.** *n.* Nonsense; empty discourse. [imit.]

pĭg *n.* & *v.* (**-gg-**). **1.** *n.* Non-ruminant omnivorous ungulate bristly mammal of family Suidae; *young pig; flesh of (usu. young or sucking) domesticated pig as food, esp. *roast pig*; (esp. in *comb.*) similar animal (GUINEA-*pig*); **in ~,** (of sow) pregnant. **2.** (colloq.) Greedy, dirty, sulky, obstinate, or annoying person, whence ~'GISH[1] *a.* (-g-); (sl., derog.) policeman; **make a ~ of** oneself, overeat etc. **3.** Oblong mass of metal (esp. iron or lead) from smelting-furnace. **4. Bleed like a (stuck) ~** (copiously); **buy a ~ in a poke,** buy thing without seeing it or knowing its value; **~s might fly,** (iron.) that is unlikely. **5. ~'headed,** obstinate; **~-iron,** crude iron from smelting-furnace; **~-jump** *n.*, & *v.i.*, (Austral. sl., of horse) jump sportively from all four legs; **~ Latin,** made-up jargon; **||~-meat,** pork, ham, or bacon; **~'nut,** = EARTH[1]-*nut* (1); ***~'pen,** = STY[1]; **~'skin,** (leather made of) pig's skin, *a football; **~-sticker,** long sharp knife; **~'sticking,** hunting of wild boar with spear on horseback, butchering of pigs; **~'sty,** = STY[1]; **in a ~'s eye,** (sl.) certainly not; **~'s wash, ~'swill, ~'wash,** swill of brewery or kitchen given to pigs; **~'weed,** herb (esp. of genus *Amaranthus*) eaten by pigs. **6.** Hence ~'LET, ~'LING[1], *ns.*, ~'LIKE *a.* **7.** *v.t.* (Of sow) bring forth (piglets, or abs.); **~ it,** live in disorderly or untidy fashion. **8.** *v.i.* Herd together like pigs; behave like pig. [ME *pigge*, f. OE **picga*, **pigga*; cf. *dog, frog*]

pĭ'geon[1] (-jĭn *or* -jon) *n.* **1.** Bird of family Columbidae, esp. variety of *Columba livia*, wild or domesticated, produced by breeding, trained to carry missives, etc., dove; **carrier ~,** HOMING *pigeon*, (trained to carry home messages tied to its neck or leg, or to fly home quickly from a distance). **2.** Simpleton, person easily swindled. **3. Clay ~,** clay saucer thrown into air from trap as mark for shooting; **~-breast,** deformed human chest laterally constricted; **~ hawk,** sparrow-hawk; **~-hearted,** cowardly; **~-hole,** (*n.*) small recess for pigeon to nest in, one of set of compartments for papers etc. in cabinet etc., (*v.t.*) deposit (document) in this, put aside (matter) for future consideration or neglect, assign (thing) to definite place in memory; **||~ pair,** (1) boy and girl twins, (2) boy and girl as sole children; **~'s milk,** partly-digested food with which pigeons feed their young, ||imaginary article for which children are sent on fool's errand; **~-toed,** having the toes turned inwards. **4.** Hence ~RY (3) *n.* [ME, f. OF *pijon* f. Rom. **pibio* f. LL *pipio -onis* (**pip-*, imit.)]

pigeon². See PIDGIN.

pĭ'ggerў (-g-) *n.* Pig-breeding establishment; = STY¹; piggishness. [f. PIG + -ERY]

pĭ'ggў¹, pĭ'ggie, (-gĭ) *n.* Little pig; ||game of tipcat; ***~back,** = PICK-A-BACK; **~ bank,** pig-shaped hollow pot for saving money in. [f. PIG + -Y³]

pĭ'ggў² (-gĭ) *a.* Like (that of) a pig. [f. PIG + -Y²]

pĭ'gment *n.*, & *v.t.* **1.** *n.* Colouring-matter used as paint or dye, usu. as insoluble suspension; natural colouring-matter of animal or plant tissue; hence ~AL (-ĕ'n-), ~ARY¹, *adjs.*, ~A'TION *n.*, (esp.) excessive colouring of tissue by deposition of pigment. **2.** *v.t.* Colour (as) with pigment. [ME, f. L *pigmentum* (**pig-* root of *pingere* paint; see -MENT)]

pĭ'gmў. See PYGMY.

pĭ'gtail *n.* Tobacco twisted into thin roll; plait of hair hanging from back of head, esp. as worn by Chinese under the Manchus, by young girls, and formerly by soldiers and sailors; hence ~ED² (-ld) *a.* [f. PIG + TAIL¹, w. ref. to shape]

pī'ka *n.* Small mammal of family Ochotonidae, akin to rabbit but small-eared. [f. Tungus *piika*]

pīke¹ *n.*, & *v.t.* **1.** *n.* (Hist.) Long wooden shaft with pointed steel or iron head, infantry weapon superseded by the bayonet. **2.** [perh. diff. wd, of Norse orig.] ||Peaked top of hill (esp. in names of hills in Lake District). **3.** *v.t.* Thrust through or kill with pike. [OE *pīc* point, prick]

pīke² *n.* Toll-bar; toll; turnpike road; **~'man,** keeper of turnpike. [abbr. of TURN¹*pike*]

pīke³ *n.* (*pl.* same). Large voracious freshwater fish (*Esox lucius*) with long narrow snout; other fish of same family; **~-perch,** pikelike perch of genus *Lucioperca* or *Stizostedion.* [ME, = PIKE¹, f. its pointed jaw]

pīke⁴ *v.i.* (colloq.) **~ on,** withdraw timidly from; hence **pī'KER¹** *n.*, cautious or timid or mean person. [ME, perh. f. PIKE¹]

pī'kelėt (-kl-) *n.* Small round teacake. [f. W. (*bara*) *pyglyd* pitchy (bread)]

pī'kestaff (-kstahf) *n.* Wooden shaft of pike; walking-stick with metal point; **plain as a ~** [orig. *packstaff*, smooth staff used by pedlar], quite plain or obvious. [f. PIKE¹ + STAFF¹]

pĭlă'ff *n.* Oriental dish of rice or wheat with meat, spices, etc. [f. Turk. *pilâv*]

pĭlă'ster *n.* Rectangular column, esp. one engaged in wall. [f. F *pilastre* f. It. *pilastro* f. med. L *pilastrum* f. L *pila* pillar]

pĭlau', pĭlaw'. Vars. of PILAFF.

pĭlch *n.* Infant's garment or wrapper worn over napkin. [OE *pyl(e)ce*, **pilece* f. LL *pellicia*; see PELISSE]

pĭ'lchard *n.* Small sea-fish (*Sardinia pilchardus*) allied to herring. [16th c. *pilcher* etc., of unkn. orig.]

pīle¹ *n.*, & *v.t.* **1.** *n.* Pointed stake or post; heavy beam driven vertically into bed of river, soft ground, etc. as support for bridge etc.; (Her.) wedge-shaped charge; **~-driver,** machine for driving piles into ground; **~-dwelling,** dwelling built on piles esp. in lake. **2.** *v.t.* Furnish with piles; drive piles into. [OE *pīl*, = OHG *pfīl*, f. L *pilum* javelin]

pīle² *n.* **1.** Heap of things laid more or less regularly upon one another; =FUNERAL *pile*; (colloq.) large quantity; (colloq.) heap of money, fortune, (*make a pile*; **make** one's **~,** amass as much money as one wants). **2.** Lofty mass of buildings. **3.** Series of plates of dissimilar metals laid one upon another alternately for producing electric current; (**atomic**) **~,** nuclear REACTOR. [ME f. OF, f. L *pila* pillar, pier, mole]

pīle³ *v.* **1.** *v.t.* **~** (**up, on**), heap up; load (table etc. *with*); **~ arms,** place (usu. four) rifles with butts on ground and muzzles supporting one another; **~ on the agony,** (colloq.) intensify painful description etc.; **~ it on,** exaggerate; **~ up,** run (ship) on rocks or aground, cause (vehicle or aircraft) to crash; **~-up** *n.*, collision of several motor vehicles. **2.** *v.i.* Crowd *in, into*, or *on* vehicle, *out of* place, etc.; **~ up,** accumulate. [f. prec.]

||**pīle⁴** *n.* (arch.) Reverse of coin; **cross or ~,** heads or tails. [ME, as PILE², orig. = lower die of minting apparatus]

pīle⁵ *n.* Soft hair, down, wool of sheep; soft surface on cloth, esp. on velvet, plush, etc., or on carpet. [ME, prob. f. AF *pyle, peile*, OF *poil* f. L *pilus* hair]

pīle⁶ *n.* Haemorrhoid; **~'wort,** lesser celandine (from reputed efficacy against piles). [ME, prob. f. L *pila* ball, f. globular form of external pile]

pī'lė|us *n.* (*pl.* **~i** *pr.* -ī). (Bot.) Caplike part of mushroom or other fungus; hence ~ATE² *a.* [L, = felt cap]

pĭ'lfer *v.t.* Steal (thing, or abs.) esp. in small quantities; hence ~AGE (3), ~ER¹, *ns.* [ME, f. AF & OF *pelfrer* pillage, of unkn. orig.; assoc. w. PILL²; cf. PELF]

pĭlgâr'lĭc *n.* (arch.) Bald head; bald-headed man; poor creature. [=*pilled* or *peeled garlic*]

pĭ'lgrĭm *n.*, & *v.i.* **1.** *n.* One who journeys to sacred place as act of religious devotion; person regarded as journeying to a future life (*The Pilgrim's Progress*); traveller; **P~ Fathers,** English Puritans who founded colony of Plymouth, Massachusetts, in 1620; hence ~IZE (2) *v.i.* **2.** *v.i.* Wander like pilgrim. [ME *pilegrim* f. Prov. *pelegrin* f. L *peregrinus* stranger; see PEREGRINE]

pĭ'lgrĭmage *n.*, & *v.i.* **1.** *n.* Pilgrim's journey, esp. *go on* (*a*) *pilgrimage*; (fig.) mortal life viewed as a journey. **2.** *v.i.* Go on a pilgrimage. [ME, f. Prov. *pilgrinatge* (as prec.; see -AGE)]

pĭlĭ'ferous *a.* (esp. Bot.) having hair; so **pĭ'lĭ**FORM *a.* [f. L *pilus* hair + -I- + -FEROUS]

pĭll¹ *n.* **1.** Small ball or flat round piece of medicinal substance for swallowing whole (**the ~,** oral contraceptive; GILD¹ *the pill*); (fig.) something that has to be done willy-nilly, a humiliation etc., (*swallow* or *sweeten the pill, a bitter pill*, etc.); **~'box,** shallow cylindrical box for holding pills, hat of similar shape, (Mil.) small isolated chiefly underground concrete fort; **~'wort,** fern with small globular involucres. **2.** (sl. or joc.) Ball, e.g. cannon-ball, tennis-ball, ||(in *pl.*) billiards. [f. MDu., MLG *pille* prob. f. L *pilula* dim. of *pila* ball]

||**pĭll²** *v.t.* (arch.) Pillage, plunder; (arch. or dial.) = PEEL³. [ME *pile, pyle*, perh. f. OE **pilian, pylan* f. L *pilare* (*pilus* hair), infl. by F *piller* plunder; in sense 'remove the bark etc. from', different. as PEEL³]

pĭ'llag|e *n.*, & *v.t.* **1.** *n.* Plundering, esp. as practised in war. **2.** *v.t.* Sack, plunder, (place, person, or abs.); hence ~ER¹ (-ĭj-) *n.* [ME f. OF (*piller* plunder; see -AGE)]

pĭ'llar *n.* Vertical structure of stone, wood, metal, etc., slender in proportion to height, used as support or ornament; post supporting a structure; (fig.) person who is a main supporter (*a pillar of the faith*); upright mass of air, water, rock, etc.; (Mining) solid mass of coal etc. left to support roof of the working; *Pillars of* HERCULES; **from ~ to post,** (*driven* etc.) to and fro, from one resource to another; ||**~-box,**

hollow pillar about 5 ft. high in which letters may be posted (~*-box red*, bright red colour of this); hence ~ED² (-*erd*) *a.*, ~ET¹ *n.* [ME & AF *piler*, OF *pilier* f. Rom. **pilare* f. L *pila* pillar; see -AR¹]

pĭ′llion (-lyon) *n.* Seating for passenger behind motor-cyclist etc. (**ride** ~, be such passenger); (Hist.) woman's light saddle, cushion attached to hinder part of saddle for second rider, usu. woman. [f. Gael. *pillean*, *pillin* dim. of *pell* cushion f. L *pellis* skin]

pĭ′llĭwĭnks *n.* (Hist.) Instrument of torture for squeezing fingers. [ME *pyrwykes*, *pyrewinkes*, of unkn. orig.]

pĭ′llorў *n.*, & *v.t.* **1.** *n.* (Hist.) Wooden framework with holes for head and hands of offender exposed to public ridicule etc. **2.** *v.t.* Put in the pillory; (fig.) expose to ridicule. [ME, f. AL *pillorium* f. OF *pilori* etc., prob. f. Prov. *espilori*, of uncert. orig.]

pĭ′llow (-ō) *n.*, & *v.t.* **1.** *n.* Cushion of linen etc. stuffed with feathers etc. as (usu. oblong) support for head in reclining esp. in bed (**take counsel of** one's ~, not decide until next day); pillow-shaped block or support. **2.** **~case, ~slip,** washable case of linen etc. for pillow; **~-fight,** children's mock fight with pillows in bedroom; **~-lace** (made on padded support); **~ lava** (forming rounded masses); hence ~Y² *a.* **3.** *v.t.* Rest, or prop up, on pillow(s). [OE **pylw*- st. of *pyle*, *pylu*, = OHG *pfuliwī*, *pfulwo* f. WG **pulwī(n)* f. L *pulvinus* cushion]

pĭ′llūle. See PILULE.

pī′lōse, pī′lous, *adjs.* Covered with hair; so **pilŏ′**SITY *n.* [f. L *pilosus* (*pilus* hair; see -OSE¹)]

pī′lot *n.*, *a.*, & *v.t.* **1.** *n.* Person qualified to take charge of ships entering or leaving a harbour (**drop the** ~, (fig.) dismiss trusted adviser); person who operates the flying controls of an aircraft; *cowcatcher; (fig.) guide; (arch.) steersman. **2.** **~ balloon,** small balloon whose movements are observed as it rises in the air, used to ascertain direction and velocity of currents at various heights; **~-bird,** rare dark-brown Austral. babbler with distinctive loud cry; **~ chute,** small parachute serving to bring main one into operation; **~-cloth,** thick blue woollen cloth for seamen's coats etc.; **~ engine** (clearing the way for another and testing the safety of the permanent way); **~-fish,** small fish said to act as pilot to food for shark; **~-house,** = WHEEL¹-*house*; **~-jacket,** = PEA-JACKET; **~-light,** (1) small gas-burner kept alight to light another, (2) electric indicator light or control light; ||**~ officer,** lowest commissioned rank in R.A.F.; hence or cogn. ~AGE (3, 4) *n.*, ~LESS *a.* **3.** *a.* Experimental, small-scale, (*pilot plant*, *scheme*). **4.** *v.t.* Conduct as pilot (lit. or fig.); act as pilot on (way, piece of water); act as pilot of (aircraft). [f. F *pilote* f. med. L *pilotus*, *pedot(t)a* f. med. Gk **pēdōtēs* f. Gk *pēdon* oar]

Pĭ′ls(e)ner (*or* -z-) *n.* Lager beer (like that) brewed at *Pilsen* (Plzeň) in Czechoslovakia.

pĭ′lūle, pĭ′llūle, *n.* Pill; small pill; hence **pĭ′lūl**AR¹, **pĭ′lūl**OUS, *adjs.* [F, f. L *pilula* (see PILL¹)]

pĭmĕ′ntō *n.* (*pl.* ~s). Allspice (tree); pimiento. [f. Sp. *pimiento* (as foll.)]

pĭmiĕ′ntō *n.* (*pl.* ~s). Sweet pepper. [Sp., f. L *pigmentum* PIGMENT, in med. L = spice]

pĭmp *n.*, & *v.i.* (Act as) one who solicits clients for prostitute or brothel, pander; ponce. [17th c., of unkn. orig.]

pĭ′mpernĕl *n.* (**Scarlet**) ~, small annual plant found in cornfields and on waste ground, with scarlet (or blue or white) flowers closing in cloudy or rainy weather. [ME, f. OF *pimpernelle*, *piprenelle* f. Rom. **piperinella* (**piperinus* pepper-like f. L *piper* PEPPER¹)]

pĭ′mpĭng *a.* Small, mean; sickly. [17th c., of unkn. orig.]

pĭ′mpl|e *n.* Small hard inflamed spot on skin; similar slight swelling on a surface; hence ~ED² (-*peld*), ~Y², *adjs.* [ME, nasalized f. OE *piplian* break out in pustules]

pĭn¹ *n.* **1.** Thin usu. cylindrical piece of (usu. tinned brass or iron) wire with sharp point and round broadened head for fastening together parts of dress, papers, etc.; thing of small value (*don't care a pin*; *for two pins I'd resign*). **2.** Peg of wood or metal for various purposes (**split** ~, metal cotter to be passed through hole and held there by the gaping of its split end); (Golf) stick with flag placed in hole to mark its position (**~-high,** (of ball) at same distance ahead as pin); peg round which one string of musical instrument is fastened; BELAY*ing-pin*, ||DRAWING-*pin*, HAIR*pin*, ||NINE*pins*, ROLL²*ing-pin*, THOLE²-*pin*. **3.** (in *pl.*, colloq.) Legs (*quick on his pins*). **4.** (Chess). Pinning of man. **5.** **~s and needles,** tingling sensation in limb recovering from numbness; **on ~s and needles,** in state of mental agitation due to suspense. **6.** **~-ball,** game in which small metal balls are shot across sloping board and strike against pins etc. with lights to indicate score; **~′cushion,** small cushion for sticking pins in to keep them ready for use; **~-feather,** ungrown feather; **~-fire,** (of cartridge) exploded by means of pin attached to it; **~-head,** (fig.) minute thing, (colloq.) stupid person; **~-headed,** (colloq.) stupid; **~-hole** (made by pin or into which peg fits); *~-hole camera* (with pin-hole aperture and no lens); **~-money,** annual allowance to woman for dress expenses etc., allowance settled on wife, or money earned by her, for private expenditure; **~-point,** (*n.*) point of pin, (fig.) something very small or sharp, (*a.*, of target) small and requiring very accurate and precise bombing and shelling, (*v.t.*) locate with high precision, designate precisely; **~′prick,** (fig.) trifling irritation; **~-stripe,** very narrow stripe in cloth; **~-table,** table used in playing pin-ball; **~′tail,** duck or grouse with pointed tail; **~-tuck,** very narrow ornamental tuck; **~-wheel,** small Catherine wheel; **~-worm,** small intestinal nematode worm of which female has pointed tail. [OE *pinn*, = MDu., MLG *pinne*, OHG *pfinn*, Icel. *pinni* f. L *pinna* point etc., assoc. w. *penna* PEN³]

pĭn² *v.t.* (-nn-). Fasten (thing *to* another, *up*, etc., things *together*) with pin(s); (fig.) fix blame or responsibility for deed *on* (person); transfix with pin, lance, etc.; ~ one's **faith** or **hopes** (rely implicitly) *on* or *to* (person etc.); seize and hold fast (*against* wall etc.); (Chess) prevent (opposing man) from moving except by exposing more valuable opposing man to capture; **~ down,** bind (person etc.) *to* (promise, arrangement), force (person) to declare his intentions, restrict actions of (enemy etc.), specify (thing) precisely; **~-up** *n.*, (colloq.) picture of attractive or famous person, pinned up on wall etc., such person. [ME, f. prec.]

pĭ′nafōre *n.* Child's or woman's washable covering worn over dress etc. to protect it from dirt; **~ dress** (without collar and sleeves, for wearing over blouse or jumper). [f. PIN² + AFORE (orig. pinned on front of dress)]

pĭnă′ster *n.* = CLUSTER *pine*. [L, = wild pine (*pinus* PINE¹; see -ASTER)]

pince-nez (pă′ńsnā) *n.* (*pl.* same). Pair of eyeglasses with spring to clip nose. [F, lit. = pinch-nose]

pĭ′ncer|s (-z) *n. pl.* (**Pair of**) **~s,** gripping-tool made of two limbs pivoted together forming pair of jaws with pair of handles to press them together with; similar organ of crustaceans etc.; ~ **movement,** (Mil.) converging movement against enemy position. [ME *pinsers, pinsours,* f. AF f. OF *pincier* PINCH²]

pincĕ'tte (pănsĕ't) *n.* Small pincers, tweezers. [F]

pĭnch¹ *n.* **1.** Pinching, squeezing; (fig.) stress (*of* poverty etc.; *feel the pinch*); **at** or **in a ~,** in an emergency, if necessary; ***~-hitter,** baseball player who bats instead of another in emergency, (fig.) person acting as substitute. **2.** As much as can be taken up with tips of finger and thumb (*a pinch of snuff, of* SALT). [ME, f. foll.]

pĭnch² *v.* **1.** *v.t.* Grip tightly between two surfaces, esp. between tips of finger and thumb, (lit., or fig. of cold, hunger, etc., esp. *pinched with cold*; **where the shoe ~es,** where one's difficulty or trouble is); (Hort.) shorten *back* or *down* by pinching; stint (person etc. *in, of, for,* food etc.); (sl.) steal (thing), rob (person), arrest. **2.** *v.i.* Be niggardly; sail (purposely or not) too close to wind. [ME, f. AF & ONF **pinchier* = OF *pincier,* f. Rom. **pinctiare,* **punctiare* f. L *pungere punct-* prick]

pĭ'nchbĕck *n.* & *a.* **1.** *n.* Goldlike alloy of copper and zinc used in cheap jewellery etc. **2.** *a.* Counterfeit, sham. [f. C. *Pinchbeck,* Engl. watchmaker d. 1732]

Pĭndă'rĭc *a.* & *n.* **1.** *a.* Of, or supposedly like the style of, the Greek poet Pindar. **2.** *n.* (usu. in *pl.*) Pindaric ode, metre, or verse. [f. L f. Gk *Pindarikos* (*Pindaros* Pindar; see -IC)]

pīne¹ *n.* **1.** Tree of genus *Pinus* with evergreen needle-shaped leaves growing in sheathed clusters of two or more (cf. FIR), many species of which afford timber, tar, and turpentine; its wood; =*pineapple*; **Chile ~,** monkey-puzzle; hence **pī'nERY** (3) *n.* **2.** **~'apple,** (large juicy edible collective fruit of) stiff-leaved tropical plant (*Ananas comosus*) [from fruit's resemblance to pine-cone], (sl.) hand-grenade; **~-beauty, ~ carpet,** moths whose larvae feed on pine-trees; **~-cone,** fruit of the pine; **~ marten,** dark-brown European or Amer. marten. [ME, f. OE *pīn* & OF *pin* f. L *pinus*]

pīne² *v.i.* Languish, waste *away,* from grief, disease, etc.; long eagerly (*for, after, to* do). [OE *pīnian,* = OHG *pīnōn,* ON *pína,* rel. to obs. E *pine* punishment, f. Gmc f. med. L *pena,* L *poena*]

pĭ'nėal *a.* (Anat.) Shaped like a pine-cone; ~ **body** or **gland,** eyelike conical gland of unknown function behind third ventricle of brain. [f. F *pinéal* f. L *pinea* PINE¹-cone; see -AL]

pīnē't|um *n.* (*pl.* **~a**). Plantation of pine-trees or other conifers. [L (*pinus* pine)]

pĭ'nfōld *n.,* & *v.t.* (Confine in) pound for stray cattle etc. [OE *pundfald* (**pund* POUND², *fald* FOLD¹)]

pĭng *n.,* & *v.i.* (Make) abrupt single ringing sound as of rifle bullet in flight, desk-bell, etc.; hence **~'ER¹** (2) *n.,* (esp.) device to ring bell after pre-set time. [imit.]

pĭ'ng-pŏng *n.* Table tennis. [***P**; imit. f. sound of bat striking ball]

pĭ'nguĭd (-nggwĭd) *a.* (usu. joc.) Fat, oily, greasy. [f. L *pinguis* fat + -ID¹]

pĭ'nguĭn (-nggwĭn) *n.* (Fruit of) tropical Amer. plant (*Bromelia pinguin*) allied to pineapple. [17th c.; orig. unkn.]

pĭ'nion¹ (-nyon) *n.* Terminal segment of bird's wing; (poet.) wing; any flight-feather of wing. [ME, f. OF *pignon* f. Rom. **pinnio -on-* augment. of L *pinna*; see PIN¹, -OON]

pĭ'nion² (-nyon) *v.t.* Cut off pinion of (wing, bird) to prevent flight; bind the arms of (person), bind (arms); bind (person etc.) fast *to* (thing). [f. prec.]

pĭ'nion³ (-nyon) *n.* Small cog-wheel engaging with larger one; cogged spindle engaging with wheel. [f. F *pignon* alt. f. obs. *pignol* f. Rom. **pineolus* f. L *pinea* PINE¹-cone]

pĭnk¹ *n.* & *a.* **1.** *n.* Garden plant of genus *Dianthus* with sweet-smelling white, pink, crimson, or variegated flowers. **2. The ~** (embodied perfection) *of elegance* etc.; **the ~** (most perfect condition) *of health* etc.; **in the ~,** (sl.) in very good health. **3.** Pale red colour slightly inclining to purple. **4.** **(Hunting-)~,** fox-hunter's red coat, cloth for this, fox-hunter. **5.** *a.* Of pale red colour of various kinds (ROSE¹-*pink,* SALMON-*pink*), whence **~'ISH¹** 2, **~'Y²,** *adjs.,* **~'LY²** *adv.,* **~'NESS** *n.*; (Polit. sl.) mildly communist. **6.** ~ **disease** (of young children, with pink discoloration of extremities); *pink* ELEPHANTS; **~-eye,** contagious fever of horse, contagious ophthalmia in man; *pink* GIN². [perh. f. obs. *pink-eyed* having small eyes]

pĭnk² *n.* Yellowish lake pigment made by combining vegetable colouring matter with a white base (*brown, French, Dutch,* etc. *pink*). [17th c.; orig. unkn.]

pĭnk³ *n.* (Hist.) Sailing-vessel, esp. with narrow stern (orig. small and flat-bottomed). [ME, f. MDu. *pin(c)ke,* of unkn. orig.]

pĭnk⁴ *v.t.* Pierce slightly with sword etc.; ~ **(out),** ornament (leather etc.) with perforations; cut scalloped or zigzag edge on; adorn, deck; **~'ing scissors** or **shears,** dressmaker's serrated shears for cutting zigzag edge. [ME perh. f. LDu.; cf. LG *pinken* strike, peck]

‖**pĭnk⁵** *n.* Young salmon; (dial.) minnow. [15th c. *penk,* of unkn. orig.]

pĭnk⁶ *v.i.* (Of vehicle engine) emit series of high-pitched explosive sounds caused by detonation of mixture following partial combustion. [imit.]

pĭ'nkĭe *n.* (U.S. & Sc.) Little finger. [cf. dial. *pink* half-shut (eye), -IE]

pĭ'nkō (*pl.* **~s**). (sl.) Politically 'pink' person. [f. PINK¹ + -O]

***Pĭ'nkster** *n.* Whitsuntide; **p~ flower,** pink azalea. [Du., = Pentecost]

pĭ'nna *n.* (*pl.* **~e**). Broad upper part of external ear; primary division of pinnate leaf; fin or fin-like structure. [L, = *penna* feather, wing, fin]

pĭ'nnace *n.* Warship's or other ship's small boat usu. motor-driven (orig. schooner-rigged or eight-oared). [f. F *pinnace, pinasse,* perh. f. Rom. **pinacea* (*navis* ship) f. L *pinus* PINE¹]

pĭ'nnacle *n.,* & *v.t.* **1.** *n.* Small ornamental turret usu. ending in pyramid or cone, crowning a buttress, roof, etc.; natural peak; (fig.) culmination, climax. **2.** *v.t.* Set (as) on pinnacle; form the pinnacle of; furnish with pinnacles. [ME *pinacle* f. OF *pin(n)acle* f. LL *pinnaculum* (*pinna* wing, point; see PIN¹, -CULE)]

pĭ'nnate *a.* (Bot., of compound leaf) with series of leaflets on each side of common petiole; (Zool.) with branches, tentacles, etc., on each side of an axis; hence or cogn. **pĭ'nnātED¹** *a.,* **~LY²** (-tlĭ) *adv.* [f. L *pinnatus* feathered (PINNA; see -ATE²)]

pĭ'nnĭ- *comb. form.* Wing, fin, as: **~grade, ~ped,** *adjs.* & *ns.,* fin-footed (animal). [f. L PINNA + -I-]

pĭ'nnūl|e *n.* (Bot.) secondary division of pinnate leaf; (Zool.) part or organ like small wing or fin; sight at end of index of astrolabe etc.; hence **~AR¹** *a.* [f. L *pinnula* dim. of PINNA; see -ULE]

pĭ'nnȳ *n.* (childish or colloq.) Pinafore. [abbr.; see -Y³]

***pĭ'nochle** (pē'nokel) *n.* Card-game with double pack of 48 cards (ace to nine only); combination of queen of spades and jack of diamonds in this game. [19th c.; orig. unkn.]

***pĭnō'lė** *n.* Flour made from parched cornflour, esp. mixed with sweet flour of mesquite beans, sugar, etc. [Amer. Sp., f. Aztec *pinolli*]

piñon (pēnyō'n) *n.* Nut-pine tree; its fruit. [Sp., f. L *pinea* PINE¹-cone]

pint *n.* Measure of capacity for liquids etc., ⅛ of gallon; ||this quantity of a liquid, esp. milk or beer; **~-pot,** (pewter) pot holding one pint; **~-sized,** (colloq.) diminutive. [ME, f. OF *pinte*, of unkn. orig.]

||**pī'nta** *n.* (colloq.) Pint of milk, beer, etc. [corrupt. of *pint of*]

pĭnta'dō (-ah'-) *n.* (*pl.* **~s**). Pigeon-sized petrel of southern seas; W. Ind. mackerel-like fish. [f. Port. *pintado* guinea-fowl, p.p. (as n.) of *pintar* f. Rom. **pinctare* (**pinctus* f. L *pictus* p.p. of *pingere* paint)]

pĭ'ntle *n.* Pin or bolt, esp. one on which some other part turns. [OE *pintel* penis, of unkn. orig.; cf. OFris. etc. *pint*]

***pĭ'ntō** (*or* pē'-) *a.* & *n.* (*pl.* **~s**). Piebald (horse). [Sp., = mottled, f. Rom. **pinctus*; see PINTADO]

pī'nў *a.* Of, like, or abounding in, pines. [f. PINE¹ + -Y²]

piolet (pyōlā') *n.* Alpinist's two-headed ice-axe. [F]

pī'ŏn *n.* (Phys.) Meson having mass about 270 times that of electron; hence **piŏ'nic** *a.* [f. PI¹ (letter used as symbol for the particle) + -ON]

pīoneer' *n.* & *v.* **1.** *n.* (Mil.) Member of infantry group serving to prepare road for main body of troops. **2.** Initiator of enterprise, original explorer, settler, etc. **3.** *v.i.* Act as pioneer. **4.** *v.t.* Open up (road etc.) as pioneer; act as pioneer to, conduct; originate (course of action etc. followed later by others). [f. F *pionnier* foot-soldier, pioneer, OF *paonier, peon(n)ier* (as PEON, -IER)]

pī'ous *a.* Devout, religious (*pious* FRAUD); hypocritically virtuous; dutiful; hence **~LY²** *adv.* [f. L *pius* dutiful, pious + -OUS]

pĭp¹ *n.* Disease of poultry, hawks, etc., marked by thick mucus in throat and often by white scale on tip of tongue; (sl.) fit of disgust, depression, or bad temper, (*he gives me the pip*). [ME, f. MDu. *pippe*, MLG *pip* f. WG **pipit* f. med. L **pip(p)ita*, prob. corrupt. of L *pituita* slime]

pĭp² *n.* Each spot on playing-cards, dice, or dominoes; ||star (1–3 acc. to rank) on shoulder of army officer's uniform; single blossom of clustered inflorescence; rhomboidal segment of surface of pineapple; image of object on radar screen. [16th c. *peep*, of unkn. orig.]

||**pĭp³** *v.* (-pp-) (colloq.) **1.** *v.t.* Blackball; hit with shot; defeat (**~ at the post,** defeat at the last moment). **2.** *v.i.* **~ out,** die. [f. prec. or foll.]

pĭp⁴ *n.*, & *v.t.* (**-pp-**). **1.** *n.* Seed of apple, pear, orange, grape, etc., whence **~'LESS** *a.*; *(sl.) excellent person or thing. **2.** *v.t.* Remove pips from (fruit). [abbr. of PIPPIN]

||**pĭp⁵** *n.* Short high-pitched sound, usu. mechanically produced (*the six pips of the time-signal*). [imit.]

pi'pa (pē'-) *n.* Toad of genus *Pipa*, female of which carries eggs and tadpoles on her back. [f. Surinam Negro *pipál* masc., *pipá* fem.]

pi'pal (pē'-) *n.* Large Indian fig-tree (*Ficus religiosa*) allied to banyan, bo-tree. [f. Hindi *pīpal* f. Skr. *pippala*]

pīpe¹ *n.* **1.** Tube of wood, metal, etc., esp. for conveying water, gas, etc. **2.** (Mus.) wind-instrument consisting of single tube, each of the tubes by which sound is produced in organ; (in *pl.*) = BAG¹*pipes*; boatswain's whistle, sounding of this. **3.** (arch.) Voice, esp. in singing; song or note of bird. **4.** Tubular organ, vessel, etc. in animal body. **5.** Cylindrical vein of ore. **6.** Cavity in cast metal. **7.** (**Tobacco-**)**~**, narrow tube of clay, wood, etc., with bowl at one end for drawing in smoke of burning tobacco; quantity of tobacco held by this (*light, smoke, a pipe*); PEACE-*pipe*; **put that in your ~ and smoke it,** consider that fact etc. and accept it if you can. **8.** Cask for wine, esp. as measure of two hogsheads, usu. = 105 gal. **9. ~'clay,** (*n.*) fine white clay used for tobacco pipes and for whitening leather etc., (*v.t.*) whiten with this, (fig.) put in order; **~-cleaner,** piece of flexible fabric-covered wire used to clean inside of tobacco-pipe; **~-dream,** groundless hope or scheme, as indulged in when smoking a pipe (orig. of opium-smoker's fantasies); **~-fish,** long slender fish of genus *Syngnatha* etc. with elongated snout; **~-light,** spill for lighting pipe; **~'line** (esp. for conveying petroleum to a distance), (fig.) channel of supply of goods, information, etc. (*in the ~line*, awaiting completion or processing); **~ major,** N.C.O. commanding regimental pipers; **~-organ,** (Mus.) organ using pipes not (only) reeds; **~-rack** (for tobacco-pipes); **~-rolls,** (Hist.) annual 12th–19th-c. records of the British Exchequer (prob. because subsidiary documents were rolled in pipe form); **~-stem,** shaft of tobacco-pipe; **~-stone,** hard red clay used by Amer. Indians for tobacco-pipes. **10.** Hence **~'FUL** 2 (-pf-) *n.*, **~'LESS** (-pl-), **pī'pY²**, *adjs.* [OE *pīpe*, = OHG *pfīfa*, ON *pípa*, f. Gmc f. Rom. **pīpa* f. L *pipare* peep, chirp]

pīpe² *v.* **1.** *v.t.* Play (tune, etc., or abs.) on pipe; lead or bring (person etc.) by sound of pipe; summon (crew *up*, *to* meal, work, etc.) by sounding whistle; whistle; utter in shrill voice; **~ down,** (Naut.) dismiss from duty; ||**~ one's eye(s),** (colloq.) weep. **2.** Propagate (pinks etc.) by cuttings taken off at joint of stem. **3.** Trim (dress etc.), ornament (cake etc.), with PIPING¹. **4.** Furnish with pipes; convey (oil, water, gas, etc.) by pipes; transmit (music, broadcast programme, etc.) by wire or cable for hearing elsewhere. **5. ~ away,** give signal for (boat) to start; **~ down,** (colloq.) be quiet, be less insistent or confident; **~ up,** begin to play, sing, speak, etc. [OE *pīpian* & OF *piper* f. L *pipare* (as prec.); in senses 2–4 f. prec.]

||**pĭp ĕ'mma** *adv.* & *n.* (colloq.) = P.M. [formerly signallers' names for letters *P.M.*]

pī'per *n.* One who plays on pipe, esp. itinerant musician; bagpipe-player; **pay the ~** (**and call the tune**), bear the cost (and have control) of a proceeding etc.; kind of gurnard whistling when caught. [OE *pīpere* (as PIPE¹, -ER¹)]

pĭpĕ'rĭdine (-ēn) *n.* (Chem.) Peppery-smelling liquid formed by reduction of pyridine. [f. L *piper* pepper + -IDE + -INE⁵]

pĭpĕ'tte *n.* Slender tube for transferring or measuring small quantities of liquids, esp. in chemistry. [F, dim. of *pipe* PIPE¹; see -ETTE]

pī'pĭng¹ *n.* In vbl senses; ornamentation of dress, upholstery, etc., usu. as edging by means of (cord enclosed in) pipelike fold; ornamental cordlike lines of sugar on cake. [f. PIPE¹,² + -ING¹]

pī'pĭng² *a.* In vbl senses; **the ~ time(s) of peace** (marked by pastoral piping as opp. to martial music); **~** (hissing or very) **hot.** [ME, f. PIPE² + -ING²]

pĭpĭstrĕ'lle *n.* Small bat of genus *Pipistrellus*. [F, f. It. *pipistrello*, *vip-*, f. L *vespertilio* bat (*vesper* evening)]

pĭ'pĭt *n.* Bird of family Motacillidae, esp. of genus *Anthus*, superficially resembling lark; MEADOW *pipit*. [prob. imit.]

pi'pkin *n.* Small earthenware pot or pan. [16th c.; orig. unkn.]
pi'ppin *n.* Apple grown from seed; red and yellow dessert apple; (sl.) excellent person or thing. [ME f. OF *pepin*, of uncert. orig.]
pi'p-squeak *n.* (sl.) Insignificant or contemptible person or thing. [imit.]
pi'qu|ant (pē'kant) *a.* Agreeably pungent, sharp, appetizing; (fig.) pleasantly stimulating, or disturbing, to the mind; hence ~ANCY *n.*, ~antLY² *adv.* [F, part. of *piquer* (as foll.; see -ANT)]
pique¹ (pēk) *v.t.*, & *n.* **1.** *v.t.* Irritate, wound the pride of; arouse (curiosity, interest); plume one*self on*. **2.** *n.* Ill-feeling, enmity, resentment, (*in a fit of pique*; *took a pique against me*). [f. F (*pique* n. f.) *piquer* v. prick, irritate, *se piquer* take offence, f. Rom. **piccare*]
pique² (pēk) *n.* & *v.* **1.** *n.* Winning of 30 points on cards and play in piquet before opponent scores anything. **2.** *v.t.* & *i.* Score pique (against). [f. F *pic*, of unkn. orig.]
pi'qué (pē'kā) *n.* Stiff ribbed cotton etc. fabric. [F, p.p. (as n.) of *piquer*; see PIQUE¹]
pĭquĕ't¹ (-kĕ't) *n.* Card game for two players with pack of 32 cards (ace to seven only). [F, of unkn. orig.]
pi'quėt² (pĭ'kĭt). Var. of PICKET 2.
pir'acy̆. See PIRATE.
pĭră'gua (-gw*a*) *n.* Long narrow canoe made from single tree-trunk; two-masted sailing--barge. [Sp. f. Carib, = dug-out]
pĭra'nha (-ah'nya), **pĭra'ya** (-ah'ya), **pėrai'** (-rī'), *n.* Voracious S. Amer. freshwater fish of genus *Serrasalmus*. [Port. f. Tupi, var. of *piraya* scissors]
pĭrarucú (-rōōkōō') *n.* = ARAPAIMA. [Port. f. Tupi, = red fish]
pir'ate *n.*, & *v.t.* **1.** *n.* (Ship used by) one who robs at sea; marauder; one who infringes another's copyright or other business rights; one who broadcasts without official authorization (freq. *attrib.*: *pirate radio station*). **2.** *v.t.* Plunder; reproduce (book etc.) without permission, for one's own benefit. **3.** Hence or cogn. **pir'**ACY *n.*, **pĭră'**TIC(AL) *adjs.* [ME, f. L *pirata* f. Gk *peiratēs* (*peiraō* attempt, assault)]
piraya. See PIRANHA.
pĭrĭpi'rĭ *n.* (N.Z.) Weed (*Acaena sanguisorbae*) having prickly burs. [Maori]
pĭrō'gue (-ō'g) *n.* = PIRAGUA. [F, prob. f. Galibi]
pĭrouĕ'tte (-rōō-) *n.*, & *v.i.* **1.** *n.* Ballet-dancer's spin round on one foot or on point of toe. **2.** *v.i.* Dance thus. [F, = spinning-top]
pis aller (pēzălā') *n.* Course of action etc. followed for want of a better. [F (*pis* worse, *aller* go)]
pi'scary̆ *n.* **Common of** ~, right of fishing in another's water in common with owner (and others). [ME, f. med. L *piscaria* neut. pl. (as n.) of L *piscarius* (*piscis* fish; see -ARY¹)]
pi'scatory̆ *a.* Of fishermen or fishing, whence **pĭscatōr'**IAL *a.*; addicted to fishing. [f. L *piscatorius* (*piscator* fisherman f. *piscis* fish)]
Pi'scēs (-z; *or* -skēz *or* pī'-) *n. pl.* Sign of the ZODIAC, the Fishes. [ME f. L, pl. of *piscis* fish]
pi'scĭcŭlture *n.* Artificial rearing of fish; hence **pĭscĭcŭ'ltur**AL *a.*, **pĭscĭcŭ'ltur**IST (3) *n.*, (-cher-). [f. L *piscis* fish, after *agriculture* etc.]
pĭscī'na (*or* -sē'-) *n.* (*pl.* ~*e or* ~*s*). Fish-pond; ancient-Roman bathing-pond; (Eccl.) perforated stone basin near altar in church for carrying away water used in rinsing chalice etc. [L (*piscis* fish)]
pĭscī'ne¹ (-ē'n) *n.* Bathing-pool. [F, f. as prec.]
pi'scīne² *a.* Of fish. [f. L *piscis* fish + -INE¹]
pĭscĭ'vorous *a.* Fish-eating. [f. as prec. + -I- + -VOROUS]
pisé (pē'zā) *n.* Rammed clay or earth (and gravel) as building-material. [F, p.p. (as n.) of *piser* pound f. L *pinsare*]
Pi'sgah (-zg*a*) *n.* ~ **sight** etc., distant view of unattainable object. [name of mountain whence Moses viewed the Promised Land (Deut. 3:27)]
pĭsh *int.* expr. contempt, impatience, or disgust. [imit.]
pĭshō'gue (-ō'g) *n.* (Ir.) Sorcery; charm, spell. [f. Ir. *pís*(*r*)*eog* witchcraft]
pi'sĭform (*or* pĭ'z-) *a.* Pea-shaped; ~ **bone,** small bone of upper row of carpus. [f. mod. L *pisiformis* (*pisum* pea; see -FORM)]
pi'smīre *n.* (dial.) Ant. [ME, f. foll. (from smell of anthill) + obs. *mire* ant]
pĭss *v.* & *n.* (vulg.) **1.** *v.i.* Urinate; ~ **off,** (sl.) go away. **2.** *v.t.* Discharge (blood etc.) with the urine; wet with urine; ~ **off,** (sl., usu. in *p.p.*) annoy; (in *p.p.*, sl.) drunk. **3.** *n.* Urine; act of urinating; ~**-pot,** chamber-pot. [ME, f. OF *pisser* f. Rom. **pišare* (imit.)]
pissoir (pēswar') *n.* Public urinal. [F]
pĭstă'chĭō (-sh-; *or* -ah'-) *n.* (*pl.* ~*s*). (Tree, *Pistacia vera*, yielding) nut with greenish edible kernel; colour of this kernel. [f. It. *pistaccio* and Sp. *pistacho* f. L f. Gk *pistakion* f. Pers. *pistah*]
piste (pēst) *n.* Ski-track of compacted snow. [F, = racetrack]
pi'stĭl *n.* Female organ of flower, comprising ovary, style, and stigma; hence ~LARY¹, ~**lĭ'**FEROUS, ~**l**INE¹, *adjs.* [f. F *pistile* or f. L *pistillum* PESTLE]
pi'stĭllate *a.* Having pistils but no stamens; having pistils. [f. prec. + -ATE²]
pi'stol *n.*, & *v.t.* (‖-ll-). **1.** *n.* Small firearm held and fired by one hand (**hold** ~ **to** person's **head,** coerce him by threats); implement of similar shape; ~**-grip,** handle of pistol-butt shape; ~**-shot,** range of, or shot fired from, pistol; ~**-whip** *v.t.*, beat with pistol; hence ~EER' *n.*, soldier armed with pistol. **2.** *v.t.* Shoot with pistol. [f. obs. F f. G *pistole* f. Czech *pišt'al*]
pĭstō'le *n.* (Hist.) Foreign gold coin, esp. Spanish coin. [f. F *pistole* abbr. of *pistolet*, of uncert. orig.]
pi'ston *n.* Disc or short cylinder of wood, metal, etc., fitting closely within tube in which it moves up and down, used in cylinder of steam or petrol engine to impart motion by means of ~**-rod,** or in pump to receive motion; sliding valve in cornet etc. [F, f. It. *pistone* var. of *pestone* augment. of *pestello* PESTLE]
pĭt¹ *n.* **1.** Natural hole in ground; hole made in digging for mineral etc. or for industrial purposes, (*chalk, clay, gravel, coal, saw, tan, -pit*); covered hole as trap for wild beasts or (esp. Bibl.) for enemies (**dig a** ~ **for,** (fig.) try to ensnare); **the** (**bottomless**) ~ (**of hell**), hell; = COCKPIT 1. **2.** Hollow in animal or plant body or on any surface (~ **of the stomach,** depression below bottom of breastbone); depressed scar, e.g. after smallpox. **3.** ‖That part of auditorium of theatre which is on floor of house, esp. the part of this behind stalls, whence ~'TITE¹ (1) *n.*; ‖people occupying this. **4.** Sunken area in workshop floor for access to underside of motor vehicles; place at which racing cars are refuelled, re-tyred, etc., during race. **5.** *Part of floor of an exchange allotted to special trading (*wheat-pit*). **6.** ~**'fall,** covered pit as trap for animals etc., (fig.) unsuspected snare or danger; ~**-head,** (area surrounding) top of coal-mine shaft; ~**'man,** collier, *connecting rod in machinery; ‖~ **pony** (kept underground for haulage in coal-mines); ~**-prop,** balk of wood used as temporary support in a mine; ~**-saw,** large saw working

in saw-pit; ~ **viper,** Amer. snake of family Crotalidae, with pit between eye and nostril. [OE *pytt*, = OS *putti*, OHG *pfuzzi*, f. WG **putti*, **putja* f. L *puteus* well]

pĭt² *v.* (-tt-). **1.** *v.t.* Put into a pit (esp. vegetables etc. for storage); set (cock, dog, etc.) to fight (orig. in pit; *against* another), (fig.) match (person *against*); (esp. in *p.p.*) make pits, esp. scars, in. **2.** *v.i.* (Path., of flesh etc.) retain impression of finger etc. when touched. [ME, f. prec.]

***pĭt³** *n.*, & *v.t.* (**-tt-**). **1.** *n.* Stone (of fruit). **2.** *v.t.* Remove pits from. [perh. Du., cogn. w. PITH]

pĭ't-a-păt *adv.* & *n.* (With) sound as of light quick steps, (with) faltering sound, (*his feet, heart, went pit-a-pat*). [imit.]

pĭtch¹ *n.*, & *v.t.* **1.** *n.* Black or dark-brown tenacious resinous substance, semi-liquid when hot, hard when cold, got from distillation of tar or turpentine, used for caulking seams of ships etc. **2. ~-black, ~-darkness,** (with no light at all); **~-pine,** pine-tree of species yielding much resin, esp. *Pinus rigida*; **~'stone,** obsidian etc. looking like pitch. **3.** *v.t.* Cover, coat, smear, with pitch. [OE *pic* (*pician* v.), = OS *pik*, OHG *peh*, ON *bik*, Gmc f. L *pix picis*]

pĭtch² *v.* **1.** *v.t.* Erect and fix (tent, camp); (abs.) encamp. **2.** Fix or plant (thing) in definite position; ~ **wickets,** (Cricket) fix stumps in ground and place bails. **3.** Pave (road) with set stones. **4. ~ed battle,** battle planned beforehand and fought on chosen ground, not casual skirmish, (fig.) vigorous argument etc. **5.** (Mus. etc.) set at particular pitch, (fig.) express in particular style or at particular level. **6.** Throw, fling; (in games) throw (flat object) towards a mark; (Cricket) cause (bowled ball) to strike ground (at specified point etc.); (sl.) tell (tale, yarn). **7.** (Golf). Play (ball) with PITCH³ shot. **8.** *v.i.* Fall heavily (on one's head, *into*, etc.); (of ship, vehicle, etc.) plunge in longitudinal direction (cf. ROLL² 4); (of bowled cricket-ball) strike the ground. **9.** ~ **in,** (colloq.) set to work vigorously; ~ **into,** (colloq.) assail forcibly with blows, words, etc., make vigorous attack on, (person, food, etc.); ~ **(up)on,** happen to select; **~-and-toss,** game of skill and chance in which coins are pitched at a mark and then tossed. [ME *pic(c)he*, perh. f. OE **picc(e)an* (cf. *picung* stigmata)]

pĭtch³ *n.* **1.** Pitching (e.g. of ship). **2.** Mode of delivering cricket-ball in bowling; delivery of baseball by pitcher; ~ **(shot),** (Golf) lofted approach shot with little run to ball after alighting. **3.** Advertising or recommendation by salesman etc. **4.** ||Place at which street performer, bookmaker, etc., is stationed (QUEER *the pitch*); (Cricket) area between or near wickets; area for playing football etc. on. **5.** Height to which falcon etc. soars before swooping on prey (*fly a high* etc. *pitch*; lit. or fig.). **6.** Height, degree, intensity, (*of* quality etc.; *affairs reached such a pitch that* etc.); (Mus.) quality of sound governed by rate of vibration of string etc., degree of acuteness or graveness of tone, (*high pitch, low pitch*); CONCERT¹ *pitch*. **7.** Degree of slope; steepness of slope of roof, stratum, etc., (**~ed roof,** not flat); (Mech.) distance between successive corresponding points or lines, e.g. between successive teeth of cog-wheel, ridges of screw, or positions of propeller before and after one rotation. **8. ~-pipe,** small pipe blown by mouth to set pitch for singing or tuning. [f. prec.]

pĭ'tchblĕnde *n.* Uranium oxide ore found in pitchlike masses and yielding radium. [f. G *pechblende* (as PITCH¹, BLENDE)]

pĭ'tcher¹ *n.* **1.** Large usu. earthenware vessel with handle or two ears and usu. a lip shaped for pouring, for holding liquids; jug; **little ~s have long ears,** children are apt to overhear. **2.** (Bot.) Modified leaf in pitcher form; **~-plant** (with such leaves, which often hold liquid secretion). **3.** Hence ~FUL 2 *n.* [ME, f. OF *pichier*, *pechier* f. Frank. **bikari* BEAKER]

pĭ'tcher² *n.* In vbl senses; player who delivers ball, esp. in baseball; stone used for paving. [f. PITCH² + -ER¹]

pĭ'tchfôrk *n.*, & *v.t.* **1.** *n.* Long-handled fork with two prongs for pitching hay etc. **2.** *v.t.* Cast (as) with pitchfork; (fig.) thrust (person) forcibly (*into* position, office, etc.). [in ME *pickfork*, prob. f. PICK¹ + FORK, assoc. w. PITCH²]

pĭ'tchȳ *a.* Of, like, dark etc. as, pitch. [f. PITCH¹ + -Y²]

pĭ'tėous *a.* Deserving or causing pity, deplorable; hence ~LY² *adv.*, ~NESS *n.* [ME *pito(u)s* etc. f. AF *pitous*, OF *pitos* f. Rom. **pietosus* (as PIETY; see -OUS)]

pĭth *n.*, & *v.t.* **1.** *n.* Spongy cellular tissue in stems and branches of dicotyledonous plants; similar tissue lining rind of orange etc.; (arch.) spinal marrow; ~ **helmet** (made from dried pith of sola etc.). **2.** (fig.) Essential part, quintessence, (*pith and marrow of*); physical strength, vigour; force, energy; **of ~** (importance) **and moment** (Shak. *Hamlet* III. i. 86). **3.** Hence ~'LESS *a.* **4.** *v.t.* Slaughter or immobilize (animal) by severing spinal cord; remove pith or marrow from. [OE *pitha*, = MDu., MLG *pitte*, *pit* f. WG **pith(th)on*, of unkn. orig.]

pĭthėcă'nthrōpe *n.* Ape-man, member of extinct genus *Pithecanthropus* of apelike men, Java MAN¹, now included in genus *Homo*. [f. Gk *pithēkos* ape + *anthrōpos* man]

pĭ'thėcoid (*or* -thē'-) *a.* Like an (esp. anthropoid) ape. [f. F *pithécoïde* (as prec.; see -OID)]

pĭ'th|os *n.* (*pl.* **~oi**). (Archaeol.) Large storage-jar. [Gk]

pĭ'th|ȳ *a.* Of, like, abounding in, pith; (fig.) condensed and forcible, terse; hence **~ĭLY²** *adv.*, **~ĭNESS** *n.* [ME, f. PITH + -Y²]

pĭ'tĭab|le *a.* Deserving or causing pity or contempt; hence **~le**NESS (-beln-) *n.*, ~LY² *adv.* [ME, f. OF *piteable*, *pitoiable* (as PITY; see -ABLE)]

pĭ'tĭful *a.* (Of thing) causing pity; contemptible; (arch.) compassionate; hence ~LY² *adv.*, ~NESS *n.* [ME, f. PITY + -FUL]

pĭ'tĭlėss *a.* Showing no pity (lit. or fig.); hence ~LY² *adv.*, ~NESS *n.* [ME, f. PITY + -LESS]

pĭ'tŏn (pē-) *n.* Peg or spike driven into rock or crack to support climber or rope. [F, = eye-bolt]

Pi'tōt (pē'tō) *n.* ~ **tube** (bent at right angles and used to measure speed of flow or of aircraft etc.). [f. H. ~, Fr. physicist d. 1771]

pĭ'tpăn *n.* Central Amer. dug-out boat. [Miskito]

pĭ'ttance *n.* Allowance or remuneration, esp. scanty one (*a mere pittance*); small number or amount; (Hist.) pious bequest to religious house for extra food etc. [ME f. OF *pitance*, f. med. L *pi(e)tantia* f. L *pietas* PITY; see -ANCE]

pĭ'tter-pătter. Var. of PIT-A-PAT.

pĭ'ttīte. See PIT¹.

pĭtū'ĭtarȳ *a.* & *n.* **1.** *a.* (arch.) Of or secreting phlegm, mucous. **2.** ~ **gland** or **body,** small ductless gland at base of brain which has important influence on growth and bodily functions, and was once thought to secrete nasal mucus. **3.** *n.* Pituitary gland. [f. L *pituitarius* (*pituita* slime; see -ARY¹)]

pĭ'turĭ *n.* (Austral.) (Narcotic drug got from) shrub *Duboisia hopwoodii*. [Aboriginal]

pĭ'tȳ *n.*, & *v.t.* **1.** *n.* Feeling of sorrow aroused by person's distress or suffering (*cannot help feeling pity for him*); **take ~ on,** feel or act compassionately towards; **for ~'s sake,** = for God's sake (GOD 7). **2.** Regrettable fact, regrettableness, ground for regret, (*what a pity!*; *it is a thousand pities you did not mention it*); **more's the ~**, so much the worse; **it is** or **was ~ of them,** (arch.) one feels sorry for them. **3.** *v.t.* Feel (often contemptuous) pity for (*he is much to be pitied*; *I pity you if you think that*); hence **~ing**LY² *adv.* [ME, f. OF *pité* f. L (as PIETY)]

pĭtyrī'as|ĭs *n.* (*pl.* **~es** *pr.* -ēz). (Path.) Skin disease characterized by shedding of branlike scales. [mod. L, f. Gk *pituriasis* (*pituron* bran; see -ASIS)]

pĭ'vot *n.* & *v.* **1.** *n.* Short shaft or pin on which something turns or oscillates; man or men about whom body of troops wheels; (fig.) cardinal or crucial person or point; hence **~**AL *a.* **2.** *v.t.* Furnish with or attach by pivot. **3.** *v.i.* Turn as on pivot; hinge (*up*)*on* (lit. or fig.). [F, of uncert. orig.]

pĭx¹. Var. of PYX.

pĭx² *n. pl.* (colloq.) Pictures. [abbr.]

pĭ'xĭe, pĭ'xȳ, *n.* Supernatural being akin to fairy; **~ hat, hood,** (with pointed crown). [17th c.; orig. unkn.]

pĭ'xĭl(l)ātėd *a.* Bewilderėd; crazy; drunk. [var. of *pixie-led* (prec., LED) + -ATE³ + -ED¹]

pi'zza (pē'tsa) *n.* Open pie containing spiced tomatoes, cheese, etc. [It., = pie]

pizzeri'a (pētserē'*a*) *n.* Place where pizzas are made or sold. [It. (as prec.; cf. -ERY)]

pizzicat|o (pĭtsĭkah'tō) *adv.*, *a.*, & *n.* (*pl.* **~os** *or* **~i** *pr.* -ē). (Mus.) (Note or passage performed by) plucking string of violin etc. with finger instead of using bow. [It., p.p. of *pizzicare* twitch (*pizzare* f. *pizza* edge)]

pĭ'zzle *n.* (vulg.) Penis of animal, esp. that of bull formerly used as flogging instrument. [f. LG *pesel*, dim. of MLG *pēse*, MDu. *pēze*]

pk. *abbr.* park; peak; peck(s).

pl. *abbr.* place; plate; (esp. Mil.) platoon; plural.

‖**P.L.A.** *abbr.* Port of London Authority.

plă'c|able *a.* Easily appeased, mild, forgiving; hence or cogn. **~**ABI'LITY *n.*, **~ab**LY² *adv.* [ME f. OF, or f. L *placabilis* (*placare* appease; see -ABLE)]

plă'cãrd *n.*, & *v.t.* **1.** *n.* Document printed on one side of single sheet for posting up, poster. **2.** *v.t.* (*or* plakar'd). Set up placards on (wall etc.); advertise (wares etc.) by placards; display (poster etc.) as placard. [ME f. OF *placquart* (*plaquier* to plaster f. MDu. *placken*; see -ARD)]

placā'te (*or* plă'kāt) *v.t.* Pacify, conciliate; hence **placā'to**RY *a.*, propitiatory. [f. L *placare* + -ATE³]

plāce¹ *n.* **1.** Particular part of space; part of space occupied by person or thing (*it has changed its place*); ***any ~**, ***some ~**, etc., = anywhere, somewhere, etc.; **in ~s**, at some places but not at others. **2.** City, town, village, etc.; group of houses in town etc.; residence, dwelling, (*he has a place in the country*; *come round to my place*); country house with surroundings; **go ~s,** (colloq.) be successful. **3.** Building or area devoted to specified purpose (*place of amusement, worship*; *bathing-place*); ‖ANOTHER *place*; ‖**the other ~**, (joc., in Cambridge Univ.) Oxford (and vice versa). **4.** Particular spot on surface etc. (*a sore place on his wrist*). **5.** Passage in book etc. **6.** Rank, station, (*servants must know their place*; *keep him in his place*); PRIDE *of place*. **7.** (Racing). Position among placed competitors, esp. other than that of winner. **8.** Position of figure in series as indicating its value in decimal or similar notation (*calculated to 50 decimal places*). **9.** Step in progression of argument, statement, etc., (*in the first, second, place*). **10.** Proper or natural position (*take your places*; *there is no place for doubt*; *is in* or *out of its* or *his place*); space, seat, accommodation, for person etc. at table, in conveyance, etc., (*take two places in the coach*; *always a place for you at our table*); **in ~ of,** in exchange or substitution for, instead of; *place in the* SUN; **take the ~ of,** be substituted for. **11.** Office, employment, esp. government appointment; duties or entitlements of office etc. (*it is not my place to inquire into that*); position as chosen member of team etc. **12. All over the ~**, in disorder (lit. or fig.); **give ~ to,** make room for, yield precedence to, be succeeded by; **in ~**, in the right position, suitable; **out of ~**, in the wrong position, unsuitable; **take ~**, (esp. of prearranged event) occur. **13. ~-bet** (that horse etc. will be among first 3 or *2 in race); **~-brick** (imperfectly burnt from being on windward side of kiln); **~ card** (marking place to be occupied by person, esp. at table); **~-kick,** (Footb.) kick made when ball is previously placed for that purpose on ground; ‖**~'man,** holder of public office, esp. one appointed from motives of self-interest rather than suitability; **~-mat,** small mat on table at person's place; **~-name,** name of town, village, hill, field, lake, etc.; **~-setting,** set of dishes and implements for one person to eat with. [ME f. OF, f. Rom. *plattja f. L f. Gk *plateia* (*hodos*) broad (way)]

plāce² *v.t.* **1.** Put (thing etc.) in particular place or state; arrange (set of things) in their proper places. **2.** Appoint (person, esp. clergyman) to post; find situation, living, etc., for. **3.** Invest (money); dispose of (goods) to customer; put (order for goods etc.) into hands of firm etc. **4.** Have (confidence etc. *in* or *on*). **5.** Assign rank to; locate; fully identify, remember circumstances of previous meeting with, assign to a class or identify (*I know that man's face but I can't place him*). **6.** State position of (usu. any of first 3 horses or runners) in race; **be ~d,** be among first three or *be second. **7.** Get (goal) by PLACE¹-*-kick*. **8.** Hence **~'**MENT (-sm-) *n.* [f. prec.]

placē'bō *n.* (*pl.* **~s**). **1.** (R.C. Ch.) Opening antiphon of the vespers for the dead. **2.** (Med.) medicine given to humour, rather than cure, the patient; dummy pill etc. used as control; blank sample in test. [L, = I shall be acceptable or pleasing (*placēre* please), first word of Ps. 114:9 in Vulgate]

placĕ'nt|a *n.* (*pl.* **~ae** *or* **~as**). Flattened circular spongy vascular organ in uterus of pregnant mammals (expelled after parturition) and helping to nourish foetus, which is attached to it by umbilical cord; (Bot.) part of carpel to which ovules are attached; hence **~**AL *a.* (**~al mammal,** mammal other than marsupial or monotreme). [L, f. Gk *plakous -ountos* flat cake f. root of *plax plakos* flat plate]

plă'cer *n.* Deposit of sand, gravel, etc., in bed of stream etc. containing valuable minerals in particles. [Amer. Sp., cogn. w. *placel* sandbank f. *plaza* PLACE¹]

placet (plā'sĕt) *n.* Affirmative vote in church or university assembly. [L, = it pleases]

plă'cĭd *a.* Mild; peaceful; serene, not easily disturbed; hence **placĭ'd**ITY *n.*, **~**LY² *adv.* [f. F *placide* or f. L *placidus* (*placēre* please; see -ID¹)]

plă'ckėt *n.* Opening or slit esp. in woman's skirt, for fastenings or access to pocket. [var. of PLACARD, assoc. w. -ET¹]

plă'coid *a.* & *n.* **1.** *a.* (Of fish-scale) plate-shaped; having placoid scales. **2.** *n.* Placoid fish. [f. Gk *plax plakos* flat plate + -OID]

plafond (plăfaw'ṅ) *n.* **1.** Ceiling, esp. one enriched with paintings; such painting. **2.** Early form of contract bridge. [F (*plat* flat, *fond* bottom)]

plā'gal *a.* (Mus.) (Of church mode) having

sounds comprised between dominant and its octave (cf. AUTHENTIC); ~ **cadence** or **close** (in which chord of subdominant immediately precedes that of the tonic). [f. med. L *plagalis* f. *plaga* plagal mode, f. L f. Gk *plagios* oblique, (in med. Gk) plagal, f. *plagos* side; see -AL]

plage (plahzh) *n.* Sea beach (esp. at fashionable resort); (Astron.) unusually bright region on sun. [F]

plā'giar|ize, ~|ise (-īz), *v.t.* Take and use another person's (thoughts, writings, inventions, or abs.) as one's own; so ~ISM (1), ~IST (1), *ns.* [f. foll. + -IZE]

plā'giarў *n.* (arch.) Plagiarism; plagiarist. [f. L *plagiarius* kidnapper (*plagium* a kidnapping f. Gk *plagion*; see -ARY¹)]

plā'gio- *comb. form.* Oblique, as: **~cepha'lic,** having anterior part of skull more developed on one side, posterior on the other; **~clase,** triclinic felspar; **~cla'stic,** (Min.) having oblique cleavage; **~stome,** fish with mouth placed transversely beneath snout, e.g. shark or ray. [f. Gk *plagios* oblique (*plagos* side) + -o-]

plāgue (-g) *n.*, & *v.t.* **1.** *n.* Affliction, esp. as divine punishment; (colloq.) unusual infestation *of* (caterpillars etc.); (colloq.) nuisance, trouble; pestilence (**the** ~ = BUBONIC *plague*, PNEUMONIC *plague*); (arch., as imprecation) *plague on it!* etc.; **~-spot,** spot on skin characteristic of plague, locality infected with plague; (fig.) source or symptom of moral corruption. **2.** *v.t.* Afflict with plague; (colloq.) annoy, bother, whence ~'SOME¹ (-gs-) *a.* (colloq.). [ME, f. L *plaga* stroke, wound, prob. f. Gk *plaga, plēgē* (**plag-* strike)]

plā'gu|ў, *plā'gu|ey, (-gĭ) *a.* & *adv.* (arch.) Annoying(ly); exceeding(ly) (*was plaguy glad to get back again*); hence **~ĭ**LY² (-gĭ-) *adv.* [f. prec. + -Y²]

plaice *n.* (*pl.* same). European flat-fish, *Pleuronectes platessa,* much used as food; similar Amer. fish. [ME, f. OF *plaïz* f. LL *platessa* app. f. Gk *platus* broad]

plaid (*or* plăd) *n.* & *a.* **1.** *n.* Long piece of twilled woollen cloth, usu. with chequered or tartan pattern, outer article of Highland costume, worn over the shoulder; cloth used for this; hence ~'ED² *a.* **2.** *a.* Made of plaid; having plaidlike pattern. [f. Gael. *plaide,* of unkn. orig.]

plain¹ *a., adv.,* & *n.* **1.** *a.* Clear, evident; simple, readily understood, (*plain words, English; plain as a* PIKESTAFF); not in code. **2.** Not intricate (*plain cooking, sewing*); unembellished, (of drawings etc.) not coloured; (of food) not rich or elaborate or highly seasoned; not luxurious (*plain* LIVING¹). **3.** Outspoken, straightforward, (**be ~ with,** tell home truths to); unsophisticated (*I am a plain man*); of homely manners, dress, or appearance; ugly (*a pity the poor girl is so plain*). **4.** Hence ~'LY² *adv.*, ~'NESS (-n-n-) *n.* **5.** *adv.* Clearly (*learn to speak plain; ah, did you once see Shelley plain?*). **6.** ~ **card** (not trump, or not court-card); **~'chant,** = *plainsong;* ~ **chocolate** (without milk added in manufacture); ~ **clothes,** unofficial dress, esp. of policeman on duty but not in uniform; ~ **cook,** person able to do plain cooking; ~ **dealing,** candour, straightforwardness; ~ **sailing,** sailing in a straightforward course, (fig.) simple situation or course of action; *plain* SERVICE¹ 6; **~'song,** traditional church music in medieval modes and in free rhythm depending on accentuation of the words, and sung in unison; **~-spoken,** outspoken; ~ **suit** (not trumps); ~ **time** (not paid for at overtime rates); ~ **weaving** (with weft alternately over and under warp). **7.** *n.* Level tract of country; **~'sman** (-z-), inhabitant of a plain. **8.** Ordinary stitch in knitting (opp. PURL¹). [ME f. OF *plain* a. & n., f. L *planus* a., *planum* n.]

plain² *v.i.* (arch. or poet.) Mourn; complain; emit plaintive sound. [ME, f. OF *plaindre* (st. *plaign-*) f. L *plangere planct-* lament]

plaint *n.* ‖(Law) accusation, charge; (literary) lamentation, complaint. [ME, f. OF *plainte* fem. p.p. (as n.) of *plaindre,* and OF *plaint* f. L *planctus* (as prec.)]

plai'ntĭff *n.* Party who brings suit into court of law (opp. *defendant*). [ME, f. OF *plaintif* a. (as foll.)]

plai'ntĭve *a.* Expressive of sorrow; mournful; hence ~LY² (-vlĭ) *adv.*, ~NESS (-vn-) *n.* [ME, f. OF (*-if, -ive*) f. *plainte* (as PLAINT; see -IVE)]

plai'ster¹,². Var. of PLASTER¹,².

plait (plăt) *n.*, & *v.t.* **1.** = PLEAT. **2.** *n.* Interlacing of three or more strands of hair, ribbon, straw, etc.; material thus interlaced. **3.** *v.t.* Form (hair, straw, etc.) into plait. [ME f. OF *pleit* fold, f. Rom. **plic(i)tum* p.p. (as n.) of L *plicare* fold]

plăn *n.* & *v.* (**-nn-**). **1.** *n.* Drawing or diagram made by projection on flat surface (cf. ELEVATION), esp. one showing relative position of parts of (one floor of) building; large-scale detailed map of town or district. **2.** Table indicating times, places, etc., of intended proceedings etc.; scheme of arrangement. **3.** Formulated or organized method by which thing is to be done (FIVE-*year plan*), project, design; way of proceeding (*the better plan is to peel them after boiling; plan of campaign*); imaginary plane perpendicular to line of vision and containing objects shown in picture. **4.** *v.t.* Make plan of (ground, existing building); design (building to be constructed etc.); scheme, arrange beforehand, (procedure etc.); (esp. in *p.p.*) conduct in accordance with plan. **5.** *v.i.* Make plans; ~ **on,** (colloq.) aim at do*ing.* **6.** Hence **~'**NER¹, **~'**NING¹ (1), *ns.* (esp. w. ref. to controlled design of buildings and development of land). [F, f. earlier *plant,* f. It. *pianta* plan of building; cf. PLANT¹]

plā'nar *a.* (Math.) Of or relating to, in the form of, a plane. [f. PLANE³ + -AR¹]

planār'ian *n.* Flatworm of family Planariidae, usu. living in fresh water. [f. mod. L *Planaria* genus-name, fem. (as n.) of L *planarius* lying flat]

plă'nchėt (-sh-) *n.* Plain disc of metal from which coin is made. [dim. of *planch* slab of metal f. OF *planche* (see PLANK¹)]

plănchĕ'tte (-sh-) *n.* Small usu. heart-shaped board supported by two castors and vertical pencil, which when person's fingers rest lightly on board is said to trace letters etc. without conscious direction. [F, dim. of *planche* PLANK¹]

Plănck *n.* ~**('s) constant,** (Phys.) fundamental constant of proportionality between energy and frequency of quanta of electromagnetic radiation. [f. M. ~, Ger. physicist d. 1947]

plāne¹ *n.* Tall spreading tree of genus *Platanus* with broad angular palmately-lobed leaves. [ME & OF, f. L f. Gk *platanos* (*platus* broad)]

plāne² *n.*, & *v.t.* **1.** *n.* Tool for smoothing surface of woodwork by paring shavings from it, consisting of wooden or metal stock from smooth bottom of which a steel blade projects; similar tool for smoothing metal. **2.** *v.t.* Smooth (wood, metal) with plane; pare *away* or *down* (irregularities) with plane; (arch.) level (*plane the way*). [n. ME & OF, f. LL *plana,* v. ME f. OF *planer,* f. L *planare* (*planus* PLAIN¹)]

plāne³ *n.*, & *v.i.* **1.** *n.* Surface such that the straight line joining any two points in it lies wholly in it; imaginary surface of this kind in which points or lines in material bodies lie; level surface. **2.** Flat thin object such as table-

-top; main supporting surface of aeroplane; aeroplane. **3.** (fig.) Level (*of* thought, attainment, knowledge, etc.; *his superstition places him on the same plane as the savage*). **4.** ~ **sailing,** art of determining ship's position on the theory that she is moving on a plane, (fig.) = PLAIN[1] *sailing*. **5.** *v.i.* Travel, glide (*down* etc.), in aeroplane; soar; (of speedboat etc.) skim over water. [f. L *planum* flat surface, neut. (as n.) of *planus* PLAIN[1]; different. f. PLAIN[1] in 17th c.]

plāne[4] *a.* (Of surface etc.) perfectly level, as a PLANE[3]; (of angle, figure, etc.) lying in a plane; ~ **chart** (on which meridians and parallels of latitude are represented by equidistant straight lines, used in PLANE[3] sailing); **~-table,** surveying instrument used for direct plotting in the field, with circular table and pivoted alidade. [var. of PLAIN[1], after F *plan plane*]

plă'nėt[1] *n.* **1.** (Astron.) heavenly body revolving in approximately circular orbit round sun; the earth; **major** ~, Jupiter, Saturn, Uranus, or Neptune; **minor** ~, asteroid; hence **~ŏ'**LOGY *n.* **2.** (Hist.) Heavenly body distinguished from fixed stars by having apparent motion of its own (including moon and sun), esp. (Astrol.) with reference to its supposed influence on persons and events; **~-stricken, ~-struck,** (arch.) bewildered, terrified. [ME, f. OF *planete* f. LL f. Gk *planētēs* wanderer, planet, (*planaomai* wander)]

plă'nėt[2] *n.* Chasuble. [f. med. L *planeta*, perh. f. LL *planetica* (*vestis*) traveller's (cloak) (*planeticus* f. as prec.; see -IC)]

plănėtār'ĭ|um *n.* (*pl.* **~ums** *or* **~ă**). Orrery; device for projecting image of night sky as seen at various times and places; building containing this. [mod. L, f. as prec.]

plă'nėtarў *a.* Of planets (*planetary influence, motions, system*); terrestrial, mundane; wandering, erratic; ~ **nebula,** ring-shaped nebula formed by shell of gas round star. [f. LL *planetarius* (as PLANET[1]; see -ARY[1])]

plănėtĕ'sĭmal *n.* One of a vast number of minute bodies which, according to the ~ **hypothesis,** formed the planets by accretion in a cold state. [f. PLANET[1], after *infinitesimal*]

plă'nėtoid *n.* Asteroid. [f. PLANET[1] + -OID]

plă'ng|ent (-nj-) *a.* (Of sound) loud and reverberating; plaintive; hence **~**ENCY *n.* [f. L *plangere* lament; see -ENT]

planĭ'|mėter *n.* Instrument for mechanically measuring the area of a plane figure; so **plănĭmĕ'tr**IC(AL) *adjs.*, **~**METRY *n.* [f. F *planimètre* f. L *planus* level; see -METER]

plă'nĭsh *v.t.* Flatten (sheet metal etc.) with smooth-faced hammer or otherwise; flatten out (coining-metal) between rollers; hence **~**ER[1] (1, 2) *n.* [ME, f. OF *planir* smooth (*plain* PLANE[4]; see -ISH[2])]

plă'nĭ|sphēre *n.* Map formed by projection of (part of) sphere on plane, esp. to show appearance of heavens at particular time and place; hence **~sphĕ'r**IC *a.* [ME, f. med. L *planisphaerium* (as PLANE[4], SPHERE); infl. by F *planisphère*]

plănk[1] *n.* Long wide piece of timber, a few inches thick; item of political or other programme (cf. PLATFORM); **walk the ~,** (Hist., of pirates' captive etc.) be made to walk blindfold into sea along plank laid over side of ship; ~ **bed** (of boards, without mattress, in prison etc.). [ME f. ONF *planke* = OF *planche* f. LL *planca* board (*plancus* flat-footed)]

plănk[2] *v.t.* Furnish, cover, or floor, with planks, whence **~'**ING[1] (2, 3) *n.*; (colloq.) put *down* roughly or violently, esp. pay (money, or abs.) *down* on the spot; *cook and serve (food) on plank with garnish. [ME, f. prec.]

plă'nktŏn *n.* (Chiefly microscopic) drifting or floating organic life found at various depths in seas, lakes, rivers, etc., taken collectively (cf. BENTHOS, NEKTON); hence **~**IC (-ŏ'n-) *a.* [G, f. Gk *plagktos* wandering (*plazomai* wander)]

plă'nner, plă'nnĭng. See PLAN 6.

plānō- *comb. form.* Level, flat, as: **~co'ncave, ~co'nvex,** (of lens etc.) with one surface plane and the other concave, convex; **~meter** (-ŏ'm-), flat plate as gauge for plane surfaces. [f. L *planus* flat + -O-]

plant[1] (-ah-) *n.* **1.** Living organism capable of living wholly on inorganic substances and having neither power of locomotion nor special organs of sensation or digestion, member of the vegetable kingdom; small plant (other than trees and shrubs). **2.** Fixtures, implements, machinery, etc., used in industrial processes; factory. **3.** (sl.) Planned swindle or burglary, hoax; thing deliberately placed for discovery by others. **4. ~-louse,** small insect that infests plants, esp. aphis. **5.** Hence **~'**LET *n.*, **~'**LIKE *a.* [f. OE *plante* & F *plante* f. L *planta* sprout, slip, cutting, or f. foll.]

plant[2] (-ah-) *v.t.* **1.** Place (tree, shoot, bulb, seed, crop, etc.) into ground or soil so that it may take root and grow; deposit (young fish, spawn, oysters) in river etc.; ~ **out,** transfer (plant) from pot or frame to open ground, set out (seedlings) at intervals. **2.** Fix (stake, feet, etc.) firmly (*in, on,* ground etc.); station (person), esp. as spy; ~ **oneself,** take up a position. **3.** Establish, found, (community, city, church); settle (person) in a place as colonist etc.; cause (idea etc.) to take root *in* (mind); furnish (land *with* plants, district *with* settlers etc.). **4.** Deliver (blow, thrust) with definite aim. **5.** (sl.) Conceal (stolen goods etc.), esp. with view to misleading a later discoverer; abandon. **6.** *Bury. **7.** Hence **~'**ABLE *a.* [OE *plantian* & OF *planter*, f. L *plantare*]

Plăntă'gėnėt *n.* & *a.* (Member) of the family founded by Geoffrey of Anjou, esp. any of the English kings from Henry II to Richard II. [surname, orig. nickname, f. sprig of broom (L *planta* plant, *genista* broom) worn as cognizance]

plă'ntain[1] (-tĭn; *or* -ah'-) *n.* Plant of genus *Plantago*, esp. low herb with broad flat leaves spread out close to ground and seeds much used as food for cage-birds; ~ **lily,** hosta. [ME & OF, f. L *plantago -ginis* (*planta* sole of foot, from its broad prostrate leaves)]

plă'ntain[2] (-tĭn; *or* -ah'-) *n.* (Fruit of) treelike tropical herbaceous plant allied to banana and bearing similar fruit. [earlier *platan*, f. Sp. *plá(n)tano* plane-tree, prob. assim. f. Galibi *palatana* etc.]

plă'ntar *a.* (Anat.) Of the sole of the foot. [f. L *plantaris* (*planta* sole; see -AR[1])]

plăntā'tion (*or* plah-) *n.* Assemblage of planted growing plants, esp. trees; estate on which cotton, tobacco, etc., is cultivated (formerly by slave labour; ~ **song,** song of the kind sung by Negroes on American plantations); (Hist.) colonization, colony. [ME f. OF, or f. L *plantatio* (as PLANT[2]; see -ATION)]

pla'nter (-ah-) *n.* Cultivator of soil; (Ir. Hist.) English settler on forfeited lands in 17th c., person settled in evicted tenant's holding in 19th c.; occupier of plantation, esp. in (sub-)tropical countries, (*coffee, cotton, sugar, tobacco, -planter*); machine for planting (*corn, potato, -planter*); container for decorative plants. [ME, f. PLANT[2] + -ER[1]]

plă'ntĭgrāde *a.* & *n.* (Animal) that walks on its soles, e.g. bear (cf. DIGITIGRADE). [F, f. mod. L *plantigradus* f. L *planta* sole + -I- + *-gradus* -walking]

plantŏ'cracy̆ (plah-) *n.* Ruling class of planters. [f. PLANTER + -O- + -CRACY]

plă'nxty̆ *n.* (Ir.) (Dance to) animated harp-tune in triplets. [18th c.; orig. unkn.]

plăque (-k; *or* -ahk) *n.* Ornamental tablet of metal, porcelain, etc., plain or decorated; small badge of rank in honorary order; (Path.) patch of eruption etc., fibrous lesion in atherosclerosis; film on teeth where bacteria proliferate; so **plaquE'TTE** (-ăkĕ't) *n.* [F, f. Du. *plak* tablet (*plakken* stick)]

plăsh[1] *n.* Marshy pool; puddle; hence ~'Y[2] *a.* [OE *plæsc*, = MDu. *plasch*, imit.; cf. foll.]

plăsh[2] *v.* & *n.* **1.** *v.t.* & *i.* Splash; strike surface of (water) so as to break it up. **2.** *n.* Splash, plunge; hence ~'Y[2] *a.* [cf. Du. *plassen*, LG *plaschen*; prob. imit.]

plăsh[3] *v.t.* Bend down and interweave (branches, twigs) to form hedge; make, renew, (hedge) thus. [ME, f. OF *pla(i)ssier* f. Rom. **plectiare* f. L *plectere* plait; cf. PLEACH]

plă'sm. Var. of foll.

plă'sm|a (-z-) *n.* **1.** Green variety of quartz. **2.** Colourless coagulable part of blood, lymph, or milk, in which the corpuscles or fat-globules float; so ~A'TIC *a.* **3.** = PROTOPLASM. **4.** (Phys.) Gas of positive ions and free electrons with approximately equal positive and negative charge, and so usu. in approximately equal numbers. [LL, = mould, f. Gk *plasma -atos* (*plassō* to shape)]

plăsmō'dĭ|um (-z-) *n.* (*pl.* ~**a**). Mass of naked protoplasm formed by fusion or aggregation of amoeboid bodies without fusion of their nuclei; parasitic protozoan of genus *Plasmodium*, causing malaria in man. [mod. L, f. PLASMA + *-odium* (see -ODE)]

plăsmŏ'ly̆sĭs (-zm-) *n.* Contraction of protoplasm of plant cell due to immersion in a solution stronger than the cell fluid; hence **plăsmolȳse, *-lȳze,** (-zm-) *v.t.*, subject to plasmolysis. [mod. L, f. as PLASMA + -O- + -LYSIS]

pla'ster[1] (-ah'-) *n.* **1.** Curative or protective application consisting of some substance spread on linen etc. and capable of adhering at the temperature of the body (COURT[1], MUSTARD, STICK[1]*ing-, plaster*). **2.** Soft plastic mixture, esp. of lime, sand, and hair, for spreading on walls etc. to form smooth surface and harden by drying; ~ **of Paris,** fine white plaster of gypsum used for making moulds or casts, in bandages for immobilizing limbs etc., or as cement etc. [prepared from gypsums of Montmartre, Paris]. **3.** ~**board,** board with core of plaster for walls etc.; ~ **saint,** person regarded as being without moral faults and human frailty. **4.** Hence ~Y[2] *a.* [OE & OF *plastre*, f. med. L *plastrum* f. L f. Gk *emplastron*]

pla'ster[2] (-ah'-) *v.t.* **1.** Cover (wall etc.) with plaster or the like, whence ~ER[1] *n.*; coat, bedaub; (fig.) load to excess (*with* praise etc.); (sl.) bomb or shell heavily; (in *p.p.*, sl.) drunk. **2.** Apply medical plaster to; stick or fix (thing) like plaster on surface; make smooth with fixative etc. (*hair plastered down*). [ME, f. prec. or f. F *plastrer* (*plastre*, as prec.)]

plă'stĭc[1] (*or* -ah'-) *a.* **1.** Moulding, giving form to clay, wax, or other yielding solid; ~ **arts,** those concerned with modelling (e.g. sculpture, ceramics) or with representation of solid objects; ~ **surgery** (repairing or replacing deficient structure esp. by transfer of tissue), so ~ **surgeon.** **2.** Causing growth of natural forms, formative of immaterial things; (Biol.) capable of forming living tissue. **3.** Produced by moulding; capable of being (easily) moulded; ~ **bomb,** one containing putty-like plastic explosive, capable of being moulded by hand. **4.** (fig.) Pliant, supple. **5.** Hence **plă'st**ICALLY *adv.*, **plăstĭ'**CITY *n.*, ~IZE (3) *v.t.*, ~**IZER**[1] (2) *n.* [f. F *plastique* or f. L f. Gk *plastikos* (*plassō* to mould; see -IC)]

plă'stĭc[2] *n.* & *a.* **1.** *n.* Synthetic resinous etc. polymeric substance that can be given any permanent shape; (in *pl.*, *attrib.*, esp.) = sense 2. **2.** *a.* Made of plastic (*plastic bag, flowers, wood*). [f. prec.]

plă'stĭcine (-ēn) *n.* Plastic substance used for modelling. [P; f. PLASTIC[1] + -INE[4]]

plă'stĭd *n.* Small body in cytoplasm of plant cell, containing pigment or food. [G, f. Gk *plastos* shaped + -ID[2]]

plă'stron *n.* Fencer's leather-covered breastplate; breast-covering of facings-cloth worn by lancers; ornamental front on woman's bodice; man's starched shirt-front; ventral part of shell of tortoise or turtle, corresponding part in other animals; (Hist.) steel breastplate. [F, f. It. *piastrone* augment. of *piastra* breastplate, f. L *emplastrum* PLASTER[1]]

plăt[1] *n.* *Plan of land ownership etc.; (arch.) patch or plot of ground. [16th c., collat. form of PLOT[1]]

plăt[2] *n.*, & *v.t.* (**-tt-**). Var. of PLAIT 2, 3.

plat[3] (plah) *n.* Dish of food; ~ ***du jour*** (-dū-zhoor'; lit. 'of the day'), dish given special prominence on day's menu. [F, = dish, flat surface, f. *plat* flat f. pop. L **plattus* f. Gk *platus*]

plă'tan *n.* Plane-tree. [ME, f. L (see PLANE[1])]

plāte[1] *n.* **1.** Flat thin usu. rigid sheet of metal etc. with even surface and more or less uniform thickness; this as part of mechanism; *anode of thermionic valve; (Geol.) rigid sheet of rock in earth's outer crust. **2.** Smooth piece of metal etc. for engraving; impression from this; illustration on special paper in book. **3.** Piece of metal with name or inscription for affixing to something (*coffin, door, name, -plate*; **put up** one's ~, begin practice as doctor etc.). **4.** Thin sheet of metal, glass, etc., coated with sensitive film for photography. **5.** Stereotype, electrotype, or plastic cast of page of composed movable types, or metal or plastic copy of filmset matter, from which sheets are printed. **6.** Horizontal timber laid along top of wall to support ends of joists or rafters (*roof*, WALL, *window, -plate*). **7.** (Biol.) Thin flat organic structure or formation. **8.** (collect. *sing.*) ‖Table and domestic utensils of silver, gold, or other metal, (*pewter plate*); (objects of) plated metal (*electroplate*). **9.** Silver or gold cup as prize for (orig. horse-)race; such race; SELL*ing plate.* **10.** Shallow usu. circular vessel, now usu. of earthenware or china, from which food is eaten or served (*cake, dessert, dinner, soup, -plate*; **on a** ~, (colloq.) to be taken without need of effort; **on** one's **plate,** (colloq.) for one to deal with or consider); contents of this (*a plate of strawberries*); *main course of meal, served on one plate; *food for one person esp. at meal to raise funds; shallow vessel used for collection in churches etc. (*put a coin in the plate*). **11.** Thin piece of plastic material, moulded to shape of gums etc., to which artificial teeth are attached; (colloq.) denture. **12.** (Baseball). Flat piece of whitened rubber marking station of batter (**home** ~) or pitcher. **13.** Light shoe for racehorse. **14.** ~ **armour** (of metal plates, for man, ship, etc.); ‖~**-basket** (for spoons, forks, etc.); ~ **clutch** (with engagement by metal plates); ~ **glass,** glass of fine quality orig. cast in plates, for shop windows etc.; ~**-holder,** light-proof container for photographic plate; ‖~**'layer,** man employed in fixing and repairing railway rails [f. flanged strip used as track in early colliery railways]; ~**-mark,** (1) = HALL*mark*, (2) impression left on margin of engraving by pressure of the plate; **~-powder** (for cleaning silver); ||**~-rack** (in which plates are kept or placed to drain); *plate* TRACERY. **15.** Hence ~'FUL 2 (-tf-) *n.* (lit. or fig.), ~'LESS *a.*, ~'LET *n.* (esp. thrombocyte), (-tl-). [ME f. OF, f. med. L *plata* plate armour (*platus* a. f. pop. L **plattus*; see PLAT[3])]

plāte[2] *v.t.* Cover (esp. ship) with plates of metal for protection, ornament, etc.; cover (other metal) with thin coat of silver, gold, or tin; make plate of (type etc.) for printing. [ME, f. prec.]

plă'teau (-tō) *n.* (*pl.* **~x** *or* **~s,** *pr.* -z). Tableland; ornamented tray or dish; decorative plaque; woman's hat with level top; state of little variation following an increase. [F, f. OF *platel* dim. of PLAT[3]]

plă'ten *n.* Plate in printing-press by which paper is pressed against type; corresponding part in typewriter etc. [f. OF *platine* flat piece (*plat* flat; see PLAT[3])]

plā'ter *n.* One who plates with silver etc.; one who makes or applies plates in shipbuilding; inferior racehorse, competing chiefly for plates (sense 9). [f. PLATE[1,2] + -ER[1]]

plăterĕ'sque (-sk) *a.* Richly ornamented in style suggesting silverware. [f. Sp. *plateresco* (*platero* silversmith f. *plata* silver); cf. -ESQUE]

plă'tfôrm *n.*, & *v.t.* **1.** *n.* Raised level surface, natural or artificial terrace; thick sole of shoe; floor area for conductor etc. at entrance to bus or tram; ||raised surface along side of line at railway station; **~ ticket** (for access to this by non-traveller). **2.** Raised flooring in hall or open air from which speaker addresses audience (**the ~**, (fig.) oratory suitable to this); (fig.) political basis of party etc., declared policy of political party. **3.** *v.t.* Place (as) on platform. [f. F *plateforme* ground-plan (PLAT[3] *plate* flat, *forme* FORM[1])]

plā'tĭng *n.* In vbl senses; coating of gold, silver, etc.; plate-racing. [f. PLATE[2] + -ING[1]]

platĭ'nĭc *a.* Of platinum, esp. (Chem.) in tetravalent form. [f. PLATINUM + -IC]

plă'tĭnīze, -īse (-īz), *v.t.* Coat with platinum. [f. PLATINUM + -IZE]

plă'tĭnoid *n.* Alloy of copper, zinc, nickel, etc.; a platinum metal. [f. PLATINUM + -OID]

plă'tĭnotȳpe *n.* (Print made by) process of photographic printing in platinum black. [f. foll. + -O- + TYPE[1]]

plă'tĭnum *n.* White heavy ductile malleable metallic element unaffected by simple acids and fusible only at very high temperature; **~ black,** platinum in form of powder like lampblack; **~ blonde,** (woman with) silvery-blonde (hair); **~ metal,** metallic element (osmium, iridium, palladium, etc.) found with and resembling platinum. [mod. L (see -IUM) f. earlier *platina* f. Sp., dim. of *plata* silver; see -INE[4]]

plă'tĭt|ūde *n.* Commonplaceness; commonplace remark, esp. one solemnly delivered; hence **~ū'dĭn**IZE (2) *v.i.*, **~ū'dĭn**OUS *a.* [F (PLAT[3]), after *certitude, multitudinous,* etc.]

plătĭtūdĭnār'ian *n.* & *a.* **1.** *n.* One who uses platitudes. **2.** *a.* Characterized by or fond of using platitudes. [f. prec., after *latitudinarian*]

Platŏ'nĭc *a.* Of Plato the Greek philosopher (d. 347 B.C.) or his doctrines; confined to words or theory, not leading to action, harmless; **~ body** or **solid,** (Geom.) one of five REGULAR solids (tetrahedron, cube, octahedron, dodecahedron, icosahedron); **~ love,** purely spiritual love usu. for one of opposite sex; **~ year,** cycle in which heavenly bodies were supposed to go through all their possible movements and return to original positions; hence or cogn. **Platŏ'n**ICALLY *adv.*, **Plā'ton**ISM (3), **Plā'ton**IST (2), *ns.*, **Plā'ton**IZE (2, 3) *v.i.* & *t.* [f. L f. Gk *Platōnikos* (*Platōn* Plato; see -IC)]

platoo'n *n.* (Mil.) subdivision of a company, a tactical unit commanded by a lieutenant and usu. divided into three sections; group of persons acting together; (Hist.) small infantry detachment, esp. a unit for volley-firing etc., volley fired by it. [f. F *peloton* small ball, dim. of *pelote*; see PELLET, -OON]

pla'tteland (plah'telahnt) *n.* (S. Afr.) = BACK[1]-*veld.* [Afrik., = flat land]

|**plă'tter** *n.* (U.S. or arch.) Flat dish or plate esp. for food (***on a ~**, = *on a* PLATE[1] 10); *gramophone record. [ME & AF *plater,* f. AF *plat* PLATE[1]]

plă'tȳ- *comb. form.* Broad, flat, as: **~he'lminth,** flatworm; **~pus,** Australian egg-laying aquatic and burrowing mammal with ducklike beak and flat tail; **~rrhine** (-rīn), (of monkey) with nostrils far apart and directed forwards or sideways, (of person) having broad nose with flat bridge. [f. Gk *platu-* (*platus* broad, flat)]

plau'dĭt *n.* (usu. in *pl.*) Round of applause; emphatic expression of approval. [shortened f. L *plaudite* applaud, imper. pl. of *plaudere plaus-* applaud, said by Roman actors at end of play]

plau's|ĭble (-z-) *a.* (Of argument, statement, etc.) specious, seeming reasonable or probable; (of person) persuasive but deceptive; hence or cogn. **~ibi'lity** *n.*, **~ĭb**LY[2] *adv.* [f. L *plausibilis* (as prec.; see -IBLE)]

play[1] *v.* **1.** *v.i.* Move about in lively or unrestrained or capricious manner, frisk, flutter, pass gently (*around, about,* etc.), strike lightly (*on* etc.), (*bees play about flowers*; *tresses play on her neck*; *smile played on his lips*; *wind plays on water*; *his fancy played round the idea*). **2.** Emit light, water, etc., (*fountains play from 10 till 4*). **3.** Amuse oneself, sport, frolic; trifle, pass time pleasantly, *with*; (sl.) act as required (*he wouldn't play*); (prov.) be away from work or on strike; **~ about** or **around,** behave irresponsibly (*with*); **~(up)on words,** make pun. **4.** Employ oneself in a game; gamble; **~ at,** engage in (game), (fig.) engage in (*fighting* etc.) in trivial or half-hearted way; **~ fair,** play or (fig.) act fairly; **false,** act deceitfully or treacherously; *play with* FIRE[1]; **~ into** person's **hands,** act so as to give him the advantage; **~ off,** play extra match to decide draw or tie; **~-off** *n.*, such extra game; **~ed out,** exhausted of energy or vitality or usefulness; **~ safe,** act with caution; *play on the* SQUARE[1]; *play for* TIME[1] 9; **~ up,** put all one's energy into game, (colloq.) behave annoyingly. **5.** (Of cricket-ground, tennis-court, etc.) be in (specified) condition. **6.** Perform *on* (musical instrument etc.); **~ by ear,** (1) perform without aid of written music, (2) proceed instinctively or step by step according to results; **~ (up)on,** make use of (person's fears, credulity, etc.). **7.** Perform role on stage (*in* drama); *play to the* GALLERY; **~ up to,** act so as to support (another actor), (fig.) flatter. **8.** *v.t.* Allow (fish) to exhaust itself by pulling against line; allow (light, water, etc.) to fall *on, over,* etc. **9.** Perform, execute, (trick, prank, joke, *on* person; stroke etc. in game). **10.** Employ oneself in game of (cricket, bridge, etc., or abs.); gamble on (**~ the market,** speculate in stocks etc.; **play the races*); pretend for fun (*that we are gipsies* etc.); *play* BALL[1]; *play* DUCK[1]*s and drakes*; *play* FAST[3] *and loose*; *play the* GAME[1]; *play* HELL *with*; **play* HOOK(E)Y; **~ off,** complete (game etc. that is to be played). **11.** Contend against (person) in game; include (person) in team for game; occupy (specified position) in team at football etc.; **~ for,** (colloq.) regard (person) as being or having; **~ oneself in,** become accustomed to prevailing conditions (in game, or fig.); ~ **off,** oppose (person etc. *against* another) esp. for one's own advantage; ~ **up,** (colloq.) annoy, tease. **12.** (Cricket etc.) Strike (ball, or abs.) in specified (esp. defensive) manner; *play* BACK³; ~ **on,** (abs., Cricket) be out by playing ball on to one's own wicket. **13.** Move (chess-man etc.); take (playing-card) from one's hand and lay it face upwards on table in one's turn; (fig.) make use of (advantage available; *play* one's *ace*, one's *trump card*); ~ one's **cards well,** (fig.) make good use of one's opportunities. **14.** Perform on (musical instrument, or abs.); ~ **by ear** (cf. sense 6); perform (piece of music etc. *on* instrument). **15.** Cause (gramophone, tape-recorder, etc.) to produce music or other sound; ~ **back,** make audible (what has previously been recorded); **~-back** *n.*, such reproduction of sound; ~ **down,** minimize; ~ **up,** make the most of, exploit. **16.** Perform (drama, role, etc.) on stage; (fig.) act in real life the part of (*play the fool*, GOD, *the* MAN¹, *truant*, etc.; *play* one's *part well*); give dramatic performance at (theatre etc.). **17.** Hence **~'**ABLE *a.* [OE *pleg(i)an, plægian* exercise, = MDu. *pleien* dance, perh. rel. to OS *plegan*, OHG *pflegan* attend to]

play² *n.* **1.** Brisk, light, or fitful movement. **2.** Activity, operation, (*lively play of fancy*; *other forces come into play*, *are in full play*, *are brought* or *called into play*); **in** ~, engaged or occupied (*hold* one's *attackers in play*); **make** ~, act effectively; **make ~ with,** use ostentatiously. **3.** Freedom of movement, space for this, scope for activity, (*bolts should have half an inch of play*; *allow full play to curiosity*). **4.** Recreation, amusement, esp. as spontaneous activity of children or young animals; **at** ~, engaged in playing; *said it only* **in** ~, not seriously; ~ **of words,** (arch.) trifling with words; ~ **on words,** pun. **5.** Playing of game; manner or style of this; action in game; *manœuvre, esp. in game (**make a ~ for,** *(sl.) seek to acquire); *ball is* **in** ~ (being used in ordinary course of game), *is* **out of** ~ (temporarily out of use according to rules); CHILD'*s*, FAIR², FOUL, *play*. **6.** (prov.) Being away from work (of workmen on strike etc.). **7.** Story to be acted on stage etc.; **as good as a ~,** very amusing or interesting; hence **~'**LET *n.* **8.** Gaming, gambling. **9. ~-acting** (lit. or fig.); **~-actor** (usu. derog.); **~'bill,** bill or placard announcing theatrical play, *theatre programme; **~'boy,** pleasure-loving usu. rich man; **~'fellow,** companion in (usu. children's) play; **~'goer,** frequenter of theatre; **~'ground,** piece of ground used for playing esp. at school, place for recreation (*playground of the idle rich*); **~-group,** group of young children who play together regularly under supervision; **~'house,** (1) theatre, (2) *toy house; **~'mate,** playfellow; **~-pen, ~-suit,** portable enclosure, garment, for young child to play in; **~'thing,** toy, (fig.) person etc. treated as mere toy; **~'time,** time assigned for playing or recreation; **~'wright,** dramatist. [OE *plega, plæga* exercise (as prec.)]

play'er *n.* In vbl senses; person engaged in or skilful in a game; performer on musical instrument; ‖(Hist.) professional cricketer etc.; actor; = RECORD-*player*; **~-piano** (fitted with apparatus enabling it to be played automatically). [OE *plegere* (as PLAY¹, -ER¹)]

play'ful *a.* Frolicsome, sportive; humorous, jocular; hence **~**LY² *adv.*, **~**NESS *n.* [ME, f. PLAY² + -FUL]

play'ĭng *n.* In vbl senses; **~-card,** oblong piece of pasteboard used in games, usu. in pack of 52, identical on one side and marked on the other side to show one of thirteen ranks in one of four suits; **~-field,** field used in outdoor games. [ME, f. PLAY¹ + -ING¹]

pla'za (-ah'-) *n.* Market-place, open square (esp. in Spanish town). [Sp., = PLACE¹]

plea *n.* Pleading, argument, excuse; appeal, entreaty, (*make a plea for*); (Law) formal statement by or on behalf of defendant, defence, (**special ~,** alleging new fact); (Hist.) action at law (*Court of Common Pleas*). [ME & AF *ple, plai*, OF *plait, plaid* agreement, discussion f. L *placitum* decree, neut. p.p. (as n.) of *placēre* please]

pleach *v.t.* Entwine, interlace; esp. = PLASH³. [ME *pleche* f. OF **plechier* var. of *ple(i)ssier, pla(i)ssier*; see PLASH³]

plead *v.* (**~'ed,** or (esp. U.S., Sc., dial.) **pled**). **1.** *v.i.* Address court as advocate on behalf of either party, whence **~'**ER¹ *n.* (SPECIAL *pleader*); put forward a plea; make appeal or entreaty; ~ **with,** make earnest appeal to, whence **~'ĭng**LY² *adv.* **2.** *v.t.* Maintain (cause) in court; allege formally as plea, (fig.) allege as excuse etc. (*I can only plead inexperience, a previous engagement*), whence **~'**ABLE *a.*; ~ **guilty,** confess liability or guilt; ~ **not guilty,** deny liability or guilt. [ME, f. AF *pleder*, OF *plaidier* (as PLEA)]

plea'dĭng *n.* In vbl senses; (usu. in *pl.*) formal (now usu. written) statement of cause of action or defence; SPECIAL *pleading*. [ME, f. prec. + -ING¹]

plea'sance (plĕ'z-) *n.* (arch.) Pleasure, enjoyment; pleasure-ground, esp. one attached to mansion. [ME, f. OF *plaisance* (as foll.; see -ANCE)]

plea'sant (plĕ'z-) *a.* (**~er, ~est**). Agreeable to mind, feelings, or senses; ‖(arch.) jocular, facetious; hence **~**LY² *adv.*, **~**NESS *n.* [ME, f. OF *plaisant* (as PLEASE; see -ANT)]

plea'santrӯ (plĕ'z-) *n.* Humorous behaviour in conversation etc., jocularity; humorous speech, joking remark. [f. F *plaisanterie* (as prec.; see -ERY)]

please (-z) *v.* **1.** *v.t.* Give pleasure to (*meant only to please the eye*; *this book will please you*); ~ **oneself,** do as one likes; **be ~d with,** derive pleasure from; **be ~d** (glad) **to** (do; esp. as polite form of consent or offer); **be ~d** (graciously willing) **to** (do; in formal or iron. deference, *Her Majesty has been graciously pleased to confer* etc., *your lordship was pleased to doubt my veracity*); (with *it* as subject, expressed or omitted, representing a prec. or foll. infinitive, clause, or sentence, now chiefly as in last use) *it has never pleased him to explain*; (*may it*) *please your honour*, *there was no moon that night*; *the matter will be cleared up some day, please God*. **2.** *v.i.* Think fit, have will or desire, (*take as many as you please*); give pleasure (*he was anxious to please*). **3. If you ~,** with your permission¹ (polite form of request esp. for trifling services; *I will take another cup, if you please*), if I may say so and be believed (iron., with implication that nothing could be more unreasonable; *and now, if you please, he expects me to pay for it!*). **4.** (in *imper.*, orig. = *may it please you*) *ring the bell, please*; *may I come in, please?*; *won't you please come in?*; *coffee for two, please*; *please return it soon*; *please don't forget the key*. **5.** Hence **pleas**ED¹ (-ēzd), **plea's**ING² (-z-), *adjs.* [ME *plaise* f. OF *plaisir* f. L *placēre*]

plea'surab|le (plĕ'zh*er*-) *a.* Causing pleasure; hence **~le**NESS (-beln-) *n.*, **~**LY² *adv.* [f. foll. + -ABLE, after *comfortable*]

plea'sure (plĕ'zh*er*) *n.* & *v.* **1.** *n.* Feeling of satisfaction or joy; sensuous enjoyment as an object of life (*a life given up to pleasure*; **man of ~,** profligate); source of pleasure (*it is a pleasure to talk to him*); gratification (*do me the* *pleasure of dining with me*); **take (a) ~ in,** like doing; **take** one's ~, (arch.) enjoy oneself (esp. sensually); **with** ~, gladly, certainly. **2.** Will, desire, (*shall consult his pleasure; can be altered at pleasure*); gracious wish (of monarch etc.). **3. ~-boat** etc. (used for pleasure, not business); **~-ground** (laid out for pleasure). **4.** *v.t.* Give (esp. sexual) pleasure to. **5.** *v.i.* Take pleasure (*in* thing, *in* doing). [ME & OF *plesir, plaisir* PLEASE, used as n.; see -URE]

pleat *n.*, & *v.t.* **1.** *n.* Fold or crease, esp. flattened fold in cloth doubled upon itself; BOX²-*pleat*; **inverted** ~, box-pleat formed on inside of material: KNIFE-*pleat*. **2.** *v.t.* Fold (cloth etc.) thus. [ME, var. of PLAIT]

plĕb *n.* (sl.) Plebeian, person of lower classes. [abbr.]

***plēbe** *n.* (colloq.) Member of lowest class at U.S. Naval or Military Academy. [shortened f. PLEBEIAN]

plėbei'an (-bē'an) *n.* & *a.* **1.** *n.* Commoner in ancient Rome (cf. PATRICIAN); commoner. **2.** *a.* Of low birth, of the common people, uncultured; coarse, base, ignoble; hence ~IZE (3) *v.t.*, ~NESS (-n-n-) *n.* [f. L *plebeius* (*plebs plebis* common people) + -AN]

plĕ'bĭscĭte *n.* Direct vote of all electors of State on important public question, e.g. change in the constitution; public expression of community's opinion, with or without binding force; (Rom. Hist.) law enacted by plebeians' assembly; hence **plėbĭ'scĭt**ARY¹ *a.* [f. F *plébiscite* f. L *plebiscitum* (*plebs plebis* commons, *scitum* decree f. *sciscere* vote for)]

plĕ'ctr|um *n.* (*pl.* ~**a** *or* ~**ums**). Small pointed piece of ivory, quill, etc., for plucking strings of guitar, zither, etc.; corresponding part of harpsichord etc. [L, f. Gk *plēktron* (*plēssō* strike)]

plĕd. See PLEAD.

plĕdge¹ *n.* **1.** Thing handed over to person as security for fulfilment of contract, payment of debt, etc., and liable to forfeiture in case of failure; thing put in pawn; (fig.) child as token of mutual love; thing given as token of favour etc. or of something to come. **2.** Drinking of a health, toast. **3.** Promise (*under pledge of secrecy*); solemn engagement to abstain from intoxicants (*take, sign, keep, the pledge*); (Polit.) leader's public promise to adopt or not adopt some course; *(person making) promise to join fraternity etc. **4.** State of being pledged (*goods lying in pledge, taken out of pledge*). [ME & OF *plege* f. Frank. L *plebium* (*plebire* assure), perh. f. Gmc **pleg*-; cf. PLIGHT]

plĕdge² *v.t.* Deposit as security, pawn; promise solemnly by pledge of (one's honour, word, etc.); bind (person, one*self*) by solemn promise; drink to the health of; hence ~'ABLE (-ja-) *a.*, **plĕdg**EE' *n.*, one who receives a pledge, **plĕ'dg**ER¹, **plĕ'dg**OR, (-jer) *ns.* [f. prec.]

plĕ'dgėt *n.* Small wad of lint etc. [16th c., of unkn. orig.]

Plei'ad (plī'-) *n.* (*pl.* ~**es** *pr.* -dēz, *or* ~**s**). **1.** (in *pl.*) Cluster of stars in constellation Taurus, usu. spoken of as 7. **2.** (fig.) Brilliant group of (usu. 7) persons or things, esp. French poets of the latter part of 16th c. [ME, f. L *Plēias* f. Gk *Pleias -ados*]

plein air (plĕnār') *a.* (Paint.) Representing effects of atmosphere and light not observable in studio; hence **pleinair'ĭst(e)** (plĕ-) *n.*, painter using this style. [F, = open air, orig. of Fr. impressionists *c.* 1870]

Plei'stocēne (plī's-) *a.* & *n.* (Geol.) (Of) division immediately following Pliocene, and forming lower part of quaternary period or system. [f. Gk *pleistos* most + *kainos* new]

plē'narў *a.* Entire, absolute, unqualified, (*plenary* INSPIRATION, *indulgence*); (of assembly) to be attended by all members. [f. LL *plenarius* (*plenus* full; see -ARY¹)]

plĕnĭpotĕ'ntiarў (-sherĭ) *a.* & *n.* (Person, esp. diplomatic envoy) invested with full power of independent action; (of power) absolute. [f. med. L *plenipotentiarius* (*plenus* full, *potentia* power); see -ARY¹]

plĕ'nĭtūde *n.* Fullness, completeness; abundance. [ME f. OF, f. LL *plenitudo* (*plenus* full; see -TUDE)]

plĕ'ntėous *a.* (rhet.) Plentiful; hence ~LY² *adv.*, ~NESS *n.* [ME f. OF *plentivous* (*plentif -ive* f. *plenté* PLENTY; see -IVE, -EOUS; cf. *bounteous*)]

plĕ'ntĭful *a.* Abundant, copious; hence ~LY² *adv.*, ~NESS *n.* [ME, f. foll. + -FUL]

plĕ'ntў *n.*, *a.*, & *adv.* **1.** *n.* Abundance, quite enough, as much as one could desire, (*of* thing, or abs.; *plenty of cake, there are plenty of apples; here is cake in plenty; we are in plenty of time*); **horn of** ~, cornucopia. **2.** *a.* (colloq.) Existing in ample quantity. **3.** *adv.* (colloq.) Fully (*it is plenty large enough*). [ME *plenteth, plente* f. OF *plentet* f. L *plenitas -tatis* (*plenus* full; see -TY¹)]

plē'num *n.* Space filled with matter (~ **system,** method of ventilation by forcing air in and out); full assembly. [L, neut. of *plenus* full]

plēochrō'|ĭc (-k-) *a.* Showing different colours when viewed in different directions; so ~ISM (2) *n.* [f. Gk *pleiōn* more + *-khroos* f. *khrōs* colour + -IC]

plēomŏr'ph|ĭc *a.* (Biol., Chem., & Min.) Exhibiting, or occurring in, more than one distinct form; so ~ISM (2) *n.* [f. as prec. + Gk *morphē* form + -IC]

plē'on|ăsm *n.* Use of more words than are needed to give the sense (*hear with* one's *ears; preceded his successor*); hence **~ă'st**IC *a.* [f. LL f. Gk *pleonasmos* (*pleonazō* be superfluous f. *pleon* more)]

plē'sĭosaur. Var. of foll.

plēsĭosaur'|us *n.* (*pl.* ~**i** *pr.* -ī, *or* ~**uses**). Extinct marine reptile with long neck, short tail, and four large paddles. [mod. L, f. Gk *plēsios* near + *sauros* lizard]

plĕ'thor|a *n.* Morbid condition marked by excess of red corpuscles in the blood; (fig.) over-supply, glut; hence or cogn. ~IC *a.*, **plėthŏ'r**IC-ALLY *adv.* [LL, f. Gk *plēthōrē* (*plēthō* be full)]

pleur'|a (ploor'*a*) (*pl.* ~**ae**). Either of the two serous membranes lining the thorax and enveloping the lungs in mammals; (also *pleuron*) lateral part of the body-wall in arthropods; hence ~AL *a.* [med. L f. Gk, = side of body, rib]

pleur'|ĭsў (ploor'-) *n.* Inflammation of the pleura, marked by pain in chest or side, fever, etc.; so **~ĭ't**IC *a.* [ME, f. OF *pleurisie* f. LL *pleurisis* alt. f. L f. Gk *pleuritis* (as prec.; see -ITIS)]

pleuro- (ploor-) *comb. form.* Pleura, side of body, as: **~dy'nia,** pain in side usu. in intercostal muscles; **~-pneumo'nia,** pneumonia complicated with pleurisy, esp. contagious disease of cattle etc. [f. as PLEURA + -O-]

pleur'|on (ploor'-) *n.* (*pl.* ~**a**). See PLEURA. [Gk, = side of body, rib]

plĕ'xĭglass (-ahs) *n.* Transparent acrylic plastic. **[P]**

plĕ'xor *n.* (Med.) Small hammer used in percussion. [irreg. f. Gk *plēxis* percussion + -OR (cf. *flexor* etc.)]

plĕ'xus *n.* Network, complication; (Anat.) network of nerves or vessels in animal body (*gastric, pulmonary,* SOLAR, *plexus*); hence **plĕ'xĭ**FORM *a.* [L (*plectere plex-* plait)]

plī'able *a.* = foll.; hence **plī**ABI'LITY *n.*, **plī'-ab**LY² *adv.* [F (*plier* bend; see PLY¹, -ABLE)]

plī'ant *a.* Bending easily, supple; (fig.) yielding, compliant; hence **plī'**ANCY *n.*, ~LY² *adv.* [ME, f. OF (as prec.; see -ANT)]

plī'cate *a.* (Biol. & Geol.) Folded; so **plĭcā'tED**¹ *a.* [f. L *plicatus*, p.p. of *plicare* fold; see -ATE²]

plĭcā'tion *n.* Folding; fold, folded condition. [ME, f. med. L *plicatio* (see -ATION) or f. L *plicare* fold, after *complication*]

plié (plē'ā) *n.* (Ballet). Bending of knees. [F, p.p. of *plier* bend (see PLY¹)]

plī'ers (-z) *n. pl.* (*Pair of*) pincers having long jaws with parallel surfaces, for holding small objects, bending wire, etc. [f. (dial.) *ply* bend (as PLIABLE) + -ER¹ + -S¹]

plīght¹ (plīt) *v.t.*, & *n.*, (arch.) **1.** *v.t.* (esp. in *p.p.*) Pledge (one's TROTH, faith, promise); engage one*self* (*to* person; *plighted lovers*). **2.** *n.* Engagement, pledging. [v. f. n., f. OE *pliht* danger, = MDu. *plicht*, OHG *pfliht* duty, f. Gmc **pleh-*; cf. PLEDGE¹]

plīght² (plīt) *n.* Condition, state, esp. unfortunate one (*sorry, evil, hopeless, plight*). [ME & AF *plit* = OF *pleit* fold; see PLAIT; *-gh-* by confus. w. prec.]

Plĭ'msoll *a.* & *n.* ~ **line,** ~ **mark,** marking on ship's side showing limit of legal submersion in summer or under various conditions; ‖(*p*~) rubber-soled canvas sports shoe. [f. S. ~, Engl. politician d. 1898, promoter of Merchant Shipping Act of 1876]

plĭnth *n.* Lower square member of base of column; projecting part of wall immediately above ground; base supporting a vase, statue, etc. [f. F *plinthe* or L *plinthus*, f. Gk *plinthos* tile, brick, squared stone]

Plī'ocēne *a.* & *n.* (Geol.) (Of) highest division of tertiary period or system. [f. Gk *pleiōn* more + *kainos* new]

plĭ'ssé (plē'sā) *a.* & *n.* (Material) treated so as to cause permanent puckering. [F, p.p. of *plisser* pleat]

plŏd *v.* (**-dd-**) & *n.* **1.** *v.i.* Walk doggedly or laboriously, trudge, (*on, along,* etc.); work steadily, drudge, slave, (*at* etc.). **2.** *v.t.* Make (one's *way*) or tread laboriously. **3.** Hence **~'d**ER¹ *n.* **4.** *n.* Laborious walk or work. [16th c., prob. imit.]

-ploid *suf.* (Biol.) forming *adjs.* denoting number of sets of chromosomes in a cell (*diploid, polyploid*). [after HAPLOID]

ploi'dȳ *n.* (Biol.) Degree of multiplicity of chromosomes in a cell. [after DIPLOIDY, POLYPLOIDY, etc.]

plŏnk¹. Var. of PLUNK.

plŏnk² *n.* (sl.) Cheap or inferior wine. [orig. Austral., perh. f. prec. or f. F *vin blanc* white wine]

plŏp *n., adv.,* & *v.* (**-pp-**). **1.** *n.* Sound as of smooth object dropping into water without splash; act of falling with this sound. **2.** *adv.* With a plop. **3.** *v.t.* & *i.* (Cause to) fall thus. [19th c.; imit.]

plō'sion (-zhon) *n.* (Phonet.) Sudden release of breath in pronunciation of stop consonant (STOP² 5). [f. EXPLOSION]

plō'sĭve (*or* -z-) *a.* & *n.* (Phonet.) (Of) stop consonant (STOP² 5). [f. EXPLOSIVE]

plŏt¹ *n.* Piece (usu. small) of ground; *plan of land ownership etc.; plan of main events or topics in play, poem, novel, etc., whence ~'LESS *a.*; conspiracy (*Gunpowder Plot*); secret plan; curve etc. found by plotting. [OE, & f. *complot* (OF, = secret plan), both of unkn. orig.)]

plŏt² *v.t.* (**-tt-**). Make plan or map of (existing object, place or thing to be laid out, constructed, etc.); mark (point etc.) on diagram; make (curve etc.) by marking out a number of points; plan, contrive, (crime etc., or abs.); plan secretly; hence **~'t**ER¹ (1, 2) *n.* [f. prec.]

plough¹ (plow), (U.S. or arch.) **plow¹**, *n.* **1.** Implement for cutting furrows in soil and turning it up, consisting of cutting blade (**~'share**) and mould-board fixed in frame drawn by tractor, horses, etc. and guided by **~'man; the P~**, constellation Ursa Major or its seven bright stars; **put** one's **hand to the ~**, undertake task (Luke 9:62). **2.** Ploughed land. **3.** Implement or device resembling plough (SNOW¹-*plough*). **4.** ‖(sl.) Rejection of candidate in examination [f. foll.]. **5. ~-beam,** central beam of plough; **~-boy,** boy who leads plough-horses etc.; **~-land,** (Hist.) as much land as could be ploughed by one team of 8 oxen in the year, unit of assessment in N. & E. counties of England; **~'man** (see sense 1; *ploughman's* SPIKENARD); **P~ Monday** (first after Epiphany); **~'share** (see sense 1); **~-shoe,** appliance for protecting or supporting ploughshare; **~-staff** (ending in small spade, used to clear earth etc. from coulter etc.); **~-tail,** rear of plough, (fig.) farm-labour (*at the plough-tail*). [OE *plōh* f. ON *plógr*, = OFris. *plōch*, OS *plōg*, OHG *pfluoc* f. Gmc **plōgaz* f. N. Italic **plōg-*]

plough² (plow), (U.S. or arch.) **plow²**, *v.* **1.** *v.t.* Turn up (earth, or abs.) with plough, esp. before sowing (~ **the sand**(**s**), labour uselessly); ~ **back,** turn (grass, etc.) with plough into soil to enrich it, (fig.) reinvest (profits) in same business etc. **2.** Root *out*, cast *up*, thrust *down*, (roots, weeds) with plough; furrow, scratch, (surface) as with plough; produce (furrow, line) thus (~ **a lonely furrow,** carry on without help); (of ship etc.) cleave (surface of water etc.); ‖(sl.) reject (candidate) in examination. **3.** *v.i.* Move like plough through or into obstacles; advance laboriously (*through* snow etc., *through* book etc.); ‖(sl.) fail in examination. [ME, f. prec.]

plo'ver (plŭ'-) *n.* Gregarious medium-sized wading bird of family Charadriidae, incl. lapwing. [ME & AF; OF *plo(u)vier*, f. Rom. **ploviarius* f. L *pluvia* rain]

plow¹,². See PLOUGH¹,².

ploy *n.* (colloq.) Expedition, undertaking; occupation, job; manœuvre to frustrate opponent etc. [orig. Sc., 18th c.; orig. unkn.]

‖**P.L.P.** *abbr.* Parliamentary Labour Party.

‖**P.L.R.** *abbr.* Public Lending Right.

plŭck¹ *n.* Plucking, twitch; ‖(arch.) rejection or failure in examination; heart, liver, and lungs, of animal as food; courage, spirit, whence (-)~ED² (-kt), ~'LESS, ~'Y², *adjs.*, **~'ĭ**LY² *adv.*, **~'ĭ**NESS *n.* [ME, f. foll.]

plŭck² *v.* **1.** *v.t.* Pull off, pick, (flower, feather, hair); (arch.) pull, drag, snatch, (*away, off, out,* etc.); pull at, twitch; sound (string of musical instrument) thus; strip (bird) of feathers (CROW¹ *to pluck*); plunder, swindle, (*pluck a pigeon*); ‖(arch.) reject (candidate) in examination; ~ **up** one's **heart, spirits, courage,** take courage. **2.** *v.i.* Tug or snatch *at*. **3.** Hence ~'ER¹ *n.* [OE *ploccian, pluccian,* cogn. w. MLG *plucken*, MDu. *plocken*, ON *plokka, plukka,* f. Gmc **plukkōn* etc., ult. f. Rom. **piluccare*]

plŭg¹ *n.* Piece of solid material fitting tightly into hole, used to fill gap or cavity or act as wedge; natural or morbid concretion acting thus; stopper for vessel or pipe; device of metal pins in insulated casing, fitting into holes in socket for making electrical connection; (colloq.) electric socket; (colloq.) release-mechanism of water-closet flushing-apparatus (*pull the plug*); = FIRE¹-*plug*; = SPARK²*ing-plug*; tobacco pressed into cake or stick, piece of this cut off for chewing; *inferior horse etc.; (colloq.) favourable reference to commercial product etc.; ***~-hat,** (colloq.) top hat; ***~-ugly,** (sl.) ruffian. [f. MDu. & MLG *plugge*, of unkn. orig.]

plŭg[2] *v.* (-gg-). **1.** *v.t.* Stop (hole etc. *up*) with plug; (sl.) shoot (person etc.); (sl.) strike (person etc.) with fist; (colloq.) seek to popularize (song, theory, policy, etc.) by constant repetition and favourable mention; ~ **in,** connect electrically by inserting plug into socket; **~-in** *a.* & *n.*, (appliance) able to be connected thus. **2.** *v.i.* (colloq.) Plod (*away at* work etc.). [f. prec.]

plŭm *n.* **1.** (Tree of genus *Prunus* bearing) roundish fleshy fruit with sweet pulp and flattish pointed stone; dried grape or raisin as used for *plum-cake* etc.; (fig.) good thing, best of a collection, prize in life etc., well-paid position. **2. ~-cake** (containing raisins, currants, etc.); ~ **duff,** plain flour pudding with raisins or currants; ~ **pudding,** (1) boiled pudding of flour, bread-crumbs, suet, raisins, currants, eggs, spices, etc., eaten esp. at Christmas, (2) ordinary suet-pudding with raisins; **~-pudding dog,** Dalmatian; **~-pudding stone,** (Geol.) conglomerate of flint or other pebbles. [OE *plūme*, = MLG *plūme*, MHG *pflūme*, ON *plóma*, f. med. L *pruna* f. L *prunum*]

plu'mag|e (-ōō'-) *n.* Bird's feathers; hence (-)~ED[2] (-ĭjd) *a.* [ME f. OF (as PLUME[1]; see -AGE)]

plumassier' (plōō-) *n.* One who trades or works in ornamental feathers. [F (*plumasse* augment. of PLUME[1]; see -IER)]

plŭmb[1] (-m) *n.*, *a.*, & *adv.* **1.** *n.* Ball of lead, esp. that attached to mason's **~-line** (string for testing perpendicularity of wall etc.; also fig.); **out of ~**, not vertical; **~-rule,** mason's plumb-line attached to board. **2.** Sounding-lead, plummet. **3.** *a.* Vertical; (fig.) downright, sheer, (*plumb nonsense*); (Cricket, of wicket) level, true. **4.** *adv.* Vertically; (fig.) exactly (*points plumb in the same direction*) *(sl.) quite, utterly, (*plumb crazy*). [ME, prob. f. OF **plombe* f. Rom. **plumba* f. L *plumbum* lead; assim. to OF *plomb* lead]

plŭmb[2] (-m) *v.t.* Sound (sea) or measure (depth, lit. or fig.) with plummet, whence ~'LESS (-ml-) *a.*; make vertical. [f. prec.]

plŭmb[3] (-m) *v.* **1.** *v.i.* Work as plumber. **2.** *v.t.* Provide with, fit as part of, plumbing system. [back form. f. PLUMBER]

plŭmbā'gō (*pl.* ~s). **1.** Graphite; hence **plŭmbă'gĭn**OUS *a.* **2.** Leadwort, plant of genus *Plumbago* with greyish-blue etc. flowers. [L *plumbago -aginis* (*plumbum* LEAD[1])]

plŭ'mbāte. See PLUMBIC.

plŭ'mbėous *a.* Of or like lead; lead-glazed. [f. L *plumbeus* (as PLUMBAGO) + -OUS]

plŭ'mb|er (-m*er*) *n.* Workman who fits and repairs water-pipes, cisterns, etc.; so ~ERY (2, 3) (-m*er*ĭ) *n.* [ME *plummer* etc., f. OF *plommier* f. L *plumbarius* (*plumbum* LEAD[1]; see -ARY[1])]

plŭ'mb|ĭc *a.* **1.** (Chem.) Containing lead, esp. in tetravalent form, whence ~ATE[1] (3) *n.*; so **~ĭ'**FEROUS *a.* **2.** (Path.) Due to presence of lead; so ~ISM (5) *n.*, lead-poisoning. [f. L *plumbum* lead + -IC]

plŭ'mbĭng (-mĭ-) *n.* Plumber's work; system of water-pipes etc. constructed by plumber. [f. PLUMBER + -ING[1]]

plume[1] (-ōōm) *n.* Feather, esp. large one used for ornament (**borrowed ~s,** pretentious display not of one's own making); ornamental feather or bunch of feathers or horsehair, esp. as attached to helmet or hat, or worn in hair; trail of smoke from chimney, blown snow from mountain, etc.; (Zool.) feather-like part or formation; hence **plu'm**ERY (1) (-ōō'-) *n.*, ~'LESS, ~'LIKE, *adjs.*, ~'LET *n.*, (-ōō'ml-). [ME f. OF, f. L *pluma* DOWN[2]]

plume[2] (-ōōm) *v.t.* Furnish with plume(s); dress one*self* with borrowed PLUME[1]S; pride one*self* (*on* esp. something trivial or to which one has no claim); (of bird) trim, dress, preen, (it*self*, its feathers). [f. prec. or L *plumare* cover with feathers]

plu'mĭcôrn (-ōō'-) *n.* Ear-tuft of owl. [f. L *pluma* plume + *cornu* horn]

plŭ'mmer-blŏck *n.* (Mech.) Metal case for supporting revolving shaft, with movable cover giving access to bearings. [perh. f. surname *Plummer* + BLOCK[1]]

plŭ'mmėt *n.*, & *v.i.* **1.** *n.* (Weight attached to) plumb-line; sounding-lead; weight attached to fishing-line to keep float upright. **2.** *v.i.* Fall rapidly. [ME f. OF *plommet* dim. (as PLUMB[1])]

plŭ'mmȳ *a.* Of, or abounding in, plums; (colloq.) good, desirable, (of voice) rich in tone. [f. PLUM + -Y[2]]

plu'mōse (-ōō'-) *a.* Feathered; feather-like. [f. L *plumosus* (as PLUME[1]; see -OSE[1])]

plŭmp[1] *a.* & *v.* **1.** *a.* (Esp. of person or animal or part of body) full, rounded, fleshy, filled out; hence ~'LY[2] *adv.*, ~'NESS *n.*, ~'Y[2] *a.* **2.** *v.t.* Make plump; fatten *up*. **3.** *v.i.* Become plump; swell *out* or *up*. [ME *plompe*, f. MDu. *plomp* blunt, MLG *plump*, *plomp* shapeless etc.]

plŭmp[2] *v.*, *n.*, *adv.*, & *a.* **1.** *v.t.* & *i.* Drop or plunge with abrupt descent (*down upon* etc.); (colloq.) utter abruptly, blurt *out*. **2.** *v.i.* ||Vote *for* (one candidate alone, when one might vote for two); (fig.) go whole-heartedly *for* one of alternative choices; *come or go abruptly. **3.** *n.* Abrupt plunge, heavy fall. **4.** *adv.* (colloq.) With sudden or heavy fall; directly, bluntly, (*I told him plump*). **5.** *a.* (colloq.) Direct, unqualified, (*answer with a plump 'No'*). [ME, f. MLG *plumpen*, MDu. *plompen*; of imit. orig.]

plŭmp[3] *n.* (arch.) Company, troop; cluster. [ME, of unkn. orig.]

plu'mūl|e (plōō'-) *n.* **1.** Rudimentary stem of embryo plant; hence ~AR[1] *a.* **2.** Little feather of down; hence ~A'CEOUS *a.* [F, or f. L *plumula*, dim. (as PLUME[1])]

plu'mȳ (-ōō'-) *a.* Plumelike; feathery; adorned with plumes. [f. PLUME[1] + -Y[2]]

plŭ'nder *v.t.*, & *n.* **1.** *v.t* Rob (place, person) forcibly of goods, esp. as in war; rob systematically; steal, embezzle, (goods, or abs.); hence ~AGE (3), ~ER[1], *ns.* **2.** *n.* Violent or dishonest acquisition of property; property so acquired; (sl.) profit, gain. [f. LG *plündern*, lit. 'rob of household goods' f. MHG *plunder* clothing etc.]

plŭnge (-nj) *v.* & *n.* **1.** *v.t.* Thrust violently (*into* liquid, cavity, etc.); (fig.) thrust (person etc. *into*, *in*, condition, action, etc.; esp. in p.p.: *plunged in gloom*); immerse completely, sink entirely (pot containing plant) in ground. **2.** *v.i.* Throw oneself, dive, (*into* water, difficulty, discussion, etc., or *in*); enter impetuously (*into* room, *up*, *down*, stairs, etc.); descend violently or suddenly; (of horse) start violently forward; (of ship) pitch; (sl.) gamble deeply, run into debt; **plunging fire** (from guns at higher level); **plunging neckline** (cut low). **3.** *n.* Plunging, dive, (**~-bath,** bath large enough to dive into; ~ **neckline,** = *plunging neckline*); (fig.) decisive step (*take the plunge*). [ME, f. OF *plungier* f. Rom. **plumbicare* sound with plummet (L *plumbum*)]

plŭ'nger (-nj-) *n.* In vbl senses; part of mechanism that works with plunging or thrusting motion; rubber cup on handle for removal of blockages by suction; (sl.) reckless gambler, speculator. [f. prec. + -ER[1]]

plŭnk *v.* & *n.* **1.** *v.t.* & *i.* Throw or fall heavily or suddenly; *hit unexpectedly; (cause to) sound with plunk. **2.** *n.* Sound made by sharply plucking strings of harp, banjo, etc.; *(colloq.) heavy blow; *(sl.) dollar. [imit.]

plupêr'fèct (-ōō-; *or* -ōō'-) *a.* & *n.* (Gram.) (Tense) denoting action completed prior to some past point of time specified or implied (expr. in E by *had* with *p.p.*: *he had called*). [f. mod. L *plusperfectum* f. L *plus quam perfectum* more than perfect, transl. Gk *hupersuntelikos*]

plur'al (-oor'-) *a.* & *n.* **1.** (Gram.) ~ **(number)**, (form or class of forms of noun, verb, etc.) denoting more than one (or, in languages with dual, more than two). **2.** *a.* More than one in number; ~ **society** (containing members of more than one race); ~ **vote, voter, voting,** (of one person in more than one constituency). **3.** Hence ~LY² *adv.* [ME, f. OF *plurel* f. L *pluralis* (*plus pluris* more; see -AL)]

plur'al|ism (-oor'-) *n.* Holding of more than one office, esp. benefice, at a time; (Philos.) system that recognizes more than one ultimate principle (cf. MONISM); form of society in which members of minority groups maintain independent traditions; so ~IST (2) *n.*, **~i'st**IC *a.* [f. prec. + -ISM]

plură'lĭtў (-oor-) *n.* State of being plural; large number, multitude; holding of two or more benefices or offices; benefice or office held with another; majority (*of* votes etc.); *majority over each other candidate etc. but not over all together. [ME, f. OF *pluralité* f. LL *pluralitas* (as PLURAL; see -ITY)]

plur'alize (-oor'-), **-īse** (-īz), *v.* **1.** *v.t.* Make plural; express in the plural. **2.** *v.i.* Hold more than one benefice. [f. PLURAL + -IZE]

plurĭ- (-oorĭ) *comb. form.* Several, as: **~li'teral,** (Heb. Gram.) having more than 3 letters in the root; **~pre'sence,** (Theol.) presence in more than one place at the same time. [f. L *plus pluris* more, *plures* several + -I-]

plŭs *prep.*, *a.*, & *n.* **1.** *prep.* With the addition of (symbol +; *3 plus 4 equals 7*); above zero (*temperatures between minus ten and plus ten degrees*); (colloq.) with, having gained, possessing; ~ **one** etc., adverse handicap assigned to golfer etc. (added to his score); **~-fours,** long wide knickerbockers worn esp. by golfers [so named because, to produce the overhang, the length is normally increased by four inches]. **2.** *a.* Additional, extra; (after number etc.) at least (*fifteen plus*); ALPHA etc. *plus*; (Math.) positive; (Electr.) having positive charge; *plus* SIGN¹. **3.** *n.* The symbol (+); additional quantity, positive quantity; advantage. [L, = more]

plŭsh *n.* & *a.* **1.** *n.* Cloth of silk, cotton, etc., with nap longer and softer than that of velvet; hence ~'Y² *a.*, stylish, luxurious. **2.** *a.* Made of plush; plushy; hence ~'LY² *adv.* [f. obs. F *pluche* contr. f. *peluche* f. OF *peluchier* f. It. *peluzzo* dim. of *pelo* f. L *pilus* hair]

plu'târchў (plōō'târkĭ) *n.* Plutocracy. [f. Gk *ploutos* wealth + *-arkhia* -rule]

Plu'tō (-ōō'-) *n.* Farthest known planet of solar system. [L, f. Gk *Ploutōn* god of the underworld]

plutŏ'cracў (-ōō-) *n.* Rule of the wealthy; State ruled by the wealthy; (ruling class of) wealthy persons; so **plu'to**CRAT *n.*, **pluto-cră'**TIC *a.*, (-ōō-). [f. Gk *ploutokratia* (as foll.; see -CRACY)]

plutŏ'latrў (-ōō-) *n.* Worship of wealth. [f. Gk *ploutos* wealth; see -LATRY]

plu'ton (-ōō'-) *n.* (Geol.) Body of rock exposed after solidification at great depth. [back form. f. PLUTONIC]

Plutō'nĭan (-ōō-) *a.* Infernal; of the infernal regions. [f. L f. Gk *Ploutōnios* (*Ploutōn* god of the underworld) + -AN]

plutŏ'nĭc (-ōō-) *a.* & *n.* **1.** *a.* (*P*~) = prec. **2.** (Geol., of rock) formed as igneous rock by solidification at great depth; ~ **theory** (attributing most geological phenomena to action of internal heat, whence **Plu'ton**ISM (3), **Plu'ton**IST (2), (-ōō'-) *ns.*). **3.** *n.* Plutonic rock. [f. as prec. + -IC]

plutō'nĭum (-ōō-) *n.* (Chem.) Radioactive metallic element formed from neptunium, used in nuclear weapons and reactors. [f. PLUTO (next planet after Neptune) + -IUM]

plu'vĭ|al (-ōō'-) *a.* & *n.* **1.** *a.* Of rain, rainy; so ~OUS *a.* **2.** (Geol.) Caused by rain. **3.** *n.* Period of prolonged rainfall; (Hist.) long cloak as ecclesiastical vestment. [f. L *pluvialis* (*pluvia* rain; see -AL); n. also f. med. L *pluviale* rain-cloak]

pluvĭ|ŏ'mèter (-ōō-) *n.* Rain-gauge; hence **~omĕ'tr**IC(AL) *adjs.* [f. L *pluvia* rain + -O- + -METER]

plȳ¹ *n.* Fold, thickness, layer, of cloth etc., strand of rope, yarn, etc., (TWO, THREE, etc., *-ply*); (fig.) turn, tendency, (*take a ply*); **~('wood),** strong thin board made by gluing layers with the grains crosswise. [ME, f. F *pli* (*plier*, *pleier* f. L *plicare* fold)]

plȳ² *v.* **1.** *v.t.* Use, wield vigorously, (tool, weapon); work at (one's business, task, trade); supply (person etc.) persistently *with* (food etc.); assail vigorously (person *with* questions, arguments). **2.** *v.i.* Work steadily; (Naut.) sail to windward; (of vessel or its master, bus, etc.) go to and fro *between* (places); (of boatman, porter, cabman) attend regularly for custom (*at* place, *for hire*). [ME *plye*, f. APPLY]

Plȳ'mouth (-muth) *n.* ~ **Brethren,** Calvinistic religious body formed at Plymouth *c.* 1830, with no formal creed and no official order of ministers; ~ **Rock,** medium-sized breed of domestic fowl of Amer. origin. [~ in Devon and in Massachusetts]

P.M. *abbr.* Prime Minister; Provost Marshal.

p.m. *abbr.* after noon. [f. L *post meridiem*]

Pm *symb.* promethium.

P.M.G. *abbr.* Paymaster General; Postmaster General.

PNdB *abbr.* perceived noise decibel(s).

||**P.N.E.U.** *abbr.* Parents' National Educational Union.

pneumă'tĭc (n-) *a.* & *n.* **1.** *a.* Of, or acting by means of, wind or (esp. compressed) air; ~ **dispatch,** conveyance of parcels etc. along tubes by compression or exhaustion of air; ~ **drill,** machine for breaking up road surface etc. and driven by force of compressed air; ~ **trough** (for collecting gases in jars over surface of water or mercury); ~ **tube** (for pneumatic dispatch); ~ **tyre** (inflated with air). **2.** Containing or connected with air-cavities esp. in fish or in bones of birds; spiritual. **3.** Hence **pneumă'**TICALLY *adv.*, **pneumatĭ'**CITY *n.*, (n-). **4.** *n.* Pneumatic tyre; (arch.) cycle with such tyres; (in *pl.*, treated as *sing.*) science of mechanical properties of gases. [f. F *pneumatique* or f. L f. Gk *pneumatikos* (*pneuma* wind f. *pneō* breathe; see -IC)]

pneu'mato- (n-) *comb. form.* Air, breath, spirit, as: **~cyst,** air-sac in body of bird etc.; **pneumato'logy** (n-;-ŏ'-), theory of spiritual beings, doctrine of the Holy Spirit, (arch.) psychology, whence **~lo'gical** *a.*; **~phore,** part of some compound hydrozoa containing air-cavity. [Gk, f. *pneuma* (as prec.)]

pneumō- (n-) *comb. form.* Lungs, as: **~conio'sis,** lung disease due to inhalation of dust etc.; **~ga'stric,** of lungs and stomach (esp. = VAGUS); **~thor'ax,** presence of air or gas in cavity between lung and chest-wall. [abbr. of *pneumono-* f. Gk *pneumōn* lung + -O-]

pneumonĕ'ctomȳ (n-) *n.* (Surg.) Excision of (part of) lung. [f. as prec. + -ECTOMY]

pneumō'nĭa (n-) *n.* Inflammation of the substance of one (**single ~**) or both (**double ~**) lungs; so **pneumŏ'nɪc** *a.* (**pneumonic plague,** virulent contagious bacterial disease affecting lungs), **pneumonɪ'tɪs** *n.*, (n-). [L f. Gk (*pneumōn* lung; see -IA[1])]

pō *n.* (*pl.* **pos**). (colloq.) Chamber-pot; **po--faced,** solemn-faced, humourless. [var. of POT[1], after F pr.]

P.O. *abbr.* Petty Officer; Pilot Officer; postal order; Post Office.

Po *symb.* polonium.

poach[1] *v.t.* Cook (egg) without shell in or with boiling water; cook (fish etc.) by simmering in water or milk; hence **~'ER**[1] (2) *n.* [ME, f. OF *pochier* (*poche* POKE[1])]

poach[2] *v.* **1.** *v.t.* Trample, cut up (turf etc.) with hoofs; trespass on (land etc.), capture (game, fish) by illicit or unsportsmanlike methods; obtain (advantage, start in race) by unfair means; (Tennis etc.) strike (ball, or abs.) in partner's court. **2.** *v.i.* (Of land) become sodden by being trampled; encroach, trespass, (*on* person's *preserves* etc., lit. or fig.). **3.** Hence **~'ER**[1] *n.* [earlier *poche*, perh. f. F *pocher* put in pocket (as prec.)]

pō'chard (*or* -k-) *n.* Diving duck esp. of genus *Aythya*, esp. European species with bright reddish-brown head and neck. [16th c.; orig. unkn.]

pŏchĕ'tte (-sh-) *n.* Woman's envelope-shaped handbag. [F, dim. of *poche* pocket; see POKE[1]]

pŏck *n.* Eruptive spot esp. in smallpox; **~--marked,** bearing marks (like those) left by smallpox. [OE *poc*, = MDu., MLG *pocke* f. Gmc **pukno-*]

pŏ'ckėt[1] *n.* & *a.* **1.** *n.* Small bag inserted in or attached to coat, trousers, etc., for carrying small articles (*watch, ticket, -pocket*); **in** person's **~**, (1) close to or intimate with him, (2) completely under his control; **put** one's **pride in** one's **~**, accept humiliation to achieve one's aim. **2.** Bag, sack, (esp. of hops); pouchlike compartment in suitcase, on interior surface of door of motor car, etc. **3.** (fig.) Pecuniary resources (*it is beyond my pocket; he will suffer in his pocket*); **put** one's **hand in** one's **~**, spend or give money; **in ~**, having gained in a transaction, (of money) available; **out of ~**, having lost in a transaction; **out-of-~ expenses,** actual outlay of cash incurred. **4.** Pouch at each corner and on each side of billiard-table into which balls are driven; cavity in earth filled with gold or other ore, whence **~Y**[2] *a.*; cavity in rock esp. (Geol.) filled with foreign matter; closed side-branch in passage etc.; (Mil.) (troops occupying) isolated area in battle (*mopping up enemy pockets; pockets of resistance*); isolated group (of unemployed persons etc.); = AIR[1] *pocket*. **5.** *a.* Of suitable size or shape for carrying in pocket (*pocket calculator, dictionary, -watch*). **6. ~ battleship,** ship armoured and equipped like, but smaller than, a battleship; **~-book,** (1) notebook, (2) booklike case for papers or paper money carried in pocket, (fig.) = sense 2 (*hurt one's pocket-book*), (3) *pocket-size book, usu. paperback, (4) *large handbag; ||*pocket* BOROUGH; **~ handkerchief** (carried in pocket; fig. of small lawn etc.); **~-knife,** knife with folding blade(s) to be carried in pocket; **~--money** (for occasional expenses, esp. that allowed regularly to children); **~-piece,** lucky coin or token carried in pocket as charm; **~-pistol,** (joc.) pocket spirit-flask; ***~ veto,** indirect veto of bill by retention in hands of President etc. until adjournment of legislature. **7.** Hence **~FUL** 2 *n.*, **~LESS** *a.* [ME f. AF *poket(e)* dim. of *poke* POKE[1]]

pŏ'ckėt[2] *v.t.* Put into one's pocket; confine as in pocket; appropriate, usu. dishonestly; submit to (affront, injury); conceal, suppress, (feelings); (Bill.) drive (ball) into pocket; *veto (bill) indirectly by retaining it; hence **~ABLE** *a.* [f. prec.]

pōcōcūrā'nt|ė *a.* & *n.* Uncaring, indifferent, (person); hence **~(ė)ISM** (2) *n.* [It., = caring little]

pŏd[1] *n.* Socket of brace and bit. [16th c., of unkn. orig.; perh. cogn. w. PAD[3]]

pŏd[2] *n.* & *v.* (**-dd-**). **1.** *n.* Long seed-vessel esp. of leguminous plants; cocoon of silkworm; case of locust's eggs; narrow-necked eel-net; compartment suspended under aircraft etc. **2.** *v.i.* Bear or form pods. **3.** *v.t.* Remove (peas etc.) from pods. [back form. f. dial. *podware, podder* field crops, of unkn. orig.]

pŏd[3] *n.*, & *v.t.* (**-dd-**). **1.** *n.* Small herd of seals or whales. **2.** *v.t.* Drive (seals) into a pod. [19th c. U.S., of unkn. orig.]

podă'gr|a (*or* pŏ'dag-) *n.* (Med.) Gout, esp. in feet; hence **~ÀL, ~IC, ~OUS,** *adjs.* [L, f. Gk *podagra* (*pous podos* foot, *agra* seizure)]

pŏ'ddėd *a.* Bearing pods; growing in pod; (fig.) well-off, snug. [f. POD[2] + -ED[2]]

pŏ'ddȳ *n.* (Austral.) Hand-fed calf. [E dial. wd, of unkn. orig.]

podestà (pŏdĕstah') *n.* Magistrate in Italian municipalities; (Hist.) chief magistrate in medieval Italian towns. [It., f. L *potestas -tatis* power]

pŏ'dgȳ *a.* (Of person) short and fat; (of face etc.) soft and fat. [f. *podge* short fat person (cf. PUDGE) + -Y[2]]

***podī'atr|ȳ** *n.* Chiropody; so **~IST** (3) *n.* [f. Gk *pous podos* foot + *iatros* physician + -Y[1]]

pō'dĭ|um *n.* (*pl.* **~a**). Continuous projecting base or pedestal round room, house, etc.; raised platform round arena of amphitheatre; continuous bench round room; conductor's or speaker's rostrum. [L, f. Gk *podion* dim. of *pous podos* foot]

pŏdophȳ'llĭn *n.* Yellow bitter cathartic resin got from root of may-apple. [f. mod. L *podophyllum* May-apple f. Gk *pous podos* foot + *phullon* leaf, + -IN]

pŏ'dzŏl, pŏ'dsŏl, *n.* Soil with certain materials leached from surface layers into a lower stratum; hence **~IZE** (3) *v.t.* [Russ. (*zola* ashes)]

pō'ė *n.* = PARSON-*bird*. [Tahitian, = 'ear-rings' from curled tufts under throat]

***P.O.E.** *abbr.* port of entry.

pō'ėm *n.* A metrical composition, esp. of elevated character; elevated composition in prose or verse (*prose poem*); (fig.) something not in words but akin or compared to a poem (*their lives are a poem*). [f. F *poème* or L f. Gk *poēma* = *poiēma* (*poieō* make)]

pō'ėsȳ (*or* -zĭ) *n.* (arch. or poet.) Art or composition of poetry; poems collectively. [ME, f. OF *poesie* f. Rom. **poesia* f. L f. Gk *poēsis* = *poiēsis* making, poetry, (as prec.)]

pō'ėt *n.* Writer of poems; writer in verse, esp. one possessing high powers of imagination, expression, etc.; *Poet* LAUREATE; **Poets' Corner,** part of Westminster Abbey containing graves and monuments of several poets; hence **~ESS**[1] *n.* [ME, f. OF *poete* f. L f. Gk *poētēs* = *poiētēs* maker, poet, (as POEM; see -ET[2])]

pōėtă'ster *n.* Paltry or inferior poet. [mod. L (as prec.; see -ASTER)]

pōĕ't|ĭc *a.* **1.** Of, or proper to, poets or poetry (*poetic* JUSTICE, LICENCE[1]). **2.** Having the good qualities of poetry. **3.** Hence **~ICALLY** *adv.*, **~ICS** *n.* [f. F *poétique* f. L *poeticus* f. Gk *po(i)ētikos* (as POET; see -IC, -AL)]

pōĕ'tĭcal *a.* = prec.; written in verse (*poetical works*). [ME, f. as prec. + -ICAL]

pōĕ'tĭcīze, -īse (-īz), *v.t.* Make (theme) poetic. [f. POETIC + -IZE]

pō'ètīze, -īse (-īz), *v.* **1.** *v.i.* Play the poet, compose poetry. **2.** *v.t.* Treat poetically; celebrate in poetry. [f. F *poétiser* (as POET; see -IZE)]

pō'ètrў *n.* Art or work of the poet; elevated expression of elevated thought or feeling in metrical or rhythmical form; quality (in any thing) that calls for poetical expression; **prose** ~, prose having all the qualities of poetry except metre. [ME, f. med. L *poetria* f. L *poeta* POET, prob. after *geometry*]

po-faced. See PO.

pō'gō *n.* (*pl.* **~s**). Stiltlike toy with cross-piece for feet, spring, and handles, used to jump about on. [20th c.; orig. uncert.]

pŏgono- *comb. form.* Beard, as: **~logy** (-ŏ'l-), study of beards; **~tomy** (-ŏ't-), shaving; **~trophy** (-ŏ't-), beard-growing. [f. Gk *pōgōn* beard + -o-]

pŏ'grom *n.* Organized massacre (orig. and esp. of Jews in Russia). [Russ., = devastation (*gromit'* destroy)]

pōhutuka'wa (-hōō-; -kah'-) *n.* (N.Z.) Evergreen tree with brilliant crimson flowers. [Maori]

poi'gn|ant (poi'na- *or* poi'nya-) *a.* Sharp or pungent in taste or smell; painfully sharp (*poignant hunger, regret, sarcasm*); pleasantly piquant; causing sympathy; hence ~ANCY *n.*, **~ant**LY[2] *adv.* [ME f. OF, part. of *poindre* prick f. L *pungere*; see -ANT]

poi'kilothĕrm *n.* Cold-blooded animal; hence ~AL, ~IC, (-ĕr'-) *adjs.* [f. Gk *poikilos* multi-coloured, changeable + *thermē* heat]

poilu (pwah'lōō) *n.* (arch.) (Nickname for) French private soldier. [F, lit. hairy (*poil* hair)]

poincĭa'na (-ah'-) *n.* Tropical tree with bright red flowers. [mod. L, f. M. de *Poinci*, 17th-c. governor in West Indies + *-ana* fem. suf. (cf. -AN)]

poind (pēnd *or* pĭnd) *v.t.*, & *n.* (Sc.) **1.** *v.t.* Distrain upon, impound. **2.** *n.* Act of poinding; animal or chattel poinded. [ME, f. OE *pyndan* impound]

poinsĕ'ttĭa *n.* Plant of genus *Euphorbia* with large scarlet bracts surrounding small yellowish flowers. [mod. L, f. J. R. *Poinsett*, Amer. diplomat d. 1851 + -IA[1]]

point[1] *n.* **1.** Very small mark on a surface. **2.** Stop or punctuation-mark (esp. FULL[1] *point*); dot, small stroke, used in Semitic languages to indicate vowels or distinguish consonants; DECIMAL *point* (*four ~ six*, 4·6; *~ one*, 0·1). **3.** Single item, detail, particular, (*we differ on these points*; *it is a point of conscience*; *point of* ORDER[1] 11; STRETCH *a point*); **possession is nine ~s of the law** (nine-tenths, almost the whole). **4.** Unit of scoring in games etc., or fig. in debate; **give ~s to,** allow handicap to (opponent), (fig.) be superior to; **score ~s off,** (fig.) worst in argument or repartee; **win on ~s,** (of boxer) win by scoring more points, not by knock-out. **5.** Unit in appraising value of bridge hand or of exhibit in show; unit of value in rationing; unit of weight (2 mg.) for diamonds; unit (of varying value) in quoting price of stocks etc.; *unit of credit for academic work. **6.** (Print.) Unit of measurement for type bodies (U.K. & U.S. 0·0138 in., European 0 0148 in.). **7.** (Geom.) That which has position but not magnitude, e.g. intersection of two lines. **8.** Precise place or spot (*point of contact*; *Bombay and points east*; **~ of no return,** point in a long-distance journey at which supplies become insufficient to return to starting-place and one must continue onwards, or in action after which one cannot withdraw); (Hunting) spot to which straight run is made, such run, (**~-to-~ race,** horse-race over course defined only by certain landmarks); (Her.) any of nine particular spots on shield used for specifying position of charges etc.; ‖= POWER *point.* **9.** Stage or degree in progress or increase (*abrupt to the point of rudeness*; *full to bursting-point*; *decided to give up at this point*); level of temperature (**boiling, freezing, melting, -point,** temperature at which liquid boils etc.). **10.** Precise moment for action etc. (*when it came to the point, he declined*); exact moment (*of* death etc.). **11.** Distinctive trait, characteristic, (*it has its points*; *singing is not his strong point*); feature of animal by which its quality is judged; *the* essential thing, *the* thing under discussion, (*that is just the point*; *come to the point*); **beside the ~,** irrelevant(ly); **carry** one's ~, secure one's object; **in ~,** apposite, relevant; **make a ~ of,** regard or treat as essential, insist on; **make** or **prove a ~,** establish proposition, prove contention; **to the ~,** relevant(ly); **you have a ~ there,** your contention is valid and relevant; *I* TAKE[1] *your point.* **12.** **~ (lace)**, thread lace made wholly with needle, (improp.) pillow-lace imitating this. **13.** Sharp or operative end of tool, weapon, pin, pen, etc., (**not to put too fine a ~ on it,** to speak bluntly); electrical contact device in distributor of motor vehicle. **14.** Tip, extreme end; **~ (of the jaw)**, (Boxing) tip of chin as spot for knock-out blow; (Ballet etc.) tip of toe; promontory; (Mil.) small leading party of advanced guard; (in *pl.*) extremities of horse, dog, etc., (*bay has black points*). **15.** Sharp-pointed tool, e.g. etching-needle; tine of deer's horn. **16.** (Railways, usu. in *pl.*) ‖tapering movable rail by which train is directed from one line to another; tapered division on backgammon board. **17.** (Hist.) Tagged lace for lacing bodice, attaching hose to doublet, etc. **18.** (Naut.) Short piece of cord at lower edge of sail for tying up a reef. **19.** One of 32 directions marked as equidistant points on compass; corresponding direction towards horizon; CARDINAL *points.* **20.** Salient feature of story, joke, remark, etc., (*don't see the point*); pungency, effectiveness, (*his remarks lack point*); purpose, value, (*there is no point in wasting time*). **21.** (Cricket). (Position of) fieldsman placed more or less in line with popping-crease a short distance on off-side of batsman; (Lacrosse) defender's position to right of and in front of goalkeeper. **22.** (Of dog) act of pointing. **23.** **At all ~s,** in every part or respect; **at the ~** (on the verge) **of** death etc.; **in ~** (as a matter) **of fact**; **(up)on the ~ of,** on the very verge of (action, do*ing*); **~ of** (thing that vitally affects one's) **honour**; **~ of view,** position from which thing is viewed, (fig.) way of looking at a matter; **up to a ~,** by no means wholly. **24.** ‖**~-duty** (of constable or traffic warden stationed at particular point to regulate traffic etc.); **~ lace** (see sense 12); ‖**~'sman,** man in charge of railway points, constable on point-duty. [ME, f. F *point* f. L *punctum*, & F *pointe* f. L *puncta*, neut. & fem. p.p. (as n.) of *pungere* prick; in sense 22 perh. f. foll.]

point[2] *v.* **1.** *v.t.* Sharpen (pencil etc.). **2.** Punctuate; insert points in (written Hebrew etc.); mark (Psalms etc.) with signs for chanting. **3.** Give point or force to (words, actions) (*pointing his remarks with apt illustrations*; *to point a* MORAL). **4.** Fill in joints of (brickwork etc.) with mortar or cement smoothed with trowel. **5.** (Of dog) indicate presence of (game, or abs.) by acting as pointer. **6.** Direct (finger, weapon, etc., *at* or *towards*; person etc. *to*); **~ out,** indicate, show, draw attention to (thing, fact, *that* etc.); ~ **up,** emphasize. **7.** *v.i.* Direct attention (*to, at*; lit. or fig.); aim or be directed *at* or *towards*; tend *towards*; ~ **to,** be evidence of. [ME, f. prec. & f. OF *pointer* (as prec.)]

point-blă'nk *a.* & *adv.* **1.** With aim or weapon level, at very close range; ~ **distance, range,** (within which gun may be aimed horizontally). **2.** (fig.). Direct(ly), flat(ly), (*point-blank refusal; told him point-blank it would not do*). [prob. f. prec. + BLANK², i.e. white spot in centre of target]

point d'appui (pwăṅ dăpwē') *n.* (*pl.* **-ts** *pr.* same). (Mil.) point of support, base, rallying-place; (fig.) basis of argument etc. [F]

point-dėvī'ce *a.* & *adv.* (arch.) **1.** *a.* Perfectly correct, extremely neat or precise. **2.** *adv.* In point-device manner. [ME *at point devis* app. f. OF or AF **à point devis* to the point arranged, or arranged to the proper point (see POINT¹, DEVICE)]

poi'ntėd *a.* Having, or sharpened to, a point; (of remark etc.) having point, penetrating, cutting; emphasized, made evident; hence ~LY² *adv.*, ~NESS *n.* [ME, f. POINT¹ + -ED², or p.p. of POINT²]

poi'nter *n.* In vbl senses; index hand of clock, balance, etc.; rod used for pointing to words etc. on blackboard, map, etc.; (colloq.) hint, suggestion; dog of breed that on scenting game stands rigidly, with muzzle stretched towards it and usu. one foot raised; (in *pl.*) two stars in Great Bear, straight line through which points nearly to pole-star. [f. POINT² + -ER¹]

pointillé (pwă'ntĭlā) *a.* (Of bound book) decorated with gilt dots; (of picture) painted by pointillism. [F, p.p. of *pointiller* mark with dots (as POINT¹)]

poi'ntĭll|ĭsm (pwă'n-) *n.* (Art). Method of producing light effects by crowding a surface with small spots of various colours, which are blended by the spectator's eye; so ~IST (3) *n.* [f. F *pointillisme* (as prec.; see -ISM)]

poi'ntĭng *n.* In vbl senses; punctuation; filling up joints of brickwork etc. with cement, facing thus given to the joints; system of signs for chanting psalms etc. [ME, f. POINT² + -ING¹]

poi'ntlėss *a.* Without a point, blunt; without point or force, meaningless; not having scored a point; hence ~LY² *adv.*, ~NESS *n.* [ME, f. POINT¹ + -LESS]

poise¹ (-z) *v.* & *n.* **1.** *v.t.* Balance; hold suspended or supported; carry (one's head etc., in specified way). **2.** *v.i.* Be balanced; hover in air etc. **3.** *n.* Equilibrium (lit. or fig.), composure, self-possession; carriage (*of* head etc.). [v. ME f. OF *peser* (st. *pois-*) f. Rom. **pesare* f. L *pensare* frequent. of *pendere pens-* weigh; n. f. OF *pois, peis* f. Rom. **pesum* f. L *pensum* weight, p.p. (as n.) of *pendere*]

poise² (-z) *n.* Unit of dynamic viscosity, such that shear of one dyne per sq. cm. causes velocity change of 1 cm. per sec. for each centimetre transverse to plane of shear. [f. J. L. M. *Poiseuille*, Fr. physician d. 1869]

poi'son (-z-) *n.*, & *v.t.* **1.** *n.* Substance that when introduced into or absorbed by a living organism destroys life or injures health, esp. one that destroys life by rapid action even when taken in small quantity; **slow** ~ (of which repeated doses are eventually injurious); **hate** person **like** ~ (bitterly); **what's your** ~**?,** (colloq.) what would you like to drink?. **2.** (fig.) Baneful principle, doctrine, etc.; (Phys. & Chem.) substance interfering with normal progress of chain reaction, catalytic reaction, etc. **3.** *Poison* GAS¹; ~ **ivy,** N. Amer. climbing plant or shrub of genus *Rhus*, secreting irritant oil from leaves; ~ **pen,** (practice of) anonymous writer of libellous or scurrilous letters. **4.** Hence ~OUS *a.* **5.** *v.t.* Administer poison to (person, animal), kill or injure thus, whence ~ER¹ *n.*; produce morbid effects in (blood etc.); infect (air, water, etc.) with poison, (esp. in *p.p.*) smear (weapon) with poison; corrupt, pervert, (person, mind); destroy, spoil, (person's pleasure etc.); render (land, furnace, etc.) foul and unfit for its purpose by noxious application etc.; (Phys. & Chem.) act as poison on (catalyst etc.). [n. ME f. OF *puison, poison* (as POTION); v. f. OF *poisonner* (*poison*)]

pōke¹ *n.* Bag, sack, (usu. dial., exc. *buy a* PIG *in a poke*). [ME, f. ONF *poke, poque*, = OF *poche*; cf. POUCH¹]

pōke² *v.* **1.** *v.t.* Thrust or push (thing *in, up, down*, etc.) with hand, arm, point of stick, etc.; thrust end of finger etc. against, stir (fire) with poker; (colloq.) shut (one*self* etc.) *up* in poky place; produce (hole etc. *in* thing) by poking; thrust forward, esp. obtrusively, (lit., or fig.: *don't poke your nose into my affairs*); ~ **fun at,** assail with ridicule; ~ one's **head,** (1) carry head thrust forward, (2) cause head to project (*through* window etc.); ~ **in the ribs,** nudge with finger or elbows in friendly manner. **2.** *v.i.* Make thrusts with stick etc. (*at* etc.); be thrust forward *through* opening, *up, down*, etc.; pry (*about, into*); move or act slowly or ineffectively, potter *about* or *around*. [ME, f. MDu., MLG *poken*, of unkn. orig.]

pōke³ *n.* Poking; thrust, nudge; device fastened on cattle etc. to prevent their breaking through fences; projecting brim or front of woman's bonnet or hat; ~(**-bonnet**), bonnet with this. [f. prec.]

pō'ker¹ *n.*, & *v.t.* **1.** *n.* Stiff metal rod with handle, for poking fire; **as stiff as a** ~ (esp. of person's carriage or manner); **red-hot** ~, plant of genus *Kniphofia* with spikes of scarlet or yellow flowers. **2.** Implement used in ~**-work,** (design made by) burning white wood etc. with heated metal rod. [f. POKE² + -ER¹]

pō'ker² *n.* Card-game for two or more persons, each of whom bets on the value of his hand and may win by holding strongest hand on agreed system of ranking, or by bluffing others into ceasing to compete; ~ **dice** (with card designs from ace to nine instead of spots); ~**-face,** (person with) impassive countenance appropriate to player of this game; so ~*-faced* a. [19th c., orig. unkn.; cf. G *pochen* to brag, *pochspiel* bragging game]

pō'keweed (-kw-) *n.* Tall Amer. plant of genus *Phytolacca* with purple berries yielding emetic and purgative. [f. *poke*, Amer. Ind. word + WEED]

pō'kȳ *a.* (Of place, room, etc.) confined, mean, shabby; (of occupation etc.) pottering, petty. [f. POKE² + -Y²]

***pŏl** *n.* (colloq., derog.) Politician. [abbr.]

***pō'lăck** *n.* (sl., derog.) Person of Polish origin. [f. F *Polaque* & G *Polack* f. Pol. *Polak*]

pola'cre (-ah'ker), **polă'cca,** *n.* Three-masted Mediterranean merchant vessel. [f. F *polacre, polaque*, It. *polacca* = Polish, Pole, as prec.; reason for name unkn.]

pō'lar *a.* & *n.* **1.** *a.* Of or near either pole of the earth or celestial body or of the celestial sphere; of species or variety living in north polar regions (*polar bear, hare*); ~ **circles** (parallel to equator at distance of 23° 27′ from the poles); ~ **distance,** angular distance of point on sphere from nearer pole; ~ **star,** = POLE²*-star*. **2.** Having polarity, magnetic; having electric charges; (of molecule) having opposite properties at its ends. **3.** (Geom. etc.) Relating to a POLE²; ~ **curve** (related in particular way to given curve and to fixed point called *pole*). **4.** (fig.) Analogous to the pole of the earth or to the pole-star; directly opposite in character or tendency. **5.** Hence ~LY² *adv.* **6.** *n.* Polar curve. [f. F *polaire* or mod. L *polaris* (as POLE²; see -AR¹)]

pōlari- *comb. form.* = prec., as: **polari'meter, pola'riscope,** instruments for measuring, showing, the polarization of light; so **polari-me'tric, polarisco'pic,** *adjs.*, **polari'metry** *n.* [f. mod. L *polaris* (as prec.) + -I-]

polă'rĭtȳ *n.* Tendency of loadstone, magnetized bar, etc., to point with its extremities to the magnetic poles of the earth; tendency of a body to lie with its mathematical axis in particular direction; possession of two poles having contrary qualities (lit. or fig.); electrical condition of body (positive or negative); (fig.) magnetic attraction towards an object. [f. POLAR + -ITY]

pō'larīz|e, -īs|e (-iz), *v.* **1.** *v.t.* Restrict vibrations of (transverse waves, esp. light) so that they have different amplitudes in different planes through their line of propagation; give magnetic or electric polarity to; reduce voltage of (electric cell) by action of electrolysis products. **2.** *v.t.* & *i.* (fig.) Divide into two groups at opposite extremes of opinion etc. **3.** Hence or cogn. ~ABLE *a.*, ~A'TION, ~ER¹ (2), *ns.* [(partly thr. F) f. POLAR + -IZE]

pōlarŏ'graphȳ *n.* (Chem.) Analysis by measurement of current-voltage relationships in electrolysis between mercury electrodes; hence **pōlarogră'ph**IC *a.* [f. POLAR + -O- + -GRAPHY]

pŏlatou'che (-ōō'ch) *n.* Small flying squirrel. [F, f. Russ. *poletuchiĭ* flying]

pō'lder *n.* Piece of low-lying land reclaimed from sea or river, esp. in Netherlands. [prob. f. MDu. *polre, polder*]

pōle¹ *n.*, & *v.t.* **1.** *n.* Long slender rounded piece of wood or metal esp. as support for tent, telegraph wires, bean-plants, etc., or propulsion of barge, punt, etc.; wooden shaft fitted to front of vehicle and attached to yokes or collars of the horses etc.; **under bare ~s,** (Naut.) with no sail set; **up the ~,** (sl.) in a difficulty, crazy, drunk; **~-jump**(**ing**), **~-vault**(**ing**), (over high crossbar with help of pole held in hands). **2.** (As measure) rod, perch, 5½ yds. or 30¼ sq. yds. **3.** *v.t.* Furnish with poles; push, move, (*off* etc.) with pole. [OE *pāl*, = MDu. *pael*, OHG *pfāl*, ON *páll*, Gmc f. L *palus* stake]

pōle² *n.* **1. North** and **South P~s,** (1) the two points in the celestial sphere about which the stars appear to revolve, (2) extremities of the earth's or other body's axis of rotation, whence ~'WARD *a.*, ~'WARD(s) *adv.*, (-lw-), (3) **magnetic ~s,** points near these extremities where magnetic needle dips vertically; **from ~ to ~,** throughout the world. **2.** (Geom.) **~s of a circle of a sphere,** the two points in which axis of that circle cuts surface of sphere; fixed point to which others are referred. **3.** Each of the two opposite points on surface of magnet at which magnetic forces are concentrated; each of two terminals (**positive** and **negative** ~) of electric cell, battery, etc.; (Biol.) extremity of main axis of any spherical or oval organ; (fig.) each of two opposed principles etc. (**be ~s apart** or **asunder,** differ greatly). **4. ~-star,** star in Little Bear, now about 1° distant from north pole of heavens, (fig.) thing serving as guide, lodestar, centre of attraction. [ME, f. L f. Gk *polos* pivot, axis, sky]

Pōle³ *n.* Native or inhabitant of Poland. [G, f. Pol. *Polanie* lit. field-dwellers (*pole* field)]

pō'le-āxe, *-ăx, (-lă-) *n.*, & *v.t.* **1.** *n.* Battleaxe; axe formerly used in naval warfare as weapon and for cutting ropes etc.; halberd; butcher's axe for slaughtering, with hammer at back. **2.** *v.t.* Slaughter or strike (as if) with pole--axe. [ME *pol(l)ax, -ex* f. MDu. *pol(l)aex*, MLG *-exe* (as POLL¹, AXE)]

pō'lecăt (-lk-) *n.* ||Small brownish-black fetid carnivorous mammal of weasel family, native of Europe; *skunk. [f. CAT¹; orig. of first syl. unkn.]

polĕ'mĭc *a.* & *n.* **1.** *a.* Controversial, disputatious; hence ~AL *a.*, **~al**LY² *adv.*, **pŏ'lĕmi**ZE (2) *v.i.* **2.** *n.* Controversial discussion, (in *pl.*) practice of this, esp. in theology; controversialist. [f. med. L f. Gk *polemikos* (*polemos* war; see -IC)]

polĕ'nta *n.* Porridge made of maize meal etc. [It., f. L, = pearl barley]

poli'ce (-ē's) *n.*, & *v.t.* **1.** *n.* Civil force responsible for maintaining public order; (as *pl.*) members of this (*several hundred police*; *the police are on his track*); force with similar functions of enforcing regulations (*military*, *railway*, *KITCHEN, *police*). **2.** ||*Police* CONSTABLE; **~ dog** (trained and used by police to track criminals etc.); **~man,** member of police force; **~-officer,** policeman or police-woman; **~ state,** totalitarian State controlled by esp. secret police supervising citizens' activities; **~ station,** office of local police force; **~woman,** woman member of police force. **3.** *v.t.* Control (country etc.) by means of police; furnish with police; (fig.) keep order in, control; ***~ (up)**, clean (barracks etc.). [F, f. med. L *politia* POLICY¹]

pŏlĭclĭ'nĭc *n.* Out-patients' department of hospital. [f. G *poliklinik* f. Gk *polis* city + G *klinik* CLINIC]

pŏ'lĭcȳ¹ *n.* Prudent conduct, sagacity; course or general plan of action (to be) adopted by government, party, person, etc., (*honesty is the best policy*); (arch.) craftiness; (Sc.) park round country seat etc. [ME f. OF *policie* f. L f. Gk *politeia* citizenship (*politēs* citizen f. *polis* city); in Sc. sense (earlier = improvement of estate) confused w. L *politus* polished]

pŏ'lĭcȳ² *n.* (Document containing) contract of insurance. [f. F *police* bill of lading, contract of insurance, f. Prov. *poliss(i)a* prob. f. med. L *apodissa*, *apodixa* f. L f. Gk *apodeixis* evidence, proof, f. APO(*deiknumi* show)]

pō'lĭō *n.* (*pl.* ~s). (colloq.) = foll. [abbr.]

pŏlĭōmȳĕlī'tĭs *n.* (Path.) Infectious viral inflammation of nerve cells in grey matter of spinal cord, with temporary or permanent paralysis. [mod. L, f. Gk *polios* grey + as MYELITIS]

pŏ'lĭsh¹ *v.t.* & *i.* Make or become smooth and glossy by friction; (fig., esp. in *p.p.*) make elegant or cultured, refine; smarten *up*; **~ off,** finish off quickly; hence ~ABLE *a.*, ~ER¹ (1, 2) *n.* [ME, f. OF *polir* (see -ISH²) f. L *polire polit-*]

pŏ'lĭsh² *n.* Smoothness or glossiness produced by friction; friction applied for this purpose; substance used to produce smooth surface; (fig.) refinement, high degree of elegance. [f. prec.]

Pō'lĭsh³ *a.* & *n.* **1.** *a.* Of Poland or the Poles. **2.** *n.* The language of Poland. [f. POLE³ + -ISH¹]

pŏ'lĭtbūrō *n.* (*pl.* ~s). Principal committee of a Communist party; (fig.) similar body with controlling power. [f. Russ. *politbyuro* (*politicheskiĭ* political, *byuro* bureau)]

poli'te *a.* (~r, ~st). Having refined manners, courteous; cultivated, cultured; well-bred; (of literature etc.) refined, elegant, (*polite letters*); hence ~LY² (-tlĭ) *adv.*, ~NESS (-tn-) *n.* [f. L *politus* (as POLISH¹)]

politesse (pŏlĭtĕ's) *n.* Formal politeness. [F, f. It. *politezza*, *pulitezza* (*pulito* POLITE)]

pŏ'lĭtĭc *a.*, & *v.i.* (**-ck-**). **1.** *a.* (Of person) sagacious, prudent, (of action etc.) judicious, expedient; scheming, crafty; **body ~**, State, or similarly organized system; hence ~LY[2] *adv.* **2.** *v.i.* Engage in politics. [ME, f. OF *politique* f. L f. Gk *politikos* (*politēs* citizen f. *polis* city; see -IC)]

polĭ'tĭcal *a.* **1.** Of or affecting the State or its government; of public affairs; of politics. **2.** (Of person) engaged in civil administration. **3.** Having an organized form of society or government. **4.** Belonging to, or taking, a side in politics; relating to person's or organization's status or influence (*a political decision*). **5.** *Political* ASYLUM, ECONOMY; **~ geography** (dealing with boundaries and possessions of States); **~ prisoner,** person imprisoned for political offence; *political* SCIENCE; **~ verse,** Byzantine and modern Greek verse composed by accent, not quantity, [f. Gk *politikos* popular]. **6.** Hence ~LY[2] *adv.* [f. L *politicus* (see prec.) + -AL]

pŏlĭtĭ'cian (-sh*a*n) *n.* One skilled in politics, statesman; one interested or engaged in politics, esp. as profession; *one who makes a trade of politics. [f. as POLITIC; see -ICIAN]

polĭ'tĭcīz|e, -īs|e (-īz), *v.* **1.** *v.i.* Act the politician; engage in or talk politics. **2.** *v.t.* Give political character to. **3.** Hence ~A'TION *n.* [f. as POLITIC + -IZE]

polĭ'tĭcō *n.* (*pl.* **~s**). One interested or engaged in politics, esp. as profession or trade. [Sp., = POLITIC (as n.)]

polĭ'tĭcō- *comb. form.* Politically, political and, as: *~-economical*, *~-geographical*, *~-moral*, *~-social*. [f. Gk *politikos* (see POLITIC) + -O-]

pŏ'lĭtics *n. pl.* (also treated as *sing.*). Science and art of government; political affairs or life (*politics is a dirty business*); political principles (*what are his politics?*; *the politics of the decision is not clear*); **not practical ~,** (1) not likely enough to be worth discussing, (2) liable to meet practical difficulties. [f. POLITIC; see -ICS]

pŏ'lĭtȳ *n.* Form or process of civil government; organized society, State; (arch.) condition of civil order. [f. L *politia* POLICY[1]]

pŏ'lka *n.*, & *v.i.* **1.** *n.* Lively dance of Bohemian origin in duple time; music for this; **~ dot,** round dot as one of many forming regular pattern on textile fabric etc. **2.** *v.i.* Dance the polka. [F & G, f. Czech *půlka* half-step (*půl* half)]

pōll[1] *n.* **1.** Human head; part of this on which hair grows (*grey, flaxen, poll*); **~-tax** (levied on every person). **2.** Counting of voters esp. at parliamentary or other election; voting at election (*exclusion of Negroes from the poll*); result of voting; number of votes recorded (*heavy, light, poll*). **3.** = GALLUP *poll*; hence ~'STER *n.* [ME, perh. f. LDu.]

pōll[2] *v.* **1.** *v.t.* (arch.) Crop hair of. **2.** Cut off top of (tree, plant), esp. make a pollard of; (esp. in *p.p.*) cut off horns of (cattle); cut evenly edge of (sheet). **3.** Take the vote(s) of, (in *pass.*) have one's vote taken; (of candidate) receive (so many votes); give (vote). **4.** *v.i.* Give one's vote. [ME, f. prec.]

pōll[3] *a.* & *n.* **1.** *a.* Polled, cut evenly. **2.** *n.* Hornless animal, esp. one of a breed of hornless oxen. [abbr. of p.p. of prec.]

pŏll[4] *n.* **~ parrot,** (1) tame parrot, (2) user of conventional or unoriginal phrases and arguments. [f. *Poll*, conventional name for parrot, alt. f. *Moll*, familiar form of *Mary*]

pŏ'llack, pŏ'llock, *n.* Marine food-fish of genus *Pollachius*, allied to cod, but with protruding lower jaw. [earlier (Sc.) *podlock*; orig. unkn.]

pŏ'llan *n.* Irish lake fish, allied to trout. [perh. f. Ir. *poll* deep water]

pŏ'llard *n.*, & *v.t.* **1.** *n.* Animal that has cast or lost its horns; ox, sheep, or goat, of hornless breed; tree polled so as to produce close rounded head of young branches; bran sifted from flour; fine bran containing some flour. **2.** *v.t.* Make (tree) a pollard. [f. POLL[2] + -ARD]

pŏ'llen *n.* Fine powdery substance discharged from anther of flower, male element that fertilizes ovules; **~ analysis,** palynology; **~ count,** index of amount of pollen in air published as warning to those allergic to it; hence ~LESS, **pollĭ'nic**, **pŏllĭnĭ'**FEROUS, *adjs.* [L *pollen pollinis* fine flour, dust]

pŏ'll|ĕx *n.* (*pl.* **~ices** *pr.* -ĭsēz). Innermost digit of fore-limb, thumb. [L, = thumb or big toe]

pollĭcĭtā'tion *n.* (Civil Law). Promise not yet formally accepted, and therefore revocable. [F, or f. L *pollicitatio* (*pollicitari* bid at auction frequent. of *polliceri* promise; see -ATION)]

pŏ'llĭn|āte *v.t.* Fertilize or sprinkle with pollen, shed pollen upon; hence ~A'TION *n.* [f. as POLLEN + -ATE[3]]

pollĭ'nĭc, pŏllĭnĭ'ferous. See POLLEN.

pŏ'llĭwŏg *n.* (dial. & U.S.) Tadpole. [earlier *polwigge*, *polwygle*, f. POLL[1] + WIGGLE]

pŏ'llock. See POLLACK.

pollu't|e (-ōō't) *v.t.* Destroy the purity or sanctity of; make foul or filthy; contaminate or defile (man's environment); hence or cogn. ~ANT *a.* & *n.*, **pollu'tion** (-ōō'-) *n.* [ME, f. L *polluere -lut-*]

pŏ'llȳ *n.* (colloq.) Apollinaris. [abbr.; see -Y[3]]

Pŏllȳă'nna *n.* Cheerful optimist; hence ~ISH[1] *a.*, ~ISM (2) *n.*, (*-aĭ*-). [character in novel (1913) by E. Porter]

pŏ'llȳwŏg. Var. of POLLIWOG.

pō'lō *n.* Game of Eastern origin like hockey played on horseback with long-handled mallet (**~-stick**); **~-neck,** high round turned-over collar; WATER[1] *polo*. [Balti, = ball]

pō'lōcrŏsse *n.* Game played on horseback with long-handled stick having net at end. [f. prec. + LACROSSE]

pŏlonai'se (-z) *n.* **1.** Woman's dress consisting of bodice with skirt open over petticoat from waist downwards. **2.** (Music for or in style of) slow processional dance of Polish origin in triple time. [F, fem. (as n.) of *polonais* Polish f. med. L *Polonia* Poland]

polō'nĭum *n.* Radioactive metallic element forming the last stage before lead in the decay of radium. [F & mod. L, f. med. L *Polonia* Poland (discoverer's native country) + -IUM]

||**polō'nȳ** *n.* Sausage of partly cooked pork etc. [app. replacing *Bologna* or *Bolognian sausage*]

pŏ'ltergeist (-gīst) *n.* Noisy mischievous ghost, esp. one manifesting itself by physical damage. [G (*poltern* create disturbance, *geist* GHOST)]

pŏ'lt-fŏŏt *n.* (*pl.* **-feet**) & *a.* (arch.) Club-foot(ed). [f. obs. *polt* pestle, club, (17th c.; orig. unkn.) + FOOT[1]]

pŏltrōō'n *n.* Spiritless coward; so ~ERY (4) *n.* [f. F *poltron* f. It. *poltrone* (perh. f. *poltro* sluggard); see -OON]

Pŏ'lȳ *n.* (*pl.*~**s**). (colloq.) Polytechnic. [abbr.]

pŏ'lȳ- *pref.* **1.** Many, much, as: **~ade'lphous,** (Bot.) with stamens united in 3 or more bundles; **~a'ndrous,** of or practising polyandry, (Bot.) having numerous stamens; **~andry,** polygamy in which woman has more than one husband; **~ato'mic,** (Chem.) consisting of many atoms, having many replaceable atoms or radicals; **~ba'sic,** (Chem.) having more than two replaceable hydrogen atoms; **~chaete** (-kēt) *a.* & *n.*, **~chae'tan, ~chae'tous,** (-kē't-) *adjs.*, (annelid worm) with many bristles on the foot-stumps; **~cry'stal(line)**, (body) consisting of several or many crystals with various orientations; **~da'ctyl** *a.* & *n.*, (animal) with more than normal number of fingers or toes; **~-**

dae'monism, belief in many supernatural powers; **~gene, ~gene'tic, ~ge'nic,** (Geol.) composed of rock formed in several ways; **~ge'nesis,** (theoretical) origination of a race or species from several independent stocks; **~graph,** (1) lie-detector, (2) writer of many or various works; **~gynous** (-ĭ'g- *or* -ĭ'j-), of or practising polygyny, (Bot.) having numerous pistils, styles, or stigmas; **~gyny** (-ĭ'g- *or* -ĭ'j-), polygamy in which man has more than one wife; **~mor'phic, ~mor'phous,** multiform, esp. (Biol.) varying in individuals, passing through successive variations, so **~mor'phism** *n.*; **~o'nymous,** called by several different names; **~o'pia,** disorder of the eyes in which one object appears as two or more; **~phagous** (-ĭ'f-), (Zool.) feeding on various kinds of food; **~phone,** letter or symbol standing for different sounds; **~phyle'tic,** formed by polygenesis; **~ptych** (-k), painting etc. with four or more folding leaves; **~sa'ccharide,** carbohydrate resolvable into two or more monosaccharides; **~synthe'tic,** (of languages) combining several or all parts of a sentence into one word; **~to'nal,** (Mus.) using more than one key; **~va'lent,** (Chem.) having a valence of more than two, or several valences; **~zo'an,** = BRYOZOAN. **2.** Polymerized, as: **~e'ster** (esp. as synthetic resin or fibre), **~e'thylene** (esp. = POLYTHENE); **~styr'ene,** hard colourless thermoplastic styrene polymer; **~ure'thane** (*or* -ūr'-) synthetic resin or plastic used esp. as foam; **~vinyl chlor'ide,** tough resistant colourless thermoplastic consisting of or made from polymer of vinyl chloride. [sense 1 f. Gk *polu-* (*polus* much, *polloi* many); sense 2 f. POLYMER]

pŏlўă'nthus *n.* Cultivated primrose from hybridized primulas. [mod. L, f. as POLY- + Gk *anthos* flower]

pŏlўchromă'tic (-kr-) *a.* Many-coloured; (of radiation) containing more than one wavelength. [f. POLY- + CHROMATIC]

pŏ'lўchrōme (-kr-) *a.* & *n.* **1.** *a.* Painted, printed, or decorated, in many colours. **2.** *n.* Work of art in several colours, esp. coloured statue; varied colouring. **3.** Hence **pŏlўchrō'm**IC, **pŏlўchrō'm**OUS, (-kr-) *adjs.* [F, f. Gk *polukhrōmos* (as POLY-, *khrōma* colour)]

polў'chromў (-kr-) *n.* Art of painting in several colours, esp. as applied to ancient pottery etc. [f. F *polychromie* (as prec.; see -Y[1])]

pŏ'lўclĭnĭc *n.* Clinic devoted to various diseases; general hospital. [f. POLY- + CLINIC]

polў'gam|ous *a.* **1.** Having more than one wife or (less usu.) husband at once; so **pŏlўgă'm**IC *a.*, ~IST (1), ~Y[1], *ns.* **2.** (Zool.) having more than one mate; (Bot.) bearing some flowers with stamens only, some with pistils only, some with both, on same or different plants. [f. Gk *polugamos* (as POLY-, *-gamos* marrying) + -OUS]

polў'gĕn|ў *n.* (Theoretical) origination of mankind from several independent pairs of ancestors; so ~ISM (3) *n.*, doctrine of polygeny, ~IST (2) *n.* [f. POLY- + -GENY]

pŏ'lўglŏt *a.* & *n.* Of many languages; (person) speaking or writing several languages; (book, esp. Bible) with text and translation into several languages; hence **pŏlўglŏ'tt**AL, **polўglŏ'tt**IC, *adjs.*, ~**t**ISM (1) *n.* [f. F *polyglotte* f. Gk *poluglōttos* (as POLY-, *glōtta* tongue)]

pŏ'lўgon *n.* Figure (usu. plane rectilinear) with many (usu. more than four) angles and sides; **~ of forces,** polygon illustrating theorem relating to several forces acting at a point; hence **polў'gon**AL *a.* [f. LL f. Gk *polugōnon* neut. a. as n. (*polu-* POLY-, *-gōnos* angled)]

pŏlўhĕ'dr|on *n.* (*pl.* **~a**). Solid figure with many (usu. more than six) faces; hence ~AL, ~IC, *adjs.* [f. Gk *poluedron*, neut. (as n.) of *poluedros* (*polu-* POLY-, *hedra* base; cf. -HEDRON)]

pŏlўhĭ'stor *n.* = foll. [f. Gk *poluistōr* (*polu-* POLY- + *histōr*; see HISTORY)]

pŏ'lўmăth *n.* Person of varied learning; great scholar; so **polў'mathy**[1] *n.* [f. Gk *polumathēs* (as POLY-, *math-* st. of *manthanō* learn)]

pŏ'lўmer *n.* (Chem.) Compound whose molecule is formed from a large number of repeated units of one or more compounds of low molecular weight (*monomers*); hence **pŏlўmĕ'r**IC *a.*, ~ISM (2) *n.*, ~IZE (2, 3) *v.i.* & *t.* [G, f. Gk *polumeros* having many parts (as POLY-, *meros* share)]

polў'merous *a.* (Biol.) Having many parts. [f. as prec. + -OUS]

Pŏlўnē'sian (-shan) *a.* & *n.* (Inhabitant or language) of Polynesia. [f. *Polynesia*, island-group including New Zealand, Hawaii, Samoa, etc. (f. as POLY- + Gk *nēsos* island + -IA[1]) + -AN]

pŏlўneur|ī'tĭs (-nūr-) *n.* Inflammation of several nerves at same time; hence **~ĭ't**IC *a.* [f. POLY- + NEURITIS]

polў'nĭa *n.* Space of open water in midst of ice, esp. in arctic seas. [f. Russ. *polyn'ya* (*pole* field)]

pŏlўnō'mĭal *a.* & *n.* (Alg.) (Expression) of more than two terms, esp. (sum) of terms containing different powers of the same variable(s). [f. POLY-, after MULTI*nomial*]

pŏ'lўp *n.* **1.** (Zool.) Individual member of coelenterate colony etc. **2.** (Path.) Small tumour of mucous membrane, with tentacle-like ramifications. [f. F *polype* f. as POLYPUS]

pŏ'lўparў *n.* Common stem or supporting structure of a colony of polyps. [f. mod. L *polyparium* (as POLYPUS; see -ARIUM)]

pŏlўpĕ'ptīde *n.* (Chem.) Peptide formed by combination of several amino-acids. [f. G *polypeptid* (as POLY- 2, PEPTONE, -IDE)]

pŏ'lўphāse (-z) *a.* (Electr.) Designed to supply or use simultaneously several alternating currents of the same voltage but with different phases. [f. POLY- + PHASE]

pŏlўphŏ'nĭc, polў'phonous, *adjs.* Having many voices; (Philol., of letter etc.) representing more than one sound; (Mus.) contrapuntal; so **polў'phony**[1] *n.* [f. Gk *poluphōnos* (as POLY-, *phōnē* voice, sound) + -IC, -OUS]

pŏ'lўploid *a.* & *n.* (Biol.) (Organism or cell) having more than two haploid sets of chromosomes; hence ~Y[1] *n.*, condition of being polyploid. [G (as POLY-, -PLOID)]

pŏ'lўpŏd *a.* & *n.* (Animal) with many feet. [f. F *polypode* a. f. Gk (as POLYPUS)]

pŏ'lўpōdў *n.* Fern of genus *Polypodium* or family Polypodiaceae, esp. common species growing on moist rocks, walls, trees, etc. [ME, f. L f. Gk *polupodion* (as POLYPUS)]

pŏ'lўp|oid *a.* Of or like a polyp; so ~OUS *a.* [f. POLYP + -OID]

pŏ'lўp|us *n.* (*pl.* **~i** *pr.* -ī, *or* **~uses**). (Path.) = POLYP 2. [ME f. L, f. Gk *pōlupos*, *polupous* cuttlefish, polyp in nose (*polu-* POLY-, *pous podos* foot)]

pŏ'lўsēm|ў *n.* (Philol.) Existence of many meanings (of word etc.); hence ~IC, ~OUS, *adjs.* [f. POLY- + Gk *sēma* sign + -Y[1]]

pŏlўsўllă'b|ĭc *a.* (Of word) having many syllables; marked by polysyllables; hence ~ICALLY *adv.* [f. med. L f. Gk *polusullabos* (as foll.) + -IC]

pŏlўsў'llable (*or* pŏ'-) *n.* Polysyllabic word. [f. med. L *polysyllaba* (*vox* word) (as POLY-, SYLLABLE)]

For other words in *poly-* see POLY-.

pŏlȳtĕ'chnĭc (-k-) *a.* & *n.* (Institution, esp. college) dealing with or devoted to various esp. technical subjects. [f. F *polytechnique* f. Gk *polutekhnos* (as POLY-, *tekhnē* art); see -IC]

pŏ'lȳthė|ĭsm *n.* Belief in, or worship of, many gods or more than one god; so ~IST (2) *n.*, ~ĭ'stIC *a.* [f. F *polythéisme* f. Gk *polutheos* of many gods (as POLY-, *theos* god); see -ISM]

pŏ'lȳthēne *n.* Tough light translucent thermoplastic polymer of ethylene. [f. POLY*ethylene*]

pŏm *n.* Pomeranian dog; = POMMY. [abbr.]

po'mace (pŭ'mĭs) *n.* Mass of crushed apples in cider-making before or after juice is pressed out; refuse of fish etc. after oil has been extracted, used as fertilizer. [ME, f. med. L *pomacium* cider f. L *pomum* apple]

poma'de (-ah'd) *n.*, & *v.t.* **1.** *n.* Scented ointment for hair and skin of head. **2.** *v.t.* Anoint with pomade. [f. F *pommade* f. It. *pomata* f. med. L **pomata* f. L *pomum* apple (see -ADE); perh. orig. made f. apples]

pomă'nder (*or* pō-) *n.* Ball of mixed aromatic substances placed in cupboard etc. or (Hist.) carried in box, bag, etc., as preservative against infection; (usu. spherical) container for this; spiced orange etc. similarly used. [earlier *pom(e)amber* f. AF **pome ambre*, OF *pome d'embre* f. med. L *pomum de ambra* apple of ambergris]

pomā'tum *n.*, & *v.t.* = POMADE. [mod. L, f. L *pomum* apple + *-atum* -ATE[1]]

pŏ'mbė *n.* Intoxicating drink made in Central and E. Africa from millet etc. [Swahili]

pōme *n.* **1.** (Bot.) Succulent fruit with firm fleshy body enclosing carpels forming the core, e.g. apple, pear, quince; so **pomĭ'**FEROUS *a.* **2.** Metal ball; (poet.) apple. [ME f. OF, f. Rom. **poma* orig. pl. of *pomum* fruit, apple]

pŏ'mėgrănate (*or* -mg-) *n.* Tropical tree (*Punica granatum*) native to N. Africa and W. Asia; its fruit, about size of orange with tough golden or orange rind and acid reddish pulp enclosing many seeds; ornamental representation of this. [ME, f. OF *pome grenate* etc. (see prec.) f. Rom. **granata* f. L (*malum*) *granatum* many-seeded (*granum* seed; see -ATE[2])]

po'melō (pŭ'm-) *n.* (*pl.* ~**s**). Shaddock or grapefruit. [19th c.; orig. unkn.]

Pŏmerā'nĭan *a.* & *n.* ~ (**dog**), small dog with long silky hair, pointed muzzle, and pricked ears. [f. *Pomerania* in Germany & Poland + -AN]

pŏ'mfrėt *n.* **1.** Food-fish of family Stromateidae, found in Indian and Pacific Oceans. **2.** Black food-fish (*Brama raii*) of northern seas. [app. f. Port. *pampo*]

||**pŏ'mfrėt-cāke** (*or* pŭ'-) *n.* Small round flat liquorice sweetmeat made at Pontefract (earlier *Pomfret*) in West Yorkshire.

pō'mĭcŭlture *n.* Fruit-growing. [f. L *pomum* fruit + -I- + CULTURE]

Pommar'd (-ar') *n.* A red burgundy wine. [~ in E. France]

po'mmel (pŭ'm-) *n.*, & *v.t.* (||-**ll**-). **1.** *n.* Knob esp. at end of sword-hilt; upward projecting front part of saddle. **2.** *v.t.* = PUMMEL. [ME, f. OF *pomel* f. Rom. **pomellum* dim. of L *pomum* fruit, apple]

pŏ'mmȳ, pŏ'mmĭe, *n.* (Austral. & N.Z. sl.) British person, esp. recent immigrant. [20th c.; orig. uncert.]

pomŏ'log|ȳ *n.* Science of fruit-growing; hence **pōmolŏ'g**ICAL *a.*, ~IST (3) *n.* [f. L *pomum* fruit + -O- + -LOGY]

pŏmp *n.* Splendid display, splendour; specious glory (esp. in *pl.*; *the pomps and vanities of this wicked world*). [ME, f. OF *pompe* f. L f. Gk *pompē* procession, pomp (*pempō* send)]

pŏ'mpadour (-oor) *n.* Woman's hair-style with hair in high turned-back roll round face. [f. Marquise de *Pompadour*, mistress of Louis XV of France d. 1764]

pŏ'mpanō *n.* (*pl.* ~**s**). W. Ind. and N. Amer. food-fish esp. of genus *Trachinotus*. [f. Sp. *pámpano*]

||**Pŏ'mpey** *n.* (sl.) Portsmouth. [corrupt.; cf. *Pompey*, Roman general d. 48 B.C.]

pŏ'm-pŏm[1] *n.* Automatic quick-firing gun esp. on ship. [imit.]

pŏ'm-pŏm[2]. Var. of foll.

pŏ'mpŏn *n.* Ornamental tuft or bunch of ribbon, flowers, etc., on women's or children's hats and shoes; round tuft on soldier's cap, front of shako, etc.; dahlia etc. with small tightly-clustered petals. [F, of unkn. orig.]

pŏ'mpous *a.* **1.** Self-important, consequential; (of language) pretentious, unduly grand in style; so **pŏmpo**'SITY *n.* **2.** (arch.) Magnificent, splendid. **3.** Hence ~LY[2] *adv.*, ~NESS *n.* [ME, f. OF *pompeux* f. LL *pomposus* (as POMP; see -OUS)]

'pŏn *prep.* = UPON (*'pon my word*). [abbr.]

pŏnce *n.*, & *v.i.* **1.** *n.* Man who lives off prostitute's earnings. **2.** *v.i.* Act as ponce; move *about* effeminately etc. [perh. f. POUNCE[1]]

pŏ'nceau (-sō) *n.* Poppy-colour, bright red; red dye. [F]

pŏ'nchō *n.* (*pl.* ~**s**). S. Amer. cloak of oblong piece of cloth with slit in middle for head; cycling-cape or other garment made to similar design. [S. Amer. Sp., f. Araucanian]

pŏnd *n.* & *v.* **1.** *n.* Fairly small body of still water formed naturally or by hollowing or embanking; (joc.) the sea (cf. HERRING-*pond*); ~**-life,** animals (esp. invertebrates) that live in ponds; ~**'weed,** aquatic herb (esp. of genus *Potamogeton*) growing in still water. **2.** *v.t.* Hold back, dam up, (stream). **3.** *v.i.* Form pond. [ME, var. of POUND[2]]

pŏ'ndage *n.* Capacity of pond; storage of water. [f. prec. + -AGE]

pŏ'nder *v.* **1.** *v.t.* Weigh mentally, think over, (matter, *how*, etc.). **2.** *v.i.* Think *on*, muse *over*. [ME, f. OF *ponderer* f. L *ponderāre* (*pondus -eris* weight)]

pŏ'nder|able *a.* Having appreciable weight (lit. or fig.); hence ~ABI'LITY *n.* [f. LL *ponderabilis* (as prec.; see -ABLE)]

pŏnderā'tion *n.* Weighing, balancing, (lit. or fig.). [f. L *ponderatio* (as PONDER; see -ATION)]

***pŏnderō'sa** *n.* (Red timber of) N. Amer. pine-tree (*Pinus ponderosa*). [mod. L, fem. of L *ponderosus* (see foll.)]

pŏ'nderous *a.* Heavy; unwieldy; laborious; (of style) dull, tedious; hence or cogn. **pŏnder-o**'SITY, ~NESS, *ns.*, ~LY[2] *adv.* [ME, f. L *ponderosus* (*pondus -eris* weight; see -OUS)]

pō'nė[1] *n.* Dealer's opponent in two-handed card games. [L, 2 sing. imper. of *ponere* place]

***pōne**[2] *n.* Maize bread, esp. as made by N. Amer. Indians; fine light bread made with milk, eggs, etc.; cake or loaf of this. [Algonquian, = bread]

pŏng *n.*, & *v.i.* (colloq.) Stink. [20th c.; orig. unkn.]

pongee' (pŭnjē') *n.* Soft usu. unbleached kind of Chinese silk fabric; imitation of this in cotton etc. [perh. f. Chin. *pun-chi* own loom, i.e. home-made]

pŏ'ngĭd (-nj-) *a.* & *n.* (Anthropoid ape) of family Pongidae. [f. mod. L *Pongidae* (*Pongo*, genus-name; see foll., -ID[3])]

pŏ'ngō (-nggō) *n.* (*pl.* ~**s**). Ape of genus *Pongo*, orang-utan; (Naut.) soldier. [f. Congolese *mpongo*, orig. of African apes]

pŏ'niard (-yerd) *n.*, & *v.t.* (Pierce or stab with) dagger. [f. F *poignard* f. OF *poignal* f. med. L *pugnale* f. L *pugnus* fist; see -ARD]

pons (pŏnz) *n.* ~ (***Varolii***), band of nerve-fibres in brain [f. C. *Varoli*, It. anatomist d.

1575]; **pons asinor'um,** bridge of asses, i.e. (1) 5th proposition of 1st book of Euclid ('the angles at the base of an isosceles triangle are equal to one another'), (2) anything found difficult by beginners. [L, = bridge]

pŏnt *n.* (S. Afr.) Ferry-boat moved by rope or cable. [Du.]

||**Pŏ'ntėfrăct-cāke.** Var. of POMFRET-CAKE.

pŏ'ntĭ|fĕx *n.* (*pl.* **~fices** *pr.* -ĭ'fĭsēz). (Rom. Ant.) Member of principal college of priests in Rome (**Pontifex Maximus,** head of this); = foll. [L *pontifex -ficis* (perh. *pons pontis* bridge, -*fex* f. *facere* make)]

pŏ'ntiff *n.* **1.** (**Sovereign** or **supreme**) ~, the pope. **2.** Bishop; chief priest. [f. F *pontife* f. as prec.]

pŏntĭ'fĭcal *a.* & *n.* **1.** *a.* Of or befitting a pontiff; pretending to infallibility, pompously dogmatic; ~ **Mass** (celebrated by bishop in full vestments); hence ~LY² *adv.* **2.** *n.* Office-book of Western Church containing forms for rites to be performed by bishops; (in *pl.*) vestments and insignia of bishop. [ME f. F, or f. L *pontificalis* (as PONTIFEX; see -AL)]

pŏntĭfĭcā'lĭa *n. pl.* Pontificals. [L, neut. pl. of *pontificalis* (see prec.)]

pŏntĭ'fĭcate¹ *n.* Office of pontifex, bishop, or pope; period of this. [f. L *pontificatus* (as PONTIFEX; see -ATE¹)]

pŏntĭ'fĭcāte² *v.i.* **1.** Play the pontiff, pretend to infallibility. **2.** Officiate as bishop, esp. at Mass. [f. med. L *pontificare* (as PONTIFEX) + -ATE³]

pŏ'ntĭfȳ *v.i.* = prec. 1. [f. F *pontifier* f. med. L *pontificare* (see prec., -FY)]

pŏntoneer', -nier', *n.* One who has charge of pontoons or of construction of a pontoon-bridge. [f. F *pontonnier* f. med. L *pontonarius* ferryman f. L *ponto* (see foll., -ARY¹)]

pŏntōō'n¹ *n.*, & *v.t.* **1.** *n.* Flat-bottomed boat used as ferry-boat or to carry lifting-gear etc.; one of several boats, hollow metal cylinders, etc., used to support temporary bridge; = CAISSON 2. **2.** *v.t.* Cross (river) by means of pontoons. [f. F *ponton* f. L *ponto -onis* (*pons pontis* bridge; see -OON)]

||**pŏntōō'n**² *n.* *Vingt-et-un*; hand at this, = NATURAL 19. [prob. corrupt.]

pō'nȳ *n.*, & *v.t.* **1.** *n.* Horse of any small breed; *small-sized motor car, liqueur-glass, etc.; *crib for translation; ||(sl.) £25; (in *pl.*, sl.) racehorses. **2.** ~ **express,** rapid postal system using ponies; **~-tail,** woman's or girl's hair drawn back, tied, and hanging behind like pony's tail; **~-trekking,** travelling across country on ponies for pleasure. **3.** *v.t.* *(sl.) Pay *up*. [perh. f. **poulney* f. F *poulenet* dim. of *poulain* foal]

***pōōch** *n.* (sl.) Dog. [20th c.; orig. unkn.]

pōōd *n.* Russian weight, 36 lb. avoirdupois. [f. Russ. *pud* f. LG or ON *pund* POUND¹]

pōō'dle *n.*, & *v.t.* **1.** *n.* Breed of dog with long curling hair often clipped and shaved in elaborate pattern. **2.** *v.t.* Clip and shave (dog) thus. [f. G *pudel(hund)* f. LG *pud(d)eln* splash in water; cf. PUDDLE²]

pōōf *n.* (colloq.) Effeminate man; male homosexual. [19th c.; cf. PUFF¹ in sense 'braggart']

pōōh (pōō) *int.* expr. impatience or contempt. [imit.]

Pōōh-Bah' (pōōb-) *n.* Holder of many offices at once. [character in W. S. Gilbert's *The Mikado*]

pōōh-pōō'h (pōōpōō') *v.t.* Express contempt for, ridicule, dismiss (idea etc.) scornfully. [redupl. of POOH]

pōō'ja. See PUJA.

pōō'ka *n.* (Ir.) Hobgoblin. [f. Ir. *púca*]

pōōl¹ *n.* & *v.* **1.** *n.* Small body of still water, usu. of natural formation; small shallow body of any liquid; deep still place in river; = SWIMMING-*pool*; ||**the P~** (**of London**), part of Thames just below London Bridge. **2.** *v.t.* Form into pool. **3.** *v.i.* Form pool; (of blood) become static. [f. OE *pōl*, MLG, MDu. *pōl*, OHG *pfuol* f. WG **pōl*-]

pōōl² *n.*, & *v.t.* **1.** *n.* (Cards). Collective amount of players' stakes and fines; receptacle for these. **2.** ||Game on billiard-table in which each player has ball of different colour with which he tries to pocket the others in fixed order, winner taking the whole stakes; *game on billiard-table with usu. 16 balls; ***~'room,** place for playing this, betting, etc. **3.** (Collective stakes in) joint gambling venture; **football ~,** form of gambling in which a proportion of the entry money for the competition is awarded in prizes to those who (most) correctly forecast the results of certain football matches; **the ~s,** various such competitions conducted week by week. **4.** Arrangement between competing parties by which prices are fixed and business shared to do away with competition. **5.** Common fund, e.g. of the profits of separate firms; common supply of persons, services, commodities, etc.; group of persons sharing duties etc. **6.** Fencing competition between two teams in which each member of one team fights each member of the other. **7.** *v.t.* Throw into common fund; share in common; (of transport organizations etc.) share (traffic, receipts). [f. F *poule* (=hen) in same sense; assoc. w. prec.]

pōōn *n.* E. Ind. tree of genus *Calophyllum*; ~ **oil** (from seeds of this, used in medicine and for lamps). [f. Sinh. *pūna*]

***pōō'ntăng** *n.* (sl.) Sexual intercourse. [f. F *putain* prostitute]

pōōp¹ *n.*, & *v.t.* **1.** *n.* Stern of ship; aftermost and highest deck. **2.** *v.t.* (Of wave) break over stern of (ship); (of ship) receive (wave) over stern. [ME, f. OF *pupe*, *pope* f. Rom. **puppa* f. L *puppis*]

pōōp² *v.t.* (esp. in *p.p.*; colloq.) Exhaust; tire *out*. [20th c.; orig. unkn.]

||**pōōp**³ *n.* (sl.) Foolish insignificant person. [abbr. of *nincompoop*]

poor *a.* **1.** Not having means to procure comforts or necessaries of life (*poor in* SPIRIT¹); ill supplied, deficient, (*in* a possession or quality); (of soil) unproductive. **2.** Scanty, inadequate, less or less good than is expected, (*the crop, visibility, was poor*; *had a poor night*; *is a poor driver*; *in poor* SPIRIT¹*s*); paltry, sorry, (*that is a poor consolation*; *it is a poor look-out if that happens*); spiritless, despicable, (*he is a poor creature*); humble, insignificant, (often iron. or joc.; *in my poor opinion*); **take a ~ view of,** regard with disfavour or pessimism. **3.** (Expr. pity or sympathy) unfortunate, hapless, (*poor fellow!*; *the poor child is inconsolable*). **4. ~-box,** money-box esp. in church for relief of the poor; **~-house,** (Hist.) workhouse; **~-law,** (Hist.) law relating to support of paupers; **~ man's,** inferior or cheaper substitute for (*cabbage* etc.); **~ man's weather-glass,** pimpernel; ||**~-rate,** (Hist.) rate or assessment for relief or support of the poor; **~ relation,** (fig.) inferior or subordinate member of group; **~-spirited,** timid, cowardly; ***~ white,** (esp. Negroes' derog.) member of socially inferior group of white people. [ME & OF *pov(e)re*, *poure*, f. L *pauper*]

poor'lȳ *adv.* & *pred. a.* **1.** *adv.* Scantily, defectively; with no great success; meanly, contemptibly. **2.** *a.* Unwell (*he is (looking) very poorly*). [ME, f. prec. + -LY²]

poor'nėss *n.* Defectiveness; lack of some good quality or constituent. [f. POOR + -NESS]

||***poort*** (pŏrt) *n.* (S. Afr.) Pass, narrower than a nek. [Du., = gate(way)]

pŏp[1] *v.* (**-pp-**). **1.** *v.i.* Make small quick explosive sound(s) as of cork when drawn; fire gun (*at* bird etc.); move, go, come, (*in, out, up,* etc.) unexpectedly or quickly or suddenly; **~ off,** (colloq.) die. **2.** *v.t.* Put (thing *in, out, down,* etc.) unexpectedly or quickly or suddenly. **3.** Put (question) abruptly; **~ the question,** (colloq.) propose marriage. **4.** Cause to burst with a pop; ||(sl.) pawn; *parch (maize) till it bursts open. **5. ~'corn,** maize so parched; **~'gun,** child's toy gun shooting pellet etc. by compression of air with piston, (derog.) inefficient firearm; ***~'over,** cake made from thin batter as hollow shell; ||**~-shop,** (sl.) pawnbroker's shop; **~-up** *a.,* (of toaster etc.) operating so as to move object (toast when ready etc.) quickly upwards. [ME; imit.]

pŏp[2] *n.* & *adv.* **1.** *n.* Abrupt explosive sound; (colloq.) effervescing drink; ||(sl.) pawning (**in ~,** in pawn). **2.** *adv.* With sound of pop (*heard it go pop*); **~ goes the weasel,** 19th-c. country dance in which dancer darted under arms of others to his partner. [as prec.]

pŏp[3] *n.* & *a.* (colloq.) **1.** *n.* Popular concert, record, music, etc. **2.** *a.* Popular; performing popular music etc. (*pop group*); **~ art** (based on modern popular culture and mass media); **~ festival** (at which popular music etc. is performed). [abbr.]

||**Pŏp**[4] *n.* Social and debating club at Eton. [perh. f. L *popina* cookshop, or E *lollipop shop* (orig. meeting-place)]

pŏp[5] *n.* (colloq., esp. as *voc.*) Father; any older man. [f. PAPA]

||**P.O.P.** *abbr.* Post Office Preferred (size of envelopes etc.).

pop. *abbr.* population.

pōpe[1] *n.* **1.** Bishop of Rome as head of Roman Catholic Church; (fig.) person pretending to or credited with infallibility etc.; = RUFF[3]. **2. P~ Joan,** card-game using compartmented tray [f. name of mythical female pope]; **~'s eye,** lymphatic gland surrounded with fat in middle of sheep's leg; **~'s head,** (arch.) round long-handled broom; *pope's* NOSE. **3.** Hence **~'**DOM (-pd-) *n.,* **~'**LESS (-pl-) *a.* [OE f. eccl. L *pāpa* bishop, pope, f. eccl. Gk *papas* = Gk *pappas* father; cf. PAPA]

pōpe[2] *n.* Parish priest of Orthodox Church in Russia etc. [f. Russ. *pop* f. OSlav. *popŭ* f. WG **papo* f. eccl. Gk (as prec.)]

pō'perў *n.* (derog.) Papal system, Roman Catholic religion. [f. POPE[1] + -ERY]

pŏ'p-eyed (-īd) *a.* (colloq.) Having bulging eyes; open-eyed (with surprise etc.). [f. POP[1] + EYE[1] + -ED[2]]

pŏ'pĭnjay *n.* **1.** (arch.) Parrot. **2.** (Hist.) Figure of parrot on pole as mark to shoot at. **3.** Conceited person; fop, coxcomb. [ME, f. AF *papeiaye,* OF *papingay* etc., f. Sp. *papagayo* f. Arab. *babağā*; assim. to JAY]

pō'pĭsh *a.* (derog.) Of popery, papistical; hence **~**LY[2] *adv.* [f. POPE[1] + -ISH[1]]

pŏ'plar *n.* Tree of genus *Populus,* of rapid growth (often w. allus. to straightness of trunk) and freq. tremulous leaves; * = TULIP-*tree* (1); **trembling ~,** aspen. [ME, f. AF *popler,* OF *poplier* (*pople* f. L *populus*)]

pŏ'plĭn *n.* Plain-woven fabric usu. of cotton, with corded surface. [f. obs. F *papeline* perh. f. It. *papalina* (fem.) PAPAL, f. the papal town Avignon where it was made]

pŏplĭ'tėal *a.* Of the hollow at back of knee. [f. mod. L *popliteus* f. L *poples -itis* this hollow; see -AL]

***pŏ'ppa.** Var. of POP[5].

pŏ'pper *n.* In vbl senses; ||(colloq.) press-stud. [f. POP[1] + -ER[1]]

pŏ'ppėt *n.* **1.** ||(colloq.) Small or dainty person, esp. as term of endearment. **2.** Lathe-head; (Naut.) short piece of wood for various purposes. **3. ~-head,** lathe-head, ||(Mining) frame at top of shaft supporting pulleys for ropes used in hoisting; **~-valve** (mushroom-shaped and lifted bodily from seat, not hinged). [ME *popet(te),* ult. f. L *pu(p)pa*; cf. PUPPET]

pŏ'ppĭng *n.* In vbl senses; **~-crease,** (Cricket) [perh. = striking-crease] line 4 ft. in front of and parallel to wicket, within which batsman must keep bat or one foot grounded to avoid risk of being stumped. [f. POP[1] + -ING[1]]

pŏ'pple *v.i.,* & *n.* **1.** *v.i.* (Of water) tumble about, toss to and fro. **2.** *n.* Rolling, tossing, ripple, (of water); hence **pŏ'ppl**Y[2] *a.* [ME, prob. f. MDu. *popelen* murmur, quiver, of imit. orig.]

pŏ'ppў *n.* Herb of genus *Papaver* having milky juice with narcotic properties and showy esp. scarlet flowers; **Californian ~,** eschscholtzia; ||**Flanders ~,** emblem of dead in World Wars, esp. artificial red poppy worn on **P~ Day** (= Remembrance Sunday) [f. *Flanders* as scene of fighting 1914–18]; **opium ~,** usu. white-flowered poppy (*Papaver somniferum*) from which opium is obtained; **~-head,** seed capsule of poppy, ornamental top to end of church seat; PRICKLY *poppy*; SHIRLEY *poppy*; **Welsh ~,** yellow-flowered plant (*Meconopsis cambrica*); hence **pŏ'ppĭ**ED[2] (-pĭd) *a.* [OE *popig, papæg, *papāg, *pāpau* f. med. L *papauum* f. L *papaver*]

pŏ'ppўcŏck *n.* (sl.) Nonsense. [f. Du. dial. *pappekak*]

***pŏ'psĭcle** *n.* Ice lolly. [P]

pŏ'psў, pŏ'psĭe, *n.* (colloq., esp. as term of endearment for) young woman. [f. POPPET + -Y[3], -IE]

pŏ'pūlace *n.* The common people; (derog.) the rabble. [F, f. It. *popolaccio* (*popolo* people + *-accio* pejorative suf.)]

pŏ'pūlar *a.* **1.** Of, or carried on by, the people (*popular election, etymology, meetings, tumult*). **2.** Adapted to the understanding, taste, or means, of the people, (*in popular language; popular science*); **~ music,** songs, folk-tunes, etc., not seeking to appeal to refined or classical taste. **3.** Liked or admired by the people or by people generally or by specified class, (*popular teachers; the popular hero; is popular with his men*); so **pŏpūlă'r**ITY *n.* **4.** Prevalent among the people (*popular fallacies,* LATIN). **5. ~ front,** (Polit.) party representing left-wing elements. **6.** Hence **~**LY[2] *adv.* [ME, f. AF *populer,* OF *populeir,* or f. L *popularis* (*populus* people; see -AR[1])]

pŏ'pūlarīz|e, -īs|e (-īz), *v.t.* Make popular; cause (person, principle, etc.) to be generally known or liked; present (technical subject etc.) in popular form; hence **~**A'TION *n.* [f. prec. + -IZE]

pŏ'pūlāte *v.t.* Inhabit, form the population of, (country, town, etc.); supply with inhabitants (*a densely populated district*). [f. med. L *populare* (as PEOPLE) + -ATE[3]]

pŏpūlā'tion *n.* **1.** Degree to which place is populated; act or process of supplying with inhabitants. **2.** Total number of inhabitants of a town, country, etc.; *the* inhabitants of a place (*the population turned out to welcome him*). **3.** Total number or quantity of things in a given place or region; (Statistics) total group of items under consideration. **4. ~ explosion,** sudden large increase of population of world or country. [f. LL *populatio* (as PEOPLE; see -ATION)]

pŏ'pūl|ĭst *n.* & *a.* (Adherent) of political party claiming to represent the whole of the people (orig. in U.S. 1892–1904, aiming at public control of railways, graduated income-tax, etc.); so ~ISM (3) *n.*, **~ĭ′stic** *a.* [f. L *populus* people + -IST]

pŏ′pūlous *a.* Thickly inhabited; hence ~NESS *n.* [ME, f. LL *populosus* (as PEOPLE; see -OUS)]

pôrbea′gle *n.* Shark of genus *Lamna*, with pointed snout. [18th c.; Corn. dial., of unkn. orig.]

pôr′celain (-slĭn) *n.* Fine kind of earthenware with translucent body and transparent glaze; thing(s) made of this; ~ **clay,** kaolin; **~-shell,** cowrie; hence or cogn. ~IZE (3) *v.t.*, ~OUS, **pôrcĕllā′nEOUS**, **pôrcĕllă′nIC**, **pôrcĕ′llanOUS**, *adjs.* [f. F *porcelaine* cowrie, porcelain, f. It. *porcellana* (*porcella* dim. of *porca* sow (cowrie being perh. likened to sow's vulva) f. L *porca* fem. of *porcus* pig)]

pôrch *n.* Covered approach to entrance of building; *veranda (~ **climber,** cat burglar); **the P~,** colonnade at Athens to which Zeno and his disciples resorted, (hence) Stoic school or philosophy (cf. ACADEMY, GARDEN, LYCEUM); hence ~ED² (-cht), ~′LESS, *adjs.* [ME, f. OF *porche* f. L *porticus* (transl. Gk *stoa*) f. *porta* passage]

pôr′cine *a.* Of or like pigs. [f. F *porcin* or f. L *porcinus* (*porcus* pig; see -INE¹)]

pôr′cūpīn|e *n.* **1.** ||Rodent of family Hystricidae with body and tail covered with erectile spines; *similar arboreal rodent of family Erethizontidae. **2.** Machine with many spikes or teeth, e.g. for hackling flax etc. **3.** (*attrib.*, applied to animals with spines, etc.) *porcupine ant-eater, crab, fish, grass.* **4.** Hence ~ISH¹, ~Y², *adjs.* [ME, f. OF *porc espin*, f. Prov. *porc espi(n)* f. Rom. **porcospinus* f. L *porcus* pig + *spina* thorn]

pôre¹ *n.* Minute opening in surface, through which fluids may pass. [ME f. OF, f. L f. Gk *poros* passage, pore]

pôre² *v.i.* **1.** ~ **over,** be absorbed in studying (book etc.), (fig.) meditate, think intently upon, (subject). **2.** (arch.) Look intently *at*, (*up*)*on*, *over*. [ME *pure* etc., perh. f. OE **pūrian*; cf. PEER³]

***pôr′gy̆** (-gĭ) *n.* Perchlike sea fish of family Sparidae. [18th c.; orig. uncert. and app. various; cf. Sp. & Port. *pargo*]

pôr′ĭfer *n.* Animal of phylum Porifera, sponge. [f. mod. L *Porifera* f. L *porus* PORE¹ + -I- + *-fer* bearing + -A 2]

pôr′ĭsm (*or* pŏ′r-) *n.* (Math.) Proposition concerned with the conditions that will render a given problem capable of innumerable solutions; corollary; so **pôrĭsmă′tIC** (-z-), **pŏrĭ′stIC**, *adjs.* [f. LL f. Gk *porisma -matos* (*porizō* deduce f. *poros* way)]

pôrk *n.* Flesh (esp. unsalted) of pig used as food; ***~-barrel,** (colloq.) government funds as source of political benefit; **~-butcher,** one who slaughters pigs for sale, or sells pork rather than other meats; ***~-fish,** yellow-striped black Atlantic fish; ~ **pie** (of minced etc. pork); **~-pie hat** (with flat rimmed crown and brim turned up all round). [ME & OF *porc* f. L *porcus* pig]

pôr′ker *n.* Pig raised for food; young fattened pig. [f. prec. + -ER¹]

pôr′kling *n.* Young or small pig. [f. PORK + -LING¹]

pôr′ky̆¹ *a.* Of or like pork, esp. (colloq.) fleshy, fat. [f. PORK + -Y²]

***pôr′ky̆²** *n.* (colloq.) Porcupine. [abbr.; see -Y³]

pôrn *n.* (colloq.) Pornography. [abbr.]

pôr′nō *n.* & *a.* (colloq.) **1.** *n.* Pornography. **2.** *a.* Pornographic. [abbr.]

pôrnŏ′cracy̆ *n.* Dominance of prostitutes, esp. in 10th-c. Rome. [f. Gk *pornē* prostitute + -O- + -CRACY]

pôrnŏ′graph|y̆ *n.* Explicit description or exhibition of sexual activity in literature, films, etc., intended to stimulate erotic rather than aesthetic feelings; literature etc. containing this; hence or cogn. ~ER¹ *n.*, **pôrnogră′phIC** *a.* [f. Gk *pornographos* (*pornē* prostitute, *graphō* write) + -Y¹]

pôroplă′stic (*or* pŏr-) *a.* (Surg.) (Of felt for splints etc.) both porous and plastic. [f. as PORE¹ + -O- + PLASTIC¹]

pôr′ous *a.* Full of pores (lit. or fig.); hence or cogn. **pôro′SITY**, ~NESS, *ns.* [ME, f. OF *poreux* f. med. L *porosus* f. L *porus* PORE¹; see -OUS]

pôrphy̆′rĭa *n.* Disease with abnormal metabolism, sometimes genetically caused, with symptoms suggesting insanity. [mod. L, f. *porphyrin* (purple substance excreted by porphyria patients; cf. foll.) + -IA¹]

pôrphy̆rŏ′gėnīte *n.* Person born in the PURPLE. [f. med. L *porphyrogenitus* f. late Gk *porphurogennētos* (Gk *porphura* purple, *gennētos* born)]

pôr′phy̆ry̆ *n.* Hard rock anciently quarried in Egypt, composed of crystals of white or red felspar in red matrix; (Geol.) unstratified or igneous rock having homogeneous base in which crystals of one or more minerals are disseminated; so **pôrphy̆rĭ′tIC** *a.* [ME, ult. f. med. L *porphyreum*, L f. Gk *porphuritēs* (*porphura* purple)]

pôr′poise (-pus) *n.* Small whale of genus *Phocaena*, with blunt rounded snout. [ME *porpays* etc. f. OF *po(u)rpois* etc. f. Rom. **porcopiscis* f. L *porcus* pig + *piscis* fish]

pŏrrā′ceous (-shus) *a.* (arch.) Leek-green. [f. L *porraceus* (*porrum* leek; see -ACEOUS)]

porrĕ′ct *v.t.* (Zool.) stretch out (part of body); (Eccl. Law) tender, submit, (document). [ME, f. L *porrigere -rect-* (*por-* PRO-¹, *regere* direct)]

pŏ′rridge *n.* Soft food of oatmeal or other meal or cereal boiled in water or milk; **save** one's **breath to cool** one's ~, keep one's advice etc. for one's own use. [16th c., alt. f. POTTAGE]

pŏ′rringer (-nj-) *n.* Small basin from which soup etc. is eaten esp. by children. [earlier *pottinger* f. OF *potager* (*potage*; see POTTAGE, -ER¹); *-n-* as in *messenger* etc.]

pôrt¹ *n.* Harbour (lit. or fig.); town or place possessing harbour, esp. one where customs officers are stationed; FREE¹ *port*; ~ **of call,** place where ship or (fig.) person stops during journey; **P~ of London Authority,** corporate body controlling London harbour and docks. [OE, f. L *portus*, & ME prob. f. OF f. L *portus*]

pôrt² *n.* **1.** (esp. Sc.) Gate, gateway, esp. of walled town. **2.** (Naut.) Opening in side of ship for entrance, loading etc.; porthole. **3.** Aperture for passage of steam, water, etc.; aperture in wall etc. for gun to be fired through. **4. ~′hole** (-t-h-), (esp. glazed) aperture in ship's or aircraft's side for admission of light and air, or (formerly) for pointing cannon through. [ME & OF *porte* f. L *porta*]

pôrt³ *n.* External deportment, carriage, bearing; (Mil.) position taken in porting arms. [ME f. OF *port*, f. as foll.]

pôrt⁴ *v.t.* (Mil.) Carry (rifle, or other weapon) diagonally across and close to the body, with barrel etc. opposite middle of left shoulder (esp. command *port arms!*). [f. F *porter* f. L *portare* carry]

pôrt⁵ *n.*, & *v.t.* (Naut. & Aeron.) **1.** *n.* Left-hand side of ship or boat or aircraft looking forward (cf. STARBOARD); *port* TACK¹; *port* WATCH¹. **2.** *v.t.* Turn (helm, or abs.) to port. [prob. orig. side turned towards PORT¹]

pôrt⁶ *n.* ~ **(wine),** strong sweet dark-red (occas. brown or white) fortified wine of Portugal. [shortened f. *Oporto*, city of Portugal, whence shipped]

pôrt⁷ *n.* (Austral.) Portmanteau. [abbr.]

pôr't|able *a.* & *n.* **1.** *a.* Easily movable, convenient for carrying, (*portable furnace, radio*); hence ~ABI'LITY *n.* **2.** *n.* Portable object, esp. radio, typewriter, etc. [ME f. OF, or f. LL *portabilis* f. L *portare* carry; see -ABLE]

pôr'tage *n.*, & *v.t.* **1.** *n.* Carrying, carriage; cost of this. **2.** Carrying of boats or goods between two navigable waters; place at which this is necessary. **3.** *v.t.* Convey (boat, goods) over portage. [ME f. OF (*porter*; see PORT⁴, -AGE)]

pôr'tal¹ *n.* Door(way), gate(way), esp. elaborate one; point of entry (*~-to-~, of time spent by workman between entrance to factory etc. and place of actual working). [ME f. OF, f. med. L *portale* neut. adj. as n. (see foll.)]

pôr'tal² *a.* (Anat.) Of the porta or transverse fissure of the liver; ~ **vein** (conveying blood to liver or other organ exc. heart). [f. mod. L *portalis* f. L *porta* gate; see -AL]

pôrtamĕ'nt|ō *n.* (*pl.* ~**i** *pr.* -ē). (Mus.) Gliding continuously from one pitch to another in singing, playing violin, etc.; piano-playing in a manner intermediate between legato and staccato. [It., = carrying]

pôr'tatĭve *a.* Serving to carry or support; (Hist.) portable (esp. of a small pipe-organ). [ME f. OF *portatif*, app. alt. of *portatil* f. med. L *portatilis* f. L *portare* carry; see -IVE, -IL]

pôrtcŭ'llĭs *n.* Strong heavy grating sliding up and down in vertical grooves, lowered to block gateway in fortress etc.; hence ~ED² (-st) *a.* [ME, f. OF *porte coleïce* sliding door (*porte* door f. L *porta*, *col(e)ïce* fem. of *couleïs* sliding f. Rom. **colaticius* f. L *colare* filter)]

Pôrte *n.* **The** (**Sublime** or **Ottoman**) ~, (Hist.) Ottoman court at Constantinople, Turkish government until 1923. [F (*la Sublime ~* = the exalted gate), transl. of Turk. title of central office of Ottoman government]

porte-cochère (pôrtkŏshār') *n.* Gateway and passage for vehicles through house into courtyard; *structure extending from entrance of building over place where vehicles stop to discharge passengers. [F (*porte* PORT², *cochère* fem. adj. f. *coche* COACH)]

pôrtĕ'nd *v.t.* Foreshow, foreshadow, as an omen; give warning of (*this portends a renewal of the conflict*). [ME, f. L *portendere -tent-* (*por-* PRO-¹, *tendere* stretch)]

pôr'tĕnt *n.* Omen, significant sign of something to come; prodigy, marvellous thing; so **pôrtĕ'nt**OUS *a.* [f. L *portentum* (as prec.)]

||**pôr'ter¹** *n.* Gate-keeper, door-keeper, esp. of large building etc. [ME & AF, OF *portier* f. LL *portarius* (*porta* door; see -ER²)]

pôr'ter² *n.* **1.** Person employed to carry burdens, esp. railway or airport or hotel employee who handles luggage, whence ~AGE (4) *n.* **2.** *Sleeping-car attendant. **3.** (Hist.) Dark-brown bitter beer brewed from charred or browned malt [app. orig. made esp. for porters]. **4.** *~**house,** (1) house at which porter and other liquors were retailed, (2) house where steaks, chops, etc., were served; ~**house steak,** choice cut of beef from between sirloin and tenderloin; ||*porter's* KNOT¹. [ME, f. OF *port(e)our* f. med. L *portator -oris* (*portare* carry; see -ER²)]

pôr'tfīre *n.* Device for firing rockets, igniting explosives in mining, etc. [after F *porte-feu* (*porter* as PORT⁴, *feu* fire)]

pôrtfō'lĭō *n.* (*pl.* ~**s**). Case for keeping loose sheets of paper, drawings, etc.; list of investments held by person, company, etc.; (fig.) office of minister of State; **Minister without ~**, Cabinet Minister who is not in charge of any department of State. [earlier *porto folio*, f. It. *portafogli* (*porta* imper. of *portare* carry, *fogli* pl. of *foglio* leaf f. L *folium*)]

pôr'tĭcō *n.* (*pl.* ~**es** *or* ~**s**). Colonnade, roof supported by columns at regular intervals, usu. attached as porch to building. [It., f. L *porticus* PORCH]

portière (pôrtyār') *n.* Curtain hung over door(way). [F (*porte* door f. L *porta*)]

pôr'tion *n.*, & *v.t.* **1.** *n.* Part, share; amount of food allotted to one person; dowry, whence ~LESS *a.*; one's destiny, one's lot; *a* (limited) quantity. **2.** *v.t.* Divide (thing) into shares, distribute *out*, assign (thing *to* person) as share; give dowry to. [ME f. OF (*portionner* v. f.) *porcion, portion* n. f. L *portio -onis*]

Pôr'tland *n.* ~ **cement,** hydraulic cement manufactured from chalk and clay, whose colour when set is similar to that of ~ **stone,** valuable building limestone. [f. Isle of ~ in Dorset, peninsula whence the stone is obtained]

pôr'tl|ȳ *a.* Bulky, corpulent; (arch.) of stately appearance; hence ~ĭNESS *n.* [f. PORT³ + -LY¹]

pôrtmă'nteau (-tō) *n.* (*pl.* ~**s** *or* ~**x,** *pr.* -z). Leather trunk for clothes etc., opening into two equal parts; ~ **word,** factitious word blending the sounds and combining the meanings of two others (*motel, Oxbridge*). [f. F *portmanteau* (*porter* carry f. L *portare*, *manteau* MANTLE¹)]

pôrtola'nō (-lah'-) *n.* (*pl.* ~**s**). (Hist.) Book of sailing directions with charts, description of harbours, etc. [It. (*porto* PORT¹)]

pôr'trait (-rĭt) *n.* Likeness of person or animal made by drawing, painting, photography, etc.; person etc. resembling or typifying another; verbal picture, graphic description. [F, p.p. (as n.) of OF *portraire* PORTRAY]

pôr'traitĭst (-rĭt-) *n.* One who paints or takes portraits. [f. prec. + -IST]

pôr'traiture (-rĭcher) *n.* Portraying; portrait; graphic description. [ME f. OF (as PORTRAIT; see -URE)]

pôrtray' *v.t.* Make likeness of; describe graphically; hence ~AL 2 *n.* [ME, f. OF *portraire* (*por-* f. L PRO-¹, *traire* draw f. Rom. **tragere* f. L *trahere*)]

pôr'treeve *n.* (Hist.) Chief officer of town or borough. [OE *portgerēfa* (*port* town = PORT¹ or PORT², *gerēfa* REEVE¹)]

pôr'trĕss *n.* Female porter. [ME, f. PORTER¹ + -ESS]

Pôrt Sălūt (pôrsălū') *n.* Pale mild type of cheese. [f. name of Trappist abbey in France]

Pôrtŭguē'se (-gē'z) *a.* & *n.* (*pl.* same). (Native, inhabitant, or language) of Portugal; ~ **man-of-war,** dangerous (sub)tropical hydrozoan of genus *Physalia*, with sail-shaped crest and poisonous sting. [f. Port. *portuguez* f. med. L *portugalensis* (see -ESE)]

pōse¹ (-z) *v.* & *n.* **1.** *v.t.* Formulate (assertion, claim, etc.); propound (question, problem); place (artist's model etc.) in certain attitude. **2.** *v.i.* Assume an attitude, esp. for artistic purposes, or to impress others; set up, give oneself out, *as* (connoisseur etc.); ~ **as,** pretend to be. **3.** *n.* Attitude of body or mind, esp. one assumed for effect (*his philanthropy is a mere pose*). [(n. f. F *pose*) f. F *poser* f. LL *pausare* PAUSE; some senses by confus. w. L *ponere* place, cf. COMPOSE]

pōse² (-z) *v.t.* Puzzle (person) with question or problem. [f. obs. *appose* f. OF *aposer* var. of *oposer* OPPOSE]

pō'ser (-z-) *n.* In vbl senses; puzzling question or problem. [f. POSE¹,² + -ER¹]

pōseur' (-zēr') *n.* (*fem.* **poseuse** *pr.* -zēr'z). Person who poses for effect or behaves affectedly. [F (*poser* POSE¹)]

pŏsh *a.* (sl.) Smart; stylish; first-rate. [orig. uncertain; perh. f. sl. *posh* money, a dandy]

pŏ'sĭt (-z-) *v.t.* Assume as fact, postulate; put in position, place, (*posited by natural agency*). [f. L *ponere posit-* place]

posi'tion (-z-) *n.*, & *v.t.* **1.** *n.* Way in which thing or its parts are placed or arranged; configuration of chess-men etc. during game. **2.** Mental attitude, way of looking at question. **3.** (Logic etc.) Proposition; statement of proposition. **4.** Place occupied by a person or thing; proper place (*in* or *out of position*); (Mil.) place where troops are posted for strategical purposes (*the position was stormed*); being advantageously placed (*manœuvring for position*); **in a ~ to,** enabled by circumstances or resources or information to *do, state,* etc. **5.** Situation of vowel in syllable, esp. (Gk & L Pros.) of short vowel before two consonants, making the syllable metrically long. **6.** (fig.) Situation in relation to other persons or things (*difficult for a person in my position*). **7.** Rank, status, (high) social standing; paid (official or domestic) employment. **8.** Hence ~AL *a.* **9.** *v.t.* Place in position; (Mil.) place or post (troops). [ME f. OF, or f. L *positio -onis* (as prec.; see -ITION)]

pŏ'sitive (-z-) *a.* & *n.* **1.** *a.* Formally or explicitly stated, definite, unquestionable, (*positive assertion; have no positive proof; here is proof positive*). **2.** (Of person) convinced, confident in opinion, cocksure. **3.** (Gram.) ~ **(degree of) adjective, adverb,** primary form expressing simple quality without comparison (cf. COMPARATIVE, SUPERLATIVE). **4.** Absolute, not relative; (colloq.) downright, out-and-out, (*it would be a positive miracle*). **5.** Dealing only with matters of fact, practical, (*positive philosophy*); constructive (*a positive suggestion*). **6.** Marked by presence, not absence, of qualities (*positive reaction;* cf. NEGATIVE[1]). **7.** (Alg., of quantity) greater than zero (cf. NEGATIVE[1]); *positive* FEEDBACK; ~ **sign** (+). **8.** Tending in the direction naturally or arbitrarily taken as that of increase or progress (*clockwise rotation is positive*). **9.** Containing or producing ~ **charge, electricity,** (of the kind produced by rubbing glass with silk; cf. NEGATIVE[1]); ~ **pole,** (of magnet) north-seeking pole; ~ **ray,** canal ray. **10.** (Photog.) Showing lights and shades as in original image cast on film etc. (opp. NEGATIVE[1]). **11.** Hence ~LY[2] (-vlĭ) *adv.*, ~NESS (-vn-), **pŏsitĭ'vity** (-z-), *ns.* **12.** *n.* Positive degree, adjective, photograph, quantity, etc. [ME f. OF *positif -ive* or f. L *positivus* (as POSIT; see -ITIVE)]

pŏ'sitiv|ism (pŏ'z-) *n.* Philosophical system of Auguste Comte, recognizing only positive facts and observable phenomena, and rejecting metaphysics and theism; religious system founded on this; **logical ~,** form of positivism in which symbolic logic is used and linguistic problems of meaning are emphasized; so ~IST (2) *n.*, **~ĭ'stic** *a.* [f. F *positivisme* (as prec.; see -ISM)]

pŏ'sitrŏn (-z-) *n.* (Phys.) Elementary particle with mass of electron and charge of same amount as electron's but positive. [f. POSITIVE + -TRON]

pŏsitrō'nium (-z-) *n.* (Phys.) System comprising a positron and an electron. [f. prec. + -IUM]

posŏ'logy̆ *n.* Study of the quantities in which drugs should be administered; hence **pŏsolŏ'gical** *a.* [f. F *posologie* f. Gk *posos* how much; see -LOGY]

pŏ'ssė *n.* Body (*of* constables); strong force or company; ~ **comitatus** (kŏmĭtā'tus), (Hist.) body of men above age of 15 in a county, summoned by sheriff to repress riot etc. [med. L, = power f. L *posse* be able; *comitatus* = of the county]

possĕ'ss (-z-) *v.t.* **1.** Hold as property, own; have (faculty, quality, etc.; *they possess a special value for us*). **2.** Maintain (one*self*, one's mind, soul, *in* patience etc.). **3.** (Of demon etc. or cause of infatuation) occupy, dominate, (person etc.) (*possessed by a devil, by* or *with an idea*; **like one ~ed,** with great energy; **what ~ed you?,** how could you be so foolish?); copulate with (woman). **4.** ~ **oneself of,** take or get for one's own; **be ~ed of,** own, have. **5.** So ~OR *n.*, ~ORY *a.* [f. OF *possesser* f. L *possidēre -sess-* (*potis* able, *sedēre* sit)]

possĕ'ssion (-zĕ'shon) *n.* **1.** Possessing or being possessed; actual holding or occupancy; (Law) visible power of exercising such control as attaches to (but may exist apart from) lawful ownership (*possession is nine* POINT[1]*s of the law*); (Footb. etc.) temporary control of ball etc. by a particular player; **in ~,** (of thing) possessed, (of person) possessing; **in ~ of,** having in one's possession; **in the ~ of,** held or owned by; **take ~,** become owner or possessor *of*. **2.** Thing possessed; (in *pl.*) property, wealth; subject territory, esp. foreign dominion. [ME f. OF, or f. L *possessio -onis* (as prec.; see -ION)]

possĕ'ssive (poz-) *a.* & *n.* **1.** *a.* Of possession; showing a desire to possess, or to retain what one possesses. **2.** (Gram.) Indicating possession; ~ **case** (e.g. *John's, the baker's*); *possessive* PRONOUN. **3.** Hence ~LY[2] (-vlĭ) *adv.*, ~NESS (-vn-) *n.* **4.** *n.* Possessive case or word. [f. L *possessivus* (as POSSESS; see -IVE), transl. Gk *ktētikē* (*ptōsis* case)]

pŏ'ssėt *n.* (Hist.) Drink made of hot milk curdled with ale, wine, etc., often flavoured with spices etc., formerly much used as remedy for colds etc. [ME *poshote*; orig. unkn.]

pŏssĭbĭ'lĭty̆ *n.* State or fact of being possible (*the possibility of miracles; cannot by any possibility be in time; there is no possibility of his coming; it is within the range of possibility*); capability of being used, improved, etc.; thing that may exist or happen (*what are the possibilities?; there are three possibilities*). [ME, f. OF *possibilité* or f. LL *possibilitas -tatis* (as foll.; see -ITY)]

pŏ'ssĭble *a.* & *n.* **1.** *a.* That can exist, be done, or happen; *that is quite possible; it is scarcely possible to say; it is possible* (*that*) *he knows* or *may know*; *there are three possible excuses* (that may be made); *provide against a possible loss of men* (that may occur); *get the greatest possible assistance; get all the assistance possible; come if possible* (if you can); *come as early as possible* (as you can). **2.** That is likely to happen etc. (*few thought his election possible*); that is acceptable for want of better (*here is a possible way of doing it*). **3.** *n.* Highest possible score esp. in shooting (*scored a possible at 800 yards*); possible candidate, member of team, etc., (**Possibles** and **Probables,** teams for football etc. trial match). [ME f. OF, or f. L *possibilis* (*posse* be able; see -IBLE)]

pŏ'ssĭbly̆ *adv.* In accordance with possibility (*cannot possibly do it; how can I possibly?*); perhaps, maybe, for all one knows to the contrary. [ME, f. prec. + -LY[2]]

pŏ'ssum *n.* (colloq.) **1.** = OPOSSUM 1; **play ~,** (1) pretend to be unconscious [from opossum's habit of feigning death if attacked], (2) feign ignorance. **2.** (Austral.) = OPOSSUM 2. [abbr.]

pōst[1] *n.*, & *v.t.* **1.** *n.* Stout piece of timber or metal usu. cylindrical or square and of considerable length, placed vertically as support in building; stake or stout pole to mark boundary, carry notices, etc. (**deaf as a ~,** completely deaf; *from* PILLAR *to post*); pole etc. marking point in race, esp. STARTING-*post* (**left at the ~,** outdistanced from the start) or WINNING[1]-*post* (**beaten at the ~,** defeated at the last moment); (Mining) vertical mass of coal left to support roof. **2. ~-mill,** windmill pivoted on post and turning to catch the wind; ***~-oak,** oak with hard durable wood used for posts etc. **3.** *v.t.* ~ **(up)**, attach (paper etc.) to post or in prominent place, advertise (fact, thing, person) by placard or in published list; publish name of of (ship) as overdue or missing; placard (wall etc.) with bills; *achieve (score in game etc.). [OE, f. L *postis*; in ME also f. OF etc.]

pōst[2] *n.* & *adv.* **1.** *n.* (Hist.) One of a series of men stationed with horses along roads at intervals, the duty of each being to ride forward with letters to next stage; courier, letter-carrier, mail-cart. **2.** ||Single dispatch of letters, letters so dispatched; letters taken from post office or postal letter-box on one occasion (*I missed the morning post*); letters etc. delivered at one place on one occasion (*the post has come*; *had a heavy post today*); official conveyance of letters, parcels, etc., (*send it by post*; GENERAL *post*); post office or postal letter-box (*take it to the post*); **by return of ~,** by next mail in opposite direction, (Hist.) by same courier who brought the dispatch. **3.** (As name of newspaper) *Evening Post* etc. **4.** Size of paper, about 500 × 400 mm. **5.** *adv.* (arch.) With post-horses, express, with haste, (*ride post*). **6.** ||**~-bag,** mail-bag; **~-box,** postal letter-box; ||**~-boy,** (1) boy or man who carries letters, (2) postilion; **~'card,** card for conveyance by post without envelope, or similar card for various purposes; **~-chaise,** (Hist.) travelling carriage hired from stage to stage or drawn by horses so hired; ||**~-code,** group of letters and figures included in postal address to assist sorting; ***~ exchange,** (Mil.) camp shop; ||**~-free,** carried free of charge by post, or with postage prepaid; **~-ha'ste** *n.* (arch.) & *adv.*, (with) great speed or haste; **~-horn** (Hist., blown to announce arrival of the post); **~-horse** (Hist., kept at inns etc. for use of post or travellers); **~'man,** one who delivers or collects letters etc.; ||*~man's knock*, parlour game in which pretended letters are delivered in exchange for kisses; **~'mark,** (*n.*) official mark stamped on letter, esp. one giving place, date, etc., of dispatch or arrival, and serving to cancel stamp, (*v.t.*) mark (envelope etc.) with this; **~'master**[1], official in charge of a post office; *P~master General*, minister at head of country's postal service; **~'mistress,** woman in charge of a post office; **P~ Office,** public department or corporation responsible for postal and telecommunication services; ~ **office,** room or building where postal business is carried on (||GENERAL *Post Office*; *~-office box*, numbered place in post office where letters are kept until called for; ||*post-office* ORDER[1] 16), *postman's knock; **~-paid,** on which postage has been paid; **~-town** (with post office, esp. one that is not sub-office of another). [f. F *poste* (fem.) f. It. *posta* f. Rom. **posta* =*posita* fem. p.p. of L *ponere posit-* place]

pōst[3] *v.* **1.** *v.i.* ||(Hist.) travel with relays of horses; travel with haste, hurry. **2.** Put (letter etc.) into post office or letter-box for transmission. **3.** (Bookk.) Carry (entry) from auxiliary book to more formal one, esp. from day-book to journal or ledger; ~ **(up)**, complete (ledger etc.) thus, (fig., esp. in *p.p.*) supply (person) with full information. [f. prec., or f. obs. F *poster*]

pōst[4] *n.*, & *v.t.* **1.** *n.* Place where soldier is stationed or which he patrols, (fig.) place of duty; position taken by body of soldiers, force occupying this; fort. **2.** **(Trading-)~,** place occupied for purposes of trade esp. in region not yet fully settled. **3.** Situation, paid employment. **4.** (Naval Hist.) Commission as officer in command of vessel of 20 guns or more; ||**~ captain,** holder of such commission (not of courtesy title or inferior command). **5.** (Mil.) **First, last, ~,** bugle-call giving notice of hour of retiring for night (*last post* also blown at mil. funerals etc.). **6.** *v.t.* Place, station, (soldiers etc.); appoint to post or command. [f. F *poste* (masc.) f. It. *posto* f. Rom. **postum* f. L neut. p.p. (as POST[2])]

pōst- *pref.* After, behind, as: **~-cla'ssic(al),** later than the classical period (usu. of Greek and Roman literature); **~-co'ital,** occurring or existing after coitus; **~-commu'nion,** part of Eucharistic office following act of communion; **~-da'te,** affix or assign a date later than the actual one to (document, event, etc.); **~-date,** such date; **~-dilu'vian** *a.* & *n.*, (person) existing, occurring, after the Flood; **~-e'ntry,** late or subsequent entry (for race, in book-keeping, etc.); **~-exi'lic,** subsequent to the Jews' exile in Babylon; **~fi'x,** append (letters) at end of word; **~'fix** *n.*, suffix; **~-gla'cial** *a.* & *n.*, (period) subsequent to a glacial period; **~-gra'duate,** (*a.*) (of a course of study) carried on after taking first degree, (*n.*) student taking such course; **P~-Impre'ssionism,** artistic aims and methods [so named as a reaction from impressionism] directed to expressing rather the individual artist's than the ordinary observer's presumable conception of the objects represented; so *P~-Impre'ssionist* n., *~-impressioni'stic* a.; **~'lude,** (Mus.) concluding voluntary [after PRELUDE[1]]; **~-mille'nnial,** following the millennium; **~-mille'nnialism,** doctrine that second Advent will follow the millennium; so *~-mille'nnialist* n.; **~-na'tal,** existing or occurring after (child)birth; **~-nu'ptial,** subsequent to marriage; **~-par'tum,** following parturition; **~-tax,** (of income) after deduction of taxes; **~-war,** occurring or existing after a war (||*~-war credits*, credits resulting from reduced income-tax allowances at time of 1939–45 war). [f. or after L *post* adv. & prep.]

pō'stage *n.* Amount charged for carriage of letter etc. by post, now usu. prepaid by **~ stamp,** small adhesive label to be affixed, or stamp embossed or impressed on envelope etc., having specified value; ~ **due,** postage not prepaid and usu. demanded by special postage stamp; ***~ meter,** franking-machine. [f. POST[2] + -AGE]

pō'stal *a.* & *n.* **1.** *a.* Of the POST[2]; by post (*postal vote*); ***~ card,** = POST[2]*card*; **~ code,** = POST[2]*-code*; ***~ meter,** franking-machine; ||*postal* ORDER[1] 16; **P~ Union,** union of governments of various countries for regulation of international postage. **2.** *n.* *Postcard. [F (*poste* POST[2]; see -AL)]

pŏstee'n *n.* Afghan sheepskin greatcoat. [f. Pers. *postin* of leather]

pō'ster *n.* In vbl senses; billposter; placard displayed in public place; ~ **paint** (gummy opaque kind). [f. POST[1] + -ER[1]]

poste restante (pōst rĕstah'ńt) *n.* Department in post office in which letters are kept until called for. [F, = letter(s) remaining (i.e., at the post office)]

pŏstēr'ior *a.* & *n.* **1.** *a.* Later, coming after in series, order, or time; so ~ITY (-ŏ'r-) *n.* **2.** Hinder; hence ~LY[2] *adv.*, as viewed from behind. **3.** *n.* (in *sing.* or *pl.*) Buttocks. [L, compar. of *posterus* following (*post* after)]

pŏstĕ'rĭtў *n.* Descendants of a person; all succeeding generations (*deserves the gratitude of posterity*). [ME, f. OF *posterité* f. L *posteritas -tatis* (*posterus*; see prec., -ITY)]

pŏ'stern *n.* Back door; side way or entrance.

For other words in *post-* see POST-.

[ME, f. OF *posterne, posterle*, f. LL *posterula* dim. f. *posterus* (see POSTERIOR)]

pō'stface *n.* Brief explanatory note or comments at end of book. [F (as POST-, PREFACE)]

pŏ'sthūmous (-tū-) *a.* (Of child) born after death of its father; (of book etc.) published after author's death; occurring after death; hence ~LY[2] *adv.* [f. L *postumus* last (superl. f. *post* after), in LL *posth-* by assoc. w. *humus* ground, + -OUS]

pŏsti'che (-ē'sh) *n.* Coil of false hair, worn as adornment. [F, = false, f. It. *posticcio*]

pŏ'stĭl *n.* (Hist.) Marginal note, comment, esp. on text of Scripture; commentary. [ME, f. OF *postille* f. med. L *postilla*, of uncert. orig.]

postĭ'lion, postĭ'llion, (-lyon) *n.* Rider on near horse drawing coach etc. without coachman. [f. F *postillon* f. It. *postiglione* post-boy (*posta* POST[2])]

pōstlĭ'mĭnȳ *n.* **1.** (Rom. Law). Right of banished person or captive to resume civic privileges on return. **2.** (Internat. Law). Restoration to their former status of persons and things taken in war, when they come again into the power of the nation they originally belonged to. [f. L POST(*liminium* f. *limen liminis* threshold)]

pō'stmaster[1] (-mah-) *n.* See POST[2].

‖**pō'stmaster**[2] (-mah-) *n.* Scholar of Merton College, Oxford; hence ~SHIP (1, 2) *n.* [16th c.; orig. unkn.]

pōst-mŏr'tĕm[1] *adv.* After death. [L]

pōst-mŏr'tem[2] *a.* & *n.* (Examination) made after death, esp. to determine its cause; (colloq.) (discussion) after conclusion (of game, election, etc.). [f. prec.]

pōst-ŏ'bĭt *a.* & *n.* **1.** *a.* Taking effect after death. **2.** *n.* Bond securing to lender a sum to be paid on death of specified person from whom borrower has expectations. [f. L *post obitum* (*post* after, *obitus* decease f. *obire* die)]

pōstpō'ne (*or* po-; *or* -sp-) *v.t.* Cause to take place at later time; treat (thing) as inferior in importance (*to* another); hence ~MENT (-nm-) *n.* [f. L POST(*ponere posit-* place)]

pōstposĭ'tion (-zĭ'-) *n.* Particle or word placed after another, usu. as enclitic, (e.g. -WARDS); hence or cogn. ~AL, **pōstpŏ'sĭtive** (-zĭ-), *adjs.* [f. LL *postpositio* (as prec.; see -ION)]

pōstprā'ndĭal *a.* (usu. joc.) After-lunch or -dinner (*post-prandial nap, eloquence*). [f. POST- + L *prandium* a meal + -AL]

pō'stscript (*or* pō'sk-) *n.* Additional paragraph esp. at end of letter after signature. [f. L *postscriptum* neut. p.p. (as n.) of POST(*scribere* write)]

pŏ'stūlant *n.* Candidate esp. for admission into religious order. [F, or f. L *postulans -antis* (as foll.; see -ANT)]

pŏ'stūlate[1] *n.* Thing claimed or assumed as basis of reasoning, fundamental condition; prerequisite; (Math.) claim to take for granted the possibility of simple operation, e.g. of drawing straight line between any two points. [f. L *postulatum*, neut. p.p. (as n.) of *postulare* demand; see -ATE[1]]

pŏ'stūl|āte[2] *v.t.* Demand, require as a necessary condition, claim, take for granted (thing, *that*, *to* do); (Eccl. Law) nominate or elect subject to superior sanction; so ~A'TION *n.*, ~**ātor** *n.*, (esp., R.C. Ch.) one who presents case for canonization or beatification. [f. L *postulare* demand + -ATE[3]]

pŏ'stur|e *n.* & *v.* **1.** *n.* Relative position of parts esp. of body, attitude of body or mind; condition, state, (*of* affairs etc.). **2.** *v.t.* Dispose limbs of (person) in particular way. **3.** *v.i.* Assume posture (lit. or fig.), esp. for effect. **4.** Hence ~AL *a.*, ~ER[1] *n.*, (-cher-). [F, f. It. *postura* f. L *positura* (*ponere posit-* place; see -URE)]

pō'sȳ (-zĭ) *n.* **1.** (arch.) Short motto, line of verse etc., inscribed within ring (**~-ring**) etc. **2.** Small bunch of flowers. [f. POESY]

pŏt[1] *n.* **1.** Rounded vessel of earthenware, metal, or glass, for holding liquids or solids; = CHAMBER-*-pot*, COFFEE-*pot*, FLOWER*pot*, GLUE-*pot*, *jam-pot*, TEA*pot*; such vessel for cooking; drinking-vessel of pewter etc.; contents of pot (*a pot of tea, of honey*). **2.** Vessel, usu. of silver, as prize in athletic sports, (sl.) any prize in these; CHIMNEY-*-pot*; LOBSTER-*pot*; (colloq.) = *pot-belly*. **3.** Size of paper, 375 × 312 mm. [from the orig. watermark of a pot]. **4.** (colloq.) Large sum (*made a pot* or *pots of money*); total amount betted. **5.** BIG *pot*; **the ~ calls the kettle black,** person blames another for fault he too has; **go to ~,** (colloq.) be ruined or destroyed (orig. of meat cut up for cooking); *keep the pot* BOIL[2]*ing*. **6.** **~-ale,** refuse from distillation, used as pig-food; **~-belly,** (person with) protuberant belly; **~-boiler,** work of literature or art done merely to make a living, writer or artist who does this; **~-bound,** (of plant) whose roots fill flowerpot and lack room to expand; **~-boy,** publican's assistant; ***~ cheese,** cottage cheese; **~ hat,** bowler; **~-herb,** any of those grown in kitchen garden; POT-HOLE; **~-hook,** hook over fireplace for hanging pot etc. on or for lifting hot pot, curved stroke in handwriting esp. as made in learning to write; **~-house,** (derog.) public house; **~-hunter,** sportsman who shoots anything he comes across, person who takes part in contest merely for sake of prize; so ~*-hunting* n. & a.; **~ luck,** whatever is to be had (for a meal, or fig.; *come and take pot luck with us*); **~'man,** publican's assistant; **~ pie,** meat or fruit pie baked in a pot; **~ plant** (grown in flowerpot); **~-roast,** (*n.*) piece of meat cooked slowly in covered dish, (*v.t.*) cook thus; **~-shot,** shot at game-bird etc. merely to provide a meal, shot aimed at animal etc. within easy reach, random shot; **~-still,** kind of STILL[2] in which heat is applied directly and not by steam-jacket; **~'stone,** granular variety of soapstone; **~-valiant,** valiant because drunk; so **~ valour;** ‖**~'wall(op)er,** householder voter (before 1832) [f. *wall (op)* boil]. **7.** Hence ~'FUL 2 *n.* [OE *pott*, corresp. to OFris., MDu., MLG *pot*, f. pop. L **pottus*]

pŏt[2] *v.* (-tt-). **1.** *v.t.* (esp. in *p.p.*) Place (butter, fish, minced meat, etc., usu. salted or seasoned) in pot or other vessel to preserve it. **2.** Place (plant) in soil in pot; (Bill.) pocket; abridge, epitomize; bag (game), kill (animal) by pot-shot; seize, secure; (colloq.) make (esp. child) sit on chamber-pot. **3.** *v.i.* Shoot (*at*, or abs.). [f. prec.]

pŏt[3] *n.* (sl.) Marijuana; **~-head,** one who smokes this. [prob. f. Mex. Sp. *potiguaya*]

pō't|able *a.* Drinkable; hence ~ABI'LITY *n.* [F, or f. LL *potabilis* f. L *potare* drink; see -ABLE]

pŏta'ge (-ah'zh) *n.* Thick soup. [F, as POTTAGE]

potă'mĭc *a.* Of rivers; so **pŏtamŏ'logy** *n.* [f. Gk *potamos* river + -IC]

pŏ'tăsh *n.* Alkaline substance (crude potassium carbonate) orig. got by leaching vegetable ashes and evaporating the solution in iron pots; **caustic ~,** potassium hydroxide. [17th c. *pot-ashes* f. Du. *pot-asschen* (as POT[1], ASH[2])]

potă'ss|ĭum *n.* Soft silver-white metallic element, one of the alkali metals; *potassium* PERMANGANATE; hence ~IC *a.* [f. prec. + -IUM]

potā'tion *n.* Drinking; (usu. in *pl.*) tippling; a drink; hence **pō'tatory** *a.* [ME f. OF, or f. L *potatio* (*potare* drink; see -ATION)]

potā'tō *n.* (*pl.* ~es). **1.** Plant (*Solanum tuberosum*) with farinaceous tubers used for food; its tuber; (colloq.) hole in stocking. **2. Hot ~,** (sl.) thing awkward to deal with; **small ~es,** insignificant person or thing; **Spanish** or **sweet ~**, (root of) tropical climbing plant (*Ipomoea batatas*) with sweet tuberous roots used for food. **3.** *Potato* CHIP[1]; ||*potato* CRISP; **~-ring,** (Hist.) Irish (usu. silver) ring used as stand for bowl etc. [f. Sp. *patata* var. of Taino *batata*]

pŏtee'n, pŏthee'n, *n.* (Ir.) Whisky from illicit still. [f. Ir. *poitín* dim. of *pota* POT[1]]

pō't|ent[1] *a.* (Of reason etc.) cogent; (of drug etc.) strong; (of a man) able to procreate, not impotent; (literary) powerful, mighty; hence or cogn. ~ENCE, ~ENCY, *ns.*, ~**ent**LY[2] *adv.* [f. L *potens -entis* part. of *posse* be able; see -ENT]

pō'tent[2] *a.* & *n.* (Her.) With crutch-head shape; (fur) formed by series of such shapes. [a. f. n., ME, f. OF *potence* crutch f. L *potentia* power (as prec.)]

pō'tentāte *n.* Monarch, ruler. [ME, f. OF *potentat* or f. L *potentatus* dominion (as prec.; see -ATE[1])]

potĕ'ntial (-sh*a*l) *a.* & *n.* **1.** *a.* Capable of coming into being or action, latent; *potential* ENERGY; **~ mood,** (Gram.) subjunctive expressing possibility; hence or cogn. ~ITY (-shiă'l-) *n.*, ~IZE (3) *v.t.*, ~LY[2] *adv.* **2.** *n.* (Phys.) Quantity determining energy of mass in gravitational field, of charge in electric field, etc.; **~ barrier,** region of high potential impeding movement of particles etc.; **~ difference,** (esp.) difference of electric potential between points. **3.** (Gram.) potential mood; possibility (*reached its highest potential*); resources that can be used. [ME, f. OF *potencial* or f. LL *potentialis* (*potentia*; as POTENT[1], see -AL)]

potĕ'ntĭāte (-shĭ-) *v.t.* Endow (esp. drug) with (more) power; make possible. [f. POTENCY, POTENCE + -ATE[3], after *substantiate*]

pōtentĭ'lla *n.* Herb or shrub of genus *Potentilla*, cinquefoil. [med. L, dim. of L *potens* POTENT[1]]

potĕntĭŏ'|mėter (-shĭ-) *n.* Instrument for measuring or adjusting electrical potential; hence **potĕntĭomĕ'tric** (-shĭ-) *a.*, ~METRY *n.* [f. POTENTIAL + -O- + -METER]

pŏthee'n. See POTEEN.

pŏ'ther (-dh-) *n.* & *v.* (literary). **1.** *n.* Choking smoke or cloud of dust; noise, din; verbal commotion (*made a pother about it*); display of sorrow. **2.** *v.t.* Fluster, worry. **3.** *v.i.* Make a fuss. [16th c.; orig. unkn.]

pŏ't-hōl|e *n.*, & *v.i.* **1.** *n.* (Geol.) deep cylindrical hole formed esp. by wearing away of rock; deep hole in ground or river-bed; depression in road surface caused by traffic etc. **2.** *v.i.* Explore pot-holes; hence ~ER[1] *n.* [f. POT[1] + HOLE[1]]

pō'tion *n.* Dose or draught of liquid medicine or of drug or poison. [ME f. OF, f. L *potio -onis* (*potus* having drunk; see -ION)]

pŏ'tlătch *n.* Tribal feast of N. Amer. Indians given by aspirant to high social standing. [Chinook, f. Nootka *patlatsh* gift]

pŏtoroō' *n.* (Austral.) Long-nosed rat-kangaroo. [Aboriginal]

pot-pourri (pōpoorē' *or* pōpoor'ĭ) *n.* Mixture of dried petals and spices kept in jar for its perfume; musical or literary medley. [F, = rotten pot]

pŏ'tsherd *n.* (esp. Archaeol.) Broken piece of earthenware. [ME, f. POT[1] + SHERD]

Pŏtt[1] *n.* **~'s fracture,** (Med.) fracture of lower end of fibula usu. with dislocation of ankle. [f. P. ~, Engl. surgeon d. 1788]

pŏtt[2]. Var. of POT[1] 3.

pŏ'ttage *n.* (arch.) Soup, stew; MESS[1] *of pottage.* [ME f. OF *potage* (as POT[1]; see -AGE)]

pŏ'tter[1] *n.* Maker of earthenware vessels; **~'s field,** burial place for paupers, strangers, etc., [after Matt. 27:7]; **~'s wheel,** horizontal revolving disc to carry clay during moulding. [OE *pottere* (as POT[1], -ER[1])]

pŏ'tter[2] *v.* **1.** *v.i.* Work in feeble or desultory manner (*at* or *in* subject or occupation); dawdle, loiter, (*about* etc.). **2.** *v.t.* Trifle *away* (one's time etc.). **3.** Hence ~ER[1] *n.* [frequent. of dial. *pote* push f. OE *potian*; see -ER[5]]

pŏ'tter|y̆ *n.* Vessels etc. made of baked clay; potter's work or workshop; ||**the P~ies,** district in N. Staffordshire, seat of English pottery industry. [ME f. OF *poterie* (*potier* POTTER[1]; see -Y[1])]

pŏ'tting *n.* In vbl senses; **~-shed** (in which delicate plants are grown in pots for later planting out). [f. POT[2] + -ING[1]]

pŏ'ttle *n.* **1.** ||(arch.) Measure for liquids, half gallon; pot etc. containing this. **2.** Small wicker or chip basket for strawberries etc. [ME f. OF *potel* (as POT[1]; see -LE 2)]

pŏ'ttō *n.* (*pl.* ~s). W. Afr. lemur (*Perodicticus potto*); kinkajou. [perh. f. Guinea dial.]

||**pŏ'tty̆**[1] *a.* (sl.) **1.** ~ (**little**), insignificant, trivial. **2.** Foolish or crazy (*about* someone or something). [19th c.; orig. unkn.]

pŏ'tty̆[2] *n.* (colloq.) Chamber-pot, esp. for child. [f. POT[1] + -Y[3]]

pouch[1] *n.* Small bag or detachable outside pocket; baggy area of skin (under eyes etc.); soldier's leather ammunition-bag; lockable bag for mail or dispatches; baglike receptacle in which marsupials carry young during lactation; baglike cavity, esp. seed-vessel, in plant; hence ~ED[2] (-cht), ~'Y[2], *adjs.* [ME, f. ONF *pouche* = OF *poche*; cf. POKE[1]]

pouch[2] *v.t.* Put into pouch; take possession of, pocket; make (part of dress) hang like pouch. [f. prec.]

pouf. Var. of POOF, POUFFE.

pouffe (pōōf) *n.* Large cushion used as low seat; soft stuffed couch; = PUFF[1] 2. [F; ult. imit.]

poular'd (pōō-) *n.* Domestic hen spayed and fattened for eating. [f. F *poularde* (*poule* hen)]

poult[1] (pōlt) *n.* Young of domestic fowl, turkey, pheasant, etc. [ME, contr. f. PULLET]

poult[2] (pōō) *n.* = foll. [abbr.]

poult-de-soie (pōōdeswah') *n.* Fine corded (usu. coloured) silk. [F, of unkn. orig.]

pou'lter (pō'l-) *n.* = foll. (now only as guild-name); **~'s measure,** (Pros.) metre with alternate lines of 12 and 14 syllables [perh. f. occasional selling of 14 instead of 12 eggs as a dozen]. [ME, f. OF *pouletier* (as PULLET; see -ER[2])]

pou'lterer (pō'l-) *n.* Dealer in poultry and usu. game. [f. prec. + -ER[1]]

pou'ltĭce (pō'l-) *n.*, & *v.t.* **1.** *n.* Soft mass of bread, bran, kaolin, etc., usu. made with boiling water and spread on muslin etc. and applied to sore or inflamed part. **2.** *v.t.* Apply poultice to. [orig. *pultes* pl. f. L *puls pultis* pottage, pap, etc.]

pou'ltry̆ (pō'l-) *n.* Domestic fowls (FOWL 1), ducks, geese, turkeys, etc., esp. as source of food. [ME, f. OF *pouletrie* (as POULTERER; see -RY)]

pounce[1] *n.*, & *v.i.* **1.** *n.* Claw or talon of bird of prey; pouncing, sudden swoop, (*make a pounce*). **2.** *v.i.* Make sudden attack (*up*)*on*, (fig.) seize eagerly (*up*)*on* (blunder etc.). [perh. f. PUNCHEON[1]]

pounce[2] *n.*, & *v.t.* **1.** *n.* Fine powder formerly used to prevent ink from spreading on unsized paper etc.; powdered charcoal etc. dusted over perforated pattern to transfer design to object beneath. **2.** *v.t.* Smooth (paper, surface of hat, etc.) with pounce or pumice; transfer (design) by use of pounce; dust (pattern) with pounce. [(v. f. F *poncer*) f. F *ponce* f. pop. L **pomice* f. L *pumex* PUMICE]

pou'ncĕt-bŏx *n.* (arch.) Small box with perforated lid for perfumes. [16th c.; perh. orig. error f. *pounced* (=perforated) *box*]

pound[1] *n.*, & *v.i.* **1.** *n.* Measure of weight, 16 oz. avoirdupois (0·4536 kilogram), 12 oz. troy (0·3732 kilogram); **~-cake,** rich cake containing a pound (or equal weights) of each chief ingredient; **~ of flesh,** [see Shak. *Merchant of Venice* IV. i] (fig.) any legal but unconscionable demand. **2.** ~ **(sterling)** (*pl.* also same), monetary unit of United Kingdom, formerly represented by gold sovereign, abbr. £ (*five pounds* or *pound* = £5); monetary unit of some other countries; PENNY *wise and pound foolish*; **~ note,** banknote for £1; **~ Scots,** (Hist.) 1s. 8d. **3.** *v.i.* ‖Test weight of coins by weighing number that ought to weigh one pound. [OE *pund*, = OS, ON, Goth. *pund*, OHG *pfunt* f. Gmc **pundo* f. L *pondo* Roman pound weight of 12 ounces]

pound[2] *n.*, & *v.t.* **1.** *n.* Enclosure for detention of stray cattle, distrained cattle or goods, officially removed vehicles, etc., till redeemed; enclosure for animals; (fig.) place of confinement; **~-lock** (with two gates to confine water). **2.** *v.t.* Shut (cattle etc.) in pound. [ME, f. OE **pund* (in *pundfald*; cf. PINFOLD); cf. POND]

pound[3] *v.* **1.** *v.t.* Crush or bruise with repeated strokes; thump, pummel, with fists etc.; knock, beat, (thing *to* pieces, *into* a jelly, etc.); **~ out,** produce (as if) with heavy blows. **2.** *v.i.* Deliver heavy blows, fire heavy shot, (*at*, *on*, *away at*); walk, run, ride, make one's way, heavily (*along* etc.); (of heart) beat heavily. [OE *pūnian*, cogn. w. Du. *puin*, LG *pün* rubbish]

pou'ndage *n.* Commission or fee of so much per pound sterling; percentage of total earnings of a business, paid as wages; payment of so much per pound weight; charge on postal order etc.; TONNAGE *and poundage.* [ME, f. POUND[1] + -AGE]

pou'ndal *n.* (Phys.) Unit of force, the force that, acting for one second on one-pound mass, gives it velocity of one foot per second. [f. POUND[1] + -*al* perh. after *quintal*]

pou'nder[1] *n.* In vbl senses; instrument for pounding with or in, pestle or mortar. [f. POUND[3] + -ER[1]]

pou'nder[2] *n.* Thing that, or gun carrying shell that, weighs a pound or (-~) so many pounds (*a three-pounder*); (-~) thing worth, or person possessing, so many pounds sterling. [f. POUND[1] + -ER[1]]

pour (pōr̂) *v.* & *n.* **1.** *v.t.* Cause (liquid, granular substance, light, etc.) to flow esp. downwards, discharge copiously, (*pour hot water over it*; *pour out the tea*; **~ oil on the flames,** aggravate passion etc.; **~ oil on the waters,** or **on troubled waters,** (fig.) calm a disturbance with soothing words etc.; *pour cold* WATER[1] *on*); discharge (missiles, crowd from building, etc.; *forth*, *out*) copiously or in rapid succession; send *forth* or *out* (words, music, etc.). **2.** *v.i.* (Of liquid etc.) flow (*forth*, *out*, *down*) in stream, (of rain) descend heavily, whence ~'ING[2] *a.*, (**it never rains but it ~s,** (fig.) events esp. misfortunes always come several together or in quick succession); pour tea into cups; (fig.) come *in*, *out*, etc., abundantly (*letters poured in from all quarters*). **3.** Hence ~'ER[1] (1, 2) *n.* **4.** *n.* Pouring; heavy fall of rain, downpour; amount of molten metal etc. poured at a time. [ME, of unkn. orig.]

pourboire (poorbwār̂') *n.* Gratuity, tip. [F, = *pour boire* (money) for drinking]

pourparler (poorpār̂'lā) *n.* (usu. in *pl.*) Informal discussion preliminary to negotiation. [F, f. OF *po(u)rparler* discuss]

pour'point (poor-) *n.* (Hist.) Stuffed and quilted doublet. [ME, f. OF p.p. of *pourpoindre* perforate, quilt (*pour* PRO-[1] for *par* PER-, *poindre* prick f. L *pungere*)]

pousse-café (po͞oskăfā') *n.* Drink of liqueur(s) taken esp. with coffee after dinner. [F, = push-coffee]

poussĕ'tte (po͞o-) *v.i.*, & *n.* **1.** *v.i.* Dance round one another with hands joined, as couple in country dance. **2.** *n.* This action. [F, dim. of *pousse* push (*pousser* PUSH[1])]

pou'ssin (po͞o'săn̊) *n.* Young chicken bred for eating. [F]

pou sto (po͞o stō') *n.* Standing-place, basis of operation, fulcrum. [f. Gk *pou stō* where I may stand, f. Archimedes' claim to be able to move the earth if given somewhere to stand while doing so]

pout[1] *n.* = BIB[1]; eel-pout. [OE **puta* in *ǣlepūta* eel-pout, app. f. WG **pūt-* inflate; cf. foll.]

pout[2] *v.* & *n.* **1.** *v.t.* & *i.* Protrude (lips), protrude lips, (of lips) protrude, esp. as sign of (mock) displeasure; *sulk. **2.** *n.* Such protrusion; **the ~s,** fit of sulking. [ME, perh. f. OE **pūtian* f. WG **pūt-* be inflated; cf. prec.]

pou'ter *n.* In vbl senses; kind of pigeon with great power of inflating crop. [f. prec. + -ER[1]]

‖**pou'tĭng** *n.* = BIB[1]. [f. POUT[1] + -ING[3]]

pŏ'vertў *n.* Being poor (POOR 1), indigence, want, (Eccl.) renunciation of right to individual ownership of property; scarcity, deficiency, (*in*, *of*); inferiority, poorness, meanness; **~ line,** minimum income level needed to get necessities of life; **~-stricken,** poor (lit., or fig., *a poverty-stricken language*). [ME, f. OF *poverte*, *poverté* f. L *paupertas -tatis* (*pauper* poor; see -TY[1])]

pow *int.* expr. sound of blow or explosion. [imit.]

P.O.W. *abbr.* prisoner of war.

pow'an (pō'-) *n.* Fish of British lakes, allied to trout. [Sc. form of POLLAN]

pow'der *n.*, & *v.t.* **1.** *n.* Mass of dry particles or granules, dust; medicine in the form of powder (**take a ~,** (sl.) depart quickly); cosmetic powder applied to face, skin, or hair. **2.** = GUN-*powder* (FOOD *for powder*; **smell of ~,** experience of fighting; **not worth ~ and shot,** not worth shooting, or fighting or striving for). **3. ~ blue,** pale blue orig. of powdered smalt for laundry use; *powder* COMPACT[3]; **~-down,** down-feathers found in definite patches on some birds; **~-flask,** (Hist.) case for carrying gunpowder; **~-horn,** (Hist.) powder-flask orig. and esp. of horn; **~ keg,** thing that may explode (lit. or fig.); **~-magazine,** place where gunpowder is stored; **~ metallurgy,** use of metal powders to form shaped objects; **~-monkey,** (Hist.) boy employed on board ship to carry powder to guns; **~-puff,** soft pad for applying powder to skin; **~-room,** ladies' cloakroom; **~ snow,** loose dry snow on ski-run etc. **4.** Hence ~Y[2] *a.* **5.** *v.t.* Sprinkle powder on, cover (*with* powder etc.); apply powder to (nose, hair, or abs.); decorate (surface) with spots or small ornamental figures; (esp. in *p.p.*) reduce to (fine) powder (*powdered milk*, *sugar*). [ME, f. OF (*poudrer* v. f.) *poudre*, *pol(d)re* f. L *pulvis pulveris* dust]

pow'er *n.*, & *v.t.* **1.** *n.* Ability to do or act (*will do all in my power*; *has the power of changing its colour*); particular faculty of body or mind (*taxes his powers to the utmost*; *man of varied powers*). **2.** Vigour, energy; **more ~ to you, to your elbow!,** (expr. encouragement or approval). **3.** Active property (*has a high heating power*). **4.** Government, influence, authority, (*over*; **in** person's **~,** under his control); personal ascendancy (*over*); political or social ascendancy (*the party now in power*; BLACK[1] *Power*; **~ politics,**

political action based on threats to use force). **5.** Authorization, delegated authority, (*a bill to extend and define their powers*; *power of* ATTORNEY). **6.** Influential person, body, or thing, (*the press had not become a power in the State*; **the ~s that be,** constituted authorities [Rom. 13:1]); State having international influence (GREAT *Power*). **7.** Deity (*merciful powers!*); (in *pl.*) sixth ORDER[1] of ninefold celestial hierarchy. **8.** (colloq.) Large number or amount (*has done me a power of good*). **9.** (Math.) **Third, tenth,** etc., ~ of a number, product obtained from three, ten, etc., factors equal to that number (*the third power of 2, or* 2^3, *is 8*; *the sixth power of* 1,000 *is* 1,000,000,000,000,000,000). **10.** Instrument for applying energy to mechanical purposes (cf. LEVER); **the mechanical ~s,** simple machines (lever, inclined plane, etc.). **11.** Mechanical or electrical energy as opp. to hand-labour; (*attrib.*) operated by this (*power lathe, shovel*); ~ **cut,** temporary withdrawal or failure of electric power-supply; **~-dive** *n.*, & *v.i.*, (of aircraft) dive without shutting off engine power; **~house,** = *power-station*, (fig.) source of drive or influence; ~ **pack,** equipment for converting alternating current (from mains) to direct current; ||~ **point,** socket for connection of electrical apparatus to mains; **~-station,** building etc. where electric power is generated for distribution; ~ **stroke** (during which piston is moved by expansion of gases in internal combustion engine). **12.** Capacity for exerting mechanical force, esp. HORSE[1]*power*. **13.** Magnifying capacity of lens. **14.** *v.t.* Supply (vehicle, vessel, etc.) with mechanical or electrical energy; HIGH, LOW[1], *-powered*. [ME & AF *poer* etc., OF *poeir* f. Rom. **potēre* be able]

pow'erful *a.* Having great (physical or other) power or influence (*powerful grasp, horse, mind, ally, book, speech, odour*); hence ~LY[2] *adv.* [ME, f. prec. + -FUL]

pow'erlėss *a.* Without power (to act etc.); wholly unable (*to* help etc.); hence ~LY[2] *adv.*, ~NESS *n.* [f. POWER + -LESS]

pow'wow *n.* & *v.* **1.** *n.* N. Amer. Ind. medicine-man or sorcerer; magic ceremonial, conference, of N. Amer. Indians; political or other meeting esp. for discussion. **2.** *v.i.* Act as powwow; hold powwow; confer, discuss, (*about* etc.). **3.** *v.t.* Doctor, treat with magic. [f. Algonquian *powah, powwaw* magician (lit. 'he dreams')]

pŏx *n.* **1.** Virus disease with pocks (usu. in *comb.*, as CHICKEN-*pox*, COW[1]*pox*, SMALL*pox*); (arch.) **a ~ on him** etc. (excl. of impatience). **2.** (colloq.) Syphilis. **3.** Plant disease causing pocklike spots. [alt. sp. of POCK*s*]

pŏzzola'na (pŏtsolah'na) *n.* Volcanic ash used for mortar or hydraulic cement. [It., f. *pozz(u)olano* a. of *Pozzuoli* near Naples]

p.p. *abbr.* *per procurationem.*

pp. *abbr.* pages.

pp *abbr.* pianissimo.

||**P.P.E.** *abbr.* philosophy, politics, and economics.

p.p.m. *abbr.* parts per million.

||**P.P.S.** *abbr.* Parliamentary Private Secretary; additional postscript [f. POST- + POSTSCRIPT].

P.Q. *abbr.* Province of Quebec; Quebec Party [f. F *Parti Québécois*].

P.R. *abbr.* proportional representation; public relations; *Puerto Rico.

pr. *abbr.* pair.

Pr *symb.* praseodymium.

P.R.A. *abbr.* President of the Royal Academy.

praam. See PRAM[1].

pră'ctĭc|able *a.* That can be done, feasible; (of road, passage, ford) that can be used or traversed; (Theatr., of window etc.) real, that can be used as such; hence ~ABI'LITY, **~able**NESS (-beln-), *ns.*, **~ab**LY[2] *adv.* [f. F *praticable* (*pratiquer* put into practice f. as foll.); see -ABLE]

pră'ctĭcal *a.* & *n.* **1.** *a.* Of, concerned with, shown in, practice (opp. *theoretical*; *practical agriculture, examination, philosophy*; *practical* JOKE[1]); available or useful in practice; engaged in practice, practising; inclined or suited to action rather than speculation (*does not appeal to practical minds*; *a practical man good at improvising*); that is such in effect though not nominally, virtual, (*a practical atheist*; *has practical control*); feasible (*practical* POLITICS); ***~ nurse** (trained in routine nursing but not registered); hence ~ITY (-ă'l-), ~NESS, *ns.* **2.** *n.* Practical examination or study. [f. earlier *practic* f. obs. F *practique* or f. LL f. Gk *praktikos* (*prattō* do, act; see -IC) + -AL]

pră'ctĭcallȳ *adv.* In a practical manner; virtually, almost, (*practically nothing*). [f. prec. + -LY[2]]

pră'ctĭce[1] *n.* **1.** Habitual action or carrying on (*the practice of advertising*; *makes a practice of saving*); action as opp. to theory; method of legal procedure; habit, custom, (*has been the regular practice*). **2.** Repeated exercise in an art, handicraft, etc., (*practice makes perfect*); spell of this (*ball, target, practice*). **3.** Professional work, business, or connection, of lawyer, doctor, etc., (*has a large practice*; *sold his practice*). **4.** (arch., esp. in *pl.*) Scheming, (usu. underhand) contrivance, artifice; SHARP[1] *practice*. **5.** (Arith.) Mode of finding value of given number of articles, or of quantity of commodity at given price, when quantity or price or both are in several denominations. **6. Good ~**, (1) satisfactory procedure, (2) means of improving one's skill; **in ~**, (1) in the realm of action (*quite useless, would never work, in practice*; **put** (plan, method) **in(to) ~**, carry it out), (2) skilled through having recently had practice (sense 2); **out of ~**, no longer possessing former skill. [ME, f. PRACTISE, after *advice, device*]

***pră'ctĭce**[2]. See PRACTISE.

prăctĭ'cian (-shan) *n.* Worker, practitioner. [f. obs. F *practicien* (*practique* f. med. L *practica* f. Gk *praktikē* fem. (as n.) of *praktikos*; see PRACTICAL)]

pră'ctĭs|e, *pră'ctĭc|e[2], *v.* **1.** *v.t.* Perform habitually, carry out in action, (*practise the same method*; *practise what you preach*); exercise, pursue, (profession or activity; **~ing** *Catholic* etc., active in religion; **~ing** *doctor, barrister*, etc., engaged in actual practice, not retired nor merely qualified); exercise oneself in or on (art, instrument, or abs.; *practise the flute, the piano, music, running*); (esp. in *p.p.*) exercise (person, one*self*, *in* action or subject). **2.** *v.i.* (arch.) Scheme, contrive, (*when first we practise to deceive*); **~e (up)on,** impose upon, take advantage of, (person, his credulity, etc.). [ME, f. OF *pra(c)tiser* or f. med. L *practizare* alt. f. *practicare* (*practica*; see prec.)]

prăctĭ'tioner *n.* Professional or practical worker, esp. in medicine (GENERAL *practitioner*). [f. obs. *practitian* = PRACTICIAN + -ER[1]]

prae- *pref.* = PRE- (esp. in wds regarded as L or relating to Rom. Ant.). [L; see PRE-]

praecipe (prē'sĭpĭ) *n.* (Law). Writ demanding action or explanation of non-action; order requesting writ. [L (first wd of writ), imper. of *praecipere* enjoin (see PRECEPT)]

praecō'cial, *prēcō'cial, (-shal) *a.* (Of bird) whose young can feed themselves as soon as hatched. [f. as PRECOCIOUS; see -AL]

praelĕ'ctor. Var. of PRELECTOR.

praemūnīr'ė *n.* (Law). Writ charging sheriff to

summon person accused of asserting or maintaining papal jurisdiction in England. [med. L, = forewarn, for L PRAE(*monēre* warn), the wds *praemunire facias* that you warn (so-and-so to appear) occurring in the writ]
praenō′mĕn *n.* (Rom. Ant.) First or personal name (e.g. *Marcus* Tullius Cicero). [L (*prae* before, *nomen* name)]
‖**praepŏ′stor,** ‖**prėpŏ′stor,** (prĭp-) *n.* (At some public schools) prefect, monitor. [f. *praepositor* alt. of L *praepositus* p.p. (as n.) of PRAE(*ponere posit-* place) set over; see -OR]
praesidium. Var. of PRESIDIUM.
prae′tor, ***prē′tor,** *n.* (Rom. Hist.) Annually elected magistrate performing some duties of consul (orig. consul as leader of army); hence **praetōr′**IAL *a.*, ~SHIP *n.* [ME, f. F *préteur* or f. L *praetor*, perh. f. as PRAE- + *ire it-* go; see -OR]
praetōr′ian, ***prė-,** (prĭt-) *a.* & *n.* **1.** *a.* Of a praetor; of bodyguard of Roman general or emperor. **2.** *n.* Man of praetorian rank; soldier of praetorian guard. [ME, f. L *praetorianus* (as prec.; see -IAN)]
prăgmă′t|ic *a.* **1.** Meddlesome; dogmatic. **2.** Of pragmatism. **3.** Treating facts of history with reference to their practical lessons; dealing with matters according to their practical significance or immediate importance. **4.** Of the affairs of a State (**~ic sanction,** imperial or royal ordinance issued as fundamental law, esp. that of Emperor Charles VI in 1724 settling Austrian succession). **5.** Hence **~ĭcă′l**ITY *n.*, ~ICALLY *adv.* [f. LL f. Gk *pragmatikos* (*pragma -matos* deed; see -IC)]
prăgmă′tĭcal *a.* = prec. 1, 2. [f. as prec. + -AL]
pră′gmat|ism *n.* Officiousness; pedantry; matter-of-fact treatment of things; (Philos.) doctrine that evaluates any assertion solely by its practical consequences and its bearing on human interests; so ~IST (2) *n.*, **~ĭ′st**IC *a.* [f. Gk *pragma* (see PRAGMATIC) + -ISM]
pră′gmatīze, -īse (-īz), *v.t.* Represent as real; rationalize (myth). [f. as prec. + -IZE]
prahu. See PROA.
prair′ĭe *n.* Large treeless tract of level or undulating grassland esp. in N. America; **~-chicken, ~-hen,** N. Amer. grouse of genus *Tympanuchus*; **~-dog,** N. Amer. rodent of genus *Cynomys*, with bark like dog's; **~ oyster,** raw egg seasoned and swallowed whole; ***~ schooner,** covered wagon used by pioneers in crossing the prairies; ***P~ State,** Illinois; **~ wolf,** coyote. [F, f. OF *praerie* f. Rom. **prataria* f. L *pratum* meadow; see -ARY¹]
praise (-z) *v.t.*, & *n.* **1.** *v.t.* Express warm approbation of, commend the merits of, (person, thing); glorify, extol the attributes of, (God etc.). **2.** *n.* Praising, commendation, (*won high praise*; *was loud in his praises*); **~ be!** (excl. of pious gratitude); **sing** person's **~s,** (fig.) commend him highly; hence ~′FUL (-zf-) *a.* [ME, f. OF *preisier* price, prize, praise, f. LL *pretiare* f. L *pretium* price; cf. PRIZE¹]
prai′seworth|ȳ (prā′zwĕrdhĭ) *a.* Worthy of praise, commendable; hence **~ĭ**LY² *adv.*, ~ĬNESS *n.* [f. prec. + -WORTHY]
Pra′krĭt (prah′-) *n.* Any of the dialects of N. and Central India anciently existing alongside Sanskrit, or derived from these. [f. Skr. *prākṛta* unrefined; cf. SANSKRIT]
pra′line (prah′lēn) *n.* Sweet made by browning nuts in boiling sugar. [F, f. Marshal de Plessis-*Praslin*, Fr. soldier d. 1675, whose cook invented it]
pra′lltrĭller (-ah′-) *n.* (Mus.) Grace consisting in one rapid alternation of written note with note immediately above it. [G (*prallen* rebound, *triller* TRILL)]
prăm¹, praam, (prahm) *n.* Flat-bottomed boat used in Baltic etc. for shipping cargo etc.; flat-bottomed boat equipped with guns; Scandinavian ship's boat corresp. to dinghy. [f. MDu. *prame, praem*, MLG *prām(e)* f. OSlav. *pramŭ*]
‖**prăm²** *n.* Carriage for one or two young children, with three or usu. four wheels, pushed by person on foot; milkman's delivery cart. [abbr. of PERAMBULATOR]
prance (-ah-) *v.i.*, & *n.* **1.** *v.i.* (Of horse) raise forelegs and spring from hind legs; (fig.) walk or behave in elated or arrogant manner. **2.** *n.* Prancing (movement). [ME, of unkn. orig.]
pră′ndĭal *a.* (joc.) Of dinner. [f. L *prandium* a meal + -AL]
‖**prăng** *v.* & *n.* (sl.) **1.** *v.t.* Bomb (target) successfully; crash (aircraft or vehicle); damage by impact. **2.** *v.i.* Crash aircraft or vehicle. **3.** *n.* Act or instance of pranging. [imit.]
prănk¹ *n.* Mad frolic, practical joke; hence ~′FUL, ~′ISH¹, ~′SOME¹, *adjs.*, ~′STER *n.* [16th c., of unkn. orig.]
prănk² *v.* **1.** *v.t.* Dress, deck, (person, one*self*, thing, often *out* or *up*); adorn, spangle, (field *with* flowers etc.). **2.** *v.i.* Show oneself off. [rel. to MLG *prank* pomp, Du. *pronk* finery]
prāse (-z) *n.* Kind of leek-green translucent quartz. [F, f. L f. Gk *prasios* a. leek-green (*prason* leek)]
prāsėodȳ′mĭum (-z-) *n.* (Chem.) Metallic element of lanthanide series. [f. G *praseodym* f. Gk *prasios* (see prec.) from its green salts, + G *didym* DIDYMIUM]
prāt|e *v.* & *n.* **1.** *v.i.* Chatter; talk too much; talk foolishly or irrelevantly. **2.** *v.t.* Tell or say (thing) in prating manner. **3.** Hence ~′ER¹ *n.*, ~′ING² *a.* **4.** *n.* Prating; idle talk. [ME, f. MDu., MLG *praten*, prob. imit.]
pră′tfall (-awl) *n.* (colloq.) Fall on buttocks; humiliating failure. [f. *prat* buttocks + FALL²]
prā′tĭe *n.* (dial., esp. Ir.) Potato. [corrupt.]
pră′tĭncōle *n.* Bird of genus *Glareola*, like swallow in appearance and habits, allied to plover. [f. mod. L *pratincola* f. L *pratum* meadow + *incola* inhabitant]
pră′tique (-ēk; *or* -ē′k) *n.* Licence to have dealings with a port, granted to ship after quarantine or on showing clean bill of health. [F, = practice, intercourse, f. It. *pratica* f. med. L *practica* (see PRACTICIAN)]
pră′ttl|e *v.* & *n.* **1.** *v.i.* Talk in childish or artless fashion. **2.** *v.t.* Say (thing) thus. **3.** Hence ~ER¹ *n.*, ~ING² *a.* **4.** *n.* Childish chatter; inconsequential talk. [f. MLG *pratelen* (as PRATE; see -LE 3)]
prau. See PROA.
prawn *n.*, & *v.i.* **1.** *n.* Marine crustacean like large shrimp. **2.** *v.i.* Fish for prawns. [ME *pra(y)ne*, of unkn. orig.]
pră′xĭs *n.* Accepted practice, custom; practising of an art etc. [med. L f. Gk, = doing (*prassō* do)]
pray *v.* **1.** *v.t.* Make devout supplication to (God, object of worship); beseech earnestly (God, person, *for* thing, *to* do, *that*); ask earnestly for (permission etc.). **2.** *v.i.* Engage in prayer, make entreaty, (*to* God, *to* person, *for* thing, *for* or *on behalf of* person, *to* do, *that*); *praying* MANTIS; **past ~ing for,** hopeless. **3.** = *I pray* (*pray God she is safe*); ~ (I beg or urge you to) *consider* etc.; *what is the use of that,* ~ (tell me)? **4. ~ in aid** (arch. ~ *in aid of*: *in* orig. adv., not prep.), summon to one's support. [ME, f. OF *preier* f. LL *precare* f. L *precari* entreat]
prayer¹ (prār) *n.* **1.** Solemn request or thanksgiving to God or object of worship; formula used in praying, e.g. *the* LORD'S *Prayer*; form of divine service consisting largely of prayers (*morning, evening, prayer*; *family prayers*); action or practice of praying; entreaty to a person; thing

prayed for; *(colloq.) slightest chance of success etc. **2. ~-book,** book of forms of prayer, esp. Book of COMMON[1] Prayer; **~-mat,** small carpet used by Muslims when praying; **~-meeting,** religious meeting at which several persons offer prayer; **~-wheel,** revolving cylindrical box inscribed with or containing prayers, used esp. by Buddhists of Tibet. **3.** Hence ~'FUL, ~'LESS, *adjs.* [ME f. OF *preiere* f. Gallo-Rom. **precaria* fem. (as n.) of L *precarius* obtained by entreaty (*prex precis* prayer; see -ARY[1])]

pray'er[2] *n.* One who prays. [ME, f. PRAY + -ER[1]]

P.R.B. *abbr.* Pre-Raphaelite Brotherhood.

prē- *pref.* Before (in time, place, order, degree, or importance). **1.** Forming *vbs.* & *vbl ns.* w. sense 'do, doing, thing done, beforehand', as: **~-arra'nge(ment)**; **~-au'dience,** right (of lawyer at Bar) to be heard before another; **~-ca'st,** (esp. in *p.p.*) cast (concrete) in blocks before use; **~-concer't; ~-condi'tion,** prior condition, one that must be fulfilled beforehand; **~-coo'k; ~-da'te,** antedate; **~dige'st,** render (food) easily digestible before ingestion, (fig.) make (reading matter) easily assimilable; **~doo'm** *v.t.*; **~-ele'ct, ~-ele'ction** (see also sense 2); **~-enga'ge(ment)**; **~-esta'blish**; **~-exi'st(ence)**; **~-hea't** *v.t.*; **~mo'tion,** motion given beforehand, esp. divine act as determining the will of the creature; **~-ordai'n,** appoint beforehand; **~-pa'ck(age)** *v.t.*, pack (goods) ready for sale before distributing them; **~-recor'd; ~-sele'ct; ~-se't; ~-shri'nk; ~-stre'ss,** (esp. in *p.p.*) strengthen (concrete) by means of stretched wires etc. in it. **2.** Forming *adjs.* & *ns.* w. sense '(person etc.) existing, dating from, before the time of', as: **~-ada'mic** *a.*, **~a'damite** *n.* & *a.*, (one of supposed race) existing before the time of Adam; **~-Ca'mbrian,** (Geol.) (of) period or system prior to Cambrian; **~-Chri'stian,** before Christ(ianity); **~-cla'ssic(al),** before the classical period (usu. of Greek and Roman literature); **~-Colu'mbian,** before discovery of America by Columbus; **~-co'nscious,** (*a.*) antecedent to consciousness, (*n.*) = FORECONSCIOUS; **~-dyna'stic,** of period before dynasties (esp. of Egypt); **~-ele'ction,** (of act, promise) done or given before election (see also sense 1); **~-exi'lic,** before the Jews' exile in Babylon; **~gla'cial,** before a glacial period; **~-hu'man,** existing before man existed; **~-lapsar'ian,** before the Fall of man; **~-ma'rital,** of the time before marriage; **~-me'nstrual,** immediately before menstruation; **~-mille'nnial(ism),** (belief that Christ's Second Advent will occur) before the millennium; so **~-mille'nnialist** *n.*; **~-na'tal,** existing or occurring before (child)-birth; **~-pra'ndial,** before-dinner; **~-school,** of time before child is old enough to attend school; **~-scienti'fic,** before the rise of modern science; **~-Socra'tic,** (philosopher) of the time before Socrates; **~-ta'x,** (of income) before deduction of taxes; **~-war'** *a.* & *adv.*, (occurring or existing) before a war. **3.** Forming *adjs.* (esp. Anat. & Zool.) w. sense 'situated in front of', as: **~-cor'dial,** in front of or about the heart; **~-co'stal,** in front of the ribs; **~-dor'sal,** anterior to the dorsal region; **~-fro'ntal,** in front of frontal bone of skull, in forepart of frontal lobe of brain; **~-maxi'llary** (*or* -mă'-), in front of the upper jaw; **~-o'cular,** in front of the eye. [f. or after L *prae-* (*prae* adv. & prep.)]

preach *v.* & *n.* **1.** *v.i.* Deliver sermon or religious address; give moral advice in obtrusive way. **2.** *v.t.* Deliver (sermon); proclaim, expound, (the Gospel, Christ, *that*, etc.) in public discourse; advocate, inculcate, (quality, conduct, principle, etc.) thus. **3.** Hence or cogn. ~'ABLE *a.*, ~'MENT (usu. derog.) *n.* **4.** *n.* (colloq.) Preaching, sermon, lecture. [ME, f. OF *prechier* f. L PRAE(*dicare* declare) proclaim, in eccl. L 'preach']

prea'cher *n.* One who preaches; minister of religion; Dominican friar; **the P~,** Solomon as supposed speaker in Ecclesiastes. [ME f. AF *prech(o)ur*, OF *prech(e)or* f. eccl. L *praedicator* (*praedicare*, as prec.; see -ER[2])]

prea'chĭfȳ *v.i.* (colloq.) Preach, moralize, or hold forth, tediously. [f. PREACH + -I- + -FY; cf. *speechify*]

prea'ch|ȳ *a.* (colloq.) Fond of preaching or moralizing or holding forth; hence ~ĬNESS *n.* [f. PREACH + -Y[2]]

prēă'mble *n.*, & *v.i.* **1.** *n.* Preliminary statement in speech or writing; introductory part of statute, deed, etc. **2.** *v.i.* Make preamble. [ME, f. OF *preambule* f. med. L *praeambulum* f. LL *praeambulus* (a.) going before (as PRE-, AMBLE)]

Preb. *abbr.* Prebendary.

prĕ'bend *n.* Part of estate revenue of cathedral or collegiate church granted to canon or member of chapter as stipend; portion of land or tithe from which this stipend is drawn; = foll.; so ~AL *a.* [ME, f. OF *prebende* f. LL *praebenda* pension, neut. pl. gerundive of L *praebēre* grant (*prae* forth, *habēre* hold)]

prĕ'bendarȳ *n.* Holder of prebend; honorary canon; hence ~SHIP *n.* [ME, f. med. L *praebendarius* (as prec.; see -ARY[1])]

prĭcār'ious *a.* Dependent on chance, uncertain, (*makes a precarious living*); insecure, perilous, (*precarious health*; *the precarious life of a fisherman*); (arch.) held during the pleasure of another (*precarious tenure*); (arch.) doubtful (assumption etc.); hence ~LY[2] *adv.*, ~NESS *n.* [f. L *precarius* (see PRAYER[1])]

prĕ'cative *a.* = foll. 1. [f. LL *precativus* f. as foll.; see -IVE]

prĕ'catorȳ *a.* **1.** (esp. Gram., of word or form) expressing request. **2. ~ words** (in a will, requesting that a thing be done); **~ trust,** precatory words that are held to be binding. [f. LL *precatorius* f. L *precari* pray; see -ORY]

prĭcau'tion *n.* Prudent foresight; action taken beforehand to avoid evil or ensure good result; hence ~ARY[1] *a.* [f. F *précaution* f. LL *praecautio -onis* f. L PRAE(*cavēre caut-* beware of); see -ION]

prĭcē'de *v.t.* (Of person or thing) go before in rank or importance (*such duties precede all others*; *sons of barons precede baronets*); come before (thing etc., or abs.) in order (*the words that precede, that precede this paragraph*); walk etc. in front of (*preceded by our guide*); come before in time (*in the years preceding his accession*); cause (thing) to be preceded *by* (*must precede this measure by milder ones*). [f. OF *preceder* f. L PRAE(*cedere cess-* go)]

prĕ'cėdence, prĕ'cėdencȳ, (*or* prĭsē'-) *ns.* Priority in time or succession; superiority, higher position; right of preceding others in ceremonies and social formalities; **takes ~ of** (has or claims right to precede, is recognized as superior to) *all others*. [ME, f. PRECEDENT[2]; see -ENCE, -ENCY]

prĕ'cėdent[1] *n.* Previous case taken as example for subsequent cases or as justification (*there is no precedent for this*; *it is without precedent*; *do not take this as a precedent*; *that would create a precedent*); (Law) decision, procedure, etc., serving as rule or pattern. [ME, f. OF n., as foll.]

prĭcē'dent[2] (*or* prĕ'sĭ-) *a.* Preceding in time,

order, rank, etc.; hence ~LY^{2} *adv.* [ME, f. OF a. & n. f. as PRECEDE; see -ENT]

prĕ′cėdĕntėd *a.* Having, or supported by, precedent. [f. PRECEDENT^{1} + -ED^{2}]

prėcĕ′nt *v.* **1.** *v.i.* Act as precentor. **2.** *v.t.* Lead singing of (psalm etc.). [back form. f. foll.]

prėcĕ′ntor *n.* One who leads singing of congregation; (in Engl. cathedrals) member of clergy in general control of musical arrangements, in old foundations ranking next to dean and having succentor as his deputy, and in new foundations being a minor canon; (in synagogue) one who leads congregation in prayer; hence or cogn. ~SHIP, **prėcĕ′n**TRIX, *ns.* [f. F *précenteur* or f. L *praecentor* f. PRAE(*cinere cent-* = *canere* sing); see -OR]

prē′cĕpt *n.* **1.** Command, maxim; so **prėcĕ′pt**IVE *a.* **2.** Moral instruction (*example is better than precept*); divine command. **3.** Writ, warrant; written order from sheriff to arrange and hold election; ||order for collection or payment of money under a RATE^{1} 2. [ME, f. L *praeceptum* neut. p.p. (as n.) of PRAE(*cipere cept-* = *capere* take) warn, instruct]

prėcĕ′pt|or *n.* Teacher, instructor; hence or cogn. **prēcĕptōr′**IAL *a.*, ~**or**SHIP, ~**r**ESS^{1}, *ns.* [f. L *praeceptor* (as prec.; see -OR)]

prėcĕ′ptorў *n.* (Hist.) Subordinate community of Knights Templars; estate or buildings of this. [f. med. L *praeceptoria* fem. (as n.) of *praeceptorius* a. (as prec.; see -ORY)]

prėcĕ′ssion (-sh*o*n) *n.* (Phys.) slow movement of axis of spinning body, gyroscope, etc., around another axis; ~ **of the equinoxes,** (Astron.) (earlier occurrence of the equinoxes in each successive sidereal year, due to) slow retrograde motion of equinoctial points along ecliptic; hence ~AL *a.* [f. LL *praecessio* (as PRECEDE; see -ION)]

prē′cĭnct *n.* **1.** Space enclosed by walls or other boundaries of a place or building, esp. around place of worship; (in *pl.*) environs. **2.** Boundary. **3.** *Subdivision of county or city or ward for election and police purposes. **4.** District in town where traffic is prohibited, esp. *pedestrian precinct*. [ME, f. med. L *praecinctum* neut. p.p. (as n.) of PRAE(*cingere* gird) encircle]

prĕ′cious (-sh*u*s) *a.* & *adv.* **1.** *a.* Of great price, costly; ~ **metals,** gold, silver, or platinum metals; ~ **stone,** piece of mineral having great value, esp. as used in jewellery. **2.** Of great non-material worth (*precious words, privilege, knowledge, blood of Christ*); beloved (person, or abs.). **3.** Affectedly refined in language, workmanship, etc.; so **prĕcĭ**o′SITY (-shĭŏ′s-) *n.* **4.** (colloq.) Very bad, considerable, (*made a precious mess of it*; *a precious sight more than you think*); worth little (*you can keep your precious raffle-tickets*). **5.** Hence ~LY^{2} *adv.*, ~NESS *n.* **6.** *adv.* (colloq.) Extremely, very, (*took precious good care of that*; *precious little of it*). [ME, f. OF *precios* f. L *pretiosus* (*pretium* price; see -OUS)]

prĕ′cĭpice *n.* Vertical or steep face of rock, cliff, mountain, etc. [f. F *précipice* or f. L *praecipitium* falling headlong, precipice (as PRECIPITOUS; see -ICE)]

prėcĭ′pĭt|ant^{1} *a.* = PRECIPITATE^{2}; hence ~ANCE, ~ANCY, *ns.* [f. obs. F *précipitant* part. of *précipiter* (as PRECIPITATE^{3}; see -ANT)]

prėcĭ′pĭtant^{2}. See PRECIPITATE^{3}.

prėcĭ′pĭtate^{1} *n.* **1.** (Chem.) Substance precipitated from solution. **2.** (Phys.) Moisture condensed from vapour by cooling and deposited, e.g. rain, dew. [f. mod. L *praecipitatum* neut. p.p. (as n.) of L *praecipitare* (see PRECIPITATE^{3}, -ATE^{1})]

prėcĭ′pĭtate^{2} *a.* Headlong, violently hurried, (*precipitate departure*); (of person or act) hasty, rash, inconsiderate; hence ~LY^{2} (-tlĭ) *adv.*, ~NESS (-tn-) *n.* [f. L *praecipitatus* p.p. of *praecipitare* (see foll., -ATE^{2})]

prėcĭ′pĭt|āte^{3} *v.t.* **1.** Throw down headlong; (fig.) hurl or fling (person etc. *into* condition etc.). **2.** Hurry, urge on, (course of events etc.); hasten occurrence of (*served to precipitate his ruin*). **3.** (Chem.) cause (substance) to be deposited in solid form from solution; (Phys.) cause (dust etc.) to be deposited from air on surface, condense (vapour) into drops and so deposit; hence ~ABLE *a.*, ~ABI′LITY, ~ANT, ~**āt**OR, *ns.* [f. L *praecipitare* f. PRAE(*ceps -cipitis* f. *caput* head) headlong, + -ATE^{3}]

prėcĭpĭtā′tion *n.* Precipitating, being precipitated; precipitateness; (Meteorol.) (quantity of) rain, snow, etc., falling to ground. [f. F *précipitation* or f. L *praecipitatio* (as prec.; see -ATION)]

prėcĭ′pĭtous *a.* Of or like a precipice; dangerously steep; = PRECIPITATE^{2}; hence ~LY^{2} *adv.*, ~NESS *n.* [f. obs. F *précipiteux* f. L *praeceps* (see PRECIPITATE^{3}, -OUS)]

précis (prā′sē) *n.* (*pl.* same *pr.* -ēz), & *v.t.* **1.** *n.* Summary, abstract, esp. of speech or written work. **2.** *v.t.* Make précis of. [F, = foll. (as n.)]

prėcī′se *a.* Accurately expressed, definite, exact; punctilious, scrupulous in observance of rules etc.; **the** ~ (exact, identical) *moment* etc.; hence ~NESS (-sn-) *n.* [f. F *précis -ise* f. L *praecisus* p.p. of PRAE(*cidere cis-* = *caedere* cut) cut short]

prėcī′selў (-slĭ) *adv.* In precise manner; in exact terms; (in emphatic or formal assent) quite so. [f. prec. + -LY^{2}]

prėcĭ′sian (-zh*a*n) *n.* One who is rigidly precise or punctilious, esp. in religious observance; hence ~ISM (3) *n.* [f. PRECISE + -IAN]

prėcĭ′sion (-zh*o*n) *n.* & *a.* **1.** *n.* Accuracy; degree of refinement in measurement etc. **2.** Hence ~IST (2) *n.* **3.** *a.* Marked by or adapted for precision (*precision bombing, instruments, tools*). [f. F *précision* or f. L *praecisio* (as PRECISE; see -ION)]

prėclu′de (-ōō′d) *v.t.* Exclude, prevent, make impracticable, (*so as to preclude all doubt*); so **prėclu′s**IVE (-lōō′-) *a.* [f. L PRAE(*cludere clus-* = *claudere* shut)]

***precocial.** See PRAECOCIAL.

prėcō′cious (-sh*u*s) *a.* (Of plant) flowering or fruiting early; (of person) prematurely developed in some faculty or characteristic; (of action etc.) indicating such development; hence or cogn. ~LY^{2} *adv.*, ~NESS, **prėcŏ′c**ITY, *ns.* [f. L *praecox -cocis* f. PRAE(*coquere* cook) ripen fully + -OUS]

prēcŏgnĭ′tion *n.* Foreknowledge; (Sc. Law) preliminary examination of witnesses etc., esp. in order to know whether there is ground for trial. [f. LL *praecognitio* f. as PRE-, COGNITION]

prēconceive (-sē′v) *v.t.* Form (idea, opinion, etc.) beforehand; anticipate in thought; so **prē**CONCE′PTION *n.* (esp. = prejudice). [f. PRE- + CONCEIVE]

prē′coniz|e, -īs|e (-īz), *v.t.* Proclaim publicly; commend publicly; summon by name; (R.C. Ch., of pope) approve publicly the appointment of (bishop); so ~A′TION *n.* [ME, f. med. L *praeconizare* f. L *praeco -onis* herald; see -IZE]

prėcûr′sor *n.* Forerunner, harbinger, esp. John the Baptist in relation to Christ; one who precedes in office etc.; substance from which another is formed by decay, chemical transformation, etc. [f. L *praecursor* f. PRAE(*currere curs-* run); see -OR]

prėcûr′s|orў *a.* Preliminary, introductory, serving as harbinger (*of*); so ~IVE *a.* [f. L *praecursorius* (as prec.; see -ORY)]

***prėdā′ceous** (-sh*u*s) *a.* (Of animal) predatory. [f. as foll. + -ACEOUS]

prĕdā′cious (-shus) *a.* (Of animal) predatory; pertaining to such animals (*predacious instincts*); hence **prĕd**A′CITY *n.* [f. L *praeda* booty + -ACIOUS; cf. *audacious*]

prĕ′dator *n.* Predatory animal. [f. L *praedator* plunderer (*praedari* seize as plunder f. *praeda* booty; see -OR)]

prĕ′datorȳ *a.* Of or addicted to plunder or robbery; (of animal) preying naturally upon others. [f. L *praedatorius* (as prec.; see -ORY)]

prēdēcea′se *v.t.*, & *n.* **1.** *v.t.* Die earlier than (another person). **2.** *n.* Death preceding that of another. [f. PRE- + DECEASE]

prē′dĕcĕssor *n.* Former holder of office or position, with respect to a later holder, (*my, William's, predecessors*; *his immediate predecessor*); thing to which another has succeeded (*will share the fate of its predecessor*); forefather. [ME, f. OF *predecesseur* f. LL PRAE(*decessor* retiring officer f. as DECEASE); see -OR]

prĕdĕ′lla *n.* (Painting on vertical face of) altar-step; (painting or sculpture on) raised shelf at back of altar. [It., = stool]

prĕdĕstĭnār′ĭan *n.* & *a.* (Holder of the doctrine) of predestination. [f. PREDESTINATION + -ARIAN]

prĕdĕ′stĭnate[1] *a.* Predestined. [ME, f. as foll.; see -ATE[2]]

prĕdĕ′stĭnāte[2] *v.t.* (Of God) ordain (person) in advance to salvation or *to* (any fate), *to* (do); determine beforehand. [f. eccl. L PRAE(*destinare* establish) + -ATE[3]]

prĕdĕstĭnā′tion *n.* God's appointment from eternity of some of mankind to salvation and eternal life; God's foreordaining of all that comes to pass; fate, destiny. [ME, f. eccl. L *praedestinatio* (as prec.; see -ATION)]

prĕdĕ′stĭne *v.t.* Determine beforehand, appoint as if by fate; (Theol.) predestinate. [ME, f. OF *predestiner* or f. eccl. L *praedestinare* PREDESTINATE[2]]

prēdētēr′mĭn|e *v.t.* Decree beforehand, predestine, so ~ATE[2] *a.*; (of motive etc.) impel (person etc. *to* thing, *to* do) beforehand; so ~A′TION *n.* [f. LL PRAE(*determinare* DETERMINE)]

prē′dĭal *a.* & *n.* **1.** *a.* Of land or farms; rural, agrarian; (of slave, tenant, etc.) attached to farms or the land; (of tithe) consisting of agricultural produce. **2.** *n.* Predial slave. [f. med. L *praedialis* f. L *praedium* farm; see -AL]

prĕ′dĭc|able *a.* & *n.* **1.** *a.* That may be predicated or affirmed; hence ~ABI′LITY *n.* **2.** *n.* Predicable thing, esp. (in *pl.*) Aristotle's classes of predicates viewed relatively to their subjects (viz. genus, species, difference, property, accident). [f. med. L *praedicabilis* a., *praedicabile* n., (thing) that may be affirmed (as PREDICATE[2]; see -ABLE)]

prĕdĭ′cament *n.* **1.** Thing predicated, esp. (in *pl.*, Philos.) Aristotle's ten categories, whence ~AL (-ĕ′n-) *a.* **2.** Unpleasant, trying, or dangerous situation. [ME, f. LL *praedicamentum* (as PREDICATE[2]; see -MENT)]

prĕ′dĭcant *a.* & *n.* **1.** *a.* (Of religious order, esp. Dominicans) engaged in preaching. **2.** *n.* Predicant person, esp. Dominican friar; *predikant*. [f. L *praedicans* part. of *praedicare* (see PREDICATE[2], -ANT)]

prĕ′dĭcate[1] *n.* **1.** (Logic). What is predicated, what is affirmed or denied of the subject by means of the copula (e.g. *mortal* in *all men are mortal*). **2.** (Gram.) What is said of the subject, including the copula (e.g. *are mortal* in prec. ex.) or other verb and its adjuncts. [f. LL *praedicatum* (transl. Gk *katēgoreumenon*), neut. p.p. of L *praedicare* (as foll.; see -ATE[2])]

prĕ′dĭc|āte[2] *v.t.* Assert or affirm as true or existent (*many truths may be predicated about humanity*; *we predicate goodness or badness of a motive*; *predicate of a motive that it is good or bad*); (Logic) assert (thing) about subject; *found or base (statement etc.) *on*; so ~A′TION *n.* [f. L PRAE(*dicare* declare) proclaim + -ATE[3]]

prĕdĭ′cative *a.* Making a predication; (Gram., of *a.* or *n.*, opp. *attributive*) forming part or the whole of the predicate (e.g. *old* in *the dog is old* but not in *the old dog*); hence ~LY[2] (-vlĭ) *adv.* [f. L *praedicativus* (as prec.; see -IVE)]

prĕ′dĭcatorȳ *a.* Of, given to, marked by, preaching. [f. LL *praedicatorius* (as PREDICATE[2]; see -ORY)]

prĕdĭ′ct *v.t.* Foretell, prophesy, (thing, *that, who*, etc.); hence or cogn. ~ABI′LITY, **prĕdĭ′ct**ION, *ns.*, ~ABLE, ~IVE, *adjs.*, **~ab**LY[2], **~ĭve**LY[2] (-vlĭ), *advs.* [f. L PRAE(*dicere dict-* say)]

prĕdĭ′ctor *n.* In vbl senses; instrument for determining height, direction, speed, and range of hostile aircraft to be attacked with anti-aircraft fire. [f. prec. + -OR]

predikant (prādēkah′nt) *n.* Minister of Dutch Protestant church, esp. in S. Africa. [Du. (as PREDICANT)]

prēdĭlĕ′ction *n.* Mental preference, liking, (*for*). [f. F *prédilection* f. med. L **praedilectio -onis* f. PRAE(*diligere*) prefer; see DILIGENT, -ION]

prēdĭspō′se (-z) *v.t.* Render liable, subject, or inclined (*to* feeling, disease, etc., *to* do). [f. PRE- + DISPOSE]

prēdĭsposĭ′tion (-zĭ′-) *n.* State of mind or body favourable *to* (mercy, bronchitis, etc.). [f. PRE- + DISPOSITION]

prĕ′dnĭsōne (-z-) *n.* Drug similar to cortisone but more active. [perh. f. *pre*gnant + *d*iene + corti*sone*]

prēdŏ′mĭn|āte *v.i.* Have or exert control (*over* person etc.), be superior; be the stronger or main element, preponderate, (*garden in which dahlias predominate*); hence or cogn. ~ANCE *n.*, ~ANT, ~ATE[2], *adjs.* [f. med. L *PRAE(*dominari* DOMINATE)]

prē-ĕ′mĭn|ent *a.* Excelling others; distinguished beyond others in some quality; hence or cogn. ~ENCE *n.*, **~ent**LY[2] *adv.* [ME f. L PRAE(*eminens* EMINENT)]

prē-ĕ′mpt *v.* **1.** *v.t.* Obtain by pre-emption; *occupy (public land) so as to have right of pre-emption; (fig.) appropriate beforehand. **2.** *v.i.* (Bridge). Make pre-emptive bid. [back form. f. foll.]

prē-ĕ′mpt|ion *n.* Purchase by one person etc. before opportunity is offered to others; right so to purchase (esp. public land); (fig.) prior appropriation. [f. med. L PRAE(*emptio* f. *emere empt-* buy); see -ION]

prē-ĕ′mptĭve *a.* Relating to pre-emption; (Mil.) intended to prevent attack by disabling threatening enemy; (Bridge, of bid) intended to be high enough to impede further bidding esp. by opponents. [f. as prec. + -IVE]

preen *v.t.* (Of bird) trim (feathers) with beak; (of person) smarten (one*self*, one's clothes, etc.); ~ one**self**, congratulate oneself, show self-satisfaction; ~ **gland** (at base of bird's tail, secreting oil used in preening). [ME, app. var. of PRUNE[3], assoc. w. Sc. & dial. *preen* pierce, pin]

pref. *abbr.* preface; preference; preferred; prefix.

prē′făb (*or* -ă′b) *n.* (colloq.) Prefabricated building. [abbr.]

prēfă′brĭc|āte *v.t.* Manufacture sections of (building etc.) prior to their assembly on a site; produce in artificially standardized way; so ~A′TION *n.* [f. PRE- + FABRICATE]

prĕ′face *n.*, & *v.t.* **1.** *n.* Introduction to book stating subject, scope, etc.; preliminary part of a speech; introduction to central part of Eucharistic service. **2.** *v.t.* Furnish (book etc.) with preface; introduce (act, speech, *with*); (of event etc.) lead up to (another). **3.** So **prĕfatōr′**IAL, **prĕ′fat**ORY, *adjs.* [ME f. OF, f. med. L *praefatia* for L *praefatio* f. PRAE(*fari* speak)]

prē′fĕct *n.* **1.** (Rom. Ant.) Chief magistrate; governor; military or naval commander. **2.** Chief administrative officer of French, Japanese, etc., department; ~ **of police,** head of Paris police. **3.** (In some schools) senior pupil authorized to maintain discipline. **4.** So **prēfĕ′ctor**AL, **~ōr′**IAL, *adjs.* [ME f. OF, f. L *praefectus* p.p. (as n.) of PRAE(*ficere fect-* = *facere* make) set in authority over]

prē′fĕcture *n.* (Period of) office, official residence, district under government, of a prefect; hence **prēfĕ′ctur**AL (-kcher-) *a.* [f. F *préfecture* or f. L *praefectura* (as prec.; see -URE)]

prēfer′ *v.t.* (-rr-). **1.** Promote (person *to* office); hence ~MENT *n.* **2.** Bring forward, submit, (statement, information, accusation, etc., *to* person in authority etc., *against* offender etc.). **3.** Choose rather, like better, (*gentlemen prefer blondes*; *prefer water to wine*; *prefer to leave it alone*; *prefer that it should be left*; *prefer to go to prison rather than pay*); hence **prĕ′fer**ABLE *a.*, **prĕ′ferab**LY[2] *adv.* [ME, f. OF *preferer* f. L PRAE(*ferre lat-* bear)]

prĕ′ference *n.* Liking *of* or *for* one thing better than (*to* or *over*) another (*do this in preference to that*); thing one prefers; prior right esp. to receive payment of debts; ‖~ **bond, share, stock,** (on which dividend is paid before any is paid on ordinary stock); favouring of one person or country before others in business relations, esp. favouring of a country by admitting its products at lower import duty. [f. F *préférence* f. med. L *praeferentia* (as prec.; see -ENCE)]

prĕferĕ′ntial (-shal) *a.* Of, giving, receiving, preference; (of customs tariff etc.) favouring particular countries, whence ~ISM (3), ~IST (2), *ns.*; hence ~LY[2] *adv.* [as prec., after *differential*; see -IAL]

prēfer′red (-er′d) *a.* In vbl senses; (of shares etc.) = PREFERENCE *shares* etc. [p.p. of PREFER]

prēfĭ′gure (-ger) *v.t.* Represent beforehand by figure or type, picture to oneself beforehand; hence or cogn. **prēfĭgūr**A′TION, ~MENT, *ns.*, **prēfĭ′gūrat**IVE *a.* [ME, f. eccl. L PRAE(*figurare* FIGURE[2])]

prē′fix[1] *n.* Verbal element placed at beginning of word to qualify meaning (e.g. *be-*, *ex-*, *re-*) or (in some languages) as inflexional formative; title placed before name, e.g. *Mr.* [f. mod. L *praefixum*, p.p. (as n.) of L PRAE(*figere* FIX[1])]

prē′fix[2] (*or* -ĭ′ks) *v.t.* Add (chapter, paragraph, etc., *to* book etc.) as introduction; join (word, verbal element) as prefix (*to* word); hence or cogn. **prēfĭ′x**ION (-kshon), **prē**FI′XTURE, *ns.* [ME, f. OF PRE(*fixer* FIX[1])]

prēfōr′m *v.t.* Form beforehand; so ~A′TION *n.* [f. PRE- + FORM[2]]

prēfōr′mative *a.* & *n.* **1.** *a.* Forming beforehand; prefixed as formative element of word. **2.** *n.* Preformative syllable or letter. [f. PRE- + FORMATIVE]

prĕ′gnable *a.* Able to be captured etc., not impregnable. [ME f. OF *prenable* takable; see IMPREGNABLE[1]]

prĕ′gnant *a.* (Of woman or female animal) having developing child(ren) or young in the womb; teeming with ideas; imaginative, inventive; fruitful in results, plentifully furnished *with* (consequences etc.); (of words or acts) having a hidden meaning, significant, suggestive, whence ~LY[2] *adv.*; ~ **construction** (Gram.) in which more is implied than the words express, e.g. *not have a chance* implying *of success* etc.); hence **prĕ′gn**ANCY *n.* [ME, f. F *prégnant* or f. L *praegnans -ntis*, earlier *praegnas* (prob. as PRAE- + (*g*)*nasci* be born)]

prēhĕ′nsile *a.* (Zool.) (Of tail or limb) capable of grasping; hence **prēhĕnsĭ′l**ITY *n.* [f. F *préhensile* f. L PRE(*hendere hens-* grasp); see -IL]

prēhĕ′nsion (-shon) *n.* Grasping, seizing; mental apprehension. [f. L *prehensio* (as prec.; see -ION)]

prēhĭstŏ′r|ic *a.* Of the period antecedent to written history; (colloq.) utterly out of date; hence ~ICALLY *adv.* [f. F *préhistorique* (as PRE-, HISTORIC)]

prēhĭ′storў *n.* Prehistoric matters or times; study of these; history (of a situation etc.); so **prē**HISTOR′IAN *n.* [f. PRE- + HISTORY, after prec.]

prē-ignĭ′tion *n.* Premature firing of explosive mixture in internal combustion engine. [f. PRE- + IGNITION]

prējŭ′dge *v.t.* Pass judgement on (person) before trial or proper inquiry; form premature judgement on (person, cause, action, etc.); so ~MENT (-jm-), **prējudĭc**A′TION (-jōō-), *ns.* [f. PRE- + JUDGE[2], after F *préjuger* or L PRAE(*judicare* JUDGE[2])]

prĕ′judĭce (-jōō-) *n.*, & *v.t.* **1.** *n.* Preconceived opinion, bias, (*against*, or *in favour of*, person or thing; *divest your mind of prejudice; has a prejudice against foreigners*; *has a prejudice in our favour*; *this is mere prejudice*); injury that results or may result from some action or judgement (*to the prejudice of*); **without** ~, without detriment to or *to* any existing right or claim. **2.** *v.t.* Impair validity of (right, claim, statement, etc.); (esp. in *p.p.*) cause (person) to have a prejudice (*against* or *in favour of*). [ME, f. OF (*prejudicier* v. f.) *prejudice* n. f. L PRAE(*judicium* judgement)]

prĕjudĭ′cial (-jōōdĭ′shal) *a.* Causing prejudice, detrimental, (*to* rights, interests, etc.); hence ~LY[2] *adv.* [ME, f. OF *prejudiciel* (as prec.; see -IAL)]

prĕ′lacў *n.* Office, rank, see, of a prelate; *the* prelates; church government by prelates (usu. derog. for *episcopacy*). [ME, f. AF *prelacie* f. med. L *prelatia* (as foll.; see -ACY)]

prĕ′lat|e *n.* High ecclesiastical dignitary, e.g. (arch)bishop, metropolitan, patriarch, (Hist.) abbot or prior; chaplain of an order; hence ~ESS[1] *n.*, **prēlă′t**IC(AL) *adjs.* [ME, f. OF *prelat* f. med. L *praelatus* p.p. (as n.); see PREFER]

prĕ′latize, -ise (-īz), *v.t.* Bring (church) under prelatical government. [f. prec. + -IZE]

prĕ′lature *n.* Office of prelate; *the* prelates. [f. F *prélature* f. med. L *praelatura* (as PRELATE; see -URE)]

prēlĕ′ct *v.i.* Discourse, lecture, (*to* audience, *on* subject); so **prēlĕ′ct**ION, **prēlĕ′ct**OR, *ns.* (**praelector,** Camb. Univ. college fellow presenting candidates for degrees etc.). [f. L PRAE(*legere lect-* read)]

prēlĭbā′tion *n.* Foretaste (usu. fig.). [f. LL PRAE(*libatio* LIBATION)]

prēlĭ′m *n.* (colloq.) Preliminary examination; (Print., in *pl.; or* prē′lĭmz) front matter, pages preceding text of book. [abbr.]

prēlĭ′minar|ў *a.* & *n.* **1.** *a.* Introductory, preparatory; hence ~ĬLY[2] *adv.* **2.** *adv.* = PREPARATORY 2. **3.** *n.* (usu. in *pl.*) Preliminary action or arrangement. [f. mod. L *praeliminaris* or F *préliminaire* f. as PRE- + L *limen liminis* threshold; see -ARY[1]]

prĕ′lūde[1] *n.* **1.** Performance, action, event, condition, serving as introduction (*to* another); introductory part of poem etc. **2.** (Mus.) Introductory movement esp. one preceding fugue or forming first piece of suite; short piece of music of similar type and on one theme. **3.** Hence or cogn. **prėlū'd**IAL *a.*, **prĕ'lūd**IZE (2) *v.i.* [f. F *prélude* or f. med. L *praeludium* (as foll.)]

prĕ'lūde² *v.t.* Serve as prelude to, introduce, foreshadow; introduce with a prelude; so **prėlū'sion** (-zhon) *n.*, **prėlū'**SIVE *a.*, (*or* -lōō'-). [f. L PRAE(*ludere lus-* play)]

prĕ'matūre *a.* & *n.* Occurring or done before the usual or proper time, too early, hasty, (*premature decision, decay*); ~ **baby** (born 3 to 12 weeks before the expected time; cf. *miscarriage*); hence or cogn. ~LY² (-ūrlĭ) *adv.*, ~NESS (-ūrn-), **prĕmatūr'**ITY, *ns.* [f. L PRAE(*maturus* MATURE¹) very early]

prēmĕ'dĭt|āte *v.t.* (esp. in *p.p.*) Think out, design, (action etc.) beforehand; so ~A'TION *n.* [f. L PRAE(*meditari* MEDITATE) + -ATE³]

prĕ'mier *a.* & *n.* **1.** *a.* First in position, importance, order, or time; of earliest creation (*premier earl*). **2.** *n.* Prime minister, esp. in Great Britain and in provinces etc. of Commonwealth countries; hence ~SHIP *n.* [ME, f. OF = first, f. L (as PRIMARY)]

première (prĕ'myār) *n.*, & *v.t.* **1.** *n.* First performance of or in play, film, etc. **2.** *v.t.* Give *première* of. [F, fem. of *premier* a. (as prec.)]

prĕ'mĭse¹ *n.* **1.** (Logic). = PREMISS. **2.** (in *pl.*) Aforesaid or foregoing matters, esp. (Law) *the* aforesaid houses, lands, or tenements. **3.** (in *pl.*) House or building with grounds and appurtenances; **on the ~s,** in the house etc. concerned. [ME, f. OF *premisse* f. med. L *praemissa* (*propositio* proposition) set in front f. L PRAE(*mittere miss-* send)]

prėmī'se² (-z) *v.t.* Say or write (thing, *that*) by way of introduction. [f. prec.]

prĕ'mĭss *n.* (Logic). Previous statement from which another is inferred, esp. MAJOR² and MINOR premisses in syllogism. [var. of PREMISE¹]

prē'mĭum *n.* **1.** Reward, prize, (**put a ~ on,** provide, or act as, incentive to); ‖**P~ (Savings) Bond,** government security with chances of cash prizes but zero interest. **2.** Amount to be paid in consideration of contract of insurance. **3.** Sum additional to interest, wages, etc., a bonus; fee for instruction in profession etc.; *charge for loan (additional to normal interest); **at a ~,** above nominal or usual price (cf. DISCOUNT¹), (fig.) in high esteem. [f. L *praemium* booty, reward, (as PRAE-, *emere* buy, take)]

prēmō'lar *a.* & *n.* (Tooth) in front of true molars (in man, bicuspid). [f. PRE- + MOLAR¹]

prēmonĭ'tion *n.* Forewarning; presentiment; so **prėmŏ'nĭt**OR *n.*, **prėmŏ'nĭt**ORY *a.* [f. F *prémonition* or f. LL *praemonitio* f. L PRAE(*monēre monit-* warn); see -ION]

Prėmŏnstratĕ'nsĭan *a.* & *n.* (Member) of order of regular canons founded at *Prémontré* in 1119, or of corresponding order of nuns. [f. med. L *Praemonstratensis* (*Praemonstratus* abbey of Prémontré, lit. foreshown, as having been prophetically indicated by St. Norbert; see -ESE) + -IAN]

prėmor'se *a.* (Bot. & Entom.) With the end abruptly terminated. [f. L PRAE(*mordēre mors-* bite) bite off]

prĕ'ntĭce *n.*, & *v.t.* (arch.) = APPRENTICE, esp. ~ (inexperienced) **hand**; hence ~SHIP (-s-sh-) *n.* (arch.). [ME, f. APPRENTICE]

prėŏccūpā'tion *n.* Prepossession, prejudice; occupation of a place beforehand; occupation, business, that takes precedence of all others; mental absorption. [f. F *préoccupation* or f. L *praeoccupatio* (as foll.; see -ATION)]

prėŏ'ccūpȳ *v.t.* Engage beforehand, engross (mind etc.); appropriate beforehand; (in *p.p.*) distrait, with thoughts elsewhere. [f. PRE- + OCCUPY, after L *praeoccupare* seize beforehand]

prĕp *n.*, *a.*, & *v.* (-pp-). (colloq.) **1.** *n.* ‖Preparation of school work; time during which this is done. **2.** *a.* Preparatory (*prep school*). **3.** *v.t.* & *i.* *Prepare. [abbr.]

prĕparā'tion *n.* **1.** Preparing; being prepared; (usu. in *pl.*) thing done to make ready (*for*); **make ~s,** prepare (*for*). **2.** ‖Work done by pupils to prepare for lessons, as part of school routine. **3.** Substance, e.g. food or medicine, specially prepared; (Mus.) (note sounded in) preparing of a discord. [ME f. OF, f. L *praeparatio -onis* (as PREPARE; see -ION)]

prėpă'rative *a.* & *n.* **1.** *a.* Preparatory; hence ~LY² (-vlĭ) *adv.* **2.** *n.* Preparatory act; (Mil. & Naut.) signal on drum, bugle, etc., as order to make ready. [ME, f. OF *preparatif -ive*, f. med. L *praeparativus* (as PREPARE; see -IVE)]

prėpă'rator|ȳ *a.* & *adv.* **1.** *a.* Serving to prepare, introductory (*to*); **~y school** (where pupils are prepared ‖for higher school, *for college or university); hence **~ĭLY**² *adv.* **2.** *adv.* In a preparatory manner (*am packing it up preparatory to sending it by post*). [ME, f. LL *praeparatorius* (as foll.; see -ORY)]

prėpār'e *v.* **1.** *v.t.* Make (person, one*self*, thing) ready (*for*); make ready (food, meal) for eating; make (person) mentally ready or fit (*for* news, *to* hear, etc.); **be ~d,** be ready or willing (*to* do). **2.** Get (lesson, speech, sermon) ready by previous study; get (person) ready by teaching (*for* college, examination, the army, etc.). **3.** Make (chemical product etc.) by regular process. **4.** (Mus.) Lead up to (discord) by sounding the dissonant note in it as consonant note in preceding chord. **5.** *v.i.* Make preparations (*for, to* do, etc.). **6.** Hence **prėpār'ĕd**NESS *n.*, readiness (esp. of preparations for possible hostilities). [ME, f. F *préparer* or f. L PRAE(*parare* make ready)]

prēpay' *v.t.* (**prepai'd**). Pay (charge) beforehand; pay (postage), pay postage of (letter, parcel, etc.) beforehand, e.g. by affixing stamp; hence ~ABLE *a.*, ~MENT *n.* [f. PRE- + PAY²]

prėpĕ'nse *a.* (usu. placed after *n.*) Deliberate, intentional; **malice ~,** intention to injure; hence ~LY² (-slĭ) *adv.* [earlier *prepensed* p.p. of obs. *prepense* v. alt. f. earlier *purpense* f. AF & OF PUR(*penser*; see PENSIVE)]

prėpŏ'nder|ant *a.* Surpassing in influence, power, number, or importance, predominant; hence ~ANCE *n.*, **~ant**LY² *adv.* [f. as foll.; see -ANT]

prėpŏ'nder|āte *v.i.* Weigh more, be heavier, (**~ate over,** exceed in number, quantity, etc.); be of greater moral or intellectual weight; be the chief element, predominate. [f. L PRAE(*ponderare* PONDER) + -ATE³]

prĕposĭ'tion (-z-) *n.* Word governing (and normally preceding) noun or pronoun, expressing latter's relation to another word (e.g. the italic wds in: found him *at* home, wait *in* the hall, what did you do it *for*?, the bed (that) he slept *on*, won *by* waiting, came *through* the roof, that is what I was thinking *of*); hence ~AL *a.* [ME, f. L *praepositio* (transl. Gk *prothesis*) f. PRAE(*ponere posit-* place); see -ION]

prėpŏ'sĭtive (-z-) *a.* (Gram.) (Of word, particle, etc.) proper to be placed before or prefixed. [f. LL. *praepositivus* (as prec.; see -IVE)]

prēpossĕ'ss (-z-) *v.t.* Imbue, inspire, (person *with* notion, feeling, etc.); (usu. in *pass.*, of idea etc.) take possession of (person); prejudice (usu.

For other words in *pre-* see PRE-.

favourably and at first sight), whence ~ING^{2} *a.*, **prēpossĕ'ssion** (-zĕ'shon) *n.* [f. PRE- + POSSESS]

prėpŏ'sterous *a.* Contrary to nature, reason, or common sense; perverse, foolish; utterly absurd; hence ~LY^{2} *adv.*, ~NESS *n.* [f. L PRAE-(*posterus* coming after) reversed, absurd + -OUS]

||**prėpŏ'stor.** See PRAEPOSTOR.

prėpō't|ent *a.* Very powerful; more powerful than others; (Biol.) having stronger fertilizing influence or power of transmitting hereditary qualities; so ~ENCE, ~ENCY, *ns.* [ME, f. L *praepotens -entis* part. of PRAE(*posse* be able)]

||**prē-prĕ'ference** *a.* (Of shares, claims, etc.) ranking before preference shares etc. [f. PRE- + PREFERENCE]

prē'print *n.* Printed document issued in advance of general publication. [f. PRE- + PRINT^{1}]

prē'pūce *n.* Foreskin; similar structure of clitoris; so **prėpū'tIAL** (-shal) *a.* [ME, f. L *praeputium*]

Prē-Ră'phaelite (*or* -fel-) *n.* Artist who aims at producing work in the spirit that prevailed before the time of Raphael; ~ **Brotherhood,** group of English artists including Holman Hunt, Millais, D. G. Rossetti; so **Prē-Ră'phāel(īt)-**ISM (3) *n.* [f. PRE- + *Raphael*, It. painter d. 1520 + -ITE^{1}]

prērĕ'quĭsĭte (-z-) *a.* & *n.* (Thing) required as previous condition (*for, of, to*). [f. PRE- + REQUISITE]

prėrŏ'gatĭve *n.* & *a.* **1.** *n.* (**Royal**) ~, right of the sovereign, theoretically subject to no restriction. **2.** Peculiar right or privilege (*it is our prerogative to ride*; *we have the prerogative of riding*); **the ~ of,** right to show (mercy etc.). **3.** Natural or divinely-given advantage, privilege, or faculty, (*reason and conscience are man's prerogatives*). **4. ~ court,** (Hist.) archbishop's court for probate of wills etc. **5.** *a.* Privileged, enjoyed by privilege; (Rom. Hist.) having the right to vote first. [n. ME f. OF or f. L *praerogativa* privilege, orig. tribe or century that voted first by lot; a. ME; both f. L PRAE(*rogativus* f. *rogare* ask; see -IVE) asked first]

Pres. *abbr.* President.

prĕ'sage^{1} *n.* Omen, portent; presentiment, foreboding; hence **prėsā'geFUL** (-jf-) *a.* [ME, f. F *présage* f. L *praesagium* f. PRAE(*sagire* perceive keenly) forebode]

prėsā'ge^{2} *v.t.* Portend, foreshadow; give warning of (event etc.) by natural means (*such ideas are held to presage insanity*); (of person) predict, or have presentiment of. [f. F *présager* or f. L *praesagire* (as prec.)]

prĕsbȳ|ō'pĭa (*or* -z-) *n.* Long-sightedness incident to old age, caused by loss of power of accommodation; hence ~**ŏ'pIC** *a.* [mod. L, f. Gk *presbus* old man + *ōps ōpos* eye; see -IA^{1}]

prĕ'sbȳter (*or* -z-) *n.* **1.** (In early Christian Church) one of several officers managing affairs of local church. **2.** (In Episcopal church) minister of second order, priest. **3.** (In Presbyterian church) elder. **4.** Hence or cogn. **prĕsbȳ'terAL, prĕsbȳtēr'IAL,** *adjs.*, **prĕsbȳ'terATE^{1},** ~SHIP, *ns.*, (*or* -z-). [eccl. L, f. Gk *presbuteros* elder (compar. as n. of *presbus* old)]

Prĕsbȳtēr'ian (*or* -z-) *a.* & *n.* **1.** *a.* ~ **Church,** one governed by elders, all (including ministers) of equal rank, esp. national Church of Scotland, (in England & Wales part of United REFORM^{1}*ed* Church from 1972); hence ~ISM (3) *n.*, ~IZE (3) *v.t.* **2.** *n.* Adherent of Presbyterian system; member of Presbyterian Church. [f. eccl. L *presbyterium* (as foll.) + -AN]

prĕ'sbȳterȳ (*or* -z-) *n.* Eastern part of chancel beyond choir, sanctuary; body of presbyters, esp. court next above kirk-session, district represented by this; (R.C. Ch.) priest's house. [ME, f. OF *presbiterie* f. eccl. L f. Gk *presbuterion* (as PRESBYTER; see -Y^{1})]

prĕ'scĭ|ent (*or* -shĭ-) *a.* Having foreknowledge or foresight; hence or cogn. ~ENCE *n.*, ~**ent**LY^{2} *adv.* [f. L PRAE(*scire* know); see -ENT]

prėscĭ'nd *v.* **1.** *v.t.* Cut off (part *from* whole) esp. prematurely or abruptly. **2.** *v.i.* ~ **from,** leave out of consideration. [f. L PRAE(*scindere* cut)]

prėscrī'be *v.* **1.** *v.t.* Lay down or impose authoritatively (*prescribe to him what he is to do* or *how to do it*; *the statutes prescribe the practice*); (Med.) advise use of (medicine etc., or abs.; *to* or *for* patient, *for* complaint; lit. or fig.); ~**d book,** = SET^{3} *book.* **2.** *v.i.* Assert prescriptive right or claim (*to* or *for* thing). [f. L PRAE(*scribere script-* write) direct in writing]

prē'script *n.* Ordinance, law, command. [f. L *praescriptum* neut. p.p. (as n.); see prec.]

prėscrĭ'ption *n.* **1.** Prescribing; physician's (usu. written) direction for composition and use of medicine; medicine thus prescribed. **2.** (Law). (**Positive**) ~, uninterrupted use or possession from time immemorial or for period fixed by law as giving title or right; **negative ~,** limitation of time within which action or claim can be raised. **3.** (fig.) Ancient custom viewed as authoritative, claim founded on long use. [ME f. OF, f. L *praescriptio -onis* (as PRESCRIBE; see -ION)]

prėscrĭ'ptĭve *a.* Prescribing; (Ling.) laying down rules of usage; based on prescription (*prescriptive right*); prescribed by custom; hence ~LY^{2} (-vlĭ) *adv.* [f. LL *praescriptivus* (as PRESCRIBE; see -IVE)]

prēsėlĕ'ctĭve *a.* (Of motor-car gear) that can be selected and set in advance; so **prē**SELE'CTOR *n.* [f. PRE- + SELECTIVE]

prĕ'sence (-z-) *n.* **1.** Being present (*your presence is requested*; *in the presence of a large company*; REAL^{2} *presence*); place where person is (*admitted to, banished from, his presence*); **in this** (*august* etc.) ~, in the presence of this (etc.) person; ||**the ~,** ceremonial attendance on person of high (esp. royal) rank (*remained in, retired from, the presence*). **2.** Personal appearance, (esp. imposing) bearing, (*a man of fine presence*); being represented with view to influence (*the British presence east of Suez*). **3.** Person or thing that is present. **4. ~ of mind,** calmness and self-command in sudden emergencies; **~-chamber** (in which great personage receives guests etc.). [ME f. OF, f. L *praesentia* (as foll.; see -ENCE)]

prĕ'sent^{1} (-z-) *a.* **1.** (usu. *pred.*) Being in the place in question (*no one else was present in* place, *at* proceedings etc.); **~ company excepted,** excluding those who are here now; **~ to,** felt or remembered by (mind, imagination). **2.** Being dealt with, discussed, etc., (*no excuse in the present case*). **3.** Existing, occurring, being such, now (*the present Duke of Fife*; *in the present fashion*; *during the present month*); **the ~** *author, writer,* etc., I who am writing; **~-day** *a.*, of this time, modern; **~ value** or **worth,** sum that with compound interest dating from now will amount to given sum in given time. **4.** (Gram.) **~ participle, tense,** etc., (denoting action etc. now going on or habitually performed in past and future). **5.** (arch.) Ready to hand, ready with assistance, (*a very present help in trouble*). [ME f. OF, f. L *praesens -entis* part. of PRAE(*esse* be) be at hand]

prĕ'sent^{2} (-z-) *n.* **1.** *The* present time, the time now passing; **at ~,** now (*do not want any more at present*; *is at present in Egypt*); **for the ~,** just now, as far as the present is concerned, (*that will do for the present*). **2.** (Gram.) Present tense. **3.**

(Law or joc.) (*Know all men* etc.) **by these ~s,** by this document. [ME, f. prec.]

prĕ'sent[3] (-z-) *n.* Gift; **make a ~ of,** present (thing *to* person). [ME, f. OF (as prec.), orig. in phr. *mettre une chose en present à quelqu'un*, put a thing into the presence of a person]

prėsĕ'nt[4] (-z-) *v.t.*, & *n.* **1.** *v.t.* Introduce (person *to* another); introduce (person) to sovereign at court; ~ one**self,** appear esp. as candidate for examination etc.; (Med., *refl.* or *abs.*, of patient or disease etc.) be the subject of initial investigation of condition. **2.** Bring or offer (actor, play or other entertainment, new product, theory, etc.) to the public. **3.** Recommend (clergyman) to bishop for institution (*to* benefice). **4.** Exhibit (thing *to* person etc.; *present a ragged appearance*; *presented its front to me*); show (quality etc.; *cases that present some difficulty*); (abs., of part of foetus) be directed towards cervix at time of delivery. **5.** (Mil.) ~ **(arms)**, hold (rifle etc.) vertically as deferential position in saluting. **6.** (Of idea etc.) offer or suggest *itself*. **7.** (Law). Bring formally under notice, submit, (complaint, offence, *to* authority). **8.** Aim (weapon *at*), hold out (weapon) in position for aiming. **9.** Offer or give (thing *to* person) as gift; offer (compliments, regards, *to*); deliver (cheque, bill, etc., *to* person etc.) for acceptance etc.; ~ person **with** thing, present it to him, cause him to have it (*this presented me with a problem*). **10.** *n.* Act of aiming weapon esp. firearm, position of weapon when aimed, position of 'present arms' in salute. [ME, f. OF *presenter* f. L *praesentare* (as PRESENT[1])]

prėsĕ'nt|able (-z-) *a.* Of decent appearance, fit to be introduced or go into company; suitable for presentation (as a gift etc.); hence ~ABI'LITY *n.*, ~**ab**LY[2] *adv.* [f. prec. + -ABLE]

prĕsentā'tion (-z-) *n.* **1.** Presenting or being presented; ~ (gratis) **copy** of book etc. **2.** Exhibition, theatrical representation, etc. **3.** Formal introduction esp. at royal court. **4.** (Philos.) Modification of consciousness due to direct cognition; hence ~AL *a.* **5.** Attitude of foetus towards cervix at time of delivery. [ME f. OF, f. LL *praesentatio -onis* (as PRESENT[4]; see -ATION)]

prĕsentā'tion|ism (-ĕz-) *n.* (Philos.) Doctrine that in perception the mind has immediate cognition of the object; so ~IST (2) *n.* [f. prec. + -ISM]

prėsĕ'ntative (-z-) *a.* (Of benefice) to which patron has right of presentation; serving to present an idea to the mind; (Philos.) of (the nature of) presentation. [prob. f. med. L **praesentativus* (as PRESENTATION; see -IVE)]

prĕsentee' (-z-) *n.* Person presented; recipient of present. [ME f. AF (as PRESENT[4]; see -EE)]

prėsĕ'ntient (-shĭ- *or* -shent) *a.* Having a presentiment (*of* event etc., or abs.). [f. L PRAE(*sentiens* SENTIENT)]

prėsĕ'ntiment (*or* -z-) *n.* Vague expectation, foreboding, (*of* coming event, esp. evil). [f. obs. F *présentiment* (as PRE-, SENTIMENT)]

prĕ'sently (-z-) *adv.* Soon, after a short time; (U.S., Sc., etc.) at the present time, now. [ME, f. PRESENT[1] + -LY[2]]

prėsĕ'ntment (-z-) *n.* (Law) statement on oath by jury of fact within their knowledge; formal complaint of offence made by parish authorities to bishop or archdeacon at his visitation; theatrical representation; delineation, portrait; statement, description, (*of*); act or mode of presenting to the mind. [ME, f. OF *presentement* (as PRESENT[4]; see -MENT)]

prĕservā'tion (-z-) *n.* Preserving or being preserved; state of being well or ill preserved (*in an excellent state of preservation*). [ME f. OF, f. med. L *praeservatio -onis* (as PRESERVE[2]; see -ATION)]

prėsėr'vative (-z-) *a.* & *n.* (Quality, course of action, etc.) tending to preserve; (substance) for preserving perishable foodstuffs. [ME, f. OF *preservatif -ive* f. med. L *praeservativus -um* (as PRESERVE[2]; see -ATIVE)]

prėsėr've[1] (-z-) *n.* **1.** (in *sing.* or *pl.*) Preserved fruit; jam. **2.** Ground set apart for protection of game or *natural resources; piece of water for fish; (fig.) sphere regarded by person as being for him alone. [f. foll.]

prėsėr'v|e[2] (-z-) *v.t.* **1.** Keep safe (*from* harm, decay, etc.); keep alive (name, memory, etc.). **2.** Maintain (state of things); retain (quality, condition); **well ~ed,** (of elderly person) showing little sign of ageing. **3.** Prepare (fruit, meat, etc.) by boiling with sugar, pickling, etc., to prevent decomposition or fermentation; keep from decomposition, by refrigeration, chemical treatment etc. **4.** Keep (game, river, or abs.) undisturbed for private use. **5.** Hence ~ABLE *a.*, ~ER[1] *n.* [ME, f. OF *preserver* f. LL PRAE(*servare* keep)]

prē'sės (-z) *n.* (*pl.* same). (Sc.) President, chairman. [f. L *praeses* (as PRESIDE)]

prėsī'de (-z-) *v.i.* Occupy chair of authority (*at* or *over* meeting of society or company); sit at head of table; exercise control, sit or reign supreme, (lit. or fig.); ~ **at** *the organ, piano*, etc., (colloq.) act as organist etc. [f. F *présider* f. L PRAE(*sidēre* = *sedēre* sit)]

prĕ'sĭdency̆ (-z-) *n.* (Period of) office of president; district administered by president, esp. (Hist.) one of three divisions of E. India Company's territory. [f. Sp. & Port. *presidencia*, It. *presidenza* f. med. L *praesidentia* (as prec.; see -ENCY)]

prĕ'sĭdent (-z-) *n.* Head of temporary or permanent body of persons, presiding over their meetings and proceedings; elected head of republican State; presiding officer of legislative body; head of some colleges and U.S. universities; person presiding over meetings of academy, literary or scientific society, etc.; *person directing general policy of bank or company; head of advisory council, board, etc., (||**Lord P~ of the Council,** Cabinet Minister presiding at meetings of Privy Council; ||**Lord P~,** chief judge of Court of Session); (Hist.) governor of province, colony, etc.; hence or cogn. **prĕsĭdĕ'nt**IAL (-z-; -sh*a*l) *a.*, ~SHIP *n.* [ME f. OF, f. L (as PRESIDE; see -ENT)]

prėsĭ'dĭarȳ *a.* Of, having, serving as, a garrison. [f. L *praesidiarius* (*praesidium* garrison f. as PRESIDE; see -ARY[1])]

prėsĭ'dĭō *n.* (*pl.* ~s). (In Spain and Sp. America) fort, garrison town. [Sp., as foll.]

prėsĭ'dĭum (*or* -z-) *n.* Standing committee in a Communist organization, esp. in Supreme SOVIET. [f. Russ. *prezidium* f. L (as PRESIDIARY)]

prĕss[1] *n.* **1.** Crowding; crowd (*of* people etc.); throng, crush, in battle; hurry, pressure of affairs, (*the press of modern life*). **2.** Pressing (*give it a slight press*). **3.** (Naut.) ~ **of sail, canvas,** (as much as wind etc. will allow). **4.** Instrument for compressing, flattening, or shaping, or for extracting juice etc. **5.** = PRINTING-*press*; printing-house or establishment; publishing firm etc. (*Oxford University Press*); *the* art, practice, of printing; **at** or **in (the)** ~, being printed; *send, go, come,* **to (the)** ~ (to be printed); ||CORRECTOR *of the press*; **freedom** or **liberty of the ~,** right to print and publish

For other words in *pre-* see PRE-.

anything without censorship (but still with liability for libel etc.; now often assoc. w. sense 6). **6.** *The* newspapers and periodicals generally (*favourably noticed by the press*); **get** or **have a good** etc. ~, receive good etc. notice; *the* GUTTER, UNDERGROUND², YELLOW, *press*; (as name of newspaper) *Aberdeen Press and Journal, Bucks Free Press.* **7.** Large usu. shelved cupboard for clothes, books, etc., esp. standing in recess in wall. **8.** ~ **agent,** person employed by theatre, actor, etc., to attend to advertising and press-publicity; *press* ATTACHÉ; ~**-box,** reporters' enclosure esp. at sports event; ~ **campaign** (by letters and articles in newspapers); ~ **conference,** interview given to journalists by some person to make announcement or answer questions; *~ **clipping,** = ||*press* CUTTING; ~**-gallery** (for reporters esp. in legislative assembly); ~**'man,** (1) ||journalist, (2) operator of printing-press; ~**'mark,** library shelf-mark showing location; *press* RELEASE². [ME f. OF *presse* (*presser*, as foll.)]

prĕss² *v.* **1.** *v.t.* Exert steady force against (thing in contact; *let a heavy weight press it; press it under* or *with a stone; press the two plates together*); do this as sign of affection etc. (*he pressed my hand, pressed her to his side*); move (thing *up, down, against,* etc.) by pressing; (of weight-lifter) raise (weight) to shoulders and then above head; ~ **the button,** set electric machinery etc. in motion, (colloq.) take decisive initial step. **2.** Squeeze (juice etc. *out of, from,* etc.); compress or squeeze (thing) to flatten or shape or smooth it, or to extract juice etc.; make (gramophone record) thus. **3.** (Of enemy, attacking force, etc.) bear heavily on (esp. in p.p.; *hard pressed*); weigh down, oppress, (feelings, mind, spirits); **be ~ed for** (have barely enough) *space, time, money,* etc. **4.** Urge, entreat, (person *to* do; person, or abs., *for* answer etc.). **5.** Use strict or strained interpretation of (words, metaphor). **6.** Urge (course of action, opinion, *upon* person); force (offer, gift, etc., *upon*); insist on (*did not press the point*). **7.** *v.i.* Exert pressure, bear with weight or force, (*on, against,* etc.); (Golf) strive too hard for long hit etc. and so strike ball imperfectly. **8.** Produce strong mental or moral impression, esp. weigh heavily, (*up*)*on* (mind, person). **9.** Be urgent, demand immediate action, (*time presses; no business that presses*); make insistent demand *for*. **10.** Crowd, throng, (*up, round,* etc.); hasten, urge one's way, *on, forward,* etc. **11.** ~**-button** *a.* = PUSH¹-*button*; ||~**-stud,** small device fastened by pressing to engage two parts; ~**-up,** (usu. in *pl.*) exercise in which prone body is raised by pressing down on hands to straighten arms. [ME, f. OF *presser* f. L *pressare* frequent. of *premere press-*]

prĕss³ *v.t.*, & *n.* (Hist. or fig.) **1.** *v.t.* Force (man, or abs.) to serve in army or navy; (fig.) bring into use as makeshift (*was pressed into service*). **2.** *n.* Compulsory enlistment esp. in navy; ~**-gang,** (*n.*) body of men employed to press men, (fig.) group using similar coercive methods, (*v.t.*) force into service (as if) by press-gang. [alt. (by assoc. w. PRESS¹,²) of obs. *prest* v. & n. f. OF (*prest* loan, advance pay f.) *prester* f. L PRAE(*stare* stand) furnish]

prĕ'ssĭng¹ *a.* In vbl senses; urgent (*pressing need, danger*); importunate, persistent, (*a pressing invitation; since you are so pressing*); hence ~LY² *adv.* [f. PRESS² + -ING²]

prĕ'ssĭng² *n.* In vbl senses; thing made by pressing (esp. part of vehicle, gramophone record or series of these made at one time). [f. PRESS² + -ING¹]

prĕ'ssure (-sher) *n.*, & *v.t.* **1.** *n.* Exertion of continuous force, force so exerted, upon or against a body by another in contact with it. **2.** Amount of this, expressed by the force on a unit area, esp. that of the atmosphere (*atmospheric pressure*); **blood** ~, varying pressure, measured for diagnosis etc., of blood in vessels, (colloq.) abnormally high value of this (*suffers from blood pressure*). **3.** Affliction, oppression; trouble, embarrassment, (*under financial pressure*). **4.** Urgency (*wrote hastily and under pressure*); constraining influence (*pressure must be brought to bear on him*). **5. High** ~, (1) condition of atmosphere with pressure above average, (2) pressure in engines higher than atmospheric, (3) pressure in engines higher than in other parts of the same machine, (4) (fig.) high degree of activity, speed, etc., (*working at high pressure; high-pressure work*); **high-~** *v.t.*, (colloq.) coerce by insistence; **low** ~, (1) condition of atmosphere with pressure below average, (2) (fig.) low degree of activity, speed, etc. **6.** ~**-cooker,** apparatus for cooking under high pressure at high temperature; ~ **gauge** (for showing pressure of steam etc.); ~ **group,** group of persons seeking to coerce legislature etc. by concerted action, propaganda, and like methods; ~ **mine** (detonated by pressure); ~ **suit,** inflatable suit for person flying at high altitude. **7.** *v.t.* Apply pressure to; coerce, persuade. [ME, f. L *pressura* (as PRESS²; see -URE)]

prĕ'ssurĭz|e, -ĭs|e, (-sherīz) *v.t.* = prec. 7; raise to high pressure; (esp. in *p.p.*) maintain normal atmospheric pressure in (aircraft cabin etc.) at high altitude; hence ~A'TION *n.* [f. prec. + -IZE]

prĕstĭdĭ'gĭt|ātor *n.* Conjurer; so ~A'TION *n.* [f. F *prestidigitateur* (*preste* nimble, as PRESTO¹, + L *digitus* finger; see -OR)]

prĕstĭ'ge (-ē'zh) *n.* & *a.* **1.** *n.* Influence or good reputation derived from past achievements, associations, etc.; hence ~FUL *a.* **2.** *a.* Having or conferring prestige. [F, = illusion, glamour, f. LL *praestigium* f. as foll.]

prĕstĭ'gious (-jus) *a.* Having or showing prestige; hence ~LY² *adv.*, ~NESS *n.* [orig. = deceptive, f. L *praestigiosus* (*praestigiae* juggler's tricks; see -OUS)]

prĕstĭ'ssĭmō *adv., a.,* & *n.* (*pl.* ~s). (Mus.) Very quick (movement or passage). [It., superl. (as foll.)]

prĕ'stō¹ *adv., a.,* & *n.* (*pl.* ~s). (Mus.) Quick (movement). [It., f. LL *praestus* f. L *praesto* ready]

prĕ'stō² *adv.* (In conjurer's formulae at moment of sudden change etc.) quickly (*hey presto!*). [= prec.]

prĕsū'm|e (-z-) *v.* **1.** *v.t.* Take the liberty, be impudent enough, venture, (*to* do). **2.** Suppose to be undoubtedly true, take for granted, (*I presume that he has seen them; I presume this decision to be final; you had better presume no such thing*); hence ~ABLE *a.*, ~**ab**LY² *adv.* **3.** *v.i.* Be impudent, take liberties; ~**e (up)on,** take advantage of, make unscrupulous use of (person's good nature, one's acquaintance with him, etc.); hence ~**ĭng**LY² *adv.* [ME, f. OF *presumer* f. L PRAE(*sumere sumpt-* take) anticipate, venture]

prĕsŭ'mption (-z-) *n.* **1.** Arrogance, assurance. **2.** Taking for granted, thing that is or may reasonably be taken for granted (*this was a mere presumption; the presumption is that he had lost it*); ground for presuming (*there is a strong presumption against its truth*). **3.** (Law). ~ **of fact,** inference of fact from known facts; ~ **of law,** (1) assumption of truth of thing until the contrary is proved, (2) inference established by law as universally applicable to certain circumstances [ME, f. OF *presumpcion* f. L *praesumptio -onis* (as prec.; see -ION)]

prĕsŭ'mptĭve (-z-) *a.* **1.** Giving grounds for presumption (*presumptive evidence*); hence ~LY[2] (-vlĭ) *adv.* **2. Heir ~** (whose right of inheritance is liable to be superseded by birth of another heir; cf. APPARENT). [f. F *présomptif -ive* f. LL *praesumptivus* (as PRESUME; see -IVE)]

prĕsŭ'mptūous (-z-) *a.* Unduly confident, presuming, forward; hence ~LY[2] *adv.*, ~NESS *n.* [ME, f. OF *presumptueux* f. LL *praesumptuosus, -tiosus* (as PRESUME; see -IOUS)]

prēsuppō'se (-z) *v.t.* Assume beforehand (thing, *that*); involve, imply, (*effects presuppose causes*). [ME, f. OF *presupposer*, after med. L *praesupponere* (as PRE-, SUPPOSE)]

prēsŭpposĭ'tion (-zĭ'-) *n.* Presupposing; thing assumed beforehand as basis of argument etc. [f. med. L PRAE(*suppositio* f. *supponere* f. as SUPPOSE); see -ITION]

prĕtĕ'nce, *prĕtĕ'nse, *n.* **1.** Claim (*to* merit etc.); **in ~,** (Her.) borne on an inescutcheon to indicate pretension or claim. **2.** Ostentation, display, (*devoid of all pretence*); false profession of purpose, pretext, (*under the pretence of helping; on the slightest pretence;* FALSE *pretences*). **3.** Pretending, make-believe. [ME, f. AF *pretense*, f. AL **pretensa* fem. sing. or neut. pl. (as n.) of med. L *pretensus* pretended (as foll.)]

prĕtĕ'nd *v.* **1.** *v.t.* Feign, give oneself out, (*to* be or do; *does not pretend to be a scholar*). **2.** Make oneself seem (*to* do), make it seem (*that*), in play. **3.** Profess falsely to have (*you should pretend illness*); allege falsely (*that*); (in *p.p.*) falsely avowed as such (*a pretended friend*). **4.** *v.i.* Venture, aspire, presume, (*to* do); lay claim *to* (right, title, etc.); **~ to,** profess to have (quality etc.), (arch.) try to win (person, person's hand) in marriage. [ME, f. F *prétendre* or f. L PRAE(*tendere tent-*, later *tens-* stretch)]

prĕtĕ'nder *n.* One who makes (esp. baseless) pretensions (*to* title etc., or abs.); **Old, Young, P~,** son, grandson, of James II as claimants to British throne; hence ~SHIP *n.* [f. prec. + -ER[1]]

***prĕtĕ'nse.** See PRETENCE.

prĕtĕ'nsion (-shon) *n.* Assertion of a claim (*to* thing, or abs.); justifiable claim (*to* thing, *to* be or do; *he has no pretensions to the name; has some pretensions to be chosen as the site*); pretentiousness. [f. med. L *praetensio, -tio*, (as PRETEND; see -ION)]

prĕtĕ'ntious (-shus) *a.* (Of person, book, speech, etc.) making claim to great merit or importance; ostentatious; hence ~LY[2] *adv.*, ~NESS *n.* [f. F *prétentieux* (as prec.; see -IOUS)]

prēter- *pref.* Beyond, outside the range of, more than, as: **~hu'man,** beyond what is human, superhuman; **~na'tural,** outside the ordinary course of nature, supernatural; **~na'turalism,** system or doctrine of the preternatural. [f. L *praeter* adv. & prep. past, beyond, compar. of *prae* before]

prĕ'terĭte, *prĕ'terĭt, *a.* & *n.* (Gram.) **~ (tense),** tense expressing past action or state; **~-present (tense),** tense originally preterite but now used as present (e.g. *can, may, shall*). [ME f. OF, or f. L *praeteritus* p.p. of *praeterire* pass (as prec., *ire it-* go)]

prēterĭ'tion *n.* Omission, disregard, (*of*); (Theol.) passing over of the non-elect. [f. LL *praeteritio* (as prec.; see -ION)]

prēter|mĭ't *v.t.* (-tt-). Omit to mention (fact etc.); omit to do or perform, neglect; leave off (custom, continuous action) for a time; so **~mĭ'ss**ION (-shon) *n.* [f. L *praetermittere* (as PRETER-, *mittere miss-* let go)]

prē'tĕxt[1] *n.* Ostensible reason, excuse; **(up)on** or **under the ~** *of* or *that*, professing as one's object etc. [f. L *praetextus* outward display f. PRAE(*texere text-* weave)]

prĕtĕ'xt[2] *v.t.* Allege (thing, *that*) as pretext. [f. F *prétexter* (*prétexte*, = prec.)]

prē'tōne *n.* Syllable or vowel preceding the stressed syllable; so **prēto'nic** *a.* [f. PRE- + TONE[1]]

***prē'tor** etc. See PRAETOR etc.

prĭ'ttĭ|fȳ *v.t.* Make pretty; represent with finical prettiness; hence ~FICA'TION *n.* [f. PRETTY + -FY]

prĭ'ttĭlȳ *adv.* In a way that pleases the eye, ear, or aesthetic sense, (*prettily dressed*). [ME, f. PRETTY + -LY[2]]

prĭ'ttĭnĕss *n.* **1.** Beauty of a dainty or graceful kind; pretty thing, ornament, etc. **2.** Affected or trivial beauty of style in literature or art; so **prĭ'ttȳ**ISM (2) *n.* [f. foll. + -NESS]

prĭ'ttȳ *a.* & *adv.* **1.** *a.* (Of woman or child) attractive in dainty or graceful way; attractive to eye, ear, or aesthetic sense, (*pretty cottage, song, scene, story*); fine, good of its kind, (*has a pretty wit; very pretty sport*); (iron.) considerable (*cost me a pretty penny; a pretty mess you have made*); (arch.) fine, stout, (*a pretty fellow*); (ellipt.) **my ~** (one, child); hence ~ISH[1] 2 *a.* **2.** *adv.* Fairly, moderately, (*am pretty well; find it pretty difficult*); **~ much** or **well,** very nearly (*the same thing* etc.); **sitting ~,** (colloq.) advantageously placed. **3.** **~-~,** overdoing the prettiness, aiming too much at prettiness. [OE *prættig*, corresp. to MLG *prattich* capricious, obs. Du. *prettig* sportive; f. WG **pratt-* trick]

prĕ'tzel *n.* Crisp knot-shaped biscuit flavoured with salt, used esp. by Germans as relish with beer. [G]

preux chevalier (prer̄ shĕvălyā') *n.* (*pl.* **~s** *pr.* same). Gallant knight. [F]

prĕvai'l *v.i.* **1.** Gain the mastery, be victorious, (*against, over*); **~ (up)on,** persuade (*to* do). **2.** Be the more usual or prominent, predominate; exist or occur in general use or experience, be current; **~ing wind** (that most frequently occurs at a place). [ME, f. L PRAE(*valēre* have power), infl. by AVAIL[1]]

prĕ'val|ent *a.* Generally existing or occurring; predominant; hence or cogn. **~ENCE** *n.*, **~ent**LY[2] *adv.* [f. as prec.; see -ENT]

prĕvă'rĭc|āte *v.i.* Speak or act evasively or misleadingly; quibble, equivocate; so ~A'TION, **~āt**OR, *ns.* [f. L PRAE(*varicari* straddle f. *varus* bent, knock-kneed) walk crookedly, practise collusion, in eccl. L transgress, + -ATE[3]]

prĕvē'nĭent *a.* Preceding something else; having in view the prevention (*of*); **~ grace** (Theol., preceding repentance and predisposing the heart to seek God). [f. L *praevenire* (see foll., -ENT)]

prĕvĕ'nt *v.t.* **1.** Hinder, stop, (*this may prevent him from writing, his* or (colloq.) *him writing; wish to prevent all dispute*). **2.** (arch.) Meet, deal with, (wish, question, etc.) before it is expressed etc.; precede, arrive before. **3.** (Theol.) **God ~s** (goes before, guides) *us with His grace.* **4.** Hence or cogn. ~ABLE, ~IBLE, *adjs.*, **prĕvĕ'nt**ION *n.* [ME = anticipate, f. L PRAE(*venire vent-* come) come before, hinder]

prĕvĕ'ntĭve *a.* & *n.* **1.** *a.* Serving to prevent, esp. (Med.) to keep off disease; ||**~ detention,** imprisonment of habitual criminal for corrective training etc.; ||**P~ Service,** department of Customs concerned with prevention of smuggling. **2.** *n.* Preventive agent, measure, drug, etc. **3.** Hence or cogn. **prĕvĕ'nt**ATIVE *a.* & *n.*, ~LY[2] (-vlĭ) *adv.* [f. prec. + -IVE]

prē'view (-vū) *n.*, & *v.t.* **1.** *n.* View or examination of a film, play, book, etc., before it is seen by the general public; *trailer of film. **2.** *v.t.* View in advance of public presentation. [f. PRE- + VIEW]

prē'vious *a.* & *adv.* **1.** *a.* Coming before in time or order; prior *to*; done or acting hastily (*you have been a little too previous*), whence ~NESS *n.*; ~ **question,** (Parl. etc.) question whether vote shall be taken on main question (put to avoid putting of main question or *to close debate on it); hence ~LY² *adv.* **2.** ~ **to,** before (*had called previous to writing*). [f. L PRAE(*vius* f. *via* way) + -OUS]

prēvī'se (-z) *v.t.* Foresee, forecast, (event etc., or abs.); so **prēvī'sION** *n.*, **prēvī'sionAL** *a.*, (-zho-). [f. L PRAE(*vidēre vis-* see)]

***prē'vūe.** Var. of PREVIEW.

***prĕ'x(y̆)** *n.* (sl.) President (esp. of college). [abbr.]

prey¹ (prā) *n.* Animal hunted or killed by other animal for food (**beast** or **bird of** ~, one that kills and devours other animals); (Bibl.) what one brings away safe from contest etc. (Jer. 21:9); person or thing that falls a victim (*to* enemy, disease, fear, etc.). [ME, f. OF *preie* f. L *praeda* booty]

prey² (prā) *v.i.* **1.** ~ **(up)on,** seek or take (animal etc.) as prey, plunder (person). **2.** (Of disease, emotion, etc.) exert harmful or destructive influence (*up*)*on*. [ME, f. OF *pre(i)er* f. LL *praedare* f. L *praedari* (as prec.)]

prī'apĭsm *n.* Licentiousness; (Path.) persistent erection of penis; so **prīăpIC** *a.*, phallic. [f. F *priapisme* f. LL f. Gk *priapismos* (*priapizō* be lewd f. *Priapos* god of procreation; see -ISM)]

price *n.*, & *v.t.* **1.** *n.* Money or other consideration for which thing is bought or sold (*what is the price of this?*; *price £5 each*; *offered at reduced prices*); odds in betting (*the* STARTING *price of a horse*); ~ **current,** ~**-list,** list of current prices of commodities; ~**-fixing,** determination of prices by agreement between sellers; ~**-ring,** RING¹ 5 of traders to maintain prices of goods; ~**-tag,** cost (lit. or fig.); **above, beyond, without,** ~, so valuable that no price can be stated; **at a** ~, at a relatively high price; **of (great)** ~, valuable; **set a** ~ **on,** announce amount for which thing will be bought or sold; **set a** ~ **on** person's **head** or **life,** offer specified reward for his capture or death. **2.** (fig.) What must be given, done, sacrificed, etc., to obtain a thing (*must be done at any price*; *peace at any price*; *every man has his price*, i.e. can be won over by some inducement); (*would not have it, do it*, etc.) **at any** ~, on any terms, for any sacrifice or consideration; ‖**what** ~ . . .?, (sl.) (1) what is the chance of . . .?, (2) the vaunted . . . has failed. **3.** *v.t.* Fix or find the price of (thing for sale); (fig.) estimate the value of; ~ one**self out of the market,** charge a prohibitive price. [n. ME f. OF *pris* f. L *pretium* (cf. PRAISE, PRIZE¹); v. var. of *prise* = PRIZE¹]

priced (-ist) *a.* To which a price is assigned (esp. in comb.: *high, low, -priced*); (of catalogue etc.) in which prices are named. [f. prec. + -ED¹,²]

prī'celėss (-sl-) *a.* Invaluable; (sl.) most amusing, incredibly absurd; hence ~NESS *n.* [f. PRICE + -LESS]

prī'c|ey *a.* (~ier, ~iest). (colloq.) Expensive. [f. PRICE + -Y²]

prĭck¹ *n.* Pricking, puncture, (~**s of conscience,** remorse); mark made by pricking; (arch.) goad for oxen, esp. (fig.) **kick against the** ~**s,** hurt oneself by useless resistance (Acts 9:5); (vulg.) penis, (sl., derog.) man; ~**-ears,** erect pointed ears of some dogs etc., conspicuous ears of person, esp. of Roundheads; ~**-eared,** having such ears. [OE *pric(c)a*, = MLG *pricke*; cf. foll.]

prĭck² *v.* **1.** *v.t.* Pierce slightly, make minute hole in, (~ **a** or **the bladder** or **bubble,** show the emptiness of a person or thing that has seemed important); (fig.) cause sharp pain to (*my conscience pricked me*); (arch.) spur, urge on, (horse). **2.** Mark off (name etc. in list) by pricking, ‖select (sheriff) thus; mark (pattern *off, out*) with pricks or dots. **3.** ~ **in, off, out,** plant (seedlings etc.) in small holes pricked in earth; ~ **up** one's **ears,** (of dog) erect the ears when on the alert, (fig., of person) become suddenly attentive. **4.** *v.i.* Feel pricking sensation; make thrust (*at, into*, etc.) as if to prick; (arch.) advance on horseback. [OE *prician*, = MLG, MDu. *prikken*]

prĭ'cker *n.* In vbl senses; pricking instrument, e.g. awl or stitch-wheel. [f. prec. + -ER¹]

prĭ'ckėt *n.* ‖Male fallow deer in second year, with straight unbranched horns; spike to stick candle on. [ME, f. AL *prikettus, -um* dim. f. PRICK¹; see -ET¹]

prĭ'ckle¹ *n.* & *v.* **1.** *n.* Small thorn; (Bot.) thorn-like process developed from, and capable of being peeled off with, epidermis of plant; hard-pointed spine of hedgehog etc. **2.** *v.t.* & *i.* Affect or be affected with sensation as of pricks. [n. f. OE *pricel*, = MDu., MLG *prickel*, cogn. w. PRICK¹; v. also dim. of PRICK², = MDu. *prickelen*]

prĭ'ckle² *n.* Wicker basket for fruit etc. [17th c., of unkn. orig.]

prĭ'cklȳ *a.* Armed with prickles (esp. in names of plants and animals); (fig., of person) ready to take offence; tingling; ~ **heat,** inflammation of skin near sweat glands with eruption of vesicles and prickly sensation, common in hot countries; ~ **pear,** (1) cactus of genus *Opuntia*, (2) its usu. pear-shaped edible fruit; ~ **poppy,** yellow-flowered plant (*Argemone mexicana*) with prickly leaves; ~ **rhubarb,** gunnera; hence **prĭ'cklĭNESS** *n.* [f. PRICKLE¹ + -Y²]

prī'cy̆. Var. of PRICEY.

pride *n.*, & *v. refl.* **1.** *n.* (Unduly) high opinion of one's own qualities, merits, etc.; arrogant bearing or conduct; ~ **of place,** exalted position, consciousness of this, arrogance. **2.** **(Proper)** ~, sense of what befits one's position, preventing one from doing unworthy thing; **false** ~, mistaken feeling of this kind; *put* one's *pride in* one's POCKET¹. **3.** Feeling of elation and pleasure due to action or circumstance that does one credit; **take a** ~ **in,** be proud of (person, thing, doing). **4.** Object of this feeling (*he is his mother's pride*; esp. in names of plants, as LONDON *pride*); best of a class etc. **5.** (Her.) **Peacock in his** ~ (with tail expanded and wings drooping). **6.** Company (of lions etc.). **7.** Best condition, prime (esp. *pride of* GREASE¹); ~ **of the morning,** mist or shower at sunrise, indicating fine day to come. **8.** Hence ~'FUL (-df-; chiefly Sc.), ~'LESS (-dl-), *adjs.* **9.** *v. refl.* ~ one**self (up)on,** be proud of (thing, quality, doing). [OE *prȳtu, prȳte, prȳde* f. *prūa* PROUD]

prie-dieu' (prēdyėr') *n.* Kneeling-desk esp. for prayer; ~ **(chair),** chair with tall sloping back for use in praying. [F, lit. 'pray God']

priest *n.*, & *v.t.* **1.** *n.* Ordained minister of R.C., Anglican, or Orthodox Church (in Anglican Church, one above deacon and below bishop with authority to administer sacraments and pronounce absolution); minister of the altar, esp. officiant at Eucharist; official minister of non-Christian religion, whence ~'ESS¹ *n.*; HIGH *priest*; ~**'craft,** ambitious or worldly policy of

For other words in *pre-* see PRE-.

priests; **~-ridden,** held in subjection by priests; **~'s hole,** (Hist.) secret hiding-place for R.C. priest; ‖**~-vicar,** minor canon in some cathedrals. **2.** Hence ~'HOOD (-t-h-), ~'LING¹, *ns.*, ~'LESS, ~'LIKE, *adjs.* **3.** *v.t.* Make (person) a priest. [OE *prēost*, = OHG *priast, prēst*, ON *prestr*, ult. f. eccl. L PRESBYTER]

prie'stl|y̆ *a.* Of, like, befitting, a priest; **P~y code,** one of the constituent elements in the Hexateuch; hence ~ĭNESS *n.* [OE *prēostlic* (as prec., -LY¹)]

prĭg *n.* Precisian in speech or morals or manners, conceited or didactic person; hence ~'**g**ERY (2), ~'**g**ISM (2), *ns.*, ~'**g**ISH¹ *a.*, (-g-). [16th c. cant, = tinker; of unkn. orig.]

prĭm *a.* & *v.* (**-mm-**). **1.** *a.* (Of person, manner, speech, etc.) formal and precise, demure; (esp. of woman) prudish; hence ~'LY² *adv.*, ~'NESS *n.* **2.** *v.i.* Assume prim air. **3.** *v.t.* Form (face, lips, etc.) into prim expression; make prim. [17th c., prob. orig. cant f. OF *prin prime* excellent f. L *primus* first]

prī'ma (prē'-) *fem. a.* First, chief; **~ balleri'na,** chief female performer in ballet; **~ do'nna** (*or* prĭ'-; *pl.* **~ donnas,** *or* **prime donne** *pr.* prēmā dŏ'nā), chief female singer in opera, (transf.) temperamental person. [It.]

prī'macy̆ *n.* Office of a primate; pre-eminence. [ME, f. OF *primatie* or f. med. L *primatia* (as PRIMATE; see -ACY)]

prīmae'val. See PRIMEVAL.

prīma fā'cĭe (*or* -shĭē) *adv.* & *a.* (Arising) at first sight, (based) on the first impression, (*has prima facie a good case*; *see a prima facie reason for it*). [ME f. L, abl. of *primus* first, *facies* FACE¹]

prī'mal *a.* Primitive, primeval; chief, fundamental; hence ~LY² *adv.* [f. med. L *primalis* f. L *primus* first; see -AL]

prī'mary̆ *a.* & *n.* **1.** *a.* Earliest, original; of the first rank in a series, not derived, (*the primary vowel sounds*; *the primary meaning of a word*). **2.** Of the first importance, chief. **3.** (Geol.) of the lowest series of strata; (Biol.) belonging to first stage of development. **4. ~ amputation** (performed before inflammation supervenes); **~ battery, cell,** (generating electricity by irreversible chemical reaction); **~ coil** (to which current is supplied in transformer); *primary* COLOUR¹; **~ education,** that which begins with the rudiments of knowledge, elementary, (cf. SECONDARY); ***~ election** (to appoint party conference delegates or to select candidates for principal election); **~ feather,** large flight-feather of bird's wing; **~ planet** (revolving directly round sun as centre; not a satellite); **~ school** (where primary education is given); **~ tense,** (L & Gk Gram.) present, future, perfect, or future perfect (cf. HISTORIC). **5.** Hence **prī'marĭ**LY² *adv.* **6.** *n.* Primary planet, period, coil, feather, election, etc. [ME, f. L *primarius* (*primus* first; see -ARY¹)]

prī'mate (*or* -āt) *n.* **1.** Archbishop (**P~ of England,** Archbishop of York; **P~ of all England,** Archbishop of Canterbury). **2.** (Zool.) Member of order Primates; hence **prīmatŏ'**LOGY *n.* **3.** Hence **prīmā'**TIAL (-shal) *a.* [ME, f. OF *primat* f. L *primas -atis* a. 'of first rank' (*primus* first), in med. L = primate]

Prīmā'tēs (-z; *or* prī'māts) *n. pl.* (Zool.) Highest order of mammals, including man, apes, monkeys, tarsiers, and lemurs. [mod. L, f. as prec.]

primavē'ra (prē-) *n.* (Hard light timber of) Central Amer. yellow-flowered tree (*Cybistax donnellsmithii*). [Sp., = spring, f. L *primus* first + *ver* SPRING² 2]

prīme¹ *n.* **1.** State of highest perfection (*in the prime of life, manhood*, etc.; *prime of* GREASE¹); *the* best part (*of* thing). **2.** Beginning or first age of anything; (Eccl.) (office of) second canonical hour of prayer, appointed for first hour of day (i.e. 6 a.m.); (arch.) this time. **3.** Prime number. **4.** (Print.) Symbol ′ added to letter etc. as distinguishing mark, or to figure as symbol for minutes or feet. **5.** First of eight parrying positions in fencing. [OE *prīm* f. L *prima* (*hora*) first (hour), & ME f. OF *prime* (as foll.), or f. foll.]

prīme² *a.* **1.** Chief, most important, (*prime agent, motive*); first-rate (esp. of cattle and provisions), excellent, whence ~'LY² (-mlĭ) *adv.*, ~'NESS (-mn-) *n.* **2.** Primary, fundamental; (Arith., of a number) divisible only by itself and unity (e.g. 2, 3, 5, 7, 11), (of numbers) having no common factor but unity. **3.** *Prime* COST¹; *prime* MERIDIAN; **~ minister,** principal minister of sovereign or State; *prime* MOVER; **~ rate,** lowest rate at which money can be borrowed commercially; **~ time** (at which highest rates are charged, esp. to advertisers on television); **~ vertical,** great circle of the heavens passing through zenith and E. and W. points of horizon. [ME f. OF, f. L *primus* first]

prīme³ *v.t.* **1.** (Hist.) supply (firearm, or abs.) with gunpowder for firing charge; prepare (explosive) for detonation. **2.** Pour liquid into (pump) to make it start working; inject petrol into (cylinder or carburettor of internal combustion engine). **3.** Equip (person *with* information etc.); ply (person *with* liquor). **4.** Cover (wood etc.) with first coat of paint or with oil etc. to prevent paint from being absorbed. [16th c.; orig. unkn.]

prĭ'mer¹ *n.* Elementary school-book for teaching children to read; small introductory book. [ME f. AF, f. med. L *primarius, -arium*, f. L *primus* first; see -ER² (2)]

prī'mer² *n.* In vbl senses; cap, cylinder, etc., used to ignite powder of cartridge etc.; substance used to prime wood etc. [f. PRIME³ + -ER¹]

prĭmēr'ō *n.* (*pl.* ~**s**). (Hist.) Gambling card-game fashionable in 16th–17th c. [f. Sp. *primera* fem. of *primero* first, f. as PRIMARY]

prīmē'val, prīmae'val, *a.* Of the first age of the world; ancient, primitive; hence ~LY² *adv.* [f. L *primaevus* (*primus* first, *aevum* age) + -AL]

prīmĭgră'vĭda *n.* (*pl.* ~**e**). Woman pregnant for the first time. [mod. L, fem. f. L *primus* first + *gravidus* GRAVID]

prī'mĭng¹ *n.* In vbl senses; gunpowder placed in pan of firearm; train of powder connecting fuse with charge in blasting etc.; mixture used by painters for preparatory coat; preparation of sugar added to beer. [f. PRIME³ + -ING¹]

prī'mĭng² *n.* Acceleration of the tides taking place from neap to spring tides (cf. LAG¹). [f. *prime* v. f. PRIME¹·² + -ING¹]

prīmĭ'par|a *n.* (*pl.* ~**ae**). Woman bearing child for the first time; hence ~OUS *a.* [L (*primus* first, *-parus* f. *parere* bring forth)]

prĭ'mĭtĭve *a.* & *n.* **1.** *a.* Early, ancient, (**the P~ Church,** Christian Church in its earliest times); old-fashioned, undeveloped, uncultured; at an early stage of civilization. **2.** Original, primary; (Gram., of words; Philol., of language) radical, not derivative; (Math., of line, figure, etc.) from which another is derived, from which some construction begins, etc.; (of colour) primary; (Geol.) of the earliest period; (Biol.) appearing in earliest or very early stage of growth or evolution; **P~ Methodist,** member of society of Methodists founded 1810 by Hugh Bourne by secession from main body, joined with other Methodists 1932. **3.** Hence ~LY² (-vlĭ) *adv.*, ~NESS (-vn-) *n.* **4.** *n.*

Painter of period before Renaissance, or modern imitator of such, or untutored painter with direct naïve style; picture by such painter; primitive word, line, etc.; (*P*~) Primitive Methodist. [ME f. OF *primitif -ive* or f. L *primitivus* first of its kind (*primitus* in the first place f. *primus* first; see -IVE)]

prĭ′mĭtĭvĭsm *n.* Primitive behaviour; belief in superiority of what is primitive. [f. prec. + -ISM]

primo (prē′mō) *n.* (*pl.* ~*s*). (Mus.) Leading or upper part in duet etc. [It.]

prīmogĕ′nĭtor *n.* Earliest ancestor; ancestor. [var. of *progenitor*, after foll.]

prīmogĕ′nĭt|ure *n.* Fact of being first-born child; (**right of**) ~**ure,** right of succession belonging to the first-born, esp. feudal rule by which whole real estate of intestate passes to eldest son; so ~AL, ~ARY[1], *adjs.* [f. med. L *primogenitura* f. L *primo* first + *genitura* (*gignere genit-* beget; see -URE)]

prīmôr′dĭal *a.* Existing at or from the beginning, primeval; original, fundamental; hence ~ITY (-ă′l-) *n.*, ~LY[2] *adv.* [ME, f. LL *primordialis* (as foll.; see -AL)]

prīmôr′dĭ|um *n.* (*pl.* ~**a**). (Biol.) Rudiment of part or organ. [L, neut. (as n.) of *primordius* original (*primus* first, *ordiri* begin)]

prĭmp *v.t.* Make (hair, clothes, etc.) tidy; make (*oneself*) smart. [dial. var. of PRIM]

prĭ′mrōse (-z) *n.* Plant of genus *Primula* (esp. *P. vulgaris*) bearing pale yellow flowers in early spring; flower of this; the colour of this flower; EVENING *primrose*; **the ~ path,** unjustified (esp. disastrous) pursuit of ease or pleasure (w. ref. to Shak. *Hamlet* I. iii. 50); ||**P~ Day, League,** anniversary of the death (19 Apr. 1881) of, Conservative association formed in memory of, Benjamin Disraeli Earl of Beaconsfield; ~ **peerless,** twin-flowered European narcissus. [ME *primerose*, corresp. to OF *primerose* and med. L *prima rosa* lit. first rose; sense unexpl.]

prĭ′mūla *n.* Herbaceous perennial of genus *Primula*, with flowers of various colours. [med. L, fem. (as n.) of *primulus* dim. of *primus* first]

prīmum mō′bĭlė *n.* Outermost sphere added in Middle Ages to Ptolemaic system, supposed to revolve round earth in 24 hours carrying with it the contained spheres; (fig.) prime source of motion or action. [med. L, lit. first moving thing, transl. Arab. *al-muḥarrik al-awwal*]

prī′mus[1] *n.* Presiding bishop of Scottish Episcopal Church; ~ ***inter pares*** (ĭnter pār′ēz), first among equals, senior or spokesman member of a group. [L, = first]

prī′mus[2] *n.* Brand of portable stove burning vaporized oil for cooking etc. [P]

prĭnce *n.* **1.** (rhet.) Sovereign ruler; **P~ of Peace,** Christ; ~ **of darkness, the air, this** or **the world,** etc., the Devil. **2.** Ruler of small State, actually or nominally feudatory to king or emperor. **3.** Male member of royal family, esp. ~ (**of the blood**), son or grandson of British king or queen; ~ **consort,** (title conferred on) husband of reigning female sovereign being himself a prince; **P~ of Denmark,** Hamlet (*Hamlet without the P~ of Denmark*, thing robbed of its essence); **P~ of Wales,** (title usu. conferred on) heir apparent to British throne. **4.** (As English rendering of foreign titles) noble usu. ranking next below duke; (as courtesy title in some connections) duke, marquis, earl; (as title of cardinal) ~ **of the** (**Holy Roman**) **Church. 5.** (fig.) The chief, the greatest, (*of novelists, liars, etc.*). **6.** ***P~ Albert,** (colloq.) frock-coat; ~ **bishop,** bishop who is also a prince; **P~ Regent,** prince who acts as regent, esp. George (afterwards IV) as regent 1811–20; ~ **royal,** eldest son of reigning monarch; (**P~**) **Rupert's drops,** pear-shaped lumps of glass bursting to pieces when thin ends are broken off; **P~ Rupert's metal,** = *prince's metal*; ~**'s feather,** tall plant (*Amaranthus hypochondriacus*) with feathery spikes of small red flowers; ~**'s metal,** brasslike alloy of copper and zinc. **7.** Hence ~′DOM (-sd-), ~′KIN (-sk-), ~′LET, ~′LING[1] 2, (-sl-), ~′SHIP (-s-sh-), *ns.*, ~′LIKE (-sl-) *a.* [ME f. OF, f. L *princeps principis* first, chief, sovereign (*primus* first, *cipere* = *capere* take)]

prĭ′ncel|ȳ (-slĭ) *a.* (Worthy) of a prince; held by a prince; sumptuous, splendid; hence ~**ĭNESS** *n.* [f. prec. + -LY[1]]

prĭ′ncĕss (*or* -ĕ′s exc. when attrib.) *n.* **1.** Wife of prince; female member of royal family, esp. ~ (**of the blood**), daughter or granddaughter of British king or queen; **P~ Regent,** (1) princess who acts as regent, (2) wife of Prince Regent; ~ **royal,** (title conferrable on) sovereign's eldest daughter. **2.** (arch.) Queen. **3.** (fig.) Pre-eminent woman or thing personified as woman. **4.** ~ **dress, petticoat, slip,** (made in panels with flared skirt and without seam at waist). [ME f. OF *princesse* (as PRINCE; see -ESS[1])]

prĭ′ncĭpal *a.* & *n.* **1.** *a.* (usu. *attrib.*) First in rank or importance, chief, (*their principal food is potatoes*; *the principal town of the district*; *the principal persons concerned*); main, leading, (*a principal cause of his failure*); ~ **boy, girl,** actress who takes leading male, female, part in pantomime. **2.** (Of money) constituting the original sum invested or lent. **3.** (Gram.) ~ **sentence, clause,** one to which another is subordinate; ~ **parts** of verb, those from which all others can be deduced. **4.** *n.* Head, ruler, superior; head of some schools, colleges, and universities, whence ~SHIP *n.*; leading performer in concert, play, etc.; ||civil servant of grade below Secretaries. **5.** Person for whom another acts as agent etc. (*I must consult my principal*); person directly responsible for crime, either (~ **in the first degree**) as actual perpetrator or (~ **in the second degree**) as aiding; person for whom another is surety; combatant in duel (opp. *second*). **6.** Main rafter supporting purlins; main girder. **7.** Capital sum as distinguished from interest or from income. **8.** Organ stop sounding octave above diapason. [ME f. OF, f. L *principalis* first, original (as PRINCE; see -AL)]

prĭncĭpă′lĭtȳ *n.* **1.** Government of a prince; State ruled by a prince; ||**the P~**, Wales. **2.** (in *pl.*) Fifth ORDER[1] of ninefold celestial hierarchy. [ME, f. OF *principalité* f. LL *principalitas -tatis* (as prec.; see -ITY)]

prĭ′ncĭpallȳ *adv.* For the most part, chiefly. [f. PRINCIPAL + -LY[2]]

prĭ′ncĭpate *n.* **1.** (Rom. Hist.) Rule of early emperors while some republican forms were retained. **2.** State ruled by a prince. [ME, f. OF *principat* or f. L *principatus* first place (as PRINCE; see -ATE[1])]

prĭ′ncĭple *n.* **1.** Fundamental source, primary element, (*held water to be the first principle of all things*). **2.** Fundamental truth as basis of reasoning etc. (*arguing from first principles*); (Phys.) general law (*Archimedes' principle*; *principle of relativity*); general law as guide to action (*moral, conservative, principles*; *a dangerous principle*); **in ~,** as regards fundamentals but not necessarily in detail. **3.** (in *pl.* or collect. *sing.*) Personal code of right conduct (*a man of high principle*; *has ability but no principles*; *principle is everything*); **on ~,** from settled moral motive (*I refuse on principle*). **4.** Law of nature forming basis for construction or working of machine etc. (*in all these instruments the principle is the same*). **5.** (Chem.)

Constituent of a substance, esp. one giving rise to some quality etc., (*bitter principle of cinchona bark*). [ME, f. AF **principle*, OF *principe* f. L *principium* source, in pl. foundations (as PRINCE)]

prĭ'ncipled (-peld) *a.* Based on or having (esp. praiseworthy) principles of behaviour. [f. prec. + -ED²]

prĭnk *v.* **1.** *v.t.* Make (one*self* etc.) smart; dress one*self up*; (of bird) preen. **2.** *v.i.* Dress oneself up. [16th c.; cf. PRANK²]

print¹ *n.* **1.** Indentation in or mark on surface preserving the form left by pressure of some body (*fingerprint*; *footprint*); hence ~'LESS *a.* **2.** Printed cotton fabric. **3.** Language embodied in printed form; printed lettering (*large*, SMALL, *clear*, *print*). **4.** State of being printed (*book is* **in** ~, (1) in printed form, (2) available from the publisher, not **out of print** (all copies sold); **appear in** ~, have one's work published; **rush into** ~, publish book, write to newspaper etc., on insufficient grounds); printed publication, esp. newspaper; quantity of a book etc. printed at one time. **5.** Picture or design printed from block or plate; (Photog.) picture produced from negative. **6.** **~-seller,** dealer in engravings etc.; **~-shop,** his shop; **~-works,** factory where cotton fabrics are printed. [ME, f. OF *priente*, *preinte*, fem. p.p. (as n.) of *preindre* press f. L *premere*]

print² *v.t.* **1.** Impress, stamp, (surface, e.g. of butter or wax, *with* seal, die, etc.; a mark or figure *on* or *in* yielding or other surface); (fig.) impress (idea, scene, etc., *on* mind, memory). **2.** Produce (book, picture, etc., or abs.) by applying inked types, blocks, or plates, to paper, vellum, etc.; (of author or editor) cause (book, MS.) to be thus produced; express or publish in print (*not bound to print every opinion you hold*); write (words, letters, or abs.) without joining, in imitation of typography; ~ **out,** (of computer etc.) produce output in printed form; **~-out,** (production of) such output. **3.** Mark (textile fabric) with decorative design in colours; transfer (coloured design) from paper etc. to unglazed surface of pottery. **4.** (Photog.) ~ (**out, off**), produce (picture) by transmission of light through negative. **5.** **~ed circuit,** electric circuit with thin strips of conductor on flat insulating sheet, usu. made by printing-like process. **6.** Hence ~'ABLE *a.* [ME *prente*, *printe*, f. prec.]

prĭ'nter *n.* In vbl senses; one who prints books, magazines, advertising matter, etc.; owner of printing business; printing instrument; **P~s' Bible** (with *Printers* for *Princes*, Ps. 119:161); *printer's* DEVIL¹; **~'s mark,** printer's device used as trade mark; **~'s pie,** = PIE³ *n.*; *printers'* REAM¹; so ***prĭ'nt**ERY (3) *n.* [f. prec. + -ER¹]

prĭ'ntĭng *n.* In vbl senses; impression of a book; **~-ink, ~-press,** (for printing on paper etc. from types etc.). [ME, f. PRINT² + -ING¹]

prī'or¹ *n.* **1.** Superior officer of religious house or order, (in abbey) officer next under abbot; so ~ESS¹ *n.* **2.** Hence or cogn. ~ATE¹ (1), ~SHIP, *ns.* [OE, & ME f. OF *pri(o)ur*, f. L *prior* (see foll.), as n.]

prī'or² *a.* & *adv.* **1.** *a.* Earlier; coming before in time, order, or importance, (*to*); ~ **art,** (Patents) relevant methods etc. known before the disclosure of an invention. **2.** *adv.* ~ **to,** before (*existing prior to his appointment*). [L, = former, elder, compar. of OL *pri* (L *prae*) before]

priŏ'rĭtȳ *n.* Being earlier or antecedent; precedence in rank etc.; an interest having prior claim to consideration. [ME, f. OF *priorité* f. med. L *prioritas -tatis* f. L *prior* (as prec.); see -ITY]

prī'orȳ *n.* Monastery or nunnery governed by prior(ess); **alien ~, ~ alien,** (dependent on abbey in another country). [ME, f. AF *priorie*, med. L *prioria* (as PRIOR; see -Y¹)]

||**prise.** See PRIZE³.

prĭ'sm *n.* Solid figure whose two ends are similar, equal, and parallel rectilinear figures, and whose sides are parallelograms (**pentagonal** etc. ~, with five etc. sides); transparent body of this form, usu. triangular, with refracting surfaces at acute angle with each other; ~ **binoculars** (in which triangular prisms are used to shorten the instrument); PRUNE¹*s and prism(s)*; hence **prĭ'sm**AL (-z-) *a.* [f. LL f. Gk *prisma prismatos* thing sawn (*prizō* saw)]

prĭsmă'tĭc (-z-) *a.* **1.** Of or like a prism; ~ **binoculars,** = PRISM *binoculars*; ~ **compass,** hand-compass used in survey work, with attached prism enabling the dial to be read while the sight is taken. **2.** (Of colours) formed, distributed, etc., (as if) by transparent prism. **3.** Hence **prĭsmă'tĭ**CALLY (-z-) *adv.* [f. F *prismatique* f. Gk *prisma* (see prec., -IC)]

prĭ'smoid (-z-) *n.* Body like prism, with similar but unequal parallel polygonal ends; hence ~AL (-oi'-) *a.* [f. PRISM + -OID]

prĭ'son (-z-) *n.*, & *v.t.* **1.** *n.* Place in which person is kept in captivity, esp. building to which person is legally committed while awaiting trial or for punishment; custody, confinement, (*in prison*); **~-bird,** = GAOL*bird*; **~-breaking,** escape from prison; **~-house,** (usu. rhet.) prison; ~ **without bars,** area to which offenders are confined although without physical restraints. **2.** *v.t.* (poet. or dial.) Imprison. [ME f. OF *prisun*, *-on*, f. L *prensio -onis* (*prehensio* f. *prehendere -hens-* lay hold of; see -ION)]

prĭ'soner (-zn-) *n.* Person kept in prison; (fig.) person or thing confined by illness, another's grasp, etc.; ~ (**at the bar**), person in custody on criminal charge and on trial; *prisoner of* CONSCIENCE; ~ **of State, state ~,** (confined for political reasons); ~ (**of war**), one who has been captured in war; **take** (person) ~, seize and hold as prisoner; **~s' base,** game played by two parties of boys etc., each occupying distinct base or home. [ME, f. AF; = OF *prisonier* (as prec.; see -ER² (2))]

prĭ'ss|ȳ *a.* Prim, prudish; hence ~ĬLY² *adv.* [perh. f. PRIM + SISSY]

prĭ'stīne (*or* -ēn) *a.* Ancient, primitive, old and unspoiled; fresh as if new. [f. L *pristinus* former; see -INE²]

prĭ'thee (-dhĭ) *int.* (arch.) Pray, please, (*tell me, prithee*). [= (*I*) *pray thee*]

prĭ'vacȳ *n.* Being withdrawn from society or public interest (*lived in absolute privacy*); being alone and undisturbed; avoidance of publicity (*in such matters privacy is impossible*). [ME, f. PRIVATE + -ACY]

privat-docent, -dozent, (prēvaht dōtsĕ'nt) *n.* (In German university) private teacher or lecturer recognized by university but not on salaried staff. [G]

prī'vate *a.* & *n.* **1.** *a.* (Of person) not holding public office or official position. **2.** Kept or removed from public knowledge or observation (*the matter was kept private*; *had private reasons*; *we are quite private here*). **3.** Not open to the public (*private carriage, door*; *news came through private channels*). **4.** One's own (*my private property*); individual, personal, not affecting the community, (*motives of private malice*). **5.** Confidential (*asked for some private conversation*; *this is for your private ear*). **6.** (Of place) retired, secluded. **7. In ~,** privately, in private company or life. **8. ~ act, ~ bill, ~ statute,** (of legislation affecting individual or corporation only); ||**~ company** (with restricted membership and limited transfer of shares); *private* DETECTIVE; ~ **enterprise,** business(es) not under State control, (fig.) individual initiative; ~ **eye,** (colloq.) private detective; ~ **hotel** (not necessarily accepting all comers); ~ **house,** dwelling-house of private person (opp. shop, office, or public building); ~ **law** (relating to private persons and property); ~ **life** (as private person, not as official, public performer, etc.); ~ **means,** income from investments etc., not earned as salary or wages; ~ **member,** (in House of Commons etc.) one not holding Government appointment; ~ **parts,** genitals; ||~ **patient,** patient treated by doctor otherwise than under National Health Service; ~ **practice** (of doctor etc. who is not only an employee); ~ **press,** printing establishment operated by private person(s) not primarily for profit and usu. on small scale; ~ **school,** ||school supported wholly by payment of fees, usu. for owner's profit, *school not supported mainly by State; *private* SECRETARY; ~ **soldier,** ordinary soldier other than officers (*and recruits); ~ **view** (of picture etc. exhibition before it is opened to the public); *private* WAR[1]; *private* WIRE; ~ **wrong,** offence against individual but not against society as a whole. **9.** Hence ~LY[2] (-tlĭ) *adv.* **10.** *n.* Private soldier (*~ **first class,** soldier ranking above ordinary private but below officers); (in *pl.*) genitals. [ME, f. L *privatus*, orig. p.p. of *privare* deprive; see -ATE[2]]

prīvateer' *n.* Armed vessel owned and officered by private persons holding commission from government (*letters of* MARQUE[1]) and authorized to use it against hostile nation esp. in capture of merchant shipping, whence ~ING[1] (1) *n.*; ~(**sman**), commander or (in *pl.*) crew of this. [f. prec. + -EER, after *volunteer*]

privā'tion *n.* Loss or absence (*of* quality; *cold is the privation of heat*); lack of the comforts or necessaries of life (*died of privation*; *suffered many privations*). [ME, f. L *privatio* (as PRIVATE; see -ATION)]

prĭ'vatĭve *a.* Consisting in or marked by the loss or removal or absence of some quality or attribute; (of term) denoting privation or absence of quality etc.; (Gram., of particle etc.) expressing privation, as Gk *a-* = 'not-'; hence ~LY[2] (-vlĭ) *adv.* [f. F *privatif -ive* or f. L *privativus* (as prec.; see -IVE)]

prĭ'vĕt *n.* Plant of genus *Ligustrum*, esp. bushy evergreen shrub (*Ligustrum vulgare*) with smooth dark-green leaves, small white flowers, and small shining black berries, much used for hedges; ~-**hawk,** large species of moth depositing eggs on privet. [16th c., of unkn. orig.]

prĭ'vĭlĕge *n.*, & *v.t.* **1.** *n.* Right, advantage, or immunity, belonging to person, class, or office, esp. freedom of members of legislative assembly when speaking therein; special advantage or benefit (*to converse with him was a privilege*); monopoly or patent granted to individual, corporation, etc.; *(St. Exch.) option. **2.** *v.t.* Invest with privilege; allow (person *to* do) as privilege; exempt (person *from* liability etc.). **3.** Hence **prĭ'vĭlĕg**ED[1] (-ĭjd) *a.* [ME; n. f. AF *privilegie, OF *privilege* f. L *privilegium* bill or law affecting an individual (*privus* private, *lex legis* law); v. f. OF *privilegier* f. med. L *privilegiare* f. L *privilegium*]

prĭ'vĭtў *n.* **1.** (Law). Relation between two parties that is recognized by law, e.g. that of blood, lease, service. **2.** Being privy (*to* designs etc.). [ME, f. OF *priveté* f. med. L *privitas -tatis* f. L *privus* private; see -ITY]

prĭ'vў *a.* & *n.* **1.** *a.* (Of thing, place, etc.) hidden, secluded; (of action) secret, whence **prĭ'vĭ**LY[2] *adv.*; ~ **to,** in the secret of (person's plans etc.). **2. P~ Council,** sovereign's or governor-general's private counsellors, (in U.K.) body of advisers chosen by sovereign (now chiefly as personal honour, most functions being performed by Cabinet, committees, etc.) together with princes of the blood, archbishops, etc.; ~ **councillor, counsellor,** private adviser, esp. member of Privy Council; ~ **parts,** (arch.) genitals; ||~ **purse,** allowance from public revenue for monarch's private expenses, keeper of this; ||~ **seal,** seal formerly affixed to documents that are afterwards to pass, or that do not require, the Great Seal; ||**Lord P~ Seal,** senior Cabinet Minister without official duties (formerly keeper of privy seal). **3.** *n.* (arch. or U.S.) Lavatory. **4.** (Law). Person having a part or interest in any action, matter, or thing. [ME, f. OF *privé* f. L *privatus* PRIVATE]

prize[1] *n.*, & *v.t.* **1.** *n.* Reward given as symbol of victory or superiority to student in school or college who excels in attainments, to successful competitor in athletic contest, to exhibitor of best specimen of manufactured products, works of art, etc., in exhibition; (fig.) anything striven for or worth striving for (*many prizes in the Church*; *missed all the great prizes of life*); money or money's worth offered for competition in lottery etc. **2.** *a.* To which prize is adjudged in show, competition, etc., (*prize bull*, *poem*, etc.); supremely excellent or outstanding of its kind. **3.** ||~ **fellowship** (given as reward for eminence in examination), ~ **fellow,** holder of this; ~-**fight,** boxing-match for money; ~-**fighter,** ~-**fighting,** (one who engages in) professional boxing; ~'**man,** winner of (often specified) prize; ~-**money** (offered as prize); ~-**ring,** enclosed area (now usu. square) for, or (fig.) practice of, prize-fighting. **4.** *v.t.* Value highly (*we prize liberty more than life*). [n. ME, var. of PRICE; v. ME, f. OF *pris-* st. of *preisier* PRAISE]

prize[2] *n.*, & *v.t.* **1.** *n.* Ship or property captured at sea in virtue of rights of war; ~-**court,** department of admiralty court concerned with prizes; ~-**money** (realized by sale of prize, esp. Hist., such money as awarded to crew of capturing ship); **make ~ of,** seize (cargo, ship, etc.) thus; **become** (*lawful* etc.) ~, be thus seized. **2.** (fig.) Find, windfall, (*see what a prize I have found!*). **3.** *v.t.* Make prize of. [ME f. OF *prise* taking, booty, fem. p.p. (as n.) of *prendre* f. L *prehendere -hens-* seize; later identified w. PRIZE[1]]

prize[3], **prise** (-z), *v.t.*, & *n.* **1.** *v.t.* Force (lid etc. *up*, *out*, box etc. *open*) by leverage. **2.** *n.* Leverage, purchase. [v. f. n., ME & OF *prise* levering instrument (as prec.)]

prō[1] *a.*, *n.*, & *prep.* **1.** *a.* ~ **and con**(**tra**), (of arguments or reasons) for and against, on both sides. **2.** *n.* (in *pl.*) ~**s and con**(**tra**)**s,** reasons for and against. **3.** *prep.* ~ **and con**(**tra**), for and against. [L, = for, on behalf of]

prō[2] *n.* (*pl.* ~s). (colloq.) A professional; ~-**am,** involving professionals and amateurs. [abbr.]

prō-[1] *pref.* denoting: **1.** Substitute(d) for, as: ~-**cathe'dral** *a.* & *n.*, (church) used as substitute for cathedral; ||~-**pro'ctor,** university proctor's assistant or deputy. **2.** (Person) favouring or siding with (opp. ANTI-), as: *pro-Communist*, *pro-Market*. **3.** Forwards (*proclaim*, *produce*). **4.** Forwards and downwards (*prolapse*, *prostrate*). **5.** Onwards (*proceed*, *progress*). **6.** In front of (*prohibit*, *protect*). [f. L *pro* in front (of), for, on behalf of, instead of, on account of]

pro-[2] *pref.* Before (in time, place, order, etc.) (*problem*, *proboscis*, *prodrome*, *prognathous*, *prophet*, *protasis*). [f. Gk *pro* before]

P.R.O. *abbr.* Public RECORD[2] Office; public relations officer.

prō'a, pra(h)u (prah'ōō), *n.* Malay boat, esp. with large triangular sail and with canoe-like outrigger. [f. Malay *prā(h)ū*]

prŏbabĭ'lĭor|ĭsm *n.* Ethical doctrine that the side on which evidence preponderates ought to be followed (cf. foll.); so ~IST (2) *n.* [f. L *probabilior* more PROBABLE + -ISM]

prŏ'babĭl|ĭsm *n.* Ethical doctrine that where authorities differ any course may be followed for which a recognized Doctor of the Church can be cited (cf. prec.); theory that there is no certain knowledge, but may be grounds of belief sufficient for practical life; so ~IST (2) *n.* [f. as PROBABLE + -ISM]

prŏbabĭ'lĭtў *n.* **1.** Quality of being probable; **in all** ~, most probably. **2.** Likelihood (*there is no probability of his coming*). **3.** (Most) probable event (*what are the probabilities?*; *the probability is that he will come*). **4.** (Math.) Extent to which an event is likely to occur, measured by the ratio of the favourable cases to the whole number of cases possible (*from a bag containing 3 red balls and 7 white balls, the probability of a red ball's being drawn first is 3/10*). [f. F *probabilité* or f. L *probabilitas* (as foll.; see -ITY)]

prŏ'bable *a.* & *n.* **1.** *a.* That may be expected to happen or prove true, likely, (*reckon the probable cost*; *it is probable that he forgot*; *gives a probable account of the matter*); hence **prŏ'bab**LY[2] *adv.* **2.** *n.* A probable candidate, member of team, etc. (cf. POSSIBLE 3). [ME f. OF, or f. L *probabilis* (*probare* prove; see -ABLE)]

prō'bănd *n.* Person forming starting-point for genetic study of family etc. [f. L *probandus*, gerundive of *probare* test]

prō'băng *n.* Surgeon's flexible strip of whalebone etc. with sponge, button, etc., at end for introducing into throat. [17th c., named *provang* by inventor; orig. unkn., perh. alt. after *probe*]

prō'bāte (or -*at*) *n.*, & *v.t.* **1.** *n.* Official proving of will; verified copy of will with certificate as handed to executors; ~ **duty,** (U.S. or Hist.) tax on personal property of deceased testator. **2.** *v.t.* *Obtain probate of (will). [ME, f. L *probatum* neut. p.p. (as n.) of *probare* PROVE]

probā'tion *n.* Testing of conduct or character of person, esp. of candidate for membership in religious body etc. (**on** ~, undergoing this before full admission etc.); moral trial or discipline; (Law) system of withholding sentence on selected offenders during good behaviour under supervision of person (~ **officer**) acting as friend and adviser (*was put on probation*). [ME f. OF, or f. L *probatio* (as PROVE; see -ATION)]

probā'tion|arў *a.* **1.** Of, serving for, done in the way of, probation; so ~AL *a.* **2.** Undergoing probation. [f. prec. + -ARY[1]]

probā'tioner *n.* Person on probation, e.g. hospital nurse at early stage of training; offender under probation; hence ~SHIP (1) *n.* [f. PROBATION + -ER[1]]

prō'batĭve *a.* Affording proof, evidential. [f. L *probativus* (as PROVE; see -IVE)]

prōbe *n.*, & *v.t.* **1.** *n.* Blunt-ended surgical instrument usu. of metal for exploring wound etc.; unmanned exploratory spacecraft transmitting information about its environment; (fig., f. v.) penetrating investigation. **2.** *v.t.* Explore (wound, part of body) with probe; penetrate (thing) with sharp instrument; (fig.) examine closely, sound, (person, motive, report, etc.); hence ~'ABLE (-ba-) *a.* [f. LL *proba* proof, in med. L = examination, f. L *probare* test]

prŏ'bĭt *n.* (Statistics). Unit of probability based on deviation from mean of standard distribution. [f. *prob*ability un*it*]

prŏ'bĭtў *n.* Uprightness, honesty. [f. F *probité* or f. L *probitas* (*probus* good; see -ITY)]

prŏ'blem *n.* **1.** Doubtful or difficult question (*how to prevent it is a problem*; *the problem of ventilation*); (*attrib.*) ~ **child** (difficult to control, unruly), ~ **play, novel,** etc., (in which social or other problem is treated). **2.** Thing hard to understand (*his whole conduct is a problem to me*). **3.** (Geom.) proposition in which something has to be constructed (cf. THEOREM); (Phys. & Math.) inquiry starting from given conditions to investigate a fact, result, or law; (Chess, Bridge, etc.) arrangement of men, cards, etc., in which solver is challenged to accomplish specified result, often under prescribed conditions. [ME, f. OF *probleme* or f. L f. Gk *problēma* -*matos* f. PRO[2](*ballō* throw)]

prŏblemă't|ĭc(al) *adjs.* Doubtful, questionable, (*its success is problematical*; *the whole question is problematical*); (Logic) enunciating or supporting what is possible but not necessarily true; hence ~ICALLY *adv.* [f. F *problématique* or f. LL f. Gk *problēmatikos* (as prec.; see -IC)]

prŏ'blemĭst *n.* One who studies or composes (esp. chess) problems. [f. PROBLEM + -IST]

prŏbŏscĭ'dean *a.* & *n.* **1.** *a.* Having a proboscis; of or like a proboscis. **2.** *a.* & *n.* (Mammal) of the order Proboscidea, containing elephants and their extinct allies. [f. mod. L *Proboscidea* (as PROBOSCIS; see -A 2) + -AN]

prŏbŏscĭ'dĭan *a.* & *n.* = prec. [f. foll. + -AN]

probŏ'scĭs *n.* Elephant's trunk; long flexible snout of tapir etc.; elongated part of mouth of some insects; sucking organ in some worms; (joc.) human nose; ~ **monkey** (with nose projecting far beyond mouth); so **probŏscĭdĭ'**FEROUS, **prŏbŏscĭ'dĭ**FORM, *adjs.* [L *proboscis -cidis* f. Gk *proboskis* f. PRO[2](*boskō* feed)]

procē'dur|e (-dy*er*) *n.* Proceeding; mode of conducting business (esp. in parliament) or legal action; hence ~AL *a.*, of or relating to procedure. [f. F *procédure* (as foll.; see -URE)]

procee'd *v.i.* **1.** Go on, make one's way, (*to* place); go on (*with* or *in* action, investigation, remarks, etc.; *to* another subject, *to* do); adopt course of action (*how shall we proceed?*); (abs.) go on to say (*'in either case', he proceeded, 'our course is clear'*). **2.** Take legal proceedings *against* person; ||~ **to** (take) *the degree of M.A.*, ~ (take degree of) *M.A.*; (of action) be carried on (further), take place, (*the case, the play, will now proceed*). **3.** Come forth, issue, originate, (*sobs heard to proceed from her bed*; *volumes proceed from the Press*; *exertions proceed from a false hope*). [ME, f. OF *proceder* f. L PRO[1](*cedere cess-* go)]

procee'dĭng *n.* In vbl senses; action, piece of conduct, (*a high-handed proceeding*); **legal** ~**s,** (steps taken in) legal action; (in *pl.*) published report of discussions or conference (*Proceedings of the Royal Society* etc.). [f. prec. + -ING[1]]

prō'ceeds (-z) *n. pl.* Money produced by sale, performance, etc., (*the proceeds will be devoted to charity*). [pl. of obs. *proceed* n. f. PROCEED]

prŏcĕleusmă'tĭc *a.* & *n.* (Pros.) (Foot) of four short syllables. [f. LL f. Gk *prokeleusmatikos* f. *prokeleusma* exhortation f. PRO[2](*keleuō* command) incite; see -IC]

prō'cĕss[1] *n.*, & *v.t.* **1.** *n.* Progress, course; **in ~ of** *construction* etc., being constructed etc.; **in ~ of time,** as time goes on. **2.** Course of action, proceeding, esp. series of operations in manufacture, printing, photography, etc. (~ **heat, steam,** etc., those got as by-products of manufacturing processes); natural or involuntary operation, series of changes. **3.** Action at law, formal commencement of this, summons or

For other words in *pro-* see PRO-.

writ (~**-server,** sheriff's officer). **4.** (Anat., Zool., & Bot.) Natural appendage, outgrowth, protuberance. **5.** *v.t.* Treat (material, food esp. to prevent decay) by particular process. **6.** Hence ~ER¹, ~OR, *ns.* [ME f. OF *proces* f. L *processus* (as PROCEED)]

procĕ'ss² *v.i.* (colloq.) Walk in procession. [back form. f. foll.]

procĕ'ssion (-sh*o*n) *n.* & *v.* **1.** *n.* Proceeding of body of persons (or of boats etc.) in orderly succession, esp. as religious ceremony or political demonstration or on festive occasion, (*go, walk, in procession*); body of persons doing this; (fig.) race in which no competitor is able to overtake another; (Theol.) emanation of the Holy Spirit; ~ **moth** (of genus *Thaumetopoea*, with caterpillars that go in processions, whence ~ARY¹ *a.*). **2.** *v.i.* Go in procession; hence ~IST (1) *n.* **3.** *v.t.* Walk along (street) or around (land) in procession. [ME f. OF, f. L *processio -onis* (as PROCEED; see -ION)]

procĕ'ssional (-sho-) *a.* & *n.* **1.** *a.* Of processions; used, carried, sung, in processions. **2.** *n.* Processional hymn; (Eccl.) office-book of processional hymns etc. [f. med. L *processionalis* a., *-ale* n., (as prec.; see -AL)]

procès-verb|al (prŏsāvārbah'l) *n.* (*pl.* **~aux** *pr.* -bō'). Written report of proceedings, minutes; (Fr. Law) written statement of facts in support of charge. [F]

prō'chronism (-k-) *n.* Referring of event etc. to an earlier than the true date (*races held in June and called by a prochronism the Mays*). [f. PRO-² + Gk *khronos* time + -ISM]

proclai'm *v.t.* Announce officially (thing, *that*); declare (war, peace); announce officially the accession of (sovereign); declare (person, thing) officially to be (a traitor etc.); declare publicly or openly (thing, *that*); make known as being (*his accent proclaimed him a Scot*); (arch.) place (district etc.) under legal restrictions, prohibit (meeting etc.), by declaration; so **prŏclama**A'TION *n.*, **proclă'mat**ORY *a.* [ME *proclame* f. L PRO¹*clamare* cry out; cf. CLAIM¹]

procli't|ic *a.* & *n.* (Gram.) (Monosyllable) closely attached in pronunciation to following word and having itself no accent, e.g. *at* in *at home*; hence ~ICALLY *adv.* [f. mod. L *procliticus* f. Gk PRO²*klinō* lean forward, after LL *encliticus* (see ENCLITIC)]

procli'vity *n.* Tendency (*to* or *towards* action or habit, esp. bad one; *to* do). [f. L *proclivitas* f. PRO¹(*clivis* f. *clivus* slope) inclined; see -ITY]

prōcŏ'nsul *n.* **1.** (Rom. Hist.) Governor of province, in later republic usu. an ex-consul. **2.** ||(rhet.) Governor of modern colony etc. **3.** Deputy consul. **4.** Hence or cogn. ~AR¹ *a.*, ~ATE¹ (1) *n.*, (-ūl-), ~SHIP *n.* [ME f. L, earlier *pro consule* (one acting) for consul]

procră'stin|āte *v.i.* Defer action, be dilatory; hence or cogn. ~A'TION, **~āt**OR, *ns.*, **~āt**IVE, **~āt**ORY, *adjs.* [f. L PRO¹(*crastinare* f. *crastinus* of tomorrow f. *cras* tomorrow) + -ATE³]

prō'crė|āte *v.t.* Bring into existence by natural process of reproduction, generate, (offspring, or abs.); hence or cogn. ~ANT, **~āt**IVE, *adjs.*, ~A'TION *n.* [f. L PRO¹(*creare* CREATE) + -ATE³]

Procrŭ'stėan *a.* Seeking to enforce uniformity by violent methods. [f. Gk *Prokroustēs*, lit. stretcher (*prokrouō* beat out), name of legendary robber who fitted victims to his bed by stretching or lopping; see -AN]

prŏ'cto- *comb. form.* Rectum, as *procto*SCOPE. [f. Gk *prōktos* anus + -O-]

prŏ'ctor *n.* **1.** ||(At Oxford & Cambridge) each of two university officers (**senior, junior,** ~) appointed annually and having various functions esp. discipline of persons *in statu pupillari*; *supervisor of students in examination etc. **2.** (Law). Person managing causes in court (now chiefly Eccl.) that administers civil or canon law; ||**Queen's** or **King's P~**, official who has right to intervene in probate, divorce, and nullity cases when collusion or suppression of facts is alleged. **3.** Representative of clergy in Church of England convocation. **4.** Hence **prŏctŏr'**IAL *a.*, ~IZE (1) *v.t.*, ~SHIP *n.* [ME, syncopation of PROCURATOR]

procŭ'mbent *a.* Lying on the face, prostrate; (Bot.) growing along the ground. [f. L PRO¹-(*cumbere* lay oneself) fall forwards; see -ENT]

prŏcūrā'tion *n.* **1.** Procuring, obtaining, bringing about; so **procūr'**AL 2, **procūr'**ANCE, *ns.* **2.** Function or authorized action of attorney; ||(Eccl.) provision of entertainment for bishop or other visitor by incumbent etc., now commuted to money payment; (fee for) negotiation of loan. **3.** Procurer's trade or offence. [ME f. OF, or f. L *procuratio* (as PROCURE; see -ATION)]

prŏ'cūrātor *n.* **1.** (Rom. Hist.) Treasury officer in imperial province. **2.** Agent, proxy, esp. one who has power of attorney; ~ **fiscal,** coroner and public prosecutor of district in Scotland; ~ **general,** high-ranking procurator, esp. ||head of law department of Treasury. **3.** Hence **procūratŏr'**IAL *a.*, ~SHIP *n.* [ME, f. OF *procurateur* or f. L *procurator* agent, collector in province (as PROCURE; see -OR)]

prŏ'cūratorў *n.* (Law). Authorization to act for another (*letters of procuratory*). [f. med. L *procuratorium* neut. (as n.) of LL *procuratorius* (as prec.; see -ORY)]

procūr'e *v.* **1.** *v.t.* Obtain by care or effort, acquire, (*must procure you a copy*; *will procure a copy for you*; *cannot procure employment*); bring about (*procured his dismissal*). **2.** *v.i.* & *t.* Act as procurer or procuress (of). **3.** Hence **procūr'**ABLE *a.*, ~MENT (-ūr'm-) *n.* [ME, f. OF *procurer* f. L PRO¹(*curare* see to) take care of, manage]

procūr'|er *n.* In vbl senses; man or woman who obtains women for gratification of another's lust, whence ~ESS¹ *n.* [ME f. AF *procurour*, OF *procureur* f. L PROCURATOR]

prŏd *v.* (**-dd-**) & *n.* **1.** *v.t.* Poke with finger, pointed instrument, end of stick, etc.; (fig.) stimulate to action. **2.** *v.i.* Make prodding motion *at*. **3.** *n.* Poke, thrust; stimulus to action; pointed instrument. [16th c., perh. imit.]

prōdėli'sion (-zh*o*n) *n.* Elision of initial vowel (as in *I'm* for *I am*). [f. L *prod-* = PRO-¹ + ELISION]

prŏ'digal *a.* & *n.* Recklessly wasteful (person); lavish *of*; ~ (**son**), repentant wastrel, returned wanderer, etc. (Luke 15:11–32); hence or cogn. ~ITY (-ă'l-) *n.*, ~IZE *v.t.*, spend lavishly, ~LY² *adv.* [f. LL **prodigalis* f. L *prodigus* lavish; see -AL]

prodi'gious (-j*u*s) *a.* Marvellous, amazing; enormous; abnormal; hence ~LY² *adv.*, ~NESS *n.* [f. L *prodigiosus* (as foll.; see -OUS)]

prŏ'digў *n.* Marvellous thing, esp. one out of the ordinary course of nature; wonderful example *of* (some quality); person endowed with surprising qualities or abilities, esp. precocious child. [f. L *prodigium* portent]

prŏ'drōme *n.* Preliminary book or treatise (*to* another); (Path.) premonitory symptom (*of*), whence **prŏ'drom**AL, **prodrŏ'm**IC, *adjs.* [F, f. mod. L f. Gk PRO²(*dromos* running) precursor]

prŏ'dūce¹ *n.* Amount produced, yield, esp. in assay of ore; what is produced, esp. agricultural and natural products collectively (*dairy produce*); result (*of* labour, efforts, etc.). [f. foll.]

produ'ce² *v.t.* **1.** Bring forward for inspection or consideration (*will produce evidence, witnesses, reasons*; *produce your tickets*). **2.** Bring (play, performer, book, etc.) before the public. **3.** (Geom.) Extend, continue, (line *to* a point). **4.** Manufacture (goods) from raw materials etc. **5.** Bring about, cause, (a reaction, a sensation, etc.); bring into existence; (of land etc.) yield (agricultural etc. produce); (of animal or plant) bear, yield, (offspring, fruit). **6.** So **prodū'**CIBLE *a.* [ME, f. L PRO¹(*ducere duct-* lead)]

prodū'cer *n.* In vbl senses; (Econ.) one who produces article for use (opp. *consumer*); person generally responsible for production of a film or play (apart from direction of the acting); ||director of play or broadcast performance; ~ **gas,** combustible gas formed by passing air, or air and steam, through red-hot carbon. [f. prec. + -ER¹]

prŏ'duct *n.* Thing or substance produced by natural process or manufacture; result (*the product of his labours*); (Math.) quantity obtained by multiplying quantities together. [ME, f. L *productum*, neut. p.p. (as n.) of *producere* PRODUCE²]

prodŭ'ction *n.* **1.** Producing; being produced; being manufactured, esp. in large quantities (*go into production*). **2.** Total yield; thing produced, esp. literary or artistic work. [ME f. OF, f. L *productio -onis* (as prec.; see -ION)]

prodŭ'ctĭve *a.* Producing, tending to produce, (*productive of figs, of great annoyance*); (Econ.) producing commodities of exchangeable value (*productive labour*); producing abundantly (*a productive soil, mine, writer*); hence ~LY² (-vlĭ) *adv.*, ~NESS (-vn-) *n.* [f. F *productif -ive* or f. LL *productivus* (as PRODUCT; see -IVE)]

prŏductĭ'vĭtў *n.* Capacity to produce; quality or state of being productive; production per unit of effort; effectiveness of productive effort, esp. in industry. [f. prec. + -ITY]

prō'ėm *n.* Preface or preamble to book or speech; beginning, prelude; hence **prōē'm**IAL *a.* [ME, f. OF *pro(h)eme* or f. L f. Gk *prooimion* prelude (as PRO-², *oimē* song)]

prŏf *n.* (colloq.) Professor. [abbr.]

Prof. *abbr.* Professor.

profā'ne¹ *v.t.* Treat (sacred thing) with irreverence or disregard; violate, pollute, (what is entitled to respect); so **prŏfan**A'TION *n.* [ME *prophane* f. L *profanare* (as foll.)]

profā'ne² *a.* **1.** Not belonging to what is sacred or biblical (*profane history, literature, writer*); not initiated into religious rites or any esoteric knowledge; (of rite etc.) heathen. **2.** Irreverent, blasphemous; so **profă'n**ITY *n.* **3.** Hence ~LY² (-nlĭ) *adv.*, ~NESS (-n-n-) *n.* [ME f. OF *prophane* or f. med. L *prophanus* f. L PRO¹(*fanus* f. *fanum* temple) before (i.e. outside) the temple, not sacred]

profĕ'ss *v.* **1.** *v.t.* Lay claim to (quality, feeling), pretend (*to* be or do), (*they profess extreme regret; does not profess to be a scholar*). **2.** Openly declare (*they profess themselves quite content*). **3.** Affirm one's faith in or allegiance to (religion, God, Christ); receive into religious order under vows. **4.** Make (law, medicine, flute-playing, the flute, etc.) one's profession or business. **5.** Teach (subject) as professor. **6.** *v.i.* Perform duties of a professor. [ME, f. L PRO¹(*fitēri fess-* = *fatēri* confess) declare publicly]

profĕ'ssed (-st) *a.* Self-acknowledged (*a professed Christian*); alleged, ostensible, whence **profĕ'ssėd**LY² *adv.*; claiming to be duly qualified (*a professed anatomist*); ~ **monk, nun,** (who has taken vows of religious order). [ME, p.p. of prec.]

profĕ'ssion (-shon) *n.* **1.** Declaration, avowal, (*accept my sincere professions of regard*); declaration of belief in a religion; vow made on entering, fact of being in, a religious order. **2.** Vocation or calling, esp. one that involves some branch of advanced learning or science (*the military profession; a carpenter by profession*); **the learned ~s** (divinity, law, medicine); **the oldest ~,** prostitution; hence ~LESS *a.* **3.** Body of persons engaged in a profession; **the ~,** (Theatr. sl.) actors and actresses. [ME f. OF, f. L *professio -onis* (as PROFESS; see -ION)]

profĕ'ssional (-shon-) *a.* & *n.* **1.** *a.* Of, belonging to, connected with, a profession, (*professional men, etiquette, jealousy*); ~ *politician, agitator*, etc., (making a trade of politics etc.); ~ *boxer, golfer*, etc., (performing for monetary reward; opp. *amateur*); hence ~LY² *adv.* **2.** *n.* Professional person, esp. professional golfer etc. [f. prec. + -AL]

profĕ'ssional|ism (-shon-) *n.* Qualities or typical features of a profession or professionals; so ~IZE (3) *v.t.* [f. prec. + -ISM]

profĕ'ssor *n.* **1.** One who makes profession (esp. of a religion). **2.** Teacher of high rank, esp. holder of a chair or *senior teaching appointment in university, whence ~ATE¹ (1), ~ESS¹ (arch.), **prŏfėssôr'ĭ**ATE¹ (1), ~SHIP, *ns.*, **prŏfėssôr'**IAL *a.* **3.** Professional teacher, sportsman, etc. [ME, f. OF *professeur* or f. L *professor* (as PROFESS; see -OR)]

prŏ'ffer *v.t.*, & *n.* **1.** *v.t.* (esp. in *p.p.*) Offer (gift, services, hand, etc., arch. *to* do). **2.** *n.* (literary). Offer, proposal. [ME; (n. f. AF *profre*) f. AF & OF *proffrir* (as PRO-¹, *offrir* OFFER¹)]

profĭ'cient (-shent) *a.* & *n.* Adept, expert, (*in* or *at* an art etc.; *in* doing); hence **profĭ'ci**ENCY (-shen-) *n.*, ~LY² *adv.* [f. L (as PROFIT¹; see -ENT)]

prō'fīle *n.*, & *v.t.* **1.** *n.* Drawing, silhouette, or other representation, of side view esp. of human face, whence **prō'fīl**IST (3) *n.*; *drawn* etc. **in ~,** as seen from one side; outline (esp. of the human face) as seen from the side. **2.** Short printed or broadcast biographical or character sketch; schematic description of person's interests for use in information retrieval etc. **3.** Vertical cross-section of structure; curve of variation of a quantity along a cross-section (**keep a low ~,** remain inconspicuous); flat outline piece of scenery on stage. **4.** *v.t.* Represent in profile; give profile to. [(n. f. obs. It. *profilo*) f. obs. It. PRO¹(*filare* spin f. L *filare* f. *filum* thread)]

prŏ'fĭt¹ *n.* **1.** Advantage, benefit, (*have studied it to my profit; no profit in such pursuits*). **2.** Pecuniary gain, excess of returns over outlay, (*sold* **at a ~,** for more than one paid to get it); ~ **and loss account,** account in which gains are credited and losses debited so as to show net profit or loss at any time; **~-sharing** (of profits esp. between employer and employed); **~-taking,** sale of shares etc. at time when profit will accrue. **3.** Hence ~LESS *a.* [ME f. OF, f. L *profectus* progress, profit f. PRO¹(*ficere fect-* = *facere* do) advance]

prŏ'fĭt² *v.* **1.** *v.t.* (Of thing) bring advantage to (person etc.; *it will not profit him to act thus*). **2.** *v.i.* Be of advantage; (of person etc.) be benefited or assisted (*hope to profit from your advice; profited by the confusion to make my escape*). [ME, f. OF *profiter* (as prec.)]

prŏ'fĭt|able *a.* Beneficial, useful; yielding profit, lucrative, (*a profitable speculation*); hence ~ABI'LITY, **~able**NESS (-beln-), *ns.*, **~ab**LY² *adv.* [ME f. OF (as prec.; see -ABLE)]

prŏfĭteer' *v.i.*, & *n.* **1.** *v.i.* (Seek to) make excessive profits out of others' needs, esp. in times

For other words in *pro-* see PRO-.

of scarcity. **2.** *n.* Person who profiteers. [f. PROFIT¹ + -EER]

profĭ'terōle *n.* Small hollow cake of choux pastry that may have sweet or savoury filling. [F, dim. of *profit* PROFIT¹]

prŏ'flĭg|ate *a.* & *n.* **1.** *a.* Licentious, dissolute; recklessly extravagant; hence ~ACY *n.*, ~**ate**LY² (-tlĭ) *adv.* **2.** *n.* Profligate person. [f. L *profligatus* dissolute, p.p. of PRO¹(*fligare* = *fligere* strike down) overthrow, ruin; see -ATE²]

prō fōr'ma *adv.*, *a.*, & *n.* **1.** *adv.* & *a.* (Done) for form's sake. **2.** *a.* & *n.* ~ (**invoice**), invoice sent to purchaser in advance of goods, for completion of business formalities. [L]

profou'nd *a.* (~er, ~est) & *n.* **1.** *a.* Having or showing great knowledge or insight (*profound statesman, inquiry, treatise*); demanding deep study or thought (*profound doctrines*). **2.** (Of state or quality) deep, intense, unqualified, (*fell into a profound sleep; take a profound interest; simulated a profound indifference*); (rhet.) having, coming from, extending to, a great depth, (*profound crevasses*); (of sigh) deep-drawn; (of disease) deep-seated. **3.** Hence or cogn. ~LY² *adv.*, ~NESS, **profŭ'nd**ITY, *ns.* **4.** *n.* (poet.) *The* vast depth (*of* ocean, futurity, the soul, etc.). [ME, f. AF, OF *profund, profond* f. L PRO¹(*fundus* bottom) deep]

profū'se *a.* Lavish, extravagant, (*in* or *of* gifts, promises, expenditure, etc.); (of thing) exuberantly plentiful (*profuse bleeding, variety*); hence or cogn. ~LY² (-slĭ) *adv.*, ~NESS (-sn-), **profū's**ION (-zhon), *ns.* [ME, f. L *profusus* p.p. of PRO¹(*fundere fus-* pour)]

||**prŏg** *n.*, & *v.t.* (-gg-). (sl.) **1.** *n.* Proctor at Oxford or Cambridge. **2.** *v.t.* Subject (undergraduate) to exercise of proctor's authority. [abbr.]

progĕ'nĭtĭve *a.* Capable of or connected with the production of offspring. [as foll.; see -IVE]

progĕ'nĭt|or *n.* Ancestor of person, animal, or plant; (fig.) political or intellectual predecessor, original of a copy; hence ~**ōr'**IAL *a.*, ~**or**SHIP, ~**r**ESS¹, **progĕ'nĭ**TRIX, *ns.* [ME, f. OF *progeniteur* f. L *progenitor -oris* f. PRO¹(*gignere genit-* beget); see -OR]

progĕ'nĭture *n.* (Begetting of) offspring. [f. L as prec.; see -URE]

prŏ'gėnў *n.* Offspring of person, animal, or plant; descendants; (fig.) issue, outcome. [ME, f. OF *progenie* f. L *progenies* f. PRO¹(*gignere* beget)]

progĕ'st|erōne *n.* (Physiol.) Steroid sex hormone inhibiting ovulation during pregnancy; so ~**o**GEN *n.*, substance having physiological effects similar to those of progesterone. [f. *progestin* (PRO-² before, GESTATION, -IN) + *luteosterone* (CORPUS *luteum*, STEROL, -ONE)]

proglŏ'tt|ĭs *n.* (*pl.* ~**ides** *pr.* -ĭdēz). Propagative segment of tapeworm. [mod. L, f. Gk PRO²-(*glōssis* f. *glōssa, glōtta* tongue), from its shape]

prŏ'gnath|ous (*or* -nā'-) *a.* With projecting jaws; (of jaws) projecting; so **prŏgnă'th**IC *a.*, ~ISM (2) *n.* [f. PRO-² + Gk *gnathos* jaw + -OUS]

prŏgnō's|ĭs *n.* (*pl.* ~**es** *pr.* -ēz). Prognostication, esp. (Med.) forecast of course of disease. [LL, f. Gk PRO²(*gnōsis* f. *gignōskō* know)]

prŏgnŏ'stĭc *n.* & *a.* **1.** *n.* Advance indication, omen, (*of*); prediction, forecast. **2.** *a.* Foretelling, predictive, (*of*). [n. ME, f. OF *pronostique* f. L f. Gk *prognōstikon* neut. (as n.) of *prognōstikos* f. PRO²(*gignōskō* learn), see -IC; a. f. med. L f. Gk *prognōstikos*]

prŏgnŏ'stĭc|āte *v.t.* Foretell, foresee, (event, *that*); (of thing) betoken; hence or cogn. ~ABLE, ~**at**IVE, ~**āt**ORY, *adjs.*, ~**A'**TION, ~**āt**OR, *ns.* [f. med. L *prognosticare* (as prec.) + -ATE³]

||**prō'grămme,** (U.S. & Computers) **prō'-grăm,** *n.*, & *v.t.* **1.** *n.* Descriptive notice of series of events, e.g. of course of study, play, concert, etc.; such series of events (*a programme of lectures*); broadcast performance; definite plan of intended proceedings; ~ **music** (intended to suggest series of scenes or events). **2.** Series of coded instructions to control operation of computer. **3.** Hence **prōgrammă'**TIC *a.* **4.** *v.t.* Make programme or definite plan of; (-**mm**-) express (problem) or instruct (computer) by means of program, whence ~**m**ER¹ *n.* [f. LL f. Gk *programma -atos* f. PRO²(*graphō* write) write publicly; sp. after F *programme*]

prō'grĕss¹ *n.*, & *v.t.* **1.** *n.* Forward or onward movement in space (*made slow progress; continued his progress*); **in** ~, in course of occurrence, going on. **2.** Advance or development esp. to better state (*made no progress in his studies; the progress of civilization; disease made rapid progress*); ~-**-chaser,** person employed to check regular progress of manufacturing work; ~ **report,** account of progress made. **3.** ||(arch.) State journey, official tour, esp. by royal person. **4.** *v.t.* Cause (work etc.) to make regular progress. [ME, f. L *progressus* f. PRO¹(*gredi gress-* = *gradi* walk)]

progrĕ'ss² *v.i.* Move forward or onward; be carried on (*the controversy, the building of the house, is progressing*); advance or develop esp. to better state (*we progress in knowledge; science progresses*). [f. prec.; readopted from U.S. after becoming obs. in England in 17th c.]

progrĕ'ssion (-shon) *n.* Progressing (*mode of progression*); succession, series; (Math.) ARITHMETICAL, GEOMETRICAL, HARMONIC, *progression*; (Mus.) passing from one note or chord to another; hence ~AL *a.* [ME f. OF, or f. L *progressio* (as PROGRESS¹; see -ION)]

progrĕ'ssionĭst (-sho-) *n.* Advocate of or believer in progress e.g. in political or social matters; one who holds that life on earth has been marked by gradual progression to higher forms. [f. prec. + -IST]

progrĕ'ssĭve *a.* & *n.* **1.** *a.* Moving forward (*progressive motion*); proceeding step by step, successive; (of card-game, dance, etc.) with periodic change of partners; (of taxation) at rates increasing with the sum taxed; (Gram., of tense) expressing action in progress (*am writing, was writing*). **2.** Advancing in social conditions, character, efficiency, etc., (*a progressive nation*); (of disease, violence, etc.) continuously increasing in severity or extent; favouring progress or reform (*progressive principles, party*), whence **progrĕ'ssĭv**ISM (3) *n.*; (of education etc.) informal and without strict discipline, stressing individualism. **3.** Hence ~LY² (-vlĭ) *adv.*, ~NESS (-vn-) *n.* **4.** *n.* Advocate of progressive policy. [f. F *progressif -ive* or f. med. L *progressivus* (as PROGRESS¹; see -IVE)]

pro hac vice (prō hahk vī'sĭ *or* vē'sĭ *or* vē'chĭ) *adv.* For this occasion (only). [L]

prohĭ'bĭt *v.t.* Forbid, debar, (action, thing, person's doing, person *from* doing); *prohibited* DEGREES; hence ~ER¹, ~OR, *ns.* [ME, f. L PRO¹(*hibēre hibit-* = *habēre* hold)]

prōhĭbĭ'tion (*or* -ōĭb-) *n.* Forbidding, being forbidden; edict or order that forbids; forbidding by law of the manufacture and sale of intoxicants, whence ~IST (2) *n.*; (Law) writ from superior court forbidding inferior court to proceed in suit deemed to be beyond its cognizance. [ME f. OF, or f. L *prohibitio* (as prec.; see -ION)]

prohĭ'bĭtĭve *a.* Prohibiting; such as to prevent the use or abuse or purchase of a thing (*prohibitive tax; published at a prohibitive price*); hence or cogn. ~LY² (-vlĭ) *adv.*, ~NESS (-vn-) *n.*, **prohĭ'bĭt**ORY *a.* [f. F *prohibitif -ive* or f. L *prohibitivus* (as PROHIBIT; see -IVE), & f. PROHIBIT + -IVE]

prŏjĕ'ct[1] *v.* **1.** *v.t.* Plan, contrive, (scheme, course of action, etc.). **2.** Cast, throw, impel, (body *into* space etc.); extrapolate (results *to* future time etc.); (Psych.) form projection of; go out of one*self into* another's feelings, the future, etc. **3.** Cause (light, shadow) to fall on surface etc.; cause (image) to be visible *on* screen etc.; (fig.) cause (idea etc.) to take shape or become known. **4.** (Geom.) Draw straight lines from a centre or parallel lines through every point of (given figure) to produce corresponding figure on a surface or line by intersecting it, draw (such lines), produce (such corresponding figure); make projection (sense 6) of (earth, sky, etc.). **5.** *v.i.* Protrude, jut out. [ME, f. L PRO[1](*jicere ject-* = *jacĕre* throw)]

prŏ'jĕct[2] *n.* Plan, scheme; planned undertaking, esp. by student(s) for presentation of results at specified time. [ME, f. L *projectum* neut. p.p. (as n.) of *projicere* (see prec.)]

projĕ'ctīle *a.* & *n.* **1.** *a.* Impelling (*projectile force*); capable of being projected by force, esp. from gun. **2.** *n.* (*or* prŏ'jĭktīl). Projectile missile. [f. mod. L *projectilis* a., *-ile* n., (as PROJECT[1]; see -IL)]

projĕ'ction *n.* **1.** Throwing; being thrown. **2.** Presentation of image on screen etc.; hence ~IST (3) *n.* **3.** Planning; thing planned. **4.** Protruding; thing that protrudes; thrusting forward. **5.** (Geom.) Projecting of a figure (see PROJECT[1] 4); ~ **of a point,** point in derived figure corresponding to point in original figure. **6.** Representation on plane surface of (any part of) surface of earth or of celestial sphere, e.g. MERCATOR'*s projection*; **conical, cylindrical,** ~ (with meridians first projected on cone, cylinder). **7.** Mental image viewed as objective reality; (Psych.) unconscious transfer of one's own impressions or feelings to external objects or persons. [f. L *projectio* (as PROJECT[1]; see -ION)]

projĕ'ctĭve *a.* **1.** (Geom.) Of or derived by projection; (of a property of a figure) unchanged by projection; ~ **geometry** (dealing with projective properties). **2.** Mentally projecting or projected (*projective imagination*). **3.** Hence ~LY[2] (-vlĭ) *adv.* [f. PROJECT[1] + -IVE]

projĕ'ctor *n.* **1.** One who forms a project; (arch.) promoter of speculative companies. **2.** Apparatus for projecting rays of light or projecting image on screen. [f. PROJECT[1] + -OR]

prolă'pse[1] *v.i.* (Path.) Slip forward or down out of place. [f. L PRO[1](*labi laps-* slip)]

prō'lăpse[2] *n.* (Path.) Prolapsing of part or organ (esp. womb or rectum). [f. foll.]

prolă'psus *n.* = prec. [mod. L, f. LL = fall (as PROLAPSE[1])]

prō'lāte *a.* (Geom., of spheroid) lengthened in direction of polar diameter (cf. OBLATE[2]); growing or extending in width; (fig.) widely spread; (Gram.) = foll.; hence ~LY[2] (-tlĭ) *adv.* [f. L *prolatus* p.p. of PRO[1](*ferre* carry) prolong; see -ATE[2]]

prolā'tĭve *a.* (Gram.) Serving to continue or complete predication, e.g. *go* (prolative infinitive) in *you may go*. [f. as prec. + -IVE]

prōle *a.* & *n.* (colloq.) Proletarian. [abbr.]

prō'lĕg *n.* Fleshy abdominal limb of caterpillar or other larva. [f. PRO-[1] + LEG]

prōlĕgŏ'mĕn|on *n.* (usu. in *pl.* ~**a**). Preliminary discourse or matter prefixed to book etc., introduction; hence ~ARY[1], ~OUS, *adjs.* [L f. Gk, neut. pass. part. of PRO[2](*legō* say)]

prolĕ'ps|ĭs *n.* (*pl.* ~**es** *pr.* -ēz). Anticipation; representation of thing as existing before it actually does or did so; (Gram.) anticipatory use of adjectives, as in *paint the town red*; so **prolĕ'pt**IC *a.* [LL f. Gk *prolēpsis* f. PRO[2](*lambanō* take) anticipate]

prōlėtār'ĭan *a.* & *n.* (Member) of the proletariat; hence ~ISM (2) *n.*, ~IZE (3) *v.t.* [f. L *proletarius* one who served the State not with property but with offspring (*proles*); see -ARY[1], -AN]

prōlėtār'ĭat *n.* (Rom. Hist., or derog. of modern society) lowest class of community; (Econ.) wage-earners, esp. those without capital and dependent on daily labour for subsistence; **dictatorship of the** ~, Communist ideal of domination by the proletariat after the suppression of capitalism and the bourgeoisie. [f. F *prolétariat* (as prec.; cf. -ATE[1])]

prolĭ'fer|āte *v.* **1.** *v.i.* Reproduce itself, grow, by multiplication of elementary parts; increase rapidly in numbers etc. **2.** *v.t.* Produce (cells etc.) thus. **3.** So ~A'TION *n.*, ~**at**IVE *a.* [back form. (see -ATE[3]) f. *proliferation* f. F *prolifération* (*prolifère* as foll.; see -ATION)]

prolĭ'ferous *a.* **1.** (Bot.) Producing leaf or flower buds from leaf or flower; producing new individuals from buds etc. **2.** (Zool.) Multiplying by budding. **3.** (Path.) Spreading by proliferation. [f. L *proles* offspring + -I- + -FEROUS]

prolĭ'fĭc *a.* Producing (much) offspring; abundantly productive (*of*), abounding *in*; hence ~ACY [irreg.], **prōlĭfĭ'**CITY, ~NESS, *ns.* [f. med. L *prolificus* (as prec.; see -FIC)]

prō'lĭx (*or* prolĭ'ks) *a.* Lengthy, tediously wordy, (*prolix speech, writer*); hence or cogn. **prolĭ'x**ITY *n.*, ~LY[2] *adv.* [ME, f. OF *prolixe* or f. L *prolixus* (as PRO-[1], *liquēre* be liquid) poured forth, extended]

prō'locūtor (*or* prolŏ'-) *n.* Chairman esp. of lower house of convocation of either province of Church of England; spokesman; hence ~SHIP *n.* [ME f. L, f. PRO[1](*loqui locut-* speak); see -OR]

prŏ'logīze, -guīze (-gīz), **-īse** (-īz), *v.i.* Write or speak a prologue. [f. med. L *prologizare* f. Gk *prologizō* speak prologue (as foll.), or f. foll. + -IZE]

prō'lŏgue (-g) *n.*, & *v.t.* **1.** *n.* Preliminary discourse, poem, etc., esp. introducing play (cf. EPILOGUE); (fig.) act or event serving as introduction (*to*). **2.** *v.t.* Introduce or furnish with a prologue. [ME *prolog* f. OF *prologue*, f. L f. Gk PRO[2](*logos* speech)]

prolŏ'ng *v.t.* Extend (action, condition, etc.) in duration; extend in spatial length; lengthen pronunciation of (syllable etc.); so **prō-lŏng**A'TION (-ngg-) *n.* [ME, f. OF *prolonger* & f. LL PRO[1](*longare* f. *longus* long)]

prolū'sion (-zhon; *or* -lōō'-) *n.* Preliminary essay, article, or attempt; so **prolū's**ORY (*or* -ōō'-) *a.* [f. L *prolusio* f. PRO[1](*ludere lus-* play) practise beforehand; see -ION]

prŏm *n.* (colloq.) Promenade (||concert). [abbr.]

prŏmena'd|e (-ah'd) *n.* & *v.* **1.** *n.* Walk, ride, drive, taken for exercise, amusement, or display, or as social ceremony; place, esp. paved public walk (||at seaside), for this; *school or university ball or dance; ~**e concert,** one at which (part of) audience is not seated and can move about; ~**e deck,** an upper deck on a passenger ship, where passengers may promenade. **2.** *v.i.* Make a promenade; hence ~ER[1] *n.* (esp. at promenade concert). **3.** *v.t.* Make a promenade through (place); lead (person) about a place esp. for display. [F (*se promener* walk, refl. of *promener* take for a walk; see -ADE)]

For other words in *pro-* see PRO-.

promē'thazine (-ēn) *n.* Drug of antihistamine group. [f. PROPYL + di*methyl*amine + phenothi*azine*]
Promē'thēan *a.* Of or like Prometheus in his skill or punishment. [f. Gk *Promētheus* (demigod in myth who stole fire from Olympus and taught men the use of it and various arts, and was punished by being chained to rock in Caucasus and preyed on by vulture) + -AN]
promē'thium *n.* (Chem.) Radioactive metallic element of lanthanide series, artificially made. [f. *Prometheus* (as prec.) + -IUM]
prŏ'minence *n.* Being prominent; prominent thing; (Astron.) cloud of incandescent gas projecting above sun's chromosphere. [obs. F, f. L *prominentia* jutting out (as foll.; see -ENCE)]
prŏ'min|ent *a.* Jutting out, projecting; conspicuous; distinguished; hence or cogn. ~ENCY *n.*, ~entLY[2] *adv.* [f. L PRO[1](*minēre*; cf. EMINENT) jut out; see -ENT]
promĭ'scūous *a.* Of mixed and indiscriminate composition or kinds; indiscriminate (*promiscuous massacre, hospitality*); (of person) having sexual relations not limited by marriage or cohabitation, (of sexual relations) of this kind; (colloq.) casual, carelessly irregular; hence **prŏmĭscū'**ITY *n.*, ~LY[2] *adv.* [f. L PRO[1](*miscuus* f. *miscēre* mix) + -OUS]
prŏ'mise[1] *n.* **1.** Assurance given that one will do or not do something or will give or procure him something (*a promise of help, to help*); BREACH[1] *of promise*; BREAK[1] one's *promise*; KEEP[1] one's *promise*; **land of** ~, = PROMISE[2]*d land.* **2.** (fig.) Ground of expectation of future achievements or good results (*a book, writer, of great promise*). [ME, f. L *promissum* neut. p.p. (as n.) of PRO[1](*mittere* send) put forth, promise]
prŏ'mise[2] *v.* **1.** *v.t.* Make (person) a promise to give or procure him (thing) (*I promise you a fair hearing*); make (person, or abs.) a promise (*to* do, *that* thing shall be done etc.; *cannot positively promise*); ~ **oneself,** look forward to (a pleasant time etc.); (colloq.) assure (*I promise you, it will not be so easy*); (fig.) afford expectation of (*these discussions promise future storms*), seem likely (*to* do). **2.** *v.i.* ~ **well** etc., hold out good etc. prospect. **3. ~d land,** Canaan (Gen. 12:7 etc.), heaven, any place of expected felicity. **4.** Hence **prŏ'mĭs**ER[1] *n.*, (esp. Law) **prŏmĭs**EE', **prŏ'mĭs**OR, *ns.* [ME, f. prec.]
prŏ'mĭsing *a.* Likely to turn out well, hopeful, full of promise, (*promising boy, sky, beginning*); hence ~LY[2] *adv.* [f. prec. + -ING[2]]
prŏ'mĭssorў *a.* Conveying or implying a promise; full of promise (*of*); ~ **note,** signed document containing written promise to pay stated sum to specified person or to bearer at specified date or on demand. [f. med. L *promissorius* f. L *promissor* (as PROMISE[1]; see -ORY)]
prŏ'montorў *n.* Point of high land jutting out into sea etc., headland; (Anat.) prominence or protuberance in the body. [f. med. L *promontorium* alt. (after *mons montis* mountain) f. L *promunturium* (perh. f. PRO-[1], *mons*); see -ORY]
promō'te *v.t.* Advance (person *to* position or higher office); help forward, encourage, (process, result), support actively the passing of (law); initiate (project), take necessary steps for passing of (private act of parliament); publicize and sell (product); (Chess) raise (pawn) to rank of queen etc. when it reaches opponent's end of board; hence or cogn. **promō'**TION *n.*, **promō'tion**AL, **promō'**TIVE, *adjs.* [ME, f. L. PRO[1](*movēre mot-* move)]
promō'ter *n.* In vbl senses; (**company**) ~, one who promotes formation of joint-stock company; one who is financially responsible for sporting event, theatrical production, etc. [earlier *promotour* f. AF, f. med. L *promotor* (as prec.; see -OR)]
prŏmpt[1] *a., adv.,* & *n.* **1.** *a.* Ready in action, acting with alacrity; made, done, etc., readily or at once (*prompt reply, decision, payment*); hence or cogn. ~'ĬTUDE, ~'NESS, *ns.*, ~'LY[2] *adv.* **2.** (Of payment) made forthwith; (of goods) for immediate delivery and payment (*prompt iron*). **3.** *adv.* Punctually (*at six o'clock prompt*). **4.** *n.* Time limit for payment of account, stated on **~-note.** [ME f. OF, or f. L *promptus* p.p. of *promere prompt-* produce (PRO-[1], *emere* take)]
prŏmpt[2] *v.t.,* & *n.* **1.** *v.t.* Incite, move, (person etc. *to* action, *to* do); help (actor, reciter, or abs.) by supplying the words that come next, assist (hesitating speaker) with suggestion; inspire, give rise to, (feeling, thought, action); hence ~'ING[1] *n.* **2.** *n.* Thing said to help the memory esp. of actor; **~-book,** copy of play for prompter's use; **~-box** (on stage, occupied by prompter); ~ **side** of stage (usu. to actor's left). [ME, f. med. L **promptare*, f. L *promptus* (see prec.)]
prŏ'mpter *n.* One who prompts, esp. (Theatr.) person placed out of sight of audience who prompts actors. [ME (as prec., -ER[1])]
prŏ'mulg|āte *v.t.* Make known to the public, disseminate (creed etc.), proclaim (decree, news); hence or cogn. ~A'TION, ~ātOR, *ns.* [f. L *promulgare* (as PRO-[1], *mulgēre* milk, cause to come forth) + -ATE[3]]
promŭ'lge *v.t.* (arch.) = prec. [f. as prec.]
pronā'|ŏs *n.* (*pl.* ~oi). (Gk Ant.) Space in front of body of temple, enclosed by portico and projecting side walls. [L, f. Gk PRO[2](NAOS) hall of a temple]
prō'n|āte *v.t.* Put (hand, foreleg) into prone position (cf. SUPINATE); so ~A'TION *n.*, ~ā'tOR *n.* (esp. muscle effecting this). [back form. f. *pronation* (as foll.; see -ATION); see -ATE[3]]
prōne *a.* **1.** Having front or ventral part downwards, (of hand) with palm downwards, lying face downwards (cf. SUPINE); lying flat, prostrate; (arch.) with downward slope or direction; hence ~'LY[2] (-nlĭ) *adv.* **2.** Disposed, liable, (*to* usu. bad quality, action, or condition; *to* do); (in *comb.*) more than usually likely to suffer (*accident-prone person; strike-prone industries*). **3.** Hence ~'NESS (-n-n-) *n.* [ME, f. L *pronus* (*pro* forwards)]
proneur (prōnér') *n.* Extoller, flatterer. [f. F *prôneur* (*prôner* eulogize f. *prône* place in church where addresses were delivered)]
prŏng *n.,* & *v.t.* **1.** *n.* Each of two or more projecting pointed parts at end of fork, whence (-)~ED[2] (-ngd) *a.* (**three-~ed attack,** on three separate points at once); **~-buck, -horn, -horn**(**ed**) **antelope,** N. Amer. deerlike ruminant (*Antilocapra americana*). **2.** *v.t.* Pierce, stab, turn up (soil etc.), with fork. [ME; also *prang*, perh. rel. to MLG *prange* pinching instrument]
pronŏ'minal *a.* Of (the nature of) a pronoun; hence ~IZE (3) *v.t.*, ~LY[2] *adv.* [f. LL *pronominalis* f. L PRO[1](*nomen nominis* noun); see -AL]
prō'noun *n.* **1.** Word used instead of (proper or other) noun to designate (without naming) person or thing already mentioned or known from context or forming the subject of inquiry; pronominal adjective. **2. Demonstrative** ~ (*this, that*); **distributive** ~ (*each, either,* etc.); **impersonal** or **indefinite** ~ (*any, some, anyone, something,* etc.); **interrogative** ~ (*who?, what?, which?*); **personal** ~ (*I, we, thou, you, he, she, it, they; me, us,* etc.); **possessive** ~, adjective representing possessive case (*my, her, our,* etc., with absolute forms *mine, hers, ours,* etc.); **reciprocal** ~ (*one another,* etc.); **reflexive** ~ (*myself, oneself,* etc.); **relative** ~ (*who, what,*

which, that). [f. PRO-[1] + NOUN, after F *pronom*, L *pronomen* transl. Gk *antōnumia* (as ANTI-, *onuma* name)]

pronou'nce *v.* **1.** *v.t.* Utter, deliver, (judgement, sentence, curse, etc.) formally or solemnly, state, declare, as one's opinion, (*apples were pronounced excellent*; *cannot pronounce him* (or *that he is*) *out of danger*); hence ~MENT (-sm-) *n.* **2.** Utter, articulate, (words, or abs.; *pronounce more distinctly*), esp. with reference to different ways (*how do you pronounce 'fulsome'?*; *cannot pronounce French*); hence ~ABLE (-sa-) *a.* **3.** *v.i.* Pass judgement, give one's opinion, (*on, for, against, in favour of*). [ME, f. OF *pronuncier* f. L PRO[1]-(*nuntiare* announce f. *nuntius* messenger)]

pronou'nced (-st) *a.* In vbl senses; strongly marked, decided, (*pronounced tendency, flavour*); hence **pronou'ncėd**LY[2] *adv.* [p.p. of prec.]

pronou'ncing *n.* In vbl senses; ~ **dictionary** (in which pronunciation is the thing chiefly indicated). [f. PRONOUNCE + -ING[1]]

***prŏ'ntō** *adv.* (sl.) Promptly, quickly. [Sp., f. L (as PROMPT[1])]

pronŭnciamĕ'ntō *n.* (*pl.* ~s). Proclamation, manifesto, esp. (in Spanish-speaking countries) one issued by insurrectionists; pronouncement. [f. Sp. *pronunciamiento* (*pronunciar* f. L as PRONOUNCE; see -MENT)]

pronŭnciā'tion *n.* Way in which a word is pronounced; a person's way of pronouncing words (*his pronunciation is often faulty*). [ME, f. OF *prononciation* or f. L *pronuntiatio* (as PRONOUNCE; see -ATION)]

proof[1] *n.*, & *v.t.* **1.** *n.* Fact or evidence or argument sufficing or helping to establish a fact (*this requires no proof*; *as* (*a*) *proof of his esteem*; *proof* POSITIVE *of his intention* or *that he intended*), whence ~'LESS *a.*; spoken or written legal evidence. **2.** Proving, demonstration, (*not capable of proof*; *in proof of my assertion*). **3.** (Sc. Law). Trial before judge instead of by jury. **4.** Test, trial, (*must be brought to the proof*; *will stand a severe proof*; *the proof of the pudding is in the eating*); **~-plane,** small flat conductor on insulating handle for measuring electrification of a body. **5.** Standard of strength of distilled alcoholic liquors (~ **spirit,** alcohol-water mixture having this standard strength; **above** ~, stronger than this). **6.** (**First**) ~, (Print.) trial impression taken from type, for making corrections etc. (cf. REVISE); **~-reader, -reading,** (person employed in) reading and correcting proofs; so *~-read* v.t.; **~-sheet,** sheet of proof. **7.** Photographic print made for selection etc. **8.** Each of a limited number of careful impressions made from engraved plate before printing of ordinary issue and usu. (also ~ *before letters*) before inscription is added; **artist's, engraver's,** ~ (taken for examination or alteration by him); **signed** ~, early proof signed by artist. **9.** *v.t.* Make proof of (printed work, engraving, etc.). [ME *prōf prōve*, earlier *prēf* etc. f. OF *proeve*, *prueve* f. LL *proba* f. L *probare* (see PROVE)]

proof[2] *a.*, & *v.t.* **1.** *a.* (Of armour) of tried strength; impervious to penetration or undesired action (*proof against the severest weather, the pricks of conscience*); able to resist or withstand damage or destruction (esp. in comb.: *bomb, bullet, burglar,* CHILD, *pilfer, sound, splinter, -proof*; FOOL[1]*proof*, WATER[1]*proof*). **2.** *v.t.* Make (*thing*) proof, esp. make (fabric etc.) waterproof, (also in comb.: *sound-proof*, WATER[1]*proof*). [a. f. prec., app. by ellipsis f. phr. *of proof* = proved to be impenetrable; v. f. a., or f. prec.]

prŏp[1] *n.* & *v.* (-pp-). **1.** *n.* Rigid support, esp. one not forming structural part of thing supported, e.g. pole; = CLOTHES-*prop*; (fig.) person etc. who upholds institution etc., (Rugby Footb.) forward at either end of front row of scrum; (esp. Austral., of horse) action of propping. **2.** *v.t.* Support (as) by prop (lit. or fig.); hold *up* thus. **3.** *v.i.* (Esp. Austral., of horse etc.) come to a dead stop with forelegs rigid. [ME, prob. f. MDu. *proppe*; v. f. n., or f. MLG, MDu. *proppen*]

prŏp[2] *n.* (Theatr., colloq.) Stage property; (in *pl.*) property-man. [abbr.]

prŏp[3] *n.* (colloq.) Aircraft propeller; **~-jet,** turbo-prop. [abbr.]

prop. *abbr.* proposition.

prōpaedeu'tic *a.* & *n.* (Subject or study) serving as introduction to higher study; (in *pl.*) preliminary learning; hence ~AL *a.* [f. PRO-[2] + *paedeutics* science of education (f. Gk *paideutikos* of teaching), after Gk *propaideuō* teach beforehand]

prŏpagă'nda *n.* **1.** Association or organized scheme for propagation of a doctrine or practice; (usu. derog.) doctrines, information, etc., thus propagated. **2.** (R.C. Ch.) (**Congregation** or **College of**) **the P~**, committee of cardinals in charge of foreign missions. [It., f. mod. L *congregatio de propaganda fide* congregation for propagation of the faith]

prŏpagă'nd|ist *n.* Member or agent of a propaganda; one who disseminates propaganda; so ~ISM (1) *n.*, **~i'stic** *a.*, ~IZE (2, 4) *v.i.* & *t.* [f. prec. + -IST]

prŏ'pag|āte *v.* **1.** *v.t.* Multiply specimens of (plant, animal, disease, etc.) by natural process from parent stock; (of plant, animal, etc.) reproduce (*itself*). **2.** Hand down (quality etc.) from one generation to another. **3.** Disseminate, diffuse, (statement, belief, practice). **4.** Extend the operation of, transmit, (vibration, earthquake, etc.). **5.** *v.i.* Undergo propagation. **6.** Hence or cogn. ~A'TION, **~ātor**, *ns.*, **~ātive** *a.* [f. L *propagare* multiply plants from layers, f. PRO[1](*pago* f. root of *pangere* fix, layer) + -ATE[3]]

prō'pāne *n.* (Chem.) Hydrocarbon of the paraffin series, C_3H_8. [f. PROPIONIC + -ANE]

prōparŏ'xȳtōne *a.* & *n.* (Gk Gram.) (Word) with acute accent on last syllable but two. [f. Gk PRO[2](*paroxutonos* PAROXYTONE)]

propĕ'l *v.t.* (-ll-). Drive or push forward, give onward motion to, (lit. or fig.); **~ling pencil** (with lead moved forward by turning outer case). [ME, = 'expel', f. L PRO[1](*pellere puls-* drive)]

propĕ'llant *n.* Propelling agent; explosive that propels bullet or shell from firearm; substance used as reagent in rocket engine to provide thrust. [f. prec. + -ANT]

propĕ'llent *a.* Propelling, propulsive. [f. PROPEL + -ENT]

propĕ'ller *n.* In vbl senses; revolving shaft with blades (usu. SCREW-*propeller*), for propelling ship or aircraft; ~ **shaft** (transmitting power from engine to propeller or to driven wheels of motor vehicle); ~ **turbine,** turbo-propeller. [f. PROPEL + -ER[1]]

propĕ'nsitȳ *n.* Inclination or tendency (*to* condition, quality, thing, *to* do, *for* doing). [f. *propense* f. L *propensus* inclined, p.p. of PRO[1]-(*pendēre* hang) + -ITY]

prŏ'per *a.* **1.** (arch., usu. w. possessive pron.) Own (*with my* (*own*) *proper eyes*). **2.** ~ **motion,** (Astron.) the part of the apparent motion of a fixed star etc. that is due to its actual movement in space relative to the sun. **3.** Belonging or relating exclusively or distinctively (*to*); ~ **psalms, lessons,** (appointed for particular day). **4.** ~ **noun** or **name,** (Gram.) name used to designate an individual person, animal, town, ship, etc. (e.g. *Jane, Neddy, London, Victory*). **5.** Accurate, correct, (*in the proper sense of the word*). **6.** (usu. placed after *n.*) Strictly so called, real, genuine, (*within the sphere of architecture proper*); ~ **fraction** (less than unity, with numerator less than denominator). **7.** (colloq.) Thorough, complete, (*there will be a proper row about this*). **8.** (arch., of person). Handsome, comely. **9.** Fit, suitable, right, (*choose the proper time; do it the proper way*). **10.** In conformity with demands of society, decent, respectable, (*she is so distressingly proper; would it be quite proper?*). **11.** (Her.) In the natural, not conventional, colours (*a peacock proper*). [ME f. OF *propre* f. L *proprius* one's own, special]

prōpĕrĭspō'mĕn|on *a.* & *n.* (*pl.* **~a**). (Gk Gram.) (Word) with circumflex accent on last syllable but one. [Gk (as PRO-², PERISPOMENON)]

prŏ'perlȳ *adv.* Fittingly, suitably, (*do it properly or not at all*); accurately, correctly, (*properly speaking*); rightly, duly, (*he very properly refused*); with decency or good manners (*behave properly*); (colloq.) thoroughly (*puzzled him properly*). [f. PROPER + -LY²]

prŏ'pertĭed (-ĭd) *a.* Having (a landed) property. [f. foll. + -ED²]

prŏ'pertȳ *n.* **1.** Owning, being owned, (*property has its duties*); thing owned, possession(s), esp. real estate, (*the book is his property; regards him as her exclusive property; a man of (great) property*); **common ~,** (fig.) = COMMON¹ *knowledge*; PERSONAL, REAL², *property*; ~ **qualification** (based on possession of property); ~ **tax** (levied directly on property). **2.** (Theatr.) Article of costume, furniture, etc., used on stage; **~-man, -master,** man in charge of stage properties. **3.** Attribute, quality, characteristic, (*the properties of soda; has the property of dissolving grease*); (Logic) quality common to a whole class but not necessary to distinguish it from others. [ME, f. AF *_propreté_, OF *proprieté* f. L *proprietas -tatis* (as PROPER; see -TY¹)]

prŏ'phĕcȳ *n.* Faculty of a prophet (*the gift of prophecy*); prophetic utterance; foretelling of future events. [ME, f. OF *profecie* f. LL f. Gk *prophēteia* (as PROPHET; see -CY)]

prŏ'phĕs|ȳ *v.* **1.** *v.i.* Speak as a prophet; foretell future events; (arch.) expound the Scriptures. **2.** *v.t.* Foretell (event, *that, who*, etc.). **3.** Hence **~ĭER**¹ *n.* [ME, f. OF *profecier* (as prec.)]

prŏ'phĕt *n.* **1.** Inspired teacher, revealer or interpreter of God's will; prophetical writer or writing in O.T. (**major ~s,** Isaiah, Jeremiah, Ezekiel, Daniel; **minor ~s,** Hosea to Malachi, whose surviving writings are not lengthy), whence **~ISM** (3) *n.*; **the P~**, (1) Muhammad, (2) Joseph Smith, founder of Mormons, or one of his successors. **2.** Spokesman, advocate, (*of* principle etc.); one who foretells events (*am no weather-prophet*); (sl.) tipster. **3.** Hence **~ESS**¹, **~HOOD** (-t-h-), **~SHIP**, *ns.* [ME, f. OF *prophete* f. L *propheta, prophetes* f. Gk PRO²(*phētēs* speaker f. *phēmi* speak) spokesman]

prophĕ'tĭc *a.* Of a prophet; predicting, containing a prediction *of* (event etc.); hence **~AL** *a.*, **~alLY**² *adv.*, **~ISM** (2, 4) *n.* [f. F *prophétique* or f. LL f. Gk *prophētikos* (as prec.; see -IC)]

prŏphȳlă'ctĭc *a.* & *n.* (Medicine or course of action) tending to prevent disease or other misfortune. [f. F *prophylactique* f. Gk *prophulaktikos* f. PRO²(*phulassō* guard)]

prŏphȳlă'x|ĭs *n.* (*pl.* **~es** *pr.* -ēz). Preventive treatment against disease etc. [mod. L, f. PRO-² + Gk *phulaxis* a guarding, after prec.]

propĭ'nquĭtȳ *n.* Nearness in place; close kinship; similarity. [ME f. OF *propinquité* or f. L *propinquitas* (*propinquus* near f. *prope* near; see -ITY)]

prōpĭŏ'nĭc *a.* ~ **acid,** colourless sharp-smelling liquid (C_4H_9COOH) found in wood-distillation products; hence **prō'pĭon**ATE¹ (3) *n.* [f. F *propionique* f. as PRO-² + Gk *piōn* fat, as being first in series of fatty acids]

propĭ'tĭāte (-shĭ-) *v.t.* Appease (offended person etc.). [f. L *propitiare* (as PROPITIOUS) + -ATE³]

propĭtĭā'tion (-shĭ-) *n.* Appeasement; (esp. Christ's) atonement; (arch.) gift etc. meant to propitiate (*Christ is the propitiation for our sins*). [ME, f. LL *propitiatio* (as prec.; see -ATION)]

propĭ'tiator|ȳ (-sha-) *a.* & *n.* **1.** *a.* Serving or intended to propitiate (*a propitiatory smile*); hence **~ĭLY**² *adv.* **2.** *n.* The mercy-seat (esp. fig. of Christ). [ME, f. eccl. L *propitiatorius* (as PROPITIATE; see -ORY)]

propĭ'tious (-shus) *a.* Well-disposed, favourable, (*the fates were propitious*); (of omen etc.) favourable; (of weather, occasion, etc.) suitable *for*, favourable *to*, (purpose); hence **~LY**² *adv.* [ME, f. OF *propicieus* or f. L *propitius*; see -OUS]

prŏ'polĭs *n.* Red or brown resinous substance got by bees from buds for use as glue etc. [L, f. Gk PRO²(*polis* city) suburb, bee-glue]

propō'nent *a.* & *n.* (Person) that puts forward a motion, theory, or proposal. [f. L *proponere* (as PROPOUND; see -ENT)]

propŏr'tion *n.*, & *v.t.* **1.** *n.* Comparative part, share, (*a large proportion of the earth's surface, of the profits*); comparative relation, ratio, (*the proportion of births to the population*); *price will be raised* **in** ~ (*to the cost* etc., or abs.), by the same factor. **2.** Correct relation of one thing to another or between parts of a thing (*windows are in admirable proportion; his success bore no proportion to his abilities; exaggerated out of all proportion*); hence **~LESS** *a.* **3.** (in *pl.*) Dimensions, size, (*athlete, building, of magnificent proportions*). **4.** (Math.) Equality of ratios between two pairs of quantities (*3, 5, 9, and 15 are in proportion*); set of such quantities, (Arith.) RULE of three; DIRECT², INVERSE, *proportion.* **5.** *v.t.* Make (thing etc.) proportionate *to* (*must proportion the punishment to the crime*); hence (-)**~ED**¹ (-shond) *a.*, **~MENT** *n.* [ME; n. f. OF, or f. L PRO¹(*portio* portion), v. f. OF *proporcioner* or f. med. L *proportionare* f. L *proportio*]

propŏr'tion|al *a.* & *n.* **1.** *a.* In due proportion, corresponding in degree or amount, (*a proportional increase in the expense; resentment proportional to his injuries*); **~al representation,** electoral system such that all parties are represented in proportion to their voting strength; hence or cogn. **~ABLE**, **~ATE**², *adjs.*, **~ablY**², **~alLY**², **~ateLY**² (-tlĭ), *advs.*, **~ă'lITY** *n.* **2.** *n.* One of the terms of a proportion (*5, 3, 10, 6 are proportionals; 6 is a mean proportional between 3 and 12*). [ME, f. LL *proportionalis* (as prec.; see -AL)]

propŏr'tionalĭst *n.* Advocate of proportional representation. [f. prec. + -IST]

propō'sal (-z-) *n.* Act of proposing something; offer of marriage (*have had a proposal*); course of action etc. proposed (*the proposal was never carried out*). [f. foll. + -AL]

propō's|e (-z) *v.* **1.** *v.t.* Put forward for consideration, propound; set up as an aim (*the object I propose to myself*); nominate (person) as member of society etc.; offer (person's health, person) as subject for drinking of toast; put forward as a plan (*we propose (to make) a change, that a change should be made*); intend, purpose, (*to* do, doing). **2.** *v.i.* Make proposal (*man proposes, God disposes*); make offer of marriage (*to*). **3.** Hence **~ER**¹ *n.* [ME, f. OF *proposer* f. L *proponere* (as PROPOUND)]

prŏposĭ'tion (-z-) *n.*, & *v.t.* **1.** *n.* Statement, assertion; (Logic) form of words consisting of subject and predicate; (Math.) formal statement of theorem or problem, often including the demonstration; hence ~AL *a.* **2.** Proposal, scheme proposed; (sl.) problem, undertaking, opponent, prospect, etc., that is to be dealt with (*a difficult, a paying, proposition*; **not a** ~, unlikely to succeed). **3.** *v.t.* (colloq.) Make proposal (esp. of sexual intercourse) to. [ME f. OF, or f. L *propositio* (as foll.; see -ITION)]

propou'nd *v.t.* Offer for consideration, propose, (question, problem, scheme, matter, etc., *to* person); produce (will etc.) before proper authority so as to establish its legality; hence ~ER[1] *n.* [earlier *propoune, propone* f. L PRO[1]-(*ponere posit-* place); cf. *compound, expound*]

prōprae'tor, *prōprē'tor, *n.* (Rom. Hist.) Ex-praetor with authority of praetor in province not under military control. [L, earlier *pro praetore* (one acting) for praetor]

proprī'etarў *a.* Of a proprietor (*proprietary rights*); holding property (*the proprietary classes*); held in private ownership; ~ **colony,** (Hist.) N. Amer. colony granted by Crown to particular person; ~ **medicines** (manufacture and sale of which is restricted by patent etc.); ~ **name** or **term** (use of which is restricted by being trade mark etc.). [f. LL *proprietarius* (as PROPERTY; see -ARY[1])]

proprī'et|or *n.* Holder of property, owner esp. of a business; hence ~**ōr'**IAL *a.*, ~**or**SHIP, ~**r**ESS[1], *ns.* [f. *proprietary* n. f. as prec.]

proprī'etў *n.* Fitness, rightness, (*doubt the propriety of the term, of refusing him*); correctness of behaviour or morals; (in *pl.*) details of correct conduct (*must observe the proprieties*). [ME, = 'ownership, peculiarity', f. OF *proprieté* PROPERTY]

prōprĭocĕ'ptĭve *a.* (Biol.) Relating to stimuli produced and perceived within an organism. [f. L *proprius* own + -O- + RECEPTIVE]

prŏptō's|ĭs *n.* (*pl.* ~**es** *pr.* -ēz). (Path.) Prolapse, protrusion, esp. of eye. [LL, f. Gk *proptōsis* f. PRO[2](*piptō* fall)]

propŭ'ls|ion (-shon) *n.* Driving or pushing forward; (fig.) impelling influence; so ~IVE *a.* [f. obs. *propulse* v. f. L *propulsare* frequent. of *propellere* PROPEL]

prō'pўl *n.* (Chem.) Radical, C_3H_7, derived from propane. [f. PROPIONIC + -YL]

prŏpўlae'|um *n.* (*pl.* ~**a**). Entrance to temple; **the P~a,** entrance to Acropolis at Athens. [L, f. Gk PRO[2](*pulaion* f. *pulē* gate)]

prŏ'pўl|ŏn *n.* (*pl.* ~**ons** *or* ~**a**). = prec. [L, f. Gk PRO[2](*pulon* f. *pulē* gate)]

pro rata (prō rā'ta; *or* rah'-) *adv.* & *a.* Proportional(ly). [L, = according to the rate]

prōrā'te *v.t.* Allocate or distribute *pro rata.* [f. prec.]

pro re nata (prō rē nā'ta; *or* rā nah'-) *adv.* & *a.* For an occasion that has arisen. [L, = for the affair born]

prorō'gue (-g) *v.* **1.** *v.t.* Discontinue meetings of (parliament etc.) without dissolving it. **2.** *v.i.* (Of parliament etc.) be prorogued. **3.** So **prōrog**A'TION *n.* [ME *proroge* f. OF *proroger, -guer* f. L PRO[1](*rogare* ask) prolong]

pros- *pref.* To, towards, in addition. [Gk (*pros* prep.)]

prosā'ĭc (-z-; *or* prō-) *a.* Like prose, lacking poetic beauty; unromantic, commonplace, dull, (*a prosaic life, person, view of things*); hence **prosā'**ICALLY (-z-) *adv.*, ~NESS *n.* [f. F *prosaïque* or f. LL *prosaicus* (as PROSE; see -IC)]

prō'sā|ĭst (-zā-) *n.* Prose-writer; prosaic person; so ~ISM (4) *n.* [f. F *prosaïste* f. L *prosa* PROSE; see -IST]

prōscē'nĭ|um (*or* pro-) *n.* (*pl.* ~**ums** *or* ~**a**). (Theatr.) Part of stage in front of drop or curtain, esp. with the enclosing arch; stage of ancient theatre. [L, f. Gk PRO[2](*skēnion* f. *skēnē* stage)]

prōsciu'ttō (-shōō'-) *n.* (*pl.* ~**s**). Spiced ham. [It.]

proscrī'be *v.t.* Put (person) outside protection of law; banish, exile, (esp. fig.); reject, denounce, (practice etc.) as dangerous etc.; so **proscrĭ'p**TION *n.*, **proscrĭ'pt**IVE *a.* [f. L PRO[1](*scribere script-* write)]

prōse (-z) *n.* & *v.* **1.** *n.* Ordinary non-metrical form of written or spoken language (*Milton's prose works*); passage of this for translation etc.; (Eccl.) = SEQUENCE 5; *prose* IDYLL; *prose* POEM; *prose* POETRY. **2.** Plain matter-of-fact quality (*the prose of existence*); tedious discourse. **3.** *v.i.* Talk tediously (*about* etc.); hence **prō'**SER[1] (-z-) *n.* **4.** *v.t.* Turn (poem etc.) into prose. [ME f. OF, f. L *prosa* (*oratio*) straightforward (discourse), fem. of *prosus*, earlier *prorsus* direct]

prosĕ'ctor *n.* One who dissects dead bodies in preparation for anatomical lecture etc. [LL, = anatomist, f. PRO[1](*secare sect-* cut), perh. after F *prosecteur*]

prŏ'sĕcūte *v.t.* Follow up, pursue, (inquiry, studies); carry on (trade, pursuit); institute legal proceedings against (person) or with reference to (claim, crime, etc.), or abs., (*trespassers will be prosecuted*; *shall not prosecute*). [ME, f. L PRO[1](*sequi secut-* follow)]

prŏsĕcū'tion *n.* Prosecuting (*of* pursuit etc.); (Law) institution and carrying on of criminal charge before court; carrying on of legal proceedings against person; prosecuting party (*the prosecution denied this*); ||**director of public** ~**s,** public PROSECUTOR. [OF, or f. LL *prosecutio* (as prec.; see -ION)]

prŏ'sĕcūtor *n.* One who prosecutes esp. in criminal court; **public** ~, law officer conducting criminal proceedings on behalf of State or in public interest; so **prŏ'sĕcū**TRIX *n.* [f. PROSECUTE or f. med. L *prosecutor* (as PROSECUTE); see -OR]

prŏ'selўt|e *n.*, & *v.t.* **1.** *n.* Person converted from one opinion, creed, or party, to another; Gentile convert to Jewish faith. **2.** *v.t.* *Make a proselyte of (person, or abs.). **3.** Hence ~ISM (1, 2) *n.*, ~IZE (3) *v.t.* (often abs.). [ME, f. LL *proselytus* f. Gk PROS(*ēluthos* f. st. *ēluth-* of *erkhomai* come) stranger, convert]

prŏsĕ'nchўm|a (-ngk-) *n.* (Bot.) Tissue of elongated cells placed with their ends interpenetrating, esp. fibro-vascular tissue; hence ~AL, ~**atous** (-ngkĭ'm-), *adjs.* [f. Gk *pros* toward + *egkhuma* infusion, after *parenchyma*]

prō'sĭfў (-z-) *v.* **1.** *v.t.* Turn into prose; make prosaic. **2.** *v.i.* Write prose. [f. PROSE + -I- + -FY]

prosit (prō'sĭt) *int.* in drinking person's health etc. [G f. L, = may it benefit]

prŏ'sod|ў *n.* Science of versification, laws of METRE[1]; study of speech-rhythms; hence **prosŏ'd**IC *a.*, ~IST (3) *n.* [ME, f. L *prosodia* accent f. Gk PROS(*ōidia* as ODE)]

prŏsōpŏ'graph|ў (*or* -so-) *n.* Description of person's appearance, personality, social and family connections, and career; study of such descriptions; hence ~ER[1] *n.*, **prŏsōpogră'ph**IC(AL) *adjs.* [f. mod. L *prosopographia* f. Gk *prosōpon* face, person (see -GRAPHY)]

prŏsōpopoe'ia (-pē'*a*) *n.* Rhetorical introduction of pretended speaker or personification of abstract thing. [L, f. Gk *prosōpopoiia* (*prosōpon* person, *poieō* make)]

For other words in *pro-* see PRO-.

prŏ'spĕct[1] *n.* **1.** Extensive view of landscape etc. (*a fine, striking, prospect*); mental view of matters (*opened a new prospect to his mind*). **2.** Expectation, what one expects, (*offers a gloomy prospect; his prospects were brilliant; no developments in prospect*); hence ~LESS *a.* **3.** (Mining). Place giving expectations of mineral deposit; sample of ore for testing; resulting yield. **4.** Possible or probable customer, subscriber, etc. [ME, f. L PROSPECTUS]

prospĕ'ct[2] *v.* **1.** *v.i.* Explore region (*for* gold etc.), whence ~OR *n.*; (fig.) look out *for*, (of mine) promise (*well, ill*). **2.** *v.t.* Explore (region) for gold etc., work (mine) experimentally; (of mine) promise (specified yield). [f. prec.]

prospĕ'ctĭve *a.* Concerned with or applying to the future (cf. RETROSPECTIVE; *the law was held to be exclusively prospective, implies a prospective obligation*); expected, future, some day to be, (*prospective peer, bridegroom, profit*); hence ~LY[2] (-vlĭ) *adv.*, ~NESS (-vn-) *n.* [f. obs. F *prospectif -ive* or f. LL *prospectivus* (as foll.; see -IVE)]

prospĕ'ctus *n.* Printed document describing chief features of school, commercial enterprise, forthcoming book, etc. [L, = prospect, f. PRO[1](*spicere spect-* = *specere* look)]

prŏ'sper *v.* **1.** *v.i.* Succeed, thrive, (*cheats never prosper; nothing will ever prosper in his hands*). **2.** *v.t.* Make successful (*Heaven prosper our attempt*). [ME, f. OF *prosperer* or f. L *prosperare* (as foll.)]

prŏ'sperous *a.* **1.** Flourishing, successful, thriving, (*a prosperous merchant, enterprise*); hence or cogn. **prŏspĕ'r**ITY *n.*, ~LY[2] *adv.* **2.** Auspicious (*a prosperous wind; in a prosperous hour*). [ME, f. obs. F *prospereus* f. L *prosper*(*us*); see -OUS]

prŏstaglă'ndĭn *n.* Any of a group of fatty acids causing contraction of muscles in mammalian (esp. uterine) tissues. [G, f. foll. + GLAND[1] + -IN]

prŏ'stāte *n.* ~ **(gland)**, large gland round neck of bladder, accessory to male genital organs, or one of several similar glands in other mammals; hence **prostă't**IC *a.* [F, f. mod. L *prostata* f. Gk PRO[2](*statēs* f. *statos* standing) one that stands before]

prŏ'sthĕs|ĭs *n.* (*pl.* ~*es pr.* -ēz). **1.** (Gram.) Addition of letter or syllable at beginning of word, e.g. *be-* in *beloved*. **2.** (Surg.) Making up of deficiencies (e.g. by false teeth or artificial limb) as a branch of surgery; part thus supplied. **3.** Hence **prŏsthĕ't**IC *a.*; **prŏsthĕ't**ICS *n. pl.* (usu. treated as *sing.*) = sense 2. [LL, f. Gk *prosthesis* f. PROS(*tithēmi* place)]

prŏ'stĭtūte *n.*, & *v.t.* **1.** *n.* Woman who offers her body to promiscuous sexual intercourse esp. for payment or as religious rite; man who undertakes homosexual actions for payment. **2.** *v.t.* Make a prostitute of (esp. one*self*); (fig.) sell (one's honour etc.) unworthily, put (abilities etc.) to wrong use, debase. **3.** So **prŏstĭtū't**ION *n.* [(n. f. L *prostituta*) f. L PRO[1](*stituere stitut-* = *statuere* set up, place) offer for sale]

prŏ'strāte[1] *a.* Lying with face to ground, esp. as token of submission or humility; lying in horizontal position; overcome, overthrown, (*prostrate with grief*); physically exhausted; (Bot.) growing along the ground. [ME, f. L *prostratus* p.p. (as foll.)]

prŏstrā'te[2] (*or* pros-) *v.t.* Lay (person etc.) flat on ground; throw one*self* down prostrate (*at* shrine, *before* person etc.); (fig.) overcome, make submissive; (of fatigue etc.) reduce to extreme physical weakness; hence **prŏstrā't**ION (*or* pros-) *n.* [ME, f. L PRO[1](*sternere strat-* lay flat)]

prō'stȳle *n.* & *a.* (That has) portico with not more than four columns. [f. L *prostylos* having pillars in front (as PRO-[2], STYLE)]

prō's|y̆ (-zĭ) *a.* Commonplace, tedious, wearisomely dull, (*prosy talk, talker*); hence ~ĬLY[2] *adv.*, ~ĬNESS *n.* [f. PROSE + -Y[2]]

Prot. *abbr.* Protectorate; Protestant.

prōtăctĭ'nĭum *n.* (Chem.) Radioactive metallic element whose chief isotope yields actinium by decay. [G, f. as PROTO- + ACTINIUM]

prōtă'gonĭst *n.* Chief person in drama or plot of story; leading person in contest, principal performer; advocate or champion *of* course, method, etc. [f. Gk *prōtagōnistēs* (as PROTO-, *agōnistēs* actor)]

prō'tamine (-ēn) *n.* Any of a group of simple proteins found esp. in fish sperm. [f. PROTO- + AMINE]

pro tanto (prō tă'ntō) *adv.* So far; to that extent. [L, = for so much]

prŏ'tas|ĭs *n.* (*pl.* ~**es** *pr.* ~ēz). Clause expressing condition in conditional sentence; so **protă't**IC *a.* [L, f. Gk PRO[2](*tasis* f. *teinō* stretch) proposition]

prō'tėa *n.* S. Afr. shrub of genus *Protea*, with conelike flower-heads. [mod. L, f. PROTEUS, w. ref. to the many species]

prō'tėan (*or* -ē'an) *a.* Variable, versatile; taking many forms. [f. PROTEUS + -AN]

protĕ'ct *v.t.* Keep safe, defend, guard, (person or thing *from* or *against* danger, injury, disadvantage etc.); (Econ.) guard (home industry) against competition by import duties on foreign goods; ||provide funds to meet (bill, draft); provide (machinery etc.) with appliances to prevent injury from it. [f. L PRO[1](*tegere tect-* cover)]

protĕ'ction *n.* Protecting, defence, (*is safe under your protection; affords protection against weather*; ||**Court of P~**, department of Supreme Court attending to affairs of the mentally unfit); protecting person or thing (*a dog is a great protection against burglars*); (arch.) keeping of woman as mistress. **2.** = SAFE[2] *conduct*. **3.** (Econ.) System of protecting home industries; hence ~ISM (3), ~IST (2), *ns.* **4.** Immunity from molestation, obtained by payment under threat of violence; ~ **(money)**, money so paid. [ME f. OF, or f. LL *protectio* (as prec.; see -ION)]

protĕ'ctĭve *a.* Serving or seeking or intended to protect; (of food) protecting against deficiency diseases; ~ **clothing** (against burns, radiation, etc.); ~ **colouring** (making animal or plant less likely to be seen or attacked by predator); ~ **custody,** detention of person actually or allegedly for his own protection; hence ~LY[2] (-vlĭ) *adv.*, ~NESS (-vn-) *n.* [f. PROTECT + -IVE]

protĕ'ctor *n.* **1.** Person who protects; regent in charge of kingdom during minority, absence, etc., of sovereign (**Lord P~ of the Commonwealth,** title of Oliver Cromwell 1653–8 and Richard Cromwell 1658–9), whence ~AL *a.*, ~SHIP *n.*; hence **protĕ'ctr**ESS[1] *n.* **2.** Thing or device that protects (*chest-protector*). [ME, f. OF *protecteur* f. LL *protector* (as PROTECT; see -OR)]

protĕ'ctorate *n.* Office of protector of kingdom or State; period of this, esp. under the Cromwells 1653–9; protectorship of weak or underdeveloped State by stronger one; State thus protected. [f. prec. + -ATE[1]]

protĕ'ctorȳ *n.* Institution for care of destitute or delinquent children. [f. PROTECT + -ORY]

protégé (prŏ'tĕzhā) *n.* (*fem.* ~*e pr.* same). Person to whom another is (usu. permanent) protector or patron. [F, p.p. of *protéger* f. L *protegere* PROTECT]

prō'tėĭd *n.* (arch.) = PROTEIN. [f. PROTEIN + -ID[4]]

prō'tėĭfŏrm *a.* Very changeable in form. [f. PROTEUS + -I- + -FORM]

prō'tein (-tēn) *n.* (Chem.) One of a class of organic compounds (containing carbon, hydrogen, oxygen, and nitrogen, freq. also sulphur, occas. phosphorus, iron, etc.) forming an important part of all living organisms, and the essential nitrogenous constituent of the food of animals; hence ~A'CEOUS, **prōtei'nic** (-tē'n-), **prōtē'ĭn**OUS, *adjs.* [f. F *protéine*, G *protein*, f. Gk *prōteios* primary; see -IN]

prō tē'm *a.* & *adv.* (colloq.) = foll. [abbr.]

pro tempore (prō tĕ'mperĭ) *a.* & *adv.* For the time being (esp. of appointment to office). [L]

prōtėŏ'lўsis *n.* Hydrolysis of proteins or peptides; hence **prōtėolў'tic** *a.* [mod. L, f. PROTEIN + -O- + -LYSIS]

prŏterozō'ic *a.* & *n.* (Geol.) (Of the) geological era containing the oldest forms of life. [f. Gk *proteros* former + *zōē* life, *zōos* living + -IC]

prō'tĕst[1] *n.* Formal statement or action of dissent or disapproval, remonstrance, (*made a protest*; *paid it under protest*); written declaration usu. by notary public that bill has been duly presented and payment or acceptance refused; solemn declaration; demonstration of objection to official policy (*marched in protest*). [ME f. OF (*protester*; see foll.)]

protĕ'st[2] *v.* **1.** *v.t.* Affirm solemnly (one's innocence etc., *that*, or abs.) esp. in reply to accusation etc.; write or obtain PROTEST[1] in regard to (bill); *object to (decision etc.). **2.** *v.i.* Make (often written) protest *against* (action, proposal). **3.** Hence ~ER[1], ~OR, *ns.* [ME, f. OF *protester* f. L PRO[1](*testari* assert f. *testis* witness)]

Prŏ'tėstant *n.* & *a.* **1.** (Member or adherent) of any of the Christian bodies that separated from the Roman communion in the Reformation (16th c.), or their offshoots; hence ~ISM (3) *n.*, ~IZE (3) *v.t.* & *i.* **2.** *n.* (Hist., in *pl.*) Those who dissented from decision of Diet of Spires (1529), adherents of Reformed doctrines in Germany. **3.** *n.* & *a.* (*p*~; *or* protĕ's-) Protesting (person). [f. mod. L *protestans*, part. of L *protestari* (see prec., -ANT)]

prŏtėstā'tion *n.* Solemn affirmation (*of*, *that*); protest (*against*). [ME f. OF, or f. LL *protestatio* (as prec.; see -ATION)]

Prō'teus (*or* -tĭus) *n.* **1.** Changing or inconstant person or thing. **2.** (*p*~). Bacterium of genus *Proteus*; olm. [L, f. Gk *Prōteus* sea-god fabled to take various shapes]

prōthalā'mĭ|um, -ĭ|ŏn, *n.* (*pl.* ~**a**). Song to celebrate forthcoming wedding. [made by Spenser on *epithalamium* (cf. PRO-[2])]

prōthă'llĭ|um *n.* (*pl.* ~**a**). = foll. [mod. L, f. PRO-[2] + Gk *thallion* dim. of *thallos*; see THALLUS, -IUM]

prōthă'll|us *n.* (*pl.* ~**i** *pr.* -ī). (Bot.) Gametophyte of fern etc.; corresponding structure in higher plant. [mod. L, f. PRO-[2] + as THALLUS]

prŏ'thės|ĭs *n.* (*pl.* ~**es** *pr.* -ēz). (Eccl.) (placing of Eucharistic elements on) credence table, part of church where this stands; (Gram.) = PROSTHESIS, whence **prothĕ'tic** *a.* [Gk, f. PRO[2](*tithēmi* place)]

prothonotary. See PROTONOTARY.

Protĭ'sta *n. pl.* Kingdom of organisms (bacteria, protozoa, etc.) not distinguished as animals or plants; hence **prōtĭstŏ'logy** *n.* [mod. L, f. Gk *prōtista*, neut. pl. superl. f. *prōtos* first]

prō'tium *n.* (Chem.) Ordinary isotope of hydrogen as dist. from heavy hydrogen (deuterium or tritium). [mod. L, f. PROTO- + -IUM]

prō'to- *comb. form.* **1.** Original, primitive (*proto-Germanic*, *proto-Slavic*). **2.** First, original, as: ~**hi'ppus,** extinct Pliocene quadruped related to horse; ~**mar'tyr,** first martyr (esp. St. Stephen, first Christian martyr); ~**pe'ctin,** pectose; ~**phyte,** unicellular plant; ~**ther'ia,** monotremes; ~**zo'ic,** (1) (of strata) containing earliest traces of living beings, (2) protozoan. [f. Gk *prōto-* (*prōtos* first)]

prō'tocŏl *n.* & *v.* (-**ll**-). **1.** *n.* Original draft of diplomatic document, esp. of terms of treaty agreed to in conference and signed by the parties; formal statement of transaction; (observance of) official formality and etiquette; official formulae at beginning and end of charter, papal bull, etc.; *record of experimental observations etc. **2.** *v.i.* Draw up protocol(s). **3.** *v.t.* Record in protocol. [orig. Sc. *prothocoll* f. OF *-cole* f. med. L f. Gk PROTO(*kollon* f. *kolla* glue) flyleaf glued to binding of book]

prō'tŏn *n.* (Phys.) Elementary particle with unit positive charge, forming part (or, in hydrogen, whole) of atomic nucleus; hence **protŏ'nic** *a.* [Gk, neut. of *prōtos* first]

prōtonō'tarў, prōthŏ-, (*or* protŏ'nŏ-) *n.* Chief clerk in some law courts (orig. in Byzantine court); **P~ Apostolic(al)**, member of college of prelates who register papal acts, direct the canonization of saints, etc. [f. med. L f. late Gk PROTO(*notarios* NOTARY)]

prō'toplăsm *n.* Viscous translucent colourless substance forming main constituent of cells in organisms, the basis of life in plants and animals; hence **prōtoplă'sm**AL, **prōtoplăsmă'tic**, **prōtoplă'smic**, (-z-) *adjs.* [f. Gk *protoplasma* (as PROTO-, PLASMA)]

prō'toplăst *n.* Mass of protoplasm within one cell; hence **prōtoplă'stic** *a.* [f. F *protoplaste* or f. LL f. Gk PROTO(*plastos* moulded f. *plassō* mould)]

prō'to|tўpe *n.* An original thing or person in relation to a copy, imitation, representation, later specimen, improved form, etc.; trial model, preliminary version, esp. of aeroplane etc.; hence ~**tўp**AL, ~**tў'pic**(AL), *adjs.* [F, or f. LL f. Gk PROTO(*tupos* TYPE[1])]

prōtozō'|on *n.* (*pl.* ~**a**). Animal of subkingdom or phylum Protozoa, usu. unicellular and microscopic; hence ~AL *a.*, ~AN *a.* & *n.*, ~**ŏ'**LOGY *n.* [mod. L, f. as PROTO- + Gk *zōion* animal; see -A 2]

protră'ct *v.t.* **1.** Prolong, lengthen, make last longer, (*protracted their stay for some weeks*); hence ~**ėd**LY[2] *adv.* **2.** Draw (plan of ground etc.) to scale. [f. L PRO[1](*trahere tract-* draw)]

protră'ctīle *a.* (Zool.) (Of organ etc.) capable of being extended. [f. prec.; see -IL]

protră'ction *n.* Protracting or being protracted; action of protractor muscle; drawing to scale. [F, or f. LL *protractio* (as PROTRACT; see -ION)]

protră'ctor *n.* Instrument for measuring angles, usu. in form of graduated semicircle; muscle serving to extend limb etc. [f. PROTRACT + -OR]

protru'de (-ōō'd) *v.* **1.** *v.t.* Thrust forth, cause to project; (fig.) obtrude. **2.** *v.i.* Extend beyond or above the surrounding surface, project. **3.** Hence **protru'd**ENT, **protru's**IBLE, **protru's**IVE, (-ōō'-) *adjs.*, **protru's**ION (-ōō'zhon) *n.* [f. L PRO[1](*trudere trus-* thrust)]

protru'sīle (-ōō'-) *a.* (Of limb etc.) capable of being thrust forth. [f. PRO-[1] + *extrusile*]

protū'ber|ant *a.* Bulging out, prominent (lit. or fig.); hence ~ANCE *n.* [f. LL PRO[1](*tuberare* f. *tuber* bump); see -ANT]

proud *a.* & *adv.* **1.** *a.* Valuing oneself highly or too highly, esp. on the ground *of* (qualities, rank, possessions, etc.); ~(**-hearted**), haughty, arrogant; PURSE[1]-*proud*. **2.** Feeling oneself greatly honoured (*am proud of his acquaintance*, *of knowing him*, *to know him*). **3.** Having a proper pride (*too proud to complain*; HOUSE[1]-*proud*). **4.** (Of action etc.) showing pride; of which one is or may be justly proud (*a proud day for us*; *a proud sight*). **5.** (Of thing) imposing, splendid; (of waters) swollen, in flood; slightly projecting; (of flesh) overgrown round healing wound. **6.** Hence ~'LY² *adv.* **7.** *adv.* (colloq.) **Do** (person, one*self*) ~, treat with great generosity or honour. [OE *prūt*, *prūd*, = ON *prúthr* f. OF *prud*, *prod* obl. case of *pruz* etc. valiant, f. Rom. **prodis* f. LL *prode*, f. L *prodesse* be of value (PRO-¹, *esse* be)]

Prov. *abbr.* Proverbs (O.T.); Province.

prov|e (prōōv) *v.* (*p.p.* **~ed** *or*, esp. U.S., Sc., & literary, **~'en**). **1.** *v.t.* (arch.) Test qualities of, try. **2.** Subject (gun etc.) to testing process; cause (dough) to rise in bread-making. **3.** (Arith.) test accuracy of (calculation); *the* EXCEPTION *proves the rule*. **4.** = PROOF¹ 9. **5.** Make certain, demonstrate by evidence or argument, (fact, *the truth of*, thing etc. *to* be, *that*), whence ~'ABLE *a.*; **~e oneself,** show one's abilities etc.; (Sc. Law, as verdict in criminal trial) **not proven,** the evidence is insufficient to establish either guilt or innocence. **6.** Establish genuineness and validity of (will). **7.** *v.i.* Be found (*to* be, *to* do); be found to be (*will prove the winner*). [ME, f. OF *prover* f. L *probare* test, approve, demonstrate (*probus* good)]

prŏ'vėnance *n.* Place of origin. [F, f. *provenir* f. L PRO¹(*venire* come); see -ANCE]

Provençal (prŏvahṅsah'l) *a.* & *n.* (Inhabitant or language) of Provence. [F (as PROVINCIAL, f. *provincia* as L colloq. name for southern Gaul under Roman rule)]

prŏ'vėnder *n.* Fodder; (joc.) food for human beings. [ME, f. OF *provendre*, *provende* f. Rom. **probenda* f. L *praebenda* (see PREBEND)]

***provē'nĭence** *n.* = PROVENANCE. [f. L PRO¹-(*venire* come); see -ENCE]

prŏ'vêrb *n.* Short pithy saying in general use, adage, saw; person or thing that is widely known (*their fickleness is a proverb*; *he is a proverb for inaccuracy*); **(Book of) P~s,** didactic poetical O.T. book of maxims ascribed to Solomon and others. [ME, f. OF *proverbe* or f. L PRO¹(*verbium* f. *verbum* word)]

provêr'bĭal *a.* Of or expressed in proverbs (*proverbial wisdom*; *the proverbial ill wind*); that has become a proverb, notorious; hence ~ITY (-ă'l-) *n.*, ~LY² *adv.* [ME, f. L *proverbialis* (as prec.; see -AL)]

provī'd|e *v.* **1.** *v.i.* Make due preparation (*for* possible event, person's safety, entertainment, etc.; *against* attack etc.); make due preparation of maintenance (*for* person). **2.** *v.t.* (Of person, law, etc.) stipulate (*that*); supply, furnish, (person *with* thing, thing *for* or *to* person); equip with necessaries (*you must provide yourselves*). **3.** (Hist.) Appoint (incumbent *to* benefice); (of pope) appoint (successor *to* benefice not yet vacant). **4. ~ing (that)** *conj.*, = foll. 2. [ME, f. L PRO¹(*vidēre vis-* see)]

provī'dėd *a.* & *conj.* **1.** *a.* In vbl senses. **2.** *conj.* ~ **(that)**, on the condition or understanding that. [p.p. of prec.]

prŏ'vĭdence *n.* Foresight, timely care; thrift; beneficent care of God or nature **(special ~,** particular instance of this); (*P~*) God in this aspect. [ME f. OF, or f. L *providentia* (as PROVIDE; see -ENCE)]

prŏ'vĭdent *a.* Having or showing foresight; thrifty (‖**P~ Society,** = FRIENDLY *Society*); hence ~LY² *adv.* [ME, f. L (as PROVIDE; see -ENT)]

prŏvĭdĕ'ntial (-shal) *a.* Of or by divine foresight or interposition; opportune, lucky; hence ~LY² *adv.* [f. PROVIDENCE + -IAL, after *evidential* etc.]

provī'der *n.* In vbl senses; breadwinner of family etc. [f. PROVIDE + -ER¹]

prŏ'vĭnce *n.* **1.** Principal administrative division of country etc.; (Eccl.) district under archbishop or metropolitan; (Rom. Hist.) territory outside Italy under Roman governor; **the ~s,** whole of a country outside capital. **2.** Sphere of action, business, (*is not within my province*); branch of learning etc. (*in the province of aesthetics*). [ME f. OF, f. L *provincia* charge, province]

provĭ'ncial (-shal) *a.* & *n.* **1.** *a.* Of a province; of the provinces; having the manners, speech, narrow views, etc., associated with or attributed to inhabitants of the provinces, whence ~ITY (-shĭă'l-) *n.*; hence ~IZE (3) *v.t.*, ~LY² *adv.* **2.** *n.* Inhabitant of a province or the provinces; countrified person; (Eccl.) head of, chief of religious order in, a province. [ME f. OF, f. L *provincialis* (as prec.; see -AL)]

provĭ'ncial|ĭsm (-sha-) *n.* Provincial manner, fashion, mode of thought, etc.; word or phrase peculiar to provincial region; attachment to one's province rather than country; so ~IST (2, 3) *n.* [f. prec. + -ISM]

provĭ'sion (-zhon) *n.*, & *v.t.* **1.** *n.* Providing (*for*, *against*; esp. *make provision*); provided amount *of* something. **2.** (in *pl.*) Supply of food, eatables and drinkables; hence ~LESS *a.* **3.** Legal or formal statement providing for something; clause of this. **4.** (Hist.) Appointment to benefice not yet vacant. **5.** *v.t.* Supply with provisions (sense 2); hence ~MENT *n.* [ME f. OF, f. L *provisio -onis* (as PROVIDE; see -ION)]

provĭ'sional (-zho-) *a.* Providing for immediate needs only, temporary; hence ~ITY (-ă'l-), ~NESS, *ns.*, ~LY² *adv.* [f. prec. + -AL]

provī'sō (-zō) *n.* (*pl.* ~**s**). Stipulation; clause of stipulation or limitation in document. [L, neut. abl. p.p. of *providēre* PROVIDE, in med. L phr. *proviso quod* it being provided that]

provī'sor (-z-) *n.* **1.** (Hist.) Holder of a provision (sense 4). **2.** (Eccl.) Deputy of (arch)-bishop. [ME, f. AF *provisour* f. L *provisor -oris* (as PROVIDE; see -OR)]

provī'sor|y̆ (-z-) *a.* Conditional; making provision (*provisory care*); hence ~ĭLY² *adv.* [f. F *provisoire* or f. med. L *provisorius* (as prec.; see -ORY)]

Prō'vō¹ *n.* (*pl.* ~**s**). Member of Dutch anarchist group seeking to provoke the authorities. [f. F *provocateur* provoker]

Prō'vō² *n.* (*pl.* ~**s**). (colloq.) Member of Provisional wing of I.R.A. [abbr.; see -O]

prŏvocā'tion *n.* Incitement esp. to anger etc., instigation, irritation, (*did it under severe provocation*; *downs tools at* or *on the slightest provocation*); cause of annoyance. [ME f. OF, or f. L *provocatio* (as PROVOKE; see -ATION)]

provŏ'catĭve *a.* & *n.* (Thing) tending to cause provocation (*of* curiosity, anger, lust, etc.); intentionally annoying. [ME, f. obs. F *provocatif -ive*, f. LL *provocativus* (as foll.; see -IVE)]

provō'k|e *v.t.* Rouse, incite, (person *to* anger, *to* do); irritate (person *into* doing); instigate, tempt, allure; call forth (indignation, inquiry, a storm, etc.); cause (*will provoke fermentation*); hence ~ING² *a.* [ME, f. OF *provoquer* f. L PRO¹(*vocare* call)]

prŏ'vost (in sense 4 provō') *n.* **1.** ‖Head of some colleges at Oxford, Cambridge, etc.; *high administrative officer in university; head of chapter in modern cathedral or of religious community. **2.** (Sc.) Head of municipal corporation or burgh (in four cities, **Lord P~**). **3.** Protestant clergyman in charge of principal church of town etc. in Germany etc. **4.** ~ **(marshal)**, head of military police in camp or on active service, master-at-arms of ship on which court martial is to be held; ***~ guard,** body of soldiers under provost marshal. **5.**

Hence ~SHIP *n.* [ME, f. OE *profost*, & f. AF *provost, prevost* f. med. L *propositus* for *praepositus*; see PRAEPOSTOR]

prow[1] *n.* Fore-part adjoining stem of boat or ship; pointed projecting front part. [f. F *proue* f. Prov. *proa* or It. dial. *prua* f. L *prora* f. Gk *prōira*]

prow[2] *a.* (arch.) Worthy, gallant. [ME, f. OF *prou, prod*, f. Rom. **prodis* (see PROUD)]

prow'ĕss *n.* Valour, gallantry; skill, expertness. [ME, f. OF *proesce* (as prec.; see -ESS[2])]

prowl *v.* & *n.* **1.** *v.i.* Go about in search of plunder or prey (lit. or fig.). **2.** *v.t.* Traverse (streets, place) thus. **3.** Hence ~'ER[1] *n.* **4.** *n.* Prowling (*on the prowl*; ***~ car,** police squad car). [ME *prolle*, of unkn. orig.]

prox. *abbr.* proximo.

prox. acc. *abbr. proxime accessit.*

prŏ'xĭmal *a.* (Anat.) Situated towards centre of body or point of attachment; hence ~LY[2] *adv.* [f. L *proximus* nearest + -AL]

prŏ'xĭmate *a.* Nearest, next before or after (in place, order, time, connection of thought, causation, etc.); approximate; hence ~LY[2] (-tlĭ) *adv.* [f. L *proximatus* p.p. of *proximare* draw near (as prec.); see -ATE[2]]

‖***proxime accessit*** (prŏksĭmĭ aksĕ'sĭt) *n.* (Person gaining) next place in merit to prize-winner(s) in examination etc. [L, = came very near]

prŏxĭ'mĭtў *n.* Nearness in space, time, etc. (*to*); **~ of blood,** kinship; **~ fuse,** radio device causing projectile to explode when near target. [ME, f. F *proximité* or f. L *proximitas* (as PROXIMAL; see -ITY)]

prŏ'xĭmō *a.* (Commerc.) Of next month (*the 3rd proximo*). [L, = in the next (*mense* month)]

prŏ'xў *n.* Agency of substitute or deputy (*voted, was married, by proxy*); person authorized to act for another (*made me his proxy; stood proxy for the godmother*); document authorizing person to vote on behalf of another, vote so given. [ME, f. obs. *procuracy* f. med. L *procuratia* (as PROCURATION; see -ACY)]

P.R.S. *abbr.* President of the Royal Society.

prud|e (prōōd) *n.* Person of extreme (esp. affected) propriety in conduct or speech, esp. as regards sexual matters; hence or cogn. ~'ERY (4) *n.*, ~'ISH[1] *a.* [F, back form. f. *prudefemme* fem. of *prud'homme* good man and true (as PROW[2], *homme* f. L *homo hominis* man)]

pru'd|ent (-ōō'-) *a.* (Of person or conduct) careful to avoid undesired consequences; circumspect, discreet; hence or cogn. ~ENCE *n.*, **~ent**LY[2] *adv.* [ME f. OF, or f. L *prudens* = *providens* PROVIDENT]

prudĕ'ntial (-ōōdĕ'nshal) *a.* & *n.* **1.** *a.* Of, involving, marked by, prudence, (*prudential motives, policy*); hence ~ISM (2), ~IST (2), *ns.*, ~LY[2] *adv.* **2.** *n.* (in *pl.*) Prudential considerations or matters, esp. *minor administrative or financial matters. [f. prec. + -IAL, after *evidential* etc.]

pru'ĭnōse (-ōō'-) *a.* (Biol.) Covered with white powdery substance, frosted. [f. L *pruinosus* (*pruina* hoar-frost; see -OSE[1])]

prune[1] (prōōn) *n.* Dried plum; (colloq.) disliked person; **~s and prism(s)** (of mincing way of speaking etc.; see Dickens's *Little Dorrit* II. v). [ME f. OF, f. Rom. **pruna* f. L *prunum* f. Gk *prou(m)non* plum]

prun|e[2] (prōōn) *v.t.* Trim (tree etc., often *down*) by cutting away dead or overgrown branches etc. with **~'ing-hook** etc., esp. to promote growth; lop (branches etc.) *off, away*; (fig.) remove (superfluities), reduce (costs etc.), clear (book etc. *of* what is superfluous). [ME *prouyne* f. OF *pro(o)ignier* f. Rom. *PRO[1](*rotundiare* cut to round shape f. *rotundus* ROUND[1])]

prune[3] (prōōn) *v.t.* (arch.) = PREEN. [ME *prune, pruyne, proyne*, f. OF *poroign-* st. of *poroindre* f. as PRO-[1] + L *ungere* anoint]

prunĕ'lla[1] (prōō-) *n.* Strong silk or worsted fabric used formerly for barristers' gowns etc. and for uppers of women's shoes; LEATHER *and prunella*. [perh. f. F *prunelle*, of uncert. orig.]

prunĕ'lla[2] (prōō-) *n.* Plant of genus *Prunella*, esp. self-heal (formerly thought to cure quinsy). [mod. L, = quinsy; earlier *brunella* dim. of med. L *brunus* brown]

prur'ĭ|ent (-oor'-) *a.* Given to or arising from indulgence of lewd ideas; hence ~ENCE, ~ENCY, *ns.*, **~ent**LY[2] *adv.* [f. L *prurire* itch, be wanton; see -ENT]

prurī'gō (-oor-) *n.* Disease of skin with violent itching; so **prurī'gin**OUS (-oor-) *a.* [L *prurigo -ginis* (*prurire* to itch)]

prur'ĭtus (-oor'-) *n.* Violent itching of skin. [L, = itching (as prec.)]

Prŭ'ssian (-shan) *a.* & *n.* (Native or inhabitant) of Prussia; **Old ~,** language spoken in Prussia until 17th c.; **~ blue,** deep blue pigment got from ferrocyanides by treatment with ferric salt; **~ carp,** crucian; hence ~IZE (3) *v.t.* (esp. w. ref. to rigid discipline). [f. *Prussi* a Balto-Slavic people + -IAN]

prŭ'ssĭc *a.* Of, or got from, Prussian blue; **~ acid,** hydrocyanic acid. [f. F *prussique* (*Prusse* Prussia; see -IC)]

prȳ[1] *v.i.* Look or peer inquisitively (*into, about* adv.); inquire impertinently *into* (person's affairs, conduct, etc.); hence ~'ING[2] *a.* [ME *prie*, of unkn. orig.]

***prȳ**[2] *v.t.* **1.** = PRIZE[3]. **2.** Get (*out of, open*, etc.) with effort. [f. PRIZE[3] taken as *pries* 3 sing.]

P.S. *abbr.* Police Sergeant; postscript; private secretary; prompt side.

Ps(s). *abbr.* Psalm(s) (O.T.).

psalm (sahm) *n.* Sacred song, hymn; **the (Book of) P~s,** book of these in O.T.; **~-book,** book containing the Psalms, esp. metrical version of these for public worship. [OE *(p)sealm* f. LL f. Gk *psalmos* song sung to harp (*psallō* pluck, sing to harp)]

psa'lmĭst (sah'm-) *n.* Author of a psalm; **the P~,** David or author of any of the Psalms. [f. LL *psalmista* (as prec.; see -IST)]

psa'lmod|ў (sah'm- *or* să'lm-) *n.* Practice or art of singing psalms, hymns, anthems, etc. esp. in public worship, whence **psălmŏ'd**IC (săl-) *a.*, ~IST (3) *n.*, ~IZE (2) *v.i.*; arrangement of psalms for singing, psalms so arranged. [ME, f. LL *psalmodia* f. Gk *psalmōidia* singing to harp (as PSALM, *ōidē* song)]

psa'lter (saw'l- *or* sŏ'l-) *n.* The Book of Psalms; version of this (*Latin, English, Prayer-Book, Scottish Metrical, Psalter*); copy of the Psalms esp. for liturgical use. [ME f. AF *sauter*, OF *sautier*, & f. OE *(p)saltere*, f. LL f. Gk *psaltērion* stringed instrument (*psallō* pluck), in eccl. L Book of Psalms]

psaltēr'ĭum (sawl- *or* sŏl-) *n.* Third STOMACH of ruminant. [L (see prec.); named from likeness to book]

psa'lterў (saw'l- *or* sŏ'l-) *n.* Ancient and medieval instrument like dulcimer but played by plucking strings with fingers or plectrum. [ME, f. OF *sauterie* etc. f. L (as PSALTER)]

psĕphŏ'|logў (*or* s-) *n.* Study of trends in elections and voting; hence ~LOGIST *n.*, **~lŏ'g**ICAL (-fo-) *a.* [f. Gk *psēphos* pebble, vote + -O- + -LOGY]

pseud (s-) *a.* & *n.* (colloq.) **1.** *a.* Not genuine;

For other words in *pro-* see PRO-.

pretentious, esp. in intellectual or social matters. **2.** *n.* Such person. [abbr. of PSEUDO]

pseud-. See PSEUDO-.

pseudĕpĭ'graph|a (s-) *n. pl.* Spurious writings, esp. Jewish writings ascribed to various O.T. prophets etc. but written in or somewhat before the early Christian period; hence ~AL, **pseudĕpĭgră'phic**(AL) (s-), *adjs.* [neut. pl. of Gk PSEUD(*epigraphos*; see EPIGRAPH) with false title]

pseu'dō (s-) *a.* & *n.* (*pl.* ~**s**). Sham, spurious, insincere, (person). [f. foll.]

pseu'dō- (s-) *comb. form.* (usu. **pseud-** bef. vowel). False, apparent, supposed but not real, as: ~**-archa'ic,** artificially archaic in style etc.; ~**carp,** (Bot.) fruit formed other than from ovary, e.g. strawberry, fig; ~**-science,** pretended science. [Gk, f. st. of *pseudēs* false, *pseudos* falsehood]

pseu'dograph (s-; -ahf) *n.* A spurious literary work. [f. LL f. Gk PSEUDO(*graphos*; see -GRAPH)]

pseu'do|mŏrph (s-) *n.* False form, esp. crystal etc. consisting of one mineral with form proper to another; hence ~**mŏr'phic**, ~**mŏr'phous**, *adjs.*, ~**mŏr'phism** (2) *n.* [f. PSEUDO- + Gk *morphē* form]

pseu'donўm (s-) *n.* Fictitious name, esp. one assumed by author. [f. F *pseudonyme* f. Gk neut. adj. (as foll.)]

pseud|ŏ'nўmous (s-) *a.* Writing, written, under a fictitious name; hence ~**onў'mity** *n.* [f. Gk PSEUD(*ōnumos* f. *onuma, onoma* name) + -OUS]

pseu'dopŏd (s-) *n.* = foll. [f. mod. L (as foll.)]

pseudopō'dĭ|um (s-) *n.* (*pl.* ~**a**). Temporary protrusion of protoplasm from cell for movement, feeding, etc. [mod. L (as PSEUDO-, PODIUM)]

pshaw (*or* sh-) *int.* expr. contempt or impatience. [imit.]

psī *n.* Twenty-third Greek letter (Ψ, ψ) = ps; parapsychological factors or faculties collectively. [Gk]

p.s.i.(g.) *abbr.* pounds per square inch (gauge).

psīlă'nthrop|ĭsm (s-) *n.* Doctrine that Christ was a mere man; so **psīlanthrŏ'pic** (s-) *a.*, ~IST (2) *n.* [f. eccl. Gk *psilanthrōpos* merely human (*psilos* bare, mere, *anthrōpos* man) + -ISM]

psīlocў'bĭn (s-) *n.* Hallucinogen found in Mexican mushrooms of genus *Psilocybe*. [f. *Psilocybe* (f. Gk *psilos* bald + *kubē* head) + -IN]

psīlō's|ĭs (s-) *n.* (*pl.* ~**es** *pr.* -ēz). (Path.) Stripping bare, e.g. of hair or flesh; = SPRUE². [f. Gk *psilōsis* (*psilos* bare; see -OSIS)]

psĭ'ttacīne (s-) *a.* Of parrots; parrot-like. [f. L *psittacinus* (*psittacus* f. Gk *psittakos* parrot; see -INE¹)]

psĭttacō's|ĭs (s-) *n.* (*pl.* ~**es** *pr.* -ēz). Contagious disease of birds transmissible (esp. from parrots) to human beings as form of pneumonia. [mod. L, f. L *psittacus* (as prec.) + -OSIS]

psō'as (s-) *n.* ~ **magnus** or **major, parvus** or **minor,** two hip-muscles. [Gk, acc. pl. of *psoa*, taken as sing.]

psorī'as|ĭs (s-) *n.* (*pl.* ~**es** *pr.* -ēz). Skin disease marked by red scaly patches. [mod. L f. Gk *psōriasis* (*psōriaō* have itch f. *psōra* itch)]

ps(s)t *int.* seeking to attract person's attention surreptitiously. [imit.]

***PST** *abbr.* Pacific Standard Time.

||**P.S.V.** *abbr.* public service vehicle.

***psўch** (sīk) *v.t.* (sl.) Psycho-analyse; analyse (problem etc.) in psychological terms. [abbr.]

psў'chē (sī'kĭ) *n.* Soul, spirit; mind. [L, f. Gk *psukhē* breath, life, soul, in Gk Myth. personified as beloved of Eros]

psўchēdĕ'l|ic (sīk-) *a.* & *n.* (Hallucinogenic drug) expanding the mind's awareness; having similar effect to such experiences; hence ~IA² *n. pl.*, psychedelic drugs, articles, etc. [irreg. f. Gk (as prec.) + *dēlos* clear, manifest + -IC]

psўchī'atr|ў (sīk-) *n.* Study and treatment of mental disease; hence or cogn. **psўchiă'tric**(AL) (sīk-) *adjs.*, ~IST (2) *n.* [f. as PSYCHE + *iatreia* healing (*iatros* healer)]

psў'chic (sī'k-) *a.* & *n.* **1.** *a.* = foll. (~ **force,** non-physical force assumed to explain spiritualistic phenomena); able to exercise psychical or occult powers; (Bridge, of bid) made by player whose hand does not have the strength normally implied by his bid. **2.** *n.* Person susceptible to psychic influence, medium; psychic bid; (in *pl.*) study of psychical phenomena. [f. Gk *psukhikos* (as PSYCHE; see -IC)]

psў'chical (sī'k-) *a.* Of the soul or mind, whence ~LY² *adv.*; of phenomena and conditions apparently outside domain of physical law (*psychical research*), so **psў'chicism** (3), **psў'chicist** (3), (sī'k-) *ns.* [f. as prec. + -AL]

psў'chō (sī'kō) *a.* & *n.* (*pl.* ~**s**). (colloq.) Psychotic (person). [abbr.]

psў'chō- (sī'kō) *comb. form.* Mind, soul, as: ~**-a'ctive,** affecting the mind; ~**-dyna'mic(s)**, (science) of the mental powers; ~**ge'nesis,** origin of the soul or mind; ~**graph,** instrument for supposed writing by spirits; ~**kine'sis,** movement of objects by mental influence without physical contact; ~**lingui'stics,** study of interrelation between use of language and speaker's and hearer's minds; ~**mo'tor,** of motion resulting from mental activity; ~**-neuro'sis,** neurosis esp. with indirect expression of emotional feelings; ~**phy'sics,** science of general relations between mind and body; ~**physio'logy,** branch of physiology dealing with mental phenomena; ~**sur'gery,** brain surgery as means of treating mental disorder; ~**the'rapy,** treatment of mental disorder by psychological means; ~**tro'pic,** (of drug) acting on the mind. [f. Gk *psukho-* (as PSYCHE, -O-)]

psўchō|-ană'lўsĭs (sīk-) *n.* Therapeutic method for treating mental disorders by investigating interaction of conscious and unconscious elements in the mind and bringing the latter into consciousness; so ~-A'NALYSE *v.t.*, ~-A'NALYST *n.*, ~-ANALY'TIC(AL) *adjs.* [f. prec. + ANALYSIS]

psўcholŏ'gical (sīk-) *a.* Of the mind; of psychology; *psychological* BLOCK¹; ~ **moment** [f. F mistransl. of G *das moment* 'potent element' as *der moment* 'moment of time'], the psychologically appropriate moment, (colloq.) the most appropriate time; ~ **warfare** (achieving aims by acting on enemy's minds); hence ~LY² *adv.* [f. as foll. + -ICAL]

psўchŏ'log|ў (sīk-) *n.* Science of the nature, functions, and phenomena, of human soul or mind; treatise on or system of this; (colloq.) mental characteristics; hence ~IST (3) *n.*, ~IZE (2, 3) *v.t.* & *i.* [f. mod. L *psychologia* (as PSYCHO-, -LOGY)]

psўchŏ'mĕtr|ў (sīk-) *n.* **1.** Divination of facts concerning an object from contact with it. **2.** Measurement of mental abilities; hence **psўchomĕ'tric** (sīk-) *a.*, ~IST (3) *n.* [f. PSYCHO- + -METRY]

psў'chopăth (sīk-) *n.* Person suffering chronic mental disorder esp. with abnormal social behaviour; mentally or emotionally unstable person; hence or cogn. **psўchopă'thic** *a.*, **psўchōpathŏ'logy**, **psўchŏ'pathy**¹, *ns.*, (sīk-). [f. PSYCHO- + -PATH]

psўch|ō'sĭs (sīk-) *n.* (*pl.* ~**oses** *pr.* -ō'sēz). Severe mental derangement involving the whole personality; hence ~**o'tic** *a.* & *n.*, of or relating to, (person) suffering from, a psychosis. [f. Gk *psukhōsis* (*psukhoō* give life to; as PSYCHE, see -OSIS)]

psȳchōsomă'tĭc (sīk-) *a.* Of mind and body; (of disease etc.) caused or aggravated by mental stress. [f. PSYCHO- + SOMATIC]
psȳchrŏ'mėter (sīk-) *n.* Wet-and-dry-bulb thermometer for measurement of atmospheric humidity. [f. Gk *psukhros* cold + -O- + -METER]
P.T. *abbr.* physical training; ***P.T. boat,** motor torpedo-boat [f. *P*atrol *T*orpedo].
pt. *abbr.* part; pint; point; port.
Pt *symb.* platinum.
P.T.A. *abbr.* parent-teacher association.
ptar'mĭgan (t-) *n.* Bird of grouse family, with black or grey plumage in summer and white in winter. [= Gael. *tàrmachan*; *p*- is pseudo-etym. after Gk wds in *pt*-]
Pte. *abbr.* Private (soldier).
ptĕrĭd|ŏ'logȳ (t-) *n.* Study of ferns; so **~olŏ'g**ICAL *a.*, **~ŏ'log**IST (3) *n.* [f. Gk *pteris -idos* fern + -O- + -LOGY]
ptĕ'rĭdophȳte (t-) *n.* Fern or similar plant (e.g. club-moss, horse-tail). [f. as prec. + Gk *phuton* plant]
ptĕ'ro- (t-) *comb. form.* Wing, as: **~da'ctyl,** extinct winged reptile; **~pod,** mollusc with middle part of foot expanded into pair of wing-like lobes; **~saur,** extinct saurian reptile. [f. Gk *pteron* wing + -O-]
ptĕ'rȳgoid (t-) *a.* **~ process,** each of two processes descending from sphenoid bone. [f. Gk *pterux -ugos* wing + -OID]
ptĭsan (tĭ'zan *or* tĭză'n) *n.* Nourishing decoction, esp. barley-water. [ME & OF *tizanne* etc. f. L f. Gk *ptisanē* peeled barley]
P.T.O. *abbr.* please turn over.
Ptŏlėmā'ĭc (t-) *a.* **1.** Of Ptolemy, 2nd-c. astronomer of Alexandria, esp. **~ system** (of astronomy, in which earth was held to be the stationary centre round which sun and stars revolved; cf. COPERNICAN). **2.** Of the Ptolemies, rulers of Egypt from death of Alexander the Great to Cleopatra. [f. L f. Gk *Ptolemaios* + -IC]
ptomaine (tō'mān *or* tomā'n) *n.* Any of various amine compounds (some toxic) in putrefying animal and vegetable matter; **~ poisoning,** (arch.) food poisoning. [f. F *ptomaïne* f. It. *ptomaina* irreg. f. Gk *ptōma* corpse; see -INE[5]]
ptō's|ĭs (t-) *n.* (*pl.* **~es** *pr.* -ēz). Drooping of upper eyelid from paralysis of a muscle; downward displacement of an organ. [Gk *ptōsis* (*piptō* fall)]
Pty. *abbr.* (Austral., N.Z., & S. Afr.) Proprietary.
ptȳ'alĭn (t-) *n.* Enzyme found in saliva of man and some animals. [f. Gk *ptualon* spittle + -IN]
Pu *symb.* plutonium.
||**pŭb** *n.* (colloq.) Public house; **~-crawl,** a journey to several pubs with one or more drinks at each. [abbr.]
pū'bertȳ *n.* Being or becoming functionally capable of procreation through natural development of reproductive organs; **age of ~** (at which puberty begins; in law usu. 14 in boys, 12 in girls); hence **pū'bert**AL *a.* [ME, f. F *puberté* or f. L *pubertas* (*puber* adult; see -TY[1])]
pū'bēs (-z) *n.* Lower part of abdomen, covered with hair at and after puberty. [L]
pūbĕ'sc|ence *n.* Arrival at puberty; soft down on leaves and stems of plants, downiness; soft down on parts of animals esp. insects; so **~**ENT *a.* [F, or f. med. L *pubescentia* f. L *pubescere* reach puberty (incept. f. prec.); see -ESCENCE]
pū'bĭc *a.* Of the pubes or pubis. [f. PUBES + -IC]
pū'b|ĭs *n.* (*pl.* **~es** *pr.* -ēz). Bone forming front of each half of pelvis. [f. L *os pubis* bone of the PUBES]
pŭ'blĭc *a.* & *n.* **1.** *a.* Of or concerning the people as a whole (*public holiday, interest, opinion*). **2.** Done by or for, representing, the people (*public assembly, expenditure*). **3.** ||Of, for, acting for, a university (*public orator, lecture, examination*). **4.** Open to or shared by the people (*public baths, lavatory,* LIBRARY, *meeting, road*). **5.** Open to general observation, done or existing in public, (*made his views public*; *made a public protest*; *gave it public utterance*); **go ~,** become public company; hence **~**LY[2] *adv.* **6.** Of or engaged in the affairs or service of the people (*public life*; *a public man*; *public money*; *public records*; NOTARY *public*). **7. ~ act, ~ bill,** (of legislation affecting the people as a whole); **~-address system,** equipment of loudspeakers etc. to enable speaker, musician, etc., to be heard by audience; ||**~ company** (with shares available to all buyers); **in the ~ domain,** belonging to the community as a whole, esp. no longer copyright; **~ enemy,** criminal whom special efforts are made to apprehend; **in the ~ eye,** receiving much publicity; *public* FIGURE[1]; **~ health,** protection of the public from disease by adequate sanitation, hygiene, etc.; **~ house,** inn, esp. ||providing alcoholic liquor for consumption on the premises; **~ law,** (1) law of relations between persons and State, (2) = *public act*; **~ lending right,** right of authors to payment when their books etc. are lent by public libraries; *public* LIBEL; **~ nuisance,** (Law) illegal act harming community rather than an individual, (colloq.) person who is obnoxious to many members of community; *public* OPINION, ||ORATOR; **~ ownership** (by the State); *public* PROSECUTOR; *Public* RECORD[2] *Office*; **~ relations,** (esp. good) relations between organization etc. and the general public (**~** *relations officer*, employee concerned with public relations and issuing information to newspapers etc.); **~ school,** ||endowed grammar (usu. boarding-) school preparing pupils esp. for universities or public services, (Sc., U.S., etc.) school managed by public authorities; **~ servant,** State official; **~ spirit, ~-spi'rited,** (being) ready to do things for the benefit of people in general; **~ transport,** buses, trains, etc., available to public and having fixed routes, as opp. to hired or private vehicles; **~ utility,** organization supplying water, gas, electricity, etc., and regarded as a public service; *public* WORK[1]*s*; **~ wrong,** offence against society as a whole. **8.** *n.* The (members of the) community in general (*the public is the best judge, are the best judges*); section of the community (*the reading public*); ||(colloq.) public house; **in ~,** openly, publicly. [ME f. OF, or f. L *publicus* (*pubes* adult; see -IC)]
pŭ'blĭcan *n.* **1.** ||Keeper of public house. **2.** (Rom. Hist., and in N.T.) Tax-farmer, tax-collector. [ME f. OF *publicain* f. L *publicanus* (*publicum* public revenue f. as prec.; see -AN)]
pŭblĭcā'tion *n.* Making publicly known; issuing of book, engraving, music, etc., to the public; book etc. so issued. [ME f. OF, f. L *publicatio -onis* (as PUBLISH; see -ATION)]
pŭ'blĭc|ĭst *n.* Writer on or person skilled in international law; writer on current public topics, esp. journalist; publicity agent; so **~**ISM (2) *n.*, **~ĭ'st**IC *a.* [f. F *publiciste* f. L (*jus*) *publicum* public law; see -IST]
pŭblĭ'cĭtȳ *n.* Being open to general observation, notoriety; the business of advertising (goods or persons); **~ agent,** person employed to keep the name of an actor etc. well known to the public. [f. F *publicité* (as PUBLIC; see -ITY)]
pŭ'blĭcīze, -ise (-īz), *v.t.* Make publicly known, esp. by advertisement. [f. PUBLIC + -IZE]
pŭ'blĭsh *v.t.* **1.** Make generally known; (Law) make (libel etc.) known to third party. **2.** Announce formally, promulgate (edict etc.); read (banns of marriage). **3.** (Of author, editor, or publisher) issue copies of (book, engraving, etc.,

or abs.) for sale to the public. **4.** Hence ~ABLE *a.* [ME *puplise* etc. f. OF *puplier*, *publier* f. L *publicare* (as PUBLIC); see -ISH²]

pŭ'blĭsher *n.* In vbl senses; one who produces copies of book, newspaper, etc., and distributes them to booksellers or to the public; *proprietor of newspaper etc. [ME, f. prec. + -ER¹]

pŭccōō'n *n.* N. Amer. plant yielding red or yellow dye. [Algonquian]

pūce *a.* Flea-colour, purple-brown. [F, = flea (-colour), f. L *pulex -icis*]

pŭck¹ *n.* Mischievous or (arch.) evil sprite; (fig.) mischievous child; hence ~'ISH¹, ~'LIKE, *adjs.* [OE *pūca* = ON *púci* mischievous demon; ult. orig. unkn.; cf. W *pwca*, Ir. *púca*]

pŭck² *n.* Rubber disc used in ice hockey. [19th c.; orig. unkn.]

pŭ'cka. Var. of PUKKA.

pŭ'cker *v.* & *n.* **1.** *v.t.* & *i.* ~ (**up**), contract, gather, (of brow, seam, material) into wrinkles, folds, or bulges, intentionally or as fault e.g. in sewing. **2.** *n.* Such bulge etc.; hence ~Y² *a.* [prob. frequent. f. as POKE¹, POCKET¹ (cf. PURSE²); see -ER⁵]

pŭd¹ *n.* Child's hand; forefoot of some animals. [17th c.; orig. unkn.]

pud² (pood) *n.* (colloq.) = foll. [abbr.]

pu'ddĭng (poo'-) *n.* **1.** Soft or fairly firm food consisting of ingredients mixed with or enclosed in flour or other farinaceous or cereal substance and cooked by boiling, steaming, or baking, (HASTY, MILK¹, PLUM, YORKSHIRE, *pudding*); sweet (course of meal); *the* PROOF¹ *of the pudding*. **2.** Intestine of pig etc. stuffed with oatmeal, blood, etc., (BLACK¹ *pudding*). **3.** Person or thing of pudding-like appearance etc. **4.** (Naut.; also **puddening**). Pad, tow binding, to prevent chafing etc. **5.** ~**-cloth,** (in which some puddings are tied up for boiling); **in the ~ club,** (sl.) pregnant; ~ **face,** large fat face; ~**-head,** stupid person; ~**-stone,** conglomerate rock of rounded pebbles in siliceous matrix. **6.** Hence ~Y² *a.* [ME *poding*, f. OF *boudin* black pudding f. Gallo-Rom. **botellinus* f. L *botellus* sausage; see BOWEL]

pŭ'ddle¹ *n.* Small dirty pool esp. of rain on road etc.; clay (and sand) mixed with water as watertight covering for embankments etc.; hence **pŭ'ddl**Y² *a.* [ME *podel*, *puddel*, dim. of OE *pudd* ditch; see -LE 1; cf. G dial. *p(f)udel* pool]

pŭ'ddle² *v.* **1.** *v.i.* Dabble or wallow in mud or shallow water; make PUDDLE¹ from clay etc.; busy oneself in untidy way. **2.** *v.t.* Make (water etc.) muddy; knead (clay and sand) into, line (canal etc.) with, PUDDLE¹; stir about (molten iron) to produce wrought iron by expelling carbon. **3.** Hence **pŭ'ddl**ER¹ (1, 2) *n.* [ME, f. prec.; cf. POODLE, Du. *poedelen*, LG *pud(d)eln* splash in water]

pū'dencў *n.* Modesty. [f. LL *pudentia* (as foll.; see -ENCY)]

pūdĕ'nd|um *n.* (usu. in *pl.* ~**a**). Genitals, esp. of woman; hence or cogn. **pūdĕ'nd**AL, **pū'd**IC, *adjs.* [f. L *pudenda* (*membra* parts), neut. pl. of gerundive of *pudēre* be ashamed]

pŭdge *n.* (colloq.) Short thick or fat person, animal, or thing; hence **pŭ'dg**Y² *a.* [cf. PODGY]

puĕ'blō (pwĕ'-) *n.* (*pl.* ~**s**). Town or village in Latin America, esp. settlement of Indians. [Sp., = people f. L *populus*]

pū'erīle *a.* Boyish, childish; suitable only for children, trivial, whence or cogn. ~LY² (-l-lĭ) *adv.*, **pūerĭ'l**ITY *n.*; ~ **breathing** (with loud pulmonary murmur as in children, usu. sign of disease in adult). [f. F *puéril* or f. L *puerilis* (*puer* boy; see -IL)]

pūer'peral *a.* Of or due to childbirth; ~ **fever** (following childbirth and caused by uterine infection). [f. L *puerperus* (*puer* child, *-parus* bearing) + -AL]

pŭff¹ *n.* **1.** Short quick blast of breath or wind; sound (as) of this; small quantity of vapour, smoke, etc., emitted at one puff. **2.** Round soft protuberant mass of material in dress (*puff sleeve*), of hair of head, etc.; *eiderdown; = POWDER-*puff*. **3.** Piece, cake, etc., of light pastry esp. of puff pastry. **4.** Unduly or extravagantly laudatory review of book, advertisement of tradesman's goods, etc., esp. in newspaper. **5.** ~**-adder,** large venomous African viper inflating upper part of body when excited; ~**-ball,** fungus with ball-shaped spore-case; ~ **pastry** (light and flaky); ||**puff-puff,** (childish for) steam-engine, train. [ME *puf*, imit.; see foll.]

pŭff² *v.* **1.** *v.i.* Emit puff of air or breath; (of air etc.) come *out* or *up* in puffs; ~ (**and blow**), breathe hard, pant; (of steam-engine, person smoking, etc.) emit puffs, move with puffs, (*puffed away at his cigar*; *train puffed out of the station*); become inflated, swell, (*up*, *out*). **2.** *v.t.* Put out of breath (*arrived somewhat puffed*); ~ **out,** utter pantingly. **3.** Blow (dust, smoke, light object, *out*, *up*, *away*, etc.) with puff; smoke (pipe) in puffs. **4.** Blow *out*, *up*, inflate; ~ **up,** elate, make proud, (esp. in *p.p.*, *with* pride etc.). **5.** Advertise (goods) with exaggerated or false praise. **6.** Hence ~'ER¹ *n.* (also in childish use, = PUFF¹-*puff*). [ME *puffe*, perh. f. OE **puffan*, imit. of sound of breath]

pŭ'fferў *n.* Advertisement, puffing. [f. prec. + -ERY]

pŭ'ffĭn *n.* N. Atlantic auk with large furrowed particoloured bill. [ME *poffin*, *pophyn*, of unkn. orig.]

pŭ'ff|ў *a.* Gusty; short-winded; puffed out, swollen; corpulent; hence ~ĬNESS *n.* [f. PUFF¹·² + -Y²]

pŭg¹ *n.* **1.** ~(**-dog**), dwarf breed of dog like bulldog, with broad flat nose and deeply wrinkled face, whence ~**'g**ISH¹, ~**'g**Y², (-g-) *adjs.*; ~**-nose(d)**, (with) short squat or snub nose. **2.** (Quasi-proper name for) fox. **3.** ||Small locomotive for shunting etc. [16th c., perh. f. LDu.]

pŭg² *n.*, & *v.t.* (**-gg-**). **1.** *n.* Loam or clay mixed and prepared for making bricks, pottery, etc.; ~**-mill** (for preparing pug). **2.** *v.t.* Prepare (clay) thus; pack (space esp. under floor, to deaden sound) with pug, sawdust, etc.; hence ~**'g**ING¹ (3) (-g-) *n.* [19th c.; orig. unkn.]

pŭg³ *n.*, & *v.t.* (**-gg-**). **1.** *n.* Footprint of animal. **2.** *v.t.* Track by pugs. [f. Hindi *pag* footprint]

pŭg⁴ *n.* (sl.) Pugilist. [abbr.]

pŭ'gg(a)ree (-rĭ) *n.* Indian's light turban; thin scarf of muslin etc. worn round hat and sometimes hanging down behind as protection against sun. [f. Hindi *pagrī* turban]

pū'gĭl|ĭst *n.* Boxer, fighter; so ~ISM (2) *n.*, ~**ĭ'st**IC *a.* [f. L *pugil* boxer + -IST]

pŭgnā'cious (-shus) *a.* Disposed to fight, quarrelsome; hence or cogn. ~LY² *adv.*, **pŭgnă'c**ITY *n.* [f. L *pugnax -acis* (*pugnare* fight, f. *pugnus* fist); see -ACIOUS]

Pŭ'gwash (-ŏsh) *n.* ~ **conferences,** regularly held international conferences of eminent scientists to discuss world problems. [~ in Nova Scotia, where first held]

pui'snė (pū'nĭ) *a.* & *n.* ~ (**judge**), judge of superior court inferior in rank to chief justices; (Law) later, subsequent (*to*), (*puisne mortgagees*; *mortgagees puisne to the plaintiff*). [OF (*puis* after f. L *postea*, *né* born f. L *natus*); cf. PUNY]

pū'ĭssance (*or* pwĭ's-) *n.* **1.** (*or* pwĭsah'ṅs). (In show-jumping) test of horse's ability to jump high obstacles. **2.** (arch.) Great power, might, or influence. [ME in sense 2, f. OF (as foll.; see -ANCE)]

pū'issant (*or* pwĭ's-) *a.* (literary). Having great power or influence, mighty; hence ~LY² *adv.* [ME f. OF, f. Gallo-Rom. **possiantem* f. L *posse* be able; cf. POTENT¹]

pu'ja (pōō'-), **pōō'ja,** *n.* Hindu religious rite. [Skr.]

pūke *v.i.* & *t.*, & *n.* Vomit. [16th c.; prob. imit.]

pukĕ'kō (po͝ok-) *n.* (*pl.* **~s**). (Austral. & N.Z.) Gallinule (*Porphyrio melanotus*) with blue, black, and white plumage. [Maori]

pŭ'kka(h) *a.* (Anglo-Ind.) Of full weight; genuine; permanent, solidly built. [f. Hindi *pakkā* cooked, ripe, substantial]

pu'ku (pōō'kōō) *n.* Red African antelope (*Adenota vardoni*). [f. Zulu *mpuku*]

pŭ'lchrĭ|tūde (-kr-) *n.* (literary). Beauty; hence **~tū'dĭn**OUS *a.* [ME, f. L *pulchritudo -dinis* (*pulcher -chri* beautiful; see -TUDE)]

pūle *v.i.* Cry querulously or weakly, whine, whimper. [16th c., prob. imit.; cf. F *piauler*]

Pū'lĭtzer (-tser; *or* po͝o-) *n.* **~ prize,** one of 13 annual awards for achievements in American journalism, literature, and music. [f. J. ~, Amer. newspaper-publisher d. 1911]

pull¹ (po͝ol) *v.* **1.** *v.t.* Exert upon (thing etc.) force tending to move it to oneself (*don't pull my hair*; *pull his sleeve* or *him by the sleeve*; *pull* person's LEG, *pull* RANK¹, *the* STRINGS, WIRES); damage (muscle etc.) by abnormal strain. **2.** Cause (thing etc.) to move towards oneself or in direction so regarded (*pull it nearer*; *pull him into the room*; *pull your cap over your ears*; *pull the trigger*); draw (knife, gun, etc.) out of its sheath etc. in order to use it (*on* person); **~ caps,** (arch.) scuffle, quarrel. **3.** Attract or secure (support, custom). **4.** ~ (thing) **apart** or **to pieces,** separate its parts forcibly, (fig.) criticize (person, thing) unfavourably. **5.** Remove (cork, tooth, etc.) by pulling; draw (quantity of liquor) from barrel etc.; pluck (plant, often *up*) by root; (colloq.) accomplish, pull off, (*pull a* FAST³ *one*). **6. ~ed bread,** pieces from inside of new loaf, rebaked till crisp; **~ed figs** (flattened before being packed). **7.** Print upon (sheet), print (copy, proof), orig. in old hand-press by pulling bar towards one. **8.** Move (boat etc., or abs.) by pulling; ~ one's **weight,** row with effect in proportion to one's weight, (fig.) do one's fair share of work. **9.** Check (horse) esp. so as to make him lose race; ~ one's **punches,** fail to give full force to one's blows in boxing (lit. or fig.). **10.** (Cricket). Strike (ball, or abs.), strike ball bowled by (bowler), to leg side. **11.** (Golf). Drive (ball, or abs.) widely to left (of right-handed player). **12.** *Pull a* FACE¹; **~ a** *sanctimonious* etc. **face,** assume such expression. **13.** *v.i.* Exert pulling force (*horse pulls well*; *engine will not pull*); tear or pluck *at* (thing). **14.** Proceed with effort (*up* hill etc.); (of horse) strain, esp. habitually, against bit. **15.** Draw or suck *at* (pipe, tankard, etc.). **16.** (Of boat, vehicle, etc.) be caused to move esp. in specified direction. **17. ~ about,** pull from side to side, treat roughly; **~ back,** (cause to) retreat; **~-back,** retarding influence, *withdrawal of troops; **~ down,** demolish (building etc.), lower in health, spirits, price, etc.; **~ in,** acquire (profit, payment, etc.), (colloq.) arrest (person), (of train) enter station, (of vehicle) move to side of road or off road, whence *~-in* n., place for doing this, ‖esp. lorry-drivers' café; **~ off,** remove garment etc. by pulling (opp. **~ on**), succeed in winning or achieving; **~ out,** depart, withdraw from an undertaking, (of train) move out of station, (of vehicle) move away from side of road, or from behind another to overtake it; *~ out of the fire*, save (game etc.) when the situation seems hopeless; *~-out* n., (1) page or plate in book that folds out from front edge of leaves to facilitate reference, (2) middle section of magazine etc. removable by pulling; ***~ over,** (of vehicle) pull in; **~ round,** (cause to) recover from illness etc.; **~ through** *adv.* & *prep.*, get (person), get oneself, safely through (danger, illness, etc., or abs.); *~-through* n., cord with which cleaning-rag is drawn through rifle; **~ together,** work in harmony; **~ oneself together,** rally, recover oneself, esp. recover one's self-control; **~ up,** cause (person, horse, vehicle) to stop, reprimand, check oneself, improve one's relative position in race etc. (and cf. sense 5); *~-up* n., house of call for travellers, *exercise of pulling oneself up to an overhead bar. **18.** Hence ~'ER¹ *n.* [OE (*ā*)*pullian*, perh. rel. to LG *pūlen*, MDu. *polen* to shell]

pull² (po͝ol) *n.* **1.** Act of pulling, wrench, tug; force thus exerted; (fig.) advantage, means of exerting influence, interest with the powerful. **2.** (Print.) Rough proof. **3.** Pulling at bridle to check horse esp. in racing. **4.** Spell of rowing. **5.** (Cricket & Golf). Pulling stroke. **6.** Deep draught of liquor. **7.** Handle etc. by which pull is applied, e.g. BELL¹-*pull*. [ME, f. prec.]

pu'llĕt (po͝o'-) *n.* Young domestic fowl, esp. hen from time she begins to lay till first moult. [ME, f. OF *poulet* dim. of *poule* f. Rom. **pulla* fem. of L *pullus* chicken]

pu'lley (po͝o'-) *n.*, & *v.t.* **1.** *n.* Grooved wheel(s) for cord etc. to pass over, mounted and used for changing direction of power; wheel or drum fixed on shaft and turned by belt, used esp. to increase speed or power. **2.** *v.t.* Hoist, furnish, work, with pulley. [ME, f. OF *polie* prob. ult. f. med. Gk **polidion* pivot dim. of *polos* POLE²]

Pu'llman (po͝o'-) *a.* & *n.* **~ (car** or **coach),** railway carriage or motor coach with especially comfortable seats etc.; sleeping-car. [f. G. M. ~, Amer. designer d. 1897]

pu'llōver (po͝o'-) *n.* (Usu. knitted) outer garment for upper part of body, put on by being pulled over head. [f. PULL¹ + OVER]

pŭ'llūl|āte *v.i.* (Of shoot or bud) sprout out, bud; (of seed) sprout; (fig., of doctrine etc.) develop, spring up; **~ate with,** abound in; hence or cogn. ~ANT *a.*, ~A'TION *n.* [f. L *pullulare* sprout (*pullulus* dim. of *pullus* young of animal) + -ATE³]

pŭ'lmonarў *a.* **1.** Of, in, connected with, the lungs (*pulmonary diseases*); **~ artery,** main artery conveying blood from heart to lungs; **~ vein** (returning this blood to heart). **2.** Having lungs or lunglike organs; so **pŭ'lmon**ATE² *a.* **3.** Affected with or subject to lung-disease. [f. L *pulmonarius* (*pulmo -onis* lung; see -ARY¹)]

pulmŏ'nĭc *a.* = prec. 1. [f. F *pulmonique* or f. mod. L *pulmonicus* f. L *pulmo* (as prec.)]

pŭlp *n.* & *v.* **1.** *n.* Fleshy part of fruit; any fleshy or soft part of animal body, e.g. nervous substance in interior cavity of tooth; soft shapeless mass, e.g. that of rags, wood, etc., from which paper is made (**~ magazine** etc., publication printed (orig.) on rough paper made from wood-pulp, often containing sensational or poor-quality writing; **~'wood,** timber suitable for making pulp); ore pulverized and mixed with water; hence ~'LESS, ~'OUS, ~'Y², *adjs.* **2.** *v.t.* Reduce to pulp; remove pulp from (coffee-beans etc.), whence ~'ER¹ (2) *n.* **3.** *v.i.* Become pulpy. [f. L *pulpa*]

pu'lpit (po͝o'-) *n.* Raised enclosed platform usu. with desk from which preacher in church or chapel delivers sermon; *the* profession of preaching; the preachers. [ME, f. L *pulpitum* scaffold, platform]

pulpĭteer′ (pŏŏ-) *n.*, & *v.i.* **1.** *n.* (usu. derog.) Professional preacher. **2.** *v.i.* Preach. [f. prec. + -EER]

pu′lque (pŏŏ′lkē; *or* -kā) *n.* Mexican fermented drink from sap of maguey; ~ **brandy,** strong intoxicant made from pulque. [17th c.; Amer. Sp., of unkn. orig.]

pŭ′lsār *n.* Cosmic source of regularly and rapidly pulsating radio signals. [f. *pulsating star,* after *quasar*]

pŭlsā′te (*or* pŭ′l-) *v.i.* Expand and contract rhythmically, beat, throb (lit. or fig.); vibrate, quiver, thrill; hence or cogn. **pŭls**A′TION, **pŭlsā′t**OR, *ns.*, **pŭ′lsat**ORY *a.* [f. L *pulsare* frequent. of *pellere puls-* drive, beat + -ATE³]

pŭ′lsatīle *a.* Of, or having the property of, pulsation; (of musical instrument) played by percussion. [f. med. L *pulsatilis* (as prec.; see -IL)]

pŭlsatĭ′lla *n.* Pasque-flower; its extract, used in pharmacy. [mod. L, dim. of *pulsata* fem. p.p. (as PULSATE), because quivering in wind]

pŭlse¹ *n.* & *v.* **1.** *n.* Rhythmical throbbing of arteries as blood is propelled along them esp. as felt in wrists, temples, etc. (FEEL person's *pulse*; *has a rapid, strong, pulse*); each successive beat of arteries or heart; (fig.) throb or thrill of life or emotion, latent sentiment. **2.** Rhythmical recurrence of strokes e.g. of oars; (Mus.) beat; single vibration of sound, light, etc.; brief variation of electric current etc. esp. as signal. **3.** Hence ~′LESS (-sl-) *a.* **4.** *v.i.* Pulsate (lit. or fig.). **5.** *v.t.* Send *out, in,* etc., by pulses or rhythmic beats. [n. ME f. OF *pous* f. L *pulsus* (*pellere puls-* drive, beat); v. f. L *pulsare* (as PULSATE)]

pŭlse² *n.* **1.** (as *sing.* or *pl.*) Edible seeds of leguminous plants, e.g. peas, beans, lentils. **2.** Any kind of these. [ME f. OF *pols* f. L *puls pultis* porridge of meal etc.]

pŭlsĭ′mēter *n.* Instrument for measuring rate or force of pulse. [f. PULSE¹ + -I- + -METER]

pŭlsŏ′mēter *n.* Steam-condensing vacuum pump. [P; f. PULSE¹ + -O- + -METER, from pulsatory action of steam]

pŭ′lverīz|e, -īs|e (-īz), *v.* **1.** *v.t.* Reduce to powder or dust, divide (liquid) into spray, whence ~**āt**OR, ~ER¹ (2), *ns.*; (fig.) demolish, crush, smash. **2.** *v.i.* Crumble to dust. **3.** Hence ~ABLE *a.*, ~A′TION *n.* [ME, f. LL *pulverizare* (*pulvis pulveris* dust; see -IZE)]

pŭlvĕrūlent (*or* -rōō-) *a.* Powdery, of dust; covered with powder; (of rock etc.) having only slight cohesion, apt to crumble. [f. L *pulverulentus* (as prec.; see -ULENT)]

pŭ′lvĭnate, -ātėd, *adjs.* (Archit.) swelling, esp. (of frieze) with convex face; (Bot. & Entom.) cushion-like, having cushion-like swelling. [f. L *pulvinatus* (*pulvinus* cushion); see -ATE², -ED¹]

pū′ma *n.* Large Amer. feline (*Felis concolor*). [Sp., f. Quechua]

pŭ′mĭce *n.*, & *v.t.* **1.** *n.* ~(**-stone**), (piece of) light porous kind of lava used for removing stains from skin etc., as powder for polishing, etc.; so **pūmĭ′ce**OUS (-shus) *a.* **2.** *v.t.* Rub or clean with pumice; (in *p.p.*, of horse's hoof) made spongy by disease. [ME f. OF *pomis* f. L *pumex pumicis* (dial. *pom-*); cf. POUNCE²]

pŭ′mmel *v.t.* (‖**-ll-**). Strike repeatedly esp. with fist. [altered f. POMMEL]

pŭmp¹ *n.* **1.** Machine, usu. cylinder in which piston etc. is moved up and down by rod, for raising water; machine of this kind or with rotary action etc. for raising or moving liquids, compressing or rarefying gases, inflating tyres, etc. (fig. of heart, insect's suckers, etc.); pumping, stroke of pump. **2.** ~**-brake,** handle of pump esp. with transverse bar for several persons to work at; ~**-handle** *v.t.*, (colloq.) shake (person's hand) effusively; ~**-priming,** (fig.) stimulation of commerce etc. by investment; ~**-room,** building where pump is worked, esp. at spa where medicinal water is dispensed. [ME *pumpe, pompe,* orig. Naut., = MDu. *pompe,* LG *pump(e)*; prob. imit.]

pŭmp² *v.* **1.** *v.i.* Work a pump. **2.** *v.t.* Raise or move (water, air, etc., esp. *in, into, out, up*) with pump; make (ship, well, etc.) *dry* by pumping; ~ **up,** inflate (pneumatic tyre), inflate tyres of (bicycle etc.). **3.** Cause to move, pour forth, be sent *out,* etc., as if by pumping; elicit information from (person) by persistent questioning. **4.** *v.t.* & *i.* Move vigorously up and down as if pumping. [f. prec.]

pŭmp³ *n.* Light shoe usu. without fastening, worn for dancing, tennis, etc.; *court shoe. [16th c.; orig. unkn.]

pŭ′mpernĭckel (*or* pōō′-) *n.* German wholemeal rye bread. [G, f. earlier sense 'lout', 'stinker' (*pumpe(r)n* break wind, *Nickel* Nicholas)]

pŭ′mpkĭn *n.* (Plant of genus *Cucurbita* bearing) large egg-shaped or globular orange-coloured fruit with edible layer next to rind, used in cookery and as food for cattle; ***some ~s,** (colloq.) important person or thing. [alt. (after -KIN) f. earler *pompon, pumpion,* f. obs. F *po(m)pon* f. L *pepo -onis* f. Gk *pepōn* large melon (see PEPO)]

pŭn¹ *n.*, & *v.i.* (**-nn-**). **1.** *n.* Humorous use of word to suggest different meanings, or of words of same or similar sound with different meanings; play on words. **2.** *v.i.* Make pun(s) (*on* word or subject); hence ~**′nĭng**LY² *adv.* [17th c., perh. f. obs. *pundigrion,* a fanciful formation]

‖**pŭn²** *v.t.* (**-nn-**). Consolidate (earth, rubble) by pounding or ramming. [dial. var. of POUND³]

pu′na (pōō′-) *n.* High bleak plateau in Peruvian Andes; = MOUNTAIN *sickness.* [Quechua, in first sense]

pŭnch¹ *n.* **1.** Instrument or machine for cutting holes in leather, metal, paper, etc., driving bolt etc. out of hole (**starting-~**), enlarging hole, etc. **2.** Tool or machine for impressing design or stamping die on material. [f. foll., or abbr. of PUNCHEON¹]

pŭnch² *v.t.*, & *n.* **1.** *v.t.* Strike esp. with closed fist; ‖**~-ball,** ***~′ing-bag,** inflated ball or bag held by elastic bands etc. and punched as form of exercise; **~-up,** fist-fight, brawl. **2.** Prod with stick etc., esp. *drive (cattle) thus. **3.** Pierce (metal, leather, bus-ticket, etc.) as or with punch; pierce (hole) thus; ~**(ed) card, tape,** etc., (perforated according to specified code, for conveying instructions to computer etc.). **4.** Hence ~′ER (1, 2) *n.* **5.** *n.* Blow with fist (*a punch on the head*; PULL¹ one's *punches*); ability to deliver this; **~-drunk,** stupefied through having been severely or repeatedly punched (lit. or fig.). **6.** (sl.) Vigour, momentum, effective force; ~ **line,** words giving point of joke etc. **7.** Hence ~′Y² *a.*, (1) having force or vigour, (2) (colloq.) punch-drunk. [ME, var. of POUNCE¹]

pŭnch³ *n.* Drink usu. of wine or spirits mixed with hot or cold water or milk, sugar, lemons, spice, etc.; **~-bowl,** (1) bowl in which punch is mixed, (2) round deep hollow in hill(s). [17th c.; orig. unkn.]

pŭnch⁴ *n.* **1.** ‖(**Suffolk**) ~, short-legged thickset draught horse. **2.** (*P~*). Grotesque humpbacked figure in puppet-show called *Punch and Judy,* esp. as title of a London weekly comic paper; **as pleased** or **as proud as P~,** showing great pleasure or pride. [abbr. of PUNCHINELLO]

pŭ'ncheon[1] (-nshon) *n.* Short post, esp. one supporting roof in coal-mine; = PUNCH[1]. [ME, f. OF *poinson*, *po(i)nchon*, f. Rom. **punctio -onis* or **punctiare* (L *pungere punct-* prick); see -ION]

pŭ'ncheon[2] (-nshon) *n.* (Hist.) Large cask for liquids etc. holding from 72 to 120 gal. [ME, f. OF *poinson*, *po(i)nchon*, of unkn. orig.]

Pŭnchĭnĕ'llō *n.* (*pl.* ~**s**). Chief character in Italian puppet-show; short stout person of comical appearance. [17th c., perh. assim. form of *Polichinello* f. Neapolitan dial. *Polecenella*, It. *Pulcinella*, perh. dim. of *pollecena* young turkey-cock with hooked beak (*pulcino* chicken f. Rom. **pullicinus* f. L *pullus*)]

pŭ'nct|āte *a.* (Biol. & Path.) Marked or studded with points, dots, or spots; hence ~A'TION *n.* [f. L (as POINT[1]; see -ATE[2])]

pŭnctĭ'liō (-lyō) *n.* (*pl.* ~**s**). Delicate point of ceremony or honour; etiquette of such points; petty formality. [f. It. *puntiglio* & Sp. *puntillo* dim. of *punto* POINT[1]]

pŭnctĭ'lious (-lyus) *a.* Attentive to punctilio(s) or to details of conduct, duties, etc.; hence ~LY[2] *adv.*, ~NESS *n.* [f. F *pointilleux* (*pointille* f. It. as prec.; see -OUS)]

pŭ'nctūal *a.* Observant of appointed time; neither early nor late; (arch.) punctilious; (Geom.) of a point; hence ~ITY (-ă'l-) *n.*, ~LY[2] *adv.* [ME, f. med. L *punctualis* f. L *punctum* POINT[1]; see -AL]

pŭ'nctūāte *v.t.* Insert stops in (writing), mark or divide with stops; (fig.) interrupt at intervals (speech *with* exclamations etc.); emphasize, accentuate. [f. med. L *punctuare* (as prec.) + -ATE[3]]

pŭnctūā'tion *n.* Insertion of vowel and other points in Hebrew etc.; practice or art of punctuating; ~ **mark,** = STOP[2] 2. [f. med. L *punctuatio* (as prec.; see -ATION)]

pŭ'nct|um *n.* (*pl.* ~**a**). (Biol. & Path.) Speck, dot, spot of colour or elevation or depression on surface. [L, = POINT[1]]

pŭ'ncture *n.* & *v.* **1.** *n.* Pricking, prick, esp. accidental piercing of pneumatic tyre; hole thus made. **2.** *v.t.* Prick, pierce, (lit. or fig.). **3.** *v.i.* Undergo puncture. [ME, f. L *punctura* (*pungere punct-* prick; see -URE)]

pŭ'ndĭt *n.* **1.** Hindu learned in Sanskrit and in philosophy, religion, and jurisprudence, of India. **2.** Learned expert or teacher; hence ~RY (5) *n.* [f. Hind. *paṇḍit* f. Skr. *paṇḍita* learned]

pŭ'ng|ent (-nj-) *a.* **1.** (Biol.) Sharp-pointed. **2.** (Of reproof, satire, etc.) biting, caustic; mentally stimulating, piquant. **3.** Affecting organs of smell or taste, or skin etc., with pricking sensation (*pungent gas, smoke, sauce*). **4.** Hence ~ENCY *n.*, ~**ent**LY[2] *adv.* [f. L *pungere* prick; see -ENT]

Pū'nĭc *a.* & *n.* Carthaginian (language); *Punic* FAITH. [f. L *Punicus*, *Poenicus* (*Poenus* f. Gk *Phoinix* Phoenician; see -IC)]

pŭ'nĭsh *v.t.* **1.** Cause (offender) to suffer for offence, chastise, inflict penalty on (offender); inflict penalty for (offence). **2.** (colloq.) Inflict severe blows on (opponent in boxing); (of race, competitor) tax severely the powers of (competitor); take full advantage of (weak bowling, bowler, stroke at tennis, etc.); subject to severe stress or depletion; hence ~ING[2] *a.* **3.** Hence ~ER[1] *n.*, ~ABLE *a.* [ME, f. OF *punir* (-ISH[2]) f. L *punire* (*poenire* f. *poena* penalty)]

pŭ'nĭshment *n.* Punishing or being punished; penalty inflicted on offender; (colloq.) severe treatment by opponent. [ME, f. AF & OF *punissement* (*punir*; see prec., -MENT)]

pū'nĭtĭve *a.* Inflicting or intended to inflict punishment (*punitive justice, expedition*); (of damages) = VINDICTIVE; (of taxation etc.) extremely severe; so **pū'nĭt**ORY *a.* [f. F *punitif -ive* or f. med. L *punitivus* (as prec.; see -IVE)]

Pŭnja'bĭ (-ah'-) *a.* & *n.* (Native or language) of the Punjab in India. [f. Hindi *pañjābi* (*Pañjāb* Punjab; see -I)]

||**pŭnk**[1] *n.* (arch.) Prostitute. [16th c., of unkn. orig.]

pŭnk[2] *n.* & *a.* **1.** *n.* Rotten wood, fungus growing on wood, used as tinder. **2.** (colloq.) Worthless stuff, nonsense; worthless person; novice; young ruffian. **3.** *a.* (colloq.) Worthless, rotten. [18th c., of unkn. orig.; cf. SPUNK]

pŭ'nkah (-ka) *n.* (Ind.) Portable fan usu. of leaf of palmyra; large swinging cloth fan on frame worked by cord or electrically. [f. Hindi *pankhā* fan f. Skr. *pakṣaka* (*pakṣa* wing)]

pŭ'nner *n.* Tool for ramming earth round post etc. to make it firm [f. PUN[2] + -ER[1]]

||**pŭ'nnėt** *n.* Small chip or plastic basket for fruit or vegetables. [19th c., perh. dim. of dial. *pun* POUND[1]; see -ET[1]]

pŭ'nster *n.* (Esp. inveterate) maker of puns. [f. PUN[1] + -STER]

pŭnt[1] *n.* & *v.* **1.** *n.* Flat-bottomed shallow boat, broad and square at both ends, propelled by long pole thrust against bottom of river etc. **2.** *v.t.* Propel with such pole; convey in punt. **3.** *v.i.* Use punt-pole; travel in punt. [ME, f. MLG *punte*, *punto*, MDu. *ponte* ferry-boat, f. L *ponto* Gaulish transport vessel]

pŭnt[2] *v.t.*, & *n.* **1.** *v.t.* Kick (football) after it has dropped from the hands and before it reaches ground; ~**-about,** kicking about of football for practice, ball so used. **2.** *n.* Such kick. [prob. f. dial. *punt* push forcibly (cf. BUNT[3])]

pŭnt[3] *v.i.*, & *n.* **1.** *v.i.* (At faro and other card-games) lay stake against bank; ||(colloq.) bet on horse etc., speculate in shares etc. **2.** *n.* Player who punts; point in faro. [f. F *ponter* (*ponte* player against bank f. Sp. *punto* POINT[1])]

pŭ'nter[1] *n.* In vbl senses. [f. PUNT[1] + -ER[1]]

pŭ'nter[2] *n.* In vbl senses. [f. PUNT[2] + -ER[1]]

pŭ'nter[3] *n.* In vbl senses; prostitute's client. [f. PUNT[3] + -ER[1]]

pū'n|ȳ *a.* Undersized; weak, feeble; petty; hence ~INESS *n.* [phonetic sp. of PUISNE]

pŭp *n.*, & *v.t.* (**-pp-**). **1.** Young dog; **in** ~, (of bitch) pregnant; **sell** person **a** ~, swindle him esp. by selling thing on prospective value. **2.** Young wolf, rat, seal, etc. **3.** Objectionable young man. **4.** ~ **tent,** small tent of simple design. **5.** *v.t.* (Of bitch etc.) bring forth (young, or abs.). [back form. f. PUPPY as if dim. in -Y[3]]

pū'p|a *n.* (*pl.* ~**ae**). Form taken by insect in torpid stage of passive development between larva and imago; hence ~AL *a.* [mod. L; in L, = girl, doll]

pū'p|āte *v.i.* Become a pupa; hence ~A'TION *n.* [f. prec. + -ATE[3]]

pū'pil *n.* **1.** One who is taught by another, schoolchild, disciple; (Law) person below age of puberty and under care of guardian; ~**-teacher,** (Hist.) boy or girl teaching in elementary school under head teacher and concurrently receiving general education from him or elsewhere. **2.** Circular opening in centre of iris of eye, varying in size to regulate passage of light to the retina. **3.** Hence or cogn. ~(**l**)AR[1], ~(**l**)ARY[2], *adjs.*, ~(**l**)**ă'r**ITY, ~SHIP, *ns.* [ME, f. OF *pupille* or f. L *pupillus*, *pupilla* ward, orphan, *pupilla* pupil of eye, dims. of *pupus* boy, *pupa* girl]

pū'pillage, pū'pilage, *n.* Nonage, minority (fig. of country, language, etc.); being a pupil. [f. prec. + -AGE]

pūpĭ'parous *a.* (Entom.) Bringing forth young already advanced to pupal state. [f. mod. L *Pupipara*, neut. pl. (as n.) of *pupiparus* (as PUPA, *parere* bring forth)]

pŭ'ppĕt *n.* Figure, usu. small, representing human being or animal and moved by various means as entertainment in **~-show;** person whose acts are controlled by another; **~ state,** country professing to be independent but actually under the control of some greater power; **~-valve,** = POPPET-*valve*; hence ~EER', ~RY (4, 5), *ns.* [later form of POPPET]

pŭ'ppў *n.* Young dog; vain empty-headed young man, coxcomb, = PUP 3; **~-dog,** (childish) = *puppy*; **~ fat,** temporary fatness of child or adolescent; **~ love,** = CALF[1]-*love*; hence ~DOM, ~HOOD, *ns.*, ~ISH[1] *a.* [ME, perh. f. OF *po(u)pee* doll, plaything, toy f. Rom. **puppata* (as POPPET)]

pur- *pref.* = PRO-[1] (*purchase, purport, pursue*). [AF, f. OF *por-, pur-, pour-* f. L *por-, pro-*]

Pura'n|a (poorah'-) *n.* Any of a class of Sanskrit sacred poems of Hindu mythology; hence ~IC *a.* [f. Skr. *purāṇa* ancient legend, ancient (*purā* formerly)]

||**Pûr'bĕck** *n.* **~ stone,** hard limestone used in building etc. [~ in Dorset]

pûr'blind *a.*, & *v.t.* **1.** *a.* Partly blind, dim-sighted; (fig.) obtuse, dull; hence ~NESS *n.* **2.** *v.t.* Make purblind. [ME *pur(e) blind* f. PURE orig. in sense 'utterly', w. assim. to PUR-]

pûr'chase[1] *n.* **1.** Buying; **~-money,** price (to be) paid; ||**~ tax,** tax on goods bought, at rate increasing with decreasing necessity of the goods. **2.** (Hist.) Practice of buying commissions in army. **3.** Thing bought. **4.** Annual rent or return from land (*sold at 20 years' purchase*); (fig.) **is not worth an hour's ~,** (of person's life etc.) cannot be trusted to last an hour longer. **5.** (Law). Acquisition of property by one's personal action, not by inheritance. **6.** Mechanical advantage, leverage, (lit. or fig.); appliance for gaining this, esp. (Naut.) rope, windlass, pulley, etc. [ME, f. AF *purchas*, OF *porchas* (as foll.)]

pûr'chas|e[2] *v.t.* **1.** Buy; acquire (victory, freedom, etc., *with* one's blood, toil, etc.). **2.** (Naut.) Haul up (anchor etc.) by means of pulley, lever, etc. **3.** Hence or cogn. ~ABLE *a.*, ~ER[1] *n.* [ME, f. AF PUR(*chacer* CHASE[2]) procure, seek]

pûr'dah (-d*a*) *n.* (Ind. etc.) Curtain, esp. one serving to screen Muslim or Hindu women from sight of men or strangers; (fig.) Indian system of secluding women of rank from public view. [f. Urdu & Pers. *pardah* veil, curtain]

pūre *a.* **1.** Unmixed, unadulterated, (*pure white, air, alcohol, water*); (of sound) not discordant, esp. (Mus.) perfectly in tune; (of vowel) not joined with another in diphthong, (Gk. Gram.) preceded by another vowel; (of consonant) not accompanied by another. **2.** Of unmixed descent (*pure-blooded, -bred*); *pure* MATHEMATICS; *pure* SCIENCE. **3.** Mere, simple, nothing but, sheer, (*knowledge pure and simple*; *pure nonsense, prejudice*). **4.** Not corrupt (*his taste was severe and pure*); morally undefiled, guiltless, sincere; sexually undefiled, chaste. **5.** Hence ~'LY[2] (pūr'lĭ) *adv.*, (esp.) merely, exclusively, solely, entirely, ~'NESS (pūr'n-) *n.* [ME, f. OF *pur pure* f. L *purus*]

purée (pūr'ā) *n.* Pulp of vegetables, meat, fruit, etc., (boiled and) passed through sieve or otherwise reduced to a uniform mass. [F]

pûr'fle *n.*, & *v.t.* **1.** *n.* Ornamental border esp. of violin etc.; (arch.) embroidered edge of garment. **2.** *v.t.* Adorn with purfle; ornament (edge of building *with* crockets etc.); beautify; hence **pûr'fl**ING[1] *n.*, (esp.) inlaid bordering on back and belly of violin etc. [ME, f. OF *porfil(er)* f. Rom. *PRO[1](*filare* f. L *filum* thread)]

pûrgā'tion *n.* Purification; purging of bowels; spiritual cleansing, esp. (R.C. Ch.) of soul in purgatory; (Hist.) clearing of oneself from accusation or suspicion by oath or ordeal. [ME f. OF or f. L *purgatio* (as PURGE; see -ATION)]

pûr'gatĭve *a.* & *n.* Strongly laxative (medicine); (thing) serving to purify. [ME, f. OF *purgatif -ive* or f. LL *purgativus* (as PURGE; see -ATIVE)]

pûr'gatorў *n.* & *a.* **1.** *n.* Condition or place of spiritual purging, esp. (R.C. Ch.) of souls departing this life in grace of God but having to expiate venial sins etc.; place or state of temporary suffering or expiation. **2.** *a.* Purifying; so **pûrgatôr'**IAL *a.* [ME, f. AF *purgatorie*, OF *-oire* f. med. L *purgatorium*, neut. (as n.) of LL *purgatorius* (as foll.; see -ORY)]

pûrge *v.t.*, & *n.* **1.** *v.t.* Make physically or spiritually clean (*of* or *from* impurities, sin, etc.); remove by cleansing process (lit. or fig.), clear *away, off, out*; (of medicine or person) clear (bowels, person, or abs.) by evacuation (**purging agaric, flax,** etc., plants yielding purgatives); clear (person, one*self, of* charge, suspicion); (Law) atone for, wipe out, (offence, esp. contempt of court, or sentence) by expiation and submission; rid (political party, army, etc.) of persons regarded as undesirable. **2.** *n.* Such clearance, purgation; purgative. [ME, f. OF *purg(i)er* f. L *purgare* purify (*purus* pure)]

pūrĭfĭcā'tion *n.* Purifying or being purified; ritual cleansing, esp. that of woman after childbirth enjoined by Jewish law; **the P~ (of the Virgin Mary),** presentation of Christ in Temple on completion of Mary's purification (Luke 2:22), feast in honour of this (2 Feb.); so **pūr'ĭfĭcāt**ORY *a.* [ME f. OF, or f. L *purificatio* (as PURIFY; see -FICATION)]

pūr'ĭfĭcātor *n.* (Eccl.) Cloth used at Eucharist for wiping chalice and paten, and fingers and lips of celebrant. [mod. var. of *purificatory* n. f. med. L *purificatorium* (as PURIFICATORY; see prec.)]

pūr'ĭf|ў *v.t.* Make pure, cleanse, (*of* or *from* impurities, sin, etc.); make ceremonially clean; clear of extraneous elements; hence ~ĪER[1] (2) *n.* [ME, f. OF *purifier* f. L *purificare* (as PURE; see -FY)]

Pūr'ĭm *n.* Jewish festival commemorating defeat of Haman's plot (Esth. 9). [Heb., pl. of *pūr*, perh. = LOT 1]

pūr'ine (-ēn) *n.* (Chem.) White crystalline base forming uric acid on oxidation. [f. G *purin* f. L *purus* pure + *uricum* uric; see -INE[5]]

pūr'|ist *n.* Stickler for or affecter of scrupulous purity esp. in language or art; so ~ISM (3) *n.*, **~ĭ'st**IC(AL) *adjs.* [f. F *puriste* (*pur* PURE; see -IST)]

pūr'ĭtan *n.* & *a.* **1.** *n.* (Hist.; *P~*). Member of the party of English Protestants who regarded reformation of Church under Elizabeth as incomplete and sought to abolish unscriptural and corrupt ceremonies etc. **2.** Purist member of any non-religious party; person practising or affecting extreme strictness in religion or morals. **3.** Hence **pūrĭtă'n**IC(AL) *adjs.*, ~ISM (3) *n.*, ~IZE (2, 3) *v.i.* & *t.* **4.** *a.* Of the Puritans; scrupulous in religion or morals. [f. LL *puritas* (as foll.) after earlier *Catharan* (as CATHAR; see -AN)]

pūr'ĭtў *n.* Pureness, cleanness, freedom from physical or moral pollution. [ME, f. OF *pureté*, w. assim. to LL *puritas -tatis* f. L *purus* pure; see -ITY]

pûrl[1] *n.*, & *v.t.* **1.** *n.* Cord of twisted gold or silver wire for bordering; ||chain of minute loops, picot, ornamenting edges of lace, ribbon, etc.; stitch in knitting with needle moved in opposite to normal (PLAIN[1]) direction. **2.** *v.t.* Border (material, or abs.) with purl; make (stitch, or abs.) purl; make stitches of (stockings etc.) purls. [orig. *pyrle*, *pirle* f. Sc. *pirl* twist; later senses perh. f. different wds]

pûrl[2] *v.i.*, & *n.* **1.** *v.i.* (Of brook etc.) flow with swirling motion and babbling sound. **2.** *n.* Such motion or sound. [16th c., prob. imit.; cf. Norw. *purla* bubble up]

pûrl[3] *n.* (Hist.) Ale or beer with wormwood infused; ‖hot beer mixed with gin as tonic. [17th c.; orig. unkn.]

pûrl[4] *v.* & *n.* (colloq.) **1.** *v.t.* & *i.* Turn upside down, upset. **2.** *n.* Cropper, heavy fall. [prob. var. of *pirl* (see PURL[1])]

‖**pûr'ler** *n.* (colloq.) Throw or blow that hurls one head foremost; **come** or **take a ~**, fall headlong. [f. prec. + -ER[1]]

pûr'lieu (-lū) *n.* ‖(Hist.) tract on border of forest, esp. one earlier included in it and still partly subject to forest laws; one's bounds, limits; one's usual haunts; (in *pl.*) outskirts, outlying region (lit. or fig.). [ME *purlew*, prob. alt. after LIEU f. AF *purale(e)*, OF *pourallee* perambulation to settle boundaries (*po(u)raler* traverse f. *po(u)r-* PUR- + *aller* go; see ALLEY[1])]

pûr'lĭn *n.* Horizontal beam running along length of roof, resting on principals and supporting common rafters or boards. [ME; AL *perlio -onis* perh. f. as PER- + L *ligare* bind]

purloi'n *v.t.* (formal or joc.) Steal, pilfer; hence **~**ER[1] *n.* [ME, f. AF PUR(*loigner* f. *loign* far f. L *longe*) put away, do away with]

pûr'ple *n.*, *a.*, & *v.* **1.** *n.* & *a.* (Of) a colour that is intermediate between red and blue; (**Tyrian**) **~**, (of) the crimson colour got from molluscs of genera *Thais*, *Purpura*, and *Murex*. **2.** *n.* Purple robe, esp. as dress of emperor, king, consul, etc.; **born in the ~**, born in reigning family, (fig.) situated in most privileged class. **3.** Scarlet official dress of cardinal. **4. ~ emperor,** large butterfly with purple wings; ‖**~ heart,** purple heart-shaped tablet of drug Drinamyl; **P~ Heart,** U.S. decoration for those wounded in action; **~heart,** purplish veneering wood from tropical Amer. tree; **~ passage** or **patch,** ornate passage in literary composition. **5.** Hence **pûr'pl**ISH[1], **pûr'pl**Y[2], *adjs.* **6.** *v.t.* & *i.* Make or become purple. [OE alt. f. *purpure purpuran* f. L PURPURA]

pûr'point. Var. of POURPOINT.

pûr'pôrt[1] *n.* Ostensible meaning; sense or tenor of document or statement. [ME, f. AF & OF *purport*, *porport* (*purporter*; see foll.)]

purpôr't[2] *v.t.* (Of document or speech) have as its meaning, convey, state, (fact, *that*); profess, be intended to seem (*to* do; *a letter purporting to be written by you, to contain your decision*); hence **~ĕd**LY[2] *adv.*, professedly. [f. AF & OF *purporter* f. med. L PRO[1](*portare* carry)]

pûr'pose[1] *n.* **1.** Object to be attained, thing intended, (*could not effect my purpose*; *this will answer* or *serve our* or *the purpose*; *what was the purpose of this law?*; *for the purpose of easier access*); **~-built, -made,** etc., built etc. for a specific purpose; **on ~**, in order (*to* do, *that*); **on ~, of set ~**, **~**LY[2] (-slĭ) *adv.*, designedly, not by accident; **serve no ~**, be useless; **to the ~**, relevant, useful for one's purpose; **to little, some, no, ~**, with little etc. result or effect. **2.** Intention to act; resolution, determination. **3.** Hence **~**LESS (-sl-), *a.* [ME, f. OF *porpos*, *purpos*, (*porposer*, *purposer*; see foll.)]

pûr'pose[2] *v.t.* Have as one's purpose, design, intend; **am ~d,** (arch.) intend (*to* do, do*ing*, *that*). [ME, f. OF *porposer*, *purposer* f. L *proponere* (as PROPOUND)]

pûr'poseful (-sf-) *a.* Having or indicating (conscious) purpose; intentional; hence **~**LY[2] *adv.*, **~**NESS *n.* [f. PURPOSE[1] + -FUL]

pûr'posĭve *a.* Having, serving, done with, a purpose; (of person or conduct) having purpose and resolution, purposeful. [f. PURPOSE[1,2] + -IVE]

pûr'pūra *n.* Disease marked by purple or livid spots on skin; mollusc of genus *Purpura*, including some yielding purple dye. [L, f. Gk *porphura* (shellfish yielding) purple]

pûr'pūre *n.*, & *a.* (usu. placed after *n.*) (Her.) Purple. [OE, & f. OF *purpre*, f. L *purpura* (as prec.)]

purpūr'ĭc *a.* Of purpura (*purpuric fever*); **~ acid,** organic acid forming purple or red salts. [f. L PURPURA + -IC]

pûr'pūrĭn *n.* Red colouring-matter got esp. from madder. [f. L PURPURA + -IN]

pûrr *v.* & *n.* **1.** *v.i.* (Of cat or other feline animal, fig. of person) make low continuous vibratory sound expressing pleasure; (of machine etc.) make similar sound. **2.** *v.t.* Utter, express, (words, contentment) thus. **3.** *n.* Such sound. [imit.]

pur sang (pūr sah'ṅ) *a.* or *adv.* (placed after *n.* or *a.*) Of the full blood, without admixture, through and through, genuine, (*is Welsh* or *a Welshman, militarist, a cynic, pur sang*). [F, = thoroughbred animal (*pur* pure, *sang* blood)]

pûrse[1] *n.* **1.** Small pouch of leather etc. for carrying money on the person, orig. closed by drawing strings together; *handbag. **2.** (fig.) Money, funds; **heavy** or **long ~**, wealth; **light ~**, poverty; ‖PRIVY *purse*; **the public ~**, national treasury. **3.** Sum collected, subscribed, or given, as present or as prize for contest. **4.** Baglike natural or other receptacle, pouch, cyst, etc. **5. ~-bearer,** one who has charge of another's or a company's money, ‖official carrying Great Seal before Lord Chancellor in purse; **~-net,** bag-shaped net for catching rabbits etc., opening of which can be closed with cords; **~-proud,** arrogant through wealth; **~-seine,** purse-net for fishing; **~-strings,** strings for closing mouth of purse (*hold the ~-strings*, have control of expenditure; *tighten, loosen, the ~-strings*, reduce, increase, expenditure). **6.** Hence **~'**FUL 2 (-sf-) *n.*, **~'**LESS (-sl-) *a.* [OE *purs* f. med. L *bursa*, *byrsa* purse f. Gk *bursa* hide, leather]

pûrse[2] *v.* **1.** *v.t.* **~ (up),** contract (lips, brow) in wrinkles. **2.** *v.i.* Become wrinkled. [ME, f. prec.]

pûr'ser *n.* Officer on ship who keeps accounts, esp. head steward in passenger vessel; hence **~**SHIP *n.* [ME, f. PURSE[1] + -ER[1]]

pûr'slane (-ĭn) *n.* Low succulent herb (*Portulaca oleracea*) formerly much used in salads and pickled. [ME, f. OF *porcelaine* (cf. PORCELAIN) alt. f. L *porcil(l)aca*, *portulaca*]

pursū'ance *n.* Carrying out, pursuing, (*of* plan, object, idea, etc.; *in pursuance of the regulations*). [f. as foll; see -ANCE]

pursū'ant *a.* & *adv.* **1.** *a.* Pursuing. **2.** *adv.* Conformably *to* (*the Act* etc.); so **~**LY[2] *adv.* [ME, = prosecuting, f. OF *po(u)rsuiant* part. of *po(u)rsu(iv)ir* (as foll.), see -ANT; assim. to AF *pursuer* and foll.]

pursūe' *v.* **1.** *v.t.* Follow with intent to overtake or attract or capture or kill; (fig., of consequences, penalty, disease, etc.) persistently attend, stick to; seek after, aim at, (pleasure etc., one's object); proceed in compliance with (plan etc.); proceed along, continue, (road, inquiry, conduct); continue to investigate or discuss (topic); follow (studies, recreation, profession); hence **pursū'**ABLE *a.* **2.** *v.i.* Go in pursuit (*after*, or abs.). [ME, f. AF *pursiwer*, *-suer*, = OF *porsivre* etc., f. Rom. *PRO[1]-, *PER(*sequere* f. L *sequi* follow); cf. SUE]

pursū′er *n.* In vbl senses; ||(Civil & Sc. Law) prosecutor. [ME, f. prec. + -ER^1]

pursui′t (-sū′t *or* -sōō′t) *n.* **1.** Pursuing, esp. **in ~** (*of* animal, person, one's object); **~ plane,** fighter aircraft; **~ race,** cycle race where riders start at intervals along track and seek to overtake others. **2.** Profession, employment, recreation, that one follows. [ME, f. OF *poursuite* (as PUR-, SUIT)]

||**pûr′suĭvant** (-sĭ- *or* -swĭ-) *n.* Officer of College of Arms below herald; (arch.) follower, attendant. [ME, f. OF *pursivant* part. (as n.) of *pursivre* (as PURSUE; see -ANT)]

pûr′s|ȳ^1 *a.* Short-winded, puffy; corpulent; hence **~ĭNESS** *n.* [ME, earlier *pursive* f. AF *porsif* f. OF *polsif* (*polser* breathe with difficulty f. L *pulsare*, as PULSATE; see -IVE)]

pûr′sȳ^2 *a.* Puckered. [f. PURSE^1 + -Y^2]

pûr′tenance *n.* (arch.) Entrails of animal. [ME, f. AF **purtinaunce* f. OF *pertinance*; cf. PERTINENCE, APPURTENANCE]

|**pūr′ul|ent** (-ōōl-) *a.* Of, full of, discharging, pus; hence or cogn. **~ENCE, ~ENCY,** *ns.*, **~entLY^2** *adv.* [F, or f. L *purulentus* (as PUS; see -ULENT)]

purvey′ (-vā′) *v.* **1.** *v.t.* Provide or supply (articles of food) as one's business. **2.** *v.i.* Make provision, act as purveyor, (*for* person, army, etc.). [ME, f. AF *purveier*, OF *porveiir* f. L *providēre* PROVIDE]

purvey′ance (-ā′a-) *n.* Purveying; ||(Hist.) right of sovereign to provisions etc. at fixed price. [ME f. OF *porveance*, f. L *providentia* PROVIDENCE]

purvey′or (-vā′-) *n.* One whose business it is to supply articles of food, esp. on large scale; (Hist.) officer exercising purveyance for sovereign. [ME, f. AF *purveour*, OF *porveour* (as PURVEY; see -OR)]

pûr′view (-vū) *n.* Enacting-clauses of statute; scope, intention, range, (*of* act, document, scheme, book, occupation, etc.); range of physical or mental vision. [ME, f. AF *purveü*, OF *porveü* p.p. of *porveiir* (as PURVEY)]

pŭs *n.* (Med.) Yellowish viscous matter produced from inflamed or infected tissue. [L *pus puris*]

Pū′sey|ism (-zĭĭ-) *n.* (Hist.) (Hostile term for) Tractarianism; so **~ITE^1** (-zĭīt) *n.* [f. E. B. *Pusey*, Engl. theologian d. 1882 + -ISM]

push^1 (pŏŏsh) *v.* **1.** *v.t.* Exert upon (thing etc.) force tending to move it away from oneself. **2.** Cause (thing etc.) to move (*up, down, away, back*, etc.) thus (lit. or fig.); thrust forward or upward; make (one's *way*) by force or persistence; *push the* BOAT^1 *out*; **~ the button** = PRESS^2 *the button*. **3.** Urge, impel, (*on, to* do, *to* effort, *into* action, etc.). **4.** Follow up, prosecute (claim etc.); engage actively in making (one's fortune); extend (one's conquests etc.). **5.** Press the adoption, use, sale, etc., of (goods etc.) esp. by advertisement; sell (drug) illegally. **6.** Press (person) hard (*do not wish to push him for payment*); tax abilities or tolerance of; **~ed for,** scarcely able to find enough (time, money, etc.); **~ one's luck,** take undue risks; **~′ing,** having nearly reached the age of (*forty* etc.). **7.** *v.t.* & *i.* (Cause to) project, thrust *out, forth*, etc., (*plants push out new roots*; *cape pushes out into sea*). **8.** *v.i.* Exert pushing force (*do not push against the fence*); make persistent demands *for*. **9.** Make one's way (*ahead, on*, etc.) forcibly or persistently. **10.** Exert oneself esp. to surpass others or succeed in business etc. **11.** **~ along,** (colloq.) depart; **~ around,** bully, treat with contempt; **~-button** *a.*, operated by pushing a button, (of warfare) conducted by guided missiles whose flight is controlled thus; **~ off,** (of person in boat) push with oar etc. against bank etc. to get boat out into stream etc., (sl.) go away; **~-over,** opponent or difficulty easily overcome; **~-pull,** operating by pushing and pulling, (Electr.) consisting of two valves etc. operated alternately by alternating current; **~ through,** bring (matter) to a conclusion, compel acceptance of (proposal etc.); **~-up,** = PRESS^2-*up*. [ME, f. AF **pusser*, OF *pousser, pou(l)ser* f. L *pulsare* (as PULSATE)]

push^2 (pŏŏsh) *n.* **1.** Act of pushing, shove, thrust; force thus exerted; (Bill.) stroke in which ball is pushed, not struck; exertion of influence to promote person's advancement. **2.** Vigorous effort (*must make a push to get it done, for home*); (Mil.) attack in force. **3.** Continuous pressure of arch etc.; pressure of affairs, crisis, pinch. **4.** Enterprise, determination to get on, self--assertion; hence **~′FUL** *a.* **5.** (sl., esp. Austral.) Gang of thieves, ruffians, etc. **6.** ||(sl.) **Give, get, the ~,** dismiss, be dismissed. **7.** **~-ball,** game played with enormous ball pushed, not kicked, towards opponents' goal; ||**~-bike,** (sl.) bicycle worked by pedalling (opp. *motor bike*); **~(-button),** button to be pushed to operate electric circuit etc.; **~-cart,** handcart; ||**~-chair,** child's folding chair on wheels; **~-rod** (opening and closing valves in internal combustion engine); **~-start** *n.*, & *v.t.*, start(ing of) motor vehicle by pushing it along to turn engine. [f. prec.]

pu′sher (pŏŏ′-) *n.* In vbl senses; illegal seller of drugs; pushing person; child's utensil for pushing food on to spoon etc. [f. PUSH^1 + -ER^1]

pu′shĭng (pŏŏ′-) *a.* In vbl senses; making (unduly) vigorous efforts to advance oneself in business etc.; hence **~LY^2** *adv.* [f. PUSH^1 + -ING^2]

Pŭ′shtu (-ōō) *n.* & *a.* (Of) the Iranian language of the Pathans. [f. Pers. *puštū*, Pushtu *păχtō*]

pu′shȳ (pŏŏ-) *a.* (colloq.) (Unpleasantly) pushing or self-assertive. [f. PUSH^{1,2} + -Y^2]

pūsĭllă′nĭmous (*or* -z-) *a.* Lacking courage, timid; hence or cogn. **pūsĭllanĭ′mITY** *n.*, **~LY^2** *adv.* [f. eccl. L *pusillanimis* (*pusillus* very small, *animus* mind) + -OUS]

puss (pŏŏs) Cat (esp. as *voc.*); (quasi-proper name for) hare; (colloq.) playful or coquettish girl; **~ in the corner,** game in which central person tries to occupy position left vacant by others changing places; **~ moth,** large European moth (*Cerura vinula*). [prob. f. MLG *pūs*, Du. *poes*, of unkn. orig.]

***pŭ′ssley, -lȳ,** *n.* Purslane. [corrupt.]

pu′ssȳ (pŏŏ′-) *n.* **~(-cat),** (childish name for) cat; (vulg.) vulva; ***~foot,** (*n.*, *pl.* **~***foots*) liquor-prohibition(ist) [f. nickname of W. E. Johnson, Amer. prohibitionist d. 1945], (*v.i.*) move stealthily, act (over-)cautiously or non--committally; **~ willow,** willow with silky catkins. [f. PUSS + -Y^3]

pŭ′stūl|āte *v.t.* & *i.* Form into pustules; hence or cogn. **~ATE^2** *a.*, **~A′TION** *n.* [f. LL *pustulare* (*pustula*; see foll.) + -ATE^3]

pŭ′stūl|e *n.* Pimple; **malignant ~e,** form of anthrax; (Bot. & Zool.) wart, wartlike excrescence; hence or cogn. **~AR^1, ~OUS,** *adjs.* [ME f. OF, or f. L *pustula*; see -ULE]

put^1 (pŏŏt) *v.* (**-tt-; put**). **1.** *v.t.* Move (thing etc.; lit. or fig.) so that it comes into some situation (*put it in your pocket, on the table, up the chimney, down the well*; *put children to* BED^1, *convict in prison*; *put matter before adviser, new life into invalid*); **not know where to ~ oneself,** be much embarrassed or uncomfortable; hurl (*the shot* or *the weight*) from hand as athletic exercise; thrust (weapon *into*), send (missile *through*); propel (tram of coal); harness (horse etc.) *to* (cart etc.); bring (animal) *to* one of opposite sex for breeding, *to* or *at* fence etc. for jumping; substitute (one thing *for* another); imagine oneself (*in* another's *place* etc.); *put the* BOOT[1] *in,* one's FOOT[1] *down, in it,* ||*the* LID *on it, words into* person's MOUTH[1], one's *hand to the* PLOUGH[1], one's SHOULDER *to the wheel,* ||*a* SOCK[1] *in it, a* SPOKE[1] *in* person's *wheel*; STAY[1] *put.* **2.** Bring into specified relation or state (*put machine out of action, goods on the market, the matter right, proposal into shape*; *put out of* COUNTENANCE[1], *out of* COURT[1], *a good* or *bold* FACE[1] *on it,* one's MIND[1] *to,* person *in* MIND[1] *of,* person's NOSE *out of joint,* STORE *by* or *on, the* WIND[1] *up,* person WISE[1]); write (words etc.) in specified position (*put your signature to it, a tick against his name*); impose the existence of (*put an* END[1] or STOP[2] *to it, a* VETO *on it*); cause (person) to go or be, habitually or temporarily, (*put* one's *child to school,* one's *daughter on the stage*; *put him at his ease, on his guard, on the right track, on antibiotics, off smoking, out of temper, to mind the sheep, through his* PACE[1]*s*); estimate (price etc.) *at*; express (thought etc.) in specified way; convert (thought etc.) *into words,* translate *into* (language); make investment of (money *into* land etc.); impose (tax etc.), lay (blame etc.), *on*; stake (money *on* horse etc.); apply *to* (use etc.); submit (case, question, etc.) *to* (person, vote, etc.; *I ~ it to you,* I appeal to you; *I ~ it to you that,* I challenge you to deny that); subject (person etc.) *to* (DEATH, *expense,* SHAME[1], *the* TEST[1], *torture,* etc.); drive (person) *to* (FLIGHT[2] etc.); HARD *put to it*; **~ it across,** (sl.) get even with or deceive (person); *not put it* PAST[2] person. **3.** *v.i.* (Naut.) Proceed, take one's course, *back, forth, in* (*to* harbour etc.), *off* (*from* shore etc.), *out, to sea,* in ship. **4.** *(Of river etc.) flow *into* or *out of.* **5. ~ and take,** gambling game played with special top that decides whether player puts money into or takes it from pool; **~ (up)on,** deceive, victimize, play joke on, (person); **~-on** *n.,* (colloq.) deception, hoax. **6.** (w. *advs.*): **~ about,** lay (sailing vessel) on opposite tack, (of vessel) go about; cause (horse, body of men) to turn round; trouble, distress; disseminate (rumour etc.). **7. ~ across,** make acceptable or effective; convey significance of; *achieve by deceit. **8. ~ away,** lay (money etc.) aside for future use; (colloq.) put into confinement; (colloq.) kill (injured, old, etc. animal); (sl.) consume (food or drink); (arch.) divorce (wife). **9. ~ back,** check advance of; move back the hands of (clock); restore to former place. **10. ~ by,** lay (money etc.) aside for future use. **11. ~ down,** suppress by force or authority; snub; write down, make a note of; enter name of (person) on list, esp. as subscriber etc.; account, reckon, (*I put him down as* or *for a fool*); attribute (*put it down to his nervousness*); preserve (eggs etc.) for future use; cease to read (book); put (baby) to bed; kill (injured, old, etc. animal); land (aircraft); allow (passenger) to alight; **~-down** *n.,* a snub. **12. ~ forth,** exert (effort, eloquence); bring into circulation; (of plant) send out (buds, leaves, or abs.). **13. ~ forward,** thrust (one*self* etc.) into prominence; advance, set forth, (theory etc.); advance hands of (clock). **14. ~ in,** install in office etc.; formally present (document etc.) in lawcourt etc.; make *an appearance*; make a claim *for,* be candidate *for,* (election, appointment, etc.); interpose (remark, blow, etc.); perform (spell of work) as part of a whole; (colloq.) spend (time). **15. ~ off,** postpone; postpone engagement with (person); evade (person etc. *with* excuse etc.); hinder or dissuade *from*; offend, disconcert; remove (clothes that one is wearing). **16. ~ on,** clothe oneself or another with; assume, take on, (character, appearance); develop additional (flesh, weight); stage (a play etc.); add (speed, amount *to* price, runs etc. *to* score); advance hands of (clock); bring into action (pressure, SCREW[1]); cause (cricketer) to bowl, (electric light) to shine, (electrical device) to operate, (train) to run, etc.; **~ it on,** (colloq.) overcharge, simulate emotion, etc. **17. ~ out,** dislocate (joint); cause (batsman, batter, etc.) to be out; extinguish (light, fire, etc.); disconcert, confuse; annoy, irritate; inconvenience; exert (strength etc.); lend (money) at interest; give (work) to be done off the premises; blind (person's eyes). **18. ~ over,** make acceptable or effective; convey significance of; *postpone; *achieve by deceit. **19. ~ through,** carry out (task); connect (person) by telephone *to* another via exchange(s); make (telephone call); complete (business transaction). **20. ~ together,** form (whole) by combination of parts, combine (parts) into whole; *put* TWO *and two together.* **21. ~ under,** render unconscious by anaesthetic etc. **22. ~ up,** construct, build; raise (price etc.); offer (prayer), present (petition, proposal), provide (money as backer etc.); propose, be candidate, for election; cause (game) to rise from cover; publish (banns); offer for sale or competition; pack up in parcel or receptacle; sheathe (sword); lodge (guest), be or become lodger *at*; concoct (**~-up** *a.,* fraudulently concocted); *put* person's BACK[1] *up*; *put up a* FIGHT[2]; *put* one's HAIR *up*; **~ up to,** inform (person) of, instruct (person) in, instigate (person) in (do*ing* etc.); **~ up with,** submit to, tolerate, (annoyance, insult, etc.). [ME, f. OE **putian* or **pūtian, potian, pȳtan,* of unkn. orig.]

put[2] (pŏŏt) *n.* **1.** Throw of the shot or weight. **2.** (St. Exch.) Option of selling stock at fixed price at given date. [ME, f. prec.]

pŭt[3]. See PUTT.

pū'tatĭve *a.* Reputed, supposed (*his putative father*); hence **~**LY[2] (-vlĭ) *adv.* [ME, f. OF *putatif -ive* or f. LL *putativus* f. L *putare* think; see -ATIVE]

pŭ'tlŏg, pŭ'tlŏck, *n.* Short horizontal timber projecting from wall, on which scaffold floor-boards rest. [17th c.; orig. uncert.]

pŭ't-pŭt *n.,* & *v.i.* (-tt-). (Make) rapid intermittent sound of small petrol engine. [imit.]

pū'trė|fȳ *v.* **1.** *v.i.* Become putrid, rot, go bad; fester, suppurate; become morally corrupt. **2.** *v.t.* Cause to putrefy. **3.** So **~**FA'CTION *n.,* **~**FA'CIENT, **~fă'ct**IVE, *adjs.* [ME, f. L *putrefacere* (*puter putris* rotten; see -FY)]

pūtrĕ'sc|ent *a.* In process of rotting; of or accompanying this process; so **~**ENCE *n.,* **~**IBLE *a.* [f. L *putrescere* incept. of *putrēre* (see foll., -ESCENT)]

pū'trĭd *a.* Decomposed, rotten; foul, noxious; (fig.) corrupt; (sl.) of poor quality, very unpleasant; hence **~**ITY (-ĭ'd-), **~**NESS, *ns.,* **~**LY[2] *adv.* [f. L *putridus* (*putrēre* rot f. *puter putris* rotten; see -ID[1])]

putsch (pŏŏch) *n.* Attempt at a revolution. [Swiss G, = thrust, blow]

pŭtt, pŭt[3], *v.* (-tt-) & *n.* **1.** *v.i.* & *t.* Strike (golf-ball) gently with club to get it into or nearer to hole on smooth grass area (**~'ing-green**). **2.** *n.* Such stroke. [different. f. PUT[1,2]]

pŭ'ttee (-ĭ) *n.* Long strip of cloth wound spirally round leg from ankle to knee for protection and support; *leather legging. [f. Hindi *paṭṭī* band, bandage]

pu'tter[1] (pŏŏ'-) *n.* In vbl senses; miner who moves loads of coal etc. into position for raising to surface. [ME, f. PUT[1] + -ER[1]]

pŭ'tter[2] *n.* In vbl sense; golf-club used in putting. [f. PUTT + -ER[1]]

pŭ'tter[3] *n.,* & *v.i.* = PUT-PUT. [imit.]

***pŭ'tter**[4]. Var. of POTTER[2].

pu'tt|ō (pŏŏ-) *n.* (*pl.* **~i**). Figure of child (esp.

cherub- or Cupid-like) in Renaissance painting or sculpture. [It., = boy, f. L *putus*]

pŭ'ttў *n.*, & *v.t.* **1.** *n.* (**Jewellers'**) ~, powder of tin (and lead) oxide for polishing glass or metal; (**plasterers'**) ~, fine mortar of lime and water without sand. **2.** (**Glaziers'**) ~, cement of whiting, raw linseed oil, etc., for fixing panes of glass, filling up holes in woodwork, etc. **3.** (fig.) Compliant person; ||~ **medal,** (joc.) fit reward for small service (*you deserve a putty medal*). **4.** *v.t.* Cover, fix, join, fill up, with putty. [f. F *potée*, lit. POT¹ful; see -Y⁴]

puy (pwē) *n.* Small volcanic cone esp. in Auvergne, France. [F, = hill, f. L PODIUM]

pŭ'zzle¹ *n.* Bewilderment, perplexity; perplexing question, enigma; problem or toy designed to test knowledge, ingenuity, or patience; **~-head(ed), -pate(d),** (person) with confused ideas. [f. foll.]

pŭ'zzle² *v.* **1.** *v.t.* Perplex; find *out* by patience and ingenuity (solution of problem etc.). **2.** *v.i.* Be perplexed (*about* or *over* problem etc.). **3.** Hence ~MENT (-zelm-), **pŭ'zzl**ER¹ (1, 2), *ns.* [16th c.; orig. unkn.]

puzzolana. Var. of POZZOLANA.

PVC *abbr.* polyvinyl chloride.

Pvt. *abbr.* Private (*soldier).

||**P.W.** *abbr.* Policewoman.

***P.X.** *abbr.* post exchange.

pyae'm|ĭa, *pyē'm|ĭa, *n.* Blood-poisoning marked by formation of abscesses in viscera; hence ~IC *a.* [mod. L, f. Gk *puon* pus + *haima* blood + -IA¹]

pў'cnĭc. Var. of PYKNIC.

pў'e-dŏg, pī'(e)-dŏg, (pī'd-) *n.* Ownerless mongrel of the East. [f. Anglo-Ind. *pye, paē*, Hindi *pāhī* outsider, + DOG¹]

pyĕlo- *comb. form.* Pelvis (of skeleton or kidney), as: **py'elogram,** X-ray picture of renal pelvis; **pyeli'tis,** inflammation of renal pelvis. [f. Gk *puelos* trough]

pў'gmў, pĭ'gmў, *n.* & *a.* **1.** *n.* One of a diminutive race of men said to have inhabited parts of Ethiopia or India; one of a group of very short people in equatorial Africa; dwarf (fig. of intellectual inferiority etc.); elf, pixie; so **pўgm(a)e'**AN (-ē'*a*n) *a.* **2.** *a.* Of the pygmies; (of person or animal) dwarf. [ME, f. L f. Gk *pugmaios* dwarf(ish) (*pugmē* length from elbow to knuckles, fist)]

||**pўja'ma|s, *paja'ma|s,** (-ah'm*a*z) *n. pl.* Loose trousers tied round waist, worn by both sexes in the East; suit of loose trousers and jacket for sleeping etc. (~ **jacket, trousers,** etc., garments forming part of this). [f. Urdu *pā(ē)jāma* f. Pers. *pae, pay*, leg + Hindi *jāma* clothing]

pў'knĭc *a.* & *n.* (Anthrop.) (Person) characterized by thick neck, large abdomen, and relatively short limbs. [f. Gk *puknos* thick + -IC]

pў'lŏn *n.* Gateway esp. of Egyptian temple; tall structure erected as support (esp. for electric-power cables) or boundary or decoration; structure marking path for aircraft. [f. Gk *pulōn* (*pulē* gate)]

pўlôr'|us *n.* (*pl.* ~**i** *pr.* -ī). (Anat.) Opening from stomach into duodenum; part of stomach where this is; hence **pўlŏ'r**IC *a.* [LL, f. Gk *pulōros, pulouros* gatekeeper (*pulē* gate, *ouros* warder)]

pўorrhoe'a, *pўorrhē'a, (-rē'*a*) *n.* Discharge of pus, esp. in disease of tooth-sockets; this disease. [f. Gk *puo-* (*puon* pus) + *rhoia* flux (*rheō* flow)]

pўracă'ntha *n.* Evergreen thorny shrub of genus *Pyracantha* with white flowers and scarlet berries. [L, f. Gk *purakantha*]

pў'ramĭd *n.* **1.** Monumental (esp. ancient Egyptian) structure of stone etc. with polygonal or (usu.) square base, and sloping sides meeting at apex. **2.** Solid of this shape with base of three or more sides (**pentagonal** etc. ~, with five etc. sides). **3.** Pyramid-shaped thing or pile of things; fruit-tree trained in pyramid shape; ~ **selling,** form of financial trickery where agents are recruited in increasing numbers at successively lower levels. **4.** ||(in *pl.*) Game played on billiard-table with (usu. 15) coloured balls and one cue-ball. **5.** Hence or cogn. **pўră'mid**AL *a.*, ~WISE *adv.* [ME, f. L f. Gk *puramis -idos*]

pўre *n.* Heap of combustible material, esp. funeral pile for burning corpse. [f. L f. Gk *pura* (*pur* fire)]

pўrē'thrum *n.* Chrysanthemum with finely divided leaves; insecticide made from dried flowers of this. [L, f. Gk *purethron* feverfew]

pўrĕ'tĭc (*or* pĭr-) *a.* Of, for, or producing, fever. [f. mod. L *pyreticus* f. Gk *puretos* fever; see -IC]

pўrĕ'x|ĭa (*or* pĭr-) *n.* (Path.) Fever; hence ~**ĭ**AL, ~IC(AL), *adjs.* [mod. L, f. Gk *purexis* (*puressō* be feverish f. *pur* fire); see -IA¹]

pyrhēlĭŏ'mĕter *n.* Instrument for measuring heat radiated by sun. [f. Gk *pur* fire + *hēlios* sun + -O- + -METER]

pў'rĭdine (-ēn) *n.* (Chem.) Colourless volatile odorous liquid base got from dry distillation of bone-oil and coal-tar, used as solvent and in chemical manufacture. [f. Gk *pur* fire + -ID⁴ + -INE⁵]

pўr'īte *n.* = *iron* PYRITES. [F, or f. L (as foll.)]

pўrī'tēs (-z) *n.* (**Iron**) ~, yellow lustrous iron sulphide mineral; **copper** ~, double sulphide of copper and iron; hence **pўrĭ'**TIC, **pўrĭtĭ'**FEROUS, **pўr'ĭt**OUS, *adjs.*, **pўr'ĭt**IZE (3) *v.t.* [L, f. Gk *puritēs* of fire (*pur*; see -ITE¹)]

pўr'ō *n.* (colloq.) = PYRO*gallic acid*. [abbr.]

pўrō- *comb. form.* **1.** Fire, as: **~-ele'ctric, ~-electri'city,** (property of) becoming electrically charged when heated; **~ga'llic acid, ~ga'llol,** weak acid used as developer in photography etc.; **~ge'nic, ~genous** (-ŏ'j-), productive of heat, esp. in the body, or of fever, (of rock) igneous, (of substance) produced by combustion of another; **~latry** (-ŏ'l-), fire-worship; **~li'gneous,** produced by action of fire or heat on wood; **pyr'omancy,** divination by fire; **~ma'nia, ~ma'niac,** (person suffering from) incendiary mania; **~pho'ric,** (of substance) that takes fire spontaneously on exposure to air. **2.** (Chem.) new substance formed from another by destructive distillation etc. (*pyrophosphate*); (Min.) mineral etc. showing some property or change under action of heat, or having fiery red or yellow colour. [f. Gk *puro-* (*pur* fire)]

pўrŏ'graphў *n.* = POKER¹-*work*. [f. prec. + -GRAPHY]

pўr'olўse, *pўr'olўze, *v.t.* Decompose by pyrolysis. [f. foll. after *analyse*]

pўrŏ'lўs|ĭs *n.* (*pl.* ~**es** *pr.* -ēz). Chemical decomposition by action of heat; so **pўrolў'**TIC *a.* [f. PYRO- + -LYSIS]

pўrŏ'mĕter *n.* Instrument for measuring high temperatures; so **pўromĕ'tr**IC *a.*, **pўrŏ'**METRY *n.* [f. PYRO- + -METER]

pўr'ōpe *n.* Deep-red garnet. [ME, f. OF *pirope* f. L f. Gk *purōpos* gold-bronze, lit. fiery-eyed (*pur* fire, *ōps* eye)]

pўrō'sĭs *n.* (Med.) Burning sensation in lower part of chest with eructation of watery fluid, heartburn, waterbrash. [mod. L, f. Gk *purōsis* (*puroō* set on fire f. *pur* fire)]

pўrotĕ'chn|ĭc (-tĕ'k-) *a.* & *n.* **1.** *a.* Of (the nature of) fireworks (*pyrotechnic display*); (fig., of wit etc.) brilliant, sensational; hence or cogn. ~**ĭ**CAL *a.*, ~IST (3), **pўr'otĕchn**Y¹ (-tĕk-), *ns.* **2.** *n.* (in *pl.*) Art of making, or display of, fireworks (lit.

or fig.). [f. *pyrotechny* (PYRO-, Gk *tekhnē* art) + -IC]

pȳrŏʹxēne *n.* Mineral composed of silicates esp. of calcium and magnesium, a common component of igneous rocks. [f. PYRO- + Gk *xenos* stranger (because supposed alien to igneous rocks)]

pȳrŏʹxȳlin *n.* Cellulose nitrate soluble in ether and alcohol to form collodion and used as basis of lacquers, artificial leather, etc. [f. F *pyroxyline* f. as PYRO- + Gk *xulon* wood + -IN]

pȳʹrrhĭc[1] (-rĭk) *n.* & *a.* **1.** ~ (**dance**), war-dance of ancient Greeks. **2.** (Based on) metrical foot consisting of two short syllables. [sense 1 f. L or Gk *purrhikhē*, said to be named from one *Purrhikhos*, the inventor; sense 2 f. L f. Gk *purrhikhios* (*pous*) pyrrhic (foot)]

Pȳʹrrhĭc[2] (-rĭk) *a.* ~ **victory** (gained at too great cost, like that of Pyrrhus king of Epirus over the Romans at Asculum in 279 B.C.). [f. Gk *purrhikos* (*Purrhos* Pyrrhus; see -IC)]

Pȳʹrrhon|ism (-ro-) *n.* Sceptic philosophy of Pyrrho of Elis (*c.* 300 B.C.), doctrine that certainty of knowledge is unattainable; scepticism, philosophic doubt; so **Pȳrrhōʹn**IAN (-rōʹ-), **Pȳrrhŏʹn**IC (-rŏʹ-), *adjs.* & *ns.*, ~IST (2) *n.* [f. Gk *Purrhōn* Pyrrho + -ISM]

pȳruʹvĭc (-ōōʹ-) *a.* ~ **acid,** organic acid important in making available energy from food in the body. [f. as PYRO- + L *uva* grape + -IC]

Pȳthăgorēʹan *a.* & *n.* (Follower) of Pythagoras, philosopher of Samos (6th c. B.C.) said to have believed in transmigration of souls and explanation of the universe in terms of numbers; **Pythaʹgoras' theorem, ~ theorem** or **proposition,** (that square on hypotenuse of right-angled triangle is equal to sum of squares on other two sides). [f. L f. Gk *Puthagoreios* + -AN]

Pȳʹthĭan *a.* & *n.* **1.** *a.* Of (Apollo's oracle and priestess at) Delphi; ~ **games** (celebrated by ancient Greeks every four years near Delphi). **2.** *n.* Apollo or his priestess at Delphi; frenzied person. [f. L f. Gk *Puthios* (*Puthō*, older name of Delphi) + -AN]

pȳʹthon *n.* Large snake (esp. of genus *Python*) that crushes its prey; hence **pȳthŏʹn**IC *a.* [L, f. Gk *Puthōn* huge serpent or monster slain near Delphi by Apollo in myth]

pȳʹthonėss *n.* Pythian priestess; witch. [ME, f. OF *phitonise* f. med. L *phitonissa* f. LL *pythonissa* fem. of *pytho* f. Gk *puthōn* soothsaying demon (cf. prec., -ESS[1])]

pȳūrʹĭa *n.* (Path.) Presence of pus in urine. [f. Gk *puon* pus + -URIA]

pȳx *n.* **1.** (Eccl.) Vessel in which consecrated bread is kept. **2.** ‖Box at Royal Mint in which specimen gold and silver coins are deposited to be tested at the annual **trial of the ~** by jury of Goldsmiths' Company. [ME, f. L (see PYXIS)]

pȳxĭʹdĭ|um *n.* (*pl.* ~**a**). (Bot.) Seed-capsule of which the top comes off like lid of box. [mod. L, f. Gk *puxidion*, dim. (as foll.)]

pȳʹx|ĭs *n.* (*pl.* ~**ides** *pr.* -ĭdēz). Small box, casket; = prec. [ME f. L, f. Gk *puxis* (*puxos* BOX[1])]

Q

Q, q, (kū) *n.* (*pl.* **Qs** *or* **Q's**). Seventeenth letter of alphabet; MIND[2] one's *P's and Q's*; **Q-boat, Q-ship,** = MYSTERY[1] *ship*; **Q department** etc. (of quartermaster).

Q. *abbr.* Queen('s); question.

Q.A.R.A.N.C. *abbr.* Queen Alexandra's Royal Army Nursing Corps.

Q.A.R.N.N.S. *abbr.* Queen Alexandra's Royal Naval Nursing Service.

Q.B. *abbr.* Queen's Bench.

Q.C. *abbr.* Queen's Counsel.

Q.E.D., Q.E.F., Q.E.I., *abbrs.* QUOD[2] *erat demonstrandum, faciendum, inveniendum.*

Q.F. *abbr.* quick-firing.

Q fēver (kūʹ-) *n.* Mild typhus-like disease. [f. Queensland, where first observed]

qibla. Var. of KIBLAH.

Qld. *abbr.* Queensland.

Q.M. *abbr.* quartermaster.

Q.M.G. *abbr.* Quartermaster General.

Q.M.S. *abbr.* Quartermaster Sergeant.

‖**Q.P.M.** *abbr.* Queen's Police Medal.

qr. *abbr.* quarter(s).

Q.S.O. *abbr.* quasi-stellar object, quasar.

q.t. *n.* (sl.) Quiet (*on the q.t.*). [abbr.]

qt. *abbr.* quart(s).

qu. *abbr.* query.

quā (*or* kwah) *conj.* As, in the capacity of, (*objects to the Church not qua Church, but qua Establishment*). [L, abl. fem. sing. of *qui* who (rel. pron.)]

quăck[1] *v.i.*, & *n.* (Utter) harsh sound made by ducks; talk loudly and foolishly; **quack-quack,** (childish name for) duck. [imit.; cf. Du. *kwakken*, G *quacken* croak, quack]

quăck[2] *n.*, *a.*, & *v.* **1.** *n.* Ignorant pretender to skill esp. in medicine or surgery; one who offers wonderful remedies or devices, charlatan; hence ~ʹERY (4) *n.*, ~ʹISH[1] *a.* **2.** *a.* Being a quack (*quack doctor*); characteristic of or used by a quack (*quack remedies*). **3.** *v.i.* Play the quack; talk pretentiously. **4.** *v.t.* Puff or advertise extravagantly (cure etc.). [abbr. of *quacksalver* f. Du. (prob. f. obs. *quacken* prattle, *salf* SALVE[1]; see -ER[1])]

quad (kwŏd) *n.* (colloq.) Quadrangle; quadrat; quadruple; QUADRUPLET 1. [abbr.]

quadragėnārʹĭan (-ŏd-) *a.* & *n.* (Person) from 40 to 49 years old. [f. LL *quadragenarius* (*quadrageni* distrib. of *quadraginta* forty; see -ARY[1]) + -AN]

Quadragĕʹsĭma (-ŏd-) *n.* ~ (**Sunday**), first Sunday in Lent. [LL, fem. (as n.) of L *quadragesimus* fortieth (*quadraginta* forty), Lent having 40 days]

quadragĕʹsĭmal (-ŏd-) *a.* (Of fast, esp. Lent) lasting forty days; Lenten. [f. prec. + -AL]

quaʹdr|ăngle (kwŏʹdrănggel) *n.* **1.** Four-cornered figure, esp. square or rectangle; so ~**ăʹngūl**AR[1] (-ngg-) *a.* **2.** Four-sided court wholly or mainly enclosed by parts of large buildings; such court with buildings round it. [ME f. OF, f. LL *quadrangulum* square, neut. (as n.) of *quadrangulus* (as QUADRI-, ANGLE[1])]

quaʹdrant (-ŏʹd-) *n.* **1.** Quarter of circle's circumference; plane figure enclosed by two radii of circle at right angles and arc cut off by them; quarter of sphere etc. **2.** Thing, esp. graduated strip of metal, shaped like quarter-circle; instrument graduated (esp. through an arc of 90°) for taking angular measurements. **3.** Hence **quadrăʹnt**AL *a.* [ME, f. L *quadrans* -*antis* quarter (*quattuor* four)]

quaʹdrat (-ŏʹd-) *n.* (Print.) Small metal block used in spacing (**em ~, en ~,** broader, narrower, size). [var. of foll.]

qua'drate[1] (-ŏ'd-) *a.* & *n.* **1.** *a.* (esp. Anat. & Zool.) Square, rectangular, (*quadrate bone, muscle*). **2.** *n.* Rectangular object; quadrate bone or muscle. [ME, f. L *quadratus* (as foll.; see -ATE[2])]

quadrā'te[2] (*or* kwŏ-) *v.* **1.** *v.t.* Make square; make conform (*with, to*, or abs.). **2.** *v.i.* Correspond or conform (*with*, or abs.). [f. L *quadrare* (as QUADRI-) + -ATE[3]]

quadră'tĭc *a.* & *n.* **1.** *a.* Square; (Math.) involving second and no higher power of unknown quantity or variable (*quadratic equation*). **2.** *n.* Quadratic equation; (in *pl.*) branch of algebra dealing with these. [f. F *quadratique* or f. mod. L *quadraticus* (as QUADRATE[1]; see -IC)]

qua'drature (-ŏ'd-) *n.* (Math.) finding of square with area equal to that of figure bounded by curve (*quadrature of the circle*); (Astron.) one of two points at which moon is 90° from sun, position of heavenly body in relation to another 90° away; (Electr.) phase difference of 90°. [F, or f. L *quadratura* (as QUADRATE[2]; see -URE)]

quadrĕ'nnĭal (-ŏd-) *a.* Lasting, recurring every four years; hence ~LY[2] *adv.* [f. as foll. + -AL]

quadrĕ'nni|um (-ŏd-) *n.* (*pl.* **~ums** *or* **~a**). Period of four years. [f. L *quadriennium* (as foll., *annus* year)]

qua'drĭ- (-ŏ'd-) *comb. form.* Four, as: **~fid** *a.*, cleft into four divisions or lobes; **~li'ngual,** using, or in, four languages; **~no'mial,** consisting of four algebraic terms; **~par'tite,** consisting of four parts, shared by or involving four parties; **~pole,** = QUADRUPOLE; **~reme,** ancient galley with four banks of oars; **~sylla'bic,** four-syllabled; **~sy'llable,** word of four syllables; **~va'lent,** (Chem.) having a valence of four. [L (*quattuor* four)]

qua'drĭc (-ŏ'd-) *a.* & *n.* (Geom.) (Surface) described by equation of second degree. [f. L *quadra* square + -IC]

qua'drĭcĕps (-ŏ'd-) *n.* (Anat.) Four-headed muscle at front of thigh. [mod. L (as QUADRI-, BICEPS)]

quadrī'ga (*or* -ē'-) *n.* (*pl.* **~e**). Ancient chariot with four horses abreast. [L (as QUADRI-, *jugum* yoke)]

quadrĭlă'teral (-ŏd-) *a.* & *n.* Four-sided (figure); area defended by four fortresses (esp. one in N. Italy). [f. LL *quadrilaterus* (as QUADRI-, *latus lateris* side) + -AL]

quadrĭ'lle[1] *n.* Fashionable 18th-c. game for four persons with forty cards. [F, perh. f. Sp. *cuartillo* (*cuarto* fourth), w. assim. to foll.]

quadrĭ'lle[2] *n.* Square dance for four couples and containing usu. five figures; piece of music for such dance. [F, f. Sp. *cuadrilla* troop, company (*cuadra* square) or f. It. *quadriglia* (*quadra* square)]

quadrĭ'llion (-yon) *n.* (for *pl.* usage see HUNDRED). ||A million raised to the fourth power; *a thousand raised to the fifth power. [F (as QUADRI-, MILLION)]

quadrĭplē'g|ĭa (-ŏd-) *n.* (Path.) Paralysis of both arms and both legs; hence ~IC *a.* & *n.* [mod. L, f. as QUADRI- + Gk *plēgē* blow, stroke + -IA[1]; cf. PARAPLEGIA]

quadrĭ'vĭum *n.* (Hist.) Medieval university course of arithmetic, geometry, astronomy, and music. [L, = place where four roads meet (as QUADRI-, *via* road)]

quadrōō'n *n.* Offspring of white and mulatto, person of quarter-Negro blood; hybrid of similarly proportioned descent between other human, animal, or plant stocks. [f. Sp. *cuarterón* (*cuarto* fourth), w. assim. to QUADRI-]

quadru'manous (-rōō'-) *a.* Four-handed; belonging to the group Quadrumana of mammals with opposable digit on all four limbs (primates other than man). [f. mod. L *quadrumana* neut. pl. (as n.) of *quadrumanus* (as foll., L *manus* hand)]

qua'drupĕd (-ŏ'drōō-) *n.* & *a.* **1.** *n.* Four-footed animal, esp. four-footed mammal; hence **quadru'pĕd**AL (-rōō'-) *a.* **2.** *a.* Four-footed. [f. F *quadrupède* or f. L *quadrupes -pedis* a. & n. (*quadru-* form of QUADRI- occas. used before *p-*, *pes* foot)]

qua'druple (-ŏ'drōō-) *a.*, *n.*, & *v.* **1.** *a.* Fourfold, consisting of four parts or involving four parties (*quadruple alliance*); **~ time** (Mus., with four beats to the bar). **2.** Amounting or equivalent to four times the amount or number of (*has a light and heat quadruple that of the earth*); hence **qua'drup**LY[2] (-ŏ'drōō-) *adv.* **3.** *n.* Number or amount four times greater than another. **4.** *v.t.* & *i.* Multiply by four. [F, f. L *quadruplus* (as prec., *-plus* as in *duplus* DUPLE)]

qua'druplėt (-ŏ'drōō-; *or* kwŏdrōō'-) *n.* **1.** One of four children born at a birth; set of four things working together. **2.** Bicycle for four; (Mus.) group of four notes to be performed in the time of three. [f. prec., after *triplet*]

quadru'plĭcate[1] (-ōō'-) *a.* & *n.* **1.** *a.* Fourfold; (esp.) of which four copies are made. **2.** *n.* **In ~**, in four exactly similar examples or copies. [f. L *quadruplicare* (*quadruplex -plicis* fourfold; cf. QUADRUPED, DUPLEX); see -ATE[2,1]]

quadru'plĭc|āte[2] (-ōō'-) *v.t.* Multiply by four; make four copies of; hence ~A'TION *n.* [f. as prec. + -ATE[3]]

quadruplĭ'cĭtȳ (-ŏdrōō-) *n.* State of being fourfold. [f. L *quadruplex -plicis* (see QUADRUPLICATE[1]), after *duplicity*]

qua'drupōle (-ŏ'drōō-) *n.* (Phys.) System of two equal and opposite dipoles. [f. as QUADRUPED + POLE[2]]

quaer'ė (kwēr'ĭ) *v.t.*, & *n.* (arch.) **1.** *v.t.* (in *imper.*) Inquire, it is a question, I should like to know, (*most interesting, no doubt; but quaere, is it true?*). **2.** *n.* Question, query. [L, imper. of *quaerere* ask]

quae'stor *n.* (Rom. Hist.) Magistrate acting as State treasurer, paymaster, etc.; treasurer; hence **quaestōr'**IAL *a.*, ~SHIP *n.* [ME f. L (*quaerere quaesit-* seek; see -OR)]

quaff (-ahf *or* -ŏf) *v.i.* & *t.* Drink deeply; drain (cup etc.) in copious or long draughts. [16th c.; perh. imit.]

quăg (*or* kwŏg) *n.* Marshy or boggy spot; quaking bog; hence **~'gy**[2] (-gĭ) *a.* [rel. to dial. *quag* v. 'shake', prob. imit.]

quă'gga *n.* Extinct S. Afr. quadruped related to ass and zebra, less striped than latter. [f. Xhosa-Kaffir *iqwara*]

quă'gmīre (*or* kwŏ'-) *n.* Quaking bog, fen, marsh, slough (lit. or fig.). [f. QUAG + MIRE[1]]

***qua'hŏg, *qua'haug,** (kwaw'-) *n.* Edible round clam of Atlantic coast of N. America. [Narraganset Indian]

quaich, quaigh, (kwāχ) *n.* (Sc.) Kind of drinking-cup, usu. of wood and having two handles. [f. Gael. *cuach* cup, prob. f. L *caucus*]

quail[1] *n.* (*pl.* **~** *or* **~s**). Migratory bird of genus *Coturnix* etc. allied to partridge and esteemed as food; **~-call, ~-pipe,** whistle with note like quail's for luring these birds; hence ~'ERY (3) *n.* [ME, f. OF *quaille* f. med. L *coacula* (prob. imit.); cf. MDu., MLG *quackele*, OHG *wahtala*]

quail[2] *v.i.* (Of person, his heart, courage, spirit, or eyes) flinch, be cowed, give way *before* or *to*. [ME, of unkn. orig.]

quaint *a.* Attractive or piquant in virtue of unfamiliar, esp. old-fashioned, appearance, ornamentation, manners, etc., daintily odd; hence ~'LY[2] *adv.*, ~'NESS *n.* [earlier senses 'wise, cunning'; ME f. OF *cointe* f. L *cognitus* p.p. of *cognoscere* ascertain]

quāk|e *v.i.*, & *n.* **1.** *v.i.* Shake, tremble, rock to and fro, (of earth with earthquake, person usu. *for* or *with* fear or cold, bog when trodden on, etc.); **~'ing-grass,** grass of genus *Briza* with slender stalks trembling in wind; hence ~'Y[2] *a.* **2.** *n.* Act of quaking; (colloq.) earthquake. [OE *cwacian*]

Quā'ker *n.* **1.** (Pop. name for) member of Society of Friends, Christian movement without written creed or ordained ministers, devoted to peaceful principles, and formerly noted for plainness of dress and simplicity of living. **2.** *~ (**gun**), dummy gun in ship or fort. **3.** **~-bird,** sooty albatross; **~(s') meeting,** religious meeting of Friends, silent till some member is moved by the Holy Spirit, (fig.) silent meeting, company in which conversation flags. **4.** Hence ~DOM, ~ESS[1], ~ISM (3, 4), *ns.*, ~ISH[1], ~LY[1], *adjs.* [f. prec. + -ER[1]]

qualĭfĭcā'tion (-ŏl-) *n.* **1.** Modification, recognition of contingency (*statement with many qualifications*), restricting or limiting circumstance (*hedged with qualifications*), detraction from completeness or absoluteness (*his delight had one qualification*). **2.** Quality or accomplishment fitting person or thing (*for* post etc., or abs.); condition that must be fulfilled before right can be acquired or office held (*the qualification for citizenship may be a specified income*); document attesting such fulfilment. **3.** Attribution of quality (*the qualification of his policy as opportunist is unfair*). **4.** Hence **qua'lĭfĭcāt**ORY (-ŏ'l-) *a.* [F, or f. med. L *qualificatio* (as prec.; see -FICATION)]

qua'lĭfȳ (-ŏ'l-) *v.* **1.** *v.t.* Attribute some quality to, describe *as*, (*qualify documents as heretical, person as a scoundrel, proposal as iniquitous; adjectives qualify nouns*). **2.** Invest or provide with the necessary qualities, make competent, fit, or legally entitled, (*for* being or doing, *to* be or do, *for* post or sphere, or abs.); **~ing examination, round,** etc., (to ensure that candidates are not below a fixed standard or that competitors do not exceed a fixed number). **3.** Modify (statement, opinion), make less absolute or sweeping, subject to reservations or limitation. **4.** Moderate, mitigate, make less complete or pleasing or unpleasing; alter strength or flavour of (spirit etc. with water, or vice versa). **5.** *v.i.* Fulfil a condition, esp. pass test or take oath, to make oneself eligible (*for* post, competition, etc., or abs.). **6.** Hence **qua'lĭfī**ER[1] (-ŏ'l-) *n.* [f. F *qualifier* f. med. L *qualificare* f. L *qualis* such as; see -FY]

qua'lĭtatĭve (-ŏ'l-; *or* -tā-) *a.* Concerned with or depending on quality (esp. Chem. of analysis, opp. *quantitative*); hence ~LY[2] (-vlĭ) *adv.* [f. LL *qualitativus* (as foll.; see -ATIVE)]

qua'lĭtȳ (-ŏ'l-) *n.* & *a.* **1.** *n.* Degree of excellence, relative nature or kind or character, (opp. *quantity*; *of good, high, poor*, etc., *quality*; *is made in three qualities*; *quality matters more than quantity*; **in the ~ of,** as); general excellence (**has ~,** is excellent). **2.** Faculty, skill, accomplishment, characteristic trait, mental or moral attribute, (**give a taste of** one's ~, show what one can do; *has many good qualities, the* DEFECTS *of his qualities, the qualities of a ruler, the quality of inspiring confidence* or *of courage*). **3.** (arch.) High rank or social standing (**people of ~, the ~,** the upper classes). **4.** (Logic). (Of proposition) being affirmative or negative. **5.** (Of sound, voice, etc.) distinctive character apart from pitch and loudness, timbre. **6.** *a.* Possessing high degree of excellence; concerned with maintenance of high quality (*quality control*). [ME, f. OF *qualité* f. L *qualitas -tatis* (*qualis* of what kind; see -ITY)]

qualm (-ahm *or* -awm) *n.* Momentary faint or sick feeling, queasiness; misgiving, sinking of heart; scruple of conscience, doubt of one's own rectitude in some matter; hence ~'ISH[1] *a.* [16th c., of uncert. orig.]

qua'ndarȳ (-ŏ'n-) *n.* State of perplexity, difficult situation, practical dilemma. [16th c., of uncert. orig.]

quand même (kahṅ mām) *adv.* Despite any consequences, even so, all the same. [F]

||**quant** (kwŏnt) *n.* & *v.* **1.** *n.* Punting-pole with projection to prevent its sinking in mud, used by Norfolk bargemen etc. **2.** *v.t.* & *i.* Propel (boat) with quant. [15th c., perh. f. L f. Gk *kontos* boat-pole]

quanta. See QUANTUM.

qua'ntĭc (-ŏ'n-) *n.* (Math.) Rational integral homogeneous function of two or more variables. [f. L *quantus* how much + -IC]

qua'ntĭ|fȳ (-ŏ'n-) *v.t.* Determine quantity of; measure or express as quantity; (Logic) define application of (term, proposition) by use of *all, some*, etc.; hence **~fī**ABLE *a.*, ~FICA'TION, **~fī**ER[1], *ns.* [f. med. L *quantificare* (as prec.; see -FY)]

qua'ntĭtatĭve (-ŏ'n-; *or* -tā-) *a.* Measured or measurable by, or concerned with, quantity (esp. Chem. of analysis, opp. *qualitative*); of or based on the quantity of syllables (*quantitative scansion, verse*, etc.); hence ~LY[2] (-vlĭ) *adv.* [f. med. L *quantitativus* (as QUANTITY; see -ATIVE)]

qua'ntĭtĭve (-ŏ'n-) *a.* = prec. [as foll.; see -IVE]

qua'ntĭtȳ (-ŏ'n-) *n.* **1.** Property of things that is estimable by some sort of measure, the having of size, extension, weight, amount, or number. **2.** Portion, sum, (of electricity, money, etc.). **3.** Specified or considerable portion or number or amount of something, *the* amount of something present, (*a small quantity of blood*; *a quantity of baskets*; *buys in quantity, in large quantities*; *the quantity of heat in a body*); (in *pl.*) large amounts or numbers, abundance, (*is found in quantities on the shore*); ||BILL[4] *of quantities*; **~ surveyor,** person who measures and prices work of builders. **4.** (Pros.) Length or shortness of vowel sounds (see LONG[1] 9); FALSE *quantity*; **~-mark** (put over vowel to indicate quantity). **5.** (Logic). Extension given to subject of proposition. **6.** (Math.) Thing having quantity; figure or symbol representing it; **negligible ~,** (fig.) person etc. that need not be reckoned with; **unknown ~,** (fig.) person or thing whose action or effect cannot be foreseen. [ME, f. OF *quantité* f. L *quantitas -tatis* (*quantus* how much; see -ITY)]

qua'ntīz|e, -īs|e, (kwŏ'ntīz) *v.t.* Form into quanta; apply quantum mechanics to; hence ~A'TION *n.* [f. foll. + -IZE]

qua'nt|um (-ŏ'n-) *n.* (*pl.* **~a**). **1.** Amount; share, portion; required, desired, or allowed amount. **2.** (Phys.) Discrete unit quantity of energy proportional to frequency of radiation; **~um mechanics, theory,** etc., (making use of assumption that energy exists in this form). [L, neut. of *quantus* how much]

quāquavẽr'sal *a.* (Geol.) Pointing in every direction. [f. LL *quaquaversus* (*quaqua* wheresoever, *versus* towards) + -AL]

qua'rantine (kwŏ'rantēn) *n.*, & *v.t.* **1.** *n.* (Period of) isolation imposed on persons or animals that have arrived from elsewhere or been exposed to, and might spread, infectious or contagious disease. **2.** *v.t.* Impose such isolation on, put in quarantine. [f. It. *quarantina* forty days (*quaranta* forty; see -INE[1])]

||***quare impedit*** (kwārĭ ĭ'mpedĭt) *n.* Writ issued against objector in case of disputed presentation to benefice. [ME f. L, = why does he hinder?]

||**qua'renden, -der,** (kwŏ'-) *n.* Deep red Devon and Somerset apple. [ME, of unkn. orig.]

quârk (*or* -ôrk) *n.* (Phys.) One of three hypothetical components of elementary particles. [f. 'Three quarks for Muster Mark' in Joyce's *Finnegans Wake*]

qua'rrel[1] (kwŏ'-) *n.* (Hist.) Short heavy arrow or bolt used in crossbow or arbalest. [ME, f. OF *quar(r)el*, f. Rom. **quadrellus* dim. of LL *quadrus* square]

qua'rrel[2] (kwŏ'-) *n.* **1.** Occasion of complaint against person or his actions (*have no quarrel against* or *with him*); **pick a ~**, contrive or eagerly accept such occasion to begin contention. **2.** Violent contention or altercation (*between* persons, of person *with* another); rupture of friendly relations; hence ~SOME[1] *a.* [ME f. OF *querele*, f. L *querel(l)a* complaint (*queri* complain)]

qua'rrel[3] (kwŏ'-) *v.i.* (‖**-ll-**). **1.** Take exception, find fault *with* (*I never quarrel with Providence*); **~ with** one's **bread and butter,** abandon employment by which one lives. **2.** Contend violently (*with* person, *about* or *for* or *over* thing); fall out, have dispute, break off friendly relations. [ME, f. prec. & f. OF *quereler* (*querele*; see prec.)]

qua'rrȳ[1] (kwŏ'-) *n.* Object of pursuit by bird of prey, hounds, hunters, etc.; intended victim or prey. [ME, f. AF **quire*, *quere* f. OF *cuiree*, *couree* (assim. to *cuir* leather and *curer* disembowel) f. Rom. **corata* entrails f. L *cor* heart (see -EE, -Y[4]); orig. = parts of deer placed on hide and given to hounds]

qua'rrȳ[2] (kwŏ'-) *n.* & *v.* **1.** *n.* Excavation made by taking stone for building etc. from its bed; place whence stone or (fig.) information etc. may be extracted; **~ (tile)**, unglazed floor-tile; **~man,** worker in quarry. **2.** *v.t.* Extract (stone) from quarry; extract (facts etc.) laboriously from books etc. **3.** *v.i.* Laboriously search documents etc. [ME, f. med. L *quare(r)ia* f. OF *quarriere* (**carre* f. L *quadrum* square)]

qua'rrȳ[3] (kwŏ'-) *n.* Diamond-shaped pane of glass as used in lattice windows. [later form of QUARREL[1]]

quart[1] (kwôrt) *n.* Measure of capacity, quarter of gallon or two pints (**put ~ into pint pot,** make less contain greater (fig.) do what is impossible); vessel containing this amount; *unit of dry measure, $\frac{1}{32}$ bushel, 1101 c.c.; **~ bottle** of wine or spirit, $\frac{1}{6}$ gal. [ME, f. OF *quarte* f. L *quarta* fem. of *quartus* fourth (*quattuor* four)]

quârt[2] (kârt) *n.* Fourth of eight parrying positions in fencing; sequence of four cards of same suit in piquet etc. (**~ major,** quart headed by ace). [f. F *quarte* f. as prec.]

quar'tan (kwôr'-) *a.* & *n.* (Fever) recurring every third (by inclusive reckoning fourth) day. [ME f. OF *quartaine* f. L (*febris* fever) *quartana* (*quartus* fourth; see -AN)]

quartā'tion (kwôr-) *n.* Combining of three parts of silver with one of gold as preliminary in purifying gold. [f. L *quartus* fourth + -ATION]

quarte. Var. of QUART[2].

quar'ter[1] (-ôr'-) *n.* **1.** One of four equal parts into which thing is or might be divided (*cut apple into quarters*; *can get it elsewhere for a quarter (of) the price*); **~ of a century,** any period of 25 years; *second* etc. **~ of the century,** 26th to 50th etc. years of it; **~ of an hour,** any consecutive 15 minutes; **bad ~ of an hour,** short but unpleasant experience; **~ mile** etc., quarter of a mile etc. **2.** (U.S. & Can.) 25 cents or quarter dollar, as amount or coin. **3.** One of four parts, each including leg or wing, into which animal's or bird's carcass is divided; (in *pl.*) similar parts of traitor quartered after execution; (in *pl.*) = HIND[3]*quarters*. **4.** Either side of ship abaft the beam; **on the ~,** between astern and abeam. **5.** (Her.) One of four divisions of quartered shield; charge occupying this, placed in chief. **6.** ‖Grain-measure of eight bushels, used in stating large quantities, prices, etc.; quarter of hundredweight, 28 lb. or *25 lb. **7.** Side of boot or shoe from back to vamp. **8.** Fourth part of year, for which payments become due on quarter-day; school or *university term. **9.** Fourth part of lunar month; moon's position between first and second (**first ~**) or third and fourth (**last ~**) of these. **10.** Point of time 15 minutes before or after any hour o'clock (*at a quarter to* or *past six*; *it is not the quarter yet*; *strikes the hours, half-hours, and quarters*). **11.** (Race over) distance of quarter mile. **12.** (Region lying about) point of compass, direction, district, locality, source of supply or help or information, (*wind blows from all quarters*; *flocked in from all quarters*; *no help to be looked for in that quarter*). **13.** Division of town, esp. one appropriated to or occupied by special class (*the Chinese*, LATIN, *manufacturing*, *residential*, etc., *quarter*). **14.** (in *pl.*) Lodgings, abode, esp. place where troops are lodged or stationed; **beat to ~s,** (Naut.) summon crew to appointed stations as for action; CLOSE[1] *quarters*; **take up** one's **~s,** lodge *in*, *with*, etc. **15.** Exemption from death offered or granted to enemy in battle who will surrender (*give* or *receive quarter*; *ask for* or *cry quarter*); **give no ~ to,** (fig.) attack relentlessly. **16.** ***~-back,** football player directing attacking play; **~-bell** (sounding the quarter-hours); **~-binding** of book (with narrow leather at back and none at corners); **~-day** (on which quarterly payments are due, tenancies begin and end, etc.: ‖Lady Day 25 Mar., Midsummer Day 24 June, Michaelmas 29 Sept., and Christmas 25 Dec., or in Scotland Candlemas 2 Feb., Whitsunday 15 May, Lammas 1 Aug., Martinmas 11 Nov.; *1 Jan., 1 Apr., 1 July, 1 Oct.); **~deck,** (1) part of upper deck between stern and after-mast, (2) the officers (cf. LOWER[3] *deck*) of ship or navy; **~-final,** match or round preceding semi-final; ***~-horse,** strong horse of breed able to run quarter mile at high speed; **~-hour,** = sense 10; **~-ill,** cattle and sheep disease causing putrefaction in one or more of the quarters; **~-jack,** (1) clock jack striking quarters, (2) (Mil. sl.) = *quartermaster*; ‖**~-light,** (1) window in body of closed carriage apart from door-window, (2) window in side of motor vehicle other than main door-window; **~master,** (Naut.) petty officer or rating in charge of steering, binnacle, signals, hold-stowing, etc., (Mil.) regimental officer with duties of assigning quarters, laying out camp, and looking after rations, clothing, etc.; **Q~master General,** head of army department controlling quartering, equipment, etc.; **Q~master Sergeant,** sergeant assisting army quartermaster; **~-miler,** runner whose distance is the quarter mile; ***~-note,** (Mus.) crotchet; **~-plate,** photographic plate or film 8·3 × 10·8 cm, photograph reproduced from it; **~ sessions,** (‖Hist.) court of limited criminal and civil jurisdiction and of appeal held usu. quarterly; **~staff,** stout pole 6–8 ft. long formerly used by peasantry as weapon; **~-tone,** (Mus.) half a semitone. [ME f. AF; OF *quartier* f. L *quartarius* fourth part (of a measure) f. *quartus* fourth; see -ER[2] (2)]

quar'ter[2] (-ôr'-) *v.t.* **1.** Divide into four equal parts; (Hist.) divide (traitor's body) into quarters. **2.** (Her.) Place or bear (charges or coats of arms) quarterly on shield; add (another's coat) to one's hereditary arms; place in alternate quarters *with*; divide (shield) into four or more parts by vertical and horizontal lines. **3.** Put (esp. soldiers) into quarters, station or lodge in specified place; impose (person *on* another) as lodger. **4.** (Of dog etc.) range or traverse (ground) in every direction. **5.** Cut (log) into quarters and these into planks so as to show the grain well. [ME, f. prec.]

quar'terage (-ôr'-) *n.* Quarterly payment; a quarter's wages, allowance, pension, etc. [ME, f. QUARTER¹ + -AGE]

quar'tering (-ôr'-) *n.* In vbl senses; (Her., in *pl.*) coats marshalled on shield to denote alliances of family with heiresses of others; square lengths of timber made by sawing planks into four lengths. [f. QUARTER² + -ING¹]

quar'terly (-ôr'-) *a.*, *n.*, & *adv.* **1.** *a.* Produced or occurring once every quarter of a year; (Her., of shield) quartered. **2.** *n.* Quarterly review or magazine. **3.** *adv.* Once every quarter of a year; (Her.) in the four, or in two diagonally opposite, quarters of shield. [f. QUARTER¹ + -LY¹,²]

‖**quar'tern** (-ôr'-) *n.* (arch.) ~(**-loaf**), four-pound loaf; quarter of a pint. [ME = quarter, f. AF *quartrun*, OF *quart(e)ron* (QUART¹(*e*) fourth or *quartier* QUARTER¹)]

quartě't, -ě'tte, (-ôr-) *n.* **1.** (Mus.) (Performers of) composition for four voices or instruments; **piano ~**, 3 stringed instruments with piano. **2.** Set of four. [f. F *quartette* f. It. *quartetto* (*quarto* fourth f. L *quartus*); see -ET¹]

quar'tic (-ôr'-) *a.* & *n.* (Math.) (Equation) involving fourth and no higher power of unknown quantity or variable. [f. L *quartus* fourth + -IC]

quar'tile (-ôr'-) *a.* & *n.* **1.** *a.* (Astrol.) Connected with or relating to an aspect of two heavenly bodies which are 90° distant from each other. **2.** *n.* Quartile aspect; (Statistics) one of 3 values of a variable dividing a population into 4 equal groups as regards the value of that variable. [f. med. L **quartilis* f. L *quartus* fourth; see -IL]

quar'tō (-ôr'-) *n.* (*abbr.* **4to**; *pl.* **~s**). Size given by folding sheet of paper twice; book consisting of sheets so folded; **~ paper** (so folded, and cut). [f. L (*in*) *quarto* (in) fourth (of sheet), abl. of *quartus* fourth]

quartz (kwôrts) *n.* Mineral form of silica, massive or crystallizing in hexagonal prisms; **~ clock** (operated by electric vibrations of quartz crystal); **~ lamp,** quartz tube containing mercury vapour as light source. [f. G *quarz* f. WSlav. *kwardy*]

quar'tzīte (-ôr'ts-) *n.* Compact granular quartz rock. [f. prec. + -ITE¹]

quā'sâr (*or* -z-) *n.* (Astron.) Starlike object having spectrum with large red-shift. [f. *quasi*-stell*ar*]

quash (kwŏsh) *v.t.* Annul, make void, reject as not valid, put an end to, (esp. by legal procedure or authority); suppress, crush, (rebellion etc.). [ME, f. OF *quasser*, *casser* annul f. LL *cassare* (*cassus* null, void, or f. L *cassare* frequent. of *quatere* shake)]

quā'sī (*or* -zī *or* kwah'zī) *adv.* (Introducing explanation) that is to say, as if it were. [L, = as if, almost]

quā'sī- (*or* -zī *or* kwah'zī) *pref.* Seeming(ly), not real(ly); half-, almost; **~-stellar object,** quasar. [f. prec.]

qua'ssia (kwŏ'sha) *n.* S. Amer., esp. Surinam, tree (*Quassia amara*); (wood, bark, or root of this or similar tree, yielding) bitter medicinal tonic and insecticide. [f. G. *Quassi*, 18th-c. Surinam Negro, who discovered its medicinal properties; see -IA¹]

quătercĕntē'narў (*or* kwŏ-) *a.* & *n.* (Festival) of the four-hundredth anniversary. [f. L *quater* four times + CENTENARY]

quatėr'narў *a.* & *n.* **1.** *a.* Having four parts, esp. (Chem.) compounded of or linked with four elements or radicals; concerned with the number four; (Geol., *Q~*) belonging to most recent period or system, subsequent to Tertiary. **2.** *n.* Set of four things; (Geol.) Quaternary period or system. [ME, f. L *quaternarius* (*quaterni* distrib. of *quattuor* four; see -ARY¹)]

quatėr'nĭon *n.* Set of four; (Math.) operator that changes one vector into another and depends on four geometrical elements. [ME, f. LL *quaternio -onis* (as prec.)]

quatėr'nĭtў *n.* Being four; set of four persons (esp. of the Godhead in contrast to *Trinity*). [f. LL *quaternitas* (as QUATERNARY; see -ITY)]

quă'torzain (kă-) *n.* Fourteen-line poem, irregular sonnet. [f. F *quatorzaine* (*quatorze* fourteen f. L *quattuordecim*)]

quatôr'ze (k-) *n.* Set of four aces, kings, queens, or jacks, in one hand at piquet, scoring 14. [F; see prec.]

qua'train (-ŏ't-) *n.* Stanza of four lines usu. with alternate rhymes. [F (*quatre* four f. L *quattuor*)]

quatre. Var. of CATER¹.

quă'trefoil (k-; *or* kă'ter-) *n.* Four-cusped figure, esp. as ornament in architectural tracery, resembling symmetrical four-lobed leaf or flower. [ME, f. AF **quatrefoil* (*quatre* four; see FOIL¹)]

quattrōcĕ'nt|ō (-ahtrōchĕ'-) *n.* Italian style of art of the 15th c.; hence **~IST** (2, 3) *n.* [It., = 400, used w. ref. to years 14—]

quā'ver¹ *v.* **1.** *v.i.* (Esp. of voice or musical sound) vibrate, shake, tremble; use trills or shakes in singing. **2.** *v.t.* Sing (note, song) with quavering; say (*out*) in trembling tones. [ME, frequent. of obs. *quave*, perh. f. OE **cwafian*, of imit. orig.; see -ER⁵]

quā'ver² *n.* **1.** Trill in singing; tremulousness in speech, whence **~Y²** *a.* **2.** ‖(Mus.) Note with one-hooked symbol, equal to half crotchet. [f. prec.]

quay (kē) *n.* Solid stationary artificial landing-place lying alongside or projecting into water for (un)loading ships; **~'side,** land forming or near quay; hence **~'AGE** (1, 4) (kē'ĭj) *n.* [ME *key(e)*, *kay* f. OF *kay* f. Gaulish *caio* f. OCelt. **kagio-*]

Que. *abbr.* Quebec.

quean *n.* (arch.) Impudent or ill-behaved girl or woman. [OE *cwene* woman, = OS *cwena*, OHG *quena*, ON *kvenna* gen. pl., Goth. *qino* f. Gmc **kwenōn*; cf. QUEEN¹]

quea's|ў (-zĭ) *a.* (Of food) unsettling the stomach, causing nausea; (of person or his stomach) (1) feeling nausea, (2) easily upset, weak of digestion; (of conscience etc.) over-scrupulous, tender; hence **~ĭLY²** *adv.*, **~ĭNESS** *n.* [ME *queysy*, *coisy*, perh. f. AF & OF **coisi* cogn. w. OF *coisier* hurt]

quebra'chō (kābrah'-) *n.* (*pl.* **~s**). S. Amer. tree (esp. *Aspidosperma quebracho*) yielding very hard timber and medicinal bark; bark of this tree, used as tonic to aid respiration. [Sp. (*quebrar* break, *hacha* axe)]

Quĕ'chu|a (kĕ'chwa) *n.* Member or language of Peruvian Indian tribe that was dominant in Inca empire; hence **~AN** *a.* [Sp., f. Quechua]

queen¹ *n.* **1.** **~ (consort)**, king's wife. **2.** Female sovereign of kingdom; **Q~ Anne is dead** (retort to stale news); *Queen Anne's* BOUNTY; **Q~ Anne's lace,** wild carrot; **Q~-Anne,** in the style of English architecture, furniture, etc., in or about Queen Anne's time, early 18th c. **3.** Worshipped female, e.g. the Virgin Mary (*Queen of grace* etc.); ancient goddess (**Q~ of heaven,** Juno, **of love,** Venus, **of night,** Diana, etc.); person's sweetheart or wife or mistress; majestic woman; belle or mock sovereign on some occasion (*Queen of the* MAY[3] etc.). **4.** Personified best example of anything that can be regarded as fem. (*the queen of watering-places, roses, nurses*); ~ **of puddings** (made with breadcrumbs and meringue). **5.** Woman, country, etc., regarded as ruling over some sphere (~ **of hearts,** any beautiful woman; ~ **of the meadows,** meadowsweet). **6.** ~ (**bee, wasp, ant**), perfect fertile female of bee etc.; adult female cat. **7.** Piece in chess (**~'s bishop, knight, pawn, rook,** those placed nearest queen at start). **8.** Court-card bearing representation of queen and usu. ranking next below king. **9.** (sl.) Male homosexual. **10. ~-cake,** small soft currant cake often heart-shaped; ~ **dowager,** widow of king; ~ **mother,** queen dowager who is mother of sovereign; **~-post,** one of two upright timbers between tie-beam and principal rafters of roof-truss; ||*Queen's* BENCH, BOUNTY, COLOUR[1], COUNSEL[1], ENGLISH[1], EVIDENCE, GUIDE[1], HIGHWAY, MESSENGER, PROCTOR, SCOUT[1], SHILLING, SPEECH; **~'s-ware,** cream-coloured Wedgwood. **11.** Hence ~'DOM, ~'HOOD, ~'SHIP, *ns.*, ~'LESS, ~'LIKE, *adjs.* [OE *cwēn*, = OS *quān*, ON *kvæn*, *kván*, Goth. *qēns* wife f. Gmc **kwǣniz*; cf. QUEAN]

queen[2] *v.* **1.** *v.t.* Make (woman) queen; ~ **it,** play the queen; (Chess) convert (pawn) to queen when it reaches opponent's end of board. **2.** *v.i.* (Of pawn) be converted thus. [f. prec.]

quee'nĭe *n.* (sl.) = QUEEN[1] 9. [f. QUEEN[1] + -IE]

quee'nl|y̆ *a.* Fit for or appropriate to a queen; majestic, queenlike; hence ~ĬNESS *n.* [f. QUEEN[1] + -LY[1]]

Quee'nsberry̆ (-z-) *n.* ~ **Rules,** standard rules esp. of boxing. [f. 8th Marquis of ~, Engl. nobleman d. 1900, who supervised preparation of boxing laws 1867]

queer *a.*, *n.*, & *v.t.* **1.** *a.* Strange, odd, eccentric; of questionable character, shady, suspect; out of sorts, giddy, faint, (*feel queer*); ||(sl.) drunk; (sl., esp. of man) homosexual; **in Q~ Street,** (sl.) in a difficulty, in debt or trouble or disrepute; hence ~'ISH[1] 2 *a.*, ~'LY[2] *adv.*, ~'NESS *n.* **2.** *n.* (sl.) (Esp. male) homosexual. **3.** *v.t.* (sl.) Spoil, put out of order; ~ **the pitch for** person, ~ person's **pitch,** spoil his chances beforehand. [perh. f. G *quer* oblique (as THWART)]

quĕll *v.t.* (literary). Suppress, forcibly put an end to, crush, overcome, reduce to submission, (fear, opposition, rebellion, rebels, etc.); hence (-)~'ER[1] *n.* [OE *cwellan* kill, = OS *quellian*, OHG *quellen*, ON *kvelja* f. Gmc **kwaljan*]

quĕnch *v.t.* **1.** Cause (fire, light, etc.) to cease burning (lit. or fig.). **2.** Cool, esp. with water (heat, heated thing); cool (hot metal or coke, etc.) rapidly in cold water, oil, air, etc. **3.** Stifle, suppress, (desire, speed, motion, electric spark or discharge); slake (thirst); (sl.) reduce (opponent) to silence. **4.** Hence ~'ABLE, ~'LESS, *adjs.*, ~'ER[1] (1, 2) *n.* [ME, f. OE *-cwencan* causative f. *-cwincan* be extinguished]

quenĕ'lle (k-) *n.* Seasoned ball of pounded fish or meat. [F; orig. unkn.]

quēr'ist *n.* (literary). Person who asks questions. [f. L *quaerere* ask + -IST]

quērn *n.* Hand-mill for grinding corn; small hand-mill for pepper etc.; **~-stone,** millstone. [OE *cweorn(e)*, = OS *quern*, OHG *quirn(a)*, ON *kvern*, Goth. *-qairnus* f. Gmc **kwern-*]

quĕ'rulous (-rōō-) *a.* Complaining, peevish; hence ~LY[2] *adv.*, ~NESS *n.* [f. LL *querulosus* or L *querulus* (*queri* complain; see -OSE[1], -OUS)]

quēr'y̆ *n.* & *v.* **1.** *n.* = QUAERE 1. **2.** A question, esp. expressing doubt or objection (*was prepared to suppress all queries*); question mark or the word *query* or *qu.* or *qy.* written against statement, or the word *query* interjected in speech, to question accuracy. **3.** *v.t.* Ask, inquire, (*whether*, *if*, etc.); call (thing) in question in speech or writing, question accuracy of; *question (person). **4.** *v.i.* Put a question. [Anglicized form of QUAERE, after *inquiry*]

quĕst[1] *n.* Seeking or thing sought by inquiry or search, esp. object of medieval knight's pursuit; **in ~ of,** seeking. [ME, f. OF *queste* f. Rom. **quaesita* fem. p.p. (as n.) of L *quaerere* seek]

quĕst[2] *v.* **1.** *v.i.* (Of dog etc.) search (*about*) for game; go (*about*) in search of or *for* something. **2.** *v.t.* (poet.) Search for, seek *out*. [ME, f. OF *quester* (as prec.)]

quĕ'stion[1] (-schon) *n.* **1.** Sentence adapted by order of words, use of interrogative pronoun or question-mark, or other means, to elicit answer, (*put a question to, ask a question of*); POP[1] *the question*; ~ **and answer,** alternation of questions and answers, as in catechism; LEADING[2], RHETORICAL, *question*; **indirect** or **oblique ~,** question made into dependent clause; ~ **mark,** punctuation mark (?) indicating question; **~-master,** chairman of broadcast quiz etc.; ||~ **time,** (Parl.) period when members may question ministers. **2.** (Raising of) doubt about or objection to thing's truth, credibility, advisability, etc. (*allowed it without question*); **beyond all ~,** certainly, undoubtedly; CALL[1] *in question*; **make no ~ of** fact etc., **but that it is so** etc., be certain of it; hence ~LESS *a.* & (arch.) *adv.* **3.** Problem requiring solution, matter or concern depending on conditions *of*; BEG *the question*; *success* **is (merely) a ~ of time,** will certainly come sooner or later; **it is (only) a ~ of,** what is required or involved is (merely). **4.** Subject being discussed or for discussion, thing to be voted on; *the person* **in ~,** that we are referring to or discussing; **come into ~,** be discussed, become of practical importance; *that* **is not the ~,** is irrelevant; **the ~ is** (introducing or recalling exact matter of debate); **Q~!** (in public assemblies, used to recall speaker from digression); OPEN[1] *question*; **out of the ~,** too impracticable to be worth discussing; *the* PREVIOUS *question*; **put the ~,** require supporters and opponents of proposal to record their votes, divide meeting etc. **5.** (arch.) Torture to elicit confession (*was put to the question*). [ME, f. AF *questiun*, OF *question* f. L *quaestio -onis* (*quaerere quaest-* seek; see -ION)]

quĕ'stion[2] (-schon) *v.t.* Ask questions of, interrogate, subject to examination, (person); seek information from study of (phenomena, facts); call in question, throw doubt upon, raise objections to, (*question the honesty, accuracy, fitness*, etc., *of*); **it cannot be ~ed but (that),** it is certain that. [ME, f. OF *questionner* (as prec.)]

quĕ'stionab|le (-schon-) *a.* Doubtful as regards its truth or quality; not clearly in accordance with honesty, honour, wisdom, etc.; hence ~LY[2] *adv.* [f. prec. + -ABLE]

quĕ'stionary̆ (-schon-) *n.* = foll. [f. med. L *quaestionarium* or f. F (as foll.); see -ARY[1]]

quĕstionnair'e (-schon-; *or* kĕstĭo-) *n.* Formulated series of questions esp. for statistical study; document containing these. [F (*questionner* QUESTION[2], *-aire* -ARY[1])]

quĕ'tzal *n.* Beautiful Central Amer. bird (*Pharomachrus mocino*), the male with long green tail-coverts; monetary unit of Guatemala. [Sp., f. Aztec *quetzalli* the bird's tail-feather]

queue (kū) *n.*, & *v.i.* **1.** *n.* Hanging plaited tail of hair or wig, pigtail; line or sequence of persons, vehicles, etc., awaiting their turn to be attended to or proceed. **2.** *v.i.* (Of persons etc.) form *up* in queue; take one's place in a queue. [F, f. L *cauda* tail]

quĭ'bbl|e *n.*, & *v.i.* **1.** *n.* Play on words, pun; equivocation, evasion, unsubstantial or purely verbal argument etc. esp. one depending on ambiguity of words. **2.** *v.i.* Use quibbles; hence ~ER[1] *n.*, ~ING[2] *a.* [dim. of obs. *quib* prob. f. L *quibus* dat. & abl. pl. of *qui* who (familiar f. use in legal documents); see -LE 1]

quiche (kēsh) *n.* Open tart with sweet or (usu.) savoury filling. [F]

Quĭ'chua (kĭ'chwa) *n.* = QUECHUA.

quĭck *a.*, *n.*, & *adv.* **1.** *a.* (arch.) Living, alive, (*the quick and the dead*); ~ **with child,** at stage of pregnancy when movements of foetus have been felt. **2.** Vigorous, lively; ready, sensitive, (*quick to take offence*); prompt to act, perceive, be affected, learn, think, or invent; ~ **ear, eye, sight,** (acute, alert); ~ **temper,** tendency to be easily irritated; **has** ~ **wits,** is ready at grasping situation, making repartees, etc., whence **~-wĭtt**ED[2] *a.* **3.** Taking only a short time to traverse a distance or do a thing, rapid, swift, done or obtained in short time or with little interval, (*in quick succession*; *at a quick trot*; *a quick way of doing it*); (of fire) burning strongly; (of oven) hot; **be** ~, act in quick manner; hence ~'LY[2] *adv.* **4. ~-change,** (of actor etc.) quickly changing costume or appearance to play another part; ~ **fire,** firing of shots in quick succession; *quick*LIME[1]; ~ **march,** (Mil.) march in quick time (esp. as word of command for starting at usual pace); ~ **one,** (colloq.) a quickly taken drink; **~'sand,** (bed of) loose wet sand readily swallowing up heavy objects placed on it; **~'set,** (hedge) formed of live (slips of) plants esp. hawthorn set in ground to grow, such slips; **~'silver,** (*n.*) mercury, (fig.) mobility of temperament or mood, (*v.t.*) coat (mirror-glass) with amalgam of tin; ~ **step,** step used in quick time; **~'step,** a fast foxtrot; **~'thorn,** hawthorn (*Crataegus oxyacantha*); ~ **time,** marching at about 120 paces per minute; ~ **trick,** (Bridge) (card that should win) trick in first two rounds of suit. **5.** Hence ~'NESS *n.* **6.** *n.* Tender or sensitive flesh below skin or esp. nails (*bites his nails to the quick*); tender part of wound or sore where healthy tissue begins (*probed it to the quick*); seat of feeling or emotion (*the insult stung him to the quick*); *mercury. **7.** *adv.* Quickly, at rapid rate, in comparatively short time, (*ran as quick as I could*; *who will be there quickest?*; *quick-drying, -fading, -forgotten*, etc.); (ellipt. for *imper.* of *go, come, be, quick*) act quickly; **~-firing,** (of gun) with special mechanism for firing shots in quick succession; **~-freeze** *v.t.*, & *n.*, freeze (food), freezing of food, rapidly so as to preserve its natural qualities. [OE *cwic(u)*, = OS *quik*, OHG *quek*, ON *kvikr*, f. Gmc **kwikwaz* f. IE **qwej-*]

quĭ'cken *v.* **1.** *v.t.* Give or restore natural or spiritual life or vigour to, animate; stimulate, rouse, inspire; (arch.) kindle, make (fire) burn brighter. **2.** *v.i.* Receive or come to life; (of woman or foetus) reach quick stage in pregnancy (see QUICK 1). **3.** *v.t.* & *i.* Accelerate, make or (of pace, motion, etc.) become quicker. [ME, f. prec. + -EN[6]]

quĭ'ckĭe *n.* (colloq.) Thing done or made quickly or hastily. [f. QUICK + -IE]

||**quĭd**[1] *n.* (*pl.* same). (sl.) One pound sterling (*at ten quid a week*); **~s in,** in a position to profit. [prob. f. *quid* nature of a thing, f. L *quid* what, something]

quĭd[2] *n.* Lump of tobacco etc. for chewing. [dial. var. of CUD]

quĭ'ddĭtў *n.* Essence of a person or thing, what makes a thing what it is; quibble, captious subtlety. [f. med. L *quidditas* f. L *quid* what; see -ITY]

quĭ'dnŭnc *n.* Newsmonger, person given to gossip. [f. L *quid* what + *nunc* now]

quĭd prō quō' *n.* (Thing given as) compensation, return made, consideration, (*must get, must find him, a quid pro quo*). [L, = something for something]

quīĕ'sc|ent *a.* Motionless, inert; silent, dormant; hence or cogn. ~ENCE, ~ENCY, *ns.*, **~ent**LY[2] *adv.* [f. L *quiescere* (*quies* QUIET[1]; see -ESCENT)]

quī'et[1] *n.* Silence, stillness; being free from disturbance or agitation or urgent tasks; peaceful state of social or political affairs; rest, repose, peace of mind; unruffled deportment, calm. [ME, f. AF *quiete* f. OF *quieté* (*quiet*; see foll.)]

quī'et[2] *a.* (**~er, ~est**). **1.** With no or slight or gentle sound or motion; of gentle or peaceful disposition; (of colour, dress, etc.) unobtrusive, not showy; **be** ~, (colloq., esp. in *imper.*) cease talk etc. **2.** Not overt, private, disguised, (*quiet resentment*; *had a quiet dig at him*); **keep** ~, say nothing (*about*); **on the** ~, unobtrusively, secretly. **3.** Undisturbed, not interfered with or interrupted, free or far from strife or uproar or vigorous action; not formal (*a quiet dinner-party, wedding*). **4.** Enjoyed in quiet, tranquil, not anxious or remorseful. **5.** Hence ~LY[2] *adv.*, ~NESS, **quī'ė**TUDE, *ns.* [ME, f. OF *quiet(e)* f. L *quietus* p.p. of *quiescere* (see QUIESCENT)]

quī'et[3] *v.* **1.** *v.t.* Reduce to quietness, soothe, calm. **2.** *v.i.* ~ (**down**), become quiet. [f. prec. & f. LL *quietare* f. L *quietus* QUIET[2]]

||**quī'eten** *v.t.* & *i.* = prec. [f. QUIET[2] + -EN[6]]

quī'et|ĭsm *n.* Passive attitude towards life with devotional contemplation and abandonment of the will, as form of religious mysticism; non-resistance principles; so ~IST (2) *n.* & *a.*, **~ĭ'stic** *a.* [f. It. *quietismo* (as QUIET[2]; see -ISM)]

quīē'tus *n.* **1.** Acquittance or receipt given on payment of account etc. **2.** Release from life; death, extinction, final riddance, (*got, gave him, his quietus*; *have given the quietus to it*). [f. med. L *quietus* (*est* he is) quit (QUIET[2]) used as receipt form]

||**quĭff** *n.* Curl plastered down on the forehead; man's tuft of hair brushed upwards over forehead. [20th c.; orig. unkn.]

quĭll[1] *n.* **1.** Hollow stem of feather; plectrum, fishing-float, or toothpick, made of this. **2.** ~(**-feather**), whole large feather of wing or tail; ~(**-pen**), pen made from this. **3.** One of porcupine's spines; bobbin esp. of hollow reed; musical pipe made of hollow stem; curled-up piece of cinnamon or cinchona bark. **4. ~-coverts,** feathers covering base of quill-feathers; **~-driver,** (arch., derog.) clerk or journalist or author. [ME, prob. f. (M)LG *quiele*]

quĭll[2] *v.* **1.** *v.t.* Form into cylindrical quill-like folds, goffer; hence ~'ING (2) *n.* **2.** *v.i.* Wind thread or yarn on bobbin. [f. prec.]

quĭ'llĕt *n.* (arch.) Quibble, fine distinction. [perh. abbr. of obs. *quillity*, app. alt. of QUIDDITY]

quilt *n.*, & *v.t.* **1.** *n.* Bed-coverlet made of padding enclosed between two layers of cloth etc. and kept in place by cross lines of stitching; bedspread of similar design (CRAZY or PATCH[1]*work quilt*). **2.** *v.t.* Cover or line with padded material; make or join together (pieces of cloth with padding between) after the manner of a quilt; sew up (coin, letter, etc.) between two layers of garment etc.; compile (literary work) out of extracts or borrowed ideas; hence ~'ING[1] (1, 3) *n.* [ME, f. OF *coilte, cuilte* f. L *culcita* mattress, cushion]

quĭn *n.* (colloq.) Quintuplet. [abbr.]
quī'nacrīne (*or* -ēn) *n.* Anti-malarial drug derived from acridine. [f. *quinine* + *acridine*]
quī'narў *a.* Of the number five; having five parts. [f. L *quinarius* (*quini* distrib. of *quinque* five; see -ARY¹)]
quī'nate *a.* (Bot.) (Of leaf) having five leaflets. [f. L *quini* (as prec.) + -ATE²]
quĭnce *n.* Hard acid yellowish pear-shaped fruit used as preserve or as flavouring; tree (*Cydonia oblonga*) bearing it; JAPANESE *quince*. [ME, orig. collect. pl. of obs. *quoyn, coyn*, f. OF *cooin* f. L *cotoneum* var. of *cydoneum* (apple) of *Cydonia* in Crete]
quĭncĕntē'narў *a.* & *n.* (Festival) of the five-hundredth anniversary. [irreg. f. L *quinque* five + CENTENARY]
quĭ'ncŭnx *n.* (Arrangement of) five objects set so that four are at corners of square or rectangle and the other at its centre (e.g. the five on dice or cards; esp. as basis of arrangement in planting trees etc.); so **quĭncŭ'nc**IAL (-shal) *a.* [L, = five-twelfths (*quinque* five, *uncia* twelfth, OUNCE¹)]
quĭngĕntē'narў (-nj-) *a.* & *n.* = QUINCENTENARY. [f. L *quingenti* 500, after CENTENARY]
quĭ'nine (-ēn; *or* -ē'n) *n.* Alkaloid found esp. in cinchona bark; salt of this, used as febrifuge and tonic. [f. *quina* cinchona bark (Sp. f. Quechua *kina* bark) + -INE⁵]
quĭ'nŏl *n.* = HYDRO*quinone*. [f. as prec. + -OL]
quĭ'noline (-ēn) *n.* Oily amine got from distillation of coal tar or by synthesis and used in preparation of drugs etc. [f. prec. + -INE⁵]
quĭnquagėnār'ĭan *a.* & *n.* (Person) from 50 to 59 years old. [f. L *quinquagenarius* (*quinquageni* distrib. of *quinquaginta* fifty; see -ARY¹) + -AN]
quĭnquagē'narў (*or* -kwă'je-) *a.* & *n.* **1.** = prec. **2.** (Festival) of the fiftieth anniversary. [as prec.]
Quĭnquagĕ'sĭma *n.* ~ (**Sunday**), Sunday before Lent. [med. L, fem. (as n.) of L *quinquagesimus* fiftieth (*quinquaginta* fifty), after QUADRAGESIMA]
quĭ'nquė- *comb. form.* Five, as: **~cente'nnial** *a.* & *n.*, = QUINCENTENARY; **~la'teral,** five-sided; **~va'lent,** (Chem.) having a valence of five. [L (*quinque* five)]
quĭnquĕ'nnial *a.* Lasting, recurring every, five years; hence ~LY² *adv.* [f. L *quinquennis* (as foll.) + -AL]
quĭnquĕ'nnĭ|um *n.* (*pl.* **~ums** *or* **~a**). Period of five years. [L (*quinque* five, *annus* year)]
quĭ'nquėrēme *n.* Ancient galley with five banks of oars. [f. L *quinqueremis* (*quinque* five, *remus* oar)]
quĭ'ns|ў (-zĭ) *n.* Inflammation of throat with abscess on, or suppuration of region around, tonsils; hence **~ĭED**² (-ĭd) *a.* [ME, f. OF *quinencie* f. med. L *quinancia* f. Gk *kunagkhē* (*kun-* dog, *agkhō* throttle)]
quĭnt (kĭnt) *n.* Sequence of five cards of same suit in piquet etc. (~ **major,** quint headed by ace). [f. F *quinte* f. L *quinta* fem. of *quintus* fifth (*quinque* five)]
quinta (kwĭ'nt*a*) *n.* Country house with vineyard etc. [Sp. & Port., orig. of house and farm let at charge of one-fifth (*quinta parte*) of produce]
quĭ'ntain (-tĭn) *n.* (Hist.) (Medieval military exercise of tilting at) post set up as mark and often provided with sandbag to swing round and strike unskilful tilter. [ME, f. OF *quintaine* perh. ult. f. L *quintana* camp market f. *quintus* (*manipulus*) fifth (maniple)]
quĭ'ntal *n.* Weight of about 100 lb.; weight of 100 kilograms. [ME f. OF; med. L *quintale*, f. Arab. *ḳinṭār*]
quĭ'ntan *a.* & *n.* (Fever) recurring every fourth (by inclusive reckoning fifth) day. [f. L (*febris* fever) *quintana* (*quintus* fifth; see -AN)]
quinte (kănt) *n.* Fifth of eight parrying positions in fencing. [F; see QUINT]
quĭntĕ'ssence *n.* **1.** Most essential part of any substance, refined extract; purest and most perfect form, manifestation, or embodiment, *of* some quality or class. **2.** (Ancient Philos.) Fifth substance (beside the four elements) forming heavenly bodies and pervading all things. **3.** Hence **quĭntėssĕ'nt**IAL (-shal) *a.* [ME in sense 2, f. F, f. med. L *quinta essentia* fifth ESSENCE]
quĭntĕ't, -ĕ'tte, *n.* **1.** (Mus.) (Performers of) composition for five voices or instruments; **piano, clarinet,** etc., ~, 4 stringed instruments plus instrument named. **2.** Set of five. [f. F *quintette* f. It. *quintetto* (*quinto* fifth f. L *quintus*); see -ET¹]
quĭntĭ'llion (-yon) *n.* (for *pl.* usage see HUNDRED). ‖A million raised to fifth power; *a thousand raised to sixth power. [f. L *quintus* fifth + MILLION]
quĭ'ntŭp|le *a., n.,* & *v.,* **~lĕt** (*or* -ū'-) *n.,* **~lў** *adv.,* **quĭntū'plĭcate,** (-*a*t) *a.* & *n.,* (-āt) *v.t.,* **quĭntūplĭcā'tion** *n.* Fivefold etc. (for detailed senses see QUADRUPLE etc., substituting *five* for *four*). [f. F *quintuple* f. L *quintus* fifth, after QUADRUPLE]
quĭp *n.,* & *v.i.* (**-pp-**). **1.** *n.* Sarcastic remark; clever saying; equivocation, quibble. **2.** *v.i.* Make quips. [abbr. of obs. *quippy* perh. f. L *quippe* forsooth]
quī'pu (kē'pōō; *or* kwē'-) *n.* Ancient Peruvians' substitute for writing by variously knotting threads of various colours. [Quechua, = knot]
quīre¹ *n.* Four sheets of paper etc. folded to form eight leaves as often in medieval MSS.; any collection of leaves one within another in MS. or book (**in ~s,** unbound, in sheets); 24 sheets of writing-paper. [ME, f. OF *qua(i)er* f. Rom. **quaternum* f. L *quaterni* set of four (as QUATERNARY)]
quīre². See CHOIR.
quīrk *n.* **1.** Quibble, quip; trick of action or behaviour; twist or flourish in drawing or writing; hence ~'Y² *a.* **2.** (Archit.) Acute hollow between convex part of moulding and soffit or fillet. [16th c., of unkn. orig.]
***quīrt** *n.,* & *v.t.* (Strike with) short-handled riding-whip with braided leather lash. [f. Sp. *cuerda* CORD]
quĭ'sle (-z-) *v.i.* (colloq.) Be a quisling. [back form. f. foll.]
quĭ'slĭng (-z-) *n.* Person co-operating with an enemy who has occupied his country; traitor; hence ~ITE¹ *a.* & *n.* [f. V. *Quisling*, renegade Norwegian Army officer d. 1945]
quĭt¹ *pred. a.* **1.** (arch.) Free, clear, absolved. **2.** Rid *of* (*glad to be quit of the trouble*). **3. ~'claim,** (*n.*) renunciation of right esp. to land, (*v.t.*) renounce claim to, give up (thing) *to*; **~'rent,** (usu. small) rent paid by freeholder or copyholder in lieu of service. [ME, f. OF *quitte* f. med. L *quittus* f. L *quietus* QUIET²]
quĭt² *v.t.* (**-tt-**; **‖~'ted, *quit**). **1.** (arch.) Rid one*self of*. **2.** Behave, acquit, conduct, one*self well* etc. (*quit yourselves*, (arch.) *you, like men*). **3.** Give up, let go, abandon (task etc., or abs.; ~ **hold of,** loose); cease, stop, (*quit grumbling*); hence **~'TER**¹ *n.*, one who deserts task or post, shirker. **4.** Depart from, leave, (place, person, etc.; *quitted Paris at midnight*; *quitted him in anger*); (abs., of tenant) leave occupied premises (esp. *give, have,* etc., *notice to quit*). **5.** (poet.) Requite, repay, clear off, (*quit love with hate*; *death quits all scores*). [ME, f. OF *quit(t)er* f. L *quietus* QUIET², QUIT¹]
quĭtch *n.* ~(**-grass**), = COUCH³-*grass*. [OE *cwice*, = MLG *kweke*, perh. cogn. w. QUICK]

quite *adv.* **1.** Completely, wholly, entirely, altogether, to the utmost extent, nothing short of, in the fullest sense, positively, absolutely, (*quite covers it*; *is quite a hero*; *was quite by myself*); NOT *quite*; ~ **other,** very different; ~ **another,** a very different; ~ (**so**), I grant the truth of that; ~ **something,** a remarkable thing; *quite the* THING 2. **2.** Somewhat, to some extent, (*it took quite a long time*); ~ **a few,** a considerable number. [ME, f. obs. *quite* a. = QUIT¹]

quits *pred. a.* On even terms by retaliation or repayment (*will be quits with him yet*; *now we are quits*); **cry** ~, acknowledge that things are now even, agree not to proceed further in quarrel etc.; DOUBLE² *or quits.* [perh. colloq. abbr. of med. L *quittus* (see QUIT¹)]

quĭ'ttance *n.* (arch. or poet.) Release *from* something; acknowledgement of payment, receipt; requital. [ME, f. OF *quitance* (*quiter* QUIT²; see -ANCE)]

quĭ'ver¹ *n.* Case for holding arrows; **have an arrow** or **shaft left in** one's ~, not be resourceless; ~ **full of children,** large family (Ps. 127:5); hence ~FUL 2 *n.* [ME, f. AF **quive(i)r*, OF *quivre* f. WG (OE *cocor*, OS *kokar(i)*, OHG *kohhar(i)*)]

quĭ'ver² *v.* & *n.* **1.** *v.i.* Tremble or vibrate with slight rapid motion (of person, leaf, wing, voice, light, etc.; *with* emotion, *in* the wind etc.). **2.** *v.t.* (Of bird, esp. skylark) make (wings) quiver. **3.** *n.* Quivering motion or sound. [ME, f. obs. *quiver* nimble; cf. QUAVER¹]

qui vive (kēvē'v) *n.* **On the** ~, on the alert, watching for something to happen. [F, = lit. (long) live who?, i.e. on whose side are you?, as sentry's challenge]

Quĭ'xote *n.* Enthusiastic visionary, pursuer of lofty but impracticable ideals, person utterly regardless of his material interests in comparison with honour or devotion; hence **quĭxŏ'tic** *a.*, **quĭxŏ'tically** *adv.*, **quĭ'xotism** (2), **quĭ'xotry** (4), *ns.* **quĭ'xotize** (2, 3) *v.t.* & *i.* [f. Don ~, hero of Cervantes' romance, f. Sp. *quixote* thigh armour]

quĭz *n.* (*pl.* ~**'zes**), & *v.t.* (**-zz-**). **1.** (arch.) Odd or eccentric person, person of ridiculous appearance; person given to quizzing. **2.** Interrogation, questionnaire, examination; test of knowledge in radio or television or other entertainment programme. **3.** Hoax, ridicule, thing done to expose or burlesque another's oddities. **4.** Hence ~**'zical** *a.* **5.** *v.t.* (arch.) Make sport of (person or his ways), regard with mocking air; look curiously at, observe the ways or oddities of, survey through an eyeglass. **6.** Examine by questioning. [18th c., of unkn. orig.]

||**quŏd¹** *n.*, & *v.t.* (**-dd-**). (sl.) **1.** *n.* Prison (*in, out of, quod*). **2.** *v.t.* Imprison. [17th c.; orig. unkn.]

quod² (kwŏd) *pron.* ~ ***erat demonstrandum, faciendum, inveniendum,*** (ĕrăt dĕmonstră'ndum, făshiĕ'ndum, ĭnvĕnĭĕ'ndum), which was the thing to be proved, made or done, found (formulae in geometrical demonstrations, and, esp. in abbr. *Q.E.D.*, in gen. use); ~ ***vide*** (vī'dĭ *or* vĭ'dā), which see (in cross and other references). [L, = which, neut. of *qui* who]

quŏ'dlĭbĕt *n.* (Hist.) (Exercise on) topic of philosophical or theological disputation. [ME f. L (*quod* what, *libet* it pleases one)]

quoin (koin) *n.*, & *v.t.* **1.** *n.* External angle of building; stone or brick forming angle, corner-stone, whence ~'ING¹ (3) *n.*; internal corner of room; wedge for locking type in forme, raising level of gun, keeping barrel from rolling, etc. **2.** *v.t.* Secure or raise with quoins. [var. of COIN¹]

quoit (koit *or* kwoit) *n.*, & *v.t.* **1.** *n.* Heavy flattish sharp-edged iron ring thrown to encircle iron peg or to fix itself in ground near it in game of ~**s**; ring of rope, rubber, etc., for use in similar game. **2.** *v.t.* Fling like a quoit. [ME, of unkn. orig.]

quŏ'ndăm *a.* That once had but no longer has the specified character, sometime, former, (*a quondam friend of mine*). [L adv., = formerly]

***Quŏ'nsĕt** *n.* ~ **hut,** building similar to Nissen hut. [**P**]

quor'um *n.* Fixed number of members that must be present to make proceedings of assembly or society or board valid. [L, = of whom (we will that you etc. be one etc.), in wording of commissions]

quō'ta *n.* **1.** Share that individual person or company is bound to contribute to or entitled to receive from a total. **2.** Quantity of goods etc. which under government controls must be manufactured, exported, imported, etc.; maximum quantity which may similarly be manufactured etc.; number of yearly immigrants allowed to enter a country, students allowed to enrol for a course, etc. [f. med. L *quota* (*pars*) how great (a part), fem. of *quotus* (*quot* how many)]

quōtā'tion *n.* **1.** Quoting or being quoted; passage quoted. **2.** Amount stated as current price of stocks or commodities; contractor's estimate. **3.** (Print.) Quadrat etc. used for filling up blanks. **4.** ~**-marks,** inverted commas and apostrophes, single (' ') or double (" "), used to mark beginning and end of quoted passage, or book etc. title, or word(s) regarded as slang, jargon, etc. [f. med. L *quotatio* (as QUOTE; see -ATION)]

quō'tative *a.* Of quoting; given to quotation. [as foll.; see -ATIVE]

quōte *v.t.*, & *n.* **1.** *v.t.* Cite or appeal to (author, book) in confirmation of some view; repeat or copy out passage(s) from. **2.** Repeat or copy out (borrowed passage) usu. with indication that it is borrowed, (abs.) make quotations, (*from* author, book, speech, etc.). **3.** Enclose (words) within quotation-marks (esp. in *imper.* in dictation etc.). **4.** Adduce or cite *as*; state price of (usu. *at* figure); (St. Exch.) regularly list price of. **5.** Hence **quō'table** *a.* **6.** *n.* (colloq.) Passage quoted; commercial quotation; (usu. in *pl.*) quotation-mark. [ME, earlier 'mark with numbers', f. med. L *quotare* (*quot* how many, or as QUOTA)]

quōth *v.t.* 1st & 3rd pers. past ind. (arch.) Said *I, he, she*, rarely *we* or *they*; ~**'a,** quoth he (used in quoting contemptuously, = *forsooth*). [OE *cwæth* past of *cwethan* say, = OS *quethan*, OHG *quedan*, ON *kuetha*, Goth. *qithan* f. Gmc **kwethan*]

quotĭ'dĭan *a.* & *n.* **1.** *a.* Daily, of every day; ~ **fever** (recurring every day). **2.** Commonplace, trivial. **3.** *n.* Quotidian fever. [ME f. OF *cotidien* & f. L *cotidianus, quotidianus* (*cotidie* daily; see -AN)]

quō'tient (-shent) *n.* (Arith.) Result given by dividing one quantity by another; INTELLIGENCE *quotient.* [ME, f. L *quotiens* how many times (*quot* how many), by confusion w. -ENT]

Qur'an (kurah'n). Var. of KORAN.

q.v. *abbr.* = QUOD² *vide.*

qy. *abbr.* query.

R

R, r, (ar) *n.* (*pl.* **Rs** *or* **R's**). Eighteenth letter of alphabet; **the r months,** those with *r* in their names (Sept.–Apr.) as season for oysters; **the three Rs,** reading, (w)riting, and (a)rithmetic, as basis of elementary education.

R. *abbr.* Railway; rand; Réaumur; Regiment; *Regina*; registered as trademark; *Republican; *Rex*; River; (Chess) rook; Royal.

r. *abbr.* recto; right; röntgen(s); run(s).

R.A. *abbr.* right ASCENSION; Royal Academician; Royal Academy; Royal Artillery.

Ra *symb.* radium.

R.A.A.F. *abbr.* Royal Australian Air Force.

ră'bbėt *n.*, & *v.t.* **1.** *n.* Step-shaped channel etc. cut along edge or face or projecting angle of wood etc. usu. to receive edge or tongue of another piece; ~ **plane** (for cutting groove along an edge). **2.** *v.t.* Join or fix with rabbet; make rabbet in. [ME, f. OF *rab(b)at* abatement, recess (*rabattre* REBATE[1]); assim. to -ET[1]]

ră'bbī *n.* Jewish scholar or teacher esp. of the law; person appointed as Jewish religious leader; **Chief R~,** religious head of British Jewish communities. [ME & OE f. eccl. L, f. Gk *rhabbi* f. Heb. *rabbî* my master (*rab* master + pronominal suf.)]

ră'bbĭn *n.* Jewish scholar or teacher of the law (**the ~s,** chief Jewish authorities on law and doctrine, most important of them 2nd–13th c.); hence ~ATE[1], ~ISM (3), ~IST (2, 3), *ns.*, **rabbĭ'n**ICAL *a.* [F, or f. mod. L *rabbinus* (as prec.); *-n* perh. f. Semitic pl.]

ră'bbĭt[1] *n.*, & *v.i.* **1.** *n.* Burrowing gregarious herbivorous mammal (*Oryctolagus cuniculus*) of hare family, brownish grey in natural state, also black or white or pied in domestication; *hare; ‖(colloq.) poor performer at any game (esp. cricket, golf, or lawn tennis); ~ **punch,** short chop with edge of hand to opponent's nape; WELSH[1] *rabbit*; hence ~Y[2] *a.* **2.** *v.i.* Hunt rabbits. [ME, perh. f. OF; cf. F dial. *rabotte*, Walloon *robète*, Flem. *robbe*]

ră'bbĭt[2] *v.t.* (vulg.) ~ **it** etc. (form of imprecation). [prob. alt. of RAT[2]]

ră'bble[1] *n.* Disorderly crowd, mob; contemptible or inferior set of people; *the* lower or disorderly classes of the populace; **~-rouser,** one who stirs up the rabble in agitation for social or political change. [ME; orig. uncert.]

ră'bble[2] *n.* Iron bar with bent end for stirring molten metal etc. [f. F *râble* f. med. L *rotabulum*, L *rutabulum* (*ruere rut-* rake up) fire-shovel]

Răbelai'sian (-zyan) *a.* & *n.* **1.** *a.* Of or like Rabelais or his writings; marked by exuberant imagination and language and coarse humour and satire. **2.** *n.* Admirer or student of Rabelais. [f. F. *Rabelais*, Fr. satirist d. 1553 + -IAN]

ră'bĭd *a.* Furious, violent, (*rabid hate*); unreasoning, insensate, headstrong, (*rabid segregationist*); (esp. of dog) affected with rabies, mad; of rabies; hence **rabĭ'd**ITY, ~NESS, *ns.*, ~LY[2] *adv.* [f. L *rabidus* (*rabere* rave; see -ID[1])]

rā'bies (-z) *n.* Contagious virus disease of dogs etc.; hydrophobia. [L (*rabere* rave)]

‖**R.A.C.** *abbr.* Royal Armoured Corps; Royal Automobile Club.

raccōō'n. See RACOON.

rāce[1] *n.* **1.** Onward sweep or movement, esp. strong current in sea or river (*tide set with a strong race*). **2.** (arch.) Course of sun or moon, course of life, (*ere he had run half his race*). **3.** Channel of stream (MILL[1]-*race*); channel for balls in ball-bearing; channel along which shuttle moves; (Austral.) fenced passageway for drafting sheep. **4.** Contest of speed between runners, ships, vehicles, horses, etc., or persons etc. doing anything; (in *pl.*) series of these for horses, dogs, etc., at fixed time on regular course; **~'card,** programme of races; **~'course,** ground for horse-racing; **~'goer,** one who frequents horse-races; **~'horse** (bred or kept for racing); **~-meeting,** horse-racing fixture; **~-track,** (usu. oval) track for horse or vehicle races; ***~'way,** track for trotting or pacing. [ME, f. ON *rás* running, race, etc., = OE *rǣs*]

rāce[2] *v.* **1.** *v.i.* Compete in speed *with*; indulge in horse-racing (*a racing man*; **the racing world,** the turf); go at full speed or (of propeller, paddle-wheel, vehicle engine, etc.) at excessive speed because of diminished resistance or load. **2.** *v.t.* Have race with, try to surpass in speed; cause (horse etc.) to race (*raced his car against a train*); make (person or thing) move or work at full or excessive speed (*raced me along at five miles an hour*; *raced the Bill through the House*). [f. prec.]

rāce[3] *n.* **1.** Group of persons or animals or plants connected by common descent, posterity *of* (person); house, family, tribe, or nation regarded as of common stock; distinct ethnical stock (*the Caucasian, Mongolian*, etc., *race*); genus or species or breed or variety of animals or plants, any great division of living creatures (*the human, feathered, four-footed*, etc., *race*). **2.** Descent, kindred, (*of noble, Oriental*, etc., *race*; *separate in language and race*). **3.** Class of persons etc. with some common feature (*the race of poets, dandies*, etc.). **4.** ~ **relations** (between members of different races in same country); **~-riot,** outbreak of violence due to racial antagonism; ~ **suicide,** gradual disappearance of a race through voluntary limitation of reproduction. [F, f. It. *razza*, of unkn. orig.]

rāce[4] *n.* Root (of ginger). [f. OF *rais, raiz* f. L *radix radicis* root]

ră'cėmāte *n.* (Chem.) Racemic mixture. [f. RACEMIC + -ATE[1] (3)]

racē'me *n.* (Bot.) Flower-cluster with the separate flowers attached by short equal stalks at equal distances along central stem. [f. L *racemus* grape-bunch]

racĕ'm|ĭc *a.* (Chem.) Composed of equal numbers of dextrorotatory and laevorotatory molecules of a compound; hence **ră'cėm**IZE (3) *v.t.* & *i.* [f. prec. + -IC, orig. of tartaric acid in grape-juice]

ră'cėmōse *a.* (Bot.) in form of raceme; (Anat., of gland etc.) clustered. [f. L *racemosus* (as RACEME; see -OSE[1])]

rā'cer *n.* In vbl senses; horse, yacht, bicycle, etc., used for racing; circular horizontal rail along which the traversing-platform of a heavy gun moves. [f. RACE[2] + -ER[1]]

rachĕ'l (-sh-) *a.* & *n.* (Of) pale fawn colour used in cosmetics. [f. *Rachel*, Fr. actress d. 1858]

rā'ch|ĭs (-k-) *n.* (*pl.* ~**ides** *pr.* -ĭdēz). Stem of grass etc. bearing flower-stalks at short intervals; axis of pinnately compound leaf or frond; vertebral column or cord from which it develops; feather-shaft, esp. the part that bears the barbs. [mod. L, f. Gk *rhakhis* spine; the E pl. *-ides* is erron.]

rach|ī'tĭs (-k-) *n.* Rickets; hence ~**ĭ'tic** *a.* [mod. L, f. Gk *rhakhitis* (as prec.; see -ITIS)]

||**Ră'chmanĭsm** (-k-) *n.* Exploitation of slum tenants by unscrupulous landlords. [f. P. *Rachman*, London landlord of early 1960s + -ISM]

rā'cial (-sh*a*l) *a.* Of, in regard to, due to, characteristic of, race; hence ~LY² *adv.* [f. RACE³ + -IAL]

rā'cial|ism (-sha-) *n.* Belief in superiority of a particular race; antagonism between different races; hence ~IST (2) *n.* [f. prec. + -ISM]

rā'c|ĭsm *n.* **1.** = prec. **2.** Theory that human abilities etc. are determined by race. **3.** Hence ~IST (2) *n.* [f. RACE³ + -ISM]

răck¹ *n.*, & *v.i.* **1.** *n.* Driving clouds. **2.** *v.i.* (Of clouds) be driven before wind. [ME, prob. of Scand. orig.; cf. Norw. and Sw. dial. *rak* wreckage etc. (*reka* drive)]

răck² *n.*, & *v.t.* **1.** *n.* Fixed or movable frame of wooden or metal bars for holding fodder; framework with rails, bars, pegs, or shelves, for keeping or placing articles on or in (*plate, luggage, hat, tool, pipe*, etc., *-rack*); instrument of torture stretching victim's joints by turning of rollers to which wrists and ankles were tied; **on the ~**, (fig.) in distress or under strain. **2.** Cogged or indented bar or rail gearing with wheel or pinion or worm, or serving with pegs etc. to adjust position of something; **~-railway** (with cogged rail between bearing rails); **~-wheel,** cog-wheel. **3.** *v.t.* ||Fill *up* (stable-rack) with hay or straw; fasten (horse) up to rack. **4.** Place in or on rack. **5.** ***~ up,** achieve (score etc.). [ME, f. Du. *rak, rek*, MLG *rek*(*ke*) rail etc., prob. f. *recken* (see foll.)]

răck³ *v.t.* **1.** Stretch joints of (person) by pulling esp. with RACK²; (of disease or bodily or mental agony) inflict torture on (*a racking headache; racked with pain*); shake violently, injure by straining, task severely, (*cough that seemed to rack his whole body*); ~ one's **brain**(**s**), make great mental effort (*for* something to say, a plan, etc.). **2.** Exact utmost possible amount of (rent), oppress (tenants) by exacting excessive rent, exhaust (land) with excessive use; **~-rent,** (*n.*) (1) rent equal to full annual value of property, (2) excessive rent, (*v.t.*) exact this from (tenant) or for (land); **~-renter,** tenant paying or landlord exacting rack-rent. [ME, f. MDu., MLG *racken, recken* stretch, = OE *reccan*, OS *rekkian*, OHG *recchan*, ON *rekja*, Goth. *ufrakjan* f. Gmc **rakjan*]

răck⁴ *n.* Arrack (esp. *rack punch*). [f. ARRACK]

răck⁵ *n.*, & *v.i.* **1.** *n.* Horse's gait between trot and canter, both legs of one side being lifted almost at once, and all four feet being sometimes off ground together. **2.** *v.i.* Progress thus. [perh. ult. rel. to Arab. *faras rikwa* easy-paced horse]

răck⁶ *v.t.* ~ (**off**), draw off (wine, beer, etc.) from the lees. [ME, f. Prov. *arracar* (*raca* stems and husks of grapes, dregs)]

răck⁷ *n.* Destruction (*go to rack and ruin*). [var. of WRACK, WRECK]

răck⁸ *n.* Joint of lamb etc. including front ribs. [perh. f. RACK²]

ră'ckėt¹, ră'cquėt (-kĭt), *n.* **1.** Stringed bat used in tennis, rackets, etc.; (in *pl.*, usu. treated as *sing.*) ball-game for two or four persons played with rackets in plain four-walled court. **2.** Snow-shoe resembling racket. **3.** **~-ball,** small hard kid-covered ball of cork and string; **~-press** (for keeping rackets taut and in shape); **~-tail,** humming-bird with racket-shaped tail. [f. F *raquette* f. It. *racchetta* f. Arab. *rāha* palm of hand]

ră'ckėt² *n.*, & *v.i.* **1.** *n.* Disturbance, uproar, din; busy activity, social excitement, gaiety; hence ~Y² *a.* **2.** (sl.) Dodge, game, line of business. **3.** Scheme for obtaining money, or effecting some other object, by fraudulent (and often violent) means. **4.** Ordeal, trying experience; **stand the ~,** (1) come successfully through test, (2) face costs or other consequences of action. **5.** *v.i.* ~ (**about**), live gay life, move *about* noisily. [16th c., perh. imit.]

răckėteer' *n.* One who operates a racket (see prec. 3); hence ~ING¹ *n.* [f. prec. + -EER]

***rā'con** *n.* Radar beacon that can be identified and located by its response to radar signal from ship etc. [f. *ra*dar + bea*con*]

răcŏnt|eur' (-tẽr') *n.* (*fem.* **~euse** *pr.* -ẽr'z). Teller of anecdotes (*good, skilful*, etc., *raconteur*). [F (*raconter* relate, RECOUNT¹)]

rac(c)ōō'n *n.* Greyish-brown furry bushy-tailed sharp-snouted N. Amer. nocturnal carnivore. [Algonquian dial.]

racquet. See RACKET¹.

rā'c|ȳ *a.* Having in high degree the qualities that characterize its kind (*racy flavour*); of distinctive quality or vigour, not smoothed into sameness or commonness, retaining traces of origin (**~y of the soil,** of homely directness, spirited, lively, piquant); **risqué*; hence ~**ĭLY**² *adv.*, ~**ĭNESS** *n.* [f. RACE³ + -Y²]

răd *n.* Unit of absorbed dose of ionizing radiation, 100 ergs per gram. [f. *rad*iation]

rad. *abbr.* radian(s); radical.

||**R.A.D.A.** (colloq. rah'd*a*) *abbr.* Royal Academy of Dramatic Art.

rā'dar *n.* System for ascertaining direction and range, or presence, of aircraft, ships, coasts, and other objects, by sending out short radio waves which they reflect; apparatus used for this; **~ trap,** arrangement using radar to detect vehicles etc. travelling faster than speed limit. [f. *ra*dio *d*etection *a*nd *r*anging]

||**R.A.D.C.** *abbr.* Royal Army Dental Corps.

ră'ddle *n.*, & *v.t.* **1.** *n.* Red ochre. **2.** *v.t.* Colour with raddle, or with much rouge crudely used; (in *p.p.*) dilapidated. [var. of RUDDLE]

rā'dĭal *a.* & *n.* **1.** *a.* Of or in rays. **2.** Arranged like rays or radii, having position or direction of a radius; **~ engine** (having cylinders arranged along radii); **~(-ply)**, (of tyre) having fabric layers parallel and tread strengthened. **3.** Having spokes or radiating lines. **4.** Acting or moving along lines that diverge from a centre; **~ symmetry,** symmetry about every line or plane through a centre; **~ velocity,** speed of motion along such line, esp. between star etc. and observer. **5.** Relating to the radius (sense 1) (*radial artery, vein, nerve*). **6.** Hence ~LY² *adv.* **7.** *n.* Radial nerve or artery; radial-ply tyre. [f. med. L *radialis* (as RADIUS; see -AL)]

rā'dĭan *n.* Unit of angle, equal to angle at centre of circle subtended by arc whose length is equal to radius. [f. RADIUS + -AN]

rā'dĭant *a.* & *n.* **1.** *a.* Emitting rays of light; (of eyes or looks) beaming with joy or hope or love; (of light) issuing in rays; (of beauty) splendid or dazzling; hence or cogn. **rā'dĭ**ANCE, **rā'dĭ**ANCY, *ns.*, ~LY² *adv.* **2.** Operating radially; (Bot. etc.) extending radially, radiating; **~ heat** (transmitted by radiation, not by conduction or convection); **~ point,** point from which rays or radii proceed, (Astron.) apparent focal point of meteor shower. **3.** *n.* Point or object from which light or heat radiates, esp. in electric or gas heater; (Astron.) radiant point. [ME, f. L *radiare* (as RADIUS); see -ANT]

rā'dĭate¹ *a.* Having divergent rays or parts radially arranged; hence ~LY² (-tlĭ) *adv.* [as foll.; see -ATE²]

rā'dĭāt|e[2] *v.* **1.** *v.i.* Emit rays of light, heat, or other electromagnetic waves; (of light or heat) issue in rays; diverge or spread from central point. **2.** *v.t.* Emit (light or heat) from centre; disseminate as from a centre; give manifest evidence of (life, love, joy, etc.); (in *p.p.*) with parts arranged in rays. **3.** Hence ~IVE *a.* [f. L *radiare* (as RADIUS) + -ATE[3]]

rādĭā'tion *n.* Radiating; emission of energy as electromagnetic waves; energy thus transmitted, esp. invisibly; ~ **chemistry,** study of chemical effects of this on matter; ~ **sickness** (caused by exposure to excessive radiation). [f. L *radiatio* (as prec.; see -ATION)]

rā'dĭātor *n.* In vbl senses; apparatus for heating room etc., consisting of metal case containing winding pipe through which steam or hot water circulates; oil or electric heater, usu. portable; engine-cooling apparatus in motor vehicle or aeroplane, with large surface for cooling circulating water; ~ **grille, mascot,** etc., (at front end of motor car, where radiator is usu. placed). [f. prec. + -OR]

ră'dĭcal *a.* & *n.* **1.** *a.* Of the root(s). **2.** Naturally inherent, essential, fundamental, (*a radical error*; *the radical rottenness of human nature*). **3.** Forming the basis, primary, (*the radical idea* or *principles of a system*). **4.** Affecting the foundation, going to the root, (*radical change, cure, reform*); (of surgery etc.) seeking to ensure removal of all diseased tissue (opp. CONSERVATIVE); (of politician) desiring radical reforms, (Hist.) ||belonging to extreme section of Liberal party, *seeking extreme anti-South action at time of Civil War; (of measure etc.) advanced by or according to principles of radical politicians, whence ~ISM (2) *n.*, ~IZE (3) *v.t.* & *i.* **5.** (Math.) Of the root of a number or quantity (~ **sign,** $\sqrt{}$, $\sqrt[3]{}$, $\sqrt[4]{}$, etc., indicating that square, cube, fourth, etc., root of number following is to be taken). **6.** (Philol.) Of the roots of words. **7.** (Mus.) Belonging to the root of a chord. **8.** (Bot.) Of, or springing direct from, the root or the main stem close to it. **9.** Hence ~LY[2] *adv.* **10.** *n.* (Philol.) root; fundamental principle; (Math.) (1) quantity forming or expressed as root of another, (2) radical sign; (Chem.) element or atom, or group of these, normally forming part of compound and remaining unaltered during compound's ordinary chemical changes; (Polit.) person holding radical views or belonging to radical party. [ME, f. LL *radicalis* f. L *radix radicis* root; see -AL]

radices. See RADIX.

ră'dĭcle *n.* Part of plant embryo that develops into primary root; rootlet; (Anat.) rootlike subdivision of nerve or vein; (Chem.) radical; so **radĭ'cūl**AR[1] *a.* [f. L *radicula* (as prec.; see -ULE)]

rā'dĭī. See RADIUS.

rā'dĭō *n.* (*pl.* ~s), *a.*, & *v.* **1.** *n.* Transmission and reception of messages etc. by electromagnetic waves without connecting wire; message so sent; (esp. sound) broadcasting; apparatus for receiving signals by radio; broadcasting station (*Radio Luxembourg*). **2.** *a.* Of or relating to, sent by, used in or using, radio; ~ **cab, car,** (equipped with radio for communication); *radio* FIX[2]; *radio* HAM[1]. **3.** Of or concerned with stars or other celestial bodies from which radio waves are received or reflected (*radio astronomy, galaxy,* TELESCOPE); ~ **star,** small celestial object emitting strong radio waves. **4.** *v.t.* Send (message), send message to (person), by radio. **5.** *v.i.* Communicate or broadcast by radio. [short for *radio-telegraphy* etc.]

rā'dĭō- *comb. form.* **1.** (Anat.) Belonging to the radius in conjunction with some other part, as: **~-car'pal,** of radius and wrist. **2.** (Phys.) Connected with rays or radiation, as: **~-assay'** (based on radiation from sample etc.); **~-bio'logy** (concerned with effects of radiation on organisms); **~meter** (-ŏ'm-), (1) instrument illustrating conversion of radiant energy into mechanical force, (2) instrument for measuring intensity of radiation; **radiopa'que,** opaque to X-rays or similar radiation; **~scopy** (-ŏ's-), examination by X-rays etc. of objects opaque to light; **~-the'rapy,** treatment of disease by X-rays or other forms of radiation. **3.** Connected with radioactivity, as: **~-cae'sium, ~-co'balt,** etc., artificially prepared radioisotopes of these elements; **~-car'bon,** radioisotope of carbon, esp. that of mass 14 used in dating ancient organic materials; **~-che'mistry,** chemistry of radioactive materials; **~-element,** natural or artificial radioisotope; **~i'sotope,** radioactive isotope; **~-nu'clide,** radioactive nuclide. **4.** Connected with radio, as: **~-controlled,** controlled from a distance by radio; **~-frequency,** (of) the frequency of radio waves, between about 10 kilohertz and 0·1 terahertz; **~-gonio'meter,** direction-finder; **~loca'tion,** = RADAR; **~-pho'nic,** pertaining to synthetic sound produced by electronic means etc.; **~sonde,** miniature radio transmitter carried up in balloon to broadcast information about pressure, temperature, etc., at various levels [f. G *sonde* probe]; **~-te'legram** (sent by radio); **~-tele'graphy, ~-tele'phony,** (using radio). [f. RADIUS + -O-]

rādĭōă'ctĭve *a.* Of or exhibiting radioactivity. [f. prec. + ACTIVE]

rādĭōăctĭ'vĭtȳ *n.* (Phys.) Property of spontaneous disintegration of atomic nuclei usu. with emission of penetrating radiation or particles. [f. RADIO- + ACTIVITY]

rādĭogĕ'n|ĭc *a.* **1.** Produced by radioactivity. **2.** Suitable for broadcasting by radio. **3.** Hence ~ICALLY *adv.* [f. RADIO- 3, 4 + -GENIC]

rā'dĭogrăm *n.* **1.** Picture obtained by X-rays, gamma rays, etc. **2.** Radio-telegram. **3.** ||Combined radio and electric gramophone. [f. RADIO- 3, 4 + -GRAM, GRAMOPHONE]

rā'dĭograph (-ahf) *n.*, & *v.t.* **1.** *n.* Instrument recording intensity of radiation. **2.** = prec. 1. **3.** *v.t.* Obtain X-ray, gamma-ray, etc., picture of. **4.** Hence **rādĭŏ'graph**ER[1] *n.*, **rādĭogră'ph**IC *a.*, **rādĭŏ'**GRAPHY *n.* [f. RADIO- + -GRAPH]

rādĭolār'ĭan *n.* Protozoan of order Radiolaria, with siliceous skeleton and radiating pseudopodia. [f. mod. L *radiolaria* f. L *radiolus* dim. of RADIUS, + -AN]

rādĭŏ'log|ȳ *n.* Scientific study of X-rays and other high-energy radiation, esp. as used in medicine; hence **rādĭolŏ'gic**(AL) *adjs.*, ~IST (3) *n.* [f. RADIO- + -LOGY]

ră'dĭsh *n.* (Cruciferous plant, *Raphanus sativus*, with) fleshy pungent root often eaten raw as relish in salads. [OE *rædic* f. L *radix radicis* root]

rā'dĭum *n.* (Chem.) Radioactive metallic element obtained from pitchblende etc., used esp. in luminous materials and in radio-therapy; ~ **emanation,** radon; ~ **therapy,** treatment of disease by the use of radium. [f. L *radius* ray + -IUM]

rā'dĭ|us *n.* (*pl.* ~i *pr.* -ī, *or* ~**uses**), & *v.t.* **1.** *n.* Thicker and shorter bone of forearm in man (cf. ULNA); corresponding bone in animal's foreleg or bird's wing. **2.** (Math.) Straight line from centre to circumference of circle or sphere; radial line from focus to any point of curve (~ **vector,** variable line drawn from fixed point to orbit or other curve, or to any point as indication of latter's position). **3.** Length of radius of circle etc.; (fig.) distance from a centre (*all within a radius of 20 miles*; *has a large radius of action*). **4.** Any of a set of lines diverging from a point like radii of circle; object of this kind, e.g. spoke. **5.** (Bot.) Outer rim of composite flower-head, e.g. daisy, also radiating branch of umbel. **6.** *v.t.* Give rounded form to (edge etc.). [L, = staff, spoke, ray]

rā'd|ĭx *n.* (*pl.* ~*ices pr.* -ĭsēz). Number or symbol used as basis of numeration scale (*ten is the radix of decimal numeration and of common logarithms*); source or origin *of*. [L, = root]

rā'dōme *n.* Dome or covering protecting radar equipment, esp. on outer surface of aircraft. [f. *ra*dar + *dome*]

rā'dŏn *n.* (Chem.) Gaseous radioactive inert element arising from the disintegration of radium. [f. RADIUM after *argon* etc.]

ră'dūla *n.* (*pl.* ~**e**). Filelike structure in molluscs for scraping off food particles and drawing them into mouth. [L, = scraper (*radere* scrape; see -ULE)]

||**R.A.F.** (colloq. răf) *abbr.* Royal Air Force.

ră'ffĭa *n.* Palm-tree (*Raphia ruffia*) orig. of Madagascar; fibre from its leaves used for tying up plants and for making hats, baskets, mats, etc. [Malagasy]

ră'ffĭnāte *n.* Product of extraction of liquid with solvent. [f. F *raffiner* + -ATE[1] (5)]

ră'ffĭsh *a.* Disreputable, dissipated, tawdry; hence ~LY[2] *adv.*, ~NESS *n.* [f. *raff* rubbish + -ISH[1]]

ră'ffle[1] *n.* & *v.* **1.** *n.* Sale of article, esp. for charity, by taking entry fee from any number of persons and assigning the article by lot to one of them. **2.** *v.i.* Enter one's name in raffle *for* article. **3.** *v.t.* Sell by raffle. [ME, kind of dice-game, f. OF *raf(f)le*, of unkn. orig.]

ră'ffle[2] *n.* Rubbish, refuse; lumber, debris. [ME, perh. f. OF *ne rifle, ne rafle* nothing at all]

raft (rah-) *n.* & *v.* **1.** *n.* Collection of logs, casks, etc., fastened together in the water for transportation; flat floating structure of timber or other materials for conveying persons or things, esp. as substitute for boat in emergencies; floating accumulation of trees, ice, etc.; *(sl.) large collection *of* things; **~'sman,** worker on raft. **2.** *v.t.* Transport as or on raft; form into a raft; cross (water) on raft(s). **3.** *v.i.* Work raft (*across* water etc.). [ME, f. ON *raptr* RAFTER[2]]

ra'fter[1] (rah'-) *n.* Man who rafts timber. [f. prec. + -ER[1]]

ra'fter[2] (rah'-) *n.*, & *v.t.* **1.** *n.* One of the sloping beams forming framework of a roof; **principal** ~, strong beam in truss, underlying **common** **~s. 2.** *v.t.* (usu. in *p.p.*) Provide with rafters. [OE *ræfter*, = OS *rehter*, MLG *rafter*, rel. to RAFT]

||**R.A.F.V.R.** *abbr.* Royal Air Force Volunteer Reserve.

răg[1] *n.* **1.** Torn or frayed piece of woven material, one of the irregular scraps to which cloth etc. is reduced by wear and tear; CHEW *the rag*; **in ~s,** much torn; RED *rag*. **2.** (in *pl.*) Old and torn clothes; GLAD[1] *rags*; **in ~s,** in old clothes; **~s to riches,** poverty to affluence. **3.** (usu. w. neg.) Smallest scrap of cloth or sail (*not a rag to cover him*; *spread every rag of sail*). **4.** (collect.) Rags used as material for paper, stuffing, etc. **5.** Remnant, odd scrap, irregular piece, (*flying rags of cloud*; *cooked* **to ~s,** till it falls to pieces; *not a rag of evidence*). **6.** (derog.) Flag, handkerchief, curtain, newspaper, etc. **7.** Jagged projection esp. on metal. **8.** ||**~-and-bone man,** itinerant dealer in old clothes etc.; **~-bag,** bag in which scraps of fabric etc., are kept for use, (fig.) miscellaneous collection; **~-bolt** (with barbs to keep it tight when driven in); **~ book,** child's book of untearable cloth; **~ doll,** stuffed cloth doll; **~ paper** (made from rags); **~-picker,** collector and seller of rags; **~'tag (and bobtail)**, the riff-raff, ragged or low or disreputable people; **~'time,** (*n.*) popular music of U.S. Negro origin with much syncopation, (*a.*) farcical (*a ragtime army*); **~ trade,** (colloq.) business of designing, making, and selling clothes; **~'weed,** (1) = *ragwort*, (2) *plant of genus *Ambrosia* with allergenic pollen; **~-wheel,** sprocket-wheel (with projections catching in links of chain that passes over it); **~'wort,** yellow-flowered ragged-leaved plant of genus *Senecio*. [ME, prob. back form. f. RAGGED, *raggy*]

răg[2] *n.* Large coarse roofing-slate; **~('stone),** hard coarse stone breaking up in thick slabs (CORAL *rag*). [ME, of unkn. orig., but assoc. w. prec.]

răg[3] *v.* (-gg-) & *n.* (sl.) **1.** *v.t.* Scold, reprove severely; tease, torment, play rough jokes on, disarrange (person's room etc.) by way of practical joke. **2.** *v.i.* ||Engage in rough play; be noisy and riotous. **3.** *n.* ||Noisy disorderly conduct or scene; rowdy celebration; annual parade etc. of students esp. to collect money for charity; prank. [18th c., of unkn. orig.; cf. BALLYRAG]

răg[4] *n.* = RAG[1]*time*. [abbr.]

rag[5] (rahg). Var. of foll.

ra'ga (rah'-) *n.* (Ind. Mus.) Pattern of notes used as basis for improvisation; piece using a particular raga. [Skr., = colour, musical tone]

ră'gamŭffĭn *n.* Person in ragged dirty clothes; hence ~LY[1] *a.* [prob. f. RAG[1] w. fanciful termination]

rāge[1] *n.* **1.** (Fit of) violent anger; violent operation of some natural force or some sentiment (*the rage of the wind, of faction*). **2.** Vehement desire or passion (*for*); object of widespread temporary enthusiasm or fashion (*the open-air cure was the*, or *all the, rage*). **3.** (poet.) Poetic or prophetic or martial ardour. [ME f. OF, f. Rom. **rabia* f. L RABIES]

rāge[2] *v.i.* Rave, storm, speak madly or furiously, (*at, against*, or abs.), be full of anger; (of wind, sea, passion, feeling, battle, pain, disease, etc.) be violent, be at its height, operate unchecked, prevail. [ME, f. OF *rager* (as prec.)]

ra'g(g)ee, ra'gi, (rah'gē) *n.* Coarse cereal (*Eleusine coracana*) forming staple food in parts of India etc. [f. Hindi *rāgi*]

ră'ggĕd (-g-) *a.* Rough, shaggy, hanging in tufts; having broken jagged outline or surface, full of rough or sharp projections; faulty, imperfect, lacking finish or smoothness or uniformity, (*ragged rhymes, time* in rowing, etc.); rent, torn, frayed; (of person) (1) in ragged clothes, (2) almost exhausted (*was run ragged*); **~ robin,** crimson-flowered campion (*Lychnis floscuculi*) with tattered petals; ||**~ school,** (Hist.) free school for poor children; hence ~LY[2] *adv.*, ~NESS *n.* [ME, f. ON *roggvathr* tufted]

ragi. See RAGEE.

ră'glan *n.* Overcoat without shoulder seams, the sleeve running up to the neck; **~ sleeve** (of this kind). [f. Lord *Raglan*, Brit. commander d. 1855]

ră'gout (-ōō) *n.*, & *v.t.* **1.** *n.* Meat in small pieces stewed with vegetables and highly seasoned. **2.** *v.t.* Cook thus. [f. F *ragoût* (*ragoûter* revive taste of; see RE-, GUST[2])]

ră'gūlȳ *a.* (Her.) Like row of sawn-off branches. [perh. f. RAGGED after *nebuly*]

***rah** *int.* expr. encouragement, approval, etc. [f. HURRAH]

raid *n.* & *v.* **1.** *n.* Sudden attack made by military party, ship(s), or aircraft; predatory incursion in which surprise and rapidity are usu. relied upon, foray, inroad; surprise visit by police etc. to arrest suspected persons or seize illicit goods; (St. Exch.) attempt to lower price by concerted selling of shares. **2.** *v.i.* Make raid *into* etc. **3.** *v.t.* Make raid on (person, place, cattle). **4.** Hence ~′ER[1] *n.* [ME, Sc. form of OE *rād* ROAD[1]]

rail[1] *n.* & *v.* **1.** *n.* Horizontal or inclined bar or continuous series of bars of wood or metal used to hang things on, as top of banisters, as part of fence, as protection against contact or falling over, or for similar purpose; **over the ~**, over side of ship. **2.** Horizontal piece (cf. STILE[2]) in frame of panelled door etc. **3.** Iron bar or continuous line of bars laid on ground usu. as one of two forming railway track (**off the ~s,** disorganized, out of order, not working right); railway (*send it by rail*; *free on rail*; *rail travel*, *unions*). **4.** **~′car,** self-propelled railway coach; ***~ fence** (made of posts and rails); **~′head,** (1) farthest point reached by railway under construction, (2) point on railway at which road transport of goods begins; **~′man,** railwayman; ***~′road,** (*n.*) railway, (*v.t.*) rush (person, thing) *to*, *into*, *through*, etc., send (person) to prison by fraud. **5.** Hence ~′AGE (4) *n.*, ~′LESS (-l-l-) *a.* **6.** *v.t.* Furnish or enclose (place) with rail(s) (*in*, *off*); provide (bench etc.) with rail(s); hence **~′ing**[1] [-ING[1] (3, 4)] *n.* **7.** Lay (railway route) with rails; convey (goods) by rail. **8.** *v.i.* Travel by rail. [ME, f. OF *reille* iron rod f. L *regula* RULE]

rail[2] *n.* Small wading bird of family Rallidae, esp. LAND[1]*rail*, WATER[1]*-rail*. [ME, f. ONF *raille* f. Rom. **rasc(u)la*, perh. imit.]

rail[3] *v.i.* Use abusive language (*at* or *against*, arch. *on* or *upon*); hence ~′ER[1] *n.*, **~′ing**[2] [-ING[1] (1)] *n.*, **~′ing**[3] [-ING[2]] *a.* [ME, f. F *railler* f. Prov. *ralhar* jest f. Rom. **ragulare* (**ragere* roar, bray, f. L *rugire* bellow & Rom. **bragere* BRAY[1])]

rai′llerў *n.* (Piece of) good-humoured ridicule, rallying. [f. F *raillerie* (as prec.; see -ERY)]

rai′lway *n.* **1.** (Hist.) Road laid with rails for carts etc. **2.** Track or set of tracks of iron or steel rails for passage of trains of carriages or trucks drawn by locomotive engine and conveying passengers and goods. **3.** Tracks of this kind worked by single company; organization and persons required for their working. **4.** Track on which wheels run (*cable railway*). **5.** **~man,** railway employee; **~-yard,** area where rolling-stock is kept and made up into trains. [f. RAIL[1] + WAY]

rai′ment *n.* (arch. or literary). Clothing. [ME, f. obs. *arrayment* (as ARRAY[1], -MENT)]

rain[1] *n.* **1.** Condensed moisture of atmosphere falling visibly in separate drops; fall of such drops; *as* RIGHT[1] *as rain*; **~ or shine,** whether it rains or not. **2.** (in *pl.*) Falls of rain; **the ~s,** rainy season in tropical countries. **3.** (Rainlike descent of) falling liquid or solid particles or objects (lit. or fig.; *a rain of ashes*, *frogs*, *pearls*, *rice*, *fire*, *of melody*, *kisses*; *congratulations*). **4.** **~-bird,** bird said to foretell rain by its cry, esp. green woodpecker; **~-check,** ticket given for later use when baseball match etc. is interrupted by rain, (fig.) promise that an offer will be maintained though deferred; **~′coat,** waterproof or water-resistant coat; **~-doctor,** sorcerer seeking to produce rain by magic; **~′drop,** single drop of rain; **~′fall,** (1) shower, (2) quantity of rain falling within given area in given time; **~ forest,** luxuriant tropical forest with heavy rainfall; **~-gauge,** instrument measuring rainfall; **~-maker,** Amer. Ind. rain-doctor; **~-making,** attempt to increase rainfall by artificial means; ‖**~-pie,** green woodpecker; **~-shadow,** region shielded from rain by mountains etc.; **~-water** (collected from rain, not got from wells etc.); **~-worm,** common earthworm. **5.** Hence ~′LESS, ~′PROOF[2], ~′TIGHT, *adjs*. [OE *regn*, *rēn*, = OS, OHG *regan*, ON *regn*, Goth. *rign*]

rain[2] *v.* **1.** *v. impers.* **It ~s** or **is ~ing,** rain comes down; **it ~ed** *blood*, *frogs*, *invitations*, etc., there was a rain of them; *it rains* CAT[1]*s and dogs*; *it never rains but it* POURS; **it ~s in,** rain penetrates house etc.; *it has rained itself* OUT 3. **2.** *v.i.* (Of the sky, the clouds, etc.) send down rain; fall in showers or like rain (*flowers rained from their hands*; *tears rained down her cheeks*; *blows rain upon him*). **3.** *v.t.* Send down like rain (*eyes rain tears*, *influence*; *he rained benefits upon us*); **~ off** or ***out,** (esp. in *p.p.*) prevent or stop (event etc.) by rain. [OE *regnian* (as prec.)]

rai′nbow (-ō) *n.* & *a.* **1.** *n.* Arch showing sequence of colours (conventionally red, orange, yellow, green, blue, indigo, violet) formed in sky (or across cataract etc.) opposite sun by reflection, twofold refraction, and dispersion of sun's rays in falling raindrops etc.; similar effect from moon, fog, sea spray, etc.; **secondary ~**, additional arch with colours in reverse order formed inside or outside rainbow by twofold reflection and twofold refraction; **all the colours of the ~**, many colours. **2.** *a.* Many-coloured; **~ trout,** large trout (*Salmo gairdnerii*) orig. of Pacific coast of N. Amer. [OE *regnboga* (as RAIN[1], BOW[1])]

rai′n|ў *a.* **1.** (Of weather, climate, day, month, season, region, etc.) in or on which rain is falling or much rain usually falls; **~y day,** (fig.) time of esp. pecuniary need. **2.** (Of clouds, wind, etc.) laden with or bringing rain. **3.** Hence ~ĭLY[2] *adv.*, ~ĭNESS *n.* [OE *rēnig* (as RAIN[1], -Y[2])]

raise (-z) *v.t.*, & *n.* **1.** *v.t.* Set upright, cause to stand up or *up*, restore to or towards vertical position, rouse, (*raised him from his knees*, *the standard of revolt*, *the country against the invader*); **~ from the dead,** restore to life; **~ a dust,** (fig.) cause turmoil, obscure the truth; **~d pastry** etc. (standing without support); ~ person's **spirits,** give him new courage or cheerfulness; **~ the wind,** (fig.) procure money for some purpose. **2.** Build up or *up*, construct, create, produce, breed, educate, utter, make audible, start, give occasion for, elicit, set up, advance, (*raise palace*, *large family*, *blister*, one's *own vegetables*, *storm*, *shout*, *hymn*, *controversy*, *prejudice*, *claim*, *demand*, *objection*, *question*, *false hopes*); *a deliverer was* **~d up,** caused by Providence to appear; **~ a laugh,** cause others to laugh; ~ one's **voice,** speak (see also sense 3). **3.** Put or take into higher position, extract from earth, direct upwards, promote to higher rank, make higher or nobler, cause to ascend, increase amount of, heighten level of, (Naut.) come in sight of (land, ship); cause (bread) to rise with yeast; make nap on (cloth); increase (stake), bet more than (another player), at poker etc.; make bid contracting for more tricks in same suit as (partner), increase (bid) thus, at bridge etc.; (Math.) multiply (quantity) *to* a power; **~d beach,** (Geol.) beach lying above water level owing to changes since its formation; ~ one's **eyebrows,** look supercilious or shocked; ~ one's **eyes,** look upwards; ~ one's **glass to,** drink health of; ~ one's **hand to,** make as if to strike (person); ~ one's **hat,** remove it as gesture of courtesy or respect; ~ one's **voice,** speak louder (see also sense 2). **4.** Levy, collect, bring together, procure, manage to get, (*raise tax*, *loan*, *subscription*, *money*, *army*, *fleet*). **5.** Relinquish, cause enemy to relinquish, (siege, blockade); remove (barrier, embargo). **6.** Cause (ghost etc.) to appear (opp. LAY[3]); (colloq.) find (person etc. wanted); **~ Cain, the devil, hell,** etc., (colloq.) make disturbance.

7. *n.* *Increase in salary. **8.** (Cards). Increase in stake or bid (cf. sense 3). [ME, f. ON *reisa* = OE *rǣran* REAR²]

rai'sin (-z-) *n.* Partially dried grape. [ME f. OF, f. Rom. **racimus* f. L *racemus* grape-bunch]

raison d'être (rāzawṅdā'tr *or* -ĕ'-) *n.* Purpose etc. that accounts for or justifies or originally caused thing's existence. [F, = reason for being]

raj (rahj) *n.* (Ind. Hist.) Sovereignty (*the British raj in India*). [Hindi *rāj* reign]

ra'ja, ra'jah, (rah'ja) *n.* (Hist.) Indian king or prince; petty dignitary or noble in India; Malay or Javanese chief; hence ~SHIP *n.* [f. Hind. *rājā* f. Skr. *rājan* king]

Ra'jpōōt, Ra'jput, (rah'jpōōt) *n.* Member of Hindu soldier caste claiming descent from Kshatriyas. [f. Hindi *rājpūt* f. Skr. *rājan* king + *putrá* son]

rāke¹ *n.* Implement consisting of pole with cross-bar toothed like comb at end, or with several tines held together by cross-piece, for drawing together hay etc. or smoothing loose soil or gravel; wheeled implement for same purpose; implement resembling rake used for other purposes, e.g. by croupier drawing in money at gaming-table. [OE *raca, racu,* = MLG, MDu. *rāke*, cogn. w. MLG *rēke*, OHG *rehho*, ON *reka*]

rāke² *v.* **1.** *v.t.* Collect, draw *together*, gather *in* or *up*, pull *out*, clear *off*, (as) with rake (*rake out the fire*; *rake up* or *together all possible charges*; *rake off the leaves*); clean or smooth with rake; search (as) with rake, ransack; make *level, clean,* etc., with rake; scratch, scrape; ~ **over** or **up,** revive memory of (past quarrels, grievances, etc.). **2.** Sweep with shot, enfilade, send shot along (ship) from stem to stern, sweep with the eyes, (of window etc.) have commanding view of. **3.** *v.i.* Use rake, search as with rake (*have been raking among* or *in* or *into old records*). **4.** **~-off,** (colloq., usu. derog.) commission, share of profits. [ME, f. ON *raka* scrape, rake, & f. prec.]

rāke³ *n.* Dissipated or immoral man of fashion; **~'s progress,** continuous deterioration through vicious indulgence [title of series of engravings by Hogarth 1735]. [f. *rakel* dial. var. of RAKEHELL]

rāke⁴ *v.* & *n.* **1.** *v.i.* (Of ship or its bow or stern) project at upper part of bow or stern beyond keel; (of mast or funnel) incline from perpendicular towards stern. **2.** *v.t.* Give backward inclination to (back of seat etc.). **3.** *n.* Amount by which thing rakes; raking position or build; slope of stage or auditorium in theatre; slope of seat-back etc.; angle of surface of cutting tool. [17th c., prob. rel. to G *ragen* project, of unkn. orig.]

rā'kehĕll (-kh-) *n.* (arch.) = RAKE³; hence ~Y² *a.* [f. RAKE² + HELL]

rā'kĭsh¹ *a.* (As) of or like a RAKE³; hence ~LY² *adv.*, ~NESS *n.* [f. RAKE³ + -ISH¹]

rā'kĭsh² *a.* (Of ship) smart and fast-looking, seeming built for speed and therefore open to suspicion of piracy. [f. RAKE⁴ + -ISH¹, assoc. w. RAKE³]

râle (rahl) *n.* (Path.) Sound additional to that of respiration heard in auscultation of unhealthy lungs. [F (*râler* to rattle)]

răllentă'nd|ō *adv.*, *a.*, & *n.* (*pl.* ~*os or* ~*i*). (Mus.) (Passage performed) with gradual decrease of speed. [It.]

ră'llĭ cār(t) *n.* Light two-wheeled horse-drawn vehicle for four persons. [f. *Ralli*, name of first purchaser 1885, + CAR, CART]

ră'llīne *a.* Of the bird-family Rallidae (see RAIL²). [f. mod. L *rallus* RAIL²; see -INE¹]

ră'llȳ¹ *v.* & *n.* **1.** *v.t.* & *i.* Reassemble, get together again, after rout or dispersion; (cause to) renew conflict. **2.** Bring or come together as support or for concentrated action (*rallied his party, his party rallied, round* or *behind* or *to him*). **3.** Revive (faculty etc.) by effort of will, pull oneself together, assume or rouse to fresh energy; throw off prostration or illness or fear, regain health or consciousness, revive; (of share-prices etc.) increase after fall. **4.** *n.* Act of reassembling forces or renewing conflict, reunion for fresh effort; recovery of energy after or in the middle of exhaustion or illness; (Tennis etc.) series of strokes before point is decided; competition for motor vehicles over public roads; mass meeting of supporters or persons having a common interest. [f. F *rallier* (as RE-, ALLY¹)]

ră'llȳ² *v.t.* Subject to good-humoured ridicule, banter. [f. F *railler* (see RAIL³)]

răm¹ *n.* **1.** Uncastrated male sheep, tup. **2.** (*R*~). *The* zodiacal sign Aries. **3.** = BATTER¹*ing-ram*; (battleship with) projecting beak at bow for piercing sides of other ships. **4.** Falling weight of pile-driving machine; rammer; hydraulic water-raising or lifting machine; piston of hydrostatic press; plunger of force-pump; **~-jet,** type of jet engine in which air is drawn in and compressed by motion through it. [OE *ram(m)*, = MDu., MLG, OHG *ram*, perh. rel. to ON *rammr* strong]

răm² *v.t.* (**-mm-**). **1.** Beat down (soil etc., or abs.) into solidity with wooden block etc.; make (post, plant, etc.) firm by ramming soil round it. **2.** Drive (pile etc.) *down, in, into,* by heavy blows; force (charge) home, pack (gun) tight with charge, by pushing with ramrod; squeeze or force into place by pressure (*rammed his clothes into a bag, his hat down on his head; had the list rammed into me by repetition*; ~ **the argument home,** lay sufficient stress on it); cram *with* stuffing etc. **3.** (Of ship, vehicle, etc.) strike (as) with ram; dash or violently impel (thing) *against, at, on, into,* (*rammed his head against the wall, his horse at a fence*). **4.** Hence **~'m**ER¹ (2) *n.* [ME, f. prec.]

‖**R.A.M.** *abbr.* Royal Academy of Music.

Rămada'n (-ah'n) *n.* Ninth month of Muslim year, during all daylight hours of which rigid fasting is observed. [f. Arab. *ramaḍān* (*ramaḍa* be hot; reason for name uncert.)]

rā'mal *a.* (Bot.) Of or proceeding from a branch. [f. L *ramus* branch + -AL]

Ra'man (rah'-) *n.* (Phys.) ~ **effect** etc. (involving change of frequency in scattering of radiation in a medium). [f. Sir C. V. ~, Ind. physicist d. 1970]

ră'mble *v.i.*, & *n.* **1.** Walk for pleasure, with or without definite route. **2.** *v.i.* Wander in discourse, talk or write disconnectedly. [prob. f. MDu. *rammelen* (of animal) wander about in sexual excitement, frequent. of *rammen* copulate with, cogn. w. RAM¹; see -LE 3]

ră'mbler *n.* In vbl senses; straggling or climbing rose, esp. red-flowered kind called **crimson** ~. [f. prec. + -ER¹]

ră'mblĭng *a.* Peripatetic, wandering; disconnected, desultory, incoherent; (of plant) straggling, climbing; (of house, street, etc.) irregularly planned; hence ~LY² *adv.* [f. RAMBLE + -ING²]

***rămbŭ'nctious** (-shus) *a.* Unruly; uncontrollably exuberant; hence ~LY *adv.*, ~NESS *n.* [19th c., of unkn. orig.]

rămbu'tan (-ōō'-) *n.* Red plum-sized fruit of an E. Ind. tree, covered with prickles and with pleasant subacid pulp; tree (*Nephelium lappaceum*) that bears this. [Malay *rambūtan* (*rambut* hair, in allusion to spines)]

‖**R.A.M.C.** *abbr.* Royal Army Medical Corps.

ră'mėkin, ră'mėquin (-kĭn), *n.* Small quantity of cheese with breadcrumbs, eggs, etc., baked and served in small mould (~ **case, dish**). [f. F *ramequin*, of LDu. orig.]

ră'mie *n.* Tall E. Asian etc. plant (*Boehmeria nivea*); strong fibre from its bast, woven into durable material. [f. Malay *rāmī*]

rămĭfĭcā'tion *n.* Ramifying, (arrangement of) tree's branches; subdivision of complex structure comparable to tree's branches (*the ramifications of a river, society, trade, plot, inquiry*, etc.). [F (*ramifier*; see foll., -ATION)]

ră'mĭfȳ *v.* **1.** *v.i.* Form branches or subdivisions or offshoots, branch out. **2.** *v.t.* (usu. in *pass.*) Cause to branch out, arrange in branching manner (*railways were ramified over the country*). [f. F *ramifier* f. med. L *ramificare* f. L *ramus* branch; see -FY]

ră'mmer. See RAM².

ră'mōse *a.* Branched, branching. [f. L *ramosus* (*ramus* branch; see -OSE¹)]

rămp¹ *n.* Slope, inclined plane joining two levels of ground, floor, etc.; stairs for entering or leaving aircraft; difference in level between opposite abutments of rampant arch; upward bend in stair-rail. [f. F *rampe* (*ramper*; see foll.)]

rămp² *v.* **1.** *v.i.* (Of lion etc.) stand on hind legs with fore-paws in air, assume or be in threatening posture; storm, rage, rush *about*. **2.** (Archit., of wall) ascend or descend to different level. **3.** *v.t.* Furnish or build with ramp. [ME, f. OF *ramper* creep]

‖**rămp**³ *n.* & *v.* (sl.) **1.** *n.* Swindle, racket, esp. conducted by levying of exorbitant prices. **2.** *v.i.* Engage in ramp. **3.** *v.t.* Subject (person etc.) to ramp. [n. f. v., 16th c.; orig. unkn.]

rămpā'ge *v.i.*, & *n.* **1.** *v.i.* Behave violently, storm, rage, rush *about*. **2.** *n.* (*or* ră'-). Violent behaviour; **on the** ~, rampaging; hence ~OUS (-jus) *a.* [18th c., perh. f. RAMP²]

ră'mpant *a.* **1.** (Her., esp. of lion; after *n.*) Ramping. **2.** Violent or extravagant in action or opinion, arrant, aggressive, unchecked, prevailing, (*rampant theorists, violence*); rank, luxuriant, (*a rich soil makes nasturtiums too rampant*); (of arch etc.) having one abutment higher than the other, climbing. **3.** Hence **ră'mp**ANCY *n.*, ~LY² *adv.* [ME f. OF, part. of *ramper* (see RAMP², -ANT)]

ră'mpart *n.*, & *v.t.* **1.** *n.* Broad-topped and usu. stone-parapeted walk on top of defensive wall; (fig.) defence, protection. **2.** *v.t.* Fortify or protect (as) with rampart. [f. F *rempart, rempar* f. *remparer* fortify (as RE-, *emparer* take possession of f. Prov. *amparer* f. Rom. **anteparare* place before another f. L *ante* before + *parare* prepare)]

ră'mpĭon *n.* Bell-flower (*Campanula rapunculus*) with white tuberous roots used as salad. [ult. f. med. L *rapuncium, rapontium*, prob. f. L *rapum* RAPE³]

ră'mrŏd *n.* Rod for ramming down charge of muzzle-loaded firearm; (fig.) thing that is very straight or rigid. [f. RAM² + ROD]

ră'mshăckle *a.* (Usu. of house or vehicle) tumbledown, crazy, rickety. [earlier *ramshackled* p.p. of obs. *ransackle* RANSACK]

ră'mson *n.* (esp. in *pl.*) (Root, eaten as relish, of) broad-leaved garlic (*Allium ursinum*). [OE *hramsan* pl. of *hramsa* wild garlic, later taken as sing.]

răn. See RUN¹.

R.A.N. *abbr.* Royal Australian Navy.

ranch (rah-) *n.*, & *v.i.* **1.** *n.* Cattle-breeding establishment esp. in U.S. and Canada; farm where other animals are bred (*mink ranch*); *DUDE *ranch*. **2.** *v.i.* Conduct ranch; hence ~'ER¹ *n.* [f. Sp. *rancho* mess, persons eating together]

ră'ncĭd *a.* Smelling or tasting like rank stale fat; hence ~ITY (-ĭ'd-), ~NESS, *ns.* [f. L *rancidus* stinking (**rancēre* be putrid; see -ID¹)]

ră'ncour (-ker), ***ră'ncor,** *n.* Inveterate bitterness, malignant hate, spitefulness; hence **ră'ncor**OUS *a.* [ME f. OF, f. LL *rancor -oris* (as prec.; see -OR)]

rănd¹ *n.* Levelling-strip of leather between heel and sides of shoe or boot. [OE, = OS *rand*, OHG *rant*, ON *rönd* edge, rim f. Gmc **rand-*]

rand² (rahnt) *n.* (S. Afr.) **1.** Ridge of high ground on either side of river. **2.** Monetary unit of S. Afr. countries. [Afrik., = edge, cogn. w. prec.; sense 2 f. *the R*~, gold-field district near Johannesburg]

R. and A. *abbr.* Royal and Ancient (Golf Club, St. Andrews).

răndă'n¹ *n.* Style of rowing for three men, the middle using pair of sculls and the others oars; boat for such use. [19th c.; orig. uncert.]

răndă'n² *n.* Spree (*on the randan*). [perh. var. of RANDOM]

R. & B. *abbr.* rhythm and blues.

R. & D. *abbr.* research and development.

ră'ndem *adv:* & *n.* **1.** *adv.* With three horses harnessed tandem. **2.** *n.* Carriage or team so driven. [prob. formed on *random* and *tandem*]

ră'ndom *n.* & *a.* **1.** *n.* **At** ~, at haphazard, without aim or purpose or principle, heedlessly. **2.** *a.* Made, done, etc., at random (*random sample, selection*); (Statistics) with equal chances for each item, given by random process, whence ~IZE (3) *v.t.*; (of masonry) with stones of irregular size and shape; hence ~LY² *adv.* [ME, f. OF *randon* great speed (*randir* gallop)]

ră'nd|ȳ *a.* Lustful, eager for sexual gratification; (Sc.) loud-tongued, boisterous, lusty; hence ~**ĭ**NESS *n.* [perh. f. obs. *rand* f. obs. Du. *randen, ranten* RANT + -Y²]

ra'nee, ra'nĭ, (rah'nĭ) *n.* (Hist.) Hindu queen; raja's wife or widow. [f. Hindi *rānī* = Skr. *rājnī* fem. of *rājan* king]

răng. See RING².

răngati'ra (-nggatē'-) *n.* (N.Z.) Maori chief or noble. [Maori]

rānge¹ (-nj) *v.* **1.** *v.t.* Place or arrange in a row or ranks or in specified situation or order or company (usu. in *pass.* or *refl.*: *ranged their troops; ranged themselves on each side; range oneself with the majority party; was ranged against, among, on the side of, with*, etc.; *trees ranged in ascending order of height*); **ra'nging-pole, -rod,** (for setting straight line in surveying); ~ **oneself,** (arch.; imit. F) take up definite position in society, settle down, e.g. by marrying. **2.** ‖(Print.) Make (type) lie flush at ends of successive lines. **3.** Traverse in all directions (*ranging the woods*). **4.** *v.i.* Run in a line, reach, lie spread out, extend, be found or occur over specified district, vary between limits, (*ranges north and south, along the sea; nightingale ranges from the Channel to Warwickshire*). **5.** Be level (*with*); (Print., of type) lie flush (see sense 2); rank or find right place *with* or *among* (*ranges with the great writers*). **6.** Rove, wander, (*over, along, through*, etc., district or region; *his thoughts range over past, present, and future*); **ranging fancy,** inconstant affections. **7.** (Of gun) throw projectile over, (of projectile) traverse, specified distance (*ranges over a mile*); obtain range of target by adjustment after firing past it or short of it. [ME, f. F *ranger* (*rang* RANK¹)]

rānge² (-nj) *n.* **1.** Row, line, tier, or series, of things, esp. of buildings or mountains. **2.** Lie, direction, (*the range of the strata is east and west*). **3.** Large open stretch of grazing or hunting ground; tract over which one ranges. **4.** Piece of ground or enclosure with targets for shooting. **5.** Area over which plant, animal, etc., is distributed, area included in or concerned with something, sphere, scope, compass, register, (region between) limits of variation, limited scale or series, distance attainable by gun or projectile, distance between gun etc. and objective, distance that can be traversed without refuelling etc., extent of time covered by forecast etc., (*gives the ranges of all species*; *the thorniest question in the whole range of politics*; *the range of her voice is astonishing*; *his reading is of very wide range*; *the range of the thermometer readings is about 10 degrees*; *Hebrew is out of my range*; *the enemy are out of range, have found the range of our camp*). **6.** Cooking fireplace usu. with oven(s), boiler(s), and iron top plate with openings for saucepans etc.; *electric or gas cooker. **7. ~-finder,** instrument for estimating distance of object, esp. one to be shot at or photographed. [ME f. OF, = row, rank (*ranger*; see prec.)]

rā'nger (-nj-) *n.* In vbl senses; keeper of a royal park, forest, etc., whence ~SHIP *n.*; *commando; member of body of mounted troops or other armed men; ||senior Guide. [ME, f. RANGE[1] + -ER[1]]

rā'ngy̆ (-njĭ) *a.* (Of person) tall and slim. [f. RANGE[1,2] + -Y[2]]

rani. See RANEE.

rănk[1] *n.* **1.** Row, line, queue; place where taxis stand to await customers; (Chess) row of squares across board (cf. FILE[3]). **2.** Number of soldiers drawn up in single line abreast; **the ~s,** or **the ~ and file,** common soldiers, i.e. privates and corporals, (fig.) ordinary undistinguished people; **close ~s,** maintain solidarity; **other ~s,** soldiers other than commissioned officers; **rise from the ~s,** advance by one's own exertions (of common soldier or sergeant who is given commission, or of self-made man). **3.** Order, array, (**keep ~, break ~,** remain, fail to remain, in line). **4.** Place in a scale; position in a hierarchy, grade of advancement; distinct social class, grade of dignity, station, high station, (*people of all ranks*; *in the front* or *top rank of performers*); **persons of ~,** members of nobility; **pull ~,** make unfair use of one's seniority etc.; **~ and fashion,** high society. [f. OF *ranc*, *renc*, f. Gmc **hrengaz* RING[1]]

rănk[2] *v.* **1.** *v.t.* Arrange (esp. soldiers) in rank; classify, give certain grade to; *take precedence of (person) in respect to rank. **2.** *v.i.* Have rank or place (*ranks among the Great Powers*, *next to the king*, etc.); *have senior position among members of hierarchy etc. [f. prec.]

rănk[3] *a.* **1.** Too luxuriant, coarse, over-productive, choked with or apt to produce weeds or excessive foliage. **2.** Foul-smelling, offensive; loathsome, indecent, corrupt. **3.** Strongly marked, unmistakable, flagrant, virulent, gross, complete, (*rank treason*, *pedantry*, *poison*, *nonsense*, *outsider*). **4.** Hence **~'**LY[2] *adv.*, **~'**NESS *n.* [OE *ranc*, = MLG *rank* long and thin, ON *rakkr* erect, f. Gmc **rankaz*]

ră'nker *n.* (Commissioned officer who has been) a soldier in the ranks. [f. RANK[1] + -ER[1]]

ră'nkle *v.i.* (Of envy, disappointment, etc., or their cause) be bitter, give intermittent or constant pain; (arch., of wound, sore, etc.) fester, continue painful. [ME in last sense, f. OF *rancler* (*rancle*, *raoncle*, *draoncle*, festering sore f. med. L *dranculus*, *dracunculus* dim. of *draco* serpent)]

ră'nsăck *v.t.* Thoroughly search (place, receptacle, person's pockets, one's conscience, etc.); pillage, plunder, (house, country, etc.). [ME, f. ON *rannsaka* (*rann* house, *-saka* f. *sœkja* seek)]

ră'nsom *n.*, & *v.t.* **1.** *n.* (Liberation of prisoner in consideration of) sum of money or value paid for release; **hold** person **to ~,** be willing to release him for such consideration, (fig.) demand concessions from by threat of damaging action; **worth a king's ~,** of immense value. **2.** *v.t.* Redeem, buy freedom or restoration of; atone for, expiate; hold to ransom, release for a ransom; exact ransom from. [ME, f. OF *ransoun(er)* f. L *redemptio -onis* REDEMPTION]

rănt *v.* & *n.* **1.** *v.i.* Use bombastic language. **2.** *v.t.* & *i.* Declaim, recite theatrically; preach noisily, whence (esp. arch. derog. of Primitive Methodist, and Hist. of sect of 17th-c. English antinomians) **~'**ER[1] *n.* **3.** *n.* Piece of ranting, tirade; empty turgid talk. [f. Du. *ranten* rave]

ranŭ'ncūl|us *n.* (*pl.* **~uses,** *or* **~i** *pr.* -ī). Plant of genus *Ranunculus*, e.g. buttercup; hence **~**A'CEOUS *a.*, of family Ranunculaceae. [L, orig. dim. of *rana* frog]

ranz-des-vaches (rahṅsdāvah'sh) *n.* Swiss herdsmen's melody played on alpenhorn or sung. [Swiss F]

||**R.A.O.C.** *abbr.* Royal Army Ordnance Corps.

răp[1] *n.* & *v.* (**-pp-**). **1.** *n.* Smart slight blow; **~ on** or **over the knuckles,** punishment inflicted on child, (fig.) reproof. **2.** (sl.) Blame, censure, punishment, etc.; **take the ~,** suffer the consequences. **3.** Sound made by knocker on door etc., or (Spiritualism) by some agency on table or floor. **4.** (sl.) A conversation. **5.** *v.t.* Strike (esp. person's knuckles) smartly; criticize adversely; **~ out,** utter (oath, pun, etc.) abruptly or on the spur of the moment, (Spiritualism) express (message, word) by raps. **6.** *v.i.* Make sound called rap (*rapped at the door*, *on the table*, etc.); (sl.) talk. [ME, prob. imit.]

răp[2] *n.* A small amount, the least bit, (*don't care a rap*). [earlier sense 18th-c. Irish counterfeit halfpenny, abbr. of Ir. *ropaire*]

rapā'cious (-shus) *a.* Grasping, extortionate, predatory; hence or cogn. **~**LY[2] *adv.*, **rapă'c**ITY *n.* [f. L *rapax -acis* (*rapere* snatch; see -ACIOUS)]

||**R.A.P.C.** *abbr.* Royal Army Pay Corps.

rāpe[1] *v.t.*, & *n.* **1.** *v.t.* (poet.) Take by force. **2.** Commit rape on (woman); hence **rā'p**IST (1) *n.* **3.** *n.* (poet.) Carrying off by force. **4.** Forcible or fraudulent sexual intercourse esp. imposed on woman; ***statutory ~,** sexual intercourse with girl below age of consent; (fig.) forcible interference with institution, country, etc., violation *of*. [ME, f. AF *rap(er)* f. L *rapere* seize]

||**rāpe**[2] *n.* (Hist.) Any of six divisions of Sussex. [OE, var. of *rāp* ROPE, w. ref. to fencing-off of land]

rāpe[3] *n.* Plant (*Brassica napus*) grown as food for sheep and for its seed from which oil is made, cole-seed; **~-cake,** rape-seed pressed into flat shape after extraction of oil and used as manure; **~-oil** (made from rape-seed and used as lubricant and in foodstuffs). [ME, f. L *rapum*, *rapa* turnip]

rāpe[4] *n.* Refuse of grapes after wine-making, used in making vinegar; vessel used in vinegar-making. [f. F *râpe*, med. L *raspa*]

ră'phĭa *n.* Var. of RAFFIA.

rā'phīde *n.* (Bot.) Needle-shaped crystal of irritant substance formed in plant. [back form. f. *raphides* pl. of *raphis* f. Gk *rhaphis -idos* needle]

ră'pĭd *a.* & *n.* **1.** *a.* Quick, swift; acting or completed in short time; (of slope) descending steeply; (Photogr.) fast; **~ eye-movement** (esp. during periods of dreaming); **~-fire,** firing shots, asking questions, etc., in quick succession; ***~ transit,** (1) high-speed urban transport of passengers, (2) lightning (chess); hence or cogn. **rapĭ'd**ITY *n.*, **~**LY[2] *adv.* **2.** *n.* (usu. in *pl.*) Steep descent in river-bed, with consequently swift current. [f. L *rapidus* (*rapere* seize; see -ID[1])]

ră'pĭer *n.* Light slender sword for thrusting only; **~-thrust,** (fig.) delicate or witty repartee.

[prob. f. Du. *rapier* or LG *rappir*, f. F *rapière*, of unkn. orig.]

ră′pīne *n.* (rhet.) Plundering, robbery. [ME f. OF, or f. L *rapina* (*rapere* seize; see -INE[4])]

rā′pĭst. See RAPE[1].

răpparee′ *n.* 17th-c. Irish irregular soldier or freebooter. [f. Ir. *rapaire* short pike]

răppee′ *n.* Coarse kind of snuff. [f. F (*tabac*) *râpé* RASPed (tobacco)]

răppĕ′l *n.*, & *v.i.* (||-ll-). (Make) descent of steep rock-face by using doubled rope fixed at higher point. [F, = recall (*rappeler* f. as RE-, APPEAL[1])]

rappōr′t (-ōr′) *n.* (Esp. useful) communication, (harmonious) relationship, or connection, (*in rapport with*); (Spiritualism) communication through medium. [F (*rapporter* f. as RE-, AP-, *porter* f. L *portare* carry)]

răppōrteur′ (-ēr′) *n.* Person who prepares account of proceedings of committee etc. for higher body. [F (as prec.)]

rapprochement (răprŏ′shmahṅ) *n.* Re-establishment or recommencement of harmonious relations, esp. between States. [F (*rapprocher* f. as RE- + APPROACH[1]; see -MENT)]

răpscă′llion (-lyon) *n.* (arch. or joc.) Rascal, scamp, rogue. [earlier *rascallion*, perh. f. RASCAL]

răpt *p.p.*, & *a.* **1.** *p.p.* Carried away bodily or in spirit from earth, from life, from consciousness, or from ordinary thoughts and perceptions (*away*, *up*, etc.). **2.** *a.* Absorbed, enraptured, intent, (*listen with rapt attention*); hence ~′LY[2] *adv.* [ME, f. L *raptus* p.p. of *rapere* seize]

ră′ptor *n.* Bird of prey (see foll.), of order Raptores. [L, = ravisher, plunderer, (*rapere rapt-* seize; see -OR)]

răptōr′ĭal *n.* & *a.* (Zool.) **1.** *n.* Bird (usu. large) which preys on other birds, mammals, etc.; bird of prey (eagle, falcon, owl, etc.); predatory animal or bird. **2.** *a.* Predatory; adapted for seizing prey. [f. L *raptor* (see prec.) + -IAL]

ră′pture *n.* **1.** Mental transport, ecstatic delight; (in *pl.*) vehement pleasure or the expression of it; **be in** or **go into ~s,** be enthusiastic, talk enthusiastically. **2.** (arch.) Act of transporting a person from one place to another. **3.** Hence **ră′ptur**OUS (-cher-) *a.* [obs. F, or f. med. L *raptura* (as RAPT; see -URE)]

ră′ptured (-cherd) *a.* (arch.) Enraptured, in ecstasy. [p.p. of obs. *rapture* v. (as prec.)]

rara avis (rār̄a ā′vĭs *or* rār̄a ă′vĭs) *n.* Rarity, kind of person or thing rarely encountered. [L, = rare bird]

rār̄e[1] *a.* **1.** With only loosely packed substance, of less than usual density (*the rare atmosphere of the mountain tops*). **2.** Few and far between, uncommon, unusual, exceptional, seldom found or occurring, (*it is rare for* person etc. *to* do; *it is rarely that* person etc. does). **3.** Of uncommon excellence, remarkably good, very amusing, (*a miracle of rare device*; *had rare fun with him*). **4. ~ bird,** *rara avis*; **~ earth,** (oxide of) lanthanide element; **~ gas,** = NOBLE *gas.* **5.** Hence ~′LY[2] (rār̄′lĭ) *adv.*, (esp.) seldom, not often, finely, in an unusual degree, ~′NESS (rār̄′n-) *n.* [ME, f. L *rarus*]

rār̄e[2] *a.* (Of meat) underdone. [var. of obs. *rear* half-cooked (of eggs), f. OE *hrēr*]

rār̄′ebĭt (rār̄′b-) *n.* See WELSH[1].

rār̄′ee-show (-ō) *n.* Show carried about in a box, peep-show; any show or spectacle. [app. = *rare show* as pronounced by Savoyard showmen]

rār̄′ė|fȳ *v.* **1.** *v.t.* Lessen density or solidity of (esp. gas); purify, refine, (person's nature etc.); make (idea etc.) subtle. **2.** *v.i.* Become less dense. **3.** So ~FA′CTION, ~FICA′TION, *ns.*, **~fă′ct**IVE *a.* [ME, f. OF *rarefier* or med. L *rarificare* f. L *rarefacere* (*rarus* rare, *facere* make); see -FY]

rār̄′ĭng *a.* (colloq.) Enthusiastic, eager, (*to go* etc.). [part. of *rare*, dial. var. of ROAR or REAR[2]]

rār̄′ĭtȳ *n.* Rareness (see RARE[1]); uncommon thing, thing valued as being rare. [f. F *rareté*, or f. L *raritas* (as RARE[1]; see -ITY)]

||**R.A.S.C.** *abbr.* (Hist.) Royal Army Service Corps.

ra′scal (rah′-) *n.* & *a.* **1.** *n.* Rogue, knave, scamp, (often joc., esp. to child: *you lucky rascal!*). **2.** *a.* (arch.) Belonging to the rabble; **the ~ rout,** the common people. **3.** Hence ~DOM, ~ISM (2), **răscă′l**ITY, *ns.*, ~LY[1] *a.* [ME, f. OF *rascaille* rabble, prob. f. ONF **rasque* f. Rom. **rasica* (**rasicare* f. L *radere ras-* scrape)]

raschĕ′l (-sh-) *n.* Fabric like tricot but more loosely knitted. [f. G *Raschelmaschine*, kind of knitting-machine f. as RACHEL]

rase. See RAZE.

răsh[1] *n.* Eruption of the skin in spots or patches; (fig.) sudden widespread onset *of* (*a rash of strikes*). [cf. OF *ra(s)che* eruptive sores, = It. *raschia* itch]

răsh[2] *a.* Hasty, impetuous, overbold, reckless, acting or done without due consideration; hence ~′LY[2] *adv.*, ~′NESS *n.* [ME, f. OE **ræsc*, = MDu. *rasch*, OHG *rasc*, ON *röskr* f. Gmc **raskuz*, perh. cogn. w. RATHE]

ră′sher *n.* Thin slice of bacon or ham. [16th c., of unkn. orig.]

rasp (rah-) *n.* & *v.* **1.** *n.* Coarse kind of file having separate teeth. **2.** *v.t.* Scrape with rasp; scrape roughly; grate upon (person or his feelings), irritate; scrape *off* or *away*; say gratingly. **3.** *v.i.* Make grating sound. **4.** Hence ~′ER[1] *n.*, (esp., Hunting) high difficult fence. [ME, f. OF *raspe(r)* f. Rom. **raspare* f. WG **raspōn* scrape together]

ra′spatorȳ (rah′-) *n.* Rasp used in surgery. [f. F *raspatoire* or f. med. L **raspatorium* (*raspare* RASP; see -ORY)]

ra′spberrȳ (rah′zb-) *n.* **1.** (Bramble *Rubus idaeus* bearing) usu. red berry of numerous drupels on conical receptacle. **2.** (sl.) Sound, gesture, or sign expressing dislike, derision, or disapproval; dismissal. **3. ~-cane,** raspberry plant; **~ vinegar,** kind of syrup made from raspberries. [f. 16th c. *rasp* (now dial.) f. obs. *raspis*, of unkn. orig., + BERRY[1]]

ră′ssė (*or* răs) *n.* Small civet. [f. Jav. *rase*]

ră′ster *n.* Pattern of scanning lines for cathode-ray tube picture. [G, = screen, f. L *rastrum* rake (*radere ras-* scrape)]

răt[1] *n.*, & *v.i.* (-tt-). **1.** *n.* Rodent of genus *Rattus* (**like a drowned ~,** (of person) wet through; **Rats!,** (sl.) nonsense!, incredible!, etc.; **smell a ~,** have suspicions of foul play etc.) similar rodent (MUSK-*rat*, WATER[1]-*rat*). **2.** (Polit.) Person who deserts his party in difficulties as rats are said to desert a doomed house or ship, turncoat. **3.** Workman who refuses to join strike, takes striker's place, or accepts less than trade-union wages. **4. ~′bag,** (Austral. & N.Z. sl.) unpleasant or eccentric person; **~-catcher** (who rids houses of rats), (sl.) unorthodox hunting dress; **~ kangaroo,** (Austral.) small ratlike marsupial; **~ race,** fiercely competitive struggle, struggle to maintain one's position in work or life; **~′sbane,** thing (esp. plant) poisonous to rats; **~′s-tail,** thing shaped like a rat's tail, e.g. kind of file; **~-tail,** (1) grenadier fish, (2) (horse with) hairless horse's tail; *~-tail(ed) spoon* (with tail-like prolongation of handle along back of bowl). **5.** *v.i.* (Of person or dog) hunt or kill rats; play the rat in politics; **~ on,** desert (person), break (promise); hence **~′t**ER[1] *n.* [OE *ræt* & OF *rat* f. Rom. **rattus*]

răt[2] *v.t.* (**-tt-;** esp. in 3 sing. pres. subj.; arch., vulg.) = DRAT. [corrupt. of ROT[2]]

ra'ta (rah'-) *n.* Large handsome New Zealand tree with crimson flowers and hard red wood. [Maori]

rā'table. Var. of RATEABLE.

rătafi'a (-ē'*a*) *n.* Liqueur flavoured with almonds or kernels of peach, apricot, or cherry; kind of biscuit similarly flavoured. [F, prob. rel. to TAFIA (Creole)]

rată'n. Var. of RATTAN.

rătaplă'n *n.* & *v.* (-**nn**-). **1.** *n.* Drumming sound. **2.** *v.t.* Play (as) on drum. **3.** *v.i.* Make rataplan. [F; imit.]

rătată't. Var. of RAT-TAT.

ratatouille (rahtahtōō'ĭ) *n.* Provençal stew of vegetables. [F dial.]

rătch *n.* Ratchet(-wheel). [perh. f. G *ratsche*; cf. foll.]

ră'tchĕt *n.*, & *v.t.* (-**tt**-). **1.** *n.* Set of teeth on edge of bar or wheel in which pawl etc. engages to ensure motion in one direction only; ~(**-wheel**), wheel with rim so toothed. **2.** *v.t.* Provide with ratchet; make into ratchet. [f. F *rochet* blunt lance-head, bobbin, ratchet, etc.; cf. It. *rocchetto* spool, ratchet, dim. f. Rom. **rokk*- f. Gmc **rukkon*]

rāte[1] *n.* **1.** Stated value of numerical proportion prevailing or to prevail between two sets of things (*moving at a rate of ten miles per hour*; *watch gains at the rate of two minutes a day*; BIRTH *rate*, DEATH *rate*); amount etc. mentioned in one case for application to all similar ones; standard or way of reckoning; (measure of) value, tariff charge, cost, (*rate of exchange*, *of interest*); speed (*travelling at a great rate*; *prices increasing at a dreadful rate*); **at that** or **this** ~, (colloq.) if this is a fair specimen, if this assumption is true, etc.; **at any** ~, in each or any possible case, even if a stronger statement is doubtfully true, etc. **2.** ||Assessment levied by local authorities for local purposes at so much per pound of assessed value of buildings and land owned; (in *pl.*) amount thus paid by householder etc. **3.** Class (*first-rate*; often derog. *second*, *third*, etc., *-rate*). **4.** ||~'**payer,** person liable to pay RATE[1]s (sense 2). [ME f. OF, f. med. L *rata* (L *pro rata parte* or *portione* according to the proportional share), f. *ratus* p.p. of *rēri* reckon]

rāte[2] *v.* **1.** *v.t.* Estimate worth or value of (*I do not rate his merits high*; *each offence is rated at a fixed penalty*; OVERRATE, UNDERRATE); assign fixed value to (coin, metal) in relation to monetary standard (*the copper coinage is rated much above its real value*); assign value to (work, power of machine, etc.). **2.** Consider, regard as, (*I rate him among my benefactors*). **3.** ||Subject to payment of a local rate; value for purpose of assessing rates on. **4.** (Naut.) Class under a certain RATING[1]. **5.** *Be worthy of, deserve. **6.** *v.i.* Rank or be rated *as*. [ME, f. prec.]

rāte[3] *v.t.* Scold angrily. [ME, of unkn. orig.]

rāte[4]. Var. of RET.

rā'te|able (-*ta*-) *a.* **1.** (arch.) Proportional. **2.** ||Liable to payment of RATE[1]s (sense 2) (**~able value,** value at which house etc. is assessed for this); hence ~ABI'LITY (-*ta*-) *n.* **3.** Hence ~**ab**LY[2] (-*ta*-) *adv.* [f. RATE[2] + -ABLE]

rā'tel (*or* rah'-) *n.* African and Indian nocturnal carnivorous burrowing mammal of genus *Mellivora*. [Afrik.; orig. unkn.]

rath (rah-) *n.* (Ir. etc. Ant.) Prehistoric hill-fort. [Ir.]

rāthe (-dh) *a.* (poet.) Coming, blooming, etc., early in the year or day; **~-ripe,** ripening early, precocious. [OE *hræth*, *hræd*, = OHG (*h*)*rad*, ON *hrathr*, Goth. **raths* f. Gmc **hrathaz*; cf. RASH[2]]

ra'ther (rah'dh-) *adv.* **1.** More truly, to a greater extent, as a more accurate description or preferable account of the matter, or to be more precise, (*is rather good than bad*; *derived rather from imagination than from reason*; *orderliness is not the result of law, rather is it the cause of it*; *late last night, or rather, early this morning*); **the ~ that,** so much the more because. **2.** In a modified way, to some extent, slightly, somewhat, (*I rather think you know him*; *the performance was rather a failure, was rather good, was rather a good one, was rather better than I expected*, *fell rather flat*). **3.** By preference, for choice, sooner, as an alternative chosen sooner *than* another (of same grammatical form, or inf. after finite v.; *would much rather not go*; *he would rather have died than refused*; *use soft water rather than hard*; *the desire to seem clever rather than honest*; *he resigned rather than act dishonestly*); **had ~,** would rather (*I had rather err with Plato than be right with Horace*). **4.** ||(colloq.) (In answer) most emphatically, yes without doubt, assuredly, (*Have you been here before?—R~!*). [ME, f. OE *hrathor*, compar. of *hræthe* adv. f. *hræth* a.; see prec.]

***ra'thskĕller** (rah'ts-) *n.* Beer-saloon or restaurant in basement. [G, = (restaurant in) town-hall cellar]

ră'tĭ|fȳ *v.t.* Confirm or accept (agreement made in one's name) by formal consent, signature, etc.; so ~FICA'TION *n.* [ME, f. OF *ratifier* f. med. L *ratificare* (as RATE[1]; see -FY)]

rā'tĭng[1] *n.* In vbl senses; ||amount fixed as local rate; (Naut.) person's position or class on ship's books, ||non-commissioned sailor; any of the classes into which racing yachts are distributed by tonnage; estimated number of audience as index of popularity of a broadcast; estimated standing etc. of person (CREDIT[1] *rating*). [f. RATE[2] + -ING[1]]

rā'tĭng[2] *n.* Angry reprimand. [f. RATE[3] + -ING[1]]

rā'tĭō (-shĭō) *n.* (*pl.* ~**s**). Quantitative relation between two similar magnitudes determined by the number of times one contains the other integrally or fractionally (*are in the ratio of three to two* or *3:2*; *the ratios 1:5 and 20:100 are the same*; INVERSE *ratio*). [L (as RATE[1]; see -ION)]

rătĭŏ'cĭn|āte (*or* răshĭ-) *v.i.* Go through logical processes, reason formally, use syllogisms; so ~A'TION *n.*, ~ATIVE *a.* [f. L *ratiocinari* (as prec.) + -ATE[3]]

ră'tion *n.*, & *v.t.* **1.** *n.* (usu. in *pl.*) Fixed daily allowance of food served out esp. for members of Services (and formerly of forage for animals). **2.** Fixed allowance of food etc. for civilians in time of shortage (~ **book, card,** document entitling holder to a ration); single portion *of* provisions, fuel, clothing, etc.; (in *pl.*) provisions; **given out with the ~s,** (sl.) awarded without regard to merit. **3.** *v.t.* Limit (persons, food, clothing) to fixed ration; ~ (**out**), share (food etc.) in fixed quantities. [F, f. It. *razione* or Sp. *ración* f. L *ratio -onis* reckoning, RATIO]

ră'tional *a.* **1.** Endowed with reason, reasoning; sensible, sane, moderate, not foolish or absurd or extreme; of or based on reasoning or reason, rejecting what is unreasonable or cannot be tested by reason in religion or custom; ~ **dress,** (Hist., esp.) knickerbockers worn by women instead of skirts; ~ **leanings,** doubts about the truth of divine revelation, the possibility of miracles, etc. **2.** (Math.) (Of quantity or ratio) expressible without radical signs (opp. *surd*). **3.** Hence or cogn. ~ITY (-ă'l-) *n.*, ~LY[2] *adv.* [ME, f. L *rationalis* (as prec.; see -AL)]

rătiona'le (-ah'l *or* -ah'lĭ) *n.* Reasoned exposition, statement of reasons; fundamental reason, logical basis, *of.* [mod. L, neut. (as n.) of L *rationalis* (see prec.)]

ră'tional|ĭsm *n.* Practice of explaining the supernatural in religion in a way consonant with reason, or of treating reason as the ultimate authority in religion as elsewhere; theory that reason is the foundation of certainty in knowledge (opp. *empiricism, sensationalism*); so ~IST (2) *n.*, ~ĭ'stIC *a.* [f. RATIONAL + -ISM]

ră'tionalīz|e, -īs|e (-īz), *v.* **1.** *v.t.* Explain (*away*) by rationalism, bring into conformity with reason; (Math.) clear of surds; make (an industry) more efficient by scientifically reducing or eliminating waste of labour, time, or materials. **2.** *v.i.* Be or act as rationalist; (colloq.) find 'reasons' for irrational or unworthy behaviour. **3.** Hence ~A'TION *n.* [f. RATIONAL + -IZE]

ră'tīte *a.* (Of bird) having keelless breastbone, e.g. ostrich, emu, cassowary, (opp. *carinate*). [f. L *ratis* raft + -ITE[2]]

ră'tlīne, -lĭn, -lĭng, *n.* (usu. in *pl.*) One of the small lines fastened across ship's shrouds like ladder-rungs. [ME; orig. unkn.]

ratoo͞'n *n.*, & *v.i.* **1.** *n.* New shoot springing from sugar-cane etc. root after cropping. **2.** *v.i.* Send up ratoons. [f. Sp. *retoño* sprout]

rattă'n *n.* E. Ind. climbing palm of genus *Calamus* etc. with long thin many-jointed pliable stems; piece of rattan stem used as cane etc. [earlier *rot(t)ang* f. Malay *rōtan* (prob. f. *raut* pare)]

răt-tă't, răt-tăt-tă't, *n.* Rapping sound, esp. of knocker. [imit.]

ră'ttle[1] *v.* **1.** *v.i.* Give out rapid succession of short sharp hard sounds, cause such sounds by shaking something (*he rattled at the door*); talk in lively thoughtless way (*on, away, along*); move or fall with rattling noise, drive vehicle or ride or run briskly, (*down, along, past,* etc.). **2.** *v.t.* Make (chain, window, crockery, etc.) rattle (~ **the sabre,** threaten war); say or recite (verses, stories, lists, oaths) rapidly (*off, out, over, away,* etc.); (sl.) excite, agitate, fluster, make nervous, frighten; make move quickly. [ME, prob. f. MDu. & LG *ratelen* (imit.)]

ră'ttle[2] *n.* **1.** Instrument or plaything made to rattle esp. in order to give alarm or to amuse babies; set of horny rings in rattlesnake's tail; plant with seeds that rattle in their cases when ripe (**red** ~, pink-flowered marsh plant *Pedicularis palustris*; **yellow** ~, yellow-flowered plant of genus *Rhinanthis*); rattling sound (DEATH-*rattle*); uproar, bustle, noisy gaiety, racket; noisy flow of words, empty chatter, trivial talk; lively incessant talker. **2.** **~-bag, -bladder, -box,** rattle constructed of bag etc. with objects inside; **~-brain, -head, -pate,** (person with) frivolous mind; **~snake,** venomous Amer. snake with rattling structure in tail; **~trap** *n.* & *a.*, rickety (vehicle etc.), (in *pl.*) curiosities, odds and ends. [f. prec.]

ră'ttler *n.* In vbl senses; remarkably good specimen of anything; *rattlesnake; *goods train. [ME, f. RATTLE[1] + -ER[1]]

ră'ttlĭng *a.* In vbl senses; brisk, vigorous, (a *rattling wind, pace*); ~ **good** etc., remarkably good etc. [f. RATTLE[1] + -ING[2]]

ră'ttȳ *a.* Relating to or infested with rats; (sl.) irritable, touchy. [f. RAT[1] + -Y[2]]

rau'cous *a.* Hoarse, harsh-sounding; hence ~LY[2] *adv.*, ~NESS *n.* [f. L *raucus* + -OUS]

***rau'nch|ȳ** *a.* Slovenly; coarsely outspoken; hence ~ĭLY[2] *adv.*, ~ĭNESS *n.* [20th c.; orig. unkn.]

ră'vage *v.* & *n.* **1.** *v.t.* & *i.* Devastate, plunder, make havoc (in). **2.** *n.* Devastation, damage; (esp. in *pl.*) destructive effect *of*. [f. F *ravage(r)* alt. f. *ravine* rush of water; see -AGE]

‖**R.A.V.C.** *abbr.* Royal Army Veterinary Corps.

rāve[1] *n.* Rail of cart; (in *pl.*) permanent or removable framework added to sides of cart to increase capacity. [var. of dial. *rathe* (15th c., of unkn. orig.)]

rāve[2] *v.* & *n.* **1.** *v.i.* Talk wildly or furiously (as) in delirium (*about, against, at, of, for*); **raving mad,** uncontrollably mad so as to rave. **2.** (Of sea, wind, etc.) howl, roar. **3.** Speak with rapturous admiration *about, of, over*; go into raptures; **raving beauty,** notably beautiful person. **4.** *v.t.* Utter with ravings (*rave* one's *grief* etc.); make one*self hoarse* etc. by raving. **5.** Hence **rā'**VING[1] (1) *n.* (usu. in *pl.*). **6.** *n.* Raving sound of wind etc.; (colloq.) highly enthusiastic review (of film, play, etc.); (sl.) infatuation; ~**(-up)**, (sl.) lively party. [ME, prob. f. ONF *raver*, rel. to (M)LG *reven* be senseless, rave]

ră'vel *v.* (‖-ll-) & *n.* **1.** *v.t.* & *i.* Entangle or become entangled or knotted, confuse, complicate, (thread etc.; (fig.) question, problem; *the ravelled skein of life*); fray out, whence ~**L**ING[1] (2) *n.* **2.** *v.t.* ~ (**out**), disentangle, unravel, distinguish the separate threads or subdivisions of. **3.** *n.* Tangle, knot, complication; frayed or loose end. [perh. f. Du. *ravelen*, tangle, fray out, unweave, LG *rebbeln* to ripple flax]

ră'velĭn (-vl-) *n.* (Hist.) Outwork of fortifications, with two faces forming salient angle. [F, f. obs. It. *ravellino*, of unkn. orig.]

rā'ven[1] *n.* & *a.* **1.** *n.* Large glossy blue-black hoarse-voiced bird (*Corvus corax*) feeding chiefly on flesh, often kept tame, sometimes thought to be of evil omen. **2.** *a.* Glossy black (~ **locks,** black hair). [OE *hræfn*, = OS *-hraban*, OHG *(h)raban*, ON *hrafn* f. Gmc **hrabhnaz*, **hrabhan*]

ră'ven[2] *v.* **1.** *v.i.* Plunder, go plundering *about*, seek *after* prey or booty, prowl for prey; have ravenous appetite (*for*). **2.** *v.t.* Devour (food, or abs.) voraciously. [f. OF *raviner* ravage f. Rom. **rapinare* f. L *rapina* RAPINE]

ră'venous *a.* Rapacious; voracious (*ravenous hunger, eagerness,* etc.); famished, very hungry; hence ~LY[2] *adv.*, ~NESS *n.* [ME, f. OF *ravineus* (as prec.; see -OUS)]

ră'vĭn *n.* (poet. or rhet.) Robbery, rapine; (seizing and devouring of) prey (**beast of** ~, beast of prey). [ME f. OF *ravine* f. L *rapina* RAPINE]

ravi'n|e (-ē'n) *n.* Deep narrow gorge, mountain cleft; hence ~ED[2] (-ē'nd) *a.* [F (as prec.)]

răvĭō'lĭ *n.* Small pasta cases containing meat etc. [It.]

ră'vĭsh *v.t.* **1.** (arch.) Carry off (person, thing) by force; (of death, circumstances, etc.) take from life or from sight. **2.** Commit rape on (woman); hence ~ER[1] *n.* **3.** Enrapture, charm, entrance, fill with delight; hence or cogn. ~ING[2] *a.*, ~MENT *n.* [ME, f. OF *ravir* f. Rom. **rapire* f. L *rapere* seize; see -ISH[2]]

raw *a.* & *n.* **1.** *a.* Uncooked; (of brick) not hardened by fire; not roasted (*raw* SIENNA, *raw* UMBER); unripe; in unwrought state, not or not completely manufactured; (of silk) as reeled from cocoons; (of cloth) unfulled; (of alcoholic spirit) undiluted; (of grain) unmalted; (of statistics etc.) not analysed or corrected. **2.** Crude in artistic quality, lacking finish. **3.** Inexperienced, untrained, fresh to a thing, (*is a raw lad; raw recruits*). **4.** Stripped of skin, having the flesh exposed, sensitive to touch from being so exposed; (of edge of cloth) without hem or selvage. **5.** (Of atmosphere, day, etc.) damp and chilly. **6.** **~-boned,** with bones almost exposed, gaunt; *raw* DEAL[2]; **~'hide,** (rope or whip of) untanned leather; ~ **material,** that out of which any process of manufacture makes the articles it produces (*the finished product of one industry is the raw material of another; the raw material of an army is men*). **7.** Hence ~'ISH[1] 2 *a.*, ~'NESS *n.* **8.** *n.* Raw place on person's or esp. horse's skin; **in the ~**, (1) in its natural state without mitigation (*life in the raw*), (2) naked; **touch** person **on the ~**, wound his feelings on the point(s) on which he is sensitive. [OE *hrēaw*, = OS, OHG (*h*)*rāo*, ON *hrár* f. Gmc **hrawaz* f. IE **krowos*]

ray[1] *n.* **1.** Single line or narrow beam of light from small or distant source; straight line in which radiation is propagated to given point; (in *pl.*) radiation of specified type (COSMIC, GAMMA, *rays*; X-RAYS); ~ **gun**, imaginary weapon causing injury by emission of rays. **2.** (fig.) Fragment or remnant or beginning of enlightening or cheering influence (*a ray of hope, truth, genius*, etc.). **3.** Any of a set of straight lines passing through one point; any of a set of radiating lines or parts or things. **4.** (Bot.) marginal part of composite flower, e.g. daisy; (Zool.) one of set of bones etc. supporting fish's fin, radial division of starfish. **5.** Hence ~ED[2] (rād), ~'LESS, *adjs.*, ~'LET *n.* [ME, f. OF *rai* f. L RADIUS]

ray[2] *v.* **1.** *v.i.* (Of light etc., or fig. of thought, hope, etc.) issue, come *forth*, *off*, or *out*, in rays. **2.** *v.t.* & *i.* Radiate. [f. prec., or F *rayer*, OF *raier* f. L *radiare* (RADIUS)]

ray[3] *n.* Large sea-fish of order Hypotremata, allied to shark, with broad flat body, used as food, esp. the skate. [ME, f. OF *raie* f. L *raia*]

ray[4], **re**[1] (rā), *n.* (Mus.) Second note of scale in movable-doh system; the note D in fixed-doh system. [ME *re* f. L *resonare*; see GAMUT]

ray'ah (rī'*a*) *n.* (Hist.) Non-Muslim subject of Ottoman empire. [f. Turk. *râya* pl. of *raiyye* f. Arab. *ra'īya* flock, subjects (*ra'ā* to pasture)]

ray'ŏn *n.* Textile fibre or fabric made from cellulose. [P; arbitr. f. RAY[1]]

rāze, rāse (-z), *v.t.* **1.** Completely destroy, level with the ground, (town, house, walls, etc.; usu. *raze to the ground*). **2.** Erase, scratch out, (esp. fig.; *raze* person's *name from remembrance*). **3.** (arch.) Wound slightly, graze. [ME *rase* in sense 3 f. OF *raser* shave close f. Rom. **rasare* f. L *radere ras-* scrape]

razee' *n.*, & *v.t.* (Hist.) **1.** *n.* Ship reduced in height by removal of upper deck(s). **2.** *v.t.* Turn into a razee; make smaller by cutting. [f. F *rasé(e)* (fem.) p.p. of *raser* (see prec.)]

rā'zor *n.*, & *v.t.* **1.** *n.* Instrument with sharp edge(s) used in cutting hair esp. from skin; SAFETY *razor*. **2.** **~-back,** back sharp as razor's edge (*~-back whale*, rorqual); **~-bill,** auk (*Alca torda*) with sharp-edged black-and-white bill; *razor*-BLADE; **~-edge,** keen edge, sharp mountain ridge, critical situation, sharp line of division (*keep on the razor-edge of orthodoxy*; *on a ~-edge* or *~'s edge*, in great danger); **~-fish, -shell,** bivalve of family Solenidae with shell like handle of cutthroat razor; **~-slasher,** criminal who attacks victims with razor. **3.** *v.t.* Use razor on; shave, cut down close. [ME, f. OF *rasor* (as RAZE; see -OR)]

***răzz** *n.*, & *v.t.* **1.** *n.* = RASPBERRY 2. **2.** *v.t.* Tease, ridicule. [f. *razzberry*, corrupt. of RASPBERRY]

ră'zzia *n.* Raid, plundering or slave-collecting expedition, orig. as carried out by African Muslims. [F, f. Algerian Arab. *ġazia*, Arab. *ġazwa* (*ġazw* make raids); Arab. *ġ* pr. like F velar *r*]

ră'zzle(-dăzzle) *n.* (sl.) Excitement, bustle, stir, spree (*on the razzle*); noisy advertising. [redupl. of DAZZLE]

răzzmată'zz *n.* (colloq.) = prec.; old-fashioned, sentimental, or insincere actions; humbug. [prob. alt. f. prec.]

Rb *symb.* rubidium.

R.C. *abbr.* Red Cross; reinforced concrete; Roman Catholic.

R.C.A. *abbr.* *Radio Corporation of America; ||Royal College of Art.

R.C.A.F. *abbr.* Royal Canadian Air Force.

||**R.C.M.** *abbr.* Royal College of Music.

R.C.M.P. *abbr.* Royal Canadian Mounted Police.

R.C.N. *abbr.* Royal Canadian Navy; ||Royal College of Nursing.

||**R.C.O.** *abbr.* Royal College of Organists.

||**R.C.P.** *abbr.* Royal College of Physicians.

||**R.C.S.** *abbr.* Royal College of Science; Royal College of Surgeons; Royal Corps of Signals.

||**R.C.T.** *abbr.* Royal Corps of Transport.

||**R.C.V.S.** *abbr.* Royal College of Veterinary Surgeons.

R.D. *abbr.* refer to drawer; ||Royal Naval Reserve Decoration.

Rd. *abbr.* road.

||**R.D.C.** *abbr.* (Hist.) Rural District Council.

re[1]. See RAY[4].

rē[2] *prep.* **1.** (Law etc.) In the matter of (as first word of headline stating matter to be dealt with). **2.** (colloq.) About, concerning. [L, abl. of *res* thing]

're *v.* (colloq., chiefly after pronouns) = *are* (see BE). [abbr.]

rè- (*or* rē, esp. in senses 8 & 9, *or* rĕ) *pref.* in vbs. and vbl derivatives (sometimes *red-* before vowels: *redeem*, *redolent*, *redound*), denoting: **1.** In return, mutual(ly), (*react*, *rebound*, *remunerate*, *resemble*, *respond*, *revenge*). **2.** Opposition (*rebel*, *rebuff*, *reluctant*, *repel*, *resist*). **3.** Behind, after, (*relic*, *remain*, *repent*, *retain*, *retard*). **4.** Retirement, secrecy, (*recluse*, *recondite*, *refuge*, *reticence*). **5.** Off, away, down, (*rebuke*, *recede*, *relegate*, *renounce*, *repress*, *resolve*). **6.** Frequentative or intensive force (*redouble*, *refine*, *regard*, *remark*, *research*, *resonant*, *revile*). **7.** Negative force (*recant*, *reprobate*, *resign*).

In senses 8 & 9 (which are not always distinguishable) *re-* can be prefixed to almost any E vb. or vbl derivative; it is often hyphenated in British use in wds made for the occasion, in wds having homonyms, and before *e* (*re-contravention*, *re-pair* = pair again, *re-entry*).

8. Once more, again, afresh, (esp. in order to alter or improve or renew): *readjust*, *reaffirm*, *reapply*, *reappraise*, *rearrange*, *reassert*, *reassess*, *reassign*, *rebaptize*, *rebroadcast*, *rebuild*, *recapitulate*, *recite*, *recoin*, *recolonize*, *recolour*, *recombine*, *recommence*, *recompose*, *redecorate*, *redesign*, *redistribute*, *redivide*, *redress*, *redye*, *re-edit*, *refashion*, *refectory*, *refurnish*, *regenerate*, *regenesis*, *regrind*, *regroup*, *rehear*, *rehouse*, *reimpose*, *reinter*, *relabel*, *remint*, *rename*, *reorder*, *reorganize*, *repack*, *repaper*, *repartition*, *repeat*, *replant*, *represent*, *repressurize*, *reprovision*, *republish*, *reread*, *rerun*, *resettle*, *reshape*, *resole*, *restart*, *restock*, *resurface*, *resurvey*, *retell*, *retrim*, *returf*, *retype*, *reuse*, *revaccinate*, *revictual*, *revise*, *revisit*, *rewind*, *rework*. **9.** Back, with return to previous state after lapse or cessation or occurrence of opposite state: *reabsorb*, *readmit*, *reafforest*, *reanimate*, *reappear*, *reappoint*, *reascend*, *reassemble*, *reassume*, *recalesce*, *recall*, *receive*, *recidivist*, *recombine*, *reconquer*, *reconvert*, *recross*, *recumbent*, *recur*, *redescend*, *rediscover*, *redissolve*, *reduce*, *re-elect*, *re-embark*, *re-emerge*, *re-enact*, *re-engage*, *re-enter*, *re-establish*, *re-export*, *reforest*, *refresh*, *refurbish*, *regain*, *regerminate*, *regild*, *regress*, *reheat*, *rehumanize*, *reignite*, *reimport*, *reimpose*, *reincorporate*, *reinsert*, *reintroduce*, *reinvigorate*, *reject*, *rekindle*, *relax*, *remilitarize*, *renationalize*, *renew*, *renovate*, *reoccupy*, *reopen*, *repatriate*, *repeople*, *replace*, *replenish*, *repolish*, *repopulate*, *repurchase*, *repurify*, *requicken*, *resilient*, *resuscitate*, *retort*, *retract*, *retrieve*, *reunite*, *reverse*, *revitalize*, *revive*. [f. L *re-*, *red-*, again, back, etc.]

||**R.E.** *abbr.* Royal Engineers.

Re *symb.* rhenium.

reach[1] *v.* **1.** *v.t.* & *i.* Stretch out, extend, (*out* etc.; *reached out his hand, its branches; a dominion reaching from the Ebro to the Carpathians*). **2.** *v.i.* Stretch out the hand etc., make reaching motion or effort (lit. or fig.; *you must reach out further; mind reaches forward to an ideal; ship reaches ahead in race*). **3.** (Naut.) Sail with wind abeam or abaft the beam. **4.** *v.t.* Get as far as, attain to, arrive at, (specified point or object of destination, or abs.), succeed in affecting with the hand or instrument or missile or influence, (*reach* BOTTOM[1] 2; *reached land; could not reach his enemy*, esp. in fencing, boxing; *how is her conscience to be reached?; is on vacation and cannot be reached; libels that the ordinary law reaches; the steps by which you reach the entrance; your letter reached me today; every syllable reached the audience; has reached agreement with them, a decision, middle age, its sixth edition; cannot reach so high, far enough, down, up to it*, etc.; *number of applications reached 200; as far as the eye could reach*, to the greatest distance visible; *my income will not reach to it*). **5.** Hand, pass or take with outstretched hand, (*reached him the book; reached down his hat*). **6.** ‖**~-me-down** *a.* & *n.*, (sl.) ready-made (garment). **7.** Hence **~'ABLE** *a.* [f. OE *rǣcan*, MDu., MLG *reiken*, OHG *reichen* f. WG **raikjan*]

reach[2] *n.* **1.** Act of reaching out. **2.** Extent to which hand etc. can be reached out, influence be exerted, motion be carried out, or mental powers be used, range, scope, compass, (**within** one's **~**, **above, out of, beyond,** one's **~**, possible, impossible, of being grasped by stretching out the hand or (fig.) of attainment or performance; *has a wide reach; within easy reach of the airport; no help was within reach*). **3.** Continuous extent, esp. part of river that can be looked along at once between two bends, or part of canal between locks. **4.** (Naut.) Distance traversed in reaching. [f. prec.]

rėă'ct[1] *v.* **1.** *v.i.* Produce reciprocal or responsive effect, act upon the agent, (*they react upon each other*); (Chem. of substance, Phys. of particle etc.) be the cause of activity or interaction *with* another (*nitrous oxide reacts with the metal*), whence **~ANT** *n.* **2.** Respond *to* stimulus, undergo change or show behaviour due to some influence. **3.** (Mil.) Make counter-attack(s). **4.** Be actuated by repulsion *against*, tend in reverse or backward direction. **5.** *v.t.* (Chem.) Cause (substance etc.) to react *with* another. [f. RE- 1 + ACT[2], & f. med. L RE(*agere* act, do)]

rē-ă'ct[2] *v.t.* Act again. [f. RE- 8 + ACT[2]]

rėă'ctance *n.* (Electr.) Component of impedance of alternating-current circuit etc. due to capacitance or inductance or both. [f. REACT[1] + -ANCE]

rėă'ction *n.* **1.** Responsive or reciprocal action (esp. *action and reaction*); (Chem. & Phys.) reacting of one substance etc. with another; CHAIN *reaction*. **2.** Response of organ etc. to external stimulus; responsive feeling (*what was his reaction to this news?*); immediate or first impression. **3.** Occurrence of condition after interval of opposite (e.g. glow felt after cold bath, depression after excitement). **4.** (Mil.) Counter-stroke. **5.** Tendency to oppose change or to return to former system esp. in politics, whence **~IST** (2) *n.* **6.** Propulsion by emission of jet of particles etc. in direction opposite to that of desired motion. [f. REACT[1] + -ION, & f. med. L RE(*actio* ACTION)]

rėă'ctionarў *a.* & *n.* (Polit.) (Person) tending to oppose change or seeking to return to former system. [f. prec. + -ARY[1]]

rėă'ctiv|āte *v.t.* Restore to a state of activity; hence **~A'TION** *n.* [f. RE- 9 + ACTIVATE]

rėă'ctĭve *a.* Showing reaction; pertaining to reactance; hence **rēăctĭ'vITY** *n.* [f. REACT[1] + -IVE]

rėă'ctor *n.* In vbl senses; (Med.) patient etc. reacting positively to foreign substance; (**nuclear**) **~**, assembly of materials in which controlled nuclear chain reaction takes place; (Electr.) component used to provide reactance, esp. inductance; apparatus for chemical reaction of substances. [f. REACT[1] + -OR]

read *v.* (**read** *pr.* rĕd) & *n.* **1.** *v.t.* Interpret mentally, declare interpretation or coming development of, (*read dream, riddle, omen, men's hearts* or *thoughts* or *faces*); **~ cards,** person's **hand,** etc., (as fortune-teller); **~ the sky** (as astrologer or meteorologist). **2.** (Be able to) convert into the intended words or meaning (written or printed or other symbols or things expressed by such symbols, or abs.; *reads* or *can read hieroglyphics, shorthand, the clock, Braille, Morse, music, several languages; cannot* or *does not read or write*); understand words intended by (person); (of computer) copy or transfer (data) from (**~ in**) or to (**~ out**) magnetic tape etc., whence **~-in, ~-out,** *ns.* **3.** Reproduce mentally or (often *aloud, out, off*, etc., or w. ind. obj.) vocally, while following their symbols with eyes or fingers, the words of (author, book, letter, etc., or abs.; *read the letter over* or *through; was reading Plato; read it to me; have no time to read; the Bible is the most read of all books*); **~** person **a lecture** or **a lesson,** reprove him; *Bill was* **~ for the first** etc. **time,** allowed its first etc. READING; TAKE[1] *as read*; **~ proof,** (Print.) check its correctness and mark changes needed; **seldom ~s French** (anything written in it); **~s well,** has good intonation etc., reads expressively. **4.** Study by reading (esp. subject at university); (in *p.p.* in act. sense as *a.*) *well, deeply, slightly, little*, etc. **~**, versed in subject by reading, acquainted with literature; **~ up,** make special study of (subject). **5.** Find (thing) recorded, find statement, in print etc. (*revenge, we read, is a kind of wild justice; I have read somewhere that . . .; have read of it*). **6.** Interpret (statement, action) in certain sense (*may be read several ways; my silence is not to be read as consent*). **7.** Assume to be intended in or deducible from writer's words, find implications, (*you read too much into the text*); **~ between the lines,** search for or discover hidden meaning in document, speech, etc. **8.** (Of editor or text) give as the word(s) probably used or intended by author (*Bentley reads 'peraeque'*); (joc. in correcting statements) *for 'white' read 'black'*, 'black' should replace 'white'. **9.** Bring into specified state by reading (*read myself to sleep*); ‖**~ oneself in,** (of incumbent) enter upon office by public reading of the 39 Articles etc.; ***~ out,** expel (from political party etc.) (as if) by reading form of dismissal. **10.** (Of recording instrument) present (figure etc.) to person reading it (*thermometer reads 20°*). **11.** *v.i.* Carry out course of study by reading (*is reading for the Bar; shall not read for honours*). **12.** Convey meaning when read (*name reads from left to right*); sound or affect hearer or reader *well, ill*, etc., when read (*play reads better than it acts; reads like a threat, translation*, etc.). **13.** *n.* Time spent in reading (*have a short, long, good, quiet, read*). [OE *rǣdan* advise, consider, discern, = OS *rādan*, OHG *rātan*, ON *rátha*, Goth. *-rēdan* f. Gmc **rǣdhan*]

rea'd|able *a.* Capable of being read with pleasure or interest; legible; hence **~ABI'LITY, ~ableNESS** (-beln-), *ns.*, **~abLY**[2] *adv.* [f. prec. + -ABLE]

For other words in *re-* see RE-.

rēaddrě'ss *v.t.* Change address of (letter). [f. RE- 8 + ADDRESS[1]]
rea'der *n.* In vbl senses; person employed by publisher to read and report on offered MSS.; printer's proof-corrector; person appointed to read aloud, esp. parts of service in church (LAY[2] *reader*); ||higher grade of lecturer in some universities etc. (*reader in Roman law* etc.); book of selections for use by students of a language etc.; device for producing image that can be read from microfilm etc.; hence ~SHIP *n.*, esp. (number of) readers of newspaper etc. [OE (as READ, -ER[1])]
rea'dilỷ (rě'-) *adv.* Without showing reluctance, willingly; without difficulty (*the facts may be readily ascertained*). [ME, f. READY + -LY[2]]
rea'dinėss (rě'-) *n.* Prompt compliance, willingness; facility, prompt resourcefulness, quickness in argument or action; ready or prepared state (*all is in readiness*). [ME, f. READY + -NESS]
rea'ding *n.* In vbl senses; literary knowledge (*a man of vast reading*); **first, second, third,** ~, successive occasions on which Bill must have been presented for acceptance to legislature before it becomes law (*first* ~, permitting introduction, *second*, ||approving general principle, *general debate on committee report, *third*, ||accepting details as amended in committee, *prior to final vote); entertainment at which something is read to audience (*poetry reading*); word(s) read or given by an editor or found in text of a passage (*the right, true, best, MS.,* etc., *reading*); (specified quality of) matter to be read (*is good, dull, reading; there is plenty of reading in it*); figure etc. shown by recording instrument (*40° difference between day and night readings*); interpretation, view taken, rendering, (*what is your reading of the facts?*; *his reading of Iago was generally condemned*); ~ **age** of child, age of average child with same reading ability; ~**-desk** (for supporting book etc., lectern); ~**-lamp, -light,** (arranged to give light for reading by); ~ **matter,** books etc. as providing something to read; ~**-room** (in club, library, etc., for persons wishing to read). [OE (as READ, -ING[1])]
rēadjŭ'st *v.t.*, **rēadjŭ'st**MENT *n.* See RE- 8.
rea'dỷ (rě'-) *a.*, *adv.*, *n.*, & *v.t.* **1.** *a.* With preparations complete (*dinner is ready*); in fit state (*are ready to march*); with resolution nerved (*am ready to risk my life*); willing, apt, inclined, (*is too ready to suspect*; *was ready to swear with rage*); about *to* (*a bud just ready to burst*); prompt, quick, facile, (*is very ready with excuses*; *has a ready pen, wit*); provided beforehand; within reach, easily secured, (*a ready source of revenue*); fit for immediate use (*found an instrument ready to hand*); unreluctant (*gave a ready consent*; *found ready acceptance*); easy (*its ready solubility in water*; *the readiest way to do it*); **make** ~, prepare (*they made ready for the attempt* or *to fight*, or *made everything ready*); ~ **money,** (1) actual coin or notes, (2) payment on the spot; ~ **reckoner,** book or table of results of arithmetical computations of kind commonly wanted in business etc.; ~**, steady, go**! (formula for starting race). **2.** *adv.* (usu. with *p.p.* & usu. hyphened). Beforehand, so as not to require doing when the time comes, (*please pack everything ready*; *boxes are ready packed* or *packed ready*). **3.** ~**-made,** ~**-to-wear,** (of clothes) made in standard shapes and sizes, not to customer's individual measure, (fig.) unoriginal, commonplace, available without special effort; ~**-to-eat,** (of food) not needing to be cooked. **4.** *n.* Position in which rifle is held before the PRESENT[4] (*come to the ready* etc.); (sl.) ready money (*planked down the ready*); **at the** ~, ready for action. **5.** *v.t.* Make ready, prepare. [ME *rædi(g)*, *re(a)di*, f. OE *rǣde*, OHG *reiti*, ON *reithr*, Goth. *garaiths* f. Gmc **raidh-* put in order, prepare, + -Y[2]]
rēaffĭr'm *v.t.*, **rēaffirm**A'TION *n.*, see RE- 8.
rēaffŏ'rėst *v.t.*, **rēaffŏrėst**A'TION *n.*, see RE- 9.
rēā'gencỷ *n.* Reactive power or operation. [f. RE- 1 + AGENCY; cf. REACT[1]]
rēā'gent *n.* (Chem.) substance used to cause reaction, esp. to detect another; reactive substance or force. [f. RE- 1 + AGENT; cf. REACT[1]]
rē'al[1] (*or* rā'- *or* rāah'l) *n.* Former silver coin and money of account in Spain and Spanish-speaking countries. [Sp., n. use of *real* a. (as ROYAL)]
rē'al[2] *a.* & *adv.* **1.** *a.* Actually existing as a thing or occurring in fact, objective, genuine, rightly so called, natural, sincere, not merely apparent or nominal or supposed or pretended or artificial or hypocritical or affected; ~ **life,** that lived by actual people, opp. fiction, drama, etc.; **a** ~ **man** etc. (worthy of the name); ~ **money,** current coin or notes, cash; **the** ~ **presence** (of Christ's body and blood in Eucharist); **the** ~ **thing,** not a makeshift or inferior article; ~ **tennis,** = TENNIS 1; ~ **time,** actual time in process analysed by computer; **for** ~, (sl.) genuine(ly). **2.** (Law). Consisting of or relating to immovable property such as land or houses (esp. *real property* or *estate*; cf. PERSONAL). **3.** (Philos.) Having an absolute and necessary and not merely contingent existence. **4.** (Econ.) valued by purchasing power, adjusted for changes in value of money, (*real income, values, wages*). **5.** (Math., of quantity) not having any IMAGINARY part; (Opt., of image etc.) such that light actually passes through it. **6.** *adv.* (Sc. & U.S. colloq.) Really, very. [AF, = OF *reel*, & f. LL *realis* (*res* thing; see -AL)]
rėă'lgar *n.* Arsenic sulphide mineral used as pigment and in fireworks. [ME f. med. L, f. Arab. *rahj al-ġār* dust of the cave]
rēalī'gn (-ī'n) *v.t.* Put into new or former alignment; (fig.) regroup (in politics etc.); hence ~MENT *n.* [f. RE- 8, 9 + ALIGN]
rē'al|ĭsm *n.* **1.** Scholastic doctrine that universals or general ideas have objective existence (cf. *nominalism, conceptualism*). **2.** Belief that matter as object of perception has real existence (cf. *idealism*). **3.** Practice of regarding things in their true nature and dealing with them as they are, freedom from prejudice and convention, practical views and policy (cf. *idealism*). **4.** Fidelity of representation, truth to nature, insistence upon details; showing of life etc. as it is without glossing over what is ugly or painful (cf. *idealism*). **5.** So ~IST (2) *n.*, ~**ĭ'stic** *a.* [f. REAL[2] + -ISM]
rėă'lĭtỷ *n.* Property of being real, resemblance to original (*reproduced with startling reality*); real existence, what is real, what underlies appearances, (**in** ~, in fact, opp. *in words, in appearance*, etc.); existent thing (*did not grasp the realities of the situation*); real nature *of*. [f. med. L *realitas*, or F *réalité* (as REAL[2]; see -ITY)]
rė'alīz|e, -īs|e (-īz), *v.t.* **1.** (usu. in *pass.*) Convert (hope, plan, etc.) into fact; (Mus.) reconstruct (part) in full from figured bass. **2.** Give apparent reality to, make realistic, present as real, (*these details help to realize the scene*). **3.** Conceive as real, apprehend clearly or in detail (fact, *that, how*, etc.). **4.** Convert (securities, property, or abs.) into money; amass (fortune, specified profit); fetch as price. **5.** Hence ~ABLE *a.*, ~A'TION *n.* [f. REAL[2] + -IZE, after F *réaliser*]
rė'allỷ *adv.* ~ **(and truly)**, in fact, in reality; positively, indeed, I assure you, I mean what I

say, I protest; **not ~,** (euphem.) no, not in fact; ~! (expr. surprise or censure); **~?,** do you mean it?, is that so?. [ME, f. REAL² + -LY²]

realm (rĕlm) *n.* **1.** (rhet. or Law). Kingdom (*coin, peer, the laws, of the realm*). **2.** Sphere, province, domain, (*the realm(s) of fancy, poetry,* etc.). [ME f. OF *realme, reaume,* f. L REGIMEN *regiminis*; infl. by OF *reiel* ROYAL]

realpolitik (rāahlpŏlĭtē′k) *n.* Politics based on realities and material needs, rather than on morals or ideals. [G]

***rē′altor** *n.* Real-estate agent (prop. one who is a member or affiliated member of the National Association of Real Estate Boards). [f. foll. + -OR]

rē′altȳ *n.* Real estate (opp. *personalty*). [f. REAL² + -TY¹]

ream¹ *n.* **1.** Twenty quires or 480 sheets of paper (or larger number, to allow for waste); **printers' ~,** 516 sheets. **2.** (usu. in *pl.*) Large quantity of paper (*wrote reams and reams of verse*). [ME *rēm, rīm,* f. OF *raime* etc., ult. f. Arab. *rīzma* bundle]

ream² *v.t.* **1.** Widen (hole in metal etc.) with borer; *squeeze juice from (fruit); hence ~′ER¹ (2) *n.* **2.** Turn over edge of (cartridge-case etc.); (Naut.) open (seam) for caulking. [19th c., of uncert. orig.]

rēă′nĭmāte *v.t.,* **rēănĭm**A′TION *n.* See RE- 9.

reap *v.t.* **1.** Cut (grain or similar crop, or abs.) with sickle in harvest; gather in thus or with machine as harvest; (fig.) receive as consequence of one's own or others' actions (*reap as* one *has sown; sow wind and reap* WHIRL*wind; reap the fruits of* one's *forethought*); **~ where one has not sown,** profit by others' toil. **2.** Harvest crop of (field etc.). **3. ~′ing-hook,** sickle; **~′ing-machine** (for cutting grain and often binding sheaves without manual labour). **4.** Hence ~′ER¹ (1, 2) *n.* (fig. of death personified). [OE *ripan, reopan,* **riopan,* **repan,* of unkn. orig.]

rēappear′ *v.i.,* **rēappear′**ANCE *n.,* **rēappoi′nt** *v.t.,* **rēappoi′nt**MENT *n.,* see RE- 9; **rēapprai′se** (-z) *v.t.,* **rēapprai′s**AL (-z-) *n.,* see RE- 8.

rear¹ *n.* **1.** Hindmost part of army or fleet (**hang on the ~ of,** follow with view to attacking); back of, space behind, position at back of, army or camp or person (**bring up the ~,** come last; **in the ~,** behind; **take in the ~,** attack from behind); back part of anything (**at the ~ of,** behind); (colloq.) buttocks; ||(colloq.) water-closet or latrine. **2.** *a.* Hinder, back-; so ~′MOST *a.* **3. ~-admiral,** flag-officer below vice-admiral; **~-commodore,** yacht-club officer below vice-commodore; **~′guard** [f. OF *rereguarde* f. L RETRO-; cf. GUARD¹], body of troops detached to protect rear esp. in retreats (*~guard action,* engagement between rearguard and enemy, lit. or fig.); **~-lamp, ~-light,** (usu. red, at rear of motor vehicle); **~ sight** (nearest to stock of firearm); *rear* VASSAL; **~-view mirror** (enabling driver of vehicle to see traffic etc. behind); **~′ward** *n.* [f. AF *rerewarde* = *rearguard*], rear (esp. in prep. phrs.; *to rearward of, in the rearward*); ~′WARD *a.* & *adv.,* ~′WARDS *adv.,* towards the rear. [prob. f. (*in the*) *rearward* or *rearguard* (see above); cf. VAN²]

rear² *v.* **1.** *v.t.* (rhet.) Raise, set upright, build, hold upwards, (*rear a monument, cathedral,* etc.; *reared his mighty stature; rear* one's *head,* one's *voice, a hand,* etc.). **2.** Bring up, breed, foster, educate, cultivate, (cattle, game, children, crops, etc.). **3.** *v.i.* (Of horse etc.) raise itself on hind legs; (rhet.) extend to great height. **4.** Hence ~′ER¹ *n.* [OE *rǣran,* = ON *reisa,* Goth. *-raisjan* f. Gmc **raizjan* causative of **reisan* raise]

rear′-ârch *n.* Inner arch of window or door opening different in size or shape from the outer. [f. REAR¹ + ARCH¹]

rēâr′m *v.t.* Provide (troops, one*self,* or abs.) with weapons again after disarming, or with weapons of more modern type; restore military strength of (country); so **rēAR′**MAMENT *n.* [f. RE- 8 + ARM³]

rēarrā′nge (-nj) *v.t.,* **rēarrā′nge**MENT (-njm-) *n.* See RE- 8.

rear′-vault (*or* -ŏlt) *n.* Vault between arched window or door head and arch in inner face of wall. [f. REAR¹ + VAULT¹]

rēascĕ′nd *v.i.* & *t.* See RE- 9.

rea′son¹ (-z-) *n.* **1.** (Fact adduced or serving as) argument, motive, cause, or justification, (*give reasons for; prove with reasons; the reason of* or *for his conduct; failed by reason of bad management; I saw reason to be suspicious; for no other reason than that I forgot, but this; there is no reason to suppose*); **~ of State,** political justification esp. for immoral proceeding; **with ~,** not unjustifiably. **2.** (Logic). Premiss of syllogism, esp. minor premiss when given after conclusion. **3.** Intellectual faculty characteristic esp. of human beings by which conclusions are drawn from premisses (*whether dogs have reason is really a question of definition; there can be no opposition between reason and common sense*). **4.** Intellect personified (*God and Reason are identical*); (as transl. of G *vernunft* in Kant) faculty transcending the understanding (G *verstand*) and providing a priori principles, intuition. **5.** Sanity (*has lost his, is restored to, reason*). **6.** Sense, sensible conduct, what is right or practical or practicable, moderation; **Age of R~,** 18th c. in England and France; **bring to ~,** induce to cease vain resistance; **in ~,** within the bounds of moderation; *without* RHYME¹ *or reason;* **it stands to ~,** it can be logically proved that, it cannot be denied without paradox, it would be generally admitted; **listen to ~,** allow oneself to be persuaded; **see ~,** (1) regard it as justifiable (*to* do, etc.), (2) be brought to reason; **within ~,** = *in reason.* **7.** Hence ~LESS *a.* [ME, f. OF *reisun, res(o)un* f. Rom. **ratione* f. L *ratio -onis* (*rēri rat-* consider; see -ION)]

rea′son² (-z-) *v.* **1.** *v.i.* Use argument *with* person by way of persuasion. **2.** Form or try to reach conclusions by connected thought silent or expressed (*from* premisses; *about,* (arch.) *of* or *upon,* subject); hence ~ER¹ *n.* **3.** *v.t.* Discuss *what, whether, why,* etc.; conclude, assume as step in argument, say by way of argument, *that.* **4.** Express in logical or argumentative form (*a reasoned exposition*), embody reasons in (amendment etc.). **5.** Persuade or bring by argument *out of* or *into* (*tried to reason him out of his fears; reasoned himself into perplexity*). **6.** Think *out* (consequences etc.). **7.** Hence ~ING¹ (1) *n.* [ME, f. OF *raisoner* (as prec.)]

rea′sonab|le (-z-) *a.* **1.** Having sound judgement, sensible, moderate, not expecting too much, ready to listen to reason. **2.** In accordance with reason, not absurd; within the limits of reason, not greatly less or more than might be expected; inexpensive, not extortionate; tolerable, fair. **3.** (arch.) Endowed with faculty of reason. **4.** Hence **~le**NESS (-beln-) *n.,* ~LY² *adv.* [ME, f. OF *raisonable* (as REASON¹; see -ABLE), after L *rationabilis*]

rēassĕ′mble *v.i.* & *t.,* **rēassĕ′mbl**Y¹ *n.,* see RE- 9; **rēassêr′t** *v.t.,* **rēassêr′**TION *n.,* **rēassĕ′ss** *v.t.,* **rēassĕ′ss**MENT *n.,* **rēassī′gn** *v.t.,* **rēassī′gn**MENT *n.,* (-ī′n) see RE- 8; **rēassū′me** *v.t.,* **rēassŭ′mp**TION *n.,* see RE- 9.

rēassur′|e (-ashoor′) *v.t.* **1.** Restore confidence

to, dispel apprehensions of; confirm in opinion or impression; hence ~**ing**LY[2] *adv.* **2.** Reinsure. **3.** So ~ANCE *n.* [f. RE- 9 & 8 + ASSURE]

Réaumur (rā′ōmūr) *a.* Pertaining to the ~ **scale** of temperature, on which water freezes at 0° and boils at 80° under standard conditions. [f. R. de ~, Fr. physicist d. 1757]

‖**reave** *v.* (**reft**). (arch. or poet.) **1.** *v.t.* (esp. in *p.p.*) Forcibly deprive *of.* **2.** Take by force, carry off, (*away, from*). **3.** *v.i.* = REIVE. [OE *rēafian,* = OS *rōbon,* OHG *roubōn,* Goth. *-raubōn* f. Gmc **raubhōjan* (**raubh-*; cf. ROB)]

rēbăptī′ze *v.t.* See RE- 8.

rėbar′bative *a.* (literary). Repellent, unattractive. [f. F *rébarbatif -ive* (*barbe* beard)]

rėbā′te[1] *v.t.* (arch.) Diminish, reduce force or effect of; blunt, dull. [ME, f. OF *rabattre* (as RE- 5, ABATE)]

rē′bāte[2] (*or* rĭbā′t) *n.* Deduction from sum to be paid, discount, drawback. [f. prec.]

rėbā′te[3] (*or* ră′bĭt) *n.,* & *v.t.* = RABBET. [re-spelling of RABBET, after prec.]

rē′běc, rē′běck, *n.* Medieval usu. three-stringed instrument played with bow. [f. F *rebec* var. of OF *rebebe, rubebe* f. Arab. *rabāb*]

rě′bel[1] *n.* & *a.* **1.** *n.* Person who rises in arms against, resists, or refuses allegiance to, the established government; person or thing that resists authority or control. **2.** *attrib. a.* Rebellious; of rebels; in rebellion. [ME, f. OF *rebelle* f. L *rebellis* (as RE- 2, *bellum* war); orig. of renewed warfare by conquered]

rėbě′l[2] *v.i.* (**-ll-**). Act as rebel (*against*); feel or manifest repugnance (*against* custom etc.). [ME, f. OF *rebeller* f. L RE(*bellare* make war) revolt]

rėbě′llion (-lyon) *n.* Organized armed resistance to established government (**the Great R~**, period of English history 1642–51); open resistance to any authority. [ME f. OF, f. L *rebellio -onis* (as REBEL[1]; see -ION)]

rėbě′llious (-lyus) *a.* In rebellion; disposed to rebel, insubordinate, defying lawful authority; (of disease) difficult to treat; (of thing) unmanageable, refractory; hence ~LY[2] *adv.,* ~NESS *n.* [ME, f. prec. + -OUS or f. earlier *rebellous* + -IOUS]

rėbě′llow (-ō) *v.i.* & *t.* (poet.) Re-echo loudly. [RE- 6, after L RE(*boare* bellow)]

rē′bĭd *v.* (**-dd-**; **re′bid**) & *n.* (Cards). **1.** *v.i.* Bid after having previously bid. **2.** *v.t.* Bid (suit) again at higher level. **3.** *n.* Act of rebidding; bid thus made. [f. RE- 8 + BID[1,2]]

rēbī′nd *v.t.* (**re-bou′nd**). Bind (esp. book) again. [f. RE- 9 + BIND[1]]

rēbĭr′th *n.* Fresh incarnation; spiritual enlightenment; revival (*the rebirth of learning*); so **rē**BOR′N *a.* [f. RE- 8 + BIRTH]

rě′bōant *a.* (poet.) Rebellowing, resounding, re-echoing. [f. L *reboare* rebellow; see -ANT]

rēbôr′e *v.t.* Make new boring in, esp. widen bore of (cylinder in internal combustion engine). [f. RE- 8 + BORE[1]]

rēbôr′n. See REBIRTH.

rėbou′nd[1] *v.i.* Spring back after impact; have reactive effect, recoil upon agent, (*their evil example will rebound upon themselves*). [ME, f. OF *rebonder, rebondir* (as RE- 1, BOUND[3])]

rē′bound[2] *n.* Act of rebounding, recoil; reaction after emotion (**take** person **on** or **at the** ~, utilize such reaction to persuade him to contrary of previously intended action etc.); (Basketball, Football, etc.) (getting possession of) ball rebounding from wall, goal-post, etc. [f. prec. or F *rebond*]

rē-bou′nd[3]. See REBIND.

rēbroa′dcast (-aw′dkah-) *v.t.,* & *n.* See RE- 8.

rėbŭ′ff *n.,* & *v.t.* **1.** *n.* Rejection of one who makes advances, proffers help or sympathy, shows interest or curiosity, makes request, etc.; repulse, snub. **2.** *v.t.* Give rebuff to. [f. obs. F *rebuffe(r)* f. It. *ribuffo, ribuffare, rabbuffo, rabbuffare,* (as RE- 2, *buffo* puff)]

rēbuĭ′ld (-bĭ′-) *v.t.* See RE- 8.

rėbū′ke *v.t.,* & *n.* **1.** *v.t.* Subject to protest or censure (*for* fault etc.); reprove. **2.** *n.* Rebuking or being rebuked; reproof. [ME, f. AF & ONF *re(buker* = OF *buchier* beat, orig. cut down wood f. *busche* log; see RE- 5)]

rē′bus *n.* Enigmatic representation of name, word, etc., by pictures etc. suggesting its syllables; (Her.) device suggesting name of its bearer. [f. F *rébus* f. L *rebus,* abl. pl. of *res* thing, in phr. *de rebus quae geruntur* concerning the things that are taking place, title in 16th-c. Picardy of satirical pieces containing such riddles]

rėbŭ′t *v.t.* (**-tt-**). Force or turn back, check; refute, disprove, (evidence, charge), whence ~TABLE *a.,* ~**t**AL 2, ~MENT, *ns.* [ME, f. AF *rebuter,* OF *rebo(u)ter* (as RE- 9, BUTT[4])]

rėbŭ′tter *n.* Refutation; (Law) defendant's reply to plaintiff's surrejoinder. [f. AF *rebuter* (as prec.; see -ER[4])]

rėcă′lcĭtr|ant *a.* & *n.* (Person) objecting to restraint or obstinately disobedient; hence ~ANCE *n.* [f. L *re(calcitrare* kick out with heels f. *calx calcis* heel); see RE- 2, -ANT]

rēcal|ě′sce *v.i.* Grow hot again (esp. of iron allowed to cool from white heat, whose temperature rises at certain point for short time); hence ~E′SCENCE *n.* [f. L *re(calescere* grow hot); see RE- 9, -ESCE]

rėca′ll[1] (-aw′l) *v.t.* Summon to return from a place or from different occupation, inattention, digression, etc.; cancel or suspend appointment of (official sent to distance, esp. overseas); bring back to or *to* memory, serve as reminder of; recollect, remember; revive, resuscitate; revoke, annul, (action, decision), take back (gift); hence ~ABLE *a.* [f. RE- 9 + CALL[1]]

rėca′ll[2] (-aw′l) *n.* Summons to come back; cancelling or suspension of appointment abroad; signal to ship etc. to return to base; possibility of recalling esp. in sense of annulling (*beyond* or *past recall*); act of remembering; ability to remember; TOTAL *recall.* [f. RE- 9 + CALL[2], after prec.]

rėcă′nt *v.* **1.** *v.t.* Withdraw and renounce (opinion, statement, etc.) as erroneous or heretical. **2.** *v.i.* Disavow former opinion, esp. with public confession of error. **3.** Hence **rēcănt**A′TION *n.* [f. L *re(cantare* sing, CHANT) revoke; see RE- 7]

***rēcă′p**[1] *v.t.* (**-pp-**). Put another cap on; partially replace worn tread of (tyre). [f. RE- 8 + CAP[2]]

rē′căp[2] *v.t.* (**-pp-**), & *n.* (colloq.) **1.** *v.t.* = foll. **2.** *n.* Recapitulation. [abbr.]

rēcapĭ′tūl|āte *v.t.* Go over main points or headings of, summarize; go briefly through again; hence ~**at**IVE, ~**at**ORY, *adjs.* [f. L *re(capitulare* f. *capitulum* CHAPTER); see RE- 8, -ATE[3]]

rēcapĭtūlā′tion *n.* Recapitulating; (Biol.) reappearance in embryos of successive type-forms in line of development; (Mus.) passage repeating exposition. [ME f. OF, or f. LL *recapitulatio* (as prec.; see -ATION)]

rēcă′pture *v.* & *n.* **1.** *v.t.* & *i.* Capture (what has been lost); (Chess) capture a man that has just captured; re-experience (past emotion etc.). **2.** *n.* Act of recapturing. [f. RE- 9 + CAPTURE]

rēca′st[1] (-kah′-) *v.t.* (**reca′st**). Put into new form; improve arrangement of; change cast of (play etc.). [f. RE- 8 + CAST[1]]

rēca′st[2] (-kah′-) *n.* Recasting; recast form. [f. RE- 8 + CAST[2]]

rě′ccė (rě′kĭ) *n.* & *v.* (sl.) **1.** *n.* Reconnaissance. **2.** *v.t.* & *i.* Reconnoitre. [abbr.]

recd. *abbr.* received.

rècē′de[1] *v.i.* Go or shrink back or farther off; be left at increasing distance by observer's motion; slope backwards; withdraw (*from* engagement, opinion, etc.); decline in character or value. [ME, f. L *re*(*cedere cess-* go); see RE- 5]

rē-cē′de[2] *v.t.* Cede back to former owner. [f. RE- 9 + CEDE]

rècei′pt (-sē′t) *n.*, & *v.t.* **1.** *n.* (arch.) Recipe. **2.** Amount of money etc. received. **3.** Fact or action of receiving or being received into person's hands or possession (*goods will be sent on receipt of remittance*; *beg to acknowledge receipt of your book*; *entrusted with the receipt of subscriptions*); written acknowledgement of this, esp. of payment of sum due. **4.** (arch.) Place where money is officially received, esp. **~ of custom,** custom-house. **5.** *v.t.* Place written receipt on (bill). [ME *receit*(*e*) f. AF & ONF *receite*, OF *reçoite*, *recete* f. med. L *recepta* fem. p.p. (as n.) of L *recipere* RECEIVE; *-p-* inserted after L]

rècei′v|e (-sē′v) *v.t.* **1.** Accept delivery of, take (proffered thing) into one's hands or possession; accept (stolen goods though knowing of the theft, or abs.); consent to hear (confession, oath) or consider (petition); **~e the sacraments,** eat and drink Eucharistic bread and wine; **~ing-order** (see foll.). **2.** Bear up against, stand force or weight of, encounter with opposition, (*received his body in their hands*; *arch receives weight of roof*; *received the sword-point with his shield*); (Tennis) be required to play against (service, or abs.). **3.** Admit, consent or prove able to hold, provide accommodation for, submit to, serve as receptacle of, (*had to receive the visits, attentions,* etc., *of*); admit to membership of church etc.; be marked (lit. or fig.) more or less permanently with (impression etc.); convert (broadcast signals) into sound or picture. **4.** Entertain (person as guest, company at formal reception, or abs.); greet, welcome, esp. in specified manner, (*you stay here and receive him*; *how did she receive his offer?*; *was received with cries of* '*Traitor*'; *news was received with horror*). **5.** (esp. in *p.p.*) Give credit to, accept as authoritative or true, (*an axiom universally received*); (in *p.p.*) generally accepted thus (*received opinions*); **~ed pronunciation, *R~ed Standard,** form of English speech used, with local variations, by majority of educated English-speaking people. **6.** Acquire, get, be given, be provided with, have sent to or conferred or inflicted on one, (*have not yet received my fee*; *receive a letter, news, a report*; *receive the name of John*; *pleasant to receive sympathy*; *deserves more attention than it receives*; *receive orders to march*; *received many insults, a thrust, a broken jaw, the contents of his pistol*); (abs.) partake *of*; **be at** or **on the ~ing end,** bear the brunt of something unpleasant. **7.** Hence **~**ABLE *a.* [ME, f. OF *receivre*, *reçoivre* f. L *re*(*cipere cept-* = *capere* take) recover; see RE- 9]

rècei′ver (-sē′v-) *n.* In vbl senses; (**official**) **~**, person appointed by court's **receiving-order** to administer property of bankrupt or insane person or property under litigation, whence **~**SHIP *n.*; person who receives stolen goods; receptacle etc. for receiving something in machine or instrument, esp. part of telephone that contains ear-piece; vessel for collecting products of distillation; radio or television receiving apparatus. [ME, f. AF **receivere*, *-our* f. OF *recevere*, *-our*, & f. prec. + -ER[1]]

rècĕ′nsion (-shon) *n.* Revision of text; revised text. [f. L *recensio* f. *re*(*censēre* review) revise; see RE- 8, -ION]

rē′cent *a.* Not long past, that happened or began to exist or existed lately, late; not long established, lately begun, modern; (Geol., *R~*) of the latter part of the Quaternary period or system, including the present time; hence **rē′**CENCY *n.*, **~**LY[2] *adv.*, **~**NESS *n.* [f. L *recens recentis* or F *récent*]

rècĕ′ptacle *n.* Containing vessel, place, or space; (Bot.) common base of floral organs, axis of cluster. [ME, f. OF, or f. L *receptaculum* (as foll.)]

rècĕ′ption *n.* **1.** Receiving or being received, esp. of person into a place or company (*the rooms were prepared for his reception*; *was honoured by reception into the Academy*); ||place where guests register on arriving at hotel etc., or where firm's clients etc. are welcomed; ||**~ order** (authorizing entry of patient into mental hospital). **2.** Formal or ceremonious welcome (*the reception of the delegates is arranged for Monday next*); occasion of receiving guests, assembly held for this purpose, (*after the review, conference, wedding, there will be a reception*); **~-room** (available or suitable for receiving company or visitors). **3.** Receiving of ideas or impressions into the mind. **4.** Welcome or greeting of specified kind, demonstration of feeling towards person or project; **warm ~**, hostile response or enthusiastic welcome. **5.** Receiving of broadcast signals; efficiency with which these are received. **6.** Hence **~**IST (3) *n.*, person employed by hotel, photographer, doctor, dentist, etc., to receive clients. [ME f. OF, or f. L *receptio* (as RECEIVE; see -ION)]

rècĕ′ptĭve *a.* Able or quick to receive impressions or ideas (*a mind more receptive than retentive or creative*); concerned with receiving stimuli etc.; hence **~**LY[2] (-vlĭ) *adv.*, **~**NESS (-vn-), **rēcĕptĭ′**VITY, *ns.* [f. F *réceptif -ive* or f. med. L *receptivus* (as prec.; see -IVE)]

rècĕ′ptor *n.* & *a.* (Biol.) (Organ) able to respond to light, heat, drug, etc., and transmit signal to sensory nerve. [f. OF *receptour* or f. L *receptor* (as prec.; see -OR)]

rècĕ′ss *n.* & *v.* **1.** *n.* Temporary cessation from work, vacation, esp. of Parliament or *lawcourt or *during school day; (arch.) receding of water, land, glacier, etc., from previous limit, amount by which it recedes. **2.** Remote or secret place (*in the inmost recesses of the Alps, of the heart*); receding part of mountain chain etc., niche or alcove of wall; (Anat.) fold or indentation in organ. **3.** *v.t.* Place in a recess, set back; provide with recess(es); *order temporary cessation from work of (court etc.). **4.** *v.i.* *Take recess, adjourn. [f. L *recessus* (as RECEDE[1])]

rècĕ′ssion (-shon) *n.* Receding or withdrawal from a place or point; receding part of object, recess; temporary decline in economic activity or prosperity; hence **~**ARY[1] *a.* [f. L *recessio* (as prec.; see -ION)]

rècĕ′ssional (-sho-) *a.* & *n.* **~** (**hymn**), hymn sung while clergy and choir withdraw after service. [f. prec. + -AL]

rècĕ′ssĭve *a.* Tending to recede; (Phonet., of accent) falling near beginning of word; (Genetics, of characteristic) found in second and later generations of hybrids, but not in first generation because there masked by dominant characteristic inherited from one parent; hence **~**LY[2] (-vlĭ) *adv.* [f. RECESS after *excessive*]

Rĕ′chabīte (-k-) *n.* Total abstainer, esp. member of a benefit society (*Independent Order of Rechabites*). [f. eccl. L *Rechabita* f. Heb. *rēkābîm* pl. (Jer. 35:6); see -ITE[1] (1)]

rē′charge[1] *n.* Renewed charge; material etc. used for this. [f. RE- 9 + CHARGE[1]]

rēchar′ge[2] *v.t.* Charge again; reload; ~ one's **batteries,** (fig.) have period of rest and recuperation. [f. RE- 9 + CHARGE[2]]

réchauffé (rĭshō′fā) *n.* Warmed-up dish; rehash. [F, p.p. of *réchauffer* (as RE-, CHAFE)]

recher′ché (reshār′shā) *a.* Devised or got with care or difficulty, (excessively) far-fetched or thought out. [F, p.p. of *rechercher* (as RE-, *chercher* seek)]

rēchrĭ′sten (-krĭ′sen) *v.t.* Christen again; (fig.) give new name to. [f. RE- 8 + CHRISTEN]

rėcĭ′dĭv|ĭst *n.* One who relapses into crime; so ~ISM (2) *n.* [f. F *récidiviste* f. *récidiver* f. med. L *recidivare* f. L *recidivus* f. RE(*cidere* = *cadere* fall); see RE- 9, -IVE, -IST]

rĕ′cĭpė *n.* Medical prescription, remedy prepared from it; statement of ingredients and procedure for preparing dish etc. in cookery; expedient, device for effecting something. [2nd sing. imper. (as used in prescriptions) of L *recipere* take, RECEIVE]

rėcĭ′pĭ|ent *a.* & *n.* **1.** *a.* Receiving; receptive; hence ~ENCY *n.* **2.** *n.* Person who receives something. [f. F *récipient* f. It. *recipiente* or L *recipiens* (*recipere* RECEIVE; see -ENT)]

rėcĭ′procal *a.* & *n.* **1.** *a.* In return (*I helped him, and had reciprocal help from him*); mutual (*reciprocal love, protection, injuries*); inversely correspondent, complementary, (*I took the chamois for a man, and it made the reciprocal mistake*); (Gram.) expressing mutual action or relation (*'each other' is a reciprocal pronoun*); hence ~LY[2] *adv.* **2.** *n.* (Math.) Function or expression so related to another that their product is unity (*1/5 is the reciprocal of 5*). [f. L *reciprocus* (ult. f. *re-* back, *pro* forward) + -AL]

rėcĭ′proc|āte *v.t.* & *i.* **1.** (Mech.) Go with alternate backward and forward motion (**~ating engine** etc., one in which work is done by part that moves thus); give such motion to. **2.** Give and receive mutually, interchange, (influence etc.); return, requite, (affection etc.), make a return (*with* thing given in return). **3.** So ~A′TION *n.* [f. L *reciprocare* (as prec.) + -ATE[3]]

rĕcĭprŏ′cĭtȳ *n.* Reciprocal condition, mutual action; principle or practice of give-and-take, esp. interchange of privileges between States, clubs, etc., as basis of commercial etc. relations. [f. F *réciprocité* (*réciproque* f. L *reciprocus*; see RECIPROCATE, -ITY)]

rėcī′tal *n.* **1.** Detailed account *of* a number of connected things or facts, relation *of* the facts of an incident etc., a narrative. **2.** Part of document stating facts. **3.** Act of reciting; performance of programme by one musician with or without accompanist (*vocal, piano,* etc., *recital*) or by small group of musicians or by solo dancer; hence ~IST (1) *n.* [f. RECITE + -AL]

rĕcĭtati′ve (-ē′v) *n.* Musical declamation of kind usual in narrative and dialogue parts of opera and oratorio; words or part given in recitative. [f. It. *recitativo* (as foll.; see -IVE)]

rėcī′te *v.t.* & *i.* Repeat aloud or declaim (poem, passage) from memory esp. before audience, give recitation (**reciting-note,** that held for indefinite number of syllables in chanting); (Law) rehearse (facts) in document; mention in order, enumerate; so **rĕcĭt**A′TION, **rėcī′t**ER[1], *ns.* [ME, f. OF *reciter* or f. L *re*(*citare* CITE); see RE- 8]

rĕck *v.* (rhet. or poet., in neg. & interrog. sents. only). **1.** *v.i.* ~ **of,** pay heed to, take account of, care about. **2.** Care, be troubled, concern oneself, (*if, though, that, how, whether,* etc., or abs.; or impers. w. ind. obj. and same construction following, *what recks it him that . . .?*); (impers.) be of importance (*it recks little*). **3.** *v.t.* Pay heed to, care about, (*recks not his own rede*). [OE *reccan*, of uncert. orig., & **rēcan*, = OS *rōkjan*, OHG *ruohhen*, ON *rœkja* f. Gmc **rōkjan*]

rĕ′cklėss *a.* Lacking caution, regardless of consequences, rash; heedless *of* danger etc.; hence ~LY[2] *adv.*, ~NESS *n.* [OE *recceléas* (as prec., -LESS)]

rĕ′ckon *v.* **1.** *v.t.* Ascertain (number, amount), ascertain number or amount of, by counting or usu. by calculation, compute; start *from*, go on *to*, in counting (things, or abs.); count *up*, sum *up* character of; arrive at as total (*I reckon 53 of them*). **2.** Include in computation, count *in*, place in class *among* or *with* or *in*, take *for*, regard *as*, consider (*to be*) (*reckon him wise, beyond redemption*). **3.** Conclude after calculation, be of the confident opinion, (*that*). **4.** *v.i.* Make calculations, cast up account or sum, (~ **with,** take into account; **to be ~ed with,** not negligible; *reckon without* one's HOST[2]); settle accounts *with* person. **5.** Rely or count or base plans (*up*)*on*. **6.** Hence ~ER[1] (1, 2) *n.* [OE (*ge*)*recenian*, = MDu., MLG *rekenen*, OHG *rehhanōn* f. WG **rekenōjan*]

rĕ′ckonĭng (-kn-) *n.* In vbl senses; bill in public house etc.; **day of** ~, time when something must be atoned for or avenged; DEAD *reckoning*; **out in** one's ~, mistaken in a calculation or expectation. [ME, f. prec. + -ING[1]]

rėclai′m *v.* & *n.* **1.** *v.t.* Win back or away from vice or error or savagery or waste condition, reform; tame, civilize; bring under cultivation esp. from state of being flooded by sea or marsh, whence ~ABLE *a.* **2.** *v.i.* (arch.) Make protest. **3.** So **rĕclam**A′TION *n.* **4.** Reclaiming or being reclaimed. [ME, f. OF *reclamer reclaim-* f. L *re*(*clamare* shout) cry out against; see RE- 2]

réclame (rā′klahm) *n.* Notoriety; art or practice by which notoriety is secured. [F (as prec.)]

rĕ′clĭnate *a.* (Bot.) Bending downwards. [f. L *reclinatus* p.p. of *reclinare* (as foll.; see -ATE[2])]

rėclī′ne *v.* **1.** *v.t.* Lay (esp. one's head, body, or limbs) in more or less horizontal or leaning position; (in *p.p.*, of person) lying thus. **2.** *v.i.* Assume, or be in, horizontal or leaning position; sit with back or side supported at considerable inclination to vertical. [ME, f. OF *recliner* or f. L *reclinare* bend back, recline; see RE- 9, DECLINE[1]]

rėclu′s|e (-lōō′s) *a.* & *n.* (Person) given to or living in seclusion or retirement or isolation, esp. as religious discipline, hermit; hence ~IVE *a.* [ME, f. OF *reclus recluse* p.p. of *reclure* f. L *re*(*cludere clus-* = *claudere* shut); see RE- 4]

rĕcognĭ′tion *n.* Recognizing or being recognized (*honour given in recognition of services; was changed out of all recognition*); hence **rėcŏ′gnĭt**ORY *a.* [f. L *recognitio* (as RECOGNIZE; see -ITION)]

rėcŏ′gnĭzance (*or* -kŏ′n-) *n.* Bond by which person engages before court or magistrate to observe some condition, e.g. to keep the peace, pay a debt, or appear when summoned; sum pledged as surety for such observance. [ME, f. OF *recon*(*n*)*issance* (as RE-, COGNIZANCE)]

rėcŏ′gnĭzant (*or* -kŏ′n-) *a.* Showing recognition (*of* favour etc.); conscious or showing consciousness of something. [f. foll. + -ANT]

rĕ′cognīz|e, -īs|e (-īz), *v.t.* **1.** Acknowledge validity or genuineness or character or claims of, accord notice or consideration or reward to; (of chairman etc.) allow to speak in debate; discover or realize nature of; treat *as*, acknowledge *for*, realize or admit *that*. **2.** Know again, identify as known before. **3.** Hence ~ABLE *a.*, ~ABI′LITY *n.*, ~**ab**LY[2] *adv.* [f. OF *recon*(*n*)*iss-* st. of *reconnaistre* f. L *re*(*cognoscere cognitum* learn), see RE- 8; assim. to -IZE]

rėcoi′l *v.i.*, & *n.* **1.** *v.i.* Retreat under enemy's attack; suddenly move or spring back, shrink mentally, in fear or horror or disgust; rebound after impact, (of gun) be driven backwards by discharge, spring back; (Phys., of atom etc.) move backwards by conservation of momentum on emission of particle; ~ **(up)on,** have adverse reactive effect upon (its source etc.; *their treason recoiled on their own heads*). **2.** *n.* Act or fact or sensation of recoiling. [ME, f. OF *reculer* f. Rom. **reculare* (as RE- 5, L *culus* buttocks)]

rēcoi'n *v.t.* See RE- 8.

rĕcollĕ'ct[1] *v.t.* Succeed in remembering, recall to mind, remember. [f. L *re(colligere collect-* COLLECT[2]); see RE- 8]

rē-collĕ'ct[2] *v.t.* Collect again; recover control of (one*self*). [f. as prec., or f. RE- 9 + COLLECT[2]]

rĕcollĕ'ct|ion *n.* Act or power of recollecting; thing recollected, reminiscence; person's memory, time over which it extends, (*happened within my recollection*); so ~IVE *a.* [F, or f. med. L *recollectio* (as RECOLLECT[1]; see -ION)]

rēcŏ'lonīze *v.t.*, **rēcŏlonīz**A'TION *n.*, **rēco'lour** (-kŭ'ler) *v.t.*, see RE- 8; **rēcombī'ne** *v.t.* & *i.*, **rēcŏmbĭn**A'TION *n.*, see RE- 8, 9; **rēcommĕ'nce** *v.t.* & *i.*, **rēcommĕ'nce**MENT (-sm-) *n.*, see RE- 8.

rĕcommĕ'nd *v.t.* **1.** Give (one*self*, one's spirit, a child, etc.) in charge *to* God or a person or his care etc. **2.** Speak or write of or suggest as fit for employment or favour or trial (*to* person, *for* post, promotion, decoration, *as* remedy, etc.). **3.** (Of qualities, conduct, etc.) make acceptable, serve as recommendation of. **4.** Advise (course of action or treatment, person *to* do, *that* thing should be done). **5.** Hence or cogn. ~A'TION *n.*, ~ABLE, ~**at**ORY, *adjs.* [ME, f. med. L *re(commendare* COMMEND); see RE- 5]

rēcommĭ't *v.t.* (**-tt-**). Commit again, esp. return (bill etc.) to committee for further consideration; hence ~**t**AL 2, ~MENT, *ns.* [f. RE- 8 + COMMIT]

rĕ'compĕnse *v.t.*, & *n.* **1.** *v.t.* Requite, reward or punish, (person, action, person *for* action, action *to* person); make amends to (person) or for (another's loss, injury etc.). **2.** *n.* Reward, requital; atonement or satisfaction given for injury; retribution. [ME, f. OF *recompense(r)* f. LL *re(compensare* COMPENSATE); see RE- 1]

rēcompō'se (-z) *v.t.* See RE- 8.

rĕ'concīl|e *v.t.* **1.** Make friendly after estrangement (persons to one another, person *to* or *with* another, person to oneself). **2.** Purify (consecrated place etc.) by special service after profanation or desecration. **3.** (usu. in *refl.* or *pass.*) Make acquiescent or contentedly submissive (*to* what is disagreeable, *to* do*ing*, or abs.). **4.** Heal, settle, (quarrel etc.). **5.** Harmonize, make compatible, show compatibility of by argument or in practice, (apparently conflicting facts, statements, qualities, actions, or one such *with* or *and* another). **6.** Hence or cogn. ~ABLE *a.*, ~ABI'LITY, ~**e**MENT (-lm-), **rĕconcĭlĭ**A'TION, *ns.* [ME, f. OF *reconcilier* or f. L *re(conciliare* CONCILIATE); see RE- 9]

rĕ'condīte (*or* rĭkŏ'n-) *a.* (Of subject or knowledge) abstruse, out of the way, little known; (of author or style) dealing in recondite knowledge or allusion, obscure; hence ~LY[2] (-tlĭ) *adv.*, ~NESS (-tn-) *n.* [f. L *re(conditus* p.p. of *condere* hide); see RE- 4]

rēcondĭ'tion *v.t.* Overhaul and refit, rehabilitate, renovate; make habitable or usable again. [f. RE- 8 + CONDITION[2]]

rĕcŏ'nnaissance (-nĭs-) *n.* Military, naval, etc., examination of region by detachment to locate enemy or ascertain strategic features; reconnoitring party; preliminary survey. [F (earlier *-oissance*) f. st. of *reconnaître* (as foll.; see -ANCE)]

rĕconnoi'tre (-t*er*), ***-ter,** *v.* & *n.* **1.** *v.t.* Make reconnaissance of (enemy, district); approach and try to learn position and condition etc. of. **2.** *v.i.* Make reconnaissance. **3.** *n.* Reconnaissance. [f. obs. F *reconnoître* f. L *recognoscere* RECOGNIZE]

rēcŏ'nquer (-ngk*er*) *v.t.*, **rēco'nquest** *n.* See RE- 9.

rēconsĭ'der *v.t.* Consider again, esp. as regards possible change of decision; hence ~A'TION *n.* [f. RE- 8 + CONSIDER]

rēconsŏ'lĭdāte *v.t.* & *i.*, **rēconsŏlĭd**A'TION *n.* See RE- 8.

rēcŏ'nstĭtūte *v.t.* Build up again from parts; restore previous constitution of (dried food etc.) by adding water; piece together (past events) into intelligible whole; reorganize; so **rē**CONSTITU'TION *n.* [f. RE- 8 + CONSTITUTE]

rēconstrŭ'ct *v.t.* Build again; restore (past event) mentally; reorganize; so **rē**CONSTRU'CTION *n.* (**R~ion,** *reincorporation of seceded states into U.S. after Civil War). [f. RE- 8 + CONSTRUCT[1]]

rēconvē'ne *v.t.*, & *i.*, **rēconver̄'t** *v.t.*, **rēconver̄'**SION (-sh*o*n) *n.*, see RE- 9.

rĕcor̄'d[1] *v.t.* **1.** Register, set down for remembrance or reference, put in writing or other legible shape, represent in some permanent form, (*his thoughts have been recorded for us by himself, his features by Watts, and his voice by the gramophone*); ~**ing angel** (who registers men's good and bad actions). **2.** (Broadcasting). Convert (sound, programme, etc.) to permanent form for later reproduction. **3.** Hence ~ABLE *a.* [ME, f. OF *recorder* f. L *recordari* remember (as RE- 9, *cor cordis* heart)]

rĕ'cord[2] *n.* & *a.* **1.** *n.* State of being recorded or preserved in writing etc.; **on** ~, in legal or other record; **go on** ~, act so that one's words etc. are recorded; **court of** ~ (whose proceedings are recorded and valid as evidence of fact); **matter of** ~, thing established as fact by being recorded. **2.** Official report of proceedings and judgement in cause before court of record, copy of pleadings etc. constituting case to be decided by court; **travel out of, keep to, the** ~, introduce, abstain from introducing, irrelevant matter. **3.** Piece of recorded evidence or information, account of fact preserved in permanent form, document or monument preserving it; **for the** ~, official(ly), for sake of recording facts; **off the** ~, unofficial(ly), secret(ly); **get, keep, put, set, the** ~ **straight,** correct a misapprehension; (**Public**) **R~ Office,** institution keeping official archives for public inspection. **4.** Object serving as memorial of something, portrait etc. **5.** Trace made by recording instrument on disc or cylinder for subsequent reproduction by gramophone; similar trace on magnetic tape etc.; disc etc. bearing such trace; **~-player,** apparatus for reproducing sound from gramophone records. **6.** Facts known about person's past (*has an honourable record of service; his record is against him*); **have a** ~, have been convicted on previous occasion. **7.** Best performance or most remarkable event of its kind on record; **break** or **beat the** ~, outdo all predecessors. **8.** *a.* Best or highest or most extreme hitherto recorded. [ME f. OF *record* remembrance (*recorder*; see prec.)]

rĕcor̄'der *n.* In vbl senses; judge, esp. ||presiding at Crown Court or sitting as circuit judge at Central Criminal Court, judge in County Court of N. Ireland, whence ~SHIP *n.*; recording instrument; recording-apparatus in instrument or machine; = TAPE-*recorder*; (Mus.) vertical (English) flute, one of family of instruments with various ranges. [ME f. AF *recordour*, OF *recordeur* (as RECORD¹, -ER²), & f. RECORD¹ + -ER¹]

rècŏr'dĭng *n.* In vbl senses; process of recording sound etc. for later reproduction; sound etc. thus recorded, television programme recorded on film, material on which it has been recorded. [f. RECORD¹ + -ING¹]

rècou'nt¹ *v.t.* Narrate, tell in detail. [f. ONF & AF *re(conter* COUNT²); see RE- 8]

rē-cou'nt² *v.t.* Count again. [f. RE- 8 + COUNT²]

rē'-count³ *n.* Recounting, esp. of election votes to preclude error. [f. RE- 8 + COUNT¹]

rècou'p (-ōō'p) *v.t.* & *i.* (Law) deduct, keep back, (part of sum due), make such deduction; compensate (person loss, person *for* loss, loss); ~(one**self**), recover what one has expended or lost; hence ~MENT *n.* [f. F *re(couper* cut); see RE- 5]

rècour'se (-ōr's) *n.* Resorting or betaking of oneself to possible source of help (**have ~ to,** adopt as adviser, helper, or expedient); person or thing resorted to; **without ~** (formula used by endorser of bill etc. to disclaim responsibility for non-payment). [ME, f. OF *recours* f. L *re(cursus* COURSE¹); see RE- 9]

rèco'ver¹ (-kŭ'-) *v.* & *n.* **1.** *v.t.* Regain possession or use or control of, acquire or find (out) again, reclaim, (*has recovered his kingdom, his friends' affection, the meaning of the hieroglyphics, the track, health, his appetite, his voice, metal from scrap, much land from the sea*); **~ oneself,** regain consciousness, calmness, control of limbs, senses, (*horse recovers itself after stumble*); ~ one's **feet** or **legs,** stand up after fall. **2.** Secure (restitution, compensation, damages, or abs.) by legal process (*plaintiff shall recover according to verdict*; *his remedy is to recover in a court of law*; *action to recover damages for illegal imprisonment*). **3.** Retrieve, make up for, cease to feel effects of, (*must try to recover lost time*). **4.** Hence ~ABLE *a.* **5.** *v.i.* & *t.* Come or (arch.) bring back to consciousness, health, or normal state or position (*have* or *am quite recovered from my illness*; *sat down to recover from his agitation*). **6.** *n.* Recovery of normal position in fencing etc. [ME, f. AF *recoverer*, OF *recovrer* f. L *recuperare* RECUPERATE]

rē-co'ver² (-kŭ'-) *v.t.* Cover again (esp. umbrella etc.). [f. RE- 8 + COVER¹]

rèco'verỳ (-kŭ'-) *n.* Act or process of RECOVER¹-ing or being recovered; (Golf) stroke bringing ball out of bunker etc. [ME, f. AF *recoverie*, OF *reco(u)vree* (as RECOVER¹; see -Y⁴)]

rĕ'crè|ant *a.* & *n.* (rhet. or poet.) Craven, coward(ly), apostate; hence ~ANCY *n.*, ~**ant**LY² *adv.* [ME f. OF, part. of *recroire* f. med. L *(se) re(credere* entrust) yield in trial by combat; see RE- 6, -ANT]

rĕ'crè|āte¹ *v.* **1.** *v.t.* (Of pastime, relaxation, holiday, employment, etc., or refl. of person indulging in them) refresh, entertain, agreeably occupy. **2.** *v.i.* Amuse oneself, indulge in recreation. **3.** Hence ~ATIVE *a.* [f. L *re(creare* create); see RE- 8, -ATE³]

rē-crèā'te² *v.t.* Create over again. [f. RE- 8 + CREATE]

rĕcrèā'tion *n.* (Means of) recreating oneself, pleasurable exercise or employment; **~ ground,** public land for games etc.; hence ~AL *a.* [ME f. OF, f. L *recreatio -onis* (as RECREATE¹; see -ATION)]

rècrĭ'mĭn|āte *v.i.* Retort accusation, indulge in mutual or counter charges; hence or cogn. ~A'TION *n.*, ~ATIVE, ~**ā**TORY, *adjs.* [f. med. L *re(criminare* accuse f. *crimen* CRIME); see RE- 1]

rēcrŏ'ss (*or* -aw's) *v.t.* See RE- 9.

rĕcrud|ĕ'sce (-ōō-) *v.i.* (Of sore, disease, etc., or fig. of discontent etc.) break out again; so ~E'SCENT *a.*, ~E'SCENCE *n.* [back form. f. *recrudescent, -ence* f. L *re(crudescere* f. *crudus* raw); see RE- 8, -ESCENT]

rècrui't¹ (-rōō't) *n.* Newly enlisted and not yet trained soldier, *soldier or sailor of lowest rank; person who joins a society etc.; (**raw**) ~, tiro. [earlier sense 'reinforcement', f. obs. F dial. *recrute* = F *recrue* fem. p.p. (as n.) of *recroître*, f. L *re(crescere* grow); see RE- 8]

rècrui't² (-rōō't) *v.* **1.** *v.t.* Enlist recruits for (army, regiment, crew, society, party); enlist (person) as recruit. **2.** Replenish, fill up deficiencies or compensate wear and tear in; refresh, reinvigorate. **3.** *v.i.* Get or seek recruits. **4.** (arch.) (Seek to) recover health etc. (*has gone into the country to recruit*); hence ~AL 2 *n.* **5.** Hence ~MENT *n.* [f. F *recruter* (*recrute*; see prec.)]

rĕ'ctal *a.* Of or by means of the rectum. [f. RECTUM + -AL]

rĕ'ctăngle (-ngg*e*l) *n.* Four-sided plane rectilinear figure with four right angles, esp. one with adjacent sides unequal. [F, or f. med. L *rectangulum* f. LL *rectiangulum* f. L *rectus* straight + *angulus* ANGLE¹]

rĕctă'ngūlar (-ngg-) *a.* Shaped, or having base or sides or section shaped, like rectangle; placed, or having parts or lines placed, at right angles; **~ co-ordinates** (measured along axes at right angles); **~ hyperbola** (with perpendicular asymptotes); hence ~ITY (-ă'r-) *n.*, ~LY² *adv.* [f. prec. + ANGULAR]

rĕ'ctĭ|fȳ *v.t.* **1.** Make right, correct, amend, reform, adjust, (method, calculation, statement, position, instrument). **2.** Abolish, get rid of, exchange for what is right, (abuse, anomaly, error, omission, grievance). **3.** (Chem.) Purify or refine by repeated distillation or other process. **4.** (Geom.) Find straight line equal in length to (curve). **5.** (Electr.) Convert (alternating current) to direct current. **6.** Hence or cogn. ~**fī**ABLE *a.*, ~FICA'TION, ~**fī**ER¹ (1, 2), *ns.* [ME, f. OF *rectifier* f. med. L *rectificare* f. L *rectus* right; see -FY]

rĕctĭlĭ'nėal *a.* = foll. [f., as foll. + -AL]

rĕctĭlĭ'nėar *a.* In or forming a straight line; bounded or characterized by straight lines; hence ~ITY (-ă'r-) *n.*, ~LY² *adv.* [f. LL *rectilineus* f. L *rectus* straight + *linea* LINE²; see -AR¹]

rĕ'ctĭtūde *n.* Moral uprightness, righteousness; correctness, rightness. [ME f. OF, or f. LL *rectitudo* f. L *rectus* right; see -TUDE]

rĕ'ctō *n.* (*pl.* ~**s**). Right-hand page of open book; front of leaf (opp. VERSO). [f. L *recto* (*folio*) on the right (leaf)]

rĕ'ctor *n.* **1.** (In Ch. of England) incumbent of parish where all tithes formerly passed to incumbent (cf. VICAR); (in R.C. Ch.) head priest of church etc.; LAY² *rector.* **2.** Head of university, college, school, or religious institution; (**Lord**) **R**~, elected representative of students on governing body of Scottish university. **3.** Hence ~ATE¹, ~SHIP, *ns.* [ME, f. OF *rectour* or f. L *rector* ruler (*regere rect-* rule; see -OR)]

rĕctŏr'ĭal *a.* & *n.* **1.** *a.* Pertaining to a rector. **2.** *n.* Election of Scottish university Rector. [f. prec. + -IAL]

rĕ'ctorỳ *n.* ‖Rector's benefice; rector's house. [f. AF & OF *rectorie* or med. L *rectoria* (as RECTOR; see -Y¹)]

rĕ'ctr|ĭx *n.* (*pl.* ~**ices** *pr.* -ĭsēz). Bird's strong tail-feather directing flight. [L, fem. of RECTOR]

rĕ'ct|um *n.* (*pl.* ~**ums** *or* ~**a**). Final section of large intestine, terminating at anus. [f. L *rectum* (*intestinum*) straight (intestine)]

rĕ'ct|us *n.* (*pl.* ~**i** *pr.* -ī). (Anat.) Straight muscle. [L, = straight]

rècŭ'mb|ent *a.* Lying down, reclining; hence

~ENCY *n.*, ~**ent**LY² *adv.* [f. L *re(cumbere* lie) recline; see RE- 9, -ENT]

rėcū'per|āte (*or* -koo'-) *v.t.* & *i.* Restore, be restored or recover, from exhaustion, illness, loss, etc.; so ~A'TION *n.*, ~ATIVE *a.* [f. L *recuperare* recover (as RE- 9, **cup-* = **cap-* take) + -ATE³]

rėcûr' *v.i.* (-rr-; *part. pr.* -ěr'ĭng *or* -ŭ'rĭng). Go back in thought or speech *to*; (of idea etc.) come back *to* one's mind etc., return to mind; (of problem etc.) present itself again; occur again, be repeated, (~**ring decimal,** decimal fraction in which same figures are repeated indefinitely). [f. L *re(currere curs-* run); see RE- 9]

rėcŭ'rrent *a.* (Of nerve, vein, branch, etc.) turning back so as to reverse direction; occurring again or often or periodically; hence **rėcŭ'r**rENCE *n.*, ~LY² *adv.* [f. as prec.; see -ENT]

rėcûr'sion *n.* Return; ~ **formula,** (Math.) expression giving successive terms of series etc.; hence **rėcûr'**SIVE *a.* [f. LL *recursio* (as RECUR; see -ION)]

rėcûr'v|e *v.t.* & *i.* Bend backwards; hence or cogn. ~ATE² *a.*, ~**at**URE *n.* [f. L *re(curvare -at-* bend); see RE- 9]

rĕ'cūs|ant (-z-) *n.* & *a.* (Hist.) (person) who refused to attend Church of England services; (person) refusing submission to authority or compliance with regulation (*against*); so ~ANCE, ~ANCY, *ns.* [f. L *recusare* refuse (as RE- 2, CAUSE¹); see -ANT]

rēcȳ'cle *v.t.* Return to previous stage of cyclic process, esp. convert (waste) to reusable material. [f. RE- 8 + CYCLE]

rĕd *a.* & *n.* **1.** *a.* Of or approaching the colour seen at least-refracted end of spectrum, of shades varying from crimson to bright brown and orange, esp. those seen in blood, rubies, glowing coals, human lips, and fox's hair, (*red as a rose* etc.; *blood, fiery, yellowish, deep*, etc., *-red*); flushed in face with shame, anger, etc.; (of hands) blood-stained; (of eyes) bloodshot, or sore with weeping; (of hair) reddish-brown, tawny; ALL-*red*; (as distinguishing epithet) *red deer, ant, cabbage*, etc. **2.** Having to do with bloodshed, burning, violence, or revolution (*red battle, ruin*; SEE¹ *red*; *a red republican*); anarchistic or communistic. **3.** (*R*~). Russian, Soviet, (*the Red Army, Air Force*). **4.** *Red* ADMIRAL; ~ **arsenic,** realgar; ~ **bark,** red kind of cinchona; ~ **biddy,** mixture of cheap red wine and methylated spirits; ~**-blind,** having retina insensitive to red rays; ~**-blooded,** virile, vigorous; ~**'breast,** robin; ||~**'brick,** (of university) of modern foundation; ~**'bud,** Amer. tree of Judas-tree genus; ~**'cap,** ||military policeman, *railway porter; ~ **carpet,** privileged treatment of important visitor; ~ **cedar,** an Amer. juniper (*Juniperus virginiana*); ~ **cell,** erythrocyte; *~ **cent,** smallest (orig. copper) coin; ~**'coat,** (Hist.) British soldier (from former scarlet uniform of most regiments); ~ **corpuscle,** erythrocyte; **Red Crescent,** organization like Red Cross in Muslim countries; ~ **cross,** (1) St. George's cross, national emblem of England, (2) Christian side in crusades; **Red Cross,** (emblem of) ambulance etc. service organized according to Geneva Convention of 1864 for treatment of sick and wounded in war and those suffering by large-scale natural disasters; *red* CURRANT; ||~ **duster,** (sl.) = *red* ENSIGN; ~**-eye,** rudd; ||~**-fish,** male salmon in spawning season; *red* FLAG⁴; ~ **gold,** (arch. or poet.) real gold, money; ||*red* GROUSE¹; **Red Guard,** young activist in Communist China; ~ **gum,** (1) teething-rash in children, (2) (kinds of eucalyptus yielding) reddish resin; ~**-ha'nded,** in the act of crime (*caught red-handed*); ~ **hat,** cardinal's hat, (symbol of) cardinal's rank; ~**'head,** person with red hair; ~ **heat,** being red-hot (lit. or fig.), temperature of red-hot thing; ~ **herring,** (1) herring(s) reddened by being cured in smoke (*neither fish, flesh, nor good* ~ *herring*, of indefinite character), (fig.) irrelevant diversion [f. use of red herring in exercising hounds]; ~**-hot,** heated to redness, highly exciting or excited, enthusiastic, furious; *red-hot* POKER¹; ||**Red Indian,** N. Amer. Indian, with reddish skin; *red* JASMINE; ||~ **lane,** (sl.) throat; ~ **lead,** pigment made from red oxide of lead; ~**-legs,** redshank, red-stemmed plant; ~**-letter,** (of day) marked with red letter(s) in calendar as saint's day or festival, (fig.) memorable as date of joyful occurrence; ~ **light,** red lamp as danger-signal on road, railway, etc. (*see the* ~ *light*, (fig.) realize approach of disaster) ~**-light district** (containing many brothels); *red* MAGGOT; ~ **man,** = *Red Indian*; ~ **meat,** beef, lamb, mutton, etc., (opp. *white meat*); ~ **orpiment,** realgar; ~ **pepper,** (1) CAYENNE pepper, (2) ripe fruit of PEPPER¹ 2; ~**'poll,** red-crested bird similar to linnet, (in *pl.*) red-haired polled cattle; ~ **rag,** thing that excites person's rage as red object enrages bull; *red* RATTLE²; ~ **ribbon,** ribbon of the Order of the Bath; *red* ROAN¹; ~ **rose,** emblem of Lancashire, or of House of Lancaster in Wars of the Roses; ~ **sanders,** red SANDAL²wood; ~**'shank,** large kind of sandpiper; ~**-shift,** (Astron.) displacement of spectral lines to longer wavelengths in radiation from distant galaxies etc.; ~**-short,** (of iron) brittle while red-hot; ~**'skin,** = *Red Indian*; ~ **snow** (reddened by snow-plant and common in Arctic and Alpine regions); ~ **spider,** mite infesting hothouse plants esp. vines; ~ **squirrel,** native English squirrel (*Sciurus leucourus*); **Red Star,** emblem of some Communist countries; ~**'start,** red-tailed song-bird of genus *Phoenicurus* [OE *steort* tail]; ~ **tape,** excessive use of or adherence to formalities esp. in public business; *Red* TERROR; ~**-water,** malarial cattle and sheep disease with red urine; ~ **wine** (coloured by grape-skins); ~**'wing,** thrush with red wing-coverts; ~**'wood,** tree yielding red wood, esp. Californian *Sequoia sempervirens*. **5.** Hence ~**'**DEN⁶ *v.t.* & *i.*, ~**'**DISH¹ 2, ~**'**DY², *adjs.*, ~'LY² *adv.*, ~'NESS *n.* **6.** *n.* Red colour; red pigment; red clothes or material (*dressed in red*); the red colour in roulette and rouge-et-noir; red light; red ball in billiards etc.; debtor side of account (**in the** ~, in debt); revolutionary radical or republican; anarchist; communist. [OE *rēad*, = OS *rōd*, OHG *rōt*, ON *rauthr*, Goth. *rauths* f. Gmc **raudhaz* f. IE **roudhos*]

rėdă'ct *v.t.* Put into literary form, arrange for publication, edit; so ~OR *n.* [f. L *red(igere act-* = *agere* drive, bring); see RE- 8]

rėdă'ction *n.* Preparing or being prepared for publication, revision, editing, rearrangement; new edition. [f. F *rédaction* f. L (as prec.; see -ION)]

rėdă'n *n.* Field-work with two faces forming salient angle. [F, f. *redent* notching (as RE-, *dent* tooth)]

rĕdd *v.t.* (**redd**). (esp. Sc.) Clear up; arrange, tidy; put right, settle, compose. [ME, = MLG, Du. *redden*]

rĕ'ddle *n.* Red ochre, ruddle. [var. of RUDDLE]

rēde¹ *n.* (arch.) Counsel, advice, whence ~'LESS (-dl-) *a.*; resolve, design; narrative. [OE *rǣd*, = OS *rād*, OHG *rāt*, ON *ráth* f. Gmc **rǣdhaz* (**rǣdhan* READ)]

For other words in *re-* see RE-.

rēde² *v.t.* (arch.) Advise (person (*to*) do); read (riddle, dream). [var. of READ, common ME sp. retained for arch. senses]

rēdĕ'corāte *v.t.*, **rēdĕcor**A'TION *n.* See RE- 8.

rėdee'm *v.t.* **1.** Buy back, recover by expenditure of effort or by stipulated payment, (*redeem* one's *rights, position, honour, mortgaged land, pawned goods*); compound for, buy off, (charge or obligation) by payment; convert (tokens etc.) into goods or cash. **2.** Fulfil (promise). **3.** Purchase the freedom of (another, one*self*); save (person's life) by ransom. **4.** Save, rescue, reclaim; (of God or Christ) deliver from sin and damnation. **5.** Make amends for, compensate, counterbalance, (fault, defect; *has one redeeming feature*); save *from* a defect (*the eyes redeem the face from ugliness*). **6.** Hence ~ABLE *a.*, ~ER¹ *n.* (esp. of Christ; see sense 4). [ME, f. OF *redimer* or L *red*(*imere -empt- = emere* buy); see RE- 8]

rėdĕ'mpt|ion *n.* **1.** Redeeming or being redeemed (**past** or **beyond ~ion,** such that there is no hope of redemption); deliverance from sin and damnation wrought by Christ's atonement (**in the year of our ~ion** *1973* etc., A.D. 1973 etc.). **2.** Thing that redeems (*that blow was* or *proved his redemption*). **3.** Hence ~IVE *a.* [ME f. OF, f. L *redemptio* (as prec.; see -ION)]

rēdėploy' *v.t.* Send (troops, workers, etc.) to new place or task; hence ~MENT *n.* [f. RE- 8 + DEPLOY]

rēdėscĕ'nd *v.i.* & *t.*, see RE- 9; **rēdėsī'gn** (-zī'n) *v.t.*, see RE- 8.

rēdī'al *v.t.* (||-ll-). Dial again. [f. RE- 8 + DIAL]

rēdĭffū'sion (-zhon) *n.* Relaying of broadcast programmes, esp. by wire from central receiver. [f. RE- 8 + DIFFUSION]

rĕ'dĭngōte (-ngg-) *n.* Woman's long coat with cut-away front or contrasting piece on front. [F, f. E *riding-coat*]

rėdĭ'ntėgr|āte *v.t.* Restore to wholeness or unity; renew or re-establish in united or perfect state; so ~A'TION *n.* [ME, f. L *red*(*integrare* INTEGRATE²); see RE- 9, -ATE³]

rēdĭrĕ'ct *v.t.* Direct again, esp. change address of (letter); hence ~ION *n.* [f. RE- 8 + DIRECT¹]

rēdĭsco'ver (-kŭ'-) *v.t.*, **rē**DISCO'VERY *n.*, **rēdĭssŏ'lve** (-z-) *v.t.* & *i.*, **rē**DISSOLU'TION *n.*, see RE- 9; **rēdĭstrĭ'būte** *v.t.*, **rēdĭstrĭbū'tı**ON *n.*, **rēdĭstrĭ'būt**IVE *a.*, **rēdĭvī'de** *v.t.*, **rē**DIVI'SION *n.*, see RE- 8.

rēdo' (-o͞o') *v.t.* (**redi'd; redo'ne** *pr.* -dŭ'n; cf. DO¹). Do again; redecorate. [f. RE- 8 + DO¹]

rĕ'dol|ent *a.* Fragrant; having a strong smell, odorous, (fig.) strongly suggestive or reminiscent or mentally associated, *of* or *with*; so ~ENCE *n.* [ME f. OF, or f. L *red*(*olēre* smell); see RE- 6, -ENT]

rēdou'ble (-dŭ'-) *v.* & *n.* **1.** *v.t.* & *i.* Intensify, increase, make or grow greater or more intense or numerous, (*redouble* one's *efforts*; *the clamour redoubled*). **2.** *v.t.* (Bridge). Double again a bid already doubled by opponent. **3.** *n.* (Bridge). Redoubling of a bid. [f. F *re*(*doubler* DOUBLE³); see RE- 6]

rėdou'bt (-ow't) *n.* Outwork or field-work usu. square or polygonal and without flanking defences. [f. F *redoute* f. obs. It. *ridotta* f. med. L *reductus* refuge f. p.p. of L *reducere* withdraw (see REDUCE); *-b-* after DOUBT¹ (cf. foll.)]

rėdou'btable (-ow't-) *a.* (Of opponent, warrior, controversialist, etc.) formidable. [ME, f. OF *redoutable* f. *re*(*douter* DOUBT²) fear; see RE- 6]

rėdou'btėd (-ow't-) *a.* (arch.) Dreaded, redoubtable. [p.p. of obs. *redoubt* f. OF *redouter* (see prec.)]

rėdou'nd *v.i.* Result in contributing, make great contribution, *to* one's advantage, credit, etc., (*this procedure will redound to our advantage*; *the tale* or *fact redounds to their credit*); come as final result *to*, come back or recoil *upon*, person (*the benefits that redound to us from his self-sacrifice*). [ME, orig. = overflow, f. OF *redonder* f. L *red*(*undare* surge f. *unda* wave); see RE- 6]

rĕ'dŏx *n.* & *a.* (Chem.) (Of) oxidation and reduction. [f. *red*uction + *ox*idation]

rēdraw' *v.t.* (**redrew'; ~n**). Draw again or differently. [f. RE- 8 + DRAW¹]

rėdrĕ'ss *v.t.*, & *n.* **1.** *v.t.* Readjust, set straight again, (~ **the balance,** restore equality); set right, remedy, make up for, get rid of, rectify, (distress, wrong, damage, grievance, abuse); hence ~AL 2, ~MENT, *ns.* **2.** *n.* Reparation for wrong, redressing *of* grievances etc. [ME, f. OF *redresse*(*r*), *redrecier* (as RE- 8, DRESS¹)]

rėdū'ce *v.* **1.** *v.t.* Convert physically or mentally *to* other (esp. simpler or more general) form (*reduce fraction to its lowest terms, oral traditions to writing, compound to components*), subject to such conversion (*reduce fractions, compound*), make suitable or conformable or adapted *to*, bring by classification or analysis *to* (*reduce observations to formula*; *the facts may all be reduced to three heads*). **2.** Bring by force or necessity *to* some state or action, subdue, bring back to obedience, (*reduce person to discipline, the Crown to submission, besieged fortress, rebels*; *reduced him to asserting an absurdity*; *was reduced to despair, to weakness, to borrowing clothes, to borrowing*). **3.** Bring lower (~ **to the ranks,** make (guilty N.C.O.) a private again); weaken (*is in a very reduced state*); diminish (*reduce liquid to two-thirds of its bulk*; *reduce the prices of the goods, the temperature of the mixture*); convert to smaller number by omission, reclassification, etc.; impoverish (**~d circumstances,** poverty after prosperity); (Photog.) make (negative) less dense. **4.** (Surg.) Restore (dislocated etc. part) to original or proper position, remedy (dislocation etc.) thus. **5.** (Chem.) Convert (oxide etc.) to metal; remove oxygen from or add hydrogen or electrons to. **6.** *v.i.* Lessen one's weight or size. **7.** Hence **rėdū'c**ER¹ (1, 2) *n.*, **rėdū'c**IBLE *a.* [ME in sense 'restore to original or proper position', f. L *re*(*ducere duct-* bring); see RE- 9]

reductio ad absurdum (rĭdŭktĭō ăd *a*bsėr'd*u*m) *n.* Proof of falsity by showing absurd logical consequence; proof of truth by thus proving falsity of alternative(s); carrying of principle to unpractical lengths. [L, = reduction to the absurd]

rėdŭ'ction *n.* Reducing or being reduced; amount by which prices etc. are reduced; reduced copy of picture, map, etc.; ~ **to absurdity,** = prec.; so **rėdŭ'ct**IVE *a.* [ME f. OF, or f. L *reductio* (as REDUCE; see -ION)]

rėdŭ'ction|ĭsm *n.* Analysis of complex things into simple constituents; view that a system can be fully understood in terms of its isolated parts, or an idea in terms of simple concepts; hence ~IST (2) *n.*, **~ĭ'st**IC *a.* [f. prec. + -ISM]

rėdŭ'nd|ant *a.* **1.** Superfluous; ||(of industrial worker) liable to dismissal as being no longer needed for any available job. **2.** Excessive, pleonastic; that can be omitted without loss of significance. **3.** Copious, luxuriant. **4.** Hence or cogn. ~ANCE, ~ANCY, *ns.* (||**~ancy payment,** by employer to redundant worker according to length of service etc.), **~ant**LY² *adv.* [f. L (as REDOUND; see -ANT)]

rėdū'plĭc|āte *v.t.* Make double, repeat; (Gram.) repeat (letter, syllable), form (tense) by reduplication; so ~ATIVE *a.* [f. LL *re*(*duplicare* DUPLICATE²); see RE- 8, -ATE³]

rėdūplĭcā'tion *n.* Doubling, repetition; counterpart; (Gram.) repetition of syllable (exactly or with change of vowel etc.: *hurly-burly, see-saw*) or letter in word-formation (esp. in perf. in Gk and L, as *leluka* from *luō*, *pependi* from *pendere*), part so repeated. [f. LL *reduplicatio* (as prec.; see -ATION)]

rēdȳe' *v.t.* (~**ing**). See RE- 8.

ree. See REEVE².

ree'bok *n.* Small S. Afr. antelope with sharp horns. [Du., = roebuck]

rē-ĕ'chō (-kō) *v.i.* & *t.* Echo; echo again and again, resound. [f. RE- 6 + ECHO²]

reed¹ *n.*, & *v.t.* **1.** *n.* (Tall straight stalk of) firm-stemmed water or marsh plant esp. of genus *Phragmites*; **broken** or (arch.) **bruised** ~, unreliable person or thing; **lean on a** ~, put trust in weak thing or person. **2.** (collect.) Reeds growing in a mass or used as material esp. for thatching, ||wheat-straw prepared for thatching. **3.** (poet.) Arrow; musical pipe of reed or straw; pastoral poetry. **4.** Vibrating part, of varying shape and material, used in some musical wind-instruments (esp. oboe, bassoon, clarinet, bagpipe, and some organ-pipes) to produce the sound; (usu. in *pl.*) reed instrument. **5.** Weaver's comblike implement for separating warp-threads and bringing weft into proper position; (in *pl.*) set of semi-cylindrical adjacent mouldings like reeds laid together. **6.** ~**-babbler** or **-bird** or **-warbler** or **-wren,** bird frequenting reed-beds, esp. *Acrocephalus scirpaceus*; ~**-bunting,** bunting frequenting reed-beds; ||~**-mace,** cat's-tail; ~**-organ,** (Mus.) harmonium etc. with wind operating metal reeds; ~**-pheasant,** bearded TIT¹; ~**-pipe,** (1) musical pipe of reed, (2) reeded organ-pipe; ~**-stop,** organ-stop consisting of reed-pipes. **7.** *v.t.* Thatch with reed; make (straw) into reed; decorate with moulding of reeds (see sense 5), whence ~'ING¹ (2) *n.*; fit (musical instrument or organ-pipe) with reed. [OE *hrēod*, = OS *hriod*, OHG (*h*)*riot* f. WG **hreudha*]

reed² *n.* Fourth STOMACH of ruminant. [OE *rēada*]

rē-ĕ'dĭt *v.t.*, **rē-**EDI'TION *n.*, **rē-ĕ'dūcāte** *v.t.*, see RE- 8.

ree'dlĭng *n.* Bearded TIT¹. [f. REED¹ + -LING¹]

ree'd|ȳ *a.* **1.** Full of reeds; (poet.) made of reed. **2.** Like a reed in weakness, slenderness, or (of grass etc.) thickness; (of voice) like reed instrument in tone, scratchy, not round and clear. **3.** Hence ~**ĭ**NESS *n.* [ME, f. REED¹ + -Y²]

reef¹ *n.*, & *v.t.* **1.** *n.* One of several strips across top of square sail or bottom of fore-and-aft sail that can be taken in or rolled up to reduce sail's surface in high wind; **take in a** ~, lit., or fig. proceed cautiously. **2.** ~**-knot,** double knot made symmetrically for secure holding and easy casting off; ~**-point,** one of short pieces of rope attached to sail to secure it when reefed. **3.** *v.t.* Take in reef(s) of (sail); shorten (topmast, bowsprit; paddles of paddle-wheel by shifting them nearer centre); ~**'ing-jacket,** thick close-fitting double-breasted jacket. [ME *riff, refe* f. Du. *reef, rif*, f. ON *rif* RIB, in same sense (cf. foll.)]

reef² *n.* **1.** Ridge of rock or shingle or sand at or just above or below surface of water; (fig.) hazardous obstacle. **2.** Lode of ore; bedrock surrounding this. [earlier *riff(e)* f. MDu., MLG *rif, ref*, f. ON *rif* (as prec.)]

ree'fer¹ *n.* One who reefs; (sl.) midshipman; REEF¹-knot; reefing-jacket. [f. REEF¹ + -ER¹]

ree'fer² *n.* Marijuana cigarette. [f. REEF¹ thing rolled + -ER¹]

***ree'fer³** *n.* (colloq.) Refrigerator. [abbr.]

reek¹ *n.* **1.** Foul or stale smell (*the reek of tobacco*); fetid atmosphere (*amid reek and squalor*). **2.** (Sc. or literary). Smoke; vapour, visible exhalation; hence ~'Y² *a.* (**Auld Reekie,** Edinburgh). [OE *rēc*, **rīec*, = OS *rōk*, OHG *rouh*, ON *reykr* f. Gmc **raukiz* (**rauk-*, **reuk-*; cf. foll.)]

reek² *v.i.* **1.** Smell unpleasantly (*of* garlic, tobacco, blood; (fig.) *of* corruption, affectation, etc.). **2.** Emit smoke, vapour, steam, etc. [OE *rēocan*, = MDu. *rieken*, OHG *riohhan*, ON *rjúka* f. Gmc **reuk-*; cf. prec.]

reel¹ *n.*, & *v.t.* **1.** *n.* Rotatory device on which thread, silk, yarn, paper, film, wire, etc., are wound; quantity of thread etc. thus wound; contrivance for winding and unwinding line as required, esp. in fishing (**off the** ~, (fig.) straight off, without hitch or pause, in rapid succession); ||small cylinder with rimmed ends on which sewing-cotton etc. is wound for convenience; revolving part in various machines. **2.** *v.t.* Wind (thread, fishing-line, etc.) on reel; take (cocoon silk etc.) *off*, draw (fish, log-line, etc.) *in* or *up*, by use of reel; rattle (story, list, verses) *off* without pause or apparent effort. [OE *hrēol*, of unkn. orig.]

reel² *v.i.*, & *n.* **1.** *v.i.* (Of eyes, mind, head) be in a whirl, be dizzy, swim; sway, stagger, stand or walk or run unsteadily, be shaken physically or mentally, rock from side to side, swing violently, (*his mind, the front rank, the ship, the tower, reeled under the shock*; *reel to and fro like a drunken man*); seem to shake (*the mountains reeled before his eyes*). **2.** *n.* Reeling motion (lit. or fig.; *without a reel or a stagger*; *the reel of vice and folly around us*). [ME, f. prec.]

reel³ *n.*, & *v.i.* **1.** *n.* Lively esp. Scottish dance, usu. of two couples in line and describing circular figures; music for this. **2.** *v.i.* Dance reel. [perh. f. prec. 2]

rē-ėlĕ'ct *v.t.*, **rē-**E'LECTION *n.*, **rē-**E'LIGIBLE *a.*, **rē-ėmbar̄'k** *v.i.* & *t.*, **rē-ĕmbar̄k**A'TION *n.*, **rē-ėmer̄'ge** *v.i.*, **rē-ėmer̄'g**ENCE *n.*, **rē-ėmer̄'g**ENT *a.*, **rē-ėnă'ct** *v.t.*, **rē-ėnă'ct**MENT *n.*, see RE- 9.

***rē-ėnfor̄'ce.** Var. of REINFORCE.

rē-ĕ'nter *v.i.* & *t.*, **rē-**E'NTRANCE *n.* See RE- 9, and cf. foll. and RE-ENTRY.

rē-ĕ'ntrant *a.* & *n.* (Angle) pointing inwards (opp. *salient*; esp. in Fortif.); reflex (angle). [f. RE- 9 + as ENTRANT]

rē-ĕ'ntrȳ *n.* Act of entering again, esp. (of spacecraft, missile, etc.) of re-entering earth's atmosphere; (Law) a retaking, possession; (**card of**) ~, card that can be relied on to give holder the lead again by winning a trick. [f. RE- 9 + ENTRY]

rē-ėstă'blĭsh *v.t.*, **rē-ėstă'blĭsh**MENT *n.* See RE- 9.

reeve¹ *n.* **1.** (Hist.) Chief magistrate of town or district; manorial supervisor of villeins. **2.** Minor local official; (Can.) president of village or town council. [OE (*ge*)*rēfa*, *girǣfa* (as Y-, **rōf* assembly)]

reeve², ree, *n.* Female of RUFF². [17th c. & 16th c., of unkn. orig.]

reeve³ *v.t.* (**rove** *or* ~**d**). (Naut.) Thread (rope, rod, etc.) *through* ring or other aperture; pass rope through (block etc.); fasten (rope, block, or other object) *in, on, round, to*, something by reeving; (of ship) thread (shoals, ice-pack). [prob. f. Du. *rēven* REEF¹]

rē-ėxă'mĭne (-gz-) *v.t.* Examine again (esp. one's witness after cross-examination by opponents); so **rē-ėxămĭn**A'TION (-gz-) *n.* [f. RE- 8 + EXAMINE]

rē-ėxpor̄'t¹ *v.t.*, **rē-ĕ'xpor̄t²** *n.* See RE- 9.

rĕf *n.* (colloq.) Referee. [abbr.]

For other words in *re-* see RE-.

ref. *abbr.* reference.
rēfā′ce *v.t.* Put new facing on (building). [f. RE- 8 + FACE²]
rēfā′shion (-shon) *v.t.* See RE- 8.
rėfĕ′ction *n.* Refreshment by food or drink (*milk and eggs were offered for our refection*); slight meal, repast. [ME f. OF, f. L *refectio -onis* f. *reficere* (as foll.); see RE- 8, -ION]
rėfĕ′ctorў (*or in monastic use* rĕ′fĭ-) *n.* Room used for meals in monasteries, colleges, etc.; ~ **table** (long and narrow). [f. LL *refectorium* f. L *re(ficere fect- = facere* make) refresh; see RE- 8, -ORY]
rėfer′ *v.* (**-rr-**). **1.** *v.t.* Trace or ascribe *to* person or thing as cause or source, consider as belonging *to* certain date or place or class, (*refer* one's *victories to Providence, miraculous tales to ignorance, ill temper to indigestion, the lake-dwellings to the sixth century, the origins of sculpture to Egypt, barnacles to the molluscs*); ~**red pain** (felt in part of body other than its true source); hence ~ABLE (*or* rĕ′fer-) *a.* **2.** Commit, hand over, (one*self*, question for decision) *to* person etc. (*I refer myself to your generosity*; *let us refer the dispute to arbitration*); ~ **to drawer** (banker's note suspending payment etc. of cheque). **3.** *v.t. & i.* Send on or direct (person), make appeal or have recourse, *to* some authority or source of information, (abs.) cite authority or passage, (*for proof I refer to your report, to the facts of human nature, to Proverbs 10:19*; *referred to his watch for the exact time*); send (person) to medical specialist etc., whence ~RAL 2 *n.*; send (proposal etc.) *back to* lower body, court, etc.; fail (examination candidate). **4.** *v.t.* Interpret (statement etc.) as being directed *to*. **5.** *v.i.* (Of statement etc.) have relation, be directed, *to* (*these remarks refer only to deliberate offences*). **6.** (Of person speaking etc.) make allusion, direct attention, *to* (*he several times referred to the increase in expenditure*; *found myself on the peak referred to*). [ME, f. OF *referer* f. L *re(ferre latum* bring) carry back; see RE- 9]
rĕferee′ *n.* & *v.* **1.** *n.* Arbitrator, person to whom dispute is to be or is referred for decision; ‖**Official R**~, person attached to Supreme Court, to whom questions arising in an action may be referred for inquiry and report or for trial where parties consent; umpire esp. in football or boxing; ‖person willing to testify to character of applicant for employment; person who assesses value of scientific paper etc. sent for publication. **2.** *v.i.* & *t.* Act as referee (for). [f. prec. + -EE]
rĕ′ference *n.*, & *v.t.* **1.** *n.* Referring of matter for decision or settlement or consideration to some authority, scope given to such authority, (*the peerage was allowed without reference to the House of Lords*; *the Commission must confine itself to, that is a question outside, the terms of reference*). **2.** Relation, respect, correspondence, *to* (*the parts of a machine all have reference to each other*; *success seems to have little reference to merit*); **in** or **with** ~ **to,** regarding, as regards, about; **without** ~ **to,** not taking account of. **3.** Allusion *to* (*made reference, a* or *no reference, several references, to our previous conversation*). **4.** Direction more or less precise *to* (page etc. of) book, file, etc. where information may be found (*gives many, verify your, does not give, references*); book, passage, etc., so cited; ~ **mark** (used to refer reader of text to note or to part of diagram, esp. asterisk *, obelisk or dagger †, double obelisk ‡, section §, parallel ‖, paragraph ¶). **5.** Act of looking up passage etc., or of referring another or applying to person, for information (*reference to the dictionary would have enlightened him*; *please give me a reference to, supply a reference from, your last employer*); ~ (**book**) (to be used not for continuous reading but to consult on occasion); *reference* LIBRARY. **6.** Person willing to testify to character of applicant for employment or of would-be credit-account customer etc.; testimonial; thing taken to have standard value etc. **7.** Hence **rĕferĕ′nt**IAL (-shal) *a.* **8.** *v.t.* Provide (book etc.) with references to authorities. [f. REFER + -ENCE]
rĕferĕ′nd|um *n.* (*pl.* ~**a** *or* ~**ums**). Referring of political question to electorate for direct decision by general vote; vote thus taken. [L, gerund or neut. gerundive of *referre* (REFER)]
rĕ′ferent *n.* What is symbolized by word etc. [f. L *referens* (as prec.; see -ENT)]
rėfer′ral. See REFER 3.
rĕ′ffō *n.* (*pl.* ~**s**). (Austral. sl.) European refugee. [abbr. + -o]
rēfĭ′ll¹ *v.t.* Fill again; provide new filling for. [f. RE- 9 + FILL]
rē′fĭll² *n.* Renewed filling; material etc. used for this. [f. prec.]
rėfī′ne *v.* **1.** *v.t.* Free from dross or impurities or defects, purify, clarify; make elegant or cultured, imbue with delicacy of feeling or taste, polish manners or appearance of; improve (up)on by refinements. **2.** *v.i.* Become pure or clear or improved in polish or delicacy; employ subtlety of thought or language, make fine distinctions. [f. RE- 6 + FINE² v., & F *raffiner*]
rėfī′nement (-nm-) *n.* Refining or being refined; fineness of feeling or taste, polished manners etc.; subtle or ingenious manifestation *of*, piece of elaborate arrangement, (*all the refinements of reasoning, torture*; *a countermine was a refinement beyond their skill*); instance of improvement (*up*)*on*; piece of subtle reasoning, fine distinction. [f. prec. + -MENT, after F *raffinement*]
rėfī′n|er *n.* In vbl senses; person whose business is to refine crude oil, metal, sugar, etc., whence ~ERY (3) *n.* [f. REFINE + -ER¹]
rēfĭ′t¹ *v.t.* & *i.* (**-tt-**). Make or become fit again (esp. of ship undergoing renewal and repairs); hence ~MENT *n.* [f. RE- 8 + FIT⁴]
rē′fĭt² *n.* Refitting. [f. prec.]
rēflā′te *v.t.* (Econ.) Cause reflation of (currency, economy, etc.). [f. RE- 9, after *inflate, deflate*]
rēflā′tion *n.* (Econ.) Inflation following deflation, to restore system to its previous condition. [f. RE- 9, after *inflation, deflation*]
rėflĕ′ct *v.* **1.** *v.t.* (Of surface or body) throw back (heat, light, sound, object, etc.), cause to rebound, (**shine with** ~**ed light,** be noticeable only because of another's brilliance). **2.** (Of mirror etc., or transf.) show image of, reproduce to eye or mind, exactly correspond in appearance or effect to, (*laws reflect the average moral attitude of half a century earlier*); ~**ing telescope,** = REFLECTOR 2. **3.** (Of action, result, etc.) bring back or cause to redound (credit, discredit, etc.), (abs.) bring discredit, (*up*)*on* person or method responsible. **4.** *v.i.* & *t.* Go back in thought, meditate, or consult with oneself (*on, upon,* or abs.), remind oneself or consider (*that, how,* etc.). **5.** *v.i.* Make disparaging remarks (*up*)*on*. [ME, f. OF *reflecter* or f. L *re(flectere flex-* bend); see RE- 9]
rėflĕ′ction, ‖**rėflĕ′xion,** (-kshon) *n.* **1.** Reflecting or being reflected (**angle of** ~, angle made by reflected ray with perpendicular to surface); reflected light, heat, colour, or image. **2.** (Piece of) censure (*on* or *upon*); thing bringing discredit (*up*)*on*. **3.** Reconsideration (*on reflection, I doubt whether I was right*). **4.** Mental faculty dealing with products of sensation and perception. **5.** Idea arising in the mind, mental or verbal; comment, apophthegm, (*on* or *upon*). **6.** Hence ~AL, ~LESS, *adjs.* [ME, f. OF *reflexion* or f. LL *reflexio* (as prec.; see -ION), w. assim. to *reflect*]

rèflĕ'ctive *a.* **1.** (Of surface etc.) giving back reflection or image; (of light etc.) reflected. **2.** (Of mental faculties) concerned in reflection or thought; (of person, mood, etc.) thoughtful, given to meditation. **3.** Hence ~LY² (-vlĭ) *adv.*, ~NESS (-vn-) *n.* [f. REFLECT + -IVE]

rèflĕ'ctor *n.* **1.** Body or surface reflecting rays, particles, objects, etc., esp. piece of glass or metal (usu. concave) for reflecting light in required direction. **2.** (Telescope etc. provided with) apparatus for reflecting images. [f. REFLECT + -OR]

reflet (reflĕ') *n.* Lustre or iridescence, esp. on pottery. [F, f. It. *riflesso* reflection, REFLEX¹]

rē'flĕx¹ *n.* **1.** Reflected light or colour or glory (*the fame of Greece was a reflex from the glory of Athens*); (Paint.) part of picture represented as affected by the light or colour of another part. **2.** Image or reflection in mirror etc. **3.** Reproduction, secondary manifestation, corresponding result, (*legislation should be a reflex of public opinion*). **4.** (Philol.) Word etc. formed by development from earlier stage of language. **5.** A reflex action (*doctor tested patient's reflexes*); CONDITION²*ed reflex*; hence **~ŏ'**LOGY *n.* [f. L *reflexus* (as REFLECT)]

rē'flĕx² *a.* **1.** Bent backwards; (of light etc.) reflected; ~ **angle** (exceeding 180°). **2.** (Of thought etc.) introspective, directed back upon itself or its own operations; (of effect or influence) reactive, coming back upon its author or source; (Radio etc.) using same amplifier for both radio-frequency and audio-frequency signal; copying by reflection from object to be copied. **3.** (Physiol.) ~ **action** (independent of the will, caused as automatic response to nerve-stimulation); ~ **arc,** sequence of nerves involved in this. **4.** ~ **(camera)**, camera in which image is reflected by pivoted mirror to allow focusing up to moment of exposure. **5.** Hence ~LY² *adv.* [f. L *reflexus* p.p. of *reflectere* REFLECT]

rèflĕ'xed (-kst) *a.* (Bot.) Bent back. [p.p. of obs. *reflex* v. = REFLECT]

rèflĕ'x|ĭble *a.* Capable of being reflected; hence ~IBI'LITY *n.* [f. as prec. + -IBLE]

reflexion. See REFLECTION.

rèflĕ'xĭve *a.* & *n.* (Gram.) (Word or form) implying subject's action on himself or itself (*pride* one*self*, *wash* one*self*, *suggest itself*, *bethought me*); (adjective) referring to subject of sentence; (verb) indicating that subject is same as object; *reflexive* PRONOUN; hence ~LY² (-vlĭ) *adv.* [f. as REFLEXED + -IVE]

rēfloa't *v.t.* Set (stranded ship) afloat again. [f. RE- 9 + FLOAT²]

rĕ'flu|ent (-ōō-) *a.* Flowing back (*refluent tide, blood*); hence ~ENCE *n.* [ME, f. L *re(fluere* flow); see RE- 9, -ENT]

rē'flŭx *n.* Backward flow; (Chem.) method of boiling in which vapour is liquefied and returned to boiler. [ME, f. RE- 9 + FLUX]

rēfŏ'rĕst *v.t.*, **rēfŏrĕst**A'TION *n.* See RE- 9.

rèfōr'm¹ *v.* **1.** *v.t.* & *i.* Make (person, institution, procedure, conduct, one*self*), or (of person or body of persons) become, better by removal or abandonment of imperfections, faults, or errors; *correct legal document; **R~ed,** of Reform Judaism; **R~ed Church,** one that has accepted the principles of the Reformation, esp. Calvinist opp. Lutheran. **2.** *v.t.* Abolish, cure, (abuse, malpractice). **3.** Hence ~ABLE *a.* [ME, f. OF *reformer* or f. L *re(formare* FORM²); see RE- 8]

rèfōr'm² *n.* Removal of abuse(s) esp. in politics (**R~ Bill, Act,** those of 1831–2 etc. amending parliamentary representation); improvement made or suggested; (*R~*) simplified and rationalized form of Judaism; ~ **school,** reformatory for young persons. [f. prec. or f. F *réforme*]

rē-fōr'm³ *v.t.* & *i.* Form again. [f. RE- 8 + FORM²]

rē-fōrmā'tion¹ *n.* Forming or being formed again. [f. RE- 8 + FORMATION]

rĕformā'tion² *n.* Reforming or being reformed, esp. radical change for the better in political, religious, or social affairs; **the R~**, 16th-c. movement for reform of doctrines and practices of Roman Church ending in establishment of Reformed or Protestant Churches, whence ~AL *a.* [ME f. OF, or f. L *reformatio* (as REFORM¹; see -ATION)]

rèfōr'matĭve *a.* = foll. [f. OF *reformatif -ive* or med. L *reformativus* (as REFORM¹; see -ATIVE)]

rèfōr'matorў *a.* & *n.* **1.** *a.* Tending or intended to produce reform. **2.** *n.* (U.S. or Hist.) Institution to which juvenile or female offenders are sent to be reformed. [f. REFORMATION + -ORY]

rèfōr'mer *n.* In vbl senses; leader in the Reformation; advocate of reform. [f. REFORM¹ + -ER¹]

rèfōr'm|ĭsm *n.* Policy of reform rather than abolition; hence ~IST (2) *n.* [f. REFORM² + -ISM]

rèfră'ct *v.t.* (Of water, air, glass, etc.) deflect (ray of light etc.) at certain angle when it enters obliquely from another medium of different density; determine refractive condition of (eye); hence or cogn. ~ION *n.* (**angle of ~ion,** angle made by refracted ray with perpendicular to surface; **double ~ion,** refraction forming two rays in different directions), ~IVE *a.* (**~ive index,** ratio of velocity of light in two adjacent media). [f. L *re(fringere fract-=frangere* break); see RE- 5]

rèfrăctŏ'mèter *n.* Instrument for measuring refractive index. [f. prec. + -O- + -METER]

rèfră'ctor *n.* Refracting medium or lens; telescope using lens to produce image. [f. REFRACT + -OR]

rèfră'ctor|ў *a.* & *n.* **1.** *a.* Stubborn, unmanageable, rebellious; (of wound, disease, etc.) not yielding to treatment; (of person etc.) resistant to infection; (of substance) hard to fuse or work. **2.** Hence ~ĭLY² *adv.*, ~ĭNESS *n.* **3.** *n.* Substance specially resistant to heat, corrosion, etc. [alt. of obs. *refractary* f. L *refractarius* (as REFRACT, -ARY¹); see -ORY]

rèfrai'n¹ *n.* Recurring phrase or line(s) esp. at end of stanzas; music accompanying this. [ME f. OF, earlier *refrait*, prob. f. Prov. *refranh*, bird song (*refranhar* f. Rom. **refrangere*, L *refringere*; see REFRACT)]

rèfrai'n² *v.* **1.** *v.t.* (arch.) Put restraint upon, curb, (one*self*, one's tears, soul, etc.). **2.** *v.i.* Abstain from doing something; abstain *from* act or do*ing*. [ME, f. OF *refrener* f. L *re(frenare* f. *frenum* bridle); see RE- 9]

rèfră'ng|ĭble (-nj-) *a.* That can be refracted; hence ~IBI'LITY *n.* [f. mod. L *refrangibilis* (*refrangere* = L *refringere*; see REFRACT, -IBLE)]

rèfrĕ'sh *v.* **1.** *v.t.* (Of food, drink, rest, amusement, etc., or person providing these, esp. in ~ one**self**) reanimate, reinvigorate; **~ing** *innocence* etc., interesting to blasé observer. **2.** Freshen up (memory, esp. by consulting source of information); restore (fire etc.) with fresh supply; make cool again. **3.** *v.i.* Take esp. liquid refreshment. [ME, f. OF *refreschi(e)r* (*fres fresche* FRESH; see RE- 9)]

rèfrĕ'sher *n.* In vbl senses; extra fee to counsel in prolonged case; (colloq.) a drink; ~ **course** (reviewing previous studies, or giving instruction in modern methods etc.). [ME, f. prec. + -ER¹]

rėfrĕ'shment *n.* Refreshing or being refreshed in mind or body; thing, esp. (usu. in *pl.*) drink or food, that refreshes (*the sight was a refreshment to him*; *take some refreshment(s)*); ~ **room** (where food and drink are available at railway station etc.); **R~ Sunday** (4th in Lent, with gospel f. John 6). [ME, f. OF *refreschement* (as REFRESH; see -MENT)]

rėfrĭ'gerant *a.* & *n.* (Substance) that cools or (Med.) allays fever. [f. F *réfrigérant* or f. L (as foll.; see -ANT)]

rėfrĭ'ger|āte *v.* **1.** *v.t.* & *i.* Make or become cool or cold. **2.** Subject (food etc.) to extreme cold in order to freeze or preserve. **3.** So ~A'TION *n.* [f. L *re(frigerare* f. *frigus frigoris* cold); see RE- 9, -ATE[3]]

rėfrĭ'gerātor *n.* Cabinet or room in which food etc. is refrigerated. [f. prec. + -OR]

rėfrĭ'geratorў *n.* & *a.* **1.** *n.* Cold-water vessel attached to still for condensing vapour. **2.** *a.* Cooling. [f. mod. L *refrigeratorium* n., L *refrigeratorius* a. (as REFRIGERATE; see -ORY)]

rėfrĭ'ng|ent (-nj-) *a.* (Phys.) Refracting; hence ~ENCE, ~ENCY, *ns.* [f. L *refringere*; see REFRACT, -ENT]

rĕft. See REAVE.

rēfū'el *v.t.* & *i.* (‖-ll-). Replenish fuel supply (of). [f. RE- 9 + FUEL]

rĕ'fūge *n.* **1.** (Place of) shelter from pursuit or danger or trouble (*seek refuge*; *has found a refuge*; *take refuge in a cave, in lying*); **city of** ~ (for those guilty of manslaughter in ancient Israel); (**house of**) ~, institution for the homeless etc. **2.** Person, thing, course, that gives shelter or is resorted to in difficulties (*he is the refuge of the distressed*; *books are the refuge of the destitute*); traffic island. [ME f. OF, f. L *re(fugium* f. *fugere* flee); see RE- 4]

rĕfūgee' *n.* Person taking refuge, esp. in foreign country from religious or political persecution, or from war, earthquake, etc. [f. F *réfugié* p.p. (as n.) of *(se) réfugier* (as prec.)]

rėfŭ'lg|ent *a.* Shining, gloriously bright; hence or cogn. ~ENCE *n.*, ~**ent**LY[2] *adv.* [f. L *re(fulgēre* shine); see RE- 6, -ENT]

rēfŭ'nd[1] *v.t.* Pay back (money received or taken, expenses incurred by another, or abs.); reimburse; hence ~MENT *n.* [ME, in sense 'pour back', f. OF *refonder* or f. L *re(fundere fus-* pour; see RE- 9); later assoc. w. FUND]

rē'fŭnd[2] *n.* Refunding; repayment. [f. prec.]

rē-fŭ'nd[3] *v.t.* Fund (debt etc.) afresh. [f. RE- 8 + FUND]

rēfûr'bĭsh *v.t.*, see RE- 9; **rēfûr'nĭsh** *v.t.*, see RE- 8.

rėfū'sal (-z-) *n.* **1.** Refusing or being refused; **will take no** ~, is importunate. **2.** (**First**) ~, right or privilege of deciding to accept or reject a thing before it is offered to others. [f. foll. + -AL 2]

rėfū's|e[1] (-z) *v.* **1.** *v.t.* Say or convey by action that one will not accept or submit to or give or grant or gratify or consent (*refuse offer, gift, chance, office, candidate*, person as husband etc.; *refuse orders, control*, etc.; *refuse obedience, compliance*; *refused me satisfaction, my request*; *refuse to* do; *car refuses to start*); not grant request made by (person); (of horse) be unwilling to jump (fence etc., or abs.); hence ~ABLE *a.* **2.** *v.i.* Make refusal; (Cards) not follow suit. [ME, f. OF *refuser* f. Rom. **refusare* prob. f. L *recusare* (see RECUSANT) after *refutare* REFUTE]

rĕ'fūse[2] *n.* & *a.* (What is) rejected as worthless or left over after use. [ME, perh. f. OF *refusé* p.p. (as prec.)]

rē-fū'se[3] (-z) *v.t.* Fuse again. [f. RE- 9 + FUSE[1,3]]

rėfū't|e *v.t.* Prove falsity or error of (statement, opinion, argument, person advancing it), rebut or repel by argument; hence or cogn. ~ABLE *a.*, ~AL 2, **rĕfūt**A'TION, *ns.* [f. L *re(futare*; cf. CONFUTE); see RE- 9]

rėgai'n *v.t.* Recover possession of (*regain confidence, consciousness*); reach (place) again; recover (one's *balance* or *feet* or *footing* or *legs*). [f. F *re(gagner* GAIN[2]); see RE- 9]

rē'gal *a.* Of or by kings (*regal government, title, office*); fit for a king, magnificent, (*lives in regal splendour*); hence ~LY[2] *adv.* [ME f. OF, or f. L *regalis* (*rex regis* king; see -AL)]

rėgā'le[1] *n.* (arch.) Choice repast (lit. or fig.), feast of some dainty; a dainty; choice flavour (*viands of higher regale*). [obs. F, f. OF *gale* pleasure]

rėgā'le[2] *v.* **1.** *v.t.* Entertain choicely (often iron.) with food or *with* talk etc.; (of beauty, flowers, etc.) give delight to. **2.** *v.i.* Feed oneself choicely (*on*). **3.** Hence ~MENT (-lm-) *n.* [f. F *régaler* (as prec.)]

rėgā'lia[1] (-lyа) *n. pl.* Insignia of royalty used at coronations; insignia of an order, e.g. of Freemasons, or of civic dignity. [med. L, = royal privileges, f. L, neut. pl. of *regalis* REGAL; see -IA[2]]

rėgā'lia[2] (-lyа) *n.* Large cigar of especially good quality. [f. Sp. *regalia* royal privilege (cf. prec.)]

rē'galĭsm *n.* Doctrine of sovereign's ecclesiastical supremacy. [f. REGAL + -ISM]

rėgă'lĭtў *n.* Attribute of kingly power, being king, (*things that touch his regality*); royal privilege. [ME, f. OF *regalité* or f. med. L *regalitas* (as REGAL; see -ITY)]

rėgâr'd[1] *v.t.* **1.** Gaze upon (usu. w. adv. phr. or adv.; *found him regarding me with curiosity, intently*). **2.** Give heed to, take into account, let one's course be affected by, (esp. w. neg.; person, advice, etc., or abs.). **3.** Look upon or contemplate mentally *with* reverence, horror, etc., or in specified manner (*regard it in that light*) or with specified sentiment (*I still regard him kindly*), or *as* being (*is to be regarded as a wild beast*; *regard it as madness* or *indispensable*, *him as among my friends*). **4.** (Of thing) concern, have relation to, have some connection with; **as ~s, ~ing** (*part.* or *prep.*), about, concerning, in respect of, so far as it concerns, (*considerations regarding peace*; *am innocent as regards* or *regarding the former*). [ME, f. F *re(garder* GUARD[2]); see RE- 6; cf. REWARD]

rėgâr'd[2] *n.* **1.** Gaze, steady or significant look. **2.** Respect, point attended to, (*in this* etc. *regard*; **in ~ to** or **of, with ~ to,** regarding, in respect of; **in** person's ~, concerning or about or towards him. **3.** Attention, heed, care, (*to* or *for*; *regard must be had* or *paid to general principles*; *the next object of regard is his conduct*; *act without regard to* or *for decency*; *pays no regard to expostulations* or *adviser*); hence ~FUL *a.* (*of*). **4.** Esteem, kindly feeling or respectful opinion, (*for*; *have little* or *a great regard for him*, *no* or *a high regard for his judgement* or *advice*); (in *pl.*) expression of friendliness in letter etc., compliments, (*kind regards to you all*; *give him my* (*best* etc.) *regards*). [ME f. OF *regard* (*regarder*; see prec.)]

rėgâr'dant *a.* (Her.) looking backwards; (arch.) observant, with steady or intent gaze. [AF & OF (as REGARD[1]; see -ANT)]

rėgâr'dlėss *a.* & *adv.* Without paying attention; without regard or consideration (*of* expense etc., or abs.); hence ~LY[2] *adv.*, ~NESS *n.* [f. REGARD[2] + -LESS]

rėgă'tta *n.* Meeting for boat or yacht races. [It. (Venetian)]

regd. *abbr.* registered.

rĕgėl|ā'te *v.i.* Freeze again (esp. of pieces of ice etc. frozen together after temporary thawing of surfaces); hence ~A'TION *n.* [f. RE- 9 + L *gelare* freeze + -ATE[3]]

rē'gency̆ *n.* Office of regent; commission acting as regent; regent's or regency-commission's period of office (**the R~**, 1810–20 in England, 1715–23 in France; **R~ dress, furniture,** etc., of the style characteristic of the Regency in England; **R~ stripes,** broad coloured stripes of equal width on fabric etc.). [ME, f. med. L *regentia* (as REGENT; see -ENCY)]

rėgĕ'ner|āte *v.* **1.** *v.t.* Invest with new and higher spiritual nature; improve moral condition of, breathe new and more vigorous and spiritually higher life into, (person, institution, etc.). **2.** Generate again, bring into renewed existence, (*must regenerate his self-respect*); form afresh (lost etc. part of body); (Electr.) increase (current) by feedback. **3.** *v.i.* Reform oneself. **4.** Come into renewed existence. **5.** Hence or cogn. ~ATE², ~ATIVE, *adjs.*, ~A'TION, ~**āt**OR, *ns.* [f. L *re(generare* GENERATE); see RE- 8]

rēgĕ'nėsĭs *n.* See RE- 8.

rē'gent *n.* & *a.* **1.** *n.* (arch.) Ruler, ruling principle. **2.** Person appointed to administer State, esp. kingdom during minority, absence, or incapacity of monarch. **3.** *Member of the governing body of a State University. **4.** **~-bird,** Austral. bower-bird; ||**R~ House,** (Cambridge Univ.) general assembly of resident senior members. **5.** *a.* (placed after *n.*) Acting as regent (*Queen, Prince,* etc., *Regent*). [ME f. OF, or f. L *regere* rule; see -ENT]

rēgẽr'mĭnāte *v.i.*, **rēgẽrmĭn**A'TION *n.* See RE- 9.

rĕ'ggae (-ā) *n.* W. Ind. style of music with strongly accented subsidiary beat. [W. Ind.]

rĕ'gĭcide *n.* Killer or participator in killing of a king (**the R~s,** those concerned in trying and executing Charles I of England or Louis XVI of France); killing of a king; hence **rĕgĭcī'd**AL *a.* [f. L *rex regis* king + -I- + -CIDE]

régie (rāzhē') *n.* State monopoly or control of tobacco, salt, etc. [F, fem. p.p. of *régir* rule]

rēgĭ'ld (-g-) *v.t.* See RE- 9.

regi'me, régi'me, (rāzhē'm) *n.* **1.** Method or system of government, prevailing system of things; ANCIEN RÉGIME. **2.** Condition(s) under which scientific, industrial, etc., process occurs. [f. F *régime* f. as foll.]

rĕ'gĭmen *n.* (Med.) prescribed course of exercise, way of life, and esp. diet; (Gram.) relation of syntactic dependence between words, government; (arch.) system of government. [L (*regere* rule)]

rĕ'gĭment (*or* -jm-) *n.*, & *v.t.* **1.** *n.* Rule, government, (*monstrous regiment of women*). **2.** Permanent recruiting and training unit of army usu. commanded by (Lieutenant-)Colonel and divided into several companies or troops or batteries and often into two or more battalions; operational unit of artillery, tanks, armoured cars, etc.; **Royal R~ (of Artillery),** Royal Artillery. **3.** Large array or number, legion, (usu. *of*). **4.** *v.t.* Form (men) into regiment(s); organize (workers, labour, data, etc., esp. oppressively) in groups or according to a system, whence **rĕgĭment**A'TION *n.* [ME f. OF, f. LL *regimentum* (as prec.; see -MENT)]

rĕgĭmĕ'ntal *a.* & *n.* **1.** *a.* Of a regiment; *regimental* COLOUR¹; hence ~LY² *adv.* **2.** *n.* (in *pl.*) Dress worn by regiment, military uniform. [f. prec. + -AL]

Regina (rĭjī'na) *n.* Reigning queen (abbr. *R.*, in signatures to proclamations: *Elizabeth R.*; in titles of Crown lawsuits: **~ v. Jones,** the Crown versus Jones; etc.). [L (*rex regis* king; see -INA)]

rē'gion (-jon) *n.* **1.** Tract of land, space, place, having more or less definitely marked boundaries or characteristics (*a desert, fertile, region; the region between the Elbe and the Rhine; the earth is divided into regions characterized by different fauna and flora*). **2.** Separate part of world or universe; layer of atmosphere or sea according to height or depth; LOWER³, UPPER, *regions.* **3.** Department of country etc. (*the North-East, Strathclyde, Region*); sphere or realm *of* (*you are getting into the region of metaphysics*); **in the ~ of,** approximately. **4.** Part of the body round or near some organ etc. (*the lumbar, abdominal,* etc., *region; the region of the eyes*). **5.** Hence ~AL *a.*, ~**al**ISM (2, 4) *n.*, ~**al**IZE (3) *v.t.* [ME f. OF, f. L *regio -onis* direction, district (*regere* direct; see -ION)]

regĭsseur' (rāzhĭsẽr') *n.* Director of ballet; ||director or *producer of stage-play. [f. F *régisseur* stage-manager]

rĕ'gĭster¹ *n.* **1.** Book etc. in which entries are made of details to be recorded for reference; official or authoritative list kept e.g. of births, marriages, and burials or deaths, of shipping, of professionally qualified persons, of qualified voters in constituency, (**~ office,** a registry). **2.** (Mus.) Sliding part in organ controlling set of pipes; set of pipes thus controlled; compass of voice or instrument, part of voice-compass (*head, lower,* etc., *register*). **3.** Form of language (colloquial, literary, etc.) customarily used in particular circumstances. **4.** Adjustable plate for widening or narrowing an opening and regulating draught esp. in fire-grate; indicator recording speed, force, etc.; CASH¹ *register.* **5.** (Print.) exact correspondence of position of printed matter on two sides of leaf (**in ~,** so corresponding); (Photog.) correspondence of position of colour-components of printed picture. **6.** Certificate of ship's ownership (*register* TON¹). [ME & OF *regestre, registre,* or f. med. L *regestrum, registrum* alt. of *regestum* (LL *regesta* pl. things recorded f. as RE- 8, L *gerere gest-* carry)]

rĕ'gĭster² *v.* **1.** *v.t.* Set down (name, fact, etc.) formally, record in writing; (fig.) make mental note of. **2.** Enter or cause to be entered in particular register; **~ letter,** entrust it to post office for transmission as **~ed post** with special precautions for safety and for compensation in case of loss; **~ed nurse** (with State certificate of competence in nursing); ~ one**self** (or abs.), put one's name on electoral etc. register, or as guest in register kept by hotel, as participant at conference, etc. **3.** (Of instrument) record automatically, indicate; express (emotion) facially or by gesture. **4.** *v.i.* & *t.* (Print. etc.) Correspond, make correspond, exactly in position. **5.** *v.i.* Make impression on person's mind (*name did not register with me*). **6.** Hence **rĕ'gĭstr**ABLE *a.* [ME, f. OF *registrer*, or f. med. L *registrare* (as prec.)]

rĕ'gĭster³ *n.* Registrar; **Lord Clerk R~,** State archivist in Scotland. [prob. f. foll.]

rĕ'gĭstrâr (*or* -âr') *n.* Official recorder, person charged with keeping register, esp. in university; ||judicial and administrative officer of High Court etc.; doctor undergoing hospital training as specialist; **R~ General,** head of office conducting population census; hence ~SHIP *n.* [f. med. L *registrarius* (*registrum* REGISTER¹; see -AR²)]

||**rĕ'gĭstrary̆** *n.* Registrar of Cambridge University. [f. as prec.; see -ARY¹]

rĕgĭstrā'tion *n.* Registering or being registered; **~ mark,** combination of letters and figures identifying motor vehicle. [f. obs. F *régistration* or f. med. L *registratio* (as prec.; see -ATION)]

rĕ'gĭstry̆ *n.* Registration; place or office where registers or records are kept; **~ (office),** place where marriages are conducted without religious ceremony, or (arch.) where lists of vacant situations and of persons seeking them are kept. [f. obs. *registery* f. med. L *registerium* (as REGISTER[1])]

||**Rē'gius** *a.* ~ **professor,** holder of chair founded by sovereign (esp. one at Oxf. or Camb. instituted by Henry VIII) or filled by Crown appointment. [L, = royal (*rex regis* king)]

rĕ'glėt *n.* (Archit.) narrow strip separating mouldings; (Print.) thin strip of wood or metal separating type. [f. F *réglet* dim. of *règle* (as RULE)]

rĕ'gnal *a.* Of a reign (~ **year,** beginning with sovereign's accession or an anniversary of it). [f. AL *regnalis* (as REIGN[1]; see -AL)]

rĕ'gnant *a.* Reigning (**Queen R~**, queen ruling in her own right and not as consort); (of things, qualities, opinions, etc.) predominant, prevalent. [f. L *regnare* REIGN[2]; see -ANT]

rėgôr'ge *v.* **1.** *v.t.* Bring or cast up again after swallowing. **2.** *v.i.* Gush or flow back from pit, channel, etc. [f. F *regorger*, or f. RE- 9 + GORGE[2]]

rėgrā't|e *v.t.* (Hist.) Buy up (goods) to retail at profit in same or neighbouring place; hence ~ER[1] *n.* [f. OF *regrater* (perh. as RE-, *grater* to scratch, of Gmc orig.)]

rē'grĕss[1] *n.* Going back; declension, backward tendency; reasoning from effect to cause. [ME, f. L *regressus* (as foll.)]

rėgrĕ'ss[2] *v.i.* Move backwards (lit. or fig.). [f. L *re(gredi gress- = gradi* step); see RE- 9]

rėgrĕ'ssion (-shon) *n.* Backward movement, retreat; (Geom.) return of curve; relapse, reversion; return to earlier stage of development; ~ **curve** (giving best fit to inexact data); so **rėgrĕ'ss**IVE *a.* [f. L *regressio* (as prec.; see -ION)]

rėgrĕ't *v.t.* (**-tt-**), & *n.* **1.** *v.t.* Feel sorrow for loss of, wish one could have again; be distressed about or sorry for (event, fact), grieve at, repent (action etc.); be sorry *to* say etc. or *that* (esp. in polite refusal of invitation etc.); hence ~**t**ABLE *a.*, ~**tab**LY[2] *adv.* **2.** *n.* Sorrow for loss of person or thing; repentance or annoyance concerning thing done or not done (*has no regrets*; *expressed regret for his misbehaviour*); (real or politely simulated) vexation or disappointment caused by occurrence or situation (*hear with regret of* or *that*; *refuse with much regret* or *many regrets*); hence (of person or feeling) ~FUL *a.*, ~**ful**LY[2] *adv.* [v. ME, n. f. F, f. OF *regreter* bewail, perh. f. as RE- 3 + Gmc **grētan*; cf. GREET[2]]

rēgrou'p (-ōō'p) *v.t.* & *i.* See RE- 8.

Regt. *abbr.* Regiment.

rĕ'gūlable *a.* Admitting of regulation. [f. REGULATE + -ABLE]

rĕ'gūlar *a.* & *n.* **1.** *a.* (Eccl.) Bound by religious rule, belonging to religious or monastic order, (opp. *secular*; *regular canon, clerk*, or *clerk, canon, regular*). **2.** (Of shape, structure, arrangement, or of objects in these respects) following or exhibiting a principle, harmonious, consistent, systematic, symmetrical, (*regular nomenclature, formation, features, curve, figure*); (of flower) having radial symmetry; **the five ~ solids,** tetrahedron or triangular pyramid bounded by 4 equal triangles, hexahedron or cube by 6 equal squares, octahedron by 8 equal triangles, dodecahedron by 12 equal pentagons, and icosahedron by 20 equal triangles. **3.** Acting, done, recurring, uniformly or calculably in time or manner, habitual, constant, not capricious or casual, orderly, (*regular working, footsteps, procedure, sequence, pulse, bowels, customer, salary, orbit, bedtime, employment*); (of person) defecating or menstruating at predictable times; **keep ~ hours,** do same thing at same time daily; **a ~ life** (lived in orderly manner, esp. without excesses). **4.** Conforming to a standard of etiquette etc., not transgressing conventions, correct, (*had no regular introduction*; *the attitude of the Government has been quite regular*). **5.** (Gram.) (Of verb, noun, etc.) following a normal type of inflexion. **6.** Properly constituted or qualified, not defective or amateur, devoted exclusively or primarily to its nominal function, (*cooks as well as a regular cook*; *has no regular profession*); ~ **army** or **soldiers** (opp. volunteers or militia or temporary levies). **7.** (colloq.) Complete, thorough, indubitable, (*he is a regular rascal, brick, hero*; *had a regular smash, overhauling*, etc.). **8.** Hence ~ITY (-ă'r-) *n.*, ~IZE (3) *v.t.*, ~LY[2] *adv.* **9.** *n.* One of the regular clergy; regular soldier; (colloq.) regular customer, visitor, etc.; (colloq.) person permanently employed. [ME f. OF *reguler*, & f. L *regularis* (*regula* RULE); see -AR[1]]

rĕ'gūl|āte *v.t.* Control by rule, subject to restrictions; moderate, adapt to requirements; alter speed of (machine, clock) so that it may work accurately; hence ~**āt**OR *n.*, ~ATIVE *a.* [f. LL *regulare* f. L *regula* RULE + -ATE[3]]

rĕgūlā'tion *n.* & *a.* **1.** *n.* Regulating or being regulated; prescribed rule, authoritative direction. **2.** *a.* In accordance with regulations, of correct pattern etc., ordinary, usual, formal, (*of the regulation size*; *exceed the regulation speed*; *a regulation sword, cap*; *the regulation mourning*). [f. prec. + -ATION]

rĕ'gūl|us *n.* (*pl.* ~**i** *pr.* -ī, *or* ~**uses**). **1.** (Chem.) Purer or metallic part of mineral separated by sinking to bottom in crucible on reduction; impure metallic product of smelting various ores; hence ~INE[1] *a.* **2.** Goldcrest. [L, dim. of *rex regis* king; sense 1 orig. of metallic form of antimony, perh. as title of honour due to its readiness to combine with gold]

rėgûr'gĭt|āte *v.* **1.** *v.i.* Gush back. **2.** *v.t.* (Of person, animal, stomach, crop, or receptacle) cast or pour out again. **3.** Hence ~A'TION *n.* [f. med. L *re(gurgitare* f. L *gurges gurgitis* whirlpool); see RE- 9, -ATE[3]]

rēhabĭ'lĭt|āte *v.t.* Restore to privileges, reputation, or proper condition; restore to effectiveness by training (esp. after imprisonment or illness); hence ~A'TION *n.* [f. med. L *re(habilitare*, see HABILITATE); see RE- 9]

rēhă'ndle *v.t.* Handle again, esp. give new form or arrangement to. [f. RE- 8 + HANDLE[2]]

rēhă'ng *v.t.* (**rehu'ng**). Hang (esp. picture or curtain) again or differently. [f. RE- 8 + HANG[1]]

rēhă'sh[1] *v.t.* Put (old material) into new form without essential change or improvement. [f. RE- 8 + HASH[1]]

rē'hăsh[2] *n.* Rehashing; material rehashed. [f. RE- 8 + HASH[2]]

rēhear' *v.t.* See RE- 8.

rėhear'sal (-hēr'-) *n.* Rehearsing; performance of play or other entertainment preparatory to public performance; DRESS[2] *rehearsal.* [ME, f. foll. + -AL 2]

rėhear'se (-hēr's) *v.t.* Recite, say over, repeat from beginning to end, give list of, recount, enumerate; have rehearsal of (play etc., part in it, or abs.), practise for later public performance; train (person) by rehearsal. [ME, f. AF *rehearser*, OF *reherc(i)er*, perh. f. as RE- + *hercer* to harrow (*herse* a harrow; see HEARSE)]

rē-hea't *n.*, & *v.t.* **1.** *n.* Obtaining of extra power by using hot exhaust to burn extra fuel in engine. **2.** *v.t.* Heat again. [f. RE- 9 + HEAT[1,2]]

rēhobō'ăm *n.* Large winebottle, twice size of jeroboam. [f. *Rehoboam* (1 Kgs. 11–14)]

rēhou'se (-z) *v.t.*, see RE- 8; **rēhū'manize** *v.t.*, see RE- 9.

Reich (rīk *or* rīχ) *n.* The German commonwealth

as a whole (**First** ~, Holy Roman Empire, 962–1806; **Second** ~, 1871–1918; **Third** ~, Nazi regime, 1933–45). [G, = empire]

Rei'chstag (rī'kstahg) *n.* (Hist.) The German parliament. [G]

rē'ĭ|fȳ *v.t.* Convert (person, abstract concept mentally) into thing, materialize; hence ~FICA'TION *n.*, ~**fĭcāt**ORY *a.* [f. L *res* thing + -I- + -FY]

reign[1] (rān) *n.* Sovereignty, rule, sway, (*under the reign of Queen Victoria*; *his reign was a gentle one*; *the reign of law in nature*; *democracy resumed her reign*; *Reign of* TERROR); (poet.) realm, sphere; period during which sovereign reigns (*in the reign of John*; *during five successive reigns*). [ME, f. OF *re(i)gne* kingdom f. L *regnum* (*rex regis* king)]

reign[2] (rān) *v.i.* **1.** Hold royal office, be king or queen (lit. or fig.; *reigned over Great Britain for 60 years*; *a king who desired to rule as well as reign*; *better to reign in hell than serve in heaven*); ~**ing beauty,** woman acknowledged as supreme beauty for the time being; ~**ing champion** etc. (who most recently won the title). **2.** Hold sway, prevail, (*dissension and improvidence reigned*); **silence ~s,** all is quiet. [ME, f. OF *reignier* f. L *regnare* (as prec.)]

rēĭgnī'te *v.t.* & *i.* See RE- 9.

Reilly. See RILEY.

rēĭmbŭr'se *v.t.* Repay (person who has expended money, person's expenses, person expenses); hence ~MENT (-sm-) *n.* [f. RE- 9 + obs. *imburse* put in purse f. med. L *imbursare* (as IM-[1], PURSE[1])]

rēĭmpŏr't[1] *v.t.*, **rēĭ'mpŏrt**[2] *n.*, see RE- 9; **rē-ĭmpō'se** (-z) *v.t.*, **rēĭmposi**'TION (-z-) *n.*, see RE- 8, 9.

rein (rān) *n.*, & *v.t.* **1.** *n.* (in *sing.* or *pl.*) Long narrow strap with each end attached to bit used to guide or check horse etc. in riding or driving, similar device to restrain child etc., (fig.) means of control; **draw** ~, stop one's horse, pull up, abandon effort, retrench expenditure, etc.; **give horse the** ~(**s**), let it go its own way; **give** (**free**) ~(**s**) **to,** let (one's imagination etc.) have free scope; **keep a tight** ~ **on,** allow little freedom to; **assume, drop, the ~s of government,** enter upon, resign, office; hence ~'LESS *a.* **2.** *v.t.* Check or manage with reins; (fig.) govern, restrain, control; pull *up* or *back* with reins, hold *in* with reins, (horse, or abs.; lit. or fig.). [ME, f. OF *rene, reigne,* earlier *resne,* f. Rom. **retina* f. L *retinēre* RETAIN]

rēĭncăr'n|āte *v.t.* Bring soul of (person) into another body after death; so ~ATE[2] *a.*, ~A'TION *n.* [f. RE- 8 + INCARNATE[2]]

rēĭncŏr'porāte *v.t.*, **rēĭncŏrpor**A'TION *n.*, (-n-k-). See RE- 9.

rei'ndeer (rā'n-) *n.* (*pl.* usu. same). Subarctic deer (*Rangifer tarandus*), with large antlers in both sexes, used for drawing sledges and kept in herds for its milk, flesh, and hide; ~ **moss,** lichen of genus *Cladonia* much eaten by reindeer. [ME, f. ON *hreindýri* (*hreinn* reindeer, *dýr* DEER)]

rēĭnfŏr'ce *v.t.* Strengthen or support by additional men or material or by increase of numbers, quantity, size, thickness, etc., (*reinforce fortress, army, provisions, party, the basses* etc. in band or chorus, person's *health* etc. with food etc., one's *argument* with fresh points); ~**d concrete** (with metal bars, gratings, or wire, embedded in it to increase its strength). [f. earlier *renforce* f. F *renforcer,* after RE- 6, *inforce* = ENFORCE]

rēĭnfŏr'cement (-sm-) *n.* Reinforcing or being reinforced; (in *pl.*) additional men, ships, etc., for military or naval force; anything that reinforces. [f. prec. + -MENT]

reins (rānz) *n. pl.* (arch.) The kidneys; the loins. [ME f. OF, f. L *renes* pl.]

rēĭnsĕr't *v.t.*, **rēĭnsĕr'**TION *n.* See RE- 9.

rēĭnstā'te *v.t.* Restore to or replace in lost position, privileges, etc.; restore to health or proper order; hence ~MENT (-tm-) *n.* [f. RE- 9; cf. INSTATE]

rēĭnsur'e (-shoor') *v.i.* & *t.* Insure again (esp. of insurer securing himself by transferring risk to another insurer); so **rē**INSUR'ANCE *n.* [f. RE- 8 + INSURE]

rēĭntĕr' *v.t.*, **rēĭntĕr'prĕt** *v.t.*, see RE- 8.

rēĭnvĕ'st *v.t.* Invest again (esp. money *in* other property, or person *with* privilege or *in* office); hence ~MENT *n.* [f. RE- 8, 9 + INVEST]

rēĭnvĭ'gorāte *v.t.*, **rēĭnvĭgor**A'TION *n.* See RE- 9.

rēĭ'ssūe[1] (*or* -shōō) *v.t.* Issue again. [f. RE- 8 + ISSUE[2]]

rēĭ'ssūe[2] (*or* -shōō) *n.* New issue, esp. of previously published book etc. [f. RE- 8 + ISSUE[1]]

rēĭ'ter|āte *v.t.* Say or do again or repeatedly; so ~A'TION *n.*, ~ATIVE *a.* [f. L *re(iterare* ITERATE); see RE- 8]

‖**reiv|e** (rēv) *v.i.* Make raids, plunder; hence ~'ER[1] *n.* [var. of REAVE]

rėjĕ'ct[1] *v.t.* Put aside or send back as not to be accepted, practised, believed, chosen, used, complied with, etc., (*reject doctrine, custom, evidence, candidate, literary contribution, food, request, suitor, vote*; *sorting-machine rejects all defective specimens*); refuse acceptance of; cast up again, vomit, evacuate; hence or cogn. ~ABLE *a.*, ~ER[1], ~OR, *ns.* [ME, f. L *re(jicere ject-* = *jacĕre* throw); see RE- 9]

rē'jĕct[2] *n.* Person or thing rejected as unfit or below standard. [f. prec.]

rėjĕctamĕ'nta *n. pl.* Refuse, waste matters; things cast up by the sea. [mod. L (as REJECT[1]; see -MENT)]

rėjĕ'ction *n.* Rejecting or being rejected; ~ **slip,** formal notice from editor or publisher accompanying rejected MS. [f. F *réjection* or f. L *rejectio* (as REJECT[1]; see -ION)]

rējĭ'g *v.t.* (**-gg-**). Re-equip (factory etc.) for new type of work. [f. RE- 8 + JIG[1]]

rėjoi'ce *v.* **1.** *v.t.* Cause joy to, make glad, (*the news rejoiced him*; *I am rejoiced to hear it, that it should be so, at it,* etc.). **2.** *v.i.* Feel great joy; be glad *that* or *to* do, take delight *in* or *at*; ~ **in,** be blessed in the possession of, (joc.) have. **3.** Make merry, celebrate some event; hence **rėjoi'cĭngs** (-z) [-ING[1]] *n. pl.* [ME, f. OF *re(joir joiss-* JOY[2]); see RE- 6]

rėjoi'n[1] *v.* **1.** *v.i.* (Law). Reply to charge or pleading, esp. to plaintiff's replication. **2.** *v.t.* Say in answer, retort. [ME, f. OF *rejoindre rejoign-* (as RE- 9, JOIN)]

rējoi'n[2] *v.t.* & *i.* Join together again, reunite; join (companion, company, etc.) again. [f. as prec. or RE- 9 + JOIN]

rėjoi'nder *n.* What is REJOIN[1]ed or said in reply, retort. [f. AF **rejoinder* v. (as n.); see REJOIN[1], -ER[4]]

rėju'ven|āte (-ōō'-) *v.t.* & *i.* Make or become young again; hence ~A'TION, ~**āt**OR, *ns.* [f. RE- 9 + L *juvenis* young + -ATE[3]]

rėjuven|ĕ'sce (-ōō-) *v.i.* & *t.* Become young again; (Biol.) (of cells) gain, fill (cells) with, fresh vitality; so ~E'SCENT *a.*, ~E'SCENCE *n.* [f. LL *re(juvenescere* f. L *juvenis* young); see -ESCENT, RE- 9]

rēkĭ'ndle *v.t.* & *i.* See RE- 9.

-rel *suf.* w. dim. or derog. force (*cockerel, doggerel, mongrel, scoundrel*). [f. or after OF *-erel(le)*]

For other words in *re-* see RE-.

rēlā'bel *v.t.* See RE- 8.

rèlă'pse *v.i.*, & *n.* **1.** *v.i.* Fall back, sink again, (*into* wrongdoing, error, heresy, weakness or illness, quiescence or indolence); **relapsing fever,** bacterial infectious disease with recurrent periods of fever. **2.** *n.* Act or fact of relapsing, esp. deterioration in patient's condition after partial recovery. [f. L *re*(*labi laps-* slip); see RE- 9]

rèlā't|e *v.* **1.** *v.t.* Narrate, recount, whence ~ER[1] *n.* **2.** Bring into relation (*to*, *with*, or abs.; *cannot relate the phenomena with* or *to anything we know* or *to each other*); establish relation between; (in *p.p.*) connected, allied, akin by blood or marriage, (*the law extends to several related groups*; *is related to the royal family*), whence ~**ėd**NESS *n.* **3.** *v.i.* Have reference *to*, stand in some relation *to*, (*notices nothing but what relates to himself*; *how parts relate to parts*); (of person) bring oneself into relation *to*. [f. L *relat-* (see REFER)]

rèlā'tion *n.* **1.** Narration, a narrative; (Law) laying of information. **2.** What one person or thing has to do with another, way in which one stands or is related to another, kind of connection or correspondence or contrast or feeling that prevails between persons or things, (*the relations primarily expressed by prepositions are those of place and time*; *the outlay seems to bear no relation, is out of all relation, to the object aimed at*; *the relation between them is that of guardian and ward*; *the report has relation to a state of things now past*); (in *pl.*) dealings *with* others (PUBLIC *relations*), sexual intercourse; **in ~ to,** as regards; hence ~AL *a.* **3.** = RELATIONSHIP. **4.** Kinsman, kinswoman, relative, (*the squire and his relations*; *is he any relation, what relation is he, to you?*; *he is no relation*). [ME f. OF, or f. L *relatio* (as prec.; see -ION)]

rèlā'tionship *n.* State of being related; condition or character due to being related; kinship (lit. or fig.). [f. prec. + -SHIP]

rĕ'latĭve *a.* & *n.* **1.** *a.* (Gram.) (Of adjective, adverb, or PRONOUN) referring, and attaching a subordinate clause, to an expressed or implied antecedent; (of clause) attached to antecedent by relative word. **2.** Having mutual relations, corresponding in some way, related to each other; (Mus., of major and minor keys) having same signature; (of rank) corresponding in grade to another in a different service etc. **3.** Pertinent, relevant, related to the subject, (*without some more relative proof*). **4.** Comparative (*what are the relative merits of the two?*; *made the next attempt with relative coolness*); in relation to something else (*their relative positions are the same though they are miles apart*; *relative density, humidity, pitch*); proportioned to something else (*supply is relative to demand*); implying comparison (*'heat', 'speed', 'strength', are relative words*); correlative or essentially involving a different but corresponding idea (*the concepts of husband and wife are relative to each other*); not having absolute existence but conditioned by relation *to* (*she is beautiful to me, but beauty is relative to the beholder's eye*). **5.** Having reference, relating, *to* (*detailed the facts relative to the matter*). **6.** Hence ~LY[2] (-vlĭ) *adv.* **7.** *n.* (Gram.) relative word, esp. pronoun, whence **rĕlātī'v**AL *a.*; (Philos.) relative thing or term. **8.** Kinsman, kinswoman; relation by blood or by marriage; species related to another by common origin (*the apes, man's closest relatives*). [ME, f. OF *relatif -ive* or f. LL *relativus* having reference or relation (as RELATE, -IVE)]

rĕ'latĭv|ĭsm *n.* Doctrine that knowledge is relative, not absolute; so ~IST (2) *n.* [f. prec. + -ISM]

rĕlatĭ'vĭtў *n.* Relativeness; (Phys.) (**special**) ~, theory based on the principle that all uniform motion is relative and that light has constant velocity in vacuum, regarding space-time as four-dimensional continuum, and modifying previous conceptions of geometry; **general ~,** theory extending this to gravitation and accelerated motion; hence **rĕlatĭvĭ'st**IC *a.*, (of phenomena etc.) accurately described only by relativity theories. [f. RELATIVE + -ITY]

rĕ'latĭvīz|e, -īs|e (-īz), *v.t.* Make relative; apply relativity theory to; hence ~A'TION *n.* [f. RELATIVE + -IZE]

rèlā'tor *n.* Relater; (Law) maker of relation (sense 1). [L (as RELATE; see -OR)]

rèlă'x *v.* **1.** *v.t.* Cause or allow to become loose or slack or limp, enfeeble, enervate, mitigate, abate, (*relax the bowels*, *the muscles*, one's *grasp*, *discipline*, *a rule*, one's *attention*, one's *efforts*); (in *p.p.*) at ease, unperturbed; **~ed throat,** form of sore throat; **~ing climate** (causing sluggish feeling, opp. *bracing*); hence ~ANT *a.* & *n.*, (drug etc.) that relaxes. **2.** *v.i.* Grow less tense or rigid or stern or ceremonious or energetic or zealous (*his hold, hands, severity, features, manner, endeavours, relaxed*; *must not relax in* one's *efforts*); cease work or effort (*take* one's *coat off and relax*). [ME, f. L *re*(*laxare* f. *laxus* LAX[1]); see RE- 9]

rēlăxā'tion *n.* Partial remission of penalty, duty, etc.; cessation from work; recreation, amusements; diminution of tension, severity, precision, etc.; (Phys.) restoration of equilibrium following disturbance. [f. L *relaxatio* (as prec.; see -ATION)]

rē'lay[1] *n.* **1.** Set of fresh horses substituted for tired ones; gang of men, supply of material, etc., similarly used (*operated in relays*); ~ (**race**), race between teams of which each person does part of the distance, the 2nd etc. members of the teams starting when the 1st etc. finish. **2.** Relayed message etc. **3.** (Electr.) Device actuating changes in circuit etc. in response to other changes affecting itself; device to receive, reinforce, and transmit telegraph message, broadcast programme, etc. [ME, f. OF *relai* (*relayer*; see foll.)]

rēlay'[2] (*or* rē'lā) *v.t.* **1.** Arrange in, provide with, replace by, relay(s). **2.** Receive (message etc. esp. by radio) and transmit to others. [f. prec. or f. OF *relayer* (as RE-, *laier* ult. f. L *laxare*; cf. RELAX)]

rē-lay'[3] *v.t.* (**re-lai'd**). Lay again. [f. RE- 8 + LAY[3]]

rèlea's|e[1] *v.t.* **1.** Set free, liberate, deliver, unfasten, (*from*); allow to move from fixed position; (Cinemat.) issue (film etc.) for (esp. general) exhibition; make (information, gramophone record, etc.) publicly or generally available. **2.** (Law). Remit (debt), surrender (right), make over (property) to another; hence ~EE', ~OR, *ns.* **3.** Hence ~ABLE *a.* [ME, f. OF *relesser*, *relaiss*(*i*)*er* f. L *relaxare* (see RELAX)]

rèlea'se[2] *n.* **1.** Deliverance, liberation, from trouble, sorrow, life, duty, restriction, or fixed position. **2.** (Law). Conveyance of right or estate to another; document effecting this. **3.** Handle, catch, etc., that releases part of machine etc. **4.** Document etc. made available for publication (*news, press, release*); film, record, etc. that is released; releasing of document, film, etc., thus. [ME, f. OF *reles* (*relesser*; see prec.)]

rĕ'lĕg|āte *v.t.* Banish to place of exile; consign or dismiss to some usu. inferior position, sphere, etc.; (Sport) transfer (team) to lower division of league etc.; transfer (matter) for decision or execution, refer (person) for information etc., *to*; hence ~ABLE *a.*, ~A'TION *n.* [f. L *re*(*legare* send); see RE- 5, -ATE[3]]

rèlĕ'nt *v.i.* Relax severity, become less stern, abandon harsh intention, yield to compassion;

hence ~LESS *a.* [ME, f. med. L **relentare* f. as RE- 9 + L *lentare* bend (*lentus* flexible)]

rĕ'lèv|ant *a.* Bearing on or pertinent *to* the matter in hand; hence ~ANCE, ~ANCY, *ns.*, ~**ant**LY² *adv.* [f. med. L *relevans*, part. of L *relevare* RELIEVE; see -ANT]

rèlī'|able *a.* That may be relied on; of sound and consistent character or quality; hence ~ABI'LITY, ~**able**NESS (-beln-), *ns.*, ~**ab**LY² *adv.* [f. RELY + -ABLE]

rèlī'ance *n.* Trust, confidence, (*upon, on, in*; *have, place, feel, reliance upon* etc.); thing depended upon (*the well is our chief reliance*); so **rèlī'**ANT *a.* [f. RELY + -ANCE]

rĕ'lĭc *n.* **1.** Part of holy person's body or belongings kept after his death as object of reverence; memento, souvenir. **2.** (in *pl.*) Dead body, remains, of person; what has survived destruction or wasting, remnant, residue, scraps. **3.** Surviving trace or memorial *of* a custom, belief, period, people, etc.; object interesting because of age or associations. [ME *relike, relique*, etc., f. OF *relique*, f. L RELIQUIAE]

rĕ'lĭct *n.* Widow *of*; geological or other object which has survived in primitive form; animal or plant known to have existed in same form in previous geological ages. [(in 1st sense f. OF *relicte* f. LL *relicta*) f. p.p. of L *re(linquere lict-* leave); see RE- 3]

rèlie'f¹ *n.* **1.** Alleviation of or deliverance from pain, distress, anxiety, etc., (*the medicine brought relief*; *gave a sigh of relief*; *it is a relief to come across an optimist*); ~ (**bus** etc.) (supplementing ordinary service); ~ **road,** road (esp. bypass) by which traffic can avoid congested area. **2.** Feature etc. that diversifies monotony or relaxes tension (*a blank wall without relief*; *a comic scene follows by way of relief*). **3.** Assistance given to the poor (esp. ||Hist. under the Poor Law) or to persons in special danger or need or difficulty (*a relief fund for the earthquake victims*; *income-tax relief*). **4.** Reinforcement (esp. raising of siege) *of* besieged town. **5.** (Replacing of person or persons on duty by) person(s) appointed to take turn of duty. **6.** (esp. Law). Redress of hardship or grievance (*sought relief of the nuisance*). [ME, f. AF *relef*, OF *relief*, (*relever reliev-* RELIEVE)]

rèlie'f² *n.* **1.** Method of moulding or carving or stamping in which design stands out from plane or curved surface with projections proportioned and more (**high** ~) or less (**low** ~) closely approximating to those of objects imitated; piece of sculpture etc. in relief. **2.** Appearance of being done in relief given by arrangement of line or colour or shading, distinctness of outline (lit. or fig.), vividness, (*stands out in relief*; *bring out the facts in full relief*); ~ **map,** (1) map-model showing elevations and depressions of area dealt with, usu. on exaggerated relative scale, (2) ordinary map indicating hills and valleys by shading, colouring, or hachures, rather than by contour lines alone; ~ **printing,** letterpress printing. [F, f. It. *rilievo* (*rilevare* raise f. L, as foll.)]

rèlie'v|e *v.t.* **1.** Bring, give, be a, RELIEF¹ to (*besieged town was relieved*; *medicine relieves pain*; *am much relieved to hear it*; *devotes himself to relieving distress* or *the distressed*; *black dress relieved with white lace*); release (person) from duty or task by taking his place or providing a substitute. **2.** ~**e** one's **feelings,** use strong language or vigorous behaviour when annoyed etc.; ~**e nature** or one**self,** urinate or defecate; ~**e** person **of,** take (load, duties, restriction, etc. or (joc.) purse, watch, etc.) from him. **3.** ~**ing arch** (built into wall to relieve pressure); ||~**ing officer,** (Hist.) official who took charge of poor or insane persons not otherwise cared for. **4.** Bring into RELIEF², make appear solid or detached. **5.** Hence ~ABLE *a.* [ME, f. OF *relever* f. L *re(levare* f. *levis* light); see RE- 9]

rèlie'vō *n.* (*pl.* ~**s**). = RELIEF² (esp. in It. forms of combs.; ALTO, BASSO, MEZZO, -RELIEVO). [f. It. *rilievo* RELIEF² w. Anglicized spelling and pronunc.]

rèlĭ'gĭō- *comb. form.* Religion; religious. [f. foll.]

rèlĭ'gion (-jon) *n.* **1.** Particular system of faith and worship (*the Christian, Muslim, Buddhist, religion*; **established** ~, that of Established CHURCH¹; **freedom of** ~, right to follow whatever religion one chooses; NATURAL, REVEAL¹*ed, religion*; *all religions are the same to him*). **2.** Human recognition of superhuman controlling power and esp. of a personal God or gods entitled to obedience and worship; effect of such recognition on conduct and mental attitude; **get** ~, (vulg. or joc.) be converted to such recognition. **3.** Thing that one is devoted to or is bound to do (*make a religion of football, of doing physical exercises*). **4.** Life under monastic conditions (*enter into, be in, religion*; *her name in religion is Sister Mary*). **5.** Hence ~LESS *a.* [ME, f. AF *religiun*, OF *religion* f. L *religio -onis* obligation, bond, reverence]

rèlĭ'gioner (-jon-) *n.* Member of monastic order; person zealous for religion. [f. prec. + -ER¹]

rèlĭ'gion|ĭsm (-jon-) *n.* Excessive religious zeal; so ~IST (2) *n.*, person (excessively) zealous for religion. [f. RELIGION + -ISM]

rèlĭ'gionīze (-jon-), **-īse** (-īz), *v.t.* Convert to or imbue with religion. [f. RELIGION + -IZE]

rèlĭ'gĭōse *a.* Excessively religious. [f. L *religiosus* (as RELIGIOUS; see -OSE¹)]

rèlĭgĭŏ'sĭtȳ *n.* Being religious or religiose. [ME, f. L *religiositas* (as foll.; see -ITY)]

rèlĭ'gious (-jus) *a.* & *n.* **1.** *a.* Imbued with religion, pious, devout; of or belonging to a monastic order; of or concerned with religion; scrupulous, conscientious, (*with religious care, exactitude*, etc.); hence ~LY² *adv.*, ~NESS *n.* **2.** *n.* (*pl.* same). Person bound by monastic vows. [ME, f. AF *religius*, OF *religious* f. L *religiosus* (as RELIGION; see -IOUS)]

rēlī'ne *v.t.* Renew lining of (esp. garment). [f. RE- 9 + LINE⁴]

rèlĭ'nquĭsh *v.t.* Give up, abandon, cease from, (habit, plan, hope, belief); resign, surrender, (right, possession); relax hold of (object held); hence ~MENT *n.* [ME, f. OF *relinquir* f. L *re(linquere* leave); see RE- 3, -ISH²]

rĕ'lĭquarȳ *n.* Receptacle for relic(s). [f. F *reliquaire* (as RELIC; see -ARY¹)]

rĕ'lĭque (-ĭk; *or* relē'k) *n.* (arch.) Relic. [F (as RELIC)]

reliquiae (rĭlĭ'kwĭē) *n. pl.* Remains; (Geol.) fossil remains of animals or plants. [L (*reliquus* remaining, f. as RE- 3 + *linquere liq-* leave)]

rĕ'lĭsh¹ *n.* **1.** Flavour, distinctive taste *of*; slight dash or tinge *of* some quality. **2.** Appetizing flavour, attractive quality, (*meat has no relish when one is ill*; *horseplay loses its relish after childhood*); thing eaten with plainer food to add flavour. **3.** Enjoyment of food or other things, zest, liking *for*, (*eat, read, appreciate jest*, etc., *with great relish*; *has no relish for poetry*). [alt. (w. assim. to -ISH²) of obs. *reles* f. OF *reles, relais* remainder (*relaisser*; see RELEASE¹)]

rĕ'lĭsh² *v.* **1.** *v.t.* Serve as relish to, make piquant etc. **2.** Get pleasure out of, like, be pleased with, (*thought he could relish a lobster*; *does not relish the prospect*); whence ~ABLE *a.* **3.** *v.i.* Taste, savour, smack, suggest presence, *of*; affect the (lit. or fig.) taste *well, badly*, etc. [f. prec.]

rēlī'̆ve *v.* **1.** *v.i.* (arch.) Come to life again. **2.** *v.t.* Live (period, experience) over again (esp. in imagination). [f. RE- 8 + LIVE²]

rēloa'd *v.t.* Load again (esp. firearm, or abs.). [f. RE- 9 + LOAD²]

rēloc|ā'te *v.t.* & *i.* Locate again; move to a new district of work or residence; so ~A'TION *n.* [f. RE- 8 + LOCATE]

rėlū'cent (*or* -ōō'-) *a.* Shining, bright. [f. L *re*(*lucēre* shine); see RE- 6, -ENT]

rėlŭ'ct *v.i.* (arch.) Show reluctance; struggle *against*. [f. L *reluctari* (see foll.)]

rėlŭ'ct|ant *a.* Unwilling, disinclined, (*to* do, or abs.; *am very reluctant to admit; gave me reluctant assistance*); hence ~ANCE *n.*, ~**ant**LY² *adv.* [f. L *re*(*luctari* struggle); see RE- 2, -ANT]

rėlū'me (*or* -ōō'm) *v.t.* (poet.) Rekindle (light or flame; lit. or fig.); make (eyes etc.) bright again; light (sky etc.) up again. [f. RE- 9, after *illume*]

rėlȳ' *v.i.* Depend with confidence or assurance (*up*)*on* person or thing (*is relying upon a broken reed; I rely on you to do it, its being done, today; you may rely upon it that he will be here; I was relying on getting there by midnight*). [ME (earlier senses 'rally, be vassal of'), f. OF *relier* bind together f. L *re*(*ligare* bind); see RE- 9]

rĕm *n.* Unit of effective absorbed dose of ionizing radiation in human tissue, equivalent to one roentgen of X-rays. [f. *r*oentgen *e*quivalent *m*an]

R.E.M. *abbr.* rapid eye-movement.

rėmai'n *v.i.* **1.** Be left over after removal of or use of or dealing with the other part(s) etc. (*the few pleasures that remain to an old man; worse things remain to be told; outcome remains to be seen; nothing remains but to draw the moral*). **2.** Be in same place or condition during further time, continue to exist, be extant, be left behind, (*remain in London till Easter; let it remain as it is; as things have been they remain; the Parthenon remains to attest* or *as a proof of; this visit will always remain in my memory; the luggage unfortunately remained on the platform; victory remained with the Thebans*). **3.** (w. compl.) Continue to be (*one thing remains certain; remain faithful* etc.); **I** ~ *yours truly* etc. (formula concluding letter). [ME, f. OF *remain-* stressed st. of *remanoir* (or f. OF *remaindre* f. Rom. **remanere*) f. L *re*(*manēre* stay); see RE- 3]

rėmai'nder *n.*, & *v.t.* **1.** *n.* (Law). Residual interest in estate when devised to another simultaneously with creation of estate (~ **man,** devisee of this); right of succession to title or position on holder's decease; hence ~SHIP *n.* **2.** Residue, remaining persons or things; (Arith.) number left after subtraction or division; copies of book left unsold when demand has almost ceased, often offered at reduced price. **3.** *v.t.* Treat or dispose of copies of (book) as remainder. [ME f. AF, = OF *remaindre*; see prec., -ER⁴]

rėmai'ns (-z) *n. pl.* **1.** What remains over, surviving members or parts or amount, (*the remains of a nation, family, meal, stock, building, of* one's *conscience* or *strength*, etc.). **2.** Relic(s) of obsolete custom or of antiquity (*Roman remains*). **3.** Works, esp. those not before or yet published, left by author (*literary remains*). **4.** Dead body, corpse. [ME f. OF (as REMAIN), & f. REMAIN]

rēmā'ke¹ *v.t.* (**rema'de**). Make again or differently. [f. RE- 8 + MAKE¹]

rē'māke² *n.* Thing that has been remade, esp. a cinema film. [f. prec.]

rēmă'n *v.t.* (**-nn-**). **1.** Equip (fleet etc.) with fresh men. **2.** Make courageous again. [f. RE- 8, 9 + MAN²]

rėma'nd (-ah'-) *v.t.*, & *n.* **1.** *v.t.* Send back *to*, reconsign, (esp. prisoner into custody to allow of further inquiry). **2.** *n.* Recommittal to custody; **on** ~, in state of being remanded; ||~ **centre** or **home,** temporary institution for juvenile offenders. [ME, f. LL *re*(*mandare* commit); see RE- 9]

rĕ'man|ent *a.* Remaining, residual; ~**ent magnetism,** magnetization remaining after removal of source of excitation; so ~ENCE *n.* [ME, f. L *remanēre* REMAIN; see -ENT]

rėmar̂'k¹ *v.* **1.** *v.t.* Take notice of, perceive, regard with attention, observe, (person, thing, fact, *that* etc.); say by way of comment (*that*). **2.** *v.i.* Make comment (*up*)*on*. [f. F *re*(*marquer* MARK²); see RE- 6]

rėmar̂'k² *n.* Noticing, observing, (**worthy of** ~, remarkable), commenting (*is the subject of general remark; let it pass without remark*); a written or spoken comment, anything said, (*his remarks are often interesting*; **make a** ~, utter a comment). [f. F *remarque* (as prec.)]

rėmar̂'kab|le *a.* Worth notice, exceptional; striking, conspicuous; hence ~**le**NESS (-beln-) *n.*, ~LY² *adv.* [f. F *remarquable* (as REMARK¹; see -ABLE)]

rēmă'rrȳ *v.i.* & *t.*, **rēma'rriage** *n.* See RE- 8.

re'mblai (rah'ṅblā) *n.* Earth used to form ramparts, parapets, etc.; earth brought to form railway embankments etc. [F, f. *remblayer* embank (as RE-, *emblayer* heap up)]

Rĕmbrandtĕ'sque (-ntĕ'sk) *a.* After the style of Rembrandt, with marked effects of light and shade. [f. *Rembrandt* van Rijn, Du. painter d. 1669 + -ESQUE]

||**R.E.M.E.** (rē'mē) *abbr.* Royal Electrical and Mechanical Engineers.

rėmē'dĭal *a.* Affording a remedy; intended to remedy disease, deficiency, etc., (*remedial measures, therapy*); hence ~LY² *adv.* [f. LL *remedialis* f. L *remedium* (as foll.); see -AL]

rĕ'mėd|ȳ *n.*, & *v.t.* **1.** *n.* Cure *for* or *against* disease, healing medicine or treatment; means of removing or counteracting or relieving any evil (*the only remedy for superstition is knowledge*); redress, legal or other reparation; hence ~**ĭ**LESS *a.* (poet. or rhet.). **2.** Margin within which coins as minted may differ from the standard fineness and weight. **3.** *v.t.* Rectify, make good; so **rėmē'dĭ**ABLE *a.* [ME; n. f. AF *remedie*, OF *remede*, v. f. OF *remedier* or L *remediare*, f. L *re*(*medium* f. *medēri* heal); see RE- 1, -Y¹]

rėmĕ'mber *v.t.* **1.** Keep in the memory, not forget, bring back into one's thoughts, know by heart, (person, thing, fact, *that, to* do, *how to* do, *when, why*, etc., or abs.); ~ one**self,** remember one's manners or intentions after a lapse; hence ~ABLE *a.* **2.** Make present to, tip, (*remembered me in his will; remember the waiter*). **3.** Mention in one's prayers. **4.** Convey greetings from (person) *to* another (*remember me kindly to them; asked to be remembered to you*). [ME, f. OF *remembrer* f. LL *re*(*memorari* f. L *memor* mindful); see RE- 9]

rėmĕ'mbrance *n.* **1.** Remembering or being remembered, memory, recollection, (*has escaped my remembrance; put in remembrance of; more than once within my remembrance; a pillar in remembrance of the exploit*); ||**R**~ **Sunday** (nearest 11 Nov., when those who were killed in the wars of 1914–18 and 1939–45 are commemorated). **2.** Keepsake, souvenir, memorial. **3.** (in *pl.*) Greetings conveyed through third person. [ME f. OF (as prec.; see -ANCE)]

rėmĕ'mbrancer *n.* **1.** ||**King's** or **Queen's R**~, officer collecting debts due to sovereign; ||**City R**~, official representing Corporation of City of London before parliamentary committees etc. **2.** Reminder, memento, (*of*). [ME, f. AF *remembrauncer* (*remembraunce*, as prec.; see -ER[1])]

rē'mĕx *n.* (*pl.* **remiges** *pr.* rĕ'mĭjēz). Primary or secondary quill in bird's wing. [L, = rower (*remus* oar)]

rēmĭ'lĭtarize *v.t.*, **rēmĭlĭtarīz**A'TION *n.* See RE- 9.

rėmī'nd *v.t.* Make (person) have recollection (*of, about, to* do, *that, how*, etc., or abs.). [f. RE- 8 + MIND[2]]

rėmī'nder *n.* Thing that reminds or is memento (*of*). [f. prec. + -ER[1]]

rėmī'ndful *a.* Acting as a remainder, reviving the memory, (*of*). [f. REMIND + -FUL]

rĕmĭnĭ'sce *v.i.* (colloq.) Indulge in reminiscence(s). [back form. f. foll.]

rĕmĭnĭ'scence *n.* **1.** Remembering, recovery of knowledge by mental effort; (Platonic Philos.) recovery of things known to the soul in previous existences. **2.** Remembered (and related) fact or incident; relating of this; (in *pl.*) collection in literary form of incidents that person remembers. **3.** Feature of a thing reminding or suggestive of other thing (*there is a reminiscence of the Greek type in her face*). **4.** Hence **rĕmĭnĭscĕ'nt**IAL (-shal) *a.* [f. LL *reminiscentia* f. L *reminisci* remember; see RE- 9, -ENCE]

rĕmĭnĭ'scent *a.* Recalling past things, given to or concerned with retrospection, mindful or having memories *of*; reminding or suggestive *of*; hence ~LY[2] *adv.* [as prec.; see -ENT]

rēmĭ'nt *v.t.* See RE- 8.

rėmi'se[1] (-ē'z) *n.*, & *v.i.* **1.** (arch.) Coach-house; carriage hired from livery-stable. **2.** (Fenc.) Second thrust made for recovery from first. **3.** *v.i.* (Fenc.) Make remise. [F, f. *remis remise* p.p. of *remettre* put back; cf. REMIT[1]]

rėmī'se[2] (-z) *v.t.* (Law). Surrender, make over, (right, property). [f. F *remis(e)* (as prec.)]

rėmĭ'ss *a.* Careless of duty, lax, negligent; (arch.) lacking force or energy; hence ~LY[2] *adv.*, ~NESS *n.* [ME, f. L *remissus* p.p. of *remittere* slacken; see REMIT[1]]

rėmĭ'ssĭble *a.* That may be remitted. [f. F *rémissible* or f. LL *remissibilis* (as REMIT[1]; see -IBLE)]

rėmĭ'ss|ion (-shon) *n.* **1.** Forgiveness (*of* sins etc.), forgiveness of sins; remitting of debt, penalty, etc.; shortening of convict's prison sentence on account of his good behaviour. **2.** Diminution of force, effect, degree, violence (esp. of disease or pain), etc. **3.** So ~IVE *a.* [ME f. OF, or f. L *remissio* (as foll.; see -ION)]

rėmĭ't[1] *v.* (**-tt-**). **1.** *v.t.* (Usu. of God) pardon (sins etc.); refrain from exacting or inflicting or executing (debt, punishment, sentence). **2.** *v.t.* & *i.* Abate, slacken, mitigate, partly or entirely cease from or cease, (*remit* one's *anger* or *efforts, the siege*; *pain, enthusiasm, begins to remit*). **3.** *v.t.* Refer (matter for decision etc.) *to* some authority, send back (case) to lower court. **4.** Send or put back (*in*)*to* previous state; postpone, defer, *to* or *till*. **5.** Transmit (money etc.), get conveyed by post etc.; hence ~TEE' *n.* **6.** Hence ~TAL 2 *n.* [ME, f. L *re(mittere miss-* send); see RE- 5]

rē'mĭt[2] (*or* rĭmĭ't) *n.* Item remitted for consideration; terms of reference of committee etc. [f. prec.]

rėmĭ'ttance *n.* Money sent to person; sending of money; ‖~ **man,** emigrant subsisting on remittances from home. [f. REMIT[1] + -ANCE]

rėmĭ'ttent *a.* & *n.* (Fever etc.) that abates at intervals. [f. as REMIT[1]; see -ENT]

rėmĭ'tter[1] *n.* In vbl senses. [f. REMIT[1] + -ER[1]]

rėmĭ'tter[2] *n.* (Law). Substitution, in favour of holder of two titles to estate, of the more valid for the other by which he entered on possession; remitting of case to other court. [f. REMIT[1] + -ER[4]]

rĕ'mnant *n.* *The* little or few that remain(s), small remaining quantity or piece or number of persons or things; surviving trace *of*; fragment, scrap, esp. piece of cloth etc. left when greater part has been used or sold. [ME, f. obs. & OF *remenant* (*remenoir* REMAIN; see -ANT)]

rēmŏ'del *v.t.* (‖-**ll**-). Model again or differently, reconstruct. [f. RE- 8 + MODEL[2]]

***remold**[1,2]. See REMOULD[1,2].

rēmo'nėtīz|e (-mŭ'n-), **-īs|e** (-īz), *v.t.* Restore (metal etc.) to former position as legal tender; hence ~A'TION *n.* [f. RE- 9 + MONETIZE]

rėmŏ'nstrance *n.* (Hist.) formal statement of public grievances (**the Grand R~**, from House of Commons to Crown 1641); remonstrating, expostulation, a protest. [ME f. obs. F, or f. med. L *remonstrantia* (as foll.; see -ANCE)]

rĕ'monstr|āte (*or* rĭmŏ'n-) *v.* **1.** *v.i.* Make protest, expostulate, (*against* course of action, *with* person, *on* or *upon* matter, or abs.). **2.** *v.t.* Urge in remonstrance (*that*). **3.** Hence or cogn. ~ANT *a.* & *n.*, **~ant**LY[2], **~āting**LY[2], *advs.*, **~at**IVE *a.*, **~āt**OR *n.* [f. med. L *re(monstrare* show); see RE- 2, -ATE[3]]

rėmŏ'ntant *a.* & *n.* (Rose) blooming more than once in year. [F (*remonter* REMOUNT[2]; see -ANT)]

rĕ'mora *n.* Fish of genus *Echeneis* etc., attaching itself to ships, sharks, etc., and formerly supposed to retard motion of ship to which it adhered; (arch.) obstruction, impediment. [L, = hindrance (as RE- 2, *mora* delay)]

rėmŏr'se *n.* **1.** Bitter regret for wrong committed; hence ~FUL (-sf-) *a.* **2.** Compunction, compassionate reluctance to inflict pain or be cruel, (esp. *without remorse*); hence ~LESS (-sl-) *a.* [ME, f. OF *remors* f. med. L *remorsus* f. L *re(mordēre mors-* bite) vex; see RE- 3]

rėmō'te *a.* (**~r, ~st**). **1.** Far apart. **2.** Far away or off in place or time (*lies remote from the road*; *came from the remotest parts of the earth*; *memorials of remote ages*); not closely related (*a remote ancestor, descendant, kinsman*); distant or widely different or by nature separate *from* (*remote causes, effects*; *introduces considerations remote from the subject*); ~ **control,** control of apparatus etc. from a distance by means of electrically operated device, radio, etc. **3.** Out-of-the-way, secluded, (*a remote village*); aloof, not friendly. **4.** (Esp. in superl., of idea etc.) slight(est), faint(est), least, (*have not the remotest, have only a very remote, conception of what he means*). **5.** Hence ~LY[2] (-tlĭ) *adv.*, ~NESS (-tn-) *n.* [ME, f. L *remotus* (as REMOVE[1])]

rēmou'ld[1] (-mō'-), ***rēmō'ld**[1], *v.t.* Mould again, refashion; reconstruct tread of (tyre). [f. RE- 8 + MOULD[3]]

rē'mould[2] (-mō-), ***rē'mōld**[2], *n.* Remoulded tyre. [f. prec.]

rē'mount[1] *n.* Fresh horse for rider; supply of fresh horses for regiment etc. [f. foll.]

rēmou'nt[2] *v.* **1.** *v.t.* Go up, get on to, (hill, ladder, horse, etc.) again; furnish (person) with fresh horse etc.; put (picture etc.) in fresh mount. **2.** *v.i.* Go up again, get on horseback again, make fresh ascent; go back *to* specified date, period, source. [ME, f. OF *re(monter* MOUNT[2]; see RE- 9) & f. MOUNT[2]]

rėmo'v|able (-mōō'-) *a.* In vbl senses; subject to removal from office; hence ~ABI'LITY *n.* [f. REMOVE[1] + -ABLE]

rėmo'val (-mōō'-) *n.* Act of removing or being removed; transfer of furniture etc. to different house, whence ~IST (3) *n.* (Austral.). [f. foll. + -AL 2]

rėmo′ve[1] (-ōō′v) *v.* **1.** *v.t.* Take off or away from place occupied, convey to another place, change situation of, get rid of, dismiss, (*remove* one's *hat, the tea-things, all traces, superfluous hair, magistrate from office; this will remove all apprehension, the last doubts*); ~ **furniture** (as special trade, for persons changing house); ~ **mountains,** do miracles; hence **rėmo′**VER[1] (1, 2) (-mōō′-) *n.* **2.** ||(arch., in *pass.*, of dish at dinner etc.) Be succeeded *by* (*boiled haddock removed by hashed mutton*). **3.** *v.i.* Change one's place of residence, go away *from*, go *to* (another place), (*am removing from London to Oxford; truth has removed from earth*). **4.** (in *p.p.*) Distant or remote *from* (*is not many degrees removed from the brute*); **once, twice,** etc., **~d** (of COUSINS). [ME, f. OF *removeir* f. L *re(movēre mot-* move); see RE- 5]

rėmo′ve[2] (-ōō′v) *n.* **1.** ||(arch.) Dish that succeeds another at table. **2.** ||Promotion to higher form at school (*has not got his remove*); ||a form or division in some schools. **3.** (arch.) Change of residence, departure, removal. **4.** Distance, degree of remoteness, (*at a certain remove its shape seems to change*). **5.** Stage in gradation, degree, (*is but one remove, a few removes, from*). [f. prec.]

rėmū′ner|āte *v.t.* Reward, pay for service rendered; serve as or provide recompense for (toil etc.) or to (person); hence or cogn. ~A′TION *n.*, **~at**IVE, **~at**ORY, *adjs.* [f. L *re-(munerari* f. *munus muneris* gift); see RE- 1, -ATE[3]]

Renai′ssance (*or* rĭ-; *or* -sahṅs) *n.* Revival of art and letters under influence of classical models in 14th–16th c., period of its progress, style of art and architecture developed by it; (*r*~) any similar revival. [F (*r*~) (as RE- 8, *naissance* birth f. L *nascentia* or *naître naiss-* be born f. Rom. **nascere*; cf. NASCENT, -ANCE)]

rē′nal *a.* Of the kidneys. [f. F *rénal* f. LL *renalis* f. L *renes* kidneys; see -AL]

rēnā′me *v.t.* See RE- 8.

rėnă′scence *n.* Rebirth, renewal; = RENAISSANCE. [f. foll. + -ENCE]

rėnă′scent *a.* Springing up anew, being reborn. [f. L *re(nasci* be born); see RE- 8, -ENT]

rĕncŏ′ntre (-*ter*) *n.* (arch.) = foll. [F (as foll.)]

rĕncou′nter *n.*, & *v.t.* (arch.) (Have) encounter, battle, skirmish, duel; meet(ing) by chance. [f. F *rencontre(r)* (as RE-, ENCOUNTER)]

rĕnd *v.* (**rent**). **1.** *v.t.* (arch. or rhet.) Tear or wrench (*off, away, out of, from, asunder, apart,* etc., or abs.; *a province rent from the empire*; ~ one's **garments** or **hair** (in grief etc.); **turn and** ~, (fig.) abuse (person) unexpectedly. **2.** *v.t.* & *i.* Split or divide in two or in pieces or into factions (*heart is rent by contending emotions; the veil was rent*); ~ **the air,** sound explosively. [OE *rendan*, = OFris. *renda*, cogn. w. MLG *rende*]

rĕ′nder *v.t.* **1.** Give in return (*render thanks, good for evil*). **2.** (arch.) Give back; hand over, deliver, give up, surrender, (*render to Caesar the things that are Caesar's*). **3.** Pay (tribute etc.), show (obedience etc.), give (assistance etc.), do (service etc.), (*to*). **4.** Produce for inspection, submit, present, send in, (account, reason, etc.); **account ~ed,** bill previously sent in and not yet paid (phr. used as substitute for repetition of items). **5.** Reproduce, portray, give representation or performance or effect of, execute, translate, (*painter has hardly rendered the expression; the quartet, Iago, the dramatist's conception, was well rendered; how would you render 'solvitur ambulando'?; poetry can never be adequately rendered in another language*); hence ~ING[1] (1, 2) *n.* **6.** (w. obj. & compl.) Make, cause to be, convert into, (*age had rendered him peevish; the tone rendered it an insult*). **7.** ~ (**down**), melt (fat) down, extract by melting, clarify. **8.** Cover (stone, brick) with first coat of plaster; hence ~ING[1] (2) *n.* **9. ~-set,** (*v.t.*) plaster (wall etc.) with two coats, (*n.* & *a.*) (plastering) of two coats. [ME f. AF; OF *rendre* f. Rom. **rendere* f. L *reddere reddit-* (as RE- 1, *dare* give)]

re′ndezvous (rŏ′ndĭvōō; *or* -dā-) *n.* (*pl.* same *pr.* -ōōz), & *v.i.* (**~es, ~ed, ~ing,** *pr.* -ōōz, -ōōd, -ōōing). **1.** *n.* Place appointed for assembling of troops or ships; place where people often meet; meeting-place agreed on, meeting by agreement. **2.** *v.i.* Meet at rendezvous. [F, f. *rendez-vous* present yourselves (*rendre*; see prec.)]

rĕndĭ′tion *n.* Interpretation, rendering, *of* dramatic role, musical piece, etc. (see RENDER 5). [obs. F (*rendre* RENDER; see -ITION)]

rĕ′nėgāde *n.*, & *v.i.* **1.** *n.* Apostate, esp. from Christianity to Islam; deserter of party or principles, turncoat. **2.** *v.i.* Be renegade. [f. Sp. *renegado* f. med. L *re(negatus* f. *negare* deny); see RE- 9]

rĕnėgā′dō *n.* (*pl.* **~es**). (arch.) = prec. [Sp., as prec.]

rėnĕ′ge, -gue, (-g) *v.* **1.** *v.i.* (Cards) *revoke; ~ **on,** fail to keep (promise etc.), disappoint (person, or abs.). **2.** *v.t.* Deny, renounce, abandon. [f. med. L *renegare* (as RE-, *negare* deny)]

rėnew′ *v.t.* **1.** Restore to original state, make (as good as) new, revive, regenerate, (*nature dies and is renewed; renew* person's *life, sorrow, energy; renew the golden age; rose from her knees renewed by the Holy Spirit*). **2.** Patch, fill up, reinforce, replace, (*coat renewed in places; renew the water in the bowl; renew garrison, tyres,* etc.). **3.** Get, begin, make, say, or give, anew, continue after intermission, (*renew attack, acquaintance, correspondence, speech, game, efforts; renew* one's *vows, statements,* etc.); grant or be granted continuation of (subscription, agreement, lease, bill, or abs.); grant or be granted continued validity of (licence etc.); recover (one's youth, strength, etc.). **4.** Hence ~ABLE *a.*, ~AL 2 *n.* [ME, f. RE- 9 + NEW[1]]

rē′nĭfŏrm *a.* Kidney-shaped. [f. L *ren* kidney + -I- + -FORM]

rĕ′nĭt|ent (*or* rĭnī′-) *a.* Resistant to force; recalcitrant; so ~ENCE, ~ENCY, *ns.* [f. F *rénitent* & L *renitens* (*reniti* resist; see -ENT)]

rĕ′nnėt *n.* Curdled milk found in stomach of unweaned calf, or preparation of stomach-membrane or of plant, used in curdling milk for cheese, junket, etc. [ME, prob. f. OE **rynet*, cogn. w. RUN[1]]

rėnou′nce *v.* & *n.* **1.** *v.t.* Consent formally to abandon, surrender, give up, (claim, right, peerage, possession). **2.** Repudiate, refuse to recognize any longer, decline association or disclaim relationship with, withdraw from, discontinue, forsake, (*renounce treaty, principles,* person's *authority, all thought of, design, attempt, son* etc., *friend, friendship*); ~ **the world,** abandon society or temporal affairs. **3.** *v.i.* (Law). Refuse or resign right or position esp. as heir or trustee. **4.** (Cards). Follow with card of another suit when having no card of suit led (cf. REVOKE). **5.** Hence ~MENT (-sm-) *n.* **6.** *n.* (Opportunity of) renouncing at cards. [ME, f. OF *renoncer* f. L *re(nuntiare* announce); see RE- 5]

rĕ′nov|āte *v.t.* Make new again, repair, restore to good condition or vigour; so ~A′TION, **~āt**OR, *ns.* [f. L *re(novare* f. *novus* new); see RE- 9, -ATE[3]]

rėnow′n *n.* Celebrity, fame, high distinction, (*man, town,* etc., *of renown* or *great* etc. *renown*).

[ME, f. AF *ren(o)un*, OF *renon*, *renom* (*renomer* make famous f. as RE- 8 + *nomer* f. L *nominare* NOMINATE)]

rėnow'ned (-nd) *a.* Famous, celebrated. [ME, f. OF *reno(u)mer* (as prec.) + -ED[1]]

rĕnt[1]. See REND.

rĕnt[2] *n.* Large tear in garment etc.; opening in clouds etc. as if torn; cleft, fissure, gorge. [f. obs. *rent* var. of REND]

rĕnt[3] *n.* & *v.* **1.** *n.* Tenant's periodical payment to owner or landlord for use of land or premises; payment for use of telephone service, machinery, etc.; ***for ~**, available to be rented; **~-free** *a.* & *adv.*, with exemption from rent; **~-roll,** register of person's lands etc. with rents due from them, sum of one's income from rent; ||**~-service,** (tenure by) personal service in lieu of or in addition to rent. **2.** *v.t.* Take, occupy, use, at a rent (*from*); let or hire (*out*) for rent (*to*); hence ~'ABLE *a.* **3.** *v.i.* Be let *at* specified rent. [ME, f. OF *rente* f. Rom. **rendita* fem. p.p. of **rendere* (see RENDER)]

rĕ'ntal *n.* Income from rents; amount paid or received as rent; act of renting; *rented house etc.; ***~ library** (lending books for a fee). [ME f. AF, or f. AL *rentale* (as prec.; see -AL 2)]

rĕ'nter *n.* In vbl senses; ||distributor of cinema films. [f. RENT[3] + -ER[1]]

rentier (rah'ntïā) *n.* Person living on dividends from property, investments, etc. [F (*rente* dividend)]

rēnŭ'mber *v.t.* Change number(s) of. [f. RE- 8 + NUMBER[2]]

rėnŭnciā'tion *n.* Renouncing, document expressing it; self-denial, giving up of things; so **rėnŭ'nci**ANT *n.* & *a.*, **rėnŭ'nci**ATIVE (-sha-), **rėnŭ'nciat**ORY (-shaterĭ), *adjs.* [ME, f. OF *renonciation* or f. LL *renuntiatio* (as RENOUNCE; see -ATION)]

rēŏ'ccūpȳ *v.t.*, **rēŏccūp**A'TION *n.*, **rēō'pen** *v.t.* & *i.*, see RE- 9; **rēôr'der** *v.t.*, & *n.*, **rēôr'ganīze** *v.t.*, **rēôrganīz**A'TION *n.*, see RE- 8.

rēôr'ĭĕnt (*or* -ŏ'r-) *v.t.* Give new orientation to; readjust, change outlook of (person). [f. RE- 8 + ORIENT[2]]

rēŏ'rĭent|āte (*or* -ôr'-) *v.t.* = prec.; hence ~A'TION *n.* [f. RE- 8 + ORIENTATE]

rĕp[1], **rĕpp,** *n.* Textile fabric with corded surface used in curtains and upholstery. [f. F *reps*, of unkn. orig.]

rĕp[2] *n.* (colloq.) Representative, esp. commercial traveller. [abbr.]

rĕp[3] *n.* (sl.) Person of immoral character. [perh. for REPROBATE[2]; cf. RIP[1]]

rĕp[4] *n.* (colloq.) Repertory (theatre or company). [abbr.]

rĕp[5] *n.* (sl.) Reputation. [abbr.]

***Rep.** *abbr.* Representative (in Congress); Republican.

rēpai'nt[1] *v.t.* Paint again or differently; restore paint or colouring of. [f. RE- 8, 9 + PAINT[2]]

rē'paint[2] *n.* Act of repainting; repainted thing, e.g. golf-ball. [f. prec.]

rėpair'[1] *v.i.*, & *n.* **1.** *v.i.* Resort, have recourse, go often or in great numbers or for a specific purpose, *to.* **2.** *n.* (arch.) Resort (*have repair to*); place of frequent resort; being visited by numbers (*a place of great, little, repair*). [ME, f. OF *repaire(r)* f. LL *repatriare* REPATRIATE]

rėpair'[2] *v.t.* **1.** Restore (building, machine, garment, tissue, strength, etc.) to good condition; renovate or mend by replacing or refixing parts or compensating loss or exhaustion; hence ~ABLE *a.*, ~ER[1] *n.* **2.** Remedy, set right again, make amends for, (loss, wrong, error). [ME, f. OF *reparer* f. L *re(parare* make ready); see RE- 9]

rėpair'[3] *n.* **1.** Restoring to sound condition (*health, bicycle, house, shoe, is beyond* or *in need of repair*); act of doing this (*shop is closed during repairs*; *repairs done while you wait*); hence ***~-man** (esp. for motor vehicles etc.). **2.** Good condition, relative condition, for working or using (*is in, out of, repair*; *must be kept in good, is in bad, repair*). [f. prec.]

rėpă'nd *a.* (Bot. & Zool.) With undulating margin, wavy. [f. L *re(pandus* bent); see RE- 9]

rēpā'per *v.t.* See RE- 8.

rĕ'parable *a.* (Of loss etc.) that can be made good. [F, f. L *reparabilis* (as REPAIR[2]; see -ABLE)]

rĕparā'tion *n.* **1.** Repairing or being repaired. **2.** Making of amends; compensation, (esp. in *pl.*, for war damage by defeated State). **3.** Hence **rĕ'parat**IVE (*or* rĭpă'r-) *a.* [ME f. OF f. LL *reparatio -onis* (as REPAIR[2]; see -ATION)]

rĕpârtee' *n.* Witty retort; (making of) witty retorts (*a great power, a storehouse, of repartee*). [f. F *repartie* fem. p.p. (as n.) of *re(partir* PART[2]) start again, reply promptly; see RE- 8]

rēpârtĭ'tion *v.t.* See RE- 8.

rēpa'ss (-ah's) *v.t.* & *i.* Pass again, esp. on the way back. [ME, f. OF *repasser* (as RE- 9, PASS[1])]

rėpa'st (-ah'-) *n.* (formal). (Food supplied for or eaten at) meal (esp. of specified kind; *rich, slight, luxurious*, etc., *repast*). [ME f. OF (*repaistre* f. LL *repascere repast-* feed; see RE- 8, PASTOR)]

rēpă'trĭ|āte *v.t.* & *i.* Restore or return to native land; hence ~ATE[1] *n.*, one who has been repatriated, ~A'TION *n.* [f. LL *re(patriare* f. L *patria* native land); see RE- 9]

rēpay' *v.* (**repai'd**). **1.** *v.t.* Pay back (money); return (blow, visit, service, etc.); give in recompense *for*; make repayment to (person); make return for, requite, (action). **2.** *v.i.* Make repayment. **3.** Hence ~ABLE *a.*, **rē**PAY'MENT *n.* [f. OF *re(paier* PAY[2]); see RE- 9]

rėpea'l *v.t.*, & *n.* **1.** *v.t.* Revoke, rescind, annul, (law etc.); hence ~ABLE *a.* **2.** *n.* Abrogation, repealing. [ME, f. AF *repeler*, OF *rapeler* (as RE- 9, APPEAL[1])]

rėpea't *v.* & *n.* **1.** *v.t.* Say or do over again, recite, rehearse, report, reproduce, give imitation of, (*repeat action, statement, poem, conversation, attempt, pattern, signal*, etc.; *action was repeated several times*, whence **~ėd**LY[2] *adv.*); **not, ~ not,** emphatically not; *language* **will not bear ~ing,** is too foul etc. to repeat; **~ itself,** recur in same form; ~ one**self,** say or do same thing over again; hence ~ABLE *a.* **2.** *v.i.* (Of watch etc.) strike last quarter etc. over again when required; (of firearm) fire several shots without reloading. **3.** Recur, appear again or repeatedly (*the last three figures repeat*; **~ing decimal,** recurring decimal); (of food) be tasted intermittently for some time after being swallowed; *illegally vote more than once in election. **4.** *n.* Repeating, esp. of item in programme in response to encore; repeated broadcast programme; (Mus.) passage intended to be repeated, mark indicating this; pattern repeated in wallpaper etc.; (Commerc.) fresh consignment similar to previous one, order given for this. [ME, f. OF *repeter* f. L *re(petere* seek); see RE- 8]

rėpea'ter *n.* In vbl senses; firearm or watch that repeats; device for automatic re-transmission or amplification of electrically transmitted message; signal lamp indicating the state of another that is invisible. [f. prec. + -ER[1]]

repêchage (rĕ'peshahzh) *n.* (Rowing etc.)

Extra contest in which runners-up in the eliminating contests compete for a place in the final. [F (*repêcher* fish out, rescue; see -AGE)]

rėpĕ'l *v.t.* (-ll-). **1.** Drive back, repulse, ward off, refuse admission or acceptance or approach to, (*repel assailant, attack, temptation, weapon, blow, moisture, suggestion, plea, offer,* person's *advances, electric charge with same sign*). **2.** Be repulsive or distasteful to. [ME, f. L *re(pellere puls-* drive); see RE- 2]

rėpĕ'llent *a.* & *n.* (Substance) that repels (esp. insects etc.). [f. L *repellere* (as prec.; see -ENT)]

rē'pent[1] *a.* (Bot.) Creeping, esp. growing along or just under surface of ground. [f. L *repere* creep; see -ENT]

rėpĕ'nt[2] *v.* **1.** *v.t.* & *i.* Think with contrition of or *of*, be regretful about or *of*, wish one had not done, resolve not to continue wrongdoing in, (action etc., or abs.; *you shall repent, repent this, repent of this*). **2.** (arch., *refl.*) Feel regret or penitence about something or *of* (*I now repent me*). **3.** (arch., *impers.*) Affect with penitence or regret (*it repents me that I did it*). **4.** So ~ANCE *n.*, ~ANT *a.* [ME, f. OF *repentir* (as RE- 3, *pentir* f. Rom. **paenitire* f. L *paenitēre*)]

rēpeo'ple (-pē'-) *v.t.* See RE- 9.

rēpercŭ'ss|ion (-shon) *n.* Echo; recoil after impact; indirect effect or reaction *of* event or act; so ~IVE *a.* [ME f. OF, or f. L *repercussio* (as RE-, PERCUSSION)]

rĕ'pertoire (-twar) *n.* Stock of pieces etc. that company or performer knows or is prepared to give; totality of regularly performed pieces, regularly used techniques, etc. [f. F *répertoire* f. LL (as foll.)]

rĕ'pertorȳ *n.* **1.** Place for finding something, store or collection, esp. of information, instances, facts, etc. **2.** = prec.; theatrical performance of various plays for short periods by one ~ **company.** [f. LL *repertorium* f. L *reperire repert-* find; see -ORY]

rĕ'pėtĕnd *n.* Recurring figures of decimal; recurring word or phrase, refrain. [f. L (as REPEAT; see -ND[1])]

répétiteur (rĕpĕtĭtėr') *n.* Tutor or coach of musicians, esp. opera-singers. [F]

rĕpėtĭ't|ion *n.* Repeating or being repeated; piece set to be learnt by heart; copy, replica; ability of musical instrument to repeat note quickly; hence or cogn. ~**ion**AL, ~**ion**ARY[1], ~**i**OUS (-shus), **rėpĕ'tĭt**IVE, *adjs.* [f. F *répétition* or f. L *repetitio* (as REPEAT; see -ITION)]

rėpī'ne *v.i.* Fret, be discontented, (*at, against,* or abs.). [f. RE- 6 + PINE[2], after *repent*]

rėpi'que (-ē'k) *n.* & *v.* **1.** *n.* Winning of 30 points on cards alone before beginning to play in piquet. **2.** *v.t.* & *i.* Score repique (against). [f. F *repic* (as RE-, PIQUE[2])]

rėplā'ce *v.t.* Put back in place; take place of, succeed, be substituted for; (in *pass.*) be succeeded or have one's or its place filled *by*, be superseded; fill up place of (*with, by*), find or provide substitute for; hence ~ABLE (-sa-) *a.* [f. RE- 9 + PLACE[2]]

rėplā'cement (-sm-) *n.* Replacing or being replaced; person or thing that takes the place of another. [f. prec. + -MENT]

rēpla'nt (-ah'-) *v.t.* See RE- 8.

rēplay'[1] *v.t.* Play (match, recording, etc.) over again. [f. RE- 8 + PLAY[1]]

rē'play[2] *n.* Replaying (of match, recording of incident in game, etc.). [f. prec.]

rėplĕ'nĭsh *v.t.* Fill up again (*with*, or abs.); (in *p.p.*) filled, fully stored, full, (*with*, or abs.); renew (supply etc.); hence ~MENT *n.* [ME, f. OF *re(plenir* f. *plein* full f. L *plenus*); see RE- 9, -ISH[2]]

rėplē'|te *a.* Filled, stuffed, fully imbued, well stocked, *with*; gorged, sated, (*with*); hence or cogn. ~**te**NESS (-tn-), ~**t**ION, *ns.* [ME, f. OF *replet replete* or f. L *repletus* p.p. of *re(plēre plet-* fill); see RE- 6]

rėplĕ'vĭn *n.* Restoration or recovery of distrained goods on security given for submission to trial and judgement; writ granting replevin; action arising out of replevin. [ME f. AF, f. OF (as foll.)]

rėplĕ'vȳ *v.t.* Recover by replevin. [f. OF *re-(plevir* f. Gmc **plegjan*; cf. PLEDGE[1]) recover; see RE- 9]

rĕ'plĭca *n.* Duplicate made by original artist of his picture etc.; facsimile, exact copy; copy, model, esp. on smaller scale. [It. (*replicare* REPLY)]

rĕ'plĭcate[1] *n.* (Mus.) Tone one or more octaves above or below given tone. [as foll.]

rĕ'plĭcate[2] *a.* (Bot.) Folded back on itself. [as foll.; see -ATE[2]]

rĕ'plĭcate[3] *v.t.* Repeat; make replica of; fold back. [f. L *re(plicare* fold); see RE- 9, -ATE[3]]

rĕplĭcā'tion *n.* **1.** Replying, rejoinder, answer, esp. reply to answer; (Law) plaintiff's reply to defendant's plea. **2.** Copy, copying; repetition. [ME, f. OF *replicacion* f. L *replicatio -onis* (as prec.; see -ATION)]

rėplȳ' *v.* & *n.* **1.** *v.i.* Make answer, respond, in word or action (*to*). **2.** *v.t.* Say in answer (*he replied that I must please myself; 'Please yourself', he replied*). **3.** *n.* Act of replying (*what he says in reply*); what is replied, response; (Law) = prec.; ~ **coupon** (for prepaying reply to letter, exchangeable for stamps in any country); ~ **paid,** (of telegram) with cost of reply prepaid by sender, (of envelope etc.) for which addressee undertakes to pay postage. [ME, f. OF *replier* f. L (as REPLICATE[3])]

rēpoi'nt *v.t.* Point (esp. brickwork) again. [f. RE- 9 + POINT[2]]

rēpŏ'lĭsh *v.t.*, **rēpŏ'pūlāte** *v.t.*, see RE- 9.

rėpôr't[1] *v.* **1.** *v.t.* Bring back or give account of, state as ascertained fact, tell as news, narrate or describe or repeat esp. as eye-witness or hearer etc. (*to*), relate as spoken by another, make official or formal statement about, name (offence, offender) *to* authorities or abs., present (one*self*) as returned or arrived, (*reports open water at pole, pole to be accessible, that he reached pole; reported all details of the scene to me; my actual words and those reported to you were quite different; was reported (to the police) for speeding*); ‖(Parl., of committee chairman) announce that committee has dealt with (bill); ‖~ **progress,** state what has been done so far; ~**ed speech,** speaker's words with changes of person, tense, etc., usual in reports; hence ~**ėd**LY[2] *adv.* **2.** Take down word for word or epitomize or write description of for publication (*report law case, proceedings, meeting,* or abs.). **3.** *v.i.* Make, draw up, or send in report. **4.** Present oneself *to* (person) as returned or arrived; be responsible *to* (superior, supervisor, etc.). **5.** Give report *of* to convey that one is *well* or *badly* impressed (*reports well of the prospects; is badly reported of*). **6.** Hence ~ABLE *a.* [ME, f. OF *reporter* f. L *re(portare* bring); see RE- 9]

rėpôr't[2] *n.* **1.** Common talk, rumour, (*mere report is not enough to go upon; the report goes that*); way person or thing is spoken of, repute, (*things of good report; faithful through good and evil report*). **2.** Account given or opinion formally expressed after investigation or consideration or collation of information, description or epitome or reproduction of scene or speech or law case esp. for newspaper publication, (‖~ **stage,** House of Commons debate on bill when reported); periodical statement on pupil's work, conduct, etc., at school. **3.** Sound of explosion (*went off with a loud report*). [ME f. OF (*reporter*; see prec.)]

rĕpŏrta'ge (-ah'zh) *n.* (Typical style of) reporting events for press etc.; factual presentation in book etc. [f. REPORT¹ + -AGE, after F]

rėpŏr'ter *n.* One who reports; person employed to report news etc. for newspaper or broadcast. [ME, f. AF **reportour*, OF *reporteur* (as REPORT¹, -ER²), & f. REPORT¹ + -ER¹]

***rĕpŏrtŏr'ĭal** *a.* Of newspaper reporter(s); hence ~LY² *adv.* [f. prec., after *editorial*]

rėpō's|e¹ (-z) *v.t.* Place (trust etc.) *in*; hence ~AL 2 *n.* [f. RE- 4 + POSE¹, after L *re(ponere posit-* place)]

rėpō'se² (-z) *v.* & *n.* **1.** *v.t.* Rest (one*self*, or abs.); lay (one's head etc.) to rest (*on* pillow etc.); give rest to, refresh with rest. **2.** *v.i.* Lie, be lying or laid, esp. in sleep or death (*in*, *on*, or abs.); be supported or based *on* (*the whole system reposes on fear*); (of memory etc.) dwell *on*. **3.** *n.* Cessation of activity or excitement, respite from toil, sleep, peaceful or quiescent state, stillness, tranquillity; restful effect, harmonious combination in art, composure or ease of manner, (*lacks repose*); **angle of ~** (beyond which inclined body will not support another on its surface by friction); hence ~FUL (-zf-) *a.* [ME, f. OF *repos(er)* f. LL *re(pausare* PAUSE); see RE- 5]

rėpŏ'sĭtorў (-z-) *n.* **1.** Receptacle; place where things are stored or may be found, museum, warehouse, store, shop, (*book*, *person*, etc., *is a repository of curious information*); burial-place. **2.** Recipient *of* confidences or secrets. [f. obs. F *repositoire* or f. L *repositorium* (as REPOSE¹; see -ORY)]

rēpossĕ'ss (-z-) *v.t.* Regain possession of (esp. forfeited hire-purchase goods); so ~ION (-shon) *n.* [f. RE- 9 + POSSESS]

rēpŏ't *v.t.* (**-tt-**). Put (plant) in another (esp. larger) pot. [f. RE- 8 + POT²]

repou'ssé (repōō'sā) *a.* & *n.* (Ornamental metalwork) hammered into relief from reverse side. [F, p.p. of *re(pousser* PUSH¹); see RE- 3]

rĕpp. See REP¹.

rĕpped (-pt) *a.* Having surface like rep. [f. REP¹ + -ED²]

repr. *abbr.* represent etc.; reprint(ed).

rĕprėhĕ'n|d *v.t.* Rebuke, blame, find fault with; so ~SIBLE *a.*, ~SION (-shon) *n.* [ME, f. L *re(prehendere* seize); see RE- 2]

rĕprėsĕ'nt (-z-) *v.t.* **1.** Call up in the mind by description or portrayal or imagination, place likeness of before mind or senses, serve or be meant as likeness of, (*can you represent infinity to yourself?*; *can only represent it to you by metaphors*; *picture represents murder of Abel*; *is represented in hunting costume*). **2.** Try to bring (facts influencing conduct) home (*to*), state by way of expostulation or incentive, (*represented the rashness of it, that it could not succeed, that it must succeed*). **3.** Make out *to* be etc., allege *that*, describe or depict *as*, (*am not what you represent me to be* or *as*; *in the corner is the Pope represented as a beggar*; *represents that he has, himself to have, seen service*). **4.** Act (play etc.), play part of on stage. **5.** Symbolize, act as embodiment of, stand for, correspond to, be specimen of, (*sovereign represents majesty of State*; *inch of rain represents 100 tons to acre*; *by-election result does not represent country's views*; *symbol χ represents guttural sound*; *camels are represented in the New World by llamas*; *Welsh football is represented in the team by Morgan*). **6.** Fill place of, be substitute or deputy for, be entitled to act or speak for, be sent as member to legislature or delegate to meeting etc. by, (*Queen was represented by the Duke*; *members representing urban constituencies*). **7.** Hence ~ABLE *a.* [ME, f. OF *representer* or f. L *re(praesentare* PRESENT⁴); see RE- 8]

rĕprėsĕntā'tion (-z-) *n.* Representing or being represented; (esp. in *pl.*) statement made by way of allegation or to convey opinion; PROPORTIONAL *representation*. [ME f. OF, or f. L *repraesentatio* (as prec.; see -ATION)]

rĕprėsĕntā'tional (-z-) *a.* Of representation; **~ art** (seeking to portray reality). [f. prec. + -AL]

rĕprėsĕntā'tion|ĭsm (-zĕ-) *n.* (Philos.) Doctrine that perceived objects are only a representation of real external objects; so ~IST (2) *n.* [f. REPRESENTATION + -ISM]

rĕprėsĕ'ntatĭve (-z-) *a.* & *n.* **1.** *a.* Serving as portrayal or symbol *of* (*a group representative of the theological virtues*); that presents or can present ideas to the mind (*imagination is a representative faculty*); (of art) representational; typical of a class or classes, containing typical specimens of all or many classes, (*the truth of an allegory is representative, not literal*; *call a meeting of representative men*; *a very representative selection, collection*); consisting of elected deputies or representatives; based on representation of nation etc. by such deputies (*representative government, institutions*); hence ~LY² (-vlĭ) *adv.*, ~NESS (-vn-) *n.* **2.** *n.* Sample, specimen, typical embodiment, analogue, *of*; person's or firm's agent; delegate, substitute, successor, heir; deputy in representative legislature (**House of R~s,** lower house of U.S. Congress and other national Parliaments). [ME, f. OF *representatif -ive* or f. med. L *repraesentativus* (as REPRESENT; see -ATIVE)]

rėprĕ'ss *v.t.* **1.** Check, restrain; keep under, quell; suppress, prevent from sounding or bursting out or rioting. **2.** (Psych.) Actively exclude (unpleasant or unwelcome thought) from conscious awareness, (usu. in *pass.*) subject (person) to repression of his thoughts. **3.** Hence or cogn. ~ION (-shon) *n.*, ~IVE *a.* [ME, f. L *re(primere = premere* PRESS²); see RE- 5]

rėprie've *v.t.*, & *n.* **1.** *v.t.* Postpone or remit execution of (condemned person); (fig.) give respite to. **2.** *n.* Reprieving or being reprieved; (warrant for) remission or commutation of capital sentence; respite. [ME as p.p. *repryed*, f. AF & OF *repris* p.p. of *re(prendre* f. L *prehendere* take; see RE- 8); 16th-c. *-v-* unexpl.]

rĕ'prĭmand (-ah-) *n.*, & *v.t.* Official(ly) or sharp(ly) rebuke (*for* fault). [f. F *réprimande(r)* f. Sp. f. L *reprimenda* neut. pl. gerundive of *reprimere* REPRESS]

rēprĭ'nt¹ *v.t.* Print again; make reprint of. [f. RE- 8 + PRINT²]

rē'prĭnt² *n.* Book reprinted, reprinting of book, in same or new form; quantity thus reprinted; article reprinted after separation from accompanying articles, = SEPARATE¹ 2. [f. prec.]

rėprī'sal (-z-) *n.* **1.** Act of retaliation. **2.** (Hist.) Forcible seizure of foreign subjects' persons or property in retaliation (**letters of ~**, official warrant authorizing this). [ME in sense 2, f. AF *reprisaille* f. med. L *reprisalia* f. *repraehensalia* (as REPREHEND; see -AL 2)]

reprī'se (-ē'z) *n.* Repeated passage in music; repeated song etc. in musical programme. [F, fem. p.p. (as n.) of *reprendre* (see REPRIEVE)]

rėproa'ch *v.t.*, & *n.* **1.** *v.t.* Scold, censure, express disapproval to (person; *with* his offence or *for* fault); rebuke (offence); (of look etc.) convey protest or censure to (*his eyes reproach me*). **2.** *n.* Thing that brings disgrace or discredit (*to*; *the*

For other words in *re-* see RE-.

state of the roads is a reproach to civilization); opprobrium, disgraced or discredited state, (*live in reproach and ignominy*; *the things that had brought reproach upon him*); **above** or **beyond ~**, perfect. **3.** Scolding, rebuke, censure, (*heap reproaches on*; *the mute reproach in his eyes*); **term of ~**, word implying censure; hence ~FUL *a.* **4.** (in *pl.*) (Chiefly R.C.) set of antiphons and responses for Good Friday, representing reproaches of Christ to people. [ME, f. OF *reproche(r)* f. Rom. **repropiare* f. as RE- 7 + L *prope* near]

rĕ'prob|āte[1] *v.t.* Express or feel disapproval of, censure; (of God) cast off, exclude from salvation; so ~A'TION *n.* [ME, f. L *re(probare* approve) disapprove; see RE- 7, -ATE[3]]

rĕ'probāte[2] *a.* & *n.* (Person who is) cast off by God, hardened in sin, of highly immoral character, or unprincipled. [f. LL *reprobatus* p.p. of L *reprobare* (see prec., -ATE[2])]

rēprodū'c|e *v.* **1.** *v.t.* Produce copy or representation of; cause to be seen, heard, etc., again; produce offspring of (*oneself, itself*); form afresh (lost etc. part of body). **2.** *v.i.* Produce further members of same species by natural means; give specified quality of result when copied (*picture does not reproduce well*). **3.** Hence ~IBI'LITY *n.*, ~IBLE *a.*, ~**ĭb**LY[2] *adv.* [f. RE- 8 + PRODUCE[2]]

rēprodŭ'ct|ion *n.* Reproducing; copy of painting etc.; (*attrib.* of furniture etc.) made in imitation of earlier style; so ~IVE *a.* [f. prec., after *production*]

rèprŏ'graphy̆ *n.* Science and practice of copying documents by photography, xerography, etc.; hence **rēprogră'phic** *a.* [f. REPRODUCE + -GRAPHY]

rèproō'f[1] *n.* Blame (*a word, glance, of reproof*); rebuke, words expressing blame. [ME f. OF *reprove* (*reprover* REPROVE)]

rēproō'f[2] *v.t.* Make fresh proof of (printed matter etc.); render (coat etc.) waterproof again. [f. RE- 8, 9 + PROOF[1,2]]

rèpro've (-ōō'v) *v.t.* Rebuke, scold, (person, conduct, etc.). [ME, f. OF *reprover* f. LL *reprobare* disapprove; see REPROBATE[1]]

rēprovĭ'sion (-zhon) *v.t.* See RE- 8.

rĕ'ptant *a.* (Biol.) Creeping. [f. L *reptare* frequent. of *repere* crawl; see -ANT]

rĕ'ptile *n.* & *a.* **1.** *n.* Member of the Reptilia or class of animals including snakes, lizards, crocodiles, turtles, and tortoises, whence **rĕptĭ'l**IAN (-lyan) *a.* & *n.*; mean, grovelling, or repulsive person. **2.** *a.* (Of animal) creeping; mean and grovelling. [ME, (n. f. OF or LL *reptile* neut.) f. LL *reptilis* f. L *repere rept-* crawl; see -IL]

rèpŭ'blĭc *n.* A State in which supreme power is held by the people or its elected representatives or by elected or nominated president, not by monarch etc.; (fig.) society of persons or animals with equality between members (*the republic of* LETTERS); **R~ Day** (commemorating foundation of republic; in India 26 Jan.). [f. F *république* f. L *respublica* (*res* concern, *publicus* PUBLIC)]

rèpŭ'blĭcan *a.* & *n.* **1.** *a.* Of, constituted as, characterizing, republic(s). **2.** *a.* & *n.* (Person) advocating or supporting republican government. **3.** (*R~*). *(Member) of political party opposed to Democratic Party and favouring only moderate degree of central power. **4.** (Of birds) social, living in large communities. **5.** Hence ~ISM (3) *n.*, ~IZE (3) *v.t.* [f. prec. + -AN]

rēpŭ'blĭsh *v.t.*, **rē**PUBLICA'TION *n.* See RE- 8.

rèpū'dĭ|āte *v.t.* **1.** Divorce (one's wife; esp. of the ancients or non-Christians). **2.** Disown, disavow, reject; refuse dealings with, deny. **3.** Refuse to recognize or obey (authority, treaty) or discharge (obligation, debt). **4.** Hence or cogn. ~A'TION, ~**ātor**, *ns.* [f. L *repudiare* (*repudium* divorce) + -ATE[3]]

rèpū'gn (-ū'n) *v.* (arch.) **1.** *v.i.* Offer opposition; strive *against*. **2.** *v.t.* Strive against; affect disagreeably, be repugnant to. [ME, f. L *re(pugnare* fight) oppose; see RE- 2]

rèpŭ'gnance *n.* Antipathy, aversion, (*to, against*); inconsistency, incompatibility, of ideas, statements, tempers, etc., (*of, between, to, with*). [ME, in second sense, f. F *répugnance* or f. L *repugnantia* (as prec.; see -ANCE)]

rèpŭ'gn|ant *a.* Distasteful (*to*); contradictory (*to*), incompatible (*with*); (poet.) refractory, resisting. [ME, f. F *répugnant* or f. L (as REPUGN; see -ANT)]

rèpŭ'lse *v.t.*, & *n.* **1.** *v.t.* Drive back (attack, attacking enemy) by force of arms, (fig.) foil in controversy; rebuff (friendly advances or their maker), refuse (request, offer, or its maker); = REPEL 2. **2.** *n.* Repulsing or being repulsed, rebuff, (*inflict, meet with, suffer*, etc., *a repulse*). [(n. f. L *repulsus* or *-sa*) f. L *repellere* (see REPEL)]

rèpŭ'lsion (-shon) *n.* Aversion, disgust; (Phys., or fig.) tendency of bodies to repel each other or increase their mutual distance (opp. *attraction*). [f. LL *repulsio* (as REPEL; see -ION)]

rèpŭ'lsĭve *a.* **1.** Causing aversion or loathing, loathsome, disgusting; hence ~LY[2] (-vlĭ) *adv.*, ~NESS (-vn-) *n.* **2.** (Phys.) Exerting repulsion. **3.** (arch.) (Of behaviour etc.) repellent, cold, unsympathetic. [f. F *répulsif -ive* or REPULSE 1 + -IVE]

rēpûr'chase *v.t.*, & *n.*, **rēpūr'ĭfȳ** *v.t.*, see RE- 9.

rĕ'pūtab|le *a.* Of good repute, respectable; hence ~LY[2] *adv.* [obs. F, or f. med. L *reputabilis* (as REPUTE; see -ABLE)]

rĕpūtā'tion *n.* What is generally said or believed about person's or thing's character (*has not justified his reputation*; *has a reputation for integrity*; *place has a bad reputation*); state of being well reported of, credit, distinction, respectability, good report, (*persons of reputation*); *the* credit or discredit *of* doing or *of* being (*has the reputation of swindling his customers, of being the best shot in England*). [ME, f. L *reputatio* (as foll.; see -ATION)]

rèpū'te *v.t.*, & *n.* **1.** *v.t.* (usu. in *pass.*) Consider, reckon. **2.** (in *pass.*) Be generally considered or reported of, (with compl. or *to* be or do; *is reputed the best doctor* or *to be the best*); be generally *well, ill*, etc., thought or spoken of. **3.** (in *p.p.* as *a.*) Passing as being but probably or possibly not being (*his reputed father, clemency*, etc.); ||**~d pint** etc., bottle of beer etc. sold as pint etc. but not guaranteed as imperial pint etc.; hence **rèpū'tèd**LY[2] *adv.* **4.** *n.* Reputation (*a philosopher of repute*; *know him by repute*). [ME, f. OF *reputer* or f. L *re(putare* think); see RE- 6]

rèquĕ'st *n.*, & *v.t.* **1.** *n.* Act of asking for something, petition made, thing asked for, (*came at his request*; *made two requests*; *you shall have your request*); **by** or **on ~**, in response to expressed wish; **~ programme** etc. (composed of items requested by audience etc.); **~ stop** (where bus etc. stops only on passenger's request). **2.** State of being sought after, demand, (*is now in great request*). **3.** *v.t.* (arch.) Seek permission *to* do. **4.** Ask to be given or allowed or favoured with (*request candid consideration*, person's *presence*, etc.); ask *that*; ask (person) *to* do. [ME, f. OF *requeste(r)* f. Rom. **requaesita* fem. p.p. (as n.) of L *requaerere* (see REQUIRE)]

rēquĭ'cken *v.t.* See RE- 9.

rĕ'quĭĕm *n.* Special Mass for repose of souls of the dead; musical setting for this; dirge. [ME f. L (acc. of *requies* repose), initial wd of the Mass]

rĕquiĕ'scăt *n.* Wish for dead person's repose. [L, = may he or she rest (in peace)]

rėquīr'e *v.t.* **1.** Order (person), demand (*of* or *from* person), *to* do (*they require me* or *of me to appear*); demand or ask in words (person's action, act *of* person, thing *at* person's *hands, that,* etc.) esp. as of right (*they require my appearance, an oath of me, a gift at my hands* or *from me, that I should appear*). **2.** Lay down as imperative (*had done all that was required by the Act*; *Gray's 'Anatomy' is required reading for nurses*). **3.** Need, depend for success, fulfilment, etc., on, (*the emergency requires it, that it should be done*; *irony requires care in its use, to be used with care*; *place would require an army to take it*; *machine requires no attention*; *it required all his authority to keep them under control*); wish to have (*do you require tea?*). **4.** Hence ~MENT (-īr'm-) *n.* [ME, f. OF *requere* f. Rom. **requaerere* f. L *re(quirere quisit- = quaerere* seek); see RE- 6]

rĕ'quĭsĭte (-z-) *a.* & *n.* **1.** *a.* Required by circumstances, necessary to success etc.; hence ~NESS (-tn-) *n.* **2.** *n.* Thing needed (*for* some purpose). [ME, f. L *requisitus* p.p. (as prec.)]

rĕquĭsĭ'tion (-z-) *n.*, & *v.t.* **1.** *n.* Requiring, demand made, esp. formal and usu. written demand that some duty should be performed; order given by authorities laying claim to use of property or materials; being called or put into service (**under** or **in** ~, being used or applied). **2.** *v.t.* Demand use or supply of esp. by requisition order. [f. F *réquisition* or f. L *requisitio* (as REQUIRE; see -ITION)]

rėquī't|e *v.t.* Make return for, reward or avenge, (service, wrong, injury, treatment; *with* what is given etc. thus); make return to, repay with good or evil, (person; *for* treatment received, *with* treatment given); give in return (*requite* person's *love, like for like*); hence ~AL 2 *n.* [f. RE- 1 + *quite* var. of QUIT[2]]

rērea'd *v.t.* (**rerea'd** *pr.* -rĕ'd). See RE- 8.

rēr'e-ârch *n.* Var. of REAR-ARCH.

rēr'e-dôrter *n.* Latrine behind dormitory of convent or monastery. [f. *rere* var. of REAR[1] + DORTER]

rēr'edŏs (rēr'd-) *n.* Ornamental screen covering wall at back of altar. [ME, f. AF **reredos* f. OF *areredos* (*arere* behind, *dos* back); cf. ARREAR]

rērou'te (-ōō't) *v.t.* (~**ing** *pr.* -tĭ-). Send or carry by different route. [f. RE- 8 + ROUTE]

rērŭ'n *v.t.* (**-nn-; -ra'n; -ru'n**), & *n.* **1.** *v.t.* Run (race, film, etc.) again. **2.** *n.* Act of re-running. [f. RE- 8 + RUN[1]]

rēsā'le *n.* Sale of thing bought. [f. RE- 9 + SALE]

rėscĭ'nd *v.t.* Abrogate, annul, revoke, cancel; so **rėscĭ'ssION** (-zhon) *n.* [f. L *re(scindere sciss-* cut); see RE- 5]

rē'script *n.* **1.** Roman emperor's written reply to appeal for guidance esp. from magistrate on legal point; pope's decretal in reply to question, any papal decision. **2.** Ruler's or government's or official edict or announcement. **3.** Thing rewritten, rewriting; palimpsest. [f. L *rescriptum*, neut. p.p. (as n.) of *re(scribere script-* write); see RE- 1]

rĕ'scū|e *v.t.*, & *n.* **1.** *v.t.* Set free or bring away from or *from* attack, custody, danger, or harm; (Law) unlawfully liberate (person), forcibly recover (property); hence ~ER[1] *n.* **2.** *n.* Rescuing or being rescued (*come* or *go to* person's or *the rescue*); succour, deliverance; illegal liberation, forcible recovery; ~**e bid,** (Bridge) bid made to get one's partner out of difficult situation. [ME *rescowe* f. OF *rescoure* f. Rom. **reexcutere* f. as RE- 6 + L EX[1](*cutere = quatere* shake)]

rėsear'ch (-sēr'-; *or* rē'-) *n.* & *v.* **1.** *n.* Careful search or inquiry *after* or *for* or *into*; endeavour to discover new or collate old facts etc. by scientific study of a subject, course of critical investigation, (*his researches have been fruitful*; *is engaged in research*). **2.** *v.i.* Make researches; hence ~ER[1] *n.* **3.** *v.t.* Make researches into or for. [f. obs. F *recerche(r)* (as RE- 6, SEARCH)]

rēsea't *v.t.* Provide (church, theatre, valve, etc.) with fresh seat(s); seat (person, one*self*) again. [f. RE- 8 + SEAT]

rėsĕ'ct *v.t.* (Surg.) Cut out part of (lung etc.); pare down (bone, cartilage, etc.); so ~ION *n.* [f. L *re(secare sect-* cut); see RE- 5]

rĕ'sėda *n.* **1.** Herbaceous plant of genus *Reseda*, e.g. mignonette. **2.** (*or* -z- *or* rĭsē'da). Pale green colour as of mignonette flowers. [L, perh. f. imper. of *resedare* assuage, used in curative charm]

rēsĕ'll *v.t.* (**reso'ld**). Sell after buying. [f. RE- 9 + SELL]

rėsĕ'mbl|e (-z-) *v.t.* **1.** Be like, have similarity to or feature(s) in common with or same appearance as; so ~ANCE (*to, between, of*) *n.*, ~ANT (*to*) *a.* **2.** (arch.) Liken *to*. [ME, f. OF *re(sembler* f. L *similare*, f. *similis* like); see RE- 1]

rėsĕ'nt (-z-) *v.t.* Show or feel indignation at or retain bitter feelings about (do*ing*, insult or injury sustained); hence or cogn. ~FUL *a.*, ~MENT *n.* [f. obs. F *resentir* (as RE- 1, L *sentire* feel)]

rėsēr'pine (-ēn) *n.* Alkaloid from plants of genus *Rauwolfia*, used as tranquillizer and in treatment of hypertension. [f. G *reserpin* f. mod. L *R*auwolfia (f. L. *Rauwolf*, Ger. botanist d. 1596) *serp*entina; see -INE[5]]

rĕservā'tion (-z-) *n.* **1.** Reserving or being reserved. **2.** (Eccl.) Right reserved to pope of nomination to vacant benefice; power of absolution reserved to superior; practice of retaining for some purpose a portion of the Eucharistic elements (esp. the bread) after celebration. **3.** (Law). (Clause reserving) right or interest retained in estate being conveyed. **4.** Strip of land between carriageways of road; *tract of land reserved esp. for exclusive occupation by Indian tribe. **5.** Express or tacit limitation or exception made about something (**mental** ~, qualification tacitly added in making statement, oath, etc.). **6.** Booking (of berth on ship, room in hotel, seat in train, etc.); place so booked. [ME f. OF, or f. LL *reservatio* (as foll.; see -ATION)]

rėsēr'v|e[1] (-z-) *v.t.* **1.** Postpone use or enjoyment or treatment of, keep back for later occasion, (~**e oneself for,** not expend one's energies till); postpone delivery of (judgement). **2.** Secure or retain possession or control or use of esp. by legal or formal stipulation (*for* or *to* one*self* or another; *management reserves the right to refuse admission*); ||~**ed list,** (Hist.) list of naval officers retired from active service but liable to be called out in emergency; ~**ed occupation** (from which person will not be taken for military service); ~**ed seat,** (at entertainment etc.) that has been or may be booked; hence ~ABLE *n.* **3.** Set apart, destine, *for* some use or fate; (in *pass.*) be left by fate *for*, fall first or only *to*. **4.** (in *p.p.* as *a.*) Reticent, slow to reveal emotions or opinions, uncommunicative; hence ~**ėd**LY[2] *adv.* [ME, f. OF *reserver* f. L *re(servare* keep); see RE- 3]

rėsēr've[2] (-z-) *n.* **1.** Thing reserved for future use, extra stock or amount, (*has a great reserve of energy, great reserves of strength*); (Banking, in *sing.* or *pl.*) assets kept readily available as cash or at central bank, or as gold or foreign exchange (~ **currency**); company's profit added

For other words in *re-* see RE-.

to capital. **2.** (Mil., in *sing.* or *pl.*) Troops withheld from action to reinforce others or to cover retreat; forces outside regular army and navy and air force liable to be called out in emergency; reservist. **3.** Extra player chosen in case substitute should be needed to make up team for game. **4.** State of being kept unused but available (*has it in reserve*). **5.** Place reserved for some special use (*game reserve*; *nature reserve*), esp. for exclusive occupation by native tribe. **6.** Limitation, exception, restriction, or qualification, attached to something; *I accept your statement* **without ~**, fully; *sale* or *auction* **without ~**, not subject to a fixed price's being reached; **~ (price)**, lowest price that will be accepted; *we publish this* **with all ~, all proper ~s,** without endorsing it. **7.** Self-restraint, abstinence from exaggeration or ill-proportioned effects, in artistic or literary expression; reticence, avoidance of plain speaking, coolness of manner, lack of cordiality; intentional suppression of truth. [f. prec.]

rē-sēr'vē[3] *v.t.* See RE- 8.

rėsēr'vĭst (rĭz-) *n.* (Mil. etc.) Member of reserve forces. [f. prec. + -IST]

rĕ'servoir (-zervwar) *n.* **1.** Receptacle constructed usu. of earthwork or masonry in which large quantity of water is stored. **2.** Any natural or artificial receptacle esp. for or of fluid, place where fluid etc. collects; part of machine or organ of body holding fluid; reserve supply or collection *of* knowledge, facts, etc. [f. F *réservoir* (*réserver* RESERVE[1]; see -ORY)]

rēsĕ't *v.t.* (**-tt-; rese't**). Set (gems, printing type, etc.) again or differently. [f. RE- 8 + SET[1]]

rēsĕ'ttle *v.t.*, **rēsĕ'ttle**MENT (-telm-) *n.*, **rē-shā'pe** *v.t.*, **rēshĭ'p** *v.t.*, see RE- 8.

rēshŭ'ffle *v.t.*, & *n.* **1.** *v.t.* Shuffle (cards) again; interchange posts of (Government ministers etc.). **2.** *n.* Reshuffling. [f. RE- 8 + SHUFFLE]

rėsī'de (-z-) *v.i.* (Of person) have one's home, dwell permanently, *at, in, abroad*, etc.; (of incumbent official) be in residence; (of power, right, etc.) rest or be vested *in* person etc.; (of quality) be present or inherent *in*. [ME, prob. back form. f. RESIDENT, infl. by F *résider* or L *re*(*sidēre* = *sedēre* sit); see RE- 3]

rĕ'sĭdence (-z-) *n.* **1.** Residing (**have, take up,** (one's) **~**, dwell, begin to dwell; **in ~**, dwelling at specified place esp. for performance of duties etc.). **2.** Place where one resides, abode *of*; house esp. of considerable pretension, mansion, (*desirable residence for sale*). [ME f. OF, or f. med. L *residentia* f. L *residēre* (see prec., -ENCE)]

rĕ'sĭdencў (-z-) *n.* (Hist.) official residence of, territory supervised by, Governor-General's representative at Indian native court, or other government agent (see RESIDENT); *period of specialized medical training. [f. as prec.; see -ENCY]

rĕ'sĭdent (-z-) *a.* & *n.* **1.** *a.* Residing (*whether resident at home or abroad*; *the resident population*); (of birds etc.) non-migratory; dwelling in a place in fulfilment of duty; having quarters on the spot (*resident housekeeper, surgeon, tutor*); inherent, located, *in* (*a right resident in the nation*; *powers of sensation resident in the nerves*). **2.** *n.* Permanent inhabitant of town or neighbourhood (opp. *visitor*); (Hist.) Indian Governor-General's political agent residing at native court, British government agent in other semi-dependent State, whence ~SHIP *n.*; *person undergoing specialized medical training. [ME f. OF, or f. L (see RESIDE, -ENT)]

rĕsĭdĕ'ntial (-z-; -shal) *a.* Suitable for or occupied by private houses (*residential area, estate, street*); used as residence (*residential hotel*); connected with residence (*a residential course of study*; *the residential qualification for voters*). [f. RESIDENCE + -IAL]

rĕsĭdĕ'ntiarў (-z-; -sherĭ) *n.* & *a.* **1.** *n.* Ecclesiastic who must officially reside in a place. **2.** *a.* Subject to, requiring, of or for, official residence (usu. after *n.*; *Canon, Canonry, Residentiary*; *at his residentiary house*). [f. med. L *residentiarius* (as RESIDENCE; see -ARY[1])]

rėsĭ'dūal (-z-) *a.* & *n.* **1.** (Quantity) remaining, left over, left as residue or residuum. **2.** (Math.) (Quantity) resulting from subtraction. **3.** (Error in calculation) still unaccounted for or not eliminated. [f. RESIDUE + -AL]

rėsĭ'dūarў (-z-) *a.* Of the residue of an estate (*residuary bequest, clause, legatee*, etc.); of or being a residuum, residual, still remaining. [f. RESIDUUM + -ARY[1]]

rĕ'sĭdūe (-z-) *n.* Remainder, rest, what is left or remains over; what remains of estate after payment of charges, debts, and bequests; (Chem. etc.) residuum. [ME, f. OF *residu* f. L *residuum* (see foll.)]

rėsĭ'dū|um (-z-) *n.* (*pl.* **~a**). What remains, esp. (Chem. etc.) substance left after combustion or evaporation; residual; residue. [L, neut. (as n.) of *residuus* remaining (*residēre*; see RESIDE)]

rėsī'gn[1] (-zī'n) *v.* **1.** *v.t.* Relinquish, surrender, hand over, (office, right, claim, property, charge, task, life, hope; *to* person, *into* person's hands etc.; one*self to* another's guidance etc.). **2.** Reconcile one*self*, one's *mind*, etc. (*to* one's *fate* etc., *to* doing). **3.** *v.i.* Accept the inevitable without repining; hence ~ED[1] (2) (-zī'nd) *a.*, ~**ėd**LY[2] *adv.* **4.** Give up office, retire, (*as* chairman etc., *from* chairmanship etc.); (Chess) discontinue play and admit defeat. [ME, f. OF *resigner* f. L *re*(*signare* SIGN[2], seal) unseal, cancel; see RE- 7]

rē-sī'gn[2] (-sī'n) *v.t.* & *i.* Sign again. [f. RE- 8 + SIGN[2]]

rĕsĭgnā'tion (-z-) *n.* Resigning esp. of an office, document conveying it (*give, send in, tender*, one's *resignation*); being resigned, uncomplaining endurance of sorrow or other evil. [ME f. OF, f. med. L *resignatio* (as RESIGN[1]; see -ATION)]

rėsī'le (-z-) *v.i.* (Of elastic body) recoil, rebound, resume shape and size after stretching or compression; have or show elasticity or buoyancy or recuperative power; withdraw *from* course of action. [f. obs. F *resilir* or f. L *re*(*silire* = *salire* jump); see RE- 9]

rėsĭ'li|ent (-zĭ'lye-) *a.* Recoiling, springing back; resuming original form after stretching, bending, etc.; (of person) readily recovering from depression etc., buoyant; so ~ENCE, ~ENCY, *ns.* [f. L (as prec.; see -ENT)]

rĕ'sĭn (-z-) *n.*, & *v.t.* **1.** *n.* Adhesive inflammable substance insoluble in water (cf. GUM[2]) secreted by most plants and exuding naturally or upon incision esp. from fir and pine; (**synthetic**) **~**, solid or liquid organic compound made by polymerization etc. and used esp. as or in plastics. **2.** Hence or cogn. ~ATE[1] (3) *n.*, ~ATE[3] *v.t.*, ~Ĭ'FEROUS, ~ĬFORM, *adjs.*, ~ĬFICA'TION *n.*, ~ĬFY *v.t.*, ~OID *a.* & *n.*, ~OUS *a.* **3.** *v.t.* Rub or treat with resin. [ME *resyn, rosyn*, f. L *resina* & med. L *rosina, rosinum*]

rĕsĭpĭ'sc|ence *n.* (arch.) Recognition of error, return to good sense; so ~ENT *a.* [f. F *résipiscence* or f. LL *resipiscentia* f. *re*(*sipiscere* f. *sapere* know); see RE- 9]

rėsĭ'st (-zĭ'-) *v.* & *n.* **1.** *v.t.* Stop course of, withstand action or effect of, prevent from reaching or penetrating, repel, abstain from, (*projectile, weapon, cutting edge, frost, heat, moisture, attack, temptation, power, infection, disease, influence, suggestion*, etc., doing); **cannot ~** *a joke* etc.,

(1) feels obliged to make it if it suggests itself, (2) is certain to be amused, attracted, etc., by it; hence ~IBLE *a.* **2.** Strive against, oppose, try to impede, refuse to comply with, (*resist arrest*). **3.** *v.i.* Offer resistance, make opposition; hence or cogn. ~ANT *a.*, ~ER[1] *n.* **4.** *n.* Composition applied to surfaces for protection from some agent employed on them, esp. to parts of calico that are not to take dye. [ME, f. OF *resister* or f. L *re(sistere* stop, redupl. of *stare* stand); see RE- 2]

rėsĭ'stance (-zĭ'-) *n.* **1.** (Power of) resisting (*showed resistance to complying, to wear and tear*); PASSIVE *resistance*; ~ (**movement**), secret organization resisting authority, esp. in a conquered country. **2.** Hindrance, impeding or stopping effect, exerted by material thing on another (*overcome the resistance of the air*); **line of ~**, direction in which this acts; **take line of least ~**, (fig.) adopt easiest method or course. **3.** (Phys.) Property of failing to conduct (electricity, heat, etc.); amount of this property in a body; (Electr.) resistor. [ME, f. F *résistance, résistence* f. LL *resistentia* (as prec.; see -ANCE)]

rėsĭstĭbĭ'lĭtў (-zĭ-) *n.* Being resistible; power of offering resistance. [f. RESIST + -IBILITY]

rėsĭ'stĭve (-zĭ'-) *a.* Able to resist; (Electr.) pertaining to resistance. [f. med. L *resistivus*, or f. RESIST + -IVE]

rēsĭstĭ'vĭtў (-zĭ-) *n.* (Electr.) Resisting power of specified material. [f. prec. + -ITY]

rėsĭ'stlėss (-zĭ'-) *a.* (arch.) Irresistible; unresisting; hence ~LY[2] *adv.* [f. RESIST + -LESS]

rėsĭ'stor (-zĭ'-) *n.* (Electr.) Device having resistance to passage of current. [f. RESIST + -OR]

rēsĭ't *v.t.* (**-tt-; resa't**). Sit (examination) a second time after failing. [f. RE- 8 + SIT]

rēsō'le *v.t.* See RE- 8.

rėsŏ'lūble[1] (-z-) *a.* That can be resolved; analysable *into*, resolvable. [f. F *résoluble* or f. LL *resolubilis* (as RESOLVE, after *soluble*)]

rē-sŏ'lūble[2] *a.* That can be dissolved again. [f. RE- 9 + SOLUBLE]

rĕ'solūte (-z-; *or* -ōōt) *a.* (Of person or his mind or action) determined, decided, bold, not vacillating, unshrinking, firm of purpose; hence ~LY[2] (-tlĭ) *adv.*, ~NESS (-tn-) *n.* [f. L *resolutus* p.p. of *resolvere* (see RESOLVE)]

rĕsolū'tion (-z-; *or* -ōō'-) *n.* **1.** Separation into components, decomposition; analysis, conversion *into* other form; (Med.) disappearance of inflammation etc. without suppuration; (Pros.) substitution of two short syllables for one long; (Mus.) causing discord to pass into concord; (Mech. etc.) replacing of single force etc. by two or more jointly equivalent to it; (Phys. etc.) resolving power, smallest interval measurable by an instrument. **2.** Solving *of* doubt, problem, question, etc. **3.** Formal expression of opinion by legislative body or public meeting; form proposed for this. **4.** Resolve, thing resolved on; **good ~s,** intentions that one formulates mentally for virtuous conduct. **5.** Resolute temper or character, boldness and firmness of purpose. [ME, f. L *resolutio* (as RESOLVE; see -ION)]

rĕ'solūtĭve (-z-; *or* -ōō-) *a.* & *n.* **1.** (Med.) Having dissolving power, disintegrating. **2.** (Law). ~ **condition,** one whose fulfilment terminates contract etc. [f. med. L *resolutivus* (as RESOLVE; see -IVE)]

rėsŏ'lv|e (-z-) *v.* & *n.* **1.** *v.t.* & *i.* Dissolve (*into*), disintegrate, analyse, break up or separate into parts, dissipate, convert or be converted *into*, reduce by mental analysis *into*, (*resolve thing, thing is resolved*, or *resolves itself*, or *resolves, into its elements*; *telescope resolves nebula into stars*; *inflammation* or *tumour resolves*, or *is resolved, without suppuration*); (Pros.) replace (long syllable) by two short syllables; (Mech. etc.) replace (force etc.) by two or more jointly equivalent to it; (Mus.) convert (discord) or be converted into concord; **~ing power,** instrument's ability to distinguish very small or very close objects. **2.** *v.t.* Solve, explain, clear up, settle, (*all doubts were resolved*; *the problem of its origin has not yet been resolved*). **3.** *v.t.* & *i.* Decide upon, make up one's mind (*up*)*on* action or do*ing* or *to* do, form mentally or (of legislative body or public meeting) pass by vote the resolution *that*, (of circumstances etc.) bring (person) to resolution *to* do or (*up*)*on* action or do*ing*, (*resolved that nothing should induce him, that he would* do, *on* or *upon* doing; *this discovery resolved us on going* or *to go*); (in *p.p.* as *a.*) resolute. **4.** Hence ~ABLE *a.* **5.** *n.* Decision come to in the mind (*and she kept her resolve*); * = RESOLUTION 3; (poet.) resoluteness, steadfastness, (*a mind, deeds, of high resolve*). [ME, f. L *re(solvere solut-* solve); see RE- 5]

rėsŏ'lvent (-z-) *a.* & *n.* (Med. etc.) (Drug, application, substance) effecting resolution of tumour etc. [f. as prec.; see -ENT]

rĕ'son|ant (-z-) *a.* & *n.* **1.** *a.* (Of sound) echoing, resounding, continuing to sound, reinforced or prolonged by vibration or reflection; (of body, room, etc.) tending to reinforce or prolong sounds esp. by vibration; (of place) resounding *with*; (Phys.) responding to vibrations of a particular frequency esp. by itself strongly vibrating; hence or cogn. ~ANCE *n.*, **~ant**LY[2] *adv.* **2.** *n.* (Phonet.) Sound involving resonance, esp. vowel or nasal. [f. F *résonnant* or f. L *re(sonare* sound); see RE- 6, -ANT]

rĕ'sonāte (-z-) *v.i.* Produce or show resonance, resound. [f. L (as prec.) + -ATE[3]]

rĕ'sonātor (-z-) *n.* Instrument responding to single note and used for detecting it in combinations; appliance for giving resonance to sounds or other vibrations. [f. prec. + -OR]

rėsŏr'b *v.t.* Absorb again; hence ~ENCE *n.*, ~ENT *n.* [f. L *re(sorbēre sorpt-* absorb); see RE- 9]

rėsŏr'cĭn (-z-) *n.* = foll. [f. RESIN + ORCIN]

rėsŏr'cĭnŏl (-z-) *n.* (Chem.) Crystalline organic compound usu. made by synthesis and used in production of dyes, drugs, resins, etc. [f. prec. + -OL]

rėsŏr'ption *n.* Resorbing or being resorbed, esp. (Path.) absorption of tissue within the body. [f. RESORB, after *absorption*]

rėsŏr't[1] (-z-) *v.i.* **1.** Turn for aid, have recourse, *to* (*resort to force, fighting, experiment*, etc.). **2.** Go in large numbers or often *to* (*visitors resorted to him*, or *to the shrine, by the hundred*; *watched the inn to which he was known to resort*). [ME, f. OF *re(sortir* come or go out); see RE- 8]

rėsŏr't[2] (-z-) *n.* **1.** Thing to which recourse is had, what is turned to for aid, expedient, (*a taxi, repetition of the experiment, was the only resort*). **2.** Recourse (*cannot be done without resort to compulsion*); **in the last ~**, when all else has failed, as final attempt. **3.** Frequenting or being frequented (*encouraged the resort of scholars*; *a place of great resort*). **4.** Place frequented usu. for specified purpose (esp. holidays) or quality (*health, holiday, resort*; *mountain, seaside, resort*). [ME f. OF (*resortir*; see prec.)]

rē-sŏr't[3] *v.t.* Sort again. [f. RE- 8 + SORT[2]]

rėsou'nd (-z-) *v.* **1.** *v.i.* (Of place) ring or echo (*with*); (of voice, instrument, sound, etc.) produce echoes, go on sounding, fill place with sound. **2.** (Of fame, event, etc.) be much talked of, produce sensation, (*through* Europe etc.).

For other words in *re-* see RE-.

3. *v.t.* Repeat loudly (the praises etc. *of*); (of place) re-echo (sound). [ME (RE- 9, SOUND² v., after OF *resoner* or L *resonare* (see RESONANT)]

rèsou'ndĭng (-z-) *a.* In vbl senses; unmistakable, emphatic, (*was a resounding success*); hence ~LY² *adv.* [f. prec. + -ING²]

rèsour'ce (-sôr's; *or* -z-) *n.* **1.** (usu. in *pl.*) Means of supplying what is needed, stock that can be drawn on, *available, assets; (in *pl.*) country's collective means for support and defence. **2.** (arch.) Possibility of aid (*lost without resource*). **3.** Expedient, device, shift, (*flight was his only resource*; *am at the end of my resources*). **4.** Leisure occupation (*reading is a great resource*); **left to** one's **own ~s,** given no help in passing time or dealing with problems. **5.** Skill in devising expedients, practical ingenuity, quick wit, (*is full of resource*). **6.** Hence ~FUL (-sf-), ~LESS (-sl-), *adjs.* [f. F *ressource, ressourse*, fem. p.p. (as n.) of OF dial. *resourdre* f. as RE- 9 + L *surgere* rise]

rèspĕ'ct¹ *n.* **1.** Reference, relation, (*to*; *the terms have respect to position alone*; *is true with respect to the French*; *with respect to possible routes, there are three*). **2.** Heed or regard *to* or *of*, attention *to*, (*have not had* or *paid respect to anything but colour*; *did it quite without respect to the results*); **~ of persons,** partiality or favour shown esp. to the powerful. **3.** Particular, detail, point, aspect, (*of*; *is admirable in respect of style*; *in all, many, some, respects*; *in one, this, respect*). **4.** (arch.) Consideration *that*; **in ~ that,** because. **5.** Deferential esteem felt or shown towards person or quality (*has won the respect of all*; *have the greatest respect for him*; *with respect, I suggest you are quite wrong*). **6.** (in *pl.*) One's polite messages or attentions (*give him my, sends his, respects*); **pay** one's **~s,** make polite visit; **pay** one's **last ~s** (by attending funeral). [ME f. OF, or f. L *respectus* (*respicere*; see foll.)]

rèspĕ'ct² *v.t.* **1.** (arch.) Pay heed to; **~ persons,** discriminate unfairly between them under influence of wealth etc., whence ~ER¹ *n. of persons*. **2.** (arch.) Relate to, be directed to or concerned with. **3.** Regard with deference, esteem, or honour; avoid degrading or insulting or injuring or interfering with or interrupting, treat with consideration, spare, refrain from offending or corrupting or tempting, (*respect* person's *feelings* or *innocence*, *the rule of the road*; *respect neutrality, privileges, property*); **~ oneself,** have self-respect. [f. L *re(spicere spect-* = *specere* look at), or f. *respectare* frequent. of *respicere*; see RE- 6]

rèspĕctabĭ'lĭtў *n.* Being, those who are, *a* person who is, socially respectable. [f. foll. + -ITY]

rèspĕ'ctab|le *a.* & *n.* **1.** *a.* Deserving respect (*did it from respectable motives*). **2.** Considerable in number, size, amount, etc., of some merit or importance, fairly good or many or much, tolerable, passable, (*a respectable hill, antiquity, painter, score, minority*; *respectable talents*). **3.** Of fair social standing, having the qualities necessary for such standing, not disreputable, honest and decent in conduct; (of activity, clothes, etc.) befitting respectable persons; hence ~LY² *adv.* **4.** *n.* Respectable person. [f. RESPECT¹ + -ABLE]

rèspĕ'ctful *a.* Showing deference (*respectful behaviour*; *stood at a respectful distance*); hence ~LY² *adv.*, ~NESS *n.* [f. RESPECT¹ + -FUL]

rèspĕ'ctĭng *a.* & *prep.* **1.** *a.* Having reference to (*legislation respecting property*). **2.** *prep.* In respect of (*am at a loss respecting his whereabouts*). [f. RESPECT² + -ING²]

rèspĕ'ctĭve *a.* Pertaining or proper to each, individual, several, comparative, (*go to your, put them in their, respective places*; *were given places according to their respective rank* or *ranks*; *he and I contributed respective amounts of £10 and £1*; *the election result depends on the respective popularity of the candidates*); hence ~LY² (-vlĭ) *adv.*, (esp.) for each separately or in turn, and in the order mentioned (*he and I contributed £10 and £1 respectively*). [f. F *respectif -ive* or f. med. L *respectivus* (as RESPECT²; see -IVE)]

rēspĕ'll *v.t.* (**respe'lt** *or* **~ed** *pr.* -lt). Spell again or differently, esp. phonetically. [f. RE- 8 + SPELL²]

rĕ'spirable (*or* rĭspīr'-) *a.* (Of air, gas, etc.) that can, or is fit to, be breathed. [F, or f. LL *respirabilis* (as RESPIRE; see -ABLE)]

rĕspirā'tion *n.* Breathing; single inspiration and expiration, a breath; plant's absorption of oxygen and emission of carbon dioxide; ARTIFICIAL *respiration*. [ME f. F, or f. L *respiratio* (as RESPIRE; see -ATION)]

rĕ'spirātor *n.* Apparatus worn over mouth and nose to warm or filter inhaled air or to prevent inhalation of poison gas etc.; apparatus for maintaining artificial respiration. [f. as foll. + -OR]

rèspīr'e *v.* **1.** *v.i.* Breathe air, inhale and exhale air, whence **rĕ'spirāt**ORY (*or* rĭspī'rat- *or* rĭspīr'at-) *a.*; breathe again, take breath, recover hope or spirit, get rest or respite. **2.** *v.t.* Breathe (air etc.); (arch.) exhale (perfume, amiability, etc.). [ME, f. OF *respirer* or f. L *re(spirare* breathe); see RE- 9]

rĕ'spīte *n.*, & *v.t.* **1.** *n.* Delay permitted in the discharge of an obligation or suffering of a penalty; interval of rest or relief. **2.** *v.t.* Grant respite to, reprieve, (condemned person); postpone execution or exaction of (sentence, obligation); give temporary relief from (pain, care) or to (sufferer). [ME, f. OF *respit* f. L *respectus* RESPECT¹]

rèsplĕ'nd|ent *a.* Brilliant, dazzlingly or gloriously bright; hence or cogn. ~ENCE, ~ENCY, *ns.*, **~ent**LY² *adv.* [ME, f. L *re(splendēre* glitter); see RE- 6, -ENT]

rèspŏ'nd¹ *v.* **1.** *v.i.* Make answer; (of congregation) make set answers to priest etc.; act or behave in answering or corresponding manner (*responded with a drop-kick, left-hander*, etc.; *horse responds to bridle, vehicle to controls, illness to treatment*); (Bridge) make bid on basis of partner's preceding bid. **2.** Show sensitiveness *to* by behaviour or change (*does not respond to kindness, to treatment*; *nerve responds to stimulus, string to note*, etc.). **3.** (arch.) Correspond, be analogous; so ~ENCE, ~ENCY, *ns.* **4.** *v.t.* Say in answer. [f. L *re(spondēre spons-* pledge) answer; see RE- 1]

rèspŏ'nd² *n.* **1.** (Eccl.) Responsory; response to versicle. **2.** (Archit.) Half-pillar or half-pier attached to wall to support arch, esp. at end of arcade. [ME f. OF (*respondre* answer f. Rom. **respondere* f. as prec.)]

rèspŏ'ndent *a.* & *n.* **1.** *a.* Making answer; responsive *to*; in position of defendant. **2.** *n.* One who makes answer, defends thesis, etc.; defendant esp. in appeal or divorce case. [f. as RESPOND¹; see -ENT]

rèspŏ'nse *n.* **1.** Answer given in word or act, reply, retort, (*in response to*; *made no response*); action, feeling, movement, change, etc., elicited by stimulus or influence (*his response was to resign*; *called forth no response in his breast*); (Bridge) bid made in responding. **2.** (Eccl.) Responsory; any part of the liturgy said or sung in answer to priest. [ME, f. OF *respons(e)* or f. L *responsum* neut. p.p. (as n.) of *respondēre* RESPOND¹]

rèspŏnsĭbĭ'lĭtў *n.* **1.** Being responsible (*refuses all responsibility for it*; *will take the responsibility of doing it*); **on** one's **own ~,** without authorization. **2.** Charge for which one is responsible (*a family is a great responsibility*). [f. foll. + -ITY]

rėspŏ'nsĭb|le *a.* **1.** Liable to be called to account (*to* person, *for* thing, or abs.); (of ruler, government) not autocratic; morally accountable for actions, capable of rational conduct; of good credit or position or repute, respectable, evidently trustworthy. **2.** Being the primary cause *for* (result etc.); involving responsibility (*a responsible task*). **3.** Hence ~LY² *adv.* [obs. F, f. L *respondēre* (see RESPOND¹, -IBLE)]

rėspŏ'nsĭve *a.* Answering, by way of answer; (of liturgy etc.) using responses; responding readily to or *to* some influence, impressionable, sympathetic; hence ~LY² (-vlĭ) *adv.*, ~NESS (-vn-) *n.* [f. F *responsif -ive* or f. LL *responsivus* (as RESPOND¹; see -IVE)]

rėspŏ'nsorў *n.* Anthem said or sung by soloist and choir after lesson. [ME, f. LL *responsorium* (as RESPOND¹; see -ORY)]

rēspray' *v.t.* Spray again (esp. to change colour of paint on vehicle). [f. RE- 8 + SPRAY²]

rĕst¹ *v.* **1.** *v.i.* Be still, cease or abstain or be relieved from exertion or action or movement or employment, lie in sleep or death, lie buried (*in* churchyard etc.), be tranquil, be let alone, (*waves that never rest*; *never let your enemy rest*; *rest from* one's *labours*; *let her rest in peace*; *is too feverish to rest*; *could not rest under the imputation, till he got his wish*); *rest on* one's OARS; *conclude calling of witnesses in law case; (of land) lie fallow; (of matter under discussion) be left without further investigation; ||**be ~ing,** (of actor) be out of work; *~ **up,** rest oneself thoroughly. **2.** Lie, be spread out, be supported or based, depend, rely, (of look etc.) alight or be steadily directed, (*up*)*on* (*shadow, light, rests on his face*; *roof rests on four arches*; *hand resting on the table*; *science rests on observation*; *I rest upon your promise*; *his gaze rested on a strange object*); be propped *against*; repose trust *in* (*be content to rest in God*). **3.** *v.t.* Give relief or repose to, allow to rest, (*stayed a day to rest myself*; *rest your men for an hour*; *says the goggles rest his eyes*; *must rest the ground*); ~ one's **case,** conclude presentation of it; (**God**) ~ **his soul,** may God give his soul repose; (in *p.p.*) refreshed or reinvigorated by resting. **4.** Place for support or foundation (*up*)*on* (*rest* one's *elbow, load, on the table*; *rest* one's *case on equity, unimpeachable evidence*). **5.** **~'ing-place,** place provided or used for resting (*last ~ing-place*, the grave). [OE *ræstan, restan,* = OHG *restan*]

rĕst² *n.* **1.** Repose or sleep esp. in bed at night (*go, retire, to rest*; *take* one's *rest*; *get a good night's rest*). **2.** Abstinence or freedom from or absence of exertion or activity or movement or worry or molestation, a period of such abstinence etc., (*a rest from work* etc.; *give* person, horse, machine, (fig.) topic of discussion, etc., *a rest*; *take a short rest*); **at ~,** not moving, not agitated or troubled (esp. of the dead); **set** *question*, person's *mind* or *heart*, **at ~** (settle, relieve); DAY *of rest*; **lay to ~,** bury in grave. **3.** Place of resting or abiding; lodging-place or shelter provided for sailors, cabmen, or other class. **4.** Prop or support or steadying-piece for resting thing on, e.g. for gun in aiming, telephone-receiver, billiard-cue, cutting-tool in lathe, foot. **5.** (Mus.) interval of silence or sign denoting it; pause in elocution, caesura in verse. **6.** **~-balk,** ridge left unploughed between furrows; **~-cure,** rest usu. of some weeks in bed as medical treatment; **~-day,** (1) day spent in rest, (2) = DAY *of rest*; **~-home,** place where old or frail people can be cared for; **~-house,** (Ind.) house for travellers to rest at; **~ mass,** (Phys.) mass of a body when at rest; **~-room,** public lavatory in factory, shop, etc. [OE *ræst, rest,* = OS, OHG *rasta*, ON *röst*, Goth. *rasta* mile (as distance after which one rests)]

rĕst³ *v.i.* **1.** (arch.) Remain over (*whatever rests of hope*). **2.** **~ with,** be left in the hands or charge of (*it rests with you to propose terms*; *the management of affairs rested with Wolsey*). **3.** Remain in specified state (*rest assured, satisfied,* etc.). [ME, f. OF *rester* f. L *re*(*stare* stand); see RE- 3]

rĕst⁴ *n.* **1.** *The* remaining part(s) or individuals *of*, *the* remainder of some quantity or number, *the* others; **and the** or **all the ~ of it,** and all else that might be mentioned; **for the ~,** as regards anything beyond what has been specially mentioned. **2.** ||(Banking) reserve fund; (Tennis etc.) = RALLY¹. [ME, f. OF *reste* (*rester*; see prec.)]

rĕst⁵ *n.* (Hist.) Check holding butt of medieval tilter's spear when couched for charging (*with, lay* or *set* one's, *lance in rest*). [ME, f. ARREST²]

rēstar't *v.* & *n.* See RE- 8.

rēstā'te *v.t.* Express again or differently, esp. more clearly or convincingly; hence ~MENT (-tm-) *n.* [f. RE- 8 + STATE²]

rĕ'staurant (-tor*ahṅ* or -tor*ŏnt*) *n.* Public premises where meals or refreshments may be had; ||**~ car,** dining-car. [F (*restaurer* RESTORE; see -ANT)]

rĕstaurateur' (-torater') *n.* Restaurant-keeper. [F (*restaurer* RESTORE)]

rĕ'stful *a.* Favourable to repose, free from disturbing influences, soothing; hence ~LY² *adv.*, ~NESS *n.* [ME, f. REST² + -FUL]

rĕ'st-hărrow (-ō) *n.* Tough-rooted herb of genus *Ononis*. [f. obs. *rest* v. or REST⁵ + HARROW¹]

rĕ'stĭff. See RESTIVE.

rĕstĭtū'tion *n.* Restoring of or *of* thing to proper owner, reparation for injury, (esp. *make restitution*); restoring of thing to its original state, esp. (Theol.) *the restitution of all things*; resumption of original shape or position because of elasticity. [ME f. OF or f. L *restitutio* f. *re*-(*stituere stitut-* = *statuere* establish) restore; see RE- 8, -ION]

rĕ'stĭve, (arch.) **rĕ'stĭff,** *a.* (Of horse) refusing to advance, stubbornly standing still or moving backwards or sideways, jibbing, refractory; (of person) unmanageable, rejecting control; fidgety, restless; hence **rĕ'stĭve**LY² (-vlĭ) *adv.*, **rĕ'stĭve**NESS (-vn-) *n.* [ME f. OF *restif -ive* f. Rom. **restivus* inclined not to move (as REST³; see -IVE)]

rĕ'stlėss *a.* Finding or affording no rest; uneasy, agitated; constantly in motion, fidgeting, etc.; **~ flycatcher,** small Austral. bird (*Seisura inquieta*); hence ~LY² *adv.*, ~NESS *n.* [OE *restlēas* (as REST², -LESS)]

rēstŏ'ck *v.t.* & *i.* See RE- 8.

rĕstorā'tion *n.* Restoring or being restored; (period of) re-establishment of monarch etc. (**the R~,** return of Charles II of England in 1660); model or drawing representing supposed original form of extinct animal, ruined building, etc. [17th c. alt. (after RESTORE) of *restauration*, ME f. OF, or f. LL *restauratio* (as RESTORE; see -ION)]

rĕstorā'tion|ĭsm *n.* Doctrine that all men will ultimately be restored to happiness in the future life; so ~IST (2) *n.* [f. prec. + -ISM]

rėstŏ'ratĭve *a.* & *n.* **1.** *a.* Tending to restore health or strength; hence ~LY² (-vlĭ) *adv.* **2.** *n.* Restorative food, medicine, etc. [ME, var. of obs. *restaurative* f. OF *restauratif -ive* (as foll.; see -ATIVE)]

rėstor'|e *v.t.* **1.** Give back, make restitution of. **2.** (Attempt to) bring back to original state by rebuilding, repairing, repainting, emending, etc., (*church, picture, text, has been restored, restored out of all recognition*, etc.); make representation of supposed original state of (extinct animal, ruin, etc.). **3.** Reinstate, bring back to dignity or right; bring back to or *to* health etc., cure (person). **4.** Re-establish, renew, bring back into use. **5.** Reinsert by conjecture (missing words in text, parts of extinct animal, etc.). **6.** Replace, put back, bring to former place or condition. **7.** Hence ~ABLE *a.*, ~ER[1] *n.* [ME, f. OF *restorer* f. L *restaurare*]

rėstrai'n[1] *v.t.* Check or hold in *from*, keep in check or under control or within bounds, repress, keep down; confine, imprison; hence ~ABLE *a.*, **~ėd**LY[2] *adv.* (esp. with self-restraint). [ME, f. OF *restrei(g)n-* st. of *restreindre* f. L *re(stringere strict-* tie); see RE- 2]

rē-strai'n[2] *v.t.* Strain again. [f. RE- 8 + STRAIN[1]]

rėstrai'nt *n.* **1.** Restraining or being restrained, stoppage, check, controlling agency or influence, confinement esp. because of insanity; **in ~ of,** in order to restrain; **~ of trade,** action seeking to interfere with free-market conditions; **without ~,** freely, copiously. **2.** Constraint or reserve of manner; self-control, avoidance of excess or exaggeration, austerity of literary expression. [ME, f. OF *restreinte* fem. p.p. of *restreindre* (see RESTRAIN[1])]

rėstrĭ'ct *v.t.* Confine, bound, limit, (*to, within*; *has a very restricted application*; *am restricted to advising*; *is restricted within narrow limits*); subject to restriction; designate as not for general disclosure; **~ed area** (||in which there is a speed limit for vehicles, *which military personnel are nót allowed to enter); hence **~ėd**LY[2] *adv.* [f. L *restringere* (see RESTRAIN[1])]

rėstrĭ'ction *n.* Restricting or being restricted; thing that restricts; limitation placed on action. [ME f. OF, or f. L *restrictio* (as prec.; see -ION)]

rėstrĭ'ctĭve *a.* Imposing restrictions; **~ practice,** agreement to limit competition or output in industry; hence ~LY[2] (-vlĭ) *adv.*, ~NESS (-vn-) *n.* [ME, f. OF *restrictif -ive* or f. med. L *restrictivus* (as RESTRICT; see -IVE)]

rēstrŭ'cture *v.t.* Give new structure to; rebuild, rearrange. [f. RE- 8 + STRUCTURE]

rēstŭ'dy̆ *v.t.* See RE- 8.

rēsty̆'le *v.t.* Remake in new style. [f. RE- 8 + STYLE]

rėsŭ'lt (-z-) *v.i.*, & *n.* **1.** *v.i.* Arise as actual or follow as logical consequence (*from* conditions, causes, premisses, etc., or abs.); have outcome or end in specified manner esp. *in* failure, success, etc. (*resulted badly, in a large profit*). **2.** *n.* Consequence, issue, or outcome of something; satisfactory outcome (*knows how to get results*; **without ~,** in vain, fruitless); (in *pl.*) list of scores, winners, etc., in sporting events or competitions; hence ~FUL, ~LESS, *adjs.* **3.** Quantity, formula etc., obtained by calculation. [ME, f. med. L f. L *re(sultare* = *saltare* frequent. of *salire* jump); see RE- 9]

rėsŭ'ltant (-z-) *a.* & *n.* **1.** *a.* Resulting, esp. as total outcome of more or less opposed forces. **2.** *n.* Force etc. equivalent to two or more acting in different directions at same point. [f. as prec.; see -ANT]

rėsū'me (-z-) *v.* **1.** *v.t.* Get or take again or back, recover, reoccupy, (*resume* one's *spirits, sway, liberty, seat*; *resume gift, grant, territory*). **2.** *v.t.* & *i.* Begin again (upon), go on (with) after interruption, begin to speak or work or use again, recommence, (*the House resumed its labours* or *resumed*; *resume the thread of* one's *discourse*; *resumed her maiden name*). **3.** Make résumé of, recapitulate, summarize. [ME, f. OF *resumer*, or f. L *re(sumere sumpt-* take); see RE- 8]

résumé (rĕ'zo͞omā) *n.* Summary; **curriculum vitae*. [F, p.p. of *résumer* (as prec.)]

rėsŭ'mpt|ion (-z-) *n.* Resuming; hence ~IVE *a.* [ME f. OF, or f. LL *resumptio* (as RESUME; see -ION)]

rėsū'pĭnate *a.* (Bot., of leaf etc.) upside down. [f. L *resupinatus* p.p. of *resupinare* bend back; see RE- 1, SUPINE[1], -ATE[2]]

rēsûr'face (-ĭs) *v.t.* See RE- 8.

rėsûr'g|ent *a.* Rising or arising again; tending to rise again; hence ~ENCE *n.* [f. L *re(surgere surrect-* rise); see RE- 9, -ENT]

rĕsurrĕ'ct (-z-) *v.t.* (colloq.) Revive practice or memory of; take from grave, exhume; dig up. [back form. f. foll.]

rĕsurrĕ'ction (-z-) *n.* **1.** (*R~*). Rising of Christ from the grave; rising again of dead at the Last Judgement. **2.** Exhumation (lit. or fig.), resurrecting, (**~ man,** (Hist.) body-snatcher), whence ~IST (1) *n.*; **~ plant,** club-moss of genus *Selaginella* or rose of Jericho, unfolding when moistened after being dried. **3.** Revival after disuse or inactivity or decay, restoration to vogue or memory. **4.** Hence ~AL *a.* [ME f. OF, f. LL *resurrectio -onis* (as RESURGENT; see -ION)]

rēsurvey' (-ā') *v.t.*, **rēsûr'vey** (-ā) *n.* See RE- 8.

rėsŭ'scĭt|āte *v.t.* & *i.* Revive from unconsciousness or apparent death, return or restore to vogue, vigour, or vividness; hence or cogn. ~A'TION, **~āt**OR, *ns.*, ~ATIVE *a.* [f. L *re(suscitare* raise); see RE- 9, -ATE[3]]

rĕt *v.* (**-tt-**). **1.** *v.t.* Soften (flax, hemp) by soaking or exposing to moisture; (in *pass.*) = sense 2. **2.** *v.i.* (Of hay etc.) be spoilt by wet, rot. [ME, = MDu. *re(e)ten, ro(o)ten*; cogn. w. ROT[2]]

ret. *abbr.* retired; returned.

rėtā'ble *n.* Shelf, or frame enclosing decorated panels, above back of altar. [f. F *rétable, retable* f. Sp. *retablo* f. med. L **retabulum* f. *retrotabulum* rear table (as RETRO-, TABLE)]

rē'tail[1] *n.*, *a.*, & *adv.* **1.** *n.* Sale of goods in small quantities at a time and usu. not for resale. **2.** *a.* & *adv.* In retail trade (*do you buy wholesale or retail?*). [ME, f. AF **retaille* f. OF *retaille* piece cut off (*retaillier*; see RE- 5, TAIL[2])]

rē'tail[2] (*or* -ā'l) *v.* **1.** *v.t.* Sell (goods) in retail trade. **2.** Recount, relate details of. **3.** Hence ~ER[1] *n.* **4.** *v.i.* (Of goods) be retailed (esp. *at* or *for* specified price). [ME, f. prec.]

rėtai'n *v.t.* **1.** Keep in place, hold fixed; **~ing wall,** wall supporting and confining mass of earth or water. **2.** Secure services of (esp. barrister) by engagement and preliminary payment; **~ing fee** (paid to secure services thus). **3.** Keep possession of, not lose, continue to have; continue to practise or recognize, allow to remain or prevail, not abolish or discard or alter. **4.** Succeed in remembering, not forget. **5.** Hence ~ABLE *a.* [ME, f. AF *retei(g)n-* f. st. of OF *retenir* f. Rom. **retenēre* f. L *re(tinēre tent-* = *tenēre* hold); see RE- 3]

rėtai'ner *n.* **1.** (Law) formal retention of something as one's own, authorization to retain thus; being retained to serve in some capacity, authorization to serve thus; retaining fee. **2.** In vbl senses; (Hist.) dependant or follower of person of rank; **old ~,** (joc.) old and faithful servant. [f. RETAIN + (sense 1) -ER[4], (sense 2) -ER[1]]

rētā'ke[1] *v.t.* (**retoo'k; reta'ken**). Take again; recapture. [f. RE- 8, 9 + TAKE[1]]

rē'tāke[2] *n.* Act of retaking; second or subsequent filming of a scene. [f. prec.]

rėtă'lĭ|āte *v.* **1.** *v.t.* Repay (injury, insult, etc.) in kind; cast (accusation) back *upon* person. **2.** *v.i.* Do as one is done by, esp. return evil, make reprisals. **3.** Hence ~A'TION *n.*, ~ATIVE, ~**at**ORY, (-lya-) *adjs.* (*retaliatory* TARIFF). [f. L *re*(*taliare* f. *talis* such); see RE- 1, -ATE³]

rėtar'd *v.t.*, & *n.* **1.** *v.t.* Make slow or late, delay progress or development or arrival or accomplishment or happening of; (in *p.p.*, esp.) backward in mental or physical development. **2.** Hence or cogn. ~ANT *a.* & *n.*, **rētardA'TION**, ~ER¹, ~MENT, *ns.*, ~ATIVE, ~**at**ORY, *adjs.* **3.** *n.* Retardation. [f. F *retarder* f. L *re*(*tardare* f. *tardus* slow); see RE- 3]

***rėtar'date** *a.* & *n.* Mentally retarded (person). [f. L *retardare* (see prec., -ATE²)]

rĕtch *v.i.*, & *n.* **1.** *v.i.* Make motion of vomiting esp. ineffectually and involuntarily. **2.** *n.* Such motion or sound of it. [var. of (now dial.) *reach*, f. OE *hrǣcan* spit, ON *hrækja* f. Gmc **hraik-*, of imit. orig.]

retd. *abbr.* retired; returned.

rētė'll *v.t.* (**reto'ld**). Tell again in same or another form. [f. RE- 8 + TELL¹]

rėtĕ'ntion *n.* Retaining or being retained; (Med.) failure to evacuate urine or other secretion; hence ~IST *n.*, one who favours retention of a policy (esp. of capital punishment). [ME f. OF, or f. L *retentio* (as RETAIN; see -ION)]

rėtĕ'ntĭve *a.* Tending to retain; (of memory) tenacious, not forgetful; ~ **of,** (of substance) apt to retain (moisture etc.); (Surg., of ligature etc.) serving to keep something in place; hence ~LY² (-vlĭ) *adv.*, ~NESS (-vn-) *n.* [ME, f. OF *retentif -ive* or f. med. L *retentivus* (as RETAIN; see -IVE)]

rē'think *v.t.* (**re'thought**), & *n.* **1.** *v.t.* Consider afresh, esp. with view to making changes. **2.** *n.* Rethinking, reassessment. [f. RE- 8 + THINK]

rĕtiar'ĭ|us *n.* (*pl.* ~**i** *pr.* -ī). Roman gladiator using net to trap opponent. [L (*rete* net)]

rē'tiarȳ (-sh*e*rĭ) *n.* Net-making or geometrical spider. [f. L (as prec.; see -ARY¹)]

rĕ'tĭc|ence *n.* Reserve in speech, avoidance of saying all one knows or feels or more than is necessary; abstinence from over-emphasis in art; holding back of some fact; disposition to silence, taciturnity; so ~ENT *a.* (*on*, *upon*, *about*). [f. L *reticentia* f. *re*(*ticēre* = *tacēre* be silent); see RE- 4, -ENCE]

rĕ'tĭcle *n.* Network of fine threads or lines in focal plane of optical instrument to help accurate observation. [f. L RETICULUM]

rėtĭ'cūl|āte *v.t.* & *i.* Divide or be divided in fact or appearance into a network; arrange or be arranged in small squares or with intersecting lines; so ~ATE² *a.*, ~A'TION *n.* [back form. f. *reticulated* f. *reticulate* a. f. L *reticulatus* (as RETICULUM; see -ATE²)]

rĕ'tĭcūle *n.* **1.** = RETICLE. **2.** (arch.) Woman's netted or other bag carried or worn to serve purpose of pocket. [f. F *réticule* f. L (as foll.)]

rėtĭ'cūl|um *n.* (*pl.* ~**a**). **1.** Ruminant's second STOMACH. **2.** Netlike structure, fine network in cytoplasm, reticulated membrane etc.; hence ~AR¹, ~OSE¹, *adjs.*, ~ŌCYTE *n.*, immature erythrocyte containing reticulum. [L, dim. of *rete* net; see -CULE]

rĕ'tĭform *a.* Netlike, reticulated. [f. L *rete* net + -I- + -FORM]

rĕ'tĭn|a *n.* (*pl.* ~**as** *or* ~**ae**). Layer at back of eyeball sensitive to light; hence ~AL *a.*, ~I'TIS *n.* [ME f. med. L, f. L *rete* net]

rĕ'tĭnūe *n.* Suite or train of persons in attendance upon great personage. [ME, f. OF *retenue* fem. p.p. (as n.) of *retenir* RETAIN]

***rėtīr'acȳ** *n.* Retirement, seclusion. [f. RETIRE + -ACY, after *privacy*]

rėtīr'al *n.* (Sc.) Retirement from office etc. [f. foll. + -AL 2]

rėtīr'e *v.* **1.** *v.i.* Withdraw, go away, retreat, seek seclusion or shelter, recede, go (as) to bed; ~ **from the world,** become recluse; ~ **into oneself,** become uncommunicative or unsociable, whence **rėtīr'ING²** *a.*; **retiring collection** (taken at end of service or concert). **2.** Cease *from* or give up office or profession or employment or candidature, (Cricket) voluntarily terminate or be compelled to suspend one's innings, (*retire from the army*, *from business*, *on a pension*; *batsman retired hurt*); **retiring age,** age at which persons normally retire. **3.** *v.t.* Compel (employee etc.) to retire; (Mil.) order (troops) to retire; (Finance) withdraw (bill, note) from circulation or currency. [f. F *retirer* (as RE- 9, *tirer* draw)]

rėtīr'ed (-īr'd) *a.* Withdrawn from society or observation, secluded, (*lives a retired life*; *in a retired valley*); who has retired (*a retired general*, *grocer*); ~ **list** (of retired officers); ~ **pay,** pension of former officer or official; hence ~NESS *n.* [f. prec. + -ED¹ (2)]

***rėtīree'** *n.* Person who retires from employment etc. [f. RETIRE + -EE]

rėtīr'ement (-īr'm-) *n.* In vbl senses; seclusion, privacy; secluded place; condition of having retired; ~ **pension** (received by person who retires from employment etc., or = *old-age* PENSION). [f. RETIRE + -MENT]

rētōō'l *v.t.* Equip (factory etc.) with new tools. [f. RE- 8 + TOOL¹]

rėtor't¹ *v.* & *n.* **1.** *v.t.* Repay (humiliation, insult, attack) in kind; cast (mischief etc.), fling (charge, sarcasm, jest), back (*on* or *upon* originator or aggressor); make (argument) tell against or *against* its user; say by way of witty reply, or counter-charge or counter-argument; (in *p.p.*) recurved, twisted or bent backwards. **2.** *v.i.* Make retort. **3.** *n.* Incisive reply, repartee; turning of charge or argument against its originator; piece of retaliation. [f. L *re*(*torquēre tort-* twist); see RE- 9]

rėtor't² *n.*, & *v.t.* **1.** *n.* Vessel usu. of glass with long downward-bent neck used in distilling liquids; vessel for heating mercury for purification, coal to generate gas, or iron and carbon to make steel. **2.** *v.t.* Purify (mercury) by heating in retort. [f. F *retorte* f. med. L *retorta* fem. p.p. (as n.) of *retorquēre* (see prec.)]

rėtor'tion *n.* Bending back (lit. or fig.); retaliation by State upon subjects of another. [f. RETORT¹ + -ION, perh. after *contortion*]

rētou'ch (-ŭ'-) *v.t.* Improve (composition, picture, photographic negative or print, etc.) by fresh touches or alterations. [prob. f. F *retoucher* (as RE- 8, TOUCH¹)]

rėtrā'ce *v.t.* Trace back to source or beginning; (arch.) look over again; recall the course of in memory; go back over (one's *steps* or *way*; lit., or fig. of undoing or reconsidering actions). [f. F *retracer* (as RE- 8, TRACE¹)]

rėtră'ct¹ *v.t.* & *i.* Draw (esp. part of one's body) or be drawn back or in (*snail retracts its horns*; *surgeon retracts skin with instrument*; *organ is retracted by muscle*); draw (undercarriage etc.) into body of aircraft; hence or cogn. ~ABLE, ~IVE, *adjs.* [f. L *re*(*trahere tract-* draw); see RE- 4]

rėtră'ct² *v.t.* Withdraw, revoke, cancel, refuse to abide by, acknowledge falsity or error of, expressly abandon, (statement, promise, opinion, chess move, or abs.); hence **rētrăctA'TION** *n.* [f. OF *retracter* or f. L *re*(*tractare* draw, frequent. of *trahere* draw); see RE- 9]

rėtră'ct|ĭle *a.* Retractable; capable of being

retracted; hence ~**i'l**ITY *n.* [f. RETRACT[1], after *contractile*]
rètră'ction *n.* Retracting or being retracted. [f. RETRACT[1,2] + -ION]
rètră'ctor *n.* Device or muscle for retracting. [f. RETRACT[1] + -OR]
rē'tral *a.* (Biol. etc.) Hinder, posterior, at the back. [f. RETRO- + -AL]
rētrănsl|ā'te (*or* -z-; *or* -trah-) *v.t.* Translate again, esp. back into the original language; so ~A'TION *n.* [f. RE- 8, 9 + TRANSLATE]
rētrea'd[1] (-ĕ'd) *v.t.* (**retro'd**; **retro'dden**). Tread again (path etc.). [f. RE- 8, 9 + TREAD]
rētrea'd[2] (-ĕ'd) *v.t.* Put fresh tread on (tyre). [f. RE- 8 + TREAD n.]
rē'tread[3] (-ĕd) *n.* Retreaded tyre. [f. prec.]
rètrea't *v.* & *n.* **1.** *v.i.* Go back, retire, relinquish a position, (esp. of army etc.); recede (*retreating chin, forehead*). **2.** *v.t.* (Chess). Move (piece) back from forward or threatened position. **3.** *n.* Act of, (Mil.) signal for, retreating (**beat a** ~, retreat, abandon undertaking; **make good** one's ~, get safely away); (Mil.) bugle-call at sunset. **4.** Withdrawing into privacy or security, (place of) seclusion; temporary retirement for religious exercises or meditation; place for reception of pensioners or alcoholics or others in need of care; lurking-place; place of shelter. [v. ME, f. OF *retraiter*; n. ME f. OF *retret(e)* f. *retraite* fem. p.p. (as n.) of *retraire* f. L *retrahere* (see RETRACT[1])]
rètrĕ'nch *v.* **1.** *v.t.* Cut down, reduce amount of, (expenses, things causing outlay); cut off, deduct, (*retrenched a year from the established period*); make excisions in or of, shorten or remove, (literary work or passages in it). **2.** *v.i.* Cut down expenses, introduce economies. **3.** Hence ~MENT *n.* [f. obs. F *retrencher* (as RE-, TRENCH)]
rētrī'al. See RETRY.
rĕtrĭbū'tion *n.* Recompense usu. for evil done, vengeance, requital; so **rètrĭ'bū**TIVE *a.* [ME, f. LL *re(tributio* f. *tribuere tribut-* assign; see RE- 1, -ION)]
rètrie'v|e *v.t.*, & *n.* **1.** *v.t.* (Of dog, esp. of special breed) find and bring in (killed or wounded game etc., or abs.); hence ~ER[1] *n.* **2.** Recover by investigation or effort of memory; find again (stored information etc.); restore to knowledge or recall to mind. **3.** Regain possession of. **4.** Rescue *from* bad state etc.; restore to flourishing state, revive, (esp. one's fortunes etc.). **5.** Make good, repair, set right, (loss, disaster, error, situation). **6.** Hence ~ABLE *a.*, ~AL 2 *n.* **7.** *n.* Possibility of recovery (*beyond* or *past retrieve*). [ME, f. OF *retroeve-* stressed st. of *re(trover* find); see RE- 9]
rētrĭ'm *v.t.* See RE- 8.
rĕ'trō- *pref.* (1) Backwards, back again, in return, (*retroact, retroflex*); (2) (Anat. & Path.) behind (~**ster'nal** *a.*, behind the breastbone), situated behind. [f. L *retro* backwards]
rĕtrōă'ct *v.i.* React; operate in backward direction; have retrospective effect; so ~IVE *a.*, ~ION *n.* [f. prec. + ACT[2]]
rĕ'tro|cēde[1] *v.i.* Move back, recede; so ~**cē'd**ENCE *n.*, ~**cē'd**ENT *a.* [f. L RETRO(*cedere cess-* go)]
rĕtrocē'de[2] *v.t.* Cede (territory) back again. [f. F *rétrocéder* (as RETRO-, CEDE)]
rĕtrocĕ'ss|ion (-sh*o*n) *n.* In vbl senses; so ~IVE *a.* [f. as RETROCEDE[1,2]; see -ION]
rĕ'trŏchoir (-kwīr) *n.* Part of cathedral or large church behind high altar. [f. med. L RETRO-(*chorus* CHOIR)]
rĕ'troflĕx, -flĕxed (-kst), *adjs.* (Anat., Path., Bot., etc.) Turned backwards; (Phonet.) cacuminal; so **rĕtroflĕ'x**ION (-ksh*o*n) *n.* [f. L RETRO(*flectere flex-* bend)]
rĕtrogradā'tion *n.* (Astron.) apparent backward motion of planet in zodiac, motion of heavenly body from E. to W., backward movement of lunar nodes on ecliptic; (arch.) retrogression. [f. LL RETRO*gradatio* (see GRADATION)]
rĕ'trogrāde *a.*, *n.*, & *v.i.* **1.** *a.* Directed backwards (*retrograde motion*), retreating; reverting esp. to inferior state, declining; inverse, reversed, (*in retrograde order*); (Astron.) in or showing retrogradation; hence ~LY[2] (-dlĭ) *adv.* **2.** *n.* Degenerate person. **3.** *v.i.* Move backwards, recede, retire; decline, revert; (Astron.) show retrogradation. [a. ME, f. L RETRO*gradus* (*gradus* step), v. f. L *retrogradi* or LL *retrogradare* (*gradi* walk)]
rĕtrogrĕ'ss *v.i.* Go back, move backwards, deteriorate; so ~IVE *a.* [f. RETRO-, after PROGRESS[2]]
rĕtrogrĕ'ssion (-sh*o*n) *n.* Backward or reversed movement; return to less advanced state, reversal of development, decline, deterioration; (Astron.) retrogradation. [f. RETRO-, after *progression*]
rĕ'trojĕct *v.t.* Throw back (usu. as opp. *project*). [f. RETRO-, after PROJECT[1]]
rĕ'tro-rŏckėt *n.* Auxiliary rocket for slowing down spacecraft etc., e.g. when re-entering earth's atmosphere. [f. RETRO- + ROCKET[2]]
rètrôr'se *a.* (Biol.) Turned back or down; hence ~LY[2] (-slĭ) *adv.* [f. L *retrorsus* = RETRO-(*versus* p.p. of *vertere* turn)]
rĕ'trospĕct *n.* Regard or reference *to* precedent or authority or previous conditions; survey of past time or events (**in** ~, when looked back on). [f. RETRO-, after PROSPECT[1]]
rĕtrospĕ'ction *n.* Action of looking back esp. into the past; indulgence or engagement in retrospect. [prob. f. *retrospect* v. (as prec.) + -ION]
rĕtrospĕ'ctĭve *a.* Of, in, proceeding by, retrospection; (of statute, award, etc.) not restricted to the future, licensing or punishing etc. past actions, having application to the past, retroactive; (of view) lying to the rear; hence ~LY[2] (-vlĭ) *adv.* [f. RETROSPECT + -IVE]
retroussé (retrōō'sā) *a.* (Of nose) turned up at tip. [F, p.p. of *retrousser* tuck up (as RE-, TRUSS)]
rĕ'trovêrt *v.t.* Turn backwards (esp. Path. in *p.p.*, of womb); so **rĕtrovêr's**ION (-sh*o*n) *n.* [f. LL RETRO(*vertere vers-* turn)]
rētrȳ' *v.t.* Try (defendant, law case) again; so **rētri'**AL *n.* [f. RE- 8 + TRY]
rĕtsi'na (-ē'-) *n.* Resin-flavoured Greek wine. [mod. Gk]
rĕ'tterȳ *n.* Flax-retting place. [f. RET + -ERY]
rētûr'f *v.t.* See RE- 8.
rètûr'n[1] *v.* **1.** *v.i.* Come or go back (*gone never to return*; *return home, by the way* one *came*; *they have returned*, (arch.) *they are returned*, cf. -ED[1] (2)). **2.** Recur, go back, *to* (*shall return to the subject*; *unto dust shalt thou return*; *return to* one's *old habits*). **3.** *v.t.* Bring, convey, give, yield, put, send, or pay, back or in return or requital (*fish must be returned to the water*; *return borrowed book* or *money, undelivered letter to sender*; *investments return a profit*; *return sword to scabbard*; *return the compliment, a blow, a visit, an answer*; *return* person's *greeting, love, gun-fire*, etc.); throw, strike, etc., (ball) back in cricket, tennis, etc.; (Cards) lead (suit) previously led or bid by partner, lead (suit or card) after taking trick; ~ **thanks,** express thanks esp. in grace at meals or in response to toast or condolence. **4.** Say in reply, retort. **5.** State, mention, or describe, officially esp. in answer to writ or formal demand (*liabilities were returned at £5000*; *were all returned guilty, unfit for work*); (of constituency) elect as M.P. etc.; ||~**ing officer,** official conducting election in constituency and announcing name

of person elected. **6.** (Archit.) Continue (wall etc.) in changed direction, esp. at right angles. **7.** Hence ~ABLE *a.* [ME, f. *retorner, returner* f. Rom. *re(tornare* TURN[1]); see RE- 9]

rėtūr'n[2] *n.* **1.** Coming or going back (*his return was the signal for riots*; POINT[1] *of no return*; *return of* POST[2]; *have had a return of the symptoms*; *died on the return voyage*); ‖~ (**ticket**), ticket for journey to place and back to starting-point (so *return fare*); **many happy ~s (of the day)** (birthday or festival greeting). **2.** (Archit.) Part receding from line of front, e.g. side of house or of window-opening (*return angle, side, wall,* etc.); termination of dripstone; ~ **crease,** (Cricket) line at right angles at each end of bowling and popping creases. **3.** (in *sing.* or *pl.*) (Coming in of) proceeds or profit of undertaking (*the returns were large*; *brings an adequate return*); **small profits and quick ~s,** motto of cheap shop etc. relying on large trade. **4.** Giving, sending, putting, or paying, back, thing so given etc., returning (of ball, suit at cards, etc.), (*must ask for the return of the book* or *loan*; *received a ticket in return for his fare, neglect in return for attention*); SALE *or return*; ~ (**match** or **game**), second match etc. between same opponents; (Electr.) conductor bringing current back to source. **5.** Formal report compiled or submitted by order (*income-tax return*); ‖sheriff's report on writ, (returning officer's announcement of) election as M.P. etc. **6.** Hence ~LESS *a.* [ME, f. AF *retorn, return* (*retorner*; see prec.)]

rėtū'se *a.* (Bot. etc.) Having broad end with central depression. [f. L *re(tundere tus-* beat); see RE- 9]

rētȳ'pe *v.t.* See RE- 8.

rēū'nion (-nyon) *n.* **1.** Reuniting or being re-united; reunited state. **2.** Social gathering, esp. of intimates or persons with common interest. [f. F *réunion* (*réunir*) or AL *reunio* (*reunire* unite); see RE- 9, UNION]

rēūni'te *v.t.* & *i.*, see RE- 9; **rēûr'ge** *v.t.*, **rēū'sable** (-z-) *a.*, **rēū'se**[1] (-z) *v.t.*, **rēū'se**[2] *n.*, see RE- 8.

rĕv *n.* & *v.* (**-vv-**). (colloq.) **1.** *n.* Revolution (of engine). **2.** *v.i.* (Of engine) revolve; ~ **up,** increase in speed of revolution. **3.** *v.t.* ~ (**up**), cause (engine) to run quickly (esp. when first starting). [abbr.]

Rev. *abbr.* Revelation (N.T.); Reverend.

rēvă'ccināte *v.t.*, **rēvă'ccinA'TION** *n.*, (-ks-). See RE- 8.

rēvă'loriz|e, -is|e (-īz), *v.t.* Establish new value of (currency etc.); hence ~A'TION *n.* [back form. f. *revalorization* f. F *révalorisation* (as RE- 8, VALORIZATION)]

rēvă'lū|e *v.t.* Give different value to (esp. currency, in sense opp. *devalue*); hence ~A'TION *n.* [f. RE- 8 + VALUE]

rēvă'mp *v.t.* Vamp or patch up again; renovate, revise, improve. [f. RE- 8 + VAMP[1]]

reva'nch|ism (-ah'-) *n.* (Polit.) Policy of seeking to recover lost territory etc.; hence ~IST (2) *n.* [f. F *revanche* (as REVENGE[2]) + -ISM]

Revd. *abbr.* Reverend.

rėvea'l[1] *v.t.* **1.** (Esp. of God) make known by inspiration or supernatural means; **~ed religion** (opp. *natural religion*). **2.** Disclose, divulge, betray; display, show, let appear; ~ **itself,** come to sight or knowledge. **3.** Hence ~ABLE *a.* [ME, f. OF *reveler* or f. L *re(velare* f. *velum* veil); see RE- 7]

rėvea'l[2] *n.* Internal side surface of opening or recess, esp. of doorway or window-aperture. [f. obs. *revale* v. lower f. OF *re(valer* f. *avaler*); see RE- 4, VAIL[1]]

rėvei'llė (-vă'lĭ *or* -vĕ'lĭ) *n.* Military waking-signal sounded in morning on bugle or drums etc. [f. F *réveillez* imper. pl. of *réveiller* awaken (as RE-, *veiller* f. L *vigilare* keep watch)]

rĕ'vel *v.* (‖**-ll-**) & *n.* **1.** *v.i.* Make merry, be riotously festive, feast, carouse, whence ~**lER**[1] *n.*; take keen delight *in.* **2.** *v.t.* Throw *away* (money, time) in revelry. **3.** *n.* Revelling; (in *sing.* or *pl.*) (occasion of indulgence in) merry-making (*the revels began*); MASTER[1] *of the Revels*; ~ **rout,** (arch.) party of revellers; hence ~RY (4, 5) *n.* [ME, f. OF *revel(er)* riot f. L *rebellare* REBEL[2]]

rĕvelā'tion *n.* **1.** Disclosing of knowledge, or knowledge disclosed, to man by divine or supernatural agency; **the R~ (of St. John the Divine)**, (colloq.) **(the) R~s,** last book of N.T., Apocalypse; hence ~AL *a.* **2.** Striking disclosure (*it was a revelation to me*; *what a revelation!*); revealing *of* some fact. [ME f. OF, or f. LL *revelatio* (as REVEAL[1]; see -ATION)]

rĕvelā'tionist *n.* **The R~,** author of the Revelation; believer in divine revelation. [f. prec. + -IST]

rĕ'venant (*or* re'venahṅ) *n.* One returned from the dead or from exile etc. [F, part. of *revenir* (see REVENUE)]

rėvĕndĭcā'tion *n.* Formal claiming back, or recovery by such claim, of lost goods, territory, etc. [F (*revendiquer* claim back; see -ATION)]

rėvĕ'nge[1] (-nj) *v.* **1.** *v.t.* Satisfy one*self*, (in *pass.*) be satisfied, with retaliation (*for* offence, *on, upon, of,* offender); retaliate, requite, exact retribution for, (offence to oneself or another; *on, upon,* offender); avenge (person). **2.** *v.i.* Take vengeance. [ME, f. OF *revenger, revencher* f. LL *re(vindicare* lay claim to); see RE- 1]

rėvĕ'nge[2] (-nj) *n.* **1.** Revenging, act done in revenging; desire to revenge, vindictive feeling, whence ~FUL (-njf-) *a.* **2.** (In games) opportunity given for reversing former result by return game (*give* person *his revenge*). [f. prec.]

rĕ'vėnūe *n.* **1.** Income, esp. of large amount, from any source; (in *pl.*) items constituting this. **2.** State's annual income from which public expenses are met (‖INLAND or *INTERNAL *revenue*); department of civil service collecting this; ~ **cutter, officer,** etc. (employed against smugglers); ~ **tax** (imposed to raise revenue, not to affect trade). [ME, f. OF *revenu(e)* masc. or fem. p.p. (as n.) of *revenir* f. L *re(venire* come) return; see RE- 9]

rėvėr'ber|āte *v.t.* & *i.* (Of sound, light, heat) be returned or echoed or reflected, return (sound etc.) thus; **~ating furnace** etc. (constructed to throw heat back on substance dealt with), so **~at**ORY *a.* & *n.*; hence or cogn. ~A'TION, **~ātor**, *ns.*, ~ANT, ~ATIVE, *adjs.* [f. L *re(verberare* lash f. *verbera* pl. scourge); see RE- 9, -ATE[3]]

rėvēr'e *v.t.* Regard as sacred or exalted, hold in deep and usu. affectionate or religious respect, venerate. [f. F *révérer* or L *re(verēri* fear); see RE- 6]

rĕ'verence *n.*, & *v.t.* **1.** *n.* Revering (*hold in, regard with, reverence*; *feel reverence for, pay reverence to*); capacity for this (*the younger generation lacks reverence*); (arch.) gesture showing that one reveres, bow, curtsy, obeisance; so **rĕverĕ'ntIAL** (-shal) *a.* **2.** Being revered; **saving your ~** (arch., apology for use of coarse term); **your** or **his ~** (arch. or Ir. or joc., title used to or of clergyman). **3.** *v.t.* Regard with reverence, venerate. [ME f. OF, f. L *reverentia* (as prec.; see -ENCE)]

rĕ'verend *a.* & *n.* **1.** *a.* Deserving reverence,

revered, (esp. as title of clergyman; **Very R~**, of dean etc.; **Right R~**, of bishop; **Most R~**, of archbishop or Irish R.C. bishop; *Rev.* or *Revd.* or *the Rev. John* or *J. Smith*, or *the Rev. Mr. Smith*); **the ~ gentleman,** the clergyman in question; **R~ Mother,** Mother Superior of convent. **2.** *n.* (colloq., usu. in *pl.*) Clergyman. [ME f. OF, or f. L *reverendus* gerundive of *reverēri* (see REVERE, -ND[1])]

rĕ'verent *a.* Feeling or showing reverence; hence ~LY[2] *adv.* [ME, f. L *reverens* (as REVERE; see -ENT)]

rĕ'verĭe *n.* (Fit of) abstracted musing (*was lost in (a) reverie*); (arch.) fantastic notion or theory, delusion; (Mus.) instrumental piece suggesting dreamy or musing state. [f. obs. F *resverie* f. OF *reverie* rejoicing, revelry (*rever* be delirious, of unkn. orig.; see -ERY)]

rėver's (-vēr') *n.* (*pl.* same *pr.* -z). Turned-back edge of garment revealing under-surface; material on this surface. [F, = REVERSE[3]]

rėvėr'se[1] *a.* Opposite or contrary (*to*, or abs.) in character or order, inverted, back or backward, upside down, (*in the reverse direction to the time before*; *the reverse side* etc. of a coin, picture, etc., cf. REVERSE[3]); **~ battery, fire,** etc., (playing on enemy's rear or into works from rear); **~ gear** (used to make vehicle etc. travel backwards); hence ~LY[2] (-slĭ) *adv.* [ME, f. OF *revers(e)* f. L *reversus* p.p. of *re(vertere vers-* turn); see RE- 9]

rėvėr's|e[2] *v.* **1.** *v.t.* Turn the other way round or up or inside-out, invert, transpose, convert to opposite character or effect, (*reverse motion, policy, order*, etc.); make (vehicle) travel backwards; make (engine etc.) work in contrary direction; **~e arms,** hold rifle(s) butt upwards; ||**~e the charge(s)**, make recipient of telephone call responsible for payment. **2.** Revoke, annul, (decree, act, etc.); ***~e oneself,** change one's mind. **3.** *v.i.* (Of dancer, esp. in waltz) revolve in opposite direction; (of vehicle etc.) travel backwards; **~ing light** (operated when vehicle is travelling backwards). **4.** Hence ~AL 2 *n.*, ~IBLE *a.*, ~IBI'LITY *n.* [ME, f. OF *reverser* f. LL *re(versare* frequent. of *vertere* turn)]

rėvėr'se[3] *n.* **1.** *The* contrary (*of*, or abs.; *with others the reverse (of this) happens*); contrary of usual manner (*name printed in reverse*); reverse gear or motion; **the ~ of,** far from (*complimentary* etc.). **2.** (Device on) subordinate side of coin etc. (lit. or fig.; opp. *obverse*). **3.** Reverse side; verso of leaf. **4.** Piece of misfortune, disaster, esp. defeat in battle, (*the reverses of fortune*; *suffered a reverse*). [ME, f. OF *revers(e)* f. L *reversus* (as REVERSE[1])]

rėvėr'sĭ *n.* Game played on draught-board with counters coloured differently above and below, which may be turned over and thereby transferred to opponent. [F]

rėvėr'sion (-shon) *n.* **1.** (Return to grantor or his heirs or passing to ultimate grantee of, right of ultimate succession to) estate granted till specified date or event, esp. death of original grantee (**in ~**, on such conditions); hence ~ER[1] *n.*, beneficiary of return by reversion. **2.** Sum payable on person's death esp. by way of life-insurance. **3.** Thing to which one has a right, or expects to succeed, when relinquished by another; such right. **4.** Return to a previous state, habit, etc., esp. (Biol.) to ancestral type. **5.** Hence ~AL, ~ARY[1], *adjs.* [ME f. OF, or f. L *reversio* (as REVERSE[1]; see -ION)]

rėvėr't *v.* **1.** *v.i.* (Of property, office, etc.) return by reversion; hence ~ER[4] *n.* (Law). **2.** Return *to* former state etc. (cf. prec.); (abs.) fall back into wild state. **3.** Recur *to* subject in talk or thought. **4.** *v.t.* Turn (eyes, steps) back. [ME, f. OF *revertir* or f. L (as REVERSE[1])]

rėvėr'tĭble *a.* (Of property) subject to reversion. [ME, f. prec. + -IBLE]

rėvĕ't *v.t.* (-tt-). Face (rampart, wall, etc.) with masonry esp. in fortification. [f. F *revêtir* f. OF *revestir* f. LL *re(vestire* clothe f. *vestis*); see RE- 8]

rėvĕ'tment *n.* Retaining-wall or facing (as prec.). [f. F *revêtement* (as prec.; see -MENT)]

rēvĭ'ctual (-vĭ'tel) *v.t.* See RE- 8.

rėview'[1] (-vū') *n.* **1.** (esp. Law). Revision (*is not subject to review*); **court of ~** (before which sentences etc. come for revision). **2.** Display and formal inspection of troops, fleet, etc.; **~ order,** dress and arrangement usu. at reviews; **pass in ~,** (lit. or fig.) examine or be examined. **3.** Retrospect, survey of the past; general survey or reconsideration of subject or thing. **4.** Published account or criticism of book etc.; periodical publication with articles on current events, new books, art, etc. **5.** Second view. [f. obs. F *reveue* (*revoir* f. as RE- 9 + *voir* see); cf. VIEW]

rėview'[2] (-vū') *v.t.* **1.** (*or* rē-) View again. **2.** Subject to esp. legal review. **3.** Survey, glance over, look back on. **4.** Hold review of (troops etc.). **5.** Write review of (book etc., or abs.); hence ~ER[1] *n.* **6.** Hence ~ABLE *a.*, ~AL 2 *n.* [f. RE- 9 + VIEW, or f. prec.]

rėvī'l|e *v.* **1.** *v.t.* Call by ill names, abuse, rail at. **2.** *v.i.* Talk abusively, rail. **3.** Hence ~EMENT (-lm-), ~ER[1], ~ING[1] (1), *ns.* [ME, f. OF *reviler* (as RE- 6, VILE)]

rėvī's|e (-z) *v.t.*, & *n.* **1.** *v.t.* Read or look over or re-examine or reconsider and correct, improve, or amend (literary matter, printers' proofs, law, constitution, etc.); **R~ed Version, R~ed Standard Version,** revisions made 1870–84, 1946–57, of Authorized Version of Bible. **2.** Re-read (work learnt or done, or abs.) to improve one's familiarity with it, its quality, etc. **3.** Hence or cogn. ~ABLE, ~ORY, *adjs.*, ~AL 2, ~ER[1], **rėvĭ'sion** (-zhon), *ns.* **4.** *n.* (Print.) Proof-sheet embodying corrections made in earlier proof. [f. F *réviser* look at, or f. L *revisere* (as RE- 8, *visere* intensive of *vidēre vis-* see)]

rėvĭ'sion|ĭsm (-zhon-) *n.* Policy of revision or modification, esp. of Marxist-Leninist doctrine; hence ~IST (2) *n.* [f. REVISION + -ISM]

rēvĭ'sĭt (-z-) *v.t.*, see RE- 8; **rēvī'talīze** *v.t.*, see RE- 9.

rėvī'val *n.* **1.** Bringing or coming back into use or vogue (**~ of learning, letters,** etc., at Renaissance); GOTHIC *Revival*; new production of old play etc. **2.** (Special effort with meetings etc. to promote) reawakening of religious fervour; hence ~ISM (3), ~IST (2), *ns.* **3.** Restoration to bodily or mental vigour or to life or consciousness. [f. foll. + -AL 2]

rėvī'v|e *v.i.* & *t.* Come or bring back to consciousness, life, existence, vigour, notice, use, activity, validity, or vogue; hence ~ABLE *a.* [ME, f. OF *revivre* or f. LL RE(*vivere* live); see RE- 9]

rėvī'ver *n.* In vbl senses; (sl.) stimulating drink; preparation used for restoring faded colour etc. [f. prec. + -ER[1]]

rėvĭ'vĭ|fȳ *v.t.* Restore to animation, activity, vigour, or life; hence ~FICA'TION *n.* [f. F *revivifier* or f. LL *re(vivificare* VIVIFY); see RE- 8]

rĕvĭvĭ'scence *n.*, **rĕvĭvĭ'scent** *a.* Returning to life or vigour. [(f. LL *reviviscentia*) f. L *re(viviscere* incept. of *vivere* live); see RE- 8, -ENCE, -ENT]

||**rėvī'vor** *n.* (Law). Proceeding for revival of suit after death of party etc. [f. REVIVE + -OR]

rėvō'ke *v.* & *n.* **1.** *v.t.* Repeal, annul, withdraw, rescind, cancel, (decree, consent, promise, permission); so **rĕ'voc**ABLE, **rĕ'vocat**ORY, *adjs.*, **rĕvoc**A'TION *n.* **2.** *v.i.* (Cards). Make revoke. **3.** *n.* Card-player's failure to follow suit when able to do so. [ME, f. OF *revoquer* or f. L *re(vocare* call); see RE- 9]

rèvō'lt *v.* & *n.* **1.** *v.i.* Cast off allegiance, make rising or rebellion, fall away *from* or rise *against* ruler, go over *to* rival power; (in *p.p.*) having revolted (*his revolted subjects*; see -ED¹ (2)). **2.** Feel revulsion or disgust *at*, rise in repugnance *against*, turn in loathing *from*, (*common sense, nature*, one's *heart*, *revolts at* or *against* or *from* it). **3.** *v.t.* Affect with strong disgust, nauseate; hence ~ING² *a.* **4.** *n.* Act of rebelling; rising, insurrection; **in ~**, having revolted. **5.** Sense of loathing; mood of protest or defiance. [f. F *révolte(r)* f. It. *rivolta(re)* f. Rom. **revolvitare* intensive of L *revolvere* (see REVOLVE)]

rĕ'volute¹ (-ōōt) *a.* (Bot. etc.) With rolled--back edge. [f. L *revolutus* p.p. of *revolvere* (see REVOLVE)]

rĕvolu'te² (-ōō't) *v.i.* (sl.) Engage in political revolution. [back form. f. foll.]

rĕvolu'tion (-lōō'-) *n.* **1.** Revolving, motion in orbit or circular course or round axis or centre, rotation, (time taken for) single completion of orbit or rotation, cyclic recurrence; **~ counter,** device for indicating number or rate of revolutions of engine etc. **2.** Complete change, turning upside down, great reversal of conditions (INDUSTRIAL *Revolution*); fundamental reconstruction, esp. forcible action by nation etc. to substitute new ruler or system of government (**the R~**, expulsion of James II of England 1688; **American R~**, overthrow of British rule 1775 etc.; **French R~**, overthrow of monarchy 1789 etc.; **Russian R~**, overthrow of monarchy 1917); hence ~IZE (1, 3) *v.t.*, ~ISM (3), ~IST (2), *ns.* [ME f. OF, or f. LL *revolutio* (as REVOLVE; see -ION)]

rĕvolu'tionarў (-ōō'-) *a.* & *n.* (Instigator or supporter) of political revolution; (*R~*) of the American etc. Revolution; involving great and usu. violent changes. [f. prec. + -ARY¹]

rèvŏ'lv|e *v.* **1.** *v.t.* & *i.* Turn round, turn round and round, rotate, move in circular orbit, (*mechanism for revolving the turntable*; *Earth revolves both round* or *about sun and on its axis*; *seasons, years, revolve*); **~ing credit** (automatically renewed as debts are paid off); **~ing door** (with several partitions turning round central axis, to exclude draughts of air). **2.** *v.t.* Ponder (problem etc.) in the mind. [ME, f. L *re(volvere* roll); see RE- 6]

rèvŏ'lver *n.* Pistol with revolving chambers enabling user to fire several shots without reloading. [f. prec. + -ER¹]

rèvūe' *n.* Theatrical entertainment reviewing (esp. satirically) current events etc. or comprising many unrelated episodes. [F, = REVIEW¹]

rèvŭ'lsion (-shon) *n.* **1.** (Med.) Counter--irritation, treatment of one disordered organ etc. by acting upon another. **2.** Sudden violent change of feeling, sudden reaction in taste, fortune, trade, etc. [F, or f. L *re(vulsio* f. *vellere vuls-* pull); see RE- 9]

rèvŭ'lsĭve *a.* & *n.* (Med.) (Substance) producing revulsion. [f. prec. + -IVE]

rèwar'd (-wŏr'd) *n.*, & *v.t.* **1.** *n.* Return or recompense for service or merit (**gone to his ~**, dead and in Heaven), requital for good or evil, retribution; sum offered for detection of criminal, restoration of lost property, etc.; hence ~LESS *a.* **2.** *v.t.* Repay, requite, recompense (service or doer of it, offender, offence); hence ~ING² *a.*, (of task, book, etc.) well worth doing, reading, etc. [ME, f. AF, ONF *reward(er)* = OF *reguard(er)* REGARD¹,²]

rĕ'wa-rēwa *n.* (N.Z.) Tall handsome timber tree (*Knightia excelsa*). [Maori]

rēwī'nd *v.t.* See RE- 8.

rēwīr'e *v.t.* (esp. Electr.) Wire again or differently. [f. RE- 8 + WIRE]

rēwor'd (-ēr'd) *v.t.* Change wording of. [f. RE- 8 + WORD²]

rēwrī'te¹ (rērī't) *v.t.* (**rewro'te; rewri'tten**). Write again or differently. [f. RE- 8 + WRITE]

rē'wrīte² (rē'rīt) *n.* Rewriting; thing rewritten; ***~ man,** journalist employed to put incoming material into form suitable for publication. [f. prec.]

Rex (rĕks) *n.* Reigning king (in use as REGINA). [L]

rĕ'xine (-ēn) *n.* Artificial leather used in upholstery, bookbinding, etc. [P]

Rey'nard (rĕ'n- *or* rā'n-) *n.* (Proper name for) the fox; a fox. [ME, f. OF *Renart* name of fox in the *Roman de Renart*]

Rey'nolds (rĕ'-; -z) *n.* **~ number,** (Phys.) quantity indicating degree of turbulence of flow past obstacle etc. [f. O. ~, Engl. physicist d. 1912]

r.f. *abbr.* radio frequency.

||**R.F.C.** *abbr.* Rugby Football Club.

***R.F.D.** *abbr.* rural free delivery.

R.G.S. *abbr.* Royal Geographical Society.

Rh *abbr.* Rhesus (factor).

r.h. *abbr.* right hand.

Rh *symb.* rhodium.

||**R.H.A.** *abbr.* Royal Horse Artillery.

rhă'bdomăncў *n.* Use of divining-rod, esp. for discovering subterranean water or ore. [f. Gk *rhabdomanteia* (*rhabdos* rod; see -MANCY)]

Rhădamă'nth|us *n.* Stern and incorruptible judge; hence ~INE² *a.* [L f. Gk, name of judge in underworld]

Rhae'tian (-shan) *a.* & *n.* = RHAETO-ROMANIC. [f. L *Rhaetia* a district of the Alps + -IAN]

Rhae'tĭc *a.* & *n.* (Of) the set of strata intermediate between Lias and Trias in Europe. [f. L *Rhaeticus* (as prec.; see -IC)]

Rhaeto-Romă'nce *a.* & *n.* = foll. [f. as foll. + ROMANCE]

Rhaeto-Romă'nĭc *a.* & *n.* (Of or in) any of the Romance dialects of S.E. Switzerland and Tyrol, esp. Romansh and Ladin. [f. L *Rhaetus* of Rhaetia in the Alps + -O- + ROMANIC]

rhă'psōde *n.* Reciter of epic poems, esp. of Homer, in ancient Greece. [f. Gk *rhapsōidos* (*rhaptō* stitch, *ōidē* song, ODE)]

rhă'psodĭst *n.* One who rhapsodizes; = prec. [f. RHAPSODY + -IST]

rhă'psodīze, -īse (-īz), *v.i.* Talk or write rhapsodies (*about, on*, etc.). [f. foll. + -IZE]

rhă'psodў *n.* **1.** Enthusiastic extravagant high--flown utterance or composition; emotional irregular piece of music; hence **rhăpsŏ'd**ICAL *a.* **2.** (Gk Ant.) Epic poem, or part of it, of length for one recitation. **3.** Hence **rhăpsŏ'd**IC *a.* [f. L *rhapsodia* f. Gk *rhapsōidia* (as RHAPSODE; see -Y¹)]

rhă'tanў *n.* (Astringent dried root of) S. Amer. shrub of genus *Krameria*. [f. mod. L *rhatania* f. Port. *ratanha*, Sp. *ratania*, f. Quechua *rataña*]

rhē'a (*or* rĭ'*a*) *n.* S. Amer. flightless bird like ostrich. [mod. L genus-name, f. L f. Gk *Rhea* mother of Zeus]

rhē'bok. Var. of REEBOK.

Rhē'mĭsh *a.* Of Rheims (**~ Bible, Testament,** etc., N.T. translated by Roman Catholics of English College at Rheims 1582). [f. obs. E *Rhemes* Rheims + -ISH¹]

Rhĕ'nĭsh *a.* & *n.* (arch.) **1.** *a.* Of the Rhine and districts on its banks. **2.** *n.* Rhine wine. [ME *rynis(ch)* etc., f. AF *reneis*, OF *r(a)inois* f. med. L **Rhenensis* f. L *Rhenanus* (*Rhenus* Rhine), assim. to L sp.; see -ISH¹]

rhē'nĭum *n.* (Chem.) Rare metallic element of manganese group. [mod. L, f. L *Rhenus* Rhine + -IUM]

rhēŏ'log|y̆ *n.* Science dealing with flow and deformation of matter; hence **rhēolŏ'g**ICAL *a.*, ~IST (3) *n.* [f. Gk *rheos* stream + -O- + -LOGY]

rhē'ostăt *n.* (Electr.) Instrument used to control current by varying resistance. [f. as prec. + -STAT]

rhėŏ'tropĭsm *n.* Tendency to be oriented in accordance with flow of water etc.; so **rhēotrŏ'p**IC *a.* [f. as RHEOLOGY + Gk *tropikos* (*tropē* a turning f. *trepō* turn, -IC) + -ISM]

rhē'sus *n.* Small catarrhine monkey (*Macaca mulatta*) common in N. India; **R~ baby,** infant with haemolytic disorder from its blood being Rhesus-positive and its mother's Rhesus-negative; **R~ factor,** antigen occurring in red blood cells of most persons and some animals (as in the rhesus monkey, in which it was first observed); **R~-positive, R~-negative,** having, not having, the Rhesus factor. [mod. L, arbitr. use of L f. Gk *Rhēsos*, mythical king of Thrace]

rhē'tor *n.* Ancient Greek or Roman teacher or professor of rhetoric; (mere) orator. [ME f. LL *rethor*, f. L f. Gk *rhētōr*]

rhĕ'torĭc *n.* (Treatise on) art of persuasive or impressive speaking or writing; language designed to persuade or impress (often with implication of its insincerity, exaggeration, etc.); persuasiveness of or *of* looks or acts. [ME, f. OF *rethorique* f. L f. Gk *rhētorikē* (*tekhnē* art) (as foll.; see -IC)]

rhėtŏ'rĭcal *a.* **1.** Expressed with a view to persuasive or impressive effect, artificial or extravagant in language, of the nature of rhetoric; ~ **question** (asked not for information but to produce effect, as *who cares?* for *nobody cares*). **2.** Of the art of rhetoric; given to rhetoric, oratorical. **3.** Hence ~LY[2] *adv.* [ME, f. L f. Gk *rhētorikos* (as RHETOR; see -IC) + -AL]

rhĕtorĭ'cian (-shan) *n.* Rhetor; rhetorical speaker or writer. [ME, f. OF *rethoricien* (as prec.; see -ICIAN)]

rheum (rōōm) *n.* (arch.) Watery secretion or discharge of mucous membrane etc. such as tears, saliva, or mucus; catarrh. [ME f. OF *reume*, f. LL f. Gk *rheuma -atos* stream (*rheō* flow)]

rheumă't|ĭc (rōō-) *a.* & *n.* **1.** *a.* Of, suffering from, subject to, producing, or produced by, rheumatism; **~ic fever,** non-infectious fever with inflammation and pain in joints; hence ~ICALLY *adv.*, **~ĭcky**[2] *a.* (colloq.), **rheu'mato-** (-ōō'-) *comb. form.* **2.** *n.* (in *pl.*, colloq.) Rheumatism. [ME, f. OF *reumatique* or f. L f. Gk *rheumatikos* (as prec.; see -IC)]

rheu'matĭsm (rōō'-) *n.* Disease marked by inflammation and pain in joints, muscles, or fibrous tissue, esp. rheumatoid arthritis; **acute** ~, rheumatic fever; **muscular** ~, myalgia. [f. F *rhumatisme* or f. L f. Gk *rheumatismos* (*rheumatizō* f. RHEUMA; see -IZE, -ISM)]

rheu'matoid (rōō'-) *a.* Having the character of rheumatism; ~ **arthritis,** chronic progressive disease causing inflammation and stiffening of joints. [f. prec. + -OID]

rheumatŏ'log|y̆ (rōō-) *n.* Study of rheumatic diseases; hence **rheumatolŏ'g**ICAL (rōō-) *a.*, ~IST (3) *n.* [f. RHEUMATISM + -O- + -LOGY]

rheu'my̆ (rōō'-) *a.* (arch.) Consisting of or flowing with rheum; (of air) damp, raw. [f. RHEUM + -Y[2]]

||**R.H.G.** *abbr.* Royal Horse Guards.

rhī'nal *a.* (Anat. etc.) Of nostril or nose. [f. Gk *rhis* (see RHINO-) + -AL]

||**rhine**[1] (rēn) *n.* (dial.) Large open ditch. [app. repr. OE *ryne* stream]

Rhīne[2] *n.* **~'land,** region adjoining the Rhine; **r~'stone,** imitation diamond; ~ **wine,** (usu. white) wine from Rhine vineyards. [f. river ~ in Germany]

rhīnī'tĭs *n.* Inflammation of (mucous membrane of) nose. [f. RHINO- + -ITIS]

rhī'nō[1] *n.* (sl.) Money. [17th c.; orig. unkn.]

rhī'nō[2] *n.* (*pl.* same *or* **~s**). (sl.) Rhinoceros. [abbr.]

rhī'no- *comb. form.* Nose, as: **~phary'ngeal,** of nose and pharynx; **~pla'stic, ~plasty,** (of) plastic surgery of the nose; ~SCOPE. [f. Gk *rhis rhinos* nostril, nose + -O-]

rhīnŏ'ceros *n.* (*pl.* **~es** *or* same). Large pachydermatous African and S. Asian quadruped with horn or two horns on nose and thick folded and plated skin; ~ **bird,** ox-pecker; so **rhīnŏcerŏ't**IC *a.* [ME, f. L f. Gk RHINO(*keros* f. *keras* horn)]

rhī'zo- *comb. form.* Root, as: **~carp,** plant with perennial root but perishing stems; **~pod,** protozoan with rootlike pseudopodia. [f. Gk *rhiza* root + -O-]

rhī'zoid *a.* & *n.* (Bot.) **1.** *a.* Rootlike. **2.** *n.* Root-hair or filament of fern etc. [f. as prec. + -OID]

rhī'zōme *n.* Prostrate or subterranean rootlike stem emitting both roots and shoots. [f. Gk *rhizoma* (*rhizoō* take root, f. as RHIZO-)]

rhō *n.* Seventeenth Greek letter (Ρ, ρ) = r. [Gk]

rhō'damine (-ēn) *n.* Brilliant red synthetic basic dye. [f. RHODO- + AMINE]

Rhōde I'sland (ī'l-) *n.* ~ **Red,** Amer. breed of reddish-black domestic fowl. [~ in U.S.]

Rhō'des (-dz) *n.* ~ **Scholar,** holder of any of a number of ~ **Scholarships** awarded annually and tenable at Oxford Univ. by students from certain Commonwealth countries, South Africa, United States, and Federal Republic of Germany. [f. C. J. ~, Brit. statesman d. 1902]

Rhō'dĭan *a.* & *n.* (Native or inhabitant) of Rhodes. [f. L *Rhodius* (*Rhodus* f. Gk *Rhodos* Rhodes, island in Aegean Sea) + -AN]

rhō'dĭum[1] *n.* ~ **(wood),** scented wood of Canary convolvulus; ~ **oil** (got from this). [mod. L *rhodium* (*lignum* wood), neut. of *rhodius* roselike f. Gk *rhodon* rose]

rhō'dĭum[2] *n.* Hard white metallic element of platinum group. [f. Gk *rhodon* rose (from colour of solution of its salts) + -IUM]

rhō'do- *comb. form.* (esp. Min. & Chem.) Rose-coloured, as: **~chro'site** (-krō'sīt), manganese carbonate occurring in rose-red crystals. [f. Gk *rhodon* rose + -O-]

rhōdodĕ'ndron *n.* Evergreen shrub of genus *Rhododendron*, with large clusters of trumpet-shaped flowers. [L, = oleander, f. Gk (as prec., *dendron* tree)]

rhōdŏ'psĭn *n.* Visual purple. [f. as RHODO- + Gk *opsis* sight + -IN]

rhodŏr'a *n.* N. Amer. pink-flowered shrub of genus *Rhodora*. [mod. L, f. L plant-name f. Gk *rhodon* rose]

rhŏmb (-m) *n.* Rhombus; object or part with such outline; (Cryst.) rhombohedron; hence **rhŏ'mb**IC *a.*, **rhŏ'mbo-** *comb. form.* [f. F *rhombe*, or f. L RHOMBUS]

rhŏmbohē'dr|on *n.* (*pl.* **~a** *or* **~ons**). (Crystal in shape of) solid bounded by six equal rhombuses; hence ~AL *a.* [f. RHOMBO- (see prec.) after *polyhedron* etc.]

rhŏ'mboid *a.* & *n.* **1.** *a.* Having or nearly having the shape of a rhombus. **2.** *n.* Quadrilateral of which only opposite sides and angles are equal. [f. F *rhomboïde* or f. LL f. Gk *rhomboeidēs* (as RHOMB; see -OID)]

rhŏmboi'dal *a.* = prec.; having the shape of a rhomboid; hence ~LY[2] *adv.* [f. prec. + -AL]

rhŏmboi'dė|us *n.* (*pl.* **~i** *pr.* -ī). (Anat.) Muscle connecting shoulder-blade to vertebrae.

[mod. L *rhomboideus* (*musculus* muscle) f. *rhomboides* (as RHOMBOID)]

rhŏ'mb|us *n.* (*pl.* **~uses,** *or* **~i** *pr.* -ī). (Geom.) Oblique equilateral parallelogram, e.g. diamond on playing-cards. [L f. Gk *rhombos*]

R.H.S. *abbr.* Royal Historical, Horticultural, or Humane Society.

rhu'bārb (rōō'-) *n.* **1.** (Purgative made from) root of Chinese and Tibetan plant of genus *Rheum.* **2.** (Fleshy leaf-stalks, used like fruit, of) garden plant of genus *Rheum.* **3.** Yellowish-brown colour like that of medicinal rhubarb. **4.** (colloq.) Murmurous hubbub or conversation (from crowd actors' repetition of the word). **5.** *(sl.) Heated dispute. [ME, f. OF *r(e)ubarbe* f. Rom. **r(h)eubarbum* f. med. L *r(h)eubarbarum, rhabarbarum* f. LL f. Gk *rha* + as BARBAROUS; assoc. w. L f. Gk *rhēon* rhubarb]

rhŭmb (-m) *n.* (Naut.) Any of 32 points of compass; angle between two successive compass-points; **~(-line)**, line cutting all meridians at same angle, line followed by ship sailing in fixed direction. [f. F *rumb* prob. f. Du. *ruim* room, assoc. w. L RHOMBUS]

rhŭ'mba. Var. of RUMBA.

rhȳme[1], **rīme**[1], *n.* **1.** Identity of sound between words or verse-lines extending from end to last fully accented vowel and (in E Pros., strictly) not further (*greet/deceit, shepherd/leopard, quality/frivolity, stationary/probationary, is it/visit,* give rhymes, but *seat/deceit, station/crustacean, visible/invisible,* strictly do not); *single* or *male* or MASCULINE, *double* or *female* or FEMININE, *treble* or *triple,* ~ (according to number of syllables included); **imperfect ~** (as in *love/move, phase/race*); **internal ~** (involving word within verse-line); **neither ~ nor reason, without ~ or reason,** (with) no reasonable character; **~-scheme,** arrangement of rhymes in piece of verse. **2.** Poem with rhymes, (in *pl.* or *sing.*) verse having rhymes, use of rhyme, (NURSERY *rhyme; prefer blank verse to rhyme; am sending you some rhymes*); **~ royal,** stanzas of seven ten-syllable lines with rhyme-scheme *ababbcc*, as in Shakespeare's *Rape of Lucrece.* **3.** Word providing a rhyme (*to* another; *can't find a rhyme to 'teacups'; English is badly off for double rhymes*). **4.** Hence **~'**LESS (-ml-) *a.* [(*rhyme* 17th c. var., w. assim. to RHYTHM, of) ME f. OF *rime* f. med. L *rithmus, rythmus* f. L f. Gk *rhuthmos* RHYTHM]

rhȳme[2], **rīme**[2], *v.* **1.** *v.i.* Write rhymes, versify; choose rhymes; **rhyming dictionary** (listing words by their terminal sounds); hence **rhȳ'm**ER[1], **rhȳ'me**STER (-ms-), **rhȳ'm**IST (3), *ns.* **2.** (Of words or lines) exhibit rhyme; (of word) supply or act as rhyme *to* or *with*; **rhyming slang** (replacing words by rhyming words or phrases, e.g. *stairs* by *apples and pears*). **3.** *v.t.* Put or make (story etc.) into rhyme (**~d verse,** opp. *blank verse*); while (time) *away* in rhyming; treat (word) as rhyming *with.* [(*rhyme* 17th c. var. of) ME *rime* f. OF *rimer* (see prec.)]

rhȳ'olite *n.* Fine-grained granitic rock. [f. G *rhyolit* f. Gk *rhuax* lava-stream + *lithos* stone; see -LITE]

rhȳ'thm (-dhem *or* -them) *n.* **1.** Metrical movement determined by various relations of long and short or accented and unaccented syllables; measured flow of words and phrases in verse or prose. **2.** Aspect of musical composition concerned with periodical accent and the duration of notes; **~ and blues,** popular music with blues themes and strong rhythm; **~ section,** part of dance band or jazz band mainly supplying rhythm. **3.** (Art etc.) Harmonious correlation of parts; regular succession of opposites. **4.** (Phys., Physiol., etc.) Movement with regular succession of strong and weak elements. **5.** Regularly recurring sequence of events; **~ method,** contraception by avoiding sexual intercourse near times of ovulation. **6.** Hence or cogn. **rhȳ'thm**IC(AL) *adjs.*, **~**LESS *a.*, **rhȳ'thm**IST (3) *n.*, (*or* -dh-). [f. F *rhythme* or L f. Gk *rhuthmos* (cf. *rheō* flow)]

R.I. *abbr.* King and Emperor [f. L *Rex et Imperator*]; Queen and Empress [f. L *Regina et Imperatrix*]; Rhode Island; Royal Institute; Royal Institution.

ri'a (rē'*a*) *n.* (Geog.) Long narrow inlet formed by partial submergence of river valley. [f. Sp. *ría* estuary]

rī'ant *a.* (Of face, eyes, etc., and esp. of landscape) smiling, cheerful. [F, part. of *rire* f. L *ridēre* laugh; see -ANT]

rĭb *n.*, & *v.t.* (**-bb-**). **1.** *n.* One of curved bones articulated in pairs to spine and protecting thoracic cavity and its organs; **true** or **sternal ~** (joined also to breastbone, opp. **false, floating,** or **short ~**); **poke** or **dig** person **in the ~s** (to draw his attention good-naturedly); **smite under the fifth ~,** (Bibl.) stab mortally. **2. ~(s)** *of beef* etc. (as joint of meat); SPARE-RIB. **3.** (joc. w. ref. to Gen. 2:21) Wife, woman. **4.** Ridge or long raised piece often of stronger or thicker material across surface or through structure, serving to support as part of framework or strengthen or adorn, e.g. vein of leaf or insect's wing, shaft of feather, spur of mountain, vein of ore, ridge between furrows, wave-mark on sand, raised pattern of lines or bands along or across rows in knitting (made by alternation of plain and purl stitches), similar line in woven fabric formed by coarser yarn, one of ship's curved timbers to which planks are nailed or corresponding ironwork, arch supporting vault, groin, raised moulding on groin or across ceiling etc., wooden or iron beam helping to carry bridge, hinged rod of umbrella frame. **5. ~-grass, ~'wort,** PLANTAIN[1] with long narrow leaves. **6.** Hence (**-**)**~b**ED[2] (-bd), **~'**LESS, *adjs.* **7.** *v.t.* Provide with ribs, act as ribs of, whence **~'b**ING[1] (3, 6) *n.*; mark with ridges; plough with spaces between furrows; (colloq.) make fun of, tease. [OE *rib(b)*, = OS *ribbi*, OHG *rippi, rippa*, ON *rif* f. Gmc **rebhja, rebhjō*]

R.I.B.A. *abbr.* Royal Institute of British Architects.

rĭ'bald *n.* & *a.* **1.** *n.* Irreverent jester, user of scurrilous, blasphemous, or indecent language; so **~**RY (4, 5) *n.* **2.** *a.* (Of language or its user) scurrilous, obscene, irreverent, coarsely humorous. [ME, earlier sense 'low-born retainer', f. OF *ribau(l)t, ribau(l)d* (*riber* pursue licentious pleasures f. Gmc, cogn. w. OHG *hriba* whore)]

rĭ'band *n.* = foll. [ME, f. OF *riban, r(e)uban*, prob. f. Gmc compd. of BAND[1]]

rĭ'bbon *n.* **1.** (Piece or length of) silk or other material woven into narrow band esp. for adorning hair or costume or for tying round a package; ribbon of special colour etc. worn to indicate award of medal etc. or membership of knightly order, club, college, athletic team, etc., (BLUE[1], RED, *ribbon*); **R~ Society,** (Hist.) Irish R.C. secret society formed in early 19th c. and associated with agrarian crime, whence **R~**ISM (3) *n.* **2.** Long narrow strip of anything, e.g. inked material struck by typewriter types to print on paper; ribbon-like object or mark; (in *pl.*) driving-reins; (in *pl.*) ragged strips (*hang in, torn to, ribbons*). **3. ~ building, ~ development,** the building of houses along main road, extending outwards from a town or village; **~-fish,** long slender flat fish of various species; **~-grass,** slender-leaved grass with white-striped leaves; **R~-man,** member of

Ribbon Society; ~ **microphone** (in which signal is produced by metal strip); ~**-worm,** nemertine. **4.** Hence (-)~ED[2] (-nd) *a.* [var. of prec.]

rīboflā'vĭn *n.* Vitamin B_2. [f. RIBOSE + L *flavus* yellow + -IN]

rībonūclē'ĭc *a.* ~ **acid,** nucleic acid yielding ribose on hydrolysis, present in cytoplasm and controlling synthesis of proteins. [f. foll. + NUCLEIC]

rī'bōse *n.* Sugar found in many nucleosides and in several vitamins and enzymes. [G (*ribon* by rearrangement f. related sugar *arabinose*; see -OSE[2])]

rī'bosōm|e *n.* Minute particle in cytoplasm concerned with formation of proteins from amino-acids; hence ~AL *a.* [f. RIBONUCLEIC + -SOME[3]]

Rĭcar'dĭan *a.* & *n.* (Adherent) of Ricardo; according to his views. [f. D. *Ricardo,* Engl. economist d. 1823 + -IAN]

rīce *n.*, & *v.t.* **1.** *n.* (Pearl-white seeds, used as staple food in many Eastern countries, and elsewhere in puddings, cakes, etc., and savoury dishes, of) chiefly oriental grass (*Oryza sativa*) grown in marshes. **2.** ~**-bird,** (1) Java sparrow, (2) bobolink; ~**-bowl,** (fig.) area producing much rice; ~**-paper,** paper made from pith of oriental tree (*Tetrapanax papyriferum*), resembling rice-straw paper and used for painting and in cookery as base for macaroons etc. **3.** *v.t.* *Pass (cooked potatoes etc.) through device to form thin strings; hence ***rī'**CER[1] (2) *n.* [ME, f. OF *ris* f. It. *riso* f. Rom. **orizum* f. L f. Gk *oruza,* of Oriental orig.]

ricercar (rēchar̄kar̄') *n.* (Mus.) Instrumental composition of study or fugue type, esp. of 16th–18th c. [It., = to seek out]

rĭch *a.* **1.** (Of person, society, State, etc.) having riches. **2.** (Of country, period, soil, etc.) abounding in or *in* natural resources or some valuable possession or production, fertile; **strike it** ~, find source of prosperity. **3.** Valuable (*rich offerings*; *a rich harvest*). **4.** (Of dress, furniture, building, banquet, etc.) splendid, costly, elaborate, (*with* lace, sculpture, etc.). **5.** (Of food or diet) containing or involving large proportion of fat, oil, butter, eggs, spice, etc. **6.** (Of colour, voice, sound, smell) mellow, deep, full, not thin. **7.** Abundant, ample, (*a rich supply of ideas*). **8.** (Of incident, assertion, etc.) highly amusing or ludicrous, full of entertainment or material for humour. **9.** (Of mixture in internal combustion engine) highly combustible, containing more than normal proportion of fuel. **10.** Hence ~'EN[6] *v.i.* & *t.*, ~'NESS *n.* [OE *rīce,* = OS *riki,* OHG *rīchi,* ON *ríkr,* Goth. *reiks,* f. an early Gmc adoption of Celt. **rīx* = L *rex* king, & f. OF *riche* rich, powerful, of Gmc orig.]

Rĭ'chard *n.* ~ **Roe,** fictitious character in law (cf. JOHN *Doe*). [man's Christian name]

rĭ'chĕs (-z) *n.* (usu. as *pl.*) Abundant means, valuable possessions; ownership of these. [ME *richesse* f. OF *richeise* (*riche* RICH; see -ESS[2]), taken as pl.]

rĭ'chlȳ *adv.* In adj. senses; fully, thoroughly, (*richly deserves a thrashing, to succeed*). [f. RICH + -LY[2]]

rĭck[1] *n.*, & *v.t.* **1.** *n.* Stack of hay, corn, peas, etc., esp. one regularly built and thatched; ~**-stand,** short wooden or stone pillars bearing joists to raise rick from ground; ~**-yard,** enclosure for ricks. **2.** *v.t.* Form into rick(s). [OE *hrēac,* = MDu. *rooc,* ON *hraukr,* of unkn. orig.]

||**rĭck**[2], **wrĭck,** *n.*, & *v.t.* Slight(ly) sprain or strain (*have a rick in my neck*; *ricked his back when digging*). [ME *wricke,* f. MLG *wricken* move about, sprain]

rĭ'ckĕt|s *n.* (as *sing.* or *pl.*) Children's disease with softening of bones, esp. of spine, and bow-legs etc., assoc. w. deficiency of vitamin D; ~- *comb. form* (*ricket-producing*). [17th c., of uncert. orig.; assoc. w. Gk *rhakhitis* RACHITIS, adopted as its scientific name]

rĭckĕ'ttsĭ|a *n.* Parasitic micro-organism of genus *Rickettsia* causing typhus etc.; hence ~AL *a.* [mod. L, f. H. T. *Ricketts,* Amer. pathologist d. 1910 + -IA[1]]

rĭ'ckĕt|ȳ *a.* **1.** Suffering from, or of (the nature of), rickets. **2.** Feeble, weak-jointed; shaky, insecure. **3.** Hence ~ĬNESS *n.* [f. RICKETS + -Y[2]]

rĭ'ckey *n.* Drink of spirit (esp. gin), lime-juice, etc. [20th c.; orig. uncert.]

rĭ'ckrăck. See RICRAC.

rĭ'ckshaw, -sha, *n.* Light two-wheeled hooded vehicle drawn by one or more persons. [abbr. of *jinricksha(w)* f. Jap. *jinrikisha* (*jin* man, *riki* power, *sha* vehicle)]

rĭ'cochet (-shā *or* -shĕt) *n.*, & *v.i.* (**-t-** *or* **-tt-,** *pr.* -shād *or* -shĕtĭd, -shāĭng *or* -shĕtĭng, etc.). **1.** *n.* Skipping or rebounding of projectile esp. shell or bullet on water, ground, wall, etc.; hit made after this. **2.** *v.i.* (Of projectile) skip or rebound once or more on water etc. [F, of unkn. orig.]

rĭ'crăc, rĭ'ckrăck, *n.* Zigzag braid trimming for garments. [redupl. of RACK[3]]

||**R.I.C.S.** *abbr.* Royal Institution of Chartered Surveyors.

rĭ'ct|us *n.* (Anat. & Zool.) Expanse or gape of mouth or beak; hence ~AL *a.* [L, = open mouth (*ringi rict-* gape)]

rĭd[1] *v.t.* (**-dd-; rid,** arch. **rĭ'dded**). Make (person or place) free, disencumber, *of* (esp. in *p.p.* with *be* or *get*; *glad to be, must get, rid of him*); (arch.) abolish, clear away, get rid of, (pest); hence ~**'**DANCE *n.* (**good** ~**dance,** thing or person one is glad to be rid of; cf. RUBBISH). [ME, earlier sense 'clear (land etc.)', f. ON *rythja*]

rĭd[2], **rĭ'dden.** See RIDE.

rĭ'ddle[1] *n.* & *v.* **1.** *n.* Question, statement, or description, designed or serving to test ingenuity or give amusement in divining its answer or meaning or reference, conundrum, enigma; puzzling or mysterious fact, thing, or person. **2.** *v.i.* Speak in or propound riddles. **3.** *v.t.* Solve (riddle); ~ **me,** (arch.) solve my riddle (if you can). [OE *rǣdels(e)* opinion, riddle, (= OS *rādisli, -lo,* OHG **rātisli*) f. **rǣdan* READ; cf. BURIAL]

rĭ'ddle[2] *n.*, & *v.t.* **1.** *n.* Coarse sieve for corn, gravel, cinders, etc. **2.** *v.t.* Pass (corn etc.) through riddle, sift, (fig.) test searchingly (evidence, truth); fill (ship, person) with holes esp. of gunshot, (fig.) pelt with questions, refute (person, theory) with facts; (in *p.p.*) filled *with* (faults etc.). [OE *hriddel,* earlier *hrīder*; cf. *hrīdrian* sift]

rĭ'ddlĭng *a.* Expressed in riddles; puzzling; hence ~LY[2] *adv.* [f. RIDDLE[1] + -ING[2]]

rīde *v.* (**rode,** arch. **rid; rĭ'dden,** arch. **rid**) & *n.* **1.** *v.i.* Sit on and be carried by horse etc., go on horseback etc. or on bicycle etc. or in train or other esp. public conveyance (cf. DRIVE[1]), sit or go or be *on* something as on horse esp. astride, sit on and manage horse, lie at anchor, float buoyantly, (of moon etc.) seem to float, (of thing normally level or even) project or overlap, rest *in* or *on* while moving, (*ride at full speed*; *riding on his father's shoulders, back, knee, foot*; *rides well, cannot ride, learn to ride, riding-lessons* or *-school*; *bird* or *ship rides on the wind* or *waves*; *ship rode at anchor*). **2.** ~ **again,** (fig.) return to vigour; *ride-a-*COCK-HORSE; ~ **for a fall,** ride or (fig.) act recklessly, risk defeat; ~ **high,** (fig.) be successful; *ride to* HOUND[1]*s*; **let** thing ~, leave it undisturbed; ~ **off on,** use (side-issue) to evade main point; ~ **over,** WALK[1] over (in horse-race); *ride* ROUGH*shod*; ~ **and tie,** (arch.) method of travel by two or more with one horse, each riding ahead in turn and leaving it tied to await other(s); ~ **up,** (of garment) work upwards when worn. **3.** *v.t.* Traverse on horseback etc., ride over or through, (*ride 50 miles, a race, a desert, a ford*); ride on, sit heavily on, oppress, haunt, dominate, tyrannize over, (*ride a horse, a bicycle; ship rides the waves; nightmare rides sleeper; ridden by fears, prejudices*, etc.; *cliché*, HAG[1], *priest*, etc. *-ridden*); be carried by, travel on; *(seek to) annoy; mount (female) in copulation; yield to (blow) so as to reduce its impact. **4.** Give ride to, cause to ride, (*ride child on* one's *back*); (of rider) cause (horse etc.) to move forward (*at* fence etc.). **5.** ~ **down,** overtake or trample on horseback; **ride* HERD[1]; ~ **off,** (Polo) edge (opponent) away from ball; ~ **out,** come safely through (storm; lit. or fig.). **6.** Hence **rī'd**ABLE *a.* **7.** *n.* Journey in esp. public conveyance, spell of riding on horse, bicycle, person's back, etc.; **take for a** ~, (sl.) (1) drive (person) away in motor vehicle prior to murdering him, (2) deceive, hoax. **8.** Path (esp. through woods) for riding on. **9.** Quality of sensations when riding (*gives a bumpy ride*). [OE *rīdan*, = OS *-rīdan*, OHG *rītan*, ON *rítha*]

rī'der *n.* **1.** In vbl senses. **2.** (Naut., in *pl.*) Additional set of timbers or iron plates strengthening ship's frame. **3.** Additional clause amending or supplementing document, esp. ‖parliamentary Bill at third reading; corollary, naturally arising supplement; ‖expression of opinion, recommendation etc., added to verdict. **4.** (Math.) Problem arising as corollary of theorem etc. **5.** Piece in machine etc. that surmounts or bridges or works on or over others. **6.** Hence ~LESS *a.* [OE *rīdere* (as prec., -ER[1])]

rĭdge *n.* & *v.* **1.** *n.* Line of junction of two surfaces sloping upwards towards each other (*ridge of roof, nose*, etc.); long narrow hill-top, mountain range, watershed; (Agric.) one of set of raised strips separated by furrows; (Hort.) raised hotbed for melons etc.; (Meteorol.) elongated region of high barometric pressure; any narrow elevation across surface. **2.** ~**-piece,** beam along ridge of roof; ~**-pole,** (1) horizontal pole of long tent, (2) = *ridge-piece*; ~**-tile** (used for roof-ridge); ~**-tree,** = *ridge-piece*; ~**'way,** road along ridge. **3.** Hence **rĭ'dg**Y[2] *a.* **4.** *v.t.* Break up (land) into ridges; mark with ridges; plant (cucumbers etc.) in ridges. **5.** *v.t.* & *i.* Gather into ridges. [OE *hrycg*, = OS *hruggi*, OHG *hrucki*, ON *hryggr* f. Gmc **hrugjaz*]

rĭ'dĭcūle *n.*, & *v.t.* **1.** *n.* Holding or being held up as object of derision or mockery; (arch.) ridiculous thing or person. **2.** *v.t.* Make fun of, subject to ridicule, laugh at. [F, or f. L *ridiculum* neut. of *ridiculus* laughable (*rīdēre* laugh)]

rĭdĭ'cūlous *a.* Deserving to be laughed at, absurd, unreasonable; hence ~LY[2] *adv.*, ~NESS *n.* [f. as prec. + -OUS, or L *ridiculosus*]

rī'dĭng[1] *n.* In vbl senses; road for riders, esp. green track through or beside wood; *riding*-HABIT[1]; ~**-lamp, -light,** (borne by ship at anchor). [ME, f. RIDE + -ING[1]]

‖**rī'dĭng**[2] *n.* (Hist.) division (**East, North,** or **West R**~) of Yorkshire; similar division of other county. [OE **thriding*, **thrithing* f. ON *thrithjungr* (*thrithi* THIRD; see -ING[3]) third part, w. loss of *th-* owing to preceding *-t(h)* of *east* etc.]

Rie'slĭng (*or* -z-) *n.* (Dry white wine made from) European variety of grape. [G]

rifacimentǀo (rĭfahchĭmĕ'ntō) *n.* (*pl.* ~*i pr.* -ē). Remodelled form of a literary or musical work. [It. (*rifare* remake)]

rīfe *pred. a.* Of common occurrence, met with in large numbers or quantities, prevailing, current, numerous; well provided *with*; hence ~'NESS (-fn-) *n.* [OE *rȳfe*, **rife*, prob. f. ON *rífr* acceptable (*reifa* enrich, *reifr* cheerful)]

rĭff *n.* Short repeated phrase in jazz and similar music. [20th c.; orig. unkn.]

rĭ'ffle *n.* & *v.* **1.** *n.* (In gold-washing) groove or slat set in trough or sluice to catch gold particles; *shallow part of stream where water flows brokenly; *patch of waves or ripples on water. **2.** *v.t.* Ruffle (water etc.); turn (pages) in quick succession; shuffle (playing-cards) rapidly, esp. by flexing and combining two halves of pack. **3.** *v.i.* Leaf (*through* pages). [perh. var. of RUFFLE[1]]

rĭ'ff-răff *n.* *The* rabble, disreputable or undesirable persons. [ME *riff and raff* f. OF *rif et raf*]

rī'fle[1] *v.t.* **1.** Search and rob, esp. of all that can be found in various pockets or storing-places; carry off as booty. **2.** Make spiral grooves in (gun or its barrel or bore) to produce rotatory motion of projectile; hence **rī'fl**ING[1] (1, 2) *n.* [sense 1 ME, f. OF *rifler* graze, scratch, plunder f. ODu. *riffelen*; sense 2 ult. f. OF *rifler*]

rī'fle[2] *n.* **1.** (arch.) Groove made in rifling a gun. **2.** ~ (**gun** arch.), firearm with rifled barrel esp. one fired from shoulder-level; (in *pl.*) troops armed with rifles. **3.** ~**-bird,** dark-green Australian bird of paradise; ~**-green** *n.* & *a.*, (of) dark green as in rifleman's uniform; *rifle*-GRENADE; ~**man,** (1) soldier armed with rifle, esp. private or other soldier in some regiments, (2) = *rifle-bird*, (3) small yellow and green N.Z. bird; ~**-pit,** excavation as cover for riflemen firing at enemy; ~**-range,** (1) distance coverable by shot from rifle, (2) place for rifle-practice; *~**scope,** telescopic sight for rifle; ~**-shot,** (1) = *rifle-range* (1), (2) *good* etc. marksman with rifle, (3) shot fired with rifle. [f. prec.]

rĭft *n.*, & *v.t.* **1.** *n.* Cleft, fissure, chasm, in earth or rock; rent, crack, split in an object, opening in cloud etc.; disagreement, dispute; ~**-valley,** steep-sided valley formed by subsidence of earth's crust; hence ~'LESS, ~'Y[2], *adjs.* **2.** *v.t.* (esp. in *p.p.*) Rend apart, cleave. [ME, of Scand. orig. (cf. Da., Norw. *rift* cleft, Icel. *ript* breach of contract); cogn. w. RIVE]

rĭg[1] *v.t.* (**-gg-**), & *n.* **1.** *v.t.* Provide (ship) with necessary spars, ropes, etc., or ~'**g**ING[1] (3) (-g-) *n.*, prepare for sea in this respect; assemble and adjust parts of (aircraft); fit (*out, up*, or abs.) with or *with* or *in* clothes or other equipment; ‖~**-out** *n.*, (colloq.) such clothes etc. **2.** Set *up* (structure) hastily or as makeshift or by utilizing odd materials. **3.** ~**'ging-loft,** gallery in dockyard for fitting rigging, (Theatr.) space over stage from which scenery is manipulated. **4.** *n.* Way ship's masts, sails, etc., are arranged, whence -~**g**ED[2] (-gd) *a.* (*ketch-, sloop-, rigged*); person's or thing's look as determined by clothes etc.; **in full** ~, (colloq.) smartly or ceremonially dressed. **5.** Equipment for constructing oil-well. [ME, perh. of Scand. orig. (cf. Norw. *rigga* bind or wrap up)]

rĭg[2] *n.*, & *v.t.* (**-gg-**). **1.** *n.* ‖Trick, dodge, way of swindling. **2.** *v.t.* Manage or conduct fraudulently (*a rigged election*; ~ **the market,** cause artificial rise or fall in prices). [19th c.; orig. unkn.]

rĭgadōō'n *n.* Lively dance for two persons; music for this. [f. F *rigodon, rigaudon*, perh. f. inventor *Rigaud*]

‖**rĭgg** *n.* Dogfish. [19th c. dial., of uncert. orig.]

rĭ'gger (-g-) *n.* In vbl senses; one who attends to rigging of aircraft; (of rowing-boat) = OUTRIGGER; = THIMBLE*rigger*; ship rigged in specified way. [f. RIG[1,2] + -ER[1]]

rīght[1] (rīt) *a.* **1.** (arch., of line) Straight. **2.** (Of angle) neither acute nor obtuse, of 90°, made by lines meeting not obliquely but perpendicularly with equal angles on either side, (**at ~ angles,** turning or placed with such angle; **~-angled,** containing or making a right angle); involving right angle(s), not oblique, (*right* ASCENSION; **~ sailing,** sailing due N., S., E., or W.; *right* SPHERE); (of cone, cylinder, prism, etc.) with base or ends perpendicular to axis. **3.** (Of conduct etc.) just, morally good, required by equity or duty, proper, (opp. *wrong*; *it is only right to tell you, that you should know*); **~-minded,** having natural inclination to favour what is right. **4.** Correct, true, (opp. *wrong*; *right use of words*; *did not give a right account of the matter*; *your opinions are right enough*); *the* preferable or most suitable, *the* less wrong or not wrong, (*which is the right way to proceed?*; *the right man in the right place*; *does not do it the right way*; *went the right way to offend us*; *a fault on the right side*; *hold it right side up*); MR. *Right*; **~ side,** (of fabric etc.) side meant for show or use; **on the ~ side of,** in favour with (person); **on the ~ side of** *forty* etc., not yet 40 etc. years old. **5.** In good or normal condition, sound, sane, satisfactory, well-advised, not mistaken, (opp. *wrong*; *all's right with the world*; *is not quite right in the head*); **are you ~?,** are you satisfied, comfortable, etc.?; **as ~ as rain, as a trivet,** etc., entirely normal; **get ~,** bring or come into right state; **in** one's **~ mind,** not mad etc.; **put** or **set ~,** restore to order, health, etc., correct mistaken ideas of (person), justify one*self* (*with* person); **she'll be ~,** (Austral. colloq.) that will be all right; **~ (you are)!,** ||**~ oh!,** (colloq. excl. of assent to order or proposal); hence **~'**EN[6] *v.t.* **6.** (arch. or colloq.) Rightful, real, veritable, properly so called (*right* WHALE; *made a right mess of it*). **7.** (Of position, opp. LEFT[1]) on or towards that side of human body of which the hand is normally more used, on or towards that part of an object which is analogous to person's right side or (with opposite sense) which is nearer to spectator's right hand, (*right side, eye*, etc.; *right flank* of army etc.); **~ about (face** or **turn)**, right turn continued to face rear, reversal of policy, hasty retreat; **~ arm,** (fig.) one's most reliable helper; *right* BANK[1]; *right* BOWER[3]; **~ field,** (Baseball) part of field on first-base side, to catcher's right; **~ hand,** hand of right side, this as the better hand (*put* one's *right hand to the work*) or w. ref. to shaking of hands (*give the right hand of fellowship*), region or direction on right side of person (*at, on, to*, one's *right hand*), indispensable or chief assistant; **~-hand,** placed on the right hand; **~-hand man,** (1) soldier on one's right hand in line, (2) indispensable or chief assistant; **~-hand screw,** = right-handed screw; **~-handed,** using right hand more than left, turning to right, (of blow etc.) struck with right hand, (of tool etc.) made to suit use of right hand, (of screw) advanced by turning to right; **~-hander,** right-handed blow or person; **~-and-left,** (of screw etc.) having right-handed and left-handed parts at opposite ends; **~ turn** (that brings one's front to face as one's right side did before); **~ wing** (of army, football etc. team, or political party, cf. RIGHT[3] 4), whence **~-wi'nger,** member of this. **8.** Hence **~'**ISH[1] 2 *a.*, **~'**LY[2] *adv.*, **~'**MOST *a.*, **~'**NESS *n.*, **~'**WARD *a.* & *adv.*, **~'**WARDS *adv.* [OE *riht*, = OS, OHG *reht*, ON *réttr*, Goth. *raihts* f. Gmc **rehtaz*]

rīght[2] (rīt) *v.t.* **1.** Restore to proper or straight or vertical position (*boat righted herself*; *could not right the boat, car*; **~ oneself,** recover one's balance); put (helm) amidships. **2.** Make reparation for or to, avenge, (wrong, wronged person); vindicate, justify, rehabilitate. **3.** Correct (mistakes etc.), correct mistakes in; (usu. *refl.*) set in order (*that is a fault that will right itself*). **4.** Hence **~'**ABLE *a.* [OE *rihtan* (*riht*; see prec.)]

rīght[3] (rīt) *n.* **1.** What is just, fair treatment; **by ~(s),** if right were done; **do** person **~, do ~ by** person, treat or think of him fairly; **the ~,** what is RIGHT[1] 3, the juster cause; **in the ~,** having justice or truth on one's side. **2.** Justification, fair claim, being entitled to privilege or immunity, thing one is entitled to, (*has a, the, no, right to* thing, *to* do, *of* doing, etc.; *belongs to him of* or *as of* or *by right*; *rights and duties*); (in *pl.*) authority to act in specified way; **in** one's **own ~,** not through marriage, adherence, etc.; *right of* SEARCH; *rights of* WAR[1]; **~ of way,** right established by usage to pass over another's ground, path subject to such right, precedence in passing granted to one vehicle etc. with regard to another, *land acquired for public use or service; **Bill of R~s,** (1) ||constitutional settlement of 1689, (2) *constitutional amendments of 1791, (3) statement of rights of a class of persons; **~s issue,** offer of new shares at reduced price in proportion to holdings of old shares; **within** one's **~s,** not exceeding one's authority or entitlement; hence **~'**LESS *a.* **3.** (in *pl.*) Right condition, true state, (**set** or **put to ~s,** arrange properly); true statement (*have not heard, do not know, the rights of the case*); ||**bang to** or ***dead to ~s,** (sl.) red-handed. **4.** Right-hand part or region or direction (*is on your, to the, right*; *to* or *from right and left*); (*R~*; Polit.) conservative members of (orig. continental) parliament etc. or other conservatives, whence **~'**ISM (3), **~'**IST (2), *ns.*; right-hand side of stage when facing audience; (Boxing) (blow with) right hand; (in marching etc.) right foot; right wing of army. [OE *riht* (as RIGHT[1])]

rīght[4] (rīt) *adv.* **1.** Straight (*go right on*; *wind was right behind us*); (colloq.) immediately (*I'll be right back*); **~ away, off,** immediately, without pausing. **2.** All the way *to, round, through*, etc., completely *off, out*, etc., (*sank right to the bottom*; *veranda right round house*; *took gate right off hinges*; *turned right round*). **3.** Exactly, quite, (*right here, now*; *right in the middle*); **~ on!** (colloq. excl. of approval). **4.** Very, to the full, (*know right well*; *banqueted right royally*; *was right glad to hear*); **~-down,** thorough(ly); ||*Right* HONOURABLE, *Right* REVEREND. **5.** Justly, properly, correctly, aright, truly, satisfactorily, (*whether they act right or wrong*; *does not hold his pen, do the sum, right*; *nothing goes right with me*; *if I remember right*; *guessed right*). **6.** On or to the right side; **~ and left,** to or on both sides, on all sides, (*he was abused right and left*); **~, left, and centre,** on all sides. [OE *rihte* (*riht*; see RIGHT[1])]

rī'ghteous (rī'chus) *a.* (Of person, life, action) morally right, just, upright, virtuous, law-abiding; hence **~**LY[2] *adv.*, **~**NESS *n.* [OE *rihtwīs* (as RIGHT[3] + -WISE or RIGHT[1] + WISE[2]), w. assim. to *bounteous* etc.]

rī'ghtful (rī't-) *a.* (Of action etc.) equitable, fair; (of person) legitimately entitled to position etc. (*the rightful king, heir, owner*); (of office, property, etc.) that one is entitled to; hence **~**LY[2] *adv.*, **~**NESS *n.* [OE *rihtful* (as RIGHT[3], -FUL)]

||**rī'ghtō** (rī'tō; *or* -ō') *int.* (colloq.) expr. assent to order or proposal. [f. RIGHT[1] + O[2]]

rĭ'gĭd *a.* Not flexible, stiff, unyielding, (*a rigid bar, stem, frame, airship*); inflexible, harsh, strict, precise, punctilious, (*rigid justice, principles, Catholics, adherence to rules, economy*); hence or cogn. **rĭgĭ'dĭ**FY *v.t.* & *i.*, **rĭgĭ'd**ITY *n.*, **~**LY[2] *adv.* [f. F *rigide* or f. L *rigidus* (as RIGOR[1])]

rĭ'gmarōle *n.* & *a.* **1.** *n.* Rambling or meaningless talk or tale. **2.** *a.* Incoherent, rambling. [alt. f. obs. *ragman roll* = catalogue, orig. unkn.]

rĭ'gŏr[1] (*or* rĭ'ger) *n.* (Path.) Sudden chill with shivering before fever etc.; rigidity of body caused by shock, poisoning, etc.; ~ **mor'tis,** stiffening of body after death. [ME f. L (*rigēre* be stiff; see -OR)]

rĭ'gour (-ger), ***rĭ'gor**[2], *n.* Severity, strictness, harshness, (in *pl.*) harsh measures; strict enforcement *of* rules etc. (*with the utmost rigour of the law*); extremity or excess *of* weather, hardship, famine, etc., great distress; austerity of life, Puritanic strictness of observance or doctrine, whence **rĭ'gor**ISM (3), **rĭ'gor**IST (2), *ns.*; logical accuracy, exactitude; so **rĭ'gor**OUS *a.* [ME, f. OF *rigour* f. L RIGOR[1]]

Rĭg-Vē'da (*or* -vā'-) *n.* The oldest and chief VEDA. [f. Skr. *ṛigvēda* (*ṛic* praise, *vēda* VEDA)]

rīle *v.t.* **1.** (colloq.) Anger, irritate. **2.** *Make (water) turbulent or muddy. [var. of ROIL]

Rī'ley, Rei'llÿ, (rī'-) *n.* **The life of** ~, (sl.) a carefree existence. [20th c.; orig. unkn.]

rilievo (rēlyā'vō) *n.* (*pl.* ~*s*). = RELIEF[2], RELIEVO. [It., = RELIEF[2]]

rĭll *n.* Small stream, runnel, rivulet; hence ~'ET[1] *n.* [prob. of LDu. orig.; cf. LG *ril(le)*]

rĭlle *n.* (Astron.) Trench or narrow valley on moon's surface. [G, as prec.]

rĭm[1] *n.*, & *v.t.* (**-mm-**). **1.** *n.* Outer ring of wheel's framework, not including tyre; (poet.) circular object (**golden** ~, crown); (Naut.) surface *of* the water. **2.** Raised edge or border, margin, verge, esp. of something more or less circular; **~-brake** (acting on rim of wheel); ***~-rock,** outcrop with steep face; hence ~'LESS, (-)~MED[2] (-md), *adjs.* **3.** *v.t.* Furnish with rim, serve as rim to, edge, border. [OE *rima*, = ON *rimi* ridge]

||**rĭm**[2] *n.* (arch.) ~ (**of the belly**), peritoneum. [OE *rēoma*, = OS, OHG *riomo* strap]

rīme[1,2] *n.* & *v.* See RHYME[1,2].

rīme[3] *n.*, & *v.t.* **1.** *n.* Frost, esp. formed from cloud or fog; hence **rī'my**[2] *a.* **2.** (poet.) Hoar-frost. **3.** *v.t.* Cover with rime. [OE *hrīm*, = MDu. *rijm*, ON *hrím*]

Rĭ'mmon *n.* **Bow down in the house of** ~, compromise one's convictions. [name of deity in ancient Damascus, 2 Kings 5:18]

rī'mōse, rī'mous, *adjs.* (Bot. etc.) Full of chinks or fissures. [f. L *rimosus* (*rima* chink; see -OSE[1], -OUS)]

rī'mu (rē'mōō) *n.* (N.Z.) Principal indigenous softwood (tree, *Dacrydium cupressinum*). [Maori]

rīnd *n.*, & *v.t.* **1.** *n.* Bark of tree or plant; peel of fruit or vegetable; harder outer layer of cheese or other substance; skin of bacon etc.; external aspect, surface; hence -~'ED[2] *a.* **2.** *v.t.* Strip bark from. [OE *rind(e)*, = OS, OHG *rinda*]

rĭ'nderpĕst *n.* Virulent infectious disease of ruminants (esp. cattle). [G (*rinder* cattle, *pest* PEST)]

rĭng[1] *n.*, & *v.t.* **1.** *n.* Circlet usu. of precious metal and often set with gem(s) worn round finger as ornament or token (esp. of betrothal or marriage) or signet, or hung from or encircling other part of body. **2.** Circular band of any material and usu. small size. **3.** Raised or sunk or otherwise distinguishable line or band round, or rim of, cylindrical or circular object. **4.** Fold, coil, bend, piece, structure, part, or mark, having form of circular band, (*has livid rings round his eyes*; *puffing out rings of smoke*; ANNUAL, FAIRY, *ring*); halo round moon etc.; (Chem.) group of atoms representable as closed sequence. **5.** Persons, trees, etc., disposed in a circle, such disposition; combination of traders, politicians, spies, etc., acting together for control of operations; PRICE-*ring*; hence ~'STER *n.* **6.** Circular or other enclosure or space for circus, boxing (PRIZE[1]-*ring*; HATS *in the ring*), betting at races (**the** ~, bookmakers), showing of cattle, etc. **7.** Circular or spiral course (**make** or **run** ~**s round,** go or do things very much better or quicker than). **8.** **~-bark** *v.t.*, cut ring in bark of (tree) to kill it or to retard its growth and improve fruit production; **~-bolt,** bolt with ring attached for fastening rope to etc.; **~-bone,** (horse-disease with) deposit of bony matter on pastern-bones; **~-cartilage,** cricoid; ~ **circuit** (Electr., serving many power points with one fuse in supply to ring); **~-cut,** remove ring of (bark; see *ring-bark*); **~-dove,** large species of pigeon (*Columba palumbus*); **~-fence** (completely enclosing estate etc.); **~-finger,** third finger esp. of left hand, on which wedding-ring is worn; **~'leader,** (one of) chief instigator(s) in mutiny, riot, etc.; **~-lock** (opened by right adjustment of several grooved rings); ~ **main,** electrical supply through cable in closed ring providing alternative paths; **~-master,** director of circus performance; **~-neck,** ring-necked pheasant, plover, duck, or (Austral.) parrot; **~-necked,** with band(s) of colour round neck; ~ **ouzel,** thrush (*Turdus torquatus*) allied to blackbird; **~-plover,** small plover of genus *Charadrius*; ~ **road,** bypass encircling town; **~'side** *a.*, (of seat, view, etc.) close to scene of action; **~-snake,** ||common European grass-snake (from its coiling), *small snake of genus *Diadophis* with ring round neck; **~-straked,** (arch.) with bands of colour round body; **~'tail,** (1) female hen-harrier, (2) golden eagle till its third year, (3) ring-tailed opossum, lemur, or phalanger; **~-tailed,** (1) with tail ringed in alternate colours, (2) with tail curled at end; **~-taw,** game with marbles in ring; **~-wall** (completely enclosing estate etc.); **~'worm,** contagious fungous disease of skin, appearing in circular patches esp. on child's scalp. **9.** Hence (-)~ED[2] (-ngd), ~'LESS, *adjs.* **10.** *v.t.* Encompass (*round, about, in*), hem in (*game, cattle*) by riding or beating in circle round them. **11.** Put ring on (bird etc.; cf. BAND[1] 2); put ring in nose of (pig, bull). **12.** = *ring-bark*. **13.** Cut (onions, apples) into rings. [OE *hring*, = OS, OHG *hring*, ON *hringr*, f. Gmc **hrengaz*]

rĭng[2] *v.* (**rang,** arch. **rung; rung**) & *n.* **1.** *v.i.* Give forth clear resonant sound (as) of vibrating metal (*bell, trumpet, coin, sound, rings,* often *out* etc.; *with a ringing laugh*; *a shot rang out*); (of bell) be sounded for specified purpose; sound in specified way; ~ **true, false,** (of coin tested by throwing on counter, (fig.) of sentiments etc.). **2.** (Of place) resound, re-echo, (*with* sound, *to* sound or its cause, *with* fame etc. or its theme, *with* talk of). **3.** (Of utterance or other sound) ~ **in** one's **ears, heart,** etc., linger in one's hearing, haunt the memory. **4.** (Of ears) be filled with sensation as of bell-ringing or with sound. **5.** Ring bell as summons; ||~ (**up**), make telephone call (~ **off,** end telephone conversation). **6.** *v.t.* Make (bell) ring; ~ **a bell,** (colloq.) begin to revive a memory; ~ **the bell,** (colloq.) be successful [from use of bell in machines for testing strength or skill], strike sympathetic or responsive note; ~ **up,** raise (church bell) over beam and ring it there; **~'ing engine,** pile-driver worked by ropes like peal of bells. **7.** Sound (peal, KNELL[1], *the* CHANGE[1]*s*) on bells (or with *bell* or *bells* as subj.). **8.** Announce (hour etc.) by sound of bell(s). **9.** Summon (*up* etc.) by ringing bell, ||esp. by telephone; ~ **back,** make telephone call to (person who has telephoned one earlier, or abs.); ~ **up,** record (sale etc.) on cash register; ~ **curtain up** or **down** in theatre, direct it by bell to be raised or lowered, (fig.) mark beginning or end of an enterprise etc. **10.** Usher *in* or *out* with bell-ringing (esp. new or old year). **11.** *n.* Set of (church) bells. **12.** Ringing sound, ringing tone in voice etc., resonance of coin or vessel; specified feeling conveyed by utterance etc. (*has a melancholy ring*). **13.** Act of ringing bell, sound so produced; (colloq.) call on the telephone (*give me a ring*). [OE *hringan*, = ON *hringja*]

rĭ'ngent (-nj-) *a.* Gaping, grinning, (esp. Bot., of wide labiate corolla). [as RICTUS; see -ENT]

rĭ'nger *n.* **1.** Quoit that falls round peg; fox that runs in ring when hunted; *substituted racehorse etc.; person's double. **2.** Bell-ringer; device for ringing bell; (Austral.) fastest shearer in shed. [f. RING[1,2] + -ER[1]]

rĭ'nghăls *n.* (S. Afr.) Snake akin to cobra with coloured ring round neck, spitting venom at victim. [Afrik. (*ring* RING[1], *hals* neck)]

rĭ'nglĕt *n.* **1.** (arch.) Small ring, fairy ring on grass, ring-shaped mark etc. **2.** Curly lock of hair, long curl; hence ~ED[2], ~Y[2], *adjs.* **3.** Butterfly of family Satyridae. [f. RING[1] + -LET]

rĭnk *n.* Stretch of ice used for game of curling; sheet of natural or artificial ice, floor, for (roller-)skating; strip of bowling green used for a match; team of four players in bowls or curling. [ME, orig. Sc., = jousting-ground; perh. orig. **renk* f. OF *renc* RANK[1]]

rĭnse *v.t.*, & *n.* **1.** *v.t.* Wash out or *out* (vessel, mouth) by filling with clean water etc., moving about or shaking, and emptying; pour liquid over or wash lightly; put (clothes) through clean water to remove soap etc.; clear (impurities) *out* or *away* by rinsing. **2.** *n.* Rinsing (*give it a rinse*); solution for temporary tinting of hair. [ME, f. OF *rincer*, *raincier*, of unkn. orig.]

rī'ot *n.*, & *v.i.* **1.** *n.* (arch.) Loose living, debauchery. **2.** Loud revelry, a revel; unrestrained indulgence in or display or enjoyment of something (*a riot of emotion, colour, sound*); (colloq.) very amusing thing or person. **3.** (Hunting). Following of any scent indiscriminately; **run ~** (orig. of hounds doing this, now usu. fig. of person or his tongue or fancy throwing off all restraint, or of luxuriant vegetation etc.). **4.** Disorder, tumult, disturbance of the peace, outbreak of lawlessness, on part of a crowd (in Law, by three or more); ‖**R~ Act** (by which persons not dispersing after official reading of part of it incur guilt of felony) (*read the R~ Act*, (joc.) insist that noise, disobedience, etc., is to cease); **~ gun, shield,** (for use in dealing with riots). **5.** *v.i.* Live wantonly, revel. **6.** Make or engage in a political riot or offence against the Riot Act; so ~ER[2] (4) *n.* [ME, f. OF *riote(r)*, *rihoter*; orig. unkn.]

rī'otous *a.* Marked by rioting or by dissolute conduct; wildly profuse; hence ~LY[2] *adv.*, ~NESS *n.* [ME f. OF (as RIOT, -OUS)]

rĭp[1] *n.* Worthless horse; dissolute person, rake; rascal. [perh. var. of REP[3]]

rĭp[2] *v.* (**-pp-**) & *n.* **1.** *v.t.* Cut or tear (thing) quickly or forcibly away from something (*rip out the lining*; *rip the boards off*); make long cut or tear in, cut or tear vigorously apart; **~ off,** (sl.) defraud, steal, whence **~-off** *n.* **2.** Split (wood, rock), saw (wood) along the grain. **3.** Strip (roof) of tiles or slates and laths. **4.** Make (fissure, passage) by ripping. **5.** Open *up* (wound, quarrel, sorrow, the past) again. **6.** *v.i.* Come violently asunder, split. **7.** Rush along (of ship, or transf.); **let ~,** not check speed of or interfere; **~ into,** attack verbally. **8.** ‖(in *part.*, arch. sl.) Fine, splendid, enjoyable, first-rate. **9.** **~-cord,** cord for releasing parachute from its pack or opening balloon gasbag; **~-roaring,** wildly noisy; **~-saw,** coarse saw used for ripping wood; **~-snorter,** (sl.) energetic person or thing. **10.** *n.* Act of ripping; long tear or cut. [ME, of unkn. orig.]

rĭp[3] *n.* Stretch of broken water in sea or river, overfall; **~ current, ~-tide,** strong surface current from shore, (fig.) conflicting psychological forces. [perh. rel. to prec.]

R.I.P. *abbr.* (May he or she or they) rest in peace. [f. L *requiesca(n)t in pace*]

rīpār'ĭan *a.* & *n.* **1.** *a.* Of or on river-bank (*riparian proprietor, rights*). **2.** *n.* Riparian proprietor. [f. L *riparius* (*ripa* bank; see -ARY[1]) + -AN]

rīpe *a.* & *v.* **1.** *a.* Ready to be reaped, gathered, eaten, drunk, used, or dealt with, fully developed, mellow, mature, prepared or able *to* undergo something, in fit state *for*, (*ripe corn, fruit, cheese, wine, seed*; *ripe scholar, scholarship, judgement, experience, understanding*; *opportunity ripe to be seized*; *time is ripe for speaking the truth*; *mood* or *person, plan, land, disease, ripe for mischief, execution, development, treatment*); (of person's age) advanced; (of age, beauty, etc.) mature; (of lips) red and full like ripe fruit; hence **rī'p**EN[6] *v.t.* & *i.*, ~'LY[2] (-plĭ) *adv.*, ~'NESS (-pn-) *n.* **2.** *v.t.* & *i.* (esp. poet.) Ripen. [OE *rīpe*, = OS *rīpi*, OHG *rīfi* f. WG]

rĭpie'n|ō (-pyā'-) *n.* (*pl.* **~os** *or* **~i**). (Mus.) Supplementary player or instrument. [It. (as RE-, *pieno* full)]

rĭpŏ'ste *n.*, & *v.i.* **1.** *n.* Quick return thrust in fencing; (fig.) quick counterstroke, retort. **2.** *v.i.* Deliver riposte. [f. F *ri(s)poste(r)* f. It. *risposta* RESPONSE]

rĭ'pper *n.* In vbl senses; tool for ripping roof; rip-saw; (arch. sl.) 'ripping' person or thing. [f. RIP[2] + -ER[1]]

rĭ'pple[1] *n.*, & *v.t.* **1.** *n.* Toothed implement used to remove seeds from flax. **2.** *v.t.* Treat with ripple. [corresp. to MDu., MLG *repel(en)*, OHG *riffila, rifilōn*]

rĭ'pple[2] *n.* & *v.* **1.** *n.* Ruffling of water's surface, small wave(s); wavy or crinkled appearance in hair, ribbons, etc.; gentle lively sound that rises and falls (*ripple of applause, conversation, laughter*); (Electr.) slight variation in strength of current etc.; *riffle in stream; **~-mark,** ridge or ridged surface left on sand or mud or rock by water or wind; hence **rĭ'ppl**ET[1] *n.*, **rĭ'ppl**Y[2] *a.* **2.** *v.i.* & *t.* Form, flow in, show, agitate or mark with, sound like, ripples. [n. 18th c., f. v. 17th c., of unkn. orig.]

***rĭ'p-răp** *n.* Loose stone as foundation for structure. [redupl. of RAP[1]]

Rĭpūār'ĭan *a.* Of the ancient Franks living on Rhine between Meuse and Moselle; **~ law,** code observed by them. [f. med. L *Ripuarius* + -AN]

Rĭp văn Wĭ'nkle *n.* Person with utterly antiquated ideas or information. [hero of tale (by W. Irving, 1820), who slept 20 years]

rīse[1] (-z) *v.i.* (**rose** *pr.* rōz; **~n** *pr.* rĭ'zen). **1.** Get up from lying or sitting or kneeling position, get out of bed, (of meeting etc.) cease to sit for business, recover standing or upright position, become erect, leave ground, (*all rose when he entered*; *found he could not, was too weak to, rise*; *rise at 5 a.m., with the lark, with the* SUN, *rise up early*; *Parliament will rise next week*; *fell never to rise again*; *the hair rose on his head*; *horse rises on its hind legs*); come to life again or *again* or *from the dead* (*Christ is risen*); stand after receiving accolade (*rise, Sir Thomas*); depart *from* (table, meal) on finishing eating; **~ and shine,** (joc.) get out of bed etc. smartly. **2.** Cease to be quiet or submissive, rebel, (*rise in arms, rebellion*, etc., *against oppression, oppressor*); (of wind) begin to blow (more strongly); **gorge** or **stomach rises,** indignation or disgust is felt; *my whole soul* **rises against it,** finds it intolerable. **3.** Come or go up, grow upwards, ascend, mount, soar, project or swell upwards, become higher, reach higher position or level or amount, increase, incline upwards, come to surface, become or be visible above or *above* surroundings or horizon, develop greater energy or intensity, be progressive, (*sun, star, morning, dawn, rises; the risen sun; smoke rises straight up; balloon rises from the ground; picture* or *idea rises before the mind; river, tide, flood, level, has risen considerably, is rising; temperatures, prices, demands, rise; a man likely to rise in his profession, to greatness; rises in a gentle curve; followed its progress with rising interest; bubbles rise; castle rises in the foreground; does not rise above mediocrity*); (of tree etc.) attain (specified height); (of blister etc.) form; (of bread etc.) swell by action of yeast etc.; (of person's spirits) become more cheerful; (of barometer etc.) show higher atmospheric pressure; (of fish) come to surface to feed; (of person's facial colour) become brighter or deeper; (of theatre curtain) be moved away to reveal scene; ~ **above,** be superior to (petty feelings etc.); *rise from the* RANK¹*s*; ~ **in the world,** attain higher social position; ~ **to,** develop powers equal to (occasion etc.). **4.** Have origin, begin to be or flow *from, in, at,* etc., (*river rises from a spring, in the Grampians,* etc.; *earth and heaven rose at His word; the difficulty rises from misapprehension*). **5.** (poet.) Arise (*a feud, rumour, rose*). [OE *rīsan,* = OS, OHG *rīsan,* ON *rísa,* Goth. *-reisan* f. Gmc]

rīse² (-z) *n.* **1.** Act or manner of rising; *going up of theatre curtain. **2.** Ascent, upward slope, knoll, hill, (*came to a rise in the road; chapel stands on a rise*). **3.** Social advancement, upward progress, increase in power, rank, value, price, amount, height, pitch, ||wages, etc., (*the rise and fall of statesmen; the rise of the tide is 30 ft.*); **on the** ~, increasing. **4.** Movement of fish to surface (*not a sign of a rise*); **get** or **take a ~ out of,** (fig.) draw (person) into display of temper or characteristic behaviour. **5.** Vertical height of step, arch, incline, etc.; = foll. 2. **6.** Origin, start, (*has* or *takes its rise in* or *from*; **give ~ to,** cause, induce, suggest). [f. prec.]

rī'ser (-z-) *n.* **1.** In vbl senses. **2.** Vertical piece between treads of staircase. **3.** Vertical pipe for flow of liquid or gas. [ME, f. RISE¹ + -ER¹]

rĭ'shĭ *n.* Hindu sage or saint. [f. Skr. *rishi*]

rĭ'sĭble (-z-) *a.* **1.** Inclined to laugh; hence **rĭsibi'lity** (-z-) *n.* **2.** Of laughter (*risible nerves, faculties,* etc.). **3.** Laughable, ludicrous. [f. LL *risibilis* f. L *ridēre ris-* laugh; see -IBLE]

rī'sĭng¹ (-z-) *n.* In vbl senses; resurrection; insurrection, revolt; boil, pimple. [f. RISE¹ + -ING¹]

rī'sĭng² (-z-) *a.* In vbl senses; advancing to maturity (*the rising generation*) or high standing (*a rising young lawyer*); approaching (specified age); (of ground) sloping upwards; ~ **butt** or **hinge** (raising door as it opens). [f. RISE¹ + -ING²]

rĭsk *n.,* & *v.t.* **1.** *n.* Hazard, chance of or *of* bad consequences, loss, etc., exposure to mischance, (*there is the risk of his catching cold; at the risk of his life*); **at** ~, exposed to danger; **at** person's ~, with him to bear any loss etc. resulting; **run ~s, a ~, the ~,** expose oneself or be exposed to loss etc. (*of*); **take ~s** etc., expose oneself so. **2.** Amount of insurance; person or thing insured or otherwise representing source of risk; **~-money,** allowance to cashier to cover accidental deficits. **3.** Hence ~'FUL, ~'LESS, *adjs.* **4.** *v.t.* Expose to chance of injury or loss; venture on, accept the chance of, (*risk the jump, a battle, a sprained ankle*). [f. F *risque(r)* f. It. *risco* danger, *riscare* run into danger]

rĭ'sk|ȳ *a.* **1.** Hazardous, full of risk. **2.** *Risqué.* **3.** Hence ~ĭLY² *adv.,* ~ĭNESS *n.* [f. prec. + -Y²]

Rĭsorgĭmĕ'ntō *n.* Movement in mid 19th c. to unite and liberate Italy. [It., = resurrection]

rĭsŏ'ttō (-z-) *n.* (*pl.* **~s**). Italian dish of rice with stock, meat, onions, etc. [It.]

risqué (rĭ'skā) *a.* (Of story etc.) slightly indecent. [F, p.p. of *risquer* RISK]

rĭ'ssōle *n.* Fried ball or cake of meat or fish mixed with bread-crumbs etc. or enclosed in pastry. [F, f. OF *ruissole, roussole* f. Rom. **russeola* (*pasta* paste) fem. of LL *russeolus* reddish f. L *russus* red]

rĭtardă'nd|ō (rē-) *adv., a.,* & *n.* (*pl.* **~os** *or* **~i**). (Mus.) = RALLENTANDO. [It.]

rīte *n.* (Form of procedure, action required or usual, in) a religious or solemn observance (*the rites of hospitality; the rite of confirmation; burial* or *funeral rites*; **conjugal** or **nuptial ~s,** (arch.) sexual intercourse between husband and wife); (body of usages characteristic of) part of a Church (LATIN *rite*); ~ **of passage** (used when person reaches new status in life, e.g. adolescence or marriage); hence ~'LESS (-tl-) *a.* [ME, f. OF *rit(e)* or f. L *ritus* (religious) usage]

ritĕnu't|ō (rētĕnōō'tō) *adv., a.,* & *n.* (*pl.* **~os** *or* **~i**). (Mus.) (Passage performed) with immediate reduction of speed. [It.]

rĭtŏrnĕ'llō *n.* (*pl.* **~os,** *or* **~i** *pr.* -ē). (Mus.) Short instrumental refrain, interlude, etc., in vocal work. [It., dim. of *ritorno* RETURN²]

rĭ'tūal *a.* & *n.* **1.** *a.* Of, with, consisting in, involving, religious or other rites; ~ **murder,** sacrifice of person to god(s); hence ~LY² *adv.* **2.** *n.* Prescribed order of performing religious etc. rites; book containing this; performance of ritual acts, whence (w. implication of excess) ~ISM (3), ~IST (2), *ns.* **~ĭ'stic** *a.,* ~IZE (2, 3) *v.i.* & *t.* [f. L *ritualis* (as RITE; see -AL)]

rĭ'tzȳ (-tsĭ) *a.* (colloq.) High-class, luxurious; ostentatiously smart. [f. *Ritz,* name of luxurious hotels f. C. *Ritz,* Swiss hotel-owner d. 1918 + -Y²]

rĭ'vage *n.* (poet.) Coast, shore, bank. [ME f. OF (*rive* f. L *ripa* bank; see -AGE)]

rĭ'val *n., attrib. a.,* & *v.* (||-ll-). **1.** *n.* Person's competitor for some prize (esp. another's love) or in some activity or quality; thing that equals another in quality; hence ~RY (2, 4), ~SHIP, *ns.* **2.** *a.* That is a rival or are rivals. **3.** *v.t.* Vie with, be comparable to, seem or claim to be as good etc. as. **4.** *v.i.* (arch.) Be in rivalry. [f. L *rivalis* (*rivus* stream; see -AL), orig. = using same stream]

rīve *v.* (**~d; ~'n** *pr.* rĭ'ven). **1.** *v.t.* (arch. or poet.) Rend, cleave, wrench *away* or *off* or *from,* strike asunder, tear with hands or claws. **2.** (Of workman) split (wood, stone), make (laths etc.) by splitting. **3.** *v.i.* Be split, gape under blow etc.; (of wood etc.) admit of being split. [ME, f. ON *rífa*]

rĭ'vel *v.i.* & *t.* (||-ll-). (arch.) Wrinkle, crumple, shrivel. [ME, back form. f. *rivelled,* OE *rifelede* app. f. **rifel* a wrinkle + -ED²]

rĭ'ven. See RIVE.

rī'ver¹ *n.* In vbl senses. [f. RIVE + -ER¹ (1)]

rĭ'ver² *n.* & *a.* **1.** *n.* Copious stream of water flowing in channel to sea or lake or marsh or another river (||*the river Thames,* **the Thames river*); copious flow or stream *of* (*a river of lava*; **~s of blood,** much bloodshed); **sell down the ~,** (colloq.) defraud or betray; ***up the ~,** (colloq.) into or in prison. **2.** *a.* (In names of animals, plants, and things) living in, situated or used on, river(s). **3.** *~ **bottom,** low-lying land beside river; **~-god,** mythological being dwelling in and personifying a river; **~-head,** source of river; **~-horse,** hippopotamus; **~-side,** ground along bank of river. **4.** Hence (-)~ED² (-*erd*), ~LESS, *adjs.* [ME, f. AF *river(e)*, OF *riviere* river (bank) f. Rom. **riparia* (*terra* land) fem. of L *riparius* (see RIPARIAN)]

rĭ'verain *a.* & *n.* **1.** *a.* Of river or its neighbourhood; situated or dwelling by river. **2.** *n.* Person dwelling by river. [F (*rivière*, as prec.)]

rĭ'verīne *a.* Of or on river or its banks, riparian. [f. RIVER² + -INE¹]

rĭ'vėt *n.*, & *v.t.* **1.** *n.* Nail or bolt for holding together metal plates etc., its headless end being beaten out or pressed down after passing through two holes. **2.** *v.t.* Clench (bolt etc.); join or fasten with rivets (*together*, *down*, etc.); fix, make immovable; concentrate, direct intently, (eyes, attention, etc., *on* or *upon*); engross (attention), engross attention of; hence ~ER¹ (1, 2) *n.* [ME f. OF (*river* clench, of unkn. orig.)]

rĭvier'a (-ār'*a*) *n.* Region with climate and scenery like that of the Riviera region on coast of S.E. France, Monaco, and N.W. Italy. [It., = sea-shore]

rĭ'vière (-ĭār; *or* rēvyār') *n.* Gem necklace, esp. of more than one string. [F, = RIVER²]

rĭ'vūlėt *n.* Small stream. [f. obs. *riveret* (F, dim. of *rivière* RIVER²), perh. after It. *rivoletto* dim. of *rivolo* dim. of *rivo* f. L *rivus* stream; see -LET]

||**R.L.** *abbr.* Rugby League.

rly. *abbr.* railway.

R.M. *abbr.* Resident Magistrate; ||Royal Mail; ||Royal Marines.

rm. *abbr.* room.

||**R.M.A.** *abbr.* Royal Military Academy.

||**R.M.S.** *abbr.* Royal Mail Steamer.

r.m.s. *abbr.* root-mean-square.

R.N. *abbr.* *registered nurse; ||Royal Navy.

Rn *symb.* radon.

RNA *abbr.* ribonucleic acid.

||**R.N.A.S.** *abbr.* Royal Naval Air Service, Station.

||**R.N.L.I.** *abbr.* Royal National Lifeboat Institution.

||**R.N.(V.)R.** *abbr.* Royal Naval (Volunteer) Reserve.

R.N.Z.A.F. *abbr.* Royal New Zealand Air Force.

R.N.Z.N. *abbr.* Royal New Zealand Navy.

roach¹ *n.* (*pl.* same). Small freshwater fish (esp. *Rutilus rutilus*) allied to carp (**sound as a ~,** in first-rate health etc.); **~-backed, ~-bellied,** (convex in profile). [ME, f. OF *roc(h)e*, of unkn. orig.]

roach² *n.* (Naut.) Upward curve in foot of square sail. [18th c.; orig. unkn.]

***roach³** *n.* Cockroach; (sl.) marijuana cigarette. [abbr.]

road¹ *n.* **1.** (usu. in *pl.*) Piece of water near shore in which ships can ride at anchor. **2.** Line of communication, esp. specially prepared track, between places for use of pedestrians, riders, and vehicles (**by ~,** using transport along roads; **one for the ~,** (colloq.) final drink before departure; **on the ~,** travelling, esp. as a commercial traveller, itinerant performer, or vagrant; **take the ~,** set out; ||**take to the ~,** (arch.) become highwayman); **rule of the ~,** custom regulating side to be taken by vehicles, riders, or ships, meeting or passing each other. **3.** Way of getting *to* (*the road to York*, *ruin*, *success*); (as name of thoroughfare) *York Road*, *Graham Road*; **royal ~ to,** way of attaining without trouble. **4.** Underground passage in mine; *railway. **5.** One's way or route; **in the, my,** etc., **~,** (colloq.) obstructing someone or something; **get out of the, my,** etc., **~,** (colloq.) cease to obstruct. **6. ~-bed,** (1) foundation structure of a railway, (2) whole material laid down of an ordinary road, (3) *part of road on which vehicles travel; **~-block,** obstruction on road set up by army or police to stop traffic for questioning etc.; **~-book** (describing roads of country etc.); ||**~ fund** (Hist., for construction and maintenance of roads and bridges); ||**~ fund licence,** (colloq.) vehicle excise tax certificate; **~-hog,** reckless or inconsiderate (*esp. obstructive) motorist or cyclist; **~-holding,** stability of moving vehicle; **~-house,** inn or club on main road in country district; **~'man** (repairing roads); **~-map** (showing roads of a country or area); **~-metal,** broken stone for road-making or railway ballast; **~'runner,** bird of New Mexico etc. like cuckoo, able to run quickly; **~ sense,** capacity for safe behaviour on the road, esp. in traffic; **~ show,** theatrical performance by company on tour; **~'side,** border of road; **~ sign** (giving information to drivers etc.); **~'stead** (= sense 1); **~ test** (of vehicle by use on road); **~'way,** road, central part of road (opp. footpath at side), part of bridge or railway used for traffic; **~-works,** construction or repair of roads; **~'worthy,** fit to be used on the road, (of person) fit to travel. **7.** Hence ~'LESS *a.* [OE *rād* (*rīdan* RIDE), = MDu. *rēd*, ON *reith*]

road² *v.t.* (Of dog) follow up (game-bird, or abs.) by scent of trail. [19th c.; orig. unkn.]

roa'dster *n.* Open car without rear seats; horse or bicycle for use on the road. [f. ROAD¹ + -STER]

roam *v.* & *n.* **1.** *v.i.* Ramble, wander. **2.** *v.t.* Walk or travel unsystematically over or through or about (country, seas). **3.** *n.* Act of roaming, ramble. [ME; orig. unkn.]

roan¹ *a.* & *n.* **1.** *a.* (Of animal) with coat of which the prevailing colour is thickly interspersed with another, esp. bay or sorrel or chestnut mixed with white or grey (*red roan*; **blue ~,** black mixed with white; **strawberry ~,** red mixed with white or grey). **2.** *n.* Roan horse or cow. [OF, of unkn. orig.]

roan² *n.* Soft sheepskin leather used in bookbinding as substitute for morocco. [ME, perh. f. *Roan*, old name of *Rouen* in N. France]

roar *v.* & *n.* **1.** *v.i.*, & *n.* (Utter, send forth) loud deep hoarse sound (as) of lion, person(s) in pain or rage or excitement, the sea, thunder, cannon, engine, furnace, etc., (*the roar of the waves*; *lions roaring after their prey*; *roared with pain* or *for mercy*); (utter) loud laughter (**set table in a ~,** make company laugh loud). **2.** *v.i.* (Of horse) make loud noise in breathing due to disease; travel in vehicle at high speed with engine roaring. **3.** *v.t.* Say, sing, utter, (words, chorus, oath, etc., *out*) in loud tone. **4.** Hence ~'ER¹ *n.* [OE *rārian*, = MDu. *reeren*, MLG *rāren*, *rēren*, OHG *rērēn*, of imit. orig.]

roar'ĭng *a.* & *adv.* **1.** *a.* In vbl senses; riotous, noisy; boisterous, brisk, (*do a roaring business* or *trade*); **~ forties** (see FORTY); **the ~ game,** curling. **2.** *adv.* ~ (very) **drunk.** [f. prec. + -ING²]

roast *v.*, *attrib. a.*, & *n.* **1.** *v.t.* Cook (esp. meat) by exposure to open fire or in oven; heat or calcine (ore) in furnace; heat (coffee-beans) in preparation for grinding; expose (victim for torture, one*self* or some part for warmth) to fire or great heat; (in *part.*) very hot; ridicule, banter, chaff; *censure. **2.** *v.i.* Undergo roasting. **3.** *a.* (Of meat, potato, chestnut, etc.) roasted. **4.** *n.* Roast meat or a dish of it (RULE *the roast*); piece of meat for roasting; operation of roasting; *party where roasted food is eaten. [ME; n. partly f. OF *rost*, partly f. a. f. obs. p.p. of v., partly f. v. f. OF *rostir* f. WG **raustjan* (**raust(a)* gridiron)]

roa'ster *n.* In vbl senses; oven or dish for roasting food in; ore-roasting furnace; coffee-roasting apparatus; pig, potato, fowl, etc., fit for roasting. [ME, f. prec. + -ER[1]]

rŏb *v.t.* (**-bb-**). Deprive (person etc.) of or *of* property by (threat of) violence, feloniously plunder (person or place, *of*), deprive *of* what is due or normal; *rob* PETER[1] *to pay Paul*; (abs.) commit robbery; so **~'b**ER[2], **~'b**ERY (2, 4), *ns.* [ME, f. OF *rob(b)er* f. Gmc **raubh-*; cf. REAVE]

rōbe *n.* & *v.* **1.** *n.* Long loose outer garment; dressing-gown; baby's outer garment esp. for christening etc.; (often in *pl.*) longer outer garment worn as indication of wearer's rank, office, profession, etc., gown, vestment; *blanket or wrap of fur etc.; *wardrobe; ***~-de-chambre*** (rōbdeshah'ňbr), dressing-gown, wrapper. **2.** *v.t.* Clothe (person) in robe; dress. **3.** *v.i.* Assume one's robes or vestments; **ro'bing-room** (in which these are donned). [ME f. OF, f. Rom. **rauba* f. Gmc (as prec., orig. sense 'booty')]

rŏ'bĭn *n.* **1.** ~ (**redbreast**), small brown red-breasted European bird (*Erithacus rubecola*); *red-breasted thrush (*Turdus migratorius*); bird of similar appearance etc. to either of these. **2.** **R~ Goodfellow,** a mischievous sportive sprite in English folklore; **R~ Hood,** (type of) medieval forest outlaw; ROUND[1] *robin.* [ME f. OF, fam. var. of man's name *Robert*]

robĭ'nĭa *n.* N. Amer. tree or shrub of genus *Robinia*, e.g. locust-tree. [mod. L, f. J. *Robin*, 17th-c. Fr. gardener; see -IA[1]]

rŏ'borant *a.* & *n.* (Med.) Strengthening (drug). [f. L *roborare* (*robur -oris* strength); see -ANT]

rō'bŏt *n.* Apparently human automaton, intelligent and obedient but impersonal machine; machine-like person; (S. Afr.) automatic traffic-signal. [Czech (in K. Čapek's play *R.U.R.* (*Rossum's Universal Robots*) 1920), f. *robota* forced labour]

robŭ'st *a.* (**~er, ~est**). (Of person) having strong health and physique; (of animal, plant, body, health, etc.) not slender or delicate or weakly; (of exercise, discipline, etc.) tending to or requiring strength, invigorating, vigorous; (of wine etc.) full-bodied; (of equipment etc.) strongly built; (of intellect etc.) sensible, straightforward, not given to nor confused by subtleties; hence ~LY[2] *adv.*, ~NESS *n.* [f. F *robuste*, or f. L *robustus* firm and hard (*robus, robur* oak, strength)]

robŭ'stĭous (*or* -schus) *a.* Boisterous, self-assertive, noisy; (arch.) robust. [f. prec. + -IOUS]

rŏc *n.* Gigantic bird of Eastern legend. [f. Sp. *rocho, ruc* f. Arab. *ruḵ*]

||**R.O.C.** *abbr.* Royal Observer Corps.

rōcai'lle (-kī') *n.* 18th-c. style of ornamentation resembling artificial rocks or shells. [F (*roc*, f. as ROCK[1])]

rŏ'cambōle *n.* Species of leek used for seasoning. [F, f. G *rockenbolle*]

rŏche moutŏ'nnée (rŏsh mōōtŏ'nā) *n.* (Geol.) Small mass of rock shaped by glacial action. [F, = fleecy rock]

rŏ'chĕt *n.* Surplice-like vestment used chiefly by bishops and abbots. [ME f. OF, dim. f. WG (cf. OE *rocc*, OS *rok*, OHG *roch*, ON *rokkr*); see -ET[1]]

rŏck[1] *n.* **1.** Solid part of earth's crust underlying soil; sure foundation, support, or protection; mass of rock projecting and forming hill, cliff, etc., or standing up into or out of sea etc. from bottom (**the R~,** Gibraltar); (fig.) source of danger or destruction; **on the ~s,** (colloq.) (1) short of money, (2) broken down, (3, of drink) served with ice cubes. **2.** Hard compact material of which rock consists (*a mass, needle, of rock*); large detached stone, boulder; (Geol.) any particular igneous or stratified mineral constituent of earth's crust, including sands, clays, etc.; *stone of any size; *(sl., in *pl.*) money; (sl.) gem, esp. diamond. **3.** Hard usu. cylindrical sweetmeat made from sugar with flavouring esp. of peppermint. **4.** (**Blue**) **~,** = *rock-pigeon.* **5.** **~-badger,** S. Afr. hyrax; **~-bed,** base of rock, rocky bottom; **~-bird,** bird frequenting rocks, esp. puffin; **~-bottom,** (colloq., of prices etc.) very lowest (level); **~-bound,** (of coast) abounding in rocks; **~-cake,** bun with rugged surface; ***~ candy** (= sense 3); **~-cork,** light variety of asbestos; **~-crystal,** transparent colourless quartz usu. in hexagonal prisms; **~-dove,** = *rock-pigeon*; **~-drill,** rock-boring tool or machine; **~-fish,** rock-frequenting goby, bass, wrasse, catfish, etc.; **~-garden,** artificial mound or bank of stones with rock-plants etc. planted in the interstices, garden in which rockeries are the chief feature; **~-goat,** ibex; **~-hewn,** cut out of the rock; **~-hopper,** small penguin of genus *Eudyptes*; **~-kangaroo,** wallaroo; **~'ling** [-LING[1]], small fish of cod family found in pools among rocks; **~ lobster,** crawfish; **~-oil,** petroleum; **~-pigeon,** wild dove frequenting rocks, supposed source of domestic pigeon; **~-plant** (growing on or among rocks); **~-rabbit,** Syrian hyrax; **~-rose,** plant of genus *Cistus, Helianthemum,* etc.; **~ salmon,** ||(trade name for) dogfish, *amberjack; **~-salt,** common salt as solid mineral; **~-snake,** large python; **~-sucker,** sea lamprey; **~-tar,** petroleum; **~-tripe,** = *tripe-de-roche*; **~-whistler,** Alpine marmot; **~-wool,** mineral wool made from limestone etc.; **~-work,** rockery or rock-garden. **6.** Hence ~'LESS, ~'LIKE, *adjs.*, ~'LET *n.* [ME, f. OF *ro(c)que, roche,* med. L *rocca,* of unkn. orig.]

rŏck[2] *n.* (Hist.) Distaff. [ME, f. MDu. *rocke*, MLG *rocken*, OHG *rocko* or f. ON *rokkr*, f. Gmc **rukkon*]

rŏck[3] *v.* & *n.* **1.** *v.t.* & *i.* Move gently to and fro (as) in cradle, set or keep or be in such motion, (*rock him to sleep*; *ship rocking on, rocked by, the waves*; *sat rocking* (*himself*) *in his chair*). **2.** Sway from side to side, shake, oscillate, reel, (*earthquake rocks house*; *house rocks*); **~ the boat,** (colloq.) disturb equilibrium of situation. **3.** **~'ing-chair** (mounted on rockers, or with seat arranged to rock); **~'ing-horse,** wooden horse on rockers for child; **~'ing-stone,** poised boulder easily rocked; **~'ing-turn,** (Skating) turn from any edge to same in opposite direction with body revolving away from convex of first curve (**counter-~ing-turn,** same turn with body revolving away from concave); **~-shaft** (that oscillates about axis without making complete revolutions); **~-staff,** part of apparatus working smith's bellows. **4.** *n.* Rocking motion; spell of rocking; rocking or swinging music; ~ (**and** or **'n' roll**), (popular dance to) music with heavy beat and simple melody, often with blues element. [OE *roccian*, prob. f. Gmc **rukk-* move, remove]

rŏ'cker *n.* In vbl senses; one of the curved bars on which cradle etc. rocks (**off** one's **~,** (sl.) crazy); rocking-chair; skate with highly curved blade; switch pivoting between 'on' and 'off' positions; = ROCK[3]*ing-turn*; ||(in 1960s) leather-jacketed teenage motor-cyclist. [f. prec. + -ER[1]]

rŏ'ckerў *n.* Pile of rough stones with soil between them for growing rock-plants on. [f. ROCK[1] + -ERY]

rŏ'ckėt[1] *n.* (**Sweet**) **~,** plant of genus *Hesperis* grown for flowers; cruciferous annual plant (*Eruca sativa*) grown for salad; **dyer's ~,** = WELD[1]; **yellow ~,** winter-cress. [f. F *roquette* f. It. *rochetta, ruchetta* dim. of *ruca* f. L *eruca* downy-stemmed plant]

rŏ'ckėt[2] *n.* & *v.* **1.** *n.* Cylindrical paper or metal case that can be projected to height or distance by ignition of contents, used in firework displays, for signalling, to carry line to ship in distress, etc.; projectile containing its own propellant and depending for its flight on reaction due to continuous jet of rapidly expanding gases released in combustion of propellant, used to propel military warhead or spacecraft, whence ~EER', ~RY (5), *ns.*; rocket-propelled bomb etc. **2.** ||(sl.) Reprimand. **3.** *v.t.* Bombard with rockets. **4.** *v.i.* Move rapidly upwards or away. [f. F *roquette* f. It. *rocchetto* dim. of *rocca* ROCK[2], w. ref. to cylindrical shape; see -ET[1]]

rŏ'cklĭng. See ROCK[1] 5.

rŏ'ck|ȳ *a.* & *n.* **1.** *a.* Of rock; full of or abounding in rocks (**the R~y Mountains,** range in western N. Amer.); like rock in ruggedness, firmness, solidity, etc. **2.** (colloq.) Unsteady, tottering. **3.** Hence **~ĭLY**[2] *adv.*, **~ĭNESS** *n.* **4.** *n.* (in *pl.*) **The R~ies,** the Rocky Mountains. [f. ROCK[1] or (sense 2) ROCK[3] + -Y[2]]

rocō'cō *a.* & *n.* (*pl.* **~s**). **1.** *a.* Of a style of decoration prevalent in 18th-c. Europe, with scroll-work, shell motifs, etc. **2.** (Of furniture, architecture, etc., also of literary style) highly ornamented, florid; (arch.) old-fashioned. **3.** *n.* Rococo style. [F, joc. alt. f. ROCAILLE]

rŏd *n.* **1.** Slender straight round stick growing as shoot on tree or cut from it or made from wood, switch, wand, (occas. as symbol of office etc.); **divining, dowsing, -~** (see DOWSE[2]). **2.** Such stick, or bundle of twigs, for use in caning or flogging (**the ~**, use of this; **make** etc. **a ~ for** one's **own back,** prepare trouble for oneself; **kiss the ~**, take punishment meekly or gladly; **have a ~ in pickle for,** be ready to punish when time comes). **3.** = FISH[2]*ing-rod*; angler using this. **4.** (As measure) = PERCH[2] or square perch. **5.** Slender metal bar, connecting bar, shaft, (*curtain, piston*, etc., *-rod*); **ride the ~s,** *(sl.) travel illicitly under railway carriage. **6.** (sl.) Penis;* = HOT[1] *rod*; *pistol or revolver. **7.** (Anat.) Rod-shaped structure in retina etc. **8.** Hence **~'LESS, ~'LIKE,** *adjs.*, **~'LET** *n.* [OE *rodd*, prob. rel. to ON *rudda* club]

rōde[1]. See RIDE.

rōde[2] *v.i.* (Of wildfowl) fly landwards in the evening; (of woodcock) fly in the evening during breeding season. [18th c.; orig. unkn.]

rō'dent *a.* & *n.* **1.** (Animal) of the order Rodentia with strong incisors and no canine teeth (e.g. rat, mouse, squirrel, beaver, porcupine); ||**~ officer,** official rat-catcher; hence **rodĕ'ntIAL** (-shal) *a.*, **rodĕ'ntĭCIDE** (1) *n.* **2.** *a.* Gnawing (esp. Path. of slow-growing ulcers). [f. L *rodere ros-* gnaw; see -ENT]

rō'dėō (*or* -dā'ō) *n.* (*pl.* **~s**). Round-up of cattle on ranch for branding etc., enclosure for this; exhibition of cowboys' skill in handling animals etc.; exhibition of motor-cycle feats etc. [Sp. (*rodear* go round ult. f. L *rotare* ROTATE)]

rŏdomontā'de *n.*, *a.*, & *v.i.* **1.** *n.* & *a.* Boastful, bragging, (saying or talk). **2.** *v.i.* Brag, talk big. [F, f. obs. It. *rodomontada* f. F *rodomont* & It. *rodomonte* f. name of boastful character in *Orlando* epics]

rōe[1] *n.* (*pl.* **~s** *or* same). **~(-deer)**, small European and Asian deer (*Capreolus capreolus*); **~'buck,** male roe. [OE *rā(ha)*, = OS, OHG *rēho*, ON *rá* f. Gmc **raih-*]

rōe[2] *n.* **(Hard) ~**, mass of eggs in female fish's ovary; **(soft) ~**, male fish's milt; **~-stone,** oolite; hence **(-)rōED**[2] (rōd) *a.* [ME *row(e)*, *rough*, f. MLG, MDu. *roge(n)*, OHG *rogo, rogan*, ON *hrogn*]

roe'ntgen (rŭ'ntyen) *n.* Unit of ionizing radiation, amount producing one electrostatic unit of positive or negative ionic charge in one c.c. of air under standard conditions. [f. W. C. *Röntgen*, Ger. physicist d. 1923, discoverer of X-rays]

roentgenŏ'|graphȳ (rŭntyen-) *n.* Photography using X-rays; so **~LOGY** *n.*, radiology. [f. as prec. + -O- + -GRAPHY]

rogā'tion *n.* **1.** (Eccl.) (Usu. in *pl.*) litany of the saints chanted on the three days (**R~ days**) in **R~ Week** before Ascension Day and following **R~ Sunday; ~ flower,** milkwort of genus *Polygala*; hence **~AL** *a.* **2.** (Rom. Ant.) Law proposed before the people by consul or tribune. [ME, f. L *rogatio* (*rogare* ask; see -ATION)]

rŏ'ger *n.*, *v.*, & *int.* **1.** *n.* (sl.) Copulation. **2.** JOLLY[1] *Roger*. **3.** *v.t.* & *i.* (sl.) Copulate (with). **4.** *int.* (In signalling etc.) your message has been received and understood; (sl.) I agree. [man's Christian name *Roger*, used in signalling code for letter *R*]

rōgue (-g) *n.*, & *v.t.* **1.** *n.* Dishonest or unprincipled person; (joc.) mischievous child or waggish or arch person; **~s' gallery,** collection of photographs of known criminals etc. **2.** Inferior or defective specimen among many that are acceptable. **3.** **~ (buffalo, elephant,** etc.) wild animal driven or living apart from the herd and of savage temper. **4.** Hence **rō'guERY** (4) (-gerĭ) *n.*, **rō'guISH**[1] (-gĭ-) *a.*, (esp.) playfully mischievous. **5.** *v.t.* Remove rogues (sense 2) from. [16th-c. cant wd, of unkn. orig.]

roil *v.t.* Make (water etc.) turbid by stirring; perturb; vex, annoy. [perh. f. OF *ruiler* mix mortar f. LL *regulare* REGULATE]

roi'ster *v.i.* Revel noisily, be uproarious, (esp. in *part.* as *a.*); hence **~ER**[1], **~ING**[1], *ns.* [f. obs. *roister* roisterer f. F *rustre* ruffian var. of *ruste* f. L *rusticus* RUSTIC]

Rō'land *n.* **A ~ for an Oliver,** effective retort, well-balanced combat or exchange. [name of legendary nephew of Charlemagne celebrated with his comrade Oliver in the *Chanson de Roland*]

rōle, rôle, (rōl) *n.* Actor's part; one's function, what person or thing is appointed or expected to do; **~-playing,** behaving in accordance with specified function etc. [f. F *rôle* and obs. F *roule*, *rolle* = foll.]

rōll[1] *n.* **1.** Cylinder formed by turning flexible fabric such as paper or cloth over and over upon itself without folding (*rolls of carpet, paper*, etc.); similar structure of pastry etc. (SAUSAGE, SWISS, *roll*); (in Ionic capital) volute. **2.** Document, esp. official record, in this form (||**Master of the R~s,** one of the judges of the Court of Appeal and Keeper of the Records at the Public Record Office); register or catalogue (*in the roll of saints*; *a long roll of heroes*; *on the rolls of fame*; **~ of honour,** esp. list of those who have died for their country in war); ||the official list of qualified solicitors (**strike off the ~s,** debar from practising after dishonesty etc.); list of persons esp. soldiers or schoolchildren (**~-call,** calling over of this to detect absentees). **3.** More or less (semi)cylindrical straight or curved mass of anything however formed (*a roll of butter, film, hair, straw, tobacco*; *has rolls of fat on him*); *money, esp. as banknotes rolled together; (Archit.) moulding of convex section. **4.** Turned-back edge of something, e.g. coat-collar. **5.** Cylinder or roller, esp. to shape metal in rolling-mill. **6.** **~ (of bread), bread ~**, small loaf esp. for one person at one meal; **egg, ham,** etc., **~** (cut open and stuffed with specified food). [ME, f. OF *ro(u)lle* f. L *rotulus, rotula* dim. of *rota* wheel]

rōll[2] *v.* & *n.* **1.** *v.t.* & *i.* Move or send or go in some direction by turning over and over on axis (cf. SLIDE[1]) esp. to lower level (*roll barrel; barrel started rolling; ball* or *coin rolled under the table* or *into a hole; river rolls stones down; rolling stone gathers no* MOSS; hence **~ing stone,** person of unsettled habits); (cause to) start moving (as if) in this manner; (make) revolve between two surfaces (*rolling a marble between his palms*); (of time) progress smoothly; *throw (dice); *rob with violence. **2.** Change direction (of) with rotatory motion (*his eyes roll strangely; rolled his eyes on us*); **~-top desk** (with flexible cover sliding in curved grooves). **3.** *v.i.* Wallow, turn about in fluid or loose medium, (of horse etc.) lie on back and kick about, esp. to dislodge rider etc.; **~'ing in,** (colloq.) plentifully supplied with (money etc.); **~'ing,** (colloq.) very rich. **4.** *v.t.* & *i.* Sway or rock; walk with swaying gait as of sailor, reel; (of ship, vehicle, etc.) sway to and fro about axis in direction of travel. **5.** Undulate, show undulating surface or motion, go or propel or carry with such motion, (*sea, river, rolls; river rolls its waters to sea; waves roll in, smoke rolls up; chimney rolls up smoke; the mist rolled away; a rolling expanse* or *plain*). **6.** Utter or be uttered, sound, with vibratory or undulating or trilling effect (*roll out verses, song,* etc.; *thunder, drum, organ, echo, rolls; roll* one's *rs*). **7.** (Of vehicle or furniture) advance or convey on wheels etc. usu. *along, by,* etc., (of person) be so conveyed, (*carriage rolled along, rolled them by; he rolled past in his carriage*); ***~'away,** bed that can be folded up and moved away on wheels; **~'ing barrage,** = CREEPING *barrage*; **~'ing-stock,** railway or *road vehicles of a company. **8.** *v.t.* Flatten by passing roller over or by passing between rollers (*roll lawn, metal, pastry for pies,* etc.); **~ed gold,** thin coating so applied on base metal; **~'ing-mill** (for rolling metal into various shapes); **~'ing-pin,** roller for pastry; **~'ing-press,** (1) copperplate-printer's press with revolving cylinder, (2) press with rollers for various purposes. **9.** *v.t.* & *i.* **~ (up),** turn over and over upon itself into more or less cylindrical shape (*hedgehog rolls itself into a ball* or *rolls up*); *roll up* one's SLEEVES. **10.** Form in(to) cylindrical or spherical shape, or accumulate into mass, by rolling (*roll a cigarette, a huge snowball, snow into ball*); **~ed into one,** combined in one person etc.; **~'mop(s),** rolled flavoured pickled herring fillet; **~-neck,** loosely turned-over neck of garment. **11. ~ back,** cause to retreat or decrease; **~ in,** arrive in great numbers or quantities; **~ on,** put on or apply by rolling; **~-on** *n.*, (1) light elastic corset, (2) liquid deodorant etc. applied by means of rotating ball in neck of container; **~ over,** send (person) rolling or sprawling; **~ up,** (Mil.) drive flank of (enemy line) back and round so that line is shortened or surrounded, (colloq.) arrive in vehicle, (colloq.) appear on the scene, and see sense 9. **12.** Hence **~'**ABLE *a.* **13.** *n.* Rolling motion (*the roll of the sea, ship*); (Aeron.) complete revolution about longitudinal axis; spell of rolling (*a roll on the grass*); rolling gait; **~-bar,** metal bar strengthening motor-car roof or acting as protection in open-top car. **14.** Quick continuous-sounding beating of drum; long peal of thunder, prolonged shout; rhythmic flow of words. [ME, f. OF *rol(l)er, rouler* f. Rom. **rotulare* f. L *rotulus* (as prec.)]

rō'ller *n.* **1.** In vbl senses; cylinder of wood, stone, metal, etc., and of various proportions used alone or as rotating part of machine for lessening friction, smoothing ground, pressing, stamping, crushing, spreading ink or paint, rolling up cloth on, etc.; **~ (bandage),** long surgical bandage rolled up for convenience of applying; small cylinder on which hair is rolled for setting; kind of tumbler-pigeon; long swelling wave; brilliant-plumaged bird allied to hoopoe, breed of canary with trilling song, [G (*rollen* to roll)]. **2. ~ bearing,** bearing like ball-bearing but with small cylinders instead of balls; **~-coaster,** switchback at fair etc.; *roller*-SKATE[2]; **~ towel,** towel with ends joined, hung on roller. [ME, f. prec. + -ER[1]]

rŏ'llĭck *v.i.*, & *n.* **1.** *v.i.* Be jovial, indulge in high spirits, enjoy life boisterously, revel, (esp. in *part.* as *a.*). **2.** *n.* Exuberant gaiety; frolic, spree, escapade. [19th c., prob. dial.; perh. f. ROMP + FROLIC]

rōlў-pō'lў *n.* & *a.* **1. ~ (pudding),** pudding made of sheet of paste covered with jam etc., formed into roll, and boiled or baked; *tumbler toy; (Austral.) bushy plant that breaks off and is rolled about by wind. **2.** *a.* (Usu. of child) podgy, plump. [prob. formed on ROLL[2]]

Rŏm *n.* (*pl.* **~'a**). Male gipsy. [Romany, = man, husband]

Rom. *abbr.* Romans (N.T.).

rom. *abbr.* roman (type).

Romā'ic *a.* & *n.* (Of) the vernacular language of modern Greece. [f. Gk *Rhōmaikos* Roman (used esp. of Eastern Empire) f. *Rhōmē* Rome]

***romai'ne** *n.* Cos lettuce. [F, fem. of *romain* (see ROMAN[1])]

rō'majĭ *n.* Roman alphabet used to transliterate Japanese. [Jap.]

Rō'man[1] *n.* **1.** Citizen, soldier, native, or inhabitant, of ancient Rome, member of ancient-Roman State; inhabitant of medieval or modern Rome. **2.** (in *pl.*) Christians of ancient Rome. **3.** (Print.; *r~*). Roman type. **4.** = ROMAN CATHOLIC. [ME, f. OF *Romain* n. & a. f. L *Romanus* (*Roma* Rome); see -AN]

Rō'man[2] *a.* **1.** Of ancient Rome or its territory, people, or (arch.) language; surviving from period of Roman rule (*Roman road*); **~ alphabet,** letters A–Z as in W. European languages; *Roman* CANDLE; **~ Empire,** that established by Augustus 27 B.C. and divided by Theodosius A.D. 395 into Western or Latin and Eastern or Greek Empire, of which the Eastern lasted till 1453, and the Western, after lapsing in 476, was revived 800 by Charlemagne and continued to exist as the **Holy ~ Empire** till 1806; **~ holiday,** enjoyment provided by others' discomfiture; **~ law,** code developed by ancient Romans and forming basis of many modern codes; **~ nose** (with high bridge, aquiline); **~ numerals,** letters I = 1, V = 5, X = 10, L = 50, C = 100, D = 500, M = 1000 used in writing numbers (opp. *arabic numerals*); *Roman* SNAIL; **r~ type,** plain upright type used in ordinary print, opp. *Gothic* or *black letter* and *italic*. **2.** Of papal Rome, esp. = ROMAN CATHOLIC, whence **~**ISH[1] 2 *a.* **3.** Of medieval or modern Rome. **4.** Of kind ascribed to Romans of early times (*Roman honesty, virtue*). [ME, f. as prec.]

roman-à-clef (rōmahnahklā') *n.* (*pl.* ***-ns-*** *pr.* same). Novel in which real persons or events appear in disguise. [F, = novel with a key]

Rōman Că'tholĭc *a.* & *n.* (Member) of part of Christian Church acknowledging the pope as its head; hence **Rōman Cathŏ'lĭc**ISM (3) *n.* [17th c., transl. L (*Ecclesia*) *Romana Catholica* (*et Apostolica*), app. orig. as conciliatory term; see ROMAN[2], CATHOLIC]

romă'nce *n.*, & *v.i.* **1.** *n.* **R~ (languages),** the languages descended from Latin (French, Spanish, Italian, etc.); (*R~*) vernacular language of old France mainly developed but distinguished from Latin, corresponding language of Italy, Spain, Provence, etc. **2.** Medieval tale usu. in verse of some hero of chivalry [named as being written in Romance]. **3.** Prose or rarely verse tale with scene and incidents remote from everyday life, class of literature consisting of such tales; set of facts, episode, suggesting such tales by its strangeness or moving nature; atmosphere characterizing such tales, mental tendency to be influenced by it, sympathetic imaginativeness. **4.** Love affair viewed as resembling a tale of romance; love-story. **5.** (An) exaggeration, (a) picturesque falsehood. **6.** (Mus.) Short simple or informal piece. **7.** *v.i.* Exaggerate or distort the truth, esp. fantastically. [ME, f. OF *romanz, -ans, -ance* f. pop. L **romanice* in the vernacular (opp. *Latine* in Latin) adv. f. L *Romanicus* ROMANIC]

romă'ncer *n.* Medieval or other writer of romances; fantastic liar. [ME, f. *romance* v. (f. prec.) + -ER[1]]

Rŏ'manĕs *n.* Gipsy language, Romany. [Romany (adv.), f. as ROMANY]

Rōmanĕ'sque (-k) *n.* **1.** = ROMANCE 1. **2.** (Archit.) Style of art and architecture prevalent in Romanized Europe between the classical and Gothic periods, esp. in period 1050–1200, with massive vaulting and round arches. [F (*roman* ROMANCE); see -ESQUE]

roman-fleuve (rōmahṅflẽr'v) *n.* Novel with leisurely description of lives of members of family etc. [F, = river novel]

Rōmā'nĭan, Rumā'nĭan (rōō-), *n.* & *a.* (Native, inhabitant, or language) of Romania. [f. *Romania, Rumania* + -AN]

Romă'nĭc *a.* & *n.* **1.** (Of) ROMANCE 1. **2.** *a.* Descended from, inheriting civilization etc. of, the Romans; Romance-speaking. [f. L *Romanicus* (as ROMAN[1]; see -IC)]

Rō'manĭsm *n.* Roman Catholicism; (partiality for) things pertaining to the Romans. [f. ROMAN[1] + -ISM]

Rō'manĭst *n.* **1.** (usu. derog.) Roman Catholic. **2.** Student of Roman history or law or of Romance languages. [f. mod. L *Romanista* (as ROMAN[1]; see -IST)]

rō'manīz|e, -īs|e (-īz), *v.t.* Make Roman or Roman Catholic in character; put into Roman alphabet or roman type; hence ~A'TION *n.* [f. ROMAN[1] + -IZE, or f. F *romaniser*]

Rōmā'nō- *comb. form.* Roman (and) (*Romano-British*). [f. ROMAN[1] + -O-]

Romă'nsh, Rou-, Ru-, (ro- *or* rōō-; *or* -ah'-) *n.* & *a.* (Of) the Rhaeto-Romanic dialects, esp. that spoken in the Grisons, E. Switzerland. [f. Romansh *Ruman(t)sch, Roman(t)sch* f. med. L *romanice* adv. (as ROMANCE)]

romă'ntĭc *a.* & *n.* **1.** *a.* Characterized by or suggestive of or given to romance, imaginative, emotional, remote from experience, visionary, (*a romantic story, scene, adventure, girl*). **2.** (Of music) subordinating form to theme, imaginative, passionate. **3.** (Of project etc.) fantastic, unpractical, quixotic, dreamy. **4.** (Of literary or artistic method etc.) preferring grandeur or picturesqueness or passion or irregular beauty to finish and proportion, subordinating whole to parts or form to matter, (opp. *classic, classical*); hence ~IST (2) *n.* **5.** Hence **romă'nt**ICALLY *adv.*, ~ISM (2, 3) *n.*, ~IZE (2, 3) *v.i.* & *t.* **6.** *n.* Romanticist; (in *pl.*) romantic ideas or talk. [f. *romant* var. of ROMAUNT f. OF (*romanz* ROMANCE) + -IC]

Rŏ'manў *n.* & *a.* Gipsy; (of) the Indo-European language of the gipsies. [f. Romany *Romani* fem. and pl. of *Romano* a. (ROM)]

romau'nt *n.* (arch.) Tale of chivalry etc. [OF (see ROMANTIC)]

Rōme *n.* **1.** Roman Empire. **2.** Roman Catholicism; hence ~'WARD (-mw-) *adv.* & *a.*, ~'WARDS (-mw-) *adv.*, **Rō'mish**[1] *a.* (usu. derog.). **3. All roads lead to ~,** the place finally reached does not depend on the route chosen; **~ was not built in a day,** achievements take time; **when in ~ do as ~ does,** one should conform to others' practices when visiting them. [OE, f. OF & f. L *Roma* Rome in Italy]

rŏ'mneya (-nĭa) *n.* Shrub of genus *Romneya*, akin to poppy. [f. T. *Romney* Robinson, Brit. astronomer d. 1882 + -A]

rŏmp *v.i.*, & *n.* **1.** *v.i.* (Of children etc.) play about together, chase each other, wrestle, etc.; (colloq.) get *along, past*, etc., without effort, come *in* or *home* as easy winner. **2.** *n.* Child or (arch.) woman fond of romping, tomboy; spell of romping, boisterous play; hence ~'Y[2] *a.* [perh. var. of RAMP[2]]

rŏ'mper *n.* (in *sing.* or *pl.*) Young child's play-garment usu. covering trunk only. [f. prec. + -ER[1]]

rŏ'ndeau (-dō) *n.* Ten-line or thirteen-line poem with only two rhymes throughout and opening words used twice as refrain. [F, earlier *rondel* (see foll.)]

rŏ'ndel *n.* = prec., esp. of specialized form. [ME f. OF (*rond* ROUND[1]; see -LE 2); cf. ROUNDEL]

rŏ'ndō *n.* (*pl.* ~s). Piece of music with leading theme which returns from time to time. [It., f. F RONDEAU]

rŏ'ndure (-dyer) *n.* (literary). Round outline or object. [f. F *rondeur* (as ROUND[1]; see -URE)]

rōne *n.* (Sc.) Gutter to carry off rain from roof. [19th c.; orig. unkn.]

rō'nėō *n.* (*pl.* ~s), & *v.t.* (Reproduce on) machine for duplicating documents etc. from stencils. [P as noun]

rŏ'nggĕng (-ng-g-) *n.* Popular dancing and singing in Malaysia. [Malay]

rō'nĭn *n.* (Hist.) Lordless wandering samurai. [Jap.]

Rö'ntgen (rŭ'ntyen) *n.* **1. ~ rays,** X-rays. **2.** (*r~*). = ROENTGEN. [f. as ROENTGEN]

röntgenography etc. Var. of ROENTGENOGRAPHY etc.

rōō *n.* (Austral. colloq.) Kangaroo. [abbr.]

rōōd *n.* **1.** (arch.) The Cross of Christ (often in oaths, as *by the Rood*). **2.** Crucifix, esp. one raised on middle of rood-screen; HOLY *Rood Day.* **3. ~-arch** (between nave and choir); **~-beam,** cross-beam, usu. as head of rood-screen, supporting rood; **~-cloth** (veiling rood in Lent); **~-loft,** gallery on top of rood-screen; **~-screen,** wooden or stone carved screen separating nave and choir. **4.** Quarter of an acre. [OE *rōd*, = OS *rōda*, cross, & OE *rōd*, = OS *rōda*, OHG *ruota* rod]

rōōf *n.*, & *v.t.* **1.** *n.* Upper covering of house or building or room usu. supported by its walls (**under one ~,** in same building; **under** person's **~,** in his house, esp. w. ref. to hospitality; **go through, hit,** or **raise the ~,** (colloq.) become very angry; **a ~ over** one's **head,** somewhere to live); overhead rock in cave, mine, etc.; branches, sky, etc., overhead; top of covered vehicle; **~ of the mouth,** palate; **~-garden** (on flat roof of building); **~-rack,** framework to carry luggage etc. on motor-car roof; **~-top,** outer surface of roof; **~-tree,** ridge-piece of roof; hence ~'AGE (1) *n.*, (-)~ED[2] (-ft), ~'LESS, *adjs.* **2.** *v.t.* Cover (*in, over*) with roof, be roof of; hence ~'ING[1] (3) *n.* [OE *hrōf*, = OFris. *hrōf*, MLG *rōf*, MDu. *roof*, ON *hróf* boat-shed]

rōō'fer *n.* In vbl senses; maker or mender of roofs; ‖(colloq.) = COLLINS[1]. [f. prec. + -ER[1]]

roo'ĭnĕk (rō'-) *n.* Newcomer, esp. British immigrant, in S. Africa. [Afrik., = red-neck]

rōōk[1] *n.*, & *v.t.* **1.** *n.* Black hoarse-voiced European and Asiatic crow, nesting in colonies; sharper, esp. at dice or cards, person who lives off inexperienced gamblers etc.; ~-**rifle** (of small bore for rook-shooting); hence ~'LET, ~'LING[1], *ns.*, ~'Y[2] *a.* **2.** *v.t.* Win money from at cards etc. esp. by swindling; charge (customer) extortionately. [OE *hrōc*, = MDu. *roec*, MLG *rōk*, OHG *hruoh*, ON *hrókr* f. Gmc **hrokaz*, prob. imit.]

rŏŏk[2] *n.* Chess piece with battlement-shaped top. [ME, f. OF *roc(k)* ult. f. Arab. *rukk*, orig. sense uncert.]

rŏŏ'kerў *n.* **1.** (Clump of trees with) colony of rooks. **2.** Colony of penguins etc. or seals. **3.** (Hist.) Crowded cluster of mean houses or tenements. [f. ROOK[1] + -ERY]

rŏŏ'kĭe *n.* (sl.) New recruit in army etc.; *new member of team etc. [corrupt. of *recruit*, after ROOK[1] + -IE]

rōōm (*or* rŏŏm) *n.*, & *v.i.* **1.** *n.* Space that is or might be occupied by something, capaciousness or ability to accommodate contents, (*takes up too much room*; *there is plenty of room*; *we have no room here for idlers*; *not room to swing a* CAT[1]); space in or on (*house-room*, *shelf-room*); **would rather have his ~ than his company,** wish he was elsewhere; **make ~,** vacate standing-ground etc. or post etc. for or *for* another, clear a space *for* person or thing by removal of others; **~ for,** (arch. *imper.*) make way for (person); **in** person's **~, in the ~ of,** (arch.) instead of, in succession to, as substitute for. **2.** Opportunity, scope, *to* do or *for* (*room to deny ourselves*; *no room for dispute*; *leave room for evasion*); **there is ~ for improvement,** things are not as good as they should or could be. **3.** Part of house enclosed by walls or partitions, floor, and ceiling; (in *pl.*) set of these occupied by person or family, apartments or lodgings; persons present in a room; **leave the ~,** (colloq.) go to lavatory; **~ and board,** = BOARD[1] and lodging; **~-divider,** piece of furniture used to divide room into separate parts; **~-mate,** person occupying same room as another; **~ service** (of food etc. to hotel guest in his room); **~ temperature,** normal temperature of a room, about 20°C. **4.** Hence *~E'TTE *n.*, private single compartment in sleeping-car; ~'FUL 2 *n.*, -~ED[2] (-md) *a.* **5.** *v.i.* *Have room(s), lodge, board; **~'ing-house,** lodging-house; hence ~'ER[1] *n.* [OE *rūm*, = OS, OHG, ON, Goth. *rūm* f. Gmc **rūmaz* spacious]

rōō'm|ў *a.* Capacious, of ample size to contain; hence ~ĭLY[2] *adv.*, ~ĭNESS *n.* [f. prec. + -Y[2]]

rōōst[1] *n.* & *v.* **1.** *n.* Bird's perching or resting place, esp. hen-house or part of it in which fowls sleep; (fig.) sleeping-accommodation; **come home to ~,** recoil upon originator; RULE *the roost.* **2.** *v.i.* (Of bird or person) settle for sleep, be perched or lodged for the night. **3.** *v.t.* Provide with sleeping-place. [OE *hrōst*, = MDu. *roest*; cf. OS *hrōst* roof-spars]

rōōst[2] *n.* Tidal race in Orkneys and Shetlands. [f. ON *röst*]

***rōō'ster** *n.* Domestic cock. [f. ROOST[1] + -ER[1]]

rōōt[1] *n.* **1.** Part of plant normally below earth's surface and serving to attach it to earth and convey nourishment from soil to it, (in *pl.*) such part divided into branches or fibres; corresponding organ of epiphyte, part attaching ivy to its support, permanent underground stock of plant, small plant with root for transplanting; (in *pl.*, fig.) what attaches one emotionally to a place etc.; **pull up by the ~s,** uproot (lit. or fig.); **put down ~s, strike** or **take ~,** begin to draw nourishment from soil, (fig.) become established; **~ and branch,** thorough(ly), radical(ly); **strike at the ~(s) of,** set about destroying; hence ~'LET *n.* **2.** (Plant, e.g. turnip or carrot, with) edible root. **3.** (Bibl.) Scion, offshoot, (*there shall be a root of Jesse*). **4.** Embedded part of bodily organ or structure (*root of hair, tongue, tooth, nail,* etc.); part of thing attaching it to a greater or more fundamental whole; (in *pl.*) base (of mountain etc.). **5.** Source or origin (*of*; *love of money is the root of all evil*; *has its roots in the distant past*); **~ fallacy, idea,** etc., the one from which the rest originated. **6.** Basis, dependence, means of continuance or growth, (*has its root(s) in selfishness*; *has no root in the nature of things*). **7.** Bottom, essential substance or nature, (*get at* or *to the root(s) of things*); **has the ~ of the matter in him,** is essentially sound, w. ref. to Job 19:28. **8.** (Math.) Value of unknown quantity satisfying given equation; **~ of,** number or quantity that when multiplied by itself a usu. specified number of times gives (specified number etc.; CUBE *root*, SQUARE[2] *root*); square root; **~-mean--square,** square root of arithmetic mean of squares of a set of numbers; **~ sign,** = RADICAL *sign.* **9.** (Philol.) Ultimate unanalysable element of language, basis (whether itself surviving as a word or not) on which words are made by addition of prefixes or suffixes or by other modification. **10.** (Mus.) Fundamental note of chord. **11.** ***~ beer,** effervescent drink made from extract of roots etc.; **~-stock,** (1) rhizome, (2) primary form whence offshoots have arisen. **12.** Hence ~'AGE (1, 3) *n.*, ~'LESS (esp. fig.), ~'Y[2], *adjs.* [OE *rōt* f. ON *rót* f. Scand. **wrōt*- cogn. w. WORT and L RADIX]

rōōt[2] *v.* **1.** *v.t.* & *i.* (Cause to) take root or grow roots, fix firmly to the spot, establish, (*some kinds root freely*; *take care to root them firmly*; *fear rooted him to the spot*); (in *p.p.*) firmly established (*her affection was deeply rooted*; *rooted objection to*). **2.** *v.t.* Drag or dig up by the roots; **~ out,** exterminate. **3.** (poet.) Uproot, tear away, *from.* [ME, f. prec.]

rōōt[3], **rout**[2], *v.* **1.** *v.i.* (Of pig etc.) turn up ground with snout, beak, etc., in search of food; rummage (*among*, *in*). **2.** *(sl.) Be active *for* another by giving encouraging applause or support; hence ~'ER[1] *n.* **3.** *v.t.* Turn *up* (ground) by rooting; search *out*, hunt *up.* [earlier *wroot* f. OE *wrōtan* & ON *róta*; MLG *wrōten*, MDu. *wroeten*, OHG *ruozzen*]

||**rōō'tle** *v.i.* & *t.* = prec. 1, 3. [f. ROOT[3] + -LE 3]

rōpe *n.* & *v.* **1.** *n.* (Piece of) stout cord made by twisting together strands of hemp, sisal, flax, cotton, nylon, wire, etc.; *lasso; **the ~,** (esp.) halter for hanging a person; **the ~s,** (1) those enclosing prize-ring etc. (*on the ~s*, near defeat), (2) the conditions in some sphere of action (*know, show* person, *the ropes*); **give** person **~, ~ enough to hang himself, plenty of ~,** etc., not check him, leave him to bring about his own discomfiture; **on the ~,** (Mount.) roped together; **~ of onions, ova, pearls,** quantity of these strung together; **~ of sand,** delusive security. **2. ~-dancer, -dancing,** performer, performing, on tightrope; **~-ladder,** two long ropes connected by short cross-pieces as ladder; **~'manship,** skill in rope-dancing or rope--climbing; **~-moulding** (cut spirally in imitation of rope-strands); **~-quoit,** ring of rope used in quoits played on board ship; **~'s end,** short piece of rope used to flog (esp. sailor) with; INDIAN *rope-trick*; **~-walk,** long piece of ground used for twisting rope; **~-walker, -walking,** = *rope-dancer, -dancing*; **~'way,** cable railway; **~-yard,** rope-making establishment; **~-yarn,** (piece of the) material (esp. after unpicking) of which rope-strands consist, (fig.) mere trifle. **3.** Hence **rō'**PING[1] (6) *n.* **4.** *v.t.* Fasten or secure or catch with rope; (Mount.) connect (party) with rope, attach (person) to rope, (abs.) put on rope; enclose, close *in* or *off*, (space) with rope; ~ **in**, persuade to take part, decoy; hence **rō'pABLE**, ~ABLE, (-pa-) *a.*, (esp., Austral. sl.) angry. **5.** *v.i.* (Mount.) Climb *down* or *up* using rope. [OE *rāp*, = MDu. *reep*, MLG *rēp*, OHG *reif*, ON *reip*, Goth. *-raip* f. Gmc **raipaz*, **raipam*]

rō'pey. Var. of foll.

rō'p|y̆ *a.* **1.** (Of wine, bread, etc.) forming viscous or gelatinous threads; like a rope. **2.** (colloq.) Poor in quality. **3.** Hence ~ĭNESS *n.* [ME, f. ROPE + -Y[2]]

***rōque** (-k) *n.* Croquet played on hard court surrounded by bank. [alt. f. ROQUET]

Rŏ'quefŏrt (-kfŏr) *n.* Blue cheese orig. made from ewes' milk. [~ in S. France]

rŏ'quelaure (-kelŏr) *n.* (Hist.) Man's cloak reaching to knees. [F (Duc de *Roquelaure*, Fr. commander d. 1738)]

rō'quet (-kā *or* -kĭ) *v.* & *n.* **1.** *v.t.* Cause one's ball to strike, (of ball) strike, (another ball at croquet). **2.** *v.i.* Strike another ball thus. **3.** *n.* Act or fact of roqueting. [app. arbitr. f. CROQUET[2]; orig. used in same sense]

rŏr'qual *n.* Whale of genus *Balaenoptera*, with dorsal fin. [F, f. Norw. *røyrkval*, f. OIcel. *reythr* the specific name + *hvalr* WHALE]

Rŏr'schach (-shahk) *n.* (Psych.) ~ **test** (in which standard ink-blots are successively presented to subject for statement of what they suggest to him). [f. H. ~, Swiss psychiatrist d. 1922]

||**rŏr'ty̆** *a.* (sl.) Enjoyable (*had a rorty time*); fond of amusement and excitement. [19th c.; orig. unkn.]

rō'sāce (-z-) *n.* Rose-window; rose-shaped ornament or design. [F, f. L *rosaceus* (see foll.)]

rosā'ceous (-zā'shus) *a.* (Bot.) Of the large family Rosaceae, of which the rose is the type. [f. L *rosaceus* (*rosa* rose; see -ACEOUS)]

rōsă'nĭlĭne (-z-; *or* -ēn) *n.* (Red dye obtained from) organic base derived from aniline; fuchsine. [f. ROSE[1] + ANILINE]

rosăr'ĭan (-z-) *n.* **1.** Rose-fancier. **2.** (R.C. Ch.) Member of a Confraternity of the Rosary. [f. L *rosarium* ROSARY + -AN]

rosăr'ĭum (-z-) *n.* Rose-garden. [L (as foll.)]

rō'sary̆ (-z-) *n.* **1.** Rose-garden; rose-bed. **2.** (R.C. Ch.) Form of devotion in which five or fifteen decades of Aves are repeated, each decade preceded by Paternoster and followed by Gloria; book containing this; string of 55 or 165 beads for keeping count in this. **3.** Similar form of bead-string used in other religions. [ME, f. L *rosarium* rose-garden, neut. (as n.) of *rosarius* (as ROSE[1]; see -ARY[1])]

Rŏ'scĭan (-shĭ-) *a.* Like Roscius; eminent as an actor. [f. L *Roscianus* (Q. *Roscius* Gallus, Roman actor d. 62 B.C.; see -AN)]

rōse[1] (-z) *n.*, *a.*, & *v.t.* **1.** *n.* (Prickly bush or shrub bearing) a beautiful and usu. fragrant flower usu. of red or pink or yellow or white colour (BRIER[1]-, CABBAGE-, DAMASK, MONTHLY, MOSS-, MUSK-, TEA-, etc., *rose*), whence **rō'sERY** (3) (-z-) *n.*; flowering plant resembling this (CHRISTMAS *rose*, ROCK[1]-*rose*); ~ **of Jericho,** a resurrection plant (*Anastatica hierochuntica*); ~ **of May,** white narcissus; ~ **of Sharon,** St. John's wort, (Bibl.) flowering plant of unknown identity. **2.** ATTAR or *otto of roses*; **no bed of** ~**s,** difficult task or condition; **gather (life's)** ~**s,** seek pleasure; **path strewn with** ~**s,** life of delights; ~ **without a thorn,** impossible happiness, unalloyed delight. **3.** Rose-flower as emblem of innocence, beauty, etc.; **under the** ~, in confidence, under pledge of secrecy; **Wars of the R**~**s,** 15th-c. civil wars between Yorkists with white and Lancastrians with red rose as emblem. **4.** Representation of the flower in heraldry or decoration (esp. as national emblem of England); **golden** ~, ornament blessed by pope on 4th Sunday in Lent and sent as compliment to some R.C. sovereign, city, etc. **5.** Rose-shaped design, e.g. on compass card or on sound-hole of lute etc. **6.** Rosette worn on shoe or clerical hat. **7.** Sprinkling-nozzle of watering-can or hose. **8.** = *rose diamond*; = *rose-window*. **9.** Light crimson colour, pink; (usu. in *pl.*) rosy complexion (*roses in her cheeks*). **10.** ~**-apple,** tropical tree of genus *Eugenia*, cultivated for foliage and fragrant fruit, its fruit; ~**-bay,** oleander, rhododendron, or a willow-herb (*Epilobium angustifolium*); ~**-bowl** (for displaying cut roses); ~**-bud,** bud of rose, thing resembling it (*rosebud mouth*), pretty girl; ~**-bush,** rose plant; ~**-chafer,** green or copper-coloured beetle frequenting roses; ~**-colour,** rosy red, pink; ~**-coloured,** rosy, (fig.) optimistic, sanguine, cheerful, (*takes rose-coloured views*; *see things through rose-coloured spectacles*); ~ **comb,** flat fleshy comb of fowl; ~**-cut,** cut as a ~ **diamond** (hemispherical with curved part in triangular facets); ~**-engine,** appendage to lathe for engraving curved patterns; ~**-gall,** excrescence of dog-rose etc. made by insect; ~ **geranium,** pink-flowered species of *Pelargonium*; *rose*-HIP[2]; ~**-leaf,** leaf or usu. petal of rose (*crumpled* ~*-leaf*, slight vexation alloying general felicity); ~**-lipped,** with rosy lips; ~ **madder,** pale pink pigment; ~**-mallow,** hibiscus or hollyhock; ~**(-head) nail** (with head shaped like rose diamond); ~ **noble,** 15th–16th c. English gold coin of varying value stamped with rose; ~**-pink,** = *rose-colour(ed)* (lit. or fig.); ~**-point,** point lace with design of roses; ~**-red** *a.* & *n.*, red as (of) a rose; ~**-root,** plant (esp. *Sedum rosea*) with root smelling like rose when dried or bruised; ~**-tree,** rose plant, esp. standard rose; ~**-water,** perfume made from roses, (fig.) compliments, gentle handling, etc.; ~**-window** (circular, usu. with roselike or spokelike tracery); ~**'wood,** valuable close-grained cabinet wood of one of various kinds named from their fragrance. **11.** Hence ~'LESS, ~'LIKE, (-zl-) *adjs.* **12.** *a.* Coloured like a pale red rose, of warm pink. **13.** *v.t.* (esp. in *p.p.*) Make (face, snow-slope, etc.) rosy. [ME f. OE *rōse*, MDu. *rōse*, OHG *rōsa*, ON *rósa*, & f. OF *rose*, f. L *rosa*]

rose[2]. See RISE[1].

rosé (rōzā') *n.* Light pink wine, coloured by only brief contact with grape-skins. [F, = pink]

rō'sėate (-z-) *a.* Rose-coloured (lit. or fig.); ~ **spoonbill, tern,** (with partly pink plumage); hence ~LY[2] (-tlĭ) *adv.* [f. L *roseus* (as ROSE[1]) rosy + -ATE[2]]

rosĕ'lla (-z-) *n.* Brightly coloured Austral. parakeet of genus *Platycercus*. [corrupt. of *Rosehill*, N.S.W., where first found]

rō'semary̆ (-zm-) *n.* Evergreen fragrant shrub with leaves used as culinary herb, in perfumery, etc., and taken as emblem of remembrance. [ME, earlier *rosmarine* f. OF *rosmarin* or MDu. *rosemarine* or f. L *ros marinus* (*ros* dew, *marinus* MARINE), w. assim. to ROSE[1] and *Mary* name of the Virgin]

rōsē'ol|a (-z-) *n.* Rosy rash in measles etc.; German measles; mild febrile disease of infants; hence ~AR[1], ~OUS, *adjs.* [mod. var. of RUBEOLA f. L *roseus* ROSE[1]-coloured]

rosery. See ROSE[1] 1.

rosĕ'tt|e (-z-) *n.* Rose-shaped ornament for dress or harness made of ribbons, leather strips, etc., esp. as supporter's badge; (Archit.) (1) carved or moulded conventional rose on wall etc., (2) rose-window; (Biol.) roselike cluster of parts, markings resembling rose; = ROSE[1] *diamond*; roselike object or symbol or arrangement of parts; hence ~ED² *a.* [F, dim. of *rose* ROSE¹; see -ETTE]

Rŏsh Hasha'nah (-ah'na) *n.* Jewish New Year. [Heb., = beginning of the year]

Rōsĭcru'cian (-zĭkrōō'shan) *n.* & *a.* (Member) of 17th–18th-c. society devoted to occult lore (said to have been founded 1484 by Christian Rosenkreuz); (member) of later organization deriving from this; hence ~ISM (3) *n.* [f. mod. L *rosa crucis* (or *crux*), as Latinization of G *Rosenkreuz*, + -IAN]

rŏ'sĭn (-z-) *n.*, & *v.t.* **1.** *n.* Resin (esp. solid residue after distillation of oil of turpentine from crude turpentine); hence ~Y² *a.* **2.** *v.t.* Smear, seal up, rub (esp. bow of violin etc.), with rosin. [ME, alt. f. RESIN]

Rŏsĭnă'ntė (-z-) *n.* Worn-out horse. [f. Sp. *Rocinante* (*rocin* worn-out horse), name of Don Quixote's horse]

rosō'lĭō (-z-) *n.* (*pl.* **~s**). Sweet cordial of spirits, sugar, and flavouring. [It., f. mod. L *ros solis* sundew]

‖**RoSPA** *abbr.* Royal Society for the Prevention of Accidents.

rŏ'ster *n.*, & *v.t.* **1.** *n.* List or plan showing turns of duty or leave for individuals or companies esp. of a military force. **2.** *v.t.* Place on roster. [f. Du. *rooster* list, orig. gridiron (*roosten* ROAST), w. ref. to parallel lines]

rŏ'stral *a.* (Of column etc.) adorned with beaks actual or sculptured etc. of ancient war-galleys; (Zool. etc.) of or on the rostrum. [f. *rostr*ATE² or f. ROSTRUM + -AL]

rŏstrā'tėd *a.* (Of column etc.) = prec.; (Zool. etc.) having, or ending in, a rostrum. [f. L *rostratus* (as foll.; see -ATE²) + -ED¹]

rŏ'str|um *n.* (*pl.* **~a** *or* **~ums**). **1.** Platform for public speaking (orig. *rostra* in Roman forum adorned with beaks of captured galleys); pulpit, office, etc., that enables one to be heard by the public. **2.** (Rom. Ant.) Beak of war-galley. **3.** (Zool. & Bot.) Beak, stiff snout, beak-like part, esp. of insect or arachnid; hence ~ATE², **~ĭ'**FEROUS, **~ĭ'**FORM, *adjs.* [L, = beak (*rodere ros-* gnaw)]

rō'sў (-zĭ) *a.* Coloured like a pink or red rose (esp. of complexion as indicating health, of blush, wine, sky, light, etc.), (fig.) = ROSE¹-*coloured*; (arch.) smelling like a rose, made of or covered or strewn with roses; **~ cross,** supposed emblem of Rosicrucians; **~-fingered** (Homeric epithet of dawn etc.); hence **rō'sĭ**LY² *adv.*, **rō'sĭ**NESS *n.*, (-z-). [ME, f. ROSE¹ + -Y²]

rŏt¹ *n.* & *int.* **1.** *n.* Decay, putrefaction, rottenness; DRY¹ *rot*; hence *rot*-PROOF² *a.*, & *v.t.* **2.** (**The**) ~, virulent liver-disease of sheep. **3.** (sl.) Nonsense, absurd statement or argument or proposal, foolish course, undesirable state of things, (*don't talk rot*; *it is perfect rot to trust him*). **4.** Sudden series of (freq. unaccountable) failures (*a rot set in*; *must try to stop the rot*). **5.** *int.* (expr. incredulity or ridicule). [ME, perh. f. Scand.; cf. Icel., Norw. *rot*]

rŏt² *v.* (**-tt-**). **1.** *v.i.* Undergo natural decomposition, decay, putrefy, (~ **off,** drop from stem etc. through rottenness); (fig., of society, institutions, etc.) gradually perish from lack of vigour or use, (of prisoner) waste away (*left to rot in gaol*). **2.** *v.t.* Cause to rot, make rotten; ‖(sl.) chaff, banter, tease. **3.** **~-gut** *a.* & *n.*, (liquor) injurious to stomach etc. [OE *rotian*, = MDu. *roten*, MLG *röten*, OS *roton*, OHG *rōzzēn*; cf. RET, ROTTEN]

rō'ta *n.* **1.** List of persons acting, or duties to be done, in rotation; roster. **2.** (R.C. Ch.; *R~*). Supreme ecclesiastical and secular court. [L, = wheel]

rō'tarў *a.* & *n.* **1.** *a.* Acting by rotation (*rotary drill, pump*). **2.** *n.* Rotary machine; *traffic roundabout. **3.** *a.* & *n.* (**The**) **R~**, **R~ International,** world-wide society of business men with many branches (**R~ Clubs**) for international service to humanity, orig. named from members entertaining in rotation; hence **Rotār'**IAN *a.* & *n.*, (member) of Rotary. [f. med. L *rotarius* (as prec.; see -ARY¹)]

rō'tate¹ *a.* (Bot.) Wheel-shaped. [f. as ROTA + -ATE²]

rōtā't|e² *v.i.* & *t.* Move round axis or centre, revolve; arrange (esp. crops) or take in rotation; hence ~ABLE, **rō'**tATIVE, **rō'tat**ORY, *adjs.* [f. L *rotare* (*rota* wheel) + -ATE³]

rōtā'tion *n.* Rotating or being rotated; recurrence, recurrent series or period, regular succession of various members of a group in office etc., (*take office in* or *by rotation*); **~ of crops,** growing of different crops in regular order to avoid exhausting soil; hence ~AL *a.* [f. L *rotatio* (as prec.; see -ATION)]

rōtā'tor *n.* (Anat.) muscle that rotates a limb etc.; revolving apparatus or part. [L (as ROTATE²; see -OR)]

***R.O.T.C.** *abbr.* Reserve Officers' Training Corps.

rŏtch(e) *n.* The little AUK. [later form of 17th-c. Du., Fris. *rotge*, of unkn. orig.]

rōte *n.* **By** ~, by mere habituation, as knowledge got by repetition, from unintelligent memory. [ME, of unkn. orig.]

rō'tĭfer *n.* Minute aquatic animal of phylum Rotifera, with rotatory organs used in swimming. [f. mod. L *rotiferus* f. L *rota* wheel + -I- + -*fer* bearing]

rotĭ'sserĭe *n.* Establishment where roast meat is sold; cooking-device for roasting food on revolving spit. [f. F *rôtisserie* (as ROAST; see -ERY)]

rōtogravūr'e *n.* Photogravure printed on rotary machine. [f. ROTARY + PHOTOGRAVURE]

rō'tor *n.* Rotary part of machine; horizontally-rotating vane of helicopter. [irreg. for ROTATOR]

rŏ'tten *a.* **1.** Decomposed or decomposing, putrid, perishing from decay, falling to pieces or friable or easily breakable or tearable from age or use. **2.** (Of sheep) affected with the rot. **3.** Morally, socially, or politically corrupt, effete; ‖*rotten* BOROUGH; **something is ~ in the state of Denmark,** (Shak. *Hamlet* I. iv. 90) things are unsatisfactory. **4.** Inefficient, worthless; (sl., of state of things, plan, etc.) disagreeable, regrettable, beastly, ill-advised. **5.** **~-stone,** decomposed siliceous limestone used as polishing-powder. **6.** Hence ~LY² *adv.*, ~NESS (-n-n-) *n.* [ME, f. ON *rotinn*, cogn. w. ROT², RET]

rŏ'tter *n.* (sl.) One who is objectionable on moral or other grounds; useless or inefficient or disliked person. [f. ROT² + -ER¹]

Rŏ'ttweiler (-wī-) *n.* Dog of tall black breed. [G (*Rottweil* in S.W. Germany)]

rotŭ'nd (*or* rō-) *a.* Circular, round; (of mouth) rounded in speaking etc., (of speech, literary style, etc.) as from rotund mouth, sonorous, grandiloquent; (of person) plump, podgy; hence or cogn. ~ITY *n.*, ~LY² *adv.* [f. L *rotundus* (*rotare* ROTATE²)]

rotŭ'nda *n.* Building with circular ground-plan, esp. one with dome; circular hall or room. [earlier *rotonda*, f. It. *rotonda* (*camera*) round (chamber), fem. of *rotondo* round f. as prec.]

roturier (rŏtūr'ĭā) *n.* Plebeian. [F (*roture* newly broken ground, plebeian tenure, f. med. L *ruptura*; see RUPTURE, -IER)]

rou'ble, ru'ble, (rōō'-) *n.* Russian monetary unit. [F, f. Russ. *rubl'*]

roucou′ (ro͞oko͞o′) *n.* Annatto. [f. F *ro(u)cou* f. Tupi *rucu, urucú*]

roué (ro͞o′ā) *n.* (Esp. elderly) debauchee, rake. [F, p.p. of *rouer* break on wheel, = one deserving this]

rouge (ro͞ozh) *a., n.,* & *v.* **1.** *a.* **R~ Croix** (krwah), **R~ Dragon,** two pursuivants of English College of Arms; **~-et-noir** (-′ānwâr), gambling game with red and black marks on table for placing of stakes; **~-royal marble** (reddish Belgian kind). **2.** *n.* Fine red powder made orig. from safflower and used for colouring cheeks and lips; powdered ferric oxide etc. as polishing agent for metal etc.; JEWELLER'*s rouge.* **3.** *v.t.* & *i.* Colour, adorn oneself, with rouge. [F, = red, f. L *rubeus* cogn. w. RED]

rough (rŭf) *a., adv., n.,* & *v.t.* **1.** *a.* Having uneven or irregular surface, not smooth or level or polished, diversified or broken by prominences, hairy, shaggy, coarse in texture, rugged, (*rough skin, hands, paper, bark, road, cloth, country*); **~ edges,** edges of original sheets in book left untrimmed; **~ rice,** = PADDY[2]. **2.** Not mild or quiet or gentle, unrestrained, violent, stormy, boisterous, disorderly, riotous, inconsiderate, harsh, unfeeling, unpleasant, severe, grating, taxing, astringent, (*rough manners, soldier, play; rough water, sea, weather, wind; rough words; rough element of the population, quarter of the town; rough usage, handling; rough remedies; rough baritone voice*); (of wine etc.) sharp or harsh in taste; *rough* BREATHING; *rough* DEAL[2]; **~ luck,** worse than one deserves; *rough* MUSIC; **~ passage,** crossing over rough sea (lit. or fig.); **~ stuff,** (sl.) boisterous or violent behaviour; **~ tongue,** habit of rudeness in speech (**~ edge** or **side of** one's **tongue,** severe or harsh words); **~ work,** violence, task requiring use of force, (and in sense 3). **3.** Deficient in finish or elaboration or delicacy, incomplete, rudimentary, entirely or partly unwrought, merely passable, inexact, approximate, preliminary, (*rough nursing, style, welcome, kindness, accommodation, sketch; rough state, attempt, makeshift, circle; rough draft, estimate, translation*); **~ coat,** first coat of plaster applied; **~ copy,** (1) original draft, (2) copy of picture etc. showing only essential features; *rough* DIAMOND; ‖**~ grazing,** pasture in natural state; **~ justice,** treatment approximating to fairness; **~ shooting** (over unprepared land). **4. ~-and-ready,** not elaborate, just good enough, not over-particular, roughly efficient or effective; **~-and-tumble,** (*a.*) irregular, scrambling, disorderly, regardless of procedure-rules, (*n.*) haphazard fight, scuffle; **~′cast,** (*a.*, of wall etc.) coated with mixture of lime and gravel, (of plan etc.) imperfectly elaborated, (*n.*) plaster of lime and gravel for walls, (*v.t.*) coat (wall) with roughcast, prepare (plan, essay, etc.) in outline; **~-dry,** dry (clothes) but not iron them etc.; **~-footed,** (of bird) having feathered feet; **~-grind,** give preliminary grinding to (edged tool etc.); **~-hew,** shape out roughly, give crude form to, (in *p.p.*) uncouth, unrefined; **~ house,** (sl.) disturbance, row, horseplay; **~-house,** (*v.t.*) handle (person) roughly, (*v.i.*) make a disturbance, act violently; **~-legged,** (of horse or bird) having hairy or feathered legs; ***~′neck,** (sl.) a rowdy; **~-rider,** horse-breaker, man who can ride unbroken horses, (Mil.) irregular cavalryman; **~′shod,** (of horse) having shoes with the nail-heads projecting (*ride ~shod over,* treat inconsiderately or arrogantly); *rough-spoken* (see SPEAK); **~-wrought,** with the earlier processes of preparation done. **5.** Hence **~′**EN[6] *v.t.* & *i.*, **~′**ISH[1] 2 *a.*, **~′**LY[2] *adv.* (*roughly* SPEAKING[2]), **~′**NESS *n.* **6.** *adv.* In rough manner (*land should be ploughed rough; play rough;* see also sense 4); **sleep ~** (not in proper bed etc., esp. out of doors). **7.** *n.* Rough ground (*over rough and smooth*); (Golf) rough ground off the fairway between tee and green; spike etc. used to rough a horse; hard part of life, piece of hardship, (*take the rough with the smooth*); rowdy, hooligan; *the* unfinished or natural state, *the* general way, (*shape it from the rough; have seen it only in (the) rough; is true in the rough*). **8.** *v.t.* Turn *up* (feathers, hair, etc.) by rubbing against the grain (**~** person **up the wrong way,** irritate him); secure (horse or its shoes) against slipping by insertion of spikes or projecting nails in shoes; break in (horse); shape or plan *out* roughly; sketch *in* roughly; give first shaping to (gem, lens, etc.); **~ it,** do without ordinary conveniences of life; **~ up,** (sl.) treat (person) with violence, attack violently. [OE *rūh,* = MLG, MDu. *rū(ch),* OHG *rūh* f. WG **rūh(w)a*]

rou′ghage (rŭ′fĭj) *n.* Coarse fodder; indigestible material eaten in food to stimulate action of intestines. [f. prec. + -AGE (1)]

roula′de (ro͞olah′d) *n.* Florid passage of runs etc. in solo vocal music, usu. sung to one syllable. [F (*rouler* ROLL[2]; see -ADE)]

rouleau′ (ro͞olō′) *n.* (*pl.* **~x** *or* **~s,** *pr.* -z). Cylindrical packet of coins; coil or roll, esp. as trimming. [F (*rôle* ROLL[1])]

roulĕ′tt|e (ro͞o-) *n.* **1.** Gambling game on table with revolving compartmented wheel in which ball rolls randomly. **2.** (Math.) Curve generated by point on curve rolling on another. **3.** Revolving toothed wheel used in engraving; similar wheel for making slits between postage stamps, whence **~**ED[1] *a.*, divided thus. [F, dim. of *rouelle* f. LL *rotella* dim. of L *rota* wheel]

Roumansh. See ROMANSH.

rou′ncў *n.* (arch.) Riding-horse. [ME, f. OF *ronci(n),* med. L *roncinus, runcinus,* of unkn. orig.]

round[1] *a.* **1.** Spherical or circular or cylindrical or approaching these forms, presenting convex or circular outline or surface, (*the round world; round limbs, post, tower; round hole, mat, shield, table*); (of face) as broad as long; (of jacket) cut level below, without skirts; (of arch) semi-circular, not pointed; (of cheeks) plump, not hollow; (Phonet., of vowel) pronounced with rounded lips. **2.** Done with or involving circular motion. **3.** Entire, continuous, all together, not broken or defective or scanty, sound, smooth, plain, genuine, candid, outspoken, (**~ dozen, score,** etc., that and no less, so many together; **~ unvarnished tale,** the plain truth); (of sum of money) considerable; (of style) flowing; (of voice) not harsh; (of statement etc.) categorical, unmistakable. **4. ~-arm,** (Cricket, of bowling) with arm swung horizontally; **~ dance,** (1) dance in which couples circulate round ballroom, (2) dance in which participants form ring; **~ figure(s),** (1) round number, (2) figure given as estimate; **~ game** (for any number of players, with no teams or partners); **~ hand,** writing with bold curves; **~-hand,** = *round-arm*; **R~′head,** member of Parliament party in English Civil War [from custom of wearing hair close-cut]; **~-house,** (Hist.) lock-up or place of detention, (Naut.) cabin or set of cabins on after part of quarterdeck esp. in sailing-ship, *locomotive repair-shed, *blow given with wide swing of arm; **~ number,** number stated without odd units etc.; *round peg in square* HOLE[1]; **~ robin,** (1) petition esp. with signatures written in circle to conceal order of writing, (2) *tournament in which each competitor plays against every other; **~ shot,** (Hist.) spherical ball for smooth-bore cannon; **~ shoulders** (bent forward so that back is convex); **R~ Table** (at which King Arthur and his knights sat so that none might have precedence); **~-table conference** (at which all present are on equal footing); **~-top,** (orig. circular) platform round mast-head; **~ towel,** roller towel; **~ trip,** circular tour or trip, *esp. by same route out and back; **~ turn,** (Naut.) single turn of rope round post etc.; **~'worm** (of rounded form, opp. *flatworm*). **5.** Hence ~'ISH 2 *a.*, ~'NESS *n.* [ME, f. OF *ro(u)nd-* st. of *ro(o)nt, reont* f. Rom. **retundus* f. L *rotundus* ROTUND]

round[2] *n.* **1.** Round object (**this earthly ~**, the earth); rung of ladder; sandwich made from whole slices of bread; **~ of beef,** thick disc from haunch as joint; **~ of bread** or **toast,** slice cut across loaf. **2.** Solid form of sculpture etc. (opp. *relief*); **in the ~**, (fig.) with all the features etc. fully shown, all things considered, (Theatr.) with audience all round stage. **3.** Circumference, bounds, extent, *of* (*in all the round of Nature*). **4.** Revolving motion, circular or circuitous or recurring course, circuit, cycle, series, (*the earth in its daily* or *yearly round*; *a continuous round of pleasure*); group of houses etc. to which goods are regularly delivered; **the daily ~**, ordinary occupations of the day; **make** or **go** one's **~s**, take customary route for inspection etc.; **make the ~ of,** go round; **go the ~(s)**, (of news etc.) be passed on from person to person. **5.** (Mil., in *pl.*) Watch that goes round inspecting sentries or circuit it makes. **6.** (Golf). Playing of all holes in course once. **7.** (Mus.) Canon for three or more voices singing at same pitch or in octaves. **8.** Allowance of something distributed or measured out esp. to each member of a group, sequence of actions by each member of a group in turn, one of set or series, one spell of play etc., one stage in competition, (*serve out a round of drinks*; *fired several rounds at us*; *round after round of cheers*; *a fight of ten rounds*; *knocked out in the third round*; *the winners in the first round are paired for the second*); (Archery) fixed number of arrows shot from fixed distance. **9. ~'sman** (-z-), ||tradesman's employee going round for orders and with goods, *police officer in charge of patrol. [ME, f. prec.]

round[3] *adv.* & *prep.* **1.** *adv.* With more or less circular motion, with return to starting-point after such motion, with rotation, with change to opposite position, (lit. or fig.; *sun goes, summer comes, round*; *brings us round to winter*; *the* CLOCK[1] *round, all the year round*; *wheels go round*; *he turned* or *looked round when I shouted*; *soon won him round*); measuring (specified distance) in girth. **2.** To or at or affecting all or many points of a circumference or area or members of a company etc., in every direction from a centre or within a radius, (*tea was served* or *handed round*; *pass* or *send the* HAT *round*; *head goes round with giddiness*; *room hung round with portraits*; *spread destruction round*; *all the neighbours for a mile round*); ALL *round*; SHOW[1] *round*; **get ~ to,** eventually deal with (task etc.). **3.** By circuitous way (*will you jump over or go round?*; *go a long way round*); **ask** person **~** (out of his house into one's own); BRING *round*; COME *round*; *order car* etc. **~**, from garage to front door etc. **4. ~ and ~**, several times round; **~ about,** in a ring (about), all round, on all sides (of), with change to opposite position, circuitously, approximately (*it will cost round about £10*); **~'about,** (*n.*) circuitous way, ||place, esp. road junction, where all traffic has to follow a curved course, piece of circumlocution, ||merry-go-round (||*lose on the swings what you make on the roundabouts*, end without net profit or loss), (*a.*) circuitous, circumlocutory, plump or stout. **5.** *prep.* So as to encircle or enclose (*tour round the world*; *has a blanket round her*; *round the* CLOCK[1]). **6.** With successive visits to, at or to points on the circumference of, (*hawks them round the cafés*; *station them round the field*; *seated round the table*). **7.** In various directions from or with regard to (*diffuses cheerfulness round her*; *the fields round Oxford*; *shells bursting round me*). **8.** Having as axis of revolution or central point (*turns round its centre of gravity*; *write book round an event*); so as to come close from various sides but not into contact (lit. or fig.; *argue round and round a matter*). **9.** So as to double or pass in curved course, having thus passed, in the position that would result from thus passing, (*go, be, find* person, *round the corner*); **~ and ~**, several times round. [ME, f. ROUND[1], as prep. perh. f. AROUND]

round[4] *v.* **1.** *v.t.* & *i.* Give or assume round shape (*rounded eyes, mouth*); pronounce (vowel) with rounded lips; crop (ears of dog etc.); make (angle) less sharp; make (number etc.) round by omitting units etc. (**~ down, up,** do so by subtracting, adding, small amount). **2.** *v.t.* **~** (**off** or **out**), bring to complete or symmetrical or well-ordered state. **3.** Gather *up* (cattle, or transf.) by riding round, gather *up* (stragglers, criminals, etc.); hence **~-up** *n.* (lit., or fig. summary of events etc.). **4.** Pass round, double, (cape, corner, etc.). **5. ~ off,** (1) = sense 2, (2) blunt the angles of; **~ on,** make unexpected retort to (friend etc.), inform against. [f. ROUND[1]; in ME perh. after OF *rondir*]

round[5] *v.i.* & *t.* (arch.) Whisper (*rounded him in the ear*). [OE *rūnian* (= OS *rūnon*, OHG *rūnēn*) f. *rūn* RUNE; *-d* as in SOUND[2]]

rou'ndel *n.* Small disc, esp. decorative medallion etc.; circular identifying mark on aircraft etc.; rondeau or rondel. [ME, f. OF *rondel(le)* (as ROUND[1]; see -LE 2)]

rou'ndėlay *n.* Short simple song with refrain; (arch.) bird's song. [f. F *rondelet* (as RONDEL; see -ET[1]), w. assim. to LAY[1] or *virelay*]

rou'nder *n.* In vbl senses; complete run of player through all the bases arranged in a round as unit of scoring in rounders; ||(in *pl.*, treated as *sing.*) game with bat and ball between two sides. [f. ROUND[4,2] + -ER[1]]

rou'ndlỷ *adv.* In thoroughgoing manner (*go roundly to work*); bluntly, with plain speech, without qualification, severely, (*told them roundly that he would not*; *roundly asserts that it is true*; *was roundly abused*); in circular way (*swells out roundly*). [f. ROUND[1] + -LY[2]]

roup[1] *v.t.*, & *n.* (Sc. & N. Engl.) (Sell by) auction. [ME 'to shout', of Scand. orig.; cf. Icel. *raupa* boast]

roup[2] (ro͞op) *n.* Infectious poultry-disease, esp. advanced coryza, or fowl pox; hence ~'Y[2] *a.* [16th c.; orig. unkn.]

rouse[1] (-z) *n.* (arch.) Draught of liquor, bumper, toast, revel, drinking-bout; **take** one's **~**, carouse; **give a ~**, propose or drink toast. [prob. for *carouse*, perh. f. wrong division of *drink carouse*]

rouse[2] (-z) *v.* **1.** *v.t.* Startle (game) from lair or cover. **2.** Bring out of sleep, stir up or *up*, startle from or *from* or *out of* sleep or inactivity or confidence or carelessness (*to* action, *to* energy, *to* do, etc.); **~ oneself,** overcome one's indolence. **3.** Provoke temper of, inflame with passion, (*is terrible when roused*). **4.** Evoke (feelings). **5.** Stir (liquid, esp. beer while brewing). **6.** (Naut.) Haul vigorously *in, out, up*. **7.** *v.i.* **~** (**up**), cease to sleep, become active. [orig. as hawking and hunting term, so prob. f. AF; orig. unkn.]

rou'seabout (-za-) *n.* = ROUSTABOUT 2. [f. prec. + ABOUT]

rou'sing (-z-) *a.* Exciting, stirring, (*a rousing cheer, sermon, song*); (of fire) blazing strongly. [f. ROUSE² + -ING²]

Rousseau'|ism (rōōsō'-) *n.* (Adherence to) views of Rousseau regarding supremacy of the popular will and degrading effects of civilization; so ~IST (2) *n.* [f. J. J. *Rousseau*, Fr. philosopher d. 1778 + -ISM]

rou'stabout *n.* **1.** *Dock labourer, deck hand; *unskilled labourer. **2.** (Austral.) Odd-job man on farm etc. [f. dial. and U.S. *roust* rout out + ABOUT]

rout¹ *n.*, & *v.t.* **1.** *n.* Assemblage or company esp. of revellers or rioters, (Law) assemblage of three or more persons proceeding to unlawful act; riot, tumult, disturbance, clamour, fuss. **2.** (arch.) ||Large evening party or reception (**~-seat,** light bench hired for use at this). **3.** Disorderly retreat of defeated army or troops (**put to ~,** utterly defeat). **4.** *v.t.* Put to rout. [ME, f. AF *rute*, OF *route* f. Rom. **rupta* (*turba*) broken (company); see ROUTE]

rout² *v.i.* & *t.* = ROOT³; force or fetch *out* (*of bed* or from bed or house or hiding-place); hence ~'ER¹ *n.*, type of plane with two handles used to cut grooves etc. [var. of ROOT³]

route (rōōt, or Mil. freq. rowt) *n.*, & *v.t.* (*part.* **~ing** *pr.* -tĭ-). **1.** *n.* Course or way taken (esp. regularly) in getting from starting-point to destination; (Mil., arch.) marching orders; *delivery etc. round; ***~ man,** roundsman; **~ march,** training march of battalion etc.; EN ROUTE. **2.** *v.t.* Send, forward, direct to be sent, by a certain route. [ME, f. OF *r(o)ute* road f. Rom. **rupta* (*via*) fem. p.p. (as n.) of L *rumpere* break]

routi'n|e (rōōtē'n) *n.* & *a.* **1.** *n.* Regular course of procedure, unvarying performance of certain acts; (Theatr.) set sequence in dance or other performance; (Computers) sequence of instructions for performing a task; hence ~ISM (3), ~IST (2), *ns.* **2.** *a.* Performed by rule (*routine duties* etc.); hence **~eLY**² (-nlĭ) *adv.* [F (as prec.; see -INE⁴)]

roux (rōō) *n.* (*pl.* same). Mixture of fat (esp. butter) and flour used in making sauces etc. [F, = browned (butter; see RUSSET)]

rōv|e¹ *v.* & *n.* **1.** *v.i.* Wander without settled destination, roam, ramble; (of eyes) look in changing directions (**~ing eye,** person's tendency to ogle); **~ing commission,** authority given to person(s) conducting an inquiry to travel as may be necessary. **2.** *v.t.* Wander over or through. **3.** *n.* Act of roving (*on the rove*); **~-beetle,** long-bodied beetle of family Staphylinidae. [ME, orig. term in archery = shoot at casual mark with range not determined, perh. f. dial. *rave* stray, prob. of Scand. orig.]

rōve² *n.*, & *v.t.* **1.** *n.* Sliver of cotton, wool, etc., drawn out and slightly twisted. **2.** *v.t.* Form into roves. [18th c.; orig. unkn.]

rōve³ *n.* Small metal plate or ring for rivet to pass through and be clenched over. [f. ON *ró*, w. excrescent *v*]

rōve⁴. See REEVE³.

rō'ver¹ *n.* In vbl senses. [f. ROVE² + -ER¹]

rō'ver² *n.* **1.** (Archery) mark chosen at undetermined range; mark for long-distance shooting. **2.** Wanderer; (Croquet) (player of) ball that has passed all hoops but not pegged out; (*R~*) senior Scout (now *Venture Scout*). [ME, f. ROVE¹ + -ER¹]

rō'ver³ *n.* Sea robber, pirate. [ME, f. MLG, MDu. *rōver* (*rōven* rob cogn. w. REAVE; see -ER¹)]

row¹ (rō) *n.* **1.** Number of persons or things in a more or less straight line (**in a ~, in ~s,** so arranged); **in a ~,** (colloq.) in succession (*two Sundays in a row*). **2.** **~ (of houses),** street with houses along one or each side; ***~-house,** terrace-house. **3.** Line of seats across theatre etc. (*in the front, third,* etc., *row*); row of plants in garden (**hard ~ to hoe,** difficult task); horizontal line of entries in table etc. [ME *raw, row*, f. OE **rāw*, *rǣw* f. Gmc **rai(g)wa*]

row² (rō) *v.* & *n.* **1.** *v.i.* & *t.* Propel boat, propel (boat), convey (passenger) in boat, with oars etc. (**~ over,** WALK¹ over in boat-race; w. cogn. obj., *row a race, a few strokes, a fast stroke, 30 to the minute*); row race with; **~ down,** overtake in rowing, esp. bumping, race; **~ out,** exhaust by rowing (*the crew were completely rowed out at the finish*); **~-boat,** ||**~'ing-boat,** boat propelled by oars; **~'ing-machine,** device for exercising muscles used in rowing; hence ~'ER¹ *n.* **2.** *n.* Spell of rowing; excursion in rowing-boat. [OE *rōwan*, = MLG *rojen*, ON *róa*; cogn. w. RUDDER, L *remus* oar]

row³ *n.* & *v.* (colloq.) **1.** *n.* Disturbance, commotion, noise, dispute; **make, kick up, a ~,** (1) raise noise, (2) make vigorous protest. **2.** Shindy, free fight, (*town-and-gown row*). **3.** Condition of being reprimanded (*shall get into a row*). **4.** *v.t.* Reprimand. **5.** *v.i.* Make, engage in, row. [18th-c. sl., of unkn. orig.]

row'an (*or* rō'-) *n.* (Sc. & N. Engl.) **~(-tree),** mountain ash (*Sorbus aucuparia*); ***~(-tree),** *S. americana*; **~(-berry),** scarlet berry of these. [f. Scand., corresp. to Norw. *rogn, raun*, Icel. *reynir*]

row'd|y̆ *n.* & *a.* Rough and disorderly and noisy (person); hence **~ĭNESS, ~y̆ISM** (2), *ns.* [19th c. U.S., orig. sense lawless backwoodsman; orig. unkn.]

row'el *n.*, & *v.t.* (||**-ll-**). **1.** *n.* Spiked revolving disc at end of spur. **2.** Circular piece of leather etc. with hole in centre inserted between horse's skin and flesh to discharge exudate. **3.** *v.t.* Urge with rowel; insert rowel in. [ME, f. OF *roel(e)* f. LL *rotella* dim. of L *rota* wheel]

***row'en** *n.* (in *sing.* or *pl.*) Aftermath. [ME, f. ONF **rewain*, OF *regain* (as RE-, GAIN¹)]

row'lock (rŏ'- *or* rŭ'-) *n.* Pair of thole-pins or other contrivance on boat's gunwale serving as fulcrum for oar and keeping it in place. [alt. of earlier OAR*lock*, OE *ārloc* (OAR, LOCK²), after ROW²]

||**Row'ton** *n.* **~ house,** type of lodging-house for poor men, providing better conditions than common lodging-house. [f. Lord ~, Engl. social reformer d. 1903]

roy'al *a.* & *n.* **1.** *a.* Of, from, suited to, worthy of, in service or under patronage of, a king or queen (after *n.* in some phrs.: BLOOD¹ *royal*, PRINCE(SS) *royal*, RHYME¹ *royal*); belonging to the king or queen (*the royal anger, hands,* etc.); of family of king or queen. **2.** *Royal* ACADEMY (*of Arts*); **R~ Air Force,** air force of Britain or Commonwealth country; *royal* ASSENT²; ||**~ blue,** deep pure vivid blue; **~ burgh** (holding charter from Crown); ||*Royal* COMMISSION¹; *royal* DUKE; **R~ Engineers,** engineering branch of British army; **~ family** (to which sovereign belongs); *Royal* HIGHNESS; **R~ Institution,** British society founded 1799 for diffusion of scientific knowledge; **R~ Marine,** member of corps trained for service at sea and on land; **R~ Navy,** navy of Britain or Commonwealth country; **~ oak,** sprig of oak worn on 29 May to commemorate restoration of Charles II (1660), who hid in oak after battle of Worcester (1651); *Royal* REGIMENT; *royal* ROAD¹; *Royal* SOCIETY; **~ standard,** banner bearing royal heraldic arms; ||*Royal* VICTORIAN *Chain, Order*;

~ **warrant** (authorizing tradesman to supply goods to royal person). **3.** Kingly, majestic, stately, splendid; first-rate, on great scale, of exceptional size etc., (*royal magnanimity*; *gave us royal entertainment*; *in royal spirits*; *had a royal time*); BATTLE¹ *royal*; ~ **fern,** osmund; *royal* FLUSH⁵; ~ **jelly,** substance secreted by honey-bee workers and fed to future queen bees; ~ **mast, sail,** (above topgallant mast and sail); ~ **stag** (with head of 12 or more points); ~ **tennis,** = TENNIS 1. **4.** Hence ~LY² *adv.* **5.** *n.* Royal stag, sail, or mast; size of paper about 620 × 500 mm; (colloq.) member of royal family; **the R~s,** (1) the Royal Scots Regiment, (2) the Royal Marines. [ME, f. OF *roial* f. L *regalis* REGAL]

roy'al|ĭst *n.* **1.** Monarchist, supporter of monarch as an institution or of the royal side in civil war etc. **2.** *Die-hard, reactionary, (esp. *economic royalist*). **3.** So ~ISM (3) *n.*, ~**ĭ'st**IC *a.* [f. prec. + -IST]

roy'altў *n.* **1.** Office or dignity or power of king or queen, sovereignty; royal persons; member of royal family. **2.** Royal right (now esp. over minerals) granted by sovereign to individual or corporation; sum paid to patentee for use of patent or to author etc. for each copy of his book etc. sold or for each public performance of his work. [ME, f. OF *roialté* (as ROYAL; see -TY¹)]

||**Roy'ston** *n.* ~ **crow,** hooded or grey crow. [~ in Herts.]

||**rŏ'zzer** *n.* (sl.) Policeman. [19th c.; orig. unkn.]

||**R.P.C.** *abbr.* Royal Pioneer Corps.

r.p.m. *abbr.* resale price maintenance; revolutions per minute.

R.P.S. *abbr.* Royal Photographic Society.

***R.R.** *abbr.* railroad; rural route.

||**R.R.C.** *abbr.* (Lady of the) Royal Red Cross.

R.S. *abbr.* Royal Scots; Royal Society.

Rs. *abbr.* rupees.

R.S.A. *abbr.* Royal Scottish Academician, Academy; Royal Society of Arts.

R.S.D. *abbr.* Royal Society of Dublin.

R.S.E. *abbr.* Royal Society of Edinburgh.

R.S.F.S.R. *abbr.* Russian Soviet Federal Socialist Republic.

||**R.Sigs.** *abbr.* Royal Corps of Signals.

R.S.M. *abbr.* Regimental Sergeant-Major.

||**R.S.P.C.A.** *abbr.* Royal Society for the Prevention of Cruelty to Animals.

***R.S.V.** *abbr.* Revised Standard Version (of Bible).

R.S.V.P. *abbr.* (In invitation etc.) please answer. [f. F *répondez s'il vous plaît*]

R.T. *abbr.* radio telegraphy; radio telephony.

rt. *abbr.* right.

||**Rt. Hon.** *abbr.* Right Honourable.

Rt. Rev(d). *abbr.* Right Reverend.

||**R.U.** *abbr.* Rugby Union.

Ru *symb.* ruthenium.

rŭb¹ *v.* (-bb-) & *n.* **1.** *v.t.* Press one's hand or an object on and slide it along over or up and down the surface of; ~ one's **hands** (each with the other usu. in sign of keen satisfaction, or for warmth); ~ **noses,** rub one's nose against another's as primitive or animal greeting; *rub* person's NOSE *in it*; ~ **shoulders,** come into contact (lit. or fig.) *with* other people; ~ **(up) the wrong way,** stroke against the grain, irritate or repel as by stroking cat upwards. **2.** Polish, clean, abrade, chafe, make dry, sore, bare, etc., by rubbing. **3.** Reproduce design of (sepulchral brass or stone) by rubbing paper laid on it with coloured chalk etc.; hence ~**'b**ING¹ (2) *n.* **4.** Slide (hand, object) *against* or *in* or *on* or *over* something, (objects) together or *together*, with friction. **5.** Bring (stain etc.) *out*, (nap etc., or fig. novelty, shyness, etc.) *off* or *away*, force (liniment etc., or fig. lesson, humiliating fact, etc.) *in* or *into*, reduce *to* powder etc., force *through* sieve, bring size or level of *down*, spread (ointment etc.) *over*, dry (horse, one*self*) *down*, polish or brush (tarnished object, or fig. one's memory, Greek, etc.) *up*, mix (pigment, etc.) *up* into paste, by rubbing (lit. or fig.); ~ **it in,** (fig.) continue to refer to person's failure etc.; ~ **out,** erase with rubber, (sl.) kill. **6.** *v.i.* Come into or be in sliding contact, exercise friction, *against* or *on*; ~ **off,** be transferred by contact (lit. or fig.). **7.** (Of BOWL²) be retarded or diverted by unevenness of ground, (fig., of person, process, etc.) go *on*, *along*, *through*, with more or less restraint or difficulty. **8.** (Of cloth, skin, etc.) get frayed or worn or sore or bare with friction. **9.** ~**-stone,** (piece of) stone used for sharpening, smoothing, etc. **10.** *n.* Spell of rubbing (*give it a rub*, *rub-up*, *rub-down*). **11.** (Bowls) inequality of ground impeding or diverting bowl, diversion etc. of bowl by this; impediment or difficulty (**there's the ~,** that is the point at which doubt or difficulty arises). **12.** ~ **of** or **on the green,** (Golf) accidental interference with course or position of ball. [ME *rubben*, perh. f. LG *rubben*; orig. unkn.]

rŭb² *n.* = RUBBER³. [abbr.]

rŭ'b-a-dŭb *n.*, & *v.i.* (**-bb-**). (Make) rolling sound of drum. [imit.]

ruba't|ō (rōōbah'-) *a.* & *n.* (*pl.* **~os,** *or* **~i** *pr.* -ē). (Mus.) (Performed at) speed momentarily varied for sake of expression. [It., = robbed]

rŭ'bber¹ *n.*, & *v.t.* In vbl senses; masseur or masseuse; Turkish-bath attendant; implement used for, part of machine operating by, rubbing. [f. RUB¹ + -ER¹]

rŭ'bber² *n.* **1.** Elastic solid made from latex of tropical plants or synthetically and used in pneumatic tyres etc.; piece of this or other substance for erasing pencil-marks; (sl.) condom; *(in *pl.*) galoshes. **2.** ~ **band,** loop of rubber to hold papers etc. together; ~ **cheque,** (joc., cf. BOUNCE¹) cheque refused by bank because of insufficiency of money in account; ~ **goods,** contraceptives; ***~-neck** *n.*, & *v.i.*, (be) gaping sightseer or inquisitive person; ~ **plant,** plant yielding rubber, esp. *Ficus elastica* grown as ornamental dwarf; ~ **solution,** liquid drying to rubber-like material, used for mending rubber articles; ~ **stamp,** device for inking and imprinting on surface, (fig.) one who mechanically copies or agrees to others' actions, indication of such agreement; **~-stamp** *v.t.*, (fig.) approve automatically without proper consideration. **3.** Hence ~IZE *v.t.*, treat or coat with rubber, ~Y² *a.* [f. prec., through its use in rubbing out pencil-marks]

rŭ'bber³ *n.* Match of three successive games between same sides or persons at whist, bridge, cricket, lawn tennis, etc.; **the ~,** winning of two games in rubber, third game when each side has won one. [orig. unkn.; as term in bowls from *c.* 1600]

rŭ'bbĭsh *n.*, *int.*, & *v.t.* **1.** *n.* Waste material, debris, refuse, litter; worthless material or articles, trash; **good riddance (to bad ~),** (said esp. at departure of person one dislikes). **2.** *n.* & *int.* Absurd ideas or suggestions, nonsense (often as excl. of contempt). **3.** Hence ~Y², (colloq.) ~ING², *adjs.* **4.** *v.t.* (Austral.) Reject as worthless; criticize severely. [ME, f. AF *rubbous* etc., perh. f. **robeus* pl. of **robel* = foll.]

rŭ'bble *n.* Waste fragments of stone, brick, etc., from old houses; pieces of undressed stone used, esp. as filling-in, for walls; (Geol.) loose angular stones etc. as covering of some rocks; water-worn stones; hence **rŭ'bbl**Y² *a.* [ME *robyl*, *rubel*, perh. f. AF **robel* f. OF *robe* spoils; see ROBE]

***rube** (rōōb) *n.* (colloq.) Country bumpkin. [abbr. of *Reuben*]

ru'bĕfȳ, -ĭfȳ, (rōō'-) *v.t.* Make red; (Med., of counter-irritant) stimulate (skin etc.) to redness, so **rubėFA'CIENT** *a.* & *n.*, **rubėFA'CTION** *n.*, (rōō-). [ME, f. OF *rubifier*, *rubefier* f. med. L *rubificare* f. L *rubefacere* (*rubeus* red; see -FY)]

rubĕ'lla (rōō-) *n.* (Path.) Acute infectious virus disease with red rash, German measles. [mod. L, neut. pl. (as n.) of L *rubellus* reddish]

ru'bellīte (rōō'-) *n.* Red variety of tourmaline. [f. L *rubellus* reddish + -ITE[1] (2)]

rubē'ola (rōō-) *n.* (Path.) Measles. [f. med. L **rubeola* dim. (as n.) of L *rubeus* red]

Ru'bĭcon (rōō'-) *n.*, & *v.t.* **1.** *n.* *The* boundary by passing which one becomes committed to an enterprise (*cross the Rubicon*). **2.** (*r*~). Winning of game in piquet before opponent has scored 100. **3.** *v.t.* (*r*~). Defeat (opponent) thus. [ancient name of stream limiting Julius Caesar's province and crossed by him in 49 B.C. as start of war with Pompey]

ru'bĭcŭnd (rōō'-) *a.* (Of face, complexion, or person in these respects) ruddy, high-coloured; hence ~ITY (-ŭ'n-) *n.* [f. F *rubicond* or f. L *rubicundus* (*rubēre* be red)]

rubĭ'dĭum (rōō'-) *n.* Soft silvery element of alkali-metal group. [f. L *rubidus* red (w. ref. to spectrum lines) + -IUM]

rubify. See RUBEFY.

rubĭ'gĭnous (rōō-) *a.* Rust-coloured. [f. L *rubigo -inis* rust + -OUS]

ru'bĭous (rōō'-) *a.* (poet.) Ruby-coloured. [f. RUBY + -OUS]

ruble. See ROUBLE.

ru'brĭc (rōō'-) *n.* **1.** Heading of chapter, section, etc., special passage, or sentence, written or printed in red or in special lettering. **2.** Direction for conduct of divine service (prop. in red) inserted in liturgical book; hence ~AL *a.*, **rubrI'CIAN** (rōō-), ~ISM (3), ~IST (2), *ns.* **3.** Explanatory words; established custom. [ME, f. OF *rubrique*, *rubric(h)e*, or f. L *rubrica* (*terra*) red (earth, ochre) as writing-material, cogn. w. *rubeus* red]

ru'brĭc|āte (rōō'-) *v.t.* Mark with, print or write in, red; furnish with rubrics; hence ~A'TION, ~**ātor**, *ns.* [f. L *rubricare* (*rubrica*; see prec.) + -ATE[3]]

ru'bȳ (rōō'-) *n.* & *a.*, & *v.t.* **1.** *n.* Rare precious stone consisting of corundum with colour varying from deep crimson or purple to pale rose (**above rubies,** of inestimable value). **2.** *a.* & *n.* (Of) glowing purple-tinged red colour. **3.** ~ **glass** (coloured with oxides of copper, iron, lead, tin, etc.); **~-tail,** insect with ruby-coloured hinder part; ~ **wedding** (fortieth anniversary). **4.** *v.t.* Dye or tinge ruby-colour. [ME, f. OF *rubi* f. med. L *rubinus* (*lapis* stone), cogn. w. L *rubeus* red]

R.U.C. *abbr.* Royal Ulster Constabulary.

ruche (rōōsh) *n.* Frill or gathering of lace etc. as trimming; hence **ruchED**[2] (rōōsht) *a.*, **ru'chING**[1] (2) (rōō'sh-) *n.* [F, f. med. L *rusca* tree-bark, of Celt. orig.]

rŭck[1] *n.* Main body of competitors not likely to overtake leaders; (fig.) undistinguished crowd of persons or things. [ME 'stack of fuel, heap, rick'; app. Scand., = Norw. *ruka* w. same meanings]

rŭck[2] *n.* & *v.* **1.** *n.* Crease, wrinkle. **2.** *v.i.* & *t.* ~ (**up**), form ruck. [f. ON *hrukka* (**hrunka*)]

||**rŭ'ckle** *n.* & *v.* = prec. [f. prec. + -LE 3]

rŭ'cksăck (*or* rōō'-) *n.* Bag slung by straps from both shoulders and resting on back for carrying walker's or climber's necessaries. [G (*rucken* dial. var. of *rücken* back, *sack* SACK[1])]

rŭ'ckus *n.* = foll. [cf. foll. and RUMPUS]

rŭ'ction *n.* (colloq.) Disturbance, tumult, row. [19th c., of unkn. orig.]

rŭdbĕ'ckĭa *n.* Composite garden plant of genus *Rudbeckia*, native to N. America. [mod. L, f. O. *Rudbeck*, Sw. botanist d. 1740 + -IA[1]]

rŭdd *n.* (*pl.* same). Red-eyed freshwater fish resembling roach. [app. rel. to *rud* red colour f. OE *rudu*, cogn. w. RED]

rŭ'dder *n.* Broad flat wooden or metal piece hinged to vessel's stern-post or rear of aeroplane for steering with; (fig.) guiding principle etc.; **~-fish** (of kind that follows ships); hence ~LESS *a.* [OE *rōther*, = MDu., MLG *rōder*, OHG *ruodar* f. WG *rōthra-* f. st. of ROW[2]]

rŭ'ddle *n.*, & *v.t.* **1.** *n.* Red ochre, esp. of kind used for marking sheep. **2.** *v.t.* Mark or colour (as) with ruddle. [rel. to obs. *rud* (see RUDD)]

rŭ'ddock *n.* Robin redbreast. [OE *rudduc* (as prec.; see -OCK)]

rŭ'dd|ȳ *a.* & *v.* **1.** *a.* (Of face or its owner) freshly or healthily red, rosy; (of health, youth, etc.) marked by ruddiness; (of light, fire, sky, object lighted up, etc., or in animal name) reddish (*ruddy duck*, *plover*, *squirrel*); ||(sl.) bloody, damnable; hence ~ĭLY[2] *adv.*, ~ĭNESS *n.* **2.** *v.t.* & *i.* Make or grow ruddy. [OE *rudig* (as RUDD, -Y[2])]

rude (rōōd) *a.* **1.** Primitive, simple, in natural state, uncivilized, uneducated, roughly made or contrived or executed, coarse, lacking subtlety or accuracy, (*rude times*, *men*, *simplicity*, *ignorance*, *chaos*; *rude plough*, *beginnings*, *methods*; *rude path*, *verses*, *drawing*; *rude fare*, *plenty*; *rude writer*, *style*; *rude observer*, *version*, *classification*). **2.** Violent, not gentle, unrestrained, startling, sudden, abrupt, (*rude passions*, *blast*, *shock*, *awakening*, *reminder*). **3.** Vigorous, hearty, (*rude health*). **4.** Insolent, impertinent, offensive, (*rude remarks*; *say rude things*); **be ~ to,** insult. **5.** Hence ~'LY[2] (-dlĭ) *adv.*, ~'NESS (-dn-), (colloq.) **ru'dERY** (4), *ns.*, **ru'dISH**[1] 2 *a.*, (rōō'-). [ME f. OF, f. L *rudis* unwrought]

Ru'desheimer (rōō'dĕs-hī-) *n.* A white Rhine wine. [f. G *Rüdesheimer* (*wein*) (*Rüdesheim* on the Rhine)]

ru'dĭment (rōō'-) *n.* **1.** (in *pl.*) Elements or first principles of or *of* knowledge or some subject. **2.** (in *pl.*) Imperfect beginning of something that will develop or might under other conditions have developed. **3.** Part or organ imperfectly developed as being vestigial or having no function (e.g. the breast in males). **4.** Hence ~ARY[1] (-ĕ'n-) *a.* [F, or f. L *rudimentum* (as RUDE, after *elementum* ELEMENT)]

rue[1] (rōō) *v.t.* (~'**ing** *or* **ru'ing,** *pr.* rōō'-), & *n.* **1.** *v.t.* Repent of, bitterly feel the consequences of, wish undone or non-existent, (*you shall rue it*; *rue the day*, *hour*, etc., *when* one did thing etc.). **2.** *n.* (arch.) Repentance, dejection at some occurrence. **3.** *n.* (arch.) Compassion, pity. [OE *hrēow(an)*, = OS *hreuwan*, OHG *(h)riuwa(n)*]

rue[2] (rōō) *n.* Perennial evergreen shrub (*Ruta graveolens*) with bitter strong-scented leaves formerly used in medicine. [ME f. OF, f. L *ruta* f. Gk *rhutē*]

rue'ful (rōō'f-) *a.* Expressing or causing (mock) sorrow or compassion; **Knight of the R~ Countenance,** Don Quixote; hence ~LY[2] *adv.*, ~NESS *n.* [ME, f. RUE[1] + -FUL]

rufĕ'sc|ent (rōō-) *a.* (Zool. etc.) Reddish; hence ~ENCE *n.* [f. L *rufescere* (*rufus* reddish; see -ESCENT)]

rŭff[1] *n.* Deep projecting frill of several folds of linen or muslin starched and separately goffered worn round neck esp. in 16th c.; projecting or conspicuously coloured ring of feathers or hair round bird's or animal's neck; domestic pigeon like jacobin. [perh. f. *ruff* = ROUGH]

rŭff² *n.* (*fem.* **reeve**). Bird of sandpiper family of which male has RUFF¹ and ear-tufts in breeding season. [f. prec.]

rŭff³, **rŭffe,** *n.* Small freshwater fish of perch family, with prickly scales. [ME, prob. f. ROUGH]

rŭff⁴ *n.*, & *v.i.* & *t.* Trump(ing) at cards; CROSS--*ruff*. [orig. name of card-game f. OF *ro(u)ffle*, = It. *ronfa* (perh. alt. of *trionfo* TRUMP²)]

rŭ'ffian *n.* Brutal violent lawless turbulent person, desperado, bully, rough; hence ~ISM (2) *n.*, ~LY¹ *a.* [f. F *ruf(f)ian* f. It. *ruffiano*, perh. f. dial. *rofia* scurf]

rŭffl|e¹ *v.* & *n.* **1.** *v.t.* Disturb smoothness or tranquillity of (feathers, hair, water, composure or temper or person in regard to it, brow); *bird* **~es up** *its feathers* (in anger or to keep out the cold); gather (lace etc.) into ruffle. **2.** *v.i.* (Of sea, hair, temper, etc.) undergo ruffling, lose smoothness or calmness. **3.** *n.* Perturbation, bustle; rippling effect on water; ornamental gathered or goffered frill of lace etc. worn at opening of garment esp. about wrist or breast or neck; RUFF¹ of bird etc.; (Mil.) vibrating drum-beat. [ME, of unkn. orig.]

rŭ'ffl|e² *v.i.* (arch.) Swagger about, behave arrogantly or quarrelsomely; hence ~ER¹ *n.* [ME, of unkn. orig.]

ru'fous (rōō'-) *a.* (Esp. of animals) reddish--brown. [f. L *rufus* red(dish) + -OUS]

rŭg *n.* **1.** Large wrap or coverlet of thick woollen stuff. **2.** Floor-mat of shaggy material or thick pile; **pull the ~ (out) from under,** (fig.) remove support or concealment of (person). [prob. f. Scand. (Norw. dial. *rugga* coverlet, Sw. *rugg* ruffled hair) & cogn. w. RAG¹]

Rŭgbei'an (-bē'an) *n.* & *a.* (Past or present member) of Rugby School. [f. *Rugby* after L adjs.]

Rŭ'gbȳ *n. Rugby* FIVES; ~ **(football)**, game played with oval ball (~ **ball**) which may be kicked or carried; ‖~ **League,** professional Rugby football with teams of 13; ~ **Union,** amateur Rugby football with teams of 15. [f. ~ School in Warwickshire (where first played)]

rŭ'ggėd (-g-) *a.* **1.** Having rough uneven surface (*rugged bark*); (of ground or country) full of abrupt ups and downs, craggy, wooded, etc.; (of features) strongly marked, irregular in outline. **2.** Unsoftened, unpolished, lacking gentleness or refinement, harsh in sound, austere, unbending, involving hardship, (*rugged manners, grandeur, individualist, kindness, honesty, character, verse, times, life*); robust, sturdy, (esp. of machine etc., whence *~IZE (3) *v.t.*). **3.** Hence ~LY² *adv.*, ~NESS *n.* [ME, prob. f. Scand.; cf. RUG, and Sw. *rugga* roughen]

‖**rŭ'gger** (-g-) *n.* (colloq.) RUGBY football. [f. RUGBY + -ER¹ (5)]

ru'gōse (rōō'-) *a.* (esp. Biol.) Wrinkled, corrugated; hence or cogn. ~LY² (-slĭ) *adv.*, **rugo**'SITY (rōō-) *n.* [f. L *rugosus* (*ruga* wrinkle; see -OSE¹)]

ru'ĭn (rōō'-) *n.* & *v.* **1.** *n.* Downfall, fallen or wrecked or impaired state, lit. (of building or structure) or fig. (*the ruin of my hopes*); complete loss of property or position (*bring to ruin*); RACK⁷ *and ruin*. **2.** (in *sing.* or *pl.*) What remains of building, town, structure, etc., or fig. of person, that has suffered ruin (*the ruins of Baalbek*; *is but the ruin of what he was*; *lies in ruins*; *lives in an old ruin*). **3.** What causes ruin, destroying agency, havoc, (*will be the ruin of us*). **4.** So [f. obs. *ruinate* v.] **ruin**A'TION (rōō-) *n.* **5.** *v.t.* (esp. in *p.p.*) Reduce (place) to ruins. **6.** Bring to ruin (*her extravagance ruined him*); utterly impair or wreck (*ruin* one's *new hat*, one's *prospects*). **7.** *v.i.* (poet.) Fall headlong or with a crash. [n. ME f. OF *ruine*, v. f. F *ruiner* or med. L *ruinare*, f. L *ruina* (*ruere* fall)]

ru'ĭnous (rōō'-) *a.* In ruins, dilapidated; bringing ruin, disastrous, (*ruinous folly, expense*), whence ~LY² *adv.*; hence ~NESS *n.* [ME, f. L *ruinosus* (as prec.; see -OUS)]

rule (rōōl) *n.* & *v.* **1.** *n.* Principle to which action or procedure conforms or is bound or intended to conform, dominant custom, canon, test, standard, normal state of things, (*deduce rules of action*; *the rules of decorum, cricket*, etc.; *rule of the* ROAD¹); **R~s,** (Austral.) = Australian Rules (football); **as a ~,** usually, more often than not; **by ~,** in regulation manner, mechanically; EXCEPTION *proves rule*; GOLDEN *rule*; **~ of three,** method of finding number in same ratio to one given as exists between two others given; **~ of thumb** (based on experience or practice, not theory); WORK² *to rule*. **2.** Government, dominion, (*under British rule*; *the rule of force, of law*; *entrusted with the rule of half the tribe*). **3.** (Eccl.) Code of discipline observed by religious order. **4.** (Law). Order made by judge or court w. ref. to particular case only (*rule* NISI); **~ absolute** (making rule nisi no longer contingent). **5. The ~s,** (Hist.) limited area outside Fleet and King's Bench prisons in London where prisoners were allowed to live on certain terms. **6.** Graduated often jointed straight measure used by carpenters etc.; *by rule and* LINE²; **run the ~ over,** (fig.) examine cursorily for correctness or adequacy; SLIDE²-*rule*. **7.** (Print.) Thin slip of metal for separating headings, columns, etc.; ‖short **(en ~)** or long **(em ~)** dash in punctuation etc. **8.** Hence ~'LESS (-l-l-) *a.* **9.** *v.t.* Exercise sway or decisive influence over, keep under control, curb, (person, conduct, one's passions; **ruling passion,** motive that habitually directs one's actions); (arch. in *pass.*) consent to follow advice, be guided *by*. **10.** *v.t.* & *i.* Be the ruler(s) or have the sovereign control of or *over*, (*rules over many millions*; *kings should rule by love*); **~ the roast** or **roost,** be in control. **11.** *v.i.* (Of prices, or goods etc. in regard to them or to quality etc.) have a specified general level, be for the most part, (*corn, prices, the market, ruled high* etc.; **ruling prices,** those current). **12.** *v.t.* Give judicial or authoritative decision (*that*; *rule* person or thing *out of order*); **~ out,** exclude, pronounce irrelevant or ineligible; hence **ru'l**ING¹ (2) (rōō'-) *n.* **13.** Make parallel lines across (paper), make (straight line), with ruler or mechanical help; hence **ru'l**ING¹ (2) (rōō'-) *n.* [ME, f. OF *reule(r)* f. Rom. **regula* & LL *regulare* f. L *regula* straight stick]

ru'ler (rọọ'-) *n.* **1.** Person or thing bearing (esp. sovereign) rule (*of*); hence ~SHIP *n.* **2.** Straight strip or cylinder of wood, metal, etc., used in ruling paper or lines. [ME, f. prec. + -ER¹]

rŭm¹ *n.* **1.** Spirit distilled from sugar-cane or molasses; *rum* BABA; *rum*-SHRUB². **2.** *Intoxicating liquor; ***~-runner,** (colloq.) smuggler of intoxicants; ***~-shop,** (colloq.) place where intoxicants are sold. [17th c., perh. abbr. of contemporary forms *rumbullion, rumbustion*; orig. unkn.]

‖**rŭm**² *a.* (sl.) Odd, strange, queer; difficult, dangerous; *rum* GO² or START²; hence **rŭ'm**LY² *adv.*, **rŭ'm**NESS *n.* [16th-c. cant, orig. = fine, spirited, perh. var. of ROM]

Rumanian. See ROMANIAN.

Rumansh. See ROMANSH.

rŭ'mba *n.*, & *v.i.* **1.** *n.* Cuban Negro dance; ballroom dance imitative of this; music for it. **2.** *v.i.* Dance rumba. [Amer. Sp.]

rŭ'mble¹ *v.* & *n.* **1.** *v.i.* Make deep continuous sound (as) of thunder, earthquake, heavy machinery, gas in the bowels, etc.; go *along, by,* etc., making or in vehicle making such sound. **2.** *v.t.* Utter, say *out,* give *forth,* with such sound. **3.** *n.* Rumbling sound; *(sl.) gang-fight; hind part of carriage arranged as extra seat or for luggage; *~ **seat,** uncovered folding seat in rear of motor car; **~-tumble,** lumbering vehicle, rough motion. [ME *romble,* prob. f. MDu. *rommelen, rummelen,* (imit.)]

rŭ'mble[2] *v.t.* (sl.) Understand fully, see through, detect. [19th c.; orig. unkn.]

rŭmbŭ'stĭous (*or* -schus) *a.* (colloq.) Boisterous, uproarious. [prob. var. of ROBUSTIOUS]

ru'm|ĕn (rōō'-) *n.* (*pl.* **~ens** *or* **~ina**). Ruminant's first STOMACH. [L *rumen ruminis* throat]

ru'mĭnant (rōō'-) *n.* & *a.* **1.** *n.* Animal that chews the cud. **2.** *a.* Belonging to the ruminants; contemplative, given to or engaged in meditation. [as foll.; see -ANT]

ru'mĭn|āte (rōō'-) *v.* **1.** *v.i.* Chew the cud. **2.** *v.i.* & *t.* Meditate, ponder, (*over, about, of, on*); hence or cogn. ~ATIVE *a.,* **~ātor** *n.* **3.** So ~A'TION *n.* [f. L *ruminari* (as RUMEN) + -ATE[3]]

rŭ'mmage *v.* & *n.* **1.** *v.t.* & *i.* Make thorough search in or *in,* make search (*through* or *among*). **2.** *v.t.* Bring *out* or *up* from among other things; disarrange, throw *about,* in searching. **3.** *n.* Things got by rummaging, miscellaneous accumulation; thorough search (esp. of ship by Customs officer); ~ **sale,** (1) clearance sale of unclaimed articles at docks etc., (2) = JUMBLE[3] *sale.* [v. f. n. in obs. sense arranging of casks etc. in hold, f. AF **rumage* f. OF *arrumage* (*arrumer* stow f. *a-* AD-, *run* ship's hold f. MDu. *ruim* ROOM; see -AGE)]

rŭ'mmer *n.* Large drinking-glass. [cf. Du. *roemer,* LG *römer,* (*roemen* praise, boast; see -ER[1])]

rŭ'mmў[1] *a.* = RUM[2]. [f. RUM[2] + -Y[2]]

rŭ'mmў[2] *n.* Card-game played usu. with two packs, each player seeking to dispose of his cards by forming sequences or sets of cards of same rank. [20th c., of unkn. orig.]

ru'mour, *ru'mor, (rōō'mer) *n.,* & *v.t.* **1.** *n.* General talk, report, or hearsay, of doubtful accuracy; *a* or *the* current but unverified statement or assertion (*that, of*). **2.** *v.t.* (usu. in *pass.*) Report by way of rumour (*it is rumoured that he will come; he is rumoured to be coming; the rumoured disaster*). [ME, f. OF *rumur, rumor* f. L *rumor -oris* noise]

rŭmp *n.* **1.** Tail-end, posterior, buttocks, of animal or bird or person; hence ~'LESS *a.,* (of fowl) tailless. **2.** Small or contemptible remnant of a parliament or similar body; **the R~,** (Hist.) remnant of Long Parliament either after its restoration 1659 or from Pride's Purge 1648 to its first dissolution 1653. **3.** ~ **steak** (cut from ox's rump). [ME, prob. f. Scand.; cf. MDa. *rumpe,* MSw. *rumpa,* Icel. *rumpr*]

rŭ'mple *v.t.* Wrinkle, crease, tousle, ruffle, disorder, (fabric, leaves, garment, hair, etc.). [f. obs. *rumple* n. f. MDu. *rompel(en)* (*rompe* wrinkle)]

rŭ'mpus *n.* (sl.) Disturbance, brawl, row, uproar; *~ **room** (esp. in basement of house for hobbies, games, etc.). [18th c.; prob. fanciful]

rŭ'mpў *n.* Manx tailless cat. [f. RUMP + -Y[3]]

rŭn[1] *v.* (**-nn-; ran; run**). **1.** *v.i.* (Of person) progress at pace faster than walk by advancing each foot alternately, never having both feet on ground at once; (of animal) go at quicker than its walking pace, amble, trot, canter, gallop, etc. **2.** (Cricket). (Start to) traverse length of pitch to score run. **3.** Flee, abscond, (*run for it;* CUT[2] *and run*). **4.** Go or travel hurriedly, precipitately, briefly, etc.; ~ **to meet,** anticipate (one's troubles etc.); *run* RIOT; **~ over** or **down** or **up** or **across** (*to* place by brief journey or for flying visit); **he who ~s may read** (said of easily intelligible exposition etc.; cf. Hab. 2:2). **5.** Be allowed to grow or stray *wild.* **6.** Compete in or *in* race (ALSO-*ran*); finish race in specified position (*ran third in the mile*); seek election etc. (*for parliament, the presidency, president,* etc.). **7.** (Of ship etc.) go straight and fast (*ship runs before the wind, into port, ashore, aground, on the rocks, foul of* another); (of salmon) go up river from sea. **8.** Advance (as) by rolling or on wheels, spin round or along, revolve (as) on axle, go with sliding or smooth or continuous or easy motion, be in action, work freely, be current or operative, have duration, (*ball, carriage, wheel, spindle, sledge, time, runs; rope runs in pulley; his life runs smoothly; kept the engine running while waiting; lease runs for 99 years;* WRIT[1] *runs*); (of play etc.) be presented (*for* specified number of performances etc.); ~ **in the family,** (of trait etc.) be found in all or many members of it; ~ **in** one's **head,** (of tune etc.) seem to be heard repeatedly, (of idea etc.) constantly recur to one. **9.** (Of public conveyance by land or water) ply (*from, to, between*), be in course of plying (*train is running late*); (of fire, news, enthusiasm, etc.) spread rapidly from point to point (*news ran like wildfire; a cheer ran down the line; a shiver ran down my spine*). **10.** (Of colour in fabric) spread from dyed parts, (of ink) spread beyond proper place. **11.** (Of thought, eye, memory, etc.) pass in transitory or cursory way (*thoughts run through* one's *head; eyes run over object*); ~ **back over the past,** survey it summarily. **12.** (Of liquid, grain, sand, etc., of vessel containing or object emitting etc., or fig.) flow, be wet, drip, flow with, (*till the blood ran; ran blood; fountains run wine; is running with oil; heavy sea is running; tide runs strong; river runs clear, thick; feeling ran* HIGH; one's **blood ~s cold,** one is horrified; SANDS *are running out*); *(of stocking) ladder; (of candle) gutter; (of nose, eyes) drop mucus or tears, so *run at the nose, run with sweat;* ~ **dry,** cease to flow, be exhausted; ~ **low, short,** become or have too little (*our tea ran short; we ran short of tea*). **13.** Extend, be continuous, have a certain course or order, progress, proceed, have a tendency or common characteristic or average price or level, (*fence runs round the house; road runs at right angles to, along, the ridge; story, title, document, runs as follows; must not run to extremes; runs to sentiment; my inclination does not run that way; prices run high*). **14.** *v.t.* (w. cogn. obj.) Pursue, follow, traverse, cover, make way (esp. swiftly) through or over, wander about in, perform, attempt or be exposed or submit to, (course, way, race, a mile, run at cricket); *run* BLOCKADE[1]; **~s a chance of being,** may be; ~ **its course,** follow natural progress, be left to itself; ~ **errands, messages,** be a messenger; *run the* GAUNTLET[2]; *run* RISK(*s*). **15.** Sew (fabric) loosely or hastily with running stitches. **16.** Chase, hunt, have running race with, (*run fox five miles*); ~ **to earth,** chase to its lair, (fig.) discover after long search; *run into the* GROUND[1] 5; ~ person **hard** or **close,** press him severely in race, competition, or comparative merit etc.; ~ **off** one's **feet,** very busy; *run* RAGGED. **17.** Make run or go (*run ship aground* or *to New York, boat down to water, car into garage, train* or *road through,* person *out of town,* one's *head against, cart into wall, sword* or *pin into,* one's *hand* or *eye along, down,* or *over* thing, *rope through eyelet, metal into mould, water into bath, fingers* or *comb through hair*); turn (cattle etc.) out to graze; smuggle (brandy, guns, etc.); enter (horse *for* race, candidate *for* election etc.); cause (machine etc.) to operate, (experiment etc.) to be conducted; own and use (vehicle etc.); *publish (article or advertisement *in* newspaper etc.); take (person) for journey in motor car etc.; keep going, manage, conduct operation(s) of, (coach, steamer, business, person, etc.); *run it* FINE[2]; ~ **the show,** (sl.) dominate in an undertaking etc.; ~ **a temperature,** be feverish. **18.** Allow (account, bill) to accumulate for some time before paying. **19.** (w. *preps.*): ~ **across,** happen to meet; ~ **after,** pursue with attentions, seek society of, give much time to (pursuit etc.); ~ **against,** happen to meet; ~ **at,** assail by charging or rushing; ~ **in,** incur (debt); ~ **into,** fall into (practice, absurdity, etc.), incur (debt), be continuous or coalesce with, have collision or chance meeting with, reach or attain (*some length, five editions,* etc.); ~ **on,** be concerned (continually) with (*talk* or *mind runs on a subject*), use as fuel (*runs on diesel oil*); ~ **over,** review, glance over, touch (notes of piano etc.) in quick succession, (of vehicle) pass over (animal, prostrate person); ~ **through,** examine or rehearse cursorily, peruse, deal successively with, consume (estate etc.) by reckless or quick spending, pervade; ~ **to,** reach (amount, number, etc.), have money or ability or (of money etc.) be enough for (some expense or undertaking), fall into (ruin), (of person) indulge or show inclination towards (coarseness, fat, etc.); *run to* SEED; ~ **upon,** (of thoughts etc.) be engrossed by, dwell on. **20.** (w. *advs.*): ~ **about,** bustle, hurry from one person etc. to another, (esp. of children) play or wander without restraint; ~**'about** *n.*, light motor car or aircraft; ~ **along,** (colloq.) depart; ~ **around,** ||take from place to place by car etc., *fob off at successive places; ~ **away,** flee, abscond, elope, (of horse) bolt, (of horse or person) get clear away *from* competitors in race; ~**'away** *n.* & *a.*, fugitive (~*away marriage* etc., wedding after elopement); ~ **away with,** carry off (person, stolen property, etc.), win (prize etc.) easily, accept (notion) hastily, (of expense etc.) consume (money etc.), (of horse etc.) bolt with (rider, carriage or its occupants); ~ **down,** (of clock etc.) stop for want of winding, (of person or his health etc.) become enfeebled from overwork, poor feeding, etc., (*had, was much, run down*), reduce numbers of (staff etc.), knock down or collide with (person, ship, etc.), overtake (game, person) in pursuit, discover after search, disparage; ~**-down,** (*n.*) reduction in numbers, detailed analysis, (*a.*) decayed, declined from prosperity; ~ **in,** (of combatant) rush to close quarters, (colloq.) arrest and take into custody, bring (new machinery, esp. car engine) into good working order by carefully running it; ~**-in,** approach to action or event, quarrel; ~ **off,** flee, flow away, digress suddenly, write or recite (poem, list, etc.) fluently, drain (liquid) off, produce (copies etc.) on machine, decide (race) after tie or trial heats; ~ **on,** (of written characters) be joined together, continue in operation, elapse, speak volubly, talk incessantly, (Print.) continue in same line as what precedes; ~ **out,** come to an end (of period, of stock of something, or of its owner; ~ *out of,* exhaust one's stock of), escape from containing vessel, (of rope) pass or be paid out, jut out, come out of contest in specified position etc. or complete required score etc., complete (race), advance (gun etc.) so as to project, put down wicket of (batsman while he is running), exhaust one*self* by running; ~ **over,** (of vessel or contents) overflow, review, glance over; ~ **through,** traverse, review, pierce with sword etc., draw line through (written words); ~ **up,** grow quickly, rise in price, amount *to,* be runner-up, accumulate (number, sum, debt) quickly, force (rival bidder) to bid higher, force up (price, or commodity in regard to price), erect or construct (wall, house, garment, etc.) to great height or in unsubstantial or hurried way, raise (flag) on mast etc., add up (column of figures); ~ **up against,** meet with (difficulty etc.); ~**-up** *n.*, approach to action or event, (Golf) low approach shot. [OE *rinnan,* = OS, OHG *rinnan,* ON *rinna,* Goth. *rinnan*]

rŭn[2] *n.* **1.** Act or spell of running; **at a** or **the** ~, running; **go and have a** ~**!,** (sl.) begone; **have a (good)** ~ **for** one's **money,** get some enjoyment etc. out of expenditure or effort [orig. w. ref. to horse's not being scratched after placing of bets]; **had a good** ~ (esp. in hunting or on ship, train, etc.); **on the** ~, (1) fleeing, (2) bustling about. **2.** Short excursion or visit; distance travelled by ship in specific time (usu. 24 hours). **3.** (Cricket). Traversing of length of pitch by both batsmen without either's being run out; (Baseball etc.) return of batter to plate after touching the other bases; point scored thus or otherwise. **4.** Rhythmical motion, way things tend to move, direction, general tendency of development; regular route. **5.** Rapid motion (**come down with a** ~, fall quickly); ladder in stocking etc. **6.** (Mus.) Rapid scale passage. **7.** Continuous stretch or spell or course, long series or succession, general demand, (*a 500 ft. run of pipe; a long run of success, of power; play had a long run; a run of luck; in the* LONG[1] *or* SHORT *run*); quantity produced in one period of operation (*print run, production run*); ~ **on,** great demand for (commodity etc.), repeated occurrence of (red in rouge-et-noir etc.); ~ **on the bank,** sudden demand from many customers for immediate repayment. **8.** Common, general, average, or ordinary type or class; the **common** or **general** or **ordinary** ~ **of men,** average men; ~ **of the mill** or **mine,** ordinary or average product or specimen, not specially selected or distributed. **9.** Class or line of goods; batch or drove of animals born or reared together; shoal of fish in motion. **10.** Regular track of some animals, enclosure for fowls etc., range of pasture (*sheep-run*); SKI-*run*. **11.** Trough for water to run in; *small stream, brook. **12.** Permission to make unrestricted use *of* (*gave me the run of their books, house*). **13.** (Of aircraft) flight on straight and even course at constant speed before or while dropping bombs. [f. prec.]

rŭ'nagāte *n.* (arch.) Vagabond. [assim. of obs. *renegate* 'renegade' to RUN[1] and obs. *agate* away]

rŭ'ncĭble *a.* ~ **spoon,** fork curved like spoon, with three broad prongs, one edged. [nonsense word used by E. Lear, Engl. humorist d. 1888, perh. after *rouncival* large pea]

rŭ'ncĭnate *a.* (Bot.) Saw-toothed, with lobes curved towards base. [f. mod. L *runcinatus* f. L *runcina* plane (formerly taken to mean saw); see -ATE[2]]

||**rŭ'ndāle** *n.* Joint occupation of (esp. Irish, earlier Scottish) land, each holder having several strips not contiguous. [f. Sc. *ryndale* (*rin* RUN[1], *dale* DOLE[1])]

rune (rōōn) *n.* **1.** Any letter of earliest Gmc alphabet used esp. by Scandinavians and Anglo-Saxons from *c.* 3rd c. and formed by modifying Roman or Greek characters to suit carving; letter of similar alphabet of 8th-c. Mongolian Turks; similar mark of mysterious or magic significance. **2.** (Division of) Finnish poem. **3.** ~**-staff,** (1) magic wand inscribed with runes, (2) runic calendar. [f. ON **rún,* pl.

rúnar magic signs, cogn. w. OE *rūn*, OS, OHG, Goth. *rūna*; see ROUND[5]]

rŭng[1] *n.* Short stick attached at each end as rail, spoke, or crossbar in chair etc.; this or corresponding piece of rope etc. in ladder (lit. or fig.; *lowest, topmost, rung of life's ladder*); hence ~ED[2] (-ngd), ~'LESS, *adjs.* [OE *hrung*, = MLG *runge*, OHG *runga*, Goth. *hrugga* rod]

rŭng[2]. See RING[2].

ru'nĭc (rōō'-) *a.* Of, in, marked with, runes; (of poetry etc.) of the ancient-Scandinavian type; (of ornament) interlacing as on runic monuments and metal-work. [f. mod. L *runicus* f. ON *rún* RUNE; see -IC]

rŭ'nlėt[1] *n.* (arch.) Cask of varying size for wine etc. [ME, f. OF *rondelet* dim. of *rondelle* dim. of *ronde* (ROUND[1])]

rŭ'nlėt[2] *n.* Small stream. [f. RUN[2] + -LET]

rŭ'nnable *a.* Suitable for being hunted (*runnable stag*). [f. RUN[1] + -ABLE]

rŭ'nnel *n.* Brook, rill; gutter. [later form (assim. to RUN[1]) of *rinel* f. OE *rynel* (as RUN[1]; see -LE 1)]

rŭ'nner *n.* **1.** In vbl senses. **2.** Messenger, scout, collector, or agent for bank etc., tout; (Hist.) police-officer (Bow STREET *runner*). **3.** Running bird, esp. water-rail. **4.** Smuggler; one who runs a blockade. **5.** Revolving millstone. **6.** (Naut.) Rope in single block with one end round tackle-block and other having hook. **7.** Creeping stem that issues from main stem of strawberry etc. and takes root, stolon; twining plant; ||~ (**bean**), twining bean, esp. SCARLET runner. **8.** Ring etc. that slides on rod, strap, etc.; one of the long pieces of wood etc. on which sledge etc. slides; groove or rod for thing to slide along; roller for moving heavy article; long narrow ornamental cloth for table etc. **9.** **~-u'p,** competitor or team taking second place. [ME, f. RUN[1] + -ER[1]]

rŭ'nnĭng[1] *n.* In vbl senses; **make, take up, the** ~, take the lead, set the pace, (lit. in race, or fig. of talk etc.); **in, out of, the** ~, (of competitor) with good, no, chance of winning; **~-board,** footboard on either side of a locomotive, motor car, etc.; ~ **powers,** right granted by railway to another to run trains over its line. [OE (as RUN[1], -ING[1])]

rŭ'nnĭng[2] *a.* In vbl senses; (after *pl. n.*) following each other without interval, in succession, (*happened three days running*); ~ **account,** current ACCOUNT[2]; ~ **bowsprit** (that can be drawn in when not needed to carry sails); ~ **commentary,** oral description of events in progress; **~-dog,** (Polit., derog.) subservient follower; *running* FIGHT[2]; *running* FIRE[1]; ~ **hand,** writing in which pen etc. is not lifted after each letter; ~ **headline** etc., repeated or varying heading of page; ~ **jump** (in which jumper runs to take-off); *take a ~ jump at yourself!*, (sl.) begone; ~ **knot** (that slips along rope etc. and changes size of noose); *~ **mate,** candidate for secondary position in election, horse from same stable as pace-setter; ~ **postman,** (Austral.) vine of genus *Kennedya*; ~ **repairs,** minor repairs and replacements; ~ **sore** (suppurating); ~ **stitch,** (one of) line of small non-overlapping stitches for gathering etc.; ~ **water** (flowing in stream or from taps etc.). [ME, f. RUN[1] + -ING[2]]

rŭ'nnȳ *a.* Tending to run or flow; excessively fluid. [f. RUN[1] + -Y[2]]

rŭ'nrĭg *n.* (Sc.) = RUNDALE. [f. RUN[1] + Sc. & N. Engl. *rig* ridge]

rŭnt *n.* Ox or cow of small esp. Scottish-Highland or Welsh breed; large breed of domestic pigeon; small pig; weakling or undersized person. [16th c.; orig. unkn.]

rŭ'nway *n.* **1.** Trail to animals' watering-place. **2.** Incline down which logs are slid. **3.** Gangway (usu. of special kind). **4.** Specially prepared surface on airfield, for taking off and landing of aircraft. [f. RUN[1] + WAY]

rupee' (rōō-) *n.* Monetary unit of India, Pakistan, Sri Lanka, Nepal, Mauritius, and Seychelles. [f. Hind. *rūpiyah* f. Skr. *rūpya* wrought silver]

rupi'ah (rōōpē'*a*) *n.* Monetary unit of Indonesia. [f. as prec.]

rŭ'pture *n.* & *v.* **1.** *n.* Breach of harmonious relations, disagreement and parting; (Path.) abdominal hernia; breaking, breach. **2.** *v.t.* Burst, break, (cell, vessel, membrane); sever (connection, marriage, etc.); affect with hernia. **3.** *v.i.* Undergo rupture. [ME f. OF, or f. L *ruptura* (*rumpere rupt-* break; see -URE)]

rur'al (roor'-) *a.* In, of, suggesting, the country (opp. *urban*), pastoral or agricultural, (*in rural seclusion*; *rural policeman, constituency, sports,* etc.); ||*rural* DEAN[1]; ~ **district,** group of country parishes governed by elected council; hence ~ITY (-ă'l-) *n.*, ~IZE (2, 3) *v.i.* & *t.*, ~LY[2] *adv.* [ME f. OF, or f. LL *ruralis* (*rus ruris* the country; see -AL)]

rurĭdėcā'nal (roor-; *or* -dĕ'k*a*-) *a.* Of rural DEAN[1] or deanery. [f. L *ruri-* (as prec., -I-) + DECANAL]

Rurĭtā'n|ĭa (roor-) *n.* Imaginary Central-European kingdom, the novelist's and dramatist's locale for court romances in a modern setting; hence ~IAN *a.* & *n.* [scene of Anthony Hope's novels *The Prisoner of Zenda* (1894) & *Rupert of Hentzau* (1898), f. as prec. after *Lusitania*]

ru'sa (rōō'-) *n.* Large E. Ind. deer, esp. sambur. [mod. L f. Malay]

ruse (rōōz) *n.* Stratagem, feint, trick. [ME f. OF (*ruser* drive back, perh. f. Rom. **ru(r)sare* f. L *rursus* backwards; cf. RUSH[2])]

rŭsh[1] *n.* **1.** Marsh or waterside plant with naked slender tapering pith-filled stems (prop. leaves) formerly used for strewing floors and still for making chair-bottoms and plaiting baskets etc., a stem of this, (collect.) rushes as a material; (arch.) thing of no value (*don't care, not worth, a rush*). **2.** ||**~-bearing,** annual N. Engl. festival on occasion of carrying rushes and garlands to strew floor and decorate walls of church; ~ **candle** (made by dipping pith of a rush in tallow); **~'light,** rush candle (usu. fig. of feeble glimmer of intelligence, scanty information, etc.). **3.** Hence ~'LIKE, ~'Y[2], *adjs.* [OE *rysc(e)*, corresp. to MLG, MHG *rusch*]

rŭsh[2] *v.* & *n.* **1.** *v.t.* Impel, drag, force, carry along, violently and rapidly, (*rushed them into danger, round the sights; patient was rushed to hospital; ball is rushed down the field; emergency legislation was rushed through Parliament*); ~ person (**off his feet**), force him to act hastily; *pay attentions to (person) with view to securing acceptance of proposal. **2.** (Mil.) take by sudden vehement assault; swarm upon and take possession of (gold-field, platform at meeting, etc.). **3.** Pass (obstacle, stream, fence, etc.) with a rapid dash; ~ one's **fences,** act with undue haste. **4.** (sl.) Charge (customer) exorbitant price. **5.** *v.i.* Run precipitately, violently, or with great speed, go or resort without proper consideration (*in*)*to*, (*rush into* or *out of the room; dark horse rushed past the favourite; rush to extremes*); ~ **at,** attack impetuously; ~ **into print,** write to newspaper, publish book, etc. without proper consideration. **6.** Flow, fall, spread, roll, impetuously or fast (*river rushes past; a rushing mighty wind; avalanches rush down; blood rushed to his face; his past life rushed into his memory*). **7.** *n.* Act of rushing, violent or tumultuous advance, spurt, charge, onslaught, period of great activity, (*the* *rush of the tide*; *carry the citadel with a rush*; *a rush of blood to the head*; *a sudden rush of business*); (Cinemat., colloq.) first print or preliminary showing of film before cutting; (Footb.) combined dash of several players with the ball, *carrying of ball; sudden migration of large numbers esp. to new gold-field; strong run *on* or *for* some commodity; **~-hour** (at which traffic is busiest); **~ job** etc. (done with minimum delay). [ME, f. AF *russher*, = OF *rus(s)er* (see RUSE)]

rŭsk *n.* Piece of bread pulled or cut from loaf and rebaked usu. as light biscuit. [f. Sp. or Port. *rosca* twist, coil, roll of bread]

Rŭss *n.* & *a.* (arch.) = RUSSIAN. [f. Russ. *Rus'* early name of Russia and Russian people]

Rŭ'ssell *n.* **~ cord,** ribbed fabric of cotton and wool used for academic gowns etc. [19th c.; orig. unkn.]

rŭ'ssėt *n.* & *a.* **1.** *n.* (Hist.) coarse homespun reddish-brown or grey cloth worn by peasants; reddish brown; kind of rough-skinned russet-coloured apple. **2.** *a.* Reddish-brown, whence ~Y[2] *a.*; (arch.) rustic, homely, simple. [ME f. AF, f. OF *ro(u)sset* dim. of *roux* red f. Prov. *ros*, It. *rosso* f. L *russus* red; see -ET[1]]

Rŭ'ssia (-sha) *n.* **~ (leather)**, durable book-binding leather from skins impregnated with birch-bark oil. [~ in E. Europe]

Rŭ'ssian (-shan) *n.* & *a.* **1.** *n.* Native, inhabitant, or language of Russia (**Little ~**, Ukrainian); GREAT *Russian*. **2.** *a.* Of or from Russia; **~ boot** (loosely enclosing calf); **~ roulette,** firing of revolver held to one's head with one chamber loaded; **~ salad** (of mixed diced vegetables with mayonnaise). **3.** Of or in Russian. **4.** Hence ~IZE (3) *v.t.* [f. med. L *Russianus* (as prec.; see -AN)]

Rŭ'ssi|fȳ *v.t.* Make Russian in character; hence ~FICA'TION *n.* [f. RUSS + -I- + -FY]

Rŭ'sskĭ *n.* (joc. or derog.) Russian person. [f. RUSSIAN after Russ. surnames ending in *-ski*]

Rŭ'ssō- *comb. form.* Russian (and); hence ~PHIL(E) *n.* & *a.*, ~PHOBE *n.* & *a.*, ~PHO'BIA *n.* [f. RUSS + -O-]

rŭst *n.* & *v.* **1.** *n.* Reddish or yellowish-brown coating formed on iron or steel by oxidation esp. as effect of moisture and gradually corroding the metal; similar coating on other metals; (fig.) impaired state due to disuse or inactivity, inaction as deteriorating influence. **2.** (Plant--disease with rust-coloured spots caused by) fungus of order Uredinales. **3.** Hence ~'LESS *a.* (esp. of chrome steel), ~-PROOF[2] *a.*, & *v.t.* **4.** *v.i.* Become rusty; undergo oxidation; (of plant) be attacked by rust; (of bracken etc.) become rust--coloured; lose quality or efficiency by disuse or inactivity. **5.** *v.t.* Affect with rust, corrode. [OE *rūst*, = OS, OHG *rost* f. Gmc **rudh-*, cogn. w. RED]

rŭ'stĭc *a.* & *n.* **1.** (arch.) Rural. **2.** Having the appearance or manners of country people, characteristic of peasants, unsophisticated, unpolished, unrefined, uncouth. **3.** Of rude or country workmanship (**~ seat, bridge, work,** structure of untrimmed branches or rough timber); (of lettering) freely formed; (Archit.) with rough-hewn or roughened surface or with sunk joints (**~-work,** such masonry); hence or cogn. **rŭ'st**ICALLY *adv.*, **rŭstĭ'**CITY *n.* **4.** *n.* Countryman, peasant. [ME, f. L *rusticus* (*rus* the country)]

rŭ'stĭc|āte *v.* **1.** *v.i.* Retire to or sojourn in the country, lead a rural life. **2.** *v.t.* Send down temporarily from university as punishment; make rural; mark (masonry) with sunk joints or roughened surface. **3.** Hence ~A'TION *n.* [f. L *rusticari* live in the country (as prec.) + -ATE[3]]

rŭ'stl|e (-sel) *v.* & *n.* **1.** *v.i.*, & *n.* (Give forth) sound (as) of dry leaves blown, rain pattering, or silk garments in motion; go with rustle (*along* etc.); be finely clad *in* (silk etc.); *(colloq.) hustle, move energetically. **2.** *v.t.* Cause to rustle by shaking etc.; *(colloq.) acquire or deal with by exerting efforts; *steal (cattle or horses); **~e up,** (colloq.) forage for, produce when needed. **3.** Hence ~ER[1] (-sl-) *n.* [ME *rustel* etc., imit.; cf. obs. Flem. *ruysselen*, Du. *ritselen*]

rŭ'st|ȳ *a.* Rusted, affected with rust; of antiquated appearance; (of voice) croaking, creaking; stiff with age or disuse, antiquated, behind the times; impaired by neglect, in need of furbishing, (*his Greek is a little rusty*); (of black clothes) discoloured by age; rust-coloured; hence ~ĬLY[2] *adv.*, ~ĬNESS *n.* [OE *rūstig* (as RUST, -Y[2])]

rŭt[1] *n.*, & *v.t.* (**-tt-**). **1.** *n.* Track sunk by passage of wheels; established mode of procedure, beaten track, groove, (**in a ~**, following a fixed pattern of behaviour difficult to change); hence ~'TY[2] *a.* **2.** *v.t.* (esp. in *p.p.*) Mark with ruts. [prob. f. OF *rote* (as ROUTE)]

rŭt[2] *n.*, & *v.i.* (**-tt-**). **1.** *n.* Periodic sexual excitement of male deer, goat, ram, etc. **2.** *v.i.* Be affected with rut; hence ~'TISH[1] *a.* [ME, f. OF *ru(i)t* f. L *rugitus* (*rugire* roar)]

rutabā'ga (rōō-) *n.* Swede turnip. [f. Sw. dial. *rotabagge*]

ruth (rōōth) *n.* (arch.) Pity, compassion. [ME, f. RUE[1] 1 + -TH[1]]

ruthē'nĭum (rōō-) *n.* Rare hard white metallic element of platinum group. [f. med. L *Ruthenia* Russia (from its discovery in ores from the Urals) + -IUM]

ru'thlėss (rōō'-) *a.* Having no pity or compassion; hence ~LY[2] *adv.*, ~NESS *n.* [ME, f. RUTH + -LESS]

ru'tīle (rōō'-) *n.* Titanium dioxide as mineral. [F, or G *rutil*, f. L *rutilus* reddish]

R.V. *abbr.* Revised Version (of Bible).

-rȳ *suf.*, = -ERY (which see for numbered meanings; *chantry*, *infantry*, *Jewry*; *gadgetry*, *rivalry*, *rocketry*). [shortened f. -ERY, or by anal.]

Ry. *abbr.* Railway.

rȳe *n.* (Grain of) a N. European cereal (*Secale cereale*) used for bread in northern Continental countries and for fodder elsewhere; **~ (whisky)**, whisky distilled from rye. [OE *ryge*, = ON *rugr* f. Gmc **rugiz*]

rȳ'e-grass (rī'grahs) *n.* Fodder grass of genus *Lolium*. [f. obs. *ray-grass*; orig. unkn.]

ryō'kăn *n.* Traditional Japanese inn. [Jap.]

rȳ'ot *n.* Indian peasant. [f. Urdu *ra'īyat* f. Arab. (as RAYAH)]

S

S, s, (ĕs) *n.* (*pl.* **Ss** *or* **S's,** *pr.* ĕ'sĭz). Nineteenth letter of alphabet; S-shaped object or curve (*S-bend*).

-s¹ (*pr.* -z after vowel or voiced consonant; see notes on Plurals, p. xv.) *suf.* denoting *pl.* of *ns.*; w. *adv.* force in *evenings* (= in the evenings), *Mondays* (= on Mondays), etc. [OE *-as* pl. ending]

-s² (*pr.* -z after vowel or voiced consonant; see notes on Verb forms, p. xvi.) *suf.* denoting 3 pers. sing. pres. ind. of vbs. [OE dial., prob. f. OE 2 pers. sing. pres. ending *-es, -as*]

-s³ (*pr.* -z after vowel or voiced consonant) *suf.* forming *advs.* (*besides, eftsoons, needs,* -WARDS, & w. changed sp. *once*), and abs. poss. *adjs.* (*hers, ours*). [f. as -'s 1]

-s⁴ (*pr.* -z after vowel or voiced consonant) *suf.* forming nicknames (*Carrots, Fats*) or pet names (*Pops, ducks*). [after -s¹]

's- (*or* z-) *pref.* (chiefly arch., in oaths). God's (*'sblood, 'sdeath, 'struth*). [abbr.]

-'s *suf.* denoting: **1.** Possessive case of *sing. ns.* etc. **2.** Plural of letter (*S's*) or symbol (*8's*). **3.** (colloq.) *is* or *has* (*he's, she's, who's, it's, Smith's*). **4.** (colloq.) *us* in *let's.* **5.** (colloq.) *does* (*what's he say?*). [sense 1 f. OE gen. sing. ending; sense 2 as -s¹; senses 3–5 abbr.]

S. *abbr.* Saint; Society; South(ern).

s. *abbr.* second(s); shilling(s) [orig. f. L SOLIDUS]; singular; son; succeeded.

S *symb.* sulphur.

S.A. *abbr.* Salvation Army; sex appeal; South Africa; South America; South Australia; (Hist.) *Sturmabteilung* (political militia of Nazi party).

săbadĭ'lla *n.* Mexican plant (*Schoenocaulon officinale*) whose seeds yield veratrine. [f. Sp. *cebadilla* dim. of *cebada* barley]

Sabae'an, Sabē'an, *a.* & *n.* (Native) of ancient Yemen; (erron.) = SABIAN. [f. L f. Gk *Sabaios* (*Saba* f. Arab. *sabā* = Heb. *šᵉḇâ* people of Yemen) + -AN]

Sā'baĭsm *n.* Worship of stars or of spirits in them, in ancient Arabia and Mesopotamia. [f. F *sabaïsme* f. Heb. *ṣābâ* host (of heaven); see -ISM]

Să'bāōth (*or* -bā'-) *n. pl.* **Lord (God) of ~** (in N.T. and *Te Deum*), Lord of Hosts. [ME f. LL f. Gk *Sabaōth* f. Heb. *ṣᵉbāōt* pl. of *ṣābâ* (see prec.)]

Săbbatār'ĭan *n.* & *a.* **1.** *n.* Strict sabbath-keeping Jew. **2.** Christian who favours observing Sunday strictly as sabbath. **3.** Christian who observes Saturday as sabbath. **4.** Hence ~ISM (3) *n.* **5.** *a.* Holding, or relating to, tenets of Sabbatarians. [f. LL *sabbatarius* f. L *sabbatum* (see foll., -ARY¹) + -AN; see -ARIAN]

să'bbath *n.* **1.** ~ **(day)**, seventh day of week as day of religious rest appointed for Israelites (~ **day's journey**, distance Israelite might travel on sabbath, about ⅔ mile, (fig.) easy journey). **2.** ~ **(day)**, Christian Sunday esp. as day of obligatory abstinence from work and play (esp. in Presbyterian use, or joc.); hence ~'LESS *a.* **3.** Period of rest. **4. (Witches')** ~, supposed general midnight meeting of the Devil and witches. [OE *sabat*, L *sabbatum*, & OF *sab(b)at*, f. Gk *sabbaton* f. Heb. *šabbāṯ* (*šāḇaṯ* to rest)]

sabbă'tĭc|(al) *adjs.* Of or appropriate to the sabbath; **~al river,** one in Jewish legend flowing except on sabbath; **~al year,** (1) seventh year in which Israelites were to cease tilling and release debtors and Israelite slaves, (2) year's leave granted at intervals to university professor etc. for study, travel, etc., (so ~*al term* etc., or as *n.*); hence **~al**LY² *adv.* [f. LL f. Gk *sabbatikos* of sabbath (as prec.; see -IC) + -AL]

să'bbatīze, -ise (-īz), *v.* **1.** *v.i.* Keep the, have a, sabbath. **2.** *v.t.* Make (day) into, keep as, a sabbath. [ME, f. LL *sabbatizare* f. Gk *sabbatizō* (as SABBATH; see -IZE)]

S.A.B.C. *abbr.* South African Broadcasting Corporation.

Sabĕ'llĭan¹ *a.* & *n.* (Rom. Hist.) (Member) of group of tribes in ancient Italy including Sabines, Samnites, Campanians, etc. [f. L *Sabellus* + -IAN]

Sabĕ'llĭan² *a.* & *n.* (Holder) of the doctrine of Sabellius that the three Divine persons are merely aspects of one. [f. LL *Sabellianus* (*Sabellius* 3rd-c. African heresiarch); see -AN]

***sā'ber.** See SABRE.

Sā'bĭan *a.* & *n.* **1.** (Member) of a sect classed in Koran with Muslims, Jews, and Christians, as believers in the true God. **2.** (erron.) (Adherent) of Sabaism. [f. Arab. *ṣābi'* + -AN]

să'bĭcu (-kōō) *n.* W. Ind. timber-tree (*Lysiloma sabicu*); its mahogany-like wood. [Cuban Sp. *sabicú*]

Să'bīne *a.* & *n.* (One) of a group of ancient Italians of central Apennines. [f. L *Sabinus*]

sā'ble¹ *n.* Small brown-furred arctic and sub-arctic carnivorous quadruped allied to martens; its skin or fur; fine paint-brush made of sable's hair; **(American)** ~, Amer. pine marten. [ME f. OF, f. med. L *sabelum* f. Slav.]

sā'ble² *n.* & *a.* **1.** *n.* (poet. or rhet.) Black; (in *pl.*) mourning garments, whence **sā'bl**ED² (-beld) *a.* **2.** ~ **(antelope)**, large stout-horned Afr. antelope of which male is mostly black. **3.** *a.* (poet. or rhet.) Black, dusky, gloomy, dread; **his ~ Majesty,** the Devil; hence **sā'b**LY² *adv.* **4.** *n.*, & *a.* (usu. after *n.*) (Her.) Black. [ME f. OF (Her.), perh. f. prec.]

să'bōt (-ō) *n.* Shoe hollowed out from one piece of wood, worn by French peasants etc.; wooden-soled shoe; hence ~ED² (-bōd) *a.* [F, blend of *savate* shoe + *botte* boot]

să'botage (-ahzh) *n.*, & *v.t.* **1.** *n.* Malicious or wanton destruction, esp. doing of damage to equipment etc. by dissatisfied workmen or by hostile agents. **2.** *v.t.* Commit sabotage on; (fig.) destroy, render useless, (*sabotaged my plans*). [F (*saboter* make noise with sabots, bungle, wilfully destroy, f. as prec.; see -AGE)]

să'boteur (-tẽr) *n.* One who commits sabotage. [F]

să'bra *n.* Native-born Israeli. [f. mod. Heb. *sābrāh* opuntia fruit]

sā'bre (-*er*), ***sā'ber,** *n.*, & *v.t.* **1.** *n.* Cavalry sword with curved blade; cavalry soldier and horse; light fencing-sword with tapering blade; **~-bill,** S. Amer. bird with curved bill; **~-cut,** (1) blow with sabre, (2) wound made or scar left by it; **~-rattling,** display of military strength (cf. RATTLE¹); **~-toothed lion** or **tiger,** extinct mammal with long sabre-shaped upper canines; **~-wing,** S. Amer. humming-bird with curved wings. **2.** *v.t.* Cut down or wound with sabre. [F, earlier *sable* f. G *sabel*, *säbel*, *schabel* f. Pol. *szabla* or Magyar *szablya*]

să'bretăche (-*er*tăsh) *n.* Cavalry officer's flat satchel on long straps from left of waist-belt. [F, f. G *säbeltasche* (as prec., *tasche* pocket)]
sabreur' (-ẽr) *n.* User of sabre, esp. cavalryman. [F (*sabrer* SABRE 2)]
săc *n.* Baglike membrane-enclosed cavity in animal or vegetable organism; membranous envelope of hernia, cyst, tumour, etc.; = SACK[1] 2. [F, or f. L *saccus* SACK[1]]
||**S.A.C.** *abbr.* Senior Aircraftman.
săcca'de (-ah'd) *n.* Brief rapid movement of eye between fixation points; hence **saccă'dIC** *a.* [F, = violent pull, f. OF *saquer, sachier* pull]
să'ccāte *a.* (Bot.) dilated into bag; contained in sac. [f. SAC + -ATE[2]]
să'ccharīde (-ker-) *n.* (Chem.) = SUGAR 3. [f. mod. L *saccharum* sugar + -IDE]
săcchari'|mĕter (-ker-) *n.* Instrument for measurement of sugar content of a solution by means of polarized light; so ~METRY *n.* [f. F *saccharimètre* (as prec., -I-, -METER)]
să'ccharĭn (-ker-) *n.* Very sweet substance used as substitute for sugar by diabetics etc. [G (as SACCHARIDE; see -IN)]
să'ccharine (-kerēn) *a.* Sugary; of, containing, like, sugar; unpleasantly over-polite etc. [f. as SACCHARIDE + -INE[1]]
să'ccharō- (-kerō) *comb. form.* Sugar (and), as ~GE'NIC (1) *a.* [f. Gk *sakkharon* sugar + -O-]
săccharŏ'|mĕter (-kar-) *n.* Instrument for measurement of sugar content of a solution; so ~METRY *n.* [f. as prec. + -METER]
să'ccharōse (-ker-) *n.* Sucrose. [f. mod. L *saccharum* sugar + -OSE]
să'ccĭfōrm (-ks-) *a.* Sac-shaped. [f. L *saccus* sac + -I- + -FORM]
să'ccūl|ar *a.* Of or like a sac; so ~ATE[2] *a.*, ~A'TION *n.* [f. L (as foll.) + -AR[1]]
să'ccūle *n.* Small sac or cyst. [f. L *sacculus* (as SAC; see -ULE)]
să'cerdōtage *n.* (joc.) Sacerdotalism; priest-ridden state. [as foll. w. ref. to *dotage*; cf. *anecdotage*]
săcerdō'tal *a.* Of priest(s) or priesthood, priestly; (of doctrine etc.) ascribing sacrificial functions and supernatural powers to ordained priests, claiming excessive authority for the priesthood; hence ~ISM (3), ~IST (2), *ns.*, ~IZE (3) *v.t.*, ~LY[2] *adv.* [ME f. OF, or f. L *sacerdotalis* (*sacerdos -dotis* priest; see -AL)]
sā'chem *n.* **1.** Supreme chief of some Amer. Ind. tribes. **2.** *Political leader. [Narraganset, = SAGAMORE]
să'chet (-shā) *n.* Small perfumed bag; (packet of) dry perfume for laying among clothes etc.; packet for small quantity of shampoo etc. [F, dim. of *sac* f. L *saccus*]
săck[1] *n.*, & *v.t.* **1.** *n.* Large usu. oblong bag for storing and conveying goods, usu. open at one end and made of coarse flax or hemp, whence ~'ING[1] (3) *n.*; ~('FUL 2 *n.*), sack with contents (usu. *of*); amount (of corn, coal, flour, wool, potatoes, etc.) usu. put in sack, as unit of measure or weight; *(sl.) bed; **the** ~, (colloq.) dismissal (*get, give* person, *the sack*). **2.** Woman's short loose dress with sacklike appearance; (arch. or Hist.) woman's loose gown, or silk train attached to shoulders of this. **3.** Man's or woman's loose-hanging coat not shaped to back. **4.** **~'cloth,** coarse fabric of flax or hemp, sacking, (fig.) mourning or penitential garb, esp. *sackcloth and ashes* (orig. Bibl.); **~-race** (between competitors tied in sacks up to waist or neck). **5.** *v.t.* Put into sack(s); (colloq.) dismiss from service etc. [OE *sacc* f. L f. Gk *sakkos*, of Semitic orig.]
săck[2] *v.t.*, & *n.* **1.** *v.t.* (Of victorious army or its commander) plunder, give over to plunder, (captured town etc.); (of burglar etc.) carry off valuable contents of. **2.** *n.* Sacking of captured place. [v. f. n., f. F. *sac* in phr. *mettre à sac* put to sack, f. It. *sacco* SACK[1]]
săck[3] *n.* (Hist.) White wine formerly imported into Britain from Spain and the Canaries (*sherry, Canary*, etc., *sack*). [16th c. *wyne seck*, f. F *vin sec* dry wine]
să'ckbut *n.* Medieval kind of trombone; (Bibl., as wrong transl.) triangular harp. [f. F *saquebute*, earlier *saqueboute* hook for pulling man off horse (*saquer* pull, *boute* as BUTT[4])]
să'cklėss *a.* (arch. or Sc.) Innocent (*of*); harmless, feeble-minded. [OE *saclēas* f. ON *saklauss* (as SAKE[1], -LESS)]
săcque (săk) *n.* = SACK[1] 2. [var. of SACK[1], w. pseudo-F sp.]
sā'cral *a.* (Anat.) of the sacrum; (Anthrop.) of or for sacred rites. [f. E or L SACRUM + -AL]
să'crament *n.*, & *v.t.* **1.** *n.* Religious ceremony or act regarded as outward and visible sign of inward and spiritual grace (applied by the Eastern, pre-Reformation Western, and R.C. Churches to the seven rites of baptism, confirmation, the Eucharist, penance, extreme unction, orders, and matrimony; restricted by most Protestants to baptism and the Eucharist); **the** ~, **the** ~ **of the altar, the Blessed** or **Holy S**~, (1) the Eucharist, (2) the consecrated elements esp. the bread or Host; **take, receive, the** ~ **to** do or **upon** (as confirmation of some promise or oath). **2.** Thing of mysterious and sacred significance, sacred influence, symbol, etc. **3.** Oath or solemn engagement taken. **4.** *v.t.* (esp. in *p.p.*) Bind by oath. [ME f. OF *sacrement* f. L *sacramentum* solemn oath etc. (*sacrare* hallow f. *sacer* SACRED; see -MENT), used in Christian L as transl. of Gk *mustērion* MYSTERY[1]]
săcramĕ'ntal *a.* & *n.* **1.** *a.* Of (the nature of) a or the sacrament, whence ~ITY (-ă'l-) *n.*; (of doctrine etc.) attaching great importance to the sacraments, whence ~ISM (3), ~IST (2), *ns.*; hence ~LY[2] *adv.* **2.** *n.* Observance analogous to but not reckoned among the sacraments, e.g. use of holy water or sign of the cross. [ME f. F, or f. LL *sacramentalis* (as prec.; see -AL)]
săcramentār'ĭan *a.* & *n.* **1.** (Hist.) Denying, one who denies, the Real Presence (holding that 'body and blood of Christ' was used only in sacramental, i.e. symbolic, sense). **2.** Holding or involving, holder of, sacramental doctrine, whence ~ISM (3) *n.* [f. mod. L *sacramentarius* (as prec.; see -ARY[1]) + -AN; see -ARIAN]
sacrār'ĭ|um *n.* (*pl.* ~**a**). Sanctuary of church; (R.C.) piscina; (Rom. Ant.) shrine, room of penates in house. [L (*sacer sacri* holy; see -ARIUM)]
sā'crėd *a.* **1.** Consecrated or held especially acceptable *to* a deity, dedicated or reserved or appropriated *to* some person or purpose; made holy by religious association, hallowed; ~ **book, writings,** (embodying laws etc. of a religion); *Sacred* COLLEGE; **S~ Heart,** the heart of Jesus as object of devotion; ~ **number** (associated with religious symbolism, e.g. 7); ~ **poetry, music,** (on religious themes); **S**~ (=HOLY) **Writ;** (as specific epithet of animal etc.) now or formerly sacred to some god (*sacred* IBIS, *monkey, beetle*). **2.** Safeguarded or required by religion or reverence or tradition, indefeasible, inviolable, sacrosanct, (*His Most Sacred Majesty the King*; *the sacred right of insurrection*; *regards it as a sacred duty*; *their property* or *persons will be held sacred*; *no place was sacred from him, from outrage*); ~ **cow,** (fig.) idea or institution unreasonably held to be immune from questioning or criticism [w. ref. to Hindus' respect for cow as holy animal]. **3.** Hence ~LY[2] *adv.*, ~NESS *n.*

[ME, p.p. of obs. *sacre* consecrate f. OF *sacrer* f. L *sacrare* (*sacer sacri* holy)]

să′crĭfice *n.* & *v.* **1.** *n.* Slaughter of animal or person, surrender of a possession, as offering to a deity, (fig.) act of prayer or thanksgiving or penitence as propitiation; what is thus slaughtered or presented or done, victim, offering; (Theol.) Christ's offering of himself in the Crucifixion, the Eucharist as either a propitiatory offering of the body and blood of Christ or an act of thanksgiving. **2.** Giving up of valued thing for the sake of another that is more worthy or more important or more urgent, thing thus given up, loss thus entailed, (*will gain nothing by the sacrifice of your principles*; *at some sacrifice of regularity*; *surplus stock for sale at a large sacrifice*; *his health was the sacrifice demanded of him*; *made sacrifices so that her son could go to university*); (in games) loss incurred deliberately to avoid greater loss or to obtain compensating advantage; SELF-*sacrifice*. **3.** So **săcrĭfĭ′c**IAL (-shal) *a.* **4.** *v.t.* & *i.* Offer (as) sacrifice (*to*, or abs.); give up, treat as secondary or of inferior importance, devote, *to* (*has sacrificed herself*, *her whole life*, *her pleasures*, *to his interest*; *sacrifice accuracy to vividness*); sell at a loss. [ME f. OF, f. L *sacrificium* (*sacrificus* as prec.; see -FIC)]

să′crĭlège *n.* Robbery or profanation of sacred building, outrage on consecrated person or thing, violation of what is sacred; so **săcrĭlē′g**IOUS (-jus) *a.* [ME f. OF, f. L *sacrilegium* (*sacrilegus* stealer of sacred things, f. *sacer sacri* sacred + *legere* take possession of)]

sā′crĭng *n.* (arch.) Consecration of Eucharistic elements; ordination and consecration of bishop, sovereign, etc.; **~-bell** (rung at elevation of Host). [ME, f. obs. *sacre* (see SACRED) + -ING[1]]

sā′crĭst *n.* Official keeping sacred vessels etc. of religious house or church. [f. OF *sacriste* or f. med. L *sacrista* (as SACRED; see -IST)]

să′crĭstan *n.* = prec.; (arch.) sexton of parish church. [ME, f. med. L *sacristanus* (as prec.; see -AN)]

să′crĭstў *n.* Repository for vestments, vessels, etc., of a church. [f. F *sacristie* or It. *sacrestia* or f. med. L *sacristia* (as SACRIST; see -Y[1])]

sā′crō- *comb. form.* Of sacrum and (*sacro-iliac*). [f. SACRUM + -O-]

să′crosănct *a.* (Of person, place, law, etc.) secured by religious sanction against outrage, inviolable; hence **săcrosă′nct**ITY *n.* [f. L *sacrosanctus* (*sacro* abl. of *sacrum* SACRED rite, *sanctus* as SAINT)]

sā′cr|um *n.* Composite triangular bone of ankylosed vertebrae forming back of pelvis. [f. L *os sacrum* transl. Gk *hieron osteon* sacred bone (from sacrificial use)]

||**S.A.C.W.** *abbr.* Senior Aircraftwoman.

săd *a.* **1.** Sorrowful, mournful, showing or causing sorrow; **a ~der and a wiser man,** one who has had a distressing but instructive experience; **in ~ earnest,** (arch.) seriously. **2.** (derog., usu. joc.) Shocking, deplorably bad, incorrigible, (*is a sad slut, coward*, etc.; *writes sad stuff*); **~ dog,** rake, scapegrace. **3.** (Of colour) dull, neutral-tinted; (of pastry etc.) heavy. **4. ~-iron,** solid flat-iron; ***~ sack,** (colloq.) very inept person. **5.** Hence **~′d**EN[6] *v.t.* & *i.*, **~′d**ISH[1] 2 *a.*, **~′**LY[2] *adv.*, **~′**NESS *n.* [OE *sæd*, = OS *sad*, OHG *sat*, ON *sathr*, Goth. *saths* f. Gmc **sadhaz* full, cogn. w. L *satis*]

să′ddle *n.*, & *v.t.* **1.** *n.* Rider's seat placed on back of horse etc. (usu. raised at front and rear, and leather-covered with side-flaps and girths and stirrups) or forming part of bicycle etc. or of agricultural machine; **in the ~,** mounted, (fig.) in office or control. **2.** Part of shaft-horse's harness that bears shafts. **3.** Part of animal's back resembling saddle in shape or marking; rear part of male fowl's back. **4.** Saddle-shaped thing, e.g. ridge between two summits, support for cable or wire on top of suspension-bridge pier or telegraph-pole, joint *of* mutton or venison consisting of the two loins. **5. ~back,** (Archit.) tower-roof with two opposite gables, saddlebacked hill, bird with saddle-like marking (esp. the grey crow or a black N.Z. bird), black pig with white stripe across back; **~backed,** with upper outline concave, (Archit.) having saddleback; **~-bag,** one of pair of bags laid across horse behind saddle, bag attached behind saddle of bicycle or motor cycle; **~-bow** (-bō), arched front or rear of saddle [BOW[1]]; **~-cloth** (laid on horse's back under saddle); **~fast,** (arch.) firmly seated in saddle; **~-horse** (for riding); ***~ shoe** (with contrasting band across upper); **~-tree,** (1) frame of saddle, (2) tulip-tree (with saddle-shaped leaves). **6.** Hence **~**LESS (-del-l-) *a.* **7.** *v.t.* Put saddle on (horse etc.); (of trainer) enter (horse) for race; burden (person) *with* task, responsibility, etc.; put (burden) *on* or *upon* (person). [(v. f. OE *sadolian*) f. OE *sadol, sadul*, MDu. *sadel*, OHG *satal, satul*, ON *söthull* f. Gmc **sadhulaz*]

să′ddl|er *n.* Maker of or dealer in saddles and other equipment for horses; (Mil.) man in charge of cavalry regiment's saddlery; hence **~**ERY (1, 2, 3) *n.* [ME, f. prec. + -ER[1]]

Să′ddūcee *n.* Member of Jewish sect or party (cf. PHARISEE, ESSENE) of time of Christ that denied resurrection of the dead, existence of spirits, and obligation of the traditional oral law; hence or cogn. **Sădduce**′AN *a.*, **~**ISM (3) *n.* [OE *sad(d)ucēas* f. LL f. Gk *Saddoukaios* f. Heb. *ṣᵉdûḳî*, prob. = descendant of Zadok (2 Sam. 8:17)]

sa′dhu (sah′dōō) *n.* (Ind.) Holy man, sage, or ascetic. [Skr., = holy man]

să′d|ĭsm (*or* sah′-) *n.* Form of sexual perversion marked by love of cruelty (opp. MASOCHISM); deriving of pleasure from inflicting or watching cruelty; so **~**IST (2) *n.*, **sadĭ′st**IC *a.* [f. F *sadisme* (Count or 'Marquis' de *Sade* Fr. author d. 1814; see -ISM)]

sădō-mă′soch|ĭsm (-k-; *or* -zo-; *or* sah-) *n.* Combination of sadism and masochism in one person; hence **~**IST (2) *n.*, **~ĭ′st**IC *a.* [f. prec. + -O- + MASOCHISM]

s.a.e. *abbr.* stamped addressed envelope.

sae′ter (sā′-) *n.* High summer-pasture in Scandinavia. [Norw., f. ON *setr* SEAT]

safar′ĭ *n.* Journey or (esp. scientific or hunting) expedition esp. in E. Africa (*go on safari*); **~ park,** area where lions etc. are kept in the open for viewing. [Swahili, f. Arab. *safara* travel]

sāfe[1] *n.* Strong locked repository or receptacle for valuables; *condom; = MEAT-*safe*; **~-blower, ~-breaker, ~-cracker,** criminal who breaks safes open. [orig. *save*, f. SAVE[1], assim. to foll.]

sāfe[2] *a.* **1.** (*pred.*, after *come, arrive, bring, keep*, etc.). **~ (and sound),** uninjured (*parcel came safe*; *saw them safe home*); secure, out of or not exposed to danger (*from*), (*now we are, can feel, safe*; *is safe from his enemies*); (Baseball) having reached a base successfully. **2.** Affording security or not involving danger (*put it in a safe place*; *is it safe to leave him?*; *maximum safe load 10 tons*; *safe custody, convoy*, etc.; *dog is not safe to touch*); **it is ~ to say,** it may be said without risk of exaggeration or falsehood; **on the ~ side,** with margin of security against risks. **3.** Debarred from escaping or doing harm (*have got him safe*). **4.** Cautious and unenterprising, consistently moderate, that can be reckoned on, unfailing, certain *to* do or be, sure to become, (*a safe critic, statesman*; *safe methods*; *a safe* CATCH[2], *winner*; *better to be safe than sorry*; *is safe to win, be there*); ~ **bet** (that is certain to succeed); ~ **seat** (in Parliament etc., that is sure to be won by a particular party). **5.** ~ **conduct,** (document conveying) privilege granted by sovereign, commander, etc., of immunity from arrest or harm on particular occasion or in district; ~ **deposit,** building containing strong-rooms and safes let separately; ~ **keeping,** preservation in safe place; ~ **period,** time during and near menstrual period (when conception is least likely). **6.** Hence ~'LY[2] (-flĭ) *adv.*, ~'NESS (-fn-) *n.* [ME f. AF *saf*, OF *sauf* f. L *salvus* uninjured]

sā'feguard (-fgard) *n.*, & *v.t.* **1.** *n.* Safe conduct; proviso, stipulation, quality, or circumstance, that tends to prevent something undesired. **2.** *v.t.* Guard or protect (rights etc.) by precaution or stipulation. [ME, f. AF *salve garde*, OF *sauve garde* (as prec., GUARD[1])]

sā'fetў (-ftĭ) *n.* **1.** Being safe, freedom from danger or risks, (*there is safety in numbers*; *cannot do it with safety*); **play for ~,** avoid risks in game (lit. or fig.); ~ **first,** motto inculcating caution. **2.** Safeness, being sure or likely to bring no danger, (*is the safety of the experiment certain?*). **3.** ~(**-catch**), contrivance for locking gun-trigger, preventing fall of lift, etc. **4.** ~(**-bicycle**), (arch.) bicycle of usual low-saddled modern form (opp. *ordinary*). **5.** (Amer. Footb.) Rearmost defensive player; touchdown behind one's own goal-line. **6.** ~**-belt,** strap securing occupant to seat in aircraft, motor car, etc., or when working at a height; ~ **curtain,** fireproof curtain that can be lowered to cut off the auditorium in a theatre from the stage; ~ **factor** or **factor of** ~, ratio of material's strength to expected strain, (fig.) margin of security against risks; ~ **film,** cinematographic film on slow-burning or non-inflammable base; ~ **fuse,** FUSE[2] containing a slow-burning composition for firing detonators from a distance, (Electr.) protective FUSE[3]; ~**-glass,** glass that will not splinter when broken; ~ **lamp,** miner's lamp so protected as not to ignite firedamp; ~ **match** (igniting only on specially prepared surface); ~ **net** (placed to catch acrobat etc. in case he falls); ~**-pin** (with point that is bent back to head and can be held in guard so that user may not be pricked nor pin come out); ~ **play,** (Bridge) play designed to give best chance of making one's contract even at cost of overtrick; ~ **razor** (with guard to prevent blade from cutting skin); ~**-valve,** (in steam-boiler) valve opening automatically to relieve excessive pressure, (fig.) means of giving harmless vent to excitement etc. (*sit on the ~-valve*, follow policy of repression); *~ **zone,** area of road marked off for pedestrians etc. to wait safely. [ME *sauvete*, f. OF *sauveté* f. med. L *salvitas -tatis* f. L *salvus* (as SAFE[2]); see -TY[1]]

să'fflower *n.* Thistle-like plant (*Carthamus tinctorius*) yielding red dye used in rouge etc.; its dried petals; dye made from them. [f. Du. *saffloer* or G *safflor* f. OF *saffleur* f. obs. It. *saffiore*; orig. unkn.]

să'ffron *n.* & *a.* **1.** *n.* Orange-coloured stigmas of a crocus (*Crocus sativus*), used for colouring and flavouring confectionery, liquors, rice, etc.; MEADOW *saffron*. **2.** *a.* & *n.* Saffron-colour(ed), whence ~Y[2] *a.*; ~ **cake** (flavoured with saffron). [ME, f. OF *safran* f. Arab. *za'farān*]

să'franin *n.* Colouring-matter of saffron; yellowish-red synthetic dyestuff. [f. F *safranine* (as prec.; see -IN)]

săg *v.i.* (-gg-), & *n.* **1.** *v.i.* Sink or subside under weight or pressure; hang sideways, be lopsided, (*gate, bridge, sags*); have downward bulge or curve in middle (*ceiling, beam, slackened rope, ladder, sags*); (Commerc.) fall in price; (of ship) drift from course (esp. to leeward); hence ~'**gy**[2] (-gĭ) *a.* **2.** *n.* Amount that rope etc. sags, distance from middle of its curve to straight line between supports; sinking, subsidence; fall in price; (Naut.) tendency to leeward. [ME, f. MLG *sacken*, Du. *zakken* subside]

sa'ga (sah'-) *n.* Medieval Icelandic or Norwegian prose narrative, esp. one embodying history of Icelandic family or Norwegian king; story of heroic achievement or adventure; series of connected books giving history of a family etc.; long involved story. [ON, = narrative, cogn. w. SAW[2]]

sagā'cious (-shus) *a.* Mentally penetrating, gifted with discernment, having practical wisdom; acute-minded, shrewd; (of saying, plan, etc.) showing sagacity; (of animal) exceptionally intelligent, seeming to reason or deliberate; hence or cogn. ~LY[2] *adv.*, **sagă'CITY** *n.* [f. L *sagax sagacis* + -OUS]

să'gamōre *n.* = SACHEM 1. [f. Penobscot *sagamo*]

sāge[1] *n.* **1.** Aromatic herb (*Salvia officinalis*) with dull greyish-green leaves; its leaves used in cookery (~ **and onions,** stuffing used for goose, duck, pork, etc.). **2.** ~**-brush,** growth of plants (esp. of genus *Artemisia*) characterizing some sterile alkaline regions of U.S.; ~ **cheese** or ~ **Derby** (flavoured and mottled by addition of sage-infusion to the curd); ~**-green,** colour of sage-leaves; ~**-grouse,** large grouse of sage-brush regions; ~ **tea,** medicinal infusion of sage-leaves. **3.** Hence **sā'gy**[2] *a.* [ME f. OF *sauge* f. L *salvia* healing plant (*salvus* safe)]

sāge[2] *a.* & *n.* **1.** *a.* Wise, discreet, judicious, having the wisdom of experience, of or indicating profound wisdom, (often iron.) wise-looking, solemn-faced; hence ~'LY[2] (-jlĭ) *adv.*, ~'NESS (-jn-) *n.* **2.** *n.* Profoundly wise man (often iron.), esp. any of the ancients traditionally reputed wisest of their time (**the Seven S~s,** 7 Greeks each credited with a notable saying); hence ~'SHIP (-jsh-) *n.* [ME f. OF, f. Gallo-Rom. **sapius* (L *sapere* be wise)]

să'ggar *n.* Case of baked fireproof clay enclosing pottery while it is baked. [prob. contr. of SAFEGUARD]

să'gĭtta *n.* (Geom.) Greatest distance of arc from its chord, measured perpendicular to the chord. [L, = arrow]

să'gĭttal *a.* (Anat.) Of suture between parietal bones; in same plane as this. [F, f. med. L *sagittalis* (as prec.; see -AL)]

Săgĭttār'ĭus *n.* Sign of the ZODIAC, the Archer. [L, = archer (as SAGITTA; see -ARY[1])]

să'gĭttāte *a.* (Bot. & Zool.) Shaped like arrow-head. [f. as SAGITTA + -ATE[2]]

sā'gō *n.* (*pl.* ~s). (Palm esp. of genus *Metroxylon*, with pith yielding) kind of starch used as food in puddings etc. [f. Malay *sāgū* (orig. thr. Port.)]

saguar'ō (-gw-) *n.* (*pl.* ~s). Giant cactus of S.W. United States & Mexico. [Mex. Sp.]

Sahar'|a (sa-h-) *n.* Arid tract (lit. or fig.); hence ~AN, ~IAN, ~IC, *adjs.* [f. ~ desert in N. Africa, f. Arab. *ṣaḥrā'* desert]

Sah'ĭb *n.* **1.** (arch.) European or other superior as spoken of or to by Indians (also used as honorific affix; *Colonel Sahib*, *Jones Sahib*). **2.** (*s*~; colloq.) Gentleman (*pukka sahib*). [Urdu, f. Arab. *ṣāḥib* friend, lord]

said. See SAY[2].

sai'ga (*or* sī'-) *n.* Antelope (*Saiga tartarica*) of steppes. [Russ.]

sail[1] *n.* **1.** Piece of canvas or other textile material extended on rigging to catch wind and propel vessel, (collect.) some or all of ship's sails (CARRY[1], CROWD[2], *hoist, lower,* MAKE[1], SET[1], SHORTEN, STRIKE, *sail*); **take in ~,** (fig.) moderate one's ambitions; *take* WIND[1] *out of* person's *sails*; **under ~,** with sails set. **2.** (collect.) Ships in squadron or company (*a fleet of twenty sail*). **3.** Ship (esp. as discerned from its sails). **4.** (in *pl.*, Naut. sl.) Maker or repairer of sails; ||(Hist.) chief petty officer in charge of rigging. **5.** Wind-catching apparatus, usu. set of boards, attached to arm of windmill. **6.** Sail-fish's dorsal fin; tentacle of nautilus; float of Portuguese man-of-war. **7. ~-arm,** arm of windmill; **~-axle** (on which sail-arms revolve); ***~-boat** (propelled by sail); **~'cloth,** (1) canvas for sails, (2) canvas-like dress-material; **~-fish,** (1) fish of genus *Istiophorus* with large dorsal fin, (2) basking shark; **~'plane,** glider designed for soaring. **8.** Hence (-)~ED[2] (-ld), ~'LESS (-l-l-), *adjs.* [OE *segel,* = OS *segel,* OHG *segal,* ON *segl* f. Gmc **seglam*]

sail[2] *v.* & *n.* **1.** *v.i.* (Of vessel or person on board) travel on water by use of sails (**~'ing-ship, -vessel,** opp. *steamer*; **~ close to** or **near the wind,** sail nearly against it, (fig.) come near transgressing a law or moral principle); (of vessel or person on board) travel on water by use of sails or engine-power, start on voyage (*we sail next week*; **~'ing orders,** instructions to captain for departure, destination, etc.). **2.** (Of bird, cloud, moon, etc.) glide in air; (esp. of woman) walk in stately manner; move smoothly; (fig.) pass easily (*sailed through the examination*); **~ into,** (sl.) attack physically or verbally. **3.** *v.t.* Travel over or along, navigate, glide through, (*the sea, Spanish main, sky,* etc.). **4.** Control navigation of (ship; PLAIN[1], PLANE[3], *sailing*; **~'ing-master,** officer navigating ship, ||esp. yacht); set (toy boat) afloat. **5.** *n.* Voyage or excursion in sailing-vessel (*go for a sail*); voyage of specified duration (*is ten days' sail from Plymouth*). [OE *segl(i)an* f. Gmc **segljan* (as prec.)]

sai'ler *n.* Ship of specified sailing-power (*fast, good, bad, sailer*). [f. prec. + -ER[1]]

sai'lor *n.* Seaman, mariner, esp. one below rank of officer; **good, bad, ~,** person not liable, very liable, to sea-sickness; **~ hat** (of straw with straight narrow brim and flat top, or with turned-up brim in imitation of sailor's worn by women or children); **~-man,** (vulg. or joc.) sailor; **~s' home,** institution for lodging sailors cheaply ashore; hence ~ING[1] (1) *n.*, ~LESS, ~LY[1], *adjs.* [var. of prec.; see -OR]

||**sain** *v.t.* (arch.) Make sign of the cross on, bless, protect by divine power or enchantment. [OE *segnian,* = OS *segnon,* OHG *seganōn,* ON *signa,* f. L *signare* mark (*signum* SIGN[1])]

sai'nfoin *n.* Pink-flowered herb (*Onobrychis viciaefolia*) grown for fodder. [f. obs. F *saintfoin,* orig. lucerne, f. mod. L *sanctum foenum* holy hay alt. of *sanum foenum* wholesome hay, based on L *herba medica* healing plant alt. of *herba Medica* grass from Media; cf. MEDICK]

saint *a.* (*or, when unstressed,* sent; usu. *abbr.* **St., S.,** in *pl.* **Sts., SS.**), *n.*, & *v.t.* **1.** *a.* Holy, canonized or officially recognized by the Church as having won by exceptional holiness a high place in heaven and veneration on earth, (usu. as prefix to name of person or archangel: *St. Paul, St. Michael*; hence ellipt. names of churches as *St. Peter's,* and of towns called after their churches often with loss of possessive sign as *St. Andrews* and *St. Albans,* and some Christian and family names taken either from patron saint or from local names as above; also in some names of churches not called after saints: *St. Saviour's, Sepulchre's, Faith, Cross*); **St. —'s day,** Church festival in memory of particular saint. **2. St. Andrew,** patron saint of Scotland; **St. Andrew's cross** (X-shaped); **St. Andrew's day,** 30 Nov.; **St. Anthony('s) cross** (T-shaped); **St. Anthony's fire,** erysipelas or ergotism; **St. Bartholomew's day,** 24 Aug.; **St. Bernard (dog),** very large dog of breed orig. kept by monks of Hospice on Great St. Bernard pass in Alps for rescue of travellers; **St. David,** patron saint of Wales; **St. David's day,** 1 Mar.; **St. Denis,** patron saint of France; **St. Elmo,** patron saint of seamen; **St. Elmo's fire,** corposant; **St. George,** patron saint of England; **St. George's cross** (+-shaped, red on white ground); **St. George's day,** 23 Apr.; **(Court of) St. James's,** the British Court; **St. John's wort,** yellow-flowered plant of genus *Hypericum*; ||**St. Leger,** horse-race at Doncaster for three-year-olds [f. founder's name]; ||*St. Luke's,* ||*St. Martin's,* SUMMER[1]; **St. Martin's day,** 11 Nov.; ||**St. Michael and St. George,** order of knighthood esp. for disguished service as diplomat etc.; *St.* MONDAY; **St. Patrick,** patron saint of Ireland; **St. Patrick's day,** 17 Mar.; **Order of St. Patrick,** Irish order of knighthood; *St. Peter's* KEY[1]*s*; ||**St. Stephen's,** House of Commons [w. ref. to former use of St. Stephen's chapel, Westminster, for its meetings]; **St. Swithin's day,** 15 July, on which rain or absence of rain is said to presage the same for 40 days; *St.* VALENTINE'*s day*; *St. Vitus's* DANCE[2]. **3.** *n.* One of the blessed dead or other member of the company of heaven; canonized person (see sense 1; PATRON *saint*); (Bibl., arch., and by Puritans, Mormons, etc.) one of God's chosen people, member of the Christian Church or one's own branch of it (**communion of ~s,** fellowship of Christians past and present); person of great real or affected holiness (*would provoke, try the patience of, a saint*); **~'s day,** Church festival in memory of a saint, often observed as holiday at schools etc.; ALL *Saints' Day*. **4.** Hence ~'DOM, ~'HOOD (-t-h-), ~'LING[1], ~'SHIP, *ns.*, ~'LIKE, ~'LY[1], *adjs.* **5.** *v.t.* Canonize, admit to the calendar of saints; call or regard as a saint; (in *p.p.*) worthy to be so regarded, of saintly life, (of place etc.) sacred; *my sainted* AUNT. [ME, f. OF *seint, saint* f. L *sanctus* holy, p.p. of *sancire* consecrate]

saintpau'lĭa (sɛn-) *n.* Blue-flowered E. Afr. herb of genus *Saintpaulia,* African violet. [mod. L, f. Baron W. von *Saint Paul,* Ger. soldier d. 1910, its discoverer + -IA[1]]

Saint-Sīmō'nĭan *a.* & *n.* (Advocate) of socialism in which State controls property and distributes profits according to value of work; hence ~ISM (3), **Saint-Sī'mon**ISM (3), *ns.* [f. C. de *Saint-Simon,* Fr. socialist d. 1825]

saith. See SAY[2].

saithe *n.* Fish akin to cod, with skin which soils fingers like wet coal. [f. ON *seithr*]

sāke[1] *n.* **For the ~ of, for my** etc. **~,** out of consideration for, in the interest of, because of, owing to, in order to please or honour or get or keep, (*for the sake of uniformity*; *for conscience' sake*; *for my own sake as well as yours*; *for both our sakes*; *persecuted for opinion's sake*); **for Christ's, God's, goodness', Heaven's,** (sl.) **Pete's,** etc., **~** (excl. of urgent supplication); **for his name's ~,** (1) because he bears the name he does, (2) in the interest of his reputation; **for old times' ~, for old ~'s ~,** in memory of old days. [OE *sacu* contention, charge, fault, sake, = OS *saka,* OHG *sahha,* ON *sök* f. Gmc **sakō* affair, accusation, (**sak-,* cogn. w. SEEK)]

sa'kė[2] (sah'-) *n.* Japanese fermented liquor made from rice. [Jap.]

sā'ker *n.* **1.** Large falcon (*Falco sacer*) used in

hawking, esp. the female (larger than the male or ~ET[1] *n.*). **2.** (Hist.) Old form of cannon. [ME, f. OF *sacre* (in both senses), f. Arab. *ṣaḳr*]

sa'kĭ (sah'-) *n.* S. Amer. monkey with long non-prehensile tail, and neck-ruff. [F, f. Tupi *çahy*]

sal (sahl) *n.* Indian tree (*Shorea robusta*), yielding timber and dammar resin. [f. Hindi *sāl*]

salaa'm (-lah'm) *n.* & *v.* **1.** *n.* Oriental salutation 'Peace'; Indian obeisance with or without this, low bow of head and body with right palm on forehead; (in *pl.*) respectful compliments. **2.** *v.t.* & *i.* Make salaam (to). [f. Arab. *salām*]

sā'lable. Var. of SALEABLE.

salā'cious (-shus) *a.* Lustful, lecherous; (of writings, pictures, talk, etc.); tending to cause sexual desire; hence or cogn. ~LY[2] *adv.*, ~NESS, **sală'**CITY, *ns.* [f. L *salax salacis* (*salire* leap) + -OUS]

să'lad *n.* Cold dish of various mixtures of raw or cooked vegetables or herbs usu. seasoned with oil, vinegar, etc., and eaten with or including cold meat, fish, hard-boiled eggs, etc.; vegetable or herb suitable for eating raw; FRUIT *salad*; ~ **days,** one's inexperienced youth; **~-dressing,** mixture of oil, vinegar, etc., used with salad; **~-oil,** olive or other vegetable oil for salad-dressing. [ME, f. OF *salade* f. Prov. *salada* f. Rom. **salata* (*herba* herb), fem. p.p. (as n.) of **salare* f. L *sal* salt]

salā'de. Var. of SALLET.

să'lamănder *n.* **1.** Lizard-like animal supposed to live in fire; elemental spirit living in fire; (Zool.) tailed amphibian of order Caudata, whence **sălamă'ndr**OID *a.* & *n.*; * = GOPHER[2] 1. **2.** Red-hot iron for firing gunpowder; hot iron plate for browning top of pudding etc. **3.** Hence **sălamă'ndr**IAN, **sălamă'ndr**INE[1], *adjs.* [ME, f. OF *salamandre*, f. L f. Gk *salamandra*]

sala'mĭ (-lah'-) *n.* Italian sausage highly salted and flavoured often with garlic. [It., pl. of *salame*, f. pop. L **salamen* (**salare* to salt)]

săl ammō'nĭăc *n.* Ammonium chloride, hard white crystalline salt, said to have been made from camels' dung near temple of Jupiter Ammon. [f. L *sal ammoniacus* (*sal* salt; see AMMONIACAL)]

să'langāne (-ngg-) *n.* Swift that makes edible nest. [F, f. *salamga* name in Luzon, Philippines]

salar'ĭăt *n.* The salaried class. [F (*salaire*, see foll.; after *prolétariat*)]

să'larў *n.*, & *v.t.* **1.** *n.* Fixed payment made by employer at regular intervals, usu. monthly or quarterly, to person doing other than manual or mechanical work (cf. WAGE[1]*s*). **2.** *v.t.* (esp. in *p.p.*) Pay salary to. [ME, f. AF *salarie*, OF *salaire* f. L *salarium* orig. soldier's salt-money (*sal* salt; see -ARY[1])]

sāle *n.* **1.** Exchange of a commodity for money or other consideration, selling; BILL[4] *of sale*; **on** or **for** ~, offered for purchase; ~ **and,** or **or, return,** arrangement by which retailer takes quantity of goods with right of returning without payment all that he fails to sell. **2.** Instance of this (*made a sale*); amount sold (*the sales were enormous*). **3.** Event at which goods are sold (~ **of work,** selling of goods made by parishioners etc. for charity; ||JUMBLE[3], RUMMAGE, WHITE[1], *sale*); public auction (**put up for** ~, offer at auction); rapid disposal at reduced prices of shop's stock at end of season etc. **4.** **~-ring,** circle of buyers at auction; **~-room** (in which auctions are held); **~s clerk,** salesman; **~s department** (of a firm, concerned with making sales as opp. manufacturing or dispatching goods); **~s engineer,** salesman with technical knowledge of his goods and their market; **~'sgirl, ~'slady,** (-z-) saleswoman; **~s resistance,** opposition or apathy of prospective customer etc., to be overcome by salesmanship; **~s talk,** persuasive talk to promote sale of goods or (fig.) acceptance of an idea; **~s tax,** tax on (receipts from) sales. [OE *sala*, f. ON, cogn. w. Gmc **saljan* SELL]

sā'le|able (-la-) *a.* Fit for sale, finding purchasers; hence ~ABI'LITY *n.* [f. prec. + -ABLE]

să'lep *n.* Nutritive meal or starch from dried tubers of orchidaceous plants esp. of genus *Orchis*. [F, f. Turk. *sālep* f. Arab. (*ḵuṣa-'l-*) *ta'lab* fox('s testicles)]

***sălerā'tus** *n.* Impure potassium or sodium bicarbonate as ingredient in baking-powder. [f. mod. L *sal aeratus* aerated salt]

Salē'sian (-zhan) *a.* & *n.* (Member) of an educational R.C. religious order. [f. St. François de *Sales*, Fr. R.C. bishop d. 1622 + -IAN]

sā'les|man (-lz-) *n.* (*fem.* **~woman**; *pl.* **~men**). Person employed to sell goods in shop or as middleman between producer and retailer or *as commercial traveller; hence **~man**SHIP (3) *n.* [f. SALE + 's 1 + MAN[1]]

Sā'lĭan[1] *a.* (Rom. Ant.) Of the Salii or priests of Mars. [f. L *Salii* n. pl. (*salire* leap) + -AN]

Sā'lĭan[2] *a.* & *n.* (Member) of 4th-c. Frankish tribe near R. Ijssel, from which Merovingians were descended. [f. LL *Salii* the tribe + -AN]

Să'lĭc *a.* = prec.; ~ **law,** (1) Frankish law-book extant in Merovingian and Carolingian times, (2) law excluding females from dynastic succession, esp. as alleged fundamental law of French monarchy (based on a quotation, not referring to such succession, from the law-book). [f. F *Salique* or f. med. L *Salicus* f. *Salii* (as prec.; see -IC)]

să'lĭcėt *n.* Organ stop like salicional but one octave higher. [f. as SALICIONAL]

să'lĭcĭn *n.* Bitter crystalline substance got from willow-bark etc. and used medicinally. [f. F *salicine* f. L *salix -icis* willow; see -IN]

salĭ'cional (-shon-) *n.* Organ stop with soft reedy tone as of willow-pipe. [G, f. L *salix* (as prec.) w. suf.]

sălĭcy̆'lĭc *a.* ~ **acid,** benzene derivative used as antiseptic and to treat rheumatism; hence **salĭ'cy̆l**ATE[1] (3) *n.* [f. *salicyl* its radical (f. F *salicyle* f. as SALICIN; see -YL) + -IC]

sā'lĭent *a.* & *n.* **1.** *a.* (arch.) Leaping or dancing; (of water etc.) jetting forth; ~ **point,** (arch.) initial stage or origin or first beginning. **2.** (Of angle, esp. in Fortif., opp. *re-entrant*) pointing outwards; jutting out, prominent, conspicuous, most noticeable, (*salient points, features, characteristics*). **3.** *n.* Salient angle or part in fortification or line of attack or defence. **4.** Hence **sā'lĭ**ENCE, **sā'lĭ**ENCY, *ns.*, ~LY[2] *adv.* [f. L *salire* leap; see -ENT]

salĭĕ'ntian (-shan) *a.* & *n.* (Member) of the order Salientia of amphibians, incl. frogs and toads. [f. mod. L *Salientia* (as prec.; see -IA[2])]

salĭ'ferous *a.* (Geol.) (Of strata) containing much salt. [f. L *sal* salt + -I- + -FEROUS]

salī'na *n.* Salt lake. [Sp., f. med. L, = salt-pit]

sā'līne (*or* salī'n) *a.* & *n.* **1.** *a.* (Of natural waters, springs, etc.) impregnated with salt or salts; containing salt; (of taste) salt; of chemical salts, of the nature of a salt; (of medicine) containing salt(s) of alkaline metals or magnesium; hence **salĭ'n**ITY, **sălĭnŏ'**METER, *ns.* **2.** *n.* Salt lake, spring, marsh, etc.; salt-pan, salt-works; saline substance, esp. medicine; solution of salt in water. [ME; a. f. L *sal* salt + -INE[1], n. f. as prec. or f. a.]

salī'v|a *n.* Colourless liquid given by mixed secretions of salivary and mucous glands discharged into mouth and assisting mastication, spittle; ~ **test** (e.g. of racehorse's saliva to determine whether the horse has been doped); so ~ARY[1] (*or* să'lĭ-) *a.* [ME f. L]

să'lĭv|āte *v.* **1.** *v.t.* Produce unusual secretion of saliva in (person) usu. with mercury. **2.** *v.i.* Secrete or discharge saliva esp. in excess. **3.** So ~A'TION *n.* [f. L *salivare* (as prec.) + -ATE[3]]

Salk (sawlk) *n.* ~ **vaccine,** first vaccine developed against poliomyelitis. [f. J. E. ~, Amer. scientist b. 1914]

să'llee *n.* (Austral.) Acacia of various species. [Aboriginal]

să'llenders, sĕ'llanders, (-z) *n. pl.* Dry eruption on front of hock of horse's hind leg. [16th c.; orig. unkn.]

să'llėt *n.* (Hist.) Light helmet with outward-curving rear part. [f. F *salade* ult. f. Rom. **caelata* fem. p.p. (as n.) of L *caelare* engrave (*caelum* chisel)]

să'llow[1] (-ō) *n.* Willow-tree, esp. of low-growing or shrubby kind, whence ~Y[2] *a.*; a shoot, or the wood, of this. [OE *salh salg-* f. Gmc **salhaz*, cogn. w. OHG *salaha*, ON *selja*, L *salix*]

să'llow[2] (-ō) *a.* & *v.* **1.** *a.* (Of skin or complexion, or person in these respects) of sickly yellow or pale brown; hence ~ISH[1] 2 *a.*, ~NESS *n.* **2.** *v.t.* & *i.* Make or grow sallow. [OE *salo* dusky, = MDu. *salu* dirty, OHG *salo* dark, ON *sölr* yellow, f. Gmc **salwa-*]

să'llȳ[1] *n.*, & *v.i.* **1.** *n.* Rush of besieged upon besiegers, sortie; a going forth, excursion; sudden start into activity, outburst; (arch.) escapade; witticism, piece of banter, lively remark esp. by way of attack upon person or thing or of diversion in argument; **~-port,** opening in fortification for making sally from. **2.** *v.i.* Make military sally (*out*); go *forth* or *out* on a journey, for a walk, etc.; (arch.) issue or come out suddenly. [f. F *saillie* fem. p.p. (as n.) of *saillir* issue, f. OF *salir* f. L *salire* leap]

să'llȳ[2] *n.* First movement of bell when set for ringing; bell's position when set; part of bell-rope prepared with inwoven wool for holding; **~-hole** (through which bell-rope passes). [perh. f. prec. in sense 'leaping motion']

Să'llȳ[3] *n.* AUNT *Sally*; ||~ **Lunn,** sweet light teacake served hot [perh. f. name of girl hawking them at Bath *c.* 1800]. [fam. form of woman's name *Sarah*; see -Y[3]]

sălmagŭ'ndĭ *n.* Dish of chopped meat, anchovies, eggs, onions, etc., and seasoning; general mixture, miscellaneous collection, of articles, subjects, qualities, etc. [f. F *salmigondis*, of unkn. orig.]

să'lmi (-ē) *n.* Ragout or casserole esp. of game-birds. [F, abbr. f. as prec.]

să'lmon (să'mon) *n.* (*pl.* usu. same) & *a.* **1.** *n.* Large silver-scaled pink-fleshed anadromous fish of genus *Salmo* etc., much prized for food and sport; (Austral. & N.Z.) barramundi or other fish resembling this; **~-colour(ed),** (of) the orange-pink colour of salmon-flesh; **~-ladder, -leap, -pass, -stair,** series of steps or other arrangement for allowing salmon to pass dam and ascend stream; **~-pink,** salmon-colour(ed); **~ trout,** trout resembling salmon; hence **să'lmon**OID *a.* & *n.* **2.** *a.* Salmon-coloured, orange-pink. [ME, f. AF *sa(u)moun*, OF *saumon* f. L *salmo -onis*]

sălmonĕ'll|a *n.* Pathogenic bacterium of genus *Salmonella*, esp. of species causing food poisoning; hence ~O'SIS *n.* [mod. L, f. D. E. *Salmon*, Amer. veterinary surgeon d. 1914 + dim. suf.]

Sălomŏ'nĭc, Sălomō'nĭan, *adjs.* Of or as of SOLOMON. [f. LL *Salomon* Solomon + -IC, -IAN]

să'lon (să'lawn) *n.* Reception-room in continental, esp. French, great house; (Hist.) (meeting of notabilities in) reception-room of (esp. Parisian) lady of fashion; room or establishment where hairdresser, couturier, etc., receives clients; (*S*~) annual exhibition of living artists' pictures; ~ **music,** light music for drawing-room. [F; see foll.]

salōō'n *n.* **1.** Hall or large room, esp. in hotel or place of public resort, fit for assemblies, exhibitions, etc. **2.** Public room for first-class or for all passengers on ship. **3.** ||Luxurious railway carriage without compartments, serving as lounge etc. **4.** ||Public room(s) or gallery for specified purpose (*billiard, dancing, hairdressing, shooting*, etc. *-saloon*). **5.** * = BAR[1] 7; || = *saloon bar*. **6.**|| = *saloon car*. **7.** ||~ **bar,** first-class bar in public house; ||~ **car,** (1) motor car with closed body and no partition behind driver, (2) = sense 3: ~ **deck** (for passengers using saloon); ***~-keeper** (of bar); ||~ **pistol, rifle,** (adapted for short-range practice in shooting-saloon). [f. F *salon*, f. It. *salone* augment. of *sala* hall; see -OON]

Salop. *abbr.* Shropshire (former name of *Salop*, county in England).

Salō'pĭan *a.* & *n.* (Native) of Salop or Shropshire; (past or present member) of Shrewsbury School. [f. AF *Salopesberia* f. ME, f. OE *Scrobbesbyrig* Shrewsbury, + -IAN]

sălpĭglŏ'ssĭs *n.* Herbaceous garden-plant allied to petunia, with trumpet-shaped flowers. [mod. L, irreg. f. Gk *salpigx* trumpet + *glōssa* tongue]

să'lpĭng- (-nj) *comb. form.* (Med.) Of Fallopian tubes, as: ~E'CTOMY, ~I'TIS, *ns.* [f. Gk *salpigx salpiggos*, lit. 'trumpet']

sălse *n.* Mud volcano. [F, f. It. *salsa* f. name of one near Modena]

să'lsĭfȳ *n.* European plant (*Tragopogon porrifolius*) with long cylindrical fleshy root cooked as vegetable; **black** ~, scorzonera. [f. F *salsifis* f. obs. It. *salsefica*, of unkn. orig.]

salt (sawlt *or* sŏlt) *n.*, *a.*, & *v.t.* **1.** *n.* (**Common**) ~, substance that gives sea-water its characteristic taste, got in crystalline forms from strata consisting of it or by evaporation of brine pumped from these or of sea-water, and used for seasoning or preserving food and other purposes, sodium chloride, (BAY[2] *salt*, ROCK[1]-*-salt*, SEA-*salt*); **table** ~ (powdered or easy to powder for the salt-cellar); **in** ~, sprinkled with salt or immersed in brine as preservative. **2. Eat ~ with,** be guest of; **eat** person's ~, be his guest or dependant; **not made of** ~, not disconcerted by wet weather; **put ~ on tail of,** capture, [w. ref. to joc. directions given children for catching bird]; **rub ~ into wound,** exacerbate humiliation etc.; **take with a grain** or **pinch of** ~, regard as exaggerated, be incredulous about, believe only part of; **the ~ of the earth,** people or classes for whose existence the world is better, those whose qualities are a model for the rest, [Matt. 5:13]; **worth** one's ~, efficient, capable, having merit. **3.** Sting, piquancy, pungency, wit, (ATTIC[1] *salt*). **4.** (in *sing.* or *pl.*) Substance resembling salt in taste, form, etc., (BATH[1] *salts*, EPSOM *salt(s)*, GLAUBER'*s salt(s)*, *salt(s) of* LEMON[1], SMELL*ing-salts*); (in *pl.*, esp.) such substance used as aperient; **like a dose of ~s,** (sl.) very fast. **5.** (Chem.) Compound of basic and acid radicals, acid with whole or part of its hydrogen replaced by a metal or metal-like radical. **6.** = *salt-cellar*; **above, below,** etc., **the** ~, (Hist.) seated at table among the family and their equals, among the servants and dependants. **7.** Marsh overflowed by sea, often used as pasture or for collecting water for salt-making. **8.** (in *pl.*) Exceptional rush of sea-water up river. **9.** (**Old**) ~, experienced sailor. **10. ~'bush,** orache; **~-cat** [*cat* unexpl.], mass of salt mixed with gravel, urine, etc., to attract pigeons and keep them at home; **~-cellar** [assim. of obs. *saler* (f. AF **saler*, OF *salier* salt-box f. L as SALARY) to CELLAR], vessel holding salt for table use, (colloq.) unusually deep hollow above collar-bone in (esp. woman's) neck; **~ dome,** mass of salt forced up into sedimentary rocks; **~-glaze,** glaze on stoneware made by throwing salt into hot kiln containing the ware; ***~-grass** (growing in salt meadows or alkaline regions); **~ lake,** lake of salt water; **~-lick,** place to which animals resort to lick earth impregnated with salt; **~-marsh,** = sense 7; **~-mine,** mine yielding rock-salt, (fig.) place of unremitting toil; **~-pan,** depression near sea, or vessel, used for getting salt by evaporation; ***~-shaker,** container of salt for sprinkling on food; **~-spoon** (usu. with short handle and roundish deep bowl for taking table salt); **~-well,** bored well yielding brine; **~-works,** manufactory of salt; **~'wort,** (1) plant of genus *Salsola*, (2) glasswort. **11.** Hence ~'LESS *a.* **12.** *a.* Impregnated with, containing, tasting of, cured or preserved or seasoned with, salt (cf. FRESH); (of plant) growing in sea or salt-marshes; (of tears, grief, etc.) bitter, afflicting; (of wit etc.) pungent; (of story, jest, etc.) indecent, spicy; **~ fish,** (W. Ind.) preserved cod; **~ horse,** (Naut. sl.) salt beef; *salt* JUNK[1]; **~ meadow** (subject to flooding with salt water); **~ water,** sea-water etc., (sl.) tears; **~-water,** of, or living in, the sea. **13.** Hence ~'ISH[1] 2 *a.*, ~'LY[2] *adv.*, ~'NESS *n.* **14.** *v.t.* Cure or preserve with salt or brine; **~ away** or **down,** (sl.) put (money etc.) by. **15.** Sprinkle (esp. snow to melt it in street) with salt. **16.** Make salt or piquant, season, (lit. or fig.); (in *p.p.*, of horse or person) proof against diseases incident to climate or special conditions by habituation, hardened. **17.** Treat with solution of salt or mixture of salts. **18.** (Commerc. sl.) **~ an account** etc., put extremely high or low price for articles, **~ the books,** show receipts as larger than they have really been; **~ a mine,** (sl., lit. or fig.) introduce extraneous ore etc. to make it seem rich. [(v. f. OE *s(e)altan*) f. OE *s(e)alt*, OS, ON, Goth. *salt*, OHG *salz* f. Gmc **saltam*, n. f. **saltaz* a., f. IE **sal-*]

S.A.L.T. *abbr.* Strategic Arms Limitation Talks.

sălterĕ'llō *n.* (*pl.* **~s**). Italian and Spanish dance for one couple, with sudden skips. [f. It. *salterello*, Sp. *saltarelo* rel. to It. *saltare*, Sp. *saltar* leap, dance f. L *saltare* (as foll.)]

săltā'tion *n.* Leaping, dancing; a jump; sudden transition or movement; so **să'ltat**ORY, **săltatŏr'**IAL, *adjs.* [f. L *saltatio* (*saltare* frequent. of *salire salt-* leap; see -ATION)]

sa'lter (saw'l- *or* sŏ'l-) *n.* Manufacturer of or dealer in salt; = DRY[1]-*salter*; workman at salt-works; person who salts fish etc. [OE *sealtere* (as SALT v., -ER[1])]

sa'ltern (saw'l- *or* sŏ'l-) *n.* Salt-works; set of pools for natural evaporation of sea-water. [OE *sealtærn* (as SALT, *ærn* building)]

să'ltĭgrāde *a.* & *n.* (Spider) with legs adapted for jumping. [f. mod. L *Saltigradae* f. L *saltus* leap (*salire salt-*) + *-gradus* walking]

săltĭmbă'ncō *n.* (*pl.* **~s**). (arch.) Mountebank, quack. [It. (*saltare* leap, *in* on, *banco* bench)]

sa'ltĭng (saw'l- *or* sŏ'l-) *n.* In vbl senses; (esp. in *pl.*) = SALT 7. [ME, f. SALT + -ING[1]]

să'ltīre *n.* (Her.) Ordinary formed by bend and bend sinister crossing like a St. Andrew's cross (**in ~,** so arranged); hence ~WISE (-īrwīz) *adv.* [ME, f. OF *sau(l)toir* etc. stirrup-cord, stile, saltire, f. med. L *saltatorium* (as SALTATION; see -ORY)]

saltpē'tre, *saltpē'ter, (sawl- *or* sŏl-; -*ter*) *n.* Potassium nitrate, nitre, white crystalline salty substance used as constituent of gunpowder, in preserving meat, and medicinally; **Chile ~,** sodium nitrate; **~-paper,** touchpaper. [ME f. OF *salpetre*, f. med. L *salpetra* prob. for **sal petrae* salt of rock (i.e. found as incrustation), w. assim. to SALT; *petrae* f. LL f. Gk *petra* rock]

să'ltus *n.* Sudden transition, breach of continuity. [L, = leap]

sa'lt|ȳ (saw'l- *or* sŏ'l-) *a.* = SALT 12; hence **~ĭ**NESS *n.* [ME, f. SALT + -Y[2]]

salū'br|ĭous (*or* -lōō'-) *a.* (Esp. of climate, air, etc.) healthy; hence or cogn. **~ĭous**LY[2] *adv.*, ~ITY *n.* [f. L *salubris* (*salus* health) + -OUS]

salu'kĭ (-lōō'-) *n.* Tall swift slender silky-coated dog, Arabian gazelle-hound. [f. Arab. *salūķī*]

să'lūtarȳ *a.* Producing good effects, beneficial; (arch.) salubrious. [ME, f. F *salutaire* or f. L *salutaris* (*salus -utis* health; see -ARY[2])]

sălūtā'tion *n.* (Use of) words spoken or written or gesture to convey interest in another's health etc., pleasure at sight of or communication with him, or courteous recognition of his arrival or departure; **the Angelic S~,** the AVE Maria; hence or cogn. ~AL, **salū'tat**ORY (*or* -lōō'-), *adjs.* [ME f. OF, or f. L *salutatio* (as foll.; see -ATION)]

salū'te (*or* -ōō't) *v.* & *n.* **1.** *v.t.* Make salutation to, greet; (arch.) hail as (king etc.). **2.** *v.t.* & *i.* Perform salute to or *to*, perform salute; (arch.) kiss (person, cheek, hand) esp. at meeting or parting. **3.** *v.t.* Accost or receive *with* smile, oath, etc.; (arch.) become perceptible to (eye, ear, person arriving). **4.** *n.* Gesture expressing respect, homage, or courteous recognition, to person esp. when arriving or departing; (arch. or joc.) kiss esp. as greeting; (Mil., Naut.) prescribed movement or position of body or weapon, or use of flag(s) or discharge of gun(s), in sign of respect (*a salute of 7 guns was fired*); **the ~,** attitude taken by individual soldier, sailor, policeman, etc., in saluting; **take the ~,** (1, of highest officer present) acknowledge it by gesture as meant for him, (2) be recipient of ceremonial salutes by members of procession. **5.** (Fenc.) Formal performance of certain guards etc. by fencers before engaging. [ME, f. L *salutare* (*salus -utis* health); n. partly f. OF *salut* (*saluer* f. L *salutare*)]

sălūtĭ'ferous *a.* (arch.) Promoting health or safety. [f. L *salutifer* (as prec.; see -FEROUS)]

să'lvage *n.*, & *v.t.* **1.** *n.* (Payment made or due for) saving of a ship or its cargo from loss by wreck or capture, rescue of property from fire, wreckage, etc.; property salvaged. **2.** Saving and utilization of waste paper, scrap-metal, etc.; materials salvaged. **3.** *v.t.* Make salvage of; save from wreck, fire, etc.; hence ~ABLE (-*ja*-) *a.* [F, f. med. L *salvagium* f. L *salvare* SAVE[1]; see -AGE]

sălvā'tion *n.* **1.** Saving of the soul; deliverance from sin and its consequences and admission to heaven brought about by Christ (**find ~,** be converted; **work out** one's **own ~,** find unaided how to avoid disaster). **2.** Preservation from loss, calamity, etc.; thing that preserves from these (*be the salvation of*). **3. S~ Army,** world-wide missionary organization on military model for charity and revival of religion among the destitute. **4.** Hence ~ISM (3), ~IST (2), *ns.* (esp. w. ref. to Salvation Army). [ME, f. OF *sauvacion, salvacion*, f. eccl. L *salvatio -onis* (*salvare* SAVE[1]; see -ATION), transl. Gk *sōtēria*]

sălve[1] (*or* sahv) *n.*, & *v.t.* **1.** *n.* (poet.) Healing ointment for sores or wounds. **2.** See LIP*salve*. **3.** Thing that is soothing *for* wounded feelings or uneasy conscience or (arch.) explains away discrepancy or palliates fault. **4.** *v.t.* (arch.) Anoint (wound etc.). **5.** (arch.) Smooth over or make good (defect, disgrace, etc.). **6.** Soothe (pride, self-love, conscience, etc.). **7.** (arch.) Account for, dispose of, harmonize, vindicate, (difficulty, doubt, discrepancy, person's honour). [n. f. OE *s(e)alf(e)*, OS OHG *salba* f. Gmc **salbhō*; v. f. OE *s(e)alfian*, in senses 5 to 7 partly f. L *salvare* SAVE¹]

Să'lvē² *n.* **S~ (Regina)**, R.C. antiphon (beginning thus) recited after Divine Office from Trinity Sunday to Advent, music for it. [ME f. L, imper. of *salvēre* = hail(, queen)]

sălv|e³ *v.t.* Save (ship, cargo) from loss at sea; save (property) from fire; hence **~'ABLE** *a.* [back form. f. SALVAGE]

să'lver *n.* Tray usu. of gold, silver, brass, or electroplate, on which refreshments, letters, cards, etc., are handed. [f. F *salve* tray for presenting certain things to king f. Sp. *salva* assaying of food (*salvar* SAVE¹); assoc. w. *platter*]

să'lvĭa *n.* Plant of genus *Salvia*, esp. cultivated species with blue or red flowers. [L, = SAGE¹]

să'lvō¹ *n.* (*pl.* **~s**). Saving clause, reservation, (*with an express salvo of their rights*); tacit reservation, quibbling evasion, bad excuse; expedient for saving reputation or soothing pride or conscience. [L, abl. of *salvus* SAFE² as used in *salvo jure* without prejudice to the right of (person)]

să'lvō² *n.* (*pl.* **~es** *or* **~s**). Simultaneous discharge of artillery or other firearms esp. as salute, or in sea-fight; number of bombs released from aircraft at same moment; round or volley of applause. [f. earlier *salve*, F f. It. *salva* salutation (as SAVE²)]

săl volă'tĭlė *n.* (Flavoured alcoholic solution, used as restorative in faintness etc., of) ammonium carbonate. [mod. L, = volatile salt]

să'lvor *n.* Person or ship making or assisting in salvage. [f. SALVE³ + -OR]

||**Săm** *n.* (sl.) **Stand ~**, bear the expense esp. of drink; **upon my ~** (excl. of asseveration). [19th c.; in second phr. prob. f. obs. cant *sal(o)mon* the Mass, perh. f. LL *Salomon* Solomon]

S.A.M. *abbr.* surface-to-air missile.

Sam. *abbr.* Samuel (O.T.).

să'mara *n.* (Bot.) Winged fruit of sycamore, ash, etc. [mod. L, f. L, = elm-seed]

Samă'rĭtan *n.* & *a.* **1.** *n.* Native or language of Samaria (**good ~**, genuinely charitable person, w. ref. to Luke 10:33 etc.); adherent of the Samaritan religious system, accepting only the (Samaritan) Pentateuch; member of an organization offering help and friendship to those in despair. **2.** *a.* Of Samaria or the Samaritans; **~ Pentateuch,** recension used by Samaritans of which MSS. are in archaic characters. **3.** Hence **~ISM** (2, 3, 4) *n.* [f. LL *Samaritanus* f. Gk *Samareitēs* (*Samareia* Samaria); see -AN]

samar̄'ĭum *n.* (Chem.) Metallic element of lanthanide series. [f. *samarskite* mineral in which its spectrum was first observed (*Samarski* 19th-c. Russ. official, -ITE¹ (2)) + -IUM]

să'mba *n.*, & *v.i.* **1.** *n.* Brazilian Negro dance; ballroom dance imitative of this; music for it. **2.** *v.i.* Dance samba. [Port., of Afr. orig.]

samb(h)ar. Var. of SAMBUR.

să'mbō *n.* (*pl.* **~s** *or* **~es**). **1.** Half-breed esp. of Negro and Indian or European blood. **2.** (*S~*). (derog.) Negro. [f. Sp. *zambo*, perh. = *zambo* bandy-legged; sense 2 perh. a diff. wd]

Săm Brow'ne *n.* Army officer's belt and strap supporting it. [f. Sir *Samuel* J. *Browne*, Brit. mil. commander d. 1901]

să'mbur̄ *n.* S.E. Asian elk (*Rusa unicolor*). [f. Hindi *sā(m)bar*]

sāme *a.*, *pron.*, & *adv.* **1.** *a.* Monotonous, uniform, unvarying (*the same old story*); hence **~'NESS** (-mn-) *n.* **2. This, these, that, those, ~,** the aforesaid, the person(s) or thing(s) previously alluded to or thought of, (*this same man was later my tutor*; *what is the use of this same patience?*; (derog.) *these same politicians would now have us believe* etc.). **3. The ~** *a.*, identical, not different, unchanged, unvarying, (*the same causes produce the same effects*; *the same car was later used in another crime*; *the difference between a body in motion and the same body at rest*; *the same observations are true of the others also*; *all planets travel in the same direction*; *either method comes* or *amounts to the same thing*; *say the same thing twice over*; *bigotry is the same in every age*; *she was always the same to me*; *he was not the same man after his illness*; **just the ~, one and the ~, the very ~,** emphatically the same; **much the ~,** not appreciably different; *at the same* TIME¹; *by the same* TOKEN), (arch.) identical *with* (*words of the same nature with those he had first heard*), (emphatic substitute—before full or ellipt. rel. clause with *that*, *where*, etc., or esp. *as* which often replaces *that* under its influence—for) the, that, those, (*at the same time that I am trying to stop it*; *to the same place where I had found it*; *on the same grounds that he would defend suicide*; *I have the same Bible my mother gave me*; *Rhenish wine at the same price as French was sold at*; *sailors received the same pay as soldiers*; *gave the same answer as before*). **4. The ~** *pron.*, the same thing (*we must all say* or *do the same*; *would do the same again*; **and the ~ to you!,** I wish you may have the same thing; **it is all** or **just the ~,** it makes no difference), (arch.) the same person (**from the ~, to the ~,** heading of poem or letter coming from or addressed to same person as previous one), (arch., colloq., or Law) the aforesaid thing or person (*grace and power faithfully to fulfil the same*; *he that shall endure unto the end, the same shall be saved*; *and never met* or *found the same again*). **5. The ~** *adv.*, in the same manner (*we take what pleasure we can get, the same as you do, the same as in the past*; ALL *the same*; **just the ~,** in spite of changed conditions; **think the ~ of, feel the ~ to,** remain in the same mind regarding). **6.** *pron.* (colloq.) = *the same* (see sense 4); **~ here,** the same applies to me. **7.** *adv.* (colloq.) = *the same* (see sense 5). [ME f. ON, = OHG, Goth. *sama* f. Gmc **samaz* f. IE **somós*]

să'mel *a.* (Of brick or tile) imperfectly baked, soft, from being outermost in the kiln. [17th c., perh. f. OE **samǣled* half-burnt]

să'mfu (-ōō) *n.* Chinese woman's suit of jacket and trousers. [Cantonese]

Sā'mĭan *a.* & *n.* (Native) of Samos; **~ ware,** fine Gaulish pottery found on Roman sites in Britain. [f. L f. Gk *Samios* (island of *Samos* in the Aegean Sea) + -AN]

să'mĭsĕn *n.* Long three-stringed Japanese guitar, played with plectrum. [Jap., f. Chin. *san-hsien* (*san* three, *hsien* string)]

să'mīte *n.* (Hist.) Rich medieval dress-fabric of silk occas. interwoven with gold. [ME, f. OF *samit* f. med. L *examitum* f. med. Gk *hexamiton* f. Gk *hexa-* six- + *mitos* thread]

să'mĭzdăt *n.* System of clandestine publication of banned literature in U.S.S.R. [Russ.]

să'mlėt *n.* Young salmon. [f. earlier *salmonet* (SALMON, -ET¹), after -LET]

Să'mnīte *n.* & *a.* (Member) of an ancient-Italian people often at war with republican Rome; their language. [ME, f. L *Samnites* pl., cogn. w. *Sabinus* SABINE; see -ITE¹]

Samō'an *a.* & *n.* (Native or language) of Samoa. [f. *Samoa* in the Pacific + -AN]

să'movar̄ *n.* Apparatus with interior heating tube to keep water at boiling-point for making tea. [Russ., = self-boiler]

Să'moyĕd (-mo-) *n.* **1.** Member of a people of northern Siberia; their language. **2.** Dog of white Arctic breed. [f. Russ. *samoed*]
Sămoyĕ'dĭc (-mo-) *a.* & *n.* **1.** *a.* Of the Samoyeds. **2.** *n.* Samoyed language. [f. prec. + -IC]
***sămp** *n.* (Porridge of) coarsely-ground maize. [f. Algonquin *nasamp* softened by water]
să'mpăn *n.* Small boat usu. with stern-oar(s), used in Far East. [f. Chin. *san-pan* (*san* three, *pan* board)]
să'mphīre *n.* Cliff plant with aromatic saline fleshy leaves used in pickles; glasswort. [earlier *samp(i)ere* f. F (*herbe de*) *Saint Pierre* St. Peter('s herb)]
sa'mple (sah'-) *n.*, & *v.t.* **1.** *n.* Small separated part of something illustrating the qualities of the mass etc. it is taken from, specimen, pattern, (esp. as offered by dealer in commodities sold by weight or measure); illustrative or typical example (*that is a fair sample of his methods*); ~ **post** (at special rates for sending trade samples). **2.** *v.t.* Take or give samples, try the qualities, get a representative experience, of. [ME, f. AF *assample*, OF *essample* EXAMPLE]
sa'mpler[1] (sah'-) *n.* In vbl senses; *a collection of samples. [f. prec. + -ER[1]]
sa'mpler[2] (sah'-) *n.* Piece of embroidery worked in various stitches as specimen of proficiency (often preserved and displayed on wall etc.). [f. OF *essamplaire* (as EXEMPLAR)]
Să'mson *n.* Person of great strength or resembling Samson in some respect; **~('s)-post,** (Naut.) strong pillar passing through hold or between decks, post in whale-boat to which harpoon rope is attached. [LL, f. Gk *Sampsōn* f. Heb. *šimšôn* (Judg. 13–16)]
să'murai (-oorī) *n.* (*pl.* same). Japanese army officer; (Hist.) military retainer of daimios, member of military caste in Japan. [Jap.]
să'native, să'natorȳ, *adjs.* Healing, of or tending to physical or moral health, curative. [ME, f. OF *sanatif* or f. LL *sanativus* (*sanare* cure; see -IVE), w. mod. var. in -ORY]
sănatōr'ĭ|um *n.* (*pl.* **~ums** *or* **~a**). Establishment for treatment of invalids, esp. of convalescents and the chronically sick; room or building for sick persons in school etc. [mod. L (as prec.; see -ORY)]
sănbeni'tō (-nē'-) *n.* (*pl.* **~s**). Penitential yellow garment shaped like monk's scapular with red St. Andrew's cross before and behind worn by confessed and penitent heretic under Spanish Inquisition; similar black garment painted with flames and devils worn by impenitent heretic at auto-da-fé. [f. Sp. *sambenito* (*San Benito* St. Benedict, as shaped like scapular introduced by him)]
să'nctĭ|fȳ *v.t.* Consecrate, set apart or observe as holy; purify or free from sin, (in *p.p.*) sanctimonious; impart sanctity to, make legitimate or binding by religious sanction, give colour of morality or innocence to, justify, sanction (*the end sanctifies the means*); make productive of or conducive to holiness; hence or cogn. **~FICA'TION** *n.*, **~fīER**[1] *n.* (esp. Holy Spirit). [ME, f. OF *saintifier* f. eccl. L *sanctificare* f. L *sanctus* holy; see -FY]
sănctĭmō'nĭous *a.* Making a show of sanctity or piety; hence **~LY**[2] *adv.*, **~NESS** *n.* [as foll. + -OUS]
să'nctĭmonȳ *n.* Sanctimoniousness. [f. L *sanctimonia* sanctity (as SAINT; see -MONY)]
să'nction *n.*, & *v.t.* **1.** *n.* (Hist.) Law, decree; PRAGMATIC *sanction*. **2.** Penalty for disobedience or reward for obedience attached to a law, clause containing this; (Eth.) consideration operating to enforce obedience to any rule of conduct; (Polit., esp. in *pl.*) economic or military action by State(s) to coerce another into conformity with international norms of conduct. **3.** Confirmation or ratification of law etc. by supreme authority, express authoritative permission, countenance or encouragement given to action etc. by custom etc. **4.** *v.t.* Ratify, invest with authority, make binding; authorize; countenance (action etc.); attach penalty or reward to (law). [F, f. L *sanctio -onis* (*sancire sanct-* make sacred; see -ION)]
să'nctĭtūde *n.* (arch.) Saintliness. [ME, f. L *sanctitudo* (as SAINT; see -TUDE)]
să'nctĭtȳ *n.* Holiness of life, saintliness, (ODOUR *of sanctity*); sacredness, being hallowed, right to reverence, inviolability; (in *pl.*) sacred obligations, feelings, etc. [ME, f. OF *sain(c)tité* or f. L *sanctitas* (as SAINT; see -ITY)]
să'nctūarȳ *n.* **1.** Place recognized as holy; church, temple, tabernacle, HOLY place, HOLY of holies; penetralia, inmost recess, (lit. or fig.); part of chancel between altar rails and east window or screen, containing high altar. **2.** (Hist.) Sacred place where fugitive from law, or debtor, was secured by medieval Church law against arrest or violence; place in which similar immunity was established by custom or law. **3.** Place of refuge (*London, the sanctuary of political refugees*); (right of affording) immunity from arrest etc.; **take ~**, resort to place of refuge. **4.** Place or time for preservation and protection of birds and wild animals. [ME, f. AF *sanctuarie*, OF *sanctuaire* f. L *sanctuarium* (as SAINT; see -ARY[1])]
să'nctum *n.* **1.** Holy place; **~ sanctor'um,** holy of holies in Jewish temple, (fig.) inner retreat, esoteric doctrine, etc. **2. ~ (sanctor'um)**, (joc.) person's private room, study, den. [L, neut. of *sanctus* holy, p.p. of *sancire* consecrate; *sanctorum* gen. pl. in transl. of Heb. *ḳōdeš haḳḳ°dāšîm* holy of holies]
să'nctus *n.* The hymn 'Holy, holy, holy' closing the Eucharistic preface; music for this; **~ bell,** bell in turret at junction of nave and chancel, or handbell, rung at the sanctus. [ME f. L, =holy]
sănd *n.*, & *v.t.* **1.** *n.* Minute fragments resulting from wearing down of esp. siliceous rocks and found covering parts of the sea-shore, river-beds, deserts, etc.; (in *sing.* or *pl.*) shoal or submarine bank of sand; (usu. in *pl.*) grain of sand; (in *pl.*) expanse or tracts of sand; **built** etc. **on ~**, unstable; **head in the ~**, refusal to acknowledge obvious danger; PLOUGH[2] *the sand(s)*; ROPE *of sand*; **the ~s are running out** etc., time of grace etc. is nearly at end [w. ref. to hour-glass etc.]. **2.** Light brown colour like that of sand. **3.** *(colloq.) Firmness of purpose, grit. **4. ~'bag,** (*n.*) bag filled with sand for use (a) in fortification for making temporary defences, or for protection of building etc. against blast and splinters, (b) as ballast esp. for boat or balloon, (c) as ruffian's weapon inflicting heavy blow without leaving mark, (d) as support for engraving-plate, (e) to stop draught from window or door, (*v.t.*) barricade or defend, provide (window, chink), with sandbag(s), fell with blow from sandbag, *persuade by harsh means; **~'bank,** deposit of sand forming shallow place in sea or river; **~-bar,** sandbank at mouth of harbour or river; **~-bath,** (Chem.) vessel of heated sand to provide uniform heating; **~-bed,** stratum of sand; **~-blast** *n.*, & *v.t.*, (treat with) jet of sand driven by compressed air or steam for cleaning or roughening glass etc.; **~-box,** mould of sand used in founding, box of sand on locomotive for sprinkling slippery rails, (Golf) container for sand used in teeing, (Hist.) device for sprinkling sand to dry ink, *sand-pit enclosed in box; **~'boy,** (prob.) boy hawking sand for sale (*jolly*

as a ~boy, in high spirits); **~-castle,** structure of sand made by child on sea-shore; **~-cloud,** driving sand in simoom; **~-crack,** disease of horses' hoofs, crack in human foot from walking on hot sand, crack in brick due to imperfect mixing; ***~ dollar,** round flat sea-urchin; *sand-*DUNE; **~-eel,** eel-like fish of genus *Ammodytes*; **~-flea,** (1) chigoe, (2) = *sand-hopper*; **~-fly,** (1) midge of genus *Simulium*, (2) biting fly of genus *Phlebotomus* transmitting a virus disease; **~-glass,** wasp-waisted reversible glass with two bulbs containing enough sand to take a definite time in passing from upper to lower bulb; **~-groper,** (Austral.) gold-rush pioneer, (joc.) Western Australian; **~-hill,** dune; **~-hopper,** small jumping crustacean burrowing on sea-shore; ***~'lot,** unoccupied sandy ground used for children's games; **~'man,** personification of tiredness causing children's eyes to smart towards bedtime; ||**~-martin,** bird (*Riparia riparia*) nesting in side of sand-pit or sandy bank; **~-painting,** Amer. Ind. ceremonial design made with coloured sands; **~'paper,** (*n.*) paper with sand or other abrasive stuck to it for smoothing or polishing, (*v.t.*) polish with sandpaper; **~'piper,** bird of family Scolopacidae haunting open wet sandy places; **~-pit,** (esp.) partly sand-filled hollow for children to play in; **~-pump** (for clearing drill-hole, caisson, etc., of wet sand); **~-shoe,** (esp. of canvas with rubber or hemp sole for use on sand); **~-skipper,** = *sand-hopper*; **~-spout,** pillar of sand raised by desert whirlwind; **~'stone,** sedimentary rock of compressed sand (*old red, new red, ~stone,* (Geol.) series of rocks below, above, Carboniferous); **~'storm,** desert storm of wind with clouds of sand; **~-table,** (Mil.) relief model in sand for explanation of tactics etc.; **~'wort,** plant of genus *Arenaria* etc. growing in sand; **~-yacht,** boat on wheels propelled over sand by wind. **5.** *v.t.* Sprinkle with sand; overlay with, bury under, sand; adulterate (sugar etc.) with sand; polish with sand or sandpaper, whence ~'ER¹ (2) *n.* [OE, = OS *sand*, OHG *sant*, ON *sandr* f. Gmc **sandam*, **sandaz*]

să'ndal¹ *n.*, & *v.t.* (||-ll-). **1.** *n.* Sole without upper, attached to foot by thongs passing over instep and round ankle (as worn orig. by ancient Greeks and Romans); strap for fastening low shoe, passing over instep or round ankle. **2.** *v.t.* (esp. in *p.p.*) Put sandals on (feet, person); fasten or provide (shoe) with sandal. [ME, f. L f. Gk *sandalion* dim. of *sandalon* wooden shoe, prob. of Asiatic orig.]

să'ndal² *n.* ~**(wood)**, scented wood esp. from E. Ind. or Australian **~-tree** of genus *Santalum*; **red ~wood,** red timber or dyewood from E. Ind. tree (*Pterocarpus santalinus*); **~wood oil,** yellow aromatic oil from sandal-tree. [ME, f. med. L *sandalum*, ult. f. Skr. *čandana*]

să'ndarăc, -ăch, (-k) *n.* **1.** Realgar. **2.** Resin of N. Afr. conifer (*Tetraclinis articulata*), used in making varnish. [f. L f. Gk *sandarakē*, of Asiatic orig.]

să'nd-blīnd *a.* (arch.) Dim-sighted, purblind. [ME, prob. f. OE **samblind* (*sam-* half f. WG **sāmi-*, BLIND¹), assim. to SAND]

să'nderlĭng *n.* Small wading bird of sandpiper family. [perh. f. OE **sandyrthling* (as SAND, *yrthling* ploughman, also name of some bird)]

să'nders, sau'nders, (-z) *n.* SANDAL²wood, esp. red sandalwood. [ME, f. OF *sandre* var. of *sandle* SANDAL²]

să'ndhĭ (-dĭ) *n.* (Gram.) Change in form of word determined by its position in an utterance (e.g. change of *a* to *an* before vowel). [f. Skr. *saṃdhi* putting together]

să'ndĭver *n.* Liquid scum formed in glass-making. [ME, app. f. F *suin de verre* exhalation (*suer* to sweat) of glass]

să'ndwĭch *n.*, & *v.t.* **1.** *n.* Two or more slices of (usu. buttered) bread with meat or other relish between (*ham, egg, jam, cucumber,* etc., *sandwich*); cake of two or more layers with jam etc. between. **2. ~-board,** one of two advertisement boards carried by sandwich-man; ||**~-boat,** boat in bumping race rowing first in lower and last in higher division on same day; **~ course** (of training with alternate periods of practical and theoretical instruction); **~-man** (walking in street with sandwich-boards hanging before and behind). **3.** *v.t.* Insert (thing, statement, etc.) between two of another character; squeeze (*in*) between others. [f. 4th Earl of *Sandwich*, Engl. nobleman d. 1792, said to have eaten only slices of bread and meat while gaming for 24 hours]

să'nd|ȳ¹ *a.* In n. senses; (of hair) yellowish-red, (of person) having sandy hair; **~y blight,** (Austral.) ophthalmia with sandlike grains in eye; hence ~INESS *n.*, ~ȲISH¹ 2 *a.* [OE *sandig* (as SAND, -Y²)]

Să'ndȳ² *n.* (Nickname for) Scotsman. [usual Sc. pet-form of man's name *Alexander*]

sāne *a.* Of sound mind, not mad; (of views etc.) moderate, sensible; hence ~LY² (-nlĭ) *adv.* [f. L *sanus* healthy]

săng. See SING.

să'nga(r) (-ngg-) *n.* Stone breastwork round hollow. [f. Pushtu *sangar*]

săngaree' (-ngg-) *n.* Cold drink of wine diluted and spiced. [f. Sp. SANGRÍA]

sang-de-bœuf (sahṅdebêr'f) *n.* & *a.* (Of) a deep red colour found on old Chinese porcelain. [F, = ox's blood]

sang-froi'd (sahṅfrwah') *n.* Composure, coolness, in danger or under agitating circumstances. [F, = cold blood]

să'ngrail (-ngg-) *n.* = GRAIL². [ME, f. OF *saint graal* (as SAINT, GRAIL²)]

sangria (sănggrē'*a*) *n.* Spanish drink of red wine with lemonade etc. [Sp., = bleeding; cf. SANGAREE]

sănguĭfĭcā'tion (-nggwĭ-) *n.* Formation of, or conversion of food into, blood. [f. mod. L *sanguificatio* (*sanguificare* form blood f. L *sanguis* blood; see -FICATION)]

să'nguĭnar|ȳ (-nggwĭ-) *a.* Accompanied by or delighting in bloodshed or slaughter; bloody, bloodthirsty, (of laws) inflicting death freely; hence ~ĬLY² *adv.*, ~ĬNESS *n.* [f. L *sanguinarius* (*sanguis -inis* blood; see -ARY¹)]

să'nguĭne (-nggwĭn) *a.*, *n.*, & *v.t.* **1.** *a.* (Her. or literary). Blood-red; (arch.) of blood, sanguinary; (Hist.) of the TEMPERAMENT in which the blood predominates over the other HUMOUR¹s, with ruddy complexion and courageous hopeful amorous disposition; (of complexion) bright, ruddy, florid; habitually hopeful, confident, expecting things to go well, whence ~LY² (-nlĭ) *adv.*, ~NESS (-n-n-) *n.* **2.** *n.* Blood-red colour; crayon coloured red with iron oxide; a drawing in red chalk. **3.** *v.t.* (poet.) Stain with blood, stain red. [ME, f. OF *sanguin -ine* f. L *sanguineus* (as prec.)]

sănguĭ'nėous (-nggwĭ'-) *a.* Sanguinary; (Med.) of blood; blood-red; full-blooded, plethoric. [f. L (as prec.) + -OUS]

Să'nhėdrĭn, Să'nhėdrĭm, (-nĭ-) *n.* Highest court of justice and supreme council in ancient Jerusalem, with 71 members. [f. late Heb. *sanhedrîn* f. Gk *sunedrion* (as SYN-, *hedra* seat)]

să'nĭcle *n.* Umbelliferous plant of genus *Sanicula*, formerly believed to have healing properties. [ME f. OF, f. med. L *sanicula* perh. f. L *sanus* healthy]

sā'nĭ|ēs (-z) *n.* (*pl.* same). (Med.) Thin discharge from wound or ulcer; hence ~OUS *a.* [L]

să'nĭfȳ *v.t.* Make healthy, improve sanitary state of, (place). [f. L *sanus* healthy + -I- + -FY]

***sănĭtār'ium** *n.* Sanatorium. [pseudo-L f. L *sanitas* health (see foll., -ARIUM)]

să'nĭtar|ȳ *a.* Of the conditions that affect health esp. with regard to dirt and infection; free from or designed to obviate influences deleterious to health; **~y engineer** (dealing with systems needed to maintain public health); ***~y napkin,** ||**~y towel,** absorbent pad used during menstruation; **~y ware,** porcelain for lavatories etc.; hence **sănĭt**AR'IAN *n.* & *a.*, ~ILY² *adv.*, **~ĭ**NESS *n.* [f. F *sanitaire* f. L *sanitas* (see SANITY, -ARY¹)]

sănĭtā'tion *n.* (Improving of) sanitary conditions; drainage and disposal of sewage and refuse from houses etc.; hence ~IST (2) *n.*, [by back form.] **să'nĭt**ATE³ *v.t.* & *i.* [irreg. f. SANITARY + -ATION]

să'nĭtīze, -īse (-īz), *v.t.* Make sanitary. [f. SANITARY + -IZE]

să'nĭtȳ *n.* Being sane, mental health; tendency to avoid extreme views. [ME, f. L *sanitas* (as SANE; see -ITY)]

să'njăk *n.* Administrative division of vilayet. [f. Turk. *sancak*, lit. 'banner']

sănk. See SINK¹.

sannya'sĭ (sŭnyah'sĭ) *n.* Hindu religious mendicant. [Hindi & Urdu *sannyāsī* f. Skr. *saṃnyāsin* laying aside (*saṃ* together, *ni* down, *as* throw)]

săns¹ (-z) *prep.* (arch. or joc.) Without (esp. w. ref. to *sans teeth, sans eyes, sans taste, sans everything*, Shak. *As You Like It* II. vii. 166). [ME, f. OF *san(z)*, *sen(s)* f. Rom. **sene* f. L *sine*; infl. by L *absentia* in the ABSENCE of]

sans² (sahṅ) *prep.* ***~-gêne*** (-zhĕ'n), absence of constraint, familiarity, making oneself at home; ***~ peur et ~ reproche*** (sahṅpẽr ā sahṅ-reprŏ'sh) *a.*, chivalrous in character. [F, as prec.; *gêne* constraint, *peur* fear, *reproche* reproach]

sănscūlŏ'tt|e (sănzk- *or* sahṅk-) *n.* Extreme republican or revolutionary; hence ~ISM (3) *n.* [F, lit. = without knee-breeches, orig. of lower--class Parisian republicans in French Revolution]

sănsĕ'rĭf *n.* & *a.* (Print.) (Form of type) without SERIFS. [app. f. SANS¹ + SERIF]

Să'nskrĭt *n.* & *a.* (Of or in) the ancient and sacred language of Hindus in India, oldest known member of Indo-European family; hence **Sănskrĭ't**IC *a.*, ~IST (3) *n.* [f. Skr. *saṃskṛta* composed, elaborated, (*saṃ* together, *kṛ* make, *-to* p.p. ending)]

sans-serif. Var. of SANSERIF.

Să'nta Claus (-z), (colloq.) **Să'nta,** *n.* Person said to fill children's stockings with presents on the night before Christmas. [orig. U.S., f. Du. dial. *Sante Klaas* St. Nicholas]

săntolī'na *n.* Aromatic shrub of genus *Santolina.* [mod. L, var. of foll.]

săntŏ'nĭca *n.* Species of wormwood (*Artemisia pauciflora*); drug made from its dried buds. [L (*Santones* Aquitanian tribe; see -IC)]

să'ntonĭn *n.* Extract of santonica used as anthelmintic. [f. prec. + -IN]

sanyasi. Var. of SANNYASI.

săp¹ *n.*, & *v.t.* (**-pp-**). **1.** *n.* Vital juice circulating in plants; (fig.) vital spirit (*the sap of youth*; *there is no sap in a written constitution*); **~-green** *n.* & *a.*, pigment made from buckthorn berries, (of) colour of this; **~('wood)**, soft outer layers of recently formed wood between heartwood and bark; hence ~'FUL, ~'LESS, **~'py²**, *adjs.* **2.** *v.t.* Drain or dry (wood) of sap; (fig.) exhaust vigour of (*his energy, constitution, belief, had been sapped by adversity*; cf. foll.); remove sapwood from (log). [OE *sæp*, = MDu., MLG *sap*, OHG *saf*, prob. f. Gmc **sap(p)am*]

săp² *n.* & *v.* (**-pp-**). **1.** *n.* Making of trenches to cover assailants' approach to besieged place, (fig.) insidious or slow undermining of belief, resolution, etc.; covered siege-trench. **2.** *v.i.* Dig sap; approach by sap. **3.** *v.t.* Undermine, make insecure by removing foundations, (fig.) destroy insidiously (cf. prec.), (*walls, cliffs, sapped by the stream, tide*; *health sapped by the damp climate*; *science was sapping old beliefs*). [n. f. F *sappe* or f. It. *zappa* spade(work), v. f. F *sap(p)er* f. It. *zappare* (*zappa*), prob. of Arab. orig.]

săp³ *n.* (sl.) Foolish person. [abbr. of *sapskull* (SAP¹ = *sapwood*, SKULL)]

să'pajou (-jōō) *n.* Capuchin or spider monkey. [F, said to be Cayenne wd]

să'pan *n.* **~-wood,** red dyewood obtained from E. Ind. tree (*Caesalpinia sappan*). [f. Du. *sapan* f. Malay *sapang*, of S. Ind. orig.]

sapē'lė *n.* (Mahogany-like hard wood of) W. Afr. tree of genus *Entandrophragma.* [W. Afr. name]

să'pĭd *a.* Having (esp. agreeable) flavour, savoury, palatable, not insipid; (of talk, writing, etc.) not vapid or uninteresting; hence **sapĭ'd**ITY *n.* [f. L *sapidus* (*sapere* taste; see -ID¹)]

sā'pĭent *a.* (literary). Would-be wise, of fancied sagacity, aping wisdom; (poet.) wise; hence or cogn. **sā'pĭ**ENCE *n.*, ~LY² *adv.* [ME f. OF, or L part. st. of *sapere* be wise; see -ENT]

săpĭĕ'ntial (-shal) *a.* Of wisdom; **~ books,** Prov., Eccles., Ecclus., Cant., Wisd., etc. [ME f. F, or f. eccl. L *sapientialis* (L *sapientia* wisdom, as prec.; see -AL)]

să'plĭng *n.* Young tree; (fig.) a youth, greyhound in first year. [ME, f. SAP¹ + -LING¹]

săpodĭ'lla *n.* Large evergreen tropical Amer. tree with durable wood and edible fruit (**~ plum**) and sap yielding chicle. [f. Sp. *zapotillo* dim. of *zapote* f. Aztec *tzápotl*]

săponā'ceous (-shus) *a.* Of, like, containing, soap, soapy (lit., or joc. fig.). [f. mod. L *saponaceus* f. L *sapo -onis* soap; see -ACEOUS]

sapŏ'nĭ|fȳ *v.* (Chem.) **1.** *v.t.* Turn (fat or oil) into soap by decomposition with alkali; convert (ester) to acid and alcohol. **2.** *v.i.* Be saponified. **3.** Hence or cogn. **~fī**ABLE *a.*, ~FICA'TION *n.* [f. F *saponifier* (as prec.; see -FY)]

să'ponĭn *n.* Plant glycoside causing foaming in solutions. [f. F *saponine* f. L *sapo -onis* soap; see -IN]

sā'pôr *n.* Quality perceptible by taste, e.g. sweetness; distinctive taste of substance; sensation of taste. [ME f. L (*sapere* taste; see -OR)]

să'ppan. Var. of SAPAN.

să'pper *n.* In vbl senses; ||soldier of Royal Engineers (esp. as official term for private). [f. SAP¹,² + -ER¹]

Să'pph|ĭc (să'fĭk) *a.* & *n.* **1.** *a.* Of Sappho or Sapphism; **s~ic verse, stanza,** (in Gk metres invented by Sappho and imitated in L by Horace, esp. four-line stanza with short fourth line copied in E light verse); hence ~ISM *n.*, homosexual relations between women. **2.** *n.* (in *pl.*; *s~ics*). Verse in sapphic stanzas. [f. F *sa(p)phique* f. L f. Gk *Sapphikos* (*Sapphō* poetess of Lesbos *c.* 600 B.C., suspected of Sapphism; see -IC)]

să'pphīr|e (să'fīr) *n.* & *a.* **1.** *n.* Transparent blue precious stone consisting of corundum; precious transparent corundum of any colour; bright blue of sapphire, azure; humming-bird with bright blue colouring; so ~INE² (să'fĭrin) *a.* **2.** Of sapphire blue; **~e wedding** (45th anniversary). [ME, f. OF *safir* f. L f. Gk *sappheiros* prob. 'lapis lazuli']

să′ppy̆. See SAP[1].

să′pro- *comb. form.* (Biol.) Rotten, putrefying, as: ~GE′NIC, causing or produced by putrefaction; **~phagous** (-ŏ′f-), living on decaying matter; ~PHILE *a.* & *n.*, (bacterium) inhabiting putrid matter; ~PHYTE, vegetable organism living on decayed organic matter, whence **~phy̆′t**IC *a.* [f. Gk *sapros* putrid + -O-]

să′rabănd *n.* Stately old Spanish dance; music for this or in its rhythm, in triple time freq. with long note on second beat of bar. [f. F *sarabande* f. Sp. & It. *zarabanda*]

Să′racen *n.* & *a.* **1.** *n.* (Hist.) Nomad of Syrian and Arabian desert; Arab or Muslim of time of Crusades. **2.** ||**~ corn,** (arch.) buckwheat; **~'s head** (as heraldic charge or inn-sign). **3.** So (esp. Islamic Archit.) **Săracĕ′n**IC *a.* **4.** *a.* Of Saracens. [ME, f. OF *Sar(r)azin, Sar(r)acin* f. LL f. late Gk *Sarakēnos* perh. f. Arab. *šarkī* eastern]

sară′ngi̇ (-nggĭ) *n.* Indian stringed instrument. [f. Hindi *sārangī*]

sarape. See SERAPE.

sar′căsm *n.* Bitter or wounding remark; taunt, esp. one ironically worded; language consisting of, faculty of uttering, use of, such remarks; so **sarcă′st**IC *a.*, **sarcă′st**ICALLY *adv.* [f. F *sarcasme* or f. LL f. late Gk *sarkasmos* f. Gk *sarkazō* tear flesh, in late Gk gnash the teeth, speak bitterly (*sarx sarkos* flesh; cf. -ISM)]

sarcĕ′lle *n.* Teal or similar duck. [ME f. OF *cercelle* f. L *querquedula*]

sarcenet. Var. of SARSENET.

sarcō′ma *n.* (*pl.* **~ta**). Malignant tumour of connective tissue; hence **~to′**SIS *n.*, **~t**OUS *a.* [mod. L f. Gk *sarkōma* (*sarkoō* become fleshy f. *sarx sarkos* flesh; see -OMA)]

sarcŏ′phag|us *n.* (*pl.* **~i** *pr.* -gī *or* -jī). Stone coffin esp. adorned with sculpture or inscription. [L, f. Gk *sarkophagos* a. (as n.) flesh-consuming (as prec., *-phagos* -eating)]

sar′coplăsm *n.* (Anat.) Interfibrillar substance of muscle. [f. Gk *sarx sarkos* flesh + -O- + PLASM]

sar′cous *a.* Consisting of flesh or muscle. [f. as prec. + -OUS]

sard *n.* Yellow or orange-red cornelian. [ME, f. F *sarde* or f. L *sarda* = LL *sardius* f. Gk *sardios* prob. f. *Sardō* Sardinia]

Sardanapā′lĭan *a.* As of, like, Sardanapalus. [f. *Sardanapalus*, legendary last king of Nineveh, notorious for effeminate luxury, + -IAN]

sardĕ′lle *n.* Sardine or similar fish. [f. It. *sardella* dim. of *sarda* f. L (as SARDINE[2])]

sar′dīne[1] *n.* Precious stone mentioned in Rev. 4:3. [ME, f. LL f. Gk *sardinos* var. of *sardios* SARDIUS]

sardi′ne[2] (-ē′n) *n.* Young pilchard, or similar young or small fish allied to herring, often tinned tightly packed in oil; **like ~s,** crowded close together. [ME f. OF, = It. f. L *sardina* (*sarda* f. Gk, perh. f. *Sardō* Sardinia)]

Sardĭ′nĭan *a.* & *n.* (Native or inhabitant or language) of the island or of the kingdom (1720–1861, including also Piedmont etc.) of Sardinia. [f. *Sardinia* island W. of Italy + -AN]

sar′dĭus *n.* (Bibl. etc.) A precious stone. [ME f. LL f. Gk *sardios* SARD]

sardŏ′n|ĭc *a.* Bitterly mocking, cynical, (laugh, laughter, humour, affected merriment, etc.); hence **~**ICALLY *adv.* [f. F *sardonique* (see -IC), earlier *sardonien* f. L f. Gk *sardonios* (= Sardinian) alt. of *sardanios*, Homeric epithet of bitter or scornful laughter]

sar′dony̆x *n.* Onyx in which white layers alternate with sard. [ME, f. L f. Gk *sardonux* (prob. as SARD, ONYX)]

sar′ee. See SARI.

sargă′ssō *n.* (*pl.* **~s** *or* **~es**). Seaweed of genus *Sargassum* with berry-like air-vessels found floating in island-like masses in Sargasso Sea etc. of N. Atlantic. [f. Port. *sargaço*, of unkn. orig.]

sarge *n.* (sl.) Sergeant. [abbr.]

sar′i, sar′ee, *n.* Length of cotton or silk draped round body, worn as main garment by Hindu women. [f. Hindi *sāṛ(h)ī*]

sark *n.* (Sc. & N. Engl.) Shirt or chemise; hence **~′**ING[1] *n.*, boarding between rafters and roof. [ME *serk* f. ON *serkr* f. Gmc **sarkiz*]

Sarmā′tian (-shan) *a.* & *n.* (Inhabitant) of ancient Sarmatia (Russia and Poland); (poet.) Pole, Polish. [f. L *Sarmatia* (*Sarmatae* its inhabitants f. Gk *Sarmatai*) + -AN]

sar′mentōse, sarmĕ′ntous, *adjs.* (Bot.) With long thin trailing shoots. [f. L *sarmentosus* (*sarmenta* pl. twigs, brushwood, f. *sarpere* prune; see -MENT, -OSE[1], -OUS)]

sarŏ′ng *n.* Malay & Javanese garment, long strip of (often striped) cloth worn by both sexes tucked round waist or under armpits; woman's garment imitating this. [Malay, lit. 'sheath']

sar′ŏs *n.* (Astron.) Period of about 18 years between repetitions of eclipses. [Gk, f. Babylonian *šār(u)* 3600 (years)]

sarrŭ′sophōne *n.* Metal wind instrument played with double reed like oboe. [f. *Sarrus*, 19th-c. Fr. inventor, + -O- + -PHONE]

sarsaparĭ′lla *n.* Tropical Amer. smilax esp. *Smilax ornata* (**Jamaica ~** [f. place whence its dried roots etc. were shipped]); dried roots, or extract of these used as tonic etc., of (esp. Jamaica) sarsaparilla. [f. Sp. *zarzaparilla* (*zarza* bramble, prob. + dim. of *parra* vine)]

sar′sen *n.* Sandstone etc. boulder, relict carried by ice in glacial period. [prob. var. of SARACEN]

sar′senet (-sn-) *n.* Fine soft silk material used esp. for linings. [ME, f. AF *sarzinett* perh. dim. of *sarzin* SARACEN (see -ET[1]) after OF *drap sarrasinois* Saracen cloth]

sartor′ĭal *a.* Of tailor, tailoring, or men's clothes. [f. L *sartor* tailor (*sarcire sart-* patch; see -OR) + -IAL]

sartor′ĭus *n.* (Anat.) Long narrow muscle across front of thigh. [mod. L, f. as prec. (being used in adopting tailor's cross-legged position)]

Sar′um *n.* (Eccl.) Salisbury; **~ use,** order of divine service used in diocese of Salisbury from 11th c. to Reformation. [med. L, prob. f. misread abbr. of L *Sarisburia* Salisbury]

săsh[1] *n.* Ornamental scarf worn by man usu. as part of uniform or insignia over one shoulder or round waist, or by woman or child round waist. [earlier *shash* f. Arab. *šāš* muslin, turban]

săsh[2] *n.* **1.** Frame usu. of wood holding pane(s) of glass and usu. made to slide up and down in grooves of window aperture; glazed sliding light of glasshouse or garden-frame. **2. ~-cord, -line,** strong cord attaching sash-weights to sash; **~-tool,** glazier's or painter's brush for work on sash-window; **~-weight** (attached to each end of sash to balance it at any height); **~-window** (with one or usu. two sashes of which one or each can be slid over the other to make opening). [f. *sashes*, corrupt. of CHASSIS, mistaken for pl.]

***săshay′** *v.i.* Walk or move ostentatiously, casually, or diagonally. [corrupt. of CHASSÉ]

săshed (-sht) *a.* In adj. senses. [f. SASH[1,2] + -ED[2]]

să′shimĭ *n.* Japanese dish of garnished raw fish in thin slices. [Jap.]

să′sĭn *n.* Common Indian antelope (*Antilope cervicapra*). [Nepalese]

sā′sĭne *n.* (Sc. Law) Possession of feudal property; act or document granting this. [var. of SEISIN]

Sask. *abbr.* Saskatchewan.

să'squătch *n.* Supposed yeti-like animal of N.W. America. [Amer. Ind.]

***săss.** Var. of SAUCE.

să'ssabȳ *n.* Large S. Afr. antelope (*Damaliscus lunatus*) like hartebeest. [f. Tswana *tsessébe, -ábi*]

să'ssafrăs *n.* (Small tree of genus *Sassafras*, esp. N. Amer. species yielding) bark used medicinally or in perfumery. [f. Sp. *sasafrás* or Port. *sassafraz*, of unkn. orig.]

Săssā'nĭan, Să'ssanĭd, *ns.* & *adjs.* (Member, esp. a king) of dynasty ruling Persian empire A.D. 211–651. [f. *Sasan* founder of dynasty + -IAN, -ID[3]]

Să'ssenăch (-k *or* -χ) *n.* & *a.* (Sc. & Ir., usu. derog.) English(man). [f. Gael. *Sasunnoch*, Ir. *Sasanach* f. L *Saxones* Saxons]

***să'ssȳ.** Var. of SAUCY.

săstru'gĭ (-ōō'gĭ) *n. pl.* Wavelike irregularities on the surface of hard polar snow, caused by winds. [f. Russ. *zastrugi* small ridges]

săt. See SIT.

S.A.T. *abbr.* South Australian Time.

Sat. *abbr.* Saturday.

Sā'tan *n.* The Devil, Lucifer. [OE f. LL f. Gk, f. Heb. *śāṭān*, lit. 'adversary' (*śaṭan* oppose)]

sată'n|ĭc *a.* Of, like, or befitting Satan; diabolical, hellish; hence ~ICALLY *adv.* [f. prec. + -IC]

Sā'tan|ĭsm *n.* **1.** Deliberate wickedness, pursuit of evil for its own sake, diabolical disposition; so ~IZE (3) *v.t.* **2.** Worship of Satan, with travesty of Christian forms; so ~IST (2) *n.* [f. SATAN + -ISM]

Sātanŏ'logȳ *n.* (History or collection of) beliefs concerning the Devil. [f. SATAN + -O- + -LOGY]

S.A.T.B. *abbr.* (Mus.) soprano, alto, tenor, bass.

să'tchel *n.* Small bag (usu. of leather and hung from shoulder with strap, for carrying books etc. esp. to and from school). [ME, f. OF *sachel* f. L *saccellus* (as SACK[1]; see -LE 2)]

sāte[1] *v.t.* Gratify (desire, desirous person) to the full; cloy, surfeit, weary with over-abundance (*sated with pleasure*); hence ~'LESS (-tl-) *a.* (poet.). [prob. f. dial. *sade*, OE *sadian* (as SAD), assim. to SATIATE[2]]

săte[2]. See SIT.

satee'n *n.* Cotton fabric woven like satin, with glossy surface. [f. *satin* after *velveteen*]

să'tellite *n.* & *a.* **1.** *n.* Person's follower or henchman or hanger-on; member of great man's retinue; underling. **2.** Heavenly body revolving round planet (lit. or fig.), whence **sătellĭ'tic** *a.*; artificial body placed in orbit round earth or other planet. **3.** *a.* Minor, secondary; ~ (**state**), country nominally independent but controlled by a greater power; ~ **town,** smaller town dependent on a larger town near it. [F, or f. L *satelles satellitis* guard]

sati. See SUTTEE.

sā'tiate[1] (-shyat) *a.* (arch.) Satiated. [f. L *satiatus* p.p. of *satiare* (*satis* enough); see -ATE[2]]

sā'ti|āte[2] (-shĭ-) *v.t.* = SATE[1]; hence **sā'tiABLE** (-sha-) *a.* (arch.), ~A'TION *n.* [f. as prec. + -ATE[3]]

satī'etȳ *n.* Glutted or satiated state, feeling of having had too much of something, cloyed dislike *of*; **to** ~, to extent beyond what is desired. [f. obs. F *societé* f. L *satietas -tatis* (*satis* enough; see -TY[1])]

să'tĭn *n.*, *a.*, & *v.t.* **1.** *n.* Silk etc. fabric with glossy surface on one side got by twill weave with weft-threads almost hidden. **2.** *a.* Smooth as satin. **3.** ~**-bird,** glossy Austral. bower-bird; ~ **finish,** polish given to silver etc. with metallic brush; ~**-flower,** (1) honesty, (2) chickweed, (3) (Austral.) a glossy-flowered umbellifer; ~ **paper,** fine glossy writing-paper; ~**-spar,** fibrous calcium carbonate; ~**-stitch,** long straight embroidery stitch giving appearance of satin; ~ **white,** white pigment of calcium sulphate and alumina; ~**wood,** (choice glossy timber of) Ind. tree (*Chloroxylon swietenia*) or one of several Austral. etc. trees. **4.** Hence ~Y[2] *a.* **5.** *v.t.* Give glossy surface to (paper). [ME f. OF, f. Arab. *zaytūnī* of Tseutung in China]

sătĭnĕ't, sătĭnĕ'tte, *n.* Satin-like fabric made partly or wholly of cotton or synthetic fibre. [f. prec. + -ET[1], -ETTE]

să'tīre *n.* **1.** (Rom. Ant.) Poetic medley, esp. poem ridiculing prevalent vices or follies. **2.** Composition in verse or prose ridiculing vice or folly or lampooning individual(s), this branch of literature; thing that brings ridicule upon something (*our lives are a satire upon our religion*); use of ridicule, irony, sarcasm, etc., in speech or writing for the ostensible purpose of exposing and discouraging vice or folly. [F, or f. L *satira* later form of *satura* medley]

satĭ'rĭc *a.* Of satires or satire, containing satire, writing satires, (*satiric verse, poem, poet, writer, intent*). [f. F *satirique* or f. LL *satiricus* (as prec.; see -IC)]

satĭ'rĭcal *a.* = prec.; given to the use of satire in speech or writing or to cynical observation of others, sarcastic, humorously critical; hence ~LY[2] *adv.* [as prec.; see -ICAL]

să'tĭrĭst *n.* Writer of satires; satirical person. [f. SATIRE + -IST]

să'tĭrīze, -īse (-īz), *v.t.* Assail with satire; write satire(s) upon; describe satirically. [f. F *satiriser* (as SATIRE; see -IZE)]

sătĭsfă'ction *n.* **1.** Payment of debt, fulfilment of obligation, atonement (*for*); thing accepted by way of satisfaction; (Eccl.) performance of penance; (Theol.) atonement by Christ for sins of mankind; **enter** ~, (Law) place on record of court that payment ordered has been made. **2.** Opportunity of fighting duel with person by whom one feels insulted (*give, demand, satisfaction*). **3.** Satisfying or being satisfied in regard to desire or want or doubt, thing that satisfies desire or gratifies feeling, (*find satisfaction in; give satisfaction; could not get, could get no, satisfaction from the dealer; to the satisfaction of; heard it with great satisfaction; their satisfaction at* or *with the results; if you can prove it to my satisfaction; the satisfaction of not having to do it; it is a great satisfaction that it need not be done; would be a satisfaction to me; thinks only of present satisfaction*). [ME f. OF, f. L *satisfactio -onis* (as SATISFY; see -ION)]

sătĭsfă'ctor|ȳ *a.* **1.** Satisfying expectations or needs, leaving no room for complaint, causing satisfaction, adequate, (*satisfactory proof, method, result, pupil, pair of shoes, marriage, compromise*). **2.** (Theol.) Serving as atonement for sin. **3.** Hence ~ĭLY[2] *adv.*, ~ĭNESS *n.* [f. F *satisfactoire* or f. med. L *satisfactorius* (as SATISFY; see -ORY)]

să'tĭsf|ȳ *v.* **1.** *v.t.* Pay (debt, creditor), fulfil (obligation), comply with (demand), (Math., of quantity) make (equation) true. **2.** Meet the expectations or desires of, be equal to (notion, preconception, etc.), be accepted by (person, his taste, etc.) as adequate, content; ~**y the examiners,** reach minimum standard to succeed in university examination. **3.** (in *pass.*) Be content or pleased (*with*), be convinced or confident *that*, demand no more than or consider it enough *to* do; REST[3] *satisfied*. **4.** Put an end to (an appetite or want), rid (person) of an appetite or want, by sufficient supply. **5.** Furnish with adequate proof, convince, (*of* fact, *that* it is so; ~**y** one**self,** attain to practical certainty). **6.** Adequately meet (objection, doubt, request, conditions). **7.** *v.i.* Give satisfaction, leave nothing to be desired; (of Christ) make atonement for sins of mankind. **8.** Hence ~IABLE, ~ȳING², *adjs.* [ME, f. OF *satisfier* f. L *satisfacere -fact-* (*satis* enough; see -FY)]

satŏr'ĭ *n.* (Buddhism). Sudden enlightenment. [Jap.]

satra'ngĭ (-ŭ'njĭ) *n.* Indian cotton carpet. [Bengali, f. Skr. *catúraṅga* chess-for four players]

să'trăp *n.* Holder of provincial governorship or ~Y¹ *n.* in ancient Persian empire, viceroy; (rhet.) subordinate ruler, colonial governor, etc. [ME, f. OF *satrape*, or f. L f. Gk *satrapēs* f. OPers. *xšaθra-pāvan* country-protector]

Să'tsuma *n.* **1.** ~ (**ware**), cream-coloured Japanese pottery. **2.** (*s*~). Kind of mandarin orange orig. grown in Japan. [~ province in Japan]

să'tūr|āte (*or* -cher-) *v.t.* Fill with moisture, soak thoroughly; imbue *with*, steep *in*, (learning, tradition, prejudice, etc.); overwhelm (defences, target area) by concentrated bombing; (Phys. etc.) cause (substance, air, vapour, metal) to absorb or hold greatest amount possible of another substance, moisture (*saturated* STEAM¹), magnetism, electricity, etc.; (Chem.) cause (substance) to combine with maximum amount of another substance, esp. hydrogen in fats; (in *p.p.*, of colour) free from admixture of white, full, rich; hence or cogn. ~ATE² *a.* (literary), ~ABLE *a.*, ~ANT *a.* & *n.* [f. L *saturare* (*satur* full) + -ATE³]

sătūrā'tion *n.* Saturating or being saturated; ~ **point,** stage beyond which no more can be absorbed or accepted. [f. LL *saturatio* or f. prec.; see -ATION]

Să'turday (*or* -dĭ) *n.* & *adv.* **1.** *n.* Day of week, following Friday; HOLY *Saturday*. **2.** *adv.* (cf. FRIDAY 2). [OE *Sætern(es)dæg* transl. of L *Saturni dies* day of Saturn]

Să'tūrn *n.* **1.** (Rom. Ant.) Italic god of agriculture later identified with Greek Kronos, father of Zeus, ruler of the world in a golden age of innocence and plenty. **2.** Planet of solar system, most distant of the 5 anciently known, with 10 moons and broad flat rings, credited in astrology with producing cold sluggish gloomy temperament in those born under its influence. **3.** (Alch.) The metal lead. [f. L *Saturnus*, perh. f. Etruscan]

săturnā'l|ia *n.* **1.** *pl.* (*S*~*ia*). Ancient-Roman festival of Saturn in December observed as time of unrestrained merry-making extending even to slaves, predecessor of modern Christmas-tide. **2.** (as *sing.* or *pl.*) Scene or time of wild revelry or tumult (*a saturnalia of crime*); hence ~IAN *a.* [L, neut. pl. (as n.) of *Saturnalis* (as prec.; see -AL)]

Satūr'nĭan *a.* & *n.* **1.** *a.* Of the god or the planet Saturn; ~ **age,** golden age; ~ **metre, verse,** metre used in early Latin poetry before introduction of Greek metres. **2.** *n.* Inhabitant of Saturn; (in *pl.*) Saturnian verse. [f. L *Saturnius* (as SATURN) + -AN]

satūr'nĭc *a.* (Path.) Affected with lead-poisoning; so **să'turn**ISM (5) *n.* [f. SATURN 3 + -IC]

să'turnīne *a.* **1.** Of sluggish gloomy temperament, (of looks etc.) suggestive of or produced by such temperament; hence ~LY² (-nlĭ) *adv.* **2.** Of the metal lead; of or affected by lead-poisoning. [ME, f. OF *saturnin* f. med. L *Saturninus* (as SATURN; see -INE¹)]

satya'graha (sahtyah'grah-hah) *n.* (Ind.) Passive resistance esp. as advocated by Gandhi. [Skr. (*satya* truth, *āgraha* obstinacy)]

să'tyr *n.* One of a class of Greek woodland deities in human form with horse's ears and tail (or, as represented by Romans, with goat's ears, tail, legs, and budding horns); lustful or sensual-minded man; satyrid butterfly. [ME, f. OF *satyre* or f. L f. Gk *saturos*]

sătyrī'as|ĭs *n.* (*pl.* ~**es** *pr.* -ēz). (Path.) Excessive sexual desire in males. [LL, f. Gk *saturiasis* (as prec.; see -ASIS)]

satȳ'rĭc *a.* Of satyrs; ~ **drama,** kind of ancient-Greek comic play with chorus of satyrs. [f. L f. Gk *saturikos* (as SATYR; see -IC)]

să'tyrĭd *n.* Butterfly of family Satyridae. [f. mod. L *Satyridae* f. genus *Satyrus* (as SATYR); see -ID³]

sauce *n.*, & *v.t.* **1.** *n.* Liquid or soft preparation taken as relish with some article of food; BREAD, **egg,** MINT³, **parsley, tomato,** etc., ~ (with these as prominent ingredient); **white** ~ (of melted butter, flour, etc.); *sauce for the* GANDER; **serve with the same** ~, subject to same usage. **2.** (fig.) Something that adds piquancy (*is tame without the sauce of danger*). **3.** *Stewed etc. fruit eaten as dessert or used as garnish;* vegetables eaten with meat etc. **4.** Impudence, impertinent speech, cheek, (*none of your sauce!*). **5.** ~**-alone,** hedge-weed formerly used to flavour salads and sauces; ~**-boat,** vessel in which sauce is served; ~**'box,** (colloq.) impudent person; ~**'pan** (-*a*n), metal cooking-vessel, usu. cylindrical with long side-handle, for use on top of stove etc. **6.** Hence ~'LESS (-sl-) *a.* **7.** *v.t.* (arch.) Season with sauces or condiments (lit. or fig.). **8.** (colloq.) Be impudent to, cheek, (person). [ME f. OF f. Rom. **salsa* fem. (as n.) of L *salsus* (*salere sals-* to salt f. *sal* salt)]

sau'cer *n.* **1.** Shallow vessel for standing cup on to catch spilt tea etc.; FLYING² *saucer*; ~ **eye** (large and round as a saucer, or wide open in surprise etc.). **2.** Vessel placed under flowerpot to prevent water from running away at once; any small shallow round vessel resembling tea-saucer. **3.** Hence ~FUL 2 *n.*, ~LESS *a.* [ME = condiment-dish, f. OF *saussier(e)* sauce-boat, prob. f. LL *salsarium* (as SAUCE; see -ER² (2))]

sau'c|ȳ *a.* Impudent to superiors, cheeky; (sl.) smart-looking; hence ~ĬLY² *adv.*, ~ĬNESS *n.* [earlier sense 'savoury', f. SAUCE + -Y²]

Sau'dĭ (sow'-) *n.* & *a.* (Native or inhabitant) of Saudi Arabia; (member) of dynasty founded by Saud. [f. A. Ibn-*Saud*, Arab. king d. 1953 + -I]

sauer'kraut (sowr'krowt) *n.* German dish of chopped pickled cabbage. [G (*sauer* SOUR, *kraut* vegetable)]

***sau'ger** (-g-) *n.* Small pike-perch. [19th c.; orig. unkn.]

Sau'mūr (sō-) *n.* White wine produced near Saumur. [~ in W. France]

sau'na (*or* sow'-) *n.* (Building for) Finnish-style steam-bath. [Finn.]

saunders. See SANDERS.

sau'nter *v.i.*, & *n.* **1.** *v.i.* Walk in leisurely way or without destination, stroll, (lit., or fig., *saunter through life*); hence ~ER¹ *n.* **2.** *n.* Leisurely ramble or gait. [ME, = muse; orig. unkn.]

saur'ĭan *a.* & *n.* (Of or like) a lizard. [f. mod. L *Sauria* f. Gk *saura* lizard + -AN]

saur'ȳ *n.* Long-beaked sea-fish (*Scombresox saurus*) of temperate waters. [perh. f. LL f. Gk *sauros* horse-mackerel]

sau'sage (sŏ's-) *n.* **1.** Pork or other meat minced, seasoned, and stuffed into long cylindrical cases prepared from entrails or synthetic material and divided when full into lengths of a few inches by twisting or tying; a length of this; **Bologna** ~, large kind made of bacon, veal, pork-suet, etc., and sold ready for eating cold; **not a** ~, (sl.) nothing at all; ~**-dog,** (colloq.) dachshund; ~**-filler, -grinder, -machine,** sausage-making appliances; ~**-meat,** meat and bread etc. minced and seasoned for use in sausages or as a stuffing etc.; ~ **roll,** sausage-meat enclosed in pastry and baked. **2.** (colloq.) Sausage-shaped object; *(derog.) a German.

[ME, f. ONF *saussiche* f. med. L *salsicia* f. L *salsus* (see SAUCE)]

sauté (sō′tā) *a.*, *n.*, & *v.t.* (~**d** *or* ~**ed** *pr.* -ād). **1.** *a.* & *n.* (Food) quickly fried in hot pan with little fat. **2.** *v.t.* Cook thus. [F, p.p. of *sauter* jump]

Sautēr′ne(s) (*or* sōtār′n) *n.* Light sweet white wine from Bordeaux region of France. [f. *Sauternes* district of Gironde]

sauve qui peut (sōvkēpēr′) *n.* Precipitate flight in various directions. [F, lit. 'save (himself) who can']

să′vage *a.*, *n.*, & *v.t.* **1.** *a.* (arch.) Uncultivated, wild, (*a savage animal, scene*). **2.** Uncivilized, in primitive state, (*savage tribes, life*). **3.** Fierce, cruel, furious, (*savage persecution, persecutor, revenge, criticism, blow*); (colloq.) angry, out of temper. **4.** (Her.) (Of human figure) naked. **5.** Hence or cogn. ~LY² (-ĭjlĭ) *adv.*, ~NESS (-ĭjn-), **să′vag**ERY (2, 4) (-ĭjrĭ), *ns.* **6.** *n.* Member of savage tribe esp. of one living by hunting and fishing, whence ~DOM (-ĭjd-) *n.*; brutally cruel or barbarous person. **7.** *v.t.* (Of horse, dog) attack and bite or trample; (of critic etc.) attack fiercely. [ME f. OF *sauvage* f. Rom. **salvaticus* f. L *silvaticus* (*silva* a wood; see -ATIC)]

savă′nnah (-na), **-nna,** *n.* Grassy plain with few or no trees in tropical and subtropical regions. [f. Sp. *zavana*, perh. of Carib orig.]

să′vant (-ahṅ) *n.* (*fem.* ~**e** *pr.* -ahṅt). Learned person, esp. distinguished scientist. [F, part. (as n.) of *savoir* know (as SAPIENT)]

sava′te (-ah′t) *n.* Form of boxing in which feet as well as fists are used. [F, orig. a kind of shoe; cf. SABOT]

sāve¹ *v.* & *n.* **1.** *v.t.* Rescue, preserve, protect, deliver, from or *from* danger or misfortune or harm or discredit (*saved my* LIFE, *me from drowning*; *save* APPEARANCES, one's BACON, *the* DAY, one's or person's FACE¹, one's SKIN¹; ~ **the situation,** find or provide way out of difficulty, avert disaster); keep in specified state (*save us alive*; *save* HARMLESS). **2.** (**God**) ~, may God preserve or protect (*God save the Queen*); (**God**) ~ **me from** *my friends* etc. (comment on well-meant but inopportune interference); (*God*) *save the* MARK¹; (**God**) ~ **us!** (excl. of surprise). **3.** Bring about spiritual salvation of, preserve from damnation, (*who then can be saved?*). **4.** Keep for future use or enjoyment; husband, reserve, abstain from expending; ~ one's **breath,** be silent; *save* one's *breath to cool* one's PORRIDGE; **you may ~ your pains** or **trouble** (need not take, will take in vain). **5.** Relieve (person, one*self*, or abs.) from need of expending (money, trouble, etc.) or from exposure to (annoyance etc.); obviate need of, reduce requisite amount of, (*that will save me, I saved myself, £50*; *his secretary saved him much time* or *labour, many interviews*; *stitch in time saves nine*; *soap saves rubbing*); ~ **the follow-on,** (Cricket) get enough runs to prevent it; ~**-all,** device to prevent waste, esp. (Hist.) pan with spike for burning-up candle-ends. **6.** Avoid losing, be in time for, succeed in catching, (*batted stubbornly and saved the game*; *write hurriedly to save the post*); ~ **the tide,** get in or out while it serves. **7.** Make reservation concerning, make reservation; *saving your* REVERENCE. **8.** Hence **sā′v**ABLE *a.* **9.** *v.i.* Save (*up*) money for future use; (Footb. etc.) prevent opponent from scoring; ‖~**as-you-earn,** method of saving by regular deduction from earnings. **10.** *n.* (Footb. etc.) act of preventing opponent from scoring; (Bridge) sacrifice-bid to prevent unnecessary losses. [ME, f. AF *sa(u)ver*, OF *salver, sauver* f. LL *salvare* f. L *salvus* SAFE²]

sāve² *prep.* & *conj.* **1.** *prep.* (arch., poet., or rhet.) Except, but, (w. n. etc. in obj. case; *forty stripes save one*; *all save him*). **2.** *conj.* (arch.) Unless, but, except, (*thou seest no beauty save thou make it*; *all the conspirators save only he*; *save where the beetle wheels his droning flight*; *I am well save that I have a cold*; *happy save for one want*). [ME f. OF *sauf sauve* f. L *salvo, salva*, abl. sing. of *salvus* SAFE²]

să′veloy *n.* Highly seasoned dried sausage. [corrupt. of F *cervelas, -at*, f. It. *cervellata* (*cervello* brain)]

sā′ver *n.* In vbl senses; person who saves money; device for economical use (of soap, time, etc.); (sl.) hedging bet. [f. SAVE¹ + -ER¹]

să′vĭn, să′vĭne, *n.* (Kind of juniper with) tips of shoots yielding a volatile oil used medicinally; *red cedar. [OE, f. OF *savine* f. L *sabina* (*herba*) Sabine (herb)]

sā′vĭng¹ *a.* & *prep.* **1.** *a.* In vbl senses; making economical use of (*labour-saving*); ~ **clause** (containing stipulation of exemption etc.); ~ **grace,** redeeming grace (of God, or fig.). **2.** *prep.* Except, with the exception of; without offence to (*saving your* REVERENCE). [ME, f. SAVE¹ + -ING²; in sense 2 prob. f. SAVE² after *touching*]

sā′vĭng² *n.* In vbl senses; (usu. in *pl.*) money saved; *~**s account,** deposit account; ~**s bank** (receiving small deposits at interest and devoting profits to benefit of depositors); ‖~**s certificate,** interest-bearing document issued by Government for benefit of savers. [ME, f. SAVE¹ + -ING¹]

sā′viour, ***sā′vior,** (-vyer) *n.* Deliverer, redeemer (**the** or **our S**~, Christ); person who saves a State etc. from destruction etc. [ME, f. OF *sauvëour* f. eccl. L *salvator -oris* (transl. Gk *sōtēr*) f. LL *salvare* SAVE¹]

savoir-faire (săvwārfār′) *n.* Quickness to see and do the right thing, address, tact. [F, = know how to do]

savoir-vivre (săvwārvē′vr) *n.* Good breeding, being at home in society. [F, = know how to live]

***sā′vor,** ***sā′vorў**¹. See SAVOUR, SAVOURY.

sā′vorў² *n.* Herb of genus *Satureia* of mint family, used in cookery. [ME *saverey*, perh. f. OE *sætherie* f. L *satureia*]

sā′vour (-ver), ***sā′vor,** *n.* & *v.* **1.** *n.* Characteristic taste, flavour, relish, or (arch.) smell, power to affect the taste (lit. or fig.); quality suggestive, perceptible admixture, suspicion, smack, *of* (*a not unpleasing savour of preciosity*); hence ~LESS *a.* **2.** *v.t.* Appreciate or perceive the (lit. or fig.) taste of, enjoy esp. lingeringly or with deliberation. **3.** *v.i.* Suggest by taste, smell, or otherwise the presence *of* (*the offer savours of impertinence*). [ME; n. f. OF, f. L *sapor -oris* (*sapere* taste; see -OR); v. f. OF *savourer* f. LL *saporare* f. L *sapor*]

sā′vour|ў (-verĭ), ***sā′vor|ў**¹, *a.* & *n.* **1.** *a.* With appetizing taste or smell; (fig.) pleasant, acceptable; (of food) having salt or piquant and not sweet flavour (*sweet or savoury omelette*); hence ~ĬLY² *adv.*, ~ĬNESS *n.* **2.** *n.* ‖Savoury dish, esp. one served at beginning or usu. end of dinner as stimulant or digestive. [ME, f. OF *savouré* p.p. (as prec.); see -Y⁴]

savoy′ *n.* Hardy cabbage with wrinkled leaves. [f. *Savoy* in S.E. France]

Savoy′ard *n.* & *a.* **1.** (Native) of Savoy. **2.** *n.* Member of the Savoy Theatre company who acted in the original productions of the Gilbert and Sullivan operas. [F (*Savoie* Savoy; see -ARD)]

să′vvў *v.*, *n.*, & *a.* (sl.) **1.** *v.i.* & *t.* Know; **no** ~, I do, he etc. does, not know or understand. **2.** *n.* Knowingness, understanding. **3.** *a.* *Knowing, wise. [orig. Negro & Pidgin E after Sp. *sabe usted* you know]

saw[1] *n.* & *v.* (*p.p.* **~n** *or* **~ed**). **1.** *n.* Tool worked by hand or mechanically and with variously shaped usu. steel blade or edge having teeth of various forms cut in or attached to it for dividing wood, metal, stone, bone, etc., by to-and-fro or rotatory motion; BAND[1]-*saw*, BOW[1]-*saw*, CIRCULAR *saw*, CROWN[1] *saw*, FRAME[2]-*saw*, FRET[1]-*saw*, HACK[2]-*saw*, HAND[1]*saw*, JIG[2]*saw*, PIT[1]-*saw*, RIP[2]-*saw*, STONE-*saw*. **2.** (Zool. etc.) Serrated organ or part. **3. ~-bill,** merganser; ***~'buck,** saw-horse, (sl.) $10 note; **~-doctor,** machine for making teeth of saw; **~'dust,** tiny wood fragments produced in sawing used in packing, pugging, stuffing, drying moisture, etc.; **~-edged,** with jagged edge like saw; **~'fish,** large sea-fish of family Pristidae with toothed flat end of snout used as weapon; **~-fly,** insect of family Tenthredinidae, injurious to plants, with serrated ovipositor; **~-frame** (in which saw-blade is held taut); **~-gate,** saw-frame; **~-gin,** cotton-GIN[1] with saw-teeth; **~-horse,** rack supporting wood for sawing; **~'mill** (driven by water or steam for mechanical sawing of wood); **~-pit** (in which lower of two men working pit-saw stands); **~-set,** tool for wrenching saw-teeth in alternate directions to give kerf wider than blade and let saw work freely; **~'tooth** *a.*, shaped like teeth of saw, esp. of roof, wave, etc., with one steep and one slanting side; **~-wort,** plant yielding yellow dye from its serrated leaves. **4.** *v.t.* Cut (wood etc.) with, make (boards etc.) with, saw; **~'bones,** (sl.) surgeon; **~ed-off, ~n-off,** (of gun) with part of barrel removed by sawing, (of person, colloq.) undersized. **5.** *v.i.* Use saw. **6.** *v.t.* & *i.* Move backward and forward, divide (the air etc.), with motion as of saw or person sawing. [OE **sagu, saga,* = OHG *saga*, ON *sög* f. Gmc **sagō*, **sagon*]

saw[2] *n.* Proverbial saying, old maxim, (esp. *old* or *wise saw*). [OE *sagu*, = OHG, ON *saga*, f. Gmc **sagō* cogn. with SAY[2]; cf. SAGA]

saw[3]. See SEE[1].

saw'der *n.*, & *v.t.* (colloq.) **1.** *n.* **Soft ~,** compliments, flattering speeches, blarney. **2.** *v.t.* Flatter. [fig. use of var. of SOLDER]

sawn. See SAW[1].

Saw'ney *n.* **1.** (derog.) Scotsman. **2.** (colloq.) Simpleton. [Sc. var. of SANDY[2]]

saw'yer *n.* **1.** Man employed in sawing timber; TOP[1]-*sawyer*. **2.** *Uprooted tree held fast by one end in river (and sawing up and down). **3.** (N.Z.) Weta. [ME, earlier *sawer* (SAW[1], -ER[1]); see -YER]

săx[1], **zăx,** *n.* Slater's chopper, with point for making nail-holes; **sa'xboard,** uppermost strake of open boat. [OE *seax* knife, = OS, OHG *sahs*, ON *sax* f. Gmc **sahsam* f. IE **sok-*, **sek-*]

săx[2] *n.* (colloq.) Saxophone. [abbr.]

să'xatĭle *a.* (Biol.) Living or growing on or among rocks. [F, or f. L *saxatilis* (*saxum* rock)]

săxe *n.* **~ (blue),** light blue with greyish tinge. [F, = Saxony, source of dye so coloured]

să'xhôrn *n.* Brass wind instrument of trumpet family made in several sizes, usu. held either with mouth upwards or with tube encircling player's body. [f. C. J. & A. *Sax*, Belgian instrument-makers d. 1865 & 1894, + HORN[1]]

săxĭ'colĭne, -lous, *adjs.* (Biol.) = SAXATILE. [f. mod. L *saxicolus* (*saxum* rock, *colere* inhabit) + -INE[1], -OUS]

să'xĭfrage (*or* -āj) *n.* Alpine or rock plant of genus *Saxifraga*, with tufted foliage and panicles of white or yellow or red flowers. [ME f. OF, or f. LL *saxifraga* (*herba*) f. L *saxum* rock + *frangere* break]

Să'xon *n.* & *a.* **1.** *n.* Member, language (usu. **Old ~**), of Germanic people that conquered parts of England in 5th–6th c.; = ANGLO-SAXON, whence **~**DOM *n.* **2.** Native of modern Saxony. **3.** Germanic (opp. Latin or Romance) elements of English. **4.** *a.* Of the Saxons (**~ architecture,** form of Romanesque preceding Norman in England); belonging to or originating from the Saxon language or Old English, whence **~**ISM (2, 4), **~**IST (2), *ns.*; **~ blue,** solution of indigo in sulphuric acid as dye; hence **~**IZE (2, 3) *v.i.* & *t.* [ME f. OF, f. LL *Saxo -onis* f. Gk *Saxones* pl. f. WG **Saxon-* (OE *Seaxan*, *Seaxe*, pl., OS, OHG *Sahso*)]

să'xonў *n.* Fine kind of wool; cloth made from it. [f. *S~* in Germany, f. LL *Saxonia* (as prec.)]

să'xophōn|e *n.* Keyed brass wind instrument made in several sizes, having reed like that of clarinet; hence **~**IST (3) (*or* -ŏ'fon-) *n.* [f. as SAXHORN + -O- + -PHONE]

să'xtūba *n.* Large saxhorn. [f. SAXHORN + TUBA]

say[1] *n.* (arch.) Fine cloth like serge. [ME, f. OF *saie* f. L *saga* pl. of *sagum* military cloak]

say[2] *v.* (**said** *pr.* sĕd; 3 *sing. pres.* **says** *pr.* sĕz, (arch.) **saith** *pr.* sĕth; 2 *sing. pres.* (arch.) **~st** *or* **~est,** *past* **saidst** *or* **saidest**) & *n.* **1.** *v.t.* Utter, make (specified remark), recite, rehearse, in ordinary speaking voice; repeat (lesson) to teacher; speak words of (prayers, grace, etc.); (ellipt.) = *that is to say* (1) (*£50 say fifty pounds*); ||**I ~** (excl. drawing attention, opening conversation, or expressing surprise); **not to ~,** and indeed (*his language was irreverent, not to say blasphemous*); **~ much, something,** etc., **for,** indicate high quality of; **~ for oneself,** utter (*something* etc.) by way of conversation or oratory (and cf. sense 4); *say* person NAY; *say* NO[4]; **~ no more,** cease speaking on a particular topic or at all; **to ~ nothing of,** even disregarding; **~ nothing to,** (fig.) leave (person) unmoved; **~ out,** express fully or candidly; **~s** or **said he** etc., **said I,** (colloq.) **~s I,** (used in reporting conversation); **~s you,** (vulg. *int.*) I disagree; **~ something,** make a short speech; *say* WHEN; *say the word, a few words, a good word for*, (see WORD[1]); *say* YES; SO[1] *to say*; **that is to ~,** (1) in other words, more explicitly, (2) or at least (*he never went, that is to say it is not recorded that he did*); **when all is said and done,** after all, in the long run; **you can ~ that (again), you said it,** (colloq.) I agree emphatically; **you don't ~ (so),** (colloq.) that is incredible. **2.** State, promise, prophesy, (*that*); have specified wording or reading (*the Bible says that thou shalt not steal*; *it says here that he was killed*); (in *pass.*) be asserted (*tree is said to be six hundred years old*), be described by a term (*in that case the loser is said to be rubiconed*); DARE *say*; HEAR *say*; **I'll ~,** (colloq.) yes indeed; **I'm not ~ing,** I refuse to answer the question; **the said,** (Law or joc.) the previously mentioned; **it is said,** the rumour is (*that*); **it ~s in the Bible,** the Bible says; **~ so,** say the thing in question; **they ~,** the rumour is (*that*). **3.** Put into words, express (*that was well said*); convey information (*spoke for an hour but didn't say much*). **4.** Adduce or allege in argument or excuse (*there is much to be said on both sides*; *have you anything to say for yourself?*). **5.** Form and give opinion or decision as to, or abs., (*there is no saying, it is hard to say, who it was*; *do say which you will have*); **I cannot** or **could not ~,** I do not know (*whether* etc., or abs.); **and so ~ all of us,** and that is our opinion too; **what do you ~ to?,** would you like?; **how ~ you?** (asking jury for verdict); **~-so** *n.*, (1) power of decision, (2) mere assertion. **6.** Select as example, assume, take (specified number etc.) as near enough, (*let us say, shall we say*, or usu. ellipt. *say*; *any country, let us say Sweden, might do the same*; *well, say it were true, what then?*; *a few of them, say a dozen or so*). **7.** *v.i.* Speak, talk; (in *imper*., poet.) tell me; *=*I say*; ~ **away,** ~ **on,** say what you have to say. **8.** *n.* (Opportunity of saying) what one has to say (*said his say*; *let him have his say*); share in decision (*had no say in the matter*); power of (final) decision. [OE *secgan*, = OS *seggian*, OHG *sagēn*, ON *segja*, f. Gmc **sagjan*, **sagǣjan*]

||**S.A.Y.E.** *abbr*. save-as-you-earn.

say'ĭng *n.* In vbl senses; sententious remark, maxim, adage; **as the ~ is** or **goes** (form used in quoting proverb or phrase); **go without ~,** be too well known or obvious to need mention; **~ and doing,** speech and action; **there is no ~,** it is impossible to know. [ME, f. SAY² + -ING¹]

Sb *symb*. antimony. [f. L *stibium*]

S.B.N. *abbr*. Standard Book Number.

S. by E., S. by W., *abbrs*. South by East, West.

S.C. *abbr*. small capitals; South Carolina; special constable.

sc. *abbr*. scilicet.

Sc *symb*. scandium.

scăb *n.*, & *v.i.* (-bb-). **1.** *n.* Dry rough incrustation formed over sore in healing; mange, itch, or similar skin-disease; fungous plant-disease causing scablike roughness. **2.** (arch.) Mean low fellow. **3.** Person who refuses to join strike or trade union or takes striker's place or breaks rules of his trade or group. **4.** Hence **~bED²** (-bd), **~'bY²**, *adjs*. **5.** *v.i.* (Of sore) form scab, heal over; act as scab. [ME, f. ON **skabbr* = OE *sceabb* (cf. SHABBY)]

scă'bbard *n.* Sheath of sword, bayonet, etc., (**throw away the ~,** commit oneself to fighting a matter out to the end); *sheath for revolver etc.; **~-fish,** silvery-white sea-fish shaped like sword-scabbard. [ME *sca(u)berc* etc., f. AF **escauberc*, *escauberge* prob. f. Frank. **skār(a)* (cf. SHEAR²) + **berg-* protect]

scā'bies (-z; *or* -ĭēz) *n.* Contagious disease, the ITCH¹. [ME f. L (*scabere* scratch)]

scā'bĭous *a.* & *n.* **1.** *a.* Scabby, affected with mange, itch, etc. **2.** *n.* Wild or cultivated annual or perennial herb of genus *Scabiosa* with blue, pink, or white, pincushion-shaped flowers. [n. ME f. med. L *scabiosa* (*herba*) named as specific against itch, a. f. F *scabieux* or f. L *scabiosus* (as prec.; see -OUS)]

scā'brous *a.* **1.** (Zool., Bot., etc.) Having rough surface, scurfy. **2.** (Of subject, situation, etc.) requiring tactful treatment, hard to handle with decency. **3.** Indecent, salacious; behaving licentiously. **4.** Hence **~LY²** *adv.*, **~NESS** *n.* [f. F *scabreux* or f. LL *scabrosus* f. L *scaber* rough; see -OUS]

scăd *n.* Fish of family Carangidae, like large mackerel. [17th c.; orig. unkn.]

***scăds** (-z) *n. pl.* (colloq.) Large quantities *of*. [19th c.; orig. unkn.]

scă'ffold *n.*, & *v.t.* **1.** *n.* Elevated platform of timber for execution of criminals (**the ~,** death by execution), for drying tobacco, etc.; scaffolding. **2.** *v.t.* Attach scaffolding to (building); hence **~ER¹** *n.* [ME, f. AF **scaffaut*, OF *(e)schaffaut*, earlier *escadafaut* f. Rom. *EX¹(*catafalcum*; cf. CATAFALQUE)]

scă'ffoldĭng *n.* Temporary structure of poles or tubes and planks providing workmen with platform(s) to stand on while building or repairing house etc.; materials for this; temporary framework (lit. or fig.) for other purposes; **~-pole,** mastlike pole helping to support scaffolding. [ME, f. prec. + -ING¹]

scăgliō'la (-lyō'-) *n.* Imitation stone of plaster mixed with glue. [f. It. *scagliuola* dim. of *scaglia* SCALE¹]

scā'lable *a.* In vbl senses. [f. SCALE¹,²,³ + -ABLE]

scā'lar *a.* & *n.* (Math.) (Quantity) having only magnitude, not direction (cf. VECTOR). [f. L *scalaris* (*scala* ladder; see SCALE³, -AR¹)]

scală'rĭfôrm *a.* (Bot. & Zool.) (Of veins in insect's wings, or of alternating thick and thin strips in structure) ladder-shaped. [f. prec. in sense 'ladder-like' + -I- + -FORM]

scalawag. See SCALLYWAG.

scald¹ (-aw- *or* -ŏ-) *v.t.*, & *n.* **1.** *v.t.* Injure or pain (skin, or person or animal or part in regard to skin) with hot liquid or vapour (*was scalded to death by the steam*); **~ing tears,** tears of bitter grief. **2.** Heat (milk) to near boiling-point; **~ed cream** (from milk scalded and allowed to stand); hence **~'ER¹** (2) *n.* **3.** Cleanse (vessel *out*) by rinsing with boiling water; treat (poultry etc.) with boiling water to remove feathers etc. **4.** *n.* Injury to skin by scalding. [ME, f. AF, ONF *escalder*, OF *eschalder* f. LL EX¹(*caldare* f. L *calidus* hot)]

scald², skald, (-aw- *or* -ŏ-), *n.* Ancient-Scandinavian composer and reciter of poems in honour of heroes and their deeds; hence **~'IC** *a.* [f. ON *skáld*, of unkn. orig.]

sca'ld-head (-aw'ld-hĕd) *n.* Scalp-disease. [f. p.p. of SCALL + HEAD¹]

scāle¹ *n.* & *v.* **1.** *n.* One of the small thin bony or horny overlapping plates protecting the skin of many fishes and reptiles. **2.** Plate or thin outer piece with some resemblance to fish-scale in organic or other object, e.g. pod, husk, rudimentary leaf or feather, bract, metamorphosed hair of Lepidoptera, bulb-layer, flake of skin, scab, lamina on surface of rusty iron; **~s fall from** one's **eyes,** one is no longer deceived. **3.** Incrustation inside boiler etc.; tartar on teeth. **4. ~-armour** (of metal scales attached to leather etc.); **~-board,** very thin wood for back of mirror, picture, etc.; **~-bug,** = *scale-insect*; **~-fern,** ceterach; **~-insect** (of family Coccidae, clinging to plants and secreting a shieldlike scale as covering); **~-leaf,** modified leaf resembling scale; **~-moss,** liverwort with scalelike leaves; **~-winged,** lepidopterous; **~-work,** overlapping arrangement. **5.** Hence **(-)scāled** (-ld), **~'LESS** (-l-l-), **scā'lY²**, *adjs*. **6.** *v.t.* Take away scale(s) from (fish, almonds, teeth, iron, etc.). **7.** *v.i.* (Of skin, metal, etc.) form, come off in, drop, scales; (of scales) come *off*. [ME, f. OF *escale* f. Gmc **skalō* (cf. foll.)]

scāle² *n.*, & *v.t.* **1.** *n.* **~(-pan),** dish of simple balance; **throw into the ~,** cause to be factor in contest or debate; **tip** or **turn the ~(s),** outweigh opposite scale (*at* specified weight), (of motive or circumstance) be decisive. **2.** (in *sing*. or *pl.*) Weighing-instrument (**hold the ~s even,** be impartial judge); (*S~s*) *the* zodiacal sign Libra; **pair of ~s,** simple balance. **3.** *v.t.* (Of thing weighed) show (specified weight) in the scales. [ME, f. ON *skál* bowl = OHG *scāla* f. Gmc **skǣlō*, cogn. w. **skalō* whence OE *scealu* SHELL¹; cf. SHALE]

scāle³ *n.* & *v.* **1.** *n.* Series of degrees, ladder-like arrangement or classification, graded system, (*is high in the scale of creation* or *the social, intellectual*, etc., *scale*; *at the top, bottom, of the scale*; *fees according to a prescribed scale*); SLIDING *scale*. **2.** (Mus.) Arrangement by pitch of all notes used in any system of music (DIATONIC, CHROMATIC, MAJOR², MINOR, PENTATONIC, *scale*); **play, sing, ~s,** perform notes in such sequence as exercise for fingers, voice, etc. **3. ~(of notation),** (Arith.) basis of numerical system as shown by ratio between units in adjacent places of number; **ordinary** or **denary** or **decimal ~** (with successive places denoting units, tens, hundreds, etc.); **binary ~** (denoting units, twos, fours, etc.); **ternary ~** (denoting units, threes, nines, etc.). **4.** Relative dimensions, ratio of reduction or enlargement in picture, map, etc., (*philanthropy, armies, on a large* or *grand scale*; *a building of small scale but fine proportions*; *large, small, -scale map*; *on a scale of one to fifty thousand, an inch to the mile*, etc.); (*attrib.*) made to scale (*scale model*); **economies of ~**, proportionate savings got by using larger quantities; **in ~**, in proportion to surroundings etc.; **to ~**, with uniform reduction or enlargement. **5.** Set of marks at measured distances on line for use in measuring or making proportional reductions and enlargements; rule determining intervals between these; piece of metal etc. or apparatus on which they are marked. **6.** *v.t.* Climb (wall, steep place, or abs.) with ladder (**scaling-ladder**) or by clambering. **7.** Represent in dimensions proportional to the actual ones, reduce to common scale; **~ up, down,** make larger, smaller, in due proportion, increase, reduce, in size. **8.** *v.i.* (Of quantities etc.) have common scale, be commensurable. [n. ME (= ladder), v. ME f. OF *escaler* or f. med. L *scalare*, f. L *scala* (*scandere* climb)]

scă'lēne *a.* & *n.* **1.** *a.* Unequal-sided; **~ cone, cylinder,** (with axis not perpendicular to base); **~ muscle,** any of several muscles connecting spine and ribs; **~ triangle** (with no two sides equal). **2.** *n.* Scalene triangle or muscle. [f. LL f. Gk *skalēnos* unequal, cogn. w. *skolios* bent]

scalē'n|us *n.* (*pl.* **~i** *pr.* ~ī). Scalene muscle. [mod. L, f. as prec.]

scā'ler *n.* In vbl senses; electronic instrument registering a fixed number of events as one unit of counting. [f. SCALE[1,2,3] + -ER[1]]

scall (-awl) *n.* (arch.) Scaly eruption on skin (**dry ~**, the itch; **moist ~**, eczema). [ME, f. ON *skalli* bald head, f. Gmc **skal-* (as SHALE, SHELL[1])]

scallawag. Var. of SCALLYWAG.

scă'llion (-yon) *n.* Shallot; long-necked onion without normal bulb. [ME, f. AF *scal(o)un* = OF *escalo(i)gne* f. Rom. **escalonia* f. L *Ascalonia* (*caepa*) (onion) of *Ascalon* in Palestine]

scă'llop (*or* skŏ'-), **scŏ'llop,** *n.*, & *v.t.* **1.** *n.* Bivalve mollusc with shell divided into grooves and ridges radiating from middle of hinge and edged with small rounded lobes. **2. ~(-shell)**, one valve of scallop used for cooking and serving various kinds of food or (Hist.) as pilgrim's badge. **3.** Small pan used like scallop-shell to hold food. **4.** (in *pl.*) Ornamental edging cut in material in imitation of scallop-edge. **5.** *v.t.* Cook in scallop; ornament (edge, material) with scallops or ~ING[1] (6) *n.* [ME, f. OF *escalope*, prob. f. Gmc]

scă'llўwăg, scă'l(l)awăg (-*a*-w-), *n.* Undersized or ill-fed animal; good-for-nothing person, scamp, scapegrace. [19th c. U.S. sl., of unkn. orig.]

scălp *n.*, & *v.t.* **1.** *n.* Skin with hair etc. of head excluding face; this or part of it cut as trophy from enemy's head by American Indian (**out for ~s,** on the warpath, (fig.) in aggressive or pugnacious or savagely critical mood); **~-lock,** single lock on Amer. Indian's shaven head left as challenge to enemies; hence ~'LESS *a.* **2.** (Sc.) Bare rock projecting above water etc. **3.** *v.t.* Take scalp of; criticize savagely; *defeat, humiliate; *(colloq.) resell (shares, tickets, etc.) at high or quick profit, whence **~'er[1]** [-ER[1]] *n.* [north. ME, prob. of Scand. orig.]

scă'lpel *n.* Surgeon's small light straight knife shaped for holding like pen. [F, or f. L *scalpellum* dim. of *scalprum* chisel (*scalpere* scratch); see -LE 2]

scă'lper[2] *n.* Engraver's tool for hollowing out the bottom of sunken designs. [f. SCALP + -ER[1] & f. L *scalper* cutting tool (*scalpere* carve)]

scă'lprĭfôrm *a.* (Of incisor teeth) chisel-shaped. [f. L *scalprum* (as prec.) + -I- + -FORM]

scă'mmonў *n.* (W. Asian plant, *Convolvulus scammonia*, yielding) a gum resin used as drastic purgative. [ME, f. OF *scamonee, escamonie* or f. L f. Gk *skammōnia*]

scămp[1] *n.* (derog. or joc.) Rascal, knave, rogue; hence ~'ISH[1] *a.* [f. *scamp* rob on highway, prob. f. MDu. *schampen* decamp f. OF *esc(h)amper* f. Rom. *EX[1](*campare* f. L *campus* field)]

scămp[2] *v.t.* Do (work etc.) in perfunctory or inadequate way. [perh. f. as prec.; cf. SKIMP]

scă'mper *v.i.*, & *n.* **1.** *v.i.* Run impulsively (*about*) like excited or frightened animal or playing child; take scamper *through*. **2.** *n.* Hasty run; gallop on horseback for pleasure; rapid tour or course of reading. [prob. f. as SCAMP[1] + -ER[5]]

scă'mpĭ *n. pl.* (Dish of) large prawns. [It.]

scăn *v.* (-nn-) & *n.* **1.** *v.t.* Test metre of (line etc. of verse) by examining number and quantity of feet and syllables; read over with emphasis on rhythm. **2.** *v.i.* Be metrically correct (*line does not scan*); admit of rhythmic reading (*line will not scan*). **3.** *v.t.* Look at all parts successively of (face, horizon, etc.), intently or quickly; examine all parts of to detect radioactivity; cause (particular region) to be traversed by controlled (radar etc.) beam. **4.** Resolve (picture) into its elements of light and shade in prearranged pattern for purposes of television transmission. **5.** Hence **~'n**ER[1] *n.* **6.** *n.* Act or process of scanning. [ME, f. L *scandere* climb, in LL scan verses, f. raising of one's foot in marking rhythm]

scă'ndal *n.* (Thing that occasions) general feeling of outrage or indignation esp. as expressed in common talk, opprobrium, (*it is a scandal that such things should be possible*; *a grave scandal occurred*; *gave rise to scandal*); malicious gossip, backbiting, whence ~MONGER *n.*; (Law) public affront, irrelevant abusive statement in court; **~ sheet,** newspaper etc. giving prominence to (malicious) gossip; so ~OUS *a.* [ME, f. OF *scandale* f. eccl. L f. Gk *skandalon* snare, stumbling-block]

scă'ndalize[1], -ise[1] (-iz), *v.t.* Offend moral feelings, sense of propriety, or ideas of etiquette, of; shock. [ME in sense 'make scandal of', f. F *scandaliser* or f. eccl. L f. Gk *skandalizō* (as prec.; see -IZE)]

scă'ndalize[2], -ise[2] (-īz), *v.t.* (Naut.) Reduce area of (fore-and-aft sail). [alt. f. obs. *scantelize* = obs. *scantle* (SCANT V.; see -LE 3)]

scăndalum măgnā'tum *n.* (Hist.) Defamation of magnates. [med. L]

Scăndĭnā'vĭan *a.* & *n.* (Native, inhabitant, family of languages) of Scandinavia (Denmark, Norway, Sweden, and Iceland). [f. L *Scandĭnavia* + -AN]

scă'nsion (-sh*o*n) *n.* Metrical scanning; way verse scans. [f. L *scansio* (LL of metre) f. *scandere scans-* climb; see SCAN, -ION]

scănsôr'ĭal *a.* (Of birds etc. or their feet) habitually climbing, adapted for climbing. [L *scansorius* (as prec.; see -ORY) + -AL]

scănt *a.*, & *v.t.* **1.** *a.* (arch. or literary). Barely sufficient, deficient, with scanty supply of, (*with scant regard for my feelings*; *scant of breath*); hence ~'LY[2] *adv.* **2.** *v.t.* (arch.) Skimp, stint, provide grudgingly, (supply, material, person). [ME, f. ON *skamt* neut. of *skammr* short]

scă'ntĭes (-ĭz) *n. pl.* (colloq.) Women's short panties. [f. prec., after *panties*]

scă'ntlĭng *n.* **1.** (arch.) Specimen, sample; modicum, small amount, one's necessary supply *of*. **2.** Timber beam of small cross-section; size to which stone or timber is to be cut. **3.** Set of standard dimensions for parts of structure esp. in shipbuilding. [alt. after -LING[1] f. obs. *scantlon* f. OF *escantillon* sample]

scă'nt|ȳ *a.* Of small extent or amount; barely sufficient; hence **~ĭLY**[2] *adv.*, **~ĭNESS** *n.* [f. obs. *scant* scanty supply f. ON *skamt* neut. a. (as n.; see SCANT) + -Y[2]]

scāpe[1] *n.*, & *v.t.* (arch.) Escape. [ME, f. ESCAPE[1,2]]

scāpe[2] *n.* (Bot.) long flower-stalk coming directly from root; (Entom.) base of antenna; shaft of column. [f. L f. Gk *skapos*, cogn. w. SCEPTRE]

-scāpe *suf.* forming *ns.* w. sense (representation of) view of (*seascape, wirescape*). [after LANDSCAPE]

scā'pegoat (-pg-) *n.*, & *v.t.* **1.** *n.* Goat allowed to escape when Jewish chief priest had laid sins of people upon it (Lev. 16). **2.** Person bearing blame that should fall on others. **3.** *v.t.* Make scapegoat of. [f. SCAPE[1] + GOAT]

scā'pegrāce (-pg-) *n.* Hare-brained person, esp. young person or child who constantly gets into trouble. [f. SCAPE[1] + GRACE = one who escapes the grace of God]

scă'phoid *a.* & *n.* (Anat.) Boat-shaped (bone in tarsus or in carpus). [mod. L, f. Gk *skaphoeidēs* (*skaphos* boat; see -OID)]

scă'pūla *n.* (*pl.* ~e). Shoulder-blade. [LL, sing. of L *scapulae*]

scă'pūlar *a.* & *n.* **1.** *a.* Of shoulder or shoulder-blade; **~ arch,** = *shoulder* GIRDLE[1]; **~ feathers** (growing near insertion of wing). **2.** *n.* Monastic short cloak covering shoulders; badge of affiliation to an ecclesiastical order, consisting of two strips of cloth hanging down breast and back and joined across shoulders. **3.** Bandage for or over shoulders. **4.** Scapular feather. [a. f. prec. + -AR[1], n. f. LL *scapulare* (as prec.; see -AR[1])]

scă'pūlarȳ *n.* = prec. 2, 4. [ME, f. AF **scapelorie*, OF *eschapeloyre* f. med. L *scapelorium, scapularium* (as SCAPULA; see -ARY[1])]

scar̄[1] *n.* & *v.* (-rr-). **1.** *n.* Mark left after healing of wound or burn or sore, (fig.) abiding effect of grief etc.; mark left by damage; mark on plant left by fall of leaf etc.; hence **~'LESS** *a.* **2.** *v.t.* (esp. in *p.p.*) Mark with scar(s). **3.** *v.i.* & *t.* Heal over, form scar (on). [ME, f. OF *eschar(r)e* f. LL f. Gk *eskhara* scab]

scar̄[2], **scaur,** *n.* Precipitous craggy part of mountain-side or cliff. [ME, f. ON *sker* low reef in sea]

scă'rab *n.* Sacred dung-beetle of ancient Egypt; = foll.; ancient-Egyptian etc. gem cut in form of beetle and engraved with symbols on flat side as signet etc. [f. L *scarabaeus* f. Gk *skarabeios*]

scărabae'ĭd *n.* Member of Scarabaeidae family of beetles, incl. dung-beetle, cockchafer, etc. [f. mod. L *Scarabaeidae* (as prec.; see -ID[3])]

scă'ramouch *n.* (arch.) Boastful poltroon, braggart. [f. It. *Scaramuccia* stock character in Italian farce (*scaramuccia* = SKIRMISH), infl. by F form *Scaramouche*]

scar̄ce *a.* & *adv.* **1.** *a.* (Usu. *pred.*, esp. of food, money, or other necessaries of life) insufficient for the demand or need, not plentiful, scanty; hence **scar̄'CITY** *n.* (*of*, or abs. = dearth of food). **2.** Seldom met with, rare, hard to find, (*a scarce book, moth*); **make** one**self ~,** (colloq.) make off, esp. surreptitiously, keep out of the way; hence **~'NESS** (-sn-) *n.* **3.** *adv.* (arch. or literary). Scarcely. [ME f. AF & ONF *(e)scars*, OF *eschars* f. Rom. **excarpsus* p.p. of **excarpere* f. L *excerpere* (see EXCERPT[2])]

scar̄'celȳ (-slĭ) *adv.* **1.** Hardly, barely, only just, (*is scarcely seventeen years old*; *had scarcely arrived when my friend left*; *I scarcely know him*). **2.** Surely not, not unless the unlikely happens or is true, (*you will scarcely maintain that*; *he can scarcely have said so*); (mild or apologetic or ironical substitute for) not (*I scarcely think so, know what to say, expected to be insulted*). [ME, f. prec. + -LY[2]]

scāre *v.* & *n.* **1.** *v.t.* Strike with sudden terror, frighten (as) with something feared; (in *p.p.*) frightened *of, to* do, (of expression etc.) betraying terror; drive *away, off, up*, etc., by fright; ***~ out** or **up,** frighten (game) out of cover, (fig.) discover, manage to find; **~'dy-cat** (-ār'dĭ-), (colloq.) timid person. **2.** Keep (birds) away from sown land etc.; **~'crow,** figure of man hung with old clothes and set up in field to keep birds away, object of baseless fear, badly dressed or grotesque-looking or skinny person. **3.** *v.i.* Become scared. **4.** *n.* Unreasoning terror, esp. baseless general apprehension of war, invasion, epidemic, etc., whence **~'MONGER** (-ār'm-) *n.*; commercial panic; **~-head(ing),** extravagantly sensational newspaper headline; hence **scār'Y**[2] *a.* [ME *skerre*, f. ON *skirra* frighten (*skjarr* timid)]

scar̄f[1] *n.* (*pl.* **scarves** *pr.* -vz, *or* ~s). Long narrow strip of material worn for ornament or warmth round neck, over shoulders, or baldric-wise; square piece of material worn round neck or over woman's hair (||**~-pin, -ring,** ornamental device for fastening this); **~-skin,** outermost layer of skin constantly scaling off (esp. of that adhering to base of nails); **~-wise,** baldric-wise; hence **~ED**[2] (-ft) *a.* [prob. f. ONF *escarpe* = OF *escherpe* sash etc., prob. same wd as *esc(h)arpe* SCRIP[1]; infl. by foll.]

scar̄f[2] *v.t.*, & *n.* **1.** *v.t.* Join ends of (pieces of timber, metal, or leather) by bevelling or notching so that they overlap without increase of thickness and then bolting, brazing, or sewing them together; cut blubber of (whale). **2.** *n.* Joint made by scarfing. [v. f. n., ME prob. f. OF **escarf* (**escarver* v. perh. f. ON)]

scă'rĭfĭcātor *n.* Surgical instrument for scarifying, in which several lancet-points protrude at once from plane surface on touching of trigger. [mod. L, f. F *scarificateur* (as SCARIFY; see -OR)]

scă'rĭfīer *n.* In vbl senses; = prec.; agricultural machine with prongs for loosening without turning soil; spiked road-breaking machine. [f. foll. + -ER[1]]

scă'rĭ|fȳ *v.t.* (Surg.) make superficial incisions in, cut off skin from; (fig.) pain by severe criticism etc.; loosen (soil) with scarifier; so **~FICA'TION** *n.* [ME, f. F *scarifier* f. LL *scarificare* f. L *scarifare* f. Gk *skariphaomai* (*skariphos* stylus); see -FY]

scār'ĭous *a.* (Bot., of bract etc.) thin, dry, and membranous. [f. F *scarieux* or mod. L *scariosus*; see -OUS]

scar̄lati'na (-tē'-) *n.* Scarlet fever. [mod. L, f. It. *scarlattina* (*febbre* fever), dim. of *scarlatto* SCARLET]

scar̄'lėt *n.* & *a.* (Of) brilliant red colour inclining to orange; scarlet clothes or material (*dressed in scarlet*); **~ fever,** infectious bacterial fever with scarlet rash; **~ hat,** cardinal's hat, (symbol of) cardinal's rank; *scarlet* PIMPERNEL; **~ rash,** roseola; **~ runner,** (scarlet-flowered climbing plant bearing) kind of bean; **~ woman,** (1) prostitute, (2) (derog.) Church of Rome. [ME, f. OF *escarlate*; ult. orig. unkn.]

scă'roid (*or* skār'-) *a.* & *n.* (Fish) of family Scaridae, incl. scarus. [f. SCARUS + -OID]

scar̄p *n.*, & *v.t.* **1.** *n.* Inner wall or slope (cf. COUNTERSCARP) of ditch in fortification; steep slope. **2.** *v.t.* Make (slope) perpendicular or steep; provide (ditch) with steep scarp and counterscarp; (in *p.p.*, of hillside etc.) steep, precipitous. [f. It. *scarpa*]

scar͡'per *v.i.* (sl.) Escape, run away. [prob. f. It. *scappare* escape, infl. by rhyming sl. *Scapa Flow* go]

scā̄r'us *n.* Bright-coloured fish with beaklike jaws, allied to wrasse family. [L, f. Gk *skaros*]

scār'ȳ. See SCARE.

scăt[1] *v.i.* (**-tt-**), & *int.* (colloq.) Depart quickly. [perh. abbr. of SCATTER]

scăt[2] *n.*, & *v.i.* (**-tt-**). (Sing) wordless jazz song using voice as instrument. [prob. imit.]

scāthe (-dh) *v.t.*, & *n.* **1.** *v.t.* (poet.) Injure esp. by blasting or withering up. **2.** (esp. in *part.*) Wither with severe speech (*scathing sarcasm, ridicule, remarks*). **3.** (w. neg.) Do the least harm to (*shall not be scathed*; cf. UNSCATHED). **4.** *n.* (arch., usu. w. neg.) Harm, injury, (*without scathe*); hence **~'LESS** (-dhl-) *a.* (usu. *pred.*). [v. ME f. ON *skatha* = OE *sceathian*, n. OE f. ON *skathi* = OE *sceatha* malefactor, injury, f. Gmc **skathōjan*, **skathon*]

scătŏ'logȳ *n.* **1.** Study of coprolites. **2.** Preoccupation with excrement. **3.** Preoccupation with obscene literature. **4.** Hence **scăto**LO'GICAL *a.* [f. Gk *skōr skatos* dung + -O- + -LOGY]

scatŏ'phagous *a.* Feeding on dung. [as prec. + Gk *-phagos* -eating + -OUS]

scă'tter *v.* & *n.* **1.** *v.t.* Throw here and there (*scatter seed*; *scatter gravel on road*); cover by scattering (*scatter road with gravel*). **2.** *v.t.* & *i.* Disperse, turn in dispersed flight, rout or be routed. **3.** *v.t.* Dissipate (cloud, hopes); (Phys.) deflect or diffuse (light, particles, etc.). **4.** *v.i.* & *t.* (Of gun) send charge, send (charge), in spreading manner. **5.** (in *p.p.*) Not situated together, wide apart, sporadic, (*scattered villages, garrisons, instances*). **6.** **~-brain,** heedless person; **~-brained,** heedless, desultory; ***~-shot** *n.* & *a.*, firing at random. **7.** *n.* Act of scattering; extent of distribution esp. of shot; ***~ cushions, rugs,** etc., (to be placed here and there in room). [ME, prob. var. of SHATTER]

scă'tt|ȳ *a.* (sl.) Feeble-minded; hare-brained; hence **~ĭLY**[2] *adv.*, **~ĭNESS** *n.* [f. SCATTER-*brained* + -Y[2]]

scaup *n.* Diving duck of genus *Aythya*. [f. *scaup*, Sc. var. of *scalp* mussel-bed, wh. it frequents]

scau'per. Var. of SCALPER[2].

scaur. See SCAR[2].

scă'vėnge (-nj) *v.t.* & *i.* Be, or act as, scavenger (of); remove unwanted products from (internal combustion engine cylinder etc.); make search for or *for* (thing) among what is unwanted by others. [back form. f. foll.]

scă'vėng|er (-nj-) *n.*, & *v.i.* **1.** *n.* ||Person employed to keep streets clean by carrying away refuse; hence **~ERY** (2, 5) *n.* **2.** Animal, esp. beetle, feeding on carrion. **3.** *v.i.* = prec. [ME *scavager* (cf. *messenger*) inspector of imports f. AF *scawager* (*scawage* f. ONF *escauwer* inspect f. Flem. *scauwen* cogn. w. SHOW[1])]

scă'zon *n.* (Pros.) Greek or Latin metre of limping character, esp. trimeter of two iambuses and spondee or trochee. [L f. Gk *skazōn* (*skazō* limp)]

Sc.D. *abbr.* Doctor of Science. [f. L *scientiae doctor*]

S.C.E. *abbr.* Scottish Certificate of Education.

scena (shā'nah) *n.* (Mus.) Scene or portion of opera; elaborate dramatic solo usu. including recitative. [It. f. L (see SCENE)]

scėnār'|iō (*or* -ar͡'-) *n.* (*pl.* **~ios**). **1.** (Table of) scene-distribution, appearances of characters, etc., in dramatic work, outline libretto. **2.** Complete plot of film play with details of scenes etc.; imagined sequence of future events. **3.** Hence **~IST** (3) *n.* [It. (as prec.)]

scĕnd. See SEND[2].

scēne *n.* **1.** (arch.) Stage of theatre. **2.** Place of action (**come on the ~**, arrive; **quit the ~**, (esp.) die); place on which something is exhibited as on the stage (*this world is a scene of strife*); (sl.) area of action, way of life. **3.** Place in which events set forth in drama or tale are supposed to occur, locality of event, (*the scene is laid in India*; *the scene of the disaster was the North Sea*). **4.** Portion of a play during which action is continuous or in which no intermediate entries or exits occur, subdivision of an act, (*in the third scene of Act II*; *the famous duel scene*); similar portion of book etc. **5.** Description with more or less abrupt beginning and end of an incident or part of person's life etc. (*scenes of clerical life, from a goldfield*, etc.); actual incident that might occasion such description (*distressing scenes occurred*), agitated conversation esp. with display of temper, stormy encounter or interview. **6.** Any of the pieces of painted canvas, woodwork, etc., used to help in representing scene of action on stage; whole of these together; **bėhind the ~s,** among the stage machinery or the actors off the stage, (fig.) not known to the public, using information of this kind; **set the ~,** (fig.) describe location of events etc.; SET[3] *scene*. **7.** Landscape or view spread before spectator like scene in theatre (*a silvan, desolate, scene*; *a scene of destruction*); **change of ~,** variety of surroundings esp. secured by travel. **8.** **~-dock,** space near stage where scenes are stored; **~-painter, -painting,** (of theatre scenes); **~-shifter, ~-shifting,** (person engaged in) changing scenes in theatre. [f. L f. Gk *skēnē* tent, stage]

scē'nerȳ *n.* Accessories used in theatre to make stage resemble supposed scene of action; general appearance of natural features of a district (*the scenery is imposing*); picturesque features of landscape; **change of ~,** = *change of* SCENE. [earlier *scenary* f. It. SCENARIO (cf. -ARY[1]); assim. to -ERY]

scē'nĭc *a.* Of or on the stage (*scenic performances*); of the nature of a show, picturesque in grouping; (of picture etc.) telling a tale, representing an incident; having fine natural scenery; **~ railway,** miniature railway running through artificial picturesque scenery at fairs etc.; hence **scē'n**ICALLY *adv.* [f. L f. Gk *skēnikos* of the stage (as SCENE; see -IC)]

scĕnt *v.* & *n.* **1.** *v.t.* Discern by smell (*scent game* etc.), (fig.) begin to suspect presence or existence of (*scent treachery*); **~ out,** discover by smelling about or search. **2.** Make fragrant or rank (*rose, carrion, scents the air*); apply perfume to (handkerchief etc.; *scented soap, tobacco*). **3.** *v.i.* & *t.* Exercise sense of smell (*goes scenting about*); apply this to (*lifts its head and scents the air*). **4.** *n.* Odour, esp. of agreeable kind, proceeding from or belonging to something (*the scent of hay*); hence (-)**~'ED**[2], **~'LESS**, *adjs.* **5.** (Hunt.) trail perceptible to hounds' sense of smell left by animal, (fig.) indications that can be followed thus, (*follow up, lose, recover*, etc., *the scent*; **on the** (**right**) **~**, having clue; **put** or **throw off the ~**, deceive by false indications; COLD[1], HOT[1], *scent*); trail laid in paper-chase; **false ~** (laid to deceive as to course, lit. or fig.). **6.** Power of detecting or distinguishing smells or of discovering presence of something, (*some dogs have practically no scent*; *keen-scented*; *has a wonderful scent for talent*). **7.** ||Liquid perfume distilled from flowers etc. **8.** **~-bag,** (1) pouch containing special odoriferous substance in some animals, (2) bag of aniseed etc. as substitute for fox in hunting; **~-bottle** (for perfume); **~-gland** (secreting musk, civet, etc.); **~-organ,** scent-bag or scent-gland. [ME *sent* f. OF *sentir* perceive, smell, f. L *sentire*]

scĕ'psĭs (sk-), ***skĕ'psĭs,** *n.* Philosophic doubt; sceptical philosophy. [f. Gk *skepsis* inquiry, doubt (*skeptomai* consider)]

***scĕ'pter.** See SCEPTRE.

scĕ'ptĭc (sk-), ***skĕ'ptĭc,** *n.* **1.** Ancient or modern adherent of Pyrrhonism. **2.** Person who doubts truth of the Christian or of all religious doctrines. **3.** Person of sceptical habit of mind, or unconvinced of truth of particular fact or theory, or who takes cynical views. **4.** Hence ~ISM (3) *n.* [f. F *sceptique* or L f. Gk *skeptikos* (as SCEPSIS; see -IC)]

scĕ'ptĭcal (sk-), ***skĕ'ptĭcal,** *a.* **1.** Inclined to suspend judgement, given to questioning truth of fact(s) and soundness of inference(s), critical, incredulous. **2.** Accepting Pyrrhonism, denying possibility of knowledge. **3.** Holding, designed to support, inspired by, the ideas of sceptics. **4.** Hence ~LY² *adv.* [f. as prec.; see -ICAL]

scĕ'ptr|e (-t*er*), ***scĕ'pter,** *n.* Staff borne as symbol of personal sovereignty; royal or imperial authority; hence ~ED² (-t*erd*) *a.* [ME, f. OF (*s*)*ceptre* f. L f. Gk *skēptron* (*skēptō* lean on)]

sch. *abbr.* scholar; school; schooner.

schadenfreude (shah'd*e*nfroid*e*) *n.* Malicious enjoyment of others' misfortunes. [G (*schade* harm, *freude* joy)]

schăppe (sh-) *n.* Fabric or yarn made from waste silk. [G, = waste silk]

schĕ'dūle (sh-) *n.*, & *v.t.* **1.** *n.* Tabulated statement of details, inventory, etc., esp. as appendix or annex to principal document; list of events, rates, etc.; *timetable; time stated in timetable (*behind, on, schedule*); **according to ~,** as planned. **2.** *v.t.* Make schedule of; include in schedule, esp. ||include (building) in list of those to be preserved and protected; **~d flight, service,** etc., (according to regular timetable); **~d territories,** = STERLING *area.* [ME f. OF *cedule* f. LL *schedula* slip of paper, dim. of *scheda* f. Gk *skhedē* papyrus-leaf; see -ULE]

schee'līte (sh-) *n.* (Min.) Calcium tungstate in native crystalline form. [f. K. W. *Scheele*, Sw. chemist d. 1786 + -ITE¹ (2)]

schē'ma (sk-) *n.* (*pl.* **~ta**). Synopsis, outline, diagram; proposed arrangement; (Logic) syllogistic figure; (Kantian Philos.) general type, essential form, conception of what is common to all members of a class. [f. Gk *skhēma -atos* form, figure]

schėmă't|ĭc (sk-; *or* -ē-) *a.* & *n.* **1.** *a.* Of a schema or scheme; representing objects by symbols etc.; hence ~ICALLY *adv.* **2.** *n.* Schematic diagram. [f. as prec. + -IC]

schē'matĭsm (sk-) *n.* Schematic arrangement or presentation. [f. mod. L f. Gk *skhēmatismos* (as foll.; see -ISM)]

schē'matiz|e, -īs|e, (sk-; -īz) *v.t.* Represent by schema or scheme; put in schematic form; hence ~A'TION *n.* [f. Gk *skhēmatizō* assume a form, or f. as SCHEMA + -IZE]

schēm|e (sk-) *n.* & *v.* **1.** *n.* Systematic arrangement proposed or in operation (COLOUR¹ *scheme*); table of classification or of appointed times, outline, syllabus; plan of construction, work, action, etc.; artful or underhand design. **2.** *v.i.* Make plans, plan esp. in secret or underhand or artful way (*to* do, *for*, or abs.), intrigue; hence ~'ER¹, ~'ING¹ (1), *ns.*, ~'ING² *a.* **3.** *v.t.* Plan to bring about. [f. L f. Gk (as SCHEMA)]

schemozzle. Var. of SHEMOZZLE.

scherză'nd|ō (skārts-) *adv.*, *a.*, & *n.* (*pl.* **~os** *or* **~i**). (Mus.) (Passage performed) in playful manner. [It., gerund of *scherzare* sport (as foll.)]

scher'zō (skār'tsō) *n.* (*pl.* **~s**). Vigorous (prop. light and playful) composition, independent or as movement in works of symphony or sonata type. [It., lit. 'sport, jest']

Schiedă'm (sk-) *n.* Hollands gin. [~ in Holland]

schĭ'llĭng (sh-) *n.* Austrian monetary unit and coin. [G (as SHILLING)]

schĭ'pperkė (sk- *or* sh-) *n.* Small black tailless breed of dog. [Du. dial., = little boatman, f. its use as watch-dog on barges]

schĭ'sm (sĭ'- *or* skĭ'-) *n.* Separation of a Church into two Churches or secession of part of a Church owing to difference of opinion on doctrine or discipline; offence of causing or promoting such separation; dividing of a group into mutually opposing parties. [ME f. OF *s*(*c*)*isme* f. eccl. L f. Gk *skhisma -atos* cleft (*skhizō* to split)]

schĭsmă'tĭc (sĭz- *or* skĭz-) *a.* & *n.*, **-ĭc|al** *a.* **1.** *a.* Tending or inclined to, guilty of, schism; hence **~al**LY² *adv.* **2.** *n.* Holder of schismatic opinions; member of schismatic faction or seceded branch of a Church. [ME, f. OF *scismatique* f. eccl. L f. eccl. Gk *skhismatikos* (as prec.; see -IC, -AL)]

schĭst (sh-) *n.* Foliated metamorphic rock presenting layers of different minerals and splitting into thin irregular plates; hence ~'OSE¹ *a.* [f. F *schiste* f. L f. Gk *skhistos* split (as SCHISM)]

schĭ'stosōme (sh- *or* sk-) *n.* Bilharzia worm. [f. Gk *skhistos* divided (as SCHISM) + -O- + *sōma* body]

schĭstosomī'as|ĭs (sh- *or* sk-) *n.* (*pl.* **~es** *pr.* -ēz). Bilharziasis. [f. mod. L *Schistosoma* (genus-name; as prec.) + -ASIS]

schĭză'nthus (sk-) *n.* Flowering annual plant of genus *Schizanthus*, with showy white, violet, or crimson flowers and finely-divided leaves. [mod. L, f. Gk *skhizō* to split + *anthos* flower]

schĭ'zō (skĭ'tsō) *a.* & *n.* (*pl.* **~s**). (colloq.) Schizophrenic. [abbr.]

schĭzocar̄p (sk-) *n.* (Bot.) Dry fruit that splits into single-seeded parts when ripe. [f. Gk *skhizō* to split + *karpos* fruit]

schĭ'zoid (sk-; *or* skĭ'ts-) *a.* & *n.* **1.** *a.* Tending to or resembling schizophrenia or a schizophrenic, but usu. without delusions. **2.** *n.* Schizoid person. [f. SCHIZOPHRENIA + -OID]

schĭzomȳ'cēte (sk-) *n.* Member of a class of minute often single-cell vegetable organisms intermediate between algae and fungi and multiplying by fission, including bacteria etc. [f. Gk *skhizō* to split + *mukēs -ētos* mushroom]

schĭzophr|ē'nĭa (sk-; *or* skĭts-) *n.* Mental disease marked by disconnection between thoughts, feelings, and actions, freq. with delusions and retreat from social life; hence **~ĕ'n**IC *a.* & *n.* [mod. L, f. Gk *skhizō* to split + *phrēn* mind; see -IA¹]

schĭzothȳ'm|ĭa (sk-; *or* skĭts-) *n.* (Psych.) Introvert character with tendency to schizophrenia; hence ~IC *a.* [mod. L, f. as prec. + Gk *thumos* temper; see -IA¹]

***schlemie'l** (shl-) *n.* Foolish or unlucky person. [f. Yiddish *shlumiel*]

schlier'en (shlēr'-) *a.* (Of apparatus etc.) producing light-patterns representing variations in physical properties of gas or other transparent medium. [G, pl. of *schliere* streak]

***schlŏck** (shl-) *a.* & *n.* Poor-quality or second--hand (material). [f. Yiddish *shlak* a blow]

schmaltz (shmawlts) *n.* Sugary sentimentalism in music etc.; hence ~'Y² *a.* [Yiddish, f. G *schmalz* dripping, lard]

schnăpps (shn-) *n.* Strong Hollands gin. [G, = dram of liquor, f. LG & Du. *snaps* mouthful (as SNAP)]

schnau'zer (shnow'ts*er*) *n.* German breed of house-dog with close wiry coat. [G (*schnauze* muzzle, SNOUT)]

schnĭ'tzel (shnĭ'ts-) *n.* Veal cutlet; **Wiener** or **Vienna ~,** one breaded, fried, and garnished. [G, = slice]

schnŏr'kel (shn-), **snŏr'kel,** *n.* Device for

supplying air to submerged submarine; breathing-tube for underwater swimmer. [f. G *schnorchel*; *snorkel* Anglicized]

schnŏr'rer (shn-) *n.* (sl.) Beggar. [Yiddish, f. G *schnurrer*]

schŏ'lar (sk-) *n.* **1.** (arch.) Schoolboy or schoolgirl. **2.** (rhet.) Person's disciple. **3.** Person who learns (*proved an apt, dull, scholar*; *at 90 he was still a scholar*); *scholar's* MATE¹. **4.** Learned person, person versed in language or literature (*is something of a Russian scholar*); (vulg. or dial.) person able to read and write; **a ~ and a gentleman,** person of good education and breeding; hence ~LY¹ *a.* **5.** Holder of scholarship (sense 2). [ME, f. OE *scol(i)ere* & OF *escol(i)er*, f. LL *scholaris* f. L *schola* SCHOOL¹; see -AR¹]

schŏ'larshĭp (sk-) *n.* **1.** Quality of having attained learning; methods and achievements characteristic of scholars. **2.** (Right to) payment from funds of school, university, etc., for education there, or from other funds for education, usu. gained by competitive examination. [f. prec. + -SHIP]

scholă'stĭc (sk-) *a.* & *n.* **1.** *a.* Of universities, schools, schooling, dons, or schoolmasters, educational, academic, pedantic, formal, (*a scholastic education, post*; *scholastic attire, manners, precision, life*); **~ agent** (finding posts for teachers). **2.** (As) of the schoolmen, dealing in logical subtleties; **~ theology** (much concerned with precise definition of and deduction from dogma). **3.** Hence or cogn. **scholă'st**ICALLY (sk-) *adv.*, ~ISM (2, 3) *n.* **4.** *n.* Schoolman; modern theologian of scholastic tendencies; Jesuit between novitiate and priesthood. [f. L f. Gk *skholastikos* studious (*skholazō* be at leisure f. as SCHOOL¹; see -IC)]

schō'lĭ|ăst (sk-) *n.* Commentator, esp. ancient grammarian who wrote scholia on the classics; hence **~ă'st**IC *a.* [f. med. Gk *skholiastēs* (*skholiazō* write scholia; see foll.)]

schō'lĭ|um (sk-) *n.* (*pl.* **~a**). Marginal note, explanatory comment, esp. one by ancient grammarian on passage in classical author. [mod. L, f. Gk *skholion* (*skholē* disputation; see foll.)]

schōōl¹ (sk-) *n.*, & *v.t.* **1.** *n.* Institution for educating children or giving instruction ||usu. of more elementary or more technical kinds than that given at universities (APPROVED, BOARDING-, COMPREHENSIVE, CONTINUATION, DAME-, DAY-, ELEMENTARY, FREE¹, *GRADE, GRAMMAR, HIGH, ||INFANT, MEDICAL, MIXED, ||MODERN, NIGHT-, NORMAL, PRIMARY, PRIVATE, PUBLIC, SECONDARY, SUMMER¹, SUNDAY, TECHNICAL, *school*; ||OLD *school tie*); *university, or department thereof; centre for archaeological research (*British School at Athens, Rome*); **keep a ~**, manage private school. **2.** Buildings of such institution (**at ~**, attending lessons), any of its rooms used for teaching in (*the fifth-form, chemistry, school*); its pupils (*the whole school knows*); time during which teaching is done (*there will be no school today*); **go to ~**, attend lessons in a school (*need not go to school today*). **3.** Being educated in a school (**at ~**, ***in ~**, in course of this; **go to, leave, ~**, begin, cease, this; **go to ~ to,** (fig.) imitate or learn from); (fig.) circumstances or occupation serving to discipline or instruct (*in the school of adversity*; *learnt his generalship in a severe school*). **4.** Medieval lecture-room (**the ~s,** medieval universities and their professors and teaching and disputations); ||branch of study with separate examinations at university (*the history, mathematical, Greats, school*); hall in which university examinations are held; (in *pl.*) such examinations. **5.** Disciples or imitators or followers of philosopher, artist, etc., band or succession of persons devoted to some cause or principle or agreeing in typical characteristics, (*left no school behind him*; *school of Epicurus, Raphael*, etc.; *Bolognese, British*, etc., *school of painters*; *Lake, Romantic*, etc., *school of literature*; *peripatetic, Hegelian*, etc., *school of philosophy*; *laissez-faire* etc. *school of economics*; *belonged to a different school of thought*); ||group of gamblers; *a gentleman* etc. **of the old ~**, according to the older acceptation of the word. **6.** (Mus.) Manual (*of* counterpoint etc.). **7. ~ age,** age-range in which children normally attend school; **~-bag** (for carrying books etc. to or from school); **~-board,** (U.S. or Hist.) local education authority; **~-book,** (for use in schools); **~'boy,** boy at school; **~ bus** (taking children to or from school); **~'child,** child at school; ||**~-dame,** keeper of dame-school; **~-days,** time of being at school esp. as looked back upon; **~ divine,** (arch.) scholastic theologian; **~ fee(s)**, amount periodically paid to school for teaching of pupil(s); **~'fellow,** past or present member of same school; **~'girl,** girl at school; **~'house,** building of esp. village school; ||**~ house,** headmaster's house at boarding-school; **~-inspector** (officially reporting on efficiency of schools); **~-kid,** (colloq.) schoolchild; ||**~-leaver,** boy or girl leaving school on reaching specified age or stage; ***~-ma'm, *~-marm,** (colloq.) schoolmistress; **~'man,** (1) teacher in medieval European university, theologian seeking to deal with religious doctrines by rules of Aristotelian logic, (2) *teacher; ***~-marmish,** (colloq.) prim and fussy; **~'master,** head or assistant male teacher in school; **~'mastering,** teaching for one's living; **~'mate,** = *schoolfellow*; **~'mistress,** head or assistant female teacher in school; **~'mistressy,** (colloq.) prim and fussy; **~'room** (used for lessons in school or private house); **~-ship,** training-ship; **~'teacher,** master or mistress in (esp. infant or primary) school; **~-time,** (1) lesson-time at school or home, (2) school-days; *school* YEAR. **8.** *v.t.* Send to school, provide for education of; hence ~'ING¹ *n.* **9.** Discipline, bring under control, deliberately train or accustom *to*, induce to follow advice, (*must school his temper*; *school oneself to patience, to take an interest*); (in *p.p.*) educated or trained *in* (habit etc.). [ME, f. OE *scōl, scolu*, & f. OF *escole* f. Rom. *scola*, f. L *schola* school f. Gk *skholē* leisure, disputation, philosophy, lecture-place]

schōōl² (sk-) *n.*, & *v.i.* **1.** *n.* Shoal of or *of* fish, porpoises, whales, etc.; **~-fish,** fish that forms school, esp. the menhaden. **2.** *v.i.* Form schools. [ME, f. MLG, MDu. *schōle*, = OS *scola*, OE *scolu* troop f. WG **skula*]

schōō'lable (sk-) *a.* Liable by age etc. to compulsory education. [f. SCHOOL¹ + -ABLE]

schōō'ner (sk-) *n.* **1.** Fore-and-aft-rigged vessel with two or more masts; *PRAIRIE *schooner*. **2.** *Tall beer-glass; ||measure for beer, sherry, etc. [18th c.; orig. uncert.]

schŏrl (sh-) *n.* Black tourmaline. [f. G *schörl*]

schŏtti'sche (shŏtē'sh) *n.* (Music for) kind of slower polka. [f. G *der schottische tanz* the Scottish dance]

schuss (shŏŏs) *n.*, & *v.i.* (Make) straight downhill run on skis. [G, lit. 'shot']

schwa (shwah *or* shvah) *n.* (Phonet.) Indistinct vowel sound as in second syllable of *common* or *comma*. [G, f. Heb. *šᵉwā*, app. f. *šaw'* emptiness]

sciă'graphy̆, ski-, *n.* Art of shading in drawing etc.; X-ray radiography; hence **sci'a**GRAM (2) *n.*, **sci'a**GRAPH (1, 2, 3) *n.*, & *v.t.*, **scia**GRA'PHIC *a.*, (*or* **ski-**). [f. F *sciagraphie* f. L f. Gk *skiagraphia* (*skia* shadow; see -GRAPHY)]

sciă'machy̆, skī-, (-kĭ) *n.* Fighting with shadows; imaginary or futile combat. [f. Gk *skiamakhia* (as prec., *-makhia* -fighting; see -Y[1])]
sciă'tic *a.* **1.** Of the hip; ~ **nerve** (from pelvis to thigh, largest nerve in human body). **2.** Of or affecting the sciatic nerve; suffering from or liable to sciatica. **3.** Hence **sciă'tically** *adv.* [f. F *sciatique* f. LL *sciaticus* f. L f. Gk *iskhiadikos* subject to sciatica (*iskhion* hip-joint)]
sciă'tica *n.* Neuralgia of hip and thigh, pain in sciatic nerve. [ME, f. LL *sciatica* (*passio*), fem. of *sciaticus* (see prec.)]
scī'ence *n.* **1.** (arch.) Knowledge. **2.** Systematic and formulated knowledge (**moral, political, natural,** etc., ~, such knowledge in reference to morals etc.); pursuit of this or principles regulating such pursuit (*man of science*). **3.** (**Natural**) ~, physical or natural sciences collectively. **4.** Branch of knowledge (esp. one that can be conducted on scientific principles), organized body of the knowledge that has been accumulated on a subject, (*the science of optics, ethics, philology*); **applied** ~ (studied for practical purposes); DISMAL *science*; EXACT *science*; **natural** ~, one dealing with material phenomena and based mainly on observation, experiment, and induction, as chemistry, biology; PHYSICAL *science*; **pure** ~, one depending on deductions from self-evident truths, as mathematics, logic, or one studied without practical applications; SOCIAL *science*. **5.** Expert's skill as opp. strength or natural ability esp. in boxing or other sport. **6.** ~ **fiction,** fanciful fiction based on postulated scientific discoveries or environmental changes, freq. dealing with space travel, life on other planets, etc. [ME f. OF, f. L *scientia* (*scrire* know; see -ENCE)]
sciĕ'nter *adv.* (Law). Intentionally, knowingly. [L (*scire* know; cf. -ENT)]
sciĕ'ntial (-shal) *a.* Pertaining to or having knowledge. [f. LL *scientialis* (as SCIENCE; see -AL)]
scienti'f|ĭc *a.* (Of investigation etc.) according to rules laid down in exact science for performing observations and testing soundness of conclusions, systematic, accurate; of, used or engaged in, (esp. natural) science (*scientific discoveries, instruments, books, terminology, men*); (of act or agent) assisted by expert knowledge (*a scientific boxer, game; scientific cruelty*); hence ~ICALLY *adv.* [f. F *scientifique* or f. LL *scientificus* (as SCIENCE; see -FIC)]
scī'ent|ĭsm *n.* (Use of) method or doctrine (deemed) characteristic of scientists; so **~ĭ'stic** *a.* [f. as foll. + -ISM]
scī'entĭst *n.* Person with expert knowledge of a (usu. physical or natural) science; person using scientific methods. [f. SCIENCE, SCIENTIFIC + -IST]
sciento̊'log|y̆ *n.* Religious system based on study of knowledge and seeking to develop the highest potentialities of mankind; hence ~IST (2) *n.* [f. L *scientia* knowledge + -O- + -LOGY; ***P**]
scī'-fī *n.* (colloq.) Science fiction. [abbr.; cf. HI-FI]
scī'lĭcĕt *adv.* To wit, that is to say, namely, (introducing word to be supplied or explanation of ambiguous one). [ME f. L, = *scire licet* one is permitted to know]
scĭ'lla *n.* Bulbous plant of genus *Scilla*, esp. blue-flowered cultivated species. [L f. Gk *skilla*]
Scĭllō'nĭan *a.* & *n.* (Native or inhabitant) of Scilly Isles. [f. *Scilly*, perh. after *Devonian*]
scĭ'mĭtar *n.* Oriental curved sword usu. broadening towards point. [f. F *cimeterre*, It. *scimitarra*, etc., of unkn. orig.]
scĭntĭ'graphy̆ *n.* Use of a radioisotope and scintillation counter to get picture of bodily organ etc. [f. SCINTILLATION + -GRAPHY]
scĭntĭ'lla (sĭ-) *n.* Spark (esp. fig.; *not a scintilla of evidence* etc.). [L]
scĭ'ntĭll|āte *v.i.* Sparkle, twinkle, emit sparks; (fig.) talk etc. cleverly or wittily; so ~ANT, **~āting**[2], *adjs.* [f. L *scintillare* (as prec.) + -ATE[3]]
scĭntĭllā'tion *n.* Scintillating; twinkling of star; (Phys.) flash produced in material by ionizing particle etc. (~ **counter,** device for detecting and recording such events). [f. as prec. + -ATION]
scī'ol|ĭst *n.* Superficial pretender to knowledge; hence ~ISM (2) *n.*, **~ĭ'stic** *a.* [f. LL *sciolus* smatterer (*scire* know) + -IST]
scī'on *n.* **1.** Shoot of plant, esp. one cut for grafting or planting. **2.** Descendant, young member of (esp. noble) family. [ME, f. OF *ciun, cion, sion*, shoot, twig, of unkn. orig.]
scire facias (sīrĭ fā'shĭăs) *n.* Writ to enforce or annul judgement, patent, etc. [L, = let (him) know]
scĭro̊'ccō. Var. of SIROCCO.
scĭ'rrh|us (sĭ'rus; *or* skĭ'-) *n.* (*pl.* ~i *pr.* -ī). (Path.) Hard carcinoma; hence or cogn. ~OID, ~OUS, *adjs.*, ~O'SITY *n.* [mod. L, f. Gk *skir(r)os* (*skiros* hard)]
scĭ'ssel *n.* Waste clippings of metal or remainder of metal plate from which discs have been punched in coining. [f. F *cisaille* (*cisailler* clip with shears)]
scĭ'ssile *a.* Able to be cut or divided. [f. L *scissilis* (*scindere sciss-* cut; see -IL)]
scĭ'ssion (-shon) *n.* Cutting, being cut; division, split. [ME f. OF, or f. LL *scissio* (as prec.; see -ION)]
scĭ'ssor (-z-) *v.t.* Cut (*off, up, into,* etc.) with scissors; clip out or *out* (cutting from newspaper, book, etc.). [f. foll.]
scĭ'ssor|s (sĭ'zerz) *n. pl.* **1.** (**Pair of**) **~s,** instrument for cutting fabrics etc., made of two blades with handles for thumb and one finger or the fingers and so pivoted that their cutting edges close on what is to be cut (*I want a pair of, some, scissors; where are my scissors?*; NAIL[1]-*scissors*); **~s and paste,** compiling of books merely out of excerpts from others. **2.** (Gymnastics) forward and backward movement of legs in manner of scissors; (Wrestling) holding of opponent's head or body with one's legs. **3.** **~-bill,** = SKIMMER 3; **~-bird, -tail,** (esp.) fork-tailed flycatcher; **~-tooth,** tooth in Carnivora acting like scissors against one in other jaw. **4.** Hence ~WISE *adv.* [ME *sisoures* f. OF *cisoires* f. LL *cisoria* pl. of *cisorium* cutting instrument (as CHISEL; see -ORY); assoc. w. L *scindere sciss-* cut]
scī'ūr|ine *a.* Of the squirrel family; squirrel-like; so ~OID *a.* [f. L f. Gk *skiouros* squirrel (*skia* shadow, *oura* tail) + -INE[1]]
sclēr'|a *n.* = SCLEROTIC 2; hence ~I'TIS, **~ŏ'tomy**, *ns.* [mod. L, f. fem. of Gk *sklēros* hard]
sclĕrĕ'nchy̆ma (-ngk-) *n.* (Zool.) hard tissue of coral; (Bot.) tissue of cells with thick woody walls. [mod. L, f. Gk *sklēros* hard + *egkhuma* infusion, after *parenchyma*]
sclēr'oid *a.* (Bot. & Zool.) Of hard texture. [f. Gk *sklēros* hard + -OID]
sclĕrō'ma *n.* (*pl.* ~ta). Morbid hardening of tissue. [f. mod. L f. Gk *sklērōma* (as SCLEROSIS; see -OMA)]
sclĕrŏ'mèter *n.* Instrument for determining hardness of materials. [f. Gk *sklēros* hard + -O- + -METER]
sclēr'ophy̆ll, sclēr'ophȳte, *ns.* Plant with large amount of sclerenchyma, preventing loss of water. [f. as prec. + Gk *phullon* leaf, -PHYTE]
sclēr'ōsed (-st *or* -zd) *a.* Affected by sclerosis. [f. foll. + -ED[1]]
sclĕrō's|ĭs (*or* -er-) *n.* (*pl.* ~es *pr.* -ēz). **1.**

Scleroma; ARTERIOSCLEROSIS; ATHEROSCLEROSIS; **disseminated ~** (spreading to many or all parts of the body); **multiple ~**, chronic progressive sclerosis of brain and spinal cord. **2.** (Bot.) Hardening of cell-wall with lignified matter. [ME f. med. L f. Gk *sklērōsis* (*skleroō* harden; see -OSIS)]

sclērŏ'tĭc *a.* & *n.* **1.** *a.* Of or having sclerosis; of the sclerotic. **2.** *n.* Membrane coating eye round iris, white of eye; hence **sclērotī'TIS** *n.* [f. med. L *sclerotica* (as prec.)]

sclēr'ous *a.* (Path., Anat., & Bot.) Indurated, bony. [f. Gk *sklēros* hard + -OUS]

S.C.M. *abbr.* State Certified Midwife; Student Christian Movement.

scŏff[1] *n.*, & *v.i.* **1.** *n.* Mocking words, taunt, gibe; object of ridicule, laughing-stock. **2.** *v.i.* Speak derisively esp. of religion or object of respect; aim scoffs or mockery *at*; hence **~'ER**[1] *n.* [perh. f. Scand.; cf. early mod. Da. *skuf, skof* jest, mockery]

scŏff[2] *n.* & *v.* (sl.) **1.** *n.* Food, meal. **2.** *v.t.* & *i.* Eat greedily. [n. f. Afrik. *schoff* repr. Du. *schoft* quarter of a day (hence, meal); v. orig. var. of dial. *scaff*, assoc. w. n.]

scōld *v.* & *n.* **1.** *v.i.* Find fault noisily, rail. **2.** *v.t.* (Esp. of parent, employer, speaking to child, servant) rebuke, whence **~'ING**[1] (1) *n.* **3.** *n.* Railing or nagging woman. [v. f. n., ME, prob. f. ON *skáld* SCALD[2]]

scō'l|ĕx *n.* (*pl.* **~eces** *pr.* -ē'sēz, *or* **~ices** *pr.* -ĭsēz). Head of larval or adult tapeworm. [mod. L, f. Gk *skōlēx* worm]

scŏlĭ|ō'sĭs *n.* (*pl.* **~o'ses** *pr.* -ō'sēz). Lateral curvature of spine; hence **~O'TIC** *a.* [mod. L f. Gk (*skolios* bent; see -OSIS)]

scŏ'llop. See SCALLOP.

scŏlopĕ'ndrĭum *n.* Hart's-tongue fern. [mod. L f. Gk *skolopendrion* (*skolopendra* millepede, f. fancied resemblance)]

scŏ'mb|er *n.* Mackerel or other fish of family Scombridae; so **~RID**[3] *n.*, **~ROID** *a.* & *n.* [L, f. Gk *skombros*]

scŏnce[1] *n.* Flat candlestick with handle; bracket candlestick to hang on wall. [ME, f. OF *esconse* lantern or f. med. L *sconsa* f. L *absconsa* fem. p.p. (as n.) of *abscondere* hide; see ABSCOND]

scŏnce[2] *n.* (arch. joc.) Head, crown of head. [perh. f. prec.]

scŏnce[3] *n.* Small fort or earthwork, usu. defending a ford, pass, etc.; (arch.) shelter, screen. [f. Du. *schans* brushwood f. MHG *schanze*]

||**scŏnce**[4] *v.t.*, & *n.* (Oxf. Univ.) **1.** *v.t.* Inflict forfeit (or penalty involving drinking) of beer etc. for offence against table etiquette upon (member of company or his offence); (Hist., of university official etc.) fine for breach of discipline. **2.** *n.* Such forfeit. [17th c., perh. f. SCONCE[2]]

scŏne *n.* Soft cake of barley-meal or oatmeal or wheat-flour of size for single portion usu. baked quickly in oven or on griddle; DROP[1] *scone.* [orig. Sc., perh. f. MDu. *schoon(broot)*, MLG *schon(brot)* fine (bread)]

scōōp *n.*, & *v.t.* **1.** *n.* Short-handled deep shovel for taking up and transferring grain, sugar, coal, coins, etc.; large long-handled ladle-shaped dipping-vessel for liquids; excavating part of digging-machine etc.; gougelike instrument e.g. for surgical use or for serving ice cream, mashed potatoes, etc.; quantity taken with scoop. **2.** Motion as of, act of, scooping; large profit made quickly or by anticipating one's competitors; piece of news published by newspaper in advance of its rivals. **3.** **~-neck,** rounded low-cut neck of garment; **~-net** (for sweeping river-bottom, or for catching bait). **4.** *v.t.* Lift (*up*), hollow (*out*), (as) with scoop; secure (large profit etc.) by sudden action or stroke of luck; forestall (rival newspaper, reporter, etc.) with news scoop. [ME, f. MDu., MLG *schōpe* bucket etc., WG f. **skōp*-, cogn. w. SHAPE[1]]

scōōt *v.i.* Run, dart, make off esp. hastily. [19th c. U.S.; earlier *scout*, of unkn. orig.]

scōō'ter *n.* Child's toy propelled by foot and consisting of footboard with wheel at front and back and long steering-handle; (**motor**) **~**, light motor vehicle of similar design for seated adult, whence **~IST** (3) *n.*; *sail-boat able to travel on both water and ice. [f. prec. + -ER[1]]

scō'pa *n.* (*pl.* **~e**). Small brushlike tuft of hairs esp. on bee's leg. [sing. of L *scopae* = twigs, broom]

scōpe[1] *n.* **1.** (arch.) End aimed at, purpose, intention. **2.** Outlook, purview, sweep or reach or sphere of observation or action, extent to which it is permissible or possible to range, opportunity, outlet, vent, (*mind, undertaking, of wide scope*; *is beyond my scope*; *give no, ample, scope for expatiating, to ability*; *seeks scope for his energies*). **3.** (Naut.) Length of cable out when ship rides at anchor. [f. It. *scopo* aim f. Gk *skopos* target (*skeptomai* look at)]

scōpe[2] *n.* (colloq.) Instrument etc. whose name ends in -SCOPE. [abbr.]

-scōpe *suf.* forming *ns.* denoting (1) thing looked at or through (*kaleidoscope, telescope*), (2) instrument for observing or showing (*gyroscope, oscilloscope*). [f. or after mod. L *-scopium* f. Gk *skopeō* look at]

-scŏ'pĭc *suf.* forming *adjs.* w. sense 'looking at' (*macroscopic*) or 'pertaining to or similar to an instrument whose name ends in -SCOPE' (*gyroscopic, oscilloscopic, telescopic*). [f. as prec. + -IC]

scopŏ'lamĭne (*or* -ēn) *n.* = HYOSCINE. [f. *Scopolia* genus-name of plants yielding it, f. G. A. *Scopoli* It. naturalist d. 1788 + AMINE]

scŏ'pūla *n.* (*pl.* **~e**). = SCOPA, esp. on bee's or spider's leg. [LL, dim. of L SCOPA; see -ULE]

-scopȳ *suf.* forming *ns.* w. sense 'looking at' (*necroscopy*) or 'use of an instrument whose name ends in -SCOPE' (*microscopy*). [f. as -SCOPE + -Y[1]]

scŏrbū't|ĭc *a.* & *n.* Of or like, (person) affected with, scurvy; hence **~ICALLY** *adv.* [f. mod. L *scorbuticus* f. med. L *scorbutus* scurvy, perh. f. MLG *schorbūk* (*schoren* break, *būk* belly) + -IC]

scôrch *v.* & *n.* **1.** *v.t.* Burn surface of with flame or heat so as to discolour or injure or pain; affect with sensation of burning; hence **~'ING**[2] *a.*; **~ed earth policy,** burning crops etc. and removing or destroying anything that might be of use to an enemy occupying the country. **2.** *v.i.* Become discoloured etc. with heat. **3.** (sl.) (Of motorist or cyclist) go at very high or excessive speed. **4.** *n.* (sl.) Spell of such driving or riding. **5.** Mark made by scorching. [ME, perh. rel. to *skorkle* in same sense]

scôr'cher *n.* In vbl senses; (colloq.) very hot day; (sl.) fine specimen of its kind. [f. prec. + -ER[1]]

scôre *n.* & *v.* **1.** *n.* Notch cut or line cut or scratched or drawn (*rock covered with scores*; *the scores of the whip showed on his back*; *made a score in the tally*; *lightning had made scores in the mountain side*); (arch.) mark showing starting-point in race or standing-place in shooting-match (**go off at ~**, start off vigorously); (Naut.) groove in block or dead-eye to hold rope. **2.** Running account kept by scores against customer's name esp. formerly for drink in inns, reckoning esp. for entertainment; **pay** one's **~**, settle reckoning; **pay off old ~s,** (fig.) pay person out for past offence. **3.** Number of points made by player or side in some games or awarded to competitor etc., list or total of items of this for each player etc., (*make a good score*; *what is the* *score now?*); ~**-board** (for publicly displaying score); ~**-book, -card, -sheet,** (prepared for entering esp. cricket scores in); **keep (the)** ~, register it as it is made; ***know the** ~, (fig.) be aware of the essential facts. **4.** (Mus.) Copy of a composition on set of staves braced and barred together (named from bar drawn through all staves); CLOSE¹, FULL¹, OPEN¹, SHORT, *score*; **in** ~, with parts arranged below each other and corresponding. **5.** (*pl.* ~ *or* ~**s**; for pl. usage see HUNDRED). Twenty, set of twenty, (esp. FOUR*score*, THREE*score*); (in *pl.*) great numbers; (arch.) weight of twenty (or twenty-one) pounds, esp. in weighing pigs or oxen. **6.** Reason, motive, (*rejected* **on the score of absurdity** etc., as being absurd etc.; **on that** ~, so far as that matter is concerned); topic, subject, (*no speculations on that score*). **7.** (colloq.) Remark or act by which person scores off another; piece of good fortune. **8.** *v.t.* Mark with notches or incisions or lines, slash, furrow, make (line etc.) with something that marks; ~ **out,** draw line through (words etc.); ~ **under,** underline. **9.** *Criticize (person) severely. **10.** Mark *up* in score (sense 2), enter (item of debt *against* or *to* customer); (fig.) mentally record (offence *against* or *to* offender); make record of (point in cricket etc. score, or abs., keep the score, whence **scŏr'**ER¹ *n.*). **11.** Win and be credited with (*has scored a success, a goal, a century at cricket*); allow scoring of (points in game; *a goal scores six points*); allot score to (competitor etc.); ~ **points off,** (colloq.) = *score off* (see sense 13). **12.** (Mus.) Orchestrate, whence **scŏr'**ING¹ (6) *n.*; arrange *for* instrument(s); write out in score. **13.** *v.i.* Make score in game (*failed to score*); secure an advantage or have good luck (*that is where he scores*); (sl.) obtain drugs illegally; ~ **off,** (colloq.) worst in argument or repartee, inflict some humiliation on. [n. f. OE **scoru*, v. partly f. ON *skora*, f. ON *skor* notch, tally, twenty, f. Gmc **skurō* (**skur-*, **sker-*, cut; see SHEAR)]

scŏr'ĭ|a *n.* (*pl.* ~**ae**). Cellular lava or fragments of it; slag or dross of metals; hence ~A'CEOUS *a.* [L, f. Gk *skōria* refuse (*skōr* dung)]

scŏr'ĭ|fȳ *v.t.* Reduce to dross, assay (precious metal) by thus treating a portion of its ore fused with lead and borax; hence ~FICA'TION, ~**fīer**¹ (2), *ns.* [f. prec. + -FY]

scorn *n.*, & *v.t.* **1.** *n.* Disdain, contempt, derision, (**think** ~ **of,** despise; LAUGH *to scorn*). **2.** Object of contempt (*a scorn to* or *the scorn of all onlookers*). **3.** *v.t.* Hold in contempt, consider beneath notice, abstain from or refuse *to* do as unworthy (*scorns lying, a lie, to lie*); hence ~'ER¹ *n.* (esp. *of*). [ME, f. OF *esc(h)arn(ir)* f. Rom. **escarnire*, **eskernire* f. Gmc **skarnjan*, **skernjan*; cf. OS *skern* mockery]

scor'nful *a.* Full of scorn, contemptuous (*of*); hence ~LY² *adv.*, ~NESS *n.* [ME, f. prec. + -FUL]

scor'per. Var. of SCALPER².

Scor'pīō *n.* Sign of the ZODIAC, the Scorpion. [ME f. L (*scorpius* f. Gk *skorpios* scorpion)]

scor'pĭoid *n.* & *a.* (Bot.) (Inflorescence) curled up at end like scorpion's tail and uncurling as flowers develop. [f. Gk *skorpioeidēs* (as prec.; see -OID)]

scor'pĭon *n.* **1.** Arachnid with lobster-like claws and jointed tail that can be bent over to inflict poisoned sting on prey held in claws, falsely reputed to sting itself to death if encircled with fire and to contain a substance serving as antidote for its poison; (**false**) ~, similar arachnid without tail. **2.** (Bibl.) Whip armed with metal points (1 Kgs. 12:11). **3.** (*S*~). *The* zodiacal sign Scorpio. **4.** (Hist.) Kind of ballista. **5.** (sl.) Native of Gibraltar. **6.** ~**-fish** (of family Scorpaenidae, with spines on head and on fins); ~**-fly** (of order Mecoptera, with curled abdomen); ~**-grass,** forget-me-not; ~**-shell,** gastropod with long spines fringing outer lip of aperture. [ME f. OF, f. L SCORPIO *-onis*]

scorzonēr'a *n.* Plant of genus *Scorzonera*, esp. species with white parsnip-like root used as vegetable. [It. (*scorzone* venomous snake f. Rom. **scurtione* f. med. L *curtio*)]

scŏt¹ *n.* **1.** (Hist.) Payment corresponding to modern tax, rate, or other assessed contribution (**pay** ~ **and lot,** share pecuniary burdens of borough etc.). **2.** ~**-free,** unharmed, unpunished, safe. [ME, f. ON *skot* & f. OF *escot*, of Gmc orig.; cf. SHOT³]

Scŏt² *n.* **1.** Native of Scotland. **2.** (Hist.) Member of Gaelic tribe that migrated from Ireland to Scotland about 6th c. [OE *Scottas* pl., f. LL *Scottus*]

Scŏtch¹ *a.* & *n.* **1.** *a.* Of Scotland or its inhabitants; in the form of English used in (esp. Lowlands of) Scotland; ~ **broth,** soup or liquid stew with pearl barley and vegetables; ~ **cap** (of shapes worn in Highland costume, glengarry, tam-o'-shanter, etc.); ~ **catch,** (Mus.) short note on the beat followed by long one; ~ **collops,** (1) beef cut small and stewed, (2) steak and onions; ~ **egg,** hard-boiled egg enclosed in sausage-meat; *Scotch* FIR (*Pinus sylvestris*), KALE, MIST; ~ **pebble,** agate, jasper, cairngorm, etc., found in Scotland; ~ **pine,** = *Scotch fir*; ~ **snap,** = *Scotch catch*; *~ **tape** (P), adhesive usu. transparent cellulose or plastic tape; ~ **terrier** (small rough-haired short-legged kind); ~ **whisky,** kind distilled in Scotland esp. from malted barley; ~ **woodcock,** eggs on anchovy toast. **2.** ~**'man,** ~**'woman,** native of Scotland. **3.** *n.* Form of English used in (esp. Lowlands of) Scotland; **the** ~, (*pl.*) the people of Scotland. **4.** Scotch whisky. [contr. of SCOTTISH]

scŏtch² *v.t.*, & *n.* **1.** *v.t.* (arch.) Make incisions in, score; wound without killing, slightly disable. **2.** Decisively put an end to; frustrate (plan etc.). **3.** *n.* Slash; line on ground for HOP²scotch. [ME; orig. unkn.]

scŏtch³ *n.*, & *v.t.* **1.** *n.* Wedge or block placed against wheel etc. to prevent motion downhill. **2.** *v.t.* Hold up (wheel, barrel) with scotch. [17th c., perh. = *scatch* stilt f. OF *escache*]

scō'ter *n.* Large sea-duck of genus *Oidemia* or *Melanitta*. [17th c.; orig. unkn.]

scō'tia (-sha) *n.* Concave moulding esp. in base of column. [L, f. Gk *skotia* (*skotos* darkness, w. ref. to shadow produced)]

scŏ'tĭcė etc. See SCOTTICE etc.

Scō't|ĭsm *n.* (Hist.) Metaphysical doctrines of Duns Scotus; so ~IST (2) *n.* [f. John Duns *Scotus*, Sc. schoolman d. 1308 (L|*Scotus* Scot) + -ISM]

Scŏtland Yar'd *n.* Headquarters of London Metropolitan Police; its Criminal Investigation Department. [f. Great & New ~, streets where it was successively situated until 1967]

scŏtodi'nĭa *n.* (Med.) Giddiness. [f. Gk *skotos* darkness + *dinē* whirl + -IA¹]

scotō'ma *n.* (*pl.* ~**ta**). (Path.) Obscuration of part of the field of vision. [LL, f. Gk *skotōma* (*skotoō* darken f. as prec.; see -OMA)]

Scŏts *a.* & *n.* (esp. Sc.) = SCOTCH¹ 3; POUND¹ *Scots*; ‖*Scots* GREYS; *Scots Guards*; ~**'man,** = SCOTCH¹*man*; ~**'woman,** = SCOTCH¹*woman*. [ME, orig. *Scottis*, north. var. of SCOTTISH]

scŏ't(t)ĭcė *adv.* In Scotch. [med. L, f. LL *Scot(t)icus* Scotch]

Scŏ't(t)ĭcism *n.* Scotch phrase, word, or idiom. [f. LL as prec. + -ISM (4)]

Scŏ't(t)ĭcize, -ise (-īz), *v.* **1.** *v.i.* Imitate the Scotch in idiom or habits. **2.** *v.t.* Imbue with, model on, Scotch ways. [f. LL (as SCOTTICE) + -IZE]

Scŏ'ttie *n.* (colloq.) Scotchman; Scotch terrier. [f. SCOT[2] + -IE]

Scŏ'ttish *a.* (esp. Sc. or literary). Of Scotland or its inhabitants (*Scottish dancing, Gaelic, islands, Nationalist*); ~ **Certificate of Education** (corresponding to GENERAL Certificate of Education). [ME, f. SCOT[2] + -ISH[1]]

scou'ndrel *n.* Unscrupulous person, villain, rogue; hence ~DOM, ~ISM (3), *ns.*, ~LY[1] *a.* [16th c., of unkn. orig.; cf. -REL]

scour[1] (-owr) *v.t.*, & *n.* **1.** *v.t.* Cleanse or brighten by friction (metal with sand etc., cloth etc. with soap or chemicals); (of water, or person with water) clear out (channel, harbour, pipe, etc.) by flushing or flowing through or over; (of drug, physician, etc.) purge (bowels) drastically; clear (rust, stain, etc.) *away, off,* by rubbing etc. (lit. or fig.); **~'ing-rush,** kind of horse-tail plant with siliceous coating used for polishing wood etc.; hence (-)~'ER[1] (1, 2) *n.* **2.** *n.* Clearing action of swift current on channel etc. (*the scour of the tide*); diarrhoea in cattle; substance used for scouring fabrics; act of scouring. [ME, f. MDu., MLG *schūren* f. F *escurer* f. LL EX[1]*curare* clean (off) f. L *curare* (see CURE[2])]

scour[2] (-owr) *v.* **1.** *v.i.* Rove, range, go along hastily, esp. in search or pursuit. **2.** *v.t.* Hasten over or along, search rapidly or thoroughly. [ME, of unkn. orig.]

scourge (skẽrj) *n.*, & *v.t.* **1.** *n.* Whip for chastising persons; person or thing regarded as instrument or manifestation of divine or other vengeance or punishment (e.g. barbarian conqueror, pestilence, war). **2.** *v.t.* Use whip on; chastise, afflict, oppress, harass. [ME, f. OF *escorge* n., *escorgier* v., f. Rom. EX[1]*corrigiare* f. L *corrigia* thong, whip]

||**scouse** *n.* & *a.* (Native) of Liverpool; Liverpool dialect. [f. LOBSCOUSE]

scout[1] *n.*, & *v.i.* **1.** *n.* Person sent out to get information (esp. Mil., about enemy or surroundings); (colloq.) fellow, person, (*a good scout*); ~ **car,** fast armoured vehicle for reconnaissance etc.; TALENT-*scout.* **2.** (*S*~). Member of boys' organization (**S~ Association**) intended to develop character by open-air activities; **King's** or **Queen's S~** (who has reached highest rank of proficiency). **3.** ||Patrolman of motoring organization. **4.** Ship or aircraft designed for reconnoitring, esp. small fast aircraft. **5.** College servant at Oxford Univ. (cf. GYP[1]). **6.** Act of seeking (esp. Mil.) information (*on the scout*). **7.** **~'master,** officer in charge of scouts or Scouts. **8.** *v.i.* Act as scout; ~ **about** or **around,** make search (*for*); hence ~'ER[1] *n.* (esp. **S~er,** adult member of Scout Association), ~'ING[1] *n.* [ME, f. OF *escoute(r)* listen(ing), earlier *ascolter* f. Rom. **ascultare* f. L *auscultare*]

scout[2] *v.t.* Reject (proposal, notion) with scorn or ridicule. [f. Scand.; cf. ON *skúta, skúti* taunt]

scow *n.* (esp. U.S.) Flat-bottomed boat used as lighter etc. [f. Du. *schouw* ferry-boat]

scowl *v.i.*, & *n.* **1.** *v.i.* Wear sullen look, look sour, frown ill-temperedly. **2.** *n.* Scowling aspect, angry frown. [ME, prob. f. Scand.; cf. Da. *skule* look down or sidelong]

||**S.C.R.** *abbr.* Senior Combination Room; Senior Common Room.

scr. *abbr.* scruple(s).

scră'bble *v.i.* Scrawl, scribble; scratch or grope *about* to find or collect something. [f. MDu. *shrabbelen* frequent. of *shrabben* SCRAPE]

scrăg *n.*, & *v.t.* (-gg-). **1.** *n.* Lean skinny person, animal, plant, etc., whence **~'gy**[2] (-gĭ) *a.*; bony part of animal's carcass as food, esp. neck of mutton or inferior part (**~-end**) of it; (sl.) person's neck. **2.** *v.t.* (sl.) Put to death by hanging, garotte, wring neck of; seize roughly by the neck; handle roughly. [perh. alt. f. dial. *crag* neck, rel. to MDu. *crāghe*, MLG *krage*]

scrăm *v.i.* (**-mm-**). (sl.) Go away, (in *imper.*) be off! [perh. f. foll.]

scră'mble *v.* & *n.* **1.** *v.i.* Make way as best one can over steep or rough ground by clambering, crawling, etc.; move hastily and anxiously; take part in physical or other struggle with competitors *for* as much as possible of something; (of aircraft or pilots) take off quickly in emergency. **2.** *v.t.* Mix together indiscriminately; deal with hastily or awkwardly (*away, through,* etc.); cook (eggs) by breaking into pan with butter, milk, etc., stirring slightly, and heating (**~d egg,** (joc.) gold braid on officer's cap); alter frequencies of transmitted speech of (telephone conversation etc.) so as to make it unintelligible except to recipient using similar process, whence **scră'mbl**ER[1] (2) *n.* **3.** *n.* Climb or walk over rough ground etc.; motor-cycle race over rough ground; eager struggle or competition for or *for* something. [16th c., imit.; cf. dial. synonyms *scamble, cramble*]

scrăn *n.* (sl.) Food, eatables; remains of food; **bad ~,** (Ir.) bad luck (*to*). [18th c., of unkn. orig.]

scră'nnel *a.* (arch.) (Of sound) weak, reedy, feeble; harsh, unmelodious (usu. w. allus. to Milton's *Lycidas* 124). [17th c.; cf. dial. synonyms *scrank(y)* & Norw. *skran* shrivelled]

scrăp[1] *n.*, & *v.t.* (-pp-). **1.** *n.* Small detached piece of something, fragment, remnant, (**~ of paper,** (fig.) treaty etc. one does not intend to honour); (w. neg.) the least piece or amount; (in *pl.*) odds and ends, fragments of uneaten food, useless remains; hence **~'py**[2] *a.* **2.** Picture, paragraph, etc., cut from book or newspaper for keeping in a collection; **~-book** (for pasting these into). **3.** Rubbish, waste material; ~(**-metal, -iron,** etc.), metal collected for re-working; **~-heap,** collection of waste material (lit. or fig.); **~-merchant,** dealer in scrap; **~-yard,** place where scrap is collected. **4.** (in *sing.* or *pl.*) Residuum of melted fat or of fish with the oil expressed; **~-cake,** compressed fish scrap. **5.** *v.t.* Consign to scrap-heap, condemn as now useless, discard. [ME, f. ON *skrap* rel. to *skrapa* SCRAPE]

scrăp[2] *n.*, & *v.i.* (**-pp-**). (sl.) **1.** *n.* Fight, scrimmage, esp. of unpremeditated kind. **2.** *v.i.* Have scrap (*with*). [perh. f. foll.]

scrāpe *v.* & *n.* **1.** *v.t.* Level surface of, clear of projections, abrade, smooth, polish, shave, or graze, by drawing sharp or angular edge breadthwise over or by causing to pass over such edge; clear (ship's bottom) of barnacles etc.; remove dirt from soles of (boots etc.) by drawing over scraper; leave no food on (plate); draw (hair) tightly *back* from forehead; ~ **away,** reduce by scraping; *scrape the* BARREL[1]. **2.** Take (projection, surface layer, stain, etc.) *off, out, away,* by scraping. **3.** Excavate (hollow) by scraping. **4.** *v.t.* & *i.* Draw or pass along with sound (as) of scraping, produce such sound from, emit such sound; draw back foot in making clumsy formal bow (**bow and ~,** behave obsequiously); (derog.) play on violin. **5.** *v.i.* Pass along something so as to graze or be grazed by it or just avoid doing so (*scraped against, along, the wall*); get *through* (adv. or prep.) etc. with a squeeze or narrow shave (lit., or fig. of passing examination etc.). **6.** *v.t.* Amass by scraping or with difficulty or by parsimony, contrive to bring (*together, up*; ~ **acquaintance with,** thrust one's acquaintance on); (abs.) practise economy (*work and scrape as one may*). **7.** Hence **scrā'p**ING[1] (esp. 2),

scrā'per[1] (1, 2), *ns.* (**~rboard,** board with blackened surface removable by scraping for making white-line drawings). **8.** *n.* Act or sound of scraping; scraped place; ||thinly applied layer of butter etc. on bread; scraping of foot in bowing; awkward predicament esp. resulting from escapade. [ME, f. ON *skrapa* or MDu. *schrapen*]

scrā'pie *n.* Virus disease of sheep with severe itching causing animals to rub against trees etc. [f. prec. + -IE]

scrătch[1] *v.t., n.,* & *a.* **1.** *v.t.* Score surface of, make long narrow superficial wounds in, with nail, claw, or something more or less pointed; **~ the surface of,** not penetrate far into (lit. or fig.). **2.** Get (some part of one) scratched (*have scratched my hands badly*); form (letters, representation), excavate (hole), by scratching; scribble (*a few lines* etc.). **3.** Scrape without marking esp. with finger-nails to relieve itching; (abs.) scratch oneself, scratch ground etc. in search (*scratch about for stray seeds, evidence,* etc.); ~ one's **head** (esp. as sign of perplexity); **~ my back and I will ~ yours** (of mutual aid or flattery). **4.** Bring *together* or *up* by scraping or with difficulty; **~ along,** (abs.) make a living etc. with difficulty. **5.** Score (written words etc.) *out* or *through,* strike *off* with pencil etc., erase (horse's name in list of entries for race, competitor's or *election candidate's name), withdraw (horse, candidate, or abs. for *refl.*) from competition. **6.** *n.* Mark or wound or sound made by scratching (**a ~ of the pen,** signature or written order easily given); spell of scratching oneself; (colloq.) trifling wound; (sl.) money; (in *pl.*) horse-disease in which pastern appears scratched. **7.** Line from which competitors not receiving handicap in race start; **start from ~,** begin from the very beginning or without advantage or preparation; **up to ~,** present at the right time, doing what is required. **8. ~-dial,** simple sundial scratched on church wall etc.; ***~ pad** (of paper for jotting or scribbling); **~(-wig),** wig covering only part of head; **~--work,** graffito decoration. **9.** *a.* Collected by haphazard, scratched together, heterogeneous, (*a scratch crew, meal, team*); with no handicap given (*scratch player, race*). [ME, prob. f. synonymous ME *scrat* & *cratch,* both of uncert. orig.; cf. MLG *kratsen,* OHG *krazzōn*]

Scrătch[2] *n.* **Old ~,** the Devil. [f. obs. *scrat* hermaphrodite f. ON *skrat(t)i* goblin, OHG *scrato* sprite]

scră'tch|y̆ *a.* (Of drawing etc.) done in scratches, careless or unskilful; (of pen) making sound of scratching or tending to catch in paper; tending to cattishness; tending to cause itching; hence **~ĭly**[2] *adv.*, **~ĭness** *n.* [f. SCRATCH[1] + -Y[2]]

scrawl *v.* & *n.* **1.** *v.i.* & *t.* Write in hurried more or less illegible way; mark (paper etc.) *over* with bad writing or lines like writing, cross (word etc.) *out* thus. **2.** *n.* Piece of hasty or illegible writing; hurried note or letter. [perh. f. obs. *scrawl* sprawl alt. of CRAWL]

scraw'ny̆ *a.* Lean, scraggy. [var. of dial. *scranny*; cf. SCRANNEL]

||**scray** *n.* Common tern. [17th c., of unkn. orig.]

scream *v.* & *n.* **1.** *v.i.* Utter piercing cry expressing terror, pain, vexation, or pretence of these, (of siren etc.) whistle or hoot shrilly; (of machine etc.) make shrill sound like scream, (of animal etc.) give shrill cry; speak or write angrily or excitedly; laugh uncontrollably; be blatantly obvious; (in *part.*, of farce, fun etc.) causing spectators to scream, intensely funny. **2.** *v.t.* Utter, say, in screaming tone (*screamed that she did not dare jump; scream out a curse, order,* etc.). **3.** *n.* Screaming cry or sound (*screams of pain, laughter*); (sl.) irresistibly comical affair or person. [OE **scrǣman* or MDu. **schreemen*]

screa'mer *n.* In vbl senses; S. Amer. bird of family Anhimidae; *large exclamatory headline; (sl.) tale etc. that raises screams of laughter, extraordinarily fine specimen of anything, exclamation mark. [f. prec. + -ER[1]]

scree *n.* (in *sing.* or *pl.*) (Mountain slope covered with) small stones that slide down when trodden on. [prob. back form. f. *screes* pl. f. **screethes* f. ON *skritha* landslip rel. to *skrítha* glide]

screech *v.i.* & *t.*, & *n.* Scream with or of fright or pain or anger, or in harsh or uncanny tones; **~-owl,** owl that screeches instead of hooting, esp. barn-owl or *small owl of genus *Otus*. [16th-c. var. of ME *scritch* (imit.)]

screed *n.* Unduly long harangue (esp. list of grievances) or writing; strip of plaster as guide to thickness; piece of wood or board for levelling concrete. [ME, prob. var. of SHRED]

screen *n.*, & *v.t.* **1.** *n.* Partition of wood or stone separating without completely cutting off one part of church (esp. ROOD-*screen*), room, etc., from another. **2.** Movable piece of furniture designed to shelter from excess of heat, light, draught, etc., or from observation; = SIGHT[1]--*screen.* **3.** Thing utilized as shelter esp. from observation (*prepared the attack behind a screen of trees*), expression of face or measure adopted for concealment, protection afforded by these, (*under screen of night*); body of cavalry detached to keep enemy's scouts from getting in touch with main body; = WIND[1]*screen.* **4.** Vertical surface for display of exhibits, notices, etc. **5.** Blank surface on which moving or televised pictures or lantern-slides or radar images are projected; piece of ground glass in camera for focussing; **~-play,** script of a film; **~ test** (of would-be film actor's suitability); **~-writer,** writer of film-scripts; **the ~,** moving pictures collectively. **6.** Body intercepting light, heat, electric or magnetic induction, etc., in physical apparatus; **~-grid** (protecting control grid from influence of anode in thermionic valve). **7.** Large sieve or riddle esp. for sorting grain, coal, etc., into sizes; *wire netting or perforated sheet in door etc. allowing flow of air; **~--printing,** process like stencilling with ink forced through prepared sheet of fine material (orig. silk). **8.** (Photog.) Transparent finely--ruled plate or film used in process of half-tone reproduction. **9.** *v.t.* Afford shelter to, hide partly or completely, (*from*); (fig.) protect another from deserved censure etc. by taking blame upon oneself or diverting it; **~ off,** shut off by or hide behind screen. **10.** Show (object, scene, film, slide, etc.) on screen. **11.** Pass (grain, coal, etc.) through screen; **~ed coal** (from which dust etc. has been removed); hence **~'ing**[1] (2) *n.*, (in *pl.*) refuse separated by sifting. **12.** Test (person) to determine presence or absence of a quality, disease, weapon, etc. **13.** Prevent from causing electrical interference. [ME, f. ONF *escren, escran* f. OFrank. **skrank,* OHG *skrank* barrier]

screw (-ōō) *n.* & *v.* **1.** *n.* Cylinder or cone with spiral ridge called THREAD[1], running round it outside (MALE or *exterior screw*) or inside (FEMALE or *interior screw*); **(wood-)~,** metal male screw with slotted head and sharp point for fastening pieces of wood together with more security than nail; **~(-bolt),** metal male screw with blunt end to receive nut and bolt things together; GRUB[1]-*screw*; wooden or metal male or female screw as part of appliance or machine acting to exert pressure in various ways; (in *sing.* or *pl.*) instrument of torture operating thus;

ENDLESS *screw*; INTERRUPTED *screw*; RIGHT¹-*and*-*left screw*; **have a ~ loose,** (colloq.) be slightly mad; **put the ~(s) on,** exert pressure esp. to extort or intimidate. **2. ~(-propeller)**, revolving shaft with twisted blades projecting from ship, boat, or aircraft, and propelling it by acting on screw principle upon water or air. **3.** One turn of a screw (*give it another screw*). **4.** ||(Bill. etc.) Oblique curling motion or tendency of ball struck below and to one side of centre. **5.** ||Small twisted-up paper *of* tobacco etc. **6.** Miser, stingy or extortionate person. **7.** ||(sl.) Amount of salary or wages. **8.** (sl.) Prison warder. **9.** (vulg.) Copulation. **10.** Worn-out horse. **11.** ***~'ball** *a.* & *n.*, (sl.) mad, crazy, (person); **~-bean,** mesquite bean; **~-bolt** (see sense 1); **~-cap,** cap screwing on to thread of container aperture; **~-coupling,** right-and-left female screw for joining ends of pipes or rods; **~-cutter,** hand-tool for cutting screws; **~'driver,** tool like narrow blunt chisel for turning screws by the slot; **~-eye,** screw with loop for passing cord etc. through instead of slotted head; **~ gear,** endless screw with cogwheel or pinion; **~-hook,** hook to hang things on with screw at end of shank to fasten it in with; **~-jack,** (1) dentist's implement for regulating distance between crowded teeth, (2) vehicle JACK¹ worked by screw; **~-pile** (with screw at lower end and sunk by rotation); **~-pine,** plant of genus *Pandanus* with leaves arranged spirally and resembling those of pineapple; **~-plate,** steel plate with threaded holes for making male screws; **~-pod,** species of mesquite with spirally twisted pods; **~-press,** press worked by simple screw used esp. by printers and binders; **~-propeller** (see sense 2); **~ steamer** (propelled by one or more screws); **~-tap,** tool for making female screws; **~-top,** = *screw-cap*; **~ valve,** stopcock opened and shut by screw; **~-wheel** (worked by endless screw); **~-wrench** (for turning screws with angular head or nuts). **12.** *v.t.* Fasten, tighten, etc., by use of screw(s); **his head is ~ed on the right way** or **straight,** he has SENSE 6. **13.** Turn (screw), twist round like screw; **~ (up)**, make tenser or more efficient (**~** one's **courage to the sticking-place, ~ up** one's **courage,** gather resolution); **~ up,** (sl.) bungle. **14.** Put the screw upon, press hard on, oppress; squeeze, extort, (consent, money, etc.) *out of*; contort, distort, contract, (*screw* one's *face into wrinkles*; *screw up* one's *eyes*). **15.** (sl.) Burgle. **16.** *v.t.* & *i.* (vulg.) Copulate (with). **17.** *v.i.* Be miserly. **18.** (Of screw) revolve (*stiffly, to the right*, etc.); twist *round*. **19.** (Of rolling ball, or of person etc.) take curling course, swerve. **20.** Hence **~'**ABLE *a.* [ME, f. OF *escroue* female screw, nut, (f. WG **scrūva* or) f. L *scrofa* sow]

screwed (-ōōd) *a.* (sl.) Drunk, drunken. [p.p. of prec.]

screw'y̆ (-ōō'ĭ) *a.* (Of horse) worn out; (sl.) crazy or eccentric or drunk. [f. SCREW + -Y²]

scrī'bal. See SCRIBE.

scrĭ'bble¹ *v.* & *n.* **1.** *v.t.* & *i.* Write hurriedly or carelessly in regard to either handwriting or composition, or simply to obliterate (*scribble out the old address*); draw carelessly or meaninglessly; (joc. or derog.) be journalist, author, poet, etc., whence **scrĭ'bbl**ER¹ *n.*; ‡||**scrĭ'bbling-pad, -paper,** (for casual jottings). **2.** *n.* Careless handwriting or thing written in it; scrawl, hasty note, etc.; hence **scrĭ'bbl**Y² *a.* [ME, f. med. L *scribillare* dim. of L *scribere* write; see -LE 3]

scrĭ'bble² *v.t.* Card (wool, cotton) coarsely. [prob. f. LG; cf. syn. G *schrubbeln*, frequent. f. LG *schrubben* (see SCRUB²)]

scribe *n.*, & *v.t.* **1.** *n.* (arch.) Person who writes or can write; **am no great ~**, do not write well. **2.** Ancient or medieval copyist of manuscripts. **3.** (Bibl.) Ancient-Jewish maker and keeper of records etc.; ancient-Jewish professional theologian and jurist. **4.** Hence **scrī'b**AL *a.* **5. ~(-awl)**, pointed instrument for marking lines on wood, bricks, etc., to guide saw etc., or for writing words on barrel etc. **6.** *v.t.* Mark with scribe; hence **scrī'b**ER¹ (2) *n.* [n. ME, f. L *scriba* (*scribere* write); in sense 5 f. v. perh. f. DESCRIBE]

scrĭm *n.* Open-weave esp. cotton fabric for lining, upholstery, *theatre curtain, etc. [18th c., of unkn. orig.]

scrĭ'mmage *n.* & *v.* **1.** *n.* Tussle, confused struggle, row, brawl, skirmish. **2.** (Amer. Footb.) Sequence of play beginning with placing of ball on ground with its longest axis at right angles to goal-line. **3.** *v.i.* Engage in scrimmage. **4.** *v.t.* Put (ball) into scrimmage. [var. of SKIRMISH]

scrĭmp *v.t.* & *i.* Skimp; hence **~'**Y² *a.* [18th c., orig. Sc.; perh. cogn. w. SHRIMP]

||**scrĭ'mshănk** *v.i.* (Mil. sl.) Shirk duty; hence **~**ER¹ *n.* [19th c.; orig. unkn.]

scrĭ'mshaw *v.* & *n.* **1.** *v.t.* & *i.* Adorn (shells, ivory, etc.), adorn shells etc., with carved or coloured designs (as sailors' amusement at sea). **2.** *n.* (Piece of) such work. [19th c.; perh. f. surname]

scrĭp¹ *n.* (arch.) Beggar's or traveller's or pilgrim's wallet, satchel. [ME, f. OF *escrep(p)e* wallet, var. of *escherpe* SCARF¹, or f. ON *skreppa*]

scrĭp² *n.* **1.** Provisional certificate of money subscribed to bank or company entitling holder to formal certificate in due time and to dividends etc.; (collect.) such certificates. **2.** Extra share(s) issued in place of dividend. [abbr. of *subscription receipt*]

scrĭpt *n.*, & *v.t.* **1.** *n.* (Law). Original document (opp. *copy*). **2.** Handwriting, written characters (opp. *print*); printed cursive characters, imitation of handwriting in type; system of writing (*cannot read Russian script*). **3.** Text of broadcaster's announcement or talk; text of play, film, etc.; **~-writer,** writer for films, broadcasting, etc. **4.** ||Examinee's written answer. **5.** *v.t.* Write script for (film etc.). [ME, f. OF *escri(p)t* f. L *scriptum* thing written, neut. p.p. (as n.) of *scribere* write]

scrĭptôr'ĭ|um *n.* (*pl.* **~a** *or* **~ums**). Room set apart for writing esp. in monastery; so **~**AL *a.*, of or for writing. [med. L (as prec.; see -ORY)]

scrĭ'ptural (-choor- *or* -cher-) *a.* Founded on, reconcilable with, laying stress on, appealing to, doctrines contained in the Bible, whence **~**ISM (3), **~**IST (2), *ns.*; of or taken from the Bible; hence **~**LY² *adv.*, **~**NESS *n.* [f. LL *scripturalis* f. L *scriptura* (see foll., -AL)]

scrĭ'pture *n.* **1.** (*S~*). The Bible with or without the Apocrypha (*a doctrine not found in* (*Holy*) *Scripture* or *the Scriptures*; *a Scripture text*); *a* or *the* quotation from the Bible. **2.** Sacred book of non-Christian religion. **3.** (arch.) Inscription. [ME, f. L *scriptura* (as SCRIPT; see -URE)]

scrĭ'vener *n.* **1.** (Hist.) Copyist, drafter of documents, notary, broker, money-lender. **2.** (arch. or derog.) Writer, author; **~'s palsy,** writer's cramp. [ME, f. obs. *scrivein* f. OF *escrivein* f. Rom. **scribano* f. L (as SCRIBE; see -AN) + -ER¹]

scrobĭ'cūlate *a.* (Bot. & Zool.) Pitted, furrowed. [f. L *scrobiculus* (*scrobis* trench; see -CULE) + -ATE²]

***scrŏd** *n.* Young cod. [19th c., of unkn. orig.]

scrŏ'fūl|a *n.* Disease with glandular swellings, prob. a form of tuberculosis; hence **~**OUS *a.* [ME, f. med. L sing. f. LL *scrofulae* pl. scrofulous swelling, dim. of L *scrofa* a sow]

scrōll *n.* & *v.* **1.** *n.* Roll of parchment or paper esp. written on; book or volume of the ancient roll form; (arch.) schedule or list. **2.** Ornamental design esp. in architecture carved or drawn or otherwise made to imitate scroll of parchment more or less exactly, scroll-shaped ornament of Ionic capital or of chair etc., head of violin etc., flourish in writing, ribbon bearing heraldic motto, etc. **3.** **~-head,** volute at ship's bow; **~-lathe** (for spiral work); **~-saw,** (1) fretsaw, (2) saw for cutting along curved lines; **~-work,** ornament of spiral lines esp. as cut by scroll-saw. **4.** *v.t.* & *i.* Curl up like paper. **5.** *v.t.* Inscribe (as) in scroll; (esp. in *p.p.*) adorn with scrolls. [ME *scrowle* alt. f. *rowle* ROLL[1], perh. after syn. *scrow* f. as ESCROW]

Scrōōge *n.* Miser. [character in Dickens's *Christmas Carol*]

scrōōp *n.*, & *v.i.* (Make) grating noise or crisp rustle of silk. [imit.]

scrō't|um *n.* (*pl.* **~a** *or* **~ums**). (Anat.) Bag containing testicles; hence **~**AL *a.*, **~**I'TIS, **~**OCELE, *ns.* [L]

scroung|e (-nj) *v.* (sl.) **1.** *v.t.* Collect by foraging; take illicitly; cadge. **2.** *v.i.* Search about; obtain things by scrounging them. **3.** Hence **~**'ER[1] *n.* [var. of dial. *scrunge* steal]

scrŭb[1] *n.* (Ground or region covered with) brushwood or stunted forest growth; stunted or insignificant person, animal, or plant; **~-fowl, ~-hen, ~-turkey,** megapode; **~-oak, ~-pine,** (dwarf kinds); **~ typhus,** rickettsial disease of W. Pacific; **~ wallaby,** pademelon; hence **~'by**[2] *a.* [ME, var. of SHRUB[1]]

scrŭb[2] *v.* (**-bb-**) & *n.* **1.** *v.t.* Rub hard to clean or brighten esp. with soap and water applied with hard-bristled brush (**~'bing-** *or* ***~-** **-brush**); (sl.) cancel, scrap; remove impurities etc. from (gas) in scrubber. **2.** *v.i.* Use scrubbing-brush or other means of cleaning by hard rubbing; **~ (up),** (of surgeon etc.) clean hands and arms by scrubbing, before operation; ***~'woman,** charwoman. **3.** *n.* Scrubbing or being scrubbed; short-bristled brush or moustache. **4.** *(colloq.) Player not belonging to regular team; second or weaker team; game of baseball with less than full complement of players. [ME, prob. f. MLG, MDu. *schrobben, schrubben*]

scrŭ'bber *n.* In vbl senses; apparatus for purifying gases by passing them through a body or stream of water. [f. prec. + -ER[1]]

scrŭff *n.* Back of the neck as used to grasp and lift or drag animal or person by (*take by the scruff of the neck*). [alt. of *scuff*, perh. f. ON *skoft* hair]

scrŭ'ff|y̆ *a.* Scurfy; shabby, slovenly, untidy; hence **~ĭLY**[2] *adv.*, **~ĭNESS** *n.* [f. *scruff* var. of SCURF + -Y[2]]

scrŭm *n.* = foll.; **~-half,** half-back who puts ball into scrum. [abbr.]

scrŭ'mmage *n.* (Rugby Footb.) Grouping of all forwards on each side to push against the other and seek possession of ball thrown on ground between them. [as SCRIMMAGE]

scrŭmp *v.i.* Steal fruit, esp. apples. [cf. SCRUMPY]

scrŭ'mptious (-pshus) *a.* (colloq.) Delightful, delicious; hence **~**LY[2] *adv.*, **~**NESS *n.* [19th c.; orig. unkn.]

scrŭ'mpy̆ *n.* (esp. dial.) Rough cider. [f. dial. *scrump* small apple + -Y[3]]

scrŭnch *v.* & *n.* = CRUNCH. [var. of CRUNCH]

scru'ple (-ōō'-) *n.* & *v.* **1.** *n.* Apothecaries' weight-unit of 20 grains; (arch.) very small quantity. **2.** (in *sing.* or *pl.*) Feeling of doubt or hesitation on grounds of morality or propriety about acting or approving of action, conscientious objection, (**make no ~ to do,** do without such hesitation or with easy conscience). **3.** *v.i.* Feel or be influenced by scruples; (esp. w. neg.) hesitate owing to scruples *to* do. **4.** *v.t.* (arch.) Be deterred from or hindered in (do*ing*, action) by scruples. [f. F *scrupule* or f. L *scrupulus* (*scrupus* rough pebble, anxiety; see -ULE)]

scru'pūlous (-ōō'-) *a.* **1.** Careful to avoid doing wrong, conscientious even in small matters, not neglectful of details, punctilious, marked by extreme thoroughness, unfailing, (*a scrupulous person*; *scrupulous honesty, cleanliness, care, methods, respect, attention,* etc.). **2.** Over-attentive to details, esp. to small points of conscience. **3.** Hence **scrupūlo**'SITY (-ōōp-) *n.*, **~**LY[2] *adv.*, **~**NESS *n.* [ME, f. F *scrupuleux* or f. L *scrupulosus* (as prec.; see -OUS)]

scrutā'tor (-ōō-) *n.* Examiner, scrutineer; person given to scrutiny. [L (as SCRUTINY; see -OR)]

scrutineer' (-ōō-) *n.* Person checking ballot papers and counting votes. [f. SCRUTINY + -EER]

scru'tĭnīze, -īse, (-ōō'tĭnīz) *v.t.* Look closely at, examine in detail. [f. foll. + -IZE]

scru'tĭnȳ (-ōō'-) *n.* Critical gaze, close investigation, examination into details; official examination of votes cast in election to check their validity or accuracy of counting. [ME, f. L *scrutinium* (*scrutari* search f. *scruta* rubbish; orig. of rag-pickers)]

scrȳ *v.i.* Use the crystal in crystal-gazing; hence **~**'ER[1] *n.* [f. DESCRY]

scū'ba *n.* Self-contained underwater breathing apparatus. [acronym]

scŭd *v.i.* (**-dd-**), & *n.* **1.** *v.i.* Run or fly straight and fast esp. with smooth or easy motion, skim along; (Naut.) run before the wind. **2.** *n.* Spell of scudding; vapoury driving clouds; driving shower; gust; wind-blown spray. [perh. alt. of SCUT]

scŭff *v.* & *n.* **1.** *v.i.* Walk with dragging feet, shuffle with the feet; *poke *at* with foot. **2.** *v.t.* Graze or brush against; wear away or mark thus. **3.** *n.* Mark of scuffing; backless slipper. [imit.]

scŭ'ffle *v.i.*, & *n.* (Engage in) confused struggle or disorderly fight at close quarters. [prob. f. Scand.; cf. Sw. *skuffa* to push, cogn. w. SHOVE]

||**scŭg** *n.* Person esp. schoolboy, lacking spirit, sociability, manners, sportsmanship, etc. [19th c.; orig. unkn.]

scŭldŭ'dderȳ, scŭldŭ'ggerȳ (-g-). Vars. of SKULDUGGERY.

scŭll *n.* & *v.* **1.** *n.* One of pair of small oars used by single rower each with one hand; oar resting on boat's stern and worked with twisting strokes to propel like ship's screw. **2.** *v.t.* & *i.* Propel (boat), propel boat, with sculls. [ME, of unkn. orig.]

scŭ'ller *n.* User of scull(s); boat intended for sculling. [f. prec. + -ER[1]]

scŭ'llerȳ *n.* Back kitchen, room for washing up dishes etc. [ME, f. AF *squillerie*, OF *escuelerie* (*escuele* dish f. L *scutella* salver dim. of *scutra* wooden platter; see -ERY)]

scŭ'llion (-yon) *n.* (arch.) Cook's boy, washer of dishes and pots. [ME, of unkn. orig.]

scŭlp *v.t.* & *i.* (colloq.) Sculpture. [f. L *sculpere*; now regarded as abbr.]

scŭ'lpĭn *n.* Small American fish of family Cottidae, with large spiny head. [perh. f. obs. *scorpene* f. L f. Gk *skorpaina* a fish]

scŭlpt *v.t.* & *i.* (colloq.) Sculpture. [f. F *sculpter* (*sculpteur* = foll.); now regarded as abbr.]

scŭ'lpt|or *n.* One who sculptures; hence **~**RESS[1] *n.* [L (as foll.; see -OR)]

scŭ'lptur|e *n.* & *v.* **1.** *n.* Art of forming representations of objects etc. or abstract designs in the round or in relief by chiselling stone, carving wood, modelling clay, casting metal, or similar processes; a work of sculpture; (Zool. & Bot.) raised or sunk markings on shell etc.; hence ~AL, ~E'SQUE, (-cher-) *adjs.* **2.** *v.t.* Represent in sculpture; shape like sculpture; adorn with sculpture; (in *p.p.*, Zool. & Bot.) having sculpture. **3.** *v.i.* Practise sculpture. [ME, f. L *sculptura* (*sculpere sculpt-* carve; see -URE)]

scŭm *n.* & *v.* (**-mm-**). **1.** *n.* Impurities that rise to surface of liquid esp. in boiling or fermentation, floating film; (fig.) worst part, refuse, offscourings, (*of*), worthless person(s); hence **~'my**[2] *a.* **2.** *v.t.* Take scum from, skim; be or form a scum on. **3.** *v.i.* (Of liquid) develop scum. [ME, f. MLG, MDu. *schūm*, OHG *scūm* f. Gmc **skūma-* (**skū-* cover)]

scŭ'mble *v.t.*, & *n.* **1.** *v.t.* Modify (painting) by applying thin opaque coat to give softer or duller effect; modify (drawing) similarly with light pencilling etc. **2.** *n.* Scumbling material or effect produced by it. [perh. frequent. of prec. 2; cf. -LE 3]

scŭ'ncheon (-nchon) *n.* Inside face of door-jamb, window-frame, etc. [ME, f. OF *escoinson* (as EX-[1], COIN[1])]

scŭ'nner *n.*, & *v.i.* **1.** *n.* Strong dislike (*take a scunner at, against*); object of loathing. **2.** *v.i.* (Sc.) Feel sick, be nauseated. [n. f. v., ME, of unkn. orig.]

scŭp *n.* E. Amer. fish of genus *Stenostomus*, kind of porgy. [f. Narraganset *mishcup* thick-scaled (*mishe* large, *cuppi* scale)]

scŭ'pper[1] *n.* Hole in ship's side to carry off water from deck. [ME, perh. f. AF, f. OF *escopir* f. Rom. **skuppire* to spit, orig. imit.]

||**scŭ'pper**[2] *v.t.* (sl.) Surprise and massacre; sink (ship, crew); defeat, discomfit. [19th c. Mil.; orig. unkn.]

***scŭ'ppernŏng** *n.* Muscadine grape; wine from it. [f. river *S~* in N. Carolina]

scûrf *n.* Flakes on surface of skin cast off as fresh skin develops below, esp. those of head, dandruff; any scaly matter on a surface; **~ pea,** plant of genus *Psoralea* used against itch etc.; hence ~'Y[2] *a.* [OE, prob. f. ON **skurfr* & earlier OE *sceorf* cogn. w. *sceorfan* gnaw, *sceorfian* cut to shreds]

scŭ'rrīle *a.* (arch.) = foll. [F, or f. L *scurrilis* (*scurra* buffoon; see -IL)]

scŭ'rrĭl|ous *a.* (Of person or language) grossly or obscenely abusive; given to or expressed with low buffoonery; hence or cogn. **~ous**LY[2] *adv.*, ~ITY (-ĭ'l-) *n.* [f. prec. + -OUS]

scŭ'rrȳ *v.i.*, & *n.* **1.** *v.i.* Run or move hurriedly esp. with short quick steps, scamper, (*the scurrying mice*). **2.** *n.* Act or sound of scurrying; haste, bustle; flurry of rain or snow. [abbr. of *hurry-scurry* redupl. of HURRY[2]]

scûr'v|ȳ *a.* & *n.* **1.** *a.* Paltry, low, mean, dishonourable, contemptible, (*a scurvy trick, fellow*); hence **~ĭ**LY[2] *adv.* **2.** *n.* Deficiency disease from lack of vitamin C, with swollen gums, livid spots, and prostration, attacking those (esp. formerly sailors etc.) who live without fresh vegetables; **~y-grass,** kind of cress used against scurvy or as salad; hence **~ĭ**ED[2] (-vĭd) *a.* [f. SCURF + -Y[2]; n. sense by assoc. w. F *scorbut* (cf. SCORBUTIC)]

scŭt *n.* Short tail esp. of hare, rabbit, or deer. [ME, orig. unkn.; cf. obs. *scut* short(en)]

scū'tage *n.* (Hist.) Money paid by feudal land-owner in lieu of personal service. [ME, f. med. L *scutagium* f. L *scutum* shield; see -AGE]

scŭtch *v.t.*, & *n.* **1.** *v.t.* Dress (fibrous material, esp. retted flax) by beating; **~-blade,** ~'ER[1] (2) *n.*, implements for scutching. **2.** *n.* Scutcher. [f. OF *escouche, escoucher* (dial.), *escousser*, f. Rom. **excussare* f. L EX[1] (*cutere cuss-* = *quatere* shake)]

scŭ'tcheon (-chon) *n.* **1.** = ESCUTCHEON. **2.** Ornamented brass etc. plate round or over key-hole; plate for name or inscription. [ME, f. ESCUTCHEON]

scūte *n.* = SCUTUM. [f. L (as SCUTUM)]

scūtĕ'll|um *n.* (*pl.* **~a**). (Bot. & Zool.) Small shield, plate, or scale, in plant, insect, bird, etc., esp. one of the horny scales on birds' feet; hence **scū'tell**ATE[2] *a.*, ~A'TION *n.* [mod. L, dim. of L SCUTUM]

scŭ'tter *v.i.*, & *n.* (colloq.) Scurry. [perh. alt. of SCUTTLE[3]; cf. -ER[5]]

scŭ'ttle[1] *n.* Coal-box; ||part of motor-car body immediately behind bonnet. [ME, f. ON *skutill*, OHG *scuzzila* f. L *scutella* dish]

scŭ'ttle[2] *n.*, & *v.t.* **1.** *n.* Hole with lid in wall or roof of house or ship's deck, side, or hatchway--covering; **~-butt,** water-butt usu. on deck with hole in top for dipping from, (sl.) rumour, gossip. **2.** *v.t.* Make hole(s) in (ship), open sea--cocks of (ship), esp. for purpose of sinking. [ME, perh. f. obs. F *escoutille* f. Sp. *escotilla* hatchway dim. of *escota* cutting out cloth (*escotar* f. as EX-[1] + Gmc **skaut-*; cf. SHEET[1])]

scŭ'ttle[3] *v.i.*, & *n.* **1.** *v.i.* Hurry along, scurry; run away, flee from danger or difficulty. **2.** *n.* Hurried gait; precipitate flight or departure. [cf. dial. *scuddle* frequent. of SCUD; see -LE 3]

scū't|um *n.* (*pl.* **~a**). (Zool. etc.) Shieldlike plate or scale, piece of bony armour in crocodile, sturgeon, turtle, armadillo, etc.; hence ~AL, ~ATE[2], ~ĭFORM, *adjs.* [L, = oblong shield]

Scȳ'lla *n.* **~ and Charybdis,** two dangers such that to avoid one increases the risk from the other. [f. names of sea-monster and whirlpool in Gk Myth.]

scȳphozō'an *a.* & *n.* (Member) of class of coelenterates comprising true marine jellyfishes. [f. as foll. + -o- + Gk *zōion* animal + -AN]

scȳ'ph|us *n.* (*pl.* **~i** *pr.* -ī). **1.** (Gk Ant.) Footless drinking-cup with two handles not higher than rim. **2.** (Bot.) Cup-shaped part as in narcissus flower or in lichens, whence ~OSE[1] *a.* **3.** Hence **~ĭ**FORM *a.* [mod. L, f. Gk *skuphos*]

scȳthe (-dh) *n.*, & *v.t.* **1.** *n.* Mowing and reaping implement of long slightly curved blade swung over ground by long usu. crooked pole with two short handles projecting at right angles from it; blade continuing axle of ancient war-chariot at each end, whence **scȳth**ED[2] (-dhd) *a.* **2.** *v.t.* Cut with scythe. [OE *sithe*, = MLG *segede*, ON *sigthr* f. Gmc **segithō* (**seg-* cut), w. sp. prob. after *scissors*]

Scȳ'thian (*or* -dh-) *a.* & *n.* (Inhabitant or language) of ancient Scythia, region north of Black Sea. [f. L f. Gk *Skuthia* Scythia + -AN]

S. D(ak). *abbr.* South Dakota.

S.D.R. *abbr.* special drawing right (from International Monetary Fund).

se- *pref.* denoting 'apart, without' (*seclude, secure*). [L, f. OL *se* prep. & adv.]

S.E. *abbr.* South-East(ern).

Se *symb.* selenium.

sea *n.* **1.** Expanse of salt water that covers most of earth's surface and encloses its continents and islands, the ocean, any part of this as opposed to dry land or fresh water, (*by sea and land*; *at the bottom of the sea*; *jumped into the sea*); **at ~,** away from (esp. out of sight of) land; **(all) at ~,** (fig.) perplexed, not knowing how to proceed; **beyond ~(s),** = OVERSEA(s)[1,2]; **by ~,** in ship(s); **follow the ~,** be sailor; **go to ~,** become sailor; HIGH *seas*; **on the ~,** (1) in ship etc., (2) situated on coast; **put (out) to ~,** leave land or port. **2.** Particular tract of sea partly or sometimes wholly enclosed by land and usu. distinguished by special name (*the North, Mediterranean, Caspian, Dead, Sea*); freshwater lake (*Sea of Galilee*); **inland ~** (entirely land-locked); **the**

seven ~s, Arctic, Antarctic, N. Pacific, S. Pacific, N. Atlantic, S. Atlantic, and Indian, Oceans. **3.** Local motion or state of the sea; swell, great billow (*seas mountains high*); HALF--*seas-over*; **heavy ~** (with great waves); **long ~** (with long regular waves); SHIP[2] *a sea*; **short ~** (choppy and irregularly agitated). **4.** Vast quantity or expanse *of* (*a sea of troubles, care, flame, upturned faces*); **~s of blood,** ruthless bloodshed. **5.** (Bibl.) = LAVER[2] 1. **6.** (*attrib.* and in *comb.*) Living or used in or on, of, near, like, the sea (often prefixed to name of animal, fruit, etc., to form name of marine thing with merely superficial resemblance to what it is named after, as *sea canary, cucumber, -fox, raven*); **~ acorn,** barnacle; **~ air,** air at seaside esp. as recommended for invalids etc.; **~ anchor,** baglike contrivance to retard drifting and maintain direction of ship or seaplane; *sea* ANEMONE; **~-angel,** angel-fish; **~-arrow,** flying squid; **~-bank,** = *sea-wall*; **~ bass,** sea-fish like bass, esp. *Centropristis striatus*; **~ bear,** (1) polar bear, (2) fur-seal; ***~'bee,** member of naval construction battalion [f. *C.B.*]; **~-bells,** seashore bindweed; **~-belt,** seaweed with beltlike fronds; **~-bird** (frequenting sea or land near sea); **~ blubber,** jellyfish; **~'board,** seashore, coast region, line of coast; **~-boat,** (1) ship etc. having (specified) sea-going qualities, (2) boat which can be lowered quickly in emergency at sea; **~-boot,** sailor's high waterproof boot; **~-born,** (poet., esp. of Aphrodite) born in the sea; **~-borne,** conveyed by sea (*sea-borne commerce, goods*); **~-bow,** rainbow effect in sea-spray; *sea*-BREAM[1]; **~-breeze** (blowing landward from sea esp. during day in alternation with land-breeze at night); **~ breeze,** any breeze at sea; **~ buckthorn,** maritime shrub (*Hippophaë rhamnoides*) with orange berries; **~ butterfly,** pteropod; **~ cabbage,** sea-kale; **~-calf,** common seal; **~ canary,** white whale (from its whistling); **~ captain,** past or present captain of ship in navy or merchant service, (poet. or rhet.) great sailor or commander at sea; **~ change,** transformation (w. ref. to Shak. *Tempest* I. ii. 400); **~-chest,** sailor's storage-chest; **~-cloth** (used in theatre to represent waves); **~ coal,** (arch.) coal (opp. *charcoal* etc.); *sea*-COAST[1]; **~-cock,** (1) grey plover, (2) valve by which sea-water can be let into ship's interior; **~ cook,** cook on board ship (esp. *son of a ~ cook* as Naut. term of abuse); **~-cow,** (1) sirenian, (2) walrus, (3) hippopotamus; **~ cucumber,** holothurian, esp. *bêche-de-mer*; **~-devil,** (1) devil inhabiting sea, (2) devil-fish or other ugly fish; **~-dog,** (1) common seal, (2) old sailor (esp. of the Elizabethan sea captains), (3) light near horizon thought to presage bad weather; **~ eagle,** fish-eating eagle esp. of genus *Haliaëtus*; **~-ear,** abalone; **~ elephant,** large seal of genus *Mirounga*, with proboscis in male; **~-fan,** fanlike polyp; **~'farer,** sailor; **~'faring** *a.* & *n.*, traversing the seas, esp. habitually; **~ fennel,** samphire; **~-fight** (between warships); **~-fish** (opp. freshwater fish); **~-flower,** sea ANEMONE; **~ fog** (caused by difference of land and sea temperatures and extending only short way inland); **~'food,** edible salt-water (shell)fish; **~-fowl,** sea-bird; **~-fox,** thresher shark; **~ front,** part of town facing sea; **~ furbelow,** a brown seaweed (*Laminaria bulbosa*); **~ gherkin,** small sea cucumber; **~ gillyflower,** sea-pink; **~-girdle,** sea-belt; **~-girt,** (poet. or rhet., of island etc.) surrounded by sea; **~'going,** (of ship) for crossing sea, not coasting or river use, (of person) seafaring; **~ gooseberry,** ctenophore; **~ grape,** (1) glasswort, (2) sargasso, (3) W. Ind. tree with grapelike fruit, (4) (in *pl.*) cuttlefish eggs; **~-grass,** grasslike plant growing in or near sea; **~-green** *a.* & *n.*, (of) bluish green as of sea; **~-gull,** = GULL[1]; **~-hare,** mollusc of genus *Tethys* with tentacles like projecting ears; **~ hedgehog,** sea-urchin; **~-hog,** porpoise; **~ holly,** spiny-leaved blue--flowered evergreen plant; **~-horse,** (1) mythical creature harnessed to sea-god's chariot having horse's head and fish's tail, (2) walrus, (3) hippocampus; **~-island (cotton),** fine quality of long-stapled cotton orig. grown on islands off Georgia and S. Carolina; **~-kale,** perennial herb (*Crambe maritima*) with young shoots used as table vegetable; **~-kale beet,** chard; **~ kidney,** kidney-shaped coelenterate; **~-king,** medieval Scandinavian pirate chief; **~ lace,** kind of seaweed with long cordlike fronds; **~ lane,** lane (sense 4) for sea traffic; **~ lawyer,** (1) shark, (2) (Naut. term of contempt for) captious person; **~-legs,** ability to walk on deck of rolling ship (*has not yet got his sea-legs*); **~ lemon,** yellow oval mollusc of family Dorididae; **~ leopard,** spotted species of seal; **~-letter,** official protective letter carried by neutral ship in wartime, describing her cargo, crew, etc.; **~-level,** level continuous with that of sea half-way between high and low water, used in reckoning height of hills etc. and as barometric standard; **~-lift,** transport of supplies etc. by sea; **~ lily,** crinoid; **~-line,** (1) coastline, (2) horizon at sea; **~-lion,** large eared seal of Pacific esp. of genus *Zalophus* or *Otaria*; **~ lizard,** gastropod of genus *Glaucus*; **~ loch,** = LOCH 2; ||**Sea Lord,** naval member of Admiralty Board; **~-mark,** beacon, lighthouse, etc., or elevated conspicuous object, used to direct course at sea; **~-mat,** bryozoan forming flat matted crust; **~ melon,** holothurian of family Pentactidae; **~-mew,** GULL[1]; *sea* MILE; **~ monster,** any huge, terrible, or strange (esp. mythical) sea-animal; **~ moss,** mosslike bryozoan or seaweed; **~'mount,** underwater mountain; **~-mouse,** iridescent sea-worm of genus *Aphrodite*; **~-mud,** saline deposit of salt marshes etc. used as manure; **~ necklace,** string of whelk egg-cases; **~ nettle,** stinging jellyfish; **~ oak,** seaweed of genus *Fucus*; **~-onion,** = SQUILL 2; **~ orange,** globose orange-coloured holothurian; **~ otter,** Pacific otter with very valuable fur; **~ parrot,** puffin; **~-pass,** = *sea-letter*; **~-pay** (for active service at sea); **~ peach, pear,** ascidians resembling these fruits; **~-pen,** feather-shaped polyp; **~ pie,** (1) sailors' pie of salt meat etc., (2) ||oyster-catcher; **~-piece,** picture of scene at sea; **~-pig,** (1) porpoise, (2) dugong; **~-pike,** sea-fish like pike, e.g. garfish, hake; **~ pilot,** oyster-catcher; **~ pincushion,** skate's egg-case; **~-pink,** seashore or Alpine plant with bright pink flowers, species of thrift; **~'plane,** aeroplane constructed for rising from and alighting on water; **~'port,** town with harbour; **~ power,** (1) ability to control and make successful use of the sea, esp. in maritime warfare, (2) State having this; **~ pumpkin,** = *sea melon*; **~-purse,** egg-case of skate or shark; **~'quake,** submarine earthquake; **~ raven,** species of sculpin (*Hemitripterus americanus*); ***~-robin,** red gurnard; **~-room,** clear space at sea allowing ship to turn etc.; **~ rover,** pirate (ship); **~-salt** (got by evaporating sea--water); **~'scape,** picture or view to sea; **Sea Scout,** maritime auxiliary to SCOUT[1]s; **~ serpent,** (1) snake of family Hydrophidae living in sea, (2) enormous serpentine sea monster often reported as seen but never identified with known species; *sea*-SHANTY[2];

~ **shell,** shell of any salt-water mollusc; **~-shore,** land close to sea, (Law) area between high and low water marks; **~'sick,** vomiting or inclined to vomit from motion of ship etc., whence **~'sickness; ~'side,** edge of sea, (place or places on) sea-coast esp. as holiday resort (*do you like the seaside?*; *must go to the seaside*); ~ **slug,** (1) sea cucumber, (2) marine gastropod with internal or no shell; ~ **snail,** (1) small slimy fish with ventral sucker, of family Liparididae, (2) spiral-shelled mollusc, e.g. whelk; ~ **snake,** = *sea serpent*; ~ **snipe,** (1) sandpiper, (2) snipe-fish; **~-squirt,** ascidian (squirting water when touched); ~ **swallow,** tern; *sea*-TANG²(*le*); **~-thrift,** = *sea-pink*; **~-toad,** the angler-fish; ~ **trout,** salmon trout; *sea*-UNICORN; **~-urchin,** marine animal of order Echinoidea, esp. globular sharp-spined kind; **~-wall,** wall or embankment made to check encroachment of sea; **~-ware,** seaweed collected for manure or other uses; **~-way,** (1) ship's progress, (2) place where ship lies in open water, (3) inland waterway open to seagoing ships; **~'weed,** any alga or other plant growing in sea; **~'whip,** = *sea-fan*; **~-wife,** species of wrasse; **~-wind,** = *sea-breeze*; **~-wolf,** (1) sea elephant, (2) bass or wolf-fish, (3) pirate; **~'worthy,** (of ship) in fit state to put to sea, strong and well rigged etc.; *sea*-WRACK. **7.** Hence ~'WARD *a.*, *adv.*, & *n.*, ~'WARDS *adv.* [OE *sǣ*, = OS, OHG *sēo*, ON *sær*, Goth. *saiws* f. Gmc **saiwiz*]

seal¹ *n.*, & *v.i.* **1.** *n.* Fish-eating amphibious marine mammal of family Phocidae or Otariidae, with short limbs modified to serve chiefly for swimming but having fur or bristles; **eared** ~ (of Otariidae, distinguished from **common** ~, *Phoca vitulina*, and other Phocidae by larger size and visible external ears, e.g. sea lion, sea elephant, and fur-seals); sealskin; **~-fishery,** ~'ERY *n.*, (place for) hunting of seals; *seal*-ROOKERY; **~'skin,** skin of seal or usu. (garment made from) prepared fur of seals as clothing material. **2.** *v.i.* Hunt seals. [OE *seolh seol-*, = MLG *sēl*, OHG *selah*, ON *selr* f. Gmc **selhaz*]

seal² *n.*, & *v.t.* **1.** *n.* Piece of wax, lead, or other such material, impressed with device and attached in some way to document usu. in addition to signature as guarantee of authenticity (**given under my hand and ~,** signed and sealed by me; **set** one's **~ to, set the ~ on,** authorize or confirm) or to envelope or to any receptacle such as box or room or house to prevent its being opened without knowledge of owner etc. (**leaden ~,** stamped piece of lead holding ends of a wire used as fastening; **under ~ of** *confession*, *confidence*, etc., subject to secrecy on stated grounds); impression stamped on or paper disc stuck to document as symbol equivalent to wax seal; adhesive stamp symbolizing a charity etc. **2.** (fig.) Significant or prophetic mark (*has the seal of death in his face*). **3.** Gem, engraved piece of metal, etc., serving as stamp to produce seal on wax etc. or paper (**~-ring,** finger-ring with seal); ||**~s of office,** those held during tenure esp. by Lord Chancellor or Secretary of State; ||**Great S~,** seal in charge of Lord Chancellor or Lord Keeper used in sealing Parliament-writs, treaties, and important State papers; ||PRIVY *seal*. **4.** Act done, thing given, event regarded, as confirmation or guarantee *of* (**~ of love,** kiss, birth of child, etc.). **5.** Substance used to close aperture etc., esp. water standing in drain-trap to prevent ascent of foul air. **6. ~-wort,** (1) SOLOMON's seal, (2) pearlwort. **7.** *v.t.* Affix seal to; stamp or fasten with seal; certify as correct with seal or stamp (**S~ed Book,** one of the presumed perfect copies of Book of Common Prayer certified by Great Seal in 1662 and deposited in cathedrals etc.; **~ed orders,** orders for procedure, not to be examined before specified time; *sealed* VERDICT); show genuineness of (devotion etc.) *with* one's life etc.; record (chess move to be made after adjournment period). **8.** Close securely or hermetically, stop up or *up*, (**my lips are ~ed,** the matter is a secret and I must not speak of it; **is a ~ed book to me,** is something of which I have and can get no knowledge); provide (pipe etc.) with water-seal by means of trap etc.; provide (road) with smooth surface of tar macadam etc.; ~ **off,** cut off (an area) to prevent entry or exit; hence ~'ANT *n.* **9.** Set significant mark on, set apart, destine, decide irrevocably, (*death has sealed her for his own*; *is sealed to* or *for salvation, damnation*, etc.; *his fate is sealed*); ||**~ed pattern,** standard pattern of equipment, clothing, etc., approved for use by armed forces. **10.** ~ (**up**), confine securely. **11. ~'ing-wax,** mixture of shellac and rosin with turpentine and pigment, used for seals. [ME, f. AF *seal*, OF *seel*(*er*) f. L *sigillum* dim. of *signum* SIGN¹]

sea'ler *n.* In vbl senses; ship or man engaged in seal-hunting; inspector of weights and measures. [f. SEAL¹,² + -ER¹]

Sea'lyham (-lĭam) *n.* ~ (**terrier**), breed of wire-haired short-legged terrier. [~ in Dyfed, Wales]

seam *n.*, & *v.t.* **1.** *n.* Line of junction between two edges esp. those of two pieces of cloth, leather, etc., turned back and sewn together or of boards fitted edge to edge; fissure left by gaping of parallel edges (*ship's seams need caulking*); scar or wrinkle; **bursting** etc. **at the ~s,** full to overflowing. **2.** Line of separation between two strata; stratum of coal etc. **3.** ~ **bowler,** ~'ER¹ *n.*, (Cricket) one who makes the ball move off its seam when it bounces. **4.** Hence ~'LESS *a.* **5.** *v.t.* Unite with seam; (esp. in *p.p.*) mark or score with seam, fissure, or scar; **~'ing-lace,** galloon or other trimming sewn over seams in upholstery etc. [OE *sēam*, = MDu. *sōm*, OHG *soum*, ON *saumr* f. Gmc **saumaz* (**sau-*, **su-* SEW)]

sea'man *n.* (*pl.* **sea'men**). Sailor, esp. below rank of officer (ABLE-*bodied*, ||LEADING², ORDINARY, *seaman*); person skilled in navigation etc.; hence ~LIKE, ~LY¹, *adjs.*, ~SHIP (3) *n.* [OE *sǣman*(*n*) (as SEA, MAN¹)]

sea'mstrèss, sĕ'mpstrèss, (sĕ'ms-) *n.* Sewing-woman. [OE *sēamestre* fem. (*sēamere* tailor, f. as SEAM + -ER¹, + -STER) + -ESS¹]

sea'mў *a.* Showing seams; ~ **side,** inside of garment etc. where rough edges of seams are visible, (esp., fig.) less presentable or attractive aspect *of life* etc. [f. SEAM + -Y²]

Sea'nad (shă'nadh) *n.* Upper house of Parliament in the Republic of Ireland. [Ir., = senate]

se'ance (sā'-), ***séance*** (sā'ahńs), *n.* Session of a society or deliberative body; meeting for exhibition or investigation of spiritualistic phenomena. [f. F *séance* f. OF *seoir* f. L *sedēre* sit; see -ANCE]

sear¹ *a.*, & *v.t.*, **sēre²** *a.* **1.** *a.* (Of leaf, flower, etc., and fig. of age etc.) withered, dried up (**the ~, the yellow leaf,** old age). **2.** *v.t.* Scorch esp. with hot iron, cauterize, brand; make callous (*a seared conscience*); (arch.) blast, wither; **~'ing-iron** (for cauterizing). [OE *sēar* a., *sēarian* v., f. Gmc **sauraz*, **saurōjan*]

sear². See SERE¹.

search (sêr-) *v.* & *n.* **1.** *v.t.* Look or feel or go over (person or his face or pockets, place, receptacle, book) for what may be found or to find something of which presence is suspected, probe (lit. or fig.; *search a wound*, one's *conscience*); ~ **me!** *int.* (colloq., implying that the speaker does not know the answer to some inquiry, what to do, etc.). **2.** Cover (area) with gun-fire. **3.** ~ **out,** (arch.) ~, look for, seek out. **4.** *v.i.* Make search or investigation (*for*, or abs.); (in *part.*, of examination etc.) thorough, leaving no loopholes, whence **~'ing**LY² *adv.* **5.** Hence ~'ER¹ (1, 2) *n.* **6.** *n.* Act of searching, investigation, quest, (*after* or *for*); **in ~ of,** trying to find; **right of ~,** belligerent's right to stop neutral vessel and search it for contraband. **7. ~'light,** (1) outdoor electric lamp with concentrated powerful beam that can be turned in any direction for use during darkness esp. for discovering hostile aircraft, enemy movements, etc., (2) light from this (lit. or fig.; cf. LIME¹-*light*); **~-party,** persons going out to look for lost or concealed person or thing; **~-warrant** (granted by Justice of the Peace etc. to enter premises of person suspected of concealing stolen property etc.). **8.** Hence ~'LESS *a.*, (poet.) inscrutable. [ME, f. AF *sercher*, OF *cerchier* f. LL *circare* go round (as CIRCUS)]

sear'ching (sẽr'-) *n.* In vbl senses; **~s of heart,** misgivings caused by guilt or otherwise. [f. prec. + -ING¹]

sea'son (-z-) *n.* & *v.* **1.** *n.* Proper time, favourable opportunity, time at which something is plentiful or in vogue or active; time of year when plant flourishes, or animal breeds or is hunted ||CLOSE¹, ||OPEN¹, *season*); time of year regularly devoted to an activity (*cricket season*) or to social activities generally (*London in the season*); time of year when a place is most frequented (HIGH, LOW¹, *season*); **compliments of the ~** (esp. w. ref. to Christmas); **in ~,** (of foodstuff) available in good condition and plentifully, (of animal) on heat, (of advice etc.) given when likely to be taken or needed (*a word in season*); **in and out of ~,** at all times indiscriminately. **2.** Period of indefinite or various length (*may endure for a season*); ~**(-ticket)** (issued at fixed charge for any number of journeys taken, performances attended, etc., within a year, six months, or other period). **3.** Division of the year with distinguishable characteristics of temperature, rainfall, vegetation, etc. (**the four ~s,** spring, summer, autumn, winter); **dry, rainy, ~,** two seasons recognized in the tropics instead of the four of temperate countries. **4.** Hence ~AL, ~LESS, *adjs.* **5.** *v.t.* Bring into efficient or sound condition by habituation, acclimatization, exposure, special preparation, use, or lapse of time, inure, mature, (*seasoned soldiers, timber*). **6.** Make palatable or piquant by introduction of salt, condiments, wit, jests, etc., give zest to, flavour, (*highly seasoned dishes*; *conversation seasoned with humour*), whence ~ER¹ (2), ~ING¹ (4), *ns.*; temper, moderate, (*let mercy season justice*). **7.** *v.i.* Become fit for use by being seasoned. [ME f. OF (*saisonner* f.) *seson* f. L *satio -onis* (*serere sat-* sow; see -ION) in Rom. sense seed-time]

sea'sonab|le (-z-) *a.* Suitable to, of the kind usual at, the season (esp. of weather, frost etc. in winter); opportune, meeting the needs of the occasion, (*seasonable aid, caution*, etc.; *the seasonable arrival of*); hence ~**le**NESS (-beln-) *n.*, ~LY² *adv.* [ME, f. prec. + -ABLE]

seat *n.*, & *v.t.* **1.** *n.* Thing used, esp. one made, for sitting on, chair, throne, stool, bench, bicycle-saddle, or other sitting-accommodation; place for one person in theatre, vehicle, etc.; occupation of a seat (*took his seat on the throne, a rock*); **take a ~,** sit down; **~-belt,** safety belt for seated person in vehicle or aircraft; ***~-mate,** person occupying seat paired with one's own in vehicle etc.; **~-mile,** distance of one mile travelled by one passenger; hence ~'ING¹ (6) *n.*, -~'ER¹ *n.*, motor car, aeroplane, etc., with seats for specified number. **2.** Part of chair etc. on which sitter's weight directly rests, part of machine that supports another part (**~ of valve,** surface etc. on which it slides or works). **3.** Buttocks, part of trousers etc. covering them; *drive* etc. **by the ~ of** one's **pants,** by instinct rather than rule. **4.** Site or location, temporary or permanent scene, abiding-place, *of* (*the liver is the seat of the disease*; *the disease has its seat in the liver*; *the seat of war is mountainous*; *an ancient seat of learning*); **~-earth,** stratum underlying coal-seam. **5.** Country mansion esp. with park or large grounds (*has a seat in Norfolk*; *the country seats of England*). **6.** Right to sitting-accommodation or to sit as member of board or esp. House of Commons (**lose** one's **~,** fail to secure re-election to Parliament); authority or dignity symbolized by sitting in particular chair or throne. **7.** Manner of sitting on horse etc. (*has a good, firm, graceful*, etc., *seat*). **8.** Hence ~'LESS *a.* **9.** *v.t.* Make sit, place or establish in seat, place one*self* in sitting posture, (in *p.p.*) sitting, (*took up the child and seated him on the bookcase*; *seated himself in state*; *found him seated on an inverted bucket*); **be ~ed,** sit down. **10.** Fit or provide (church, room, etc.) with seats; (of room etc.) have seats for (specified number). **11.** Mend seat of (chair, trousers). **12.** Establish in position, fix in particular place; put (machinery) on its supports; DEEP³-*seated*. [ME, f. ON *sæti* = OE *gesete*, MDu. *gesæte*, OHG *gasāzi* f. Gmc **gasǣtjam* (**sæt-*, **set-* SIT)]

S.E.A.T.O. (sē'tō) *abbr.* South-East Asia Treaty Organization.

sėbā'ceous (-sh*u*s) *a.* Of tallow or fat, fatty; ~ **gland, follicle, duct,** (secreting or conveying oily matter to lubricate skin and hair). [f. L *sebaceus* (*sebum* tallow); see -ACEOUS]

sėbě'sten *n.* (Plumlike fruit of) an E. Ind. tree (*Cordia myxa*). [ME f. med. L, f. Arab. *sabastān* f. Pers. *sapistān*]

sěborrhoe'|a, *sěborrhē'|a, (-rē'*a*) *n.* (Path.) Excessive discharge from sebaceous glands; hence ~IC *a.* [f. foll. after *gonorrhoea* etc.]

sē'bum *n.* Secretion of sebaceous glands. [mod. L, f. L *sebum* grease]

sec (sěk) *a.* (Of wine) dry. [F, f. L *siccus*]

***S.E.C.** *abbr.* Securities & Exchange Commission.

Sec. *abbr.* Secretary.

sec *abbr.* secant.

sec. *abbr.* second(s); secondary.

sē'cant *a.* & *n.* (Math.) **1.** *a.* Cutting (*secant line*). **2.** *n.* Secant line, esp. radius of circle produced through one end of arc to meet tangent to other end; ratio of this to radius; ~ **of angle,** ratio of greater to less of its containing lines as bounded by a perpendicular to either. [f. F *sécant(e)* f. L *secare* cut; see -ANT]

||**sē'cateurs** (-ẽrz) *n.* Pair of pruning clippers used with one hand. [f. F *sécateur* cutter, irreg. f. L *secare* cut]

sě'cco *n.* (*pl.* ~s). Painting on dry plaster with pigments suspended in water. [It., = dry, f. L *siccus*]

sėcē'd|e *v.i.* Withdraw formally from membership of some body, esp. a Church or federation of States; hence ~ER¹ *n.* [f. L SE(*cedere cess-* go)]

sėcě'ssion (-sh*o*n) *n.* Act of seceding (**War of S~,** American civil war of 1861–5, caused by secession of eleven Southern States); hence ~AL *a.*, ~ISM (3), ~IST (2), *ns.* [f. F *sécession* or f. L *secessio* (as prec.; see -ION)]

sėclū'de (-ōō'd) *v.t.* Keep (person, place, esp.

one*self*) retired or away from company, screen from view, (*seclude* one*self from society*; *a secluded spot, life*, etc.). [ME, f. L SE(*cludere clus-* = *claudere* shut)]

sēclu'sion (-ōō'zhon) *n.* **1.** Secluding or being secluded; retirement, privacy; hence ~IST (2) *n.* **2.** Secluded place. [f. med. L *seclusio* (as prec.; see -ION)]

sēclu'sĭve (-lōō'-) *a.* Serving or tending to seclude (oneself). [f. SECLUDE after *inclusive* etc.]

sĕ'cond *a., n.,* & *v.t.* **1.** *a.* Next after first (*the second man*; *the second man you meet*; *was the second to come*; *the world's second largest city*); *second* BASE[1] 9, -CHOP[5]; ~ **class,** set of persons or things ranking after others, next-to-best accommodation in train, ship, etc., mail delivered less quickly than first class, (place in) next to highest division in examination-list, and cf. sense 4; **come in** ~, be next to winner in race; ~ **day,** Monday; *second* FLOOR, FORM[1] 6; ~ **gear,** next-to-lowest gear in motor vehicle or bicycle; **second* GRADE 1; ~ **master** or **mistress,** deputy to head teacher; ~ **to none,** surpassed by no other; *second* PERSON 5, 6; **in the** ~ **place,** secondly; *second* READING. **2.** Other besides one or the first (*a second man now arrived*), additional, supplementary; ~ **advent** or **coming,** return of Christ, esp. as preliminary to his expected personal reign on earth; ~ **ballot,** electoral method by which, if winner on first ballot has not polled more than half the votes cast, a second ballot is taken in which only he and the next candidate are eligible; ~ **chamber,** upper house in bicameral parliament; ~ **coming,** = *second advent*; ~ **home,** subsidiary place of residence; *second* HONEYMOON; *second* LESSON; ~ **name,** surname; ~ **nature,** acquired tendency that has become instinctive (*habit is second nature*; *self-sacrifice is now second nature with him*); *second* SELF; *second* SIGHT[1], STRING; ~ **teeth,** those of adults (cf. MILK[1]-*teeth*); ~ **thoughts,** opinion or resolution formed on reconsideration; *second* WIND[1]. **3.** Of secondary kind, subordinate, derived, unoriginal, imitative, metaphorical; such as to be comparable to (*Daniel, Solomon*, etc.); (Mus., of instrument or voice) performing next to highest part or part subordinate to principal one; ~ **cause** (that is itself caused); *second* CHILDHOOD, COUSIN, FIDDLE; **at** ~ **hand,** by hearsay, not actual observation etc.; *second* INTENTION; ~ **lieutenant,** army officer below (*first) lieutenant; ~ **officer,** assistant mate on merchant ship; **the** ~ **sex,** women. **4.** ~**-best,** (what is) of second quality (*come off* ~*-best*, get the worst of it); ~**-class,** (*a.*) of second or of inferior class or position or quality, (of passenger, ticket) using, entitling to use of, second-class railway-carriage etc., (*adv.*; -ah's) by the second class (*travels second-class*); ~**-generation,** having parents belonging to first GENERATION; *~**-guess,** know only by hindsight; ~**-hand,** (*a.*) (of clothes, books, furniture, etc.) bought after use by a previous owner, (of shop etc.) where such goods can be bought, (of information etc.) taken on another's authority and not got by original observation or research, (*adv.*) at second hand; ~**-rate,** not of superior quality, rated in second class; *~**-storey man,** cat burglar. **5.** *n.* Second person etc. in race etc. (**a good** ~, close to winner); second day of month; second form; second gear; (person having) place in second class in examination (**upper, lower,** ~, in upper, lower, division of second class). **6.** Another person or thing besides the previously mentioned or principal, whether regarded as next, inferior, or equal. **7.** (Mus.) Interval of which the span involves two alphabetical notes, harmonic combination of notes thus separated. **8.** (in *pl.*) Goods of second quality, esp. coarse flour or bread made from it; second helping of food; second course of meal. **9.** Supporter chosen by principal in duel or boxing-match. **10.** Sixtieth part of a minute of time or angular measurement [see etym.]; (colloq.) short time (*wait a second*). **11.** ~ **in command,** officer next in rank to commanding or chief officer; ~**(s) hand,** extra hand in some watches and clocks recording seconds; ~**-mark,** mark (″) used with figures denoting seconds in statements of angular measurement or time (*1° 6′ 40″*; *1h. 35′ 15″*), or denoting linear inches. **12.** *v.t.* Supplement, support, back up, (*second words with deeds*; *will you second me if I ask him?*). **13.** (Of member of society or debating body) give the necessary formal support to (nomination, motion, etc., or its proposer) by rising with or without speech or otherwise acting to show that move is not isolated; hence ~ER[1] *n.* **14.** (*pr.* sĭkŏ'nd). ‖(Mil.) put (officer) into temporary retirement with a view to staff or other extra-regimental appointment; ‖transfer (official) temporarily to another department; hence ~MENT *n.* [a. ME f. OF, f. L *secundus* (*sequi* follow); n. (time etc.) ME f. OF *seconde* f. med. L *secunda* (*minuta*) secondary (minute), i.e. minute of a minute; v. f. F *seconder* f. L *secundare*]

sĕ'condarȳ *a.* & *n.* **1.** *a.* Next below, coming in place or time after, depending on or derived from, of less importance or originality than, what is primary; of the second or inferior rank or class etc. (*to*), supplementary, indirectly caused; (Geol., *S*~) mesozoic. **2.** ~ **battery, cell,** storage cell; ~ **coil** (from which current is taken in transformer); *secondary* COLOUR[1]; ~ **education** (for those who have received primary education but not yet proceeded to university or occupation); ~ **feather** (growing from second joint of bird's wing); ~ **planet,** planet's satellite; ~ **school** (where secondary education is given) ~ **sexual characteristics** (distinctive of one sex but not directly related to reproduction). **3.** Hence **sĕ'condarĭ**LY[2] *adv.* **4.** *n.* Deputy or delegate; ‖minor cathedral dignitary; secondary planet, period, coil, feather, etc. [ME, f. L *secundarius* (as prec.; see -ARY[1])]

seco'nde (-aw'nd) *n.* Second of eight parrying positions in fencing. [F, fem. of *second* SECOND]

sĕ'condlȳ *adv.* In the second place, as second item, (in enumerating topics, arguments, etc.). [ME, f. SECOND + -LY[2]]

second|o (sĭkŏ'ndō) *n.* (*pl.* ~*i pr.* -ē). (Mus.) Second or lower part in duet etc. [It.]

sē'crēcȳ *n.* Keeping of, ability to keep or habit of keeping, secrets (*he promised secrecy*; *can rely on his secrecy*; *done with great secrecy*); tendency to concealment, secretiveness; unrevealed state, being kept secret, (*there can be no secrecy about it*; **in** ~, secretly). [ME, f. *secretie* (obs. *secre* or SECRET adjs.; see -TY[1], -Y[1])]

sē'crĕt *a.* & *n.* **1.** *a.* (To be) kept private, not (to be) made known or exposed to view, (*secret treaty, understanding, errand, door, dovetail, passage, sin, process, influence*); ~ **ballot** (in which voters' choices are not made public); ~ **parts,** (arch.) genitals; ~ **service** (done to Government by securing information etc. without public disclosure); hence ~LY[2] *adv.* **2.** Given to or having faculty of secrecy; ~ **agent,** spy; ~ **ink,** invisible ink; ~ **police** (operating in secret esp. for political purposes); **S**~ **Service,** Government intelligence department; ~ **society** (whose members are sworn to secrecy about it). **3.** Secretive, close, reticent; (of place etc.) secluded, retired. **4.** *n.* Thing (to be) kept secret (**keep a** ~ or **the** ~, not reveal it); thing known only to a limited number (**in the ~,** among the number of those allowed to know it; **open ~,** thing secret only to those who do not trouble to learn it); mystery, thing of which explanation is sought in vain, (*the secrets of nature*); true but not generally understood method for attainment *of* (*the secret of health, success, happiness, salvation, is temperance, to try again,* etc.); (R.C. Ch.) celebrant's private prayer in Mass; **in ~,** secretly. [ME f. OF, f. L *secretus* f. SE(*cernere cret-* sift) separate, set apart]

sĕcrĕtair'e *n.* Escritoire. [F, as SECRETARY]

sĕcretār'ĭat *n.* Office of secretary; members of a government administrative office collectively; (premises of) administrative office or department headed by Secretary(-General). [f. F *secrétariat* f. med. L *secretariatus* (as foll.; see -ATE¹)]

sĕ'cretarў *n.* **1.** (**Private**) **~,** person employed by another to assist him in correspondence, literary work, getting information, and other confidential matters. **2.** Official appointed by society or company or corporation to conduct its correspondence, keep its records, and deal in the first instance with its business; HONORARY *secretary.* **3.** Principal assistant of government minister or ambassador etc.; **S~-General,** principal administrator of an organization; **S~ of State,** ||head of a major government department, * = FOREIGN Secretary, *head of general records department in a state; ||**Parliamentary Private S~,** ||**Parliamentary (Under-)S~,** members of parliament assisting head of government department; ||**Permanent (Under-)S~,** ||**Assistant (Under-)S~,** senior civil servants in government department. **4.** Escritoire. **5.** (Print.) Type-fount imitating secretary-hand. **6. ~-bird,** long-legged African raptorial bird, with crest likened to quill-pens stuck over writer's ear; **~-hand,** 15th–17th-c. style of handwriting esp. in legal documents. **7.** Hence **sĕcretār'**IAL *a.*, **~**SHIP (1, 2) *n.* [ME, f. LL *secretarius* (as SECRET; see -ARY¹)]

sėcrē't|e *v.t.* **1.** Put (object, person, one*self*) into place of concealment. **2.** (Physiol., of gland or organ or the person etc. of which it is part) produce by secretion, whence **~**OR *n.*, **~**ORY *a.* [sense 1 f. obs. *secret* v. f. SECRET; sense 2 f. as SECRET or by back form. f. foll.]

sėcrē'tion *n.* **1.** Act of concealing (*the secretion of stolen goods*). **2.** (Physiol.) Process by which substances are separated in gland etc. from blood or sap for function in the organism or for excretion; substance produced by such process, e.g. saliva, urine, resin. [f. F *sécrétion* or f. L *secretio* separation (as SECRET; see -ION)]

sē'crėtĭve (*or* sĭkrē'-) *a.* Inclined to make secrets, intentionally uncommunicative, needlessly reserved; hence or cogn. **~**LY² (-vlĭ) *adv.*, **~**NESS (-vn-) *n.* [back form. f. *secretiveness* after F *secrétivité* (as SECRET; see -IVE)]

sĕct *n.* Body of persons agreed upon religious doctrines usu. different from those of an established or orthodox Church from which they have separated and usu. having distinctive common worship; nonconformist or other Church as described by opponents; party or faction in a religious body; religious denomination; followers of a particular philosopher or philosophy or school of thought in politics etc. [ME, f. OF *secte* or f. L *secta* f. stem of *sequi secut-* follow]

sect. *abbr.* section.

sĕctār'ĭan *a.* & *n.* (Person) adhering to a sect, esp. in bigoted fashion; hence **~**ISM (3) *n.*, **~**IZE (3) *v.t.* [f. foll. + -AN; see -ARIAN]

sĕ'ctarў *n.* Member of a sect, esp. (Hist.) of the Independents, Presbyterians, etc., at time of the English Civil War. [f. med. L *sectarius* adherent (as SECT; see -ARY¹)]

sĕ'ction *n.*, & *v.t.* **1.** *n.* (Surg.) Separation by cutting. **2.** Part cut off from something; one of the parts into which something is divided arbitrarily or may naturally be considered as divided (e.g. length of cane-stem between two rings; *subject falls into five sections*; *last section of the journey*); one part of structure such as boat or wooden house that is made in parts for transportation; minor subdivision of book, statute, etc.; *one square mile of land; area of land, region; (Mil.) subdivision of platoon; part of the community or of a society etc. having separate interests or functions or characteristics; *particular district of a town (*residential section*); *division of sleeping-car; **microscopic ~,** thin slice cut from something for examination with microscope. **3.** Cutting of solid by plane (CONIC *section*); (area of) resulting figure; (CROSS-)**~**, representation of internal structure of something supposed to be cut thus (**vertical, horizontal, longitudinal, oblique,** etc., **~,** according to position chosen for plane). **4.** (Biol.) Group, esp. subgenus. **5. ~(-mark),** sign (§) used as reference mark or (with or without number) to indicate beginning of section of book etc. **6.** *v.t.* Arrange in or divide into sections. [F, or f. L *sectio* (*secare sect-* cut; see -ION)]

sĕ'ctional *a.* **1.** Pertaining to a section, esp. of the community; hence **~**ISM (3) *n.*, **~**IZE (3) *v.t.*, **~**LY² *adv.* **2.** Made in parts for transportation. [f. prec. + -AL]

sĕ'ctor *n.* **1.** (Geom.) Plane figure enclosed between two radii of circle, ellipse, etc., and the arc cut off by them (**~ of sphere,** solid generated by revolution of sector of circle round one radius). **2.** (Mil.) portion of a front controlled by one commander or headquarters; similar portion of any activity (*the private sector of industry*). **3.** Mathematical instrument of two stiffly-hinged flat pieces with lines representing sines, tangents, etc., radiating from centre of joint for use in making diagrams etc. **4.** Hence **~**AL *a.* [LL, = sector f. L = cutter (as prec.; see -OR)]

sĕctōr'ĭal *a.* & *n.* **1.** *a.* Of or like sector(s). **2.** (Of carnivore's premolar teeth) adapted for cutting. **3.** *n.* Sectorial tooth. [sense 1 f. prec. + -IAL; sense 2 f. mod. L *sectorius* (as prec.) + -AL]

sĕ'cūlar *a.* & *n.* **1.** *a.* Occurring once in or lasting for an age or a century; **~ games,** ancient-Roman festival held at long intervals. **2.** Lasting or going on for ages, occurring over an indefinitely long time (opp. *periodical, short-term*); **~ change** (going on slowly but persistently); **~ fame** (enduring); *secular* VARIATION (Astron.). **3.** Concerned with the affairs of this world, worldly, not sacred, not monastic, not ecclesiastical, temporal, profane, lay, (*secular affairs, education, music*); **the ~ arm,** (Hist.) civil jurisdiction to which criminal was transferred by ecclesiastical courts for severer punishment; **~ clergy,** parish priests etc. (opp. *regular clergy*). **4.** Sceptical of religious truth or opposed to religious education etc.; hence **~**ISM (3) *n.*, **~**IST (2) *n.*, **~**IZE (3) *v.t.* **5.** Hence **sĕcūlă'**RITY *n.*, **~**LY² *adv.* **6.** *n.* Secular priest. [ME (in senses 3 & 4 f. OF *seculer*) f. L *saecularis* (*saeculum* generation, age)]

sėcŭ'nd *a.* (Bot. & Zool.) Arranged on one side only (as flowers in lily-of-the-valley); hence **~**LY² *adv.* [f. L (as SECOND)]

sėcūr'e *a.*, & *v.t.* **1.** *a.* Untroubled by danger or apprehension (*a quiet secure existence*; *dwell secure*); (arch.) confident or unsuspecting (*the secure hope of salvation*). **2.** Safe against attack, impregnable;

reliable, certain not to fail or give way, (*a secure foundation, fastening, foothold, grasp*); (usu. *pred.*) in safe keeping, firmly fastened, (*have got him secure*; *are you sure it is secure?*). **3.** Having sure prospect *of*, safe *against* or *from*, (*secure of victory, against assault, from interruption*). **4.** Hence ~LY[2] (-ūr′lĭ) *adv.* **5.** *v.t.* Fortify (town, harbour, etc., usu. *with* wall etc.); confine, enclose, fasten, or close, securely (*secure prisoner, valuables, buckle, window*); compress (blood-vessel) to prevent bleeding; ~ **arms,** (Mil.) hold rifle's muzzle down with lock in armpit to guard from rain. **6.** Guarantee, make safe against loss, (*loan secured on landed property* etc.; *how can I secure myself against the consequences?*). **7.** Succeed in getting, obtain, (esp. something coveted or competed for; *have secured front seats, a first-class cook, the prize, my ends*). **8.** Hence **sėcūr′**ABLE *a.*, ~MENT (-ūr′m-) *n.* [f. L SE(*curus* f. *cura* care)]

sėcūr′ĭtў *n.* In adj. senses; confidence; thing that guards or guarantees (**in** ~ **for,** as guarantee for); (organization for ensuring) safety of State, company, etc., against espionage, theft, or other danger (~ **risk,** person of doubtful loyalty); thing deposited or pledged as guarantee of fulfilment of undertaking or payment of loan, to be forfeited in case of failure; document as evidence of loan, certificate of stock, bond, etc.; **S~ Council,** permanent body of United Nations seeking to maintain peace and security. [ME, f. OF *securité* or f. L *securitas* (as prec.; see -ITY)]

sėdă′n *n.* **1.** ~**(-chair)**, 17th–18th-c. vehicle seating one and carried by two chairmen with poles. **2.** *Enclosed motor car for four or more persons including driver. [perh. f. It. dial., ult. f. L *sella* saddle (*sedēre* sit)]

sėdā′te[1] *a.* (Of person or his manner, look, speech, or writing) tranquil, equable, composed, settled, not impulsive or lively or agitated; hence ~LY[2] (-tlĭ) *adv.*, ~NESS (-tn-) *n.* [f. L *sedatus* p.p. of *sedare* settle (*sedēre* sit); see -ATE[2]]

sėdā′te[2] *v.t.* (Med.) Put under sedation. [back form f. foll.]

sėdā′tion *n.* (Med.) Calming esp. by use of sedative drug. [f. F *sédation* or f. L *sedatio* (as SEDATE[1]; see -ATION)]

sĕ′datĭve *a.* & *n.* (Drug, influence, etc.) tending to calm or soothe. [ME, f. OF *sedatif* or f. med. L *sedativus* (as SEDATE[1]; see -IVE)]

sĕ′dentar|ў *a.* Sitting (*sedentary posture, statue*); (of person) inclined by nature or driven by occupation to, (of occupation) involving, (of life etc.) characterized by, much sitting and little physical exercise, whence ~ĭLY[2] *adv.*, ~ĭNESS *n.*; (Zool. etc.) not migratory or free-swimming etc., (of spider) lying in wait till prey is in web. [f. F *sédentaire* or f. L *sedentarius* (*sedēre* sit; see -ENT, -ARY[1])]

Se′der (sā′-) *n.* Ritual for the first night or first two nights of the Passover. [f. Heb. *sēder* order]

sėdēr′unt *n.* (Sc.) Sitting of ecclesiastical assembly or other body, or of a company over the wine or in talk (*had a long sederunt*). [L, = (the following persons) sat (*sedēre* sit)]

sĕdge *n.* Grasslike plant of genus *Carex* with jointless stems growing in marshes or by waterside; bed of such plants; ~**-warbler, -wren,** small warbler breeding among sedge; hence **sĕ′dg**Y[2] *a.* [OE *secg* f. Gmc **sagjaz* (**sag-*; cf. SAW[1])]

sėdī′l|ė *n.* (*pl.* ~**ia** *pr.* -ĭ′lĭa). (usu. in *pl.*) One of usu. three stone seats for priests in S. wall of chancel, often canopied and otherwise decorated. [L, = seat (*sedēre* sit)]

sĕ′dĭment *n.* Matter that settles to bottom of liquid; lees, dregs; (Geol.) water-borne or wind-borne matter that settles and may become consolidated into rock; hence ~ARY[1] (-ĕ′n-) *a.*, ~A′TION *n.* [f. F *sédiment* or f. L *sedimentum* (as prec.; see -MENT)]

sėdĭ′ti|on *n.* Agitation against the authority of a State; conduct or speech tending to rebellion or breach of public order; so ~OUS (-shus) *a.* [ME f. OF, or f. L *seditio* (*sed-* = SE-, *ire it-* go; see -ION)]

sėdū′c|e *v.t.* Lead astray, tempt into sin or crime, corrupt; persuade (person) into abandonment of principles, esp. chastity or allegiance; persuade by temptingness or attractiveness; hence ~ER[1] *n.*, ~IBLE *a.* [f. L SE(*ducere duct-* lead)]

sėdŭ′ction *n.* Seducing or being seduced; thing that tends to seduce; tempting or attractive quality *of.* [f. F *séduction* or f. L *seductio* (as prec.; see -ION)]

sėdŭ′ctĭve *a.* Alluring, enticing; hence ~LY[2] (-vlĭ) *adv.*, ~NESS (-vn-) *n.* [f. prec. after *inductive* etc.]

sėdŭ′ctrėss *n.* Female seducer. [f. obs. *seductor* male seducer (as SEDUCE; see -OR) + -ESS[1]]

sĕ′dūlous *a.* Diligent, persevering, assiduous, (*with sedulous care*); (of action etc.) deliberately and consciously continued, painstaking, (*sedulous flattery, attentions*); **play the** ~ **ape,** acquire literary style by imitation; hence or cogn. ~LY[2] *adv.*, **sėdū′l**ITY, ~NESS, *ns.* [f. L *sedulus* zealous + -OUS]

sē′dum *n.* Fleshy-leaved plant of genus *Sedum*, with pink, white, or yellow flowers, e.g. stonecrop. [L, = houseleek]

see[1] *v.* (**saw**; **seen**). **1.** *v.i.* Have or exercise the power of discerning objects with the eyes (*sees best at night*; *cannot see till the ninth day*); ~**′ing** *n.*, (Astron.) quality of observed images as determined by atmospheric conditions; ~**ing eye,** dog trained to guide blind person; ~**ing is believing,** one's own observation is the best evidence; *see* DOUBLE[1] 5; ~ **over,** tour and examine (house etc.); ~ **red,** see things as blood-coloured, be filled with fury; ~ **through,** (fig.) not be deceived by, penetrate, detect nature of; ~**-through** *a.*, (esp. of clothing) transparent; ~ **through a brick wall** etc., have superhuman acuteness. **2.** *v.t.* Descry, discern by sight, observe, look at or over, (*come where we cannot be seen*; *children should be seen and not heard*; *please see whether it is there, where it is*; *was seen to fall* or *falling*; *saw him fall* or *falling*; *cannot see my way*); ~ **the back of,** be rid of (visitor, invader, etc.); ~ **the light (of day)**, be born or (fig.) published; ~ **the light,** (fig.) undergo conversion etc., realize one's errors etc.; ~ **the sights, town,** etc., be SIGHT[1]seer; *see* SOMETHING *of*; ~ **stars,** have dancing lights before eyes from blow on head; ~ **things,** have hallucinations; **things** ~**n** (not imaginary etc.); ~ **visions,** be seer etc.; ~ one's **way (clear) to** do or **to** do*ing*, manage or feel able or entitled to do; **worth** ~**ing,** notable. **3.** Look at for information (usu. in imper.: *see page 15*); watch, be spectator of, (film, game, etc.); meet (or be near) and recognize (person; *saw her in church today*); **see you (later)!, (I'll) be seeing you!,** (colloq.) *au revoir.* **4.** Learn from newspaper etc. (*I see that another speed record was broken yesterday*). **5.** Discern mentally, attain to comprehension of, apprehend, ascertain by search or inquiry or reflection, consider, foresee, (*cannot see a* or *the joke, the point*; *see* REASON[1]; *do you see what I mean?*; *justice is seen to be done*; *can't think what he sees in her*; *must see what can be done*; *do not see the good, fun, advantage*, etc., *of* doing; *do not see how to do it*; *you see what it is to have faith*; *saw myself obliged to resign*; *saw myself having to continue indefinitely*); ~**?,** (colloq.) do you understand what I mean?;

as far as I can ~, to the best of my understanding or belief; **I ~,** I understand your explanation; **you ~,** (1) you understand, (2) you will understand when I explain. **6.** Experience, go through more or less observantly, have presented to one's attention, (*shall never see death*; *have seen five reigns*; *see little of them now*; *never saw such a mess*; *1839 saw him in Mesopotamia*); **we shall ~** (the outcome etc.); **will never ~** *50* etc. **again,** is over that age; **have ~n the day when** (in drawing attention to past state of affairs); **has ~n better** or **its** etc. **best days,** has declined from former prosperity etc.; **~ life,** mix freely with others, gain experience of men and manners esp. by dissipation etc.; *see* SERVICE[1] 2, 4. **7.** Grant interview or be at home to, pay visit to, have meeting with, secure interview with, (*refused to see me*; *can I see you on business?, for lunch?*; *when will you come and see us?*; *must see the lawyer, doctor,* etc.; *can see you for five minutes*); (in gambling, esp. poker) accept (challenge to bet etc.), accept challenge of (person). **8.** Call up picture of, imagine, (*cannot see him agreeing to it*). **9.** Recognize as tolerable, consent willingly to, (*do not see going all that way for nothing*). **10.** Escort, conduct, (*may I see you home?*; *mind you see him off the premises*; *saw him off at Southampton*; *will you see me through* or *through the difficulty?*); be witness of (event etc.) (*see the New Year in*; *has seen his income gradually decrease*); supervise (action etc.) (*stay and see the doors locked*; *saw the book through the press*); contemplate without interfering with (*are you going to see me treated like this?*; **~** person **blowed, damned, further,** etc., (**first**), refuse categorically to do what he asks or trouble about it); **~** person **out,** be present at, or last until, his death; **~** thing **out** or **through,** not abandon it or depart before its completion; **~** person **right,** make sure that he is safe, rewarded, etc. **11.** Take view of, have opinion of, (*I see life, things, it, differently now*; *I see it as being quite possible*; *see* EYE[1] *to eye*; *see* FIT[3] *to*); **as I ~ it,** in my opinion. **12.** *v.t.* & *i.* Make provision, take care, give attention, make sure, (*see that it is done*; *see* (*that*) *you don't catch your foot*; *see to* one's *business*); **~ about, ~ after,** take care of; **~ here!,** = LOOK *here!*; **~ into,** investigate; **~ to it that,** take care that. **13.** *v.i.* Reflect, take time to consider; **let me ~** (appeal for time to think before making answer or giving particulars, or confession that coming statement may need reconsideration); **will ~ about it** (form for declining to act at once). [OE *sēon*, = OS, OHG *sehan*, ON *séa*, Goth. *saihwan* f. Gmc **sehwan* f. IE **seqʷ-*]

see[2] *n.* What is committed to (arch)bishop, (archi-)episcopal unit, (*fill a vacant see*; *several new sees were created*; *the see of Norwich, Canterbury,* etc.; **Holy See, See of Rome,** the papacy or papal court). [ME, f. AF *se(d)* = OF *sie(d)* f. Rom. **sede* f. L *sedes* seat (*sedēre* sit)]

seed *n.* & *v.* **1.** *n.* Flowering plant's unit of reproduction (esp. in form of grain) capable of developing into another such plant, (collect.) seeds in any quantity esp. as collected for sowing, (*its seeds are* or *seed is black*; *is full of seed*; *drops its seeds* or *seed everywhere*; *to be kept for* or *as seed*); **go** or **run to ~,** cease flowering as seed develops, (fig.) become habitually unkempt, ineffective, etc. **2.** Semen, milt. **3.** (Bibl.) Offspring, progeny, descendants; **raise up ~,** beget children; **the ~ of Abraham,** Hebrews. **4.** Germ, prime cause, beginning, *of* (*seeds of doubt, strife, vice*; **sow the ~(s) of,** first give rise to). **5.** (colloq.) Seeded player. **6.** Small seedlike container for application of radium etc. **7. ~-bed,** (fig.) place of development; **~-cake** (containing whole seeds esp. of caraway as flavouring); **~-coat,** outer integument of seed; **~-corn** (kept for seed); **~ crystal** (used to initiate crystallization); **~-eater,** bird (esp. finch) living mainly on seeds; **~-fish** (ready to spawn); **~-leaf, ~-lobe,** cotyledon; **~-lip,** basket for seed in sowing by hand [OE *lēap* basket]; **~ money** (to initiate a project); **~-oysters,** young oysters for planting; **~-pearl** (very small); **~-plot,** = *seed-bed*; **~-potato** (kept for seed); **~'sman** (-z-), dealer in seeds; **~-time,** sowing season; **~-vessel,** pericarp. **8.** Hence **~'**LESS *a.* **9.** *v.i.* Go to seed; produce or let fall seed; sow seeds. **10.** *v.t.* Place seed(s) in; sprinkle (as) with seed; place crystal etc. in (solution etc.) to cause crystallization or condensation (esp. in cloud to produce rain). **11.** Remove seeds from (fruit etc.). **12.** (Sport). Designate stronger among (competitors in knock-out tournament), arrange (order of play) thus, so that they are not matched against one another till later rounds; designate (competitor) thus. [OE *sǣd*, = OS *sād*, OHG *sāt*, ON *sáth*, Goth. *-seths* f. Gmc **sǣdh-* (**sǣ-* SOW[1])]

see'der *n.* In vbl senses; = DRILL[2] 2; apparatus for seeding raisins etc.; ‖spawning fish. [f. prec. + -ER[1]]

see'dlĭng *n.* Plant raised from seed and not from cutting etc.; young tender plant. [f. SEED + -LING[1]]

see'd|ȳ *a.* Full of seed, going to seed; (colloq.) shabby-looking, in worn clothes, out of sorts, feeling ill, whence **~ĭLY**[2] *adv.*; hence **~ĭNESS** *n.* [f. SEED + -Y[2]]

see'ĭng[1] *conj.* **~** (**that**), considering that, inasmuch, as, (*seeing that you do not know it yourself*; *seeing no other course is open to us*). [f. SEE[1] + -ING[2]]

see'ĭng[2]. See SEE[1] 1.

seek *v.* (**sought** *pr.* sawt). **1.** *v.t.* Make search or inquiry for, try or be anxious to find or get, ask (thing *of* person), aim at, pursue as object, endeavour *to* do, make for or resort to (place, person, for advice, health, etc.), (*seeks a situation as cook, wealth, scope for his energies,* etc.; *sought help from him*; *seeks my aid*; *sought his bed, a fortune-teller, the shore*); **~ dead** (order to retriever to find killed game); **~ out,** single out for pursuit etc. (esp. make special efforts to secure society of), search for and find. **2.** *v.i.* Make search or inquiry (*after* or *for*); **sought-after,** much in demand, generally desired or courted. **3.** (arch.) Resort *to* (person, place). **4. Is** etc. **to ~** or **much to ~,** is deficient, lacking, or not yet found (*an efficient leader is yet to seek*). **5.** Hence (-)**~'**ER[1] *n.* [OE *sēcan*, = OS *sōkian*, OHG *suohhan*, ON *sœkja*, Goth. *sōkjan* f. Gmc **sōk-*]

seel *v.t.* (arch.) Close (person's eyes). [f. obs. *sile* f. F *ciller, siller* or f. med. L *ciliare* f. L *cilium* eyelid]

seem *v.i.* **1.** Have the air or appearance or sensation of being, appear or be apparently perceived or ascertained *to* do or have done, (*be what you seem to be* or *seem*; *the man who seemed* (*to be*) *the ringleader*; *seems to be tired, a hopeless absurdity*; *seems to be a good fellow*; *seems certain to win*; *not the angel she seems to be*; *I seem* (*to be*) *deaf today*; *I seem to see him still*; *seems to have died at 35*); **can't ~ to,** (colloq.) seem(s) unable to; **do not ~ to,** (colloq.) somehow do not (*I do not seem to like him, to fancy it*); **~ good to,** be adopted as best course of action by; **what ~eth him good,** (arch.) what he chooses. **2.** (With anticipatory *it* and following *that*-clause, or parenth. with *it* only, often with implication of anger or remonstrance) appear to be true or the fact (*it seems to me that it will rain, that such talk is absurd,* *that we had better make up our minds to do it; so we are to get nothing, it seems; it seems you were lying*); **it would** or (arch.) **should** ~ (in guarded or ironical statement); MESEEMS. [ME, f. ON *sœma* honour (*sœmr* fitting)]

see'mĭng[1] *a.* Ostensible, apparent only, apparent but perhaps not real, apparent and perhaps real, (*the seeming and the real*; *a seeming friend*; *with seeming sincerity*); **~-virtuous** etc. (usu. w. suggestion of falsity); hence ~LY[2] *adv.* [ME, f. prec. + -ING[2]]

see'mĭng[2] *n.* Appearance, aspect (*to* OUTWARD *seeming*); deceptive appearance. [ME, f. SEEM + -ING[1]]

see'ml|ȳ *a.* & *adv.* **1.** *a.* Decent, decorous, becoming; hence ~ĬNESS *n.* **2.** *adv.* (arch.) Decorously. [ME, f. ON *sœmiligr* (as SEEM, -LY[1])]

seen. See SEE[1].

seep *v.i.* Ooze out, percolate slowly, (lit. or fig.); hence ~'AGE (3) *n.* [perh. dial. form of OE *sipian* to soak]

seer[1] *n.* In vbl senses; (esp.) prophet, person who sees visions, person of preternatural insight esp. as regards the future. [ME, f. SEE[1] + -ER[1]]

seer[2] *n.* Indian (varying) measure of weight (about one kilogram) or liquid measure (about one litre). [f. Hindi *ser*]

seer[3], **seir** (sēr), *n.* Large Indian scombroid fish of genus *Cybium*. [corruption of Port. *serra* SAW[1]]

seer'sŭcker *n.* Striped material of linen, cotton, etc., with puckered surface. [f. Pers. *šir o šakar*, lit. 'milk and sugar']

see-saw *a.*, *adv.*, *n.*, & *v.i.* **1.** *a.* & *adv.* With backward-and-forward or up-and-down motion as of a saw (*see-saw motion*; **go** ~, vacillate or alternate). **2.** *n.* Game in which persons sit at each end of long board balanced on central support and move up and down alternately; board thus balanced; (fig.) contest in which the advantage repeatedly changes from one side to the other. **3.** *v.i.* Play at see-saw; move up and down as in see-saw; vacillate in policy etc. [redupl. of SAW[1]]

seethe (-dh) *v.* (~**d**; arch. *past* **sod** & *p.p.* SODDEN). **1.** *v.t.* & *i.* (arch.) Cook by boiling. **2.** *v.i.* (fig.) Boil, bubble over, be agitated, (*the seething waters*; *India was seething with discontent*; *I was seething inwardly*; *madness, enthusiasm, seething in his brain*). [OE *sēothan*, = OS **siothan*, OHG *siodan*, ON *sjótha* f. Gmc **seuth-*]

sĕ'gment *n.*, & *v.* (*or* -mĕ'-). **1.** *n.* Part cut off or separable or marked off as though separable from the other parts of something (e.g. one ring of worm, one division of limb or skull, one wedge of orange-pulp); smallest distinct part of a spoken utterance. **2.** (Geom.) Part cut off by line or plane from any figure (~ **of circle,** part enclosed between arc and chord; ~ **of sphere,** part cut off by any plane not passing through centre); ~ **of line,** part included between two points. **3.** **~-gear, -rack, -wheel,** (with cogs occupying arc of circle only). **4.** Hence ~AL (-ĕ'n-), ~ARY[1], *adjs.* **5.** *v.i.* & *t.* Divide into segments. **6.** *v.i.* (Biol., of cell) undergo cleavage or divide into many cells. **7.** Hence ~A'TION *n.* [f. L *segmentum* (*secare* cut; see -MENT)]

sē'gō *n.* (*pl.* ~**s**). ~ (**lily**), N. Amer. plant (*Calochortus nuttallii*) with green and white campanulate flowers. [Paiute]

sĕ'grĕg|āte[1] *v.* **1.** *v.t.* Put apart from the rest, isolate; enforce racial segregation on (persons) or in (community etc.). **2.** *v.i.* Separate from a mass and collect together; (Biol., of genes) separate into dominant and recessive groups; so ~ATIVE *a.* [f. L SE(*gregare* f. *grex gregis* flock) + -ATE[3]]

sĕ'grĕgate[2] *a.* **1.** (arch.) Set apart, separate. **2.** (Zool.) Simple or solitary, not compound. [f. L *segregatus* p.p. (as prec.); see -ATE[2]]

sĕgrĕgā'tion *n.* Segregating or being segregated; enforced separation of different racial groups in a community etc., whence ~IST (2) *n.* [f. LL *segregatio* (as SEGREGATE[1]; see -ATION)]

sĕguidĭ'lla (-gĭdĭ'lya) *n.* Spanish dance in triple time; music for it. [Sp. (*seguida* following f. *seguir* follow)]

sei (sā) *n.* Small rorqual (*Balaenoptera borealis*). [f. Norw. *sejhval* sei whale]

seicĕ'nt|ō (sāchĕ'-) *n.* Italian style of art of the 17th c.; hence ~(ō)IST (2, 3) *n.* [It., = 600, used w. ref. to years 16—]

seiche (sāsh) *n.* Oscillation of lake etc. waters due usu. to changes in barometric pressure. [Swiss F]

Sei'dlĭtz (sĕ'dlĭts) *n.* ~ **powder,** *~ **powders,** aperient medicine of two powders mixed separately with water and then poured together to effervesce. [named w. ref. to mineral water of *Seidlitz* in Bohemia]

seigneur' (sānyẽr'), **sei'gnior** (sā'nyer), *n.* Feudal lord, lord of manor, whence **seigneur'**IAL (sānyẽr'-), **seigniôr'**IAL (sānyôr'-), *adjs.*; **grand seigneur** (grahṅ-), person of high rank or whose demeanour etc. correspond to popular ideal of great nobleman. [ME, f. OF *seigneur*, *seignor* f. L SENIOR *-oris*]

sei'gn(i)orage (sā'nyerĭj) *n.* **1.** (Hist.) Something claimed by sovereign or feudal superior as prerogative. **2.** Crown's right to percentage on bullion brought to mint for coining; profit made by issue of coins rated above intrinsic value. [ME, f. OF *seignorage*, *seigneurage* (as prec.; see -AGE)]

sei'gniorȳ (sā'nyerĭ) *n.* Lordship, sovereign authority; seigneur's domain. [ME, f. OF *seignorie* (as SEIGNEUR; see -Y[1])]

seine (sān) *n.* & *v.* **1.** *n.* ~(**-net**), fishing-net for encircling fish, with floats at top and weights at bottom edge, and usu. hauled ashore. **2.** *v.i.* & *t.* Fish or catch with seine; hence **sei'n**ER[1] (sā'-) *n.* [ME, f. OF *saïne*, & f. OE *segne*, OS, OHG *segina* f. WG **sagina*, f. L f. Gk *sagēnē*]

seir. See SEER[3].

seise. See SEIZE.

sei'sĭn (sē'z-) *n.* (Law). Possession of land by freehold; act of taking such possession; what is so held. [ME, f. AF *sesine*, OF *seisine*, *saisine* (as SEIZE; see -INE[4])]

sei'sm|ĭc (sī'z-) *a.* Of earthquake(s); hence or cogn. ~(IC)AL *adjs.*, ~ICALLY *adv.* [f. Gk *seismos* earthquake (*seiō* shake) + -IC]

sei'smo- (sī'z-) *comb. form.* Earthquake, as: ~**gram,** record given by ~**graph** or ~**meter** (-ŏ'm-) or ~**scope,** instruments showing force, direction, etc., of earthquake; so ~GRAPHY, ~GRAPHER, (-ŏ'g-) *ns.*, ~GRA'PHIC(AL) *adjs.*, ~METRY (-ŏ'm-) *n.*, ~ME'TRIC(AL), ~SCO'PIC, *adjs.*, ~LOGY, ~LOGIST, (-ŏ'l-) *ns.*, ~LO'GICAL *a.* [f. as prec. + -O-]

seize (sēz) *v.* **1.** *v.t.* (Law; *or* **seise** *pr.* same). Put in possession of (esp. in *p.p.*; ~**d** or **seised of,** having in legal possession, (fig.) aware or informed of). **2.** Take possession of (contraband goods, documents, etc.) by warrant or legal right, confiscate, impound, attach; hence **sei'z**ABLE (sē'-) *a.* **3.** Lay hold of forcibly or suddenly, snatch, grasp with hand or mind, comprehend quickly or clearly, (*seize fortress*, *power*, person *by the neck* etc., person's *hand*, *opportunity* or *occasion*, *an idea*, *a distinction*, *the point*, *the essence of the matter*; *was seized by apoplexy*, *with remorse* or *panic*); (Naut.) fasten or attach by binding with turns of yarn etc., whence **sei'z**ING[1] (4) (sē'-) *n.* **4.** *v.i.* Lay hold eagerly (*up*)*on* (*seize upon a chance* or *pretext*). **5.** ~ (**up**), (of moving part in machine) become stuck, jam, from undue heat or friction. [ME, f. OF *seizir, saisir* give seisin f. Frank. L *sacire* f. Gmc **sakjan* quarrel, claim at law, (**sak-* process, perh. infl. by **satjan* SET¹)]

seizin. Var. of SEISIN.

sei'zure (sē'zh*er*) *n.* In vbl senses; esp., sudden attack of apoplexy etc., stroke. [ME, f. SEIZE + -URE]

sē'jant *a.* (Her.) (Of animal) sitting upright on haunches. [prop. *seiant* f. OF var. of *seant* sitting (*seoir* f. L *sedēre* sit; see -ANT)]

sėlā'chĭan (-k-) *n.* & *a.* (Fish) of order Selachii, including sharks and dogfishes. [f. mod. L *Selachii* f. Gk *selakhos* shark + -IAN]

sela'dăng (-ah'-) *n.* Malayan gaur. [Malay]

sē'lah *int.* (In Psalms and Habakkuk, at end of verse; supposed to be a musical direction.) [f. Heb. *se·lāh*]

sĕ'ldom *adv.* & *a.* (occas. **~er, ~est**). **1.** *adv.* Rarely, not often, (*seldom or never*; *seldom, if ever*; *very seldom*). **2.** *a.* Rare, uncommon. [OE *seldan* (OHG *seltan*, ON *sjaldan*), dat. f. Gmc **selda-*]

sėlĕ'ct *a.*, & *v.t.* **1.** *a.* Chosen for excellence, choice, picked, got by rejection or exclusion of what is inferior; (of society etc.) exclusive, cautious in admitting members; hence ~NESS *n.* **2.** ~ **committee,** small parliamentary committee appointed to conduct some special investigation; ***~man,** elected councillor in New England town. **3.** *v.t.* Pick out as best or most suitable; hence *~EE' *n.*, conscript. [f. L SE(*ligere lect-* = *legere* pick)]

sėlĕ'ction *n.* **1.** Selecting, choice; being selected; what is selected (*a fine selection of summer goods*; *what is your selection for the Derby?*; *the new headmaster is a good selection*). **2.** (Biol.) Sorting out in various ways (*natural, physical, artificial*, etc., *selection*) of the types of animal or plant better fitted to survive or multiply, regarded as a factor in evolution. [f. L *selectio* (as prec.; see -ION)]

sėlĕ'ctĭve *a.* Using selection; characterized by selecting; (Electr.) able to respond to one particular frequency; ‖~ **employment tax** (on employees in certain industries only); *~ **service,** service in armed forces under conscription; hence ~LY² (-vlĭ) *adv.*, ~NESS (-vn-) *n.* [f. SELECT 2 + -IVE]

sėlĕctĭ'vĭtў (*or* sĕl-) *n.* Quality of being selective; (esp., of radio receiver) ability to respond to a chosen frequency without interference from others. [f. prec. + -ITY]

sėlĕ'ctor *n.* Person who selects, esp. representative team; device that selects appropriate material, vehicle-gear, etc. [f. SELECT 2 + -OR]

sĕ'lėnīte *n.* **1.** Gypsum occurring as transparent crystals or thin plates; hence **sĕlėnĭ'tic** *a.* **2.** (Chem.) Salt of selenious acid. [sense 1 f. L f. Gk *selēnitēs* (*lithos*) moon(-stone) f. *selēnē* moon; sense 2 f. SELENIUM + -ITE¹]

sėlē'nĭum *n.* (Chem.) Non-metallic element of sulphur group, characterized by variation of its electrical resistivity with intensity of illumination; ~ **cell,** piece of this used as photoelectric device; hence **sĕ'lėn**ATE¹ (3) *n.*, **sėlĕ'n**IC, **sėlē'nĭ**OUS, *adjs.* [mod. L, f. Gk *selēnē* moon + -IUM]

sėlē'no- *comb. form.* Moon, as: **~ce'ntric,** as seen etc. from centre of moon; **~dont** *n.* & *a.*, (mammal) with crescent-ridges on crowns of teeth; **~graphy** (sĕlĭnŏ'g-), study of or mapping of the moon, whence ~GRAPHER (sĕlĭnŏ'g-) *n.*, ~GRA'PHIC *a.*; **~logy** (sĕlĭnŏ'l-), science of the moon, whence ~LOGIST (sĕlĭnŏ'l-) *n.* [f. Gk *selēnē* moon + -O-]

sĕlf *n.* (*pl.* **selves** *pr.* sĕlvz), *a.*, & *pron.* **1.** *n.* Person's or thing's own individuality or essence, person or thing as object of introspection or reflexive action, (*the study of the self*; *the consciousness of self*); one's **former, better,** etc., ~, oneself as one formerly was, one's nobler impulses, etc.; one's **second** ~, intimate friend, right-hand man; **my humble** ~, **your good selves, our noble selves** (as joc. toast), etc., **his, its,** etc., **own** or **very** ~ (forms of *myself, himself* etc. when divided); **Caesar's, pity's,** etc., ~, (rhet.) Caesar himself, pity itself. **2.** One's own interests or pleasure, concentration on these, (*cares for nothing but, refers everything to, self*; *self is a bad guide to happiness*). **3.** (*pl.* **~s**). Flower of uniform, or of the natural wild, colour. **4.** (Commerc., vulg., or joc.) Myself, yourself, himself, etc., (*cheque drawn to self*; *ticket admitting self and friend*). **5.** *a.* (Of colour) uniform, the same throughout, (of flower) self-coloured. **6.** *pron.* See HERSELF, HIMSELF, ITSELF, MYSELF, ONE*self*, OURSELF, OURSELVES, THEMSELVES, THYSELF, YOURSELF. [OE, = OS *self*, OHG *selb*, ON *sjálfr.*, Goth. *silba* f. Gmc **selbha-*]

sĕlf- *pref.* **1.** Expr. direct reflexive action, (w. *part.*) acting on oneself or itself (*self-accusing, self-closing*), (w. *p.p.*) acted on by oneself or itself (*self-accused, self-propelled*), (w. vbl derivs.) of oneself or itself (*self-accuser, self-accusation, self-accusatory, self-fertilization, self-explanatory*). **2.** Expr. action or condition (a) occurring without external agency or assistance (*self-acting, self-evident*), (b) relating to oneself or itself (*self-confident, self-inflicted, self-righteous*). **3.** Denoting 'uniform' or 'natural' (*self-coloured, self-faced*). **4.** **~-aba'ndonment, -aba'sement, -abho'rrence,** -ABNEGA'TION, sense 1; **~-absor'bed** 2b; **~-absor'ption** 2b, (1) absorption in oneself, (2) (Phys.) absorption, by a body, of radiation emitted within it; **~-abu'se** 1, (1) reviling of oneself, (2) masturbation; **~-accusa'tion, -accu'satory,** etc., 1; **~-a'cting, -a'ction, -acti'vity,** 2a, automatic (action); **~-addre'ssed** 2b, (of envelope for return communication); **~-adhe'sive** 2b; **~-adju'sting, -adju'stment,** 1, (of machinery etc.); **~-admira'tion, -adver'tisement,** 1; **~-affirma'tion** 1, (Psych.) recognition and assertion of the existence of the conscious self; **~-aggra'ndizement,-ana'lysis,-appoi'nted, -apprecia'tion, -approba'tion, -appro'val,** 1; ~-ASSER'TING, **-asser'tion, -asser'tive,** etc., 1; **~-assur'ance, -assur'ed,** 2b; **~-bego'tten** 2a; **~-betray'al** 1; **~-bi'nder** 2a, reaping-machine with automatic arrangement for binding sheaves; **~-born** 1; **~-ce'ntred** 2b, preoccupied with one's own personality or affairs; **~-clea'ning, -clo'sing,** 1; **~-co'cking** 1, (of gun) with hammer raised by trigger, not by hand; **~-colle'cted** 2b, having or showing presence of mind or composure; **~-co'lour(ed)** 3, (of flower or material whose colour is uniform throughout, or flower whose colour has not been changed by cultivation etc.); **~-comma'nd** 1, power of controlling one's emotions; **~-commu'nion** 2b, meditation esp. upon one's own character or conduct; **~-compla'cent, -compla'cency,** 2b, (of person too easily pleased with himself); **~-concei't(ed)** 2b; **~-condemna'tion, -conde'mned,** 1; **~-confe'ssed** 2b, openly admitting oneself to be; **~-co'nfidence, -co'nfident(ly),** 2b; **~-congratula'tion, -co'nquest,** 1; **~-co'nscious(ness)** 2b, (esp. of person embarrassed or unnatural in manner from knowing he is observed by others, or (Philos. etc.) of man as having faculty of self-contemplation); **~-consi'stency, -consi's-**

tent, 2b; ~**-co'nstituted** 1, (esp. of person who or body which assumes function without right to it); ~**-consu'ming** 1; ~**-contai'ned** 1, (1) not communicative or dependent on others, (2) (||esp. of living accommodation) complete in itself; ~**-conte'mpt, -conte'mptuous**(**ly**), 1; ~**-conte'nt** *n.*, **-conte'nted,** 2b; ~**-contra-di'ction, -contradi'ctory, -contro'l, -convi'cted, -crea'ted, -crea'tion, -cri'tical, -cri'ticism, -cu'lture, -decei'ving, -decei'ver, -decei't, -dece'ption, -defea'ting,** 1; ~**-defe'nce** 1, (esp. of judo etc.; *in ~-defence,* not by way of aggression; *noble art of ~-defence,* boxing); ~**-delu'sion, -deni'al,** 1; ~**-**DENY**'ing** 1 (*~-denying ordinance,* (w. allus. to) resolution of Long Parliament 1645 depriving members of Parliament of civil and military office); ~**-depe'ndence, -depe'ndent,** 2b; ~**-deprecia'tion, -depre'ciative,** 1; ~**-despair'** 2b; ~**-destroy'ing,** ***-destru'ct, -destru'ction,** etc., 1; ~**-determina'tion** etc., 1, (esp. w. ref. to free will as opp. fatalism etc., or (Polit.) a nation's right to determine its own allegiance or form of government); ~**-deve'lopment** 1; ~**-devo'tion** 1, devoting of oneself to person or cause; ~**-di'scipline, -dispa'ragement, -display', -disprai'se, -distru'st**(**ful**), **-dou'bt,** 1; ~**-dri've** 1, (of hired vehicle) driven by hirer; ~**-e'ducated, -educa'tion, -effa'cement,** 1; ~**-ele'ctive** 1, (esp.) proceeding etc. by co-optation; ~**-employ'ed** 1, working as owner of business etc.; ~**-estee'm** 1; ~**-e'vident**(**ly**) 2a, without need of demonstration; ~**-examina'tion** 1; ~**-e'xecuting** 1, not needing legislation etc. to enforce it; ~**-exi'stent** 2a; ~**-explai'ning, -expla'natory, -expre'ssion,** 1; ~**-fa'ced** 3, (of stone) unhewn, undressed; ~**-fee'ding, -fee'der,** 1, (furnace, machine, etc.) that renews its own fuel or material automatically; ~**-fertiliza'tion, -fer'tilized, -fer'tilizing,** 1, ~**-fer'tile, -ferti'lity,** 2a, (of plants fertilized by their own pollen, not from others); ~**-fla'ttering, -fla'ttery,** 1; ~**-forge'tful**(**ness**) 1, unselfish(ness); ~**-fulfi'lling, -fulfi'lment, -ge'nerating,** 1; ~**-gla'zed** 3, (of porcelain) covered with glaze of one tint; ~**-glorifica'tion** 1; ~**-go'verning, -go'vernment,** 1, (esp. of colony etc.); ~**-gratula'tion** 1; ~**-heal** 1, plant (esp. *Prunella vulgaris*) believed to have great healing properties; ~**-he'lp** 1, providing for oneself without waiting for external aid; ~**-humilia'tion** 1; ~**-i'mage** 2b, one's idea of what one is; ~**-immola'tion** 1; ~**-impor'tance, -impor'tant,** having high opinion of oneself, pompous(ness); ~**-impo'sed** 2b, (of task etc.); ~**-i'mpotent** 2a, = *self-sterile*; ~**-impro'vement** 1; ~**-indu'ced** 2b; ~**-indu'ctive, -indu'ction,** 2a, (Electr.) (capable of) production of electromotive force in circuit when current in that circuit is varied; ~**-indu'lgence, -indu'lgent,** etc., 1, yielding to temptations of ease or pleasure; ~**-infli'cted** 2b; ~**-i'nterest**(**ed**) 2b, (actuated by or absorbed in) what one conceives to be for one's own interests; ~**-invi'ted** 1, having had to ask for, having come without, an invitation; ~**-invo'lved** 2b, wrapped up in oneself; ~**-justifica'tion, -ki'ndled, -know'ledge, -loa'ding, -lo'cking,** 1; ~**-lo've** 1, selfishness, impulse towards self-indulgence; ~**-lu'minous** 2a; ~**-made** 1, (of person who has risen from poverty or obscurity by his own exertions); ~**-ma'stery,** -MATE[1], **-mortifica'tion, -mo'tion, -mo'ving, -mur'der**(**er**), 1; ~**-opi'nion, -opi'nionated,** 2b, (of stubborn adherence to one's own opinions); ~**-par'tial, -partia'lity,** 2b; ~**-perpe'tuating, -pi'ty, -plea'sing** *a.* & *n.*, 1; ~**-poi'sed** 2a; ~**-pollu'tion** 1, masturbation; ~**-por'trait** 2a, portrait (literary or pictorial) made by a person of himself; ~**-posse'ssed, -posse'ssion,** 1, cool(ness), composed, composure, in agitating circumstances etc.; ~**-prai'se** 1; ~**-preserva'tion** 1, (esp.) the primary instinct impelling conscious being to go on living and avoid injury; ~**-pro'fit** 2b; ~**-pro'pagating, -prope'lled,** 1; ||~**-rai'sing** 1, (of flour) not needing addition of baking-powder etc.; ~**-realiza'tion** 1, development of one's faculties esp. as ethical first principle; ~**-recor'ding** 2a, (of scientific instrument etc.); ~**-regar'd** 1, (proper) regard for oneself (opp. *altruism*); ~**-re'gistering** 2a, (of scientific instrument etc.); ~**-re'gulating** 1, (of machinery); ~**-reli'ance, -reli'ant,** 2b; ~**-renuncia'tion** 1, unselfishness; ~**-repre'ssion, -reproa'ch**(**ful**), 1; ~**-repu'gnant** 2b, inconsistent; ~**-respe'ct, -respe'ctful, -respe'cting,** 1, (of person who has, and adheres to, a standard of dignity and worthy conduct); ~**-restrai'ned, -restrai'nt, -revea'ling** *a.*, **-revela'tion,** 1; ~**-ri'ghteous**(**ness**) 2b, (being) righteous in one's own estimation; ~**-ri'ghting** *a.* 1, (of boat); *~**-ri'sing** 2a, = *self-raising*; ~**-sa'crifice, -sa'crificing,** 1, subordinating one's own interests and desires to those of others; ~**'same** 3, (emphatic form of *same*); ~**-satisfa'ction, -sa'tisfied,** 2b, showing (undue) satisfaction with oneself or one's achievements; ~**-sea'ling** *a.* 1, (of pneumatic tyre, fuel tank, etc.) having means of automatically sealing small punctures; ~**-see'king** *a.* & *n.* 2b, seeking one's own welfare before that of others; ~**-ser'vice** 1, (esp. *attrib.*) system by which customers serve themselves with food or goods and pay a cashier or put money into and take food or goods from a machine; ~**-ser'ving** *a.* 1, placing one's own interests before others'; ~**-slau'ghter** 1; ~**-sow'n** 1, grown from seed that has dropped by chance; ~**-star'ter** 2a, electric appliance for starting engine of motor vehicle without use of crank; ~**-ste'rile, -steri'lity,** 2a, not self-fertile; ~**-styled** 1, having taken the name or description without right etc., pretended, would-be; ~**-suffi'cient, -suffi'cing,** 2b, (1) requiring nothing from outside, independent, (2) sufficient in one's own opinion, presumptuous; ~**-sugge'stion** 2b, reflexive suggestion of the mesmeric or hypnotic kind; ~**-suppor't**(**ing**), **-surre'nder, -sustai'ning, -sustai'ned, -tau'ght, -torme'nting** etc., **-tor'ture** etc., 1; ~**-vi'olence** 2b, (esp.) suicide; ~**-wi'll**(**ed**) 2b, (of obstinate pursuit of one's own desires or opinions); ~**-wi'nding** 1, (of watch etc. with automatic winding apparatus); ~**-wor'ship** 1. [f. prec.]

sĕ'lfhood *n.* Personality, separate and conscious existence. [f. SELF + -HOOD]

sĕ'lfĭsh *a.* Deficient in consideration for others, thinking chiefly of one's own personal profit or pleasure, actuated by self-interest; (of motive etc.) appealing to self-interest; ~ **theory of morals** (that pursuit of personal profit or pleasure is the ultimate motive of every action); hence ~LY[2] *adv.*, ~NESS *n.* [f. SELF + -ISH[1]]

sĕ'lflèss *a.* Oblivious of oneself, incapable of or resisting selfishness; hence ~LY[2] *adv.*, ~NESS *n.* [f. SELF + -LESS]

sĕ'lfnèss *n.* Selfishness; self-regard. [f. SELF + -NESS]

Sĕ'ljuk (-ŏŏk) *a.* & *n.* (Member) of 11th–13th-c. Turkish dynasties in central and Western Asia; hence ~IAN (-jōō'k-) *a.* & *n.* [f. Turk. *seljūq* (name of reputed ancestor)]

sĕll *v.* (**sold** *pr.* sō-) & *n.* **1.** *v.t.* Make over or dispose of in exchange for money; *sell the* DUMMY, *the* PASS³, *a* PUP, *down the* RIVER², SHORT 7; ~ one's **life** etc. **dear**(**ly**), (fig.) do great injury before being killed etc.; **~'ing-race** etc. (in which winning horse must be auctioned); hence ~'ABLE *a.* **2.** Cause to be sold (*the author's name alone will sell many copies*); keep stock of for sale or be a dealer in (*do you sell candles?*; *book-selling* etc.). **3.** Betray for money or other reward (*sell* one's *country* etc.). **4.** Offer dishonourably for money or other consideration, make a matter of corrupt bargaining, (*sell justice*, one*self*, one's *honour* or *chastity*). **5.** (sl.) Disappoint by not keeping engagement etc., by failing in some way, or by trickery; **sold again!** (excl. used by or to disappointed person). **6.** Advertise or publish merits of; give (person) information on value of something, inspire with desire to buy or acquire or agree to something; **sold on,** enthusiastic about. **7.** *v.i.* (Of goods) find purchasers (*will never sell*; *selling like wildfire*, *hot* CAKES), have specified price (*it sells at* or *for £5*). **8.** ~ **off,** sell remainder of (goods), clear out (stock), at reduced prices; ~ **out,** (1) sell (all or some of one's shares in company, whole stock-in-trade, etc., or abs.), (2) betray; *~-out* n., (1) selling of all tickets etc. for a show etc., commercial success, (2) betrayal; ||~ **up,** sell one's business, house, etc., sell goods of (debtor) by distress or legal process. **9.** Hence (-)~'ER¹ *n.*; **~er's** or **~ers' market,** one in which goods are scarce and expensive. **10.** *n.* (colloq.) Deception, disappointment; manner of selling (HARD, SOFT, *sell*). [OE *sellan*, =OS *sellian*, OHG *sellen*, ON *selja*, Goth. *saljan* offer sacrifice f. Gmc **saljan*]

sellanders. See SALLENDERS.

Sĕ'llōtāpe, s-, *n.*, & *v.t.* (Fix with) adhesive usu. transparent cellulose or plastic tape. [**P** as noun]

sĕ'ltzer (-ts-) *n.* ~ (**water**), medicinal mineral water from Nieder-Selters in Germany; artificial substitute for this, soda-water. [f. G *Selterser* a. (*Selters*)]

sĕ'lvage, sĕ'lvėdge, *n.* Edge of cloth so woven that it cannot unravel (e.g. by return of weft in loom-weaving); border of different material or finish along edge of cloth intended to be removed or hidden; edge-plate of lock with opening for the bolt. [ME, f. SELF + EDGE¹, after Du. *selfegghe*]

selves. See SELF.

sėmă'ntēme *n.* (Ling.) Element expressing image or idea. [f. F *sémantème* (as foll.; see -EME)]

sėmă'nt|ĭc *a.* & *n.* **1.** *a.* Relating to meaning in language; relating to connotations of words; hence ~ICALLY *adv.* **2.** *n.* (in *pl.*, usu. treated as *sing.*) Branch of philology concerned with meanings; hence **~ĭc**IST (3) *n.* [f. F *sémantique* f. Gk *sēmantikos* significant (*sēmainō* signify f. *sēma* sign; see -IC)]

sĕ'maphōre *n.* & *v.* **1.** *n.* Signalling apparatus of post with movable arm(s), arrangement of lanterns, etc., for use (esp. on railways) by day or night; military etc. signalling by operator's two arms or by flag in each hand according to alphabetic code; hence **sĕmaphŏ'r**IC *a.* **2.** *v.i.* & *t.* Signal or send by semaphore. [f. F *sémaphore*, irreg. f. Gk *sēma* sign + *-phoros* -PHORE]

sėmāsĭ|ŏ'logy̆ *n.* Semantics; hence ~**o**LO'GICAL *a.* [f. G *semasiologie* f. Gk *sēmasia* meaning (*sēmainō* signify); see -LOGY]

sėmă'tĭc *a.* (Zool.) (Of coloration, markings, etc.) significant, serving to warn off enemies or attract attention. [f. Gk *sēma sēmatos* sign + -IC]

sĕ'mblable *a.* (arch.) Having semblance of something, seeming. [ME f. OF (as foll.; see -ABLE)]

sĕ'mblance *n.* What looks like, the outward appearance of, something (*put on a semblance of anger*; *bears the semblance of an angel and the heart of a devil*); resemblance. [ME f. OF (*sembler* f. L *similare*, *simulare* SIMULATE)]

semée, semé, (sĕ'mĭ) *a.* (Her.) Covered with small bearings of indefinite number (e.g. stars, fleurs-de-lis) arranged all over field. [F, fem. or masc. p.p. of *semer* to sow]

semeiology, semeiotics. See SEMIOLOGY.

sĕ'mēme *n.* (Ling.) Unit of meaning carried by morpheme. [f. SEMANTIC + -EME]

sē'mĕn *n.* Generative fluid of male animals, containing spermatozoa in suspension. [ME f. L *semen seminis* seed (*serere* to sow)]

sėmĕ'ster *n.* Half-year course or term in (esp. German and U.S.) universities. [G, f. L *semestris* six-monthly (*sex* six, *mensis* month)]

||**sĕ'mĭ** *n.* (colloq.) Semi-detached house. [abbr.]

sĕ'mĭ- *pref.* denoting: **1.** A half of (*semicircle*). **2.** On one of two sides (*semi-detached*); in one of two directions (*semi-infinite*); in some particular (*semivowel*). **3.** Little more or better than (*semi-barbarism*). **4.** Rather less than (*semi-official*); in low degree (*semi-civilized*); not quite deserving the description (*semi-smile*). **5.** Imperfect(ly) (*semi-bull*, *semi-double*). **6.** Occurring, published, etc., twice in a specified period (*semi-annual*; cf. BI- 1(e)). **7.** **~-a'nnual(ly)**, sense 6; **~-automa'tic** 2; **~-barbar'ian,-bar'barism,** 3; **~-ba'sement** 4, inhabited storey partly below ground level; **~-bo'ld** 4, (Print.; cf. BOLD 3); ||**~breve** 1, (Mus.) longest note in common use, = two minims (see BREVE); **~-bull** 5, (issued by pope after election and before coronation with one side of seal left blank); **~-cente'nnial** 6, occurring etc. every fifty years; **~-chor'us** 1, part of chorus, passage performed by it; **~circle, ~cir'cular** *a.*, 1, (amounting to, arranged as or in, shaped like) half of a circle or of its circumference, set of objects ranged in or object forming a semicircle, (*~circular canal*, one of three fluid-filled channels in ear giving information to brain to help maintain balance); **~-ci'vilized** 4; **~co'lon** 4, punctuation-mark (;) of intermediate value between comma and full stop; **~condu'cting** *a.*, **~condu'ctor,** 4, (solid substance) that is non-conductor when pure or at low temperature but has conductivity between that of insulators and that of most metals when containing suitable impurity or at higher temperature; **~-co'nscious** 5; **~cy'linder, ~cyli'ndrical,** 1, (of forming, etc.) half of a cylinder cut longitudinally; ||**~demisemiquaver** 1; **~-depo'nent** 4, (L Gram.) having active forms in present tenses and passive forms with active sense in perfect tenses; **~-deta'ched** 2, (of house) joined to another by party-wall on one side only; **~dia'meter** 1; **~-docume'ntary** *a.* & *n.* 4, (cinema film) having a factual background and a fictitious story; **~-dome** 1, 4, half-dome formed by vertical section, part of structure more or less resembling dome; **~-dou'ble** 5, (Bot.) having only outer stamens converted to petals; **~fi'nal** 4, match or round preceding the final (*~fi'nalist*, competitor in this); **~-fi'nished** 4, prepared for final stage of manufacture; **~-fi'tted** 4, (of garment) shaped to the body but not closely fitted; **~flu'id** *a.* & *n.* 4, (fluid) of consistency between solid and liquid; **~-i'nfidel** 3; **~-i'nfinite** 2, limited in one direction and stretching to infinity in the other; **~-i'nvalid** 4; **~-li'quid** *a.* & *n.* 4, = *semifluid*; **~-lu'nar** 1, 4, half-moon-shaped, crescent-shaped, (esp. Anat., as *~-lunar bone* in carpus, *cartilage* in knee, *valve* in heart); **~-me'tal,** substance with some of the properties of metals; **~-mo'nthly** 6; **~-offi'cial(ly)** 4, (esp. of communications made to newspapers by official with stipulation that they shall not be formally attributed to him); **~-opa'que, ~-per'manent,** 4; **~-per'meable** 4, (esp. of membrane allowing small molecules to pass through but not large molecules); **~-plume** 2, feather with firm stem but downy web; **~-pre'cious** 4, (of gems less valuable than precious stones); ||**~quaver** 1, (Mus.) note with two-hooked symbol, equal to half a quaver; **~-ri'gid** 4, (of airship) having stiffened keel attached to flexible gas container; **~-ski'lled** 4, having or requiring some training but less than skilled work(er); **~-smile, ~-so'lid,** 4; **~-sweet** 4, (of biscuit etc.) slightly sweetened; **~tone** 1, (Mus.) smallest interval used in classical European music, half of tone; **~-trai'ler** 4, trailer having wheels at back but supported by towing vehicle at front; **~-transpar'ent** 4; **~tro'pical** 4, (as) of regions bordering on the tropics; **~-u'ncial** 5, between uncial and minuscule; **~vowel** 2, sound, or letter representing sound, intermediate between vowel and consonant (e.g. y, w); **~-wee'kly** 6. [F etc. or L, corresp. to Gk HEMI-, Skr. *sāmi*]

sĕ'mĭnal *a.* Of seed or semen or reproduction, germinal, reproductive, propagative, (~ **fluid,** semen; **in the ~ state,** rudimentary, still undeveloped); providing a basis for future development (*seminal ideas, mind*); hence ~LY² *adv.* [ME f. OF, or f. L *seminalis* (as SEMEN; see -AL)]

sĕ'mĭnar *n.* Small class at university for discussion and research; *conference of specialists; short intensive course of study. [G, f. as foll.]

sĕ'mĭnar|ў *n.* **1.** (arch. or fig.) Place of education or development. **2.** Training college for priests, rabbis, etc.; hence ~IST (3) *n.* [ME, f. L *seminarium* seed-plot neut. (as n.) of *seminarius* a. (as SEMEN; see -ARY¹)]

sēmĭnĭ'ferous *a.* Bearing seed; conveying semen. [f. SEMEN + -I- + -FEROUS]

sēmĭŏ'logў, sēmĭŏ'tĭcs, sēmeiŏ'- (-mĭŏ'-), *ns.* Branch of linguistics concerned with signs and symbols; (Path.) symptomatology; hence **sēmĭo**LO'GICAL, **sēmĭŏ'tic**(AL), *adjs.* [f. Gk *sēmeion* sign (*sēma* mark), *sēmeiōtikos* of signs + -LOGY, -ICS]

Sĕ'm|ite *n.* & *a.* (Member) of any of the races supposed to be descended from Shem, son of Noah (Gen. 10:21 ff.), including esp. the Jews, Phoenicians, Arabs, and Assyrians; so **Sėmĭ'tic** *a.* (esp. of (1) languages of family including Hebrew and Arabic, (2) the Jews), **~ĭtism** (2, 4), **~ĭtist** (3) *ns.*, **~ĭtize** (3) *v.t.* [f. mod. L *Semita*, f. LL f. Gk *Sēm* Shem; see -ITE¹]

sĕ'mmĭt *n.* (Sc.) Undershirt. [ME; orig. unkn.]

sĕmoli'na (-lē'-) *n.* Hard grains left after milling of flour, used in puddings etc. and in pasta. [f. It. *semolino* dim. of *semola* bran f. L *simila* flour]

sĕmpĭter'nal *a.* (rhet.) Eternal, everlasting. [ME, f. OF *sempiternel* f. LL *sempiternalis* f. L *sempiternus* (*semper* always, *aeternus* eternal); see -AL]

semplice (sĕ'mplĭchā) *adv.* (Mus.) In a simple style of performance. [It., = SIMPLE]

sempre (sĕ'mprā) *adv.* (Mus.) Throughout, always, (*sempre forte, rallentando*). [It.]

sempstress. See SEAMSTRESS.

||**S.E.N.** *abbr.* State Enrolled Nurse.

Sen. *abbr.* Senate; Senator; Senior.

sėnār'ĭ|us *n.* (*pl.* ~**i** *pr.* -ī). (L Pros.) Verse of six feet, esp. iambic trimeter. [L (see foll.)]

sĕ'narў *a.* Of six, by sixes; *senary* SCALE³. [f. L *senarius* (*seni* distrib. of *sex* six; see -ARY¹)]

sĕ'nate *n.* **1.** (Rom. Hist.) State council of the republic and empire sharing legislation with the popular assemblies, administration with the magistrates, and judicial power with the knights. **2.** Upper and less numerous branch of the legislative assembly in U.S., France, and other countries, in states of U.S., etc.; (rhet.) any legislature or its proceedings or members. **3.** Governing (academic) body of university or *college. [ME, f. OF *senat* f. L *senatus* (*senex* old man; see -ATE¹)]

sĕ'nator *n.* Member of senate; hence or cogn. **sĕnator'**IAL *a.*, ~SHIP *n.* [ME, f. OF *senateur* f. L *senator -oris* (as prec.; see -OR)]

sėnā'tus *n.* ~ **(acade'micus),** senate of Scottish university; ~ **consu'ltum,** decree of ancient Roman senate, or of French senate under Napoleon I or III. [L (see SENATE)]

sĕnd¹ *v.* **(sent). 1.** *v.t.* Order or cause to go, bring about conveyance of, (*to* some destination, *into* place, *out, away*, etc.; *send message* or *messenger to; sent me a book; will send an army; send goods all over* or *round the world*); ~ **in,** enter for competition etc.; ~ **on,** transmit to further destination or in advance of one's own arrival; ~ **up,** transmit to higher authority (see also sense 4); *send* WORD¹ 4. **2.** (Of God, providence, etc.) grant, bestow, inflict, bring about, cause to be, (*send rain, a judgement, pestilence; God send it may not be so!; send her victorious!*). **3.** Propel, cause to move, (*send bullet; send* person *flying, packing; sent his temperature up, down; send out* or *forth leaves, steam, odour*); cause to go (*into* raptures etc., *to* sleep etc.). **4.** Dismiss with or without force (*sent him away, about his business*); *send to* COVENTRY; ||~ **down,** rusticate or expel from university, put in prison, (Cricket) bowl (ball, over); ~ **off,** get (letter, parcel, etc.) dispatched, attend departure of (person) as sign of respect etc., (Footb., of referee) order (player) to take no further part in a game; ~*-off* n., sending off of person, laudatory review of book etc.; ~ **up,** (colloq.) satirize, ridicule by mimicking, *(sl.) put in prison, (see also sense 1); ~*-up* n., (colloq.) a satire. **5.** Drive *mad* etc.; (sl.) affect emotionally, put into ecstasy. **6.** *v.i.* Send message or letter (*sent to warn me*); ~ **for,** tell (person) to come, order (book etc.) from elsewhere. **7.** Hence ~'ER¹ *n.* [OE *sendan*, = OS *sendian*, OHG *sendan, senten*, ON *senda*, Goth. *sandjan* f. Gmc **sandhjan* (**sandh-*, **santh* causative of **senth*)]

sĕnd², scĕnd, *n.*, & *v.i.* (Naut.) **1.** *n.* Impulse given by wave(s) (*scend of the sea*); plunge of vessel. **2.** *v.i.* (Of vessel) plunge or pitch owing to impulse of wave. [f. prec. or f. DESCEND]

sĕ'ndal *n.* (Hist.) (Garment of) thin rich silk material. [ME, f. OF *cendal*, ult. f. Gk *sindōn*]

Sĕnėgalē'se (-z) *a.* & *n.* (*pl.* same). (Native or inhabitant) of Senegal. [f. *Senegal* in W. Africa + -ESE]

sėnĕ'sc|ent *a.* Growing old; hence ~ENCE *n.* [f. L *senescere* (*senex* old; see -ESCENT)]

sĕ'nėschal (-shal) *n.* Steward or major-domo of medieval great house; ||cathedral official; judge in Sark. [ME f. OF, f. med. L *seniscalus* f. Gmc **siniskalkaz* (**seni-* old, **skalkaz* servant; cf. MARSHAL¹)]

senhor, senhora, senhorita, (sānyor', -or'a, -erē'ta) *ns.* (used of or to Portuguese or Brazilians as SIGNOR etc.). [Port., f. L SENIOR]

sē'nīle *a.* Showing the feebleness etc. of, incident to, old age (*senile apathy, decay, garrulity*, etc.); hence **sėnĭ'l**ITY *n.* [f. F *sénile* or f. L *senilis* (*senex* old man; see -IL)]

sē'nĭor *a.* & *n.* **1.** *a.* More advanced in age, older or oldest in standing, superior in age or standing *to*, of higher or highest position, (opp. JUNIOR); (of school) having pupils in an older age-range; *of final year at university, high school, etc.; ||~ **citizen,** old person (above specified age); *~ **college** (offering four-year course for baccalaureate); ||~ **combination** or **common room** (for use by senior members of college); ~ **officer** (esp. one to whom a junior is responsible); ~ **partner,** head of firm; ||~ **service,** Navy as opp. Army; ||~ **tutor,** college tutor in charge of teaching arrangements; *senior* WRANGLER; so **sēnĭŏ'r**ITY *n.* **2.** (Appended to name for distinction, opp. JUNIOR) senior to another of same name. **3.** *n.* Person of advanced age or comparatively long service etc.; one's elder or superior in length of service, membership, etc., (*is my senior*); senior student. [ME f. L, = older, old(ish) man, compar. of *senex senis* old (man)]

sĕ'nna *n.* (Dried pods or leaflets, used as laxative, of) cassia plant. [f. med. L *sena* f. Arab. *sanā*]

sĕ'nnėt *n.* (Hist.) Signal call on trumpet or cornet (in stage-directions of Elizabethan plays). [perh. var. of SIGNET]

sĕ'nnight (-īt) *n.* (arch.) Week. [OE *seofon nihta* seven nights]

sĕ'nnĭt, sĭ'nnėt, *n.* (Naut.) Braided cordage made in flat or round or square form from 3–9 cords. [17th c., of unkn. orig.]

señor (*pl.* ***señores***)**,** ***señora, señorita,*** (sĕnyŏr', -ŏr'*a*, -*erē'ta*) *ns.* (used of or to Spaniards or Spanish-speakers as SIGNOR etc.). [Sp., f. L SENIOR]

Senr. *abbr.* Senior.

sĕnsā'tion *n.* **1.** Consciousness of perceiving or seeming to perceive some state or condition of one's body or its parts or senses or of one's mind or its emotions, contents of such consciousness, (*had a sensation of giddiness, heat, pain, comfort, thirst, falling, sourness, deafness, pride, stupidity; pressing the eyeball in the dark will produce the sensation of light* or *of seeing light; in search of a new sensation*). **2.** Stirring of the emotions of many people or of eager interest among them, display of intense common emotion or interest, literary or other use of material calculated to cause such effect; event, person, etc., causing such effect. **3.** Hence ~AL *a.*, ~**al**LY² *adv.* [f. med. L *sensatio* f. L *sensus* SENSE; see -ATION]

sĕnsā'tional|ism *n.* **1.** (Philos.) Theory that ideas are derived solely from sensation (opp. *rationalism*). **2.** Pursuit of the sensational in literature, political agitation, etc. **3.** So ~IST (2) *n.* [f. SENSATIONAL + -ISM]

sĕnse *n.*, & *v.t.* **1.** *n.* Any of the special bodily faculties by which sensation is roused (*has quick, keen, senses, a dull sense of smell*); **the five ~s,** sight, hearing, smell, taste, and touch, by which the external world is perceived; **sixth ~,** (supposed faculty giving) intuitive or extra-sensory knowledge; **~-datum,** element of experience received through the senses; **~-organ,** bodily organ conveying external stimuli to the sensory system. **2.** (in *pl.*) Sanity or ordinary state of mind regarded as attested by possession of senses; **in one's ~s,** sane; **has taken leave of, is out of, his ~s,** has gone mad; **frightened out of his ~s** (into loss of faculties); **come, bring** (person), **to his ~s** (out of unconsciousness or folly). **3.** Ability to perceive or feel or to be conscious of the presence or properties of things, sensitiveness of all or any of the senses (*sense-perception*); **errors of ~,** mistakes in perception; **the pleasures of ~,** those depending on sensation. **4.** Consciousness *of* (*a* or *the sense of pleasure, pain, gratification, having done well,* one's *own importance, shame, responsibility*); **under a ~ of wrong,** feeling wronged. **5.** Quick or accurate appreciation *of*, instinct regarding or insight into specified matter, habit of basing one's conduct on such instinct, (*sense of locality,* DIRECTION, *distance, the ridiculous,* HUMOUR¹, *duty, beauty, gratitude; a keen sense of honour;* ROAD¹ *sense; the religious, moral, aesthetic, sense*). **6.** Practical wisdom, judgement, COMMON¹ sense, conformity to these, (*sound, good, sense; had not the sense to* do; *has plenty of sense; what is the sense of talking like that?; has more sense than to* do; *now you are talking sense*); **a man of ~** (sagacious). **7.** Meaning, way in which word etc. is to be understood, intelligibility or coherence or possession of a meaning, (*in what exact sense we shall rise again is doubtful; the sense of the word is clear; in the strict, literal, figurative, moral, metaphorical, legal, proper, full, sense; in a vague, in every, sense*); **in a** or **one ~,** provided that the statement is taken in a particular way, under limitations, (*what you say is true in a sense*); **make ~,** be intelligible or practicable; **make ~ of,** show to have a meaning. **8.** Prevailing sentiment among a number of people (**take the ~ of the meeting,** ascertain this by putting question etc.). **9.** (Math. etc.) Direction of movement; position of line etc. in one of two opposite directions. **10.** *v.t.* Perceive by sense; be vaguely aware of; *understand; (of machine etc.) detect. [ME, f. L *sensus* faculty of feeling, thought, meaning (*sentire sens-* feel)]

sĕ'nselėss (-sl-) *a.* Unconscious; incapable of sensation; wildly foolish; meaningless, purposeless; hence ~LY² *adv.*, ~NESS *n.* [f. prec. + -LESS]

sĕnsĭbĭ'lĭtў *n.* **1.** Capacity to feel (*skin lost its sensibility*). **2.** Exceptional openness to emotional impressions (*sense and sensibility*); delicacy of feeling, susceptibility (*sensibility to kindness* etc.); (over-)sensitiveness. **3.** (in *pl.*) Susceptibility, tendency to feel offended etc. [ME, f. LL *sensibilitas* (as foll.; see -ITY)]

sĕ'nsĭble *a.* **1.** Perceptible by the senses (*sensible phenomena, things*); great enough to be perceived, appreciable, (*a sensible difference, increase*). **2.** (arch.) Sensitive (*to*). **3.** Aware, not unmindful, *of*, (*was sensible of his peril, your kindness*). **4.** Having or showing good sense, reasonable, judicious, moderate, practical, (*a sensible man, course of action, compromise; that is very sensible of him*); (of clothing) unpretentiously practical. **5.** Hence **sĕ'nsĭb**LY² *adv.*, ~NESS (-beln-) *n.* [ME f. OF, or f. L *sensibilis* (as SENSE; see -IBLE)]

sĕ'nsĭtĭve *a.* **1.** Having sensibility *to*, very open *to* or acutely affected by external stimuli or mental impressions; (of topic etc.) subject to restriction of discussion because of embarrassment, to ensure security, etc. **2.** (Of instrument etc.) readily responding *to* or recording slight changes of condition; ~ **market** (liable to quick changes of price). **3.** (Of material) readily affected by or responsive *to* external action; ~ **paper,** (Photog.) paper prepared to respond to action of light; ~ **plant,** mimosa or other plant whose leaves curve downwards and leaflets fold together when touched. **4.** Hence ~LY² (-vlĭ) *adv.*, ~NESS (-vn-), **sĕnsĭtĭ'v**ITY *ns.*, **sĕnsĭtŏ'**METER *n.*, device for measuring sensitivity. [ME, = sensory, f. OF *sensitif -ive* or f. med. L *sensitivus*, irreg. f. L *sentire sens-* feel; see -IVE]

sĕ'nsĭtīz|e, -īs|e (-iz), *v.t.* Make sensitive; (Photog.) make sensitive to light; make (organism etc.) abnormally sensitive to foreign substance; hence ~A'TION, ~ER¹ (2), *ns.* [f. prec. + -IZE]

sĕ'nsor *n.* Device giving signal for detection or measurement of a physical property to which it responds. [f. SENSORY, after *motor*]

sĕnsŏr'ĭ|um *n.* (*pl.* ~**a** *or* ~**ums**). The seat of sensation, the brain, brain and spinal cord, or grey matter of these; (Biol.) whole sensory apparatus including nerve-system etc.; hence ~AL *a.* [LL, f. L *sentire sens-* feel; see -ORY]

sĕ'nsorȳ *a.* Of sensation or the senses. [f. as prec. + -ORY]

sĕ'nsūal (*or* -shōō-) *a.* **1.** Of sense or sensation, = prec. **2.** Of or depending on the senses only and not on the intellect or spirit, carnal, fleshly, (*sensual pleasures*); given to the pursuit of sensual pleasures or gratification of the appetites, self-indulgent in regard to food and drink and sexual enjoyment, voluptuous, licentious; indicative of sensual nature (*sensual lips, mouth*). **3.** (Philos.) Holding the doctrine of, according to, of, sensationalism. **4.** Hence or cogn. ~ISM (2, 3), ~IST (1, 2), ~ITY (-ă'l-), *ns.*, ~IZE (3) *v.t.*, ~LY² *adv.* [ME, f. LL *sensualis* (as SENSE; see -AL)]

sĕ'ns|um *n.* (*pl.* **~a**). (Philos.) Sense-datum. [mod. L, neut. p.p. (as n.) of L *sentire* feel]

sĕ'nsūous *a.* Of, derived from, affecting, the senses esp. in neutral or aesthetic manner (opp. SENSUAL 2); hence ~LY² *adv.*, ~NESS *n.* [f. L *sensus* sense + -OUS]

sĕnt. See SEND¹.

sĕ'ntence *n.*, & *v.t.* **1.** *n.* (arch.) Opinion for or against some course or conclusion (*my sentence is for war*). **2.** (arch.) Pithy or pointed saying, briefly expressed thought, maxim, proverb. **3.** Decision of lawcourt, esp. (declaration of) punishment allotted to person convicted in criminal trial (lit. or fig.); **under ~ of,** having been condemned to (death etc.). **4.** (Gram.) Set of words complete in itself as expression of thought, containing subject and predicate (either, or part of either or both, of which may be omitted by ellipsis), and conveying a statement, question, exclamation, or command (e.g. *I go, will you go?*, *go* = go thou or you, *what?* = what did you say?, *fire!* = there is a fire; *hearts trumps* = hearts are trumps); **simple ~** (with single subject and predicate); **compound ~** (with more than one of either or both); **complex ~** (with subordinate clause or clauses); so **sĕntĕ'nt**IAL (-sh*a*l) *a.* **5.** Part of writing or speech between two full stops or equivalent pauses and often including several grammatical sentences (e.g. *I went and he came*); (Mus.) unit of two or more phrases. **6.** *v.t.* Announce sentence of (convicted criminal or transf.), declare condemned *to.* [ME f. OF, f. L *sententia* (*sentire* be of opinion; see -ENCE)]

sĕntĕ'ntious (-sh*u*s) *a.* Aphoristic, pithy, given to the use of maxims, affecting a concise impressive style; (of style) affectedly formal; (of person) fond of pompous moralizing; hence ~LY² *adv.*, ~NESS *n.* [f. L *sententiosus* (as prec.; see -OUS)]

sĕ'ntĭ|ent (-shĭ-; *or* -shent) *a.* Having the power of sense-perception; hence ~ENCE, ~ENCY, *ns.*, ~**ent**LY² *adv.* [f. L *sentire* feel; see -ENT]

sĕ'ntĭment *n.* **1.** A mental feeling, the sum of what one feels on some subject, a tendency or view based on or coloured with emotion, such feelings collectively as an influence, (*the sentiment of pity, patriotism*; *my sentiment towards him is one of respect*; *animated by noble sentiments*; *sentiment unchecked by reason is a bad guide*); **those are,** (joc.) **them's, my ~s,** that is what I think about it. **2.** Emotional feeling conveyed in literature or art. **3.** Tendency to be swayed by feeling rather than by reason, emotional weakness, false or unworthy tenderness or the display of it, nursing of the emotions. **4.** (Sense intended to be conveyed by) the expression of some desire or view esp. as formulated for a toast etc. (*the sentiment is good though the words are injudicious* etc.; *conclude* one's *speech with a sentiment*). [ME, f. OF *sentement*, f. med. L *sentimentum* (L *sentire* feel; see -MENT)]

sĕntĭmĕ'ntal *a.* (Of person or action) characterized by sentiment (esp. sense 3); pertaining to sentiment; appealing to sentiment (**~ value,** value of a thing to particular person because of its associations); hence ~ISM (3), ~IST (2), ~ITY (-ă'l-), *ns.*, ~IZE (2, 3) *v.i.* & *t.*, ~LY² *adv.* [f. prec. + -AL]

sĕ'ntĭnel *n.*, & *v.t.* (||**-ll-**). **1.** *n.* Soldier etc. posted to keep guard (lit. or fig.). **2. ~ (crab),** Indian-Ocean crab with long eye-stalks. **3.** *v.t.* (poet.) Keep guard over or in. **4.** Station sentinels at or in. [f. F *sentinelle* f. It. *sentinella*, of unkn. orig.]

sĕ'ntrȳ *n.* **1.** (esp. Mil.) = prec. 1. **2. ~-box,** wooden cabin large enough to hold sentry standing; **~-go,** duty of pacing up and down as sentry. [perh. f. obs. *centrinel*, var. of prec.]

Sĕnu'ssĭ (-ōō'-) *n.* (*pl.* usu. same). Member of N. Afr. Muslim sect noted for fanaticism and belligerence. [f. Sidi Muhammad ibn 'Alī *as-Sanūsī*, founder of the sect d. 1859]

sĕ'pal *n.* (Bot.) One of the divisions or leaves of the calyx. [f. F *sépale*, mod. L *sepalum*, formed by N. J. de Necker 1790, perh. f. as SEPARATE¹ + PETAL]

sĕ'par|able *a.* Able to be separated; (Gram., of prefix, or verb in respect of it) written as separate word in some collocations; hence ~ABI'LITY, **~able**NESS (-beln-), *ns.*, **~ab**LY² *adv.* [f. F *séparable* or f. L *separabilis* (as SEPARATE²; see -ABLE)]

sĕ'parate¹ *a.* & *n.* **1.** *a.* Physically disconnected, forming a unit that is or may be regarded as apart or by itself, distinct, individual, of individuals, (*from*, or abs.; *the separate members of the body*; *the separate volumes may be had singly*; *live in separate rooms*; *live separate*; *the two questions are essentially separate*; *one is quite separate from the other*; *separate and corporate* or *common ownership*); **~ estate,** married woman's property when not subject to husband's control; **~ maintenance,** husband's allowance to wife from whom he lives separate by consent (cf. ALIMONY); hence ~LY² (-tlĭ) *adv.*, ~NESS (-tn-) *n.* **2.** *n.* Copy of single article etc. reprinted from proceedings of society, magazine, etc., for separate distribution. **3.** (in *pl.*) Separate articles of dress suitable for wearing together in various combinations. [f. L *separatus* p.p. (as foll.); see -ATE²]

sĕ'par|āte² *v.* **1.** *v.t.* Make separate, sever, disunite, keep from union or contact; *discharge, dismiss. **2.** Sort or divide (milk, grain, ore, fruit, light, etc.) into constituent parts or sizes, get (cream, waste product, etc.) by such process for use or rejection, whence **~āt**OR *n.* **3.** *v.i.* Secede *from*, go different ways, disperse; cease to live together as married couple. **4.** Hence ~ATIVE, **~at**ORY, *adjs.* [ME, f. L SE(*parare* make ready) + -ATE³]

sĕparā'tion *n.* Separating or being separated; **judicial** or **legal ~** (of man and wife under **~ order** made by court). [ME f. OF, f. L *separatio -onis* (as prec.; see -ATION)]

sĕ'parat|ĭst *n.* One who favours separation, esp. for political or ecclesiastical independence (opp. *unionist*); so ~ISM (3) *n.* [f. SEPARATE¹ + -IST]

Sĕphar'd|ĭ *n.* (*pl.* **~im**). Jew of Spanish or Portuguese descent (cf. ASHKENAZI); hence ~IC *a.* [LHeb., f. *sᵉpārad*, country mentioned in Obad. 20 and taken to be Spain]

sē'pĭa *n.* Black fluid of cuttlefish; brown pigment prepared from this used in monochrome drawing and in water-colours; rich reddish-brown colour; drawing done in sepia. [L, f. Gk *sēpia* cuttlefish]

sē'poy *n.* (Hist.) Native Indian soldier under

European, esp. British, discipline; *Sepoy* MUTINY. [f. Urdu & Pers. *sipāhī* soldier (*sipāh* army)]

sĕppu'ku (-ōō'kōō) *n.* Hara-kiri. [Jap.]

sĕps *n.* Skink of genus *Chalcides*, with serpent-like body. [L, f. Gk *sēps* (*sēpō* make rotten)]

sĕ'ps|ĭs *n.* (*pl.* ~**es** *pr.* -ēz). Bacterial contamination from festering wound etc., blood-poisoning. [mod. L, f. Gk *sēpsis* (as prec.)]

sĕpt *n.* Clan, esp. in Ireland. [prob. alt. of SECT]

sĕpt-, sĕ'pt|ĭ-, *comb. forms.* Seven, as: ~**e'nnial,** lasting, recurring every, seven years; ~**e'nnium** (pl. *-iums* or *-ia*), period of seven years; ~**ila'teral,** seven-sided; ~**iva'lent,** (Chem.) having a valence of seven. [L (*septem* seven)]

Sept. *abbr.* September; Septuagint.

sĕ'pta. See SEPTUM.

sĕ'ptal *a.* Of sept(s); of septum or septa. [f. SEPT, SEPTUM + -AL]

sĕ'pt|āte *a.* (Bot., Zool., & Anat.) Having septum or septa, partitioned; hence ~A'TION *n.* [f. SEPTUM + -ATE[2]]

Sĕptĕ'mber *n.* Ninth month of year. [ME, f. L *September* (*septem* seven; orig. seventh month of Roman year)]

sĕptėnār'ĭ|us *n.* (*pl.* ~**i** *pr.* -ī). (Pros.) Verse of seven feet, esp. trochaic or iambic tetrameter catalectic. [L (*septeni* distrib. of *septem* seven; see -ARY[1])]

sĕptē'narў (*or* sĕ'ptĭn-) *a.* & *n.* **1.** *a.* Of seven, by sevens, on basis of seven. **2.** *n.* Group or set of seven (esp. years); septenarius. [f. L (as prec.; see -ARY[1])]

sĕ'ptėnate *a.* (Bot.) Growing in sevens; having seven divisions. [f. L *septeni* (as SEPTENARIUS) + -ATE[2]]

sĕptĕ't, -ĕ'tte, *n.* **1.** (Mus.) (Performers of) composition for seven voices or instruments. **2.** Set of seven. [f. G *septett* f. L *septem* seven; see -ET[1], -ETTE]

sĕ'ptfoil (sĕ't-) *n.* **1.** (arch.) Tormentil. **2.** Seven-lobed ornamental figure. [f. LL *septifolium* after *cinquefoil, trefoil*]

sĕ'ptĭ-. See SEPT-.

sĕ'pt|ĭc *a.* Of or involving sepsis, putrefying; ~**ic tank** (in which organic matter in sewage is disintegrated through bacterial activity); hence ~ICALLY *adv.*, ~**ĭ'**CITY *n.* [f. L f. Gk *sēptikos* (*sēpō* make rotten; see -IC)]

sĕptĭcae'm|ĭa (-sē'm-), ***-cē'm|ĭa,** *n.* (Path.) Blood-poisoning; hence ~IC *a.* [mod. L, f. Gk *sēptikos* + *haima* blood + -IA[1]; see prec., -AEMIA]

sĕptĭ'llion (-yon) *n.* (for *pl.* usage see HUNDRED). ||A million raised to seventh power; *a thousand raised to eighth power. [F (*sept* seven, after *billion* etc.)]

sĕ'ptĭmal *a.* Of the number seven. [f. L *septimus* seventh (*septem* seven) + -AL]

sĕ'ptime (-ēm) *n.* Seventh of eight parrying positions in fencing. [f. L *septimus* (as prec.)]

sĕptūagėnār'ĭan *a.* & *n.* (Person) from 70 to 79 years old. [f. L *septuagenarius* (*septuageni* distrib. of *septuaginta* seventy; see -ARY[1]) + -AN]

sĕptūagē'narў *a.* & *n.* Of seventy; = prec. [as prec.]

Sĕptūagĕ'sĭma *n.* ~ **(Sunday)**, Sunday before Sexagesima. [ME f. L, = seventieth (day), f. as foll. (w. ref. to period of 70 days from Septuagesima to Saturday after Easter)]

Sĕ'ptūagĭnt *n.* Greek version of O.T. including the Apocrypha, said to have been made about 270 B.C. by seventy-two translators. [f. L *septuaginta* seventy]

sĕ'pt|um *n.* (*pl.* ~**a**). (Anat., Bot., & Zool.) Partition such as that between the nostrils or the chambers of a poppy-fruit or shell. [f. L *s(a)eptum* (*saepire saept-* enclose f. *saepes* hedge)]

sĕ'ptūple *a.*, *n.*, & *v.* **1.** *a.* & *n.* Sevenfold (amount). **2.** *v.t.* & *i.* Multiply by seven. [f. LL *septuplus* f. L *septem* seven]

sĕ'ptūplėt (*or* -ū'-) *n.* **1.** One of seven children born at a birth. **2.** (Mus.) Group of seven notes to be played in the time of four or six. [f. as prec., after *triplet* etc.]

sėpŭ'lchral (-kral) *a.* Of sepulchre(s) or sepulture (*sepulchral mound, pillar,* etc.; *sepulchral customs*); suggestive of the tomb, funereal, gloomy, dismal, (*a sepulchral look, voice*); hence ~LY[2] *adv.* [f. F *sépulchral* or f. L *sepulchralis* (as foll.; see -AL)]

sĕ'pulchre, *sĕ'pulcher, (-ker) *n.*, & *v.t.* **1.** *n.* Tomb esp. cut in rock or built of stone or brick, burial vault or cave; **the Holy S~** (in which Christ was laid); **whited** ~, hypocrite (w. ref. to Matt. 23:27). **2.** *v.t.* Lay in sepulchre; serve as sepulchre for. [ME f. OF, f. L *sepulc(h)rum* (*sepelire sepult-* bury)]

sĕ'pulture *n.* Burying, putting in the grave. [ME f. OF, f. L *sepultura* (as prec.; see -URE)]

seq(q). *abbr.* the following. [f. L *sequens* etc.]

sėquā'cious (-shus) *a.* (arch.) Inclined to follow, lacking independence or originality, servile; (of reasoning or reasoner) not inconsequent, coherent; hence ~LY[2] *adv.*, **sėquă'**CITY *n.* [f. L *sequax* (*sequi* follow); see -ACIOUS]

sē'quel *n.* What follows (esp. as result); continuation or resumption of a story or process or the like after a pause or intended or provisional ending (**in the** ~, as things developed afterwards). [ME, f. OF *sequelle* or f. L *sequel(l)a* (*sequi* follow)]

sėquē'la *n.* (*pl.* ~**e**). (Path., esp. in *pl.*) Morbid condition or symptom following upon some disease. [L (*sequi* follow)]

sē'quence *n.* **1.** (Order of) succession, coming after or next, set of things that belong next to each other on some principle of order, series without gaps, (*shall follow the sequence of events; give the facts in historical sequence; calamities in rapid sequence*); set of poems on one theme; part of cinema film dealing with one scene or topic; set of three or more cards next to each other in value. **2.** Succession without implication of causality (opp. *consequence*). **3.** (Mus.) Repetition of phrase or melody at higher or lower pitch. **4.** (Gram.) ~ **of tenses,** dependence of subordinate verb tense according to certain rules on tense of principal verb (e.g. *I think you* are, *thought you* were, *wrong*). **5.** (Eccl.) Hymn said or sung after the Gradual or Alleluia that precedes the Gospel. [ME, f. LL *sequentia* f. part. of *sequi* follow; see -ENCE]

sē'quent *a.* Following as sequence or consequence; consecutive. [OF, or f. L *sequens* (*sequi* follow; see -ENT)]

sėquĕ'ntial (-shal) *a.* Forming a sequence or consequence or sequela; hence ~ITY (-shĭă'l-) *n.*, ~LY[2] *adv.* [f. SEQUENCE after *consequential*]

sėquĕ'ster *v.* **1.** *v.t.* Seclude, isolate, set apart, (*sequester oneself from the world*; esp. in *p.p.*: *a sequestered life, retreat, cottage*); (Chem.) bind (metal ion) so that it cannot react. **2.** (Law) seize temporary possession of (debtor's estate etc.); (Eccl.) apply (income of benefice) to clearing of incumbent's debts or accumulating fund for next incumbent. **3.** Confiscate, appropriate. [ME, f. OF *sequestrer* or f. LL *sequestrare* commit for safe keeping f. L *sequester* trustee]

sėquĕ'str|āte (*or* sē'kwĭs-) *v.t.* = prec. 2, 3; hence or cogn. ~ABLE *a.*, **sēquėstr**A'TION, **sē'quėstrāt**OR, *ns.* [f. LL *sequestrare* (as prec.) + -ATE[3]]

sėquĕ'str|um *n.* (*pl.* ~**a**). Piece of dead bone or other tissue detached from surrounding parts;

hence ~AL *a.*, **sēquèstrŏ'**TOMY *n.* [mod. L, neut. (as n.) of L *sequester* standing apart]

sē'quĭn *n.* **1.** Circular spangle on dress; hence ~(**n**)ED² (-nd) *a.* **2.** (Hist.) Venetian gold coin. [F, f. It. *zecchino* (*zecca* a mint f. Arab. *sikka* a die)]

sèquoi'a *n.* Californian coniferous tree of great height. [mod. L genus-name, f. *Sequoiah*, name of a Cherokee]

sēr'a. See SERUM.

sĕră'c *n.* One of the castellated masses into which a glacier is divided at steep points by the crossing of crevasses. [f. Swiss F *sérac*, orig. name of a compact white cheese]

sera'glio (-ah'lyō) *n.* (*pl.* ~**s**). Harem; (Hist.) Turkish palace, esp. that of Sultan with government offices etc. at Constantinople. [f. It. *serraglio* f. Turk. f. Pers. *sarāy* palace; cf. foll.]

serai (-rī' *or* -rah'ĭ) *n.* = CARAVANSERAI. [f. Turk. f. Pers. (as prec.)]

seră'ng *n.* (Anglo-Ind.) Native head of Lascar crew. [Hindi, f. Pers. *sarhang* commander]

sĕra'pe, săra'pe, zăra'pe, (-ah'pā) *n.* Shawl or blanket worn as cloak by Spanish-Americans. [Mexican Sp.]

sĕ'raph *n.* (*pl.* ~**im** *or* ~**s**). Celestial being, one of the highest ORDER¹ of ninefold celestial hierarchy gifted esp. with love and associated with light, ardour, and purity. [back formation f. *seraphim* (cf. CHERUB) pl. f. LL f. Gk *seraphim* f. Heb. *śᵉrāpīm*]

seră'ph|ĭc *a.* Of or like seraphim; ecstatically adoring or fervent; **S~ic Doctor,** St. Bonaventura; hence ~ICALLY *adv.* [f. med. L *seraphicus* f. LL (as prec.; see -IC)]

sĕraskier' *n.* (Hist.) Turkish commander-in-chief and minister of war. [Turk., f. Pers. *sar'askar* head of army]

Sērb, Sēr'bĭan, *adjs.* & *ns.* (Native, inhabitant, or language) of Serbia. [f. Serbo-Croatian *Srb* Serb + -IAN]

Sēr'bō- *comb. form.* Serbian, as: **~-Cro'at, ~-Croa'tian,** (of the) Slavonic language of the Serbs and Croats. [f. prec. + -o-]

Sērbō'nĭan *a.* ~ **bog,** difficult position with no way of escape. [f. Gk *Serbōnis* (*limnē* lake) in Nile delta, in which whole armies were said to have disappeared (Milton *Paradise Lost* ii. 592)]

sēre¹, sear², *n.* Catch of gun-lock holding hammer at half or full cock. [prob. f. OF *serre* lock, bolt, grasp (*serrer*; see SERRIED)]

sēre². See SEAR¹.

sēre³ *n.* (Ecol.) Sequence of animal or plant communities. [f. SERIES]

serein (serā'ṅ) *n.* Fine rain falling at evening in tropical climates from cloudless sky. [F, f. OF *serain* f. Gallo-Rom. **seranum* f. L *serum* evening (*serus* late)]

sĕrenā'd|e *n.*, & *v.t.* **1.** *n.* Evening song or instrumental piece sung or played esp. by lover at his lady's window, or suitable for this; = foll. **2.** *v.t.* Sing or play serenade to; hence ~ER¹ *n.* [f. F *sérénade* f. It. *serenata* (*sereno* SERENE); see -ADE]

sĕrena'ta (-nah'-) *n.* (Mus.) Cantata with pastoral subject; simple form of orchestral or wind-band suite. [It. (as prec.)]

sĕrendĭ'pĭt|ȳ *n.* The faculty of making happy and unexpected discoveries by accident; hence ~OUS a. [coined by Horace Walpole (1754) after *The Three Princes of Serendip* (Sri Lanka), a fairy-tale]

sèrē'ne (*or* ser-) *a.* (**-er, -est**), *n.*, & *v.t.* **1.** *a.* (Of sky, air, etc.) clear and calm, (of sea etc.) unruffled; placid, tranquil, unperturbed, (*a serene temper, look, life*); **all ~,** ||(sl.) all right; **His, Her, Their, Your, S~ Highness**(**es**) (titles used of or to members of some European royal families); hence or cogn. ~LY² (-nlĭ) *adv.*, **serĕ'n**ITY *n.* (**your** etc. **Serenity,** title of reigning prince or similar dignitary). **2.** *n.* Serene expanse of sky, sea, etc. **3.** *v.t.* (poet.) Make (sky, brow, etc.) serene. [f. L *serenus*]

sērf *n.* Villein, person whose service is attached to the soil and transferred with it (cf. SLAVE); oppressed person, drudge; hence ~'AGE, ~'DOM, ~'HOOD, *ns.* [OF, f. L *servus* slave]

sērge *n.* Durable twilled worsted etc. fabric. [ME f. OF *sarge, serge* f. Rom. **sarica* f. L *serica* (*lana*); see SILK]

ser'geant (sār'jant) *n.* **1.** (Mil.) Non-commissioned officer above corporal; **~-major,** *highest-ranking non-commissioned officer; ||(**regimental**) **~-major,** warrant officer assisting adjutant of regiment or battalion; **company ~-major,** highest non-commissioned officer of company. **2.** Police officer ranking below ||inspector or *captain. **3. S~ Baker,** (Austral.) large brightly-coloured sea-fish; **~-fish,** sea-fish with lateral stripes suggesting chevron. **4.** Hence ~SHIP *n.* [ME, f. OF *sergent* f. L *serviens -entis* servant (*servire* SERVE; see -ENT)]

Sergt. *abbr.* Sergeant.

sēr'ĭal *a.* & *n.* **1.** *a.* Of, in, forming, a series, whence ~ITY (-ă'l-) *n.*; (of story etc.) issued in instalments (~ **rights,** copyright in regard to story etc. so issued), whence ~IST (1) *n.*; (of publication) appearing in successive parts published usu. at regular intervals, periodical; (Mus.) of composition using transformations of a fixed SERIES of notes, whence ~ISM (3), ~IST (2), *ns.*; ~ **number** (showing position in a series); hence ~LY² *adv.* **2.** *n.* Serial story; a serial publication, periodical. **3.** Hence ~IZE *v.t.* [f. SERIES + -AL]

sēr'ĭate¹ *a.*, **sēr'ĭāte²** *v.t.* (Arrange) in the form of a series, in orderly sequence; so **sērĭA'**TION *n.* [f. SERIES + -ATE²,³]

sĕrĭā'tĭm (*or* sēr-) *adv.* Point by point, taking one subject etc. after another in regular order, (*consider, examine, discuss, take,* etc., *seriatim*). [med. L f. L *series*, after LITERATIM etc.]

Sēr'ĭc *a.* (rhet. etc.) Chinese. [f. L *sericus*; see SILK]

sèrĭ'ceous (-shus) *a.* (Bot. & Zool.) Covered with glossy down. [f. as prec.; see -EOUS]

sĕ'rĭcŭltur|e *n.* Silkworm-breeding; production of raw silk; hence ~AL *a.*, ~IST (3) *n.*, (-ŭ'lcher-). [f. F *sériciculture* f. LL *sericum*; see SILK, -I-, CULTURE]

sĕrĭē'ma *n.* Long-legged loud-voiced crested Brazilian or Argentinian bird. [mod. L, f. Tupi *siriema* etc. crested]

sēr'ies (-z; *or* -ĭz) *n.* (*pl.* same). **1.** Number of things of which each is similar to the preceding or in which each successive pair are similarly related, sequence, succession, order, row, set, (*a series of kings, misfortunes*; **in** ~, in ordered succession); group of stamps, coins, etc., of different denominations but issued at one time, in one reign, etc.; group of successive games between same teams, programmes with same actors etc. but each complete in itself, lectures by same speaker or on same subject, etc. **2.** Set of successive issues of a periodical, of articles on one subject or by one writer, etc., esp. (*first, second,* etc., *series*) when numbered separately from a preceding or following set; set of independent books in common format or under common title or supervised by common general editor. **3.** (Geol.) Set of strata with common characteristic. **4.** (Chem.) Set of elements with common properties or of compounds related in composition or structure. **5.** (Math.) Set of quantities constituting a progression or having the several values determined by a common relation (**arithmetical, geometrical, ~**, one in ARITHMETICAL, GEOMETRICAL, progression). **6.** (Electr.) Set of batteries etc. having positive electrode of each connected with negative electrode of next; set of circuits arranged **in ~**, so that same current passes through each circuit. **7.** (Zool.) Number of connected genera, families, etc. **8.** (Mus.) Arrangement of twelve chromatic notes as basis for serial music. [L, = row, chain (*serere* join, connect)]

sĕ'rĭf *n.* (Typogr.) Cross-line finishing off a stroke of a letter as in T (compare SANSERIF T). [perh. f. Du. *schreef* dash, line f. Gmc **skrebh-*]

serĭ'graph|ȳ *n.* Art or process of printing designs by means of a silk screen; so **sĕ'rĭ**GRAPH, ~ER¹, *ns.* [irreg. f. L *sericum* SILK + -GRAPHY]

sĕ'rĭn *n.* Small green Mediterranean finch of genus *Serinus*, esp. the wild canary. [F, of uncert. orig.]

sĕrĭnĕ'tte *n.* Instrument for teaching cage-birds to sing. [F (as prec.; see -ETTE)]

serĭ'nga (-ngg*a*) *n.* **1.** Syringa. **2.** Brazilian rubber-tree. [F, f. as SYRINGA]

sēr̃ĭō-cŏ'm|ĭc *a.* Combining the serious and the comic, jocular in intention but simulating seriousness or vice versa; hence ~ICALLY *adv.* [f. foll. + -O- + COMIC]

sēr̃'ĭous *a.* **1.** Thoughtful, earnest, sober, sedate, responsible, not frivolous or reckless or given to trifling, (*has a serious look, air*; *a serious young person*); **~ music, play,** etc., (not merely for amusement); **~ thought,** real deliberation. **2.** Important, demanding consideration, not to be trifled with, not slight, (*this is a serious matter, question, step*; *make a serious alteration*; *have a serious rival in her affections*; *serious illness, danger, wound, damage, accident, defeat*); **~ charge, offence,** (esp. of rape etc.) **3.** Sincere, not ironical or jesting or perfunctory, in earnest, (*are you serious?*; *and now to be serious*). **4.** Concerned with religion or ethics, not worldly or secular, (*serious subjects* etc.); (joc. or arch.) religious-minded, with thoughts concentrated on salvation. **5.** Hence ~LY² *adv.* (esp. as preface to sentence implying that irony etc. is now to cease), ~NESS *n.* [ME, f. OF *serieux* or LL *seriosus* (L *serius*; see -OUS)]

sĕ'rĭph. Var. of SERIF.

ser'jeant (sar̃'j*a*nt) *n.* **1.** ~**(-at-law)**, (Hist.) barrister of highest rank. **2. ~-at-arms,** court, parliamentary, or city official with ceremonial duties. **3.** ‖**Common S~**, circuit judge of Central Criminal Court. **4.** ‖ = SERGEANT 1 (in official lists). **5.** Hence ~SHIP *n.* [var. of SERGEANT]

sēr̃'mon *n.* **1.** Discourse usu. based on Scripture text and delivered from pulpit by way of religious instruction or exhortation; similar discourse on religious or moral subject delivered elsewhere or published; **S~ on the Mount,** discourse of Christ recorded in Matt. 5–7. **2.** Moral reflection suggested by natural objects etc. (esp. *sermons in stones*); piece of admonition or reproof, lecture. **3.** Hence ~IZE (1, 2) *v.t.* & *i.* [ME, f. AF *sermun*, OF *sermon* f. L *sermo -onis* discourse, talk]

sērŏ'log|ȳ *n.* Scientific study of sera and their effects; hence **sēro**LO'GICAL *a.*, ~IST (3) *n.* [f. SERUM + -O- + -LOGY]

serō'sa *n.* (Med.) Serous membrane. [mod. L, fem. of med. L *serosus* SEROUS]

sĕ'rotĭne *n.* Chestnut-coloured European bat (*Eptesicus serotinus*). [f. F *sérotine* f. L *serotinus* late, of the evening (*serus* late)]

sērotō'nĭn *n.* Compound present in blood serum, with vaso-constrictive action. [f. SERUM + -O- + TONIC + -IN]

sēr̃'ous *a.* Of or like serum, watery; **~ gland, membrane,** (with serous secretion); so **sēr**O'SITY *n.* [f. F *séreux* or f. med. L *serosus* (as SERUM; see -OUS)]

sēr̃'pent *n.* **1.** Scaly limbless reptile, snake esp. of large kind, or in rhet. use (**the, the old, S~**, the Devil, w. ref. to Gen. 3 & Rev. 20); (fig.) treacherous person esp. one who worms himself into favour for base ends; kind of firework with serpentine motion; PHARAOH'*s serpent*. **2.** (Mus.) Old wind instrument of long leather-covered wooden tube with several bends, giving powerful deep note. **3. ~-charmer,** snake-charmer; **~-eater,** (1) secretary-bird, (2) markhor; **~-grass,** Alpine bistort; **~ lizard,** seps; **~'s-tongue,** adder's-tongue. **4.** Hence **serpĕ'ntĭ**FORM, ~-LIKE, *adjs.* [ME f. OF, f. L *serpens -entis* part. of *serpere* creep; see -ENT]

sēr̃'pentīne *a.* & *n.*, & *v.i.* **1.** *a.* Of or like a serpent (lit. or fig.), writhing, coiling, tortuous, sinuous, meandering, cunning, subtle, treacherous, (*serpentine windings* of stream, road, etc., or of insinuation); **~ verse,** metrical line beginning and ending with same word; **~ wisdom** (profound, w. ref. to Matt. 10:16). **2.** *n.* Soft rock mainly of hydrated magnesium silicate, usu. dark green and sometimes mottled or spotted like serpent's skin, taking high polish and used as decorative material; (Skating) figure of three circles in line. **3.** *v.i.* Move sinuously, meander. [v. f. a., ME, f. OF *serpentin* f. LL *serpentinus* (as prec.; see -INE¹); n. f. med. L *serpentina, -um* abs. use of a.]

serpĭ'gĭnous *a.* (Of skin-disease etc.) creeping from one part to another. [f. med. L *serpigo -ginis* ringworm f. L *serpere* creep, + -OUS]

sēr̃'pūla *n.* (*pl.* ~**e**). Marine worm of genus *Serpula*, inhabiting beautifully coloured tortuous calcareous tubes often massed together. [LL, = small serpent, f. L *serpere* creep]

sĕ'rra *n.* (*pl.* ~**e**). (Anat., Bot., & Zool.) Serrated organ, structure, or edge. [L, = saw]

sĕrradĭ'lla *n.* Clover of genus *Ornithopus*, grown as fodder. [Port., dim. of *serrado* serrated]

sĕ'rran *n.* Carnivorous sea-fish of family Serranidae. [f. mod. L *serranus* f. L *serra* saw; see -AN]

sĕ'rrāte¹ *a.* (esp. Anat., Bot., & Zool.) Notched like saw. [f. L *serratus* (as prec.; see -ATE²)]

sĕrr|ā'te² *v.t.* (esp. in *p.p.* as *a.*) Provide with sawlike edge; hence ~A'TION *n.* [f. LL *serrare* f. L *serra* saw, + -ATE³]

sĕ'rrĭed (-rĭd) *a.* (Of ranks of soldiers, rows of trees, etc.) pressed together, without gaps, close. [f. p.p. of *serry* press close prob. f. F *serré* p.p. of *serrer* close f. Rom. **serrare* f. L *-serare* (*sera* lock), or f. p.p. of obs. *serr* f. OF *serrer*]

sĕ'rrul|āte (-rōō-) *a.* Finely serrate, with series of small notches; hence ~A'TION *n.* [f. mod. L *serrulatus* f. L *serrula* (SERRA; see -ULE); see -ATE²]

sēr̃'|um *n.* (*pl.* **~a** *or* **~ums**). Whey; amber-coloured liquid which separates from clot when blood coagulates; blood serum as antitoxin or therapeutic agent; watery animal fluid; **~um sickness** etc., skin eruption, fever, etc., sometimes following injections of serum. [L, = whey]

sēr̃'val *n.* Tawny black-spotted long-legged African tiger-cat (*Felis serval*). [F, f. Port. *cerval* deerlike (*cervo* deer f. L *cervus*)]

sēr̃'vant *n.* **1.** Person who has undertaken usu. in return for stipulated pay to carry out the orders of an individual or corporate employer; (esp.) one who lives in house of master or mistress, receiving board and lodging and wages and performing domestic duties; CIVIL, PUBLIC, *servant*; **~s' hall,** room in which servants of large household have meals etc.; ~ **of ~s,** lowest of dependants, esp. ~ *of the ~s of God,* title assumed by popes, transl. of *servus servorum Dei*; **a good ~ but a bad master** (of things that should be treated as means and not ends). **2.** Devoted follower, person willing to serve another, (*a servant of Jesus Christ*); ||**your humble ~** (arch., in subscription of letter or as form of ironical courtesy); ||**your obedient ~** (epistolary form preceding signature, now used only in letters of official type). [ME f. OF (as foll.; see -ANT)]

sẽrve *v.* & *n.* **1.** *v.t.* & *i.* Be servant (to), do service (to), be useful (to); render obedience to (deity etc.); be employed *in* (organization, esp. armed forces, or country etc., esp. abroad); be soldier etc. (*in* war, *against* enemy, etc.); ~ **at table,** act as waiter; ~ **two masters,** seek to obey two conflicting principles. **2.** Meet needs (of), avail, suffice, satisfy, perform function, be suitable, do what is required for, (*serve a purpose*; *to serve some private ends*; *that excuse will not serve you*; *his attempt served only to postpone the inevitable*; *it serves to show the folly of*; *one packet serves him for a week*; *nothing would serve (him) but absolute submission*; *a sofa serving (him) as* or *for (a) bed*; *buses serve the area*; *one curate serves two parishes*); go through due period of (office, apprenticeship, prison sentence, etc.); (Mil.) keep (gun, battery, etc.) firing; copulate with (mare etc.; esp. of stallion etc. hired for purpose); (Naut.) bind (rope etc.) with small cord to strengthen it; (of tide) be suitable for getting out of harbour etc.; **it will ~** (do what is absolutely necessary); **as memory ~s,** whenever one remembers; ~ **the** or one's **need(s)** or **turn,** be adequate; **as occasion ~s,** when circumstances are favourable; ~ **the purpose of,** take the place of, be used as; ~ (one's) **time,** undergo imprisonment, apprenticeship, etc.; ~ one's **time,** hold office for normal period. **3.** Dish *up*, set (food) on table, set out ready, distribute, supply (person *with*), make legal delivery of (writ etc.), (Eccl.) act as server (at), (Tennis etc.) set ball or set (ball) in play, (*fish served up nearly cold*; *asparagus served with butter*; *serve up dinner*; *ladies and gentlemen, dinner is served*; *serve ammunition, rations,* etc., *out* or *round*; *was serving a customer (with stockings)*, *serving in the shop*; *serve* person, *town,* etc., *with gas, water*); *serve with the same* SAUCE; ~ person **with** (warrant, writ, notice, process, attachment, etc.), ~ (writ) etc. **on** person, deliver document to person concerned in legally formal manner. **4.** Treat, treat to, pay (person) out, (*has served me shamefully*; *you may serve me as you will*); play (trick etc.) on; ~ **out,** retaliate on; ~(s) **him right!** (excl. of satisfaction at sight of offender getting his deserts). **5.** Hence (-)**sẽr'**VER[1] (1, 2) *n.*, (esp., Eccl.) celebrant's assistant, **sẽr'**VERY (3) *n.*, room from which meals etc. are served and in which utensils are kept, **sẽr'**VING[2] *a.* (*serving-man*, male servant). **6.** *n.* (Tennis etc.) = SERVICE[1] 10. [ME, f. OF *servir* f. L *servire -it-* (*servus* slave)]

Sẽr'vian[1]. Var. of SERBIAN.

Sẽr'vian[2] *a.* ~ **wall** (built by Servius Tullius, king of Rome in 6th c. B.C.). [f. *Servius* + -AN]

sẽr'vĭce[1] *n.*, & *v.t.* **1.** *n.* Being servant, servant's status; master's or mistress's employ; **be in** or **go into** (esp. domestic) ~; **take ~ with,** become servant to; **take into** one's ~, employ (person) as servant. **2.** Department of royal or public employ or of work done to meet some general need, persons engaged in it, employment in it, (*the* CIVIL, *consular*, DIPLOMATIC, ||PREVENTIVE, SECRET, *service*; *the bus, railway, telephone,* etc., *service*; *the public services*); ||(in *pl.*) public supply of water, electricity, etc.; **the (fighting) ~s,** navy, army, and air force; **on (active) ~,** employed in the fighting services; **see ~,** have experience esp. in the fighting services; (*attrib.*) of the kind issued to the services (*service rifle*). **3.** Person's disposal or behalf; **at your** etc. ~, ready to obey orders or be used; ||**on His** or **Her Majesty's ~** (frank stamped on official envelopes etc.). **4.** What employee or subordinate or vassal is bound to, work done, or doing of work, on behalf of employer, benefit conferred on or exertion made on behalf of someone, expression of willingness to confer or make these, performance of functions by machine etc., (*has a right to my service*; *asks for my services*; *will you do me a service?*; *typewriter, typist, has given good service*); **has seen ~,** has been much used, shows signs of wear; **my ~ to him** (arch. form of respectful message); YEOMAN *service*. **5.** Use, assistance, (*can I, will it, be of service to you?*). **6.** Liturgical form or office appointed for use on some occasion, (whole proceedings, usu. including one such service or more, of) single meeting of congregation for worship, musical setting of all or several of the invariable parts of a liturgy adapted for such treatment (*the communion, burial,* etc., *service*; *special services were held*; *holds four services every Sunday*; *are you going to (the) service?*); DIVINE *service*; **full ~** (performed by choir without solos, or performed with music wherever possible); **plain ~** (read or monotoned). **7.** Legal serving of or *of* writ etc.; **personal ~,** delivery with announcement of contents to person affected; ~ **by publication, substitution,** publishing of writ etc. by posting up or insertion in newspaper or by handing to neighbour etc., recognized as sufficient under some conditions. **8.** Serving of food etc.; set of dishes, plates, etc., required for serving meal (*dinner, dessert, tea,* etc., *-service*). **9.** System of trains, steamers, buses, etc., plying at stated times; transport thus provided (*a fast service to London*). **10.** (Single act of) serving in tennis etc., manner of serving, person's turn to serve, game in which one serves, (*his service is weak, terrific*; *whose service is it?*; *he lost his service*). **11.** Provision of what is necessary for due maintenance of thing or operation; assistance or advice given to customers after sale by manufacturers or vendors of goods. **12.** Serving of mare etc. **13.** ~ **area,** (1) area for supply of petrol, refreshments, etc., near road, (2) area round broadcasting station where reception is normally satisfactory; **~-book,** book of offices of a Church; ~ **bus** or **car,** (Austral. & N.Z.) motor coach; ~ **charge,** additional charge for service rendered; **~-court,** (Tennis etc.) area within which validly served ball must fall; ~ **dress,** ordinary military etc. uniform; ~ **engineer** (who maintains and services equipment already in use); ||~ **flat** (in which domestic service and sometimes meals are provided by the management); ~ **industry** (providing services, not goods); **~-line** (bounding service-court); **~man** (-sm-), (1) man in fighting services, (2) man providing service (sense 11); ~ **module** (containing main engine and power supplies of spacecraft); ~ **pipe** (conveying water or gas from main to building); ~ **road** (to serve houses lying back from main road, not for through traffic); ~ **station,** place where service (esp. of petrol etc.) is available; **~woman** (-sw-), woman in fighting services. **14.** *v.t.* Provide service (sense 11) for (machine etc.); supply with service; pay interest on (debt etc.). [ME f. OF, or f. L *servitium* (*servus* slave; see -ICE)]

sẽr'vĭce[2] *n.* ~ (**tree**), European tree of genus *Sorbus,* esp. *S. domestica* with leaves like those of mountain ash, cream-coloured flowers, and small round or pear-shaped fruit eaten when overripe; **~-berry,** (1) fruit of service tree, (2) (edible fruit of) Amer. shrub of genus *Amelanchier.* [earlier *serves*, pl. of obs. *serve* f. OE *syrfe* f. Gmc *surbhjōn* f. pop. L **sorbea* f. L *sorbus*]

ser'vice|able (-sa-) *a.* Of use, useful or usable, willing and able to render or capable of rendering service, (*a serviceable person, reminder, instrument*); durable, suited for rough use or ordinary wear rather than for ornament; hence ~ABI'LITY, **~able**NESS (-beln-), *ns.*, **~ab**LY² *adv.* [ME, f. OF *servisable* (as SERVICE¹, -ABLE)]

servie'tte *n.* Table-napkin. [ME f. OF (*servir* SERVE; see -ETTE)]

ser'vile *a.* **1.** Of or being a slave or slaves; ~ **war** (between slaves in revolt and their owners). **2.** As of a slave, slavish, cringing, fawning, menial, completely dependent, (*servile spirit, creature, submission, flattery, fear, imitation*); hence **servi'l**ITY *n.* **3.** ~ **works,** (Eccl.) menial or mechanical work forbidden on Sundays and major Church festivals. **4.** Hence ~LY² (-l-lĭ) *adv.* [ME, f. L *servilis* (*servus* slave; see -IL)]

ser'ving *n.* In vbl senses; quantity of food served to one person, helping. [f. SERVE + -ING¹]

ser'vitor *n.* **1.** (arch. or poet.) Attendant, henchman, servant. **2.** (Hist.) Oxford undergraduate assisted from college funds and performing menial duties in return; hence ~SHIP *n.* [ME f. OF f. LL (as SERVE; see -OR)]

ser'vitūde *n.* **1.** Slavery (lit. or fig.); subjection (esp. involuntary) to a master, bondage; PENAL *servitude.* **2.** (Law). Subjection of property to an easement. [ME f. OF, f. L *servitudo -inis* (*servus* slave; see -TUDE)]

ser'vō *n.* (*pl.* **~s**). Servo-motor or servo-mechanism. [abbr.]

ser'vō- *comb. form* denoting means of powered automatic control of a larger system (*servo-assisted, -mechanism, -motor*). [f. *servo-motor* f. F. *servo-moteur* f. L *servus* slave + F *moteur* MOTOR]

se'samė *n.* Annual E. Ind. herbaceous plant (*Sesamum indicum*) with seeds used in various ways as food and yielding an edible oil; its seeds; (**open**) ~, [w. ref. to Arabian-Nights tale] magical or mysterious means of commanding access to what is usu. inaccessible. [f. L f. Gk *sēsamon, sēsamē*, of Oriental orig.]

se'samoid *a.* & *n.* **1.** *a.* Shaped like a sesame-seed, nodular, (esp. of small independent bones developed in tendons passing over angular structure such as the kneecap and the navicular bone). **2.** *n.* Sesamoid bone. [f. prec. + -OID]

se'squi- *pref.* denoting one and a half. **1.** (Chem.) (Of compound) in which there are three equivalents of a named element or radical to two others (*sesquioxide, sesquisulphide*). **2.** **~a'ltera** (-ă'l-), (Mus.) interval or group of notes having ratio 2:3 to another; **~cente'nary, ~cente'nnial,** (festival) of the one-hundred-and-fiftieth anniversary; **~peda'lian** (-ā'l-), (of word) many-syllabled [f. L *sesquipedalis* (Horace), lit. 1½ feet long], cumbrous and pedantic; **sesqui'plicate,** in ratio of square roots of cubes. [L, f. **semis-que* a half in addition]

sess. Var. of CESS¹.

se'ssile *a.* (Bot. & Zool.) (Of flower, leaf, eye, etc.) attached directly by the base without stalk or peduncle; fixed in one position, immobile; ~ **oak,** durmast. [f. L *sessilis* (*sedēre sess-* sit; see -IL)]

se'ssion (-shon) *n.* **1.** (arch.) Being seated, sitting posture. **2.** Being assembled esp. for transaction of deliberative or judicial business; single uninterrupted meeting for such purpose; period during which such meetings are held daily or at short or regular intervals; period between meeting and prorogation or final adjournment of legislative body; period spent continuously in an activity; **in** ~, sitting or assembled for business, not on vacation. **3.** ||Academic year; *university term. **4.** Governing body of a Presbyterian church. **5.** **Court of S~,** supreme civil court in Scotland; ||KIRK-*-session*; LORDS *of Session*; **petty ~s,** meeting of two or more magistrates for summary trying of certain offences; QUARTER¹ *sessions.* **6.** Hence ~AL *a.* (**~al order,** one valid only for, renewable each, session of Parliament). [ME f. OF, or f. L *sessio -onis* (as prec.; see -ION)]

se'sterce, sester'tius (-shus; *pl.* **-tii** *pr.* -shĭī), *ns.* Ancient-Roman silver (and later bronze) coin and money of account = ¼ denarius or 2½ (later 4) asses. [f. L *sestertius* (*nummus* coin) = 2½ (*semis* half, *tertius* third)]

sester't|ium (-shum) *n.* (*pl.* **~ia**). Ancient-Roman money of account = 1000 sesterces. [L, orig. gen. pl. of prec., w. ellipsis of *mille* thousand]

seste't *n.* Sextet; last six lines of sonnet. [f. It. *sestetto* (*sesto* f. L *sextus* sixth; see -ET¹)]

sesti'na (-tē'-) *n.* Form of rhymed or unrhymed poem with six stanzas of six lines and final triplet, each stanza having same words to end its lines but in different order. [It. (as prec.; cf. -INE⁴)]

set¹ *v.* (-tt-; **set**). **1.** *v.t.* Put, lay, stand, (usu. w. *adv.* or *adv. phr.*: *set load* or *passenger down, ashore*, etc., *statue up, food before person, flowers in water, one brick on another*); ~ (thing) **against** another, balance, reckon as counterpoise or compensation for it; ~ **apart,** reserve, separate; ~ **aside,** reserve, reject, disregard, annul; ~ **by,** (arch.) reserve, save for future use; *set* FOOT¹ 12, SEAL², *on*; ~ *stone* **out,** lay with edge projecting beyond one below; ~ person **over** others or thing, put in authority. **2.** Apply (thing) *to* (*set pen to paper, bugle to* one's *lips, spurs to horse*); *set* FIRE¹ *to*; ~ one's **hand to,** sign (document), begin (task); *set* SEAL² *to*; *set* one's SHOULDER *to the wheel*; ~ one's **wits to,** try to solve (problem); ~ one's **wits to** another's, argue with him. **3.** Station, place ready, place or turn in right or specified position or direction, dispose suitably for use or action or display; put hands of (clock or watch) to right time; arrange for (alarm-clock) to sound at desired time; cause (hen) to sit on eggs; place (eggs) for hen to sit on; put (seed, plant, etc.) in ground to grow (QUICK*set*); arrange (butterfly etc.) as specimen; make (trap) ready to catch victim; *start (a fire); (Bridge) defeat (contract); give sharp edge to (razor); give teeth of (saw) alternate outward inclination; lay (table) for meal; place (chairs etc.) for visitors etc.; *set* one's CAP¹ *at*; ~ **sail,** (1) hoist sail, (2) begin voyage; *set the* SCENE; ~ **a** or (Naut.) **the watch,** station sentinels etc.; SHARP¹-*set.* **4.** Join, attach, fasten; fix, determine, decide; appoint, settle, establish; put parts of (bone, limb, etc.) into right relative position for healing after fracture or dislocation, deal thus with (fracture or dislocation); give (person, *oneself*) permanent feeling *against* person or thing; fix (hair) while damp so that it dries in desired style; insert (jewel) in gold etc. as frame or foil; ~ **eyes on,** catch sight of; ~ one's **face against,** steadfastly oppose; ~ one's **heart, hopes,** etc., **on,** long for, be resolved to get; ~ one's **life on a chance** etc., risk it [metaph. from gambling]; *set* PRICE *on*; ~ (STORE, **little, much,** etc.) **by,** estimate at specified value; ~ one's **teeth,** clench them, (fig.) make up one's mind inflexibly. **5.** (Print.) ~ (**up**), arrange (type) in words etc., construct words of (book etc.) in type; print in specified manner (~ **close,** print with small spaces between words or letters; ~ **out** or **wide,** print with these spaces large). **6.** Bring by placing, arranging, impelling, or other means, into specified state (*set things right, to rights, in order, in motion*; *set* person *on his feet* (lit. or fig.), *box on its end*; *set machine going*, person *laughing*); *set* persons *by the* EAR[1]*s*; *set* person *at* EASE; *set on* FIRE[1], *on* FOOT[1] 12; *set* one's HOUSE[1] *in order*; *set question*, person's *mind* or *heart*, *at* REST[2]; *set* person RIGHT[1] 5; *set* person's *teeth on* EDGE[1]; *set at* DEFIANCE, *at* NAUGHT; ~ **free,** release, liberate. **7.** Make sit down *to* task, order to apply energies *to* doing, cause *to* WORK[1], apply oneself *to* WORK[1], (*set him to dictation, wood-chopping, work at his Greek*); ~ one**self** *to* do, make up one's mind, resolve or undertake. **8.** Exhibit or arrange as pattern or as material to be dealt with (often w. ind. obj.; *set, set* person, *an example, task, problem*, etc., to be followed, done, solved, by him); compose (puzzle, questions, etc.) to be answered; *establish (a record etc.); ~ **the fashion, the pace,** determine it by leading. **9.** ~ **(to music),** provide (poem, words) with music usu. composed for the purpose. **10.** Ornament or provide (surface) *with* (*gold, field, sky, set with gems, daisies, stars*; *shall set top of wall with broken glass, this bed with geraniums*). **11.** *v.t.* & *i.* Turn to solid or hard or rigid from liquid or soft or mobile state; curdle, solidify, harden, (*cement, jelly, has* or *is set*); take shape, develop into definiteness or maturity; (of egg) become solid by cooking or incubation; (of blossom) form into fruit, (of fruit) develop out of blossom, (of tree) develop fruit; (of face) take hard expression; (of eyes) become motionless in death, swoon, etc. **12.** *v.i.* Be brought towards or below horizon by earth's rotation (*sun, moon, sets*); one's **star ~s,** greatness departs. **13.** (Of tide, current, etc., and fig. of feeling, custom, etc.) have motion, gather force, sweep along, show or feel tendency, (*tide sets in, out*; *current sets strongly, eastwards*; *opinion is setting against it*; *his soul set to grief*). **14.** (Of hunting dog) take rigid attitude indicating presence of game; ~ **(to partner),** (of dancer) take position facing partner. **15.** (dial. or vulg.) Sit. **16.** (w. *preps.*): ~ **about,** begin, take steps towards, (task, do*ing*), attack; ~ **(up)on,** urge (dog etc.) to attack (person etc.), attack. **17.** (w. *advs.*): ~ **back,** place farther back in space or time, impede or reverse advance of, (sl.) cost (person) specified amount; ~*-back* n., reversal or arrest of progress, relapse, placing of building etc. farther back than it might have been; ~ **down,** put in writing, record, allow (passenger) to alight, attribute *to*, explain or describe to oneself *as*; ~*-down* n., rebuff; ~ **forth,** make known, declare, expound, adorn, begin journey or expedition; ~ **forward,** (arch.) assist progress of, begin going forward; ~ **in,** arise, come into vogue, become established, (*reaction, rain, set in*; *it set in to rain*), fit (part of garment) into remaining part; ~ **off,** act as adornment or foil to, enhance, make more striking, detonate, use as compensating item *against*, start (person) laughing or talking on pet subject, begin journey; ~*-off* n., thing set off against another, thing of which the amount or effect may be deducted from that of another of opposite tendency, counterpoise, counter-claim, thing that embellishes, adornment to something, (Archit. & Print.) = OFFSET; ~ **on,** instigate, advance to the assault; ~ **out,** embellish, demonstrate, exhibit, declare, begin journey, mark out design of (work to be done); ~*-out* n., commencement, things set out, equipment, display; ~ **to,** begin doing something vigorously, esp. (usu. w. pl. subj.) fighting or arguing; ~*-to* n. (pl. ~*-tos*), combat esp. conducted with fists or verbally; ~ **up,** develop figure of by physical training (esp. in p.p.; *a well set-up man*), start (institution, HOUSE[1], business, etc.), cause (soreness etc.), establish (person) or provide with means of establishment or establish oneself in some capacity (*his father, £5000, set him up as a tobacconist* or *in the tobacco trade*; *shall set up as a dentist*), provide adequately *in* or *with* some article (*am set up with novels for the winter*), place (standard, notice, etc.) in view, prepare (task etc. for another; type etc., see sense 5), begin uttering (protest, shriek, etc.) loudly, propound (theory), restore after ill-health or depression; ~*-up* n., manner or position of setting up, erectness of carriage of body, (colloq.) structure or arrangement of an organization etc., *artificially easy task etc.; ~ **up as** or **for,** (colloq.) make pretensions to being (scholar, moralist, etc.). [OE *settan*, = OS *settian*, OHG *sezzan*, ON *setja*, Goth. *satjan* f. Gmc **satjan* causative of **setjan* SIT]

sĕt[2] *n.* **1.** Number of things or persons that belong together as essentially similar or as complementary to each other, group, collection, (*set of studs, chairs, stamps, novels by Dickens* etc., *golf-clubs, fire-irons, lectures*; *a fine set of men, players, officers*, etc.); = SERVICE[1] 8 (*dinner* etc. *set*); TOILET-*set*; section of society consorting together (*the fast, jet, racing, smart*, etc., *set*); ~ **(of quadrilles),** figures that make up a quadrille; ~ **(of dancers),** number needed to make up square dance; ~ **(of teeth),** person's or animal's natural or artificial teeth collectively; radio or television receiver; (Tennis etc.) group of games counting as unit towards match for side that wins greater number of games in it (~ **point,** state of a set in lawn tennis when one side needs only one more point to win it, this point); (Math. etc.) collection of things having a common property (~ **theory,** study of sets without regard to nature of their individual constituents). **2.** Slip or shoot for planting; young fruit just set. **3.** (poet.) Setting *of* sun. **4.** Way current or wind or opinion etc. sets, drift or tendency *of*, (*the set of the current, public feeling*, etc.; *the set of his mind is towards intolerance*); (Psych.) predisposition to a response etc. **5.** Configuration, conformation, habitual posture, way head etc. is set on or carried, way dress etc. sits or flows, (*the set of the hills, his head, the drapery*); warp or bend or displacement caused by continued pressure or position (*has got a set to the right*); setting of damp hair; (Austral. & N.Z. colloq.) grudge. **6.** (Amount of) alternate deflection of saw-teeth. **7.** Last coat of plaster on wall. **8.** Adjustment of reeds in weaving; (square in) tartan pattern. **9.** Amount of spacing in type causing letters to be close or wide set; width of piece of type. **10.** Number of eggs in nest, or number laid before bird sits, clutch. **11.** (**Dead**) ~, setter's pointing in presence of game; **make a dead ~ at,** attack esp. by argument or ridicule, (esp. of woman) try to win affections of. **12.** Badger's burrow. **13.** Granite paving-block. **14.** (Theatr.) set scene; setting, stage furniture, etc., in production of film or play. [sense 1 f. OF *sette* f. L *secta* SECT; other senses f. prec.]

sĕt[3] *a.* In vbl senses; unmoving, fixed (*set smile, eyes, look, purpose*); (Cricket, of batsman) fully accustomed to prevailing type of bowling, light, etc.; (of book etc.) specified for reading in preparation for examination; (of meal) served according to fixed menu; **all ~,** (colloq.) ready to start; **close-~,** placed with only small intervals between; ~ **fair,** (of weather etc.) fine without sign of breaking; ~ **form** *of prayer* etc.

(not extempore); *~ **line,** trawl-line; ~ **(up)-on,** determined to get etc., absorbed in; ~ **phrase,** invariable or customary arrangement of words; ~ **piece,** (1) fireworks arranged on scaffolding etc., (2) formal or elaborate arrangement esp. in art or literature; **of ~ purpose,** intentionally, deliberately; ~ **scene** (built up of more or less solid material); ~ **screw** (for adjusting or clamping parts of machine); ~ **scrum** (in Rugby Footb., ordered by referee); ~ **speech** (composed beforehand); ~ **square,** draughtsman's right-angled triangular plate for drawing lines esp. at 90°, 60°, 45°, or 30°; ~ **time** (prearranged). [p.p. of SET[1]]

sē't|a *n.* (*pl.* ~**ae**). (Bot. & Zool.) Stiff hair, bristle; so ~A'CEOUS *a.* [L, = bristle]

sėtĭ'ferous, sėtĭ'gerous, sē'tōse, *adjs.* Having bristles. [f. L *seta* bristle, *setiger*, *setosus*, bristly; see -FEROUS, -GEROUS, -OSE[1]]

sē'ton *n.* (Surg.) Skein of cotton etc. passed below skin and left with ends protruding to promote drainage etc. [ME, f. med. L *seto*, *seta*, silk, app. f. L *seta* bristle]

sĕtt. Var. of SET[2] (esp. in senses 2, 8, 12, 13).

sĕttee'[1] *n.* Long seat for more than one person, with back and usu. with arms. [18th c., perh. fanciful var. of SETTLE[1]; see -EE]

sĕttee'[2] *n.* (Hist.) Mediterranean sharp-prowed lateen-sailed vessel with two or three masts. [f. It. *saettia* (*saetta* arrow f. L *sagitta*)]

sĕ'tter *n.* In vbl senses; breed (*English*, *Irish*, *Gordon*, etc., *setter*) of long-haired dog trained to stand rigid on scenting game (cf. SET[1] 14). [ME, f. SET[1] + -ER[1]]

sĕ'tterwort (-wẽrt) *n.* Bear's-foot plant. [f. MLG *siterwort* etc. (see WORT); first element of unkn. orig.]

sĕ'ttĭng *n.* **1.** In vbl senses. **2.** Music to which words of a song etc. are set. **3.** Metal or other frame in which jewel is set; surroundings of any object regarded as its framework or as accessories setting it off, environment, (Theatr.) way a play is put on the stage, scenery, properties, costumes, etc.; cutlery etc. for one person at table. **4.** ~**-board** (on which entomological specimens are set); ~**-lotion** (used to prepare hair for being set); ~**-needle,** needle in wooden handle used in setting specimens; ~**-rule,** brass rule or steel plate with which type is kept temporarily in place as it is set up in the stick; ~**-stick,** compositor's STICK[2]. [ME, f. SET[1] + -ING]

sĕ'ttle[1] *n.* Bench with high back and arms and often with chest from seat to floor. [OE *setl*, = OHG *sezzal*, Goth. *sitls* f. Gmc **setlaz*, **setlam*]

sĕ'ttle[2] *v.* **1.** *v.t.* & *i.* ~ **(down)**, establish or become established in more or less permanent abode or place or way of life (*shall settle in London*, *Australia*; *settle feet in stirrups*, *plant's roots well down in ground*, *invalid among pillows*, *oneself in chair*); ~ **in,** become established in a place. **2.** (Cause to) sit down or *down* to stay for some time (*settle down to dinner*, *a game of chess*, *reading*); (of bird, fog, darkness, etc.) come down and remain for some time; (of disease etc.) establish itself *in* or *on* specified part; **cannot ~ to work, to anything,** (of restless or excited or desultory person). **3.** ~ **(down)**, (cause to) cease from wandering or motion or change or disturbance or turbidity (*things will soon settle into shape*; *marry and settle down*; *settle down to married life*, *to defensive play*; *let excitement settle down*; *settle beer by leaving to stand*, *coffee with egg-white*); aid digestion of (meal); remedy disordered state of (nerves, stomach, etc.). **4.** Bring to or attain fixity or composure or certainty or clarity or decision; (in *p.p.*) fixed, not rapidly changing, (*man of settled convictions*; *settled habitation*, *weather*); ~ **up,** finally arrange (a matter). **5.** Determine, agree upon, decide, appoint; resolve (quarrel, question, doubts, etc.); terminate (lawsuit) by mutual agreement; ~ one's **affairs,** (esp.) make will etc. when death is imminent; ~ **the day,** fix date; ~ **for** or **on,** agree on, accept; ~ **the matter** or **it,** leave no more to be discussed. **6.** *v.t.* Colonize, establish colonists in, become dwellers in, people, (country etc.). **7.** *v.i.* Subside, come down to the bottom or on a surface, (*dust*, *solid matter*, *soon settles*); (of soil, house, foundation, etc.) come gradually to lower level; (of ship) show loss of buoyancy, begin to sink. **8.** *v.t.* Deal effectually with, dispose of, get rid of; get rid of importunity or obstruction of (person) by argument or conflict or killing; *settle* person's HASH[2]. **9.** *v.t.* & *i.* Pay money owed according to (account, bill, etc.); pay (money owed); ~ **up,** draw up and settle (account etc.); ~ **with,** pay (agreed proportion of) bills of (creditor etc.); ‖**se'ttling day,** (St. Exch.) day of settlement. **10.** *v.t.* Bestow legally for life *on* (*settled an annuity on him*; *settled all his property on his wife*); ~**d estate** (held by tenant for life under specified conditions). [OE *setlan* (as prec.)]

sĕ'ttlement (-telm-) *n.* In vbl senses; ‖(St. Exch.) regular settling of accounts; (Law) conveyance of, or creation of estate(s) in, property to make provision for one or more beneficiaries differing from what would result from simple conveyance or statutory inheritance (**marriage ~,** usu. made at time of marriage and in favour of wife, her children, etc.); group of social workers from a college etc. who establish themselves in poor or crowded district to provide education, recreation, etc., for the inhabitants; newly settled tract of country, colony; subsidence of wall, house, soil, etc.; **Act of S~,** statute of 1701 vesting British crown in Sophia of Hanover and her heirs. [f. prec. + -MENT]

sĕ'ttler *n.* In vbl senses; one who settles in new colony, early colonist; (sl.) decisive blow, argument, or event; ~**'s clock,** (Austral.) laughing JACK[1]ass. [f. SETTLE[2] + -ER[1]]

sĕ'ttlor *n.* (Law). One who makes a settlement esp. of property. [f. prec.; see -OR]

sĕ'twall (-awl) *n.* Valerian plant, *Valeriana officinalis*. [ME f. AF *zedewal*, OF *citoual* f. med. L **zedoale*, var. of *zedoarium* ZEDOARY]

sĕ'ven *a.* & *n.* **1.** One more than six; symbol for this (7, vii, VII); card with seven pips; time of seven o'clock; size etc. denoted by seven; set of seven; (in *pl.*) gloves, shoes, etc., of seventh size; ‖(in *pl.*) Rugby Football matches with seven players on each side. **2.** ~**-league boots** (in fairy-tale, giving wearer the power of going seven leagues at each stride); *the Seven* SAGE[2]*s*, or *Wise Men*; *the seven* SEA*s*, *deadly* SIN[1]*s*, *cardinal* VIRTUE*s*, WONDER[1]*s of the world*; ~**-year itch,** alleged tendency to infidelity after seven years of marriage; **S~ Years' War** (of France, Austria, and Russia against Britain and Prussia, 1756–63). **3.** Hence ~FOLD *a.* & *adv.* [OE *seofon*, = OS, OHG *sibun*, ON *sjau*, Goth. *sibun* f. Gmc **sebhun* f. IE **septm*]

sĕventee'n (*or* sĕ'-) *a.* & *n.* One more than sixteen; symbol for this (17, xvii, XVII); size etc. denoted by seventeen; **sweet ~,** age of girlish beauty; hence ~TH[2] *a.* & *n.* [OE *seofontiene*, = OHG **sibunzehan*, ON *sjautján* (as prec., -TEEN)]

sĕ'venth *a.* & *n.* **1.** *a.* Next after sixth; ~ **part,** one of seven equal parts into which thing is or might be divided. **2.** *n.* Seventh part, thing, etc.;

(Mus.) interval of which the span involves seven alphabetical notes, harmonic combination of notes thus separated. **3.** ~ **day,** Saturday (esp. when kept as sabbath); **S~-day Adventists,** millenarian and Sabbatarian sect; *seventh* *GRADE 1; *seventh* HEAVEN. **4.** Hence ~LY² *adv.*, in the seventh place. [f. SEVEN + -TH²]

sĕ'ventў *a.* & *n.* **1.** Seven times ten; symbol for this (70, lxx, LXX); set of seventy persons or things (**the** ~, (1) the disciples in Luke 10, (2) the Sanhedrin, (3) the Septuagint translators); ~ **times seven,** large indefinite number (Matt. 18:22); (in *pl.*) numbers, esp. years of a century or a life, from 70 to 79; hence ~FOLD *a.* & *adv.*, **sĕ'ventĭ**ETH¹ *a.* & *n.* **2.** ~**-one** etc. (arch.) **one-and-~** etc., seventy plus one etc., w. corresp. ordinals ~**-first** etc. [OE *-seofontig*, = OS *sivuntig*, OHG *sibunzug*, ON *sjautigr* (as SEVEN, -TY²)]

sĕ'ver *v.* **1.** *v.t.* & *i.* Separate, divide, part, disunite, (*sever husband and wife*, *friends* or *friendship*, *rope*, *neck*, *connection*; *sea severs England and* or *from France*; *the rope severed under the strain*); (Law) make (oneself) separate party in suit. **2.** *v.t.* Cut or break off, take away, (part) from or *from* whole (*severed his head*, *his head from his body*; *sever oneself from the Church*). **3.** Terminate employment contract of (person). **4.** Hence or cogn. ~ABLE *a.*, ~ANCE *n.* (~**ance pay,** amount paid to employee on termination of contract). [ME, f. AF *severer*, OF *sevrer* f. Rom. **seperare* f. L *separare* SEPARATE²]

sĕ'veral *a.* & *pron.* **1.** *a.* Separate, diverse, distinct, individual, respective, (*all of us in our several provinces*; *went their several ways*; *indicted on three several counts*; *the several members of the Board*; *each several ship sank her opponent*); **collective and ~ responsibility** (of persons as a body and as individuals); **joint and** ~, (of bond etc.) signed by more than one person, of whom each is liable for whole sum; hence ~LY² *adv.* **2.** A few, more than two but not many, (*have called several times*; *myself and several others*). **3.** *pron.* A moderate number, more than two but not many, of the previously mentioned or implied persons or things (*several of you have seen him*; *went salmon-fishing and caught several*). [ME f. AF, f. AL *separalis* f. L *separ* SEPARATE¹; see -AL]

sĕ'veraltў *n.* Separateness; individual or unshared tenure of estate etc. (esp. *in severalty*). [ME, f. AF *severalte* (as prec.; see -TY¹)]

sėvēr'e *a.* (~**r**, ~**st**). **1.** Austere, strict, harsh, rigorous, unsparing, (*severe look*, *discipline*, *critic*, *master*, *sentence*, *inspection*, *self-control*); ~ **(up)on,** harsh in judgement of. **2.** Violent, vehement, extreme, (*a severe winter*, *attack of influenza*); (of weather) very cold or stormy. **3.** Making great demands on endurance, energy, skill, or other quality, (*severe test*, *pain*, *competition*, *requirements*); serious, not slight, (*severe haemorrhage*, *shortage*). **4.** Unadorned, stripped of all that is unessential, without redundancy, restrained, terse, (*severe architecture*, *beauty*, *simplicity*, *style*). **5.** Hence or cogn. ~LY² (-ēr'lĭ) *adv.* (**leave** or **let ~ly alone,** abstain from dealing with as mark of disapproval, (joc.) avoid meddling with as too formidable or difficult), **sėvĕ'r**ITY *n.* [f. F *sévère* or f. L *severus*]

sĕ'verў *n.* (Archit.) Compartment of vaulted ceiling. [ME, f. AF **civorie*, OF *civoire* (as CIBORIUM)]

Sĕ'vĭlle *n.* ~ **orange,** small bitter orange used for marmalade. [~ in S. Spain]

Sèvres (sāvr) *n.* Fine porcelain made at Sèvres. [~ in N. France]

sew (sō) *v.* (*p.p.* ~**n** *pr.* sōn, *or* ~**ed** *pr.* sōd). **1.** *v.t.* Fasten (material, pieces) by passing thread again and again through holes made with threaded needle or with awl etc. (*sew cloth*, *calico*, *leather*, *pieces together*, *sheets of book*); hence ~'ING¹ (5) *n.* **2.** Make by sewing (*sew seam*, *pleat*, *shirt*, *book*, *boot*, *buttonhole*); fasten *on* or *in*, attach, by sewing (*sew on a button*; *can you sew buttons?*; *sew in a patch*, *band*, *gusset*, *rib*, etc.); close *up* (hole, rent, wound, bag) by sewing. **3.** Enclose, fasten *up*, by sewing receptacle (*sew up money in a bag*; *sew money into* one's *belt*); ~ **up,** (colloq., esp. in *p.p.*) ||utterly exhaust, ||intoxicate, finish dealing with (a matter), *obtain exclusive use of. **4.** *v.i.* Use needle and thread or sewing-machine. **5.** ~**'ing-machine,** machine for sewing or stitching; ~**'ing-press,** apparatus for sewing books. [OE *si(o)wan*, = OHG *siuwen*, ON *sýja*, Goth. *siujan* f. Gmc **siwjan* f. IE **siw-*, **sju-*]

sew'age *n.* Matter conveyed in SEWER³s; ~**-farm** (on which sewage is treated and used as manure, esp. one that utilizes and disposes of a town's sewage); ~**-works** (for artificial purification of sewage before discharge to river etc.). [formed f. SEWER³ by change of (supposed) -ER¹ to -AGE]

sėwĕ'llel *n.* Small burrowing rodent of the W. coast of U.S. [Amer. Ind.]

sew'er¹ (sō'-) *n.* In vbl senses. [f. SEW + -ER¹]

sew'er² *n.* (Hist.) Person who set out table, placed guests, carried and tasted dishes, etc. [ME, f. AF *asseour* f. OF *asseoir* to seat, set, f. L AS(*sidēre* = *sedēre* sit) sit beside]

sew'er³ *n.*, & *v.t.* **1.** *n.* Conduit or channel usu. covered over for carrying off the drainage waters and excrementitious matter of a town, factory, house, etc., public drain; ~**-gas,** foul air of sewers; ~ **rat,** common brown rat; hence ~AGE (1) *n.* **2.** *v.t.* Drain with sewers; provide with sewers. [ME, f. AF *sever(e)*, ONF *se(u)wiere* channel to carry off overflow from a fish-pond f. Rom. *EX¹*aquaria* (*aqua* water; see -ARY¹); cf. EWER]

sew'ĭn *n.* Salmon trout of Welsh etc. rivers. [16th c., of unkn. orig.]

sewn. See SEW.

sĕx *n.*, *a.*, & *v.t.* **1.** *n.* Being male or female or hermaphrodite (*what is its sex?*; *my sex does not matter*; *without distinction of age or sex*); hence ~'LESS *a.* (lit. or fig.). **2.** Males or females collectively (*all ranks and both sexes*); **the fair, gentle, second, softer, weaker,** ~, (arch. joc.) **the** ~, women; **the sterner** ~, men. **3.** Sexual instincts, desires, etc., or their manifestation; (colloq.) sexual intercourse (*have sex with*). **4.** *a.* Pertaining to sex (*sex education*); arising from difference or consciousness of sex (*sex antagonism*, *instinct*, *urge*); ~ **act,** sexual intercourse; ~ **appeal,** attractiveness arising from difference of sex; ~ **change,** (esp.) apparent change of sex by surgical means; ~ **chromosome** (concerned in determining the sex of an organism); ~ **kitten,** young woman mischievously exploiting her sex appeal; ~ **life,** person's activities relating to sex (sense 3); ~**-limited,** (Genetics) appearing only in one sex; ~**-linked,** (Genetics) carried on or by a sex chromosome; ~ **maniac,** person needing excessive gratification of sex instincts; ~**'pot,** (colloq.) sexy woman; ~**-starved,** deprived of sexual gratification. **5.** *v.t.* Determine sex of, whence ~'ER¹ *n.*; (in *p.p.*) equipped with sexual characteristics (esp. *highly* etc. *sexed*). [ME, f. OF *sexe* or f. L *sexus*]

sĕx-, sĕ'x|ĭ-, *comb. forms.* Six, as: ~**a'ngular**(**ly**), hexagonal(ly); ~**cente'nary** (*or* -sĕ'-) *a.* & *n.*, (festival) of the six-hundredth anniversary; ~**di'gitate,** six-fingered; ~**e'nnial,** lasting, recurring every, six years; ~**'foil,** six-lobed ornamental figure; ~**isylla'bic,** ~**isy'llable,**

(word) of 6 syllables; ~(i)**va'lent,** (Chem.) having a valence of six; ~**par'tite,** divided into six. [f. L *sex* six, -I-]

sĕxagėnār'ĭan *a.* & *n.* (Person) from 60 to 69 years old. [f. L *sexagenarius* (*sexageni* distrib. of *sexaginta* sixty; see -ARY[1]) + -AN]

sĕxagē'narў *a.* & *n.* Of sixty; = prec. [as prec.]

Sĕxagĕ'sĭma *n.* ~ (**Sunday**), Sunday before Quinquagesima. [ME f. eccl. L, = sixtieth (day), prob. named loosely as preceding QUINQUAGESIMA]

sĕxagĕ'sĭmal *a.* & *n.* Of sixtieths or sixty; reckoning or reckoned by sixtieths; ~ (**fraction**) (with denominator equal to power of 60 as in the divisions of the degree and hour); hence ~LY[2] *adv.* [f. L *sexagesimus* (as prec.) + -AL]

sĕxŏ'log|ў *n.* Study of sexual life or relationships, esp. in human beings; hence **sĕxolŏ'g**ICAL *a.*, ~IST (3) *n.* [f. SEX + -O- + -LOGY]

sĕxt *n.* (Eccl.) (Office of) canonical hour of prayer appointed for sixth daytime hour (i.e. noon). [ME, f. L *sexta* (*hora* hour) fem. of *sextus* sixth]

sĕ'xtain *n.* Sestina. [perh. alt. f. obs. F *sestine*, after *quatrain*, *sixain*]

sĕ'xtan *a.* (Fever) recurring every fifth (by inclusive reckoning sixth) day. [f. med. L *sextana* (*febris* fever) f. *sextus* sixth; cf. QUARTAN]

sĕ'xtant *n.* Instrument with graduated arc of 60° used in navigation and surveying for measuring the angular distance of objects by means of mirrors. [f. L *sextans -ntis* sixth part (*sextus* sixth; see -ANT)]

sĕxtĕ't, -ĕ'tte, *n.* **1.** (Mus.) (Performers of) composition for six voices or instruments. **2.** Set of six. [alt. of SESTET after L *sex* six]

sĕxtĭ'llion (-lyon) *n.* (for *pl.* usage see HUNDRED). ||A million raised to the sixth power; *a thousand raised to the seventh power. [F, f. L *sex* six, after *septillion* etc.]

sĕ'xtō *n.* (*pl.* ~**s**). Book-size in which each leaf is $\frac{1}{6}$ of printing-sheet; book of this size. [f. L *sextus* sixth, as QUARTO]

sĕxtōdĕ'cĭmō *n.* (*pl.* ~**s**). Book-size in which each leaf is $\frac{1}{16}$ of printing-sheet; book of this size. [f. L *sextus decimus* 16th, as QUARTO]

sĕ'xton *n.* Officer charged with care of church and churchyard, and often with duties of bell-ringer and grave-digger; ~ **beetle** (of genus *Necrophorus*, burying carrion to serve as nidus for eggs). [ME *segerstane* etc., f. AF, OF *segerstein*, *secrestein* f. med. L *sacristanus* SACRISTAN]

sĕ'xtūple *a.*, *n.*, & *v.* **1.** *a.* & *n.* Sixfold (amount). **2.** *v.t.* & *i.* Multiply by six. [f. med. L *sextuplus*, rreg. f. L *sex* six, after LL *quintuplus* QUINTUPLE]

sĕ'xtūplėt (*or* -ŭ'-) *n.* **1.** One of six children born at a birth. **2.** (Mus.) Group of six notes to be played in the time of four. [f. prec., after *triplet* etc.]

sĕ'xūal (*or* -kshŏŏ-) *a.* **1.** Of sex, a sex, or the sexes; pertaining to relations between the sexes, esp. w. ref. to mutual attraction and to gratification of resulting desires; ~ **intercourse** or (arch.) **commerce,** copulation esp. of man and woman; ~ **organs,** reproductive organs, esp. genitals. **2.** (Bot., of classification) based on the distinction of sexes in plants; hence ~IST (2) *n.* **3.** (Biol.) Having sex; (of reproduction) occurring by fusion of male and female gametes. **4.** Hence ~ITY (-ă'l-) *n.*, ~IZE (3) *v.t.*, ~LY[2] *adv.* [f. LL *sexualis* (as SEX; see -AL)]

sĕ'x|ў *a.* Unduly engrossed in or concerned with sex; sexually stimulating, attractive, or provocative; hence ~ĬNESS *n.* [f. SEX + -Y[2]]

sĕz *v.i.* = SAY[2]*s*; ~ **you** (see SAY[2] 1). [phonetic repr.]

S.F. *abbr.* science fiction.

sf *abbr.* sforzando.

s.f. *abbr.* *sub finem.*

S.F.A. *abbr.* Scottish Football Association.

sfōrză'ndō (-ts-), **sfōrză'tō** (-tsah'-), *adjs.* & *advs.* (Mus.) With sudden emphasis. [It., gerund & p.p. of *sforzare* use force]

sfumato (sfōōmah'tō) *a.* (Paint.) With indistinct outlines. [It., p.p. of *sfumare* shade off (*s-* = EX-[1], *fumare* smoke)]

sfz *abbr.* sforzando.

S.G. *abbr.* *senior grade; Solicitor-General; specific gravity.

sgd. *abbr.* signed.

sgraffi't|ō (-ahfē'-) *n.* (*pl.* ~**i** *pr.* -ē). = GRAFFITO 2. [It., p.p. of *sgraffire* scratch (*s-* = EX-[1], *graffio* scratching)]

Sgt. *abbr.* Sergeant.

sh. Var. of HUSH[2] *int.*

||**sh.** *abbr.* shilling(s).

shă'bb|ў *a.* Contemptible, paltry, dishonourable, (*played me a shabby trick*); niggardly, mean; faded, worn, threadbare, dilapidated, poorly dressed; of poor quality, in bad repair or condition; ~**y-gentee'l,** showing signs of shabbiness but attempting to keep up genteel appearances (so ~**y-genti'lity**); hence ~ĬLY[2] *adv.*, ~ĬNESS *n.*, ~ЎISH[1] 2 *a.* [f. *shab* scab f. OE *sceabb* f. ON **skabbr* (cf. SCAB) + -Y[2]]

shă'brăck *n.* (Hist.) Cavalry saddle-cloth. [f. G *schabracke*, of E. Eur. orig. (cf. Russ. *shabrak*)]

Shabu'ōt(h), Shevu'ōt(h), (-vōō'-) *n.* = PENTECOST 1. [f. Heb. *šāḇû'ôṯ*, = weeks, w. ref. to weeks between Passover and Pentecost]

shăck *n.*, & *v.i.* **1.** *n.* Roughly built cabin etc. **2.** *v.i.* (sl.) ~ **up,** cohabit *with.* [perh. f. Mex. *jacal*, Aztec *xacatli* wooden hut]

shă'ckle *n.*, & *v.t.* **1.** *n.* Metal loop or staple, link closed by bolt for connecting chains etc., coupling link; long link joining pair of wrist or ankle rings; (in *pl.*) fetters, (fig.) impediments or restraints (*the shackles of convention*). **2.** ~**-bolt,** (1) bolt for closing shackle, (2) bolt with shackle at its end; ~**-joint** (in some fishes, formed by bony ring passing through hole in another bone). **3.** *v.t.* Fetter, impede, trammel. [OE *sc(e)acul* fetter, corresp. to LG *shäkel* link, coupling, ON *skökull* wagon-pole f. Gmc **skak-*]

shăd *n.* (*pl.* ~**s** *or* ~). Anadromous deep-bodied fish of genus *Alosa*, much esteemed as food; ***~'berry,** ***~'bush,** = SERVICE[2]-*berry* (2). [f. OE *sceadd*, of unkn. orig.]

shă'ddock *n.* (Tree, *Citrus grandis*, bearing) largest citrus fruit, of which small round varieties are called grapefruit. [f. Capt. *Shaddock*, introducer to W. Indies in 17th c.]

shāde[1] *n.* **1.** Comparative darkness (and usu. coolness) caused by interception of light (and usu. heat) rays; (fig.) comparative obscurity (**put in the** ~, **throw into the** ~, outshine); (in *pl.*) darkness *of* night or evening. **2.** (in *sing.* or *pl.*) Place sheltered from sun, cool or sequestered retreat; ||(in *pl.*) wine-vaults; **in the** ~, (of temperature) measured at position not directly exposed to sun. **3.** Darker part of picture; **without light and** ~, (of painting, or fig. of description or character) monotonous, uniformly glaring or sombre. **4.** A colour esp. with regard to its depth, or as distinguished from one nearly like it, or made darker by admixture of black, gradation of colour, material so coloured, (*in all shades of purple*; *I want the same colour in a lighter shade*; *all the newest shades in stock*); (fig.) slightly differing variety (*people of all shades of opinion*; *delicate shades of meaning*). **5.** Slight difference, small amount, (*am a shade better today*). **6.** Unsubstantial or unreal thing; **is the shadow of a** ~, (rhet.) is delusive. **7.** Ghost of person after death (*spoke with the shade* *of Homer*); **the ~s,** Hades; **S~ of** *Priscian* etc.! (excl. at grammatical blunder etc., that would have outraged person invoked). **8.** Screen excluding or moderating light, heat, etc.; eye-shield; translucent cover for lamp etc.; *window-blind; *(in *pl.*) sun-glasses. **9.** Hence ~′LESS (-dl-) *a.* [OE *sc(e)adu*, = OS *scado*, OHG *scato*, Goth. *skadus* f. Gmc **skadhw-* f. IE **skotw-* or **skatw-*]

shād|e² *v.* **1.** *v.t.* Screen from excessive light (*shaded his eyes with his hand*; *trees shade the street*). **2.** Cover, keep off, or moderate power of (luminous object, light) with or as intervening object. **3.** Make dark or gloomy (*a sullen look shaded his face*). **4.** Darken (parts of drawing etc.) esp. with parallel pencil lines to give effects of light and shade or gradations of colour, whence ~′ING¹ (6) *n.* **5.** *v.i.* & *t.* (Of colour or light, and fig. of opinion, practice, etc.) pass *off* by degrees into (or *into*) other colour or variety; make (colour etc.) pass thus into another; reduce (prices etc.) slightly. [ME, f. prec.]

shadōō′f *n.* Pole with bucket and counterpoise used esp. in Egypt for raising water. [f. Egypt. Arab. *šādūf*]

shă′dow¹ (-dō) *n.* **1.** = SHADE¹ 1, 2, 3 (*sitting in the shadow*; *the shadow of death is on his face*; VALLEY *of the shadow of death*; *the shadows of night*; *under the shadow of misfortune*); substance used to darken painting, eyes, etc. **2.** Patch of shade, region not reached by light, sound, etc., because of intervening object; dark figure projected by body that intercepts light rays, this regarded as person's or thing's appendage (**afraid of** one's **own** ~, very timid; **may your ~ never grow less,** wish for person's increasing prosperity); (fig.) one's inseparable attendant or companion; **cast a long ~,** (fig.) be significant. **3.** Reflected image. **4.** Type, faint representation, foreshadowing, premonition, (*coming events cast their shadows before*). **5.** Slightest trace (*without a shadow of doubt*). **6.** Unsubstantial or unreal thing or counterfeit (*catch at shadows*; *having only the shadow of freedom*); phantom, ghost, (lit., or fig.: *worn to a shadow*); **the ~ of** one's **former self,** much weakened or emaciated. **7.** Shelter, protection, (*under the shadow of the Almighty*). **8.** **~-bird,** = HAMMER¹-*-head* (3); **~-boxing** (against imaginary opponent as form of training); ‖**S~ Cabinet, Chancellor,** etc., (of members of Opposition party who would be Cabinet ministers if that party became the Government); **~ factory,** one planned or built for possible reserve production against the emergency of war; **~graph,** shadow-like picture made esp. with X-rays; **~ roll,** thick piece of material on horse's head to prevent seeing shadow on ground. **9.** Hence ~LESS, ~Y², *adjs.* [repr. OE *scead(u)we*, obl. case of *sceadu* SHADE¹]

shă′dow² (-dō) *v.t.* Cast shadow over; set *forth* dimly, in outline, allegorically, or prophetically; secretly follow and watch all movements of. [OE *sceadwian* (as prec.)]

shā′d|ȳ *a.* Giving, situated in, shade; (of action, conduct, etc.) avoiding the light, disreputable, of dubious honesty; **on the ~y side of** *forty* etc., more than; hence **~ĭLY²** *adv.*, **~ĭNESS** *n.* [f. SHADE¹ + -Y²]

shaft (-ah-) *n.* **1.** (Slender pole of) lance or spear. **2.** Arrow, esp. of longbow; (fig.) remark aimed like arrow (*shafts of satire, wit, ridicule, envy*). **3.** Ray *of* light; bolt or stroke *of* lightning. **4.** Stem, stalk; column between base and capital, one of group of clustered columns; spire; part of chimney above roof; central stem of feather; part more or less long and narrow and straight supporting or connecting part(s) of greater thickness etc.; part of golf-club between handle and head. **5.** (Mech.) Large axle, revolving bar transferring force by belts or cogs; hence ~′ING¹ (3, 6) *n.* **6.** Handle of tool etc. **7.** One of pair of bars between which horse of vehicle is harnessed. **8.** Vertical or inclined excavation giving access to mine; tunnel of blast-furnace; upward vent for smoke or foul air from tunnel, drain, etc.; **~-grave** (in deep rectangular pit). [OE *scæft, sceaft,* = OS, OHG *scaft*, ON *skapt* f. Gmc **skaft-*]

shăg¹ *n.* **1.** Rough growth or mass of hair etc.; (arch.) long-napped rough cloth. **2.** Coarse kind of cut tobacco. **3.** Cormorant, esp. crested cormorant (*Phalacrocorax aristotelis*). [OE *sceacga*, cogn. w. ON *skegg* beard, OE *sceaga* coppice, SHAW¹ f. Gmc **skag-*]

shăg² *v.t.* (**-gg-**). (sl.) Copulate with; (in *p.p.*) exhausted, tired *out*. [18th c.; orig. unkn.]

***shă′gbârk** *n.* (Wood of) hickory with thick curling bark. [f. *shag* a. = foll. + BARK¹]

shă′gg|ȳ (-gĭ) *a.* Hairy, rough-haired; (of hair) coarse and abundant, unkempt; (of land etc.) overgrown with forest or rough vegetation; (of tree etc.) having rough branches or twigs; (Biol.) having hairlike covering; **~y-do′g story,** long detailed inconsequential narrative amusing only to its teller or by its pointlessness; hence **~ĭLY²** *adv.*, **~ĭNESS** *n.*, (-g-). [f. SHAG¹ + -Y²]

shagree′n *n.* Kind of untanned leather with artificially granulated surface made from skin of horse, ass, shark, etc., and usu. dyed green; shark-skin rough with natural papillae used for rasping and polishing. [var. of CHAGRIN in sense 'rough skin']

shah *n.* King of Iran. [f. Pers. *šāh* f. OPers. *kšāyṯiya* king]

shaik(h). See SHEIKH.

shāke¹ *v.* (**shook** *pr.* -ŏŏk; **sha′ken,** arch. or colloq. **shook**). **1.** *v.t.* Move (thing, person) violently or quickly up and down or to and fro with the hand(s) etc. (*like a terrier shaking a rat*; *shook the mat to get the dust out*; *deserves a good shaking*); **~ hands, ~** person **by the hand,** clasp right hands with or without shaking at meeting or parting, in reconciliation or congratulation, or over concluded bargain. **2.** *v.t.* & *i.* (Cause to) tremble or rock or quiver or vibrate or wave, jolt, jar, brandish, (*explosion shook the house*; *the earth shook*); tremble violently (*with* cold, fear, etc.); **hand ~s** (is unsteady); *shake* one's FINGER *at*; **~** one's **fist, stick,** etc., **at,** threaten with fist etc.; **~** one's **head,** move it from side to side in refusal, denial, disapproval, or concern (*over* or *at*, or abs.); *shake a* LEG; **~ in** one's **shoes,** tremble with apprehension. **3.** *v.t.* Agitate, shock, disturb, (*was much shaken by, with, at, the news*; *shake him out of his lethargy*; *shaken but unhurt in the accident*; *shook my composure*); (colloq.) upset composure of (person); (Austral. sl.) steal, rob. **4.** Weaken, impair, make less convincing or firm or stable or courageous, (*the firm's credit was shaken*; *could not shake the witness's evidence*; *his faith in Providence was greatly shaken*; *the ranks were shaken but not broken*). **5.** *v.i.* (Of voice, musical note, singer, etc.) make tremulous sounds, change pitch or power with rapid alternations, trill, (*his voice shook with emotion*; *must learn to shake*). **6.** (colloq.) Shake hands (*we shook on the bargain*). **7.** **~ down,** fetch or send down by shaking (fruit from tree; straw or blankets etc. on floor for bed, whence *~′down* n.; grain etc. in vessel into least volume), *(sl.) extort money from, become compact, get comfortably settled or into harmony with associates or circumstances (*~down* *cruise* of new ship, to run the engines in and accustom the crew to the ship); ~ **off,** get rid of (dust etc.; fig., illness, bad habit, undesirable companion, worry) by shaking (*shake the* DUST[1] *off* one's *feet*); ~ **out,** empty (vessel, garment, etc.) of contents or dust, (contents) from vessel etc., spread or open (sail, flag, reef) by shaking; *~-out* n., radical upheaval or reorganization; ~ **up,** mix (ingredients), restore (pillow etc.) to shape, by shaking, rouse from stagnant or lethargic or convention-ridden state, whence *~-up* n. **8.** Hence ~ABLE (-ka-), **shā'k**ABLE, *adjs.* [OE *sc(e)acan*, = OS *skakan*, ON *skaka* f. Gmc **skakan*]

shāke[2] *n.* **1.** Shaking or being shaken (*with a shake of the head*; *give it, had, a shake*); **all of a ~,** trembling; **no great ~s,** (sl.) not very good or efficient; **the ~s,** fit of trembling or shivering. **2.** Jolt, jerk, shock; = MILK[1] *shake*; (U.S. & N.Z.) earthquake. **3.** (Mus.) Trill. **4.** Moment; **in two** etc. **~s** (**of a lamb's tail** etc.), **in a brace of ~s,** very quickly, in no time. **5.** Crack in growing timber. [f. prec.]

shā'ker *n.* In vbl senses; vessel for shaking together ingredients of cocktails etc.; SUGAR--*shaker*; (*S~*) member of Amer. religious sect with simple life in celibate mixed communities [named from religious dances], whence **Shā'ker**ESS[1], **Shā'ker**ISM (3), *ns.* [ME, f. SHAKE[1] + -ER[1]]

Shākespear'ĭ|an, -ks-, -ēr-, (-kspēr'-) *a.* & *n.* **1.** *a.* (In the style) of Shakespeare. **2.** *n.* Student of Shakespeare's works. **3.** So ~A'NA *n. pl.* [f. W. *Shakespeare*, Engl. dramatist d. 1616 + -IAN]

shă'kō *n.* (*pl.* ~s). Form of military hat, more or less cylindrical with peak and upright plume or tuft. [f. F *schako* f. Magyar *csákó* (*süveg*) peaked (cap) f. *csák* peak f. G *zacken* spike]

shā'k|ȳ *a.* Unsteady, apt to shake, trembling, unsound, infirm, (*a shaky hand, table, old man, house*); unreliable, tottering, wavering, (*shaky credit, voters, courage*); (of timber) containing shakes; hence **~ĭ**LY[2] *adv.*, **~ĭ**NESS *n.* [f. SHAKE[1,2] + -Y[2]]

shāle *n.* Finely stratified stone splitting readily into thin plates and resembling slate but softer and less solid, consisting of consolidated mud or clay; **~-oil** (got from bituminous shale); hence **shā'l**Y[2] *a.* [prob. f. G *schale* f. OE *sc(e)alu* cogn. w. ON *skál* SCALE[2]]

shall (shal *or, when stressed,* shăl) *v. aux.* (*pres.* **shall,** *or* **'ll** (after *I* or *we*), exc. 2 *sing.* (arch.) **shalt,** *neg.* **shall not,** (colloq.) **shan't** *pr.* shahnt; *past* **should** *pr.* shŏŏd *or* shud, *or* **'d** (after *I* or *we*), exc. 2 *sing.* (arch.) **shouldst** *pr.* shŏŏdst, *or* **shouldest** *pr.* shŏŏ'dĭst, *neg.* **should not,** (colloq.) **shouldn't** *pr.* shŏŏ'dent; no other parts used). **1.** In first person (the others having *will, would*) forming simple future or conditional statement or question (*we shall hear about it tomorrow*; *I should have been killed if I had let go*; *shall I hear from you soon?*; *should I hear from you in that case?*) or emphatic intention (*I shall return*). **2.** In 2nd and 3rd persons (1st having *will, would*) forming future or conditional statement expressing speaker's will or intention (*you shall not catch me again*; *he should not have gone if I could have prevented it*). **3.** (Less often than *will, would*) in sentences of type 1 changed in reporting from 1st to other person (*he says* or *said, you say* or *said, that he, you, shall* or *should never manage it*). **4.** Replacing *will* or *would* in sentences of type 1 changed in reporting from 2nd or 3rd person to 1st (*he says I shall never manage it*, reporting *you will never*). **5.** In reporting sentences of type 2 that contained *shall* or *should* (*you promised I, he, should not catch you at it again*). **6.** In 2nd-person questions corresponding to type 1, by attraction to expected answer (*shall you be going to church?*) or to avoid implication of request in *will.* **7.** In any person to form statements or questions involving the notions of command and future or conditional duty, obligation, likelihood, etc., (*thou shalt not steal*; *any person failing to display the licence shall be guilty of an offence*; *I, you, he, should really have been more careful*; *shall I, he, open the door?*; *we should be safe now*; *why should I, you, he, obey?*; (iron.) *I should* WORRY). **8.** In any person to form conditional protasis or indefinite clause (*if, when, we shall be defeated* or *defeat shall overtake us*; *anyone who should say*; *it is surprising that I, you, they, should be* or *have been so foolish*; *if you should happen to be there*; *should I, she, be there I will tell her*; (in tentative or modest expression) *I should like to disagree, I should say it is time*). **9.** Alternatively with *may, might,* in any person in purpose--clause (*in order that I, you, he, shall* or *should not be able*). **10.** *It should* SEEM; **you ~ find,** (arch.) be sure you will find. [OE *sceal*, = OHG *scal*, OS, ON, Goth. *skal*, preterite-present v. f. Gmc **skal-*, **skul-* owe f. IE **skel-* etc.]

shallōō'n *n.* Light twilled woollen cloth for coat-linings etc. [f. *Châlons*-sur-Marne in N.E. France]

shă'llop *n.* Light open boat for shallow water. [f. F *chaloupe* f. Du *sloep* SLOOP]

shallŏ't *n.* Onion-like plant (*Allium ascalonicum*) with cloves like, but of milder flavour than, those of garlic. [f. *eschalot* f. F *eschalotte* alt. of OF *eschaloigne* (see SCALLION)]

shă'llow (-ō) *a., n.,* & *v.* **1.** *a.* Of little depth (*shallow water*; *a shallow stream, dish*); (fig.) superficial, trivial, (*a shallow mind, argument, love, man*); hence ~LY[2] *adv.*, ~NESS *n.* **2.** *n.* Shallow place, shoal. **3.** *v.i.* & *t.* Become or make shallow. [ME, prob. rel. to *schald*, OE *sceald* SHOAL[1]]

shalō'm *n.* & *int.* (Excl. of) salutation at meeting or parting, used among Jews. [f. Heb. *šālôm* peace]

shălt. See SHALL.

sha'lwār (-ŭ'lv-) *n.* Loose trousers worn by both sexes in some S. Asian countries. [f. Pers. *šalwār*]

shăm *v.* (**-mm-**), *n.,* & *a.* **1.** *v.t.* & *i.* Feign, simulate, (*sham illness, sleep, a faint, fear*; *is only shamming*); pretend to be (*shammed ill, dead, asleep*); hence **~'**MER[1] *n.* **2.** *n.* Imposture, pretence, humbug, (*this age of shams*); person or thing pretending or pretended to be something that he or it is not; (arch.) embroidered linen laid on bed in day for show. **3.** *a.* Pretended, counterfeit; ~ **fight,** imitation battle for training troops or for display; ~ **plea** etc. (Law, advanced only to gain time); **~-Tudor** etc. (simulating an architectural or other style). [perh. north. dial. var. of SHAME[1,2]]

shă'man *n.* Priest or witch-doctor of class claiming to have sole contact with gods etc.; hence ~ISM (3) *n.*, **~ĭ'st**IC *a.* [f. G *schamane* & Russ. *shaman* f. Tungusian *samán*]

shă'mateur (-tūr *or* -tēr) *n.* Sports player classed as amateur though often profiting like professional; hence ~ISM (3) *n.* [f. SHAM + AMATEUR]

shă'mbl|e *v.i.,* & *n.* **1.** *v.i.* Walk or run in shuffling or awkward or decrepit way; **~ing gait** (of person who shambles). **2.** *n.* Shambling gait. [prob. f. dial. *shamble* a. ungainly, perh. f. *shamble legs* w. ref. to straddling trestles (see foll.)]

shă'mbles (-belz) *n. pl.* (usu. treated as *sing.*) Butcher's slaughter-house; scene of carnage (*the place became a shambles*); (colloq.) mess, muddle. [pl. of *shamble* stool, stall f. OE *sc(e)amul*, = OS *skamel*, OHG *scamil* f. WG f. L *scamellum* dim. of *scamnum* bench]

shāme[1] *n.* **1.** Feeling of humiliation excited by consciousness of (esp. one's own) guilt or shortcoming, of having made oneself or been made ridiculous, or of having offended against propriety, modesty, or decency, (*flushed with shame*; *begin with shame to take the lowest room*). **2.** Restraint imposed by, desire to avoid, such humiliation (*cannot do it for very shame*; *has no sense of shame*, *is quite without* or *dead to* or *lost to shame*); **for ~!** (appeal to person not to disregard, or reproof for disregarding, this restraint or desire). **3.** State of disgrace or regret or ignominy or discredit (*shame on you!*; **put** person **to ~**, disgrace him esp. by exhibiting one's superior qualities etc.); person or thing that brings disgrace etc. (*is a shame to his parents*; *would think shame to do it*; *is a sin and a shame*); **what a ~!**, (1) that is disgraceful!, (2) how unlucky!. [OE *sc(e)amu*, = OS, OHG *skama*, ON *skömm* f. Gmc **skamō*]

shāme[2] *v.* **1.** *v.i.* (arch., usu. w. neg.) Be ashamed, refuse from shame *to* (*he shamed not to say*). **2.** *v.t.* Bring shame on, be a shame to, make ashamed; put to shame by outdoing (*a sanctity which shames our religions*); force by shame *into* or *out of* doing, conduct, etc. [OE *sc(e)amian*, = OS *skamon*, OHG *skamōn*, Goth. *skaman* (as prec.)]

shā'mefāced (-mfāst) *a.* Bashful, shy; displaying shame; (poet., of virtue, flowers, etc.) modest, retiring, inconspicuous; hence **~LY**[2] (-sĭd-) *adv.*, **~NESS** *n.* [16th c. etym. misinterpretation of *shamefast* f. OE *sc(e)amfæst* (as SHAME[1], FAST[3]), after FACE[1]]

shā'meful (-mf-) *a.* That causes or ought to cause shame (sense 1); disgraceful, degrading; hence **~LY**[2] *adv.*, **~NESS** *n.* [OE *sc(e)amful* (as SHAME[1], -FUL)]

shā'melėss (-ml-) *a.* Having or showing no sense of shame, impudent; hence **~LY**[2] *adv.*, **~NESS** *n.* [OE *sc(e)amlēas* (as SHAME[1], -LESS)]

shă'mmy̆ *n.* = CHAMOIS 2. [repr. corrupted pronunc.]

shămpōō' *v.t.*, & *n.* **1.** *v.t.* Lather, wash, and rub (head, hair); clean (hair) with dry shampoo; clean surface of (carpet, car, etc.) with soap or chemical. **2.** Shampooing; substance used for this; DRY[1] *shampoo*. [f. Hind. *chhāmpo*, imper. of *chhāmpnā* to press]

shă'mrŏck *n.* Trefoil (esp. *Trifolium minus*) used as national emblem of Ireland. [f. Ir. *seamróg* trefoil, dim. of *seamar* clover]

Shă'ndėan *a.* Having characteristics of (the family portrayed in) Sterne's novel *Tristram Shandy*. [f. *Shandy* + -AN]

shă'ndry̆dăn *n.* Chaise with hood; old rickety vehicle. [19th c.; orig. unkn.]

shă'ndy̆(găff) *n.* Mixed drink of beer and ginger-beer or lemonade. [19th c.; orig. unkn.]

shănghai' (-hī') *v.t.* (Naut. sl.) Ship as sailor while unconscious from drugs etc.; trick into awkward situation. [f. *S~* in China]

Shă'ngrĭ-La (-nggrĭlah; *or* -ah') *n.* Imaginary paradise on earth. [name of hidden valley in J. Hilton's *Lost Horizon*]

shănk *n.* & *v.* **1.** *n.* Leg (**on S~s's mare** or **pony,** walking as opp. riding etc.); lower part of leg, leg from knee to ankle; lower part of animal's foreleg, esp. as cut of meat; shin-bone; upright part of bird's foot; footstalk of flower; ‖leg of stocking. **2.** Shaft of pillar etc., shaft of tool between head etc. and handle, stem of key, spoon, anchor, etc., straight part of nail or fish-hook, narrow middle of sole of shoe etc., whence (-)**~ED**[2] (-kt) *a.*; *first or last part *of* (afternoon etc.). **3.** *v.i.* **~ off,** (of flower) fall off by decay of shank. **4.** *v.t.* (Golf). Strike (ball) with heel of club. [OE *sceanca*, = LG *schanke* f. WG **skanka*, cogn. w. MHG *schenkel* thigh]

shă'nny̆ *n.* Oblong olive-green European sea-fish, the smooth blenny. [19th c., of unkn. orig.; cf. 18th c. *shan*]

shan't. See SHALL.

shăntŭ'ng *n.* Soft undressed Chinese silk (usu. undyed). [f. *S~*, Chin. province]

shă'nty̆[1] *n.* Hut, cabin; mean roughly-built dwelling; **~ town** (consisting of shanties). [19th c., orig. N. Amer., of uncert. orig.]

shă'nty̆[2] *n.* (**Sea-**)**~**, sailor's song (with alternating solo by **~man,** and chorus) sung while pulling etc. [prob. F *chantez*, imper. pl. of *chanter* sing; see CHANT]

shāpe[1] *v.* (arch. *p.p.* **sha'pen**). **1.** *v.t.* Create, form, construct; model, mould, fashion, bring into desired or definite figure or form; (in *p.p.*) having such figure (*shaped like a pear*); hence **shā'pER**[1] (1, 2) *n.* **2.** Adapt, make conform, *to*; plan, devise; direct, aim, (one's course etc.); frame mentally, imagine, call up image of. **3.** Hence **~ABLE** (-pa-), **shā'pABLE**, *adjs.* **4.** *v.i.* Assume form, develop into shape, give signs of future shape (**~ (up) well,** be promising); **~ up,** take (specified) form. [ME, back form. f. p.p.; orig. f. OE *sceppan*, Goth. *gaskapjan* create, f. Gmc **skap-*]

shāpe[2] *n.* **1.** Configuration, external form, total effect produced by thing's outlines, (*spherical in shape*; *has the shape of a boat*). **2.** Appearance, guise, (*monster in human shape*). **3.** Specific form, embodiment, (*intention took shape in action*; *showed me politeness in the shape of an invitation*). **4.** Kind, description, sort, (*made no approach in any shape or form*). **5.** Symmetrical or definite form, orderly arrangement, proper form or condition, (*get* one's *ideas into shape*; *knock* or LICK *into shape*; *give shape to*); **in bad, good, poor,** etc., **~** (condition); hence **~'LESS** (-pl-) *a.* **6.** Person considered as impressing the sight, and esp. as indistinctly seen or imagined, apparition, ghost, (*a shape loomed through the mist*; *a grim mysterious shape stalked towards me*). **7.** Pattern for workman etc., mould for shaping hat, jelly, etc.; untrimmed hat; jelly, blancmange, etc., shaped in mould; piece of material made in a particular form. **8.** Hence (**-**)**shāpED**[2] (-pt) *a.* [OE *gesceap* creation, = OS *giskapu* creatures, ON *skap* condition f. as prec.]

SHAPE (shāp) *abbr.* Supreme Headquarters Allied Powers Europe.

shā'pel|y̆ (-plĭ) *a.* Well formed or proportioned, of the right or a pleasing shape; hence **~ĭNESS** *n.* [ME, f. SHAPE[2] + -LY[1]]

shārd[1]. Var. of SHERD, = potsherd. [OE *sceard*, = MLG *skart* crack, ON *skarthr* notch f. Gmc **skardaz* notched (**skar-*, **sker-* SHEAR[1])]

shārd[2] *n.* Beetle's wing-case. [back form. f. *shard-borne* (Shak.) = born in shard (dial. = cow-dung), misinterpreted as 'borne on shards']

shāre[1] *n.* **1.** Portion detached for individual from jointly owned amount (*must get a share of the plunder*); part one gets or contributes (*had a large share in bringing it about, but no share of the credit*; *has his share of conceit*). **2.** Part one is entitled to have or bound to contribute, equitable portion, (*that is your fair share*; LION'*s share*; *took, bore, my* or *more* or *less than my* (*fair*) *share of the burden*); **go ~s,** make equitable division (*with* others); **~ and ~ alike,** with equal division. **3.** Part-proprietorship of property held by joint owners (*has a share in the bank, estate*, etc.), esp. one of the equal parts into which company's capital is divided entitling holder to proportion of profits; DEFER[1]*red*, ‖ORDINARY, ‖PREFERENCE or *preferred*, *shares*; **~'holder,** owner of shares; ‖**~-list** (of current prices of shares in various companies); **~-pusher,** (colloq.) one who peddles shares by circular or advertisement. [ME, f. OE *scearu* division, OS, OHG *scara* troop, cogn. w. SHEAR[1]]

shāre[2] *v.* **1.** *v.t.* Apportion (food, property, task, etc.) among others, give each a share of; give away part of (*would share his last crust*); get or have share of, benefit from or possess or use or endure jointly with others. **2.** *v.i.* Have share(s), be sharer(s), (*will share with you in the undertaking*); ~ **and** ~ **alike,** make equal division; **~-cropper,** tenant farmer who pays part of crop as rent, whence *~-crop* v.i. & t.; ~ **out,** distribute, whence *~-out* n., distribution esp. of profits, booty, etc., in shares. **3.** Hence **shār'**ER[1] *n.* [f. prec.]

shāre[3] *n.* Ploughshare; blade of seeding-machine or cultivator; **~-beam,** part of plough in which share is fixed. [OE *scear, scær,* = OHG *scar(o),* WG f. Gmc **skar-, *sker-* SHEAR[1]]

sharif. Var. of SHERIF.

shārk *n.* Long-bodied lateral-gilled inferior-mouthed elasmobranch sea-fish, esp. if large and voracious; rapacious person, swindler; *(sl.) brilliant student; **~-skin,** (1) skin of shark, shagreen, (2) dull-surfaced smooth usu. heavy fabric; **~'s-mouth,** opening in awning for mast etc. [16th c., of unkn. orig.]

shārp[1] *a., n.,* & *adv.* **1.** *a.* Having edge or point able to cut or pierce, not blunt; peaked, pointed, edged, (*sharp gable, summit, ridge*); (of sand etc.) composed of angular grains. **2.** Well-defined, clean-cut, (*sharp outline, distinction, contrast, impression, features*). **3.** Abrupt, angular, (*sharp fall, turn, incline*). **4.** Keen, pungent, acid, tart, shrill, piercing, biting, harsh, acrimonious, severe, intense, painful, (*sharp appetite, flavour, wine, sauce, voice, cry, frost, air, words, tongue, temper, reproof, contest, attack of cramp*). **5.** Acute, sensitive, quick to see or hear or notice, keen-witted, vigilant, clever, (*sharp eyes, ears, intelligence, wits, attention*; *sharp-eyed, -witted,* etc.; *keep a sharp look-out*; *a sharp remark, child*); (sl.) stylish or flashy with regard to dress; **as ~ as a needle,** very intelligent; **~'shooter,** skilled marksman. **6.** Quick to take advantage, bent on winning, artful, unscrupulous, dishonest; **be too ~ for,** outwit; **~ practice,** dishonest or barely honest dealings. **7.** Vigorous, brisk, speedy, not loitering, impetuous, (*take a sharp walk*); **~'s the word** (exhortation to be quick); **~ work,** matter quickly dispatched, fight etc. that takes all one's energy. **8.** (Mus.) Above true pitch (**C, F,** etc., ~, a semitone higher than C, F, etc.); (of key) having sharp(s) in signature. **9.** Hence ~'LY[2] *adv.,* ~'NESS *n.* **10.** *n.* Sewing-needle of slender make; (Mus.) note raised a semitone above natural pitch, sign indicating this raising; (colloq.) swindler, cheat; *(joc.) expert; ||(in *pl.*) middlings (between flour and bran). **11.** *adv.* Punctually (*at six o'clock sharp*); suddenly (*pulled up sharp*); at a sharp angle (*turn sharp right*); (Mus.) above true pitch (*sings sharp*); **~-set,** (1) set with sharp edge, (2) hungry; **~-shod,** shod with sharp iron to prevent slipping. [OE *sc(e)arp,* = OS *skarp,* OHG *skarf, scarpf,* ON *skarpr* f. Gmc **skarpaz*]

shārp[2] *v.* **1.** *v.t.* *(Mus.) Make sharp. **2.** *v.i.* (arch.) Play unfairly, swindle, at cards etc. [f. OE **scierpan* sharpen f. Gmc **skarpjan,* & prob. partly f. prec.]

shār'pen *v.t.* & *i.* Make or become sharp; hence (-)~'ER[1] (1, 2) *n.* [ME, f. SHARP[1] + -EN[6]]

shār'per *n.* Swindler, esp. at cards etc. [f. SHARP[2] + -ER[1]]

shār'pĭsh *a.* & *adv.* (colloq.) Somewhat or fairly sharp(ly). [f. SHARP[1] + -ISH[1]]

Shă'sta *n.* ~ **daisy,** large-flowered daisy (*Chrysanthemum maximum*) like ox-eye. [~ in California]

Sha'stra (-ah'-) *n.* Hindu sacred writings. [f. Hindi *śāstr,* Skr. *śāstra*]

shă'tter *v.t.* & *i.* **1.** Break suddenly and violently in pieces; hence ~-PROOF[2] *a.* **2.** *v.t.* Utterly destroy, dissipate, (*shattered nerves, health, hopes*); (colloq.) severely discompose. [ME, rel. to SCATTER]

shāve[1] *v.* (*p.p.* **~d** or, esp. as *a.,* **sha'ven**). **1.** *v.t.* Remove (hair), free (chin etc.) of hair, remove hair from chin etc. of (person), with razor (*has shaved off* or *shaved his beard*; *a shaven chin*). **2.** Pare surface of (wood etc.) with spokeshave, plane, etc., whence **shā'**VING[1] (2) *n.*; (fig.) reduce amount of, reduce by (amount). **3.** Pass close to without touching, skirt, miss narrowly, nearly graze. **4.** *v.i.* Shave oneself (*he does not shave every day*). **5.** **~-hook,** tool for scraping surface of metal before soldering; ***~-tail,** newly broken-in mule, (fig.) newly commissioned officer; **sha'ving-brush** (for lathering chin etc. before shaving); **sha'ving-cream** (for applying to chin etc. with or without brush, to assist shaving); **sha'ving-soap** (for making lather to assist shaving); **sha'ving-stick,** cylindrical piece of shaving-soap. [OE *sc(e)afan,* = OS **scaban,* OHG *scaban,* ON *skafa,* Goth. *skaban* f. Gmc **skabhan*]

shāve[2] *n.* **1.** Having one's beard etc. shaved (*must have a shave*). **2.** Close approach without contact, narrow miss or escape or failure, (*had a close shave of it*). **3.** Tool (e.g. knife-blade with handle at each end) for shaving wood etc. **4.** ||(arch.) Trick, deception, hoax. [f. prec.; sense 3 f. OE *sceafa,* = OHG *scaba,* ON *skafa* f. Gmc **skabhōn* (as prec.)]

shā'velĭng (-vl-) *n.* (arch.) Shaven person; monk, friar, priest. [f. SHAVE[1] + -LING[1]]

shā'ven. See SHAVE[1].

shā'ver *n.* In vbl senses; electrically driven razor; (colloq.), lad, youngster, (*young shaver*). [ME, f. SHAVE[1] + -ER[1]]

Shā'vĭan *a.* (In the manner) of G. B. Shaw, Brit. dramatist etc. d. 1950. [f. *Shavius* L form of *Shaw* + -IAN]

||**shaw**[1] *n.* (arch. or dial.) Thicket, wood. [OE *sceaga,* = ON *skagi* promontory; cf. SHAG[1]]

||**shaw**[2] *n.* Stalks and leaves of potatoes, turnips, etc. [perh. = SHOW[2]]

shawl *n.,* & *v.t.* **1.** *n.* Rectangular piece of fabric often folded into triangle, worn over shoulders, round neck, etc., or wrapped round baby; ~ **collar,** rolled collar extended downwards to meet or cross at waist; **~-pattern,** variegated design like that of Oriental shawl. **2.** *v.t.* (esp. in *p.p.*) Put shawl on (person). [f. Urdu etc. f. Pers. *šāl,* prob. f. *Shāliāt* in India]

shawm *n.* Obsolete musical instrument of oboe type. [ME, f. OF *chalemie, chalemel, chalemeaus* pl., f. Rom. **calamellus* dim. of L f. Gk *kalamos* reed]

shay *n.* (arch. or dial.) = CHAISE 1. [back form. f. CHAISE taken as pl.]

shē (*or, when unstressed,* shĭ) *pron.* (*obj.* HER[1], *refl.* HERSELF *or* arch. HER[1], *poss.* HER[2], HERS, *pl.* THEY etc.), *n.,* & *a.* **1.** *pron.* The female (or thing personified as female, e.g. the moon, nation, ship, motor vehicle) previously mentioned or implied as easily identified; the or any female person *who*; (Austral. colloq.) it, the state of affairs (*she'll be* RIGHT[1] 5). **2.** *n.* Female, woman, (**the not impossible** ~, woman one might love; *is the child, the puppy, a he or a she?*). **3.** *a.* (usu. w. hyphen). Female (*she-goat, -ass, -bear,* etc.); **~-cat, ~-devil,** malignant or spiteful woman; **~-oak,** Australian casuarina tree; **~-pine,** Australian evergreen tree yielding yellow timber. [ME *scæ, sche,* etc., f. OE fem. demonstr. pron. & a. *sīo, sēo,* acc. *sīe*]

shea *n.* W. Afr. tree whose fatty nut yields a vegetable butter (**~-butter**). [f. Mandingo *si, se, sye*]

shea'dĭng *n.* Any of the six administrative divisions of the Isle of Man. [f. SHED¹ + -ING¹]

sheaf *n.* (*pl.* **sheaves** *pr.* -vz), & *v.t.* **1.** *n.* Bundle of things laid lengthwise together and usu. tied (*sheaf of papers, arrows*, etc.), esp. armful of corn-stalks tied after reaping (**~-binder,** tool for tying these). **2.** *v.t.* Make into sheaves. [OE *scēaf*, = OS *skōf*, OHG *scoub*, ON *skauf* fox's brush, f. Gmc **skaubhaz* (as SHOVE)]

shea'lĭng. Var. of SHIELING.

shear¹ *v.* (*past* **~ed,** arch. **shore;** *p.p.* **shorn** *or* **~ed**). **1.** *v.t.* & *i.* (arch. or poet.) Cut with sword etc. (*shore off his plume; shore through the bone*). **2.** *v.t.* Clip, cut with scissors or shears; clip wool off (sheep, or abs.); remove or reduce nap of (cloth) by clipping; (fig.) fleece, strip bare, (*come home shorn; shorn of his glory* etc.); hence ~'ER¹ *n.* **3.** Distort or break by SHEAR² (sense 2). **4.** *v.i.* (Of structure, material, etc.) be distorted or broken by SHEAR² (sense 2). [OE *sceran*, = OS, OHG *sceran*, ON *skera* f. Gmc **sker-*, **skar-*, **skǣr-*, **skur-*, cut, shear]

shear² *n.* **1.** (in *pl.*) Clipping or cutting instrument with two meeting blades pivoted as in scissors or connected by spring and passing close over each other edge to edge (*a pair of shears*); **~'bill,** = SKIMMER 3; **~-grass** (with sharp-edged leaves); **~-legs,** SHEER⁴S; **~ steel** (of special quality for shears and other cutting tools); **~'tail,** humming-bird with tail like shears. **2.** (Mech. & Geol.) Strain produced by pressure in structure of a substance, its successive layers being shifted laterally over each other. [OE *scērero* & *scēara* pl., = OHG *skari*, ON *skæri* f. Gmc **skǣr-* (as prec.)]

shear'lĭng *n.* (Wool from) sheep shorn once. [ME, f. SHEAR¹ + -LING¹]

shear'water (-waw-) *n.* Long-winged sea-bird of genus *Puffinus*, usu. flying close to surface of water; = SKIMMER 3. [f. SHEAR¹ + WATER¹]

shea't-fĭsh *n.* (*pl.* usu. same). Large catfish (*Silurus glanis*), largest European freshwater fish. [earlier SHEATH-*fish*, prob. after G *scheid*]

sheath *n.* (*pl. pr.* -dhz *or* -ths). Close-fitting cover esp. for blade of weapon or tool; (Bot., Zool., & Anat.) investing membrane, tissue, skin, horny case, etc.; sheathing of cable etc.; condom; woman's close-fitting dress; **~-bill,** Antarctic sea-bird with horny sheath at base of bill; **~-knife** (dagger-like, carried in sheath); hence ~'LESS *a.* [OE *scǣth, scēath*, = OS *skēthia*, OHG *sceida*, ON *skeithir* pl. f. Gmc **skaithiz*, **skaithjo*, prob. cogn. w. SHED¹]

sheathe (-dh) *v.t.* Put into sheath (**~ the sword,** cease from war, lit. or fig.); encase, protect with casing or **shea'th**ING¹ (3) (*or* -dh-) *n.* [ME, f. prec.]

sheave¹ *n.* Grooved wheel in pulley-block etc. for rope to run on. [ME, f. OE **scife, scīfe*, = OS, OHG *sciba* f. Gmc **skibh* disc, quoit, wheel, pane, slice of bread]

sheave² *v.t.* Gather (corn etc.) into sheaves. [f. SHEAF]

sheaves. See SHEAF.

***shĕbă'ng** *n.* (sl.) House, hut; matter, affair, business (*the whole shebang*). [19th c.; orig. unkn.]

shĕbee'n *n.* (Ir.) Unlicensed house selling alcoholic liquor. [f. Anglo-Ir. *síbín* (*séibe* mugful; see -EEN)]

Shechinah. Var. of SHEKINAH.

shĕd¹ *v.t.* (**-dd-; shed**). Part with, let fall off, (*tree sheds leaves; stag sheds horns; snake sheds skin; bather sheds clothes*); reduce (electrical power load) by disconnection etc.; drop (**~ tears,** weep; **~** one's **blood,** be wounded or killed *for* one's *country* etc.); cause (blood) to flow by injury; disperse, diffuse, spread abroad, (*shed* LIGHT¹ *on; shed love, radiance, perfume*, etc., *around* one); hence **~'d**ER¹ *n.*, (esp.) female salmon after spawning. [OE *sc(e)adan*, = OS *skēdan, skēthan*, OHG *sceidan*, Goth. *skaidan* f. Gmc **skaithan*, **skaidhan*]

shĕd² *n.* One-storeyed building for storing goods or vehicles or keeping cattle etc. or for use as workshop etc. and consisting of roof with some or all or no sides open; hence **~'d**ING¹ (3) *n.* [app. var. of SHADE¹]

sheen *n.* Splendour, radiance, brightness; gloss etc. on surface. [f. obs. *sheen* beautiful, resplendent, f. OE *scēne*, = OS, OHG *scōni*, Goth. *skauns* f. Gmc **skau-* behold (cf. SHOW¹); sense assim. to SHINE²]

shee'nў¹ *a.* Covered with sheen; bright and shiny. [f. prec. + -Y²]

shee'nў² *n.* (sl., derog.) Jew. [19th c.; orig. unkn.]

sheep *n.* (*pl.* same). **1.** Wild or domesticated (for its meat, wool, and leather) timid gregarious woolly often horned ruminant of genus *Ovis*; **~ and goats,** the good and the wicked (Matt. 25:33); BLACK¹ *sheep; cast* or *make sheep's* EYE¹*s*; **like ~** (of person(s) with no initiative or independence); *as well be hanged for a sheep as a* LAMB¹; WOLF *in sheep's clothing.* **2.** Bashful or docile person; (usu. in *pl.*) member of minister's flock, parishioner etc. **3.** Sheepskin leather. **4. ~-bot,** fly and larva injurious to sheep; **~-cote,** (arch.) = *sheep-fold*; **~-dip,** preparation for cleansing sheep of vermin or preserving their wool, place where this is used; **~-dog,** dog trained to guard and herd sheep, esp. (1) collie, (2) (*Old English*) *~-dog*, breed of rough-coated short-tailed dog used by shepherds; ‖**~-farmer,** breeder of sheep; **~-fold,** enclosure for penning sheep; ***~-herder,** shepherd; **~-hook,** shepherd's crook; **~-ked, -louse, -tick,** kinds of parasite on sheep; ***~'man,** ‖**~-master,** breeder of sheep; **~-pen,** = *sheep-fold*; **~-pox,** sheep-disease akin to smallpox; **~-run,** extensive sheep-walk, esp. in Australia; **~'s-bit,** plant (*Jasione montana*) resembling scabious; **~'s fescue,** a pasture grass (*Festuca ovina*); **~'shank,** bight and hitches used to shorten rope's length temporarily; **~'s-head,** (1) head of sheep (esp. as food), (2) large marine food-fish with sheeplike head; **~-shearing,** (festival at) shearing of sheep; **~'skin,** (1) garment or rug of sheep's skin with wool on, (2) leather of sheep's skin used in bookbinding etc., (3) *parchment of it or deed or diploma engrossed on this; ‖**~-walk,** tract of land on which sheep are pastured; **~-wash,** lotion for killing vermin or preserving wool on sheep, place where this is used. **5.** Hence ~'LIKE *a.* [OE *scēp, scǣp, scēap*, = OS *scāp*, OHG *scāf* f. WG **skǣpa*]

shee'pĭsh *a.* Bashful; embarrassed through shame; hence ~LY² *adv.*, ~NESS *n.* [f. prec. + -ISH¹]

sheer¹ *a.* & *adv.* **1.** *a.* Mere, simple, unassisted, undiluted, uncompounded, neither more nor less than, absolute, (*did it by sheer force; is sheer waste, nonsense, folly; a sheer impossibility*); (of rock, fall, ascent, etc.) perpendicular, unrelieved by more gradual slope; (of textile) diaphanous. **2.** *adv.* Plumb, perpendicularly, outright, (*fell sheer downward 3000 ft.; torn sheer out by the roots; rises sheer from the water*). [ME *schere* prob. f. dial. *shire* pure, clear f. OE *scīr*, = OS *skīr(i)*, ON *skírr*, Goth. *skeirs* f. Gmc **skīraz* etc. (**skī-*; see SHINE¹)]

sheer² *v.i.*, & *n.* **1.** *v.i.* (Naut.) Deviate from course. **2. ~ off,** part company, depart, esp.

from person or topic one dislikes or fears or is offended by. **3.** *n.* (Naut.) Deviation from course. [perh. f. MLG *scheren* = SHEAR[1]]

sheer[3] *n.* Upward slope of ship's lines towards bow and stern. [prob. f. SHEAR[2]]

sheer[4] *n.* **~s, ~-legs,** hoisting-apparatus of two (or more) poles attached at or near top and separated at bottom for masting ships or putting in engines etc., used in dockyards or on **~-hulk,** dismasted ship used for the purpose. [var. of SHEAR[2]]

sheet[1] *n.* **1.** Rectangular piece of linen used in pairs as inner bedclothes (**between the ~s,** in bed), whence ~'ING[1] (3) *n.*; WHITE[1] (*as a*) *sheet.* **2.** Broad more or less flat piece of some thin material (*a sheet of iron, glass, paper,* etc.); set of postage stamps printed on one piece of paper for later division into units; CLEAN[1] *sheet.* **3.** Wide expanse *of* water, snow, ice, flame, colour, etc. **4.** Complete piece of paper of the size in which it was made; (Print.) such piece before or after printing and folding (**in ~s,** printed and folded but not bound); (esp. scurrilous etc.) newspaper. **5. ~ copper, iron, metal,** etc., (spread by rolling, hammering, etc., into thin sheets); **~ glass** (made by drawing and cutting into sheets when cool); *sheet* LIGHTNING; **~ music** (published in sheets, not bound). [OE *scēte, sciete* f. Gmc **skautjōn* (**skaut-* SHOOT[1])]

sheet[2] *v.* **1.** *v.t.* Furnish with sheets; cover with sheet (*the sheeted dead*); form into sheets (*sheeted rain*). **2.** *v.i.* (Of rain etc.) move in sheets. [f. prec.]

sheet[3] *n.,* & *v.t.* **1.** *n.* Rope or chain at lower corner of sail for regulating its position etc.; (in *pl.*) space at bow or stern of open boat; **flowing ~** (not close-hauled, eased for free wind); **a ~, three ~s, in the wind,** (sl.) rather, very, drunk; **~-anchor,** second anchor orig. carried outside waist of ship for use in emergencies, (fig.) thing depended on for ultimate security, one's best or only hope or expedient; **~-bend,** method of temporarily fastening rope in bight of another. **2.** *v.t.* **~ home,** extend (sail) fully with sheet. [ME f. OE *scēata,* ON *skaut* (as SHEET[1])]

sheikh, sheik, shaik(h), (-āk *or* -ēk) *n.* Chief, head of Arab tribe, family, or village; Muslim leader; (colloq.) romantic lover; hence ~'DOM *n.* [ult. f. Arab. *šayḵ* old man, sheikh (*šāḵa* be or grow old)]

shei'la (-ē'-) *n.* (Austral. & N.Z. sl.) Young woman; girl. [orig. *shaler,* of unkn. orig., assim. to name *Sheila*]

shėkă'rrў. See SHIKAREE.

shĕ'kel *n.* Ancient Jewish etc. weight and silver coin; (in *pl.,* colloq.) money, riches. [f. Heb. *šeḳel* (*šāḳal* weigh)]

Shėkī'nah (-*a*) *n.* Visible glory of God resting over mercy-seat, or seen in other natural or supernatural phenomena. [f. Heb. *šᵉḵīnāh* (*šāḵan* rest, dwell)]

shĕ'ldrāke *n.* (*fem.* & *pl.* **she'lduck** *or* **sheld duck**). Bright-plumaged coastal wild duck of genus *Tadorna.* [ME, prob. f. dial. *sheld* pied, cogn. w. MDu. *schillede* variegated, + DRAKE[2]]

shĕlf *n.* (*pl.* **shelves** *pr.* shĕlvz). **1.** Projecting slab of stone or board let into or hung on wall to support things, one of the boards in cabinet, bookcase, etc., on which books etc. stand; **on the ~,** put aside, done with, (esp. of person past work or of unmarried woman now growing old and regarded as unlikely to be married). **2.** Ledge, horizontal steplike projection in cliff face etc.; reef or sandbank under water; CONTINENTAL *shelf.* **3. ~-life,** time for which stored thing remains usable; **~-mark,** mark etc. on book showing its place in library; **~-room,** available space on shelf. **4.** Hence **shĕlv**ED[2] (-vd) *a.,* ~-FUL 2 *n.* [ME, f. (M)LG *schelf,* cogn. w. OE *scylfe* partition, *scylf* crag]

shĕll[1] *n.* **1.** Hard outer case enclosing nut-kernel, seed, fruit, egg, animal (esp. marine mollusc) or part of it; husk, crust, pod, carapace, scale, conch, wing-case, pupa-case; **come out of** one's **~,** throw off reserve, become communicative. **2.** Walls of unfinished or gutted building, ship, etc. **3.** Inner or roughly-made coffin; light racing-boat; hollow case of pastry etc.; metal framework of vehicle body etc. **4.** Hollow metal or paper case to contain explosives for fireworks, cartridges, etc.; explosive projectile or bomb for use in big gun or mortar, whence ~'PROOF[2] *a.*; *cartridge. **5.** Handguard of sword. **6.** Building shaped like conch; ||intermediate form in school [f. such building at Westminster School]. **7.** Outward show, mere semblance. **8.** (Phys.) Group of electrons with almost equal energy in atom. **9. ~'back,** (Naut. sl.) old sailor; **~-bark,** hickory with bark in long narrow plates; **~-bit,** gouge-shaped boring-bit; **~ company,** unimportant firm made subject of take-over bid because of its status on Stock Exchange etc.; **~ egg** (still in its shell, not dried etc.); **~'fish,** aquatic shelled mollusc (oyster etc.) or crustacean (crab, shrimp, etc.); ***~ game,** thimblerig; **~-heap, ~-mound,** kitchen MIDDEN; **~-jacket,** army officer's tight-fitting undress jacket reaching only to waist behind; **~-lime,** fine quality lime produced by burning sea-shells; **~-money,** shells as medium of exchange (wampum etc.); **~-pink,** delicate pale pink; **~-shock,** nervous breakdown resulting from exposure to bombardment and other battle conditions; **~-work,** ornamentation of shells cemented on wood etc. **10.** Hence (-)~ED[2] (-ld), ~-LESS, ~'Y[2], *adjs.* [OE *sc(i)ell,* = MDu., MLG *schelle,* ON *skel,* Goth. *skalja* f. Gmc **skaljō* (**skal-* SCALE[1,2])]

shĕll[2] *v.* **1.** *v.t.* Take out of shell, remove shell or pod from, (*shell peas*). **2.** Provide or cover with shell(s). **3.** Bombard (town etc.), fire at (troops), with shells. **4.** *v.i.* (Of metal etc.) come *off* in scales; (of seed etc.) be released from shell. **5. ~ out,** (sl.) pay up (money or abs.), hand over (required sum); ~-*out* n., (1) act of shelling out, (2) snooker etc. played by three or more persons. [f. prec.]

shellă'c *n.,* & *v.t.* (-ck-). **1.** LAC[1] melted into thin flakes, used for making varnish. **2.** *v.t.* Varnish with shellac; *(sl.) defeat or thrash soundly. [f. SHELL[1] + LAC[1], transl. F *laque en écailles* lac in thin plates]

Shĕ'lta *n.* Ancient hybrid cant language of Irish gipsies and pipers, Irish and Welsh travelling tinkers, etc. [19th c.; orig. unkn.]

shĕ'lter[1] *n.* Thing serving as shield or barrier against attack, danger, heat, wind, etc.; screen or cabin built to keep wind and rain off persons (*bus, cabman's, shelter*); place of safety or immunity esp. as provided for the homeless, *animals, etc.; shielded condition (*find, take, shelter*); **~-belt,** line of trees etc. to protect crops from wind; hence ~LESS *a.* [16th c., perh. f. obs. *sheltron* phalanx f. OE *scieldtruma* (as SHIELD, *truma* troop)]

shĕ'lter[2] *v.* **1.** *v.t.* Act or serve as shelter to, protect, conceal, harbour; defend *from* blame, trouble, etc.; protect (industry, trade, etc.) from competition; **~** one**self** *under, beneath, behind,* etc., use the protection available. **2.** *v.i.* Take shelter *under, in, from,* etc. [f. prec.]

shĕ'ltie, shĕ'ltў, *n.* Shetland pony. [prob. repr. ON *Hjalti* Shetlander as pr. in Orkney]

shĕlve[1] *v.t.* Put (books etc.) on shelf, (fig.)

abandon or defer consideration of (plan etc.), remove (person) from employment etc.; fit (cupboard etc.) with shelves, whence **shĕ'lv**ING[1] (3) *n.* [f. *shelves* pl. of SHELF]

shĕlve[2] *v.i.* (Of ground etc.) slope gently. [perh. f. *shelvy* a. having underwater reefs f. *shelve* n. ledge, f. prec.]

shelves. See SHELF.

shėmŏ'zzle *n.* (sl.) Rumpus, brawl; muddle. [f. Yiddish, after LHeb. *šel-lō'-mazzāl* of no luck]

***shėnă'nĭgan** *n.* (colloq.) Nonsense; trickery; high-spirited behaviour. [19th c.; orig. unkn.]

Shē'ōl *n.* Hebrew underworld abode of the dead. [f. Heb. *šᵉ'ōl*]

shĕ'pherd (-perd) *n.*, & *v.t.* **1.** *n.* Man who tends sheep esp. at pasture (lit., or fig. esp. of minister in relation to his flock; **the Good S~**, Christ); **~ dog,** sheep-dog; **~'s crook,** staff with hook at one end used by shepherds; **~'s needle,** white-flowered common weed with spiny fruit; **~'s pie,** minced meat baked under mashed potatoes; **~'s plaid,** (woollen cloth with) small black and white check pattern; **~'s purse,** white-flowered hairy cornfield weed with triangular or cordate pods; hence ~ESS[1] *n.* **2.** *v.t.* Tend (sheep, lit. or fig.) as shepherd; marshal or conduct or drive (crowd etc.) like sheep. [OE *scēaphierde* (as SHEEP, HERD[2])]

shĕ'rardīze, -īse (-iz), *v.t.* Coat (iron or steel) with zinc by heating in contact with zinc dust. [f. *Sherard* Cowper-Coles, Engl. inventor d. 1936 + -IZE]

Shĕ'raton *n.* Style of furniture introduced in England *c.* 1790, with delicate and graceful forms. [f. T. ~, Engl. furniture-maker d. 1806]

shẽr'bet *n.* Oriental cooling drink of sweetened diluted fruit-juices; effervescing sweet flavoured drink or powder; water-ice. [f. Turk. & Pers. *šerbet* f. Arab. *šarba* drink (*šariba* to drink); cf. SHRUB[2], SYRUP]

shẽrd *n.* Potsherd. [var. of SHARD]

sheri'f (-ē'f), **-ee'f,** *n.* Descendant of Muhammad through his daughter Fatima, entitled to wear green turban or veil; Muslim leader. [f. Arab. *šarīf* noble (*šarafa* be exalted)]

shĕ'rĭff *n.* ||(**High**) ~, chief executive officer of Crown in county, charged with keeping the peace, administering justice under direction of the courts, executing writs by deputy, presiding over elections, etc.; ||honorary officer elected annually in some towns; ~(**-depute**), (in Scotland) chief judge of county or district; *elective officer responsible for keeping the peace in his county, executing court orders, and supervising county jail; **~ court,** (Sc.) county court; hence **~al**TY[1], ~DOM, ~HOOD, ~SHIP, *ns.* [OE *scīr-gerēfa* (as SHIRE, REEVE[1])]

Shẽr'lŏck *n.* ~ (**Holmes**) (hōmz), skilful detective, acute reasoner. [f. *Sherlock Holmes*, character in stories by Sir A. Conan Doyle]

Shẽr'pa *n.* (One of) a Himalayan people living on the borders of Nepal and Tibet. [native name]

shĕ'rrȳ *n.* White usu. fortified wine orig. from S. Spain; *sherry* COBBLER; **~-glass,** small wine-glass for sherry; *sherry* SACK[3]. [earlier *sherris* f. Sp. (*vino de*) *Xeres* (now Jerez de la Frontera) in Andalusia]

Shĕ'tland *a.* **~ lace,** open-work woollen trimming; **~ pony** (small hardy rough-coated breed); **~ sheep-dog,** breed of dog like small collie; **~ wool,** fine loosely twisted wool from Shetland sheep; hence ~ER[1] (4) *n.* [f. ~ Islands N.N.E. of Scotland]

sheva. Var. of SCHWA.

Shevuot(h). See SHABUOT(H).

shew, shewbread. See SHOW[1].

Shi'ah (shē'*a*) *n.* Muslim sect esp. in Iran that regards Ali as first successor of Muhammad and rejects first three Sunnite Caliphs; hence **Shi'**ITE[1] (1) (shē'-) *n.* [f. Arab. *ši'a* party (of Ali, Muhammad's cousin and son-in-law)]

shĭ'bbolĕth *n.* Test word or principle or behaviour or opinion, the use of or inability to use which reveals one's party, nationality, orthodoxy, etc. (see Judg. 12:6); catchword, esp. old-fashioned and generally abandoned doctrine or formula of a party or sect. [ME, f. Heb. *šibbōleṯ* ear of corn]

shield *n.*, & *v.t.* **1.** *n.* Variously shaped and sized detached piece of armour made of leather, wood, or metal, for carrying in hand or on arm to receive thrust or stroke, esp. one of elongated form large enough to cover most of body. **2.** Protective plate or screen in machinery etc.; person or thing that protects one; shieldlike part in animal or plant; (Her.) drawing etc. of shield used for displaying person's coat of arms; trophy in form of shield; *policeman's shield-shaped badge. **3. ~'bug,** flat insect with large scutellum; **~-fern,** common handsome fern with buckler-shaped indusia. **4.** Hence ~'LESS *a.* **5.** *v.t.* Protect, screen, esp. from censure or punishment (often with implication of illegitimate concealment of facts). [(v. f. OE *sceldan*) f. OE *sc(i)eld*, = OS, OHG *scild*, ON *skjöldr*, Goth. *skildus* f. Gmc **skelduz*, prob. orig. = board, cogn. w. SCALE[1]]

shie'lĭng *n.* (Sc.) Grazing-ground for cattle; roughly constructed hut for shepherds or sportsmen. [f. Sc. *shiel* hut, ME, of unkn. orig., + -ING[1]]

shī'er, shī'ėst. See SHY[1].

shĭft[1] *v.* **1.** *v.t.* & *i.* Change or move from one position to another, (of cargo) get shaken out of place; substitute one specimen of for another, undergo such substitution; change form or character; *change gear in vehicle; ~ one's **ground,** take up new position in argument etc.; **~ the scene, the scene ~s,** (in drama, novel, etc.); ~ (**off**), get rid of (responsibility etc.) to another. **2.** (sl.) Move quickly; consume (food or drink). **3.** *v.i.* Use expedients, take whatever course is available, contrive to do something, manage or get along or make a livelihood; **~ for oneself,** depend on one's own efforts. **4.** (arch.) Be evasive or indirect. [OE *sciftan* arrange, divide, etc., = MLG *schiften*, *schichten*, ON *skipta* f. Gmc **skip-*]

shĭft[2] *n.* **1.** Change of position or form or character, substitution of one thing for another, vicissitude, rotation. **2.** Relay of workers (*night shift*); time for which they work. **3.** New device, expedient, stratagem, resource. **4.** Dodge, trick, artifice, piece of evasion or equivocation. **5. Make ~,** manage or contrive (*to* do, or abs.), get along somehow (*must make shift without it*). **6.** Woman's dress of oblong form; (arch.) chemise. **7.** Arrangement by which joints of successive rows in brickwork etc. do not coincide. **8.** Displacement of spectral lines (RED-*shift*); (**sound**) ~, systematic change in pronunciation as a language evolves; (Bridge) change of suit in bidding or *play; change of position of typewriter type-bars to type capitals etc.; *gear-change in motor vehicle. [ME, f. prec.]

shĭ'ftlėss *a.* Lacking resourcefulness; lazy, inefficient; hence ~LY[2] *adv.*, ~NESS *n.* [f. prec. + -LESS]

shĭ'ft|ȳ *a.* Not straightforward, evasive; deceitful; hence **~ĭ**LY[2] *adv.*, **~ĭ**NESS *n.* [f. SHIFT[2] + -Y[2]]

shĭgĕ'lla (-g-) *n.* Aerobic bacterium of genus *Shigella*, causing dysentery. [mod. L, f. K. *Shiga*, Jap. bacteriologist d. 1957 + dim. suf.]

shih-tzu' (shētsōō') *n.* (Breed of) long-haired short-legged dog. [Chin., = lion]

Shiite. See SHIAH.

shĭkar' *n.* (Ind.) Hunting. [f. Urdu f. Pers. *šikār*]

shĭkar'ee (-rĭ), **shĭkar'i, shėkă'rrȳ,** *n.* (Ind.) Hunter, esp. native professional hunter or guide. [f. as prec.]

***shill** *n.* Person employed to decoy or entice others. [prob. f. earlier *shillaber*, of unkn. orig.]

shĭlle'lagh (-ā'l*a* *or* -ā'lĭ) *n.* Irish cudgel of blackthorn or oak. [f. *S*~ in Co. Wicklow, Ireland]

shĭ'llĭng *n.* **1.** Former British monetary unit and coin = $\frac{1}{20}$ of pound or twelve pence; **take King's** or **Queen's ~,** enlist as soldier [w. ref. to now obs. method of recruiting]; CUT² *off* one's heir etc. *with a shilling*; **~-mark,** solidus; **~s-worth** (-z-), as much as can be bought for a shilling. **2.** Monetary unit in E. Afr. countries. [OE *scilling*, = OS, OHG *scilling*, ON *skillingr*, Goth. *skilliggs* f. Gmc **skillingaz*]

shĭ'llȳ-shăllȳ *n., a.,* & *v.i.* **1.** *n.* Inability to make up one's mind, indecision, vacillation. **2.** *a.* Vacillating. **3.** *v.i.* Vacillate, be undecided, hesitate to act or choose one's course of action. [orig. *shill I, shall I*, redupl. of SHALL *I?*]

shĭ'lȳ. Var. of *shyly* (see SHY¹).

shĭm *n.,* & *v.t.* (**-mm-**). **1.** *n.* Thin slip or wedge used in machinery etc. to make parts fit. **2.** *v.t.* Fit or fill up thus. [18th c.; orig. unkn.]

shĭ'mmer *v.i.,* & *n.* (Shine with) tremulous or faint diffused light. [OE *scymrian*, = MDu., MLG *schēmeren*, f. Gmc **skim-*, **ski-* SHINE¹; cf. -ER⁵]

***shĭ'mmȳ** *n.,* & *v.i.* **1.** *n.* Kind of foxtrot accompanied by oscillation of body; abnormal vibration of (front) wheels of motor car. **2.** *v.i.* Dance a shimmy; move in similar manner; vibrate abnormally. [20th c.; orig. unkn.]

shĭn *n.* & *v.* (**-nn-**). **1.** *n.* Front of leg below knee; **~ of beef,** ox's (esp. fore-)shank; **~-bone,** tibia; **~-guard, ~-pad,** protective pad worn at football or hockey. **2.** *v.i.* Climb *up* (tree, wall, etc.) by using arms and legs, not on ladder etc. **3.** *v.t.* Kick on shin. [OE *sinu*, = MLG, MDu. *schēne*, OHG *scina*]

shĭ'ndĭg *n.* (colloq.) Festive gathering (esp. boisterous one). [prob. f. foll.]

shĭ'ndȳ *n.* Brawl, disturbance, row, noise, (KICK² *up a shindy*); = prec. [perh. alt. f. SHINTY]

shīne¹ *v.* (in sense 1 **shone** *pr.* shŏn; in other senses or arch. **~d**). **1.** *v.i.* Emit or reflect light, be bright, glow, (lit. or fig.; *lamp was shining*; *face shone with soap* or *with gratitude* etc.); (of sun, star, etc.) be visible, not be obscured by clouds etc.; be brilliant, be a luminary, excel, in some respect or sphere (*does not shine in conversation*; *is a shining example*). **2.** ***~ up to,** seek to ingratiate oneself with. **3.** *v.t.* (colloq.) Make bright, polish, (shoes, brass, etc.). [OE *scīnan*, = OS *skīnan*, OHG *scīnan*, ON *skína*, Goth. *skeinan* f. Gmc **skīnan* f. **skī-*, **skĭ-*]

shīne² *n.* **1.** Light, brightness, (RAIN¹ *or shine*); *polishing (of shoes etc.); high degree of polish; **take the ~ out of,** (1) impair brilliance or newness of, (2) throw into the shade by surpassing. **2.** (sl.) Disturbance, shindy, sensation; ***take a ~ to,** (sl.) take a fancy to. [f. prec.]

shī'ner *n.* **1.** (sl.) Black eye; (in *pl.*) money. **2.** *Small silvery freshwater fish of genus *Notropis* etc. [f. SHINE¹ + -ER¹]

shĭ'ngle¹ (-ngg*e*l) *n.,* & *v.t.* **1.** *n.* Rectangular slip of wood used like roof-tile on roofs, spires, etc.; *small signboard esp. of doctor, lawyer, etc.; shingled hair, shingling of hair. **2.** *v.t.* Roof with shingles; cut (hair of head) so that all ends are exposed like roof-shingles, cut hair of (head, person) thus. [ME, app. f. L *scindula*, earlier *scandula*]

shĭ'ngle² (-ngg*e*l) *n.* Small rounded pebbles, esp. lying on sea-shore; hence **shĭ'nglY²** (-ngg-) *a.* [16th c., of uncert. orig.]

shĭ'ngles (-ngg*e*lz) *n. pl.* (usu. treated as *sing.*) Acute painful viral inflammation of nerve ganglia, with skin eruption often forming girdle round middle of body. [ME, f. med. L *cingulus* f. L *cingulum* girdle (*cingere* gird)]

***shĭ'nnȳ¹** *v.i.* (colloq.) Shin *up* tree etc. [f. SHIN]

shĭ'nnȳ². Var. of SHINTY.

Shĭ'ntō *n.* Japanese religion revering ancestors and nature-spirits; hence **~ISM** (3), **~IST** (2), *ns.* [Jap., f. Chin. *shin tao* way of the gods]

||**shĭ'ntȳ** *n.* Game like hockey played with ball and curved sticks, and goal-posts as in rugby football; stick or ball used in it. [earlier *shinny*, app. f. cry used in the game *shin ye, shin you, shin t' ye*, of unkn. orig.]

shī'n|ȳ *a.* Glistening, polished, rubbed bright; (of coat, trousers, etc.) with nap worn off; hence **~ĭNESS** *n.* [f. SHINE² + -Y²]

shĭp¹ *n.* **1.** Vessel with bowsprit and three, four, or five square-rigged masts; any large seagoing vessel; *aircraft; (sl.) boat, esp. racing-boat. **2.** BREAK¹ *ship*; *when my* etc. **~ comes home,** fortune is made; **~ of the desert,** camel; *ship of the* LINE² 19; **take ~,** embark. **3.** **~('s) biscuit,** hard coarse kind made for keeping, formerly used on board ship; **on ~'board,** on board ship; **~-breaker,** contractor who breaks up old ships; **~-broker,** agent in shipping goods and insuring ships; **~'builder, ~'building,** (person engaged in) business of constructing ships; **~ burial** (Archaeol., in ships under mound); **~-canal** (to allow ships to go inland); *ship('s)*-CHANDLER(*y*); **~-fever,** typhus; **~'lap,** fit (boards) together for cladding etc. by rabbeting so that each overlaps the one below; **~'load,** quantity of something forming whole cargo; **~'master,** captain of ship; **~'mate,** person belonging to or sailing on same ship as another, esp. fellow sailor; **~-money,** (Hist.) impost for providing ships for navy (revival of which by Charles I was a cause of Great Rebellion); **~'owner,** person owning (shares in) ship(s); **~-railway** (for transportation of ships overland from water to water); **~-rigged,** square-rigged; **~'s articles,** terms on which seamen take service on ship; *ship's* COMPANY; ||*ship's* CORPORAL³; **~'shape** *adv.* or *pred. a.*, in good order, trim and neat; **~'s husband,** agent appointed by owners to see that ship in port is well provided in all respects; **~'s papers,** documents establishing ownership, nationality, nature of cargo, etc., of ship; **~-way,** inclined structure on which ship is built and down which it slides to be launched; **~-worm,** worm-shaped mollusc boring into ship timbers; **~'wreck,** (*n.*) destruction of ship by storm, foundering, stranding, striking rock, etc., (fig.) ruin *of* one's *hopes* etc., (*v.t.*) inflict shipwreck (lit. or fig.) on (person, hopes, etc.), (*v.i.*) suffer shipwreck; **~'wright,** shipbuilder, ship's carpenter; **~'yard,** shipbuilding establishment. **4.** Hence **~'LESS** *a.* [OE *scip*, = OHG *skif*, OS, ON, Goth. *skip*, f. Gmc **skipam*]

shĭp² *v.* (**-pp-**). **1.** *v.t.* Put, take, or send away (goods, passengers, sailors) on board ship; (Commerc.) deliver (goods) to forwarding agent for conveyance by land or water or air; step (mast), fix (rudder etc.), in its place on ship; take (oars) from rowlocks and lay inside boat; **~ a sea,** (of ship or boat) be flooded by wave. **2.** *v.i.* Take ship, embark; (of sailor) take service on ship. [OE *scipian* (as prec.)]

||**'shĭp** *n.* (Print. sl.) Companionship. [abbr.]

-shĭp *suf.* forming abstract *ns.* f. *adjs.* (*hardship*) or *ns.* (*courtship, friendship, scholarship*), w. senses (1) being so-and-so, status, office, honour, (2) tenure of office, (3) skill in certain capacity, (4) (number of) those who are. [OE *-scipe* etc. f. Gmc **skapiz* (**skap-*; see SHAPE[1])]

shĭ'pment *n.* Putting of goods etc. on ship; amount shipped, consignment. [f. SHIP[2] + -MENT]

||**shĭ'ppen, -on,** *n.* (dial.) Cow-house, cattle-shed. [OE *scypen* f. Gmc **skupinī* (**skup-*; cf. SHOP, -EN[2])]

shĭ'pper *n.* Merchant etc. who sends or receives goods by ship, or *by land or air. [OE *scipere* (as SHIP[1], -ER[1])]

shĭ'ppĭng *n.* In vbl senses; ships, esp. the ships of a country, port, etc.; **~-agent,** person acting for ship or line of ships at a port etc.; **~-articles,** = SHIP[1]'s *articles*; ||**~-bill,** manifest of goods shipped; ||**~-master,** official in whose presence ship's articles are signed, paying off is done, etc.; **~-office** (of shipping-agent or -master). [ME, f. SHIP[2] + -ING[1]]

shirā'lee *n.* (Austral.) Tramp's swag. [20th c.; orig. unkn.]

||**shīre** *n.* County; (Austral.) rural area with its own elected council; KNIGHT *of the shire*; **the ~s,** (1) band of English counties with names (formerly) in *-shire* extending N.E. from Hampshire and Devon, (2) midland counties of England, (3) fox-hunting district of England comprising mainly Leics. and Northants.; **~-horse,** heavy powerful breed of draught-horse bred chiefly in midland counties of England. [OE *scīr*, OHG *scīra* care, official charge; orig. unkn.]

||**-shire** (-sher *or* -shīer) *suf.* forming names of counties and districts (*Derbyshire, Hallamshire, Hampshire*). [f. prec.]

shîrk *v.t.*, & *n.* **1.** *v.t.* Avoid meanly, get out of, shrink selfishly from, (duty, responsibility, fighting, etc., or abs.); hence **~'**ER[1] *n.* **2.** *n.* Shirker. [f. obs. *shirk* n. sponger, perh. f. G *schurke* scoundrel]

Shîr'ley *n.* **~ poppy,** cultivated variety of common corn poppy with variously coloured single or double flowers. [f. ~ Vicarage, Croydon, Surrey, where first produced]

shîrr *n.*, & *v.t.* **1.** *n.* Elastic webbing; elastic thread woven into fabric; gathered trimming, gathering in garment etc. **2.** *v.t.* Gather (material) with parallel threads run through; hence **shîr'**RING[1] *n.* **3.** *Bake (eggs) without shells. [19th c., of unkn. orig.]

shîrt *n.* **1.** Man's loose sleeved garment of linen, silk, etc., for upper part of body, usu. worn inside jacket and trousers; NIGHT-*shirt*; **in** one's **~-sleeves,** not wearing jacket (**~-sleeve** *a.*, informal, direct); **keep** one's **~ on,** (sl.) keep one's temper; **the ~ off** one's **back,** one's last remaining possessions; **put** one's **~ on,** (sl.) bet all one has upon; **~-front,** breast of shirt esp. if stiffened and starched (*~-front wicket*, absolutely true and smooth cricket pitch). **2. ~ (blouse), *~'waist,** woman's blouse resembling man's shirt; **~ dress, *~'maker, ~'waister,** woman's dress with bodice like shirt. **3.** Hence -**~'**ED[2], **~'**LESS, *adjs.*, **~'**ING[1] (3) *n.* [OE *scyrte*, corresp. to ON *skyrta* (cf. SKIRT), f. Gmc **skurt-* SHORT]

shîr'tў *a.* (sl.) Angry, annoyed. [f. prec. + -Y[2]]

shĭ'sh kebăb *n.* Pieces of marinated meat and vegetable cooked on skewers. [f. Turk. *şiş kebabi* (*şiş* skewer, KEBAB roast meat)]

shĭt *v.i.* (**-tt-**; **shit**), & *n.* (vulg.) **1.** *v.i.* Defecate. **2.** *n.* Faeces; act of defecating; nonsense; contemptible person. [OE **scītan* f. Gmc **skit-*, **skĭt-*]

Shiva. Var. of SIVA.

shĭ'ver[1] *v.i.*, & *n.* **1.** *v.i.* Experience or show quick slight vibrating movement (such as is) caused by sensation of cold, tremble with cold or fear. **2.** *n.* Momentary shivering movement; (in *pl.*) attack of shivering, feeling of fear or horror (*gave me the cold shivers*); hence **~**Y[2] *a.* [ME *chivere*, perh. f. *chavele* chatter (f. as JOWL) + -ER[5]]

shĭ'ver[2] *n.* (usu. in *pl.*) & *v.* **1.** *n.* (One of) the many small pieces into which thing is shattered by blow or fall. **2.** *v.t.* & *i.* Break into shivers; **~ my timbers** (reputed naut. imprecation). [ME *scifre*, cogn. w. OHG *scivaro* splinter f. Gmc **skif-*, **skif-* split]

shoal[1] *a.*, *n.*, & *v.* **1.** *a.* (Of water) shallow, not deep. **2.** *n.* Shallow place, submerged sandbank esp. one that shows at low water; (fig., usu. in *pl.*) hidden danger(s) or impediment(s); hence **~'**Y[2] *a.* **3.** *v.i.* Get shallower. **4.** *v.t.* (Of ship) come into shallower part of (water). [OE *sceald* f. Gmc **skaldaz*, rel. to SHALLOW]

shoal[2] *n.*, & *v.i.* **1.** *n.* Multitude, crowd, great number, esp. of fish swimming in company (cf. SCHOOL[2]), (*shoals of people*; *gets letters in shoals*). **2.** *v.i.* (Of fish) form shoals. [prob. re-adoption of MDu. *schōle* SCHOOL[2]]

***shoat** *n.* Young (esp. weanling) pig. [ME; cf. W. Flem. *schote*]

shŏck[1] *n.* **1.** Violent collision, concussion, or impact (*clashed with a mighty shock*); violent shake or tremor of earth's surface as part of earthquake; **~ absorber,** device on vehicle etc. for absorbing shocks, vibrations, etc.; **~ tactics,** (Mil.) use of cavalry to charge in masses, (fig.) sudden and violent action; **~ troops,** troops specially trained for assault. **2.** Sudden and disturbing physical or mental impression (*news came upon me with a shock, was a great shock*; ELECTRIC *shock*); (Path.) acute state of prostration following over-stimulation of nerves by sudden pain as of wound etc. or violent emotion (*died of shock*; *the shock is more dangerous than the loss of blood*); **~ therapy, treatment,** method of treating psychiatric patients by means of an electric shock or powerful drug inducing coma or convulsions. **3.** Injury inflicted on credit, stability, etc., great disturbance of organization or system. **4. ~-brigade, -workers,** (in U.S.S.R.) body of workers engaged in especially arduous task; *shock*-PROOF[2]; **~ stall,** excessive strain produced by air resistance on aircraft when speed approximates to that of sound; **~ wave,** sharp change of pressure in narrow region travelling through air etc., caused by explosion or by body moving faster than sound. [f. F *choc* (*choquer*; see foll.)]

shŏck[2] *v.* **1.** *v.t.* Affect with indignation, sorrow, disgust, or horror, appear improper or outrageous or scandalous to (*was shocked at, by, to hear*, etc.); affect with electric or pathological shock. **2.** *v.i.* Cause shock; (arch.) collide violently. [f. F *choquer*, of unkn. orig.]

shŏck[3] *n.*, & *v.t.* **1.** *n.* Group of usu. twelve corn-sheaves stood up close together in field. **2.** *v.t.* Arrange (corn) in shocks. [ME, = OS *scok*, MDu., MLG *schok* shock of corn, sixty]

shŏck[4] *n.* Unkempt or shaggy mass of hair; **~ head,** rough head of hair; **~-headed,** having a shock of hair. [cf. obs. *shock*(*-dog*), earlier *shough*, shaggy-haired poodle]

shŏ'cker *n.* (colloq.) Shocking or very bad specimen of anything; sordid or sensational novel etc. [f. SHOCK[2] + -ER[1]]

shŏ'ckĭng *a.* & *adv.* **1.** *a.* Causing indignation or disgust; (colloq.) very bad (*shocking weather*); hence **~**LY[2] *adv.*, **~**NESS *n.* **2.** *adv.* (colloq.) Shockingly. [f. SHOCK[2] + -ING[2]]

shŏd. See SHOE².

shŏ'dd|ў *n.* & *a.* **1.** *n.* Fibre made from old cloth etc. shredded; inferior cloth made partly of such fibre; anything of worse quality than it claims or seems to have. **2.** *a.* Counterfeit, pretentious, trashy, shabby, poorly done; hence ~ĭLY² *adv.*, ~ĭNESS *n.* [19th c., of unkn. (dial.) orig.]

shoe¹ (-ōō) *n.* (arch. *pl.* **shoon**). **1.** Outer foot-covering of leather etc. with fairly stiff sole and ||not reaching above ankle; **another pair of ~s,** a different matter; **dead men's ~s,** property or position as looked forward to by expectant successor; ***if the ~ fits,** if the CAP¹ fits; **be in** person's **~s,** be in his situation or plight; DIE² *in* one's *shoes*; *where the shoe* PINCH²*es*; **put the ~ on the right foot,** apportion blame etc. truly; **shake in** one's **~s,** be filled with apprehension. **2.** Metal rim nailed to hoof of horse etc., horseshoe. **3.** Thing like shoe in shape or use, e.g. wheel-drag, BRAKE⁵-shoe, socket, ferrule, mast-step. **4. ~'black,** person who cleans shoes of passers-by for payment; **~-buckle** (for fastening shoe over instep, or worn only as ornament); **~'horn,** curved piece of horn, metal, etc., for helping heel into shoe; **~-lace,** cord for lacing shoes; **~-leather,** leather for shoes, wearing-out of shoes by walking (*save shoe-leather*); **~'maker,** maker of boots and shoes; ***~'shine,** polishing of shoes; **~-string,** (1) shoe-lace, (2, colloq.) a small or inadequate amount of money, (*attrib.*) precarious, just adequate, (*a shoe-string majority*); **~-tree,** shaped block for keeping shoe in shape. **5.** Hence ~'LESS *a.* [OE *scōh*, = OS *scōh*, OHG *scuoh*, ON *skór*, Goth. *skōhs* f. Gmc **skōh(w)az*]

shoe² (-ōō) *v.t.* (**shod**; **~'ing**). Fit (esp. horse etc.) with shoe(s); protect (end of pole etc.) with metal shoe; (in *p.p.*) having shoes etc. of specified kind (DRY¹-*shod*, ROUGH*shod*, SLIP¹*shod*; *car shod with radial tyres*). [OE *scōg(e)an*, = OHG *scuohōn*, ON *skúa* (as prec.)]

shō'far *n.* (*pl.* **sho'froth** *pr.* -rōt). Ram's-horn trumpet used by Jews in religious ceremonies and as ancient battle-signal. [f. Heb. *šôp̄ār*, pl. *šôp̄ārôṯ*]

shō'gun (-ōōn) *n.* (Hist.) Japanese hereditary commander-in-chief and virtual ruler before 1868; hence ~ATE¹ *n.* [Jap., = general]

shŏne. See SHINE¹.

shoo *int.*, & *v.i.* & *t.* (Utter) sound used to frighten birds etc. away; drive *away* thus; ***~'fly,** temporary road or railway, policeman etc. detailed to watch others; ***~'fly pie,** very sweet treacly dessert; ***~-in,** something easy or certain to succeed. [imit.]

shook¹. See SHAKE¹.

***shook²** *n.*, & *v.t.* **1.** *n.* Set of staves and headings for cask ready for putting together. **2.** *v.t.* Pack in shooks. [18th c., of unkn. orig.]

shoon. See SHOE¹.

shoot¹ *v.* (SHOT²). **1.** *v.i.* Come or go vigorously or swiftly *out*, *forth*, *along*, etc., or abs., (*boat shot out from the creek*; *flash shoots across sky*); (of plant) put forth buds, (of bud) appear; (of cricket-ball) dart along ground after pitching; (of pain) pass with stabbing sensation (*through*, *up*, arm etc.), (of part of body) be intermittently painful; **~ ahead,** come quickly to front of competitors etc.; **~ up,** rise suddenly, (of person) grow rapidly; **~'ing star,** small meteor appearing like star, moving rapidly and disappearing. **2.** Project abruptly *out* (*mountain-spur*, *cape*, *shoots out*). **3.** *v.t.* Send out, discharge, propel, emit, violently or swiftly (*bow shoots arrow*; *gun shoots missile*, or abs. *shoots*, *shoots straight*; *coaches collided and passengers were shot out*; *sun shoots its rays*; *tree shoots out branches*; *shot a glance at his neighbour*); let (rubbish etc.) fall or slide from container; move (door-bolt) so as to fasten or unfasten door; **~** one's **cuffs** or **linen,** display shirt-cuffs by shaking or pulling them down; **~ out,** (arch.) protrude (lips etc.) esp. in mockery. **4.** *v.t.* & *i.* Discharge (bullet etc.) from gun etc., (fig., sl.) inject (drug); cause (bow, gun, etc.) to discharge missile; discharge gun etc., make use of gun etc. (*shoots well*, *straight*); kill or wound (person, animal) with missile from gun etc.; kill (person) thus as punishment; hunt game etc. habitually or on one occasion with gun, shoot the game *over* estate etc., shoot game in or on (coverts, estate, etc.); (Footb. etc.) score (goal), take shot at goal; (Golf, colloq.) make (specified score) for round; (esp. Cinemat.) photograph; *(colloq.) play game of (craps etc.); ***~!,** (sl.) say what you have to say; **~ the cat,** (sl.) vomit; **~ down,** kill (person) cold-bloodedly by shooting, cause (aircraft or its pilot) to fall to ground by shooting, (fig.) argue effectively against (proposal etc.); **~ it out,** (sl.) engage in decisive gun-battle or **~-out** *n.*; **~ a line,** (sl.) tell a tall story; **||~ the moon,** (sl.) remove one's goods by night to avoid paying rent; ***~ off** one's **mouth,** (sl.) talk freely; **~ the sun,** take its altitude with the sextant at noon; **~ up,** terrorize (district) by indiscriminate shooting. **5.** *v.t.* Be, have one's boat, swept swiftly under or down (bridge, rapids, falls); (sl.) pass (traffic-lights at red). **6.** Plane (edge of board) accurately. **7.** Hence ~'ABLE *a.* [OE *scēotan*, = OS *skietan*, OHG *sciozzan*, ON *skjóta* f. Gmc **skeut-*, **skaut-*, **skut-*; cf. SHEET¹, SHOT¹, SHUT]

shoot² *n.* Young branch or sucker, new growth of plant; rapid in stream; = CHUTE 1; shooting-party or -expedition or -practice or -land; **the whole ~,** (sl.) everything. [f. prec.]

shoo'ter *n.* In vbl senses; (Cricket) ball that shoots; shooting-implement (esp. in comb.: PEA-, SIX-, *shooter*). [ME, f. SHOOT¹ + -ER¹]

shoo'tĭng *n.* In vbl senses; right of shooting over particular land; estate etc. rented to shoot over; **||~-box,** sportsman's lodge for use in shooting-season; **||~-brake** or **-break,** estate car; **~-coat, -jacket,** (as worn when shooting game); **~-gallery,** place for shooting at targets with rifles etc.; **~-iron,** (sl.) firearm; **~-range,** ground with butts for rifle practice; **~-stick,** walking-stick which may be adapted to form a seat; **~ war,** one in which there is shooting (opp. *cold war* or *war of nerves*). [f. SHOOT¹ + -ING¹]

shŏp *n.* & *v.* (**-pp-**). **1.** *n.* Building, room, etc., for retail sale of some commodity or service (*chemist's*, *butcher's*, *fruit-*, *betting-*, *shop*; **come to the wrong ~,** (sl.) apply to wrong person etc.), or in which manufacture or repairing is done (*engineering-shop*; *fitting*, *pattern*, etc., *-shop*; CLOSED *shop*). **2.** (sl.) Institution, establishment, place of business, etc. **3.** One's profession, trade, or business, things connected with it, or talk of it esp. when inopportune; **shut up ~,** cease business for the day or permanently; hence **~'PY²** *a.* **4. All over the ~,** (sl.) in disorder (*my books are all over the shop*), in every place (*have looked for it all over the shop*), wildly (*hitting*, *steering*, etc., *all over the shop*). **5. ||~ assistant** (in retail shop); **~-bell** (on door of shop, to give notice of customer's entrance); **~-boy, -girl,** assistant in shop; **~-floor,** (fig.) workers as dist. from management; **~'keeper,** owner and manager of shop (*nation of ~keepers*, the English); **~-lifter, ~-lifting,** (customer) stealing goods in shop; **~'man,** ||shopkeeper or his assistant, *workman in repair-shop; **||~-soiled,** soiled or faded by display in shop (lit. or fig.); **~-steward,** person elected by fellow-workers in a factory or branch of it as their spokesman in dealings with employer; ||**~'walker,** attendant in large shop who directs customers, supervises assistants, etc.; *shop*-WINDOW; **~-worn,** = *shop-soiled.* **6.** *v.i.* Go to shop(s) to make purchases (*or inspect goods); **~ around,** look for best bargain; hence **~'PER**[1], **~'PING**[1], *ns.* **7.** *v.t.* (sl.) Imprison; inform against. [ME, f. AF & OF *eschoppe* booth f. MLG *schoppe*, OHG *scopf* porch, rel. to SHIPPEN]

shōr'an *n.* System of aircraft navigation using return of two radar signals by two ground stations. [f. *short range navigation*]

shōre[1] *n.* Land that adjoins sea or large body of water (**in ~,** on the water near or nearer to shore, cf. INSHORE; **on ~,** ashore; **these ~s,** the island where one is); (Law) land between ordinary high and low water marks; **~-based,** operating from a base on shore; **~ leave,** (Naut.) permission to go ashore; hence **~'LESS** (-ōr'l-) *a.*, **~'WARD** *a.* & *adv.*, **~'WARDS** *adv.*, (-ōr'w-). [ME, f. MDu., MLG *schōre*, perh. f. root of SHEAR[1]]

shōre[2] *n.*, & *v.t.* **1.** *n.* Prop, beam set obliquely against ship, wall, tree, etc., as support. **2.** *v.t.* Support, hold *up*, with shore(s); hence **shōr'ING**[1] (3) *n.* [ME, f. MDu., MLG *schōre* prop, of unkn. orig.]

shōre[3], **shōrn.** See SHEAR[1].

shōrt *a.*, *adv.*, *n.*, & *v.t.* **1.** *a.* Measuring little from end to end in space or time, soon traversed or finished, (*a short line, journey, way off*; *a short time ago*; *he, his joy* etc., *had but a short life*). **2.** Of small stature, not tall, (usu. of human being, or of upright thing, as chimney, tower, tree). **3.** Not far-reaching, acting near at hand; deficient, scanty, having partial or total lack *of*, below the degree *of* (*nothing short of miraculous*), abruptly finished; (seemingly) less than the stated amount etc. (*after a few short years of happiness*); (of bill of exchange) maturing at early date; (Cricket, of ball) pitching relatively near bowler, (of fieldsman or his position) relatively near batsman; (of person's memory) retaining only things from the immediate past; **~ of breath,** panting, short-winded; **come ~,** be inadequate or disappointing; **come ~ of,** fail to reach or amount to; CUT[2], FALL[1], *short*; **go ~,** not have enough (*of*); *run short* (RUN[1] 12). **4.** Concise, brief, curt, sullenly or snappishly reticent, uncivil; *the* LONG[1] *and the short of it*; **in ~,** to use few words, without circumlocution, to give conclusion briefly; *is called Bob* **for ~,** by way of short name; **something ~,** drink of spirits etc. **5.** (Phonet. & Pros.) (Of vowel or syllable) having the less of the two recognized durations, unstressed; (of vowel) having sound other than that called LONG[1] (e.g. those in *met*, *pill*, *cut*). **6.** (Of pastry, clay, etc.) friable, crumbling, not tenacious; COLD-SHORT. **7.** (St. Exch. etc.; of stocks, stockbroker, crops, etc.) sold, selling, etc., when the amount is not in hand, with reliance on getting the deficit in time for delivery; **sell ~,** (fig.) disparage. **8.** **~-arm,** (of blow etc.) delivered with arm not fully extended; **~'bread,** crisp dry crumbly cake made with flour, butter, and sugar; **~'cake,** (1) shortbread, (2) cake of short pastry usu. served with fruit; **~ change,** insufficient money given as change; **~-change** v.t., rob by giving short change, cheat; **~ circuit,** electric circuit through small resistance, esp. instead of resistance of normal circuit; **~-circuit** v.t., cause short circuit in, (fig.) shorten or avoid by taking more direct route; **~'coming,** failure to come up to a standard, deficiency, defect; *short* COMMONS; **~-coupled,** (of animal) having short body between fore and hind legs; *short* CUT[1]; **~ date,** early date for maturing of bill etc.; **~-dated,** due for early payment or redemption; **~-day,** (of plant) needing regular cycle of light and dark to cause flowering; *short* DIVISION; **~ drink,** cocktail etc., e.g. before meal; **~'fall,** deficit below what was expected; **~ for,** an abbreviation of ('*Bob*' *is short for* '*Robert*'); **~ game,** (Golf) approaching and putting; **get** or **have by the ~ hairs,** be in complete control of (person); **~'hand,** method of rapid writing for keeping pace with speaker etc., (fig.) abbreviated or symbolic mode of expression; **~-ha'nded,** undermanned or understaffed; **~ haul,** transport of goods, or other effort made, over a short distance; **~ head,** (Racing) distance less than length of horse's head; **~-head** v.t., beat by a short head; **~'horn,** one of a breed of cattle with short horns; *short* HUNDREDWEIGHT; ||**~ list** (of selected candidates, from which final choice will be made); ||**~-list** v.t., put on short list; **~-lived** (-ĭvd), having a short life, ephemeral; **~ mark,** = BREVE 3; *short* MEASURE[1]; **~ metre,** hymn stanza of four lines with 6, 6, 8, and 6 syllables; *at short* NOTICE; **~ odds,** nearly even chances in betting; **~ on,** (colloq.) having partial or total lack of; ***~ order** (for food quickly prepared, at lunch-room etc.); ***in ~ order,** immediately; **~-pitched,** (Cricket, of ball) pitching relatively near bowler; **~-range,** having a short range, relating to a short period of future time; *short* RIB; **in the ~ run,** over a short period of time; **~ score,** (Mus.) one not giving all parts; *short* SEA; **~ ~ story,** very brief story with immediate point; *short* SHRIFT; **~ sight,** ability to see clearly only what is comparatively near; **~-sighted,** having short sight, (fig.) lacking imagination or foresight; **~-sleeved,** with sleeves not reaching below elbow; **~-sta'ffed,** not adequately provided with staff; **~ stop,** (Baseball) fielder near second base; **~ story** (with fully developed theme but shorter than novel); **~ suit** (of less than four cards); **in ~ supply,** scarce; **~ and sweet,** brief and pleasant (usu. iron.); **~ temper,** self-control soon or easily lost; **in the ~ term,** over a short period of time; **~-term,** occurring in or relating to a short period of time; **~ time,** condition of working fewer than the regular hours per day or days per week; **~ title,** abbreviated form of title; *short* TON[1]; **~ view,** consideration of the present time only, not the future; **~ waist,** high or shallow waist of dress; **~ wave,** radio wave of about 10 to 100 metres wavelength; **~ weight** (less than it is alleged to be); *short* WHIST[3]; **~ wind,** easily exhausted breathing-power; **~-winded,** having short wind, (fig.) unable or unwilling to discourse or perform at length; **make ~ work of,** accomplish, dispose of, destroy, consume, etc., quickly. **9.** Hence **~'ISH**[1] 2 *a.*, **~'NESS** *n.* **10.** *adv.* Abruptly, before the natural or expected time or place, in short manner; **bring** or **pull up ~,** check or pause abruptly; **stop ~,** suddenly cease, not go on to the end; **take up ~,** interrupt (person); **be taken ~,** be put at disadvantage, esp. (colloq.) by sudden desire to defecate; **~ of,** without going so far as, except, putting out of the question, (*all aid short of war*; *short of committing suicide he does his best to keep out of the way*). **11.** *n.* Short syllable or vowel; mark indicating that vowel is short; short film; (St. Exch. etc.) person who sells short; (colloq.) short circuit, short drink esp. of neat spirits; (in *pl.*) trousers reaching only to knees or higher, *underpants; (in *pl.*) short-dated stocks; (in *pl.*) mixture of bran and coarse flour; see also LONG[1]

14, 15. **12.** *v.t.* (colloq.) Short-circuit. [OE *sceort*, = OHG *scurz* f. Gmc **skurtaz*; cf. SHIRT, SKIRT]

shor'tage *n.* (Amount of) deficiency (*there is no shortage*; *a shortage of 100 tons*). [f. prec. 11 + -AGE]

shor'ten *v.i.* & *t.* Become or make actually or apparently shorter or short, curtail; reduce the amount of (sail spread); (of prices, odds, etc.) become shorter, decrease; hence ~ING[1] (3) *n.*, fat used for making pastry (short). [f. SHORT + -EN[6]]

shor'tlỹ *adv.* Before long, a short time *before* or *after*; in few words, briefly; curtly. [OE *scortlice* (as SHORT, -LY[2])]

shor'tỹ, -ie, *n.* (colloq.) Person or garment shorter than the average. [f. SHORT + -Y[3], -IE]

shŏt[1] *n.* (*pl.* in sense 2 usu. same). **1.** Single missile for cannon or gun, non-explosive projectile, (CHAIN-*shot*, GRAPE-*shot*, ROUND[1] *shot*, etc.); heavy ball thrown by athletes; *not a shot in* one's or *the* LOCKER. **2.** Small lead pellet of which several are used for single charge or cartridge, esp. in sporting guns; such pellets collectively. **3.** Discharge of cannon or gun (*several shots were fired, heard*, etc.), firing of space-rocket (MOON[1]-*shot*); remark aimed at a person; stroke in golf, tennis, cricket, billiards, etc.; attempt to hit with projectile or missile or fig. to make stroke in game or guess or do something (*at each shot he was nearer the bull's-eye*; *a beautiful shot from cover-point took off the bails*; *a lucky shot at goal*; *had a shot at learning Greek*); **like a ~,** willingly, without hesitation; **make a bad ~,** guess wrong; LONG[1], PARTHIAN, SNAP, *shot*; **~ in the dark,** a mere guess. **4.** Range, reach, distance to or at which thing will carry or act, (*within* EAR[1]*shot*). **5.** Possessor of specified skill with rifle, gun, pistol, etc., (*is a good, bad, crack* or *first-class*, or *no, shot*); BIG *shot*. **6.** Hypodermic injection of drug, vaccine, etc. (**~ in the arm,** (fig.) stimulus or encouragement); (colloq.) dram of spirits. **7.** Photograph; film sequence photographed continuously by one camera. **8. ~-blasting,** cleaning of metal etc. by impact of stream of shot; **~-firer** (who fires blasting-charge in mine etc.); **~'gun,** smooth-bore gun for firing small shot at short range (*~gun marriage* or *wedding*, wedding enforced esp. because of bride's pregnancy); **~-tower** (in which shot was made from molten lead poured through sieves at top and falling into water at bottom). **9.** Hence ~'PROOF[2] *a.* [OE *sc(e)ot, gesc(e)ot*, = OS *-scot*, OHG *scoz*, ON *skot* f. Gmc **skutaz* (**skut-* SHOOT[1])]

shŏt[2] *v.* & *a.* **1.** *v.t.* & *i.* Past tense of SHOOT[1]. **2.** *a.* In vbl senses; (of coloured material) woven or dyed so as to show different colours at different angles; (of board-edge) accurately planed; (sl.) exhausted, finished, drunk; **~ through,** permeated or suffused (*with*); FOOL[1]*'s bolt is soon shot*; **I'll be ~ if** (form of neg. asseveration). [sense 2 p.p. of SHOOT[1]]

shŏt[3] *n.* Reckoning, (one's share of) bill at inn etc., (*pay* one's *shot*). [ME, = SHOT[1] (cf. OE *scēotan* shoot, pay, contribute); cf. SCOT[1]]

shŏ'tten *a.* **~ herring,** one that has spawned, (fig., arch.) weakened or dispirited person. [ME, arch. p.p. of SHOOT[1]]

should. See SHALL.

shou'lder (shō'l-) *n.* & *v.* **1.** *n.* Part of body at which arm or foreleg or wing is attached, either lateral projection below or behind neck; ~(**-joint**), combination of end of upper arm with those of collarbone and blade-bone, upper foreleg and adjacent parts of butchered animal (COLD[1] *shoulder*); (in *pl.*) upper part of back, (fig.) body regarded as bearing burden, blame, etc.; **broad ~s,** ability to bear heavy load or responsibility; HEAD[1] *and shoulders*; **old head on young ~s,** (person displaying) youthful wisdom; RUB[1] *shoulders with*; **~ to ~,** side by side, with closed ranks or united effort; **put** or **set** one's **~ to the wheel,** make effort; **straight from the ~** (of well-delivered blow or frank verbal attack). **2.** Part of mountain, bottle, tool, etc., projecting like human shoulder; part of garment covering shoulder; strip of land adjacent to metalled surface of road. **3. ~-bag,** woman's handbag that can be hung from shoulder; **~-belt,** bandolier or other band passing over one shoulder and under opposite arm; **~-blade,** either large flat bone of upper back, scapula; **~-high,** up to or as high as shoulders; **~-holster** (in armpit); **~-knot** (of ribbon, metal lace, etc., worn on shoulder by officer in full dress, livery servant, etc.); ***~ loop,** shoulder-strap of army, air-force, or marines officer; ***~ mark,** shoulder-strap of naval officer; **~-note** (Print., at top corner of page); **~-of-mutton sail,** = LEG-*of-mutton sail*; **~-pad** (used to elevate shoulder of garment); **~-strap,** (1) piece of cloth from shoulder to collar of military uniform, bearing indication of rank etc., (2) one of two strips of fabric suspending garment from wearer's shoulders. **4.** Hence (-)~ED[2] (*-erd*) *a.* **5.** *v.t.* & *i.* Push with shoulder, jostle, make way thus. **6.** *v.t.* Take (burden, lit. or fig.) on one's shoulders; **~ arms,** (Mil.) hold rifle vertical with barrel against shoulder and butt in hand. [OE *sculdor*, = OFris. *skuldere*, OHG *sculter(r)a* f. WG **skuldr-*]

shouldn't. See SHALL.

shout *v.* & *n.* **1.** *v.i.* Make loud articulate or inarticulate cry or vocal sound, speak loudly, (*shouted to attract attention, with laughter, for joy*); **~ at,** speak loudly to etc.; **~ for,** call for by shouting; **all is over but** or **bar the ~ing,** contest is virtually decided. **2.** *v.t.* Say loudly, call out, express in loud tones, (*shout approbation*; *shouted that the coast was clear*; *shouted to* or *for me to come*; *'Go back', he shouted*); **~ down,** reduce to silence by shouting. **3.** *v.t.* & *i.* (Austral. & N.Z. colloq.) Treat (another person, or abs.) to drinks etc. **4.** *n.* Loud utterance or vocal sound from individual or group expressing joy, (dis)approval, defiance, etc., or calling attention; (Austral. & N.Z. colloq.) one's turn to order drink etc. for the company, free drink. [ME, perh. cogn. w. SHOOT[1]; cf. ON *skúta* SCOUT[2]]

shove (-ŭv) *v.* & *n.* **1.** *v.t.* & *i.* Push vigorously, cause to move along by hard or rough pushing; make one's way *along, past, through*, etc., by pushing, jostle (person); (colloq.) put somewhere (*shove it in the drawer*); **~-halfpenny,** form of shovelboard with coins etc. on table; **~ off,** start from shore in boat, (colloq.) depart. **2.** *n.* Act of shoving. [OE *scūfan*, = MDu., MLG *schūven*, OHG *sciuban*, ON *skúfa*, Goth. *-skiuban* f. Gmc **skeubh-*, **skaubh-*, **skubh-*]

sho'vel (-ŭ'v-) *n.*, & *v.t.* (‖-ll-). **1.** *n.* Scooping implement for shifting coal, earth, etc., often in form of spade with sides of blade turned up; machine (part) of similar form and function; **~ hat,** broad-brimmed hat as worn by some clergymen; **~-head,** (1) shark like hammerhead but with smaller head, (2) flat-headed species of catfish; hence ~FUL 2 *n.* **2.** *v.t.* Shift or clear (coal etc.) with or as with shovel; move roughly in large quantities (*shovel food into mouth*). [OE *scofl*, = MLG *schuffel*, cogn. w. OHG *scūvala*, f. Gmc **skuf-*, **skubh-* (see prec.)]

sho'velboard (-ŭ'v-) *n.* Game played esp. on ship's deck by impelling discs with hand or long-handled shovel-like implement over marked surface. [earlier *shoveboard*, *-groat* f. SHOVE + BOARD[1], GROAT]

sho'veller, -eler, (-ŭ'v-) *n.* **1.** In vbl senses. **2.** Duck with broad shovel-like beak. [f. SHOVEL + -ER[1]; sense 2 earlier *shovelard* f. -ARD, perh. after *mallard*]

show[1], (arch.) **shew,** (-ō) *v.* (*p.p.* **~n,** *or* **~ed** *pr.* -ōd). **1.** *v.t.* Allow or cause to be seen, disclose, manifest, offer (thing, thing *to* person) for inspection, exhibit, produce, give (treatment, treatment *to* person), reveal, (*clothes show signs of wear*; *white muslin shows the dirt*; *an aperture shows the inside*; *showed bad judgement in refusing*; *film was shown only once*; *show me, I was shown, a specimen*; *show your tickets, please*; *showed a profit on the year's business*; *show favour, mercy, to*; *showed me kindness* or *unkindness*); indicate by one's behaviour the presence or extent of (one's feelings); exhibit (animal, flower, etc.) in show; ~ one's **cards,** = *show* one's *hand*; *show* CAUSE[1], CLEAN[1] *pair of heels, cloven hoof* (see CLEAVE[1]), one's COLOUR[1]*s*, one's FACE[1], FIGHT[2]; ~ thing **the fire,** heat it slightly; *show the* FLAG[4]; ~ one's **hand,** reveal one's cards, (fig.) disclose one's plans; **~ a leg,** get out of bed; **nothing to ~ for,** no visible result of (effort etc.); ~ one**self,** be seen in public, let it be seen that one is (honest, a rogue, etc.); *show the white* FEATHER[1]. **2.** *v.i.* Be visible or noticeable, come into sight, appear in public, have specified appearance, (*the blood shows through her skin*; *stain will never show*; *he dislikes me and it shows*; *buds are just showing*; *film now showing*; *shows white, like a disc, from here*); *finish third (or better) in horse-race. **3.** *v.t.* Demonstrate, prove, expound, point out, cause (person) to understand (thing), (*has shown the falsity of the tale, that it is false, how false it is, it to be false*; *show* person *how to write, what to do*, etc.; *it only shows how little you know*; (abs.) *it all* or *just goes to show*); *show* person *the* DOOR; ~ **the way** (by words, pointing, accompanying, or preceding, or by doing thing first). **4.** Conduct (*showed us round the house*); ~ person **out** or **in,** (esp.) open door for his exit or entrance; ~ person **round,** take him to all points of interest. **5. ~-down,** (Poker) laying down of cards with faces up, (fig.) final test, disclosure of achievements or possibilities; ~ **forth,** (arch.) exhibit, expound; ~ **off,** (*v.t.*) display to advantage, (*v.i.*) try to make impression by exhibiting one's wealth or skill (whence *~-off* n., person who shows off); ~ **through,** be visible (lit. or fig.) although behind something else; ~ **up,** make or be conspicuous or clearly visible, expose (fraud, impostor, inferiority of another), (colloq.) appear, be present. **6. Shew'bread,** twelve loaves displayed in Jewish temple and renewed each sabbath; **~-card** (for advertising); **~-case,** glazed case for exhibiting goods, curiosities, etc.; **~-place** (that tourists etc. go to see); **~-room, -window,** (in which wares are kept, hung up, for inspection). [OE *scēawian*, = OS *skawon*, OHG *scouwōn* f. WG **skauwōjan* (**skau-* behold); cf. SHEEN]

show[2] (-ō) *n.* **1.** Showing or being shown; DUMB *show*; ~ **of force,** proof that one is prepared to use force; ~ **of hands,** raising of hands to vote for or against. **2.** Spectacle, exhibition, pageant, display (*a fine show of blossom*; *is on show today*), collection of things shown esp. in competition or to entertain (*dog, flower, horse, motor*, etc., *-show*; ||**Lord Mayor's Show,** procession of decorated vehicles etc. in London on day of Lord Mayor's coming into office); (colloq.) any public entertainment or performance; (sl.) concern, undertaking, business, (RUN[1], STEAL, *the show*; **give the** (**whole**) ~ **away,** betray inadequacies or pretensions; **good ~!,** well done!; **poor** or **bad ~!,** that was badly done or unfortunate). **3.** Outward appearance, semblance, impression produced, parade, ostentation, pomp, mere display, (*pierce beneath the shows of things*; *there is a show of reason in it*; *made a good show in the high jump*; *good enough in outward show*; *made a* (*great*) *show of being reasonable about it*; *did it for show*; *is fond of show*). **4.** (sl.) Opportunity of acting, defending oneself, etc., (*give him a fair show*). **5.** Discharge of blood from vagina at approach of childbirth or onset of menstruation. **6. ~'boat,** (river) steamboat in which theatrical performances are given; ~ **business,** (sl.) **~'biz,** the entertainment (esp. theatrical) profession; **~'girl,** actress whose role is decorative rather than histrionic; **~-jumping,** competitive jumping on horseback with points deducted for errors; **~'man,** proprietor or manager of menagerie or other such show; **~'manship,** the art of the showman, (fig.) capacity for exhibiting one's wares or capabilities to the best advantage; **~-piece,** excellent specimen used for show; **~-stopper,** (colloq.) performance receiving prolonged applause; ~ **trial,** judicial trial allegedly designed to make a favourable impression on public opinion. [ME, f. prec.]

show'er *n.* & *v.* **1.** *n.* Brief fall of rain, hail, sleet, or snow, or of arrows, bullets, water, dust, stones, etc. or (fig.) of incoming gifts, honours, letters, etc.; hence ~-PROOF[2], ~Y[2], *adjs.* **2.** ~(**-bath**), bath in which water is sprayed from above, apparatus or premises for this. **3.** *Party for giving presents to prospective bride etc. **4.** Group of meteors moving like a shower; group of particles initiated by cosmic-ray particle in earth's atmosphere. **5.** *v.t.* Discharge (water, missiles, etc.) in a shower; lavishly bestow (gifts etc. *on* or *upon*). **6.** *v.i.* Descend or come in a shower; use shower-bath. [OE *scūr*, = OS *skūr*, OHG *scūr*, ON *skúr*, Goth. *skūra* storm f. Gmc **skūr-*]

show'ĭng (-ō'-) *n.* In vbl senses; quality of performance (*made a poor showing*; *on this showing he will fail*); evidence, putting of case, (*on present showing, on your own showing, it must be true*). [OE *scēawung* (as SHOW[1], -ING[1])]

shown. See SHOW[1].

show'|ȳ (-ō'ĭ) *a.* Striking, making good display; brilliant, gaudy; hence **~ĭLY**[2] *adv.*, **~ĭNESS** *n.* [f. SHOW[2] + -Y[2]]

s.h.p. *abbr.* shaft horsepower.

shrănk. See SHRINK.

shră'pnel *n.* Hollow projectile containing bullets or pieces of metal and timed to burst slightly short of objective and release them in shower; fragments of bomb etc. thrown out by explosion. [f. Gen. H. *Shrapnel*, Brit. soldier d. 1842, inventor of the projectile]

shrĕd *n.*, & *v.t.* (**-dd-**). **1.** *n.* Scrap, fragment, rag, strip, torn or broken piece, small remains, least amount, (*tore it to shreds*; *without a shred of clothing on him*; *not a shred of evidence, reputation*, etc.); **tear** *an argument* etc. **to ~s,** completely refute. **2.** *v.t.* Tear or cut into shreds; hence **~'DER**[1] (2) *n.* [OE **scrēad* piece cut off (*scrēadian* v.), = OS *skrōd*, OHG *scrōt* f. WG **skraud-*, **skreud-*, **skrud-*; see SHROUD]

shrew (-ōō) *n.* **1.** Scolding woman; hence ~'ISH[1] *a.* **2.** ~(**-mouse**), small long-snouted mouselike insectivore of family Soricidae. [OE *scrēawa*, *scrǣwa* shrew-mouse; cf. OHG *scrawaz* dwarf, MHG *schrawaz* etc. devil]

shrewd (-ōōd) *a.* **1.** (arch. or literary). (Of pain, cold, etc.) sharp, biting; (of blow, thrust, etc.) severe, hard; mischievous, malicious. **2.** Sagacious, sensible, discriminating, astute, judicious, (*can make a shrewd guess*; *a shrewd observer*); (of face etc.) sagacious-looking. **3.** Hence ~'LY[2] *adv.*, ~'NESS *n.* [ME, f. prec. in sense 'evil person or thing' + -ED², or p.p. of obs. *shrew* to curse, f. prec.]

shriek *v.i.* & *t.*, & *n.* (Utter) shrill and usu. inarticulate cry of terror, pain, etc., screech, scream; (make) high-pitched piercing sound; ~ (**with laughter**), laugh uncontrollably; ~ (**out**), say in shrill agonized tones. [imit.; cf. dial. *screak*, ON *skrækja*, and SCREECH]

shrie'v|altȳ *n.* Sheriff's office or jurisdiction; tenure of this; so ~AL *a.*, of sheriff. [f. *shrieve*, obs. var. of SHERIFF, + *-alty* as in *mayoralty* etc.]

shrĭft *n.* **1.** (arch.) Confession to priest; confession and absolution. **2. Short** ~, little time between condemnation and execution or punishment, (fig.) curt treatment. [OE *scrift*, = OHG *scrift*, ON *skrift*, vbl. n. f. SHRIVE]

shrīke *n.* Bird of family Laniidae, with strong hooked and toothed bill and habit of impaling its prey of small birds and insects on thorns. [perh. cogn. w. OE *scric* thrush, MLG *schrik* corncrake, imit.; cf. SHRIEK]

shrĭll *a.* & *v.* **1.** *a.* Piercing and high-pitched in sound; (fig.) sharp, unrestrained; hence **shrĭ'l**LY² (-l-lĭ) *adv.*, ~'NESS *n.* **2.** *v.i.* (Of cry etc.) sound shrilly. **3.** *v.t.* (Of person etc.) utter, send out, (song, complaint, etc.) shrilly. [ME, rel. to LG *schrell* sharp in tone or taste f. Gmc **skral-*, **skrel-*]

shrĭmp *n.*, & *v.i.* **1.** *n.* (*pl.* ~**s** *or* ~). Small aquatic (esp. marine) edible decapod crustacean, grey-green when alive, pink when boiled. **2.** (usu. derog.) Diminutive person. **3.** *v.i.* Go catching shrimps; hence ~'ER¹ *n.* [ME, prob. cogn. w. MLG *schrempen* wrinkle, MHG *schrimpfen* contract, and SCRIMP]

shrīne *n.*, & *v.t.* **1.** *n.* Casket, esp. one holding sacred relics; tomb (usu. sculptured or highly ornamented) of saint etc.; altar or chapel with special associations; place hallowed by some memory. **2.** *v.t.* (poet.) Enshrine. [OE *scrīn*, = OHG *scrini*, ON *skrín*, Gmc f. L *scrinium* case for books etc.]

shrĭnk *v.* (**shrank; shrunk** *or*, esp. as *a.*, **shru'nken**), & *n.* **1.** *v.i.* Become of less dimensions, grow smaller, esp. by action of heat or cold or moisture; hence ~'AGE (3) *n.* **2.** Recoil, retire from observation, (~ **into oneself,** become reserved), cower, flinch *from*, whence ~**'ing**LY² *adv.*; be averse *from* doing. **3.** *v.t.* Make smaller (esp. in *pass.*; *his face has a shrunken look*), cause to shrink (esp. fabric etc., in order that it may not do so later); ~ (metal tyre etc.) **on,** slip it on while expanded with heat and let it tighten as it cools; ~**-wrap,** enclose (article) in material that shrinks tightly round it; hence ~'ABLE *a.* **4.** *n.* Act of shrinking; shrinkage, whence ~-PROOF², ~**-resistant,** *adjs.*; (sl.) psychiatrist, 'head-shrinker'. [OE *scrincan*; cf. *skrynka* to wrinkle]

shrīve *v.t.* (**shrove** *pr.* -ōv; **shriven** *pr.* -ĭ'ven). (arch.) Hear confession of, assign penance to, and absolve; (of penitent) submit one*self* to priest for this purpose. [OE *scrīfan* impose as penance, = OS *skrīban*, OHG *scrīban* write, prescribe, WG f. L *scribere* write]

shrĭ'vel *v.t.* & *i.* (||**-ll-**). Contract or wither into wrinkled, folded, rolled-up, contorted, or dried-up, state. [perh. f. ON; cf. Sw. dial. *skryvla* to wrinkle]

shrĭ'ven. See SHRIVE.

shrŏff *n.*, & *v.t.* (arch.) **1.** *n.* Banker or money-changer in the East; (in Far East) native expert employed to detect base coin. **2.** *v.t.* Examine (coin) for genuineness. [Anglo-Ind., ult. f. Arab. *ṣarrāf* (*ṣarafa* exchange)]

shroud *n.*, & *v.t.* **1.** *n.* Winding-sheet, garment for the dead, whence ~'LESS *a.*; concealing agency (*wrapped in a shroud of mystery*); (in *pl.*) set of ropes forming part of standing rigging and supporting mast or topmast; ~**-laid,** (of rope) having four strands laid right-handed on a core. **2.** *v.t.* Clothe (corpse) for burial; cover and conceal or disguise. [OE *scrūd*, = ON *skrúth* fittings, fabric, f. Gmc **skrūdh-*, **skreudh-* cut; see SHRED]

Shrōve¹ *n.* ~ **Tuesday,** day before Ash Wednesday, on which and the two preceding days (~**-tide**) it was customary to be shriven. [ME, abnormally f. foll.]

shrōve². See SHRIVE.

shrŭb¹ *n.* Woody plant smaller than tree and usu. divided into separate stems from near the ground; hence ~**'b**Y² *a.*, ~**'b**ERY (3) *n.* [ME, f. OE *scrubb*, *scrybb* shrubbery; cf. NFris. *skrobb* brushwood, WFlem. *schrobbe* vetch, Norw. *skrubba* dwarf cornel, and SCRUB¹]

shrŭb² *n.* Cordial made of sweetened fruit-juice and spirit (esp. rum). [f. Arab. *šurb*, *šarāb* (*šariba* to drink); cf. SHERBET, SYRUP]

shrŭg *v.* (**-gg-**) & *n.* **1.** *v.t.* & *i.* Slightly and momentarily raise (shoulders), raise shoulders, to express indifference, helplessness, contempt, vexation, etc.; ~ **off,** dismiss as unimportant (as) by shrugging. **2.** *n.* This motion (*of the shoulders*, or abs.). [ME, of unkn. orig.]

shrŭnk('en). See SHRINK.

shŭck *n.*, & *v.t.* **1.** *n.* Husk, pod; *shell of oyster or clam; *(in *pl.*, as *int.* of disgust or regret). **2.** *v.t.* Remove shucks of, shell. [17th c., of unkn. orig.]

shŭ'dder *v.i.*, & *n.* (Experience) sudden shivering due to fear, horror, repugnance, or cold; feel strong repugnance etc. (*I shudder to think what might happen*); (have) quivering or vibrating motion. [ME *shod(d)er* f. MDu. *schūderen*, MLG *schōderen* f. Gmc. **skūd-* shake; see -ER⁵]

shŭ'ffle *v.* & *n.* **1.** *v.t.* & *i.* Move with scraping or sliding or dragging or difficult motion (*shuffles along rheumatically*; *shuffles his* or *with his feet*); ~**-board,** = SHOVELBOARD. **2.** *v.t.* Slide or flick (cards etc., or abs.) over one another so as to change their relative positions; rearrange, intermingle, confuse; ~ **the cards,** (fig.) change the parts, try new policy, etc. **3.** Slip (clothes, burden, etc., esp. clumsily or evasively) *off* or *on* (*shuffle off responsibility on to others*; *shuffled on his clothes*). **4.** *v.i.* Keep shifting one's position (lit. or fig.); get *out of* evasively; fidget, vacillate, prevaricate; hence **shŭ'ffl**ER¹ *n.* **5.** *n.* Shuffling movement; shuffling of cards, general change of relative positions; piece of equivocation or sharp practice; quick scraping movement of feet in dancing (**double** ~, this executed twice, with one and then with the other foot). [f. or cogn. w. LG *schuffeln* walk clumsily f. Gmc **skuf-*; cf. SHOVE, -LE 3]

shŭn *v.t.* (**-nn-**). Avoid, keep clear of, eschew, esp. by habit. [OE *scunian*, of unkn. orig.]

||**'shŭn!** *int.* (as word of command) = Attention! [abbr.]

shŭnt *v.* & *n.* **1.** *v.t.* & *i.* Divert (train), ||(of train etc.) diverge, on to a side track, esp. to clear line for more important traffic, whence ~'ER¹ *n.* **2.** *v.t.* (Electr.) Provide (current) with shunt. **3.** Postpone or evade discussion of (subject), lay aside (project), leave (person) inactive. **4.** *n.* Turning or being turned on to side track; (Electr.) conductor joining two points of circuit, through which more or less of current may be diverted; (Surg.) alternative path for circulation of blood; (sl.) collision of vehicles. [ME, perh. f. SHUN]

shŭsh *int.* & *v.* **1.** *int.* = HUSH² 2. **2.** *v.i.* Call for silence by saying *shush*; be silent. **3.** *v.t.* Call or reduce to silence. [imit.]

shŭt *v.* (**-tt-; shut**). **1.** *v.t.* Move (door, window, lid, lips, etc.) into position to block an aperture; ~ **the door on,** refuse to consider, make impossible. **2.** Shut door etc. of (room, window, box, eye, mouth, etc.); bar access to (place etc.); ~ one's **eyes** or (fig.) **ears** or **heart** or **mind to,** pretend not, or refuse, to see or hear or feel sympathy for or think about; ~ **your head** or **mouth** or **trap,** (vulg.) stop talking; **~-eye,** (sl.) sleep. **3.** *v.i.* Become or admit of being closed, swing or fall or contract into closed position, (*the door shut with a bang*; *what time do the shops shut?*; *lid shuts automatically*, *won't shut*; *pimpernels shut in rainy weather*). **4.** *v.t.* Keep (person, sound, etc.) *out* or *in* by shutting door etc.; keep (person) *in* or *out of* room etc. by fastening door etc. **5.** (in *p.p.*, sl.) *Be* or *get* rid *of* (person, thing). **6.** Catch (finger, dress, etc.) by shutting something on it (*shut finger in door*, between it and jamb). **7.** Bring parts of together (*shut a book, a knife*, etc.). **8.** ~ **down,** push or pull (window-sash etc.) down into closed position, terminate operation of (factory, nuclear reactor, etc.), (of factory etc.) cease working, whence *~-down* n.; ~ **in,** (of hills, houses, sea, etc.) encircle, prevent free prospect of egress from or access to (see also sense 4); ~ **off,** stop flow of (water, gas, etc.) by shutting valve, separate *from* society etc.); ~ **out,** exclude (landscape etc.) from view, *prevent (opponent) from scoring, prevent (possibility etc.) (see also sense 4); **~-out bid,** (Bridge) pre-emptive bid; ~ **to,** close (door etc.), (of door etc.) close as far as it will go; ~ **up,** close all doors and windows of or bolt and bar (house; *shut up* SHOP), close (box etc.) securely or decisively or permanently, imprison (person), put (thing) away in box etc., reduce to silence by rebuke or refutation, (sl. esp. in *imper.*) stop talking. [OE *scyttan* f. WG **skuttjan* (**skut-* SHOOT¹)]

shŭ'tter *n.*, & *v.t.* **1.** *n.* In vbl senses; one of a set of wooden panels or iron plates, hinged, sliding, folding, or detachable, placed inside or outside glass of window to keep out light or burglars or ensure privacy (**put up the ~s,** cease business for the day or permanently); structure of jointed laths or metal slats on rollers serving same purpose; blind of swell-box in organ for regulating loudness; device that opens and closes lens aperture of photographic camera; hence ~ING¹ (3) *n.* (esp. = FORM¹ 15), ~LESS *a.* **2.** *v.t.* Provide with shutters; put up shutters of. [f. prec. + -ER¹]

shŭ'ttle *n.* & *v.* **1.** *n.* Weaving-implement with two pointed ends by which weft-thread is carried or thrown across between threads of warp; carrier of lower thread in sewing-machine; train, bus, etc., going to and fro over short route on ~ **service**; **space** ~, rocket for repeated use, e.g. between earth and space station; ~ **armature,** (Electr.) armature with single coil wound on elongated iron bobbin; **~cock,** cork with ring of feathers, struck to and fro in badminton and in battledore-and-shuttlecock [COCK¹, prob. f. flying motion], (fig.) thing passed repeatedly back and forth. **2.** *v.t.* & *i.* (Cause to) move to and fro like shuttle. [OE *scytel* dart f. Gmc **skutilaz* (**skut-* SHOOT¹; see -LE 1)]

shȳ¹ *a.* (**~'er** *or* **shi'er, ~'est** *or* **shi'est,** *pr.* -ī'-). (Of animal, bird, fish, etc.) easily startled, timid, avoiding observation; diffident or uneasy in company; avoiding company *of* person, chary *of* doing, (FIGHT¹ *shy of*); (sl.) short (*of*), in the position of having lost (*I'm shy three quid*); (as *suf.*) showing fear of or distaste for (GUN-*shy*, WORK¹-*shy*); hence ~'LY² *adv.*, ~'NESS *n.* [OE *sceoh*, = MHG *schiech*, OHG **scioh* f. Gmc **skeuh(w)az*]

shȳ² *v.i.*, & *n.* Start suddenly aside (*at* object or noise, or fig. *at* or *away from* proposal etc.) in alarm (usu. of horse, or fig. of person); hence ~'ER¹ *n.* [f. prec.]

shȳ³ *v.t.*, & *n.* (colloq.) **1.** *v.t.* Fling, throw, (stone etc., or abs.). **2.** *n.* Act of shying (**have a ~ at,** try to hit with missile, jeer at, make an attempt to get). [18th c., of unkn. orig.]

Shȳ'lŏck *n.* Hard-hearted money-lender. [character in Shak. *Merchant of Venice*]

***shȳ'ster** *n.* (sl.) Person without professional honour, esp. tricky lawyer. [19th c.; orig. unkn.]

si (sē) *n.* (Mus.) = TE. [F f. It., perh. f. initials of *Sancte Iohannes*; see GAMUT]

S.I. *abbr.* (Order of the) Star of India; international system of units of measurement [f. F *Système International*].

Si *symb.* silicon.

sī'ăl *n.* (Geol.) Lighter upper layer of earth's crust. [f. SILICA + ALUMINA (main constituents)]

sī'alagŏgue (-g) *n.* & *a.* (Medicine) inducing flow of saliva. [F, f. Gk *sialon* saliva + *agōgos* leading]

sī'amăng (*or* sē'-) *n.* Large black gibbon of Sumatra and Malay peninsula. [f. Malay *si(y)āmang* (*āmang* black)]

Sīamē'se (-z) *a.* & *n.* (*pl.* same). (Native or language) of Siam (Thailand); ~ (**cat**), cream-coloured short-haired breed of cat with brown face etc.; ~ **twins,** two Siamese men (d. 1874) joined by fleshy band at waist, any conjoined twins, any pair of very closely associated persons or things. [f. *Siam* + -ESE]

sĭb *a.* & *n.* **1.** *a.* (esp. Sc.) Related, akin, (*to*). **2.** *n.* Brother or sister; hence ~'LING¹ *n.*, one of two or more children having one or both parents in common, ~'SHIP *n.*, group of children having the same two parents. [OE *sib(b)*, = MDu. *sib(be)*, OHG *sibbi*, *sippi*, Goth. *-sibjis*]

Sĭ'bbald *n.* **~'s rorqual,** blue whale. [f. Sir R. ~, Sc. scientist d. 1722]

Sībēr'ĭan *a.* & *n.* (Native or inhabitant) of Siberia; ~ **dog** (of breed much used for sledging). [f. *Siberia* + -AN]

sĭ'bĭl|ant *a.* & *n.* **1.** *a.* Hissing, sounded with a hiss (esp. of letter or set of letters, as *s*, *sh*); hence ~ANCE, ~ANCY, *ns.* **2.** *n.* Sibilant letter(s). [f. L *sibilare* hiss; see -ANT]

sĭ'bĭl|āte *v.t.* & *i.* Pronounce with or utter hissing sound; hence ~A'TION *n.* [f. as prec. + -ATE³]

sĭ'blĭng, sĭ'bshĭp. See SIB.

sĭ'bȳl *n.* One of the women who in ancient times acted in various places as reputed mouthpiece of a god, uttering oracles and prophecies; pagan prophetess; fortune-teller, witch. [ME, f. OF *Sibile* or f. med. L *Sibilla* f. L f. Gk *Sibulla*]

sĭ'bȳllīne *a.* Issuing from an ancient sibyl, oracular, mysteriously prophetic; **the S~ books,** collection of oracles belonging to ancient-Roman State and often consulted by its magistrates for guidance. [f. L *Sibyllinus* (as prec.; see -INE¹)]

sic (sĭk) *adv.* (usu. parenth.) Thus used, spelt, etc., (confirming, or calling attention to, form of quoted words). [L, = so, thus]

sĭ'ccatīve *a.* & *n.* (Substance etc.) having drying properties, esp. one mixed with oil-paint to dry it. [f. LL *siccativus* (*siccare* to dry; see -ATIVE)]

sīce¹ *n.* The six on dice. [ME, f. OF *sis* f. L *sex* six]

sīce², sȳce, *n.* (Anglo-Ind.) Groom. [f. Hind. f. Arab. *sā'is*, *sāyis*]

Sĭcĭl'ĭan (*or* -lyan) *a.* & *n.* (Native or inhabitant) of Sicily. [f. L *Sicilia* Sicily, island in Mediterranean S. of Italy, + -AN]

sĭck[1] *a.*, & *v.t.* **1.** *a.* Ill, incapacitated by illness, feeling effects of some disease, (*a sick man*; *sick of a fever*); **the** ~, those who are ill; **go** ~, (Mil.) report oneself as ill; **take** ~, (colloq.) be taken ill. **2.** ||~ (**at* or **to* one's *stomach*), vomiting or inclined to vomit (*be*, *feel*, *make* person, *sick*; AIR[1]*sick*, *carsick*, SEA*sick*); **lo͝ok** ~, (sl.) be unimpressive or discomfited. **3.** Disordered, perturbed, suffering effects (of surfeit) *of*, disgusted, pining *for*, (*am sick at heart*; HEART-*sick*; LOVE[1]*sick*; *makes me sick to think of it*; *is awfully sick at being beaten*; *sick for a sight of home*; HOME[1]*sick*; *am sick* (*and tired*) *of being told off*, *of this bad weather*); (of humour) finding amusement in, or making fun of, misfortune and macabre things (*sick joke*). **4.** (Of ship) needing repair (esp. of specified kind; *nail-sick*, *paint-sick*). **5.** *Sick*-BAY[3]; **~-bed,** invalid's bed, state of being an invalid; ||**~-benefit,** allowance made to person absent from work through illness; **~-call,** visit to sick person by doctor etc., (Mil.) summons for sick men to attend; **~-flag,** yellow flag indicating presence of disease at quarantine station or on ship; **~ headache,** migraine; **~-leave,** leave of absence granted because of illness; **~-list,** list of those sick, esp. in regiment, ship, etc., (*on the ~-list*, ill); **~-making,** (colloq.) sickening; **the S~ Man (of Europe),** (Hist.) the Turkish Empire; **~-nurse,** = NURSE[1] 4; **~-pay,** (to employee etc. on sick-leave); **~-room** (occupied by sick person, or kept ready for the sick). **6.** *v.t.* ~ **(up),** (colloq.) vomit. [OE *sēoc*, = OS *siok*, OHG *sioh*, ON *sjúkr*, Goth. *siuks* f. Gmc **seukaz*]

sĭck[2] *v.t.* (usu. in *imper.*) Set upon; ~ **him!** etc. (urging dog to worry rat etc.). [19th c., dial. var. of SEEK]

sĭ'cken *v.* **1.** *v.i.* Begin to be ill, show symptoms of illness (*child is sickening for measles* etc.); feel nausea or disgust *at*, *to see*, etc. **2.** *v.t.* Affect with inclination to vomit, loathing, or disgust (*a sickening sight*) or with weariness or despair *of* (*was sickened of trying to make peace*). [ME, f. SICK[1] + -EN[6]]

sĭ'ckle *n.* Short-handled semicircular-bladed implement used for lopping and trimming, or for cutting corn; sickle-shaped object (e.g. crescent moon); HAMMER[1] *and sickle*; **~bill,** bird with sickle-shaped bill, e.g. curlew; ~ **cell,** sickle-shaped erythrocyte, esp. as found in a severe hereditary anaemia; **~-feather,** one of long middle feathers of cock's tail. [OE *sicol*, *sicel*, = MDu., MLG *sekele*, OHG *sichila*, f. L *secula* (*secare* cut)]

sĭ'ckl|ȳ *a.*, & *v.t.* **1.** *a.* Apt to be ill, chronically ailing, of weak health; suggesting sickness, as of sick person, languid, faint, pale, (*sickly colour*, *look*, *smile*, *complexion*); causing ill health (*sickly climate*); inducing or connected with nausea (*sickly smell*, *taste*); mawkish, weakly sentimental; hence **~ĭNESS** *n.* **2.** *v.t.* (arch.) Cover *over* or *o'er* with a sickly hue, (w. ref. to Shak. *Hamlet* III. i. 85). [ME, prob. after ON *sjukligr* (as SICK[1], -LY[1])]

sĭ'cknėss *n.* **1.** Being ill, disease; *sickness* BENEFIT[1]. **2.** A disease (FALL[1]*ing*, SLEEP[2]*ing*, SLEEPY, *sickness*). **3.** Vomiting or inclination to vomit. [OE *sēocnesse* (as SICK[1], -NESS)]

sīde[1] *n.* **1.** One of the more or less flat surfaces bounding an object (*cube has six sides*; *carry it with this side up*), esp. more or less vertical outer or inner surface (*side of house*, *cave*, *mountain*, etc.); such surface as dist. from top and bottom, or front and back, or ends (*four*, or *two*, *sides of box*; *two sides of house*). **2.** Either surface of thing that is regarded as having only two (*two sides of sheet of paper*, *board*, *gramophone record*, etc.; *the inside and outside of a bowl*); amount of writing filling one side of sheet of paper; RIGHT[1], WRONG, *side*; BACK[1]*side*. **3.** (Math.) Bounding line of plane rectilinear figure (*opposite sides of a parallelogram*; *hexagon has six sides*); one of two quantities stated to be equal in an equation. **4.** Part of person or animal that is on his or its right or left, esp. such part of trunk; corresponding half of carcass (*side of mutton*, *bacon*, etc.); BLIND[1] *side*; **~ by ~,** standing close together, esp. for mutual support; **shake** or **split** one's **~s,** laugh heartily. **5.** Part of object turned in same direction as observer's right or left and not directly towards or away from him, or turned in specified direction (*right*, *left*, *side*; *north*, *south*, *seaward*, *side*; **debit, credit,** ~, (in account book); EPISTLE, GOSPEL, PROMPT[2], *side*. **6.** Part or region near margin and remote from centre or axis of thing, subordinate or less essential or more or less detached part, (*side of room*, *road*, *table*, etc.); corner (of mouth); **on one** ~, not in the main or central position; *set* or *take on one* ~ (= ASIDE); **on the** ~, as a sideline, in addition to one's regular work or activity, *as a side-dish. **7.** Region external but contiguous to, specified direction with relation to, person or thing (SEA-*side*, *Merseyside*; *look on all sides*; *came from all sides* or *every side*; *standing at my side*; *on the north side of*); **by the ~ of,** close to (and compared with). **8.** Partial aspect of thing, aspect differing from or opposed to other aspects (*study all sides of the question*; *has many sides to his character*; *the side of the moon visible to us*); department of school etc. (*the classical side*); **on the** SAFE[2], *high*, *fat*, etc. ~, fairly, somewhat. **9.** (Cause represented by, position in company with) one of two sets of opponents in war, politics, games, etc., (*the Lord is on my side*; *the side that bats first*; *there is much to be said*, *there are faults*, *on both sides*); NO[1] *side*, ON[1]*side*, OFF*side*; **let the ~ down,** (fig.) frustrate one's colleagues' efforts; **take ~s,** decide to espouse one or other cause. **10.** Position nearer or farther than, right or left of, dividing line (*on this side of*, or *on this side*, *the Alps*, *idolatry*; *on the other side of the road*, *the river*); **on this ~ the grave,** in life; *on the* RIGHT[1], WRONG, *side of*. **11.** Line of descent through father or mother (*well descended on the mother's* or *maternal side*; DISTAFF or *spindle*, SPEAR, *side*). **12.** ||(Bill.) Spinning motion given to ball by striking it on one side, not centrally. **13.** ||(sl.) Assumption of superiority, swagger, (*puts on*, *has too much*, *side*). **14. ~-arms,** swords or bayonets; **~-band,** range of frequencies near carrier frequency of radio wave, concerned in modulation; **~-bet,** bet between opponents, freq. in card-games, over and above the ordinary stakes; **~'board,** table or flat-topped chest at side of dining-room for supporting and containing dishes, decanters, etc., (in *pl.*, sl.) side-whiskers; **~-bone,** (in carving fowls) either small forked bone under wing; **~'burns,** side-whiskers cut short; **~-car,** (1) jaunting-car, (2) car for passenger(s) attachable to side of (motor) cycle, (3) cocktail of orange liqueur, lemon juice, and brandy; **~-chapel** (in aisle or at side of church); **~-dish,** extra food subsidiary to main dish; **~-door,** door in or at side of building, (fig.) indirect means of access; **~-drum,** small double-headed drum in jazz or military band (orig. hung at drummer's side); **~-effect,** secondary (usu. undesirable) effect; **~-glance,** sideways or brief glance (lit. or fig.); ***~'hill,** hillside; **~-issue,** point that distracts attention from what is important; ***~'kick,** (colloq.) close associate; **~'light,** light from side, (fig.) incidental information etc., light at side of front of motor vehicle to warn of its presence, (Naut.) red port or green starboard light on ship under way; **~'line,** (*n.*) work etc. carried on in addition to one's main activity, (in *pl.*) (space immediately outside) lines bounding football-pitch, tennis--court, etc., at sides, place for spectators as opp. participants, *(*v.t.*) remove (player) from team by injury, suspension, etc.; **~-note,** marginal note; **~-road,** minor or subsidiary road, road joining or diverging from main road; **~-saddle,** (*n.*) saddle for rider, esp. woman, with both feet on same side of horse, (*adv.*) sitting thus on horse; **~-seat** (in vehicle etc., in which occupant has back against side of vehicle); **~-show,** minor show attached to principal one, minor incident or affair; **~-slip** *v.i.*, & *n.*, skid(ding), (Aeron.) move, motion, sideways instead of forward; **~'sman** (-z-), deputy churchwarden; **~-splitting,** causing violent laughter; **~-step,** (*n.*) step taken sideways, (*v.t.*) avoid by stepping sideways (esp. in football), (fig.) evade; **~-street,** street lying aside from main streets or roads; **~-stroke,** stroke towards or from a side, incidental action, swimming action in which swimmer lies on side; ***~--swipe,** (hit with) glancing blow along side; **~-table** (placed at side of room or apart from main table); **~-track,** (*n.*) siding, (*v.t.*) turn into siding, shunt, (fig.) postpone or evade treatment or consideration of; **~-trip,** minor excursion during a voyage; **~ valve** (in vehicle engine, operated from side of cylinder); **~--view,** view obtained sideways, profile; ***~'walk,** path at side of road for pedestrians (*~walk superintendent,* (joc.) spectator at building-site); ***~-wheeler,** steamer with paddle-wheels; **~-whiskers** (growing on cheek); **~ wind,** wind from a side, (fig.) indirect agency or influence; ***~-winder** (-wi-), (1) sideways blow, (2) small rattlesnake with lateral motion. **15.** Hence (-)**sī'd**ED² *a.*, **-sī'dèd**LY² *adv.*, (-)**sī'dèd**NESS *n.*, ~'LESS (-dl-) *a.* [OE *sīde,* = OS *sīde,* OHG *sīta,* ON *sítha* f. Gmc **sīdhō,* prob. f. **sīdhaz* extending lengthways]

sīde² *v.i.* Take part, be on same side, *with* disputant etc. [f. prec.]

sī'delŏng (-dl-) *adv.* & *a.* Inclining to one side, oblique(ly), (*move sidelong; a sidelong glance*). [f. *sideling* (SIDE¹, -LING²); see -LONG]

sidēr'ėal *a.* Of the constellations or the fixed stars; ~ **clock** (showing sidereal time); ~ **day,** time between successive meridional transits of star or esp. of first point of Aries, about four minutes shorter than solar day; ~ **time** (measured by apparent diurnal motion of stars); *sidereal* YEAR. [f. L *sidereus* (*sidus sideris* star) + -AL]

sī'derīte *n.* **1.** Ferrous carbonate as mineral. **2.** Meteorite consisting mainly of nickel and iron. [f. Gk *sidēros* iron + -ITE¹]

sī'derostăt *n.* (Astron.) Instrument for keeping image of heavenly body in fixed position. [f. L (as SIDEREAL) after *heliostat*]

sī'deward(s) (-dwerd(z)) *adv.* & *a.* = foll. [f. SIDE¹ + -WARD(S)]

sī'deways (-dwāz) *adv.* & *a.* To or from a side (*moved sideways; sideways movement*); with one side facing forward (*sit sideways in the bus*). [f. SIDE¹ + -WAYS]

sī'dewise (-dwiz) *adv.* & *a.* = prec. [f. SIDE¹ + -WISE]

sī'dĭng *n.* Short track by side of railway line and opening into it at one end or both for shunting purposes; *cladding material for outside of building. [f. SIDE¹ + -ING¹]

sī'dle *v.i.* Walk obliquely (*along, up*), esp. in timid or furtive or cringing manner. [back form. f. *sideling,* SIDELONG; cf. -LE 3]

siege *n.* Operations of encamped attacking force to take, or compel surrender of, fortified place, period during which these last, besieging or being besieged (**raise the ~ of,** abandon, or cause abandonment of, attempt to take by siege; **lay ~ to,** begin besieging); (fig.) persistent attack or attempt to persuade; **~-gun,** (Hist.) gun used in sieges, too heavy for field use; *siege--*TRAIN 14. [ME f. OF *sege* seat (*assegier* f. Rom. *Assedicare* f. L **sedicum* siege)]

sie'mens (-z) *n.* (Electr.) Unit of conductance, reciprocal of ohm. [f. W. von *Siemens,* Ger. electrical engineer d. 1892]

sĭĕ'nna *n.* Ferruginous earth used raw or burnt as pigment of brownish-yellow (**raw ~**) or reddish-brown (**burnt ~**) colour. [f. It. (*terra di*) *Sienna* (earth of) Siena in Tuscany]

sĭĕ'rra *n.* Long jagged mountain-chain in Spain or Spanish America; Spanish mackerel. [Sp., f. L *serra* saw]

sĭĕ'sta *n.* Afternoon nap or rest esp. in hot countries. [Sp., f. L *sexta* (*hora*) sixth hour]

sieve (sĭv) *n.*, & *v.t.* **1.** *n.* Sorting utensil with meshed or perforated bottom through which liquids or fine particles can pass while solid or coarser matter is retained (**head like a ~,** memory that retains little), or soft solid be passed to reduce it to uniform pulp etc.; person who cannot keep secrets. **2.** *v.t.* Put through or sift with sieve; (fig.) (examine in order to) select or separate. [OE *sife,* = MDu., MLG *seve,* OHG *sib, sip* f. WG **sibhi*]

sĭfa'ka (-ah'-) *n.* Long-tailed black and white lemur of genus *Propithecus.* [Malagasy]

siffleur (sēflẽr') *n.* (*fem.* ***-euse*** *pr.* -ẽr'z). Whistling artiste. [F (*siffler* whistle)]

sĭft *v.* **1.** *v.t.* Separate into finer and coarser parts with sieve, separate (finer parts) *from* material or its coarser parts or *out,* sprinkle (sugar etc.) from perforated spoon etc.; closely examine details of (evidence, facts, etc.) with regard to credibility or authenticity or relevance, analyse character of. **2.** *v.i.* (Of snow, light, etc.) fall as from sieve. **3.** Hence (-)~'ER¹ (1, 2) *n.* [OE *siftan,* = MDu., MLG *siften* f. WG **sibh-* (see SIEVE)]

Sig. *abbr.* Signor.

sigh (sī) *v.* & *n.* **1.** *v.i.* Draw long deep audible breath expressive of sadness, weariness, longing, relief from tension, cessation of effort, etc.; yearn *for* (person or thing desired or lost); (of wind etc.) make sound like sighing. **2.** *v.t.* Utter or express with sighs. **3.** *n.* Act of, sound made in, sighing (*a sigh of relief*). [ME *sihen* etc. prob. back form. f. *sihte* past of *sīhen* f. OE *sīcan*]

sight¹ (sīt) *n.* **1.** Faculty of perception through response of brain to action of light on eye; LONG¹, *near* or SHORT, *sight*; **know by ~,** be familiar with appearance (only) of; **loss of ~,** becoming blind; **second ~,** power of mental vision by which future or distant occurrences are perceived; hence (-)~'ED² *a.* **2.** Seeing or being seen, way of looking at or considering thing; **catch, lose, ~ of,** begin, cease, to see or (fig.) be aware of; **have lost ~ of,** no longer know whereabouts of (person); **get a ~ of,** manage to see; LINE² *of sight*; **at** or **on ~,** as soon as person or thing has been seen (*plays music at ~,* without preliminary study of score or practice of piece); **at first ~,** on first glimpse or impression. **3.** Range or unobstructed space within which person etc. can see or object be seen; **in ~,** visible, (fig.) clearly near at hand; **(with)in ~ of,** so as to see (lit. or fig.) or be seen from; **out of ~,** not visible; **put out of ~,** hide, ignore; **out of ~ out of mind,** we forget the absent; **out of my ~!** (rhetorical order to depart). **4.** Thing seen, visible, or worth seeing, display, show, spectacle, (*a sad sight awaited us*; *the daffodils were a beautiful sight, a sight to see, a sight worth seeing*; **a ~ for the gods** or **for sore eyes,** person or thing one is glad to see, esp. welcome visitor); (in *pl.*) noteworthy or attractive features of town etc. (*see the sights*); **a** (**perfect** etc.) **~**, person or thing of ridiculous, repulsive, dishevelled, etc., appearance; **~ unseen,** without previous inspection. **5.** (colloq.) Great quantity (*will cost a sight of money*; *is a long sight better*). **6.** (Device for assisting) precise aim with gun or observation with optical instrument; **set** one's **~s on,** (fig.) aim at. **7. ~-glass,** transparent device for observing interior of apparatus etc.; **~-line** (from person's eye to what is seen); **~-reading, ~-singing,** etc., reading music, singing, etc., at sight; **~-screen,** (Cricket) large movable white structure placed near boundary in line with wicket to help batsman see ball; **~'seer, ~'seeing,** (person) visiting sights of town etc.; ||**~ translation,** unseen; **~'worthy,** worth seeing. [OE (*ge*)*sihth*, = OS *gisicht*, OHG *sicht*, WG (as SEE¹)]

sight² (sīt) *v.t.* Get sight of, esp. by coming near (*sight land, game*); observe presence of (esp. aircraft or unidentified flying object, or unusual species etc.); take observation of (star etc.) with instrument; provide (gun, quadrant, etc.) with sights; adjust sight of (**~'ing shot,** experimental one to guide rifleman etc. in this); aim (gun etc.) with sights. [f. prec.]

sī'ghtless (sī't-) *a.* Blind; (poet.) invisible; hence **~**LY² *adv.*, **~**NESS *n.* [ME, f. SIGHT¹ + -LESS]

sī'ghtl|y̆ (sī't-) *a.* Attractive to the sight, not unsightly; hence **~ĭ**NESS *n.* [f. SIGHT¹ + -LY¹]

sĭ'gillate *a.* (Of pottery) with impressed patterns; (Bot.) having seal-like marks. [f. L *sigillatus* (*sigillum* seal dim. of *signum* sign; see -ATE²)]

sĭ'gl|um *n.* (*pl.* **~a**). Letter (esp. initial) or other character used to denote word, esp. for source of an edition of a text. [f. LL *sigla* pl., perh. f. *singula* neut. pl. of *singulus* single]

sĭ'gma *n.* Eighteenth Greek letter (Σ, σ or, when final, ς) = s. [L f. Gk]

sĭ'gmate *a.* Sigma-shaped; S-shaped. [f. prec. + -ATE²]

sĭ'gmoid *a.* & *n.* **1.** *a.* Curved like the uncial sigma (C) or like S; **~ flexure,** (Anat.) curved part of intestine between colon and rectum. **2.** *n.* Sigmoid flexure. [f. Gk *sigmoeidēs* (as SIGMA; see -OID)]

sīgn¹ (sīn) *n.* **1.** Mark traced on surface etc.; **~ of the cross** (made by Christian priest in blessing, or layman in reverence with finger between forehead and breast and across breast); **~ manual,** (arch. or Hist.) signature written with person's own hand, gesture of command etc. **2.** Written mark conventionally used for word or phrase, symbol, thing used as representation of something, (*words are the signs of ideas*; *a sacrament is an outward and visible sign of an inward and spiritual grace*); **positive** or **plus ~**, +; **negative** or **minus ~**, −; ROAD¹ *sign.* **3.** (Thing serving as) presumptive evidence or indication or suggestion or symptom *of* or *that*, distinctive mark, token, guarantee, password, miracle evidencing supernatural power, portent, (*violence is a sign of weakness* or *that one is weak*; *gave little* or *no sign of being aware of it*; *shows all the signs of decay*; *bowed down in sign of submission*; *by this sign ye shall know them*; *did signs and wonders*); *trail of wild animal; **~ and counter~**, secret words etc. by which confederates recognize each other; **~ of the times,** thing showing the tendency of affairs. **4.** (Path.) Objective symptom of disease (usu. w. defining word: *Babinski's, Oppenheim's, sign*). **5.** (Math.) Positiveness or negativeness of a quantity. **6.** **~('board)**, more or less fanciful device usu. painted on a board displayed formerly by all traders and still by many inns, board indicating nature of business and placed in front of shop etc. **7.** Natural or conventional motion or gesture used instead of words to convey information and esp. order or request (*conversed by signs, in sign language*; *gave him a sign to withdraw*); DEAF*-and-dumb signs*; **make no ~**, seem unconscious, not protest, etc. **8.** Any of twelve divisions of ZODIAC named from constellations formerly situated in them. **9. ~-painter, -writer,** (of signboards); **~'post** (at crossroads etc. with arms showing names of places on each road), (*v.t.*) provide with signpost(s) (lit. or fig.). [ME f. OF *signe*, f. L *signum* mark, token]

sīgn² (sīn) *v.* **1.** *v.t.* Mark with sign (esp. infant etc. *with the sign of the cross* in baptism). **2.** Acknowledge or guarantee (letter, deed, picture, book, article, petition, bill, etc., or abs.) as one's own production or as having one's authority or consent by affixing or having affixed one's name or initials or recognized mark (*the will had never been signed*; *a signed masterpiece of Turner's*; *signed as usual with a double cross*; *does not sign his contributions to the press*; *nothing shall induce me to sign*); hence **~'**ABLE *a.* **3.** Write (one's name) as signature; convey (right, property, etc.) *away* by signing deed etc. **4.** *v.t.* & *i.* **~** (**on** or **up**), engage, acknowledge being engaged, for some undertaking to which person binds himself by signature; **~ off,** end such engagement (of). **5.** Communicate by gesture (*sign assent*); give order or make request by gesture *to* person *to* do (*signed to me to come*). **6. ~ off,** (Bridge) indicate by conventional bid that one is seeking to end the bidding; so **~***-off* n. **7. ~ off, on,** end, begin, work, broadcasting, etc., esp. by writing, announcing, etc., one's name. [ME, f. OF *signer* f. L *signare* (*signum*; see prec.)]

sĭ'gnal¹ *a.* Remarkably good or bad, conspicuous, noteworthy, exemplary, condign, (*signal victory, defeat, reward, punishment, virtue, example*); hence **~**LY² *adv.* [f. F *signalé* f. It. p.p. *segnalato* distinguished (*segnale* SIGNAL²)]

sĭ'gnal² *n.* & *v.* (||**-ll-**). **1.** *n.* Intelligible (esp. prearranged) sign conveying information or direction esp. to person(s) at a distance, message made up of such signs, (*the signal was to be the dropping of a handkerchief*; *train stopped at the red signal*; *signals are made by day with flags and by night with lights*; *gave the signal for advance*); **~ of distress,** appeal for help, esp. from ship made by firing guns; **code of ~s, ~-book,** body of signals arranged for sending complicated messages esp. in naval and mil. use; **~s department** etc. (concerned with arrangements for these). **2.** Immediate occasion for some general movement (*the earthquake was the signal for an outbreak of the primitive instincts*); (Bridge) prearranged mode of bidding or play to convey information to one's partner; (Electr.) (sequence of) electrical impulse(s) or radio wave(s) transmitted as signal. **3.** ||**~-box,** railway building with signalling-apparatus; **~man** (responsible for display of naval, railway, etc., signals); ***~-tower,** signal-box. **4.** *v.i.* Make signals. **5.** *v.t.* Make signals to; transmit (order, information) by signal; announce (event, *that*) by signal; direct (person *to* do) by signal. **6.** Hence **~(l)**ER¹ *n.* [ME f. OF, f. Rom. & med. L *signale* neut. (as n.) of LL *signalis* f. L *signum* SIGN¹; see -AL]

sĭ'gnalize, -ise (-īz), *v.t.* Make noteworthy or

remarkable, lend distinction or lustre to, (*his accession was signalized by an amnesty*). [f. SIGNAL¹ + -IZE]

sĭ'gnarў *n.* List of signs constituting syllabic or alphabetic symbols of a language. [f. L *signum* SIGN¹ + -ARY¹, after *syllabary*]

sĭ'gnatorў *a.* & *n.* (Party, esp. State) that has signed an agreement esp. a treaty (*the signatories, or signatory powers, to the Treaty of Rome*). [f. L *signatorius* of sealing (*signare -at-* mark; see -ORY)]

sĭ'gnature *n.* **1.** (arch.) Significant appearance or mark (*has the signature of passion, of early death, in his face; herb's yellow flowers are a signature indicating that it will cure jaundice*). **2.** Person's name or initials or mark used in signing. **3.** (Print.) Letter or figure placed at foot of one or more pages of each sheet of book as guide in making up for binding; such sheet after folding. **4.** (Mus.) **Key ~**, sharps or flats after clef at beginning of each staff; **time ~**, fraction placed at beginning of composition, numerator giving number of beats in each bar and denominator duration of each beat. **5.** *Directions to patient as part of medical prescription. **6. ~ tune,** special tune used in broadcasting to announce a particular programme etc. [f. med. L *signatura* (LL = marking of sheep), as prec.; see -URE]

sĭ'gnėt *n.* Private seal for use instead of or with signature as authentication (**the ~**, royal seal formerly used for special purposes in England & Scotland, in Scotland later as seal of Court of Session; ||WRITER *to the Signet*); **~-ring,** finger-ring with seal set in it. [ME f. OF, or f. med. L *signetum* (as SIGN¹; see -ET¹)]

sĭgnĭ'fĭcance *n.* Being significant (*with a look of deep significance*); covert or real import, what is meant to be or may be inferred, (*those were the words, but what is their significance?*); importance, noteworthiness, (*what he thinks about it is of no significance*). [OF, or f. L *significantia* (as SIGNIFY; see -ANCE)]

sĭgnĭ'fĭcancў *n.* Expressiveness (*brought out with great force and significancy*); = prec. [f. as prec. + -ANCY]

sĭgnĭ'fĭcant *a.* Having a meaning (*'-kin' is a significant termination*); expressive, suggestive, with unstated or secret sense, inviting attention; noteworthy, of considerable amount or effect or importance, not insignificant or negligible, (*a little man may be a very significant man*); **~ figure,** (Math.) digit conveying information about a number containing it, and not a zero used simply to fill vacant place at the beginning or end; hence **~**LY² *adv.* [f. L *significare* (see SIGNIFY) + -ANT]

sĭgnĭfĭcā'tion *n.* Act of signifying; exact meaning or sense (*of*, esp. *of* word or phrase). [ME f. OF, f. L *significatio -onis* (as SIGNIFY; see -ATION)]

sĭgnĭ'fĭcatĭve *a.* Signifying; having a meaning; serving as sign or presumptive evidence *of*. [ME, f. OF *significatif -ive*, or f. LL *significativus* (as foll.; see -ATIVE)]

sĭ'gnĭfў *v.* **1.** *v.t.* Be a sign or indication or presage of (*a long upper lip signifies obstinacy; a lunar halo signifies rain*); mean, have as meaning, (*'D.D.' signifies 'Doctor of Divinity'*); communicate, make known, (*he signified his agreement, that he could not consent*). **2.** *v.i.* Be of importance, matter, (esp. w. neg.; *it does not signify*). [ME, f. OF *signifier* f. L *significare* (as SIGN¹; see -FY)]

signor (*pl.* ***signori***), ***signora, signorina,*** (sē'nyor̂, sēnyor̂'ē; sēnyor̂'*a*; sēnyerē'na) *ns.* (Titles used of or to Italians corresponding to) Mr. or sir, Mrs. or madam, Miss or madam (to unmarried woman). [It., f. L SENIOR]

si'gnorў (sē'nyerĭ) *n.* **1.** Seigniory. **2.** (Hist.) Governing body of medieval Italian republic. [ME f. OF *s(e)ignorie* (as SEIGNEUR)]

si'ka (sē'-) *n.* Species of deer (*Cervus sika*) from Japan. [f. Jap. *shika*]

Sikh (sēk *or* sĭk) *n.* Member of Indian monotheistic sect founded in 16th c.; hence **~'**ISM *n.*, the (religious) tenets of the Sikhs. [Hindi, = disciple, f. Skr. *sishya*]

sī'lage *n.*, & *v.t.* **1.** *n.* Ensilage. **2.** *v.t.* Put into silo. [alt. f. ENSILAGE after *silo*]

sī'lence *n.*, & *v.t.* **1.** *n.* Abstinence from speech or noise, being silent, taciturnity, non-betrayal of secret etc., fact of not mentioning a thing, not communicating any message, etc., (*the silence of Scripture on the subject; silence gives consent*); **~ is golden,** saying nothing is often best; **keep, break, ~**, abstain from speaking, speak; **pass over in ~**, not mention; **put** or **reduce to ~**, (esp.) refute in argument. **2.** Absence of sound, stillness, (**in ~**, without speech or other sound); **S~!** (order to cease from speech or noise); ||(**two minutes'**) **~**, ceremony observed at 11 a.m. on Remembrance Sunday. **3.** Oblivion, state of not being mentioned, (*have passed into silence*); **tower of ~**, structure on which Parsees place their dead. **4.** *v.t.* Make silent by force, superior argument, etc., (*silenced the enemy's batteries, the best debaters in the House, the voice of conscience*); hence **sī'lenc**ER¹ *n.*, device for reducing noise of escape of gas from gun, ||vehicle engine, etc., or of shutting of door etc. [ME f. OF, f. L *silentium* (*silēre* be silent; see -ENCE)]

sī'lent *a.* **1.** Not speaking, not uttering or making or accompanied by any sound; (of letter) written but not pronounced, e.g. *b* in *doubt*; (of film) without sound-track accompaniment; ***~ butler,** device for gathering up crumbs, cigarette ash, etc.; **~ majority,** those of moderate opinions who rarely make themselves heard; ***~ partner,** = SLEEP²*ing partner*; **~ system** (in prisons, by which prisoners are never allowed to speak). **2.** Taciturn, speaking little; saying or recording nothing on some subject (*history is silent upon it*); (of spirits) unflavoured. **3.** Hence **~**LY² *adv.* [f. L *silēre* be silent; see -ENT]

silē'n|us *n.* (*pl.* **~i** *pr.* -ī). (Gk Myth.) Bearded old man like satyr, sometimes with tail and legs of horse. [L, f. Gk *seilēnos*]

sĭlē'sia (-sh*a*) *n.* Thin twilled cotton or linen cloth for dress-linings etc. [f. *S~* in E. Germany, where orig. made]

sĭlhouĕ'tte (-lo͞o-) *n.*, & *v.t.* **1.** *n.* Portrait of person in profile showing outline only, all inside the outline being usu. black, on white ground or cut out in paper; appearance of person or object as seen against light so that outline only is distinguishable (**in ~**, so seen or placed). **2.** *v.t.* Represent or (usu. in *pass.*) exhibit in silhouette. [f. Étienne de *Silhouette*, Fr. author and politician d. 1767]

sĭ'lĭc|a *n.* Silicon dioxide, occurring as quartz etc. and as principal constituent of sandstone and other rocks; hence **sĭlĭ'c**IC, **~ĭ'**FEROUS, **sĭlĭ'c**EOUS or **sĭlĭ'c**IOUS (-sh*u*s), *adjs.*, **sĭlĭ'c**IFY *v. t.* & *i.* [f. L *silex -icis* flint, after *alumina* etc.]

sĭ'lĭcāte *n.* One of many insoluble compounds of metal(s), silicon, and oxygen, occurring widely in rocks of earth's crust. [f. prec. + -ATE¹ (3)]

sĭ'lĭc|on *n.* Non-metallic element occurring widely in silica and silicates; hence **~o-** *comb. form.* [f. L *silex -icis* flint (after *carbon, boron*), replacing earlier *silicium*]

sĭ'lĭcōne *n.* One of many polymeric organic compounds of silicon with high resistance to cold, heat, water, and passage of electricity. [f. prec. + -ONE]

silĭc|ō'sĭs *n.* (*pl.* **~o'ses** *pr.* -ō'sēz). Lung fibrosis caused by inhalation of dust containing silica; hence ~o'TIC *a.* [f. as SILICA + -OSIS]

sĭ'lĭqu|a (*pl.* **~ae**), **sĭli'qu|e** (-ē'k), *n.* Long narrow seed-vessel of cruciferous plants; so ~OSE¹, ~OUS, (sĭ'lĭkw-) *adjs.* [L]

sĭlk *n.* **1.** Fine strong soft lustrous fibre produced by silkworm in making cocoon; similar fibre spun by some spiders etc.; **artificial ~**, rayon. **2.** Thread or cloth made from silk fibre (||**take ~**, become K.C. or Q.C. and so have right to wear silk gown); (in *pl.*) kinds, or garments made, of such cloth, esp. jockey's cap and jacket in horse-owner's colours. **3.** ||(colloq.) K.C. or Q.C. **4.** Silky styles of female maize-flower. **5.** (*attrib.*) Made of silk (*silk stockings* etc.); **make a ~ purse out of a sow's ear,** get better results from a person than his qualities admit of. **6.** **~ cotton,** kapok or similar substance; **~-fowl,** breed of fowl with silky plumage; **~-gland** (secreting the substance produced as silk); **~ hat,** tall cylindrical hat covered with silk plush; **~-screen printing** (with silk SCREEN used like stencil); **~'worm,** caterpillar of moth (esp. *Bombyx mori*) which spins its cocoon of silk. [OE *sioloc, seol(e)c* (cf. ON *silki*) f. LL *sericum* neut. (as n.) of L *sericus* (*seres* f. Gk *Seres* an oriental people; see -IC)]

sĭ'lken *a.* Made of silk; clad in silk; soft or lustrous as silk; (of manner etc.) suave, insinuating. [OE *seol(o)cen* (as prec., -EN⁵)]

sĭ'lk|ȳ *a.* Like silk in smoothness, softness, fineness, or lustre; (of manner etc.) suave, insinuating; hence ~ĬLY² *adv.*, ~ĬNESS *n.* [f. SILK + -Y²]

sĭll *n.* Shelf or slab of stone or wood or metal at foot of doorway or esp. window; horizontal timber at bottom of dock or lock entrance, against which gates close; (Geol.) sheet of igneous rock intruded between other rocks. [OE *syll(e)*, = MDu., MLG *sulle* cogn. w. ON *svill, syll*, OHG *swelli*]

sĭ'llabŭb, sȳ'-, *n.* Dish made of cream or milk curdled with wine etc. and sometimes whipped or solidified with gelatin. [16th c., of unkn. orig.]

sĭ'ller *n.* (Sc.) Silver; money. [= SILVER]

sĭ'llĭmanīte *n.* (Min.) Aluminium silicate in orthorhombic crystals, often fibrous. [f. B. *Silliman*, Amer. chemist d. 1864 + -ITE¹]

sĭ'll|ȳ *a.* & *n.* **1.** (arch.) Innocent, simple, helpless. **2.** Foolish, imprudent, unwise; feeble-minded, imbecile; (Cricket) placed (dangerously) close to batsman (*silly mid-off, point*, etc.); **~y-billy,** foolish person; ||**the ~y season,** August and September as season when newspapers start trivial discussions for lack of important news. **3.** Hence ~ĬLY² *adv.*, ~ĬNESS *n.* **4.** *n.* (colloq.) Foolish person. [later form of ME *sely* (dial. *seely*) happy f. OE **sǣlig*, = OS, OHG *sālig* f. WG **sǣliga* (**sǣli* luck, happiness)]

sī'lō *n.* (*pl.* **~s**), & *v.t.* **1.** *n.* Pit or airtight structure in which green crops are pressed and kept for fodder, undergoing fermentation; pit or tower for storage of ||grain, cement, etc.; underground place where guided missile is kept ready for firing. **2.** *v.t.* Make ensilage of. [Sp., f. L f. Gk *siros* pit for corn]

sĭlt *n.* & *v.* **1.** *n.* Sediment deposited by water in channel, harbour, etc.; **~'stone,** rock of hardened silt; hence ~'Y² *a.* **2.** *v.t.* & *i.* Choke or be choked (*up*) with silt (*the channel has* or *is silted up*); hence ~A'TION *n.* [ME, perh. cogn. w. Da., Norw. *sylt*, OLG *sulta*, OHG *sulza* salt marsh, f. as SALT]

Sīlūr'ĭan *a.* & *n.* **1.** *a.* Of the Silures, a people of ancient S.E. Wales. **2.** *a.* & *n.* (Geol.) (Of) palaeozoic period or system above Ordovician and below Devonian. [f. L *Silures* + -IAN]

sĭ'lvan, sȳ'lvan, *a.* Of the woods; having woods; rural. [f. F *sylvain*, obs. *silvain*, or f. L *Silvanus* woodland deity (*silva* a wood; see -AN)]

sĭ'lver¹ *n.* & *a.* **1.** *n.* White lustrous malleable ductile precious metallic element used chiefly with admixture of harder metals for coin, plate, and ornaments, as subordinate monetary medium, and in compounds for photography etc., (GERMAN¹, NICKEL, *silver*; OXIDIZE*d silver*); colour of silver. **2.** Silver or cupro-nickel coins (*have you any silver on you?*); (esp. Sc.) money. **3.** Silver vessels or implements (esp. cutlery) or articles of furniture (*melted down all his silver in the king's service*); household cutlery of any material; = *silver medal*. **4.** *a.* Made of silver; second-best (opp. *golden*); silvery; **every cloud has a ~ lining,** misfortune has its consolations or hopeful prospects. **5.** **~ age,** period inferior to GOLDEN *age*, e.g. period of Latin literature corresp. to silver LATIN; ||**~ band** (playing silver-plated brass instruments); **~-bath,** (Photog.) solution of silver salt used for sensitizing; **~ birch,** common birch (*Betula alba*) with silver-coloured bark; **~ fir** (with silver-coloured under-sides of leaves); **~-fish,** (1) silver-coloured fish, esp. a colourless variety of goldfish, (2) silvery bristletail found in books and damp places; *silver* FOIL¹; **~ fox,** variety of red fox with black white-tipped fur; **~ gilt,** (1) gilded silver, (2) imitation gilding of yellow lacquer over silver leaf; **~-grey,** lustrous grey; **~ jubilee,** 25th anniversary of sovereign's accession or other event; *silver* LATIN, LEAF; **~ medal,** medal of silver usu. awarded as second prize; **~ paper,** (1) fine white tissue-paper for wrapping silver, (2) tin foil; **~ plate,** vessels, spoons, etc., of silver or of copper etc. plated with silver; **~-point,** (process of sketching on prepared paper with) silver-pointed stylus (*a head in silver-point*); **~ print,** photographic positive print on paper sensitized with silver salt; **~ salmon,** coho; **~ sand,** fine pure kind used in gardening; **~ screen,** (1) superior type of cinematographic screen, (2) motion pictures collectively; ||**~side,** upper (best) side of round of beef; **~smith,** worker in silver, manufacturer of silver articles; **~ solder,** solder containing silver; *silver* SPOON¹; *silver* STANDARD; ||**S~ Stick,** (1) field-officer of Life Guards when on palace duty, (2) official of Queen's bodyguard for Scotland; ||**~ streak,** *the* English Channel; **~ thaw,** glassy coating of ice on the ground, exposed woodwork, etc., caused when rain freezes as it falls, or when a sudden thaw (after hard frost) is succeeded by a light frost; **~ tongue,** eloquence; **~-top,** disease of grasses with whitening caused by mites etc.; **~ware,** articles made of silver; **~ wedding,** 25th anniversary of wedding; **~weed,** plant with silvery leaves, esp. a potentilla with silver-coloured under-sides of leaves. [OE *seolfor*, = OS *silubar*, OHG *sil(a)bar*, ON *silfr*, Goth. *silubr* f. Gmc **silubr-*, of uncert. orig.]

sĭ'lver² *v.* **1.** *v.t.* Coat or plate with silver; provide (mirror-glass) with backing of tin amalgam etc.; (of moon or white light) give silvery appearance to; turn (hair) grey or white. **2.** *v.i.* (Of hair) turn grey or white. [ME, f. prec.]

sĭ'lvern *a.* (arch. or poet.) = SILVER¹ 4. [OE *seolfren, silfren* (as SILVER¹, -EN⁵)]

sĭ'lver|ȳ *a.* Resembling silver in whiteness, lustre, ringing sound, etc.; (of hair) white and lustrous; hence ~ĬNESS *n.* [f. SILVER¹ + -Y²]

sĭ'lvĭcŭlture, sȳ'-, *n.* Growing and tending of

trees as branch of forestry. [F, f. L *silva* a wood + F CULTURE]

sī'ma *n.* (Geol.) Denser lower layer of earth's crust. [f. SILICA + MAGNESIA (main constituents)]

sĭ'mĭan *a.* & *n.* **1.** (Zool.) (Of) one of the anthropoid apes. **2.** Ape(like), monkey(-like). [f. L *simia* ape (perh. f. *simus* flat-nosed f. Gk *simos*) + -AN]

sĭ'mĭlar *a.* & *n.* **1.** *a.* Like, alike; having mutual resemblance or resemblance *to*; of the same kind, nature, or amount; (Geom.) shaped alike; hence or cogn. ~ITY (-ă'r-) *n.*, ~LY[2] *adv.* **2.** *n.* (arch.) Thing resembling another. [f. F *similaire* or f. med. L *similaris* f. L *similis* like; see -AR[1]]

sĭ'mĭlė *n.* Writer's or speaker's reference to thing or person with explicit comparison to it of what is being discussed, as illustration or ornament; words by which this is done (*the kingdom of heaven is like to a grain of mustard seed*; *as dead as a doornail*; *life, like a dome of many-coloured glass*). [ME f. L, neut. of *similis* like]

sĭmĭ'lĭtūde *n.* Likeness, guise, outward appearance, (*in, assume, the similitude of*); (expression of) comparison (*talks in similitudes*); (arch.) counterpart, facsimile, (*is the very similitude of*). [ME f. OF, or f. L *similitudo* (as prec.; see -TUDE)]

sĭ'mmer *v.* & *n.* **1.** *v.i.* Be on the point of boiling, boil very gently; (fig.) be in a state of suppressed anger, indignation, or laughter; ~ **down,** calm oneself, become less agitated. **2.** *v.t.* Keep simmering. **3.** *n.* Simmering state. [alt. f. ME (now dial.) *simper*, perh. imit.; see -ER[5]]

||**sĭ'mnel** *n.* ~ (**cake**), rich ornamental cake baked esp. at Easter, Christmas, and Mid-Lent, often with marzipan layer and decoration. [ME, f. OF *simenel*, ult. f. L *simila* or Gk *semidalis* fine flour]

sīmō'nĭăc *n.* Person guilty of simony. [ME, f. OF *simoniaque* or f. med. L *simoniacus* (as SIMONY; see -AC)]

sīmonī'acal *a.* Guilty, or of the nature, of simony; hence ~LY[2] *adv.* [f. prec. + -AL]

Sīmon Pūr'e *n.* & *a.* **1.** *n.* (**The real**) ~, the real or genuine person or article. **2.** *a.* (*simon-pure*). Real, genuine. [character in Centlivre's *Bold Stroke for a Wife*]

sī'monȳ *n.* Buying or selling of ecclesiastical preferment. [ME, f. OF *simonie* f. LL *simonia* f. *Simon* Magus (Acts 8:18); see -Y[1]]

sĭmōō'm, sĭmōō'n, *n.* Hot dry suffocating dust-laden wind blowing at intervals esp. in Arabian desert. [f. Arab. *samūm* (*samma* to poison)]

***sĭmp** *n.* (colloq.) Simpleton. [abbr.]

sĭ'mper *v.* & *n.* **1.** *v.i.* Smile affectedly, smirk. **2.** *v.t.* Express by or with simpering (*simpered her consent*). **3.** *n.* Affected self-conscious smile, smirk. [16th c.; cf. Da., Norw., Sw. dial. *semper, simper*, G *zimp(f)er* elegant, delicate]

sĭ'mple *a.* & *n.* **1.** *a.* Not compound, consisting of one element, all of one kind, involving only one operation or power, not divided into parts, not analysable, (*simple* INTEREST[1]; *simple* SENTENCE); ~ **eye** (of insect, having only one lens); ~ **fracture** (of bone, only); (*simple*) HARMONIC *motion*; ~ **idea** (not analysable into elements); ~ **machine,** any of the mechanical POWERS. **2.** (Bot.) ~ **fruit** (formed from one pistil); ~ **leaf** (of one blade); ~ **pistil** (of one carpel). **3.** (Mus.) ~ **interval** (of an octave or less); ~ **time** (with two to four crotchets, quavers, etc., in the bar). **4.** Not complicated or elaborate or adorned or involved or highly developed (*the style is simple and devoid of ornament*; *simple diet*; *a simple form of pump*; *the greatest works of art are the simplest*); **in ~ beauty,** unadorned; **the ~ life,** practice of doing without luxuries and artificial amusements, attempt to return to more primitive conditions; ~ **forms of life,** creatures low in scale of evolution. **5.** Absolute, unqualified, mere, neither more nor less than, just, (*tell the simple truth*; *a simple majority of votes decides*; *story was a simple invention*; FEE *simple*; cf. PURE 3). **6.** Plain in appearance or manner, unaffected, unsophisticated, ingenuous, natural, artless, (*a simple person*; *simple attire*; *a simple heart* or *mind*). **7.** Foolish, ignorant, inexperienced, (*am not so simple as to suppose*); feeble-minded. **8.** Easily understood or done, presenting no difficulty, (*gave a simple explanation*; *the problem is very simple*; *can be cured by a simple device*). **9.** Of low rank, humble, insignificant, trifling, (*simple people*; *her simple efforts to please*). **10.** ~**-minded,** (1) natural, unsophisticated, (2) feeble-minded; **S~ Simon,** (fig.) foolish person [f. nursery-rhyme character]. **11.** Hence or cogn. ~NESS (-peln-), **sĭmplĭ'**CITY, *ns.*; **be simplicity itself,** (colloq.) be extremely easy to do etc. **12.** *n.* (arch.) Herb used medicinally; medicine made from it. [ME f. OF, f. L *simplus*]

S

sĭ'mpleton (-pelt-) *n.* Foolish, gullible, or half-witted person. [f. prec. after surnames f. place-names in *-ton*]

sĭ'mplĕx *a.* & *n.* Simple, uncompounded, (thing, esp. word). [L, = single, var. of *simplus* simple]

simpliciter (sĭmplĭ'sĭter) *adv.* Absolutely, universally, without limitation, not relatively or in certain respects only. [L]

sĭ'mplĭ|fȳ *v.t.* Make simple, make easy or easier to do or understand; so ~FICA'TION *n.* [f. F *simplifier* f. med. L *simplificare* (as SIMPLE; see -FY)]

sĭ'mpl|ĭsm *n.* Affected simplicity; unjustifiable simplification of problem etc.; hence ~**ĭ'stic** *a.* [f. SIMPLE + -ISM]

sĭ'mplȳ *adv.* In adj. senses; absolutely, without doubt or possibility of argument, (*he simply doesn't understand*; *I simply can't afford it*). [ME, f. SIMPLE + -LY[2]]

sĭmūlā'cr|um *n.* (*pl.* ~**a**). Image of something; shadowy likeness, deceptive substitute, mere pretence. [L (as foll.)]

sĭ'mūl|āte *v.t.* Feign, pretend to have or feel, put on, (*simulate virtue, indignation,* etc.); pretend to be, act like, resemble, wear the guise of, mimic, (of word) take or have an altered form suggested by (word wrongly taken to be its source), (*actor simulates king* etc.; *art simulating nature*; *chameleon simulates its surroundings*; '*amuck*', *for* '*amok*', *simulates the English* '*muck*'); imitate conditions of (situation etc.) with model, for convenience or training; (in *p.p.*) made to resemble the real thing but not genuinely such (*simulated fur, pearl*); hence or cogn. ~A'TION, ~**āt**OR, *ns.* [f. L *simulare* (*similis* like) + -ATE[3]]

sĭ'mulcast (-ah-) *n.* Simultaneous transmission on radio and television. [f. foll. + BROADCAST]

sĭmultā'nėous *a.* Occurring or operating at the same time (*with*); ~ **display,** playing of several games of chess at the same time; ~ **equations** (involving two or more variables that are to have same values in each equation); hence **sĭmŭltanē'**ITY, ~NESS, *ns.*, ~LY[2] *adv.* [f. med. L *simultaneus* f. L *simul* at the same time, prob. after *instantaneus* etc., + -OUS]

sĭmūr'g *n.* Monstrous bird of Persian myth, with power of reasoning and speech. [f. Pers. *simurġ* f. Pahlavi *sīn* eagle + *murġ* bird]

sĭn[1] *n.* & *v.* (**-nn-**) **1.** *n.* (Act of) transgression against divine law or principles of morality; *ugly* etc. **as ~,** exceedingly; BESET*ting sin*; **deadly** or **mortal ~** (such as causes death of the soul or is fatal to salvation); **the seven deadly ~s,** pride, covetousness, lust, anger, gluttony, envy, sloth; ~ **against the Holy Ghost,** worst possible offence [w. ref. to Matt. 12:31–32]; **like** ~, (sl.) vehemently, forcefully; **live in** ~, (esp. colloq.) cohabit without marriage; **man of** ~, (1, arch. or joc.) reprobate, (2) Antichrist; **for my** ~**s,** (joc.) as a judgement on me for something or other; *sins of* OMISSION; ORIGINAL, VENIAL, *sin.* **2.** Offence against good taste, propriety, etc. **3.** ~**-eater,** (Hist.) one hired to take on himself a dead person's sins by eating and drinking near the corpse; ~**-offering,** sacrifice etc. in expiation of sin. **4.** Hence ~′LESS *a.* **5.** *v.i.* Commit sin; offend *against.* **6.** *v.t.* Commit (sin); ~ one's **mercies,** be ungrateful for good luck. **7.** Hence ~′**n**ER[1] *n.* (lit., or joc. = rascal etc.). [OE *syn(n)*, rel. to OS *sundea*, OHG *sunt(e)a*, ON *synd*]

sin[2] *abbr.* sine.

Sīnăī′tic *a.* Of Mount Sinai or the peninsula of Sinai. [var. of *Sinaic* (*Sinai* f. Heb. *sīnay*, -IC), w. euphonic *t*]

sĭnă′nthropus *n.* Apelike man of extinct genus *Sinanthropus.* [mod. L, f. as SINO- (remains having been found near Peking) + Gk *anthrōpos* man]

sĭ′napĭsm *n.* Mustard plaster. [f. F *sinapisme* or LL f. Gk *sinapismos* (*sinapi* mustard; see -ISM)]

sĭnce *adv.*, *prep.*, & *conj.* **1.** *adv.* After specified or implied past time, throughout or at some or any point in the period between such time and that which is present or being dealt with, (*has* or *had been healthy* (*ever*) *since*; *more flourishing at that time than ever before or since*; *has since been cut down*; *have* or *had not seen him since*); ago (*happened many years since*; *how long since is it?*; *saw him not long since*). **2.** *prep.* After (specified past time or event), through or in period between (such time) and time present or being dealt with, (*has* or *had been going on*, *has happened*, *since 1960* or *Christmas*; *have eaten nothing since yesterday*; *since seeing you I have* or *had heard nothing*). **3.** *conj.* From the past time when, through or in the period before time present or being dealt with and after that when (*what have you been doing since we met?*; *nothing has happened*, *there had been a disturbance*, *since we parted*). **4.** For the reason that, seeing that, inasmuch as, (*since it is so*, *there is no more to be said*); (ellipt.) as being (*a more dangerous*, *since unknown*, *foe*). [ME, reduced form of obs. *sithence* (or f. dial. *sin* (f. *sithen*) + -S[3]) f. OE *siththon*, earlier **sīth thon* after that (OS *sīth*, OHG *sīd*, ON *síthr* less) + -S[3]]

sĭncēr′e *a.* (~**r**, ~**st**). Free from pretence or deceit, the same in reality as in appearance or seeming or profession, not assumed or put on, genuine, honest, frank; hence or cogn. ~NESS (-ēr′n-), **sĭncĕ′r**ITY, *ns.*, ~LY[2] (-ēr′lĭ) *adv.* (**yours** ~**ly,** customary formula for closing letter to acquaintance or friend). [f. L *sincerus* clean, pure]

sĭ′ncĭpŭt *n.* (Anat.) Front of head from forehead to top. [L (*semi-* half, *caput* head)]

sīne *n.* (Math.) ~ (**of arc**), line drawn from one end of arc perpendicularly to radius through other end; ~ (**of angle**), ratio of sine of arc to radius; this quantity as generalized function of any argument; ~ **curve, wave,** (representing periodic oscillations of constant amplitude as given by sine function); **versed** ~, unity minus cosine. [f. L *sinus* curve, fold of toga, used in med. L as transl. of Arab. *jayb* bosom, sine]

sī′nĕcūr|e *n.* Office of profit or honour without duties attached, esp. benefice without cure of souls; hence ~ISM (3), ~IST (2), *ns.* [f. L *sine cura* without care]

sine die (sīnĭ dī′ē *or* sĭnā dē′ā) *adv.* (Of business adjourned indefinitely) with no appointed date. [L, = without day]

sine qua non (sīnĭ kwā nŏ′n *or* sĭnā kwah nō′n) *n.* Indispensable condition or qualification. [L, = without which not]

sĭ′new *n.*, & *v.t.* **1.** *n.* (Piece of) tough fibrous tissue uniting muscle to bone, tendon; (in *pl.*) muscles, bodily strength, wiriness, (fig.) what forms the strength or sustains or holds together, framework, resources, (**the** ~**s of war,** money); hence ~LESS, ~Y[2], *adjs.* **2.** *v.t.* (poet.) Serve as sinews of, sustain, hold together. [OE *sin(e)we* etc., obl. forms of *sinu*, *seonu*, = MHG, MLG, MDu. *sene*, ON *sin* f. Gmc **senawō*]

sĭnfonī′a (-ē′*a*) *n.* (Mus.) Symphony; (in early Italian opera) overture. [It., = SYMPHONY]

sĭnfōnĭĕ′ttă *n.* (Mus.) Short or simple symphony; small symphony-orchestra. [It., dim. of prec.]

sĭ′nful *a.* (Of person) full of sin, wicked; (of act) involving or characterized by sin; highly reprehensible; hence ~LY[2] *adv.*, ~NESS *n.* [OE *synfull* (as SIN, -FUL)]

sĭng *v.* (**sang,** arch. **sung; sung**) & *n.* **1.** *v.i.* & *t.* Utter words, utter (words), in tuneful succession, esp. in accordance with a set tune (*sing* person's PRAISES); (sl.) turn informer; hence ~′ABLE *a.* **2.** Produce vocal melody, utter (song, tune), (*birds were singing*; *sing another song* or TUNE); ~ **small,** become more humble, be crestfallen. **3.** Make inarticulate melodious or humming or buzzing or whistling sounds (*wind*, *kettle*, *bee*, *sings*; *singing* HINNY[2]); (of ears) be affected as with buzzing sound; ~**ing saw,** = MUSICAL *saw.* **4.** Compose poetry; ~ (**of**), celebrate (hero, beauty, great event, etc.) in verse. **5.** Usher (esp. old or new year) *out* or *in* with singing; put *to sleep*, *into good humour*, etc., with singing. **6.** ~ **out,** call out loudly, shout; ~ **up,** sing more loudly. **7.** Hence ~′ER[1] *n.* **8.** *n.* *Meeting for amateur singing. [OE *singan*, = OS, OHG *singan*, ON *syngva*, Goth. *siggwan* f. Gmc **sengwan*]

sĭnge (-nj) *v.* (*part.* ~′**ing** *pr.* -njĭ-) & *n.* **1.** *v.t.* & *i.* Burn superficially or lightly (~ person's **hair,** burn off tips as hairdressing operation; ~ **pig, fowl,** burn off bristles, down, after killing, plucking; ~ one's **wings,** take some harm esp. in venturesome attempt). **2.** *n.* Superficial burn. [OE *sencgan*, = OS *bisengian*, MHG *sengen*, f. WG **sangjan*]

Sĭngh (-ng) *n.* (Title given to) great Indian warrior; title of member of warrior caste, esp. Rajput or Sikh. [Hind., f. Skr. *sinhá* lion]

Singhalese. See SINHALESE.

sĭ′ngle[1] (-nggel) *a.* & *n.* **1.** *a.* One only, not double or multiple, united, undivided, designed for or used or done by one person etc. or one set or pair; ‖(of ticket) valid for outward journey only, not return. **2.** One by itself, not one of several (*a single tree stands on the ridge*; *paid in a single sum*); unmarried (*single* BLESSEDNESS); lonely, unaided. **3.** Taken separately (*every single thing*); (w. neg. or interrog.) even one, not to speak of more (*did not see a single one*, *a single person*; *can a single argument be advanced for it?*). **4.** Free from duplicity, sincere, consistent, guileless, ingenuous, (**a** ~ **eye,** devotion to one purpose; ~ **heart** or **mind,** simplicity of character or devotion to one purpose). **5.** *Single* ACROSTIC; ~**-acting,** (of engine etc.) with steam admitted only to one side of piston; ~ **bed** (for one person); ~**-breasted,** (of coat etc.) with only one set of buttons and buttonholes, not overlapping; *single* COMBAT; ~**-cut,** (of file) with grooves cut in one direction only, not crossing; *single*-DECKER; *single* ENTRY; *single* FILE[3]; ~**-fire,** (of cartridge) not meant to be recharged after use; ~ **flower** (having only one set of petals); ~**-handed** *a.* & *adv.*, (1) (done etc.) without help from other persons (*by his single-handed* *efforts*; *cannot be done single-handed*), (2) with or for one hand (*the men played single-handed against the women with both hands*; *two-handed and single-handed swords*); **~-line,** (of traffic) moving in only one direction at a time; **~-loader,** breech-loading rifle without magazine; **~-minded,** having a single mind (see sense 4); *single* RHYME[1]; **~ room,** bedroom for one person; **~-seater,** vehicle with one seat; **~stick,** (one-handed fencing with) basket-hilted stick of about sword's length; *single* TRACK[1]; ***~-tree,** = SWINGLE*tree*; **~ wicket,** form of cricket in which only one batsman is in at one time. **6.** Hence ~NESS *n.*, **sĭ'ng**LY[2] *adv.*, (-ngg-). **7.** *n.* Single ticket; single issue of journal etc.; pop record with one piece of music etc.; ||£1 note; *$1 note; hit for one run in cricket; (usu. in *pl.*) game with one player on each side. [ME f. OF, f. L *singulus*, cogn. w. *simplus* simple]

sĭ'ngle[2] (-ngg*e*l) *v.t.* Choose *out* as an example or as distinguishable or to serve some purpose. [f. prec.]

sĭ'nglĕt (-ngg-) *n.* **1.** ||Garment worn under or instead of shirt, vest. **2.** Single unresolvable line in spectrum. [f. SINGLE[1] + -ET[1], after *doublet*, garment being unlined]

sĭ'ngleton (-ngg*e*lt-) *n.* One card only of a suit (dealt to a player); single thing, only child, etc; single child or animal born, not twin etc. [f. SINGLE[1], after *simpleton*]

sĭ'ngsŏng *a.*, *n.*, & *v.* **1.** *a.* In or recited with monotonous rhythm. **2.** *n.* Monotonous rhythm; monotonous cadence in speaking; ||impromptu vocal concert, meeting for amateur singing; **~ girl,** Chinese performer like geisha. **3.** *v.t.* & *i.* Recite (verse etc.), speak, in singsong manner. [f. SING + SONG]

sĭ'ngūlar (-ngg-) *a.* & *n.* **1.** (Gram.) **~ (number),** (form of noun, verb, etc.) denoting a single person or thing, not dual or plural. **2.** *a.* Single, individual, (esp. **all and ~**, all whether taken together or separately); unique; unusual, remarkable from rarity, much beyond the average in degree, extraordinary, surprising; eccentric, unconventional, strangely behaved; (Math.) possessing unique properties; hence ~IZE (3) *v.t.*, distinguish, individualize, ~LY[2] *adv.* [ME f. OF *singuler* f. L *singularis* (as SINGLE[1]; see -AR[1])]

sĭngūlă'rĭtȳ (-ngg-) *n.* In adj. senses; uncommonness, being remarkable, odd trait or peculiarity. [ME, f. OF *singularité* f. LL *singularitas* (as prec.; see -ITY)]

sinh (shīn *or* sīnā'ch) *abbr.* hyperbolic sine.

Sĭ'nhala (*or* -na-) *n.* & *a.* = foll. (esp. of language). [Sinh.]

Sĭnhalē'se (-z; *or* -na-), **Sĭnghalē'se** (-ngg*a*lē'z), *a.* & *n.* (*pl.* same). (Member or language) of an Aryan people deriving from N. India and now forming the majority of the population of Sri Lanka. [f. Skr. *siṁhalam* Sri Lanka (Ceylon) + -ESE]

sĭ'nĭster *a.* **1.** (Her.) of or on left-hand side of shield etc. (i.e. to the spectator's right; BAR[1], BATON, BEND[1], *sinister*); (arch.) left(-hand). **2.** Of evil omen; (usu. of person in regard to his appearance, or of his face or look) suggestive of evil, looking malignant or villainous; wicked, criminal, (*a sinister motive*); hence ~LY[2] *adv.* [ME, f. OF *sinistre* or f. L *sinister* left]

sĭ'nĭstral *a.* & *n.* **1.** Left-handed (person). **2.** *a.* Of or on the left; (of flat-fish) with left side uppermost; (of spiral shell) with whorls rising to left and not as usu. to right. **3.** Hence ~ITY (-ă'l-) *n.*, ~LY[2] *adv.* [f. prec. + -AL]

sĭ'nĭstrorse *a.* Rising towards the left (esp. Bot. of spiral stem). [f. L *sinistrorsus* (**sinistrovorsus* f. *sinister* left + *vertere* turn)]

sĭnk[1] *v.* (**sank** *or* **sunk; sunk** *or*, esp. as *a.* w. *pass.* sense, **sunken**). **1.** *v.i.* Fall slowly downwards, decline, disappear partly or wholly below surface of liquid or granular solid or below horizon, come gradually to lower level or pitch, droop, despond, subside, settle down, gradually expire or perish or cease, (*sun is sinking, sank*; *my heart, spirits, sank*; *sank under the burden*; *sink in the social scale*; *his head, chin, sank on his shoulder, chest*; *sink into feebleness, degradation, the grave, sleep, a quicksand, a chair* (in weariness or luxury)); (of ship) go to bottom of sea etc.; (of eyes) be turned downwards, or shrink inwards; (of cheeks) shrink inwards, become hollow; (of voice) become lower-pitched or quieter; (of sick person) approach death; (of price etc.) become lower; (of storm or river) subside; (of ground) slope down, or reach lower level by subsidence; (of darkness) descend (*up*)*on* (place etc.); **~ in** person's **estimation,** become less highly esteemed by him; *here goes*, **~ or swim,** even at the risk of complete failure. **2.** Penetrate, make way, *in* or *into* (*bayonet sank in to the hilt*); be absorbed *in* or *into* (mind etc.; *paused to let his words sink in*). **3.** *v.t.* Cause or allow to sink, send below surface of liquid etc. or ground, lower level of, keep in obscurity or background, conceal, ignore, put out of sight, make no reference to, (*would sooner sink the ship than surrender*; *sink* one's *head on* one's *chest*; *sunk in thought*; *drought had sunk the streams*; *must sink our differences if we are to make progress*; *sank its teeth into my leg*); dig (well), bore (shaft); engrave (die); invest (money), lose (money) by investment; cause failure of (plan etc.) or discomfiture of (person); cause (ball) to enter pocket at billiards, hole at golf, etc., achieve this by (stroke etc.); *sunk* FENCE[1]; **sunken garden** (below general level of surroundings). **4.** Hence ~'ABLE *a.*, ~'AGE (3) *n.* [OE *sincan*, = OS, OHG *sinkan*, ON *sökkva*, Goth. *sigqan* f. Gmc]

sĭnk[2] *n.* **1.** Place in which foul liquid collects; (fig.) place of rampant vice etc. **2.** Basin or box of porcelain etc. with outflow pipe, esp. with water supply in KITCHEN etc. for washing-up. **3.** Pool or marsh in which river's water disappears by evaporation or percolation. **4.** (Phys.) Place of disappearance of flux-lines (cf. *source*); body used to absorb or dissipate heat. **5.** **~(-hole),** (Geol.) cavity in limestone etc. into which water disappears. [ME, f. prec.]

sĭ'nker *n.* In vbl senses; weight used to sink fishing or sounding line (HOOK[1], *line, and sinker*); *doughnut; DIE[1]-*sinker*. [f. SINK[1] + -ER[1]]

sĭ'nkĭng *n.* In vbl senses; internal bodily sensation caused by hunger or apprehension; **~-fund,** moneys set aside for the purpose of sinking or wiping out a State's or corporation's debt by degrees. [ME, f. SINK[1] + -ING[1]]

sĭ'nner. See SIN.

sĭ'nnĕt. See SENNIT.

Sinn Fein (shĭn fā'n) *n.* Patriotic movement (founded 1905) and party in Ireland aiming at national revival in language etc. as well as political independence for the island; hence ~ER[1] *n.* [Ir., = we ourselves]

Sī'no- *comb. form.* Chinese (and), as: *Sino-Ame'rican*, ~MA'NIA *n.*, ~PHIL(E), ~PHOBE, *ns.* & *adjs.*, ~PHO'BIA *n.* [f. Gk *Sinai* the Chinese + -O-]

sī'nolŏgue (-ŏg) *n.* Person skilled in sinology. [F, f. as prec. + Gk *-logos* -speaking]

sīnŏ'log|ȳ *n.* Study of Chinese language, history, customs, etc.; hence ~IST (3) *n.* [f. SINO- + -LOGY]

sĭ'nter *n.* & *v.* **1.** *n.* Siliceous or calcareous rock formed by deposit from springs; substance produced by sintering. **2.** *v.t.* & *i.* (Cause to) coalesce from powder into solid by heating. [G, = E *sinder* CINDER]

sĭ'nūate *a.* (esp. Bot.) Wavy-edged, with distinct inward and outward bends along edge. [f. L *sinuatus* p.p. of *sinuare* (SINUS) bend; see -ATE²]

sĭnūŏ'sĭtȳ *n.* Being sinuous; a bend, esp. in a stream or road. [f. F *sinuosité* or f. med. L *sinuositas* (as foll.; see -ITY)]

sĭ'nūous *a.* With many curves, serpentine, tortuous, undulating; hence ~LY² *adv.* [f. F *sinueux* or f. L *sinuosus* (as SINUS; see -OUS)]

sī'nus *n.* (Anat. & Zool.) cavity of bone or tissue, esp. in skull communicating with nostrils, whence ~I'TIS *n.*; (Path.) fistula esp. to deep abscess; (Bot.) curve between lobes of leaf. [L, = bosom, recess]

sī'nusoid *n.* Curve having form of sine wave; hence ~AL *a.* [f. F *sinusoïde* f. L SINUS; see -OID]

Sī'on. Var. of ZION.

-sion (-shon *or* -zhon) *suf.* forming *ns.* (see -ION) from L *p.p.* stems in *-s-* (*mansion, mission, persuasion*).

Sioux (sōō) *n.* (*pl.* same) & *a.* (Member or language) of a group of N. Amer. Indian tribes; hence **Siou'**AN (sōō'*an*) *a.* [F, f. native name]

sĭp *v.* (**-pp-**) & *n.* **1.** *v.t.* & *i.* Drink in repeated small mouthfuls or by spoonfuls. **2.** *n.* Small mouthful of liquid imbibed (*a sip of brandy*). [ME, perh. modification of SUP]

sīpe *n.* Small groove or channel in tyre-tread to improve grip. [f. dial. *sipe* to ooze f. OE *sīpian*, MLG *sipen*, of unkn. orig.]

sī'phon *n.* & *v.* **1.** *n.* Pipe or tube shaped like inverted V with unequal legs for conveying liquid over edge of vessel and delivering it at lower level by utilizing atmospheric pressure; ~(**-bottle**), aerated-water bottle from which liquid is forced out through tube by pressure of gas; (Zool.) canal or conduit esp. in cephalopods, sucking-tube of some insects etc. **2.** ~ **barometer** (with tube bent at bottom like inverted siphon); ~**-cup,** lubricating apparatus with oil led over edge of reservoir by capillary action through wick; ~ **gauge,** glass siphon attached to reservoir and containing mercury for indicating pressure etc. inside reservoir. **3.** Hence ~AGE (3) *n.*, ~AL, **sīphŏ'n**IC, *adjs.* **4.** *v.t.* & *i.* Conduct or flow (as) through siphon (*water is siphoning from the vase on to the tablecloth; money was siphoned off illegally from the fund*). [F, or f. L *sipho -onis* f. Gk *siphōn* pipe]

sī'phonĕt *n.* Honey-tube of aphis. [f. prec. + -ET¹]

sīphŏ'nophōre *n.* Compound usu. translucent marine animal of order Siphonophora, e.g. Portuguese man-of-war. [f. Gk *siphōno-* (as SIPHON, -O-) + -PHORE]

sī'phŭncle *n.* (Zool.) = SIPHON. [f. L *siphunculus* dim. of *sipho* SIPHON]

sĭ'ppėt *n.* Small piece of bread etc. soaked in liquid; piece of toast or fried bread as garnish; (fig.) fragment. [app. dim. of SOP; see -ET¹]

si quis (sī kwĭ's) *n.* Notice posted in ordination-candidate's parish church to give opportunity for objection. [L, = if anyone, opening wds of notice when in L]

sĩr *n.*, & *v.t.* (**-rr-**). **1.** *n.* (Used esp. in *sing.* as voc. in addressing man who is superior in rank or age, Speaker of legislative assembly either in his own person on point of order or as embodiment of the House in ordinary debate, whose name is or is to be understood to be unknown to speaker, or inferior who is to be rebuked) *please sir, may I go now?; excuse me, sir, have you the time?; you shall pay for this, sir!.* **2.** (*S~*; usu. *pr. ser*). (Used as titular prefix to name of knight or baronet, always followed by Christian name, or its initial and surname, or the whole name) *Sir John Moore, Sir J. Moore,* (esp. as voc.) *Sir John.* **3.** (**Dear**) **Sir**(**s**) (words used to begin formal letter). **4.** Person with title of, or addressed as, 'Sir'. **5.** *v.t.* Address as 'Sir' (*don't sir me*). [ME, reduced form of SIRE]

sĩr'cãr, sĩr'kãr, *n.* (Ind.) The Government; head of government or household; house-steward; Indian accountant. [f. Urdu *sirkar* f. Pers. *sarkār* (*sar* head, *kār* agent)]

sĩr'dãr *n.* (Ind. etc.) Person in command, leader; Sikh. [f. Urdu *sardār* f. Pers. *sar* head + *dār* possessor]

sīre *n.*, & *v.t.* **1.** *n.* (poet.) Father or male ancestor. **2.** (arch., as *voc.* to king) = *Your* MAJESTY. **3.** Male parent of animal, esp. stallion kept for breeding. **4.** *v.t.* (Esp. of stallion) beget. [ME f. OF, f. Rom. **seior* f. L SENIOR]

sĩr'en *n.* **1.** (Gk Myth.) Any of several women, or creatures half woman and half bird, living on rocky isle to which they lured unwary seafarers with enchanting singing. **2.** Sweet singer. **3.** Dangerously fascinating woman, temptress, a tempting pursuit etc.; (*attrib.*) irresistibly tempting, as of a siren. **4.** Eel-like tailed amphibian of family Sirenidae. **5.** Instrument used in acoustic experiments or for making loud sound for information, warning, etc., by revolution of perforated disc over jet of compressed air or steam; (instrument giving) warning of air raids or of approach of police etc. vehicle; ~ **suit,** one-piece garment for whole body, easily put on or taken off. [ME, f. OF *sereine, sirene* f. LL *Sirena* fem. f. L f. Gk *Seirēn*]

sīrē'nĭan *a.* & *n.* (Member) of the order Sirenia of large aquatic herbivorous mammals, e.g. manatee and dugong. [f. mod. L *Sirenia* (as prec.); see -IA², -AN]

sĩr'găng *n.* Green Asian bird with red wings (*Kitta chinensis*). [name in E. Indies]

sĩr'kãr. See SIRCAR.

sĩr'loin *n.* ||Upper and choicer part of loin of beef; *rump steak. [f. OF **surloigne* var. of *surlonge* (as SUR-, LOIN)]

sĭrŏ'ccō *n.* (*pl.* ~s). Sahara simoom reaching Italy etc.; warm sultry rainy wind in S. Europe. [F, f. It. *scirocco*, ult. f. Arab. *šarūḳ* east wind]

sĭ'rrah (*-a*) *n.* (arch., as *voc.*) = SIR (in imperious or contemptuous use). [prob. f. ME *sĭrĕ* SIR]

***sirree'** *n.* (as *voc.*) = SIR (in emphatic use). [f. SIR + emphatic suf.]

***sĭ'rup.** See SYRUP.

sirvente (sẽrvah'ṅt) *n.* Medieval usu. satirical lay of special metrical form. [F, f. Prov. *sirventes*, taken as pl.; of unkn. orig.]

***sĭs** *n.* (colloq.) Sister. [abbr.]

sī'sal *n.* Fibre prepared from leaves of an agave, used for cordage, ropes, etc.; plant (*Agave sisalana*) yielding this. [*S~*, port of Yucatan]

sĭ'skĭn *n.* Olive-green song-bird (*Spinus spinus*) allied to goldfinch. [f. MDu. *siseken* dim., rel. to MLG *sisek*, MHG *zīse(c)*, of Slav. origin]

sĭ'ssōō *n.* (Valuable Indian timber from) tree of genus *Dalbergia*. [f. Urdu (Hindi) *sīsū*]

sĭ'ssȳ *n.* & *a.* (Typical of) effeminate or cowardly person. [f. SIS + -Y²]

sĭ'ster *n.* **1.** Daughter of same parents or (also **half-~**) same parent as another person; **the Fatal S~s** or **S~s three** or **three S~s,** the Fates. **2.** Woman who is a close friend, female fellow member of class or sect or human race. **3.** Member of religious community of women; LAY² *sister*; **S~ of Mercy,** member of educational or charitable order, esp. that founded in Dublin 1827. **4.** ||Female hospital nurse in authority over others; (colloq.) any female nurse. **5.** Personified quality or thing regarded as female that closely resembles another (*prose, younger sister of verse*); ~ **ship** (built on same design as another). **6.** ~ **german,** (having same parents); ~ **uterine** (having same mother only); **~-in-law,** sister of one's husband or wife, wife of one's brother. **7.** Hence ~LY[1,2] *a.* & *adv.* [ME, f. ON *systir*; OE *sweoster* etc., = OS *swestar*, OHG *swester*, Goth. *swistar* f. Gmc **swestr* f. IE **swes(o)r-*]

sĭ'sterhood *n.* Relationship (as) between sisters; society of women bound by monastic vows or devoting themselves to religious or charitable work. [ME, f. prec. + -HOOD]

Sĭ'stīne (*or* -ēn) *a.* Of one of the popes called Sixtus, esp. Sixtus IV (~ **chapel,** in Vatican, with frescoes by Michelangelo). [f. It. *Sistino* (*Sisto* Sixtus; see -INE[1])]

sĭ'str|um *n.* (*pl.* **~a**). Jingling metal instrument used by ancient Egyptians esp. in worship of Isis. [ME f. L, f. Gk *seistron* (*seiō* shake)]

Sĭsȳphē'an *a.* As of Sisyphus (in Gk Myth., king of Corinth condemned in Hades to push a heavy stone up hill and begin again when it rolled down); everlastingly laborious. [f. L f. Gk *Sisupheios* (*Sisuphos* Sisyphus) + -AN]

sĭt *v.* (**-tt-**; **sat,** arch. **sate** *pr.* săt). **1.** *v.i.* Take or be in position in which body is supported more or less upright by buttocks resting on ground or raised seat; *sit on the* FENCE[1]; ~ **on** one's **hands,** take no action, not applaud; ~ **tight,** (colloq.) remain firmly in one's place, not be shaken off or move away or yield to distractions; ~ **well,** have good seat in riding. **2.** Be engaged in some occupation in which this position is usual (~ **in judgement,** assume right of judging others, be censorius); pose *for* portrait etc., *to* painter etc.; be candidate *for* (award by) examination; be member of Parliament etc. *for* (constituency); act as baby-sitter; (of Parliament, Courts, committee, etc.) be in session; ~ **at** person's **feet,** be his pupil; ~ **at home,** be inactive. **3.** (Of birds and some animals) rest with (hind) legs bent and body close to ground or perch; remain on nest to hatch eggs. **4.** Be in more or less permanent position or condition (esp. of inactivity or being out of use or out of place); **~s the wind there?,** is it in that quarter?, is that the state of affairs?; *food* **~s heavy on the stomach,** is not soon digested; *her dress, imperiousness,* etc., **~s well on** *her*, suits, fits; *his principles* ~ **loosely on him,** do not bind him much. **5.** *v.t.* Keep or have one's seat on (horse etc.; *he could not sit his mule*). **6.** Undergo, be candidate at, (examination etc.). **7.** Cause to sit, place in sitting position. **8.** ~ **back,** relax one's efforts; ~ **by,** look on without interfering; ~ **down,** take seat after standing, seat one*self*, cause to sit, (Mil.) encamp *before* place to besiege it; *~-down meal* etc. (taken seated); *~-down strike*, one in which strikers refuse to leave the place where they were working; ~ *down under*, submit tamely to (insult etc.); ~ **in,** occupy place as protest esp. against (alleged) activities there (whence *~-in* n.), (colloq.) act as baby-sitter; ~ *in on*, be present as guest etc. at (meeting etc.); ~ **on,** (see also sense 4) (of jury etc.) hold session concerning, be member of (committee etc.), (colloq.) delay action concerning (*Government has been sitting on the report*), (sl.) repress or rebuke or snub (*he wants sitting on*); ~ **out,** take no part in something, esp. in particular dance (*decided to sit out; sat out the next dance*), sit outdoors, outstay (other visitors), stay till end of (performance, ordeal, etc.); ~ **over,** (Cards) be (in advantageous position) on left of (player); ~ **under,** be one of congregation preached to by (minister), (Cards) be on right of (player); ~ **up,** rise from lying to sitting posture, remain (*late, nursing,* etc.) out of bed, sit erect without lolling; *make* person ~ *up*, (colloq.) subject him to surprise, hard work, pain, etc.; ~ *up and take notice*, (colloq.) have one's interest (suddenly) aroused; ~ **upon,** = *sit on*; *~-upon*, (colloq.) buttocks. **9.** **~'fast,** horny sore caused by saddle on horse's back. [f. OE *sittan*, OS *sittian*, OHG *sizzen*, ON *sitja* (Goth. *sitan*), f. Gmc **sitjan*, **setjan* (**set-* f. IE **sed-* etc.)]

sĭ'tar̄ (*or* -ar̄') *n.* Long-necked Indian guitar-like instrument. [f. Hindi *sitār*]

sĭ'tcŏm *n.* (colloq.) Situation comedy. [abbr.]

site *n.*, & *v.t.* **1.** *n.* Ground on which town or building stood, stands, or is to stand; place where some activity is or has been conducted (*camping site; caravan site; launching site; prehistoric burial site*). **2.** *v.t.* Locate, place; provide with site. [ME f. AF, or f. L *situs* local position]

sĭth *conj.* (arch.) Since. [OE *siththa* (as SINCE)]

Sĭ'tka *n.* ~ **cypress,** yellow cedar; ~ **spruce,** tall spruce (*Picea sitchensis*) yielding valuable timber. [~ in Alaska]

sītophō'bĭa *n.* Morbid aversion to food. [f. Gk *sitos* food + -O- + -PHOBIA]

sĭ'trĕp *n.* Report on current military situation. [f. *sit*uation *rep*ort]

sĭ'tter *n.* In vbl senses; person sitting for portrait; sitting hen; **~(-i'n),** baby-sitter; (sl.) easy catch, shot, etc., thing easily done. [ME, f. SIT + -ER[1]]

sĭ'ttĭng[1] *n.* In vbl senses; time during which one sits continuously (*wrote, read, the whole poem at a sitting; all-night sitting of House of Commons; lunch is served in two sittings*); ‖(Law) = TERM[1] 2; clutch of eggs; seat in church appropriated to a person; **~-room,** (1) space enough to accommodate seated persons, (2) room used for sitting in (opp. *bedroom*). [ME, f. SIT + -ING[1]]

sĭ'ttĭng[2] *a.* In vbl senses; (of game-bird) not flying (*shot a sitting pheasant*); (of animal) not running; (of hen) engaged in hatching; ~ **duck, target,** person or thing easily attacked; ~ **tenant,** one already in occupation of house etc. [f. SIT + -ING[2]]

sĭ'tūāte[1] *v.t.* Place or put in (specified) position, situation, etc., (*is situated on the top of the hill*); (in *p.p.*) in (specified) circumstances (*am awkwardly situated at the moment*). [f. med. L *situare* f. L *situs* site + -ATE[3]]

sĭ'tūate[2] *a.* (arch. or Law). Situated. [f. LL *situatus* (as prec.; see -ATE[2])]

sĭtūā'tion *n.* Place, with its surroundings, occupied by something (*house stands in a fine situation*); set of circumstances, position in which one finds oneself, (*came out of a difficult situation with credit*); critical point or complication in drama (*curtain falls on a strong situation*); employee's place or paid office (*cannot find a situation*); ~ **comedy** (in which humour derives from characters' misunderstandings and embarrassments); **~s vacant, wanted,** (headings of lists of employment offered and sought); hence ~AL *a.* [ME, f. F, or f. med. L *situatio* (as SITUATE[1]; see -ATION)]

sĭ'tz-bath (-tsbahth; *pl. pr.* -ths *or* -dhz). Hip-bath. [partial transl. of G *sitzbad* (*sitzen* sit, *bad* bath)]

Si'va (sē'- *or* shē'-) *n.* Hindu god held supreme by his special votaries, and by others associated as principle of destruction with Brahma and Vishnu in a triad; hence ~ISM (3) *n.*, ~ITE[1] (1) *n.* & *a.*, (-a-). [Skr. *Śiva*, = propitious]

sĭx *a.* & *n.* **1.** One more than five; symbol for this (6, vi, VI); card etc. with six pips; time of six o'clock; size etc. denoted by six; set of six; hit at cricket scoring six runs (**hit** or **knock for** ~, utterly surprise or defeat); (in *pl.*) gloves, shoes, etc., of sixth size, candles weighing six to the pound; **it is ~ of one and half-a-dozen of the other,** difference is merely nominal; **at ~es and sevens,** in confusion. **2. Six Counties** (of N. Ireland); **~-footer,** person 6 ft. in height, thing 6 ft. long; **~-gun,** = *six-shooter*; ||**~'pence,** sum of 6p., (coin worth) 6d.; ||**~'penny,** (*a.*) costing or worth 6p. or 6d.; *~penny bit*, *~penny* (*n.*), the coin sixpence; **~-shooter,** six-chambered revolver. **3.** Hence ~'FOLD *a.* & *adv.* [OE *siex* etc., = OS, OHG *sehs*, ON *sex*, Goth. *saihs* f. Gmc **seks* f. IE **s(w)eks*]

sĭ'xain *n.* Six-line stanza. [F (*six* six)]

sĭ'xer *n.* Hit for six runs in cricket; leader of group of six Brownies or Cubs. [f. SIX + -ER[1]]

sĭxte *n.* Sixth of eight parrying positions in fencing. [F, f. L *sextus* sixth]

sĭxtee'n (*or* sĭ'-) *a.* & *n.* One more than fifteen; symbol for this (16, xvi, XVI); size etc. denoted by sixteen; **~mo,** sextodecimo; hence ~TH[2] *a.* & *n.* (***~th-note,** semiquaver). [OE *siextiene* (as SIX, -TEEN)]

sĭxth *a.* & *n.* **1.** *a.* Next after fifth; **~ part,** one of six equal parts into which thing may be divided. **2.** *n.* Sixth part, thing, etc.; (Mus.) interval of which the span involves six alphabetical notes, harmonic combination of notes thus separated. **3. ~ day,** Friday; **~ form,** highest form in secondary school; *sixth* SENSE. **4.** Hence ~'LY[2] *adv.*, in the sixth place. [f. SIX + -TH[2]]

Sĭ'xtīne (*or* -ēn) *a.* = SISTINE. [f. mod. L *Sixtinus* (*Sixtus*; see -INE[1])]

sĭ'xtȳ *a.* & *n.* **1.** Six times ten; symbol for this (60, lx, LX); set of sixty persons or things; (in *pl.*) numbers etc., esp. years of a century or a life, from 60 to 69; hence ~FOLD *a.* & *adv.*, **sĭ'xtĭ**ETH[1] *a.* & *n.* **2. ~-one** etc., (arch.) **one-and-~** etc., sixty plus one etc., w. corresp. ordinals **~-first** etc.; **~-four (thousand) dollar question,** difficult and crucial question [f. top prize in broadcast quiz shows]; **~-four'mo** (-fôr'mō), (size of) book in which each leaf is $\frac{1}{64}$ of printing-sheet [after *duodecimo* etc.]. [OE *siextig* (as SIX, -TY[2])]

sī'zable. Var. of SIZEABLE.

||**sī'zar** *n.* Student at Cambridge or at Trinity College, Dublin, paying reduced fees and formerly having certain menial duties; hence ~SHIP *n.* [f. foll. = ration + -AR[3]]

sīze[1] *n.*, & *v.t.* **1.** *n.* Relative bigness, dimensions, magnitude, (*is of vast, diminutive, size*; *size matters less than quality*); **cut down to ~,** (fig.) reduce to proper degree of (un)importance; **of a ~,** having the same size; **of some ~,** fairly large; *is* **the ~ of,** as big as; **the ~ of it,** (colloq.) a true account of the matter; **try** (thing) **for ~,** test to determine whether it fits (lit. or fig.); **what ~?,** how big?; see OUTSIZE. **2.** One of the usu. numbered classes into which things, esp. garments, otherwise similar are divided in respect of size (*is made in several sizes*; *takes size 7 in gloves*; *is three sizes too big*). **3. ~-stick,** shoemaker's measure for taking length of foot. **4.** Hence (-)**sīz**ED[2] (-zd) *a.* **5.** *v.t.* Group or sort in sizes or according to size, whence **sī'z**ER[1] (2) *n.*; **~ up,** estimate size of, (colloq.) form judgement of (person etc.). [ME, f. OF *sise* f. *assise* ASSIZE, or f. ASSIZE]

sīze[2] *n.*, & *v.t.* **1.** *n.* Gelatinous solution used in glazing paper, stiffening textiles, etc.; hence **sī'z**Y[2] *a.* **2.** *v.t.* Glaze or stiffen or treat with size. [ME, perh. = prec.]

sī'zeable (-za-) *a.* Of (fairly) large size. [f. SIZE[1] + -ABLE]

sĭ'zzl|e *v.i.*, & *n.* (colloq.) (Make) sputtering sound as of frying; (be in) state of great heat or excitement or marked effectiveness; hence ~ING[2] *a.* & *adv.* (*sizzling hot*). [imit.]

S.J. *abbr.* Society of Jesus.

||**S.J.A.(A., B.)** *abbr.* St. John Ambulance (Association, Brigade).

sjă'mbŏk (sh-) *n.*, & *v.t.* (Flog with) rhinoceros-hide whip. [Afrik., f. Malay *samboq*, *chambok* f. Urdu *chābuk*]

skald. See SCALD[2].

skat (-aht) *n.* Three-handed card-game with bidding for contract. [G, f. It. *scarto* a discard (*scartare* discard)]

skāte[1] *n.* (*pl.* also same). Cartilaginous fish of family Rajidae, esp. *Raja batis*, large flat rhomboidal food-fish. [ME, f. ON *skata*]

skāte[2] *n.* & *v.* **1.** *n.* One of pair of implements, each with steel blade or set of rollers, attached beneath boots or shoes and enabling wearer to glide over ice or (**roller-~**) hard floor or pavement etc.; **get** one's **~s on,** (sl.) make haste. **2.** *v.i.* & *t.* Move, perform (specified figure), on skates; pass lightly *over* (esp. fig.); **~ on thin ice,** deal with subject needing tactful treatment; **skā'ting-rink,** piece of ice artificially made, or floor used, for skating; hence **skā't**ER[1] *n.* [orig. *scates* pl. f. Du. *schaats* sing. f. ONF *escace*, OF *eschasse* stilt]

skean, skēne, *n.* Gaelic dagger formerly used in Ireland and Scotland; **~-dhu'** (-doo'), dagger stuck in stocking as part of Highland costume. [f. Gael. *sgian* knife, *dubh* black]

skėdă'ddle *v.i.*, & *n.* (colloq.) **1.** *v.i.* Run away, disperse in flight. **2.** *n.* Hurried flight or dispersal. [19th c., of unkn. orig.]

***skee'sĭcks** (-z-), **-zĭcks,** *n.* Rascal, good-for--nothing. [19th c., of unkn. orig.]

skeet *n.* Shooting sport in which clay target is thrown from trap to simulate flight of bird. [f. ON *skjóta* SHOOT[1]]

skein (-ān) *n.* Loosely coiled bundle of yarn or thread; flock of wild geese etc. in flight; (fig.) tangle, confusion. [ME, f. OF *escaigne*, of unkn. orig.]

skĕ'lėton *n.* **1.** Hard internal or external framework of bones, cartilage, shell, woody fibre, etc., supporting or containing animal or vegetable body; hence **skĕ'lėt**AL *a.* **2.** Dried bones of human being or other animal fastened together in same relative positions as in life (**~ at the feast,** something that spoils one's pleasure, intrusive worry; **~ in the** ||**cupboard** or ***closet,** discreditable or humiliating fact concealed from strangers); very thin or emaciated person or animal; remaining part of anything after its life or usefulness is gone. **3.** Framework or essential part of anything; **~ crew** etc., permanent nucleus ready for supplementing; **~ key** (fitting many locks by having interior of bit hollowed); **~ staff** (minimum needed to do essential work). **4.** Outline sketch, epitome, abstract. **5.** Hence ~IZE (3) *v.t.* [mod. L f. Gk, neut. (as n.) of *skeletos* dried-up (*skellō* dry up)]

skēne. See SKEAN.

skĕp, skĭp[5], *n.* Wooden or wicker basket of various forms; quantity contained in this; straw or wicker beehive. [ME, f. ON *skeppa*, rel. to OHG *sceffil*]

***skĕ'psĭs, *skĕ'ptĭc,** etc. See SCEPSIS etc.

skĕ'rrĭck *n.* (Austral. & U.S. colloq.) Smallest bit (usu. w. neg.; *not a skerrick left*). [N. Engl. dial. wd]

skĕ'rrȳ *n.* Reef, rocky isle. [Orkney dial., f. ON *sker*; cf. SCAR[2]]

skĕtch *n.* & *v.* **1.** *n.* Preliminary, rough, slight, merely outlined, or unfinished drawing or painting often as experiment for or to assist in making of regular picture; brief account without many details conveying general idea of something, rough draft, general outline; slight usu. one-scene play often of comic kind; short descriptive article; musical composition of single movement; **~-block, -book,** arrangements of drawing-paper leaves for doing series of sketches on; **~-map** (with outlines but little detail). **2.** *v.t.* Make or give sketch of; ~ (**in, out**), indicate briefly or in outline. **3.** *v.i.* Make sketches esp. of landscape (*went out sketching*). **4.** Hence ~'ER[1] *n.* [f. Du. *schets* or G *skizze* f. It. *schizzo* (*schizzare* make sketch f. Rom. **schediare* f. L f. Gk *skhedios* extempore)]

skĕ'tch|y̆ *a.* Giving only slight or rough outline, like a sketch; (colloq.) unsubstantial or imperfect esp. through haste; hence **~ĭLY**[2] *adv.*, ~ĭNESS *n.* [f. prec. + -Y[2]]

skew *a.*, *n.*, & *v.* **1.** *a.* Oblique, slanting, sideways, distorted; **~ arch, bridge,** (with line of arch not at right angles to abutment); **~ chisel** (with oblique edge); **~ wheel,** bevel wheel with oblique teeth. **2.** (Math.) Lying in three dimensions (*skew curve*); (of lines) not coplanar; (of statistical distribution) not symmetrical. **3.** **~'back,** sloping face of abutment on which extremity of arch rests; **~'bald** *a.* & *n.*, (animal, esp. horse) with irregular patches of white and another colour (prop. not black; cf. PIEBALD); ||**~-eyed,** squinting; ||**~-whi'ff,** (colloq. or dial.) askew; hence ~'NESS *n.* **4.** *n.* Slant; **on the ~**, askew. **5.** *v.t.* Make skew; distort. **6.** *v.i.* Move obliquely; twist. [a. & n. f. v. f. ONF *eskiu(w)er* = OF *eschuer* (see ESCHEW)]

skew'er *n.*, & *v.t.* **1.** *n.* Pin for holding meat compactly together while cooking. **2.** *v.t.* Fasten together, pierce, (as) with skewer. [17th c., var. of dial. *skiver*, of unkn. orig.]

ski (skē) *n.* (*pl.* **~s** *or* ~), & *v.i.* (**~'d** *or* **~ed,** *pr.* -ēd). **1.** *n.* One of pair of long narrow pieces of wood etc. usu. pointed and turned up at front, fastened under feet for travelling over snow; similar device on vehicle; WATER[1]-*ski*. **2.** **~-bob,** machine like bicycle with skis instead of wheels; **~ boots, pants,** etc., (for wear when skiing); **~ heil!** (hīl), good skiing!; **~-jump,** steep slope levelling off before sharp drop to allow skier to leap through the air; **~-lift,** device for carrying skiers up slope, usu. on seats hung from overhead cable; **~-run,** slope suitable for skiing as sport. **3.** *v.i.* Travel on skis. [Norw., f. ON *skíth* billet, snow-shoe]

skiă'graphy̆ etc. See SCIAGRAPHY etc.

skĭd *n.* & *v.* (-dd-). **1.** *n.* Piece of frame or timber serving as support, inclined plane, (Naut.) fender, etc.; **on the ~s,** (colloq.) ready for launching or discarding; **put the ~s under,** cause to hasten esp. to downfall. **2.** Braking device, esp. wooden or metal shoe preventing wheel from revolving or used as drag; runner on aircraft for use when landing. **3.** Slip or slide, esp. of wheel on slippery ground; **~-lid,** (sl.) crash-helmet; ||**~-pan,** (1) slippery road surface prepared for vehicle-drivers to practise control of skids, (2) braking device (see sense 2); ***~ road,** (1) road for hauling logs along, (2) part of town frequented by loggers; hence ***~ row,** part of town frequented by vagrants, alcoholics, etc. **4.** *v.t.* Support or move or protect or check with skid; cause (vehicle etc.) to skid. **5.** *v.i.* (Of wheel or vehicle, also of its driver) slide forwards or backwards or sideways on slippery ground; slip, slide. [17th c., of unkn. orig.]

***skĭddōō'** *v.i.* (sl.) Go away, depart. [perh. f. SKEDADDLE]

ski'er[1] (skē'*er*) *n.* Person using skis. [f. SKI + -ER[1]]

skī'er[2]. Var. of SKYER.

skī'ey. Var. of SKYEY.

skĭff *n.* Light rowing or sculling boat. [f. F *esquif* f. It. *schifo* f. Lombardic **skif* = OHG *skif* SHIP[1]]

skĭ'ffle *n.* Kind of folk music played by group, mainly with rhythmic accompaniment to singing guitarist etc. [perh. imit.]

ski'-jōring (skē'-; *or* shēyer'-) *n.* Winter sport in which skier is towed by horse or vehicle. [f. Norw. *skikjøring* (as SKI, *kjøre* drive, -ING[1])]

skĭ'lful, *skĭ'llful, *a.* Having or showing skill (*at, in*); practised, expert, adroit, ingenious; hence ~LY[2] *adv.* [f. foll. + -FUL]

skĭll[1] *n.* Expertness, practised ability, facility *in* an action or *in* do*ing* or *to* do something; dexterity, tact. [ME, f. ON *skil* distinction, cf. foll.]

skĭll[2] *v.i.* *impers.* (arch.) Avail; (w. neg. or interrog.) matter, make a difference, (*it skills not which*). [ME, f. ON *skila* give reason for, *skilja* distinguish]

skĭlled (-ld) *a.* Having or showing skill, skilful, *in*; (of work) requiring skill; (of worker) highly trained or experienced. [f. SKILL[1] + -ED[2]]

skĭ'llĕss (-l-l-) *a.* (arch.) Without skill; knowing nothing *of*. [f. SKILL[1] + -LESS]

skĭ'llĕt *n.* ||Small metal pot with long handle and usu. legs used in cooking; *frying-pan. [ME, perh. f. OF *escuelete* dim. of *escuele* platter f. pop. L *scutella*]

***skĭ'llful.** See SKILFUL.

||**skĭ'lly̆** *n.* Thin broth or soup or gruel (usu. of oatmeal and water flavoured with meat). [abbr. f. *skilligalee*, prob. fanciful]

skĭm *v.* (-mm-), *a.*, & *n.* **1.** *v.t.* Take scum or cream or floating layer from surface of (liquid), take (cream etc.) from surface of liquid; **~ the cream off,** (fig.) take the best part of. **2.** Keep touching lightly or nearly touching (surface) in passing over. **3.** *v.i.* Go thus *over* or *along* surface, glide along in air. **4.** *v.t.* & *i.* Read superficially (*through*), look over cursorily, gather salient facts contained (in). **5.** *a.* **~ milk** (from which cream has been skimmed). **6.** *n.* Act of skimming; thin covering on liquid. [ME, back form. f. foll.]

skĭ'mmer *n.* **1.** Ladle etc. for skimming liquids. **2.** Flat (straw) hat. **3.** Long-winged marine bird of genus *Rynchops* that feeds by skimming over water with knifelike lower mandible immersed. [ME, f. OF *escumoir* (*escumer* f. *escume* scum f. Gmc; see SCUM); assim. to -ER[1]]

skĭ'mmĭa *n.* E. Asian evergreen shrub of genus *Skimmia*, with red fruit. [mod. L, f. Jap.; see -IA[1]]

skĭmp *v.* **1.** *v.t.* Supply meagrely, stint, (person with or *in* food, money, etc.; material, expenses, etc.). **2.** *v.i.* Be parsimonious. [19th c.; orig. unkn. (cf. 18th-c. *skimp* a. scanty, and SCRIMP)]

skĭ'mp|y̆ *a.* Meagre, not ample; hence **~ĭLY**[2] *adv.*, ~ĭNESS *n.* [f. *skimp* a. + -Y[2]; cf. prec.]

skĭn[1] *n.* **1.** Flexible continuous covering of human or other animal body; **change** one's ~, undergo impossible change of character etc.; **get under** person's ~, (colloq.) take strong hold on him, interest or annoy him intensely; **jump out of** one's ~, be extremely surprised, delighted, etc.; **save** one's **skin,** avoid loss or injury; *is only* **~ and bone,** very thin; **the ~ off your nose** (colloq. toasting formula); **no ~ off** one's **nose,** (colloq.) a matter of indifference or even benefit to one; *escape* **by** or **with the ~ of** one's **teeth,** narrowly; **thick, thin, ~,** imperviousness, sensitiveness, to affront or reproach; *wet* **to the ~**, through all one's clothing; **with a whole ~**, unwounded. **2.** Colour of skin, complexion (*has a fair, dark, skin*); (Anat.) one layer of the skin (**true** or **inner ~**, dermis; **outer ~**, epidermis). **3.** Skin of flayed animal with or without the hair etc.; material prepared from skins esp. of smaller animals (opp.

hide); vessel for wine or water made of animal's whole skin. **4.** Outer coating of plant, fruit, sausage, etc.; film like skin on surface of liquid etc. **5.** Planking or plating of ship or boat inside or outside ribs; outer covering of aeroplane. **6.** = GOLD-*beater's skin*; thin sheet for use as typewriter stencil. **7.** **~-deep,** (of wound, or of emotion, impression, beauty, etc.) superficial, not deep or lasting; **~-diver,** one who dives and swims under water, usu. in deep water with flippers and aqualung; **~ effect,** (Electr.) tendency of high-frequency alternating current to flow through the outer layer only of a conductor; **~-flick,** (sl.) explicitly pornographic film; **~-food,** cosmetic intended to improve condition of skin; **~ friction** (at surface of solid and fluid in relative motion); **~'ful** (*of wine* etc., or abs.), as much liquor as one can hold; ***~ game,** (sl.) swindling game; **~-graft,** skin cut from another part or person and surgically substituted for damaged part; **~'head,** ‖young gangster esp. with close-cropped hair, *recruit in Marines; **~-tight,** (of garment) very close-fitting. **8.** Hence (-)~NED[2] (-nd), ~'LESS, *adjs.* [OE *scin(n)* f. ON *skinn*; cf. OHG *scinden* flay]

skĭn[2] *v.* (**-nn-**). **1.** *v.t.* & *i.* ~ (**over**), cover (sore etc.) as with skin, (of wound etc.) form or become covered with new skin. **2.** *v.t.* Strip of skin, withdraw or scrape skin from, flay; (sl.) fleece, swindle; *keep* one's EYE[1]*s skinned*; **~ a flint,** be miserly or avaricious; **~'flint,** niggard, miser. [f. prec.]

skĭnk *n.* Small lizard of family Scincidae. [f. F *scinc* or f. L f. Gk *skigkos*]

skĭ'nner *n.* In vbl senses; dealer in skins, furrier. [ME, f. SKIN[1,2] + -ER[1]]

skĭ'nn|ȳ *a.* Made of or like skin; (of person) thin, emaciated; niggardly; hence ~ĬNESS *n.* [f. SKIN[1] + -Y[2]]

skĭnt *a.* (sl.) Having no money. [=*skinned*, p.p. of SKIN[2]]

skĭp[1] *v.* (**-pp-**) & *n.* **1.** *v.i.* (Of young animal, child, etc.) jump about, gambol, caper, frisk, move lightly from one foot on to the other; use skipping-rope. **2.** Shift quickly *from* or *off* one subject or occupation *to* another, be desultory; (sl.) make off, disappear. **3.** *v.t.* & *i.* Omit, make omissions, in dealing with a series or in reading (*do them all without skipping any* or *skipping*; *always skips the small print*; *skips as he reads*; *skip every tenth row*); (colloq.) not participate in; (colloq.) flee, depart quickly (from); **~ it!,** (sl.) abandon topic etc. **4.** **~'jack,** (1) jumping toy made of bird's wishbone, (2) fish that jumps above water surface, (3) click beetle; **~'ping-rope, *~-rope,** length of rope with handle at each end, revolved over head and under feet during jumping as game or exercise; **~ zone,** annular region round broadcasting station where neither direct nor reflected waves are received. **5.** *n.* Skipping movement, esp. quick shift from one foot to other (HOP[3], *skip, and jump*). [ME, prob. f. Scand.]

‖**skĭp**[2] *n.* College servant, esp. at Trinity College, Dublin. [prob. f. obs. *skip-kennel* lackey (as prec., KENNEL[2])]

skĭp[3] *n.* Captain or director of side at bowls or curling. [abbr. of SKIPPER[2]]

skĭp[4] *n.* Cage, bucket, etc., in which men or materials are lowered and raised in mines and quarries; large container for builder's refuse etc. [var. of SKEP]

skĭp[5]. See SKEP.

skĭ'pper[1] *n.* In vbl senses; small dark thick-bodied butterfly. [ME, f. SKIP[1] + -ER[1]]

skĭ'pper[2] *n.*, & *v.t.* **1.** *n.* Sea captain, esp. master of small trading or fishing vessel; **~'s daughters,** tall white-crested waves. **2.** Captain of an aircraft; captain of side in games. **3.** *v.t.* Act as captain of. [ME, f. MDu., MLG *schipper* (*schip* SHIP[1]; see -ER[1])]

skĭ'ppėt *n.* Small round wooden box to enclose and protect seal attached to document. [ME, of unkn. orig.]

skîrl *v.i.*, & *n.* (Make) shrill sound characteristic of bagpipes. [prob. Scand., ult. imit.]

skîr'mĭsh *n.*, & *v.i.* **1.** *n.* Piece of irregular or unpremeditated fighting esp. between small or outlying parties, slight engagement; encounter of wit, argument, etc. **2.** *v.i.* Engage in skirmish; hence ~ER[1] *n.* [ME, f. OF *eskirmir, escremir*, f. Frank. **skirmjan* defend; see -ISH[2]]

skîrr *v.i.* Move rapidly esp. with whirring sound. [perh. rel. to SCOUR[1]]

skĭ'rrėt *n.* Perennial umbelliferous plant (*Sium sisarum*) formerly cultivated in Europe for its edible root. [ME *skirwhit(e)* perh. f. as SHEER[1], WHITE[1]]

skîrt *n.* & *v.* **1.** *n.* Part of coat etc. that hangs below waist; woman's outer garment hanging from waist (**divided ~,** culotte); (vulg. sl.) woman (esp. *bit of skirt*); **~-dance** (with graceful manipulation of full skirt). **2.** Flap of saddle; hanging part round base of hovercraft. **3.** (in *sing.* or *pl.*) Edge, border, extreme part; **~ of beef** etc., (1) diaphragm and other membranes as food, (2) ‖cut of meat from lower flank. **4.** Hence -~'ED[2], ~'LESS, *adjs.* **5.** *v.t.* Go along or round or past the edge of; be situated along. **6.** *v.i.* Go *along* coast, wall, etc.; ‖**~'ing(-board),** board etc. along bottom of room-wall. [ME, f. ON *skyrta* shirt, corresp. to OE *scyrte*; see SHIRT]

skĭt[1] *n.* Light piece of satire, burlesque, (*on*). [rel. to *skit* move lightly and rapidly, perh. f. ON **skyt-* cogn. w. *skjóta* SHOOT[1]]

skĭt[2] *n.* (colloq.) A number, crowd (esp. in *pl.*, heaps, lots). [20th c.; cf. SCADS]

skĭ'tter *v.i.* (Of wildfowl) go splashing along water in rising or settling; fish by drawing bait jerkily along surface of water; hurry about, dart off. [app. frequent. of dial. *skite*, perh. f. as SKIT[1]]

skĭ'ttĭsh *a.* (Of horse etc.) nervous, inclined to shy, excitable, playful, fidgety; (of person, esp. woman) frivolous, coquettish, excessively lively; hence ~LY[2] *adv.*, ~NESS *n.* [ME, perh. f. as SKIT[1] + -ISH[1]]

skĭttle *n.*, & *v.t.* **1.** *n.* (in *pl.*) Game played with usu. nine wooden pins set up at end of alley to be bowled down with wooden ball or disc (**beer and ~s,** amusement; *life is not all beer and skittles*); **(table) ~s,** game played with similar pins set up on board to be knocked down by swinging suspended ball; (colloq.) chess not played seriously. **2.** Pin used in skittles. **3.** *v.t.* **~ out,** (Cricket) get (batsmen) out in rapid succession. [17th c. (also *kittle-pins*), of unkn. orig.]

skīve *v.* **1.** *v.t.* Split or pare (hide, leather); (sl.) evade (a duty). **2.** *v.i.* (sl.) Evade a duty; **~ off,** depart evasively. [f. ON *skífa*, rel. to ME *schive* slice]

skī'ver *n.* In vbl senses; knife for skiving leather; thin leather got by skiving. [f. prec. + -ER[1]]

skĭ'vvȳ *n.* **1.** ‖(colloq., derog.) Female domestic servant. **2.** *Thin high-necked long-sleeved garment; *(in *pl.*) underwear of vest and underpants. [20th c.; orig. unkn.].

skū'a *n.* Large predatory sea-bird of genus *Stercorarius* etc. which pursues other birds and makes them disgorge the fish they have caught. [mod. L, f. Faroese *skúgvur*, ON *skúfr*]

skŭldŭ'ggerȳ, -ŭll-, (-g-) *n.* (joc.) Trickery; unscrupulous behaviour. [earlier *sculduddery*, orig. Sc. = unchastity (18th c., of unkn. orig.)]

skŭlk[1] *v.i.* Move stealthily, lurk, keep oneself

concealed esp. in cowardice or because intending mischief; stay or sneak away in time of danger; shirk duty, avoid observation; hence ~′ER[1] *n.* [ME, f. Scand.; cf. Norw. *skulka* lurk, Da. *skulke*, Sw. *skolka* shirk]

skŭlk[2] *n.* Person who skulks; company of foxes. [ME, f. prec.]

skŭll *n.* Bony case of brain of vertebrates; part of skeleton corresponding to head; (representation of) this with skin and soft internal parts removed; head as seat of intelligence; ~ **and cross-bones,** representation of bare skull with two thigh-bones crossed below it as emblem of death, prison, or piracy; **thick** ~, slowness of comprehension; **~-cap,** (1) close-fitting brimless cap, (2) top part of skull, (3) plant of genus *Scutellaria* with helmet-shaped bilabiate flowers; hence (-)~ED[2] (-ld) *a.* [ME *scolle*, of unkn. orig.]

skullduggery. See SKULDUGGERY.

skŭnk[1] *n.* Black white-striped bushy-tailed American carnivorous animal of genus *Mephitis* etc., about size of cat and able to emit powerful stench from liquid secreted by anal glands as defence; its fur; thoroughly contemptible person; ***~-bear,** wolverine; ***~-cabbage,** herb with offensive-smelling spathe. [f. Amer. Ind. *segankw, segongw*]

***skŭnk**[2] *v.t.* (sl.) Defeat; fail to pay (bill etc.). [f. prec.]

skȳ *n.*, & *v.t.* **1.** *n.* (in *sing.* or *pl.*) (The vault of) heaven, weather or climate evidenced by it, (*blue, clear, cloudy, overcast, starry,* etc., *sky* or *skies*); **the ~ is the limit,** there is practically no limit; **to the skies,** (1) very highly (*praised to the skies*), (2) into heaven (*raised to the skies*); **under the open ~**, out of doors. **2. ~-blue** *a.* & *n.*, colour(ed) like clear sky; **~-born,** (poet.) of divine birth; **~-diving,** sport of falling freely from aircraft and opening parachute only at last safe moment; **~-high** *adv.* & *a.*, (as if) reaching the sky, very high(ly); **~′jack** *v.t.*, (sl.) hijack (aircraft); **~′lark,** (*n.*) lark that soars while singing, (*v.i.*) (w. pun on LARK[1,2], and perh. of naut. orig. w. ref. to clambering about rigging), frolic, play tricks or practical jokes, ballyrag, etc.; **~′light,** window set in plane of roof or ceiling; **~′line,** outline of hills, buildings, etc., defined against sky, visible horizon; ~ **marker,** parachute flare dropped to mark target area; ~ **pilot,** (sl.) clergyman; **~-rocket,** (*n.*) rocket exploding high in air, (*v.i.*, esp. fig. of prices etc.) rise steeply; **~′sail** (*or* -sal), light sail above royal in square-rigged ship; **~′scape,** picture chiefly representing sky; **~′scraper,** very tall building; **~-sign,** advertisement on roof of building; ~ **wave,** radio wave reflected from ionosphere; **~′way,** (route in) sky as medium of transport; **~-writing,** legible smoke-trails made by aeroplane esp. for advertising. **3.** Hence **~′ey**[2], ~′LESS, *adjs.*, ~WARD(s) *adv.* & *a.* **4.** *v.t.* Hit (cricket-ball) high up; hang (picture) high on wall, treat picture by (artist) so. [ME *ski(es)* cloud(s) f. ON *ský* (f. **skiuja*), rel. to OE *scēo*, OS *scio*]

Skȳe *n.* ~ **(terrier)**, small long-bodied short-legged long-haired slate or fawn coloured variety of Scotch terrier. [~, island of Inner Hebrides]

skȳ′er *n.* High hit at cricket. [f. SKY + -ER[1]]

slăb[1] *n.*, & *v.t.* (**-bb-**). **1.** *n.* Flat broad fairly thick usu. square or rectangular piece of stone or other solid material; large flat piece of cake, chocolate, etc.; (of timber) outer cut sawn from log; ***~-sided,** long and lank; **~-stone,** (1) slab of stone, (2) kind of stone that splits readily into slabs. **2.** *v.t.* Remove slabs from (log, tree) to prepare it for sawing into planks. [ME, of unkn. orig.]

slăb[2] *a.* (arch.) Viscous, (of liquid) thick and sticky, (usu. *thick and slab* after Shak. *Macbeth* IV. i. 32). [rel. to *slab* ooze, sludge, prob. f. Scand.; cf. ODa. *slab* mud, Norw., Sw., Icel. *slabb* wet filth]

slăck[1] *a.*, *adv.*, *n.*, & *v.* **1.** *a.* Sluggish; remiss; relaxed, languid; loose; inactive, negligent; (of rope etc.) not taut; (of trade, business, market) with little happening; (of weather) inclining one to indolence; (Phonet.) lax; ~ **hand** or **rein,** lack of full control in riding or (fig.) governing; ~ **lime,** slaked lime; *~ **suit,** casual clothes of slacks and jacket or shirt; ~ **water,** time near turn of tide, esp. at low tide; hence ~′LY[2] *adv.*, ~′NESS *n.* **2.** *adv.* Slackly; (*dry, bake,* etc.) slowly or insufficiently. **3.** *n.* Slack part of rope (*haul in the slack*); slack time in trade etc.; (colloq.) spell of inactivity or laziness; (in *pl.*) full-length loosely-cut trousers for informal or sports wear. **4.** *v.t.* & *i.* Slacken; loosen (rope etc.); (colloq.) take a rest, be indolent, whence ~′ER[1] *n.*; slake (lime); ~ **off,** loosen, (cause to) lose vigour; ~ **up,** reduce speed of train etc. before stopping. [OE *slæc*, = OS *slak*, OHG *slah*, ON *slakr* f. Gmc **slakaz*]

slăck[2] *n.* Coal-dust. [ME, prob. f. LDu.]

slă′cken *v.t.* & *i.* Make or become slack; ~ **off,** = SLACK[1] *off.* [f. SLACK[1] + -EN[6]]

slăg *n.*, & *v.i.* (**-gg-**). **1.** *n.* Dross separated in fused state in reduction of ores, vitreous smelting-refuse, clinkers, (BASIC *slag*); volcanic scoria; **~-heap,** hill of refuse from mine etc.; **~-wool,** = *mineral* WOOL; hence **~′gy**[2] (-gĭ) *a.* **2.** *v.i.* Form slag; cohere into slaglike mass. [f. MLG *slagge*, perh. f. *slagen* strike, w. ref. to fragments formed by hammering]

slain. See SLAY[1].

slāke *v.t.* Assuage, satisfy, (thirst, or fig. revenge etc.), whence ~′LESS (-kl-) *a.* (poet.); disintegrate (LIME[1]) by combining chemically with water. [OE *slacian* (*slæc* SLACK[1])]

slā′lom (*or* -ah′-) *n.* Ski-race down zigzag course defined by artificial obstacles (**giant** ~, long-distance slalom); obstacle race in canoes. [Norw., lit. 'sloping track']

slăm *v.* (**-mm-**), *n.*, & *adv.* **1.** *v.t.* & *i.* Shut with loud bang (*slammed the door*; *door slammed to* or *shut*); put down (object) with similar sound; move violently (*he slammed out of the room*); put or come into sudden action (*slam the brakes on*); (sl.) criticize severely; (sl.) hit, beat, gain easy victory over. **2.** *n.* Sound (as) of slammed door; shutting of door etc. with loud bang; gaining of every trick at cards; **grand, little** or **small,** ~, winning of 13, 12, tricks in bridge; **grand** ~, (fig.) winning of all of a group of championships in tennis, golf, etc. **3.** *adv.* **~(ba′ng)**, with sound of slam. [prob. f. Scand.; cf. ON *slam(b)ra*]

sla′nder (-ah′-) *n.*, & *v.t.* **1.** *n.* False report maliciously uttered to person's injury; uttering of such reports, calumny; (Law) false oral defamation (cf. LIBEL); so ~OUS *a.* **2.** *v.t.* Utter slander about, defame falsely; hence ~ER[1] *n.* [ME *sclaundre* f. AF (OF) *escla(u)ndre*, alt. f. OF *escandle* f. LL *scandalum* (see SCANDAL)]

slăng *n.* & *v.* **1.** *n.* Words and phrases, or particular meanings of these, that are in common informal use, but generally considered not to form part of standard English, and often used deliberately for picturesqueness or novelty or unconventionality; words etc. either entirely peculiar to or used in special senses by some class or profession, cant, (*racing, thieves', theatrical, schoolboy,* etc., *slang*). **2.** *v.i.* & *t.* Use abusive language (to); **~′ing-match,** prolonged exchange of insults. [18th c. cant, of unkn. orig.]

slă′ng|ȳ *a.* Of the character of slang; fond of

using slang; hence ~ĭLY² *adv.*, ~ĭNESS *n.* [f. prec. + -Y²]

slant (-ah-) *v.*, *a.*, & *n.* **1.** *v.i.* & *t.* Slope, diverge from a line, (cause to) lie or go obliquely to a vertical or horizontal line; present (news etc.) from a particular angle esp. in biased or unfair way. **2.** *a.* Sloping, inclined, oblique; **~-eyed,** having slanting eyes, esp. Mongoloid; **~ height** (of cone, from vertex to periphery of base); hence ~'WISE *adv.* **3.** *n.* Slope, oblique position, (**on the** or **on a** ~, aslant); way of regarding a thing, point of view, aspect, bias. [1 later var. of ME (now dial.) *slent*, f. ON **slenta, sletta* dash, throw, prob. infl. by ASLANT; 2 f. ME *aslonte, o-slante* ASLANT *adv.*; 3 17th c. f. v.]

slantendĭ'cūlar (-ahnt-) *a.* (joc.) Slanting, oblique. [f. prec. after *perpendicular*]

slăp *v.* (**-pp-**), *n.*, & *adv.* **1.** *v.t.* & *i.* Strike (as) with palm of hand, smack; ~ (**down**), (colloq.) reprimand; lay forcefully (*slapped the money on the table; slapped a writ, a large fine, on the offender*); put hastily or carelessly (*slap some paint on the walls*); **~ on the back,** congratulate. **2.** *n.* Such stroke (**~ in the face,** lit., or fig. rebuff, insult; **~ on the back,** congratulations; ||**~ and tickle,** (colloq.) boisterous esp. amorous amusement). **3.** *adv.* With the suddenness or effectiveness or true aim of a blow, suddenly, just, quite, full, (*ran slap into him; hit me slap in the eye*). **4.** **~-(-bang)**, violently, noisily, headlong; **~'dash,** (*adv.*) vehemently, recklessly, (*a.*) impetuous, random, careless, happy-go-lucky, (*n.*) (1) such action or work, (2) roughcast, (*v.t.*) roughcast; **~-happy,** (colloq.) (1) punch-drunk, (2) cheerfully casual; **~-up** *a.*, (sl.) (1) quite up to date, (2) done regardless of expense. [v. f. n. & adv. f. LG *slapp* (imit.)]

***slă'pjăck** *n.* Kind of pancake cooked on a griddle, = FLAPJACK. [f. prec. 1 + JACK¹]

slă'pstĭck *n.* Flexible divided lath used by Harlequin; (fig.) boisterous knockabout comedy. [f. SLAP 1 + STICK²]

slăsh *v.* & *n.* **1.** *v.i.* Make sweeping or random cut(s) with sword, knife, whip, etc.; (in *part.*, fig.) vigorously incisive or effective. **2.** *v.t.* Make long narrow gash(es) in (**~ed** *sleeve* etc., with slits cut to show lining or puffing of other material); make (one's *way*) by slashing; reduce or cut drastically (prices etc.); lash (person etc.) with whip, crack (whip); censure vigorously. **3.** *n.* (Wound or slit made by) slashing cut; (colloq.) = SOLIDUS 2; *debris resulting from the felling or destruction of trees; (vulg.) act of urinating. [ME, perh. f. OF **esclaschier, esclachier* break in pieces]

slăt *n.* Thin narrow piece of wood, esp. used in sets in Venetian blind, bedstead, etc. [ME *s(c)lat* f. OF *esclat* splinter etc. (*esclater* split f. Rom. *EX¹*clatare*, imit.)]

slāte¹ *n.*, *a.*, & *v.t.* **1.** *n.* Fine-grained grey, green, or bluish-purple metamorphic rock easily split into flat smooth plates; piece of such plate used as roofing-material; piece of it usu. framed in wood used for writing on with **~-pencil** (small rod of soft slate); **clean** ~, no discreditable history; **clean the** ~, rid oneself of or renounce obligations; **wipe the ~ clean,** forgive past offences; ||**on the** ~, recorded as debt to be paid. **2.** *List of nominees for office etc. **3.** **~-black, -blue, -grey,** modifications of these colours such as occur in slate; ||**~-club,** benefit society with small weekly contributions and accounts nominally kept on slate; **~-colour(ed)**, (of) dark bluish or greenish grey; hence **slā'tY²** *a.* **4.** *a.* (Made) of slate. **5.** *v.t.* Cover with slates esp. as roofing. **6.** *Nominate, propose (for office etc.), make arrangements for (event etc.). [ME *s(c)late* f. OF *esclate*, fem. form of *esclat* SLAT]

||**slāte²** *v.t.* (colloq.) Criticize severely, scold. [app. f. prec.]

slā'ter *n.* One who slates roofs etc.; wood-louse or similar crustacean. [ME, f. SLATE¹ + -ER¹]

slă'ther (-dh-) *n.*, & *v.t.* **1.** *n.* *(colloq., usu. in *pl.*) Large amount. **2.** (Austral. & N.Z. sl.) (**Open**) ~, unrestricted scope for action. **3.** *v.t.* *(colloq.) Spread thickly; squander. [19th c.; orig. unkn.]

slă'ttern *n.* Sluttish woman; hence ~LY¹ *a.* [17th c., rel. to *slattering* (woman etc.) slovenly, f. dial. *slatter* to spill, slop, waste, frequent. of *slat* strike; see -ER⁵]

slau'ghter (-aw't-) *n.*, & *v.t.* **1.** *n.* Killing of animal(s) for food; killing of many persons or animals at once or continuously, carnage, massacre; **~house,** place for killing animals for food, place of carnage; hence ~OUS *a.* (literary). **2.** *v.t.* Kill (people) in ruthless manner or on great scale; butcher, kill for food; (colloq.) defeat utterly; hence ~ER¹ *n.* [ME *slahter* f. ON **slahtr* (ON *slátr* butcher's meat), f. **slah-* (see SLAY¹)]

Slav (-ahv) *n.* & *a.* **1.** *n.* Member of group of peoples in Central & Eastern Europe speaking languages of Slavonic group; hence **~'o**PHIL(E), **~'o**PHOBE, *ns.* & *adjs.*, ~'ISM (2, 3) *n.* **2.** *a.* Of the Slavs; Slavonic. [ME *Sclave* f. med. L *Sclavus*, late Gk *Sklabos*, & f. med. L *Slavus*]

slāve *n.*, & *v.i.* **1.** *n.* Person who is the legal property of another or others and is bound to absolute obedience, human chattel (WHITE¹ *slave*); helpless victim *to* or *of* some dominating influence (*is a slave to duty, to drink, the slave of his wife's caprices*, etc.; *the slaves of fashion*); drudge, person having no leisure; (arch.) contemptible person; part of machine directly dependent on another; ant captured by others and made to serve them. **2.** **~-bangle** (of gold, glass, etc., worn by woman usu. above elbow); **~-born** (in slavery, of slave parents); **~-driver,** overseer of slaves at work, (fig.) hard task-master; hence **~-drive** *v.t.*; **~-hunter,** person who hunted esp. Negroes to sell them as slaves; **~-ship** (employed in slave-trade); **~ state,** (Hist.) southern State of U.S.A. in which slavery was legal before Civil War; **~-trade,** procuring, transporting, and selling as slaves, of human beings, esp. African Negroes. **3.** *v.i.* Work like slave, drudge, (*at, over*). [ME, f. OF *esclave* = med. L *sclavus, sclava* Slav (captive); see prec.]

slā'ver¹ *n.* Ship or person engaged in slave-trade. [f. prec. + -ER¹]

slă'ver² *v.* & *n.* **1.** *v.i.* Let spittle flow from mouth. **2.** *v.t.* (arch.) Let one's spittle fall upon (garment etc., or another's cheek in kissing). **3.** *n.* Spittle running from mouth, (fig.) fulsome or servile flattery. [ME, prob. f. LDu.; cf. SLOBBER]

slā'verў *n.* Condition of a slave; existence of slaves as an institution; exhausting labour, drudgery. [f. SLAVE + -ERY]

slā'vey *n.* (colloq.) Maid-servant, esp. hard-worked one. [f. SLAVE + -Y³]

Sla'vĭc (-ah'-) *a.* & *n.* (Language-group) of the Slavs, Slavonic. [f. SLAV + -IC]

slā'vĭsh *a.* As of or having the characteristics of slaves; abject, servile, base; showing no attempt at development or originality; hence ~LY² *adv.*, ~NESS *n.* [f. SLAVE + -ISH¹]

Slavō'nian *a.* & *n.* Slovene; (arch.) Slavic. [f. med. L *S(c)lavonia* country of Slavs (*Sclavus* SLAV) + -AN]

Slavŏ'nĭc *a.* & *n.* **1.** *a.* Of the Slavs; **~ languages,** group of Indo-European languages including Russian, Polish, Czech, etc. **2.** *n.*

Slavonic language-group; **Church** or **Old** (**Church**) ~, earliest written Slavonic language, surviving as liturgical language in Orthodox Church. [f. med. L *S(c)lavonicus* (as prec.; see -IC)]

slaw *n.* Cole-slaw. [Du. *sla*, shortened f. *salade* SALAD]

slay[1] *v.t.* (**slew** *pr.* -ōō; **slain**). (esp. literary or joc.) Kill; hence (-)~'ER[1] *n.* [OE *slēan*, = OS, OHG *slahan*, ON *slá*, Goth. *slahan*, f. Gmc **slah-*, **slag-*]

slay[2]. Var. of SLEY.

S.L.B.M. *abbr.* submarine-launched ballistic missile.

slea'z|ȳ *a.* (Of textile etc.) flimsy; (colloq.) shoddy, slatternly, tawdry, squalid; hence ~ĭLY[2] *adv.*, ~ĭNESS *n.* [17th c., of unkn. orig.]

***slĕd** *n.* & *v.* = foll. [f. MLG *sledde*, = MHG *slitte*, OHG *slito*, *slita*, ON *slethi*, cogn. w. SLIDE[1]]

slĕdge[1] *n.* & *v.* **1.** *n.* Vehicle on runners instead of wheels for conveying loads or passengers esp. over snow, drawn by horses or dogs or reindeer or pushed or pulled by person(s); toboggan. **2.** *v.i.* & *t.* Travel, go, convey, in sledge. [f. MDu. *sleedse*, rel. to SLED]

slĕdge[2] *n.* ~(**-hammer**), blacksmith's large heavy hammer; **~-hammer** *a.*, (as if) given by or using this (*sledge-hammer blows, arguments, style*). [OE *slecg*, = MDu. *slegge*, ON *sleggja*, f. **slagj-* (as SLAY[1])]

sleek *a.*, & *v.t.* **1.** *a.* (Of hair, fur, skin, or animal or person with such hair etc.) smooth and glossy; looking well-fed and comfortable; (fig.) ingratiating; (of thing) smooth and polished; hence ~'LY[2] *adv.*, ~'NESS *n.* **2.** *v.t.* Make sleek, esp. by stroking or pressing down. [later var. of SLICK]

sleep[1] *n.* Bodily condition such as that which normally recurs for several hours every night, in which nervous system is inactive, eyes closed, postural muscles relaxed, and consciousness nearly suspended, (BEAUTY *sleep*; **fall on** ~, (arch.) fall asleep (lit., or fig. = die); **get to** ~, manage to fall asleep; **go to** ~, enter state of sleep, (of limb) be numbed by pressure; **in** one's ~, while asleep; **the ~ of the just,** sound sleep; **last** ~, death; **put to** ~, anaesthetize, (euphem.) kill (animal) painlessly); *a* period of or single indulgence in sleep (*shall try to get a sleep*); prolonged inert condition of hibernating animals; (fig.) rest, quiet, negligence, death, etc.; **~-walker, -walking,** (person) walking or performing other actions during sleep. [OE *slēp*, *slǣp*, = OS *slāp*, OHG *slāf*, Goth. *slēps* f. Gmc **slǣpaz*]

sleep[2] *v.* (**slept**). **1.** *v.i.* Be in state of sleep, fall or be asleep, (**let ~ing dogs lie,** avoid stirring up trouble; **~ like a log** or **top,** sleep soundly); **~ in,** (1) sleep by night at one's place of work, (2) sleep late (intentionally or not); **~ on, over,** not decide (question) till next day. **2.** *v.t.* Spend in or affect by sleeping (*sleep the hours away*; *slept off his vexation, hangover*). **3.** *v.i.* Be inactive or dormant (*sword sleeps in the scabbard*; *passed through the sleeping village*); (of top) spin so steadily as to seem motionless; **~ing partner** (not sharing in actual work of a firm). **4.** Lie in the grave. **5.** Spend the night *at, in*, etc.; have sexual intercourse in bed *together* or *with*; **~ around,** (colloq.) be sexually promiscuous. **6.** *v.t.* Provide sleeping accommodation for (*lodging-house sleeps 300 men*). **7. ~'ing-bag** (for sleeping esp. out of doors in); **S~ing Beauty,** fairy-tale heroine who slept for 100 years; **~'ing-car**(**riage**), railway coach provided with beds or berths; **~'ing--draught, ~'ing-pill,** (to induce sleep); **~ing sickness,** disease with extreme lethargy caused by trypanosome transmitted by tsetse-fly bite; **~'ing-suit,** child's one-piece night-garment. [OE *slēpan*, *slǣpan*, = OS *slāpan*, OHG *slāfan*, Goth. *slēpan* f. Gmc **slǣpan*]

slee'per *n.* In vbl senses; ||wooden beam or piece of other material used as support for rails etc.; (berth in) SLEEP[2]*ing-car*; ring worn in place of ear-ring in pierced ear; thing that is suddenly successful after being undistinguished; *sleeping--suit. [ME, f. prec. + -ER[1]]

slee'plėss *a.* Unable to sleep; such that sleep is absent (*a sleepless night*); continually active or moving; hence ~LY[2] *adv.*, ~NESS *n.* [ME, f. SLEEP[1] + -LESS]

slee'p|ȳ *a.* Drowsy, ready for sleep; habitually indolent, unobservant, etc.; without stir or bustle (*a sleepy little town*); (of fruit, esp. pear) insipid and dry with incipient decay; **~yhead,** sleepy or inattentive person (esp. in *voc.*); ***S~y Hollow chair** (deeply upholstered); **~y sickness,** ENCEPHALITIS lethargica; hence ~ĭLY[2] *adv.*, ~ĭNESS *n.* [ME, f. SLEEP[1] + -Y[2]]

sleet *n.*, & *v.i. impers.* **1.** *n.* Snow and rain together; hail or snow melting while falling; *thin coating of ice; hence ~'Y[2] *a.* **2.** *v.i.* **It ~s** or **is ~ing,** sleet falls. [ME, prob. f. OE **slēte*, **slīete*, rel. to MLG *slōten* pl. hail, MHG *slōz(e)* f. Gmc **slautan-*]

sleeve *n.* **1.** Part of garment that covers arm; *wear* one's HEART *on* one's *sleeve*; LAUGH *in* or *up* one's *sleeve*; *have* (card, plan, etc.) **up** one's ~, in reserve, concealed but ready for use; **roll up** one's **~s,** prepare to fight or work. **2.** Tube enclosing rod or smaller tube. **3.** Wind-sock; drogue towed by aircraft. **4.** Cover of gramophone record. **5. ~-board,** small ironing-board for pressing sleeves; **~-coupling,** tube for connecting shafts or pipes; **~-link,** cuff-link; **~-nut,** long nut with right-hand and left-hand screw-threads for drawing together pipes or shafts conversely threaded; **~-valve** (in the form of a cylinder with sliding movement). **6.** Hence (-)**sleeve**ED[2] (-vd) *a.* [OE *slēfe*, *slīefe*, *slȳf*, = NFris. *slēv*, *sliv*]

slee'velėss (-vl-) *a.* Having no sleeves; futile, unprofitable, (*sleeveless errand*). [OE *slīeflēas* (as prec., -LESS)]

sleigh (slā) *n.* & *v.* = SLEDGE[1] (esp. for travelling over snow); **~-bell,** one of tinkling bells often attached to harness of sleigh-horse etc. [orig. U.S., f. Du. *slee*, = OHG *slito* (see SLED)]

sleight (slīt) *n.* **1.** (arch.) Dexterity, cunning, deceptive trick or device or movement. **2.** **~ of hand,** conjuring, display of dexterity, quickness of hand in fencing etc. [ME *sleghth*, f. ON *slœgth* (*slœgr* SLY; see -TH[1])]

slĕ'nder *a.* Of small girth or breadth, (gracefully) slim, not stout, (*slender stem, waist, pillar,* LORIS, *girl, hand*); scanty, slight, meagre, inadequate, relatively small, (*slender hopes, means, store, income, acquaintance with subject, foundations for belief*); hence ~LY[2] *adv.*, ~NESS *n.* [ME, of unkn. orig.]

slĕ'nderīze, -īse (-īz), *v.t.* & *i.* Make or become slender (esp. in regard to human body). [f. prec. + -IZE]

slĕpt. See SLEEP[2].

sleuth (slōō-) *n.* Detective; **~-hound,** bloodhound (lit. or fig.). [orig. in *~-hound*, ME f. *sleuth* f. ON *slóth* track, trail (cf. SLOT[2]), + HOUND[1]]

slew[1], **slue,** (slōō) *v.* & *n.* **1.** *v.t.* & *i.* Turn or swing forcibly or with effort out of the forward or ordinary position (*round, to the left*, etc.). **2.** *n.* Such change of position. [18th c., Naut., of unkn. orig.]

slew[2]. See SLAY[1].

***slew**[3] (slōō) *n.* (colloq.) Large number or quantity. [f. Ir. *sluagh*]

sley (slā) *n.* Weaver's REED[1]. [OE *slege*, = OS *slegi*, cogn. w. SLAY[1]]

slīce *n.* & *v.* **1.** *n.* Thin broad piece or wedge cut off or out esp. from meat, bread, large fruit, or cake; share, part taken or allotted or gained, (*a slice of territory, of the profits, of luck*, etc.); implement with thin broad blade for serving fish etc. or for scraping or chipping; (Golf) slicing stroke; ~ **of life,** realistic representation of everyday experience. **2.** *v.t.* Cut (*up*) into slices; cut (piece) *off* thing or *off*; go through (air etc.) with cutting motion; (Golf) strike (ball, or abs.) so that it deviates away from the striker; **~d bread** (esp. sliced and wrapped before being sold); hence ~ABLE (-sa-) *a.* **3.** *v.i.* Cut (*into* or *through*) as if to remove slice. **4.** Hence (-)**slī'**CER[1] (1, 2) *n.* [ME, f. OF *esclice* n., *esclicier* v. splinter, f. Frank. *slītjan* = OHG *slīzan*; cf. SLIT]

slĭck *a.*, *n.*, & *v.t.* **1.** *a.* (colloq.) Dextrous, not marred by bungling, carried smoothly through; superficially or pretentiously smooth and dextrous; slippery; smooth, sleek; glib. **2.** *n.* Smooth patch of oil etc. on road or sea. **3.** *v.t.* Make sleek. [ME *slike(n)*, prob. f. OE **slice*, *-slician* polish; cf. SLEEK]

***slĭ'cker** *n.* Plausible rogue; sprucely-dressed townsman; raincoat of smooth material; = SILVER[1]-*fish* (2). [f. prec. + -ER[1]]

slĭd. See foll.

slīde[1] *v.* (**slid**). **1.** *v.t.* & *i.* (Cause to) progress along smooth surface with continuous friction on same part of object progressing (cf. ROLL[2]) (*slid in sitting position down a grass slope; piston slides noiselessly up and down; slide the drawer into place*). **2.** *v.i.* Glide over ice on one or both feet without skates under gravity or with momentum got by running; move quietly, glide, go smoothly along; ~ **over,** barely touch upon (delicate subject etc.). **3.** Take its own course (*let it slide*); **let things ~**, be negligent, allow deterioration. **4.** Go unconsciously or by imperceptible degrees (*slide into sin; slide from one note to another* in music). **5.** *v.t.* Cause to move (*into* position) quietly or unobtrusively. **6.** Hence **slī'd**ABLE *a.*, **slī'd**ER[1] (1, 2) *n.* [OE *slīdan*, = LG *slīden*, MHG *slīten*]

slīde[2] *n.* **1.** Track on ice made by persons sliding; slope prepared with snow or ice for tobogganing. **2.** Act of sliding. **3.** Inclined plane down which children, goods, etc., slide to lower level, chute. **4.** ~**(-way)**, part(s) of machine on or between which sliding part works. **5.** Part of machine or instrument that slides; **~-rule,** ruler with sliding central piece, graduated logarithmically to allow easy multiplication and division of numbers; ~**(-valve)**, sliding piece that opens and closes aperture by sliding across it. **6.** Thing slid into place, esp. glass holding object for microscope; mounted picture placed usu. in projector for viewing on screen etc.; ‖ = HAIR-*slide*; *~ **fastener,** zip-fastener. [f. prec.]

slī'dĭng *a.* In vbl senses; ~ **door** (drawn across aperture on slide, not turning on hinges); ~ **keel,** centre-board; ~ **roof,** part of roof (esp. in motor car) made able to slide and so form aperture; ~ **scale,** scale of fees, taxes, wages, etc., that varies as a whole in accordance with variation of some standard; ~ **seat,** seat able to slide to and fro on runners etc., esp. in racing-boat to adjust length of stroke. [f. SLIDE[1] + -ING[2]]

slight[1] (-īt) *a.* **1.** Slender, frail-looking, (*saw a slight figure approaching; supported by a slight framework*). **2.** Inconsiderable (*has a slight cold; took a slight repast; have made a slight inquiry, some slight inquiries, into it; the damage is very slight*); perceptible but not great (*a* or *the slight smell of gas; I have some slight acquaintance with the matter*). **3.** Not much or great or thorough, inadequate, scanty, (*after slight inquiry; did it well with but slight inconvenience to himself; a conclusion based on very slight observation; a structure raised on slight foundations; paid him slight attention*); (in *superl.*, w. neg. or interrog.) any whatever (*paid not the slightest attention*; **not in the ~est,** not at all). **4.** Hence ~'ISH[1] 2 *a.*, ~'LY[2] *adv.*, ~'NESS *n.* [ME *slyght, sleght*, f. ON **slehtr, sléttr*, level, smooth, = OS *sliht*, OHG *sleht*, Goth. *slaihts* f. Gmc **slehtaz*]

slight[2] (-īt) *v.t.*, & *n.* **1.** *v.t.* Treat or speak of (person etc.) as not worth attention, fail in courtesy or respect towards, markedly neglect. **2.** *n.* Marked piece of neglect, omission of due respect etc., (**put a ~ upon,** slight). [f. prec.]

slī'lȳ. Var. of SLYLY.

slĭm *a.*, & *v.i.* (**-mm-**). **1.** *a.* Of small girth or thickness, slenderly built (and graceful), of long narrow shape; small, insufficient, (*a slim chance of success*); clever, artful, crafty, unscrupulous; hence ~'LY[2] *adv.*, **~'m**ISH[1] 2 *a.*, ~'NESS *n.* **2.** *v.i.* Make oneself slimmer by dieting, exercise, etc.; hence **~'m**ER[1], **~'m**ING[1], *ns.* [Du. or LG, = MLG *slim(m)* slanting, MHG *slimp* f. Gmc **slimbaz*]

slīme *n.*, & *v.t.* **1.** *n.* Fine oozy mud or other substance of similar consistency, e.g. liquid bitumen or mucous exudation of fish etc.; ~ **mould,** spore-bearing micro-organism living in slime. **2.** *v.t.* Cover with slime (esp. of snake preparing prey for gorging). [OE *slīm*, = MDu., MLG, MHG *slīm*, ON *slím*, rel. to L *limus* mud, Gk *limnē* marsh]

slī'm|ȳ *a.* Of the consistency of slime; covered or smeared with or full of slime; slippery, hard to hold; disgustingly dishonest, meek, or flattering; hence **~ĭ**LY[2] *adv.*, **~ĭ**NESS *n.* [ME, f. prec. + -Y[2]]

slĭng[1] *v.t.* (**slung**), & *n.* **1.** *v.t.* Hurl (stone etc., or abs.) from sling; (colloq.) throw (~ **ink,** be author, journalist, etc.); suspend with sling, allow to swing suspended, arrange so as to be supported from above, hoist or transfer with sling; *sling* one's HOOK[1]; **~-cart** (in which load is slung from axle-tree); ***~-shot,** boy's catapult; **slung shot,** metal ball attached by thong etc. to wrist and used esp. by criminals as weapon. **2.** *n.* Strap or string used with the hand to give impetus to small missile; belt, strap, etc., used to support hanging weight, e.g. rifle, ship's boat, goods being transferred; bandage looped round neck to support injured arm; **~-back,** shoe without quarters, held in place by strap above heel. [sense 1 ME, prob. f. ON *slyngva*; 2 ME, prob. f. LDu.]

***slĭng**[2] *n.* Sweetened drink of spirits (esp. gin) and water. [18th c., of unkn. orig.]

slĭ'nger *n.* In vbl senses; user or operator of sling. [ME, f. SLING[1] + -ER[1]]

slĭnk[1] *v.i.* (**slunk**). Go in stealthy manner or with guilty or ashamed or sneaking air (*off, away, by*, etc.); hence ~'Y[2] *a.*, gracefully slender, (of garment) close-fitting and flowing, sinuous. [OE *slincan* crawl, = MLG *slinken* subside]

slĭnk[2] *v.t.*, & *n.* **1.** *v.t.* (Of animal) produce (young, or abs.) prematurely. **2.** *n.* Animal, esp. calf, so born; its flesh; **~-butcher** (who deals in slink); **~'weed,** plant believed to cause slinking. [app. f. prec.]

slĭp[1] *v.* (**-pp-**). **1.** *v.i.* Slide unintentionally esp. for short distance, lose footing or balance or place by unintended sliding, (*slipped in the mud* or *over the edge and fell; blanket slipped off bed; foot slips out of stirrup, ring slips off finger*). **2.** Go with sliding motion (*as the door closes the catch slips into place; slipped into her night-dress*); *slipped* DISC. **3.** Escape restraint or capture by being slippery or

hard to hold or by not being grasped (*eel, opportunity, slipped through his fingers; let reins slip out of his hands*); **let ~,** release from leash, utter inadvertently, miss (opportunity); **let ~ the dogs of war,** (poet.) begin war. **4.** Make one's way unobserved or quietly or quickly (*how time slips away!; slip by, past; slip out of the room; just slip across to the baker's; errors will slip in*); **~ off** or **away,** depart without leave-taking etc. **5.** Make careless mistake (*slips now and then in his grammar*); fall below normal standard, deteriorate, lapse; **~ up,** (colloq.) fail, make a mistake, whence *~-up* n., (colloq.) failure, blunder. **6.** *v.t.* Let go from restraint of some kind (*slip greyhounds from leash*); detach (anchor) from ship, ||(carriage) from moving train; (of animal) produce (young) prematurely; release (clutch of motor vehicle) for a moment. **7.** Pull (garment etc.) hastily *on, off.* **8.** Insert or transfer stealthily or casually or with gliding motion (*slipped a coin into the porter's hand, a white powder into her glass, the papers into his pocket, a marker between the pages*); move (stitch) to the other needle without knitting it; **~ something over on,** outwit. **9.** Escape from, give the slip to, (*dog slips his collar, prisoner his guard; the point had slipped my mind, memory, attention*). **10.** ||**~-carriage, -coach,** railway carriage on express for detaching at station where rest of train does not stop; **~-case,** close-fitting case for book; **~-cover,** (1) calico etc. cover for furniture out of use, *LOOSE[1] cover, (2) jacket or slip-case for book; **~-hook** (with contrivance for loosing it readily when necessary); **~-knot,** (1) knot that can be undone by a pull, (2) = RUNNING[2] *knot*; **~-on, ~-over,** (shoe, garment, etc.) that can be easily slipped on and off; **~-ring** (for sliding contact in dynamo or electric motor); ||**~-road** (for entering or leaving motorway etc.); **~-rope** (with both ends on board so that casting loose either end frees ship from moorings); **~'shod,** having shoes down at heel, slovenly, (fig., of speech, writing, speaker, writer, method of work, etc.) negligent, careless, unsystematic, casual, loose in arrangement; **~'slop,** (*a.*) = *slipshod* (fig.), (*n.*) slipshod writing etc., (as redupl. of *slop*) washy stuff (lit. or fig.), weak drink, slops, sentimental talk or writing; **~-stitch** (1) *n.*, & *v.t.*, (sew with) loose stitch joining layers of fabric and not visible externally, (2) = slipped stitch (see sense 8); **~'way,** shipbuilding or landing slip. **11.** Hence **~'PAGE** (3, 6) *n.* [ME, prob. f. MLG *slippen* = MHG *slipfen*; cf. SLIPPERY]

slĭp[2] *n.* **1.** Act of slipping, blunder, accidental piece of misconduct, (*a slip on a piece of orange-peel may be fatal*); **there's many a ~ 'twixt the cup and the lip,** nothing is certain till it has happened; **give** person **the ~,** escape from or evade him; **~ of the tongue, pen,** thing said, written, accidentally for something else. **2.** Loose covering or garment, e.g. pillowcase, petticoat; GYM-*slip*. **3.** Leash for slipping dogs; device for suddenly loosing clip or attachment. **4.** Artificial slope of stone as landing-stage; inclined structure on which ships are built or repaired. **5.** Long narrow strip of thin wood, paper, etc.; printer's proof on such paper, galley proof; small piece of paper for making notes etc. **6.** Cutting taken from plant for grafting or planting, scion; **a ~ of a,** slim (girl etc.). **7.** (Cricket). Fieldsman stationed for balls glancing off bat to off side behind wicket; (in *sing.* or *pl.*) this part of ground (*was caught in the slips* or *at slip*). **8.** Finely ground clay in creamy mixture with water for coating or making pattern on earthenware; **~-ware,** ware coated with slip. **9.** Loss of distance travelled by ship or aircraft arising from nature of medium in which its propeller revolves; loss of movement of pulley etc. due to slipping of belt; **~-stream,** current of air or water driven backward by revolving propeller. [ME, f. prec.; sense 8 f. OE *slipa, slyppe* slime (cf. COWSLIP); senses 5 & 6 prob. f. MDu., MLG *slippe* cut, strip, etc.]

slĭ'pper *n.*, & *v.t.* **1.** *n.* Light loose comfortable indoor shoe (HUNT[1] *the slipper*), whence **~ED**[2] (-erd) *a.*; light slip-on shoe for dancing etc.; skid or shoe placed under wagon-wheel as drag; **~ animalcule,** paramoecium; **~-bath** (shaped like slipper, with covered end); **~wort,** calceolaria. **2.** *v.t.* Chastise (child etc.) with slipper; hence **~ING**[1] (1) *n.* [ME f. SLIP[1] + -ER[1]]

slĭ'pper|y̆ *a.* (Of ground) difficult to stand on, causing slips by its smoothness or muddiness, (fig., of subject) requiring tactful handling; (of object or person) hard to hold firmly owing to polish or sliminess or elusive motion, (fig.) unreliable, incalculable, shifty, unscrupulous; **~y elm,** (medicinal inner bark of) N. Amer. red elm; hence **~ĭLY**[2] *adv.*, **~ĭNESS** *n.* [prob. made by Coverdale (1535) after Luther's *schlipfferig*, MHG *slipferig* (*slipfern, slipfen* f. Gmc **slip-*); partly f. (now dial.) *slipper* slippery f. OE *slipor*, MLG *slipper* f. Gmc **slip-*; see -Y[2]]

slĭ'ppy̆ *a.* (colloq.) Slippery; ||**look** or **be ~,** look sharp, make haste. [f. SLIP[1] + -Y[2]]

slĭt *v.t.* (-tt-; **slit**), & *n.* **1.** *v.t.* Cut or tear lengthwise, make long straight narrow incision or rent in, cut into strips, (*threatened to slit his nose, tongue, etc.; slit hide into thongs, sheet of metal into strips* or *rods; slit the envelope* (*open*)*; has slit my coat-sleeve from shoulder to wrist*). **2.** *n.* Long straight narrow incision; long narrow opening comparable to cut (*a slit is provided for the coin to drop through; his eyes, the windows, are mere slits; light passes through slit into spectroscope; the slits on the neck are gill-openings*); **~-eyed,** having long narrow eyes; **~-pocket** (with vertical opening giving access to pocket or to garment beneath); **~ trench,** narrow trench for soldier or weapon. [ME *slitte*, rel. to OE, OS *slītan*, OHG *slīzan*, ON *slíta*]

slĭ'ther (-dh-) *v.i.*, & *n.* **1.** *v.i.* Slide unsteadily, go with irregular slipping motion; hence **~Y**[2] *a.* **2.** *n.* Act of slithering. [ME var. of (now dial.) *slidder* f. OE *slid(e)rian* frequent. f. *slid-*, weak grade of *slīdan* SLIDE[1]]

slĭ'ver *n.* & *v.* **1.** *n.* Long thin piece cut or split off; piece of wood torn from tree or timber, splinter (esp. of exploded shell); strip of loose textile fibres after carding. **2.** *v.t.* & *i.* Break off as sliver; break up into slivers; form into slivers. [ME, cogn. w. (now dial.) *slive* cleave f. OE **slīfan*]

slĭ'vovĭtz (-ts) *n.* Balkan plum brandy. [f. Serbo-Croatian *šljivovica* (*šljiva* plum)]

slŏb *n.* Stupid or careless person; (Ir.) muddy land. [f. Ir. *slab* mud f. SLAB[2]]

slŏ'bber *v.* & *n.* **1.** *v.i.* & *t.* Slaver. **2.** *v.t.* Do (task) badly, botch, bungle. **3.** *n.* SLAVER[2]; hence **~Y**[2] *a.* [ME, = Du. *slobbern*, of imit. orig.]

slōe *n.* (Small bluish-black wild plum, fruit of) blackthorn; **~-eyed,** (1) having eyes of this colour, (2) slant-eyed; **~-gin,** liqueur of sloes steeped in gin. [OE *slā(h)*, = MDu., MLG *slē*, OHG *slēha, slēwa* f. Gmc **slaihwōn*]

slŏg *v.* (-gg-) & *n.* **1.** *v.i.* & *t.* Hit hard and freq. wildly esp. in boxing or at cricket; walk or work doggedly (*on, away*); hence **~'GER**[1] (-g-) *n.* **2.** *n.* Hard random hit; (spell of) hard steady work. [19th c., orig. unkn.; cf. SLUG[2]]

slō'gan *n.* Scottish Highland war-cry; party cry, watchword, motto; short catchy phrase used in advertising. [f. Gael. *sluagh-ghairm* (*sluagh* army, *gairm* shout)]

sloid, sloyd, *n.* System (orig. Swedish) of manual

training, esp. by means of wood-carving. [f. Sw. *slöjd* f. ON *slægth* SLEIGHT]

slo͞op *n.* Small one-masted fore-and-aft-rigged vessel with mainsail and jib; ||~ (**of war**), (Hist.) small warship with guns on upper deck only; **~-rigged,** rigged like sloop. [f. Du. *sloep(e)*, of unkn. orig.]

slo͞ot. See SLUIT.

slŏp[1] *n.* & *v.* (**-pp-**). **1.** *n.* (in *pl.*) Dirty water or liquid, waste contents of kitchen or bedroom vessels; (in *pl.* or *sing.*) unappetizing weak liquid food. **2.** Quantity of liquid spilled or splashed; weakly sentimental utterance. **3.** ||**~-basin** (for receiving dregs of cups at table); **~-pail** (for removing bedroom slops). **4.** *v.i.* & *t.* Spill, (allow to) flow over or *over* edge of vessel; carry slops *out* (in prison etc.); make mess with slops on, spill or splash liquid on, (clothes, floor, etc.); **~ over,** (fig.) gush, be maudlin. [earlier sense 'slush', prob. repr. OE **sloppe*, rel. to *slyppe*; cf. COWSLIP]

slŏp[2] *n.* **1.** (in *pl.*) Workman's loose outer clothes; ready-made or cheap clothing; clothes and bedding supplied to sailors in navy; (arch.) wide baggy trousers esp. as worn by sailors. **2.** **~-room** (from which slops are issued aboard ship); **~-seller, -shop,** (of ready-made clothes). [ME; cf. OE *oferslop* surplice, MDu. *(over)slop*, ON *(yfir)sloppr* f. Gmc **slup-*]

slōpe *n.* & *v.* **1.** *n.* Inclined position or direction, state in which one end or side is at higher level than the other, difference in level between two ends or sides of thing, rate at which this increases with distance etc., position in a line neither parallel nor perpendicular to level ground or a line serving as standard, (*there is always a certain slope in a ship's deck*; *cut this side straight and the other with a slope to the right*; *the whole slope may amount to 2 ft.*); piece of rising or falling ground, incline; skiing-ground on side of hill or mountain; hence **~'**WISE (-pwīz) *adv.* **2.** *v.i.* Have or show slope; lie or tend obliquely esp. to ground level; slant esp. up or down; (sl.) make *off*, go away. **3.** *v.t.* Place or arrange or make in or at a slope; **~ arms,** place rifle at a slope over shoulder. [f. ASLOPE]

slŏ'pp|y̆ *a.* **1.** (Of ground) wet with rain, full of puddles; (of food etc.) watery and disagreeable; (of floor, table, etc.) wet with slops, having water etc. spilt on it. **2.** (Of work) unsystematic, not thorough; (of garment) ill-fitting or untidy; **~y Joe,** woman's loose sweater. **3.** (Of sentiment or talk) weakly emotional, maudlin. **4.** Hence **~ĭ**LY[2] *adv.*, **~ĭ**NESS *n.* [f. SLOP[1] + -Y[2]]

slŏsh *n.* & *v.* **1.** *n.* Slush; heavy blow; quantity of liquid; sound or act of splashing; hence **~'**Y[2] *a.* **2.** *v.t.* & *i.* Splash about, move with splashing sound; (colloq.) pour (liquid) clumsily, pour liquid on; ||(sl.) hit, beat; ||(in *p.p.*, colloq.) drunk. [var. of SLUSH]

slŏt[1] *n.*, & *v.t.* (**-tt-**). **1.** *n.* Groove, channel, slit, or long aperture, made in machine etc. to admit some other part, esp. slit for coin to operate **~-machine** (for automatic retail of small articles, allowing spell of play at pin-table, etc., * = FRUIT *machine*); place in hierarchy, in scheme, in regularly broadcast programme, etc. **2.** *v.t.* Provide with slot(s). **3.** *v.t.* & *i.* Place or be placed (as if) into slot. [ME, = hollow of the breast, f. OF *esclot*, of unkn. orig.]

slŏt[2] *n.* Track of deer etc. esp. as shown by foot-prints; deer's foot. [f. OF *esclot* hoof-print of horse, prob. f. ON *slóth* trail; cf. SLEUTH]

slōth *n.* **1.** Laziness, indolence, whence **~'**FUL *a.* **2.** S. Amer. long-haired slow-moving arboreal edentate mammal with curved long-clawed feet. **3.** **~-bear,** large-lipped black shaggy honey-eating bear (*Melursus ursinus*) of India etc.; **~-monkey,** slow LORIS. [ME, f. SLOW + -TH[1]]

slouch *v.* & *n.* **1.** *v.i.* Droop, hang down loosely; go or stand or sit with loose ungainly attitude. **2.** *v.t.* Bend one side of brim of (hat) downwards (opp. *cock*). **3.** *n.* Slouching attitude or walk, stoop, downward bend of hat-brim (opp. *cock*); (sl.) incompetent or slovenly worker or operator or performance (esp. neg., *is no slouch at* etc.), whence **~'**Y[2] *a.*; **~ hat** (with wide flexible brim). [v. f. *slouching* a. f. n. (+ -ING[2]), 16th c., of unkn. orig.]

slough[1] (-ow) *n.* Quagmire, swamp, miry place; (**the S~ of Despond,** state of hopeless depression). [OE *slōh*, *slō(g)*, of unkn. orig.]

slough[2] (slŭf) *n.* & *v.* **1.** *n.* Snake's cast skin, any part that an animal casts or moults; dead tissue that drops off from living flesh etc.; (fig.) habit etc. abandoned. **2.** *v.t.* Cast off as slough. **3.** *v.i.* Drop off or *off* as slough; cast off slough. [ME, perh. rel. to LG *slu(we)* husk]

slou'ghy̆[1] (-ow'ĭ) *a.* Like a slough; miry, muddy. [f. SLOUGH[1] + -Y[2]]

slou'ghy̆[2] (slŭ'fĭ) *a.* (Path.) Being or resembling a slough. [f. SLOUGH[2] + -Y[2]]

Slō'văk *n.* & *a.* (Member or language) of Slavonic people inhabiting Slovakia etc. [f. Slovak etc. *Slovák*, rel. to SLOVENE]

slo'ven (-ŭ'v-) *n.* Person who is untidy or dirty in personal appearance, careless and lazy, or unmethodical; hence **~**LY[1] *a.*, **~**LY[2] *adv.*, **~**RY (4) *n.* [ME, perh. f. Flem. *sloef* dirty, or Du. *slof* careless]

Slō'vēne (*or* slovē'n), **Slovē'nĭan,** *adjs.* & *ns.* (Member or language) of Slavonic people in Slovenia etc. [f. G *Slowene* f. Styrian etc. *Slovenec* f. OSlav. *Slov-*, perh. cogn. w. *slovo* word; -IAN]

slow (-ō) *a.*, *adv.*, & *v.* **1.** *a.* Not quick, deficient in speed, taking a relatively long time to traverse a distance or do a thing, (*slow and steady wins the race*; *slow music, train*; **~ handclap** (by spectators as sign of boredom); **~ and sure,** haste is risky; **~ but sure,** successful in the end); done or obtained over a long time, gradual (*slow growth, progress*); not producing or allowing quick motion; hence **~'**LY[2] *adv.* **2.** Tardy, reluctant, lingering, (*was not slow to defend himself*); not hasty or easily moved (*is slow to anger*); (of clock etc.) showing time earlier than correct time; dull-witted, stupid, (*is slow of speech, of wit*); (of fire) burning feebly; (of oven) not very hot; deficient in interest or liveliness, dull, tedious, (*business is very slow today*); **~(-moving)**, (of goods) not finding ready sale; (of photographic film) needing long exposure, (of lens) having small aperture; (of cricket-pitch, tennis-court, putting-green, etc.) on which ball bounces or runs slowly. **3.** **~'coach,** person slow in action, dull of wit, or behind the times in opinions etc.; *slow* LORIS; **~ march** (of troops in funeral procession etc.); **~-match** (slow-burning, for igniting explosives); **~ motion,** operation or speed of film in which actions etc. appear much slower than usual because of more rapid exposure or slower projection, simulation of this in real action; **~ neutron** (with low kinetic energy, esp. after moderation); **~ poison** (of which repeated doses are eventually injurious); ***~'poke,** = *slowcoach*; **~ puncture** (causing only slow deflation of tyre); **~ reactor,** nuclear reactor using slow neutrons. **4.** Hence **~'**NESS *n.* **5.** *adv.* At slow pace, slowly, (esp. when *slow* gives the essential point: *how slow he climbs!*; *please read* or *go slow* or *slower*; *watch goes slow*; *slow-moving traffic*); see GO[1] 2. **6.** *v.i.* & *t.* **~** (**down, up, off**), reduce one's speed, reduce speed of (train, ship, etc.); **~-down** *n.*, action of slowing down, go-slow. [OE *slāw*, = OS *slēu*,

OHG *slēo*, ON *slær*, *sljár*, *sljór* f. Gmc **slǣwaz* f. IE **slēwos*]

slow-worm (slō'-wẽrm) *n.* Small European legless lizard (*Anguis fragilis*), blindworm. [OE *slā-wyrm*; first element of uncert. orig., cf. OSw. *slā*, Norw. *slo*, etc., slow-worm; see WORM[1]]

sloyd. See SLOID.

slŭb[1] *n.* & *a.* **1.** *n.* Thick place or lump in yarn or thread. **2.** *a.* (Of material etc.) with irregular appearance caused by uneven thickness of warp. [19th c., of unkn. orig.]

slŭb[2] *n.*, & *v.t.* (**-bb-**). **1.** *n.* Wool slightly twisted as preparation for spinning. **2.** *v.t.* Twist thus. [n. f. v., 18th c., of unkn. orig.]

slŭbberdėgŭ'llion (-lyon) *n.* (arch.) Worthless slovenly fellow. [f. *slubber* v. = SLOBBER, + fanciful ending]

slŭdge *n.* Thick greasy mud; sewage (ACTIVATE*d sludge*); muddy or slushy sediment or deposit; accumulation of dirty oil, esp. in sump of internal combustion engine; sea-ice newly formed in small pieces; hence **slŭ'dg**Y[2] *a.* [cf. SLUSH]

slue. See SLEW[1].

slŭg[1] *n.* **1.** Shell-less gastropod often destructive to small plants. **2.** Bullet of irregular shape; missile for airgun; roundish lump of metal; (Print.) metal bar used in spacing; line of type in linotype printing. **3.** Unit of mass, given acceleration of 1 ft. per sec. per sec. by force of 1 lb. **4.** *Tot of liquor. [ME *slugg*(*e*) sluggard, prob. f. Scand.]

***slŭg**[2] *v.* (**-gg-**) & *n.* = SLOG. [19th c., orig. unkn.; cf. SLOG]

slŭ'g-abĕd *n.* (arch.) Lazy person who lies late in bed. [f. *slug* v. (see foll.) + ABED]

slŭ'ggard *n.* Lazy sluggish person. [ME, f. *slug* v. be slothful (prob. f. Scand.; cf. SLUG[1]) + -ARD]

slŭ'ggish (-gĭ-) *a.* Inert, inactive, torpid, indolent, slow-moving, (*a sluggish stream, circulation, market, temper, person*); hence ~LY[2] *adv.*, ~NESS *n.* [ME, f. SLUG[1] or *slug* v. (see prec.) + -ISH[1]]

sluice (-ōōs) *n.* & *v.* **1.** ~(**-gate, -valve**), sliding gate or other contrivance for controlling volume or flow of water, floodgate; water above or below or issuing through floodgate; ~(**-way**), artificial water-channel esp. for washing ore; (place for) rinsing. **2.** *v.t.* Provide with sluice(s); flood with water from sluice; rinse; pour or throw water freely upon; wash *out* or *away* with flow of water. **3.** *v.i.* (Of water) rush out etc. (as) from sluice. [ME, f. OF *escluse* f. Gallo-Rom. **exclusa* (*aqua* water), fem. p.p. (as n.) of L *excludere* EXCLUDE]

sluit (-ōōt), **slōōt,** *n.* (S. Afr.) Deep gully formed by heavy rain. [Afrik. *sluit* f. Du. *sloot* ditch]

slŭm *n.*, & *v.i.* (**-mm-**). **1.** *n.* Overcrowded and squalid back street, district, etc., of city, inhabited by very poor people; ~ **clearance,** demolition of slums and movement of their inhabitants to better housing; hence **~'m**Y[2] *a.* **2.** *v.i.* Go about the slums to visit philanthropically or examine condition of inhabitants; behave like inhabitant of slums. [19th c. cant]

slŭ'mber *v.i.* & *t.*, & *n.* Sleep (esp. with kind or manner specified or implied, or in poet. or rhet. or fig. use; *fell into a troubled slumber*; *his slumbers were interrupted by a knock*; *his eyes with heavy slumber overcast*; *successors of Alaric had slumbered in a long peace*); ~ **away,** spend (time) in slumber; **~-wear,** (Commerc.) night-clothes; hence ~ER[1] *n.*, **slŭ'mb(e)r**OUS *a.* [ME *slūmere* etc., f. *slūmen* v. or *slūme* n. (OE *slūma*) + -ER[5]; *-b-* as in *number*]

slŭmp *n.*, & *v.i.* **1.** *n.* Sudden or rapid or great fall in prices or values, or diminution of demand for commodity or interest taken in subject or undertaking. **2.** *v.i.* Undergo slump; fall in price; fall through, fail utterly; subside limply (*he slumped to the ground, into a chair*). [17th c., orig. 'sink in bog', imit.]

slŭng. See SLING[1].

slŭnk. See SLINK[1].

slûr *v.* (**-rr-**) & *n.* **1.** *v.t.* & *i.* Write or pronounce indistinctly with letters or sounds running into one another. **2.** *v.t.* (Mus.) Perform (notes) legato; mark (notes) with slur. **3.** Pass (fault, fact, etc.) lightly *over*, conceal or minimize; (arch. or U.S.) put slur upon (person, character), make insinuations against. **4.** *n.* Imputation, blame, stigma, (*he put a slur upon me*; *it is no slur on his reputation*); piece of slurring in handwriting, pronunciation, or singing; (Mus.) curved line to show that two or more notes are to be sung to one syllable or played or sung legato. [17th c., of unkn. orig.]

slûrp *n.*, & *v.t.* (colloq.) Eat(ing) or drink(ing) noisily. [f. Du. *slurpen*, *slorpen*]

slŭ'rrȳ *n.* Thin liquid cement; suspension of fine solid material in liquid, esp. water; thin mud; sticky muddy residue separated from coal at pit-head washing plants. [ME, rel. to dial. *slur* thin mud]

slŭsh *n.* Watery mud or thawing snow; (fig.) silly sentiment; *~ **fund,** money used to bribe public servants; hence ~'Y[2] *a.* [17th c., also *sludge* and *slutch*; orig. unkn.]

slŭt *n.* Slovenly woman, slattern; hussy; (arch., joc.) girl; hence **~'t**ERY (4) *n.*, **~'t**ISH[1] *a.* [ME; orig. unkn.]

slȳ *a.* (**~'er, ~'est**). Cunning, wily, hypocritical; practising secrecy or stealth (~ **dog,** person who keeps his peccadilloes or pleasures quiet), done etc. in secret (**on the** ~, privately, covertly, without publicity); (Austral. sl.) illicit (liquor etc.); knowing, arch, bantering, insinuating, ironical; **~'boots,** (colloq.) sly person; hence ~'LY[2] *adv.*, ~'NESS *n.* [ME *sleh* etc. f. ON *slœgr* cunning, orig. 'able to strike' f. *slóg-* past stem of *slá* strike; cf. SLEIGHT]

slȳpe *n.* Covered way or passage from cathedral etc. transept to chapter-house or deanery. [perh. = *slipe* long narrow piece of ground, = SLIP[2] 5]

S.M. *abbr.* Sergeant-Major; short metre.

Sm *symb.* samarium.

smăck[1] *n.*, & *v.i.* **1.** *n.* Flavour, taste that suggests presence of something; barely discernible amount *of* some food-material etc. or *of* a quality etc. present in dish or person's character, tinge, tincture, spice, dash, *of*, (*has a smack of ginger, of the cask, in it, of recklessness, of the old Adam, in him*). **2.** *v.i.* Taste slightly *of*, suggest by taste or otherwise the presence or effects *of*, (*wine smacking of the cork*; *his manner smacked of superciliousness*). [OE *smæc*, = MDu., MLG *smak*, OHG *-smac*]

smăck[2] *n.*, *v.*, & *adv.* **1.** *n.* Slight sharp sound as of surface struck with palm of hand, of lips parted suddenly, or of whip cracked; blow with palm of hand or flat object, slap; hard hit at cricket; loud kiss (*gave her a hearty smack*); **have a ~ at,** (colloq.) attempt, attack; ~ **in the eye** or **face,** (fig.) rebuff. **2.** *v.t.* Slap (person's face etc., or abs.) with palm etc.; part (lips) noisily in eager anticipation or enjoyment of food or other delight; crack (whip). **3.** *v.t.* & *i.* Move with sound of smack. **4.** *adv.* (colloq.) With a smack; in sudden direct violent way, outright, exactly, (*went smack through windows, into ditch*; *hit him smack on the nose*). [f. MDu. *smack*(*en*), of imit. orig.]

smăck[3] *n.* Single-masted sailing-boat for coasting or fishing. [f. Du. *smak*, earlier *smacke*, of unkn. orig.]

smă'cker *n.* (sl.) **1.** Loud kiss; resounding blow. **2.** ||£1; *$1. [f. SMACK² + -ER¹]

smăckeroō' *n.* (sl.) = prec. 2. [alt. f. prec.]

small (-awl) *a.*, *n.*, & *adv.* **1.** *a.* Not large, of deficient or comparatively little size or strength or power or number, (usu. without emotional implications of *little*); (of agent) not doing thing on large scale (*small farmer*, *shopkeeper*); consisting of fine particles (*small gravel*, *shot*); young, far from fully grown or developed; *small* DEER; *small* FRY¹; *small* HOURS; *small profits and quick* RETURN²*s*; **the ~est room,** (colloq.) lavatory in house; STILL¹ *small voice*; *in a small* WAY 12. **2.** (As distinctive epithet) of the smaller kind; **feel, look,** ~, be humiliated; *small* ARM²*s*; *small* BEER; **~-bore** (of firearm, esp. of ·22 inch calibre); **~ capital,** letter shaped like capital but only about as high as lower-case letter; **~ change,** coins opp. notes, (fig.) trivial remarks; *small* CIRCLE¹; **~ claim** (as *small debt*); **~-clothes,** (arch.) knee-breeches; **~ craft,** boats; ||**~ debt** (not too large to be recovered by action in county or sheriff court); **~'goods,** (Austral.) delicatessen meats; **~ gross,** ten dozen; ||**~'holder,** owner or user of **~'holding,** agricultural holding smaller than farm; **~ letter** (not capital); **~'pox,** acute contagious virus disease, with fever and pustules usu. leaving permanent scars; **~ print,** matter printed in small type, (fig.) inconspicuous unfavourable limitations etc. in a contract; **~-scale,** made or occurring on a small SCALE³ or in small amounts; *small* SLAM; **~-sword,** light tapering thrusting-sword, esp. for duelling; **~ time,** (colloq.) unimportant or petty activities; ||**~'wares,** haberdashery. **3.** Not much (*paid small attention to etiquette*); **no ~,** considerable, a good deal of, (*there was no small excitement about it*); **has ~ Latin,** knows little of it; **~ wonder,** that is not very surprising. **4.** Unimportant, trifling, (*grew from small beginnings*; *the small worries of life*; *is only a small matter*); **~ card** (of low rank in suit); **~ talk,** unimportant social conversations. **5.** Socially undistinguished, poor, obscure, humble; **great and ~,** all classes; *in a small* WAY 12. **6.** Morally mean, ungenerous, petty, paltry, (*his small spiteful nature*; *only a small man would think of that at such a time*; *I call it small of him to remind me of it*); **~-minded,** petty or rigid in one's views. **7.** Hence ~'ISH¹ 2 *a.*, ~'NESS *n.* **8.** *n. The* slenderest part of something, esp. **~ of the back,** hinder part of waist; ||(in *pl.*, colloq.) small articles of laundry. **9.** *adv.* Into small pieces (*chop it small*); SING *small*. [OE *smæl*, = OS, OHG *smal*, ON *smalr*, Goth. *smals* f. Gmc **smalaz*]

sma'llage (-aw'l-) *n.* Wild celery. [ME, f. SMALL + obs. *ache* f. OF *ache* f. L f. Gk *apion* parsley]

smalt (-awlt *or* -ŏlt) *n.* Glass coloured blue with cobalt; pigment made by pulverizing this. [F, f. It. *smalto* f. Gmc, cogn. w. SMELT¹]

smârm *v.t.* (colloq.) Smooth, plaster *down*; flatter fulsomely; hence ~'Y² *a.* [orig. dial., also *smalm*, of uncert. orig.]

smârt¹ *v.i.*, & *n.* **1.** *v.i.* (Of person or part of body, or of wound lit. or fig. or the missile or insult etc. that has inflicted it) feel or give acute pain, rankle, (*my finger smarts*; *smarting with nettle-stings*, *under disappointment*, etc.; *with the gibe yet smarting in his brain*); **~ for,** be paid out for, suffer consequences of, (esp. as threat; *you shall smart for this*). **2.** *n.* Bodily or mental sharp pain, stinging sensation. **3. ~-money** (paid or exacted as penalty or compensation); **~'weed,** the water-pepper. [v. f. OE *smeortan* = MDu. *smerten*, OHG *smerzan* f. WG **smert-*; n. ME, app. f. OE **smiertu* (as foll.)]

smârt² *a.* & *adv.* **1.** *a.* Severe enough to cause pain, sharp, vigorous, lively, brisk, (*gave him a smart rap over the knuckles*; *had a smart skirmish*, *walk*, *bout of toothache*; *went off at a smart pace*). **2.** Clever, ingenious, showing quick wit or ingenuity, keen in bargaining, quick to take advantage, (*a smart talker*, *retort*, *saying*, *device*, *invention*); (of employee etc.) ready and intelligent; (of transaction) selfishly clever to verge of dishonesty; unscrupulously clever; **look ~!,** make haste; **~ a'lec(k), a'lick,** (ă'lĭk), ~'Y³, ***~'y-pants,** (derog.) would-be clever person. **3.** Bright and fresh in appearance, neat, in perfect order or repair, in gay or fashionable clothes, well groomed, showing bright colours or new paint, (*smart clothes*; *a smart garden*; *person*, *house*, *ship*, *looks very smart*). **4.** Conspicuous in society, leading the fashion, stylish, (*smart people*; *the smart set*). **5.** *adv.* Smartly. **6.** Hence ~'EN⁶ *v.t.* & *i.*, ~'ISH¹ *a.* & *adv.*, ~'LY² *adv.*, ~'NESS *n.* [OE *smeart*, rel. to *smeortan* (see prec.)]

smăsh *v.*, *n.*, & *adv.* **1.** *v.t.* & *i.* ~ (**up**), break utterly to pieces, shatter; break *in* with crushing blow; **~-and-grab** *a.*, (colloq., of robbery) by breaking shop-window and snatching goods etc.; **~-up** *n.*, complete smash, violent collision of motor vehicles. **2.** *v.t.* Utterly rout and disorganize (enemy); hit (lawn-tennis etc. ball) downwards over net with great force; move with great force (*smashed his fist down on the table*). **3.** *v.i.* (Of business firm) break, go bankrupt, come to grief; (of vehicle etc.) crash *into* another or an obstacle. **4.** Hence ~'ER¹ *n.*, ~'ING² *a.*, (colloq.) unusually good, superlative, (person or thing). **5.** *n.* Breaking to pieces; violent fall or collision or disaster (**go to ~,** be spoilt or disorganized or ruined); smashing stroke in lawn tennis etc.; violent blow with fist etc.; bankruptcy, series of commercial failures; drink of spirit (esp. brandy) and water iced and flavoured; **~ hit, *~,** (sl.) notably successful thing. **6.** *adv.* (With vbs. of motion) with a smash (*went smash into a goods train*). [18th c., prob. imit., after *smack*, *smite*, and *bash*, *mash*, etc.]

smătch *n.* = SMACK¹ *n.* [ME, app. f. OE *smæc* SMACK¹, infl. by *smatch* v. f. OE *smæccan*]

smă'tter|ing *n.* Slight superficial knowledge of a language or subject; so ~ER¹ *n.* [f. ME *smatter* talk ignorantly, prate, of unkn. orig., + -ING¹]

smāze *n.* Mixture of smoke and haze. [portmanteau wd; cf. SMOG]

smear *v.t.*, & *n.* **1.** *v.t.* Daub with greasy or sticky substance or with something that stains, (of grease etc.) make marks on; blot, obscure outline of, (writing, drawing); defame character of, (seek to) discredit publicly. **2.** *n.* Blotch made by smearing; (specimen of) material smeared on microscope slide etc. for examination; (colloq.) attempt at defamation; hence ~'Y² *a.* [OE *smierwan*, = OHG *smirwen*, ON *smyrva*, *smyrja* f. Gmc **smerwjan*]

smĕ'gm|a *n.* Sebaceous secretion in folds of the skin, esp. of the foreskin; hence ~A'TIC *a.* [L, f. Gk *smēgma -atos* detergent (*smēkhō* cleanse)]

smĕll *n.* & *v.* (**smelt** *or* **~ed**). **1.** *n.* Faculty of perception through response of brain to action of odour on nose (*smell is less acute in man than in most animals*; *has a fine sense of smell*; *is perceptible to smell as well as sight*); quality in substances that affects this sense, odour, (*has no*, *a sweet*, *pungent*, *disgusting*, *peculiar*, *smell*; *the smell of thyme*, *carrion*); unpleasant odour, whence ~'Y² *a.* (colloq.); act of inhaling in order to ascertain smell (*take a smell at it*); hence ~-LESS *a.* **2.** *v.t.* Perceive smell of, detect presence of by smell, (*am sure I smell gas*; *horses smelt the water a mile off*; *smell a* RAT¹), whence ~'ABLE *a.*; inhale smell of, set one's sense of smell to work at (*smelt it* *to see if it was high*); (of dog) hunt *out* by smell, (fig. of person) find *out* (secret, plotter, etc.) by investigation. **3.** *v.i.* Perceive smells, have sense of smell; emit smell (usu. of kind specified by *a.* or *adv.*), suggest or recall the smell *of*, (*flowers that do not smell*; *smells sweet, nice, disgustingly, of garlic, of brandy*); (of dog or fig. of person) sniff or search *about*; ~ **at,** inhale smell of; ~ **of,** (fig.) be suggestive of (~ **of the lamp,** seem to have been composed laboriously; ~ **of the shop,** be over-anxious to sell one's wares, or over-technical). **4.** Stink, be rank, (*his breath smells*); seem from the smell to be (*food smells good*; *milk smells sour*). **5.** **~'ing-bottle,** small bottle of **~'ing-salts,** ammonium carbonate mixed with scent to be sniffed as restorative in faintness etc. [ME *smel*(*le*), prob. f. OE, of unkn. orig.]

smĕ'ller *n.* In vbl senses; (sl.) nose. [f. prec. + -ER[1]]

smĕlt[1] *v.t.* Extract metal from (ore) by melting; extract (metal) from ore by melting. [f. MDu., MLG *smelten*, = OHG *smelzan*, cogn. w. MELT[2]]

smĕlt[2] *n.* (*pl.* **~s** *or* ~). Small green and silver fish of genus *Osmerus* etc. allied to salmon and prized as food. [OE, of uncert. orig.; cf. SMOLT]

smĕlt[3]. See SMELL.

smew *n.* Small species of merganser (*Mergus albellus*). [17th c., cogn. w. *smeath* & *smee* = smew, widgeon, etc.]

***smĭ'dgen, *smĭ'dgin,** *n.* (colloq.) Small bit or amount. [perh. f. syn. *smitch*; cf. dial. *smitch* wood-smoke]

smī'lăx *n.* Climbing shrub of genus *Smilax*, root-stocks of some species of which yield sarsaparilla; climbing kind of asparagus much used in decoration. [L f. Gk, = bindweed]

smile *v.* & *n.* **1.** *v.i.* Relax features, often with parting of lips and upward turning of their ends, into pleased or kind or gently amused or indulgently contemptuous or sceptical expression or forced imitation of these, look (*up*)*on* or *at* with such expression, (*smile sweetly, indulgently, cynically, bitterly*); ~ **at,** (fig.) ridicule or show indifference to; **come up smiling,** (colloq.) recover from adversity and cheerfully face what is to come (like boxer rising at start of new round). **2.** Be or appear propitious, have bright aspect (*the smiling countryside*); seem to look propitiously (*up*)*on* (*fortune smiled on us*). **3.** *v.t.* Express by smiling (*smile a welcome*, one's *consent, appreciation*, etc.); give (smile) of specified kind (*smiled an ironical, a curious, smile*); drive (person's vexation etc.) *away*, bring (person) *into* or *out* of a mood, by smiling. **4.** *n.* Act of smiling; smiling expression or aspect; hence **smī'**LER[1] *n.*, **~'**LESS (-l-l-) *a.* [ME. perh. f. Scand., cogn. w. SMIRK; cf. OHG **smīlan* (part. *smīlenter*)]

smîrch *v.t.*, & *n.* Stain, soil, smear, spot, (lit., or fig., *a smirched reputation*). [ME, of unkn. orig.]

smîrk *v.i.*, & *n.* (Put on or wear) affected or conceited or silly smile. [OE *sme*(*a*)*rcian* f. **smar-*, **smer-* as in OE *smerian* laugh at]

smīte *v.* (**smote** *pr.* smōt; **smĭ'tten** or arch. **smit,** *pr.* smĭ-) & *n.* **1.** *v.t.* (arch., literary, or joc.) Strike, hit, (*whosoever shall smite thee on thy right cheek*; *smote his hands together*; *smote the harp-strings*; *smite off his head*; *smote the first ball for four*); inflict severe defeat on (*smite* person HIP[1] *and thigh*); chastise (*God shall smite thee*); have sudden effect on (*an idea, his conscience, smote him*); (esp. in *p.p.*) strike or seize or infect or possess *with* disease or desire or emotion or fascination (*city, person, smitten with plague, palsy*; *am smitten with her charms* or *her* or abs.; *smitten with a desire to*). **2.** *v.i.* (arch., literary, or joc.) Come forcibly or abruptly (*up*)*on* (*wave smote upon the cliff*; *sun's rays smiting upon him*; *sound smites upon the ear*). **3.** *n.* (colloq.) Blow, stroke, attempt. [OE *smītan* smear, = MDu., MLG *smīten*, OHG *smīzan*, Goth. *-smeitan* f. Gmc **smītan*]

smĭth *n.* Worker in metal (esp. in comb., as GOLD*smith*, TIN*smith*); one who forges iron, blacksmith; (fig.) one who creates (*song-smith*). [OE, = MDu. *smid, smit*, OHG *smid*, ON *smithr*, Goth. *-smitha* f. Gmc **smithaz*]

smĭtheree'ns (-dherē'nz), **smĭ'thers** (-dherz), *ns. pl.* Small fragments (*smash* etc. *to* or *into smither*(*een*)*s*). [*smithereens* f. *smithers* (19th c., of unkn. orig.) + -EEN]

smĭ'therў *n.* Smith's work; ‖(esp. in naval dockyards) smithy. [f. SMITH + -ERY]

smĭ'thў (-dhĭ) *n.* Blacksmith's workshop, forge. [ME, f. ON *smithja*, = OE *smiththe*, MLG *sme*(*d*)*e*, MDu. *smisse*, OHG *smidda, smitta*]

smĭ'tten. See SMITE.

smŏck *n.*, & *v.t.* **1.** *n.* Child's overall; **~(-frock),** (esp. European) field-labourer's former outer linen garment of shirtlike shape and with upper part closely gathered; similar garment worn by artists etc.; **~-mill,** (Hist.) windmill of which the cap only and not the body revolves. **2.** *v.t.* Adorn with smocking. [OE *smoc*, = OHG *smoccho*, ON *smokkr*, prob. rel. to OE *smūgan* creep, ON *smjúga* put on a garment]

smŏ'ckĭng *n.* Honeycomb ornamentation on garment of which the basis is close gathers as on smock-frock. [f. prec. + -ING[1]]

smŏg *n.* Fog intensified by smoke; hence **~'gY**[2] (-gĭ) *a.* [portmanteau wd]

smōke[1] *n.* **1.** Visible volatile products of burning, esp. with carbon etc. in suspension, (*a column, cloud, of smoke*); *the* (BIG) *smoke*; **end, go up, in** ~, come to nothing; *no smoke without* FIRE[1]; **from** ~ **into smother,** (arch.) from one evil to another or a worse; **like** ~, (sl.) without hindrance or difficulty, rapidly, easily. **2.** Spell of tobacco-smoking (*must have a smoke*); break for smoking during work. **3.** (sl.) Cigar(ette). **4.** ~ **abatement,** reduction of amount of smoke from chimneys etc. in towns; **~-ball,** (1) puff-ball, (2) projectile filled with material emitting dense smoke used to conceal military operations etc.; **~-bomb** (emitting dense smoke on bursting); **~-bush,** = *smoke-plant*; **~-dried,** cured in smoke; **~-ho,** (Austral. & N.Z. colloq.) = SMOKO; **~-jack,** machine for turning roasting-spit by use of current of hot air in chimney; **~-plant, -tree,** ornamental shrub of genus *Cotinus* with feathery smokelike fruit-stalks; *smoke-*RING[1] 4; **~-rocket,** contrivance for injecting smoke into drain to discover leak; **~-screen,** cloud of smoke (lit. or fig.) diffused to hide operations; *smoke-*STACK; **~-stone,** cairngorm; **~-tunnel,** form of wind-tunnel using smoke filaments to detect motion of air. **5.** Hence **~'**LESS (-kl-) *a.* free from smoke, producing little or no smoke, (esp. of areas where smoke from chimneys is not allowed, or of fuel for use in such conditions). [OE *smoca*, f. weak grade of st. of *smēocan* emit smoke]

smōke[2] *v.* **1.** *v.i.* Emit smoke or steam or vapour (*smoking ruins, horse*); (of lamp etc.) burn badly with emission of smoke, (of chimney or fire) discharge smoke into room. **2.** *v.t.* Colour or darken or obscure, spoil taste of in cooking, preserve or cure, suffocate, rid of insects etc., by action of smoke; (arch.) make fun of; **~d glass** (darkened with smoke for looking at sun etc.); ~ **out,** discover by thorough investigation, destroy (wasps, their nest, etc.) by injecting smoke. **3.** Breathe in and out smoke from (tobacco-pipe, cigar, cigarette, tobacco, opium, marijuana, etc.; *put that in your* PIPE[1] *and smoke* *it*); bring oneself into specified state by smoking; hence **smō'kABLE** *a.* **4.** *v.i.* Smoke tobacco (*smokes too much* or *like a chimney*; *do you, will you, smoke?*); ||**~-room,** smoking-room. [OE *smocian* (as prec.)]

smō'ker *n.* In vbl senses; person who habitually smokes tobacco (**~'s cough, heart, throat,** ailments due to excessive smoking); smoking-compartment on train; smoking-concert, men's informal entertainment. [f. prec. + -ER[1]]

smō'kĭng *n.* In vbl senses; **~-cap, -jacket,** (of ornamental kind formerly worn while one smoked); **~-compartment** (to be used by smokers on railway-train); ||**~-concert,** concert at which smoking is allowed; **~-mixture,** blend of tobaccos for smoking in pipe; **~ room** (in hotel or house, kept for smoking in); **~-room** a., (of talk etc., esp.) such as is suited for men only. [f. SMOKE[2] + -ING[1]]

smō'kō *n.* (*pl.* **~s**). (Austral. & N.Z. colloq.) Stoppage of work for rest and smoke; tea-break; smoking-concert. [f. SMOKE[1] + -O]

smō'k|ў *a.* Emitting, veiled or filled with, obscured (as) with, stained or coloured like, smoke (*a smoky fire, city, room, hue, ceiling*); hence **~ĭLY**[2] *adv.*, **~ĭNESS** *n.* [ME, f. SMOKE[1] + -Y[2]]

***smō'lder.** See SMOULDER.

smōlt *n.* Young salmon migrating to sea for first time. [ME, orig. Sc. & N. Engl.; of unkn. orig.]

smōōch *v.i.* (colloq.) Engage in kissing and caressing. [f. dial. *smouch*, imit.]

smōōth[1] (-dh) *a.* & *adv.* **1.** *a.* Having relatively even and regular surface, free from perceptible projections or lumps or indentations or roughness or (of liquid) undulations, not wrinkled or pitted or scored or hairy, that can be traversed without hindrance, (*smooth skin, surface, chin, paste, tyre, path*); **~ muscle** (without striations, usu. in thin sheet and performing involuntary functions); **in ~ water,** having passed obstacles or difficulties. **2.** Not harsh in sound or taste (*smooth* BREATHING); (of verse) having easy and correct rhythm; (of movement etc.) not suddenly varying, not jerky; (of movement, journey, etc.) unaffected by difficulties or adverse conditions. **3.** Equable, unruffled, polite, conciliatory, complimentary, flattering, (*smooth person, temper, manners, speech*); **~ face** (esp. hypocritically friendly); **~ things,** (esp.) flattery or insincere encouragement; **~ tongue,** insincerely flattering speech. **4. ~-bore,** gun with unrifled barrel. **5.** Hence **~'ISH**[1] 2 *a.*, **~'LY**[2] *adv.*, **~'NESS** *n.* **6.** *adv.* Smoothly (*course of true love never did run smooth*). [OE *smōth*, of unkn. orig.]

smōōth[2] (-dh) *v.* & *n.* **1.** *v.t.* & *i.* Make or become smooth; remove accidental minor variations of (statistics etc.); free from impediments or discomforts (*smooth the way*; *will smooth his declining years*); **~ over** or **away,** reduce or get rid of (differences, perplexities, difficulties, faults, etc.) in fact or appearance; **~'ing-iron,** implement usu. heated to smooth linen etc.; **~'ing-plane,** small plane for finishing the planing of wood. **2.** *n.* Smoothing touch or stroke (*gave his hair a smooth*). [ME, f. prec.]

smōō'thĭe (-dhĭ) *n.* (colloq.) Person who is smooth (sense 3). [f. SMOOTH[1] + -IE]

smörgåsbord (smēr'gōsboord), **smōr'gasbōrd,** *n.* Swedish hors-d'œuvres; buffet meal with variety of dishes. [Sw. (*smör* butter, *gås* goose, lump of butter, *bord* table)]

smōte. See SMITE.

smo'ther (-ŭ'dh-) *n.* & *v.* **1.** *n.* Smouldering ashes etc.; cloud of dust, spray, smoke, etc., or obscurity caused by it (*from* SMOKE[1] *into smother*). **2.** *v.t.* Suffocate, stifle, kill by stopping breath of or excluding air from; **~ed mate** (Chess, when king having no vacant space to move to is checkmated by knight). **3.** Overwhelm *with* kisses, gifts, kindness, etc.; *defeat quickly; deaden or extinguish (fire) by heaping with ashes etc.; **~ (up),** suppress, conceal or secure concealment of, keep from notice or publicity, (*smother a yawn*; *with smothered curses*; *the facts, the recommendations of the committee, were smothered up*); cover entirely *in* (*strawberries smothered in cream*). **4.** *v.i.* Perish of suffocation, have difficulty in breathing. [ME *smorther* f. st. of OE *smorian* suffocate, = MDu., MLG *smoren*]

smo'therў (-ŭ'dh-) *a.* Tending to smother, stifling. [f. prec. + -Y[2]]

smou'lder (smō'l-), ***smō'lder,** *v.i.*, & *n.* **1.** *v.i.* Burn with smoke but without flame, burn inwardly or in suppressed way or unseen; (of feelings etc.) exist, operate, be nursed, undetected or without conspicuous effects (*smouldering discontent, hatred, rebellion*). **2.** *n.* Smouldering combustion (*the smoulder will soon be a flame*). [ME, cogn. w. LG *smöln*, MDu. *smölen*]

smrĭ'tĭ *n.* Hindu traditional religious etc. teachings. [f. Skr. *smṛti* what is remembered]

smŭdge[1] *v.* & *n.* **1.** *v.t.* Smear or blur lines of (writing, drawing); make dirt-mark or confused blot or smear on (face, paper, surface); defile, sully, stain with disgrace, impair purity of, (person's record, fame, etc.). **2.** *v.i.* (Of ink, drawing, etc.) become smeared or blurred (*smudges easily*). **3.** *n.* Dirt-mark, smear, blot, (lit. or fig.); smudged line or mark; hence **smŭ'dgy**[2] *a.* [ME, of unkn. orig.]

***smŭdge**[2] *n.* Outdoor fire with dense smoke made to keep off insects, protect plants against frost, etc.; **~-pot** (containing burning material that produces smudge). [f. *smudge* v. cure (herring) by smoking, 16th c., of unkn. orig.]

smŭg *a.* Consciously respectable, self-satisfied, unambitious, in character or appearance; hence **~'LY**[2] *adv.*, **~'NESS** *n.* [16th c., orig. 'neat', f. LG *smuk* pretty]

smŭ'ggl|e *v.t.* Import or export (goods, or abs.) illegally, esp. without payment of customs duties, whence **~ER**[1], **~ING**[1], *ns.*; convey secretly *in, out*, etc., or put *away* etc. into concealment. [17th c., also *smuckle*, f. LG *smukkeln, smuggelen*]

smŭt *n.* & *v.* (**-tt-**). **1.** *n.* (Spot or smudge made by) small flake of soot; lascivious talk or pictures or stories; fungous disease of cereals in which parts of the ear change to black powder; fungus causing this; **~-ball,** grain affected by smut; **~-mill,** machine for freeing grain from smut; hence **~'ty**[2] *a.* **2.** *v.t.* Mark with smut(s); infect (plant) with smut. **3.** *v.i.* (Of plant) contract smut. [rel. to LG *smutt*, MHG *smutz(en)*, etc.; cf. OE *smitt(ian)* smear, and SMUDGE[1]]

smŭtch. Var. (arch.) of SMUDGE[1].

Sn *symb.* tin. [f. L *stannum*]

snăck *n.* Slight or casual or hurried meal (**~-bar,** place where snacks may be obtained); **go ~s,** (arch.) go shares. [ME, orig. a snap or bite, f. MDu. *snac(k)* (*snacken* v., var. of *snappen* SNAP)]

snă'ffle[1] *n.* Bridle consisting of **~-bit,** or plain slender jointed bit without curb, and single rein; **ride** person **on the ~,** (fig.) manage him gently. [prob. f. LDu.; cf. MLG, MDu. *snavel* beak, mouth]

snă'ffle[2] *v.t.* Put snaffle on; (sl.) appropriate, steal, seize. [f. prec.]

***snăfu'** (-fōō') *a.* & *n.* (sl.) (In state of) utter confusion. [acronym f. '*s*ituation *n*ormal, *a*ll *f*ouled *u*p']

snăg *n.*, & *v.t.* (**-gg-**). **1.** *n.* Jagged projecting point, e.g. irregular or broken tooth, stump of branch remaining on tree, pointed root or stump poking out of ground, piece of rough timber or rock embedded in river or sea bottom and impeding navigation; short tine of antler; tear in material caused by a snag; (fig.) unexpected obstacle or drawback; hence ~GED[2] (-gd), **~'gy**[2] (-gĭ), *adjs.* **2.** *v.t.* Catch on snag; tear on or pierce with snag; clear (land, waterway, tree-trunk) of snags; *catch by prompt action. [prob. f. Scand.; cf. Norw. dial. *snag(e)* sharp point]

snă'ggle-tōōth (-gel-) *n.* (*pl.* **-teeth**). Irregular or projecting tooth; hence ~ED[2] (-tht) *a.* [f. prec. + -LE 1 + TOOTH]

snail *n.* **1.** Gastropod with spiral shell able to enclose whole body, esp. slow-moving kind destructive in gardens; **Roman ~,** the chief edible kind; **~'s pace,** (arch.) **gallop,** very slow movement. **2.** ~(**-wheel**), spiral cam in clock, resembling snail in outline; ~(**-clover**), plant like lucerne, with spiral pods; **~-fish,** = *sea snail* (1); hence ~-LIKE *a.* [OE *snæg(e)l* etc., = OS, OHG *snegil*, ON *snigill* f. Gmc **snag-*, **sneg-*]

snāke *n.*, & *v.i.* **1.** *n.* Limbless reptile of suborder *Ophidia*; limbless lizard or amphibian; ~ (**in** one's **bosom**), ungrateful or treacherous person; **~ in the grass,** hidden danger or secret enemy; **see ~s,** have delirium tremens; **~s and ladders,** game in which players move their counters along board towards goal with periodic sudden advances by 'ladders' or returns by 'snakes' depicted on the board. **2. ~-bird,** fish-eating bird of genus *Anhinga*, with long slender neck; **~-charmer, -charming,** (person giving) exhibition of control of venomous snake by music etc.; ***~-fence** (of horizontal rails laid zigzag with overlapping ends); **~-root,** plant having roots reputed to be snake-poison antidotes; **~'s-head,** plant with some part resembling head of snake; **~-weed,** bistort or other plant resembling snake; **~-wood,** (1) (wood of) S. Amer. timber-tree (from its snakelike markings), (2) (wood of) E. Ind. plant of genus *Strychnos* (used as snake-poison antidote). **3.** *v.i.* Move, twist, etc., like a snake. [f. OE *snaca*, = MLG *snake*, ON *snákr*, *snókr*]

snā'k|ȳ *a.* Infested with snakes; snakelike in appearance or in such attributes as venom, guile, coldness, ingratitude; composed of snakes (esp. of the hair of the Furies); (Austral. sl.) angry, irritable; hence ~ĬLY[2] *adv.*, ~ĬNESS *n.* [f. prec. + -Y[2]]

snăp *v.* (**-pp-**), *n.*, *adv.*, & *a.* **1.** *v.i.* Make sudden audible bite (*dog snapped viciously*); **~ at,** (1) try to bite, (2) speak irritably to, (3) accept (bait, offer, chance, etc.) eagerly; **~'ping turtle,** large Amer. freshwater tortoise seizing prey with snap of jaws. **2.** *v.i.* & *t.* Say ill-tempered or spiteful things; **~ out,** say irritably. **3.** *v.t.* Bite *off*; ~ person's **head** or **nose off,** (esp., fig.) interrupt him angrily or rudely. **4.** Pick *up* (scraps, or fig. bargain, catch at cricket, etc.) hastily or smartly; take *up* (interlocutor) without letting him finish. **5.** *v.t.* & *i.* Break with sharp crack (*snap the string, a stick; oar, wire, snaps*). **6.** Produce report from, emit report or crack, (*snap pistol, whip*); ~ one's **fingers,** make audible fillip esp. *at* person etc. in contempt; ~ one's **fingers at,** (fig.) defy. **7.** Close etc. with snapping sound (*snap the clasp*, one's *teeth together*; *the door snapped to*); move smartly (*snapped to attention*); **~ out of,** (sl.) get rid of (mood, habit, etc.). **8.** *v.t.* Take snapshot of. **9.** (Amer. Footb.) Put (ball) into play on ground by quick backward movement. **10.** *n.* Act or sound of snapping. **11.** Catch that fastens with a snap; small crisp brittle cake or biscuit (BRANDY-*snap*); snapshot. **12.** ||Card-game in which first player to call 'snap' when two cards of equal rank are exposed has right to take cards from other player(s) (also as *int.* at instance of unexpected similarity of two things). **13.** (**Cold**) ~, sudden usu. brief spell of frost. **14.** Crispness of style, fresh vigour or liveliness in action, zest, dash, spring. **15.** *(sl.) Easy task. **16.** *adv.* With sound of snap. **17.** *a.* (Of decision etc.) taken on the spur of the moment; (Parl. etc.) taken unexpectedly, brought on without notice, etc., (*a snap decision, election, vote*, etc.). **18.** ***~ bean** (eaten as young pods broken into pieces); **~-bolt, -lock,** (going home automatically with spring on closing of door etc.); **~-brim,** (of hat) with brim that can be turned up and down at opposite sides; **~'dragon,** (1) plant of genus *Antirrhinum* with bag-shaped flower like dragon's mouth, (2) Christmas game of plucking raisins from dish of burning brandy; **~-fastener,** = PRESS[2]-*stud*; **~-hook, -link,** (with spring allowing entrance but barring escape of cord, link, etc.); **~ shot,** shot taken with little or no delay in aiming; **~'shot,** rapid casual photograph taken with small hand-camera. [prob. f. MDu. or MLG *snappen*; partly imit.]

snă'pper *n.* In vbl senses; carnivorous food-fish of family Lutianidae; Australasian food-fish of genus *Pagrosomus*; snapping turtle; PRESS[2]-stud; *cracker (toy); **~-up,** one who snaps up bargains etc. [f. prec. + -ER[1]]

snă'ppĭsh *a.* Inclined to speak in ill-tempered or spiteful way; (of dog etc.) inclined to snap; hence ~LY[2] *adv.*, ~NESS *n.* [f. SNAP + -ISH[1]]

snă'pp|ȳ *a.* (colloq.) Brisk, full of zest; neat and elegant; **make it ~y,** be quick about it; hence ~ĬLY[2] *adv.* [f. SNAP + -Y[2]]

snâre *n.*, & *v.t.* **1.** *n.* Trap for catching birds or animals, esp. one made with noose of wire or cord; (Surg.) wire loop for catching and extracting polyps etc.; device for tempting enemy or dupe to expose himself to capture, defeat, failure, disgrace, loss, etc.; thing that acts as a temptation (*popularity is often a snare*). **2.** (in *pl.*) Twisted strings of gut or hide stretched across lower head of side-drum to produce rattling sound; ~ (**drum**), drum thus fitted. **3.** *v.t.* Catch (bird etc.) in snare, whence (-)**snâr'**ER[1] *n.*; get (person) into snare, ensnare. [OE *sneare* f. ON *snara*, = OS *snari*, OHG *snarahha*; sense 2 prob. f. MLG or MDu.]

snârk *n.* Chimerical animal of ill-defined characteristics and potentialities. [from *The Hunting of the S~* by Lewis Carroll (1876)]

snârl[1] *v.* & *n.* **1.** *v.i.* (Of dog) make high-pitched quarrelsome growl with bared teeth; (of person) speak cynically, make ill-tempered complaints or criticisms. **2.** *v.t.* ~ (**out**), utter in snarling tone, express (discontent etc.) by snarling. **3.** Hence ~'ER[1] *n.* **4.** *n.* Act or sound of snarling; hence ~'Y[2] *a.* [earlier *snar*, f. (M)LG, MHG *snarren*; see -LE 3]

snârl[2] *v.* & *n.* **1.** *v.t.* & *i.* Twist, entangle, become entangled; **~ up,** confuse and hamper movement of (traffic etc.). **2.** *v.t.* Adorn exterior of (narrow metal vessel) with raised work made by indirect internal hammering with **~'ing-iron. 3.** *n.* Knot, tangle. [ME, f. *snare* n. or v. (see -LE 3); sense 2 perh. f. n. in dial. sense 'knot in wood']

snătch *v.* & *n.* **1.** *v.t.* Seize quickly, eagerly, or unexpectedly, esp. with suddenly outstretched hand(s) or by way of robbery, rescue narrowly *from*, secure with difficulty, carry suddenly *away* or *from*, (*snatched his gun up, down*; *wind snatched my cap off*; *child snatches its food*; *snatch a kiss, an early breakfast, an opportunity*, etc.; *handbag was snatched from its owner, baby from its pram*;

was snatched from the jaws of death; *snatch half an hour's rest*; *snatch victory out of defeat*; *snatched away, from us, by premature death*). **2.** *v.i.* ~ **at,** shoot out hand(s) to seize, (fig.) take (offer etc.) eagerly. **3.** **~-block,** (Naut.) block with hinged flap admitting rope to sheave. **4.** *n.* Act of snatching (*made a snatch at it*); (Weight-lifting) rapid raising of weight from floor to above head; (usu. in *pl.*) fragment(s) or short burst(s) of song or recitation or talk, short spell(s) of action (*only works* **in** or **by ~es,** in fits and starts), whence ~'Y² *a.* [ME *snecchen*, *sna(c)che*, of unkn. orig.; perh. rel. to SNACK]

snăth *n.* (U.S. or dial.) Pole of scythe. [var. of *snead* f. OE *snǣd*, of unkn. orig.]

snă'zz|ȳ *a.* (sl.) Smart, attractive, excellent; hence **~ĭLY²** *adv.* [20th c.; orig. unkn.]

sneak *v.*, *n.*, & *a.* **1.** *v.i.* & *t.* Slink, go or take furtively, (*in*, *out*, *past*, *away*, etc.); hence **~'ers** (-z) *n. pl.*, (sl.) soft-soled shoes. **2.** *v.i.* (in *part.*) Furtive, not avowed, (*have a sneaking affection for him*); persistent in one's mind (*have a sneaking feeling it is not right*). **3.** ‖(school sl.) Turn informer, tell tales. **4.** *v.t.* (sl.) Make off with, steal unobserved. **5.** *n.* Mean-spirited cowardly underhand person; ‖(school sl.) informer, telltale; hence ~'Y² *a.* **6.** *a.* Acting or done without warning (*sneak attack*, *raider*); secret (**~-thief,** one who steals without breaking in, using open doors or windows). [16th c., prob. dial.; perh. rel. to ME *snike*, OE *snīcan* creep]

snĕck *n.*, & *v.t.* (Sc. & N. Engl.) Latch. [ME; cogn. w. SNATCH]

sneer *v.* & *n.* **1.** *v.i.* Smile derisively (*at*); utter derisive words esp. of a covert or ironical kind (*at*); hence ~'ER¹ *n.* **2.** *v.t.* Utter sneeringly. **3.** *n.* Sneering look or remark. [16th c., perh. f. LDu.]

sneeze *v.i.*, & *n.* **1.** *v.i.* Make explosive sound in sudden involuntary expiration to expel anything that irritates interior of nostrils (**not to be ~d at,** passable, not contemptible); **~'wort,** kind of yarrow whose dried leaves are used to induce sneezing. **2.** *n.* Act or sound of sneezing. [ME *snese*, app. alt. f. obs. *fnese* f. OE **fnēosan*, *-fnēsan*, ON *fnýsa*, & repl. earlier and less expressive *nese*]

Snĕll *n.* **~'s law,** (Phys.) constancy of ratio of sines of angles of incidence and refraction between two given media. [f. W. ~, Du. mathematician d. 1626]

snĭb *n.*, & *v.t.* **(-bb-)**. (Sc.) **1.** *n.* Bolt, fastening, catch, of door, window, etc. **2.** *v.t.* Bolt, fasten. [19th c.; orig. uncert.]

snĭck *v.t.*, & *n.* (Cut) small notch in, (make) small incision in; (Cricket) (cause) slight deflection of course of (ball) with bat. [18th c., prob. suggested by SNICKERSNEE etc.]

snĭ'cker *v.i.*, & *n.* Whinny, neigh; snigger. [imit.]

snĭckersnee' *n.* (joc.) Large knife, esp. one usable as weapon. [alt. f. obs. *snick-or-snee* a fight with knives, earlier *stick or snee*, f. Du. *steken* thrust, *snij(d)en* cut]

snīde *a.* & *n.* (colloq.) **1.** *a.* Counterfeit, bogus; insinuating, sneering, slyly derogatory; *mean (trick etc.). **2.** *n.* Counterfeit jewellery or coin(s); snide person. [19th c. cant, of unkn. orig.]

snĭff *v.* & *n.* **1.** *v.i.* Draw up air audibly through nose to stop it from running or as expression of contempt; ~ **at,** (1) try the smell of, (2) show contempt for or discontent with. **2.** *v.t.* Draw up or *up* (air, liquid, scent, drug), draw up scent of (flower, brandy, meat, etc.), into nose. **3.** *n.* Act or sound of sniffing; amount of air etc. sniffed up. [ME; imit.]

snĭ'ffle *v.i.*, & *n.* **1.** *v.i.* Sniff slightly or repeatedly. **2.** *n.* Act of sniffling; (in *pl.*) cold in the head causing running nose and sniffling. [imit.; cf. SNIVEL]

snĭ'ff|ȳ *a.* (colloq.) Disdainful, contemptuous; hence **~ĭLY²** *adv.*, **~ĭNESS** *n.* [f. SNIFF + -Y²]

snĭ'fter *n.* **1.** (sl.) Small drink of intoxicating liquor; *balloon glass for brandy. **2.** **~-valve** (in steam-engine, to allow air in or out). [f. dial. *snift* sniff, perh. f. Scand.; imit.]

snĭ'ftĭng *a.* **~-valve,** = prec. 2. [f. as prec. + -ING²]

snĭ'gger (-g-) *v.i.*, & *n.* (Utter) half-suppressed secretive laugh. [var. of SNICKER]

snĭ'ggle *v.i.* Fish (for eels) by pushing bait into hole. [f. *snig* small eel, ME, of unkn. orig.]

snĭp *v.* **(-pp-)** & *n.* **1.** *v.t.* & *i.* Cut with scissors or shears esp. in small quick strokes (*snip cloth, a hole*; *snip off the ends*; ~ **at,** make snipping strokes at); hence **~'PING¹** (2) *n.* **2.** *n.* Act of snipping; piece snipped off; ‖(sl.) something easily done or cheaply acquired; (in *pl.*) hand-shears for metal-cutting. [f. LG & Du. *snippen* (imit.)]

snīpe *n.* (*pl.* **~s** *or* **~**) & *v.* **1.** *n.* Wading bird of genus *Gallinago*, with long straight bill, frequenting marshes; GUTTER*snipe*; **~-eel** (with long slender snout); **~-fish** (of family Macrorhamphosidae, with long tubular snout). **2.** *v.i.* Go snipe-shooting. **3.** *v.i.* & *t.* (Mil.) Fire shots from hiding usu. at long range into enemy's camp or *at* individuals; (fig.) make sly critical attack *at*; kill or hit by sniping; hence **snī'PER¹** *n.* [ME, prob. f. Scand.; cf. Icel. *mýrisnípa*, & MDu., MLG *snippe*, OHG *snepfa*]

snĭ'ppĕt *n.* Small piece cut off, snipping; (in *pl.*) detached fragments *of* knowledge or information, short extracts from books, odds and ends, whence ~Y² *a.* [f. SNIP + -ET¹]

snĭtch *v.* (sl.) **1.** *v.i.* Act as informer. **2.** *v.t.* Steal. [17th c. in sense (fillip on) nose; orig. unkn.]

snĭ'vel *v.i.* (‖-ll-), & *n.* **1.** *v.i.* Run at the nose; make repeated sniffing sound; be tearful, show maudlin emotion; hence **~LER¹** *n.*, **~LING²** *a.* **2.** *n.* Running mucus; whining and weeping; hypocritical talk, cant. [ME, f. OE **snyflan* (*snofl* mucus); cf. SNUFFLE]

snŏb *n.* Person with exaggerated respect for social position or wealth and a disposition to be ashamed of socially inferior connections, behave with servility to social superiors, and judge of merit by externals; person despising those whose attainments or tastes he considers inferior to his own (*intellectual snob*; *the snob appeal of an address in Belgravia*; *has snob value but no more*); hence **~'BISH¹** *a.*, **~'BERY** (4, 5), **~ŏ'CRACY,** *ns.* [18th c. (now dial.) 'cobbler'; orig. unkn.]

snoek (-ōōk) *n.* (S. Afr.) Barracouta. [Afrik., f. Du., = PIKE³, f. MLG *snōk*, prob. rel. to SNACK]

snŏg *v.i.* **(-gg-)**. (sl.) Engage in kissing and caressing. [20th c., orig. unkn.]

***snŏ'llȳgŏster** *n.* (sl.) Shrewd unscrupulous person. [perh. f. *snallygaster*, a mythical creature]

snōōd *n.* **1.** (Sc. or literary). Fillet worn by maidens in Scotland to confine hair. **2.** Loose net for woman's back hair. **3.** Short line attaching hook to a main line in sea fishing. [OE *snōd*, of unkn. orig.]

snōōk¹ *n.* = SERGEANT-fish. [f. Du. SNOEK]

snōōk² *n.* (sl.) Contemptuous gesture with thumb to nose and fingers spread out (**cock a ~,** make this gesture, lit. or fig.). [19th c.; orig. unkn.]

snōō'ker (*or* -ŏŏ'-) *n.*, & *v.t.* **1.** *n.* ~ **(pool),** form of POOL² 2, with 15 red and 6 other coloured balls; position in this game where direct shot would lose points. **2.** *v.t.* Subject (player) to a snooker; (sl., esp. in *pass.*) thwart, defeat. [19th c.; orig. unkn.]

snōōp *v.i.*, & *n.* (colloq.) **1.** *v.i.* Pry into matters one need not be concerned with; sneak *about* or *around* looking for infractions of the law; hence ~'ER[1] *n.*, ~'Y[2] *a.*; *~**'erscope,** device for revealing objects in the dark. **2.** *n.* Act of snooping. [f. Du. *snoepen* eat on the sly]

snōōt *n.* (sl.) Nose. [var. of SNOUT]

snōō't|y̆ *a.* (colloq.) Supercilious, conceited; hence **~ĭ**LY[2] *adv.*, **~ĭ**NESS *n.* [20th c.; orig. unkn.]

snōōze *v.i.*, & *n.* (Take) short sleep esp. in day-time. [18th c. cant, of unkn. orig.]

snōre *v.i.* & *t.*, & *n.* (Make) hoarse rattling or grunting noise in breathing esp. during sleep; pass (time) *away* in snoring; bring one*self* awake, etc., by snoring; hence **snōr'**ER[1] *n.* [ME, prob. imit.; cf. SNORT[1]]

snōr'kel. See SCHNORKEL.

snōrt[1] *v.* & *n.* **1.** *v.i.* Make explosive noise due to sudden forcing of breath through nose and usu. expressing anger or indignation or incredulity, or (of steam-engine etc.) noise resembling this. **2.** *v.t.* Express (defiance etc.) by snorting; throw *out* (words) with snorting. **3.** *n.* Noise made in snorting; small drink of liquor. [ME, prob. imit.; cf. SNORE]

||**snōrt**[2] *n.* = SCHNORKEL. [substituted for S(CH)NORKEL]

snōr'ter *n.* In vbl senses; (sl.) boisterous gale, performance etc. conspicuous for vigour or violence, difficult task. [f. SNORT[1] + -ER[1]]

snŏt *n.* (vulg.) Nasal mucus; contemptible person; **~-rag,** handkerchief. [prob. f. MDu., MLG *snotte*, MHG *snuz*, cogn. w. SNOUT]

snŏ'tt|y̆ *a.* & *n.* **1.** *a.* (vulg.) Running or foul with nasal mucus; contemptible. **2.** (colloq.) Annoyed, short-tempered; cheeky. **3.** Hence **~ĭ**LY[2] *adv.*, **~ĭ**NESS *n.* **4.** *n.* (Naval sl., arch.) Midshipman. [f. prec. + -Y[2]]

snout *n.* Projecting nose (and mouth) of animal; (derog.) human nose; pointed front of thing, nozzle, (*snout of glacier*, *of battleship's ram*, etc.); (sl.) tobacco; **~-beetle,** weevil; hence (-)~'ED[2] *a.*, ~'Y[2] *a.*, like a snout, having a (prominent) snout. [ME, f. MDu., MLG *snūt*(*e*)]

snow[1] (-ō) *n.* & *v.* **1.** *n.* Atmospheric vapour frozen into ice crystals and falling to earth in light white flakes, or spread on it as a white layer after falling; (in *pl.*) falls or accumulations of snow (*where are the snows of yester-year?*). **2.** Skin, hair, etc., resembling snow esp. in whiteness; dessert or other dish resembling snow; frozen carbon dioxide; (sl.) cocaine. **3.** **~'ball,** (*n.*) mass of snow pressed into hard ball esp. for use as missile, anything that grows or increases rapidly like snowball rolled on snow, (*v.t.* & *i.*) pelt or have pelting-match with snow-balls, (fig.) increase rapidly; **~'ball-tree,** guelder rose; **~-berry,** garden shrub of genus *Symphoricarpos*, with white berries; **~-bird,** white or partly white bird, esp. the snow bunting, (sl.) cocaine addict; **~-blind**(**ness**), unable, inability, to see owing to effects on the eye of reflection of light endured in traversing snow-fields etc.; **~-blink,** reflection in sky of snow or ice fields; **~-boot,** overboot of rubber and cloth; **~-bound,** prevented by snow from going out or travelling; **~-broth,** melted or melting snow; **~ bunting,** mainly white species of finch; **~-cap,** white-crowned humming-bird; **~-capped,** (of mountain) covered at top with snow; **~-drift,** bank of snow heaped by wind; **~'drop,** bulbous plant (*Galanthus nivalis*) with white drooping flowers in early spring; **~'fall,** (esp.) amount of snow that falls on one occasion or on given area within given time; **~-field,** (esp.) permanent wide expanse of snow in mountainous or polar regions; **~'flake,** (1) one of the small collections of crystals in which snow falls; (2) (white flower of) plant of genus *Leucojum*; **~-goggles,** darkened spectacles worn by mountaineers etc. to prevent snow-blindness; **~-goose,** arctic white goose with black-tipped wings; **~-grouse,** ptarmigan; **~-ice,** opaque white ice formed from melted snow; *~ **job,** (sl.) attempt at deception by overwhelming with many details; **~-leopard,** OUNCE[2]; **~-line,** level above which snow lies permanently at a place; **~'man,** figure made of snow by children etc. and set up; ABOMINABLE *Snowman*; ***~'-mobile** (-ēl), motor vehicle to travel over snow, esp. with skis and caterpillar track; **~ owl,** = *snowy owl*; **~-plant,** microscopic alga growing in snow and colouring it red; **~--plough,** contrivance for clearing road or track by pushing snow aside; **~-shoe,** racket--head or ski attached to foot and enabling wearer to traverse snow without sinking in; **~-shovel,** large esp. wooden shovel for moving snow; **~-slip,** avalanche; **~'storm,** heavy fall of snow esp. with wind; **~-white,** white as snow. **4.** Hence ~'LESS, ~'Y[2], *adjs.*; **~y owl,** large white owl (*Nyctea nyctea*). **5.** *v.i. impers.* **It ~s** or **is ~ing,** snow falls. **6.** *v.t.* & *i.* Sprinkle or scatter or fall as or like snow. **7.** *v.t.* *(sl.) Overwhelm, impress greatly. **8.** **~ under,** cover (as) with snow, overwhelm with numbers etc. (*esp. in *pass.* of election candidate defeated by huge majority). **9.** **~ed up** or **in,** snow-bound, blocked up with snow. [OE *snāw*, = OS, OHG *snēo*, ON *snær* etc., Goth. *snaiws* f. Gmc **snaiwaz*]

snow[2] (-ō) *n.* Small briglike sailing vessel with supplementary trysail mast. [f. Du. *sna*(*a*)*uw* or LG *snau*, of unkn. orig.]

S.N.P. *abbr.* Scottish National Party.

Snr. *abbr.* Senior.

snŭb[1] *v.t.* (**-bb-**), & *n.* **1.** *v.t.* Rebuff, reprove, humiliate, with sharp words or marked lack of cordiality; check movement of (boat, horse, etc.) esp. by rope wound round **~'bing-post** or bollard, tree, etc.; hence **~'b**ER[1] *n.*, (esp.) *shock absorber. **2.** *n.* Act of snubbing, rebuff. [ME, f. ON *snubba* chide]

snŭb[2] *a.* & *n.* **1.** *a.* (Of nose) short and stumpy or turned up; **~-nosed,** having a snub nose. **2.** *n.* Snub nose. [f. prec. in sense 'check growth of']

snŭff[1] *v.* & *n.* **1.** *v.i.* & *t.* = SNIFF; take snuff. **2.** *n.* = SNIFF. **3.** Powdered tobacco taken by sniffing up nostrils (**up to ~**, (sl.) ||not childishly ignorant or innocent, *reaching normal standard); medicinal powder taken by sniffing; **~-colour**(**ed**), (of) dark yellowish-brown. [n. sense 2 f. v., sense 3 f. Du. *snuf*(*tabak* tobacco), both f. MDu. *snuffen* snuffle]

snŭff[2] *v.* & *n.* **1.** *v.t.* Trim snuff from (candle) with fingers or scissors or snuffers; **~ out,** extinguish thus or with snuffer, (fig.) kill, put an end to, (*I was nearly*, *his hopes were*, *snuffed out*). **2.** *v.i.* **~ it,** **~ out,** (sl.) die. **3.** *n.* Charred part of candle-wick, esp. when obscuring light. [v. f. n., ME *snoffe*, *snuffe*, of unkn. orig.]

snŭ'ffer *n.* **1.** Person who takes snuff. **2.** Small hollow cone with handle used to extinguish candle; (in *pl.*) implement like scissors used to snuff candle. [f. SNUFF[1,2] + -ER[1]]

snŭ'ffle *v.* & *n.* **1.** *v.i.* Sniff; make sniffing sounds; speak nasally, whiningly, or like one with a cold; breathe noisily as through partly blocked nose; hence **snŭ'ffl**ER[1] *n.* **2.** *v.t.* **~ (out),** utter with snuffling. **3.** *n.* Sniff; snuffling sound, tone, or talk. [prob. f. LG & Du. *snuffelen* (as SNUFF[1], -LE 3); cf. SNIVEL]

snŭ'ffy̆[1] *a.* Like snuff in colour or substance. [f. SNUFF[1] + -Y[2]]

snŭ'ffy̆[2] *a.* Annoyed; irritable; supercilious, contemptuous. [f. SNUFF[2] + -Y[2]]

snŭg *a.* & *n.* **1.** *a.* Protected from weather and cold, well enclosed or packed in or fixed in place, closely fitting, comfortably situated, cosy; (of income etc.) allowing comfort and comparative ease; hence ~'LY[2] *adv.*, ~'NESS *n.* **2.** *n.* ‖Bar-parlour of inn. [16th c., orig. Naut.; prob. of LDu. orig.]

snŭ'ggerў (-g-) *n.* Snug place, esp. person's private room or den; ‖=prec. 2. [f. prec. + -ERY]

snŭ'ggle *v.* **1.** *v.i.* Shift one's position or lie close *up to* for warmth. **2.** *v.t.* Draw (child etc.) close *to* one, cuddle. [f. SNUG + -LE 3]

sō[1] *adv., conj.,* & *pron.* **1.** *adv.* To the extent or in the manner set forth by preceding or following *as*-clause or implied in context, thus, equally, similarly, analogously, (now used to express degree before *as*-clause only with negative: *I am not so eager as you, I am as eager as you*; *as the tree falls, so must it lie*; occas. used twice correlatively: *so many men so many minds*; *when he saw her so frightened*; *why are you panting so?*; with a gesture, *have known him since I was so high*; *so, and so only, can it be done*; *stand just so*; *could show me so divine a thing*; *did not expect to live so long*; *did not get it by force and ought not to be so deprived of it*; *can stand only so much of it*; often in sentence appended as explanation: *I paid him double, I was so pleased*; *were it* EVER OR NEVER *so bad* etc.; MORE *so*; EVERY *so often*); **so be it** (expr. acceptance or being resigned); **so far,** to such an extent or distance, until now, (*so far it has not happened*; *so far you are right*); **(in) so far as,** to the extent that; *so* FAR[1] *from*; **so far so good,** progress has been satisfactory; **and so forth, and so on,** et cetera, and the like; **so long!,** (colloq.) goodbye till we next meet; **so long as,** with the proviso that, on the condition that; **so many,** nothing but (*went down like so many skittles*); **so much,** nothing but (*rubbish* etc.); **so much for,** that is all that need be done or said about; *so much* THE *worse* etc.; *at* **so much** *a week, a head,* etc., **so much** *of one ingredient and* **so much** *of another*, a definite but unspecified sum, quantity, etc.; **not so (very)** *difficult* etc. (as had been expected or predicted); **not so much as,** less . . . than (*is not so much discontented as unsatisfied*), not even (*did not so much as glance at it*); *so* SOON *as*. **2.** To the degree or in the manner or with the intent or result set forth by following *that*-clause or *but*-clause or *as to* (*so high that you cannot reach it*; *so run that ye may obtain*; **so much so that,** to such an extent that; *warned him so that*, or **so, he might avoid the danger*; *all precautions have been taken, so that we expect to succeed*; *not so deaf but he can, that he cannot, hear a gun*; *not so big a fool as to believe that*; *was so fortunate as to escape*; *put it so as not to offend him*; *it so happens that he was not there*). **3.** To a degree that demands exclamatory emphasis (*so many worlds, so much to do!*; *I am so glad, so tired!*; *she is so beautiful!*; *so kind of you!*; *cricket is so boring*); EVER *so easy* etc.; **so sorry!,** (colloq.) I beg your PARDON[1]. **4.** (arch.) On condition that or *that*, on condition set forth in *as*-clause or implied, (*so that* or *so it is done, it matters not how*; *so may you find forgiveness as now you forgive me!*); **so help me (God)!** (form of asseveration; see HELP[1]). **5.** *adv.* & *conj.* Accordingly, consequently, therefore, as appears or results from preceding or implied statements or fact, (*he says he was not there, so* or *and so he doubtless was not*; *so* or *and so I cannot come*; *so* that's *what he meant*; *so you are back again*); **so that's that** (colloq., concluding statement or discussion or piece of work); *so* (WHAT)? **6.** *adv.* (Accompanying emphasis on some later word) moreover, also, as well, in actual fact, (*well, so I did*; *you said it was good, and so it is*; *yes, I denied it, but* or *and so did you*; *'your birthday? yes, so it is'*). **7.** *adv.* & *pron.* (As substitute, often preceding v., for obj. of vbs. of saying, thinking, etc.) it, this, that, the same, this is what, (*so he said*; *do you think so?*; *and so say all of us*; *so saying, he departed*; *so am I*; *so spake Achilles*, i.e. what precedes, *and Patroclus so*, i.e. what follows; *she is ill and he thinks himself so*; arch., ellipt.: *So Satan, whom the archangel thus rebukes*); **I suppose so** (expr. hesitant agreement); **I told you so,** I warned you in vain; **so-called** (epithet calling attention to, or questioning accuracy of, description); **so to say** or **speak** (apology for exaggeration, metaphor, neologism, imprecision, bluntness, etc.); *you don't* SAY[2] *so*. **8.** In that state or condition, actually the case, (*he, it, is better so*; *God said Let there be light, and it was so*; *must it be so?*; *but perhaps it is not so*; *even if it were so*); EVER *so*; (with omission of *it is* etc.: *how so?, why so?, if so, not so*; JUST[2] *so*, QUITE *so*). **9.** (arch.) **And so,** after which I, they, etc., proceeded (*and so to dinner, to bed*, etc.); **so please you,** by your favour, if you please. **10. -so** = -SOEVER. **11. So-and-so** (*pl.* **so-and-so's**), particular person or thing not needing to be specified (*never mind what so-and-so says*; *tells me to do so-and-so*), (colloq.) disliked or contemptible person; **so so, so-so,** *pred. a.* or *adv.*, not more than passable, -bly, indifferent(ly), not very good or well; **or so,** or thereabouts (after expressions of quantity or numbers: *send me ten or so*; *a pound or so will do*). [OE *swā* etc., = OS, OHG *sō*, ON *svá*, Goth. *swa, swe*]

sō[2]. See SOH.

‖**S.O.** *abbr.* Stationery Office.

***So.** *abbr.* South.

soak *v.* & *n.* **1.** *v.t.* (Of absorbent substance) take *up* or suck *in* (liquid). **2.** *v.t.* & *i.* Place or leave or lie in or *in* liquid for saturation, steep, (lit., or fig. in sunshine, one*self* in subject of study, etc.); make or be wet through, (of rain etc.) drench, whence ~'ING[1] (1) *n.* **3.** (Of moisture or fig. of understanding etc.) make way *in(to)* or *through*, make its *way*, by saturation, whence ~'AGE (3) *n.*; ‖**~-away,** arrangement for disposal of rain-water by percolation through soil. **4.** *v.t.* (sl.) Extract money from by extortionate charge, taxation, etc., (*soak the rich*). **5.** *v.i.* Drink persistently, booze; (in *p.p.*) very drunk. **6.** *n.* Soaking; drinking-bout; hard drinker. [OE *socian* cogn. w. *soc* sucking at breast, f. weak grade of *sūcan* SUCK]

soa'ker *n.* In vbl senses; hard drinker; drenching rain. [f. prec. + -ER[1]]

soap *n.*, & *v.t.* **1.** *n.* Cleansing agent that is compound of fatty acid with soda or potash or (**insoluble ~**) with another metallic oxide, of which the soluble kinds when rubbed in water yield a lather used in washing; **no ~,** (colloq.) nothing doing; **soft ~,** semifluid soap made with potash, (fig.) flattery. **2. ~-bark, -berry, -nut, -plant, -pod, -root, -wort,** plants yielding substances serving purposes of soap. **3. ~-boiler, -boiling,** manufacture(r) of soap; **~-box,** (packing-)box for holding soap, makeshift stand for street orator, crude vehicle; **~-bubble,** globe of air enclosed in iridescent film of soapy water made esp. by blowing through pipe or ring dipped in soapsuds; **~-dish,** holder for soap in bathroom etc.; **~-earth,** steatite; **~-flakes** (specially prepared for washing clothes etc.); ***~ opera,** sentimental domestic broadcast serial; **~ powder** (esp. with additives); **~'stone,** steatite; *soap*-SUDS; **~-works,** manufactory of soap. **4.** Hence ~'LESS *a.* **5.** *v.t.* Apply soap to; scrub or rub with soap. [OE *sāpe*, = MDu. *seepe*, OHG *seifa* f. WG **saipo*]

soa'p|ў *a.* Like, smeared or impregnated with, suggestive of, soap; (fig., of person or his manners or talk) unctuous, flattering; hence ~ĭLY[2] *adv.*, ~ĭNESS *n.* [f. prec. + -Y[2]]

soar *v.i.* Fly high (lit. or fig.), mount to or be at a great height above earth or normal position, hover or sail in the air without flapping of wings or use of engine, (*soaring eagle, spire, thoughts, prices, glider, ambition, ideals*). [ME, f. OF *essorer* f. Rom. *EX[1](*aurare* f. *aura* breeze)]

sŏb *v.* (-**bb**-) & *n.* **1.** *v.i.* Draw breath in convulsive gasps usu. with weeping under mental distress or physical exhaustion. **2.** *v.t.* ~ (**out**), utter with sobs. **3.** *n.* Convulsive drawing of breath esp. in weeping; **~-sister,** writer of sentimental stories; ***~-story,** narrative designed mainly to evoke sympathy; ***~-stuff,** pathos, sentimental writing or behaviour. [ME *sobbe(n)*, prob. imit.]

***S.O.B.** *abbr.* SON of a bitch (or *silly old bastard* etc.).

sō'ber *a.* & *v.* **1.** *a.* Not drunk (**as ~ as a judge,** entirely sober; **appeal from Philip drunk to Philip ~,** suggest that opinion etc. represents passing mood only); temperate in regard to drink (*is a sober man*); moderate, well-balanced, sane, tranquil, self-controlled, sedate, not vehement or passionate or excited or wayward or fanciful or exaggerated, (of colour) quiet and inconspicuous; **in ~ fact,** in fact as opp. fancy; **~-sided,** sedate, solemn, earnest; **~-sides,** sedate person; hence ~LY[2] *adv.* **2.** *v.t.* & *i.* ~ (**down** or **up**), make or become sober or less wild, reckless, enthusiastic, visionary, etc. [ME, f. OF *sobre* f. L *sobrius*]

sobrī'etў *n.* Being sober. [ME, f. OF *sobrieté* or L *sobrietas* (as SOBER; see -TY[1])]

sō'brĭquet (-kā), **sou'-** (sōō'-), *n.* Nickname; assumed name. [F, orig. = 'tap under chin']

Soc. *abbr.* Socialist; Society.

sŏ'cage, sŏ'ccage, *n.* Feudal tenure of land involving payment of rent or other non-military service to superior. [ME f. AF *socage* (*soc* f. OE *sōcn* SOKE; see -AGE)]

sŏ'ccer (-k-) *n.* (colloq.) Association football. [f. Assoc. + -ER[1]]

sō'ciab|le (-sh*a*-) *a.* & *n.* **1.** *a.* Fitted for companionship, ready and willing to converse, not averse to society, communicative, liking company; (of meeting etc.) marked by friendliness, not stiff or formal; hence **sōci**ABI'LITY (-sh*a*-) *n.*, ~LY[2] *adv.* **2.** *n.* Open carriage with facing side seats; S-shaped couch for two occupants partly facing each other; *social. [F, or f. L *sociabilis* (*sociare* to unite f. *socius* companion; see -ABLE)]

sō'cial (-sh*a*l) *a.* & *n.* **1.** *a.* Living in companies or organized communities, gregarious, (*man is a social animal*); not fitted for or not practising solitary life; interdependent, co-operative, practising division of labour; existing only as member of compound organism, (of insects) having common nests etc., (of birds) building near each other in communities; (of plants) growing thickly together and monopolizing ground they grow on. **2.** Concerned with the mutual relations of (classes of) human beings (*social problems, morality, students, philosophers*); **the ~ contract** or **compact,** agreement to co-operate for social benefits, e.g. to exchange the individual freedom of the state of nature for legal restriction (assumed by 18th-c. thinkers as basis of political society); **~ credit,** economic theory that profits of industry should be distributed to the general public; **S~ Democrat,** politician aiming at improving condition of lower classes by gradual advance towards socialism; **~ disease,** venereal disease; **the ~ evil,** (arch.) prostitution; **~ history,** history of social behaviour; **~ order,** network of human relationships in society; **~ realism,** expression of social views in art etc.; **~ science,** scientific study of human society and social relationships, branch of this (e.g. politics, economics); **~ security,** State assistance to those lacking economic security and welfare; **~ service,** philanthropic activity; **~ services,** education, health, housing, insurance, pensions, etc., as State-provided welfare services; **~ worker,** person trained for social service(s). **3.** Of or in or towards society (*social intercourse, life, etiquette, pleasures, duties*; one's *social superiors and inferiors*; *social rank, position, distinctions*; *has social tastes*; *a social club, evening, gathering*); **~ climber,** person seeking to gain higher rank in society; **~ secretary** (making arrangements for social activities of a group). **4.** (Rom. & Gk Hist.) Of or with allies (*the Social War*). **5.** Hence or cogn. **sōcĭă'l**ITY (-shĭ-) *n.*, ~LY[2] *adv.* **6.** *n.* Social gathering, esp. one organized by club, congregation, etc. [F, or f. L *socialis* allied (*socius* friend; see -AL)]

sō'cial|ism (-sh*a*-) *n.* Political and economic theory of social organization which advocates that community as a whole should own and control the means of production, distribution, and exchange; policy or practice based on this theory; **Christian S~ism,** attempt to apply Christian precepts in ordinary life resulting in some approximation to the aims of socialism; hence ~IST (2) *n.*, **~ĭ'st**IC *a.* [f. F *socialisme* (as prec.; see -ISM)]

sō'cialīte (-sh*a*-) *n.* Person prominent in fashionable society. [f. SOCIAL + -ITE[1]]

sō'cializ|e (-sh*a*-), **-is|e** (-īz), *v.* **1.** *v.t.* Make social; arrange in socialistic manner; ***~ed medicine,** provision of medical services for all from public funds; hence ~A'TION *n.* **2.** *v.i.* Act in sociable manner. [f. SOCIAL + -IZE]

socī'etў *n.* **1.** Social mode of life, the customs and organization of a civilized nation, (*the progress of society is an evolution*); hence **socī'et**AL *a.* **2.** A social community (*no society can retain members who flout its principles*); (Ecol.) plant community; ***~ finch,** small white weaver-bird. **3.** Members of a community whose movements and entertainments and other doings are more or less conspicuous, the socially distinguished, fashionable, leisured, well-to-do, and well-connected people, (*was welcomed by society*; *the customs of polite society*; *society does not approve*; *leaders of society*; *society people, gossip, news*). **4.** Participation in hospitality, other people's homes or company, (*goes a great deal into, avoids, is at his best* or *embarrassed in, society*). **5.** Companionship, company, (*society and solitude*; *always enjoy his society*; *seek, avoid, the society of*). **6.** Association of persons united by a common aim or interest or principle (**S~ of Friends,** Quakers; **S~ of Jesus,** Jesuits; ||BUILDING *society*; ||FRIENDLY *Society*); **Royal S~,** (**of London,** founded 1662 to promote scientific discussion). [f. F *société* f. L *societas -tatis* (*socius* companion; see -TY[1])]

Socĭ'nĭan *a.* & *n.* (Holder) of the doctrine of the 16th-c. Italian rationalist theologians Laelius and Faustus Socinus, who denied the existence of the Trinity and the divinity of Christ; hence ~ISM (3) *n.* [f. *Socinus*, Latinized f. *Sozzini*, + -IAN]

sōcĭō- (*or* -shĭ-) *comb. form.* Of society or sociology (and), as: **~-cu'ltural,** combining social and cultural factors; **~-econo'mic,** relating to social status and economic position; **~-lingui'stic,** pertaining to language in its social context; **~-linguis'tics,** study of language in relation to social factors. [f. L *socius* companion (cf. SOCIETY) + -O-]

sōcĭŏ'log|ў̆ (*or* -shĭ-) *n.* Science of the development and nature and laws of human (esp. civilized) society; study of social problems; hence **sōcĭo**LO'GICAL (*or* -shĭ-) *a.*, ~IST (3) *n.* [f. F *sociologie* f. as prec. + -LOGY]

sōcĭŏ'mĕtr|y̆ (*or* -shĭ-) *n.* Study of relationships within a group of people; hence **sōcĭomĕ'tr**IC (*or* -shĭ-) *a.*, ~IST (3) *n.* [f. SOCIO- + -METRY]

sŏck[1] *n.* **1.** (*pl.* ~**s** *or* ***sox**). Short stocking not reaching knee; ‖**pull** one's ~**s up,** (colloq.) make an effort; ‖**put a ~ in it,** (sl.) be quiet. **2.** Removable inner sole put into shoe for warmth etc. **3.** Ancient comic actor's light shoe; (fig.) comic drama. [OE *socc*, = OHG *soc*, ON *sokkr*, Gmc f. L *soccus* comic actor's shoe, light low-heeled slipper, f. Gk *sukkhos*]

sŏck[2] *v.t.*, & *n.* (sl.) **1.** *v.t.* Hit (person) with fist or hand-flung missile; ~ **it to,** attack (person) vigorously. **2.** *n.* Blow inflicted by missile or fist; *power to deliver a blow. [*c.* 1700, cant, of unkn. orig.]

***sŏckdŏ'loger, -lager,** *n.* (sl.) Decisive blow or argument; remarkable thing. [19th c., prob. fanciful]

sŏ'ckĕt *n.*, & *v.t.* **1.** *n.* Natural or artificial hollow for something to fit into or stand firm or revolve in (*socket of eye, hip, tooth*; *candle too large for socket*; BALL[1] *and socket*); (Electr.) device receiving plug, light-bulb, etc., to make connection; (Golf) part of iron club into which shaft is fitted. **2.** *v.t.* Place in, fit with, socket; (Golf) hit (ball) with socket of club. [ME f. AF, dim. of OF *soc* ploughshare, prob. of Celt. orig.]

sŏ'ckeye (-kī) *n.* Blue-back salmon of Alaska etc. (*Oncorhynchus nerka*). [f. Salish *sukai* fish of fishes]

sŏ'cle *n.* (Archit.) Plain low block or plinth serving as support for column, vase, statue, etc., or as foundation of wall. [F, f. It. *zoccolo* orig. 'wooden shoe' f. L *socculus* (*soccus* SOCK[1]; see -ULE)]

Socră't|ĭc *a.* & *n.* **1.** *a.* Of, like, following, etc., Socrates, Gk philosopher d. 399 B.C.; *Socratic* ELENCHUS; ~**ic irony,** pose of ignorance assumed in order to confute others by enticing them into display of supposed knowledge; ~**ic method,** dialectic, procedure by questions and answer; hence ~ICALLY *adv.* **2.** *n.* Follower of Socrates. [f. L f. Gk *Sōkratikos* (*Sōkratēs* Socrates; see -IC)]

sŏd[1] *n.*, & *v.t.* (-dd-). **1.** *n.* = TURF 1; **the old ~,** (colloq.) one's native land; **under the ~,** in the grave. **2.** *v.t.* Cover (ground) with sods. [ME, f. MDu., MLG *sode*, = OFris. *sātha, sāda*, of unkn. orig.]

sŏd[2]. See SEETHE.

sŏd[3] *n.* & *v.* (-dd-). **1.** *n.* (vulg., & derog. or joc.) Person, fellow. **2.** *v.t.* (vulg.) = DAMN 2; (in *part.*) = DAMNED 2. **3.** *v.i.* (vulg.) ~ **off,** go away. [abbr. of SODOMITE]

sō'da *n.* **1.** Compound of sodium in common use, esp. the carbonate (**washing-~**), bicarbonate (**baking-~**), or hydroxide (**caustic ~**). **2.** ~(**-water**), water made effervescent by impregnation with carbon dioxide under pressure and used alone or with spirits etc. as a drink (orig. made with sodium bicarbonate; *some soda-water*; *some* or *a brandy and soda*). **3.** ~**-bread** etc. (leavened with baking-soda); ~**-fountain,** vessel in which soda-water is stored under pressure to be drawn out, shop etc. equipped with this apparatus; ***~-jerk(er),** (sl.) attendant at soda-fountain. [med. L, perh. f. *sodanum* glasswort (used as remedy for headaches) f. *soda* headache f. Arab. *ṣudā'* (*ṣada'a* split)]

sodă'lĭtў̆ *n.* Confraternity or association, esp. R.C. religious guild or brotherhood. [f. F *sodalité* or f. L *sodalitas* (*sodalis* comrade; see -ITY)]

sŏ'dden *a.* & *v.* **1.** *a.* Saturated with liquid, soaked through; (of bread etc.) doughy, heavy and moist; stupid or dull in fact or appearance with habitual drunkenness; hence ~NESS (-n-n-) *n.* **2.** *v.i.* & *t.* Become or make sodden. [p.p. of SEETHE]

sō'dĭum *n.* Soft silver-white metallic element, one of the alkali metals, found in soda, salt, and other compounds; ~ **chloride,** common SALT; ~ **lamp** (using electrical discharge in sodium vapour and giving yellow light); hence **sō'd**IC *a.* [f. SODA + -IUM]

Sŏ'dom *n.* (Type of) a wicked town. [~ in ancient Palestine (Gen. 18, 19)]

sŏ'domite *n.* Person practising sodomy. [ME f. OF, f. LL f. Gk *Sodomitēs* inhabitant of Sodom (*Sodoma* Sodom; see -ITE[1])]

sŏ'domў̆ *n.* Anal or other copulation-like act esp. between male persons or between human being and animal. [ME, f. med. L *sodomia* f. LL *peccatum Sodomiticum* sin of SODOM; see -Y[1]]

sōĕ'ver *adv.* (usu. as *suf.* to *rel. prons.*, *advs.*, or *adjs.*) Of any possible kind or extent (*whosoever, howsoever*, etc.; *how great soever it may be*; *with what end soever he did it*). [f. SO[1] + EVER; cf. WHATSOEVER]

sō'fa *n.* Couch with raised ends and back, on which several persons can sit or one lie; ~ **bed,** piece of furniture able to serve as either sofa or bed. [F, ult. f. Arab. *ṣuffa*]

sŏ'ffĭt *n.* Under-surface of architrave, arch, balcony, etc. [f. F *soffite* or It. *soffitta, -itto* f. Rom. **suffictus -a* f. L *suffixus* (as SUFFIX[2])]

S. of S. *abbr.* Song of Songs (O.T.).

sŏft (*or* saw-) *a.*, *n.*, *adv.*, & *int.* **1.** *a.* Comparatively lacking in hardness, yielding to pressure, malleable, plastic, easily cut, (*soft as butter*; *soft toy*; *book in soft cover*; *soft stone, iron*); ***~'ball,** (modified form of baseball using) ball like baseball but softer and larger; ~**-boiled,** (of egg) boiled but not hard-boiled; ~**-centred,** (of a chocolate) with centre having soft consistency; ~ **coal** (bituminous); ~ **corn,** moist thickening of skin between toes; ~ **currency** (not convertible to gold or supported by gold reserves, or not easily exchangeable for other currencies, and therefore likely to depreciate); ~ **detergent** (biodegradable); ‖~ **fruit,** small stoneless fruit (strawberry, currant, etc.); ‖~ **furnishings,** curtains, rugs, etc.; ‖~ **goods,** textiles; ~ **palate,** rear part of palate; ~ **roe** (of male fish); *soft* SAWDER; ~**-shell(ed),** (of crab etc.) having soft shell esp. after recent moult, (fig.) moderate in one's attitude; *soft* SOAP; *soft* SOLDER; ~ **sugar** (granulated or powdered); ~ **tack,** bread or other good fare (opp. HARD *tack*); ~ **tissues** (of body, not bony or cartilaginous); ~**'ware,** programs etc. for computer, or other interchangeable material for performing operations, opp. HARD*ware*; ~ **wicket** (Cricket, with moist or sodden turf); ~**'wood** (of coniferous tree). **2.** Having smooth surface or fine texture, not rough or coarse, (*soft skin, hair, raiment*). **3.** Mellow, mild, balmy, not noticeably cold or hot, (*soft air*; *a soft winter*). **4.** ‖Rainy or moist or thawing (*soft weather*; *a soft day*). **5.** (Of water) free from mineral salts and hence good for washing or cooking. **6.** Not crude or brilliant or dazzling (*soft colours, light, eyes*); not sharply defined (*soft outline*); not strident or loud, low-toned, (*a soft voice*; *soft whispers, murmurs*; *soft music*); ~ **focus,** (Photog.) slight deliberate blurring of picture; *soft* PEDAL[1]; ~**-pedal** *v.i.* & *t.*, play with soft pedal down, tone down, refrain from emphasizing. **7.** (Phonet.) Sibilant (*c is soft in 'ice', and g in 'age'*); voiced or unaspirated. **8.** Gentle, quiet, conciliatory, complimentary or amorous, (*soft rain,* *manners*); (of shares etc.) low-priced; ~ **answer** (esp. good-tempered one to abuse or accusation); ~ **drink** (non-alcoholic); ~ **drug** (not likely to cause addiction); ~ **landing** (in which spacecraft etc. reaches ground without being destroyed); ~ **nothings,** amorous talk; ~ **on,** (colloq.) in love with; ~ **radiation** (with little penetrating power); ~ **sell,** persuasive salesmanship; **~-spoken,** having a soft voice. **9.** Sympathetic, compassionate, (*has a soft heart*); **~-hearted,** easily affected by others' pain or grief; ~ **spot,** sentimental affection *for*. **10.** Tranquil (*soft slumbers*). **11.** (sl.) Easy (*has a soft job*; *a soft option*); *soft* TOUCH² 9. **12.** Flabby, feeble, effeminate, silly, (*the national character has gone soft*; *a soft luxurious people*; *soft muscles*); **~-headed, ~-witted,** half idiotic. **13.** Hence ~'ISH¹ 2 *a.*, ~'LY² *adv.*, ~'NESS *n.* **14.** *n.* Silly weak person. **15.** *adv.* (esp. in *compar.*) Softly (*play soft* or *softer*; *soft-whispering* etc.). **16.** *int.* (arch.) Wait a moment; hush! [OE *sōfte* agreeable, earlier *sēfte* = OS *sāfti*, OHG *semfti* f. WG **samfti*]

sŏ'fta *n.* Muslim student of sacred law and theology. [Turk., f. Pers. *sūkta* burnt, afire]

sŏ'ften (-fen; *or* saw'-) *v.i.* & *t.* Become or make soft or softer; ~ (**up**), reduce strength of (defences) by bombing or other preliminary attack; **~ing** (morbid, esp. senile, degeneration) **of the brain;** hence ~ER¹ (1, 2) *n.* [ME, f. SOFT + -EN⁶]

sŏ'ftie, sŏ'ftў, (*or* saw'-) *n.* = SOFT 14. [f. SOFT + -IE, -Y³]

‖**SOGAT** (sō'găt) *abbr.* Society of Graphical and Allied Trades.

sŏ'gg|ў (-gĭ) *a.* Sodden, saturated, dank; hence ~ĭLY² *adv.*, ~ĭNESS *n.* [f. dial. *sog* a swamp + -Y²]

soh (sō), **sō²,** *n.* (Mus.) Fifth note of scale in movable-doh system; the note G in fixed-doh system. [f. *sol*, ME, f. L *solve*; see GAMUT]

sohō'¹ *int.* announcing discovery e.g. of hare or unexpected event. [ME, f. AF hunting-cry]

Sō'hō² *n.* District of central London with many strip clubs and foreign-style restaurants. [perh. f. prec.]

soi-disant (swahdē'zahṅ) *a.* Self-styled, pretended. [F (*soi* oneself, *disant* saying)]

soigné (swah'nyā) *a.* (*fem.* ~*e pr.* same). Carefully finished or arranged, well-groomed. [p.p. of F *soigner* take care of (*soin* care)]

soil¹ *n.* The ground, upper layer of earth in which plants grow, consisting of disintegrated rock usu. with admixture of organic remains, mould, (*good*, *poor*, *clayey*, *alluvial*, *light*, *rich*, etc., *soil*); ground belonging to (esp. one's own) nation (*on British soil*); ~ **science,** pedology; hence ~'LESS (-l-l-) *a.* [ME f. AF, perh. f. L *solium* seat, taken in sense of L *solum* ground]

soil² *v.t.*, & *n.* **1.** *v.t.* Make dirty, smear or stain with dirt, tarnish, defile, (*soiled linen*; (fig.) *would not soil my hands with it*); so ~'URE *n.* (arch.). **2.** *n.* Dirty mark, stain, smear, defilement; filth, refuse matter, (NIGHT-*soil*). **3.** **~-pipe,** discharge-pipe of water-closet. [ME, f. OF *suill(i)er*, *soill(i)er*, etc., f. Rom. **suculare* f. L *sucula* dim. of *sus* pig]

soil³ *v.t.* Feed (cattle) on fresh-cut green fodder (orig. for purging). [perh. f. prec.]

soirée (swar̄'ā) *n.* Social evening, evening gathering esp. for music, conversation, the advancement of some society's objects, or the like. [F (*soir* evening)]

sŏ'journ (-ẽrn *or* -ern) *v.i.*, & *n.* (Make) temporary stay in or *in* place or *with* or *among* person(s); hence ~ER¹ *n.* [ME, f. OF *so(r)jorn(er)* etc., f. Rom. **subdiurnare* f. LL SUB- + *diurnum* day]

‖**sōke** *n.* (Hist.) Right of local jurisdiction; district under a particular jurisdiction and administration (*Soke of Peterborough*). [ME, f. AL *sōca* f. OE *sōcn* prosecution, = ON *sókn* attack, Goth. *sōkns* inquiry f. Gmc **sōkniz* (**sōk-* SEEK)]

Sŏl¹ *n.* (joc. or Rom. Myth.) The sun (personified). [ME f. L]

sŏl². Var. of SOH.

sŏl³ *n.* Liquid solution or suspension of a colloid. [abbr. of SOLUTION]

sō'la¹ *n.* Pithy-stemmed E. Ind. swamp plant (~ **topi,** Indian sun-helmet made from its pith). [f. Urdu & Bengali *solā*, Hindi *sholā*]

sō'la². See SOLUS.

sŏ'lace *n.*, & *v.t.* Comfort in distress or disappointment or tedium (~ **oneself with,** find compensation or relief in). [ME, f. OF (*solacier* f.) *solas* f. L *solatium* (*solari* CONSOLE¹)]

sō'lan *n.* ~ (**goose**), gannet. [prob. f. ON *súla* gannet + *önd and-* duck]

solă'nder *n.* Book-shaped box for papers, specimens, etc. [f. D. C. *Solander*, Sw. botanist d. 1782]

sō'lar *a.* & *n.* **1.** *a.* Of, concerned with, determined by, the sun (*solar eclipse*, *spectrum*, *time*, YEAR); ~ **battery** or **cell,** device to convert solar radiation into electricity; ~ **constant,** quantity of heat reaching earth from sun; ~ **day,** interval between successive meridian transits of sun at a place; ~ **month,** one-twelfth of solar year; ~ **myth,** tale explained as symbolizing solar phenomena; ~ **plexus,** complex of radiating nerves at pit of stomach; ~ **system,** sun and the heavenly bodies whose motion is governed by it; ~ **wind,** continuous flow of charged particles from sun. **2.** *n.* Solarium; upper chamber in medieval house. [ME, f. L *solaris* (*sol* sun; see -AR¹)]

sō'lar|ĭsm *n.* Belief in solar myths as chief source of mythology; so ~IST (2) *n.* [f. prec. + -ISM]

solar̄'ĭ|um *n.* (*pl.* ~**a**). Place, often enclosed in glass, for enjoyment, or esp. medical use, of sun's rays. [L, = sundial, sunning-place, (as SOLAR; see -ARIUM)]

sō'lariz|e, -īs|e (-īz), *v.i.* & *t.* (Photog.) Cause or undergo change in relative darkness of parts of image by long exposure; hence ~A'TION *n.* [f. SOLAR + -IZE]

solā'tĭ|um (-shĭ-) *n.* (*pl.* ~**a**). Thing given as compensation or consolation. [L, = SOLACE]

sōld. See SELL.

sŏldanĕ'lla *n.* Dwarf Alpine plant of genus *Soldanella*, often with fringed leaves. [mod. L, f. It.]

sŏ'lder *n.*, & *v.t.* **1.** *n.* Fusible alloy used to join edges of less fusible metals (**hard, soft,** ~, fusible at higher, lower, temperature and serving for different metals); (fig.) cementing agency. **2.** *v.t.* Join with solder; **~ing-iron,** tool used hot for applying solder. [ME, f. OF *soudure* (*souder* f. L *solidare* fasten f. *solidus* SOLID; see -URE)]

sō'ldier (-ljer) *n.*, & *v.i.* **1.** *n.* Member of army (lit. or fig.; *soldiers and sailors*; *children play at soldiers*; *tin*, *toy*, *soldier*); OLD *soldier*; ~ **of Christ,** active or proselytizing Christian; ~ **of fortune,** adventurous person ready to take service under any State or person that will hire him; **~'s wind,** (Naut.) fair wind for going in either direction; UNKNOWN *Soldier*. **2.** (**Common**) ~, private or N.C.O. in army (*both officers and soldiers*); PRIVATE *soldier*. **3.** Military commander of specified ability (*a great*, *fine*, *poor*, *soldier*; *no soldier*); hence ~SHIP (3) *n.* **4.** Hence ~-LIKE *a.*, ~LY¹,² *a.* & *adv.* **5.** ~ (**ant**), (1) one of fighting section of ant or termite colony, (2) large red Austral. ant; ~ (**beetle**), reddish-coloured insect of family

Cantharidae, with carnivorous larvae; ~ (**crab**), hermit-crab; ~ (**fish**), (Austral.) small red fish of genus *Apogon*; ~ **orchis,** military orchis. **6.** *v.i.* Serve as soldier (*go soldiering*); (sl.) shirk one's work; ~ **on,** (colloq.) persevere doggedly. [ME *souder* etc., f. OF *soud(i)er, so(l)dier* (*sou(l)de* pay f. L SOLIDUS; see -ARY[1])]

sō'ldierў (-ljerĭ) *n.* *The* soldiers (of a State, in a district, etc.); *a* set of troops of specified character (*a wild, licentious,* etc., *soldiery*). [f. prec. + -Y[1]; cf. -ERY]

sōle[1] *n.*, & *v.t.* **1.** *n.* Lower surface of human or other foot that rests flat on ground in walking or standing; part of shoe, sock, etc., below foot, esp. part other than heel; bottom or foundation or lower surface of plough, carpenter's plane, wagon, golf-club head, etc.; floor of ship's cabin; **~-plate,** bedplate of engine etc.; hence **-sōl**ED[2] (-ld) *a.* **2.** *v.t.* Provide (shoe etc.) with sole. [OE **solu*, **sole*, = OS, OHG *sola* f. pop. L **sola* f. L *solea* sandal]

sōle[2] *n.* Flat-fish of genus *Solea*, much esteemed as food; LEMON[2] *sole*. [ME f. OF, f. Prov. *sola* f. Rom. **sola* f. L *solea* (as prec., named from its shape)]

sōle[3] *a.* One and only, exclusive, (*his sole reason is this*; *he is the sole heir, has the sole right*; *on my own sole responsibility*); (arch. or Law, esp. of woman) unmarried (FEME *sole*); (arch.) alone, unaccompanied, (*went forth sole*); CORPORATION *sole*; hence ~LY[2] (-l-lĭ) *adv.* [ME, f. OF *soule* f. L *sola* fem. of *solus* alone]

sŏ'lėc|ĭsm *n.* Offence against grammar or idiom, blunder in the manner of speaking or writing; piece of bad manners or incorrect behaviour; so ~IST (1) *n.*, **~ĭ'st**IC *a.* [f. F *solécisme* or f. L f. Gk *soloikismos* (*soloikos* speaking incorrectly; see -ISM)]

sŏ'lemn (-m) *a.* Accompanied with religious or other ceremony, done etc. in due form, formally regular, (*solemn feast-day, sacrifice, oath*; *the Solemn League and* COVENANT; *probate in solemn form*); mysteriously impressive (*solemn silence*; *a solemn cathedral*); full of importance, weighty, (*a solemn occasion, truth, warning*); grave, sober, deliberate, slow in movement or action, (*solemn music*; *a solemn promise, solemn looks*; *a solemn pace*); pompous, pretending to gravity or importance, dull, (*put on a solemn face*; *a solemn fool*); ~ **mass,** = *high* MASS[1]; hence ~LY[2] *adv.* [ME f. OF *solem(p)ne*, f. L *so(l)lemnis* customary, celebrated at fixed date (*sollus* entire)]

solĕ'mnĭtў *n.* Rite, celebration, festival, piece of ceremony; being solemn, solemn character or feeling or behaviour. [ME, f. OF *solem(p)nité* f. L *sollem(p)nitas -tatis* (as prec.; see -ITY)]

sŏ'lemnīz|e, -īs|e (-īz), *v.t.* Celebrate (festival etc.); duly perform (marriage ceremony); make solemn; so ~A'TION *n.* [ME, f. OF *solem(p)niser* f. med. L *solem(p)nizare* (as SOLEMN; see -IZE)]

sō'len *n.* Razor-shell esp. of genus *Solen*. [L, f. Gk *sōlēn* tube, shellfish]

sō'lėnoid *n.* Cylindrical coil of wire which, when an electric current is passed through it, behaves as a bar magnet. [f. F *solénoïde* (as prec.; see -OID)]

sŏl-fa' (-ah') *v.i.* & *t.*, & *n.* = SOLMIZATE, SOLMIZATION; TONIC *sol-fa*. [f. SOL[2] + FA]

sŏlfatār'a *n.* Volcanic vent emitting only sulphurous and other vapours. [name of volcano near Naples, f. It. *solfo* sulphur]

sŏlfĕ'gg|iō (-jō) *n.* (*pl.* **~i** *pr.* -jē). Solmization, sol-fa; sol-fa exercise for voice. [It., (as SOL-FA)]

soli. See SOLO.

solĭ'cĭt *v.* **1.** *v.t.* Invite, make appeals or requests to, importune, ask importunately or earnestly for, (*events solicit his attention*; *we solicit your custom, you for your custom*; *was known to have solicited the judges*); (of prostitute) accost (man, or abs.) for immoral purpose. **2.** *v.i.* Make request or petition (*for*). **3.** So ~A'TION *n.* [ME, f. OF *solliciter* f. L *sollicitare* agitate (*sollicitus* anxious f. *sollus* entire + *citus* p.p. set in motion)]

solĭ'cĭtor *n.* **1.** One who solicits; *canvasser. **2.** ||Member of the legal profession qualified to advise clients and instruct barristers but not to appear as advocate except in certain lower courts; *law officer of city etc.; **S~-General,** ||Crown law officer below Attorney-General (in Scotland below Lord Advocate), *law officer below Attorney-General. [ME, f. OF *solliciteur* (as prec.; see -OR)]

solĭ'cĭtous *a.* Eager *to* do; desirous *of*; anxious, troubled, (*about, for,* etc., or abs.); hence ~LY[2] *adv.* [f. L *sollicitus* (see SOLICIT, -OUS)]

solĭ'cĭtūde *n.* Being solicitous; anxiety, concern. [ME, f. OF *sollicitude* f. L *sollicitudo* (as prec.; see -TUDE)]

sŏ'lĭd *a.* & *n.* **1.** *a.* Of stable shape, not liquid or fluid, having some rigidity, (*solid food*; *water becomes solid at 0°C*); ~ **solution,** solid material containing one substance uniformly distributed in another; ~ **state,** state of matter that retains its boundaries without support; **~-state** *a.*, (esp.) using electronic properties of solids to replace those of valves. **2.** Of solid substance throughout, not hollow, without internal cavities or interstices, uninterrupted, whole, (*solid sphere or ball*); (of tyre) without central tube; (of printing) without spaces between words or without leads between lines; (colloq., of time) complete, uninterrupted, (*worked for two solid hours at it*); **~-drawn,** (of tube etc.) pressed or drawn out from solid bar of metal. **3.** Strongly constructed, not flimsy, (*solid house, pier, furniture*; *man of solid build*). **4.** Homogeneous, alike all through, (*of solid silver* etc.); (fig.) staunch, reliable, (*a solid Tory*); *(colloq.) on good terms *with*; ~ **colour** (covering the whole of an object, without pattern etc.); ~ **vote** etc. (unanimous, undivided); **go** or **be ~ for,** be united in favour of. **5.** Well grounded, sound, reliable, real, genuine, not fancied or pretended or showy, (*solid reasons, arguments, sense, comfort*); (of person or his work) sensible but not brilliant; of sound financial position. **6.** Of three dimensions; cubic (foot etc.); ~ **angle** (formed by planes etc. meeting at point). **7.** Concerned with solids (*solid geometry*; *solid measure*). **8.** Hence or cogn. **solĭ'dĭ**FY *v.t.* & *i.*, **solĭdĭ**FICA'TION *n.*, **solĭ'd**ITY *n.*, ~LY[2] *adv.* **9.** *n.* Solid substance or body; (Geom.) body or magnitude having three dimensions (REGULAR *solid*); (in *pl.*) solid food. [ME; a. f. OF *solide* or f. L *solidus* rel. to *salvus* safe, *sollus* entire; n. f. F *solide* f. L *solidum* neut. (as n.) of *solidus*]

sŏlĭdă'rĭtў *n.* Holding together, mutual dependence, community of interests, feelings, and action. [f. F *solidarité* (*solidaire* f. *solide* = prec.; see -ARY[1], -ITY)]

solĭdŭ'ngūlate (-ngg-) *a.* (Zool.) Solid-hoofed, of horse family. [f. L *solidus* solid + *ungulatus* ungulate; see -ATE[2]]

sŏ'lĭd|us *n.* (*pl.* **~i** *pr.* -ī). **1.** (Hist.) Gold coin introduced by Roman Emperor Constantine. **2.** Oblique stroke / used in writing fractions (*3/4*), or to denote alternatives (*and/or*), ratios (*miles/day*), shillings (*7/6*), etc. **3.** ~ (**curve**), curve in graph of temperature and composition of a mixture, below which the substance is entirely solid. [ME, f. L (see SOLID)]

sōlĭfĭ'dĭan *a.* & *n.* (Holder) of doctrine that faith by itself suffices for salvation. [f. mod. L *solifidius* f. L *solus* alone + -I- + *fides* faith, + -IAN]

sŏlĭflŭ'ction *n.* Gradual movement of wet soil

etc. down slope. [f. L *solum* soil + -I- + L *fluctio* flowing (*fluere fluct-* flow; see -ION)]

solĭ'loqu|ȳ *n.* Talking without, or regardless of the presence of, hearers; piece of this esp. by character in play; hence ~IST (1) *n.*, ~IZE (2) *v.i.* [f. LL *soliloquium* f. L *solus* alone + -I- + *loqui* speak]

sŏ'lĭpĕd *a.* & *n.* Solidungulate (animal). [f. F *solipède* or mod. L *solipes -pedis* f. L *solidipes* (*solidus* solid, *pes* foot)]

solĭ'ps|ĭsm (*or* sŏ'-) *n.* (Metaphys.) View that the self is the only knowable, or the only existent, thing; so ~IST (2) *n.* [f. L *solus* alone + *ipse* self + -ISM]

sŏlĭtair'e *n.* Diamond or other gem set by itself; ear-ring etc. having a single gem; game played on special board by one person with marbles etc. removed one at a time by jumping others over them; * = PATIENCE 2; extinct bird like dodo; Amer. thrush of genus *Myadestes*; (arch.) = foll. 2. [F, f. L *solitarius* (see foll.)]

sŏ'lĭtar|ȳ *a.* & *n.* **1.** *a.* Living alone, not gregarious, without companions, unfrequented, secluded, single, lonely, sole, (*a solitary life, walk, valley, instance*); (of insect) not living in communities; **~y confinement,** isolation in separate cell as punishment; hence ~ĭLY[2] *adv.*, ~ĭNESS *n.* **2.** *n.* Recluse, anchorite. **3.** (sl.) Solitary confinement. [ME, f. L *solitarius* (*solus* alone; see -ARY[1])]

sŏ'lĭtūde *n.* Being solitary; lonely place. [ME f. OF, or f. L *solitudo* (*solus* alone; see -TUDE)]

sŏlmĭzā'tion *n.* (Mus.) System of associating each note of scale with particular syllable, now usu. *doh ray me fah soh lah te*, in fixed-doh system C always being doh and other syllables accordingly, in movable-doh or tonic sol-fa system key-note always being doh and other syllables accordingly; so **sŏ'lmĭz**ATE[3] *v.i.* & *t.* [f. F *solmisation* (as SOL[2], MI, -IZE, -ATION)]

sō'lō *n.* (*pl.* **~s** *or, in sense 1,* **so'li** *pr.* -ē), *a.*, & *adv.* **1.** *n.* Vocal or instrumental piece or passage, or dance, performed by one person with or without subordinate accompaniment; hence ~IST (1) *n.* **2.** ~ **(whist)**, card-game like whist in which one player may oppose the others; declaration or playing to win five tricks at this. **3.** An unaccompanied flight by pilot in aircraft. **4.** *a.* Performed as solo; ~ **stop,** organ-stop especially suitable for imitating solo performance on another instrument. **5.** *a.* & *adv.* Unaccompanied, alone, (*for solo flute*; *solo flight*; *flying solo*). [It., f. L *solus* alone]

Sŏ'lomon *n.* **1.** Profoundly wise person; **is no ~**, (iron.) is stupid; hence **Sŏlomŏ'n**IC *a.* **2. Judgement of ~** (see 2 Kgs. 3:16–28); **~'s seal,** (1) figure like Star of David, (2) plant of genus *Polygonatum*, esp. one with drooping green and white flowers; SONG *of Solomon*. [~, king of Israel in 10th c. B.C., famed for his wisdom]

Sō'lon *n.* Sage; wise legislator. [f. *Solon*, Athenian lawgiver d. *c.* 558 B.C.]

sŏ'lstĭce *n.* **1.** Either time (**summer, winter,** ~, about 21 June, 22 Dec.) at which sun is farthest from equator and appears to pause before returning. **2.** Point in ecliptic reached by sun at solstice. **3.** So **sŏlstĭ'tɪ**AL (-shal) *a.* [ME f. OF, f. L *solstitium* (*sol* sun, *sistere stit-* make stand)]

sŏ'lūbĭlĭz|e, -ĭs|e (-īz), *v.t.* Make (more) soluble; hence ~A'TION *n.* [f. SOLUBILITY + -IZE, after *stabilize*]

sŏ'lūble *a.* That can be dissolved (*in* liquid etc., esp. in water); that can be solved; **~ glass,** = WATER[1]-*glass* (2); hence **sŏlu**BI'LITY *n.* [ME f. OF, f. LL *solubilis* (as SOLVE; see -UBLE)]

sō'l|us *pred. a.* (*fem.* **~a**). Alone, unaccompanied, (esp. in stage direction: *enter king, solus,* or joc.: *found myself solus*). [L]

sŏ'lūte *n.* Dissolved substance. [f. L *solutum*, neut. (as n.) of *solutus* (see SOLVE)]

solū'tion (*or* -lōō'-) *n.* **1.** Dissolving or being dissolved, esp. conversion of solid or gas into liquid form by mixture with liquid solvent; state resulting from this (*held in solution*); liquid etc. and solid or gas so mixed (*a solution of alum*); = RUBBER[2] *solution*; SOLID *solution*. **2.** Resolution, solving, explanation, method for the solving, *of, for, to*, a problem, puzzle, question, doubt, difficulty, etc. **3.** Separating, breaking; **~ of continuity,** breach, interruption, (Med.) separation of normally contiguous parts. [ME f. OF, f. L *solutio -onis* (as SOLVE; see -ION)]

Solū'trėan, -ĭan, (*or* -lōō'-) *a.* & *n.* (Culture) of the palaeolithic period in Europe following the Aurignacian and preceding the Magdalenian. [f. *Solutré* in E. France, where remains of it were found, + -AN, -IAN]

sŏ'lv|āte *v.t.* & *i.* (Cause to) enter into combination with solvent; hence ~A'TION *n.* [f. foll. + -ATE[3]]

sŏlve *v.t.* Find answer to (problem, puzzle) or way out of (difficulty); (arch.) loosen, unravel, dissolve, (knot, tangle, cohesion, etc.); hence **sŏ'lv**ABLE *a.*, **sŏ'lv**ER[1] *n.* [ME, = loosen, f. L *solvere solut-* unfasten, release]

sŏ'lv|ent *a.* & *n.* **1.** *a.* Having the power of dissolving or forming a solution with something; (fig.) weakening the hold of traditions or beliefs; having money enough to meet all pecuniary liabilities, whence ~ENCY *n.* **2.** *n.* Solvent liquid etc. (*water is the commonest solvent*; *alcohol is a solvent of resinous substances*); dissolving or weakening agent (*science as a solvent of superstition*). [f. as prec.; see -ENT]

-som. See -SOME[1].

Som. *abbr.* Somerset.

sō'ma[1] *n.* Body as opp. soul; body other than germ-cells. [f. Gk *sōma -atos* body]

sō'ma[2] *n.* Intoxicating drink used in Vedic ritual; plant yielding it. [f. Skr. *sōma*]

Soma'lĭ (-ah'-) *a.* & *n.* (Member or language) of Hamitic Muslim people of Somalia. [native name]

somă'tĭc *a.* Of the body, corporeal, physical, (opp. *mental, spiritual, psychic*); **~ cell,** body cell as opp. germ-cell; **~ death** (of the body as a whole). [f. Gk *sōmatikos* (as SOMA[1]; see -IC)]

sō'mato- *comb. form.* (The human) body, as: ~GE'NIC, originating in the body; ~LOGY (-ŏ'l-), science of living bodies physically considered; **~to'nic,** like mesomorph in temperament, with predominantly physical interests; **~type,** physique expressed in relation to various extreme types. [f. as SOMA[1] + -O-]

sŏ'mbre (-ber), ***sŏ'mber,** *a.* Dark, gloomy, dismal, (*a sombre sky, prospect*; *man of sombre character*); hence ~LY[2] *adv.*, ~NESS *n.*, **sŏ'mbr**OUS *a.* (literary). [F *sombre* f. OF *sombre* n. f. Rom. *subombrare* f. L SUB- + *umbra* shade]

sŏmbrer'ō (-ār'ō) *n.* (*pl.* **~s**). Broad-brimmed felt or straw hat worn esp. in S.W. of U.S. [Sp. (*sombra* shade, f. as prec.)]

some (sŭm *or* sum) *a., pron.,* & *adv.* **1.** *a.* & *pron.* Particular but unknown or unspecified (person or thing), (*some fool has locked the door*; *saw it in some book (or other)*; *will tell you some day*; *is true to some extent*; *ask some experienced person*; *some (people) say yes and some* (or *others* or *other people*) *say no*). **2.** A certain quantity or number of (thing) (*drink some water*; *eat some bread*; *buy some apples*; *I have some already*; *have some more*; *some* (but not all) *of it is spoilt*; *some* (but not all) *of them were late*; *if I find some I will send them*); **and the'n ~,** (sl.) and (plenty) more than that. **3.** *a.* **~ (little, small,** etc.), an appreciable or considerable quantity of (*went some miles out of our* *way; had some (little) trouble in arranging it; have been waiting (for) some time; some years ago; that is some help*). **4.** Such to a certain extent (*that is some guide, test, proof*); (U.S. or sl.) such in the fullest sense, truly worthy of the name, (*this is some war; I call that some poem*). **5.** (Usu. stressed) at least a small amount of (*do have some mercy on our nerves; has after all some sense of decency*). **6.** Approximately so many or much of (thing) (*waited some 20 minutes; weighs some 15 stone; we were some dozen, 60, in all*). **7.** *adv.* (colloq.) In some degree (*we talked some; do it some more*). [OE *sum*, = OS, OHG *sum*, ON *sumr*, Goth. *sums* f. Gmc **sumaz* f. IE **smmos*]

-some[1], **-som,** *suf.* **1.** Forming *adjs.* (1) f. *ns.*, w. sense 'adapted to, productive of' (*gamesome, cuddlesome, quarrelsome, fearsome*), (2) f. *adjs.*, w. sense 'characterized by being' (*lithesome, lissom, blithesome, fulsome*), (3) f. transitive *vbs.*, w. sense 'apt to' (*tiresome, winsome, wearisome*). [OE *-sum*, = OS, OHG *-sam*, ON *-samr*, Goth. **-sams*]

-some[2] *suf.* forming *ns.* f. numerals w. sense 'group of' (*foursome*). [OE *sum* (see prec.) after numerals in gen. pl.]

-sōme[3] *suf.* (Biol.) denoting portion of a body, esp. of a cell, (*chromosome, ribosome*). [f. Gk *sōma* body]

so'mebodў (sŭ'mb-) *n.* & *pron.* Some person; a person of importance. [ME, f. SOME + BODY (= person)]

so'mehow (sŭ'mh-) *adv.* In some unspecified or unexplained manner, for some reason or other, (*he somehow dropped behind; somehow or other I never liked him*); no matter how (*must get it finished somehow*). [f. SOME + HOW]

so'meone (sŭ'mwŭn; *or -un*) *n.* & *pron.* Somebody. [ME, f. SOME + ONE]

***so'meplāce** (sŭ'mp-) *adv.* Somewhere. [f. SOME + PLACE[1]]

so'mersault (sŭ'-; *or* -ŏlt) *n.*, & *v.i.* **1.** *n.* Acrobatic movement in which person turns head over heels in the air or on the ground and lands on feet; **turn a ~,** perform this. **2.** *v.i.* Perform somersault. [f. OF *sombresau(l)t* alt. f. *sobresault* f. Prov. **sobresaut* f. L *supra* above + *saltus* leap (*salire* to leap)]

so'methĭng (sŭ'mth-) *n.*, *pron.*, & *adv.* **1.** *n.* & *pron.* Some thing (*have something to tell you; has lost something or other; his temper is something awful*); **~ (or other)** (as substitute for unknown or forgotten description: *she is a lecturer in something or other; he is something in the City*); some quantity etc. of thing expressed or understood (*have seen something of his work; there is something* (of truth etc.) *in what you say; take a drop of something* (liquor); *has something* (impressive) *about him; it is something* (praiseworthy etc.) *to have got so far; you have something* (a valid point) *there*); an important thing (*thinks himself something; the party was quite something*). **2.** *adv.* (arch.) In some degree (*was something impatient, troubled*). **3. Or ~,** or some unspecified alternative possibility (*has lost a glove or something; is called a 'strike-out' or something; must have run away or something*); **see ~ of,** meet (person) for short time or occasionally; **~ like,** approximately (*he left something like a million*), a thing like, somewhat like (*it is something like a cross between a rabbit and a cat; shaped something like a cigar*); **~ li'ke,** (colloq.) impressive, a fine specimen of; **~ of,** to some extent, in some sense, (*is something of an expert on dogs*). [OE *sum thing* (as SOME, THING)]

so'metīme (sŭ'mt-) *adv.* & *a.* Former(ly) (*was sometime mayor of this city; the sometime sheriff*). [f. SOME + TIME[1]]

so'metimes (sŭ'mtīmz) *adv.* At some times (*have sometimes thought about it; is sometimes hot and sometimes cold*). [f. SOME + TIME[1] + -S[1]]

so'mewhat (sŭ'mwŏt) *n.* & *adv.* **1.** *n.* (arch.) Something (*loses somewhat of its force*). **2.** *adv.* In some degree (*it is somewhat difficult; answered somewhat hastily*); **more than ~,** (colloq.) very (*was more than somewhat perplexed*). [ME, f. SOME + WHAT]

so'mewhĕn (sŭ'mw-) *adv.* At some time. [ME, f. SOME + WHEN]

so'mewhere (sŭ'mwār) *adv.* & *pron.* (In or to) some place; (euphem.) in hell etc. (*will see him somewhere first*); **~ about,** approximately; **get ~,** (sl.) achieve success. [ME, f. SOME + WHERE]

sō'mīte *n.* Each body-division of a segmented animal; hence **sōmĭ'tic** *a.* [f. Gk *sōma* body + -ITE[1] (2)]

sŏmnă'mbūl|ĭsm *n.* Sleep-walking; condition of brain inducing this; so **~ANT** *a.*, **~IST** (3) *n.* [f. L *somnus* sleep + *ambulare* walk + -ISM]

sŏmnĭ'ferous *a.* Inducing sleep, soporific. [f. L *somnifer* (*somnium* dream; see -FEROUS)]

sŏ'mnol|ent *a.* Sleepy, drowsy; inducing drowsiness; (Path.) in state between sleeping and waking; hence or cogn. **~ENCE, ~ENCY,** *ns.*, **~entLY**[2] *adv.* [ME, f. OF *sompnolent* or f. L *somnolentus* (*somnus* sleep; see -LENT)]

son (sŭn) *n.* **1.** Male child in relation to his parents; **~ and heir,** (esp.) eldest son; **~-in-law,** daughter's husband; *he is* **his father's ~,** like, or worthy of, his father. **2. The Son of Man,** (N.T.) Christ, the Messiah, (O.T.) descendant of Adam, esp. as form of address in Ezekiel; **the ~s of men,** mankind; **the Son (of God),** Second Person of the Trinity; **~ of God,** (1) angel, (2) person spiritually attached to God. **3. ~ of a bitch,** (vulg.) disliked person or thing; *son of a* GUN; (*every*) MOTHER[1]*'s son.* **4.** Male descendant, male member of family, nation, etc. **5.** (**My**) **~** (as form of address esp. by old man to young man, confessor to penitent, etc.). **6.** Person viewed as inheriting an occupation, quality, etc., (*sons of toil, freedom, darkness,* etc.); **~ of the soil,** native of a district, worker on the land, dweller in the country. **7.** Hence **~'LESS** *a.*, **~'SHIP** *n.* [OE *sunu*, = OS, OHG *sunu*, ON *sunr, sonr*, Goth. *sunus* f. Gmc **sunuz*]

sō'n|ant *a.* & *n.* (Phonet.) (Sound) accompanied by vocal vibration, voiced, (e.g. *b, d, g, v, z*); hence **~ANCY** *n.* [f. L *sonare* sound; see -ANT]

sō'nār *n.* System for underwater detection of objects by reflected or emitted sound; apparatus for this. [f. *so*und *na*vigation (and) *r*anging, after *radar*]

sona'ta (-nah'-) *n.* (Mus.) Composition for one instrument (e.g. piano) or two (e.g. piano and violin), normally with three or four movements (one or more being usu. in sonata form) contrasted in rhythm and speed but related in key; **~ form,** type of composition in which two themes ('subjects') are successively set forth, developed, and restated. [It., fem. p.p. of *sonare* sound]

sŏnati'na (-tē'-) *n.* Simple or short sonata. [It., dim. of prec.]

sŏnde *n.* Device sent up to obtain information about atmospheric conditions, esp. RADIO*sonde*. [F, = sounding(-line)]

sōne *n.* Unit of subjective loudness, equal to 40 phons. [f. L *sonus* sound]

son et lumière (sŏn ā lōō'myār) *n.* Entertainment given by night at historic building etc. with recorded sound and lighting effects to give dramatic narrative of its history. [F, = sound and light]

sŏng *n.* **1.** Singing, vocal music, (*burst forth into song*); musical cry of some birds. **2.** Short poem set to music or meant to be sung; short poem in rhymed stanzas; poetry, verse, (*renowned in* *song*); (Mus.) composition suggestive of a song (*Mendelssohn's 'Songs without Words'*). **3. For a ~** or **an old ~,** very cheaply; **nothing to make a ~ about,** (colloq.) of very trifling importance; **~ and dance,** (colloq.) rigmarole, commotion; **S~ of Degrees** or **Ascents** (in O.T., Psalms 120–134; name variously explained); **S~ of S~s, S~ of Solomon,** poetic O.T. book traditionally attributed to Solomon. **4. ~-bird** (with musical cry); **~-book,** collection of songs; *song*-CYCLE; **~-smith,** composer of songs; **~-sparrow,** N. Amer. sparrow of genus *Melospiza*; *song*-THRUSH[1]. **5.** Hence **~'LESS** *a.* [OE *sang*, = OS *sang*, OHG *sanc*, ON *songr*, Goth. *saggws* f. Gmc **sangwaz* f. as SING]

sŏ'ngst|er *n.* Singer; song-bird; poet; *song-book; hence **~RESS**[1] *n.* [OE *sangestre* (as prec., -STER)]

sŏ'nĭc *a.* Of or relating to or using sound or sound-waves; **~ bang** or **boom,** loud noise heard when shock wave from supersonic aircraft reaches hearer; **~ barrier,** = SOUND[2] *barrier*; **~ mine** (exploded by sound of ship). [f. L *sonus* sound + -IC]

sŏ'nnėt *n.* Poem of 14 lines with lengths and rhymes in accordance with one of various definite schemes, in English usu. having 10 syllables per line and rhyming *abbaabba* + varying sestet of 3 rhymes, or *ababcdcdefefgg*, or *ababbcbccdcdee*; **~ sequence,** set of sonnets on one theme; so **~EER'**, (usu. derog.) (*n.*) composer of sonnets, (*v.i.*) compose sonnets, (*v.t.*) celebrate in sonnets, address sonnets to. [F, or f. It. *sonetto* dim. of *suono* SOUND[2]; see -ET[1]]

so'nnў (sŭ'-) *n.* (colloq., as familiar form of address to) boy or younger man. [f. SON + -Y[3]]

sō'nobuoy (-boi) *n.* Buoy for detecting underwater sounds and transmitting them by radio. [f. L *sonus* sound + -O- + BUOY[1]]

sonofabitch. Var. of SON *of a bitch*.

sonŏ'mėter *n.* Instrument for measuring vibration frequency of string etc.; audiometer. [f. L *sonus* sound + -O- + -METER]

sonōr'ous (*or* sŏ'ner-) *a.* Resonant; loud-sounding; (of speech, style, etc.) pretentious, imposing; hence or cogn. **sonŏ'RITY, ~NESS,** *ns.*, **~LY**[2] *adv.* [f. L *sonorus* (*sonor* sound) + -OUS]

sŏ'nsў, sŏ'nsie, *a.* (Sc.) Plump, buxom; of cheerful disposition (*sonsy lass*); bringing good fortune. [ult. f. Ir. & Gael. *sonas* good fortune (*sona* fortunate); see -Y[2]]

sōōl *v.t.* (Austral.) Set (dog) to attack; (of dog) worry (animal). [f. (now dial.) *sowl*, 17th c., of unkn. orig.]

sōōn *adv.* **1.** Not long after the present time or time in question or *after* specified time, in a short time, (*shall soon know the result*; *was soon convinced of his error*; *arrived soon after four*, *soon after the gate was closed*; *least said soonest mended*). **2. As** (or **so,** esp. after neg. or when causality or other close connection is suggested) **~ as,** at the moment that, not later than, as early as, (*came as* (or *so*) *soon as I heard of it*; *he will get there as soon as they* (*do*); *did not arrive so* (or *as*) *soon as I expected*; *drops his fine theories so* (or *as*) *soon as they clash with his interests*; *as soon as* (*ever*) *there is any talk of paying he cools down*). **3.** (With expressed or implied comparison) willingly (*I would just as soon stay at home* (*as go*); *would sooner die than let him* (or *than that he should*) *find it out*; *which would you sooner* or *soonest do?*). **4.** Early (*what makes you come so soon?*; *you spoke too soon*); **no ~er . . . than,** at the very moment that (*no sooner said than done*, it was done the moment it was proposed etc.); **~ or late, ~er or later,** at some future time, eventually. **5.** Hence **~'ISH**[1] 2 *adv.* [OE *sōna*, = OS, OHG *sān* f. WG **sǣno*]

sōōt *n.*, & *v.t.* **1.** *n.* Black carbonaceous substance rising in fine flakes in the smoke of wood, coal, oil, etc., and deposited on sides of chimney etc. **2.** *v.t.* Cover with soot. [OE *sōt*, = MLG *sōt*, MDu. *soet*, ON *sót* f. Gmc **sōtam* that which settles]

sōō'terkĭn *n.* (arch.) Dutch woman's afterbirth allegedly produced by sitting over stove; (fig.) abortive scheme, imperfect literary composition. [perh. f. prec.; cf. obs. *sooterkin* sweetheart, app. f. early Du. **soetekijn* (*soet* sweet)]

sōōth *n.* (arch.) Truth, fact; **in** (**good**) **~,** really, truly. [OE *sōth*, orig. a. = true, = OS *sōth*, ON *sannr*, *sathr* f. Gmc **santhaz* f. IE **sontos*]

sōōthe (-dh) *v.t.* Calm (person, nerves, passions); soften, mitigate, (pain); flatter, humour, (person, his vanity). [OE *sōthian* verify (*sōth* true; see prec.)]

sōō'thfast (-ah-) *a.* (arch.) Truthful; true; loyal, steadfast. [OE *sōthfæst* (as SOOTH, FAST[3]); cf. *steadfast*]

sōō'thsayer *n.* **1.** One who foretells the future; diviner; hence **sōō'thsay** *v.i.* **2.** Mantis. [ME, f. SOOTH + *sayer* (SAY[2], -ER[1])]

sōō't|ў *a.* Covered with or full of soot; (esp. of animal or bird) coloured like soot, brownish-black, (*sooty albatross*, *kangaroo*, *tern*); hence **~ĬLY**[2] *adv.*, **~ĬNESS** *n.* [ME, f. SOOT + -Y[2]]

sŏp *n.* & *v.* (**-pp-**). **1.** *n.* Piece of bread etc. dipped or steeped in liquid before being eaten or cooked; MILK[1]*sop*; something given (*to* formidable or troublesome animal, person, etc., esp. *to* CERBERUS) to pacify, bribe. **2.** *v.t.* Soak (bread etc. in liquid); take *up* (water etc.) by absorption in towel etc.; wet thoroughly. **3.** *v.i.* Be drenched (*am sopping with rain*; *clothes are sopping wet*). [OE *sopp*, corresp. to MLG *soppe*, OHG *sopfa* bread and milk, prob. f. weak grade of base of OE *sūpan* SUP]

***sŏph** *n.* (colloq.) Sophomore. [abbr.]

sŏ'phĭsm *n.* False argument, esp. one intended to deceive (cf. PARALOGISM). [ME, f. OF *sophime* f. L f. Gk *sophisma* clever device (*sophizomai* become wise f. *sophos* wise; see -ISM)]

sŏ'phĭst *n.* **1.** Captious or fallacious reasoner, quibbler. **2.** (Gk Ant.) Paid teacher of philosophy and rhetoric. **3.** So **sophĭ'stIC(AL)** *adjs.*, **~RY** (4, 5) *n.* [f. L f. Gk *sophistēs* (*sophizomai*; see prec., -IST)]

sŏ'phĭster *n.* = prec. 1; (esp. Hist.) student of varying seniority at some English and American universities. [ME, f. OF *sophistre* f. L (as prec.)]

sophĭ'stĭc|āte[1] *v.* **1.** *v.t.* Involve (subject) in sophistry; mislead (person) thus. **2.** Deprive (person, thing) of natural simplicity, make artificial by worldly experience etc.; (in *p.p.*, of person) worldly-wise, cultured. **3.** Tamper with (text etc.) for purposes of argument etc.; adulterate (wine etc.). **4.** (In *p.p.*, of equipment, techniques, etc.) elaborate, using advanced methods, highly developed or complicated. **5.** *v.i.* Use sophistry. **6.** So **~A'TION** *n.* [f. med. L *sophisticare* tamper with (*sophisticus* f. *sophista*; see SOPHIST, -ATE[3])]

sophĭ'stĭcate[2] *a.* & *n.* Sophisticated (person). [f. med. L *sophisticatus* p.p. of *sophisticare* (as prec.; see -ATE[2])]

***sŏ'phomōr|e** *n.* Second-year university or high-school student; hence **~IC** (-ŏ'r-) *a.* [app. f. *sophom* obs. var. of SOPHISM + -OR]

Sō'phў *n.* (Hist.) Ruler of Persia in 16th–17th c. [f. Pers. *ṣafī* surname of dynasty, f. Arab *ṣafī-ud-dīn* pure of religion, title of founder's ancestor]

sŏpor|ĭ'fĭc *a.* & *n.* (Drug) tending to produce sleep; so **~ĭ'FEROUS** *a.* [f. L *sopor* sleep + -I- + -FIC]

sŏ'pp|ў *a.* Soaked with water; ||(colloq.) mawkishly sentimental (**~ on,** foolishly enamoured of); hence **~ĬNESS** *n.* [f. SOP + -Y[2]]

sōpranī'nō (-nē'-) *n.* (*pl.* **~s**). (Mus.) Instrument higher than soprano, occas. added to group of recorders etc. [It., dim. of foll.]

sopra'n|ō (-rah'-) *n.* (*pl.* **~os,** *or* **~i** *pr.* -ē). (Mus.) Highest female or boy's voice, treble; singer with soprano voice; part written for soprano voice; (usu.) highest-pitched member of a group of similar instruments; **~o clef** (placing middle C on lowest line of staff); hence ~IST (3) *n.*, (esp.) male adult singer retaining boy's soprano voice. [It. (*sopra* above f. L *supra*)]

sôr'a *n.* **~ (rail)**, bird frequenting marshes of N. & S. Carolina etc. in autumn and used as food. [prob. native name]

sôrb[1] *n.* = SERVICE[2] *tree*; **~(-apple)**, its fruit. [f. F *sorbe* or f. L *sorbus* service tree, *sorbum* service-berry]

Sôrb[2] *n.* = WEND[2]; hence ~'IAN *a.* & *n.* [f. G *Sorbe* var. of *Serbe* SERB]

sôrbėfā'cient (-shent) *a.* & *n.* (Med.) (Drug etc.) causing absorption. [f. L *sorbēre* suck in + -FACIENT]

sôr'bėt *n.* Flavoured water-ice; sherbet. [F, f. It. *sorbetto* f. Turk. *şerbet*, f. Arab. *šarba* drink; cf. SHERBET]

||**sôr'bō** *n.* (*pl.* **~s**). **~ (rubber)**, sponge rubber. [f. ABSORB + -O]

sôr'cer|er *n.* User of magic arts, wizard, enchanter (lit. or fig.); so ~ESS[1], **sôr'c**ERY (4, 5), *ns.* [f. obs. *sorcer* f. OF *sorcier* f. Rom. **sortiarius* caster of lots (*sors sortis* lot; see -ARY[1]), + -ER[1]]

sôr'dĭd *a.* Mean, niggardly; ignoble, base; mercenary; dirty, squalid; dull-coloured; hence ~LY[2] *adv.*, ~NESS *n.* [f. F *sordide* or f. L *sordidus* (*sordēre* be dirty; see -ID[1])]

sôrdi'n|ō (-ē'-) *n.* (*pl.* **~i** *pr.* -ē). (Mus.) Mute for bowed or wind instrument. [It. (*sordo* mute f. L *surdus*)]

sôr'dor *n.* Sordidness. [f. SORDID after *squalor*]

sôre *a.*, *n.*, & *adv.* **1.** *a.* (Of part of body) causing pain from injury or disease (*has a sore arm*; FOOT[1]-*sore*; *sore* THROAT; *touched him on a sore place*, lit. or fig.); (of person) suffering pain; *a* SIGHT[1] *for sore eyes*; *like a* BEAR[1] *with a sore head*; ***~'head,** grumpy person; STICK[1] *out like a sore thumb*. **2.** Irritated, aggrieved, touchy, (*is very sore about his defeat*); *vexed (*at*); arousing painful feelings, irritating, (*a sore point, subject*). **3.** Distressing, grievous, severe, (arch. or poet.) (*in sore distress*; *a sore struggle*; *affliction sore long time he bore*); hence ~'LY[2] (sôr'lĭ) *adv.* **4.** Hence ~'NESS (sôr'n-) *n.* **5.** *n.* Sore place on body e.g. where skin or flesh is bruised or inflamed; (fig.) sore subject, painful memory, (*reopen old sores*). **6.** *adv.* (arch.) Grievously, severely, (*sore oppressed*, *afflicted*). [OE *sār*, n. & a., *sāre* adv., = OS, OHG *sēro*, ON *sár* n., *sárr* a., Goth. *sair* n., f. Gmc **sairam*, *sairaz*]

||**sō'rel** *n.* Male fallow deer in third year. [var. of SORREL[2]]

sôr'ghum (-gum) *n.* Tropical cereal grass of genus *Sorghum*, e.g. durra. [mod. L, f. It. *sorgo*, perh. f. Rom. **syricum* (*gramen*) Syrian (grass)]

sorī'tēs (-z) *n.* (*pl.* same). Series of propositions in which predicate of each is subject of next; form of sophism leading by gradual steps from truth to absurdity and based on the absence of precise, esp. numerical, limits to terms such as 'heap'; hence **sorĭ't**ICAL *a.* [L f. Gk *sōreitēs* in heaps (*sōros* heap)]

sôrn *v.i.* (Sc.) Obtrude oneself *on* (person) for bed and board; hence ~'ER[1] *n.* [f. *sorren* free hospitality given to one's lord, f. obs. Ir. *sorthan* free quarters]

sorŏ'ptĭmĭst *n.* Member of an international association of women's clubs. [app. f. L *soror* sister + OPTIMIST]

sorŏ'rĭcīd|e *n.* Killing of one's sister; one who kills his sister; hence ~AL *a.* [f. LL *sororicidium*, L *sororicida*, (*soror* sister; see -CIDE)]

sorŏ'rĭtȳ *n.* Devotional sisterhood; *women's society in university or college. [f. med. L *sororitas* or f. L *soror* sister, after *fraternity*]

sorō's|ĭs *n.* (*pl.* **~es** *pr.* -ēz). (Bot.) Fleshy compound fruit, e.g. pineapple, mulberry. [mod. L, f. Gk *sōros* heap + -OSIS]

sôr'ption *n.* Absorption and adsorption considered jointly. [f. ab*sorption*, ad*sorption*]

sŏ'rra *n.* (Sc. & Ir.) Var. of SORROW 4.

sŏ'rrel[1] *n.* Acid-leaved herb of genus *Rumex*, used in salads etc. [ME, f. OF *surele*, *sorele* (*sur* f. Gmc **sūraz* SOUR; see -LE 1)]

sŏ'rrel[2] *a.* & *n.* (Of) light reddish-brown colour; sorrel animal, esp. horse; ||sorel. [ME, f. OF *sorel* (*sor* yellowish f. Frank. **saur* dry; see -LE 2)]

sŏ'rrow (-ō) *n.*, & *v.i.* **1.** *n.* Grief, sadness, caused by loss of good or occurrence of evil. **2.** Occasion of sorrow, misfortune, trouble, (*has had many sorrows, much sorrow*); **the Man of S~s,** Christ. **3.** Lamentation (*his sorrow was loud and long*). **4.** (Sc. & Ir.) **(The) ~**, not at all, never (*sorrow a one, a bit*, etc.). **5.** *v.i.* Grieve, feel sorrow, (*at, over, for*, misfortune, etc.; *for*, i.e. on behalf of, person etc.); mourn (*after, for*, lost person or thing); hence ~ER[1] *n.*, ~ING[2] *a.* [OE *sorh*, *sorg*, = OS, OHG *sorga*, ON *sorg*, Goth. *saurga*]

sŏ'rrowful (-ōf-) *a.* Showing or feeling sorrow; distressing, lamentable; hence ~LY[2] *adv.*, ~NESS *n.* [OE *sorhful* (as prec., -FUL)]

sŏ'rrȳ *a.* **1.** (*pred.*) Feeling regret (*am sorry to hear it, that you must go, about your accident*); **~ for,** regretful concerning (thing) or concerning unhappiness etc. of (person); **~ for oneself,** (colloq.) dejected; **~!**, (colloq.) I beg your PARDON[1]. **2.** (literary). Wretched, paltry, shabby, of poor quality, (*a sorry fellow, nag*; *in a sorry plight*; *a sorry excuse*); hence **sŏ'rrĭ**LY[2] *adv.*, **sŏ'rrĭ**NESS *n.* [OE *sārig*, = OS, OHG *sērag*, f. WG **sairag-*, *-ig-* (as SORE, -Y[2])]

sôrt[1] *n.* **1.** Group of things etc. with common attributes, class, kind, species, variety, (*biscuits of several sorts*; *a new sort of bicycle*; *people of every sort and kind*; *all sorts and conditions of men*). **2.** = KIND[1] (*nothing of the sort*; *coffee of a sort*; *what sort of tree?*; *she's not the sort to make a fuss*; (colloq.) *these sort of men*, *a sort of stockbroker* etc., *I sort of expected it*). **3. A ~ of** *war* etc., *a war* etc. **of a ~** or (colloq.) **of ~s,** not fully deserving the name. **4.** (colloq.) Person of specified sort (*a good sort*). **5.** (arch.) Manner, way, (*in seemly, courteous*, etc., *sort*); **after** or **in a ~** (= FASHION); **in some ~**, to a certain extent. **6.** (Print.) Any letter or piece in fount of type. **7. Out of ~s,** slightly unwell, in low spirits, or irritable. [ME, f. OF *sorte* f. Rom. **sorta* alt. f. L *sors sortis* lot, condition]

sôrt[2] *v.* **1.** *v.t.* **~ (out, over)**, separate into sorts according to size, quality, destination, etc. **2. ~ out,** disentangle (lit. or fig.), select (things of one or more sorts) from miscellaneous group (*sorted out those of largest size*), (sl.) deal with, punish. **3.** Hence ~'ABLE *a.*, ~'ER[1], ~'ING[1], *ns.* **4.** *v.i.* (arch.) Correspond or agree *with* (*his actions sort ill, well, with his protestations*). [ME, f. OF *sortir* or f. L *sortiri* divide or obtain by lot (as prec.), or f. prec. or f. ASSORT]

sortes (sôr'tēz) *n. pl.* Divination by chance selection of passages: **~ *Biblicae*** (bĭ'blĭsē) from the Bible, **~ *Homericae*** (hōmĕ'rĭsē) from Homer, etc. [L, pl. of *sors* lot]

sôr'tĭe (*or* -ē) *n.* **1.** Sally esp. of beleaguered garrison. **2.** Operational flight by a military aircraft. [F, fem. p.p. (as n.) of *sortir* go out]

sôr'tĭlėge *n.* Divination by lots. [ME f. OF, f.

med. L *sortilegium* sorcery f. L *sortilegus* sorcerer (as SORT¹, *legere* choose)]

sortĭ'tion *n.* Casting of lots. [f. L *sortitio* (*sortiri* cast lots; see SORT², -ITION)]

sōr'|us *n.* (*pl.* ~i *pr.* -ī). (Bot.) Heap, cluster, esp. of spore-cases on under-surface of fern-leaf, or in fungus or lichen. [mod. L, f. Gk *sōros* heap]

SOS (ĕsōĕ'ṡ) *n.* International code-signal of extreme distress; ‖broadcast appeal to (otherwise untraceable) person (to visit dying relative etc.); urgent appeal for help. [chosen as being easily transmitted and recognized in Morse code]

sō-sō. See SO¹ 11.

sŏstenu'tō (-nōō'-) *adv.*, *a.*, & *n.* (*pl.* ~s). (Mus.) (Passage performed) in sustained or prolonged manner. [It., p.p. of *sostenere* SUSTAIN]

sŏt *n.*, & *v.i.* (-tt-). **1.** *n.* Confirmed drunkard, person stupefied by habitual drunkenness; hence ~'TISH¹ *a.* **2.** *v.i.* Tipple. [OE *sott* & OF *sot* foolish, f. med. L *sottus*, of unkn. orig.]

sotērĭŏ'logy̆ *n.* (Theol.) Doctrine of salvation. [f. Gk *sōtēria* salvation + -o- + -LOGY]

Sō'thĭc *a.* Of the dog-star; ~ **year,** ancient Egyptian year of 365¼ days, fixed by heliacal rising of dog-star; ~ **cycle** (of 1460 Sothic years, after which 365-day calendar year gives same date for this rising). [f. Gk *Sōthis* f. Egypt. name of dog-star + -IC]

sotto voce (sŏtō vō'chĭ) *adv.* In an undertone, aside. [It. (*sotto* under, *voce* voice)]

sou (sōō) *n.* (Hist.) French coin of various values; (colloq.) very small amount of money (**not a** ~, no money at all). [F, orig. pl. *sous* f. OF *sout* f. L SOLIDUS]

soubrĕ'tte (sōō-) *n.* Maidservant or similar character (esp. w. implication of pertness, coquetry, intrigue, etc.) in comedy. [F, f. Prov. *soubreto* fem. of *soubret* coy (*sobrar* f. L *superare* be above)]

soubriquet. See SOBRIQUET.

sou'chŏng (sōō'sh-) *n.* Fine black kind of China tea. [f. Chin. *hsiao* small + *chung* sort]

Soudanese. Var. of SUDANESE.

souffle (sōō'fel) *n.* (Med.) Low murmur heard in auscultation of various organs etc. [F (*souffler* blow f. L SUF*flare*)]

soufflé (sōō'flā) *a.* & *n.* **1.** *a.* Made light and frothy (*omelette soufflé*); (of pottery) decorated with small spots. **2.** *n.* Light spongy dish usu. made with stiffly beaten whites of eggs. [F, p.p. (as prec.)]

soufrière (sōōfrĭăr') *n.* Solfatara. [F (*soufre* sulphur)]

sough (sŭf *or* sow) *n.*, & *v.i.* (Make) moaning, whistling, or rushing sound as of wind in trees etc. [f. OE *swōgan* resound]

sought. See SEEK.

souk (sōōk) *n.* Market-place in Muslim countries. [f. Arab. *sūḳ*]

soul (sōl) *n.* **1.** Spiritual or immaterial part of man, held to survive death (*immortality of the soul*; ALL *Souls' Day*; COMMEND one's *soul to God*); *lost soul* (see LOSE); **sell** one's ~ **for,** make any sacrifice to get; **upon my** ~ (form of asseveration). **2.** Moral and emotional part of man (*his whole soul revolted from it*; CURE¹ *of souls*; *has a soul above such trivialities*); ~ **kiss,** deep kiss; ~ **mate,** person ideally suited to another; ~**-searching,** examination of one's own conscience. **3.** Intellectual part of man, vital principle and mental powers of animals including man, (*keep* BODY¹ *and soul together*); **cannot call his** ~ **his own,** is dominated by another; ~**-destroying,** deadeningly monotonous etc. **4.** Animating or essential part, person viewed as this, (*he was the* (*life and*) *soul of the enterprise*, *of the party*). **5.** Person viewed as embodying moral or intellectual qualities (*the greatest souls of antiquity*; *left that to meaner souls*). **6.** Emotional or intellectual energy e.g. as revealed in work of art (*the fellow has no soul*; *his pictures lack soul*). **7.** (Of person) personification or pattern *of*; **the** ~ **of honour,** person incapable of dishonourable conduct. **8.** Person (*not a soul to speak to for miles around*; *ship went down with 200 souls*); person regarded with familiarity, patronage, pity, contempt, etc., (*my, good soul*; *there's a good soul*; *the poor little soul had lost her way*; *a simple soul*). **9.** American Negrohood or Black culture; ~ **brother,** fellow Negro; ~ **food,** traditional food of American Negroes; ~ **music,** style of jazz playing with strong emotional fervour; ~ **sister,** fellow Negress. **10.** Hence (-)~ED² (sōld) *a.* [OE *sāwol*, *sāw(e)l*, = Goth. *saiwala* f. Gmc **saiwalō*; cf. OS *sēola*, OHG *sē(u)la*]

sou'lful (sō'l-) *a.* Having, expressing, appealing to, the (esp. higher) emotional or intellectual qualities; (colloq.) over-emotional; hence ~LY² *adv.*, ~NESS *n.* [f. prec. + -FUL]

sou'llĕss (sō'l-l-) *a.* Having no soul; destitute of noble qualities; dull, uninteresting; hence ~LY² *adv.*, ~NESS *n.* [f. SOUL + -LESS]

sound¹ *a.* & *adv.* **1.** *a.* Healthy, not diseased or injured or rotten, (*a sound mind in a sound body*; *sound fruit*, *timbers*, *ship*); correct, orthodox, logical, well-founded, judicious, (*sound doctrine*, *theologian*, *argument*, *views*, *policy*); financially secure (*sound company*, *investment*); thorough, unqualified, (*sound sleep*, *sleeper*, *thrashing*); hence ~'LY² *adv.*, ~'NESS *n.* **2.** *adv.* Soundly (*will sleep the sounder for it*); fast *asleep*. [ME *sund*, *isund* f. OE *gesund*, = OS *gisund*, OHG *gisunt* f. WG **gasunda*]

sound² *n.* & *v.* **1.** *n.* Sensation caused in ear by vibration of surrounding air; what is or may be heard; vibrations causing sensation of sound; similar vibrations whether audible or not; (**musical**) ~ (produced by continuous and regular vibrations, opp. *noise*); any of a series of articulate utterances (*vowel and consonant sounds*); music, speech, etc., accompanying film or other visual presentation; mere words (*sound and fury*); (fig.) mental impression produced by oral or other statement etc., (*will have a strange sound*; *don't like the sound of it*). **2.** ~ **barrier,** high resistance of air to objects moving at speeds near that of sound; ~**-board,** = SOUNDING²-*board*; ~**-bow,** thick edge of bell against which tongue strikes; ~**-box** (carrying a recording or reproducing acoustic gramophone-stylus); ~ **broadcasting,** ~ **radio,** (opp. television); ~ **effect,** sound other than speech or music made artificially for use in play, film, etc.; ~ **engineer** (dealing with acoustics etc.); ~**-film,** cinema film with audible dialogue, songs, etc., recorded on sound-track; ~**-hole, -post,** aperture in belly, small prop between belly and back, of some stringed instruments; *sound*-PROOF² *a.*, & *v.t.*; ~**-ranging,** determination of position by timing arrival of sounds from known points; ~ **shift** (see SHIFT² 8); ~ **spectrograph,** instrument for analysing sound into frequency components; ~**-track,** narrow strip on side of cinema film for recording sound; ~**-wave** (of condensation and rarefaction, by which sound is propagated in elastic medium e.g. air). **3.** Hence ~'LESS *a.* **4.** *v.i.* Give forth sound (*the trumpet shall sound*); convey an impression by sound (lit. or fig.; *sounds to me like something cracking*; *sounds as if a tap were running*; *sounds as if he wanted to back out of it*; *will sound very strange to say you hadn't time*; *that* (*excuse* etc.) *sounds very hollow*); ~ **in,** (Law) be concerned with (damages etc.); *~ **off,** (colloq.) talk loudly, express one's opinions forcefully. **5.** *v.t.* Cause to sound; utter (*sound a note of alarm*); pronounce (*the h in 'hour' is not sounded*); give notice of (*an alarm, the retreat,* etc.) with bell, trumpet, etc.; cause to resound, make known, (*sound his praises far and wide*); test (railway-carriage wheel etc., lungs etc.) by noting sound produced by hammer, on auscultation, etc. [ME; n. f. AF *s(o)un*, OF *son* f. L *sonus* (*-d* as in ROUND[5]), v. f. AF *suner*, OF *soner* f. L *sonare* (*sonus*)]

sound[3] *v.* & *n.* **1.** *v.t.* Test depth or quality of bottom of (sea, channel, pond, etc., or abs.) with **~'ing-line** etc.; find depth of water in (ship's hold) with **~'ing-rod**; get records of temperature, humidity, pressure, etc., from (upper atmosphere) with **~'ing-balloon** or sonde; (Med.) examine (bladder etc.) with probe; **~ (out)**, inquire esp. in cautious or reserved manner into sentiments or inclination of (person *about* etc.). **2.** *v.i.* (Of whale or fish) dive to the bottom. **3.** *n.* Surgeon's probe. [ME, f. OF *sonder* f. Rom. **subundare*, f. L SUB- + *unda* wave]

sound[4] *n.* **1.** Narrow passage of water connecting two seas or sea with lake etc.; arm of sea. **2.** Fish's air-bladder. [OE *sund*, = ON *sund* swimming, strait, f. Gmc **sundam* (as SWIM)]

sou'nder[1] *n.* (arch.) Herd of wild swine. [ME, f. OF *sonre, sundre* f. Gmc]

sou'nder[2] *n.* In vbl senses; telegraphic receiving instrument for reading message by sound. [f. SOUND[2] + -ER[1]]

sou'nder[3] *n.* In vbl senses; ECHO-*sounder*. [f. SOUND[3] + -ER[1]]

sou'nding[1] *n.* Measurement of depth of water; (in *pl.*) region near enough to shore to admit of this; **~-balloon, -line, -rod,** (see SOUND[3]). [ME, f. SOUND[3] + -ING[1]]

sou'nding[2] *n.* In vbl senses; **~-board,** (1) canopy over pulpit etc. to direct sound towards audience, (2) thin plate of wood increasing sound from musical instrument, (3, fig.) means of causing opinions etc. to be more widely known. [ME, f. SOUND[2] + -ING[1]]

sou'nding[3] *a.* Giving forth (esp. loud or resonant) sound (*sounding brass*); (fig.) having more sound than sense or truth (*sounding rhetoric, promises*), imposing (*sounding titles*). [ME, f. SOUND[2] + -ING[2]]

soup (sōōp) *n.*, & *v.t.* **1.** *n.* Liquid food made of stock from stewed meat etc. and other ingredients; **in the ~,** (sl.) in difficulties. **2.** *(sl.) Nitro-glycerine, esp. for safe-breaking. **3. ~ and fish,** (sl.) evening dress; **~-kitchen,** public establishment for supplying soup free to the poor or in times of distress; **~ maigre** (*-ger*), (arch.) thin soup chiefly of vegetables; **~-plate,** large deep plate for soup. **4.** Hence **~'Y**[2] *a.* **5.** *v.t.* **~ (up),** (colloq.) increase power of (engine), supercharge. [f. F *soupe* sop, broth, f. LL *suppa* (**suppare* soak f. Gmc; cf. SOP, SUP)]

sou'pçon (sōō'psawṅ) *n.* Very small quantity, dash, (*of* flavouring, quality, etc.; *add a soupçon of garlic; a soupçon of grey in his hair*). [F, f. OF *sou(s)peçon* f. LL *suspectio -onis* (see SUSPICION)]

sour (sowr) *a., n.,* & *v.* **1.** *a.* Of acid taste like lemon or vinegar, esp. as result of unripeness (*sour apples; sour* GRAPES) or of fermentation (*sour milk, bread*); (of smell) suggestive of fermentation; (of soil) deficient in lime and usu. dank; (of person or temper) harsh, peevish, morose; (of thing) unpleasant, distasteful; **go** or **turn ~,** (fig.) turn out badly. **2. ~ cream** (deliberately fermented by adding bacteria); ***~'dough,** old-timer in Alaska etc. [dial., = leaven]; ***~ mash,** brewing- or distilling-mash made acid to promote fermentation; **~'puss,** (sl.) sour-tempered person [*puss* = face]; **~-sop,** (large succulent fruit of) W. Ind. tree, *Anona muricata*. **3.** Hence **~'ISH**[1] 2 *a.* **~'LY**[2] *adv.*, **~'NESS** *n.* **4.** *n.* Acid solution used in bleaching etc.; *acid drink esp. of whisky with lemon-juice or lime-juice. **5.** *v.t.* & *i.* Make or become sour (lit., or fig.: *soured by misfortune*). [OE *sūr*, = OS, OHG *sūr*, ON *súrr* f. Gmc **sūraz*]

source (sōrs) *n.* Spring, fountain-head, from which stream issues (*the sources of the Nile*); body emitting radiation etc.; (Phys.) place where flux-lines begin; origin, place from which thing comes or is got, (*the source of all our woes; reliable sources of information*); document etc. providing evidence; **at ~,** at point of origin or issue; **~-book** [transl. of G *quellenbuch*], book or collection of original documents serving as material for the historical study of a subject; **~-criticism** [transl. of G *quellenkritik*], evaluation of different (esp. successive) literary or historical sources. [ME, f. OF *sors, sourse*, p.p. (as n.) of *sourdre* rise f. L *surgere*]

sou'saphōne (sōō'z-) *n.* Large brass wind instrument shaped like French horn. [f. J. P. *Sousa*, Amer. bandmaster d. 1932, after *saxophone*]

souse[1] *n.* & *v.* **1.** *n.* Pickle made with salt; *food in pickle, esp. pig's head, feet, and ears; dip, plunge, drenching, in water. **2.** *v.t.* Put in pickle (*soused mackerel*). **3.** *v.t.* & *i.* Plunge into liquid; soak (thing *in* liquid), throw (liquid *over* thing); (in *p.p.*, sl.) drunk. [ME, f. OF *sous, souz* pickle f. OS *sultia*, OHG *sulza* brine f. Gmc **sult-*, **salt-* SALT]

souse[2] *adv.* (arch. or dial.) With swift descent, headlong, (*came souse into our midst*). [f. obs. *souse* swoop of hawk on rising bird, alt. f. SOURCE in obs. sense 'rising of hawk etc.']

sou'tache (sōō'tahsh) *n.* Narrow flat ornamental braid. [F, f. Magyar *sujtás*]

souta'ne (sōōtah'n) *n.* Cassock of Roman Catholic priest. [F, f. It. *sottana* (*sotto* under f. L *subtus*)]

souteneur (sōōtenēr') *n.* Man living on earnings of prostitute(s). [F, = protector]

sou'ter (sōō'-) *n.* (Sc. & N. Engl.) Shoemaker, cobbler. [OE *sūtere* f. L *sutor* (*suere sut-* sew)]

sou'terrain (sōō'-) *n.* (esp. Archaeol.) Underground chamber or passage. [F (*sous* under, *terre* earth)]

south *adv., n., a.,* & *v.i.* **1.** *adv., n.,* & *a.* (Towards, at, near) point of horizon to right of person facing east; **(to the) ~ (of),** in a southward direction (from); compass point opposite NORTH 3; **~ wind,** wind blowing from the south; *south* BY[1] *east* or *west*. **2.** (w. uses & derivs. like those of *south*) **~-east, ~-west,** compass point midway between south and east or west; **~-~-east, -west,** compass point midway between south and south-east or south-west. **3.** *n.* (usu. *S~*). Part of world or country or town lying to the south; *the *Southern* STATE[1]*s* (**Deep S~**, States bordering Gulf of Mexico); card-player occupying position designated 'south'. **4. S~ African,** (native or inhabitant) of Republic of South Africa; **~'bound,** travelling southwards; **S~'down,** (one of) breed of sheep raised esp. for mutton, orig. on South Downs of Hampshire and Sussex; **~'paw** *n.* & *a.*, (colloq.) left-handed (person) esp. in sport; *South* POLE[2]; **S~ Sea,** southern Pacific Ocean; **S~ Sea Bubble,** scheme for trading in southern hemisphere to repay British national debt, started and collapsed 1720. **5.** Hence **~'WARD** *a.* & *n.*, **~'WARD(S)** *adv.* **6.** *v.i.* Move towards south; (of heavenly body) cross meridian. [OE *sūth*, = OS *suth*, OHG *sunt*, ON *suthr*]

southea'ster, sou'ther, *ns.* Wind from S.E., from S. [f. SOUTH(*-east*) + -ER[1]]

sou'therly̆ (sŭ'dh-) *a., adv.,* & *n.* In a southern position or direction; (wind) blowing (nearly) from the south; ~ (**buster**), (Austral. & N.Z.) cool southerly gale. [f. SOUTH, as *easterly* etc.]

sou'thern (sŭ'dh-) *a.* & *n.* **1.** *a.* Of or (dwelling) in the south; lying or directed towards the south; *Southern* CROSS^1, HEMISPHERE; ~ **lights,** aurora australis; *Southern* STATE^1*s*; ~**wood,** species of wormwood (*Artemisia abrotanum*) with scented leaves; hence ~ER^1 (4) *n.*, ~MOST *a.* **2.** *n.* Inhabitant of the south, esp. of the Southern States. [OE *sūtherne* (as SOUTH, -ERN)]

sou'thĭng *n.* In vbl senses; (Naut. etc.) distance travelled or measured southward, southerly direction. [f. SOUTH + -ING^1]

sou'thron (sŭ'dh-) *a.* & *n.* (arch. Sc.) English-(man). [Sc. var. of SOUTHERN]

southwĕ'ster *n.* Wind from S.W. [f. SOUTH-*west* + -ER^1]

souvenir (sōōvenēr') *n.* Thing given, bought, kept, etc., to recall the past, memento (*of* occasion, place, etc.). [F, inf. (as n.) of *souvenir* f. L SUB(*venire* come) occur to the mind]

sou'wĕ'ster *n.* Wind from S.W.; waterproof hat with broad flap at back. [f. SOUTHWESTER]

||**sov.** *abbr.* sovereign.

sŏ'vereign (-vrĭn) *a.* & *n.* **1.** *a.* Supreme (*sovereign power*; **the ~ good,** *summum bonum*); unmitigated (*with sovereign contempt*). **2.** Possessing sovereign power (*sovereign States*); royal (*our sovereign* LORD); *sovereign* PONTIFF; so ~TY^1 *n.* **3.** Very good or effective (*a sovereign remedy*). **4.** Hence ~LY^2 *adv.* **5.** *n.* Supreme ruler, esp. monarch; ||British gold coin (now rarely used) worth nominally £1. [ME, f. OF *so(u)verain* f. Rom. *SUPER(*anus* -AN); *-g-* by assoc. w. *reign*]

sŏ'vĭet *n.* & *a.* **1.** *n.* Council elected in district of U.S.S.R.; **Supreme S~,** governing council of U.S.S.R. or one of its constituent republics; **S~ Union, Union of S~ Socialist Republics, the S~(s),** the Russian nation since 1917. **2.** *a.* (*S~*). Russian; of the Soviet Union. **3.** Hence ~IZE (3) *v.t.*, ~ŏ'LOGIST *n.*, one who makes a special study of the Soviet Union. [f. Russ. *sovet* council]

sŏ'vran. Var. (poet.) of SOVEREIGN.

sow^1 (sō) *v.t.* (~**ed** *pr.* sōd; ~**n** *or* ~**ed**). **1.** Scatter (seed, or abs.) on or in the earth for purpose of growth; (fig.) initiate, arouse, (*must reap what you have sown*); *sow the* SEED(*s*) *of*; ~ **the wind** (see WHIRL*wind*). **2.** Plant (field etc. *with* seed) by sowing; (fig.) cover thickly *with*. **3.** Hence ~'ER^1 (1, 2), ~'ING^1, *ns.* [OE *sāwan*, = OS *sāian*, OHG *sāwen* etc., ON *sá*, Goth. *saian* f. Gmc **sǣjan* f. IE **sē(j)*-]

sow^2 *n.* **1.** Adult female pig (esp. after farrowing) or guinea-pig; **get the wrong ~ by the ear,** fix on wrong person or thing, reach wrong conclusion; **as drunk as a ~,** completely drunk; SILK *purse out of sow's ear*. **2.** ~(**-bug**), wood-louse. **3.** Main trough through which molten iron runs into side-channels to form pigs; large block of iron that solidifies in this. **4.** ~'**back,** low ridge of sand etc.; ~'**bread,** kind of cyclamen whose roots are eaten by pigs; ~'**thistle,** plant of genus *Sonchus* with thistle-like leaves and milky juice. [OE *sugu*, = OS *suga*, MDu., MLG *soge*, rel. to OE, OHG *sū*, ON *sýr*, f. IE **su*-]

sown. See SOW^1.

soy *n.* Sauce made in Japan and China from pickled soya beans; ~ (**bean**), soya bean. [Jap., colloq. f. *sho-yu* f. Chin. *shi-yu* (*shi* salted beans, *yu* oil)]

soy'a *n.* ~ (**bean**), (seed of) widely cultivated leguminous plant (*Soja hispida*) orig. of S.E. Asia, yielding edible oil and flour. [f. Du. *soja* f. Malay *soi* f. as prec.]

sŏ'zzled (-zeld) *a.* (sl.) Very drunk. [p.p. of dial. *sozzle* mix sloppily (prob. imit.)]

S.P. *abbr.* starting price.

spa (-ah) *n.* (Place where there is a) curative mineral spring. [f. *Spa* in Belgium]

spāce^1 *n.* **1.** Continuous extension viewed with or without reference to the existence of objects within it. **2.** Interval between points or objects viewed as having one, two, or three dimensions (*separated by a space of 10 ft.*; *clear a space in that corner*; *box occupies too much space*); amount of paper used in writing etc. (*would take too much space to discuss in detail*; *bought space in the newspapers to advertise the idea*); large region (*the wide open spaces*). **3.** = OUTER *space*; ~ **age,** era when space travel has become possible; ~'**craft,** vehicle for travelling in space; ~ **flight,** = *space travel*; ~'**man,** = *space traveller*; ~ **medicine** (dealing with effects of space travel on human body); *~ **opera,** science-fiction drama etc. dealing with interplanetary travel; ~ **probe** (used to investigate conditions in outer space); ~ **rocket** (used to launch spacecraft); ~'**ship,** spacecraft (esp. controlled by its crew); *space* SHUTTLE; ~ **station,** artificial satellite used as base for operations in space; ~'**suit,** garment designed to allow wearer to breathe etc. in space; ~ **travel(ler),** (person) going from one place to another through space; ~ **vehicle,** = *spacecraft*; ~ **walk,** physical activity by astronaut in space outside spacecraft. **4.** Blank between printed, typed, or written words etc.; piece of metal providing this. **5.** Interval of time (*in the space of an hour*; *after a short space*; *let us rest a space*). **6.** ~**-bar,** bar in typewriter for making space between words etc.; ~**-heater,** self-contained unit for heating room etc. in which it is; ~**-saving,** occupying little space; ~**-time,** fusion of concepts of space and time, esp. as a four-dimensional continuum in which the existent exists. [ME, f. OF *espace* f. L *spatium*]

spāce^2 *v.t.* Set or arrange at intervals, put spaces between (esp. words, letters, lines, or abs., in printing, typing, or writing); ~ **out,** put more or wider spaces or intervals between; hence **spā'**CING^1 (1, 6) *n.* [f. prec.]

spacial. Var. of SPATIAL.

spā'cious (-shus) *a.* Enclosing a large space; having ample space, roomy; hence ~LY^2 *adv.*, ~NESS *n.* [ME, f. OF *spacios* or f. L *spatiosus* (as SPACE^1; see -IOUS)]

spāde^1 *n.*, & *v.t.* **1.** *n.* Tool for digging or cutting ground, turf, etc., with sharp-edged broad metal blade and wooden handle used with both hands; **call a ~ a ~,** call things by their names, speak plainly or bluntly; hence ~'FUL 2 (-df-) *n.* **2.** Tool of similar shape for various purposes, e.g. for removing blubber from whale; ~ **beard,** beard of more or less oblong shape; ~ **foot,** square spadelike enlargement at end of chair-leg; ~'**work,** (fig.) hard preparatory work. **3.** *v.t.* Dig over (ground) with spade. [OE *spadu, spada*, = OFris. *spada*, OS *spado*]

spāde^2 *n.* **1.** Playing-card of suit (~**s**) denoted by black figures shaped like inverted heart with small handle; ~ **guinea** (of George III with spade-shaped shield on reverse); ***in ~s,** (sl.) to a high degree, with great force. **2.** *(sl.) Negro. [f. It. *spade* pl. of *spada* sword f. L *spatha* f. Gk *spathē*, cogn. w. prec.; assoc. w. shape of pointed SPADE^1]

||**spă'dger** *n.* (sl.) Sparrow. [fanciful alt.]

spadĭ'lle *n.* (Highest trump, esp.) ace of spades in ombre and quadrille. [F, f. Sp. *espadilla* dim. of *espada* sword; see SPADE^2]

spā'd|ix *n.* (*pl.* ~**ices** *pr.* -ĭsēz). (Bot.) Spike of flowers closely arranged round fleshy axis and usu. enclosed in a spathe; hence or cogn. **~i'**CEOUS (-shus), **~i**COSE[1], *adjs.* [L, f. Gk, = palm-branch]

spā'dō *n.* (pl. **~s**). Castrated or otherwise sexually impotent man. [ME f. L, f. Gk *spadōn* eunuch]

spae (spā) *v.i.* & *t.* (Sc.) Foretell, prophesy; **~'wife,** female fortune-teller. [ME, f. ON *spá*]

spaghĕ'ttĭ (-gĕ'-) *n.* Pasta made in solid strings, between macaroni and vermicelli in thickness. [It., pl. of dim. of *spago* string]

spahi (spah'hē) *n.* (Hist.) Member of Turkish irregular cavalry; member of native Algerian cavalry in French service. [f. Turk. *sipāhī* f. as SEPOY]

spāke. See SPEAK.

spall (-awl) *v.t.* & *i.*, & *n.* Splinter, chip; (Mining) prepare (ore) for sorting by breaking it up; hence **~A'TION** *n.*, (Phys.) break-up of bombarded nucleus into several parts. [ME, also *spale,* of unkn. orig.]

spălpee'n *n.* (Ir.) Mean fellow, rascal; youngster. [f. Ir. *spailpín,* of unkn. orig.; cf. -EEN]

spăm *n.* Tinned meat product made mainly from ham. [**P**; f. *sp*iced *ham*]

spăn[1] *v.* (**-nn-**). **1.** *v.t.* (Of bridge, arch, etc., fig. of memory etc.) stretch from side to side of, extend across, (river etc., fig. period etc.), (of builder etc.) bridge (river etc.); measure, cover, the extent of (thing) with one's hand with fingers stretched. **2.** *v.i.* *Move in distinct stretches like span-worm. [f. foll.]

spăn[2] *n.* **1.** Full extent from end to end (*span of a bridge, of an arch, our brief span* (*of life*), *the whole span of Roman history*). **2.** Each part of a bridge etc. between piers or supports. **3.** Maximum lateral extent of aeroplane or its wing. **4.** Maximum distance between tips of thumb and little finger, esp. as a measure = 9 in. **5.** Short distance or time (*our life is but a span*). **6.** ~ **roof** (with two inclined sides, opp. *penthouse* or *lean-to*); ***~-worm,** caterpillar of geometer moth. [OE *span*(*n*), = MDu. *spanne,* OHG *spanna,* ON *spann-* or f. OF *espan*]

spăn[3] *n.* **1.** (Naut.) Rope with both ends fastened to take purchase in loop. **2.** *Matched pair of horses, mules, etc. **3.** (S. Afr.) Team of two or more pairs of oxen. [f. LG & Du. *span* (*spannen* unite = OE, OHG *spannan*)]

spăn[4]. See SPICK.

spăn[5]. See SPIN[1].

spă'ndrel *n.* Space between shoulder of arch and surrounding rectangular moulding or framework, or between shoulders of adjoining arches and moulding above; ~ **wall** (built on curve of arch, filling in spandrel). [perh. f. AF *spaund*(*e*)*re,* or f. *espaundre* EXPAND]

***spăng** *adv.* (colloq.) Exactly, completely, (*spang in the middle*). [20th c.; orig. unkn.]

spă'ngle (-nggel) *n.*, & *v.t.* **1.** *n.* Small thin piece of glittering material esp. one of many as ornament of dress etc.; small sparkling object; spongy excrescence on oak-leaves; hence **spă'ngl**Y[2] (-ngg-) *a.* **2.** *v.t.* Cover with spangles (esp. in *p.p.*: STAR[1]-*spangled*). [ME, f. *spang* (f. MDu. *spange,* OHG *spanga,* ON *spöng* brooch f. Gmc **spangō*) + -LE 3]

Spă'niard (-yerd) *n.* Native of Spain; (N.Z.) species of spear grass. [ME, f. OF *Espaignart* (*Espaigne* Spain; see -ARD)]

spă'niel (-yel) *n.* (Breed of) dog with long silky coat, drooping ears, and docile and affectionate disposition, used by sportsmen or kept as pet; (fig.) fawning or cringing person. [ME, f. OF *espaigneul* Spanish (dog) f. Rom. *(*hi*)*spaniolus* f. *Hispania* Spain]

Spă'nĭsh *a.* & *n.* **1.** *a.* Of Spain or the Spaniards or their language; ~ **America,** parts of America orig. settled by Spaniards, incl. most of S. America and part of W. Indies; *Spanish* ARMADA; ~ **bayonet,** yucca with stiff sharp-pointed leaves; *Spanish* CHESTNUT; ~ **fly,** bright green beetle (*Lytta vesicatoria*) dried and used for raising blisters, as aphrodisiac, etc.; ~ **Main,** (Hist.) N.E. coast of S. America between Orinoco river and Panama, and adjoining part of Caribbean Sea; ~ **omelette** (with chopped vegetables and often not folded); ~ **onion** (large and mild-flavoured); *Spanish* POTATO; ~ **windlass,** use of stick as lever for tightening ropes etc. **2.** *n.* Language of the Spaniards. [ME (*Spain*; see -ISH[1])]

spănk *v.* & *n.* **1.** *v.t.* Slap on buttocks with open hand or slipper etc. **2.** *v.i.* (Of horse etc.) move briskly, esp. at step between trot and gallop. **3.** *n.* Slap, blow with open hand etc., on buttocks. [perh. imit.]

spă'nker *n.* In vbl senses; fast horse; (colloq.) person or thing of notable size or quality; (Naut.) fore-and-aft sail set on after side of mizen-mast. [f. prec. + -ER[1]]

spă'nkĭng *a.* & *adv.* In vbl senses; (colloq.) striking(ly), excellent(ly), (*had a spanking time; a spanking fine woman*), moving quickly (*a spanking trot, breeze*), lively, brisk. [f. SPANK + -ING[2]; perh. partly symbolic (cf. *whacking, thumping*)]

spă'nner *n.* **1.** ‖Instrument for turning nut on screw etc.; **throw a ~ into the works,** (fig.) introduce upsetting element or influence. **2.** Cross-brace of bridge etc. [G (*spannen* draw tight; see SPAN[3], -ER[1])]

spar̂[1] *n.* Stout pole esp. such as is used for mast, yard, etc., of ship; main longitudinal beam of aeroplane wing; **~-buoy** (made of a spar with one end moored so that the other stands up); **~-deck,** light upper deck in vessel. [ME *sparre, sperre,* f. OF *esparre* or ON *sperra* or direct f. Gmc; cf. MDu., MLG *sparre,* OS, OHG *sparro*]

spar̂[2] *n.* Crystalline easily cleavable and non-lustrous mineral, e.g. calcite, FLUORSPAR, ICELAND *spar.* [MLG, cogn. w. OE *spæren* of plaster, *spærstān* gypsum]

spar̂[3] *v.i.* (**-rr-**), & *n.* **1.** *v.i.* Make motions of attack and defence with closed fists, use the hands (as) in boxing, (*at* opponent); (of game-cock) fight with feet or spurs; (fig.) engage in argument (*they are always sparring*); **~'ring partner,** boxer employed to practise with another in training for a fight, (fig.) person with whom one enjoys arguing. **2.** *n.* Sparring motion; boxing-match; cock-fight. [ME, f. OE *sperran, spyrran,* of unkn. orig.; cf. ON *sperrask* kick out]

spă'rable *n.* Headless nail for soles and heels of shoes. [f. SPARROW-*bill*]

spară'xis *n.* S. Afr. iridaceous plant of genus *Sparaxis,* with showy flowers and jagged spathes. [mod. L f. Gk, = laceration (*sparassō* tear)]

spār̂e[1] *a.* & *n.* **1.** *a.* Scanty, frugal, (*spare diet*); lean, thin, (*man of spare frame*); not copious (*a spare style of prose*); hence **~'**LY[2] (-ār'lĭ) *adv.*, **~'**NESS (-ār'n-) *n.* **2.** That can be spared, not required for ordinary use, (*how to use your spare time; have no spare cash*); (colloq.) not wanted by others (*is this seat going spare?*); reserved for emergency or occasional use (*always take a spare cap; visitors sleep in the spare room*); ‖**go ~,** (sl.) become very annoyed or baffled; ~ **part,** duplicate part to replace lost or damaged part of machine etc.; ‖**~ tyre,** (fig., colloq.) obesity just above waist. **3.** *n.* ‖Spare part. **4.** (Bowling). Knocking-down of all pins with first two balls. [OE *spær,* = OHG *spar,* ON *sparr,* cogn. w. foll.]

spār̂e[2] *v.* **1.** *v.t.* Be frugal or grudging of (*spare the rod and spoil the child; must not spare expense*); **not ~ oneself,** exert one's utmost efforts. **2.**

Dispense with, do without, (*cannot spare him just now*; *can you spare me a moment, a pound?*; *could have spared the explanation*); **to ~**, left over, additional to what is needed, (*arrived with an hour to spare*; ENOUGH *and to spare*). **3.** Abstain from inflicting, relieve of the necessity of doing etc., (w. double obj.; *spare me these protestations, this task*); abstain from killing, hurting, wounding, etc., (*spare me, my life, my feelings*; **if I am ~d,** if I live so long); abstain from causing (*spare his blushes*). **4.** *v.i.* Be frugal. [OE *sparian*, = OS, OHG *sparōn*, ON *spara* f. Gmc **sparōjan*]

spār'e-rĭb (*or* spār'ĭb) *n.* Part of closely-trimmed ribs of meat, esp. pork. [prob. f. MLG *ribbesper*, by transposition and assoc. w. SPARE[1]]

spārg|e *v.t.* Moisten by sprinkling (esp. in brewing); hence **~'ER**[1] (2) *n.* [app. f. L *spargere* sprinkle]

spār'ĭng *a.* Inclined to save, economical; restrained, limited; hence **~LY**[2] *adv.*, **~NESS** *n.* [f. SPARE[2] + -ING[2]]

spārk[1] *n.* **1.** Fiery particle thrown off from burning substance, or still visibly alight in ashes, or struck out by impact from flint etc., (**as the ~s fly upward,** with the certainty of a law of nature). **2.** Small bright object or point e.g. in gem. **3.** (fig.) Flash of wit etc.; **strike ~s out of** person, provoke him to lively or original conversation. **4.** (usu. w. neg.) Particle of fire or (fig.) *of* a quality etc. (*not a spark of life remained*; *if you had a spark of generosity in you*). **5.** (Electr.) Luminous effect of sudden disruptive discharge through air etc.; such discharge serving to fire explosive mixture in internal combustion engine; **advance, retard, the ~** (in cycle of engine operation); *spark* CHAMBER; **~-gap,** space between electric terminals where sparks occur; **~-plug,** = SPARK[2]*ing-plug*, *(fig.) person providing impetus in an undertaking. **6.** **S~s,** (colloq. nickname for) radio operator on ship. **7.** Hence **~'LESS** *a.*, **~'LET** *n.*, (1) small spark, (2) capsule of compressed carbon dioxide for siphons (**P**). [OE *spærca*, *spearca*, = MDu., MLG *sparke*, of unkn. orig.]

spārk[2] *v.* **1.** *v.i.* Emit sparks of fire or electricity; ||**~'ing-plug,** device for firing explosive mixture in internal combustion engine. **2.** (Electr.) Produce sparks at point where circuit is interrupted. **3.** *v.t.* ~ (**off**), stir into activity. [ME, f. prec.]

spārk[3] *n.*, & *v.i.* **1.** *n.* Gay fellow; gallant; hence **~'ISH**[1] *a.* **2.** *v.i.* Play the gallant. [prob. fig. use of SPARK[1]]

spār'kl|e *v.i.*, & *n.* **1.** *v.i.* (Seem to) emit sparks, (of gem, star, eye, water, etc. and fig. of wit etc.) glitter, glisten, scintillate; **~ing wine** (giving off carbon dioxide in small bubbles, opp. *still*). **2.** *n.* Sparkling; gleam, spark. [ME, f. SPARK[1] + -LE 1, 3]

spār'kler *n.* In vbl senses; sparkling firework; (sl.) diamond. [f. prec. + -ER[1]]

spār'lĭng *n.* European species of smelt, *Osmerus eperlanus*. [ME, f. OF *esperlinge*, of Gmc orig.]

spă'roid *a.* & *n.* (Fish) of family Sparidae, e.g. porgy. [f. mod. L *Sparoides* f. L f. Gk *sparos* sea-bream; see -OID]

spă'rrow (-ō) *n.* Small brownish-grey bird, of genus *Passer*; bird of similar appearance (HEDGE[1]-*sparrow*); **~-bill,** sparable; **~-grass,** (dial. or vulg.) asparagus; **~-hawk,** small hawk (*Accipiter nisus*) preying on small birds. [OE *spearwa*, = OHG *sparo*, ON *spörr*, Goth. *sparwa* f. Gmc **sparwon*, **sparwaz*]

spār'rȳ *a.* Of, like, rich in, SPAR[2]. [f. SPAR[2] + -Y[2]]

spārse *a.* (Of population etc.) thinly scattered, not dense; (Bot. & Zool.) placed or occurring at wide or irregular intervals; hence **~'LY**[2] (-slĭ) *adv.*, **spār'SITY**, **~'NESS** (-sn-), *ns.* [f. L *sparsus* p.p. of *spargere* scatter]

Spār'tacĭst *n.* Member of extreme socialist party in Germany in 1918. [f. *Spartacus*, pen-name of leader, after leader of slave revolt against Rome 73–71 B.C., + -IST]

Spār'tan *a.* & *n.* (Native or inhabitant) of Sparta in ancient Greece (esp. w. allus. to supposed characteristics of Spartans: *Spartan endurance, frugality, simplicity*). [ME, f. L *Spartanus* (*Sparta* f. Gk *Sparta*, *-tē*; see -AN)]

spă'sm *n.* Excessive muscular contraction (CLONIC, TONIC, *spasm*); sudden convulsive movement, wrench, or strain, (*a spasm of coughing*; (fig.) *spasms of grief* etc.). [ME, f. OF *spasme* or f. L f. Gk *spasmos*, *spasma* (*spaō* pull)]

spăsmŏ'd|ĭc (-z-) *a.* Of, caused by, subject to, spasm(s) (*a spasmodic jerk*; *spasmodic asthma*); occurring or done by fits and starts, (*spasmodic efforts*); hence **~ICALLY** *adv.* [f. mod. L *spasmodicus* f. Gk *spasmōdēs* (as prec.; see -ODE, -IC)]

spă'st|ĭc *a.* & *n.* (Med.) **1.** (Person) suffering from cerebral palsy, with tonic spasm of muscles. **2.** *a.* = prec. **3.** Hence **~ICALLY** *adv.*, **~ĭ'CITY** *n.* [f. L f. Gk *spastikos* pulling (*spaō* pull; see -IC)]

spăt[1] *n.* & *v.* (-tt-). **1.** *n.* Spawn of shellfish esp. oyster. **2.** *v.i.* & *t.* (Of oyster etc.) spawn; shed (spawn). [AF, of unkn. orig.]

spăt[2] *n.* (usu. in *pl.*) Short gaiter covering instep and reaching little above ankle; cover for aircraft wheel. [abbr. of SPATTER*dash*]

spăt[3]. See SPIT[2].

***spăt**[4] *n.*, & *v.i.* (-tt-). (colloq.) **1.** *n.* Petty quarrel; slight amount. **2.** *v.i.* Quarrel pettily. [prob. imit.]

spă'tchcŏck *n.*, & *v.t.* **1.** *n.* Fowl killed and then plucked, dressed, split open, and cooked immediately. **2.** *v.t.* Treat (fowl) thus; (colloq.) insert, interpolate, esp. incongruously. [orig. in Ir. use, expl. by Grose (1785) as f. *dispatch-cock*, but cf. SPITCHCOCK]

spāte *n.* River-flood (*river is in spate*); (fig.) large or excessive amount (*a spate of inquiries, of words*). [ME, Sc. & N. Engl., of unkn. orig.]

spāthe (-dh) *n.* (Bot.) Large bract or pair of bracts enveloping spadix or flower-cluster; hence **spath**A'CEOUS, **spā'th**OSE[1], *adjs.* [f. L f. Gk *spathē* broad blade etc.]

spă'thĭc *a.* Of SPAR[2]; like spar esp. in cleavage; **~ iron ore,** = SIDERITE 1. [f. *spath* spar f. G *spath*, + -IC]

spā'tial (-shal) *a.* Of space (*spatial relations, extent*); hence **spātiă'l**ITY (-shĭ-) *n.*, **~IZE** (3) *v.t.*, **~LY**[2] *adv.* [f. L *spatium* space + -AL]

spātio-tĕ'mporal (-shĭ-) *a.* Belonging to both space and time or to space-time; hence **~LY**[2] *adv.* [f. as prec. + -O- + TEMPORAL]

spă'tter *v.* & *n.* **1.** *v.t.* Scatter (liquid, mud, etc.) here and there in small drops; splash (person *with* mud, slander, etc.) thus. **2.** *v.i.* (Of liquid) fall here and there in drops. **3.** *n.* Spattering, splash (*of* mud etc.); quick succession of light sounds, pattering. **4.** **~dash,** *roughcast, (usu. in *pl.*) cloth or other legging to protect stocking etc. from mud etc. [frequent. f. base as in Du., LG *spatten* burst, spout; see -ER[5]]

spă'tūla *n.* Broad-bladed instrument for working pigments, picking up powder, etc.; surgeon's instrument for pressing tongue down or to one side. [L, var. of *spathula*, dim. of *spatha* SPATHE]

spă'tūlate *a.* Spatula-shaped; having broad rounded end. [f. prec. + -ATE[2]]

spă'vĭn *n.* Disease of horse's hock with hard bony tumour or excrescence; **blood, bog, ~,** distension of the joint by effusion of lymph or fluid; **bone ~**, deposit of bony substance uniting the bones; hence ~ED² (-nd) *a.* [ME, f. OF *espavin*, var. of *esparvain* f. Gmc **spadwāni*]

spawn *v.* & *n.* **1.** *v.t.* (Of fish, frog, mollusc, crustacean) produce (eggs, or abs.); (derog.) produce (offspring), (fig.) produce or generate esp. in large numbers. **2.** *v.i.* (Of eggs or young of fish etc.) be produced, issue. **3.** *n.* Eggs of fish, frogs, etc.; (derog.) human or other offspring; white fibrous matter from which fungi are produced, mycelium, (*mushroom spawn*). [ME, f. AF *espaundre* shed roe, OF *espandre* EXPAND]

spay *v.t.* Remove ovaries of (female animal). [ME, f. AF *espeier*, OF *espeer* cut with a sword (*espee* sword f. L *spatha*; see SPATHE)]

S.P.C.K. *abbr.* Society for Promoting Christian Knowledge.

speak *v.* (**spoke** *pr.* -ōk, arch. **spake** *pr.* -āk; **spo'ken,** arch. or joc. **spoke,** *pr.* -ōk-). **1.** *v.i.* Use articulate utterance in ordinary (not singing-)voice (*unable to speak after his stroke*; *wish you would speak distinctly*; (on telephone) *hallo, Grose speaking*). **2.** Hold conversation (*with* or *to* person; *of* or *about* thing; so¹ *to speak*; *have heard him speak of it*; *will speak to him about it*); make mention in writing *of*. **3.** Make oral address, deliver speech, before assembly, magistrate, tribunal, etc., (*Prime Minister spoke for an hour*; *shall speak for* or *against the resolution*; *has a good speaking voice*). **4.** (Of hound) bark, bay; (of musical instrument, gun, etc.) sound. **5.** *v.t.* Utter (words); make known (one's opinion, the truth, etc.) thus; use (specified language) in speaking (*cannot speak French*); ~ one's **mind** (bluntly, frankly, etc.). **6.** Hail and hold communication with (ship). **7.** (arch.) (Of conduct, circumstance, etc.) show (person) to be (*his conduct speaks him generous*); be evidence of (*the loud laugh that speaks the vacant mind*). **8.** (Of fact etc.) ~ **volumes,** be very significant; ~ **volumes** etc. **for,** ~ **well for,** be abundant evidence of, place in favourable light, (*speaks volumes for his forbearance*); ~ **for itself,** need no supporting evidence. **9.** *Speak by the, like a, without,* BOOK¹; *speak* person FAIR³; ~ **for,** (1) act as spokesman of, state the sentiments of, (2) bespeak; ~ **for oneself,** give one's own opinions (only); **not** or **nothing to** ~ **of,** not or nothing worth mentioning, practically not or nothing; ~ **out,** speak loudly or freely, give one's (whole) opinion; ~ **to,** address (person etc.), speak in confirmation of or in reference to, (*I can speak to his having been there*; *will speak to that point later*); ~ **up,** = *speak out.* **10.** FAIR³, *smooth,* SOFT, *ill, well,* etc., **-spoken** [as if -*speech*ED²], (given to) using such language. **11.** *~**-easy,** (sl.) illicit liquor shop. [OE *sprecan*, later *specan*, = OS *sprekan*, OHG *sprehhan*]

spea'ker *n.* One who speaks esp. in public; one who speaks specified language (*speaker of French*; *French-speaker*); (*S~*) presiding officer in legislative assembly charged with preservation of order etc., whence ~SHIP *n.*; = LOUD*speaker*. [ME, f. prec. + -ER¹]

spea'kĭng¹ *n.* In vbl senses; ~ **acquaintance,** person one knows well enough to exchange conversation with him, this degree of familiarity; **not on ~ terms,** not, esp. no longer, having speaking acquaintance with (usu. implying estrangement); **~-trumpet,** instrument for conveying voice to a distance; **~-tube,** tube for conveying voice from one room, building, etc., to another. [ME, f. SPEAK + -ING¹]

spea'kĭng² *a.* In vbl senses; ||~ **clock,** telephone service giving correct time in words; ~ **likeness,** lifelike portrait; **strictly, roughly, generally,** ~, in the strict etc. sense of the word(s) (*am not strictly speaking a member of the staff*); **legally** etc. ~, from the legal etc. point of view. [ME, f. SPEAK + -ING²]

spear *n.*, & *v.t.* **1.** *n.* Hunter's or foot-soldier's thrusting or hurling weapon consisting of long shaft with point usu. of steel; (arch.) spearman; sharp-pointed and barbed instrument for stabbing fish etc.; pointed stem of asparagus etc.; ~ (long stiff) **grass;** ~ **gun** (used to propel spear in underwater fishing); **~'head,** (*n.*, esp. fig.) individual or group chosen to lead a thrust or attack, (*v.t.*) act as spearhead of (attack etc.); **~'man,** person esp. soldier who uses spear; **~'mint,** a common garden mint (*Mentha spicata*), used in cookery and to flavour chewing-gum; ~ **side,** male branch of family. **2.** *v.t.* Pierce or strike (as if) with spear. [OE *spere*, = OS, OHG *sper*, ON *spjör* pl.]

spĕc¹ *n.* (colloq.) Speculation, speculative enterprise, (*it turned out a good spec*; *did it on spec*). [abbr. of SPECULATION]

spĕc² (-s) *n.* (colloq.) Specification (of patent etc.). [abbr.]

spĕ'cial (-sh*a*l) *a.* & *n.* **1.** *a.* Of a particular kind, peculiar, not general, (*lacks the special qualities required*; *word used in a special sense*; *what is your special work?*; *its special charm did not appeal to him*). **2.** For a particular purpose (*appointed special agents*; *received special instructions*). **3.** Especial, exceptional in amount, degree, intensity, etc., (*took special trouble*; *find no special excellence in his work*). **4.** ||~ **area,** district for which special provision is made in legislation, because of depression etc.; ||**S~ Branch,** police department dealing with political security; ~ **case,** (1) written statement of facts submitted by litigants to court, (2) exceptional or peculiar case; ||~ **constable** (sworn in to assist in maintaining public peace in time of emergency); ~ **correspondent** (appointed by newspaper to report on special event or facts); ~ **delivery** (of mail in advance of regular delivery); ~ **drawing rights** (to purchase extra foreign currency from International Monetary Fund); ~ **edition** (including later news than ordinary edition of newspaper); *special* INTENTION; *special* JURY; ||~ **licence** (allowing marriage to take place without publication of banns or at time or place other than those usually required by law); *special* PLEA; ~ **pleader,** counsel employed to give verbal or written opinions on matters submitted to him and to deal with various proceedings out of usual course; ~ **pleading,** (Law) allegation of special or new matter as opp. to denial of allegations of other side, (pop.) specious but unfair argument, statement of case designed to favour speaker's point of view rather than to discover the truth; *special* VERDICT. **5.** Hence ~LY² *adv.* **6.** *n.* Special constable, train, examination, edition of newspaper, dish on menu, etc. [ME, f. OF *especial* (ESPECIAL) or f. L *specialis* (as SPECIES; see -AL)]

spĕ'cial|ĭst (-sh*a*-) *n.* One who devotes himself to particular branch of a profession (esp. of medicine), science, etc.; hence or cogn. ~ISM (1) *n.*, **~ĭ'st**IC *a.* [f. prec. + -IST]

spĕcĭă'lĭtȳ (-shĭ-) *n.* **1.** Special feature or characteristic. **2.** Special pursuit, product, operation, etc., thing to which a person gives special attention. [ME, f. OF *especialité* or f. LL *specialitas* (as SPECIAL; see -ITY)]

spĕ'cializ|e (-sh*a*-), **-is|e** (-īz), *v.* **1.** *v.t.* Make specific or individual; modify, limit, (idea, statement); (Biol.) adapt, set apart, (organ etc.) for particular purpose, differentiate. **2.** *v.i.* Be differentiated, become individual in character; be(come) a specialist. **3.** Hence ~A'TION *n.* [f. F *spécialiser* (as SPECIAL; see -IZE)]

spĕ'cialtȳ (-sh*a*l-) *n.* **1.** (Law). Instrument under seal, sealed contract. **2.** = SPECIALITY 2. [ME, f. OF (*e*)*specialté* (as SPECIAL; see -TY[1])]

spēciā'tion (*or* -shĭ-) *n.* (Biol.) (Cause of) formation of new species by evolutionary process. [f. SPECIES + -ATION]

spē'cie (-shē *or* -shĭ) *n.* Coin as opp. to paper money (*specie payments*; *paid in specie*; *shortness of specie*). [L, abl. of foll. in phr. *in specie*]

spē'cies (-shēz *or* -shĭz) *n.* (*pl.* same). **1.** (Biol.) Group of animals or plants subordinate in classification to genus and having members that can interbreed and that differ only in minor details; **the** or **our** ~, mankind. **2.** Class of individuals having common qualities or characteristics; (Logic) group subordinate to genus and containing individuals agreeing in some common attribute(s) and called by a common name. **3.** Kind, sort, (*has a species of cunning*; *a species of dogcart*). **4.** (Law). Form or shape given to materials. **5.** (Eccl.) Visible form of each of the elements of consecrated bread and wine used in the Eucharist. [L, = appearance, kind, beauty, (*specere* look)]

spėcĭ'fĭc *a.* & *n.* **1.** *a.* Definite, distinctly formulated, (*a specific statement*; *has no specific aim*). **2.** Of a species (*the specific name of a plant* etc.); ~ **difference,** what differentiates a species. **3.** Possessing, or concerned with, the properties that characterize a species (*the specific forms of animals*; *draws a specific distinction between them*). **4.** Relating to particular subject; peculiar (*has a specific style*; *a style specific to that school of painters*); (of a duty or tax) assessed by quantity or amount, not by value of goods. **5.** ~ **cause** (producing a particular form of disease); ~ **disease** (caused by one identifiable agent); *specific* GRAVITY; *specific* HEAT[1]; ~ **medicine** (having distinct effect in curing a certain disease); ~ **performance** (of contractual duty, as ordered in cases where damages would not be adequate remedy). **6.** Hence **spėcĭ'f**ICALLY *adv.*, **spěcĭfĭ'**CITY, ~NESS, *ns.* **7.** *n.* Specific medicine or remedy; specific aspect or factor. [f. LL *specificus* (as SPECIES; see -FIC)]

spěcĭfĭcā'tion *n.* Specifying or being specified; specified detail, esp. (in *pl.*) detailed description of construction, workmanship, materials, etc., of work (to be) undertaken, prepared by architect, engineer, etc.; description by applicant for patent of the construction and use of his invention; (Law) conversion of materials into a new product not held to be the property of the owner of the materials. [f. med. L *specificatio* (as foll.; see -FICATION)]

spě'cĭf|ȳ *v.t.* Name expressly, mention definitely, (items, details, ingredients, etc., or abs.); include in (e.g. architect's) specifications (*a French window was not specified*); hence ~**ĭ**ABLE *a.* [ME, f. OF *specifier* or f. LL *specificare* (as SPECIFIC; see -FY)]

spě'cĭmen *n.* Individual or part taken as example of a class or whole, esp. individual animal or plant or piece of a mineral etc. used for investigation or scientific examination, (*specimens of copper ore*; *zoological specimens*; *fine specimen of the swallow-tail*, *of mosaic work*; *a specimen of his handwriting*, *skill*, *generosity*); (Med.) sample of urine etc. for testing; (colloq., usu. derog.) person of specified sort; ~ **page** (of book, printed in prospectus etc.). [L (*specere* look)]

spēcĭ|ŏ'logȳ (-shĭ-) *n.* Science of (origin etc. of) species; hence ~OLO'GICAL *a.* [f. SPECIES + -O- + -LOGY]

spē'cious (-sh*u*s) *a.* Of good appearance, plausible, fair or right on the surface but not in reality, (*specious argument*, *tale*, *pretence*, *person*, *appearance*); hence or cogn. **spēcĭ**o'SITY (-shĭ-), ~NESS, *ns.*, ~LY[2] *adv.* [ME, = beautiful f. L *speciosus* (as SPECIES; see -IOUS)]

spěck *n.*, & *v.t.* **1.** *n.* Small spot, dot, stain; particle (*of* dirt etc.); spot of rottenness in fruit; hence ~'LESS *a.* **2.** *v.t.* (esp. in *p.p.*) Mark with specks. [OE *specca*; cf. foll.]

spě'ckle *n.*, & *v.t.* **1.** *n.* Small spot or stain, esp. one of many irregular natural markings of skin etc. **2.** *v.t.* (esp. in *p.p.*) Mark with speckles or patches. [ME, f. MDu. *spekkel*]

spěcktioneer' *n.* Chief harpooner on whaling-ship. [f. Du. *speksnijer*, for *-snijder* (*spek* blubber, *snijden* cut; see -ER[1])]

spěcs *n. pl.* (colloq.) (Pair of) spectacles; specifications. [abbr.]

spě'ctacle *n.* **1.** Public show. **2.** Object of sight, esp. of public attention, (*a charming spectacle*; *a drunken woman is a deplorable spectacle*); **make a** ~ (= EXHIBITION) **of oneself. 3.** (**Pair of**) ~**s,** pair of lenses to correct or assist defective sight, or to protect eyes, set in springless frame constructed to rest on nose and ears (ROSE[1]-*-coloured spectacles*); frame containing a green and a red piece of glass in railway signal; ||**pair of** ~**s,** (Cricket) score of 0 in each innings of match. [ME f. OF, f. L *spectaculum* (*spectare* frequent. of *specere* look)]

spě'ctacled (-k*e*ld) *a.* Wearing spectacles; (of animal) marked in a way that suggests spectacles; ~ **bear,** S. Amer. bear (*Tremarctos ornatus*); ~ **cobra,** INDIAN cobra. [f. prec. + -ED[2]]

spěctă'cūlar *a.* & *n.* **1.** *a.* Of or like a public show; striking, amazing, lavish; hence ~LY[2] *adv.* **2.** *n.* Spectacular performance etc. [f. SPECTACLE, after *oracular* etc.]

spěctā'tor *n.* One who looks on esp. at a show, game, incident, etc.; ~ **sport** (attracting many spectators). [f. F *spectateur* or f. L *spectator* (*spectare*; see SPECTACLE, -OR)]

***spě'cter.** See SPECTRE.

spě'ctral *a.* **1.** Ghostlike, of ghosts. **2.** Of spectra or the SPECTRUM (*spectral colours*, *analysis*). **3.** Hence ~LY[2] *adv.* [f. foll. + -AL]

spě'ctre (-t*er*), ***spě'cter,** *n.* **1.** Ghost, thing that is thought to be seen but has no material existence; haunting presentiment (*of* ruin, war, madness, etc.); ~ **of the Brocken,** huge shadowy image of the observer projected on mists about mountain-top, first observed on the Brocken in Germany. **2.** (In names of animals compared to spectres from thinness of body etc.) *spectre-bat*, *-crab*, *-insect*, *-lemur*, *-shrimp*. [F, or f. L SPECTRUM]

spě'ctrō- *comb. form.* Spectrum, as: ~**che'mistry,** chemistry based on the study of spectra of substances; ~**he'liograph,** instrument for taking photographs of the sun in light of one wavelength only; ~**he'lioscope,** similar device for visual observation; ~**photo'meter,** instrument for measuring intensity of light in various parts of the spectrum. [f. SPECTRUM + -O-]

spě'ctro|grăm *n.* Record obtained with ~GRAPH (2), apparatus for photographing or otherwise reproducing spectra; so ~GRA'PHIC *a.*, ~GRAPHY (-ŏ'g-) *n.* [f. prec. + -GRAM]

spěctrŏ'|mėter *n.* Spectroscope that can be used for measurement of observed spectra; hence ~**mě'tr**IC *a.*, ~METRY *n.* [f. G *spektrometer* or F *spectromètre* (as SPECTRO-, -METER)]

spě'ctro|scōpe *n.* Instrument for producing and examining spectra; hence ~**scŏ'p**IC(AL) *adjs.*, ~**scop**IST (3), ~**scop**Y[1], (-ŏ's-) *ns.* [f. G *spektroskop* or F *spectroscope* (as SPECTRO-, -SCOPE)]

spě'ctr|um *n.* (*pl.* ~**a**). **1.** Image formed by rays of light or other radiation or sound in which the parts are arranged in a progressive series according to their refrangibility, i.e. according to wavelength; this as characteristic of a body or substance when emitting or absorbing radiation; similar arrangement of component parts according to mass etc.; **~um** (or **~al) analysis,** chemical analysis by means of spectroscope. **2. (Ocular) ~um,** after-image. **3.** Entire range of wavelengths of electromagnetic radiation; (fig.) entire range of anything arranged by degree, quality, etc. [L, = image, apparition (*specere* look)]

spĕ'cūlar *a.* Of (the nature of) a speculum; reflecting (*specular surface*); **~ iron (ore),** lustrous haematite. [f. L *specularis* (as SPECULUM; see -AR[1])]

spĕ'cūl|āte *v.i.* **1.** Pursue an inquiry, meditate, form theory or conjectural opinion, (*on, upon, about*, subject, the nature, cause, etc., of a thing, or abs.). **2.** Make investment, engage in commercial operation, that involves risk of loss, (*has been speculating in stocks, in rubber*; esp. w. implication of rashness: *is believed to speculate a good deal*); so **~ātor** *n.* [f. L *speculari* spy out, observe, (*specula* watch-tower f. *specere* look) + -ATE[3]]

spĕcūlā'tion *n.* **1.** Meditation on, inquiry into, theory or conjecture about, a subject (*much given to speculation*). **2.** Speculative investment or enterprise, practice of speculating, in business (*ruined by (a single unlucky) speculation*; *bought it as a speculation*). **3.** Game in which trump cards are bought and sold. [ME f. OF, or f. LL *speculatio* (as prec.; see -ATION)]

spĕ'cūlative *a.* Of or based on speculation; given to or engaging in speculation; involving risk of loss; hence **~**LY[2] (-vlĭ) *adv.*, **~**NESS (-vn-) *n.* [ME, f. OF *speculatif -ive* or f. LL *speculativus* (as SPECULATE; see -ATIVE)]

spĕ'cūl|um *n.* (*pl.* **~a**). **1.** (Surg.) Instrument for dilating cavities of human body for inspection. **2.** Mirror, usu. of polished metal e.g. **~um-metal** (alloy of copper and tin), esp. in reflecting telescope. **3.** (Ornith.) Lustrous coloured area on wing of some birds. [L, = mirror (*specere* look)]

spĕd. See SPEED.

speech *n.* **1.** Faculty of speaking (*recover* one's *speech*); act of speaking (**have ~ with,** speak with); **freedom of ~,** right to express one's views freely. **2.** Thing said, remark (*after this unlucky speech he remained silent*); manner of speaking (*a man of blunt speech*). **3.** Public address (*after-dinner, impromptu,* MAIDEN, SET[3], *speech*; *speech for the defence*); **make** (deliver) **a ~**; ||**Queen's** or **King's (gracious) ~, ~ from the throne,** brief statement on foreign and domestic affairs and on the chief measures to be considered by Parliament, prepared by Government and read by sovereign in person or by commission at opening of Parliament. **4.** Language of a nation, region, group, etc. **5.** Act of sounding in organ-pipe etc. **6.** FIGURE[1] *of speech*; PART[1]*s of speech*; ||**~-day,** annual day for presenting prizes in schools usu. marked by speeches etc.; **~-reading,** lip-reading; **~ therapy,** treatment to improve defective speech. **7.** Hence **~'**FUL *a.*, talkative. [OE *sprǣc*, later *spēc*, = OS *sprāka*, OHG *sprāhha* f. WG (see SPEAK)]

spee'chĭ|fȳ *v.i.* (joc. or derog.) Make speeches, hold forth in public; hence **~**FICA'TION, **~fīer**[1], *ns.* [f. prec. + -I- + -FY]

spee'chlėss *a.* Dumb; temporarily deprived of speech by emotion etc. (*speechless with rage*); hence **~**LY[2] *adv.*, **~**NESS *n.* [OE *spǣclēas* (as SPEECH, -LESS)]

speed *n.* & *v.* **(sped** exc. in senses 8 & 9). **1.** *n.* Rapidity of movement (*with all speed*; *more haste less speed*; *at full speed*); rate of progress or motion, rate of change of distance with time (*attains a high speed*; *depends on the speed required*); gear appropriate to a range of speeds of bicycle, (U.S. or arch.) motor car, etc.; (Photog.) sensitivity of film to light, light-gathering power of lens, duration of exposure; **at ~,** moving quickly; AIR[1], GROUND[1], *speed*. **2.** (arch.) Success, prosperity, (*send me good speed*). **3.** (sl.) Methedrine. **4. ~'ball,** (sl.) mixture of cocaine with heroin or morphine; **~'boat,** motor boat designed for high speed; **~ limit,** maximum permitted speed of vehicle on road etc.; **~-merchant,** (colloq.) motorist etc. who travels at high speed; **~'way,** (1) arena for motor-cycle racing, (2) *road or track reserved for fast motor traffic. **5.** *v.i.* Go fast (*sped down the street*). **6.** *v.t.* Send fast, send on the way, (*speed an arrow from the bow*; *speed the parting guest*). **7.** *v.i.* & *t.* (arch.) Be or make prosperous, succeed, give success to, (*how have you sped?*; *God speed you!*). **8.** *v.t.* Regulate speed of (engine etc.), cause to go at fixed speed; **~ up,** cause to work at greater speed (*the service wants speeding up*); **~-up** *n.*, increase in rate of working, esp. by employees without corresponding additional pay. **9.** *v.i.* (Of motorist etc.) travel at illegal or dangerous speed; **~ up,** move at greater speed. [n. f. OE *spēd*, earlier *spǣd*, = OS *spōd*, OHG *spuot* f. Gmc **spōan* prosper; v. f. OE *spēdan*, = OS *spodian*, OHG *spuoten* f. Gmc st. **spōd-*]

spee'dō *n.* (*pl.* **~s**). (colloq.) = foll. [abbr.]

speedŏ'mėter *n.* Appliance indicating speed of vehicle. [f. SPEED + -O- + -METER]

***spee'dster** *n.* Person who travels at high speed, esp. illegally. [f. SPEED + -STER]

spee'dwĕll *n.* Small herb of genus *Veronica*, with creeping or ascending stem and small usu. bright-blue flowers. [app. f. SPEED 7 + WELL[3]]

spee'd|ȳ *a.* Moving quickly, rapid; expeditious, prompt, coming without delay, (*speedy answer, vengeance*); hence **~ĭ**LY[2] *adv.*, **~ĭ**NESS *n.* [ME, f. SPEED + -Y[2]]

speiss (-ĭs) *n.* Compound of arsenic, iron, etc., formed in smelting some lead ores. [f. G *speise* food, amalgam]

spēlėŏ'log|ȳ *n.* Scientific study of caves; hence **spēlėolŏ'g**ICAL *a.*, **~**IST (3) *n.* [f. F *spéléologie* f. L f. Gk *spēlaion* cave; see -LOGY]

spĕ'lĭcan. Var. of SPILLIKIN.

spĕll[1] *n.* Words used as charm, incantation or its effect (**break the ~,** make it ineffectual; **under a ~,** mastered by or as by a spell); attraction, fascination, exercised by person, activity, quality, etc.; **~'bind,** bind (as) by a spell; **~'binder,** (esp.) political speaker who can hold audiences spellbound; **~'bound,** bound (as) by a spell. [OE *spel(l)*, = OS, OHG *spel*, ON *spjall*, Goth. *spill* tale, f. Gmc **spellam*]

spĕll[2] *v.t.* (**spelt** *or* **~ed** *pr.* -lt). **1.** Write or name (in correct sequence) the letters that form (a word, or abs.; *how do you spell 'analyse'?*; *'surprise' must not be spelt with a z*; *can't spell his own name*; *wish you would learn to spell (correctly)*); **~ out** or **over,** make out (words, writing) laboriously letter by letter, (fig.) explain in detail. **2.** (Of letters) make up, form, (word; *what does c a t spell?*); (fig., of circumstances, scheme, etc.) have as necessary result, involve, (*these changes spell ruin to the farmer*). [ME, f. OF *espel(l)er*, **espeldre* f. Frank. **spellōn* discourse (as prec.)]

spĕll[3] *n.*, & *v.t.* **1.** *n.* Turn of work (*did a spell of carpentering*); short or fairly short period (*wait (for) a spell*; *had a spell of hay fever*; *a cold spell in April*); (Austral.) period of rest from work. **2.** *v.t.* Relieve, take the place of, (person) in work etc.; allow to rest briefly. [n. f. v., later form of dial. *spele* take place of f. OE *spelian*, of unkn. orig.]

spĕll[4] *n.* Splinter of wood etc.; trap in game of knur and spell (N. Engl. game like trap-ball). [perh. f. obs. *speld*]

spĕ'ller *n.* In vbl senses; spelling-book. [ME, f. SPELL[2] + -ER[1]]

spĕ'llĭcan. Var. of SPILLIKIN.

spĕ'llĭng *n.* In vbl senses (*his spelling is weak*; *not sure of the spelling of* '*aneurysm*'; *another spelling of the same word*); **~-bee,** competition in spelling; **~-book** (for teaching spelling); **~-pronunciation,** artificial pronunciation based on spelling, e.g. *forehead* pr. fŏr'hĕd instead of fŏ'rĭd. [ME, f. SPELL[2] + -ING[1]]

spĕlt[1] *n.* Species of wheat (*Triticum spelta*) giving very fine flour. [OE f. OS *spelta* (OHG *spelza*), ME f. MLG, MDu. *spelte*]

spĕlt[2]. See SPELL[2].

spĕ'lter *n.* (Esp. commercial) zinc. [corresp. to OF *espeautre*, MDu. *speauter*, G *spialter*, rel. to PEWTER]

***spėlŭ'nk|er** *n.* One who explores caves for sport; so ~ING[1] *n.* [f. obs. *spelunk* cave (f. L *spelunca*) + -ER[1]]

spĕnce *n.* (arch.) Buttery, larder. [ME, f. OF *despense* f. L *dispensa* fem. p.p. (as n.) of *dispendere* (see DISPENSE)]

spĕ'ncer[1] *n.* Short close-fitting jacket; thin jumper worn under dress etc. [prob. f. 2nd Earl *Spencer*, Engl. politician d. 1834]

spĕ'ncer[2] *n.* (Naut.) Trysail. [perh. f. K. *Spencer* (early 19th c.)]

Spĕncēr'ĭan *a.* & *n.* (Follower) of the doctrines of continual mechanical evolution of the universe, propounded by Spencer; hence ~ISM (3) *n.* [f. H. *Spencer*, Engl. philosopher d. 1903 + -IAN]

spĕnd *v.t.* (**spent**). **1.** Pay out (money, or abs.; *on* or **for* a thing; *on* person or thing so as to improve etc.) in making a purchase etc.; **~ a penny,** (colloq.) urinate or defecate [f. coin-operated lock of public water-closet]; ***~'ing money,** pocket-money. **2.** Use, use up, consume, (*our ammunition was all spent*; *shall spend no more breath, trouble*, etc., *on him*; *how do you spend your time?*; *spent a pleasant day*; *night is far spent*); exhaust, wear out, (*his anger will soon spend itself*); (in *p.p.*) having lost its original force or strength (*storm is spent*; *spent cannon-ball, tan, fish after spawning*). **3. ~'thrift,** extravagant person, prodigal. **4.** Hence ~'ABLE *a.*, ~'ER[1] *n.* [OE *spendan*, = OHG *spentōn*, ON *spenna*, f. L *expendere* (see EXPEND); in ME perh. also f. obs. *dispend* f. OF *despendre* expend f. L *dispendere* (see DISPENSE)]

Spĕnsēr'ĭan *a.* (In the style) of Spenser; **~ stanza,** that used by Spenser in the *Faerie Queene*, with eight iambic pentameters and an alexandrine, rhyming *ababbcbcc*. [f. E. *Spenser*, Engl. poet d. 1599 + -IAN]

spĕnt. See SPEND.

spērm[1] *n.* (*pl.* **~s** *or* **~**). Male generative fluid; (Biol.) spermatozoon. [ME, f. LL f. Gk *sperma -matos* seed (*speirō* sow)]

spērm[2] *n.* **~ (whale),** large whale (*Physeter catodon*) yielding spermaceti; = SPERMACETI; **~-oil,** lubricant found together with spermaceti. [abbr. of foll.]

spērmacĕ'tĭ *n.* White waxy substance contained in head of sperm whale etc., used for candles and ointments. [ME f. med. L, f. LL *sperma* SPERM[1] + *ceti* of whale (*cetus* f. Gk *kētos*), it being regarded as whale-spawn]

spēr'marў *n.* Organ in which spermatozoa are generated. [f. mod. L *spermarium* (as SPERM[1]: see -ARY[1])]

spērmă'tĭc *a.* Of SPERM[1] or the spermary; **~ cord** (supporting testicle within scrotum). [f. LL f. Gk *spermatikos* (as SPERM[1]; see -IC)]

spēr'matĭd *n.* (Biol.) Cell that develops into spermatozoon. [f. as SPERM[1] + -ID[2]]

spēr'mato- *comb. form.* Seed, SPERM[1], as: **~blast,** spermatid; **~cyte,** cell that is ancestor of spermatozoa; **~ge'nesis,** development of spermatozoa; **~go'nium,** cell from which male gametes are ultimately formed; **~phore,** capsule containing spermatozoa; **~phyte,** plant producing seeds; **~zo'on** (*pl.* **~zo'a**), male fertilizing element contained in semen of animals, (or **~zo'id**) similar element in lower plants. [f. as SPERM[1] + -O-]

spēr'mĭcīd|e *n.* Substance able to kill spermatozoa; hence ~AL *a.* [irreg. f. SPERM[1] + -I- + -CIDE (1)]

spēr'mo-. Var. of SPERMATO-.

spew, (arch.) **spūe,** *v.t.* & *i.* Vomit (lit. or fig.). [OE *spīwan*, *spēowan*, = OS, OHG *spīwan*, ON *spýja*, Goth. *speiwan*, Gmc f. IE **spjūj-*, imit.]

sp. gr. *abbr.* specific gravity.

sphă'gn|um *n.* (*pl.* **~a**). Moss of genus *Sphagnum*, growing in bogs and peat, and used as packing etc. [mod. L, f. Gk *sphagnos* a moss]

sphă'lerīte *n.* = BLENDE. [f. Gk *sphaleros* deceptive (cf. BLENDE) + -ITE[1]]

sphē'no- *comb. form.* Of the sphenoid bone (*spheno-ethmoidal*). [Gk (*sphēn* wedge; see -O-)]

sphē'noid *a.* & *n.* Wedge-shaped, esp. **~ (bone),** compound bone between temporal bone and eye; hence **sphēnoi'd**AL *a.* [f. mod. L f. Gk *sphēnoeidēs* (*sphēn* wedge; see -OID)]

sphēre *n.*, & *v.t.* **1.** *n.* (Surface of) solid figure generated by revolution of semicircle about its diameter, every point on whose surface is equidistant from its centre. **2.** Ball, globe; (poet.) the heavens, the sky; any heavenly body; globe representing the earth; globe representing the surface on which heavenly bodies appear to lie (**oblique, right, parallel, ~,** sphere of apparent heavens at place where there is oblique angle, right angle, zero angle, between equator and horizon). **3.** Each of the revolving globe-shaped shells in which the heavenly bodies were formerly supposed to be set; **music** or **harmony of the ~s** (supposed to be produced by movements of these shells). **4.** One's field of action, influence, or existence, one's natural surroundings, one's place in society, (*has done much within his own sphere*; *great mistake to take him out of his sphere*; *moves in quite another sphere*); claimed or recognized area *of* State's *influence*. **5.** Hence **sphēr'**Y[2] *a.* (poet.). **6.** *v.t.* Enclose (as) in sphere; make sphere-shaped; (poet.) exalt to the (celestial) spheres. [ME *sper(e)* f. OF *espere* f. LL *sphera*, L f. Gk *sphaira* ball]

sphĕ'r|ĭc *a.* = foll., whence **~ĭ'**CITY *n.*; (poet.) of the heavens, celestial, exalted. [f. LL f. Gk *sphairikos* (as prec.; see -IC)]

sphĕ'rĭcal *a.* Shaped like a sphere, globular, whence ~LY[2] *adv.*; of spheres (*spherical geometry, trigonometry*); (of triangle etc.) bounded by arcs of great circles of sphere; **~ aberration** (due to spherical form of lens or mirror). [f. as prec.; see -ICAL]

sphēr'oid *n.* Spherelike but not perfectly spherical body; solid generated by half-revolution of ellipse about its major axis (PROLATE *spheroid*) or minor axis (OBLATE[2] *spheroid*); hence **sphĕroid'**AL *a.*, ~I'CITY *n.* [f. L f. Gk *sphairoeidēs* (as SPHERE; see -OID)]

sphērŏ'mėter *n.* Instrument for finding radius of sphere and for exact measurement of thickness of small bodies. [f. F *sphéromètre* (as SPHERE, -O-, -METER)]

sphĕ'rul|e (-ōōl) *n.* Small sphere; hence ~AR[1] *a.* [f. LL *sphaerula* dim. of L *sphaera* (see SPHERE, -ULE)]

sphĕ'rulīte (-rōō-) *n.* Vitreous globule as constituent of volcanic rocks. [f. as prec. + -ITE[1]]

sphĭ'ncter *n.* Ring of muscle surrounding and serving to guard or close an opening or tube; hence ~AL, **sphĭnctĕ'ric**, *adjs.* [L, f. Gk *sphigktēr* (*sphiggō* bind tight)]

sphĭ'ngĭd (-ngg-) *a.* & *n.* (Member) of the hawk-moth family Sphingidae. [f. foll. + -ID[3]]

sphĭnx *n.* **1.** (Gk Myth.; *S*~) Winged monster of Thebes with woman's head and lion's body who proposed a riddle to the Thebans, killed all who could not guess it, and on Oedipus' solving it threw herself from the rock on which she sat, and died. **2.** (Egypt. Ant.) Figure with lion's body and man's or animal's head, esp. colossal one near the Pyramids at Giza. **3.** Enigmatic or inscrutable person. **4.** Hawk-moth; species of baboon (*Papio sphinx*). [L, f. Gk *Sphigx*, app. f. *sphiggō* draw tight]

sphragĭ'stĭcs *n. pl.* (also treated as *sing.*) Study of engraved seals. [f. F *sphragistique* n. & a. f. Gk *sphragistikos* (*sphragis* seal; see -IC)]

sphȳ'gmo- *comb. form.* (Physiol.) Pulse, pulsation, as: ~**graph,** instrument for showing character of pulse in series of curves; ~**gram,** record so produced; ~**mano'meter,** instrument for measuring blood pressure. [f. Gk *sphugmo-* (*sphugmos* pulse f. *sphuzō* throb)]

spī'c|a *n.* **1.** (Bot.) Spike; hence ~ATE[2], ~**āt**ED[1], *adjs.* **2.** (Surg.) Spiral bandage with reversed turns, suggesting ear of corn. [L, = spike, ear of corn, rel. to *spina* SPINE; in sense 2 after Gk *stakhus*]

spīce *n.*, & *v.t.* **1.** *n.* Aromatic or pungent vegetable substance used to flavour food, e.g. cloves, pepper, mace; spices collectively (*dealer in spice*; *sugar and spice and all that's nice*), so **spī'**CERY (1) *n.*; (fig.) touch, dash, flavour, (*of* malice etc. *in* person's character, writings, etc.); ~**'bush,** aromatic Amer. shrub of genus *Lindera* or *Calycanthus*. **2.** *v.t.* Flavour with spice. [ME, f. OF *espice(r)* f. L *species* specific kind, in LL pl. = merchandise]

spĭck *a.* ~ **and span,** smart and new, brand-new, very neat. [16th c. *spick and span new*, emphatic extension of ME *span new* f. ON *spán-nýr* (*spánn* chip, *nýr* new)]

spĭ'cknel *n.* Baldmoney. [var. of SPIGNEL]

spĭ'cūl|e *n.* Small sharp-pointed body; (Zool.) small hard calcareous or siliceous body esp. in framework of sponge; (Bot.) small or secondary spike; (Astron.) spikelike prominence; hence ~AR[1], ~ATE[2], *adjs.* [f. mod. L *spicula*, *spiculum*, dims. of SPICA; see -ULE]

spī'c|ȳ *a.* Of, flavoured or fragrant with, spice; (fig.) piquant, pungent, sensational, improper (*spicy story*), (sl.) showy, smart; hence ~**ĭ**LY[2] *adv.*, ~**ĭ**NESS *n.* [f. SPICE + -Y[2]]

spī'der *n.* **1.** Eight-legged arthropod of the order Araneida, many species of which spin webs esp. for capture of insects as food (~ **and fly,** (fig.) ensnarer and ensnared); kinds of arachnid like spider (RED *spider*). **2.** Thing compared to spider esp. as having prominent legs or radiating spokes etc.; *iron frying-pan (orig. with legs or feet). **3.** High-built cart etc. with very large light wheels. **4.** ~**-crab,** crab of superfamily Oxyrhyncha, with long thin legs; ~**-line,** thread of spider's web substituted for wire in reticle etc.; ~**-man,** one who works at great height in construction of buildings; ~ **monkey,** Amer. monkey with long limbs and long prehensile tail; ~**-wasp,** wasp that stores its nest with spiders as food for its young; ~**wort,** plant of genus *Tradescantia*, whose flowers have slender hairy stamens. **5.** Hence ~Y[2] *a.*, (esp., of handwriting, legs, spokes, etc.) very thin. [OE *spīthra* (as SPIN[1])]

spie'geleisen (-gelīzen) *n.* Kind of pig-iron containing manganese, used in Bessemer process of steel-making. [G (*spiegel* mirror, *eisen* iron)]

***spiel** *n.* & *v.* (sl.) **1.** *n.* Speech, story, esp. glib or persuasive one. **2.** *v.i.* Hold forth, orate. **3.** *v.t.* Reel off (patter, yarn, tale of misfortune). [G, = play, game]

spie'ler *n.* (sl.) *One who spiels; (Austral.) gambler, swindler. [G (as prec.; see -ER[1])]

spies. See SPY.

spĭ'ffȳ, spĭ'ffĭng, *adjs.* (colloq.) Smart, handsome; excellent. [19th c.; orig. unkn.]

spĭ'f(f)lĭcāte *v.t.* (usu. joc.) Trounce, castigate, destroy. [18th c.; fanciful]

spĭ'gnel *n.* Baldmoney. [perh. f. ME *spigurnel*, plant-name, f. med. L *spigurnellus*, of unkn. orig.]

spĭ'got *n.* Small peg or plug, esp. one for insertion into vent-hole of cask; (similar device controlling flow of liquor in) faucet; plain end of pipe-section fitting into socket of next one. [ME, perh. f. Prov. *espigou(n)* f. L *spiculum* dim. of *spicum* = SPICA]

***spĭk** *n.* (derog.) Spanish American, esp. Mexican. [f. SPEAK as allegedly used in 'no spik English' etc.]

spīke[1] *n.*, & *v.t.* **1.** *n.* Sharp point; pointed piece of metal e.g. one of set forming top of iron fence etc. or worn on bottom of running-shoe to prevent slipping; (in *pl.*) running-shoes fitted with spikes; large stout nail esp. as used for railways; pointed metal rod standing upright on base and used e.g. to hold postponed matter in newspaper office; (sl.) hypodermic needle; ~ **heel** of shoe (high and tapering to narrow base). **2.** *v.t.* Fasten with or furnish with spikes; fix on or pierce with spikes; plug up vent of (gun) with spike, (fig.) make useless, *put an end to (idea etc.); (colloq.) add alcohol to (drink). [ME, perh. f. MLG, MDu. *spiker*, rel. to SPOKE[1]]

spīke[2] *n.* (Bot.) Flower-cluster of many sessile flowers arranged closely on long common axis; separate sprig of any plant in which flowers form spikelike cluster; hence ~'LET (-kl-) *n.* [ME, = ear of corn, f. L SPICA]

spī'kenârd (-kn-) *n.* (Ancient costly aromatic ointment made chiefly from) Indian plant (*Nardostachys jatamansi*); **ploughman's** ~, composite fragrant plant (*Inula squarrosa*) with purplish-yellow flower-heads. [ME, (ult.) f. med. L *spica nardi* (as SPIKE[2], NARD), after Gk *nardostakhus*]

spī'k|ȳ[1] *a.* Like a spike; having spike(s); (colloq., derog.) holding rigid high-church or ritualistic views; hence ~**ĭ**LY[2] *adv.*, ~**ĭ**NESS *n.* [f. SPIKE[1] + -Y[2]]

spī'kȳ[2] *a.* Having spikes or ears. [f. SPIKE[2] + -Y[2]]

spīle *n.*, & *v.t.* **1.** *n.* Wooden peg, spigot; large timber for driving into ground, pile; *small spout for conducting sap from sugar-maple etc. **2.** *v.t.* Make spike-hole in (cask etc.). [MDu., MLG, = wooden peg etc.; in sense 'pile' app. alt. f. PILE[1]]

spĭll[1] *v.* (**spilt** *or* ~**ed**) & *n.* **1.** *v.t.* Allow (liquid, substance in small particles) to fall or run out from vessel esp. accidentally or wastefully (*spilt the salt*; *no use crying over spilt* MILK[1]); ~ **blood,** be guilty of bloodshed; ~ **the blood of,** kill; ~**'way,** passage for surplus water from dam; hence ~'AGE (3) *n.* **2.** (Naut.) Empty (sail) of wind; lose (wind) from belly of sail. **3.** (sl.) Disclose (information etc.); ~ **the beans,** give the show away, divulge information indiscreetly. **4.** Throw from saddle or vehicle (*horse spilt him*). **5.** *v.i.* (Of liquid etc.) be spilt, fall or run out from vessel; ~ **over** (of surplus population of towns; cf. OVERSPILL). **6.** *n.* Spilling or being spilt; throwing or being thrown from saddle etc.

(*had a nasty spill*); tumble, fall. [OE *spillan* kill, = MDu., MLG *spillen*, rel. to OE *spildan* destroy = OS *spildian*, OHG *spilden*, ON *spilla*, of unkn. orig.]

spĭll² *n.* Thin strip of wood, folded or twisted paper, for lighting candles, pipe-tobacco, etc. [ME, rel. to SPILE]

spĭ'llĭkĭn *n.* Splinter of wood, bone, etc.; (in *pl.*) game in which heap of these is to be removed by taking one at a time without disturbing others. [f. prec. + -KIN]

spĭlt. See SPILL¹.

spĭlth *n.* What is spilt; act of spilling; excess, surplus. [f. SPILL¹ + -TH¹]

spĭn¹ *v.* (**-nn-**; **spun** or arch. **span**; **spun**). **1.** *v.t.* Draw out and twist (wool, cotton, or abs.) into threads; make (yarn) thus. **2.** (Of spider, silkworm, etc.) make (web, gossamer, cocoon, or abs.) by extrusion of fine viscous thread; make (artificial fibre) thus. **3.** (fig.) Produce, compose, (narrative, literary article, etc.); ~ **a yarn,** (orig. Naut.) tell a story. **4.** ~ **out,** spend, consume, (time, one's life, etc., *by* discussion etc., *in* occupation etc.), prolong (discussion etc.), narrate etc. at great length, (Cricket) dismiss (batsman, side) by spin bowling. **5.** Cause (top etc.) to whirl round; shape (metal) on mould in lathe etc.; turn (person, thing) quickly round; toss (coin); **~-dry,** dry (washed articles) in rapidly rotating drum (**~-drier,** machine for doing this). **6.** Fish in (stream, pool) with spinner or spinning bait. **7.** (in *p.p.*) Converted into threads for subsequent use (*spun glass, gold, silver*); **spun silk,** cheap material of short-fibred and waste silk often mixed with cotton; **spun yarn,** (Naut.) line formed of rope-yarns twisted together. **8.** ~ **off,** throw off by centrifugal force in spinning; **~-off** *n.*, incidental result(s), esp. as benefit from industrial or technological development. **9.** *v.i.* (Of top etc.) whirl round; (of person or thing) turn *round* quickly, e.g. as result of being struck; (of person's head etc.) be in a whirl through dizziness or astonishment. [OE *spinnan*, = OHG, Goth. *spinnan*, ON *spinna*]

spĭn² *n.* Spinning motion, whirl; aircraft's diving descent combined with rotation (FLAT² *spin*); secondary revolving motion esp. as developed in rifle bullet, or in billiard or tennis ball struck aslant; (Cricket) twisting motion given to ball when bowled (~ **bowler,** expert at this); brisk or short run or spell of driving, rowing, cycling, etc., (*went for a spin*); (Phys.) intrinsic angular momentum of elementary particle; (Austral. colloq.) piece of good or bad luck. [f. prec.]

spīna bĭ'fĭda *n.* Congenital defect of spine allowing meninges to protrude. [mod. L (as SPINE, BIFID)]

spĭ'nach (-nĭj) *n.* Garden vegetable (*Spinacia oleracea*) with succulent leaves cooked as food; other plant similarly used; *unwanted or unnecessary thing; ~ **beet,** kind of beet grown for its leaves and used like spinach; hence **spĭn**A'CEOUS *a.* [prob. f. MDu. *spinaetse*, *spinag*(*i*)*e*, f. OF *espinage*, *espinache* f. med. L *spinac*(*h*)*ia* etc. f. Arab. *'isfānāḵ* f. Pers. *ispānāḵ*; perh. assim. to L *spina* SPINE, w. ref. to prickly seeds]

spī'nal *a.* Of the spine, (*spinal curvature, disease*); ~ **canal,** cavity between vertebrae containing spinal cord; ~ **column,** spine; ~ **cord,** cylindrical structure within spine, a part of the central nervous system; *spinal* MARROW. [f. LL *spinalis* (as SPINE; see -AL)]

spĭ'ndle *n.*, & *v.i.* **1.** *n.* Pin in spinning-wheel used for twisting and winding the thread; small bar with tapered ends serving same purpose in hand-spinning; pin bearing bobbin of spinning-machine; pin or axis that revolves or on which a thing revolves; (Biol.) spindle-shaped configuration in mitosis; slender thing or person; varying measure of length for yarn. **2. ~-berry,** fruit of spindle-tree; **~-shanked,** with long thin legs; **~-shanks,** person with such legs; **~-shaped,** of circular cross-section and tapering towards each end; ~ **side,** = DISTAFF *side*; **~-tree,** shrub or small tree of genus *Euonymus*, esp. *E. europaeus* with greenish-white flowers, pink or red berries, and hard wood used for spindles. **3.** Hence **spĭ'ndl**Y² *a.*, slender, attenuated. **4.** *v.i.* Have, or grow into, long slender form. [OE *spinel*, = OS *spinnila*, OHG *spin*(*n*)*ila*, f. as SPIN¹ + -LE 1]

spĭ'ndrĭft *n.* Spray blown along surface of sea. [Sc. var. of *spoondrift* (*spoon* run before wind or sea, DRIFT¹)]

spīne *n.* **1.** Series of vertebrae extending from skull, backbone; central feature, main support or source of strength. **2.** (Bot. & Zool.) stiff sharp-pointed process; (Anat.) sharp-pointed slender process of bone; hence **spīn**ED² (-nd), **spī'n**OSE¹, **spī'n**OUS, *adjs.* **3.** Sharp ridge or projection. **4.** Part of book's cover or jacket that encloses its page-fastening part and usu. faces outwards on shelf. **5. ~-chiller, -chilling,** (book, film, etc.) causing thrill of terror. [ME, f. OF *espine* or f. L *spina* thorn, backbone]

spĭ'nel *n.* Hard crystalline mineral of various colours consisting chiefly of magnesia and alumina; substance of similar composition or properties; ~ **ruby,** valuable deep-red variety of spinel. [f. F *spinelle*, f. It. *spinella* dim. of *spina* (as prec.; see -LE 2)]

spī'nelėss (-nl-) *a.* Having no spine, invertebrate; (of fish) having no fin-spines; (fig.) lacking energy or resolution, weak, having no backbone, whence ~LY² *adv.*, ~NESS *n.* [f. SPINE + -LESS]

spĭnĕ't (*or* spĭ'nĭt) *n.* (Hist.) Small harpsichord with one string to each note. [f. obs. F *espinette* f. It. *spinetta* virginal, spinet, dim. of *spina* thorn etc. (as SPINE), both instruments having plucked strings]

spĭ'nĭfĕx *n.* Coarse spiny-leaved Austral. grass of genus *Spinifex*. [mod. L, f. L *spina* spine + -I- + *-fex* maker (*facere* make)]

spĭ'nnaker *n.* Large triangular sail carried opposite mainsail of racing-yacht running before wind. [fanciful f. *Sphinx*, name of yacht first using it, perh. after *spanker*]

spĭ'nner *n.* In vbl senses; manufacturer engaged in (esp. cotton-) spinning; (arch.) spider; real or artificial fly for (esp. trout-)fishing, revolving bait; (Cricket) spin bowler, ball given spin; spinneret. [ME, f. SPIN¹ + -ER¹]

spĭ'nnerĕt *n.* Spinning-organ in spider, silkworm, etc.; device for forming filaments of synthetic fibre. [f. prec. + -ET¹]

||**spĭ'nney** *n.* Small wood, thicket. [f. OF *espinei* f. Rom. **spineta* f. L *spinetum* thicket (*spina* thorn)]

spĭ'nnĭng *n.* In vbl senses; **~-house,** (Hist.) house of correction for prostitutes; **~-jenny,** early machine for spinning with more than one spindle at a time; **~-machine,** (esp.) machine that spins fibres continuously; **~-top,** = TOP³; **~-wheel,** household implement for spinning yarn or thread, with spindle driven by wheel driven by crank or treadle. [ME, f. SPIN¹ + -ING¹]

spī'nōse, spī'nous. See SPINE.

Spĭnō'z|ĭsm *n.* Doctrine of Spinoza that there is one sole and infinite substance of which extension and thought are attributes and individual beings are changing forms; so ~IST (2) *n.*, **~ĭ'st**IC *a.* [f. B. de *Spinoza*, Du. philosopher d. 1677 + -ISM]

spĭ′nster *n.* Unmarried woman; (elderly) woman thought unlikely to marry; hence ~HOOD *n.* [ME, orig. = woman who spins, f. SPIN¹ + -STER]

spĭnthă′rĭscōpe *n.* Instrument with fluorescent screen showing incidence of alpha particles by flashes. [irreg. f. Gk *spintharis* spark + -SCOPE]

spī′nūl|e *n.* (Bot. & Zool.) Small spine; hence ~OSE¹, ~OUS, *adjs.* [f. L *spinula* dim. of *spina* spine; see -ULE]

spī′nȳ *a.* **1.** Full of spines, prickly; ~ **eel,** eel-shaped fish with dorsal fin of free spines; ~ **lobster,** lobster-like crustacean with spiny shell and no claws; ~ **rat,** bristly rat of S. America. **2.** (fig.) Perplexing, troublesome, thorny. **3.** Hence **spī′nĭ**NESS *n.* [f. SPINE + -Y²]

spīr′acle *n.* (Zool.) External respiratory orifice in insects; blow-hole of whale etc.; hence **spīră′cūl**AR¹ *a.* [f. L *spiraculum* (*spirare* breathe)]

spīră′cūl|um *n.* (*pl.* ~**a**). = prec. [L; see prec.]

spīrae′a *n.* Shrub or plant of genus *Spiraea*, with small white or pink flowers. [L, f. Gk *speiraia* (*speira* coil)]

spīr′al *a.*, *n.*, & *v.* (‖-ll-). **1.** *a.* Coiled; winding continually about and constantly receding from or moving towards a centre, whether remaining in same plane like watch-spring or rising in a cone; winding continually and advancing as if along cylinder, like thread of screw; ~ **balance** (measuring weight by torsion of spiral spring); ~ **nebula** (in which matter is mainly in one or more spiral arms); ~ **staircase** (rising circularly round central axis). **2.** Hence ~ITY (-ă′l-) *n.*, ~LY² *adv.* **3.** *n.* Plane or other spiral curve; spiral spring; spiral formation in shell etc.; spiral nebula; (fig.) gradual but progressive rise or fall of two or more interdependent quantities alternately (*the vicious spiral of rising prices and wages*). **4.** *v.t.* Make spiral. **5.** *v.i.* Move in a spiral course. [F, or f. med. L *spiralis* (as SPIRE²; see -AL)]

spīr′ant *a.* & *n.* (Phonet.) (Consonant) uttered with continuous expulsion of breath, esp. fricative. [f. L *spirare* breathe; see -ANT]

spīre¹ *n.* & *v.* **1.** *n.* Tapering structure in form of tall cone or pyramid rising above tower; continuation of tree trunk above point where branching begins; any tapering body, e.g. spike of flower; hence **spīr′**Y² *a.* **2.** *v.i.* Shoot up. **3.** *v.t.* Furnish with spire. [OE *spīr*, = MLG, MDu. *spier*, *spīr*, MHG *spīr*]

spīre² *n.* Spiral, coil; single twist of this; upper part of spiral shell. [F, f. L f. Gk *speira* coil]

spīrĭ′ll|um *n.* (*pl.* ~**a**). Bacterium of genus *Spirillum* characterized by a spiral structure. [mod. L, irreg. dim. of L *spira* (see prec.)]

spĭ′rĭt¹ *n.* **1.** Animating or vital principle of man; intelligent or immaterial part of man, soul; **in** (**the**) ~, inwardly (*groaned in spirit*; *was vexed in spirit*; *shall be with you in* (*the*) *spirit*). **2.** Person viewed as possessing this, esp. w. ref. to particular mental or moral qualities, (*one of the most ardent spirits of his time*; *a meeting of choice spirits*); KINDRED *spirit*. **3.** Rational or intelligent being not connected with material body (*God is a spirit*; HOLY *Spirit*; *spirit* MOVE²*s* person); disembodied soul, incorporeal being, elf, fairy, (*spirits must have been at work*; FAMILIAR *spirit*; *peace to his departed spirit*). **4.** Person's mental or moral nature or qualities (*a man of unbending spirit*); **the poor in** ~, (arch.) the meek. **5.** (**High**) ~, courage, self-assertion, vivacity, energy, dash, (*if you had the spirit of a mouse*; *do show a little spirit*; *went at it, played the waltz, with spirit*; *infused spirit into his men*; *people of spirit*). **6.** Person viewed as supplying this (= SOUL 4, but usu. w. adj.; *was the animating spirit of the rebellion*). **7.** Mental or moral condition or attitude, mood, (*took it in a wrong spirit*; *depends on the spirit in which it is done*; *did it in a spirit of mischief*; *enter into the spirit of the thing*; PUBLIC *spirit*; *objections made in a captious spirit*). **8.** Real meaning opp. to verbal expression (*must consider the spirit of the law, not the letter*; *have followed out the spirit of his instructions*). **9.** Animating principle or influence, mental or moral tendency (*cannot resist the spirit of the age* or *times*). **10.** Immaterial principle formerly thought to govern vital phenomena; ANIMAL *spirits*; **high** or **great** ~**s,** cheerfulness and buoyancy; **poor** or **low** ~**s,** depression. **11.** Volatile liquid got by distillation (‖MOTOR *spirit*; WOOD *spirit*); purified alcohol (METHYLATED *spirit*); (usu. in *pl.*) strong distilled liquor esp. alcohol, e.g. brandy, whisky, gin, rum, (*a glass of spirits and water*; ARDENT *spirits*; *touches no spirit but gin*). **12.** Solution (*of* volatile principle) in alcohol, tincture; ~**s of salt,** (arch.) hydrochloric acid; ~(**s**) **of wine,** (arch.) purified alcohol. **13.** ~ **blue,** blue aniline dye soluble in alcohol; ~ **duck,** bufflehead or golden-eye (diving rapidly at flash of gun etc.); ~ **duplicator** (using alcoholic solution to produce copies from master sheet); ~ **gum,** quick-drying solution of gum used esp. for attaching false hair; ~**-lamp** (burning methylated or other volatile spirit instead of oil); ~**-level,** glass tube nearly filled with spirit, used to test horizontality by position of air-bubble; ~**-rapper,** person professing to converse with departed spirits by means of their raps on table etc.; so ~**-rapping.** [ME, f. AF (*e*)*spirit*, OF *esp*(*e*)*rit*, f. L *spiritus* breath, spirit (*spirare* breathe)]

spĭ′rĭt² *v.t.* Convey (*away*, *off*, etc.) rapidly and secretly (as) by agency of spirits; ~ **up,** animate, cheer, (person). [f. prec.]

spĭ′rĭtėd *a.* Full of spirit, animated, lively, brisk, courageous, (*a spirited translation, attack, reply*); having specified spirit(s) (*high, low, mean, proud, jealous, -spirited*); hence (-)~LY² *adv.*, ~NESS *n.* [f. SPIRIT¹ + -ED²]

spĭ′rĭtĭsm *n.* = SPIRITUALISM 1. [f. SPIRIT¹ + -ISM]

spĭ′rĭtlėss *a.* Lacking courage, vigour, or vivacity; hence ~LY² *adv.* [f. SPIRIT¹ + -LESS]

spĭ′rĭtūal *a.* & *n.* **1.** *a.* Of spirit as opp. to matter; of the soul esp. as acted on by God (*spiritual life*); of or proceeding from God, holy, divine, inspired, (*spiritual songs*; *the spiritual law*); concerned with sacred or religious things (*our spiritual interests*); ~ (ecclesiastical) **courts**; ‖**lords** ~, bishops and archbishops in House of Lords (cf. TEMPORAL). **2.** Having the higher qualities of the mind; concerned with or based on the spirit (*spiritual relationship*; one's *spiritual home*). **3.** Hence ~LY² *adv.*, ~NESS *n.* **4.** *n.* Religious song characteristic of Amer. Negroes. [ME, f. OF *spirituel* f. L *spiritualis* (as SPIRIT¹; see -AL)]

spĭ′rĭtūal|ĭsm *n.* **1.** Belief that departed spirits communicate with and show themselves to men, esp. through mediums, or at seances by means of spirit-rapping, -handwriting, etc.; system of doctrines or practices founded on this. **2.** (Philos.) Doctrine that spirit exists as distinct from matter or that spirit is the only reality (cf. MATERIALISM). **3.** Hence or cogn. ~IST (2) *n.*, ~**ĭ′st**IC *a.* [f. prec. + -ISM]

spĭrĭtūă′lĭtȳ *n.* Spiritual quality; (Hist., usu. in *pl.*) what belongs or is due to the Church or to an ecclesiastic as such (*the spiritualities of his office*). [ME, f. OF *spiritualité* or LL *spiritualitas* (as SPIRITUAL; see -ITY)]

spĭ′rĭtūalīz|e, -īs|e (-īz), *v.t.* Make spiritual, elevate, (character, person, thoughts); attach spiritual as opp. to literal meaning to; hence ~A′TION *n.* [f. SPIRITUAL + -IZE, or f. F *spiritualiser*]

spĭrĭtūĕ'l(le) *a.* Marked by refinement and sprightliness of mind. [f. F *spirituel*, fem. *-elle* (as SPIRITUAL)]
spĭ'rĭtūous *a.* Containing much alcohol, distilled and not only fermented (*spirituous liquor*); hence ~NESS *n.* [f. L *spiritus* spirit + -OUS, or f. F *spiritueux*]
spĭ'rĭtus *n.* (Gk Gram.; arch.) ~ **a'sper, le'nis** (lē'nĭs), = *rough, smooth,* BREATHING. [L]
spīr'ĭvălve *a.* (Esp. of gastropod) having spiral shell; (of shell) spiral. [F, f. L *spira* SPIRE² + *valva* (see VALVE)]
spîr'kėtĭng *n.* (Naut.) Inside planking between top of waterways and lower sills of ports. [f. obs. *spirket, spurket,* space between timbers of ship's side, of unkn. orig., + -ING¹ (6)]
spīr'o-¹ *comb. form.* Coil, as: ~**chaete,** *~**chete,** (-kēt), spiral-shaped bacterium; ~**gyr'a** (-jīr'*a*), freshwater alga with spiral bands of chlorophyll. [f. L *spira*, Gk *speira* coil + -O-]
spīr'o-² *comb. form.* Breath, as: ~**graph,** instrument for recording breathing movement; ~**meter** (-ŏ'm-), instrument for measuring lung capacity. [irreg. f. L *spirare* breathe + -O-]
spîrt. See SPURT².
spīr'y̆. See SPIRE¹.
spĭt¹ *n.*, & *v.t.* (**-tt-**). **1.** *n.* Slender bar on which meat that is to be roasted is fixed before fire etc.; skewer; small point of land projecting into sea; long narrow underwater bank. **2.** *v.t.* Thrust spit through (meat etc.); (fig.) pierce or transfix with sword etc. [OE *spitu*, = MDu., MLG *spit, spet,* OHG *spiz* f. WG **spitu*]
spĭt² *v.* (**-tt-; spat** *or* **spit**) & *n.* **1.** *v.i.* Eject saliva; ~ **and polish,** cleaning and polishing work of soldier etc., (fig.) exaggerated neatness and smartness. **2.** *v.t.* Eject (saliva, blood, food, etc. *out*) from mouth; (fig.) utter (oaths, threats, etc.) vehemently; ~ **it out,** (colloq.) speak louder or without further delay. **3.** *v.i.* (Of cat etc., or fig. of person) make noise as of spitting as sign of anger or hostility; (of rain) fall lightly; (of fire, candle, pen) send out sparks, stray ink, etc. **4.** *~**'ball** (of chewed paper as missile, or baseball moistened by pitcher to impart spin); ~**'fire,** person of fiery temper; ~**ting cobra** (ejecting venom without striking); ~**ting image,** = sense 7. **5.** *n.* Spitting (esp. of cat). **6.** Spittle; saliva-like secretion of some insects; CUCKOO-*spit*. **7. The** (**dead** or **very**) ~ (**and image**), exact counterpart *of*, likeness *of*, (*he is the very spit of his father*). [OE *spittan* = G dial. *spützen*, of imit. orig.; cf. SPEW]
spĭt³ *n.* Spade-depth of earth (*dig it two spits* or *spit deep*). [MDu. & MLG, = OE *spittan* dig with spade, prob. rel. to SPIT¹]
spĭ'tchcŏck *n.*, & *v.t.* **1.** *n.* Eel split and broiled. **2.** *v.t.* Prepare thus (eel, fish, bird). [16th c., of unkn. orig.; cf. SPATCHCOCK]
spite *n.*, & *v.t.* **1.** *n.* Ill will, malice, (*did it from pure spite* or *in* or *out of spite*); grudge (*has a spite against me*); **in** ~ **of,** (arch.) ~ **of,** notwithstanding; **in** ~ **of oneself,** though one would rather have done otherwise. **2.** *v.t.* Thwart, mortify, annoy, (*does it to spite me*); **cut off** one's **nose to** ~ one's **face,** injure oneself by vindictive or resentful conduct. [ME, f. OF *despit* DESPITE]
spī'teful (-tf-) *a.* Animated by spite, malevolent; hence ~LY² *adv.*, ~NESS *n.* [ME, f. prec. + -FUL]
spĭ'ttle *n.* Saliva esp. as ejected from mouth. [alt. f. ME (now dial.) *spattle* (OE *spātl* f. *spǣtan* to spit) after SPIT²]
spĭttōō'n *n.* Vessel to spit into, usu. round metal or earthenware vessel with funnel-shaped top. [f. SPIT² + -OON]
spĭtz (-ts) *n.* Small dog with pointed muzzle, esp. Pomeranian. [G *spitz*(*hund*) (*spitz* pointed, *hund* dog)]
‖**spĭv** *n.* (sl.) Person living by his wits without regular work; one who engages in petty black--market dealings etc.; hence ~**'**VERY (5) *n.*, ~'ISH¹ *a.* [20th c.; orig. unkn.]
splă'nchn|ĭc (-ngk-) *a.* Of the viscera, intestinal; so ~O- *comb. form,* ~**ŏ'**LOGY, ~**ŏ'**TOMY, *ns.* [f. mod. L f. Gk *splagkhnikos* (*splagkhna* entrails; see -IC)]
splăsh *v.* & *n.* **1.** *v.t.* Cause to be struck by small drops (person etc. *with* water, mud, etc.); throw small drops of (liquid *about, on,* or *over* person etc.); decorate with scattered colour (*white robe splashed with red*); display (news) prominently; spend (money) ostentatiously. **2.** *v.i.* (Of liquid) fly about in drops or scattered portions; (of person) cause liquid to do this, move *across, along,* etc., thus; step, fall, plunge, etc., *into* (water etc.) so as to splash it. **3.** *n.* Splashing; quantity of liquid splashed; resulting noise (*we heard a splash*; **make a** ~, attract much attention); prominent display of news etc.; WATER¹-*splash*; ‖(colloq.) small quantity of soda-water etc. (diluting whisky etc.); spot of dirt etc. splashed on to thing; daub or patch of colour esp. on animal's skin. **4.** ~**'back,** panel behind sink etc. to protect wall from splashes; ~**-board,** guard in front of vehicle or over or beside wheel of vehicle to keep mud etc. off occupants; ~**-down,** alighting of spacecraft on sea. **5.** Hence ~'Y² *a.* [alt. f. PLASH²]
splăt *n.* Flat piece of thin wood in centre of chair-back. [f. *splat* v. split up, rel. to SPLIT¹]
splă'tter *v.i.* & *t.*, & *n.* Splash esp. with continuous and noisy action; *spatter. [imit.]
splay *v.*, *n.*, & *a.* **1.** *v.t.* Construct (aperture) with divergent sides; make (window, doorway) wider at one side of wall; spread (elbows, feet, etc., *out*). **2.** *v.i.* (Of aperture or its sides) be divergent in shape or position. **3.** *n.* Surface making oblique angle with another, e.g. splayed side of window, embrasure. **4.** *a.* Wide and flat, turned outward; ~**-foot** *n.* & *a.*, ~**-footed** *a.*, (having) broad flat foot turned outward. [ME, f. DISPLAY¹]
spleen *n.* **1.** Abdominal organ involved in maintaining proper condition of blood in most vertebrates, situated in mammals at left of stomach. **2.** Lowness of spirits, moroseness, ill temper, spite, (*a fit of spleen*; *vented his spleen*); hence ~'FUL, ~'Y², *adjs.* **3.** ~**'wort,** fern of genus *Asplenium*, formerly used as remedy for spleen disorders. [ME, f. OF *esplen* f. L f. Gk *splēn*]
splēn- *comb. form.* = prec. 1, as: ~**e'ctomy,** excision of spleen; ~**ī'tis,** inflammation of spleen; ~**o'logy** (-ŏ'l-), study of spleen; ~**ome'galy,** enlargement of spleen; ~**o'tomy** (-ŏ't-), incision into, or dissection of, spleen. [Gk (as prec.)]
splĕ'ndent *a.* Shining, lustrous; illustrious. [ME, f. L *splendēre* shine; see -ENT]
splĕ'ndĭd *a.* Magnificent, gorgeous, sumptuous, glorious, brilliant, (*a splendid palace, gift, achievement, victory*); dignified, impressive, (*splendid isolation*); (colloq.) excellent, very fine, (*here is a splendid chance of escape*); hence ~LY² *adv.* [f. F *splendide* or f. L *splendidus* (as prec.; see -ID¹)]
splĕndĭ'ferous *a.* (colloq.) Splendid. [irreg. f. foll. + -FEROUS]
splĕ'ndour (-der), ***splĕ'ndor,** *n.* Great or dazzling brightness; magnificence, grandeur; **sun in** ~ (Her., with rays and human face). [ME, f. AF *splendeur* or f. L *splendor* (as SPLENDENT; see -OR)]
splėnĕ't|ĭc *a.* & *n.* **1.** Ill-tempered, peevish, (person); hence ~ICALLY *adv.* **2.** *a.* Of the spleen. [f. LL *spleneticus* (as SPLEEN; see -ETIC)]

splĕ'nĭc *a.* Of or in the spleen; ~ **fever,** anthrax; so **splē'n**OID *a.* [f. F *splénique* or f. L f. Gk *splēnikos* (as SPLEEN; see -IC)]

splē'nĭ|us *n.* (*pl.* ~**i** *pr.* -ī). (Either section of) muscle on back and sides of neck serving to draw back the head; hence ~AL *a.* [mod. L, f. Gk *splēnion* bandage]

splīce *v.t.*, & *n.* **1.** *v.t.* Join ends of (ropes) by interweaving strands; join (pieces of timber, magnetic tape, film, etc.) in overlapping position; (colloq., esp. in *pass.*) join in marriage; *splice the* MAIN³ *brace.* **2.** *n.* Junction of two ropes or pieces of wood etc. (e.g. handle and blade of cricket-bat) made by splicing; **sit on the** ~, (Cricket sl.) play a cautious defensive game, stonewall. [prob. f. MDu. *splissen*, of uncert. orig.]

splīne *n.*, & *v.t.* **1.** *n.* Rectangular key fitting into grooves in hub and shaft of wheel and allowing longitudinal play; slat; flexible wood or rubber strip, e.g. used in drawing large curves esp. in railway work. **2.** *v.t.* Fit with spline. [orig. E. Anglian dial., perh. rel. to SPLINTER]

splint *n.*, & *v.t.* **1.** *n.* Strip of rigid or flexible material to protect part of body (e.g. for holding broken bone when set) or for basketwork etc.; tumour or bony excrescence on inside of horse's leg; ~**(-bone)**, (1) either of two small bones in horse's foreleg lying behind and close to cannon-bone, (2) human fibula; ~**-coal,** hard bituminous laminated coal burning with great heat. **2.** *v.t.* Secure (broken limb etc.) with splint(s). [ME *splent(e)*, f. MDu. *splinte* or MLG *splinte*, *splente* metal plate or pin, rel. to foll.]

splĭ'nter *v.* & *n.* **1.** *v.t.* & *i.* Break into splinters; = SHIVER². **2.** *n.* Sharp-edged or thin piece broken off from wood, stone, etc.; ||~**-bar,** crossbar in vehicle to which traces are attached, swingle-tree; ~ **group** or **party,** (Polit.) party (esp. one that is very small in numbers) that has broken away from a larger one; ~**-proof** (against splinters of bursting shells or bombs). **3.** Hence ~Y² *a.* [ME, f. MDu. (= LG) *splinter*, *splenter*; rel. to prec.]

splĭt¹ *v.* (**-tt-; split**). **1.** *v.t.* & *i.* Break forcibly, be broken into parts esp. longitudinally or with the grain or plane of cleavage; (of ship) be wrecked; cause fission of (atom). **2.** Divide into parts, thicknesses, etc. (*split it into three layers*; *the job, sum*, etc., *was split* (*up*) *among 6 of us*; *the three of them split a bottle of wine*); *dilute (whisky etc.) with water; remove or be removed by breaking or dividing (*off*); *split the* DIFFERENCE; ~ **hairs,** draw over-subtle distinctions; ~ ***the ticket** or one's **vote,** vote for opposed candidates; ||~ **the vote,** (of candidate) attract votes from another so that both are perhaps defeated by a third. **3.** Divide into disagreeing or hostile parties (*on* or *over* question etc.). **4.** ~ (one's **sides**), be convulsed with laughter; so SIDE¹- *-splitting.* **5.** *v.i.* (Of headache etc., in *part.*) acute; **my head is** ~**ting** (feels acute pain). **6.** (sl.) Betray secrets, inform *on* (accomplice etc.). **7.** (in *p.p.*) ~ **gear, pulley, wheel,** (made in halves for removal from shaft); ~ **infinitive** (with adverb etc. inserted between *to* and verb, e.g. *seems to partly correspond*); ~**-level,** (of building) having some room(s) a fraction of a storey higher than the adjacent part; ~ **mind,** schizophrenia; ~ **moss** (of genus *Andreaea*, of which capsules split at maturity); ~ **pea** (dried and split in half for cooking); ~ **personality,** alteration or dissociation of personality such as may occur in some mental illnesses esp. schizophrenia and hysteria; *split* PIN¹; ~ **ring** (usu. of steel with two helical turns, on the pattern of those used for bunches of keys); ~ **second,** a very brief moment of time; ~ **shift** (comprising two or more separate periods of duty); ~ **shot, stroke,** stroke at croquet driving two touching balls in different directions. **8.** Hence (**-**)~**'**TER¹ (1, 2) *n.* [orig. Naut., f. MDu. *splitten*, rel. to *spletten*, *splīten*, MHG *splīzen*]

splĭt² *n.* **1.** Splitting or being split; fissure, rent, crack, cleft. **2.** Separation into parties, schism, rupture, breach. **3.** Split osier etc. for parts of basketwork; each strip of steel, cane, etc., of reed in loom; single thickness of split hide. **4.** Turning up of two cards of equal value in faro, so that stakes are divided. **5.** Half bottle of mineral water; half glass of liquor. **6.** (||in *pl.*) Feat of sitting down or leaping with legs widely spread out at right angles to body. **7.** Sweet dish of split fruit, ice cream, etc., (*banana split*). [f. prec.]

||**splŏdge.** Var. of SPLOTCH.

splŏsh *n.* & *v.* (colloq.) **1.** *n.* A quantity of water suddenly dropped or thrown down. **2.** *v.t.* & *i.* Move with splashing. [imit.]

splŏtch *n.*, & *v.t.* Daub, blot, smear; (make) large irregular spot or patch (on); hence ~'Y² *a.* [perh. f. SPOT¹ + obs. *plotch*, BLOTCH]

splûrge *n.*, & *v.i.* (Make) noisy or ostentatious display or effort. [19th c. U.S.; prob. imit.]

splŭ'tter *v.* & *n.* = SPUTTER (esp. of speech); hence ~ER¹ *n.* [f. SPUTTER by assoc. w. *splash*]

Spōde *n.* Type of fine pottery or porcelain. [f. J. ~, Engl. maker of china d. 1827]

spoil¹ *n.* **1.** (usu. in *pl.* or collect. *sing.*) Plunder taken from enemy in war, or seized by force; (fig.) profit, advantage accruing from success in contest etc., (joc.) emoluments of public office etc.; ***~s system,** practice of giving public offices to adherents of successful party; ***~'sman** (-z-), advocate of, one who seeks to profit by, this. **2.** Earth etc. thrown up or brought up in excavating, dredging, etc. [ME, f. OF *espoille* (*espoillier*; see foll.)]

spoil² *v.* (~**t** (exc. sense 1), *or* ~**ed** *pr.* -ld *or* -lt). **1.** *v.t.* (arch. or literary). Plunder, deprive (person *of* thing), by force or stealth; ~ **the Egyptians** (persons regarded as one's natural enemies etc.; Exod. 12:36). **2.** Damage, diminish the good qualities of, reduce person's enjoyment of, (*was quite spoilt by the rain*; *will spoil all the fun*; *always spoils a joke in the telling*; *the news spoilt his dinner*). **3.** Injure character of (person etc.) by indulgence (*spare the rod and spoil the child*; *are determined to spoil me*; *is the spoilt child* or *darling of fortune*). **4.** *v.i.* (Of fruit, fish, etc., fig. of joke etc.) become unfit for use, decay, go bad, (*will not spoil with keeping*); **be** ~**'ing for,** desire eagerly (*a fight* etc.). **5.** ~**-five,** card-game in which deal is 'spoilt' if no player takes three of the five tricks; ~**-sport,** one who spoils others' sport or enjoyment. [ME, f. OF *espoillier* f. L *spoliare* (*spolium* spoil, plunder), or f. DESPOIL]

spoi'lage *n.* Paper spoilt in printing; spoiling of food by decay. [f. prec. + -AGE]

spoi'ler *n.* In vbl senses; device on aircraft or vehicle to retard it by interrupting air flow. [f. SPOIL² + -ER¹]

spōke¹ *n.*, & *v.t.* **1.** *n.* Each of the bars running from hub to rim of wheel, whence ~'WISE (-kw-) *adv.*; rung of ladder; each radial handle of steering-wheel of vessel; **put a** ~ **in** person's **wheel,** thwart his purposes; ~**-bone,** radius of forearm; ~**'shave,** blade set between two handles, used for spokes and other esp. curved work where ordinary plane is not suitable. **2.** *v.t.* Furnish with spokes; obstruct (wheel etc.) by thrusting spoke in. [OE *spāca*, = OS *spēca*, OHG *speihha* f. WG **spaika*, Gmc **spaik-* (cf. SPIKE¹)]

spōke², **(-)spō'ken.** See SPEAK.

spō'kes|man (-ks-) *n.* (*pl.* **~men,** *fem.* **~-woman**). One who speaks for others; person deputed to express a group's views. [irreg. f. SPOKE² after *craftsman* etc.]

spōlĭā'tion *n.* Plunder, pillage, esp. of neutral vessels by belligerent; (fig.) extortion; (Eccl.) taking of fruits of benefice under pretended title etc.; (Law) destruction, mutilation, alteration, of document to prevent its being used as evidence; so **spō'lĭāt**OR *n.*, **spō'lĭat**ORY *a.* [ME, f. L *spoliatio* (as SPOIL²; see -ATION)]

spŏndā'ĭc *a.* Of spondees; (of hexameter) having spondee as fifth foot. [f. F *spondaïque* or LL *spondaicus* = LL f. Gk *spondeiakos* (as foll.; see -AC, -IC)]

spŏ'ndee (*or* -dĭ) *n.* (Pros.) Foot consisting of two long syllables. [ME f. OF, or f. L f. Gk *spondeios* (*pous* foot) f. *spondē* libation, as being characteristic of music accompanying libations]

spŏndū'lĭcks *n. pl.* (sl.) Money. [19th c.; orig. unkn.]

spŏ'ndȳl- *comb. form.* Vertebra(e), as **~ī'tis** *n.* [f. L f. Gk *spondulos* vertebra]

sponge¹ (-ŭnj) *n.* **1.** Aquatic animal of phylum Porifera, with pores in body-wall and tough elastic skeleton. **2.** Skeleton of a sponge or colony of sponges, esp. soft light elastic kind used as absorbent in bathing, cleansing surfaces, etc.; piece of porous rubber used similarly; **throw up the ~,** (of boxer or his attendant) throw into the air as token of defeat the sponge used between rounds, (fig.) abandon contest, admit oneself beaten; **pass the ~ over,** (arch.) agree to forget (offence etc.). **3.** Thing of sponge-like absorbency or consistency, e.g. piece of leavened dough, sponge-cake, absorbent pad used in surgery, kind of mop for cleaning bore of big gun, iron or other metal in finely divided condition. **4.** (fig.) Parasite, person who contrives to live at another's expense; one who drinks heavily. **5.** ||**~-bag,** waterproof bag for toilet articles; ||*~-bag trousers* (of checked material); **~ biscuit, ~-cake,** (light, of sponge-like consistency); **~ cloth,** soft loosely woven cotton fabric with wrinkled surface; **~ cucumber, -gourd, vegetable ~,** loofah; **~ pudding,** light pudding of spongelike consistency; **~ rubber** (made porous like a sponge); **~-tree,** spiny tropical acacia with globose heads of fragrant yellow flowers yielding a perfume. [OE, f. L f. Gk *spoggia, spoggos*]

sponge² (-ŭnj) *v.* & *n.* **1.** *v.t.* Wipe or cleanse with sponge; sluice water over (parts of body etc., or abs.; *down, over*) with sponge; wipe *out* or efface (writing, fig. memory of thing etc.) (as) with sponge; absorb, take *up*, (water etc.) with sponge; obtain (food etc., or abs.) by mean or parasitic behaviour. **2.** *v.i.* Gather sponges; **~ on,** live as the parasite of, be meanly dependent on (person *for* thing). **3.** Hence **spo'ng**ER¹ (1, 2) (-ŭ'nj-) *n.* **4.** *n.* Sponging, bath with sponge, (*had a sponge down*). [ME, f. prec., or OF *esponger* (*esponge* f. L *spongia*, as prec.)]

spo'ngĭng (-ŭ'nj-) *n.* In vbl senses; **~-house,** (Hist., f. arch. sense 'extortion') bailiff's house for initial confinement of arrested debtor. [f. prec. + -ING¹]

spo'ng|ȳ (-ŭ'njĭ) *a.* Like sponge; porous, compressible, elastic, absorbent, as sponge; (of metal) finely divided and loosely coherent; hence **~ĭ**NESS *n.* [f. SPONGE¹ + -Y²]

spŏ'nsion (-shon) *n.* Being surety for another; engagement made on behalf of State by agent not authorized to do so. [f. L *sponsio* (*spondēre spons-* promise solemnly; see -ION)]

spŏ'nson *n.* Projection from side of warship or tank to enable gun to be trained forward and aft; triangular platform before and abaft paddle-box; short subsidiary wing to stabilize seaplane. [19th c.; orig. unkn.]

spŏ'nsor *n.*, & *v.t.* **1.** *n.* Person who makes himself responsible for another; person who presents candidate for baptism and makes responses on behalf of infant etc. being baptized; person who introduces proposal for legislation; person who subscribes to charity in return for specified activity by another; advertiser who pays for a broadcast programme into which advertisements of his wares are introduced; organization lending support to election candidate; hence **spŏnsôr'**IAL *a.*, **~**SHIP *n.* **2.** *v.t.* Be sponsor for. [L (as SPONSION; see -OR)]

spŏntā'nėous *a.* **1.** Acting, done, occurring, without external cause; voluntary, without external incitement, (*made a spontaneous offer of his services*); (of sudden movement, etc.) involuntary, not due to conscious volition; growing naturally without cultivation; (Biol., of structural changes in plants, muscular activity in esp. young animals) instinctive, automatic, prompted by no motive; (of bodily movement, literary style, etc.) gracefully natural and unconstrained. **2. ~ combustion,** ignition of mineral or vegetable substance (e.g. heap of rags soaked with oil, mass of wet coal) from heat engendered by rapid oxidation; **~ generation,** supposed production of living from non-living matter as inferred from appearance of life (due in fact to bacteria etc.) in some infusions; **~ suggestion** (from association of ideas without conscious volition). **3.** Hence or cogn. **spŏntanē'**ITY, **~**NESS, *ns.*, **~**LY² *adv.* [f. LL *spontaneus* (*sponte* of one's own accord; see -ANEOUS)]

spŏntōō'n *n.* (Hist.) Kind of halberd used by some British infantry officers. [f. obs. F *sponton* f. It. *spuntone* (*spuntare* to blunt f. *s-* EX-¹ + *punto* POINT¹; see -OON)]

spōōf *v.t.*, & *n.* (sl.) Swindle, hoax; parody; hence **~'**ER¹ *n.* [invented by A. Roberts, Engl. comedian d. 1933]

spōōk *n.* (joc.) Ghost; hence **~'**ISH¹, **~'**Y², *adjs.* [Du., = MLG *spōk*, of unkn. orig.]

spōōl *n.*, & *v.t.* **1.** *n.* Reel for winding yarn, *thread, photographic film, etc., on; revolving cylinder of angler's reel. **2.** *v.t.* Wind on spool. [ME, f. OF *espole* or f. MLG *spōle*, MDu. *spoele*, OHG *spuolo*, of unkn. orig.]

spōōn¹ *n.* & *v.* **1.** *n.* Utensil consisting of round or usu. oval bowl and a handle for conveying esp. liquid food to mouth, usu. of silver or plated metal for table use (**tea~, dessert-~, table~,** of small, medium, large size, also as recognized measure for medicine, culinary ingredients, etc.; APOSTLE *spoon*; EGG¹, SALT, *-spoon*) or of wood or iron for cooking etc.; **born with a silver ~ in** one's **mouth,** destined to be wealthy; **wooden ~,** (Hist.) (wooden spoon given to) last man in Cambridge mathematical tripos, (fig.) booby prize; EGG¹-*-and-spoon race*; hence (-)**~'**FUL 2 *n.* **2.** Spoon--shaped thing, esp. (oar with) broad curved blade, wooden-headed golf-club with more loft than driver and brassie. **3. ~(-bait),** bright revolving spoon-shaped piece of metal used as lure in fishing; **~'beak,** shoveller duck; **~'bill,** wading-bird of family Plataleidae, with very broad flat tip of bill; ***~-bread,** soft maize bread; **~-feed,** feed by means of liquid food from spoon, (fig.) artificially encourage (industry) by bounties or import duties, provide information etc. to without requiring any effort on recipient's part; **~-meat,** liquid food, food for infants (lit. or fig.). **4.** *v.t.* Take (liquid etc., *up, out*) with spoon; hit (ball) feebly upwards. **5.** *v.i.* Fish with spoon-bait. [OE *spōn* chip of wood, = MLG *spān*, OHG *spān*, ON *spánn*, *spónn*]

spōōn[2] *n.* & *v.* (sl.) **1.** *n.* Simpleton; silly or demonstratively fond lover. **2.** *v.i.* Behave in silly amorous way. **3.** *v.t.* Woo in silly or sentimental way. [f. prec.]

spōō'nerĭsm *n.* Accidental or deliberate transposition of initial letters etc. of two or more words (*you have hissed the mystery lectures*). [f. Rev. W. A. *Spooner*, Engl. scholar d. 1930, reputed to make such errors in speaking, + -ISM]

spōō'n|ў *a.* & *n.* (sl.) **1.** *a.* Foolish, silly; sentimental, amorous, sweet (*up*)*on*; hence **~ĭLY**[2] *adv.*, **~ĭNESS** *n.* **2.** *n.* Simpleton. [f. SPOON[2] + -Y[2]]

spoor *n.* & *v.* **1.** *n.* Track or scent of animal. **2.** *v.t.* & *i.* Follow by spoor; hence ~'ER[1] *n.* [Afrik., f. MDu. *spo*(*o*)*r*, = OE, OHG, ON *spor*]

sporă'd|ĭc *a.* Occurring only here and there, separate, scattered; hence ~ICALLY *adv.* [f. med. L f. Gk *sporadikos* (*sporas -ados* scattered, cf. *speirō* sow; see -IC)]

sporă'ngĭ|um (-nj-) *n.* (*pl.* ~**a**). (Bot.) Receptacle in which spores are formed. [mod. L, f. Gk *spora* SPORE + *aggeion* vessel]

spōre *n.* (Bot.) Minute reproductive cell of cryptogamous plants; resistant form of bacterium etc. [f. mod. L f. Gk *spora* sowing, seed (*speirō* sow)]

spōr'o- *comb. form.* Spore, as: **~ge'nesis,** spore-formation; **~genous** (-ŏ'j-), producing spores; **~phyte** (-fīt), spore-producing form of plant with alternation of generations; hence **~phy'tic** (-fĭ't-) *a.* [f. Gk *spora* (as prec.) + -O-]

spŏ'rran *n.* Pouch, usu. of skin covered with fur etc., worn by Highlander in front of kilt. [f. Gael. *sporan* f. med. L *bursa* PURSE[1]]

spōrt *n.* & *v.* **1.** *n.* Amusement, diversion, fun; **in** ~, jestingly; **make ~ of,** turn into ridicule, make fun of; **be the** ~ (plaything, butt) *of Fortune* etc. **2.** Pastime, game; outdoor pastime, e.g. hunting, fishing, racing, cricket, football; these collectively (*the world of sport*); **have good** ~, (esp.) make good bag or basket when shooting etc.; ||(**athletic**) **~s,** (1) running, jumping, throwing discus, etc., (2) meeting of athletes to compete in these (*school sports*); **~s car** (of open low-built fast type); **~s coat,** ***~ coat,** (suitable for outdoor sports or informal wear); **~s writer,** one who writes (esp. as journalist) on sports. **3.** (sl.) Good fellow, sportsman; *playboy. **4.** Animal or plant deviating suddenly or strikingly from normal type. **5.** *v.i.* Divert oneself, take part in pastime; (Biol.) become or produce a sport. **6.** *v.t.* Wear, exhibit, produce, esp. ostentatiously, (*sported a gold tie-pin*); ||*sport* one's OAK. [ME, f. DISPORT]

spōr'ting *a.* Interested in sport (*a sporting man*); sportsmanlike (*a sporting offer*; *will give you* **a ~ chance,** some possibility of success); concerned in sport (*sporting dog, news*); ***~ house,** brothel; hence ~LY[2] *adv.* [f. prec. + -ING[1,2]]

spōr'tĭve *a.* Playful; hence ~LY[2] (-vlĭ) *adv.*, ~NESS (-vn-) *n.* [f. SPORT + -IVE]

spōr'tsman *n.* (*pl.* **spōr'tsmen,** *fem.* **spor'tswoman**). Person fond of sports, esp. of hunting etc.; person who behaves fairly and generously; hence ~LIKE *a.*, ~SHIP *n.* [f. SPORT + MAN[1]]

spōr't|ў *a.* (colloq.) Fond of sport; gay, rakish, showy; hence **~ĭLY**[2] *adv.*, **~ĭNESS** *n.* [f. SPORT + -Y[2]]

spŏ'rūl|e *n.* Spore; small spore; hence ~AR[1] *a.* [F, or f. mod. L *sporula* (as SPORE; see -ULE)]

spŏt[1] *n.* **1.** Particular place, definite locality, (*dropped it on this precise spot*; *the spot where William III landed*); place used for a particular activity (NIGHT-*spot*); particular part of one's body or (fig.) character (TOUCH[1] *the spot*; SOFT, TENDER[3], *spot*); (fig., colloq.) one's (regular) position in an organization, programme of events, etc. **2.** Small part of the surface of a thing distinguished by colour, texture, etc., usu. round or less elongated than a streak or stripe (*a blue tie with pink spots*; *can the* LEOPARD *change his spots?*); small mark or stain; pimple; small circle, SPADE[2], etc., used in various numbers to distinguish faces of dice, playing-cards in suit, etc.; (fig.) moral blemish, stain, (*without a spot on his reputation*); SUN*spot*; **knock ~s off,** defeat easily. **3.** Fish of various species with noticeable spot on skin. **4.** ||(colloq.) Small quantity of anything (*a spot of leave, lunch, whisky, culture*); drop (*of* rain etc.); a drink. **5.** (Bill. etc.) Small round black patch to mark position where ball is placed at certain times; ||**~-stroke,** pocketing red ball from spot where it is usually placed after previous pocketing; ||**~-barred game** (in which successive spot-strokes are not allowed); ~(**-ball**), white ball distinguished from the other by two black spots. **6. On the ~,** without delay or change of place, then and there, at scene of action or event, (of person) wide awake, equal to the situation, in good form at game etc., (colloq.) in difficult position, compelled to take some action; **put on the** ~, *(sl.) decide to murder; **running on the** ~, raising feet alternately as in running but without moving forwards or backwards; **in a** (**tight** etc.) ~, (colloq.) in difficulties; **~-o'n,** (colloq.) precise(ly). **7.** (Commerc.) Money paid or goods delivered immediately after sale (*spot cash*; *spot silver*). **8.** ~(**'light**), (*n.*) (projector giving) beam of light on particular part of theatre stage or on particular part of road in front of vehicle, (fig.) receiving of full attention or publicity; *~'light*, (*v.t.*) illuminate with spotlight (lit. or fig.). **9. ~ check,** test made on the spot or on randomly selected subject; **~ height,** (figure on map showing) altitude of a point; **~ welding** (between points of metal surfaces in contact). [ME, perh. f. MDu. *spotte*, LG *spot*, ON *spotti* small piece]

spŏt[2] *v.* (-tt-). **1.** *v.t.* Mark, stain, soil, with spot(s) (lit., or fig. of character etc.); (Bill. etc.) place (ball) on spot. **2.** (colloq.) Single out beforehand (winner of race etc., horse etc. as winner *for* event); detect, recognize identity, nationality, etc., of, (*spotted him at once as the murderer, as an American*); catch sight of; (Mil.) locate (enemy's position), esp. from the air; watch for and take note of (trains, talent, etc.); hence **(-)~'tER**[1] *n.* **3.** (in *p.p.*, esp. Zool.) Marked or decorated with spots; **~ted Dick** or **dog,** Dalmatian dog, ||(sl.) plum duff; **~ted fever,** (1) cerebro-spinal meningitis, (2) typhus. **4.** *v.i.* Make spots (*it's spotting with rain*). [ME, f. prec.]

spŏ'tlĕss *a.* Free from spot or stain (lit. or fig.); hence ~LY[2] *adv.*, ~NESS *n.* [ME, f. SPOT[1] + -LESS]

spŏ'tt|ў *a.* Marked with (many) spots; patchy, irregular; hence **~ĭLY**[2] *adv.*, **~ĭNESS** *n.* [ME, f. SPOT[1] + -Y[2]]

spouse (-z) *n.* Husband or wife. [ME *spūs*(*e*) f. OF *sp*(*o*)*us* masc., *sp*(*o*)*use* fem., vars. of *espous*(*e*) f. L *sponsus sponsa* p.p. of *spondēre* betroth]

spout *v.* & *n.* **1.** *v.t.* & *i.* Discharge or issue forcibly in a jet (*blood spouts from wound*; *wound spouts blood*; *whale spouts water*); utter (verses etc., or abs.) in declamatory manner, speechify. **2.** *n.* Projecting tube through which liquid etc. is poured from teapot, kettle, roof-gutter, etc., or issues from fountain, pump, etc.; sloping trough down which thing may be shot into receptacle; lift serving pawnbroker's store-room; **up the ~,** (1) in pawn, (2) useless, hopeless. **3.** Jet or column of liquid or grain etc.; WATER[1]-

spout; ~(**-hole**), whale's blow-hole. **4.** Hence ~′ER[1] *n.*, ~′LESS *a.* [ME, f. MDu. *spouten*, f. imit. base **spūt-*; cf. ON *spýta* SPIT[2]]

S.P.Q.R. *abbr.* Roman Senate and people [f. L *Senatus Populusque Romanus*]; small profits and quick RETURN[2]s.

||**Spr.** *abbr.* Sapper.

sprăg *n.* Billet of wood or similar device for braking wheel of car etc.; support-prop in coal-mine. [19th c.; orig. unkn.]

sprain *v.t.*, & *n.* **1.** *v.t.* Wrench (ankle, wrist, etc.) violently so as to cause pain and swelling but not dislocation. **2.** *n.* Such wrench; resulting inflammation and swelling. [17th c.; orig. unkn.]

sprainţs *n. pl.* Otter's dung. [ME, f. OF *espreintes* f. *espraindre*, **espriembre* squeeze out f. Rom. **expremere* f. L EX[1](*primere* = *premere* press)]

sprăng. See SPRING[1].

sprăt *n.*, & *v.i.* (**-tt-**). **1.** *n.* Small European herring-like fish (*Sprattus sprattus*) much used as food; other similar fish, e.g. sand-eel, young herring; **a ~ to catch a herring** or **mackerel** or **whale,** a little risked to gain much. **2.** *v.i.* Fish for sprats; hence **~′TER[1]**, **~′TING[1]**, *ns.* [earlier *sprot*, OE, = MDu., MLG *sprot*, of unkn. orig.]

sprawl *v.* & *n.* **1.** *v.i.* & *t.* Spread oneself, spread (one's limbs), out in careless or ungainly way; (of writing, plant, town, etc.) be of irregular or straggling form. **2.** *n.* Sprawling movement or attitude; straggling group or mass. [OE *spreawlian*; cf. NFris. *spraweli*, Da. *sprelle* kick about]

spray[1] *n.* Branch of tree with branchlets or flowers, esp. slender or graceful one, sprig of flowers or leaves; ornament in similar form (*a spray of diamonds* etc.); **~-drain,** drain in field etc. made by filling trench with branches; hence **~′ey[1]** *a.* [cf. CLAYEY]. [ME, f. OE **sprǣg*, of unkn. orig.]

spray[2] *n.*, & *v.t.* **1.** *n.* Water or other liquid flying in small drops from force of wind, dashing of waves, or action of atomizer etc.; medical or other liquid preparation to be applied in this form with atomizer etc.; instrument or apparatus for such application. **2.** *v.t.* Throw (liquid, or abs.) in form of spray; sprinkle (object) thus, esp. (fruit-trees etc.) with insecticides. **3.** **~-dry,** dry (milk etc.) by spraying into hot air etc.; **~-gun,** gunlike device for spraying paint etc. **4.** Hence ~′ER[1] (1, 2) *n.*, **~′ey[2]** *a.* [cf. CLAYEY]. [earlier *spry*, perh. rel. to MDu. *spra(e)yen*, MHG *spræjen* sprinkle]

spread[1] (-ĕd) *v.* (**spread**). **1.** *v.t.* ~ (**out**), extend the surface of, cause to cover larger surface, by unrolling, unfolding, smearing, flattening out, etc., (fig.) display thus to eye or mind, (*peacock spreads its tail*; *spread* one's WINGS; *spread a banner*; *spread out a rug on the grass*; *spread butter on bread*; *map lay spread out on the table*; *the view spread out before us*); ~ one**self,** be lavish or discursive; hence ~′ER[1] (2) *n.* **2.** *v.i.* ~ (**out**), show or acquire extended or extensive surface (*river here spreads out to a width of half a mile*; *on every side spread a vast desert*; *spreading yews*; *spreads like butter*). **3.** *v.t.* & *i.* (Cause to) become widely felt, known, etc., (*his name spread fear in every quarter*; *rumour spread from mouth to mouth*; *why not spread a little happiness?*). **4.** *v.t.* Cover surface of (*slices of bread spread with jam*; *a table spread with every luxury*; *meadow spread with daisies*). **5.** ~ **eagle,** (1) figure of eagle with legs and wings extended as emblem; (2, Naut.) person lashed in rigging with arms and legs spread out as punishment; **~-ea′gle,** (*v.t.*) lash (man) thus, spread out, defeat utterly, (*a.*) *bombastic, esp. noisily patriotic. [OE -*sprǣdan*, = OS -*spreidan*, MDu., MLG *sprēden*, OHG *spreitan* f. WG **spraidjan* causative of **sprīdan* be extended]

spread[2] (-ĕd) *n.* **1.** Spreading; capability of expanding (*inferior to the eagle in spread of wings*); span of aeroplane's wings; increased bodily girth (*middle-age(d) spread*); breadth, compass, (*arches of equal spread*); diffusion (*of* education etc.). **2.** = BED[1]*spread*; (colloq.) feast, meal; difference between two rates, prices, etc.; sweet or savoury paste for spreading on bread; printed matter spread across two facing pages or across more than one column. [f. prec.]

spree *n.*, & *v.i.* (colloq.) **1.** *n.* Lively frolic, bout of drinking etc.; **on the ~**, engaged in this; **buying, shopping, spending, ~,** bout of lavish spending. **2.** *v.i.* Have a spree. [19th c.; orig. unkn.]

sprĕnt *a.* (arch.) Sprinkled, overspread, (*with* drops, particles, etc.). [p.p. of obs. *sprenge* f. OE *sprengan* f. Gmc **sprangjan* causative of **springan* SPRING[1]]

sprĭg[1] *n.*, & *v.t.* (**-gg-**). **1.** *n.* Small branch, shoot; ornament of sprig form, esp. on fabric (*sprig muslin*); (usu. derog.) youth, young man, (*a sprig of* (*the*) *nobility*); **~′tail,** pintail; hence **~′GY[2]** (-gĭ) *a.* **2.** *v.t.* Ornament with sprigs (*sprigged muslin*). [ME, f. or cogn. w. LG *sprick*]

sprĭg[2] *n.* Small tapering headless tack. [ME, of unkn. orig.]

sprī′ghtl|ȳ (-ī′t-) *a.* Vivacious, lively, gay; hence **~INESS** *n.* [f. *spright* var. of SPRITE + -LY[1]]

sprĭng[1] *v.* (**sprang; sprung**). **1.** *v.i.* Jump, move rapidly or suddenly, (*up*, *down*, *out*, *over*, *through*, *away*, *back*, etc.; *sprang* (*up*) *from his seat*; *sprang through the gap*, *at his throat*, *to their assistance*; *blood sprang to her cheeks*). **2.** Move rapidly as from constrained position or by action of a spring (*branch sprang back*; *door sprang to*). **3.** Come (*up*) into being, originate or arise (*from* source), appear, (*a breeze sprang up*; *the piers from which the arches spring*; *is sprung from* or *of a royal stock*; *the buds are springing*; *the belief has sprung up*; *his actions spring from a false conviction*); **where did you ~ from?** (to person arriving suddenly or unexpectedly or whose presence is only now realized). **4.** Become warped or split. **5.** *v.t.* Rouse (game) from earth or covert; (sl.) contrive escape of (person *from* prison etc.). **6.** Split, crack, (wood or wooden implement). **7.** Cause to act suddenly by means of a spring, produce or develop or make known suddenly or unexpectedly, (*spring a trap*; *has sprung a new theory*; *loves to spring surprises on us*). **8.** (usu. in *p.p.*) Provide (motor vehicle etc.) with springs. **9.** Cause (mine) to explode. **10.** **~ a leak,** develop leak (orig. Naut., from starting of timbers). **11.** **Sprung rhythm,** poetic metre approximating to speech, each foot having one stressed syllable followed by a varying number of unstressed. [OE *springan*, = OS, OHG *springan*, ON *springa* f. Gmc **sprengan*]

sprĭng[2] *n.* **1.** Jump (*took a spring*; *rose with a spring*). **2.** Season in which vegetation begins to appear, first season of the year, in N. hemisphere March–May (Astron., from vernal equinox to summer solstice); (fig.) early stage *of* life etc. **3.** Place where water, oil, etc., wells up from earth, basin or flow so formed, (*hot*, *mineral*, *springs*). **4.** Backward movement from constrained position, recoil, e.g. of bow. **5.** Elasticity (*these mattresses have no spring in them*). **6.** Elastic contrivance usu. of bent or coiled metal used esp. as motive power in clockwork etc. or for preventing vibration as in vehicle. **7.** (fig.) Motive actuating person etc., source, origin, (*the springs of human action*; *the custom had its spring in another country*). **8.** Upward curve of beam etc. from horizontal line. **9.** Splitting or yielding of plank etc. under strain. **10.** ~ **balance** (measuring weight by tension of spring); ~ **bed** (with spring mattress); **~'-board,** elastic board giving impetus in leaping, diving, etc., (fig.) source of impetus in any activity; ~ **chicken,** young fowl for eating (orig. available only in spring); **~-clean** *n.*, & *v.t.*, clean(ing) (house, room) thoroughly, esp. in spring; ~ **gun** (contrived to go off when trespasser or animal stumbles on it); **~-halt,** spasmodic movement of horse's hind leg; ~ **mattress** (containing or consisting of springs); ~ **onion** (taken from ground before bulb has formed, and eaten raw in salad); **~'tail,** wingless insect of order Collembola, leaping by means of springlike caudal part; *spring* (TIDE^1); **~'tide** (poet.), **~'time,** season of spring; ~ **water** (from spring, opp. to river or rain water). **11.** Hence ~'LESS, ~'LIKE, *adjs.*, ~'LET *n.* [OE, f. as prec.]

sprĭ'ngal(d) *n.* (arch.) Youngster, stripling. [ME, perh. f. SPRING^1]

sprĭ'ngbŏk *n.* S. Afr. gazelle (*Antidorcas marsupialis*) with habit of springing in play or when alarmed; **S~s,** (nickname for) S. Africans, S. African Rugby football etc. touring team etc. [Afrik., f. Du. *springen* SPRING^1 + *bok* antelope]

sprĭnge (-nj) *n.* Noose or snare for catching small game. [ME, repr. OE **sprencg*, rel. to obs. *sprenge* (see SPRENT)]

sprĭ'nger *n.* In vbl senses; (Archit.) part of arch where curve begins, lowest stone of this, bottom·stone of coping of gable, rib of groined roof or vault; small spaniel used to spring game; springbok. [f. SPRING^1 + -ER^1]

sprĭ'ng|ȳ *a.* (Of movement or substance) elastic; hence ~ĬNESS *n.* [f. SPRING^{1,2} + -Y^2]

sprĭ'nkle *v.t.*, & *n.* **1.** *v.t.* Scatter (liquid, ashes, crumbs, etc.) in small drops or particles, whence **sprĭ'nkl**ER^1 (2) *n.* (esp. as lawn-waterer or fire-extinguisher); (fig.) distribute in small amounts; subject (ground, object) to sprinkling (*with* liquid etc., or fig.); (of liquid etc.) fall thus on; hence **sprĭ'nkl**ING^1 (2) *n.*, (esp., fig.) *a* few here and there *of*. **2.** *n.* Light shower (*of* rain etc.). [ME, perh. f. MDu. *sprenkelen*]

sprĭnt *v.* & *n.* **1.** *v.i.* & *t.* Run short distance, run (specified distance), at full speed; hence ~'ER^1 *n.* **2.** *n.* Such run; similar short spell of maximum effort in cycling, swimming, etc. [f. ON **sprinta*, of unkn. orig.]

sprĭt *n.* Small spar reaching diagonally from mast to upper outer corner of sail; **~'sail** (*or* -*sal*), sail extended by sprit, (formerly) sail extended by yard set under bowsprit. [OE *sprēot* pole, = MDu., MLG *spr*(*i*)*et*, cogn. w. SPROUT]

sprīte *n.* Elf, fairy, goblin. [ME, f. *sprit* var. of SPIRIT^1]

sprŏ'ckėt *n.* Each of several teeth on wheel engaging with links of chain; **~-wheel,** such wheel, e.g. for engaging bicycle chain. [16th c., of unkn. orig.]

sprout *v.* & *n.* **1.** *v.i.* Begin to grow, shoot forth, put forth shoots; spring up, grow to a height. **2.** *v.t.* Produce by sprouting (lit., or fig.: *has sprouted horns, a moustache*). **3.** *n.* Shoot of plant; (in *pl.*, colloq.) = BRUSSELS *sprouts*. [OE **sprūtan*, = OS *sprūton*, MLG *sprūten* f. WG **sprūtan*]

spruce^1 (-ōōs) *a.*, & *v.t.* **1.** *a.* Neat in dress and appearance, trim, smart; hence ~'LY^2 (-slĭ) *adv.*, ~'NESS (-sn-) *n.* **2.** *v.t.* Smarten (one*self* etc., usu. *up*). [perh. f. foll. in obs. sense 'Prussian', in the collocation *spruce* (*leather*) *jerkin*]

spruce^2 (-ōōs) *n.* Conifer of genus *Picea*, with dense foliage in conical shape; its wood; **~-beer** (made from leaves and small branches of spruce). [alt. f. obs. *Pruce* Prussia; cf. PRUSSIAN]

sprue^1 (-ōō) *n.* Passage through which metal is poured into mould; metal filling sprue. [19th c., of unkn. orig.]

sprue^2 (-ōō) *n.* Tropical deficiency disease with ulcerated mucous membrane of mouth and chronic enteritis. [f. Du. *spruw* THRUSH^2; cf. Flem. *spruwen* sprinkle]

spruit (-rāt) *n.* (S. Afr.) Small watercourse, usu. almost dry except in the wet season. [Du., cogn. w. SPROUT]

sprŭng. See SPRING^1.

sprȳ *a.* (**~'er, ~'est**). Active, lively; hence ~'LY^2 *adv.*, ~'NESS *n.* [18th c., dial. & U.S., of unkn. orig.]

spŭd *n.* & *v.* (**-dd-**). **1.** *n.* Small narrow spade for cutting roots of weeds etc.; (sl.) potato; **~-bashing,** (Services' sl.) task of peeling potatoes. **2.** *v.t.* Remove (weeds *up* or *out*) with spud. **3.** *v.i.* Make initial drilling for oil-well. [ME; orig. unkn.]

spūe. See SPEW.

spūm|e *n.*, & *v.i.* Froth, foam; hence or cogn. ~'OUS, ~'Y^2, *adjs.* [ME, f. OF (*e*)*spume* or f. L *spuma*]

spŭn. See SPIN^1.

spunge. Var. (arch.) of SPONGE.

spŭnk *n.* Touchwood; (colloq.) courage, mettle, spirit, whence ~'Y^2 *a.* [16th c., of unkn. orig.; cf. PUNK^2]

spûr *n.* & *v.* (**-rr-**). **1.** *n.* Pricking instrument with point or rowel worn on horseman's heel (**put** or **set ~s to,** = sense 5; **win** one's **~s,** (Hist.) gain knighthood, (fig.) gain distinction, make a name for oneself); (fig.) stimulus, incentive; **on the ~ of the moment,** impromptu, on a momentary impulse. **2.** Spur-shaped thing, e.g. hard projection on cock's leg, steel point fastened to leg of gamecock, projection from mountain (range), branch road or railway, climbing-iron; (Bot.) slender hollow projection from some part of flower, group of fruit-buds. **3.** ~ **royal,** 15-shilling coin of James I bearing spurlike sun with rays; **~-wheel, ~-gear,** cog-wheel with radial teeth; **~'wort,** plant with whorls of leaves like rowel of spur. **4.** Hence ~'LESS *a.* **5.** *v.t.* Prick (horse) with spurs; incite (person *on to* effort, *to* do, etc.); stimulate (interest etc.); (esp. in *p.p.*) furnish (person, boots, gamecock) with spurs. **6.** *v.i.* Ride horse hard (*on*, *forward*, etc.; lit. or fig.). [OE *spora*, *spura*, = OS, OHG *sporo*, ON *spori* f. Gmc **spuron* f. IE **sper-* strike with foot; cf. SPURN]

spûrge *n.* Plant of genus *Euphorbia*, with acrid milky juice; ~ **laurel,** shrub of genus *Daphne*, esp. yellow-flowered *D. laureola*. [ME, f. OF *espurge* (*espurgier* f. L EX^1*purgare* PURGE)]

spūr'ious *a.* Not genuine, not being what it pretends to be, not proceeding from the pretended source, (*spurious pregnancy*, *coin*, (*reading in*) *MS.*, *anger*); (of offspring) illegitimate; having outward similarity of form or function only; hence ~LY^2 *adv.*, ~NESS *n.* [f. L *spurius* false + -OUS]

spûrn *v.* & *n.* **1.** *v.t.* Repel, thrust back, with foot; reject with disdain, treat with contempt, (offer, advances, person, etc.). **2.** *v.i.* (arch.) ~ **at,** spurn. **3.** *n.* Spurning, contemptuous rejection. [OE *spurnan*, *spornan*, = OS, OHG *spurnan*, ON **spurna*; cf. SPUR]

spûr'rier (*or* spŭ'r-) *n.* Spur-maker. [ME, f. SPUR + -IER]

spŭ'rrȳ, -rey, *n.* Slender plant of genus *Spergula*, esp. **corn-~,** white-flowered weed in cornfields etc. [f. Du. *spurrie*, prob. rel. to med. L *spergula*]

spûrt^1 *v.i.*, & *n.* (Make) short sudden violent effort esp. in racing. [= foll.]

spûrt², **spîrt**, *v.* & *n.* **1.** *v.i.* Gush out in a jet or stream. **2.** *v.t.* Cause (liquid etc.) to do this. **3.** *n.* Sudden gushing out, jet. [16th c., of unkn. orig.]

spu'tnĭk (-ŏŏ't-) *n.* Russian artificial earth satellite. [Russ., = travelling companion]

spŭ'tter *v.* & *n.* **1.** *v.t.* Emit with spitting sound; speak, utter, (words, threats, a language, etc.) rapidly or incoherently; (Phys.) deposit (metal) by using fast ions etc. to eject particles of it from target. **2.** *v.i.* Speak in hurried or vehement fashion (*at* person etc.); (of thing) emit spitting sounds, esp. when being heated (*sausages sputtered in the pan*). **3.** Hence ~ER¹ *n.* **4.** *n.* Sputtering speech. [f. Du. *sputteren* (imit.)]

spū't|um *n.* (*pl.* ~**a**). Saliva, spittle; expectorated matter esp. as diagnostic of disease. [L, neut. p.p. (as n.) of *spuere* spit]

spȳ *n.* & *v.* **1.** *n.* Person who goes secretly into enemy's camp or territory to observe activities, watch movements, etc., and report the result; person who keeps (esp. secret) watch on movements of others (*refuse to be a spy on his conduct*). **2.** *v.t.* Discern, make out, esp. by careful observation, (*spied a horseman approaching*); **I** ~, children's game of guessing visible object from initial letter of its name; ||*I spy* STRANGERS; ~ **out,** explore secretly, discover by this means. **3.** *v.i.* Play the spy, keep close and secret watch (*on* person, movements, etc.); pry (*into* secret etc.). **4.** ~**'glass,** small telescope; ~**'hole,** peep-hole. [ME, f. OF (*espie* n. f.) *espier* espy f. Gmc **spekh-* f. IE **spek-*]

sq. *abbr.* square.

Sqn. Ldr. *abbr.* Squadron Leader.

squab (-ŏb) *a.* & *n.* **1.** *a.* Short and fat, squat. **2.** *n.* Short fat person, whence ~**'by**² *a.*; young esp. unfledged pigeon or other bird; stuffed cushion, esp. ||as part of seat in motor car; sofa, ottoman. **3.** ~**-chick,** unfledged bird; ~ **pie,** (1) pigeon pie, (2) pie of mutton, pork, onions, and apples. [17th c., of unkn. orig.; cf. obs. *quab* shapeless thing, Sw. dial. *sqvabba* fat woman]

squa'bbl|e (-ŏ'-) *v.i.*, & *n.* (Engage in) petty or noisy quarrel (*with* person *about* thing); hence ~ER¹ *n.* [prob. imit.; cf. Sw. dial. *sqvabbel* a dispute]

squă'ccō *n.* (*pl.* ~**s**). Small crested heron of S. Europe, Africa, and Asia. [f. It. dial. *sguacco*]

squad (-ŏd) *n.* **1.** (Mil.) Small number of men assembled for drill etc.; **awkward** ~ (of raw recruits not yet competent to take place in regimental line, or fig.). **2.** Small party of persons with common task etc.; FLYING² *squad*; *~ **car,** police car having radio link with headquarters. [f. F *escouade* var. of *escadre* f. It. *squadra* SQUARE¹]

squa'dron (-ŏ'd-) *n.* **1.** *n.* Principal division of cavalry regiment or armoured formation, consisting of two troops. **2.** Organized body of persons. **3.** Detachment of warships employed on particular service; FLYING² *squadron.* **4.** Unit of Royal Air Force (10 to 18 aircraft); ~ **leader,** officer commanding this. [f. It. *squadrone* (as prec.; see -OON)]

squail *n.* (in *pl.*) Game with small wooden discs (~**s**) propelled across table or board (~**-board**). [19th c., of unkn. orig.; cf. dial. *kayles* skittles]

squa'lĭd (-ŏ'l-) *a.* Dirty; repulsively filthy; mean or poor in appearance; (fig.) wretched; hence or cogn. ~ITY (-ĭ'd-), ~NESS, **squa'lOR** (-ŏ'l-), *ns.*, ~LY² *adv.* [f. L *squalidus* (*squalēre* be rough or dirty; see -ID¹)]

squall (-awl) *v.* & *n.* **1.** *v.i.* Cry out, scream, violently as in fear or pain. **2.** *v.t.* Utter in screaming or discordant voice. **3.** Hence ~'ER¹ *n.* **4.** *n.* Sudden or violent gust or successive gusts of wind, esp. with rain or snow or sleet; **arched** ~ (occurring near equator with sudden collection of black clouds in form of arch and usu. violent thunderstorm); **black** ~ (with dark cloud); **line** ~ (occurring along cold front); **white** ~ (arising in fair weather without formation of clouds); **look out for** ~**s,** (fig.) be on one's guard against danger or trouble; hence ~'Y² *a.* **5.** Discordant cry, scream (esp. of baby). [prob. f. SQUEAL, assoc. w. *bawl*]

squā'loid *a.* & *n.* (Fish) like shark, esp. of suborder Squaloidea. [f. L *squalus*, a sea-fish + -OID]

squalor. See SQUALID.

squā'm|a *n.* (*pl.* ~**ae**). (Bot. & Zool.) Scale; scalelike feather or part of bone; hence ~OSE¹, ~OUS, *adjs.*, ~ULE *n.* [L]

squa'nder (-ŏ'n-) *v.t.* Spend (money, time, etc.) wastefully; dissipate (fortune etc.) thus; hence ~ER¹ *n.*, ~MANIA *n.*, craze for extravagant expenditure. [16th c., of unkn. orig.]

squāre¹ *n.* **1.** Equilateral rectangle; object of (approximately) this shape; square scarf; small square area on game-board; **back to** ~ **one,** (colloq.) back to starting-point with no progress made. **2.** Area (usu. quadrilateral) planted with trees etc. or ornamentally laid out and surrounded with buildings esp. dwelling-houses, (*Berkeley, Trafalgar, Times, Square*); *block of buildings bounded by four streets; area of cricket-field suitable for use as wicket; area within barracks etc. for drill; ~**-bashing,** (Services' sl.) drill on barrack-square. **3.** L-shaped or T-shaped instrument for obtaining or testing right angles; **out of** ~, not at right angles; SET³ *square.* **4.** (arch., usu. fig.) Standard, pattern. **5. On the** ~, fair(ly), honest(ly), (*can be trusted to act on the square*); **is on the** ~, is a Freemason. **6.** Product of a number multiplied by itself (*the square of 9 is 81, of* x^2 *is* x^4); INVERSE *square law*; *9* **is a perfect** ~, has integral square root. **7.** Body of infantry drawn up in rectangular form; **hollow** ~, (Hist.) body so drawn up with space in middle. **8.** Square arrangement of letters, figures, etc., (MAGIC *square*; WORD¹-*square*). **9.** (sl.) Conventional or old-fashioned person, one ignorant of or opposed to current trends. **10.** Unit of 100 sq. ft. as measure of flooring etc. [ME, f. OF *esquire, esquar(r)e* f. Rom. **exquadra* (*exquadrare*; see SQUARE³)]

squāre² *a.* & *adv.* **1.** *a.* Of square shape; ~ **foot, metre, mile,** etc., (area equal to that of) square whose side is one foot etc.; ~ **measure** (expressed in square feet etc.). **2.** Rectangular (*table with square corners*); at right angles *to*; (Cricket) on line through stumps at right angles to the wicket. **3.** ~ **number,** square of an integer e.g. 1, 4, 9, 16, etc.; ~ **root** *of a given number*, number of which it is the square (*the square root of 9 is 3, of* x^6 *is* x^3, *of 2 is irrational*). **4.** ~ **dance, game** (in which four couples, players, face inwards from four sides). **5.** Having the breadth more nearly equal to the length or height than is usual (*a man of square frame*). **6.** Of square section (*square peg in round* HOLE¹; *has a square jaw*). **7.** Properly arranged, in good order, (*must tidy up and get things square*). **8.** Thorough, uncompromising, (*was met with a square refusal; made a square meal*). **9.** Fair, honest, (*his dealings are not always quite square*); **a** ~ **deal,** fair bargain, fair treatment. **10.** (sl.) Conventional or old-fashioned (cf. SQUARE¹ 9). **11.** On a proper footing, even, quits, (*am now square with all the world*); **get** ~ **with,** pay, compound with, (creditor); (**all**) ~, with no debit remaining, (Golf) having won same number of holes as opponent. **12.** ~ **brackets** (of [ ] shape);

~-built, of comparatively broad shape; ***~'head,** (derog.) Scandinavian, German, or Dutch immigrant; **~ leg,** (Cricket) (position of) fieldsman at some distance on batsman's leg-side and nearly opposite stumps; **~ piano** (early type with low oblong shape like clavichord); **~-rigged,** with principal sails at right angles to length of ship and extended by horizontal yards slung to mast by middle, opp. to *fore-and-aft rigged*; **~ sail,** four-cornered sail extended on yard slung to mast by middle; **~-shouldered,** with broad and not sloping shoulders, esp. opp. to *round-shouldered*; **~-toed,** (having boots or shoes) with square toes, (fig.) formal, prim. **13.** Hence ~'LY[2] (-ār'lĭ) *adv.*, ~'NESS (-ār'n-) *n.*, **squār'**ISH[1] *a.* **14.** *adv.* Squarely (*sat square on his seat*; *hit him square on the jaw*); fairly (*do you think he plays square?*); FAIR[2] *and square*. [ME, f. OF *esquarré* p.p. (as foll.)]

squāre[3] *v.* **1.** *v.t.* Make rectangular, give rectangular cross-section to (timber etc.); mark out in squares (**~d paper,** esp. for plotting graphs); place (shoulders etc.) squarely facing forwards; **~ the circle,** construct square equal in area to given circle (problem incapable of purely geometrical solution), (fig.) do what is impossible. **2.** Multiply (number) by itself (*3 squared is 9*; *x squared is written* x^2). **3.** *v.t.* & *i.* Adjust, make or be suitable *to* or consistent *with*, reconcile, (*decline to square my conduct to* or *with his interests*; *his practice does not square* or *he does not square his practice with his principles*). **4.** *v.t.* Settle, pay, (bill etc., or abs. *up*); *square* ACCOUNT[2]*s with*. **5.** (colloq.) Pay, esp. bribe, (*can you square the porter?*; *has been squared to hold his tongue*); secure acquiescence etc. of (person) thus. **6.** (Golf). Make score of (match, or abs.) all square. **7.** (Naut.) Lay (yards) at right angles with keel making them at same time horizontal, get (dead-eyes) horizontal, get (ratlines) horizontal and parallel to one another. **8.** *v.i.* **~ (*off),** assume attitude of boxer; **~ up to,** move towards (person) in this attitude, face and tackle (difficulty etc.) resolutely. **9.** ***~ away,** tidy up. [ME, f. OF *esquarrer* f. Rom. *EX[1](*quadrare* f. *quadra* square)]

squa'rrōse (-ŏ'r-) *a.* (Bot. & Zool.) Rough with scalelike processes. [f. L *squarrosus* scurfy, scabby; see -OSE[1]]

||**squār'son** *n.* (joc.) Squire and parson in one. [portmanteau wd]

squash[1] (-ŏ-) *v.* & *n.* **1.** *v.t.* Crush, squeeze flat or into pulp; pack tight, crowd; (fig.) silence (person) with crushing retort. **2.** *v.i.* Make one's way (*into*) by squeezing. **3.** *n.* Squashed thing or mass, whence ~'Y[2] *a.*; crowd, crowded assembly; (sound of) fall of soft body; **~ (rackets),** game played with rackets and small fairly soft ball in closed court; drink made of crushed fruit; **~ hat** (of soft felt etc.). [alt. f. QUASH]

squash[2] (-ŏ-) *n.* (Gourd, used as vegetable etc., of) trailing herbaceous annual plant of genus *Cucurbita*. [f. obs. (*i*)*squoutersquash* f. Narraganset *asquutasquash* (*asq* uncooked)]

squat (-ŏt) *v.* **(-tt-),** *a.*, & *n.* **1.** *v.i.* Sit on ground etc, with knees drawn up and heels close to or touching hams, crouch with hams resting on backs of heels; (of animal) crouch close to ground; (colloq.) sit (*down*, *on*, etc.); act as squatter. **2.** *v.t.* Put (*oneself*, person) into squatting position. **3.** *a.* In squatting posture; (of person etc.) short and thick, dumpy. **4.** *n.* Squatting posture; being squatter; place occupied by squatter(s). [ME, f. OF *esquatir* flatten (*es-* EX-[1] + *quatir* press down, crouch f. Rom. **coactire* f. L *coactus* p.p.; see COGENT)]

squa'tter (-ŏ't-) *n.* In vbl senses; person who settles on new esp. public land without title; person who takes unauthorized possession of unoccupied premises; (Austral.) (1) person who gets right of pasturage from government on easy terms, (2) sheep-farmer esp. on large scale. [f. prec. + -ER[1]]

squaw *n.* N. Amer. Ind. woman or wife; **~-man,** white married to squaw; ***~ winter,** brief wintry spell before Indian summer. [f. Narraganset *squaws*, Massachusetts *squaw* woman]

squawk *v.i.*, & *n.* **1.** *v.i.* Make squawk. **2.** *n.* (Usu. bird's) loud harsh cry; loud complaint; **~-box,** (colloq.) loudspeaker. [imit.]

squeak *v.* & *n.* **1.** *v.i.* Utter short shrill cry as of mouse; make slight high-pitched sound as of unoiled hinge; (sl.) turn informer. **2.** *v.t.* Utter (words) shrilly. **3.** *n.* Short shrill sound, whence ~'Y[2] *a.*; **(narrow) ~,** narrow escape, success barely attained; BUBBLE[1] *and squeak*. [ME; imit., cf. *squeal*, *shriek*, and Sw. *skväka* croak]

squea'ker *n.* In vbl senses; young bird, esp. pigeon. [f. prec. + -ER[1]]

squeal *v.* & *n.* **1.** *v.i.* Utter shrill cry as of child from pain, fear, anger, joy, etc.; (sl.) protest excitedly e.g. against taxation; (sl.) turn informer. **2.** *v.t.* Utter (words) with squeal. **3.** Hence ~'ER[1] *n.* **4.** *n.* Shrill prolonged cry of child, pig, etc. [ME; imit.]

squea'mish *a.* Easily nauseated; fastidious, overscrupulous in questions of propriety, honesty, etc.; hence ~LY[2] *adv.*, ~NESS *n.* [ME var. of (now dial.) *squeamous*, f. AF *escoymos*, of unkn. orig.]

squeegee' *n.*, & *v.t.* **1.** *n.* Rubber-edged implement for sweeping wet deck, road, etc.; small similar instrument or roller used in photography. **2.** *v.t.* Treat with squeegee. [f. *squeege*, strengthened form of foll.]

squeeze *v.* & *n.* **1.** *v.t.* Exert pressure on (sponge, lemon, etc.) esp. in order to extract moisture, compress with hand or between two bodies: ~ person's **hand** (as sign of sympathy, affection, etc.); **~d orange,** (fig.) person or thing from whom or which no more is to be had. **2.** Thrust (*oneself*, person, thing, *into* vehicle, room, etc., *out of*, etc.) by pressure. **3.** Harass by exactions, extort money etc. from; constrain, bring pressure to bear on; (Bridge) subject (player) to squeeze; get (money etc. *out of* person etc.) by extortion, entreaty, etc. **4. ~ (out),** produce with effort (*a tear* etc.). **5.** Hence **squee'z**ABLE *a.*, **squee'z**ER[1] (1, 2) *n.* **6.** *v.i.* & *t.* Make one's way or *way* by pressure (*into* etc.). **7.** *n.* Application of pressure by squeezing (lit. or fig.); small quantity produced by squeezing; (pressure of) crowd, crush, (*we all got in, but it was a* (*tight*) *squeeze*); ||close embrace; impression of coin etc. taken by pressing damp paper, wax, etc., against it; (Econ.) restriction imposed on borrowing, investment, etc.; forced exaction by Asian official, illicit commission, percentage on goods purchased extorted by native servant. **8. ~ bottle,** flexible container whose contents are extracted by squeezing it; **~ (play),** (Bridge) leading winning cards until opponent is forced to discard important card, (Baseball) hitting ball short to infield to enable runner on third base to start for home as soon as ball is pitched. [earlier *squise*, intensive of obs. *queise*, of unkn. orig.]

squĕlch *v.* & *n.* (colloq.) **1.** *v.t.* Stamp on, crush flat, put an end to; disconcert, silence. **2.** *v.i.* Make sucking sound as of treading in thick mud. **3.** *n.* Act or sound of squelching. [imit.]

squĭb *n.* & *v.* **(-bb-). 1.** *n.* Small firework burning with hissing sound and usu. with final explosion (**damp ~**, unsuccessful attempt to impress etc.); short satirical composition, lampoon. **2.** *v.i.* & *t.* Write, attack with, lampoons. [16th c., of unkn. orig., perh. imit.]

squĭd *n.*, & *v.i.* (**-dd-**). **1.** *n.* Ten-armed cephalopod esp. of genus *Loligo* used as bait or food; artificial bait imitating this. **2.** *v.i.* Fish with squid as bait. [17th c., of unkn. orig.]

squĭ'ffȳ *a.* (sl.) Slightly drunk. [19th c., of unkn. orig.]

squĭ'ggl|e *n.* Short curly line, esp. in handwriting; hence ~Y² *a.* [imit.]

squĭll *n.* **1.** Bulbous plant of genus *Scilla.* **2.** Sea-shore plant (*Urginea maritima*) whose bulbs are dried and used as diuretic, purgative, etc. **3.** Crustacean of genus *Squilla.* [ME, f. L *squilla*, *scilla* f. Gk *skilla*]

squĭnch *n.* Straight or arched structure across interior angle of square tower to carry dome etc. [var. of obs. *scunch* abbr. of SCUNCHEON]

squĭnt *v.*, *n.*, & *a.* **1.** *v.i.* Have the eyes turned in different directions, have squint; look obliquely (*at* etc.). **2.** *v.t.* Close (eyes) quickly, hold (eyes) half-shut. **3.** *n.* Abnormality of eyes in which their axes are differently directed; stealthy or sidelong glance; (colloq.) glance, look, (*let's have a squint at it*); leaning, inclination, (*to*, *towards*, policy etc.). **4.** Oblique opening through wall of church affording view of altar. **5.** *a.* Squinting; looking different ways; **~-eyed,** (fig.) malignant. [f. ASQUINT; adj. perh. f. *squint-eyed* f. obs. *squint* adv. f. *asquint*]

squīre *n.*, & *v.t.* **1.** *n.* Country gentleman, esp. *the* chief landed proprietor in a district; *magistrate or lawyer; woman's escort or gallant (**~ of dames,** man who is attentive to or frequents company of women); (Hist.) attendant on knight; hence ~'DOM (-īr'd-), ~'HOOD (-īr'h-), ~'LET, ~'LING, (-īr'l-), ~'SHIP (-īr'sh-), *ns.*, ~'LY¹ (-īr'lĭ) *a.* **2.** (Austral.) Young snapper fish. **3.** *v.t.* (Of man) attend upon, escort, (woman). [ME, f. OF *esquier* ESQUIRE]

squīr'(e)|ârchȳ (-īr'ârkĭ) *n.* The class of landed proprietors, esp. as having political or social influence; hence [by back form. after *monarch*] **~ârch** (-k) *n.*, **~ârch**AL, **~âr'ch**ICAL, (-k-) *adjs.* [f. prec., after *hierarchy* etc.]

||**squīree'n** *n.* Owner of small landed property esp. in Ireland. [f. SQUIRE + -EEN]

squīrm *v.i.*, & *n.* **1.** *v.i.* Wriggle, writhe; (fig.) show or feel embarrassment or discomfiture. **2.** *n.* Wriggling movement. [imit., prob. assoc. w. WORM¹]

squĭ'rrel *n.*, & *v.t.* **1.** *n.* Rodent of family Sciuridae, usu. of arboreal habits, with bushy tail carried over back, and pointed ears; its fur; **barking ~**, prairie-dog; GREY, GROUND¹-, RED, *squirrel*; **~-cage** (for squirrel etc., with revolving cylinder resembling treadmill; fig. of similar structure in electric motor or of monotonous repetition); ***~-hawk,** large hawk preying on squirrels; **~-monkey,** small soft-haired S. Amer. monkey of genus *Saimiri*; **~(-tail) grass** (of barley genus, with bushy spikelets). **2.** *v.t.* Hoard *away.* [ME, f. AF *esquirel*, OF *esquireul*, f. Rom. **scuriolus*, dim. of L f. Gk *skiouros*, f. *skia* shade + *oura* tail]

squīrt *v.* & *n.* **1.** *v.t.* Eject (liquid, powder) in a jet as from syringe. **2.** *v.i.* (Of liquid etc.) be discharged thus. **3.** *n.* Syringe; jet of water etc.; **~(-gun)**, kind of toy syringe; (colloq.) insignificant self-assertive fellow. [ME, imit.]

squĭsh *v.i.*, & *n.* (Move with) slight squelching sound; hence ~'Y² *a.* [imit.]

||**squĭt** *n.* (sl.) Small insignificant person. [cf. dial. *squirt* in same sense, and *squit* to squirt]

squitch *n.* = COUCH³-*grass.* [alt. f. QUITCH]

Sr. *abbr.* Senior; Señor.

sr *abbr.* steradian(s).

Sr *symb.* strontium.

||**S.R.C.** *abbr.* Science Research Council.

S.R.N. *abbr.* State Registered Nurse.

S.R.O. *abbr.* *standing room only; ||Statutory Rules and Orders.

SS. *abbr.* Saints.

S.S. *abbr.* steamship; (Hist.) Nazi special police force [f. G *Schutz-Staffel*].

||**S.S.A.F.A.** *abbr.* Soldiers', Sailors', and Airmen's Families Association.

S.S.C. *abbr.* (Sc.) Solicitor to the Supreme Court.

S.S.E. *abbr.* south-south-east.

||**S.S.R.C.** *abbr.* Social Science Research Council.

S.S.S. *abbr.* *Selective Service System; (Golf) standard scratch score.

S.S.T. *abbr.* supersonic transport.

S.S.W. *abbr.* south-south-west.

-st. See -EST².

St. *abbr.* Saint; stokes; Street.

st. *abbr.* stone; (Cricket) stumped by.

Sta. *abbr.* Station.

stăb *v.* (**-bb-**) & *n.* **1.** *v.t.* & *i.* Pierce, wound, with (usu. short) pointed tool or weapon e.g. knife or dagger; aim blow with such weapon (*at*); (fig.) inflict sharp pain on (person, his feelings, conscience, etc.), aim blow *at* (reputation, person, etc.); **~ in the back,** slander or betray; hence **~'b**ER¹ *n.* **2.** *n.* Act of stabbing; blow or thrust with knife etc., wound thus made, blow or pain inflicted on person's feelings; (colloq.) attempt, try; **~-culture** (of bacteria inoculated by deep-thrust needle). [ME; cf. dial. *stob* in first sense]

Sta'bat Mater (stah'-; mah-) *n.* (Musical setting for) Latin hymn on agony of the Virgin Mary at the Crucifixion. [f. the opening wds, L *Stabat mater dolorosa* 'Stood the Mother, full of grief']

stā'bĭle *n.* Abstract sculpture or structure of wire etc. [f. L *stabilis* STABLE¹]

stā'bĭlīz|e, -īs|e (-īz), *v.t.* & *i.* Make or become stable; hence ~A'TION *n.*, ~ER¹ (1, 2) *n.* (esp. gyroscope device to prevent rolling of ship, or *horizontal tailplane of aircraft). [f. STABILITY (see foll.) + -IZE]

stā'ble¹ *a.* Firmly fixed or established, not easily to be moved or changed or destroyed or altered in value, (*doubt whether the building, the government, is stable*; *element forms stable compounds, has no stable isotope*); firm, resolute, not wavering or fickle, (*a stable and steadfast friend*); *stable* EQUILIBRIUM; hence or cogn. **stabĭ'l**ITY, ~NESS (-beln-), *ns.*, **stā'b**LY² *adv.* [ME f. AF; OF *estable* f. L *stabilis* (*stare* stand; see -ABLE)]

stā'ble² *n.* & *v.* **1.** *n.* Building set apart and adapted for lodging and feeding horses; race-horses of particular stable; (fig.) (persons, products, etc., having) common origin or affiliation; **~-boy, ~-lad, ~man,** person employed in stable; **~-companion, ~-mate,** horse of same stable, (fig.) member of same school, club, etc.; **lock ~-door when horse is stolen,** take preventive action too late. **2.** *v.t.* Put or keep (horse) in stable. **3.** *v.i.* (Of horse etc., or fig. of person) be stabled. [ME, f. OF *estable* f. Rom. **stabula* & L *stabulum* (*stare* stand)]

stā'blĭng *n.* In vbl senses; accommodation for horses etc. [f. prec. + -ING¹]

stă'blĭsh *v.t.* (arch.) Fix firmly, establish, set up. [var. of ESTABLISH]

stacca'to (-ah'tō) *a.*, *adv.*, & *n.* (*pl.* **~s**). **1.** (Mus.) *a.* & *adv.* (To be played) in abrupt sharply detached manner (cf. LEGATO, TENUTO); **~ mark,** dot or stroke above or below staccato note in score. **2.** *a.* & *n.* (Uttered etc. with) delivery or presentation in separate short bursts. [It., p.p. of *staccare* = *distaccare* DETACH]

stăck *n.*, & *v.t.* **1.** *n.* Circular or rectangular pile of grain in sheaf or of hay, straw, etc., usu. with sloping thatched top, rick; **~-yard,** enclosure for these. **2.** ||(As measure of wood) pile of 108 cu. ft. **3.** Pile or heap of anything, esp. in orderly arrangement; (colloq.) large quantity, (*has stacks of money, a whole stack of work to get through*); stacked group of aircraft; pyramidal group of rifles, pile; **~(-room)**, part of library where books are compactly stored and to which public does not have direct access. **4.** **(Chimney-)~**, number of chimneys standing together. **5.** Isolated tall factory chimney; **(smoke-)~**, chimney or funnel to discharge smoke of locomotive or steamer; *BLOW[1] one's *stack*. **6.** ||High detached rock esp. off coast of Scotland and Orkneys. **7.** *v.t.* Pile in stack(s); arrange (cards, or fig. circumstances etc.) secretly for cheating; instruct to fly round at different levels (aircraft waiting to land at airport); ~ (= PILE[3]) **arms.** [ME, f. ON *stakkr* haystack, f. Gmc **stakkaz*]

stă'ctē *n.* Sweet spice used by ancient Jews in making incense. [ME, f. L f. Gk *staktē* (*stazō* drip)]

stă'ddle *n.* Platform or framework supporting rick etc.; **~-stone** (used similarly). [OE *stathol* base, = OS *stathal*, OHG *stadal*, ON *stöthull* f. Gmc **stathlaz* (**sta-* STAND[1])]

stā'dĭ|um *n.* **1.** (Gk Ant.; *pl. also* **~a**). Measure of length, about 220 metres; course for foot-race and chariot-race. **2.** Enclosed athletic or sports ground with tiers of seats for spectators. **3.** Stage or period of development etc. [ME f. L, f. Gk *stadion*]

sta'd(t)hōlder (stah'd- *or* stah't-; *or* stă'-) *n.* (Hist.) Viceroy or governor of province or town in Netherlands; chief magistrate of United Provinces of Netherlands; hence ~SHIP *n.* [f. Du. *stadhouder* deputy (*stad* STEAD, *houder* HOLDER, after med. L LOCUM TENENS)]

staff[1] (-ahf) *n.* (*pl.* **~s** *or* (arch. exc. Mus.) **staves** *pr.* stāvz), & *v.t.* **1.** *n.* Stick or pole for use in walking or climbing or as weapon (lit., or fig.: *bread is the staff of life*; *you are the staff of his old age*); QUARTER[1]*staff*. **2.** This as sign of office or authority; **pastoral ~**, crosier. **3.** Shaft, pole, as support or handle (FLAG[4]*staff*); spindle in watch. **4.** Rod for measuring distances, heights, etc., in surveying. **5.** Token given to engine-driver on single-line railway as authority to proceed over a given section of line (**~ system,** this method of working). **6.** (Mil. etc.) Body of officers assisting officer in high command and concerned with army or regiment or fleet or air force as a whole; GENERAL *staff*; ||**~ college** (in which officers are prepared for staff duties); **~ officer** (serving on staff). **7.** Body of persons carrying on work under manager etc. (*editorial staff of newspaper*; *diplomatic staff*; ||**~ nurse,** nurse ranking just below a sister); those in authority within an organization, opp. students, pupils, etc.; hence (-)~ED[2] (-ft) *a.*, *~'ER[1] *n.*, member of staff esp. of newspaper. **8.** (Mus.) Set of usu. five parallel lines on any one or between any adjacent two of which a note is placed to indicate its pitch; **~ notation** (by means of staff, esp. opp. to TONIC *sol-fa*). **9.** *v.t.* Provide (institution etc.) with staff. [OE *stæf*, = OS *staf*, OHG *stap*, ON *stafr* f. Gmc **stabhaz*]

staff[2] (-ahf) *n.* Mixture of plaster of Paris, cement, etc., as temporary building-material. [19th c.; orig. unkn.]

staffa'ge (-ah'zh) *n.* Accessory items in painting, esp. figures in landscape picture. [G (*staffieren* decorate, perh. f. OF *estoffer*; see STUFF, -AGE)]

Staffs. *abbr.* Staffordshire.

stăg *n.* **1.** Male of red deer or of other large kinds of deer, esp. in fifth year. **2.** ||(St. Exch.) person who applies for shares of new issue with a view to selling at once at a profit. **3.** *Man who attends social gathering unaccompanied by woman. **4.** **~-beetle** (with branched mandibles like stag's antlers); **~-horn,** (1) horn of stag used for knife-handle etc., (2) club-moss or coral resembling antlers; **~'hound,** large hound hunting deer by sight or scent; **~ film,** ***~ movie,** (suitable for men only); **~-party** (of men only). [ME f. OE **stacga*, **stagga*; cf. *docga* dog, *frogga* frog, **picga* pig]

stāge[1] *n.* **1.** Raised floor or platform, e.g. scaffold for workmen's use in building; LANDING-*-stage*. **2.** Surface on which object is placed for inspection through microscope. **3.** Platform on which plays etc. are performed before an audience; (fig.) the drama, dramatic art or literature, actor's profession; **go on the ~,** become actor or actress. **4.** Scene of action (*quitted the stage of politics*); **hold the ~,** dominate conversation etc. **5.** Point or period in development, process, etc., (*reached a critical stage*; *at this stage an interruption occurred*; *passed through a long stage of inactivity*; *is in the tomboy stage, the larval stage*). **6.** (Regular) stopping-place on route, distance between two of these, (*travelled by easy stages*); **(fare-)~**, section of bus etc. route for which fixed fare is charged, stopping-place at end of this. **7.** (Geol.) Range of strata forming subdivision of series. **8.** (Electr.) Single amplifying transistor or valve with associated equipment. **9.** Section of rocket with separate engine, jettisoned when its propellant is exhausted. **10.** **~-coach,** (Hist.) large closed coach running regularly by stages between places; **~'craft,** skill or experience in writing or staging plays; **~ direction,** instruction in text of play as to movement, position, tone, etc., of actor, or sound effects etc.; **~ door,** actors' and workmen's entrance from street to theatre behind stage; **~ effect,** effect produced in acting or on the stage, artificial or theatrical effect produced in real life; **~ fever,** inordinate desire to go on the stage; **~ fright,** nervousness on facing audience esp. for first time; **~-hand,** person handling scenery etc. during performance on stage; **~-manage,** be stage-manager of, (fig.) arrange and control for effect in manner of stage-manager; **~-manager,** person responsible for lighting and other mechanical arrangements, costumes, etc. of play; **~ play** (opp. broadcast etc.); **~ rights,** exclusive rights to perform particular play; **~-struck,** struck with stage fever; **~-wait,** hitch or delay in theatrical performance; **~ whisper,** aside, whisper meant to be heard by others than the person addressed. [ME, f. OF *estage* dwelling f. Rom. **staticum* standing-place (*stare* stand); see -AGE]

stāge[2] *v.t.* Present (play) on stage; arrange occurrence of, esp. dramatically (*stage a come-back*). [f. prec.]

stā'ger *n.* **Old ~,** experienced person, old hand. [f. STAGE[1] + -ER[1]]

stā'gey. Var. of STAGY.

stăgflā'tion *n.* Period in which inflation occurs without corresponding increase of production. [f. STAGNATION + INFLATION]

stă'ggard *n.* (arch.) Stag in fourth year. [ME, f. STAG + -ARD]

stă'gger (-g-) *v.* & *n.* **1.** *v.i.* Walk or stand unsteadily, totter; hesitate, waver in purpose. **2.** *v.t.* Cause to totter (*was staggered by the blow*); cause to hesitate or waver (*the question, the news, staggered him, his resolution*). **3.** Arrange in zigzag order, esp. set (spokes of wheel) to incline alternately to right and left; arrange (holidays, hours of work, etc.) so that they do not coincide with those of others; arrange (road-crossing) so that side roads are not in line. **4.** Hence ~ER[1] *n.* **5.** *n.* Tottering movement; overhanging or slantwise or zigzag arrangement of like parts in a structure etc. **6.** (in *pl.*) Disease of brain and spinal cord esp. in horses and cattle; giddiness. [alt. of ME (now dial.) *stacker* f. ON *stakra* frequent. of *staka* push, stagger]

stă'ggering (-g-) *a.* In vbl senses; bewildering, astonishing; hence ~LY[2] *adv.* [f. prec. + -ING[2]]

stā'ging *n.* In vbl senses; driving or running stage-coaches; scaffolding, temporary platform or support; shelves for plants in greenhouse; ~ **area,** intermediate assembly point for troops in transit; ~ **post,** regular stopping-place, esp. on air route. [ME, f. STAGE[2,1] + -ING[1]]

Stă'girīte *n.* **The** ~, Aristotle. [f. L f. Gk *Stag(e)iritēs* native of *Stagira* in Macedonia, birthplace of Aristotle; see -ITE[1]]

stăgn|ā'te *v.i.* (Of liquid) be(come) motionless, have no current, cease to flow; (of life, action, mind, business, person) be(come) dull or sluggish; hence or cogn. ~ANCY, ~A'TION, *ns.*, ~ANT *a.* [f. L *stagnare* (*stagnum* pool) + -ATE[3]]

stăgnĭ'colous *a.* Living in swamps or stagnant water. [f. mod. L *stagnicolus* f. L *stagnum* pool + *colere* inhabit, + -OUS]

stā'g|y̆ *a.* Theatrical in manner, style, appearance, etc.; hence ~ĬLY[2] *adv.*, ~ĬNESS *n.* [f. STAGE[1] + -Y[2]]

staid *a.* Of steady and sober character; of quiet and serious demeanour; sedate; hence ~'LY[2] *adv.*, ~'NESS *n.* [=*stayed*, p.p. of STAY[1]]

stain *v.t.*, & *n.* **1.** *v.t.* Discolour, soil, (*cigarettes stain the fingers*; *wine will stain the cloth*; *guaranteed not to stain clothes*); (fig.) sully, blemish, (reputation, name, person); colour (wood, glass, etc.) by process other than painting or covering the surface; impregnate (substance) for microscopic examination with colouring matter that makes structure visible by being deposited in some parts more than in others; print colours on (wallpaper); hence ~'ABLE *a.*, ~'ER[1] *n.* **2.** *n.* Discoloration, spot or mark caused esp. by contact with foreign matter and not easily removed (*cloth is covered with tea-stains*); staining-material; (fig.) blot, blemish, (*without a stain on his character*); hence ~'LESS *a.* (esp. of reputation); ~**less steel,** chrome steel not liable to rust or tarnish under ordinary conditions. [ME, f. *distain* f. OF *desteindre desteign-* f. Rom. **distingere* (as DIS-, TINGE)]

stair *n.* **1.** Each of a set of fixed indoor steps (*on the top stair but one*). **2.** (in *pl.* exc. arch. or Sc.) Set of these (*passed him on the stairs*; *down a winding stair*); FLIGHT[1] or PAIR[1] *of stairs*; BACK[1] *stairs*; **below** ~**s,** in basement of house esp. as part occupied by servants; DOWNSTAIRS; UPSTAIRS. **3.** (in *pl.*) Landing-stage. **4.** ~**'case,** (part of building containing) flight(s) of stairs (MOVING *staircase*; SPIRAL *staircase*); ~**'head,** level space at top of stairs; ~**-rod** (for securing stair-carpet in angle between two steps); ~**'way,** (1) way up a flight of stairs, (2) staircase. [OE *stǣger* f. Gmc **staig-*, **stig-* to climb; cf. (M)Du., (M)LG *steiger* landing-stage]

||**staithe** (-dh) *n.* Waterside coal depot equipped for loading vessels. [ME, f. ON **stathwō*, *stöth* landing-stage, = OS *stath*, OHG *stad* bank, shore f. Gmc **stathaz*, **-am* (**sta-* STAND[1])]

stāke *n.*, & *v.t.* **1.** *n.* Stout stick or post sharpened at one end and driven into ground as support, boundary mark, etc.; post to which person was tied to be burnt alive, (fig.) punishment of death by burning, (*was condemned to*, *suffered at*, *the stake*); long vertical rod in basket-making; ***pull (up)** ~**s,** depart, go to live elsewhere. **2.** Metal-worker's small anvil fixed on bench by pointed prop. **3.** Money etc. wagered on an event, esp. deposited with third party (~**'holder**) by each of those who make a wager; (in *pl.*) money to be contended for esp. in horse-race, such race (*maiden*, *trial*, *stakes*); **have a** ~ **in the country,** be materially concerned in its welfare, e.g. as land-owner; **at** ~, at issue, in question, risked, (*life itself is at stake*). **4.** ~**-boat** (anchored to mark course for boat-race etc.); ~**-net,** fishing-net hung on stakes. **5.** *v.t.* Fasten, secure, or support with stake(s); mark *off*, *out*, (area) with stakes (*stake out a claim*, lit. or fig.); *(colloq.) give financial or other support to; *~ **out,** (colloq.) place under, or for purpose of, surveillance. **6.** Wager, risk, (money etc. *on* event etc.). [OE *staca*, = MDu., (M)LG *stake*, f. WG **stak-*, **stek-* pierce, cogn. w. STICK[2]; senses 3 and 6 16th c., perh. of different orig.]

Stăkha'nov|ite (-kah'n-) *n.* (Esp. Russian) worker who increases his output to an exceptional extent, and so gains special awards; hence ~ISM (3) *n.* [f. A. G. *Stakhanov*, Russ. coal-miner d. 1977 + -ITE[1] (1)]

stă'lactīte *n.* Deposit of calcium carbonate, usu. in form like large icicle, hanging from roof of cave etc. and formed by trickling of water; hence **stală'ct**IC, **stală'ctĭ**FORM, **stălactĭ't**IC, *adjs.* [f. mod. L *stalactites* f. Gk *stalaktos* dripping (*stalassō* drip; see -ITE[1])]

Stă'lăg *n.* German prison camp, esp. for non-commissioned officers and privates. [G (*stamm* base, main stock, *lager* camp)]

stă'lagmīte *n.* Deposit like stalactite standing on floor of cave etc. and often uniting with stalactite; hence **stălagmĭ't**IC *a.* [f. mod. L *stalagmites* f. Gk *stalagma* dripping (as STALACTITE)]

stāle[1] *a.* & *v.* **1.** *a.* Musty, insipid, or otherwise the worse for age or use, not fresh; ~ **bread** (musty, or not quite new: *stale bread is best for toast*). **2.** Lacking novelty, trite, (*stale joke*, *news*, *tricks*); (of athlete or other performer) having ability impaired by over-exertion; (Law, esp. of claim) having been left dormant for an unreasonably long time. **3.** Hence ~'LY[2] (-l-lĭ) *adv.*, ~'NESS (-ln-) *n.* **4.** *v.t.* & *i.* Make or become stale or common. [ME, prob. f. AF & OF **estale* (*estaler* halt; cf. STALL[1])]

stāle[2] *v.i.* (arch. or dial.), & *n.* **1.** *v.i.* (Esp. of horses and cattle) urinate. **2.** *n.* Urine of horses and cattle. [ME, perh. f. OF *estaler* adopt position (cf. prec.)]

stā'lemāte (-lm-) *n.*, & *v.t.* **1.** *n.* (Chess) drawn position resulting from player's having no move available, his king not being in check; (fig.) deadlock, drawn contest. **2.** *v.t.* Bring (player) to stalemate; (fig.) bring to a standstill. [f. obs. *stale* (f. AF *estale* f. *estaler* be placed; cf. STALE[1]) + MATE[1]]

Sta'lĭn|ĭsm (-ah'-) *n.* Policy followed by Stalin in government of U.S.S.R.; so ~IST (2) *n.* [f. J. V. *Stalin* (Dzhugashvili), Soviet statesman d. 1953 + -ISM]

stalk[1] (-awk) *v.* & *n.* **1.** *v.i.* Stride, walk in stately or imposing manner (*along* etc.); steal up to game under cover. **2.** *v.t.* Pursue (game, enemy) stealthily; ~**'ing-horse,** horse behind which hunter conceals himself, (fig.) pretext concealing one's real actions or intentions; hence (-)~'ER[1] *n.* **3.** *n.* Stalking of game; imposing gait. [OE **stealcian* f. Gmc **stalkōjan*, frequent. of **stal-*, **stel-* STEAL]

stalk[2] (-awk) *n.* Main stem of herbaceous plant; slender attachment or support of leaf, flower, fruit, etc.; similar support of organ etc. in animals; stem of wineglass etc.; tall chimney of factory etc.; ~**-eyed,** (of crab etc.) having the eyes mounted on stalks; hence (-)~ED[2]

(-kt), ~'LESS, *adjs.*, ~'LET *n.* [ME *stalke*, prob. dim. of (now dial.) *stale* rung of ladder, long handle, f. OE *stalu*]

stall[1] (-awl) *n.* & *v.* **1.** *n.* (Single compartment for one animal in) stable, cow-house; **~-feed,** fatten (cattle) in stall. **2.** Trader's booth in bazaar, market, etc., compartment in a building for sale of goods, table in this on which goods are exposed; ||BOOK[1]*stall.* **3.** Fixed seat in choir or chancel of church more or less enclosed at back and sides and often canopied, esp. one appropriated to clergyman (*canon's, dean's, stall*); (fig.) office, dignity, of canon etc. (*how long has he had his stall?*). **4.** ||Each of a set of seats in theatre usu. between pit and stage. **5.** Compartment for occupation by one person in shower-baths etc.; compartment for one horse at start of race. **6.** Receptacle for one object (FINGER-*stall*). **7.** (Condition resulting from) stalling of engine or aircraft. **8.** *v.t.* Put or keep (cattle etc.) in stall esp. for fattening (*a stalled ox*); furnish (stable etc.) with stalls. **9.** Cause (engine, vehicle, aircraft) to stall. **10.** *v.i.* (Of horse or cart) stick fast as in mud or snow; *be snow-bound; (of motor vehicle or its engine) stop because of overload on engine or inadequate supply of fuel to it; (of aircraft or its pilot) reach condition where speed is too low to allow effective operation of controls. [OE *steall*, = MDu., OHG *stal*, ON *stallr* f. Gmc **stalla-* prob. f. **stadhlaz* (**sta-* STAND[1]); partly f. OF *estal* f. Frank. **stal*]

stall[2] (-awl) *v.* **1.** *v.i.* Play for time when being questioned etc. **2.** *v.t.* Block, delay, obstruct; ~ **off,** evade or deceive. [f. *stall* pickpocket's confederate, orig. 'decoy' f. AF *estal(e)*, prob. cogn. w. prec.]

||**sta'llage** (-aw'l-) *n.* Space for, rent for, right to erect, stall(s) in market etc. [ME, f. OF *estalage* (*estal* STALL[1]; see -AGE)]

stă'llion (-yon) *n.* Uncastrated male horse, esp. one kept for breeding. [ME, f. OF *estalon* thr. Rom. f. Gmc **stall-* STALL[1]]

sta'lwart (-aw'l-) *a.* & *n.* **1.** *a.* Strongly built, sturdy; courageous, resolute, determined, (*stalwart supporters*); hence ~LY[2] *adv.*, ~NESS *n.* **2.** *n.* (esp. Polit.) Resolute uncompromising partisan. [Sc. var. of obs. *stalworth* f. OE *stǣlwierthe* (*stǣl* place, WORTH[1])]

stā'mĕn *n.* Male fertilizing organ of flowering plants, including anther containing pollen; hence **stămĭnĭ'**FEROUS *a.* [L *stamen staminis* warp in upright loom, thread]

stă'mĭna *n.* Staying-power, power of endurance; ability to undergo prolonged strain on body or mind. [L, pl. of prec., in sense warp, threads spun by the Fates]

stă'mĭnal *a.* Of stamens or stamina. [f. as STAMEN + -AL]

stă'mĭnate *a.* Having stamens but no pistils; having stamens. [f. as STAMEN + -ATE[2]]

stă'mmer *v.* & *n.* **1.** *v.i.* Speak (habitually, or on occasion from embarrassment etc.) with halting articulation esp. with pauses or rapid repetitions of same syllable; hence ~ER[1] *n.* **2.** *v.t.* ~ (**out**), utter (words) thus (*stammered out an excuse*). **3.** *n.* Stammering speech; tendency to stammer. [OE *stamerian*, = OS *stamaron*, MLG, MDu. *stameren* f. WG **stamrōjan*]

stămp *v.* & *n.* **1.** *v.t.* Impress pattern, mark, etc., upon (metal, butter, paper, etc.) with die or similar instrument of metal, wood, rubber, etc.; produce by cutting *out* with die etc.; impress *on* the memory etc.; affix postage or other stamp to (envelope, document); crush, pulverize, (ore etc.). **2.** *v.i.* & *t.* Bring down one's foot, bring down (foot), heavily on ground; bring into specified state thus (*stamp down earth around plant*); ~ **on,** suppress; ~ **out,** put an end to, crush, destroy; **~'ing-ground,** favourite place of resort or action. **3.** *v.t.* Assign a character to, characterize, (*this alone stamps the story (as) an invention, stamps him as a genius*). **4.** Hence (-)~'ER[1] (1, 2) *n.* **5.** *n.* Instrument for stamping pattern or mark; mark made by this; impression of official mark required to be made for revenue purposes on deeds, bills of exchange, etc., as evidence of payment of tax; piece of paper impressed with official mark as evidence of payment of tax or fee and meant to be affixed to letter, postcard, deed of transfer of property, etc. (||INSURANCE *stamp*; POSTAGE *stamp*); mark impressed on, label etc. affixed to, commodity as evidence of quality etc. **6.** (fig.) Characteristic mark, impress, (*bears the stamp of genius*); character, kind, (*avoid men of that* or *his stamp*). **7.** Block that crushes ore in stamp-mill; (sound made by) heavy downward blow with foot. **8.** **S~ Act,** act concerned with stamp-duty, esp. that imposing duty on American colonies in 1765 and repealed in 1766; **~-collecting, ~-collector,** (of postage stamps as objects of interest or value); **~-duty** (imposed on certain kinds of legal instrument); *stamp*-HINGE; **~-machine** (for selling postage stamps); **~-mill** (for crushing ore etc.); **~-office** (for issue of government stamps and receipt of stamp-duty etc.); **~-paper,** (1) paper with government revenue stamp, (2) gummed marginal paper of sheet of postage stamps. [v. prob. f. OE **stampian*, OHG *stampfōn* pound, ON *stappa* f. Gmc **stampōjan* (**stamp-*, prob. cogn. w. **stap-* STEP[2]); n. partly f. v., partly f. OF *estampe* f. same Gmc source]

stămpē'de *n.* & *v.* **1.** *n.* Sudden fright and scattering of a number of horses, cattle, etc.; sudden flight or hurried movement of people due to panic; *(Polit.) unconcerted movement of many persons by common impulse. **2.** *v.i.* & *t.* (Cause to) take part in stampede or act hurriedly or unreasoningly. [f. Sp. *estampida* crash, uproar, fem. p.p. (as n.) f. Rom. **stampire* f. Gmc **stampjan* (as prec.)]

stănce *n.* (Golf, Cricket, etc.) position taken for stroke; pose, attitude. [F, f. It. STANZA]

stanch[1], **staunch**[2], (-ah- *or* -aw-) *v.t.* Check the flow of (esp. blood); check the flow from (esp. wound). [ME, f. OF *estanchier* f. Rom. **stancare* (**stancus* dried up, of unkn. orig.)]

stanch[2] etc. See STAUNCH[1] etc.

sta'nchion (-ah'nshon) *n.*, & *v.t.* **1.** *n.* Post, pillar, upright support, vertical strut; upright bar, pair of bars, or frame, for confining cattle in stall. **2.** *v.t.* Supply with stanchion; fasten (cattle) to stanchion. [ME, f. AF *stanchon*, OF *estanchon*, *-son* (*estance* prop, f. Rom. **stantia*; see STANZA)]

stănd[1] *v.* (**stood** *pr.* -ŏŏd). **1.** *v.i.* Have or take or maintain upright position, esp. on feet or base, be set upright, (*stood there till I was tired*; *was too weak to stand*; *chair will not stand on two legs*; *hair stood on end with fright*); *stand at* EASE[1], ||EASY, (Mil.); *stand in* person's LIGHT[1], *in the* BREACH[1], *on* one's HEAD[1], *in the* WAY *of.* **2.** Be of specified height (*stands six foot three*). **3.** Be situated, be, (*on each side stand two pillars*; *a stranger stood in the doorway*; *the cups stand on the top shelf*; *here once stood a village, a huge oak*). **4.** Assume stationary position, cease to move, (*now stand still*; *was commanded to stand*); ~ (**and deliver**)! (highwayman's order); **~'still,** stoppage, inability to proceed. **5.** Maintain position, avoid falling or moving or being moved, (*don't stand there arguing*; *house will stand for another century*; *whether we stand or fall*; *has stood through worse storms*; *stand on* one's *own feet*

(FOOT[1] 12); *stand fast*; *stand firm*); *not a* LEG *to stand on*; *stand* PAT[3]. **6.** Hold good, remain valid or unaltered, (*the former conditions may stand*; *the wording must stand*; *the same remark stands good*). **7.** Be, find oneself, in specified situation, rank, etc., (*stands convicted of treachery*, *in need of help*, *in an awkward position*, *under heavy obligations*; *thermometer stood at 90°*; *the matter stands thus*; *he stands first on the list*, *in the same relation to both parties*; *I stand prepared to dispute it*, *in awe of*); act in specified capacity (*stand proxy for*; *have often stood his friend*). **8.** ~ **alone,** be unequalled; *stand at* BAY[4]; ~ **corrected,** accept correction from another person; ~ **high,** be high in status, price, etc.; *stand* person *in good* STEAD; ~ **well,** be on good terms or in good repute *with*; **as it ~s,** in its present condition, unaltered; ~ **to,** be certain or likely to (win, lose, etc.). **9.** Move to and remain in specified position (lit. or fig.; *stand back*, *clear*, *aside*, *aloof*, *away*, **from under*); (Naut.) hold specified course (*stand in for the shore*; *you are standing into danger*); (of dog) point, set. **10.** *v.t.* Place or set in upright or specified position (*stand the jug on the table*; *stand it against the wall*; *shall stand you in the corner as punishment*). **11.** Endure without yielding or complaining, tolerate, (*her nerves could not stand the strain*; *how does he usually stand pain?*; *could never stand the fellow*; *shall stand no* (*more*) *nonsense*; *stood the enemy's fire*; *failed to stand the test*); ~ one's **ground,** maintain one's position (lit., or fig. in argument etc.). **12.** Undergo (trial); *stand a* CHANCE[1]. **13.** Provide for another or others at one's own expense (*stood him a drink*; *stood a bottle to the company*; *who is going to stand treat?*). **14.** Hence ~EE′ *n.*, (colloq.) one who stands, esp. when all seats are occupied. **15.** (w. *preps.*): ~ **by,** uphold, support, side with, (person), adhere to, abide by, (terms, promises), (Naut.) stand ready to take hold of or operate (anchor etc.); ~ **for,** represent, signify, imply, (*U.S. stands for 'United States'*; *Liberalism stands for a great deal more than that*), ||be candidate for (office), ||be candidate for representation of (constituency) in Parliament, espouse the cause of (free trade etc.), (colloq.) endure, tolerate, acquiesce in; ||~ (person) **in,** (arch.) cost (specified sum); ~ **on,** insist on, observe scrupulously, (*stand on ceremony*, one's *dignity*, one's *rights*); ~ **over,** stand close to person to watch, control, threaten, etc.; ~ **to,** = *stand by*; *it stands to* REASON[1]; ~ **upon,** = *stand on*. **16.** (w. *advs.*): ~ **by,** stand near, be a bystander, look on without interfering (*will not stand by and see him ill-treated*), stand ready, be on the alert; ~*-by* n. (pl. *-bys*), thing or person that one can depend on, equipment kept for emergency; ~ **down** *v.t.* & *i.*, retire from team, witness-box, or similar position, ||cease to be candidate etc., ||(Mil.) go off duty; ~ **in,** deputize *for*; ~*-in* n., deputy, substitute, esp. for actor when latter's acting ability is not needed; ~ **in with,** be in league with; ~ **off,** move or keep away, keep one's distance, ||dispense with services of (employee) temporarily; ~*-off* n., *deadlock; **~-off** (**half**), (Rugby Footb.) half-back who forms link between scrum-half and three-quarters; **~-o′ffish,** cold or distant in manner; ~ **on,** (Naut.) continue on same course; ~ **out,** hold out, persist in opposition (*against*) or support (*for*) or endurance, be prominent or conspicuous or outstanding; *~*-out* n., remarkable person or thing; ~ **over,** be postponed, be left for later settlement etc.; ~ **to,** (arch.) fall to, set to work, (Mil.) take post in preparation for an attack (esp. before dawn or after dark); ~ **up,** rise to one's feet from sitting or other position, maintain erect position (*have only the clothes I stand up in*), be valid (*that argument does not stand up on examination*), (colloq.) fail to keep appointment with; ~ **up for,** side with, maintain, support, (person, cause); ~ **up to,** meet, face, (opponent) courageously, (of thing) remain unimpaired despite the effects of (hard wear etc.); ~*-up* a., (of collar) upright, high, opp. to *turn-down*, (of meal) eaten standing, (of fight) thorough, fair and square. [OE *standan*, = OS, Goth. *standan*, OHG *stantan*, ON *standa* f. Gmc **standan* (**sta-*, **sto-*, f. IE **sth'-*, **sthā-* (cause to) stand)]

stănd[2] *n.* **1.** Cessation from motion or progress, stoppage, (*came*, *was brought*, *to a stand*); **be at a** ~, (arch.) be unable to proceed, be in perplexity. **2.** Stationary condition assumed for purpose of resistance, esp. **make a** ~ (*against* enemy, *for* or *against* principle, etc.); (Cricket) prolonged stay at wicket by two batsmen. **3.** Position taken up (*took his stand near the door*); **take** one's ~, base argument etc., rely, *on*. **4.** Table, set of shelves, rack, etc., on or in which things may be placed, (*music*, *hat*, *umbrella*, *-stand*; HALL-*stand*; INK*stand*; ||WASH[1]-*hand stand*); ~ **camera** (for use on tripod, not hand-held). **5.** Stall in market etc. (*fruit-stand*, NEWS-*stand*). **6.** Standing-place for vehicles etc. (*cab-stand*). **7.** Raised structure for persons to sit or stand on (BAND[1]*stand*; GRAND*stand*); *witness-box (*take the stand*). **8.** Standing growth (*of* trees, clover, etc.). **9.** (Theatr. etc.) Each halt made on a tour to give performances (*a one-night stand*). **10.** ||(Mil.) ~ **of arms,** complete set of weapons for one man; ~ **of colours,** regiment's flags. [ME, f. prec.]

stă′ndard *n.* **1.** Distinctive flag, esp. flag of cavalry regiment, opp. to *colours* of infantry; (fig.) rallying principle (*raise the standard of revolt*). **2.** Weight or measure to which others conform or by which the accuracy or quality of others is judged (*by present-day standards*; DOUBLE[1] *standard*; *standard pound*, *yard*, etc.; **S~ English,** form of English speech used, with local variations, by majority of educated English-speaking people); thing serving as basis of comparison; document specifying (inter)nationally agreed properties for manufactured goods etc. (*British Standard*); *standard* DEVIATION. **3.** Degree of excellence etc. required for particular purpose (*does not come up to* (*the*) *standard*; *set a low standard*; ~ **of living,** degree of material comfort available to person or class or community); thing recognized as model for imitation etc. (~ **book** etc., one recognized as meritorious or authoritative); ||grade of classification in primary schools. **4.** Average quality (*work was of a low standard*); ordinary procedure, or quality or design of a product, without added or novel features. **5.** Prescribed proportion of weight of fine metal, establishment of monetary basis, in gold or silver coin (**gold, silver,** ~) or in both (DOUBLE[1] *standard*); **multiple, tabular,** ~, standard of value obtained by averaging prices of a number of products. **6.** Measure (165 cu. ft.) of timber. **7.** Upright support; upright water or gas pipe; tree or shrub that stands alone without support; shrub grafted on upright stem and trained in tree form (*standard rose*). **8.** **~-bearer,** soldier who bears standard, (fig.) prominent leader in cause; ***S~bred,** (member of) breed of race-horses able to attain a specified speed; ||~ **lamp** (set on tall pillar standing on floor); ~ **time** (uniform for places in approximately same longitude, and established in a country or region by law or custom). [ME, f. AF *estaundart*, OF *estendart* (*estendre*, as EXTEND; see -ARD); in sense 7 affected by assoc. w. STAND[1]]

stă'ndardīz|e, -īs|e (-īz), *v.t.* Make conform to standard; determine properties of by comparison with a standard; hence ~A'TION *n.* [f. prec. + -IZE]

stă'nding[1] *n.* In vbl senses; estimation in which one is held, repute, position, (*men of high standing; is of no standing*; **in good** ~, fully paid-up as member etc.); length of service, membership, etc.; duration (*a dispute of long standing*); **~-room,** space to stand in. [ME, f. STAND[1] + -ING[1]]

stă'nding[2] *a.* In vbl senses; established, permanent, (*a standing rule; has become a standing* JOKE[1]; **long-~,** that has long existed, not recent); not made, raised, etc., for the occasion (*a standing army*; ~ **order,** instruction to banker to make regular payments, or to bookseller etc. for regular supply of a periodical; ~ **orders,** those governing manner in which all business shall be conducted in Parliament, council, society, etc.); (of race, jump, start, etc.) performed from rest, without run-up; **all** ~, (Naut. or transf.) without time to lower sails, taken by surprise; **leave** person ~, make far more rapid progress than he; ~ **corn** (unreaped); ~ **rigging** (fixed in position); ~ **type** (Print., not yet distributed after use); ~ **water** (stagnant); ~ **wave,** vibration of system in which some particular points remain fixed while others between them vibrate with the maximum amplitude. [ME, f. STAND[1] + -ING[2]]

stă'ndish *n.* (arch.) Inkstand. [ME, prob. f. STAND[1]]

***stăndpă'tter** *n.* (esp. Polit.) One who opposes changes in policy. [f. *stand* PAT[3] + -ER[1]]

stă'nd-pipe *n.* Vertical pipe for fluid to rise in. [f. STAND[1] + PIPE[1]]

stă'ndpoint *n.* Point of view (lit. or fig.). [f. STAND[1] + POINT[1], after G *standpunkt*]

stă'nhope (-nop) *n.* Light open carriage for one, with 2 or 4 wheels. [f. Hon. & Rev. Fitzroy *Stanhope*, Engl. clergyman d. 1864, for whom first made]

stă'niel (-yel) *n.* Kestrel. [OE *stāngella* (*stān* stone, **gella* yeller f. *gellan* YELL)]

stănk. See STINK.

||**stă'nnarў** *n.* Tin-mine; (usu. in *pl.*) tin-mining district of Cornwall and Devon; ~ **court** (for regulation of tin-mines in the stannaries). [f. med. L *stannaria* n. pl. f. LL *stannum* tin; see -ARY[1]]

stă'nn|ic *a.* (Chem.) Of tin esp. in its higher valence (*stannic acid*); so ~ATE[1] (3) *n.* [f. LL *stannum* tin + -IC]

stă'nn|ous *a.* (Chem.) Of tin esp. in its lower valence (*stannous salts*); so ~ITE[1] (2) *n.* [f. as prec. + -OUS]

stă'nza *n.* Group of (usu. four or more) rhymed lines occurring as repeated metrical unit (SPENSERIAN *stanza*); group of four lines in some Greek and Latin metres (SAPPHIC *stanza*); hence (-)~'D[2], ~ED[2] (-ad), **stănzā'**IC, *adjs.* [It., = standing-place, chamber, stanza, f. Rom. **stantia* abode f. L *stare* stand; see -ANCE]

stăp *v.t.* (-pp-). (arch.) = STOP[1] (~ **my vitals, me,** excl. of surprise or anger). [affected pronunc. in Vanbrugh's *The Relapse* (1697)]

stapē'lĭa *n.* S. Afr. plant of genus *Stapelia*, with evil-smelling flowers. [mod. L, f. J. B. van *Stapel*, Du. botanist d. 1636 + -IA[1]]

stā'pēs (-z) *n.* (*pl.* same). Small stirrup-shaped bone in ear of mammal. [mod. L, f. med. L *stapes* stirrup]

stăph *n.* (colloq.) = foll. [abbr.]

stăphўlocŏ'cc|us *n.* (*pl.* ~i *pr.* -kī). Form of pus-producing bacterium characterized by forming grapelike clusters; hence ~AL *a.* [mod. L, f. Gk *staphulē* bunch of grapes + *kokkos* berry]

stā'ple[1] *n.*, & *v.t.* **1.** *n.* U-shaped piece of metal bar or wire with ends pointed for driving into wood etc. to take hasp of padlock or hook, or for driving through and clenching, to secure papers, netting, electric wire, etc. **2.** *v.t.* Furnish or fasten with staple; hence **stā'pl**ER[1] (1, 2) *n.* [OE *stapol*, = OHG *staffal* foundation, ON *stöpull* pillar f. Gmc **stapulaz*; see -LE 1]

stā'ple[2] *n.*, *a.*, & *v.t.* **1.** *n.* Important or principal article of commerce (*the staples of that country, of British industry*); raw material; (fig.) chief element or material (*formed the staple of conversation*); fibre of cotton, wool, etc., regarded as determining its quality, (*cotton of fine, short, long, staple*). **2.** *a.* Principal (*staple commodities*); important as product or export. **3.** *v.t.* Sort, classify, (wool etc.) according to fibre; WOOL-*-stapler*. [ME, f. OF *estaple* market f. MLG, MDu. *stapel* market, f. as prec.]

stâr[1] *n.* **1.** Celestial body appearing as luminous point in night sky; (**fixed**) ~, such body so far from earth as to appear motionless except for diurnal revolution of the heavens (opp. *planet, comet*, etc.); this as subject of astronomical study, large self-luminous gaseous ball such as the sun is; BINARY, DOUBLE[1], MULTIPLE, *star*; DAY-*star*; EVENING, MORNING, *star*; FALL[1]*ing*, SHOOT[1]*ing*, *star*; POLE[2]-*star*. **2.** Thing suggesting star by its shape, esp. figure or object with radiating points e.g. as insignia of an order or mark of rank (**S~s and Stripes,** U.S. national flag; **S~s and Bars,** flag of Confederate States); asterisk; star-shaped mark esp. as indicating category of excellence; white spot on forehead of horse etc.; (Electr.) Y-shaped arrangement of three-phase windings; SEE[1] *stars*. **3.** Famous actor or actress or other performer (**the ~ system,** that of relying on stars to make film or play attractive; ~ **turn,** principal item in an entertainment or performance), whence ~'DOM *n.*; brilliant or prominent person, (*literary star; star pupil*; **bright particular** ~, object of one's devotion); ||convict serving first prison sentence. **4.** Heavenly body regarded as influencing person's fortunes etc. (*born under an unlucky star; his star was in the ascendant; you may thank your (lucky) stars you were not there; the stars were against it*; ILL-*starred*). **5. ~-apple,** edible purple apple-like fruit (with starlike cross-section) of a tropical evergreen tree (*Chrysophyllum cainito*); **S~ Chamber,** ||(Hist.) court of civil and criminal jurisdiction primarily concerned with offences affecting crown interests, noted for summary and arbitrary procedure, and abolished 1640, (fig.) arbitrary oppressive tribunal; **~-crossed,** (arch.) ill-fated; **~-dust,** a multitude of stars looking like dust, (fig.) twinkling mass, romantic mystical sensation; **~'fish,** echinoderm of class Asteroidea with five or more radiating arms; **~-gazer,** (joc.) astronomer; **~'light,** (*n.*) light of stars (*walked home by starlight*), (*a.*) with stars visible, lighted by the stars, (*a starlight night*); **~'lit,** = *starlight* (*a.*); ~ **of Bethlehem** [f. Matt. 2:9], starlike flower, esp. of *Ornithogalum umbellatum*, which has white starlike flowers striped with green on outside; **S~ of David,** figure of two interlaced equilateral triangles used as Jewish and Israeli symbol; **S~ of India,** (Hist.) order instituted 1861 to commemorate assumption of direct government of India; ||~ **prisoner** (see sense 3); *~ **route,** postal delivery route served by private contractors; ~ **sapphire** (cabochon); ~ **shell,** kind designed to burst in air and light up enemy's position; **~-spangled,** spangled with stars (esp. of U.S. flag); **~-stone,** = *star sapphire*; **~-stream,** systematic drift of stars; **~-studded,** containing many stars (esp. in sense 4); **~'wort,** plant of genus *Stellaria*, with starlike flowers. **6.** Hence ~'LET *n.*, little star, esp. young film actress who shows promise of becoming a star, ~'LESS, ~'LIKE, **~'ry**^{2}, *adjs.*; **~'ry-eyed,** (colloq.) visionary, enthusiastic but impractical. [OE *steorra*, = OS, OHG *sterro* f. WG **sterro*; cf. OHG *sterno*, ON *stjarna* Goth. *stairnō* f. Gmc **sternōn* f. IE **ster-*]

star^2 *v.* (**-rr-**). **1.** *v.t.* (esp. in *p.p.*) Set or adorn (as) with stars. **2.** Affix asterisk or star symbol to (name in list etc.); present as theatrical, film, etc., star. **3.** *v.i.* Appear as star actor. [f. prec.]

star'board (-berd) *n.*, & *v.t.* (Naut. & Aeron.) **1.** *n.* Right-hand side of ship or boat or aircraft looking forward (cf. PORT^5); *starboard* TACK^1; *starboard* WATCH^1. **2.** *v.t.* Turn (helm, or abs.) to starboard. [OE *stēorbord* (*stēor* rudder, as STEER^1, *bord* BOARD^1), early Teut. ships being steered with a paddle over the right side]

starch *a.*, *n.*, & *v.t.* **1.** *a.* (arch.) Precise, prim; hence ~'LY^2 *adv.*, ~'NESS *n.* **2.** *n.* White odourless tasteless carbohydrate obtained chiefly from cereals and potatoes but found in all plants except fungi, an important constituent of human food (**~-reduced,** containing less than normal proportion of starch). **3.** Preparation of this for stiffening linen etc. before ironing; (fig.) stiffness of manner, formality. **4.** *v.t.* Stiffen with starch (lit., or fig. esp. in *p.p.*); hence ~'ER^1 *n.* [a. f. n. f. v., ME *sterche* f. OE **stercan* stiffen, = OS *sterkian*, OHG *sterken* f. WG **starkjan* f. Gmc **starkaz*; cf. STARK]

star'ch|y *a.* Of or like starch; containing much starch; (of person) precise, prim; hence ~ILY^2 *adv.*, ~INESS *n.* [f. prec. + -Y^2]

stare *v.* & *n.* **1.** *v.i.* Look fixedly with eyes wide open (*at*, *upon*, etc., or abs.) from or *with* surprise, admiration, bewilderment, stupidity, horror, impertinent curiosity, etc.; (of eyes) be wide open and fixed (*staring mad*); be unpleasantly prominent or striking. **2.** *v.t.* Reduce (person) to specified condition by staring (*stared him out of countenance*, *into silence*); **~ down,** outstare; ~ (person) **in the face,** be evident or imminent, (*the facts stare us in the face*; *ruin stared him in the face*). **3.** *n.* Staring gaze. [OE *starian*, = OHG *starēn*, ON *stara* f. Gmc **star-* be rigid]

stark^1 *a.* & *adv.* **1.** *a.* Stiff, rigid, (*lies stark in death*); (arch.) strong; desolate, bare; sharply evident (*in stark contrast*); downright, sheer, (*stark madness*); stark naked; hence ~'LY^2 *adv.*, ~'NESS *n.* **2.** *adv.* Quite, wholly, (*stark mad*, *naked*). [OE *stearc*, = OS, OHG *stark*, ON *sterkr*, Goth. **starks* f. Gmc **starkaz*; *stark naked* f. earlier *start-naked* f. obs. *start* tail (cf. RED*start*)]

Stark^2 *n.* **~ effect,** (Phys.) splitting of spectrum line into several components by electric field. [f. J. ~, Ger. physicist d. 1957]

star'kers (-z) *a.* (sl.) Stark naked. [f. STARK^1; see -ER^1 (5)]

star'ling^1 *n.* Small gregarious partly migratory bird (*Sturnus vulgaris*) with blackish-brown speckled lustrous plumage inhabiting chiefly cultivated areas; bird of family Sturnidae or *Icteridae. [OE *stærlinc* (*stær* starling = OHG *star(a)*, ON *stari* f. Gmc **staraz*, **starōn*; see -LING^1)]

star'ling^2 *n.* Protective piling round pier of bridge. [perh. corrupt. of (now dial.) *staddling* (STADDLE, -ING^1)]

star'ry. See STAR^1 6.

start^1 *v.* **1.** *v.i.* Make sudden movement from pain, surprise, etc., (*started in his seat*; *started at the sound of my voice*); change position abruptly from shock or sudden impulse (*start aside*, *from one's chair*). **2.** (Of thing) move suddenly (*out* etc.; *tears started to her eyes*); (of eyes, usu. w. exagg.) burst *from* (their sockets etc.); (of timbers etc.) spring from proper position, give way. **3.** Set out, begin journey (*we start at six*); make a beginning (*on* journey, undertaking, book, meal, etc.); (of engine etc.) begin running; **~ at** or **with,** have as initial member of sequence etc. (*prices start at ten dollars*; *we started with prawn cocktail*); **to ~ with,** in the first place, before anything else is considered (*you have no right to be here, to start with*), at the beginning (*had six members to start with*). **4.** *v.t.* Begin, commence, (work etc., do*ing*, *to* do); **~ life,** be born, begin one's career, etc.; **~ school,** attend it for first time. **5.** Rouse (game) from lair etc.; *start a* HARE. **6.** Originate, set going, (undertaking, business, publication, fire, quarrel, race, etc.); cause (engine, clock, etc.) to begin operating; cause (person) to make a beginning (*on*); cause to begin do*ing* (*the smoke started me coughing*); conceive (baby), cause (baby) to be conceived; cause or enable (person) to commence business etc.; give signal to (persons) to start in race; **~ something,** (colloq.) cause trouble. **7.** Cause or experience the starting or loosening of (timbers etc.). **8.** (Naut.) Pour out (liquor) from cask. **9. ~ in,** (colloq.) begin (*to* do), *make a beginning *on*; **~ off,** begin to move; **~ out,** (colloq.) proceed as intending (*to* do), *begin journey; **~ up,** rise suddenly e.g. from seat, arise, come into existence or action, occur to the mind, (*many difficulties*, *rivals*, *have started up*), originate (undertaking etc.), start (engine). [OE **stiertan*, **styrtan*, etc., = OHG *sturzen* overthrow, rush f. Gmc **sturt-*, **start-*, **stert-*]

start^2 *n.* **1.** Sudden movement of surprise, pain, etc., (**give** person **a ~,** cause him to move thus); (in *pl.*) intermittent or spasmodic efforts or movements (esp. *by fits and starts*). **2.** Beginning of journey or action or race (*shall make an early start for town*; *is difficult work at the start*; *the start is fixed for 3 p.m.*; *saw it from start to finish*); starting or starting-place of race; **for a ~,** (colloq.) to start with. **3.** Advantage conceded in race (*will give you 60 yards start*, *15 seconds start*); advantageous initial position gained in business etc. (*got a good start in life*); **get the ~ of,** gain advantage over. **4.** (colloq.) Surprising occurrence (*queer*, *rum*, *start*). [ME, f. prec.]

star'ter *n.* In vbl senses; one who gives signal to start in race; horse or competitor starting in race (*list of probable starters*); (esp. automatic) apparatus for starting engine of motor vehicle etc.; initial action etc., first course of meal; **for ~s,** *(sl.) to start with; **under ~'s orders,** (of racehorses etc.) in position to start race and awaiting starting-signal. [f. START^1 + -ER^1]

star'ting *n.* In vbl senses; **~-block,** shaped rigid block for bracing feet of runner at start of race; **~-gate,** removable barrier for securing fair start in horse-races; ||**~-handle,** crank for starting motor engine; **~-pistol** (used to give signal for start of race); **~-point** (from which a journey, process, argument, etc., begins); **~-post** (from which competitors start in race); **~ price,** final odds before start of horse-race etc.; *starting*-PUNCH^1; *starting*-STALL^1. [ME, f. START^1 + -ING^1]

star'tle *v.t.* Cause (person etc.) to start with surprise or sudden alarm, give shock to, take by surprise. [OE *steartlian* (as START^1, -LE 3)]

star'tling *a.* Surprising, alarming, (*startling news*, *discovery*, *development*); hence ~LY^2 *adv.* [f. prec. + -ING^2]

starve *v.* **1.** *v.i.* Die of hunger; suffer from lack of food; suffer extreme poverty; (colloq.) feel very hungry (*am simply starving*); (arch. or dial.) perish with or suffer from cold; (fig.) suffer mental or spiritual want, feel strong craving *for* (sympathy, amusement, knowledge, etc.). **2.** *v.t.*

Cause to perish with hunger; deprive *of*, keep scantily supplied with, food (lit. or fig.); compel (garrison etc. *into* surrender, *out*, etc.) thus; (arch.) cause to perish, affect severely, with cold; cause to starve mentally or spiritually (SEX-*starved*). **3.** Hence **stãrvA'TION** *n.* [OE *steorfan* die, = OS, OHG *sterban* f. Gmc **sterbh-*, perh. = 'be rigid']

stãr'veling (-vl-) *n.* & *a.* **1.** *n.* Starving or ill-fed person or animal. **2.** *a.* Starving; (fig.) meagre. [f. prec. + -LING¹]

stăsh *v.t.*, & *n.* (sl.) **1.** *v.t.* Conceal, put *away* in safe place. **2.** *n.* *House; hiding-place; thing hidden. [18th c.; orig. unkn.]

stă's|ĭs *n.* (*pl.* **~es** *pr.* -ēz). **1.** State of stopped flow, stagnation, (lit. or fig.). **2.** (Path.) Stoppage of circulation of any of the fluids of the body. [mod. L f. Gk (*sta-* STAND¹)]

-stă's|ĭs *suf.* (*pl.* **~es** *pr.* -ēz), forming *ns.* w. sense 'slowing or stopping of flow of or growth of or deviation from' (*haemostasis*, *bacteriostasis*, *homoeostasis*). [f. prec.]

-stăt *suf.* forming *ns.* w. ref. to keeping fixed or stationary (*coelostat*, *rheostat*, *thermostat*). [first in *heliostat*; f. Gk *statos* stationary and agent-suf. *-statēs* (*sta-* stand)]

stā'tal *a.* Pertaining to State(s). [f. foll. + -AL]

stāte¹ *n.* & *a.* **1.** *n.* Condition in which a thing is, mode of existence as determined by circumstances, (*precarious state of health*; *found him in the same state*; *in a state of deep depression*; *things were in an untidy state*; *in a bad state of repair*); **~ of the art,** current stage of development or knowledge of a subject; *state of* GRACE; **~ of life,** rank and occupation; *in a state of* NATURE; **~ of things** or **affairs** or (fig.) **play,** conditions existing for the time being; **~ of war** (when war has been declared or hostilities are in progress); CIVIL *state*; **in a ~,** (colloq.) untidy, excited, anxious, etc. **2.** (Often *S~*). Organized political community under one government, commonwealth, nation; such community forming part of federal republic, esp. **the** (**United**) **S~s** (of America); **of S~,** = sense 11 (‖MINISTER¹, SECRETARY, *of State*); **State's* EVIDENCE; FREE¹, POLICE, SLAVE, *state*; **Northern S~s** (in N. of U.S.); PAPAL *States*; **Southern S~s** (in S., esp. S.E., of U.S.); ***S~s' Rights,** rights and powers not assumed by United States but reserved to its individual states. **3.** (in *pl.*) Legislative body in Jersey, Guernsey, and Alderney; **S~s General,** legislative body in Netherlands, and in France before 1789. **4.** Civil government (*Church and State*). **5.** Rank, dignity, (*in a style befitting his state*). **6.** Pomp (*arrived in great state*); **keep ~,** maintain one's dignity, be difficult of access; **in ~** (with all due ceremony); **lie in ~,** (of deceased great personage) be laid in public place of honour before burial. **7.** (Bibliog.) One of two or more variant forms within a single edition of a book. **8.** (Impression taken from) an etched or engraved plate at a particular stage of its progress. **9. ~'craft,** art of conducting affairs of State; ***~-house,** building where legislature of a state meets; **~ house,** (N.Z.) private house built at government's expense; **~'room,** (1) state apartment, (2) private compartment in passenger ship or *train; ***S~'side,** (colloq.) of, in, or towards the U.S.; ***~'wide,** so as to include or cover a whole State. **10.** Hence **~'HOOD** (-t-h-) *n.*, **~'LESS** (-tl-) *a.* (esp. of person having no nationality or citizenship). **11.** *a.* Of, for, concerned with, the State (*state documents*, *service*); **S~ capitalism,** policy of State control of use of capital; ***S~ Department** (of foreign affairs); *state* PRISONER; **S~ socialism,** policy of State control of industries and services in order to benefit all equally; **‖S~ school** (managed by public authorities); **~ trial,** prosecution by State esp. for political offence; ***~ university** (managed by public authorities of a State of U.S.). **12.** Reserved for or done on occasions of ceremony (*state apartments*, *carriage*, *visit*); involving ceremony (*state opening of Parliament*). [ME; partly f. ESTATE, partly f. L STATUS]

stāte² *v.t.* Express, esp. fully or clearly, in speech or writing (*have stated my opinion*; *must state full particulars*; *this condition was expressly stated*; *no precise time was stated*; *did not state why*; *states that arrangements are complete*); fix, specify, (date, etc.; *at stated intervals*), whence **stā'tĕdLY²** *adv.*; (Law) specify facts of (case) for consideration by court; (Mus.) play (theme etc.) so as to make it known to the listener; hence **stā'tABLE** *a.* [f. prec.]

stā'tel|ȳ (-tlĭ) *a.* (Of manner, language, person, literary style, rhythm, building, proportions, etc.) dignified, imposing, grand; **‖~y home,** large magnificent house, esp. one open to visits by public; hence **~ĭNESS** *n.* [ME, f. STATE¹ + -LY¹]

stā'tement (-tm-) *n.* Stating or being stated, expression in words; thing stated (*that statement is unfounded*); formal account of facts, e.g. of liabilities and assets (*the Bank issues monthly statements to each customer*) or of amount due to tradesman. [f. STATE² + -MENT]

stā'ter *n.* Ancient Greek coin of one of various values, esp. gold coin worth 20 drachmas or silver coin worth 4 drachmas. [ME f. LL, f. Gk *statēr*]

stā'tesman (-ts-) *n.* (*pl.* **-men**). Person skilled, esp. one taking prominent part, in management of State affairs; sagacious far-sighted practical politician; **elder ~,** (1) one of the Japanese statesmen who mainly directed the evolution of Japan between the re-establishment of the Mikado (1868) and the end of the 19th c., (2) person of ripe years and experience whose counsel is therefore sought and valued; hence **~LIKE,** **~LY¹,** *adjs.*, **~SHIP** (3) *n.* [=*state's man*, after F *homme d'état*]

stă'tĭc *a.* & *n.* **1.** *a.* Concerned with bodies at rest or forces in equilibrium (opp. *dynamic*); of statics; acting as weight but not moving (*static pressure*); passive, not acting or changing. **2. ~ electricity,** electric charges at rest, not flowing as current; **~ line,** length of cord attached to aircraft etc. and releasing parachute without use of rip-cord. **3.** *n.* Atmospherics; static electricity. [f. mod. L f. Gk *statikos* (*sta-* stand; see -IC)]

-stă'tĭc *suf.* forming *adjs.*, esp. corresp. to *ns.* in -STASIS (*bacteriostatic*). [f. as prec.]

stă'tĭcal *a.* = STATIC 1; hence **~LY²** *adv.* [f. as STATIC + -ICAL]

stă'tĭcs *n. pl.* (usu. treated as *sing.*) Science of bodies at rest or forces in equilibrium (opp. *dynamics*); = STATIC 3. [f. STATIC n. in same senses + -ICS]

stā'tion *n.*, & *v.t.* **1.** *n.* Place, building, etc., in which person or thing stands or is placed esp. habitually or for definite purpose (*was assigned a station in the valley*; *returned to their several stations*; *took up a convenient station*; *Oxford won the toss and chose the Surrey station*; ACTION *stations*). **2.** Establishment where a public service is provided (*broadcasting*, *coastguard*, FILLING, FIRE¹, POLICE, *polling*, *station*) or which is used as a base for some activity (*air*, *lifeboat*, *naval*, *research*, *station*); POWER-, SERVICE¹, *station*; *subsidiary post office. **3.** Stopping-place on railway with buildings for temporary accommodation of passengers and goods or ‖of goods only; buildings of railway station; **bus ~,** similar stopping-

-place for a number of buses etc. **4.** Position in life, (high) rank, status, employment, (*occupied a humble station; men of (exalted) station; she married beneath, has ideas above, her station; the duties of his station*). **5.** (Surv.) Point from which measurements are made. **6.** Military or naval post esp. (Hist.) in India; officers or society residing there. **7.** (Austral.) Large pastoral or mixed farming estate; sheep-run or its buildings. **8.** (Eccl.) ~ (**of the Cross**), each of series of usu. 14 images or pictures representing events in Christ's passion before which devotions are performed in some churches etc., such devotions; church esp. in Rome to which pilgrims etc. go for devotions. **9.** (Bot. & Zool.) Nature of the habitat of plant or animal in respect of climate, soil, etc. **10.** (arch.) Standing, being still; (place of) halting. **11.** **~-bill,** (Naut.) list of appointed emergency posts of ship's company; ***~ break,** pause between broadcast programmes for identification of station transmitting them; **~-house,** police station; **~-keeping,** maintenance of one's proper relative position in a moving body of ships etc.; **~-master,** official in charge of railway-station; **~-pointer,** three-armed protractor for locating place on chart from certain data; ||**~ sergeant** (in charge of police station); ***~-wagon,** estate car. **12.** *v.t.* Assign station to; place (person, one*self*) in specified location. [ME, = standing, f. OF, f. L *statio -onis* (*stare* stand; see -ATION)]

stā'tionarў *a.* Remaining in one place, not moving, (*balloon was now stationary*); not meant to be moved, not portable, (*stationary engine, troops*); (of planet) having no apparent motion in longitude; not changing in magnitude, number, quality, efficiency, etc., (*stationary temperature, population*); **~ air** (remaining in lungs during ordinary respiration); **~ wave,** = STANDING[2] *wave*; hence **stā'tionarĭ**NESS *n.* [ME, f. L *stationarius* (as prec.; see -ARY[1])]

stā'tioner *n.* One who sells writing-materials etc.; ||**S~s' Hall** (of Stationers' Company in London, at which book was formerly *entered*, i.e. registered, for purposes of copyright). [ME, = bookseller (as prec. in med. L sense 'shopkeeper' (esp. bookseller) as opp. pedlar)]

stā'tionerў *n.* Articles sold by stationer; materials for writing on or with; CONTINUOUS *stationery*; ||**S~ Office,** Government's publishing house (also providing Government offices with stationery). [f. prec. + -Y[1]]

stā'tĭsm *n.* State administration and control of social and economic affairs. [f. STATE[1] + -ISM]

stā'tĭst *n.* Statistician; supporter of statism. [orig. 'politician', f. It. *statista* (as STATE[1], -IST)]

statĭ'stĭc *a.* & *n.* **1.** *a.* = foll. **2.** *n.* Statistical fact or item. [f. G *statistisch, statistik*, (*statist*, as prec.)]

statĭ'stĭcal *a.* Of or pertaining to statistics; **~ physics** (concerned with systems of large numbers of particles etc., to which statistics is applicable); hence ~LY[2] *adv.* [f. prec. + -AL]

statĭ'stĭcs *n. pl.* **1.** Numerical facts systematically collected (*statistics of population, crime*; VITAL *statistics*). **2.** (usu. treated as *sing.*) Science of collecting, classifying, and using statistics, esp. in or for large quantities or numbers. **3.** So **stătĭstĭ**'CIAN *n.* [f. STATISTIC + -ICS]

stā'tor *n.* (Electr.) Stationary part of machine, esp. of electric generator or motor. [f. STATIONARY after ROTOR]

stă'toscōpe *n.* Aneroid barometer for showing minute variations of pressure, esp. to indicate altitude of aircraft. [f. Gk *statos* fixed (*sta-* stand) + -SCOPE]

stă'tūarў *a.* & *n.* **1.** *a.* Of or for statues (*statuary art*); **~ marble,** fine-grained white kind. **2.** *n.* Sculptor; (art of making) statues. [f. L *statuarius* (as foll.; see -ARY[1])]

stă'tū|e (*or* -choo) *n.* Sculptured or cast or moulded figure of person or animal (esp. one not much below life size, opp. to ~E'TTE *n.*); hence ~ED[2] (-ūd) *a.* [ME, f. OF, f. L *statua* (*stare* stand)]

stătūĕ'sque (-k; *or* -choo-) *a.* Like, or having the dignity or beauty of, a statue; hence ~LY[2] (-klĭ) *adv.*, ~NESS (-kn-) *n.* [f. prec. + -ESQUE, after *picturesque*]

stă'tur|e (-yer) *n.* Height of (esp. human) body; (fig.) stage of advancement, degree of eminence; hence (-)~ED[2] (-yerd) *a.* [ME f. OF, f. L *statura* (*stare stat-* stand; see -URE)]

stā'tus *n.* **1.** Social position, rank, relation to others, relative importance, (*his status is a matter of doubt; their status is wholly different; his status among novelists*); superior social etc. position (**~ symbol,** possession etc. indicating person's high status). **2.** (Law). Person's relation to others as fixed by law. **3.** Position of affairs; **~ *quo,*** unchanged position; **~ *quo (ante),*** the previous position. [L, = standing (*stare* stand) (*quo* in which, *ante* before)]

stă'tūtab|le *a.* = STATUTORY; hence ~LY[2] *adv.* [f. foll. + -ABLE]

stă'tūte *n.* **1.** A written law of a legislative body, e.g. Act of Parliament; **~s at large** (in full as originally enacted, regardless of later modifications); **~ law,** a statute, (collect.) the statutes (opp. to CASE[1]-*law* and COMMON[1] *law*); *statute* MILE. **2.** Ordinance of corporation, founder, etc., intended to be permanent (*University Statutes*). **3.** (Bibl.) Divine law (*kept, teach me, thy statutes*). **4.** **~-barred,** barred by the statute of LIMITATIONS; **~-book,** book(s) containing the statute law; **~-roll,** (1) engrossed statute, (2) statute-book. [ME, f. OF *statut* f. LL *statutum* neut. p.p. (as n.) of L *statuere* set up (STATUS)]

stă'tūtor|ў *a.* Enacted, required, imposed, by statute (*statutory provisions, minimum*; **statutory* RAPE[1]); hence ~ĭLY[2] *adv.* [f. prec. + -ORY]

staunch[1], stanch[2], (-aw- *or* -ah-) *a.* Trustworthy, loyal, (*staunch friend, supporter*); (of ship, joint, etc.) watertight, airtight; hence ~'LY[2] *adv.*, ~'NESS *n.* [ME, f. OF *estanche* fem. of *estanc* f. Rom. **stancus*; see STANCH[1]]

staunch[2]. See STANCH[1].

stāve[1] *n.* Each of the curved pieces of wood forming sides of cask, pail, etc.; rung of ladder; stanza, verse; (Mus.) = STAFF[1] 8; **~-rhyme,** alliteration esp. in old Gmc poetry. [ME, var. of STAFF[1], due to pl. *staves*]

stāve[2] *v.t.* (**stove** *pr.* -ōv, *or* **~d**). **1.** **~** (**in**), break a hole in (cask, boat), crush or bash (hat, ribs, box) out of shape. **2.** Furnish, fit, (cask etc.) with staves. **3.** **~ off,** avert, ward off, defer, (ruin, exposure, etc.). [f. prec.]

staves. See STAFF[1].

stā'vesācre (-vzāker) *n.* Species of larkspur (*Delphinium staphisagria*) whose emetic seeds are used as poison for vermin. [ME, f. L *staphisagria* f. Gk *staphis agria* wild raisin]

stay[1] *v.* & *n.* **1.** *v.t.* (arch. or literary). Check, stop, (progress, inroads of disease, etc.). **2.** Appease hunger of (person, his stomach), esp. temporarily. **3.** Postpone (judgement, decision). **4.** Support, prop (*up*) as or with buttress etc. **5.** *v.i.* Continue to be in same place or state, not depart or change, (*stay here till I return; will not stay where it is put* or (colloq.) *stay put; will not stay clean; stayed away from the meeting; stayed behind* or *on when others left*); **has come to ~, is here to ~,** (colloq.), must be regarded as permanent; **~-at-home** *a.* & *n.*, (person) remaining habitually at home; **~ for** or **to,**

(colloq.) wait long enough to partake of (*can you stay for* or *to supper?*); **~-in strike,** = SIT-DOWN *strike*; **~ up,** not go to bed. **6.** Dwell temporarily (*at* hotel etc., *in* town etc., *with* person). **7.** Pause in movement, action, speech (esp. in *imper.*), etc., (*get him to stay a minute*; *stay! you forget one thing*). **8.** *v.i.* & *t.* Show endurance (to end of) esp. in race; **~'ing-power,** endurance; **~ the course,** be able to reach end of race, (fig.) struggle, etc.; hence **~'ER**[1] *n.* **9.** *n.* Staying, esp. dwelling, in one place, duration of this, (*made a long stay in London*; *your stay has been very short*). **10.** Suspension of judicial proceedings; **~ of execution,** postponement of carrying out judgement given. **11.** (arch. or literary). Check, restraint, (*will endure no stay*; *a stay upon his activity*). **12.** Endurance, staying-power. **13.** Prop, support, (*you have been the stay of my old age*). **14.** (in *pl.*) Corset, esp. with whalebone etc. stiffening and laced. **15. ~-bar, -rod,** support in building or machinery; **~-lace, -maker,** (of corsets). [f. AF *estai-* st. of OF *ester* f. L *stare* stand; sense 'support' (4, 13–15) f. OF *estaye(r)* prop, f. as foll.]

stay[2] *n.*, & *v.t.* (Naut.) **1.** *n.* Rope supporting mast or spar; **in ~s,** (of ship) going about from one tack to another; **miss ~s,** fail in endeavour to go about in tacking; **~'sail** (*or* -sal), sail extended on stay. **2.** Guy or rope supporting flagstaff etc.; tie-piece in aircraft etc. **3.** *v.t.* Support (mast etc.) by stays; put (ship) on other tack. [OE *stæg*, = MLG *stach*, ON *stag* f. Gmc **staga-* (**stag-*, **stah-* be firm; cf. STEEL)]

S.T.C. *abbr.* short-title catalogue.

S.T.D. *abbr.* Doctor of Sacred Theology [f. L *Sanctae Theologiae Doctor*]; subscriber trunk dialling.

stead (stĕd) *n.* **Stand** (person) **in good ~,** be advantageous or serviceable to; **in** person's or thing's **~,** instead of him or it, as substitute. [OE *stede*, = OS *stad, stedi*, OHG *stat*, ON *stathr*, Goth. *staths* f. Gmc **stadhiz* f. IE **st(h)'tís* (**st(h)'-*, **st(h)a-* STAND[1])]

stea'dfast (stĕ'd-) *a.* Constant, firm, unwavering; hence **~LY**[2] *adv.*, **~NESS** *n.* [OE *stedefæst* (as prec., FAST[3])]

‖**stea'dĭng** (stĕ'd-) *n.* Farmstead. [f. STEAD + -ING[1]]

stea'dȳ (stĕ'dĭ) *a., adv., n.,* & *v.* **1.** *a.* Firmly fixed or supported or standing or balanced, not tottering or rocking etc., (*is steady on his legs*; *must level table's legs to make it steady*; *steady as a rock*; *has not acquired steady seat on bicycle*); firmly directed, not faltering, (*steady eye, hand*). **2.** Done, moving, acting, happening, in uniform and regular manner (*went off at a steady pace*; *had a steady wind behind us*; *requires a steady light*; *observe a steady increase in the numbers*); **~!,** (as command or warning) be steady, abstain from erratic or boisterous behaviour, premature action, hasty inference, etc.; **(keep her) ~!,** (Naut.) keep direction of ship's head unchanged; **~ on!,** slow! or stop!; **~ state,** unvarying condition (esp. in physical process, e.g. of universe not created by any past event). **3.** Constant in mind or conduct, not changeable, (*steady in his principles, allegiance*); of industrious and temperate habits. **4.** Hence **stea'dĭLY**[2] *adv.*, **stea'dĭNESS** *n.*, (stĕ'd-). **5.** *adv.* Steadily; **go ~ with,** (colloq.) be regular sweetheart of; **~-going,** staid, sober. **6.** *n.* *(colloq.) Regular sweetheart. **7.** *v.t.* & *i.* Make or become steady (*steady the boat*; *boat steadied*; *adversity will steady him*; *he will soon steady (down)*). [f. STEAD + -Y[2]]

steak (stāk) *n.* Thick slice of meat (esp. beef) or fish, cut for grilling, frying, etc.; **~-house,** restaurant specializing in serving steaks. [ME, f. ON *steik*, cogn. w. *steikja* roast on spit, *stikna* be roasted]

steal *v.* (**stole; sto'len;** *pr.* stō-) & *n.* **1.** *v.t.* Take away (thing, or abs.) esp. secretly for one's own use without right or leave, take feloniously; **~ the show,** unexpectedly outshine other performers; *steal* person's THUNDER. **2.** Obtain surreptitiously or by surprise (*stole a kiss*; *a stolen interview*); (Baseball) reach (base) by deceiving fielders. **3. ~ (away),** win, get possession of, (esp. person's *heart* fig.) by insidious arts, attractions, etc.; **~ a march on,** get an advantage over by surreptitious means, anticipate. **4.** *v.i.* Move (*in, out, away, up,* etc.) secretly or silently (*stole out of the room*; *mist stole over the valley*); (of sound etc.) become gradually perceptible. **5.** Hence (-)**~'ER**[1] *n.* **6.** *n.* *(colloq.) Stealing; (unexpectedly) easy task or good bargain. [OE *stelan*, = OS, OHG *stelan*, ON *stela*, Goth. *stilan* f. Gmc **stel-*]

stealth (stĕl-) *n.* Secrecy, secret procedure; **by ~,** surreptitiously. [ME, f. OE **stǣlth* (as prec., -TH[1])]

stea'lth|ȳ (stĕ'l-) *a.* (Of action) done with stealth, proceeding imperceptibly; (of person or thing) moving with stealth; hence **~ĭLY**[2] *adv.*, **~ĭNESS** *n.* [f. prec. + -Y[2]]

steam[1] *n.* **1.** Invisible gas into which water is changed by boiling, used as motive power by virtue of its elasticity; **saturated ~** (in contact with, and at same temperature as, boiling water); **superheated ~** (having higher temperature at given pressure than saturated steam); **wet, dry, ~** (containing, not containing, suspended particles of water). **2.** Visible particles of water resulting from condensation of steam; any vaporous exhalation. **3.** Energy or power provided by or (colloq.) as if by steam (*full steam ahead*); **get up ~,** generate enough power to work steam-engine, (fig.) work oneself into energetic or angry state; **let off ~,** (fig.) relieve one's pent-up energy or feelings; **run out of ~,** lose one's impetus; **under** one's **own ~,** without external motive power (lit. or fig.). **4. ~-bath** (in which bather or substance to be heated is immersed in steam); **~'boat,** boat propelled by steam; **~-boiler,** vessel in which water is boiled to generate steam esp. for working an engine; **~-box, -chest,** (through which steam passes from engine boiler to cylinder); **~-coal** (used in heating steam-boilers); **~-cylinder** (in which piston of steam-engine moves); **~-engine,** locomotive or stationary engine in which the motive power depends on elasticity and expansion or rapid condensation of steam; **~-gauge** (attached to boiler to show pressure of steam); **~-hammer,** forging-hammer worked by steam; **~-heat,** heat given out by steam from radiators etc.; **~ iron,** electric iron emitting steam from its flat surface; **~-jacket,** casing round cylinder etc. with space between to be filled by steam for heating the cylinder etc.; ‖**~ navvy,** = *steam-shovel*; **~-organ,** set of steam whistles producing musical notes, played by keyboard like that of organ; **~-power,** force of steam applied to machinery etc.; **~ radio,** (colloq.) radio broadcasting regarded as antiquated by comparison with television; **~-roller,** (*n.*) heavy slow-moving locomotive engine with wide wheels and roller used in road-making, (fig.) a crushing power or force, (*v.t.*) crush or move along as with a steam-roller; **~'ship** (propelled by steam); **~-shovel,** excavator worked by steam; **~-tight,** capable of resisting passage of steam; **~ train** (esp. opp. electric or diesel train); **~ tug,** steamer for towing ships etc.; **~**

turbine (in which a high-velocity jet of steam rotates a bladed disc or drum); *steam* WHISTLE. **5.** Hence ~'Y² *a.* [OE *stēam*, = WFris. *steam*, Du. *stoom* f. Gmc **staumaz*]

steam² *v.* **1.** *v.t.* Cook (food) by steam; treat with steam, soften (timber) for bending by steam, get (envelope) *open* by treating its gum with steam; ~ **up,** cover with condensed steam, (sl., esp. in *p.p.*) make (person) excited or angry. **2.** *v.i.* Give out steam or vapour (*kettle steaming on the hob*; *horses steaming after a gallop*; *water steaming hot*); rise as or like vapour; move by agency of steam (*we, the vessel, steamed down the river*); (colloq.) work vigorously, make great progress, (*steam ahead, away*). [OE *stȳman*, *stēman*, f. Gmc **staumjan* (as prec.)]

stea'mer *n.* In vbl senses; vessel propelled by steam; vessel in which things are steamed, esp. cooked by steam; *~ **rug,** travelling-rug. [f. prec. + -ER¹]

stėă'rĭc *a.* Derived from stearin; ~ **acid,** white crystalline fatty acid obtained from animal or vegetable fats; hence **stē'ar**ATE¹ (3) *n.* [f. F *stéarique* f. Gk *stear steatos* tallow; see -IC]

stē'arĭn *n.* Ester of glycerol and stearic acid, esp. white crystalline constituent of tallow etc.; mixture of fatty acids used for candles. [f. F *stéarine* f. as prec. + -IN]

stē'atīte *n.* Kind of usu. grey talc, soapstone; hence **stēatĭ't**IC *a.* [f. L f. Gk *steatitēs* (as STEARIC; see -ITE¹)]

stēatopȳ'g|ĭa *n.* Excessive development of fat on the buttocks, esp. of Hottentot women; hence ~OUS (-ī'g- *or* -ŏ'pĭg-) *a.* [mod. L, f. as STEARIN + Gk *pugē* rump + -IA¹]

steed *n.* (poet., rhet., or joc.) Horse, esp. war-horse; hence ~'LESS *a.* [OE *stēda* stallion, cogn. w. STUD²]

steel *n.*, & *v.t.* **1.** *n.* Malleable alloy of iron and carbon much used as material for tools, weapons, etc., and capable of being tempered to many different degrees of hardness; **cold** ~, cutting or thrusting weapons; **pressed** ~ (moulded under pressure); *a grip, muscles, a heart,* **of** ~, very tight, strong, hard, etc. **2.** Rod of steel, usu. tapering and roughened, for sharpening knives; FLINT *and steel*; strip of steel for stiffening corset or expanding skirt; (poet. or rhet.; not in *pl.*) sword (*foemen worthy of their steel*). **3.** ~ **band** (of W. Ind. musicians with instruments made from oil-drums); **~-clad,** wearing armour; ~ **engraving,** engraving on, impression taken from, steel plate; **~'head,** large N. Amer. rainbow trout; ~ **plate,** sheet of steel for engraving, armour of warships, etc.; ~ **wool,** fine shavings of steel massed together, used as abrasive; **~'work,** steel articles; **~'works,** place where steel is manufactured. **4.** *v.t.* Harden, make resolute, (oneself, one's heart, etc., *to* do, *to* action, *for* disappointment etc., *against* compassion etc.). [OE *stȳle*, **stēle*, *stēli*, = OS *stēhli*, WG **stahlja* a. f. Gmc **stahla-* prob. f. **stah-*, **stag-* be rigid; see STAY²]

stee'l|ȳ *a.* Of, or hard as, steel; inflexibly severe (*steely glance, composure*); hence ~ĬNESS *n.* [f. prec. + -Y²]

stee'lyărd *n.* Kind of balance with short arm to take the thing weighed and long graduated arm along which a weight is moved till it balances this. [f. STEEL + YARD¹]

stee'nbŏk (*or* stā'n-) *n.* Small African antelope (*Raphicerus campestris*). [Du. (*steen* STONE, *bok* BUCK¹)]

stee'nĭng *n.* Stone lining of well. [f. *steen* v. f. OE *stǣnan* to stone, + -ING¹]

stee'nkĭrk, stei'nkĭrk, (stē'n-k-) *n.* (Hist.) Man's or woman's neck-cloth with long lace ends. [f. F (*cravate à la*) *Steinkerke*, named after French defeat of English at *Steenkerke* in Belgium (1692)]

steep¹ *a.* & *n.* **1.** *a.* Having a marked slope, almost perpendicular, (*steep hill, stairs*); (of rise or fall) rapid; (colloq., of demand, price, etc.) exorbitant, unreasonable, (*seems a bit steep that we should have both the trouble and the expense*), (of story etc.) exaggerated, incredible; hence ~'EN⁶ *v.i.* & *t.*, ~'ISH¹ 2 *a.*, ~'LY² *adv.*, ~'NESS *n.*, ~'Y² (poet.) *a.* **2.** *n.* Steep slope, precipice. [OE *stēap* f. WG **staupa-*, rel. to STOOP¹]

steep² *v.t.*, & *n.* **1.** *v.t.* Soak in liquid; bathe with liquid; ~ **in,** (fig.) impregnate with, pervade with, (*steeped in the classics, misery, slumber*). **2.** *n.* Process of steeping (*barley in steep*); liquid in which thing is steeped. [ME, f. OE **stīepan*, **stēpan* f. Gmc **staupjan* (as STOUP)]

stee'ple *n.* Lofty structure, esp. tower surmounted by spire, rising above roof of church; **~chase,** (1) horse-race (orig. with steeple as goal) across tract of country or on racecourse with ditches, hedges, etc., to jump, (2) cross-country foot-race; **~chaser,** rider or runner in, or horse trained for, steeplechase; **~chasing,** the sport of riding in steeplechases; **~-crowned,** (of hat) with tall pointed crown; **~jack,** man who climbs tall chimneys, steeples, etc., to do repairs etc.; **~-top,** Greenland whale, with spout-holes ending in cone; hence **stee'pl**ED² (-pėld) *a.* [OE *stēpel*, *stȳpel* f. Gmc **staupilaz* (as STEEP¹; see -LE 1)]

steer¹ *v.t.* & *i.* **1.** Guide (vessel) by rudder or helm, guide vessel in specified direction, guide (motor vehicle, aircraft, etc.) by wheel etc.; **~'ing-wheel,** (1) vertical wheel with handles along rim for controlling rudder, (2) wheel for controlling front wheels of motor vehicle, mounted on **~'ing-column,** (3) wheel of cycle etc. by which it is steered. **2.** Direct (one's course), direct one's course, in specified direction (*steered his flight heavenwards*; *we steered* (*our course*) *for the railway station*); guide movement or trend of (*steer them into the garden*; *steer him* or *the conversation away from that subject*); ~ **clear of,** take care to avoid; **~'ing committee** (deciding order of dealing with business, or priorities and general course of operations). **3. ~'sman** (-z-), one who steers vessel. **4.** Hence ~'ABLE *a.*, ~'ER¹ (1, 2) *n.* [OE *stieran*, = OHG *stiuren*, ON *stýra*, Goth. *stiurjan* settle f. Gmc **steurjan* (**steurō* rudder)]

steer² *n.* Young male of bovine animal, esp. one castrated and raised for beef. [OE *stēor*, = OHG *stior*, ON *stjórr*, Goth. *stiur*, f. Gmc **steuraz*]

steer'age *n.* Act of steering; (Naut.) effect of helm on ship (*ship went with easy steerage*); part of ship allotted to passengers travelling at cheapest rate; (Hist., in warship) quarters assigned to midshipmen etc. just forward of wardroom; **~-way,** amount of headway required by vessel to enable her to be controlled by helm. [ME, f. STEER¹ + -AGE]

steeve¹ *v.* & *n.* (Naut.) **1.** *v.i.* (Of bowsprit) make angle with horizontal. **2.** *v.t.* Cause (bowsprit) to do this. **3.** *n.* Such angle. [17th c.; orig. unkn.]

steeve² *n.*, & *v.t.* (Naut.) **1.** *n.* Long spar used in stowing cargo. **2.** *v.t.* Stow with steeve. [ME, f. OF *estiver* or f. Sp. *estivar* f. L *stipare* pack tight]

***stein** (stīn) *n.* Large earthenware mug esp. for beer. [G, lit. 'stone']

stei'nbŏck (stī'n-) *n.* Alpine ibex; steenbok. [G (*stein* STONE, *bock* BUCK¹)]

steinkirk. See STEENKIRK.

stē'la *n.* (*pl.* ~*e*). (Archaeol.) Upright slab or pillar usu. with inscription and sculpture, esp. as gravestone. [L, f. as foll.]

stēle (*or* stē'lĭ) *n.* **1.** (Bot.) Axial cylinder in stem or root of vascular plant. **2.** (Archaeol.) = prec. [f. Gk *stēlē* standing block]

stĕ'll|ar *a.* Of star(s); so **~ĭform** *a.* [f. LL *stellaris* f. L *stella* star; see -AR[1]]

stĕ'llate, stĕllā'tĕd, *adjs.* Arranged like a star, radiating; (Bot., of leaves) surrounding stem in a whorl. [f. L *stellatus* (*stella* star; see -ATE[2]), -ED[1]]

||**stĕ'llenbŏsch** (-sh) *v.t.* (arch. Mil. sl.) Supersede without formal disgrace by appointing to unimportant command. [f. *S*~ in S. Africa, military base so utilized]

stĕ'llūlar *a.* Shaped like, or set with, small stars. [f. LL *stellula* dim. of L *stella* star + -AR[1]]

stĕm[1] *n.* & *v.* (**-mm-**). **1.** *n.* Main body or stalk (usu. rising into light and air but occas. subterranean) of tree, shrub, or plant; slender stalk supporting fruit, flower, or leaf, and attaching it to main stalk or branch or twig. **2.** Stem-shaped part, e.g. slender part of wineglass between body and foot, vertical line upwards or downwards from head of note in music, upright stroke of written or printed letter, winding-shaft of watch (***~-winder,** watch wound by turning head on end of stem, not by key), tubular part of tobacco-pipe. **3.** (Gram.) Part of noun, verb, etc., to which case-endings etc. are added, part that appears or would originally appear unchanged throughout the cases and derivatives of a noun, persons of a tense, etc. **4.** Line of ancestry, branch of family, (*descended from an ancient, a collateral, stem*). **5.** Curved timber or metal piece to which ship's sides are joined at fore end, piece joined to and forming upright continuation of keel at fore end; **from ~ to stern,** from end to end of ship. **6. ~ cell,** (Biol.) undifferentiated cell from which specialized cells develop; **~ stitch,** embroidery stitch used for narrow stems etc.; ***~'ware,** glasses with stems. **7.** Hence **~'less,** (-)**~med**[2] (-md), *adjs.*, **~'let** *n.* **8.** *v.t.* Remove stem(s) from (tobacco etc.); make headway against (tide etc.). **9.** *v.i.* Spring *from*, originate *in*. [OE *stemn, stefn*, f. Gmc **stamniz* (cogn. w. OHG *stam*, ON *stamn, stafn*) f. root **sta-* STAND[1]]

stĕm[2] *v.* (**-mm-**) & *n.* **1.** *v.t.* Check, dam up, (stream etc., lit. or fig.). **2.** *v.i.* Retard oneself by forcing heel of ski(s) outwards. **3.** *n.* Act of stemming on skis; **~-turn,** turn on skis made by stemming with one ski. [f. ON *stemma* = OHG *stemmen*, f. Gmc **stamjan* (**stam-* check; cf. STAMMER)]

stĕ'mma *n.* (*pl.* **~ta**). Family tree, pedigree; lineal descent; (Zool.) simple eye, facet of compound eye. [L, f. Gk *stemma* wreath (*stephō* wreathe)]

stĕ'mple *n.* Each of several crossbars in shaft of mine serving as supports or steps. [17th c., of uncert. orig.; cf. MHG *stempfel*]

Stĕn *n.* ~ (**gun**), type of lightweight sub-machine-gun. [f. *S* and *T* (initials of inventors' surnames) + *-en* after BREN]

stĕnch *n.* Offensive or foul smell; **~-trap** (in sewer etc., to prevent upward passage of gas). [OE *stenc* (any) smell, = OS *stanc*, OHG *stank* f. Gmc **stankw-* var. of **stinkw-* STINK]

stĕ'ncil *n.*, & *v.t.* (||**-ll-**). **1.** *n.* **~(-plate)**, thin sheet of metal etc. in which pattern (interrupted when necessary by thin bar of material left to prevent piece from falling out) is cut out, used to produce corresponding pattern on a surface beneath it by applying paintbrush etc.; decoration, lettering, etc., produced by stencil; waxed sheet etc. from which stencil is made by means of typewriter. **2.** *v.t.* Produce (pattern) on or *on* surface, ornament (surface) with pattern, by brushing paint etc. over a stencil-plate laid on the surface. [n. f. v. in sense 'ornament', ME, f. OF *estanceler* sparkle, cover with stars, (*estencele* spark f. pop. L **stincilla* for L *scintilla*)]

***stĕ'nō** *n.* (*pl.* **~s**). (colloq.) Stenographer. [abbr.]

stĕnŏ'graph|ȳ *n.* Shorthand writing; hence **~er**[1] *n.*, **stĕnogră'phic** *a.* [f. Gk *stenos* narrow + -GRAPHY]

stĕnō's|is *n.* (*pl.* **-es** *pr.* -ēz). (Path.) Narrowing of a passage in the body. [mod. L, f. Gk *stenōsis* narrowing (*stenoō* make narrow f. as prec.; see -OSIS)]

stĕ'notȳp|e *n.* Letter(s) representing syllables or phonemes; machine like typewriter for writing these; hence **~ist** (3) *n.* [f. STENOGRAPHY + TYPE[1]]

||**stĕ'nter** *n.* = TENTER[2]. [f. *stent* v. perh. f. *stend*, = EXTEND]

Stĕ'ntor *n.* Person with powerful voice; hence **stĕntŏr'ian** *a.* [f. Gk *Stentōr*, herald in Trojan War (Homer, *Iliad* v. 785)]

stĕp[1] *v.* (**-pp-**). **1.** *v.i.* Lift and set down foot or alternate feet as in walking; **~ out, short,** take long, short, steps; **~ out,** (fig.) be active socially; **~ through a dance,** perform its steps; **~ high,** (esp. of trotting horse) lift feet high. **2.** Go short distance or progress in some direction (as) by stepping or steps (lit. or fig.; *step aside, back, forward, up, down, across the road, into the boat, into the breach, into a fortune*); **~ in, out,** enter, leave, room or house; **~ in,** (fig.) intervene to help or hinder; *step on the* GAS[1] or (colloq.) *on it*; **~ this way** (deferential formula for 'come this way, follow me'). **3.** *v.t.* Perform (dance); **~ it,** dance. **4.** Measure (distance *off* or *out*) by stepping. **5.** (Naut.) Set up (mast) in step. **6. ~ up,** increase rate, volume, etc., of; **~ up, down,** (Electr.) increase, decrease, (voltage) by transformer. **7. ~-in** *n.* & *a.*, (garment, esp. arch. of woman's undergarment) put on by being stepped into without unfastening; **~'ping-stone,** raised stone usu. as one of set in stream or muddy place to help in crossing, (fig.) means or stage of progress to an end. [OE *stæppan, steppan*, = OS **steppian*, OHG *stepfen* f. Gmc **stap-* (as foll.)]

stĕp[2] *n.* **1.** Complete movement of one leg in walking or running or unit of movement in dancing (*took a step back*; ONE*step*, TWO-*step*); distance gained by stepping (*a long step towards success*; *do not move a step*); short distance (*but a step from my door*). **2.** Mark left by foot on ground; sound made by setting foot down (*do you hear a step?*), manner of stepping as seen or heard (*recognized her step*; *walks with a rapid step*). **3.** Simultaneous stepping with corresponding legs by two or more persons or animals; **in, out of, ~,** stepping, not stepping, in time with others or with drum-beat etc., (fig.) conforming, not conforming, to what others are doing; **break ~,** get out of step; **change ~,** begin to keep step with opposite leg; **keep ~,** remain in step (*with* person, *to* drum, etc.). **4.** Measure taken esp. as one of a series in some course of action (*must take steps in the matter, to prevent it*, etc.; *a rash, prudent,* FALSE, *step*). **5. ~ by ~,** gradually, cautiously, by degrees; **in** person's **~s,** following his example; **turn** one's **~s,** go in specified direction; **watch** or **mind your ~,** be careful. **6.** Surface provided or utilized for placing foot on in ascending or descending, e.g. tread, or rise and tread, of staircase, block of stone or other platform before door or altar etc., rung of ladder, notch cut for foot in ice-climbing, attached piece of vehicle for stepping up or down by; (**pair of**) **~s, ~-ladder,** short ladder with flat steps and prop used without being leant against wall etc. **7.** (fig.) One of the degrees in some scale of precedence or advancement, going from one of these to another e.g. by promotion or increase of pay; *(Mus.) interval of one tone. **8.** (Naut.) block or socket or platform supporting mast; (Carpentry) piece of timber with another fixed upright in it; (Mech.) lower socket or bearing for shaft. **9.** **~-cut,** (of gem) cut in straight facets round centre; **~-dance** (in which the steps are peculiar or difficult or of more importance than the figure, usu. danced as display by one performer). **10.** Hence ~PED² (-pt) *a.*, ~'WISE *adv.* [OE *stæpe, stepe,* f. WG **stapiz* f. Gmc **stap-*]

stĕ'p- *pref.* denoting nominal relationship analogous to one specified, resulting from remarriage of a parent: **~'child, ~'son, ~'daughter,** one's wife's or husband's child by previous marriage; **~'father,** STEPMOTHER, **~'parent,** one's parent's later husband or wife; **~'brother, ~'sister,** child of one's stepparent; **~'dame,** (arch.) stepmother. [OE *stēop-*, = OS, OHG *stiof-*, ON *stjúp-*, cogn. w. OHG *stiufen* bereave]

stĕphanō'tĭs *n.* Climbing tropical plant of genus *Stephanotis*, with fragrant white waxy flowers. [mod. L, f. Gk fem. adj. = fit for a wreath (*stephanos*)]

stĕ'pmother (-mŭdh-) *n.* One's father's later wife; harsh or neglectful mother (lit. or fig.); hence ~LY¹ *a.* [OE *stēopmōdor* (as STEP-, MOTHER¹)]

stĕppe *n.* Level grassy plain devoid of forest esp. in S.E. Europe and Siberia. [f. Russ. *step'*]

-ster *suf.* forming *ns.* denoting agents, orig. fem. (*spinster*) & f. *vbs.* (*brewster*), now often f. *ns.* (*gangster, maltster*) or *adjs.* (*youngster*) & w. *fem.* in *-stress* (*seamstress, songstress*); occas. derog. (*rhymester, trickster*). [OE *-estre* etc., = MLG, MDu. *-ster* f. WG *-*strja* f. Gmc *-*astrijōn*]

sterā'dĭan *n.* Unit of solid angle, equal to angle at centre of sphere subtended by part of surface whose area is equal to square of radius. [f. as STEREO- + RADIAN]

stẽrcorā'ceous (-shus), **stẽ'coral,** *adjs.* Of, produced by, living in, dung or faeces. [f. L *stercus -oris* dung + -ACEOUS, -AL]

stēre *n.* Unit of volume equal to one cubic metre. [f. F *stère* f. Gk *stereos* solid]

stĕ'rėō (*or* -ēr'-) *n.* (*pl.* ~s) & *a.* (colloq.) Stereophonic, stereophony; stereoscope, stereoscopic; stereotype. [abbr.]

stĕ'rėō- (*or* -ēr'-) *comb. form.* Solid, having three dimensions, as: **~che'mistry,** branch of chemistry dealing with composition of matter as affected by relations of atoms in space; **~graphy** (-ŏ'g-), art of depicting solid bodies in a plane; **~-i'somer,** (Chem.) one of two or more compounds differing only in spatial arrangement of atoms; **~metry** (-ŏ'mĭ-), measurement of solid bodies. [f. Gk *stereos* solid + -O-]

stĕ'rėobāte *n.* (Archit.) Solid mass of masonry as foundation for building. [f. F *stéréobate* f. L f. Gk *stereobatēs* (as prec., *bainō* walk)]

stĕrėophŏ'n|ĭc (*or* -ēr-) *a.* (Of sound-reproduction) using two or more transmission channels so that sound reaches listener from more than one direction and thus seems more realistic; hence ~ICALLY *adv.*, ~Y¹ (-ŏ'fonĭ) *n.* [f. STEREO- + PHONIC]

stĕ'rėoscōp|e (*or* -ēr'-) *n.* Device for viewing pair of photographs etc. taken at slightly different angles, looking at each with one eye, the combined images giving an impression of depth and solidity; hence ~IC (-ŏ'p-) *a.*, ~Y¹ (-ŏ'skopĭ) *n.* [f. STEREO- + -SCOPE]

stĕ'rėotȳpe (*or* -ēr'-) *n.*, & *v.t.* **1.** *n.* Printing-plate cast from mould of piece of printing composed in type; making or use of such plates; (fig.) unduly fixed mental impression. **2.** *v.t.* Make stereotype(s) of; print by use of stereotypes; (fig., esp. in *p.p.*) make unchangeable, impart monotonous regularity to, fix in all details, formalize. [f. F *stéréotype* a. (as STEREO-, TYPE¹)]

stĕ'rĭc *a.* (Chem.) Pertaining to arrangement in space of atoms in a molecule; ~ **hindrance** (of chemical reaction because of spatial arrangement of reacting atoms). [irreg. f. Gk *stereos* solid + -IC]

stĕ'rīle *a.* Unfruitful, unproductive, barren, not producing crop or fruit or young or complete seed or result (*sterile land, cow, plant, year, effort, discussion*); free from living germs esp. bacilli or bacteria or microbes; mentally barren, lacking originality or emotive force; hence or cogn. ~LY² (-l-lĭ) *adv.*, **sterĭ'lITY** *n.* [f. F *stérile* or f. L *sterilis*]

stĕ'rīlīz|e, -īs|e (-īz), *v.t.* Make sterile; deprive of power of reproduction by removal etc. of organs; make free from micro-organisms, whence ~ER¹ (2) *n.*; hence ~A'TION *n.* [f. prec. + -IZE]

stẽ'rlėt *n.* Small sturgeon (*Acipenser ruthenus*) found in Caspian Sea area and yielding fine caviare. [f. Russ. *sterlyad'*]

stẽ'rlĭng *a.* & *n.* **1.** *a.* (Of coin or precious metal) genuine, of standard value or purity; ~ **silver** (of 92½ per cent purity). **2.** Of solid worth, not showy, that is what it seems to be, (*is a sterling fellow; sterling sense, qualities, character*), whence ~NESS *n.* **3.** *n.* British money, as dist. from foreign money (*pound sterling*); ~ **area,** those countries whose currency is tied to British pound and which keep their reserves mainly in sterling and not in gold or dollars, and transfer money freely between themselves; ~ **balance** etc. (repayable in sterling). [prob. f. OE **steorling* coin with a star (*steorra*; see -LING¹), some of the early Norman pennies having on them a small star]

stẽrn¹ *a.* Severe, grim, rigid, strict, enforcing discipline or submission, not compassionate or indulgent or yielding, (*stern countenance, ruler, treatment, rebuke, virtue, father, tutor; ambition should be made of sterner stuff*; **the ~er sex,** men); hence ~'LY² *adv.*, ~'NESS (-n-n-) *n.* [OE *styrne*, **stierne* f. WG **sternja*, prob. f. **ster-*, **star-* be rigid (cf. STARE)]

stẽrn² *n.* **1.** Hind part of ship or boat (opp. *bow, head, stem; from* STEM¹ *to stern*), esp. part projecting behind stern-post; **~-chase,** pursuit of ship by another straight behind it; ~ **foremost,** moving backwards; ~ **on,** with stern presented; BY¹ *the stern.* **2.** Buttocks, rump; tail esp. of foxhound. **3.** **~-fast,** rope or chain securing stern to quay etc.; **~-post,** central upright timber or iron of stern usu. bearing rudder; ~ **sheets,** space in boat aft of rowers' thwarts often with seats for passengers; **~-way,** backward motion or impetus of ship; **~-wheeler,** steamer propelled by one large paddle-wheel at stern. **4.** Hence (-)~ED² (-nd), ~'MOST, *adjs.*, ~'WARD *a.* & *adv.*, ~'WARDS *adv.* [ME, prob. f. ON *stjórn* steering (*stýra* STEER¹)]

stẽ'rn|um *n.* (*pl.* **~ums** *or* **~a**). = BREAST¹*bone*; hence ~AL *a.* (*sternal* RIB), ~O- *comb. form.* [mod. L, f. Gk *sternon* chest]

stẽrnūtā'tion *n.* (Med. or joc.) Sneezing, sneeze. [f. L *sternutatio* (*sternutare* frequent. of *sternuere* sneeze; see -ATION)]

stẽ'rnūtātor *n.* Substance (esp. poison gas) causing irritation of nose. [f. as prec. + -OR]

sternū'tatorȳ *a.* & *n.* (Substance, e.g. snuff) causing sneezing. [f. as STERNUTATION + -ORY]

stẽ'roid (*or* -ĕ'r-) *n.* (Chem.) One of large group of organic compounds with four carbon rings, incl. some hormones and other physiological substances; hence **steroi'd**AL *a.* [f. foll. + -OID]

stĕr'ŏl (*or* -ĕr'-) *n.* (Chem.) One of group of complex solid alcohols important in vitamin synthesis. [f. CHOLESTEROL, ERGOSTEROL, etc.]

stĕr'torous *a.* (Of breathing or breather, esp. in apoplexy etc.) making snorelike sounds; hence ~LY² *adv.*, ~NESS *n.* [f. *stertor*, mod. L f. L *stertere* snore + -OR, + -OUS]

stĕt *v.* (-tt-). **1.** *v.i.* (as *imper.*, written in margin of proof or MS.) Ignore correction or alteration, let original form stand. **2.** *v.t.* Write 'stet' against, cancel correction of. [L, = let it stand, 3 pres. sing. subj. of *stare* stand]

stĕ'tho|scōpe *n.*, & *v.t.* **1.** *n.* Instrument used in auscultation esp. of heart and lungs. **2.** *v.t.* Examine with stethoscope. **3.** Hence ~**scop**IST (1), ~**scop**Y¹, (-ŏ's-) *ns.*, ~**scŏ'p**IC *a.* [f. F *stéthoscope* f. Gk *stēthos* breast; see -SCOPE]

stĕ'tson *n.* Slouch hat with very wide brim and high crown. [f. *Stetson*, name of maker]

stē'vedōre *n.* Man employed in loading and unloading ships. [f. Sp. *estivador* (*estivar* stow a cargo f. L *stipare*; see STEEVE²)]

stē'vengraph (-n-grahf) *n.* Colourful woven silk picture. [f. T. *Stevens*, Engl. weaver d. 1888, whose firm made them, + -GRAPH]

stew¹ *n.* (arch.; esp. in *pl.*) Brothel. [ME, orig. 'heated bath(-house)' f. OF *estuve*, rel. to foll.]

stew² *v.* & *n.* **1.** *v.t.* & *i.* Cook by long simmering in closed vessel with liquid; ~ **in** one's **own juice,** (be left unaided to) undergo consequences of one's own actions etc.; (in *p.p.*, of tea) bitter or strong with too long infusing; (in *p.p.*, sl.) drunk. **2.** *v.i.* (fig.) Be oppressed by close or moist warm atmosphere; (sl.) study hard; *(colloq.) be worried or anxious (*over*). **3.** *n.* Dish of meat etc. made by stewing (**Irish** ~, of mutton, potato, and onion); **in a** ~, (colloq.) agitated with perplexity, anxiety, or anger; ~**-pan,** ~**-pot,** shallow saucepan, covered crock, used for stewing. [ME, f. OF *estuver* f. Rom. **extupare*, **extufare* prob. f. EX-¹ + **tūfus* f. Gk *tuphos* smoke, steam]

stew³ *n.* ||Fish-pond, tank for keeping fish alive in; artificial oyster-bed. [ME, f. F *estui* (*estoier* confine f. Rom. **studiare* take care of f. as STUDY¹)]

stew'ard *n.* **1.** Person entrusted with management of another's property, esp. paid manager of great house or estate. **2.** Purveyor of provisions etc. for a college, club, guild, ship, etc. **3.** Passengers' attendant and waiter on ship or aircraft or train. **4.** Any of the officials managing race-meeting, ball, show, etc. **5.** ||**Lord High S~ of England,** high officer of state presiding at coronations; ||**Lord S~ of the Household,** high court officer in charge of kitchen etc. and presiding at Board of GREEN¹ Cloth; **High S~,** judicial officer at Oxford and Cambridge Universities; (**Lord High**) **S~ of Scotland,** (Hist.) chief officer of Scottish royal court. **6.** Hence ~ESS¹, ~SHIP, *ns.* [OE *stīweard* (*stig* (prob.) house, hall, *weard* WARD¹)]

stg. *abbr.* sterling.

Sth. *abbr.* South.

sthĕ'nĭc *a.* (Path.) (Of disease etc.) with morbid increase of vital action esp. of heart and arteries. [f. Gk *sthenos* strength + -IC, after *asthenic*]

stĭchomȳ'thĭa (-k-) *n.* Dialogue in alternate lines of verse esp. in ancient Greek plays. [mod. L, f. Gk *stikhomuthia* (*stikhos* line of verse, *muthos* speech)]

stĭck¹ *v.* (**stuck**). **1.** *v.t.* Thrust point of *in*(*to*) or *through* (*stick the spurs in*; *stick bayonet, pin, into* or *through*); **get stuck into,** (sl.) make serious start on (job etc.). **2.** Insert pointed thing(s) into, stab, (*will pull out a knife and stick you*; *tipsy-cake stuck over*, or *stuck, with almonds*; *pin-cushion stuck full of pins*); ~ **pigs,** engage in PIG-sticking. **3.** Fix (*up*)*on* pointed thing, be fixed (as) by point *in*(*to*) or *on* (*to*), (colloq.) put in specified position, (*heads were stuck on spikes of gateway*; *arrows stick in target*; *piece of needlework with needle sticking in it*; *stick feather, rose, in cap, buttonhole*; *stick pen behind* one's *ear*; *stick up a target*; *have stuck their prices up, I see*; *stick it on the bill*; *stick your cap on*; *stick them in your pocket*; *stick a few commas in it*; *just stick it on the table, down anywhere*). **4.** *v.i.* & *t.* ~ **out** or **up,** protrude, (cause to) project, be or make erect, (*stick* one's *head out of window*; *his hair sticks straight up*; *stick out* one's *chest*; *how his stomach sticks out!*); ~ one's **chin** (or **neck**) **out,** (colloq.) ask for trouble, expose oneself to danger; ~ **out a mile** (sl.), ~ **out like a sore thumb** (colloq.), be very obvious; ~ **up,** (sl.) rob (person etc.) by threatening with gun (~ **'em up!,** (sl.) hands up!; ~**-up** *n.*, hold-up); **stuck-up,** conceited, insolently exclusive, [prob. f. carriage of head]; ~ **up to,** not humble oneself before, offer resistance to; ~ **up for,** maintain cause or character of (esp. absent person). **5.** Fix or become or remain fixed (as) by glue, suction, or other means of adhesion of surfaces (*stick label, postage stamp, on*; *this envelope will not stick*; *was referred to as 'Winnie' and the nickname stuck*; *memory of it sticks in my mind*; *friends should stick together*; *limpet sticks to rock*; *stick photographs in album*); (colloq.) remain in same place (*are you going to stick indoors all day?*); ||post (*bill*) as placard on wall; (colloq., of accusation etc.) be regarded as valid (*could not make the charges stick*); ||(sl.) endure, tolerate (*cannot stick that fellow*; *could not stick it* (*out*) *any longer*); ~ **around,** (sl.) linger, remain near same place; ~ **at it,** (colloq.) be persistent; ~ **it on,** (sl.) make high charges, tell exaggerated story; **stuck on,** (sl.) captivated by; ~ **out for,** insist on (price etc., refusing anything less); ~ **to,** remain fixed on or to, remain faithful to (friend, promise, etc.), abide by, (~ *to business*, avoid distractions; ~ *to the point*, not digress); ~ **to** person's **fingers,** (of money) be embezzled etc. by him; *stick to* one's GUNS; ~ **to it,** persist, not cease trying (*~*-to--it-ive*, persistent); ~ **with,** remain in touch with or faithful to; **stuck with,** (colloq.) unable to get rid of. **6.** Lose or deprive of power of motion through friction, jamming, suction, difficulty, or other impediment, (*is stuck on a sandbank*; *got up to the fourth form, through some ten lines, and then stuck*); ~ **at nothing,** allow nothing, esp. no scruples, to deter one; ~ **fast,** be hopelessly bogged etc.; **stuck for,** at a loss for, unable to think of; ~ **in the mud,** lit., or fig. be unprogressive; ~*-in-the-mud*, slow, unprogressive, (person) ~ **in** one's **throat** etc., be unable to be swallowed (lit. or fig.). **7.** *v.t.* Provide (plant) with stick as support or to climb up. **8.** ||~**'ing-piece,** beef from lower part of neck; ~**'ing-place, -point,** (at which screw becomes jammed; usu. fig. w. ref. to Shak. *Macbeth* I. vii. 60); ~**'ing-plaster,** adhesive plaster for cuts etc.; ~**'jaw,** toffee etc. hard to masticate because it makes jaws stick together; *~**'pin,** tie-pin; *~**'weed,** = RAG¹*weed* (2). [OE *stician*, = OHG *stehhan* prick f. Gmc **stik*- f. IE **st*(*e*)*ig*-]

stĭck² *n.* **1.** Shoot of tree cut to convenient length for use in walking or as bludgeon (BIG *stick*) or as fuel or to support plant; staff, wand, rod; piece of wood etc. (whether as part of something or separate) more or less resembling these in shape and size (BROOM*stick*, DRUM¹*stick*, FIDDLE*stick*, ||GOLD *Stick*, JOY¹*stick*, SHOOTING-*stick*, ||SILVER¹

Stick, SINGLE[1]*stick*, SWORD-*stick*); (colloq.) such piece of wood as part of house or furniture (*house pulled down and not a stick left standing*; *has only a few sticks of furniture*); implement used to propel ball in hockey, polo, etc.; gear-lever, conductor's baton; cane used in punishing; (**the**) ~, (caning as) punishment (lit. or fig.); compositor's instrument with compartment of adjustable width for setting type before transfer to galley; (in *pl.*) raising of stick above shoulder in hockey; (in *pl.*, sl.) rural areas, hurdles, football goal; (Naut., joc.) mast or spar; (colloq.) person, esp. one lacking vigour or intelligence or social qualities; slender more or less cylindrical piece of sealing-wax, shaving-soap, rhubarb, celery, chocolate, dynamite; number (of bombs or paratroops) released in rapid succession from aircraft. **2.** *In a cleft stick* (see CLEAVE[1]); *as* CROSS[3] *as two sticks*; HOP[2] *the stick*; *the* WRONG *end of the stick*. **3.** ~ **figure,** drawing of human figure with single straight lines for body and limbs; **~-insect,** (usu. wingless) insect of family Phasmidae with twiglike body; ~ **lac** (in natural state, encrusting insects and small twigs). [OE *sticca*, = OHG *stecko* f. WG **stikka* (**stik-* **stek-* pierce)]

stĭ'cker *n.* In vbl senses; adhesive label; difficult problem; wooden rod transmitting motion between ends of levers in piano or organ; persistent person; BILL[4]*sticker*; PIG-*sticker*. [f. STICK[1] + -ER[1]]

stĭ'ckit *a.* (Sc.) Not proceeding with one's intended profession; ~ **minister,** licentiate who has failed to get a pastoral charge. [Sc. form of p.p. of STICK[1]]

stĭ'cklebăck (-kelb-) *n.* Small fish of family Gasterosteidae, with sharp spines on back. [ME, f. OE *sticel* thorn, sting (as STICK[2], -LE 1) + *bæc* BACK[1]]

stĭ'ckler *n.* ~ **for,** person who insists on or pertinaciously supports or advocates (*is a great, am no, stickler for authority, precision*, etc.). [f. obs. *stickle* be umpire, ME *stightle* control, frequent. of *stight* f. OE *stiht(i)an* set in order]

stĭ'ck|y̆ *a.* Tending or intended to stick to what is touched; glutinous, viscous; (of weather) humid; unbending, critical, making or likely to make objections (*he was very sticky about giving me leave*); (sl.) highly unpleasant and painful (*he'll come to a sticky end*); **~ybeak,** (Austral. sl.) inquisitive person; **~y wicket,** (colloq.) **~y dog,** (Cricket, or fig.) pitch drying after rain and difficult for batsmen; hence **~ĭLY**[2] *adv.*, **~ĭNESS** *n.* [f. STICK[1] + -Y[2]]

stĭff *a.* & *n.* **1.** *a.* Rigid, not flexible, unbending, unyielding, uncompromising, obstinate, (*stiff collar*; *lies stiff in death*; *put up a stiff resistance*; *answered with a stiff refusal*); (of leg) incapable of bending at knee; (of ship) heeling little under sail; (of market) with prices remaining firm; *stiff upper* LIP; **~-necked,** obstinate or haughty; ~ **with,** (sl.) abundantly provided with. **2.** Lacking ease or grace or graciousness or spontaneity, constrained, reserved, haughty, formal, (*stiff manners*; *a stiff reception, bow*, etc.; *stiff movement, attitude*, etc.; *writes in a stiff style*). **3.** Not working freely, sticking, offering resistance, (*a stiff hinge, piston*, etc.); ~ **neck,** rheumatic affection in which head cannot be turned without pain. **4.** (Of muscle, limb, etc., or person in regard to them) aching when in action, as result of previous exertion. **5.** Hard to cope with, calling for strength or effort of some kind, trying, (*stiff examination, climb, slope, breeze*); (of price or penalty) high; (of a drink) strong. **6.** (Of moist clay, batter, etc.) thick and viscous, not fluid, in or approaching plastic state. **7.** (*pred.*, colloq.) To the point of exhaustion, almost to death, (*bore, scare, stiff*). **8.** Hence **~'ISH**[1] 2 *a.*, **~'LY**[2] *adv.*, **~'NESS** *n.* **9.** *n.* (sl.) Negotiable paper, money; corpse; (**big**) ~, hopeless or intractable or incorrigible person. [OE *stīf*, = MLG, MDu. *stīf*, ON *stífr* f. Gmc **stifaz* f. IE **stīpos*]

stĭ'ffen *v.t.* & *i.* Make or become stiff(er); (Mil.) bring in better soldiers to improve quality of (a force); hence **~ER**[1] (2), **~ING**[1] (1, 4), *ns.* [f. prec. + -EN[6]]

stī'fle[1] *v.t.* & *i.* Smother; constrain breathing or suppress utterance of, be thus constrained. [perh. alt. of ME *stuff(l)e* f. OF *estouffer* f. Rom. **extuffare*]

stī'fle[2] *n.* ~(**-joint**), joint of horse's, dog's, etc., leg between hip and hock; **~-bone,** bone of stifle-joint, like knee-cap. [ME; orig. unkn.]

stĭ'gma *n.* (*pl.* **~s** *or* **~ta**). **1.** (arch.) Mark branded on slave, criminal, etc. **2.** Imputation attaching to person's reputation; stain on one's good name. **3.** Characteristic feature *of*; (Path.) definite characteristic of some disease; (Anat. & Zool.) spot, pore, small natural mark on skin etc.; insect's spiracle. **4.** Small red spot on person's skin that bleeds periodically or under mental stimulus. **5.** (Bot.) Part of style or ovary-surface that receives pollen in impregnation. **6.** (Eccl., usu. in *pl.* **~ta**). Mark(s) corresponding to those left on Christ's body by the nails and spear at the Crucifixion, said to have been impressed on the bodies of St. Francis of Assisi and others and attributed to divine favour. [L, f. Gk *stigma -atos* mark made by pointed instrument, brand (**stig-*, cogn. w. STICK[2])]

stĭgmă't|ĭc[1] *a.* Pertaining to stigma(s); [by back form.] anastigmatic, not astigmatic; hence **~ICALLY** *adv.* [f. as prec. + -IC]

stĭgmă'tĭc[2], **stĭ'gmatĭst,** *ns.* (Eccl.) Person bearing stigmata. [f. as prec., -IST]

stĭ'gmatīz|e, -is|e (-īz), *v.t.* Use opprobrious terms against, describe opprobriously *as*, (*shall not stigmatize him as he deserves*; *stigmatize him, it, as a coward, cowardice*); (Eccl.) produce stigmata on; hence **~A'TION** *n.* [f. F *stigmatiser* or med. L f. Gk *stigmatizō* (as STIGMA; see -IZE)]

stī'lbēne *n.* (Chem.) Aromatic hydrocarbon forming phosphorescent crystals. [f. Gk *stilbō* glitter + -ENE]

stĭlboe'strol (-ē's-), ***-ē'strol,** *n.* Powerful synthetic oestrogen derived from stilbene. [f. prec. + OESTRUS + -OL]

stīle[1] *n.* Steps, rungs, etc., arranged to allow person to get over or through fence or hedge or wall but excluding cattle etc.; *help lame* DOG[1] *over stile*. [OE *stigel*, = OS, OHG *stigilla* f. Gmc **stig-* climb]

stīle[2] *n.* Vertical piece (cf. RAIL[1]) in frame of panelled door, wainscot, etc. [prob. f. Du. *stijl* pillar, door-post]

stĭlĕ'ttō *n.* (*pl.* **~s** *or* **~es**). **1.** Short thick-bladed dagger. **2.** Pointed implement for making eyelets etc.; ~ **heel** of shoe (long and pointed). [It., dim. of *stilo* dagger (as STYLUS); see -ET[1]]

stĭll[1] *a.*, *n.*, *v.*, & *adv.* **1.** *a.* Without or almost without motion (*stand, sit, lie, keep, still*); (of water) without surface movement (*still waters run* DEEP[3]). **2.** Without or almost without sound (*still as the grave*; *a still evening*; *how still everything is!*; *in still meditation*); (of sounds) hushed, stilled; ~ **small voice,** that of conscience (w. ref. to 1 Kgs. 19:12). **3.** (Of wine etc.) not sparkling or effervescing (*still hock, lemonade*). **4.** ~ **birth,** birth of dead child; **~'born,** born dead, (fig.) abortive; ***~-hunt,** silent pursuit of quarry (lit. or fig.); ~ **life** (*pl.* ~ *lifes* or *lives*), (a) painting of inanimate things such as fruit and cut flowers; ~ **picture,** = sense 6. **5.** Hence **~'NESS** *n.* **6.** *n.* Ordinary static photograph (as distinct from a motion picture), esp. single shot from cinema film. **7.** Deep silence (*in the still of night*). **8.** *v.t.* (literary). Quiet, calm, appease, assuage, silence. **9.** *v.i.* (literary). Grow calm (*when the tempest stills*). **10.** *adv.* Then or now or for the future as before, even to this or that past or present or future time, (*Pyramids are still standing*; *what, are you still here so late?*; *had still not realized the truth*); nevertheless, for all that, on the other hand, all the same; (w. *compar.* etc.) even, yet, (*still greater efforts*; *still* LESS; *greater efforts still*; *still another possible explanation*); (arch.) constantly, habitually. [OE *stille* a. & adv., *stillan* v., = OS, OHG *stilli* f. WG **stillja*, **stellja* (**stel-* be fixed)]

still² *n.* Distilling-apparatus, esp. for making spirituous liquors, consisting essentially of a closed boiler and a condensing chamber; ||**~-room,** (1) room for distilling, (2) housekeeper's store-room in large house. [f. *still* v., ME f. DISTIL]

stĭ'llage *n.* Bench, frame, etc., for keeping articles off floor while draining, drying, waiting to be packed, etc. [app. f. Du. *stellagie* scaffold (*stellen* to place + F *-age*; see -AGE)]

stĭ'llĭcīde *n.* (Law). (Right or duty relating to) dropping of water from eaves on to another's land. [f. L *stillicidium* (*stilla* drop, *cid-* f. *cadere* fall)]

stĭ'llȳ¹ (-l-lĭ) *adv.* In adj. senses. [OE *stillīce* (as STILL¹, -LY²)]

stĭ'llȳ² *a.* (poet.) Still, quiet. [f. STILL¹ after *vasty* etc.]

stilt *n.* **1.** Pole with rest for foot used generally in pairs with upper part of pole bound to leg or held with hand or arm, enabling user to walk at a distance above the ground (**on ~s** lit., or fig. = bombastic, stilted). **2.** One of set of piles or posts supporting building etc. **3.** Long-legged slender-billed marsh bird of genus *Himantopus*; **~-petrel, -sandpiper,** (long-legged kind). [ME & LG *stilte* f. Gmc **steltjōn*, cogn. w. MDu., MLG *stelte*, OHG *stelza* f. **steltōn*; cf. STOUT]

stĭ'ltėd *a.* (As) on stilts; (of literary style etc.) artificially lofty, pompous, bombastic, whence ~LY² *adv.*, ~NESS *n.*; (of arch) with pieces of upright masonry between imposts and springers. [f. prec. + -ED²]

Stĭ'lton *n.* Rich blue-veined cheese with added cream. [~ in Cambridgeshire, where formerly sold]

stī'lus. Var. of STYLUS.

stĭ'mūlant *a.* & *n.* **1.** *a.* Stimulating (esp. Med., producing increase of activity in the body or some part of it). **2.** *n.* Stimulant agent or substance, as warmth, electricity, joy, etc., or quickening drug or article of food esp. alcoholic drink. [f. L (as foll.; see -ANT)]

stĭ'mūl|ate *v.t.* Apply stimulus to, act as stimulus upon, animate, spur on, excite (person etc., or abs.) to (more vigorous) action; hence or cogn. ~A'TION, **~ātor**, *ns.*, ~ATIVE *a.* [f. L *stimulare* (as foll.) + -ATE³]

stĭ'mūl|us *n.* (*pl.* **~i** *pr.* -ī). **1.** Thing that rouses to activity or energy (*so lethargic that no stimulus affects him*); rousing effect (*under the stimulus of hunger*). **2.** (Physiol.) Thing that evokes specific functional reaction in organ or tissue. [L, = goad, spur, incentive]

stī'mȳ. Var. of STYMIE.

stĭng *v.* (**stung**) & *n.* **1.** *v.t.* Wound with sting (*a bee, nettle, stung him, his finger*); affect with tingling physical or sharp mental pain (*pepper stings one's tongue*; *the cane, his bat-handle, the blow, his conscience, the imputation, stung him*; *stung by reproaches, with envy* or *desire*; *a stinging insult*); incite by such mental effect (*was stung into replying*); (sl.) charge heavily, involve in expense, swindle. **2.** *v.i.* (Of part of one's body) feel or be seat of acute pain (*my hand stings*); be able to sting, have a sting, (*some bees do not sting*; **~'ing-nettle,** opp. DEAD nettle). **3.** *n.* Sharp-pointed wounding organ often tubular and connected with poison-gland of insect etc.; snake's poison-fang; stiff sharp hair of nettle etc. causing rash or inflammation on contact with skin; infliction of wound with sting, wound so made, pain caused by it, wounding quality or effect, rankling or acute pain of body or mind, keenness or vigour, (*was hurt by a sting*; *face covered with stings*; *the sting of hunger*; *stings of remorse*; *this air, bowling, has no sting in it*); **~ in the tail,** (fig.) unexpected final pungency. **4. ~-moth,** (Austral.) moth with stinging larva; **~-nettle,** stinging-nettle; **~-ray,** ray esp. of family Dasyatidae, with long tapering tail having sharp serrated projecting spine(s) used by it as weapon; **~-winkle,** beaked shellfish that bores holes in other shellfish. **5.** Hence ~'LESS *a.* [OE *stingan* v., *sting* n., = ON *stinga* f. Gmc **steng-* pierce]

stĭ'ngaree (-ngg-) *n.* (U.S. & Austral.) = STING-*ray*. [corrupt.]

stĭ'nger *n.* In vbl senses; smart painful blow. [f. STING + -ER¹]

||**stĭ'ngō** (-nggō) *n.* (arch. sl.) Strong beer. [f. STING, w. ref. to sharp taste, + -O]

stĭ'ng|ȳ (-njĭ) *a.* Meanly parsimonious, niggardly; hence **~ĭLY**² *adv.*, **~ĭNESS** *n.* [perh. f. dial. *stinge* sting + -Y²]

stĭnk *v.* (**stank** or **stunk**; **stunk**) & *n.* **1.** *v.i.* Emit strong offensive smell (*stink in the* NOSTRILS *of*); (fig.) be or seem very unpleasant or unattractive or unsavoury; **~ of money,** (sl.) be notoriously rich. **2.** *v.t.* Drive (person) *out* etc. by stink; fill (place) with stink; (sl.) perceive stink of (*can stink it a mile off*). **3.** *n.* Strong offensive smell, stench; ||(in *pl.*, sl.) chemistry or natural science as subject of study; (colloq.) loud complaint (*kick up, raise, a stink about*); **like ~,** (sl.) intensely. **4. ~-alive,** the BIB¹ [from rapid putrefaction after death]; **~-ball,** missile containing explosives etc. generating noxious vapours used formerly in naval warfare; **~-bomb,** small bomb emitting nauseating smell on exploding; **~-horn,** ill-smelling fungus of order Phallales; **~'pot,** (1) any receptacle containing something that stinks, (2) stink-ball, (3) objectionable person or thing; **~-stone,** kind of limestone giving off fetid smell when quarried; **~-trap,** stench-trap; **~'wood,** (ill-smelling timber of) Afr. tree (*Ocotea bullata*). [OE *stincan*, = MDu., MLG *stinken*, OHG *stinkan* f. WG **stinkwan*; cf. STENCH]

stĭ'nkard *n.* Stinking person or animal, esp. teledu. [f. prec. + -ARD]

stĭ'nker *n.* Stinkard, stinkpot; petrel feeding on carrion; (sl.) anything peculiarly offensive, irritating, or severe, (esp. of a letter: *I wrote him a stinker*), difficult task. [f. STINK + -ER¹]

stĭ'nkĭng *a.* & *adv.* **1.** *a.* In vbl senses; having typical usu. disagreeable smell (**~ badger,** teledu; **~ cedar** or **yew,** evergreen Amer. tree of genus *Torreya*, with yewlike leaves stinking when bruised; **~ weed** or **wood,** a rank-scented cassia); (sl.) objectionable; **cry ~ fish,** condemn one's own products etc. **2.** *adv.* (sl.) Extremely and objectionably (*stinking rich*). [OE *stincende* (as STINK, ING²)]

stĭ'nkō *a.* (sl.) Drunk. [f. STINK + -O]

stĭnt *v.t.*, & *n.* **1.** *v.t.* Keep on limited allowance (*stint* oneself or person or animal *of* food etc.); supply or give in niggardly amount or grudgingly (*stint food, money, service*, etc.). **2.** *n.* Limitation of supply or effort (usu. *without, no, stint*); hence ~'LESS *a.* **3.** Fixed or allotted amount of or *of* work (*do* one's *daily stint*). **4.** Small sandpiper, esp. dunlin. [OE *styntan* to blunt, dull, f. Gmc **stuntjan* (**stunt-*; cf. STUNT¹)]

stīpe *n.* (Bot. & Zool.) Stalk or stem (esp. support of carpel, stalk of frond, stem of fungus, eye-stalk); hence **stī'pi**FORM, **stī'pĭt**ATE², **stīpĭ'tĭ**FORM, *adjs.* [F, f. L STIPES]

stī'pel *n.* (Bot.) Secondary stipule at base of leaflets of compound leaf; hence **~late**² *a.* [f. F *stipelle* f. mod. L *stipella* dim. (as STIPULE)]

stī'pĕnd *n.* Fixed money allowance at regular intervals for work done, salary, esp. clergyman's official income. [ME, f. OF *stipend(i)e* or f. L *stipendium* (*stips* wages, *pendere* to pay)]

stīpĕ'ndĭarȳ *a.* & *n.* (Person) receiving stipend, paid, not serving gratuitously; ||**~ (magistrate)**, paid professional magistrate in large provincial town. [f. L *stipendiarius* (as prec.; see -ARY¹)]

stī'p|ēs (-z) *n.* (*pl.* **~ites** *pr.* stĭ'pĭtēz). Stipe. [L, = log, tree-trunk]

stĭ'ppl|e *v.* & *n.* **1.** *v.t.* Engrave (plate, thing portrayed), paint or draw, in stipple, not lines; roughen smooth surface of (paint, cement, etc.). **2.** *v.i.* Use such method. **3.** Hence **~**ER¹ (1, 2), **~**ING¹, *ns.* **4.** *n.* Dotted engraving, painting, etc., giving gradation of shade etc.; effect (as) of this. [f. Du. *stippelen* frequent. of *stippen* to prick (*stip* point)]

stĭ'pūlate¹ *a.* (Bot.) Having stipules. [f. L *stipula* (as STIPULE) + -ATE²]

stĭ'pūl|āte² *v.* **1.** *v.i.* **~ate for,** mention or insist upon as essential condition. **2.** *v.t.* Demand as part of bargain or agreement *that*; (in *p.p.*) laid down as part of the terms of an agreement (*is not of the stipulated quality*). **3.** *v.i.* & *t.* *Agree *to*, agree on, (evidence etc. to figure in legal proceedings). **4.** So **~**A'TION, **~āt**OR, *ns.* [f. L *stipulari* + -ATE³]

stĭ'pūl|e *n.* Small leaflike appendage to leaf usu. at base of leaf-stem; hence **~**AR¹ *a.* [F, or f. L *stipula* straw]

stir¹ *v.* (-rr-) & *n.* **1.** *v.t.* & *i.* Set, keep, or (begin to) be, in motion (*not a breath of wind stirs the lake, the leaves*; *sit without stirring a foot etc.* or *stirring*; *if you stir, I shoot*); rise from bed (*is not stirring yet*), go *out* (*of house* etc.). **2.** *v.t.* Use poker to ventilate and assist burning of (fire etc.); arouse (wrath etc.); move spoon etc. round and round in (tea, porridge, soup, etc.) to mix ingredients, keep from burning in pot, etc.; **~ the blood,** inspire enthusiasm etc.; **~** one's **stumps,** (colloq.) make haste, walk etc. faster; **~ up,** mix well by stirring, make (mud, sediment, etc.) rise from bottom of liquid by stirring, (fig.) rouse, excite, animate, inspirit, (*stir up strife, mutiny, discontent, curiosity*). **3. ~-about,** (1) porridge made by stirring oatmeal etc. in boiling water or milk, (2) bustling person. **4.** Hence **~'r**ER¹ (1, 2) *n.* **5.** *n.* Commotion, bustle, disturbance, excitement, sensation, (*full of stir and movement*; **make a great ~,** be much discussed etc.); slightest movement (*not a stir*), whence **~'**LESS *a.*; act of stirring (*give the fire a stir*). [OE *styrian*, = OS *-sturian*, MHG *stürn* f. Gmc **sturjan*]

stir² *n.* (sl.) Prison; **~-crazy,** mentally abnormal from being imprisoned (lit. or fig.). [19th c.; orig. unkn.]

||**stirk** *n.* (prov.) Yearling bullock or heifer. [OE *stirc*, perh. dim. of *stēor* STEER²; see -OCK]

stir'pĭcūlture *n.* Breeding of special stocks or strains. [f. as foll. + -I- + CULTURE]

stirp|s *n.* (*pl.* **~es** *pr.* ster'pēz). **1.** (Law). (Progenitor of) branch of family. **2.** (Zool.) Classificatory group. [L, = stock]

stir'rĭng *a.* In vbl senses; actively occupied (*lead a stirring life*); exciting, stimulating, inspiring, (*stirring events, music, tales*), whence **~**LY² *adv.* [OE *styrende* (as STIR¹, -ING²)]

stĭ'rrup *n.* Horse-rider's foot-rest usu. consisting of metal or leather loop with flattened base hung by **~-strap** or **~-leather** from **~-bar,** iron attachment let into saddle; part of garment etc. passing under instep; (Naut.) rope with eye giving hold in reefing; **~(-bone)**, stapes; **~-cup** (of wine etc. presented to person about to depart, orig. on horseback); **~-iron,** metal loop of stirrup; **~-jar,** ancient Greek jar with arched supported handle at top; **~-pump,** hand-operated pump with foot-rest and nozzle for producing either jet or spray of water, used for extinguishing small fires. [OE *stigrāp* (*stigan* climb f. as STILE¹, ROPE)]

stĭtch *n.* & *v.* **1.** *n.* Sudden acute pain in side of body. **2.** Single pass of needle in sewing (*a stitch in time* SAVE¹*s nine*); result of it or of single complete movement in knitting, crocheting, embroidery, etc., (*if one stitch gives the rest will*); thread etc. between two successive needle-holes; least bit of material, esp. of clothing; **drop a ~,** let loop fall off end of knitting-needle by accident; **in ~'es,** (colloq.) laughing uncontrollably. **3.** Fastening through sheets of book etc.; (Surg.) movement of needle, loop of material formed, in sewing up a wound with gut, silk, wire, etc. **4.** Method followed in making stitches or kind of work produced (*am learning a new stitch*; LOCK²*-stitch*, CROSS*-stitch*, etc.). **5. ~-wheel,** harness-maker's notched wheel for pricking leather in places where stitches are to go; **~'wort,** plant of genus *Stellaria*, esp. one with erect stem and white starry flowers, named as curing stitch in side. **6.** *v.t.* & *i.* Sew, make stitches (in), join or close with stitches; **~ up,** join or mend by sewing; hence **~'**ER¹, **~'**ERY (1), *ns.* [OE *stice*, = OS *stiki*, OHG *stih*, Goth *stiks* f. Gmc **stikiz* (**stik-* STICK¹)]

stĭ'thȳ (-dhĭ) *n.* (arch. or poet.) Smith's shop, forge. [ME, f. ON *stethi* (**stathjon* f. Gmc **sta-* STAND¹)]

stī'ver *n.* Even the smallest coin (usu. *don't care, has not, a stiver*). [f. Du. *stuiver* small coin, prob. cogn. w. STUB]

stō'a *n.* (*pl.* **~e**). Portico or roofed colonnade in ancient-Greek architecture; **the S~,** = *the* PORCH (cf. STOIC). [Gk]

stoat *n.* Ermine, esp. when in its brown summer coat. [ME, of unkn. orig.]

stochă'st|ĭc (-k-) *a.* Governed by the laws of probability; hence **~**ICALLY *adv.* [f. Gk *stokhastikos* (*stokhazomai* aim at, guess f. *stokhos* aim; see -IC)]

stŏck *n.*, *a.*, & *v.* **1.** *n.* Stump, butt, main trunk, (**~s and stones,** inanimate things, lethargic persons; LAUGHING¹*-stock*); plant into which graft is inserted; body-piece serving as base or holder or handle for working parts of implement or machine (e.g. for barrel of rifle or for ploughshare); headstock or tailstock; cross-bar of anchor; LOCK², *stock, and barrel.* **2.** (Source of) family or breed, raw material of manufacture (e.g. of paper or cinema film), store ready for drawing on, equipment for trade or pursuit, (*renew* one's *stock*, *lay in a stock*, *has a great stock*, *of information*, *of hardware*); ROLL²*ing-stock*; **in ~,** ready without needing to be procured specially; **out of ~,** not thus available; **comes of** (*a*) *good*, *Puritan*, *treacherous*, etc., **~** (family of distinct character); **take ~,** review one's stock for accurate knowledge of what one has; **take ~ of,** (fig.) observe with a view to estimating character etc. of. **3.** (Zool.) Aggregate organism of polyp etc. **4.** Liquor made by stewing bones, meat, fish, vegetables, etc., as basis for soup, stew, sauce, or gravy. **5.** Farm animals (*livestock*) and implements (*deadstock*); FAT*stock*. **6.** Cruciferous fragrant-flowered plant of genus *Matthiola*; TEN-*week stock*, VIRGINIA *stock* [orig. ~-*gillyflower*, named as having stronger stem than clove-gillyflower]. **7.** (in *pl.*, Hist.) Timber frame with holes for feet and occas. hands in which petty offenders were confined in sitting position in public. **8.** (in *pl.*) Timbers on which ship rests during building; **on the ~s,** in construction or preparation. **9.** Stiff wide band of leather or other material worn round neck esp. in riding-kit; piece of black or purple silk etc. worn below clerical collar. **10.** ||Money lent to a government and involving payment of fixed interest to lenders or their successors in title; right to receive such interest (*buy, hold, stock*); ||**the ~s,** State's funded debts as a whole; **take ~ in,** (fig.) concern oneself with. **11.** Capital of corporation or company contributed by individuals for prosecution of some undertaking and divided into shares entitling holders to proportion of profits (DEFER¹*red*, ||ORDINARY, ||PREFERENCE or *preferred stock*); *share(s) of stock; one's ~ **rises, falls,** (fig.) one is more, less, popular or highly regarded. **12.** ||Hard solid brick pressed in a mould. **13.** ||**~-account, -book,** (showing amount of goods laid in and amount disposed of); **~-breeder,** raiser of livestock; **~'broker, ~'broking,** (person engaged in) buying and selling for clients stocks held by stockjobbers; **~-car,** (1) *railway cattle-truck, (2) racing car with basic chassis of ordinary commercial model, but sometimes partly made from old cars, used in racing where deliberate bumping is allowed; **~ company,** one semi-permanently engaged at a particular theatre; **~'dove,** European wild pigeon (*Columba oenas*) smaller and darker than ring-dove [prob. named from breeding in stocks of trees]; **~ exchange,** place where stocks and shares are publicly bought and sold; **the S~ Exchange,** (building occupied by) association of dealers in stocks conducting business according to fixed rules (*on the S~ Exchange*, a member of this association); **~'fish,** cod or similar fish split and dried in open air without salt; **~'holder,** holder of stock or shares; **~-in-trade,** all requisites for a trade (lit. or fig.: *the politician's stock-in-trade of a dozen catchwords*); **~'jobber, ~'jobbing,** ||(person engaged in) dealing in stocks so as to profit by fluctuations in price, *(unscrupulous) stock-broker, -broking; **~'list,** daily or periodical publication giving current prices of stocks etc. or stating dealer's stock of goods; **~ lock** (enclosed in wooden case, usu. on outer door); **~'man,** (Austral.) man in charge of livestock, *owner of livestock, *person in charge of stock of goods in warehouse etc.; **~-market,** stock exchange or transactions on it; **~'pile,** accumulate(d) stocks of commodities, raw materials, nuclear weapons, etc., to be held in reserve; **~-pot** (for making or keeping stock, sense 4); **~'rider,** (Austral.) herdsman on unfenced station; **~-room** (for storage of goods kept in stock); **~ saddle,** cowboy's (ornamental) saddle; **~-still,** motionless; **~-taking,** review of stock in shop etc. or fig.; **~-whip** (with short handle and long lash for herding cattle); **~'yard,** enclosure with pens etc. for sorting or temporary keeping of cattle. **14.** Hence ~'LESS *a.* **15.** *a.* Kept in stock and regularly available (*a stock item, size*); (fig.) always available and perpetually repeated without fresh thought or originality (*stock argument, comparison, joke, response, role*). **16.** *v.t.* Fit (gun etc.) with stock. **17.** (Hist.) Confine in the stocks. **18.** Provide (shop, farm, etc.) with goods or livestock or requisites (*a well-stocked larder, library,* etc.); keep (goods) in stock. **19.** *v.i.* **~ (up),** take in stocks of goods. [OE *stoc(c)*, = OS *stok*, ON *stokkr* trunk f. Gmc **stukkaz*]

stŏckā'de *n.*, & *v.t.* (Fortify with) breastwork or enclosure of upright stakes. [f. obs. F *estocade*, alt. of *estacade* f. Sp. *estacada* (rel. to STAKE)]

Stŏ'ckhōlm (-hōm) *n.* ~ **pitch, tar,** (prepared from resinous pinewood, used esp. in ship-building). [~ in Sweden]

stŏckĭnĕ't, -ĕ'tte, *n.* Elastic knitted material used esp. for bandages. [prob. f. *stocking-net*]

stŏ'ckĭng *n.* Tight covering usu. knitted or woven of wool or cotton or silk or nylon for foot and (part of) leg (*pair of stockings*); *is* or *stands six feet* **in** one's **~s** or **~(ed) feet** (when measured) without shoes; **elastic ~,** surgical appliance of elastic webbing like stocking or part of it worn for varicose veins, strained muscles, etc.; **white** etc. **~,** lower part of leg of horse etc. differently coloured from rest of leg; **~ cap,** knitted usu. conical cap; **~-filler,** small present for adding to stocking hung up for Santa Claus; **~-frame, -loom, -machine,** knitting-machine; **~ mask,** nylon stocking worn over head as criminal's disguise; **~-stitch** (of alternate rows plain and purl, giving uniform surface); hence ~LESS *a.* [f. STOCK, in (now dial.) sense 'stocking' + -ING¹]

||**stŏ'ckĭst** *n.* One who stocks (certain) goods for sale. [f. STOCK + -IST]

stŏ'ck|ȳ *a.* (Of person, plant, or animal) thick-set, relatively short and strongly built; hence ~ĬLY² *adv.*, ~ĬNESS *n.* [f. STOCK + -Y²]

stŏdge *n.* & *v.* (colloq.) **1.** *n.* Food esp. of thick heavy kind; unimaginative person or work. **2.** *v.i.* Eat greedily; trudge through mud etc. **3.** *v.t.* Stuff with food etc. [n. f. v., imit., after *stuff* and *podge*]

stŏ'dg|ȳ *a.* (Of food) heavy, filling, indigestible; (of book, style, etc.) over-full of facts or details, lacking lightness or originality or interest; dull, drab; hence ~ĬLY² *adv.*, ~ĬNESS *n.* [f. prec. + -Y²]

stoep (-ōōp) *n.* (S. Afr.) Terraced veranda in front of house. [Du. cogn. w. STEP¹˒ ²]

***stō'gȳ, -gĭe,** (-gĭ) *n.* Rough heavy boot; long narrow roughly-made cigar. [orig. *stoga*, short for *Conestoga* in Pennsylvania]

stō'ĭc *n.* & *a.* **1.** (*S~*). (Typical of) philosopher of the school founded at Athens *c.* 308 B.C. by Zeno making virtue the highest good, concentrating attention on ethics, and inculcating control of the passions and indifference to pleasure and pain (*Stoic doctrines, indifference*); hence **S~**ISM (2, 3) *n.* **2.** (Person) having great self-control or fortitude or austerity; hence ~AL *a.*, **~al**LY² *adv.*, ~ISM (2, 3) *n.* [ME, f. L f. Gk *stōikos* (STOA porch, w. ref. to Zeno's teaching in the *Stoa Poikilē* or Painted Porch at Athens; see -IC)]

stoichĭŏ'|mĕtrȳ, ||**-cheiŏ'|-,** (-kĭ-) *n.* Determination of equivalent weights of substances in chemical reactions; quantitative relationship between reacting substances; hence **~mĕ'tr**IC (-kĭo-) *a.* [f. Gk *stoikheion* element + -O- + -METRY]

stōke *v.* **1.** *v.t.* ~ **(up),** feed with fuel and tend (furnace or colloq. fire), feed furnace or fire-box of (engine etc.). **2.** *v.i.* Act as stoker; ~ **(up),** (colloq.) take food esp. steadily and in large quantity. **3. ~'hold,** compartment in which steamer's fires are tended; **~'hole,** space for stokers in front of furnace. [back form. f. foll.]

stō'ker *n.* Man who feeds and tends furnace or fire-box esp. that of steamer or steam-engine; machine for doing this. [Du. f. *stoken* stoke f. MDu. *stoken* push cogn. w. STICK¹, + -ER¹]

stōkes (-ks) *n.* (*pl.* same). Unit of kinematic viscosity, corresponding to dynamic viscosity of

1 poise and density 1 gram per c.c. [f. Sir G. G. *Stokes*, British physicist d. 1903]

S.T.O.L. *abbr.* short take-off and landing (aircraft).

stō'la *n.* (*pl.* ~e). = foll. 1. [L, f. Gk *stolē* equipment, clothing (*stellō* put, array)]

stōle¹ *n.* **1.** (Rom. Ant.) Woman's long loose outer dress. **2.** (Eccl.) Strip of silk or other material hanging from back of neck over shoulders and down to knees (worn by deacon over left shoulder only). **3.** Woman's wrap of similar shape. [OE *stol(e)* f. as prec.]

stōle², **stō'len.** See STEAL.

stŏ'lĭd *a.* Phlegmatic, unemotional, lacking or seeming to lack animation, not easily excited, hard to stir, obstinate, apparently stupid; hence or cogn. **stolĭ'd**ITY *n.*, ~LY² *adv.* [f. obs. F *stolide* or f. L *stolidus*]

stō'lon *n.* (Bot.) reclined or prostrate branch that strikes root and develops new plant; (Zool.) rootlike creeping growth; hence ~ATE², ~ĭ'FEROUS, *adjs.* [f. L *stolo -onis*]

stō'ma *n.* (*pl.* ~s *or* ~ta). **1.** (Zool.) Small mouthlike opening of lower animals. **2.** (Bot.) Minute orifice in epidermis of leaf etc. [mod. L, f. Gk *stoma -atos* mouth]

sto'mach (-ŭ'mak) *n.*, & *v.t.* **1.** *n.* Internal organ in which first part of digestion occurs, in man a pear-shaped enlargement of the alimentary canal extending from end of gullet to beginning of gut (**on an empty** ~, not having recently eaten; **on a full** ~, after large meal); one of several digestive organs of animal, esp. ruminant, either of similar character or differing in action or function (*ruminant's* **first** ~ or paunch or rumen, **second** ~ or honeycomb or reticulum, **third** ~ or psalterium or omasum or manyplies, **fourth** or **true** ~ or reed or maw or abomasum; **muscular** ~ (acting by grinding or squeezing, as the gizzard). **2.** Belly, abdomen, lower front of body, (PIT¹ *of the stomach*); protuberant belly (*what a stomach he has got!*). **3.** Appetite for or *for* food (STAY¹ one's *stomach*). **4.** Taste or readiness or sufficient spirit *for* (or arch. *to*) controversy, conflict, danger, or an undertaking (*had no stomach for the fight*). **5.** **~-ache,** pain in belly, esp. in bowels; **~-pump,** syringe for emptying stomach or forcing liquid into it; **~-tooth,** lower canine milk-tooth in infants, cutting of which often disorders stomach; **~-tube** (for introducing through gullet into stomach to wash it out or empty it by siphon action); ~ **upset, upset** ~, temporary slight disorder of digestive system. **6.** Hence ~AL, ~LESS, *adjs.*, ~FUL 2 *n.* **7.** *v.t.* Eat with relish or toleration, find sufficiently palatable to swallow or keep down, (fig.) submit to or put up with (affront etc.), (usu. w. neg.; *cannot stomach it*). [ME *stomak* f. OF *stomaque*, *estomac* f. L f. Gk *stomakhos* gullet (*stoma* mouth)]

sto'macher (-ŭ'mak-) *n.* Ornament worn on bodice-front; (Hist.) front-piece of 15th–17th-c. woman's dress covering breast and pit of stomach, ending downwards in point often lapping over skirt, and often set with gems or richly embroidered. [ME, prob. f. OF *estomachier* (as prec.; see -ER²)]

stomă'chĭc (-k-) *a.* & *n.* **1.** *a.* Of the stomach; aiding stomach action, promoting digestion or appetite. **2.** *n.* Stomachic medicine or stimulant. [f. F *stomachique* or f. L f. Gk *stomakhikos* (as STOMACH; see -IC)]

stōmatī'tis *n.* Inflammation of the mucous membrane of the mouth. [f. as STOMA + -ITIS]

stōmatŏ'log|ȳ *n.* Science of (diseases of) the mouth; hence **stōmato**LO'GICAL *a.*, ~IST (3) *n.* [f. as STOMA + -O- + -LOGY]

stŏmp *n.*, & *v.i.* **1.** *n.* Lively jazz dance with heavy stamping. **2.** *v.i.* Dance stomp; tread heavily; *stamp one's feet. [U.S. dial. var. of STAMP]

stōne *n.*, *a.*, & *v.t.* **1.** *n.* Piece of rock of any shape usu. detached from earth's crust and of no great size, esp. a pebble, a cobble, or a single piece used or usable in building or road-making or as missile (*built of great stones*; *as hard as a stone*; ROCK³*ing-stone*; ROLL²*ing stone*; SERMONS *in stones*; STOCKS *and stones*); **~s will cry out,** wrong is great enough to move inanimate things; **give a ~ for bread,** offer a mockery of help; **mark with a white ~,** record as a joyful day [w. ref. to ancient-Roman use of chalk]; **meteoric** ~, meteorite; **leave no ~ unturned,** try every possible means (*to* do); **break ~s,** get living by preparing road-metal, (fig.) be reduced to extremities; **cast** or **throw ~s** or **a ~ at,** or **the first** ~, lit., or fig. = make aspersions on character etc. (of); **those who live in glass houses should not throw ~s,** aspersion by the vulnerable provokes damaging retort; *kill two* BIRDS *with one stone*; **~'s throw,** distance stone can be thrown, short or moderate distance. **2.** = PRECIOUS *stone* (*no stone in it worth less than £100*). **3.** Stones or rock as a substance or material (LIME¹*stone*, SAND*stone*; HOLYSTONE; PHILOSOPHERS' *stone*), esp. for building (PORTLAND *stone*); ~ **jar** etc. (of stoneware); **has a heart of** ~, is hard-hearted; **harden into** ~, petrify (lit. or fig.). **4.** Piece of stone of definite and designed shape (often with purpose specified by word in comb. or by context: GRAVE¹*stone*, GRIND*stone*, HEARTH*stone*, MILL¹*stone*, OIL¹*stone*, TOMB*stone*, WHET*stone*); (Print.) smooth flat surface on which type is imposed in pages. **5.** Thing resembling stone in hardness or pebble in shape, e.g. hard morbid concretion in the body (or disease in which these occur), hard case of kernel in stone-fruit, seed of grape, pellet of hail, (arch. or vulg.) testicle. **6.** (*pl.* same). ||Weight of 14 lb. (or of other amounts varying with the commodity) esp. as unit weighing person or large animal; **give a ~ and a beating to,** (orig. Racing sl.) surpass easily. **7. S~ Age,** stage of civilization in which tools and weapons were of stone not metal; **~-axe** (with two blunt edges for hewing stone); **~-blind,** completely blind; ***~ boat,** flat sledge carrying stones; **~-boiling,** primitive method of boiling by putting heated stones into water; **~-borer,** mollusc of genus *Lithophaga*; **~-brash,** subsoil of broken stones; ***~-broke,** = STONY 2; **~-cast,** = *stone's throw* (see sense 1); **~'chat,** small black and white European song-bird (*Saxicola torquata*), with alarm-note like knocking of pebbles; **~-coal,** anthracite; **~-cold,** completely cold; **~'crop,** plant of genus *Sedum*, esp. yellow-flowered plant growing on walls and rocks; **~-curlew,** large-headed bird of family Burhinidae; **~-dead, -deaf,** completely so; **~-eater,** = *stone-borer*; ***~-fence,** (sl.) whisky and cider, or similar mixed drink; **~-fern,** ceterach; **~-fish,** venomous tropical fish with erect dorsal spines; **~-fly,** insect of order Plecoptera, with aquatic larvae found under stones, used as bait; **~-fruit,** drupe (e.g. plum, peach, cherry); **~-ground** *a.*, ground with millstones; ||**~'-hatch,** ring-plover; *stone* JUG¹; ~ **lily,** fossil crinoid; **~-marten,** = BEECH-*marten*; **~'mason,** dresser of or builder in stone; **~-parsley,** umbelliferous hedge plant with aromatic seeds; **~-pine,** S. European pine-tree with branches at top spreading like umbrella; **~-pit,** quarry; **~-plover,** = *stone-curlew*; **~-saw,** untoothed iron blade stretched in saw-frame for cutting stone with aid of sand; **~-snipe,** (1) = *stone-curlew*, (2) large N. Amer. snipe; **~'wall** *v.i.*

& *t.*, obstruct by stonewalling; **~wa'lling,** (Cricket) excessively cautious batting, ||(Polit. etc.) obstruction of discussion; **~'ware,** pottery made from very siliceous clay or from composition of clay and flint; **~'weed,** gromwell; **~'work,** masonry; **~'wort,** (1) = *stone-parsley*, (2) plant of genus *Chara*, with calcareous deposit on stem. **8.** Hence **(-)stōn**ED² (-nd), ~'LESS (-nl-), *adjs.* **9.** *a.* Made of stone. **10.** *v.t.* Pelt with stones; ~ **the crows** (sl. excl. of surprise or disgust). **11.** Remove stones from (fruit). **12.** Face, pave, etc., with stone. **13.** (sl.; esp. in *p.p.*) Stupefy or stimulate with drink, drug, etc. [OE *stān*, = OS *stēn*, OHG *stein*, ON *steinn*, Goth. *stains* f. Gmc **stainaz*]

stŏnk *v.t.*, & *n.* Bombard(ment) with artillery. [20th c.; cf. dial. *stonk* game of marbles]

stŏ'nker *v.t.* (Austral. & N.Z. sl.) Baffle, tire, defeat. [20th c.; orig. unkn.]

stō'n|ȳ *a.* & *adv.* **1.** *a.* Full of, covered with, having many, stones; hard, rigid, fixed, as stone; (of stare etc.) refusing response or recognition; (of fear, grief, etc.) stupefying; **~y heart,** (1) obdurate or unfeeling heart, (2) hard core or interior; hence **~ĭ**LY² *adv.*, **~ĭ**NESS *n.* **2.** *a.* & *adv.* **~y(-broke)**, (sl.) entirely without money. [OE *stānig* (as STONE, -Y²)]

stŏŏd. See STAND¹.

stōōge *n.*, & *v.i.* (sl.) **1.** *n.* Butt, foil, esp. for a comedian; deputy, subordinate, esp. for routine or unpleasant work. **2.** *v.i.* Move, esp. fly, *about*, *around*, etc.; act as stooge *for*. [20th c., orig. U.S.; of unkn. orig.]

stŏŏk (*or* -ōōk) *n.*, & *v.t.* (chiefly Sc. & N. Engl.) = SHOCK³. [ME *stouk*, f. or cogn. w. MLG *stūke*]

stōōl *n.*, & *v.i.* **1.** *n.* (Usu. moveable) seat for one, having no back or arms and often consisting of wooden slab on three or four legs; CAMP¹-*stool*; MUSIC-*stool*; ~ **of repentance,** that on which fornicators etc. were set to receive rebuke in churches in Scotland, (fig.) humble position of repentance; **fall between two ~s,** fail from vacillation between two courses etc. **2.** = FOOT¹-*stool*; low bench for kneeling on; seat as symbol of authority; (Archit.) window-sill. **3.** (Place for) evacuation of bowels (*go to stool*); faeces evacuated. **4.** Root or stump of felled tree etc. from which shoots spring. **5.** *Decoy-bird. **6.** **~-ball,** old game resembling cricket still played in Sussex etc. esp. by girls; **~-pigeon,** pigeon used, person acting, as decoy, *police informer. **7.** *v.i.* Throw up shoots from root; (arch.) evacuate bowels; *(sl.) act as stool-pigeon. [OE *stōl*, = OS *stōl*, OHG *stuol*, ON *stóll*, Goth. *stōls* chair, throne f. Gmc **stōlaz* (**stō-*, **stā-* STAND¹)]

***stōō'lie** *n.* (sl.) Person acting as stool-pigeon. [f. prec. + -IE]

stōōp¹ *v.* & *n.* **1.** *v.i.* Bring one's head nearer the ground by bending forwards and down from standing position, (fig.) deign or condescend *to* do, descend or lower oneself *to* (some conduct, or abs.; ~ **to conquer,** gain power or one's end by preliminary self-abasement). **2.** Carry one's head and shoulders bowed forward. **3.** (Of hawk etc., or fig.) swoop, pounce, (*on*). **4.** *v.t.* Incline (head, neck, shoulders) forwards and down. **5.** *n.* Stooping carriage of body; (arch.) swoop of hawk etc. [OE *stūpian*, = MDu. *stūpen*, ON *stúpa* f. Gmc **stūp-*, rel. to STEEP¹]

stōōp². Var. of STOUP.

***stōōp³** *n.* Porch or small veranda in front of house. [f. Du. STOEP]

stŏp¹ *v.* (-pp-). **1.** *v.t.* Close or almost close up or *up* by plugging, obstructing, etc., prevent or forbid passage through, make impervious or impassable, close, bar, stifle, stanch, (*stop a leak*, *hole*, etc.); plug upper end of (organ-pipe), giving note an octave lower; (Bridge) be able to prevent opponents from taking all tricks in (suit); ||FILL (tooth) with **~'p**ING¹ *n.* of gold, amalgam, cement, etc.; ~ one's **ears,** put one's fingers in them to avoid hearing, (fig.) refuse to listen; ~ **a gap,** serve to meet a temporary need; ~ person's **mouth,** (fig.) induce him by bribery or other means to keep silence about something; ~ **the way,** be or act as obstruction, prevent progress. **2.** Put an end to (motion etc.), completely check progress or motion or operation of, effectively hinder or prevent, discontinue (one's action), (*stop cricket-ball*, *runaway horse*, *progress*; *stop* person's *doing*, person *from* doing; *stop me if I talk for too long*; *stop that noise!*; *shall stop their misbehaviour at once*; *shall stop playing*, *subscribing*, *my visits*, *my endeavours*; *do stop grumbling*, *your complaints*, *that noise*; ~ **it!,** desist from your action; ~ **thief!,** cry of pursuer); (Boxing) parry (blow), knock out (opponent); (sl.) receive (blow, bullet, etc.); make (sound) inaudible; (Hort.) pinch back (plant); make (clock, factory, etc.) cease working; **enough to ~ a clock,** (colloq., of face etc.) very ugly. **3.** Cut off, suspend, decline customary giving of or permission for, (*shall stop your wages*, *holidays*, *meetings*; *the cost must be stopped out of his salary*); ~ **(payment of)**, direct one's banker not to honour (cheque); ~ **payment,** declare oneself insolvent. **4.** Obtain desired pitch from (string of violin etc.) by pressing at appropriate point with finger, so shortening vibrating length; DOUBLE¹-*-stopping*. **5.** *v.i.* Cease, come to an end, (*noise*, *annuity*, *stops*; ~ **dead** or **short,** cease abruptly); cease from motion or speaking or action, make a halt or pause, (*car stopped outside the house*; *he stopped in the middle of a sentence*; *my watch*, *his heart*, *has stopped*; *train does not stop at* or *before Exeter*; *he never stops to think*); ~ **at nothing,** be ruthless; ||**~'ping train** (stopping at many intermediate stations). **6.** (colloq.) Remain, stay, sojourn, (*shall stop in bed*, *at home*; *shall you stop for the sermon?*; *have been stopping in Cornwall with friends*). **7.** *v.t.* ||Provide with stops, punctuate, (*a badly spelt and stopped letter*). **8.** (Naut.) Make fast, stopper, (cable etc.). **9.** *~ **by,** call at (place, or abs.); ~ **down,** (Photog.) reduce aperture of (lens, or abs.) with diaphragm; ~ **off,** fill in (part of mould not to be used) with sand; ~ **off,** ~ **over,** break one's journey; **~'off, ~'over,** a break in one's journey; ~ **out,** cover (part of area) to prevent printing, etching, etc., there. **10.** Hence **~'p**AGE (3) *n.* **11.** **~'cock,** externally-operated valve inserted in pipe to regulate passage of contents; **~'gap,** temporary substitute; **~-go,** alternate cessation and recommencement of progress; **~-lamp,** light on rear of motor vehicle showing when brakes are applied; **~-light,** (1) red traffic-light, (2) = *stop-lamp*; ||**~-press,** (late news) inserted in newspaper after printing has begun; ~ **valve** (closing pipe against passage of liquid); **~-volley,** (Lawn Tennis) checked volley close to net, dropping ball dead on other side; **~-watch** (with mechanism for instantly starting and stopping it at will, used in accurate timing of races etc.). [ME, f. OE *-stoppian*, = MLG *stoppen*, OHG *stopfōn*, WG f. LL *stuppare* STUFF 5 (see ESTOP)]

stŏp² *n.* **1.** Stopping or being stopped, pause, check, (*put a stop to*; *make*, *come to*, *bring to*, *a stop*; *train runs from London to Edinburgh without a stop*); place of regular stopping of bus, train, etc. **2.** Sign used to clarify meaning in written matter, punctuation-mark, esp. comma, semicolon, colon, or FULL¹ stop; (in telegrams etc.) = PERIOD 5. **3.** (Mus.) change of pitch effected by stopping (see prec. 4), (in organ) row of pipes of one character, knob etc. by which these are brought into action; (fig.) manner of speech adopted to produce particular effect (*can put on* or *pull out the pathetic, blustering, virtuous*, etc., *stop at will*; **with all the ~s out,** exerting extreme effort). **4.** Batten, peg, or the like, meant to stop motion of something at fixed point; (Bridge) card(s) stopping suit. **5.** (Opt. & Photog.) diaphragm, (device reducing) effective diameter of lens; (Phonet.) consonant sound made by closure of organs followed by audible release of air, as *g, k, t, p*; (Naut.) small line used as lashing. **6. ~-drill** (with shoulder limiting depth of penetration); **~-knob** (controlling organ-stop); **~-order** (to stockbroker to buy or sell on stock's reaching specified price, or preventing payment of funds in custody of law-court). **7.** Hence ~′LESS *a.* [ME, f. prec.]

stōpe *n.* Steplike part of mine where ore etc. is being extracted. [app. cogn. w. STEP²]

stŏ′ppage. See STOP¹ 10.

stŏ′pper *n.*, & *v.t.* **1.** *n.* In vbl senses; plug for closing bottle etc. usu. of same material as the vessel (**put a ~ on,** bring about cessation of); implement for pressing down tobacco in pipe-bowl; (Naut.) rope, clamp, double claw, etc., for checking and holding rope cable or chain cable; (Bridge) = prec. 4. **2.** *v.t.* Close or secure with stopper. [ME, f. STOP¹ + -ER¹]

stŏ′pple *n.*, & *v.t.* **1.** *n.* Stopper of bottle or other vessel; *ear-plug. **2.** *v.t.* Close with stopple. [ME; partly f. STOP¹ + -LE 1, partly f. ESTOPPEL]

stōr′age *n.* Storing of goods, data, etc., method of doing this (COLD¹ *storage*); space available for it; cost of warehousing; **~ battery, cell,** apparatus for storing electrical energy in a chemical form, accumulator; **~ heater,** electric heater accumulating heat outside peak hours, for later release. [f. STORE + -AGE]

stōr′ăx *n.* (Tree of genus *Styrax* yielding) fragrant resin formerly used as perfume; (**liquid**) ~, balsam got from Oriental tree of genus *Liquidambar*. [L f. Gk, var. of STYRAX]

stōre *n.*, *a.*, & *v.t.* **1.** *n.* Abundance, provision, stock of something ready to be drawn upon, (*has a store, a good store, stores, of wine, wit, anecdotes, wisdom*); **in ~,** kept in readiness, about to come, destined or intended *for* (*I have, tomorrow has, a surprise in store for you*). **2.** Place where things are kept for sale, *shop, ||large commercial establishment selling goods of many different kinds (**the ~s,** such establishment(s) opp. ordinary shops); warehouse for temporary keeping of furniture etc. **3.** Device in computer for storing and retrieving data or instructions. **4.** (in *pl.*) Articles of particular kind or for special purpose accumulated for use, supply of things needed, (*military, naval, etc., stores*; MARINE *stores*). **5. Lay, put,** or **set ~ by** or **on,** reckon precious or important (esp. *set no great store by*). **6.** *a.* Kept for future use; (of cattle etc.) not yet (being) fattened; *bought at shop, esp. (of clothes) ready-made. **7.** ***~-front,** (rooms etc. at) street front of a store; **~′house,** place where things are stored up, granary etc., (esp. fig.; person, *book, is a storehouse of information* etc.); **~′keeper,** person in charge of store(s), *shopkeeper; **~′man** (in charge of, or employed to handle, stored goods); **~-room** (in which household or other supplies are kept); **~-ship** (carrying stores for fleet, garrison, etc.). **8.** *v.t.* Stock or furnish adequately with or *with* something useful (usu. with knowledge or the like; *store your mind with facts*; *a well-stored memory*). **9.** Put in store, lay up or *up* or *away* for future use; deposit (furniture etc.) in a warehouse for temporary keeping. **10.** (Of receptacle) hold, keep, contain, have storage-accommodation for (*a single cell can store enough energy for 12 months' operation*). **11.** Hence **stōr′**ABLE *a.* [ME, f. obs. *astore* n. & v. f. OF (*estore* f.) *estorer* v. f. L *instaurare* renew; cf. RESTORE]

stōr′ey, stōr′ȳ², *n.* Any of the parts into which a house or building is divided horizontally, the whole of the rooms etc. having a continuous floor, (*fell from a third-storey window*; *a house of five storeys*); thing forming horizontal division; **upper ~,** (joc.) the brain or intellect; hence **(-)stōr′ey**ED², **(-)stōr′ied**², (-rĭd) *a.* [ME, f. AL *historia* HISTORY (perh. orig. meaning a tier of painted windows or sculpture)]

stōr′ĭ|ātėd *a.* Decorated with artistic historical, legendary, or emblematic designs; hence ~A′TION *n.* [f. HISTORIATED]

stōr′ied¹ (-rĭd) *a.* Celebrated in legend, associated with legends or stories or history; adorned with legendary or historical representations. [f. STORY¹ and *story* v. adorn thus + -ED¹,²]

storied². See STOREY.

stōrk *n.* Tall stately wading bird of family Ciconiidae, the best-known species pure white except for black wing-tips, long reddish bill, and red feet, sometimes nesting on buildings, and in the nursery the pretended bringer of babies; KING¹ *Stork*; **~'s-bill,** plant of genus *Pelargonium* or *Erodium*. [OE *storc*, = OS *stork*, OHG *stor(a)h*, ON *storkr* f. Gmc **sturkaz* (prob. rel. to STARK¹, from its rigid posture)]

stōrm *n.* & *v.* **1.** *n.* Violent disturbance of the atmosphere with thunder (THUNDER*storm*), strong wind, or heavy rain or snow (SNOW¹*storm*) or hail (HAIL¹*storm*), a tempest; **~ in a teacup,** great excitement over trivial matter. **2.** (Meteorol.) Wind intermediate between gale and hurricane (on Beaufort scale, of 55–72 m.p.h.). **3.** Violent disturbance of the established order in human affairs, tumult, agitation, war, invasion, dispute, etc. (**~ and stress,** period of fermenting ideas and unrest in person's or nation's life [f. G. *sturm und drang*, used as title of a play characteristic of the literary movement in Germany *c.* 1770–82]). **4.** Violent shower *of* missiles or outbreak *of* hisses, applause, indignation, etc. **5.** Direct assault by troops on fortified place, capture *of* place by such assault; **take by ~,** capture thus, (fig.) rapidly captivate audience or person. **6. ~-belt,** tract in which storms are frequent or regular; **~-bird,** stormy PETREL; **~-bound,** prevented by storms from leaving port or continuing voyage; **~-centre,** point to which wind blows spirally inward in cyclonic storm, (fig.) subject etc. upon which agitation or disturbance is concentrated; **~-cloud,** heavy rain-cloud, (fig.) state of affairs that threatens disturbances; **~-cock,** missel-thrush; **~-collar,** high coat-collar that can be turned up and fastened; ||**~-cone,** tarred-canvas cone hoisted as warning of high wind, upright for north and inverted for south; **~-door,** additional outer door for protection in bad weather or winter; ||**~-finch,** stormy PETREL; **~-glass,** sealed tube containing a solution of which the clarity is thought to change when storms approach; ||**~-lantern,** hurricane lamp; *storm* PETREL; **~-sail** (of smaller size and stouter canvas than the corresponding one used in ordinary weather); **~-signal,** device warning of an approaching storm; **~-troops,** (1) shock-troops, (2) Nazi political militia (**~-trooper,** member of this); **~-window,** additional outer sash-window used like storm-door; **~-zone,** = *storm-belt*. **7.** Hence ~′LESS, ~′PROOF², *adjs.* **8.** *v.i.* (Of wind, rain, etc.) rage, be violent; move violently or angrily (*stormed out of the meeting*). **9.** Talk violently, rage, bluster, (*at* or *against*). **10.**

v.t. & *i.* Attack or capture by storm (**~'ing--party,** detachment ordered to begin assault). [OE, = OS *storm*, OHG *sturm*, ON *stormr* f. Gmc **sturmaz* prob. f. **stur-* STIR¹]

stŏr'm|ў *a.* Of marked violence, raging, vehement, boisterous, (*stormy wind, sea, waves, passions, temper, abuse*); subject to or troubled with storms (lit. or fig.; *a stormy coast, sea, night, debate, life*); associated with or threatening storms (*a stormy sunset*; *stormy* PETREL); hence ~ĭLY² *adv.*, ~ĭNESS *n.* [ME, f. prec. + -Y²]

stŏr'ў¹ *n.* **1.** Past course of person's or institution's life (*his story is an eventful one*; *in our rough island-story*). **2.** Account given of an incident or series of events (*they all tell the same story*; *according to his own story, which may or may not be true*); **the (old,) old** (or **same old**) ~, (fig.) the very familiar course of events; **to cut** or **make a long ~ short** (formula excusing omission of details); **it is quite another ~ now,** (fig.) things have greatly changed; **the ~ goes,** it is said. **3.** Piece of narrative, tale of any length told or printed in prose or verse of actual or fictitious events, legend, myth, anecdote, novel, romance, (*tell me a story*; *but is the story true?*); narrative or descriptive item of news; **good** or **funny ~,** amusing anecdote often embodying witticism or ludicrous situation; SHORT *story*; **but that is another ~** (formula for breaking off and tantalizing reader with allusion). **4.** Main facts or plot of novel or epic or play (*reads only for the story*; *the story is the least part of the book*). **5.** Facts or experiences that deserve narration (*that face must have a story belonging to it*). **6.** (colloq. or childish). Lie, fib; liar (*oh, you story!*). **7.** **~-book** (containing story or stories); *~-book ending* etc. (romantically happy); **~-line,** = sense 4; **~--teller,** (1) person esp. in Orient making a living by telling stories to audiences, person who tells stories to audience of children, (2) writer of stories, (3) retailer of anecdotes in society, (4, colloq.) liar. [ME *storie* f. AF *estorie* (OF *estoire*) f. L (as HISTORY)]

stŏr'ў². See STOREY.

stoup (-ōōp) *n.* Flagon, beaker, drinking-vessel; holy-water basin. [ME, f. ON *staup* = OE *stēap*, OHG *stouf* f. Gmc **staupaz, -am*, cogn. w. STEEP²]

stout *a.* & *n.* **1.** *a.* Brave, doughty, resolute, vigorous, sturdy, stubborn, staunch, (*made a stout resistance*; *a stout opponent*); **~ fellow,** (arch. or colloq.) brave fighter etc.; **a ~ heart,** courage; **~-hear'ted,** courageous. **2.** Of considerable thickness or strength (*a stout stick, ship*, etc.); corpulent, bulky, tending to fatness. **3.** Hence ~'ISH¹ 2 *a.*, ~'LY² *adv.*, ~'NESS *n.* **4.** *n.* Strong dark beer brewed with roasted malt or barley. [ME, f. AF & dial. OF *(e)stout* f. WG **stult-*, perh. rel. to STILT]

stōve¹ *n.*, & *v.t.* **1.** *n.* Closed apparatus in which heat is produced by combustion of fuel or electrically for use in warming rooms, cooking, etc.; ||(Hort.) hothouse with artificial heat; **~-enamel** (heat-proof kind produced by treatment of enamelled objects in stove); **~-pipe** (conducting smoke and gases from stove to chimney); ***~-pipe hat,** tall silk hat. **2.** *v.t.* ||Force or raise (plants) in stove. [ME = sweating-room, f. MDu., MLG *stove*, OHG *stuba* f. Gmc **stubh-*, perh. rel. to STEW²]

stōve². See STAVE².

stow (-ō) *v.t.* Pack (goods etc.) in right or convenient places without waste of room; (Naut.) place (cargo, provisions) in proper place and order; fill (receptacle) with articles compactly arranged; (sl., esp. in *imper.*) abstain from, cease to indulge in (**~ it,** cease talking etc.); **~ away,** place (thing) where it will not cause obstruction, conceal oneself on board ship etc. so as to travel without charge or escape unseen; **~'away,** (1) person who does this, (2) place where things may be stowed away; hence ~'AGE (1, 3, 4) *n.* [ME, f. *bestow*; in Naut. use perh. infl. by Du. *stouwen*]

S.T.P. *abbr.* Professor of Sacred Theology [f. L *Sanctae Theologiae Professor*]; standard temperature and pressure.

str. *abbr.* strait; stroke (oar).

strabĭ'sm|us (-z-) *n.* (Path.) Squinting, squint; hence ~IC, ~AL, *adjs.* [mod. L, f. Gk *strabismos* (*strabizō* squint f. *strabos* squinting; see -ISM)]

Străd *n.* (colloq.) Stradivarius. [abbr.]

stră'ddle *v.* & *n.* **1.** *v.i.* Take or be in attitude with legs wide apart, (of legs) be wide apart. **2.** *v.t.* Stand or sit across (thing) thus (*cannot straddle his horse*; *stood straddling the ditch*); part (one's legs) widely; drop shots or bombs short of and beyond (target etc.); (fig.) vacillate between two policies etc. regarding (an issue). **3.** *n.* Act of straddling (lit. or fig.); doubling of stakes in poker; (St. Exch.) option giving holder the right of either calling for or delivering stock at fixed price. [alt. of *striddle*, back form. f. *striddlings* astride f. *strid-* = STRIDE; see -LE 3]

|**Strădĭvār'ĭus** (*or* -âr'-) *n.* Violin or other stringed instrument made by Antonio Stradivari of Cremona (d. 1737) or his followers. [Latinized f. *Stradivari*]

strafe (-ahf) *v.t.*, & *n.* (sl.) **1.** *v.t.* Bombard, harass with shells, bombs, sniping, etc.; reprimand; abuse; thrash. **2.** *n.* Piece of strafing. [joc. adaptation of G 1914 catchword *Gott* ~ (God punish) *England*]

stră'ggl|e *v.i.*, & *n.* **1.** *v.i.* Stray from the main body, fail to remain compact (*straggling village*), get dispersed, proceed in scattered irregular order (*crowd straggled along*), be sporadic, occur here and there, (of plant, beard, etc.) grow long and loose; hence ~ER¹ *n.*, ~Y² *a.* **2.** *n.* Body or group of straggling or scattered persons or things. [ME, perh. alt. f. **strackle* frequent. of dial. *strake* go, rel. to STRETCH; see -LE 3]

straight (-āt) *a.*, *n.*, & *adv.* **1.** *a.* Without curve or bend, extending uniformly in same direction, (of line, Geom.) lying evenly between any two of its points; (of arch) flat-topped; (of person's back) not bowed; (of hair) not curly or wavy; (of knee) not bent; (of legs) not bandy or knock--kneed; (of skirt) not flared; coming direct from its source; undiluted, unmodified; successive (*ten straight wins*). **2.** (Of aim, look, blow, course) going direct to the mark; upright, honest, candid, not evasive, (*straight dealings, answer, speaking*; *is perfectly straight, straight as a die, in all his dealings*); (of thinking) logical, not swayed by emotion; (of drama etc.) without music and not portraying abnormal behaviour etc. **3.** In proper order or place or condition, duly arranged, level, symmetrical, (*are the pictures, is my tie, hair, straight?*); (sl.) heterosexual; **put things ~,** get rid of disorder; *get, keep, put, set, the facts* or RECORD² *straight*. **4.** **~ bat,** (Cricket) bat held vertically, (fig.) honourable behaviour; **~-edge,** bar with one edge accurately straight, used for testing; **~-eight,** motor vehicle with eight cylinders in line; **~ eye,** ability to detect deviation from the straight; **~ face** (intentionally expressionless, esp. avoiding smile though amused); ||**~ fight,** (Polit.) direct contest between two candidates; *straight* FLUSH⁵ (cf. sense 6); **~ man,** person who says things so that comedian can make jokes about them; ***~ razor** (cut-throat); ***~ ticket,** (voting for) party programme or candidate-list without modification; **~ tip,** hint (esp. as to likely winner of race or prospects of investment) got from good authority; **~'way,** (arch.) at once, immediately. **5.** Hence ~'EN[6] *v.t.* & *i.* (**~en up,** stand erect after bending), ~'LY[2] *adv.*, ~'NESS *n.* **6.** *n.* Straight condition (**on the ~**, opp. *on the* BIAS[1]; **out of the ~**, crooked); straight part of something, esp. concluding stretch of racecourse (*they were level as they reached the straight*); (sl.) straight person; sequence of five cards in poker. **7.** *adv.* In a straight line, direct, without deviation or hesitation or circumlocution, (*comes straight from Paris*; *is making straight for a precipice*; *I told him straight, told it him straight out*); **go ~**, (fig.) not be dishonest or criminal; *straight from the* SHOULDER. **8.** In right direction, with good aim, (*shoot straight*); correctly (*does not see straight*); (arch.) at once, immediately. **9.** ~ **away,** (colloq.) immediately; ***~'away,** straight (course etc.), straightforward; ~ **off,** without hesitation, deliberation, etc., (*cannot tell you straight off*). **10.** **~-bred,** not cross-bred; **~-cut,** (of tobacco) cut lengthwise into long silky fibres; ***~-out,** (Polit. etc.) uncompromising. [ME, p.p. of STRETCH]

straightfŏr'ward (-ăt-) *a.* Honest, open, frank; (of task etc.) presenting no complications; hence ~LY[2] *adv.*, ~NESS *n.* [f. prec. 7 + FORWARD[1]]

strain[1] *v.* **1.** *v.t.* Stretch tightly, make taut; exercise to greatest possible or beyond legitimate extent, press to extremes, wrest or distort from true intention or meaning, = STRETCH 2; *strain every* NERVE; ~ one's **ears, eyes, voice,** etc., listen etc. to best of one's power (see also sense 4); ~ one's **authority, powers, rights,** etc., or **the law** etc., apply them beyond their province or in violation of their true intention. **2.** Hug (person) *to* oneself or one's breast etc. **3.** (in *p.p.*) Produced under compulsion or by effort, artificial, forced, constrained, not spontaneous or natural, (*strained manner, laugh, cordiality,* etc.); **~ed interpretation** etc. (involving unreasonable assumption as to grammar etc.). **4.** Overtask, injure or try or imperil by over-use or making of excessive demands, (*take care not to strain your eyes, voice,* etc.; *for fear of straining his followers' loyalty*; *has strained a muscle, his leg, his heart,* etc.); ~ **oneself,** injure oneself by effort, (fig.) make undue exertions; **~ed relations,** dangerous or unpleasant tension between parties who have tried each other's forbearance too far. **5.** *v.i.* Make intense effort, strive intensely *after*, tug *at*, hold out with difficulty under or *under* pressure, (*the straining horses, masts*; *plants straining upwards to the light*; *dogs, horses, rowers, strain at the leash, collar, oar*; *porter straining under his load*; *strains too much after epigram, effect,* etc.). **6.** *v.t.* & *i.* Clear (liquid) of solid matter by passing through sieve or other ~'ER[1] (2) *n.*; filter (solids) *out* from liquid; (of liquid) percolate; ~ **at a gnat,** be unduly scrupulous or fussy about trifles (w. ref. to Matt. 23:24, where sense is prop. 'strain a liquid if it contains even a gnat'). **7.** Hence ~'ABLE *a.* [ME, OF *estreindre estrei(g)n-* f. L *stringere strict-* draw tight]

strain[2] *n.* **1.** Pull, stretching force, tension, demand upon or force that tries cohesion or strength or stability or resources, exertion required to meet such demand or to do something difficult, injury or change of structure resulting from such exertion or force, (*the strain on the rope was tremendous*; *was a great strain on my resources, attention, credulity*; *could not stand* or *take the strain,* lit. or fig.; *the strains of modern life*; *has a strain in his leg*; *is suffering from strain* or *overstrain*); **at (full)** ~ or **on the ~**, exerted to the utmost. **2.** (Phys.) Condition of a body subjected to stress, molecular displacement; quantity measuring this, equal to amount of deformation usu. divided by original dimension. **3.** (in *sing.* or *pl.*) Burst or snatch or spell of music or poetry (*martial, inspiriting, pathetic,* etc., *strains*; *heard strains of 'Tosca' from the bathroom*). **4.** Tone or style adopted in talking or writing, tendency of discourse, (*he went on in another strain*; *and much more in the same strain*). **5.** Moral tendency forming part of a character (*there is a strain of weakness, ferocity, mysticism, in him*). **6.** Breed of animals, plants, cells, etc.; human stock or family, (*comes of a good strain*). [ME, f. prec.; sense 6 f. OE **strēon* gain, progeny]

strait *a.* & *n.* **1.** *a.* (arch.) Narrow, limited, confined or confining. **2.** ~ **gate,** limitation of access (w. ref. to Matt. 7:14); **~-jacket** or ‖**-waistcoat,** (*n.*) strong garment put on violent person to confine arms, (fig.) restrictive measures, (*v.t.*) confine thus (lit. or fig.); **~-laced,** (fig.) severely virtuous, morally scrupulous, puritanic. **3.** (arch.) Strict, rigorous, (*straitest sect,* w. ref. to Acts 26:5). **4.** Hence ~'LY[2] *adv.* ~'NESS *n.*, (arch.) **5.** *n.* (in *sing.* or *pl.*) Narrow passage of water connecting two seas or large bodies of water; (usu. in *pl.*) difficult position, need, distress, (*in desperate, dire, straits*). [ME *streit,* f. OF *estreit* tight, narrow (place), f. L *strictus* STRICT]

strai'ten *v.t.* & *i.* **1.** (arch.) Make or become narrow. **2.** *v.t.* Restrict in range or scope; **~ed circumstances,** inadequate means of living, poverty; **~ed for** or **in,** (arch.) not amply supplied with. [f. prec. + -EN[6]]

strāke *n.* Continuous line of planking or plates from stem to stern of ship (GARBOARD *strake*); section of iron rim of wheel. [ME, app. f. **strak-*, cogn. w. OE *streccan* STRETCH]

stramō'nĭum *n.* (Drug, much used in asthma, from dried leaves of) datura. [mod. L, perh. f. Tartar *turman* horse-medicine]

strănd[1] *n.* & *v.* **1.** *n.* (rhet. or poet.) Margin of sea, lake, or river, esp. foreshore. **2.** *v.t.* & *i.* Run aground; (in *p.p.*) in difficulties, unable to get along esp. for want of funds or other resources, left behind while others advance. [OE, = MLG *strand-*, ON *strönd*]

strănd[2] *n.*, & *v.t.* **1.** *n.* One of the strings or wires that are twisted together to make a rope etc.; constituent filament in necklace, hair, DNA, etc.; (fig.) element or strain in any composite whole. **2.** *v.t.* Break a strand in (rope); arrange in strands. [ME; orig. unkn.]

strānge (-nj) *a.* **1.** Foreign, alien, (*in a strange land*), not one's own (*worship strange gods*), not familiar or well known (*to*), (*cannot play on a strange ground, with a strange racket*; *the place, work, handwriting, is strange to me*). **2.** Novel, queer, peculiar, eccentric, singular, surprising, unaccountable, unexpected, (*it is a strange thing, story*; *how strange that you should not have heard!*; *wears the strangest clothes*; *truth is stranger than fiction*; *repeating the question with strange persistence*); **feel ~**, not be in one's usual condition, esp. feel dizzy etc. (see also sense 4); **it feels ~**, it is an unaccustomed sensation; ~ **particle,** (Phys.) elementary particle classified according to a property conserved in strong interactions; ~ **to say,** (parenth.) it is surprising that. **3.** Hence ~'LY[2] (-njlĭ) *adv.* **4.** Fresh or unaccustomed *to*, unacquainted, bewildered, (*am strange to the work*); **am quite ~ here,** do not know my way about or the people etc.; **feel ~**, feel not at home, out of one's element etc. (see also sense 2). **5.** Hence ~'NESS (-njn-) *n.* [ME, f. OF *estrange* f. L *extraneus* EXTRANEOUS]

strā'nger (-nj-) *n.* **1.** Foreigner, person in a country or town or company that he does not belong to, person unknown to or *to* oneself or another; person entirely unaccustomed *to* some feeling or practice or experience; floating tea-

-leaf etc. held to foretell arrival of a visitor. **2. Am a ~ here, to the town,** etc., do not know my way about etc.; ||**I spy ~s,** (in House of Commons) I demand withdrawal of all but members and officials; **make a, no, ~ of,** treat distantly, cordially; **you are quite a ~,** you are seldom seen here now; **he is no, a, ~ to me,** I know, do not know, him; **is a, no, ~ to,** has had no, much, experience of; **the little ~,** (joc.) new-born child. [ME, f. OF *estrangier* f. Rom. **extranearius* f. L (as prec.; see -ER² (2))]

stră'ngle (-ngg*e*l) *v.t.* Throttle, kill by external compression of throat; (of collar etc.) squeeze (neck); (fig.) hamper or suppress (movement, impulse, cry, etc.); **~hold,** wrestling hold that throttles opponent, deadly grip (lit. or fig.). [ME, f. OF *estrangler* f. L *strangulare* f. Gk *straggalaō* (*straggalē* halter; cf. *straggos* twisted)]

stră'ngler *n.* In vbl senses; ||throttle of petrol engine. [f. prec. + -ER¹]

stră'ngles (-ngg*e*lz) *n. pl.* (usu. treated as *sing.*) Infectious streptococcal fever of horse, ass, etc. [pl. of *strangle* n. f. STRANGLE]

stră'ngūl|āte (-ngg-) *v.t.* (Path. & Surg.) Prevent circulation through (vein, intestine, etc.) by compression; remove (tumour) etc. by binding with cord; **~ated hernia** (in which constriction arrests circulation in protruding part). [f. L (as STRANGLE) + -ATE³]

străngūlā'tion (-ngg-) *n.* Strangling or being strangled; strangulating. [f. L *strangulatio* (as prec.; see -ATION)]

stră'ngūrȳ (-ngg-) *n.* Disease in which urine is passed painfully and in drops; so **străngūr'ĭous** (-ngg-) *a.* [ME, f. L f. Gk *straggouria* (*stragx -ggos* drop squeezed out, *ouron* urine; see -Y¹)]

străp *n.*, & *v.t.* (-pp-). **1.** *n.* Strip of leather; strip of leather or other flexible material with buckle or other fastening for holding things together or other purpose (CHIN-*strap*, SHOULDER-*strap*); loop for grasping to steady oneself in moving vehicle; strip of metal used to secure or connect, leaf of hinge, etc.; (Bot.) tongue-shaped part in floret; (**the**) ~, chastisement with a strap. **2. ~'hanger,** bus or train passenger who has to stand and hold strap for lack of sitting-space; **~-laid,** (of rope) made by laying ropes side by side and joining them into a flat band; **~-oil,** (sl.) beating given with strap; **~-work,** ornamentation imitating plaited straps. **3.** Hence ~'LESS *a.*, (of garment) without (shoulder-)straps. **4.** *v.t.* Secure with strap (*up, down,* etc.); (colloq., esp. in *p.p.*) subject to dearth; close (wound), bind (part), up or *up* with adhesive plaster or **~'p**ING¹ (4) *n.*; flog with strap; (in *part.* as *a.*) big, tall, sturdy, (*a strapping girl, fellow*), whence **~'p**ER¹ *n.* [dial. form of STROP]

strappā'dō *n.* (*pl.* ~s), & *v.t.* (Hist.) **1.** *n.* Torture inflicted by securing person's hands or other part in ropes, raising him, and letting him fall till brought up with jerk by taut rope. **2.** *v.t.* Subject to strappado. [f. F (*e*)*strapade* f. It. *strappata* (*strappare* snatch)]

străss *n.* = PASTE¹ 6. [G, f. name of inventor, Josef *Strasser* (18th c.)]

strata(l). See STRATUM.

stră'tagem *n.* (An) artifice, trick(ery), device(s) for deceiving enemy, (*devised a stratagem; must be effected by stratagem*). [ME, f. F *stratagème* f. L *stratagema* f. Gk *stratēgēma* f. *stratēgeō* be a general (*stratēgos*, f. *stratos* army + *agō* lead)]

stratē'g|ĭc *a.* Of, dictated by, serving the ends of, strategy (*strategic skill, considerations, movement, position*); (of materials) essential in war; (of bombing) designed to disorganize the enemy's internal economy and to destroy morale (opp. *tactical*); hence ~ICAL *a.*, ~ICALLY *adv.*, ~ICS *n.* [f. F *stratégique* f. Gk *stratēgikos* (as prec.; see -IC)]

stră'tėg|ȳ *n.* Generalship, the art of war, (lit. or fig.); management of an army or armies in a campaign, art of so moving or disposing troops or ships or aircraft as to impose upon the enemy the place and time and conditions for fighting preferred by oneself, (cf. TACTICS); instance of, or plan formed according to, this; hence ~IST (3) *n.* [f. F *stratégie* f. Gk *stratēgia* generalship (*stratēgos*; see STRATAGEM, -Y¹)]

străth *n.* (Sc.) Broad mountain valley; **~spey'** (-ā'), (music for) a lively Scottish dance (named f. *Strathspey* valley of the river Spey). [f. Gael. *srath*]

stratĭ'cūlate *a.* (Geol.) Arranged in thin layers. [f. STRATUM, after *vermiculate* etc.]

stră'tĭ|fȳ *v.t.* (esp. in *p.p.*) Arrange in strata; construct in layers, social grades, etc.; so ~FICA'TION *n.* (**~ficational grammar,** treating language as comprising several structural layers with different syntactic rules). [f. F *stratifier* (as STRATUM; see -FY)]

stratĭ'graphȳ *n.* (Geol.) (Study of) order and relative position of strata; hence **străti**GRA'PHIC(AL) *adjs.* [f. STRATUM + -I- + -GRAPHY]

stră'tō- *comb. form.* **1.** Stratus, as: **~ci'rrus, ~cu'mulus,** clouds combining features of stratus and cirrus or cumulus. **2.** Stratosphere, as: **~-cruiser,** jet air-liner travelling in stratosphere; **~pause,** interface between stratosphere and ionosphere. [f. STRATUS or STRATUM + -O-]

stratŏ'cracȳ *n.* Military government, domination by soldiers. [f. Gk *stratos* army + -CRACY]

stră'tosph|ēre *n.* Layer of atmospheric air above troposphere, in most of which the temperature ceases to fall with increasing height, remaining constant; hence **~ĕ'r**IC *a.* [f. foll. + -O- + SPHERE, after *atmosphere*]

strā't|um (*or* -ah'-) *n.* (*pl.* ~a). (Geol. etc.) layer, or set of successive layers, of any deposited substance; layer of atmosphere, biological tissue, or other structure; social grade (*the various strata of society*); hence ~AL *a.* [L, = something spread or laid down, neut. p.p. (as n.) of *sternere* strew]

strā't|us (*or* -ah'-) *n.* (*pl.* ~i *pr.* -ī). Continuous horizontal sheet of cloud. [L, p.p. of *sternere* (see prec.)]

straw¹ *n.* **1.** Dry cut stalks of grain as material for bedding, thatching, packing, hats, fodder, etc., (*made of, thatched* etc. *with, straw; a load of straw; straw mattress, hat, rope,* etc.; **in the ~,** (arch.) in parturition; **man of ~,** stuffed effigy, imaginary person set up as opponent, surety, etc., person undertaking financial commitment without adequate means, sham argument set up for demolition); straw hat. **2.** Single stalk or piece of straw; insignificant trifle (*is not worth a straw; don't care a straw*); hollow tube orig. of straw for sucking drink through; CHEESE¹ *straw*; **make bricks without ~,** try to work without adequate means (w. ref. to Exod. 5:7); **catch** or **grasp at a ~,** resort to utterly inadequate expedient, like a drowning man; **the last ~,** slight addition that makes something no longer bearable (as with camel's load), limit of tolerance or controllable vexation; **~ in the wind,** slight hint that suggests much. **3. ~-board,** coarse cardboard made of straw pulp; ***~ boss,** assistant foreman; **~-colour(ed),** (of) pale yellow; ***~ poll** or **vote,** unofficial balloting as test of strength of support; **~-worm,** caddis-worm. **4.** Hence ~'Y² *a.* [OE *strēaw*, = OS, OHG *strō*, ON *strá* f. Gmc **strawam*, cogn. w. STREW]

straw² *v.t.* (arch.) Strew. [f. var. of OE *stre(o)wian* STREW]

straw'berrў *n.* (Plant of genus *Fragaria,* with white flowers, trifoliate leaves, and) pulpy red fruit having surface studded with yellow seeds; **crushed ~,** dull crimson colour; **~ blonde,** (woman with) yellowish-red (hair); ||**the ~ leaves,** ducal rank, w. ref. to ornamentation of duke's coronet; **~-mark,** soft reddish birthmark; **~ pear,** (fruit of) W. Ind. cactaceous plant (*Hylocereus undatus*); *strawberry* ROAN[1]; **~ tongue,** red swollen tongue as in scarlet fever; **~-tree,** (1) evergreen tree (*Arbutus unedo*) bearing strawberry-like fruit, (2) Amer. spindle-tree with crimson pods. [OE *strēa(w)berige, strēowberige* (as STRAW[1], BERRY[1]; reason for name unknown)]

stray *v.i., n.,* & *a.* **1.** *v.i.* Wander, go aimlessly, deviate from the right way or from virtue, lose one's way, get separated from flock or companions or proper place; (in *p.p.*) that has gone astray. **2.** *n.* Strayed domestic animal; strayed thing or person (WAIF*s and strays*); (esp. in *pl.*) electrical phenomena interfering with radio reception. **3.** *a.* Strayed; scattered, sporadic, occurring or met with now and then or casually or unexpectedly, (*a few stray instances; a stray customer or two came in; hit by a stray bullet; lucky enough to find a stray taxi*); (Phys.) wasted or unwanted (*eliminate stray magnetic fields*). [ME, f AF & OF *estrayer* v., AF *(a)strey* n. & a. f. OF *estraié* (as ASTRAY)]

streak *n.* & *v.* **1.** *n.* Long narrow irregular line or band or layer-edge, esp. one distinguished by colour or substance and visible on a surface (*black with red streaks; a streak of light above the horizon*); line of bacteria etc. placed on culture medium; **~ of lightning,** flash (*like a ~ of lightning, like a ~,* swiftly); ||*the* SILVER[1] *streak.* **2.** (fig.) Strain, element, (*has a streak of humour, superstition,* etc., *in him*); spell, series, (*had a long winning streak*). **3.** Hence **~'**Y[2] *a.*; **~y bacon** (having alternate streaks of fat and lean). **4.** *v.t.* (usu. in *p.p.*) Mark with streak(s). **5.** *v.i.* Move very rapidly (like a streak of lightning); (colloq.) run through public place while indecently unclothed, whence ~'ER[1], ~'ING[1] (1), *ns.* [OE *strica* pen-stroke, = OHG *strich,* Goth. *striks* f. Gmc **strik-* STRIKE]

stream *n.* & *v.* **1.** *n.* Body of water flowing in bed, river or (esp.) brook, (*on the banks of a stream;* UPSTREAM, DOWNSTREAM); hence ~'LESS *a.,* ~'LET *n.* **2.** Flow of any liquid, onward moving fluid mass or crowd, (in *sing.* or *pl.*) large quantity of or *of* something that flows or moves along, (*saw a stream of lava; came out, went by, in a stream* or *streams; a stream* or *streams of blood, tears, people*); ||group of schoolchildren selected as being of similar ability for a given age; **~ of consciousness,** (literary style depicting) continuous flow of person's thoughts and conscious reactions to events. **3.** Current, direction of flow, (*with, against, the stream; the stream of tendency, thought, is the other way*); **go with the ~,** do as others do. **4. ~-anchor** (intermediate in size between bower and kedge esp. for use in warping); **~'line,** (*n.*) natural course of water or air currents, shape of aircraft, motor car, etc., calculated to cause least resistance to motion, (*v.t.*) give a streamline form to, (fig.) simplify, make more efficient or better organized. **5.** *v.i.* Flow or move as a stream; run with liquid (*streaming eyes, nose, cold, windows, umbrella*); (of banner, loose hair, etc.) float or wave in the wind. **6.** *v.t.* Emit stream of (blood etc.); ||arrange (pupils of school) in streams. [OE *strēam,* = OS *strōm,* OHG *stroum,* ON *straumr* f. Gmc **straumaz* f. IE **srou-* flow]

strea'mer *n.* Pennon, ribbon attached at one end and floating or waving at the other; narrow strip of paper thus used; banner headline; (in *pl.*) aurora borealis. [ME, f. prec. + -ER[1]]

street *n.* **1.** Town or village road that has (mainly) contiguous houses on one side or both, this with the houses, (*go down, across, the street; lives in the next street; window looks on the street; in Oxford Street,* **on 57th Street;* HIGH, MAIN[3], SIDE[1]-, etc., *street*); **in the ~,** outside the houses, (of St. Exch. business) done after closing-time; KEY[1] *of the street;* MAN[1] *in* or **on the street;* **not in the same ~ with,** (colloq.) utterly inferior to in ability etc.; **on the ~s,** living by prostitution; **~s ahead (of),** (colloq.) much superior (to); **(right) up** one's **~,** (colloq.) familiar or acceptable; WOMAN *of the streets.* **2.** Persons who live or work in a street; **the S~,** street or district associated with particular occupation etc., esp. ||FLEET[2] Street or *WALL STREET. **3.** *Street* ARAB; ***~'car,** tram; ||**~ cries** (of hawkers); **~ door,** main outer house-door opening on street; **~-sweeper,** person, or machine with revolving brush, employed for cleaning streets; **~-walker,** prostitute seeking customers in street. **4.** Hence (-)~'ED[2] *a.,* ~'WARD *adv.* & *a.* [OE *strǣt,* = OS *strāta,* OHG *strāz(z)a,* f. LL *strāta (via)* paved (way), fem. p.p. of *sternere* lay down]

strĕngth (*or* -ngkth) *n.* **1.** Being strong, degree or respect in which person or thing is strong, (*the strength of a man, rope, fortress, current, magnetic field, argument, fleet; the strength of wine, acid, tea, evidence; strength of body, mind, will, memory, judgement; his strength is in endurance; tensile, compressive, strength of a beam; has not the strength to lift a cup, to walk upstairs; that is beyond human, too much for my, strength*); *argue* etc. **from ~,** from a strong position; **from ~ to ~,** with ever-increasing success; MEASURE[2] one's *strength with;* **on the ~ of,** encouraged by or relying on or arguing from (*I did it on the strength of your promise*). **2.** What makes strong (*God is our strength; his strength is patience*). **3.** Proportion of whole number present (*were there in great, full, strength*); full complement (*up to, below, strength*); **in ~,** in large numbers; **on the ~,** (Mil. etc.) on the muster-roll. **4.** Hence ~'LESS *a.* [OE *strengthu,* = OHG *strengida* f. Gmc **strangithō* (as STRONG; see -TH[1])]

strĕ'ngthen (*or* -ngkth-) *v.t.* & *i.* Make or become stronger; **~** person's **hand(s),** (fig.) encourage him to vigorous action. [ME, f. prec. + -EN[6]]

strĕ'nūous *a.* Energetic, unrelaxing, ardently persistent; requiring exertion; hence ~LY[2] *adv.,* ~NESS *n.* [f. L *strenuus* brisk + -OUS]

strĕp *n.* (colloq.) = foll. [abbr.]

strĕptocŏ'cc|us *n.* (*pl.* **~i** *pr.* -kī). Bacterium of genus *Streptococcus* that remains attached after fission and is usu. found in chains; hence ~AL *a.* [f. Gk *streptos* twisted (*strephō* turn) + COCCUS]

strĕptomȳ'cĭn *n.* Antibiotic produced by *Streptomyces griseus* bacteria, effective against some groups of disease-producing bacteria. [f. Gk *streptos* (as prec.) + *mukēs* fungus + -IN]

Strĕ'pўan *a.* & *n.* (Of) a palaeolithic culture of N. Europe. [f. *Strépy* in Belgium, where remains of it were found, + -AN]

strĕss *n.,* & *v.t.* **1.** *n.* Constraining or impelling force of (*under, driven by, stress of weather, poverty,* etc.). **2.** Effort, demand upon physical or mental energy, (STORM *and stress; subjected to great stress; times of slackness and times of stress*); **~ disease** (suffered by managers etc. subjected to continual stresses); hence ~'FUL *a.* **3.** Emphasis (**lay ~ on,** convey that one attaches importance to); accentuation, emphasis laid on syllable or word, *a* or *the* accent, (*stress and quantity are different metrical principles; the stress is on the first* *syllable, on the adjective*). **4.** (Mech.) Force per unit area exerted between contiguous bodies or parts of a body. **5.** Hence ~′LESS *a.* **6.** *v.t.* Lay (the) stress on, accent, emphasize; subject to mechanical or physical or mental stress. [ME, f. DISTRESS¹ or partly f. OF *estresse* narrowness, oppression, f. Rom. **strictia* f. L *strictus* STRICT]

strĕtch *v., n., & a.* **1.** *v.t.* Make taut, tighten, straighten, place somewhere in tight-drawn or outspread state, (*the rope must be stretched tight*; *stretch a wire across the road*; *with a canopy stretched over them*); (in *p.p.*) lying at full length; ~ (one-**self,** or abs.), tighten muscles after sleeping etc. by extending limbs etc. in various directions; ~ one's **legs,** straighten them by walking as relief from sitting etc.; *stretch* one's WINGS; ~ person **on the ground,** knock him sprawling; ~ **out,** extend (hand, foot, etc., or abs.) by straightening arm or leg. **2.** Strain, exert to utmost or beyond legitimate extent, make the most of, do violence to, exaggerate, (*stretch a principle*, one's *powers*, one's *credit*); ~ **a point,** agree to something beyond the limit normally allowed; ~ (**the truth,** or abs.), exaggerate, lie. **3.** *v.i.* Have specified length or extension, be continuous between points or to or from a point, (*stretches from end to end, across the sky, to infinity*; *road stretches away, memory stretches down, from* or *to* place, period). **4.** *v.t.* & *i.* Draw, be drawn or admit of being drawn, out into greater length or extension or size (*gloves, shoes, need stretching*; *it stretches like elastic*). **5.** *n.* Stretching or being stretched (*by a stretch of authority, the imagination, language*, etc.; *with every faculty on the stretch*); ~ **marks** (esp. on abdomen after pregnancy); hence ~′Y² *a.* (colloq.). **6.** Continuous expanse or tract or spell (*a stretch of road, open country*, etc.; *works ten hours at a stretch*); (Naut.) distance covered on one tack; (sl.) imprisonment for a year or other term, period of service; *straight side of race-track. **7.** *a.* Able to stretch, elastic, (*stretch fabric*). [OE *streccan*, = OHG *strecken*, f. WG **strakkjan*; cf. STRAIGHT]

strĕ′tcher *n.* In vbl senses; brick or stone laid with side in face of wall (cf. HEADER); board in boat against which rower presses feet; appliance, often of canvas stretched on oblong frame, for carrying disabled or dead person on; rod or bar as tie between chair-legs etc.; wooden frame over which canvas of picture is stretched; (sl.) exaggeration, lie; **~-bearer,** person who helps to carry stretcher; **~-bond,** method of building in which all bricks are stretchers but joints of contiguous courses do not coincide. [ME, f. prec. + -ER¹]

stretto (strĕ′tō) *adv.* (Mus.) In quicker time. [It., = narrow]

strew (-o͞o) *v.t.* (*p.p.* **~n** *or* **~ed**). Scatter (sand, flowers, small objects) over a surface; (partly) cover (surface, object) *with* small objects scattered. [OE *stre(o)wian*, = OS *strōian*, OHG *strewen*, ON *strá*, Goth. **straujan*, prob. f. IE **ster-* spread]

′strewth. Var. of ′STRUTH.

strī′|a *n.* (*pl.* **~ae**). **1.** (Anat., Zool., Bot., & Geol.) Linear mark on surface, slight ridge or furrow or score. **2.** (Archit.) Fillet between flutes of column. **3.** Hence ~ATE² *a.*, ~ATE³ *v.t.*, ~A′TION, **~at**URE, *ns.* [L]

strĭ′cken *a.* Struck, esp. so as to afflict, (lit. or fig.; *stricken with fever*; PANIC²-*stricken*); levelled with strickle; *deleted (*from* etc.); ~ **field,** (scene of) pitched battle; ~ **heart** (afflicted by strokes of grief); ~ **in years,** (arch.) enfeebled by age. [arch. p.p. of STRIKE]

strĭ′ckle *n.* Rod used in strike-measure; whetting tool. [OE *stricel* (cogn. w. STRIKE)]

strĭct *a.* Precisely limited or defined, accurate, tense, without irregularity or exception or deviation, requiring or giving implicit obedience or exact performance, not lax, (*in the strict sense*; *keep strict watch*; *lives in strict seclusion*; *was told me in strict confidence*; *gave strict orders*; *a strict code of laws* or *customs*; *strict parents, schoolmaster, Muslim, discipline, morals*); hence ~′LY² *adv.* (**~ly speak-ing,** if one uses words in their strict sense), ~′NESS *n.* [f. L *strictus* p.p. of *stringere* tighten]

strĭ′ctur|e *n.* **1.** (usu. in *pl.*) Piece of censure, critical remark (*on* or *upon*). **2.** (Path.) Morbid narrowing of some canal or duct in the body; hence ~ED² (-kcherd) *a.* [ME, f. L *strictura* (as prec.; see -URE)]

strīde *v.* (**strode** *pr.* -ōd; **strĭ′dden** *pr.* -ĭ′d-) & *n.* **1.** *v.i.* & *t.* Walk with long steps. **2.** *v.t.* Pass over (ditch etc.) with one step; bestride, straddle. **3.** *n.* Single step esp. in respect of length, gait as determined by length of stride, (*walks with vigorous strides* or *a vigorous stride*); (fig., usu. in *pl.*) progress (*has made great strides towards self-sufficiency*); **take in** (one's) ~, clear (obstacle) without changing gait to jump, (fig.) find no serious impediment in; **get into** one's ~, (fig.) settle down steadily to the job in hand; **be thrown out of** one's ~, (fig.) be disconcerted. **4.** Distance between feet parted either laterally or as in walking. [OE *strīdan*, = MLG *strīden* straddle]

strī′dent *a.* Loud and harsh in sound; hence **strī′d**ENCY *n.*, ~LY² *adv.* [f. L *stridere* creak; see -ENT]

strĭ′dūl|āte *v.i.* (Esp. of cicada, grasshopper, etc.); make shrill jarring sound; so ~ANT *a.*, ~A′TION *n.* [f. F *striduler* f. L *stridulus* creaking (as prec.) + -ATE³]

strīfe *n.* Contention, state of conflict, struggle between opposed persons or things. [ME, f. OF *estrif*; cf. OF *estriver* STRIVE]

strĭ′gĭl *n.* **1.** (Gk & Rom. Ant.) Skin-scraper used by bathers or after exercise. **2.** Structure used by insect to clean antennae etc. [f. L *strigilis* (*stringere* graze)]

strī′gōse *a.* **1.** (Bot.) With short stiff hairs or scales. **2.** (Entom.) Streaked. [f. L *striga* swath, furrow + -OSE¹]

strīke *v.* (**struck**; **struck** *or* arch. STRICKEN) & *n.* **1.** *v.t.* & *i.* Subject to impact of blow or missile, hit upon or (*up*)*on*, deliver blow(s) or stroke(s), come sharply into contact with, (*struck me in the mouth, with his fist, with a dart*; *strike* one's *foot against a stone*, one's *hand on the table, while the* IRON¹ *is hot*; *struck by lightning*; *lightning never strikes twice in same place*; *strike a blow, strike, for freedom*; *hammer strikes on* or *strikes bell*; *ship strikes rock* or *on rock* or *strikes*; *his head struck the kerb*); send with blow (*strike ball out of court*); divert by blow (*strike weapon up, down, aside*); jerk tackle in order to secure hook in (fish, or abs.); discover (track etc.); encounter (unusual thing etc.); (of serpent) wound with fangs; ~ **hands,** (arch.) touch or clasp hands in sign of agreement made; ~ **lucky,** have lucky success; *strike* OIL¹; *strike it* RICH; ~ **at,** aim blow at; *strike at the* ROOT¹(*s*) *of*; ~ **back,** return blow or attack, (of gas-burner) burn from internal point before gas has become mixed with air; ~ **home,** get blow right to target; ~ **out,** (1) hit from the shoulder or violently, (2) use arms and legs in swimming, (3) take vigorous action; ~ **upon,** have (idea etc.) luckily occur to one, (of light) illuminate; **struck on,** (sl.) infatuated with. **2.** Produce or record or bring into specified state by stroke(s) or striking (*strike sparks, fire, light, out of flint* or fig. *out of* person); (of clock) indicate (time, or abs.), (of time) be indicated, by sounding of bell etc. (*clock strikes, strikes the hour, five*, etc.; *the hour has struck*); produce (musical note) by touching key etc.; make (coin) by stamping; make (bargain) as if by striking hands; ignite (match) by rubbing against something; make (person *blind, deaf,* etc.) at one stroke; **~ me dead!** (vulg. form of asseveration); *strike* (arrive at) *the* HAPPY *medium*; **~ a light,** produce light by striking match, (sl., as int. expr. disgust etc.); **~ me pink!** (vulg. int. expr. surprise); *strike the right* NOTE[1]; **~ all of a heap,** (colloq.) dumbfound; **~ down,** fell with blow (lit., or fig. of illness etc.); **~ off,** remove (head etc.) with stroke, delete (name etc., esp. from register of solicitors etc. because of misconduct), produce (copies of document); **~ out,** forge or devise (plan etc.), delete (item, name, etc.), (Baseball) dismiss (batter) by means of three strikes; **~ through,** delete (word etc.) with stroke of pen; **~ up,** start (acquaintance, conversation, etc.) rapidly or casually, (of band or performer) begin playing or singing (tune etc., or abs.). **3.** Arrest attention of, occur to mind of, produce mental impression on, impress *as,* (*what struck me was the generosity of the offer*; *struck my eye as I glanced over the letter*; *it strikes me he* or *that he may have misunderstood*; *an idea suddenly struck me*; *it strikes me as ridiculous*); **how does it ~ you?,** what do you think about it?. **4.** Lower or take down (flag, sail, mast, tent); signify surrender by striking flag, surrender; **~ one's flag,** surrender ship or fortress to enemy, (of admiral) resign command; **~ tents,** break up camp. **5.** Cease (work), cease work, (of employees) enter upon or be on a strike (sense 12; *strike for higher pay, against long hours,* etc.), *act thus against (employer). **6.** (Cause to) penetrate (*struck a knife, terror, into his heart*; *ink strikes through paper in printing*; *cold struck through his clothes,* (*in*)*to his marrow*; *the wind strikes cold*; *rays strike through fog*; *plant strikes its roots into the soil, strikes root,* or *strikes*); (of oysters), attach themselves to bed; suddenly fill (person) *with* (terror, panic, dizziness, etc.); insert (cutting of plant) in soil to take root. **7.** Direct one's course somewhere, take specified direction, diverge *to,* start *into,* (*then strike to the right*; *strike into* or *out of a track, subject,* etc.); **~ in,** intervene in talk, often *with* suggestion etc., (of disease) attack interior of body from surface. **8.** Level (grain etc. or the measure) in *strike-measure* (see sense 13). **9.** Ascertain (balance) by deducting credit or debit from the other; arrive at (average, state of balance) by equalizing all items; compose (jury) esp. by allowing both sides to reject same number. **10.** Suddenly and dramatically assume (attitude). **11.** Hence **strī'k**ABLE *a.* **12.** *n.* Employees' concerted refusal to work till some grievance is remedied; similar refusal to participate in other expected activity; **on ~,** acting on such refusal; **~'bound,** immobilized by strike; **~-breaker,** employee brought in to replace striker; **~ pay,** allowance for subsistence made by trade union to employees on strike; GENERAL, HUNGER[1]-, LIGHTNING, SIT-*down* or *stay-in,* SYMPATHETIC, UNOFFICIAL, *strike.* **13.** Strickle; **~-measure** (when grain etc. is measured by passing a rod across top of heaped vessel to secure that it shall be full and no more). **14.** Sudden success at finding petroleum, gold, etc., or in financial operations; sudden success or good luck. **15.** (Baseball). Batter's unsuccessful attempt to hit pitched ball, or other event counting equivalently against him. **16.** Act of striking (*lightning strike*; BIRD-*strike*); knocking-down of all bowling-pins with first ball; horizontal direction in geological structure; attack, esp. from the air. [OE *strīcan* go, stroke, = OHG *strihhan,* f. WG **strīk-*]

strī'ker *n.* In vbl senses; player who is (next) to strike the ball in games; (Footb. etc.) player whose main function is to seek to score goals; device striking primer in gun. [ME, f. prec. + -ER[1]]

strī'kĭng[1] *n.* In vbl senses; **~-circle,** (Hockey) elongated semicircle in front of goal from within which ball must be hit in order to score; **within ~-distance,** near enough to strike (lit. or fig.); **~-force,** (esp.) military body ready to attack at short notice; **~-plate** (against which end of spring-lock bolt strikes in closing). [ME, f. STRIKE + -ING[1]]

strī'kĭng[2] *a.* In vbl senses; sure to be noticed, arresting, impressive; (of clock) making sound to indicate hours etc.; hence ~LY[2] *adv.,* ~NESS *n.* [f. STRIKE + -ING[2]]

Strīne *n.* Comic transliteration of (alleged) Australian speech, e.g. *Emma Chissitt* = 'How much is it?'. [= *Australian* in Strine]

strĭng *n.* & *v.* (**strung**). **1.** *n.* Narrow cord; piece of this or of leather, ribbon, webbing, or other material, used for tying up, lacing, drawing or holding together, actuating puppet, etc., (*want some string and brown paper*; APRON-*strings*; BOW[1]-*string*); *two strings to* one's BOW[1], hence **first, second, ~,** person or thing that one's chief, alternative, reliance is set on; *have* person **on a ~,** entirely under one's influence; **pull (some) ~s,** exert (esp. hidden) influence; **pull the ~s,** be the real actuator of what another does; SHOE[1]-*string*; **without ~s, with no ~s attached,** not subject to conditions. **2.** Tough piece connecting two halves of pod in bean etc. **3.** Piece of catgut, cord, wire, etc., yielding musical tone(s) when stretched and caused to vibrate in piano, harp, violin, or other instrument (**harp on one ~,** dwell on single subject; **touch the ~s,** play; **touch a ~,** (fig.) excite particular feeling in person's heart); (in *pl.*) stringed instruments in a band or orchestra, part contributed by them to the effect; (*attrib.*) relating to or consisting of or imitative of stringed instruments (*string quartet, orchestra, tone*); hence (-)~ED[2] (-ngd) *a.* **4.** Set of or usu. *of* objects strung together or persons or things of one kind coming one after another (*a string of beads, onions, pearls, symbols*; *filed past in a long string*; *a string of porters, cars, oaths, lies*); string-course; racehorses, collectively, under training at a particular stable. **5.** **~ alphabet,** code for blind readers in which special knots on string represent letters; **~ bag** (esp. for carrying parcels etc.); **~ band** (esp. of stringed instruments only); **~-bark,** stringy-bark; ***~ bass,** double-bass; ***~ bean,** French or kidney bean with strings; **~(-board)**, supporting timber in which ends of staircase steps are set; **~-course,** raised horizontal band or course of bricks etc. on a building; **~-halt,** = SPRING[2]-*halt*; **~-piece,** long timber supporting and connecting the parts of a framework; **~ tie,** very narrow necktie; **~ vest** (made of large meshes). **6.** Hence ~'LESS *a.* **7.** *v.t.* Supply with string(s); tie with string. **8.** Secure (bow) in state ready for use by bending it and slipping loop of string into notch; (fig., esp. in *p.p.*) tighten *up* or make ready or sensitive or excited (senses, nerves, resolution, or person in regard to them; *was strung up to do the deed*); HIGH(*ly*)-*strung*. **9.** Thread (beads etc.) on a string; arrange in or as a string; remove strings from (beans). **10.** *(colloq.) Hoax. **11.** *v.t.* & *i.* (colloq.) **~ along,** deceive (person); **~ along with,** accompany; **~ up,** (1) kill by hanging, (2) make tense. **12.** *v.i.* (Of glue etc.) become stringy. **13.** (Bill.) Make the preliminary strokes that decide which player shall begin. [OE *streng,* OHG *stranc,* ON *strengr* f. Gmc **strangiz*; cf. STRONG]

strĭngĕ'ndō (-nj-) *adv.* (Mus.) With increasing speed. [It. (*stringere* press, f. as foll.)]

strĭ'ng|ent (-nj-) *a.* (Of rule, stipulation, etc.) strict, precise, requiring exact performance, leaving no loophole or discretion; (of money-market etc.) tight, hampered by scarcity, unaccommodating, hard to operate in; hence ~ENCY *n.*, **~ent**LY² *adv.* [f. L *stringere* draw tight; see -ENT]

strĭ'nger *n.* In vbl senses; string-board; longitudinal structural member in framework esp. of ship or aircraft; newspaper correspondent not on regularly paid staff. [f. STRING + -ER¹]

strĭ'ng|ȳ *a.* **1.** Fibrous, like string; **~y-bark,** (Austral.) eucalyptus with tough fibrous bark. **2.** (Of liquid) viscous, ropy. **3.** Hence **~ĭ**NESS *n.* [f. STRING + -Y²]

strĭp¹ *v.* (**-pp-**) & *n.* **1.** *v.t.* Denude, lay bare, deprive of or *of* covering or (all) clothing or appurtenance or property or rank (**~ped to the waist,** wearing nothing above waist); deprive (house) of furniture, (bed) of bedclothes, (ship) of rigging, (tree) of bark and branches; ~ (**down**), remove accessory fittings of or take apart (machine etc.) to inspect or adjust it; milk (cow) to last drop; remove the old hair from (dog); remove stems from (tobacco); tear thread from (screw), cogs from (gearwheel), etc.; remove (paint), remove paint from, with solvent. **2.** Pull or tear (covering lit. or fig., appurtenance, property) off or *off* from or *from* something. **3.** *v.i.* Take off or *off* one's clothes, undress; **~-tease** *n.*, & *v.i.*, (perform in) entertainment in which woman or occas. man gradually undresses before an audience. **4.** (Of screw) lose thread; (of bullet) issue from rifled gun without spin owing to loss of surface. **5.** *n.* Act of stripping, esp. of undressing in strip-tease; ~ **club** (at which strip-tease performances are given); *~ **mine** (worked by removing material that overlies ore etc.). [ME, f. OE **strȳpan, -striepan* despoil, = MDu. *stroopen,* OHG *stroufen* f. WG **straupjan*]

strĭp² *n.* Long narrow piece (*a strip of card, paper, cloth, garden, territory, board*); ~ (**cartoon**), sequence of small drawings telling comic or serial story in newspaper etc.; (colloq.) clothes worn by members of football etc. team; AIR¹-*strip*; **tear** person **off a** ~, (sl.) rebuke him angrily; ~ **light,** tubular fluorescent lamp; ~ **mill** (in which steel slabs are rolled into strips). [ME, f. or cogn. w. MLG *strippe* strap, thong, prob. rel. to foll.]

strīpe *n.* **1.** Long narrow band usu. of uniform breadth on a surface from which it differs in colour or texture (*black with a red stripe*; STAR¹*s and Stripes*; *stripes on soldier's trousers*; *zebra's stripes*); (Mil.) chevron etc. on sleeve denoting rank (**get, lose, a** ~, be promoted, demoted); *category of character, opinion, etc., (*a man of that stripe*; *men of all political stripes*); hence **(-)strip**ED² (-pt), **strī'p**Y², *adjs.* **2.** (arch., usu. in *pl.*) Blow with scourge or lash. **3.** (in *pl.*, treated as *sing.*; colloq.) Tiger. [perh. back form. f. *striped*; cf. MDu., MLG *stripe*, MHG *strīfe*; sense 2 ME, of unkn. orig.]

strĭ'pling *n.* Youth approaching manhood. [ME, prob. f. STRIP² + -LING, in sense of having figure not yet filled out]

strĭ'pper *n.* In vbl senses; device or solvent for removing paint etc.; strip-tease performer. [f. STRIP¹ + -ER¹]

strīve *v.i.* (**strove** *pr.* -ōv; **strĭ'ven** *pr.* -ĭ'ven). Struggle, endeavour, try hard, make efforts, contend, vie (*to* do, *for* or *after* desired end, *with* or *against* opponent or temptation or difficulty); ~ **together,** or **with each other,** quarrel, dispute pre-eminence etc. [ME, f. OF *estriver* rel. to *estrif* STRIFE]

strōbe *n.* (colloq.) Stroboscope; stroboscopic lamp. [abbr.]

strobī'la *n.* (*pl.* **~e**). = foll. 2. [mod. L, f. Gk *strobilē* twisted lint-plug (*strephō* twist)]

strō'bīle *n.* **1.** Cone of pine etc.; imbricated flower of hop. **2.** Chain of segments in tapeworm; section of jellyfish larva developing into new individual. [F, or f. LL f. Gk *strobilos* (*strephō* twist)]

strŏ'bĭl|us *n.* (*pl.* **~i** *pr.* -ī). = prec. 1. [LL (as prec.)]

strŏ'bo|scōpe *n.* Instrument for determining speeds of rotation etc. by intermittent vision with intervals adjusted to make the rotating object appear stationary; lamp made to flash intermittently esp. for this purpose; hence **~scŏ'p**IC *a.* [f. Gk *strobos* whirling + -o- + -SCOPE]

strōde. See STRIDE.

Strŏ'ganŏff *a.* (Of meat) cut into strips and cooked in sour-cream sauce (*beef Stroganoff*). [f. P. ~, 19th-c. Russ. diplomat]

strōke¹ *n.*, & *v.t.* **1.** *n.* Blow, shock given by blow, (*to receive 20 strokes of the birch*; *with one stroke of his sword*; *killed by a stroke of lightning* or *lightning stroke*); **at a** ~, by a single action; **finishing** ~, *coup de grâce*, final and fatal blow. **2.** Sudden disabling attack esp. of apoplexy; SUN*stroke.* **3.** Single effort put forth, one complete performance of a recurrent action or movement, time or way in which such movements are done; slightest such action (*has not done a stroke of work*); whole of motion (of wing, oar, etc.) till starting-position is regained; whole motion (of piston) in either direction; (Golf) action of hitting (at) ball with club, as unit of scoring; (Rowing) mode or action of moving oar (*row a fast, slow, long, etc., stroke*; *second boat is gaining at every stroke*); mode of moving arms and legs in swimming; **off** one's ~, not performing as well as usual. **4.** Method of striking in games etc., specially successful or skilful effort, (*invented a new stroke in cricket*; *stroke of wit, diplomacy, etc.*; ~ **of business,** profitable transaction; ~ **of genius,** original or strikingly successful idea; ~ **of (good) luck,** unforeseen opportune occurrence; MASTER¹-*stroke.* **5.** Mark made by movement in one direction of pen or pencil or paintbrush, similar mark printed, detail contributing to general effect in description, (UP, DOWN⁵, HAIR, *-stroke*; *thick, thin, horizontal, oblique,* etc., *stroke*; *dash off picture with a few strokes*; *description is full of strokes from the life*); **with a** ~ **of the pen,** merely by writing signature etc.; **finishing ~s,** finishing touches. **6.** Sound made by a striking clock (**it is on the** ~ **of nine,** clock is about to strike 9; *was there* **on the** ~, punctually). **7.** ~ (**oar**), oar or oarsman nearest stern, setting time of stroke. **8.** *v.t.* Act as stroke of (boat, crew). [ME, f. OE **strāc* f. Gmc **straikaz,* cogn. w. STRIKE]

strōke² *v.t.*, & *n.* **1.** *v.t.* Pass the hand gently, and usu. repeatedly in same direction, along surface of (~ person or **his hair the wrong way,** irritate him; ~ person **down,** appease his anger etc.). **2.** *n.* Act or spell of stroking. [OE *strācian,* = MDu., MLG *strēken,* OHG *streihhōn* f. Gmc **straik-* (as prec.)]

strōll *v.i.*, & *n.* **1.** *v.i.* Saunter, go for short leisurely walk; go from place to place giving performances etc. (*strolling players*). **2.** *n.* Short leisurely walk (*go for, take, a stroll*). [orig. of vagrant, prob. f. G *strollen, strolchen* (*strolch* vagabond, of unkn. orig.)]

strō'ller *n.* In vbl senses; *push-chair. [f. prec. + -ER¹]

strō'ma *n.* (*pl.* **~ta**). (Biol.) Framework of an organ or cell, usu. of connective tissue; fungous tissue containing spore-producing bodies; hence **stromă'**TIC *a.* [mod. L, f. LL f. Gk *strōma* coverlet]

strŏng *a.* (**~'er, ~'est,** *pr.* -ngg-). **1.** Having power of resistance, not easily broken or torn or worn or injured or captured, tough, healthy, firm, solid, (*strong china, stick, cloth, fortress, conviction, faith, character, foundation*); (of constitution) able to overcome, or not liable to, disease; (of nerves) proof against fright, irritation, etc.; (of patient) restored to health; (of market) having steadily high or rising prices. **2.** Capable of exerting great force or of doing much, muscular, powerful by size or numbers or resources or quality or ability, well equipped (*in*), convincing, striking, powerfully affecting the senses, (*strong to do, suffer, labour, save,* etc.; *is strong enough to lift a horse*; *strong in judgement, Greek, numbers, health*; *strong eyes, memory, army*; *strong evidence, argument, case*; *strong light, perfume, cigar, colour*; **as ~ as a horse** or **an ox,** able to do or stand much work); (of company) numerous, having specified number (*we were 200 strong*); capable of doing much when united (*a strong combination*); formidable, likely to win, (*a strong candidate*); (of tea etc.) made with large proportion of the flavouring element; (of solution) containing relatively little solvent; (of situation in play or story) calculated to move audience deeply; (of voice) loud or penetrating; (of food or its flavour) pungent; (of breath) ill-smelling. **3.** Energetic, effective, vigorous, decided, (*a strong tide, attraction, influence, inclination to, suspicion*; *strong feelings, support*(*er*)); (of literary style) vivid and terse; (of wind) very fresh; (of measure) drastic; **going ~,** (sl.) continuing race or other action vigorously, in good health or trim; **come it** or **go it ~,** (sl.) go to great lengths in something, use exaggeration. **4.** (Gmc Gram.) (Of verb) forming inflexions by vowel-change within stem rather than by addition of suffix (e.g. *swim swam, give gave, break broke*; cf. *float floated*), (of noun or adjective declension) corresponding to original vowel-stems, opp. WEAK 7; **~ grade,** stressed ablaut-form. **5. ~ arm,** use of force or sheer strength (so *~-arm a.*); **~-box,** strongly made small chest for valuables; *strong* DRINK[2]; **~'hold,** fortified place, secure refuge, centre of support for a cause etc.; **~ interaction,** (Phys.) interaction between certain elementary particles that is very strong but is effective only at short distances; **~ language,** forcible (esp. profane or abusive) expressions; **~ man,** muscular person, masterful or capable person; **~ meat,** doctrine or action acceptable only to vigorous or instructed minds; **~-mi'nded,** having a vigorous or determined mind; **~ point,** specially fortified defensive position, (fig.) thing at which one excels; **~-room** (designed to protect valuables against fire and theft); **~ stomach** (not easily affected by nausea); **~ suit,** suit at cards in which one can take tricks, (fig.) thing at which one excels; **~ waters,** (arch.) alcoholic liquor. **6.** Hence **~'**ISH[1] 2 *a.*, **~'**LY[2] *adv.* [OE, = OS *strang*, ON *strangr* f. Gmc **strangaz*; cf. STRING]

strŏ'ntia (-sha) *n.* Strontium oxide. [f. *strontian* native strontium carbonate f. *Strontian* in Highland Region of Scotland, where it was discovered; see -IA[1]]

strŏ'ntĭum (*or* -shum) *n.* (Chem.) Soft silver-white metallic element; **~ 90,** radioactive isotope of strontium concentrating selectively in bones when ingested. [f. prec. + -IUM]

strŏp *n.*, & *v.t.* (**-pp-**). **1.** *n.* Strip of leather on which razor is sharpened, implement or machine serving same purpose; (Naut.) collar of leather or spliced rope or iron used for handling cargo. **2.** *v.t.* Sharpen on or with strop. [ME f. MDu., MLG; OHG *strupf*, WG f. L *stroppus, struppus*]

strophă'nthĭn *n.* White crystalline poisonous glucoside extracted from various species of the genus *Strophanthus* of tropical plants and used as a heart-tonic. [f. mod. L *strophanthus* f. Gk *strophos* twisted cord + *anthos* flower, + -IN]

strō'phė *n.* (Lines recited during) turn made in dancing by ancient-Greek chorus (**~, antistrophe, epode,** three sections of a choral ode or of one division of it, strophe and antistrophe exactly corresponding in metre); group of lines forming section of lyric poem; hence **strŏ'ph**IC *a.* [f. Gk *strophē*, lit. turning (*strephō* turn)]

‖**strŏ'ppў** *a.* (sl.) Bad-tempered, awkward to deal with. [20th c.; orig. unkn.]

strōve. See STRIVE.

strow (-ō) *v.t.* (*p.p.* **~n** *or* **~ed**). (arch.) Strew. [var. of STREW]

strŭck. See STRIKE.

strŭ'ctural (-kch*er*-) *a.* Of structure; **~ engineering,** design and construction of dams, bridges, etc.; **~ formula,** (Chem., showing arrangement of atoms in the molecule of a compound); **~ linguistics,** study of language as system of interrelated elements; **~ psychology,** study of arrangement and composition of mental states and conscious experiences; **~ steel,** strong mild steel in shapes suited to construction work; hence **~**LY[2] *adv.* [f. STRUCTURE + -AL]

strŭ'ctural|ĭsm (-kch*er*-) *n.* Doctrine that structure rather than function is important; structural linguistics or psychology; hence **~**IST (2) *n.* [f. prec. + -ISM]

strŭ'ctur|e *n.*, & *v.t.* **1.** *n.* Manner in which a building or organism or other complete whole is constructed, supporting framework or whole of the essential parts of something, make, construction, (*the structure of a house, machine, animal, poem, sentence, society*; *a sentence of loose, a rock of columnar, structure*; *its structure is ingenious*; *demanded a new wages structure*; *ornament should emphasize and not disguise the lines of a structure*); hence **~e**LESS (-kch*er*l-), (-)**~**ED[2] (-kch*er*d), *adjs.* **2.** Thing constructed, complex whole, a building, (*a fine marble structure*; *a lumbering structure pulled by six horses*). **3.** *v.t.* Give structure to, organize. [ME f. OF, or f. L *structura* (*struere struct-* build; see -URE)]

stru'del (-ōō'-) *n.* Confection of thin pastry rolled up round a filling and baked (*apple strudel* = APFELSTRUDEL). [G]

strŭ'ggle *v.i.*, & *n.* **1.** *v.i.* Throw one's limbs or body about in violent effort to get free or escape grasp (*child struggled and kicked*); make violent or determined efforts under difficulties, strive hard *to* do or *for* thing, contend *with* or *against* opponent or obstacle or difficulty, (*struggled to express himself, to control his feelings, for supremacy*; *struggling with his infirmity, against superior numbers* or *the forces of nature*); make one's way with difficulty *through, up, along, in,* etc., (*light struggled in through dirty panes*; *struggled to his feet*); (esp. in *part.*) experience difficulty in making a living or getting recognition (*a struggling artist* etc.); hence **strŭ'ggl**ER[1] *n.* **2.** *n.* Spell of struggling, confused wrestle or jostling, hard contest, determined effort under difficulties; **the ~ for existence** or **life,** the competition between organisms esp. as an element in natural selection, or between persons seeking livelihood. [ME *strugle, strogel,* etc., frequent. (see -LE 3) of uncert. orig.; perh. imit.]

strŭm *v.* (**-mm-**) & *n.* **1.** *v.i.* Touch keys or twang strings of piano or other stringed instrument (esp. carelessly or unskilfully). **2.** *v.t.* Strum on (piano, guitar, etc.). **3.** *n.* Sound made by strumming (*the strum of a guitar*). [imit.; cf. THRUM²]

stru'm|a (-ōō'-) *n.* (*pl.* ~**ae**). Scrofula; goitre; (Bot.) cushion-like dilatation of an organ; so ~OSE¹, ~OUS, *adjs.* [L, = scrofulous tumour]

strŭ'mpėt *n.* (arch. or rhet.) Prostitute. [ME, of unkn. orig.]

strŭng. See STRING.

strŭt¹ *v.i.* (-**tt**-), & *n.* (Walk with) pompous or affected stiff erect gait. [ME 'bulge, swell, strive', earlier *stroute* f. OE *strūtian* be rigid (?)]

strŭt² *n.*, & *v.t.* (-**tt**-). **1.** *n.* Bar of wood or iron inserted in a framework and intended to bear weight or pressure in the direction of its length, brace, e.g. one set obliquely from rafter to king-post or queen-post. **2.** *v.t.* Brace with strut(s). [16th c., prob. f. prec.]

'struth (-ōō-) *int.* (colloq., used as mild oath). [f. *God's truth*]

stru'thĭous (-ōō'-) *a.* Of or like an ostrich. [f. L *struthio* ostrich + -OUS]

strȳ'chn|ine (-knēn) *n.* Vegetable alkaloid got from plants of genus *Strychnos* (esp. nux vomica), very bitter to the taste and highly poisonous, used as stimulant and tonic; hence ~IC *a.*, ~(**in**)ISM (5) *ns.* [F, f. L f. Gk *strukhnos* kind of nightshade; see -INE⁵]

Sts. *abbr.* Saints.

Stū'art *n.* & *a.* (Member) of the royal family of England and Scotland from James I to Anne. [name of royal house of Scotland from accession (1371) of Robert II, a hereditary STEWARD of Scotland]

stŭb *n.*, & *v.t.* (-**bb**-). **1.** *n.* Stump of tree, tooth, etc.; remnant of pencil, cigar, or similar object after use; stunted tail etc.; counterfoil of cheque, receipt, etc.; ~**-axle** (supporting only one wheel of a pair); ~**-mortise, -tenon,** (going only part of the way through); hence ~**'BY**² *a.* **2.** *v.t.* Grub *up* by the roots; clear (land) of stubs; ~ one's **toe,** hurt it by striking against something; ~ (**out**), extinguish (cigar, cigarette) by pressing lighted end against some hard object. [OE *stub(b)*, = MDu., MLG *stubbe*, ON *stubbr, stubbi* f. Gmc **stubbaz*, **stubbon*]

stŭ'bble *n.* Cut stalks of cereal plants left sticking up after harvest; cropped hair or beard, hair on unshaven chin or cheek; hence **stŭ'bblY**² *a.* [ME, f. AF *stuble*, OF *estuble* f. L *stup(u)la* var. of *stipula* straw]

stŭ'bborn *a.* Unreasonably obstinate; unyielding, obdurate, inflexible; refractory, intractable, (*facts* **are** ~ **things,** will not adapt themselves to theory); hence ~LY² *adv.*, ~NESS (-n-n-) *n.* [ME *stiborn, stoburn*, etc., of unkn. orig.]

stŭ'ccō *n.* (*pl.* ~**es**), & *v.t.* **1.** *n.* Plaster or cement used for coating wall surfaces or moulding into architectural decorations. **2.** *v.t.* Coat with stucco. [It., of Gmc orig.]

stŭck. See STICK¹.

stŭd¹ *n.*, & *v.t.* (-**dd**-). **1.** *n.* Large-headed nail, boss, or knob, projecting from a surface esp. for ornament; small object projecting slightly from road-surface as marker etc.; rivet, cross-piece in each link of chain-cable. **2.** Double button esp. for use with two button-holes in shirt-front (‖COLLAR¹-*stud*); ‖PRESS²-*stud*. **3.** Post to which laths are nailed; *height of room as indicated by length of this; hence ~**'DING**¹ *n.*, woodwork of lath-and-plaster wall. **4.** *v.t.* Set with studs to strengthen or usu. to decorate; (in *p.p.*) thickly set or strewn *with* (*door, lawn, sea, sky, studded with nails, daisies, islands, stars*); be scattered over or about (surface). [OE *studu, stuthu*, = MHG *stud*, ON *stoth*, cogn. w. G *stützen* to prop]

stŭd² *n.* Number of horses kept for breeding etc.; place where these are kept; **at** ~, (of male horse) publicly available for breeding on payment of fee; ~**-book** (containing pedigrees of horses); ~**-farm,** place where horses are bred; ~(**-horse**), stallion; ~(**-horse**) **poker,** form of poker with betting after dealing of successive rounds of cards face up. [OE *stōd*, = OHG *stuot*, ON *stóth* f. Gmc **stōdh*- (**stō*-, **sta*- STAND¹)]

stŭ'dding-sail (stŭ'nsəl) *n.* Sail set on small extra yard and boom beyond leech of square sail in light winds. [16th c., of uncert. orig.; perh. f. MLG, MDu. *stōtinge* a thrusting]

stū'dent *n.* **1.** Person studying in order to qualify himself for some occupation, or devoting himself to some branch of learning or investigation, or observation, or under instruction at university or other place of higher education or technical training (*medical, theological, historical, theology, history, student*; *a student of archaeology, law, botany, manners, society*; *numbers its students in thousands*); (*attrib.*) studying in order to become (*student teacher*). **2.** Person of studious habits. **3.** ‖Graduate recipient of stipend from foundation of college, esp. fellow of Christ Church, Oxford; hence ~SHIP *n.* [ME, f. L *studēre* (*studium* STUDY¹); see -ENT]

stū'dĭō *n.* (*pl.* ~**s**). **1.** Working-room of painter, sculptor, photographer, etc., often with skylights or windows specially designed to secure suitable light. **2.** Room in which cinema-play is staged for filming; (in *pl.*) such premises of a film company with auxiliary buildings. **3.** Room used for making recordings or in broadcasting station for transmissions. **4.** ~ **couch,** couch that can be converted into a bed; ~ **flat** (containing room suitable as artist's studio). [It., f. L (as STUDY¹)]

stū'dĭous *a.* Assiduous in study, much occupied with reading; taking care *to* do or *in* doing; anxiously desirous *of* doing; studied, deliberate, intended, zealous, anxious, painstaking, (*with studious care, attention, politeness*); hence ~LY² *adv.*, ~NESS *n.* [ME, f. L *studiosus* (as foll.; see -OUS)]

stŭ'dȳ¹ *n.* **1.** (arch.) Thing to be secured by pains or attention (*it shall be my study to please*); **make a** ~ **of,** try to secure (see also sense 3). **2. In a brown** ~, in a reverie, too intent on one's thoughts to observe what is passing. **3.** (in *sing.* or *pl.*) Devotion of time and thought to acquiring information esp. from books, pursuit of some branch of knowledge, (*gives his time to study*; *my studies have convinced me of its truth*; *the study of mathematics, morals*; *continued his studies abroad*; *Institute of Advanced Studies*); **make a** ~ **of,** investigate carefully (see also sense 1); (Theatr.) memorizing or memorizer of roles; ~**-group** (of persons meeting from time to time to study a particular subject or topic). **4.** Thing that is or deserves to be investigated or carefully examined (*the proper study of mankind is man*; *his face was a study*). **5.** Drawing etc. made for practice in technique or as preliminary experiment for picture or part of it (*his studies are exquisite, but his finished work disappointing*; *a study of a head*); (Mus.) composition designed to develop skill in some particular branch of execution; literary portrayal of an aspect of behaviour, character, etc. **6.** Room used for literary occupation, transaction of business, etc., (*you will find him in his* or *the study*). [ME, f. OF *estudie* f. L *studium* zeal, study]

stŭ'dȳ² *v.* **1.** *v.t.* Make a study of, take pains to investigate or acquire knowledge of (subject), scrutinize or earnestly contemplate (visible object), (*study law, French, philosophy*; *study* person's *face* or *character, a map, the stars*); read (book) attentively; try to learn (role) by heart; take pains to achieve (result) or pay regard to (*studies others' convenience, his own interests*). **2.** *v.i.* Apply oneself to study esp. reading (~ **for the Bar,** cf. READ 11). **3.** *v.t.* (arch.) Be on the watch, try constantly to manage, *to* do (*studies to avoid disagreeable topics*). **4.** (in *p.p.*) Deliberate, intentional, affected, (*a studied insult*; *with studied politeness, rudeness, unconcern, abandon*); hence **stŭ'dĭed**LY² (-dĭd-) *adv.* [ME, f. OF *estudier* f. med. L *studiare* f. L (as prec.)]

stŭff *n.* & *v.* **1.** *n.* Material that thing is made of or that is or may be used for some purpose (*such stuff as dreams are made on*; *the stuff that heroes are made of*; *Conrad's books are good stuff*; *always eating sweet stuff*; *lots of stuff about it in the newspapers*); **the ~,** (colloq.) available supply of something, (sl.) money; BIT² *of stuff.* **2.** Woollen fabric (opp. silk, cotton, linen); ‖~ **gown** (worn by barrister who has not taken silk). **3.** Valueless matter, refuse, trash, nonsense, (*take that stuff away*; *stuff and nonsense!*; *what stuff he writes!*). **4.** (sl.) **Do** one's ~, perform one's tricks, get on with one's assigned task; HOT¹ *stuff*; **know** one's ~, be a master of one's subject, trade, etc.; ROUGH *stuff*; **the ~ to give 'em** or **to give the troops,** the absolutely correct way to proceed etc. **5.** *v.t.* Pack, cram, stop up, fill, distend, (*stuff* one's *ears with wool, cushion with feathers, doll with padding*; *head stuffed with romantic ideas*); fill out skin of (animal, bird, etc.) with material to restore original shape (**~ed shirt,** (colloq.) pompous but incompetent person; **get ~ed,** (sl.) take oneself away); fill (fowl, rolled meat, etc.) with minced seasoning etc. before cooking; make (person, goose, etc.) eat to repletion (~ **oneself,** gorge, eat greedily); (usu. in *pass.*) block *up* (nose etc. with secretions); *place bogus votes in (ballot-box); (vulg.) copulate with (woman). **6.** Ram or press into receptacle (*stuffed his things into a small bag, his fingers into his ears, the food into his mouth*), push hastily (*stuffed the note behind the cushion*), (sl.) dispose of as unwanted (*you can stuff the job so far as I'm concerned*). **7.** *v.i.* Stuff oneself. **8.** Hence (-)~'ER¹ *n.* [ME *stoffe* f. OF (*estoffe* n. f.) *estoffer* equip, furnish f. Gk *stuphō* draw together]

stŭ'ffĭng *n.* Material used for stuffing (sense 5); **~-box** (in machinery, packed with material to allow working of axle while remaining airtight); **knock** or **take the ~ out of,** (colloq.) make feeble or weak, defeat utterly. [f. prec. + -ING¹]

stŭ'ff|ȳ *a.* (Of room etc., or atmosphere in it) lacking fresh air or ventilation, close, hard to breathe in, fusty; dull, uninteresting; (of nose etc.) stuffed up; angry, sulky; narrow-minded, prim; hence ~ĬLY² *adv.*, ~ĬNESS *n.* [f. STUFF + -Y²]

stŭ'ltĭ|fȳ *v.t.* (Of act, statement, agent, speaker) reduce (previous act etc.) to foolishness or absurdity; make (act etc.) of no effect, neutralize (one*self*) as agent, by later inconsistent act etc.; impair, render inefficient through frustration etc.; hence ~FICA'TION *n.* [f. LL *stultificare* f. L *stultus* foolish; see -FY]

stŭm *n.*, & *v.t.* (**-mm-**). **1.** *n.* Unfermented grape-juice, must. **2.** *v.t.* Prevent from fermenting, secure (wine) against further fermentation in cask, by use of sulphur etc.; renew fermentation of (wine) by adding stum. [f. Du. (*stommen* v. f.) *stom* n. f. *stom* a. dumb]

stŭ'mble *v.* & *n.* **1.** *v.i.* Lurch forward, have partial fall, from catching or striking foot or making false step (~ **along,** go with frequent stumbles); make blunder(s) in doing something (*stumbles in his speech*; *stumble through a recitation*); (arch.) be offended, feel scruples, *at*; come accidentally (*up*)*on* or *across*; **stumbling--block,** obstacle, circumstance that causes difficulty or hesitation or scruples. **2.** *v.t.* (arch.) Cause to stumble or pause, nonplus. **3.** *n.* Act of stumbling. [ME *stomble, stumble,* (w. euphonic *b*) corresp. to Norw. *stumla,* cogn. w. STAMMER]

‖**stū'mer** *n.* (sl.) Worthless cheque, counterfeit coin or note; sham, fraud; failure. [19th c.; orig. unkn.]

stŭmp *n.* & *v.* **1.** *n.* Projecting remnant of cut or fallen tree, corresponding remnant of broken branch or tooth or amputated limb, stub of cigar or pencil, worn-down brush or other implement, (***up a ~,** in difficulties); (in *pl.*, joc.) legs (STIR¹ one's *stumps*). **2.** Stump of tree, or other place, used by orator to address meeting from; **on the ~,** (colloq.) engaged in political speech-making or agitation; ~ **oratory** (of kind suitable for such speeches). **3.** (Cricket). One of the three uprights of a wicket (*off, middle, leg, stump*; DRAW¹ *stumps*). **4.** Cylinder of rolled paper or other material with conical ends for softening pencil-marks and other uses in drawing. **5.** *v.i.* Walk stiffly or noisily as on wooden leg. **6.** *v.t.* (Of question etc., colloq.) be too hard for; (in *p.p.*) at a loss, at one's wit's end; hence ~'ER¹ (2) *n.* **7.** (Cricket). (Of wicket-keeper) put (batsman who is not in his ground and not running) out by dislodging bail(s) with ball or while holding ball; hence ~'ER¹ (1) *n.*, (colloq.) wicket-keeper. **8.** *v.i.* & *t.* *Make stump speeches (see sense 2); traverse (district) doing this. **9.** *v.t.* Use stump on (drawing, line, etc.). **10.** *v.i.* & *t.* ‖~ **up,** (sl.) pay over the money required, produce (sum). [ME *stompe,* f. MDu. *stomp,* OHG *stumpf* n. & a.; sense 4 prob. thr. F *estompe*]

stŭ'mp|ȳ *a.* Thickset, stocky, of small height or length in proportion to girth, (*stumpy man, book, tail, pencil*); hence ~ĬLY² *adv.*, ~ĬNESS *n.* [f. prec. + -Y²]

stŭn *v.t.* (**-nn-**). (Of sound) deafen temporarily, bewilder; (of blow, lit. or fig.) knock senseless, reduce to insensibility or stupor, benumb, overwhelm. [ME, f. OF *estoner* ASTONISH]

stŭng. See STING.

stŭnk. See STINK.

stŭ'nnĭng *a.* In vbl senses; (colloq.) extremely attractive, delightful, splendid; hence or cogn. **stŭ'nn**ER¹ *n.*, ~LY² *adv.* [f. STUN + -ING²]

stŭ'nsail, stŭ'ns'l, *n.* = STUDDING-SAIL. [repr. pronunc.]

stŭnt¹ *v.t.* (esp. in *p.p.*) Retard growth or development of, dwarf, cramp. [f. (now dial.) *stunt* foolish, MHG *stunz,* ON *stuttr* short f. Gmc **stuntaz,* perh. rel. to STUMP]

stŭnt² *n.*, & *v.i.* (colloq.) **1.** *n.* Special effort, feat, show performance (~ **man,** man employed to take actor's place in performing dangerous stunts), display of concentrated energy; advertising device. **2.** *v.i.* Perform stunts, esp. aerobatics. [orig. unkn.; first in 19th-c. U.S. college athletics]

stū'pa *n.* Round usu. domed building erected as Buddhist shrine. [f. Skr. *stūpa*]

stūpe¹ *n.*, & *v.t.* (Treat with) flannel etc. soaked in hot water, wrung out, and applied as fomentation. [ME, f. L f. Gk *stup(p)ē* tow]

stūpe² *n.* (sl.) Foolish person. [f. STUPID]

stū'pė|fȳ *v.t.* Make stupid or torpid, deprive of sensation, (*stupefied with drink, narcotics, grief,* etc.); hence or cogn. ~FA'CIENT *a.* & *n.*, ~FA'CTION, ~**fĭer**¹ (1, 2), *ns.*, ~**făct**IVE *a.* [f. F *stupéfier* f. L *stupefacere* (*stupēre* be amazed; see -FY)]

stūpĕ'ndous *a.* Amazing, prodigious, astounding, esp. by size or degree (*a stupendous structure, error, achievement*; *stupendous folly*); hence ~LY² *adv.*, ~NESS *n.* [f. L *stupendus* gerundive of *stupēre* be amazed at, + -OUS]

stū'pĭd *a.* & *n.* **1.** *a.* In a state of stupor or

lethargy; slow-witted, lacking in sensibility, obtuse, characteristic of persons of this nature, (*a stupid person, joke, idea, book*; *what a stupid place to put it in!*), so **stūpĭ'd**ITY *n.*; uninteresting, dull; hence ~LY[2] *adv.* **2.** *n.* (colloq.) Stupid person. [f. F *stupide* or f. L *stupidus* (as prec.; see -ID[1])]

stū'por *n.* Dazed state, torpidity, whence ~OUS *a.*; helpless amazement. [ME f. L (as STUPENDOUS; see -OR)]

stûr'd|ў[1] *a.* Robust, hardy, vigorous, lusty, strongly built, (*sturdy child, opponent, legs, frame, resistance, courage*); **~y beggar,** (arch.) able-bodied but idle beggar; hence ~ĭLY[2] *adv.*, ~ĭNESS *n.* [ME 'reckless, violent', f. OF *est(o)urdi* p.p. of *estourdir* stun, daze f. Rom. **exturdire* f. L *ex-* EX-[1] + *turdus* thrush (taken as type of drunkenness)]

stûr'd|ў[2] *n.* Vertigo in sheep caused by tapeworm in brain; hence ~ĭED[2] (-ĭd) *a.* [f. prec.]

stûr'geon (-jon) *n.* Large anadromous fish of genus *Acipenser* etc., resembling shark in general shape, having mailed body and head, yielding caviare and isinglass, and esteemed as food. [ME f. AF; OF *esturgeon* f. Rom. **sturio -onis* f. Gmc **sturjon*]

Sturm und Drang (shtoorm ŏŏnt drah'ng) *n.* = STORM *and stress*. [G]

stŭ'tter *v.* & *n.* **1.** *v.i.* Stammer; involuntarily repeat parts, esp. initial consonants, of words in effort to articulate. **2.** *v.t.* ~ **(out)**, utter (words) thus. **3.** Hence ~ER[1] *n.* **4.** *n.* Act or habit of stuttering. [frequent. of (now dial.) *stut*, ME f. Gmc **stut-* knock; see -ER[5]]

stȳ[1] *n.* & *v.* **1.** *n.* Pen or enclosure for pig(s); filthy abode or dwelling; place of debauchery. **2.** *v.t.* & *i.* Lodge in sty. [OE *sti*, prob. = *stig* hall (cf. STEWARD), f. Gmc **stijam*]

stȳ[2], **stȳe,** *n.* Inflamed swelling on edge of eyelid. [f. (now dial.) *styany* = *styan eye* f. OE *stigend* sty, lit. riser (*stīgan* rise) + EYE[1], shortened as though = *sty on eye*]

Stў'gian *a.* (As) of the Styx or Hades; murky, gloomy. [f. L f. Gk *Stugios* (STYX) + -AN]

stȳle *n.*, & *v.t.* **1.** *n.* Ancient writing-implement, small rod with pointed end for scratching letters on wax-covered tablets and blunt end for obliterating; thing of similar shape esp. for engraving, tracing, etc.; gnomon of sundial; (Bot.) narrow extension of ovary supporting stigma. **2.** Manner of writing, speaking, or doing, esp. as contrasted with the matter to be expressed or thing done (*the style is better than the matter*; *written in a florid, cumbrous, lucid,* or *delightful style*; *different styles of rowing, swimming*; *slashed about him in fine style*; CRAMP[3] person's *style*; **good, bad, ~,** = *good, bad,* FORM[1]). **3.** Collective characteristics of the writing or diction or way of presenting things or artistic expression or decorative methods (in painting, architecture, furniture, dress, etc.) proper to a person or school or period or subject, manner exhibiting these characteristics, (*in the style of Shakespeare, Raphael, Wagner*; *the epic, lyric, dramatic, classical, style*; *buildings in Romanesque, Early English, Tudor, style*; *fried chicken Southern style*; *flattery is not his style*); ***old ~,** = OLD *face*; (as *suf.*) = -WISE (*dressed cowboy-style*). **4.** Descriptive formula, designation of person or thing, full title, (*is entitled to the style of 'Right Honourable'*; *did not recognize him under his new style*; *my style is plain John Smith*; *regret that I am not acquainted with your proper style*); **old, new, ~,** (of date) reckoned by the Julian, Gregorian, calendar. **5.** Noticeably superior quality or manner esp. in regard to breeding or fashion, distinction, (*let us do the thing in style if we do it at all*); **has no ~,** is commonplace. **6.** Kind, sort, esp. with regard to appearance (*what style of house do you require?*; *a gentleman of the old style*). **7.** Make, shape, pattern, (*in all sizes and styles*). **8.** *v.t.* Design, arrange, make, etc., in (esp. fashionable) style; hence ***stȳ'l**ER[1] *n.* **9.** (usu. in *pass.*) Use specified designation of (*is styled king, folly*). [ME f. OF *stile, style* f. L *stilus*; sp. *style* due to assoc. w. Gk *stulos* column]

stȳ'lĕt *n.* Slender pointed instrument, stiletto; (Surg.) stiffening wire of catheter, probe. [f. F *stilet* f. It. STILETTO]

stȳ'lĭsh *a.* Noticeable for (fashionable) elegance or superior quality or manner; hence ~LY[2] *adv.*, ~NESS *n.* [f. STYLE + -ISH[1]]

stȳ'lĭst *n.* Person with or aiming at good literary style; person who designs fashionable styles or makes things according to these. [f. STYLE + -IST]

stȳlĭ'st|ic *a.* Of literary style; hence ~ICALLY *adv.*, ~ICS *n.*, study of literary style. [f. as prec. + -IC, after G *stilistisch*]

stȳ'līte *n.* Medieval ascetic living on top of a pillar. [f. eccl. Gk *stulitēs* (*stulos* pillar; see -ITE[1])]

stȳ'līze, -īse (-īz), *v.t.* (usu. in *p.p.*) Make (artistic representation) conform to the rules of a conventional style. [f. STYLE + -IZE, after G *stilisieren*]

stȳ'lō *n.* (*pl.* ~s). (colloq.) = STYLOGRAPH. [abbr.]

stȳ'lobāte *n.* (Archit.) Continuous base supporting row of columns. [f. L f. Gk *stulobatēs* (*stulos* pillar, *bainō* walk)]

stȳ'lo|graph (-ahf) *n.* Kind of pen containing reservoir of ink and marking with point instead of split nib; hence **~gră'ph**IC *a.* [f. STYLUS + -O- + -GRAPH]

stȳ'loid *a.* & *n.* (Anat.) ~ **(process)**, spine of bone, esp. that projecting from base of temporal bone. [f. mod. L *styloides* f. Gk *stuloeidēs* (*stulos* pillar; see -OID)]

stȳ'l|us *n.* (*pl.* ~*i pr.* -ī). **1.** = STYLE 1. **2.** Tracing-point producing indented groove in gramophone record, or following such groove in reproducing sound. [erron. sp. of L *stilus*; cf. STYLE]

stȳ'mie *n.*, & *v.t.* **1.** *n.* (Golf) situation on putting-green when one ball lies between the other ball and the hole, formerly a possible obstruction to the play of the farther ball (*lay a stymie*); (fig.) difficult situation. **2.** *v.t.* (Golf) put (opponent, his ball, *oneself*) into position of having to negotiate a stymie; (fig.) obstruct, thwart. [19th c.; orig. unkn.]

stў'ptic *a.* & *n.* (Substance) that checks bleeding. [ME, f. L f. Gk *stuptikos* (*stuphō* contract; see -IC)]

stȳr'ăx *n.* Storax resin; tree or shrub of genus *Styrax*, e.g. storax-tree. [L, f. Gk *sturax*; cf. STORAX]

stȳr'ēne *n.* Liquid hydrocarbon easily polymerized and used in making plastics etc. [f. prec. + -ENE]

Stўx *n.* (Gk Myth.) River encompassing Hades (**cross the ~**, die; *black* etc. *as Styx*). [ME f. L, f. Gk *Stux -ugos* (*stugnos* hateful, gloomy)]

sū'able (*or* sōō'-) *a.* That can be sued; hence **sūabĭ'lity** (*or* sōō-) *n.* [f. SUE + -ABLE]

suā'sion (swā'zhon) *n.* Persuasion as opposed to force (*moral suasion*); so **suā's**IVE (sw-) *a.* [ME f. OF, or f. L *suasio* (*suadēre suas-* urge; see -ION)]

suav|e (swahv) *a.* Bland, soothing, mollifying, (superficially) polite, (*suave person, speech, manners, wine, medicine*); hence or cogn. ~**e**LY[2] (-vlĭ) *adv.*, ~ITY *n.* [F, or f. L *suavis* agreeable, cogn. w. SWEET]

sŭb *n.* & *v.* **(-bb-)**. (colloq.) **1.** *n.* Subaltern; sub-editor; submarine; subscription; substitute. **2.** *v.i.* Act as substitute *for* someone. **3.** *v.t.* Sub-edit. [abbr.]

sŭb- (*or* sub) *pref.* denoting: **1.** Lower position (*subordinate, subscribe*); to lower position (*submerge, subside*); from lower position (*subtract*). **2.** Covertness, secrecy, (*suborn*). **3.** Inclusion (*subsume*). **4.** Closeness (*subsequent, suburb*). **5.** Inferiority (*subserve*). **6.** Support (*subsidy, subvention*). **7.** (forming *adjs.*) Under as regards (1) position (esp. Anat.; *subabdominal*), (2) degree (*subnormal*), or (3) quality (*subhuman*); (4) somewhat (*subacid*), more or less (*subaquatic*), (5) approximately (*subcylindrical*), (6) incipiently (*subdelirious*), (7) nearly (*suberect*), (8) immediately adjacent in space or time (*subalpine; subapostolic*). **8.** (forming *ns.*) (1) Subordinate, secondary, deputy, (*sub-editor, subheading, subdean*); (2) secondary part of (*subculture, subsection*); (3) incipient (*subdelirium*); (4) lying below (*subsoil*); (5) (Chem., of salt) basic (*subacetate*); (6) smaller than or inferior to (*subshrub, sub-man*). **9.** (forming *vbs.*) Subordinately, secondarily, (*subdivide, sublet*). [f. or after L *sub-* (*sub* under, close to, towards)]

sŭbăbdŏ'mĭnal *a.* See SUB- 7(1).

sŭbă'cĭd *a.* Moderately acid or tart (lit. or fig.); hence **sŭbacĭ'd**ITY *n.* [f. L *subacidus* (see SUB- 7 (4), ACID¹)]

sŭbacū'te *a.* (Med.) Between acute and chronic. [f. SUB- 7 (2) + ACUTE]

sŭbā'gencȳ, sŭbā'gent, *ns.* See SUB- 8 (1).

subahdar' (sōōba-) *n.* (Hist.) Chief native officer of company of sepoys. [f. Urdu *ṣūbaʰdār* (*ṣūbah* province + Pers. *dār* master)]

sŭbă'lpīne *a.* Of higher slopes of mountains just below timberline. [f. SUB- 7 (8) + ALPINE]

sŭ'baltern *a.* & *n.* **1.** *a.* Of inferior rank; (Logic, of proposition) particular, not universal. **2.** *n.* ‖(Mil.) Officer below rank of captain. [f. LL SUB(*alternus* ALTERNATE¹)]

sŭbăpostŏ'lĭc *a.* Of period immediately after that of the Apostles. [f. SUB- 7 (8) + APOSTOLIC]

sŭbă'qua *a.* (Of sport etc.) taking place under water. [f. SUB- 1 + L *aqua* water]

sŭbaquă'tĭc *a.* Of more or less aquatic habits or kind; underwater. [f. SUB- 7 (4, 1) + AQUATIC]

sŭbā'queous *a.* Underwater. [f. SUB- 7 (1) + AQUEOUS]

sŭbar'ctĭc *a.* Of or like regions somewhat south of Arctic Circle. [f. SUB- 7 (8) + ARCTIC]

sŭbă'stral *a.* Terrestrial. [f. SUB- 7 (1) + ASTRAL]

sŭbatŏ'mĭc *a.* Occurring in or smaller than an atom. [f. SUB- 7 (3) = ATOMIC]

sŭbaudĭ'tion *n.* Mental supplying of omitted word(s), understanding of what is not expressed, reading between the lines. [f. LL *subauditio* f. SUB(*audire* hear) understand; cf. AUDITION]

sŭbă'xĭllarȳ *a.* See SUB- 7 (1).

sŭb-bā'sement (-sm-) *n.* Storey below basement. [f. SUB- 8 (4) + BASEMENT]

sŭb-branch (-ah-), **sŭ'b-breed,** *ns.*, see SUB- 8 (1); **sŭ'bcătėgorȳ** *n.*, see SUB- 8 (2); **sŭbcau'dal** *a.*, see SUB- 7 (1); **sŭ'bclass** (-ahs) *n.*, see SUB- 8 (2).

sŭbclā'vĭan *a.* & *n.* (Artery etc.) lying or extending under collar-bone. [f. mod. L *subclavius* (as SUB- 7 (1), *clavis* key; cf. CLAVICLE) + -AN]

sŭbclĭ'nĭcal *a.* (Med., of disease) not yet presenting definite symptoms. [f. SUB- 7 (6) + CLINICAL]

sŭ'bcommĭssion(er) (-shon-), **sŭ'bcommĭttee** (-tĭ), *ns.*, see SUB- 8 (1); **sŭbcŏ'nĭcal** *a.*, see SUB- 7 (5).

sŭbcŏ'nscious (-shus) *a.* & *n.* (Of) part of mind that is not fully conscious but is able to influence actions etc.; hence ~LY² *adv.*, ~NESS *n.* [f. SUB- 7 (7) + CONSCIOUS]

|**sŭbcŏ'ntĭnent** *n.* Land-mass that is large, but smaller than those generally called continents; large geographically or politically independent part of a continent. [f. SUB- 8 (2) + CONTINENT²]

sŭbcŏ'ntrăct¹ *n.*, **sŭbcontră'ct**² *v.t.* & *i.*, **sŭbcontră'ctor** *n.* See SUB- 8 (1), 9.

sŭbcŏ'ntrarȳ *a.* & *n.* (Logic). (Proposition) that cannot be false at the same time as another. [f. LL SUB(*contrarius* CONTRARY), transl. Gk *hupenantios*]

sŭbcor'dāte *a.*, see SUB- 7 (5); **sŭbcor'tĭcal, sŭbcŏ'stal, sŭbcrā'nĭal,** *adjs.*, see SUB- 7 (1).

sŭbcrĭ'tĭcal *a.* (Phys.) Of less than critical mass etc. [f. SUB- 7 (2) + CRITICAL]

sŭ'bcŭlture *n.* (Sociol.) Cultural group within a larger culture; hence **sŭ'bcŭltural** (-cher-) *a.* [f. SUB- 8 (2) + CULTURE]

sŭbcūtā'nėous, sŭbcūtĭ'cūlar, *adjs.*, see SUB- 7 (1); **sŭbcȳlĭ'ndrĭcal** *a.*, see SUB- 7 (5).

sŭbdea'con *n.* (Eccl.) Minister of order next below deacon; epistoler; so **sŭb**DIA'CONATE *n.* [f. SUB- 8 (1) + DEACON²]

sŭbdea'n *n.* Official ranking next below, or acting as deputy for, dean; so **sub**DEA'NERY *n.*, **sub**DECA'NAL *a.* [f. SUB- 8 (1) + DEAN¹]

***sŭ'bdĕb** *n.* (colloq.) = foll. [abbr.]

***sŭbdĕ'būtante** (-ahnt) *n.* Girl who is about to become a débutante, or one of corresponding age. [f. SUB- 8 (3) + DÉBUTANTE]

sŭbdėcā'nal. See SUBDEAN.

sŭbdėlĭ'rĭous *a.*, **sŭbdėlĭ'rĭum** *n.* See SUB- 7 (6), 8 (3).

sŭ'bdĭvīde (*or* -ī'd) *v.t.* & *i.* Divide again after first division. [ME, f. L *subdividere* (as SUB- 9, DIVIDE¹)]

sŭ'bdĭvĭsion (-zhon; *or* -vĭ'-) *n.* Subdividing; subordinate division; *area of land divided into plots for sale. [f. LL *subdivisio* (as SUB- 8 (1), DIVISION)]

sŭbdŏ'mĭnant *n.* (Mus.) Fourth note of diatonic scale of any key. [f. SUB- 8 (1) + DOMINANT]

subdŭ'ct *v.t.* (arch.) Withdraw, remove; deduct, subtract; hence **subdŭ'ct**ION *n.* [f. L SUB(*ducere duct-* draw)]

subdūe' *v.t.* Conquer, subjugate, (*subdue enemies, nature, rough land*); tame, bring into subjection, discipline, (*subdue* one's *passions; subdued by kindness*); (esp. in *p.p.*) soften, make gentle or less intense, tone down, mitigate, (*subdued colours, light, mood, manners, satisfaction*); hence **subdū'**ABLE *a.*, **subdū'**AL *n.* [ME *sodewe* f. AF **soduer*, **su(b)duer* = OF *so(u)duire* deceive, seduce, f. L *subducere*, (see prec.), used w. sense of SUB(*dere* = *dare* put) conquer]

sŭb-ĕ'dĭtor *n.* Assistant editor; ‖person who prepares material for printing in book, newspaper, etc.; hence (as back form.) **sŭb-ĕ'dĭt** *v.t.* [f. SUB- 8 (1) + EDITOR]

sŭbėrĕ'ct *a.* (Bot.) See SUB- 7 (7).

sŭbēr'ėous, sūbĕ'rĭc, sū'berōse, *adjs.* Corky, of or like cork. [f. L *suber* cork(-oak) + -EOUS, -IC (F *subérique*), -OSE¹]

sŭ'bfămĭlȳ *n.* Taxonomic category between family and tribe or genus. [f. SUB- 8 (2) + FAMILY]

sŭbfē'brīle *a.* See SUB- 7 (4).

sub finem (sŭb fī'nem *or* sōōb fē'nĕm) *adv.* Towards the end (of specified chapter etc.). [L]

sŭ'bfloor (-or) *n.* Foundation for floor in building. [f. SUB- 8 (4) + FLOOR]

sŭ'bform *n.* See SUB- 8 (1).

sŭ'bfŭsc *a.* & *n.* Dusky, dull-coloured (formal clothing in some universities). [f. L *subfuscus* (as SUB- 7 (4), *fuscus* dark brown)]

sŭ'bgēnus *n.* (*pl.* **su'bgenera**). Taxonomic category between genus and species. [f. SUB- 8 (2) + GENUS]

For other words in *sub-* see SUB-.

sŭbglā'cĭal (*or* -shal) *a.*, see SUB- 7 (8); **sŭ'b-group** (-ōōp) *n.*, see SUB- 8 (2).

sŭ'bhead, sŭ'bheadĭng, (-ĕd-) *ns.* Subordinate division in classification; subordinate heading or title in chapter, article, etc. [f. SUB- 8 (1) + HEAD¹, HEADING]

sŭbhėpă'tĭc *a.*, see SUB- 7 (1); **sŭb-Hĭmalay'an** *a.*, see SUB- 7 (8).

sŭbhū'man *a.* Less than human; not fully human. [f. SUB- 7 (3) + HUMAN]

||**sŭbĭnfeudā'tion** *n.* See SUB- 8 (1).

subjā'cent *a.* Underlying, situated below. [f. L SUB(*jacēre* lie); see -ENT]

sŭ'bjėct¹ (*or* -ĕ-) *a.* & *adv.* **1.** *a.* Under government, not independent, in subjection, owing obedience *to*, (*a subject province, tribe*; *is held subject*; *has long been subject to France*; *States subject to foreign rule*; *we are all subject to the laws of nature, the law of the land*). **2.** Liable or exposed or prone *to* (thing; *persons subject to gout*; *is very subject to damage, envy*, etc.). **3.** *a.* & *adv.* ~ **to,** conditional(ly) upon (for validity etc.), on the assumption of, without precluding, (*the arrangement is made*, or *is*, *subject to your approval*; *subject to your consent, I propose to try again*; *subject to correction, these are the facts*). [ME f. OF *suget* etc., f. L *subjectus* p.p. of SUB(*icere* = *jacere* throw)]

sŭ'bjėct² (*or* -ĕ-) *n.* **1.** Person subject to political rule, any member of a State except the Sovereign, any member of a subject State, (*rulers and subjects*; *the subjects of the Crown, of the Sultan*; *the* LIBERTY *of the subject*); person owing obedience to another. **2.** (Logic & Gram.) Member of a proposition about which something is predicated, noun or noun-equivalent with which verb of sentence is made to agree in number etc., (*subject and predicate are the essential parts of a sentence*; *every verb has a subject expressed or understood*). **3.** (Philos.) Thinking or feeling entity, the mind, *the* ego, the conscious self, as opp. all that is external to the mind (~ **and object,** the ego and the non-ego, self and not-self, the consciousness and what it is or may be conscious of); substance or substratum of anything as opp. its attributes. **4.** Theme of or *of* discussion or description or representation, matter (to be) treated of or dealt with, (*never talks on serious subjects*; *proposed a subject for the debate*; *a difficult, interesting, dull, subject*; *what is the subject of the poem, story, picture?*; *constantly wanders from the subject*; *he, it, was made the subject of an experiment*; *cannot think of a subject to write about*); department of study (*was examined in six subjects*); (Mus.) theme of fugue or sonata, leading phrase, motif; ~ (**for dissection**), dead body; **change the** ~, talk of something else, esp. as way out of embarrassment; **on the** ~ **of,** concerning, about. **5.** Circumstance, person, or thing, that gives occasion *for* specified feeling or action (*is a subject for ridicule, pity, rejoicing, congratulation*). **6.** (esp. Med.) Person of specified usu. undesirable bodily or mental tendencies (*a sensitive, bilious, hysterical, subject*). **7.** ~ **catalogue** etc. (arranged according to subjects treated); **~-heading** (in index, collecting references to a subject); **~-matter,** matter treated of in book, lawsuit, etc.; **~-object,** (Philos.) object of sense or thought as it is conceived of (opp. *object-object*). **8.** Hence **~LESS** *a.* [ME f. OF *suget* etc. f. L *subjectus -um* masc. and neut. p.p. (as prec.)]

subjĕ'ct³ *v.t.* Subdue (nation etc. usu. *to* one's sway etc.); expose, make liable, treat, *to* (*rudeness subjects one to retorts in kind*; *must be subjected to great heat*; *shall subject it to criticism, to chemical analysis*); so **subjĕ'ction** *n.* [ME, f. OF *subjecter* or f. L *subjectare* frequent. (as SUBJECT¹)]

subjĕ'ctĭve *a.* & *n.* **1.** *a.* (Philos.) belonging to, of, due to, the consciousness or thinking or perceiving subject or ego as opp. real or external things; due to one's own feelings or capacities rather than being actually existent; imaginary. **2.** (Of art and artists, literature, and history) giving prominence to or depending on personal idiosyncrasy or individual point of view, not producing the effect of literal and impartial transcription of external realities; hence ~NESS (-vn-), **sŭbjėctĭ'vITY,** *ns.* **3.** (Gram.) Of the subject; ~ **case,** nominative; ~ **genitive** (as in 'by the act of God'; cf. OBJECTIVE). **4.** Hence ~LY² (-vlĭ) *adv.* **5.** *n.* Subjective case. [ME, f. L *subjectivus* (as SUBJECT¹; see -IVE)]

subjĕ'ctĭv|ism *n.* Doctrine that knowledge is merely subjective and that there is no external or objective test of truth; so ~IST (2) *n.* [f. prec. + -ISM]

subjoi'n *v.t.* Add at the end, append, (illustration, anecdote, etc.). [f. obs. F *subjoindre* f. L SUB(*jungere junct-* join)]

sŭ'bjoint *n.* Secondary joint (e.g. in insect's leg). [f. SUB- 8 (1) + JOINT¹]

sub judice (sŭb jōō'dĭsĭ *or* sōōb ū'dĭkā) *a.* Under judicial consideration (*newspaper comment on cases sub judice is prohibited*); not yet decided, still debatable, (*the matter is still sub judice*). [L, = under a judge]

sŭ'bjug|āte (-jōō-) *v.t.* Subdue, vanquish, bring under bondage or into subjection; hence or cogn. ~ABLE *a.*, ~A'TION, **~ātor,** *ns.* [ME, f. LL SUB(*jugare* f. *jugum* yoke) bring under the yoke + -ATE³]

subjŭ'nctĭve *a.* & *n.* ~ (**mood**), (Gram.) mood of verbs used esp. to denote what is imagined or wished or possible (*if I were you*; *God help you*; *suffice it to say*; *be that as it may*), in some languages also in subordinate clauses; hence ~LY² (-vlĭ) *adv.* [f. F *subjonctif -ive* or f. LL *subjunctivus* f. L (as SUBJOIN; see -IVE), transl. Gk *hupotaktikos*, as being used in subjoined clauses]

sŭ'bkĭngdom *n.* Taxonomic category below kingdom; phylum. [f. SUB- 8 (2) + KINGDOM]

sŭblăpsār'ĭan *a.* & *n.* = INFRALAPSARIAN. [f. mod. L *sublapsarius* (as SUB- 7 (1), *lapsus* LAPSE¹; see -ARIAN)]

sŭ'blease¹ *n.*, **sŭblea'se²** *v.t.*, **sŭblĕ't** *v.t.* (**-tt-; suble't**). Lease to subtenant. [f. SUB- 8 (1), 9 + LEASE, LET²]

||**sŭb-lieutĕ'nant** (see LIEUTENANT) *n.* Officer ranking next below lieutenant. [f. SUB- (1) + LIEUTENANT]

sŭ'blĭm|āte¹ *v.t.* **1.** Convert (substance) from solid state directly to its vapour by heat (and usu. allow to solidify again). **2.** (fig.) Refine, purify, idealize; (Psych.) divert energy of (primitive impulse) into culturally higher activity. **3.** Hence ~A'TION *n.* [f. as foll. + -ATE³]

sŭ'blĭmate² *a.* & *n.* Sublimated (substance); CORROSIVE *sublimate.* [f. L *sublimare* SUBLIME² + -ATE²]

sublī'me¹ *a.* Of the most exalted kind, so distinguished by elevation or size or nobility or grandeur or other impressive quality as to inspire awe or wonder, aloof from and raised far above the ordinary, (*sublime mountain, scenery, tempest, ambition, virtue, love, thought, beauty, genius, poet*, etc.); (of indifference, impudence, etc.) like that of one too exalted to fear consequences; *Sublime* PORTE; hence or cogn. ~LY² (-mlĭ) *adv.*, **sublĭ'mITY** *n.* [f. L *sublimis*]

sublī'me² *v.t.* & *i.* **1.** = SUBLIMATE¹ 1; undergo sublimation. **2.** Purify or elevate, become pure, as by sublimation; make sublime. [ME, f. OF *sublimer* or f. L *sublimare* lift up, in med. L sublimate, f. as prec.]

sŭblĭ'mĭnal *a.* (Psych.) Below the threshold of sensation or consciousness; ~ **advertising** (presented by very brief television picture etc.

so as to influence opinion or behaviour without being consciously perceived); ~ **self,** part of one's personality outside conscious awareness. [f. SUB- 7 (1) + L *limen -inis* threshold + -AL]

sŭblĭ'ngual (-nggwal) *a.* Under the tongue. [f. SUB- 7 (1) + L *lingua* tongue + -AL]

sŭblĭ'ttoral *a.* See SUB- 7 (8).

||**Sub-Lt.** *abbr.* Sub-Lieutenant.

sŭblū'narȳ (*or* -lōō'-) *a.* Beneath the moon; within the moon's orbit; subject to the moon's influence; of this world, earthly. [f. LL *sublunaris* (as SUB- 7 (1), LUNAR); see -ARY²]

sŭb-machi'ne-gŭn (-shē'-) *n.* Lightweight machine-gun held by hand for firing. [f. SUB- 8 (1) + MACHINE-*gun*]

sŭ'b-|măn *n.* (*pl.* ~**men**). Markedly inferior man; brutal or stupid man. [f. SUB- 8 (6) + MAN¹]

sŭbmari'ne (-ē'n; *or* sŭ'-) *a.* & *n.* **1.** *a.* Existing, occurring, done, or used, under the surface of the sea, (*submarine plant, earthquake, travel, cable*). **2.** *n.* Submarine vessel, esp. warship capable of operating either on or under the water surface, equipped with torpedo-tubes, guns, and periscope, and propelled by diesel engines or electric motors or nuclear power. [f. SUB- 7 (1) + MARINE]

sŭ'bmaster (-mah-) *n.* Assistant (head)master in school. [f. SUB- 8 (1) + MASTER¹]

sŭbmă'xĭllarȳ (*or* -ĭ'l-) *a.* Under the lower jaw. [f. SUB- 7 (1) + MAXILLARY]

sŭbmē'dĭant *n.* (Mus.) Sixth note of diatonic scale of any key. [f. SUB- 8 (1) + MEDIANT]

sŭbmĕ'ntal *a.* Under the chin. [f. SUB- 7 (1) + MENTAL²]

submer'ge *v.* **1.** *v.t.* Place below water, flood with water, inundate (lit. or fig.); **the ~d tenth,** the part of the population that is sunk in poverty or permanently in distress. **2.** *v.i.* (Of submarine or its crew or commander) dive, go below surface. **3.** Hence or cogn. **submer'g**ENCE, **submer's**ION (-shon), *ns.* [f. L SUB(*mergere mers-* dip)]

submer'sĭble *a.* Capable of being submerged. [f. *submerse* v. = prec., + -IBLE]

sŭbmīcroscŏ'pĭc *a.* Too small to be seen by an ordinary microscope. [f. SUB- 7 (3) + MICROSCOPIC]

sŭbmĭ'nĭature (*or* -nĭcher) *a.* Of greatly reduced size; (of camera) miniature and using 16-mm film. [f. SUB- 7 (2) + MINIATURE]

submĭ'ssion (-shon) *n.* **1.** Submitting or being submitted (*shall be satisfied with nothing short of complete submission*; *demands the submission of the signature to an expert*). **2.** (Law). Theory etc. submitted by counsel to judge or jury. **3.** Humility, meekness, resignation, acceptance of authority, obedient conduct or spirit. [ME f. OF, or f. L *submissio* (as SUBMIT; see -ION)]

sŭbmĭ'ssĭve *a.* Willing to submit; yielding to power or authority; humble, obedient; hence ~LY² (-vlĭ) *adv.*, ~NESS (-vn-) *n.* [f. prec. after *remissive* etc.]

submĭ't *v.* (-tt-). **1.** *v.t.* Surrender one*self* for control etc. *to* (*submit ourselves entirely to the Divine Will*); subject *to* operation or process. **2.** Present for consideration or decision (*should like to submit it to your inspection*; *fifteen entries were submitted*; *submit a case to court*); urge or represent deferentially (*that*; *I submit that a material fact has been overlooked*; *that, I submit, is a false inference*). **3.** *v.i.* Give way, resign oneself, yield, cease or abstain from resistance, (*to*; *will never submit, submit to indignity, submit to being parted from you*; *had to submit to defeat*). [ME, f. L SUB(*mittere miss-* send)]

sŭbmŭ'ltĭple *n.* & *a.* (Number) that is an aliquot part of another specified number. [f. SUB- (3) + MULTIPLE]

sŭbnor'mal *a.* Less than normal; below normal (esp. as regards intelligence); hence ~ITY (-ă'l-) *n.* [f. SUB- 7 (2) + NORMAL]

sŭbnū'clėar *a.* (Phys.) Occurring in or smaller than an atomic nucleus. [f. SUB- 7 (3) + NUCLEAR]

sŭbŏ'cūlar, sŭboesophă'gėal (-ēs-; *or* -ēsŏfajē'-), *adjs.* See SUB- 7 (1).

sŭbor'bĭtal *a.* **1.** Situated below the orbit of the eye. **2.** Not completing a full orbit round the earth etc. [f. SUB- 7 (1), (2) + ORBITAL]

sŭ'border *n.* Taxonomic category between order and family; so **sub**OR'DINAL *a.* [f. SUB- 8 (2) + ORDER¹]

subor'dĭnate¹ *a.* & *n.* **1.** *a.* Of inferior importance or rank, secondary, subservient, (*to*); ~ **clause,** sentence made by inclusion of a conjunction or by position to serve as *n.* or *a.* or *adv.* in another sentence; hence ~LY² (-tlĭ) *adv.* **2.** *n.* Person working under another's control or orders. [f. med. L SUB(*ordinatus* p.p. f. L *ordinare* ordain); see -ATE²]

subor'dĭn|āte² *v.t.* Make subordinate, treat or regard as of minor importance, bring or put into subservient relation, (*to*); hence or cogn. ~A'TION *n.*, ~ATIVE *a.* [f. med. L *subordinare* (as prec.) + -ATE³]

subor'n *v.t.* Induce by bribery or otherwise to commit perjury or other unlawful act; hence or cogn. **sŭborn**A'TION, ~ER¹, *ns.* [f. L SUB(*ornare* equip) incite secretly]

sŭbŏ'xīde *n.* (Chem.) Oxide containing smallest proportion of oxygen. [f. SUB- 8 (1) + OXIDE]

sŭ'bphȳl|um *n.* (*pl.* ~**a**). Taxonomic category between phylum and class. [f. SUB- 8 (2) + PHYLUM]

sŭ'b-plŏt *n.* Subordinate plot in play etc. [f. SUB- 8 (1) + PLOT¹]

subpoe'na (-ē'-; *or* sup-) *n.*, & *v.t.* (~**ed** *pr.* -*ad*, *or* ~'**d**). **1.** *n.* Writ commanding person's attendance in lawcourt. **2.** *v.t.* Serve subpoena on. [ME, f. L *sub poena* under penalty (first wds in the writ)]

sŭbprī'or *n.* Prior's assistant or deputy. [f. SUB- 8 (1) + PRIOR¹]

sŭ'brēgion (-jon) *n.* Division of faunal region; hence ~AL (-ē'-) *a.* [f. SUB- 8 (2) + REGION]

subrĕ'ption *n.* Obtaining of thing by surprise or misrepresentation. [f. L *subreptio* purloining f. SUB(*ripere rept-* = *rapere* snatch); see -ION]

sŭbrogā'tion *n.* (Law). Substitution of one party for another as creditor, with transfer of rights and duties. [f. LL *subrogatio* f. SUB(*rogare* ask) choose as substitute; see -ATION]

sub rosa (sŭb rō'za) *a.* (Of communication, consultation, etc.) in confidence, under express or implied pledge of secrecy. [L, lit. under the rose, as emblem of secrecy]

sŭ'broutine (-rōōtēn) *n.* (Computers). Routine designed to perform a frequently used mathematical operation within a program. [f. SUB- 8 (1) + ROUTINE]

sŭbsă'tŭrātėd (*or* -cher-) *a.*, **sŭbsătŭrā'tion** *n.* See SUB- 7 (2).

subscrī'b|e *v.* **1.** *v.t.* Write (esp. one's name) at foot of document etc. (*the subscribed names carry weight*; *someone has subscribed a motto*); write one's name at foot of, sign, (document, picture, etc.); ~**e oneself,** sign one's name. **2.** *v.i.* Express one's adhesion *to* an opinion or resolution (*cannot subscribe to that*). **3.** *v.i.* & *t.* Enter one's name in a list of contributors, make or promise a contribution, contribute (specified sum), to or *to* a common fund or *for* a common object, raise or guarantee raising of by subscribing thus; **~e for,** engage before publication to take copy or copies of (book); **~e to,** engage to take (newspaper etc.) for specified time. **4.** Hence or cogn. ~ER[1] *n.*, (esp.) person paying regular sum for hire of telephone line operated by commercial company (**~er trunk dialling,** making of trunk-calls by subscriber without assistance of operator). [ME, f. L SUB(*scribere script-* write)]

sŭ'bscrĭpt *a.* & *n.* **1.** *a.* (Gk Gram.) **Iota ~,** small ι written below ᾱ, η, or ω. **2.** *a.* & *n.* (Math. etc.) (Symbol) written below and to the right of another symbol. [f. L *subscriptus*, p.p. of *subscribere* (see prec.)]

subscrĭ'ption *n.* Thing, esp. money, subscribed; act of subscribing; fee for membership of society etc.; offering of reduced price to those ordering book before publication; **~ concert** etc. (paid for mainly by those who subscribe (sense 3) for tickets to attend). [ME, f. L *subscriptio* (as SUBSCRIBE; see -ION)]

sŭ'bsĕction *n.* See SUB- 8 (2).

subsĕ'llĭ|um *n.* (*pl.* **~a**). = MISERICORD 3. [L (as SUB- 1, *sella* seat)]

sŭ'b-sēquence *n.* Sequence forming part of a larger one. [f. SUB- 8 (2) + SEQUENCE]

sŭ'bsėqu|ent *a.* That follow(s) or followed a specified event etc., of later time or date than something, posterior in time *to*; hence ~ENCE *n.*, **~ent**LY[2] *adv.* [ME f. OF, or f. L SUB(*sequi* follow); see -ENT]

subsẽ'rve *v.t.* Serve as means in furthering (purpose, action, etc.). [f. L SUB(*servire* SERVE)]

subsẽ'rvĭ|ent *a.* Serving as means, having merely instrumental relation, (*to*); subordinate *to*; cringing, obsequious; hence ~ENCE, ~ENCY, *ns.*, **~ent**LY[2] *adv.* [f. L (as prec.; see -ENT)]

sŭ'bsĕt *n.* See SUB- 8 (2).

sŭ'bshrŭb *n.* Low-growing or small shrub. [f. SUB- 8 (6) + SHRUB[1]]

subsī'd|e *v.i.* **1.** (Of water, esp. flood) sink to low(er) level; (of ground) cave in, sink; (of building, ship, etc.) settle down lower in ground or water; (of suspended matter) fall to bottom, be precipitated; (of swelling etc.) become less; (of person, usu. joc.) sink into sitting or kneeling or lying posture (*subsided into an armchair*). **2.** Cease from activity or agitation, become tranquil, abate, (*storm, tumult, apprehension, excitement, subsides*). **3.** So ~ENCE (*or* sŭ'bsĭ-) *n.* [f. L SUB(*sidere* settle cogn. w. *sedēre* sit)]

subsĭ'dĭar|ў *a.* & *n.* **1.** *a.* Serving to assist or supplement, auxiliary, supplementary; hence ~ĬLY[2] *adv.* **2.** (Of company) controlled by another on basis of voting power or issued share capital. **3.** (Of troops) paid for by subsidy, hired by another nation. **4.** *n.* Subsidiary thing or person, accessory; subsidiary company. [f. L *subsidiarius* (as SUBSIDY; see -ARY[1])]

sŭ'bsĭdīze, -īse (-īz), *v.t.* Pay subsidy to. [f. foll. + -IZE]

sŭ'bsĭdў *n.* **1.** (Hist.) Parliamentary grant of money to the sovereign for State needs; tax levied on particular occasion. **2.** Money grant from one State to another in return for military or naval aid or other equivalent. **3.** Money contributed by State or public body to keep down price of commodities etc. (*food, housing, subsidy*) or to expenses of commercial undertaking, charitable institution, etc., held to be of public utility. [ME, f. AF *subsidie*, OF *subside* f. L *subsidium* assistance; see -Y[1]]

subsĭ'st *v.* **1.** *v.i.* Exist, continue to exist, remain in being; keep oneself alive, support life, be kept alive, find sustenance, (*on vegetables, charity*, etc., *by begging* etc.). **2.** *v.t.* Provide sustenance for (*undertook to clothe, arm, and subsist 1000 men*). [f. L SUB(*sistere* set, stand) stand firm]

subsĭ'stence *n.* Subsisting; means of supporting life, livelihood, what one lives on or by; **~ allowance** or **money,** allowance or advance of pay granted for maintenance esp. while travelling on business; **~ farming** (in which almost all produce is consumed by farmer's household); **~ level, ~ wage,** (merely enough to provide the bare necessities of life). [f. LL *subsistentia* substance (as prec.; see -ENCE)]

sŭ'bsoil *n.* Soil lying immediately under surface soil. [f. SUB- 8 (4) + SOIL[1]]

sŭbsŏ'n|ic *a.* Relating to speeds less than that of sound; hence ~ICALLY *adv.* [f. SUB- 7 (2) + SONIC]

sŭ'bspēcies (-shēz *or* -shĭz) *n.* (*pl.* same). (Biol.) Taxonomic category below species, usu. a more or less permanent variety geographically isolated; so **sŭb**SPECĬ'FIC *a.* [f. SUB- 8 (2) + SPECIES]

sŭ'bstance *n.* **1.** (Metaphys.) The substratum that the cognizable properties or qualities or attributes or accidents of things are conceived as inhering in or affecting, the essential nature underlying phenomena, (*substance and accidents in metaphysics correspond to subject and predicate in logic*); essential nature (*the Son being of one substance with the Father*); essence or most important part of anything, pith, purport, real meaning, (*can give you the substance of his remarks*); *I agree with you* **in ~,** generally, apart from details. **2.** Theme, subject, material as opposed to form, (*the substance is good, but the style is repellent*). **3.** Reality, solidity, (arch.) wealth and possessions, (*sacrifice the substance for the shadow; there is no substance in him; an argument of little substance*); *a man* **of ~,** with much property, wealthy; **waste** one's **~,** be spendthrift. **4.** Particular kind of material having more or less uniform properties (*a heavy, porous, yellow, transparent, substance; the small number of substances that make up the world*). [ME f. OF, f. L SUB(*stantia* essence f. *stare* stand; see -ANCE)]

sŭbstă'ndard *a.* Of less than required or normal quality or size; inferior; (of language usage) existing in a community but not accepted in the standard language. [f. SUB- 7 (3) + STANDARD]

substă'ntial (-sh*a*l) *a.* Having substance, actually existing, not illusory, (*the ghost proved substantial after all*); of real importance or value, of considerable amount, (opp. *nominal, verbal*; *a substantial argument, point; awarded substantial damages; made a substantial contribution; made substantial progress, concessions*); of solid material or structure, not flimsy, stout, (*a substantial house; a man of substantial build*); possessed of much property, well-to-do, commercially sound, (*a substantial yeoman; deal only with substantial firms*); deserving the name in essentials, virtual, practical, (*substantial truth, agreement, success, performance of contract*); hence or cogn. ~ITY (-shĭă'l-) *n.*, ~LY[2] *adv.* [ME, f. OF *substantiel* or LL *substantialis* (as SUBSTANCE; see -AL)]

substă'ntial|ĭsm (-sh*a*-) *n.* (Philos.) Doctrine that behind phenomena there are substantial realities; so ~IST (2) *n.* [f. prec. + -ISM]

substă'ntialīze (-sh*a*-), **-īse** (-īz), *v.t.* & *i.* Invest with or acquire substance or actual existence. [f. SUBSTANTIAL + -IZE]

substă'ntĭ|āte (-shĭ-) *v.t.* Prove the truth of, give good grounds for, (charge, statement, claim); hence ~A'TION (*or* -sĭ-) *n.* [f. med. L *substantiare* give substance to, f. as SUBSTANCE, + -ATE[3]]

sŭ'bstantīve (*or*, in sense 2, substă'-) *a.* & *n.* **1.** *a.* Expressing existence (**the ~ verb,** 'to be'). **2.** Having separate and independent existence, not merely inferential or implicit or subservient or parasitic; (of enactment, motion, etc.) made in due form as such; (of dye) not needing mordant; (of law) relating to rights and duties; (Mil., of rank etc.) permanent (not brevet, honorary, acting, or temporary). **3.** (arch.) Denoting a substance (NOUN *substantive*). **4.** Hence ~LY² (-vlĭ) *adv.*, (esp. Gram., as a substantive). **5.** *n.* = NOUN 1; hence **sŭbstantī'vAL** *a.* [ME, f. OF *substantif -ive*, or f. LL *substantivus* (as SUBSTANCE; see -IVE)]

sŭ'bstātion *n.* Subordinate station, esp. reducing high voltage of electric power transmission to that suitable for supply to consumers. [f. SUB- 8 (1) + STATION]

substĭ'tūent *a.* & *n.* (Chem.) (Group of atoms) replacing another atom or group in a compound. [f. L (as foll.; see -ENT)]

sŭ'bstĭt|ūte *n.*, *a.*, & *v.* **1.** *n.* & *a.* (Person or thing) acting or serving in place of another; artificial food used in place of a natural food (*butter substitute*); (Sc. Law) deputy (*sheriff substitute*). **2.** *v.t.* Make (person or thing) fill a place or discharge a function for or *for* another; (vulg.) replace (person or thing) *by* or *with* another; put in exchange (*for*). **3.** *v.i.* Act as substitute (*for*). **4.** Hence or cogn. **~ūt**ABLE *a.*, **~ū'tION** *n.*, **~ū'tionAL**, **~ū'tionARY¹**, **~ūt**IVE, *adjs.* [ME, f. L *substitutus* p.p. of SUB(*stituere* = *statuere* set up)]

sŭ'bstrāte *n.* = foll.; surface to be painted, printed, etc., on; nutrient medium for bacteria culture. [Anglicized f. foll.; see -ATE¹]

sŭ'bstrāt|um (*or* -ah-) *n.* (*pl.* ~**a**). Underlying layer or substance; foundation, basis, (lit., or fig.: *there is a substratum of truth in it*). [mod. L, p.p. (as n.) of L SUB(*sternere* strew); cf. STRATUM]

sŭ'bstrŭctur|e *n.* Underlying or supporting structure; hence ~AL *a.* [f. SUB- 8 (4) + STRUCTURE]

subsū'me *v.t.* Include (instance etc.) under a rule or class; hence **subsŭ'mpt**ION *n.* [f. med. L SUB(*sumere sumpt-* take)]

sŭ'btĕnancў, sŭ'btĕnant, *ns.* See SUB- 8 (1).

subtĕ'nd *v.t.* (Geom.) (Of line, arc, figure, etc.) form (angle) *at* a point when its extremities are joined to that point; (of angle or chord) have bounding lines or points that meet or coincide with those of (line or arc). [f. L SUB(*tendere* stretch); cf. TEND¹]

sŭ'bterfūge *n.* Attempt to escape censure or defeat in argument by evading the issue or using deception; statement etc. resorted to for such purpose; use of such statements etc. [F, or f. LL *subterfugium* f. L *subterfugere* escape secretly (*subter* beneath, *fugere* flee)]

sŭbter'mĭnal *a.* Nearly at the end. [f. SUB- 7 (7) + TERMINAL]

sŭbterrā'nean *a.* Existing, occurring, or done under the earth's surface; underground. [f. L SUB(*terraneus* f. *terra* earth) + -AN]

subtil(e), subtilty. Vars. (arch.) of SUBTLE(TY).

sŭ'btĭliz|e, -is|e, (sŭ'tĭlīz) *v.* **1.** *v.t.* Make subtle; elevate, refine. **2.** Argue or reason subtly (*upon*). **3.** Hence ~A'TION *n.* [f. F *subtiliser* or f. med. L *subtilizare* (as SUBTLE; see -IZE)]

sŭ'btītle *n.*, & *v.t.* (Provide with) subordinate or additional title of book etc., or caption of cinema film. [f. SUB- 8 (1) + TITLE]

sŭ'btle (sŭ'tel) *a.* Pervasive or elusive owing to tenuity (*the subtle air*; *a subtle vapour*; *of subtle texture*; *a subtle perfume*); evasive, mysterious, hard to grasp or trace, (*subtle magic, charm, power, art, poison*; *a subtle distinction*); making fine distinctions, having delicate perception, acute, (*subtle senses, perception, insight*; *a subtle observer, philosopher, intellect, mind*); ingenious, elaborate, clever, (*a subtle device, fancy, workman, explanation, policy*; *subtle fingers*); crafty, cunning (*now the serpent was more subtle than any beast of the field*; *a subtle enemy*); hence **sŭ'bt**LY² (sŭ't-) *adv.* [ME f. OF *sotil*, f. L *subtilis*]

sŭ'btletў (sŭ'teltĭ) *n.* In adj. senses; a fine distinction, piece of hair-splitting. [ME, f. OF *s(o)utilté* f. L *subtilitas -tatis* (as prec.; see -TY¹)]

sŭbtŏ'nĭc *n.* (Mus.) Note below tonic, seventh note of diatonic scale of any key. [f. SUB- 8 (4) + TONIC]

||**sŭbtō'pĭ|a** *n.* (derog.) Suburban and rural areas disfigured by ill-planned and ugly building development; unsightly suburbs regarded as encroaching upon the natural scene; hence ~AN *a.* [f. SUBURB + UTOPIA]

sŭ'btōtal *n.* Total of part of a group of figures to be added. [f. SUB- 8 (2) + TOTAL]

subtră'ct *v.t.* Deduct (part, quantity, number) from or *from* whole or greater quantity or number, esp. in arithmetic or algebra; hence or cogn. ~ION *n.*, ~IVE *a.* [f. L SUB(*trahere tract-* draw)]

sŭ'btrahĕnd (-*a*-h-) *n.* (Math.) Quantity or number to be subtracted. [f. L *subtrahendus* gerundive of *subtrahere* (see prec.)]

sŭbtrŏ'pĭcal *a.* (Characteristic) of regions bordering on the tropics. [f. SUB- 7 (8) + TROPICAL]

sŭ'būlate *a.* (Bot. & Zool.) Slender and tapering. [f. L *subula* awl + -ATE²]

sŭ'bûrb *n.* Outlying district of city. [ME, f. OF *suburbe* or f. L SUB(*urbium* f. *urbs urbis* city)]

subûr'ban *a.* Of suburb(s); (derog.) provincial in outlook; hence ~ITE¹ (1) *n.*, ~IZE (3) *v.t.* [f. L *suburbanus* (as prec.; see -AN)]

Subûr'bĭa *n.* (usu. derog.) The suburbs (esp. of London) and their inhabitants. [f. SUBURB + -IA¹]

subvĕ'ntion *n.* Grant of money from government etc., subsidy. [ME f. OF, f. LL *subventio -onis* f. L SUB(*venire vent-* come) assist; see -ION]

subvêr'sĭve *a.* & *n.* (Person) seeking to subvert (esp. government); hence ~LY² (-vlĭ) *adv.*, ~NESS (-vn-) *n.* [f. med. L *subversivus* (as foll.; see -IVE)]

subvêr't *v.t.* Overturn, upset, effect destruction or overthrow of, (religion, monarchy, the constitution, principles, morality); so **subvêr's**ION (-shon) *n.* [ME, f. OF *subvertir* or f. L SUB(*vertere vers-* turn)]

sŭ'bway *n.* Underground passage for pipes etc. or for pedestrians to cross below road(s) etc.; *underground railway. [f. SUB- 8 (4) + WAY]

sŭbzēr'ō *a.* Less than zero (esp. on scale of temperature). [f. SUB- 7 (2) + ZERO]

suc- *pref.*, assim. form of SUB- 1–6 before *c*.

sŭccēdā'nē|um (-ks-) *n.* (*pl.* ~**a**). Substitute, thing (or occas. person) that one falls back on in default of another; so ~OUS *a.* [mod. L, neut. (as n.) of L *succedaneus* (as foll.; see -ANEOUS)]

succee'd (-ks-) *v.* **1.** *v.t.* Take the place previously filled by. **2.** *v.t.* & *i.* Follow in order, come next to or *to*, ensue, be subsequent (to), come by inheritance or in due order to or *to* office or title or property, (*day succeeds day* or *to day*; *agitation succeeded calm*; *succeeding ages will reverence his memory*; *Elizabeth I succeeded Mary, succeeded to the throne, succeeded*). **3.** *v.i.* Have success (*in doing* etc.); be successful, prosper, accomplish one's purpose; (of plan etc.) be brought to successful outcome. [ME, f. OF *succeder* or f. L SUC(*cedere cess-* go)]

succĕ'ntor (-ks-) *n.* Precentor's deputy in some cathedrals; hence ~SHIP *n.* [LL, f. L SUC(*cinere cent-* = *canere* sing); see -OR]

For other words in *sub-* see SUB-.

succès de scandale (sŏŏksā de skahñdah'l) *n.* Cordial reception given to work because of its scandalous nature or associations. [F]

succès d'estime (sŏŏksā dĕstē'm) *n.* Passably cordial reception given to performance or work from respect for performer or author rather than appreciation of its merits; *cordial reception by the critics but not by the general public. [F]

succès fou (sŏŏksā fōō') *n.* Success marked by wild enthusiasm. [F]

succĕ'ss (-ks-) *n.* **1.** Outcome of undertaking (*ill success*); favourable outcome, accomplishment of what was aimed at, attainment of wealth or fame or position, (*have inquired for it without success*; *military successes*; *spoilt by success*); **nothing succeeds like ~,** one success leads to others; **~ story,** person's rise from poverty etc. to fame; hence **~**FUL *a.*, **~ful**LY² *adv.* **2.** Thing or person that turns out well (*the experiment is a success*; *was a great success as a bishop*). [f. L *successus* (as SUCCEED)]

succĕ'ssion (-ksĕ'shon) *n.* **1.** A following in order; **in ~,** one after another, without intervention of anything else; **in quick ~,** following one another at short interval(s). **2.** Series of things in succession (*a succession of defeats*). **3.** (Right of) succeeding to the throne or any office or inheritance, set or order of persons having such right, (*laws regulating the succession*; *claimed, was excluded from, the succession*; *the succession must not be broken*; *is second in the succession*); **in ~ to,** as successor of; **apostolic ~,** uninterrupted transmission of spiritual authority through successive popes and other bishops from the Apostles; **law of ~** (regulating inheritance esp. in cases of intestate's decease); **settle the ~,** determine who shall succeed; **S~ State** (resulting from partition of previously existing country). **4.** (Biol.) Order of development of species or community; = SERE³. **5.** Hence **~**AL *a.* [ME f. OF, or f. L *successio* (as SUCCEED; see -ION)]

succĕ'ssive (-ks-) *a.* Following one after another, in uninterrupted succession, running, consecutive; hence **~**LY² (-vlĭ) *adv.* [ME, f. med. L *successivus* (as SUCCEED; see -IVE)]

succĕ'ssor (-ks-) *n.* Person or thing that succeeds to another (*successor of* or *to his father*; *his immediate successor*). [ME, f. OF *successour* f. L *successor* (as SUCCEED; see -OR)]

succĭ'nct (-ks-) *a.* Terse, concise, briefly expressed; hence **~**LY² *adv.*, **~**NESS *n.* [ME, f. L *succinctus* p.p. of SUC(*cingere* gird) tuck up]

succĭ'n|ic (-ks-) *a.* (Chem.) **~ic acid,** crystalline dibasic acid derived from amber etc.; hence **~**ATE¹ (3) (sŭ'ks-) *n.* [f. F *succinique* f. L *succinum* amber; see -IC]

sŭ'ccorÿ *n.* CHICORY plant. [alt. f. *cicoree* etc., early forms of CHICORY]

***sŭ'ccotăsh** *n.* Dish of green maize and beans boiled together. [f. Narraganset *msiquatash*]

Su'ccōth (sŏŏ'kōt) *n.* Jewish autumn thanksgiving festival commemorating sheltering in the wilderness. [f. Heb. *sukkôṯ* pl. of *sukkāh* thicket, hut]

sŭ'ccour (-ker), ***sŭ'ccor,** *v.t.*, & *n.* **1.** *v.t.* Come to the assistance of, give aid to, (person in danger or difficulty). **2.** *n.* Aid given at time of need; (in *pl.*, arch.) reinforcements, troops coming to the rescue; hence **~**LESS *a.* [ME, f. OF *socorre* v., *socours n.* f. med. L *succursus*, f. L SUC(*currere curs-* run)]

sŭ'ccūb|a *n.* (*pl.* **~ae**), **sŭ'ccūb|us** *n.* (*pl.* **~i** *pr.* -i). Female demon supposed to have sexual intercourse with sleeping men. [f. LL *succuba* prostitute, med. L *succubus*, f. SUC(*cubare* lie)]

sŭ'ccūl|ent *a.* & *n.* **1.** *a.* Juicy (of food, lit. or fig.); (Bot.) thick and fleshy, having such leaves or stems; hence **~**ENCE *n.*, **~ent**LY² *adv.* **2.** *n.* (Bot.) Succulent plant. [f. L *succulentus* (*succus* juice; see -ULENT)]

succŭ'mb (-m) *v.i.* Be overcome, have to cease from resistance or competition or other effort, be forced to give way *to*, die owing *to*, die, (*succumb to* one's *enemies, superior numbers, grief, temptation*, one's *injuries*). [ME, f. OF *succomber* or f. L SUC(*cumbere* lie)]

succŭr'sal *a.* (esp. Eccl., of chapel etc.) Subsidiary. [f. F *succursale* f. med. L *succursus* (as SUCCOUR; see -AL)]

sŭch *a.* (no *compar.* or *superl.*; placed not between *a* or *an* and *n.* but before or after them), & *pron.* **1.** *a.* Of the same kind or degree *as* (*such people, people such, as these*; *such beauty as yours*; *there is such a thing as divorce, you know*; *experiences such as this are rare*; *such grapes as you never saw*); **~ as,** (1) of the or a kind that (*a scarlet such as makes the eyes ache*), (2) for example (*insects, such as moths and bees*); **~ as it is,** if indeed it is good etc. enough to be called that. **2.** So great, having a quality in so high a degree, *as to* do or *that* (*is such as to make one despair*; *had such a fright that she hardly survived it*; *not such a fool as to believe that*). **3.** Of the kind or degree already described or implied in context (*never had such sport*; *there are no such doings now*; *it is no such thing*; *such things make one despair*; *such are the privileges of fatherhood*; *such is life*; *no such* LUCK; *don't be in such a hurry*; *how could you leave him at such a time?*; *saw just such* ANOTHER *yesterday*; *long may he continue such!*); (colloq. preceding *a.* & *n.* w. effect of *so* modifying the adjective: *don't use such horrid language*; *was it such a long time ago?*; *don't want such a big one* or *such big ones*); (occas. used twice correlatively, = LIKE¹ 1:) **~ master ~ man,** the servant is such as the master is. **4.** (Law or formal). The aforesaid, of the aforesaid kind (*whoever shall make such return falsely*). **5.** So great!, of a kind that demands exclamatory description, (*we have had such sport!*; (EVER) *such an enjoyable evening!*; *house has such a lot of windows*). **6.** Of a kind or degree sufficient to explain the preceding or following statement (*he cannot come too often, he gives such pleasure*; *there was such a draught, it is no wonder she caught cold*). **7.** **~(-and-~),** particular, of particular kind, but not needing to be specified (*will be in such-and-such a place at such-and-such a time*); **~-and-~ a person,** someone, so-and-so. **8.** **~ a one,** such a person or thing (*as*), (arch.) some person or thing unspecified. **9.** *pron.* **~ as,** those who, persons such as. **10.** That, the thing or action referred to, (*such being the case, we can do nothing*; *I may have offended, but such was not my intention*). **11.** **As ~,** as being what has been named (*in country places a stranger is welcome as such*); **all ~,** all persons of such character (*so perish all such!*). **12.** **~'like,** (colloq.) (things) of such kind. **13.** (vulg. or Commerc.) The aforesaid thing(s), it, they or them, (*those who leave parcels in the train cannot expect to recover such*). [OE *swilc*, *swylc*, = OS *sulik*, OHG *solih*, ON *slíkr*, Goth. *swaleiks* f. Gmc **swa* SO¹ + **lĭk* form (cf. LIKE¹)]

sŭck *v.* & *n.* **1.** *v.t.* Draw (milk, liquid) into mouth by making partial vacuum with muscles of lips etc., (fig.) imbibe or gain (*knowledge, advantage*, etc. *from*; *suck in knowledge*; *suck advantage out of*). **2.** Draw milk or liquid or sustenance or advantage from (*suck the breast, the mother*; **~ dry,** exhaust of contents thus); roll the tongue round, squeeze in the mouth, (*suck sweets*, one's *teeth*, etc.); (sl.) perform fellatio on. **3.** (Of substance) **~ in** or **up,** absorb;

(of whirlpool etc.) ~ **in,** engulf. **4.** *v.i.* Suck the breast or udder; suck something, use sucking action, make sucking sound, (*sat sucking at his pipe*); (of pump etc.) make gurgling or drawing sound; ~ **up,** (sl.) play toady (*to*). **5.** *n.* Opportunity of sucking the breast; **give** ~ (of mother or nurse or dam). **6.** Drawing action of whirlpool etc.; spell of sucking with lips or in mouth (*take a suck at it*); small draught of or *of* liquor; (sl., esp. in *pl.*) disappointment, fiasco, (**what a** ~!, ~**s!,** *ints.* expr. amusement at another's failure after confidence). [OE *sūcan*, = L *sugere* f. IE **sūg*-]

sŭ'cker *n.* & *v.* **1.** *n.* Person or thing that sucks, esp. sucking-pig or new-born whale; (sl.) person easily deceived, greenhorn, (**be a** ~ **for,** be unable to resist attractions of); fish that has mouth suggesting suction or adheres by suction; *lollipop. **2.** Piston of suction-pump; pipe through which liquid is drawn by suction. **3.** Flat or concave animal organ or artificial device of rubber etc. that adheres by suction and atmospheric pressure to what it is placed against. **4.** (Bot.) Shoot springing from subterranean part of stem, from part of root remote from main stem, from axil, or abnormally from bole or branch. **5.** *v.t.* & *i.* (Bot.) Remove suckers from; produce suckers. [ME, f. prec. + -ER¹]

sŭ'ckĭng *a.* In vbl senses; not yet weaned (*sucking child, sucking-pig*), unfledged (*sucking dove*); ~**-disc,** = prec. 3; ~**-fish,** remora. [f. SUCK + -ING²]

sŭ'ckle *v.* **1.** *v.t.* Give suck to; (fig.) nourish. **2.** *v.i.* Feed by sucking at breast or udder. [ME, prob. back form. f. foll.]

sŭ'cklĭng *n.* Unweaned child or animal; BABES *and sucklings*. [ME, f. SUCK + -LING¹]

sū'crōse *n.* (Chem.) Sugar obtained from sugar-cane, sugar-beet, etc. [f. F *sucre* SUGAR + -OSE²]

sŭ'ction *n.* Sucking; production of partial vacuum by removal of air etc. for purpose of enabling external atmospheric pressure to force in liquid or produce adhesion of surfaces; ~**-pump** (drawing liquid through pipe into chamber exhausted by piston). [f. LL *suctio* f. L *sugere suct-* SUCK; see -ION]

sŭctŏr'|ĭal *a.* (Zool.) Adapted for or capable of sucking; having sucker for feeding or adhering; so ~IAN *n.* [f. mod. L *suctorius* (as prec.; see -ORY) + -AL]

Sudanē'se (sōōdanē'z) *a.* & *n.* (*pl.* same). (Native or inhabitant) of (the) Sudan. [f. *Sudan*, republic in N.E. Africa, or the *Sudan*, region of Africa S. of Sahara desert, + -ESE]

sūdār'ĭ|um (*or* sōō-) *n.* (*pl.* ~**a**). Cloth for wiping face, esp. St. Veronica's kerchief miraculously impressed with face of Christ; = VERONICA 2. [L, = napkin (*sudor* sweat; see -ARY¹)]

sūdatŏr'ĭ|um (*or* sōō-) *n.* (*pl.* ~**a**). (esp. Rom. Ant.) Hot-air or steam bath taken in order to induce sweating. [L, neut. of *sudatorius* (see foll.)]

sū'datorў (*or* sōō'-) *a.* & *n.* **1.** *a.* Promoting perspiration. **2.** *n.* Sudatory drug; = prec. [f. L *sudatorius* (*sudare* sweat; see -ORY)]

sŭdd *n.* Floating plants, trees, etc., impeding navigation of White Nile. [Arab., = obstruction]

sŭ'dden *a.* & *n.* **1.** *a.* Occurring or come upon or made or done unexpectedly or without warning, abrupt, abnormally rapid, hurried, (*sudden need, fear; a sudden resolve, departure, change, turn of the wrist, bend in the road; is very sudden in his movements*); ~ **death,** (fig., colloq.) decision by a single toss of a coin, decision of draw or tie by result of next game, next hole won, etc.; hence ~LY² *adv.*, ~NESS (-n-n-) *n.* **2.** *n.* (**All**) **of a** or **on a** ~, suddenly. [ME, f. AF *sodein*, *sudein*, OF *soudain* f. LL *subitanus* f. L *subitaneus* (*subitus* sudden; see -ANEOUS)]

sūdorĭ'ferous (*or* sōō-) *a.* (Of gland etc.) secreting sweat. [f. LL *sudorifer* f. L *sudor* sweat; see -FEROUS]

sūdorĭ'fĭc (*or* sōō-) *a.* & *n.* (Drug) causing sweating. [f. mod. L *sudorificus* f. L *sudor* sweat; see -FIC]

Su'dra (sōō'-) *n.* Lowest of four great Hindu castes. [f. Skr. *çūdra*]

sŭds (-z) *n.*, & *v.i.* **1.** *n. pl.* (**Soa'p**)~, froth of soap and water; hence ~'Y² *a.* **2.** *v.i.* Form suds. [orig. = fen waters etc., of uncert. orig.; cf. MDu., MLG *sudde*, MDu. *sudse* marsh, bog, prob. rel. to SEETHE]

sūe (*or* sōō) *v.t.* & *i.* **1.** Institute legal proceedings against (person, or abs.); make application to or *to* lawcourt *for* redress; ~ (**out**), make petition in lawcourt for and obtain (writ, pardon, etc.). **2.** Entreat (person, or abs.); make entreaty *to* (person), *for* a favour. [ME, f. AF *suer*, *siwer*, etc. f. OF *siu-* etc. st. of *sivre* f. Rom. **sequere* f. L *sequi* follow]

suede (swād) *n.* Kid or other skin with flesh side rubbed to a nap; ~(**-cloth**), woven fabric with short nap imitating this. [f. F (*gants de*) *Suède* (gloves of) Sweden]

sū'ĕt (*or* sōō'-) *n.* Hard fat of kidneys and loins of oxen, sheep, etc.; ~ **pudding** (made with suet and usu. boiled or steamed); hence ~Y² *a.* [ME, f. AF **suet*, **sewet* f. OF *seu* f. L *sebum* tallow; see -ET¹]

suf- *pref.*, assim. form of SUB- 1–6 before *f*.

sŭ'ffer *v.* **1.** *v.t.* Undergo, experience, be subjected to, (pain, loss, grief, defeat, change, punishment, wrong, etc.). **2.** *v.i.* Undergo pain or grief or damage or disablement (*suffers acutely; suffering mortals; was suffering from neuralgia; your reputation will suffer; the engine suffered severely; trade is suffering from the war*); undergo martyrdom; hence ~ER¹, ~ING¹ (1), *ns.* **3.** *v.t.* Permit *to* do, allow to go on, put up with, tolerate, (*suffer them to come; should not suffer it for a moment; does not suffer fools gladly*); hence ~ABLE *a.* [ME, f. AF *suffrir*, *soeffrir*, OF *sof*(*f*)*rir* f. Rom. **sufferire* f. L SUF(*ferre* bear)]

sŭ'fferance *n.* Tacit consent, permission or toleration implied by abstinence from objection, (**on** ~, in virtue of such toleration); (arch.) submissiveness. [ME, f. AF, OF *suffraunce* f. LL *sufferentia* (as prec.; see -ENCE)]

suffī'ce *v.* **1.** *v.i.* Be enough (*to* do, *for* person or purpose, or abs.), be adequate, (*your word will suffice; that suffices to prove it*); ~ **it to say,** I will content myself with saying *that*. **2.** *v.t.* Satisfy, meet the needs of, (*half a dozen sufficed him*). [ME, f. OF *suffire* (*suffis-*) f. L SUF(*ficere* = *facere* make)]

suffĭ'ciencў (-shen-) *n.* Adequate resources, a competence, a sufficient amount of or *of* something; (arch.) being sufficient, ability, efficiency. [f. LL *sufficientia* (as foll.; see -ENCY)]

suffĭ'cient (-shent) *a.* & *n.* **1.** *a.* Sufficing, adequate esp. in amount or number to the need, enough, (*is sufficient to feed a hundred men; had not sufficient courage for it; has impudence sufficient for anything; have you sufficient provisions?*); SELF-*-sufficient*; hence ~LY² *adv.* **2.** (arch.) Competent, of adequate ability or resources. **3.** *n.* Enough, a sufficient quantity, (*have you had sufficient?; am not sufficient of an expert to decide*). [ME f. OF, or f. L *sufficiens* (as SUFFICE; see -ENT)]

suffĭ'x¹ (*or* sŭ'-) *v.t.* Append, esp. as suffix; hence ~A'TION *n.* [f. foll. & L *suffixus* p.p. (see foll.)]

sŭ'ffix² *n.* Verbal element added at end of word to form derivative (e.g. *-ation, -fy, -ing, -itis*); (Math.) = SUBSCRIPT 2. [f. mod. L *suffixum* neut. p.p. (as n.) of L SUF(*figere fix-* fasten)]

sŭ'ffoc|āte *v.* **1.** *v.t.* (Of person, overlying mass, fumes, etc.) choke or kill by stopping breathing; produce choking sensation in, impede breath or utterance of, (*suffocated by* or *with grief, excitement*, etc.). **2.** *v.i.* Be or feel suffocated, gasp for breath. **3.** So ~A'TION *n.* [f. L SUF(*focare* f. *fauces* throat) + -ATE[3]]

Sŭ'ffolk (-ok) *n.* Breed of black-faced sheep; =*Suffolk* PUNCH[4]. [~ in England]

sŭ'ffragan *a.* & *n.* ~ (**bishop**), **bishop** ~, (1) bishop appointed to help diocesan bishop in administration of diocese, (2) bishop in relation to his archbishop or metropolitan; ~ **see** etc. (of suffragan bishop); hence ~SHIP *n.* [ME f. AF & OF, repr. med. L *suffraganeus* assistant (bishop) f. L *suffragium* (see foll., -AN)]

sŭ'ffrage *n.* **1.** Vote, view expressed by voting, (*the electors gave their suffrages for and against*); opinion in support of proposal etc. **2.** Right of voting in political elections; **manhood** ~ (extended to all adult males other than those disqualified e.g. as being criminals, without property tests etc.); **female** or **woman** ~ (extended to women as well as men); **universal** ~ (extended to all adults with minor exceptions). **3.** (Eccl., esp. in *pl.*) Intercessory petition of priest in liturgy; short petition of congregation, esp. one said in response to priest; (arch.) an intercessory prayer. [ME, f. L *suffragium*, partly thr. F *suffrage*]

sŭffragĕ'tte *n.* (Hist.) Woman who agitated, esp. with violence, for woman suffrage. [f. prec. + -ETTE, after foll.]

sŭ'ffragist *n.* One who advocates extension of the suffrage, esp. to women. [f. SUFFRAGE + -IST]

suffū'se (-z) *v.t.* (Of colour or moisture) well up from within and colour or moisten (*a blush, tears, suffused her cheeks, eyes*); (fig.) overspread with colour etc.; so **suffū'sion** (-zhon) *n.* [f. L SUF(*fundere fus-* pour)]

Su'f|ĭ (sōō'-) *n.* Muslim ascetic (and pantheistic) mystic; hence ~IC *a.*, ~ISM (3) *n.* [f. Arab. *ṣūfī*, perh. f. *ṣūf* wool (from his woollen garment)]

sug- *pref.*, assim. form of SUB- 1–6 before *g*.

su'gar (shŏŏ'-) *n.*, & *v.t.* **1.** *n.* Sweet crystalline substance obtained from various plants, esp. the sugar-cane and sugar-beet, for use in cookery, confectionery, brewing, etc.; **cane, beet, maple,** etc., -~ (named from plant of origin); BROWN[1], WHITE[1], CASTOR[2], LUMP[1], *sugar*. **2.** Sweet words, flattery, anything comparable to sugar put round pill in reconciling person to what is unpalatable; *(sl.) money; *(as colloq. term of address) dear, darling. **3.** (Chem.) Soluble usu. sweet-tasting simple crystalline carbohydrate of group found esp. in plants, e.g. glucose; ~ **of lead,** lead acetate. **4.** ‖**~-basin** (holding sugar for table use); **~-beet** (from which sugar is extracted); **~-bird** (of kind that sucks nectar from flowers); **~-bowl,** = *sugar-basin*; *sugar-*CANDY; **~-cane,** a perennial tropical grass with stout jointed stems 18–20 ft. high from which sugar is made; **~-coated,** (of food) enclosed in sugar, (fig.) made superficially attractive; ***~-daddy,** (sl.) elderly man who lavishes gifts on a young woman; **~-gum,** Australian gum-tree with sweet foliage eaten by cattle; **~-house,** establishment in which raw sugar is made; *sugar-*LOAF[1]; **~-maple,** *Acer saccharum* etc. (from sap of which sugar is made); **~-mill** (for crushing sugar-cane and extracting sugar); **~-mite** (infesting unrefined sugar); **~-pea,** kind of pea eaten with pod; **~plum,** (arch.) sweetmeat, esp. small ball of boiled sugar; **~-refiner(y),** (establishment of) manufacturer who refines raw sugar; **~-shaker, ~-sifter,** (for sprinkling powdered sugar); ~ **soap,** abrasive compound for cleaning or removing paint; **~-tongs,** small tongs for picking up lump sugar at table. **5.** Hence ~LESS *a.* **6.** *v.t.* Sweeten with sugar (lit. or fig.); coat with sugar (*sugar the pill*); spread sugar mixture on (tree) to catch moths. [ME, f. OF *çukre, sukere* f. It. *zucchero* prob. f. med. L *succarum* f. Arab. *sūkkar*]

su'gar|ỹ (shŏŏ'-) *a.* Containing or resembling sugar; (fig.) attractively or excessively sweet or pleasant; hence ~ĬNESS *n.* [f. prec. + -Y[2]]

suggĕ'st (suj-) *v.t.* **1.** Cause (idea) to present itself, call up the idea of by mention or association; (of thing) ~ **itself,** come into the mind. **2.** Propose (theory, plan, *that*) for acceptance or rejection, set up the hypothesis *that*, (*suggested a retreat, that they should retreat, that the calculation was incorrect*); **I ~ that** (formula of examining counsel in imputing motives etc.: *I suggest that you had a secret understanding with them*). [f. L SUG(*gerere gest-* bring)]

suggĕ'st|ĭble (suj-) *a.* That may be suggested; open to (esp. hypnotic) suggestion; hence ~IBI'LITY *n.* [f. prec. + -IBLE]

suggestio falsi (sujĕstĭō fă'lsī) *n.* Positive misrepresentation not involving direct lie but going beyond concealment of the truth (cf. SUPPRESSIO VERI). [L]

suggĕ'stion (sujĕ'schon) *n.* Suggesting or being suggested; theory or plan suggested; suggesting of lewd ideas; insinuation of a belief or impulse into the mind, such belief or impulse; hint, slight trace, (*not a suggestion of condescension about her*); **~(s)-book, ~(s)-box,** (to receive written suggestions for improvements etc.). [ME f. OF, f. L *suggestio -onis* (as SUGGEST; see -ION)]

suggĕ'stive (suj-) *a.* Conveying a suggestion (*of*); suggesting something indecent; hence ~LY[2] (-vlĭ) *adv.*, ~NESS (-vn-) *n.* [f. SUGGEST + -IVE]

sū'ĭcidal (*or* sōō'- *or* -ī'd-) *a.* Pertaining to suicide; (of person) tending to commit suicide; (fig.) destructive or fatal to one's own interests etc.; hence ~LY[2] *adv.* [f. foll. + -AL]

sū'ĭcide (*or* sōō'-) *n.*, & *v.i.* **1.** *n.* Person who intentionally kills himself. **2.** Intentional self-slaughter; **commit ~,** kill oneself intentionally; ~ **pact,** agreement between persons to commit suicide together; ~ **pilot** etc. (on dangerous mission in war, or undertaking a mission involving his own death). **3.** Action destructive to one's own interests or continuance in some capacity; **commit political ~,** ruin one's prospects as a politician, political party, etc.; RACE[3] *suicide*. **4.** *v.i.* Commit suicide. [f. mod. L *suicida, suicidium*, f. L *sui* of oneself; see -CIDE]

sui generis (sūī jĕ'nerĭs; *or* sōōē g-) *a.* Of its own kind, peculiar, unique. [L]

sui juris (sūī joor'ĭs; *or* sōōē ūr'-) *a.* Of full age and capacity, independent. [L]

sū'illine *a.* Of the pig family. [f. L *suillus* (*sus* pig) + -INE[1]]

sū'i-māte. See MATE[1].

suint (swĭ-) *n.* Natural grease in sheep's wool. [F (*suer* sweat)]

suit (sūt *or* sōōt) *n.* & *v.* **1.** *n.* Suing, petition, seeking of woman's hand in marriage, (*pay suit to; press, push*, etc., one's *suit; prosper in* one's *suit*). **2.** ~ (**at law**), lawsuit (*criminal, civil*, etc., *suit*). **3.** Any of the four sets (spades, hearts, diamonds, clubs) into which pack of cards is divided (**follow** ~, play card of suit that was led, fig. conform to another's actions); player's holding in it (LONG[1], SHORT, STRONG, *suit*); (Bridge) one of the suits as proposed trumps in bidding, opp. no trumps. **4.** Set of outer clothes esp. when of same cloth, consisting usu. of coat (and for men sometimes waistcoat) and trousers or skirt; costume for use in particular circumstances (PLAY²-*suit*, SPACE¹*suit*, SWIM-*suit*); **~'case,** oblong case for carrying clothes, usu. with handle and flat hinged lid; hence ~'ING¹ (3) *n.* **5.** Set *of* sails, set *of* armour, for simultaneous use. **6.** *v.t.* Accommodate, adapt, make fitting or appropriate, *to* (*suit* one's *style to* one's *audience*; **~ the action to the word,** carry out promise or threat at once); (in *p.p.*) appropriate *to*, well adapted or having the right qualities *for*, (*is not suited to be* or *for an engineer*). **7.** Satisfy, meet the demands or requirements or interests of, (*does not suit all tastes*; *it suits me* or *my* BOOK¹ *to put up with him*; **~ yourself,** (1) do as you choose, (2) find something that satisfies you); (of food, climate, etc.) improve or not impair the health of, agree with, (*cold*, *asparagus*, *does not suit me*). **8.** *v.t.* & *i.* Go well with or *with* appearance or character of, become, (*red does not suit with*, *suits*, *her complexion*; *the part suits him admirably*; *mercy suits a king*). **9.** *v.i.* Be convenient (*that date will suit*). [ME, f. AF *siute*, OF *si(e)ute* f. Gallo-Rom. **sequita* fem. p.p. (as n.) of Rom. **sequere* follow; see SUE]

sui't|able (sū't- *or* sōō't-) *a.* Suited *to* or *for*, well fitted for the purpose, appropriate to the occasion; hence ~ABI'LITY, **~able**NESS (-beln-), *ns.*, **~ab**LY² *adv.* [f. prec. + -ABLE, after *agreeable*]

suite (swēt) *n.* Retinue, set of persons in attendance; set of things, esp. rooms or furniture, belonging together; (Mus.) set of instrumental compositions with related themes, orig. succession of movements in dance style. [F (as SUIT)]

sui'tor (sū't- *or* sōō't-) *n.* Plaintiff or petitioner in lawsuit; wooer, man who seeks to marry a (specified) woman. [ME, f. AF *seutor*, *suitour*, etc., f. L *secutor -oris* (*sequi secut-* follow; see -OR)]

suk(h). Vars. of SOUK.

sukĭya'kĭ (sōō-; -ah'-) *n.* Japanese dish of sliced meat fried with vegetables and sauce. [Jap.]

sŭ'lcāte *a.* (Bot. & Anat.) Grooved, fluted, channelled. [f. L *sulcatus* p.p. of *sulcare* furrow (as foll.); see -ATE²]

sŭ'lc|us *n.* (*pl.* **~i** *pr.* -sī). Groove, furrow, esp. between two convolutions of brain. [L]

sŭ'lfa. See SULPHA.

***sŭ'lfur** etc. See SULPHUR etc.

sŭlk *n.*, & *v.i.* **1.** *n.* (usu. in *pl.*) Sulky fit. **2.** *v.i.* Be sulky. [n. f. v., perh. back form. f. foll.]

sŭ'lk|ў *a.* & *n.* **1.** *a.* Sullen, morose, silent or inactive or unsociable from resentment or ill temper; (of thing) sluggish; hence **~ĭ**LY² *adv.*, **~ĭ**NESS *n.* **2.** *n.* Light two-wheeled one-horse vehicle for single person, esp. as used in trotting-races. [perh. f. obs. *sulke* hard to dispose of + -Y²]

sŭ'llage *n.* Filth, refuse, sewage. [perh. f. AF *s(*o)uillage* (*souiller* SOIL²; see -AGE)]

sŭ'llen *a.* & *n.* **1.** *a.* Passively resentful, unforgiving, gloomy-tempered, unsociable, not responding to friendliness or encouragement or urging, stubbornly ill-humoured, morose; dismal, melancholy; hence ~LY² *adv.*, ~NESS (-n-n-) *n.* **2.** *n.* (in *pl.*, arch.) Sullen frame of mind, ill temper, depression. [16th c. alt. f. ME *solein* f. AF **solein* (*sol* SOLE³)]

sŭ'llў *v.t.* Diminish the purity or splendour of (reputation, character, victory, etc.), disgrace; (poet.) soil, tarnish. [perh. f. F *souiller* (as SOIL²)]

sŭ'lpha, sŭ'lfa, *a.* Sulphonamide (*sulpha drug*). [abbr. of SULPHANILAMIDE]

sŭlphă'mĭc, *sŭlf-, *a.* **~ acid,** strong acid used as weed-killer, an amide of sulphuric acid; hence **sŭ'lpham**ATE¹ (3) *n.* [f. SULPHUR + AMIDE + -IC]

sŭlphanĭ'lamīde, *sŭlf-, *n.* Colourless sulphonamide drug with anti-bacterial properties. [f. *sulphanilic* (SULPHUR, ANILINE, -IC) + AMIDE]

sŭ'lphāte, *sŭ'lf-, *n.* Salt of sulphuric acid. [f. F *sulfate*, f. L *sulphur*; see -ATE³]

sŭ'lphīde, *sŭ'lf-, *n.* Binary compound of sulphur. [f. SULPHUR + -IDE]

sŭ'lphīte, *sŭ'lf-, *n.* Salt of sulphurous acid. [f. F *sulfite* alt. of *sulfate* SULPHATE; cf. -ITE¹ (2)]

sŭlphŏ'namīde, *sŭlf-, *n.* & *a.* ~ (**drug**), substance derived from amide of a sulphonic acid, able to prevent multiplication of some pathogenic bacteria. [f. foll. + AMIDE]

sŭ'lphōne, *sŭ'lf-, *n.* Organic compound containing SO_2 group united directly to two carbon atoms; hence **sŭ'lphon**ATE¹ (3), **sŭlphon**A'TION, *ns.*, **sŭlphŏ'n**IC *a.* [f. G *sulfon* (as SULPHUR, -ONE)]

sŭ'lphur, *sŭ'lfur, *n.*, *a.*, & *v.t.* **1.** *n.* Pale-yellow non-metallic element having crystalline and amorphous forms, burning with blue flame and suffocating smell, and used in making gunpowder, matches, and sulphuric acid, in vulcanizing, and in medical treatment of skin-diseases; FLOWER*s*, LIVER¹, MILK¹, *of sulphur*. **2.** Yellow butterfly of family Pieridae. **3.** Material of which hell-fire and lightning were held to consist. **4. ~-bottom** (**whale**), Pacific rorqual with yellow belly; **~ candle** (burnt to produce sulphur dioxide for fumigating); **~-spring** (of water impregnated with sulphur or its compounds); **~-wort,** yellow-flowered herb, hog's fennel. **5.** Hence ~Y² *a.* **6.** *a.* Containing or like sulphur; of pale slightly greenish yellow. **7.** *v.t.* Apply sulphur to; fumigate with sulphur. [ME, f. AF *sulf(e)re*, OF *soufre* f. L *sulfur*, *sulp(h)ur*]

sŭ'lphūr|āte, *sŭ'lf-, *v.t.* Impregnate or fumigate or treat with sulphur, esp. in bleaching; hence ~A'TION, **~āt**OR, *ns.* [f. prec. + -ATE³]

sŭlphūr'ėous, *sŭlf-, *a.* Of, like, suggesting, sulphur; sulphur-coloured. [f. L *sulphureus* (SULPHUR); see -EOUS]

sŭlphūrĕ'ttėd, *sŭlfūrĕ'ttėd, *a.* Containing sulphur in combination; **~ hydrogen,** hydrogen sulphide. [f. *sulphuret* sulphide f. mod. L *sulphuretum* (cf. -URET), + -ED²]

sŭlphūr'ĭc, *sŭlf-, *a.* (Chem.) Containing sulphur in a higher valency (cf. SULPHUROUS); **~ acid,** H_2SO_4, dense oily colourless highly acid and corrosive fluid much used in chemical industry; **~ ether,** = ETHER 3. [f. F *sulfurique* (as SULPHUR; see -IC)]

sŭ'lphūriz|e, -is|e (-īz), ***sŭ'lf-,** *v.t.* = SULPHURATE; hence ~A'TION *n.* [f. F *sulfuriser* (as SULPHUR; see -IZE)]

sŭ'lphūrous, *sŭ'lf-, *a.* **1.** = SULPHUREOUS. **2.** (*or* -ūr'-) (Chem.) Containing sulphur in a lower valency (cf. SULPHURIC); **~ acid,** H_2SO_3, unstable weak acid used as reducing and bleaching agent. [f. L SULPHUR(*osus* -OUS), or f. SULPHUR + -OUS]

sŭ'ltan *n.* **1.** Muslim sovereign; **the S~,** (Hist.) sultan of Turkey; hence ~ATE¹ *n.* **2.** Gorgeously coloured bird of genus *Porphyrio*; variety of white domestic fowl from Turkey; (**sweet**) ~, sweet-scented plant, *Centaurea moschata* or *C. suaveolens*. [F, or f. med. L *sultanus*, f. Arab. *sulṭān* power, ruler (*saluṭa* rule)]

sŭlta'na (-tah'-) *n.* **1.** Sultan's mother, wife, concubine, or daughter. **2.** Mistress of king etc. **3.** Sultan-bird. **4.** Seedless raisin used in puddings and cakes; small pale yellow grape yielding it. [It., fem. of *sultano* = prec.]

sŭ'ltanėss *n.* (arch.) = prec. 1. [f. SULTAN + -ESS¹]

sŭ'ltr|ў *a.* (Of atmosphere or weather) hot and close or oppressive; (of temper etc. or person) passionate, sensual; hence **~ĭ**LY² *adv.*, **~ĭ**NESS *n.*

[f. obs. *sulter* swelter prob. f. **swulter* cogn. w. SWELTER + -Y²]

sŭm *n.* & *v.* (**-mm-**). **1.** *n.* ~ (**total**), total amount resulting from addition of items, brief expression that includes but does not specify details, substance, summary, (*the sum of two and three is five*; *the sum of all my wishes is happiness*; *the sum of his objections is this*); **in ~**, briefly but comprehensively put. **2.** Particular amount of money (*what sum would you give for it?*; *for the sum of £15*; *a good, round, considerable, sum*; LUMP¹ *sum*). **3.** (Working out of) an arithmetical problem (*good at sums*; *did a rapid sum in his head*). **4.** *v.t.* Find sum of; ~ (**up**), collect into or express or include as one total or whole; gather *up* (evidence, points of argument etc., already treated in detail) into brief review; **~ up,** form or express idea of character of (person). **5.** *v.i.* **~ up,** (esp. of judge after both sides have been heard) make recapitulation of evidence or argument, whence ~*ming¹-u'p n.* [ME, f. OF *summe, somme,* f. L *summa* main part, fem. of *summus* highest; v. f. OF *sommer* or f. med. L *summare* f. L *summa*]

sū'măc, -ăch, (-k; *or* sōō'- *or* shōō'-) *n.* (Dried and ground leaves, used in tanning and dyeing, of) shrub of genus *Rhus*. [ME f. OF *sumac* or f. med. L *sumac(h)* f. Arab. *summāk*]

Sūmēr'ĭan *a.* & *n.* (Archaeol.) **1.** *a.* Of the early and non-Semitic element in the civilization of ancient Babylonia. **2.** *n.* The Sumerian language; Sumerian person. [f. F *sumérien* (*Sumer* in Babylonia; see -IAN)]

sŭ'mma *a.* (*pl.* ~**e**). Summary of what is known of a subject. [ME, f. L (see SUM)]

sŭ'mmar|ize, -ise (-īz), *v.t.* Make or be a summary of, sum up; so ~IST (1) *n.* [f. foll. + -IZE]

sŭ'mmar|y̆ *a.* & *n.* **1.** *a.* Compendious, brief, dispensing with needless details or formalities, done with despatch or (Law) without formalities required by common law, (*a summary account*; *summary methods*); **~y jurisdiction,** authority of a court to use summary proceedings and arrive at judgement or conviction; **~y offence** (within scope of summary court); hence **~ĭLY²** *adv.* **2.** *n.* Brief account, abridgement, epitome. [ME, a. f. med. L *summarius*, n. f. L *summarium*, f. L *summa* SUM; see -ARY¹]

summā'tion *n.* Addition, finding of total or sum; summing-up; hence ~AL a. [f. SUM 4 + -ATION]

sŭ'mmer¹ *n.*, *a.*, & *v.* **1.** *n.* Warmest season of the year, in N. hemisphere June–August (Astron., from summer solstice to autumnal equinox); INDIAN *summer*; ||**St. Luke's ~**, ||**St. Martin's ~**, period of fine weather expected about 18 Oct., 11 Nov. **2.** Weather typical of summer; (fig.) mature stage of life etc. **3.** (poet., usu. in *pl.* with number etc.) Year of life or age (*a child of ten summers*). **4.** *a.* Characteristic of or fit for summer; **~-house,** light building in garden etc. providing cool shade in summer; *summer* LIGHTNING; **~ pudding** (of chopped usu. soft fruit in bread or sponge-cake); **~ school,** long-vacation meeting for lectures etc., esp. at university; *summer* SOLSTICE; **~-time** or **~time,** the weather or season of summer: ||**~ time** (shown by clocks advanced in summer for DAYLIGHT saving); **~-weight,** (of clothes) suitable in weight for use in summer. **5.** Hence ~LESS, ~LY¹, ~Y², *adjs*. **6.** *v.i.* Pass the summer (*at* or *in* place). **7.** *v.t.* Pasture (cattle) *at* or *in*. [OE *sumor*, = OS, OHG, ON *sumar*]

sŭ'mmer² *n.* ~(**-tree**), horizontal bearing beam, esp. one supporting joists or rafters. [ME, f. AF *sumer, somer* pack-horse, beam, OF *somier* f. Rom. **saumarius* f. LL *sagmarius* (*sagma* f. Gk *sagma* pack-saddle)]

summersault, -set. Vars. of SOMERSAULT.

sŭ'mmĭt *n.* Highest point, top, apex, highest degree, (*the icy summits of the Alps*; *at the summit of power*; *the summit of my ambition is*); ~ (**meeting, talks,** etc.), discussion taking place between heads of governments, whence ~RY (5) *n.*; hence ~LESS *a.* [ME, f. OF *somet, som(m)ete,* (*som* top f. L *summum* neut. of *summus*; see -ET¹)]

sŭ'mmon *v.t.* Demand the presence of, call upon to appear, esp. as defendant or witness in lawcourt, so ~ER² (4) *n.* (Hist.); call together by authority for action or discussion; call upon (*to* do, esp. town etc. to surrender); **~ up,** gather (courage, spirit, etc.) usu. *to* do or *for* undertaking. [ME, f. OF *somondre* f. pop. L **summonere* f. L *summonēre* (as SUB- 2, *monēre* warn)]

sŭ'mmons (-z) *n.*, & *v.t.* **1.** *n.* Authoritative call or urgent invitation to attend on some occasion or do something. **2.** Call to appear before judge or magistrate. **3.** *v.t.* Serve with summons. [ME, f. OF *somonce, sumunse* f. Gallo-Rom. **summonsa* f. L *summonita* fem. p.p. (as n.) of *summonēre* (see prec.)]

summum bonum (sŭmum bō'num) *n.* The chief good, esp. as the end or ultimate determining principle in an ethical system. [L]

su'mō (sōō'-) *n.* (*pl.* ~**s**). (Participant in) Japanese wrestling where defeat follows touching of ground except with feet, or failure to keep within marked area. [Jap.]

sŭmp *n.* Pit or well for the reception of (esp. superfluous) water, oil, or other liquid in mines, machines, etc.; cesspool. [ME = marsh, f. MDu., MLG *sump*, or (mining) G *sumpf*, rel. to SWAMP]

sŭ'mpter *n.* (arch.) Pack-horse; pack-animal (*sumpter-horse, -mule, -pony*). [ME, f. OF *som(m)etier* f. Rom. **saumatarius* f. LL f. Gk *sagma -atos* pack-saddle; cf. SUMMER², -ER² (2)]

sŭ'mptūary̆ *a.* Regulating expenditure; (of law, edict, etc.) limiting private expenditure, in the interests of the State. [f. L *sumptuarius* (*sumptus* cost f. *sumere sumpt-* take)]

sŭ'mptūous *a.* Rich and costly; suggesting lavish expenditure; hence ~LY² *adv.*, ~NESS, **sŭmptūŏ'SITY**, *ns.* [ME, f. OF *somptueux* f. L *sumptuosus* (as prec.; see -OUS)]

sŭn *n.* & *v.* (**-nn-**). **1.** *n.* The star that the earth travels round and receives warmth and light from, such light or warmth or both (*keep out, let in, the sun*). **2. ~ rises, sets,** (is brought by earth's rotation above, below, the horizon); *his, its,* etc., **~ is set,** time of prosperity or existence is over; **rise with the ~**, get up early; **hail** or **adore the rising sun,** curry favour with new or coming power; *empire* etc. **on which the ~ never sets,** world-wide; **let not the ~ go down upon your wrath,** limit it to one day. **3. Against the ~**, counter-CLOCK¹*wise*; **hold a candle to the ~**, do something quite superfluous; **catch the ~**, (1) be in sunny position, (2) become sunburnt; *make* HAY¹ *while the sun shines*; **in the ~**, exposed to sun's rays (*place in the ~*, (fig.) favourable situation or condition); MIDNIGHT *sun*; **mock ~**, parhelion; **Sun of Righteousness,** Christ; **see the ~**, be alive; **take the ~**, expose oneself to sun's light and heat; **take,** (sl.) **shoot, the ~**, (Naut.) ascertain its altitude in order to fix latitude; **touch of the ~**, slight attack of sunstroke; **beneath** or **under the ~**, anywhere in the world; **with the ~**, = CLOCK¹*wise*. **4. ~ and planet,** system of gearing in which cogged wheel on reciprocating rod both rotates on its axis and travels round the wheel that it engages and communicates motion to. **5.** Any fixed star with or without planets. **6.** (poet.) Day or year. **7.** **~-bath,** exposure of body to sun; **~'bathe,** take sun-bath; **~'beam,** ray of sun; **~-bear,** small black bear of S.E. Asia; **~-bird,** small bright-plumaged Old-World bird of family Nectariniidae, with resemblance to humming-birds; ||**~-blind,** window awning; **~-bonnet,** (of cotton etc., with projection and pendent back to shade face and neck); **~-bow,** effect like rainbow given by sunlight on spray etc.; **~'burn** *n.*, & *v.i.*, (undergo) tanning or inflammation of skin by exposure to sun; so **~'burnt** or **~'burned** *a.*; **~'burst,** firework or ornament or piece of jewellery imitating sun and rays; **~-dance** (of N. Amer. Indians in honour of sun); **~-deck,** upper deck of steamer; **~'dew,** small insectivorous bog-plant of genus *Drosera*, with hairs secreting drops of moisture; *sun*DIAL; **~-disc,** winged disc emblematic of sun-god; **~-dog,** parhelion; **~'down,** sunset; **~'downer,** (Austral.) tramp who times his arrival at a station for the evening, ||(colloq.) a drink at sunset; **~-dress** (allowing arms, shoulders, and back to be exposed to sunlight); **~-dried,** dried by sun and not by artificial heat; ***~'fast,** (of dye) not subject to fading by sunlight; **~'fish,** fish of almost spherical shape, esp. a large ocean fish (*Mola mola*); **~'flower,** tall garden-plant of genus *Helianthus* with showy golden-rayed flowers, grown also for its seeds which yield an edible oil; **Sunflower State*, Kansas; **~-glasses** (tinted to protect the eyes from direct sunlight or glare); **~-god,** the sun worshipped as a deity; **~-hat, ~-helmet,** (adapted by material or shape to keep sun off); **~-lamp,** (1) large lamp with parabolic reflector used in film-making, (2) lamp giving ultra-violet rays for therapy or artificial sun-tan; **~'light, ~'lit,** (illuminated by) light from the sun; **~ lounge,** room in house for sun-bathing etc.; **~-myth,** solar myth; ***~ parlor,** sun lounge; **~-rays,** (1) sunbeams, (2) ultra-violet rays used therapeutically as substitute for sunlight; **~'rise,** (moment of) sun's rising; **~-roof,** = *sunshine roof*; **~'set,** (moment of) sun's setting, western sky with colours characterizing sunset, (fig.) declining period of life; **~'shade,** (1) parasol, (2) awning; **~'shine,** light of sun (*~shine recorder*, instrument recording duration of sunshine; *~shine roof*, sliding roof of saloon motor car), area illuminated by it, fair weather, (fig.) cheerfulness or bright influence, hence **~'shiny** *a.*; **~'spot,** one of the dark patches, changing in shape and size and lasting for varying periods, observed on sun's surface; **~-star,** red starfish with many rays; **~-stone,** cat's eye gem, felspar with embedded flecks of haematite etc.; **~'stroke,** acute prostration or collapse from excessive heat of sun; **~-suit,** play-suit suitable for sunbathing; **~-tan** *n.*, & *v.i.*, tan(ning of) skin by exposure to sun; **~-trap,** place (esp. sheltered from wind) suitable for catching the sunshine; ***~-up,** sunrise; **~ visor,** = VISOR 3. **8.** Hence ~'LESS, ~'LIKE, ~'PROOF^2, *adjs.*, ~'WARD *a.* & *adv.*, ~'WARDS *adv.*, ~'WISE *adv.* (opp. WITHERSHINS). **9.** *v.t.* Expose to the sun; ~ one**self,** bask in sunlight (lit. or fig.). **10.** *v.i.* Sun oneself. [OE *sunne*, *sunna*, = OS, OHG *sunna*, *sunno*, f. Gmc **sunnōn* f. IE **su*-]

Sun. *abbr.* Sunday.

sŭ'ndae (-dā *or* -dĭ) *n.* Confection of ice cream topped or mixed with crushed fruit, nuts, syrup, etc. [perh. f. SUNDAY, w. ref. to sale of left-over ice cream during the week]

Sŭndanē'se (-z) *n.* & *a.* (Member or language) of a people of Western Java. [f. *Sunda* name of W. Java + -ESE, after *Chinese*]

Sŭ'nday (*or* -dĭ) *n.* & *adv.* **1.** *n.* Day of week, following Saturday, Lord's day, observed by Christians as day of rest and worship; newspaper published on Sundays; **month of ~s,** indefinite long period; **~ best, ~ go-to-meeting clothes,** (usu. joc.) best clothes (kept for Sunday use); **~ letter,** dominical letter; **~ painter,** one who paints purely for pleasure; **~ school** (for religious instruction of children on Sundays). **2.** *adv.* (cf. FRIDAY 2). [OE *sunnandæg*, = OS *sunnundag*, OHG *sunnuntag*, ON *sunnudagr*, transl. of L *dies solis*, Gk *hēmera hēliou* day of the sun]

sŭ'nder *v.* & *a.* (arch. or literary). **1.** *v.t.* & *i.* Separate, sever. **2.** *a.* **In ~,** apart. [v. f. OE *sundrian*, f. *āsundrian* etc., = OHG *sund(e)rōn*, ON *sundra*; a. ME, f. *o(n)sunder* ASUNDER]

sŭ'ndrў *a.* & *n.* **1.** *a.* Various, several; ALL *and sundry*. **2.** *n.* (Austral.) an extra in cricket; (in *pl.*) oddments, accessories or items not needing special mention; ||**su'ndriesman** (-rĭzm-), dealer in sundries. [OE *syndrig* separate, = OHG *sunt(a)ric*, cogn. w. prec.; see -Y^2]

sŭng. See SING.

sŭnk('en). See SINK^1.

sŭnn *n.* **~ (hemp),** E. Ind. hemplike fibre. [f. Hindi *san* f. Skr. *çāṇá* hempen]

Sŭ'nn|a *n.* Traditional portion of Muslim law based on Muhammad's words or acts, but not written by him, accepted as authoritative by the orthodox (~ITE^1, ~I, *ns.*) but rejected by the Shiites. [Arab., = form, course, rule]

sŭ'nn|ў *a.* Bright with or as sunlight; exposed to, warm with, the sun (**the ~y side,** side of house etc. that gets sun, (fig.) the more cheerful aspect of circumstances etc.); cheery, bright in disposition, diffusing cheerfulness; hence ~ĬLY^2 *adv.*, ~ĬNESS *n.* [ME, f. SUN + -Y^2]

sŭp *v.* (-pp-) & *n.* **1.** *v.t.* & *i.* Take (soup, tea, etc.) by sips or spoonfuls (**he must have a long spoon that ~s with the devil,** having dealings with doubtful characters is risky). **2.** *v.i.* Take supper (*on* or *off* specified food). **3.** *n.* Mouthful of liquid (esp. *neither bite nor sup*). [senses 1 and 3 f. OE *sūpan*, = MLG *sūpen*, OHG *sūfan*, ON *súpa*; sense 2 ME, f. OF *soper*, *super* f. Gmc **sup*- (as SOP, SOUP)]

sup- *pref.*, assim. form of SUB- 1–6 before *p*.

sū'per (*or* sōō'-) *n.* & *a.* **1.** *n.* (colloq.) Supernumerary actor, (fig.) extra or unwanted or unimportant person etc.; superintendent; superphosphate; (Commerc.) superfine cloth or manufacture. **2.** *a.* (Commerc.) Superfine; (of measure) superficial, in square (not lineal or solid) measure (*120 super ft.*, or *120 ft. super*). **3.** **~(-duper),** (sl.) exceptional, splendid. [abbr.]

sū'per- (*or* sōō'-) *pref.* denoting: **1.** (forming *adjs.*) (1) situated directly over (*superincumbent*), (2) not in or under but above (*superaqueous*, *supernatant*), (3) exceeding, going beyond, more than, transcending, too exalted for contact or connection with, (*superfine*, *superhuman*, *supernatural*). **2.** (forming *vbs.*) (1) on the top of something (*superimpose*, *superscribe*), (2) observation from above (*superintend*), (3) besides, in addition, (*superadd*), (4) to a degree beyond what is usual or right (*supersaturate*). **3.** (forming *ns.*) (1) upper or outer (*superstratum*, *superstructure*), (2) of higher kind, higher in degree, superior in quality, expressing addition, in higher than the ordinary sense, esp. in names of classificatory divisions (*superclass*). [f. or after L *super*- (*super* on top (of), above, beyond)]

sū'perable (*or* sōō'-) *a.* That can be overcome;

For other words in ***super-*** **see** SUPER-.

not insuperable. [f. L *superabilis* (*superare* overcome; see -ABLE)]

sūperabou'nd (*or* sōō-) *v.i.* Be very or too abundant. [f. LL *superabundare* (as SUPER- 2 (4), ABOUND)]

sūperabŭ'nd|ant (*or* sōō-) *a.* Abounding beyond what is normal or right; hence or cogn. ~ANCE *n.*, **~ant**LY² *adv.* [ME, f. LL *superabundare* (see prec., -ANT)]

sūper|ă'dd (*or* sōō-) *v.t.* Add over and above; hence ~ADDI'TION *n.* [ME, f. L *superaddere* (as SUPER- 2 (3), ADD)]

sū'peraltar (-awl- *or* -ŏl-; *or* sōō'-) *n.* (Eccl.) Slab of stone consecrated for use on unconsecrated altar etc. [ME, f. med. L *superaltare* (as SUPER- 3 (1), ALTAR)]

sūperă'nnū|āte (*or* sōō-) *v.t.* Declare too old for work or use or continuance, dismiss or discard as too old; send into retirement with pension; (in *p.p.*) too old for work or use; hence ~ABLE *a.*, ~A'TION *n.*, (esp.) (payment made to obtain) pension granted to superannuated person. [back form. f. *superannuated* f. med. L *superannuatus* f. L SUPER- + *annus* year; see -ATE², -ED¹]

sūperā'quėous (*or* sōō-) *a.* Above water. [f. SUPER- 1 (2) + AQUEOUS]

sūpẽr'b (*or* sōō-) *a.* Of the most impressive or splendid or exalted kind, grand, majestic, (*superb beauty, courage, impudence; a superb view, display, collection, specimen, voice, binding*); (colloq.) of very high quality, excellent; hence ~LY² *adv.* [f. F *superbe* or f. L *superbus* proud]

sūpercă'lėnder (*or* sōō-) *v.t.* Give highly glazed finish to (paper) by extra calendering. [f. SUPER- 2 (4) + CALENDER¹]

sū'percar̃gō (*or* sōō'-) *n.* (*pl.* **~es**). Person in merchant ship managing sales etc. of cargo. [earlier *supracargo* f. Sp. *sobrecargo* (*sobre* over, CARGO)]

sūpercėlĕ'stĭal (*or* sōō-) *a.* Above the heavens; more than heavenly. [f. LL *supercaelestis* (as SUPER- 1 (2, 3), CELESTIAL)]

sū'perchar̃ge (*or* sōō'-) *v.t.* Charge to excess (*with* energy, emotion, etc.); use supercharger on. [f. SUPER- 2 (4) + CHARGE²]

sū'perchar̃ger (*or* sōō'-) *n.* Device supplying air or fuel to internal combustion engine at above normal pressure to increase efficiency. [f. prec. + -ER¹]

sūperci'lĭarў (*or* sōō-) *a.* Of the eyebrow; over eye. [f. L *supercilium* eyebrow (SUPER-, *cilium* eyelid) + -ARY¹]

sūperci'lĭous (*or* sōō-) *a.* Contemptuous, showing haughty indifference; assuming an air of superiority; hence ~LY² *adv.*, ~NESS *n.* [f. L *superciliosus* (as prec.) + -OUS]

sū'perclass (-ahs; *or* sōō'-) *n.* See SUPER- 3 (2).

sūper|colŭ'mnar *a.* (*or* sōō-) (Archit.) Having one order or set of columns above another; so **~colŭmnĭ**A'TION *n.* [f. SUPER- 1 (1) + COLUMNAR]

sūper|cŏndŭctĭ'vĭtў (*or* sōō-) *n.* (Phys.) Property of zero electrical resistance in some substances at temperatures near absolute zero; hence **~condŭ'ct**ING², **~condŭ'ct**IVE, *adjs.*, **~condŭ'ct**OR *n.*, (substance) having this property. [f. SUPER- 3 (2) + CONDUCTIVITY]

sūpercŏ'nscious (-shus; *or* sōō-) *a.* Transcending human consciousness; hence ~LY² *adv.*, ~NESS *n.* [f. SU ER- 1 (3) + CONSCIOUS]

sū'percōōl (*or* sōō'-) *v.t.* Cool (liquid) below its freezing-point without solidification or without crystallization. [f. SUPER- 2 (4) + COOL²]

sūpercrĭ'tĭcal (*or* sōō-) *a.* (Phys.) Of more than critical mass etc. [f. SUPER- 1 (3) + CRITICAL]

sūper-ĕ'gō (*or* sōō-) *n.* (*pl.* **~s**). (Psych.) Part of mind that exerts conscience and responds to social rules. [f. SUPER- 3 (2) + EGO]

sūperĕlėvā'tion (*or* sōō-) *n.* Amount by which outer edge of curve on road or railway is above inner edge. [f. SUPER- 3 (2) + ELEVATION]

sūperĕ'mĭn|ent (*or* sōō-) *a.* Supremely eminent or remarkable; hence or cogn. ~ENCE *n.*, **~ent**LY² *adv.* [f. L *supereminēre* rise above (as SUPER- 2 (4), EMINENT)]

sūper|ĕrogā'tion (*or* sōō-) *n.* Doing of more than duty requires; **works of ~erogation,** (R.C. Theol.) actions such as form a reserve fund of merit that can be drawn on in favour of sinners; so **~ėrŏ'gat**ORY *a.* [f. LL *supererogatio* f. SUPER- (*erogare* pay out, orig. public money after formal request for permission, f. as E- + *rogo* ask); see -ATION]

sūperĕ'xcell|ent (*or* sōō-) *a.* Very or supremely excellent; hence ~ENCE *n.*, **~ent**LY² *adv.* [f. LL *superexcellens* (as SUPER- 1 (3), EXCELLENT)]

sū'perfămĭlў (*or* sōō'-) *n.* Taxonomic category between family and order. [f. SUPER- 3 (2) + FAMILY]

sūperfă'ttėd (*or* sōō-) *a.* (Of soap) containing extra fat. [f. SUPER- 2 (4) + FAT + -ED²]

sūperfĕcundā'tion (*or* sōō-) *n.* = foll. 1. [f. SUPER- 3 (2) + FECUNDATION]

sūperfētā'tion (*or* sōō-) *n.* **1.** (Med. & Zool.) Second conception during gestation. **2.** (Bot.) Fertilization of same ovule by different kinds of pollen. [f. F *superfétation* or f. mod. L *superfetatio* f. L SUPER(*fetare* f. *fetus* FOETUS); see -ATION]

sūperfĭ'cial (-shal; *or* sōō-) *a.* Of or on the surface only, not going deep, without depth, (*superficial colour, resemblance, knowledge, wound, accomplishments*); (of person) having no reserve of knowledge or feeling beyond what he shows; (of measure) square (cf. SUPER 2); hence ~ITY (-shĭă'l-) *n.*, ~LY² *adv.* [f. LL *superficialis* f. L (as foll.; see -AL)]

sūperfĭ'ciēs (-shĭēz; *or* sōō-) *n.* (*pl.* same). (Geom. etc.) Surface. [L (as SUPER- 3 (1), *facies* face)]

sū'perfīne (*or* sōō'-) *a.* Affecting great refinement; (Commerc.) of extra quality. [f. med. L *superfinus* (as SUPER- 1 (3), FINE²)]

sūperflu'ĭtў (-lōō'-; *or* sōō-) *n.* Being superfluous; superfluous amount or thing. [ME, f. OF *superfluité* f. LL *superfluitas -tatis* f. L *superfluus* (see foll., -ITY)]

sūpẽr'fluous (-flōō-; *or* sōō-) *a.* More than enough, redundant, needless; hence ~LY² *adv.*, ~NESS *n.* [ME, f. L SUPER(*fluus* f. *fluere* flow) + -OUS]

sū'pergīant (*or* sōō'-) *n.* (Astron.) Star of very great luminosity and size. [f. SUPER- 3 (2) + GIANT]

sūper|hea't (*or* sōō-) *v.t.* Heat (liquid) above its boiling-point without vaporization; heat (vapour) above the boiling-point (*superheated* STEAM¹); hence ~HEA'TER *n.* [f. SUPER- 2 (4) + HEAT²]

sūperhĕ't (*or* sōō-) *n.* (colloq.) = foll. [abbr.]

sūperhĕ'terodўne (*or* sōō-) *n.* & *a.* (Using) system of radio reception in which a local variable oscillator is tuned to beat at a constant ultrasonic frequency with carrier-wave frequencies, thus making it unnecessary to vary the amplifier tuning and securing great selectivity. [f. SUPERSONIC + HETERODYNE]

*__sū'perhīghway__ (-īwā; *or* sōō'-) *n.* Broad main road for fast traffic. [f. SUPER- 3 (2) + HIGHWAY]

sūperhū'man (*or* sōō-) *a.* Beyond (normal) human capacity or power; higher than man; hence ~LY² *adv.* [f. LL *superhumanus* (as SUPER- 1 (3), HUMAN)]

sūperhū'meral (*or* sōō-) *n.* (Eccl.) Vestment worn over shoulders, e.g. amice, ephod, or pallium. [f. LL *superhumerale* (as SUPER- 1 (1), HUMERAL)]

sūper|impō'se (-z; *or* sōō-) *v.t.* Lay (thing) on or *on* something else; so ~IMPOSI'TION *n.* [f. SUPER- 2 (1) + IMPOSE]

sūperincŭ'mbent (-n-k-; *or* sōō-) *a.* Lying on something else. [f. SUPER- 1 (1) + INCUMBENT²]

sūperindū'ce (*or* sōō-) *v.t.* Introduce or induce in addition. [f. L SUPER(*inducere*, as INDUCE) cover over, bring from outside]

sūperintĕ'nd (*or* sōō-) *v.t.* & *i.* Have the management (of), arrange and inspect working (of); so ~ENCE, ~ENCY, *ns.* [f. eccl. L SUPER-(*intendere*, as INTEND), transl. Gk *episkopō*]

sūperintĕ'ndent (*or* sōō-) *n.* Person who superintends; director of institution etc.; ||police officer above rank of inspector, *head of police department; *caretaker of building. [f. eccl. L (as prec.); see -ENT]

sūpēr'ior (*or* sōō-) *a.* & *n.* **1.** *a.* Upper, in higher position, of higher rank, (*superior officer, rank, court*); (of planet) having orbit outside the earth's; (of insect's wings) folding over others; (of figures or letters) written or printed above the line; (Bot., of calyx) above ovary, (of ovary) above calyx. **2.** Better or greater in some respect, related as the better or greater *to*, (*by superior wisdom, cunning*, etc.; *is superior in speed to any other machine*); ~ **numbers,** (esp.) more men or their strength (*was overcome by superior numbers*). **3.** Of quality or qualities above the average, having or showing consciousness of such qualities, (*made of superior leather; he remarked with a superior air*); ~ **persons,** the better educated etc., (iron.) prigs. **4.** Above giving attention or yielding or making concessions *to* (*superior to bribery, temptation, revenge, fortune*); **rise ~ to,** be unaffected by. **5.** Hence or cogn. **superiŏ'r**ITY (*or* sū- *or* sōō-) *n.* (**~ity complex,** undue conviction of one's own superiority to others, (colloq.) aggressive behaviour to compensate for one's supposed inferiority to others), ~LY² *adv.* **6.** *n.* One's better, person superior to another, in rank or *in* some respect (*is deferential to his superiors; has no superior in courage*). **7.** Head of monastery or other religious house (esp. *Father, Mother, Lady, Superior*); hence ~ESS¹ *n.* **8.** Superior letter or figure. [ME, f. OF *superiour* f. L *superior -oris*, compar. of *superus* that is above (*super* above)]

sūperjā'cent (*or* sōō-) *a.* Overlying, superincumbent. [f. L SUPER(*jacēre* lie); see -ENT]

sūpēr'lative (*or* sōō-) *a.* & *n.* **1.** *a.* Of the highest degree (*superlative wisdom, beauty*, etc.); (Gram.) ~ **adjective, adverb,** one in the ~ **degree,** expressing the highest or a very high degree of a quality (*bravest; most absurdly*); hence ~LY² (-vlĭ) *adv.*, ~NESS (-vn-) *n.* **2.** *n.* Superlative degree or form (*not used in the superlative; what is the superlative of* '*shy*'?); word in the superlative or expressing high degree (**his talk is all ~s,** he expresses extreme opinions or exaggerates). [ME, f. OF *superlatif -ive* f. LL *superlativus* f. L SUPER(*latus* p.p. of *ferre* take); see -IVE]

sūperlū'narў (*or* sōō-, -lōō'-) *a.* Beyond the moon; celestial. [f. med. L *superlunaris* (as SUPER- 1 (2), LUNAR); see -ARY²]

sū'per|măn (*or* sōō'-) *n.* (*pl.* **~men**). Ideal superior man of the future; man of superhuman powers or achievement. [f. SUPER- 3 (2) + MAN¹, formed by G. B. Shaw after Nietzsche's G *übermensch*]

sū'permārkėt (*or* sōō'-) *n.* Large self-service store selling foods and some household goods. [f. SUPER- 3 (2) + MARKET¹]

sūpermŭ'ndāne (*or* sōō-) *a.* Superior to earthly things. [f. med. L *supermundanus* (as SUPER- 1 (2), MUNDANE)]

sūpernă'cŭlum (*or* sōō-) *adv.* & *n.* **1.** *adv.* To the last drop (*drink supernaculum*). **2.** *n.* Wine etc. of high quality. [mod. L, tr. G *auf den nagel* on to the nail, w. ref. to upturning of glass on thumb to prove emptiness]

sūpēr'nal (*or* sōō-) *a.* (poet. or rhet.) Heavenly, divine; of the sky; lofty. [ME f. OF, or f. med. L *supernalis* f. L *supernus* (*super* above); see -AL]

sūpernā'tant (*or* sōō-) *a.* & *n.* (Substance) floating on surface of liquid. [f. SUPER- 1 (2) + *natant* swimming (as NATATION; see -ANT)]

sūpernă'tural (-cher-; *or* sōō-) *a.* Due to or manifesting some agency above the forces of nature; outside the ordinary operation of cause and effect; hence ~ISM (2, 3), ~IST (2), *ns.*, ~IZE (3) *v.t.*, ~LY² *adv.*, ~NESS *n.* [f. med. L *supernaturalis* (as SUPER- 1 (3), NATURAL)]

sūpernōr'mal (*or* sōō-) *a.* Beyond what is normal or natural. [f. SUPER- 1 (3) + NORMAL]

sūpernō'va (*or* sōō-) *n.* (*pl.* **~e** *or* **~s**). (Astron.) Star that suddenly increases very greatly in brightness because of explosion ejecting most of its mass. [f. SUPER- 3 (2) + NOVA]

sūpernū'merarў (*or* sōō-) *a.* & *n.* (Person or thing) in excess of normal number, (person) engaged for extra work, (actor) who appears on stage but does not speak. [f. LL *supernumerarius* (soldier) added to legion already complete, f. L *super numerum* beyond the number; see -ARY¹]

sū'per|ōrder (*or* sōō'-) *n.* Taxonomic category between order and class; so ~OR'DINAL *a.* [f. SUPER- 3 (2) + ORDER¹]

sūperōr'dinate (*or* sōō-) *a.* Of superior importance or rank (*to*). [f. SUPER- 1 (2), after *subordinate*]

sūperphŏ'sphāte (*or* sōō-) *n.* Fertilizer made by treating phosphate rock with sulphuric or phosphoric acid. [f. SUPER- 3 (2) + PHOSPHATE]

sūperphў'sical (-z-; *or* sōō-) *a.* Beyond what is physical; unexplainable by physical causes. [f. SUPER- 1 (3) + PHYSICAL]

sūper|pō'se (-z; *or* sōō-) *v.t.* Place (thing) on or *on* or above something else; bring into same position so as to coincide; so ~POSI'TION *n.* [f. F *superposer* (as SUPER- 2 (1), *poser* place, POSE¹)]

sū'perpower (*or* sōō'-) *n.* Extremely powerful nation, esp. one of only a few such. [f. SUPER- 3 (2) + POWER]

sūpersă'tūr|āte (*or* sōō-; *or* -cher-) *v.t.* Add to (esp. solution) beyond saturation point; hence ~A'TION *n.* [f. SUPER- 2 (4) + SATURATE]

sū'per|scribe (*or* sōō'-) *v.t.* Write (inscription) at top of or on outside of document etc.; write inscription over or on (thing); so **~scrĭ'pt**ION *n.*, (esp.) words superscribed. [f. L SUPER-(*scribere script-* write)]

sū'perscrĭpt (*or* sōō'-) *a.* & *n.* (Math. etc.) (Symbol) written above and to the right of another symbol. [f. L *superscriptus* p.p. of *superscribere* (see prec.)]

sūper|sē'de (*or* sōō-) *v.t.* Set aside, cease to employ, adopt or appoint another person or thing in place of, (of such person or thing) take the place of; hence or cogn. **~sē'd**ENCE, **~sē'd**URE, ~SE'SSION, *ns.* [f. OF *superseder* f. L SUPER(*sedēre sess-* sit) be superior to]

sūpersŏ'n|ic (*or* sōō-) *a.* Relating to speeds greater than that of sound; (arch.) ultrasonic; hence ~ICALLY *adv.* [f. SUPER- 1 (3) + SONIC]

sūperstĭ't|ion (*or* sōō-) *n.* Credulity regarding the supernatural, irrational fear of the unknown or mysterious; misdirected reverence; religion or practice or particular opinion based on such tendencies; widely held but unjustified idea of

For other words in *super-* see SUPER-.

the effects or nature of a thing; so ~IOUS (-shus) *a.* [ME f. OF, or f. L *superstitio* f. SUPER(*stare stat-* stand); see -ION]

sū'perstōre (*or* sōō'-) *n.* Hypermarket; large supermarket. [f. SUPER- 3 (2) + STORE]

sū'perstrāt|um (*or* sōō'-; *or* -ah-) *n.* (*pl.* ~**a**). Overlying stratum. [f. SUPER- 3 (1) + STRATUM]

sū'perstrŭctur|e (*or* sōō'-) *n.* Building with respect to its foundation; structure resting on something else; upper part of building etc.; concept etc. based on others; hence ~AL *a.* [f. SUPER- 3 (1) + STRUCTURE]

sūpersubstă'ntial (-shal; *or* sōō-) *a.* Transcending material substance or all substance. [f. eccl. L SUPER(*substantialis* f. *substantia* SUBSTANCE; see -AL)]

sūper|sŭ'btle (-ŭ'tel; *or* sōō-) *a.* Excessively subtle; so ~SU'BTLETY *n.* [f. SUPER- 1 (3) + SUBTLE]

sū'pertănker (*or* sōō'-) *n.* Very large tanker ship. [f. SUPER- 3 (2) + TANKER]

sū'pertăx (*or* sōō'-) *n.*, & *v.t.* = SURTAX. [f. SUPER- 2 (3), 3 (2) + TAX[1,2]]

sūpertĕ'mporal (*or* sōō-) *a.* **1.** Above the temples of the head. **2.** Transcending time. [f. SUPER- 1 (1, 3) + TEMPORAL]

sūperterrā'nėan (*or* sōō-) *a.* Existing or dwelling on the earth's surface. [f. SUPER- 1 (2), after SUBTERRANEAN]

sūpertĕrrē'ne (*or* sōō-) *a.* **1.** = foll. **2.** = prec. [f. SUPER- 1 (2), after *subterrene* f. L SUB(*terrenus* TERRENE)]

sūperteŗrĕ'strĭal (*or* sōō-) *a.* Belonging to a region above the earth, celestial. [f. SUPER- 1 (3) + TERRESTRIAL]

sūpertŏ'nĭc (*or* sōō-) *n.* (Mus.) Note above tonic, second note of diatonic scale of any key. [f. SUPER- 3 (2) + TONIC]

sūper|vē'ne (*or* sōō-) *v.i.* Occur as interruption to or change from some condition or process; so ~**vĕ'nt**ION *n.* [f. L SUPER(*venire vent-* come)]

sū'per|vīse (-z; *or* sōō'-) *v.t.* Oversee, superintend execution or performance of (thing) or actions or work of (person); hence ~**vĭ'**SION (-zhon) *n.*, ~**vīs**ORY (-z-) *a.* [f. med. L SUPER(*vidēre vis-* see)]

sū'pervīsor (-z-; *or* sōō'-) *n.* Person who supervises; *administrative or advisory official in town, school, etc. [med. L (as prec.; see -OR), or f. prec. + -OR]

sū'pĭn|āte (*or* sōō'-) *v.t.* Put (hand, foreleg) into supine position (cf. PRONATE); so ~A'TION *n.*, ~**ā'**TOR *n.* (esp. muscle effecting this). [back form. f. *supination* f. L *supinatio* (*supinare* f. *supinus*; see foll., -ATE[3])]

sū'pine[1] (*or* sōō'-; *or* -ī'n) *a.* Having front or ventral part upwards, (of hand) with palm upwards, lying face upwards (cf. PRONE); disinclined for moral or mental action, indolent, lethargic; hence ~LY[2] (-nlĭ) *adv.*, ~NESS (-n-n-) *n.* [f. L *supinus* (st. of *super* above; see -INE[1])]

sū'pine[2] (*or* sōō'-) *n.* (L Gram.) Verbal noun comprising accusative in *-um* and ablative in *-u* formed from stem of past participle and used to denote purpose or make adj. specific (e.g. *mirabile dictu* wonderful to relate). [f. LL *supinum* neut. (as n.) of *supinus* (see prec.); reason for name unknown]

sŭ'pper *n.* Meal taken at the end of the day, esp. evening meal less formal and substantial than dinner; LAST[3] *Supper*; LORD'*s Supper*; **sing for** one's ~, (be required to) do something in return before or immediately after receiving a benefit; hence ~LESS *a.* [ME, f. OF *soper, super,* (*soper* SUP; see -ER[4])]

suppla'nt (-ah'-) *v.t.* Dispossess and take the place of, esp. by underhand means; hence ~ER[1] *n.* [ME, f. OF *supplanter* or f. L SUP(*plantare* f. *planta* sole) trip up]

sŭ'pple *a.* & *v.* **1.** *a.* Easily bent, pliant, flexible; compliant, avoiding overt resistance, artfully or servilely submissive; **~-jack,** (walking-cane of) strong twining tropical shrub; hence ~LY[2] (-pel-lĭ *or* -plĭ) *adv.*, ~NESS (-peln-) *n.* **2.** *v.t.* & *i.* Make or become supple. [ME f. OF *souple,* f. Rom. **supples* f. L SUP(*plex -plicis* f. **plic-* bend) submissive]

sŭ'pplėment[1] *n.* Thing added to remedy deficiencies; part added to book etc. with further information, or to periodical for treatment of particular matter(s); ~ **of an angle,** (Math.) its deficiency from 180° (cf. COMPLEMENT[1]); hence ~AL, ~ARY[1], (-mĕ'n-) *adjs.* (*supplementary* BENEFIT[1]). [ME, f. L SUP(*plementum* f. *-plēre* fill; see -MENT)]

sŭ'pplėmĕnt[2] (*or* -ĕ'nt) *v.t.* Make supplement to; hence ~A'TION *n.* [f. prec.]

supplē't|ion *n.* Supplementing, esp. (Ling.) occurrence of unrelated forms as part of same conjugation etc. (*go, went*); so ~IVE *a.* [ME f. OF, f. med. L *suppletio -onis* (as SUPPLY[1]; see -ION)]

sŭ'pplĭant *a.* & *n.* (literary). **1.** *a.* Supplicating, expressive of supplication; hence ~LY[2] *adv.* **2.** *n.* Humble petitioner. [ME f. F (*supplier* f. L as foll.; see -ANT)]

sŭ'pplĭc|āte *v.t.* & *i.* Make humble petition to or *to* person, for or *for* thing; so ~A'TION *n.*, ~**at**ORY (*or* -āt-) *a.* [ME, f. L SUP(*plicare* f. **plic-* bend) + -ATE[3]]

supplȳ'[1] *v.t.*, *n.*, & *a.* **1.** *v.t.* Furnish, provide, (thing needed, or person, receptacle, etc., with or *with* thing needed); hence **supplī'**ER[1] *n.* **2.** Make up for, meet, serve to obviate, (deficiency, need, loss); fill (place, vacancy, pulpit) as substitute. **3.** *n.* Providing of what is needed (**Committee of S~,** House of Commons discussing details of estimates for public service). **4.** Stock, store, amount of something provided or available or accessible, (*an inexhaustible supply of fish, coal,* etc.; *water* etc. *-supply*); *in* SHORT *supply*; ~ **and demand,** (Econ.) factors regarded as regulating price of commodities. **5.** (in *pl.*) Collected necessaries for army etc.; grant of money by Parliament for cost of government; money allowance to person (*his father cut off the supplies*). **6.** Person, esp. clergyman or schoolteacher, who acts as temporary substitute for another; **on** ~, acting thus. **7.** *a.* Providing supply or supplies (*supply officer, pipe, teacher*). [ME, f. OF *so(u)pleer* etc. f. L SUP(*plēre* fill)]

sŭ'pplȳ[2] *adv.* Supplely. [f. SUPPLE + -LY[2]]

suppōr't *v.t.*, & *n.* **1.** *v.t.* Carry (part of) weight of, hold up, keep from falling or sinking, (*foundation, buttress, supports house, wall*; *supported by a lifebelt*; *had to be supported home*). **2.** Enable to last out, keep from failing, give strength to, encourage, (*what supported him* or *his strength was a glass of brandy, a good conscience, hope, your approval*; *too little food to support life*). **3.** Endure, tolerate, (*supports fatigue well*; *I can support life, such insolence, no longer*); hence ~ABLE *a.*, ~**ab**LY[2] *adv.* **4.** Supply with necessaries, provide for, (*support oneself, a family*). **5.** Lend assistance or countenance to, back up, second, further, (*support a cause, policy, team, leader, candidate*); take secondary part to (actor or other performer); speak in favour of (resolution etc.); assist (lecturer etc.) by one's presence; subscribe to funds of (institution); **~ing film, picture,** etc., less important part of cinema programme.

6. Bear out, tend to substantiate or corroborate, bring facts to confirm, (statement, charge, theory, etc.). **7.** Keep up or represent (part, character) adequately. **8.** Hence ~IVE *a.* **9.** *n.* Supporting or being supported (*give support to*; *needs support*; *gets no support*; *troops stationed in support*); ~ **price,** minimum price guaranteed to farmers etc. by Government subsidy; **in ~ of,** in order to support, advocate, etc. **10.** Person or thing that supports (*shelf must have another support*; *he is the chief support of the cause*). **11.** Hence ~LESS *a.* [ME, f. OF *supporter* f. L SUP(*portare* carry)]

suppor'ter *n.* In vbl senses; (Her.) representation of living creature holding up or standing beside an escutcheon (usu. as one of pair on either side); one who takes an interest in a particular team or sport. [ME, f. prec. + -ER[1]]

suppō's|e (-z) *v.t.* **1.** Assume as a hypothesis (*let us suppose it to be true*; *well, suppose it was so*); (in *part.* or *imper.*, with conjunctional force =) if (*supposing white were black you would be right*; *suppose your father saw you what would he say?*); (in *imper.* as formula of proposal: *suppose we went for a walk*; *suppose we try another*). **2.** (Of theory, result, etc.) involve or require as a condition, presuppose, (*that supposes a mechanism without flaws*; *design in creation supposes a creator*). **3.** Take for granted, presume, assume in default of knowledge, be inclined to think, accept as probable, (*I suppose we shall be back in an hour*; *you cannot suppose*, *it is not to be supposed*, *that*; *I suppose he won't come* or *I don't suppose he will come*; *what do you suppose he meant?*); *I suppose* so[1] 7; (abs. in parenth.: *you will not be there, I suppose*). **4.** (in *pass.*) Have as a duty (*he is supposed to clean the shoes*); **not be ~ed,** (1) not have as a duty, (2, colloq.) have duty not (*you are not supposed to kick people*). **5.** (in *p.p.*) Believed to exist, believed to have specified character, (*the supposed music of the spheres*; *his supposed brother*, *generosity*; *he is supposed to be very rich*); hence **~ĕd**LY[2] *adv.* **6.** Hence or cogn. ~ABLE *a.*, **sŭpposi'**TION *n.*, **sŭpposi'tion**AL *a.*, (-z-). [ME, f. OF SUP(*poser* POSE[1])]

sŭpposi'tious (-zĭ'shus) *a.* Hypothetical, assumed; = foll.; hence ~LY[2] *adv.*, ~NESS *n.* [partly f. foll., partly f. SUPPOSITION + -OUS]

suppŏsitĭ'tious (-zĭtĭ'shus) *a.* Substituted for the real, spurious, (*supposititious child*, *writings*); hence ~LY[2] *adv.*, ~NESS *n.* [f. L *supposititius*, *-icius* f. SUP(*ponere posit-* place) substitute; see -ITIOUS[1]]

suppŏ'sitorў (-z-) *n.* (Med.) Cone or cylinder of medicinal substance introduced into rectum or vagina or urethra and left to melt. [ME, f. med. L *suppositorium*, neut. (as n.) of LL *suppositorius* placed underneath (as prec.; see -ORY)]

supprĕ'ss *v.t.* Use force or authority to make cease, quell, put an end to activity or existence of, (rebellion, sedition, agitators, haemorrhage, conscience, piracy, monasteries, etc.); restrain, keep in, not give vent to, withhold or withdraw from publication, keep secret, not reveal, (groan, yawn, feelings, name, book, evidence, facts); (Psych.) keep out of one's consciousness; (Electr.) partly or wholly eliminate (unwanted frequencies, interference), equip (device) so as to reduce interference due to it; hence or cogn. ~IBLE, ~IVE, *adjs.*, ~ION (-shon), ~OR, *ns.* [ME, f. L SUP(*primere press-* = *premere* press)]

suppressio veri (suprĕsĭō vēr'ī) *n.* Suppression of truth, misrepresentation by concealment of facts that ought to be made known (cf. SUGGESTIO FALSI). [L]

sŭ'ppūr|āte *v.i.* Form pus, fester; so ~A'TION *n.*, ~ATIVE *a.* [f. L SUP(*purare* f. PUS) + -ATE[3]]

supra (sū'pra; *or* sōō'-) *adv.* Above; previously, before (in a book or writing). [L, = above]

sū'pra- (*or* sōō'-) *pref.* Above (opp. INFRA-, SUB-). **1.** (Anat.) = SUPER- 1 (1) (**~or'bital,** above the orbit of the eye; **~re'nal,** = ADRENAL); upper (**~maxi'llary,** (of) the upper jaw). **2.** Over, beyond; **~lapsar'ian(ism),** (holder of, holding) Calvinist doctrine that predestination preceded the Creation and the Fall; **~mu'ndane,** above or superior to the world; **~na'tional,** transcending national limits; **~segme'ntal,** (Phonet.) relating to features of phonemes as assembled in an utterance. [f. or after L *supra-* (*supra* above, beyond, before in time)]

sūprĕ'mac|ў (*or* sōō-) *n.* Being supreme, highest authority; **Act of S~y** (securing ecclesiastical supremacy to the Crown and excluding the authority of the pope); hence ~IST *n.*, advocate of some group's (esp. WHITE[1]) supremacy. [f. foll. + -ACY]

sūprē'me (*or* sōō-) *a.* & *n.* **1.** *a.* Highest in authority or rank; **the S~ (Being),** God; **S~ Court,** highest judicial court in State etc. (cf. JUDICATURE); ~ **end** or **good,** *summum bonum*; *supreme* PONTIFF; *Supreme* SOVIET. **2.** Greatest possible, uttermost, extreme, last and greatest or most important, (*supreme wisdom*, *courage*, etc.; *the supreme test of fidelity*; *a* or *the supreme hour*, *moment*, etc.); (of penalty, sacrifice, etc.) involving one's death. **3.** *n.* (Dish served in) rich cream sauce. **4.** Hence ~LY[2] (-mlĭ) *adv.* [f. L *supremus* superl. of *superus* that is above (*super* above)]

suprême (sūprĕ'm) *n.* = prec. 3. [F]

sūprĕ'mō (*or* sōō-) *n.* (*pl.* ~s). Supreme leader or ruler. [Sp., = SUPREME]

Supt. *abbr.* Superintendent.

suq. Var. of SOUK.

sur- *pref.* **1.** Assim. form of SUB- 1–6 before *r* (*surreptitious*, *surrogate*). **2.** = SUPER- (*surcharge*, *surface*, *surprise*, *surrealism*, *surrender*) [OF].

sur'a, sur'ah[1], (soor'*a*) *n.* Chapter or section of Koran. [f. Arab. *sūra*]

sūr'ah[2] (-*a*) *n.* Soft twilled silk for scarves etc. [f. F pr. of SURAT]

sūr'al *a.* Of the calf of the leg (*sural artery* etc.). [f. mod. L *suralis* f. L *sura* calf; see -AL]

sūră't *n.* (Hist.) Kind of cotton grown, kind of coarse cotton cloth made, in the Bombay Presidency. [f. *S~* in India]

surcea'se *n.* & *v.* (arch.) **1.** *n.* Cessation. **2.** *v.i.* & *t.* Cease. [ME, f. OF *sursis*, *-ise* (cf. AF *sursise* omission), p.p. of OF *surseoir* refrain, delay f. L (as SUPERSEDE), w. assim. to CEASE[1,2]]

sûr'chârge[1] *n.* Excessive or additional load or burden or amount of money charged; additional charge made by assessors as penalty for false returns of taxable property; mark printed on postage stamp changing its value; ||amount in official account not passed by auditor and having to be refunded by person responsible; showing of omission in account for which credit should have been given. [f. foll.]

surchâr'ge[2] *v.t.* Overload, fill or saturate to excess; (of assessor or auditor) exact surcharge from, exact (sum) as surcharge, fine (person sum) as surcharge; show omission of credit in (account); print surcharge on (postage stamp). [ME, f. OF SUR(*charger* CHARGE[2])]

sûr'cingle *n.* Band round horse's body usu. to keep pack etc. in place. [ME, f. OF SUR(*cengle* girth f. L *cingula* f. *cingere* gird)]

sûr'coat *n.* **1.** (Hist.) loose robe worn over armour; similar sleeveless garment worn as part of insignia of order of knighthood. **2.** (Hist.) outer coat of rich material; man's belted jacket. [ME, f. OF SUR(*cot* COAT)]

sûr'cūlōse *a.* (Bot.) Producing suckers. [f. L *surculosus* (*surculus* twig; see -OSE[1])]

sûrd *a.* & *n.* **1.** (Math.) Irrational (number, esp. root of integer). **2.** (Phonet.) (Sound) uttered with breath and not voice (e.g. *f, k, p, s, t*). [f. L *surdus* deaf, mute; sense 1 by mistransl. into L of Gk *alogos* irrational, speechless, thr. Arab. *jadr asamm* deaf root]

sure (shoor) *a.* & *adv.* **1.** *a.* Having or seeming to have adequate reason for belief, convinced *of* or (*that*), having certain prospect or confident anticipation or satisfactory knowledge *of*, free from doubts *of*, (*you may be sure of his honesty, he is* or *that he is honest; he feels* or *is sure of success; I did not feel sure of my position, could not feel sure about it; if one could be sure of living to 70*); **I'm ~** *I didn't mean to hurt you* (form of asseveration); **well, I'm ~!** (excl. of surprise). **2.** Safe, reliable, trusty, unfailing, (*sent it by a sure hand; there is only one sure way; put it in a sure place*); **~ card,** scheme etc. certain to succeed; **~-footed,** never stumbling or making false step (lit. or fig.); **~ shot,** marksman who never misses; SLOW *and, but, sure.* **3.** To be relied on, certain, *to* do (*is sure to turn out well; would be sure to dislike him*); (in *imper.* or *inf.*) take care, not fail, (*be sure you* or *to* or *and finish it*); ***~-fire,** certain (to succeed); ***~ thing,** (*n.*) a certainty, (*int.*) certainly! **4.** Undoubtedly true or truthful (*one thing is sure*); **to be ~,** (formula of concession =) to avoid overstatement (*to be sure she is not perfect, is pretty*), (as excl. of surprise: *so it is, to be sure!; well, to be sure!*); **make ~,** ascertain absolutely that something is as supposed, take measures to secure that something is as desired, establish the truth or ensure the existence or happening *of*, (in *past*) have confident (but often false) anticipation *of* or *that* (*he suspected nothing, and made sure of succeeding*); hence **~'NESS** (shoor'n-) *n.* **5.** *adv.* (arch.) Undoubtedly, with certainty. **6.** *(colloq.) Certainly (*it sure was cold*). **7.** *As* certainly *as* (*as sure as eggs are eggs, as sure as I stand here*, etc., colloq. forms of asseveration); **~ enough,** in fact as well as in prospect (*I said it would be, and sure enough it is*), with practical certainty (*he will come sure enough*). [ME, f. OF *sur sure*, earlier *sëur* f. L *securus* SECURE]

sure'ly (shoor'lĭ) *adv.* With certainty or safety (*will diminish slowly but surely; mule plants its feet surely*); if strong belief or experience or probability or right is to count for anything (*it surely cannot have been he; surely I have met you before; there is no truth in it, surely; surely you will not desert me*); (as answer) certainly, undoubtedly, ('*May I use your telephone?*' '*Surely*'). [ME, f. prec. + -LY²]

sure'ty (shoor'tĭ) *n.* **1.** (arch.) Certainty; **for** or **of a ~,** certainly. **2.** Person who makes himself responsible for another's appearance in court or payment of debt or performance of undertaking (**stand ~,** become so responsible, go bail, *for* another); hence **~SHIP** *n.* [ME, f. OF *surté, sëurté* f. L *securitas -tatis* SECURITY]

sûrf *n.*, & *v.i.* **1.** *n.* Foam and swell of sea breaking on shore or reefs; **~-bird,** Pacific coast-bird related to sandpiper; **~-board,** long narrow board used in surf-riding; **~-boat** (of buoyant build for use in surf); **~-man** (skilled in managing surf-boats); **~-riding,** sport of being carried over surf to shore on boards etc.; hence **~'Y²** *a.* **2.** *v.i.* Go surf-riding; hence **~'ER¹** *n.* [app. f. obs. *suff*, perh. assim. to *surge*; orig. applied to the Indian coast]

sûr'face (-ĭs) *n.*, *a.*, & *v.* **1.** *n.* The outside of a material body, area of this, (any of) the limits that terminate a solid, the upper boundary of soil, water, etc., outward aspect of material or immaterial thing, what is apprehended of something on casual view or consideration, (*has a smooth, uneven, surface; presents a large surface to view; its upper surface is as cold as ice; looks only at the surface of men and things; his politeness is only of* or *on the surface; one never gets below the surface with him*); **come to the ~,** (fig.) become perceptible after being hidden; hence **(-)sûr'faceD²** (-fĭst) *a.* **2.** (Geom.) That which has length and breadth but no thickness. **3.** *a.* Of the surface only (*surface plausibility, impressions*); of the surface of the sea, opp. the air above or the water beneath; of the surface of the earth, opp. underground. **4.** **~-active,** (of substance) able to affect wetting properties of a liquid; ***~-car** (running on road, opp. underground or elevated transport); **~ craft,** ship travelling only on surface of sea (opp. *submarine*); **~ density,** amount of mass etc. per unit area of surface; **~ mail** (carried by sea or *land and not by air); **~ noise** (in playing gramophone record, due to roughness of groove); **~-printing** (from raised surface such as letterpress type, not from incised plate); **~ tension,** (Phys.) tension of surface-film of liquid tending to minimize its surface area; **~-water** (that collects on and runs off from surface of ground etc.). **5.** *v.t.* Put special surface on (paper etc.); bring (submarine) to the surface. **6.** *v.i.* Come to the surface; (fig.) wake, *become visible or known. [F (as SUR-, FACE¹)]

surfă'ctant *n.* Surface-active agent. [abbr.; see -ANT]

sûr'feit (-fĭt) *n.* & *v.* **1.** *n.* Excess esp. in eating or drinking; oppression or satiety resulting. **2.** *v.t.* & *i.* Overfeed, (cause to) take too much of something; cloy, satiate *with.* [ME, f. OF *sorfe(i)t, surfe(i)t*, f. Rom. **superfactum* neut. p.p. (as n.) of **superficere* (as SUPER-, L *facere fact-* do); cf. LL *superficiens* excessive]

surfĭ'cial (-shal) *a.* (Geol.) Of the earth's surface; hence **~LY²** *adv.* [f. SURFACE after *superficial*]

sûrge *v.i.*, & *n.* **1.** *v.i.* (Of sea, crowd, standing corn, emotion, etc.) move up and down or to and fro (as) in waves; (Naut., of rope or chain or windlass) slip back with a jerk; move suddenly and powerfully *forwards, upwards*, etc.; (of electric current etc.) increase suddenly. **2.** *n.* Waves, a wave; surging motion, (fig.) impetuous onset; **~ tank** (to neutralize sudden changes of pressure in flow of liquid). [f. OF *sourdre sourge-*, or *sorgir* f. Cat., f. L *surgere* rise]

sûr'geon (-jon) *n.* Person skilled in surgery; medical practitioner qualified to practise (esp. one who specializes in) surgery (**~ dentist,** dentist thus qualified for dental surgery); medical officer in navy or army or military hospital; TREE *surgeon*; **~-fish,** fish of genus *Acanthurus* with movable lancet-shaped spines on each side of tail; ***~ general,** head of public health service or of medical service in army etc.; **~'s knot,** reef-knot with double twist. [ME, f. AF *surgien*, etc., f. OF *serurgien, sirurgien* (*sirurgie* f. L *chirurgia* f. Gk *kheirourgia* handiwork, surgery f. *kheir* hand, -O-, *-ergō* to work; see -Y¹)]

sûr'gerў *n.* **1.** Manual or instrumental treatment of injuries or disorders of the body, (*antiseptic, clinical, plastic*, etc., *surgery*). **2.** ‖Place where doctor, dentist, etc., gives advice and treatment; (colloq.) place where M.P., lawyer, etc., is available for discussion of person's problems; period during which doctor etc. is present at surgery. [ME, f. OF *surgerie*, contr. f. *sirurgerie* (*sirurgien*; see prec., -ERY)]

sûr'gĭcal *a.* Of surgeons or surgery (*surgical skill, operations, instruments*); resulting from surgery (*surgical fever*); used for purposes of surgery (*surgical boot*); ‖**~ spirit,** methylated spirits used in surgery for cleansing etc.; hence **~LY²** *adv.* [f. earlier *chirurgical* f. *chirurgy* f. OF *sirurgie* (see SURGEON)]

sur'icāte (soor'-) *n.* S. Afr. burrowing mammal (*Suricata suricatta*) like mongoose, grey with black stripes. [F, f. S. Afr. native name]

Surĭnă'm (soor-) *n.* ~ **toad,** pipa. [~ in S. America]

sûr'l|ȳ *a.* Uncivil, given to making rude answers, showing unfriendly temper, churlish; hence ~ĭLY² *adv.*, ~ĭNESS *n.* [alt. sp. of obs. *sirly* haughty f. SIR + -LY¹]

surmī'se (-z) *n.* & *v.* **1.** *n.* Conjecture, suspicion of the existence or guess at the nature of something. **2.** *v.t.* Infer doubtfully, suspect the existence of. **3.** *v.i.* Make a guess, try to divine something. [ME f. AF & OF fem. p.p. of *surmettre* accuse f. LL SUPER(*mittere miss-* send)]

surmou'nt *v.t.* **1.** (esp. in *pass.*) Cap, be on the top of, (*peaks surmounted with snow*). **2.** Overcome, get over, (difficulty, obstacle); hence ~ABLE *a.* [ME, f. OF SUR(*monter* MOUNT²)]

surmŭ'llĕt *n.* Red mullet. [f. F *surmulet* f. OF *sor* red + *mulet* MULLET]

sûr'nāme *n.*, & *v.t.* **1.** *n.* Name common to all members of a family; (Rom. Ant.) cognomen; (arch.) additional name of descriptive or allusive kind attached to a person and occas. becoming hereditary. **2.** *v.t.* Give surname to; give (person surname); (in *p.p.*) called by way of additional name, having as family name. [ME, alt. of *surnoun* f. AF (as SUR-, NOUN name)]

surpa'ss (-ah's) *v.t.* Go beyond (another, or one*self* previously) in degree, amount, or quality; be or do more or better than; hence ~ING² *a.*, greatly excelling or exceeding others, of very high degree. [f. F SUR(*passer* PASS¹)]

sûr'plĭc|e *n.* Loose full-sleeved white-linen vestment descending usu. to knees or ankles and worn usu. over cassock by clergy and choristers at divine service; ||~**e-fee** (paid to clergy for marriages, funerals, etc.); hence ~ED² (-st) *a.* [ME, f. AF *surplis*, OF *sourpelis*, f. med. L *superpellicium* (as SUPER-, *pellicia* PELISSE)]

sûr'plus *n.* & *a.* **1.** *n.* What remains over, what is not required for the purpose in hand, esp. excess of public revenue over expenditure for the financial year, (opp. *deficit*); so ~AGE (1) *n.* **2.** *a.* That is in excess of what is taken, used, needed, or acceptable; ~ **value,** difference between value of work done and wages paid. [ME f. AF; OF *s(o)urplus* f. med. L SUPER(PLUS)]

surprī'se (-z) *n.*, & *v.t.* **1.** *n.* Catching of person(s) unprepared (*the fort was taken, the truth must be elicited, by surprise*; *determined to attempt a surprise*); **a** ~ **visit** (without notice). **2.** Emotion excited by the unexpected, astonishment, (*full of surprise*; *his surprise was visible*); **to my great** ~, much against my expectations; ||~ **package, packet,** (with unexpected contents, e.g. sweets with coin; often fig.). **3.** Event etc. that excites surprise (*was a great surprise to me*); piece of unexpected news, unexpected gift, etc. **4.** *v.t.* Capture (place, person) by surprise; attack without warning; come upon (person) off his guard (*surprised him in the act*). **5.** Affect with surprise, astonish, turn out contrary to expectations of, be a surprise to, (*it may surprise you to learn of this*; *more surprised than frightened*); ~**d at,** scandalized by (*I am surprised at you, your behaviour*); hence **surprī'sING**² *a.*, **surprī'sĭngLY**² *adv.*, (-z-). **6.** Hurry (person) by surprise *into* conduct or act or do*ing* (*surprised me into rudeness, consent, dropping the reins*); discover (secret etc.) by unexpected action. **7.** Hence **surprī'sAL** 2 (-z-) *n.* [OF, fem. p.p. (as n.) of SUR(*prendre* f. L *praehendere* seize)]

sŭ'rra (*or* soor'*a*) *n.* Febrile disease affecting horses and cattle in the tropics. [Marathi]

sŭrrē'al|ĭsm *n.* (Twentieth-century movement in) art and literature purporting to express the subconscious mind by phenomena of dreams etc.; so ~ *a.*, ~IST (2) *a.* & *n.*, ~**ĭ'st**IC *a.* [f. F SUR(*réalisme* REALISM)]

sŭrrēbŭ'tter *n.* (Law). Plaintiff's reply to defendant's rebutter. [f. SUR- 2 + REBUTTER, after foll.]

sŭrrējoi'nder *n.* (Law). Plaintiff's reply to defendant's rejoinder. [f. SUR- 2 + REJOINDER]

surrĕ'nder *v.* & *n.* **1.** *v.t.* Hand over, give into another's power or control, relinquish possession of, esp. upon compulsion or demand, (*surrender fortress, army, ship, freedom, hopes, chastity, privilege, office*, etc.); give up rights under (insurance policy) in return for smaller sum payable immediately; give one*self* over *to* habit, emotion, influence, etc. **2.** *v.i.* (Of fortress, ship, or force, or its commander) accept enemy's demand for submission; give oneself up, cease from resistance, submit; ||~ **to** one's **bail,** duly appear in court after being released on bail. **3.** *n.* Surrendering or being surrendered; ~ **value,** amount payable to one who surrenders insurance policy. [ME f. AF, f. OF SUR(*rendre* RENDER)]

sŭrreptĭ'tious (-sh*us*) *a.* Underhand, kept secret, done by stealth, clandestine; hence ~LY² *adv.* [ME, f. L *surrepticius -itius* f. SUR(*ripere rept-* = *rapere* seize); see -ITIOUS¹]

***sŭ'rrey** *n.* Light four-wheeled carriage with two seats facing forwards. [f. *S*~ in England, where first made]

sŭ'rrogate *n.* Deputy, substitute; ||deputy of bishop or his chancellor for granting licences for marriages without banns; *judge in charge of probate, inheritance, and guardianship; hence ~SHIP (-tsh-) *n.* [f. L *surrogatus* p.p. of SUR(*rogare* ask) elect as substitute; see -ATE²]

surrou'nd *v.t.*, & *n.* **1.** *v.t.* Come or be all round, invest, enclose, encompass, encircle, environ; ~**ed by** or **with,** having on all sides; **the** ~**ing country,** the neighbouring district. **2.** *n.* ||Border, edging, esp. floor-covering between walls and carpet; *driving of wild animals into place of no escape. [ME = overflow, f. AF *sur(o)under*, OF *s(o)uronder* f. LL SUPER(*undare* flow f. *unda* wave)]

surrou'ndĭngs (-z) *n. pl.* Sum total of things or conditions in the neighbourhood of a person or thing (*picturesque, healthy, degraded, cultured, surroundings*). [f. prec. + -ING¹ + -S¹]

sûr'tăx *n.*, & *v.t.* (Impose) additional tax (on) (esp. of graduated tax on incomes above a certain figure in addition to ordinary income tax). [f. F SUR(*taxe* TAX²)]

sûrtou't (-ōō't; *or* -ōō' *or* sêr'-) *n.* (Hist.) Greatcoat; frock-coat. [F (*sur* over, *tout* everything)]

survei'llance (-vā'l-) *n.* Supervision, close observation, invigilation, esp. of suspected person. [F, f. SUR(*veiller* f. L *vigilare* keep watch)]

survey'¹ (-vā') *v.t.* Let the eyes pass over, take general view of, form general idea of the arrangement and chief features of, make or present survey of; examine condition of (building etc.); determine boundaries, size, position, shape, contour, etc., of (land, coast, district, estate, etc.) by measuring distances and angles. [ME, f. AF *survei(e)r*, OF *so(u)rveeir -vey-* f. med. L SUPER(*vidēre* see)]

sûr'vey² (-vā) *n.* General view, casting of eyes or mind over something; inspection or investigation of the condition, amount, etc., of something, account given of result of this; department carrying on, operations constituting, piece of, surveying of land etc.; map or plan setting forth results of such work; ||ORDNANCE *survey*. [f. prec.]

survey'or (-vā'-) *n.* Official inspector *of* (*surveyor of weights and measures* etc.), official in charge of a department, whence ~SHIP *n.*; person professionally engaged in surveying (QUANTITY *surveyor*); *exciseman. [ME, f. AF & OF *surve(i)our* (as SURVEY¹; see -OR)]

survī'val *n.* **1.** Surviving (~ **of the fittest,** process or result of natural selection); ~ **kit,** emergency rations etc. carried by airmen. **2.** Person or thing that has remained as a relic of an earlier time. [f. foll. + -AL 2]

survī've *v.* **1.** *v.t.* Outlive, be still alive or in existence after the passing away of, (*survive* one's *children, contemporaries,* etc.; *survive* one's *usefulness*); come alive through or continue to exist in spite of (*survive all perils*). **2.** *v.i.* Continue to live or exist, be still alive or existent. **3.** Hence **survī'**VOR *n.*, one who survives, (Law) joint tenant who has right to whole estate on other's death. [ME, f. AF *survivre,* OF *sourvivre* f. L SUPER(*vivere* live)]

sŭs *n.*, & *v.t.* (-ss-). (sl.) Suspect; suspicion; ~ **out,** reconnoitre. [abbr.]

sus- *pref.*, assim. form of SUB- 1–6 before *c, p,* or *t.*

suscĕptĭbĭ'lĭtў *n.* Being susceptible; (in *pl.*) sensitive feelings of a person; (Phys.) ratio of magnetization to magnetizing force. [f. foll. + -ITY; see -IBILITY]

suscĕ'ptĭb|le *a.* **1.** (*pred.*) Admitting *of* (*words are susceptible of another interpretation*; *facts not susceptible of proof*), open or liable or accessible or sensitive *to* (*very susceptible to pain, injury, kindness, women's charms*). **2.** Impressionable, sensitive, readily touched with emotion, touchy. **3.** Hence ~LY² *adv.* [f. LL *susceptibilis* f. L SUS(*cipere cept-* = *capere* take); see -IBLE]

suscĕ'ptĭve *a.* Concerned with the receiving of emotional impressions or ideas, receptive; = prec. [f. LL *susceptivus* (as prec.; see -IVE)]

su'shĭ (sōō'-) *n.* Japanese snack of cold rice flavoured and garnished. [Jap.]

sŭ'slĭk *n.* E. European & Asian rodent like gopher, of genus *Cittellus.* [Russ.]

suspĕ'ct¹ *v.t.* **1.** Have an impression of the existence or presence of (*danger, a plot, foul play, collusion, a causal relation*); believe without adequate proof *to be* (*suspect him to be my brother, a liar, dying*); be inclined to think that or *that* (*I suspect you once thought otherwise*; *you, I suspect, don't care*). **2.** Incline to mentally accuse *of* or inculpate, doubt the innocence of, distrust, (*I suspect him of lying, of deep designs*; *suspected persons*; *the ignorant suspect everybody*); ~**ed** *criminal, connection,* etc., person or thing suspected of being (such). **3.** Hold to be uncertain, mistrust, doubt the genuineness or truth of, (*suspect the authenticity of the evidence*). [ME, f. L *suspicere* (see foll.)]

sŭ'spĕct² *a.* & *n.* **1.** *a.* Of suspected character, subject to suspicion or distrust, not unimpeachable, (*the statement of an interested party is naturally suspect*). **2.** *n.* Suspected person (*political suspects are kept under surveillance*). [ME, f. L *suspectus* p.p. of *suspicere* (as SUB- 1, 2, *specere* look)]

suspĕ'nd *v.t.* **1.** Hang up; (in *p.p.*, of solid particles or body in fluid medium) sustained somewhere between top and bottom (*a balloon suspended in mid-air*; *suspended particles of dust*); so **suspĕ'ns**IBLE *a.* **2.** Keep in undecided or inoperative state for a time, defer, temporarily annul, adjourn, debar temporarily from office or function or privilege or membership, (*suspend judgement, hostilities, the rules, the proceedings, a player, a clergyman*); ~ **payment,** (of company) fail to meet financial engagements, admit insolvency; ~**ed animation,** state of cessation of vital functions without death; ~**ed sentence** (Law, remaining unenforced subject to good behaviour during specified period). [ME, f. OF *suspendre* or L SUS(*pendere pens-* hang)]

suspĕ'nder *n.* In vbl senses; (in *pl.*) *pair of braces, ||pair of (sets of) attachments to hold up socks or stockings by their tops; ||~ **belt,** woman's undergarment carrying suspenders for holding up stockings. [f. prec. + -ER¹]

suspĕ'nse *n.* **1.** State of usu. anxious uncertainty or expectation or waiting for information; **keep** person **in** ~, delay telling him what he is eager to know; hence ~FUL (-sf-) *a.* **2.** (Law) suspension, temporary cessation of right etc.; ~ **account** (in which items are temporarily entered till proper place is determined). [ME, f. AF & OF *suspens,* f. p.p. (as n.) of L *suspendere* SUSPEND]

suspĕ'nsion (-sh*o*n) *n.* Suspending or being suspended; substance consisting of particles suspended in a medium; means by which vehicle is supported on its axles; (Mus.) prolongation of note of chord to form discord with following chord; ~ **bridge** (in which roadway is hung across river etc., usu. on wire or chain cables passing over towers and anchored, without support from below). [F, or f. L *suspensio* (as SUSPEND; see -ION)]

suspĕ'nsĭve *a.* Having the power or tendency to suspend or postpone; causing suspense; *suspensive* VETO; hence ~LY² (-vlĭ) *adv.*, ~NESS (-vn-) *n.* [f. F *suspensif -ive* or f. med. L *suspensivus* (as SUSPEND; see -IVE)]

suspĕ'nsorў *a.* (Of ligament, muscle, bandage, etc.) holding (organ etc.) suspended. [f. F *suspensoire* (as SUSPENSION; see -ORY)]

suspĭ'cion (-sh*o*n) *n.* Feeling or state of mind of one who suspects (*have a suspicion that all is not well*); suspecting or being suspected (**above** ~, too obviously good etc. to be suspected; **under** ~, suspected); partial or unconfirmed belief esp. that something is wrong or someone guilty; soupçon *of*; hence ~LESS *a.* [ME, f. AF *suspeciun* (OF *sospeçon*) f. med. L *suspectio -onis* f. L *suspicere* (see SUSPECT¹, -ION), assim. to F *suspicion* & L *suspicio*]

suspĭ'cious (-sh*u*s) *a.* Prone to, feeling, indicating, suggesting or justifying, suspicion (*the ignorant are suspicious of everybody*; *his silence made me suspicious*; *with a suspicious glance*; *under suspicious circumstances*); hence ~LY² *adv.*, ~NESS *n.* [ME f. AF & OF, f. L *suspiciosus* (as prec.; see -OUS)]

suspīr'e *v.i.* (esp. poet.) Sigh (*for*); breathe; so **sŭspĭr**A'TION *n.* [f. L *suspirare* (as SUB- 1, *spirare* breathe)]

sŭss. Var. of SUS.

Sŭ'ssĕx *n.* Speckled or red domestic fowl of English breed; ~ **spaniel** (dark golden breed with short legs and neck). [~ in England]

sustai'n *v.t.* **1.** Carry weight of, hold up, keep from falling or sinking, esp. for prolonged period. **2.** = SUPPORT 2; ~**ing food** (that keeps up one's strength); ~**ing member** (making regular contributions to funds of institution etc.); *~**ing programme,** broadcast programme without commercial sponsor. **3.** Endure without giving way, stand, bear up against, (*sustained the shock of the enemy's attack*; *will not sustain comparison with*). **4.** Undergo, experience, suffer, (*sustain a defeat, a broken leg, severe bruises, loss,* etc.). **5.** (Of court or other authority) allow validity of, give decision in favour of, uphold, (*sustain the objection, the applicant in his claim,* etc.). **6.** = SUPPORT 6. **7.** Keep up or represent (part, character) adequately. **8.** Keep (sound, effort, etc.) going continuously (*a sustained note, effort*; *the interest is well sustained*). **9.** Hence ~ABLE *a.*, ~MENT *n.* [ME, f. AF *sustein-*, OF *so(u)stein-* stressed st. of *so(u)stenir* f. L SUS(*tinēre tent-* = *tenēre* hold)]

sŭ'stenance *n.* Nourishing, nourishment; nourishing quality, subsistence, food (lit. or fig.; *there is no sustenance in it*; *how shall we get sustenance?*; *lived a week without sustenance of any kind*); means of support. [ME, f. AF *sustenaunce*, OF *so(u)stenance* (as prec.; see -ANCE)]

sŭstentā'tion *n.* Support of life; maintenance; ~ **fund** (collected to support indigent clergy, esp. in Church of Scotland). [ME f. OF, or f. L *sustentatio* (*sustentare* frequent. of *sustinēre* SUSTAIN; see -ATION)]

sūsurrā'tion, sūsŭ'rrus, (*or* sōō-) *ns.* (literary). Whispering, rustling. [(ME, f. LL *susurratio* f. L *susurrare* f.) L *susurrus* a. or n.; see -ATION]

sŭ'tler *n.* (Hist.) Camp-follower selling provisions etc. to soldiers. [f. obs. Du. *soeteler* (*soetelen* befoul, perform mean duties f. Gmc **sudh*-; cf. SUDS)]

Su'tra (sōō'-) *n.* (Set of) aphorism(s) in Hindu literature; narrative part of Buddhist literature; Jainist scripture. [f. Skr. *sūtra* thread, rule (*siv* SEW)]

suttee', satī', (-ē') *n.* (Hist.) Hindu widow who immolated herself on her husband's funeral pyre; (custom requiring) such immolation. [Hindi & Urdu, f. Skr. *satī* faithful wife (*sat* good)]

su'tur|e (sōō'-) *n.*, & *v.t.* **1.** *n.* (Anat.) seamlike line of junction of two bones at their edges, esp. in the skull; (Bot. & Zool.) similar junction of parts; (Surg.) uniting of edges of wound by stitching, thread or wire used for this; hence ~AL (-cher-), ~ED[2] (-cherd), *adjs.* **2.** *v.t.* Stitch (wound). [F, or f. L *sutura* (*suere sut*- sew; see -URE)]

sū'zerain (*or* sōō'-) *n.* Feudal overlord; sovereign or State having some control over another State that is internally autonomous; hence ~TY[1] *n.* [F, app. f. *sus* above f. L *su(r)sum* upward, after *souverain* SOVEREIGN]

s.v. *abbr.* side valve; under the word (*for 'span' see s.v. 'spick'*) [f. L *sub voce* or *sub verbo*].

svĕlte *a.* (Of human figure) slim, slender, lissom; graceful. [F, f. It. *svelto*]

S.W. *abbr.* South-West(ern).

swab (-ŏb) *n.*, & *v.t.* (**-bb-**). **1.** *n.* Mop or other arrangement of absorbent material on handle for cleaning or mopping up; absorbent pad used in surgery; specimen of morbid secretion etc. taken with a swab for bacteriological examination. **2.** (sl.) Contemptible person. **3.** *v.t.* Clean with swab; take *up* (moisture) with swab. [n. f. v., back form. f. *swabber* f. early mod. Du. *zwabber* f. Gmc base = 'splash, sway']

swă'cked (-kt) *a.* (sl.) Drunk. [p.p. of Sc. *swack* drink heavily]

swa'ddl|e (-ŏ'-) *v.t.*, & *n.* **1.** *v.t.* Swathe in bandages or many or thick wraps or garments; **~ing-bands, -clothes,** (in which infants were formerly wrapped to restrain them, (fig.) influences that restrain freedom of action or thought). **2.** *n.* *Swaddling-clothes. [ME, f. SWATHE[2] + -LE 3]

swa'ddy̆ (-ŏ'-) *n.* (sl.) Soldier. [f. dial. *swad* soldier, bumpkin, perh. of Scand. orig., + -Y[3]]

Swade'shĭ (-ahdā'-) *n.* (Hist.) Movement in India, originating in Bengal, advocating the production of home-manufactured, and the boycott of foreign, goods. [Bengali, = own-country things]

swăg[1] *n.* **1.** Ornamental festoon of flowers etc.; carved or moulded representation of this; drapery of similar appearance. **2.** (sl.) Booty carried off by burglars etc., gains made by political or other jobbery; large quantity. **3.** (Austral.) Tramp's, miner's, or bush-traveller's bundle; hence **~'man,** tramp. [f. foll.]

swăg[2] *v.* (**-gg-**). **1.** *v.i.* Sway from side to side; hang heavily. **2.** *v.t.* Cause to sway or sag; arrange (curtain etc.) in swags; (Austral.) carry in swag. [16th c., prob. f. Scand.]

swāge *n.*, & *v.t.* **1.** *n.* Die or stamp for shaping wrought iron etc. by hammering or pressure; tool for bending metal etc.; **~-block** (with variety of perforations, grooves, etc., for shaping metal). **2.** *v.t.* Shape with swage. [f. F *s(o)uage* decorative groove, of unkn. orig.]

swă'gger[1] (-g-) *v.i.*, *n.*, & *a.* **1.** *v.i.* Walk like a superior among inferiors; show self-confidence or self-satisfaction by gait; go *about*, *in*, *out*, etc., with such walk; behave in domineering or defiant way; talk boastfully (*about* thing) or in hectoring manner; hence ~ER[1] *n.* **2.** *n.* Swaggering gait or manner or talk; dashing or confident air or way of doing something, freedom from tameness or hesitancy, smartness; ‖**~-cane, ~-stick,** short cane carried by soldiers in town etc. or by officers. **3.** *a.* (colloq.) Smart, fashionable, (*swagger clothes*, *society*, etc.); (of coat) cut with loose flare from shoulders. [app. f. SWAG[2] + -ER[5]]

swă'gger[2], **swă'ggĭe,** (-g-) *n.* (Austral.) Tramp travelling with swag. [f. SWAG[1] + -ER[1], -IE]

Swahi'lĭ (swahhē'-) *n.* Bantu people of Zanzibar and the adjacent coasts; their language, widely used in E. Africa. [f. Arab. *sawāḥil* pl. of *sāḥil* coast; see -I]

swain *n.* Young rustic; bucolic lover; (joc.) lover, suitor. [ME *swein* f. ON *sveinn* lad = OE *swān* swine-herd, OHG *swein* f. Gmc **swainaz*]

swa'llow[1] (-ŏ'lō) *v.* & *n.* **1.** *v.t.* Cause or allow (food etc.) to pass down one's throat; = EAT (one's *words*); repress (tears, resentment, etc.); pronounce (sounds) indistinctly or not at all; **~ a camel,** make no difficulty about something incredible or impossible or outrageous (w. ref. to Matt. 23:24). **2.** ~ (**up**), engulf, absorb, exhaust, draw in, make away with, (*the earth swallowed them up*; *the expenses more than swallow up the earnings*; *death is swallowed up in victory*). **3.** Accept (statement) with ready credulity (*will swallow anything you tell him*); accept meekly, put up with, (affront, insult). **4.** Hence ~ABLE *a.* **5.** *v.i.* Perform muscular action (as) of swallowing something. **6.** *n.* Gullet; act of swallowing; amount swallowed at once; ‖~(**-hole**), = SINK[2]-*hole*. [OE *swelg* n., *swelgan* v., = OHG *swel(a)han*, ON *svelga* f. Gmc **swelg*-etc.]

swa'llow[2] (-ŏ'lō) *n.* **1.** Bird of genus *Hirundo* etc., esp. migratory, long-winged, swift-flying, wide-gaped, weak-legged, fork-tailed, insectivorous bird associated with summer; **one ~ does not make a summer** (warning against hasty inference from one instance). **2.** ‖**~-dive** (with arms outspread till close to water); **~-hawk,** = *swallow-tailed kite*; **~-tail,** deeply forked tail, butterfly etc. having this, two-pointed end of flag, (in *sing.* or *pl.*, colloq.) swallow-tailed coat; **~-tailed,** (of bird etc.) with deeply forked tail (*~-tailed coat*, tailcoat; *~-tailed kite*, Amer. white kite (*Elanoides forficatus*) with black deeply forked tail), dovetailed; **~-wort,** (1) milkweed, (2) greater celandine. [OE *swealwe*, = OS *swala*, OHG *swal(a)wa*, ON *svala* f. Gmc **swalwōn*]

swăm. See SWIM.

swa'mĭ (-ah'-) *n.* Hindu idol; Hindu religious teacher (esp. as form of address to Brahmin); (fig.) = PUNDIT 2. [f. Hindi *swāmī* master, prince, f. Skr. *svāmin*]

swamp (-ŏ-) *n.* & *v.* **1.** *n.* Piece of wet spongy ground, bog, marsh, (*attrib.*, in many names of plants and animals found in swamps); hence ~'Y[2] *a.* **2.** *v.t.* (Of water) overwhelm, flood, soak, (boat or its crew or contents, house, provisions, etc.); make helpless with excessive supply of something (*am swamped with* or *in* *letters, applications, work*); (of greater quantity or numbers) swallow up, make invisible etc., prevent from being noticed or taking effect; *defeat decisively. **3.** *v.i.* Become swamped. [17th c.; usu. referred to Gmc root **swamp-*, **swamb-*, **swamm-* sponge, fungus]

swan (-ŏn) *n.*, & *v.i.* (**-nn-**) **1.** *n.* Large water-bird of genus *Cygnus* etc. with long flexible neck, webbed feet, and in most species snow-white plumage, formerly supposed to sing melodiously at point of death; **black ~**, (1) something extremely rare, (2) Australian swan with mainly black plumage; *all his geese are swans* (see GOOSE). **2.** (fig., w. ref. to sweetness of swan's dying song.) Poet (esp. **S~ of Avon,** Shakespeare). **3.** ***~-dive,** = SWALLOW²-*dive*; **~-flower,** S. Amer. orchid with flower shaped like swan's neck; **~-goose,** long-necked China goose, esp. = CHINESE *goose*; **~-herd,** (esp. royal) officer having charge of swans; **~-maiden** (in Gmc Myth., able to change herself into swan); **~-mark** (cut in skin of swan's beak to show ownership); **~-neck,** curved structure shaped like swan's neck; **~'sdown** (-z-), (1) down of swan used in trimmings and esp. in powder-puffs, (2) kind of thick cotton cloth with soft nap on one side; **~-shot** (of large size for shooting swans); **~-skin,** kind of fine twilled flannel; **~-song,** fabled song of dying swan, (fig.) person's last composition, performance, etc.; ||**~-upping,** annual taking up and marking of Thames swans. **4.** Hence **~'LIKE** *a.* & *adv.*, **~'nERY** (3) *n.* **5.** *v.i.* (sl.) Move aimlessly or majestically (*around*) like swan. [OE, = OS, OHG *swan*, ON *svanr* f. Gmc **swanaz*]

swănk *n.*, & *v.i.* (colloq.) **1.** *n.* Ostentation, swagger, bluff; ||**~'pot,** person behaving with swank; hence **~'Y²** *a.*, marked by swank, ostentatiously smart. **2.** *v.i.* Behave with swank. [orig. 19th c. Midland Engl. wd]

swap (-ŏp), **swŏp,** *v.* (**-pp-**) & *n.* (colloq.) **1.** Exchange by way of barter (lit. or fig.; *swapped my knife for bread*; *swap blows, jokes*; *will you swap places* etc.?, *will you swap?*, *shall we try a swap?*); **never ~ horses while crossing the stream,** leave changes till crisis is past. **2.** *n.* Thing suitable for swapping. [ME, orig. = 'hit', prob. imit.]

swara'j (-ah'j) *n.* (Hist.) Self-government, independence, for India; hence **~IST** (2) *n.* [Skr., = self-ruling (cf. RAJ)]

sward (-ŏrd) *n.* (literary). Expanse covered with short grass, lawnlike ground; turf, whence **~'ED²** *a.* [OE *sweard* skin, = MDu., MLG *swarde*, MHG *swarte*, ON *svörthr*, of unkn. orig.]

swāre. See SWEAR.

swarf (-ŏrf) *n.* Chips or filings of wood, metal, etc.; wax etc. removed in cutting gramophone record. [f. ON *svarf* file-dust]

swarm¹ (-ŏrm) *n.*, & *v.i.* **1.** *n.* Large number or dense group of insects, birds, small animals, persons, etc., moving about in a cluster or irregular body esp. round prey or enemy; (in *pl.*) great numbers *of* children, stars, people, bills, etc.; cluster of honey-bees emigrating from hive with queen bee to establish new home; group of zoospores (**~-cell, -spore,** zoospore or other mobile spore). **2.** *v.i.* Move in a swarm (*round, about, over*, etc., thing or person, *in, out*); (of bees) cluster for emigration; congregate in large numbers, be very numerous; (of place) be overrun, be crowded, abound, *with* (*road, hills, house, swarming with beggars, rebels, fleas*). [OE *swearm*, = OS *swarm*, OHG *swar(a)m*, ON *svarmr* f. Gmc **swarmaz*]

swarm² (-ŏrm) *v.* **1.** *v.i.* **~ up,** climb (rope or tree or pole) by clasping with arms and legs alternately, climb (steep slope) by clinging with hands and knees. **2.** *v.t.* Swarm up (rope etc.). [16th c., of unkn. orig.]

swart (-ŏrt) *a.* (arch.) Dark-hued, swarthy. [OE *sweart*, = OS *swart*, OHG *swarz*, ON *svartr*, Goth. *swarts* f. Gmc **swartaz*]

swar'th|y̆ (-ŏr'dhĭ) *a.* Dark, esp. dark-complexioned; hence **~ĭLY²** *adv.*, **~ĭNESS** *n.* [var. of obs. *swarty* (as prec.; see -Y²)]

swash¹ (-ŏ-) *v.* & *n.* **1.** *v.t.* (arch.) Strike violently. **2.** *v.i.* (Of water etc.) wash about, make sound of washing or rising and falling; (arch.) swagger. **3. ~'buckler, ~'buckling,** swaggering (bully or ruffian). **4.** *n.* Motion or sound of swashing water. [imit.]

swash² (-ŏ-) *a.* **1.** Inclined obliquely; **~-plate,** inclined disc revolving on axle and giving reciprocating motion to part in contact with it. **2.** (Typogr., of letter) having flourished stroke(s). [17th c., of unkn. orig.]

swa'stĭka (swŏ's-) *n.* Ancient symbol formed by cross with equal arms when all arms are continued as far again at right angles clockwise (esp. as symbol of Nazis) or counter-clockwise. [f. Skr. *svastika* (*svastí* well-being f. *sú* good + *astí* being)]

swat (-ŏt) *v.t.* (**-tt-**). Hit hard; crush (fly etc.) with blow, whence **~'tER¹** (2) *n.* [17th c. in sense 'sit down', N. Engl. dial. & U.S. var. of SQUAT]

swatch (-ŏ-) *n.* Sample (esp. of cloth or fabric); a collection of samples. [17th c., of unkn. orig.]

swath (-aw-; *pl. pr.* -dhz), **swāthe¹** (-dh), *n.* Ridge of grass, corn, etc., lying after being cut; space left clear after one passage of mower etc.; broad strip; **cut a wide ~,** (fig.) be effective in destruction. [OE *swæth, swathu*, = MHG *swade*]

swāthe² (-dh) *v.t.*, & *n.* **1.** *v.t.* Bind with bandages; enclose in wraps or cloths or warm garments or many garments. **2.** *n.* Bandage, wrapping. [OE *swathian* (**swæth* n.; cf. SWADDLE)]

sway *v.* & *n.* **1.** *v.i.* Lean unsteadily to one side or in different directions by turns, have unsteady swinging motion, oscillate irregularly; waver, vacillate. **2.** *v.t.* Give swaying motion to (*wind sways trees*); govern the motion of; wield, control direction of, have influence over, govern, (poet.) rule over, (*his speech swayed votes*; *is too much swayed by the needs of the moment*; *sways a fifth of mankind*); **~-back(ed),** (with) back (esp. of horse) abnormally hollowed, (having) lordosis. **3.** *n.* Swaying motion or position; rule, government, (*hold sway*). [ME; cf. LG *swājen* be blown to and fro, Du. *zwaaien* swing, wave]

swear (swār) *v.* (**swore,** arch. **sware; sworn**) & *n.* **1.** *v.t.* & *i.* State something on oath, take oath (*to*, that or *that*), promise (conduct, *to* do) on oath, take (oath), (*will you swear, swear it, swear to it*, (*that*) *you were not there?*; *swear eternal fidelity*; *had sworn*, or *sworn a solemn oath, to return*); (colloq.) say emphatically that (*swore he hadn't touched it*); **~ by** or **to,** appeal to as witness and guarantee of oath; **~ by,** (colloq.) profess or have great belief in, regularly resort to or recommend; **~ off,** take oath to abstain from (drink etc.). **2.** *v.i.* Use profane oaths to express anger or as expletives (*at* person etc.); **~ at,** (of colours etc.) fail to harmonize with. **3.** *v.t.* Cause to take oath, administer oath to, (*swear a witness* etc.; *swear person to secrecy*); **sworn brothers** or **friends,** intimates; **sworn enemies** (open and irreconcilable); **~ evidence** etc. (given on oath); **~ in,** induct into office by administering oath; ***~ out,** obtain (warrant etc.) by making charge on oath. **4.** Make sworn affirmation of (offence) *against* (*swear treason against*); **~ the peace against,**

make oath that one is in danger of bodily harm from. **5.** Hence ~′ER[1] *n.* **6.** *n.* Spell of profane swearing; ~(**-word**), (colloq.) a profane oath. [OE *swerian,* = OS *swerian,* OHG *swer(i)en,* ON *sverja* f. Gmc **swarjan* (**swar-,* cogn. w. ANSWER[1])]

sweat (-ĕt) *n.* & *v.* (~′**ed** *or* *~). **1.** *n.* Moisture exuded from the skin esp. when one is hot, perspiration, (*running, dripping, wet, with sweat*); **in** or **by the ~ of** one's **brow** or **face,** by dint of toil; **bloody ~,** exudation of blood mixed with sweat. **2.** Sweating state, spell of sweating, piece of exercise that induces sweat (*in a,* (colloq.) *all of a, sweat; night sweats; a sweat will do him good*); **a cold ~** (as in death, fainting, terror, etc.). **3.** (colloq.) State of anxiety (*in a sweat*); drudgery, toil, effort, laborious task or undertaking; ***no ~,** there is no need to worry; ||**old ~,** old soldier, person with much experience. **4.** Drops exuding from or condensing on any surface. **5.** **~-band,** leather or other lining of hat or cap, band round wrist, head, etc., for wiping away or absorbing sweat; **~-cloth,** (esp.) thin blanket under horse's saddle or collar; **~-duct** (by which sweat exudes from **~-gland,** spiral tubular gland secreting sweat below skin); **~-house, ~-lodge,** Amer. Ind. steam-bath; **~-shirt,** sleeved cotton sweater worn esp. by athletes before or after exercise; **~-shop** (in which sweated workers are employed); **~-suit** (of sweat-shirt and close-fitting trousers). **6.** Hence ~′LESS, ~′Y[2], *adjs.* **7.** *v.i.* Exude sweat, perspire; (fig.) be in state of terror or suffering or repentance (**~ it out,** endure to the end); (of wall etc.) exhibit surface moisture; toil, drudge. **8.** *v.t.* Emit (blood, gum, etc.) like sweat; make (horse, athlete, etc.) sweat by exercise; **~ blood,** (fig.) work strenuously, be extremely anxious. **9.** *v.t.* & *i.* Employ (labour, workers) at starvation wages for long hours under poor conditions; (in *p.p.*, of clothes etc.) made by sweated workers; (of workers) work on such terms. **10.** *v.t.* Subject (hides, tobacco) to fermentation in manufacturing; fasten (metal part) *on* or *in* by partial fusion of metal or solder. **11.** **~′ing-bath** (for producing sweat); **~′ing-room** (in Turkish bath, or for drying cheeses); **~′ing-sickness,** epidemic fever with sweating prevalent in England in 15th–16th c. [ME *swet(e),* alt. (after *swete* v. f. OE *swǣtan,* OHG *sweizzen* roast) f. *swote* f. OE *swāt,* OS *swēt,* OHG *sweiz* f. Gmc **swait-*]

swea′ter (-ĕ′t-) *n.* In vbl senses; employer who sweats workers; jersey worn during or before or after exercise to prevent chills, or as informal garment; **~ girl,** (colloq.) girl or woman with well-developed bust and wearing sweater to emphasize it. [f. prec. + -ER[1]]

swēde *n.* **1.** (*S~*). Native of Sweden. **2.** ~ (**turnip**), large yellow-fleshed turnip brought from Sweden to Scotland in 18th c. [f. MLG & MDu. *Swēde,* prob. f. ON *Svíthjóth* (*Svíar* Swedes, *thjóth* people)]

Swēdenbôr′gĭan *a.* & *n.* (Adherent) of the 'New Church' and religious doctrines of E. Swedenborg, Sw. philosopher d. 1772; hence ~ISM (3) *n.* [f. *Swedenborg* + -IAN]

Swē′dĭsh *a.* & *n.* (Language) of Sweden or its inhabitants; **~ drill,** system of therapeutic muscular exercises. [f. SWEDE or *Sweden* + -ISH[1]]

***swee′nȳ** *n.* Atrophy of muscle, esp. of shoulder, in horse. [prob. f. G dial. *schweine* atrophy]

sweep[1] *v.* (**swept**) & *n.* **1.** *v.i.* Glide swiftly, speed along with impetuous unchecked motion, go majestically, extend in continuous curve or line or slope, (*eagle sweeps past; wind sweeps along; cavalry sweeps down on the enemy; she swept out of the room; his glance sweeps from right to left; with a sweeping stroke; coast sweeps northward; plain sweeps away to the sea*). **2.** *v.t.* Impart sweeping motion to, carry *along* or *down* or *away* or *off* in impetuous course or forceful action, clear *off* or *away* or *out of* existence etc. or *from,* (*swept his hand across; flood sweeps away bridge, sweeps logs down with it; was swept away by an avalanche; the plague swept off thousands*); **~ away,** (fig.) abolish swiftly. **3.** Traverse swiftly or in all directions (*wind sweeps the hillside; epidemic, new fashion, sweeping America*); pass lightly across or along, pass eyes or hand quickly along or over (**~ the strings** etc., play musical instrument); drag (river-bottom etc.) to find something. **4.** (Of artillery etc.) include in line of fire, cover, enfilade, rake, (*battery sweeps the approaches, glacis, street*). **5.** ~ (**up**), clear everything from, clear of dust or soot or litter with broom or sweeper, (*sweep floor, carpet, chimney; sweep up the room*); **swept and garnished,** generally renovated, w. ref. to Luke 11:25; **~ the board,** win all cards or money on gaming-table, (fig.) win all possible prizes etc.; **~ a constituency** etc., receive nearly all votes, have large majority; **~ the seas,** drive all enemies from them. **6.** Gather *up* or collect (as) with broom or brush, push *aside, away,* etc., thus; *sweep under the* CARPET; **~ everything into** one's **net,** seize all that comes; **swept-back,** (of aircraft wing) having outer part aft of inner part; **swept-up,** (of hair) = UPSWEPT; **swept-wing,** (of aircraft) having swept-back wings; hence ~′ING[1] (2) *n.* (usu. in *pl.*; lit. or fig.). **7.** Propel (barge etc.) with sweeps. **8.** **~′back,** angle at which aircraft's wing is set back from position at right angles to body; **~-net, ~-seine,** large fishing-net; **~-second hand** (on clock or watch, moving on same dial as other hands); **~′stake(s),** (prize won in) race or contest in which all competitors' stakes are taken by winner(s), form of gambling on horse-races etc. in which the sum of participators' stakes goes to drawer(s) of winning or placed horse(s) etc. [ME *swepe,* earlier *swōpe* f. OE *swāpan*]

sweep[2] *n.* **1.** Sweeping motion or extension, curve in road etc., piece of curving road etc., (*with a sweep of his arm, eyes, scythe; a sweep of mountain country; river makes a great sweep to the left; house is approached by a fine sweep*). **2.** Range or compass of something that has sweeping motion (lit. or fig.; *within* or *beyond the sweep of the scythe, net, telescope, eye, human intelligence*). **3.** Act of sweeping (as) with broom (*give it a thorough sweep, sweep-up, sweep-out*; **make a clean ~,** (1) have complete riddance of old or outdated material, staff, etc., (2) win all prizes etc.); sortie by aircraft. **4.** Long oar worked by rower(s) standing on barge, becalmed sailing-ship, etc.; sail of windmill. **5.** Long pole mounted as lever for raising buckets from well. **6.** = CHIMNEY-*sweep.* **7.** (colloq.) Sweepstake. **8.** Movement of beam across screen of cathode-ray tube. [f. prec.]

swee′per *n.* In vbl senses; = CARPET-*sweeper,* MINE[1]*sweeper*; person whose work is to clean a place by sweeping; (Footb. etc.) player positioned just in front of goalkeeper. [f. SWEEP[1] + -ER[1]]

swee′pĭng *a.* In vbl senses; of wide range, regardless of limitations or exceptions, (*sweeping condemnation, generalization,* etc.); far-reaching, comprehensive, (*sweeping changes, success,* etc.); hence ~LY[2] *adv.*, ~NESS *n.* [f. SWEEP[1] + -ING[2]]

sweet *a.* & *n.* **1.** *a.* Tasting like sugar or honey (*sweet apples* etc.); **~-and-sour,** cooked in sauce containing sugar and vinegar or lemon; **~ stuff,** sweetmeats; **~ tea** etc. (with much sugar); **a ~ tooth,** liking for sweet things; **~ wine** (opp. DRY[1]); **tastes ~,** has sweet taste. **2.** Smelling pleasant like roses or perfumes, fragrant, (*smells sweet; has a sweet scent; air is sweet with jasmine; sweet breath*). **3.** Melodious or harmonious in sound (*has a sweet voice; sounds sweet; sweet song, singer*, etc.). **4.** Fresh and sound, not salt or salted or sour or bitter or rancid or high or stinking, (*is the milk, butter, still sweet?; keep the room clean and sweet*); (of water) fresh and drinkable. **5.** Highly agreeable or attractive or gratifying, inspiring affection, dear, beloved, amiable, gentle, easy, (colloq.) pretty or charming or delightful, (*'tis sweet to hear one's own praises; a sweet nature, face, girl; sweet* SEVENTEEN; *sweet love, dalliance, idleness, dreams, sleep; what a sweet blouse, moustache, collie!; how sweet of you to bring me a present!*); **keep** person **~,** ingratiate oneself with him; **~ on,** (colloq.) fond of or in love with. **6.** Pleasing to oneself merely; **at** one's **own ~ will,** just as or when one pleases, arbitrarily, at random. **7.** *Sweet* BASIL; **~ bay,** (1) = BAY[1] 1, (2) N. Amer. magnolia (*M. virginiana*); **~'bread,** pancreas or thymus gland of animal, esp. as food; *sweet*-BRIER[1]; *sweet* CHESTNUT; **~ cicely,** white-flowered plant (*Myrrhis odorata*); **~ corn,** kind of maize with sweet-flavoured grains; *sweet*-GALE[1]; **~'heart,** *n.*, & *v.t.*, (act as) one of pair of lovers; **~ herb,** fragrant culinary herb; **~'meal,** sweet wholemeal (biscuit etc.); **~'meat,** small shaped piece of confectionery usu. consisting chiefly of sugar or chocolate with flavouring or filling, or of fruit preserved in sugar; **~ oil,** (esp.) olive oil; **~ pea,** climbing garden annual (*Lathyrus odoratus*) with showy variously-coloured sweet-scented flowers; *sweet* PEPPER[1] 2; *sweet* POTATO; **~-root,** liquorice; **~ rush, ~ sedge,** kind of sedge with thick creeping aromatic rootstock used in medicine and confectionery; ||**~-shop** (where sweetmeats are sold); **~-sop,** (sweet-pulped green-rinded fruit of) a tropical Amer. evergreen shrub (*Annona squamosa*); *sweet* SULTAN; ***~-talk,** blandish(ment); **~-tempered,** amiable; *sweet* VIOLET; **~-wi'lliam,** cultivated species of pink with close-clustered sweet-smelling flowers often particoloured in zones. **8.** Hence ~'ISH[1] 2 *a.*, ~'LY[2] *adv.*, ~'NESS *n.* (**~ness and light,** display of mildness and reason). **9.** *n.* Sweet part (*the sweet and the bitter* or *sweets and bitters of life*); sweetmeat; ||sweet dish such as pudding, tart, ice cream, jelly, forming course of meal; (arch., usu. in *pl.*) fragrance; (in *pl.*) delights, gratifications, pleasures, (*the sweets of office, domestication, flattery, success*); (esp. in *voc.*) darling. [OE *swēte*, = OS *swōti*, OHG *s(w)uozi*, ON *sætr*, f. Gmc **swōtja-*, **swōti-*, f. IE **swād-*]

swee'ten *v.t.* & *i.* Make or become sweet(er); make agreeable or less painful; hence ~ER[1] *n.*, (esp.) bribe, substitute for sugar, ~ING[1] (4) *n.* [f. prec. + -EN[6]]

swee'tĭe *n.* (colloq.) ||Sweetmeat; **~(-pie),** sweetheart. [f. SWEET + -IE]

swee'tĭng *n.* Sweet-flavoured variety of apple; (arch.) darling. [ME, f. SWEET + -ING[3]]

swĕll *v.* (*p.p.* **swo'llen** *pr.* swō'-, *or* **~ed**), *n.*, & *a.* **1.** *v.t.* & *i.* (Cause to) grow bigger or louder, dilate, expand, rise or raise up from surrounding surface, bulge out, increase in volume or force or intensity, (*river swollen with melted snow; the injured wrist began to swell* or *swell up; the swelling sails, wind swells the sails; the swelling tide; expenditure swollen by extravagance; items swell the total; frog swelled himself to size of ox; a thousand voices swell the sound; sound swells on the breeze; murmur swelled into a roar; ground swells into an eminence*); (of heart) feel like bursting with emotion; **~ with** *pride, indignation*, etc., be or seem hardly able to restrain; **~ like a turkey-cock,** put on blustering air; **~ed** or **swollen head,** (sl.) conceit. **2.** *n.* Act or condition of swelling; heaving of sea with waves that do not break, after storm etc.; protuberant part of column etc. **3.** (Mus.) Gradual increase of loudness, with or without subsequent gradual decrease; mechanism in organ etc. for obtaining crescendo or diminuendo by opening or closing slats in front of **~-box** containing pipes of the **~-organ. 4.** (colloq.) Person of distinction or ability; person of good social standing; person of dashing or fashionable appearance; hence ~'DOM *n.* **5. ~-fish,** globe-fish; **~-rule,** (Print.) rule or dash widening in middle and tapering towards ends. **6.** *a.* (colloq.) That is a swell (sense 4); fine, splendid; ||**~ mob(sman),** (arch. sl.) (class of) criminal dressing fashionably as disguise; hence ~'ISH[1] 2 *a.* [OE *swellan*, = OS **swellan*, OHG *swellan*, ON *svella* f. Gmc **swellan*]

swĕ'llĭng *n.* In vbl senses; protuberance, esp. abnormal enlargement of part of body. [f. prec. + -ING[1]]

swĕ'lter *v.i.*, & *n.* **1.** *v.i.* (Of atmosphere etc., or of thing or person suffering from it) be faint or sweating or languid or oppressive with heat. **2.** *n.* Sweltering atmosphere or conditions. [f. base of (now dial.) *swelt*, f. OE (= OS) *sweltan* perish, = OHG *swelzan*, ON *svelta*, Goth. *swiltan* f. Gmc **swelt-* etc.]

swĕpt. See SWEEP[1].

swẽrve *v.* & *n.* **1.** *v.i.* Diverge from regular line of motion, go off in changed direction, dodge, (*never swerves an inch from the path, from his duty; bird, ball, swerves in the air; horse, right-half, swerved suddenly*). **2.** *v.t.* Cause to swerve, esp. cause (ball) to swerve in the air. **3.** *n.* Divergence from course, swerving motion; hence ~'LESS (-vl-) *a.* [ME, repr. OE *sweorfan* scour, = OS, OHG *swerban* wipe etc., ON *sverfa* file, Goth. *-swairban*]

S.W.G. *abbr.* standard wire gauge.

swĭft *a.*, *adv.*, & *n.* **1.** *a.* (literary). Rapid, QUICK 3, soon coming or passing, not long delayed, (*swift runner, movement, feet, retribution, anger, laughter, response, riddance*). **2.** Prompt, quick *to* do, (*has a swift wit; swift to anger; be swift to hear, slow to speak*). **3.** Hence ~'LY[2] *adv.*, ~'NESS *n.* **4.** *adv.* (arch. exc. in comb.) Swiftly (*swift-coming, -passing*). **5.** *n.* Very long-winged and swift-flying insectivorous bird of family Apodidae with superficial resemblance to swallow; hence ~'LET *n.*, small swift of genus *Collocalia*. **6.** Swift-running small lizard. **7.** Revolving frame for winding yarn etc. from. [OE, cogn. w. *swīfan* move in a course]

swĭg *v.* (**-gg-**) & *n.* (colloq.) **1.** *v.t.* & *i.* Take deep draughts (of). **2.** *n.* (Act of taking) a (deep) draught of liquor. [v. f. n. (16th c.) in obs. sense 'liquor', of unkn. orig.]

swĭll *v.* & *n.* **1.** *v.t.* Rinse, pour water over or through, flush, (*out*). **2.** *v.t.* & *i.* Drink greedily. **3.** *n.* Rinsing (*give it a swill* or *swill out*); inferior liquor; (partly) liquid refuse as pig-food. [OE *swillan, swilian*, of unkn. orig.]

swĭm *v.* (**-mm-; swam; swum**) & *n.* **1.** *v.i.* Float on or at surface of liquid (SINK[1] *or swim; vegetables swimming in butter; with bubbles swimming on it*). **2.** Progress at or below surface of water by working legs, arms, tail, webbed feet, fins, flippers, wings, body, etc.; (fig.) go with gliding motion; **~ with the tide** or **stream,** act with the majority. **3.** *v.t.* Traverse or accomplish (stream, distance, etc.) thus, compete in (race) thus, compete with thus, cause (horse, dog, etc.) to progress thus. **4.** Hence

~'mER[1] *n.* **5.** *v.i.* Appear to undulate or reel or whirl, have dizzy effect or sensation, (*everything swam before his eyes*; *my head swims*; *have a swimming in the head*). **6.** Be flooded or overflow with or *with* or *in* moisture (*eyes, deck, swimming with tears, water*; *swimming eyes*; *floor swimming in blood*). **7.** ||**~'ming-bath,** indoor swimming-pool; **~'ming-bell,** bell-shaped swimming-organ of jellyfish etc.; **~'ming-bladder,** fish's air-bladder; **~'ming-pool,** artificial pool for swimming in; **~'ming-stone,** float-stone. **8.** *n.* Spell of swimming; deep pool frequented by fish in river; (fig.) main current of affairs (**in the ~**, engaged in or acquainted with what is going on); **~-suit,** bathing-suit. [OE *swimman*, = OS, OHG *swimman*, ON *svim(m)a* f. Gmc. **swemjan*]

swi'mmerĕt *n.* Swimming-foot in crustaceans. [f. SWIMMER + -ET[1]]

swi'mmingly *adv.* With easy and unobstructed progress (*going on swimmingly*). [f. SWIM + -ING[2] + -LY[2]]

swi'ndl|e *v.t.*, & *n.* **1.** *v.t.* Cheat (person, money *out of* person, person *out of* money etc., or abs.); so **~ER**[1] *n.* **2.** *n.* Fraudulent scheme, imposition, piece of swindling, person or thing represented as what it is not; **~e-sheet,** (colloq.) expense account. [back form. f. *swindler* f. G *schwindler* extravagant maker of schemes, swindler (*schwindeln* be dizzy)]

swine *n.* (*pl.* same). **1.** (U.S., formal, or Zool.) = PIG 1, whence **swi'nERY**[3] *n.*; PEARL[1]*s before swine.* **2.** Person of greedy or bestial habits; (colloq.) unpleasant thing. **3.** **~-fever,** infectious intestinal virus disease of pigs; **~-herd,** one who tends pigs; **~-plague,** infectious bacterial lung-disease of pigs. **4.** Hence **swi'nISH**[1] *a.* (esp. of persons or their habits). [OE *swīn*, = OS, OHG *swīn*, ON *svín*, Goth. *swein* f. Gmc **swīnam*, neut. (as n.) of a. f. IE **suw*-pig]

swing *v.* (**swung** *or rarely* **swang**; **swung**) & *n.* **1.** *v.t.* & *i.* Move with to-and-fro or curving motion as of object having fixed point(s) or side but otherwise free; sway, hang so as to be free to sway, like a pendulum or door or branch or tree or hammock or anchored ship; oscillate, revolve (propeller etc.), rock, wheel. **2.** *v.t.* Suspend (hammock) by its ends; have decisive influence on (voting, *jury, etc.); *(sl.) be competent to deal with; *not room to swing a* CAT[1]; ||**~ the lead,** (sl.) malinger, shirk duty; **swung dash,** (Typ.) dash (~) with alternate curves. **3.** *v.i.* Go with swinging gait (*he swung out of the room*; *swing along, past, by*, etc.); move by gripping something and leaping etc. (*swing from bough to bough*); (sl.) be executed by hanging; (sl.) be lively or up-to-date. **4.** *v.t.* & *i.* Play (music) with swing rhythm; (Cricket etc.) (cause ball to) deviate from straight flight. **5.** Hence **~'ER**[1] *n.* **6.** *n.* Act of swinging, oscillation, swinging movement; *circular tour; **in full ~**, at height of activity; *swing of the* PENDULUM. **7.** Swinging gait or rhythm (*goes with a swing*; *get into the swing of things*); vigorous continued action. **8.** **~ (music)**, easy rhythmic jazz, esp. with freely varied melody and simple harmonic accompaniment in strict rhythm. **9.** Seat slung by ropes or chains for swinging in (||*swings and* ROUND[3]*abouts*); spell of swinging in this. **10.** Extent to which thing swings; amount by which votes, points scored, etc., change from one side to the other. **11.** **~-boat,** boat-shaped carriage hung from frame for swinging in at fair etc.; **~ bridge** (that can be swung aside as a whole or in sections to let ships etc. pass); **~-door** (able to open in either direction and close itself when released); **~ plough** (without wheels); **~-wing,** aircraft wing that can be moved backwards and forwards. [OE *swingan*, = OHG *swingan* f. Gmc **sweng*-, **swang*-]

swinge (-nj) *v.t.* (*part.* **~'ing** *pr.* -nji-). **1.** (arch.) Strike hard, beat. **2.** (in *part.*) ||(Of blow) forcible; huge, daunting, (majority, lie, taxation, damages). [alt. f. ME *swenge* f. OE *swengan* shake, shatter, f. Gmc **swangwjan*]

swi'nging *a.* In vbl senses; (of gait, melody, etc.) vigorously rhythmical; (sl.) lively, up to date, excellent; hence **~LY**[2] *adv.* [f. SWING + -ING[2]]

swi'ngle (-nggel) *n.*, & *v.t.* **1.** *n.* Wooden instrument for beating flax and removing woody parts from it; swinging part of flail; ||**~tree,** crossbar pivoted in middle, to ends of which traces are fastened in cart, plough, etc. **2.** *v.t.* Clean (flax) with swingle; **swi'ngling-tow,** coarse part of flax. [ME, f. MDu. *swinghel* (as SWING; see -LE 1)]

swink *v.i.*, & *n.* (arch.) Toil. [OE *swinc* n. f. *swincan* v., parallel form. to *swingan* SWING]

swipe *v.* & *n.* **1.** *v.i.* & *t.* Hit *at* or hit (cricket-ball etc., or fig.) hard and recklessly; (sl.) steal esp. by snatching; hence **swi'pER**[1] *n.* **2.** *n.* (colloq.) Reckless hard hit or attempt to hit (at cricket etc., or fig.). [perh. var. of SWEEP[1]]

||**swipes** (-ps) *n. pl.* (sl.) Poor weak or otherwise inferior beer. [f. prec. in sense 'drink off']

swi'pple *n.* Swingle of flail. [ME, prob. f. as SWEEP[1] + -LE 1]

swirl *v.* & *n.* **1.** *v.i.* & *t.* Eddy, carry (object) or be carried with eddying motion. **2.** *n.* Eddying motion of water, air, etc., commotion made by fish etc. rushing through water; twist, curl. [ME, v. f. n., orig. Sc., perh. of LDu. orig.]

swish[1] *v.* & *n.* **1.** *v.t.* & *i.* Audibly cut the air with (cane etc.); cut (flower etc.) *off* thus; make such audible cut *with* cane etc.; flog with birch or cane. **2.** *v.i.*, & *n.* (Make, move with) sound as of cane or lash or swift bird cutting the air or of scythe cutting grass. **3.** Hence **~'Y**[2] *a.* [imit.]

swish[2] *a.* (colloq.) Smart, fashionable. [perh. f. prec.]

Swiss *a.* & *n.* (*pl.* same). (Native) of Switzerland (**~ French, German,** dialects of French and German spoken in Switzerland; **~ chard,** = CHARD; **~ cheese** (esp. with internal holes); **~ guards,** body of soldiers at Vatican serving the pope; **~ milk** (condensed and sweetened); **~ roll,** thin flat sponge-cake spread with jam and rolled up). [f. F *Suisse* f. MHG *Swīz*]

switch *n.* & *v.* **1.** *n.* Flexible shoot cut from tree; tapering rod or whip resembling this. **2.** Tress of detached or false hair tied at one end used in hairdressing. **3.** Mechanism for making and breaking connection between corresponding parts of a system, by which railway trains are diverted from one line to another, electric circuits completed or interrupted, etc. **4.** Switching of positions, roles, tactics, etc.; deviation from usual procedure. **5.** **~'back,** zigzag railway or road for ascending or descending steep slopes, ||road with alternate ascents and descents, ||railway (chiefly used for amusement at fairs etc.) in which train's ascents are effected solely by momentum acquired in previous descents; **~-blade,** pocket-knife with blade released by spring; **~'board,** arrangement for varying the connections between a number of electric circuits, esp. in telephony; **~('ing)-engine,** shunting-engine; **~-man** (in charge of railway switches); **~-signal,** flag or lantern or semaphore board indicating position of railway signal; ***~-tower,** signal-box; ***~-yard,** area where railway-carriages are switched between lines. **6.** *v.t.* Whip with switch. **7.** Swing (thing, or abs.) round quickly, snatch suddenly, whisk, (*cow switches her tail; I switched my head round; he switched it out of my hand*). **8.** Transfer (train, current, etc.) with switch, (fig.) direct (thoughts, talk) to another subject; ~ (**over**), change or exchange (positions, roles, tactics, etc., or abs.), whence **~-over** *n.* **9.** Turn (electric light, current, radio or television set, or abs.) *off* or *on* by switch; **~ed on,** (sl.) (1) under the influence of marijuana etc., (2) aware of what is going on, up to date. **10.** *v.i.* (Bridge). Change to another suit in bidding or play. [early forms *swits, switz*, prob. f. LG; cf. Hanoverian dial. *swutsche*, LG *swukse* long thin stick]

***swĭ'tcheroō** *n.* (sl.) Unexpected change of behaviour etc. [fanciful f. prec.; cf. SMACKEROO]

swĭ'ther (-dh-) *v.i.*, & *n.* (Sc.) **1.** *v.i.* Hesitate, be uncertain. **2.** *n.* Flurry, doubt, uncertainty. [16th c., of unkn. orig.]

Swĭ'tzer (-ts-) *n.* (||arch.) A Swiss. [f. MHG *Switzer*, or MDu. *Switser*, (*Swiz* Switzerland)]

swĭ'vel *n.* & *v.* (||**-ll-**). **1.** *n.* Coupling between two parts enabling one of them to revolve without turning the other; ~ **chain, gun,** etc., (provided with swivel); ~ **chair** (with seat turning horizontally); **~-eye(d),** (with) squinting eye. **2.** *v.t.* & *i.* Turn (as) on swivel (*swivelled the gun, his eyes, round*). [ME, f. weak grade *swif-* of OE *swifan* sweep + -LE 1; cf. SWIFT]

||**swĭz(z)** *n.* (*pl.* **-zzes**). (sl.) Swindle, disappointment. [20th c.; orig. unkn.]

swĭ'zzle *n.* (colloq.) Compounded intoxicating drink esp. of rum or gin and bitters made frothy; ||(sl.) = prec.; **~-stick** (used for frothing or flattening drinks). [19th c.; orig. unkn.]

swŏb. Var. of SWAB.

swō'llen. See SWELL.

swoōn *v.i.*, & *n.* (literary). (Have) fainting-fit (*swooned for joy, with pain*, etc.); (of sound) die languidly away. [ME *swoune* perh. back form. f. *swogning* n. (*iswogen* f. OE *geswogen* overcome p.p. of **swogan* suffocate, of unkn. orig.); see -ING[1]]

swoōp *v.* & *n.* **1.** *v.i.* Come down or *down* with the rush of a bird of prey, make sudden attack from a distance, (*on* prey, place, etc.). **2.** *v.t.* (colloq.) Snatch (*up*) the whole of at one swoop. **3.** *n.* Sudden attack or downward plunge (as) of bird of prey; snatching action carrying off many things at once; *at one* FELL[3] *swoop*. [perh. dial. var. of obs. *swōpe* f. OE *swāpan*; see SWEEP[1]]

swoōsh *v.i.*, & *n.* (Make, move with) noise of sudden rush of liquid, air, etc. [imit.]

swŏp. See SWAP.

sword (sord) *n.* **1.** Offensive weapon consisting of long variously shaped blade for cutting or thrusting or both and hilt with hand-guard, also worn with court dress; **the ~,** war, military power, war as means of deciding disputes; *sword of* DAMOCLES; **the ~ of justice,** judicial authority; ||**S~ of State** (borne before sovereign on state occasions); CROSS[2] *swords*; **draw, sheathe, the ~,** begin, cease from, war; FIRE[1] *and sword*; MEASURE[2] *swords*; **put to the ~,** (esp. of victor or captor) kill; **throw** one's **~ into the scale,** back claim etc. with arms. **2. ~-arm,** right arm; **~-bayonet,** kind with short sword-blade and hilt; ||**~-bearer,** person carrying sovereign's or other great person's sword on some occasions; **~-belt** (to which scabbard is attached); **~-bill,** long-billed humming-bird; **~-cane,** = *sword-stick*; **~-cut,** wound given with sword-edge, scar left by it; **~-dance** (in which swords are brandished, or performer treads about swords laid on ground); **~'fish,** sea-fish (*Xiphias gladius*) with upper jaw prolonged into sharp swordlike weapon; **~-flag,** yellow iris; **~-grass,** (1) gladiolus, (2) grass or sedge with swordlike leaves; **~-guard,** part of sword-hilt that protects hand; **~-hand,** right hand; **~-knot,** ribbon or tassel attached to sword-hilt orig. for securing it to wrist; **~-law,** military domination; **~-lily,** gladiolus; **~-play,** fencing, (fig.) repartee, cut-and-thrust argument; **~'sman** (-z-), person of (usu. specified) skill with sword; **~-stick,** hollow walking-stick containing blade that can be used as sword; **~-swallower,** one who (ostensibly) swallows a sword-blade as entertainment; **~-tail,** (1) = KING[1]-*crab* (1), (2) tropical fish of genus *Xiphophorus*. **3.** Hence (-)~'ED[2], ~'LESS, ~'LIKE, ~'PROOF[2], *adjs.* [OE *sw(e)ord*, = OS *swerd*, OHG *swert*, ON *sverth* f. Gmc **swerdham*]

swore, sworn. See SWEAR.

||**swŏt** *v.* (**-tt-**) & *n.* (school sl.) **1.** *v.i.* Work hard esp. at books. **2.** *v.t.* ~ (subject) **up,** study it hurriedly. **3.** *n.* Hard study; (thing that demands) effort; person who works hard esp. at learning. [dial. var. of SWEAT]

swound *n.*, & *v.i.* (arch.) Swoon. [f. ME *swoune* SWOON]

swŭm. See SWIM.

swŭng. See SWING.

swȳ *n.* (Austral.) Two-up. [f. G *zwei* two]

sȳ- *pref.*, assim. form of SYN- before *s* + consonant & before *z*.

S.Y. *abbr.* steam yacht.

sȳ'bar|ite *n.* & *a.* Luxurious and effeminate (person); hence **~ĭ'tic**(AL) *adjs.*, **~ītism** (2) *n.* [orig. native or inhabitant of Sybaris in S. Italy, noted for luxury, f. L f. Gk *Subaritēs* (*Subaris* Sybaris; see -ITE[1])]

sȳ'bĭl. Var. of SIBYL.

sȳ'camīne *n.* (Bibl.) The black mulberry-tree. [f. L f. Gk *sukaminos* mulberry-tree f. Heb. *šikmāh* sycamore, assim. to Gk *sukon* fig]

sȳ'camore *n.* **1.** ~ (**maple**), large maple (*Acer pseudoplatanus*) grown for its shade and timber. **2.** *Plane-tree. **3.** (Bibl.) Species of fig-tree (*Ficus sycomorus*) growing in Egypt, Syria, etc. [var. of SYCOMORE]

sȳce. See SICE[2].

sȳ'comore *n.* = SYCAMORE 3. [ME, f. OF *sic(h)amor* f. L f. Gk *sukomoros* (*sukon* fig, *moron* mulberry)]

sȳcō'nĭ|um *n.* (*pl.* **~a**). (Bot.) Fleshy hollow receptacle developing into multiple fruit as in fig. [mod. L, f. Gk *sukon* fig]

sȳ'coph|ant (*or* -ănt) *n.* Servile flatterer, toady, parasitic person; so **~ancy** *n.*, **~ă'ntic** *a.* [f. F *sycophante* or f. L f. Gk *sukophantēs* informer (*sukon* fig, *phainō* show; reason for name uncert.)]

sȳcō's|ĭs *n.* (*pl.* **~es** *pr.* -ēz). Skin-disease of bearded part of face, with inflammation of hair-follicles. [mod. L, f. Gk *sukōsis* (*sukon* fig; see -OSIS)]

sȳ'ĕn|ite *n.* Grey crystalline rock of felspar and hornblende with or without quartz; hence **~ĭ'tic** *a.* [f. F *syénite* f. L *Syenites* (*lapis* stone) of *Syene* in Egypt; see -ITE[1]]

sȳl- *pref.*, assim. form of SYN- before *l*.

sȳ'llabarȳ *n.* List of characters representing syllables and serving the purpose, in some languages or stages of writing, of an alphabet. [f. mod. L *syllabarium* (as SYLLABLE; see -ARY[1])]

sȳllă'b|ĭc *a.* Of syllable(s); (Pros.) based on number of syllables; (of symbol) representing a whole syllable; articulated in syllables; hence **~ically** *adv.*, **~ĭ'city** (-a-) *n.* [f. F *syllabique* or f. LL f. Gk *sullabikos* (as SYLLABLE; see -IC)]

sȳllăbĭ(fĭ)cā'tion *ns.* Division into or articulation by syllables. [f. (med. L *syllabicatio* f. *syllabicare* f.) L *syllaba*; see SYLLABLE, -ATION, -FICATION]

sȳ'llabīze, -īse (-īz), *v.t.* Divide into or articulate by syllables. [f. med. L *syllabizare* f. Gk *sullabizō* (as foll.; see -IZE)]

sў'llabl|e *n.*, & *v.t.* **1.** *n.* Unit of pronunciation uttered without interruption as word or part of word and containing usu. one vowel sound with or without consonant(s) preceding or following (*'inferno' has three syllables*); character(s) representing syllable; (transf.) so much as a word, the least amount of speech (*did not utter a syllable*); **in words of one ~e,** expressed plainly or bluntly; hence (-)~ED² (-beld) *a.* **2.** *v.t.* Pronounce by syllables, articulate distinctly; (poet.) utter (name, word). [ME, f. AF *sillable* f. OF *sillabe* f. L. f. Gk *sullabē* (as SYL-, *lambanō* take)]

sў'llabŭb. See SILLABUB.

sў'llab|us *n.* (*pl.* **~uses,** *or* **~i** *pr.* -ī). **1.** Concise statement of main subjects of lecture, course of teaching, etc.; conspectus or programme of hours of work etc. **2.** (R.C. Ch.) Summary of points decided by an ecclesiastical decree, esp. catalogue of 80 heretical doctrines or practices or institutions condemned by Pius IX in 1864, or of 65 heretical doctrines condemned by Pius X in 1907. [mod. L, orig. misreading of L *sittybas* acc. pl. of *sittyba* f. Gk *sittuba* title-slip or label]

sўllĕ'ps|ĭs *n.* (*pl.* **~es** *pr.* -ēz). Figure of speech applying a word to two others in different senses (e.g. *took the oath and his seat*) or to two others of which it grammatically suits one only (e.g. *neither you nor he knows*); cf. ZEUGMA; so **sўllĕ'pt**IC *a.* [LL, f. Gk *sullēpsis* taking together (*sullambanō*; see SYLLABLE)]

sў'llog|ĭsm *n.* **1.** Form of reasoning in which from two given or assumed propositions called the premisses and having a common or middle term a third is deduced called the conclusion, from which the middle term is absent; **false ~ism,** one whose conclusion does not necessarily follow from its premisses because it fails to fulfil the rules of logic regarding the nature and mutual relations of the major and minor terms and middle term that are necessary if the inference is to be sound. **2.** Deductive reasoning as opp. induction. **3.** So **~ĭ'st**IC *a.* [ME, f. OF *silogi(s)me* or f. L f. Gk *sullogismos* f. *sullogizomai* (as SYL-, *logizomai* to reason f. *logos* reason); see -ISM]

sў'llogīze, -īse (-īz), *v.* **1.** *v.i.* Use syllogisms. **2.** *v.t.* Put (facts, argument) in syllogistic form. [ME, f. OF *sil(l)ogiser* or LL *syllogizare* f. Gk *sullogizomai* (as prec.; see -IZE)]

sўlph *n.* Elemental spirit of the air in Paracelsus's system; slender graceful woman or girl; humming-bird with long forked tail; hence ~'LIKE *a.* [f. mod. L *sylphes*, G *sylphen* (pl.), perh. based by Paracelsus on L *sylvestris* of the woods + *nympha* nymph]

sў'lvan. See SILVAN.

sў'lvĭcŭlture. See SILVICULTURE.

sўm- *pref.*, assim. form of SYN- before *b*, *m*, *p*, as: **sympe'talous,** having petals united, **symphy'llous,** having leaves united.

sў'mbĭŏnt *n.* Organism living in symbiosis. [f. Gk *sumbiōn -ountos* part. of *sumbioō* live together (as foll.)]

sўmbĭ|ō'sĭs *n.* (*pl.* **~o'ses** *pr.* -ō'sēz). Association of two different organisms living attached to each other or one within the other to their mutual advantage, e.g. fungus and alga in lichen; hence ~O'TIC *a.* [mod. L, f. Gk *sumbiōsis* a living together (*sumbioō* live together, *sumbios* companion f. as SYM- + *bios* life; see -OSIS)]

sў'mbol *n.*, & *v.t.* (‖-**ll**-). **1.** *n.* Thing regarded by general consent as naturally typifying or representing or recalling something (esp. an idea or quality) by possession of analogous qualities or by association in fact or thought (*white, the lion, the thunderbolt, the cross, are symbols of purity, courage, Zeus, Christianity*). **2.** Mark or character taken as the conventional sign of some object or idea or process, e.g. the astronomical signs for the planets, the letters standing for chemical elements, musical notation, the mathematical signs for addition and infinity, the asterisk. **3.** (Eccl.) Creed. **4.** Hence or cogn. **sўmbŏ'l**IC(AL) *adjs.* (**~ic logic,** use of symbols to denote propositions etc. in order to assist reasoning; **~ic theology,** study of the creeds of various churches), **sўmbŏ'lĭcal**LY² *adv.*, **sўmbŏ'l**ICS, **sўmb(ol)ŏ'**LOGY, *ns.* **5.** *v.t.* Symbolize. [ME in sense 3, f. L f. Gk *sumbolon* mark, token, (as SYM-, *ballō* throw)]

sў'mbol|ĭsm *n.* Use of symbols to represent things; symbols collectively; school of painters and of (esp. French) poets seeking special symbols to express essence of things by suggestion; hence ~IST (2) *n.* [f. prec. + -ISM]

sў'mbolīz|e, -īs|e (-īz), *v.t.* Be symbol of; represent by means of symbols; so ~A'TION *n.* [f. F *symboliser* (*symbole* SYMBOL; see -IZE)]

sў'mmĕtr|ў *n.* **1.** (Beauty resulting from) right proportion between the parts of the body or any whole, balance, congruity, harmony. **2.** Such structure as allows of an object's being divided by a point or line or plane or radiating lines or planes into two or more parts exactly the same in size and shape and similar in position relatively to the dividing point etc., repetition of exactly similar parts facing each other or a centre; RADIAL *symmetry*; hence (in Art) **~o-**PHO'BIA *n.* **3.** Approximation to such structure, possession by a whole of corresponding parts correspondingly placed; (Bot.) possession by flower of sepals and petals and stamens and pistils in (multiples of) the same number. **4.** Hence or cogn. **sўmmĕ'tr**IC(AL) *adjs.*, **sўmmĕ'trĭcal**LY² *adv.*, ~IZE (3) *v.t.* [f. obs. F *symmétrie* or f. L f. Gk *summetria* (as SYM-, *metron* measure)]

sўmpathĕ'ctomў *n.* Surgical removal of sympathetic ganglion etc. [f. foll. + -ECTOMY]

sўmpathĕ'tĭc *a.* & *n.* **1.** *a.* Of, full of, exhibiting, expressing, due to, effecting, sympathy (*to* or *towards*; *sympathetic heart, person, conduct, words*); (of landscape etc.) that touches the feelings by association etc.; (of pain etc.) caused by pain or injury to someone else or in another part of the body; (of sound, resonance, string) sounding by vibration communicated through the air or other medium from vibrating object; **~ ganglion, ~ nerve,** parts of a system of nerves uniting viscera and blood-vessels and passing along vertebral column; **~ ink,** invisible ink; **~ magic** (seeking to affect person etc. by means of associated thing); **~ strike** (by workers in support of other strikers). **2.** Capable of evoking sympathy, likeable, appealing to reader etc.; **~ to,** inclined to favour (proposal etc.). **3.** Hence **sўmpathĕ'**TICALLY *adv.* **4.** *n.* Sympathetic nerve or system. [f. SYMPATHY, after *pathetic*]

sў'mpathīz|e, -īs|e (-īz), *v.i.* Feel or express sympathy, share feeling or opinion *with* person etc., agree *with* sentiment; hence ~ER¹ *n.* [f. F *sympathiser* (as foll.; see -IZE)]

sў'mpathў *n.* (Capacity for) being simultaneously affected with the same feeling as another; ~ (*with* person, thing, or state etc.), tendency to share or state of sharing another person's or thing's emotion or sensation or condition; (in *sing.* or *pl.*) mental participation *with* another in his trouble or *with* another's trouble; compassion (*for*); (in *sing.* or *pl.*) agreement (*with*) in opinion or desire; **in ~,** having, or as a result of, sympathy with another, by way of sympathetic action. [f. L f. Gk *sumpatheia* f. SYM(*pathēs* f. *pathos* feeling) sympathetic; see -Y¹]

sўmphŏ'n|ĭc *a.* Pertaining to or like a symphony or symphonies; **~ic ballet** (danced to symphony); **~ic dance,** orchestral piece in dance style; **~ic poem,** orchestral piece in one movement, usu. descriptive or rhapsodic; hence ~ICALLY *adv.* [f. SYMPHONY + -IC]

sўmphō'nĭous *a.* (literary). Harmonious, concordant; hence ~LY² *a.* [f. L *symphonia* (see SYMPHONY) + -OUS]

sў'mphonĭst *n.* Composer of symphonies. [f. foll. + -IST]

sў'mphonў *n.* (Mus.) Passage for instruments alone in vocal work; elaborate composition for full orchestra, usu. in sonata form; *symphony orchestra; ~ **orchestra** (playing symphonies and other serious orchestral works). [ME, = harmony of sound, f. OF *symphonie* f. L f. Gk *sumphōnia* f. SYM(*phōnos* f. *phōnē* sound) harmonious]

sў'mphўs|ĭs *n.* (*pl.* **~es** *pr.* -ēz). Growing together; (place or line of) union between two bones esp. in median plane of body; hence ~ėAL, ~IAL, (-fĭ'z-) *adjs.* [mod. L, f. Gk SYM(*phusis* growth)]

sўmpō'dĭ|um *n.* (*pl.* **~a**). (Bot.) Apparent main axis or stem made up of successive secondary axes, as in vine; hence ~AL *a.* [mod. L, f. as SYM- + Gk *pous podos* foot; see -IUM]

sўmpō'sĭarch (-z-; -k) *n.* President of symposium. [f. Gk *sumposiarkhos* (as SYMPOSIUM, *arkhos* ruler f. *arkhō* rule)]

sўmpō'sĭăst (-zĭ-) *n.* Participant in symposium. [f. Gk *sumposiazō* drink together (as foll.), after *enthusiast* etc.]

sўmpō'sĭ|um (-z-) *n.* (*pl.* **~a**). **1.** Drinking--party, esp. of ancient Greeks with conversation etc. after banquet. **2.** Philosophical or other friendly discussion; set of contributions on one subject from various authors and points of view at meeting or in magazine etc. **3.** Hence ~AC, ~AL, *adjs.* [f. L f. Gk *sumposion* f. SYM(*potēs* drinker); see -IUM]

sў'mptom *n.* **1.** Perceptible change in the body or its function indicating injury or disease; **subjective, objective,** ~ (directly perceptible to patient only, to others). **2.** Sign or token of the existence of something. **3.** Hence or cogn. ~A'TIC *a.* (*of*), **~atŏ'**LOGY *n.* [ME *synthoma*, f. med. L *sinthoma*, & f. LL f. Gk *sumptōma -atos* chance, symptom, f. SYM(*piptō* fall) happen]

sўn- *pref.* With, together, alike, as: **synallagma'tic,** (of treaty or contract) imposing reciprocal obligations [f. Gk *allassō* exchange]; **syna'ntherous,** having stamens joined by anthers; **syna'nthous,** with flowers and leaves appearing simultaneously; **sy'ncarp** (-n-k-), compound fruit from flower with several carpels, e.g. blackberry; **synda'ctyl(ous)** *adjs.*, **synda'ctylism, synda'ctyly,** *ns.*, having digits united as in webbed feet etc.; **syndesmo'sis,** articulation by ligaments; **syneco'logy,** study of ecological communities in their environment; **sy'ngamy** (-ngg-), (Biol.) fusion of gametes or nuclei in reproduction; **synge'nesis** (-nj-), sexual reproduction from combined male and female elements; **sy'ngnathous,** (of fish) with jaws united in tubular snout; **synosto'sis,** joining of bones by ankylosis etc. [f. or after Gk *sun-* (*sun* with)]

sўnaer'ės|ĭs (-ēr'-), ***sўnēr'ės|ĭs,** *n.* (*pl.* **~es** *pr.* -ēz). Contraction of two vowels into diphthong or single vowel. [LL, f. Gk SYN(*airesis* f. *haireō* take)]

sўnaes|thē'sĭa (-nĭ-), ***-ės|th-,** (-zĭa) *n.* Sensation produced in part of body by stimulus elsewhere; production of mental sense-impression by stimulation of another sense; hence **~thĕ'**TIC *a.* [mod. L, f. SYN- after *anaesthesia*]

sў'nagŏg|ue (-ŏg) *n.* Jewish assembly or congregation for religious observance and instruction; its place of meeting; hence ~AL, ~ICAL (-gŏ'g- *or* -gŏ'j-), *adjs.* [ME, f. OF *sinagoge* f. LL f. Gk *sunagōgē* f. SYN(*agō* bring)]

sў'năpse *n.* Place where nerve-cells join. [f. as foll.]

sўnă'ps|ĭs *n.* (*pl.* **~es** *pr.* -ēz). **1.** = prec. **2.** (Biol.) Fusion of chromosome-pairs at start of meiosis. **3.** Hence **sўnă'pt**IC *a.* [f. Gk SYN(*apsis* = *hapsis* f. *haptō* join)]

sўnarthrō's|ĭs *n.* (*pl.* **~es** *pr.* -ēz). (Anat.) Articulation with bones immovably fixed, e.g. sutures of skull. [f. SYN- + Gk *arthrōsis* jointing (*arthron* joint; see -OSIS)]

sўnc, sўnch (-ngk), *n.*, & *v.t.* (colloq.) **1.** *n.* Synchronization. **2.** *v.t.* Synchronize. [abbr.]

sўnchŏndrō's|ĭs (-ngk-) *n.* (*pl.* **~es** *pr.* -ēz). Nearly immovable articulation of bones by layer of cartilage, as in spinal vertebrae. [f. SYN- + Gk *khondros* cartilage + -OSIS]

sў'nchrō- (-ngkr-) *comb. form.* Synchronized, synchronous, as: **~-cy'clotron,** cyclotron reaching higher energies by decreasing electric field frequency with increasing particle energy and mass. [abbr.]

sў'nchromĕsh (-ngkr-) *a.* & *n.* (System of gear--changing, esp. in motor vehicles) in which the sliding gear-wheels are provided with small friction clutches which make contact with the non-sliding wheels before engagement, thus facilitating gear-changing by making both wheels revolve at meshing speed during engagement. [abbr. of *synchronized mesh*]

sўnchrŏ'n|ĭc (-ngkr-) *a.* Describing a subject (esp. a language) as it exists at one point in time (opp. *diachronic*); hence ~ICALLY *adv.* [f. LL *synchronus* (see SYNCHRONOUS) + -IC]

sў'nchronĭsm (-ngkr-) *n.* Synchrony; synchronizing of sound and picture in cinematography, television, etc. [f. Gk *sugkhronismos* (as SYNCHRONOUS; see -ISM)]

sў'nchronīz|e (-ngkr-), **-īs|e** (-īz), *v.* **1.** *v.i.* Occur at the same time, be simultaneous (*with*). **2.** *v.t.* Make occur at same time; carry out synchronism of (film); ascertain or set forth the correspondence in date of (events). **3.** *v.t.* & *i.* Cause (clocks etc.) to show, (of clocks etc.) show, a standard or uniform time. **4.** Hence ~A'TION *n.* [f. prec. + -IZE]

sў'nchronous (-ngkr-) *a.* Existing or occurring at same time (*with*); ~ **motor,** (Electr.) motor having speed exactly proportional to current frequency; hence ~LY² *adv.* [f. LL *synchronus* f. Gk *sugkhronos* (as SYN-, *khronos* time) + -OUS]

sў'nchronў (-ngkr-) *n.* Being synchronic or synchronous; treatment of events etc. as being synchronous. [f. Gk *sugkhronos* (see prec., -Y¹)]

sў'nchrotrŏn (-ngkr-) *n.* (Phys.) Cyclotron in which magnetic field strength increases with energy of particles to keep their orbital radius constant. [f. SYNCHRO- + -TRON]

sў'nclīn|e *n.* (Geol.) Rock-bed forming a trough; so ~AL (*or* -ī'n-) *a.* [f. SYN(*clinal* f. Gk *klinō* lean; see -AL)]

sў'ncop|āte *v.t.* Shorten (word) by dropping interior letter(s) or syllable(s), as *symbology* for *symbolology*, *Gloster* for *Gloucester*; (Mus.) displace beats or accents in (passage) so that what was 'strong' becomes 'weak', and vice versa; so ~A'TION *n.* [f. LL *syncopare* swoon (as foll.) + -ATE³]

sў'ncop|ė *n.* (Gram.) syncopated spelling or

For other words in *syn-* see SYN-.

pronunciation; (Med.) temporary loss of consciousness from fall of blood-pressure, whence ~AL *a.* [ME, f. LL f. Gk *sugkopē* (as SYN-, *koptō* strike, cut off)]

sy̆'ncrėt|ism *n.* **1.** (Philos. & Theol.) Attempt to unify or reconcile differing schools of thought, sects, etc.; (derog.) inconsistency of accepting incompatible principles or beliefs. **2.** (Philol.) Merging of inflected forms of a word. **3.** Hence or cogn. **sy̆ncrĕ'ti**C *a.*, ~IST (2) *n.*, **~ĭ'sti**C *a.*, ~IZE (2, 3) *v.i.* & *t.* [f. mod. L *syncretismus* f. Gk *sugkrētismos* (*sugkrētizō* combine as two parties against a third; see -ISM)]

sy̆ncy̆'ti|um *n.* (*pl.* **~a**). Mass of protoplasm with several nuclei but forming one cell; hence ~AL *a.* [f. as SYN- + -CYTE + -IUM]

sy̆'ndės|ĭs *n.* (*pl.* **~es** *pr.* -ēz). = SYNAPSIS 2. [mod. L, f. Gk SYN*desis* binding together (*sundeō* bind together)]

sy̆ndĕ'tĭc *a.* (Gram.) Of or using conjunctions. [f. Gk SYN*detikos* (as prec.; see -IC)]

sy̆'ndĭc *n.* Government official, esp. chief magistrate in Andorra etc.; ‖(Camb. Univ.) member of special committee of senate. [F, f. LL f. Gk SYN(*dikos* f. *dikē* justice) advocate]

sy̆'ndĭcalĭsm *n.* Movement among industrial workers (esp. in France) aiming at transfer of means of production and distribution from their present owners to unions of workers. [f. F *syndicalisme* (*syndical* f. as prec., -AL; see -ISM)]

sy̆'ndĭcate[1] *n.* **1.** Body of syndics; office of syndic. **2.** Combination of commercial firms etc. associated to promote some common interest; combination of persons for the acquisition of literary articles etc., and their simultaneous publication in a number of periodicals; group of people who combine to buy or rent property, gamble, organize crime, etc. [f. F *syndicat* f. med. L *syndicatus* f. LL *syndicus* (see SYNDIC, -ATE[1])]

sy̆'ndĭc|āte[2] *v.t.* Form into syndicate; publish (material) through syndicate; hence ~A'TION *n.* [f. prec.; see -ATE[3]]

sy̆'ndrōm|e (*or* -dromĭ) *n.* Concurrent symptoms in disease; characteristic combination of opinions, behaviour, etc.; hence ~IC (-ŏ'm-) *a.* [mod. L, f. Gk SYN(*dromē* f. *dramein* to run)]

sy̆ne. See AULD.

sy̆nĕ'cdochė (-kĭ) *n.* Figure of speech in which part is named but whole is understood (*50 sail* for *50 ships*) or whole is named but part is understood (*England beat Australia at cricket*). [ME f. L, f. Gk SYN(*ekdokhē* f. *ekdekhomai* take up)]

sy̆'nerg|ĭsm, sy̆'nerg|y̆, *ns.* Combined effect of drugs, organs, etc. that exceeds the sum of their individual effects; hence or cogn. ~E'TIC, **sy̆nêr'g**IC, **~ĭ'sti**C, *adjs.* [f. Gk SYN*ergos* working together (-*ergō* to work) + -ISM, -Y[1]]

sy̆nĭzē's|ĭs *n.* (*pl.* **~es** *pr.* -ēz). (Gram. & Pros.) Coalescence of two vowels into one syllable other than as recognized diphthong. [LL, f. Gk *sunizēsis* f. SYN(*izanō* = *hizanō* settle down f. *hizō* sit)]

sy̆'nod *n.* Ecclesiastical council attended by bishop(s) and delegated clergy (**General S~**, highest governing body in Church of England); Presbyterian ecclesiastical court above presbyteries and subject to General Assembly; any meeting for debate; so ~AL *a.* [ME, f. LL f. Gk *sunodos* (as SYN-, *hodos* way) meeting]

sy̆nŏ'dĭc|(al) *adjs.* Synodal; (Astron.) pertaining to conjunction of planets etc. (**~ period,** time between successive conjunctions of planet with sun). [f. LL f. Gk *sunodikos* (as prec.; see -IC, -ICAL)]

sy̆noe'cious (-ē'sh*us*) *a.* (Bot.) with male and female organs in same inflorescence or receptacle; (Biol.) symbiotic with benefit to one partner. [f. SYN- after *dioecious* etc.]

sy̆'nony̆m *n.* Word or phrase identical and coextensive in sense and usage with another of the same language (as *caecitis* with *typhlitis*); word denoting the same thing(s) as another but suitable to different context (as *serpent*, *slay*, cf. *snake*, *kill*) or containing different emphasis (as *blindworm*, cf. *slow-worm*); word equivalent to another in some only of either's senses (as *ship* to *vessel*); hence or cogn. **sy̆nony̆'mi**C *a.*, **sy̆nony̆'mi**TY *n.*, **sy̆nŏ'ny̆m**OUS *a.* (*with*). [ME, f. L f. Gk *sunōnumon* neut. (as n.) of *sunōnumos* (as SYN-, -*ōnum*- name; cf. ANONYMOUS)]

sy̆nŏ'ny̆my̆ *n.* Synonymity; collocation of synonyms for emphasis (as *in any shape or form*); system or collection of, treatise on, synonyms. [f. LL f. Gk *sunōnumia* (as prec.; see -Y[1])]

sy̆nŏ'ps|ĭs *n.* (*pl.* **~es** *pr.* -ēz). Summary; brief general survey. [LL, f. Gk SYN(*opsis* seeing)]

sy̆nŏ'ptĭc *a.* & *n.* **1.** *a.* Of or forming a synopsis; taking or affording a comprehensive mental view; of the synoptic Gospels; giving a general view of weather conditions; **~ Gospels,** those of Matthew, Mark, and Luke, describing events from same point of view; hence ~AL *a.*, **~al**LY[2] *adv.* **2.** *n.* (Writer of) a synoptic Gospel. [f. Gk *sunoptikos* (as prec.; see -IC)]

sy̆nŏ'ptĭst *n.* Writer of a synoptic Gospel. [f. prec. + -IST]

sy̆nō'vĭ|a *n.* (Physiol.) Viscous fluid lubricating joints and tendon sheaths; hence ~AL *a.* (**~al membrane,** dense membrane of connective tissue secreting synovia), **sy̆novi**'TIS *n.*, inflammation of synovial membrane. [mod. L, formed prob. arbitrarily by Paracelsus]

sy̆ntă'ctĭc *a.* Of, according to, syntax; hence ~AL *a.*, **~al**LY[2] *adv.* [f. Gk *suntaktikos* (as SYNTAX; see -IC)]

sy̆ntă'gm|a *n.* Word or phrase forming syntactic unit; orderly collection of statements; hence ~A'TIC, ~IC, *adjs.* [LL, f. Gk *suntagma* (as foll.)]

sy̆'ntăx *n.* Sentence-construction, (analysis of) the grammatical arrangement of words in speech or writing to show their connection and relation; set of rules governing this arrangement. [f. F *syntaxe* or f. LL f. Gk SYN(*taxis* f. *tassō* arrange) marshalling, syntax]

sy̆'nthės|ĭs *n.* (*pl.* **~es** *pr.* -ēz). Combination, composition, putting together, (opp. *analysis*); building up of separate elements esp. of conceptions or propositions or facts, into a connected whole, esp. a theory or system; (Chem.) artificial production of compounds from their constituents as opp. extraction from plants etc.; (Gram.) making of compound and derivative words, preference of composition and inflexion to use of prepositions etc.; (Surg.) joining of divided parts; hence ~IST (1) *n.*, ~IZE (1) *v.t.* [L, f. Gk *sunthesis* (as SYN-, THESIS)]

sy̆nthĕ'tĭc *a.* & *n.* **1.** *a.* Made by synthesis (*synthetic drugs*), esp. to imitate a natural product (*synthetic cream, rubber*); *synthetic* RESIN; (colloq.) artificial, affected, insincere; (Philos.) having truth or falsity determinable by recourse to experience; **~ philosophy,** Spencerianism. **2.** Hence ~AL *a.*, **~al**LY[2] *adv.* **3.** *n.* Synthetic substance. [f. F *synthétique* or mod. L *syntheticus* f. Gk *sunthetikos* f. *sunthetos* f. SYN(*tithēmi* put); see -IC]

sy̆'nthėtĭst, sy̆'nthėtīze. Vars. of SYNTHESIST, SYNTHESIZE.

sy̆'phĭl|ĭs *n.* Contagious venereal disease affecting first some local part (**primary ~is**), secondly the skin and mucous membrane (**secondary ~is**), and thirdly the bones and muscles and brain (**tertiary ~is**); **congenital ~is** (contracted by unborn child from mother's blood); hence **~i'tic**, ~OID, *adjs.*, ~IZE (5) *v.t.* [mod. L, f. title (*Syphilis, sive Morbus Gallicus*) of L poem (1530), f. *Syphilus,* a character in it, supposed first sufferer from the disease]

sȳ'phon, sȳr'en. Vars. of SIPHON, SIREN.

Sȳ'rĭăc *n.* & *a.* (In) the language of ancient Syria, western Aramaic. [f. L f. Gk *Suriakos* (*Suria* Syria; see -AC)]

Sȳ'rĭan *a.* & *n.* (Native or inhabitant) of Syria in S.W. Asia. [ME, f. OF *sirien* f. L f. Gk *Surios*; see -AN]

sȳrĭ'nga (-ngg*a*) *n.* **1.** Mock ORANGE[1]. **2.** (Bot.) Plant of genus *Syringa,* lilac. [mod. L, f. as SYRINX (w. ref. to use of stems cleared of pith as pipe-stems) + -A]

sȳ'rĭnge (-nj; *or* -rĭ'-) *n.*, & *v.t.* **1.** *n.* Tube with nozzle and piston or bulb for drawing in liquid by suction and then ejecting it in fine stream used in surgery, gardening, etc.; HYPODERMIC *syringe.* **2.** *v.t.* Sluice or spray (ear, plant, etc.) with syringe. [ME, f. med. L *syringa* (as foll.)]

sȳ'rĭn|x *n.* (*pl.* **~xes,** *or* **~ges** *pr.* -njēz). Pan-pipe; (Archaeol.) narrow gallery cut in rock in ancient Egyptian tomb; lower larynx or song-organ of birds, whence **sȳrĭ'ngėal** (-nj-) *a.* [L *syrinx -ngis,* f. Gk *surigx suriggos* pipe, channel]

Syrō- *comb. form.* Syrian (and), as: *~-Ara'bian, ~-Phoeni'cian.* [f. Gk *Suro-* (*Suros* a Syrian; see -O-)]

sȳ'rup, *sĭ'rup, *n.* **1.** Water (nearly) saturated with sugar; this combined with flavouring as beverage or with drug(s) as medicine. **2.** Condensed sugar-cane juice, part of this remaining uncrystallized at various stages of refining, molasses, treacle; ||**golden ~**, trade name for pale kind; **maple ~** (made by evaporating maple sap or dissolving maple sugar). **3.** (fig.) Excessive sweetness of literary style etc. **4.** Hence ~Y[2] *a.* [ME, f. OF *sirop* or med. L *siropus* f. Arab. *šarāb* beverage; cf. SHERBET, SHRUB[2]]

sȳssarcō's|ĭs *n.* (*pl.* **~es** *pr.* -ēz). Connection between bones by intervening muscle. [mod. L, f. Gk *sussarkōsis* (as SYN-, *sarx sarkos* flesh, -OSIS)]

sȳstă'ltĭc *a.* Contracting and dilating by turns, having systole and diastole, pulsatory. [f. LL f. Gk *sustaltikos* (as SY-, *staltos* f. *stellō* put; see -IC)]

sȳ'stem *n.* **1.** Complex whole, set of connected things or parts, organized body of material or immaterial things; *the* established political or social order; **mountain ~**, range or connected ranges; **river, railway, ~**, (1) river, railway, with its tributaries or branches, (2) rivers, railways, of a country, continent, etc.; **~s analysis,** technique of analysing an operation etc. in order to use a computer in seeking ways to improve its efficiency etc. **2.** (Phys.) Group of associated bodies moving under mutual gravitation etc.; SOLAR *system*; **~ of pulleys** (several arranged to work together). **3.** (Biol.) Set of organs or parts in animal body with common structure or function (*digestive, muscular, nervous, reproductive, system*); **the ~**, animal body as a whole; **get** thing **out of** one's **~**, (fig.) be rid of its effects. **4.** Method, organization, considered principles of procedure, (principle of) classification; body of theory or practice pertaining to a particular form of government, religion, etc.; method of choosing one's procedure in gambling etc.; one of six general types of crystal structure; METRIC *system*; **Ptolemaic** etc. **~**, set of hypotheses or principles composing Ptolemy's etc. theory; (Geol.) **Devonian** etc. **~**, major group of strata etc. so named; **~ of philosophy,** set of co-ordinated doctrines; hence ~LESS *a.* **5.** (Mus.) Braced staves of score. [f. F *système* or f. LL f. Gk *sustēma -atos* (as SY-, *histēmi* set up)]

sȳstemă't|ĭc *a.* Methodical, according to a plan, not casual or sporadic or unintentional, classificatory, (*systematic worker, liar, insolence, nomenclature*); **~ic theology** (arranging religious truths in a self-consistent whole); hence or cogn. ~ICALLY *adv.*, ~ICS *n.*, taxonomy, **sȳ'stemat**ISM (1), **sȳ'stemat**IST (1), *ns.*, **sȳ'stemat**IZE (3) *v.t.* [f. F *systématique* f. LL f. late Gk *sustēmatikos* (as prec.; see -IC)]

sȳstĕ'm|ĭc *a.* (Physiol.) of the bodily system as a whole, not confined to a particular part, (of blood circulation) other than pulmonary; (of insecticide, fungicide, etc.) entering the plant via roots or shoots and passing through the tissues; hence ~ICALLY *adv.* [irreg. f. SYSTEM + -IC]

sȳ'stolė *n.* (Physiol.) Contraction of heart rhythmically alternating with DIASTOLE; hence **sȳstŏ'l**IC *a.* [LL, f. Gk *sustolē* (*sustellō* contract, as SYSTALTIC)]

sȳ'zȳgȳ *n.* **1.** (Astron.) Conjunction or opposition, esp. of moon with sun. **2.** Pair of connected or correlated things. [f. LL f. Gk *suzugia* (*suzugos* yoked, paired, f. as SY- + *zugon* yoke; see -Y[1])]

T

T, t, (tē) *n.* (*pl.* **Ts** *or* **T's**). Twentieth letter of alphabet; T-shaped thing (esp. *attrib.*: *T-bandage, -bar, -bolt, -joint, -junction, -pipe*); *suits me, hit it off,* etc., **to a T,** exactly, to a nicety; **cross the t's,** (fig.) be minutely accurate, emphasize details; **T-bone,** T-shaped bone esp. in steak from thin end of loin; **T-shirt,** short-sleeved shirt having shape of T when spread out flat; **T-square,** T-shaped SQUARE[1] 3.

't *pron.* = IT[1] (*'tis*). [contr.]

-t[1] *suf.* = -ED[1] (*bought, crept, sent*).

-t[2] *suf.* = -EST[2] (*shalt, wert*).

T *abbr.* tera-; tesla.

t. *abbr.* ton(s); tonne(s).

T *symb.* tritium.

||**ta** (tah) *int.* (childish or colloq.) Thank you. [infantile form]

||**T.A.** *abbr.* Territorial Army.

Ta *symb.* tantalum.

taal (tahl) *n.* **The ~**, (Hist.) early form of Afrikaans. [Du., = language, cogn. w. TALE]

tăb *n.*, & *v.t.* (**-bb-**). **1.** *n.* Small flap, strip, tag, or tongue, as appendage for grasping, suspending, fastening, or identifying garment etc.; similar object as part of garment etc.; ||(Mil.) mark on collar distinguishing staff officer; (loop for suspending) stage-curtain; (colloq.) account, tally, *bill, *price; **keep ~(s)** or **a ~ on,** keep account of, have under observation or in check. **2.** *v.t.* Provide with tab(s). [prob. f. dial.; cf. TAG[1]]

T.A.B. *abbr.* Typhoid-paratyphoid A and B vaccine; (Austral.) Totalizator Agency Board.

tă'bard *n.* **1.** (Hist.) Knight's short emblazoned garment worn over armour. **2.** Herald's official coat emblazoned with arms of sovereign. [ME, f. OF *tabart*, of unkn. orig.]

tă'barėt *n.* Upholstery fabric of alternate satin and plain stripes. [prob. f. TABBY]

tabă'scō *n.* (*pl.* **~s**). Pungent pepper made from fruit of *Capsicum annuum*; (*T~*; **P**) sauce made from tabasco pepper. [f. *T~* in Mexico]

tă'bbў *n.* Plain weave; watered fabric, esp. of silk; ~ (**cat**), brindled or mottled or streaked cat, esp. of grey or brownish colour with dark stripes; cat, esp. female; (derog.) gossiping woman, ||esp. old maid. [f. F *tabis* f. Arab. *al-'attabiya* quarter of Baghdad where tabby was manufactured; connection of remaining senses uncert.]

||**tă'berdar** *n.* Scholar of Queen's College, Oxford; hence ~SHIP *n.* [f. L *tabardarius* (as TABARD; see -AR[2]; from former dress)]

tă'bernăcl|e *n.* & *v.* **1.** *n.* (Bibl.) Fixed or movable habitation usu. of light construction; **Feast of T~es,** Succoth. **2.** (Jewish Hist.) Tent used as sanctuary before final settlement of Jews in Palestine. **3.** Place of public worship other than church. **4.** (Eccl.) Receptacle for pyx or Eucharistic elements; canopied niche; **~e-work,** ornamental carving or tracery over pulpit etc.; hence ~ED[2] (-keld) *a.* **5.** Socket or double post for hinged mast that requires lowering to pass under bridges. **6.** *v.t.* Place in tabernacle. **7.** *v.i.* Dwell temporarily. [ME f. OF, or f. L *tabernaculum* tent dim. of *taberna* hut; see -CULE]

tā'bēs (-z) *n.* (Med.) Emaciation; ~ **dorsalis,** locomotor ATAXY; hence **tabĕ'tɪc** *a.* [L, = wasting away]

tă'bĭnėt *n.* Watered fabric of silk and wool. [app. f. TABBY]

tă'bla (*or* tah'-) *n.* (Ind. Mus.) Pair of small drums played with hands. [Urdu, f. Arab. *tabla* drum]

tă'blature *n.* (Mus.) early form of notation indicating point of string etc. to be stopped; (arch.) mental picture. [F, f. It. *tavolatura* (*tavolare* set to music; see -URE)]

tā'ble *n.*, & *v.t.* **1.** *n.* Piece of furniture consisting of flat top of wood, marble, etc. and one or more usu. vertical supports esp. one on which meals are laid out, articles of use or ornament kept, work done, or games played; **breakfast, dinner, tea,** etc., -~, table used for such meals or on which such meal is laid out; **at** ~, while taking meal at table (see also SERVE, WAIT[1]); **under the** ~, (esp.) drunken after dinner. **2.** Company seated at table for dinner etc.; (quantity and quality of) food provided at table (*keeps a good table*; *expenses of his table*). **3.** Part of machine tool on which work is put to be operated on. **4.** Slab of wood, stone, etc.; matter written on this; **the two ~s** or **the ~s of the law** etc., the Ten COMMANDMENTS; **the Twelve T~s,** laws promulgated in Rome 451–450 B.C., principal source of Roman jurisprudence. **5.** = *tableland*. **6.** (Archit.) Flat usu. rectangular vertical surface; horizontal moulding esp. cornice. **7.** Flat surface of gem; cut gem with two flat faces. **8.** Each half or quarter of folding board for backgammon; (Bridge) *the* dummy hand. **9.** List of facts, numbers, etc., systematically arranged esp. in columns (MULTIPLICATION *table*; *tables of weights and measures*; *table of contents*); matter contained in this; **learn** one's ~ (of multiplication, weights and measures, etc.); **mathematical ~s** (of logarithms, trigonometrical ratios, etc.). **10. Lay** (measure, report, etc., in Parliament etc.) **on the** ~, (1) postpone indefinitely, (2) ||submit for discussion; **turn the ~s** (*on* person, or abs.), reverse relations (between), esp. pass from inferior to superior position [f. interchange of positions at backgammon; see sense 8]. **11. ~-cloth** (of white linen etc. for use at meals, or of coloured material esp. for use at other times); **~-cut,** (of gem) cut with large flat top; **~-flap,** hinged end of table-top, lowered when not in use; **~-knife** (for use at meals, esp. for cutting meat small); **~land,** extensive elevated region with level surface, plateau; **~-leaf,** (1) piece that may be inserted in top of table to increase its length, (2) = *table-flap*; ~ **licence** (to serve alcoholic liquor with meals only); **~-lifting, -rapping, -turning,** lifting etc. of table apparently without physical force, as spiritualistic phenomenon; **~-linen,** table-cloths, napkins, etc.; ~ **manners,** ability to behave properly while eating at table; **~-mat** (to protect surface of table from hot dishes etc.); **~-money,** allowance to higher officers in army etc. for official hospitality, charge to members of club for use of dining-room; *table*-NAPKIN; *table* SALT; *table*-SPOON[1], whence ~*spoon*FUL 2 *n.*; **~-talk,** miscellaneous informal talk at table; ~ **tennis,** game like lawn tennis with net across table; **~-tomb,** flat-topped chestlike tomb in Roman catacombs; **~-to**[illegible]se on table; **~ware,** dishes etc. for use [illegible] **~-water,** mineral water bottled for use a[illegible]able; ~ **wine** (for drinking with meal). **12.** Hence ~FUL 2 *n.* **13.** *v.t.* Lay (measure etc.; see sense 10) on the table; strengthen (sail) with wide hem; hence **tā'bl**ING[1] (1, 2) *n.* [ME f. OF, f. L *tabula* plank, tablet, list]

tă'bleau (-lō) *n.* (*pl.* **~x** *pr.* -ōz). **1.** Picturesque presentation; ~ (**vivant** *pr.* vē'vahṅ; *pl.* **~x** *vivants pr.* same; lit. 'living picture'), silent and motionless group of persons etc. arranged to represent a scene. **2.** Dramatic or effective situation suddenly brought about; ~ **curtains,** (Theatr.) pair of curtains drawn open by diagonal cord. [F, = picture, dim. of *table* (see prec.)]

table d'hôte (tahbl-dō't) *n.* Meal at fixed time and price for guests at hotel; ~ **dinner** etc. (served in hotel etc. at fixed price, with less choice of dishes than à la carte). [F, = host's table]

tă'blėt *n.* **1.** Thin sheet of ivory, wood, etc., for writing on, esp. each of a set fastened together; (usu. in *pl.*) such set. **2.** Small slab esp. with or for inscription (*votive tablet*). **3.** Small flat piece of prepared substance, e.g. soap; small fixed weight or measure of a drug compressed into convenient shape. **4.** (Archit.) = TABLE 6. [ME, f. OF *tablete* f. Rom., dim. of L *tabula* TABLE; see -ET[1]]

tă'blier (-lyā) *n.* (Hist.) Apron-like part of woman's dress. [F]

tă'bloid *n.* Newspaper, usu. popular in style, printed on sheets of half normal size; anything in compressed or concentrated form. [orig. **P,** name of compressed and concentrated drug-preparation; see TABLET, -OID]

taboo', tabu' (-ōō'), *n.*, *a.*, & *v.t.* **1.** *n.* (Among Polynesians etc.) system or act of setting apart person or thing as accursed or sacred; ban, prohibition. **2.** *a.* Prohibited, consecrated; avoided or prohibited by social custom (*taboo word*). **3.** *v.t.* Put (thing, practice, etc.) under taboo; exclude or prohibit by authority or social influence (*the subject was tabooed*). [f. Tongan *tabu*]

tā'bor *n.* (Hist.) Small drum, esp. one used to accompany pipe. [ME, f. OF *tab(o)ur*; cf. TABLA, Pers. *tabīra* drum]
tă'bourĕt (-b*er*-), ***tă'borĕt,** *n.* Low seat usu. without arms or back. [F, = stool, dim. as prec.]
tabu. See TABOO.
tă'būlar *a.* **1.** Of, arranged in, computed etc. by means of, tables (*tabular statement, values, results, computations; arranged in tabular form*); *tabular* STANDARD. **2.** Broad and flat like a table (*tabular surface*); (of crystal) with two broad flat faces; (formed) in thin plates (*tabular structure*). **3.** Hence ~LY² *adv.* [f. L *tabularis* (as TABLE; see -AR¹)]
tabula rasa (tăbūl*a* rā'*sa*; *or -za*; *or* -ah'-) *n.* Erased tablet, (fig.) human mind (esp. at birth) viewed as having no innate ideas. [L, = scraped tablet]
tă'būl|āte *v.t.* Arrange (figures, facts) in tabular form; hence ~A'TION *n.* [f. LL *tabulare* (*tabula* table) + -ATE³]
tă'būlātor *n.* Person who tabulates; attachment to typewriter for advancing to sequence of set positions in tabular work; machine that tabulates data. [f. prec. + -OR]
tă'camahăc (-*a*mah-) *n.* Gum resin from tropical Amer. tree esp. of genus *Bursera* or *Protium*; (resin of) balsam poplar. [f. obs. Sp. *tacamahaca* f. Aztec *tecomahiyac*]
tă'c-au-tăc (-ō-) *n.* (Fencing). Parry combined with riposte. [F, imit.]
tacet (tă'sĭt) *v.i.* (as *imper.* in Mus. score). Be silent (of voice or instrumental part). [L, = is silent]
tă'chĭsm(e) (-shĭzem) *n.* = ACTION *painting.* [F *tachisme* (*tache* stain; see -ISM)]
tachĭ'sto|scōpe (-k-) *n.* Instrument for very brief measured exposure of objects to the eye; hence ~**scŏ'pic** *a.* [f. Gk *takhistos* swiftest + -O- + -SCOPE]
tă'chō (-kō) *n.* (*pl.* ~**s**). (colloq.) Tachometer. [abbr.]
tă'chograph (-k*o*grahf) *n.* Device in motor vehicle for automatic recording of its speed and travel-time. [f. Gk *takhos* speed + -O- + -GRAPH]
tachŏ'mėter (-k-) *n.* Instrument for measuring velocity or speed of rotation (esp. of vehicle engine). [f. Gk *takhos* speed + -O- + -METER]
tăchўcar'dĭa (-kĭ-) *n.* (Path.) Abnormally rapid heart-action. [f. Gk *takhus* swift + *kardia* heart]
tachў'graph|ў (-k-) *n.* **1.** Stenography, esp. that of ancient Greeks and Romans; hence ~ER¹ *n.*, **tăchўgră'phic(al)** (-k-) *adjs.* **2.** Abbreviated medieval writing of Greek and Latin. [f. Gk *takhus* swift + -GRAPHY]
tachў'mėter (-k-) *n.* Surveyor's instrument for rapid location of points. [f. as prec. + -METER]
tă'cĭt *a.* Understood, implied, or existing, without being stated, (*tacit consent, agreement, understanding*); hence ~LY² *adv.* [f. L *tacitus* silent (*tacēre* be silent)]
tă'cĭturn *a.* Reserved in speech, saying little, uncommunicative; so ~ITY (-ûr'-) *n.* [f. F *taciturne* or f. L *taciturnus* (as prec.)]
tăck¹ *n.* & *v.* **1.** *n.* Small sharp broad-headed easily removed nail of iron, copper, etc., for securing carpet etc.; * = THUMB*tack*; BRASS *tacks.* **2.** Long stitch as slight or temporary fastening in needlework. **3.** (Naut.) Rope for securing corner of some sails, corner to which this is fastened; direction in which vessel moves as determined by position of sails (**port, starboard,** ~, with wind on port, starboard, side); temporary change of direction in sailing to take advantage of side wind etc., esp. each of several alternate movements to port and starboard. **4.** (fig.) Course of action or policy (*must change our tack; is on the right* or *wrong tack; try another tack*). **5.** ||Extraneous clause appended to bill in Parliament. **6.** Sticky condition of varnish etc. **7.** ~**-driver,** machine that automatically places and drives tacks; ~**-hammer,** light hammer for driving tacks, usu. with claw for extracting them. **8.** *v.t.* Fasten (carpet etc. *down*) with tacks; stitch (pieces or parts of cloth etc.) lightly together; (fig.) annex, append, (thing *to* or *on to* another); ||append (clause; see sense 5). **9.** *v.i.* Change ship's course (*about*) by turning head to wind (cf. WEAR³); (fig.) change one's conduct, policy, etc. **10.** Hence ~'ER¹ (1, 2) *n.* [ME *tak* etc., of uncert. orig.; cf. Bibl. *tache* clasp, link f. OF *tache*]
tăck² *n.* Riding-harness, saddles, etc.; ~**-room** (where this is kept). [f. TACKLE]
tăck³ *n.* Food (HARD, SOFT, *tack*); (derog.) stuff, rubbish. [19th c.; orig. unkn.]
tă'ckle (*or* Naut. tā'k*e*l) *n.*, & *v.t.* **1.** *n.* (**Block and**) ~, mechanism esp. of ropes, pulley-blocks, hooks, etc., for lifting weights, managing sails or spars, etc.; windlass with its ropes and hooks; requisites for a task or sport (*fishing-tackle*). **2.** Act of tackling in football etc.; (Amer. Footb.) (player in) position next to end of forward line. **3.** ~**-block,** pulley over which rope runs; ~**-fall,** rope for applying force to blocks of a tackle. **4.** *v.t.* Grapple with, grasp with endeavour to hold or manage or overcome, (opponent, awkward thing or problem); enter into discussion with (person esp. *on* awkward matter); (Footb. etc.) obstruct, intercept, or seize and stop (player running with ball); secure by means of tackle. **5.** Hence **tă'ckl**ING¹ (1, 3, 6) *n.* [ME, prob. f. MLG *takel* (*taken* lay hold of; see -LE 1)]
tă'ck|ў¹ *a.* (Of varnish etc.) slightly sticky, not quite dry; hence ~INESS *n.* [f. TACK¹ + -Y²]
***tă'ckў²** *a.* Showing poor taste or style; tatty, seedy. [19th c.; orig. unkn.]
ta'cō (tah'-) *n.* (*pl.* ~**s**). Mexican food of meat etc. in folded or rolled tortilla. [Mex. Sp.]
tăct *n.* Intuitive perception of what is fitting esp. of the right thing to do or say in order to avoid giving offence or to gain goodwill, adroitness in dealing with persons or circumstances; hence ~'FUL, ~'LESS, *adjs.* [F, f. L *tactus* (sense of) touch (*tangere tact-* touch)]
tă'ctĭc *n.* (Piece of) tactics. [f. mod. L *tactica* f. Gk *taktikē* (*tekhnē* art), f. as TACTICS]
tă'ctĭcal *a.* Of tactics; (of bombing) carried out in immediate support of (esp. brief or local) military or naval operations (opp. *strategic*); adroitly planning or planned; hence ~LY² *adv.* [f. Gk *taktikos* (as foll.) + -AL]
tă'ctĭcs *n. pl.* (also treated as *sing.*) Art of disposing military or naval or air forces esp. in actual contact with enemy (cf. STRATEGY); procedure calculated to gain some end, skilful device(s), (*cannot approve of these tactics*); hence **tăctĭ'**CIAN *n.* [f. mod. L f. Gk *taktika* neut. pl. (*taktos* ordered f. *tassō* arrange; see -IC)]
tă'ctĭle *a.* **1.** Of, perceived by, connected with, the sense of touch, (*tactile impression, organ*); so **tă'ctū**AL *a.* **2.** Tangible; (Paint.) producing or having to do with the effect of solidity (*tactile values* etc.). **3.** Hence **tăctĭ'l**ITY *n.* [f. L *tactilis* (*tangere tact-* touch; see -IL)]
tă'dpōle *n.* Larva of amphibian, esp. frog or toad from time it leaves egg till loss of gills and tail. [ME *taddepolle* (as TOAD, POLL¹, f. size of head)]
taedium vitae (tēdĭum vī'tē *or* vē'tī) *n.* (Path.) Weariness of life (with tendency to suicide). [L]
tae'nĭ|a *n.* (*pl.* ~**ae** *or* ~**as**). (Archit.) fillet between Doric architrave and frieze; (Anat.) ribbon-like part esp. of brain or colon; (Zool.) tapeworm of genus *Taenia*; (Gk Ant.) fillet, headband; hence ~OID *a.* [L, f. Gk *tainia* ribbon]

tă'ffėta *n.* Fine plain-woven silk or silklike fabric. [ME, f. OF *taffetas* or med. L *taffata*, ult. f. Pers. *tāfta* p.p. (as n.) of *tāftan* twist]

tă'ffrail (*or* -rĭl) *n.* (Naut.) Rail round stern of vessel. [f. earlier *tafferel* f. Du. *taffereel* panel, dim. of *tafel* (as TABLE); assim. to RAIL[1]]

Tă'ffy̆[1] *n.* (colloq.) (Nickname for) Welshman. [supposed W pronunc. of *Davy* = *David*]

***tă'ffy̆**[2] *n.* Sweetmeat like toffee; insincere flattery. [19th c., of unkn. orig.]

tă'fĭa *n.* (W. Ind.) Rum distilled from molasses etc. [18th c.; orig. uncert.]

tăg[1] *n.* & *v.* (-gg-). **1.** *n.* Metal or plastic point at end of lace etc. to assist insertion. **2.** Loop at back of boot used in pulling it on. **3.** Label, esp. one for tying on, to show address, price, etc.; *motor-vehicle licence-plate. **4.** Loose or ragged end of anything; ragged lock of wool on sheep. **5.** Appendage; (Theatr.) closing speech addressed to audience; trite quotation, stock phrase; refrain of song. **6.** (Tip of) animal's tail. **7.** ***~ day,** = FLAG[4]-*day* (but with tags not flags); **~-end,** last remnant of anything; **~'rag,** = RAG[1]*tag*. **8.** *v.t.* Furnish (lace etc., literary composition) with tag(s); label with radioactivity. **9.** Join (thing, esp. piece of writing, *to* or *on to* another, things *together*), find rhymes for (verses), string (rhymes) together. **10.** Shear away tags from (sheep). **11.** *v.t.* & *i.* (colloq.) Follow closely; trail behind; go *along with*. [ME, of unkn. orig.]

tăg[2] *n.*, & *v.t.* **1.** *n.* Children's game in which one chases the rest until he touches another, who then becomes pursuer; (Baseball) tagging of runner. **2.** *v.t.* Touch in game of tag; (Baseball) put (runner) out or *out* by touching with ball or with hand holding ball. [18th c.; orig. unkn.]

Taga'log (-ah'-) *n.* (Member or language) of principal people of Philippine Islands. [Tagalog (*taga* native, *ilog* river)]

tagē'tēs (-z) *n.* Plant of genus *Tagetes*, with showy yellow or orange flowers. [mod. L, f. L *Tages*, Etruscan divinity]

tagliatĕ'llĕ (tahlyah-), **-lli** (-ē), *n.* Ribbon-shaped form of pasta. [It.]

Tahi'tian (ta-hē'shan) *a.* & *n.* (Native, inhabitant, or language) of Tahiti. [f. *Tahiti* in S. Pacific + -AN]

tahr. Var. of THAR.

tahsi'l (-ē'l) *n.* Territorial subdivision in India for revenue purposes; hence **~dar̄** *n.*, native collector of revenue in tahsil. [f. Hindi *tahsil* f. Arab., = collection; Pers. *dār* holder]

tai'ga (tī'gah) *n.* Coniferous forest lying between tundra and steppe esp. in Siberia. [Russ.]

tail[1] *n.* & *v.* **1.** *n.* Hindmost part of animal esp. when prolonged beyond (rest of) body; **on** person's **~**, closely following him; **with ~ between legs,** showing alarm or dejection; **with ~ up,** (of person, fig.) in good spirits; **turn ~,** turn one's back, run away; *twist the* LION'*s tail*; *put* SALT *on tail of*; cf. WAG[1]. **2.** Thing like or suggesting tail in shape or position, hind or lower or subordinate or inferior part, slender part or prolongation; luminous train of comet, outer corner *of the eye*, rear part of aeroplane containing rudder etc., part of shirt below waist, hanging part of back of coat, end of procession etc., weaker members of cricket etc. team, foot of page, long train of attendants etc., back of a cart, string and paper appendage at lower end of kite, stem of musical note, part of letter *g* etc. below line, exposed end of slate or tile in roof, unexposed end of brick or stone in wall, slender backward prolongation of butterfly's wing, comparative calm at end *of a gale*, calm stretch following rough water in a stream, (sl.) person following or shadowing another. **3.** (in *pl.*, colloq.) (Evening dress with) tailcoat. **4.** (usu. in *pl.*) Reverse of coin turned upwards after toss (cf. HEAD[1] 5). **5. ~-bay,** part of canal lock between tail-gate and lower pond; **~-board,** hinged or removable back of cart, lorry, etc.; **~'coat,** man's morning or evening coat with long skirt divided at back into tails and cut away in front; *tail*-COVERT[2]; **~-end,** hindmost or lowest or last part; **~-gate,** (1) lower end of canal lock, (2) = *tail-board*, (3) (*v.i.*) drive too close behind another vehicle; **~-lamp, ~-light,** (carried at back of train, car, bicycle, etc.); **~'piece,** (1) decoration in blank space at end of chapter etc., (2) triangular piece of wood to which lower ends of strings are fastened in some musical instruments, (3) appendage at the end of a thing; **~'pipe,** suction-pipe of pump, exhaust-pipe of motor vehicle; **~'plane,** horizontal stabilizing surface of aeroplane tail; **~-race,** part of mill-race below water-wheel; **~-skid,** support for tail of aeroplane when on ground; **~-spin,** spin of aircraft, (fig.) state of panic; **~'stock,** adjustable part of lathe holding fixed spindle; **~ wind** (blowing in direction of one's travel). **6.** Hence (-)ED[2] (-ld), **~'**LESS (-l-l-), *adjs.* **7.** *v.t.* Furnish with tail; remove stalks of (fruit); dock tail of (lamb etc.). **8.** (sl.) Shadow, follow closely. **9.** Join (thing *on to* another). **10. ~ after,** follow closely; **~ away** or **off,** fall behind or away in scattered line, become fewer or smaller or slighter, end inconclusively; **~ in,** fasten (timber) by one end into wall etc. [OE *tæg(e)l*, = OHG *zagal*, ON *tagl*, Goth. *tagl* hair, f. Gmc **taglaz*]

tail[2] *n.* & *a.* (Law). **1.** *n.* Limited ownership, esp. of estate limited to a person and heirs of his body; **in ~,** under such limitation. **2.** *a.* So limited (esp. *estate tail*, FEE-*tail*). [ME, f. OF *taille* notch, cut, tax, (*taillier* cut f. Rom. **tal(l)iare* f. L *talea* twig)]

tai'lĭng *n.* In vbl senses; (in *pl.*) refuse or inferior part of grain, ore, etc. [f. TAIL[1] + -ING[1]]

tai'lor *n.* & *v.* **1.** *n.* Maker of (esp. men's) garments esp. to order; **~-bird,** small Asian bird sewing leaves together to form nest; **~-made,** (*a.*, esp. of woman's dress) made by tailor usu. with little ornament and with special attention to exact fit, (fig.) perfectly suited for purpose, (*n.*) tailor-made garment, (sl.) ready-made cigarette; **~'s chair** (without legs, for sitting cross-legged like tailor at work); **~'s twist,** fine strong silk thread used by tailors. **2.** Hence **~**ESS[1] *n.* **3.** *v.i.* Be, work as, a tailor; hence **~**ING[1] (1, 2) *n.* **4.** *v.t.* Make (esp. tailor-made clothes) as tailor; (esp. in *p.p.*) make clothes for. [ME & AF *taillour*, OF *tailleur* cutter f. Rom. **tal(l)iator -oris* (**tal(l)iare*; see TAIL[2], -OR)]

taint *n.* & *v.* **1.** *n.* Spot or trace of decay or corruption or disease (lit. or fig.), corrupt condition, infection, (*there was a taint of insanity in the family*; *the moral taint had spread among all classes*; *without taint of commercialism*); hence **~'**LESS *a.* **2.** *v.t.* Introduce corruption or disease into, infect, (*tainted meat*); affect slightly *with*. **3.** *v.i.* Be infected or corrupted (*meat will taint readily in hot weather*). [ME, partly f. OF *teint(e)* f. L *tinctus*, *tincta* masc. & fem. p.p. (as n.) of *tingere* dye, partly f. ATTAINT]

tai'păn[1] (tī'-) *n.* Head of a foreign business in China. [Chin.]

tai'păn[2] (tī'-) *n.* Largest venomous snake in Australia. [Aboriginal]

taj (tahj) *n.* Tall conical cap of dervish. [f. Arab. *tāj*]

ta'kahė (tah'ka-hĭ) *n.* Notornis. [Maori]

tāke[1] *v.* (**took** *pr.* to͝ok; **ta'ken**). **1.** *v.t.* Lay hold of with the hand(s) or other part of the body or with any instrument (lit. or fig.), grasp, seize, capture, catch by pursuit or surprise, captivate, win, gain, (*take it between your finger and thumb*; *took him by the throat*; *take it up with the tongs*; *take the* BULL[1] *by the horns*; *the devil take it, him!*; *take the* BIT[1] *between* one's *teeth*; *take a fortress*; *take by* STORM; *took 113 prisoners, six wickets*; *was taken prisoner* or *captive*; *the woman taken in adultery*; *rabbit taken in trap*; *took him in the act, at a disadvantage*; *took rook with pawn, king with ace, first five tricks*; *takes £100 a week in fees, in salary, at the box-office*; *take* person's FANCY[1]; *took the first set 6-3*; *took first prize*; *taken* ABACK, SHORT); ~ **the biscuit** or **bun** or **cake,** (sl.) carry off the honours; **~n ill** or (colloq.) **bad,** suddenly affected by illness; **~n by** or **with,** attracted or charmed by. **2.** *v.i.* Be successful or effective (*novel, inoculation, skin-graft, did not take*); (of plant, seed, etc.) begin to grow. **3.** *v.t.* Assume possession of, acquire, avail oneself of, use, (*takes whatever he can lay his hands on*; *wish you would not take my bicycle*; *quotation taken from Pope*; *shall take a bath, a holiday*; (in recipe) *take a dozen eggs and beat them well*; *has taken a partner, a wife*; *take* LEAVE[1] *to, take the* LIBERTY; *take* ADVANTAGE[1] *of*; *take the opportunity to* do, *of* doing; ~ one's **time,** not hurry; ~ person **all his time,** (colloq.) tax his powers); occupy (position) esp. as one's right (*take a* or *the* CHAIR; *take* one's *seat, a* BACK[1] *seat*); copulate with (woman); obtain after fulfilling necessary conditions (*take a degree,* ORDER[1]*s*, ‖SILK); regularly buy (periodical etc.); obtain use of by purchase etc. (*took tickets, seats, for the ballet*; *must take lessons, lodgings, a taxi, a train to London*; *will take two pairs of these socks, please*; *took the cure at Bath*); use as instance (*take Hitler, now*); consume (*will take some food, a cup of tea*; *takes too much alcohol*; *took poison*; *do you take sugar?*); have as necessary condition or accompaniment or part (*these things take time*; *it takes a poet to translate Virgil*; *transitive verbs take an object*; *in German 'folgen' takes the dative*; *this cake takes six eggs*; *takes a large size in hats*; ~ **a lot of** or **some doing,** be hard to do; **have what it ~s,** possess necessary qualities esp. for success). **4.** Cause to come or go with one, carry with one, conduct, convey, remove, dispossess person etc. of, (*take the letters to the post, the dog for a walk, the children to the pantomime, the corkscrew from the shelf*; *take for a* RIDE; *my business often takes me abroad*; *route, bus, takes you past the station*; *took him into partnership*; *takes all the fun out of it*; *take to* TASK; *was taken from us by a stroke*); ~ **in hand,** undertake, start doing or dealing with, undertake the control or reform of (*the boy wants taking in hand*); **you can't ~ it with you,** (colloq.) your possessions will pass to others when you die. **5.** Catch, be infected with or affected by, (cold, fever, fire, etc.; ~ **ill** or ***sick,** (colloq.) be taken ill); conceive, experience, indulge, give play to, exert, (*take comfort, courage, offence, umbrage, a dislike to,* EXCEPTION *to, a* FANCY[1] *to,* FRIGHT; *take* one's *revenge, takes a pride in his work, a pleasure in contradicting*; *take pity on him*; *take no notice*; *take heed, pains, trouble*). **6.** Ascertain and record (person's measure, height, temperature, name, address, etc.) by inquiry, measurement, etc. **7.** Apprehend, grasp mentally, infer, conclude, understand, interpret, (*I take your meaning* or (arch.) *you*; *I take this to be ironical*; *I take it that we are to wait here*; *took his reply as a denial, him to be* or *for a fool*; *would you take this passage literally?*); *take* person *at his* WORD[1]; *take it for* GRANTed; **I ~ your point,** I grant the validity of what you say. **8.** Treat or regard in specified manner, adopt specified attitude towards, (*take things coolly*; *take it easy*; *take to* HEART); **~n all in all, taking one thing with another,** when the matter is viewed as a whole; ~ **it badly,** be very upset; ~ **it ill,** resent it; ~ **as read,** dispense with the actual reading of (minutes etc.); ~ **it well,** not be upset or resentful. **9.** Accept, put up with, submit to, adopt, choose, receive, accommodate, derive, (*take the offer*; *take what you can get*; *took a risk in doing that*; *I took his bet* or *him*; *took a beating from his opponent*; *cannot take a joke in good part*; *cannot take coffee without suffering from insomnia*; *must take us as you find us*; *will take no nonsense*; *will not take this treatment*; *took it like a lamb*; *will not take a hint*; *takes its name from the inventor*); **(you may)** ~ **it from me** or ~ **my word for it,** I, a well-informed person, assure you; ~ **it,** (colloq.) endure adversity, punishment, etc., bravely; ~ **it or leave it,** please yourself, I do not care whether you accept or not; ~ **sides,** join one of two parties; ~ **that!** (accompanying a blow etc.); ~ (hold, adopt) **a different view. 10.** Perform, execute, make, undertake, negotiate, deal with, (*took work for a friend*; *take notes, dictation*; *took a decision, a sudden leap*; *horse will not take the fence*; *take a walk*; *take a look at this, around you*; *took a deep breath*; *take a* BOW[4], *an oath*; *took the corner too fast*); be taught or examined in (subject), be teacher of (subject) in school etc.; conduct (religious service). **11.** Make (photograph); photograph (person etc.). **12.** *Take (no)* ACCOUNT[2] *of*; *take into* ACCOUNT[2]; *take* ACTION; *take* ADVICE; *take* AIM[2]; *take* CARE[1] *(of)*; *take a* CHANCE[1], one's CHANCE[1]; *take into* CONSIDERATION; *take* EFFECT[1]; *take* HEART *(of grace)*; *take* HOLD[2]; **~-home,** (of pay etc.) available to employee after deduction of taxes etc.; *take* one's HOOK[1]; *take* LEAVE[1] *(of)*; *take* LIFE, one's LIFE *(in* one's *hands)*; ~ person's (esp. **God's**) **name in vain,** use it lightly or profanely, (joc.) mention it; *take* PART[1]; *take* PLACE[1], *the* PLACE[1] *of*, one's PLACE[1]; *take* POSSESSION; *take* PRECEDENCE; *take* STOCK *(of, in)*; *take the* WALL, *(the)* WIND[1]. **13.** (w. *advs.*): ~ **away,** subtract (number), remove, buy (food etc.) at restaurant for eating elsewhere; ~ **back,** retract (statement etc.), (Print.) transfer to previous line, carry (person) back in thought to past time; ~ **down,** write down (spoken words), humiliate (*take* person *down a* PEG[1]), remove (building, structure) by taking it to pieces. **14.** ~ **in,** admit, receive, (lodger, guest, etc.); conduct (esp. lady) to dinner; undertake (work) to be done at one's home; include, comprise; (colloq.) visit (place) *en route*; make (garment) smaller; furl (SAIL[1]); understand, digest mentally; deceive, cheat; ‖regularly buy (newspaper etc.); *~-in* n., deception. **15.** ~ **off,** remove (clothes, HAT, etc.) from the body; remove, lead away; deduct (part of price); ridicule by imitation, mimic; jump, spring, (*from* or *at* place); (of aircraft or pilot) become airborne from ground etc.; regard (day etc.) as holiday; ~ **oneself off,** depart; *~-off* n., caricature, place from which one jumps, act of becoming airborne. **16.** ~ **on,** undertake (work, responsibility); acquire (*takes on a new meaning*); engage (employee); agree to oppose (person *at golf* etc.); (colloq.) show violent emotion, make a fuss. **17.** ~ **out,** cause to come out, bring or convey out, (*take him out for a walk*; *books must not be taken out of the library*); *= *take away* (food); remove (stain etc.); (Bridge) remove (partner or his call) from suit by bidding a different one or no trumps; procure, get issued, (patent, summons, etc.); ~ **it out of,** have revenge on, exhaust strength of; ~ **it out on,** work off one's frustration etc. by attacking or maltreating; ~ person **out of himself,** make him forget his worries etc. **18.** ~ **over,** succeed to management or ownership of (business), assume control, (Print.) transfer to next line; *~-over* n., assumption of control (esp. of business etc.). **19.** ~ **up,** lift up; absorb, occupy, engage (*sponges take up water*; *takes up all my time, my attention*); take (person) into vehicle (*train stops to take up passengers*); adopt as protégé or pursuit; begin (residence etc.); interrupt or correct or question (speaker); pursue (matter, idea, inquiry) further; shorten (garment); accept (offer etc.); ~ person **up on,** accept his (offer, bet, etc.); ~ **up with,** begin to consort with; *take up the* CUDGELS, GAUNTLET[1], GLOVE. **20.** (w. *preps.*): ~ **after,** resemble (ancestor etc., esp. parent) in character, features, etc.; ~ **against,** oppose, begin to dislike; ~ **from,** subtract (*take 4 from 6*), diminish, weaken, detract from; ~ (person) **into** one's **confidence,** confide in him; ~ **it into** one's **head,** get the idea *that*, resolve *to* do; ~ **to,** begin, have recourse to, fall into the habit of (using), begin to busy oneself with, adapt oneself to, conceive liking for (person); *take to* one's HEEL[1]*s*; ~ **it (up)on** one(**self**), venture or presume *to*. **21.** Hence **tā'k**ABLE *a.* [OE *tacan* f. ON *taka*]

tāke[2] *n.* Amount (*of* fish, game, etc.) taken or caught; (Print.) amount of copy set up at one time; takings, esp. money received at theatre for seats; (Cinemat.) scene or sequence of actions photographed at one time without interruption. [f. prec.]

tā'ker *n.* In vbl senses; one who takes a bet etc. (*there were no takers*). [ME, f. TAKE[1] + -ER[1]]

ta'kĭn (tah'-) *n.* Tibetan horned ruminant (*Budorcas taxicolor*). [Mishmi]

tā'kĭng[1] *n.* In vbl senses; (in *pl.*) money taken in business, receipts; (arch.) state of agitation (*was in a great taking*). [ME, f. TAKE[1] + -ING[1]]

tā'kĭng[2] *a.* Attractive, captivating; catching, infectious; hence ~LY[2] *adv.*, ~NESS *n.* [ME, f. TAKE[1] + -ING[2]]

ta'la (tah'-) *n.* Rhythmic pattern of Indian music. [Skr.]

tă'lapoin *n.* **1.** Buddhist monk or priest. **2.** Small W. Afr. monkey (*Cercopithecus talapoin*). [f. Port. *talapão* f. Talaing *tala pói* my lord]

talăr'ĭa *n. pl.* (Rom. Myth.) Winged sandals as attribute of Mercury, Iris, and others. [L, neut. pl. of *talaris* (*talus* ankle; see -AR[1])]

ta'lbot (taw'- *or* tŏ'-) *n.* Extinct breed of large white hunting-hound. [perh. f. family name *Talbot*]

tălc *n.*, & *v.t.* (**-ck-**). **1.** *n.* A magnesium silicate usu. found in flat smooth often transparent plates and used as lubricator etc.; talcum powder; mica esp. as glazing-material; hence **tă'lck**Y[2], ~'OSE[1], ~'OUS, *adjs.* **2.** *v.t.* Treat with talc. [F, or f. med. L *talcum*, f. Arab. f. Pers. *talk*]

tă'lcum *n.* = prec.; ~ (**powder**), powdered talc for toilet use, usu. perfumed. [med. L; see prec.]

tāle *n.* **1.** True or usu. fictitious narrative esp. one imaginatively treated, story, (*tell me a tale*; *a true tale of the Crusades*; *marvellous legendary tales*); THERE*by hangs a tale*; ~ **of a tub,** idle fiction; TELL[1] *a* or *the tale*; TELL[1] one's or *its own tale*; *old wives' tale* (see WIFE). **2.** Malicious report whether true or false (*all sorts of tales will get about*); TELL[1] *tales* (*out of school*); **~'bearer,** person who maliciously reveals secrets; so **~'bearing** *a.* & *n.*; **~'teller,** one who tells tale(s) (in either sense). **3.** (arch. or literary). Number, total, (*the tale is complete*); **shepherd tells his** ~ (of sheep). [OE *talu*, = OS, ON *tala*, OHG *zala*, f. Gmc **talō* (**tal-*; cf. TELL[1])]

tă'lent *n.* **1.** Special aptitude, faculty, gift, (*for* music etc.; *for* do*ing*; see Matt. 25:14-30); high mental ability; hence ~ED[2], ~LESS, *adjs.* **2.** Persons of talent (*all the talent of the country*; *looking out for local talent*; *ministry of all the talents*); **~-scout, ~-spotter,** seeker-out of talent esp. for entertainment industries. **3.** Ancient weight and money of account among Assyrians, Greeks, Romans, etc., of varying value. [OE *talente* & OF *talent* f. L *talentum* inclination of mind f. Gk *talanton* balance, weight, sum of money]

tales (tā'lēz) *n.* (Law). Writ for summoning jurors, list of persons who may be so summoned, to supply deficiency; **pray a** ~, plead for completion of jury thus; **~'man** (*or* tā'lz-), person so summoned. [ME f. L ~ (*de circumstantibus*) such (of the bystanders), first wds of writ]

Tălĭacō'tian (-shan) *a.* ~ **operation,** formation of new nose by means of flap taken from upper arm but severed only after union has taken place. [f. *Taliacotius*, Latinized f. *Tagliacozzi*, It. surgeon d. 1599 + -AN]

tă'lĭon *n.* = LEX TALIONIS. [ME f. OF, f. L *talio -onis* (*talis* such)]

tă'lĭpēs (-z) *n.* Club-foot(edness). [mod. L f. L *talus* ankle + *pes* foot]

tă'lĭpŏt *n.* Very tall S. Ind. fan palm with huge leaves used as sunshades etc. [f. Malayalam *tālipat*, Hindi *tālpāt* f. Skr. *tālapattra* (*tāla* palm, *pattra* leaf)]

tă'lĭsman (-z-) *n.* Charm, amulet, thing supposed capable of working wonders; inscribed stone or ring supposed to ensure safety or good fortune; hence ~IC (-ă'n-) *a.* [F & Sp., = It. *talismano*, f. med. Gk *telesmon*, Gk *telesma* completion, religious rite (*teleō* complete f. *telos* end)]

talk (tawk) *v.* & *n.* **1.** *v.i.* Converse, communicate ideas, by spoken words (*was talking with* or *to a friend*; *what are you talking about?*); communicate by radio; *talk* BIG; *talk* TALL; **people will** ~, there will be gossip or scandal; **now you're ~'ing,** (sl.) I welcome that offer etc.; **you can** or **can't** ~, (colloq.) you are just as bad yourself; **do the ~'ing,** be spokesman; **know what** one **is ~'ing about,** be expert; **money ~s** (has influence). **2.** Have the power of speech (*child is learning to talk*; *this parrot can talk*); betray secrets (*we have ways of making you talk*). **3.** *v.t.* Express, utter, discuss, in words, (*you are talking nonsense*; *talk treason, scandal, philosophy*, SHOP, *cricket*); *~ **turkey,** (colloq.) be straightforward and realistic. **4.** Use (language) in speech (*they were talking French*). **5.** Bring into specified condition etc. by talking (*talked himself hoarse*; *talk* one*self out of a difficulty*; *talked him out of his resolution, into his grave*); *talk the hind leg off a* DONKEY. **6.** ~ **about,** discuss, make subject of gossip, (~ **about** *trouble* etc.!, (colloq.) there was a great deal of it); ~ **at,** address to one of a company remarks covertly hostile and meant to be heard by (another), address pompously; ~ **away,** consume (time) in talking; ~ **back,** (1) reply defiantly, (2) respond on two-way radio system; ~ **down,** silence (person) by superior loudness or persistency, bring (pilot or aircraft) to a landing by radio instructions from the ground, speak patronizingly or condescendingly *to*; ~ **of,** (1) discuss, mention, (2) express some intention of (do*ing*); ~ **out,** get rid of (bill in Parliament etc.) by prolonging discussion till time of adjournment; ~ **over,** discuss at some length; ~ person **over** or **round,** win him over by talking; ~ **round,** discuss (subject) at length without reaching conclusion; *talk through* one's HAT, one's NECK[1]; ~ **to,** speak to, (colloq.), reprove (*gave him a talking-to*); ~ **to oneself,**

soliloquize; ~ **up,** discuss (subject) in order to rouse interest in it. **7.** Hence ~'ER¹ *n.* **8.** *n.* Conversation (*let us have some talk*); discussion (*talks were held*); SMALL, TABLE-, TALL, *talk*; **it will end in ~,** nothing will be done; ~ **show** (of interviews on television). **9.** Short address or lecture in conversational style (esp. when broadcast). **10.** (Theme of) gossip (*there is talk of a new appointment*; *they, their quarrels, are the talk of the town*). **11.** Mode of speech (BABY-, *sailors'*, *talk*). [ME *talk(i)en* frequent. v. f. TALE or TELL¹]

ta'lkathon (taw'k-) *n.* Prolonged public oral discussion. [f. prec. + MARATHON]

ta'lkatĭve (taw'k-) *a.* Fond of talking; hence ~LY² (-vlĭ) *adv.*, ~NESS (-vn-) *n.* [ME, f. TALK + -ATIVE]

ta'lkee-talkee (taw'kĭtawkĭ) *n.* Incessant chatter; broken English of W. Ind. Negroes etc. [redupl. & dim. f. TALK]

ta'lkfĕst (taw'k-) *n.* Talkathon; informal meeting for general discussion. [f. TALK + FEST]

ta'lkĭe (taw'kĭ) *n.* (sl.) = SOUND²-*film*. [f. *talking film*, after *movie*]

ta'lkĭng¹ (taw'k-) *n.* In vbl senses; ~ **point,** topic for discussion or argument; **~-shop,** (derog.) Parliament etc. regarded as place of argument rather than action. [ME, f. TALK + -ING¹]

ta'lkĭng² (taw'k-) *a.* In vbl senses; having the power of speech (*talking parrot*); expressive (*talking eyes*); ~ **book,** recorded reading of book esp. for the blind; ~ **film** or **picture,** = SOUND²-*film*; ~ **of,** while we are discussing (*talking of food, what time is dinner?*). [f. TALK + -ING²]

tall (tawl) *a.* & *adv.* **1.** *a.* (Of person) of more than average height, or of specified height (*he is six feet tall*); (of tree, steeple, mast, ship, stag, etc.) higher than the average or than surrounding objects; **~'boy,** tall chest of drawers sometimes in lower and upper sections or mounted on legs; ~ **drink** (served in tall glass); ~ **hat,** = TOP¹ *hat*; hence ~'NESS *n.* **2.** (sl.) Extravagant, boastful, excessive, (*a tall story*; *tall talk*); **a ~ order,** an exorbitant or unreasonable demand. **3.** Hence ~'ISH 2 *a.* **4.** *adv.* (sl.) In a tall way; **talk ~,** boast; **walk ~,** be proud. [ME, repr. OE *getæl* swift, prompt, = OS *gital*, OHG *gizal* quick]

tă'llage *n.* (Hist.) Form of taxation on towns etc., abolished in 14th c.; tax on feudal dependants etc. [ME f. OF *taillage* (*tailler* cut; see TAIL², -AGE)]

tă'llĭth *n.* Scarf worn by Jews esp. at prayer. [f. Rabbinical Heb. *ṭallīt* (*ṭillel* to cover)]

tă'llow (-ō) *n.*, & *v.t.* **1.** *n.* Substance got by melting the harder and less fusible kinds of (esp. animal) fat, used for making candles and soap, greasing machinery, etc.; **vegetable ~,** vegetable fat similarly used; **~-chandler,** maker or vendor of tallow candles; **~-drop,** style of cutting precious stones with dome on one or both sides; **~-tree,** tree esp. of genus *Stillingia* yielding vegetable tallow; hence ~ISH¹, ~Y², *adjs.* **2.** *v.t.* Grease with tallow. [ME *tal(u)g*, f. MLG *talg*, *talch*, of unkn. orig.]

tă'llȳ *n.* & *v.* **1.** *n.* (Hist.) Piece of wood scored across with notches for the items of an account and then split into halves of which each party kept one; account so kept. **2.** Score, reckoning; mark made to register a fixed number of objects delivered or received, such number used as unit. **3.** Ticket, label of wood or metal or paper with name etc. attached to thing for identification. **4.** Corresponding thing, counterpart, duplicate, (*of*). **5.** ~ **clerk,** one who keeps a tally of goods, esp. those loaded or unloaded in docks; ||**~man,** one who keeps a tally or tally-shop, one who sells goods on credit; **~-sheet,** paper on which tally is kept; ||**~-shop** (conducted on tally system); ||~ **system, trade,** (of sales on short credit or instalments with account kept by tally). **6.** *v.t.* Record or reckon by tally. **7.** *v.i.* Agree, correspond, (*with*; *goods do not tally with invoice*). **8.** Hence **tă'llĭ**ER¹ *n.* [ME, f. AF *tallie*, AL *tal(l)ia* f. L *talea*; cf. TAIL²]

tăllȳ-hō' *int.*, *n.* (*pl.* ~s), & *v.* **1.** *int.* & *n.* Huntsman's cry to hounds on viewing fox. **2.** *v.i.* & *t.* Utter, indicate (fox) or urge (hounds) with, this. [cf. F *taïaut*]

Tă'lmud (*or* -ŏŏd) *n.* Body of Jewish civil and ceremonial law and legend comprising the Mishnah and the Gemara; hence **Tălmŭ'd**IC(AL) *adjs.*, ~IST (2, 3) *ns.* [f. late Heb. *talmûḏ* instruction f. Heb. *lāmaḏ* learn]

tă'lon *n.* **1.** Claw esp. of bird of prey. **2.** Cards left after deal; last part of dividend-coupon sheet, entitling to new sheet on presentation. **3.** Shoulder of bolt against which key presses in shooting it; ogee moulding. **4.** Hence (-)~ED² (-nd) *a.* [ME, f. OF, = heel, f. Rom. **talo -onis* f. L (see foll.)]

tā'l|us¹ *n.* (*pl.* **~i** *pr.* -ī). (Anat.) Ankle(-bone). [L, = ankle, heel]

tā'lus² *n.* Slope of wall that tapers to top or rests against bank; (Geol.) sloping mass of fragments at foot of cliff. [F, of unkn. orig.]

tăm *n.* Tam-o'-shanter. [abbr.]

TAM *abbr.* television audience measurement.

tā'mable. Var. of TAMEABLE.

tama'lė (-ah'-) *n.* Mexican food of seasoned meat and maize flour steamed or baked in maize husks. [f. Mex. Sp. *tamal*, pl. *tamales*]

tamă'ndūa *n.* Arboreal ant-eater (*Tamandua tetradactyla*) of Central & S. America. [Port., f. Tupi *tamanduà*]

tă'manoir (-nwâr) *n.* Great ant-eater (*Myrmecophaga jubata*) of S. America. [F, f. Carib *tamanoà* (cf. prec.)]

tă'marăck *n.* Amer. larch, esp. *Larix laricina*; its wood. [Amer. Ind.]

tă'marĭn *n.* S. Amer. marmoset of genus *Leontocebus*. [F, f. Carib]

tă'marĭnd *n.* (Tropical tree, *Tamarindus indica*, with) fruit whose acid pulp is used in making cooling or medicinal drinks etc. [f. med. L *tamarindus* f. Arab. *tamr-hindī* DATE¹ of India]

tă'marĭsk *n.* Plant of genus *Tamarix*, esp. **common** or **French ~,** evergreen shrub (*T. gallica*) with feathery branches, tiny leaves, and small white or pink flowers, suitable for planting near sea. [ME, f. LL *tamariscus*, L *tamarix*]

tă'mbour (-oor) *n.*, & *v.t.* **1.** *n.* Drum; circular frame on which silk etc. is stretched to be embroidered, material so embroidered; (Archit.) cylindrical stone in shaft of column, circular part of various structures, lobby with ceiling and folding doors in church porch etc. to obviate draught; drum-fish or globe-fish; sloping buttress or projection in fives-court etc. **2.** *v.t.* Decorate, embroider, (material, or abs.) on tambour. [F, f. *tabour* TABOR]

tămbour'a (-oor'*a*) *n.* Indian stringed instrument used as drone. [f. Arab. *ṭanbūra*]

tă'mbourĭn (-ber-) *n.* Long narrow drum used in Provence; (music for) dance accompanied by this. [F, dim. of TAMBOUR]

tămbouri'ne (-berē'n) *n.* **1.** Small musical instrument made of wooden or metal hoop with parchment stretched over one side and loose jingling metal discs. **2.** Afr. pigeon with tambourine-like note. [f. as prec.]

tāme *v.t.*, & *a.* **1.** *v.t.* Make gentle and tractable, domesticate, (wild animal, bird, etc.); subdue, curb, reduce to submission, humble, (person, spirit, courage, ardour, etc.); hence ~'LESS (-ml-; literary) *a.*, **(-)tā'm**ER[1] *n.* **2.** *a.* Made tractable, domesticated, not wild; (joc., of person) kept available for one's domestic or private use; ~ **cat,** (fig.) person tolerated as useful hanger-on. **3.** *(Of land or plant) cultivated, produced by cultivation. **4.** Submissive, spiritless, inert, unexciting, insipid, (*tame acquiescence*, *scenery*, *description*). **5.** Hence ~'LY[2] (-mlĭ) *adv.*, ~'NESS (-mn-) *n.* [v. f. a., f. OE *tam*, = OHG *zan*, ON *tamr* f. Gmc **tamaz* f. IE **dom-*]

tā'meable (-ma-) *a.* Capable of being tamed; hence **tāme**ABI'LITY (-ma-), ~NESS (-beln-), *ns.* [f. prec. + -ABLE]

Tă'mĭl *n.* & *a.* (Language or member) of a Dravidian people inhabiting S. India and Sri Lanka; hence **Tamĭ'l**IAN *a.* [f. native name *Tamil*, cogn. w. DRAVIDIAN]

***Tă'mmanỳ** *n.* Organization of Democratic party notorious in 19th c. for political corruption; hence ~ISM (3) *n.* [orig. name of benevolent society in New York, f. 17th-c. Indian chief friendly to whites]

tăm-o'-shă'nter, tă'mmỳ, *ns.* Round woollen or cloth cap fitting closely round brows but large and full above. [f. hero of Burns's *Tam o' Shanter*]

tămp *v.t.* Pack (blast-hole) full of clay etc. to get full force of explosion, whence ~'ING[1] (3) *n.*; ram down (road material etc.); hence ~'ER[1] (1, 2) *n.* [perh. back form. f. *tampin* (var. of TAMPION) taken as = *tamping*]

tă'mpăn *n.* Venomous S. Afr. tick. [perh. f. Tswana]

tă'mper *v.i.* **1.** ~ **with,** meddle with, make unauthorized changes in (will, MS., etc.), exert secret or corrupt influence upon, bribe. **2.** Hence ~ER[1] *n.*, ~-PROOF[2] *a.* [var. of TEMPER[1]]

tă'mpĭon *n.* Wooden stopper for muzzle of gun; plug e.g. for top of organ-pipe. [ME, f. F *tampon*, nasalized var. of *tapon* f. Frank. **tappo* (as TAP[1])]

tă'mpon *n.*, & *v.t.* **1.** *n.* Plug used to stop haemorrhage or absorb secretions. **2.** *v.t.* Plug (wound etc.) with tampon. [F; see prec.]

tămponā'de, tă'mponage, *ns.* Use of tampon for wound etc. [f. prec. + -ADE, -AGE]

tă'm-tăm *n.* Large metal gong. [Hindi; see TOM-TOM]

tăn[1] *v.* (-nn-), *n.*, & *a.* **1.** *v.t.* Convert (raw hide) into leather by soaking in liquid containing tannic acid or by use of mineral salts etc., whence ~'**n**ABLE *a.*, ~'**n**AGE (3), ~'**n**ER[1], ~'**n**ERY (2, 3), *ns.* **2.** *v.t.* & *i.* Make or become brown by exposure to sun; (sl.) beat, thrash. **3.** Hence ~'**n**ING[1] (1) *n.* **4.** *n.* Bark of oak or other tree bruised and used for tanning hides (FLOWERs *of tan*); colour of this, yellowish-brown; bronze of sunburnt skin; **the** ~, (sl.) (1) the circus, (2) floor of riding-school; (**spent**) ~, tan from which tannic acid has been extracted, used for covering roads etc. **5.** ~**-liquor, -ooze, -pickle,** liquid used in tanning; ~**-pit,** ~**-vat,** (for containing tan-liquor); ~**-yard,** tannery. **6.** *a.* Of tan colour; BLACK[1] *and Tans*. [OE *tannian*, prob. f. med. L *tan(n)are*, perh. f. Celt.]

tăn[2] *abbr.* tangent.

tă'nager *n.* Amer. bird of family Thraupidae, the males mostly with brilliant plumage. [f. mod. L *tanagra* f. Tupi *tangara*]

Tă'nagra (*or* tană'g-) *n.* ~ (**statuette, figurine**), terracotta statuette found in ancient tombs near Tanagra. [~, town in ancient Greece]

||**T. & A.V.R.** *abbr.* Territorial and Army Volunteer Reserve.

tă'ndem *adv.* & *n.* **1.** *adv.* (Of horses in harness) one behind another; **drive** ~ (with horses so harnessed). **2.** *n.* (Carriage with) horses tandem; bicycle or tricycle with seats for two or more one behind another; group of two or more persons, machines, etc., with one behind or following another; **in** ~, thus arranged. [L, = at length (of time), used punningly]

tăng[1] *n.*, & *v.t.* **1.** *n.* Projecting point; part of chisel, knife, sword, etc., by which blade etc. is held firm in handle. **2.** Strong taste or flavour or smell, characteristic property, whence ~'Y[2] *a.* **3.** *v.t.* Furnish or affect with a tang. [ME, f. ON *tange* point, tang of knife]

tăng[2] *n.* Large coarse seaweed, esp. of genus *Fucus*. [f. Scand., = Norw. & Da. *tang*, Icel. *thång*]

tăng[3] *v.* & *n.* **1.** *v.t.* & *i.* Ring, clang, sound loudly. **2.** *n.* Tanging sound. [imit.]

tă'ngelō (-nj-) *n.* (*pl.* ~**s**). Hybrid between tangerine and grapefruit. [f. TANGERINE + POMELO]

tă'ngent (-nj-) *a.* & *n.* **1.** *a.* (Of line or surface) meeting a curved line or surface at a point and having same direction there, thus touching it but not (usually) intersecting it; (of surface) meeting a curved surface along a curve or line of such points; hence **tă'ng**ENCY (-nj-) *n.* **2.** *n.* Line etc. that is tangent (**fly, go, off at a** ~, diverge impetuously from matter in hand or from normal line of thought or conduct); ~ **of an angle,** (Math.) ratio of the perpendicular subtending it in any right-angled triangle to the base; ~ **galvanometer** (for which strength of current measured is proportional to tangent of angle of deflection). **3.** Upright piece that strikes string of clavichord. [f. L *tangere* touch; see -ENT]

tăngĕ'ntial (-njĕ'nshal) *a.* Of or along a tangent; divergent; peripheral; hence ~LY[2] *adv.* [f. prec. + -IAL]

Tăngeri'ne (-njerē'n) *a.* & *n.* **1.** (Native) of Tangier. **2.** **t**~ (**orange**), small flattened kind, its deep orange-yellow colour. [f. *Tanger*, *Tangier* + -INE[1]]

tă'nghĭn (-nggĭn) *n.* Madagascar tree, the large purple fruit of which has poisonous kernel formerly used in ordeals; this poison. [F, f. Malagasy *tangena*]

tă'ng|ĭble (-nj-) *a.* Perceptible by touch; definite, clearly intelligible, not elusive or visionary, (*tangible advantages*, *scheme*, *distinction*); (Law) corporeal; hence ~IBI'LITY, ~**ĭble**NESS (-beln-), *ns.*, ~**ĭb**LY[2] *adv.* [F, or f. LL *tangibilis* (*tangere* touch; see -IBLE)]

tă'ngle[1] (-nggel) *v.* & *n.* **1.** *v.t.* & *i.* Intertwine (threads, hair, etc.), become involved, in confused mass; entrap, entangle; complicate (*a tangled affair*); become involved (esp. in conflict) *with*. **2.** *n.* Confused mass of intertwined threads etc.; confused state (*skein*, *business*, *is in a tangle*); hence **tă'ngl**Y[2] (-ngg-) *a.* [ME var. of obs. *tagle*, of uncert. orig.]

tă'ngle[2] (-nggel) *n.* = TANG[2]; leathery seaweed of genus *Laminaria*. [prob. f. Norw. *taangel* f. ON *thöngull*]

tă'ngō (-nggō) *n.* (*pl.* ~**s**), & *v.i.* **1.** *n.* S. Amer. slow ballroom dance of Central Afr. origin; music for it. **2.** *v.i.* Dance the tango. [Amer. Sp.]

tă'ngrăm (-ngg-) *n.* Chinese puzzle square cut into seven pieces to be combined into various figures. [19th c.; orig. unkn.]

tanh (thăn *or* tănsh *or* tănā'ch) *abbr.* hyperbolic tangent.

tă'nĭst *n.* (Hist.) Successor-apparent to Celtic chief, usu. most vigorous adult of his kin, chosen by election; hence ~RY (5) *n.* [f. Ir. & Gael. *tánaiste* heir]

tănk *n.*, & *v.i.* **1.** *n.* Large metal, wooden, glass etc., vessel for liquid, gas, etc.; part of locomotive tender containing water for boiler; (Ind.) storage-pond, artificial lake, reservoir for water. **2.** (Mil.) Armoured motor vehicle carrying guns and moving on caterpillar tracks. **3.** **~-car,** railway truck with large tank for carrying liquids; **~ drama,** sensational drama in which water is used for representing rescue from drowning etc.; **~-engine,** railway engine carrying fuel and water receptacles on its own frame, not in tender; **~ farm,** area where petroleum is stored in tanks; **~-farming,** growing plants in tanks of water without soil; **~ top,** short tight sleeveless scoop-necked upper garment; **~-trap,** obstacle able to stop a military tank. **4.** Hence ~'FUL 2 *n.* **5.** *v.i.* ~ (**up**), fill tank of vehicle etc., (sl.) drink heavily. [f. Gujarati *tānkh* etc., perh. f. Skr. *tadāga* pond]

tă'nka *n.* Japanese poem in five lines and 31 syllables giving complete picture of event or mood. [Jap.]

tă'nkage *n.* (Charge for) storage in tanks; cubic content of tank(s); kind of fertilizer got from refuse bones etc. [f. TANK + -AGE]

tă'nkard *n.* Large one-handled drinking-vessel usu. of silver or pewter and often with cover; contents of, amount held by, this (*a tankard of ale*). [ME, of unkn. orig.; cf. MDu. *tanckaert*]

tă'nker *n.* Ship or aircraft with tank(s) for carrying liquids, esp. mineral oils, in bulk; road vehicle with large tank for conveying milk etc. in bulk. [f. TANK + -ER[1]]

tă'nner. See TAN[1].

tă'nn|ic *a.* Of tan; **~ic acid,** tannin; so ~ATE[1] (3) *n.* [f. F *tannique* (as foll.; see -IC)]

tă'nnĭn *n.* Any of several astringent substances got from oak-galls and various tree-barks, used in preparing leather and in making ink etc. [f. F *tanin* (as TAN[1]; see -IN)]

tă'nrĕc. See TENREC.

tă'nsȳ (-zĭ) *n.* Herb of genus *Tanacetum*, esp. common species with yellow flowers and finely--toothed bitter aromatic leaves formerly used in medicine and cookery. [ME, f. OF *tanesie* f. med. L f. Gk *athanasia* immortality (*a-* not, *thanatos* death)]

tă'ntalīte *n.* Rare heavy black mineral, principal source of tantalum. [f. G & Sw. *tantalit* (as TANTALUM; see -ITE[1])]

tă'ntalīz|e, -īs|e (-īz), *v.t.* Torment, tease, (person etc.) by sight or promise of desired thing withheld or kept just out of reach; hence ~A'TION *n.* [f. as TANTALUS + -IZE]

tă'ntalum *n.* Rare hard white metallic element highly resistant to heat and to action of acids; hence **tăntă'lɪc** *a.* [f. as foll. w. ref. to its non--absorbent quality + -UM]

tă'ntalus *n.* Spirit-stand in which decanters are locked up but visible; wood ibis. [L, f. Gk *Tantalos* mythical king of Phrygia, condemned to stand in Tartarus surrounded by inaccessible water and fruit]

tă'ntamount *pred. a.* Equivalent *to* (*his message was tantamount to a flat refusal*). [f. obs. v. f. It. *tanto montare* amount to so much]

tă'ntara *n.* Fanfare of notes on trumpet or horn. [imit.]

tăntĭ'vȳ *n.* & *a.* (arch.) **1.** *n.* Hunting cry; swift movement, gallop, rush; (*T~*; Hist.) English High Churchman or Tory of 1660–1688. **2.** *a.* Swift; of Tantivies. [perh. imit. of hoof-beats]

tant pis (tahṅ pē') *adv.* So much the worse. [F]

tă'ntr|a *n.* Each of a class of Hindu or Buddhist mystical and magical writings; hence ~IC *a.*, ~ISM (3), ~IST (2), *ns.* [Skr., = loom, groundwork, doctrine (*tan* stretch)]

tă'ntrum *n.* Outburst of bad temper or petulance (*is in a tantrum*; *went into her tantrums*). [18th c., of unkn. orig.]

T.A.N.U. *abbr.* Tanganyika African National Union.

Taoiseach (tē'shaχ) *n.* Prime Minister of Irish Republic. [Ir., = chief, leader]

Tao|ism (tah'ō- *or* tow'-) *n.* Religious doctrine orig. based on writings attributed to Lao-tse, Chinese philosopher (*c.* 500 B.C.); hence ~IST (2) *n.* [f. Chin. *tao* (right) way + -ISM]

tăp[1] *n.*, & *v.t.* (**-pp-**). **1.** *n.* Device through which liquid is drawn from cask or flows from pipe in controllable manner; plug used to close opening in cask; liquor of a particular brewing etc. w. ref. to quality; taproom; act of tapping telephone etc.; **on ~**, ready to be drawn, (fig.) ready for immediate use, (of government bonds etc.) freely available. **2.** Instrument for cutting thread of female screw. **3.** **~ bill, issue,** etc., (available on tap); **~-borer,** auger for boring tapering hole in cask; **~'room** (in which liquor on tap is sold and drunk); **~-root,** chief descending root of plant; **~-water** (esp. supplied through pipes to taps in house etc.). **4.** *v.t.* Furnish (cask) with tap; pierce (cask etc.) to let out liquid, let out thus; (Surg.) release (fluid accumulated in body), operate thus on (person); draw sap from (tree) by cutting into it; penetrate to, get into communication with, establish trade etc. in, (district etc.); apply to, solicit, (person *for* subscription etc.); broach (subject); divert part of current from (telegraph or telephone wires etc.) to detect message; make female screw-thread in. [OE (*tæppian* v. f.) *tæppa*, = OHG *zapho*, ON *tappi* f. Gmc **tappon*]

tăp[2] *v.* (**-pp-**) & *n.* **1.** *v.t.* Strike lightly (*tap the door with your knuckles, the pavement with your stick*; *tapped his forehead knowingly*); cause (thing) to strike lightly *against* etc. (*tapped his stick against the window*); *apply leather to (heel or sole of shoe). **2.** *v.i.* Strike gentle blow, rap, (*at* or *on* door etc.). **3.** *n.* Light blow, rap; sound of this (*heard a tap at the door*); *(in *pl.*, usu. treated as *sing.*) signal on drum or bugle for lights to be put out in soldiers' quarters, similar signal at military funeral; **~-dance, -dancer, -dancing,** (on stage, characterized by rhythmical tapping of the feet). [ME *tappe*, imit., perh. thr. F *taper*]

ta'pa (tah'-) *n.* Bark of paper-mulberry tree, used in Pacific islands for clothes, mats, etc.; cloth made from it. [Polynesian]

tāpe *n.*, & *v.t.* **1.** *n.* Narrow woven cotton etc. strip used for tying up parcels or papers, fastening or labelling garments, etc., (RED *tape*); such strip stretched across racing-track at finishing-line (**breast the ~**, win race); narrow band of strong fabric rotating on pulleys etc. in machinery; (**adhesive**) **~**, strip of paper, transparent film, etc., coated with adhesive for fastening packages etc.; continuous strip of paper on which messages are printed in tape-machine; (**magnetic**) **~**, impregnated or coated plastic strip or ribbon for electromagnetic recording and reproduction of signals; tape-measure; tape-recording; tapeworm. **2.** **~-machine** (for receiving and recording telegraph messages); **~-measure,** strip of tape or thin flexible metal marked for use as distance-measure, and often coiled up in cylindrical case; **~-recorder,** apparatus for recording sounds etc. on magnetic tape and afterwards reproducing them; **~-recording,** such record or reproduction; **~'worm,** tape-like many-jointed cestode of genus *Taenia* etc. parasitic in alimentary canal in man and most vertebrates. **3.** Hence ~'LESS, ~'LIKE, *adjs.* **4.** *v.t.* Furnish, tie up, with tape; join sections of (book) with bands of tape; record on magnetic tape; fasten with adhesive tape; ‖**have** person or thing **~d,** (sl.) have summed him up, fully understand it. [OE *tæppa, -e,* of unkn. orig.]

tā'per *n., a.,* & *v.* **1.** *n.* Slender candle, wick coated with wax etc. (**~-stick,** holder for this). **2.** *a.* (esp. poet. or rhet.) Growing gradually smaller towards one end like cone or pyramid (*taper fingers*). **3.** *v.t.* & *i.* ~ (**off**), make or become taper, (cause to) grow gradually less, (*the upper part tapers* or *is tapered* (*off*) *to a point*). [OE *tapur, -or, -er* wax candle, f. L PAPYRUS, whose pith was used for candle-wicks]

tă'pėstr|ў *n.* Thick hand-woven textile fabric in which design is formed by weft stitches across parts of warp, used for covering walls, furniture, etc.; machine-made fabric imitating or resembling this; hence (-)~IED[2] (-rĭd) *a.* [ME, alt. f. *tapissery* f. OF *tapisserie* (*tapissier* tapestry-worker or *tapisser* to carpet, f. TAPIS; see -RY)]

tăpĭō'ca *n.* Starchy substance in hard white grains got from cassava and used for puddings etc. [f. Tupi & Guarani *tipioca* (*tipi* dregs, *og, ok* squeeze out)]

tā'pir (*or* -ēr) *n.* Hoofed piglike mammal with short proboscis, allied to rhinoceros; hence ~OID *a.* & *n.* [f. Tupi *tapira*]

tapis (tă'pē; *or* -ĭs) *n.* **On the ~,** (of subject) under consideration or discussion. [ME, a kind of cloth, f. OF *tapiz* f. Rom. **tappetium* f. LL f. Gk *tapētion* dim. of *tapēs -ētos* tapestry]

tapō'tement (-tm-) *n.* (Med.) Percussing as part of massage treatment. [F (*tapoter* to tap; see -MENT)]

tă'ppėt *n.* Arm, collar, cam, etc., used in machinery to impart intermittent motion; ~ **loom** (in which hammers are worked by tappets); ~ **rod** (carrying tappet, e.g. to open or close valve). [app. f. TAP[2] + -ET[1]]

tă'ppĭt *a.* (Sc.) Topped; ~ **hen,** crested hen, large drinking-vessel with knob on lid. [= *topped,* p.p. of TOP[2]]

tă'pster *n.* Person employed at a bar to draw and serve liquor. [OE *tæppestre,* orig. fem. (as TAP[1], -STER)]

tapu (tah'pōō) *n.* & *a.* (N.Z.) = TABOO. [Maori]

tar̄[1] *n.,* & *v.t.* (**-rr-**). **1.** *n.* Thick dark inflammable liquid got by dry distillation of wood, coal, etc., and used as preservative of timber and iron, antiseptic, etc.; similar substance formed in combustion of tobacco etc.; ***beat the ~ out of,** (colloq.) knock the STUFFING out of; **a touch of the ~-brush,** admixture of Negro or Indian blood as shown by colour of skin; ***~'heel,** native of N. Carolina; ~ **macadam,** road-materials of stone or slag bound with tar; **~-paper,** tar-coated thick paper as building-material; **~-seal,** (N.Z. & Austral.) surface (a road) with tar macadam, road thus surfaced; **~-water,** cold infusion of tar formerly used as medicine. **2.** *v.t.* Cover with tar; ~ **and feather,** smear with tar and then cover with feathers as punishment; **~red with the same brush** or **stick,** having the same faults. [OE *te(o)ru,* = MLG *ter(e),* ON *tjara* f. Gmc **terw-* (**trew-* TREE)]

tar̄[2] *n.* (colloq.) Sailor. [abbr. of TARPAULIN]

tă'r(r)adĭddle *n.* (colloq.) Petty lie; pretentious nonsense. [18th c.; cf. DIDDLE]

taraki'hi (tar̄akē'hē), **tĕrakihi** (tĕrakē'), *n.* (N.Z.) Species of morwong widely used as food. [Maori]

tară'ntara. Var. of TARATANTARA.

tărantă'ss *n.* Springless four-wheeled Russian vehicle. [f. Russ. *tarantas*]

tărantĕ'lla, -ĕ'lle, *n.* (Music for) rapid whirling S. Ital. dance once held to be a cure for or effect of tarantism. [(F *tarantelle* f.) It. *tarantella* dim. f. as foll.]

tă'rantĭsm *n.* (Hist.) Dancing mania, esp. that originating in S. Italy among those who (thought they) had been bitten by the tarantula. [f. mod. L *tarantismus,* It. *tarantismo* (*Taranto* in S. Italy f. L *Tarentum*; see -ISM)]

tară'ntūla *n.* Large black spider of S. Europe whose bite was formerly held to cause tarantism; large hairy tropical spider. [med. L, f. It. *tarantola* (as prec.)]

tărată'ntara (*or* -ăntar̄'*a*) *n.* Sound of trumpet or bugle. [imit.; cf. TANTARA]

tară'xacum *n.* Herb of genus *Taraxacum,* e.g. dandelion; drug prepared from dried roots of dandelion. [med. L, f. Arab. *ṭarakšakūk* f. Pers. *talk* bitter + *chakūk* purslane]

tar̄bōō'sh *n.* Cap like fez, worn alone or as part of turban. [f. Egypt. Arab. *ṭarbūš,* ult. f. Pers. *sar-būš* head cover]

Tar̄denoi'sĭan (-z-) *a.* & *n.* (Archaeol.) (Of) a mesolithic culture using small flint implements. [f. *Tardenois* in N.E. France, where remains of it were found, + -IAN]

tar̄'dĭgrāde *a.* & *n.* (Zool.) **1.** Slow-moving (animal). **2.** (Minute aquatic arthropod) of order Tardigrada. [F, or f. L *tardigradus* (*tardus* slow, *gradi* walk)]

tar̄'d|ў *a.* Slow-moving, slow, sluggish; late, coming or done late, (*tardy retribution, amends, reform,* **to school*); (of person etc.) reluctant, hanging back; hence ~ĬLY[2] *adv.,* ~ĬNESS *n.* [f. F *tardif -ive* f. Rom. **tardivus* f. L *tardus* slow; see -IVE]

tar̄e[1] *n.* Vetch, esp. as corn-weed or fodder; (Bibl., in *pl.* in Matt. 13:25, 36) an injurious corn-weed. [ME, of unkn. orig.]

tar̄e[2] *n.,* & *v.t.* **1.** *n.* Allowance made for weight of box etc. in which goods are packed; weight of motor vehicle without fuel etc.; ~ **and tret,** arithmetical rule for computing tare etc. **2.** *v.t.* Ascertain weight of (box etc.). [ME f. F, = deficiency, tare, f. med. L *tara* f. Arab. *ṭarḥa* what is rejected (*ṭaraḥa* reject)]

tar̄e[3]. See TEAR[1].

tar̄ge *n.* (arch.) = foll. 4. [ME f. OF; see foll.]

tar̄'gėt (-g-) *n.* **1.** Circular stuffed pad with concentric circles painted on surface as mark in archery; similar usu. rectangular mark for firearms; anything that is fired at or made an objective of warlike operations; substance bombarded with particles, e.g. to generate X-rays; (fig.) objective, (minimum) result aimed at, (*export, fuel, savings, target*; *our target date is next July*); (fig.) person or thing serving as object *for* (scorn etc.). **2.** *Circular railway signal e.g. at a switch. **3.** Neck and breast of lamb as joint. **4.** Shield, buckler, esp. small round one. **5.** **~-card** (coloured like target, for keeping archer's score); ~ **practice** (in shooting at target). [ME, dim. of ME and OF *targe* f. Frank. **targa* shield, cogn. w. OE *targe, -a,* OHG *zarga,* ON *targa*]

Tar̄'gum *n.* Any of various ancient Aramaic paraphrases or interpretations of the Hebrew scriptures; hence ~IST (3) *n.* [f. Chald. *trgūm* interpretation (*trgēm* interpret)]

tă'rĭff *n.,* & *v.t.* **1.** *n.* List of duties or customs to be paid on imports or exports; such duties collectively; law imposing these; duty on particular class of goods; **preferential ~,** reduced duties on imports from favoured country; **retaliatory ~,** import duties levied by a nation to balance foreign duties imposed on its exports; ~ **reform,** (Hist.) removal of inequalities etc. in tariff, esp. with general aim of ‖increasing or *decreasing import duties; ~ **wall,** tariff-created national trade barrier.

2. List of charges (*railway, postal, hotel, tariff*); standard charges agreed between insurers etc. **3.** *v.t.* Make tariff of duties on (goods). [f. F *tarif* f. It. *tariffa* f. Turk. *tarife* f. Arab. *ta'rif(a)* (*'arrafa* notify)]

tar'latan *n.* Thin stiff open kind of muslin. [f. F *tarlatane*, earlier *tarn-*; prob. of Ind. orig.]

tar'măc *n.*, & *v.t.* (-ck-). **1.** *n.* = TAR[1] *macadam*; part of airfield surface made of tarmac. **2.** *v.t.* Apply tarmac to. [abbr.; **P** as noun]

tarn *n.* Small mountain lake. [ME *terne, tarne* f. ON **tarnu, tjörn*]

***tar'nal, *tarnā'tion,** *adjs.* & *advs.* (sl.) = DAMNED 2, 3. [dial. pr. of ETERNAL, DAMNATION]

tar'nish *v.* & *n.* **1.** *v.t.* Lessen or destroy the lustre of (*has been tarnished by damp*; (fig.) *a tarnished reputation*); hence ~ABLE *a.* **2.** *v.i.* Lose lustre (*will tarnish if exposed*; *does not easily tarnish*). **3.** *n.* Loss of lustre, blemish, stain; film of colour formed on exposed surface of mineral. [f. F *ternir* (*terne* dark); see -ISH[2]]

tar'ō *n.* (*pl.* ~**s**). Tropical plant (*Colocasia esculenta*) of arum family with tuberous root used as food esp. in Pacific islands. [Polynesian]

tă'rŏc, tă'rōt (-ō), *n.* Game played with, each card of, a pack of 78 cards used also for fortune--telling; (esp.) one of 22 trumps in this. [f. It. *tarocchi*, F *tarot*, of unkn. orig.]

tarp *n.* (U.S. & Austral. colloq.) Tarpaulin. [abbr.]

tar'păn *n.* Wild horse of central Asia. [Kirghiz Tartar]

tarpau'lin *n.* Waterproof cloth esp. of tarred canvas; sheet of this as covering; sailor's tarred or oilskin hat; (arch.) sailor. [prob. f. TAR[1] + PALL[1] + -ING[1] (3)]

Tarpei'an (-pē'an) *a.* ~ **rock,** cliff from which ancient-Roman criminals were hurled. [f. L *Tarpeius* (*Tarpeia*, who was said to be buried at foot of the rock) + -AN]

tar'pon *n.* Large silvery game-fish (*Megalops atlanticus*) common in Gulf of Mexico. [f. Du. *tarpoen*; orig. unkn.]

tă'rradiddle. See TARADIDDLE.

tă'rragon *n.* Plant (*Artemisia dracunculus*) allied to wormwood, with leaves used for flavouring salads etc. and in making a vinegar. [= med. L f. med. Gk *tarkhōn*, perh. thr. Arab. f. Gk *drakōn* dragon]*

Tărragō'na *n.* Spanish wine like port. [~ in Spain]

tarră's. See TRASS.

tar'rў[1] *a.* Of, like, smeared with, tar. [f. TAR[1] + -Y[2]]

tă'rrў[2] *v.* (literary). **1.** *v.i.* Remain, stay, lodge, (*at, in*, etc.); wait (*for*); delay in coming or appearing, be late. **2.** *v.t.* Wait for. [ME; orig. uncert.]

tar'sal. See TARSUS.

tar'sia *n.* = INTARSIA. [It.]

tar'sier *n.* Small large-eyed arboreal nocturnal E. Ind. animal like lemur. [F (as foll., from structure of foot)]

tar's|us *n.* (*pl.* ~**i** *pr.* -ī). **1.** Collection of bones between lower leg and metatarsus, ankle; shank of bird's leg; (Entom.) terminal segment of limb. **2.** Plate of connective tissue in eyelid. **3.** Hence ~AL *a.*, ~I-, ~O-, *comb. forms.* [mod. L, f. Gk *tarsos* flat of the foot, rim of eyelid]

tart[1] *a.* Sharp-tasting, acid; cutting, biting, (*a tart rejoinder*); hence ~'LY[2] *adv.*, ~'NESS *n.* [OE *teart*, of unkn. orig.]

tart[2] *n.* & *v.* **1.** *n.* ||Pie containing fruit or sweet filling (*apple, cherry, tart*); piece of pastry with jam etc. on top; so ~'LET *n.* **2.** (sl.) Girl or woman, esp. of immoral character; hence ~'Y[2] *a.* **3.** *v.t.* & *i.* (colloq.) ~ **up,** dress up like a tart (sense 2), deck gaudily, (fig.) smarten up. [ME f. OF *tarte*, = med. L *tarta*, of unkn. orig.; sense 2 prob. abbr. of *sweetheart*]

tar'tan[1] *n.* & *a.* Woollen fabric with stripes of various colours crossing at right angles esp. as worn by Scottish Highlanders; (other fabric) so striped; (Scottish plaid with) distinctive pattern of a clan. [perh. f. OF *tertaine, tiretaine*]

tar'tan[2] *n.* Lateen-sailed single-masted vessel used in Mediterranean. [f. F *tartane* f. It. *tartana*, perh. f. Arab. *ṭarida*]

tar'tar[1] *n.* **1.** Pink or red deposit of acid potassium tartrate from completely fermented wine, forming hard crust on side of cask, whence ~IZE (5) *v.t.*; ~ **emetic,** potassium antimony tartrate used as mordant and in medicine (formerly as emetic); CREAM[1] *of tartar.* **2.** Incrustation of saliva, calcium phosphate, etc., forming on the teeth. [ME, f. med. L f. med. Gk *tartaron*]

Tar'tar[2] *a.* & *n.* **1.** (Native) of Central Asia E. of Caspian Sea; (member) of a group of peoples including Turks, Mongols, etc.; ~ **fox,** corsac; **t~ sauce** (of mayonnaise, chopped gherkins, etc.); so **Tartar'IAN** *a.* **2.** *n.* Turkic language of Tartars. **3.** Violent-tempered or intractable or savage person (**catch a ~,** meet with person who is unexpectedly more than a match for one). [ME *tartre* f. OF *Tartare* or f. med. L *Tartarus*]

tar'tare *a.* ~ **sauce,** = TARTAR[2] *sauce.* [F, = prec.]

tartă'ric *a.* (Chem.) Of TARTAR[1] 1; ~ **acid,** organic acid present in numerous plants, esp. unripe grapes. [f. F *tartarique* f. med. L *tartarum*; see TARTAR[1], -IC]

Tar'tarus *n.* (Gk Myth.) Abyss below Hades where Titans were confined; place of punishment in Hades; so **Tartar'ean** *a.* [L, f. Gk *Tartaros*]

tar'trāte *n.* Salt of tartaric acid. [F (as TARTAR[1], -ATE[1])]

Tartu'f(f)|e (-ōō'f) *n.* Religious hypocrite; hence ~IAN *a.*, ~ISM (3) *n.* [character in Molière]

Tar'zan *n.* Man of great agility and powerful physique. [name of white man reared by African apes, in stories by E. R. Burroughs, Amer. writer d. 1950]

Tas. *abbr.* Tasmania.

task (tah-) *n.*, & *v.t.* **1.** *n.* Piece of work imposed; lesson to be learnt at school; piece of work voluntarily undertaken (*undertook the task of classification*); **take** person **to ~,** accuse him of fault, rebuke him *for* (do*ing*); ~ **force,** ~ **group,** specially organized unit for a special task; **~'master, ~'mistress,** one who imposes task or burden. **2.** *v.t.* Assign task to; exact labour from, put strain upon, tax, (person's powers, intellect, etc.). [ME, f. ONF *tasque* = OF *tasche* f. med. L *tasca*, perh. f. *taxa* f. L *taxare* TAX[1]]

Tăsmā'nian (-z-) *a.* & *n.* (Inhabitant or native) of Tasmania; ~ **devil,** savage-looking nocturnal carnivorous marsupial now confined to Tasmania; ~ **wolf,** wolflike nocturnal carnivorous marsupial now confined to Tasmania. [f. *Tasmania* f. A. J. *Tasman*, Du. navigator d. 1659 who discovered the island, + -IA[1], + -AN]

tăss[1] *n.* (Sc.) Small draught (*of* brandy etc.). [ME, f. OF *tasse* cup f. Arab. *ṭāsa* basin f. Pers. *tast*]

Tăss[2] *n.* Telegraphic news-agency of the Soviet Union. [f. initials of Russ. title]

tă'ssel[1] *n.* & *v.* (||-ll-). **1.** *n.* Tuft of loosely hanging threads or cords as ornament for cushion, cap, etc.; tassel-like head of some plants, esp. staminate inflorescence at top of maize stalk. **2.** *v.t.* Furnish with tassel. **3.** *v.i.* *(Of maize etc.) form tassels. [ME, f. OF *tas(s)el* clasp, of unkn. orig.]

tă'ssel[2] *n.* Small piece of stone, wood, etc., supporting end of beam or joist. [OF, f. pop. L **tassellus* f. L *taxillus* small die & *tessella* (see TESSELLATE)]

tă'ssĭe *n.* (Sc.) Small cup. [f. TASS[1] + -IE]

tāste[1] *v.* **1.** *v.t.* Learn flavour of (food etc., or abs.) by taking it into the mouth (*do taste this cheese*); examine (teas, wines, etc.) thus. **2.** (esp. w. neg.) Eat (even a) small portion of (*has not tasted food for days*). **3.** Perceive the flavour of (*can taste nothing when you have a cold; fancy I taste garlic*). **4.** (arch.) Relish, enjoy, (*cannot taste a joke against himself*). **5.** Experience, have experience of, (*shall not taste death; has never tasted success*). **6.** Hence ~'ABLE (-ta-) *a.* **7.** *v.i.* Have specified flavour (*tastes sour*); ~ **of,** (of food etc., or fig.) have flavour or smack of (*tastes of mint*), (arch.) = sense 2 or 5. [ME, = touch, taste, f. OF *taster* touch, try, taste, f. Rom. **tastare*, perh. f. L *tangere* touch + *gustare* taste]

tāste[2] *n.* **1.** Sensation caused in tongue etc. by contact of some soluble things, flavour, (*cannot endure the taste of onions; white of egg has no taste*); **bad** or **nasty ~ in the mouth,** (fig.) unpleasant after-feeling. **2.** Faculty of perceiving this sensation; **~-bud,** group of cells in epithelium of tongue etc. through which this faculty operates. **3.** Small portion (*of* food, or fig.) taken as sample; slight sensation or experience thus received (**a** ~ *of the whip* etc., enough to show how it feels). **4.** Liking, predilection, (*has no taste for sweet things; a taste for drawing, scenery, argument; is not to my taste; tastes differ; there is no accounting for tastes*); *add pepper, garnish,* **to ~**, in the amount that gives the desired result. **5.** Faculty of discerning and enjoying beauty or other excellence esp. in art and literature, or appropriateness of conduct, (*a man of taste; good, bad, taste*). **6.** Disposition or execution of work of art, choice of language, conduct, etc., dictated by or seen in the light of this faculty, (*composed in admirable taste; the remark was in bad taste*). [ME, f. OF *tast* (*taster*; see prec.)]

tā'steful (-tf-) *a.* (Of person, work of art, etc.) having, showing, done in, good taste; hence ~LY[2] *adv.*, ~NESS *n.* [f. prec. + -FUL]

tā'stelėss (-tl-) *a.* Having no flavour; uninteresting; lacking artistic taste; (of language, conduct, etc.) not in good taste; hence ~LY[2] *adv.*, ~NESS *n.* [f. TASTE[2] + -LESS]

tā'ster *n.* In vbl senses; person employed to judge teas, wines, etc., by taste (COPY[1]-*taster*); (Hist.) person employed to taste food before it was touched by his employer, esp. as precaution against poison; small shallow cup used by wine-taster; instrument for extracting small sample from within a cheese. [ME, f. AF *tastour*, OF *tasteur* (*taster*; see TASTE[1])]

tā'st|y̆ *a.* (colloq.) Savoury, of pleasant flavour, appetizing; hence ~ĬLY[2] *adv.*, ~ĬNESS *n.* [f. TASTE[2] + -Y[2]]

tăt[1] *v.* (-tt-). **1.** *v.i.* Do tatting. **2.** *v.t.* Make by tatting. [19th c.; orig. unkn.]

tăt[2] *n.* Tattiness; tatty thing(s) or person. [back form. f. TATTY[2]]

tăt[3]. See TIT[2].

ta-ta' (tătah') *int.* (childish or colloq.) Goodbye. [19th c.; orig. unkn.]

tata'mĭ (-ah'-) *n.* Japanese standard-sized mat; unit of room-size in Japan. [Jap.]

Tatar. Var. of TARTAR[2] 1.

tā'ter *n.* (vulg.) Potato. [abbr.]

tă'tler. Var. (arch.) of TATTLER 1.

ta'tou (tah'tōō) *n.* Armadillo. [Tupi]

tă'tter *n.* (usu. in *pl.*) Rag, irregularly torn piece, of cloth, paper, etc.; (fig.) useless remains (*left his argument in tatters*); **~dema'lion** (-dĭmā'lĭon), ragamuffin; hence ~ED[2] (-erd), ~Y[2], *adjs.* [ME, f. ON **taturr*, pl. *tötrar* rags]

Tă'ttersall *n.* ~ **(check)**, pattern of coloured lines forming squares like tartan. [f. R. ~, Engl. horseman d. 1795]

tă'tting *n.* Kind of knotted lace made by hand with small shuttle and used for trimming etc. [19th c.; orig. unkn.]

tă'ttle *v.* & *n.* **1.** *v.i.* Prattle, chatter, gossip idly. **2.** *v.t.* Utter (words) idly; **~-tale,** telltale. **3.** *n.* Trivial talk. [ME, f. MFlem. *tatelen, tateren*, imit.]

tă'ttler *n.* **1.** Prattler, gossip, (arch. **tatler,** esp. (*T*~) as name of periodical). **2.** Vociferous sandpiper of genus *Totanus* etc. [f. prec. + -ER[1]]

tattōō'[1] *n.*, & *v.i.* **1.** *n.* Evening drum or bugle signal recalling soldiers to quarters; elaboration of this with music and marching as entertainment; drumming or rapping; **devil's** ~, idle drumming or tapping with fingers etc. **2.** *v.i.* Rap quickly and repeatedly; beat the devil's tattoo (*on*). [17th c. *tap-too* f. Du. *taptoe*, lit. 'close the tap' (of the cask)]

tattōō'[2] *v.t.*, & *n.* **1.** *v.t.* Mark (skin etc.) with indelible patterns by inserting pigments in punctures; make (pattern) thus; hence ~ER[1], ~IST (3), *ns.* **2.** *n.* Such mark. [v. f. n. f. Polynesian]

tattōō'[3] *n.* (Anglo-Ind.) Native-bred pony. [f. Hindi *ṭaṭṭū*]

tă'tty̆[1] *n.* (Anglo-Ind.) Matting of cuscus-grass roots hung and kept wet to cool and perfume the air. [f. Hindi *ṭaṭṭi* wicker frame]

tă'tt|y̆[2] *a.* Ragged, untidy, shabby; tawdry, fussily ornate; inferior; hence ~ĬLY[2] *adv.*, ~ĬNESS *n.* [orig. Sc., = shaggy, app. rel. to OE *tættec* rag, TATTER]

tau (*or* -ow) *n.* Nineteenth Greek letter (T, τ) = t; ~ **cross** (T-shaped). [ME f. Gk]

taught. See TEACH.

taunt *v.t.*, & *n.* **1.** *v.t.* Reproach, upbraid, (person etc. *with* conduct etc.) contemptuously. **2.** *n.* Contemptuous reproach. [16th c., in phr. *taunt for taunt* f. F *tant pour tant* tit for tat, hence smart rejoinder]

taupe (tōp) *n.* Grey colour with brownish or other tinge. [F, = MOLE[2]]

taur'ine *a.* Bull-like, bovine. [f. L *taurinus* (*taurus* bull; see -INE[1])]

taurŏ'machy̆ (-kĭ) *n.* (arch.) Bullfight(ing). [f. Gk *tauromakhia* (*tauros* bull, *makhē* fight); see -Y[1]]

Taur'us *n.* Sign of the ZODIAC, the Bull. [ME f. L, = bull]

taut *a.* (Of rope etc.) tight, not slack; (of ship etc.) in good order or condition; (of nerves etc.) tense; strict or severe as regards duty; hence ~'EN[6] *v.t.* & *i.*, ~'LY[2] *adv.*, ~'NESS *n.* [ME *touht, togt*, perh. = TOUGH, infl. by *tog-* p.p. st. of obs. *tee* (OE *tēon*) pull]

tau'to- *comb. form.* The same, as: **~chrone** (-krōn) [f. Gk *khronos* time], curve on which body starting from state of rest under given force will reach fixed point in same time from whatever point it starts; **~phony** (-ŏ'f-), repetition of same sound. [Gk, f. *tauto, to auto* the same]

tautŏ'g *n.* Food and game fish (*Tautoga onitis*) of Atlantic coast of N. America. [f. Narraganset *taut-auog* pl.]

tautŏ'log|y̆ *n.* Saying of the same thing twice over in different words, esp. as fault of style, (e.g. *arrived one after the other in succession*); statement necessarily true; hence **tautolŏ'g-IC(AL)** *adjs.*, ~IST (1) *n.*, ~IZE (2) *v.i.*, ~OUS *a.* [f. LL f. Gk TAUTO(*logia* -LOGY)]

tau'tomer̃ *n.* (Chem.) Organic compound reacting as if its molecule had more than one structure; hence ~IC (-mĕ'r-) *a.*, ~ISM (2) (-ŏ'm-) *n.* [f. TAUTO- + -MER]

tă'vern *n.* (literary). Inn or public house. [ME, f. OF *taverne* f. L *taberna* hut, tavern]

||**T.A.V.R.** Var. of T. & A.V.R.

taw[1] *v.t.* Make (hide) into leather without use of tannin, esp. by soaking in solution of alum and salt; hence ~'ER[1], ~'ERY (3), *ns.* [OE *tawian*, = MDu., MLG *touwen*, OHG *zouwen*, Goth. *taujan* do, f. Gmc **taw(ō)jan*]

taw[2] *n.* Large streaked etc. marble for shooting in game of marbles; game played with taws; line from which players propel marbles. [18th c.; orig. unkn.]

taw'dr|y̆ *a.* & *n.* **1.** *a.* Showy but worthless, gaudy, having too much or ill-judged ornament; hence ~ĭLY[2] *adv.*, ~ĭNESS *n.* **2.** *n.* Cheap or excessive or tasteless finery. [a. f. n., short for *tawdry lace*, orig. *St. Audrey's lace*, (*Audrey = Etheldrida*, patron saint of Ely)]

taw'n|y̆ *a.* Brownish-yellow, brownish-orange, tan-coloured; **~y eagle,** brownish Afr. & Asian eagle (*Aquila rapax*); **~y owl,** reddish-brown European owl; hence ~ĭNESS *n.* [ME, f. AF *tauné*, OF *tané* (*tan* TAN[1])]

taws(e) (-z) *n. sing.* or *pl.* (Sc.) Thong with slit end for chastising children. [app. pl. of obs. *taw* tawed leather, f. TAW[1]]

tăx[1] *v.t.* **1.** Impose tax on (subjects, citizens, etc., commodity, land, etc.) pay tax on (*income taxed at source*); **~ed cart,** (Hist.) type of open cart for trade etc., on which little or no tax was payable. **2.** Make demands upon, demand exertion from, (person's resources, powers, ingenuity, etc.). **3.** (Law). Examine and (dis)allow items of, assess, (costs etc.); ||**~'ing-master,** law-court official who taxes costs. **4.** Charge (person *with* fault, *with* doing); call to account. **5.** Hence ~ABI'LITY, **~able**NESS (-beln-), *ns.*, ~'ABLE *a.* [ME, f. OF *taxer* f. L *taxare* censure, charge, compute, perh. f. Gk *tassō* fix]

tăx[2] *n.* Contribution levied on or *on* persons, property, or business, for support of national or *local government, oppressive or burdensome obligation, (DIRECT[2], INCOME, INDIRECT, POLL[1]-, ||PURCHASE[1], VALUE-*added*, *tax*); strain, heavy demand, (*up*)*on* (person, his energies etc.); **~-collector,** official who collects taxes; **~-deductible,** (of expenses) that may be paid out of income before deduction of income tax; **~-dodger,** (colloq.) one who evades paying taxes; **~-farmer,** one who buys from government the right to collect certain taxes; **~-free,** exempt from taxes; **~-gatherer,** (arch.) tax-collector; **~ haven,** country etc. where income tax is low; **~'payer,** one who pays taxes; **~ return,** declaration of income for taxation purposes; *tax* YEAR; hence ~'LESS *a.* [ME, f. prec.]

tăxā'tion *n.* Imposition or payment of tax(es); taxing of costs. [ME, f. AF *taxacioun*, OF *taxation* f. L *taxatio -onis* (*taxare*; see TAX[1], -ATION)]

tă'xĭ *n.* & *v.* (**~ing** *or* **ta'xying**). **1.** *n.* **~(-cab),** motor car plying for hire and usu. fitted with taximeter; other motor car of similar pattern; boat etc. similarly used; **~-dancer,** dance-partner whose services may be hired; **~-driver, ~-man,** driver of taxi. **2.** *v.i.* & *t.* Go or convey in taxi. **3.** *v.i.* (Aeron., of aircraft or pilot) go along ground or water under machine's own power before or after flying. [abbr. of *taximeter cab*]

tă'xĭderm|y̆ *n.* Art of preparing and mounting skins of animals with lifelike effect; hence **tăxĭder'm**AL, **tăxĭder'm**IC, *adjs.*, ~IST (3) *n.* [f. Gk TAXIS + *derma* skin; see -Y[1]]

tă'xĭmēter *n.* Automatic device fitted to taxi-cab etc. and indicating fare due for distance travelled up to present moment in journey. [f. F *taximètre* (*taxe* tariff, TAX[2]; see -METER)]

tă'xĭs *n.* (Surg.) manual pressure applied to restore parts to their place; (Gk Ant.) variously sized division of troops; (Gram. & Rhet.) arrangement; (Biol.) movement of organism in particular direction in response to external stimulus. [Gk (*tassō* arrange)]

tă'x|on *n.* (*pl.* **~a**). Taxonomic group, esp. genus or smaller group. [back form. f. foll.]

tăxŏ'nom|y̆ *n.* (Principles of) classification, esp. in biology; hence or cogn. ~IST (3) *n.*, **tăxonŏ'm**IC(AL) *adjs.* [f. F *taxonomie* f. as TAXIS + Gk *-nomia* distribution]

ta'zza (tah'tsa) *n.* Saucer-shaped cup, esp. one mounted on a foot. [It.]

T.B. *abbr.* torpedo-boat; tubercle bacillus, hence (colloq.) tuberculosis.

Tb *symb.* terbium.

T-bone. See T.

tbsp. *abbr.* tablespoonful.

Tc *symb.* technetium.

T.C.D. *abbr.* Trinity College, Dublin.

T.D. *abbr.* Territorial (Officer's) Decoration; (Ir.) Teachta Dala, Member of the Dáil.

tē, ti[2] (tē), *n.* (Mus.) Seventh note of scale in movable-doh system; the note B in fixed-doh system. [alt. f. *si*, F f. It., perh. f. *S*ancte *I*ohannes; see GAMUT]

tea *n.* & *v.* **1.** *n.* **~(-plant),** evergreen shrub or small tree of camellia genus with fragrant white flowers grown in China, India, etc. **2.** Leaves of this dried and prepared for use in various ways; (sl.) marijuana. **3.** Infusion of tea-leaves as beverage; infusion etc. of leaves of other plants or of other substance (*beef*, *camomile*, *tea*); **~ and sympathy,** (colloq.) friendly treatment of the unhappy. **4.** (**Afternoon**) ~, light afternoon meal with tea; (**early morning**) ~ (usu. drunk before getting up); ||(**high**) ~, evening meal with tea and usu. meat etc. **5. ~-bag,** small permeable bag of tea-leaves for infusion; **~-ball** (of perforated metal, to contain tea for infusion); **~-bread,** light or sweet bread for eating at tea; *tea*-BREAK[2]; *tea*-CADDY[1]; **~'cake,** ||light flat usu. sweet bun eaten at tea, often toasted, *small sweet cake; **~ ceremony,** elaborate Japanese ritual of serving and drinking tea; **~-chest,** light cubical wooden box lined with sheets of lead or tin, in which tea is exported; **~-cloth,** (1) cloth for tea-table, (2) tea-towel; *tea*-COSY; **~'cup,** cup from which tea is drunk (STORM *in a teacup*), whence ~'*cup*FUL 2 *n.*; **~ dance,** *thé dansant*; **~-fight,** (colloq.) tea-party; **~-garden** (in which tea is grown, or served to the public); **~-gown,** woman's long loose ornamental gown worn at tea etc.; **~-house** (in which tea etc. is served in China and Japan); **~-kettle** (used in making tea); **~-leaf,** leaf of tea esp. (in *pl.*) after infusion or soaking; **~-party** (at which tea is served); **~-planter,** proprietor or cultivator of tea plantation; **~'pot,** spouted vessel in which tea is made and from which it is poured; **~-room** (for serving tea etc. to public); **~-rose** (with scent compared to that of tea); *tea*-SERVICE[1] or **~-set**; **~-shop,** (1) = *tea-room*, (2) shop selling tea (sense 2); *tea*SPOON[1], whence ~'*spoon*FUL 2 *n.*; *tea*-TABLE; **~-things,** things used for serving tea; **~-time** (at which tea is served); **~-towel** (for drying washed crockery etc.); **~-tray** (on which tea-set is used or carried); **~-tree,** (Austral.) tree of genus *Leptospermum* etc. whose leaves are used as substitute for tea; **~-trolley,** small wheeled table to carry tea-things; **~-urn** (for boiling or holding water for tea); **~-wagon,** = *tea-trolley*. **6.** *v.i.* Take tea. **7.** *v.t.* Give tea to (person). [17th c. *tay*, *tey*, prob. f. Du. *tee* f. Chin. (Amoy dial.) *t'e*, = Mandarin dial. *ch'a*]

teach *v.* (**taught** *pr.* tawt). **1.** *v.t.* Enable or cause (person etc. *to* do) by instruction and training (*teach him to swim*; *dog was taught to beg*; *misfortune has taught him to be thankful for small mercies*); compel (person) by punishment etc. *to* do (*this will teach you to speak the truth*); (colloq.) make (person) disinclined (*to* offend etc.; *I will teach him to meddle in my affairs*). **2.** Give lessons at school or elsewhere in or on (subject, game, instrument, etc., *to* person, or w. double obj.; *taught him Greek*; *teaches Greek for a living*; *teaches the violin*; *teach me bridge*; *was never taught music*; *music was never taught to a more unwilling pupil*; *it is time the boy was taught something*); *~ **school,** be a teacher in a school. **3.** Give instruction to, educate; **~-in,** series of lectures and discussions on subject of public interest. **4.** Explain, show, state by way of instruction, (fact etc., *how, that,* etc., *to* person, or w. double obj.; *taught that we must forgive our enemies*; *teach him how to swim*; *I was taught that two sides of a triangle were greater than the third*; *was taught otherwise*; *was never taught this*; *who taught you that?*). **5.** *v.i.* Be a teacher, give lessons esp. at school. **6.** Hence ~′ER[1] *n.* [OE *tǣcan* f. Gmc **taikjan* (**t(a)ik-* show f. IE **d(e)ig-*)]

tea′ch|able *a.* Apt to learn, docile; (of subject etc.) that can be taught; hence ~ABI′LITY, **~able**NESS (-bəln-), *ns.* [ME, f. prec. + -ABLE]

tea′chĭng *n.* In vbl senses; what is taught, doctrines, (*the teachings of the Church*); profession of teacher; ~ **hospital** (where medical students are taught); **~-machine,** mechanical device for giving instruction. [ME, f. TEACH + -ING[1]]

teak *n.* (Orig. E. Ind. tree, *Tectona grandis*, with) heavy durable timber that does not warp or shrink, much used in shipbuilding. [f. Port. *teca* f. Malayalam *tēkka*]

teal *n.* (*pl.* same). Small freshwater duck of genus *Anas* etc. [rel. to MDu. *tēling*, of unkn. orig.]

team *n.* & *v.* **1.** *n.* Two or more draught animals harnessed together; one animal or more with harness and vehicle. **2.** Set of players forming one side in game (*cricket, golf, team*); set of persons working together; **~-mate,** fellow member of a team; ~ **spirit,** willingness to act for group rather than individual benefit; **~-work,** combined effort, organized co-operation. **3.** *v.t.* Harness (horses etc.) in team; ~ **(up)**, join (one) as team *with* (another). **4.** *v.i.* ~ **(up),** join in team or in common action (*with*). [OE *tēam* offspring, = OS *tōm*, OHG *zoum*, ON *taumr* bridle, f. Gmc **taumaz* prob. f. **taug-* pull; cf. TOW[1]]

tea′mster *n.* Driver of a team; *lorry-driver. [f. prec. + -STER]

tea′poy *n.* Small three- or four-legged table esp. for tea. [f. Hindi *tīn, tir-* three + Pers. *pāī* foot; sense and spelling infl. by TEA]

tear[1] (tār) *v.* (**tore** *or* arch. **tare; torn**) & *n.* **1.** *v.t.* Pull apart with some force, rend, lacerate, (*tore up the letter*; *has torn his coat*; *tear it in half, in two, in pieces*; *torn to pieces by a tiger*; (fig.) *country was torn by factions, heart torn by conflicting emotions, was torn* (distracted at having to make a choice) *between love and duty*); make (hole, rent) thus; ~ **it,** (sl.) spoil one's chances, foil one's plans, (*that's torn it*). **2.** Pull violently or with some force (lit. or fig.) esp. *down, off,* etc., (*tore down the notice*; *tear out a page*; *tear off the cover*; *tree torn up by the roots*); remove (person) forcibly *from*; ~ one**self away,** go away despite strong allurement to stay; ~ one's **hair,** pull it in anger or perplexity or despair. **3.** *v.i.* Pull violently or with some force *at* etc.; run or walk or travel hurriedly or impetuously (*tore down the hill*); undergo tearing (*tore down the middle*). **4. ~′away,** (*a.*) impetuous, (*n.*) hooligan, ruffian; **~-sheet,** sheet torn from magazine etc. to provide copy of one page. **5.** *n.* Hole made or damage caused by tearing; torn part of cloth etc. [OE *teran*, = OHG *zeran*, Goth. *-tairan* f. Gmc **teran* f. IE **der-*]

tear[2] *n.* **1.** ~**(-drop)**, drop of clear saline liquid ordinarily serving to moisten and wash the eye but falling from it as result of grief or other emotion or of coughing or laughter, (*the tears fell* or *rolled down her cheeks*; *wept bitter tears of remorse*; *laughed till the tears came*; *tears were her only argument*; *a tear-stained face*); **in ~s,** weeping; **without ~s,** (fig.) presented so as to be easily learned etc.; CROCODILE *tears*. **2.** Tearlike thing, e.g. drop of fluid, solid drop of resin etc. **3. ~-duct** (carrying tears to eye or from eye to nose); **~-gas,** lachrymatory gas used in warfare etc. to disable opponents or make crowds disperse; **~-jerker,** (colloq.) song, story, film, etc., calculated to evoke sadness or sympathy. [OE *tēar*, = OHG *zah(h)ar*, ON *tár*, Goth. *tagr* f. IE **dakru-*]

tear′ful *a.* Shedding tears; (of event, news, etc.) mournful, sad; hence ~LY[2] *adv.*, ~NESS *n.* [f. prec. + -FUL]

tear′ĭng (tār′-) *a.* In vbl senses; violent, overwhelming, (*tearing hurry, pace, rage*). [f. TEAR[1] + -ING[1]]

tear′lĕss *a.* Not shedding tears; hence ~LY[2] *adv.*, ~NESS *n.* [f. TEAR[2] + -LESS]

tear′ȳ *a.* (colloq.) Tearful. [ME, f. TEAR[2] + -Y[2]]

tease (-z) *v.t.*, & *n.* **1.** *v.t.* Irritate playfully or maliciously, vex, with jests, questions, or petty annoyances; *importune (person *for* thing, *to* do); pick into separate fibres, comb, card, (wool, flax, etc.); dress (cloth etc.) with teasels; ~ **out,** separate by disentangling (lit. or fig.). **2.** *n.* (colloq.) Person fond of teasing others. [OE *tǣsan*, = MDu., MLG *tēzen*, OHG *zeisan* f. WG **taisjan*]

tea′sel (-z-), **tea′zel, tea′zle,** *n.*, & *v.t.* **1.** *n.* Plant of genus *Dipsacus* with large prickly heads that are dried and used in dressing cloth to form nap; such head; device used as substitute for teasels. **2.** *v.t.* Dress (cloth) with teasels; hence **tea′sel**ER[1] (-z-) *n.* [OE *tǣs(e)l*, = OHG *zeisala* (as prec.; see -LE 1)]

tea′ser (-z-) *n.* In vbl senses; teasing person; (colloq.) difficult question or problem or task, thing hard to deal with. [ME, f. TEASE + -ER[1]]

teat *n.* Mammary nipple esp. of animal; thing resembling this, esp. device of rubber etc. for sucking milk from bottle. [ME f. OF *tete*, prob. of Gmc orig., replacing TIT[3]]

tea′zel, -zle. See TEASEL.

tĕc *n.* (sl.) Detective (novel). [abbr.]

Tĕc(h) (-k) *n.* (colloq.) Technical college, institute, or school. [abbr.]

tĕchnē′tium (-knē′shum) *n.* (Chem.) Artificially produced radioactive metallic element. [mod. L, f. Gk *tekhnētos* artificial (*tekhnē* art) + -IUM]

tĕ′chnĭc (-k-) *n.* Technique; (usu. in *pl.*) technology; (in *pl.*) technical terms, details, methods, etc.; hence ~IST (3) *n.* [f. L f. Gk *tekhnikos* (*tekhnē* art; see -IC)]

tĕ′chnĭcal (-kn-) *a.* Of or in a particular art, science, handicraft, etc., (*technical terms, skill, difficulty*); of, for, in, applied science or vocational training (*technical college, education, school*); (of book etc.) (1) dealing with applied science, (2) using technical terms; legally such, in the strict legal interpretation, (*technical assault*); ~ **hitch,** interruption or breakdown due to mechanical failure; ~ **knock-out,** (Boxing) referee's termination of fight on grounds of boxer's inability to continue, his opponent being declared winner; hence ~LY² *adv.*, ~NESS *n.* [f. as prec. + -AL]

tĕchnĭcă'lĭtў (-kn-) *n.* Technicalness; technical expression, (merely) technical distinction, etc., (*legal technicalities*; *was acquitted on a technicality*). [f. prec. + -ITY]

tĕchnĭ'cian (-knĭ'shan) *n.* Person skilled in technique of an art or craft; person expert in practical application of science. [f. TECHNIC + -IAN]

Tĕ'chnĭcolor (-knĭkŭl-) *n.* Process of colour cinematography in which colours are separately but simultaneously recorded and then transferred to a single positive print; (fig.) vivid colour, artificial brilliance; hence ~ED² (-*erd*) *a.* [*P; f. TECHNICAL + COLOR¹]

tĕchni'que (-knē'k) *n.* Mode of artistic execution in music, painting, etc.; mechanical skill in art; means of achieving one's purpose, esp. skilfully. [F, as TECHNIC]

tĕchnŏ'cracў (-kn-) *n.* Organization and management of a country's industrial resources by technical experts for the good of the whole community; hence **tĕ'chno**CRAT (-kn-) *n.*, advocate of this, **tĕchnocră'tic** (-kn-) *a.* [f. Gk *tekhnē* art + -O- + -CRACY]

tĕchnŏ'log|ў (-k-) *n.* (Science of) practical or industrial art(s); ethnological study of development of such arts; application of science; hence **tĕchno**LO'GICAL (-kn-) *a.*, ~IST (3) *n.* [f. Gk *tekhnologia* systematic treatment (*tekhnē* art; see -LOGY)]

tĕ'chў. See TETCHY.

tĕctŏ'n|ĭc *a.* Of building or construction; (Geol.) relating to deformation of earth's crust or to structural changes caused thereby; hence ~ICALLY *adv.*, ~ICS *n.*, whole art of producing useful and beautiful buildings, (Geol.) structural features as a whole. [f. LL f. Gk *tektonikos* (*tektōn -onos* carpenter; see -IC)]

tĕctŏr'ĭal *a.* Forming a covering, esp. ~ **membrane** (of inner ear, covering organ of CORTI). [f. L *tectorium* a cover (as foll.) + -AL]

tĕ'ctrĭ|x *n.* (*pl.* **~ces** *pr.* -sēz, *or* -ī'-). (Ornith.), = COVERT². [mod. L, f. L *tegere tect-* cover; see -TRIX]

tĕd¹ *v.t.* (-dd-). Turn over and spread out (grass, hay) to dry; hence **~'d**ER¹ (1, 2) *n.* [ME, f. ON *tethja* spread manure, (*tad* dung, *toddi* small piece)]

‖**Tĕd²** *n.* Teddy boy. [abbr.]

Tĕ'ddў *n.* **1.** ‖~ (**boy**), (colloq.) youth affecting Edwardian (sense 2) style of dress. **2.** ~ **bear,** child's toy bear. [f. pet-name *Teddy* for (sense 1) *Edward*, or (sense 2) *Theodore* Roosevelt, U.S. President d. 1919 famous as bear-hunter]

Te Deum (tē dē'*um or* tā dā'-) *n.* (Music for) hymn beginning *Te Deum laudamus*, 'Thee, God, we praise', sung at morning service, or on special occasions as thanksgiving; expression of thanksgiving or exultation. [L]

tē'dĭous *a.* Wearisome, irksome, tiresomely long; hence ~LY² *adv.*, ~NESS *n.* [ME, f. OF *tedieus* or f. LL *taediosus* (as foll.; see -OUS)]

tē'dĭum *n.* Tediousness. [f. L *taedium* (*taedēre* to weary)]

tee¹. Var. of T.

tee² *n.* & *v.* **1.** *n.* Mark aimed at in quoits, bowls, curling. **2.** (Golf). Cleared space from which ball is struck at beginning of play for each hole; small pile of sand or small appliance of wood, rubber, etc., on which ball is placed before being thus struck. **3.** *v.t.* Place (ball) on golf tee. **4.** *v.i.* ~ **off,** play ball from tee, (fig.) start, begin; ~ **up,** place ball on tee. [sense 1 perh. = prec.; sense 2 f. obs. *teaz*, of unkn. orig.]

tee³ *n.* Umbrella-shaped usu. gilded ornament crowning stupa or pagoda. [f. Burm. *h'ti* umbrella]

teehee'. Var. of TEHEE.

teem¹ *v.i.* Be prolific, be stocked to overflowing *with*, (*forests teem with snakes*; *book teems with blunders*); be abundant (*fish teem in these waters*). [OE *tēman* etc. f. **taumjan* f. Gmc **taumaz* TEAM]

teem² *v.* **1.** *v.t.* (dial. or tech.) Empty, discharge, pour out, (vesssel, cart, coal, molten metal, etc.); hence ~'ER¹ *n.* **2.** *v.i.* (Of water etc.) flow copiously, pour. [ME *tēmen* f. ON *tœma* (*tómr* a. empty)]

teen *n.* (arch.) Grief, misfortune. [OE *tēon*(*a*), = OS *tiono*, ON *tjón*]

-teen *suf.* = TEN, added to the numerals 3 to 9 to form the names of those from 13 to 19. [OE *-*tiene*, -*tēne*, -*tȳne*, = OS -*tein*, OHG -*zehan*, Goth. -*taihun*]

tee'n-āg|e *a.* Pertaining to or characteristic of teenagers; so ~ED¹ (-jd) *a.* [f. TEENS + AGE¹]

tee'nāger *n.* Person in teens. [f. as prec. + -ER¹]

teens (-z) *n. pl.* Years of one's age from 13 to 19 (*boy in his teens*). [f. -TEEN + -S¹]

tee'nsў(**-weensў**), **tee'nў**(**-weenў**), *adjs.* (childish or colloq.) Tiny. [var. of TINY]

tee'nў-bŏpper *n.* (colloq.) Teen-age girl who follows latest fashions in clothes, pop music, etc. [f. TEENS + -Y³ + BOPPER]

tee'pee. See TEPEE.

tee'ter *v.i.*, & *n.* **1.** *v.i.* Totter; move unsteadily; *see-saw. **2.** *n.* *See-saw. [var. of dial. *titter*]

teeth. See TOOTH.

teeth|e (-dh) *v.i.* Grow or cut (esp. milk-) teeth; hence ~'ING¹ *n.* (**~ing-ring,** small ring for infant to bite on while teething; **~ing troubles,** initial difficulties in an enterprise etc.). [ME, f. prec.]

teetō'tal *a.* Of or advocating total abstinence from intoxicants, whence ~ISM (3) *n.*; (U.S. colloq., or dial.) total, entire, whence ~LY² *adv.* [redupl. of TOTAL]

teetō'taller, *-aler, *n.* Total abstainer, advocate of total abstinence, from intoxicants. [f. prec. + -ER¹]

teetō'tum *n.* Children's four-sided top with sides lettered to determine gain or loss by the spinner; any top spun with the fingers (**like a** ~, spinning). [f. *T* (the letter on one side) + L *totum* the whole (stakes), for which this letter stood]

tĕff *n.* African cereal (*Eragrostis abyssinica*). [f. Amh. *têf*]

tĕg *n.* Sheep in its second year. [ME **tegge* (in place-names), f. OE **tegga*, OSw. *takka* ewe]

tĕ'gūlar *a.* Of or (arranged) like tiles; hence ~LY² *adv.* [f. L *tegula* tile (*tegere* cover) + -AR¹]

tĕ'gūment *n.* Natural covering of (part of) animal body; hence ~AL, ~ARY¹, (-ĕ'n-) *adjs.* [f. L *tegumentum* (*tegere* cover; see -MENT)]

tēhee' *n.*, & *v.i.* **1.** *n.* Restrained or contemptuous laugh. **2.** *v.i.* Laugh thus, titter. [imit.]

tehsil. Var. of TAHSIL.

teind (tēnd) *n.* (Sc. & N. Engl.) Tithe; (Sc., usu. in *pl.*) portion of laity's estates assessable for clergy stipend. [ME *tende* = TENTH]

tĕknŏ'nўm|ў *n.* (Anthrop.) Practice of naming parent from child; hence ~OUS *a.* [f. Gk *teknon* child + -*ōnumos* -named (cf. ANONYMOUS) + -Y¹]

tĕ'ktīte *n.* Small roundish glassy body of unknown origin such as occur in various regions of the earth. [f. G *tektit* f. Gk *tēktos* molten (*tēkō* melt); see -ITE¹]

Tel. *abbr.* Telegraph(ic); Telephone.

tĕlaesth|ē'sĭa (-lĭ-), ***tĕlĕsth|ē'sĭa,** (-zĭa), *n.* (Psych.) Direct perception of distant occurrences or objects that is not effected by the recognized senses; so ~ĕ'tic *a.* [mod. L, f. as TELE- + Gk *aisthēsis* perception + -IA[1]]

tĕlamon *n.* (*pl.* **~es** *pr.* -ō'nēz). (Archit.) Male figure used as pillar to support entablature. [f. L f. Gk *telamōnes* pl. of *Telamōn*, name of a mythical hero]

tĕ'lė- *comb. form.* **1.** Far (esp. in names of instruments producing or recording results etc. at a distance; *telemeter, telethermo'meter*). **2.** Television, as: **~cast,** (transmit) television broadcast programme or item: **~caster,** television broadcaster; **~cine, ~film,** cinema film transmitted by television; **~ge'nic,** suitable for being televised; **~prompter,** device that slowly unrolls (television) speaker's text, in large print, out of view of audience [*P]; **~record** *v.t.*, record (item or programme to be televised), whence *~recording* n.; **~vi'sual,** pertaining to television. [sense 1 f. Gk *tēlē-* (*tēle* far off); sense 2 f. TELEVISION]

tĕ'lėcămera *n.* Television camera; telephotographic camera. [f. TELE- + CAMERA]

tĕlėcommūnĭcā'tion *n.* Communication over long distances by cable, telegraph, telephone, or radio; (usu. in *pl.*) branch of technology concerned with this. [f. F *télécommunication* (as TELE-, COMMUNICATION)]

tĕ'ledu (-ōō) *n.* Stinking badger of Java and Sumatra. [Jav.]

tėlĕ'gonў *n.* (Biol.) Supposed influence of previous sire seen in subsequent sire's progeny by same dam; hence **tĕlėgŏ'nic** *a.* [f. TELE- + Gk *-gonia* begetting]

tĕ'lėgrăm *n.* Message sent by telegraph and usu. then written etc. for delivery to addressee. [f. TELE- + -GRAM, after foll.]

tĕ'lėgraph[1] (-ahf) *n.* **1.** (Apparatus for) transmitting messages or signals to a distance esp. by making and breaking electrical connection; BUSH[1] *telegraph.* **2.** Semaphore apparatus. **3.** Newspaper (used in titles, as *Daily Telegraph*). **4.** **~(-board)**, board on which numbers of horses running in race, cricket scores, etc., are put up so as to be visible at distance; **~-key,** device for making and breaking electric circuit of telegraph; **~-line, -pole** or **-post, -wire,** (used in providing telegraphic connection); **~ money order,** money ORDER[1] for which authority to pay is transmitted by telegraph; **~-plant,** E. Ind. plant (*Desmodium gyrans*) whose leaves have spontaneous jerking motion. [f. F *télégraphe* (as TELE-, -GRAPH)]

tĕ'lėgraph[2] (-ahf) *v.* **1.** *v.t.* Send (message *to* person, or abs.) by telegraph (*telegraph the news to your father*; *telegraph me the result*; *telegraph to him to come, that we cannot come*). **2.** *v.i.* Make signals (*to* person *to* do, *that*, etc.). [f. prec.]

tėlĕ'graph|er (*or* tĕ'lĭgrah-) *n.* Person skilled in, or employed in, telegraphy; so ~IST (3) *n.* [f. prec. + -ER[1]]

tĕlėgraphē'se (-z) *n.* (colloq. or joc.) Elliptical style usual in telegrams. [f, TELEGRAPH[1] + -ESE]

tĕlėgră'ph|ĭc *a.* Of telegraphs or telegrams; of telegraphic brevity, economically worded, with unessential words omitted; **~ic address,** abbreviated or other registered address for use in telegrams; hence ~ICALLY *adv.* [f. TELEGRAPH[1] + -IC]

tėlĕ'graphў *n.* Art of construction of, practice of communicating by, telegraph; WIRELESS *telegraphy.* [f. TELEGRAPH[1] + -Y[1]]

tĕlėkīnē's|ĭs *n.* (*pl.* **~es** *pr.* -ēz). (Psych.) Movement at a distance from the motive cause or agent without material connection. [mod. L, f. as TELE- + Gk *kinēsis* motion (*kineō* move)]

tĕ'lėmark *n.*, & *v.i.* (Make) swing turn in skiing used to change direction or to stop short. [f. *T~* in Norway]

tĕ'lėmēter (*or* tĭlĕ'mĭ-) *n.* & *v.* **1.** *n.* Apparatus to record readings of an instrument at a distance usu. by means of radio. **2.** *v.i.* Record readings thus. **3.** *v.t.* Transmit (readings etc.) to a distant receiving set or station. **4.** So **tėlĕ'**METRY *n.* [f. TELE- + -METER]

tĕlėŏ'log|ў *n.* Doctrine of final causes, view that developments are due to the purpose or design that is served by them; hence **tĕlėolŏ'g**IC(AL) *adjs.*, ~ISM (3), ~IST (2), *ns.* [f. mod. L *teleologia* f. Gk *telos teleos* end + -O- + -LOGY]

tĕ'lėŏst *n.* (Zool.) Fish of order Teleostei, with skeleton (usu.) completely ossified. [f. Gk *teleo-* complete (*telos*; see prec.) + *osteon* bone]

tĕ'lėpăth *n.*, & *v.i.* **1.** *n.* Telepathic person. **2.** *v.i.* Practise telepathy. [back form. f. foll.]

tėlĕ'path|ў *n.* Communication from one mind to another at a distance other than through known senses; hence **tĕlėpă'th**IC *a.*, ~IST (2) *n.*, ~IZE (1, 2) *v.t.* & *i.* [f. TELE- + -PATHY]

tĕ'lėphōne *n.* & *v.* **1.** *n.* Apparatus for transmitting sound (esp. speech) to a distance by wire or cord or radio, esp. by converting acoustic vibrations to electrical signals for transmission; (transmitting and) receiving instrument used in this, with bell to indicate incoming call, (*the telephone is ringing*; *pick up the telephone*); **the ~**, system of communication by a network of telephones; **on the ~**, (1) having an instrument connected to this, (2) by use of or (while) using the telephone; **over the ~**, by use of the telephone. **2.** **~ book, directory,** (listing names and numbers of telephone subscribers); **~ booth,** ‖**~-box, ~ kiosk,** (containing telephone for public use); *telephone* CALL[2]; *telephone* EXCHANGE[1] 5; **~ number** (assigned to a particular subscriber and used in making connections to his telephone). **3.** *v.t.* Send (message etc.), by telephone; speak to (person) by telephone. **4.** *v.i.* Make telephone call. **5.** Hence **tĕlėphŏ'n**IC *a.*, **tėlĕ'phon**IST (3) (esp. operator in telephone exchange), **tėlĕ'phon**Y[1], *ns.* [f. TELE- + -PHONE]

tĕlėphō'tō *a.* Telephotographic; **~ lens** (for telephotography). [abbr.]

tĕlėphotŏ'graphў *n.* Photographing of distant objects by means of a combination of telescopic and ordinary photographic lens giving large image; so **tĕlėphōtogră'ph**IC *a.* [f. TELE- + PHOTOGRAPHY]

tĕ'lėpôrt *v.t.* Move by telekinesis; hence ~A'TION *n.* [f. TELE- + PORT[4]]

tĕ'lėprĭnter *n.* Telegraph instrument for transmitting messages by typing. [f. TELE- + PRINTER]

tĕ'lergў *n.* (Psych.) Force conceived as operating on the brain in telepathy. [f. TELE- + ENERGY]

tĕ'lėscōpe *n.* & *v.* **1.** *n.* Optical instrument using lenses or mirrors or both to make distant objects appear nearer and larger; **radio ~**, directional aerial system for collecting radio waves from celestial objects and recording their intensity etc. **2.** *v.t.* Press, drive, (sections of tube, colliding trains, etc.) together so that one slides into another like sections of small telescope; compress (lit. or fig.) forcibly. **3.** *v.i.* Close, be driven, be capable of closing, thus. [f. It. *telescopio* or mod. L *telescopium* (as TELE-, -SCOPE)]

tĕlėscŏ'p|ĭc *a.* Of, or made with, a telescope (*telescopic observations*); visible only through telescope (*telescopic stars*); consisting of sections that telescope (*telescopic funnel of steamer*; *telescopic umbrella*); **~ic sight,** telescope used for sighting on rifle etc.; hence ~ICALLY *adv.* [f. prec. + -IC]

***telesthesia,** etc. See TELAESTHESIA, etc.

For other words in *tele-* **see** TELE-.

***tĕ'lĕthon** *n.* Very long television programme, esp. to raise money for a fund. [f. TELE- + MARATHON]
tĕ'lĕtȳpe, *tĕlĕtȳ'pewrīter (-prī-) *ns.* Teleprinter. [f. TELE- + TYPE¹(WRITER)]
tĕ'lėview (-vū) *v.t.* Watch by means of television; hence ~ER¹ *n.* [f. TELE- + VIEW]
tĕ'lėvīs|e (-z) *v.t.* Transmit by television; hence ~OR *n.*, apparatus for televising. [back form. f. foll.]
tĕ'lėvĭsion (-zhon; *or* -vĭ'-) *n.* System for reproducing actual or recorded scene at a distance on a screen etc. by radio transmission, usu. with appropriate sounds; vision of distant objects obtained thus; televised programmes etc.; ~ (**set**), apparatus for displaying pictures transmitted thus. [f. TELE- + VISION]
tĕ'lĕx, Tĕ'lĕx, *n.*, & *v.t.* **1.** *n.* System of telegraphy in which printed signals or messages are sent from and to teleprinters connected to public telecommunication network. **2.** *v.t.* Send, communicate with, by telex. [f. TELEPRINTER + EXCHANGE¹]
tĕll¹ *v.* (**told** *pr.* tō-). **1.** *v.t.* Give detailed account of (as) in spoken or written words (*tell me a tale*; *every picture tells a story*); ~ **a tale,** be significant or revealing; ~ **the tale,** (sl.) relate marvellous or incredible story, esp. tale of woe to evoke sympathy; ~ **its own tale,** be significant, explain itself, need no comment; ~ one's **own tale,** give one's own account of the matter; ~ **tales** (**out of school**), report esp. maliciously what is meant to be secret. **2.** Make known, divulge, state, express in words, (*tell me your name, what you want, what to do*; *tell me all about it*; *will tell you a secret, that he has failed, my candid opinion*; *cannot tell you how glad I was*); tell FORTUNE¹*s*; ~ **it not in Gath,** (usu. joc.) let this news not reach and gladden the enemy [w. ref. to 2 Sam. 1:20]; *~ (person) **goodbye,** say goodbye to; *tell that to the* (*horse*) MARINES; **don't ~ me** *it's here already* (expr. incredulity); **you're ~ing me,** (sl.) I am fully aware of that; **I ~ you** (emphatic or impatient assurance); *I told you* SO¹ 7; *I'll tell you* WHAT; ~ **the world,** announce openly, assert emphatically. **3.** Utter (*you told me a lie*; *are you telling the truth?*). **4.** *v.i.* Give information or description (*of* or *about*); reveal a secret; HEAR *tell* (*of*); **time will ~,** we shall know eventually; ~ **on,** (colloq.) inform against (person). **5.** *v.t.* & *i.* Decide, determine, (*how do you tell which button to press?*); ~ **the time,** read it from face of clock etc.; **as far as** one **can ~,** judging from the available evidence; **you never can ~,** appearances and probabilities are deceptive. **6.** Distinguish (*cannot tell them apart, him from his brother*). **7.** Assure (*it is not easy, I can tell you*; cf. sense 2). **8.** *v.i.* Produce marked effect (*every blow tells*; *strain began to tell on him*); have influence *in favour of* or *against*. **9.** *v.t.* Count (votes esp. in House of Commons, one's BEAD¹*s*; *we were 18 men all told*); ~ **off,** count off or detach for duty (*six of us were, I was, told off to get fuel*), reprimand, scold, (person). **10.** Direct, order, (person) *to* do something (*tell him to wait for me*). **11.** Hence ~'ABLE *a.* [OE *tellan,* = OS *tellian,* OHG *zellen,* ON *telja* f. Gmc **taljan* (**talō* TALE)]
tĕll² *n.* Artificial mound in Middle East etc. formed by accumulated remains of ancient settlements. [f. Arab. *tall* hillock]
tĕ'ller *n.* In vbl senses; any of four persons appointed (two for each side) to count votes in House of Commons; person appointed to receive or pay out money in bank etc.; hence ~SHIP *n.* [ME, f. TELL¹ + -ER¹]
tĕ'llĭng *a.* Having marked effect, striking; hence ~LY² *a.* [f. TELL¹ + -ING²]
tĕ'll-tāle *n.* One who tells about another's private affairs, tattler; (fig.) thing, circumstance, that reveals person's thoughts, conduct, etc., (esp. *attrib.*: *tell-tale blushes*; *the tell-tale clay on his shoes*); mechanical device for recording person's attendance at specified time etc., giving warning that cistern is full, etc.; (Naut.) index near wheel to show position of tiller, compass hung usu. in captain's cabin for checking ship's course. [f. TELL¹ + TALE]
tĕllūr'ĭan *a.* & *n.* (Inhabitant) of the earth. [f. L *tellus -uris* earth + -IAN]
tĕllūr'ĭc *a.* **1.** Of the earth as a planet; of the soil. **2.** (Chem.) Of tellurium, esp. in its higher valency; hence **tĕ'llūr**ATE¹ (3) *n.* [sense 1 f. as prec.; sense 2 f. foll.]
tĕll|ūr'ĭum *n.* (Chem.) Rare brittle lustrous silver-white element; hence **~'ūr**IDE, **~'ūr**ITE¹ (Chem., Min.), *ns.*, **~'ūr**OUS *a.* [f. L *tellus -uris* earth + -IUM, prob. named in contrast to *uranium*]
‖**tĕ'llȳ** *n.* (colloq.) Television (set). [abbr.]
tĕ'lpher *a.* & *n.* (Container) serving to transport (esp. goods) by electric power; so ~AGE (1, 2) *n.* [f. **telephore* f. TELE- + -PHORE]
tĕ'lson *n.* Last segment in abdomen of Crustacea etc. [Gk, = limit]
Tĕ'lugu (-ōō) *n.* Language or member of Dravidian people in S.E. India. [Telugu]
***tĕ'mblor** *n.* Earthquake. [Sp.]
tĕmerār'ĭous *a.* (literary). Reckless, rash. [f. L *temerarius* (*temere* rashly) + -OUS]
tėmĕ'rĭtȳ *n.* Rashness. [f. L *temeritas* (*temere* rashly; see -ITY)]
tĕmp *n.* (colloq.) Temporary employee. [abbr.]
temp. *abbr.* In the time of (*temp. Henry I*) [f. L *tempore* abl. of *tempus* time]; temperature.
tĕ'mper¹ *v.* **1.** *v.t.* Bring (clay etc.) to desired consistency by moistening, mixing, and kneading. **2.** *v.t.* & *i.* Bring (metal, esp. steel), (of metal) come, to proper hardness and elasticity by heating after quenching. **3.** *v.t.* Modify, mitigate, (justice etc.) by blending *with* (mercy, etc.); moderate, restrain, tone down. **4.** (Mus.) Tune, modulate, (piano, organ) in particular temperament. **5.** Hence ~ABLE, ~ATIVE, *adjs.*, ~ER¹ *n.* [OE *temprian* f. L *temperare* mingle; infl. by OF *temprer, tremper*]
tĕ'mper² *n.* **1.** Mixture, esp. suitable combination of ingredients (*of* mortar etc.); resulting condition or consistency. **2.** Condition of metal as regards hardness and elasticity. **3.** Habitual or temporary disposition of mind (*person of a saturnine, fiery, placid, temper*; *persons of congenial temper*); **in a good ~,** not irritable or angry; **in a bad ~,** peevish, angry. **4.** Irritation, anger, (*fit of temper*; *what a temper he is in!*); **have a ~,** be prone to become angry; **lose** one's **~,** become angry; **keep, control,** one's **~,** not lose it; **out of ~,** angry; **show ~,** be petulant. **5.** Hence (-)~ED² *a.*, (**-)ed**LY² *adv.*, (-erd-). [ME, f. prec.]
tĕ'mpera *n.* Method of painting like DISTEMPER³, esp. as technique of fine art on canvas etc. [It.]
tĕ'mperament *n.* **1.** Individual character of one's physical constitution permanently affecting the manner of acting, feeling, and thinking, (*a nervous temperament*; *the artistic temperament*); SANGUINE, **lymphatic** or **phlegmatic, choleric** or **bilious, melancholic** or **atrabilious, ~** (formerly attributed to predominance of blood, lymph or phlegm, yellow bile, black bile). **2.** (Mus.) Adjustment of intervals in tuning of piano etc. so as to fit the scale for use in all keys,

For other words in *tele-* see TELE-.

esp. **equal** ~ (in which the 12 semitones are at equal intervals). **3.** Hence ~AL (-ĕ'n-) *a.*, (esp., of person) liable to peculiar moods, having or giving way to erratic or neurotic temperament, behaving unpredictably. [ME, f. L *temperamentum* (as TEMPER[1]; see -MENT)]

tĕ'mperance *n.* Moderation, self-restraint, in speech, conduct, etc., esp. in eating and drinking; moderation in use of, or total abstinence from, alcoholic liquors as beverages; ~ **hotel** (not supplying alcoholic drinks); ~ **society** etc. (for restriction or abolition of use of alcoholic drinks). [ME, f. AF *temperaunce* f. L *temperantia* (as TEMPER[1]; see -ANCE)]

tĕ'mperate *a.* Moderate; self-restrained, abstemious; of mild temperature; *temperate* ZONE; hence ~LY[2] (-tlĭ) *adv.*, ~NESS (-tn-) *n.* [ME, f. L *temperatus*, p.p. of *temperare* (see TEMPER[1], -ATE[2])]

tĕ'mperature *n.* Degree or intensity of heat of a body in relation to others, esp. as shown by thermometer or perceived by touch etc.; (Med.) degree of internal heat of the body (**take** person's ~, ascertain any variation from normal value, in illness etc.); (colloq.) body temperature above normal (*have*, RUN[1], *a temperature*); (fig.) degree of excitement in discussion etc.; ~-**-humidity index,** quantity giving measure of discomfort due to combined effects of temperature and humidity of air. [f. F *température* or f. L *temperatura* (as TEMPER[1]; see -URE)]

tĕ'mpersome *a.* Having a quick temper. [f. TEMPER[2] + -SOME[1]]

tĕ'mpėst *n.* Violent storm of wind often with rain, snow, etc.; (fig.) violent tumult or agitation; ***~ in a teapot,** = STORM *in a teacup*. [ME, f. OF *tempest(e)* f. Rom. **tempesta*, **tempestum* f. L *tempestas* season, storm (*tempus* time)]

tĕmpĕ'stūous *a.* (Of weather, time, etc., or fig. of person or mood) stormy, violent; hence ~LY[2] *adv.*, ~NESS *n.* [f. LL *tempestuosus* (as prec.; see -OUS)]

Tĕ'mplar *n.* **1.** Member of religious and military order (**Knights T~s**) for protection of pilgrims to Holy Land, suppressed in 1312. **2.** Lawyer or law student with chambers in the Temple, London. [ME, f. AF *templer*, OF *templier*, = med. L *templarius* (as TEMPLE[1]; see -AR[2])]

tĕ'mplate (-ĭt), **tĕ'mplėt,** *n.* Pattern, gauge, usu. thin board or metal plate, used as guide in cutting or drilling metal, stone, wood, etc.; timber or plate used to distribute weight in wall or under beam etc.; molecular pattern governing assembly of protein etc. [orig. *templet*, prob. f. TEMPLE[3] + -ET[1], alt. after *plate*]

tĕ'mple[1] *n.* **1.** Edifice dedicated to accommodation or service of (esp. ancient Egyptian, Greek, Roman, or modern Hindu, Buddhist, etc.) god(s) or other objects of religious reverence. **2.** Any of three successive religious buildings of the Jews in Jerusalem; *synagogue. **3.** Place of Christian public worship, esp. Protestant church in France. **4.** (fig.) Place in which God is regarded as residing, esp. Christian's person or body. **5. Inner, Middle, T~**, two Inns of Court on site of the Temple (establishment of Knights Templars) in London; **T~ Bar,** gateway (removed 1879) that marked the westward limit of the City Corporation's jurisdiction, at junction of Fleet Street and Strand in London. [OE *temp(e)l*, reinforced in ME by OF *temple*, f. L *templum* open or consecrated space]

tĕ'mple[2] *n.* Flat part of either side of head between forehead and ear. [ME f. OF, f. Rom. **temp(u)la*, f. L *tempora* pl. of *tempus* temple]

tĕ'mple[3] *n.* Device in loom for keeping cloth stretched. [ME f. OF, orig. same wd as prec.]

tĕ'mplėt. See TEMPLATE.

tĕ'mp|ō *n.* (*pl.* **~os,** *or* **~i** *pr.* -ē). **1.** (Mus.) Time, rapidity of movement; characteristic speed and rhythm of movement (*waltz tempo*). **2.** (fig.) Rate of motion or activity (*the tempo of the war is quickening*). [It., f. L *tempus* time]

tĕ'mporal *a.* **1.** Of this life, secular, esp. opp. to *spiritual* (*temporal affairs, interests*); ||~ **lords** or **lords** ~, peers of realm (cf. SPIRITUAL); ~ **power** (of ecclesiastic esp. pope in temporal matters); hence ~LY[2] *adv.* **2.** Of or in or denoting time; ~ **conjunction,** *when* etc. **3.** Of the temple(s) of the head (*temporal artery, bone*). [ME, f. OF *temporel* or f. L *temporalis* (*tempus -oris*; see TEMPORARY, TEMPLE[2], -AL)]

tĕmporă'lĭtў *n.* Temporariness; (usu. in *pl.*) a secular possession, esp. properties and revenues of religious corporation or ecclesiastic. [ME, f. LL *temporalitas* (as prec.; see -ITY)]

tĕ'mporaltў *n.* (arch.) The laity. [ME, f. TEMPORAL + -TY[1]]

tĕ'mporar|ў *a.* & *n.* **1.** *a.* Lasting, meant to last, only for a time, (*temporary buildings, relief, possession, office*); hence **~ĭLY**[2] *adv.*, **~ĭNESS** *n.* **2.** *n.* Person employed temporarily. [f. L *temporarius* (*tempus -oris* time; see -ARY[1])]

tĕ'mporiz|e, -is|e (-īz), *v.i.* Adopt indecisive or time-serving policy; avoid committing oneself, act so as to gain time; comply temporarily with requirements of occasion; hence ~A'TION, ~ER[1], *ns.* [f. F *temporiser* bide one's time f. med. L *temporizare* delay (*tempus -oris* time; see -IZE)]

tĕmpt *v.t.* **1.** (arch.) Make trial of, try the resolution of, (*God did tempt Abraham*). **2.** Provoke, defy, (*shalt not tempt the Lord*; *would be tempting Providence* or *fate to try it*). **3.** Entice, incite esp. to sin, (*to* do, *to* action esp. evil one); *I am* **~ed** (strongly disposed) *to question this.* **4.** Allure, attract. **5.** Hence or cogn. ~ABI'LITY *n.*, ~ABLE *a.* [ME, f. OF *tenter*, *tempter*, f. L *temptare* handle, test, try]

tĕmptā'tion *n.* Tempting or being tempted (**the T~**, esp. of Christ, see Matt. 4); incitement esp. to sin; thing that attracts, attractive course of action. [ME, f. OF *tentacion*, *temptacion* f. L *temptatio -onis* (as prec.; see -ATION)]

tĕ'mpt|er *n.* One who tempts; **the T~er,** the Devil; so ~RESS[1] *n.* [ME, f. OF *tempteur*, f. eccl. L *temptator -oris* (as TEMPT; see -OR)]

tĕ'mptĭng *a.* Enticing to evil; attractive, inviting; hence ~LY[2] *adv.* [f. TEMPT + -ING[2]]

tĕ'mpura (-oor*a*) *n.* Japanese dish of fish or shellfish, fried in batter. [Jap.]

tĕn *a.* & *n.* **1.** One more than nine; symbol for this (10, x, X); card with ten pips; time of ten o'clock; size etc. denoted by ten; set of ten; (as round number: *ten times as easy*; *ten to one he forgets it*); HART *of ten*; UPPER *ten*. **2.** *Ten* COMMANDMENTS; **~-gallon hat,** cowboy's large broad-brimmed hat; **~'pins** (usu. treated as *sing.*), game similar to ninepins; *Ten* TRIBES; **~-week stock,** garden flower (*Matthiola incana annua*) said to bloom ten weeks after sowing of seed. **3.** Hence ~'FOLD *a.* & *adv.*, ~TH[2] *a.* & *n.* (**~th-rate,** of extremely poor quality), **~'th**LY[2] *adv.* [OE *tīen*, *tēn*, = OS *tehan*, OHG *zehan*, ON *tíu*, Goth. *taihun* f. Gmc **tehan*, *-un* f. IE **dekm̥*]

ten. *abbr. tenuto.*

tĕ'nable *a.* That can be maintained or defended against attack (*a tenable position, fortress, theory*); (of office etc.) that can be held *for* specified time, *by* class of person, etc.; hence **tĕn**ABI'LITY, ~NESS (-beln-), *ns.* [F (*tenir* hold f. L *tenēre*; see -ABLE)]

tĕ'nace *n.* (Holding of) two cards, one ranking next above, the other next below, card held by opponent. [F f. Sp. *tenaza*, lit. pincers]

tėnā'cious (-sh*u*s) *a.* Holding fast; keeping firm

hold (*of* property, rights, principles, life, etc.), not readily relinquishing; persistent, resolute; (of memory) retentive; adhesive, sticky; strongly cohesive; hence or cogn. ~LY² *adv.*, ~NESS, **tėnă'city**, *ns.* [f. L *tenax -acis* (*tenēre* hold; see -ACIOUS)]

tėnă'cūl|um *n.* (*pl.* ~**a**). Surgeon's sharp hook for picking up arteries etc. [L, = holding instrument (*tenēre* hold)]

tĕ'nant *n.*, & *v.t.* **1.** *n.* One who occupies land or tenement under a landlord; (Law) person holding real property by private ownership; occupant (*of* any place); ~ **farmer** (cultivating farm he does not own); ||~ **right,** right of tenant to continue tenancy at termination of lease; hence or cogn. **tĕ'nancy** *n.*, ~LESS *a.*, ~RY (1, 2) *n.* **2.** *v.t.* Occupy as tenant; hence ~ABLE *a.* [ME f. OF, part. of *tenir* hold f. L *tenēre*; see -ANT]

tĕnch *n.* (*pl.* same). European freshwater fish (*Tinca tinca*) of carp family. [ME, f. OF *tenche* f. LL *tinca*]

tĕnd¹ *v.i.* Be moving, be directed, hold a course, (lit. or fig.; *tends in our direction, downwards, this way, towards the coast, to the same conclusion*); be apt or inclined, serve, conduce, (*to* action, quality, etc.; *to* do). [ME, f. OF *tendre* stretch f. L *tendere tens-* or *tent-*]

tĕnd² *v.* **1.** *v.t.* Take care of, look after, (sheep, invalid, machine). **2.** *v.i.* Wait (*up*)*on*; *give attention *to*. **3.** So ~'ANCE *n.* (arch.). [ME, f. ATTEND]

tĕ'ndency̆ *n.* Bent, leaning, inclination, (*towards, to*, thing; *to* do). [f. med. L *tendentia* (as TEND¹; see -ENCY)]

tĕndĕ'ntious (-shus) *a.* (derog.) (Of writing etc.) having an underlying purpose, calculated to promote a particular cause or viewpoint; hence ~LY² *adv.*, ~NESS *n.* [f. as prec. + -OUS]

tĕ'nder¹ *n.* In vbl senses; vessel or vehicle attending larger one to supply stores, convey passengers or orders, etc.; carriage attached to steam-locomotive and carrying fuel, water, etc. [ME, f. TEND² + -ER¹, or f. ATTENDER]

tĕ'nder² *v.* & *n.* **1.** *v.t.* Offer, present, (one's services, apologies, resignation, etc.); offer (money etc.) as payment. **2.** *v.i.* Make a tender (*for* supply of thing or execution of work). **3.** *n.* Offer, esp. offer in writing to execute work or supply goods at fixed price; **put out to** ~, seek tenders in respect of (work etc.). **4. Plea of** ~ (that defendant has always been ready to satisfy plaintiff's claim and now brings the sum into court); **legal** ~, currency that cannot legally be refused in payment of debt (usu. up to limited amount for baser coins etc.). [f. OF *tendre* (see TEND¹); for *-er* cf. RENDER and -ER⁴]

tĕ'nder³ *a.* **1.** Soft, not tough or hard, (*tender steak*). **2.** Easily touched or wounded, susceptible to pain or grief, (*a tender heart, conscience*); ~ **place** (on skin etc.); ~ **spot,** (fig.) subject on which one is touchy. **3.** Delicate, fragile, (lit., or fig. of reputation etc.); **of** ~ **age,** immature, young. **4.** Loving, affectionate, fond, (*tender parents*; *wrote tender verses*); solicitous, considerate, (*of* one's honour, good name, etc.). **5.** Requiring careful handling, ticklish, (*a tender subject*). **6.** ~**-eyed,** (1) having gentle eyes, (2) weak-eyed; ~**foot,** newcomer in bush etc., novice (esp. in Scouts); ~**-hearted,** having tender heart, easily moved by pity etc.; ~**loin,** ||middle part of pork loin, *undercut of sirloin, *(*T~loin*) district of city where vice and corruption are prominent. **7.** Hence ~IZE (3) *v.t.*, ~LY² *adv.*, ~NESS *n.* [ME, f. OF *tendre* f. L *tener*]

tĕ'ndon *n.* Strong band or cord of tissue forming termination and attachment of fleshy part of muscle; **Achilles** ~ (connecting heel [where alone Achilles was vulnerable] with calf muscles); so **tĕndĭnĭ'tis** *n.*, **tĕ'ndĭnous** *a.* [F, or f. med. L *tendo -dinis* f. Gk *tenōn* sinew (*teinō* stretch)]

tĕ'ndrĭl *n.* Slender leafless plant-organ attaching itself to or round another body for support; (fig.) slender curl of hair etc. [prob. f. obs. F *tendrillon* dim. of obs. *tendron* young shoot f. Rom. **tenerumen* f. L *tener* TENDER³]

Tĕ'nėbrae *n. pl.* (R.C. Ch.) Matins and lauds for last three days of Holy Week, at which candles are successively extinguished. [L, = darkness]

tĕnėbrĭ'fĭc *a.* (arch.) Causing darkness. [f. as prec.; see -FIC]

tĕ'nėbrous *a.* (arch.) Dark, gloomy. [ME, f. OF *tenebrus* f. L *tenebrosus* (as TENEBRAE; see -OUS)]

tĕ'nėment *n.* Piece of land held by an owner; (Law) any kind of permanent property, e.g. lands or rents, held from a superior; dwelling-place; dwelling-house, esp. (Sc.) containing several dwellings; set of apartments used by one family; *~**(-house)**, house containing several such tenements; so ~AL, ~ARY¹, (-mĕ'n-) *adjs.* [ME f. OF, f. med. L *tenementum* (*tenēre* hold; see -MENT)]

tėnĕ'smus (-z-) *n.* (Path.) Continual inclination to evacuate bowels or bladder accompanied by painful straining. [med. L, f. Gk *teinesmos* straining (*teinō* stretch)]

tĕ'nėt *n.* Principle, dogma, doctrine, of a person or school. [L, = he holds (*tenēre* hold)]

tĕ'nfōld. See TEN.

***tē'nĭa.** See TAENIA.

Tenn. *abbr.* Tennessee.

tĕ'nné (-nĭ) *n.*, & *a.* (usu. placed after *n.*) (Her.) Brown. [obs. F, var. of *tanné* TAWNY]

tĕ'nner *n.* (colloq.) ||Ten-pound or *ten-dollar note. [f. TEN + -ER¹]

tĕ'nnĭs *n.* **1.** Game (**real** or ***court** ~) for 2 or 4 persons played by striking ball with rackets over net stretched across walled court. **2.** = LAWN² *tennis*. **3.** ~ **arm, elbow,** sprain caused by playing tennis; ~**-ball, -court, -racket,** (used in playing tennis). [ME *tenetz, tenes*, etc., app. f. OF *tenez* 'take, receive', called by server to his opponent, imper. of *tenir* take]

Tĕnny̆sō'nĭan *a.* & *n.* **1.** *a.* (In the style of) Tennyson. **2.** *n.* Student or admirer of Tennyson. [f. Alfred (Lord) *Tennyson*, Engl. poet d. 1892 + -IAN]

tĕ'non *n.*, & *v.t.* **1.** *n.* Projecting piece of wood made for insertion into corresponding cavity (esp. MORTISE) in another piece; ~**-saw** (small, with strong brass or steel back, for fine work). **2.** *v.t.* Cut as tenon; join by means of tenon; hence ~ER¹ (1, 2) *n.* [ME f. F (*tenir* hold f. L *tenēre*; see -OON)]

tĕ'nor *n.* **1.** Settled or prevailing course or direction, esp. fig. *of* one's *life, way*, etc.; general purport, drift, (*of* speech, writing, etc.); (Law) (1) actual wording, (2) exact copy. **2.** (Mus.) Highest ordinary adult male voice, between baritone and alto or counter-tenor; singer with this voice; part written for tenor voice; instrument, esp. viola, of which range is roughly that of tenor voice; ~ **bell** (largest of peal or set); ~ **clef** (placing middle C on second highest line of staff). [ME, f. AF *tenur*, OF *tenour* f. L *tenor -oris* (*tenēre* hold; see -OR)]

tenŏ'tomy̆ *n.* Tendon-cutting, esp. as remedy for club-foot. [f. F *ténotomie*, irreg. f. Gk *tenōn -ontos* tendon; see -TOMY]

tĕ'nrĕc, tă'nrĕc, *n.* Hedgehog-like tailless insectivorous mammal of Madagascar. [F *tanrec*, f. Malagasy *t*(*r*)*àndraka*]

tĕnse¹ *n.* (Gram.) Form taken by verb to indicate the time (also continuance or completeness) of the action etc. (*present, future, past, imperfect, perfect, tense*; PRIMARY, HISTORIC, *tense*); set of such forms for the various persons and numbers; SEQUENCE *of tenses*; hence ~'LESS (-sl-) *a.* [ME, f. OF *tens* f. L *tempus* time]

tĕnse[2] *a.* & *v.* **1.** *a.* (Of cord, membrane, or fig. of nerve, mind, emotion) stretched tight, strained to stiffness; causing tenseness (*a tense moment*); (Phonet.) pronounced with vocal muscles tense; hence ~'LY[2] (-slĭ) *adv.*, ~'NESS (-sn-), **tĕ'ns**ITY, *ns.* **2.** *v.t.* & *i.* Make or become tense; ~ **up,** become tense. [f. L *tensus* p.p. of *tendere* stretch (TEND[1])]

tĕ'nsīle *a.* **1.** Of tension (*tensile force, stress*); ~ **strength,** resistance to breaking under tension. **2.** Capable of being drawn out or stretched; hence **tĕnsĭ'l**ITY *n.* [f. med. L *tensilis* (as prec.; see -IL)]

tĕnsĭ'mėter *n.* Instrument for measuring vapour pressure; manometer. [f. foll. + -METER]

tĕ'nsion (-sh*o*n) *n.*, & *v.t.* **1.** *n.* Stretching, being stretched; tenseness; mental strain or excitement; strained (political, social, etc.) state or relationship. **2.** (Mech.) Stress by which bar, cord, etc. is pulled when it is part of a system in equilibrium or motion; expansive force of gas or vapour; SURFACE *tension*; electromotive force (*high, low, tension*). **3.** Hence ~AL *a.* **4.** *v.t.* Subject to tension. [F, or f. L *tensio* (as TEND[1]; see -ION)]

tĕ'nson, tĕ'nzon, *n.* Contest in verse-making between troubadours; piece of verse composed for this. [F *tenson*, = Prov. *tenso*]

tĕ'nsor *n.* **1.** (Anat.) Muscle that tightens or stretches a part. **2.** (Math.) Generalized form of vector involving two or more directions for each of its components. [mod. L (as TEND[1]; see -OR)]

tĕnt[1] *n.* & *v.* **1.** *n.* Portable shelter of canvas, cloth, etc., supported by pole(s) and stretched by cords secured to **~-pegs** driven into ground; (Med.) tentlike enclosure for control of air supply to patient. **2. ~-bed** (with tentlike canopy, or for patient in tent); ~ **coat, dress,** (cut very full); **~-fly,** (1) flap at entrance of tent, (2) piece of canvas stretched over ridge-pole of tent leaving open space but keeping off sun and rain; **~-pegging,** cavalry exercise or sport in which rider tries at full gallop to carry off on point of lance tent-peg fixed in ground; **~-stitch,** (one of) series of parallel diagonal stitches [perh. f. another wd]. **3.** *v.t.* Cover (as) with tent. **4.** *v.i.* Encamp in tent; dwell temporarily. [ME f. OF *tente* f. Rom. **tenta* neut. pl. p.p. (as fem. n.) of L *tendere* stretch]

tĕnt[2] *n.*, & *v.t.* **1.** *n.* (Surg.) Piece, bunch, roll, of lint, linen, etc., inserted into wound or natural opening to keep it open. **2.** *v.t.* (arch.) Keep open thus. [ME f. OF *tente* (*tenter* probe, as TEMPT)]

tĕnt[3] *n.* Deep red sweet wine chiefly from Spain, used esp. as sacramental wine. [f. Sp. *tinto* deep--coloured f. L *tinctus* p.p. (see TINGE)]

tĕ'ntacl|e *n.* Long slender flexible process or appendage of animal, used for feeling, grasping, or moving; (Bot.) sensitive hair or filament; (fig.) thing used like tentacle as feeler etc.; so (-)~ED[2] (-keld), **tĕntă'cūl**AR[1], **tĕntă'cūl**ATE[2], *adjs.* [f. mod. L *tentaculum*, f. L *tentare* = *temptare* (TEMPT) + *-culum* -CULE]

tĕ'ntatĭve *a.* & *n.* **1.** *a.* Done by way of trial, experimental; hesitant, not definite, (*tentative suggestion, acceptance*); hence ~LY[2] (-vlĭ) *adv.* **2.** *n.* Experimental proposal or theory. [f. med. L *tentativus* (as prec.; see -IVE)]

‖**tĕ'nter**[1] *n.* Person in charge of something, esp. of machinery in factory; workman's unskilled attendant. [f. obs. and Sc. *tent* pay attention perh. f. *tent* attention f. INTENT[1] or obs. *attent* (as ATTEND), + -ER[1]]

tĕ'nter[2] *n.* Machine for stretching cloth to dry in shape; ~(**hook**), each of the hooks that hold the cloth; **on ~hooks,** (arch.) **on the ~hooks,** in state of suspense or mental agitation due to uncertainty. [ME, f. AF **tentur* f. med. L *tentorium* (as TEND[1]; see -ER[2], -OR)]

tĕnth. See TEN.

tĕ'nū|ĭs *n.* (*pl.* **~es** *pr.* -ēz). (Phonet.) Voiceless stop, e.g. *k, p, t.* [L, = thin, transl. Gk *psilos* smooth]

tėnū'ĭtȳ *n.* Slenderness; (of air, fluid) rarity, thinness. [f. L *tenuitas* (as prec.; see -ITY)]

tĕ'nūous *a.* Thin, slender, small; rarefied; (of distinction etc.) subtle, over-refined; hence ~LY[2] *adv.*, ~NESS *n.* [f. L *tenuis* + -OUS]

tĕ'nure (-ny*er*) *n.* Condition, form of right or title, under which (esp. real) property is held; (period of) holding, possession, enjoyment, (*during his tenure of office*; *has tenure of the estate*); *permanent appointment as teacher etc.; hence **tĕnūr'**IAL *a.* [ME f. OF (*tenir* hold f. L *tenēre*; see -URE)]

tenuto (tenōō'tō) *a.* & *adv.* (Mus., of note etc.) sustained, given its full time-value (cf. STACCATO). [It., = held]

tĕ'nzon. See TENSON.

tēocă'llĭ *n.* Temple of Aztec or other Mex. aborigines, usu. on truncated pyramid. [Nahuatl (*teotl* god, *calli* house)]

tē'pee, tee'pee, *n.* Conical tent or wigwam of the Amer. Indians, made of skins, cloth, or canvas, on frame of poles. [f. Dakota *tipi*]

tĕ'pĭd *a.* Slightly warm, lukewarm (lit. or fig.); hence or cogn. **tėpĭ'd**ITY, ~NESS, *ns.*, ~LY[2] *adv.* [f. L *tepidus* (*tepēre* be lukewarm; see -ID[1])]

tėqui'la (-kē'-) *n.* Mescal or redistilled mescal. [f. *T*~ in Mexico]

ter- *pref.* Thrice, threefold, (*tercentenary*; *tervalent*). [f. L *ter* thrice]

tĕ'ra- *pref.* denoting factor of 10^{12}, as ~METRE[2]. [f. Gk *teras* monster]

terai' (-ī') *n.* Wide-brimmed felt hat, often with double crown, worn by travellers etc. in subtropical regions. [f. *T*~, belt of marshy jungle between Himalayan foothills and plains, f. Hindi *tarāī* moist (land)]

terakihi. See TARAKIHI.

tĕ'raph *n.* (*pl.* **~im,** also used as *sing.*) Small image as domestic deity or oracle of ancient Hebrews. [ME, f. LL *theraphim*, Gk *theraphin* f. Heb. *t^erāpīm*]

tĕrato- *comb. form.* Monster, as: **~ge'nic** *a.*, **~geny** (-ŏ'j-) *n.*, (of) production of monstrosities; **~logy** (-ŏ'l-), tale(s) of the marvellous, (Biol.) study of animal or vegetable monstrosities; so ~LO'GICAL *a.*, ~LOGIST (-ŏ'l-) *n.*; **~ma** (-ō'-), tumour of heterogeneous tissues. [f. Gk *teras -atos* monster + -O-]

tėr'bĭum *n.* (Chem.) Metallic element of lanthanide series. [mod. L, f. *Ytterby* in Sweden + -IUM]

tėrce *n.* (Eccl.) (Office of) canonical hour of prayer appointed for third daytime hour (i.e. 9 a.m.) [var. of TIERCE]

tėr'cel, tier'cel, *n.* Male of hawk, esp. peregrine or goshawk; **tercel-gentle,** male falcon. [ME, f. OF *tercel* etc., f. Rom. **tertiolus* dim. of L *tertius* third, perh. because believed to come from third egg of clutch]

tėrcĕntē'narȳ (*or* -sĕ'ntĭ-) *a.* & *n.* (Festival) of the three-hundredth anniversary. [f. TER- + CENTENARY]

tėrcĕntĕ'nnĭal *a.* & *n.* **1.** *a.* Lasting, occurring every, three hundred years. **2.** *n.* = prec. [f. TER- + CENTENNIAL]

tẽr'cĕt, tier'cĕt, *n.* (Pros.) = TRIPLET. [F, f. It. *terzetto* dim. of *terzo* third f. L *tertius*; see -ET[1]]

tĕ'rĕbēne *n.* Mixture of terpenes prepared by treating oil of turpentine with sulphuric acid, used as expectorant etc. [f. foll. + -ENE]

tĕ'rĕbĭnth *n.* Small S. Eur. tree (*Pistacia terebinthus*) yielding turpentine. [ME, f. OF *t(h)erebinte* or f. L f. Gk *terebinthos*]

tĕrĕbĭ'nthīne *a.* Of the terebinth; of turpentine. [f. L f. Gk *terebinthinos* (as prec.; see -INE[2])]

tĕ'rĕbr|a *n.* (*pl.* ~ae). Boring ovipositor of Hymenoptera; so ~ANT *a.*, having a terebra. [L, = borer]

terē'dō *n.* (*pl.* ~s). Ship-worm of genus *Teredo*, mollusc that bores ships etc. [L, f. Gk *terēdōn* (*teirō* rub hard, wear away, bore)]

terē'te *a.* (Biol.) Smooth and rounded. [f. L *teres -etis*]

tẽr'gal *a.* Of the back, dorsal. [f. L *tergum* back + -AL]

tẽr'gĭvẽrs|āte *v.i.* Turn one's back on something; be apostate, change one's party or principles; equivocate, make conflicting or evasive statements; hence or cogn. ~A'TION, ~ātor, *ns.* [f. L *tergiversari* turn one's back (*tergum* back, *vertere vers-* turn) + -ATE[3]]

-tẽr'ia *suf.* forming *ns.* denoting self-service establishments. [f. CAFETERIA]

tẽrm[1] *n.* **1.** (arch.) Boundary, limit, esp. of time, (*set a term to his encroachments, his existence*); hence ~'LESS *a.* **2.** Limited period (*for a term of 5 years*; *his term of office expired*); (**full**) ~, completion of (normal) pregnancy; period of tenure; period of some weeks, alternating with holiday or vacation, during which instruction is given in school or university, or ‖during which lawcourt holds sessions (‖EAT one's *terms*), whence ~'LY[1] *a.*, ~'LY[2] *adv.*; period of imprisonment; period over which operations are conducted or results contemplated (*in the short, medium, long, term*). **3.** Appointed day, esp. Scottish QUARTER[1]-*day*. **4.** (Law). ~ (**of** or **for years**), estate or interest in land to be enjoyed for fixed period. **5.** = TERMINUS 4. **6.** (Math.) Each of two quantities in ratio; each quantity in a series; part of expression joined to the rest by + or − ($3ax^2 - b + cz$ has three terms). **7.** (Logic). Word(s) that may be subject or predicate of a proposition (MAJOR[2], MIDDLE[1], MINOR, *term*). **8.** Word used to express a definite concept esp. in particular branch of study etc., (*technical, scientific, law, term*); **in ~s of,** in the language peculiar to, using as basis of expression or thought; CONTRADICTION *in terms*; **in set** (definite) **~s. 9.** (in *pl.*) Language employed, mode of expression, (*in the most flattering, no* UNCERTAIN, *terms*); *state* etc. **in ~s,** explicitly. **10.** (in *pl.*) Conditions, stipulations, (*cannot accept his terms*; *do it on your own terms*; *surrendered on terms*); (esp.) charge, price, (*his terms are £5 a lesson*; *hire-purchase on easy terms*; INCLUSIVE *terms*); **bring** person **to ~s,** cause him to accept conditions; **come to ~s,** yield, give way; **come to** or **make ~s,** conclude agreement (*with*), reconcile oneself *with* difficulties etc.; **on ~s** (fig. of friendship or equality); ‖**~s of reference,** points referred to an individual or body of persons for decision or report, (definition of) scope of inquiry etc.; **~s of trade,** ratio between prices paid for imports and received for exports. **11.** (in *pl.*) Relation, footing, (*am on good, bad, familiar, terms with him*; *not on* SPEAKING[1] *terms*). [ME f. OF *terme* f. L TERMINUS]

tẽrm[2] *v.t.* Denominate, call, (*the music termed plainsong*; *I forget how* or *what he terms it*; *this he termed sheer robbery*). [f. prec.]

tẽr'magant *n.* & *a.* **1.** *n.* (Hist.; *T~*). Imaginary deity of violent and turbulent character, often appearing in morality plays. **2.** Brawling overbearing woman, shrew. **3.** *a.* Violent, turbulent, shrewish. [ME *Tervagant* f. OF *Tervagan* f. It. *Trivigante*]

tẽr'mĭnable *a.* That may be terminated; coming to an end after certain time (*terminable annuity*); hence ~NESS (-bəln-) *n.* [f. TERMINATE[1] + -ABLE]

tẽr'mĭnal *a.* & *n.* **1.** *a.* Of or forming a limit or terminus (*terminal station*); (Med.) forming or undergoing last stage of fatal disease; (Bot.) borne at end of stem etc.; (Zool. etc.) ending a series (*terminal joints*); of, done etc., each term, (*terminal accounts, examinations*); ~ **figure,** = TERMINUS 4; ~ **velocity** (of falling body, such that resistance of air etc. prevents further increase of speed under gravity); hence ~LY[2] *adv.* **2.** *n.* Terminating thing, extremity, esp. point of connection for closing electric circuit; terminus for railway trains or long-distance buses; departure and arrival building for air passengers; ornament at end of column etc.; apparatus for transmission of messages to and from computer, communications system, etc. [f. L *terminalis* (as TERMINUS; see -AL)]

tẽr'mĭnāte *v.* **1.** *v.t.* Bound, limit. **2.** *v.t.* & *i.* Bring or come to an end; end (pregnancy) before term by artificial means. **3.** *v.i.* (Of word) end *in* (specified letter(s) or syllable). [f. L *terminare* (as TERMINUS) + -ATE[3]]

tẽrmĭnā'tion *n.* In vbl senses; word's final syllable or letter(s) esp. as element in inflexion or derivation, whence ~AL *a.*; **put a ~ to, bring to a ~,** make an end of. [ME, f. OF, or f. L *terminatio* (as prec.; see -ATION)]

tẽr'mĭnātor *n.* Person or thing that terminates; dividing line between light and dark part of heavenly body. [f. TERMINATE + -OR, or f. LL *terminator*]

tẽr'mĭner. See OYER.

tẽr'mĭn|ĭsm *n.* Doctrine that everyone has limited term for repentance; = NOMINALISM; so ~IST (2) *n.* [f. L TERMINUS + -ISM]

tẽrmĭnolŏ'gĭcal *a.* Of terminology; ~ **inexactitude,** (joc.) a lie; hence ~LY[2] *adv.* [f. foll. + -ICAL]

tẽrmĭnŏ'log|ў *n.* Science of proper use of terms; system of terms used in a science, art, etc.; hence ~IST (3) *n.* [f. G *terminologie* f. med. L TERMINUS term; see -LOGY]

tẽr'mĭn|us *n.* (*pl.* ~i *pr.* -ī, *or* ~**uses**). **1.** Final point, goal; starting-point. **2.** Point at end of railway or bus route, pipeline, etc. **3.** (Math.) End-point of vector etc. **4.** Figure of human bust ending in square pillar, orig. as boundary-marker. **5.** *~us ad que'm, a quo'* (ahkwō'), finishing-, starting-, point (of argument, policy, period, etc.). [L, = end, limit, boundary]

tẽrmĭtār'ĭum, tẽr'mĭtarў, *ns.* Nest of termites. [f. foll. + -ARIUM, -ARY[1]]

tẽr'mīte *n.* Social insect of order Isoptera, chiefly tropical and very destructive to timber, white ant. [f. LL *termes -mitis* alt. f. L *tarmes* after *terere* rub]

tẽr'mor *n.* (Law). One who holds lands etc. for a term of years, or for life. [ME, f. AF *termer* (as TERM[1]; see -ER[2], -OR)]

tẽrn[1] *n.* Sea-bird of genus *Sterna*, like gull but usu. smaller and with long forked tail. [of Scand. orig.; cf. Da. *terne*, Sw. *tärna* f. ON *therna*]

tẽrn[2] *n.* Set of three, esp. three lottery numbers that when drawn together win large prize; such prize. [f. F *terne* f. L *terni* three each]

tẽr'narў *a.* Composed of three parts; (Math.) using three as base (*ternary* SCALE[3]); ~ **form,** (Mus., of movement) having subject repeated after interposed second subject in related key. [ME, f. L *ternarius* (*terni* three each; see -ARY[1])]

tēr'nate *a.* Arranged in threes, esp. (Bot., of leaf) having three leaflets, whorled in threes; hence ~LY[2] (-tlĭ) *adv.* [f. mod. L *ternatus* (as prec.; see -ATE[2])]

tērne *n.* ~**(-plate)**, inferior tin-plate alloyed with much lead. [prob. f. F *terne* dull; cf. TARNISH]

tērōtĕchnŏ'logy̆ (-k-; *or* tĕ'r-) *n.* Branch of technology dealing with installation and maintenance of equipment. [f. Gk *tēreō* take care of + -O- + TECHNOLOGY]

tēr'pēne *n.* (Chem.) Any of large group of hydrocarbons found in essential oils esp. from conifers and oranges. [f. *terpentin* obs. var. of TURPENTINE + -ENE]

Tērpsĭchorē'an (-k-) *a.* Pertaining to dancing. [f. *Terpsichore* Muse of dancing + -AN]

terra (tĕ'ra) *n.* ~ ***alba*** (ă'lba), pipeclay or similar white mineral [L *albus* white]; ~***firma*** (fēr'ma), dry land, firm ground [L *firmus* firm]; ~ ***incognita*** (ĭn-kŏ'gnĭta), unknown or unexplored region [L *incognitus* unknown]; ~ ***sigillata*** (sĭjĭlā'ta), (1) astringent clay from Lemnos, (2) Samian ware, [med. L *sigillatus* sealed]. [L, = earth]

tĕ'rrace (*or* -ĭs) *n.*, & *v.t.* **1.** *n.* Raised level space, natural or artificial, esp. for walking or standing; (Geol.) raised beach, or similar formation beside river etc. **2.** Row of housing along top or face of slope, row of contiguous uniform houses; ~**-house,** one of row of houses joined by party-walls. **3.** *v.t.* Form into or furnish with terrace(s); ~**d house,** = *terrace-house*; ~**d roof,** flat roof esp. of an Indian or Eastern house. [OF, f. Rom. **terracea* (as prec.; see -ACEOUS)]

tĕrracŏ'tta *n.* Unglazed usu. brownish-red fine pottery used as ornamental building-material and in statuary, pottery, etc.; statuette of this; its colour. [It. *terra cotta* baked earth]

terrae fili|us (tĕrī fĭ'lĭus) *n.* (*pl.* ~***i*** *pr.* -ī). Person of humble or obscure parentage; (Hist.) satirical orator at Oxford Univ. [L, = son of the earth]

tĕrrai'n *n.* Tract of land as regarded by the physical geographer or the military tactician. [F, f. Rom. **terranum*, f. L *terrenum* neut. (as n.) of *terrenus* TERRENE]

tĕrramār'|a *n.* (*pl.* ~**e** *pr.* -ā). = foll. [It. dial.; see foll.]

tĕrramār'ė (*or* -ār') *n.* (Ammoniacal earthy deposit found in mounds in) prehistoric lake-dwelling or -settlement esp. in Italy. [F, f. It. dial. *terra* (*mara* = *marna* marl)]

tĕ'rrapĭn *n.* N. Amer. edible freshwater tortoise of family Emydidae; type of prefabricated one-storey building. [Algonquian]

tĕrrā'quėous *a.* (Of the earth) comprising both land and water; living in or extending over land and water. [f. L *terra* earth + AQUEOUS]

tĕrrār'ĭ|um *n.* (*pl.* ~**a** *or* ~**ums**). **1.** Vivarium for terrestrial animals. **2.** Sealed transparent globe etc. containing growing plants. [mod. L, f. L *terra* earth, after *aquarium*]

tėrră'zzō (-tsō) *n.* (*pl.* ~**s**). Flooring-material of stone chips set in concrete and given a smooth surface. [It., = terrace]

tĕrrē'ne *a.* Of earth, earthy: terrestrial. [ME f. AF, f. L *terrenus* (TERRA)]

terr'eplein (tār'plān) *n.* Level space where battery of guns is mounted. [orig. = talus behind rampart, f. F *terre-plein* f. It. *terrapieno* (*terrapienare* fill with earth f. *terra* earth + *pieno* f. L *plenus* full)]

terrĕ'strĭal *a.* & *n.* **1.** *a.* Of the earth, esp. opp. to *celestial*; **the** ~ **globe,** the earth; **a** ~ **globe** (representing the earth); *terrestrial* MAGNETISM; ~ **planet,** Mercury, Venus, Earth, or Mars; ~ **telescope** (giving erect image for observation of terrestrial objects). **2.** Of this world, worldly, (*terrestrial aims, interests*). **3.** Of land opp. to water; (Zool.) living on the ground, (Bot.) growing in the soil, opp. to *aquatic, arboreal* or *epiphytic, aerial.* **4.** Hence ~LY[2] *adv.* **5.** *n.* Inhabitant of earth. [ME, f. L *terrestris* (*terra* earth) + -IAL]

tĕ'rrėt, -ĭt, *n.* Each of loops or rings on harness-pad for driving-reins to pass through. [ME, var. of (now dial.) *toret* f. OF *to(u)ret* dim. of TOUR]

terre-verte (tārvār't) *n.* Soft green earth used as pigment. [F, = green earth]

tĕ'rrĭble *a.* Causing terror, fit to cause terror, awful, dreadful, formidable; (colloq.) very great or bad (*he is a terrible bore*); (colloq.) incompetent (*I'm terrible at tennis*); ENFANT TERRIBLE; hence ~NESS (-beln-) *n.* [ME f. F, f. L *terribilis* (*terrēre* frighten; see -IBLE)]

tĕ'rrĭbly̆ *adv.* In adj. senses; (sl.) very, extremely, (*he was terribly nice about it*). [f. prec. + -LY[2]]

tĕrrĭ'colous *a.* Living on or in the earth. [f. L *terricola* earth-dweller (*terra* earth, *colere* inhabit) + -OUS]

tĕ'rrĭer[1] *n.* **1.** Small active hardy dog able to pursue fox etc. into earth. **2.** (*T*~; colloq.) ||Member of Territorial Army etc. [ME, f. OF (*chien*) *terrier* f. med. L *terrarius* f. L *terra* earth; see -ER[2] (2)]

tĕ'rrĭer[2] *n.* Book recording site, boundaries, etc., of land of private persons or corporations; rent-roll; (Hist.) collection of acknowledgements of vassals or tenants of a lordship. [ME, f. OF *a.* (as *n.*) = med. L *terrarius* (*liber* book); see prec.]

terrĭ'f|ĭc *a.* Causing terror; (colloq.) of great size, excellent (*did a terrific job*), excessive (*making a terrific noise*); hence ~ICALLY *adv.* [f. L *terrificus* (*terrēre* frighten; see -FIC)]

tĕ'rrĭfy̆ *v.t.* Fill with terror, frighten (q.v. for constructions). [f. L *terrificare* (as prec.; see -FY)]

tĕrrĭ'gėnous *a.* Produced by the earth or land (*terrigenous deposits*). [f. L *terrigenus* earth-born + -OUS]

terri'ne (-ē'n) *n.* (Earthenware vessel, esp. containing and sold with) table delicacy such as pâté. [orig. form of TUREEN]

tĕ'rrĭt. See TERRET.

tĕrrĭtōr'ĭal *a.* & *n.* **1.** *a.* Of territory (*territorial possessions, acquisitions*); limited to a district (*the right was strictly territorial*); (*T*~) of (any of) the U.S. Territories; ||**T**~ **Army,** volunteer force organized 1908–67 according to localities to provide reserve of trained and disciplined man-power for use in emergency, now **T**~ **and Army Volunteer Reserve**; ~ **waters,** marginal waters under the jurisdiction of a State, esp. that part of the sea within three (or other number of) miles of shore measured from low-water mark; hence ~IZE (3) *v.t.*, ~LY[2] *adv.* **2.** *n.* ||Member of Territorial Army etc. [f. LL *territorialis* (as TERRITORY; see -AL)]

tĕrrĭtōr'ĭalĭsm *n.* System of Church government in which civil power has supreme authority. [f. prec. + -ISM]

tĕ'rrĭtory̆ *n.* Extent of land under jurisdiction of sovereign, State, city, etc.; (fig.) sphere, province; area over which goods-distributor or commercial traveller operates; large tract of land; (*T*~) organized division of a country, esp. (U.S. etc.) one not yet admitted to full rights of a State; (Zool.) area held by animal(s) against others of same species; area defended by team etc. in game. [ME, f. L *territorium* (*terra* land; see -ORY)]

tĕ´rror *n.* **1.** Extreme fear; **~-stricken, ~-struck,** affected with terror. **2.** Person or thing that causes terror; (**holy**) ~, (colloq.) formidable person, troublesome child, etc.; **king of ~s,** Death (Job 18:14); **Reign of T~, the T~,** period of French Revolution 1793–4, similar period marked by remorseless sanguinary excesses of revolutionaries (also **Red T~**) or reactionaries (also **White T~**). [ME f. OF *terrour* f. L *terror -oris* (*terrēre* frighten; see -OR)]

tĕ´rror|ĭst *n.* One who favours or uses terror-inspiring methods of governing or of coercing government or community; hence or cogn. ~ISM (2, 3) *n.*, ~ĭ´STIC *a.* [f. F *terroriste* (as prec.; see -IST)]

tĕ´rrorīz|e, -is|e (-īz), *v.t.* Fill with terror; coerce by terrorism; hence ~A´TION *n.* [f. TERROR + -IZE]

tĕ´rrȳ *n.* & *a.* (Pile fabric) with the loops uncut, used esp. for towels. [18th c., of unkn. orig.]

Tēr̃să´nctus *n.* (Eccl.) = SANCTUS. [L (*ter* thrice, SANCTUS)]

tēr̃se *a.* (Of speech, written matter, style, writer) free from cumbrousness and superfluity, smooth and concise; curt; hence ~´LY^{2} (-slĭ) *adv.*, ~´NESS (-sn-) *n.* [f. L *tersus* p.p. of *tergēre* wipe, polish]

tēr̃´tian (-shan) *a.* & *n.* (Fever) recurring every other (by inclusive reckoning every third) day. [ME (*fever*) *tersiane* f. L (*febris*) *tertiana* (as foll.; see -AN)]

tēr̃´tiarȳ (-sherĭ) *a.* & *n.* **1.** *a.* Of the third order, rank, formation, etc.; next after secondary. **2.** *n.* Bird's flight-feather of third row, borne on humerus; (*T~*) member of third order of monastic body, (Geol.) period or system subsequent to Secondary. [f. L *tertiarius* (*tertius* third; see -ARY^{1})]

tertium quid (tēr̃shĭum kwĭ´d) *n.* A third something, esp. intermediate between mind and matter or between opposite things. [L, app. transl. Gk *triton ti*]

tēr̃´valent (*or* -vā´-) *a.* (Chem.) = TRI*valent*. [f. TER- + *valent-* part. st. f. as VALENCE^{2}]

tĕ´rȳlēne *n.* Synthetic polyester used as textile fibre. [P; f. *terephthalic* acid (f. *terebic* f. TEREBINTH, + PHTHALIC) + ETHYLENE]

terza rima (tār̃tsa rē´ma) *n.* (Pros.) Arrangement of (esp. iambic pentameter) triplets rhyming *aba bcb cdc* etc. as in Dante's *Divina Commedia*. [It., = third rhyme]

terzett|o (tār̃tsĕ´tō) *n.* (*pl.* *~i pr.* -ē, *or* *~os*). (Mus.) Vocal trio. [It.; see TERCET]

Tĕ´sla *n.* **1.** ~ **coil,** form of induction coil for producing high-frequency alternating currents. **2.** (*t~*). Unit of magnetic induction, = 10,000 gauss. [f. N. ~, Amer. scientist d. 1943]

tĕ´ssell|āte *v.t.* (esp. in *p.p.*) Make from tesserae (*tessellated pavement*); (Bot. & Zool., in *p.p.*) regularly chequered; hence ~A´TION *n.* [f. L *tessellare* (*tessella* dim. of foll.) + -ATE^{3}]

tĕ´sser|a *n.* (*pl.* *~ae*). Small square usu. cubical block used in mosaic, whence ~AL *a.*; (Rom. & Gk Ant.) small square of bone etc. used as token, ticket, etc. [L f. Gk, neut. of *tesseres*, *tessares* four]

tessitura (tĕsĭtoor´a) *n.* (Mus.) Range within which most tones of a voice-part fall. [It., = TEXTURE]

tĕst^{1} *n.* **1.** Critical examination or trial of person's or thing's qualities (ACID^{2} *test*; BLOOD^{1} *test*; BREATH *test*; MEAN^{1}*s test*; M.O.T. *test*); **put to the ~,** cause to undergo this; STAND^{1} *the test*. **2.** Means of so examining, standard for comparison or trial, circumstances suitable for this, (*success is not a fair test*). **3.** Ground of admission or rejection (*is excluded by our test*). **4.** (Chem.) Reagent, substance employed to reveal presence of another in a compound. **5.** ||Movable hearth in reverberating furnace with cupel used in separating gold or silver from lead. **6.** (colloq.) Test match. **7.** **T~ Act** (of 1672–1828, requiring all persons before holding office in Britain to **take the ~**, i.e. the oaths of supremacy and allegiance or equivalent test, or act of 1871 relaxing conditions for university degrees); ~ **bed,** equipment for testing aircraft engines before acceptance for general use; ~ **case,** (Law) case whose decision is taken as settling other cases involving same question of law; ~ **drive** (to determine qualities of motor vehicle with view to regular use); ~ **flight** (to determine performance of aircraft); ~ **match** (in cricket tour etc., usu. between different countries and as one of series); ~ **meal** (of specified quantity and composition, eaten to assist tests of gastric secretion); ~ **paper,** minor examination-paper, (Chem.) paper impregnated with substance changing colour under known conditions; **~-piece** (performed by entrant in musical etc. competition); ~ **pilot** (undertaking test flights); **~-tube** (of thin glass closed at one end, for tests or other chem. purposes); *~-tube baby*, (colloq.) one conceived by artificial insemination, or developing elsewhere than in a mother's body. [ME f. OF, f. L *testu(m)* earthen pot, collateral form of *testa* TEST^{3}; in mod. use mainly f. foll.]

tĕst^{2} *v.t.* Put to the test or a test, make trial of, (person, thing, quality); try severely, tax, (one's powers of endurance etc.); ||refine or assay (metal); (Chem.) examine by means of reagent; ~ **out,** put (theory etc.) to practical test; hence ~ABI´LITY *n.*, ~´ABLE *a.*, ~EE´ *n.* [f. prec.]

tĕst^{3} *n.* External shell etc. of invertebrate, esp. tunicate. [f. L *testa* tile, jug, shell, etc.; cf. TEST^{1}]

tĕ´sta *n.* (*pl.* *~e*). (Bot.) Seed-coat. [L (as prec.)]

tĕstā´ceous (-shus) *a.* Of shells or shellfish; with hard continuous shell; (Bot. & Zool.) of brick-red colour. [f. L *testaceus* (as TEST^{3}; see -ACEOUS)]

tĕ´stacȳ *n.* Being testate. [f. TESTATE, after *intestacy*]

tĕ´stament *n.* **1.** = WILL^{2} 8; so ~ARY^{1} (-ĕ´n-) *a.* **2.** (Bibl.) Covenant, dispensation; **Old, New, T~,** portion of the Bible dealing with Mosaic, Christian, dispensation; (*T~*) copy of the N.T. **3.** (colloq.) (Written) statement of one's beliefs, principles, etc. [ME, f. L *testamentum* will (as TESTATE; see -MENT); in early Christian L rendering Gk *diathēkē* covenant]

tĕ´stāte (*or* -at) *a.* & *n.* (Person) who has left a valid will at death. [f. L *testatus* p.p. of *testari* testify, make will, (*testis* witness); see -ATE^{2}]

tĕstā´|tor *n.* One who has made a will, esp. one who dies testate; so ~TRIX *n.* [ME, f. AF *testatour* f. L *testator* (as prec.; see -OR)]

tĕ´ster^{1} *n.* In vbl senses. [f. TEST^{2} + -ER^{1} (1, 2)]

tĕ´ster^{2} *n.* Canopy, esp. over four-poster bed. [ME, f. med. L *testerium*, *testrum*, *testura* f. Rom. **testa* head f. L *testa* tile]

||**tĕ´ster^{3}** *n.* (Hist.) Shilling of Henry VIII, esp. depreciated one; sixpence. [var. of earlier & F *teston* f. Rom. (as prec.; see -OON)]

tĕ´stĭcle *n.* Male organ that secretes spermatozoa etc., esp. one of ovoid pair enclosed in scrotum behind penis of man and most mammals; so **tĕstĭ´cūlAR^{1}** *a.* [ME, f. L *testiculus* dim. of *testis* witness (of virility)]

tĕstĭ´cūlate *a.* Having or shaped like testicles; (Bot., esp. of orchid) having pair of tubers so shaped. [f. LL *testiculatus* (as prec.; see -ATE^{2})]

tĕ´stĭfȳ *v.* **1.** *v.i.* (Of person or thing) bear witness (*to* fact, state, assertion, *against* person etc., (arch.) *of* or *concerning* matter); (Law) give evidence. **2.** *v.t.* Affirm, declare, (one's regret etc., *that, how,* etc.); (of thing) be evidence of, evince. [ME, f. L *testificari* (*testis* witness; see -FY)]

tĕstĭmō'nĭal *n.* Certificate of character, conduct, or qualifications; gift or money presented to person, esp. in public, as mark of esteem, in acknowledgement of services, etc. [ME, f. OF *testimoignal* a. f. *tesmoin* or f. LL *testimonialis* (as foll.; see -AL)]

tĕ'stĭmonў *n.* Evidence, demonstration, (*called him in testimony; produce testimony* (*to* or *of*); *we have his testimony for that; in testimony whereof*); (Law) oral or written statement under oath or affirmation; declarations, statements, (*must rely on the testimony of history, of historians*); (arch.) solemn protest or confession; (Bibl.) the decalogue, esp. *the tables of the testimony*; (in *sing.* or *pl.*) the Scriptures. [ME, f. L *testimonium* (*testis* witness; see -MONY)]

tĕ'st|ĭs *n.* (*pl.* ~**es** *pr.* -ēz). (Anat. & Zool.) Testicle. [L, = witness (cf. TESTICLE)]

tĕstŏ'sterōne *n.* Steroid androgen formed in testicles. [f. TESTIS + -O- + STEROL + -ONE]

tĕstū'dĭnal *a.* Of or shaped like a tortoise. [f. as foll. + -AL]

tĕstū'd|ō (*or* -ōō'-) *n.* (*pl.* ~**os,** *or* ~**ines** *pr.* -ĭnēz). (Rom. Ant.) screen formed by body of troops in close array with overlapping shields; movable screen to protect besieging troops. [L *testudo -dinis* tortoise etc. (as TEST³)]

tĕ'st|ў *a.* Irritable, touchy; hence ~**ĬLY²** *adv.*, ~**ĬNESS** *n.* [ME f. AF *testif,* f. OF *teste* head (as TEST³); see -IVE]

tėtă'n|ĭc *a.* Of, such as occurs in, tetanus (*tetanic spasm*); hence ~ICALLY *adv.* [f. L f. Gk *tetanikos* (as foll.; see -IC)]

tĕ'tan|us *n.* Bacterial disease marked by tonic spasm of voluntary muscles, e.g. lockjaw; prolonged contraction of muscle caused by rapidly repeated stimuli; hence ~IZE (3) *v.t.*, ~OID *a.* [ME f. L, f. Gk *tetanos* muscular spasm (*teinō* stretch)]

tĕ'tanў *n.* Disease with intermittent muscular spasms caused by malfunction of parathyroid glands and consequent deficiency of calcium. [f F *tétanie* (as prec.; see -Y¹)]

tĕ'(t)ch|ў *a.* Peevish, irritable; hence ~**ĬLY²** *adv.*, ~**ĬNESS** *n.* [prob. f. *tecche, tache* blemish, fault, f. OF *teche, tache,* + -Y²]

tête-à-tête (tātahtā't) *adv.*, *a.*, & *n.* **1.** *adv.* & *a.* Together in private. **2.** *a.* Private, confidential; concerning only two persons. **3.** *n.* Private interview or conversation usu. between two; sofa for two face to face. [F, lit. head-to-head]

tête-bêche (tātbā'sh) *a.* (Of postage stamp) printed upside down or sideways relative to another. [F (*tête* head, *bêche* f. *bêchevet* double bed--head)]

tĕ'ther (-dh-) *n.*, & *v.t.* **1.** *n.* Rope, chain, halter, by which grazing animal is confined; (fig.) scope, extent of one's knowledge, authority, etc.; **at the end of** one's ~, having reached the limit of one's abilities, resources, patience, etc. **2.** *v.t.* Tie (esp. grazing animal) with tether. [ME, f. ON *tjóthr,* = OHG *zeotar* wagon-pole f. Gmc **teudr-* (**teu-* fasten)]

tĕ'tra- *comb. form.* **1.** Four, as: ~**chord,** scale series of four notes in half-octave (esp. in ancient music), musical instrument with four strings; ~**cy'clic,** (Bot.) having four circles or whorls; ~**da'ctyl** *a.* & *n.*, ~**da'ctylous** *a.*, four-toed (animal); ~**gon,** plane figure with four angles and four sides; ~**gram, T~gra'mmaton,** word of four letters, esp. Hebrew name of God written in four letters; ~**gynous** (tĭtră'jĭ-), having four pistils; ~**logy** (tĭtră'l-), group of four related literary or operatic works, esp. (Gk Ant.) three tragedies (trilogy) and satyric drama; ~**merous** (tĭtră'm-), having four parts; ~**meter** (tĭtră'm-), (Pros.) verse of four measures; ~**morph,** (Christian Art) union of attributes of four evangelists in one winged figure; **tetra'ndrous** (tĭtră'-), having four stamens; ~**ploid,** having four times the haploid set of chromosomes; ~**pod** *a.* & *n.*, ~**podous** (tĭtră'p-) *a.*, (animal or structure) with four feet; ~**pterous** (tĭtră'p-), having four wings; ~**stich** (-k), (Pros.) group of four lines of verse; ~**style** *a.* & *n.*, (building) with four pillars esp. forming portico in front or supporting ceiling; ~**sy'llable,** word of four syllables (so ~*sylla'bic a.*); **tetrato'mic,** (Chem.) having four atoms (of a specified kind) in the molecule; ~**va'lent,** (Chem.) having a valence of four. **2.** (Chem., forming names of compounds) containing four atoms or groups of a specified kind (*tetroxide*; ~**e'thyl lead,** liquid added to petrol as anti-knock). [Gk (*tettares* four)]

tĕ'trăd *n.* The number four; group of four. [f. Gk *tetras -ados* (as prec.; see -AD 1)]

tėtră'gonal *a.* Of a TETRAgon; (Cryst.) having three axes at right angles, two of them equal; hence ~LY² *adv.* [f. TETRA*gon* + -AL]

tĕtrahĕ'dr|on (-*a*-h-) *n.* (*pl.* ~**a** *or* ~**ons**). Four--sided solid, triangular pyramid; so ~AL *a.* [f. late Gk *tetraedron* neut. (as n.) of TETRA(*edros* f. *hedra* base) four-sided; cf. -HEDRON]

tĕ'trarch (-k) *n.* One of 4 joint rulers; (Rom. Hist.) governor of fourth part of country or province, subordinate ruler; hence or cogn. ~ATE¹ (1), ~Y¹, *ns.*, ~ICAL (-ar'k-) *a.* [ME, f. LL *tetrarcha* f. L *tetrarches* f. Gk *tetrarkhēs* (as TETRA-, *arkhō* rule)]

tĕ'trōde *n.* Thermionic valve having four electrodes. [f. TETRA- + Gk *hodos* way]

tĕ'tter *n.* (arch. or dial.) Pustular skin-eruption, e.g. eczema; ~**wort,** greater celandine (supposed to cure tetters). [OE *teter*; cf. OHG *zittaroh,* G dial. *zitteroch,* Skr. *dadru*]

Teut. *abbr.* Teutonic.

Teuto- *comb. form.* = foll., as: ~MANIA(C), ~PHIL(E), ~PHOBE, ~PHOBIA, *adjs.* & *ns.* [irreg. f. foll. + -O-]

Teu'ton *n.* Member of a Teutonic nation, esp. a German; (Hist.) member of a N. Eur. tribe mentioned in 4th c. B.C. and attacking Roman republic *c.* 110 B.C. [f. L *Teutones, Teutoni,* f. IE base meaning 'people' or 'country']

Teutŏ'nĭc *a.* & *n.* **1.** *a.* Of the Teutons; of the Germanic peoples or their languages; having characteristics attributed to these peoples; German; hence ~ISM (4), **Teu'ton**ISM (2, 4), *ns.*, **Teu'ton**IZE (3) *v.t.* **2.** *n.* Germanic language. [f. F *teutonique* f. L *Teutonicus* (as prec.; see -IC)]

Tex. *abbr.* Texas.

Tĕ'xan *a.* & *n.* (Native or inhabitant) of Texas. [f. *Texas* in U.S. + -AN]

tĕxt *n.* **1.** Original words of author esp. opp. to paraphrase of or commentary on them (*there is nothing about this in the text; the text is hopelessly corrupt*). **2.** Passage of Scripture quoted as authority or esp. chosen as subject of sermon etc.; subject, theme. **3.** Main body of book opp. to notes, pictures, etc.; *textbook; (in *pl.*) books prescribed for study. **4.** ~(**-hand**), fine large kind of handwriting esp. for manuscripts. **5.** ~**'book,** (*n.*) manual of instruction, standard book in a branch of study, (*a.*) = COPY¹-*book* (2). [ME f. ONF *tixte, texte* f. L *textus* tissue, literary style (in med. L = Gospel) f. L *texere text-* weave]

tĕ'xtīle *a.* & *n.* **1.** *a.* Of weaving (*the textile art, industry*); woven, suitable for weaving, (*textile fabrics, materials*). **2.** *n.* Textile material; any cloth. [f. L *textilis* (as prec.; see -IL)]

tĕ'xtūal *a.* Of or in the text (*textual* CRITICISM, *errors*); hence ~LY² *adv.* [ME, f. med. L *textualis* (as TEXT; see -AL)]
tĕ'xtūal|ist *n.* One who adheres strictly to the letter of the text; person learned in scriptural texts; so ~ISM (3) *n.* [f. prec. + -IST]
tĕ'xtur|e *n.*, & *v.t.* **1.** *n.* Arrangement of threads etc. in textile fabric, characteristic feel due to this; arrangement of small constituent parts, perceived structure, (*of* skin, rock, soil, organic tissue, literary work, etc.); representation of structure and detail of objects in art; (Mus.) quality of sound formed by combining parts; hence ~AL (-scher- *or* -tūr-), ~eLESS (-cher-), *adjs.* **2.** *v.t.* Make by weaving; provide with texture. [ME, f. L *textura* weaving (as TEXT; see -URE)]
||**T.G.W.U.** *abbr.* Transport & General Workers' Union.
-th¹ *suf.* forming *ns.* (a) f. *vbs.* (*birth, growth, tilth*) [f. or after OE & ON, f. IE *-*tos* etc.], (b) f. *adjs.* (*breadth, filth, length*) [f. or after OE *-thu, -tho, -th* f. Gmc *-*ithō* f. IE *-*itā*].
-th², -ėth¹ (after *-ty*), *suf.* forming ordinal and fractional numbers with all simple numbers from *four* onwards (*4th, fifth, twentieth*). [OE *-tha, -the,* or *-otha, -othe,* f. IE *-*tos*]
-th³. See -ETH².
Th *symb.* thorium.
Thai (tī) *a.* & *n.* (Native, inhabitant, or language) of Thailand; (member) of a Mongolian people in S.E. Asia or the group of languages spoken by them. [Thai, = free]
thă'lam|us *n.* (*pl.* **~i** *pr.* -ī). (Gk Ant.) inner room, women's apartment; (Anat.) interior region of brain where sensory nerves originate, esp. *optic thalamus*; (Bot.) receptacle of flower. [L, f. Gk *thalamos*]
thală'ssĭc *a.* Of sea(s), esp. small or inland seas. [f. F *thalassique* f. Gk *thalassa* sea; see -IC]
tha'ler (tah'-) *n.* (Hist.) German silver coin. [G *t(h)aler*; see DOLLAR]
thalĭ'domīde *n.* Sedative drug found in 1961 to cause malformation of limbs of foetus when taken by mother early in pregnancy; ~ **baby** or **child** (born deformed, esp. without limb(s), through effects of this drug). [f. ph*thalimido*-glutar*imide*]
thă'll|ium *n.* Rare soft white metallic element; hence ~IC, ~OUS, *adjs.* [f. as THALLUS (from green line in its spectrum) + -IUM]
thă'llogėn, thă'llophȳte, *ns.* (Bot.) Plant having thallus, e.g. alga or fungus or lichen. [f. mod. L *Thallophyta* (as foll., -GEN, -PHYTE)]
thă'll|us *n.* (*pl.* **~i** *pr.* -ī). Plant-body without vascular tissue and not differentiated into root, stem, and leaves; hence ~OID *a.* [L, f. Gk *thallos* green shoot (*thallō* bloom)]
tha'lwĕg (tah'lv-) *n.* **1.** (Geog.) Line where opposite slopes meet at bottom of valley or river or lake. **2.** (Law). Boundary between States along centre of river etc. [G (*thal, tal* valley, *weg* way)]
Thames (tĕmz) *n.* ||*Set the Thames on* FIRE¹; FATHER¹ *Thames.* [river ~ in England]
than (dhan *or, when stressed,* dhăn) *conj.* (& quasi-*prep.*) introducing second member of comparison (*you are taller than he* (*is*), (colloq.) *taller than him*; *I know you better than he* (*does*), *better than* (*I know*) *him*; *it is better to use hot water than cold*; *would do anything rather than let him get hurt, rather than this*; *would do anything rather than that he should get hurt*; *a man than whom no one is better able to judge*) or statement of difference (*any person other than himself*; *not known elsewhere than in Britain*). [OE *thanne* etc., orig. same wd as THEN]
thā'nage *n.* (Hist.) Rank of or land granted to thane. [ME, f. AF *thanage* (as THANE; see -AGE)]
thănato- *comb. form.* Death, as: **~logy** (-ŏ'l-), scientific study of phenomena accompanying and practices relating to death. [f. Gk *thanatos* death + -o-]
thāne *n.* (Engl. Hist.) One holding land from king etc. by military service, ranking between ordinary freemen and hereditary nobles; (Sc. Hist.) one holding land from king, ranking with earl's son, chief of clan; hence ~'DOM (-nd-), ~'SHIP (-nsh-), *ns.* [OE *theg(e)n* servant, soldier, = OS *thegan,* OHG *degan,* ON *thegn* freeman, liegeman f. Gmc **thegnaz* f. IE **teknos*]
thănk *v.t.* Express gratitude to (person *for* thing); ~ **God, goodness, heaven**(**s**), etc. (expr. pious gratitude, or (colloq.) pleasure or relief); (**I**) ~ **you,** (colloq.) **~'ing you,** (polite formula acknowledging gift, service, offer accepted or refused); ~ **you for nothing** (as contempt. denial that any thanks are due from one); ~ **you for,** (anticipatory) please give me etc.; **I will ~ you** (as polite formula, now usu. iron. implying reproach: *I will thank you to shut the door, wipe your shoes, leave my affairs alone*); **he may ~ himself, has only himself to ~, for that,** it is his own fault; **~-you** *n.*, (colloq.) expressing of thanks. [OE *thancian,* = OS *thankon,* OHG *dankōn* f. Gmc **thankōjan* (as THANKS)]
thă'nkful *a.* Grateful; (of words or act) expressive of thanks; hence ~LY² *adv.*, ~NESS *n.* [OE *thancful* (as THANKS, -FUL)]
thă'nklėss *a.* Not feeling or expressing gratitude; (of task etc.) not likely to win thanks, unprofitable; hence ~LY² *adv.*, ~NESS *n.* [f. as foll. + -LESS]
thănk|s *n. pl.* **1.** (Expression of) gratitude (*give thanks to Heaven*; *expressed his heartfelt thanks*; *she smiled her thanks*; *small,* iron. *much, thanks I got for it*; *many thanks for your help*); **give ~s,** say grace at meal; RETURN¹ *thanks*; **~-offering,** offering made as act of thanksgiving. **2.** (As formula) thank you (esp. colloq., *thanks awfully, very much,* etc.); **~s to** (as the good or bad result of) *my foresight, your obstinacy*; **small** or **no ~s to,** despite. [pl. of obs. *thank* f. OE *thanc,* = OS *thank,* OHG *danc,* Goth. *thagks* f. Gmc **thankaz,* cogn. w. THINK]
thă'nksgĭvĭng (-g-) *n.* Expression of gratitude esp. to God; form of words for this (**General T~**, in Book of Common Prayer); ***T~** (**Day**) (set apart for giving thanks to God, usu. fourth Thursday in November in U.S., second Monday in October in Canada). [f. prec. + GIVE¹ + -ING¹]
thâr (târ) *n.* Goat-antelope of Nepal; Himalayan wild goat. [native name in Nepal]
that¹ *a., pron.,* & *adv.* **1.** *dem. a.* & *pron.* (*pr.* dhăt; *pl.* **those** *pr.* dhōz). The (person, thing), the person or thing, pointed to or drawn attention to or observed by the speaker at the time, or already named or understood or in question or familiar, (*observe that dog in the next field*; *who is that* (*woman*) *in the garden?*; *what was that* (*noise*)*?*; *what bird is that?*; *don't roll your eyes in that imbecile fashion*; *I knew all that before*; *that* (*action of yours* or *of which you speak*) *is not fair*; *I use that term in a special sense*; *much to the disgust of that monarch*; *was cured from that hour*; *things were easier in those days*); (expr. strong feeling: *I will not see that boy bullied*; *why will you bring that woman here?*; *when you have done thumping that piano*; *shall not easily forget that day*; '*Are you glad?*' '*I am that*'); (coupled or contrasted with THIS, and applied esp. to the farther, less immediate or obvious, etc., of two; *this poker is much heavier than that* (*one*)); (on telephone) ||the person spoken to (*who is that?*); **and** (**all**) **that,** and all or various things associated with or similar to what has been mentioned, and so forth; AT *that*;

wouldn't give ~ (a snap of the fingers) **for it**; HOW'*s that?*; **like ~**, of that kind, in that manner, as you are doing, as he has been doing, etc., (*don't roll your eyes like that*; *wish he would not talk like that*), without effort (*did the job just like tha't*), of that character (*he wouldn't accept any payment—he is like that*); TAKE[1] *that!*; THIS *and that*; THIS, *that, and the other*; WITH *that*; **~ is (to say)** (introducing explanation of preceding word or words); *that's* IT[1]; **~'s more like it,** you are improving; **~'s right!** (expr. approval or (colloq.) assent); **~'s** *a dear, a good boy*, etc., (colloq.) you are (by virtue of present or future obedience etc.); (SO[1]) **~'s ~** (concluding a narrative or discussion, or completing a task); **~ there,** (vulg.) = *that* a.; **~ will do,** no more is needed or desirable. **2.** *pron.* (replacing *the* w. noun, w. sense completed by *rel. pron.* expressed or omitted: *those who drink water think water*; *those may try it who choose*; *hold fast that which is good*; *had that in his eye which forbade further trifling*; *all those* (*that*) *I saw*; *all those specimens that I saw*; or by *a.* or equivalent: *those unfit for use*; *those below the standard*; *a tunic like that described above*; *those persons most affected by the tax*; *like most of those coming from abroad*; *cost of oil is less than that of gas*); (arch. or colloq., foll. by THAT[2]) such, such a, (*has that confidence in his theory that he would put it into practice tomorrow*; *was wounded to that degree that he resigned*). **3.** *adv.* (*pr.* dhăt). (colloq.) To such a degree, so, (*will go that far*; *have done that much*); (**all**) ~, very (*not all that expensive*). **4.** *rel. pron.* (*pr.* dhat; *pl.* same; used, exc. arch., rhet., or poet., only to introduce defining-clause essential or rhet. viewed as essential to identification; often omitted esp. after antecedent in obj. case; cf. WHICH, WHO: *the book* (*that* or *which*) *I sent you*; *the box* (*that* or *which*) *you put them in*; *the man* (*that* or *whom*) *you saw*; *the people* (*that*) *you got it from* or *from whom you got it*; *the meanest flower that blows*; *the best* (*that*) *you can do*; *no one* (*that*) *I ever heard of could see any difference*; *there's a man* (*that* or *who*) *wants to speak to you*; *what is it* (*that*) *makes you sad?*; *this is all* (*that*) *I have*; *there is nothing here that matters*). **5.** *rel. adv.* = *prep.* + sense 4 (*the day* (*that*) *I first met her*; *at the speed* (*that*) *he was going he could not stop*). [OE *thæt*, nom. & acc. sing. neut. of dem. pron. & a. *se, sēo, thæt* (see THE); *those* f. OE *thās* pl. of *thes* THIS]

that[2] (dhat, *or, when stressed,* dhăt) *conj.* (introducing subord. clause): (statement or hypothesis) *they say* (*that*) *he is better*; *there is no doubt* (*that*) *he meant it*; *it is suggested that the mistake was intentional*; *it is hoped that all will go well*; *it is monstrous that he should expect further help*; *the result was that the handle fell off*; (purpose) *he lives that he may eat*; *he withdrew* (*in order*) *that the dispute might cease*; (result) *am so sleepy* (*that*) *I cannot keep my eyes open*; *his language was such that we refused to see him again*; *what have I done that you should treat me like this?*; *where is he, that you come without him?*; (reason or cause) *it is rather that he has not the time*: (wish) (*O*) *that this were all!*; *Oh! that we two were maying*; IN[1] *that*; NOT *that*; NOW *that*. [uses of THAT[1] dem. or rel. pron., in which it becomes a mere rel. or conj. particle]

thătch *n.*, & *v.t.* **1.** *n.* Roof-covering of straw, reeds, palm-leaves, etc.; (colloq.) hair of the head. **2.** *v.t.* Cover (roof, house, or abs.) with thatch; hence **~'**ER[1] *n.* [n. late collateral form of (now dial.) *thack* (OE *thæc*, = OHG *dach* roof f. Gmc **thakam*), after v. f. OE *theccan*, = OS *thekkian*, OHG *decchen*, ON *thekja* f. Gmc **thakjan*, assim to *thack*]

thau'matrōpe *n.* Disc etc. with two different pictures on its two sides, which combine into one by persistence of visual impressions when disc is rapidly rotated; zoetrope. [irreg. f. Gk *thauma* marvel + *-tropos* -turning]

thau'matûrg|e, thau'matûrg|ist, *ns.* Worker of miracles, wonder-worker; hence or cogn. **thaumatûr'gic**(AL) *adjs.*, **~**Y[1] *n.* [f. med. L f. Gk *thaumatourgos* a. (*thauma -matos* marvel + *-ergos* -working)]

thaw *v.* & *n.* **1.** *v.i.* (Of ice, snow, frozen thing) pass into liquid or unfrozen state; (of weather, *it*) become warm enough to melt ice etc.; become warm enough to lose numbness etc.; (fig.) become less cold or stiff in manner, become genial. **2.** *v.t.* Cause to thaw (lit. or fig.). **3.** *n.* Thawing; warmth of weather that thaws (*a thaw has set in*); hence **~'**LESS, **~'**Y[2], *adjs.* [OE *thawian*, = OHG *douwen* f. WG **thawōjan*, of unkn. orig.]

the (*before vowel* dhĭ, *before consonant* dhe, *when stressed* dhē) *a.* & *adv.* **1.** *a.* (Called the *definite article*; placed before *ns.* to denote person(s) or thing(s)) already mentioned or under discussion, or from the nature of the case actually or potentially existent, or unique (as class or individual), or familiar, or otherwise sufficiently identified, (*tried to soothe the child*; *gave the man a tip*; *shall let the matter drop*; *called on everyone in the building*; *got there and back in the day, within the week*; *how is the game* or *score?*, *what is the score, the time?*; *depends on the weather*; *the Devil, sun, moon, stars, Himalayas, Thames*; *hanged by the neck*; *inflammation of the lungs*; *pulled the trigger*; *what was the result?*; *generally correct, but there is the occasional error*; *you will be the loser*; *revised by the author*; *flowers that bloom in the spring*; *came into the garden*; *find their way to the sea*; *went to the baths, the theatre*; **is in the hospital with a broken leg*; *the Queen, President, Prime Minister, Earl of Norfolk*; *the difficulty is to avoid slipping*; *if you want a quick survey, this is the book*; *story does not lose in the telling*); ||(colloq.) my, our, (*the wife, the dog*). **2.** (w. *sing. n.* as repr.) Species, class, etc., (*the lion, domestic cat, philosopher, cucumber, gavotte, general reader, man in the street*; *was quite the philosopher about his misfortunes*; *has the novel a future?*; *the pen is mightier than the sword*; *plays the harp superbly*; *we have the television*; (rhet., esp. Bibl.) *the oppressor, years that the locust hath eaten*). **3.** (w. *n.* as fig. repr.) Occupation, pursuit, etc., (*the stage, theatre, platform, pulpit, hustings, table, bottle*); **the Macnab** etc., chief of clan of that name; (w. names of diseases etc.) *the itch, the fidgets*, (colloq.) *the measles, the toothache*, (arch.) *the smallpox*; (w. names of units) = a, per, (*£5 the square foot*; *allow 8 minutes to the mile*; *16 ounces go to the pound*); (w. units of time) present, current, (*man of the moment, hero of the hour, questions of the day, book of the month, best-dressed woman of the year, painter of the century*). **4.** (w. sense completed by *a.* or rel. clause or equivalent: *the book* (*that*) *you borrowed*; *the best* (*that*) *I can do for you*; *has not the nerve for motoring*; *wonder you have the impudence* (*to ask it*), (excl.) *the impudence of the fellow!*; *the cup on the top shelf*; *the one with a broken handle*; *the bottom of a well*; *the England of today*; *the best way*; *the only way*; *the way out*; *the upper classes*; *the better man of the two*). **5.** (w. *adjs.* used abs.) That which is, those who are, etc., (*from the sublime to the ridiculous*; *none but the brave deserve*(*s*) *the fair*; *your letter of the ninth* (day of the month)). **6.** (w. *adjs.* used rhet. etc. as part of definition) Which is, who are, etc., (*gave details of the shocking disaster*; *scored past the unsighted Smith*; *Alfred the Great, Edward the Seventh, the Honourable James Jones*; ||*the High Street*). **7.** (Stressed; of person or thing) best known or best entitled to the name (*no relation to* the *Kipling*). **8.** *adv.* (a) *rel.*, only in comb. w. (b). In whatever degree. (b) In that degree, by that amount, on that account, (*the more he gets, the more he wants; I play the worse, the more I practise; am not* (or *none*) *the more inclined to help him because he is poor, on that account, for what you tell me; none the better for seeing you*); *that makes it* **all** ~ *worse* (in the full degree to be expected from what you say etc.); (tautologically) **so much** ~ *worse for him,* = the worse (*or* so much worse) for him. [a. OE, replacing *se, sēo, thæt,* (= THAT¹), = ON *sá, sú, that,* OHG *der, diu, daz,* Goth. *sa, sō, thata,* f. Gmc **sa, *so, *that*; adv. f. OE *thȳ, thē,* instrumental case]

thēă'ndrĭc *a.* Of union, or by joint agency, of divine and human nature in Christ. [f. eccl. Gk *theandrikos* (*theos* god, *anēr andros* man; see -IC)]

thēanthrŏ'pĭc *a.* Both divine and human; tending to embody deity in human form. [f. eccl. Gk *theanthrōpos* god-man (*theos* god, *anthrōpos* man) + -IC]

thē'ārchȳ (-kĭ) *n.* Government by god(s); system or order of gods (*the Olympian thearchy*). [f. eccl. Gk *thearkhia* rule of god (*theos* god, *-arkhia* f. *arkhō* rule)]

thė'atre (-*ter*), ***thė'ater,** *n.* **1.** Building or outdoor area for dramatic representations; cinema; **~-goer, -going,** frequenter, frequenting, of theatres; **~-in-the-round,** dramatic performance on stage surrounded by spectators. **2.** Room or hall for lectures etc. with seats in tiers; ‖(**operating-**)~, room for surgical operations and demonstrations (~ **sister,** nurse assisting in this). **3.** Dramatic literature or art; effective material for stage (*makes good theatre*). **4.** Scene or field of action (*the theatre of war*). **5.** Natural land-formation in gradually rising part-circle like ancient Gk & Rom. theatres. [ME, f. OF *t*(*h*)*eatre* or f. L f. Gk *theatron* (*theaomai* behold)]

thėă'trĭc *a.* = foll. [f. as foll.; see -IC]

thėă'trĭcal *a.* & *n.* **1.** *a.* (Of manner, speech, gesture, person) calculated for effect, showy, artificial, affected; of or suited to the theatre, of acting or actors; hence ~ISM (2, 4), ~ITY (-ă'l-), *ns.,* ~IZE (3) *v.t.,* ~LY² *adv.* **2.** *n.* (in *pl.*) Theatrical actions; theatrical performances, esp. *private* or *amateur theatricals.* [f. LL f. Gk *theatrikos* (*theatron* THEATRE) + -ICAL]

Thē'ban *a.* & *n.* (Inhabitant or native) of Thebes in ancient Egypt or ancient Greece. [ME, f. L *Thebanus* (*Thebae* Thebes f. Gk *Thēbai*)]

thē'ca *n.* (*pl.* ~*e pr.* -sē). (Bot.) part of plant serving as receptacle; (Zool.) case or sheath enclosing organ or part. [L, f. Gk *thēkē* case]

thé dansant (tā dahǹsah'ǹ) *n.* Afternoon tea with dancing. [F]

thee. See THOU.

thĕft *n.* (Act or instance of) stealing; (Law) dishonest appropriation of another's property with intent to deprive him of it permanently. [OE *thīefth, thēofth,* later *thēoft,* = ON *thȳft*(*h*) f. Gmc **thiubhithō* (as THIEF, -TH¹)]

thegn (-ān) *n.* (Engl. Hist.) = THANE. [OE; see THANE]

thē'ĭne *n.* = CAFFEINE. [f. mod. L *thea* tea + -INE⁵]

their (dhār) *poss. pron. attrib.* Of them(selves); for phrs. see HER², OUR. [ME, f. ON *their*(*r*)*a* of them, gen. pl. of *sá* THE, that]

theirs (dhārz) *poss. pron. pred.* (& abs.) = prec.; for phrs. see HERS. [ME, f. prec. + -s³]

thē'|ĭsm *n.* Belief in existence of gods or a god, esp. a God supernaturally revealed to man (cf. DEISM) and sustaining a personal relation to his creatures; so ~IST (2) *n.,* **~ĭ'stIC(AL)** *adjs.* [f. Gk *theos* god + -ISM]

them. See THEY.

thėmă't|ĭc *a.* **1.** (Mus.) Of themes (*thematic treatment*); **~ic catalogue** (giving opening themes of works as well as names etc.). **2.** (Gram.) Of or belonging to a theme (*thematic vowel, form*); (of form of verb) having thematic vowel. **3.** Hence ~ICALLY *adv.* [f. Gk *thematikos* (as foll.; see -IC)]

thēme *n.* Subject on which one speaks, writes, or thinks; *school composition, essay, on given subject; (Gram.) stem of noun or verb, part to which inflexions are added, esp. composed of root and added vowel; (Mus.) melodic subject usu. developed with variations (~ **song,** recurrent melody in musical play or film; ~ **song** or **tune,** signature tune of performer etc.); (Hist.) any of 29 provinces in Byzantine empire. [ME *teme* f. OF **teme* f. L f. Gk *thema -matos* (*tithēmi* set, place)]

themsĕ'lves (dhemsĕ'lvz) *pron.* Emphat. & refl. form corresp. to THEY or THEM (for uses cf. HERSELF, ITSELF). [f. THEM + pl. of SELF]

thĕn (dh-) *adv., conj., a.,* & *n.* **1.** *adv.* At that time (*was then too much occupied; then comes the trouble; the then existing laws; Sir Winston, then Mr., Churchill*); NOW *and then*; ~ **and there,** immediately and on the spot. **2.** Next, afterwards, after that, and also, (*it must then soak for two hours; and then the operation is complete; then* (*again,*) *there are the children to consider*); *it is a problem, but then* (after all) *that is what he is here for.* **3.** *conj.* In that case, therefore, it follows that, (*then you should have said so; then it is no use your going*); (*but*) *then* (if what you say is true) *why did you take it?*; (of grudging or impatient concession) if you must have it so (*take it then; 'Between you and I'* . . . *'me', then*); (resumptively, not as first word) accordingly (*the new Governor, then, came prepared*); NOW *then*; WELL⁴ *then*; WHAT *then?* **4.** *a.* Existing etc. at that time (*the then Duke, secretary*). **5.** *n.* That time (*before, till, by, from, then*); *every* NOW *and then.* [OE *thanne, thonne,* etc., = OS *than*(*na*), OHG *danne, denne,* adv. form. f. dem. root **tha-*; cf. THAT¹, THE]

thē'nar *n.* (Anat.) Palm of hand, sole of foot; ball of thumb. [mod. L f. Gk]

thĕnce (dh-) *adv.* & *n.* (arch. or literary). (**From**) ~, from that place or source, for that reason, (*a discrepancy thence results; it thence appears*); (**from**) **~for'th, ~for'ward,** from that time forward. [ME *thannes, thennes,* (*thanne, thenne* adv. f. OE *thanon*(*e*) etc., = OS & OHG *danan*(*a*) f. WG **thanana*) + -s³]

thē'o- *comb. form.* God or god, as: **~ce'ntric,** having God as its centre; **~cracy** (thĭŏ'k-), form of government by God or god directly or through a priestly order etc. (**the Theocracy,** Jewish commonwealth from Moses to the monarchy), so ~CRAT *n.*; **~crasy** (-krāsĭ; *or* thĭŏ'kra-), (1) mingling of deities into one personality, (2) union of soul with God through contemplation (among Neo-Platonists, Buddhists, etc.), [f. Gk *krasis* mingling]; **~dicy** (thĭŏ'd-), vindication of divine providence in view of existence of evil [f. Gk *dikē* justice], whence **~dice'an** *a.*; **~gony** (thĭŏ'g-), (account of) genealogy of the gods; **~machy** (thĭŏ'makĭ), strife against or among the gods [f. Gk *makhē* fight]; **~ma'nia,** (1) insane belief that one is God, (2) religious insanity; **~phany** (thĭŏ'f-), visible manifestation of god to man; **~phor'ic,** bearing the name of a god; **~pneust,** divinely inspired. [Gk (*theos* god; see -o-)]

thēobrō'mĭne (*or* -ēn) *n.* Bitter white alkaloid from cacao seeds, related to caffeine. [f. *Theobroma* cacao genus, mod. L f. Gk *theos* god + *brōma* food, + -INE⁵]

thėŏ'dol|īte *n.* Surveying-instrument for measuring horizontal and vertical angles by means of rotating telescope; hence **~ĭ'tIC** *a.* [16th c. *theodelitus,* of unkn. orig.]

thēolō′gian *n.* Person skilled in theology. [ME, f. OF *theologien* (as foll.; see -IAN)]

thėŏ′log|ȳ *n.* Study of or system of (esp. Christian) religion; rational analysis of a religious faith; hence or cogn. **thēolŏ′g**ICAL *a.* (*theological* VIRTUE*s*), ~IST (3) *n.*, ~IZE (1, 2) *v.t.* & *i.* [ME f. OF *theologie* f. L f. Gk THEO(*logia* -LOGY)]

thēophȳ′llīne (*or* -ēn) *n.* Alkaloid similar to theobromine, found in tea-leaves. [irreg. f. mod. L *thea* tea + Gk *phullon* leaf + -INE[5]]

thėor′bō *n.* (*pl.* ~**s**). Two-necked musical instrument of lute class much used in 17th c. [f. It. *tiorba*, of unkn. orig.]

thē′orem *n.* (Math.) proposition not self-evident but to be proved by chain of reasoning, a truth to be established by means of accepted truths, (cf. PROBLEM); algebraical or other rule, esp. one expressed by symbols or formulae, (BINOMIAL *theorem*); so ~A′TIC *a.* [f. F *théorème* or f. LL f. Gk *theōrēma* speculation, proposition (*theōreō* behold)]

thēorĕ′tĭc *a.* & *n.* **1.** *a.* = foll. **2.** *n.* (in *sing.* or *pl.*) Speculative part of a science etc. [f. LL f. Gk *theōrētikos* (as THEORY; see -ETIC)]

thēorĕ′tical *a.* Concerned with knowledge but not with its practical application, speculative; based on mere theory, not dealing with facts as presented by experience; hence ~LY[2] *adv.* [f. as prec. + -AL]

thēorėtĭ′cian (-sh*a*n) *n.* Person concerned with theoretical part of a subject. [f. THEORETIC + -IAN]

thē′or|ȳ *n.* Supposition or system of ideas explaining something, esp. one based on general principles independent of the facts, phenomena, etc., to be explained, opp. to HYPOTHESIS, (*atomic theory*; *theory of gravitation, evolution*); speculative (esp. fanciful) view (*one of my pet theories*); the sphere of abstract knowledge or speculative thought (*this is all very well in theory, but how will it work in practice?*); exposition of the principles of a science etc. (*the theory of music*); (Math.) collection of propositions to illustrate principles of a subject (*probability theory*; *theory of equations*); hence ~IST (3) *n.*, ~IZE (2) *v.i.* [f. LL f. Gk *theōria* (*theōros* spectator f. *theōreō* behold)]

thėŏ′soph|ȳ *n.* Any of various philosophies professing to achieve a knowledge of God by spiritual ecstasy, direct intuition, or special individual relations, esp. a modern movement following Hindu and Buddhist teachings and seeking universal brotherhood; hence or cogn. **thē′osŏph,** ~ER[1], ~IST (2), *ns.*, **thēosŏ′phɪ**C(AL), **thēosophĭ′st**IC(AL), *adjs.*, ~IZE (2) *v.i.* [f. med. L f. late Gk *theosophia* f. THEO(*sophos* wise) wise concerning God]

thĕrapeu′t|ĭc *a.* & *n.* **1.** *a.* Curative; of the healing art; hence ~**ĭ**CAL *a.*, ~**ĭcal**LY[2] *adv.*, ~IST (3) *n.* **2.** *n.* (in *pl.*, usu. treated as *sing.*) Branch of medicine concerned with treatment of disease and action of remedial agents in disease or health. [orig. n., f. F *thérapeutique* or f. LL f. Gk *therapeutika* neut. pl. (as *n.*) of *therapeutikos* (*therapeuō* wait on, cure; see -IC)]

thĕ′rap|ȳ *n.* Medical treatment of disease; hence ~IST (3) *n.* [f. mod. L f. Gk *therapeia* healing]

Thĕrava′da (-ah′-) *n.* = HINAYANA. [f. Pali *theravāda* (*thera* elder, old, *vāda* speech, doctrine)]

there (dhār; in sense 3 usu. dh*er*) *adv.*, *n.*, & *int.* **1.** *adv.* In or at that place or position (*put it there*; *put it down, in, out, over, through, under, up, there*; *what is that dog doing there?*; *lived there for some years*; ALL *there*; **have been ~ before,** (sl.) know all about it; HERE *and there*; *neither* HERE *nor there*; **~ and then,** = THEN *and there*; (calling attention) **hallo ~!, you ~!, move along ~!, ~ goes the bell,** *there's courage* etc. FOR *you*, ~ (= THAT[1])'**s** *a dear* etc.); in that respect, at that point in argument, progress of affairs, situation, etc., (*there I agree with you*; *there you go misquoting me again*; *ay, there's the* RUB[1]); **so ~**, that is my final decision (whether you like it or not); **~ it is,** (1) that is the trouble, (2) nothing can be done about it; **~ you are,** this is what you wanted etc. (& see sense 5). **2.** To that place or position (*goes there every day*; *got there, there and back, in two minutes*); **get ~,** (sl.) succeed, understand what is meant; **~ or ~abouts,** about that place, amount, time, etc., (‘*Was it two years ago?*’ ‘*There or thereabouts*’). **3.** (Merely expletive or introductory, preceding, or in interrog. or neg. or quasi-neg. sentence following, vb., which normally precedes its subject, esp. *be*; in poet. or excl. use, subject may stand first: *there was a cart close by*; *there was nothing in it*; *there was plenty to eat*; *what is there for supper?*; *not a sound was there to indicate their presence*; *seldom has there been more fuss*; *there fell a deep silence*; *a fool there was*; *a nice mess there is* or *seems to be!*). **4.** *n.* That place (*was brought from there*; *lives somewhere near there*; *tide comes up to there*; *passed by there*). **5.** *int.* expr. confirmation, triumph, dismay, etc., (*there* (*you are*)! *what did I tell you?*) or used to soothe child etc. (*there, there, never mind*). **6. ~abou′t(s)** (cf. sense 2), near that place (*ought to be somewhere thereabouts*), near that number, quantity, etc., (*two gallons or thereabouts*); **~a′fter,** (formal) after that; **~ane′nt,** (Sc.) about that matter; **~a′t,** (arch.) at that place, on that account, after that; **~by′** (*or* dhār′bī), by that means, as result of that (*~by hangs a tale*, in which connection there is something to be told); **~for′,** (arch.) for that object or purpose; **~′fore,** for that reason, accordingly, consequently, [= *therefor*]; **~fro′m,** (arch.) from that or it; **~i′n,** (formal) in that place, in that respect; **~ina′fter, ~inbefor′e,** later, earlier, in same document etc.; **~i′nto,** (arch.) into that place; **~o′f,** (formal) of that or it; **~o′n,** (arch.) on that or it (of motion or position); **~ou′t,** (arch.) out of that, from that source; **~throu′gh,** (arch.) through that; **~to′,** (formal) to that or it, in addition, to boot; **~tofor′e,** (formal) before that time; **~u′nto,** (arch.) to that or it; **~upo′n,** in consequence of that, soon or immediately after that, (arch.) upon that (of motion or position); **~wi′th,** (arch.) with that, thereupon; **~witha′l,** (arch.) in addition, besides. [OE *thǣr, thēr,* = OS *thār*, OHG *dār*, ON, Goth. *thar* f. dem. root **tha-* (cf. THAT[1], THE)]

thēr′ĭac *n.* (arch.) Antidote to bites of poisonous animals, esp. snakes. [f. L f. Gk *thēriakē* antidote, fem. (as n.) of *thēriakos* (as foll.; see -AC)]

thērĭănthrŏ′pĭc *a.* Of or worshipping beings represented in combined form of man and animal. [f. Gk *thērion* dim. of *thēr* wild beast + *anthrōpos* man + -IC]

thērĭomor′phĭc *a.* (Esp. of deity) having animal form. [f. as prec. + Gk *morphē* form + -IC]

therm *n.* Unit of heat, esp. ||statutory unit of calorific value in gas-supply (100,000 British THERMAL units). [f. Gk *thermē* heat]

ther′mae *n. pl.* (Gk & Rom. Ant.) Public baths. [L, f. Gk *thermai* pl. (as prec.)]

ther′mal *a.* & *n.* **1.** *a.* Of heat; **~ capacity,** number of heat units needed to raise temperature of a body by one degree; **~ equator,** line along which greatest heat occurs on earth's surface; **~ reactor,** nuclear reactor using **~ neutrons** (in thermal equilibrium with surroundings); **~ unit** (for measuring heat); *British ~ unit*, amount of heat needed to raise 1 lb. of water at maximum density one degree F.; hence ~LY[2] *adv.* **2.** *n.* Rising current of heated air (used by gliders to gain height). [F (as THERM; see -AL)]

ther'mic *a.* = prec. [f. as THERM + -IC]

ther'midor *n.* **Lobster ~,** mixture of lobster meat, mushrooms, cream, egg yolks, and sherry, cooked in lobster shell. [*T* ~, name of eleventh month of Fr. revolutionary calendar, f. as THERM + Gk *dōron* gift]

ther'mion *n.* Ion or electron emitted by incandescent substance; hence **thermiŏ'nic** *a.* (**~ic** ||**valve** or ***tube,** device giving flow of thermionic electrons in one direction, used esp. in rectification of current and in radio reception). [f. THERMO- + ION]

thermi'stor *n.* (Electr.) Resistor whose resistance is greatly reduced by heating, used for measurement and control. [f. *thermal resistor*]

ther'mite, ther'mit, *n.* Mixture of finely powdered aluminium and oxide of iron that produces a very high temperature on combustion (used in welding and as a composition for incendiary bombs). [G *thermit* (as foll.; see -ITE[1])]

ther'mō- *comb. form.* Heat, as: **~che'mistry,** branch of chemistry dealing with the quantities of heat evolved or absorbed during chemical reactions; **~electri'city,** electricity produced by difference of temperature, so **~ele'ctric** *a.*; **~ge'nesis,** production of heat esp. in human or animal body; **~gram,** record made by **~graph** (self-registering thermometer); **~-la'bile,** unstable when heated; **~lumine'scent,** luminescent when heated; **~lysis** (-ŏ'l-), decomposition by action of heat; **~nu'clear,** relating to nuclear reactions that occur only at very high temperatures, (of bomb etc.) using such reactions; **~phil(e),** (bacterium etc.) growing at high temperatures; **~pile,** set of thermocouples esp. arranged for measuring small quantities of radiant heat; **~pla'stic,** (substance) becoming plastic on heating, hardening on cooling, and able to repeat these processes; **~se'tting,** (of plastics) setting permanently when heated; **~sphere,** region of atmosphere beyond mesosphere; **~sta'ble,** stable when heated; **~ta'xis,** regulation of heat or temperature esp. in warm-blooded animals, so **~ta'ctic, ~ta'xic,** *adjs.*; **~tropism** (-ŏ't-), involuntary movement of animal or plant towards or away from source of heat, so **~tro'pic** *a.* [Gk (*thermos* hot, *thermē* heat)]

ther'mocouple (-kŭ-) *n.* Pair of different metals in contact at a point, generating thermoelectric voltage that can serve as measure of temperature at this point relative to their other parts. [f. THERMO- + COUPLE[1]]

thermodynă'm|ics *n. pl.* (usu. treated as *sing.*) Science of relations between heat and other (mechanical, electrical, etc.) forms of energy; so ~IC(AL) *adjs.*, **~ical**LY[2] *adv.* [f. THERMO- + DYNAMICS]

thermŏ'mèter *n.* Instrument for measuring temperature, esp. graduated glass tube with small bore containing mercury or alcohol which expands when heated; **clinical ~** (small, with range of 25° or less, for taking temperature of esp. patient's body); MAXIMUM, MINIMUM, *thermometer*; hence **thermo**ME'TRIC(AL) *adjs.*, **thermŏ'**METRY *n.* [f. F *thermomètre* or mod. L *thermometrum* (as THERMO-, -METER)]

ther'mŏs *n.* ~ (**flask** etc.), (brand of) vacuum flask. [P]

ther'mostăt *n.* Device which automatically maintains constant temperature or actuates appropriate equipment when temperature varies beyond fixed limit; hence ~IC (-ă't-) *a.* [f. THERMO- + Gk *statos* standing]

thèsaur'|us *n.* (*pl.* **~i** *pr.* -ī). Storehouse of information, esp. dictionary or encyclopaedia; list of concepts or words arranged according to sense or chosen for use in indexing etc. [L, f. Gk *thēsauros* treasure]

these. See THIS.

thē's|is (*or* thĕ'- in sense 2) *n.* (*pl.* **~es** *pr.* -ēz). **1.** Proposition to be maintained or proved; dissertation, esp. by candidate for degree. **2.** Unstressed syllable in or part of metrical foot (opp. ARSIS). [ME f. LL f. Gk, = putting, placing, a proposition etc., f. *the-* root of *tithēmi* place]

Thĕ'spian *a.* & *n.* **1.** *a.* Of tragedy or the drama. **2.** *n.* Actor or actress. [f. Gk *Thespis* traditional originator of Gk tragedy + -AN]

Thess. *abbr.* Thessalonians (N.T.).

thē'ta *n.* Eighth Greek letter (Θ, θ) = th. [Gk]

thē'urg|y̆ *n.* Supernatural or divine agency esp. in human affairs; art of securing this; magical science of Neo-Platonists; hence **theur'g**IC(AL) *adjs.*, ~IST (3) *n.* [f. LL f. Gk *theourgia* (*theos* god, *-ergos* working; see -Y[1])]

thew *n.* (usu. in *pl.*) Bodily strength; sinew, muscle; (fig.) mental or moral vigour. [OE *thēaw* usage, conduct, = OS *thau*, OHG *dau* discipline, of unkn. orig.]

they (dhā) *pron.* (*obj.* **them** *pr.* dhem *or, when stressed,* dhĕm; *refl.* THEMSELVES *or* arch. *them*; *poss.* THEIR, THEIRS). Pl. of HE[1], SHE, IT[1]; he and she etc.; the or any persons *who*; people in general (*they say*); those in authority (*they have raised the fees*; WE *and they*); **them** (colloq., cf. HER[1] 2); (joc.) **them's** (those are) **my** SENTIMENTS; (vulg.) *not like* **them** (those) *Pharisees* etc. [ME *thei*, obj. *theim*, f. ON *their* nom. pl. masc., *theim* dat. pl., of *sá* THE, that]

***THI** *abbr.* temperature-humidity index.

thī'amine (*or* -ēn) *n.* Vitamin B_1, aneurin. [f. THIO- + VITAMIN*e*]

Thibetan. Var. of TIBETAN.

thĭck *a.*, *n.*, & *adv.* **1.** *a.* Of great or specified depth (between opposite surfaces) or diameter (*bread is* (*cut*) *too thick*; *spread the butter thick*; *a board, a rope, two inches thick*; *how thick was it?*); (of line etc.) broad, not fine; (of script, type, etc.) consisting of thick lines. **2.** Arranged closely, crowded together, dense, (*thick hair, forest, fog*; *crowd grew thicker*); numerous (*fell thick as peas*); abounding, packed *with* (*trees thick with leaves*; *air thick with snow*); of firm consistency (*thick paste*); containing much solid matter (*thick soup*); turbid, muddy, cloudy, not clear, (*thick puddles, weather*); impenetrable by the sight (*thick darkness*). **3.** Stupid, dull; (of voice) muffled, indistinct. **4.** (colloq.) Intimate (esp. *thick as thieves*). **5. Lay it on ~,** (sl.) flatter or exaggerate grossly; ||**a bit ~,** (sl.) going beyond what is reasonable, excessive in some disagreeable quality; ||**~ ear,** (sl.) external ear swollen as result of blow (esp. *give* person *a thick ear*); **~ end of the stick,** the worst of a bargain etc. **6. ~ head,** (1) stupidity, (2) muzziness; **~'head,** blockhead; **~-headed,** stupid; **~-knee,** stone-curlew; **~'set,** (*a.*) set or growing close together, heavily or solidly built, (*n.*) thicket; **~-skinned,** (fig.) not sensitive to reproach or rebuff, stolid; **~-skulled, -witted,** stupid; hence ~'ISH[1] 2 *a.*, ~'LY *adv.* **7.** *n.* Thick part of anything (**in the ~ of it** or **of things,** in busiest part of fight, activity, etc.; **through ~ and thin,** under all conditions, in spite of all difficulties, resolutely). **8.** *adv.* Thickly (*snow was falling thick*; *blows came thick and fast*). [OE *thicce* a. & adv., = OS *thikki, thikko*, OHG *dicki, diccho*, ON *thykkr* f. Gmc **theku-*, of unkn. orig.]

thĭ'cken *v.t.* & *i.* Make or become thick(er); give (gravy etc.) more solid consistency, whence

~ING[1] (3) *n.*; **plot ~s** (becomes more intricate). [ME, f. prec. + -EN[6]]

thĭ'ckėt *n.* Number of shrubs, trees, etc., growing close together. [OE *thiccet* (as THICK, + -ET[1] denominative suf.)]

thĭ'cknėss *n.* Being thick; dimension other than length and breadth; layer of material of known thickness (*three thicknesses of cardboard will suffice*); part that is thick or lies between opposite surfaces (*steps cut in the thickness of the wall*). [OE *thicness* (as THICK, -NESS)]

thie|f *n.* (*pl.* **~ves** *pr.* -vz). **1.** One who steals esp. secretly and without violence; *thieves'* LATIN; hence **~'VERY** (4), **~'VISH**[1] *a.* **2. ~f ant** (stealing food from others); ‖**~f-taker,** (Hist.) member of group undertaking to arrest thieves. [OE *thēof*, = OS *thiof*, OHG *diob*, ON *thjófr*, Goth. *thiubs* f. Gmc **theubhaz*]

thieve *v.* **1.** *v.i.* Be a thief, engage in stealing. **2.** *v.t.* Steal (thing). [f. OE *thēofian* (as prec.)]

thigh (thī) *n.* Part of human leg between hip and knee; corresponding part in other animals; *smite* HIP[1] *and thigh*; **~-bone,** bone of thigh, femur; **~-boot** (reaching to thigh); hence (-)~ED[2] (-id) *a.* [f. OE *thē(o)h*, *thīoh*, OHG *dioh*, ON *thjó* f. Gmc **theuham*]

thill *n.* Shaft of cart or carriage, esp. one of pair; **~-horse,** ~'ER[1] *n.*, (put between thills). [ME, of unkn. orig.]

thĭ'mble *n.* Metal or plastic cap with closed or open end, worn to protect finger and push needle in sewing; (Mech.) short metal tube, ferrule, etc.; (Naut.) metal ring concave on outside and fitting in loop of spliced rope to prevent chafing; hence ~FUL 2 (-bėlf-) *n.*, (esp.) small quantity (*of* brandy etc.) to drink; **~rig** *n.*, & *v.i.*, (play) swindling sleight-of-hand trick with three thimble-shaped cups and pea, and bystanders betting which cup covers pea; **~rigger,** one who conducts this, sharper. [OE *thȳmel* (as THUMB; see -LE 1)]

thĭn[1] *a.* & *adv.* **1.** *a.* Having opposite surfaces close together, of small thickness or diameter, slender, (*thin board, sheet,* ICE[1], *wire, string*); not dense or copious (*thin haze, hair*); not full or closely packed (*a thin audience*); of slight consistency (*thin paste, gruel*); lacking an important ingredient (*thin beer, blood, voice, humour, eloquence*); (fig.) shallow, transparent, scanty, flimsy, (*thin disguise, excuse*; *patience is wearing thin*); lean, not plump; (of line) narrow, fine, (of script, type, etc.) consisting of thin lines; (sl.) uncomfortable, wretched, (*have a thin time*); *through* THICK *and thin*; **~ air,** (fig.) condition of invisibility or non-existence (*appear out of, disappear into, thin air*); **~ on the ground,** few in number; **~ on top,** balding; *thin end of the* WEDGE; **~-skinned,** (fig.) sensitive to reproach or rebuff; hence ~'LY[2] *adv.*, ~'NESS (-n-n-) *n.*, **~'n**ISH[1] 2 *a.* **2.** *adv.* Thinly (*cut the bread very thin*). [OE *thynne*, = OS *thunni*, OHG *dunni*, ON *thunnr* f. Gmc **thunnuz* f. IE **tn-*, **ten-* stretch]

thĭn[2] *v.t.* & *i.* (**-nn-**). Make or become thin(ner), reduce in bulk or numbers (*his hair is thinning*; *crowd began to thin out*); remove some young fruit from (vine, tree) to improve growth of rest; **~ out,** treat (seedlings etc.) similarly; hence **~'n**ER[1] *n.*, (esp., also in *pl.* treated as *sing.*) volatile liquid used to make paint etc. thinner. [OE *thynnian* (as prec.)]

thine (dhīn) *poss. pron.* See THY. [OE *thīn*, = OS *thīn*, OHG *dīn*, ON *thínn*, Goth. *theins* f. Gmc **thīnaz* f. IE **t(w)einos* (as THOU; cf. MINE[3])]

thing *n.* **1.** Whatever is or may be an object of thought (including or opp. to *person*), as: (of animate object, esp. person, expr. contempt, pity, affection, etc.) *poor thing, you spiteful thing, a dear old thing, dumb things,* (sl.) OLD *thing*; (of inanimate material object) *take those things off the table, platinum is a costly thing*; (of act, fact, idea, course of action, task, affair, circumstance) *a foolish thing to do, it is a strange thing that you cannot understand that, that is not the same thing, the only thing now is to shout for help, it is a big thing to undertake, is likely to achieve great things, a reputation for getting things done, things begin to look brighter, has made a mess of things, takes things too seriously, asked me how things were*); (of specimen or type of work etc.) *the latest thing in hats, a little thing of mine I should like to read to you*; one's special interest or concern (esp. colloq. *do* one's *own thing*); (colloq.) something remarkable (*now* there's *a thing!*); (in *pl.*) personal belongings (*pack up your things*), (esp. outer) clothing, equipment, (Law) property (*things personal, real*), the world in general (*is impossible in* or *by the nature of things*), (w. following *a.*, often joc.) all that is so describable (*things Japanese, political, feminine, scholastic,* etc.); **and ~s,** (colloq.) and the like; **do ~s to,** affect remarkably; (**just**) **one of those ~s,** something ordained by fate or unavoidable; SEE[1] *things.* **2. The ~,** (1) what is conventionally proper or fashionable, (2) what is to be aimed at (*the thing is to improve the pace*), (3) what is needed (*your suggestion was just the thing*), (4) what is in question (*for the fun, the look, of the thing*), (5) what is most important (*the thing about him is his complete integrity*; *the thing is, will she come?*); *am not feeling* **the ~,** quite well. **3. And another ~,** moreover; **do the decent** etc. **~ by,** treat decently etc.; (*the*) FIRST *thing*; **for one ~,** as one of several reasons; GOOD *thing*; **have a ~ about,** (colloq.) be obsessed or prejudiced about; **know a ~ or two,** be experienced or shrewd; LAST[3] *thing(s)*; **make a ~ of,** regard as essential, get excited about; **not a ~,** nothing (*did not mean a thing to me*); *SURE *thing*; **~ in itself** (viewed in the abstract, not in relation to others). [OE, = OS *thing*, OHG *ding* deliberative assembly, ON *thing* f. Gmc **thingam*]

thĭ'ngamy̆, thĭ'ngumajĭg, thĭ'ngum(a)bŏb, thĭ'ngummy̆, *ns.* (colloq.) Person or thing whose name one forgets or does not know or does not wish to mention; what's-his-name, what-d'you-call-it. [f. prec., w. meaningless suf.]

think *v.* (**thought** *pr.* thawt) & *n.* **1.** *v.t.* Consider, be of opinion, (*we think* (*that*) *he will come*; *we do not think it probable*; *I think it a shame*; *thinks himself very fine*; *to think* (*that*) *he should treat me like this!*; *it is not thought proper*; *is thought to be a fraud*; *what do you think of* or *about my idea?*); **I do'n't ~** (sl. addition to ironical statement; *you are a model of tact, I don't think*). **2.** Intend, expect, (*thinks to deceive us*); (colloq.) remember (*did not think to lock the door*). **3.** Form conception of (*cannot think the infinite*; (colloq.) *I can't think how you do it*). **4.** Recognize presence or existence of (*the child thought no harm*). **5.** Reduce to specified condition etc. by thinking (*cannot think away a toothache*). **6.** *v.i.* Exercise the mind otherwise than by passive reception of another's ideas; **~ for** one**self,** have independent mind; **let me ~** (appeal for time before answering etc.). **7.** Have half-formed intention (*I think I'll try*). **8. ~ about,** consider, esp. consider the practicability of (scheme, doing); **~ again,** change one's mind; **~ aloud,** utter one's thoughts immediately as they occur; **~ back to,** recall (past event or time); **~ big,** be ambitious; *think* FIT[3]; **~ of,** consider, be aware of in the mind, imagine, propose to oneself, entertain the idea of, hit upon, (*have many things to think of*; *think of you constantly*; *must be thinking of going*; *couldn't think of* (*doing*) *such a thing*; *think of a word beginning with B*; *would have telephoned if I had thought of it*);

(**just** or **to**) ~ **of it!,** one can hardly imagine it; ~ **better of,** (1) decide on second thoughts to abandon (intention), (2) have higher opinion of (person, esp. *than to believe* etc.); ~ **little** or **nothing of,** consider insignificant or contemptible, (*thinks nothing of walking 30 miles a day; I think nothing of your friend Jones*); ~ **much, a lot, well, highly, of,** esteem; *think no small* BEER *of*; ~ **on,** (arch.) think of or about; ~ **out,** consider carefully, devise (plan etc.); ~ **over,** reflect upon in order to reach decision (*think over what I have said; will think it over*); ~ **through,** reflect fully upon (problem etc.); ~ **twice,** use careful consideration, avoid hasty action etc.; ~ **up,** (colloq.) devise, produce by thought; ~ **upon,** (arch.) think of or about. **9.** Hence ~′ABLE *a.* **10.** *n.* (colloq.) Act of thinking (*must have a think about that*); ~**-piece,** piece of writing dealing with general assessment and interpretation of news etc.; ~**-tank,** organization providing advice and ideas on national and commercial problems, *(sl.) the brain. [OE *thencan thōhte gethōht,* = OS *thenkian,* OHG *denken,* ON *thekkja,* Goth. *thagkjan,* factitive f. Gmc **thank-* f. IE **teng-* etc.]

thi′nker *n.* In vbl senses; one who thinks in a specified way (*original thinker*); person with skilled or powerful mind. [ME, f. prec. + -ER¹]

thi′nking¹ *n.* In vbl senses; opinion, judgement, (*the best, to my thinking; what is your thinking on this question?*); **put on** one's ~**-cap,** meditate on a problem. [ME, f. THINK + -ING¹]

thi′nking² *a.* In vbl senses; thoughtful, intellectual. [f. THINK + -ING²]

thi′nner. See THIN²; *compar.* of THIN¹.

thi′ō- *comb. form.* Sulphur, as: ~**-acid,** ~**-su′lphate,** ~**ure′a,** etc., compounds in which (some) oxygen is replaced by sulphur. [f. Gk *theion* sulphur + -O-]

third *a.* & *n.* **1.** *a.* Next after second; ~ **part,** one of three equal parts into which thing is or might be divided. **2.** *n.* Third part; third thing etc.; third day of month; (person having) place in third class in examination; third gear; (Mus.) interval of which the span involves three alphabetical notes, harmonic combination of notes thus separated; (Hist., in *pl.*) third of deceased husband's property falling to widow. **3.** *Third* BASE¹ 9; ~**-best,** (what is) of third quality; ~ **class,** next after second class in accommodation, examination-list, etc.; ~ **day,** Tuesday; *third* DEGREE; *third* ESTATE; *third* FLOOR; ~ **force,** party etc. acting as check on conflict between two others; *third* FORM¹ 6; ~ **gear,** next above second gear in motor vehicle or bicycle; **third* GRADE 1; ~ **man,** (Cricket) fieldsman beyond slip(s) and point, his place; ~ **party,** another party besides the two principals, bystander etc., (~*-party insurance,* against damage or injury to person other than the insured); ~ **person,** (1) = *third party,* (2) see PERSON 5, 6; ~ **rail** (carrying current to electric train); ~**-rate,** inferior, poor; *third* READING; **T**~ **World,** countries of Asia, Africa, and Latin America not politically aligned with Communist or with Western nations. **4.** Hence ~′LY² *adv.,* in the third place. [OE *third(d)a, thridda,* = OS *thriddio,* OHG *dritto,* ON *thrithi,* Goth. *thridja* f. Gmc **thridhjaz* f. IE **tritjós*]

thirst *n.,* & *v.i.* **1.** *n.* Suffering caused by lack of drink; desire for a drink; (fig.) ardent desire, craving, (*of, for, after,* glory, person's blood, etc.). **2.** *v.i.* Feel thirst, be thirsty, (fig. *for, after,* or arch. lit.). [OE *thurst, thyrstan,* = OS *thurst(ian)* f. WG **thurstu* (**thurs-* f. IE **t(o)rs-*)]

thir′st|y̆ *a.* Feeling thirst (*am very thirsty*); (of country or season) dry, parched; (fig.) eager (*for, after*); (colloq.) causing thirst (*this is thirsty work*); hence ~ILY² *adv.,* ~INESS *n.* [OE *thurstig, thyrstig* (as prec., -Y²)]

thirtee′n (*or* ther′-) *a.* & *n.* One more than twelve; symbol for this (13, xiii, XIII); size etc. denoted by thirteen; hence ~TH² *a.* & *n.* [OE *thrēotīene,* = OS *thriutein,* OHG *drīzehan,* ON *threttán* (as THREE, -TEEN)]

thir′ty̆ *a.* & *n.* **1.** Three times ten; symbol for this (30, xxx, XXX); (in *pl.*) numbers, esp. years of a century or life, from 30 to 39; hence ~FOLD *a.* & *adv.,* **thir′tieth**¹ *a.* & *n.* **2.** ~**-one** etc., (arch.) **one-and-**~ etc., thirty plus one etc., w. corresp. ordinals ~**-first** etc.; **T**~**-nine Articles** (assented to by person taking orders in Church of England); *~**-second-note,** demisemiquaver; ~**-two-mo,** book with 32 leaves to the printing-sheet. [OE *thrītig,* = OS *thritig,* OHG *drīzzug,* ON *thrírtegr* (as THREE, -TY²)]

this (dh-) *dem. a.* & *pron.* (*pl.* **these** *pr.* dhēz), & *adv.* **1.** *dem. a.* & *pron.* The (person, thing), the person or thing, close at hand or touched or pointed to or drawn attention to or observed by the speaker at the time, or already named or understood or in question or familiar (seldom idiomatically interchangeable with THAT¹, but often only equally applicable to the facts, the implication of greater nearness, familiarity, etc., being purely idiomatic: *observe this dog on the hearth-rug; who are these people in the next room?; what is all this (noise)?; what flower is this?; fold it like this; I knew all this before; this (action of yours* or *of which I speak) is not fair; this term is liable to much abuse; at this time Caesar was in Gaul; things are easier (in) these days; am not going to leave this house, this country*); (of time) the present (*day,* etc.; *this day* FORTNIGHT, WEEK, *month; shall be* or *have been busy all this week; ought to be ready by this (time), before this (time)*), of today (*this morning, this evening*), just past or to come (*have been asking for it these three weeks; will not be wanted these ten years*); (on telephone) ‖the person speaking, *the person spoken to, (*who is this?*); (colloq., in narrative) a previously unspecified (*yesterday I was arguing with this bus-conductor, when . . .*); ~ **and that,** various ones, various things, (*went to this doctor and that* or *to this and that doctor; talked of this and that*); ~, **that, and the other,** various things; ~ **here,** (vulg.) = *this* a.; ~ **much,** this amount, esp. = what I am about to state (*I know this much, that the thing is absurd*); *this* WORLD. **2.** *adv.* (colloq.) To such a degree, so, (*knew him when he was this high*); so as to correspond to the present time, place, etc., (*not likely to get this far*). [OE, neut. of *thes,* = OS **these,* OHG *dese,* WG (**tha-* THE, THAT¹, *-*se* dem. suf.)]

thi′sness (dh-) *n.* Quality of being this, = HAECCEITY. [f. prec. + -NESS]

thi′stle (-sel) *n.* Prickly composite herbaceous plant of genus *Carduus* etc. usu. with globular heads of purple flowers; (figure of this as) Scottish national emblem; **Order of the T**~, Scottish order of knighthood; ~**down,** DOWN² of thistle, esp. w. ref. to its lightness or flimsiness; hence **thi′stly**² (-slĭ) *a.* [OE *thistel,* = OS *thistil,* OHG *distil,* ON *thistill* f. Gmc **thistilaz, -ilō*]

thi′ther (dhĭ′dh-) *adv.* (arch.) To that place; ~**to,** up to that time; hence ~WARD(s) *adv.* [OE *thider,* alt. (after HITHER) f. *thæder* f. root **tha-* (THAT¹, THE) + suf. *-ther* denoting motion towards; cf. HITHER, WHITHER]

thixŏ′tropy̆ *n.* Property of becoming temporarily liquid when shaken, stirred, etc., and returning to gel state on standing; so **thixotrŏ′pic** *a.* [f. Gk *thixis* touching + -O- + *tropē* turning + -Y¹]

tho′. See THOUGH.

‖**thōle**¹ *v.t.* (arch. or Sc.) Undergo, endure,

suffer, (pain, grief, etc., or abs.); permit, admit of. [OE *tholian*, = OS *tholon*, *tholian*, OHG *dolōn*, *dolēn*, ON *thola*, Goth. *thulan* f. Gmc **thul-* f. IE **tol-* etc. raise]

thōle[2] *n.* ~(**-pin**), pin in gunwale of boat as fulcrum for oar; each of two such pins forming rowlock, between which oar works. [OE *thol*(*l*), = MDu., MLG *dolle*, ON *thollr* fir-tree, peg]

thō'l|os *n.* (*pl.* ~**oi**). (Gk Ant.) Dome(-shaped tomb). [Gk]

Thŏ'mas (t-) *n.* ~ (**Atkins**), = TOMMY 1; DOUBT[2]*ing Thomas*. [OE f. L, f. Gk *Thōmas*]

Thō'm|ism (tō'-) *n.* Doctrine of Thomas Aquinas, It. scholastic philosopher and theologian d. 1274, or of his followers; so ~IST (2) *n.*, ~**ĭ'st**IC(AL) *adjs.* [f. prec. + -ISM]

thŏng *n.*, & *v.t.* **1.** *n.* Narrow strip of hide or leather used as halter, reins, lash of whip, etc. **2.** *v.t.* Furnish with thong; strike with thong. [OE *thwang*, *thwong*, = OHG *dwang* rein f. Gmc **thwang-* restrain]

thōr'ă|x *n.* (*pl.* ~**ces** *pr.* -*asēz*, *or* ~**xes**). **1.** (Anat. & Zool.) Part of trunk between neck and abdomen; hence **thōră'**CIC *a.* **2.** (Gk Ant.) Breastplate, cuirass. [L, f. Gk *thōrax -akos*]

thōr'ium *n.* Radioactive metallic element, the oxide of which (**thor'ia**) is used in gas-mantles. [f. *Thor*, Scand. god of thunder + -IUM]

thōrn *n.* **1.** Stiff sharp-pointed process on plant, esp. abortive branch; thorn-bearing shrub or tree; **a** ~ **in** one's **flesh** or **side,** constant source of annoyance; **on** ~**s,** continuously uneasy esp. in expectation of being detected etc. at any moment. **2.** Name of OE & Icel. runic letter, = th. **3.** ~**-apple,** (prickly fruit of) *Datura stramonium*; ~**'back,** (1) ray with spines on back and tail, (2) Eur. spider crab (*Maia squinado*); ~**'bill,** S. Amer. humming-bird of genus *Ramphomicron*; ~**-bush,** bush bearing thorns, e.g. hawthorn; ~**-lizard,** moloch; ~**'tail,** Amer. humming-bird of genus *Popelairia*; ~**-tree,** tree bearing thorns, esp. hawthorn or (S. Afr.) spiny acacia; hence ~'LESS, ~'PROOF[2], ~'Y[2] (often fig. of affair, = hard to handle), *adjs.* [OE, = OS, ON *thorn*, OHG *dorn*, Goth. *thaurnus* f. Gmc **thurnuz* f. IE **trnus*]

tho'rough (thŭ'ro) *a.*, *n.*, *prep.*, & *adv.* **1.** *a.* Complete, unqualified, not superficial, out-and-out, (*his work is seldom thorough*; *has caught a thorough chill*; *want a thorough change*; *a thorough scoundrel*). **2.** *n.* (Hist.) Uncompromising policy of Strafford and Laud under Charles I. **3.** *prep.* & *adv.* (arch.) Through (*thorough bush*, *thorough brier*). **4.** *Thorough* BASS[3]; ***~-brace,** leather strap supporting body of vehicle; ~**bred** *a.* & *n.*, (animal, esp. horse, or fig. person) of pure breed, high-spirited, mettlesome, (*T*~) (member of) breed of racehorses originating from Engl. mares and Arab stallions; ~**fare,** road or street or path open at both ends, esp. one through which much traffic passes; *no* ~*fare*, (as notice in obstructed or private road) no public right of way; ~**going,** not superficial, uncompromising, extreme, out-and-out; ~**-paced,** (lit., of horse) trained to all paces, (fig.) complete, unqualified, (*a thoroughpaced rascal*); ~**-pin,** swelling in hollow or horse's hock; ~**wax,** umbelliferous herb with stem appearing to grow through leaves [f. WAX[2]]. **5.** Hence ~LY[2] *adv.*, ~NESS *n.* [orig. prep., f. OE *thuruh*, var. of *thurh* THROUGH]

thōrp(**e**) *n.* (arch.) Village, hamlet. [OE *thorp*, *throp*, = OS, ON *thorp*, OHG *dorf*, Goth. *thaurp* land f. Gmc **thurpam*]

Thos. *abbr.* Thomas.

those. See THAT[1].

thou[1] (dh-) *pron.* (*obj.* **thee** *pr.* dhē; *poss.* THY, THINE; *pl.* YE[1], YOU) & *v.* **1.** Sing. *pron.* of 2nd pers. (arch. or poet. or dial. exc. in addressing God and (usu. *thee* as subj. w. 3rd pers. v.) as used by Quakers). **2.** *v.t.* Address (person) as *thou*. **3.** *v.i.* Use *thou* instead of *you*. [OE *thu*, = acc. & dat. *thē*, OS *thu*, *thī*, OHG *du*, *dih*, *dir*, ON *thú*, *thik*, *thér*, Goth. *thu*, *thuk*, *thus* f. Gmc **thu*, **theke*, **thez* f. IE **tu*, **te*(*s*)]

thou[2] *n.* (*pl.* ~**s** *or* ~). (colloq.) Thousand(th). [abbr.]

though, thō', (dhō) *conj.* **1.** Notwithstanding the fact that (*he finished first though he began last*; *though it was late, late though it was, we decided to go*; (ellipt.) *though annoyed, I consented*). **2.** (Even) on the supposition that (*it is better to ask him* (*even*) *though he* (*should*) *refuse* or *refuses*); **as** ~, as IF; **what** ~, what does it matter if (*the way is* or arch. *be long?*). **3.** (Introducing what is virtually an independent sentence) and yet, nevertheless, (*I have no doubt he will understand—though you never know*; *she read on, though not to the very end*). **4.** (abs. or as *adv.*) However (*I wish you had told me, though*). [ME *thoh* etc. f. ON **thóh*, *thó*, **thauh*, corresp. to OE *thēah*, OS *thoh*, OHG *doh*, Goth. *thauh* or, yet, f. Gmc **thauh* (**tha-* THAT[1], THE)]

thought[1] (thawt) *n.* **1.** Process or power of thinking; way of thinking characteristic of a person or class; faculty of reason; sober reflection (**in** ~, meditating); consideration (*after serious thought*; *acts without thought*); **give** ~ **to,** consider; **take** ~, consider matters; **have** or **take no** ~ **for,** neglect, not heed; TRAIN *of thought*. **2.** Idea, conception, chain of reasoning, etc., produced by thinking (*an essay full of striking thoughts*; **a** (**happy**) ~, a well-timed or apposite idea or suggestion); half-formed intention (*had* (*some*) *thoughts of resigning*; *had no thought of offending him*); (usu. in *pl.*) what one thinks, one's opinion, (*will tell you my thoughts on the matter*); subject of one's thinking (*his one thought is how to get away*; *a* PENNY *for your thoughts*); **in** person's ~**s,** thought of by him. **3.** **A** ~, a little, somewhat, (*cut it a thought shorter*; *seems to me a thought arrogant*); **quick as** ~, very quick; SECOND *thoughts*; ~**-provoking,** giving rise to serious thought; ~**-reader, -reading,** (person capable of) direct perception of what another is thinking; ~**-transference,** telepathy; ~**-wave,** undulation of the supposed medium of thought-transference. **4.** Hence (-)~'ED[2] *a.* [OE *thōht*, = OS *githāht*, OHG *gidāht* f. Gmc **gathanht-* (**thankjan*; cf. THINK)]

thought[2]. See THINK.

thou'ghtful (-aw't-) *a.* Engaged in or given to meditation; (of book, writer, remark, etc.) giving signs of original thought; (of person or conduct) considerate (*of*), not haphazard or unfeeling; hence ~LY[2] *adv.*, ~NESS *n.* [ME, f. THOUGHT[1] + -FUL]

thou'ghtless (-aw't-) *a.* Careless of consequences or of others' feelings; due to lack of thought; hence ~LY[2] *adv.*, ~NESS *n.* [f. THOUGHT[1] + -LESS]

thou'sand (-z-) *a.* & *n.* (*pl.* ~ *or* ~**s**; for pl. usage see HUNDRED). Ten hundred; symbol for this (1000, m, M); set of 1000, £1000, etc.; very many (*a thousand times easier*; see PITY); **one in a** ~, (fig.) a rare or excellent one; (**a**) ~ **and one** etc., one thousand plus one etc., w. corresp. ordinals ~**-and-first** etc.; (**a**) ~ **and one,** myriad, numberless, (*the thousand and one small worries of life*; *made a thousand and one excuses*); **a** ~ *thanks*, *pardons*, *apologies*, etc., (forms of polite exaggeration); UPPER *ten thousand*; hence ~FOLD *a.*, *adv.*, & *n.*, (-)~TH[2] *a.* & *n.* [OE *thūsend*, = OS *thūsundig*, OHG *dūsunt*, ON *thúsund*, Goth. *thūsundi* f. Gmc **thūsundi*]

thrall (-awl) *n.*, *a.*, & *v.t.* **1.** *n.* Slave (*of*, *to*, person or thing, lit. or fig.); bondage (*in thrall*); hence **thra'l**DOM (-aw'l-), *~'DOM, *n.* **2.** *a.* (arch.) Enslaved (*to*). **3.** *v.t.* Enslave. [OE *thrǣl* f. ON *thrǣll*, perh. f. **thrahilaz* (Gmc **thrah-* run)]

thrăsh *v.* **1.** *v.t.* = THRESH 1; ~ **out,** arrive at, obtain, (truth etc.) by repeated trial, discuss (problem etc.) exhaustively. **2.** *v.i.* (Of paddle-wheel, branch, etc.) act like flail, deliver repeated blows, (of ship) keep striking the waves, make way against wind or tide (*thrash to windward*), move violently *about* or *around* (*in* water etc.). **3.** *v.t.* Beat esp. with stick or whip, conquer, surpass; hence ~'ING[1] (1) *n.* [OE *therscan*, later *threscan*, = OHG *dreskan*, ON *threskja*, Goth. *thriskan* f. Gmc **thersk-* f. IE **tersk-*]

thră'sher[1] *n.* In vbl senses; = THRESHER. [f. prec. + -ER[1]]

thră'sher[2] *n.* Long-tailed N. Amer. thrushlike bird of family Mimidae. [perh. f. E dial. *thrusher* = THRUSH[1]]

thrasŏ'nĭcal *a.* Bragging; hence ~LY[2] *adv.* [f. L *Thraso -onis*, braggart soldier in Terence's *Eunuchus*, f. Gk *thrasus* bold, + -ICAL]

thrawn *a.* (Sc.) Perverse, ill-tempered; misshapen. [Sc. form of THROW[1]*n*, in obs. senses]

thread[1] (-rĕd) *n.* **1.** Spun-out filament of cotton, flax, silk, wool, glass, etc., yarn, (**has not a dry ~ on him,** is wet through); piece of this; thin cord of twisted yarns; **gold ~** (of silk etc. with gold wire wound round it); *thread and* THRUM[1]. **2.** Thread-shaped thing, long slender body, e.g. spiral ridge of screw, or one turn of this; thin seam or vein of ore. **3.** (fig.) **The ~** (course) **of life; hang by a ~,** (of person's life etc.) be in a precarious state, (of momentous issue etc.) be determinable either way by something still in doubt; **lose the ~** (sequence, connection) *of an argument*; **resume** or **take up the ~ of,** proceed with after interruption; **gather up the ~s,** bring divisions of subject etc. into relation after separate treatment. **4. ~'bare,** (of cloth) worn so that nap is lost and thread visible, (of person) wearing such clothes, (fig.) well-worn, hackneyed; **~'fish,** small tropical fish with long streamers from fins; **~ lace** (made of linen etc. thread, not silk); **~-mark,** mark made in bank-note paper with highly coloured silk fibres to prevent photographic counterfeiting; **~-paper,** (strip of) soft thin paper used for rolling up thread, (fig.) slender person; **~'worm,** threadlike nematode worm, esp. one infesting rectum of children. **5.** Hence ~'Y[2] *a.* (esp., of person's pulse) scarcely perceptible. [OE *thrǣd*, = OS *thrād*, OHG *drāt*, ON *thráthr* f. Gmc **thrǣdhuz* (*thrǣ-* twist, THROW[1])]

thread[2] (-rĕd) *v.t.* Pass thread through eye of (needle); arrange (material in strip form, e.g. film, recording-tape) in proper position in camera, recorder, etc.; string (beads etc.) on thread, make (chain etc.) thus; pick one's way through (maze, streets, crowded place, etc.), make one's *way* thus; streak (hair etc.) as with threads; form screw-thread on. [ME, f. prec.]

threat (-rĕt) *n.* Declaration of intention to punish or hurt; (Law) menace of bodily hurt or injury to reputation or property, such as may restrain person's freedom of action; indication of something undesirable coming (*there is a threat of rain*). [OE *thrēat* affliction etc., f. Gmc **threut-*, **thraut-*, **thrut-*]

threa'ten (-rĕ't-) *v.t.* Use threats towards (person etc., or abs., *with* harm etc.; *threatened me with death*; *am threatened with a visit*); give warning of the infliction of (harm etc., or abs.), announce one's intention (*to* do), as punishment or in revenge etc., (*threatens every kind of torment*; *threaten to resign*, (fig.) *clouds threaten* (*rain, an interruption, to interrupt us*), *the practice threatens to become general*). [OE *thrēatnian* (as prec.; see -EN[6])]

three *a.* & *n.* **1.** One more than two; symbol for this (3, iii, III); card etc. with three pips; time of three o'clock; size etc. denoted by three; set of three; (in *pl.*) gloves, shoes, etc., of third size; (Rugby Footb.) = *three-quarter*; *three* CHEER[1]*s*; **~ parts** (quarters); **~ times ~,** three cheers thrice repeated; *the three* Rs; RULE *of three*. **2. ~-ball,** golf match between three players each with his own ball; **~-card trick** (in which bets are made on which is the queen among three cards lying face downwards); **~-colour process** (of reproducing natural colours by combining photographs in red, blue, and yellow or other primary colours); **~-cornered,** triangular, (of contest etc.) between three parties each for himself; **~-decker,** warship with three gun-decks, novel in three volumes, sandwich with three slices of bread, three-tiered pulpit; **~-dimensional,** having or appearing to have length, breadth, and depth; **~-handed,** with three hands, (of card-game) played by three persons; ||**~ halfpence,** $1\frac{1}{2}$d. or $1\frac{1}{2}$p.; **T~ in One,** the Trinity; **~-lane,** (of road) marked out for three lines of traffic; **~-legged race** (-gd- *or* -gĭd-), race between pairs having one runner's right leg tied to other's left leg; ||*three-line* WHIP[2]; **~-ma'ster,** vessel (esp. schooner) with three masts; ||**~'pence** (thrĕ'p- *or* -ĭ'p-), sum of three pence; ||**~'penny** (same pr.), costing or worth 3p. or 3d.; ||**~'penny (bit)** (same pr.), former coin worth three pence; ||**~-per-ce'nts,** (Hist.) (government) bonds bearing interest at 3%; *three*-PHASE; **~-ply,** (*a.*) of three strands, webs, or thicknesses, (*n.*) three-ply wool, three-ply wood made by gluing together three layers with grain in different directions; **~-point landing,** (Aeron.) landing of an aircraft on the two main wheels and the tail wheel or skid simultaneously; ||**~-point turn,** method of turning vehicle round in narrow space by moving forwards, backwards, and forwards; **~-quarter(s),** of three-fourths of normal size or numbers, (of portrait) going down to hips or showing three-fourths of face (between full face and profile); **~-quarter (back),** (Rugby Footb.) any of 3 or 4 players just behind half-backs; **~-quarter (length),** (of coat etc.) having three-fourths of normal length; **~-ring circus,** circus having three rings, (fig.) extravagant performance; **~'score,** (arch.) sixty (*~score and ten*, age of 70 as normal limit of life); **~-way,** involving three ways or participants (*resulted in a three-way tie*); **~-wheeler,** vehicle with three wheels. **3.** Hence ~'FOLD *a.* & *adv.* [OE *thrī*, = OS *thria*, OHG *drī*, ON *thrír* f. Gmc **thrijiz* f. IE **trejes*]

three'some *n.* & *a.* **1.** *n.* Set of three persons; game etc. for three, esp. (Golf) of one against two. **2.** *a.* Of three. [f. prec. + -SOME[2]]

thrĕmmatŏ'logy̆ *n.* Science of breeding animals and plants. [f. Gk *thremma -matos* nursling + -O- + -LOGY]

thrĕ'n|ōde, thrĕ'n|ody̆, *n.* (Song of) lamentation esp. on person's death; hence or cogn. **~ō'dĭ**AL, **~ŏ'dĭ**C, *adjs.*, **~od**IST (3) *n.* [f. Gk *thrēnōidia* (*thrēnos* wailing, *ōidē* ODE)]

thrĕsh *v.* **1.** *v.t.* Beat out or separate grain from (corn etc.) on threshing-floor or in threshing-machine; go *over* (problem etc.) in search of solution; **~ out,** = THRASH *out*; **~'ing-floor,** hard level floor for threshing; **~'ing-machine,** power-driven machine for separating grain from straw or husk. **2.** *v.i.* = THRASH 2. [var. of THRASH]

thrĕ'sher *n.* In vbl senses; shark lashing at enemies with very long upper lobe of tail. [f. prec. + -ER[1]]

thrĕ'shōld *n.* Plank or stone at bottom of door in dwelling-house, church, etc.; (fig.) point of entry (*on the threshold of a revolution, of a new century*); (Physiol. & Psych.) limit below which a stimulus ceases to be perceptible; (Phys.) limit below which no reaction etc. occurs, esp. minimum dose of radiation producing a specified effect. [OE *therscold, threscold,* etc., = ON *thresk(j)öldr,* OHG *thriscūfli,* cogn. w. THRASH in sense 'tread']

threw. See THROW[1].

thrīce *adv.* (arch. or literary). Three times; (esp. in comb.) highly (*thrice-blessed*). [ME *thries* (*thrie* adv. f. OE *thrīwa, thrīga* f. as THREE, -S[3])]

thrĭd *v.t.* (**-dd-**). (arch.) = THREAD[2].

thrĭft *n.* **1.** Frugality, economical management; ***~ account,** deposit account; hence ~'LESS *a.* **2.** *n.* Plant of genus *Armeria*, esp. sea-pink. [ME f. ON (as THRIVE)]

thrĭ'ft|y̆ *a.* Frugal, economical; thriving, prosperous; hence **~ĭLY**[2] *adv.*, **~ĭNESS** *n.* [ME, f. prec. + -Y[2]]

thrĭll *v.* & *n.* **1.** *v.t.* Penetrate (person etc.) with thrill of emotion or sensation (*his voice thrilled the listeners*); hence ~'ER[1] (2) *n.* (esp. sensational or exciting play, story, etc.), ~'ING[2] *a.* **2.** *v.i.* Be thus penetrated or agitated (*with* horror, excitement, etc.); (of emotion etc.) pass *through, over, along,* (*fear thrilled through my veins*); quiver, throb, (as) with emotion. **3.** *n.* Wave or nervous tremor of emotion or sensation, (*a thrill of joy, of recognition*); throb, pulsation; (Med.) vibratory movement or resonance observed in auscultation. [f. (now dial.) *thirl* f. OE *thyrlian* pierce (*thȳrel* hole f. *thurh* THROUGH; see -LE 1)]

thrĭps *n.* Insect of order Thysanoptera, esp. pest injurious to plants. [L f. Gk, = woodworm]

thrīve *v.i.* (**throve** *pr.* -ōv, *or* **~d**; **thri'ven** *pr.* -ĭ'ven, *or* **~d**). Prosper, flourish; grow rich; (of animal or plant) grow vigorously. [ME, f. ON *thrífask* refl. of *thrífa* grasp]

thro'. See THROUGH.

throat *n.* **1.** Front of neck between chin and collar-bone, corresponding part of animal, (**cut** person's ~, slash this esp. with intent to kill him; **cut** one's **own** ~, (fig.) bring about one's own defeat; **cut one another's ~s,** compete ruinously; **take by the ~,** try to throttle); windpipe (*the words* STICK[1] *in* one's *throat*; LIE[2] *in* one's *throat*; **give** person **the lie in his ~,** accuse him of lying grossly); (literary) voice esp. of song-bird; gullet (CLEAR[2] one's *throat*; JUMP[2] *down* person's *throat*; **ram** or **thrust down** person's ~, force (thing) on his attention; **sore ~,** inflammation of lining membrane of gullet etc.; **clergyman's (sore) ~,** chronic form of this affecting those who speak much in public); **~ lozenge** etc. (sucked to alleviate sore throat) **~ microphone** (suspended at neck of speaker etc. and actuated by vibrations of larynx). **2.** Throat-shaped thing, e.g. narrow part of chimney or blast-furnace, narrow part of river between rocks, narrow passage esp. in or near an entrance; (Naut.) forward upper corner of fore-and-aft sail. **3.** Hence (-)~'ED[2] *a.* [OE *throte, throtu,* = OHG *drozza,* f. Gmc **thrut-,* **thrŭt-* swell]

throa't|y̆ *a.* Guttural, uttered in the throat; hoarse; having prominent or capacious throat; hence **~ĭLY**[2] *adv.*, **~ĭNESS** *n.* [f. prec. + -Y[2]]

thrŏb *v.i.* (**-bb-**), & *n.* **1.** *v.i.* (Of heart, bosom, temples, etc.) palpitate, pulsate esp. with more than usual force or rapidity; (fig.) quiver, vibrate, (as) with emotion or with persistent rhythm. **2.** *n.* Throbbing; palpitation, (esp. violent) pulsation, (HEART-*throb*; *throbs of pleasure*). [ME, app. imit.]

thrōe *n.* (usu. in *pl.*) Violent pang(s), esp. of childbirth or death, or fig. of authorship etc.; anguish; **in the ~s,** (colloq.) struggling with the task *of* (*spring-cleaning* etc.). [ME *throwe* perh. f. OE *thrēa, thrawu* calamity, alt. perh. by assoc. w. *woe*]

thrŏ'mbĭn *n.* Enzyme promoting clotting of blood. [f. as THROMBUS + -IN]

thrŏ'mbocȳte *n.* Blood platelet, small plate of protoplasm concerned in coagulation of blood. [f. as THROMBUS + -O- + -CYTE]

thrŏmbō'se *v.t.* & *i.* Affect with or undergo thrombosis. [back form. f. foll.]

thrŏmb|ō'sĭs *n.* (*pl.* **~oses** *pr.* -ō'sēz). Coagulation of blood in blood-vessel or organ during life; hence **~O'TIC** *a.* [mod. L, f. Gk *thrombōsis* curdling (as foll.; see -OSIS)]

thrŏ'mb|us *n.* (*pl.* **~i** *pr.* -ī). Blood-clot formed in vascular system and obstructing circulation. [mod. L, f. Gk *thrombos* lump, blood-clot]

thrōne *n.*, & *v.t.* **1.** *n.* Chair of state for sovereign, pope, bishop, etc., usu. decorated and raised on dais; sovereign power (*came to the throne*; *lost his throne*); (in *pl.*) third ORDER[1] of ninefold celestial hierarchy; hence ~'LESS (-nl-) *a.* **2.** *v.t.* Enthrone (lit. or fig.). [ME f. OF *trone* f. L f. Gk *thronos* high seat]

thrŏng *n.* & *v.* **1.** *n.* Crowd of people; multitude (*of* people or things) esp. in small space. **2.** *v.i.* Come, go, press, (*round* etc.) in multitudes. **3.** *v.t.* Fill (street etc.) with a crowd or as crowd does; (arch.) crowd round, press hard upon, (person). [ME *thrang(e), throng(e),* OE *gethrang,* f. vbl st. *thring-, thrang-*]

thrŏ'stle (-sel) *n.* **1.** Song-THRUSH[1]. **2.** **~(-frame)**, machine for continuously spinning wool, cotton, etc. [OE; OS *throsla,* OHG *drōscala* f. Gmc **thrau(d)st-,* cogn. w. THRUSH[1]]

thrŏ'ttle *n.*, & *v.t.* **1.** *n.* Throat, gullet, windpipe; **~(-valve)**, valve controlling flow of steam, fuel, etc., in engine; **~(-lever)**, lever etc. operating this valve. **2.** *v.t.* Choke, strangle; prevent utterance etc. of; control (steam etc., engine) with throttle-valve; **~ back** or **down,** reduce speed of (engine, vehicle) thus. [v. ME, perh. f. THROAT + -LE 3; n. perh. dim. of THROAT (see -LE 1)]

through, thro', *thru, (-rōō) *prep.*, *adv.*, & *a.* **1.** *prep.* From end to end or side to side of, between the sides or walls or parts of, (*marched through the town*; *arrow went through his arm*; *see through a telescope*; *look through the window*; *pass through the doorway*; *swam through the waves*; *pushes his fingers through his hair*; *read through the whole book*; (fig.) *went through many trials, got through his examinations, bill passed through Parliament, I saw through his hypocrisy, wait through ten long years, flashed through his mind*). **2.** By reason of, by agency, means, or fault of, (*it all came about through his not knowing the way*; *concealed it through shame*; *it was all through you that we were late*). **3.** *Up to and including (*Friday through Tuesday*). **4.** *adv.* Through a thing, from side to side, from end to end, from beginning to end, (*let us stroll through*; *would not let us through* (the gate etc.); *ice gave and I went through*; *read it carefully through*); **~ and ~,** through again and again, thoroughly, completely; **be ~,** have finished (*with*), be connected to desired telephone etc., cease to have dealings (*with*), have no further prospects. **5.** *a.* Going or concerned with going through (*a through bolt*; **~-stone,** = BOND[1]*stone*); (of travel by rail, ship, air, etc.) going or concerned with going all the way without change of line or vehicle etc., going over different companies' lines with same ticket (*through carriage, train, passenger, ticket*); (of traffic) passing through a place to its destination; **no ~ road,** = *no* THOROUGH*fare.* **6. ~'put,**

amount of material put through a manufacturing etc. process; **~'way,** thoroughfare, esp. motorway. [OE *thurh,* = OS *thurh, thuru,* OHG *duruh* f. WG **thurh*]

throu'ghlў (-ōō'lĭ) *adv.* (arch.) Thoroughly. [ME, f. prec. + -LY²]

throughou't (-rōō-ow't) *adv.* & *prep.* **1.** *adv.* Right through, in every part, in all respects, (*timber was rotten throughout; followed a sound policy throughout*). **2.** *prep.* Right through, from end to end of, (*throughout the length and breadth of the land; throughout the 18th century*). [ME, f. THROUGH + OUT]

thrōve. See THRIVE.

throw¹ (-ō) *v.* (**threw** *pr.* -ōō; **~n**). **1.** *v.t.* Release (thing) after imparting motion, propel through space, send forth or dismiss esp. with some violence, (fig.) compel to be in specified condition, (*threw the ball at the stumps, over his head, to him, threw him the ball; mortars throw shells; hose throws water; threw himself down, on his knees; ship was thrown upon the coast; thrown from his horse; was thrown out of work, into prison, into a dilemma, upon his own resources*); project (rays, light; **~ light on the matter,** help to explain it); (Cricket) bowl (ball) with illegitimate sudden straightening of elbow; cast (line etc. in fishing, shadow, spell); *throw cold* WATER¹ *on,* DUST¹ *in* person's *eyes*; **~ good money after bad,** incur further loss in hopeless attempt to recoup previous loss; **~** one**self at,** blatantly seek as spouse, friend, etc.; *throw a* SOP *to*; **~'ing-stick,** = THROW²-*stick* (2); **~ stones,** (fig.) cast aspersions. **2.** (Of wrestler) bring (antagonist) to the ground; (of horse) unseat (rider); (colloq.) disconcert (*his question threw me for a moment*). **3.** Put (clothes etc.) carelessly or hastily *on, off, over* one's *shoulders* etc.; (of snake) cast (skin). **4.** (Of animal, e.g. bitch, rabbit, pigeon) give birth to (young). **5.** Cause (dice) to fall on table etc., obtain (specified number) thus. **6.** Twist (silk etc.) into thread or yarn. **7.** Shape (round pottery) on potter's wheel; turn (wood etc.) on lathe. **8.** Turn, direct, move esp. quickly (esp. part of body), (*threw his eyes to the ground, a glance backwards, his arms up, his head back*); cause to pass or extend suddenly to another state or position (*threw army* or *bridge across river; throw switch to 'on'; throw* OPEN¹); put into a form or *into* another form, language, etc. **9.** *Lose (contest, race, etc.) intentionally. **10.** Have (fit, tantrum, etc.); (sl.) give (a party). **11. ~ about** or **around,** throw in various directions, spend (one's money) ostentatiously, make vigorous use of (one's WEIGHT¹, lit. or fig.); **~ away,** (fig.) part with as unwanted, part with needlessly or recklessly, lose by neglect (*threw away all his advantages, an excellent chance*), discard (card), (Theatr.) speak (lines) with deliberate under-emphasis, (in *p.p.*) wasted (*the advice was thrown away on him*); *~-away* a. & n., (1) (thing) to be thrown away after (one) use, (2) deliberately under-emphasized; **~ back,** revert to ancestral character, (usu. in *pass.*) compel to rely *on*; *~-back* n., (instance of) reversion to ancestral character; **~ down,** cause to fall; *throw down the* GAUNTLET¹ or GLOVE; **~ in,** add (thing) to a bargain without extra charge, interpose (word, remark) by way of parenthesis or casually, (Footb. etc.) throw (ball) from edge of pitch etc. after it has gone out of play there, (Cricket etc.) return (ball) from outfield, (Cards) give (player) the lead to his disadvantage; **~** one's **hand in,** (lit.) abandon one's chances in card game esp. poker, (fig.) give up, withdraw from a contest; **~ in** one's **lot with,** decide to share fortunes of; *throw in the* TOWEL; **~** one**self into,** engage vigorously in; **~ off,** discard (acquaintance etc.), contrive to get rid of (illness, troublesome companion), abandon (disguise), produce, deliver, (poem, epigram) in offhand manner, (of hounds or hunt) begin hunting, make a start, (and see sense 3); *~-off* n., start in hunt or race; **~** one**self on** *or* **upon,** attack, place one's reliance on (*the mercy of the court* etc.); **~ out,** put out forcibly or suddenly, expel (trouble-maker etc.), build (wing of house, pier, projecting or prominent thing), suggest, put forward tentatively, reject (proposal, bill in Parliament), confuse or distract (person speaking, thinking, or acting) from the matter in hand so that he blunders or stops, (Cricket & Baseball) put out (opponent) by throwing ball to wicket or base; **~ over,** desert, abandon; **~ together,** (1) assemble hastily, (2) bring into casual contact; **~ up,** lift (sash-window) quickly, erect (building), bring to notice, renounce (task), resign (office), (*v.t.* & *i.*) vomit; **~ up** one's **eyes** (as sign of horror or outraged propriety); *throw up the* SPONGE¹. **12.** Hence (-)**~'ER**¹ *n.* [OE *thrāwan* twist, turn, = OS *thrāian,* OHG *drāen,* WG f. IE **ter-*]

throw² (-ō) *n.* **1.** Throwing; cast of dice; cast of fishing-line etc.; distance a missile is or may be thrown (*record throw with the hammer; a* STONE'*s throw*); fall in wrestling; (Cricket) bowler's illegitimate delivery by throwing. **2.** (Geol. & Mining). Fault or leap in strata; amount of vertical displacement so caused. **3.** Machine or device giving rapid rotary motion; (extent of) movement of crank, cam, etc.; distance moved by pointer of instrument etc. **4.** ***~ (rug),** light cover for furniture, light wrap; **~-stick,** (1) club or stick meant to be whirled from the hand (e.g. boomerang), (2) device for throwing spear etc. more forcibly. [f. prec.]

throw'ster (-rō'-) *n.* One who throws silk. [ME, f. THROW¹ + -STER]

***thru.** See THROUGH.

thrŭm¹ *n.,* & *v.t.* (**-mm-**). **1.** *n.* Fringe of warp-threads remaining on loom when web has been cut off; single thread of this; any loose thread or tuft; **thread and ~,** all alike, good and bad; hence **~'my**² *a.* **2.** *v.t.* Make of or cover with thrums. [OE, = OHG *drum* remnant, end-piece, f. Gmc **thrum-,* **thram-* f. IE **trm-*]

thrŭm² *v.* (**-mm-**) & *n.* **1.** *v.t.* & *i.* Play monotonously or unskilfully on or *on* (stringed instrument); drum, tap, idly on or *on* (table etc.). **2.** *n.* Such playing; resulting sound. [imit.]

thrŭsh¹ *n.* Small or medium-sized bird of family Turdidae, e.g. blackbird, nightingale, or esp. **song-~** (*Turdus philomelos*) or MISSEL-*thrush.* [OE *thrysce* f. Gmc **thruskjōn*; cf. THROSTLE]

thrŭsh² *n.* Disease, esp. of children, marked by whitish fungous vesicles in mouth and throat; inflammation affecting frog of horse's foot. [17th c., of unkn. orig.]

thrŭst *v.* (**thrust**) & *n.* **1.** *v.t.* Push with sudden impulse or with force (lit. or fig.; *thrust his fist into my face, the letter into my hand* or *his pocket; thrust a pin into the cushion; I thrust out my hand; some have greatness thrust upon them; was thrust from his rights; my objections were thrust aside*); **~** one**self** or one's **nose in,** obtrude, interfere. **2.** Pierce (person etc.) *through*; make one's *way* by force. **3.** *v.i.* Make sudden push *at* (person etc. *with* dagger etc.); force oneself *through, past,* etc. **4.** Hence **~'ER**¹ *n.,* (esp.) ‖foxhunter who endangers others or the hounds in securing a forward place, pushing person, reaction-propulsion system. **5.** *n.* Sudden or forcible push; forward force exerted by propeller, jet, etc.; strong attempt to penetrate enemy's line or territory; attack with point of weapon; remark aimed at a person; stress between two contiguous bodies esp. parts of structure, e.g. arch, rafters. **6. ~-block,** (esp.) casting or frame carrying or containing bearings on which collars of propeller-shaft press; **~-hoe** (worked by thrust, not pull); **~ stage** (Theatr., extending into audience). [ME *thruste* etc. f. ON *thrýsta*]

***thruway.** See THROUGH*way*.

thŭd *v.i.* (**-dd-**), & *n.* (Make, fall with) low dull sound as of blow on non-resonant thing. [prob. f. OE *thyddan* thrust]

thŭg *n.* **1.** (*T~*; Hist.). Member of religious organization of robbers and assassins in India suppressed about 1825. **2.** Vicious or brutal ruffian. **3.** Hence **~'g**ERY (5) (-g-) *n.* [f. Hindi & Marathi *ṭhag* swindler]

thŭ'gg|ee (-gē) *n.* (Hist.) The practice of the Thugs; so ~ISM (3) (-g-) *n.* [f. Hindi *ṭhagī* (as prec.)]

thū'ja, thū'ya, *n.* Coniferous tree of genus *Thuja* or *Thuya*, arbor vitae. [mod. L, f. Gk *thu(i)a*, an Afr. tree]

thū'lĭum *n.* (Chem.) Metallic element of lanthanide series. [mod. L, f. L *Thule* name of a region in the uttermost north + -IUM]

thŭmb (-m) *n.* & *v.* **1.** *n.* Short thick finger set apart from and opposable to the others on human hand; digit of other animals corresponding to this; part of glove etc. that holds thumb; **~s down,** gesture of rejection; **~s up!** (sl. excl. of satisfaction); RULE *of thumb*; STICK[1] *out like a sore thumb*; **he has ten ~s,** his FINGERS are all thumbs; **under** person's **~** (influence, domination). **2. ~-index** *n.*, & *v.t.*, (provide with) set of lettered grooves cut or tabs fixed in fore-edges of book's leaves to facilitate reference; **~-mark** (made by thumb, esp. dirty thumb on leaf of book); **~-nail,** nail of thumb; *~-nail sketch*, portrait of small size or hastily made, brief word-picture; **~-nut** (Mech., shaped for thumb to turn); **~-pot,** flower-pot of smallest size; **~-print,** impression of thumb esp. as used for identification; **~'screw,** instrument of torture for squeezing thumbs, (Mech.) screw with flattened head for thumb to turn; **~-stall,** cover like finger-stall to protect thumb; **~-sucking,** infantile habit of sucking one's thumb; ***~'tack,** drawing-pin. **3.** Hence (-)~ED[2] (-md), ~'LESS, *adjs.* **4.** *v.t.* Wear, soil, (pages etc.) with thumb; (try to) get (a lift in a vehicle) by signal with thumb to indicate movement in desired direction; **~** one's **nose,** cock a SNOOK[2] (*at*). **5.** *v.i.* Turn over pages (as if) with thumb (*thumbed through the directory*). [OE *thūma*, = OS *thūma*, OHG *dūmo* f. WG **thōmo* f. IE **tum-* swell]

thŭ'mmĭm. See URIM.

thŭmp *v.* & *n.* **1.** *v.t.* & *i.* Beat or strike heavily esp. with fist; deliver blows *at*, *on*, etc., esp. to attract attention; **~ (out)**, play (tune) on piano etc. with thumping of keys. **2.** *n.* Heavy blow, bang. [imit.]

thŭ'mp|er *n.* In vbl senses; (colloq.) large, striking, or impressive person or thing, esp. lie, so ~ING[2] *a.* [f. prec. + -ER[1]]

thŭ'nder *n.* & *v.* **1.** *n.* Loud noise heard after flash of lightning and due to disturbance of air by discharge of electricity; (rhet. or fig.) thunderbolt; (fig.) resounding loud deep noise (*thunders of applause*); (in *sing.* or *pl.*) authoritative censure or threats; BLOOD[1]*-and-thunder*; (sl.) = HELL (*what the* or *in thunder . . . ?*); **steal** person's **~**, (fig.) forestall him (by telling the story he meant to tell, making profitable use of his invention before he can, and the like) [f. remark of John Dennis (*c.* 1710) when stage thunder he had intended for his own play was used for another]. **2. ~bolt,** flash of lightning with crash of thunder, imaginary bolt or shaft viewed as destructive agent in lightning esp. as attribute of god, stone or fossil supposed to be such bolt, formidable threat etc.; **~-box,** primitive lavatory; **~clap,** crash of thunder (esp. fig., or in simile, of sudden terrible event or news); **~-cloud,** storm-cloud charged with electricity and producing thunder and lightning; **~ egg,** rounded concretion of chalcedony; **~-head,** rounded cumulus cloud projecting upwards and heralding thunder; **~-shower** (accompanied by thunder); **~storm** (with thunder and lightning and usu. heavy rain or hail); **~struck,** struck by lightning, (fig.) amazed. **3.** Hence ~LESS, ~OUS, ~Y[2], *adjs.* **4.** *v.i.* Give forth thunder (esp. *it thunders, is thundering*); make noise like thunder, sound very loudly, (*voice thundered in my ears*); move with loud noise (*train thundered past*); make violent threats etc. *against* etc. **5.** *v.t.* Utter (threats etc.) in loud or impressive manner. [OE *thunor*, = OS *thunar*, OHG *donar*, ON *thórr* f. Gmc f. IE **t(o)n-*]

thŭ'nderer *n.* In vbl senses; **the T~**, Jupiter (Tonans), ||(arch. or joc.) *The Times* newspaper. [ME, f. prec. + -ER[1]]

thŭ'ndering *a.* & *adv.* In vbl senses; (colloq.) unusual(ly), remarkable, remarkably, decided(ly), (*a thundering nuisance*; *a thundering great fish*); **the T~ Legion,** Roman legion containing Christian soldiers whose prayers were held to have procured a thunderstorm that terrified the enemy; hence ~LY[2] *adv.* [f. THUNDER + -ING[2]]

thūr'ible *n.* Censer. [ME f. OF, or f. L *t(h)uribulum* (as foll.)]

thūr'ĭ|fer *n.* Acolyte carrying censer; so ~FEROUS (-ĭ'f-) *a.*, incense-bearing, ~FICA'TION *n.*, burning of incense. [LL (*thus thuris* incense f. Gk *thuos* sacrifice, *-fer* -bearing)]

Thur(s). *abbr.* Thursday.

Thūr'sday (-z-; *or* -dĭ) *n.* & *adv.* **1.** *n.* Day of week, following Wednesday; HOLY *Thursday*. **2.** *adv.* (cf. FRIDAY 2). [OE *thunres-*, *thur(e)sdæg*, day of thunder, representing LL *Jovis dies* day of Jupiter]

thŭs (dh-) *adv.* (formal). In this way, in the way (to be) indicated; accordingly, as a result or inference; to this extent, so, (*thus far*; *thus much*). [OE, = OS *thus*, of unkn. orig.]

thŭ'snėss (dh-) *n.* (joc.) State of being thus. [f. prec. + -NESS]

thū'ya. See THUJA.

thwăck *v.t.*, & *n.* = WHACK 1, 2. [imit.]

||thwaite *n.* (dial.) Piece of wild land made arable. [f. ON *thveit(i)* paddock (**thvíta* = OE *thwītan* to cut)]

thwart (-ôrt) *adv.*, *prep.*, *a.*, *v.t.*, & *n.* **1.** *adv.* & *prep.* (arch.) Across, athwart; (Naut.) **~-ship** *a.*, **-ships** *adv.*, (Naut.) (lying) across ship. **2.** *a.* (arch.) Lying across, transverse. **3.** *v.t.* Frustrate, foil, (person, wish, purpose). **4.** *n.* Oarsman's bench placed across boat. [ME *thwert* f. ON *thvert* adv., neut. of *thverr* transverse = OE *thwe(o)rh*, OHG *twerh*, Goth. *thwairhs* angry f. Gmc **thwerhwaz* f. IE **twerk-*, **twork-*]

thȳ (dhī) *poss. pron. attrib.* (arch. or poet. or dial. exc. as described at THOU). Of thee (in *pred.* & abs. use, & usu. before vowel, **thine**: *thy lips*; *the fault is thine*; *thine eyes*); for phrs. see HER[2], HERS. [ME *thī*, reduced f. *thīn* THINE]

thȳ'lacine *n.* = TASMANIAN *wolf*. [F, f. mod. L *thylacinus* f. Gk *thulakos* pouch; see -INE[1]]

thȳme (tīm) *n.* Herb of genus *Thymus* with aromatic leaves; **garden ~**, shrub with pungent aromatic leaves used in cookery; **lemon ~**, lemon-scented wild thyme; **wild ~** (species with mildly aromatic leaves); hence **thȳ'm**Y[2] (tī'-) *a.* [ME, f. OF *thym* f. L f. Gk *thumon* (*thuō* burn sacrifice)]

thȳ'mine (-ēn) *n.* (Chem.) Crystalline base

found as constituent of DNA or derived from thymus gland. [f. *thymic* (as THYMUS; see -IC) + -INE[5]]

thȳ'mŏl *n.* (Chem.) White crystalline phenol obtained from oil of thyme and used as antiseptic. [f. as THYME + -OL]

thȳ'm|us *n.* (*pl.* **~i** *pr.* -ī). **~us (gland)**, (Anat.) ductless gland situated near base of neck (in man becoming much smaller at approach of puberty). [mod. L, f. Gk *thumos*]

thȳr'oid *a.* & *n.* (Anat. & Zool.) Shield-shaped (~ **cartilage,** large cartilage of larynx, projection of which in man forms Adam's apple); connected with the thyroid cartilage (*thyroid artery*); ~ **(gland)**, (1) large ductless gland lying near larynx and trachea secreting hormone which regulates growth and development through rate of metabolism, (2) extract prepared from the thyroid gland of animals and used in treating goitre, cretinism, etc.; hence **thȳr'ėo-, thȳr'o-,** *comb. forms.* [f. obs. F *thyroide* or mod. L *thyroides*, irreg. f. Gk *thureoeidēs* (*thureos* oblong shield; see -OID)]

thȳrŏ'xine *n.* White crystalline active principle of thyroid gland. [f. prec. + OX- + -INE[5]]

thyr's|us (-ēr'-) *n.* (*pl.* **~i** *pr.* -ī). (Gk & Rom. Ant.) staff tipped with ornament like pine-cone, an attribute of Bacchus; (Bot.) inflorescence as in lilac, with primary axis racemose and secondary axis cymose. [L, f. Gk *thursos*]

thȳsĕ'lf (dh-) *pron.* Emphat. & refl. form corresp. to THOU or THEE (for uses cf. HERSELF). [ME, f. THY + SELF]

ti[1] (tē) *n.* Tree of genus *Cordyline*, esp. *C. terminalis* with edible roots. [Tahitian, Maori, etc.]

ti[2]. See TE.

Ti *symb.* titanium.

tiār'a *n.* Ancient Persian turban worn erect by king, depressed by others; pope's diadem pointed at top and surrounded by three crowns, (fig.) the papal office; woman's ornamental coronet; hence ~ED[2] (-rad), ~'D[2], *adjs.* [L f. Gk, of unkn. orig.]

Tībĕ'tan *a.* & *n.* (Native, inhabitant, or language) of Tibet. [f. *Tibet* + -AN]

tĭ'bi|a *n.* (*pl.* **~ae**). (Anat.) inner and usu. larger of two bones from knee to ankle; tibiotarsus of bird; fourth segment of leg in insects; so ~AL *a.* [L, = shin-bone, flute]

tĭbiotār's|us *n.* (*pl.* **~i** *pr.* -ī). Bone in bird corresponding to tibia, fused at lower end with some bones of tarsus. [f. prec. + -O- + TARSUS]

tĭc *n.* Habitual spasmodic contraction of muscles esp. of face; ~ (**douloureux** *pr.* dōolerēr' *or* dŏlerōō'), trigeminal neuralgia. [F, f. It. *ticchio*]

tīce *n.* (Cricket) = YORKER; (Croquet) stroke tempting opponent to aim at one's ball. [f. (now dial.) *tice* v. (= ENTICE)]

tĭck[1] *v.* & *n.* **1.** *v.i.*, & *n.* (Make) slight recurring click, esp. that of watch or clock (‖**to** or **on the** ~, with exact punctuality; **what makes** person ~, his motivation; ~ **over,** (of engine, or fig.) idle); ‖(colloq.) moment, instant; **~-tack,** pulsating sound esp. of the heart, kind of manual semaphore signalling practised by racecourse bookmakers; ***~-tack-toe,** noughts and crosses; **~-tick,** ticking of watch etc.; **~-tock,** ticking of large clock etc. **2.** *n.* Small mark set against items in list etc. in checking. **3.** *v.t.* Mark (item, usu. *off*) with tick. **4.** (Of clock etc.) ~ **away** (the time etc.); ~ **off,** (sl.) reprimand; (of tape-machine) ~ **out** (news etc.). [n. ME; cf. Du. *tik*, LG *tikk* touch, tick; v. 16th c.; cf. Du. *tikken*, OHG *zekōn* pluck]

tĭck[2] *n.* Arachnid parasitic on dogs, cattle, etc.; insect parasitic on sheep, birds, etc.; (colloq.) unpleasant or despicable person; ~ **fever** (transmitted by bite of tick). [OE **tīca*, **ticca*, ME *teke*, *tyke*; cf. MDu., MLG *tēke*, OHG *zēcho*]

tĭck[3] *n.* Cover or case of mattress or pillow; = TICKING. [ME *tikke*, *tēke* = MDu., MLG *tēke*, OHG *ziehha*, f. WG **teka*, **tika*, f. L f. Gk *thēkē* case]

tĭck[4] *n.* (colloq.) Credit (*buy goods on tick*). [app. abbr. of TICKET in phr. *on the ticket*]

tĭ'cker *n.* In vbl senses; (colloq.) watch, tape-machine; (joc.) the heart; ***~-tape,** paper strip from tape-machine, this or similar material thrown from windows to greet a celebrity. [f. TICK[1] + -ER[1]]

tĭ'ckėt *n.*, & *v.t.* **1.** *n.* Written or printed piece of card or paper entitling holder to admission to place of entertainment etc., participation in event, conveyance by train etc., or other right, (*concert, theatre, library, lottery, railway, bus, cloakroom, pawn, -ticket*); (Mil.) certificate of discharge; certificate of qualification as ship's master, pilot, etc.; label attached to thing and giving price or other particulars; official notification of traffic offence etc. (*parking ticket*); *(Polit.) list of candidates put forward by a party, (fig.) principles of a party, (SPLIT[1] *the ticket*; STRAIGHT *ticket*); **the** ~, (sl.) the correct or desirable thing. **2.** ‖~ **of leave** (Hist., allowing liberty with certain restrictions to ~*-of-leave man*, i.e. prisoner or convict who had served part of his time); **~-collector,** railway official who takes or checks passengers' tickets; ‖**~-day,** (St. Exch.) day before settling day, when names of actual purchasers are handed to stockbrokers; **~-office,** place where tickets for transport, entertainment, etc., are sold; **~-porter,** (Hist.) licensed London porter identified by badge; **~-punch** (for making hole in ticket to show that it has been used). **3.** *v.t.* Put ticket on (article for sale etc.). [f. obs. F *étiquet* f. OF *estiquet(te)* (*estiquier*, *estechier* fix f. MDu. *steken*; see -ET[1])]

‖**tĭckėtȳ-bōō'** *a.* (sl.) All right, satisfactory. [perh. f. prec. + -Y[2] + BOO]

tĭ'cking *n.* Stout usu. striped linen or cotton material for bed-ticks. [f. TICK[3] + -ING[1]]

tĭ'ckle *v.* & *n.* **1.** *v.t.* Apply light touches or stroking to (person, part of his body, or abs.) so as to excite the nerves and usu. produce laughter and spasmodic movement (*tickle him with a feather*; *tickle the soles of her feet*; *don't tickle*); ~ person's **ribs,** (fig.) cause him great amusement. **2.** *v.i.* Feel this sensation (*my foot tickles*). **3.** *v.t.* Excite agreeably, amuse, divert, (person, his sense of humour, vanity, etc.; *I was highly tickled at the idea*; *this will tickle his palate*; **~d pink** or **to death,** (colloq.) extremely amused etc.); catch (trout etc.) with the hand. **4.** *n.* Act or sensation of tickling; so **tĭ'cklȳ**[2] *a.* [ME, prob. frequent. of TICK[1]; see -LE 3]

tĭ'ckler *n.* In vbl senses; puzzling or delicate question or matter; *memorandum book. [f. prec. + -ER[1]]

tĭ'cklĭsh *a.* Easily tickled, sensitive to tickling; (of person or question or thing to be dealt with) difficult, critical, requiring careful handling; hence ~LY[2] *adv.*, ~NESS *n.* [f. TICKLE + -ISH[1]]

tĭcpolŏ'nga (-ngga) *n.* Venomous serpent of India and Sri Lanka [f. Sinh. *titpolongā* spot-viper]

tĭ'c-tăc. Var. of TICK[1]*-tack.*

tī'dal *a.* Of tide(s); actuated by tide(s); ~ **air** (passing in and out of lungs at each respiration); ~ **basin, dock,** etc., (subject to rise and fall of tide); ~ **flow** (of traffic moving mainly in opposite directions at different times of day); ~ **friction** (of tide wave, retarding diurnal rotation of earth); ~ **river** (affected by tide to considerable distance from mouth); ~ **wave,** (1) exceptionally large ocean wave e.g. one attributed to earthquake, (2) widespread manifestation of feeling etc., (3) tide wave; hence ~LY[2] *adv.* [f. TIDE[1] + -AL]

***tĭ'dbĭt.** See TITBIT.

***tiddledy-wink.** See TIDDLY-WINK.

‖**tĭ'ddler** *n.* (childish or colloq.). Small fish, esp. stickleback; unusually small thing. [perh. rel. to *tiddly* 'little' and TITTLEBAT]

‖**tĭ'ddl(e)ȳ** (-lĭ) *a.* (sl.) Slightly drunk. [earlier sense 'a drink', 19th c.; orig. unkn.]

tĭ'ddlȳ-wĭnk, *tĭ'ddledȳ- (-dəld-), *n.* Counter flicked into cup or other receptacle on centre of table in game of ~**s.** [19th c., perh. rel. to prec.]

tīde[1] *n.* **1.** Time, season, (arch. exc. in *Whitsuntide, Christmas-tide, yule-tide,* etc.). **2.** Periodical rise (**flood-~**) and fall (**ebb-~**) of sea due to attraction of moon and sun; water as moved by this (~ **is in, out,** water is at high, low, level); **high, low,** ~, completion of flood, ebb, -tide; **spring, neap, -~,** tide of maximum, minimum, height when solar and lunar attractions are combined or at right angles; **work double ~s** (twice normal time, or as hard as possible); **meteorological** ~ (due to regular alternations of wind etc.). **3.** (fig.) Trend of opinion or fortune or events (*go with, against, the tide;* TURN[1,2] (*of*) *the tide; roll back the tide of war*). **4.** ~**-gate** (opened to admit water or let vessels pass during rising tide, closed to keep water in during ebb); ~**-gauge** (showing extremes or present level of tide); ~**-lock** (between tidal harbour etc. and basin or canal behind it); ~**-land** (submerged at high tide); ~**-mark,** mark made by tide at high water, (colloq.) line on body to which person has washed, or on bath to which water has risen when person was in it; ~**-mill** (with water-wheel driven by tide); ~**-rip(s),** rough water caused by opposing tides; ~**-table,** list of times of high tide at a place; ~**-waiter,** (Hist.) customs officer who boarded ship on arrival to enforce customs regulations; ~ **water** (brought by or affected by tides); ~ **wave,** undulation of water passing round earth and causing high and low tides; ~**'way,** channel where tide runs, tidal part of river, ebb or flow in such channel. **5.** Hence ~'LESS (-dl-) *a.* [OE *tīd* time, = OS *tīd,* OHG *zīt,* ON *tīth* f. Gmc **tīdiz* (**tī-;* cf. TIME[1])]

tīde[2] *v.* **1.** *v.i.* Drift with tide, esp. work in or out of harbour with help of tide. **2.** *v.t.* & *i.* (Enable or assist to) get *over* (difficulty etc., or abs.). [f. prec.]

tī'dĭngs (-z) *n.* (literary; treated as *sing.* or *pl.*) (Piece of) news, information. [OE *tīdung,* prob. f. ON *títhindi* events (*títhr* occurring)]

tī'd|ȳ *a., n.,* & *v.t.* **1.** *a.* (Of dress, room, person, habits) neatly arranged, neat, orderly; (colloq.) pretty large, considerable, (*left a tidy sum when he died; a tidy day's work*); hence ~ĬLY[2] *adv.,* ~ĬNESS *n.* **2.** *n.* Detachable usu. ornamental cover for chair-back etc.; receptacle for odds and ends, e.g. in kitchen sink. **3.** *v.t.* ~**y** (**up**), make (room, table, etc., one*self,* or abs.) neat, put in good order. [ME, = timely etc., f. TIDE[1] + -Y[2]]

tīe[1] *v.* (*part.* **ty'ing** *pr.* tī'ĭ-). **1.** *v.t.* Attach or fasten with cord or the like (*tie the dog to the railings;* HAND[1]*s are tied;* RIDE *and tie; tie his legs together; tie on a label*); secure (shoe etc.) by tightening and knotting its strings; arrange (string, ribbon, tie, etc.) to form knot, bow, etc. (~ **and dye,** method of producing dyed patterns by tying string etc. to protect parts of fabric from dye), form (knot, bow) thus; bind (rafters etc.) by cross-piece etc.; restrict, bind, (person etc. *to, down to,* conditions, occupation, place, etc.); **fit to be ~d,** (sl.) very angry; ~ **in** or **up,** (cause to) agree or be closely associated *with;* ~ **up,** fasten with cord etc., obstruct, make (money etc.) not immediately available e.g. by investment, restrict, esp. annex conditions to (bequest etc.) to prevent its being sold or diverted from its purpose; hence ~*-up* n. **2.** (Mus.) Unite (notes) by tie. **3.** *v.t.* & *i.* Make tie with or *with* (competitor; *for* place or prize), equal (feat etc.). [OE *tīgan, tēgan* f. Gmc **taugian*]

tīe[2] *n.* **1.** Cord, chain, etc., used for fastening. **2.** = NECK[1]*tie;* ‖OLD *school tie.* **3.** (fig.) Thing that unites or restricts persons, bond, obligation, (*ties of blood, friendship*). **4.** Rod or beam holding parts of a structure together, *rail sleeper. **5.** (Mus.) Curved line above two notes of same pitch that are to be joined as one. **6.** Equality of score or draw or dead heat among competitors in game or contest; **play, shoot,** etc., **off a** ~, play further game etc. to decide between such competitors. **7.** Match between any pair of several competing players or teams; **cup-~,** match in competition for a cup. **8.** *Laced shoe. **9.** ~**-bar,** metal rod holding parts of building together; ~**-beam,** horizontal beam connecting rafters; ~**-break,** (means of) deciding winner as between competitors tying; ~**-clip,** ~**-pin,** (to hold necktie in place); ~**-piece,** ~**-rod,** connecting member; ~**-wig** (tied at back with ribbon). [OE *tēah, tēg,* = ON *taug* rope f. Gmc **taugō* (**tauh-;* cf. TEAM, TOW[1])]

‖**tīed** (tīd) *a.* (Of public house etc.) bound to supply only a particular brewer's liquor; (of dwelling-house) occupied subject to tenant's working for house's owner. [p.p. of TIE[1]]

tier *n.* Row or rank, esp. one of several placed one above another as in theatre; one of several units of a structure placed one above another; (Naut.) circle of coiled cable, place for coiled cable; hence (-)~ED[2] (-ērd) *a.* [earlier *tire* f. F (*tirer* draw, elongate f. Rom. **tirare*)]

tierce *n.* **1.** (arch.) One third of a pipe as wine-measure; cask containing certain quantity (varying with the goods) esp. of provisions. **2.** (Mus.) Interval of two octaves and a major third. **3.** Sequence of three cards; third of eight parrying positions in fencing, or corresponding thrust. **4.** (Eccl.) = TERCE. [ME, f. OF *t(i)erce* f. L *tertia* fem. (as n.) of *tertius* third]

tier'cel. See TERCEL.

tier'cėt. See TERCET.

tiers état (tyārzātah') *n.* (Fr. Hist.) = *third* ESTATE. [F]

tĭff[1] *v.i.* (Ind.) = TIFFIN. [abbr.]

tĭff[2] *n.* Fit of peevishness; slight or petty quarrel. [18th c.; orig. unkn.]

tĭ'ffanȳ *n.* Thin gauze muslin. [orig. (dress for) Twelfth-night, f. OF *tifanie* f. eccl. L *theophania* f. Gk THEO*phaneia* manifestation of God, Epiphany]

|**tĭ'ffĭn** *n.,* & *v.i.* (Ind.) (Take) light meal esp. of curried dishes and fruit, lunch. [app. f. *tiffing* taking slight drink]

tĭg *n.* Game of TAG[2]. [var. of TICK[1]]

tī'ger (-g-) *n.* **1.** Large Asian yellow-brown black-striped carnivorous maneless feline (*Felis tigris*); **American** ~, jaguar; **paper** ~, person or thing threatening in appearance but ineffectual. **2.** Fierce or energetic person; (colloq.) formidable opponent in a game; ‖dissolute swaggerer or bully; ‖(arch.) groom accompanying master in light vehicle; *(sl.) yell supplementary to three cheers, final burst. **3.** ~**-beetle,** carnivorous beetle of family Cicindelidae, with spotted or striped wing-covers; ~**-cat,** any moderate-sized feline resembling the tiger, e.g. ocelot, serval, margay, (Austral.) carnivorous marsupial of genus *Dasyurus;*

~('s)-eye, yellow-brown gem of brilliant lustre, *pottery-glaze of similar appearance; **~-lily,** tall garden lily with flowers of dull orange spotted with black or purple; **~-moth** (with richly spotted and streaked wings suggesting tiger's skin); **~-wood,** striped or streaked wood for cabinet-making. **4.** Hence ~ISH[1] *a.*, **ti'gr**ESS[1] *n.* [ME, f. OF *tigre* f. L f. Gk *tigris*]

tight (tīt) *a.*, *n.*, & *adv.* **1.** *a.* Closely and firmly put together (*tight joint, ship*); impermeable, impervious, esp. (in *comb.*) to specified thing (*airtight, watertight*). **2.** Closely held, drawn, fastened, fitting, etc., (*tight knots*; *cork is too tight*); (of shoe) too closely fitting; (of control etc.) strictly imposed. **3.** Tense, stretched so as to leave no slack, (*tight cord*; **~'rope,** one on which acrobats, rope-dancers, etc., perform). **4.** (colloq.) Drunk. **5.** (Of money or materials) not easily obtainable; (of money-market) in which money is tight. **6.** Produced by or requiring great exertion or pressure (*a tight squeeze*); (of precautions, programme, etc.) stringent, demanding; **~ corner** or **place** or (colloq.) **spot,** (fig.) difficult situation. **7. ~-fisted,** stingy; **~-lipped,** with lips compressed to restrain emotion or speech; **~'wad,** (sl.) close-fisted or stingy person. **8.** Hence ~'EN[6] *v.t.* & *i.*, (~*en* one's *belt*, go without food, lit. or fig.), ~'LY[2] *adv.*, ~'NESS *n.* **9.** *n.* (in *pl.*) Close-fitting elastic garments as worn by dancers, acrobats, etc.; woman's one-piece stretchable under-garment covering legs and body up to waist, worn in place of stockings. **10.** *adv.* Tightly (*squeeze it tight*; *hold me tight*); SIT *tight*; **~-fitting,** (of garment) fitting (too) close to body. [prob. alt. f. *thight* f. ON **thehtr, théttr* watertight, of close texture]

ti'gon *n.* Offspring of tiger and lioness. [portmanteau wd]

ti'gress. See TIGER.

tike. See TYKE.

ti'ki *n.* (N.Z.) Large wooden or small ornamental greenstone image of creator of man or of an ancestor. [Maori]

til (tēl) *n.* Portuguese tilde. [Port.]

ti'lbury *n.* (Hist.) Light open two-wheeled carriage. [f. inventor's name]

ti'lde (-*e or* -ā) *n.* Mark (~) put over letter, e.g. Spanish *n* when pronounced *ny* (so *señor*) or Portuguese *a* or *o* when nasalized (so *São Paulo*). [Sp., var. of **tidlo* f. L *titulus* TITLE]

tile *n.*, & *v.t.* **1.** *n.* Thin slab of baked clay for roof, pavement, drain, etc.; similar slab glazed and often decorated for hearth, fireplace, wall, etc.; **have a ~ loose,** (sl.) be slightly crazy; **on the ~s,** (sl.) on a debauch. **2.** (sl.) Hat, esp. silk hat. **3. ~'stone,** flagstone suitable to be split for use instead of tiles. **4.** *v.t.* Cover (roof etc., or abs.) with tiles; **~ in,** enclose in tiles. **5.** (Freemasonry). Guard (lodge, meeting) against intrusion by placing tiler at door. **6.** Hence **ti'l**ING[1] (1, 2, 6) *n.* [OE *tigule, -ele,* = OS *tiegla*, OHG *ziagal(a)*, ON *tigl*, f. L *tegula* f. IE *teg-* cover]

ti'ler *n.* **1.** One who makes or lays tiles. **2.** (Freemasonry). Door-keeper of lodge. [ME, f. prec. + -ER[1]]

till[1] *v.t.* Prepare and use (land) for crops; hence ~'ABLE *a.*, ~'AGE (3) *n.* [OE *tilian* strive for, cultivate, = OS *tilian, tilon* obtain, OHG *zilōn*, Goth. *gatilon* f. Gmc **tilōjan* (**tilam* aim, goal)]

till[2] *prep.* & *conj.* **1.** *prep.* Up to, as late as, (specified time; *wait till evening, four o'clock, then, Monday, next week*); up to the time of (event expected to happen sooner or later; *was true till death*; *waited till the end, till his return, arrival, departure*). **2.** *conj.* Up to the time when (*ring till you get an answer*; *walk on till you come to the gate*). [f. OE & ON *til* to, prob. orig. f. Gmc **tilam* n. (see prec.) used as adv.]

till[3] *n.* Money-receptacle behind counter in shop, bank, etc. [ME, of unkn. orig.]

till[4] *n.* Stiff clay containing boulders, sand, etc., boulder clay; hence ~'Y[2] *a.* [17th c. Sc.; orig. unkn.]

ti'ller[1] *n.* (literary or arch.) One who tills. [ME, f. TILL[1] + -ER[1]]

ti'ller[2] *n.* Horizontal bar fitted to head of rudder for steering; **~-chain, -rope,** (connecting tiller with wheel). [ME, f. AF *telier* weaver's beam f. med. L *telarium* f. L *tela* web; see -ER[2] (2)]

ti'ller[3] *n.*, & *v.i.* **1.** *n.* Shoot of plant springing from bottom of original stalk; sapling; sucker. **2.** *v.i.* Put forth tillers. [app. repr. OE *telgor* extended (*telga* bough)]

tilt[1] *v.* & *n.* **1.** *v.i.* & *t.* (Cause to) assume sloping position from vertical or horizontal, heel over, (*table is apt to tilt*; *don't tilt the table*; *tilt the cask so as to drain it*); (Geol. of strata, in *act.* or *pass.*) turn *up* at steep angle. **2.** *v.i.* Strike, thrust, run, *at* with weapon; engage in contest *with*; **~ at the ring** (suspended for horseman to carry off on point of lance); *tilt at* WINDMILLS. **3.** *v.t.* Forge or work (steel etc.) with tilt-hammer. **4.** Hence ~'ER[1] (1, 2) *n.* **5.** *n.* Tilting; sloping position. **6.** Charging on horseback with lance etc. against opponent or mark (**~-yard,** place used for this); encounter between opponents; **full ~,** at full speed, with full force, (*come* or *run full tilt against*). **7.** ~**(-hammer)**, heavy pivoted hammer used in forging. [ME *tilte* perh. f. OE **tyltan, *tieltan* (*tealt* unsteady) f. Gmc **taltjan*; sense 2 f. 6, of unkn. orig.]

tilt[2] *n.*, & *v.t.* **1.** *n.* Covering of canvas etc. esp. for cart. **2.** *v.t.* Furnish with tilt. [ME, var. of *telde*, OE *teld*, OHG *zelt*, perh. infl. by TENT[1]]

tilth *n.* Tillage, cultivation (lit. or fig.); depth of soil affected by this; condition of soil under cultivation. [OE *tilth(e)* (as TILL[1], -TH[1])]

Tim. *abbr.* Timothy (N.T.).

ti'mbal *n.* (arch.) Kettledrum. [f. F *timbale*, earlier *tamballe* f. Sp. *atabal* f. Arab. *aṭ-ṭabl* the drum]

timbale (tǎṅbah'l) *n.* Drum-shaped dish of minced meat or fish in pastry shell. [F; see prec.]

ti'mber *n.* **1.** Wood prepared for building, carpentry, etc.; trees suitable for this; woods, forest; piece of wood, beam, esp. (Naut.) any of the curved pieces forming ribs of vessel, (SHIVER[2] *my timbers*); (esp. as *int.*) tree about to fall. **2.** ||**~-cart** (high-wheeled, with tackle for lifting timber); **~-head,** top end of timber rising above deck and used for belaying ropes etc.; **~-hitch,** knot used in attaching rope to log or spar; ***~-land,** land covered with forest yielding timber; **~-line** (above which no trees grow); **~-toe(s)**, (sl.) (person with) wooden leg; **~-wolf,** large N. Amer. grey wolf. **3.** Hence (-)~ED[2] (-*erd*) *a.*, ~ING[1] (2, 3) *n.* [OE, = building; OS *timbar*, OHG *zimbar*, ON *timbr* f. Gmc **timram* f. IE **dem-* build]

timbre (tǎṅbr *or* tǎ'mber) *n.* Characteristic quality of sounds produced by a particular voice or instrument, depending on the number and character of the overtones. [F, f. Rom. **timbano* f. med. Gk *timbanon* f. Gk *tumpanon* drum]

ti'mbrel *n.* (arch.) Tambourine or similar instrument. [dim. of ME *timbre* f. OF (as prec.; see -LE 2)]

Timbŭctoo' *n.* Very remote place. [f. *Timbuktu* in W. Africa]

time[1] *n.* **1.** Duration, indefinitely continued existence, progress of this viewed as affecting persons or things, (*time will show who is right*; *will stand for all time*; *has stood the test of time*;

time and tide wait for no man; *take time by the* FORELOCK); **(Father) T~** (personified esp. as old man with scythe and hourglass). **2.** More or less definite portion of time associated with particular events or circumstances, historical or other period, (*the times of the Stuarts*; *the time of the Black Death*; *for the time* (BE*ing*); *prehistoric times*; *those godless times*; *the good old times*; *things have changed since those times*; *the scientists of the time*); **the ~(s)**, the age now (or then) present (BEHIND *the times*); **~ was,** there has been a time *when*. **3.** Allotted or available portion of time, the time at one's disposal, (*had no time to discuss it*; *spend, lose, waste, time*; *gave a lot of his time to relief work*; *cannot find the time to write*; *give me time and I will pay*; *the cure is bound to take* (*some*) *time*); one's lifetime (*will last my time*); prison sentence (*is doing time*); period of apprenticeship (*served his time*); duration of boxing-round, drinking-hours, etc. (*time is up*; *referee* or *landlord called* '*Time!*'). **4.** Moment or definite portion of time destined or suitable for a purpose etc. (*there is a time for everything*; *will fix a time for seeing him*; *now is the time* (*to buy, to press your point*); *I must* BIDE *my time*; *it is* (HIGH) *time to go, time for lunch, time for a change, time* (*that*) *I was going* or *for me to go*; BEHIND *time*; *till such time as they return home*); period of gestation (*is far on in her time*), date of childbirth (*is near her time*) or death (*my time is drawing near*). **5.** (in *sing.* or *pl.*) Conditions of life, prevailing (esp. economic) circumstances, of a period (*hard, bad, good, times*; *times have changed*); **have a ~ (of it)**, undergo trouble or difficulty; **have a good ~**, enjoy oneself. **6.** Occasion (*the first time* (*that*) *I saw him*; *admitted at twopence a time*; *cannot do it this time, wait till next time*; *did it seven times running*; *have told you a dozen times*; *for the last time of asking*); **~s out of number, ~ and (~) again, many a ~, ~ after ~**, on many occasions, in many instances; (expressing multiplication: *three times four is twelve, one-and-a-half times four is six*; *is three times the size of mine*; *ten times easier* or *as easy*). **7.** (Amount of) time as reckoned by conventional standards (*the time allowed was four months*; *did a mile in record time*); point of time esp. stated in hours and minutes of the day (*the time fixed was 4.30*; *what is the time?, what time is it?*; *is that the correct time?*); measured time spent in work etc. (*workmen on* SHORT *time*); **~ and a half,** DOUBLE[1] *time*, etc., (paid at that much more than the normal rate); GREENWICH, MEAN[2], SIDEREAL, STANDARD, SUMMER[1](-), *time*. **8.** (Mus.) Duration of note as indicated by semibreve, minim, etc.; style of movement depending on number and accentuation of beats in a bar (*time* SIGNATURE); rate of execution, = *tempo*; DOUBLE[1] *time*. **9. Against ~**, with utmost speed so as to reach a goal by a specified time (*working, riding, against time*); **ahead of ~**, earlier than expected or promised; **ahead of** one's **~**, having ideas too enlightened to be accepted by one's contemporaries; **all the ~**, during the whole of the time referred to (*they were laughing all the time*; *I thought you were serious, but all the time you were only teasing me*), at all times (*is a business man all the time*); *one, two*, etc., **at a ~**, in such groups (separately); **at the same ~**, at a time which is the same for both or all, simultaneously, notwithstanding, all the same; **at ~s,** intermittently; **at one ~**, during a known but unspecified past period (*at one time we met frequently*), simultaneously (*ran three businesses at one time*); BEAT[1] *time*; **before** (one's) **~**, = *ahead of* (one's) *time*; **before** one's **~**, prematurely (*old* etc.); **between ~s,** in the intervals between other actions, occasionally; EVERY *time*; **from ~ to ~**, occasionally; GAIN[2] *time*; (*all*) *in* GOOD *time*; **half the ~**, (colloq.) as often as not; **have no ~ for,** not wish or be able to spend time on, dislike; **have the ~**, (1) be able to spend time needed, (2) know from watch etc. what time it is; **in ~**, not late, early enough (*to* do, *for* thing), eventually, sooner or later, in accordance with or following the time of music etc.; **in (less than) no ~**, rapidly, in an instant; **in** one's **~**, at some previous period of one's life (*in his time he was the world's greatest hurdler*); **in** one's **own ~**, outside working hours; **in** one's **own (good) ~**, at a rate decided by oneself only; **keep ~**, walk, dance, sing, etc., in time; **keep good** or **bad ~**, (of clock etc.) record time accurately or not; KILL[1] *time*; **lose no ~**, (1) not waste time *in doing, on* thing, (2) act immediately; MAKE[1] *time*; *in the* NICK[1] *of time*; **no ~**, (colloq.) a very short interval (*it was no time before she was back*); **on ~**, in accordance with timetable etc., *on hire-purchase; **out of ~**, unseasonable, unseasonably, too late, (of singing etc.) not in time; **play for ~**, seek to gain time by delaying etc.; TAKE[1] (one's, *all* one's) *time*; **~ immemorial** or **out of mind,** (for, from) a longer time than anyone can remember or trace; **the ~ of day,** hour by clock; **at this ~ of day,** (fig.) at this late stage in history, in the negotiations, etc.; **know the ~ of day,** be well informed; **pass the ~ of day,** (colloq.) exchange greeting or casual remarks (*with* person); *so that's* **the ~ of day!** (sl., the state of affairs, your little game, etc.); **the ~ of** one's **life,** a period of exceptional enjoyment or pleasant or unpleasant excitement (*have the time of* one's *life*; *give* person *the time of his life*); **~ off** or ***out,** time used for rest or for a different activity, *brief intermission in game; **what ~**, (poet., arch., or joc.) while, when; **The T~s,** (as name of newspaper, esp. *The Times* of London, *The New York Times*, or the *Financial Times*). **10. ~-and-motion** *a.*, concerned with measuring efficiency of industrial etc. operations; **~-ball** (dropped from top of pole at observatory to indicate fixed moment of mean time); **~-bargain,** a contract for sale of stock etc. at future time (often a form of gambling); **~ bomb** (designed to explode at a set time after being dropped or put in position); **~-book, -card, -clock,** (for recording workmen's hours of work); **~ capsule** (buried in foundations of new building etc. and containing objects typical of the present time, for discovery in the future); **~-consuming** *a.*, using much time, wasteful of time; ***~ deposit,** bank deposit not repayable before set date; **~-expired,** (of soldier) having completed period of military service; **~ exposure** (of photographic film for longer than an instant); **~ factor,** passage of time as limitation on what can be achieved; **~-fuse** (calculated to burn for or explode at a given time); **~-honoured,** venerable because of antiquity, traditional, customary; **~'keeper,** one who records time esp. of workmen or in game (*watch* etc. *is good, bad, ~keeper*, keeps good, bad, time); **~-lag,** interval of time between cause etc. and result or consequence; **~-lapse** *a.*, (of film etc.) containing frames taken at long intervals but shown at normal pace to accelerate view of events; **~-limit** (within which something must be done); **~'piece,** time-measuring instrument, esp. non-striking portable but stationary clock; **~-scale,** sequence of events as measure of historical etc. duration; **~-server,** one who, esp. for selfish ends, adapts himself to opinions of the times or of persons in power; **~-sharing,** operation of computer by several users simultaneously; **~-sheet** (for recording hours of work etc.); **~-signal,** visible or audible announcement of exact time of day; **~-switch** (acting automatically at set time); **~'table,** scheme of school work, etc., table showing times of public transport services; **~-travel,** hypothetical movement through time; **~-work** (paid for by time, not piece-work); *time* ZONE. [OE *tīma*, = ON *tími*, f. Gmc root **tī-* extend]

time[2] *v.* **1.** *v.t.* Choose the time for, do at chosen or correct time, (*must time your blows*; *time the opening of the valves*; *remark was ill, well, timed*); arrange time of arrival of, regulate rate of travelling of, (train etc.); ascertain the time taken by (race, runner, process, etc.), whence **tī'm**ER[1] (1, 2), **tī'm**ING[1], *ns.* **2.** *v.i.* Keep time, harmonize, *with.* [ME, f. prec.]

tī'melėss (-ml-) *a.* (rhet. or poet.) Not subject to or affected by the passage of time; (arch.) untimely; hence ~LY[2] *adv.*, ~NESS *n.* [f. TIME[1] + -LESS]

tī'mel|y̆ (-mlĭ) *a.* & *adv.* **1.** *a.* Seasonable, opportune; hence **~ĭ**NESS *n.* **2.** *adv.* (arch.) Opportunely. [ME, f. TIME[1] + -LY[1]]

||**tī'meous** (-m*us*), ||**tī'mous,** *a.* (chiefly Sc.) Timely; hence ~LY[2] *adv.* [f. TIME[1] + -OUS]

tī'mer. See TIME[2].

tĭ'mĭd *a.* Easily alarmed; indicating fear; shy; hence or cogn. **tĭmĭ'd**ITY, ~NESS, *ns.*, ~LY[2] *adv.* [f. F *timide* or f. L *timidus* (*timēre* fear; see -ID[1])]

tī'mĭng. See TIME[2].

timŏ'cracy̆ *n.* Form of government in which there is a property qualification for office; form of government in which rulers are motivated by love of honour; hence **tīmocră'**TIC *a.* [f. OF *timocracie* f. med. L f. Gk *timokratia* (*timē* honour, worth, value; see -CRACY)]

tĭ'morous *a.* Frightened; timid, easily alarmed; hence ~LY[2] *adv.*, ~NESS *n.* [ME, f. OF *temoreus* f. med. L *timorosus*, f. L *timor* (*timēre* fear; see -OR, -OUS)]

tĭ'mothy̆ *n.* ~ **(grass)** a fodder-grass, *Phleum pratense*. [f. *T~* Hanson, who introduced it in Carolina *c.* 1720]

||**tī'mous.** See TIMEOUS.

tĭ'mpan|ō *n.* (usu. in *pl.* **~i** *pr.* -ē). Kettledrum; hence ~IST *n.*, one who plays the timpani in an orchestra. [It., = TYMPANUM]

tĭn *n.*, & *v.t.* (**-nn-**). **1.** *n.* White malleable metallic element, taking high polish and resisting corrosion, used mainly in alloys with lead, copper, or antimony to form solder, white-metal, pewter, bronze, etc., or in plating thin steel sheets to form tin plate for containers, kitchen utensils, toys, etc.; CRY[1] *of tin.* **2.** ||Vessel etc. of tin or tinned iron esp. for preserving meat, fish, fruit, etc.; tinned iron as material for this; ||(sl.) money. **3.** ~ **fish,** (Naut. sl.) torpedo; ~ **foil,** foil of tin or aluminium or tin alloy for wrapping etc.; ~ **god,** object of unjustified veneration; ~ **hat,** (Army sl.) modern soldier's steel helmet; ***~'horn** *n.* & *a.*, pretentious but unimpressive (person); ||*put the tin* LID *on*; ~ **Lizzie,** small cheap motor car; **~'man,** tinsmith; ||**~-opener,** tool for opening tins; **~-pan alley,** (fig.) the world of the composers and publishers of popular music; ~ **plate,** sheet iron or sheet steel coated with tin; **~-plate** *v.t.*, coat with tin; **~'pot** *a.*, (derog.) cheap, inferior; **~'smith,** worker in tin and tin plate; ~ **soldier,** toy soldier made of tin etc.; **~'stone,** cassiterite; **~-tack,** tinned iron tack; **~'ware,** vessels etc. of tin or tin plate; ~ **whistle,** = *penny* WHISTLE. **4.** *v.t.* Cover or coat with tin; ||pack (meat etc.) in a tin for preservation. [OE, = OHG *zin*, ON *tin*, f. Gmc **tinam*, of unkn. orig.]

tĭ'namou (-ōō) *n.* S. Amer. bird of family Tinamidae, resembling grouse but related to rhea. [F, f. Galibi *tinamu*]

tĭnct *a.* (poet.) Coloured, tinted. [f. L *tinctus* p.p. (see TINGE)]

tĭnctōr'ial *a.* Of colour or dyeing; producing colour. [f. L *tinctorius* (*tinctor* dyer); see TINGE, -ORY, -AL]

tĭ'ncture *n.*, & *v.t.* **1.** *n.* Alcoholic solution of some (usu. vegetable) principle used in medicine (*tincture of quinine*); slight flavour, spice, smack, (*of* thing, fig. *of* moral quality etc.); tinge (*of* colour); (Her.) inclusive term for the metals, colours, and furs used in coats of arms. **2.** *v.t.* Colour slightly, tinge, flavour; (fig.) affect slightly (*with* quality). [ME, f. L *tinctura* dyeing (as TINGE; see -URE)]

tĭ'ndal *n.* (Ind.) Native petty officer of Lascars. [f. Hind. *taṇdel* f. Malayalam *taṇḍal*]

tĭ'nder *n.* Dry substance readily taking fire from spark, esp. charred linen etc. used in **~-box** (containing tinder, flint, and steel, for kindling fire); hence ~Y[2] *a.* [OE *tynder*, *tyndre* f. Gmc **tund-* etc. kindle]

tīne *n.* Point, prong, e.g. of antler, harrow, or fork; hence (**-**)**tīn**ED[2] (-nd) *a.* [OE *tind*, = OHG *zint*, ON *tindr*]

tĭ'nėa *n.* (Path.) Ringworm. [L, = moth, worm]

tĭng *n.*, & *v.i.* & *t.* (Make, cause to make) tinkling sound as of bell. [imit.]

tĭnge (-nj) *v.t.* (*part.* **~ing** *pr.* -njĭ-), & *n.* **1.** *v.t.* Colour slightly (*with* red etc.); (fig.) modify by mixture (*with* envy etc.). **2.** *n.* Tint, slight colouring or admixture, flavour (lit. or fig.). [ME, f. L *tingere tinct-* dye, stain]

tĭ'ngle (-ngg*e*l) *v.* & *n.* **1.** *v.i.*, & *n.* (Feel) slight prickling or stinging or throbbing sensation esp. in ears or hands; cause this (*the reply tingled in his ears*). **2.** *v.t.* Make (ear etc.) tingle. [ME, perh. var. of TINKLE]

tĭ'nker *n.* & *v.* **1.** *n.* Mender (esp. itinerant) of kettles, pans, etc. (*don't care* **a ~'s damn** or **cuss,** at all); (Ir.) gipsy; rough-and-ready worker, botcher; act of tinkering (*had an hour's tinker at it*); *small mackerel. **2.** *v.t.* Repair (metal-work), patch (anything, lit. or fig.) roughly or temporarily. **3.** *v.i.* Work in amateurish or clumsy or desultory fashion *at* or *with* (thing) in the way of repair or alteration. [ME, of unkn. orig.]

tĭ'nkle *v.* & *n.* **1.** *v.i.*, & *n.* (Make) succession of short light ringing sounds; ||**give** person **a** ~, (colloq.) telephone him. **2.** *v.t.* Make (small bell etc.) tinkle. [ME, f. obs. *tink* to chink (imit.) + -LE 3]

tĭ'nner *n.* In vbl senses; tin-miner; tinsmith. [f. TIN + -ER[1]]

tĭnnī'tus *n.* (Med.) Ringing in the ears. [L (*tinnire -it-* ring, tinkle, of imit. orig.)]

tĭ'nn|y̆ *a.* Of or like tin; having metallic taste or thin metallic sound; hence **~ĭ**LY[2] *adv.*, **~ĭ**NESS *n.* [f. TIN + -Y[2]]

tĭ'nsel *n.*, *a.*, & *v.t.* (||**-ll-**). **1.** *n.* Glittering metallic substance made in thin sheets and used in strips, threads, etc., to give inexpensive sparkling effect; fabric adorned with tinsel; (fig.) superficial brilliancy or splendour. **2.** *a.* Showy, gaudy, cheaply splendid. **3.** *v.t.* Adorn with tinsel (lit. or fig.). [prob. f. AF *(*satin*) *estincelé* f. OF (*estincele* spark f. pop. L **stincilla* for L *scintilla*)]

tĭnt *n.*, & *v.t.* **1.** *n.* A variety of a colour, esp. one made lighter by admixture of white; tendency towards, admixture of, a different colour (*red of* or *with a blue* or *bluish tint*); background of faint colour for printing on; set of parallel engraved lines to give uniform shading; **~-block,** block bearing design to be printed in faint colour as background; hence **~'**LESS *a.* **2.** *v.t.* Apply tint to, colour (lit. or fig.); hence **~'**ER[1] *n.* [alt. f.

earlier *tinct* f. L *tinctus* dyeing (as TINGE), perh. infl. by It. *tinto*]

tĭntĭnnăbūlā'tion *n.* Ringing or tinkling of bells. [f. as foll. + -ATION]

tĭntĭnnă'būl|um *n.* (*pl.* ~**a**). Bell, esp. small tinkling one; hence ~AR(Y)[1], ~OUS, *adjs.* [L, = bell (*tintinnare* redupl. form, as TINNITUS)]

tĭntŏ'mėter *n.* Instrument for determining tints. [P; f. TINT + -O- + -METER]

tī'n|ȳ *a.* Very small or slight; hence ~**ĭ**LY[2] *adv.*, ~**ĭ**NESS *n.* [f. obs. *tine, tyne* (a. & n., small, a little; ME, of unkn. orig.) + -Y[2]]

-tion (-sh*u*n) suf. forming *ns.* of action, condition, etc.; cf. -ATION, -ITION, -UTION, and -ION. [f. or after F, or f. L *-tio -tionis* f. p.p. stems in *-t-* + as -ION]

tĭp[1] *n.*, & *v.t.* (**-pp-**). **1.** *n.* Extremity, end, esp. of small or tapering thing (*the tips of the fingers*; *walk on the tips of your toes*; *tip of a cigarette*, *of a bird's* or *aeroplane's wing*; **on the ~ of** one's **tongue,** just about to be said, or on the point of being remembered and spoken); leaf-bud of tea, whence ~**'p**Y[2] *a.*; thin flat brush used in gilding; small piece or part attached to end of thing, e.g. ferrule, leather cap on billiard-cue, cork filter on cigarette. **2.** ~**'staff** (*pl.* ~*staffs* or ~*staves*), (metal-tipped staff as badge of) sheriff's officer; ~**-tilted,** (of nose) turned up at tip; ~**'toe,** (*n.*) the tips of the toes, (*adv.*) on tiptoe, with heels off the ground, (*v.i.*) walk (as if) on tiptoe; ~**'top** (*or* -ŏ'p), (*n.*) highest point of excellence, (*a.* & *adv.*) excellent(ly). **3.** *v.t.* Furnish with tip; paste (sheet as part of book) *in* at inside edge of page. [ME, f. ON *typpi* n., *typpa* v., *typptr* tipped f. Gmc **tupp-* TOP[1]; prob. reinforced by MDu. & MLG *tip*]

tĭp[2] *v.* (**-pp-**) & *n.* **1.** *v.t.* & *i.* (Cause to) lean or slant, tilt, topple, (*over, up*, etc.) esp. with slight effort; ~ **the balance** or SCALE[2](*s*); ~ one's ***hat** or ||(sl.) **lid,** raise one's hat. **2.** *v.t.* Strike or touch lightly; ||~ **and run,** form of cricket in which batsman must run if bat touches ball (~*-and-run raid*, one in which the raider appears suddenly and makes off immediately after attacking; cf. HIT[1]); ~ **off,** (Basketball) start play by throwing ball up between two opponents. **3.** Overturn, cause to overbalance, (person *into* pond etc.); ||discharge (contents of truck, jug, etc. *out, into*, etc.) thus. **4.** (sl.) Throw lightly, hand, give, communicate, in informal manner; mention as likely winner of horse-race or other contest; ~ (= SHOW[1]) one's **hand**; ~ person **the wink,** give him private warning or information; ~ **off,** give (person) warning, hint, or inside information, so ~*-off* n., a hint. **5.** Make usu. small present of money to (esp. for service given or expected; *must tip the porter, the waiter*). **6.** Hence ~**'p**ER[1] (1, 2) *n.* **7.** *n.* Small money present (cf. sense 5). **8.** Private or special information about horse-racing, stock-market, etc., (STRAIGHT *tip*); piece of advice, good way of doing something; **miss** one's ~, fail in one's object. **9.** Slight push or tilt; light stroke esp. in baseball; ||place where material, esp. refuse, is tipped. **10.** ~**-cart** (pivoted for tipping); ~**'cat,** (game with) short piece of wood tapering at ends and struck with stick; ~**-up,** able to be tipped, (of seat) as used in theatres etc. to allow of free passing. [ME, perh. f. Scand.; partly f. prec.]

tĭ'ppėt *n.* Cape or muffler of fur etc. covering shoulders and coming down some distance in front, worn by women (arch.) and as part of official costume by judges, clergy, etc.; (Hist.) long narrow strip of cloth as part of or attachment to hood etc. [ME, prob. f. TIP[1]; see -ET[1]]

tĭ'ppl|e *v.* & *n.* **1.** *v.i.* Drink intoxicating liquor habitually. **2.** *v.t.* Drink (liquor) repeatedly in small amounts. **3.** So ~ER[1] *n.* **4.** *n.* (colloq.) (Esp. strong) drink. [ME, back form. f. *tippler*, of unkn. orig.]

tĭ'pster *n.* One who gives tips about horse-races etc. [f. TIP[2] + -STER]

tĭ'ps|ȳ *a.* Slightly intoxicated; caused by or showing intoxication (*a tipsy lurch*); ~**y-cake,** sponge-cake soaked in wine or spirits and served with custard; hence ~**ĭ**FY *v.t.*, ~**ĭ**LY[2] *adv.*, ~**ĭ**NESS *n.* [prob. f. TIP[2], = inclined to lean, unsteady; cf. *tricksy, flimsy*]

||**TIR** *abbr.* Transport International Routier (F, = international road transport).

tĭrā'de (*or* tĭr-) *n.* Long vehement speech esp. of censure; long passage of declamation etc. [F, = long speech, f. It. *tirata* volley (*tirare* f. Rom. **tirare* draw; see -ADE)]

tĭrailleur (-ralẽr'; *or* tērahyẽr') *n.* Sharpshooter, skirmisher. [F (*tirailler* shoot independently f. *tirer* shoot, draw f. Rom. **tirare* draw)]

tīre[1] *v.t.* & *i.* Make or grow weary; exhaust patience or interest of, bore; (in *p.p.*) having had enough *of*, sick *of*, (thing, do*ing*), exhausted *with*, (fig.) hackneyed; hence ~'LESS (tīr'l-) *a.*, untiring. [OE *tēorian*, of unkn. orig.]

tīre[2] *n.*, & *v.t.* **1.** *n.* Band of metal placed round rim of wheel to strengthen it. **2.** *v.t.* Place tire on (wheel). [ME, perh. = TIRE[4]]

***tīre**[3]. See TYRE.

tīre[4] *n.*, & *v.t.* (arch.) **1.** *n.* Head-dress; attire; ~**'woman** (employed to dress another woman). **2.** *v.t.* Adorn (one's hair or head); **tīr'ing-room,** dressing-room (esp. in theatre). [ME, f. ATTIRE]

tīr'esome (tīr's-) *a.* Wearisome, tedious; (colloq.) annoying (*how tiresome!—I have left my watch behind*); hence ~LY[2] (-mlĭ) *adv.*, ~NESS (-mn-) *n.* [f. TIRE[1] + -SOME[1]]

tīr'ō, tȳr'ō, *n.* (*pl.* ~**s**). Beginner, novice. [L *tiro*, med. L *tyro*, recruit]

'tĭs (-z) (arch. or poet.) It is. [contr.]

tĭsă'ne (-z-) *n.* Ptisan; infusion of dried herbs etc. [F, f. as PTISAN]

tĭ'ssue (-sū, -shū, *or* -shōō) *n.* Fine woven esp. gauzy fabric; (Biol.) substance of animal or plant body, mass of cells of one kind (*adipose, connective, muscular, nervous, tissue*); (fig.) interwoven series, set, collection, (*of* lies, absurdities, etc.); ~(**-paper**), thin soft unsized paper for wrapping or protecting delicate articles, engravings in book, etc.; (**paper**) ~, disposable piece of thin soft absorbent paper for wiping, drying, etc., with. [ME, f. OF *tissu* rich material, p.p. (as n.) of *tistre* f. L *texere* weave]

tĭt[1] *n.* Small bird of family Paridae, including titlark and titmouse; **bearded** ~, similar bird (*Panurus biarmicus*), the male having black face-tufts; **blue** ~, *Parus caeruleus*, with bright blue tail, wings, and top of head. [prob. f. Scand.]

tĭt[2] *n.* ~ **for tat,** blow for blow, retaliation. [= earlier TIP[2] *for tap*]

tĭt[3] *n.* (vulg.) Nipple (esp. of woman); (in *pl.*) woman's breasts. [OE; cf. MLG *titte*]

Tit. *abbr.* Titus (N.T.).

Tī'tan *n.* (Gk Myth.) member of a gigantic race, the children of Uranus and Gaea; sun-god; person of superhuman size, strength, intellect, etc.; hence ~E'SQUE *a.*, ~ESS[1] *n.* [ME f. L f. Gk]

tītă'n|ĭc[1] *a.* Of or like the Titans; gigantic, colossal; hence ~ICALLY *adv.* [f. Gk *titanikos* (as prec.; see -IC)]

tĭtă'nĭc[2] *a.* (Chem.) Of titanium, esp. in tetravalent form; hence **tĭ'tan**ATE[1] (3) *n.* [f. foll. + -IC]

tĭtā'nĭum *n.* Grey metallic element occurring in many clays etc.; ~ (**di**)**oxide,** a white pigment. [f. Gk (as TITAN) + -IUM, after *uranium*]

tĭ'tbĭt, *tĭ'dbĭt, *n.* Delicate bit, choice morsel

(of food, news, etc.). [perh. f. dial. *tid* tender + BIT²]

***ti'ter.** See TITRE.

||**tĭ'tfer** *n.* (sl.) Hat. [abbr. of *tit for tat*, rhyming sl.]

tīthe (-dh) *n.*, & *v.t.* **1.** *n.* (Hist.) Tax of one-tenth, esp. tenth part of annual produce of land or labour taken for support of clergy and church; hence ~ **barn** (built to hold tithes paid in kind). **2.** (rhet.) Tenth part (esp. *not a tithe of*). **3.** *v.t.* Subject to tithes; hence **tī'th**ABLE (-dh-) *a.* [OE (*teogothian, tēothian* v.f.) *teogotha, tēotha* TENth]

tī'thĭng (-dh-) *n.* Taking tithe; (Hist.) (area occupied by) ten householders living near together and bound over as sureties for each other's peaceable behaviour. [f. as prec. + -ING¹]

ti'ti (tē'tē) *n.* S. Amer. monkey of genus *Callicebus*. [Tupi]

ti-ti (tē'tē) *n.* (N.Z.) Mutton-bird. [Maori]

Tĭ'tian (-sh*a*n) *a.* ~ **(red)**, (esp. of hair) bright golden auburn; so ~E'SQUE *a.*, in the style of Titian. [name of *Tiziano* Vecelli, It. painter d. 1576]

tĭ'tĭll|āte *v.t.* Tickle, excite pleasantly; so ~A'TION *n.* [f. L *titillare* + -ATE³]

tĭ't(t)ĭv|āte *v.t.* (colloq.) Adorn, smarten, put finishing touches to, (one*self* etc., or abs.); hence ~A'TION *n.* [earlier *tid*-, perh. f. TIDY after *cultivate*]

tĭ'tlârk *n.* Pipit, ||esp. meadow pipit. [f. TIT¹ + LARK¹]

tī'tle *n.*, & *v.t.* **1.** *n.* Distinguishing appellation placed at head of chapter, poem, etc.; contents of title-page of book, short essential part of these used in reference (e.g. *Gone with the Wind, Shakespeare's Plays*); book or publication as distinguished from others; HALF-*title*. **2.** Formula at head of legal document, statute, etc.; division of statute etc.; caption or CREDIT¹ title in film. **3.** Distinctive name; personal appellation, hereditary or not, denoting or implying office (e.g. *king, queen, judge, mayor, rector, professor, captain*) or nobility (e.g. *duke, duchess, marquis, earl, viscount, baron, lord*; COURTESY *title*) or distinction or merit (e.g. *baronet, knight*) or (usu. degree) qualification (e.g. *D.D., M.A.*), or used in addressing or referring to person (e.g. *Lord, Lady, Sir, Miss, Doctor, Professor*, prefixed to name; *Your* or *Her* or *His Majesty, Grace*, etc.). **4.** (Law) right to ownership of property with or without possession, the facts constituting this; ~**(-deed)**, legal instrument as evidence of right; just or recognized claim (*to*); service, merit, etc., that constitutes this. **5.** Championship in sport. **6.** (Eccl.) Fixed sphere of work and source of income as condition to ordination; parish church in Rome under cardinal. **7.** ~**-deed** (see sense 4); ~**-page,** page at beginning of book giving particulars of subject, authorship, publication, etc.; ~**-piece,** essay etc. with same title as book that contains it and others; ~**-role,** part in a play that gives it its name (e.g. *Othello*). **8.** Hence ~LESS (-tel-l-) *a.* **9.** *v.t.* Give title to; (esp., in *p.p.*) having title of nobility. [ME f. OF, f. L *titulus* placard, title]

tĭ'tlĭng¹ *n.* Titlark or titmouse. [ME, f. TIT¹ + -LING¹]

tī'tlĭng² *n.* Impressing of title in gold leaf etc. on cover of book. [f. TITLE + -ING¹]

tĭ't|mouse *n.* (*pl.* ~**mice**). Tit esp. of genus *Parus*. [ME *titmōse* (TIT¹, OE *māse* titmouse, = OHG *meisa* f. WG **maisō*); assim. to MOUSE¹]

Tī'tō|ĭsm (tē'-) *n.* Independent form of Communism e.g. as initiated by President Tito in Yugoslavia, as dist. from that of U.S.S.R. and its satellite countries; so ~IST (2) *n.* [f. *Tito*, assumed name of Josip Broz (b. 1892) + -ISM]

tī'tr|āte (*or* -ā't) *v.t.* (Chem.) Determine quantity of given constituent in (solution) by observing volume of a standard solution necessary to convert this constituent entirely into another form; hence ~A'TION *n.* [f. F *titrer* (as foll.) + -ATE³]

tī'tre (-ter), ***tī'ter,** *n.* (Chem.) Strength of solution or quantity of constituent as determined by titration. [F, = TITLE]

tĭ'tter *v.i.*, & *n.* **1.** *v.i.* Laugh or giggle in restrained or covert manner. **2.** *n.* Such laugh. [imit.]

tĭ'ttĭvāte. See TITIVATE.

tĭ'ttle *n.* Small written or printed stroke or dot; particle, whit, (esp. *not one jot or tittle*). [ME, f. L (as TITLE)]

||**tĭ'ttlebăt** (-telb-) *n.* Stickleback. [var., of childish orig.]

tĭ'ttle-tăttle *n.*, & *v.i.* (Engage in) petty gossip. [redupl. f. TATTLE]

tĭ'ttup *v.i.* (**-p-** *or* **-pp-**), & *n.* **1.** *v.i.* Go *along* etc., move, conduct oneself, in lively or frisky fashion; prance or canter. **2.** *n.* Canter; spring, prance; hence ~**(p)**Y² *a.* [perh. imit. of hoof-beats]

tĭ'ttȳ *n.* (vulg.) = TIT³; (childish) a teat, breast. [f. TEAT + -Y³]

tĭtūbā'tion *n.* (Med.) Unsteadiness esp. as caused by nervous disease. [f. L *titubatio* (*titubare* totter; see -ATION)]

tĭ'tūlar *a.* & *n.* **1.** *a.* Held by virtue of a title (*titular possessions*); relating to a title (*titular hero of book*); existing, that is such, only in name (*titular sovereign(ty)*); ~ **bishop,** (R.C. Ch.) bishop bearing name of a former Christian see esp. in Muslim countries; ~ **saint,** patron saint of church; hence ~LY² *adv.* **2.** *n.* Holder of office etc. esp. benefice without corresponding functions or obligations; titular saint. [f. F *titulaire* or mod. L *titularis* (*titulus* TITLE; see -AR¹)]

tĭ'zzȳ *n.* (sl.) State of nervous agitation (*in a tizzy; all of a tizzy*). [20th c.; orig. unkn.]

T-junction. See T.

T.K.O. *abbr.* technical knock-out.

Tl *symb.* thallium.

T.L.S. *abbr.* *Times Literary Supplement*; typed letter signed.

T.M. *abbr.* transcendental meditation.

Tm *symb.* thulium.

tmē's|ĭs *n.* (*pl.* ~**es** *pr.* -ēz). (Gram.) Separation of parts of compound word by intervening word(s) (e.g. *what things soever*, sl. *abso-bloody-lutely*). [Gk *tmēsis* cutting (*temnō* cut)]

T.M.O. *abbr.* telegraph money order.

tn *abbr.* *ton(s); town.

T.N.T. *abbr.* trinitrotoluene.

to¹ (before vowel to͝o, before consonant *t*o, when stressed to͞o) *prep.* **1.** In the direction of (place, person, thing, condition, quality, etc.; with or without implication of intention or of arrival; *was walking over to the town; on his way to the station; fled to Rome; throw it to me; got to the house by four; to bed with you!; fluttered to the ground; was committed to the flames; invited them to dinner; house looks to the south; held it (up) to the light; to arms!; fought hand to hand; back to back; told him to his face; was carried to destruction; letter has come to hand; fell to work; fell to musing; tends to, has a tendency to, indolence; slow to anger; appointed to the post; born to a great fortune; all to no purpose; to his shame be it said*). **2.** As far as, not short of, (*true to the end; cut him to the heart; a patriot to the core; rooted to the spot; goods to the value of £10; increased from 10 to 20*, cf. FROM; *fought to the last gasp; to a* MAN¹; *hit it to the boundary; correct to a hair's breadth; suits him to a T; much to my surprise; loves her to distraction; acted his part to perfection;*

might run to £5; drank himself to death; might argue to all eternity; don't know to this day how it ended; and so on to the end of the chapter). **3.** (Of comparison, ratio, adaptation, reference, etc.: *this is nothing to what it might be; won by 3 goals to 2; 3 is to 4 as 6 is to 8; ten to one he will find it out; two to one is not fair play;* ||*it is five minutes to two; 100 miles to London; not up to the mark; equal to the occasion; made to order; drawn to scale; not to the point; true to life; will speak to that question later; sang to a small guitar; cannot do it to his liking; corresponding, compared, inferior,* etc., *to*). **4.** (arch.) For, by way of, (*took her to wife; has a duke to his father-in-law*). **5.** (Introducing indirect object of verb, recipient, possessor, etc., or person or thing affected by the action, quality, etc.: *lend it* or *this* or *your knife to John* or *to him; write to me; explain it to me; talking to oneself; this does not apply to the secretary; please apply to the secretary; seems to me absurd; to my mind* or *thinking; revolting to sane minds; I object to that remark; secretary to the governor; pleasant to the taste; impervious to weather; caverns measureless to man; obedient to command; duty to one's neighbour; unkind to him; has been a good father to them; a room to myself; what's that to you?; drink to me only with thine eyes;* HERE'S *to you; to goods* etc., in debit entries; *broken in to the saddle; accustomed to it; next door to us; ready to his hand; has not a shilling to his name;* (arch.) *takes no wine to his dinner; weigh four to the pound; there is a moral to it; there is no end to it; that is all there is to it; I wish to God he would stop*). **6.** (Before vb. as sign of infinitive, expressing purpose, consequence, etc., limiting meaning of adj., or forming vbl n.: *he proposes to stay, declines to go, wants to know, began to sing, failed to understand, does it to annoy; shoot to kill; the rubber floor is to prevent noise; the matter is difficult to explain; it is useless to rebel, to rebel is useless; allow me to remind you; was seen to fall; was heard to complain; I'm not one to complain; floor was felt to tremble; was never known* or *found to fail; have sometimes known* or *found it (to) fail; he was made to repeat it; help me (to) lift this; you are pleased to be facetious; I prefer to go; lived to be 100; had my work to do, had to do my work; was about to protest; awoke to find her gone; for a year, in years, to* COME; *the first to arrive; to be honest, I can't face it; to hear him talk, you would think he invented it; to* WIT¹); cf. BE 3. **7.** (As substitute for infinitive: *meant to call but forgot to, had no time to, did not promise to*). [OE *tō* adv. & prep., = OS *tō*, OHG *zō, zuo* f.WG **tō* adv.]

to² (to͞o) *adv.* To or in the normal or required position or condition, esp. to a standstill, (COME, FALL¹, GO¹, HEAVE¹, *to*); (of door) just not shut; **to and fro,** backwards and forwards, repeatedly between same places. [f. prec.]

toad *n.* **1.** Amphibian of genus *Bufo*, like frog but with clumsy and usu. warty body and not aquatic except when breeding; detestable or disgusting person. **2.** ~ **in a** (or **the**) **hole,** beef or sausages baked in batter; **~-eater,** toady; **~-fish,** Amer. fish of family Batrachoididae, with large head; **~'flax,** perennial plant with flaxlike leaves and spurred yellow flowers marked with orange spot (*ivy-leaved ~flax*, related plant with lilac flowers and ivy-shaped leaves); **~'stone,** stone, occas. precious, supposed to resemble or to have been formed in body of toad, formerly used as amulet etc., intrusive volcanic rock in limestone; **~'stool,** (esp. poisonous) fungus with round top and slender stalk. **3.** Hence ~'ISH¹ *a.* [OE *tādige, tādde, tāda*, of unkn. orig.]

toa'dy̆ *n.* & *v.* **1.** *n.* Sycophant, obsequious hanger-on; hence ~ISH¹ *a.*, ~ISM (2) *n.* **2.** *v.t.* & *i.* ~ (**to**), behave servilely to, fawn upon, (person, or abs.). [f. TOAD-*eater* + -Y³]

toast *n.*, & *v.t.* **1.** *n.* Bread slice(s) browned on each side before fire or by electric etc. heat (FRENCH, MELBA, *toast; sardines* etc. **on** ~, laid on this and served at table; **have** person **on** ~, (sl.) have him at one's mercy; **as warm as (a)** ~, glowing with warmth). **2.** Person (Hist. esp. woman) or thing in whose honour company is requested to drink; call to drink or instance of drinking thus. **3.** **~-list, ~-master,** (person who announces) toasts at public dinner; **~-rack** (for holding slices of toast at table); ~ **and water,** = **~-water** (arch., in which toast has stood, used as cooling drink). **4.** *v.t.* Brown, cook, (bread, teacake, cheese, bacon) before fire or by electric etc. heat; warm (one's feet, one*self*) thus. **5.** Drink to the health or in honour of. **6.** Hence ~'ER¹ (1, 2) *n.*, (esp.) electrical device for toasting bread. [ME, n. f. v. f. OF *toster* roast f. Rom. **tostare* f. L *torrēre tost-* parch; sense 2 f. notion that woman's name flavours drink as spiced toast would]

toa'sting *n.* In vbl senses; **~-fork,** long-handled fork for making toast, (arch., joc.) sword. [f. prec. + -ING¹]

tobă'ccō *n.* (*pl.* ~s). **1.** ~(**-plant**), plant of genus *Nicotiana*, of Amer. orig. with narcotic leaves used for smoking, chewing, or snuff; its leaves esp. as prepared for smoking etc. **2.** ~ **heart,** disorder of heart caused by excessive use of tobacco; ~ **mosaic virus** (causing mosaic disease in tobacco, etc., and much used in biochemical research); *tobacco*-PIPE¹; **~-pouch** (for carrying about small quantity of tobacco); **~-stopper,** instrument for pressing down tobacco in pipe. [f. Sp. *tabaco*, of Amer. Ind. orig.]

tobă'cconist *n.* Dealer in tobacco, esp. by retail. [f. prec. + -IST, w. euphonic *n*]

tobŏ'ggan *n.*, & *v.i.* **1.** *n.* Long light narrow sledge curved upwards at front, used for going downhill esp. over prepared snow or ice. **2.** *v.i.* Ride on toboggan; hence ~ER¹, ~ING¹, *ns.* [f. Can. F *tabaganne* f. Algonquian]

tō'by̆ *n.* ~ (**jug**), jug or mug for ale etc. usu. in form of old man with three-cornered hat; ||~ **collar,** broad turned-down goffered collar like the frill of Punch's dog Toby. [familiar form of name *Tobias*]

tocca'ta (-kah'-) *n.* (Mus.) Composition for piano, organ, etc., designed to display performer's technique. [It., fem. p.p. (as n.) of *toccare* touch]

||**Tŏc H** (-ā'ch) *n.* Society of (orig. ex-service)men and women for Christian fellowship and social service. [*toc* = signallers' former name for letter *T*, + *H*, for *T*albot *H*ouse, soldiers' club started by Rev. P. T. B. Clayton (d. 1972) in Ypres Salient in 1915 in memory of Gilbert Talbot]

Tochār'ian (-k-) *a.* & *n.* (Of or in) extinct Indo-European language of central Asian people in first millennium A.D. [f. F *tocharien* f. L *Tochari* f. Gk *Tokharoi* a Scythian tribe]

tŏ'cher (-χ-) *n.* (Sc.) Marriage portion, dowry. [f. Ir. & OGael. *tochar*]

||**tō'cō** *n.* (*pl.* ~s). (sl.) A thrashing; chastisement. [f. Hind. *ṭhōkō*, imper. of *ṭhoknā* thrash]

tocŏ'pherŏl *n.* Oily liquid compound of vitamin E group, found in seed and fish oils. [f. Gk *tokos* offspring + *pherō* bear + -OL]

tŏ'csin *n.* (Bell rung as) alarm-signal (lit. or fig.). [F, f. OF *touquesain, toquassen* f. Prov. *tocasenh* (*tocar* TOUCH¹, *senh* signal-bell)]

||**tŏd¹** *n.* (arch.) Bush; mass of foliage; weight of wool, usu. 28 lb. [ME; cf. LG *todde* bundle, pack, ON *toddi* bit, piece]

||**tŏd²** *n.* (Sc. & N. Engl.) Fox. [ME, of unkn. orig.]

||**tŏd**³ *n.* (sl.) **On** one's ~, alone, on one's own. [perh. f. *on* one's *Tod Sloan*, rhyming sl.]

today', to-day', *adv.* & *n.* (On) this present day, (*saw* or *shall see him today*; *today is her birthday*); nowadays; *today* WEEK; HERE *today, gone tomorrow.* [OE *tō dæg* on (this) day (as TO¹, DAY)]

tŏ'ddle *v.* & *n.* **1.** *v.i.* Walk with short tottering steps, as child learning to walk; take casual or leisurely walk (*round, to,* etc.); (colloq.) depart; hence **tŏ'ddl**ER¹ *n.* **2.** *v.t.* Make (one's *way*), perform (distance), thus. **3.** *n.* Toddling walk. [16th c., orig. Sc. & N. Engl. *todle*, of unkn. orig.]

tŏ'ddў *n.* Sap of some kinds of palm, fermented to produce arrack; sweetened and spiced drink of spirits and hot water. [f. Hindi *tāṛī* (*tār* palm f. Skr. *tâla* palmyra)]

to-do' (-dōō') *n.* Bustle, fuss. [f. *to* DO¹, dat. form of inf. = '*to be done*', as in *What's to do?*]

tō'dў *n.* Small insectivorous W. Ind. bird of genus *Todus*, related to kingfisher. [f. F *todier* f. L *todus*, a small bird]

tōe *n.* & *v.* (*part.* **~'ing** *pr.* tō'ĭ-). **1.** *n.* One of five terminal members of foot; part of stocking, shoe, or boot, that covers the toes. **2.** Fore part of hoof; piece of iron under front of horseshoe to prevent slipping. **3.** Toelike object; projection from foot of buttress etc. to give stability; outer end of head of golf-club. **4.** BALL¹ *of* (*big*) *toe*; BIG or *great toe*; **the light fantastic ~**, (joc.) dancing; LITTLE *toe*; **on** one's **~s,** alert, eager; *from* TOP¹ *to toe*; TREAD¹ *on* person's *toes*; **turn up** one's **~s,** (sl.) die; *heel-and-toe* WALKING¹. **5. ~-cap,** outer covering of toe in boot or shoe; **~-clip** (on bicycle pedal, to prevent foot from slipping); **~-dance** (performed on tiptoe); **~-hold,** slight foothold (lit. or fig.); **~-nail,** nail of human toe, metal nail driven obliquely through end of board etc. **6.** Hence **(-)tō**ED² (tōd), **~'**LESS (tō'l-), *adjs.* **7.** *v.t.* Furnish with toe, mend toe of, (stocking, shoe); touch (*the line, mark*) with toe before starting in race (**~ the line** or ***mark,** (fig.) conform esp. under pressure to the requirements of one's party); (Golf) strike (ball) with part of club too near toe. **8.** *v.i.* **~ in, out,** turn toes in, out, in walking, (of vehicle wheels) be set with slight convergence forwards, backwards. [OE *tā*, = ON *tá*, OHG *zēha* f. Gmc **taih(w)ōn*]

||**tŏff** *n.*, & *v.t.* (sl.) **1.** *n.* Distinguished person, swell. **2.** *v.t.* Dress *up* like a toff. [perh. perversion of TUFT 3]

tŏ'ffee (-fĭ), **tŏ'ffў,** *n.* Sweetmeat made with sugar, butter, etc., often with nuts; ||small piece of this; **can't** *shoot* etc. **for ~,** (sl.) is incompetent at shooting etc.; **~-apple,** toffee-coated apple on stick; ||**~-nose(d),** (sl.) snob(bish), pretentious (person). [f. TAFFY²]

||**tŏft** *n.* Homestead; land once occupied by this. [OE, f. ON *topt*]

tŏg *n.*, & *v.t.* **(-gg-).** (sl.) **1.** *n.* (usu. in *pl.*) Garment. **2.** *v.t.* Dress (person, one*self, out* or *up*); hence **~'g**ERY (5) (-g-) *n.* [app. abbr. of 16th-c. cant *togeman(s), togman*, f. F *toge* or L TOGA]

tō'ga *n.* Ancient Roman citizen's loose flowing outer garment; **~ *praetexta*** (prētĕ'-) (with wide purple border, worn by boys, magistrates, etc.); **~ *virilis*** (vĭrī'lĭs), white toga donned as sign of manhood (at age of 14); hence **~'**D², **~**ED² (-*ad*) *a.* [L, cogn. w. *tegere* cover]

togĕ'ther (-gĕ'dh-) *adv.* In company or conjunction (*walking together*; *lived together*; *were at school together*); simultaneously (*both together exclaimed*); one with another (*compared together*; *fighting together*); into conjunction, so as to unite, (*sew them together*; *tied together*; *put* TWO *and two together*); into company or companionship; (colloq.) well organized or controlled; uninterruptedly (*he would talk for hours together*); **~ with,** as well as, and also; hence **~**NESS *n.*, (esp.) feeling of belonging together. [OE *tōgædere* (*tō* TO¹, *gædre* together f. **gad-*; cf. GATHER)]

tŏ'ggle *n.*, & *v.t.* **1.** *n.* Device for fastening with cross-piece which can pass through hole or loop in one position but not in another; pin or other cross-piece through eye of rope, link of chain, etc., to keep it in place; pivoted barb of harpoon; **~(-joint),** device for exerting pressure along two rods hinged together by transverse force at the hinge; **~-switch,** electric switch with projecting lever to be moved usu. up and down. **2.** *v.t.* Furnish, or fasten, with toggle. [18th c. Naut., of unkn. orig.]

Tōgōlē'se (-z) *a.* & *n.* (*pl.* same). (Native or inhabitant) of Togo. [f. *Togo*, republic in W. Africa; cf. CONGOLESE]

toil *v.i.*, & *n.* **1.** *v.i.* Work long or laboriously (*at, on, through*, task); move painfully or laboriously (*up* hill etc., *along*). **2.** *n.* Hard or continued labour, drudgery; **~-worn,** worn (out) by toil. **3.** Hence **~'**ER¹ *n.*, **~'**FUL, **~'**SOME¹, *adjs.* [ME, f. AF *toiler* v., *toil* n., dispute, OF *tooilier, tooil*, f. L *tudiculare* stir about (*tudicula* machine for bruising olives, cogn. w. *tundere* beat)]

toile (twahl) *n.* Cloth esp. for garments; pattern of garment in muslin etc. for fitting or for use in making copies; **~ de Jouy** (-dezhwē'), cotton or linen printed fabric with light-coloured background. [F, f. as TOILS]

toi'lĕt *n.* **1.** Process of dressing, arranging the hair, etc., (*make* one's *toilet*); (arch.) (style of) dress, costume, (*an elaborate toilet*; *a toilet of white satin*). **2. ~(-table),** dressing-table usu. with looking-glass. **3.** (Room containing) lavatory. **4.** (Med.) Cleansing of part after an operation or at time of childbirth. **5. ~-cover,** (for toilet-table); **~-paper,** thin soft paper for use in lavatory; **~ powder,** dusting powder used in making one's toilet; **~-roll** (of toilet-paper); **~-set** (of utensils for making one's toilet); **~ soap** (mild and usu. perfumed and coloured); **~-training** (of child, to control urination and defecation and use lavatory); **~ water,** scented liquid used after washing oneself. [f. F *toilette* cloth, wrapper, dim. of prec.]

toi'lĕtrў *n.* Article(s) used in making one's toilet. [f. prec. + -RY]

toilĕ'tte (twah-) *n.* = TOILET 1. [F; see TOILET]

toils (-z) *n. pl.* Net, snare, (lit. or fig.; *taken in the toils*). [pl. of *toil* f. OF *toile* cloth, f. L *tela* web]

to'ĭng (tōō'-) *n.* **~ and froing** (-ō'ĭ-), movement to and fro. [f. TO² + -ING¹]

Tokay' *n.* Sweet aromatic dessert wine made near *Tokaj* in Hungary; similar Californian wine.

tō'ken *n.* & *a.* **1.** *n.* Sign, symbol, evidence, (*of* affection etc.; *as a* or *in token of my esteem*); memorial of friendship, keepsake; ring, coin, etc., serving as proof of authenticity; voucher that can be exchanged for specified kind of goods or at specified shop(s) (||BOOK¹ *token*). **2.** (Hist.) piece of metal like and used instead of coin, but worth much less than nominal value and issued by tradesmen, bank, etc., without sanction of government; device like coin bought for use with machines etc. or for other payments where money itself is not to be handled. **3. By (this** or **the same) ~,** (arch.) **more by ~,** (1) similarly, (2) moreover, (3) in corroboration of what I say. **4.** *a.* Serving as token(s) or as sample; perfunctory; **~ money,** coins of higher nominal than intrinsic value but exchangeable for full-standard money at the higher rate; **~**

payment, (1) payment of small proportion of sum due as indication that debt is not repudiated, (2) nominal payment; **~ resistance, ~ strike,** (brief, to demonstrate strength of feeling only); **~ vote,** Parliamentary vote of money in which the amount stated pro forma to allow discussion is not meant to be binding; hence ~ISM *n.*, policy of making only a token effort or of doing no more than is minimally necessary. [OE *tāc(e)n*, = OS *tēcan*, OHG *zeihhan*, ON *teikn* f. Gmc **taiknam* (**taik*- TEACH)]

||**tō'kō.** Var. of TOCO.

tolbooth. See TOLL¹.

tōld. See TELL¹.

Tolē'dō *n.* (*pl.* **~s**). Fine sword(-blade) made at *Toledo* in Spain.

tŏ'lerab|le *a.* Endurable; fairly good, not bad, (*am in tolerable health*); hence **~le**NESS (-beln-) *n.*, ~LY² *adv.* [ME f. OF, f. L *tolerabilis* (as TOLERATE; see -ABLE)]

tŏ'ler|ance *n.* Willingness to tolerate, forbearance; (esp. Med.) capacity to tolerate; permissible variation in dimensions, weight, etc.; REMEDY of coinage; so ~ANT *a.* [ME f. OF, f. L *tolerantia* (as foll.; see -ANCE)]

tŏ'ler|āte *v.t.* Endure, permit, (practice, action, person's do*ing*); allow (person, religious sect, opinion) to exist without interference or molestation; endure with forbearance; sustain, endure, (suffering etc.), esp. (Med.) sustain use of (drug, radiation, etc.) without harm; so ~A'TION *n.*, (esp.) allowing of differences in religious opinion without discrimination. [f. L *tolerare* endure + -ATE³]

tōll¹ *n.* **1.** Tax or duty paid for use of market, public road, etc., or for service rendered; *charge for long-distance telephone call. **2.** (Law). ||**~ thorough** (taken by town for use of highway, bridge, etc.), ||**~ traverse** (for passing over private land). **3.** Cost or damage necessarily and regrettably caused by disaster or incurred in achieving something; **take its ~,** be accompanied by loss, injury, etc. **4. ~-bar, -gate,** bar or usu. gate across road to prevent passage of person, vehicle, etc., until toll is paid; **to'l(l)booth,** (arch., Sc.) town hall, town gaol; **~-bridge** (at which toll is charged for passage); **~-call,** telephone call for which charge is higher than for local call; **~-house** (occupied by collector at toll-gate or toll-bridge); **~-road** (maintained by means of tolls collected on it). [OE, = OHG *zol*, ON *tollr* f. med. L *toloneum* f. LL *teloneum* f. Gk *telōnion* toll-house (*telos* tax)]

tōll² *v.* & *n.* **1.** *v.t.* Cause (bell, or abs.) to ring with slow uniform strokes; (of bell or clock) give out (stroke, knell, hour of day) thus, be tolled on account of (person, his death, etc.). **2.** *v.i.* (Of bell) Give out slow measured sounds. **3.** *n.* Tolling or stroke of bell. [ME, spec. use of (now dial.) *toll* entice, pull, f. OE **tollian*]

Tŏ'ltĕc *n.* Member of language of Amer. Ind. people that flourished in Mexico before the Aztecs; hence ~AN *a.* [Amer. Ind.]

tolū' (*or* tŏ'-) *n.* Fragrant brown balsam got from a S. Amer. tree (*Myroxylon balsamum*) and used in perfumery and medicine. [f. (Santiago de) *T~* in Colombia]

tŏ'lū|ēne *n.* Colourless aromatic liquid hydrocarbon derivative of benzene, orig. got from tolu; so ~IC *a.*, ~OL *n.*, commercial grade of toluene. [f. prec. + -ENE]

Tŏm *n.* **1. ~, Dick, and Harry,** (usu. derog.) persons taken at random, ordinary people, *every* ordinary person; PEEP²*ing Tom.* **2.** (*tom*). Male animal, esp. **tom(-cat)**; male turkey. **3. ~ o' Bedlam,** (Hist.) deranged beggar released from hospital of St. Mary (see BEDLAM); **to'mboy,** wild romping girl who behaves like boy; ***to'mcod,** small fish of genus *Microgadus*; **~ Collins,** Collins made with gin; **tomfoo'l,** (*n.*) fool, trifler, (*a.*) extremely foolish, (*v.i.*) play the fool, act in trifling manner; **tomfoo'lery,** foolish trifling, foolish ornaments etc.; **~ and Jerry,** drink of hot rum, water, and beaten eggs; **tomno'ddy,** stupid person, fool; **~ Thumb,** a legendary dwarf, any diminutive person, dwarf variety of various plants; **~ Tiddler's ground,** children's game, place where money can be had for the picking up; **to'mtit,** small bird, esp. blue tit. [abbr. of name THOMAS]

tŏ'mahawk (-*a*-h-) *n.*, & *v.t.* **1.** *n.* War-axe of N. Amer. Indian, with head of horn, stone, or iron (*BURY *the tomahawk*); (Austral.) hatchet. **2.** *v.t.* Strike, cut, or kill, with tomahawk; criticize savagely in reviewing. [f. Renape *tämähāk* (*tämäham* he cuts)]

tomă'lley *n.* Fat (called 'liver') in lobster, cooked to make a green sauce. [Carib]

toma'tō (-ah'-) *n.* (*pl.* **~es**). (Plant, *Lycopersicon esculentum*, with) glossy red or yellow pulpy edible fruit; **currant ~,** plant of same genus with small fruit about size of currant; **tree-~,** S. Amer. shrub of same family with lemon-shaped red fruit. [17th c. *tomate*, = F (2 syl.) or Sp. & Port. (3 syl.), f. Mex. *tomatl*]

tomb (tōōm) *n.* Hole (made) in earth or rock to receive dead (esp. human) body, grave; subterranean or other vault for the dead; sepulchral monument; **the ~,** state of death; **~'stone,** monumental stone placed over grave; hence ~'LESS *a.* [ME *t(o)umbe* f. AF *tumbe*, OF *tombe* f. LL *tumba* f. Gk *tumbos*]

tŏ'mbăc *n.* Alloy of copper and zinc used esp. as material for cheap jewellery. [F, f. Malay *tambāga* copper]

tŏ'mbola (*or* -bō'-) *n.* Kind of lottery resembling lotto. [F or f. It. (*tombolare* tumble)]

tōme *n.* Book, volume, esp. large heavy one. [F, f. L f. Gk *tomos* section, volume (*temnō* cut)]

-tōme *suf.* forming *ns.* w. sense (1) section, segment [f. Gk *tomē* a cutting], (2) instrument for cutting (*microtome*), esp. (Surg.) for operation w. name in -TOMY [f. Gk -*tomos* -cutting].

tomĕ'nt|um *n.* (*pl.* **~a**). (Bot.) kind of pubescence composed of matted woolly hairs; (Anat.) flocculent inner surface of pia mater; hence ~OSE¹ (*or* tō'-), ~OUS, *adjs.* [L, = cushion-stuffing]

tŏ'mmў *n.* **1.** (usu. *T~*). British private soldier [f. *T~ Atkins*, orig. *Thomas Atkins*, name randomly chosen and used in specimens of completed official forms 1815–]. **2.** (Mech.) Spanner or screw-driver; **~(-bar),** short bar for use with box-spanner. **3.** ||Bread, provisions, esp. as carried by workman or given to workman in lieu of wages; truck system of payment. **4. ~-gun,** (type of) sub-machine-gun [f. co-inventor J. T. *Thompson*, U.S. Army officer d. 1940]; **~ rot,** = ROT¹ 3. [f. TOM + -Y³]

tomŏ'graphў *n.* Method of radiography displaying details in a selected plane within the body. [f. Gk *tomē* a cutting + -O- + -GRAPHY]

tomŏ'rrow, to-mŏ'rrow, (-ō) *adv.* & *n.* (On) the day after today (*will write tomorrow*; *tomorrow is her birthday*); the (near) future; **like there's no ~,** (sl.) with complete disregard of future needs; **~ come never,** a day that will never arrive; **~ morning, afternoon,** etc., (*ns.* & *advs.*) (in) the morning etc. of tomorrow; *tomorrow* WEEK. [f. TO¹ + MORROW; cf. TODAY]

tŏ'mpĭon. Var. of TAMPION.

tŏ'm-tŏm *n.*, & *v.i.* (**-mm-**). **1.** *n.* Indian, Chinese, African, etc., hand-beaten drum. **2.** *v.i.* Beat tom-tom. [f. Hindi *tamtam*, imit.]

-tomy̆ *suf.* forming *ns.* w. sense 'cutting' (*anatomy*, *dichotomy*) and esp. names of surgical operations of incision (*laparotomy*). [f. (mod. L f.) Gk *-tomia* cutting (*temnō* cut)]

ton[1] (tŭn) *n.* **1.** Measure of weight, (**long**) ~ of 2240 or (**short**) ~ of 2000 lb. avoirdupois; **metric ~**, tonne. **2.** Measure of capacity for various materials, esp. 40 cu. ft. of timber; **~-mile,** one ton of goods carried one mile, as unit of traffic. **3.** Unit of volume in shipping (**deadweight, displacement, ~**, 2240 lb. of total load, 35 cu. ft. of total water displaced, with load-line just immersed; **freight ~**, 40 cu. ft. of cargo; **gross, net** or **register, ~**, 100 cu. ft. of gross, net, internal capacity). **4.** Unit of refrigerating power able to freeze 2000 lb. of ice at 0°C in 24 hours. **5.** (colloq.) Large number or amount (*tons of money*; *bag* **weighs** (**half**) **a ~**, is very heavy); **~s of,** very many (*tons of people*; *have asked him tons of times*). **6.** ||(sl.) £100; speed of 100 m.p.h. (**~-up boys,** motor-cyclists who travel at this speed). [different. f. TUN in 17th c.]

ton[2] (tawṅ) *n.* Prevailing mode, fashion; fashionable style or society. [F]

tō'nal *a.* Of tone or tones; of tonality; (of fugue etc.) having repetitions of subject at different pitches in same key; hence **~LY**[2] *adv.* [f. med. L *tonalis* (as TONE[1]; see -AL)]

tonă'lĭty̆ *n.* (Mus.) character of tone, (relationships constituting) key; colour scheme of picture. [f. prec. + -ITY]

tŏ'nd|ō *n.* (*pl.* **~i** *pr.* -ē). Painting, or relief, of circular form. [It., = round (plate), f. *rotondo* f. L *rotundus* round]

tōne[1] *n.* **1.** Sound, esp. w. ref. to pitch, quality, and strength. **2.** Modulation of voice to express emotion, sentiment, etc., (*impatient*, *lively*, *imploring*, *despondent*, *bantering*, *suspicious*, *tone*); corresponding style in writing etc. **3.** (Phonet.) Accent on one syllable of word; way of pronouncing word to distinguish it from others of similar sound (*Mandarin Chinese has four tones*). **4.** (Mus.) Musical sound, esp. of definite pitch and character; ||interval of major second, e.g. C–D, E–F sharp (**whole-~ scale,** scale consisting entirely of tones, with no semitones); FUNDAMENTAL *tone*; GREGORIAN *tones*. **5.** (Med.) Proper firmness of the bodily organs; state of health in which natural functions are duly performed. **6.** Prevailing character of morals, sentiments, etc., in a group (*raise* or *lower the tone of the nation* etc.; *tone of the market is confident*; *gave a flippant tone to the debate*; *set the tone with a dignified speech*). **7.** General effect of colour or of light and shade in picture; tint, shade of colour; degree of luminosity of colour; (Photog.) colour of monochrome picture. **8. ~-arm,** tubular arm connecting sound-box of gramophone to horn, or pick-up of record-player to amplifier; **~ control,** variation of proportion of high and low frequencies in reproduced sound; **~-deaf,** unable to perceive accurately differences of musical pitch; **~-poem,** (1) musical composition for orchestra illustrating or translating a poetic idea, (2) painting in which the tones are harmonized poetically; **~-row,** = SERIES 8. **9.** Hence **~'LESS** (-nl-) *a.* [ME, f. (OF *ton* f.) L f. Gk *tonos* tension, tone (*teinō* stretch)]

tōne[2] *v.* **1.** *v.t.* Give tone or quality (of sound or colour) to; **~d paper** (having slight, esp. pale amber, tint). **2.** (Photog.) Give (monochrome picture) altered colour in finishing by means of chemical solution. **3.** *v.i.* Undergo change in colour by toning; harmonize (*does not tone* (*in*) *with the wallpaper*). **4. ~ down,** (*v.t.*) soften colouring of (picture), render (statement, expression of views, etc.) less pronounced or confident, (*v.i.*) become softer, less pronounced, etc.; **~ up,** provide with or receive higher tone or pitch or character or greater vigour. **5.** Hence **tō'NER**[1] (1, 2) *n.* [ME, f. prec.]

tō'nēme *n.* (Phonet.) Phoneme distinguished from another only by its tone; hence **tōnē'MIC** *a.* [f. TONE[1] after *phoneme*]

tŏng *n.* A Chinese guild, association, or secret society. [f. Chin. *t'ang* meeting-place]

tŏ'nga (-ngg*a*) *n.* (Ind.) Light two-wheeled vehicle. [f. Hindi *tāngā*]

tŏngkă'ng *n.* Junklike boat used in E. Indies. [Malay]

tŏngs (-z) *n. pl.* (**Pair of**) ~, instrument for more conveniently grasping and holding usu. with two limbs pivoted together near either end or connected by spring piece, esp. **fire-~** (for grasping coal etc.); LAZY, SUGAR, *-tongs*; HAMMER[1] *and tongs*; **would not touch** (repulsive person or thing) **with a pair of ~** (still less without). [pl. of *tong* f. OE *tang*(*e*), = OS *tanga*, OHG *zanga*, ON *töng*, f. Gmc **tang-* f. IE **dank-*]

tongue[1] (tŭng) *n.* **1.** Fleshy muscular organ in the mouth, serving purposes of tasting, licking, swallowing, and (in man) of speech; **put out** one's ~, protrude it from mouth as grimace, or for doctor's inspection; **with** one's **~ hanging out,** thirsty or (fig.) expectant. **2.** This organ of ox etc. as article of food. **3.** Faculty of, tendency in, speech (*has a ready* or *fluent tongue*; *sharp*, LONG[1], *caustic*, *dangerous*, *tongue*); **have, speak with,** one's **~ in** one's **cheek,** speak insincerely or with sly irony; **keep a civil ~ in** one's **head,** avoid rudeness; **have lost, find,** one's ~, be too bashful or surprised to speak, recover power of speech after this; **give ~**, (of hounds) bark esp. on finding scent, speak so as to be widely heard; **hold** one's ~, be silent; *on the* TIP[1] *of* one's *tongue*; **wag** one's ~, talk indiscreetly or volubly. **4.** Language of a nation etc. (*the German tongue*; MOTHER[1] *tongue*); CONFUSION *of tongues*; **gift of ~s,** power of speaking in unknown languages, esp. as claimed by some modern sects or as miraculously conferred on early Christians (Acts 2). **5.** Thing like tongue in shape (esp. tapering) or function, e.g. long low promontory, strip of leather closing gap under laces or buckle of shoe, clapper of bell, pin of buckle, projecting edge of matchboard, slip connecting two grooved boards etc., index of scale or balance, vibrating slip in reed of some musical instruments, jet of flame, pointed movable rail in railway-switch. **6. ~-bit** (with plate preventing horse from getting tongue over mouthpiece); **~-bone,** hyoid; **~-lashing,** severe rebuke; **~-tie,** impediment in speech due to shortness of fraenum of tongue; **~-tied,** having this, (fig.) debarred from speaking out esp. through shyness; **~-twister,** sequence of words difficult to pronounce quickly and correctly, e.g. *she sells sea shells*. **7.** Hence **(-)tongueD**[2] (tŭngd), **~'LESS**, *adjs.*, **~'LET** *n.* [OE *tunge*, = OS, ON *tunga*, OHG *zunga*, Goth. *tuggō* f. Gmc **tungōn*, cogn. w. L *lingua* (f. **dingua*)]

tongue[2] (tŭng) *v.t.* & *i.* Produce staccato etc. effects with (flute etc.) by use of tongue, use tongue thus; **~ and groove,** furnish (matchboard etc.) with tongue and groove. [f. prec.]

tŏ'nĭc *a.* & *n.* **1.** *a.* (Of medicine, medical treatment, etc., or fig. of success, misfortune, punishment) serving to invigorate, bracing; producing tension, esp. of muscles, or normal tone of organs etc.; **~ spasm,** continuous muscular contraction (cf. CLONIC); **~ water,** non-alcoholic carbonated drink. **2.** (Mus.) of tones, esp. of the keynote; **~ accent,** accent on syllable; **~ major** and **minor,** keys with same keynote; **~ sol-fa,** system of sight-singing and notation in which keynote of all major keys is doh and keynote of all minor keys is lah, with time-values shown by vertical lines, colons, etc. **3.** Hence **tŏ'n**ICALLY *adv.* **4.** *n.* Tonic medicine etc. (lit. or fig.); tonic water; (Mus.) keynote. [f. F *tonique* f. Gk *tonikos* (as TONE[1]; see -IC)]

tonĭ'cĭtȳ *n.* Being tonic; healthy elasticity of muscles etc. [f. prec. + -ITY]

tonī'ght, to-nī'ght, (-nī't) *adv.* & *n.* (On) the present evening or night, (on) the evening or night of today. [f. TO[1] + NIGHT; cf. TODAY]

tŏ'nĭsh *a.* Fashionable, stylish. [f. TON[2] + -ISH[1]]

tŏ'nka bean *n.* Black fragrant seed of S. Amer. tree of genus *Dipteryx,* used in perfumery etc. [*tonka,* name in Guyana + BEAN]

to'nnage (tŭ'-) *n.* Internal cubic capacity, or freight-carrying capacity, of ship in TON[1]s; total carrying capacity esp. of country's mercantile marine; charge per ton on cargo or freight; ~ **and poundage,** (Hist.) customs duties on each tun of wine and pound's-worth of merchandise imported or exported, usu. granted as subsidies and levied unconstitutionally by Charles I without consent of Parliament; **~-deck** (second upwards from keel). [in Hist. sense ME f. OF (*tonne* TUN); otherwise f. TON[1] + -AGE]

tonne (tŭn *or* tŭ'nĭ) *n.* Metric ton of 1000 kg. [F (see TUN)]

tŏ'nneau (-nō) *n.* Part of motor car that contains the back seats. [F, lit. cask, tun]

tonŏ'mèter *n.* Tuning-fork or other instrument for measuring pitch of tones; instrument for measuring pressure of fluid. [f. as TONE[1] + -O- + -METER]

tŏ'nsil *n.* Either of two small organs on each side of root of tongue; hence **tŏ'nsillAR**[1] *a.*, **~LE'CTOMY, ~lI'TIS,** *ns.* [f. F *tonsilles* or f. L *tonsillae* pl.]

tŏnsōr'ĭal *a.* (joc.) Of a barber or his work. [f. L *tonsorius* f. *tonsor* barber (*tondere tons-* shave; see -OR) + -AL]

tŏ'nsure (-sher) *n.*, & *v.t.* **1.** *n.* Rite of shaving the crown (R.C. Ch. until 1972) or whole head (Orthodox Ch.) esp. of person entering priesthood or monastic order; shaved part of monk's or priest's head. **2.** *v.t.* Shave head of; give tonsure to. [ME f. OF, or f. L *tonsura* (as prec.; see -URE)]

tŏntī'ne (-ē'n; *or* tŏ'-) *n.* Annuity shared by subscribers to loan, the shares increasing as subscribers die till last survivor gets all, or till specified date when remaining survivors share the proceeds. [F, f. name of Lorenzo *Tonti* of Naples, originator of tontines in France *c.* 1653]

***Tō'nȳ**[1] *n.* Annual award for outstanding theatrical performance. [f. nickname of Antoinette Perry, Amer. actress d. 1946]

***tō'nȳ**[2] *a.* Stylish, fashionable. [f. TONE[1] + -Y[2]]

too *adv.* **1.** In a higher degree than is admissible or desirable for a specified or understood purpose, standard, etc., (*too ripe for cooking*; *too good to be true*; *allows too long an interval, too long intervals*; *too large for me, my taste, my purpose*; *the rumour was all too true*; *is too fond of comfort*); *too* MANY *for*; ~ **much (of a good thing),** intolerable; *too* MUCH *for*; **none ~,** rather less than (*good* etc.); ONLY[2] *too*; **~-too** *a.* & *adv.*, extreme, excessive(ly). **2.** (colloq.) Very (*you are too kind*; *he is not too well today*; *they did not perform too well*). **3.** Also, as well, (*take the others too*; *mean to do it too* (as well as threaten)). **4.** Moreover (*achieved, too, at small cost*). [stressed form of TO[1], f. 16th-c. sp. *too*]

took. See TAKE[1].

tool[1] *n.* **1.** Mechanical implement, usu. held in hand, for working upon something (*carpenter's, gardener's, mason's, tools*); simple machine, e.g. lathe; (cutting part of) MACHINE tool; EDGE[1]- or *edged tool.* **2.** (fig.) Thing used in an occupation or pursuit (*literary tools*; *the tools of* one's *trade*; *the computer as a research tool*); person used as mere instrument by another, cat's-paw. **3.** Separate figure in tooling of book; small stamp or roller to make this. **4.** (sl.) Penis. **5. ~-bag, -box,** (to hold workman's tools); **~-holder,** (1) device for holding tool in lathe, (2) handle for use with different tools; **~-post, -rest,** devices to support cutting-tool in lathe; **~-shed** (in which garden etc. tools are kept). [OE *tōl,* = ON *tól* pl., f. Gmc **tōwlam* (**tōw-*; cf. TAW[1])]

tool[2] *v.* **1.** *v.t.* Dress (building-stone) with chisel; ornament (sides and back of book-cover) with tooling; ~ **(up),** equip with tools. **2.** *v.i.* Work with tool. **3.** *v.t.* & *i.* (sl.) Drive (vehicle), drive, ride, (*along* etc.), esp. in casual or leisurely manner. **4.** Hence ~'ER[1] *n.* [f. prec.]

too'ling *n.* **1.** Stone-dressing with chisel. **2.** Ornamentation of book-cover with designs impressed by heated tools; BLIND[1] *tooling.* [f. prec. + -ING[1]]

toon *n.* E. Ind. tree (*Cedrela toona*) with close-grained red wood used for furniture etc. [f. Hindi *tūn*]

toot *v.* & *n.* **1.** *v.t.* Sound, esp. produce short sound with, (horn, cornet, whistle, etc.); ~ one's **own horn,** praise oneself. **2.** *v.i.* Sound horn etc. thus; (of horn etc.) give out such sound; (of grouse) call. **3.** *n.* Sound of tooted horn, trumpet, etc. [prob. f. MLG *tūten,* or imit.]

tooth *n.* (*pl.* **teeth**) & *v.* **1.** *n.* Each of several hard dense structures growing in rows in jaws of most vertebrates and used for biting and chewing; **false, artificial,** ~ (made by or for dentist to replace missing one). **2.** Tooth-shaped projection or thing, e.g. cog, point, etc., of gear-wheel, saw, comb, rake; pointed part of leaf-margin. **3.** Sense of taste, liking (*for* a food); SWEET *tooth.* **4. Armed to the teeth** (completely, elaborately); **cast** or **fling** thing **in** person's **teeth,** reproach him with it; *cut* one's EYE[1]-*teeth*; **escape by** or **with the skin of** one's **teeth** (narrowly); **fight ~ and nail** (fiercely, with utmost effort); **get** one's **teeth into,** begin serious work upon; **in the teeth of,** in spite of (opposition etc.), in opposition to (instructions etc.), directly against (the wind etc.); **kick in the teeth,** (colloq.) treat(ment) with brutal contempt; LIE[2] *in* one's *teeth*; **long in the ~,** old (orig. of horses, from recession of gums with age); **put teeth into** (law, regulation, etc.), make it effective; SET[1] one's *teeth*; *set* person's *teeth on* EDGE[1]; **show** one's **teeth,** adopt threatening manner; *take the* BIT[1] *between* one's *teeth.* **5. ~'ache,** ache in tooth or teeth; **~-billed,** (of bird) having toothlike process(es) on cutting edges of bill; **~-brush** (for cleaning teeth); *~-brush moustache* (bristly); ||**~-comb** (with fine close-set teeth; prop. FINE[2]-*tooth comb,* taken as *fine tooth-comb*); **~-glass, -mug,** (used when cleaning teeth); **~'paste, -powder,** (for cleaning teeth); **~'pick,** small sharp instrument of quill, wood, etc., for removing food etc. lodged between teeth; **~-shell,** (long tubular tusk-shaped shell of) mollusc of class Scaphopoda; **~'wort,** (1) parasitic plant with tooth-like root-scales, (2) plant of genus *Dentaria,* with toothed root-stock. **6.** Hence (-)~ED[2] (-tht), ~'LESS *adjs.*, ~'LET *n.* **7.** *v.t.* Furnish with teeth. **8.** *v.i.* (Of cog-wheels) interlock. [OE *tōth,* pl. *tēth,* = OS *tand,* OHG *zan(d),* ON *tönn,* Goth. *tunthus* f. Gmc **tanthuz* f. IE **dont-,* **dent-*]

too'thful (-ŏŏl) *n.* Small draught of spirit etc., thimbleful. [f. prec. + -FUL 2]

too'thing *n.* In vbl senses; projecting bricks or stones left at end of wall to provide for continuation; **~-plane** (with serrated blade for roughening surface). [f. TOOTH + -ING¹]

too'thsome *a.* Pleasant to eat; hence ~LY² (-mlĭ) *adv.*, ~NESS (-mn-) *n.* [f. TOOTH + -SOME¹]

too'thy̆ *a.* Having numerous, large, or prominent teeth. [f. TOOTH + -Y²]

too'tle *v.i.* Toot gently or repeatedly esp. on flute; (colloq.) move casually *along*, *around*, etc. [f. TOOT + -LE 3]

too'tsy̆(-wootsy̆) *n.* (joc. or childish). Foot. [cf. FOOTSIE]

tŏp¹ *n.* & *a.* **1.** *n.* Highest point or part; **at the ~ (of the tree)**, (fig.) in highest rank in profession etc.; **come to the ~**, win distinction; **from ~ to toe,** from head to foot, completely; **on ~**, above, in superior position, in addition, on upper part of head (*going bald on top*); **on ~ of,** (fig.) (1) fully in command of, (2) in close proximity to, (3) in addition to; **on ~ of the world,** exuberant; **over the ~**, over parapet of trench, (fig.) into final or decisive state or state of excess. **2.** (usu. in *pl.*) Leaves etc. of plant grown mainly for its root (*turnip-tops*); bundle of long wool fibres prepared for spinning. **3.** Surface (of ground), upper surface (of table etc.). **4.** Upper part of shoe; cover of carriage; folding roof of car or pram; lid of saucepan etc. (BLOW¹ one's *top*); stopper of bottle; creamy part of milk; upper part of page in book; upper edges of book's leaves (*gilt top*); garment worn on upper part of body; turned-down part of leg of sock or stocking, (broad band of light-coloured material on) corresponding part of high boot. **5.** (Person occupying) highest rank, foremost place, (*came out* (*at the*) *top of the school* or *form*); upper or more honourable end, head, (*top of the table*). **6.** Utmost degree, height, (*realized the top of my ambition*; *called at the top of his voice*; *ran at the top of his speed*); **the ~ of the morning (to you)** (Irish morning greeting); (in *pl.*, *pred.*) person or thing of very best quality. **7.** (Naut.) Platform round head of lower mast, serving to extend topmast rigging or carry guns. **8.** (in *pl.*) Two or three highest cards of a suit in bridge etc. **9.** ‖ = *top* GEAR in motor vehicle (*climbed the hill in top*). **10.** *a.* Highest in position or degree or importance (*the top rail*; *at top speed*; *top prices paid*; *the country's top chess-player*; *was given top priority*; *singer reached her top note*); hence ~'MOST *a.* **11. ~-boot,** boot with high top usu. of different material or colour and made to look as if turned down; *top* BRASS; **~'coat,** overcoat, outer coat of paint etc.; **~ copy** (in typing, opp. *carbon copy* etc.); **~ dog,** (sl.) victor, master; **~ drawer,** uppermost drawer in a chest etc., (fig.) high social position or origin; **~-dress,** apply manure or fertilizer on the top of (earth) instead of ploughing it in; **~-dressing,** this process, manure so applied, (fig.) superficial show; **~-flight,** in highest rank of achievement; ‖**~ fruit** (grown on trees, not bushes); **~ga'llant** (*or* tog-), mast, sail, yard, rigging, immediately above topmast and topsail; ‖*top* GEAR; **~-hamper,** encumbrance on top, esp. upper sails and rigging; **~ hat,** tall silk hat; **~-heavy,** overweighted at top so as to be in danger of falling (lit., or fig. of scheme etc.); ‖**~-hole,** (sl.) first-rate; **~'knot,** (1) knot, bow, of ribbon etc., tuft, crest, worn or growing on head, (2) kind of small flounder; **~'man,** top-sawyer, (Naut.) man doing duty in a top; **~'mast** (*or* -*ast*) (next above lower mast); **~-notch,** (colloq.) first-rate; **~'sail** (*or* -*sal*), square sail next above lowest, fore-and-aft sail on gaff; **~-sawyer,** sawyer in upper position in saw-pit; **~ secret,** of the highest secrecy; **~'side,** outer side of round of beef, side of ship above water-line; **~'soil,** top layer of soil, opp. *subsoil*. [OE *topp*, = OHG *zopf* plait, ON *toppr* f. Gmc **toppaz*]

tŏp² *v.t.* (**-pp-**). **1.** Furnish with top or cap (*cake topped with icing*). **2.** Remove top of (plant) to improve growth etc.; remove withered calyx of (fruit); (sl.) execute by hanging. **3.** Reach top of (hill etc.). **4.** Be higher than; be superior to, surpass; be at top of (*top the list*); **~ one's part,** act or discharge it to perfection. **5.** (Golf). Hit (ball) above centre; make (stroke) thus. **6. ~ (off** or **up),** put an end or a finishing touch to (thing, or abs.); **~ out,** put highest stone on (building); **~ up,** fill up (partly empty container). [ME, f. prec.]

tŏp³ *n.* Wooden or metal toy, usu. conical, spherical, or pear-shaped, rotating on sharp point at bottom when set in motion by hand, spring, or string; SLEEP² *like a top*; **old ~**, (sl.) old chap, old fellow, (see OLD 5); **~-shell,** shellfish of family Trochidae with short conical shell. [OE, of uncert. orig.]

tō'păz *n.* **1.** Transparent or translucent aluminium silicate mineral, yellow, white, green, blue, or colourless, used as gem; **false ~**, transparent yellow variety of quartz; **oriental ~**, yellow sapphire. **2.** S. Amer. humming-bird of genus *Topaza*. [ME, f. OF *topace*, *topaze* f. L f. Gk *topazos*, *-zion*]

topă'zolīte *n.* Yellow or green kind of garnet. [f. prec. + -O- + -LITE]

tōpe¹ *v.i.* (arch. or literary). Drink intoxicating liquor to excess, esp. habitually; hence **tō'pER¹** *n.* [perh. f. obs. *top* quaff]

tōpe² *n.* (Ind.) Grove, esp. of mangoes. [f. Telugu *tōpu*, Tamil *tōppu*]

tōpe³ *n.* = STUPA. [f. Punjabi *tōp* f. Prakrit & Pali *thūpo* f. Skr. STUPA]

tōpe⁴ *n.* Small shark of genus *Galeorhinus*. [perh. f. Corn.]

topee. See TOPI.

Tō'phėt *n.* Hell. [name of place in Valley of Hinnom near Jerusalem used for idolatrous worship and later for depositing refuse, for consumption of which fires were kept burning, f. Heb. *tōpeṯ*]

tō'ph|us *n.* (*pl.* ~**i** *pr.* -ī). **1.** Gouty deposit of calcareous matter round teeth and at surface of joints; dental tartar. **2.** Tufa. [L, name of loose porous stones]

tō'pĭ, tō'pee, (-ī) *n.* (Anglo-Ind.) Hat, esp. SOLA¹ *topi*. [f. Hindi *ṭopī*]

tō'pĭar|y̆ *a.* Concerned with or formed by clipping shrubs etc. into ornamental shapes; hence **tōpĭār'ĭAN** *a.*, ~IST (1) *n.* [f. F *topiaire* f. L *topiarius* landscape-gardener (*topia opera* fancy gardening f. Gk *topia* pl. dim. of *topos* place + OPERA¹)]

tŏ'pĭc *n.* Theme for discussion, subject of conversation or discourse. [f. L f. Gk (*ta*) *topika* topics, as title of a treatise by Aristotle (*topos* a place, a commonplace; see -IC)]

tŏ'pĭcal *a.* Of topics; dealing with esp. current or local topics (*topical allusion*, *song*); local, esp. (Med.) affecting a part of the body; hence ~ITY (-ă'l-) *n.*, ~LY² *adv.* [f. as prec. + -AL]

tŏ'plėss *a.* (Seemingly) without a top; (of clothes) having no upper part, (of person) wearing such clothes, bare-breasted. [f. TOP¹ + -LESS]

topŏ'graph|y̆ *n.* Detailed description, representation on map etc., of natural and artificial features of a town, district, etc.; such features; (Anat.) mapping of surface of body with reference to the parts beneath; hence ~ER¹ *n.*, **tŏpogră'phIC(AL)** *adjs.* [ME, f. LL f. Gk *topographia* (*topos* place; see -GRAPHY)]

topŏ'log|y̆ *n.* (Math.) Study of geometrical properties and spatial relations unaffected by continuous change of shape or size of figures; hence **tŏpolŏ'gical** *a.*, ~ist (3) *n.* [f. G *topologie* f. Gk *topos* place; see -logy]

topŏ'nўmў *n.* Study of the place-names of a region; so **tŏ'ponўm** *n.*, place-name. [f. Gk *topos* place + *onoma* name + -y[1]]

tŏ'p|os *n.* (*pl.* ~**oi**). Stock theme in literature etc. [Gk, = commonplace]

tŏ'pper *n.* In vbl senses; (colloq.) = top[1] *hat*; (colloq.) a good fellow, good sort. [f. top[2] + -er[1]]

tŏ'pping *a.* Pre-eminent in position, rank, etc.; ||(sl.) excellent. [f. top[2] + -ing[2]]

tŏ'pple *v.i.* & *t.* (Cause to) fall headlong or as if top-heavy, or to totter and fall (*over, down*; lit. or fig.) [f. top[2] + -le 3]

tŏpsў-tur'v|ў *adv.*, *a.*, & *n.* Upside down; (in) utter confusion; hence ~**ily**[2] *adv.*, ~**iness**, ~**ўdom**, *ns.* [app. f. top[1] + obs. *terve* overturn]

tōque (-k) *n.* **1.** (Hist.) small cap or bonnet for man or woman; woman's small hat with little or no or turned-up brim. **2.** Bonnet-monkey; small macaque with caplike arrangement of hair. [F, app. = It. *tocca*, Sp. *toca*, of unkn. orig.]

toqui'lla (-kē'ya) *n.* (Fibre from leaves of) S. Amer. palmlike tree (*Carludovica palmata*). [Sp., = small gauze head-dress, dim. of *toca* toque]

tor *n.* Hill, rocky peak, esp. in Devon and Cornwall. [OE *torr*; cf. Gael. *tòrr* bulging hill]

Tor'ah (-*a*) *n.* Revealed will of God, esp. Mosaic law; *the* Pentateuch; scroll containing this. [f. Heb. *tōrāh* instruction]

torc. Var. of torque 1.

torch *n.* Piece of resinous wood or twisted flax etc. soaked in tallow etc. for carrying lighted in hand; other appliance for this purpose, e.g. oil-lamp on pole; ||(**electric**) ~, electric lamp with battery etc. in portable case; *blowlamp; *arsonist; (fig.) source of heat or illumination; **carry a ~ for,** have (esp. unreturned) admiration of; **hand on the ~,** keep tradition of knowledge etc. alive; **~-fishing,** catching fish by torchlight at night; **~'light,** (light of) torch; **~-race,** (Gk Ant.) festival performance of runners handing lighted torches to others in relays; **~-singer,** woman who sings **~-songs** (sentimental songs of unrequited love); **~-thistle,** cactus of genus *Cereus*. [ME, f. OF *torche* f. Rom. **torca* f. L *torqua* (*torquēre* twist)]

torchère (-shar') *n.* Tall stand with small table for candlestick etc. [F (as prec.)]

tor'chŏn (-sh-; *or* -awn) *n.* ~ (**lace**), coarse bobbin lace with geometrical designs. [F, = duster, dishcloth (*torcher* wipe)]

tore[1]. See tear[1].

tore[2] *n.* = torus 1, 4. [F, f. L torus]

tŏ'reador *n.* Bullfighter, esp. on horseback. [Sp. (*torear* fight bulls f. *toro* bull f. L *taurus*)]

torer'ō (-ar'ō) *n.* (*pl.* ~**s**). Bullfighter. [Sp. (*toro*; see prec.)]

toreu't|ic (-rōō'-) *a.* Of chasing, carving, and embossing, esp. metal; hence ~**ics** *n.* [f. Gk *toreutikos* (*toreuō* work in relief; see -ic)]

tor'gŏch (-χ) *n.* Red-bellied char[1] in Welsh lakes. [W (*tor* belly, *coch* red)]

tor'ic *a.* Having form of (part of) torus. [f. torus + -ic]

tŏ'rii *n.* (*pl.* same). Gateway of Shinto shrine, with two uprights and two cross-pieces. [Jap.]

tor'mĕnt[1] *n.* Severe bodily or mental suffering (*was in torment; suffered torments*); cause of this. [ME f. OF, f. L *tormentum* missile-engine (*torquēre* twist; see -ment)]

tormĕ'nt[2] *v.t.* Subject to torment (*tormented with neuralgia, suspense, inquiries*); tease or worry excessively; hence ~**or** *n.* [ME, f. OF *tormenter* (*torment*; see prec.)]

tor'mentil *n.* Low herb with bright yellow flowers and highly astringent root-stock used in medicine. [ME, f. OF *tormentille* f. med. L *tormentilla*, of unkn. orig.]

torn. See tear[1].

tornā'dō *n.* (*pl.* ~**es**). Violent storm of small extent with whirling winds, esp. in W. Africa at beginning and end of rainy season and in U.S. etc. over narrow track often accompanied by funnel-shaped cloud; (fig.) outburst or volley *of* cheers, hisses, missiles, etc.; hence **tornă'dic** *a.* [app. assim. of Sp. *tronada* thunderstorm (*tronar* to thunder) to Sp. *tornar* to turn; see -ado]

tor'oid *n.* Figure of toroidal shape. [f. torus + -oid]

toroi'dal *a.* Of or resembling torus; hence ~**ly**[2] *adv.* [f. as prec. + -al]

tor'ōse *a.* (Bot.) cylindrical with bulges at intervals; (Zool.) knobby. [f. L *torosus* (torus; see -ose[1])]

torpē'dō *n.* (*pl.* ~**es**), & *v.t.* **1.** *n.* (Zool.) Electric ray. **2.** Cigar-shaped self-propelled submarine missile that can be aimed at a ship etc. and explodes on impact with it; **aerial ~,** similar missile discharged from aircraft. **3.** *Explosive device, e.g. petard or detonator. **4. ~-boat,** small fast lightly armed warship for carrying or discharging torpedoes; **~-net(ting)** (of steel wire, hung round ship to intercept torpedoes); **~-tube** (from which torpedoes are discharged). **5.** *v.t.* Destroy or attack with torpedo; (fig.) paralyse, make (policy, institution, etc.) ineffective. [L, = numbness, electric ray (*torpēre* be numb)]

tor'pefў *v.t.* Make numb or torpid. [f. L *torpefacere* (*torpēre* be numb; see -fy)]

tor'pid *a.* & *n.* **1.** *a.* (Of hibernating animal) dormant; numb; sluggish, inactive, dull, apathetic; hence ~**ity** (-ĭ'd-), ~**ness**, *ns.*, ~**ly**[2] *adv.* **2.** *n.* (*T*~; in *pl.*) ||Hilary-term boat-races at Oxford between (orig. second crews of) colleges; (in *sing.*) boat or crew in these. [f. L *torpidus* (as foll.; see -id[1])]

tor'por *n.* Torpidity; hence ~**ĭ'fic** *a.* [L (*torpēre* be sluggish; see -or)]

tor'quāte *a.* (Zool.) With ring of peculiar colour or texture of hair or plumage round neck. [f. L *torquatus* (as foll.; see -ate[2])]

torque (-k) *n.* **1.** Necklace of twisted metal, esp. of ancient Gauls and Britons. **2.** (Mech.) Moment of system of forces tending to cause rotation; ~ **converter,** device to transmit correct torque from engine to axle in motor vehicle. [(sense 1 F f. L *torques*) f. L *torquēre* twist]

torr *n.* Unit of pressure in measuring partial vacuum, equal to 1/760 of standard atmosphere. [f. *Torricelli* (see Torricellian)]

tŏ'rre|fў *v.t.* Parch or scorch with heat; roast, dry, (metallic ore, drug); hence ~**fa'ction** *n.* [f. F *torréfier* f. L *torrefacere* (*torrēre* scorch; see -fy)]

tŏ'rrent *n.* Rushing stream of water, lava, etc.; (in *pl.*) great downpour of rain (*rain came down in torrents*); (fig.) violent flow (*of* abuse, grief, questions); hence **torrĕ'ntial** (-shal) *a.* [F, f. It. *torrente* f. L *torrens -entis* scorching, boiling, roaring (*torrēre* scorch; see -ent)]

Tŏrrĭcĕ'llian (*or* -chĕ'-) *a.* ~ **experiment** (with mercury in tube, leading to principle on which barometer is made); ~ **tube** (used for this); ~ **vacuum** (above liquid in Torricellian tube). [f. E. *Torricelli*, It. physicist d. 1647 + -an]

tŏ'rrid *a.* (Of land etc.) parched by sun, very hot; (fig.) intense, zealous; *torrid* zone; hence ~**ity** (-ĭ'd-), ~**ness**, *ns.*, ~**ly**[2] *adv.* [f. F *torride* or f. L *torridus* (*torrēre* parch; see -id[1])]

tŏrse *n.* (Her.) = WREATH. [obs. F *torse, torce* wreath f. Rom. **torsa* for L *torta* fem. p.p. (as TORT)]

tŏr'sel. Var. of TASSEL².

tŏr'sion (-shon) *n.* Twisting, esp. of one end of body while other end is held fixed; (Math.) departure of curve from planar form; (Bot.) state of being spirally twisted; (Med.) twisting of cut end of artery after operation etc. to stop haemorrhage; ~ **balance** (for measuring minute horizontal forces by means of fine twisted wire); ~ **pendulum** (rotating, not swinging); hence ~AL, ~LESS, *adjs.* [ME f. OF, f. LL *torsio -onis* f. L *tortio* (as TORT; see -ION)]

tŏrsk *n.* Fish of cod family. [Norw. *to(r)sk* f. ON *tho(r)skr* prob. cogn. w. *thurr* dry]

tŏr'sō *n.* (*pl.* ~**s**). Trunk of human statue apart from head and limbs; human trunk; (fig.) unfinished or mutilated work. [It., = stalk, stump, torso, f. L THYRSUS]

tŏrt *n.* (Law). Breach of duty (other than under contract) leading to liability for damages; so ~**'feasor** (-z-), person guilty of tort. [ME f. OF, f. med. L *tortum* wrong, neut. p.p. (as n.) of L *torquēre tort-* twist]

tŏr'te (-te) *n.* (*pl.* ~**n** *or* ~**s**). Large flat confection of pastry covered with chocolate etc. [G]

tŏrticŏ'llis *n.* (Path.) Rheumatic etc. disease of muscles of neck, causing twisting and stiffness. | [mod. L, f. *tortus* crooked (see TORT) + *collum* neck]

tŏrti'lla (-ēlya) *n.* Thin flat maize cake eaten hot in Latin America. [Sp. dim. of *torta* cake f. LL]

tŏr'tious (-shus) *a.* (Law). Constituting a tort, wrongful; hence ~LY² *adv.* [f. AF *torcious* (*torcion* extortion f. LL *tortio* torture; see TORSION, -OUS)]

tŏr'toise (-tus) *n.* **1.** Land (or freshwater) slow-moving reptile of order Chelonia, encased in two scaly or leathery shields forming a box and having retractile head and legs; ALLIGATOR *tortoise*; (Rom. Ant.) = TESTUDO. **2.** ~**(-shell)** (*or* -tesh-), yellowish-brown mottled and clouded outer shell or scale of some sea-turtles used for combs etc.; ~**-shell butterfly, cat,** (with black and yellow markings suggesting tortoise-shell). [ME *tortuce* etc., OF *tortue,* f. med. L *tortuca,* of uncert. orig.]

tŏr'trix *n.* Moth of genus *Tortrix,* rolling leaves up to make its nest. [mod. L, fem. of L *tortor* twister (see TORT, -OR, -TRIX)]

tŏr'tūous *a.* Full of twists and turns; (fig., of policy etc.) devious, circuitous, crooked, not straightforward; hence or cogn. **tŏrtūo'**SITY, ~NESS, *ns.*, ~LY² *adv.* [ME f. OF, f. L *tortuosus* (*tortus* a twist f. as TORT; see -OUS)]

tŏr'tur|e *n.*, & *v.t.* **1.** *n.* Infliction of severe bodily pain e.g. as punishment or means of persuasion (*was put to the torture; instruments of torture*); severe physical or mental pain. **2.** *v.t.* Subject to torture (*tortured to extract a confession; tortured with neuralgia* or *anxiety*); (fig.) force out of natural position or state, pervert meaning of (words). **3.** Hence ~ABLE, ~OUS, *adjs.*, ~ER¹ *n.* [F, f. LL *tortura* twisting (as TORT; see -URE)]

tŏ'rūla *n.* (*pl.* ~**e**). Yeast or yeastlike fungus without spores and not causing alcoholic fermentation. [mod. L, dim. of TORUS; see -ULE]

tŏr'|us *n.* (*pl.* ~**i** *pr.* -ī). **1.** Large moulding of convex semicircular profile esp. as lowest member of base of column. **2.** (Bot.) Receptacle of flower. **3.** (Anat.) Smooth ridge of bone or muscle. **4.** (Geom.) Surface or solid formed by rotating closed curve, esp. circle, about line in its plane but not intersecting it. [L, = swelling, bulge, cushion, etc.]

Tŏr'ȳ *n.* & *a.* **1.** (colloq. or derog.) = CONSERVATIVE 2, 5. **2.** (Hist.) (Member) of party that opposed the exclusion of the Duke of York (James II), inclined to the Stuarts after 1689, but after 1760 accepted George III and the established order in Church and State, opposed Reform Bill of 1832, and gave rise to Conservative party (opp. WHIG); *loyal colonist during American Revolution. **3.** Hence ~ISM (3) *n.* [orig. = Irish outlaw, prob. f. Ir. **tóraighe* pursuer (*tóir* pursue)]

tŏsh *n.* (sl.) Rubbish, nonsense. [19th c., of unkn. orig.]

tŏss (*or* taws) *v.* (~**ed,** arch. or poet. **tost**) & *n.* **1.** *v.t.* Throw up (ball etc.) with the hand; (of bull etc.) throw (person etc.) up with the horns. **2.** Throw (thing *to* person, *away, aside, out,* etc.) lightly or carelessly. **3.** Throw (coin) into air to decide choice etc. by way it falls; settle question or dispute with (person *for* thing) thus (*will toss you for* (or *who has*) *the armchair*). **4. Toss** (person) **in blanket,** jerk him upwards out of it by pulling suddenly on all corners; *toss the* CABER; ~ one's **head,** throw it back esp. in contempt or impatience; ~ **oars,** raise them to upright position in salute; ~ **a pancake,** jerk it up so that it returns upside-down to pan; ~**'pot,** (arch.) toper. **5.** *v.t.* & *i.* Throw (thing, one*self*) about from side to side, throw oneself about thus in bed etc., roll about restlessly; (of sea, ship, branch, etc.) roll or swing with fitful to-and-fro motion. **6.** *v.t.* Coat (food) with dressing etc. by gentle shaking. **7.** ~ **off,** (*v.t.*) drink off at a draught, dispatch (work) rapidly or without apparent effort, (sl., *v. refl.* & *i.*) masturbate; ~ **up,** toss coin (see sense 3), prepare (food) hastily; ~*-up* n., tossing of coin, doubtful matter (*it is a toss-up whether he comes or not*). **8.** *n.* Tossing of coin, head, etc., (**win, lose, the** ~, have, not have, its decision in one's favour; **argue the** ~, dispute about a choice); **full** ~, a full pitch at cricket; PITCH²*-and-toss.* **9.** ||Throw from horse-back etc. (**take a** ~, be thrown). [16th c., of unkn. orig.]

tŏt¹ *n.* Small child, esp. *a tiny tot*; (colloq.) dram of liquor. [18th c., of dial. orig.]

tŏt² *n.* & *v.* (-tt-). **1.** *n.* ||Set of figures to be added. **2.** *v.t.* Add (usu. *up*); ~**ting-u'p,** adding of separate items (||esp. of convictions for driving offences to cause disqualification). **3.** *v.i.* (Of items) mount up (~ **up to,** amount to). [abbr. of TOTAL or of L *totum* the whole]

||**tŏt**³ *n.* (sl.) Bone or other article retrieved from refuse-heap etc.; hence ~**'**TING¹ *n.*, collecting of valuable items from among refuse. [19th c., of unkn. orig.]

tō'tal *a.*, *n.*, & *v.* (||-ll-). **1.** *a.* Complete, comprising the whole, (*the total number of persons, total population,* SUM *total, total tonnage*); absolute, unqualified, (*was in total ignorance of it; resulted in total loss of his fortune; total* ABSTINENCE, *abstainer*); ~ **eclipse** (in which whole disc etc. is obscured); ~ **internal reflection** (without refraction, of light-ray meeting interface between two media at more than a certain critical angle to the normal); ~ **recall,** ability to remember every detail of one's experience clearly; ~ **war** (in which all available weapons and resources are employed); hence or cogn. **totă'l**ITY *n.* (e.g. time for which an eclipse is total), ~LY² *adv.* **2.** *n.* Total number or amount. **3.** *v.t.* Find the total of (things, set of figures); amount in number to (*the visitors totalled 131*). **4.** *v.i.* Amount *to,* mount *up to.* [ME f. OF, f. med. L *totalis* (*totus* entire; see -AL)]

tōtălĭtār'ian *a.* Relating to a form of government that permits no rival loyalties or parties, usu. demanding entire subservience of the individual to the State; hence ~ISM (3) *n.* [f. TOTALITY + -ARIAN]

tō'talizātor *n.* Device showing number and

amount of bets staked on race with a view to dividing the total among those betting on winner; system for dealing with bets in this way. [f. foll. + -ATE³ + -OR]

tōtaliz|e, -is|e (-īz), *v.t.* Collect into a total, find the total of; hence ~A'TION *n.*, ~ER¹ *n.* = prec. [f. TOTAL + -IZE]

tōte¹ *n.* (sl.) Totalizator. [abbr.]

tōte² *v.t.* (colloq.) Convey, carry as load, (gun, supplies, timber, etc.); ~ **bag,** woman's large bag for carrying parcels etc.; *~ **box,** small container for goods. [17th c. U.S., prob. of dial. orig.]

tō'tem *n.* Natural object esp. animal adopted among N. Amer. Indians as emblem of clan or individual on ground of kinship; image of this; **~-pole,** pole on which totems are carved or hung, often in tall vertical array, (fig.) hierarchy; hence **totĕ'm**IC, **~ĭ'st**IC, *adjs.*, ~ISM (3), ~IST (2), *ns.* [Algonquian]

t'o'ther, to'ther, (tŭ'dh-) *a.* & *pron.* The other; **tell ~ from which,** (joc.) tell one from the other. [ME *the tother*, for earlier *thet other* 'the other'; now understood as = *the other*]

toties quoties (tŏtiēz kwŏ'tiēz *or* tŏshiēz kwŏ'shiēz) *adv.* On each occasion, every time. [L, = as often as]

toto caelo (tōtō sē'lō *or* kī'lō) *adv.* By an immense amount (*differ toto caelo*). [L, = by the whole heaven]

tŏ'tter¹ *v.i.*, & *n.* **1.** *v.i.* Stand or walk unsteadily or feebly (esp. of child learning to walk); (of tower etc., or fig. of State, system, etc.) be shaken, be on the point of falling; hence ~ER¹ *n.*, ~Y² *a.* **2.** *n.* Unsteady or shaky movement or gait. [ME, f. MDu. *touteren* to swing, f. OS **taltron*]

‖**tŏ'tter²** *n.* (sl.) Rag-and-bone man. [f. TOT³ + -ER¹]

tŏ'tting. See TOT²,³.

tou'can (tōō'-) *n.* Tropical Amer. fruit-eating bird of family Ramphastidae, with immense beak. [f. Tupi *tucana*, Guarani *tucā*]

touch¹ (tŭch) *v.* **1.** *v.t.* Be placed or move so as to meet (thing etc.) at one or more points without intervening space or object, be in or come into contact with; bring part of body esp. hand into contact with, establish this relation towards (thing *with* one's hand, stick, etc.), cause (two things) to come into contact; (w. neg.) move or harm in any degree; *touch* BOTTOM¹; ~ one's **hat** (as salutation); ~ **pitch,** (fig.) have to do with shady transaction or person; ~ **the spot,** find out or do exactly what was needed; *wouldn't touch him* (unpleasant person) *with a* BARGE-*pole* or *a pair of* TONGS; *touch* WOOD. **2.** *v.i.* (Of two things etc.) be in or come into contact with one another. **3.** *v.t.* (Geom.) Be tangent to (circle etc.). **4.** Apply slight force to; strike (keys, strings, of musical instrument), strike keys or strings of. **5.** Delineate, mark lightly, put *in*, (features etc.) with brush, pencil, etc. **6.** Reach, rise as far as (*thermometer touched 90°*); (fig.) approach in excellence etc. (*no one can touch him in light comedy, for purity of style*). **7.** Affect with tender feeling, soften, (*it touched me to the heart*; *was visibly touched by her appeal*); rouse painful or angry feelings in (*touched him to the quick*). **8.** Deal with (subject) lightly or in passing; (arch.) concern (*the matter touches you closely*). **9.** (usu. w. neg.) Have to do with, (*dare not touch alcohol*; *has not touched her breakfast*; *is forbidden to touch the money for ten years*; *never touches his violin now*). **10.** Injure slightly (*blossom is a little touched by the frost*). **11.** (in *p.p.*) Slightly crazy. **12.** Affect slightly, modify, (*morality touched with emotion*); (w. neg.) produce slightest effect on, cope with, (*brass polish won't touch these candlesticks*; *couldn't touch the algebra paper*). **13.** (Hist., of monarch) lay hand on (person) as supposed cure for scrofula. **14.** (sl.) ~ person **for,** get (sum of money) from him as loan or gift (*touched me for £5*). **15.** ~ **at,** (Naut.) call at (port etc.); ~ **down,** (Rugby & Amer. Footb.) touch ball on ground behind either one's own or the opponent's goal, (of aircraft) alight; *~'down* n., act of touching down; ~ **off,** make (sketch) hastily, make hasty sketch of, explode by touching with match etc., (fig.) initiate (process) suddenly; ~ **on** or **upon,** treat (subject) briefly, refer to or mention casually, verge on; ~ **up,** correct, give finishing touches to or retouch (picture, writing, etc.), strike (horse) lightly with whip, jog (memory). **16. ~-and-go,** (*a.*) uncertain as regards result, risky, (*n.*) touch-and-go situation; **~-me-not,** plant of genus *Impatiens* with ripe seed-capsules jerking open when touched. **17.** Hence ~'ABLE *a.* [ME, f. OF *tochier*, *tuchier*, f. Rom. **toccare*, prob. imit., f. **toc* imitating a knock]

touch² (tŭch) *n.* **1.** Act or fact of touching, contact, (*felt a touch on my arm*; *goalkeeper got a touch to the ball*); game of TAG²; **at a ~,** if touched, however lightly; **to the ~,** when touched. **2.** Faculty of perception through response of brain to contact esp. with fingers or lips. **3.** Light stroke with pencil, brush, etc., in drawing etc. (*added a few touches*); **finishing ~es** (lit., or fig. of writing, management of affairs, etc.); *touch of the* SUN. **4.** Small amount, slight tinge or trace, (*wants a touch of salt*; *has a touch of flu*; *a touch of colour in her cheeks, of frost in the air*; *an occasional touch of irony*); = SHAVE²; **a ~,** (*adv.*) slightly. **5.** Performer's manner of touching keys or strings of musical instrument, manner or degree in which keys etc. respond to this, manner or style of workmanship in carving etc. or in writing, (*has a light* or *firm touch on piano*; *writer has light touch*); **the Nelson ~,** Nelson's or a Nelson-like masterly handling of a situation; **personal ~,** way of treating a matter characteristic of or designed for an individual. **6.** Mental correspondence, sympathy, communication; **keep in ~,** (1) remain in sympathy, (2) continue correspondence or personal relations, (*with*); **get, put, in(to) ~ with,** come, cause to come, into communication with; **out of ~,** no longer in touch (*with*). **7.** (arch.) Test (as) with touchstone (*put it to the touch*). **8.** (Footb.) Part of field outside the side limits (**~-lines**) and between continuations of goal-lines; **~-in-goal,** each of the four outside corners enclosed by touch-lines and goal-lines. **9.** (sl.) Act of getting money from person; **easy** or **soft ~,** person readily parting with money. **10. ~-body, -corpuscle,** (concerned in sense of touch); *~ **football** (with touching in place of tackling); **~-hole,** small hole in cannon for firing it; **~-judge,** linesman in Rugby football; **~-line** (see sense 8); **~-mark,** maker's mark on pewter; **~-needle,** needle of gold or silver alloy of known composition used as standard in testing other alloys on touchstone; **~ of nature,** natural trait, (pop.) exhibition of feeling with which others sympathize (f. misinterpretation of Shak. *Troilus & Cressida* III. iii. 175); **~-paper** (impregnated with nitre, for firing gunpowder etc.); **~'stone,** fine-grained dark schist or jasper used for testing alloys of gold etc. by marking it with them, (fig.) standard, criterion; **~-typing,** use of typewriter without looking at keys; **~'wood,** readily inflammable wood, esp. soft substance into which wood is changed by some fungi, used as tinder. [ME, f. OF *touche* (*tochier*; see prec.); partly f. prec.]

touché (tōō'shā) *int.* acknowledging hit by fencing-opponent or justified accusation or valid point made by another person in discussion. [F, p.p. of *toucher* TOUCH¹]

tou'cher (tŭ'-) *n.* In vbl senses; (Bowls) wood that touches jack. [ME, f. TOUCH¹ + -ER¹]

tou'chĭng (tŭ'-) *a.* & *prep.* **1.** *a.* Affecting, pathetic, (*a touching incident*; *shows the most touching confidence in us*); hence ~LY² *adv.*, ~NESS *n.* **2.** *prep.* (arch. or literary). (**As**) ~, concerning, about. [ME, f. TOUCH¹ + -ING¹; in sense 2 f. OF *touchant* part. (as TOUCH¹)]

tou'ch|ȳ (tŭ'-) *a.* Apt to take offence, over-sensitive; hence ~ĭLY² *adv.*, ~ĭNESS *n.* [perh. alt. f. TETCHY after TOUCH²]

tough (tŭf) *a.* & *n.* **1.** *a.* Hard to break or cut, not brittle or tender; (of clay etc.) stiff, tenacious; able to endure hardship, hardy; unyielding, stubborn, difficult, (*he's a tough customer*; *found it a tough job*); (colloq.) acting sternly or vigorously (*get tough with*); (colloq., of luck etc.) hard, severe, unpleasant; *ruffianly, violent and criminal; ~ **guy,** (colloq.) person not easily injured or thwarted; **~-minded,** realistic, not sentimental; hence ~'EN⁶ *v.t.* & *i.*, *~'IE *n.*, tough person or problem, ~'ISH¹ 2 *a.*, ~'LY² *adv.*, ~'NESS *n.* **2.** Tough person, esp. ruffian. [OE *tōh,* = OHG *zāh* f. Gmc **tanhuz*]

tou'pee, ***toupet,*** (tōō'pā) *n.* Wig or artificial patch of hair worn to cover bald spot. [F *toupet* hair-tuft dim. of OF *toup* tuft (as TOP¹); see -ET¹]

tour (toor) *n.* & *v.* **1.** *n.* Journey through a country from place to place; GRAND *tour*; **on** ~, going from place to place to give performances, play matches, etc. **2.** Rambling excursion, journey, walk, (*a tour of observation through the town*); spell of duty on military or diplomatic service, time to be spent at a station. **3.** ~ ***de force*** (-defôr's), feat of strength or skill [F]. **4.** *v.i.* Make tour (*through* etc.); **~'ing-car** (with room for passengers and much luggage). **5.** *v.t.* Make tour of, travel through, (country etc.). **6.** Hence ~'ER¹ *n.*, touring-car. [ME, f. OF *to(u)r*, f. L f. Gk *tornos* lathe]

tour'acō (toor'-) *n.* (*pl.* ~**s**). Large Afr. bird of family Musophagidae, with crimson and green plumage and prominent crest. [F, f. native name in W. Africa]

tour'ĭsm (toor'-) *n.* Organized touring; operation of tours as a business; provision of things and services that attract tourists. [f. TOUR + -ISM]

tour'ĭst (toor'-) *n.* & *a.* **1.** *n.* Person who makes a tour, traveller, esp. for recreation; ~ **trap,** place that exploits tourists; hence ~Y² *a.*, (derog.) suitable for or visited by tourists. **2.** *a.* Of or for tourists; ~ **class,** lowest class of passenger accommodation in ship, train, etc. **3.** Hence ~IC (-ĭ's-) *a.* [f. TOUR + -IST]

tour'malĭne (toor'-; *or* -ēn) *n.* Boron aluminium silicate mineral of various colours possessing unusual electric properties and used as gem. [F, f. Sinh. *toramalli* cornelian]

tour'nament (toor'-) *n.* **1.** (Hist.) Pageant in which two parties of mounted and armed men contended with usu. blunted weapons; appointed meeting for jousting etc. **2.** Any contest of skill between a number of competitors (*chess, lawn-tennis, tournament*). [ME, f. OF *torneiement* (*torneier* TOURNEY; see -MENT)]

tour'nedōs (toor'nedō) *n.* (*pl.* same). Small fillet of beef with strip of suet round it. [F]

tour'ney (têr'- *or* toor'-) *n.*, & *v.i.* (Take part in) tournament (esp. sense 1). [ME, f. (OF *tornei* n. f.) OF *torneier* v. f. Rom. **tornidiare* f. L *tornus* a turn]

tour'nĭquet (toor'nĭkā) *n.* Bandage etc. for stopping flow of blood through artery by compression effected with screw or twisted bar. [F, prob. f. OF *tournicle* coat of mail, TUNICLE, infl. by *tourner* TURN¹]

tou'sle (-zel) *v.t.* Handle roughly or rudely; make (esp. hair) untidy. [frequent. of (now dial.) *touse*, ME f. OE **tūsian* cogn. w. OHG *-zuson*; see -LE 3]

tous-les-mois (tōōlāmwah') *n.* Food starch got from tubers of species of canna. [F, lit. = every month, prob. corrupt. of W. Ind. *toloman*]

tout *v.* & *n.* **1.** *v.i.* Solicit custom, pester possible customers with requests (*for* orders); ||spy out movements and condition of race-horses in training; *offer racing tips for share of resulting gains. **2.** *v.t.* Solicit custom of (person) or for (thing). **3.** *n.* Person employed in touting. [ME *tūte* look out (OE **tūtian*) = ME (now dial.) *toot* (OE *tōtian*) f. Gmc **tūt-*, **tōt-* project]

tout court (tōō koor') *adv.* (Of name etc.) without addition of title or explanation. [F, lit. quite short]

tout ensemble (tōōt ahṅsah'ṅbl) *n.* See ENSEMBLE. [F (*tout* whole, ENSEMBLE)]

tovar'ish *n.* Comrade. [Russ. *tovarishch*]

tow¹ (tō) *v.t.*, & *n.* **1.** *v.t.* (Of vessel, horse on bank, etc.) pull (boat, barge, etc.) along in water by rope or chain; (of vehicle) pull another running behind it; pull (person, thing) along behind one. **2.** *n.* Towing or being towed; **take** or **have in** or **on** ~, (fig.) be accompanied by, assume direction of, take possession of, (person). **3.** **~('ing)-line, -rope,** (used in towing); **~('ing)-net** (for dragging through water to collect specimens); **~('ing)-path** (along river or canal for use in towing); hence ~'ABLE *a.*, ~'AGE (3, 4) (tō'ĭj) *n.* [OE *togian,* = OHG *zogōn*, ON *toga* f. Gmc **togōjan* (**tog-* pull; cf. TUG)]

tow² (tō) *n.* Coarse and broken part of flax or hemp prepared for spinning; loose bunch of rayon etc. strands; **~-coloured,** (of hair) light in colour; **~-head,** tow-coloured or unkempt hair; hence ~'Y² (tō'ĭ) *a.* [ME, f. MLG *touw*, f. OS *tou*, rel. to ON *tó* wool f. **tāw-* (cf. TOOL¹)]

tow'ard¹ (tō'*erd*) *a.* (arch.) Docile, apt; promising, auspicious; about to take place, being planned; hence ~LY¹ *a.*, ~NESS *n.* [as foll.]

towards, toward², (tôrd(z) *or* twôrd(z) *or* towôr'd(z)) *prep.* In the direction of (*looks towards the sea*; *set out towards town*); as regards, in relation to, (*felt some animosity toward him*; *his attitude towards death*); for, for the purpose of, (*saved something towards his education*); near (*towards noon*; *toward the end of our journey*). [OE *tōweard* a. future, = OS *tōward*, OHG *zuowart* (as TO¹, -WARD; see -S³)]

tow'el *n.* & *v.* (||-ll-). **1.** *n.* Absorbent cloth, paper, etc., for drying oneself or thing after washing; **throw in the** ~, (Boxing or fig.) admit defeat; ROLLER, ||SANITARY, TEA-, *towel*; **~-horse, -rail,** frame for hanging towels on. **2.** *v.t.* Wipe or dry (one*self* etc.) with towel; ||(sl.) thrash. **3.** *v.i.* Wipe or dry oneself with towel. **4.** Hence ~LING¹ (1, 3) *n.* [ME, f. OF *toail(l)e* f. Gmc **thwahljō* (**thwaham* to wash)]

tow'er *n.*, & *v.i.* **1.** *n.* Tall usu. equilateral (esp. square) or circular structure, often forming part of church or other large building; similar structure housing machinery, apparatus, operators, etc., (*control, cooling, tower*); tall building containing offices or dwelling-places; fortress etc. comprising or including a tower; (fig.) place of defence, protector, (~ **of strength,** champion, comforter, etc.); IVORY *tower*; MARTELLO *tower*; WATER¹-*tower*; *tower of* SILENCE; ||**the T~ (of London),** assemblage of buildings now used as repository of crown jewels etc., orig. fortress, palace, and State prison; hence ~ED[2] (-*erd*), ~Y[2], *adjs.* **2.** *v.i.* Reach high (*above* or *over* surroundings, lit., or fig. of eminent person: *towers above his contemporaries*), (of eagle etc.) soar or be poised aloft, (of wounded bird) shoot straight up; (in *part.*) high, lofty, (fig., of rage etc.) violent. [OE *torr*, & ME *tūr*, AF & OF *tur* etc., f. L f. Gk *turris*]

town *n.* **1.** Considerable collection of dwellings etc. (larger than *village*), esp. one not created a city. **2.** Densely populated settlement, esp. opp. country or suburbs. **3.** The people of a town (*the whole town knows of it*); **the talk of the ~**, what is being talked about generally in the town. **4.** London or the chief city or town in one's neighbourhood, (*went up to town from York*; *is not in town, is out of town*; *the best coffee in town*); central business area of one's neighbourhood (*went into town today*). **5.** * = TOWNSHIP 2. **6. Go to ~**, act or work with energy and enthusiasm; **man about ~**, fashionable idler; *woman* etc. **of the ~**, belonging to the disreputable side of town life; **on the ~**, in carefree pursuit of urban pleasures; PAINT[2] *the town red*; *town and* GOWN. **7.** ~ **clerk,** officer of corporation of a town, in charge of records etc., ||(until 1974) secretary and legal adviser of town corporation; ||~ **council(lor)**, (member of) elective governing body in municipality; *town* CRIER; ~ **gas,** inflammable gas for domestic and commercial use; ~ **hall,** building for transaction of official business of town, often also used for public entertainment etc.; ~ **house,** (1) one's town (as opp. to country) residence, (2) ||town hall, (3) house in planned group in town, (4) terrace-house; **~-major,** (Hist.) chief executive officer in garrison-town or fortress; ||~ **mayor,** chairman of town council; *~ **meeting** (of voters of town for transaction of public business); ~ **planning,** preparation of plans for regulated growth and improvement of towns; **~'scape,** (1) picture of a town, (2) visual appearance of town(s); **~'sfolk** (-z-), inhabitants of particular town(s); **~'sman, ~'swoman,** (-z-), inhabitant of town, fellow citizen; **~'speople** (-z-), the people of a town; ~ **talk,** (arch.) the talk of the town (see sense 3). **8.** Hence ~'LESS, ~'WARD, *adjs.*, ~'LET *n.*, ~'WARD(s) *adv.* [OE *tūn* enclosure, = OS *tūn*, ON *tún*, OHG *zūn* fence, hedge f. Gmc **tunaz*, **tunam*, rel. to Celt. **dun*-]

townee', *tow'nĭe, *tow'nȳ, *n.* (derog.) Townsman, esp. opp. countryman or (in university town) member of the university. [f. prec. + -EE, -IE, -Y[3]]

tow'nshĭp *n.* **1.** (Hist.) Community inhabiting a manor, parish, etc.; manor or parish as territorial division; small town or village forming or having formed part of a large parish. **2.** (U.S. & Can.) Division of county with some corporate powers; district six miles square. **3.** (Austral. & N.Z.) Small town, town-site. [OE *tūnscipe* (as TOWN, -SHIP)]

towy. See TOW[2].

tŏxae'm|ĭa, *-ē'm|ĭa, *n.* Blood-poisoning; disease of pregnancy with increased blood-pressure; hence ~IC *a.* [f. as foll. + -AEMIA]

tŏ'x|ĭc *a.* Of poison (*toxic symptoms*); poisonous; caused by poison (*toxic anaemia*); hence ~ICALLY *adv.*, **~ĭ'**CITY, **~ĭco**MA'NIA, *ns.*, ~I-, **~ĭco**-, ~O-, *comb. forms.* [f. med. L *toxicus* poisoned f. L *toxicum* f. Gk *toxikon pharmakon* poison for arrows (*toxa* arrows; see -IC)]

tŏxĭcŏ'log|ȳ *n.* Science of poisons; hence **tŏxĭcolŏ'g**ICAL *a.*, ~IST (3) *n.* [f. prec. + -O- + -LOGY]

tŏ'xĭn *n.* Poison esp. of animal or vegetable origin; (Path.) poison formed in body by pathogenic organism. [f. TOXIC + -IN]

tŏxŏ'phĭl|īte *n.* & *a.* (Student or lover) of archery; hence ~Y[1] *n.* [f. Ascham's *Toxophilus* (1545) f. Gk *toxon* bow + *-philos* -PHIL, + -ITE[1]]

toy *n.*, *a.*, & *v.i.* **1.** *n.* Thing to play with, esp. for child; thing meant rather for amusement than for serious use; occupation followed in trifling or unpractical manner. **2. ~-box** (for keeping one's toys in); ~ **soldier** (of lead etc., or of an army that has no fighting to do). **3.** *a.* That is a toy; (of dog etc.) of diminutive breed or variety. **4.** *v.i.* Trifle, amuse oneself; ~ **with,** deal with or handle in trifling or fondling or careless manner. [16th c.; earlier = dallying, fun, jest, whim, trifle; orig. unkn.]

Tpr. *abbr.* Trooper.

trābėā'tion *n.* Use of beams (not arches or vaulting) in construction; so **trā'bė**ATE[2] *a.* [f. L *trabs trabis* beam + -ATION]

trabĕ'cūl|a *n.* (*pl.* **~ae**). (Anat.) supporting band or bar of connective tissue etc.; (Bot.) beamlike projection or process; so ~AR[1], ~ATE[2], *adjs.* [L, dim. of *trabs* beam; see -CULE]

tracă'sserĭe *n.* State of annoyance; fuss, petty quarrel. [F (*tracasser* bustle; see -ERY)]

trāce[1] *v.t.*, & *n.* **1.** *v.t.* ~ **(out)**, delineate, mark out, sketch, write esp. laboriously, (*traced* (*out*) *a plan of the district*; *traced the words with a shaking hand*; (fig.) *the policy he traced* (*out*) *was never followed*). **2.** ~ **(over)**, copy (drawing etc.) by following and marking its lines on superimposed sheet (esp. of transparent **tracing-paper**) through which they are visible or on sheet placed below with carbon paper etc. between; hence **trā'**CING[1] (1, 2) *n.* **3.** Follow or mark track or path of (person, animal, footsteps, etc., *along*, *through*, *to*, etc.). **4.** Ascertain position and dimensions etc. of (ancient road, wall, etc.) by its remains. **5.** Observe or find vestiges or signs of (*his resentment can be clearly traced in many passages*; *cannot trace any letter of that date*). **6.** ~ **back,** go back over the course of (*have traced my genealogy back to* (*the time of*) *William I*; *the report has been traced back to you*). **7.** Pursue one's way along (path etc.). **8.** Hence ~ABLE (-*sa*-) *a.* **9.** *n.* Track left by person or animal walking or running or by moving pen of instrument etc.; (esp. in *pl.*) footprints or visible signs of course pursued; line on screen of cathode-ray tube showing path of moving spot; projection of curve on plane etc. **10.** Visible or other sign of what has existed or happened (*of these buildings no trace remains*; *sorrow has left its traces on her face*; *has vanished, sunk, without trace*; *traces of Italian influence abound in his earlier works*); change in the brain as result of learning; small quantity (*contains traces of soda*); amount of substance, rainfall, etc., too small to be measured; ~ **element** (occurring or required, esp. in soil, only in minute amounts). **11.** Hence ~'LESS (-sl-) *a.* [ME; (n. f. OF *trace*) f. OF *tracier* f. Rom. **tractiare* f. L *tractus* drawing (see TRACT[1])]

trāce[2] *n.* Each of the two side-straps or chains or ropes by which horse draws vehicle; **kick over the ~s,** (fig., of person) become insubordinate or reckless; **~-horse** (that draws in traces or by single trace, esp. one hitched on to help up hill etc.). [ME f. OF *trais*, pl. of TRAIT]

trā'cer *n.* In vbl senses; (Mil.) projectile whose course is made visible by flame etc. emitted; artificially produced radioactive isotope capable of being followed in its course in the human body etc. by the radiation it produces. [f. TRACE[1] + -ER[1]]

trā'cer|ȳ *n.* Stone ornamental open-work esp. in head of Gothic window; decorative pattern or natural outline (e.g. in insect's wing) suggesting this; **bar ~y** (with strips of stone across aperture); **geometric ~y** (with openings of geometrical form); **plate ~y** (with perforations in otherwise continuous stone); hence **~ĭed**[2] (-ĭd) *a.* [f. TRACE[1] + -ERY]

trachē'a (-k-; *or* trā'kĭa) *n.* (*pl.* ~e). Principal air-passage of body from larynx to bronchial tubes; (Zool.) each of the passages by which air is conveyed through body of insect, arachnid, etc.; (Bot.) duct, vessel; hence **trā'chė**AL, **trā'chė**ATE[2], *adjs.*, **trachē'**O- *comb. form*, (-k-). [ME f. med. L, = LL *trachia* f. Gk *trakheia* (*artēria*) 'rough artery', f. *trakhus* rough]

trāchėŏ'tomy̆ (-k-) *n.* Incision of trachea; ~ **tube,** breathing-tube inserted in opening so made. [f. TRACHEO- + -TOMY]

trach|ō'ma (-k-) *n.* Contagious disease of eye with inflamed granulation on inner surface of lids; hence **~ŏ'mat**OUS *a.* [f. mod. L f. Gk *trakhōma* (*trakhus* rough; see -OMA)]

tră'chȳte (-k-) *n.* Light-coloured volcanic rock rough to the touch; hence **trachy̆'t**IC (-k-) *a.* [F, f. Gk *trakhutēs* roughness (as prec.) + -ITE[1]]

trăck[1] *n.* & *v.* **1.** *n.* Mark or series of marks left by person, animal, or thing, in passing along; (in *pl.*) such marks, esp. footprints; **in** one's **~s,** (sl.) where one stands, there and then; **off the** ~, (fig.) away from subject; **on** person's ~, in pursuit of him, (fig.) in possession of clue to his conduct, plans, etc.; **on the wrong** ~, following wrong line of inquiry etc.; **cover** one's **~s,** conceal evidence of what one has done; **keep, lose,** ~ **of,** follow, fail to follow, the course or development of; **make ~s,** (sl.) go or run away; **make ~s for,** (sl.) go in pursuit of or towards. **2.** Course taken (*followed in his track*; *indicated the track in which we were to go*; *track of ionizing particle, of comet*); ONE-*track mind.* **3.** Path, esp. one beaten by use, (fig.) course of life or routine, (*a rough track runs round the hillside*; *covered with sheep-tracks*; *road has only a single track*; BEATEN *track*). **4.** Prepared racing-path (*grass track*; *running-track*); racecourse for horses etc. **5.** Continuous line of railway; **single, double,** ~, one pair, two pairs, of rails; ***across, *on the wrong side of, the ~s,** in socially inferior part of town; hence *~'AGE (1) *n.* **6.** Band round wheels of tank, tractor, etc.; hence **~-laying,** (of vehicle) having caterpillar tread. **7.** Transverse distance between a vehicle's wheels. **8.** = SOUND[2]-*track*; groove on gramophone record; section of gramophone record with a recorded sequence; lengthwise strip of magnetic tape containing one sequence of signals. **9.** ~ **events,** (Athletics) running-races as opp. throwing etc. (FIELD *events*); ***~'layer, ~'man,** platelayer; ~ **record,** (fig.) person's past achievements; ~ **shoe,** spiked shoe worn by runner; ~ **suit** (worn by athlete etc. during training); ***~ system,** streaming in education; **~'way,** beaten path, ancient roadway. **10.** Hence ~'LESS *a.* (***~less trolley,** trolleybus). **11.** *v.t.* Follow the track of (animal, person, *to* lair etc.; spacecraft etc.); ~ **down,** reach or capture by tracking. **12.** Trace, make out, (course, development, etc.) by vestiges. **13.** *Make track with (dirt etc.) from feet; *leave such track on (floor etc.). **14.** *v.i.* (Of wheels) run so that the hinder is exactly in the first's track; (of gramophone stylus) follow groove; (of cine--camera) move along set path while taking picture. [ME, f. OF *trac*, perh. f. LDu. *tre(c)k* draught etc.]

trăck[2] *v.* **1.** *v.t.* Tow (boat) by rope etc. from bank. **2.** *v.i.* Travel by being towed. [app. f. Du. *trekken* to draw etc., assim. to prec.]

tră'cker *n.* In vbl senses; wooden connecting--rod in organ mechanism; police dog tracking by scent; BLACK[1] *tracker.* [f. TRACK[1,2] + -ER[1]]

trăct[1] *n.* Region or area of indefinite (usu. large) extent, (*a tract of sand*; *pathless tracts*); (Anat.) area of organ or system (*olfactory, respiratory, tract*); ||(arch.) period (*of* time etc.). [f. L *tractus* drawing (*trahere tract-* draw, pull)]

trăct[2] *n.* Short treatise or discourse or pamphlet esp. on religious subject; **T~s for the Times, Oxford T~s,** (see TRACTARIANISM). [app. abbr. of L *tractatus* TRACTATE]

trăct[3] *n.* (R.C. Ch.) Anthem replacing alleluia in some masses. [f. med. L *tractus* (*cantus*) drawn-out (song), p.p. of L *trahere* draw]

tră'ct|able *a.* (Of person, material, etc.) easily handled, manageable, pliant, docile, malleable; hence ~ABI'LITY, **~able**NESS (-beln-), *ns.*, **~ab**LY[2] *adv.* [f. L *tractabilis* (*tractare* handle, frequent. of *trahere tract-* draw; see -ABLE)]

Trăctār'ĭan *a.* & *n.* (Adherent or promoter) of ~ISM (3) *n.*, 19th-c. English High-Church movement towards primitive sacramental Catholicism and against liberalism, voiced by Newman, Pusey, Keble, Froude, etc., in 90 tracts (*Tracts for the Times*) published at Oxford 1833–41. [f. TRACT[2] + -ARIAN]

tră'ctāte *n.* Treatise. [f. L *tractatus* (*tractare*; see TRACTABLE, -ATE[1])]

tră'ction *n.* Drawing of a body along a surface, esp. of vehicle along road or track (*electric, steam, traction*); grip of tyre on road, wheel on rail, etc.; (Med.) sustained pull on limb etc. for therapeutic purpose; contraction e.g. of muscle; *public transport service; **~-engine,** steam or diesel engine for drawing heavy load on ordinary road or across fields etc.; **~-wheel,** driving-wheel of locomotive etc.; hence or cogn. ~AL, **tră'ct**IVE, *adjs.* [F, or f. med. L *tractio* f. L *trahere tract-* draw; see -ION]

tră'ctor *n.* Traction-engine; stationary or movable engine for hauling; self-propelled vehicle for hauling other vehicles, farm machinery, etc. [f. as prec. + -OR]

trăd *a.* & *n.* (colloq.) Traditional (jazz). [abbr.]

trāde *n.* & *v.* **1.** *n.* Business, esp. mechanical or mercantile employment opp. to *profession*, carried on as means of livelihood or profit (*a carpenter, a butcher, by trade*); skilled handicraft (*learn a trade*); **be in** ~, be a retailer, keep a shop; JACK[1] *of all trades*; **trick of the** ~, device for attracting custom, gaining advantage over rival by special technique, etc. **2.** Exchange of commodities for money or other commodities, commerce; business done with specified class or at specified time (*tourist, Christmas, trade*); *a transaction; **foreign** ~, exportation and importation of goods from and to home country or exchange of commodities of different countries; **domestic** or **home** ~ (carried on within a country); **is good, bad, for** ~, induces, discourages, buying; **carrying-~,** transportation of goods from one country to another by water or air as a business. **3.** *The* persons engaged in one trade (*the trade will never agree to it*; *is unpopular with the book trade*), esp. ||(colloq.) *the* licensed victuallers, (Nav. sl.) *the* submarine service. **4.** BALANCE[1] *of trade*; ||BOARD[1] *of Trade*; FREE[1] *trade*; TERM[1]*s of trade.* **5.** (usu. in *pl.*) Trade wind. **6.** ||**T~ Board,** (Hist.) statutory body for the settlement of disputes, wage claims, etc., in certain industries; ||**~ cycle,** recurring succession of trade conditions alternating between prosperity and depression; ~ **journal** (containing articles and information on a particular trade); ~ **mark,** device or word or words legally registered (or, formerly, established by use) as distinguishing a manufacturer's or trader's goods, (fig.) distinctive feature of person's activities etc.; ~ **name,** (1) that by which a thing is called in the trade, (2) name given by manufacturer to proprietary article,

(3) name under which business is carried on; ~ **paper,** = *trade journal*; ~ **plates,** number-plates used by dealer etc. on various unlicensed cars; ~ **price** (charged by manufacturer etc. to dealer for goods that are to be sold again); ~ **secret,** device or technique used in trade and giving advantage because not generally known; **~'sman** (-z-), person engaged in trade, esp. shopkeeper or craftsman; **~'speople** (-z-), tradesmen (and their families); **T~s Union Congress,** official representative body of British trade unions, meeting annually; ~ **union,** **~s union,** organized association of workmen of a trade or group of allied trades formed for protection and promotion of their common interests; **~-u'nionism,** this system of association; **~-u'nionist,** advocate of this or member of trade union; ~ **wind,** wind blowing continually towards equator within parallels 30° N. and 30° S. and deflected westwards by rotation of earth [f. obs. *blow trade* = blow regularly]. **7.** *v.i.* Buy and sell, engage in trade (*in* commodity or (fig.) *in* favours etc., *with* person); have a transaction (*with* person *for* thing); carry merchandise (*to* place); ~ **on,** take (esp. unscrupulous) advantage of (person's credulity, one's reputation, etc.). **8.** *v.t.* Exchange in commerce, barter, (goods); ~ **(in),** give (used car etc.) in (part) payment or exchange *for*; *~-in* n., (thing given in) such transaction; ***~-last,** compliment from a third person to be reported in exchange for one to the reporter; ~ **off,** exchange esp. by way of compromise, so *~-off* n. [ME, f. MLG *trade* track, f. OS *trada*, OHG *trata* (**trad-* TREAD)]

trā'der *n.* Person engaged, vessel regularly employed, in trade. [f. prec. + -ER[1]]

trădėscă'ntĭa *n.* Perennial herb of genus *Tradescantia*, with large blue, white, or pink flowers. [mod. L, f. J. *Tradescant*, Engl. naturalist d. 1638 + -IA[1]]

trā'dĭng *n.* In vbl senses; ~ **estate,** area designed to be occupied by a group of industrial and commercial firms; *trading*-POST[4]; ~ **stamp** (given by tradesman to customer and exchangeable in quantity for various articles). [f. TRADE + -ING[1]]

tradĭ'tion *n.* **1.** Opinion or belief or custom handed down, handing down of these, from ancestors to posterity esp. orally or by practice. **2.** (Theol.) Doctrine etc. supposed to have divine authority but not committed to writing, esp. (1) laws held by Pharisees to have been delivered by God to Moses, (2) oral teaching of Christ and Apostles not recorded in writing by immediate disciples, (3) words and deeds of Muhammad not in Koran. **3.** Artistic or literary principle(s) based on accumulated experience or continuous usage (*stage tradition*; *the traditions of the Dutch School*). **4.** (Law). Formal delivery. **5.** Hence ~ARY[1] *a.*, ~IST (2) *n.*, = TRADITIONALIST. [ME, f. OF *tradicion* or f. L *traditio* f. *tradere* (*tra-* = TRANS-, *dare* give) hand on, betray; see -ION]

tradĭ'tional *a.* Of or based on or obtained by tradition; (of jazz) in style descending from the early period of jazz history; hence ~LY[2] *adv.* [f. prec. + -AL]

tradĭ'tional|ĭsm *n.* (Excessive) respect for tradition esp. in religion; philosophical system referring all religious knowledge to divine revelation and tradition; so ~IST (2) *n.* [f. F *traditionalisme* or f. prec. + -ISM]

tră'dĭtor *n.* (*pl.* **~s,** *or* **~es** *pr.* -ōr'ēz). Early Christian who to save his life surrendered copies of Scripture, or Church property, to persecutors. [L (see TRAITOR)]

tradū'ce *v.t.* Calumniate, misrepresent; hence **tradū'**CER[1], ~MENT (-sm-), *ns.* [f. L *traducere* disgrace (*tra-* = TRANS-, *ducere duct-* lead)]

tradū'cĭan|(ĭst) *ns.* One who believes that soul as well as body is propagated; so ~ISM (3) *n.* [f. LL *traducianus* transmitting f. L *tradux -ucis* vine-shoot trained for propagation; see -IAN]

tră'ffĭc *v.* (**-ck-**) & *n.* **1.** *v.i.* Trade (*in* commodity, lit. or fig.), esp. deal or bargain in something that should not be the subject of trade. **2.** *v.t.* Deal in, barter. **3.** Hence **~k**ER[1] *n.* **4.** *n.* Trade, esp. trafficking (*in* commodity; *the traffic in drugs*; *unscrupulous traffic in lucrative appointments*); transportation of goods, coming and going of persons or goods by road, rail, air, sea, etc.; number or amount of persons or goods conveyed; (amount of) use of a service (*telephone traffic*); dealings or communication between persons etc. **5.** *~ **circle,** roundabout; *~ **cop,** (colloq.) policeman controlling road traffic; ~ **island,** paved etc. area in road to direct the traffic and provide refuge for pedestrians crossing; ~ **jam,** condition in which road traffic cannot proceed freely and comes to a standstill; **~-light**(**s**), **~-signal,** mechanical signal controlling road traffic (esp. at junctions) by coloured lights; ~ **sign** (conveying information, warning, etc., to vehicle-drivers); ||~ **warden,** person appointed to assist police in controlling movement of road traffic and esp. parking of vehicles. **6.** Hence ~LESS *a.* [f. F *traf*(*f*)*ique*(*r*), Sp. *traficar*, *tráfico*, It. *trafficare*, *traffico*, of unkn. orig.]

||**tră'ffĭcātor** *n.* Movable device on road vehicle to indicate intended change of direction of travel. [f. prec. + INDICATOR]

tră'gacănth *n.* White or reddish gum from plants of genus *Astragalus*, used in pharmacy, calico-printing, etc. [f. F *tragacante* f. L f. Gk *tragakantha*, name of shrub (*tragos* goat, *akantha* thorn)]

tragē'dĭan *n.* Writer of tragedies; actor in tragedy. [ME, f. OF *tragediane* (as TRAGEDY; see -IAN)]

tragēdĭĕ'nne *n.* Actress in tragedy. [F, fem. f. as prec.]

tră'gėdў *n.* **1.** Drama in prose or verse of elevated theme and diction and with unhappy events or ending (cf. COMEDY). **2.** Sad event, calamity; serious accident or crime. [ME, f. OF *tragedie* f. L f. Gk *tragōidia* app. goat-song (*tragos* goat, *ōidē* song)]

tră'g|ĭc *a.* **1.** Of, in the style of, tragedy (*tragic drama*; *in a tragic voice*; *tragic actor*); **~ic irony** (in Gk tragedy, of words having an inner esp. prophetic meaning for audience, unsuspected by speaker). **2.** Sad, calamitous, distressing, (*a tragic tale, event, scene*). **3.** Hence ~ICALLY *adv.* [f. F *tragique* f. L f. Gk *tragikos* (*tragos* goat; see prec., -IC)]

tră'gĭcal *a.* = prec. 2. [f. as prec. + -AL]

trăgĭcŏ'm|ėdў *n.* Drama of mixed tragic and comic elements; so ~IC *a.*, ~ICALLY *adv.* [f. F *tragicomédie* or f. It. *tragicomedia* f. LL *tragicomoedia* f. L *tragico-comoedia* (as TRAGIC, COMEDY)]

tră'gopăn *n.* Asian horned pheasant of genus *Tragopan*. [L f. Gk (*tragos* goat, *Pan* the god Pan)]

trahison des clercs (trahĭzawṅ dā klār') *n.* Betrayal (of standards) by the intellectuals. [F, title of book by J. Benda (1927)]

trail *n.* & *v.* **1.** *n.* Part drawn behind or in the wake of a thing, long (real or apparent) appendage, (*engine left a trail of smoke behind it*; CONDENSATION *trail*; *the trail of a meteor*); hinder end of gun-carriage stock; track left by what has moved or has been drawn over surface (*vandals left a trail of wreckage*; *slimy trail of a slug*). **2.** Track, scent followed in hunting, (*on*, *off*, *the* *trail*); beaten path esp. through wild region (BLAZE[4] *a trail*, whence **~-blazer,** esp. fig.); **at the ~**, (Mil.) with arms trailed; **~-net,** drag-net. **3.** *v.t.* Draw along behind one esp. on the ground, (*trailed her dress through the mud*; *trailing clouds of glory*); drag (one*self*, one's limbs) along wearily etc.; follow the trail of, pursue, shadow; (Mil.) **~ arms,** let rifle etc. hang balanced in one hand and ||parallel to ground; *trail* one's COAT. **4.** *v.i.* Be drawn along behind (*skirt trails on the ground*); hang loosely; walk wearily, lag, straggle; be losing in game or other contest; tail *away* or *off*; (of plant) grow to some length over ground, wall, etc. **5. ~'ing edge,** rear edge of aircraft's wing etc., (Electr.) part of pulse in which amplitude diminishes; **~'ing wheel** (not given direct motive power). [ME, n. f. v. f. OF *traillier* to tow, or f. MLG *treilen* haul, f. Rom. **tragulare* f. L *tragula* drag-net]

trai'ler *n.* In vbl senses; trailing plant; set of short extracts from cinema or television film, exhibited to advertise it in advance; wheeled vehicle (esp. caravan) drawn by another. [f. prec. + -ER[1]]

train *v.* & *n.* **1.** *v.t.* Bring (person, animal, etc.) to desired state or standard of efficiency etc. by instruction and practice (*train up a child in the way he should go*; *was trained for the ministry*; *a trained nurse, soldier*; *trained faculties*; *did not escape his trained eye*). **2.** Teach and accustom (person, animal, *to* do, *to* action; *dog is trained to jump through hoop*; *trained to all outdoor exercises, to obey* or *obedience*). **3.** *v.t.* & *i.* Bring (horse, athlete, one*self*) or come to physical efficiency by exercise and diet (*is training for the boat-race*; *trains horses*; *is only half-trained*); **~ down** (to lower weight). **4.** *v.t.* Cause (plant) to grow in required shape (*up* or *over wall* etc.). **5.** Point, aim, (gun, camera, *on* object etc.). **6.** (arch.) Entice, lure, (*away* etc.); draw along (esp. heavy thing). **7.** *v.i.* & *t.* (colloq.) Go by train; perform (journey) thus. **8.** Hence **~'ABLE** *a.*, **~EE'** *n.* **9.** *n.* Thing drawn along behind or forming hinder part, esp. elongated part of woman's skirt trailing on ground or of official robe, long or conspicuous tail of bird. **10.** Body of followers, retinue, (*formed part of his train*; *a train of admirers*); **in the ~ of,** as a sequel of. **11.** Succession or series of persons or things (*long train of sight-seers, of camels*; *wagon train*; *by an unlucky train of events*; *suggested a whole train of ideas*; *train of thought*); **in ~**, properly arranged or directed. **12.** Series of railway carriages or trucks drawn by same engine(s). **13.** Line of combustible material to lead fire to charge of explosive. **14.** (Mil.) Artillery and other equipment for siege or battle, with their vehicles and attendants. **15.** Series of connected wheels or parts in machinery. **16. ~'band,** (Hist.) each division of London citizen soldiery esp. in Stuart period; **~-bearer,** (1) person employed to hold up train of another's robe, (2) long-tailed S. Amer. humming-bird; **~-ferry,** vessel that conveys a railway train across a piece of water; **~-mile,** one mile travelled by one train, as unit of traffic; **~'sick,** affected with nausea caused by motion of train; **~-spotter,** collector of locomotive numbers. **17.** Hence **~'LESS** *a.* [ME, (n. f. OF *train(e)*) f. OF *traïner*, *trahiner*, f. Rom. **traginare*, ult. f. L *trahere* draw]

trai'ner *n.* In vbl senses; one who trains horses, athletes, etc., for races etc., or sees to physical fitness of footballers etc.; aircraft or device simulating it used to train pilots. [f. prec. + -ER[1]]

trai'ning *n.* In vbl senses; PHYSICAL *training*; **in ~**, (1) undergoing physical training (so **go into ~**), (2) physically fit as result of this, opp. **out of ~**; **~-college, -school,** (for training persons, formerly esp. teachers); **~-ship** (on which boys are taught seamanship etc.). [ME, f. TRAIN + -ING[1]]

trai'n-oil *n.* Oil got from blubber of whale (esp. of the right whale). [f. obs. *train, trane* train-oil f. MLG *trān*, MDu. *traen*, app. = TEAR[2]]

traipse *n.*, & *v.i.* (colloq. or dial.) **1.** *n.* Slattern; tedious journey on foot. **2.** *v.i.* Tramp or trudge wearily; go *about* on errands. [16th c. *trapes* v.; orig. unkn.]

trait (trā) *n.* Distinguishing feature in character, appearance, habit, or portrayal. [F, f. L *tractus* (as TRACT[1])]

trai'tor *n.* One who is false to his allegiance or acts disloyally (*to* country, king, cause, religion, principles, him*self*, etc.); so **~OUS** *a.*, **trai'tRESS**[1] *n.* [ME, f. OF *traït(o)ur* f. L *traditor -oris* (*tradere*; see TRADITION, -OR)]

tră'jèctorў (*or* trajĕ'-) *n.* Path described by projectile moving or object developing under given forces; (Geom.) curve or surface cutting system of curves or surfaces at constant angle. [orig. a., f. med. L *trajectorius* f. L *traicere traject-* (*tra-* = TRANS-, *jacere* throw); see -ORY]

tra-la' (-ah') *int.* expr. joy or gaiety. [imit. of song]

trăm[1] *n.* ||**~('car)**, passenger car running on rails laid in public road; four-wheeled car used in coal-mines; ||**~-lines,** rails for tramcar, (fig.) immovable principle etc., (colloq.) either pair of long parallel lines at side of lawn-tennis doubles court, similar lines at side or back of badminton court; **~-road,** (Hist.) road with wooden, stone, or metal wheel-tracks; **~'way,** (1) tram-road, (2) ||rails for tramcar. [f. MLG & MDu. *trame* balk, beam, barrow-shaft]

trăm[2] *n.* **~ (silk)**, double silk thread used for weft of some velvets and silks. [f. F *trame* f. L *trama* weft]

tră'mmel *n.*, & *v.t.* (||-ll-). **1.** *n.* Triple drag-net for fish, which are trapped in a pocket formed when they attempt to swim through; *hook in fireplace for kettle etc.; instrument for drawing ellipses etc. with bar sliding in perpendicular grooves; beam-compass; (usu. in *pl.* and fig.) impediment(s) to free movement or action (*trammels of etiquette, of official routine*). **2.** *v.t.* (usu. fig.) Confine, hamper, with trammels. [in sense 'net' ME, f. OF *tramail* f. med. L *tramaculum, tremaculum*, perh. f. as TRI- + *macula* (MAIL[1]); later history uncert.]

tramonta'na (trah-; -ah'-) *n.* Cold north wind in Adriatic. [It.; see foll.]

tramŏ'ntāne *a.* & *n.* **1.** *a.* (Situated or living) on other side of mountains, esp. the Alps; (fig., from It. point of view) foreign, barbarous. **2.** *n.* Tramontane person; = prec. [ME, f. It. *tramontano* f. L TRANS(*montanus* f. *mons montis* mountain) beyond the mountains; cf. -ANE]

trămp *v.* & *n.* **1.** *v.i.* Walk heavily and firmly (*heard him tramping about overhead*); walk, go on foot; be a tramp. **2.** *v.t.* Perform (journey), traverse (country), on foot (usu. reluctantly, wearily, etc.); stamp (*down* etc.), tread on, trample. **3.** *n.* Sound of person(s) walking or marching or of horse's steps. **4.** Journey on foot, walk. **5.** Iron plate protecting sole of boot from wear and tear of spade in digging; part of spade that it strikes. **6.** Person who tramps the roads in search of work or as vagrant; this mode of life; (sl.) dissolute woman. **7. (Ocean) ~**, freight-vessel, esp. steamer, running on no regular line. [ME *trampe* f. Gmc **tremp-*, **tramp-*]

tră'mpl|e *v.* & *n.* **1.** *v.t.* Tread under foot, press down or crush thus, (*trampled to death by elephants*). **2.** *v.i.* **~e on,** tread heavily on, (fig.) treat roughly or with contempt, show no consideration for, (person, feelings, etc.). **3.** Hence ~ER[1] *n.* **4.** *n.* Sound or act of trampling. [ME, f. prec. + -LE 3]

tră'mpoline (-ēn) *n.*, & *v.i.* **1.** *n.* Canvas sheet connected by springs to horizontal frame, used by acrobats etc. **2.** *v.i.* Use trampoline. [f. It. *trampolino* (*trampoli* stilts)]

trance (-ah-) *n.*, & *v.t.* **1.** *n.* Sleeplike state without response to stimuli; half-conscious state; ecstasy, rapture, extreme exaltation; catalepsy; hypnotic state. **2.** *v.t.* (poet.) = ENTRANCE[2]. [ME, f. OF *transe* (*transir* depart, fall into trance f. L *transire*; see TRANSIT)]

tranche (-ahnsh) *n.* Portion, esp. of income, or of block of shares. [F, = slice (as TRENCH)]

tră'nquĭl *a.* Calm, serene, unruffled, not agitated, (*preserved a tranquil mind*; *tranquil surface of pond*); hence or cogn. ~**lITY** (-ĭ'l-) *n.*, ~LY[2] *adv.* [f. F *tranquille* or f. L *tranquillus*]

tră'nquĭllīz|e, -īs|e (-īz), ***-ĭlĭ-,** *v.t.* Make tranquil, esp. by drug etc.; hence ~ER[1] *n.*, drug used to diminish anxiety. [f. prec. + -IZE]

trăns- (*or* -z; *or* trah-) *pref.* w. sense 'across, beyond' (*transcontinental, transgress, trans-Siberian*), 'on or to the other side of' (*transatlantic, translunary*; opp. *cis-*), 'through' (*transonic, transpierce*), 'into another state or place' (*transcribe, transform, transliterate*), 'surpassing, transcending' (*transfinite*); (Chem.) (1) having two atoms or groups on opposite sides of plane of symmetry, (2) having higher atomic number than (*transuranic*). [f. or after L *trans* across]

trănsă'ct (*or* -z-; *or* trah-) *v.t.* Perform, carry through, (business); hence ~OR *n.* [f. L TRANS-(*igere act-* = *agere* do)]

trănsă'ction (*or* -z-; *or* trah-) *n.* Management of business (*left the transaction of the matter to him*); piece of esp. commercial business done (*the transactions of a firm*; *the transaction will not bear looking into*; *mixed up in shady transactions*); (in *pl.*) reports of discussions, papers read etc., at meetings of learned society (*Philosophical Transactions of the Royal Society*). [ME, f. LL *transactio* (as prec.; see -ION)]

trănsă'lpīne (*or* -z-; *or* trah-) *a.* Beyond the Alps (usu. from It. point of view). [f. L TRANS(*alpinus* ALPINE)]

trănsatlă'ntĭc (*or* -z-; *or* trah-) *a.* Beyond the Atlantic, ||American, *European; crossing the Atlantic (*transatlantic flight, line, steamer*). [f. TRANS- + ATLANTIC]

trănscei'ver (-nsē'v-; *or* -ah-) *n.* Combined radio transmitter and receiver. [f. TRANSMITTER + RECEIVER]

trănscĕ'nd (*or* -ah-) *v.t.* Be beyond the range or domain or grasp of (human experience, reason, description, belief, etc.); excel, surpass. [ME, f. OF *transcendre* or f. L *transcendere* (TRANS-, *scandere* climb)]

trănscĕ'nd|ent (*or* -ah-) *a.* & *n.* **1.** *a.* Excelling, surpassing, (*transcendent merit, genius*); transcending human experience. **2.** (Scholastic Philos.) Higher than, not included under any of, Aristotle's ten categories. **3.** (Kantian Philos.) Not realizable in experience. **4.** (Esp. of God) existing apart from, not subject to limitations of, the material universe, opp. *immanent*. **5.** Hence or cogn. ~ENCE, ~ENCY, *ns.*, ~**ent**LY[2] *adv.* **6.** *n.* (Philos.) Transcendent thing. [as prec.; see -ENT]

trănscendĕ'ntal (*or* trah-) *a.* & *n.* **1.** *a.* = prec. 2. **2.** (Kantian Philos.) Of a priori character, presupposed in and necessary to experience; ~ **cognition,** a priori knowledge; ~ **object,** real (unknown and unknowable) object; ~ **unity** (brought about by cognition). **3.** Explaining matter and objective things as products of the subjective mind (esp. in Schelling's philosophy); regarding the divine as guiding principle in man (esp. in Emerson's philosophy). **4.** (pop.) Abstruse, vague, obscure, visionary, abstract; ~ **meditation** (seeking to induce detachment from problems and relief from anxiety etc.). **5.** (Math.) (Of function) not capable of being produced by the algebraical operations of addition, multiplication, and involution, or the inverse operations. **6.** Hence ~LY[2] *adv.* **7.** *n.* Transcendental term, conception, etc. [f. med. L *transcendentalis* (as prec.; see -AL)]

trănscendĕ'ntal|ĭsm (*or* trah-) *n.* Transcendental philosophy; exalted or visionary language; so ~IST (2) *n.*, ~IZE (3) *v.t.* [f. prec. + -ISM]

trănscŏntĭnĕ'ntal (*or* -z-; *or* trah-) *a.* (Of railway etc.) extending across a continent. [f. TRANS- + CONTINENTAL]

trănscr|ī'be (*or* trah-) *v.t.* Make copy of, esp. in writing; transliterate; write out (shorthand) in ordinary characters; record for subsequent reproduction; broadcast in this form; arrange (music) for different instrument etc.; hence or cogn. ~**ī'b**ER[1], ~**ĭ'pt**ION, *ns.*, ~**ĭ'ption**AL, ~**ĭ'pt**IVE, *adjs.* [f. L *transcribere* (TRANS-, *scribere script-* write)]

tră'nscrĭpt (*or* trah'-) *n.* (Written or recorded) copy. [ME f. OF *transcrit* f. L *transcriptum* neut. p.p. (as n.); see prec.]

trănsdū'cer (*or* -z-; *or* -ah-) *n.* Device that converts variations of one quantity into those of another (e.g. pressure into voltage). [f. L TRANS(*ducere* lead) + -ER[1]]

trănsĕ'ct (*or* -z-; *or* -ah-) *v.t.* Cut across or transversely; so ~ION *n.* [f. TRANS- + L *secare sect-* cut]

tră'nsĕpt (*or* -ah'-) *n.* Transverse part of cruciform church; either arm (**north, south,** ~) of this; hence ~AL (-ĕ'p-) *a.* [f. mod. L *transeptum* (as TRANS-, SEPTUM)]

transexual. Var. of TRANSSEXUAL.

trănsfer'[1] (*or* -ah-) *v.* (**-rr-**). **1.** *v.t.* Convey, remove, hand over, (thing etc. *from* person or place *to* another); make over possession of (property, ticket, rights, etc., *to* person). **2.** Convey (drawing etc.) from one surface to another esp. to lithographic stone by means of transfer-paper; remove (picture) from one surface to another esp. from wood or wall to canvas. **3.** Move (person) to another group, (esp. Footb.) club, etc.; change (sense of word etc.) by extension or metaphor. **4.** *v.i.* Change from one station, route, etc., to another to continue journey; change or be moved to another group, club, etc. **5.** Hence ~EE', ~OR, ~RER[1], *ns.* [ME, f. F *transférer* or f. L TRANS(*ferre lat-* bear)]

tră'nsfer[2] (*or* -ah'-) *n.* **1.** Transferring or being transferred; conveyance of property or right, document effecting this; *ticket allowing journey to be continued on another route etc. **2.** Design etc. (to be) conveyed from one surface to another; small usu. coloured picture or design on paper from which it is transferable to other surface. **3.** ~**-book,** register of transfers of property, shares, etc.; *~ **company** (conveying passengers or luggage between usu. nearby stations); ~ **fee** (paid for transfer esp. of professional footballer); ~**-ink** (for making designs on lithographic stone or transfer-paper); ~ **list** (of footballers available for transfer); ~**-paper** (specially coated to receive impression of transfer-ink and transfer it to stone); ~ **RNA** (conveying amino-acid molecule from cytoplasm to ribosome for use in protein synthesis); *~ **table,** railway traverse-table. [f. prec.]

tră'nsfer|able (*or* -ah'-; *or* -ẽr'-) *a.* Capable of being transferred; ~**able vote,** indication on ballot-paper of candidate to whom vote shall be transferred if candidate for whom it is first cast is eliminated in one of successive counts or has more votes than are needed for election; hence ~ABI'LITY *n.* [f. TRANSFER¹ + -ABLE]

tră'nsference (*or* -ah'-) *n.* Action of transferring; (Psych.) redirection of desires etc. to new object. [f. TRANSFER¹ + -ENCE]

trănsfĕ'rrĭn (*or* -ah-) *n.* Protein transporting iron in blood of animals. [f. TRANS- + L *ferrum* iron + -IN]

trănsfĭgūrā'tion (*or* trah-) *n.* Change of form or appearance, esp. that of Christ (Matt. 17:2, Mark 9:2–3); (*T*~) festival of Christ's transfiguration, 6 Aug. [ME f. OF, or f. L *transfiguratio* (as foll.; see -ATION)]

trănsfĭ'gure (-ger; *or* trah-) *v.t.* Change in form or appearance, esp. so as to elevate or idealize. [ME, f. OF *transfigurer* or f. L TRANS(*figurare* FIGURE²)]

trănsfī'nīte (*or* -ah-) *a.* Beyond or surpassing what is finite; (Math., of number) exceeding all finite numbers. [f. TRANS- + FINITE]

trănsfĭ'x (*or* -ah-) *v.t.* Pierce with lance etc.; (of horror etc.) root (person) to the spot, paralyse faculties of; hence ~ION (-kshon) *n.* [f. L TRANS(*figere fix-* fix)]

trănsfôr'm¹ (*or* -ah-) *v.* **1.** *v.t.* Make (esp. considerable) change in the form, outward appearance, character, disposition, etc., of (*caterpillar is transformed into butterfly*; *10 years in India have transformed him* (in character or physique); *a beard may transform a man beyond recognition*); (Electr.) change voltage etc. of (current); hence ~ABLE, ~ATIVE, *adjs.* **2.** *v.i.* Undergo transformation (*to, into*). [ME, f. OF *transformer*, or f. L TRANS(*formare* FORM²)]

tră'nsfôrm² (*or* -ah'-) *n.* (Math. & Ling.) Product of transformation. [f. prec.]

trănsformā'tion (*or* trah-) *n.* Transforming or being transformed (*has undergone a great transformation*); (Zool.) change of form esp. of insects; change from solid to liquid or from liquid to gaseous state or vice versa; (Math.) change from one (geometrical) figure or expression or function to another of same magnitude, value, etc.; (Phys.) transmutation of element; (Ling.) statement of basic equivalence of differently-structured sentences; woman's wig; ~ **scene,** elaborate spectacular scene in pantomime with scenery etc. changing in sight of audience; hence ~AL *a.* [ME f. OF, or f. LL *transformatio* (as TRANSFORM¹; see -ATION)]

trănsfôr'mer (*or* -ah-) *n.* In vbl senses; apparatus for reducing or increasing voltage of alternating current. [f. TRANSFORM¹ + -ER¹]

trănsfū's|e (-z; *or* -ah-) *v.t.* Cause (fluid, or fig. quality etc.) to pass from one vessel etc. to another; permeate (lit. or fig.); (Med.) transfer (blood) from veins of person or animal to those of another, inject (liquid) into blood-vessel to replace lost fluid; so ~ION (-zhon) *n.* [ME, f. L TRANS(*fundere fus-* pour)]

trănsgrĕ'ss (*or* -z-; *or* -ah-) *v.t.* Violate, infringe, go beyond bounds set by, (commandment, law, limitation, or abs.); so ~ION (-shon), ~OR, *ns.*, ~IVE *a.* [f. F *transgresser* or f. L TRANS(*gredi gress-* = *gradi* go)]

tranship. Var. of TRANS-SHIP.

trănshū'mance (-s-h-; *or* trah-) *n.* Seasonal moving of livestock to another region. [F (*transhumer* f. L TRANS- + *humus* ground; see -ANCE)]

tră'nsĭ|ent (*or* -z-; *or* -ah'-) *a.* & *n.* **1.** *a.* Not permanent (*the transient affairs of this life*); quickly passing away, fleeting; of short duration, momentary, hasty, (*a transient gleam of hope*); (Mus.) unessential, serving only to connect (*transient chord, note*); hence ~ENCE, ~ENCY, *ns.*, ~**ent**LY² *adv.* **2.** *n.* Temporary visitor, worker, etc.; (Electr.) brief current etc. [f. L TRANS(*ire* go).; see -ENT]

trănsĭllu'mĭn|āte (-ōō'-; *or* trah-) *v.t.* Pass strong light through in order to inspect, esp. for diagnosis; so ~A'TION *n.* [f. TRANS- + ILLUMINATE]

||**trănsīr'ē** *n.* Custom-house permit for passage of goods. [L TRANS(*ire* go) go across]

trănsĭ'stor (*or* -z-; *or* -ah-) *n.* Semiconductor device with three electrodes, performing same functions as thermionic valve but smaller, stronger, and consuming less power; ~ (**radio**), portable radio set equipped with transistors; hence ~IZE *v.t.*, design with transistors (rather than valves). [portmanteau wd, f. TRANSFER¹ + RESISTOR]

tră'nsĭt (*or* -z-; *or* -ah'-) *n.* & *v.* **1.** *n.* Going, conveying, being conveyed, across or over or through (*allowed 2 days for the transit of the lake*; *improved methods of transit by rail*; *goods delayed in transit*); passage, route, (*the overland transit*); *local conveying of passengers on public routes; apparent passage of heavenly body across meridian of place; apparent passage of heavenly body across disc of sun or planet. **2.** ~ **camp** (for temporary accommodation of soldiers, refugees, etc.); ~**-circle, -instrument,** (for observing transit of heavenly body across meridian); ~**-compass, -theodolite,** surveyor's instrument for measuring horizontal angle; ~**-duty** (paid on goods passing through a country); ~ **visa** (allowing only passage through country). **3.** *v.t.* & *i.* Make transit (across). [ME, f. L *transitus* f. TRANS(*ire it-* go)]

trănsĭ'tion (*or* -z-; *or* -ah-) *n.* Passage or change from one place or state or act or set of circumstances to another (*came by an abrupt transition into hilly country*; *we live in an age of transition*; *is subject to frequent transitions from high spirits to depression*); (Mus.) momentary modulation; (Art) change from one style to another, esp. (Archit.) from Norman to Early English; ~ **point** (Phys., at which different phases of same substance can be in equilibrium); hence ~AL, ~ARY¹, *adjs.* [F, or f. L *transitio* (as prec.; see -ION)]

tră'nsĭtĭv|e (*or* -z-; *or* -ah'-) *a.* **1.** (Gram.) Taking a direct object expressed or understood (e.g. *pick* in: *pick peas*, *pick till you are tired*; opp. to *intransitive* as in *picked at the hole to make it bigger*). **2.** (Logic, of relation) such as to be valid for any two members of a sequence if it is valid for every pair of successive members. **3.** Hence ~**e**LY² (-vlĭ) *adv.*, ~**e**NESS (-vn-), ~ITY (-ĭ'v-), *ns.* [f. LL *transitivus* (as TRANSIT; see -ITIVE)]

tră'nsĭtor|ȳ (*or* -z-; *or* -ah'-) *a.* Not permanent, lasting only a short time; ~**y action,** (Law) one that can be brought in any country irrespective of where the transaction etc. occurred; hence ~ĬLY² *adv.*, ~ĬNESS *n.* [ME, f. AF *transitorie*, OF *transitoire* f. L *transitorius* (as TRANSIT; see -ORY)]

trănsl|ā'te (*or* -z-; *or* trah-) *v.t.* **1.** Express the sense of (word, sentence, speech, book, poem, etc., or abs.) in or *into* another language, in or *to* another form of representation, in plainer words, etc. **2.** Infer or declare the significance of, interpret, (signs, movements, conduct, hint, etc.; *I translated this as a protest*; *translated his gestures to the bystanders*). **3.** Move from one person, place, or condition to another; (Eccl.) remove (bishop) to another see, (saint's relics etc.) to another place; (Bibl.) convey to heaven without death; transform. **4.** (Mech.) Cause (body) to move so that all its parts travel in the same direction, impart motion without rotation to. **5.** Hence or cogn. **~ā'**TABLE, **~ā'tion**AL, *adjs.*, ~A'TION, **~ā'**TOR, *ns.* [ME, f. L *translatus*, p.p. of *transferre* (see TRANSFER[1]) + -ATE[3]]

trănslĭ'ter|āte (*or* -z-; *or* trah-) *v.t.* Represent (word etc., or abs.) in the more or less corresponding characters of a different alphabet or language; hence ~A'TION, **~ā**TOR, *ns.* [f. TRANS- + L *littera* letter + -ATE[3]]

trănslocā'tion (*or* -z-; *or* trah-) *n.* Movement from place to place, esp. (Bot.) of substances in a plant. [f. TRANS- + LOCATION]

trănslū'c|ent (*or* -ah-; *or* -z-; *or* -ōō'-) *a.* Transmitting light but not transparent; transparent; hence ~ENCE, ~ENCY, *ns.*, **~ent**LY[2] *adv.* [f. L TRANS(*lucēre* shine); see -ENT]

trănslū'narȳ (*or* -z-; *or* trah-; *or* -lōō'-) *a.* Lying beyond the moon; (fig.) insubstantial, visionary. [f. TRANS-, after *sublunary*]

trănsmari'ne (-ē'n; *or* -z-; *or* trah-) *a.* Situated or going beyond the sea. [f. L TRANS(*marinus* MARINE)]

tră'nsmĭgr|āte (*or* -ī'g-; *or* -z-; *or* trah-). *v.i.* (Of soul) pass into, become incarnate in, a different body, undergo metempsychosis; migrate; hence or cogn. ~ANT *a.* & *n.* (esp. alien passing through one country on way to another), ~A'TION, **~ā**TOR, *ns.*, **~at**ORY (-ī'g-) *a.* [ME, f. L TRANS(*migrare* MIGRATE)]

trănsmĭ'ssion (-shon; *or* -z-; *or* -ah-) *n.* Transmitting or being transmitted; broadcast programme; gear by which power is transmitted from engine to axle in motor vehicle; ~ **line,** conductor(s) carrying electricity over large distances with minimum losses. [f. L TRANS(*missio*; see MISSION)]

trăns|mĭ't (*or* -z-; *or* -ah-) *v.t.* (**-tt-**). **1.** Pass on, hand on, transfer, communicate, (*will transmit the message, the parcel, the title, the disease, the faculty; his writings have transmitted the principle to posterity*). **2.** Allow to pass through, be a medium for, serve to communicate, (heat, light, sound, electricity, emotion, signal, news); hence or cogn. **~mĭ'**SSIBLE, **~mĭ'**SSIVE, **~mĭ'tt**ABLE, *adjs.* [ME, f. L TRANS(*mittere miss-* send)]

trănsmĭ'tter (*or* -z-; *or* -ah-) *n.* In vbl senses; equipment used to transmit message, signal, etc.; substance transferring message at junction of nerve fibre. [f. prec. + -ER[1]]

trănsmŏ'grĭ|fȳ (*or* -z-; *or* -ah-) *v.t.* (joc.) Transform esp. in magical or surprising manner; hence ~FICA'TION *n.* [17th c., of unkn. orig.]

trănsmŏ'ntāne (*or* -z-; *or* trah-; *or* -ā'n) *a.* Tramontane. [f. L *transmontanus* (see TRAMONTANE)]

trănsmūtā'tion (*or* -z-; *or* trah-) *n.* Transmuting; change into another form, nature, or substance; (Alch.) supposed change of baser metals into gold etc.; (Phys.) change of one element into another by nuclear bombardment etc.; (Geom.) change of figure or body into another of same area or volume; (Biol.) Lamarck's theory of change of one species into another, whence ~IST (2) *n.* [ME f. OF, or f. LL *transmutatio* (as foll.; see -ATION)]

trănsmū't|e (*or* -z-; *or* -ah-) *v.t.* Change the form, nature, or substance of; subject to transmutation; hence or cogn. ~ABI'LITY, ~ER[1], *ns.*, ~ABLE, ~ATIVE, *adjs.* [ME, f. L TRANS(*mutare* change)]

trănsnă'tional (*or* -z-; *or* trah-) *a.* Extending beyond national boundaries. [f. TRANS- + NATIONAL]

trănsōcēă'nĭc (*or* -z-; *or* trah-; *or* -ōshĭ-) *a.* Situated beyond the ocean; (concerned with) crossing the ocean (*transoceanic flight of birds*). [f. TRANS- + OCEANIC]

tră'nsom *n.* **1.** Horizontal (cf. MULLION) bar of wood or stone across window or top of door; ~ **window** (divided by transom, or placed above transom of door or larger window). **2.** Each of several beams fixed across stern-post of ship; beam across saw-pit; strengthening crossbar. **3.** Hence ~ED[2] (-md) *a.* [ME *traversayn, transyn, -ing*, f. OF *traversin* (TRAVERSE)]

trănsŏ'nĭc (*or* -z-; *or* -ah-) *a.* Relating to speeds close to that of sound. [f. TRANS- + SONIC, after *supersonic* etc.]

trănspacĭ'fĭc (*or* -z-; *or* trah-) *a.* Beyond the Pacific; crossing the Pacific. [f. TRANS- + PACIFIC]

tră'nspadāne (*or* trah'-) *a.* Situated beyond (usu. = north of) the Po. [f. L TRANS(*padanus* f. *Padus* river Po in N. Italy; see -ANE)]

transparence. Var. of foll. 1.

trănspār'encȳ (*or* -ă'r-; *or* trah-) *n.* **1.** Being transparent. **2.** Picture, inscription, etc., made visible by light behind it; (Photog.) positive picture on glass as ornament or lantern-slide, or otherwise to be viewed by light from behind it; **his** etc. **T~** (arch. burlesque title = G *Durchlaucht*; cf. SERENITY). [f. med. L *transparentia* (as foll.; see -ENCY)]

trănspār'ent (*or* -ă'r-; *or* trah-) *a.* **1.** Transmitting rays of light without diffusion so that bodies behind can be distinctly seen (cf. *translucent*); transmitting heat or other electromagnetic rays without distortion. **2.** (fig.) (Of disguise, pretext, etc.) easily seen through, (of motive, quality, etc.) easily seen through attempted disguise; evident, obvious, (*transparent sincerity*); easily understood; free from affectation or disguise, frank. **3.** Hence ~LY[2] *adv.*, ~NESS *n.* [ME f. OF, f. med. L *transparens* f. L TRANS(*parēre* appear) shine through; see -ENT]

trănspier'ce (*or* -ah-) *v.t.* Pierce through. [f. TRANS- + PIERCE]

trănspīr'|e (*or* -ah-) *v.* **1.** *v.t.* Emit through skin or lungs; send off in vapour. **2.** *v.i.* Be emitted thus; pass off as perspiration; (Bot., of plant or leaf) exhale watery vapour. **3.** (fig.) (Of secret etc.) leak out, come to be known; (colloq.) occur, happen. **4.** Hence or cogn. ~ABLE, **~at**ORY, *adjs.*, **trănspĭr**A'TION (*or* trah-) *n.* [f. F *transpirer* or f. med. L *transpirare* f. L TRANS- + *spirare* breathe]

trănspla'nt[1] (-lah'-; *or* trah-) *v.t.* Plant in another place; remove and establish, esp. cause to live, in another place; (Surg.) transfer (living tissue or organ) and implant in another part of body or in another person's body; hence or cogn. ~ABLE *a.*, ~A'TION, ~ER[1] (1, 2), *ns.* [ME, f. LL TRANS(*plantare* PLANT[2])]

tră'nsplant[2] (-lah-; *or* trah'-) *n.* Transplanting of tissue or organ; thing transplanted. [f. prec.]

trănspŏ'nder (*or* -z-; *or* -ah-) *n.* Device for receiving radio signal and automatically transmitting a different signal. [f. TRANSMIT + RESPOND[1] + -ER[1]]

trănspŏ'ntīne (*or* -z-; *or* -ah-) *a.* On the other side of a bridge, esp. on south side of Thames; cheaply melodramatic, like the plays in 19th-c. Surrey-side theatres. [f. TRANS- + L *pons pontis* bridge + -INE[1]]

trănspōr't[1] (*or* -ah-) *v.t.* **1.** Convey (person, goods, troops, baggage, etc.) from one place to another, whence ~ER[1] *n.*; **~er bridge** (carrying vehicles etc. across water on suspended moving platform). **2.** (Hist.) Convey (criminal) to penal

For other words in ***trans-*** **see** TRANS-.

colony, deport. **3.** (esp. in *p.p.*) Affect with strong emotion (*transported with joy, anger, fear*). [ME, f. OF *transporter*, or f. L TRANS(*portare* carry)]

tră'nspôrt[2] (*or* -ah'-) *n.* **1.** Conveyance or transportation from place to place, means of this (*the transport has arrived*); ~ **café** (providing meals for (esp. commercial) motor-vehicle drivers). **2.** Vessel employed to carry soldiers, stores, etc., to destination. **3.** (Hist.) Transported convict. **4.** Vehement emotion (*in a transport of rage*; *was in transports* (of joy etc.)). [ME, f. prec.]

trănspôr'tǀable (*or* trah-) *a.* **1.** That may be transported; hence ~ABI'LITY *n.* **2.** (Hist.) (Of offender or offence) punishable by transportation. [f. TRANSPORT[1] + -ABLE]

trănsportā'tion (*or* trah-) *n.* Conveying or being conveyed from place to place; *means of this; (Hist.) removal to penal colony. [f. TRANSPORT[1] + -ATION]

trănspō'sǀe (-z; *or* -ah-) *v.t.* Cause (two or more things) to change places; change position of (thing) in series; (Alg.) transfer (term) with changed sign to other side of equation; change natural or existing order or position of (words, a word) in sentence; (Mus.) write or play in different key; **~ing instrument** (producing notes different in pitch from the written notes); **~ing piano** etc. (on which transposition may be effected mechanically); hence ~AL, ~ER[1], *ns.* [ME, = transform, f. OF TRANS(*poser*, see COMPOSE)]

trănsposi'tion (-zĭ'-; *or* -ah-) *n.* Transposing, being transposed; hence or cogn. ~AL, **trănspŏ'sĭt**IVE (-zĭ-; *or* -ah-), *adjs.* [F, or f. LL TRANS(*positio*; see POSITION)]

trănssĕ'xūal (-zs-; *or* trah-; *or* -kshōō-) *a.* & *n.* (Person) having physical characteristics of one sex and psychological characteristics of the other; hence ~ISM (2) *n.* [f. TRANS- + SEXUAL]

trăns-shĭ'p (-nsh-; *or* -ns-sh- *or* -nzsh-; *or* -ah-) *v.t.* & *i.* (-**pp**-). Transfer from one ship or conveyance to another; hence ~MENT *n.* [f. TRANS- + SHIP[2]]

trans-sonic. Var of TRANSONIC.

trănsubstă'ntiǀāte (-shĭ-; *or* trah-) *v.t.* Change from one substance into another, esp. (Theol.) convert whole substance of Eucharistic elements into body and blood of Christ by consecration; so ~A'TION (*or* -sĭ-) *n.* [f. med. L *transubstantiare* (as TRANS-, SUBSTANCE) + -ATE[3]]

trănsū'dǀe (*or* -ah-) *v.i.* (Of fluid) pass through pores or interstices of membrane etc.; so ~A'TION *n.*, **~at**ORY *a.* [f. F *transsuder* f. OF *tressuer* f. Gallo-Rom. *TRANS(*sudare* sweat)]

trănsūră'nĭc (*or* trah-) *a.* (Chem.) (Of element) having higher atomic number than uranium. [f. TRANS- + URANIC]

Trănsvaa'l (-ah'l; *or* trah-; *or* -z-) *n.* ~ **daisy,** orange-flowered S. Afr. herb (*Gerbera jamesoni*). [~ in S. Africa]

trănsvêr'sal (-nz-; *or* trah-) *a.* & *n.* **1.** *a.* (Of line) cutting a system of lines; hence ~ITY (-ă'l-) *n.*, ~LY[2] *adv.* **2.** *n.* Transversal line. [ME, f. med. L *transversalis* (as foll.; see -AL)]

trănsvêr'se (-z-; *or* -ah-; *or* tră'-) *a.* Situated, arranged, acting, in crosswise direction (*transverse artery, ligament, section, stress*); ~ **magnet** (whose poles are at sides and not ends); ~ **wāve** (vibrating at right angles to direction of propagation); hence ~LY[2] (-slĭ) *adv.* [f. L TRANS(*vertere vers-* turn)]

trănsvĕ'st (*or* -ah-) *v.t.* (Psych.) Clothe (usu. one*self*) in other garments esp. those of opposite sex; hence or cogn. ~ISM (3), ~IST (2), ~ITE[1] (1), *ns.* [f. TRANS- + L *vestire* clothe]

tră'nter *n.* (dial.) Carrier; hawker. [app. f. AF *traventer*, AL *trave(n)tarius*, of unkn. orig.]

trăp[1] *n.*, & *v.t.* (-**pp**-). **1.** *n.* Pitfall or enclosure or mechanical structure for catching animals, affording entrance but not exit and often baited and having door or lid actuated by spring; device for pigeons to enter but not leave loft; arrangement to measure speed of motorist without his knowledge, for detecting infringement of speed limit; golf bunker; (fig.) trick or arrangement for betraying person into speech or act (*is always setting traps for me*; *is this* (*question* etc.) *a trap?*). **2.** Device for suddenly releasing bird, or throwing ball etc. into air, to be shot at; compartment from which greyhound is released at start of race; shoe-shaped wooden device with pivoted bar that sends ball from its heel into air on being struck at other end with bat (**~-ball,** game played with this). **3.** Device for preventing passage of steam etc.; U-shaped or other section of pipe so arranged as to prevent return flow of gas by means of permanent barrier of liquid. **4.** Two-wheeled carriage with springs, e.g. dogcart. **5.** = *trapdoor*; (sl.) mouth (*shut your trap*). **6.** (colloq., esp. in *pl.*) Percussion instrument esp. in jazz band. **7. ~'door,** door flush with surface of floor or roof (~*door spider*, kind that makes hinged trapdoor at top of nest); **~-shooting,** sport of shooting at objects released from trap. **8.** *v.t.* Catch (animal, fig. person) in trap; furnish (place) with traps; stop and retain (as) in trap. [OE *treppe, træppe*; cf. syn. MDu. *trappe*, med. L *trappa*; ult. orig. uncert.]

trăp[2] *n.* (Min.) ~(**-rock**), dark-coloured igneous rock of often columnar structure. [f. Sw. *trapp* (*trappa* stair, the rock freq. presenting a stairlike appearance)]

trăp[3] *v.t.* (-**pp**-). Furnish with trappings. [f. obs. *trap* n., ME f. OF *drap*; see DRAPE]

trăp[4] *n.* **1.** (Sc.) Ladder leading to a loft. **2. ~-cut,** = STEP[2]*-cut*. [app. = Du., MFlem. *trap* flight of steps]

trapes. Var. of TRAIPSE.

trapē'ze *n.* Crossbar(s) suspended by cords used as swing for acrobatics etc. [f. F *trapèze* f. LL *trapezium* (see foll.)]

trapē'ziǀum *n.* (*pl.* ~**a** *or* ~**ums**). ǁQuadrilateral with one pair but not two pairs of sides parallel; *trapezoid. [LL, f. Gk *trapezion* (*trapeza* table)]

tră'pėzoid *n.* ǁQuadrilateral with no two sides parallel; *trapezium; hence ~AL (-oi'd-) *a.* [f. mod. L *trapezoides* f. Gk *trapezoeidēs* (as prec.; see -OID)]

tră'ppėan *a.* Of the nature of the rock TRAP[2]. [f. TRAP[2] + -EAN]

tră'pper *n.* One engaged in trapping wild animals esp. for furs. [f. TRAP[1] + -ER[1]]

tră'ppĭngs (-z) *n. pl.* Harness of horse esp. when ornamental; (fig.) ornamental accessories (*of* office etc.). [ME, f. as TRAP[3] + -ING[1] + -S[1]]

Tră'ppĭst *n.* Member of a Cistercian order founded 1664 at La Trappe and noted for silence and other austerities; hence ~INE[3] *n.*, member of affiliated order of nuns. [f. F *trappiste* (La *Trappe* in Normandy; see -IST)]

tră'ppǀy̆ *a.* (colloq., esp. of things). Tricky, treacherous; hence **~ĭ**NESS *n.* [f. TRAP[1] + -Y[2]]

trăps *n. pl.* (colloq.) Personal belongings, baggage. [perh. contr. f. TRAPPINGS]

trăsh *n.*, & *v.t.* **1.** *n.* Worthless or waste stuff, rubbish, refuse; fragments or loppings of trees etc.; (**cane-**)~, (W. Ind.) refuse of crushed sugar-canes and dried stripped leaves and tops of sugar-cane used as fuel. **2.** Thing, e.g. literary production, of bad workmanship or

For other words in *trans-* see TRANS-.

material; nonsensical talk; worthless person(s). **3.** ***~-can,** dustbin; **~-ice,** broken ice mixed with water; ***white ~,** (derog.) the poor white population in the Southern States. **4.** Hence ~'ERY (1) *n.*, ~'Y[2] *a.* **5.** *v.t.* Strip (sugar-canes) of outer leaves to hasten ripening; discard as worthless; wreck. [16th c., of unkn. orig.]

trăss, tarră's, *n.* Light-coloured tuff used as cement-material. [f. Du. *trass*, earlier *terras, tiras* f. Rom.; cf. TERRACE]

trăttori'a (-ē'*a*) *n.* Italian eating-house. [It.]

trau'ma *n.* (*pl.* **~ta** *or* **~s**). (Morbid condition of body produced by) wound or external violence; (Psych.) emotional shock. [Gk *trauma -matos* wound]

traumă't|ĭc *a.* Of or for wounds; of or causing trauma, (colloq.) unpleasant (*a traumatic experience*). [f. LL f. Gk *traumatikos* (as prec.; see -IC)]

trau'matĭsm *n.* (Condition produced by) action of trauma. [f. as TRAUMA + -ISM]

tră'vail *n.*, & *v.i.* **1.** (arch.) (Suffer) pangs of childbirth. **2.** (literary). (Make) painful or laborious effort. [ME, f. OF (*travail* n. f.) *travaillier* f. Rom. **trepaliare* f. med. L *trepalium* instrument of torture f. L *tres* three + *palus* stake]

tră'vel *v.* (||-ll-) & *n.* **1.** *v.i.* Make a journey esp. one of some length to distant countries (*ordered to travel for his health*); (colloq.) withstand long journey (*wines that travel badly*); act as COMMERCIAL traveller (*for* firm, *in* commodity); (of machine or part) move (*along* bar etc., *in* groove etc.); pass esp. in deliberate or systematic manner from point to point (*his eye travelled over the scene*); (of deer etc.) move onwards in feeding; move or proceed in specified manner or at specified rate (*horse travels slowly*; *light travels faster than sound, travels at thousands of miles per second*; **~ out of the record,** (fig.) wander from subject); (colloq.) move quickly along road etc. **2.** *v.t.* Journey along or through; travel over, traverse, (distance). **3.** (in *p.p.*) Experienced in travelling. **4.** **~ling-bag,** small bag carried in hand, for traveller's requisites; **~ling-cap, -rug,** etc., (of form suitable for travelling); **~ling clock,** small clock in a case; **~ling crane** (moving on esp. overhead support); **~ling fellowship** etc. (enabling holder to travel in order to study); ***~ing salesman,** commercial traveller; **~ling wave** (in which particles of medium move in direction of propagation). **5.** *n.* Travelling esp. in foreign countries (*has returned from his travels*; *cannot read books of travel*(*s*) or *travel books*); range, rate, or mode of motion of part in machinery; **~ agency, agent, bureau,** (making arrangements for travellers); **~-sick**(**ness**), suffering from nausea induced by motion; **~-stained** etc. (as result of travel). [ME, orig. = prec.]

||**tră'veller, *-eler,** *n.* In vbl senses; moving mechanism (esp. TRAVELling crane); = COMMERCIAL *traveller*; **~'s cheque** or ***check** (for fixed amount, encashable on signature in many countries); **~'s joy,** wild clematis; **~'s tale,** incredible and probably untrue story. [ME, f. prec. + -ER[1]]

tră'velŏgue (-ŏg) *n.* Film or illustrated lecture with narrative of travel. [f. TRAVEL, after *monologue* etc.]

tră'verse *n.* & *v.* (*or* travěr's). **1.** *n.* Thing, esp. part of structure, that crosses another; gallery from side to side of church etc.; single line of survey (usu. plotted from compass bearings and chained or paced distances between angular points); tract thus surveyed; (Naut.) zigzag line taken by ship owing to contrary winds or currents; skier's similar movement on slope; sideways movement of part in machine; sideways motion across face of precipice from one practicable line of ascent or descent to another, place where this is necessary; (Mil.) pair of right-angle bends in trench to avoid enfilading fire; (Law) denial esp. of allegation of matter of fact; horizontal turning of large gun to required direction; **~-table,** (1) nautical table for computing distance in traverses, (2) platform for shifting engine etc. from one line of rails to another. **2.** *v.t.* Travel or lie across (*must traverse a vast extent of country*; *district traversed by canals*; *well traversed by beam*); (fig.) consider, discuss, the whole extent of (subject); turn (large gun) horizontally; deny esp. (Law) in pleading; thwart, frustrate, oppose, (plan, opinion). **3.** *v.i.* (Of needle of compass etc.) turn (as) on pivot; (of horse) walk obliquely; make traverse in climbing. **4.** Hence **travěr'sAL** 2 *n.* [n. f. OF *travers*(*e*), v. f. OF *traverser*, f. LL *traversare*, *transversare* (as TRANSVERSE)]

tră'verser *n.* In vbl senses; railway traverse-table. [f. prec. + -ER[1]]

tră'vertĭne (*or* -ēn) *n.* White or light-coloured calcareous rock deposited from springs. [f. It. *travertino, tivertino* f. L *tiburtinus* of Tibur (Tivoli), near Rome; see -INE[1]]

tră'vėstȳ *v.t.*, & *n.* **1.** *v.t.* Make (person or thing) ridiculous (intentionally or not) by grotesque representation. **2.** *n.* Such treatment or imitation (*of*), esp. in literature. [orig. a., f. F *travesti* p.p. of *travestir* disguise, change the clothes of, f. It. *travestire* (*tra-* TRANS-, *vestire* clothe)]

travoi's (-oi') *n.* (*pl.* same *pr.* -oi'z). N. Amer. Ind. vehicle of two joined poles pulled by horse etc. and carrying burden. [f. earlier *travail* f. F, perh. same wd as TRAVAIL]

trawl *v.* & *n.* **1.** *v.i.* Fish with trawl-net or seine-net. **2.** *v.t.* Catch by trawling. **3.** *n.* Act of trawling (lit. or fig.); **~(-net),** large bag-net with wide mouth held open, dragged along the bottom by boat; ***~(-line),** long sea-fishing line buoyed and supporting short lines with baited hooks. [prob. f. MDu. *traghelen* to drag, cf. *traghel* drag-net, perh. f. L *tragula*]

traw'ler *n.* Person who trawls; boat for use with trawl-net or trawl-line. [f. prec. + -ER[1]]

tray *n.* Flat utensil usu. of wood or metal and usu. with raised edge, for placing or carrying esp. small articles on; metal or other container on desk for correspondence (*in, out, pending, -tray*); shallow lidless box forming compartment in trunk; hence ~'FUL 2 *n.* [OE *trīg*, **trieg* f. Gmc **traujam* (**trau-*, **treu-* wood; see TREE)]

trea'cherous (-ĕ'ch-) *a.* Violating faith or allegiance, betraying trust, perfidious; not to be relied on, deceptive, likely to fail or give way when used; hence or cogn. ~LY[2] *adv.*, ~NESS, **trea'cherY**[1] (-ĕ'ch-), *ns.* [ME, f. OF *trecherous* (*trecheor* a cheat f. *trechier, trichier*; see TRICK, -OUS)]

trea'cle *n.* ||Syrup got in process of refining sugar; molasses; (fig.) cloying blandishments etc.; hence **trea'clY**[2] *a.* [ME *triacle*, in sense 'theriac', f. OF f. L *theriaca* THERIAC]

tread (-ĕd) *v.* (**trod** *pr.* -ŏd, arch. **trode** *pr.* -ōd; **trŏ'dden** *or* **trod**) & *n.* **1.** *v.i.* Set down one's foot, walk, step, (of foot) be set down, (*do not tread on the grass, in the mud*; *trod on a snake*; *where no foot may tread*; *fools rush in where angels fear to tread*); *tread in* person's FOOT[1]*steps*; **~ lightly,** (fig.) deal cautiously with delicate subject; **~ on air** (of buoyant or jubilant person); **~ on** person's **corns** or **toes,** (fig.) offend against his feelings or privileges; **~ on eggs** (of person who needs to be very tactful); **~ on the heels of,** (fig., of event etc.) come closely or immediately after; **~** (set one's foot lit. or fig. as sign of supremacy) **on the neck of** person. **2.** *v.t.* Walk on, press or crush with the feet, (*treads a perilous path*; *trod the room from end to end*); *tread grapes* (in making wine); make track with (dirt etc.) from feet. **3.** Perform, execute, in walking etc. (*trod a dozen hurried paces*); make (hole etc.) by treading; **~ a measure,** (arch.) execute a dance. **4.** (Of male bird) copulate with (hen, or abs.). **5. ~ down,** press down with feet, trample on, crush, destroy; **~ in,** press in or into earth etc. with feet; **~ out,** stamp out (fire, fig. insurrection etc.), press out (wine, grain) with feet; **~ the stage** or **boards,** be an actor, appear on stage; **~ under foot,** trample on, destroy, treat contemptuously; **~ water,** maintain upright position in water with head above surface by action as if walking upstairs. **6.** *n.* Manner or sound of walking (*recognized his heavy tread*; *approached with cautious tread*). **7.** (Of male bird) copulation; chalaza. **8. ~(-board)**, top surface of step or stair. **9.** Part of wheel that touches ground or rails, thick moulded part of vehicle tyre, part of rail that wheels touch; CATERPILLAR *tread*; part of sole that rests on ground. **10. ~'mill,** appliance for producing motion by stepping of man or horse etc. on movable steps on revolving cylinder, esp. kind formerly used in prisons as punishment, (fig.) monotonous routine; **~-wheel,** treadmill or similar appliance. [OE *tredan*, = OS *tredan*, OHG *tretan*, f. WG **tredhan*]

trea'dl|e (-ĕ'd-) *n.*, & *v.i.* **1.** *n.* Lever moved by foot and imparting motion to machine, e.g. lathe, sewing-machine, bicycle, reed-organ. **2.** *v.i.* Work treadle; hence ~ER[1] *n.* [OE *tredel* stair (as prec.; see -LE 1)]

trea'son (-z-) *n.* **1.** (**High**) ~, violation by subject of allegiance to sovereign or to chief authority of State (e.g. by plotting sovereign's death or engaging in war against him); (**petit** or **petty**) ~, (Hist.) similar offence against a subject, e.g. murder of one's master or husband. **2.** Breach of faith, disloyalty, (*to* cause, friend, etc.). **3.** ‖**~-felony,** attempt to depose sovereign or make war in order to compel change of policy etc. **4.** Hence ~OUS *a.* [ME, f. AF *treisoun* etc., OF *traïson*, f. L (as TRADITION)]

trea'sonab|le (-z-) *a.* Involving the crime of treason; guilty of treason; hence **~le**NESS (-bəln-) *n.*, ~LY[2] *adv.* [ME, f. prec. + -ABLE]

trea'sure (-ĕ'zher) *n.*, & *v.t.* **1.** *n.* (literary). Precious metals or gems, hoard of these, accumulated wealth, (*buried treasure*; *had amassed great treasure(s)*; *a voyage in quest of treasure*). **2.** Thing valued for rarity, workmanship, associations, etc., (*art treasures*); (colloq.) beloved or highly valued person. **3.** *v.t.* Store (*up*) as valuable; receive or regard as valuable, store (*up*) in memory, (person's words, looks, etc.). **4. ~-house,** place where treasures (esp. fig.) are kept; **~-hunt,** search for treasure, game in which players seek hidden object(s); **~ trove** [f. AF *trové* p.p. of TROVER], gold etc. found hidden of unknown ownership, (fig.) valuable object(s) found or collected. [ME, f. OF *tresor* f. Rom. **tresaurus* for L THESAURUS]

trea'surer (-ĕ'zher-) *n.* Person in charge of funds of municipality, society, company, club, etc.; officer authorized to receive and disburse public revenues; **Lord High T~,** (Hist.) Crown officer controlling sovereign's revenues; ‖**T~ of the Household,** official ranking next to Lord Steward; HONORARY *treasurer*; hence ~SHIP *n.* [ME, f. AF *tresorer*, OF *-ier* (*tresor*; see prec., ~ARY[1], ~ER[2]), after LL *thesaurarius*]

trea'surў (-ĕ'zherĭ) *n.* **1.** Place or building where treasure (lit. or fig.) is stored; (fig.) book, person, etc., viewed as repository of information etc. **2.** Place where public revenues are kept; department managing public revenue of a country, officers of this; ‖**Lords of the T~,** board in charge of British public revenue, viz. Prime Minister (*First Lord of the T~*), Chancellor of the Exchequer, and 5 junior lords; ‖**T~ bench,** front bench on right hand of Speaker in House of Commons, occupied by Prime Minister, Chancellor of Exchequer, and other ministers. **3. ~ bill,** bill of exchange issued by the government to raise money for temporary needs; **~ note,** note issued by Treasury for use as currency. **4.** Hence ~SHIP *n.*, treasurership. [ME, f. OF *tresorie* (as TREASURE; see -Y[1])]

treat *v.* & *n.* **1.** *v.t.* Act towards, behave to, (*treated me abominably, kindly, as if I were a child*; *better treat it as a joke*). **2.** Deal with or act upon (person, thing) with view to obtaining particular result, apply process to, subject to chemical agent etc., (*treated him for sunstroke*; *how would you treat a sprained ankle?*; *must next be treated with acid*). **3.** Manipulate, present, express, (subject) in literature or art. **4.** Give (person, or abs.) access to or *to* food and drink or entertainment (lit. or fig.) at one's own expense (*I will treat you all*; *think you might treat me to an ice cream, a visit to the theatre*; *treated myself to a new hat*); (of candidate for election) give food etc. or cause these to be given to (electors) in order to influence election. **5.** *v.i.* Negotiate terms (*with* person); **~ of,** handle, discuss, (subject). **6.** Hence or cogn. ~'ABLE *a.*, ~'ER[1], ~'ING[1], *ns.* **7.** *n.* Thing that gives great pleasure (*what a treat it is not to have to get up early*); entertainment designed to do this, e.g. picnic etc. for schoolchildren; treating of others to food etc. (**stand** ~, bear expense of entertainment). [ME, f. AF *treter*, OF *traitier* f. L *tractare* handle frequent. of *trahere*, *tract-* draw, pull]

trea'tĭse (*or* -z) *n.* Literary composition dealing more or less formally and methodically with definite subject. [ME, f. AF *tretis*, OF **traitiz* (*traitier*; see prec.)]

trea'tment *n.* (Mode of) dealing with or behaving towards a person or thing (*received rough treatment from him*; *must follow the prescribed treatment*; *is now ready for treatment with acid*); mode of treating a subject in literature or art; **the** (**full** etc.) ~, (colloq.) the customary way of dealing with a particular type of person etc. [f. TREAT + -MENT]

trea'tў *n.* Formally concluded and ratified agreement between States; agreement between persons (*to* do etc.), esp. for purchase of property at price agreed by them alone, not by auction; **in ~,** negotiating *with* (person *for* purchase etc.); **~ port,** one that a country is bound by treaty to keep open to foreign trade (esp. in Far East). [ME, f. AF *treté* f. L *tractatus* TRACTATE; see -Y[4]]

trĕ'ble *a.*, *n.*, & *v.* **1.** *a.* Threefold, triple, whence **trĕ'b**LY[2] *adv.*; three times as much or many (*treble the amount*); (esp. ‖of boy's voice or boy, or of instrument) = SOPRANO; (of voice etc.) high-pitched; **~ chance,** method of competing in football pool in which there are (orig.) three different possible scores from one's forecast of each match; **~ clef** (placing G above middle C on second lowest line of staff); *treble* RHYME[1]. **2.** *n.* Treble quantity or thing; (Darts) throw on narrow ring enclosed between two middle circles of dartboard, scoring treble; (Racing) bet on three horses etc. as in DOUBLE[2]; soprano; high-pitched voice etc. **3.** *v.t.* & *i.* Multiply, be multiplied, by three (*has trebled its value*; *its value has trebled*). [ME f. OF, f. L *triplus* TRIPLE]

trĕ'būchĕt (-sh-), **trĕ'bŭckĕt,** *n.* (Hist.) military engine for throwing stones etc.; tilting balance for accurately weighing light articles. [ME f. OF (*trebucher* overthrow f. pop. L *TRANS*bucare* f. Frank. **buk* belly)]

trecĕ'nt|ō (-āchĕ'-) *n.* Italian style of art and literature of the 14th c.; hence ~IST (2, 3) *n.* [It., = 300, used w. ref. to years 13—]

tree *n.*, & *v.t.* **1.** *n.* Perennial plant with single woody self-supporting stem or trunk usu. unbranched (cf. SHRUB[1]) for some distance above ground (CHRISTMAS *tree*); piece or framework of wood for various purposes, e.g. AXLE, ROOF, SHOE[1], SWINGLE, *-tree*; (arch. or poet.) gibbet, cross used for (esp. Christ's) crucifixion; (Math.) diagram of branching connecting lines; = *family* or GENEALOGICAL *tree*; **grow on ~s,** (fig.) be plentifully available without effort; **up a ~,** (fig.) cornered, nonplussed; *at the* TOP[1] *of the tree*. **2. ~ agate** (with treelike markings); **~ calf,** calf binding for books stained with treelike design; **~-creeper,** bird of family Certhiidae; **~-dozer,** bulldozer for felling trees; **~-fern,** fern with upright stem attaining size of tree; **~-frog,** = *tree-toad*; **~-goose,** BARNACLE 1; **~-hopper,** insect of family Membracidae; **~-line,** = TIMBER-*line*; **~-milk,** juice of tree or shrub used instead of milk; **~'nail,** pin of hard wood for securing planks etc.; **~ of heaven,** ornamental Asian tree of genus *Ailantus*, with ill-scented flowers; **~ of knowledge,** branches of knowledge as a whole; **~ of liberty** (dedicated to liberty and set up in public place); **~ of life,** arbor vitae; **~ onion** (producing bulbs on stems, not flowers); **~-ring,** ANNUAL ring in tree; **~-shrew,** squirrel-like arboreal mammal of family Tupaiidae; **~ sparrow,** ||small sparrow (*Passer montanus*), large sparrow (*Spizella arborea*), found among trees; **~ surgeon,** one who treats decayed trees in order to preserve them; so **~ surgery**; **~-toad,** arboreal amphibian climbing by means of adhesive discs on digits; *tree*-TOMATO; **~-top,** topmost branches of tree. **3.** Hence ~'LESS *a.* **4.** *v.t.* Force (animal, fig. person) to take refuge in tree; put into difficult position; stretch on shoe-tree. [OE *trēow*, = OS *treo*, ON *tré*, Goth. *triu* f. Gmc **trewam* f. weak grade of IE **deru-*, **doru-*]

treen *n.* Small domestic wooden objects, esp. antiques. [f. *treen* a. wooden f. OE *trēowen* (as prec., -EN[5])]

tre'fa (-ā'-) *a.* Not kosher. [f. Heb. *ṭᵉrēpāh* flesh of animal torn (*ṭārap* rend)]

trĕ̆'foil *n.* & *a.* **1.** *n.* Leguminous plant of genus *Trifolium* with leaves of three leaflets and flowers of various colours, clover; plant with similar leaves; three-lobed ornamentation in tracery etc. **2.** *n.* & *a.* (Thing) arranged in three lobes, whence ~ED[2] (-ld) *a.* [ME, f. AF *trifoil* f. L TRI(*folium* leaf)]

trėha'la (-ah'-) *n.* Manna-like substance of cocoon formed by a beetle of Asia Minor. [f. Turk. *tıgala*]

trĕk *v.i.* (**-kk-**), & *n.* (orig. S. Afr.) **1.** *v.i.* (Of ox) draw vehicle, pull load; travel by ox-wagon or similarly with animals; travel arduously; migrate. **2.** *n.* Such journey, each stage of it; organized migration, esp. of Boers 1835–7. [f. S. Afr. Du. (*trek* n. f.) *trekken* draw, travel]

trĕ'llĭs *n.*, & *v.t.* **1.** *n.* ~(**-work**), lattice or grating of light wooden crossbars nailed together where they cross, similar structure of wire or metal, as screen or to support climbing plants, etc. **2.** *v.t.* Furnish, support (vine etc.), with trellis. [ME, f. OF *trelis*, *trelice* f. Rom. **trilicius* f. L TRI(*lix* f. *licium* warp-thread) three-ply]

trĕ'matōde *n.* Parasitic flatworm of class Trematoda, e.g. fluke. [f. mod. L *Trematoda* f. Gk *trēmatōdēs* perforated (*trēma* hole; see -ODE)]

trĕ'mble *v.i.*, & *n.* **1.** *v.i.* Shake involuntarily from fear, agitation, physical weakness, etc., (*he was trembling with anger*; *voice trembled with excitement*); (fig.) be in state of extreme agitation, fear, suspense, etc., (*I tremble for his safety, to think what has become of him*; *tremble at the thought*; *no cause to tremble before his judge*); move in quivering manner (*leaves tremble in the breeze*); (fig., of person's fate, life, etc.); **~ in the balance,** have reached a critical point, be in extreme danger. **2.** Hence or cogn. ~MENT (-belm-) *n.*, **trĕ'mbl**Y[2] *a.* (colloq.). **3.** *n.* Trembling, quiver, (*there was a tremble in her voice*); **all of a ~,** (colloq.) trembling all over. **4.** (in *pl.*) Disease (esp. of cattle) marked by trembling. [ME, f. OF *trembler* f. med. L *tremulare* f. L *tremulus* TREMULOUS]

trĕ'mbler *n.* In vbl senses; automatic vibrator for making and breaking electric circuit; W. Ind. bird with continually shaking tail. [f. prec. + -ER[1]]

trĕ'mblĭng *a.* In vbl senses; **~ bog** (formed over water etc. and shaking at every step); **~ poplar,** aspen. [f. TREMBLE + -ING[2]]

trėmĕ'ndous *a.* Awe-inspiring, fearful, overpowering, (colloq.) remarkable, considerable, excellent, (*a tremendous explosion*; *makes a tremendous difference*; *gave a tremendous performance*); hence ~LY[2] *adv.*, ~NESS *n.* [f. L *tremendus* gerundive of *tremere* tremble + -OUS]

trĕ'molō *n.* (*pl.* ~s). (Mus.) Tremulous effect in singing or playing bowed instruments etc.; rapid continuous change of pitch during singing of note; device in organ producing tremulous effect; cf. VIBRATO. [It., as TREMULOUS]

trĕ'mor *n.*, & *v.i.* **1.** *n.* (Of leaf, part of body, voice, person) shaking, quivering; thrill (of fear, exultation, etc.); (**earth**) ~, slight earthquake; **intention ~** (in part of body when it moves to do something). **2.** *v.i.* Undergo tremor(s). [ME, f. OF *tremour* & f. L *tremor* (*tremere* tremble; see -OR)]

trĕ'mūlous *a.* Trembling, quivering, (*tremulous leaves, voice, hand*); (of line etc.) drawn by tremulous hand; timid, vacillating; hence ~LY[2] *adv.*, ~NESS *n.* [f. L *tremulus* (*tremere* tremble) + -OUS]

trē'nail. Var. of TREE*nail*.

trĕnch *v.* & *n.* **1.** *v.t.* Dig ditch(es) or trench(es) in (ground); turn over earth of (field etc.) by digging succession of contiguous ditches. **2.** *v.i.* Encroach (*up*)*on* (person's rights, privacy, etc.); verge or border closely (*up*)*on* (heresy, vulgarity, etc.). **3.** *n.* Long narrow usu. deep furrow or ditch; (Mil.) ditch with earth thrown up to form parapet, (in *pl.*) defensive system of these; long narrow deep area in ocean. **4. ~-cart,** handcart on low wheels for use in trenches; **~ coat,** (soldier's) lined or padded waterproof coat; **~ fever,** form of fever affecting soldiers in trenches, spread by lice; **~ foot,** disease of feet caused by much standing in water; **~ mortar,** light simple mortar throwing bomb from one's own into enemy trenches; **~ warfare,** hostilities carried on from more or less permanent trenches. [ME, f. OF *trenchier* v., *trenche* n., cut f. Rom. **trincare* for L *truncare* TRUNCATE]

trĕ'nchant *a.* **1.** (arch. or poet.) Sharp, keen, (*trenchant sword*). **2.** (Of style, language, policy, etc.) penetrating, incisive, decisive, vigorous; hence **trĕ'nch**ANCY *n.*, ~LY[2] *adv.* [ME f. OF, part. of *trenchier* (see prec.)]

trĕ'ncher *n.* (arch.) Wooden platter for serving food; **~ (cap),** stiff square academic cap, mortar-board; ||**~-fed,** (of hound) kept by a member of the hunt, not as one of a pack; **good, poor,** etc., **~man,** one who eats much, little, etc. [ME, f. AF *trenchour*, OF *-eoir* (*trenchier*; see TRENCH, -ER[2])]

trĕnd *v.i.*, & *n.* **1.** *v.i.* Have specified general direction, bend or turn away in specified direction; (fig.) be chiefly directed, have general and continued tendency, (*towards* etc.). **2.** *n.* General direction and tendency (esp. fig. of events, opinion, etc.); **~-setter,** person who leads the way in fashion etc. [ME 'revolve' etc. f. OE *trendan* f. Gmc **trend-*, **trand-*, **trund-*; cf. TRUNDLE]

‖**trĕ'nd|ȳ** *a.* & *n.* (colloq.) **1.** *a.* Fashionable, following the latest trend of fashion; hence ~ĭLY² *adv.*, ~ĭNESS *n.* **2.** *n.* Trendy person. [f. prec. + -Y²]

trĕ'ntal *n.* (R.C. Ch.) Set of 30 successive usu. daily masses for the dead. [ME, f. OF *trentel* & med. L *trentalis* f. pop. L **trenta* for L *triginta* thirty + -AL]

trente-et-quarante (trahṅtākărah'ṅt) *n.* = ROUGE-*et-noir*. [F, = 30 and 40]

trėpă'n¹ *n.*, & *v.t.* (-nn-). **1.** *n.* Surgeon's cylindrical saw for removing part of bone of skull; borer for sinking shafts. **2.** *v.t.* Perforate (skull) with trepan; hence **trĕpan**A'TION, ~**n**ING¹, *ns.* [ME, (f. OF *trepaner* v. f. *trepan* n.) f. med. L *trepanum* f. Gk *trupanon* (*trupaō* bore f. *trupē* hole)]

trėpă'n² *v.t.* (-**nn**-), & *n.* Trap, snare, lure. [17th c., earlier *trapan* n., prob. thieves' sl. f. TRAP¹]

trėpă'ng *n.* = BÊCHE-DE-MER 1. [f. Malay *tripang*]

trėphī'ne (*or* -ē'n) *n.*, & *v.t.* **1.** *n.* Improved form of trepan with guiding centre-pin. **2.** *v.t.* Operate on (skull, cornea, person) with this; hence **trĕphĭn**A'TION *n.* [orig. *trafine*, f. L *tres fines* three ends, app. formed after TREPAN¹]

trĕpĭdā'tion *n.* Alarm, flurry; tremulous agitation; trembling of limbs e.g. in paralysis. [f. L *trepidatio* (*trepidare* be agitated, tremble, f. *trepidus* alarmed; see -ATION)]

trĕ'spass *v.i.*, & *n.* **1.** *v.i.* Make unlawful or unwarrantable intrusion (*on* or *upon* land, rights, etc., or abs.; ~ **on** person's **preserves,** (fig.) meddle in a matter that he has made his own); make unwarrantable claim *on* (*shall trespass on your hospitality*; *may I trespass on your valuable time?*); (literary or arch.) offend (*against* person, law, principle, rights; *forgive them that trespass against us*); hence ~ER¹ *n.* **2.** *n.* Transgression of law or right; (Law) any transgression that is not (misprision of) treason or felony, wrongful entry on another's land with damage, tort against person or property, action arising from this. [ME, f. (OF *trespas* n. f.) *trespasser* pass over, trespass, f. med. L TRANS-(*passare* PASS¹)]

trĕss *n.*, & *v.t.* **1.** *n.* Portion, lock, plait, of hair of human (esp. woman's or girl's) head; (in *pl.*) hair of (esp. woman's or girl's) head; hence (-)~ED² (-st), ~'Y², *adjs.* **2.** *v.t.* (esp. in *p.p.*) Arrange (hair) in tresses. [ME, f. OF *tresce, tresse* n., *tresser* v., perh. ult. f. Gk *trikha* three-fold]

trĕ'ssure (-sher) *n.* (Her.) Narrow orle. [ME, orig. = hair-ribbon, f. OF *tressour* etc. (as prec.; see -URE)]

trĕ'stle (-sel) *n.* Supporting structure for table etc., consisting of bar supported by two divergent pairs of legs or of two frames fixed at an angle or hinged; ~**(-table)**, table of board(s) laid on trestles or other supports; ~**(-work)**, open braced framework of wood or metal or concrete for supporting bridge etc.; ~**(-tree)**, (Naut.) each of a pair of horizontal pieces on lower mast supporting topmast etc. [ME, f. OF *trestel* f. Rom. **transtellum* beam, dim. of L *transtrum*; see -LE 2]

trĕt *n.* (Hist.) Allowance of extra weight formerly made to purchasers of some goods for waste in transportation; TARE² *and tret.* [ME f. AF & OF, var. of *trait* draught; see TRAIT]

trėvă'llȳ *n.* Austral. food-fish of genus *Caranx*. [app. f. CAVALLY]

‖**trews** (-ōōz) *n. pl.* Close-fitting usu. tartan trousers. [f. Ir. *trius*, Gael. *triubhas* (sing.); cf. TROUSER]

trey (trā) *n.* The three on dice or (arch.) cards. [ME, f. OF *trei(s)* three f. L *tres*]

T.R.H. *abbr.* Their Royal Highnesses.

trī- *comb. form.* Three, triple, thrice, (Chem., forming names of compounds) containing three atoms or groups of a specified kind, as: **~a'cetate** (containing 3 acetate groups, esp. as base for fabrics); **~ade'lphous,** (Bot.) with stamens united in 3 bundles; **~a'ndrous,** having 3 stamens; **~a'xial,** having 3 axes; **~ba'sic,** (Chem.) having 3 replaceable hydrogen atoms; **~cente'nary,** = TERCENTENARY; **~chlor'ide,** compound of element or radical with 3 atoms of chlorine; **~'chord** *a.* & *n.*, 3-stringed (instrument esp. lute), (of piano) with 3 strings to most notes; **~chroma'tic,** having or using 3 colours (*~chromatic photography*, THREE-colour process), (of vision) having the normal 3 colour-sensations, i.e. red, green, and purple; so *~chro'matism* n.; **~cor'poral, ~cor'porate,** (Her.) having 3 bodies and one head; **~cotyle'donous,** with 3 cotyledons; **~cro'tic** (-ŏ't-), (of pulse) with triple beat; **~cu'spid,** (tooth) with 3 cusps or points, heart-valve formed of 3 triangular segments; **~da'ctyl(ous)**, with 3 fingers or toes; **~de'ntate,** with 3 teeth or prongs; **~di'gitate,** = *tridactyl*; **~dime'nsional,** of 3 dimensions; **~fa'cial,** = TRIGEMINAL; **~fo'cal,** (of lens) having 3 parts with different focal lengths; **~fo'liate,** (of compound leaf) with 3 leaflets, (of plant) having such leaves; **~fo'liated,** (Bot.) trifoliate, (Archit.) trefoiled; **~'form(ed)**, formed of 3 parts, having 3 forms or bodies; **~fur'cate¹** (-*at*) *a.*, divided into 3 branches; **~'furcate²** (-āt) *v.t.* & *i.*, divide into 3 branches; **~'glot,** written in 3 languages; **~goneu'tic,** (Entom.) having 3 broods in a year; **~'gram, ~'graph,** group of 3 letters representing one sound, figure of 3 lines; **~'gynous** (trĭ'j-), having 3 pistils; **~he'dral,** with 3 surfaces; **~he'dron,** figure of 3 intersecting planes; **~hy'dric,** (Chem.) containing 3 hydroxyl groups; **~la'biate,** 3-lipped; **~la'minar,** of 3 layers; **~la'teral** *a.* & *n.*, (figure) having 3 sides, affecting or between 3 parties; **~le'mma,** choice between 3 (unwelcome) things; **~li'near,** of 3 lines; **~li'ngual,** using, or in, 3 languages; **~li'teral,** of 3 letters, (of Semitic language) having (most) roots with 3 consonants; **~lo'bate,** 3-lobed; **~lo'cular,** with 3 cells or compartments; **~me'str(i)al,** occurring every 3 months; **~'merous** (-ĭ'-), having 3 parts; **~mor'phism, ~mor'phic** *or* **~mor'phous,** (Bot., Zool., & Cryst.) existence, existing, in 3 distinct forms; **~no'mial** *a.* & *n.*, (scientific name, algebraic expression) consisting of 3 terms; **~no'mialism,** use of 3 terms in scientific naming of objects; **~oe'cious** (-ē'sh-), (Bot.) with male, female, and hermaphrodite organs each on separate plants; **~o'xide,** (Chem.) oxide containing 3 oxygen atoms; **~pe'talous,** having 3 petals; **~phy'llous,** three-leaved; **~pi'nnate,** thrice pinnate; **~'stichous** (-ĭ'stĭk-), (Bot.) arranged in 3 vertical rows **~stigma'tic, ~sty'lous,** (Bot.) having 3 stigmas, styles; **~su'lcate,** (Bot.) 3-grooved, (Zool.) divided

For other words in *tri-* see TRI-.

into 3 digits or hoofs; **~ter'nate,** (Bot.) thrice ternate, having 27 leaflets; **~'tone,** (Mus.) interval of 3 tones, augmented fourth; **~-va'lent** (*or* -ī'-), (Chem.) having a valence of 3; **~-wee'kly** *a.*, produced or occurring 3 times in a week or every 3 weeks. [L & Gk, f. L *tres*, Gk *treis* three]

trī'able *a.* That may be tried. [ME f. AF (as TRY; see -ABLE)]

trī'ăd (*or* -*ad*) *n.* The number three; group of three; (Mus.) chord of three notes, esp. common chord without octave; Welsh form of literary composition with arrangement in groups of three; hence **triă'dic** *a.* [f. F *triade* or LL f. Gk *trias -ados* (*treis* three; see -AD)]

trī'age *n.* Sorting according to quality; assignment of degrees of urgency to decide order of treatment of wounded etc. [F (*trier*; cf. TRY, -AGE)]

trī'al *n.* **1.** Process or mode of testing the qualities of a thing, experimental treatment, investigation by means of experience, test, attempt, (*made trial of his strength*; *was found on trial to be incompetent*; *shall subject* or *put it to further trial*; *trial of the* PYX); *bicycle is hired, clerk employed,* **on ~** (to be retained only if efficient); *will* **give** *you* or *it* **a ~** (employ on trial); **~ and error,** process of succeeding by repeated trying with or without improvement of method by learning from failures; **~ of strength** (to find who is the stronger). **2.** Trying thing or experience or person, esp. hardship, trouble, (*old age has many trials*; *fear you will find the boy, the piano next door, a great trial*). **3.** Judicial examination and determination of issues between parties by judge with or without jury or by referee etc. (*was* (*put*) *on* (*his*) *trial* or *stood* or *was brought to* or *underwent trial for murder*). **4.** = *trial match*; test of individual ability on motor cycle over rough ground or on road; hence ~IST (3) *n.* **5. ~ balance** (of ledger in double-entry bookkeeping), comparison of totals on either side, inequality of which reveals error in posting; **~ balloon,** *ballon d'essai*; **~ court** (opp. appellate court); **~ eights,** two experimental rowing crews tried against each other with a view to selection of crew for boat-race; *trial* HEAT[1]; *trial* JURY; **~ (match)**, game of cricket, football, etc., in which players who may be selected for an important team take part; **~ run, ~ trip,** new vessel's or vehicle's trip to test its performance, (fig.) experiment. [AF *trial, triel* (*trier* TRY; see -AL 2)]

trī'ăngle (-nggel) *n.* **1.** Figure (esp. plane) bounded by three (esp. straight) lines (SPHERICAL *triangle*); any three points not in one straight line, together with the imaginary lines joining them; ETERNAL *triangle*. **2.** Implement etc. of this shape; right-angled triangle of wood etc. as drawing-implement; (Naut.) device of three spars for raising weights; (Mus.) steel rod in form of triangle open at one angle sounded by striking with small steel rod; (Hist.) frame of three halberds joined at top to which soldier was bound for flogging; **~ of forces,** triangle whose sides represent in magnitude and direction three forces in equilibrium. [ME f. OF, or f. L *triangulum* neut. (as n.) of TRI(*angulus* ANGLE[1]) three-cornered]

triă'ngūlar (-ngg-) *a.* Of the shape of a triangle, three-cornered, (of contest, treaty, etc.) between three persons or parties; **~ compasses** (with three legs, for marking out triangles); **~ numbers,** sums of the series 1, 2, 3, etc., taken to any number of terms, e.g. 1, 6, 28, 55 [w. ref. to arrangement of such numbers of points in equilateral triangle]; **~ pyramid** (with triangular base); hence ~ITY (-ă'r-) *n.*, ~LY[2] *adv.* [f. LL *triangularis* (as prec.; see -AR[1])]

triă'ngūl|āte[1] (-ngg-) *v.t.* Make triangular; divide (area etc.) into triangles for surveying; measure and map (area) by use of triangles with known base length and base angles, determine (height, distance, etc.) thus; hence ~A'TION *n.* [f. L (as TRIANGLE) + -ATE[3]]

triă'ngūlate[2] (-ngg-) *a.* (Zool.) Marked with triangles; hence ~LY[2] (-tlĭ) *adv.* [f. med. L *triangulatus* (as prec.; see -ATE[2])]

triă'ntėlōpe *n.* Large flat-bodied Austral. spider. [corrupt. of TARANTULA]

Trī'as *n.* (Geol.) Earliest mesozoic period or system, above Permian and below Jurassic; hence **Triă'ssic** *a.* & *n.* [f. LL (as TRIAD), f. threefold subdivision in Germany]

trīatŏ'mĭc *a.* (Chem.) Having three atoms (of a specified kind) in the molecule; having three replaceable atoms or radicals. [f. TRI- + ATOM + -IC]

trĭ'bad|e *n.* Woman who engages with another in simulation of sexual intercourse; hence ~ISM (2) *n.* [F, or f. L f. Gk *tribas* (*tribō* rub)]

trī'bal *a.* Of tribe(s); hence ~LY[2] *adv.* [f. TRIBE + -AL]

trī'bal|ism *n.* Tribal organization; so ~IST (2) *n.*, **~ĭ'stic** *a.* [f. prec. + -ISM]

trībe *n.* **1.** Group of (primitive) clans under recognized chief and usu. claiming common ancestor; (Rom. Hist.) each of the political divisions (orig. three, probably representing clans, ult. 35) of the Romans; any similar division whether of natural or political origin, e.g. **the Twelve T~s** of the Israelites (**the Ten T~s,** these without Judah and Benjamin; **the Lost T~s,** the Ten Tribes after deportation by Shalmaneser). **2.** (Biol.) Group of plants or animals usu. ranking between genus and subfamily. **3.** (in *pl.*) Large numbers. **4.** (usu. derog.) Set, number, of persons esp. of one profession etc. or family (*the whole tribe of parasites, actors*; *the scribbling tribe*). **5. ~'sman** (-z-), member of a tribe or of one's own tribe. [ME, orig. in pl. form *tribuz, tribus* f. OF or f. L *tribus* sing. & pl.]

trĭ'blėt *n.* Mandrel used in making tubes, rings, etc. [f. F *triboulet*, of unkn. orig.]

trĭ'bō- *comb. form.* Rubbing, friction, as: **~-electri'city,** generation of electric charge by friction; **~logy** (-ŏ'l-), study of friction, wear, lubrication, and design of bearings, science of interacting surfaces in relative motion; **~-lumine'scence,** emission of light from a substance when rubbed, scratched, etc.; **~meter** (-ŏ'm-), instrument for measuring friction in sliding. [f. Gk *tribos* rubbing + -o-]

trī'brăch[1] (-k) *n.* (Pros.) Foot of three short syllables; hence **trĭbră'chic** (-k-) *a.* [f. L f. Gk TRI(*brakhus* short)]

trī'brăch[2] (-k) *n.* Object with three arms, esp. prehistoric flint implement. [f. TRI- + Gk *brakhiōn* arm]

trĭbūlā'tion *n.* Great affliction or oppression (*trials and tribulations*); cause of this. [ME f. OF, f. eccl. L *tribulatio -onis* f. L *tribulare* press, oppress, (*tribulum* sledge for threshing, f. *terere trit-* rub); see -ATION]

trībū'nal *n.* Judgement-seat, seat or bench for judge(s) or magistrate(s); court of justice; (fig.) place of judgement, judicial authority (*before the tribunal of public opinion*); board appointed to adjudicate regarding fair rents, exemption from military service, etc. [F, or f. L (as foll.; see -AL)]

trĭ'būn|e[1] *n.* **1.** (Rom. Hist.) **~e (of the people)**, each of (orig. two, ultimately ten) officers chosen by the people to protect their liberties against senate and consuls; **(military) ~e,** officer commanding legion for two-month periods. **2.** Popular leader or demagogue. **3.** Hence or cogn. ~ATE[1] (1), ~**e**SHIP (-nsh-), *ns.*, ~**ĭ'ci**AL, ~**ĭ'ti**AL, (-shal), ~I'CIAN, *adjs.* [ME, f. L *tribunus*, prob. f. *tribus* tribe]

trĭ'būne[2] *n.* Raised floor for magistrate's chair in apse of Roman basilica; bishop's throne, apse containing this, in basilica; platform, stage, pulpit, esp. that used by speakers in French Chamber of Deputies; raised area with seats. [F, f. It. f. med. L *tribuna* for L TRIBUNAL]

trĭ'būtar|ȳ *a.* & *n.* **1.** *a.* Paying or subject to tribute (*tributary States*); contributory, auxiliary; (of river) flowing into larger river or into lake; hence ~ĭLY[2] *adv.*, ~ĭNESS *n.* **2.** *n.* Tributary State, person, or stream. [ME, f. L *tributarius* (as foll.; see -ARY[1])]

trĭ'būte *n.* **1.** Money or equivalent paid periodically by one State or ruler to another in acknowledgement of submission or as price of peace or protection, or by virtue of treaty; obligation to pay this (*was laid under tribute*). **2.** (fig.) Contribution, esp. thing done, said, given, etc., as mark of respect, affection, etc., (*paid tribute to his great services*; *many floral tributes to actress, at funeral*); **a ~ to,** an indication of (some praiseworthy quality). **3.** (Mining). Proportion of ore or its equivalent paid to miner for his work, or to owner of mine. [ME, f. L *tributum* neut. p.p. (as n.) of *tribuere -ut-* assign, orig. divide between tribes (*tribus*)]

||**trī'câr** *n.* Three-wheeled motor car. [f. TRI- + CAR]

trīce[1] *v.t.* (Naut.) ~ (**up**), haul up (and secure in place); tie up. [ME, f. MDu. & MLG *trīsen*]

trīce[2] *n.* **In a ~,** in an instant. [ME, f. prec.]

trī'cĕps *a.* & *n.* **1.** *a.* (Of muscle) having three heads or points of attachment. **2.** *n.* Triceps muscle, esp. large muscle at back of upper arm. [L, = three-headed, f. TRI- + *-ceps* (*caput* head)]

trĭchī'asĭs (-k-) *n.* (Path.) Inversion of eyelashes. [LL, f. Gk *trikhiasis* (*trikhiaō* be hairy; see -ASIS)]

trĭchī'n|a (-k-) *n.* (*pl.* ~**ae**). Hairlike nematode worm parasitic in body of man and carnivores; hence ~IZE (3) *v.t.*, ~O'SIS (-kĭ-) *n.*, disease caused by eating meat containing trichinae, **trĭ'chin**OUS (-k-) *a.* [mod. L, f. Gk *trikhinos* of hair (as foll.; see -INE[2])]

trĭ'cho- (-k-) *comb. form.* Hair, as: ~**genous** (-ŏ'j-), causing or promoting growth of hair; ~**logy** (-ŏ'l-), study of the structure, functions, and diseases of hair; ~**pa'thic** *a.*, ~**pathy** (-ŏ'p-) *n.*, (treatment) of diseases of hair. [f. Gk *thrix trikhos* hair + -O-]

trī'chōme (-k-) *n.* (Bot.) Hair, scale, prickle, or other outgrowth from epidermis of plant. [f. Gk *trikhōma* (*trikhoō* cover with hair f. as prec.; see -OMA)]

trĭchomŏ'n|ăd (-k-) *n.* Flagellate protozoan of genus *Trichomonas*; ~**ī'**ASIS *n.*, disease caused by this as parasite in man, cattle, or fowls. [f. TRICHO- + MONAD]

trĭchŏ'tom|ȳ (-k-) *n.* Division (esp. sharply defined) into three, esp. of human nature into body, soul, and spirit; so **trĭchotŏ'mic** (-k-), ~OUS, *adjs.*, ~IZE (1, 3) *v.t.* & *i.* [f. Gk *trikha* threefold (*treis* three), after *dichotomy*]

trīchrō'|ic (-k-) *a.* (Esp. of crystal viewed in different directions) showing three colours; so ~ISM (2) *n.* [f. Gk TRI(*khroos* f. *khrōs* colour) + -IC]

trĭck *n.*, & *v.t.* **1.** *n.* Fraudulent device or stratagem (*I suspect some trick*; *trick of the* TRADE); optical or other illusion (*misled by a trick of vision*). **2.** Feat of skill or dexterity, trained animal's unusual action; knack, precise or best mode of doing or dealing with a thing; (*attrib.*) thus made to deceive or mystify (*trick photograph*); BAG[1] *of tricks*; **do the ~,** (sl.) accomplish one's purpose, achieve desired result; **a ~ worth two of that,** a better expedient; **how's ~s?,** (sl.) how are you?, how are things? **3.** Peculiar or characteristic practice, habit, mannerism, (*has a trick of repeating himself*; *style is spoilt by tricks*). **4.** Mischievous or foolish or discreditable act, practical joke, prank, (*is always playing mad tricks*; *a dirty* or *shabby trick to play*); **up to** one's **~s,** misbehaving; **up to** person's **~s,** aware of what he is likely to do by way of mischief. **5.** (Cards). The cards played in a round, one from each player; such round, point gained as result of this; hence ~'LESS *a.* **6.** (Naut.) Man's turn at helm, usu. two hours. **7. ~ cyclist,** cyclist who performs tricks, (sl.) psychiatrist; ***~ or treat,** Hallowe'en children's game of calling at houses with threat of pranks if sweets etc. are not given them; **~ wig** (of which hair can be made to stand on end). **8.** *v.t.* Deceive by trick, cheat, (person; *out of* thing, *into* doing, etc.); (of thing) foil, baffle, disappoint the calculations of, take by surprise; ~ (**out** or **up**), dress, decorate, deck. **9.** Hence ~'ER[1], ~'ERY (4, 5), ~'STER, *ns.*, ~'ISH[1] *a.* [ME, f. OF dial. *trique*, OF *triche* (*trichier* deceive, of unkn. orig.)]

trĭ'ckle *v.* & *n.* **1.** *v.i.* (Of liquid) flow in drops or in small stream (*tears trickled down her cheeks*; *water trickles through crevice*); (fig.) come or go slowly or gradually (*ball trickled into hole*; *audience, information, trickled out*). **2.** *v.t.* Cause (liquid etc.) to trickle; pour out in drops. **3.** *n.* Trickling stream; **~ charger,** accumulator-charger that works at a steady low rate from the mains. [ME *trekel*, *trikle*, prob. imit.; see -LE 3]

trĭ'cks|ȳ *a.* Playful, frolicsome; full of tricks; hence ~ĭLY[2] *adv.*, ~ĭNESS *n.* [f. TRICK; for *-sy* cf. *tipsy*]

trĭ'ck|ȳ *a.* Crafty, deceitful; skilful at evasion, resourceful, adroit; (of task etc.) requiring caution or adroitness, full of pitfalls, ticklish; hence ~ĭLY[2] *adv.*, ~ĭNESS *n.* [f. TRICK + -Y[2]]

trīclī'nĭc *a.* (Cryst.) Having three unequal oblique axes. [f. Gk TRI- + *klinō* incline + -IC]

trĭclī'nĭ|um *n.* (*pl.* ~**a**). (Rom. Ant.) Dining-table with couches along three sides; room containing this. [L, f. Gk TRI(*klinion* f. *klinē* couch)]

trĭ'colour, *-or, (-ŭler) *a.* & *n.* **1.** *a.* Having three colours. **2.** *n.* Flag of three colours, esp. French national standard of blue, white, and red, adopted during Revolution. [f. F *tricolore* f. LL TRI(*color* COLOUR[1])]

trī'coloured (-kŭlerd) *a.* = prec. [f. TRI- + COLOURED]

trī'côrn, -ne, *a.* & *n.* (Imaginary animal) with three horns; (cocked hat) with brim turned up on three sides. [f. F *tricorne* or f. L TRI(*cornis* f. *cornu* horn)]

trĭ'cōt (-kō; *or* trē'-) *n.* Hand-knitted woollen fabric; imitation of this; ribbed woollen cloth. [F, = knitting (*tricoter* knit, of unkn. orig.)]

trī'cȳcl|e *n.*, & *v.i.* (Ride on) three-wheeled pedal-driven road vehicle; three-wheeled motor vehicle for disabled driver; hence ~IST (1) *n.* [f. TRI- + CYCLE]

trī'dent *n.* Three-pronged implement e.g. fish-spear or gladiator's weapon; such spear or sceptre as attribute of Poseidon (Neptune) or Britannia. [f. L TRI(*dens dentis* tooth)]

Trīdĕ'ntine *a.* & *n.* **1.** *a.* Of the Council of Trent

For other words in *tri-* see TRI-.

(1545–63) esp. as basis of Roman Catholic doctrine and practice. **2.** *n.* Orthodox Roman Catholic. [f. med. L *Tridentinus* (*Tridentum* Trent = Trento in N. Italy; see -INE[1])]

trĭ'dūum *n.* (R.C. Ch.) Three days' prayer in preparation for saint's day or other religious occasion. [L, neut. of *TRI(*duus* f. *dies* day)]

trĭ'dȳmīte *n.* (Min.) Form of silica occurring in cavities of igneous rocks. [f. G *tridymit* f. Gk *tridumos* threefold (as TRI-, *didumos* twin), f. its occurrence in groups of three crystals, + -ITE[1]]

tried. See TRY.

triĕ'nnĭal *a.* & *n.* **1.** *a.* Lasting, recurring every, three years; hence ~LY[2] *adv.* **2.** *n.* (Bot.) Triennial plant; visitation of diocese by Anglican bishop every three years. [f. LL TRI(*ennis* f. *annus* year) + -AL]

triĕ'nnĭ|um *n.* (*pl.* **~ums** *or* **~a**). Period of three years. [L (as prec.)]

trī'er *n.* In vbl senses; person appointed to decide whether challenge to juror is well founded; tester esp. of foodstuffs; one who perseveres in his attempts. [ME, f. TRY + -ER[1]]

trī'erarchȳ (-kĭ) *n.* (Gk Ant.) (Athenian formation of fleet at expense of) body of citizens compelled to provide triremes at their own expense. [f. Gk *triērarkhia* (*triērarkhos* such citizen f. *triērēs* trireme + *-arkhos* ruler)]

trī'fĭd *a.* (esp. Biol.) Partly or wholly cleft into three divisions or lobes. [f. L TRI(*fidus* f. root of *findere* split)]

trī'fle *n.* & *v.* **1.** *n.* Thing, fact, circumstance, of only slight value or importance (*wastes time on trifles*; *the merest trifle puts him out*; (iron.) *shall probably break our necks, but that is a trifle*); small amount esp. of money (*was sold for a mere trifle*); **a ~** *adv.*, somewhat (*seems a trifle angry*). **2.** Confection of sponge-cake with custard or cream or white of eggs and fruit, jam, jelly, wine, almonds, etc. **3.** *v.i.* Talk or act frivolously; **~ with,** treat (person, thing, matter) with flippancy or derision, refuse to take seriously, occupy oneself carelessly with, toy with, (novel, cigarette, etc.). **4.** *v.t.* Throw or fool *away* (time, energies, money, etc., *on* object). **5.** Hence **trī'flER**[1] *n.* [ME f. OF *truf(f)le* by-form of *truf(f)e* deceit, of unkn. orig.]

trī'flĭng *a.* In vbl senses; frivolous; unimportant, petty; hence ~LY[2] *adv.* [f. prec. + -ING[2]]

trifŏr'ĭ|um *n.* (*pl.* **~a**). Gallery or arcade above arches of nave and choir (and transepts) of church. [AL, of unkn. orig.]

trĭg *a.*, & *v.t.* (**-gg-**). (arch. or dial.) (Make) trim, spruce, smart. [ME, = trusty, f. ON *tryggr*, = Goth. *triggws* TRUE]

trĭ'gam|ous *a.* **1.** Thrice married or having three wives or husbands at once; so ~IST (3), ~Y[1], *ns.* **2.** (Bot.) Having male, female, and hermaphrodite flowers in same head. [f. Gk TRI(*gamos* -married) + -OUS]

trigĕ'mĭnal *a.* & *n.* (Of) cranial nerve of fifth pair, dividing into three branches (ophthalmic, maxillary, mandibular); **~ neuralgia** (involving one or more of these branches, and often causing severe pain). [f. as foll. + -AL]

trigĕ'mĭn|us *n.* (*pl.* **~i** *pr.* -ī). Trigeminal nerve. [L, = born as a triplet (TRI-, *geminus* born at same birth)]

trĭ'gger (-g-) *n.*, & *v.t.* **1.** *n.* Movable device for releasing spring or catch and so setting mechanism in action, esp. projecting tongue in firearm that liberates hammer of lock; agent that sets off a chain reaction; HAIR-*trigger*; **pull the ~,** initiate a process; **quick on the ~,** (fig.) quick to respond; **~-fish** (whose first dorsal fin-spine can be depressed by pressing on second); **~-happy,** apt to shoot on slight provocation; hence (-)~ED[2] (-*erd*) *a.* **2.** *v.t.* Fire (gun) by use of trigger; **~ (off)**, set in action, initiate or precipitate (process). [17th c. *tricker* f. Du. *trekker* (*trekken* pull; cf. TREK, -ER[1])]

trī'glȳph *n.* (Archit.) Each of the three-grooved tablets alternating with metopes in Doric frieze; hence **triglȳ'phIC(AL)** *adjs.* [f. L f. Gk TRI(*gluphos* f. *gluphē* carving)]

trī'gon *n.* Triangle; ancient triangular lyre or harp; cutting region of upper molar tooth. [f. L f. Gk *trigōnon* neut. (as n.) of TRI(*gōnos* -cornered); cf. -GON]

trĭ'gonal *a.* Of a triangle; (Biol.) triangular in cross-section; (Cryst.) having axis with threefold symmetry; hence ~LY[2] *adv.* [f. med. L *trigonalis* (as prec.; see -AL)]

trigon|ŏ'mĕtrȳ *n.* Branch of mathematics dealing with relations of sides and angles of a triangle, and with relevant functions of any angles; hence **~omĕ'trIC(AL)** *adjs.* [f. mod. L *trigonometria* (as TRIGON, -O-, -METRY)]

trīke *n.*, & *v.i.* (colloq.) Tricycle. [abbr.]

trĭ'lbȳ *n.* **1.** ||**~ (hat)**, (colloq.) soft felt hat with lengthwise dent in crown and narrow brim. **2.** (sl., in *pl.*) Feet. [f. name of fair-footed heroine of G. du Maurier's novel *Trilby*, in stage version of which such a hat was worn]

trī'lĭth, trī'lĭthon, *n.* Monument of three stones, esp. two uprights and a lintel; hence **trilĭ'thIC** *a.* [Gk *trilithon* neut. of TRI(*lithos* stone)]

trĭll *v.* & *n.* **1.** *v.i.* (Of person or thing) give forth sound with tremulous vibration (*trilling laughter*). **2.** *v.t.* & *i.* Sing in quavering manner, esp. (Mus.) with trill. **3.** *n.* Quavering or tremulous sound, esp. (Mus.) quick alternation of two notes a (semi)tone apart, shake; (consonant pronounced with) vibration of tongue etc. [f. It. (*trillo* n. f.) *trillare*]

trĭ'llĭng *n.* Compound crystal of three individuals. [f. TRI- + -LING[1], app. after Da., Sw. *trilling*, Du. *drieling*]

trĭ'llion (-lyon) *n.* (for *pl.* usage see HUNDRED). ||A million million millions; *a million millions; hence ~TH[2] *a.* & *n.* [F, or It. *trilione* (as TRI-, MILLION, after *billion*)]

trī'lobīte *n.* Fossil marine arthropod of palaeozoic times, characterized by a three-lobed body. [f. mod. L *Trilobites* (TRI-, Gk *lobos* lobe; see -ITE[1])]

trĭ'logȳ *n.* Group of three related literary or operatic works, esp. (Gk Ant.) set of three tragedies to be performed in immediate succession. [f. Gk TRI(*logia* -LOGY)]

trĭm *a.*, *v.* (**-mm-**), & *n.* **1.** *a.* In good order, well arranged or equipped, neat, spruce; hence ~'LY[2] *adv.*, ~'NESS *n.* **2.** *v.t.* Set in good order, make neat or tidy, remove irregular or superfluous or unsightly parts from (lamp or strictly its wick, hedge, beard, folded sheets of book, etc.); remove (such parts; *off, away*) by clipping, pruning, planing, etc.; **~ (up)**, make (person, one*self*) neat in dress and appearance; ornament (dress etc. *with* ribbon, lace, etc.); adjust balance of (ship, boat, aircraft) by distribution of ballast, cargo, or passengers, arrange (yards, sails) to suit wind (lit. or fig.), (*trim* BY[1] *the head, stern*); (colloq.) rebuke sharply, thrash, cheat out of money, worst in bargain etc. **3.** *v.i.* Hold middle course in politics or opinion; attach oneself to temporarily prevailing views, or to neither of contesting parties; be time-server. **4.** *n.* State or degree of adjustment or readiness or fitness (*found everything in perfect trim*); **in ~,** suitably dressed, healthy, etc., (Naut.) in good order; **in fighting ~,** (of ship, or fig.) ready for battle. **5.** Adornment; dress, equipment; decorative material on furniture, vehicle, etc. **6.** Trimming of hair etc. **7.** Inclination of aircraft to horizontal. [a. & n. f. v., formally repr.

OE *trymman*, *trymian* make firm, arrange; but there is no clear evidence for the verb from OE to 1500]

trī'marăn *n.* Vessel like catamaran, with three hulls side by side. [f. TRI- + CATAMARAN]

trī'mer *n.* (Chem.) Compound like DIMER but with three times the monomer atoms; hence **trīmĕ'ric** *a.* [f. TRI- + -MER]

trīmĕ'ster *n.* Period of three months. [f. F *trimestre* f. L TRI(*mestris* f. *mensis* month)]

trĭ'mėter *n.* (Pros.) Verse of three measures; hence **trīmĕ'tric(al)** *adjs.* [f. L f. Gk TRI(*metros* f. *metron* measure)]

trĭ'mmer *n.* In vbl senses; one who trims articles of dress; person who trims in politics etc., time-server; instrument for clipping etc.; (Archit.) short piece of timber across opening (e.g. for hearth) to carry ends of truncated joists; small capacitor etc. used to tune radio set. [f. TRIM + -ER¹]

trĭ'mmĭng *n.* In vbl senses; ornamentation of lace, braid, etc., on dress etc.; (in *pl.*) pieces cut off in trimming, (colloq.) usual accompaniments esp. of meat-joint etc. [f. TRIM + -ING¹]

trīne *a.* & *n.* **1.** *a.* Threefold, triple, made up of three parts; ~ **aspersion** or **immersion,** thrice sprinkling in baptism; hence **trī'nal** *a.* **2.** *a.* & *n.* (Astrol.) (Of) aspect of two planets 120° (one-third of zodiac) apart; **in** ~, so related (*to*). [ME, f. OF *trin trine* f. L *trinus* threefold (*tres* three)]

trīnītrotŏ'lūēne, -ūŏl, *n.* High explosive formed from toluene by substitution of nitro (NO_2) groups for three hydrogen atoms. [f. TRI- + NITRO- + TOLUENE]

trĭ'nĭtў *n.* Being three; group of three; **the (Holy) T~,** (Theol.) union of three Persons (Father, Son, Holy Spirit) in one Godhead, doctrine of this, whence **Trĭnĭtar'ian(ism)** *ns.*; **T~ (Sunday),** Sunday next after Whit Sunday; ||**T~ Brethren,** members of **T~ House,** association concerned with licensing of pilots, erection and maintenance of lighthouses, buoys, etc., in England, Wales, etc.; ||**T~ term** (in university etc., beginning after Easter). [ME, f. OF *trinité* f. L *trinitas -tatis* triad f. as TRINE; see -ITY]

trĭ'nkėt *n.* Trifling ornament, jewel, etc., worn on the person; small fancy article; hence ~RY (1, 5) *n.* [16th c., of unkn. orig.]

trī'ō (-ē'ō) *n.* (*pl.* ~s). **1.** (Mus.) (Performers of) composition for three voices or instruments (**piano** ~, violin, violoncello, and piano); second division of minuet, scherzo, march, etc. (perh. orig. performed by trio of instruments). **2.** Set of three; three aces, kings, queens, or jacks, in one hand at piquet. [F & It., f. L *tres* three, after *duo*]

trī'ōde *n.* Thermionic valve having three electrodes; semiconductor rectifier having three terminals. [f. TRI- + ELECTRODE]

trī'olėt (*or* trē'-) *n.* Poem of 8 (usu. 8-syllabled) lines rhyming *abaaabab*, first line recurring as fourth and seventh and second as eighth. [F (as TRIO; see -LET)]

trī'or. Var. of TRIER (Law).

trĭp *v.* (-pp-) & *n.* **1.** *v.i.* Walk or dance with quick light steps; (fig., of rhythm etc.) run lightly. **2.** Take a trip (*to* a place, or esp. with drugs); hence ||**~'per**¹ *n.*, person who goes on a trip esp. for a day's pleasure. **3.** Make false step, stumble, (*on* or *over* obstacle, difficulty, etc.); make mistake, commit inconsistency or inaccuracy or moral delinquency. **4.** *v.t.* ~ (**up**), (of person or obstacle) cause (person) to stumble by entangling or suddenly catching his feet, (fig.) detect (person) in blunder. **5.** (Naut.) release and raise (anchor) from bottom by means of cable, turn (yard etc.) from horizontal to vertical position for lowering; release (part of machine) suddenly by knocking aside catch etc. **6.** *n.* Journey, voyage, excursion esp. for pleasure (ROUND¹ *trip*); (colloq.) visionary experience caused by drug; EGO-*trip*. **7.** Nimble step. **8.** Stumble (lit. or fig.); tripping or being tripped up. **9.** Contrivance for tripping mechanism etc. **10.** **~-hammer,** large TILT¹-*hammer* operated by tripping; **~-wire** (stretched near ground to trip up enemy etc. and often operating warning device, mine, etc.). [ME, f. OF *treper*, *trip(p)er*, f. MDu. *trippen* skip, hop]

trīpar'tīte *a.* Consisting of three parts; (Bot., of leaf) divided into three segments almost to the base; shared by or involving three parties; ~ **indenture** (with three corresponding parts or copies); hence ~LY² (-tlĭ) *adv.*, **trīparti'tion** *n.* [ME, f. L TRI(*partitus* p.p. of *partiri* divide)]

trīpe *n.* First or second stomach of ox etc. as food; (in *pl.*, vulg.) entrails, belly; (sl.) worthless or trashy thing; ***~-de-roche*** (trēpderō'sh) [F, lit. rock-tripe], bitter slightly nutritive vegetable substance obtained from some lichens and used at a pinch by Canadian hunters etc. as food; **~'man,** man who prepares and sells tripe; hence **trī'pery** (3) *n.* [ME f. OF, of unkn. orig.]

trīphĭ'bĭous *a.* (Of military operations) on land, on sea, and in the air. [irreg. f. TRI- after *amphibious*]

trĭ'phthŏng *n.* Union of three vowels (letters or sounds) pronounced in one syllable (as in *fire*); three vowel characters representing sound of single vowel (as in *beau*); hence ~AL (-ŏ'ngg-) *a.* [f. F *triphtongue* (as TRI-, DIPHTHONG)]

trī'plāne *n.* Aeroplane with three sets of wings. [f. TRI- + PLANE³]

trĭ'ple *a.* & *v.* **1.** *a.* Threefold, consisting of three parts or involving three parties (*triple entente*); *triple* ACROSTIC; **T~ Alliance,** alliance of three States etc., esp. (1) between England, Sweden, and Netherlands in 1668 against Louis XIV, (2) between France, Great Britain, and Netherlands in 1717 chiefly against Spain, (3) between Germany, Austria, and Italy, in 1882–3 against Russia and France; ~ **crown,** (1) pope's tiara, (2) winning of all three of group of important events in horse-racing, rugby football, etc.; ~ **fugue** (with three subjects); ~ **jump,** = HOP³, *step, and jump*; ~ **play,** (Baseball) putting out three runners; *triple* RHYME¹; ~ **time** (Mus., with three beats to the bar). **2.** Amounting or equivalent to three times the amount or number of; hence **trĭ'ply**² *adv.* **3.** *n.* Set of three; number or amount three times greater than another; (in *pl.*) peal of changes on seven bells. **4.** *v.t.* & *i.* Multiply by three. [OF, or f. L *triplus* f. Gk *triplous*; v. ME, f. LL *triplare* f. L *triplus*]

trĭ'plėt *n.* Set of three things; three verses rhyming together; (Mus.) group of three notes performed in the time of two; one of three children or animals born at a birth. [f. prec. + -ET¹, after *doublet*]

trĭ'plĕx *a.* Triple, threefold; ~ **(glass), (P)** unsplinterable glass consisting of transparent sheet of plastic material between two sheets of glass. [L TRI(*plex -plicis* f. *plic-* fold)]

trĭ'plĭcate¹ *a.* & *n.* **1.** *a.* Threefold; (esp.) of which three copies are made. **2.** *n.* Each of a set of three copies or corresponding parts; state of being triplicate (*document drawn up in triplicate*). [ME, f. L *triplicatus* p.p. of *triplicare* (as prec.; see -ATE²)]

trĭ'plĭc|āte² *v.t.* Treble, make triplicate; so ~A'TION *n.* [f. as prec. + -ATE³]

trĭplĭ'cĭtȳ *n.* State of being triple; group of three things; (Astrol.) set of three zodiacal signs 120° apart. [ME, f. LL *triplicitas* f. L TRIPLEX; see -ITY]

trĭ'ploid *a.* & *n.* (Biol.) (Organism or cell) having three times the haploid set of chromosomes; hence ~Y¹ *n.*, condition of being triploid. [f. mod. L *triploides* f. Gk (as TRIPLE; see -OID)]

trī'pŏd *n.* Stool, table, utensil, resting on three feet or legs; three-legged stand for supporting camera etc.; (Gk Ant.) bronze altar at Delphi on which priestess sat to utter oracles; hence **trĭ'pod**AL *a.* [f. L *tripus tripodis* f. Gk TRI(*pous podos* foot)]

trĭ'polĭ *n.* = ROTTEN-stone. [F, f. *T~* in N. Africa or in Syria]

‖**trī'pŏs** *n.* (Camb. Univ.) Honours examination for degree of Bachelor of Arts. [as TRIPOD, w. ref. to stool on which B.A. sat to deliver satirical speech at Commencement]

‖**trĭ'pper.** See TRIP 2.

trĭ'ptȳch (-k) *n.* Picture or carving on three panels with sides able to fold over centre, set of three associated pictures so placed, esp. as altar-piece; set of three writing-tablets hinged or tied together; set of three artistic works. [f. TRI- after *diptych*]

trĭpty'que (-ē'k) *n.* Customs permit serving as passport for motor vehicle. [F, as prec. (orig. having three sections)]

trĭquĕ'tr|a *n.* (*pl.* **~ae**). Symmetrical ornament of three interlaced arcs; so ~AL, ~OUS, *adjs.*, (esp. Biol.) triangular in cross-section etc. [L, fem. of *triquetrus* three-cornered]

trī'rēme *n.* Ancient esp. Greek warship with three banks of oars. [f. F *trirème* or f. L TRI(*remis* f. *remus* oar)]

Trĭsă'giŏn (-g-) *n.* Hymn esp. in Eastern Churches with triple invocation of God as holy. [ME f. Gk, neut. of *trisagios* (*tris* thrice, *hagios* holy)]

trīsĕ'ct *v.t.* Cut or divide into three (usu. equal) parts; hence or cogn. ~ION, ~OR, *ns.* [f. TRI- + L *secare sect-* cut]

trī'shaw *n.* Light three-wheeled pedalled vehicle used in Far East. [f. TRI- + RICKSHAW]

trĭskĕ'lĭon *n.* Symbolic figure of three legs or lines from common centre. [f. Gk TRI- + *skelos* leg]

trĭ'smus (-z-) *n.* (Path.) = LOCK³*jaw*. [mod. L, f. Gk *trismos* = *trigmos* a scream, grinding]

triste (-ē-) *a.* Sad, melancholy, dreary. [F, f. L *tristis*]

trĭ'stful *a.* (arch.) = prec. [f. obs. *trist* a. (as prec.) + -FUL]

trĭsȳ'llable *n.* Word or metrical foot of three syllables; so **trĭsȳllă'bĭ**C *a.* [f. TRI- + SYLLABLE]

trĭtă'gonĭst *n.* Third actor in Greek play (cf. DEUTERAGONIST). [f. Gk *tritagōnistēs* (*tritos* third, *agōnistēs* actor)]

trīte *a.* (Of expression, sentiment, quotation, etc.) commonplace, hackneyed, worn out by constant repetition; hence ~'LY² (-tlĭ) *adv.*, ~'NESS (-tn-) *n.* [f. L *tritus* p.p. of *terere* rub]

trī'thē|ĭsm *n.* Doctrine that there are (esp. that Father, Son, and Holy Spirit are) three Gods; hence ~IST (2) *n.*, **~ĭ'stĭ**C(AL) *adjs.* [f. TRI- + THEISM]

trĭ'tĭ|āte *v.t.* Replace ordinary hydrogen in (substance) by tritium; hence ~A'TION *n.* [f. foll. + -ATE³]

trĭ'tĭum *n.* (Chem.) Heavy radioactive isotope of hydrogen with mass about three times that of ordinary hydrogen. [mod. L, f. Gk *tritos* third + -IUM]

trĭ'tō- *comb. form.* Third, as: **T~Isaiah,** supposed later author of Isaiah 56–66. [f. Gk *tritos* third + -O-]

Trī'ton¹ *n.* **1.** (Gk Myth.) minor sea-god usu. represented as man with fish's tail and carrying trident and shell-trumpet; *Triton among the* MINNOWS. **2.** (*t~*). Marine gastropod of family Cymatiidae, with long conical shell; newt. [L, f. Gk *Tritōn*]

trī'tŏn² *n.* Nucleus of tritium atom, consisting of proton and two neutrons. [f. TRITIUM + -ON]

trĭ'tūr|āte *v.t.* Grind to fine powder; masticate thoroughly; hence or cogn. ~ABLE *a.*, ~A'TION, **~āt**OR, *ns.* [f. L *triturare* thresh corn (*tritura* rubbing, as TRITE; see -URE) + -ATE³]

trī'umph *n.*, & *v.i.* **1.** *n.* (Rom. Ant.) Procession into Rome and ceremony in honour of victory and victorious general. **2.** State of being victorious or successful, signal success, great achievement, thing that constitutes this, (*returned home in triumph*; *has achieved great triumphs*; *the triumphs of science*); joy at success, manifestation of this, exultation, (*great was his triumph on hearing this*; *could detect no triumph in his eye*). **3.** *v.i.* (Rom. Ant.) enjoy a triumph; gain victory, be successful, prevail, (*over* enemy, opposition, obstacles, etc.); exult (*over* fallen enemy etc., or abs.). [ME; n. f. OF *triumphe*, v. f. OF *triumpher* f. L *triumphare*, f. L *triump(h)us*, prob. f. Gk *thriambos* hymn to Bacchus]

trīŭ'mphal *a.* Of, used in, celebrating, a triumph (*triumphal car*, *progress*, *hymn*); **~ arch** (built to commemorate victory etc.). [ME f. OF, or f. L *triumphalis* (as prec.; see -AL)]

trīŭ'mphant *a.* Victorious, successful, (CHURCH¹ *triumphant*); (of person, speech, voice, etc.) exulting; hence ~LY² *adv.* [ME f. OF, or f. L *triumphare*; see TRIUMPH, -ANT]

trīŭ'mvir *n.* (*pl.* **~s,** *or* **~i** *pr.* -ī). (Rom. Hist. etc.) Each of three men united in office; each member of first or second triumvirate; hence ~AL *a.* [L, orig. in pl. *triumviri*, back form. f. *trium virorum* gen. of *tres viri* three men]

trīŭ'mvirate *n.* Office of a triumvir; set of triumvirs or of any three persons (esp. in authority); (Rom. Hist.) **first ~,** (coalition 60 B.C. between) Pompey, Julius Caesar, and Crassus, **second ~,** (that in 43 B.C. between) Mark Antony, Octavian, and Lepidus. [f. L *triumviratus* (as prec.; see -ATE¹)]

trī'ūne *a.* Three in one (*triune Godhead*); hence **trīū'n**ITY *n.* [f. TRI- + L *unus* one]

trĭ'vėt *n.* Iron tripod for holding cooking-vessels over heat; iron bracket designed to hook on to bars of grate for similar purposes; *metal plate on three feet for hot dish; **as right** (orig. = steady) **as a ~,** (*a.* & *adv.*, colloq.) in perfectly good health or position or circumstances; **~ table** (with three feet). [ME *trevet*, app. f. L TRI(*pes pedis* foot) three-footed]

trĭ'vĭa *n. pl.* Trifles, trivialities. [mod. L, pl. of TRIVIUM, infl. by foll.]

trĭ'vĭal *a.* Of small value or importance, trifling, (*trivial matters*, *offence*, *loss*; *raised trivial objections*); (of person) concerned only with trivial things; (arch.) commonplace, humdrum, (*the trivial round of daily life*); (Biol. & Chem., of name) (1) popular, not scientific, (2) specific, opp. to generic; (Math.) giving rise to no difficulty or interest; hence ~ITY (-ă'l-), ~NESS, *ns.*, ~IZE (3) *v.t.*, ~LY² *adv.* [f. L *trivialis* commonplace (*trivium*; see foll., -AL)]

trĭ'vĭum *n.* (Hist.) Medieval university course of grammar, rhetoric, and logic. [L, = place where three roads meet (as TRI-, *via* road)]

-trĭx *suf.* (*pl.* **-trices** *pr.* -trĭsĭz *or* -trī'sēz, *or* **-trixes**), forming *fem.* agent *ns.* corresp. to *masc. ns.* in *-tor*, esp. in Law (*executrix*, *administra-*

trix) & Geom. = straight line (*directrix*). [f. L -*trix* -*tricis*]

troat *v.i.*, & *n.* (Make) cry of rutting buck. [cf. OF *tr(o)ut*, int. for urging on hunting dogs etc.]

trō'căr *n.* (Surg.) Instrument used in dropsy etc. for withdrawing fluid from body. [f. F *trois-quarts*, *trocart* (*trois* three + *carre* side, face of instrument), f. its triangular form]

trochā'ĭc (-k-) *a.* & *n.* (Pros.) **1.** *a.* Of or using trochees (*trochaic dimeter*, *tetrameter*). **2.** *n.* (usu. in *pl.*) Trochaic verse. [f. L f. Gk *trokhaikos* (as TROCHEE; see -IC)]

trō'chal (-k-) *a.* (Zool.) Wheel-shaped; ~ **disc,** flattened end of rotifer serving to draw in food or to propel. [f. Gk *trokhos* wheel + -AL]

trochă'nter (-k-) *n.* (Anat. & Zool.) Each of several bony processes for attachment of muscles on upper part of thigh-bone; second segment of leg in insects. [F, f. Gk *trokhantēr* (*trekhō* run)]

trōche (-k, -sh, -ch, *or* trō'kē) *n.* Small usu. circular medicated tablet or lozenge. [f. obs. *trochisk* f. OF *trochisque* f. LL f. Gk *trokhiskos* dim. of *trokhos* wheel]

trō'chee (-kĭ) *n.* (Pros.) Foot consisting of one long followed by one short syllable. [f. L f. Gk *trokhaios* (*pous*) running (foot) (*trekhō* run)]

trŏ'chĭlus (-k-) *n.* Small Egyptian bird mentioned by ancient writers as picking crocodiles' teeth. [f. L f. Gk *trokhilos* (*trekhō* run)]

trŏ'chlė|a (-k-) *n.* (*pl.* **~ae**). (Anat.) Pulley--like part or arrangement; hence ~AR¹ *a.* [L, = pulley, f. Gk *trokhilia*]

trō'choid (-k-) *a.* & *n.* **1.** *a.* (Anat.) rotating on its own axis; (of curve) generated by a point moving with one curve that rolls on another; (of shell) top-shaped. **2.** *n.* Trochoid joint or curve; top-shell. **3.** Hence ~AL (-koi'-) *a.* [f. Gk *trokhoeidēs* wheel-like (*trokhos* wheel; see -OID)]

trō'chus (-k-) *n.* Top-shell, esp. of genus *Trochus*. [L, f. Gk *trokhos* wheel]

trŏd('den), trōde. See TREAD.

trŏ'glodўt|e *n.* Cave-dweller, esp. of prehistoric times; (fig.) hermit; anthropoid ape; hence or cogn. **trŏglodў'tic**(AL) *adjs.*, ~ISM (2) *n.* [f. L f. Gk *trōglodutēs* f. name of Ethiopian people, after *trōglē* hole]

trō'gŏn *n.* Tropical bird of genus *Trogon*, with brilliantly coloured plumage. [mod. L, f. Gk *trōgōn* (*trōgō* gnaw)]

troi'ka *n.* (Russian vehicle with) team of three horses abreast; group of three persons, esp. as administrative council. [Russ. (*troe* three)]

Trō'jan *a.* & *n.* **1.** (Inhabitant) of Troy; ~ **War** (legendary ten years' struggle between Greeks under Agamemnon and Trojans under Priam); ~ **Horse,** hollow wooden horse used by Greeks to enter Troy, (fig.) person or device that is insinuated to bring about enemy's downfall. **2.** *n.* (fig.) Person who works or fights or endures courageously (*like a Trojan*). [ME, earlier *Troyan*, *Troian*, f. L *Troianus* (*Troia* Troy, ancient city in N.W. Asia Minor)]

trōll¹ *v.* & *n.* **1.** *v.t.* & *i.* Sing out in carefree jovial spirit; fish for, fish in (water), fish, with rod and running line and dead bait or with spoon-bait drawn along behind boat. **2.** *n.* Trolling for fish; line or bait used in this. [ME 'stroll, roll'; cf. OF *troller* to quest, MHG *trollen* stroll]

trōll² *n.* (Scand. & Gmc Myth.) Supernatural being, giant or (now usu.) friendly but mischievous dwarf. [f. ON & Sw. *troll*, Da. *trold*]

trŏ'lley, trŏ'llў, *n.* ||Low truck running on rails; ||small table or stand on wheels or castors for use in serving food, transporting light objects, luggage, etc.; ~**(-wheel)**, wheel attached to pole etc. used for collecting current from overhead electric wire to drive vehicle (||~**bus,** electric bus running on road and using trolley; *~**-car,** electric tram using trolley); * = *trolley-car*. [of dial. orig., perh. f. TROLL¹]

trŏ'llop *n.* Slatternly woman, slut; prostitute; hence ~ISH¹, ~Y², *adjs.* [17th c.; perh. rel. to TRULL]

trŏmbō'n|e (*or* -ŏ'm-) *n.* Large brass wind instrument with sliding tube, whence ~IST (3) *n.*; its player; organ reed-stop of similar quality. [F or f. It. (*tromba* trumpet; see TRUMP¹, -OON)]

trŏ'mmel *n.* (Mining). Revolving cylindrical sieve for cleaning ore. [G, = drum]

tromŏ'mėter *n.* Instrument for measuring very slight earthquake shocks. [f. Gk *tromos* trembling + -METER]

trŏmpe *n.* Apparatus for producing blast in furnace by using falling water to displace air. [F, = trumpet; see TRUMP¹]

trompe-l'œil (trŏmp lŭ'ē) *n.* & *a.* (Still-life painting etc.) designed to make spectator think objects represented are real. [F, lit. 'deceives the eye']

-trŏn *suf.* forming *ns.* w. sense (1) thermionic valve etc. (*dynatron*, *klystron*), (2) elementary particle (*positron*), (3) particle accelerator (*betatron*, *cyclotron*, *synchrotron*). [f. ELECTRON]

trōōp *n.* & *v.* **1.** *n.* Assembled company, assemblage of persons or animals, (*a troop of children*, *of antelopes*; *surrounded by troops of friends*); (in *pl.*) soldiers, armed forces, (||HOUSEHOLD *troops*); cavalry unit commanded by captain; unit of artillery and armoured formation; grouping of three or more Scout patrols. **2.** ~**-carrier,** large aircraft, *or armoured vehicle, for transporting troops; ~**-ship,** = TRANSPORT² 2. **3.** *v.i.* Assemble, flock together; move in a troop (*along*, *in*, *out*, etc.); (colloq.) go, walk, *off* or *away*. **4.** *v.t.* Form (regiment) into troops; ||~**ing the colour**(**s**), ceremony of transferring flags and carrying them along ranks of soldiers at public mounting of garrison guards. [f. F *troupe*, back form. f. *troupeau* dim. of med. L *troppus* flock, prob. of Gmc orig.]

trōō'per *n.* **1.** Cavalry soldier; private soldier in cavalry or armoured unit; **swear like a** ~ (extensively or forcefully). **2.** Cavalry horse; troop-ship; (Austral. & U.S.) mounted or motor-borne policeman. [f. prec. + -ER¹]

tropae'olum *n.* S. Amer. trailing or climbing plant of genus *Tropaeolum*, with spurred yellow or scarlet flowers. [mod. L, f. L *tropaeum* TROPHY, w. ref. to likeness of flower and leaf to helmet and shield]

trōpe *n.* Figurative (e.g. metaphorical or ironical) use of a word. [f. L f. Gk *tropos* turn, way, trope, (*trepō* turn)]

trŏ'phĭc *a.* Concerned with nutrition (*trophic nerves*). [f. Gk *trophikos* (*trophē* nourishment f. *trephō* nourish; see -IC)]

trŏ'pho- *comb. form.* Nourishment, as: ~**blast,** layer of tissue on outside of mammalian blastula thought to nourish embryo; ~**neuro'sis,** defective nutrition due to derangement of nerves. [f. Gk *trophē* (see prec.) + -O-]

trō'ph|ў *n.* **1.** (Gk & Rom. Ant.) Arms etc. of vanquished enemy set up on field of battle or elsewhere to commemorate victory. **2.** Thing made or kept or awarded as memorial of victory (lit. or fig.); memorial or token of valour, skill, etc.; ornamental group or symbolic or typical objects arranged on wall etc. **3.** Hence (-)~**ĭED²** (-ĭd) *a.* [f. F *trophée* f. L *trop(h)aeum* f. Gk *tropaion* (*tropē* rout f. *trepō* turn)]

trŏ'pĭc *n.* & *a.* **1.** *n.* Parallel of latitude 23° 27′ north (~ **of Cancer**) or south (~ **of Capri-**

For other words in *tri-* see TRI-.

corn) of the equator (**the ~s,** region between these); each of the two corresponding circles on celestial sphere where sun appears to turn after reaching greatest declination; **~-bird,** ternlike sea-bird of genus *Phaethon*. **2.** *a.* = foll. 1. **3.** (as *suf.*) = -TROPHIC. [ME, f. L f. Gk *tropikos* (*tropē* turning f. *trepō* turn; see -IC)]

trŏ'pĭcal *a.* **1.** Of, peculiar to, suggestive of, the tropics, (*tropical fish, plants, diseases, heat; tropical* YEAR); (fig.) very hot, passionate, luxuriant. **2.** Of trope(s), figurative. **3.** Hence ~LY[2] *adv.* [f. as prec. + -AL]

trŏ'pĭsm *n.* (Biol.) Turning of (part of) organism in particular direction in response to external stimulus. [f. second element of *heliotropism* etc.]

tropŏ'logy̆ *n.* Figurative use of words; figurative interpretation esp. of the Scriptures; hence **trŏpolŏ'g**ICAL *a.* [f. LL f. Gk *tropologia* (as TROPE; see -LOGY)]

trŏ'popause (-z) *n.* Interface between troposphere and stratosphere. [f. foll. + PAUSE]

trŏ'posph|ēre *n.* Layer of atmospheric air extending about seven miles upwards from earth's surface, in which temperature falls with increasing height (cf. STRATOSPHERE); hence **~ĕ'r**IC *a.* [f. Gk *tropos* turning + -O- + SPHERE]

troppo (trŏ'pō) *adv.* (Mus.) Too; *andante* etc. ***ma non*** **~**, but not too much so. [It.]

trŏt *v.* (-tt-) & *n.* **1.** *v.i.* (Of horse etc.) proceed at steady pace faster than walk lifting each diagonal pair of legs alternately, often with brief intervals during which body is unsupported; (of person) run at moderate pace esp. with short strides (*along* etc.), (colloq.) walk, go. **2.** *v.t.* Cause (horse, person) to trot; traverse (distance) by trotting; **~ out,** cause (horse) to trot to show his paces, (fig.) produce, introduce, (person, thing, information, subject) for or as if for inspection and approval. **3.** *n.* Action or exercise of trotting (*proceed at a trot; went for a trot*); (fig.) brisk steady movement or occupation; ||toddling child; *(sl.) student's crib; (in *pl.*, Austral. colloq.) (meeting for) trotting-races; (in *pl.*, sl.) diarrhoea; **on the ~**, (colloq.) (1) continually busy (*kept him on the trot*), (2) in succession (*for five weeks on the trot*). [ME, f. OF (*trot* n. f.) *troter* f. Rom. & med. L *trottare*, of Gmc orig.]

trōth *n.* (arch.) **1.** Truth; **(in) ~, by my ~,** truly, upon my word. **2.** Faith, loyalty, (*pledge one's troth*); **plight** one's **~**, pledge one's word esp. in betrothal. [ME *trowthe*, for OE *trēowth* TRUTH]

Trŏ'tsky̆|ĭsm *n.* Political or economic principles of Trotsky, esp. as urging world-wide socialist revolution; so ~IST (2), ~ITE[1], *ns.* [f. L. *Trotsky* (L. D. Bronstein), Russ. politician d. 1940 + -ISM]

trŏ'tter *n.* In vbl senses; horse of special breed trained for trotting; (usu. in *pl.*) animal's foot used as food (*pigs' trotters*), (joc.) human foot. [ME, f. TROT + -ER[1]]

trŏ'ttĭng *n.* In vbl senses; harness racing for trotting horses. [f. TROT + -ING[1]]

trottoir (trŏtwar̄') *n.* Pavement at side of street. [F (*trotter* TROT)]

trŏ'ty̆l *n.* Trinitrotoluene. [f. trini*tro*toluene + -YL]

trou'badour (-ōō'badoor) *n.* Lyric poet in S. France etc. 11th–13th c., singing in Provençal mainly of chivalry and courtly love. [F, f. Prov. *trobador* (*trobar* find, invent, compose in verse)]

trou'ble (trŭ'b-) *v.* & *n.* **1.** *v.t.* & *i.* Agitate, disturb, be disturbed or worried, (FISH[2] *in troubled waters; don't let it trouble you, don't trouble about it; has been troubled about* or *with money matters; a troubled conscience, countenance*). **2.** *v.t.* Afflict, cause pain etc. to, (*am troubled with neuralgia; how long has it been troubling you?*). **3.** *v.t.* & *i.* Subject or be subjected to inconvenience or unpleasant exertion (esp. in polite or ironically polite speech: *may I trouble you to shut the door?, to mind your own business?; sorry to trouble you; don't trouble (to explain* etc., or abs.)). **4.** *n.* Vexation, affliction, (*has been through much trouble; am having trouble with the ignition, with my teeth*); (in *pl.*) public disturbances; faulty operation (*engine trouble*); disease (*suffers from kidney trouble*); cause of vexation etc. (*the trouble with him is that he always wants to win*); **ask for** or **look for ~**, (colloq.) meddle, be rash, etc.; **in ~**, subject to censure, punishment, etc., (colloq.) pregnant but unmarried; so **get** (*v.t.* & *i.*) **into ~; make ~**, cause disturbance or disagreement. **5.** Inconvenience or unpleasant exertion (*did it to spare you trouble; shall not put you to any trouble in the matter; might have saved myself the trouble*; **give** one**self (the) ~, go to the, some,** etc., **~, take (the) ~**, exert oneself to do something), cause of this (*fear that the child is a great trouble to you*; **be no ~**, cause no inconvenience etc.). **6. ~-maker,** troublesome person, esp. deliberate fomenter of disagreement; **~-shooter,** (1) person who traces and corrects faults in machinery etc., (2) mediator in diplomatic, industrial, etc., disputes; **~-spot,** place where trouble frequently occurs. [ME, f. OF (*truble* n. f.) *trubler, turbler* f. Rom. **turbulare* (**turbulus* for L *turbidus* TURBID)]

trou'blesome (trŭ'bels-) *a.* (Of person or thing) causing trouble, vexatious; hence ~LY[2] (-mlĭ) *adv.*, ~NESS (-mn-) *n.* [f. prec. + -SOME[1]]

trou'blous (trŭ'b-) *a.* (arch. or literary). Full of troubles, agitated, disturbed, (*troublous times*). [ME, f. OF *troubleus* (as TROUBLE; see -OUS)]

trough (-ŏf *or* -awf) *n.* Long narrow open wooden or other receptacle for holding water or food for sheep etc., kneading dough, washing ore, etc. (BOOK[1]-, PNEUMATIC, *trough*); wooden or other channel for conveying liquid; hollow between two waves; (Meteorol.) elongated region of low barometric pressure; region near minimum on curve of variation of a quantity. [OE *trog*, = OS, ON *trog*, OHG *troc* f. Gmc **trugaz* f. IE **drukós* (**dru-* wood, tree)]

trounce *v.t.* Beat severely, castigate, (lit. or fig.). [16th c. 'afflict', of unkn. orig.]

troup|e (-ōōp) *n.* Company of actors, acrobats, etc.; hence ~'ER[1] *n.*, member of a theatrical troupe, (fig.) staunch colleague. [F, = TROOP]

trou'ser (-z-) *n.* **1. (Pair of) ~s,** two-legged outer garment reaching from waist usu. to ankles; WEAR[1] *the trousers*. **2. ~-clip,** = BICYCLE-*clip*; **~(s) pocket** (esp. as holding one's money, or hand when idle); **~-press** (to make or keep crease in legs of trousers); **~-suit,** woman's suit of trousers and jacket. **3.** Hence ~ED[2] (-zerd) *a.*, ~ING[1] (3) *n.* [in pl. as extended pl. form, after *drawers*, of arch. *trouse* sing., f. Ir. (& Gael.) *triubhas* TREWS]

trousseau (trōō'sō *or* trōōsō') *n.* (*pl.* **~s** *or* **~x** *pr.* -z). Bride's outfit of clothes etc. to begin married life. [F, lit. bundle, dim. of *trousse* TRUSS]

trout *n.* (*pl.* usu. same). Small fish of genus *Salmo* in northern rivers and lakes, esteemed as food and game; similar fish of family Salmonidae (SALMON or *sea trout*); (sl., derog.) *old* etc. woman; hence ~'LET, ~'LING[1], *ns.*, ~'Y[2] *a.* [OE *truht* f. LL *tructa*]

trouvaille (trōō'vīl) *n.* Lucky find, windfall. [F (*trouver* find)]

trouvère (trōōvar̄') *n.* Epic poet in N. France in 11th–14th c. [f. OF *trovere* (*trover* find); cf. TROUBADOUR]

trōve *n.* = TREASURE *trove*.

trō'ver *n.* (Law). Finding and keeping personal property; common-law action to recover value of personal property wrongfully taken or detained. [AF, f. OF *trover* to find; see -ER[4]]

trow (*or* -ō) *v.t.* (arch.) Think, believe. [OE *trūwian, trēowian*, cogn. w. TRUCE]

trow'el *n.*, & *v.t.* (‖-ll-). **1.** *n.* Mason's or bricklayer's flat-bladed short-handled tool for spreading mortar etc.; **lay it on with a ~**, (fig.) flatter lavishly. **2.** Gardener's short-handled scoop for lifting plants etc. **3.** *v.t.* Apply (plaster etc.), dress (wall etc.), with trowel. [ME, f. OF *truele* f. med. L *truella* f. L *trulla* scoop dim. of *trua* ladle etc.]

troy *n.* ~ **(weight)**, system of weights used for precious metals and gems, with pound of twelve ounces or 5760 grains. [ME, prob. f. *Troyes* in France]

trs. *abbr.* transpose.

tru'ant (-ōō'-) *n., a.,* & *v.i.* **1.** *n.* One who absents himself from place of work, esp. child who stays away from school without leave; **play ~**, stay away thus. **2.** *a.* (Of person, conduct, character, thoughts, etc.) shirking, idle, loitering, wandering. **3.** *v.i.* Play truant. **4.** Hence **tru'**ANCY (-ōō'-) *n.* [ME f. OF, f. Gallo-Rom. **trugant-* prob. f. Celt. (W *truan*, Gael. *truaghan* wretched)]

truce (-ōōs) *n.* (Agreement for) temporary cessation of hostilities (FLAG[4] *of truce*); respite from pain etc., rest from work etc. (**a ~ to,** (arch.) let us have done with); **~ of God,** (Hist.) suspension of war or of private feuds esp. during certain church festivals etc.; hence ~'LESS (-sl-) *a.* [ME *trew(e)s* etc. pl. of *tru(w)e* f. OE *trēow*, OS *treuwa*, OHG *triuwa*, Goth. *triggwa* covenant]

tru'cial (-ōō'shal) *a.* (Hist.) Of or bound by truce of 1835 between Britain and Arab sheikhs of Oman Peninsula. [f. prec. + -IAL, app. after *fiducial*]

trŭck[1] *v.* & *n.* **1.** *v.i.* Make an exchange, trade, bargain, (*with* person *for* thing). **2.** *v.t.* Exchange, barter, (thing *for* another). **3.** *n.* Exchange, barter, traffic, (**have no ~ with,** avoid dealing with); small wares; *market-garden produce (*truck farm, garden*); (colloq.) rubbish, nonsense. **4.** ~ **(system)**, (Hist.) practice of paying workmen in goods instead of money or in money on the understanding that they will buy provisions etc. in ~ **shop** from their employers. [ME, f. AF **truquer*, OF **troquer*, = med. L *trocare*, of unkn. orig.]

trŭck[2] *n.* & *v.* **1.** *n.* Strong usu. four- or six-wheeled vehicle for heavy goods, lorry; ‖open railway wagon; motor vehicle for transporting goods, troops, etc.; porter's two-, three-, or four-, wheeled barrow for luggage at railway station etc.; railway bogie; wheeled stand for transporting goods; (Naut.) wooden disc at top of mast with holes for halyards; small solid wheel. **2.** *v.t.* Convey on or in truck. **3.** *v.i.* *Drive truck. **4.** Hence ~'AGE (1, 3, 4) *n.* [perh. short for TRUCKLE in sense 'wheel, pulley']

***trŭ'cker** *n.* **1.** Market-gardener. **2.** Driver of truck. [f. TRUCK[1,2] + -ER[1]]

trŭ'ckle *v.i.*, & *n.* **1.** *v.i.* Submit obsequiously, cringe, (*to*); hence **trŭ'ckl**ER[1] *n.* **2.** *n.* ~**(-bed)**, low bed on wheels that may be pushed under another, esp. as formerly used by servants etc. [n. ME f. AF *trocle* f. L *trochlea*; v. orig. = to sleep in truckle-bed]

trŭ'cūl|ent *a.* Fierce, cruel; aggressive, savage; pugnacious; hence or cogn. ~ENCE, ~ENCY, *ns.*, ~**ent**LY[2] *adv.* [f. L *truculentus* (*trux trucis* fierce; see -ULENT)]

trŭdge *v.* & *n.* **1.** *v.i.* Walk esp. laboriously. **2.** *v.t.* Traverse (distance) by trudging. **3.** *n.* Trudging walk. [16th c., of unkn. orig.]

trŭ'dgen *n.* Swimming stroke like crawl with scissors movement of legs. [f. J. *Trudgen*, 19th-c. Engl. swimmer]

true (-ōō) *a., adv.,* & *v.t.* **1.** *a.* In accordance with fact or reality, not false or erroneous, (*his story is true*; *that is only too true*; *is it true that he refused?*); **come ~**, be realized in fact; **(it is) ~**, certainly, admittedly, (*true, it would cost more*). **2.** In accordance with reason or correct principles or accepted standard, rightly so called, genuine, not spurious or hybrid or counterfeit or merely apparent, having all the attributes implied in the name, (*could not form a true judgement*; *frog is not a true reptile*; *is a true benefactor, the true heir*); *true* HORIZON; *true* RIB; *true* SKIN[1]; ~ **north** etc. (geographical, not magnetic). **3.** Accurately conforming *to* (type etc.); **~ to life,** showing life as it really is. **4.** (Of voice etc.) in good tune. **5.** Loyal, constant, adhering faithfully, (*to* one's word, friend, one*self*, etc.). **6.** (Of wheel, post, beam, etc.) in correct position, balanced or upright or level; **out of (the) ~**, not in correct or exact position. **7.** (arch.) Not given to lying, veracious; honest (*true men*). **8. ~ bill,** (Hist. & U.S.) bill of indictment endorsed by grand jury as being sustained by evidence, (fig.) true statement or allegation; **~-blue** *a.* & *n.*, (person, esp. ‖Conservative or Presbyterian) of uncompromising orthodoxy or loyalty; **~-born,** of genuine or legitimate birth, truly such by birth (*a true-born Englishman*); **~-breed,** of genuine or good breed; **~-hearted,** faithful, loyal; **~-love,** (1) person truly loved or loving, sweetheart, (2) herb Paris, with four leaves arranged like **~-love(r's) knot** (kind of double knot with interlacing bows on each side, symbolizing true love); **~'penny,** (arch.) honest fellow. **9.** Hence ~'NESS *n.* **10.** Truly (*tell me true*; RING[2] *true*); accurately (*aim true*); without variation (*breed true*). **11.** *v.t.* Bring (tool, wheel, frame, etc.) into exact position or form required. [OE *trēowe*, *trȳwe*, = OS, OHG *triuwi*, ON *tryggr*, Goth. *triggws*, f. n. repr. by TRUCE]

trŭ'ffle *n.* Edible subterranean fungus of genus *Tuber*, esteemed for its rich flavour; globular sweetmeat of chocolate mixture covered with cocoa etc.; **~-dog, -pig,** (trained to discover truffles). [prob. f. Du. *truffel*, f. obs. F *truffle* perh. f. pop. L **tufera* for L *tubera* pl. of TUBER]

‖**trŭg** *n.* Wooden milk-pan; shallow garden basket made of wood strips. [perh. dial. var. of TROUGH]

tru'ism (-ōō'-) *n.* A self-evident or indisputable truth; proposition that states nothing not already implied in one of its terms (e.g. *I don't like my tea too hot* = *I don't like it hotter than I like it*); hackneyed truth, platitude. [f. TRUE + -ISM]

trŭll *n.* (arch.) Prostitute. [16th c.; cf. G *trulle*, TROLLOP]

tru'lȳ (-ōō'-) *adv.* Sincerely, genuinely, (*am truly grateful*; *a truly alarming state of affairs*; *a truly courageous act*; YOURS *truly*); (usu. parenth.) really, indeed, (*truly, I should be puzzled to say*); faithfully, loyally, (*has served his master truly*); accurately, truthfully, (*it has been truly stated*; *is not truly represented*); rightly, properly, (WELL[3] *and truly*). [OE *trēowlīce* (as TRUE, -LY[2])]

trumeau' (trōōmō') *n.* (*pl.* **~x** *pr.* -z). Piece of wall, pillar, between two openings, e.g. pillar dividing large doorway. [F]

trŭmp[1] *n.* (arch. or poet.) (Sound of) trumpet (LAST[3] *trump*; *trump of doom*). [ME f. OF *trompe*, f. Frank. **trumpa*, prob. imit.]

trŭmp[2] *n.* & *v.* **1.** *n.* Playing-card of a suit temporarily ranking above others; (colloq.) person of great excellence; **~ card,** card turned up to determine which suit shall be trumps, any card of this suit, (fig.) valuable resource; NO[1] *trump(s)*; **put** person **to his ~s,** (fig.) reduce him to his last resources; ||**turn up ~s,** (colloq.) turn out better than was expected, have a stroke of luck. **2.** *v.t.* Take (card, trick) with a trump; **~ up,** fabricate, invent, (story, excuse, accusation, etc.). **3.** *v.i.* Play a trump. [corrupt. f. TRIUMPH in same (now obs.) sense]

trŭ'mperў *n.* & *a.* **1.** *n.* Worthless finery; rubbish; nonsense. **2.** *a.* Showy but worthless, delusive, shallow, (*trumpery jewels, arguments*). [ME, f. OF *tromperie* (*tromper* deceive; see -ERY)]

trŭ'mpėt *n.* & *v.* **1.** *n.* Metal tubular or conical wind instrument with flared mouth and bright penetrating ringing tone, used for military etc. signals, by heralds, and in orchestral form having valves etc. to give additional notes; organ reed-stop with similar tone; trumpeter, esp. (Hist.) one sent as envoy; EAR[1], SPEAKING[1], *-trumpet*; trumpet-shaped thing, e.g. tubular corona of daffodil; sound (as) of trumpet; BLOW[1] one's *own trumpet*; **Feast of T~s,** Jewish festival celebrating beginning of year; FLOURISH[2] *of trumpets*; **marine ~,** large single-stringed viol with trumpet-like tone. **2.** **~-call,** call by sound of trumpet, (fig.) urgent summons to action; **~-creeper, -vine,** N. Amer. creeper with large red trumpet-shaped flowers; **~-flower, -leaf,** plant with trumpet-shaped flowers, leaves; **~-major,** head trumpeter of cavalry regiment; **~-shell,** = TRITON[1] 2, esp. of genus *Triton*. **3.** *v.t.* Proclaim (as) by sound of trumpet, (fig.) celebrate. **4.** *v.i.* Blow trumpet; (of enraged elephant etc.) make loud sound as of trumpet. [ME, f. OF *trompette* dim. (as TRUMP[1]; see -ET[1])]

trŭ'mpėter *n.* **1.** One who sounds a trumpet, esp. cavalry soldier giving signals with trumpet; **be** one's **own ~,** = BLOW[1] one's *own trumpet*. **2.** Bird making trumpet-like sound, esp. variety of domestic pigeon, or large S. Amer. cranelike bird of genus *Psophia*; **~ (swan),** large N. Amer. wild swan. **3.** Fish making trumpet-like sound when taken from water, esp. Austral. & N.Z. food-fish of genus *Latris*. [f. prec. + -ER[1] or f. F *trompeteur*]

trŭ'ncal *a.* Of the trunk of a body or tree. [f. TRUNK + -AL]

trŭ'nc|āte *v.t.*, & *a.* **1.** *v.t.* (*or* -ā't). Cut top or end from (tree, body, screw-thread, cone, pyramid, (fig.) sequence, quoted passage, etc.); (Cryst.) replace (edge or angle) by plane; hence **~A'TION** *n.* **2.** *a.* Truncated; (Bot. & Zool., of leaf, feather, etc.) ending abruptly as if cut off at tip, whence **~āteLY**[2] (-tlĭ) *adv.* [f. L *truncare* maim + -ATE[2,3]]

trŭ'ncheon (-shon) *n.* Short club or cudgel e.g. that carried by policeman; baton, staff of authority, esp. (Her.) that of Earl Marshal. [ME, f. OF *tronchon* stump f. Rom. **truncio -onis* f. L *truncus* trunk]

trŭ'ndle *n.* & *v.* **1.** *n.* Small broad wheel, e.g. castor; set of parallel rods between two discs, serving as pinion; **~(-bed),** truckle-bed. **2.** *v.t.* Roll, move on wheel(s), (hoop, truck, etc., *along, down*, etc.). **3.** *v.i.* (Of hoop etc.) move thus. [var. of obs. or dial. *trendle, trindle*, f. OE *trendel* circle (as TREND)]

trŭnk *n.* **1.** Main stem of tree opp. to branches and roots; human or animal body apart from head and limbs (and tail); main part of any structure. **2.** Main body of artery, nerve, etc.; **~(-line),** main line of railway or canal, main telephone line (esp. from town to town). **3.** Large box with hinged lid, for carrying clothes etc. on journey (WARDROBE *trunk*); *boot of motor car. **4.** Shaft, conduit, or trough, usu. rectangular and of wood, for ventilation, separation of ores, etc. **5.** Long flexible nose of elephant etc. **6.** (in *pl.*) Short breeches worn with tights etc.; short close-fitting breeches worn by men for swimming, boxing, etc.; men's short underpants. **7.** **~-call,** telephone call on trunk-line with charges according to distance; **~ hose,** 16th–17th-c. puffed breeches from waist to middle of thigh; **~-nail,** nail with large ornamental head for trunk, coffin, etc.; **~-road,** important main road. **8.** Hence **~'FUL** 2 *n.*, **~'LESS** *a.* [ME f. OF *tronc* f. L *truncus*]

trŭ'nnion (-yon) *n.* Supporting cylindrical projection on each side of cannon or mortar; hollow gudgeon supporting cylinder in steam-engine and giving passage to steam. [f. F *trognon* core, tree-trunk, of unkn. orig.]

trŭss *v.t.*, & *n.* **1.** *v.t.* Support (roof, bridge, etc.) with truss (sense 3). **2.** Fasten (wings of fowl etc.), fasten wings etc. of (fowl etc.), before cooking; **~ (up),** tie arms of (person) to his sides; **~(up),** (arch.) fasten, tighten, (garment), hang (criminal). **3.** *n.* Supporting structure or framework of roof, bridge, etc., e.g. pair of rafters with tie-beam, king-post, and struts. **4.** ||Bundle of old (56 lb.) or new (60 lb.) hay or (36 lb.) straw. **5.** Compact terminal cluster of flowers or fruit. **6.** Large corbel supporting monument etc. **7.** (Naut.) Heavy iron ring securing lower yards to mast. **8.** Padded belt or encircling spring used to support hernia. [ME, f. OF *trusser* v., *trusse* n., of unkn. orig.]

trŭst *n.* & *v.* **1.** *n.* Firm belief in reliability, honesty, veracity, justice, strength, etc., of person or thing, (*our trust is in God*; *I have* or *place* or *put considerable trust in him*; *put no trust in him*); confident expectation (*that*). **2.** Person or thing confided in (*he is our sole trust*). **3.** Reliance on truth of statement etc. without examination; **take on ~,** accept without evidence. **4.** Commercial credit (*obtained goods on trust*). **5.** Responsibility arising from confidence reposed in one (*am in a position of trust*). **6.** (Law). Confidence reposed in person by making him nominal owner of property to be used for another's benefit; right of the latter to benefit by such property; property so held, legal relation between holder and property so held; **in ~,** so held. **7.** Thing or person committed to one's care, resulting obligation, (*would not desert his trust*; *have fulfilled my trust*). **8.** Organized association of several companies for purpose of reducing or defeating competition etc., esp. one in which all or most stock is transferred to central committee and shareholders lose voting power while remaining entitled to profits; hence **~IFICA'TION** *n.*, **~'IFY** *v.t.* **9.** BRAIN(*s*) *trust*; **~ company** (formed to act as trustee or deal with trusts); **~-deed,** deed by debtor conveying property to trustee for payment of creditor, deed conveying property to creditor to sell and pay himself and restore the residue, any instrument of conveyance that creates a trust; **~ territory,** one under trusteeship of (State designated by) United Nations; ||UNIT *trust*. **10.** *v.t.* Place trust in, believe in, rely on the character or behaviour of, (*have never trusted him*; *if we may trust this account*; *can trust him to do his best*; (in *imper.*, colloq., iron.) *trust him to get it wrong*); **~** person **with,** allow him to use (thing) because one is confident that he will not misuse it; hence **~'ING**[2] *a.* **11.** Consign (thing *to* person etc.), place or leave (thing *with* person etc., *in* place etc.), without misgivings. **12.** Allow credit to (customer *for* goods). **13.** Entertain an earnest or (occas.) confident hope (*I trust he is not hurt(?)*; *I trust to hear better news*). **14.** *v.i.* Place reliance *in*; **~ to,** place (esp. undue) reliance on (*we must trust to meeting someone who knows*; *decided to trust to* *luck; does not do to trust to memory for these things*). [ME *troste, truste* n. f, ON *traust* (*traustr* strong); v. f. ON *treysta* w. assim. to n.]

trŭstee′ *n.* Person who holds property in trust for another (||**the Public T~,** State official executing wills and trusts when invited); each of a body of persons, often elective, managing affairs of institution; State made responsible for government of an area; one who is responsible for preservation and administration of a thing; hence ~SHIP *n.* [f. prec. + -EE]

trŭ′stful *a.* Full of trust, confiding; hence ~LY² *adv.*, ~NESS *n.* [f. TRUST + -FUL]

trŭ′stworth|y̆ (-ẽrdhĭ) *a.* Worthy of trust, reliable; hence ~ĭLY² *adv.*, ~ĭNESS *n.* [f. TRUST + -WORTHY]

trŭ′st|y̆ *a.* & *n.* **1.** *a.* (arch.) Trustworthy (*trusty steed, sword, servant*), whence ~ĭLY² *adv.*, ~ĭNESS *n.*; ||~**y and well-beloved** (in sovereign's epistolary form of address to subjects). **2.** *n.* Well-behaved and privileged convict. [ME, f. TRUST + -Y²]

truth (-ōō-) *n.* (*pl. pr.* -dhz *or* -ths). Quality or state of being true or accurate or honest or sincere or loyal or accurately shaped or adjusted (*the truth of the rumour is doubted; there is* (*some*) *truth in what he says; may depend on his truth; wheel is out of truth*); what is true (*have told you the* (*whole*) *truth; the truth is that I forgot; am a lover of truth; fundamental truths*); GOD'*s*, GOSPEL, HALF-, HOME¹, *truth*; **in ~** (literary), **of a ~** (arch.), truly, really; MOMENT *of truth*; **to tell the ~, ~ to tell,** (introducing a confession); **~ drug,** substance administered in supposition that it will make person tell the truth; **~ table,** list indicating truth or falsity of various propositions in logic etc.; hence ~′LESS *a.* [OE *triewth, trēowth* (as TRUE; see -TH¹)]

tru′thful (-ōō′-) *a.* Habitually speaking the truth, veracious; (of tale etc.) true; hence ~LY² *adv.*, ~NESS n. [f. prec. + -FUL]

trȳ *v.* & *n.* **1.** *v.t.* Test (quality), test the qualities of (person, thing), by experiment, subject (person etc.) to suffering or hard treatment (as if) for this purpose, (*try your skill, strength; try it on the* DOG¹; *rope must be tried before it is used; each machine is tried before it leaves the shops; try for* SIZE¹; *this will try his courage; my patience has been sorely tried; should not try your eyes with that small print*); examine the effectiveness or usefulness of for a purpose (*try soap and water, Woolworths, our ginger ale, quinine, the top shelf, the back door, shaking it*); ascertain state of fastening of (door, window, etc.); ~ one's **hand,** see how skilful one is, esp. at first attempt. **2.** Make experiment in order to find out (*try how far you can throw; let us try which takes longest, whether it will break*); *try* CONCLUSIONS, *a* FALL². **3.** Investigate and decide (case, issue) judicially; subject (person) to trial (*for* murder, etc., or *for his life*); (arch.) settle (question) by investigation; *(of lawyer) submit (case) for judgement. **4.** *v.t.* & *i.* Attempt to achieve or perform (*tried a jump and fell; better try something easier*); attempt, endeavour, (*to* do, or abs.; *do try to be in time; must try to get it finished tonight; if at first you don't succeed try, try, try again; no use trying to persuade him; try harder next time; tried my best* or *hardest; don't try to excuse yourself; have often tried to mend it*); **~ and,** (colloq.; rarely w. neg. or in past tense) = *try to* do. **5.** *v.t.* ~ (**out**), extract (oil) from fat by heating, treat (fat) thus, render (fat); ~ (**up**), smooth (roughly-planed board) with **~′ing-plane** to give accurately flat surface. **6. ~ back** *v.i.*, = HARK *back* (lit. or fig.); **~ for,** apply or compete for (appointment etc.), seek to reach or attain; **~ on,** put (clothes etc.) on to test fit, ||begin (*it*, one's *games, tricks*, etc., *with* person) experimentally to see how much will be tolerated (*no use trying it on with me*); ~-*on* n., (colloq.) act of trying (it) on, an attempt to deceive; **~ out,** put to the test, test thoroughly; ~-*out* n., experimental test of efficiency, popularity, etc. **7. ~-sail** (-s*a*l), small strong fore-and-aft sail set with gaff in heavy weather on mainmast or foremast or supplementary mast instead of mainsail or foresail [f. obs. naut. sense of v. = LIE³ to]; **~-square,** carpenter's square usu. with one wooden and one metal limb. **8.** *n.* Attempt (*made a good try; have a try at it, for it, to catch it*). **9.** (Rugby Footb.) (points scored for) touching-down of ball by player behind opponents' goal-line, entitling his side to a kick at goal; (Amer. Footb.) attempt to score extra point in various ways after touchdown. [ME 'separate', 'distinguish', etc. f. OF *trier* sift, of unkn. orig.]

trȳ′ing *a.* In vbl senses, esp. severely testing, hard to endure; hence ~LY² *adv.* [f. prec. + -ING²]

try̆′panosōm|e *n.* Flagellate protozoan parasite infesting blood etc. and causing **~ī′**ASIS *n.*, disease of group including sleeping sickness, kala-azar, etc. [f. Gk *trupanon* borer + -SOME³]

try̆′psĭn *n.* Chief digestive enzyme present in pancreatic juice. [f. Gk *tripsis* friction (*tribō* rub; because first obtained by rubbing down the pancreas with glycerine) + -IN]

try̆′ptophăn *n.* Crystalline amino-acid needed by animals for proper growth and formed by action of trypsin. [f. as prec. + Gk *phainō* show]

try̆st *n.* & *v.* (arch. or literary). **1.** *n.* Appointed meeting, appointment, (*keep, break, tryst*). **2.** *v.t.* Engage to meet (person), appoint (time, place) for meeting. **3.** *v.i.* Make a tryst (*with*). [ME, = obs. *trist* (= TRUST) f. OF *triste* appointed station in hunting]

tsâr, czâr (z-), *n.* **1.** (Hist.) Emperor of Russia; hence ~′ISM (3), ~′IST (2), *ns.* **2.** Person with great authority. [f. Russ. *tsar'*, ult. f. L *Caesar*]

tsâr′ėvĭch, cz- (z-), *n.* (Hist.) Eldest son of emperor of Russia. [Russ. *tsarevich* son of a tsar]

tsari′na, czari′na (z-), (-ē′n*a*) *n.* (Hist.) Empress of Russia. [It. & Sp. (*c*)*zarina* f. G (*c*)*zarin* fem. of (*c*)*zar* TSAR; cf. -INA]

tsĕ′tsė *n.* Afr. fly of genus *Glossina* carrying disease (esp. sleeping sickness) to man and animals by biting. [Tswana]

T.S.H. *abbr.* Their Serene Highnesses; thyroid-stimulating hormone.

T-shirt, T-square. See T.

tsp. *abbr.* teaspoonful.

tsuna′mi (tsōōnah′mĭ) *n.* Series of long, high sea waves caused by disturbance of ocean floor or seismic movement; = TIDAL *wave* (1). [Jap. (*tsu* harbour, *nami* wave)]

Tswa′na (-ah′-) *n.* (Bantu language of) Bechuana people. [native name]

T.T. *abbr.* teetotal(ler); ||Tourist Trophy; tuberculin-tested.

T.U. *abbr.* Trade Union.

tua′n (tōōah′n) *n.* (As respectful term of address by Malay-speakers) sir, master. [Malay *tu*(*w*)*an*]

tuatâr′a (tōō*a*-) *n.* Large iguana-like reptile, peculiar to New Zealand, having dorsal row of yellow spines. [Maori (*tua* on the back, *tara* spine)]

tŭb *n.* & *v.* (**-bb-**). **1.** *n.* Open flat-bottomed usu. round vessel of wooden staves held together by hoops, or of metal or plastic, used for washing (WASH-*tub*) or holding butter, liquids, soil for plants, etc.; varying measure of capacity for butter, corn, tea, etc. **2.** (||colloq.) Bath (vessel or process; *jumped into his tub; seldom has a tub*). **3.** (Mining). Bucket or wheeled box for conveying ore, coal, etc. **4.** (derog. or joc.) Clumsy slow boat. **5.** Boat (esp. stout roomy one) for practice rowing. **6.** ~ **chair** (with solid arms continuous with usu. semicircular back); ~-**-thumper,** (derog. or joc.) ranting preacher or orator. **7.** Hence ~ʹFUL 2 *n.* **8.** *v.t.* & *i.* Plant, row, coach (oarsmen), bathe, wash, in tub; line (mine-shaft) with wooden or iron casing; hence ~ʹ**b**ABLE *a.*, ~ʹ**bing**[1] (1, 2) *n.* [ME, prob. f. LDu. (MDu., MLG *tubbe*)]

tūʹba *n.* Brass wind instrument in bass range of saxhorn family; its player; sonorous organ reed-stop. [It., f. L, = trumpet]

tūʹbal *a.* (Anat.) Of (esp. bronchial or Fallopian) tube(s). [f. mod. L *tubalis* (as TUBE) or f. TUBE; see -AL]

tŭʹbb|ȳ *a.* Tub-shaped, short and fat, corpulent; (of violin etc.) dull-sounding, lacking resonance; so ~ISH[1] *a.* [f. TUB + -Y[2]]

tūbe *n.*, & *v.t.* **1.** *n.* Long hollow cylinder esp. for conveying or holding liquids etc.; cylinder of thin flexible metal with screw cap for holding semi-liquid substance ready for use; cylindrical body of wind instrument; (Anat. & Zool.) hollow cylindrical vessel or organ; = INNER *tube*, whence ~ʹLESS (-bl-) *a.* **2.** *Thermionic valve; cathode-ray tube, e.g. in television set; ***the** ~, television. **3.** (colloq.) Cylindrical tunnel of some electric railways in London etc.; railway system of this kind. **4.** CROOKES, PNEUMATIC, TEST[1]-, *tube.* **5.** ~-**flower,** ornamental E. Ind. shrub (*Clerodendron siphonanthus*) with long tubular corolla; ~-**foot,** tubular grasping projection of starfish etc.; ~-**shell,** bivalve forming shelly tube; ~-**well,** hollow iron pipe with sharp point and perforations at bottom for getting water from underground. **6.** *v.t.* Furnish with or enclose in tube(s); ~**d horse** (that has had a metallic tube inserted to help breathing). **7.** Hence **tūʹ**BING[1] (2) *n.* [F, or f. L *tubus*]

tūbĕʹctomȳ *n.* (Surg.) Removal of Fallopian tube(s). [f. prec. + -ECTOMY]

tūʹber *n.* Short thick rounded part of stem or rhizome, usu. underground, covered with modified buds, e.g. in potato; similar root of dahlia etc.; (Anat.) swelling part, prominence. [L, = hump, swelling]

tūʹbercle *n.* Small rounded projection esp. of bone; (Path.) small rounded swelling on body or in organ, esp. as characteristic of tuberculosis in lungs etc.; (Bot.) wartlike excrescence, small tuber; ~ **bacillus** (causing tuberculosis); so **tūberʹcūl**ATE[2], **tūberʹcūl**OUS, *adjs.* [f. L *tuberculum* dim. of TUBER; see -CULE]

tūberʹcūlar *a.* & *n.* **1.** *a.* Of or having tubercle(s); of tuberculosis. **2.** *n.* Tuberculosis patient. [f. L (as prec.) + -AR[1]]

tūbercūlāʹtion *n.* Formation, or a growth, of tubercles. [f. L (as TUBERCLE) + -ATION]

tūberʹcūlin *n.* Sterile liquid from cultures of tubercle bacillus, used in diagnosis (and treatment) of tuberculosis; ~ **test,** hypodermic injection of tuberculin to detect tubercular infection; ~-**tested,** (of milk) from cows giving negative response to tuberculin test. [f. L (as TUBERCLE) + -IN]

tūbercūlōʹsis *n.* Infectious bacterial disease marked by tubercles, esp. in lungs (**pulmonary** ~). [mod. L, f. as TUBERCLE; see -OSIS]

tūʹber|ōse[1] *a.* Covered with tubers, knobby; of the nature of a tuber; bearing tubers; so ~OʹSITY *n.* [f. L *tuberosus* (TUBER; see -OSE[1])]

tūʹberōse[2] (-z) *n.* Tropical tuberose plant (*Polianthes tuberosa*) with creamy-white fragrant funnel-shaped flowers. [f. L *tuberosa* fem. (as prec.), pop. regarded as = TUBE + ROSE[1]]

tūʹberous *a.* = TUBEROSE[1]; ~ **root** (thick and fleshy like tuber but without buds). [f. F *tubéreux* or f. L *tuberosus* (TUBER; see -OUS)]

tūʹbĭ- *comb. form.* Tube, as: ~**colous** (-bĭʹ-), (of worm, spider, etc.) living in or constructing tubes; ~**corn** *a.* & *n.*, (ruminant) with hollow horns; ~FORM *a.*; ~**liʹngual,** (of bird) with tubular tongue. [f. L *tubus* tube + -I-]

tūʹbūlar *a.* Tube-shaped; having, consisting of, contained in, tube(s); (of furniture etc.) made of tubular pieces; ~ **boiler** (in which heat or water to be heated passes through many tubes); ~ **bridge,** rectangular hollow bridge through which railway etc. passes; so **tūʹbūl**OUS *a.* [f. as foll. + -AR[1], but without dim. force]

tūʹbūle *n.* Small tube; hence **tūʹbūlɪ-** *comb. form.* [f. L *tubulus* dim. of *tubus* tube; see -ULE]

||**T.U.C.** *abbr.* Trades Union Congress.

tŭck[1] *v.* & *n.* **1.** *v.t.* Put tuck(s) in (material), shorten or ornament with tuck(s); draw or thrust or roll the outer parts of (cloth etc. *up, in*) close together or so as to be held in place (*tuck in the blankets, the loose ends*; *tucked up his shirt-sleeves, her petticoats*); draw together into small compass (*tucked his legs under him like a tailor*; *bird tucks head under wing*); cover (person, one*self*) snugly and compactly *up* or *in*, (*tucked him, himself, up in bed*); stow away (thing *in* corner etc., *away, out of sight,* etc.); empty (seine) by means of smaller one. **2.** *v.i.* & *t.* ~ **in** or **into,** ~ **away,** (sl.) eat heartily. **3.** *n.* Flat fold, often one of several parallel folds, in fabric fixed in place by stitches for shortening or ornament; = *tuck-net*; (Naut.) part of vessel's hull where planks meet under stern. **4.** ||(sl.) Eatables esp. pastry and sweets; ~-**in, -out,** large meal; ~-**box,** ~-**shop,** (where tuck is kept esp. for school-children). **5.** ~-**in,** (part) that can be tucked in (e.g. of blouse to be tucked inside top of skirt); ~-**net, -seine,** small net for taking fish from larger one; ~-**pointing,** method of pointing brickwork with coloured mortar, a central groove in which is filled with fine white lime putty, projecting slightly. [ME *tukke, tokke,* f. MDu., MLG *tucken,* = OHG *zucchen* pull, pluck, cogn. w. TUG]

tŭck[2] *n.* (arch.) Beat (*tuck of drum*). [f. ME (now dial.) *tuck* v. f. ONF *toquer,* OF *toucher* TOUCH[1]]

tŭʹcker[1] *n.* In vbl senses; piece of lace, linen, etc., in or on woman's bodice in 17th–18th c. (*best* BIB[2] *and tucker*); (Austral. colloq.) food. [ME, f. TUCK[1] + -ER[1]]

***tŭʹcker**[2] *v.t.* ~ (**out**), (colloq.) tire, weary. [f. TUCK[1] + -ER[5]]

tŭʹckėt *n.* (arch.) Flourish on trumpet. [f. as TUCK[2] + -ET[1]]

tuʹcum (tōōʹ-) *n.* Brazilian palm with fibre used for cordage etc. [f. Tupi *tucumá*]

-tūde *suf.* forming abstract *ns.* (*altitude, attitude, desuetude, exactitude, solitude*). [f. or after F *-tude* f. L *-tudo -tudinis*]

Tūʹdor *n.* & *a.* (Member) of the royal family of England from Henry VII to Elizabeth I; ~ **arch,** flattened four-centred arch; ~ **flower,** ornament of upright stalked trefoil; ~ **rose,** conventional five-lobed figure of rose, esp. combination of red and white roses; ~ **style** (late Perpendicular, or half-timbered elaborately decorated design of houses). [f. Owen ~ of Wales, grandfather of Henry VII]

Tue(s). *abbr.* Tuesday.

Tūeʹsday (tūʹz-; *or* -dĭ) *n.* & *adv.* **1.** *n.* Day of week, following Monday; SHROVE[1] *Tuesday.* **2.** *adv.* (cf. FRIDAY 2). [OE *Tīwesdæg* (transl. of L *dies Martis* day of Mars) f. *Tīwes* gen. of *Tīw* Gmc god identified w. Roman Mars]

tūʹf|a *n.* Porous rock formed round mineral springs; = foll.; hence ~AʹCEOUS *a.* [It., var. of *tufo* (see foll.)]

tŭff *n.* Rock formed by consolidation of volcanic ashes; hence ~AʹCEOUS *a.* [f. F *tuf(fe)* f. It. *tufo* f. LL *tofus,* L TOPHUS]

tŭ'ffĕt. Var. of foll. 1.

tŭft *n.* & *v.* **1.** *n.* Bunch or collection of threads, grass, feathers, hair, etc., held or growing together at the base; hence ~'Y[2] *a.* **2.** (Anat.) bunch of small blood-vessels; (arch.) imperial (beard). **3.** ||(arch.) Titled undergraduate [from gold tassel formerly worn on cap]. **4.** **~-hunter, -hunting,** one who seeks, practice of seeking, society of titled persons, snob(bery). **5.** *v.t.* Furnish with tuft(s); make depressions at regular intervals in (mattress etc.) by passing thread through. **6.** *v.i.* Grow in tufts. [ME, prob. f. OF *tof(f)e*, of unkn. orig.; for *-t* cf. GRAFT[1]]

tŭ'ftėd *a.* Having or forming tuft(s); (of bird) with tuft of feathers on head. [f. prec. + -ED[1,2]]

tŭg *v.* (**-gg-**) & *n.* **1.** *v.t.* Pull with great effort or violently (lit. or fig.); tow (vessel) by means of tugboat. **2.** *v.i.* Make vigorous pull *at.* **3.** *n.* Tugging, violent pull, (*gave a tug at the bell*); violent or painful effort (esp. fig.; *felt a great tug at parting*). **4.** **~('boat)**, small powerful steam-vessel for towing others. **5.** Aircraft towing glider; loop from saddle supporting shaft or (in double harness) trace. **6.** **~ of war,** contest in which each of two teams holding same rope tries to pull the other across line marked between them; decisive or severe contest. [ME *togge, tugge*, intensive f. Gmc **teuh-*; see TOW[1]]

tu'ī (tōō'ĭ) *n.* (N.Z.) Bird with dark plumage and white throat-tuft, parson-bird. [Maori]

tūĭ'tion *n.* Teaching, instruction, esp. as a thing to be paid for; fee for this; hence ~AL, ~ARY[1], *adjs.* [ME f. OF, f. L *tuitio -onis* (*tuēri tuit-* watch, guard; see -ITION)]

tūlarae'm|ĭa, *-ē'm|ĭa, *n.* Severe infectious bacterial disease of man and domestic animals, carried by contact or by insect bites; hence ~IC *a.* [mod. L, f. *Tulare* County, California (where first observed) + -AEMIA]

tŭ'lchan (-χ-) *n.* (Sc.) Calf-skin stuffed with straw or spread on mound beside cow to make her give milk; ~ **bishops,** (Hist.) titular bishops in whose names revenues of Scottish sees were drawn by lay barons after Reformation. [Gael., = mound]

tū'lĭp *n.* (Flower of) bulbous spring-flowering plant of genus *Tulipa*, esp. one of many cultivated forms with showy cup-shaped flowers of various colours and markings; **~-root,** disease of oats etc. causing base of stem to swell; **~-tree,** (1) N. Amer. tree (*Liriodendron tulipifera*) with flowers like large greenish-yellow tulips and soft white wood (**~-wood**), (2) similar tree of genus *Magnolia* etc. [orig. *tulipa(n)* f. mod. L *tulipa* f. Turk. *tul(i)band* f. Pers. *dulband* TURBAN (f. shape of expanded flower)]

tūlle *n.* Fine silk etc. net used for veils and dresses. [f. *T~* in S.W. France, where first made]

tŭ'lwār *n.* Sabre of N. India etc. [f. Hindi *talwār*]

tŭm[1] *n.* Sound of banjo or similar instrument. [imit.]

tŭm[2] *n.* (childish or joc.) Stomach. [abbr. of TUMMY]

tŭ'mble *v.* & *n.* **1.** *v.i.* Fall esp. helplessly (*down, over, off, from*, etc.) suddenly or violently; (of waves, sick person, etc.) roll, toss, irregularly up and down or from side to side or over and over; move, walk, run, in headlong or blundering fashion (*came tumbling along*; *tumbled up the stairs*; *tumbled into* or *out of bed*); fall rapidly in amount etc.; (of pigeon) turn over backwards in flight; perform acrobatic feats. **2.** *v.t.* Cause to tumble; pull about, disorder, rumple, (clothes, hair, etc.); overturn, fling headlong, throw or push (*down, out, in*, etc.) roughly or carelessly; dry in tumbler-drier; clean in tumbling-barrel. **3.** ~ **home** or **in,** (Naut., of ship's sides) incline inwards above extreme breadth, whence ~*-home* n., amount of this inclination; ~ **to,** (sl.) understand, grasp, (hidden idea etc.). **4.** *n.* Fall (*had a slight, nasty*, etc. *tumble*); somersault or other acrobatic feat; untidy or confused state (*things were all in a tumble*). **5.** **~-bug,** dung-beetle rolling up balls of dung; **~down,** falling or fallen into ruin, dilapidated; **~-drier,** = TUMBLER-*drier*; ***~-weed,** plant forming globular bush that breaks off in late summer and is rolled about by the wind. [ME *tumbel*, f. MLG *tummelen*, OHG *tumalōn*, frequent. of *tūmōn*; see -LE 3]

tŭ'mbler *n.* In vbl senses; one who turns somersaults etc., acrobat; variety of pigeon that tumbles; flat-bottomed drinking-glass without handle or foot (formerly with rounded bottom so as not to stand upright), whence ~FUL 2 *n.*; electrical switch worked by pushing small sprung lever; pivoted piece in lock that holds the bolt until lifted by key; notched pivoted plate in gun-lock; toy figure that rocks when touched; tumbling-barrel etc.; **~(-drier)**, machine for drying washing in heated drum rotating on horizontal axis. [ME, f. prec. + -ER[1]]

tŭ'mblĭng *n.* In vbl senses; **~-barrel, -box,** etc., revolving device containing abrasive substance, in which castings etc. are cleaned by friction against each other or the walls of the box; **~-bay,** (pool receiving) outfall of river, reservoir, etc. [ME, f. TUMBLE + -ING[1]]

tŭ'mbrel, -ĭl, *n.* (Hist.) Two-wheeled covered cart for carrying tools, ammunition, etc.; tip-cart, esp. dung-cart; open cart used in French Revolution to convey victims to the guillotine; instrument of punishment, usu. = cucking-stool. [ME, f. OF *tumberel, tomberel* (*tomber* fall)]

tū'mė|fȳ *v.t.* & *i.* (Cause to) swell, inflate, be inflated, (lit. or fig.); so (Path.) ~FA'CIENT *a.*, ~FA'CTION *n.* [f. F *tuméfier* f. L *tumefacere* (*tumēre* swell; see -FY)]

tūmĕ'sc|ent *a.* Becoming tumid, swelling; showing such response to sexual stimulation; hence ~ENCE *n.* [f. L *tumescere* (as prec.; see -ESCENT)]

tū'mĭd *a.* (Of parts of the body etc.) swollen, inflated; (fig., of style etc.) inflated, bombastic; hence or cogn. ~ITY (-ĭ'd-) ~NESS, *ns.*, ~LY[2] *adv.* [f. L *tumidus* (*tumēre* swell; see -ID[1])]

tŭ'mmȳ *n.* (childish or colloq.) Stomach; ~ **button,** (colloq.) navel. [childish pr.; see -Y[3]]

tū'mour (-m*er*), ***tū'mor,** *n.* Local swelling esp. from morbid or abnormal growth. [f. L *tumor* (*tumēre* swell; see -OR)]

tŭ'mtŭm[1] *n.* (Anglo-Ind.) Light vehicle, dog-cart. [19th c.; orig. unkn.]

tŭ'mtŭm[2]. Var. of TUM[1,2].

tū'mult *n.* Commotion of a multitude esp. with confused cries etc.; public disturbance, riot; din, uproar; confused and excited state of mind. [ME, f. OF *tumulte* or f. L *tumultus*]

tūmŭ'ltūarȳ *a.* (Of troops) hastily brought together, undisciplined; done hurriedly, haphazard; = foll. [f. L *tumultuarius* (as prec.; see -ARY[1])]

tūmŭ'ltūous *a.* Full of or making tumult; disorderly, agitated; hence ~LY[2] *adv.*, ~NESS *n.* [OF, or f. L (as TUMULT; see -OUS)]

tū'mūl|us *n.* (*pl.* ~i *pr.* -ī). Ancient sepulchral mound, barrow; so ~AR(Y)[1] *adjs.* [L (*tumēre* swell)]

tŭn *n.*, & *v.t.* (**-nn-**). **1.** *n.* Large cask for wine, beer, etc.; measure of capacity (252 wine gallons); brewer's fermenting-vat; **~'dish,** wooden funnel esp. in brewing, intermediate reservoir in metal-founding. **2.** *v.t.* Store (liquor) in tun. [OE *tunne*, = OHG, ON *tunna*, f. med. L *tunna*, prob. of Gaulish orig.]

tū'na[1] *n.* (*pl.* **~s** *or* same). Tunny; **~(-fish)**, its flesh as food. [Amer. Sp., perh. f. Sp. *atún* tunny]

tū'na[2] *n.* Prickly pear, esp. (fruit of) *Opuntia tuna.* [Sp. f. Haitian]

tū'na[3] (*or* tōō'-) *n.* (N.Z.) Common species of eel (*Anguilla sucklandii*). [Maori]

tŭ'ndra (*or* tōō'-) *n.* Vast level treeless Arctic region where subsoil is frozen. [Lappish]

tūne *n.* & *v.* **1.** *n.* Melody with or without harmony (**call the ~**, have control of events; see PIPER); correct pitch or intonation in singing or playing (*sings in, out of, tune*); due adjustment of instrument to obtain this (*piano is out of tune*). **2.** Agreement, concord, harmonious relation (*in, out of, tune with* one's *surroundings* or *company*); *in, out of,* proper condition; suitable mood (*for* purpose etc.). **3. Change** one's **~**, **sing another ~**, assume a different style of language or manner, e.g. change from insolent to respectful tone; **to the ~** (considerable or exorbitant amount) **of** *£500* etc.; **to some ~**, to a remarkable degree. **4.** *v.t.* Put (violin, piano, etc.) in tune; adjust (radio receiver etc.) to particular wavelength of signals; adjust (engine etc.) to run smoothly and efficiently; hence **tū'n**ER[1] (1, 2) *n.* **5.** (fig.) Adjust, adapt, (thing *to* standard, purpose, circumstances, etc.); (poet.) produce music from (instrument), produce (music) (*lark tunes his song*), express, celebrate, in music. **6.** *v.i.* Be in harmony (lit. or fig., *with*). **7. ~ in,** set radio receiver to right wavelength to receive transmitted signal; **~ out,** cut out (radio etc. signal) by tuning; **~ up,** (of orchestra) bring instruments to proper or uniform pitch, begin to play or sing, bring to most efficient condition. **8.** Hence **tū'n**ABLE, **tū'ne**ABLE, (-na-) *a.* [ME; unexpl. var. of TONE[1]]

tū'neful (-nf-) *a.* Melodious, musical; hence ~LY[2] *adv.*, ~NESS *n.* [f. prec. + -FUL]

tū'nelėss (-nl-) *a.* Not in tune; unmelodious, unmusical; (arch.) making no (musical) sound; hence ~LY[2] *adv.*, ~NESS *n.* [f. TUNE + -LESS]

tŭng *n.* **~(-tree)**, Chinese tree of genus *Aleurites*, esp. a species whose seeds yield **~ oil** used for varnishing etc. [f. Chin. *t'ung*]

tŭ'ngst|en *n.* Steel-grey heavy metallic element with very high melting-point, used for the filaments of electric lamps and for alloying steel etc.; hence ~ATE[1] (3) *n.*, ~IC, ~OUS, *adjs.* (Chem.) [Sw. (*tung* heavy, *sten* stone)]

tū'nĭc *n.* **1.** Ancient Greek or Roman short-sleeved body-garment reaching about to knees; woman's or child's loose blouse or coat gathered or belted at waist; close-fitting short coat of uniform of soldier, policeman, etc.; GYM-*tunic.* **2.** (Zool.) leathery envelope of ascidian etc.; (Anat.) membrane enclosing or lining an organ; (Bot.) any of the layers of a bulb, integument of a part; (Eccl.) tunicle. [f. F *tunique* or f. L *tunica*]

tū'nĭca *n.* (*pl.* **~e**). (Zool. & Anat.) = prec. [L]

tū'nĭcate *a.* & *n.* **1.** *a.* (Zool.) enclosed in tunic; (Bot.) having concentric layers. **2.** *a.* & *n.* (Member) of subphylum Urochorda of marine animals with hard outer coat. [f. L *tunicatus* p.p. of *tunicare* clothe with tunic (as prec.; see -ATE[2])]

tū'nĭcle *n.* (Eccl., esp. R.C. Ch.) Short vestment of bishop or subdeacon at Eucharist etc. [ME f. OF, or f. L *tunicula* dim. of TUNICA]

tū'nĭng *n.* In vbl senses; **~-fork,** two-pronged steel fork designed to give particular note (esp. middle C) when struck; **~-peg, -pin,** (attached to strings in piano etc. and turned to alter their tension in tuning). [f. TUNE + -ING[1]]

Tūnĭ'sĭan (-z-) *a.* & *n.* (Native or inhabitant) of Tunisia or Tunis. [f. *Tunisia* in N. Africa or its capital *Tunis* + -IAN]

tŭ'nnel *n.* & *v.* (||-ll-). **1.** *n.* Artificial subterranean passage through hill etc. or under road or river etc., esp. for railway; subterranean passage dug by burrowing animal; tube containing propeller-shaft etc.; WIND[1]-*tunnel*; **~-net,** fishing-net wide at mouth and narrow at other end; **~ vision** (defective in lateral directions). **2.** *v.t.* Make a tunnel through (hill etc.); furnish with tunnel; make one's *way* by tunnelling. **3.** *v.i.* Make one's way by tunnelling (*through, into,* etc.); (Phys.) pass through potential barrier. [ME, f. OF *tonel* dim. of *tonne* TUN; see -LE 2]

tŭ'nnў *n.* Large marine scombroid fish esp. of genus *Thunnus,* used as food-fish and game-fish. [f. F *thon* f. Prov. *ton,* f. L f. Gk *thunnos*]

tŭp *n.*, & *v.t.* (-pp-). **1.** *n.* Male sheep, ram; striking-head of steam-hammer, pile-driver, etc. **2.** *v.t.* Copulate with (ewe). [ME *toje, tupe,* of unkn. orig.]

Tupamar̂'ō (tōō-) *n.* (*pl.* **~s**). Left-wing urban guerrilla in Uruguay. [f. *Tupac Amaru,* name of two Inca leaders]

tu'pėlō (tōō'-) *n.* (*pl.* **~s**). Large N. Amer. swamp tree of genus *Nyssa*; its wood. [Creek (*ito* tree, *opilwa* swamp)]

Tu'pĭ (tōō'-) *n.* & *a.* (Member or language) of Amer. Ind. people in Amazon valley etc. [Tupi]

||**tŭ'ppence, tŭ'ppennў.** Vars. of TWO*pence,* TWO*penny.*

tūque (-k) *n.* Canadian stocking cap. [Can. F form of TOQUE]

tu quoque (tūkwō'kwĭ *or* tōōkwŏkwā) *n.* The retort *So are* (or *did* etc.) *you.* [L, = you too]

turaco(u), turako. Vars. of TOURACO.

Tūrā'nĭan *a.* & *n.* (The group) of Asian languages that are neither Semitic nor Indo--European, esp. the Ural-Altaic family of languages. [f. Pers. *Tūrān* region beyond Oxus + -IAN]

tûr'ban *n.* Man's head-dress of scarf wound round cap, worn esp. by Muslims and Sikhs; modification of this, esp. (1) woman's head--dress resembling turban, (2) woman's or child's close-fitting hat with narrow or no brim; **~ lily** (with deep-red spotted turban-shaped flowers); **~-shell,** mollusc of genus *Turbo* with thick spiral shell; **~-stone,** Muslim pillar tombstone with turban carved on top; hence ~ED[2] (-nd) *a.* [16th c. also *tulbant* etc., ult. f. Turk. *tülbent* f. Pers. *dulband*; cf. TULIP]

||**tûr'barў** *n.* Right of digging turf on common or on another's ground; place where turf or peat is dug. [ME, f. AF *turberie,* OF *tourberie* (*tourbe* TURF; see -ARY[1])]

tûrbĕllâr'ĭan *a.* & *n.* (Flatworm) of class Turbellaria, with external cilia causing eddies in water. [f. mod. L *Turbellaria* f. L *turbella* dim. of *turba* crowd (see foll., -ARY[1]) + -AN]

tûr'bĭd *a.* (Of liquid or colour) muddy, thick, not clear; (fig.) confused, disordered; hence ~ITY (-ĭ'd-), ~NESS, *ns.*, ~LY[2] *adv.* [f. L *turbidus* (*turba* crowd, disturbance; see -ID[1])]

tûr'bĭn|ate *a.* Shaped like a top or inverted cone; (of shell) with whorls decreasing rapidly in size; (Anat., esp. of some nasal bones) of scroll-like formation; whirling like a top; so ~AL *a.*, ~A'TION *n.* [f. L *turbinatus* (as foll.; see -ATE[2])]

tûr'bĭne *n.* Water-wheel driven by impact or reaction or both of a stream of water; similar machine driven by flow of gas (esp. *gas turbine, steam turbine*); **~ boat** etc. (driven by turbines). [F, f. L *turbo -binis* spinning-top, whirlwind]

tûr'bĭt *n.* Variety of domestic pigeon with stout build, neck frill, and short beak. [app. f. L *turbo* top, from its figure]

tûr'bō- *comb. form.* Turbine, as: **~-fan,** = FAN¹-*-jet*; **~-jet (engine),** (aircraft with) jet engine in which jet gases also operate turbine-driven compressor for supplying compressed air to combustion chamber; **~-prop (engine),** (aircraft with) jet engine in which turbine is used as in turbo-jet and also to drive propeller. [f. TURBINE + -O-]

tûr'bot *n.* Large Eur. flat-fish (*Scophthalmus maximus*) esteemed as food; similar fish, e.g. halibut. [ME f. OF, f. OSw. **törnbut* (*törn* thorn, *but* BUTT²)]

tûr'bŭl|ent *a.* Disturbed, in commotion; tumultuous; insubordinate, riotous; (Phys., of flow) having irregular variations in the course of time; hence or cogn. **~**ENCE *n.*, **~ent**LY² *adv.* [f. L *turbulentus* (*turba* crowd; see -ULENT)]

Tûr'cō *n.* (*pl.* **~s**). (Hist.) Algerian soldier in French army. [Sp., Port., & It., = TURK]

Tûr'cō-, Tûr'kō-, *comb. form.* Turkish (and); hence **~**PHIL(E), **~**PHOBE, *ns.* & *adjs.* [f. med. L (as TURK) + -O-]

Tûr'coman. See TURKOMAN.

tûrd *n.* (vulg.) Ball or lump of excrement; contemptible person. [OE *tord*, = ON *tord(ýfill)* dung(-beetle) f. Gmc **turdam*]

tûr'doid *a.* Thrushlike. [f. L *turdus* THRUSH¹ + -OID]

tŭree'n *n.* Deep covered dish from which soup, gravy, etc., is served at table. [earlier *terrine*, *-ene* f. F *terrine* large circular earthenware dish, fem. (as n.) of OF *terrin* earthen f. Rom. **terrinus* f. L *terra* earth; see -INE¹]

tûrf *n.* (*pl.* **~s,** *or* **turves** *pr.* -vz), & *v.t.* **1.** *n.* Covering of grass etc. with earth and matted roots as surface layer of grassland; piece of this cut from ground; **the ~** the racecourse, occupation or profession of horse-racing; hence **~**'Y² *a.* **2.** Slab or block of peat for fuel. **3. ~ accountant,** bookmaker; **~ drain** (covered with turf); **~**'ITE¹, **~'man,** person interested in horse-racing. **4.** *v.t.* Plant (ground) with turf; (sl.) throw (person or thing) *out*. [OE, = OS *turf*, ON *torf(a)*, OHG *zurf*, *zurba*, f. Gmc **turbh-* f. IE **drbh-*]

tûr'g|ĭd *a.* Swollen, inflated, enlarged; (fig., of language) pompous, bombastic; hence or cogn. **~**E'SCENCE, **~ĭ'd**ITY, *ns.*, **~**E'SCENT *a.*, **~ĭd**LY² *adv.* [f. L *turgidus* (*turgēre* swell; see -ID¹)]

tûr'gor *n.* (Bot.) Rigidity of cells due to uptake of water. [LL (as prec.; see -OR)]

tûr'ĭon *n.* (Bot.) Young scaly shoot rising from underground bud as in asparagus etc. [F, f. L *turio -onis* shoot]

Tûrk *n.* **1.** Native of Turkey; native or inhabitant of Ottoman empire; member of the Central Asian people from whom the Ottomans derived, speaking Turkic languages; ferocious, wild, or unmanageable person; (arch.) Muslim; Turkish horse; see YOUNG 2. **2. ~'s cap,** martagon lily or other plant with turban-like flowers; **~'s head,** turban-like ornamental knot. [ME, = F *Turc*, It. etc. *Turco*, med. L *Turcus*, Pers. & Arab. *Turk*, of unkn. orig.]

tûr'key¹ *n.* **1.** Large (esp. domestic) orig. Amer. gallinaceous bird of genus *Meleagris*, esteemed as food and associated with festivities of ||Christmas or *Thanksgiving; *TALK *turkey*. **2.** Flesh of turkey as food; COLD¹ *turkey*. **3. ~ buzzard, vulture,** Amer. carrion vulture (*Cathartes aura*); **~cock,** male of turkey (*red as a ~cock*, flushed with anger etc.), (fig.) pompous or self-important person. [16th c., short for *turkeycock*, *-hen*, orig. applied to the guinea-fowl, as imported through Turkey, and then erron. to the Amer. bird]

Tûr'key² *n.* **~ carpet** (made of wool with thick pile and bold design); ||**~ leather** (treated with oil before hair side is removed); **~ red,** (cotton cloth dyed with) scarlet pigment from madder or alizarin. [~ in Asia Minor & S.E. Europe, country of the Turks]

Tûr'k|ĭ *a.* & *n.* (Of) a group of Ural-Altaic (incl. Turkish) languages and peoples; so **~**IC *a.* [f. Pers. *turkī* (as TURK; see -I)]

Tûr'kĭsh *a.* & *n.* **1.** (Language) of Turkey or the Turks. **2. ~ bath,** hot-air or steam bath followed by washing, massage, etc., (in *sing.* or *pl.*) building used for this; **~ carpet,** TURKEY² carpet; **~ coffee,** strong usu. sweet black coffee made from very finely ground beans; **~ delight,** sweetmeat in flavoured gelatinous lumps coated with powdered sugar; **~ tobacco** (aromatic kind grown mainly in Turkey and Greece); **~ towel,** cloth of cotton terry. [f. TURK + -ISH¹]

Tûr'kō-. See TURCO-.

Tûr'koman, Tûr'coman, Tûr'kmen, *n.* Member or language of any of various Turkic tribes in Turkmenistan etc.; **~ carpet,** rich-coloured kind with soft long nap. [f. Pers. *Turkumān* (as TURK, *mānistan* resemble)]

tûr'merĭc *n.* E. Ind. plant (*Curcuma longa*) of ginger family; its large aromatic root powdered as dyestuff, stimulant, and condiment esp. in curry-powder; **~-paper** (saturated with turmeric and used as test for alkalis). [16th-c. forms *tarmaret* etc., perh. f. F *terre mérite* and mod. L *terra merita*, of unkn. orig.]

tûr'moil *n.*, & *v.t.* **1.** *n.* Agitation, trouble. **2.** *v.t.* (arch.; esp. in *p.p.*) Agitate, trouble. [16th c., of unkn. orig.]

tûrn¹ *v.* **1.** *v.t.* & *i.* Move round so as to keep at same distance from a centre or axis, give rotary motion to, receive such motion, (*crank turns wheel*; *wheel turns*; *turn the key in the lock*; *turn the tap*; *tap will not turn*; *make* person *turn in his* GRAVE¹; *turn on* one's HEEL¹). **2.** *v.t.* Execute (somersault etc.) with rotary motion. **3.** *v.t.* & *i.* Change from one side to another, invert, reverse, (fig.) revolve mentally, (*turn upside down*, *inside out*, *back to front*; *whole world has turned topsy-turvy*; *turned the body with its face upwards*; *have turned the matter over and over in my mind*); (Print.) invert (type) so that it appears upside down (**~ed comma,** inverted comma; **~ed period,** ˙); make (profit); convert less soiled inside of (dress etc.) to serve as outside; *turn* one's COAT; *not turn a* HAIR; *turn an* HONEST *penny*, *the* SCALE²(*s*), *the* TABLES (*on*), TURTLE². **4.** Give new direction to, take new direction, adapt, be adapted, (*turn your face this way*; *river turns to the right*; *turned his flight northwards*; *turn into a side-road*; *turned the hose on them*; *cricket-ball turns on pitching*; *turned to God in her trouble*; *turn your attention to this*; *have often turned my thoughts*, *thoughts have often turned*, *to the subject*); (Golf) begin second half of round; resist or divert (bullet); blunt (edge of knife etc. or fig. of remark etc.); *turn to* ACCOUNT²; *turn* one's BACK¹ *on*, *a* DEAF *ear* (*to*), one's HAND¹ *to*; *turn* TAIL¹; **~ the tide,** (fig.) reverse trend of events, so **tide ~s** (also lit.); *not know* **where** or **which way to ~,** (fig.) what course to follow, how to proceed, where to seek help; *a* WORM¹ *will turn*. **5.** *v.t.* Move to other side of, go round, flank, (*turn the* CORNER); **~ (the flank** or **position of) an army,** pass round so as to attack it from flank or rear; **~** person's **flank,** outwit him, defeat him in argument etc. **6.** Pass age or time of (*is* or *has turned 40*, *noon*). **7.** Cause to go, send, put, (*was turned into a field*, *adrift in the world*; *turn it out into a basin*; *never turned* (*away*) *a beggar from his door*). **8.** *v.t.* & *i.* Change in nature, form, condition, etc., change for the worse, (cause to) become, (*turned water into wine*; *has been turned into a theatre*, *a frog*, *a millionaire*; *fear he will turn awkward*; *has turned traitor*, *informer*, *Queen's* EVIDENCE, *Muslim*, *botanist*; *joy is* or *has turned to bitterness*; *my luck has turned at last*; *turned pale at the thought*; *very thought turns me pale*); (of leaves, hair, etc.) change colour; translate (*turn it into French*); make or become sour (of milk), nauseated (of stomach), giddy (of head); ~ person's BRAIN or **head,** etc. **9.** Shape (object) in lathe; give (esp. elegant) form to (*can turn a compliment*; *could turn a Latin verse in my day*; *well-turned phrase, leg*). **10.** (w. *advs.*): ~ **about,** turn so as to face in new direction; *~ **around** = *turn round*; ~ **away,** refuse to look (at) or accept; ~ **down,** fold down, fold down corner of sheet of (bed, page), place (playing-card) face downwards, reduce volume of (sound etc.) by turning knob etc., reduce flame of (gas, lamp, etc.) by turning tap etc., reject (proposal, its maker, etc.); ~ **in,** fold inwards, hand in, surrender, register (score, performance, etc.), deliver, incline inwards (*his toes turn in*), (colloq.) go to bed, (colloq.) abandon (plan etc.); ~ **off,** enter side-road, stop flow or working of (water, radio, etc.) by means of tap, switch, etc., (colloq.) cause to lose interest, dismiss (servant etc.) from employment; ~ **on,** start flow or working of (water, radio, etc.) by means of tap, switch, etc., (colloq.) arouse interest of (person sexually, with drugs, etc.); ~ **out,** expel, extinguish (electric light etc.), incline outwards (*turn out your toes*), equip, dress (*well turned out*), produce (manufactured goods etc.), ||empty (room etc. for cleaning), expose contents of (*made him turn out his pockets*), (colloq.) get out of bed, (colloq.) go out of doors or to vote etc., (Mil.) call (guard) from guard-room, be found, prove to be the case (*this turns out to be true*; *he turned out a humbug*; *it turns out that he was never there*; *we shall see how things turn out*); ~ **over,** (cause to) fall over, upset, expose or bring uppermost the other side of (page etc., *a new* LEAF, or abs.), cause (engine etc.) to revolve, consider thoroughly, transfer the conduct of (thing *to* person), do business to the amount of (*turns over £5,000 a week*); ~ **round** = *turn about*, adopt new opinions or policy, unload and reload (ship etc.); ~ **to,** begin work; ~ **up,** disinter (*plough turns up mouse's nest*), make one's appearance (*turned up an hour late, unexpectedly*), (of event, opportunity, etc.) happen, present itself, (colloq.) cause to vomit (*the sight turned me up*), give upward turn to (NOSE, TOES, etc.), increase volume of (sound etc.) by turning knob etc., increase flame of (gas, lamp, etc.) by turning tap etc., place (playing-card) face upwards. **11.** (w. *preps.*): ~ **against,** make or become hostile to; ~ **on,** depend on, face hostilely, become hostile to; ~ **to,** apply oneself to, set about (work, do*ing*), go on to consider next; ~ **upon,** = *turn on*. **12.** ~**-about,** turning about, (fig.) abrupt change of policy etc.; ~**-bench,** watch-maker's portable lathe; ~**-buckle,** device for tightly connecting parts of metal rod or wire; ~**-cap,** revolving chimney-top; ~**'coat,** one who turns his COAT; ~**'cock,** person employed to turn on water for mains etc.; ~**-down,** (of collar) doubled down; ~**'key,** (*n.*) person in charge of prison keys, (*a.*, of contract etc.) providing for supply of equipment ready for operation; ~**-out,** turning out esp. for duty, strike of employees, number of persons who go to vote, see spectacle, etc., equipage, quantity of goods manufactured etc. in given time; ~**'over,** turning over, semicircular or triangular pie or tart made by turning half of pastry over filling, amount of money turned over in business, numbers of persons etc. entering and leaving employment etc.; ~**'pike,** (Hist.) defensive frame of spikes, (Hist.) toll-gate, (Hist. & U.S.) road on which toll is collected at gates; ~**-round,** (of ship etc.) process of arriving at destination, unloading, reloading, and leaving; ~**-screw,** screwdriver; ~**'sick,** = STURDY[2]; ~**'side,** giddiness in dogs and cattle; ~**'sole,** plant supposed to turn with the sun [ult. f. L *sol* sun]; ~**'spit,** person or long-bodied short-legged dog, formerly used to turn spit; ~**'stile,** post at entrance of building esp. where admission fee is charged or numbers entering are counted, with arms that move round as person passes through; ~**'stone,** bird of genus *Arenaria*, allied to plover, seeking small animals under stones as food; ~**'table,** circular revolving platform for reversing a locomotive etc., circular revolving support for gramophone record being played; ~**-up,** thing turned up, ||esp. lower end of trouser leg, (colloq.) commotion, (colloq.) unexpected event. [OE *tyrnan, turnian*, in ME reinforced f. OF *turner, torner*, f. L *tornare* turn in lathe (*tornus* f. Gk *tornos*)]

tûrn[2] *n.* **1.** Turning, rotary motion, changed or change of direction or position or tendency, deflection, deflected part, bend, (*a single turn of the handle*; *with a neat turn of the wrist*; *took a sudden turn to the left*; *his illness, events, took a favourable turn*; *gave a new turn to the argument*; *path is full of twists and turns*; *walked along a turn of the river*); turning of road; point at which turning or change occurs; change of tide (lit. or fig.) from ebb to flow or vice versa; **at every** ~, continually; HAND[1]*'s turn*; **on the** ~, changing, at the turning-point; ||THREE-*point turn*; **to a** ~, (roasted etc.) precisely right. **2.** Character, tendency, disposition, formation, (*was of a humorous turn, a mechanical turn of mind*; *do not like the turn of the sentence*; *the turn of an ankle*); ~ **of speed,** ability to go very fast on occasion. **3.** Short walk, stroll, drive, ride, (*take a turn in the garden, on a bicycle*); short performance on stage, in circus, etc. **4.** Opportunity, occasion, privilege, obligation, coming successively to each of several persons etc. (*it is your turn to watch*; *it was now my turn to be angry*; *you must wait your turn*; *be patient, your turn will come*); **by** ~**s,** in rotation of individuals or groups, alternately; **in** ~, in succession; **in** one's ~, when one's turn comes; **out of** ~, before or after one's turn, (fig.) at an inappropriate moment; **take** ~**s,** work etc. alternately; (~ **and**) ~ **about,** alternately. **5.** Purpose (*did not serve my, its turn*; service of specified kind (*did me a good, an ill, turn*); *one good turn deserves another*). **6.** (Mus.) Grace consisting of principal note with those above and below it, in various sequences. **7.** Each round in coil of rope, wire, etc. **8.** (Print.) Inverted type as temporary substitute for missing letter; letter turned wrong side up. **9.** (colloq.) Momentary nervous shock (*gave me quite a turn*). **10.** (Profit made by) difference between the buying and selling prices of stocks etc. [ME, partly f. AF **torn*, **turn*, = OF *torn* f. L *tornus* (see prec.); partly f. prec.]

tûr'n|er *n.* In vbl senses; one who works with lathe, so ~ERY (1, 2, 3) *n.*; *member of society of gymnasts. [ME, f. OF *tornere -eor* f. LL *tornator* (as TURN[1]; see -ER[2])]

tûr'ning *n.* In vbl senses; use of lathe, (in *pl.*) chips or shavings formed by this; place where road meets another, such road, (*stop at the next turning*; *take the second turning to the left*); ~**-circle,** smallest circle in which vehicle can be turned round without reversing; ~**-point,** point in place, time, development, etc., at which decisive change occurs (*has reached the turning-point*; *this may be the turning-point of his life*). [ME, f. TURN[1] + -ING[1]]

tûr'nĭp *n.* (Biennial plant of genus *Brassica* with) fleshy globular white root used as vegetable and for feeding cattle etc.; (sl.) large thick old-fashioned watch; **~-top,** sprouting leaves of turnip used as vegetable; hence ~Y² *a.*, (esp.) tasting of turnips. [earlier *turnep(e)*, f. Sc. & N. Engl. dial. *neep* (OE *næp* f. L *napus* turnip); first element of uncert. orig.]

tûr'pentine *n.*, & *v.t.* **1.** *n.* Oleo-resin secreted by several coniferous trees and (**Chian** ~) by terebinth; (**oil of**) ~, volatile pungent oil distilled from this, used in mixing paints and varnishes and in medicine; **~-tree,** terebinth or other tree yielding turpentine. **2.** *v.t.* Apply turpentine to. [ME f. OF *ter(e)bentine* f. L *ter(e)binthina* (*resina* resin) (as TEREBINTH; see -INE²)]

tûr'pėth *n.* Cathartic root of an E. Ind. jalap; ~ (**mineral**), yellow basic mercury sulphate. [ME, f. med. L *turbit(h)um* f. Arab. & Pers. *turbid*]

tûr'pĭtūde *n.* Baseness, depravity, wickedness. [F, or f. L *turpitudo* (*turpis* disgraceful, base; see -TUDE)]

tûrps *n.* (colloq.) Oil of turpentine. [abbr.]

tûr'quoise (-z; *or* -koiz; *or* -kwahz) *n.* Opaque or translucent sky-blue or greenish-blue precious stone, hydrated copper aluminium phosphate; ~ **blue, green,** colours between green and blue. [ME *turkeis* etc., f. OF *turqueise*, later *-oise* Turkish (stone) (*Turc* TURK; f. being orig. known in Turkestan or coming through Turkish dominions)]

tŭ'rrėt *n.* Small tower connected with main building whether rising from ground or projecting from wall or corbels esp. at angle of main building; low flat usu. revolving armoured tower for gun and gunners in ship or aircraft or fort or tank; (Mech.) rotating holder for various dies and cutting tools in lathe, drill, etc.; hence ~ED² *a.*, having turret(s), (of shell) having long conical spiral part. [ME, f. OF *to(u)rete* dim. of *to(u)r* TOWER; see -ET¹]

tûr'tle¹ *n.* (arch.) = **~-dove,** wild dove of genus *Streptopelia*, esp. *S. turtur*, noted for soft cooing and affection for mate and young. [OE *turtla*, *turtle*, = OHG *turtulo*, *-la*, & OE *turtur*, = ON *turturi*, & ME *turture*, OF *turtre*, all f. L *turtur*]

tûr'tle² *n.* Marine or *freshwater reptile of order Chelonia with structure of tortoise and with flippers used in swimming; flesh of turtle, much used for soup; MOCK² *turtle soup*; **turn** ~, capsize; **~-neck,** high close-fitting neck of knitted garment, *polo-neck; **~-shell,** (1) tortoise-shell, esp. dark kind used for inlaying, (2) large handsome kind of cowrie. [app. alt. of *tortue* (see TORTOISE), assim. to prec.]

Tŭ'scan *a.* & *n.* (Classical Italian language, inhabitant) of Tuscany; *Tuscan* ORDER¹; ~ **straw,** fine yellow wheat-straw used for hats etc. [ME f. F, f. L *Tuscanus* (*Tuscus* Etruscan; see -AN)]

tŭsh¹ *int.* (arch.) = PSHAW. [ME; imit.]

tŭsh² *n.* Long pointed tooth, esp. canine tooth of horse; elephant's short tusk. [OE *tusc* TUSK]

tŭ'sherў *n.* (literary). Use of affected archaisms such as TUSH¹. [-ERY; wd made by R. L. Stevenson]

tŭsk *n.*, & *v.t.* **1.** *n.* Long pointed tooth, esp. protruding from closed mouth as in elephant, walrus, etc.; tusklike tooth or other object; hence (-)~ED² (-kt), ~'Y², *adjs.* **2.** *v.t.* Gore, thrust, tear up, with tusk(s). [ME alt. of OE *tux* var. of *tusc*; cf. TUSH²]

tŭ'sker *n.* Elephant or wild boar with developed tusks. [f. prec. + -ER¹]

tŭ'sser, tŭ'ssôre, *tŭ'ssah (*-a*), *n.* Indian or Chinese silkworm yielding strong but coarse brown silk; ~(**-silk**), silk of this and of some other silkworms. [f. Urdu f. Hindi *tasar* f. Skr. *tasara* shuttle]

tŭ'ssīve *a.* (Med.) Of a cough. [f. L *tussis* cough + -IVE]

tŭ'ssle *n.*, & *v.i.* Struggle, scuffle, (*with* person, *for* thing). [orig. Sc. & N. Engl., perh. dim. of *touse*; see TOUSLE]

tŭ'ssock *n.* Clump, hillock, of grass etc.; ~(**-moth**) (of genus *Orgyia* etc., with tufted larvae); **~-grass** (growing in tussocks, esp. *Poa flabellata* from Patagonia etc.); hence ~Y² *a.* [16th c., perh. alt. f. dial. *tusk* tuft; see -OCK]

tŭ'ssôre. See TUSSER.

tŭt¹**(-tŭ't)** *int.*, *n.*, & *v.i.* (-tt-). **1.** *int.* expr. impatience, contempt, or rebuke. **2.** *n.* Such exclamation. **3.** *v.i.* Exclaim thus. [imit. of click of tongue against teeth]

‖**tŭt**² *n.* (Mining). Job; **~-work,** piece-work. [18th c. in Cornwall, of unkn. orig.]

tū'tėlage *n.* Guardianship; (period of) being under this; instruction, tuition. [f. L *tutela* (*tuēri tuit-* or *tut-* watch) + -AGE]

tū'tėlarў, tū'tėlar, *adjs.* Serving as guardian, protective, (*tutelary saint, god*); of a guardian (*tutelary authority*). [f. LL *tutelaris*, L *-arius* (*tutela*; see prec., -AR¹, -ARY¹)]

tū'tėnăg *n.* Zinc imported from China and E. Indies; white alloy like German silver. [f. Marathi *tuttināg* perh. f. Skr. *tuttha* copper sulphate + *nāga* tin, lead]

tū'tor *n.* & *v.* **1.** *n.* Private teacher, esp. one having general charge of person's education; ‖university graduate, usu. a college fellow, supervising studies and welfare of assigned undergraduates; *college teacher below instructor; (Law) guardian of minor; ‖book of instruction in a subject; hence or cogn. ~AGE (2), ~ESS¹, ~SHIP, *ns.* **2.** *v.t.* Act as tutor to, instruct; discipline, school. **3.** *v.i.* Work as tutor; *study under tutor. [ME, f. AF, OF *tutour* or f. L *tutor* (*tuēri tut-* watch; see -OR)]

tūtôr'ĭal *a.* & *n.* **1.** *a.* Of a tutor; hence ~LY² *adv.* **2.** *n.* Period of individual instruction given by college tutor. [f. L *tutorius* (as prec.) + -AL]

tŭ'tsan *n.* A St. John's wort once thought to heal wounds etc. [ME, f. AF *tutsaine* all healthy]

tutti (tŏŏ'tē) *adv.* & *n.* (Mus.) All voices or instruments together; passage thus performed. [It., pl. of *tutto* all]

tutti-fru'tti (tŏŏtēfrŏŏ'tē) *n.* Confection, esp. ice-cream, of or flavoured with mixed fruits. [It., = all fruits]

tŭ'ttў *n.* Impure zinc oxide used as polishing-powder. [ME, f. OF *tutie* f. med. L *tutia* f. Arab. *tūtiyā*]

tu'tu¹ (tōō'tōō) *n.* Ballet dancer's skirt, esp. short projecting skirt of stiff frills in layers. [F]

tu'tu² (tōō'tōō) *n.* (N.Z.) Shrub of genus *Coriaria*, with black berries containing poisonous seeds. [Maori]

tuum. See MEUM.

tu-whĭ't (tōō-), **tu-whōō'** (tōō-), *n.*, & *v.i.* (-tt-). (Make) cry of owl. [imit.]

***tŭx** *n.* (colloq.) = foll. [abbr.]

***tŭxē'dō** *n.* (*pl.* ~*s or* ~*es*). Dinner-jacket; man's evening dress including this. [f. country club at *T*~ Park, N.Y.]

tuyère, -ere, (twēyār' *or* tōōyār' *or* twēr) *n.* Nozzle through which air is forced into furnace etc. [F (*tuyau* pipe)]

T.V. *abbr.* television (set).

T.V.A. *abbr.* Tennessee Valley Authority.

twa'ddl|e (-ŏ'-) *v.i.*, & *n.* (Indulge in) senseless, feeble, or prosy talk; hence ~ER¹ *n.*, ~Y² *a.* [alt. f. earlier *twattle*, alt. of TATTLE]

twain *a.* & *n.* (arch. or poet.) Two; two persons or things; *cut* etc. **in** ~, in two. [OE *twegen*, masc. nom. & acc. of *twā* TWO]

twăng *v.* & *n.* **1.** *v.i.* & *t.* (Cause to) make sharp ringing sound as of string of musical instrument or bow when plucked, (derog.) play *on* or on (fiddle etc.) thus; hence ~'LE 3 (-ă'nggel) *v.i.* & *t.* **2.** Speak or utter with nasal sound. **3.** *n.* Sound of tense string when plucked; nasal tone of voice. [imit.]

'twas (-ŏz) (arch. or poet.) It was. [contr.]

twăt *n.* (vulg.) Female genitals; (derog.) person, esp. woman. [17th c.; orig. unkn.]

tway'blāde *n.* Orchid of genus *Listera* etc., with green or purple flowers and single pair of leaves. [f. *tway* var. of TWAIN + BLADE]

tweak *v.t.*, & *n.* **1.** *v.t.* Pinch and twist sharply, pull with sharp jerk, twitch. **2.** *n.* Twitch, sharp pull, pinch. [prob. alt. f. dial. *twick* & TWITCH[1]]

||**twee** *a.* (**tweer** *pr.* twē'*er*; **tweest** *pr.* twē'ĭst). (Esp. affectedly) dainty or quaint. [f. childish pr. of SWEET]

tweed *n.* Twilled woollen or wool-and-cotton fabric with roughish surface and usu. two colours combined in the yarn, used esp. for men's clothes and orig. made in S. Scotland; (in *pl.*) cloths or clothes of tweed; hence ~'Y[2] *a.*, (colloq.) fond of wearing tweed, (fig.) heartily informal. [orig. a misreading of *tweel*, Sc. form of TWILL, helped by assoc. w. the river *Tweed*]

twee'dle *n.* Sound as of fiddle; **~du'm and ~-dee'** (-deld-), persons or things differing only or chiefly in name (orig. of rival musicians). [imit.]

'tween *prep.* Between, esp. **~-decks,** (space) between decks. [ME, f. BETWEEN]

||**twee'nȳ** *n.* (colloq.) Between-maid. [f. as prec. + -Y[3]]

tweet *n.*, & *v.i.* Chirp (of small bird); hence ~'ER[1] *n.*, small loudspeaker for accurately reproducing high-frequency signals (cf. WOOF[2]*er*). [imit.]

twee'zer *n.*, & *v.t.* **1.** *n.* **(Pair of) ~s,** small pair of tongs for taking up small objects, plucking out hairs, etc. **2.** *v.t.* Extract (hair, thorn, etc.) with tweezers. [extended form of *tweezes* (cf. *pincers* etc.) pl. of obs. *tweeze* case for small instruments, f. *etweese* = *étuis*, pl. of ÉTUI]

twĕlfth *a.* & *n.* **1.** *a.* Next after eleventh; ||**the** ~ (of August, as beginning of legal grouse-shooting); ~ **man,** reserve member of cricket team; ~ **part,** one of twelve equal parts. **2.** **T~-day** (after Christmas, festival of Epiphany); **T~-night,** night before this, formerly celebrated with various festivities etc.; **T~-cake** (prepared for Twelfth-night, often with bean or coin to determine 'ruler' of the feast). **3.** Hence ~LY[2] *adv.* **4.** *n.* Twelfth part; twelfth thing etc.; (Mus.) interval of an octave and a fifth. [OE *twelfta*, = OHG *zwelifto*, ON *tólfti* (as foll.; see -TH[2])]

twĕlve *a.* & *n.* **1.** One more than eleven; symbol for this (12, xii, XII); time of twelve o'clock; size etc. denoted by twelve; set of twelve; **the T~** (Apostles); *Twelve* TABLES; *Twelve* TRIBES; (in *pl.*) duodecimo sheet of book; hence ~'FOLD (-vf-) *a.* & *adv.* **2.** **~'mo,** duodecimo; **~'month,** period of twelve months, year (*today* etc. *~month*, a year before or esp. after today etc.); **~-note, ~-tone,** (Mus.) using twelve chromatic notes of octave arranged in chosen order without conventional key; ||**~'penny** *a.*, (Hist.) costing or worth a shilling. [OE *twelf(e)*, = OS *twelif*, OHG *zwelif*, ON *tólf*, Goth. *twalif* f. Gmc, prob. f. **twa* TWO + **lif-* as in ELEVEN]

twĕ'ntȳ *a.* & *n.* Twice ten; symbol for this (20, xx, XX); set of twenty persons or things; (in *pl.*) numbers, esp. years of a century or life, from 20 to 29; large indefinite number (*have told him twenty times*); **~-one** etc., (arch.) **one-and-~** etc., twenty plus one etc., w. corresp. ordinals **~-first** etc.; **~-five,** (Rugby Footb. & Hockey) line drawn across ground 25 yards from either goal, ground between this and goal-line; **~mo, ~fourmo,** leaf of sheet folded into 20, 24, equal parts, book made up of such leaves; hence **twĕ'ntiETH**[1] *a.* & *n.*, ~FOLD *a.* & *adv.* [OE *twentig*, = OS *twēntig*, OHG *zweinzug*, perh. f. as TWO + -TY[2]]

'twere (-*er*) (arch. or poet.) It were. [contr.]

twẽrp *n.* (sl.) Stupid or objectionable person. [20th c.; orig. unkn.]

twi-, twȳ-, *comb. form.* (arch.) Two, double, twice, as: **~'bill,** double-bladed battle-axe; **~'fold** *a.* & *adv.*, twofold; **~'formed,** having two forms or parts. [OE, = OHG *zwi-*, ON *tví-*, cogn. w. L BI-, Gk DI-[2]]

twice *adv.* Two times (esp. of multiplication), on two occasions, (*twice 3 is 6*; *told him twice*; THINK *twice*); doubly, in double degree or quantity, (*twice as strong*; *has twice the strength*); *is* ~ **the man** *he was* (twice as strong etc.); *did it* **at** or **in** ~, (colloq.) in two attempts or instalments; **~-laid,** (of rope) made from yarns of old rope; **~-told,** (fig.) trite. [ME *twiges*, f. OE *twige* + -S[3]]

||**twi'cer** *n.* (sl.) Double-dealing person, cheat. [f. prec. + -ER[1]]

twĭ'ddle *v.* & *n.* **1.** *v.t.* Twirl randomly or idly, esp. ~ one's **thumbs** (for lack of occupation). **2.** *v.i.* Trifle *with* (object); move twirlingly. **3.** *n.* Slight twirl; twirled mark or sign; hence **twĭ'ddlY**[2] *a.* [app. imit., after *twirl*, *twist*, and *fiddle*, *piddle*]

twĭg[1] *n.* Small shoot or branch of tree or plant; (Anat.) small branch of artery etc.; divining-rod, esp. *work the twig*; **hop the ~,** (colloq.) die; hence **(-)~GED**[2] (-gd), ~'LESS, **~'GY**[2] (-gĭ), *adjs.* [OE *twigge*, rel. to OE *twig*, *twī*; cf. OHG *zwīg* f. Gmc as TWI-]

twĭg[2] *v.t.* (-gg-). (colloq.) Understand, catch the meaning of, (person, words, plan, *that* etc., or abs.); perceive, observe. [18th c., of unkn. orig.]

twī'light (-īt) *n.* Light from sky when sun is below horizon in morning or (usu.) evening; period of this; faint light; (fig.) state of imperfect knowledge, understanding, etc.; ~ **arc(h)** or **curve** (dividing the earth's shadow from part of sky lit by direct rays of sun); ~ **of the gods,** (Norse Myth.) conflict in which gods and giants destroy each other; ~ **sleep,** partial narcosis esp. as means of making childbirth less painful; ~ **zone,** (1) area between two others in position and character, (2) urban area becoming decrepit. [ME (TWI-, LIGHT[1])]

twī'lighted (-īt-), **twī'lĭt,** *adjs.* Dimly illuminated (as) by twilight. [p.p. of *twilight* v., f. prec.]

twĭll *n.*, & *v.t.* **1.** *n.* Textile fabric in which weft-threads pass alternately over one warp-thread and under (not one as in plain weaving but) two or more thus producing diagonal lines. **2.** *v.t.* (esp. in *p.p.*) Weave (material) thus. [N. Engl. var. of obs. *twilly*, OE *twili* = OHG *zwilih*, f. TWI- after L BI(*lix* f. *licium* thread)]

'twĭll (arch. or poet.) It will. [contr.]

twĭn *a.*, *n.*, & *v.* (-nn-). **1.** *a.* Forming, or being one of, a closely related or associated pair esp. of children or animals born at a birth (*twin children*, *brother(s)*, *sister(s)*); (Bot.) growing in pairs; consisting of two closely connected and similar parts; ~ **bed,** one of a pair of single beds; **~-engined,** having two engines; ***~'flower,** plant of genus *Linnaea* with paired flowers; **~-screw,** (steamer) with two propellers on separate shafts having opposite twists; ~ **set,** woman's matching cardigan and jumper; ~ **towns,** two towns (usu. in different countries) establishing special links. **2.** *n.* Each of a closely related or associated pair esp. of children or animals born at a birth; exact counterpart of person or thing; compound crystal one part of which is in a reversed position with reference to the other; **the T~s,** zodiacal sign Gemini; hence ~'LING[1], ~'SHIP, *ns.* **3.** *v.t.* & *i.* Join intimately together, couple, pair, (*with*); hence ~'**n**ING[1] *n.*, formation of twin crystals. **4.** *v.i.* Bear twins; grow as twin crystal. [OE *twinn* double, f. TWI-; cf. ON *tvinnr*]

twīne *n.* & *v.* **1.** *n.* Strong thread or string of two or more strands of hemp, cotton, etc., twisted together; coil, twist; interlacing, tangle. **2.** *v.t.* Form (thread) by twisting strands together; form (garland etc.) of interwoven material, garland (brow etc.) *with*; interweave; coil, wind, (thing *about, round,* another). **3.** *v.i.* & *t.* (Of plant, snake, etc.) coil or twist itself or it*self* (*round*). [OE *twin, twigin* linen, ult. f. stem of TWI-]

twĭnge (-nj) *n.* Sharp momentary local pain (lit. or fig.; *a twinge of toothache, rheumatism, conscience, remorse*). [f. *twinge* v. pinch, wring f. OE *twengan,* = MLG *twengen,* OHG *zwengen* f. Gmc **twang-*]

twĭnk *v.i.*, & *n.* **1.** Twinkle, sparkle. **2.** *n.* **In a ~,** in an instant. [ME, f. OE **twincan*; cf. MHG *zwinken,* and foll.]

twĭ'nkle *v.* & *n.* **1.** *v.i.* (Of light, star, etc.) shine with rapidly intermittent gleams, sparkle; (of feet in dancing, etc.) move rapidly up and down or to and fro; (of eyes) sparkle (*at* jest etc.). **2.** *v.t.* Blink, wink, (one's eyes); emit (light, signal) in quick gleams. **3.** Hence **twĭ'nkl**ER[1] *n.* **4.** *n.* Twitching of eyelid, blink, wink, (**in a ~,** in an instant); sparkle, gleam, of the eyes, (*a humorous, mischievous, twinkle*); short rapid movement e.g. of feet in dancing; quick tremulous light, glimmer. [OE *twinclian,* frequent. of **twincan*; see prec., -LE 3]

twĭ'nklĭng *n.* In vbl senses; **in a ~, in the ~ of an eye,** (joc.) **of a teacup,** etc., in an instant. [ME, f. prec. + -ING[1]]

twĭrl *v.* & *n.* **1.** *v.t.* & *i.* Revolve rapidly, spin, whirl, twist, (*round*). **2.** *v.t.* Turn (one's *thumbs* etc.) round and round in purposeless way, twiddle. **3.** *n.* Twirling, rapid or idle circular motion; twirling thing; flourish or curl made with pen etc.; hence ~'Y[2] *a.* [16th c., prob. alt., after *whirl,* f. obs. *tirl* TRILL]

twĭrp. Var. of TWERP.

twĭst *n.* & *v.* **1.** *n.* Thread, rope, etc., made by winding two or more strands etc. about one another; fine strong silk thread used by tailors etc.; roll of bread, tobacco, etc. in form of twist; ||paper packet with screwed-up ends; curled piece of lemon etc. peel to flavour a drink. **2.** Act of twisting, condition of being twisted, (*give it a twist; has a curious twist; full of twists and turns*); dance with vigorous bodily contortions; unexpected development of events in story etc.; *change from usual procedure. **3.** Manner or degree in which thing is twisted, e.g. inclination of rifle-grooves, whirling motion given to ball in cricket etc. to make it take special curve. **4.** Peculiar tendency of mind, character, etc., (freq. derog.); **round the ~,** (sl.) crazy. **5.** Twisting strain; (angle showing) amount of twisting of rod etc.; forward motion combined with rotation about an axis. **6.** ||(sl.) Drink made of two ingredients mixed. **7.** ||(colloq.) Hearty appetite; swindle. **8.** (sl.) Young woman, esp. disreputable one. **9.** *v.t.* Wind (strands etc.) one about another; form (rope etc.) thus; interweave (thing *with* or *in with* another). **10.** Give spiral form to (rod, column, cord, etc.) as by rotating the ends in opposite directions; break *off* thus; *twist* person *round* one's (*little*) FINGER. **11.** Cause (ball, esp. in billiards) to rotate while following curved path. **12.** Twine (flowers etc. *into* garland etc.); make (garland etc.) thus. **13.** Make one's *way* (*through* crowd, etc., *along,* etc.) in winding manner. **14.** Pull out of natural shape, distort, (*limbs twisted on the rack; fell and twisted her ankle; features twisted with pain*; (fig.) *wants to twist my words into an admission of error*; ~ person's **arm,** force his hand or wrist round as torture, (fig.) coerce him by moral pressure; ||(colloq.) cheat; (in *p.p.*, of mind etc.) warped, (Geom., of curve) extending in three dimensions. **15.** Hence ~'ABLE *a.* **16.** *v.i.* Be given, grow in, spiral form; move (*along, through,* etc.) in winding manner; take twisted position (*twisted round in his seat*); dance the twist. [ME; cogn. w. TWIN, TWINE]

twĭ'ster *n.* In vbl senses; untrustworthy person, swindler; twisting ball in cricket or billiards; *tornado, waterspout, etc.; TONGUE[1]-*twister.* [f. prec. + -ER[1]]

twĭ'stȳ *a.* Full of twists; (fig.) dishonest. [f. TWIST + -Y[2]]

twĭt[1] *v.t.* (-tt-). Reproach, upbraid, taunt, (person *with* **fau**lt etc.). [16th c. *twite,* f. *atwite* f. OE *ætwītan* reproach with (*æt* at, *wītan* blame)]

twĭt[2] *n.* (sl.) ||Foolish or insignificant person; state of jumpiness. [orig. dial., perh. f. prec.]

twitch[1] *v.* & *n.* **1.** *v.t.* Pull (thing *off* etc.) with light jerk; pull sharply at, jerk at, (person's sleeve etc.) esp. to call attention. **2.** *v.i.* Pull sharply, jerk, *at*; (of features, muscles, limbs) move or contract spasmodically. **3.** *n.* Sudden involuntary contraction or movement, sudden pull or jerk; (colloq.) state of nervousness, whence ~'Y[2] *a.*; noose and stick for quietening horse during veterinary operation. [ME, = LG *twikken,* MHG *zwicken* f. Gmc **twik-*; cf. OE *twiccian,* dial. *twick*]

twitch[2] *n.* **~(-grass),** = COUCH[3]-*grass.* [var. of QUITCH]

twite *n.* Mountain linnet (*Acanthis flavirostris*). [imit. of its note]

twĭ'tter *v.* & *n.* **1.** *v.i.* (Of bird, or fig. of person) utter succession of light tremulous sounds, chirp. **2.** *v.t.* Utter or express thus. **3.** *n.* Twittering; (colloq.) tremulously excited state. [ME, imit.; cf. -ER[5]]

'twĭxt *prep.* (poet. or arch.) = BETWIXT. [abbr.]

two (tōō) *a.* & *n.* **1.** One more than one; symbol for this (2, ii, II); card etc. with two pips; time of two o'clock; size etc. denoted by two; (in *pl.*) gloves, shoes, etc., of second size; **a . . . or ~,** one or two . . .s, a few . . .s; *two* CHEER[1]*s*; *cut, divide,* etc., **in ~,** into two parts; *in two* SHAKE[2]*s*, ||**in ~ ticks,** ||**in ~ ~s,** (colloq.) in a very short time; ONE *or two*; **~ can play at that game,** cf. GAME[1] *that two can play*; **~ and ~, ~ by ~,** in pairs; **put ~ and ~ together,** make inference from known facts; **that makes ~ of us,** (colloq.) that is true of myself also; *two a* PENNY; *two* TABLE*s*; hence ~'FOLD *a.* & *n.*, ~'NESS *n.* **2.** ***~-bit,** costing 25 cents, (fig.) petty; **~-by-four,** (*n.*) timber with cross-section 2″ by 4″, *(*a.*, fig.) petty; **~-dimensional,** having or appearing to have length and breadth but no depth; **~-edged,** (of sword etc.) having an edge on each side, (fig., of argument, compliment, etc.) cutting both ways, ambiguous; **~-faced,** having two faces, (fig.) insincere; **~-fisted,** ||clumsy, *vigorous; **~-handed,** having two hands, (of sword) requiring to be used with both hands, (of saw, game, etc.) to be worked, played, etc., by two persons; **~-line(d),** (Print.) having a depth double that of the normal size of letters; | ||**~pence** (tŭ'pens), sum of two pence (*~pence coloured,* cheap and, as opp. *penny plain,* gaudy), thing of little value (*don't care twopence*); ||**~-penny** (tŭ'penĭ), costing or worth 2p. or 2d., cheap, worthless; ||**~penny-halfpenny** (tŭpnĭhā'pnĭ), contemptible, insignificant, trumpery; **~-piece,** suit of clothes or woman's bathing-suit comprising two separate parts; **~-ply,**

(wool etc.) of two strands, layers, or thicknesses (*two-ply rope, carpet*); ~**-seater,** vehicle or aircraft with two seats; ~**-sided,** having two sides, aspects, etc.; ~**-step,** round dance with sliding step in march or polka time; ~**-stroke,** (of internal combustion engine) having power cycle completed in one up-and-down movement of piston; ~**-sui'ter,** (Bridge) hand containing two long suits; ~**-time** *v.t.*, (sl.) swindle, deceive (esp. spouse by infidelity); ~**-tone,** having two colours or sounds; ~**-up,** gambling game with tossing of two coins; ~**-way,** involving two ways or participants, (Electr., of switch) permitting current to be switched on or off from either of two points, (of tap etc.) permitting fluid etc. to flow in either of two channels or directions, (of traffic etc.) moving in two esp. opposite directions; ~**-whee'ler,** vehicle with two wheels. [OE *twā* fem. & neut., *tū* neut. (cf. TWAIN), = OS *twā, twō*, OHG *zwā, zwō*, ON *tvær*, Goth. *twōs*, cogn. w. Skr. *dwau, dwe*, Gk & L *duo*]

***two'fer** (tōō'-) *n.* Free ticket entitling holder to buy theatre-tickets at half price. [f. *two for one*]

two'some (tōō'-) *a.* & *n.* (Game, dance, etc.) for two persons; pair or couple of persons. [f. TWO + -SOME²]

'twould (-ŏŏd) (arch. or poet.) It would. [contr.]

twȳ-. See TWI-.

twȳ'er. Var. of TUYÈRE.

-tȳ¹ *suf.* forming *ns.* denoting quality or condition (*bounty, cruelty, faculty, plenty, puberty, safety, subtlety*). [ME *-tie, -tee, -te* f. OF *-té, -tet* f. L *-tas -tatis*; cf. -ITY]

-tȳ² *suf.* = tens (*twenty, thirty, ninety*, etc.). [OE *-tig*, = OS *-tig*, OHG *-zug*; cf. ON *tigr*, Goth. *tigus* ten]

tȳ'chĭsm (-k-) *n.* Theory that chance controls the universe. [f. Gk *tukhē* chance + -ISM]

Tȳchō'nĭan, Tȳchŏ'nĭc, (-k-) *adjs.* Of (the astronomical system) of Tycho Brahe. [f. *Tycho -onis* Latinized name of *Tyge* Brahe, Da. astronomer d. 1601 + -IAN, -IC]

tȳcōō'n *n.* Title applied by foreigners to shogun of Japan 1854–68; (colloq.) business magnate. [f. Jap. *taikun* great prince]

tȳ'ĭng. See TIE¹.

tȳke, tīke, *n.* Cur; ||low fellow; **(Yorkshire)** ~, Yorkshireman; *small child. [ME, f. ON *tík* bitch]

tyle(r). Var. of TILE 5, TILER 2.

tȳ'lopŏd *a.* & *n.* (Animal) with padded not hoofed digits, e.g. camel; hence **tȳlŏ'pod**ous *a.* [f. Gk *tulos* knob or *tulē* callus, cushion + -o- + *pous podos* foot]

tȳ'mpan *n.* (Print.) apparatus to equalize pressure between platen etc. and printing-sheet; (Archit.) tympanum. [F, or f. L TYMPANUM]

tȳmpă'nĭc *a.* (Acting) like a drumhead; (Anat.) of the tympanum (*tympanic membrane*); ~ **(bone)**, bone of ear supporting tympanic membrane. [f. TYMPANUM + -IC]

tȳ'mpanĭst, tȳ'mpanō. Var. of TIMPANIST, TIMPANO.

tȳmpan|ī'tēs (-z) *n.* Swelling of abdomen caused by gas in intestine etc.; hence ~**ĭ'tic** *a.* [LL, f. Gk *tumpanitēs* of drum (as TYMPANUM; see -ITE¹)]

tȳ'mpan|um *n.* (*pl.* ~**a** *or* ~**ums**). **1.** (Anat.) Middle ear; ear-drum; hence ~I'TIS *n.* **2.** (Zool.) Bony labyrinth at base of trachea in some ducks; membrane covering hearing-organ on leg etc. of insect. **3.** (Archit.) Vertical triangular space forming centre of pediment; (carving on) similar space over door between lintel and arch. **4.** Drum-wheel for raising water from stream. [L, f. Gk *tumpanon* drum (*tuptō* strike)]

Tȳ'nwald (-ŏld) *n.* Isle of Man annual assembly proclaiming newly enacted laws. [f. ON *thing-völlr* place of assembly (*thing* assembly, *völlr* field)]

tȳpe¹ *n.* **1.** Person, thing, event, serving as illustration, symbol, prophetic similitude, or characteristic specimen, of another thing or of a class (*water may serve as a type of instability; paschal lamb is a type of Christ; the treatment he received is but a type of what patriots must expect; he is an admirable type of modern athleticism* or *of the modern athlete*); (colloq.) person, esp. of a specified character. **2.** Class of things etc. having common characteristics (*her beauty was of* or *belonged to another type; dislike men of that type*); (as *suf.*) made of, resembling, functioning by or as, (*ceramic-type materials; Cheddar-type cheese*). **3.** (Biol. etc.) Plan of structure (*deviates from the type*; TRUE *to type*); main division of animal or vegetable kingdom characterized by this (*the vertebrate type*); organism (chosen as) having the essential characteristics of its group (~ **genus,** genus giving its name to and having the characteristics of a higher group, e.g. a family); ~ **site,** (Archaeol.) site where objects regarded as defining the characteristics of a period etc. are found. **4.** Biblical event regarded as symbolic or foreshadowing a later one (cf. ANTITYPE). **5.** Object, conception, work of art serving as model for subsequent artists. **6.** Device on either side of medal or coin. **7.** (Print.) Piece of metal or wood having on its upper surface a raised letter or character for use in printing, a kind or size of such pieces, (collect. *sing.*) set or supply of these, (*wooden types are* or *type is now used only for posters; ran short of type; short of certain types; printed in large type*); **in** ~, composed and ready for printing. **8.** ~**-bar,** (1) bar in typewriter carrying one pair of letters etc., (2) line of types in solid bar as cast in some type-setting machines; *type* BASKET; ~**-cast** *v.t.*, cast (actor) in role appropriate to his nature or of a kind in which he has been successful; ~**-face,** (impression made by) inked part of type, set of types in one design; ~**-founder,** one who designs and makes metal type for printing; ~**-high,** (of block etc.) set at proper height to print with accompanying type; ~**-metal,** alloy of lead etc. used for printing-types; ~**'script,** typewritten document; ~**-setter,** (1) compositor, (2) composing-machine: ~**-setting,** setting of types in proper order for printing; ~*-setting machine* (for simplifying this process, now usu. including the making of types as they are needed); ~**-wheel,** wheel bearing letters in relief as used in some typewriters and telegraphs. **9.** Hence **tȳ'p**AL *a.* [ME f. F, or f. L f. Gk *tupos* impression, figure, type (*tuptō* strike)]

tȳpe² *v.t.* & *i.* Be a type or example of; write with typewriter; assign to a type; type-cast. [f. prec.]

tȳ'pewrīte (-prīt) *v.t.* & *i.* (**-wrote; -written;** usu. in *p.p.*) Write with typewriter. [back form. f. foll.]

tȳ'pewrīter (-prī-) *n.* Machine for writing in characters like those used in printing, by pressing keys to actuate steel types that strike paper through inked ribbon; (arch.) typist. [f. TYPE¹ + WRITER]

tȳphl|ī'tĭs *n.* Inflammation of caecum; hence ~**ĭ'tic** *a.* [mod. L, f. Gk *tuphlon* caecum or blind gut (*tuphlos* blind) + -ITIS]

tȳ'phoid *a.* & *n.* Like typhus; ~ **(fever)**, infectious bacterial fever with eruption of red spots on chest and abdomen and severe intestinal irritation, similar disease of animals; ~ **condition** or **state** (of depressed vitality, occurring in many acute diseases); hence **tȳphoi'd**AL *a.* [f. TYPHUS + -OID]

tȳphōō'n *n.* Violent hurricane in E. Asian seas; so **tȳphŏ'n**IC *a.* [partly f. Port. *tufão* f. Arab.

ṭūfān perh. f. Gk *tuphōn* whirlwind; partly f. Chin. dial. *tai fung* big wind]

tȳ'ph|us *n.* Rickettsial infectious fever with eruption of purple spots, great prostration, and usu. delirium; hence ~OUS *a.* [mod. L, f. Gk *tuphos* smoke, stupor (*tuphō* to smoke)]

tȳ'pĭc *a.* (arch. or poet.) = foll. 1. [f. F *typique* f. LL f. Gk *tupikos* (as TYPE[1]; see -IC)]

tȳ'pĭcal *a.* **1.** Serving as a type or characteristic example, representative, symbolical, emblematic, (*of*), (*a typical genus, plant, Scotsman, shingles rash*; *is typical of the genus*). **2.** Characteristic of, serving to distinguish, a type (*typical markings, structure, phraseology*). **3.** Hence ~LY[2] *adv.*, ~ITY (-ă'l-), ~NESS, *ns.* [f. med. L *typicalis* f. LL *typicus* (see prec., -AL)]

tȳ'pĭ|fȳ *v.t.* Represent by a type, foreshadow; be a type or example of, embody the characteristics of; hence ~FICA'TION, **~fīer**[1], *ns.* [f. L *typus* TYPE[1] + -FY]

tȳ'pĭst *n.* One who uses a typewriter, esp. professionally; **shorthand** ~ (who can also write shorthand). [f. TYPE[1] + -IST]

tȳ'pō *n.* (*pl.* ~s). (colloq.) Typographer; *typographical error. [abbr.]

tȳpŏ'graph|ȳ *n.* **1.** Art of printing; so ~ER[1] *n.* **2.** Style or appearance of printed matter (*faults of typography*; *the typography was admirable*). **3.** Hence **tȳpogră'phic**(AL) *adjs.* [f. F *typographie* or mod. L *typographia* f. as TYPE[1] + -O- + -GRAPHY]

tȳpŏ'log|ȳ *n.* Study and interpretation of (esp. biblical) types; hence **tȳpolŏ'gical** *a.*, ~IST (3) *n.* [f. Gk *tupos* TYPE[1] + -O- + -LOGY]

tȳ'ponȳm *n.* (Biol.) Name based on a type. [f. as prec. + Gk *onum-* = *onoma* name]

tȳră'nnĭcal *a.* Acting like, characteristic of, a tyrant; arbitrary, imperious, despotic; hence ~LY[2] *adv.* [f. OF *tyrannique* f. L f. Gk *turannikos* (as TYRANT; see -IC) + -AL]

tȳră'nnĭ|cīde *n.* Killer or killing of a tyrant; hence **~cī'dal** *a.* [F, f. L *tyrannicida, -cidium* (as TYRANT; see -CIDE)]

tȳ'rannize, -ise (-īz), *v.* **1.** *v.i.* Play the tyrant, rule despotically or cruelly (*over* person etc.). **2.** *v.t.* Rule (person etc.) despotically. [f. F *tyranniser* (as TYRANT; see -IZE)]

tȳră'nnosaur *n.* Fossil biped dinosaur (*Tyrannosaurus rex*), largest known carnivore. [f. as TYRANT, after *dinosaur*]

tȳ'rann|ȳ *n.* **1.** Despotic or cruel exercise of power; instance of this, tyrannical act or behaviour; hence ~OUS *a.* **2.** Rule of (Greek) tyrant; State thus ruled; period of this. [ME, f. OF *tyrannie* f. med. L *tyrannia* f. Gk *turannia* (as foll.; see -Y[1])]

tȳr'ant *n.* **1.** Oppressive or cruel ruler; person exercising power or authority arbitrarily or cruelly. **2.** (Gk Hist.) Absolute ruler who seized power without legal right; one of 30 oligarchs ruling Athens 404–403 B.C. **3. ~-bird, ~ flycatcher,** Amer. bird of genus *Tyrannus*, driving all other birds from near its nest. [ME *tyran, -ant*, f. OF *tiran, tyrant* f. L f. Gk *turannos*]

||**tȳre, *tīre**[3], *n.* Solid, or hollow inflated, rubber ring placed round wheel of vehicle to prevent jarring; **~-chain** (fastening over tread of tyre to improve grip on ice etc.); **~-gauge,** portable device for measuring air-pressure in tyre. [var. of TIRE[2]]

Tȳ'rĭan *a.* & *n.* (Native or inhabitant) of ancient Tyre in Phoenicia; *Tyrian* PURPLE. [f. L *Tyrius* (*Tyrus* Tyre) + -AN]

tȳr'ō. See TIRO.

Tȳrol|ē'an *a.* Of or characteristic of the Tyrol; so ~E'SE *a.* & *n.* [f. *Tyrol*, Tirol, Alpine province of W. Austria + -EAN]

tȳr'osine (-ēn) *n.* (Chem.) Crystalline amino-acid obtained by decomposition of proteins. [f. Gk *turos* cheese + -INE[5]]

Tȳ'rrhēne, Tȳrrhē'nĭan, (-rē-) *adjs.* & *ns.* Etruscan. [f. L *Tyrrhenus* + -IAN]

tzar. Var. of TSAR.

tzĭga'ne (tsĭgah'n) *a.* & *n.* **1.** *a.* Of the Hungarian gipsies or their music. **2.** *n.* Hungarian gipsy. [F, f. Magyar *c(z)igány*]

U

U[1], u, (ū) *n.* (*pl.* **Us** *or* **U's**). Twenty-first letter of alphabet; **U-bolt, -tube,** etc., (shaped like U); **U-turn,** driving of vehicle so as to face in opposite direction without reversing, (fig.) complete reversal of policy etc.

U[2] (ōō) *n.* Burmese title of respect before man's name. [Burm.]

U[3] (ū) *a.* (colloq.) Upper-class; supposedly characteristic of the upper class. [abbr.]

U. *abbr.* universal (of cinema film open to all persons); university.

u *pref.* = μ (symbol for MICRO- 2).

U *symb.* uranium.

ūbī'etȳ *n.* Being in definite place, local relation. [f. med. L *ubietas* f. L *ubi* where; see -TY[1]]

-ūbĭ'lĭtȳ *suf.* forming *ns.* f. *adjs.* in -UBLE (*dissolubility*). [f. L *-ubilitas*; see -ITY]

ūbĭquĭtār'ĭan *a.* & *n.* (Theol.) Of, believer in, the omnipresence of Christ's body; hence ~ISM (3) *n.* [f. mod. L *ubiquitarius* (as foll.; see -ARIAN)]

ūbĭ'quĭt|ȳ *n.* Being everywhere or in an indefinite number of places at same time; (joc., of person) being frequently encountered; ||**~y of the king,** (Law) his official presence in all courts in the person of his judges; hence ~OUS *a.* [f. mod. L *ubiquitas* f. L *ubique* everywhere (*ubi* where; see -ITY)]

-ūble *suf.* forming *adjs.* w. senses as -ABLE (*soluble, voluble*); hence **-ūbly**[2] *adv. suf.* [F, f. L *-u-* of vbs. in *-vere* + *-bilis* (see -BLE)]

U'-boat (ū'b-) *n.* German submarine. [f. G *U-boot* (*Unterseeboot* under-sea boat)]

U.C. *abbr.* University College.

u.c. *abbr.* upper case.

||**U.C.C.A.** *abbr.* Universities Central Council on Admissions.

ū'dal *n.* Kind of freehold right based on uninterrupted possession prevailing in N. Europe before feudal system and still in Orkney and Shetland; **~ler, ~man,** holder of property by udal. [f. ON *óthal*, = OE *ǣthel, ēthel, ōthel*, OS *ōthil*, OHG *uodal* f. Gmc *ōth-]

U.D.C. *abbr.* Universal Decimal Classification; ||(Hist.) Urban District Council.

ŭ'dder *n.* Mammary glands of cattle etc. in pendulous baggy organ having more than one teat; hence (-)~ED[2] (-erd), ~LESS, *adjs.* [OE *ūder*, = OS *ūder*, OHG *ūter* f. WG *ūdhr-]

U.D.I. *abbr.* unilateral declaration of independence.

ūdŏ'mėter *n.* Rain-gauge. [f. F *udomètre* f. L *udus* damp; see -O-, -METER]

U.F.O. *abbr.*, **ū'fō** *n.* (*pl.* ~s), unidentified flying object, esp. 'flying saucer'.

ugh (ŭh *or* ŏŏh) *int.* expr. disgust or horror, or sound of cough or grunt. [imit.]

ŭ'glĭ *n.* Mottled green and yellow citrus fruit, hybrid of grapefruit and tangerine. [f. foll.]

ŭ'glȳ *a.* & *n.* **1.** *a.* Unpleasing or repulsive to sight or hearing (*an ugly beast of a bulldog*; *must not make ugly faces*; *the ugliest house I have seen*; *has an ugly scar on his forehead*; *produced an ugly discord*); morally repulsive, vile, discreditable, unpleasant, unpleasantly suggestive, threatening, unpromising, (*ugly vices*; *his conduct has an ugly look*; *ugly rumours are about*; *cloud has an ugly look*; *have had ugly weather*; *an ugly gash*); ~ **customer,** unpleasantly formidable person; ~ **duckling,** person who turns out to be the genius etc. of the family after being thought the dullard etc. [w. ref. to cygnet in brood of ducks in tale by Andersen]; hence **ŭ'glĭ**FY *v.t.*, **ŭ'glĭ**LY[2] *adv.*, **ŭ'glĭ**NESS *n.* **2.** *n.* = prec.; silk shade worn as appendage to bonnet about middle of 19th c. [ME, f. ON *uggligr* to be dreaded (*ugga* to dread; see -LY[1])]

U'grĭan, U'grĭc, (ŏŏ'-) *adjs.* & *ns.* (Language or member) of (orig.) E. branch of Finnic peoples, esp. Magyar. [f. Russ. *Ugry* name of race dwelling E. of Urals + -IAN, -IC]

U.H.F. *abbr.* ultra-high frequency.

uh'lan (ōō'- *or* ū'-) *n.* (Hist.) Cavalryman armed with lance in some European armies, esp. former German army. [F & G, f. Pol. (*h*)*ulan* f. Turk. *oğlan* youth, servant]

Ui'tlander (ā'tlŏnd*er*) *n.* (S. Afr.) Foreigner, alien, esp. before Boer War. [Afrik., f. Du. *uit* out + *land* land; see -ER[1]]

U.K. *abbr.* United Kingdom.

U.K.A.E.A. *abbr.* United Kingdom Atomic Energy Authority.

ūkā'se *n.* Edict of Tsarist Russian government; any arbitrary order. [f. Russ. *ukaz* ordinance, edict (*ukazat'* show, decree)]

ukiyō-e' (ōōkēyōyā') *n.* School of Japanese art using subjects from everyday life and simple treatment. [Jap., = genre picture]

Ukrai'nĭan (ū-) *a.* & *n.* (Native or language) of the Ukraine, a constituent republic of U.S.S.R. [f. *Ukraine* f. Russ. *ukraina* frontier region (*u* at, *krai* edge) + -IAN]

ūkule'lė (-lā'-) *n.* Small four-stringed Hawaiian (orig. Portuguese) guitar. [Hawaiian]

-ūlar *suf.* forming *adjs.*, sometimes corresp. to *ns.* in -ULE (*pustular*) but often without dim. force (*angular*, *cellular*, *globular*, *granular*, *tubular*); so **-ūlă'**RITY *n. suf.*, ~LY[2] *adv. suf.* [f. or after L *-ularis* (as -ULE, -AR[1])]

ŭ'lcer *n.* Open sore on external or internal surface of body with suppuration etc.; (fig.) moral blemish, corroding or corrupting influence, etc.; hence or cogn. ~ED[2] (-erd), ~OUS, *adjs.* [ME, f. L *ulcus -eris*, rel. to Gk *helkos*]

ŭ'lcer|āte *v.i.* & *t.* Form, convert or be converted into, affect with, an ulcer (lit. or fig.); hence or cogn. ~ABLE, ~ATIVE, *adjs.*, ~A'TION *n.* [ME, f. L *ulcerare* (as prec.) + -ATE[3]]

-ūle *suf.* forming dim. *ns.* (*capsule*, *globule*, *granule*, *pustule*). [f. or after L *-ulus*, *-ula*, *-ulum*]

u'lėma (ōō'-) *n.* (Member of) body of Muslim doctors of sacred law and theology esp. in former Turk. empire. [f. Arab. *'ulamā* pl. of *'ālim* learned (*'alama* know)]

-ūlent *suf.* forming *adjs.* w. sense 'abounding in, full of' (*flatulent*, *fraudulent*, *turbulent*); so **-ūl**ENCE *n. suf.*, ~LY[2] *adv. suf.* [f. L *-ulentus*]

ūlĭ'gĭnōse, -ous, *adjs.* (Bot.) Growing in wet or swampy places. [f. L *uliginosus* (*uligo -ginis* moisture; see -OSE[1], -OUS)]

ŭ'llage *n.* Amount by which cask etc. falls short of being full, loss by evaporation or leakage. [ME, f. AF *ulliage*, OF *ouillage* (*ouiller* fill up f. Gallo-Rom. **oculare* f. L *oculus* eye, w. ref. to bung-hole; see -AGE)]

ŭ'ln|a *n.* (*pl.* ~ae). Large thinner bone of forearm in man (cf. RADIUS); corresponding bone in animal's foreleg or bird's wing; hence ~AR[1] *a.* [L, rel. to Gk *ōlenē* and ELL]

ūlŏ'trĭchan *a.* & *n.*, **-chous** *a.*, (-k-). Woolly-haired; (member) of the crisp- or woolly-haired division of mankind. [f. mod. L *Ulotrichi* f. Gk *oulos* woolly, crisp + *thrix trikhos* hair + -AN, -OUS]

-ūlous *suf.* forming *adjs.* (*fabulous*, *garrulous*, *populous*, *tremulous*); hence ~LY[2] *adv. suf.*, ~NESS *n. suf.* [f. L *-ulosus* & *-ulus* + -OUS]

ŭ'lster *n.* Long loose overcoat of rough cloth, often with belt, [orig. sold in Belfast]; **U~ custom,** form of tenant right in Ireland; **U~-man, U~woman,** native or inhabitant of Ulster. [f. *U~* in Ireland]

ult. *abbr.* ultimo.

ŭltēr'ĭor *a.* Situated beyond; more remote, not immediate, in the future; in the background, beyond what is seen or avowed, (*ulterior motive*, *plans*); hence ~LY[2] *adv.* [L, compar. of **ulter*; cf. ULTRA-]

ŭ'ltĭma *n.* Last syllable of word. [L *ultima* (*syllaba*), fem. of *ultimus* last]

ŭ'ltĭmate *a.* Last, final, beyond which no other exists or is possible, (*ultimate result*, *analysis*); fundamental, primary, (*ultimate basis*, *principles*, *truths*); maximum (*ultimate tensile strength*); ~ **cause** (beyond which no other can be found); **the ~ facts of nature** (beyond reach of analysis); hence ~LY[2] (-tlĭ) *adv.*, ~NESS (-tn-) *n.* [f. LL *ultimatus* p.p. of *ultimare* come to an end (*ultimus* last); see -ATE[2]]

ultĭma Thule (ŭltĭma thū'lē) *n.* Far-away unknown region. [L, = farthest Thule (as prec., THULIUM)]

ŭltĭmā't|um *n.* (*pl.* ~ums *or* ~a). Final proposal or statement of terms, rejection of which by opposite party may lead to end of harmonious relations, declaration of war, etc.; final point; fundamental principle. [neut. p.p. (as n.); see ULTIMATE]

ŭ'ltĭmō *a.* (Commerc.) Of last month (*the 28th ultimo*). [L, = in the last (*mense* month)]

ŭltĭmogĕ'nĭture *n.* System in which youngest son (cf. PRIMOGENITURE) has right of inheritance. [f. L *ultimus* last, after *primogeniture*]

ŭ'ltra *a.* & *n.* (Person) favouring extreme views or measures, esp. in religion or politics. [orig. as abbr. of F *ultra-royaliste*; see foll.]

ŭ'ltra- *pref.* Beyond, on the other side of; extreme(ly), excessive(ly), (*ultra-conservative*, *ultra-fashionable*, *ultra-modern*). [f. L *ultra* beyond]

ŭltracĕ'ntrĭfūge *n.* High-speed centrifuge to determine size of small particles and large molecules by their rate of sedimentation. [f. ULTRA- + CENTRIFUGE]

ŭ'ltra-high (-hī) *a.* (Of frequency) in range 300 to 3000 megahertz. [f. ULTRA- + HIGH]

ŭ'ltra|ĭst *n.* Holder of extreme opinions in politics, religion, etc.; so ~ISM (3) *n.* [f. ULTRA + -IST]

ŭltramarī'ne (-ē'n) *a.* & *n.* **1.** *a.* Situated beyond the sea. **2.** *n.* (Colour of) blue pigment got from lapis lazuli; imitation of this from powdered fired clay, sodium carbonate, sulphur, and resin. [f. obs. It. *oltramarino* & med. L ULTRA(*marinus* MARINE); sense 2 from fact that lapis lazuli was brought from beyond sea]

ŭltramī'croscōpe *n.* Instrument revealing, by

scattered light, objects too small to be seen with ordinary microscope. [f. ULTRA- + MICROSCOPE]

ŭltramīcroscŏ'pĭc *a.* Of ultramicroscope; too small to be seen with ordinary microscope. [f. ULTRA- + MICROSCOPIC]

ŭltramŏ'nt|āne *a.* & *n.* **1.** *a.* Situated south of the Alps; Italian; favourable to the absolute authority of the pope in matters of faith and discipline, whence **~an**ISM (3), **~an**IST (2), *ns.* **2.** *n.* One who resides south of the Alps; person holding ultramontane views. [f. med. L ULTRA(*montanus* f. L *mons montis* mountain; see -ANE)]

ŭltramŭ'ndāne *a.* Lying beyond the world or the solar system. [f. L ULTRA(*mundanus* f. *mundus* world; see -ANE)]

ŭltrasŏ'n|ĭc *a.* Of sound waves with pitch above upper limit of human hearing; hence ~ICALLY *adv.*, ~ICS *n.*, (science and application of) ultrasonic waves. [f. ULTRA- + SONIC]

ŭ'ltrasound *n.* Sound having ultrasonic frequency; ultrasonic waves. [f. ULTRA- + SOUND²]

ŭ'ltrastrŭcture *n.* (Biol.) Structure not visible with optical microscopes. [f. ULTRA- + STRUCTURE]

ŭltravī'olet *a.* (Phys.) having wavelength (just) beyond violet end of visible spectrum; of or using such radiation. [f. ULTRA- + VIOLET]

ultra vires (ŭltra vīr'ēz *or* ŏŏltrah vēr'āz) *adv.* & *pred. a.* Beyond one's (legal) power or authority. [L]

ū'lūl|āte *v.i.* Howl, wail; give prolonged cry of joy; hoot; so ~ANT *a.*, ~A'TION *n.* [f. L *ululare* (imit.) + -ATE³]

-um. See -IUM.

ŭ'mbel *n.* (Bot.) Flower-cluster in which stalks nearly equal in length spring from common centre and form a flat or curved surface as in parsley; so **~l**AR¹, **~l**ATE², *adjs.*, **ŭmbĕ'll**ULE *n.* [f. obs. F *umbelle* or f. L *umbella* sunshade dim. of UMBRA]

ŭmbĕ'llĭfer *n.* Plant of order Umbelliferae, bearing umbels; hence **ŭmbellĭ'**FEROUS *a.* [f. obs. F *umbellifère* f. L (as prec., *-fer* bearing)]

ŭ'mber *n.*, *a.*, & *v.t.* **1.** *n.* Natural pigment like ochre but darker and browner (**raw ~**, this in natural state, of dark yellow colour; **burnt ~**, redder and deeper in colour); **~-bird,** dark-brown Afr. bird allied to stork and heron. **2.** *a.* Of umber colour; dark, dusky. **3.** *v.t.* Colour (as) with umber. [f. F (*terre d'*)*ombre* or It. (*terra di*) *ombra* = shadow (earth), f. L UMBRA or *Umbra* fem. of *Umber* Umbrian]

ŭmbĭ'lĭcal (*or* -ī'kal) *a.* **1.** Of, situated near, affecting, the umbilicus; **~ cord,** ropelike structure attaching foetus to placenta, (fig.) essential connecting-line in various technologies. **2.** Centrally placed. [obs. F, or f. UMBILICUS + -AL]

ŭmbĭ'lĭcate *a.* Shaped like a navel; having an umbilicus. [f. foll. + -ATE²]

ŭmbĭ'lĭcus (*or* -ī'kus) *n.* Navel; (Bot. & Zool.) navel-like formation; (Geom.) point in a surface through which all cross-sections have same curvature. [L, rel. to Gk *omphalos* and NAVEL]

ŭ'mbles (-belz) *n. pl.* Edible offal of deer etc. (cf. HUMBLE *pie*). [ME var. of NUMBLES]

ŭ'mbō *n.* (*pl.* **~s,** *or* **~nes** *pr.* -ō'nēz). Boss of shield, esp. in centre; (Bot. & Zool.) boss, knob, protuberance; hence **ŭ'mbon**AL, **ŭ'mbon**ATE², *adjs.* [L *umbo -onis*]

ŭ'mbr|a *n.* (*pl.* **~ae** *or* **~as**). **1.** (Astron.) Total shadow (cf. PENUMBRA) cast by earth or moon in eclipse; dark central part of sunspot (cf. PENUMBRA). **2.** (Rom. Ant.) Uninvited guest brought by an invited guest. **3.** Hence **~**AL *a.* [L, = shade]

ŭ'mbrage *n.* **1.** Sense of slight or injury, offence, (*give, take, umbrage* (*at*)). **2.** (arch. or poet.) Shade; what gives shade. **3.** So **ŭmbrā'ge**OUS (-jus) *a.* [ME f. OF, f. Rom. **umbraticum* neut. (as n.) of L *umbraticus* (UMBRA; see -AGE)]

ŭmbrĕ'lla *n.* **1.** Light usu. circular screen of silk etc. in collapsible form raised on radial ribs attached to central stick, used for protection against sunshine or as symbol of authority in some Oriental and African countries or as portable protection against rain; (fig.) screen of fighter aircraft or curtain of fire put up as protection against enemy aircraft; protection, patronage, co-ordinating agency; gelatinous disc of jellyfish etc. by contraction and expansion of which it swims; **~(-shell)**, gastropod with umbrella-like shell. **2.** **~-bird,** S. Amer. bird of genus *Cephalopterus*, with radiating crest; **~ pine,** (1) = STONE-*pine*, (2) tall Japanese evergreen with leaves in umbrella-like whorls; **~-stand** (for holding closed umbrellas, usu. with pan at bottom to catch drippings); **~-tree,** small magnolia with leaves in umbrella-like whorl at end of branch. **3.** Hence **~**ED² (-*a*d) *a.* [f. It. *ombrella*, dim. of *ombra* shade f. L UMBRA]

ŭmbrĕ'tte *n.* = UMBER-*bird*. [f. mod. L *umbretta* or f. F *ombrette* (*ombre* shade f. L UMBRA); see -ETTE]

U'mbrĭan (ŭ'-) *a.* & *n.* **1.** *a.* Of (ancient or modern) Umbria in central Italy; **~ school,** Renaissance school of painting to which Raphael and Perugino belonged. **2.** *n.* Language or inhabitant of ancient Umbria. [f. L *Umber* Umbrian or *Umbria* + -IAN]

ŭmbrĭ'ferous *a.* Affording shade. [f. L *umbrifer* (UMBRA; see -FEROUS)]

u'miăk (ŏŏ'myăk) *n.* Eskimo skin-and-wood open boat worked by women with paddles. [Eskimo]

u'mlaut (ŏŏ'mlowt) *n.*, & *v.t.* **1.** *n.* (In Germanic languages) vowel change due to *i*, *j*, etc., (now usu. lost or altered) in following syllable (e.g. German *mann männer*, *fuss füsse*, English *man men*); diaeresis used to mark this in German etc. **2.** *v.t.* Modify (form, sound) by umlaut. [G (*um* about, *laut* sound)]

ŭ'mpīre *n.* & *v.* **1.** *n.* (Law) third person called in to decide between arbitrators who disagree; person chosen to give final decision on disputed question; person chosen to enforce rules and settle disputes in cricket, hockey, baseball, etc.; hence **ŭ'mpīr**AGE (3), ~SHIP (-īrsh-), *ns.* **2.** *v.i.* Act as umpire (*for* persons, *in* game etc.). **3.** *v.t.* Act as umpire in (game). [ME, later form of *noumpere* f. OF *nonper* not equal (*non* NON-, *per* PEER¹); for loss of *n-* cf. ADDER]

ŭ'mpteen *a.* (sl.) Indefinitely many, a lot of; or cogn. ~TH², **ŭ'mp**TY², *adjs.* [joc. form. on -TEEN]

'un *pron.* (colloq.) One (*that's a good 'un*; *he's a tough 'un*); WRONG *'un*. [dial. var.]

---

un-. This prefix has limitless applications in English, and only a selection of the existing words formed by it is given here. Its two broad categories of use are described under UN-¹ and UN-², which convey the respective senses of contrary action and absence of a quality, and which are not identical in etymology. Within each of these, more than one category of use is explained. Many vbl adjs. in *-able*, *-ed*, and *-ing* can be formed from either prefix; for example, *undressed* may mean 'having had the clothes removed (after being dressed)' or 'not having been dressed', and *unbending* may mean 'that unbends' or 'that does not bend'. Usually only the form with *un-*² is listed here, the form with *un-*¹ being implied as a derivative of the corresponding verb. The stress shown for *un-* words is the normal one, but the prefix is sometimes stressed for emphasis or in attrib. use (*an u'nmasked villain*; *u'ntold wealth*). Words in *un-* are rarely hyphened except when they are formed from a capitalized word (*un-American*) or when they are made for the occasion (*un-suburban*).

ŭn-¹ *pref.* w. neg. sense, usu. denoting a contrary or annulling or depriving or removing action. **1.** To *vbs.*, forming *vbs.* w. contrary sense (*unlock*; cf. COME 13); occas. w. intensified sense (*unloose, unrip*). **2.** To *ns.* forming *vbs.*, w. sense 'deprive of' (*unfrock*), 'separate from' (*unlimber*). **3.** To *ns.* forming *vbs.*, w. sense 'release from' (*uncage*), 'take out of' (*unearth*), 'displace from' (*unhorse*). **4.** To *ns.* forming *vbs.*, w. sense 'cause to be no longer' (*unman*), 'degrade from position of' (*unking*). (Words in 2, 3, and 4 may sometimes be regarded as formed from a verb, e.g. *cage*, and thus as belonging in 1.) [OE *un-*, *on-*, = OS *ant-*, OHG *ant-*, *int-*, Goth. *and-*]

ŭn-² *pref.* w. neg. sense, usu. denoting absence of a quality. **1.** To *adjs.* & *advs.*, either simply w. sense 'not' (*unconscious, undoubted, unmistakable, unofficial, unsuspecting*), or often w. sense 'the reverse of', implying praise or blame (*unfair, ungracious, unremitting, unselfish, untimely* a. & adv., *untrue*); cf. IN-², NON-. A few such as *unsplinterable* are included here even though their rare positive forms have not been listed elsewhere. Most *adjs.* in UN-² can form *advs.* in -LY² and *ns.* -NESS, even where these are not listed. **2.** To *ns.*, w. similar senses to those given in 1, (*unrest, untruth*). These may sometimes be regarded as derivs. of a word in 1 (*unchastity*). [OE, = OS, OHG, Goth. *un-*, ON *ú-*, *ó-* f. IE **-n̥*, ablaut var. of *ne* not]

U.N. *abbr.* United Nations.

U.N.A. *abbr.* United Nations Association.

ŭnabă'shed (-sht), **ŭnabā'tėd,** *adjs.* See UN-² 1.

ŭnā'ble *a.* Not able (*to* do), lacking ability. [ME, f. UN-² 1 + ABLE]

ŭnabrĭ'dged (-jd), **ŭnabsor̄'bed** (-bd; *or* -z-), **ŭnăccĕ'ntėd** (-ks-), **ŭnaccĕ'ptable** (-ks-), **ŭnaccŏ'mmodāting,** *adjs.* See UN-² 1.

ŭnacco'mpanĭed (-ŭ'mpanĭd) *a.* Not accompanied; (Mus.) without accompaniment. [f. UN-² 1; see ACCOMPANY]

ŭnaccŏ'mplĭshed (-sht; *or* -ŭ'm-) *a.* Not accomplished or completed; lacking accomplishments. [f. UN-² 1 + ACCOMPLISHED]

ŭnaccou'nt|able *a.* That cannot be explained; strange in behaviour; not responsible; hence ~ABI'LITY, **~able**NESS (-beln-), *ns.*, **~ab**LY² *adv.* [f. UN-² 1 + ACCOUNTABLE]

ŭnaccou'ntėd *a.* Of which no account is given; ~ **for,** unexplained, not included in account. [f. UN-² 1; see ACCOUNT¹]

ŭnaccŭ'stomed (-md) *a.* Not accustomed (*to*); not usual (*his unaccustomed silence*). [f. UN-² 1 + ACCUSTOMED]

ŭnacknow'lėdged (-nŏ'lĭjd), **ŭnacquai'ntėd,** *adjs.* See UN-² 1.

ŭnadŏ'ptėd *a.* Not adopted; ||(of road) not taken over for maintenance by local authority. [f. UN-² 1; see ADOPT]

ŭnador̄'ned (-nd), **ŭnadŭ'lterātėd, ŭnadvĕ'nturous** (-cher-), *adjs.* See UN-² 1.

ŭnadvī'sable (-z-) *a.* Not open to advice; (of thing) inadvisable. [f. UN-² 1 + ADVISABLE]

ŭnadvī's|ed (-zd) *a.* Indiscreet, rash; not having had advice; hence **~ėd**LY² *adv.* [ME, f. UN-² 1 + ADVISED]

ŭnaffĕ'ctėd *a.* Not affected (*by*); free from affectation, genuine, sincere; hence ~LY² *adv.*, ~NESS *n.* [f. UN-² 1 + AFFECTED]

ŭnaffĭ'lĭātėd, ŭnafrai'd, ŭnai'dėd, ŭnā'lĭenable, ŭnallow'able, *adjs.* See UN-² 1.

ŭnă'lloyed (-oid; *or* -aloi'd) *a.* Not alloyed; (fig.) pure, unmixed, (*unalloyed joy*). [f. UN-² 1; see ALLOY²]

ŭna'lterable (-aw'- *or* -ŏ'-), **ŭnaltered** (-aw'lterd; *or* -ŏ'-), **ŭnamā'zed** (-zd), **ŭnambĭ'gūous, ŭnămbĭ'tious** (-shus), **ŭnamē'nable,** *adjs.* See UN-² 1.

ŭn-Amĕ'rĭcan (-am-) *a.* Not in accordance with American characteristics; contrary to the interests of the U.S.A. [f. UN-² 1 + AMERICAN]

ŭnā'mĭable, ŭnă'nalȳsable (-z-), **ŭnă'nalȳsed** (-zd), *adjs.*, see UN-² 1; **ŭnă'nchor** (-k-) *v.t.* & *i.*, UN-¹ 1.

ŭnanē'led (-ld) *a.* (arch.) Not having received extreme unction. [f. UN-² 1; see ANELE]

ūnă'nĭmous *a.* All agreeing in opinion (*we were, the meeting was, unanimous* (*for reform, as to the policy to be pursued, in protesting,* etc.)); (of opinion, vote, etc.) formed, held, given, by general consent; hence or cogn. **ūnanĭ'm**ITY, ~NESS, *ns.*, ~LY² *adv.* [f. LL *unanimis*, L *unanimus* (*unus* one, *animus* mind) + -OUS]

ŭnannou'nced (-st) *a.* See UN-² 1.

ŭna'nswerab|le (-ah'nser-) *a.* That cannot be answered; that cannot be refuted; hence ~LY² *adv.* [f. UN-² 1 + ANSWERABLE]

ŭna'nswered (-ah'nserd), **ŭnăntĭ'cĭpātėd,** *adjs.* See UN-² 1.

ŭnăpostŏ'lĭc *a.* Contrary to apostolic usage; not having apostolic authority. [f. UN-² 1 + APOSTOLIC]

ŭnappă'rent *a.* See UN-² 1.

ŭnappea'lable *a.* That cannot be appealed against. [f. UN-² 1 + APPEALABLE]

ŭnappea'lĭng, ŭnappea'sable (-z-), **ŭnappea'sed** (-zd), **ŭnă'ppėtīzĭng, ŭnapprē'cĭātėd** (-shĭ-), **ŭnapprē'cĭatĭve** (-shĭ-), **ŭnapproa'chable, ŭnapprō'prĭātėd, ŭnappro'ved** (-oo'vd), *adjs.* See UN-² 1.

ŭnă'pt *a.* Not suitable (*for*); not apt (*to* do); hence ~LY² *adv.*, ~NESS *n.* [ME, f. UN-² 1 + APT]

ŭnar̄'gūable *a.* See UN-² 1.

ŭnar̄'m *v.t.* Deprive or free of arms or armour. [ME, f. UN-¹ 2 + ARM²]

ŭnar̄'med (-md) *a.* See UN-² 1.

ŭnar̄tĭ'stĭc *a.* Not artistic, esp. not concerned with art. [f. UN-² 1 + ARTISTIC]

ŭnăscertai'nable, ŭnăscertai'ned (-nd), **ŭnashā'med** (-md), *adjs.*, **ŭnashā'mėdlȳ** *adv.* See UN-² 1.

ŭna'sked (-ah'skt) *a.* Not asked (*for*), requested, or invited. [ME, f. UN-² 1; see ASK]

ŭnassai'lab|le *a.* That cannot be attacked or questioned; hence ~LY² *adv.* [f. UN-² 1 + ASSAILABLE]

ŭnassī'gnable (-ī'n-), **ŭnassī'gned** (-ī'nd), **ŭnassĭ'stėd,** *adjs.* See UN-² 1.

ŭnassū'mĭng *a.* Not pretentious or arrogant; modest; hence ~LY² *adv.* [f. UN-² 1 + ASSUMING]

ŭnattă'ched (-cht) *a.* Not attached (*to*); not attached to a particular regiment, church, college, club, etc.; not engaged or married. [f. UN-² 1; see ATTACH]

ŭnattai'nable, ŭnattĕ'mptėd, *adjs.* See UN-² 1.

ŭnattĕ'ndėd *a.* Not attended (*to*); (of person,

For other words in *un-* see UN-, UN-¹, UN-².

vehicle, etc.) having no person accompanying; (of thing) not accompanied or followed *by*. [f. UN-[2] 1; see ATTEND]

ŭnattră'ctīve *a.*, see UN-[2] 1; hence ~LY[2] (-vlĭ) *adv.*, ~NESS (-vn-) *n.*

ū'nau *n.* Brazilian two-toed sloth. [Tupi]

ŭnau'thorīzed (-zd), **ŭnavai'lable, ŭnavoi'dable,** *adjs.* See UN-[2] 1.

ŭnavai'lĭng *a.* Achieving nothing, ineffectual; hence ~LY[2] *adv.* [f. UN-[2] 1; see AVAIL[1]]

ŭnavow'ed (-ow'd) *a.* See UN-[2] 1.

ŭnawār'e (-aw-) *a.* & *adv.* **1.** *a.* Not aware, ignorant, (*of, that*); hence ~NESS (-ār'n-) *n.* **2.** *adv.* = foll. [f. UN-[2] 1 + AWARE]

ŭnawār'es (-awār'z) *adv.* Unexpectedly (*came upon them unawares*); inadvertently (*must have dropped it unawares*); **at** ~, unexpectedly. [f. earlier *unware(s)* f. OE *unwær(es)*; see UN-[2], WARE[2], -S[3]]

ŭnbă'cked (-kt) *a.* Not supported; having no backers in betting etc.; having no back(ing). [f. UN-[2] 1; see BACK[2]]

ŭnbă'g *v.t.*, see UN-[1] 3; **ŭnbă'lance** *v.t.*, UN-[1] 1.

ŭnbălanced (-st) *a.* Not balanced; (of mind or person) unstable or deranged. [f. UN-[2] 1; see BALANCE[2]]

ŭnbar' *v.t.* (-rr-). Remove bar from (gate etc.); unlock, open, (lit. or fig.). [f. UN-[1] 1 + BAR[2]]

ŭnbear'able (-ār'-), **ŭnbea'table,** *adjs.* See UN-[2] 1.

ŭnbea'ten *a.* Not beaten; (of record etc.) not surpassed. [f. UN-[2] 1 + BEATEN]

ŭnbėco'mĭng (-kŭ'-) *a.* Indecorous (*an unbecoming speech*); not befitting (person, *to* or *for* person); not suited to the wearer (*an unbecoming hat*); hence ~LY[2] *adv.*, ~NESS *n.* [f. UN-[2] 1 + BECOMING]

ŭnbĕ'd *v.t.*, see UN-[1] 3; **ŭnbėfĭ'ttĭng, ŭnbėfrie'ndėd** (-ĕ'-), **ŭnbėgŏ'tten,** *adjs.*, UN-[2] 1.

ŭnbėknow'n(st) (-ĭnō'-) *a.* (colloq.) Not known; ~ **to,** without the knowledge of. [f. UN-[2] 1 + BE*known* (arch.) = KNOWN]

ŭnbėlie'f *n.* Incredulity, disbelief esp. in divine revelation or in a particular religion; so **ŭn**BELIE'VER *n.*, **ŭn**BELIE'VING *a.* [f. UN-[2] 2 + BELIEF]

ŭnbėlie'vable, ŭnbėlo'ved (-ŭ'vd), *adjs.*, see UN-[2] 1; **ŭnbĕ'lt** *v.t.*, UN-[1] 2.

ŭnbĕ'nd *v.t.* & *i.* (**unbe'nt**). Change from bent position, straighten; relax from strain or exertion or constraint or severity; become affable; (Naut.) unfasten (sails) from yards and stays, cast (cable) loose, untie (rope). [f. UN-[1] 1 + BEND[3]]

ŭnbĕ'ndĭng[1] *a.* Relaxing from one's exertion or constraint. [f. prec. + -ING[2]]

ŭnbĕ'ndĭng[2] *a.* Not bending, inflexible; firm; austere; hence ~LY[2] *adv.*, ~NESS *n.* [f. UN-[2] 1; see BEND[3]]

ŭnbĕ'nt *a.* See UN-[2] 1.

unberufen (o͝onberōō'fen) *int.* deprecating Nemesis after boastful remark etc. [G, = unsummoned]

ŭnbėsee'm *v.t.* (arch.; impers.) Be unbecoming to. [f. UN-[1] 1 + BESEEM]

ŭnbėsee'mĭng, ŭnbėsou'ght (-saw't), **ŭnbėspō'ken, ŭnbī'as(s)ed** (-st), *adjs.* See UN-[2] 1.

ŭnbĭ'blĭcal *a.* Not in or authorized by the Bible. [f. UN-[2] 1 + BIBLICAL]

||**ŭnbĭ'ddable** *a.* Disobedient, not docile. [f. UN-[2] 1 + BIDDABLE]

ŭnbĭ'dden *a.* Not commanded or invited. [f. UN-[2] 1 + BIDDEN]

ŭnbi'nd *v.t.* (**unbou'nd**). Release from bonds or binding. [f. UN-[1] 1 + BIND[1]]

ŭnbir'thday *a.* (joc., of a present). Given other than on a birthday. [f. UN-[2] 1 + BIRTH*day*]

ŭnbĭ'tt *v.t.* (Naut.), see UN-[1] 3 and BITTS;

ŭnblea'ched (-cht), **ŭnblĕ'mĭshed** (-sht), **ŭnblĕ'ssed** (-st), **ŭnblĕ'st, ŭnblĭ'nkĭng,** *adjs.*, UN-[2] 1.

ŭnblŏ'ck *v.t.* Remove obstruction from; (Cards) allow later unobstructed play of (suit, or abs.) by playing high card. [f. UN-[1] 1 + BLOCK[2]]

ŭnblow'n (-ō'n) *a.*, see UN-[2] 1 and BLOW[1,3]; **ŭnblŭ'shĭng,** UN-[2] 1.

ŭnbō'lt *v.t.* Release (door etc.) by drawing back the bolt. [f. UN-[1] 1 + BOLT[2]]

ŭnbō'ltėd *a.*, see UN-[2] 1 and BOLT[2,5].

ŭnbŏ'nnėt *v.* **1.** *v.i.* (arch.) Remove one's bonnet esp. as mark of respect. **2.** *v.t.* Remove bonnet from. [f. UN-[1] 2 + BONNET]

ŭnboo'kĭsh *a.*, see UN-[2] 1; **ŭnboo't** *v.t.* & *i.*, UN-[1] 2; **ŭnbor'n** *a.*, UN-[2] 1.

ŭnbo'som (-o͝o'z-) *v.t.* Disclose (thoughts etc.); ~ **oneself,** disclose one's thoughts, secrets, etc. [f. UN-[1] 3 + BOSOM]

ŭnbou'nd *a.*, see UN-[1] 1, UN-[2] 1, BIND[1], and UNBIND.

ŭnbou'ndėd *a.* Not bounded (*by*, or abs.); infinite. [f. UN-[2] 1; see BOUND[2]]

ŭnbrā'ce *v.t.* Remove brace(s) of, free from tension, relax (nerves etc.). [f. UN-[1] 1 + BRACE[2]]

ŭnbrea'kable (-ā'-), **ŭnbrī'bable,** *adjs.* See UN-[2] 1.

ŭnbrī'dle *v.t.* Remove bridle from (horse, or fig. person, tongue, etc.). [f. UN-[1] 1 + BRIDLE[2]]

ŭnbrī'dled (-deld) *a.* Not bridled (esp. fig. of insolence, tongue, etc.). [f. UN-[2] 1; see BRIDLE[2]]

ŭnbrō'ken *a.* Not broken; not subdued (*unbroken horse*); not interrupted (*unbroken sleep, peace*); not surpassed (*unbroken record*); hence ~LY[2] *adv.*, ~NESS (-n-n-) *n.* [f. UN-[2] 1 + BROKEN]

ŭnbŭ'ckle *v.t.* Release the buckle of (strap, shoe, etc.). [f. UN-[1] 1 + BUCKLE[2]]

ŭnbuĭ'ld (-bĭ'-) *v.t.* (**unbui'lt**). Demolish, destroy, (building, or fig.). [f. UN-[1] 1 + BUILD[1]]

ŭnbuĭ'lt (-bĭ'-) *a.* Not (yet) built (on). [f. UN-[2] 1; see BUILD[1]]

ŭnbur'den *v.t.* Relieve of burden; relieve (one-*self*, one's conscience, etc.) by confession etc. *to* person. [f. UN-[1] 1 + BURDEN[2]]

ŭnbur'dened (-nd), **ŭnbu'rĭed** (-ĕ'rĭd), *adjs.* See UN-[2] 1.

ŭnbu'rў (-bĕ'-) *v.t.* Remove from ground etc. after burial (lit. or fig.). [f. UN-[1] 1 + BURY]

ŭnbŭ'tton *v.t.* Open (coat etc.), open coat etc. of (person), by taking buttons out of buttonholes. [f. UN-[1] 1 + BUTTON[2]]

ŭnbŭ'ttoned (-nd) *a.* Not buttoned; (fig.) communicative, informal. [f. UN-[2] 1; see BUTTON[2]]

ŭncā'ge (ŭn-k-) *v.t.* See UN-[1] 3.

ŭnca'lled (ŭn-kaw'ld) *a.* Not summoned or invited; ~**-for,** impertinently or unnecessarily offered or intruded. [f. UN-[2] 1; see CALL[1]]

ŭncă'ndĭd (ŭn-k-) *a.* See UN-[2] 1.

ŭncă'nn|ў (ŭn-k-) *a.* Seemingly supernatural; mysterious; hence ~**ĭLY**[2] *adv.*, ~**ĭ**NESS *n.* [orig. Sc. & N. Engl., f. UN-[2] 1 + CANNY]

ŭncanŏ'nĭcal (ŭn-k-), **ŭncă'nonīzed** (ŭn-k-; -zd), *adjs.*, see UN-[2] 1; **ŭncă'p** (ŭn-k-) *v.t.*, UN-[1] 2.

ŭncar'ed-for (ŭn-kār'd-) *a.* Disregarded, neglected. [f. UN-[2] 1; see CARE[2]]

ŭncā'se (ŭn-k-) *v.t.* & *i.* Remove from cover or case; (arch.) undress. [f. UN-[1] 3 + CASE[2]]

ŭncau'sed (ŭn-kaw'zd) *a.* Having no cause; not created. [f. UN-[2] 1; see CAUSE[2]]

ŭncea'sĭng *a.* See UN-[2] 1.

ŭncĕrėmō'nĭous *a.* Lacking ceremony or formality; abrupt in manner, discourteous; hence ~LY[2] *adv.*, ~NESS *n.* [f. UN-[2] 1 + CEREMONIOUS]

ŭncer'tain (-tan *or* -tĭn) *a.* Not certainly knowing or known (*am uncertain which he means, whether*

I should go or not; *is of uncertain age*; *result is uncertain*); not to be depended on (*his aim is uncertain*), changeable (*uncertain temper, weather*); **in no ~ terms,** clearly and forcefully; hence ~LY² *adv.*, ~TY¹ *n.*; **~ty principle,** (Phys.) principle that momentum and position of a particle cannot both be precisely determined at same time, or one of other similar restrictions on accuracy of measurement. [ME, f. UN-² 1 + CERTAIN]

ŭncertĭ'fĭcatėd, uncer'tĭfied (-id), *adjs.*, see UN-² 1; **ŭnchai'n** *v.t.*, UN-¹ 1; **ŭnchă'llėngeable** (-nj*a*-), **ŭnchă'llėnged** (-njd), *adjs.*, UN-² 1.

ŭncha'ncy̆ (-ah'-) *a.* (Sc.) Ill-omened; dangerous. [f. UN-² 1 + CHANCY]

ŭnchā'ngeable (-nj*a*-), **ŭnchā'nged** (-njd), **ŭnchā'ngĭng** (-nj-), **ŭnchar'ged** (-jd), *adjs.* See UN-² 1.

ŭnchă'rĭtab|le *a.* Not charitable; severe in judgement; hence **~le**NESS (-b*e*ln-) *n.*, ~LY² *adv.* [f. UN-² 1 + CHARITABLE]

ŭnchar'tėd, ŭnchar'tered (-*e*rd), **ŭnchā'ste,** *adjs.*, see UN-² 1; **ŭnchă'stĭty̆** *n.*, UN-² 2; **ŭnchě'cked** (-kt), **ŭnchĭ'valrous** (-sh-), *adjs.*, UN-² 1.

ŭnchrĭ'stian (ŭn-krĭ'sty*a*n) *a.* Not Christian; contrary to Christian principles; (colloq.) outrageous. [f. UN-² 1 + CHRISTIAN]

ŭnchur'ch *v.t.* Excommunicate; deprive of status as church. [f. UN-¹ 3, 4 + CHURCH¹]

ū'ncĭal (*or* -sh*a*l) *a.* & *n.* **1.** *a.* Of or written in majuscule writing with rounded unjoined letters found in MSS. of 4th–8th c., from which modern capitals are largely derived. **2.** *n.* Uncial letter or style or MS. [f. L *uncialis* (*uncia* inch; see -AL), in LL sense (Jerome, of uncert. orig.)]

ū'ncĭnate, ū'ncĭform, *adjs.* (Anat. etc.) Hooked, crooked. [f. L (*uncinatus* f. *uncinus* hook f.) *uncus* hook; see -INE¹, -ATE², -FORM]

ŭncir'cumcised (-zd) *a.* Not circumcised; (fig.) spiritually impure, heathen. [ME, f. UN-² 1; see CIRCUMCISE]

ŭncircumcĭ'sion (-zh*o*n) *n.* State of being uncircumcised; **the ~,** (N.T.) the Gentiles. [f. UN-² 2 + CIRCUMCISION]

ŭncĭ'vĭl *a.* Ill-mannered, impolite; contrary to civic well-being; hence ~LY² *adv.* [f. UN-² 1 + CIVIL]

ŭncĭ'vĭlized (-zd), **ŭnclă'd** (ŭn-k-), **ŭnclai'med** (ŭn-klā'md), *adjs.* See UN-² 1.

ŭncla'sp (ŭn-klah'-) *v.t.* Loosen clasp(s) of, release grip of (hand etc.). [f. UN-¹ 1 + CLASP²]

ŭnclă'ssĭfied (ŭn-k-; -id) *a.* See UN-² 1.

ŭ'ncle *n.* **1.** Father's or mother's brother; aunt's husband; (colloq.) unrelated man friend of children; ||BOB⁵'*s your uncle*; DUTCH¹ *uncle*; **U~ Sam,** (colloq.) federal government or typical citizen of U.S.; ***U~ Tom,** Negro subservient to whites [f. hero of Mrs. Stowe's *Uncle Tom's Cabin*]. **2.** (sl.) Pawnbroker. [ME f. AF; OF *oncle* f. LL *aunculus*, f. L *avunculus* maternal uncle (see AVUNCULAR)]

-ŭncle *suf.* forming *ns.* usu. dim. (*carbuncle*). [f. OF *-uncle, -oncle* or f. L *-unculus, -la*, a special form of *-ulus* -ULE]

ŭnclea'n (ŭn-k-) *a.* Not clean; foul; unchaste; (Bibl., of spirit) wicked; unfit to be eaten, ceremonially impure; hence ~NESS (-n-n-) *n.* [OE *unclǣne* (as UN-² 1, CLEAN¹)]

ŭnclea'nly̆ (ŭn-klě'-) *a.*, see UN-² 1; **ŭnclě'nch, ŭnclĭ'nch,** (ŭn-k-) *vbs. t.* & *i.*, UN-¹ 1; **ŭncloa'k** (ŭn-k-) *v.t.*, UN-¹ 2; **ŭnclŏ'g** (ŭn-k-) *v.t.*, UN-¹ 1; **ŭncloi'ster** (ŭn-k-) *v.t.*, UN-¹ 3.

ŭnclō'se (ŭn-klō'z) *v.t.* & *i.* Open. [ME, f. UN-¹ 1 + CLOSE³]

ŭnclō'the (ŭn-klō'dh) *v.t.*, see UN-¹ 1; **ŭnclō'thed** (ŭn-klō'dhd), **ŭnclou'dėd** (ŭn-k-), **ŭnclŭ'ttered** (ŭn-k-; -*e*rd), *adjs.*, UN-² 1.

ŭ'ncō *a.*, *n.* (*pl.* **~s**), & *adv.* (Sc.) **1.** *a.* Strange, unusual; notable. **2.** *n.* Stranger; (in *pl.*) news. **3.** *adv.* Remarkably, very; **the ~ guid,** (usu. derog.) rigidly religious people. [ME, var. of UNCOUTH]

ŭncoi'l (ŭn-k-) *v.t.* & *i.*, see UN-¹ 1.

ŭnco'loured, *-ored, (ŭn-kŭ'l*e*rd) *a.* Having no colour(s); not exaggerated; not influenced *by*. [f. UN-² 1 + COLOURED]

ŭncome-ă't-able (ŭn-kŭm-) *a.* (colloq.) Inaccessible, unattainable. [f. UN-² 1 + COME-*at-able*]

ŭnco'mely̆ (ŭn-kŭ'mlĭ) *a.* Improper, unseemly; not pleasant in appearance. [ME, f. UN-² 1 + COMELY]

ŭnco'mfortable (ŭn-kŭ'-) *a.* See UN-² 1.

ŭncommer'cial (ŭn-k-; -sh*a*l) *a.* Not commercial; contrary to commercial principles. [f. UN-² 1 + COMMERCIAL]

ŭncommĭ'ttėd (ŭn-k-) *a.* See UN-² 1.

ŭncŏ'mmon (ŭn-k-) *a.* & *adv.* **1.** *a.* Not common, unusual, remarkable; remarkably great etc.; hence ~LY² *adv.*, ~NESS (-n-n-) *n.* **2.** *adv.* (arch. colloq., or dial.) Uncommonly. [f. UN-² 1 + COMMON¹]

ŭncommū'nĭcatĭve (ŭn-k-) *a.* Not inclined to give information, taciturn, reserved; hence ~LY² (-vlĭ) *adv.*, ~NESS (-vn-) *n.* [f. UN-² 1 + COMMUNICATIVE]

ŭncompă'nionable (ŭn-k-; -ny*o*-), **ŭncomplai'nĭng, ŭncomplē'tėd, ŭncŏ'mplĭcātėd, ŭncŏmplĭmě'ntary̆, ŭncompou'ndėd,** (ŭn-k-) *adjs.* See UN-² 1.

ŭncŏ'mpromīsĭng (ŭn-k-; -z-) *a.* Not allowing or seeking compromise; unyielding, stubborn; hence ~LY² *adv.* [f. UN-² 1; see COMPROMISE²]

ŭnconcea'led (ŭn-k-; -ld) *a.* See UN-² 1.

ŭnconcer'n (ŭn-k-) *n.* Freedom from anxiety, indifference, apathy. [f. UN-² 2 + CONCERN²]

ŭnconcer'n|ed (ŭn-k-; -nd) *a.* Not concerned (*in* or *with*); free from anxiety or agitation; hence **~ėd**LY² *adv.* [f. UN-² 1; see CONCERN¹]

ŭncondĭ'tional (ŭn-k-) *a.* Not subject to conditions (*unconditional refusal, surrender*); hence ~ITY (-ă'l-) *n.*, ~LY² *adv.* [f. UN-² 1 + CONDITIONAL]

ŭncondĭ'tioned (ŭn-k-; -nd) *a.* Not subject to conditions; not determined by previous conditions; **~ reflex,** instinctive response to stimulus. [f. UN-² 1; see CONDITION²]

ŭnconfī'ned (ŭn-k-; -nd), **ŭnconfir'med** (ŭn-k-; -md), *adjs.* See UN-² 1.

ŭnconfor'mab|le (ŭn-k-) *a.* Not conformable or conforming, esp. (Hist.) to provisions of Act of UNIFORMITY; (Geol.) not having same direction of stratification, whence **ŭnconfor'm**ITY (ŭn-k-) *n.*; hence **~le**NESS (-b*e*ln-) *n.*, ~LY² *adv.* [f. UN-² 1 + CONFORMABLE]

ŭncongē'nĭal (ŭn-k*o*nj-), **ŭnconně'ctėd** (ŭn-k-), **ŭncŏ'nquerable** (ŭn-kŏ'ngk-), **ŭncŏ'nquered** (ŭn-kŏ'ngk*e*rd), *adjs.* See UN-² 1.

ŭncŏ'nscionab|le (ŭn-kŏ'nsh*o*n-) *a.* **1.** Having no conscience; contrary to the dictates of conscience. **2.** Not right or reasonable; unreasonably excessive. **3.** Hence **~le**NESS (-b*e*ln-) *n.*, ~LY² *adv.* [f. UN-² 1 + obs. *conscionable* (*conscions* obs. var. of CONSCIENCE, -ABLE)]

ŭncŏ'nscious (ŭn-kŏ'nsh*u*s) *a.* & *n.* **1.** *a.* Not conscious (*was unconscious of any change*; *lay unconscious for some hours*; *has an unconscious prejudice*; *examples of unconscious humour*); hence ~LY² *adv.*, ~NESS *n.* **2.** *n.* Part of mind whose content is not normally accessible to consciousness but which is found to affect behaviour; COLLECTIVE *unconscious*. [f. UN-² 1 + CONSCIOUS]

ŭnconsĭ'dered (ŭn-k-; *-erd*) *a.* Disregarded; not based on consideration. [f. UN-² 1; see CONSIDER]
ŭncŏnstĭtū'tional (ŭn-k-) *a.* Not in accordance with the political constitution or with procedural rules; hence ~ITY (-ă'l-) *n.*, ~LY² *adv.* [f. UN-² 1 + CONSTITUTIONAL]
ŭnconstrai'ned (ŭn-k-; -nd) *a.* See UN-² 1.
ŭnconstrai'nt (ŭn-k-) *n.* Freedom from constraint. [f. UN-² 2 + CONSTRAINT]
ŭnconsū'med (ŭn-k-; -md), **ŭncontai'nable, ŭncontă'mĭnātėd, ŭncontĕ'stėd, ŭncŏntradĭ'ctėd, ŭncontrō'llable,** (ŭn-k-), **ŭncontrō'lled** (ŭn-k-; -ld); **ŭncŏntrovêr'sial** (ŭn-k-; -sh*a*l), **ŭncŏntrovêr'tėd, ŭncŏntrovêr'tĭble,** (ŭn-k-; *or* -kŏ'-) *adjs.* See UN-² 1.
ŭnconvĕ'ntional (ŭn-k-) *a.* Not bound by convention or custom; unusual; hence ~ITY (-ă'l-) *n.*, ~LY² *adv.* [f. UN-² 1 + CONVENTIONAL]
ŭnconvêr'tėd (ŭn-k-), **ŭnconvĭ'nced** (ŭn-k-; -st), **ŭnconvĭ'ncing** (ŭn-k-), **ŭncoo͝'ked** (ŭn-koo͝'kt), *adjs.* See UN-² 1.
ŭncoo͞'l (ŭn-k-) *a.* (sl.) Not cool (in Jazz sense); unrelaxed; unpleasant. [f. UN-² 1 + COOL¹]
ŭncō-ŏ'peratĭve, ŭncōôr'dĭnātėd, (ŭn-k-) *adjs.*, see UN-² 1; **ŭncôr'd** (ŭn-k-) *v.t.*, UN-¹ 1.
ŭncôr'k (ŭn-k-) *v.t.* Draw cork from (bottle); (fig.) give vent to (feelings etc.). [f, UN-¹ 1 + CORK]
ŭncorrŏ'borātėd, ŭncorrŭ'ptėd, ŭncou'ntable, (ŭn-k-) *adjs.* See UN-² 1.
ŭncou'ple (ŭn-kŭ'-) *v.t.* Release (dogs, wagons, etc.) from couples or couplings. [ME, f. UN-¹ 2 + COUPLE¹]
ŭncou'pled(ŭn-kŭ'p*e*ld), **ŭncour'tlȳ** (ŭn-kôr'-), *adjs.* See UN-² 1.
ŭncou'th (ŭn-koo͞'th) *a.* **1.** (Of person, conduct, etc.) strange, awkward, clumsy, uncultured, (of language) harsh, rugged. **2.** (arch.) Not known, unfamiliar, unusual, (of place) unfrequented, desolate, wild, (of life) uncivilized, comfortless. **3.** Hence ~LY² *adv.*, ~NESS *n.* [OE *uncūth* unknown (as UN-² + *cūth* p.p. of *cunnan* know, CAN²)]
ŭnco'venantėd (ŭn-kŭ'-) *a.* Not promised by or based on (esp. God's) covenant; not bound by covenant. [f. UN-² 1 + COVENANTED]
ŭnco'ver (ŭn-kŭ'-) *v.* **1.** *v.t.* Remove cover(ing) from; lay bare, disclose, make known. **2.** *v.i.* Remove one's hat, cap, etc. [ME, f. UN-¹ 1, 3 + COVER¹·²]
ŭnco'vered (ŭn-kŭ'v*erd*) *a.* Not covered by roof, clothing, etc.; wearing no hat. [ME, f. UN-² 1; see COVER¹]
ŭncrėā'te¹ (ŭn-k-) *v.t.* Annihilate. [f. UN-¹ 1 + CREATE]
ŭncrėā'te² (ŭn-k-) *a.* (arch.) = foll. [f. UN-² 1 + obs. *create* f. L *creatus* p.p. of *creare*; see CREATE, -ATE²]
ŭncrėā'tėd (ŭn-k-) *a.* Existing without having been created; not created. [f. UN-² 1; see CREATE]
ŭncrĭ'tĭcal (ŭn-k-) *a.* Not critical, disinclined or not competent to criticize; not in accordance with principles of criticism; hence ~LY² *adv.* [f. UN-² 1 + CRITICAL]
ŭncrŏ'pped (ŭn-krŏ'pt) *a.* See UN-² 1.
ŭncrŏ'ss (ŭn-k-; *or* -aw's) *v.t.* Remove (legs, arms, knives, etc.) from crossed position. [f. UN-¹ 1 + CROSS²]
ŭncrŏ'ssed (ŭn-krŏ'st; *or* -aw'st) *a.* Not wearing a cross; not thwarted; ‖(of cheque) not crossed. [f. UN-² 1; see CROSS²]
ŭncrow'n (ŭn-k-) *v.t.* Deprive (king etc.) of crown (lit. or fig.). [f. UN-¹ 2 + CROWN¹]
ŭncrow'ned (ŭn-k-; -nd) *a.* Not crowned; having power but not name of (*king* etc.). [f. UN-² 1; see CROWN²]
ŭncrŭ'shable (ŭn-k-) *a.* See UN-² 1.
UNCTAD *abbr.* United Nations Conference on Trade and Development.
ŭ'nction *n.* Anointing with oil or unguent for medical purposes or as religious rite or ceremonial (EXTREME *unction*); thing used in anointing, unguent, (fig.) soothing or flattering words or thought or circumstance (see FLATTER); fervent or sympathetic quality in words or tone caused by or causing deep religious or other emotion; simulation of this, affected enthusiasm; keen enjoyment of a situation or activity. [ME, f. L *unctio* (*ung*(*u*)*ere unct-* anoint; see -ION)]
ŭ'nctūous *a.* Full of (esp. simulated) unction; greasy, oily, esp. (of minerals) having a soapy feel when touched; hence ~LY² *adv.*, ~NESS *n.* [ME, f. med. L *unctuosus* f. L *unctus* anointing (as prec.); see -OUS]
ŭncŭ'lled (ŭn-kŭ'ld) *a.*, see UN-² 1; **ŭncûr'b** (ŭn-k-) *v.t.*, UN-¹ 1; **ŭncûr'bed** (ŭn-kêr'bd), **ŭncūr'ed** (ŭn-kūr'd), *adjs.*, UN-² 1; **ŭncûr'l** (ŭn-k-) *v.t.*, UN-¹ 1; **ŭncûrtai'led** (ŭn-k-; -ld), **ŭncûr'tained** (ŭn-kêr't*a*nd), *adjs.*, UN-² 1.
ŭncŭ'stomed (ŭn-k; -md) *a.* Not liable to customs duty; on which no duty has been paid. [ME, f. UN-² 1 + p.p. of obs. *custom* v. pay duty on, f. OF *costumer* (as CUSTOM)]
ŭncŭ't (ŭn-k-) *a.* Not cut; (of book) with leaves not cut open or with untrimmed margins; (of book, film, etc.) not shortened, e.g. by censor; (of diamond) not shaped by cutting; (of fabric) having pile-loops intact. [ME, f. UN-² 1; see CUT²]
ŭndă'maged (-ĭjd), **ŭndā'tėd, ŭndau'ntėd,** *adjs.* See UN-² 1.
ŭndĕ'cagon *n.* Hendecagon. [f. L *undecim* eleven, after *decagon*]
ŭndėcei've (-sē'v) *v.t.* Free (person) from deception or *of* error. [f. UN-¹ 1 + DECEIVE]
ŭndėcī'dėd *a.* Not settled or certain (*the point is still undecided*); hesitating, irresolute, (*he stood undecided*); hence ~LY² *adv.* [f. UN-² 1 + DECIDED]
ŭndėcī'pherable, ŭndėclār'ed (-ār'd), *adjs.* See UN-² 1.
ŭndėfĕ'ndėd *a.* Not defended (esp. of lawsuit where no defence is entered). [f. UN-² 1; see DEFEND]
ŭndėfī'led (-ld), **ŭndėfī'ned** (-nd), *adjs.*, see UN-² 1; **ŭndē'ĭfȳ** *v.t.*, UN-¹ 1; **ŭndėlĭ'vered** (-*erd*), **ŭndėma'ndĭng** (-ah'-), **ŭndĕmocră'tĭc, ŭndĕ'monstrātėd,** *adjs.*, UN-² 1.
ŭndėmŏ'nstratĭve *a.* Not given to or making outward expression of one's feelings; hence ~LY² (-vlĭ) *adv.*, ~NESS (-vn-) *n.* [f. UN-² 1 + DEMONSTRATIVE]
ŭndėnī'ab|le *a.* That cannot be denied or disputed; unexceptionable, excellent; hence ~LY² *adv.* [f. UN-² 1 + DENIABLE]
ŭ'nder *prep.*, *adv.*, & *a.* **1.** *prep.* In or to a position lower than, below, (*it lay* or *fell under the table*; *struck him under the left eye*); at foot of (high wall etc.), sheltered by (island etc.); *under* CANVAS; *under the* COUNTER¹; *under* COVER² (*of.*); *under* FOOT¹; *under* one's HAT; *under* HATCH¹*es*; *under the* LEE *of*; *under* person's NOSE; *under the* ROSE¹; ~ **the sun,** anywhere in the world; ~ **water** (in and covered by it); *take under* one's WING. **2.** Within, on the inside of, (surface etc.; *inserted a knife-blade under the bark*; *was seen to blush under his dusky skin*); *under* one's ARM¹, BELT¹; ~ **separate cover,** in another envelope. **3.** Inferior to, less than, (*no one under a bishop*; *did it in under an hour*; *incomes under £4000*; *those under 18*

cannot vote; total is under what was expected); at lower cost than; *under* AGE[1], one's BREATH. **4.** In the position or act of supporting or sustaining, subjected to, undergoing, liable to, on condition of, subject to, governed or controlled or bound by, in accordance with, in the form of, in the reign of, (*sank under the load* (lit. or fig.); *groaning under tyranny; is now under repair; under examination; forbidden under pain of death; a criminal under* SENTENCE *of death; born under Saturn; fought under Wellington; country prospered under him* or *his rule; might succeed under other conditions; is under a delusion; was under the impression that; under the circumstances; is permissible under the agreement; was under a vow; is classified under biology; known under an assumed name; appears under various forms; under pretence of ignorance; lived under the Stuarts*); planted with (crop); propelled by (power, sail, etc.); attested by (one's *hand*, i.e. signature, *and seal*); following (another player in turn at cards); *under* ARM[2]*s*; *under a* CLOUD; *under* CONTROL[1]; *under* FIRE[1]; *under* WAY; *under the* WEATHER[1]. **5.** *adv.* In or to a lower position or subordinate condition; in or into state of unconsciousness; BRING, GO[1], KEEP[1], KNUCKLE, SNOW[1], *under*; DOWN[3] *under*. **6.** Lower (*under jaw, layers, servants*); hence ~MOST *a.* [OE, = OS *undar*, OHG *untar*, ON *undir*, Goth. *undar* f. Gmc **undher-* f. IE **ndhero-*]

ŭ'nder- *pref.* = prec. **1.** As *prep.* to *ns.*, forming *adjs.* w. sense 'below' (*underground*). **2.** As *adv.* or *prep.* to *vbs.* & vbl derivs., w. sense 'beneath, lower than, below' (*underseal, undersell, undersigned*). **3.** As *adv.* to *adjs.*, *vbs.*, & vbl derivs., w. sense 'insufficiently, incompletely' (*undercook, underdeveloped, underfeed, undernourished, underpay, underpopulated, underripe, understock, underuse*). **4.** As *a.* to *ns.*, w. sense 'situated beneath, subordinate', often equivalent to UNDER *a.* (*undercarriage, underfelt, under-king, under-*SECRETARY, *undersoil*). [OE (as prec.)]

ŭnderachie'v|e *v.i.* Do less than was expected (esp. scholastically); hence ~ER[1] *n.* [f. UNDER- 3 + ACHIEVE]

ŭnderă'ct *v.t.* & *i.* Act (part etc.), act part, with insufficient force. [f. UNDER- 3 + ACT[2]]

ŭ'nderârm *a.* & *adv.* (Cricket) = UNDERHAND[1,2]; (Lawn Tennis) with racket below shoulder-level. [f. UNDER- 1 + ARM[1]]

ŭ'nderbĕllȳ *n.* Under surface of animal or thing, esp. as area vulnerable to attack. [f. UNDER- 4 + BELLY[1]]

ŭnderbĭ'd[1] *v.t.* (**-dd-**; **underbi'd**). **1.** Make lower bid than (person); hence ~**der**[1] *n.*, person who makes the bid next below the highest. **2.** (Bridge etc.) Bid less on (hand, or abs.) than is justified. [f. UNDER- 2 + BID[1]]

ŭ'nderbĭd[2] *n.* Act of underbidding; bid thus made. [f. UNDER- 4 + BID[2]]

ŭ'nderbŏdȳ *n.* Under surface of body of animal, vehicle, etc. [f. UNDER- 4 + BODY[1]]

ŭnderbrĕ'd *a.* Ill-bred, vulgar; not of pure breeding. [f. UNDER- 3 + BRED]

***ŭ'nderbrŭsh** *n.* Undergrowth in forest. [f. UNDER- 4 + BRUSH[1]]

ŭ'ndercărrĭage (-rĭj) *n.* **1.** Supporting frame of vehicle. **2.** Structure beneath aircraft, usu. retractable when not in use, to receive impact on landing and support aircraft on ground etc. [f. UNDER- 4 + CARRIAGE]

||**ŭ'ndercârt** *n.* (colloq.) = prec. 2. [f. UNDER- 4 + CART]

ŭnderchâr'ge *v.t.* Charge too little for (thing) or to (person); give less than proper charge to (gun, electric battery, etc.). [f. UNDER- 3 + CHARGE[2]]

ŭ'nderclay *n.* Clay bed under coal seam. [f. UNDER- 4 + CLAY]

ŭ'ndercliff *n.* Terrace or lower cliff formed by landslip. [f. UNDER- 4 + CLIFF]

ŭ'nderclōthes (-dhz; *or* -ōz), **ŭ'nderclōthing** (-dh-), *ns.* Clothes worn under others, esp. next to skin. [f. UNDER- 4 + CLOTHES, CLOTHING]

ŭ'ndercoat *n.* Coat worn under another; animal's under layer of hair or down; layer of paint under finishing coat; paint thus used, so ~ING[1] (3) *n.* [f. UNDER- 4 + COAT]

ŭnderco'ver (-kŭ'-) *a.* Surreptitious; engaged in spying esp. by working with or among those to be observed. [f. UNDER- 1 + COVER[2]]

ŭ'ndercrŏft (*or* -awft) *n.* Crypt. [ME, f. UNDER- 4 + *croft* crypt f. MDu. *crofte* cave f. med. L *crupta* for L *crypta*; see CRYPT]

ŭ'ndercŭrrent *n.* Current below the surface; (fig.) unperceived influence or feeling of different or contrary tendency, suppressed or underlying activity. [f. UNDER- 4 + CURRENT[2]]

ŭndercŭ't[1] *v.t.* (**-tt-**; **undercu't**). Cut away material to show (carved design etc.) in relief; (Golf etc.) strike (ball) so as to make it rise high; sell or work at lower price or wages than. [f. UNDER- 2 + CUT[2]]

ŭ'ndercŭt[2] *n.* *Notch cut in tree-trunk to guide its fall when felled; ||under-side of sirloin. [f. UNDER- 4 + CUT[1]]

ŭnderdėvĕ'lop|ed (-pt) *a.* Not fully developed; (Photog.) not developed enough to give a normal image; (of country etc.) below its potential economic level; so ~MENT *n.* [f. UNDER- 3; see DEVELOP]

ŭ'nderdŏg *n.* Dog, or usu. (fig.) person, losing a fight; one who is in a state of inferiority or subjection. [f. UNDER- 4 + DOG[1]]

ŭnderdo'ne (-ŭ'n; *or* ŭ'-) *a.* Not thoroughly done; (of meat etc.) lightly or insufficiently cooked. [f. UNDER- 3 + DONE]

ŭnderdrĕ'ss *v.t.* & *i.* Dress too plainly or too lightly. [f. UNDER- 3 + DRESS[1]]

ŭnderĕ'mphas|ĭs *n.* (*pl.* ~**es** *pr.* -ēz). Insufficient degree of emphasis; so ~IZE (1) *v.t.* [f. UNDER- 3 + EMPHASIS]

ŭnderėmploy'|ed (-oi'd) *a.* Not fully employed; so ~MENT *n.* [f. UNDER- 3; see EMPLOY]

ŭnderĕ'stĭmate[1] *n.* Estimate that is too low. [f. UNDER- 3 + ESTIMATE[1]]

ŭnderĕ'stĭm|āte[2] *v.t.* Form too low an estimate of; hence ~A'TION *n.* [f. UNDER- 3 + ESTIMATE[2]]

ŭnderėxpō's|e (-z) *v.t.* (esp. Photog.) Expose for too short a time; so ~URE (-zh*er*) *n.* [f. UNDER- 3 + EXPOSE]

ŭ'nderfĕlt *n.* Felt for laying under carpet. [f. UNDER- 4 + FELT[1]]

ŭ'nderfloor (-ōr) *a.* Situated beneath the floor (esp. of source of domestic heating). [f. UNDER- 1 + FLOOR]

ŭ'nderflow (-ō) *n.* Undercurrent. [f. UNDER- 4 + FLOW]

ŭnderfoo't *adv.* Under one's feet; on the ground; (fig.) in state of subjection; (fig.) so as to obstruct one's progress. [ME, f. UNDER- 1 + FOOT[1]]

ŭ'ndergârment *n.* Piece of underclothing. [f. UNDER- 4 + GARMENT]

ŭndergĭr'd *v.t.* Make secure underneath; (fig.) strengthen, support. [f. UNDER- 2 + GIRD[1]]

ŭ'nderglāze *a.* (Of painting on porcelain etc.) done before the glaze is applied. [f. UNDER- 1 + GLAZE]

ŭndergō' *v.t.* (**underwe'nt**; **undergo'ne** *pr.* -gŏ'n *or* -gaw'n; cf. GO[1]). Be subjected to, suffer, endure esp. with firmness, (*has undergone many trials; underwent a rapid change, an operation*). [OE UNDER(*gān* GO[1])]

ŭndergră'd *n.* (colloq.) = foll. [abbr.]

ŭndergră'dū|ate *n.* Member of university who has not taken the first degree; hence ~E'TTE *n.*, (joc.) female undergraduate. [f. UNDER- 1 + GRADUATE¹]

ŭndergrou'nd¹ *adv.* Beneath surface of ground; in or into secrecy or hiding. [f. UNDER- 1 + GROUND¹]

ŭ'nderground² *a.* & *n.* (Railway) situated underground; (fig.) secret, hidden, (group or activity), esp. aiming to subvert the established order; ~ **press,** production of unconventional and experimental publications. [f. prec.]

ŭ'ndergrowth (-ōth) *n.* Shrubs or small trees growing under larger ones. [f. UNDER- 4 + GROWTH]

ŭ'nderhănd¹ *a.* Clandestine, secret, not above-board; crafty, deceptive; (Cricket, of bowling) performed with hand underneath both shoulder and ball. [f. foll.]

ŭnderhă'nd² *adv.* In underhand manner. [OE (as UNDER-, HAND¹)]

ŭnderhă'ndėd *a.* & *adv.* = UNDERHAND¹,². [f. UNDERHAND¹ + -ED¹]

ŭ'nderhŭng *a.* (Of lower jaw) projecting beyond upper jaw; having underhung jaw. [f. UNDER- 2 + HUNG]

ŭnderlay'¹ *v.t.* (**underlai'd**). Lay something under (thing) as support or to raise it. [OE *underlecgan* (as UNDER- 2, LAY³)]

ŭ'nderlay² *n.* Thing laid under another, esp. paper under types, (material for) sheet under carpet or mattress as protection or support. [f. UNDER- 2 + LAY³]

ŭnderlay'³. See UNDERLIE.

ŭ'nderlease *n.*, & *v.t.* Sublease. [f. UNDER- 2, 4 + LEASE]

ŭnderlĕ't *v.t.* (-tt-; **underle't**). Sublet; let at less than the true value. [f. UNDER- 2, 3 + LET²]

ŭnderlie' *v.t.* (**underly'ing; underlay'; underlai'n**). Lie, be situated, under (stratum etc., or abs.); (arch.) be subject to (challenge etc.); (fig., of principle, reason, etc.) be the basis of (doctrine, law, conduct, etc., or abs., esp. in part.); exist beneath the superficial aspect of. [OE UNDER(*licgan* LIE³)]

ŭnderlī'ne¹ *v.t.* Draw line under (word etc.) to give emphasis or draw attention or indicate italic or other special type; stress, emphasize. [f. UNDER- 2 + LINE³]

ŭ'nderlīne² *n.* Line drawn under word etc.; caption below illustration. [f. UNDER- 4 + LINE²]

ŭ'nderlĭnėn *n.* Underclothes of linen etc. [f. UNDER- 4 + LINEN]

ŭ'nderlĭng *n.* (usu. derog.) Subordinate. [ME, f. UNDER 5 + -LING¹]

ŭnderlȳ'ing. See UNDERLIE.

ŭndermă'nned (-nd) *a.* (Of ship etc.) having too few men to operate it properly; understaffed. [f. UNDER- 3; see MAN²]

‖**ŭndermĕ'ntioned** (-shond; *or* ŭ'-) *a.* Mentioned at later place in book etc. [f. UNDER- 2; see MENTION²]

ŭndermī'ne *v.t.* Make mine or excavation under, wear away base or foundation of, (*rivers undermine their banks*); injure (person, reputation, influence, etc.) by secret or insidious means; weaken, injure, wear out, (health etc.) insidiously or imperceptibly. [ME, f. UNDER- 2 + MINE²]

ŭndernea'th *adv.*, *prep.*, *a.*, & *n.* **1.** *adv.* & *prep.* At or to a lower place (than), below; within, on the inside (of), (surface etc.). **2.** *a.* & *n.* Lower (surface, part). [OE *underneothan* (as UNDER, *neothan*; cf. BENEATH)]

ŭ'nderpănts *n. pl.* Undergarment covering lower part of body and part of legs. [f. UNDER- 4 + PANTS]

ŭ'nder-pärt *n.* Lower or under part; subordinate part in play etc. [f. UNDER- 4 + PART¹]

ŭ'nderpass (-ahs) *n.* (Crossing that has) road etc. passing under another. [f. UNDER- 4 + PASS²]

ŭnderpĭ'n *v.t.* (-nn-). Support from below with masonry etc.; (fig.) support, strengthen. [f. UNDER-2 + PIN²]

ŭ'nderplŏt *n.* Subordinate plot in play etc. [f. UNDER- 4 + PLOT¹]

ŭnderprĭ'vĭlėged (-jd) *a.* Less privileged than others; not enjoying the normal standard of living or rights in a society. [f. UNDER- 3; see PRIVILEGE]

ŭnderprodŭ'ction *n.* Production of less than is usual or required. [f. UNDER- 3 + PRODUCTION]

ŭ'nderproof *a.* Containing less alcohol than proof spirit does. [f. UNDER- 1 + PROOF¹]

ŭnderprŏ'p *v.t.* (-pp-). Support with prop; (fig.) support, sustain. [f. UNDER- 2 + PROP¹]

ŭnderquō'te *v.t.* Quote lower price than (person); quote lower price than others for (goods etc.). [f. UNDER- 2 + QUOTE]

ŭnderrā'te (-*er*-r-) *v.t.* = UNDERESTIMATE². [f. UNDER- 3 + RATE²]

ŭnderscôr'e¹ *v.t.* = UNDERLINE¹. [f. UNDER- 2 + SCORE]

ŭ'nderscôre² *n.* = UNDERLINE². [f. UNDER- 4 + SCORE]

ŭ'ndersea *a.* Below (surface of) the sea, submarine. [f. UNDER- 1 + SEA]

ŭ'nderseal *v.t.* Seal under-part of (esp. motor vehicle against dirt etc.). [f. UNDER- 2 + SEAL²]

ŭndersĕ'll *v.t.* (**underso'ld**). Sell at lower price than; sell at less than the true value. [f. UNDER- 2, 3 + SELL]

ŭndersĕ't¹ *v.t.* (-tt-; **underse't**). Underprop; place something under (thing). [ME, f. UNDER- 2 + SET¹]

ŭ'ndersĕt² *n.* (Naut.) Undercurrent. [f. UNDER- 4 + SET²]

ŭnder-sĕ'xed (-kst) *a.* Having less than the normal degree of sexual desire. [f. UNDER- 3 + SEX + -ED²]

ŭ'ndershĭrt *n.* Undergarment worn under shirt, vest. [f. UNDER- 1 + SHIRT]

ŭndershoo't *v.t.* (**undersho't**). (Of aircraft) land short of (runway); shoot short of or below. [f. UNDER- 3 + SHOOT¹]

***ŭ'ndershôrts** *n.* Short underpants. [f. UNDER- 4; see SHORT]

ŭ'ndershŏt *a.* (Of water-wheel) turned by water flowing under it; = UNDERHUNG. [f. UNDER- 2 + SHOT²]

ŭ'nder-shrŭb *n.* Subshrub. [f. UNDER- 4 + SHRUB¹]

ŭ'nder-sīde *n.* Lower or under side or surface. [f. UNDER- 4 + SIDE¹]

ŭ'ndersīgned (-īnd) *a.* Whose signature is appended in document etc. (*we, the undersigned, wish to state* . . .). [f. UNDER- 2; see SIGN²]

ŭ'ndersīzed (-zd; *or* -ī'-) *a.* Of less than the usual size; dwarfish. [f. UNDER- 3 + SIZE¹ + -ED²]

ŭ'nderskĭrt *n.* Skirt worn under another, petticoat. [f. UNDER- 4 + SKIRT]

ŭ'nderslŭng *a.* Supported from above; (of vehicle chassis) hanging lower than axles. [f. UNDER- 2 + SLUNG]

ŭndersta'ffed (-ah'ft) *a.* Having less than the necessary number of staff. [f. UNDER- 3; see STAFF¹]

ŭnderstă'nd *v.* (**understoo'd,** arch. *p.p.* **understa'nded**). **1.** *v.t.* Perceive the meaning of (words, person, language, etc.; *does not under-*

stand what you say, you, French); ~ **each other,** know each other's views or feelings, be in agreement or collusion; **tongue not ~ed of the people,** (arch.) foreign language. **2.** Grasp mentally, perceive the significance or explanation or cause or nature of, know how to deal with, (*do not understand why he came, what the noise is about, the point of his remark; quite understand your difficulty; cannot understand him, his conduct, his wanting to go; thoroughly understands children; could never understand mathematics*). **3.** Infer esp. from information received, take as implied, take for granted, (*I understand that it begins at noon, that they are almost destitute, him to be* or *that he is a distant relation; but I understood that expenses were to be paid; no one could understand that from my words*); (expr. uncertainty or surprise or indignation: *do I understand* (*you to say*) *that* or *am I to understand that you refuse?*); GIVE¹ person *to understand.* **4.** Supply (word) mentally (*the verb may be either expressed or understood*). **5.** Hence ~ABLE *a.* **6.** *v.i.* Have understanding (in general or particular); believe or assume from knowledge or inference (*he is coming tomorrow, I understand*). [OE UNDER(*standan* STAND¹)]

ŭnderstă'nding¹ *a.* Having understanding or insight or good judgement; able to be sympathetic to others' feelings; hence ~LY² *adv.* [ME, f. prec. + -ING²]

ŭnderstă'nding² *n.* In vbl senses; intelligence (*has an excellent understanding*); power of apprehension, power of abstract thought, (often opp. to *reason*); agreement, harmony, convention, thing agreed upon, (*must come to an understanding with him; disturbed the* (*good*) *understanding between them; had a secret understanding with other firms; consented only on this understanding, on the distinct understanding that*). [OE (as UNDERSTAND, -ING¹)]

ŭnderstā'te *v.t.* Express in (unduly) restrained terms; represent as being less than it actually is; so ~MENT (-tm-) *n.* [f. UNDER- 3 + STATE²]

ŭ'ndersteer *v.i.*, & *n.* (Of motor vehicle) (have) tendency to turn less sharply than was intended. [f. UNDER- 3 + STEER¹]

ŭ'nderstrăpper *n.* Underling, subordinate agent. [f. UNDER- 4 + STRAP + -ER¹; cf. dial. *strapper* groom]

ŭ'nderstŭdy̆ *n.*, & *v.t.* **1.** *n.* One who studies another's theatrical etc. role or duties in order to act at short notice in absence of the other. **2.** *v.t.* Study (role etc.) thus; act as understudy to (person). [n. f. v., f. UNDER- 2 + STUDY²]

ŭ'nder-sûrface (-ĭs) *n.* Lower or under surface. [f. UNDER- 4 + SURFACE]

ŭndertā'ke *v.t.* (**undertoo'k; underta'ken**). Bind oneself to perform, make oneself responsible for, engage in, enter upon, (work, enterprise, responsibility); accept an obligation, promise, (*to* do); guarantee, affirm, (*I will undertake that he has not heard a word, that you shall* or *will not be the loser by it*). [ME, f. UNDER- 2 + TAKE¹]

ŭ'ndertāker *n.* In vbl senses; one whose business is to carry out arrangements for funerals; (Hist.) influential person in 17th-c. England who undertook to procure particular legislation, esp. to obtain supplies from House of Commons if king would grant some concession. [ME, f. prec. + -ER¹]

ŭ'ndertāking (*or* -ā'-) *n.* In vbl senses; work etc. undertaken, enterprise, (*a serious undertaking*); pledge, promise; management of funerals. [ME, f. UNDERTAKE + -ING¹]

ŭ'ndertĕn|ant *n.* Subtenant; so ~ANCY *n.* [f. UNDER- 4 + TENANT]

ŭ'ndertĭnt *n.* Subdued tint. [f. UNDER- 4 + TINT]

ŭ'ndertōne *n.* Subdued tone of sound or colour; underlying quality; undercurrent of feeling. [f. UNDER- 4 + TONE¹]

ŭ'ndertow (-ō) *n.* Current below sea-surface moving in opposite direction to surface current. [f. UNDER- 4 + TOW¹]

ŭ'ndertrĭck *n.* (Bridge). Trick by which declarer falls short of contract. [f. UNDER- 4 + TRICK]

ŭndervă'lū|e *v.t.* Rate at too low a value; underestimate; hence ~A'TION *n.* [f. UNDER- 3 + VALUE]

ŭ'ndervĕst *n.* = VEST¹ 2. [f. UNDER- 4 + VEST¹]

ŭnderwa'ter (-aw'-) *a.* & *adv.* (Situated, carried on, etc.) under water. [f. UNDER- 1 + WATER¹]

ŭ'nderwear (-ār) *n.* Underclothes. [f. UNDER- 4 + WEAR²]

ŭ'nderweight (-wāt) *n.* & *a.* **1.** *n.* Insufficient weight. **2.** *a.* Weighing less than is normal or desirable. [f. UNDER- 3 + WEIGHT¹]

ŭnderwĕ'nt. See UNDERGO.

ŭnderwhĕ'lm *v.t.* (joc.) Be far from overwhelming. [f. UNDER- 2, after *overwhelm*]

ŭ'nderwĭng *n.* Moth with conspicuous markings on under-side of wings. [f. UNDER- 1 + WING]

ŭ'nderwŏŏd *n.* Undergrowth. [f. UNDER- 4 + WOOD]

ŭ'nderworld (-wêr-) *n.* (Myth.) abode of the dead under the earth; antipodes; part of society comprising those who live by (organized) crime and immorality. [f. UNDER- 4 + WORLD]

ŭnderwrī'te (-*er*ī't) *v.* (**underwro'te; underwri'tten**). **1.** *v.t.* Sign, and accept liability under, (policy of insurance esp. on marine property), accept (liability) thus; engage to buy all stock in (company etc.) not bought by the public; undertake to finance or support; write below (*the underwritten names*). **2.** *v.i.* Practise (marine) insurance. **3.** Hence **ŭ'nderwrīt**ER¹ (-*er*ī-) *n.* [ME, f. UNDER- 2 + WRITE]

ŭndėscĕ'ndėd *a.* Not having descended; (of testicle) remaining in abdomen instead of descending normally into scrotum. [f. UN-² 1 + DESCENDED]

ŭndėsêr'v|ed (-zêr'vd) *a.* Not deserved (as reward or punishment); hence ~**ėd**LY² *a.* [ME, f. UN-² 1; see DESERVE]

ŭndėsêr'vĭng (-z-) *a.* See UN-² 1.

ŭndėsī'gn|ed (-zī'nd) *a.* Unintentional; hence ~**ėd**LY² *adv.* [f. UN-² 1; see DESIGN²]

ŭndėsīr'|able (-z-) *a.* & *n.* **1.** *a.* Not desirable, objectionable, unpleasant; hence ~ABI'LITY, ~**able**NESS (-beln-), *ns.*, ~**ab**LY² *adv.* **2.** *n.* Undesirable person, esp. drunkard etc. [f. UN-² 1 + DESIRABLE]

ŭndėsīr'ed (-zīr'd), **ŭndėsīr'ous** (-z-), **ŭndėtĕ'ctable, ŭndėtĕ'ctėd,** *adjs.* See UN-² 1.

ŭndėtêr'mĭned (-nd) *a.* = UNDECIDED. [ME, f. UN-² 1 + DETERMINED]

ŭndėtêr'red (-êr'd), **ŭndėvĕ'loped** (-pt), **ŭndē'vĭātĭng, ŭndī'agnōsed** (-zd), *adjs.* See UN-² 1.

ŭ'ndĭes (-dĭz) *n. pl.* (colloq.) (Esp. women's) underclothing. [abbr.; cf. -Y³]

ŭndĭfferĕ'ntĭātėd (-shĭ-), **ŭndĭgĕ'stėd, ŭndĭ'gnĭfĭed** (-īd), **ŭndĭlū'tėd, ŭndĭmĭ'nĭshed** (-sht), **ŭndĭ'mmed** (-md), *adjs.* See UN-² 1.

ŭ'ndĭne (-ēn) *n.* Female water-spirit. [f. mod. L *undina* (wd invented by Paracelsus) f. L *unda* wave: see -INE¹]

ŭndĭplomă'tĭc, ŭndĭschâr'ged (-jd), *adjs.*, see UN-² 1; **ŭndĭ'scĭplĭne** *n.*, UN-² 2; **ŭndĭ'scĭplĭned** (-nd), **ŭndĭsclō'sed** (-zd), **ŭndĭsco'verable** (-kŭ'-), **ŭndĭsco'vered** (-kŭ'verd), **ŭndĭscrĭ'mĭnātĭng, ŭndĭsguī'sed** (-gī'zd), **ŭndĭsmay'ed** (-ā'd), **ŭndĭspū'tėd, ŭndĭssŏ'lved** (-zŏ'lvd), **ŭndĭstĭ'nguĭshed** (-nggwĭsht), *adjs.*, UN-² 1.

For other words in ***un-*** **see** UN-, UN-¹, UN-².

ŭndĭstrĭ'būtėd *a.* Not distributed; ~ **middle,** (Logic) fallacy resulting from failure of middle term to refer to all members of a class. [ME, f. UN-² 1; see DISTRIBUTE]

ŭndĭstûr'bed (-bd), **ŭndĭvī'dėd, ŭndĭvŭ'lged** (-jd), *adjs.* See UN-² 1.

ŭndo' (-ōō') *v.t.* (**undi'd**; UNDONE; cf. DO¹). Unfasten, untie, (coat, button, parcel); unfasten garment(s) of (person); annul, cancel, (*cannot undo the past, our past actions*); ruin prospects or reputation of; hence ~ING¹ *n.* [OE *undōn* (as UN-¹, DO¹)]

ŭndŏ'ck *v.t.* See UN-¹ 1, 3 and DOCK⁴.

ŭndo'ne (-ŭ'n) *a.* Not done (up) (*left the job, the buttons, undone*). [ME, f. UN-² 1 + DONE]

ŭndou'btėd (-ow't-) *a.* Not regarded as doubtful, unaffected by doubt; hence ~LY² *adv.*, without any doubt. [ME, f. UN-² 1; see DOUBT²]

ŭndrā'ped (-pt) *a.* See UN-² 1.

ŭndrea'med (-md), **ŭndrea'mt** (-ĕ'mt), *a.* Not (even) dreamed; not thought *of.* [f. UN-² 1; see DREAM²]

ŭndrĕ'ss¹ *v.* **1.** *v.t.* Take off the clothes of. **2.** *v.i.* Take off one's clothes. [f. UN-¹ 1 + DRESS¹]

ŭndrĕ'ss² *n.* Ordinary dress opp. full dress or uniform; informal dress, négligé. [f. UN-² 2 + DRESS²]

ŭndrĕ'ssed (-st), **ŭndrĭ'nkable,** *adjs.* See UN-² 1.

UNDRO *abbr.* United Nations Disaster Relief Organization.

ŭndūe' *a.* Not owed or suitable; excessive, disproportionate; ~ **influence** (Law; by which person is induced not to act of his own free will); so **ŭndū'**LY² *adv.* [ME, f. UN-² 1 + DUE¹]

ŭ'ndūlant *a.* Moving like waves; ~ **fever,** brucellosis in humans. [f. foll. + -ANT]

ŭ'ndūlāte¹ *v.i.* & *t.* (Cause to) have wavy motion or look. [f. as foll. + -ATE³]

ŭ'ndūlate² *a.* Wavy, going alternately up and down or in and out (*leaves with undulate margins*); hence ~LY² (-tlĭ) *adv.* [f. LL *undulatus* f. L *unda* wave; see -ULE, -ATE²]

ŭndūlā'tion *n.* Wavy motion or form, gentle rise and fall, each wave of this; set of wavy lines. [f. mod. L *undulatio* or UNDULATE²; see -ATION]

ŭ'ndūlātorў *a.* Undulating, wavy; of or due to undulation; ~ **theory** (that light is propagated through the ether by wave-motion imparted to the ether by molecular vibrations of the radiant body). [f. UNDULATE¹ + -ORY]

ŭndū'tĭful, ŭndȳ'ĭng, *adjs.* See UN-² 1.

ŭnear'ned (-ẽr'nd) *a.* Not earned; ~ **income** (from interest payments etc., opp. wage or salary or fees); ~ **increment,** increase in value of property not due to owner's labour or outlay. [ME, f. UN-² 1; see EARN]

ŭnear'th (-ẽr'-) *v.t.* Drive (fox etc.) from earth; dig up; (fig.) bring to light, find by searching. [f. UN-¹ 3 + EARTH¹]

ŭnear'thl|ў (-ẽr'-) *a.* Not earthly; supernatural, mysterious; (colloq.) absurdly early or inconvenient (*getting up at this unearthly hour?*); hence ~ĬNESS *n.* [f. UN-² 1 + EARTHLY]

ŭnea'se (-z) *n.* Lack of ease, discomfort, distress. [f. UN-² 2 + EASE¹]

ŭnea's|ў (-zĭ) *a.* Disturbed or uncomfortable in body or mind (*passed an uneasy night*); disturbing (*had an uneasy suspicion*); hence ~**ĬLY²** *adv.*, ~ĬNESS *n.* [ME, f. UN-² 1 + EASY]

ŭnea'table *a.* Not able to be eaten, esp. because of its condition (cf. INEDIBLE). [f. UN-² 1 + EATABLE]

ŭnea'ten *a.* See UN-² 1.

ŭnea'th *adv.* (arch.) With difficulty; scarcely. [OE *unēathe* (as UN-², *ēathe* easily, = OS *ōtho*, OHG *ōdo*, ON *auth-*)]

ŭnĕconŏ'm|ĭc *a.* Not economic, incapable of being profitably operated etc.; hence ~ICALLY *adv.* [f. UN-² 1 + ECONOMIC]

ŭnĕconŏ'mĭcal *a.* See UN-² 1.

ŭnĕ'dĭfўĭng *a.* Not edifying, esp. uninformative or degrading. [f. UN-² 1; see EDIFY]

ŭnĕ'dĭtėd, ŭnĕ'dūcātėd, ŭnėmbă'rrassed (-st), **ŭnėmō'tional, ŭnėmphă'tĭc,** *adjs.* See UN-² 1.

ŭnėmploy'able *a.* & *n.* (Person) unfitted by character, age, etc., for paid employment. [f. UN-² 1 + EMPLOYABLE]

ŭnėmploy'ed (-oi'd) *a.* Not in use; having no employment; temporarily out of work. [f. UN-² 1; see EMPLOY]

ŭnėmploy'ment *n.* Lack of employment; inability to find paid work; ~ **benefit** (paid by State or *trade union to unemployed worker). [f. UN-² 2 + EMPLOYMENT]

ŭnėnclō'sed (-n-klō'zd) *a.* See UN-² 1.

ŭnėncŭ'mbered (-n-k-; -*erd*) *a.* Having no encumbrance; (of estate) free from mortgage etc. [f. UN-² 1; see ENCUMBER]

ŭnĕ'ndĭng *a.* Having (apparently) no end; hence ~LY² *adv.*, ~NESS *n.* [f. UN-² 1; see END²]

ŭnėndow'ed (-ow'd), **ŭnėndûr'able, ŭnėngā'ged** (-n-gā'jd), *adjs.* See UN-² 1.

ŭn-E'nglĭsh (-ĭ'ngg-) *a.* Not (characteristic of the) English. [f. UN-² 1 + ENGLISH¹]

ŭnėnjoy'able, ŭnėnlī'ghtened (-ī'tend), **ŭnĕ'nterprisĭng** (-z-), **ŭnėnthūsĭă'stĭc** (-zĭ-; *or* -ōōz-), **ŭnĕ'nvĭable, ŭnĕ'nvĭed** (-ĭd), *adjs.* See UN-² 1.

ŭnē'qual *a.* Not equal (*to*); of varying quality; not with equal advantage to both sides (*unequal bargain, contest*). [f. UN-² 1 + EQUAL¹]

ŭnē'qualīze *v.t.*, see UN-¹ 1; **ŭnē'qualled** (-ld), UN-² 1.

ŭnėquĭ'vocal *a.* Not ambiguous, plain, unmistakable; hence ~LY² *adv.*, ~NESS *n.* [f. UN-² 1 + EQUIVOCAL]

ŭnẽr'rĭng *a.* Not erring or failing or missing the mark; hence ~LY² *adv.*, ~NESS *n.* [f. UN-² 1; see ERR]

ŭnėscā'pable *a.* See UN-² 1.

UNESCO, Unĕ'scō, (ūnĕ'skō) *abbr.* United Nations Educational, Scientific, & Cultural Organization.

ŭnėspī'ed (-ī'd) *a.* See UN-² 1.

ŭnėssĕ'ntial (-sh*a*l) *a.* & *n.* **1.** *a.* Not essential; not of the first importance. **2.** *n.* Unessential part or thing. [f. UN-² 1 + ESSENTIAL]

ŭnėstă'blĭshed (-sht) *a.* See UN-² 1.

ŭnĕ'thĭcal *a.* Not ethical, esp. unscrupulous in business or professional conduct; hence ~LY² *adv.* [f. UN-² 1 + ETHICAL]

ŭnēvăngĕ'lĭcal (-nj-) *a.* See UN-² 1.

ŭnē'ven *a.* Not level or smooth; not uniform or equable; hence ~LY² *adv.*, ~NESS (-n-n-) *n.* [OE *unefen* (as UN-², EVEN²)]

ŭnėvĕ'ntful, ŭnėxă'mĭned (-gz-; -nd), *adjs.* See UN-² 1.

ŭnėxa'mpled (-gzah'mp*e*ld) *a.* Having no precedent or parallel. [f. UN-² 1; see EXAMPLE]

ŭnėxcĕ'lled (-ld) *a.* See UN-² 1.

ŭnėxcĕ'ptionab|le *a.* With which no fault can be found; entirely satisfactory; hence ~**le**NESS (-beln-) *n.*, ~LY² *adv.* [f. UN-² 1 + EXCEPTIONABLE]

ŭnėxcĕ'ptional *a.* Not out of the ordinary; hence ~LY² *adv.* [f. UN-² 1 + EXCEPTIONAL]

ŭnėxcī'tĭng, ŭnĕ'xėcūtėd, ŭnėxĕ'mplĭfīed (-gz-; -īd), **ŭnėxhau'stėd** (-gzaw'-), **ŭnėxpĕ'ctėd, ŭnĕ'xpĭātėd, ŭnėxpīr'ed** (-īr'd), **ŭnėxplai'nable, ŭnėxplai'ned** (-nd), **ŭnėxplôr'ed** (-ôr'd), **ŭnėxpō'sed** (-zd), **ŭnėxprĕ'ssed** (-st), **ŭnĕ'xpurgātėd,** *adjs.* See UN-² 1.

ŭnfā'dĭng *a.* See UN-² 1.

ŭnfai'lĭng *a.* Not failing; never ending, constant; reliable; hence ~LY[2] *adv.*, ~NESS *n.* [ME, f. UN-[1] 2; see FAIL[2]]
ŭnfair' *a.* Not equitable or honest or impartial or according to rules (*an unfair advantage*; *procured by unfair means*; *unfair play*); hence ~LY[2] *adv.*, ~NESS *n.* [OE *unfæger* (as UN-[2] 1, FAIR[2])]
ŭnfai'th *n.* See UN-[2] 2.
ŭnfai'thful *a.* Not loyal; treacherous; adulterous; hence ~LY[2] *adv.*, ~NESS *n.* [ME, f. UN-[2] 1 + FAITHFUL]
ŭnfa'ltering (-aw'l- *or* -ŏ'l-), **ŭnfamĭ'liar** (-lyer), **ŭnfă'shionable** (-shon-), *adjs.* See UN-[2] 1.
ŭnfă'shioned (-shond) *a.* Not wrought into shape. [f. UN-[2] 1; see FASHION]
ŭnfa'sten (-ah'sen) *v.t.* Make loose; detach; open fastening(s) of. [ME, f. UN-[1] 1 + FASTEN]
ŭnfa'stened (-ah'send) *a.* See UN-[2] 1.
ŭnfa'thered (-ah'dherd) *a.* Fatherless; (fig.) of unknown origin (*unfathered rumours*). [f. UN-[2] 1; see FATHER[2]]
ŭnfa'therlў (-ah'dh-), **ŭnfă'thomable** (-dh-), **ŭnfă'thomed** (-dhomd), **ŭnfā'vourable** (-ver-), **ŭnfea'sĭble** (-z-), *adjs.*, see UN-[2] 1; **ŭnfea'ther** (-ĕ'dh-) *v.t.*, UN-[1] 2; **ŭnfĕ'd** *a.*, UN-[2] 1.
ŭnfee'd *a.* Paid no fee. [f. UN-[2] 1 + FEED[3]]
ŭnfee'lĭng *a.* Lacking sensation or sensitivity; unsympathetic, harsh, not caring about others' feelings; hence ~LY[2] *adv.*, ~NESS *n.* [OE *unfelende* (as UN-[2], FEELING[2])]
ŭnfei'gned (-ā'nd), **ŭnfĕ'lt, ŭnfĕ'mĭnĭne, ŭnfĕ'nced** (-st), **ŭnfermĕ'ntėd, ŭnfer'tĭlīzed** (-zd), *adjs.*, see UN-[2] 1; **ŭnfĕ'tter** *v.t.*, UN-[1] 1; **ŭnfĕ'ttered** (-erd), **ŭnfĭ'lĭal, ŭnfĭ'lled** (-ld), **ŭnfĭ'ltered** (-erd), **ŭnfĭ'nĭshed** (-sht), *adjs.*, UN-[2] 1.
ŭnfĭ't[1] *a.* Not fit (*to* do, *for* purpose); hence ~LY[2] *adv.*, ~NESS *n.* [f. UN-[2] 1 + FIT[3]]
ŭnfĭ't[2] *v.t.* (-tt-). Make unsuitable (*for*). [f. UN-[1] 1 + FIT[4]]
ŭnfĭ'ttėd *a.* Not fit; not fitted; not furnished with fittings. [f. UN-[2] 1; see FIT[4]]
ŭnfĭ'ttĭng *a.*, see UN-[2] 1; **ŭnfĭ'x** *v.t.*, UN-[1] 1; **ŭnfĭ'xed** (-kst), **ŭnflă'ggĭng** (-g-), *adjs.*, UN-[2] 1.
ŭnflă'pp|able *a.* (colloq.) Imperturbable; remaining cool in a crisis; hence ~ABI'LITY *n.* [f. UN-[2] 1 + FLAP + -ABLE]
ŭnflă'ttering, ŭnflā'voured (-erd), *adjs.* See UN-[2] 1.
ŭnflĕ'dged (-jd) *a.* Not yet fledged; (of person) inexperienced. [f. UN-[2] 1; see FLEDGE]
ŭnflĕ'shed (-sht), **ŭnflĭ'nchĭng,** *adjs.* See UN-[2] 1.
ŭnfō'ld[1] *v.t.* & *i.* Open folds (of), spread out, develop; (fig.) reveal (thoughts etc.). [OE *unfealdan* (as UN-[1], FOLD[2])]
ŭnfō'ld[2] *v.t.* Release (sheep) from fold(s). [f. UN-[1] 3 + FOLD[1]]
ŭnfor'ced (-st), **ŭnfor'dable, ŭnforesee'n** (-ōrs-), **ŭnforgĕ'ttable** (-g-), **ŭnforgĭ'vable** (-g-), **ŭnforgĭ'vĭng** (-g-), **ŭnforgŏ'tten,** *adjs.* See UN-[2] 1.
ŭnfor'med (-md) *a.* Not formed; not developed; shapeless. [ME, f. UN-[2] 1; see FORM[2]]
ŭnfor'mūlatėd, ŭnforthco'mĭng (-kŭ'-), **ŭnfor'tĭfīed** (-īd), *adjs.* See UN-[2] 1.
ŭnfor'tūnate (*or* -choo-) *a.* & *n.* **1.** *a.* Having bad fortune, unlucky; disastrous; regrettable; hence ~LY[2] (-tlĭ) *adv.*, (also, qualifying whole sentence) it is unfortunate that. **2.** *n.* Unfortunate person. [f. UN-[2] 1 + FORTUNATE]
ŭnfou'ndėd *a.* See UN-[2] 1.
ŭnfree'ze *v.t.* & *i.* (**unfro'ze**; **unfro'zen**). (Cause to) thaw. [f. UN-[1] 1 + FREEZE]
ŭnfrėquĕ'ntėd *a.* See UN-[2] 1.
ŭnfrie'ndėd (-rĕ'n-) *a.* Without friends. [f. UN-[2] 1 + FRIEND + -ED[2]]
ŭnfrie'ndlў (-rĕ'n-) *a.* See UN-[2] 1.
ŭnfrŏ'ck *v.t.* Deprive (priest etc.) of frock or ecclesiastical rank. [f. UN-[1] 2 + FROCK]
ŭnfrui'tful (-oo't-), **ŭnfulfĭ'lled** (-oolfĭ'ld), **ŭnfŭ'ndėd,** *adjs.* See UN-[2] 1.
ŭnfŭ'nnў *a.* Not amusing (though meant to be). [f. UN-[2] 1 + FUNNY]
ŭnfur'l *v.t.* & *i.*, see UN-[1] 1; **ŭnfur'nĭshed** (-sht) *a.*, UN-[2] 1.
ŭngai'nl|ў (ŭn-g-) *a.* (Of person or animal, or movements thereof) awkward-looking, clumsy; hence ~ĬNESS *n.* [f. UN-[2] 1 + obs. *gainly* ME f. obs. *gain* a., OE f. ON *gegn* straight, + -LY[1]]
ŭngă'llant (ŭn-g-), **ŭngar'bled** (ŭn-gar'beld), **ŭngĕ'nerous** (ŭnj-), **ŭngē'nĭal** (ŭnj-), **ŭngĕ'ntle** (ŭnj-), **ŭngĕ'ntlemanlў** (ŭn-jĕ'ntelm-), *adjs.* See UN-[2] 1.
ŭngĕt-ă't-able (ŭn-g-) *a.* (colloq.) Inaccessible. [f. UN-[2] 1 + GET[1]-*at-able*]
ŭngĭ'ld (ŭn-g-) *v.t.*, see UN-[1] 1; **ŭngĭ'mmĭckў** (ŭn-g-) *a.*, UN-[2] 1; **ŭngir'd** (ŭn-g-) *v.t.*, UN-[1] 1; **ŭnglā'zed** (ŭn-glā'zd) *a.*, UN-[2] 1.
ŭnglo've (ŭn-glŭ'v) *v.t.* & *i.* Remove gloves (of). [ME, f. UN-[1] 2 + GLOVE]
ŭnglo'ved (ŭn-glŭ'vd) *a.* See UN-[2] 1.
ŭngŏ'dl|ў (ŭn-g-) *a.* Impious, wicked; (colloq.) outrageous; hence ~ĬNESS *n.* [f. UN-[2] 1 + GODLY]
ŭngo'vernab|le (ŭn-gŭ'-) Uncontrollable, violent; hence ~LY[2] *adv.* [f. UN-[2] 1 + GOVERNABLE]
ŭngrā'ceful (ŭn-grā'sf-) *a.* See UN-[2] 1.
ŭngrā'cious (ŭn-grā'shus) *a.* Not kindly or courteous or attractive; hence ~LY[2] *adv.*, ~NESS *n.* [ME, = graceless, unlucky, f. UN-[2] 1 + GRACIOUS]
ŭngrammă'tĭcal (ŭn-g-) *a.* Contrary to rules of grammar; hence ~LY[2] *adv.* [f. UN-[2] 1 + GRAMMATICAL]
ŭngrā'teful (ŭn-grā'tf-), **ŭngrŭ'dgĭng** (ŭn-g-), *adjs.* See UN-[2] 1.
ŭ'ngual (ŭ'nggw-) *a.* Of, like, bearing, a nail or hoof or claw. [f. L UNGUIS + -AL]
ŭnguar'd (ŭn-gar'd) *v.t.* Deprive of guard or defence; (Cards) discard a low card that was protecting (a high card) from capture. [f. UN-[1] 2 + GUARD[1]]
ŭnguar'dėd (ŭn-gar'-) *a.* Not guarded; incautious; thoughtless; hence ~LY[2] *adv.* [f. UN-[2] 1; see GUARD[2]]
ŭ'nguent (ŭ'nggw-) *n.* Soft substance used as ointment or for lubrication. [f. L *unguentum* (*unguere* anoint)]
ŭnguĭ'cūlate (ŭnggw-) *a.* Having nail(s) or claw(s). [f. mod. L *unguiculatus* (*unguiculus* dim. of UNGUIS; see -CULE, -ATE[2])]
ŭ'ngu|ĭs (ŭ'nggw-) *n.* (*pl.* ~**es** *pr.* -ēz). (Bot.) narrow base of petal; (Zool.) nail, claw. [L]
ŭ'ngūl|a (ŭ'ngg-) *n.* (*pl.* ~**ae**). Hoof, claw, talon; so ~ATE[2] (2) *a.* & *n.*, (Zool.) hoofed (mammal). [L, dim. of UNGUIS]
ŭngŭ'm (ŭn-g-) *v.t.*, see UN-[1] 2; **ŭnhă'ckneyed** (-nĭd) *a.*, UN-[2] 1; **ŭnhair'** *v.t.*, UN-[1] 2.
ŭnhă'llowed (-ōd) *a.* Not consecrated; not sacred, unholy, wicked. [f. UN-[2] 1; see HALLOW[2]]
ŭnhă'mpered (-erd) *a.* See UN-[2] 1.
ŭnhă'nd *v.t.* Take one's hands off; release from one's grasp. [f. UN-[1] 3 + HAND[1]]
ŭnhă'ndsome (-ns-), **ŭnhă'ndў,** *adjs.* See UN-[2] 1.
ŭnhă'ng *v.t.* (**unhu'ng**). Take down from a hanging position. [ME, f. UN-[1] 1 + HANG[1]]
ŭnhă'nged (-ngd) *a.* See UN-[2] 1.
ŭnhă'pp|ў *a.* Not happy, miserable; causing misfortune; disastrous; inauspicious; unsuccessful; hence ~ĬLY[2] *adv.*, ~ĬNESS *n.* [ME, f. UN-[2] 1 + HAPPY]

||**ŭnhar′bour** (-ber) *v.t.* Dislodge (deer) from covert. [f. UN-[1] 3 + HARBOUR]

ŭnhar′med (-md) *a.*, see UN-[2] 1; **ŭnhar′nėss, ŭnha′sp** (-ah′-), *vbs. t.*, UN-[1] 1; **ŭnhea′lthful** (-ĕ′l-) *a.*, UN-[2] 1.

ŭnhea′lth|ȳ (-ĕ′l-) *a.* Not in good health; unwholesome; (of place etc.) harmful to health, (sl.) dangerous to life; hence **~ĭLY**[2] *adv.*, **~ĭNESS** *n.* [f. UN-[2] 1 + HEALTHY]

ŭnhear′d (-er′d) *a.* Not heard; **~(-of)**, unknown, unprecedented. [ME, f. UN-[2] 1 + HEARD]

ŭnhee′dėd, ŭnhee′dful, ŭnhee′dĭng, *adjs.* See UN-[2] 1.

ŭnhĕ′lm *v.t.* & *i.* (arch.) Remove helmet (of). [ME, f. UN-[1] 2 + HELM[1]]

ŭnhĕ′lpful, ŭnhĕ′raldėd, ŭnhėrō′ĭc, ŭnhĕ′sĭtātĭng (-z-), *adjs.* See UN-[2] 1.

ŭnhĭ′nge (-nj) *v.t.* Take (door etc.) off its hinges; (fig., esp. in *p.p.*) unsettle or disorder (person's mind etc.). [f. UN-[1] 1 + HINGE]

ŭnhĭstŏ′rĭc(al) *adjs.*, see UN-[2] 1; **ŭnhĭ′tch** *v.t.*, UN-[1] 1.

ŭnhō′l|ȳ *a.* Not holy; impious, profane, wicked; (colloq.) dreadful, outrageous, (*made an unholy row about it*); hence **~ĭNESS** *n.* [OE *unhālig* (as UN-[2], HOLY)]

ŭnhŏ′noured (ŭnŏ′nerd) *a.* See UN-[2] 1.

ŭnhoo′k *v.t.* Detach from hook(s); unfasten by releasing hook(s). [f. UN-[1] 3 + HOOK[1]]

ŭnhō′ped (-pt) *a.* **~(-for)**, not hoped for or expected. [ME, f. UN-[2] 1; see HOPE[2]]

ŭnhor′se *v.t.* Throw or drag from horse; (of horse) throw (rider); (fig.) dislodge, overthrow. [ME, f. UN-[1] 3 + HORSE[1]]

ŭnhou′se (-z) *v.t.* Deprive of shelter, turn out of house. [ME, f. UN-[1] 3 + HOUSE[1]]

ŭnhou′seled (-zeld) *a.* (arch.) Not having received the Eucharist. [f. UN-[2] 1 + obs. *housel* v. & n. (give) consecrated elements f. OE *hūsl(ian)*, of unkn. orig., + -ED[1]]

ŭnhū′man *a.* = INHUMAN 1; superhuman; non-human. [f. UN-[2] 1 + HUMAN]

ŭnhū′manīze *v.t.*, see UN-[1] 1; **ŭnhŭ′ng, ŭnhŭ′rrĭed** (-ĭd), **ŭnhur′t,** *adjs.*, UN-[2] 1; **ŭnhŭ′sk** *v.t.*, UN-[1] 3.

ū′nĭ- *comb. form.* One, having or consisting of one, as: **~a′xial,** having a single axis; **~ca′meral,** of only one (legislative) chamber; **~ce′llular,** one-celled; **~co′lour(ed),** of one colour; **~cu′spid** *a.* & *n.*, (tooth) with one cusp; **~cycle,** single-wheeled vehicle esp. as used by acrobats; **~dime′nsional,** having (only) one dimension; **~dire′ctional,** having only one direction of motion, operation, etc.; **~li′ngual,** of only one language; **~li′teral,** consisting of one letter; **~lo′cular,** (Bot. & Zool.) single-chambered; **~nu′cleate,** having one nucleus; **~parous** (-ĭ′-), producing one at a birth, (Bot.) having one axis or branch; **~ped** *n.* & *a.*, single-footed (person); **~per′sonal,** (of Deity) existing only as one person; **~pla′nar,** lying in one plane; **~pod,** one-legged support; **~po′lar,** (Biol., of cell etc.) having only one pole, (Electr.) showing only one kind of polarity; **~ser′ial,** set in one row; **~valent** (-ĭ′-), (Chem.) having a valence of one; **~valve** *a.* & *n.*, (mollusc) with one valve; **~vocal** (-ĭ′-) *a.* & *n.*, (word) of only one proper meaning. [L (*unus* one; see -I-)]

U′nĭat, -ate, (ū′-) *n.* & *a.* (Member) of any community of Christians in E. Europe and Near East that acknowledge papal supremacy but retain own liturgy etc. [f. Russ. *uniyat* (*uniya* f. L *unio* UNION)]

UNICEF (ū′nĭsĕf) *abbr.* United Nations Children's (orig. International Children's Emergency) Fund.

ū′nĭcorn *n.* **1.** Fabulous animal with horse's body and single straight horn (in O.T. transl. Heb. *rᵉ'em*, a two-horned animal); heraldic representation of this, with twisted horn, deer's feet, goat's beard, and lion's tail. **2. ~(-fish), ~ whale, sea-~,** narwhal. **3. ~ moth** (having caterpillar with hornlike prominence on back). **4.** Pair of horses with third horse in front; equipage with these. **5. ~(-shell),** gastropod with spine on lip of shell. [ME, f. OF *unicorne* f. L UNI(*cornis* f. *cornu* horn), transl. Gk *monocerōs*]

ŭnīdė′a′d *a.* Having no ideas. [f. UN-[2] 1 + IDEA'D]

ŭnīdė′al, ŭnīdĕ′ntĭfīed (-īd), *adjs.* See UN-[2] 1.

UNIDO (ūnē′dō) *abbr.* United Nations Industrial Development Organization.

ūnĭfĭcā′tion etc. See UNIFY.

ū′nĭform *a.*, *n.*, & *v.t.* **1.** *a.* Not changing in form or character, the same, unvarying, (*present a uniform appearance*; *all of uniform size and shape*; *keeps a uniform temperature*; *behaved with uniform moderation*); constant in the course of time (*uniform acceleration*); (of tax, law, etc.) not varying with time or place; conforming to same standard or rules or pattern; hence **~LY**[2] *adv.* **2.** *n.* Uniform distinctive dress worn by members of same body, e.g. by soldiers, sailors, policemen, nurses, schoolchildren. **3.** *v.t.* Make uniform; clothe in uniform (*a uniformed officer*). [f. F *uniforme* or f. L UNI(*formis* f. *forma* FORM[1])]

ūnĭformĭtar′ian *a.* & *n.* (Holder) of theory that geological processes are always due to continuously and uniformly operating forces; hence **~ISM** (3) *n.* [f. foll. + -ARIAN]

ūnĭfor′mĭtȳ *n.* Being uniform, sameness, consistency; **Act of U~** (for securing uniformity in public worship and use of a particular Book of Common Prayer, esp. that of 1662). [ME, f. OF *uniformité* or f. LL *uniformitas* (as UNIFORM; see -ITY)]

ū′nĭ|fȳ *v.t.* Reduce (things, or abs.) to unity or uniformity; hence or cogn. **~FICA′TION, ~fīer**[1], *ns.* [f. F *unifier* or f. LL UNI(*ficare*; see -FY)]

ūnĭlă′teral *a.* One-sided; performed by or affecting only one person or party (*unilateral declaration of independence, disarmament*); (of parking of vehicles) restricted to one side of street; (of leaves) all on same side of stem; hence **~LY**[2] *adv.* [f. UNI- + LATERAL]

ŭnĭllu′mĭnātėd (-oō′-), **ŭnĭmă′gĭnable, ŭnĭmă′gĭnatĭve, ŭnĭmpair′ed** (-ar′d), **ŭnĭmpă′ssioned** (-shond), *adjs.* See UN-[2] 1.

ŭnĭmpea′chab|le *a.* Giving no opportunity for censure; beyond reproach or question; hence **~LY**[2] *adv.* [f. UN-[2] 1 + IMPEACHABLE]

ŭnĭmpē′dėd *a.*, see UN-[2] 1; **ŭnĭmpor′tance** *n.*, UN-[2] 2; **ŭnĭmpor′tant, ŭnĭmpō′sĭng** (-z-), **ŭnĭmprĕ′ssionable** (-shon-), **ŭnĭmprĕ′ssĭve,** *adjs.*, UN-[2] 1.

ŭnĭmpro′ved (-oō′vd) *a.* Not made better; not made use of; (of land) not used for agriculture or building. [f. UN-[2] 1; see IMPROVE]

ŭnĭmpū′gned (-ū′nd), **ŭnĭ′ndĕxed** (-kst), **ŭnĭnflĕ′ctėd, ŭnĭ′nfluenced** (-ooenst), *adjs.* See UN-[2] 1.

ŭnĭnfor′med (-md) *a.* Not informed or instructed; uneducated, ignorant. [f. UN-[2] 1 + INFORMED]

ŭnĭnhă′bĭtable, ŭnĭnhă′bĭtėd, ŭnĭnhĭ′bĭtėd, ŭnĭnĭ′tĭātėd (-shĭ-), **ŭnĭ′njured** (-jerd), *adjs.* See UN-[2] 1.

ŭnĭnspīr′ed (-īr′d) *a.* Not inspired; (of oratory etc.) commonplace. [f. UN-[2] 1; see INSPIRE]

ŭnĭnspīr′ĭng, ŭnĭnstrŭ′ctėd, ŭnĭnsur′able

(-shoor'-), **ŭninsur'ed** (-shoor'd), **ŭnintĕ'llĭgent, ŭnintĕ'llĭgĭble, ŭnintĕ'ntional,** *adjs.* See UN-² 1.

ŭnĭ'nterĕstĕd (*or* -tr-) *a.* Not interested, esp. unconcerned, indifferent; hence ~LY² *adv.*, ~NESS *n.* [f. UN-² 1; see INTEREST]

ŭnĭ'nterĕstĭng (*or* -tr-), **ŭninterrŭ'ptĕd, ŭninvĕ'ntĭve, ŭninvĕ'stĭgātĕd, ŭninvī'tĕd,** *adjs.* See UN-² 1.

ŭninvī'tĭng *a.* Not inviting, unattractive, repellent; hence ~LY² *adv.* [f. UN-² 1 + INVITING]

ŭninvō'ked (-kt), **ŭninvŏ'lved** (-vd), *adjs.* See UN-² 1.

ū'nion (-yon) *n.* **1.** Uniting, being united, coalition, junction, (*the union of the parts was imperfect*; *union by first* or *second* INTENTION); **the U~** (of English and Scottish crowns in 1603 or parliaments in 1707, or of Great Britain and Ireland in 1801). **2.** Matrimony, marriage. **3.** Concord, agreement, (*lived together in perfect union*). **4.** A whole resulting from combination of parts or members, esp. (1) the U.S., (2) the United Kingdom, (3) South Africa, (4) the Union of SOVIET Socialist Republics; (Math.) totality of members of two or more sets; = TRADE *union*; ~ **catalogue** (showing combined holdings of several libraries). **5.** ‖(Hist.) Two or more parishes consolidated for administration of poor-laws; ~ (**workhouse**), workhouse erected by this. **6.** ‖Association of independent (esp. Congregational or Baptist) churches for purposes of co-operation. **7.** (*U~*). General social club and debating society at some universities; buildings of such society. **8.** Part of flag with device emblematic of union normally occupying upper corner next to staff; ~ **down,** hoisted with union below as signal of distress; **U~ Jack** or **flag,** national ensign of United Kingdom formed by union of crosses of St. George, St. Andrew, and St. Patrick; *~ **jack,** JACK³ comprising union from national flag. **9.** Joint or coupling for pipes etc. **10.** Fabric of mixed materials, e.g. cotton with linen or silk or jute. **11.** *~ **suit,** single undergarment for body and legs, combinations. [ME f. OF, or f. eccl. L *unio* unity f. L *unus* one; see -ION]

ū'nion|ist (-yo-) *n.* **1.** Member of a trade union; advocate of trade unions. **2.** (Polit.) One who supports union, esp. one opposed to rupture of parliamentary union between Great Britain and (Northern) Ireland; (arch.) Conservative; *(Hist.) one who during the civil war opposed secession. **3.** One who supports union of churches. **4.** So ~ISM (3) *n.*, ~**ĭ'stic** *a.* [f. prec. + -IST]

ū'nioniz|e, -is|e, (-yonīz) *v.t.* Bring under trade-union organization or rules; hence ~A'TION *n.* [f. UNION + -IZE]

ŭn-ī'onized, -īsed, (-zd) *a.* See UN-² 1.

ūni'que (-ē'k) *a.* & *n.* **1.** *a.* Of which there is only one, unequalled, having no like or equal or parallel, (*his position was unique*; *this vase is so far as is known unique*); (colloq.) remarkable, unusual, (*the most unique man I ever met*); hence ~LY² (-klĭ) *adv.*, ~NESS (-kn-) *n.* **2.** *n.* Unique thing or person. [F, f. L *unicus* (*unus* one; see -IC)]

ū'nĭsĕx *n.* & *a.* **1.** *n.* Tendency of human sexes to become indistinguishable in dress etc. **2.** *a.* (Of clothes) designed to be worn by either sex. [f. UNI- + SEX]

ūnĭsĕ'xūal *a.* Of one sex; (Bot.) having stamens or pistils but not both; hence ~ITY (-ă'l-) *n.*, ~LY² *adv.* [f. UNI- + SEXUAL]

ū'nĭson *a.* & *n.* **1.** *a.* (Mus.) Coinciding in pitch; hence or cogn. ~AL, ~ANT, ~OUS, (-ĭ's-) *adjs.*; ~ **string** (tuned in unison with another string and meant to be sounded with it). **2.** *n.* (Mus.) Coincidence in pitch of sounds or notes, this regarded as an interval; state of sounding at same pitch (esp. *in unison*). **3.** Concord, agreement, (*acted in perfect unison*). [OF, or f. LL UNI(*sonus* SOUND²)]

ŭnĭ'ssūed (-sūd; *or* -shōōd) *a.* See UN-² 1.

ū'nĭt *n.* **1.** Individual thing or person or group regarded for purposes of calculation etc. as single and complete, each of the (smallest) separate individuals or groups into which a complex whole may be analysed, (*the family as the unit of society*). **2.** Quantity chosen as a standard in terms of which other quantities may be expressed; quantity of electricity etc. for which stated charge is made; ‖smallest share in unit trust. **3.** Device with specified function forming element in complex mechanism; piece of furniture for fitting with others like it or made of complementary parts; group with special function in an organization. **4.** ‖~-**-holder,** person with holding in unit trust; ~ **price** (charged for each unit of goods supplied); ‖~ **trust,** investment company investing combined contributions from many persons in various securities and paying them dividends in proportion to their holdings; ~ **volume** (etc.), volume taken as unit in calculation or expression of other quantities. [1570 (J. Dee's preface to Billingsley's transl. of Euclid), f. L *unus* repl. UNITY, prob. after *digit*]

ūnĭtār'ĭan *n.* & *a.* **1.** *n.* (*U~*). One who, member of a religious body that, maintains against the doctrine of the Trinity that God is one person; advocate of general freedom of belief; hence **U~**ISM (3) *n.*, **U~**IZE (3) *v.t.* **2.** Advocate of unity or centralization e.g. in politics. **3.** *a.* (*U~*). Of the Unitarians. **4.** = foll. 2. [f. mod. L *unitarius* f. L *unitas* UNITY; see -ARIAN]

ū'nĭtarў *a.* **1.** Of a unit or units. **2.** Marked by unity or uniformity. [f. UNIT or UNITY + -ARY¹]

ūnī'te *v.* **1.** *v.t.* & *i.* Join together, make or become one, combine, consolidate, amalgamate, (*unite the parts with cement*; *give the parts time to unite*; *the two nations gradually* (*became*) *united*; *oil will not unite with water*); **U~d Brethren,** the (sect of) MORAVIANS; **U~d Kingdom,** Great Britain and (since 1922 Northern) Ireland; **U~d Nations,** (orig., in 1942) those united against the Axis powers in the war of 1939–45, (later) a peace-seeking organization of these and many other States; **U~d Provinces,** (Hist.) (1) seven provinces united in 1579 and forming basis of republic of Netherlands, (2) major Indian administrative division, comprising Agra and Oudh; **U~d Reformed Church** (formed 1972 from English Presbyterian and Congregational churches); *United* STATE¹*s*. **2.** *v.i.* Agree, combine, co-operate, (*in* sentiment, conduct, do*ing*). **3.** Hence **ū'nĭt**IVE *a.* [ME, f. L *unire -it-* (*unus* one) + -ITE²]

ū'nĭtў *n.* **1.** Oneness, being one or single or individual, being formed of parts that constitute a whole, due interconnection and coherence of parts, (*disturbs the unity of the idea*; *pictures lack unity*; *national unity*). **2.** Thing showing such unity, thing that forms a complex whole, (*a person regarded as a unity*); (Math.) the number one, factor that leaves unchanged the quantity on which it operates; **the dramatic unities, the unities of time, place, and action,** limitation of supposed time of drama to that occupied in acting it or to a single day, use of same scene throughout, and abstention from all that is irrelevant to development of single plot. **3.** Harmony, concord, between persons etc., (*dwell together in unity*; *at unity with*). [ME, f. OF *unité* f. L *unitas -tatis* (*unus* one; see -ITY)]

Univ. *abbr.* University.

ūnĭvẽr'sal *a.* & *n.* **1.** *a.* Of or belonging to or done etc. by all persons or things in the world or in the class concerned, applicable to all cases, (*the terror was universal*; *met with universal applause*; *has the universal sanction of philosophers*; *the rule does not pretend to be universal*). **2.** ~ **agent** (empowered to do all that can be delegated); ~ **compass** (with legs that may be extended for large circles); ~ **coupling** or **joint** (transmitting power by a shaft at any selected angle); ~ **language,** artificial language intended for use by all nations; ~ **proposition** (in which predicate is affirmed or denied of the entire subject; opp. *particular proposition*); *universal* SUFFRAGE; ~ **time** (used for astronomical reckoning at all places). **3.** Hence or cogn. ~ITY (-ă'l-) *n.*, ~IZE (3) *v.t.*, ~LY[2] *adv.* **4.** *n.* (Logic) universal proposition; (Philos.) general notion or idea, thing that by its nature may be predicated of many. [ME f. OF, or f. L *universalis* (as UNIVERSE; see -AL)]

ūnĭvẽr'sal|ĭst *n.* One who holds, esp. member of an organized body of Christians who hold, that all mankind will eventually be saved; hence or cogn. ~ISM (3) *n.*, **~ĭ'st**IC *a.* [f. prec. + -IST]

ū'nĭvẽrse *n.* All existing things; the whole creation (and the Creator); the COSMOS[1]; the world, all mankind; ~ **(of discourse)**, (Logic) all the objects under consideration; (Statistics) = POPULATION 3. [f. F *univers* f. L *universum* neut. (as n.) of UNI(*versus* p.p. of *vertere* turn) combined into one, whole]

ūnĭvẽr'sĭtȳ *n.* Educational institution designed for instruction or examination or both of students in all or many of the more important branches of advanced learning, conferring degrees in various faculties, and often embodying colleges and similar institutions; members of this collectively; team, crew, etc., representing a university; **at** ~, studying there; *University* EXTENSION. [ME, f. OF *université* f. L *universitas -tatis* the whole (world), in LL college, guild (as prec.; see -ITY)]

ŭnjau'ndĭced (-st) *a.*, see UN-[2] 1; **ŭnjoi'n** *v.t.*, UN-[1] 1; **ŭnjoi'ned** (-nd) *a.*, UN-[2] 1.

ŭnjoi'nt *v.t.* Separate joints of; (fig.) disunite. [f. UN-[1] 1 + JOINT[3]]

ŭnjŭ'st *a.* Not just, contrary to justice or fairness; hence ~LY[2] *adv.* [ME, f. UN-[2] 1 + JUST[1]]

ŭnjŭ'stĭfīable *a.* See UN-[2] 1.

ŭnkĕ'mpt (ŭn-k-) *a.* Uncombed, dishevelled; untidy, of neglected appearance. [f. UN-[2] 1 + arch. *kempt* p.p. of *kemb* COMB[2] f. OE *cemban* (as COMB[1])]

ŭnkĕ'nnel (ŭn-k-) *v.t.* (||-ll-). Dislodge (fox) from its hole; (fig.) bring to light. [f. UN-[1] 3 + KENNEL[1]]

ŭnkī'nd (ŭn-k-) *a.* Not kind; harsh, ungentle, unpleasant; hence ~LY[2] *adv.*, ~NESS *n.* [ME, f. UN-[2] 1 + KIND[2]]

ŭnkĭ'ng (ŭn-k-) *v.t.*, see UN-[1] 4; **ŭnkĭ'nglȳ** (ŭn-k-) *a.*, UN-[2] 1.

ŭnkĭ'nk (ŭn-k-) *v.t.* Remove kinks from, straighten. [f. UN-[1] 1 + KINK]

ŭnknī'ghtlȳ (ŭn-nī't-) *a.*, see UN-[2] 1; **ŭnknĭ't, ŭnknŏ't,** (ŭn-n-) *vbs. t.*, UN-[1] 1.

ŭnknow'able (ŭn-nō'-) *a.* & *n.* **1.** *a.* That cannot be known. **2.** *n.* Unknowable thing; **the U~**, postulated absolute or ultimate reality. [ME, f. UN-[2] 1 + KNOWABLE]

ŭnknow'ĭng (ŭn-nō'-) *a.* Not knowing; unconscious or ignorant (*of*, or abs.); hence ~LY[2] *adv.* [ME, f. UN-[2] 1 + KNOWING[2]]

ŭnknow'n (ŭn-nō'n) *a.*, *n.*, & *adv.* **1.** *a.* Not known, unfamiliar, (*to*; *he, his purpose, what he wanted, that district, was unknown to me*); *unknown* COUNTRY, QUANTITY; **U~ Soldier** or **Warrior,** unidentified representative member of a country's armed forces killed in war, given burial with special honours in national memorial. **2.** *n.* Unknown thing or person; unknown quantity (*equation in two unknowns*). **3.** *adv.* ~ **to,** without the knowledge of. [ME, f. UN-[2] 1 + KNOWN]

ŭnlā'belled (-ld), **ŭnlā'boured** (-*erd*), *adjs.* See UN-[2] 1.

ŭnlā'ce *v.t.* Undo laces of; unfasten or loosen thus. [ME, f. UN-[1] 1 + LACE[2]]

ŭnlā'de *v.t.* See UN-[1] 1.

ŭnlā'den *a.* Not laden; ~ **weight** (of vehicle without goods etc.). [f. UN-[2] 1; see LADE]

ŭnlā'dȳlike, ŭnlai'd, ŭnlamĕ'ntėd, *adjs.* See UN-[2] 1.

ŭnlă'sh *v.t.* Unfasten (thing lashed down etc.). [f. UN-[1] 1 + LASH[1]]

ŭnlă'tch *v.t.* & *i.*, see UN-[1] 1; **ŭnlaw'ful** *a.*, UN-[2] 1.

ŭnlay' *v.t.* (**unlai'd**). (Naut.) Untwist (rope). [f. UN-[1] 1 + LAY[3]]

ŭnlea'dėd (-lĕ'-) *a.* See UN-[2] 1.

ŭnlear'n (-ẽr'n) *v.t.* (for forms see LEARN). Cause to be no longer in one's knowledge or memory. [ME, f. UN-[1] 1 + LEARN]

ŭnlear'nėd[1] (-ẽr'-) *a.* Not LEARNED, untaught, ignorant; hence ~LY[2] *adv.* [ME, f. UN-[2] 1 + LEARNED]

ŭnlear'ned[2] (-ẽr'nd), **ŭnlear'nt** (-ẽr'-), *adjs.* That has not been learnt. [f. UN-[2] 1; see LEARN]

ŭnlea'sh *v.t.* Release from leash or restraint; set free to engage in pursuit or attack (lit. or fig.). [f. UN-[1] 3 + LEASH]

ŭnlea'vened (-lĕ'vend) *a.* See UN-[2] 1.

unlĕ'ss *conj.* If not, except when, (*shall go, shall not go, unless I hear from him, unless absolutely compelled*; *always walked unless I had a bicycle*). [f. LESS preceded by *on* or *in*, unstressed & assim. to UN-[2]]

ŭnlĕ'ttered (-*erd*) *a.* Not instructed in learning from books; illiterate. [ME, f. UN-[2] 1 + LETTER + -ED[2]]

ŭnlī'censed (-st) *a.* See UN-[2] 1.

ŭnlĭ'cked (-kt) *a.* Not licked into shape; unpolished, rude. [f. UN-[2] 1; see LICK]

ŭnlī'ghtėd (-ī't-) *a.* See UN-[2] 1.

ŭnlī'ke *a.* & *adv.* Not like, different(ly) (from), dissimilar, (*is unlike both his parents*; *the two are unlike*; *portrait is utterly unlike*; *sings quite unlike anyone I have heard before*); not characteristic of (*such behaviour is unlike him*); ~ **signs,** (Math.) plus and minus; hence ~NESS (-kn-) *n.* [perh. f. ON *úlíkr*, OE *ungelic*; see UN-[2], LIKE[1]]

ŭnlī'kel|ȳ (-klĭ) *a.* Improbable (*unlikely tale*); unpromising (*unlikely errand*); hence **~ĭ**HOOD, **~ĭ**NESS, *ns.* [ME, f. UN-[2] 1 + LIKELY]

ŭnlĭ'mber *v.t.* Remove (gun, or abs.) from limber for action. [f. UN-[1] 2 + LIMBER[1]]

ŭnlĭ'mĭtėd *a.* Without limit, unrestricted, very great in number or quantity, (*has unlimited scope, possibilities*; *unlimited expanse of sea*; *drinks unlimited coffee*); hence ~LY[2] *adv.*, ~NESS *n.* [ME, f. UN-[2] 1; see LIMIT[2]]

ŭnlī'ned[1] (-nd) *a.* Without lining. [f. UN-[2] 1; see LINE[4]]

ŭnlī'ned[2] (-nd) *a.* Without lines; (of face etc.) without wrinkles. [f. UN-[2] 1; see LINE[3]]

ŭnlĭ'nk *v.t.*, see UN-[1] 1; **ŭnlĭ'quĭdātėd** *a.*, UN-[2] 1.

|**For other words in** *uni-* **see** UNI-.

ŭnlĭ'stėd *a.* Not included in (published) list, esp. of Stock Exchange prices or of telephone numbers. [f. UN-[2] 1; see LIST[1]]
ŭnlĭ't *a.* See UN-[2] 1.
ŭnloa'd *v.t.* Remove load from (ship, cart, etc., or abs.); remove (load) from ship etc.; (fig.) get rid of; remove charge from (firearm etc.). [f. UN-[1] 1 + LOAD[2]]
ŭnlŏ'ck *v.t.* Release lock of (door, box, etc., or fig.); release (thing) by unlocking (lit. or fig.). [ME, f. UN-[1] 1 + LOCK[3]]
ŭnlŏ'cked (-kt) *a.* See UN-[2] 1.
ŭnlo͝o'ked (-kt) *a.* **~-for,** unexpected, unforeseen. [f. UN-[2] 1; see LOOK]
ŭnlo͞o'se *v.t.* = LOOSE[2] 1. [ME, f. UN-[2] 1 + LOOSE[2]]
ŭnlo͞o'sen *v.t.* = LOOSE[2] 1. [ME, f. UN-[2] 1 + LOOSEN]
ŭnlo'vable (-ŭ'-), **ŭnlo'ved** (-ŭ'vd), *adjs.* See UN-[2] 1.
ŭnlo'vel|ȳ (-ŭ'vlĭ) *a.* Not attractive, unpleasant, ugly; hence **~ĭness** *n.* [ME, f. UN-[2] 1 + LOVELY]
ŭnlo'vĭng (-ŭ'-) *a.* See UN-[2] 1.
ŭnlŭ'ck|ȳ *a.* Not fortunate or successful; wretched; bringing bad luck; ill-judged; hence **~ĭly**[2] *adv.* [f. UN-[2] 1 + LUCKY[1]]
ŭnmā'de, ŭnmai'denlȳ, *adjs.* See UN-[2] 1.
ŭnmā'ke *v.t.* (**unma'de**). Undo the making of, destroy, depose, annul. [ME, f. UN-[1] 1 + MAKE[1]]
ŭnmă'n *v.t.* (**-nn-**). Deprive (ship etc.) of men; deprive of manly qualities, discourage, (person). [f. UN-[1] 2, 4 + MAN[1]]
ŭnmă'nageab|le (-nĭj*a*-) *a.* Not (easily) managed or manipulated or controlled; hence **~leness** (-b*e*ln-) *n.*, **~ly**[2] *adv.* [f. UN-[2] 1 + MANAGEABLE]
ŭnmă'nlȳ *a.* See UN-[2] 1.
ŭnmă'nnerl|ȳ *a.* Without good manners; showing lack of good manners; hence **~ĭness** *n.* [ME, f. UN-[2] 1 + MANNERLY]
ŭnmar̂'ked (-kt) *a.* Not marked; not noticed. [f. UN-[2] 1; see MARK[2]]
ŭnmar̂'kėtable, ŭnmă'rriageable (-rĭj*a*-), **ŭnmă'rrĭed** (-ĭd), **ŭnmă'scūlĭne** (*or* -mah'-), *adjs.* See UN-[2] 1.
ŭnma'sk (-ah'-) *v.* **1.** *v.t.* Remove mask from; (fig.) expose true character of. **2.** *v.i.* Remove one's mask. [f. UN-[1] + MASK[2]]
ŭnmă'tchable, ŭnmă'tched (-cht), *adjs.* See UN-[2] 1.
ŭnmea'nĭng *a.* Having no significance, meaningless; hence **~ly**[2] *adv.*, **~ness** *n.* [f. UN-[2] 1 + MEANING[2]]
ŭnmea'nt (-ĕ'-), **ŭnmea'surable** (-ĕ'zh*er*-), *adjs.* See UN-[2] 1.
ŭnmea'sured (-ĕ'zh*er*d) *a.* Not measured; limitless. [ME, f. UN-[2] 1 + MEASURED]
ŭnmee't *a.* (arch.) Not suitable (*to* do, *for* a purpose); hence **~ly**[2] *adv.*, **~ness** *n.* [OE *unmǣte* (as UN-[2], MEET[3])]
ŭnmėlō'dious, ŭnmĕ'ltėd, ŭnmĕ'morable, *adjs.* See UN-[2] 1.
ŭnmĕ'ntionable *a.* & *n.* **1.** *a.* That cannot (properly) be mentioned. **2.** *n.* (in *pl.*, arch., joc.) Trousers; undergarments. [f. UN-[2] 1 + MENTIONABLE]
ŭnmer̂'chantable, ŭnmer̂'cĭful, ŭnmĕ'rĭtėd, ||**ŭnmĕ'talled** (-ld), **ŭnmėthŏ'dĭcal, ŭnmĕ'trĭcal, ŭnmĭ'lĭtarȳ, ŭnmī'ndful,** *adjs.* See UN-[2] 1.
ŭnmĭstā'kab|le *a.* That cannot be mistaken or doubted, quite clear; hence **~ly**[2] *adv.* [f. UN-[2] 1 + MISTAKABLE]
ŭnmĭ'tĭgātėd *a.* Not mitigated or modified; absolute, unqualified, (*an unmitigated scoundrel*). [f. UN-[2] 1; see MITIGATE]
ŭnmĭ'xed (-kst), **ŭnmŏ'dĭfīed** (-īd), **ŭnmŏ'dūlātėd, ŭnmolĕ'stėd,** *adjs.* See UN-[2] 1.
ŭnmoor' (*or* -ōr') *v.t.* Release moorings of (vessel, or abs.); weigh all but one anchor of (vessel). [f. UN-[1] 1 + MOOR[3]]
ŭnmŏ'ral *a.* Not concerned with morality; hence **ŭnmoră'lity** *n.* [f. UN-[2] 1 + MORAL]
ŭnmor̂'tise *v.t.*, see UN-[1] 1; **ŭnmo'therlȳ** (-ŭ'dh-), **ŭnmou'ntėd, ŭnmour'ned** (-ōr'nd), *adjs.*, UN-[2] 1.
ŭnmo'ved (-o͞o'vd) *a.* Not moved; not changed in one's purpose; not affected by emotion. [ME, f. UN-[2] 1; see MOVE[2]]
ŭnmow'n (-ō'n) *a.* See UN-[2] 1.
ŭnmŭ'ffle *v.t.* Remove muffler from (face, bell, etc.). [f. UN-[1] 1 + MUFFLE[3]]
ŭnmur̂'murĭng *a.* Not complaining; hence **~ly**[2] *adv.* [f. UN-[2] 1; see MURMUR[2]]
ŭnmū'sĭcal (-z-) *a.* Not pleasing to the ear; unskilled in or indifferent to music; hence **~ly**[2] *adv.*, **~ness** *n.* [f. UN-[2] 1 + MUSICAL]
ŭnmū'tĭlātėd *a.* See UN-[2] 1.
ŭnmŭ'zzle *v.t.* Remove muzzle from; (fig.) relieve of obligation to remain silent. [f. UN-[1] 2 + MUZZLE[1]]
ŭnnai'l (ŭn-n-) *v.t.* See UN-[1] 2.
ŭnnā'meable (ŭn-nā'm*a*-) *a.* That cannot be named, esp. too bad to be named. [f. UN-[2] 1 + NAMEABLE]
ŭnnā'med (ŭn-nā'md), **ŭnnă'tional** (ŭn-n-), *adjs.* See UN-[2] 1.
ŭnnă'tural (ŭn-nă'ch*er*-) *a.* Contrary to (the usual course of) nature; extremely cruel or wicked; lacking natural feelings; artificial; hence **~ly**[2] *adv.*, **~ness** *n.* [ME, f. UN-[2] 1 + NATURAL]
ŭnnĕ'cėssar|ȳ (ŭn-n-) *a.* Not necessary; more than is necessary (*with unnecessary care*); hence **~ĭly**[2] *adv.* [f. UN-[2] 1 + NECESSARY]
ŭnnei'ghbourlȳ (ŭn-nā'b*er*-) *a.* See UN-[2] 1.
ŭnner̂'ve (ŭn-n-) *v.t.* Deprive of strength or resolution. [f. UN-[1] 1 + NERVE]
ŭnnō'tĭced (ŭn-nō'tĭst) *a.* See UN-[2] 1.
ŭnnŭ'mbered (ŭn-n-; -*er*d) *a.* Not marked with a number; not counted; not able to be counted. [ME, f. UN-[2] 1; see NUMBER[2]]
U.N.O. (ū'nō) *abbr.* United Nations Organization.
ŭnobjĕ'ctionable, ŭnobscūr'ed (-ūr'd), **ŭnobser̂'vant** (-z-), **ŭnobser̂'ved** (-zer̂'vd), **ŭnobstrŭ'ctėd, ŭnobtai'nable, ŭnobtru'sĭve** (-o͞o'-), **ŭnŏ'ccūpied** (-īd), *adjs.* See UN-[2] 1.
ŭnoffĕ'ndĭng *a.* Not offending; harmless, innocent. [f. UN-[2] 1; see OFFEND]
ŭnoffĭ'cial (-sh*a*l) *a.* Not having official character or authorization; **~ strike** (not formally approved by trade union of those striking); hence **~ly**[2] *adv.* [f. UN-[2] 1 + OFFICIAL]
ŭnoi'led (-ld), **ŭnō'pened** (-nd), **ŭnoppō'sed** (-zd), **ŭnor̂'dinarȳ, ŭnor̂'ganized** (-zd), *adjs.* See UN-[2] 1.
ŭnorĭ'gĭnal *a.* Not having originality, derivative; hence **~ity** (-ă'l-) *n.*, **~ly**[2] *adv.* [f. UN-[2] 1 + ORIGINAL]
ŭnor̂'namĕntėd, ŭnor̂'thodŏx, ŭnŏstĕntā'tious (-sh*u*s), **ŭnow'ned** (-ō'nd), *adjs.* See UN-[2] 1.
ŭnpă'ck *v.t.* Open and remove contents of (package, luggage, etc., or abs.); take out (thing) from package etc. [f. UN-[1] 1 + PACK[2]]
ŭnpā'ged (-jd) *a.* With pages not numbered. [f. UN-[2] 1; see PAGE[3]]
ŭnpai'd *a.* (Of debt or person) not (having been) paid; ||**the great ~**, unpaid magistrates or justices. [ME, f. UN-[2] 1 + PAID]
ŭnpair'ed (-ār'd), **ŭnpă'latable,** *adjs.* See UN-[2] 1.

For other words in *un*- see UN-, UN-[1], UN-[2].

ŭnpă′rallĕled (-ld) *a.* Having no parallel or equal. [f. UN-² 1; see PARALLEL²]

ŭnpâr′donable *a.* See UN-² 1.

ŭnpârliamĕ′ntarў (-lam-) *a.* Contrary to parliamentary usage; ~ **language,** oaths or abuse. [f. UN-² 1 + PARLIAMENTARY]

ŭnpă′tentėd, ŭnpătriŏ′tĭc, ŭnpā′ved (-vd), **ŭnpee′led** (-ld), *adjs.*, see UN-² 1; **ŭnpĕ′g** *v.t.*, UN-¹ 1; **ŭnpeo′ple** (-ē′-) *v.t.*, UN-¹ 2; **ŭnpercei′ved** (-sē′vd), **ŭnperfôr′med** (-md), *adjs.*, UN-² 1.

ŭ′npêrson *n.* Person whose name or existence is denied or ignored. [f. UN-² 2 + PERSON]

ŭnpersuā′dėd (-sw-), **ŭnpersuā′sĭve** (-sw-), **ŭnpertûr′bed** (-bd), *adjs.* See UN-² 1.

ŭnphĭlosŏ′phĭc(al) *adjs.* Not according to philosophical principles; lacking philosophy. [f. UN-² 1 + PHILOSOPHIC(AL)]

ŭnphўsĭolŏ′gĭc(al) (-z-) *a.* Not in accordance with normal physiological functioning. [f. UN-² 1 + PHYSIOLOGIC(AL)]

ŭnpĭ′ck *v.t.* Undo sewing of (stitches, garment, etc.). [f. UN-¹ 1 + PICK²]

ŭnpĭ′cked (-kt) *a.* Not selected; (of flower) not plucked. [f. UN-² 1; see PICK²]

ŭnpĭcturĕ′sque (-kch*e*rĕ′sk) *a.* See UN-² 1.

ŭnpĭ′n *v.t.* (-nn-). Unfasten or detach by removing pins; (Chess) make (man) no longer pinned. [ME, f. UN-¹ 1 + PIN²]

ŭnpĭ′tĭed (-ĭd), **ŭnpĭ′tўĭng,** *adjs.* See UN-² 1.

ŭnplā′ced (-st) *a.* Not placed, esp. in race etc. [f. UN-² 1; see PLACE²]

ŭnplă′nned (-nd), **ŭnpla′ntėd** (-ah′-), **ŭnpla′stered** (-ah′st*e*rd), **ŭnplau′sĭble** (-z-), *adjs.* See UN-² 1.

ŭnplay′able *a.* (Esp. of ball in games) that cannot be played, returned, etc. [f. UN-² 1 + PLAYABLE]

ŭnplea′sant (-ĕ′z-) *a.* Not pleasant, disagreeable; hence ~LY² *adv.*, ~NESS *n.* (**the late ~ness,** a recent war). [f. UN-² 1 + PLEASANT]

ŭnplea′sĭng (-z-) *a.*, see UN-² 1; **ŭnplea′sure** (-ĕ′zh*e*r) *n.*, UN-² 2; **ŭnplĕ′dged** (-jd), **ŭnplou′ghed** (-ow′d), **ŭnplŭ′cked** (-kt), *adjs.*, UN-² 1; **ŭnplŭ′g** *v.t.*, UN-¹ 1; **ŭnplŭ′mbed** (-md), **ŭnpōĕ′tĭc(al),** *adjs.*, UN-² 1.

ŭnpoi′ntėd *a.* Having no point(s); not punctuated; (of written Hebrew etc.) having no vowel points marked; (of brickwork etc.) not pointed. [f. UN-² 1 + POINTED]

ŭnpŏ′lĭshed (-sht) *a.* See UN-² 1.

ŭnpolĭ′tĭcal *a.* Not concerned with politics. [f. UN-² 1 + POLITICAL]

ŭnpō′lled (-ld), **ŭnpollu′tėd** (-ōō′-), *adjs.* See UN-² 1.

ŭnpŏ′pūlar *a.* Not popular, not liked by the public or by people in general; hence ~ITY (-ă′r-) *n.*, ~LY² *adv.* [f. UN-² 1 + POPULAR]

ŭnpossĕ′ssed (-zĕ′st) *a.* Not possessed; not in possession *of.* [f. UN-² 1; see POSSESS]

ŭnpō′stėd *a.* See UN-² 1.

ŭnpră′ctĭcal *a.* Not practical; (of person) not having practical skill; hence ~ITY (-ă′l-) *n.*, ~LY² *adv.* [f. UN-² 1 + PRACTICAL]

ŭnpră′ctĭsed, *-ĭced, (-st) *a.* Not experienced or skilled; not put into practice. [f. UN-² 1; see PRACTISE]

ŭnprĕ′cėdĕntėd *a.* For which there is no precedent, unparalleled; novel; hence ~LY² *adv.* [f. UN-² 1 + PRECEDENTED]

ŭnprėdĭ′ctable, ŭnprĕ′jŭdĭced (-jōōdĭst), *adjs.* See UN-² 1.

ŭnprėmĕ′dĭtātėd *a.* Not previously thought over, not deliberately planned, unintentional; hence ~LY² *adv.* [f. UN-² 1; see PREMEDITATE]

ŭnprėpâr′ed (-âr′d) *a.* Not prepared (in advance), not ready; hence ~NESS *n.* [f. UN-² 1; see PREPARE]

ŭnprēpossĕ′ssĭng (-zĕ′-), **ŭnprėsĕ′ntable** (-z-), **ŭnprėsū′mĭng** (-z-), **ŭnprėsŭ′mptūous** (-z-), *adjs.* See UN-² 1.

ŭnprėtĕ′ndĭng, ŭnprėtĕ′ntious (-sh*u*s), *adjs.* Not making a great display; hence ~LY² *adv.*, ~NESS *n.* [f. UN-² 1; see PRETEND, PRETENTIOUS]

ŭnprī′ced (-st) *a.* Not having price(s) fixed or marked or stated. [f. UN-² 1 + PRICED]

ŭnprie′st *v.t.*, see UN-¹ 4; **ŭnprī′med** (-md) *a.*, UN-² 1.

ŭnprĭ′ncĭpled (-p*e*ld) *a.* Not having or based on good moral principles of conduct. [f. UN-² 1 + PRINCIPLED]

ŭnprĭ′ntable *a.* That cannot be printed, esp. because too blasphemous, indecent, etc. [f. UN-² 1 + PRINTABLE]

ŭnprĭ′ntėd, ŭnprĭ′vĭlėged (-jd), **ŭnprocūr′able, ŭnprodŭ′ctĭve,** *adjs.* See UN-² 1.

ŭnprofĕ′ssional (-sh*o*n-) *a.* Not belonging to one's or a profession; contrary to professional standards of behaviour etc. [f. UN-² 1 + PROFESSIONAL]

ŭnprŏ′fĭtable, ŭnprogrĕ′ssĭve, ŭnprŏ′mĭsĭng, ŭnprŏ′mptėd, ŭnpronou′nceable (-ns*a*-), **ŭnprophĕ′tĭc, ŭnpropĭ′tious** (-sh*u*s), **ŭnprŏ′sperous, ŭnprotĕ′ctėd, ŭnpro′vable** (-ōō′-), **ŭnpro′ved** (-ōō′vd), **ŭnpro′ven** (-ōō′-), **ŭnprovī′dėd,** *adjs.* See UN-² 1.

ŭnprovō′ked (-kt) *a.* (Of person or act) having no provocation. [f. UN-² 1; see PROVOKE]

ŭnpŭ′blĭshed (-sht), **ŭnpŭ′nctūal, ŭnpŭ′nctūātėd, ŭnpŭ′nĭshable, ŭnpŭ′nĭshed** (-sht), **ŭnpūr′ĭfĭed** (-id), *adjs.* See UN-² 1.

ŭnputdow′nable (-pŏŏ-) *a.* (colloq.) (Of book) so engrossing that reader cannot put it down. [f. UN-² 1 + PUT¹ *down* + -ABLE]

ŭnqua′lĭfĭed (ŭn-kwŏ′lĭfīd) *a.* Not competent (*am unqualified to serve*); not legally or officially qualified (*an unqualified practitioner*); not modified or restricted (*gave his unqualified assent*; *was an unqualified success*). [f. UN-² 1; see QUALIFY]

ŭnquee′n (ŭn-kw-) *v.t.*, see UN-¹ 4; **ŭnquĕ′nchable** (ŭn-kw-), **ŭnquĕ′nched** (ŭn-kwĕ′ncht), *adjs.*, UN-² 1.

ŭnquĕ′stionab|le (ŭn-kwĕ′sch*o*n-) *a.* That cannot be disputed or doubted; hence ~LY² *adv.* [f. UN-² 1 + QUESTIONABLE]

ŭnquĕ′stioned (ŭn-kwĕ′sch*o*nd) *a.* That is not disputed or doubted; not interrogated. [f. UN-² 1; see QUESTION²]

ŭnquĕ′stionĭng (ŭn-kwĕ′sch*o*n-) *a.* Asking no questions; done etc. without asking questions. [f. as prec.]

ŭnquī′et (ŭn-kw-) *a.* Restless, agitated, stirring; perturbed, anxious. [f. UN-² 1 + QUIET²]

ŭnquō′table (ŭn-kw-) *a.* See UN-² 1.

ŭnquō′te (ŭn-kw-) *v.i.* Terminate passage placed within quotation-marks (esp. in *imper.* in dictation etc.). [f. UN-¹ 1 + QUOTE]

ŭnquō′tėd (ŭn-kw-), **ŭnră′nsomed** (-md), *adjs.* See UN-² 1.

ŭnră′vel *v.* (||-ll-). **1.** *v.t.* Cause to be no longer ravelled, tangled, or intertwined, (lit. or fig.); undo (fabric, esp. knitted one). **2.** *v.i.* Become disentangled or unknitted. [f. UN-¹ 1 + RAVEL]

ŭnră′vĭshed (-sht), **ŭnrā′zored** (-*e*rd), **ŭnrea′chable,** *adjs.* See UN-² 1.

ŭnrea′d (-ĕ′d) *a.* Not read; (of person) not well-read. [f. UN-² 1; see READ]

ŭnrea′dable *a.* See UN-² 1.

ŭnrea′d|ў¹ (-ĕ′-) *a.* Not ready; not prompt in action; hence ~ĬNESS *n.* [f. UN-² 1 + READY]

ŭnrea′dў² (-ĕ′-) *a.* Lacking good advice, rash, (*Ethelred the Unready*). [f. UN-² 1 + REDE¹ + -Y², assim. to prec.]

ŭnrē′al *a.* Not real; imaginary; hence ~ITY (-ĭă′l-) *n.* [f. UN-² 1 + REAL²]

ŭnrēalĭ'stĭc, ŭnrė'alīzable, ŭnrė'alized (-zd), **ŭnrea'ped** (-pt), *adjs.* See UN-² 1.
ŭnrea'sonab|le (-z-) *a.* Not reasonable; going beyond the limits of what is reasonable or equitable; hence ~**le**NESS (-beln-) *n.*, ~LY² *adv.* [ME, f. UN-² 1 + REASONABLE]
ŭnrea'soned (-zond), **ŭnrea'sonĭng** (-z-), **ŭnrėcĕ'ptĭve, ŭnrėcĭ'procātėd, ŭnrĕ'ckoned** (-nd), **ŭnrėclai'med** (-md), **ŭnrĕ'cognīzable, ŭnrĕ'cognīzed** (-zd), **ŭnrĕ'compĕnsed** (-st), **ŭnrĕ'concīled** (-ld), **ŭnrėcôr'dėd, ŭnrĕ'ctĭfīed** (-īd), **ŭnrėdee'med** (-md), **ŭnrėdrĕ'ssed** (-st), *adjs.* See UN-² 1.
ŭnree'l *v.t.* & *i.* Unwind from reel. [f. UN-¹ 1 + REEL¹]
ŭnree've *v.t.*, see UN-¹ 1; **ŭnrėfī'ned** (-nd), **ŭnrėflĕ'ctĭng, ŭnrėfôr'med** (-md), **ŭnrē'gal, ŭnrėgâr'dėd, ŭnrėgĕ'nerate, ŭnrĕ'gĭstered** (-*er*d), **ŭnrėgrĕ'ttėd, ŭnrĕ'gūlātėd, ŭnrėhear'sed** (-êr'st), *adjs.*, UN-² 1; **ŭnrei'n** (-ā'n) *v.t.*, UN-¹ 3; **ŭnrėlā'tėd, ŭnrėlă'xed** (-kst), **ŭnrėlĕ'ntĭng, ŭnrėlī'able, ŭnrėlie'ved** (-vd), *adjs.*, UN-² 1.
ŭnrėlĭ'gious (-j*u*s) *a.* Irreligious; not concerned with religion. [ME, f. UN-² 1 + RELIGIOUS]
ŭnrėmâr'kable, ŭnrėmĕ'mbered (-*er*d), *adjs.* See UN-² 1.
ŭnrėmĭ'ttĭng *a.* Never relaxing or slackening, incessant; hence ~LY² *adv.* [f. UN-² 1; see REMIT¹]
ŭnrėmū'nerative *a.* Bringing no, or not enough, profit; hence ~LY² (-vlĭ) *adv.*, ~NESS (-vn-) *n.* [f. UN-² 1 + REMUNERATIVE]
ŭnrėnou'nced (-st), **ŭnrėpea'led** (-ld), **ŭnrėpea'table, ŭnrėpĕ'ntant, ŭnrėpôr'tėd, ŭnrĕprėsĕ'ntatĭve** (-z-), **ŭnrĕprėsĕ'ntėd** (-z-), **ŭnrėpro'ved** (-o͞o'vd), *adjs.* See UN-² 1.
ŭnrėquī'tėd *a.* (Of love etc.) not given in return. [f. UN-² 1; see REQUITE]
ŭnrėsêr've (-z-) *n.* See UN-² 2.
ŭnrėsêr'ved (-zêr'vd) *a.* Not reserved (*unreserved seats*); without reservations (*unreserved confidence*); free from reserve (*an unreserved nature*); hence ~LY² (-vĭdlĭ) *adv.*, ~NESS *n.* [f. UN-² 1; see RESERVE¹]
ŭnrėsĭ'stėd (-zĭ'-), **ŭnrėsĭ'stĭng** (-zĭ'-), **ŭnrėsŏ'lved** (-zŏ'lvd), **ŭnrėspŏ'nsĭve,** *adjs.* See UN-² 1.
ŭnrĕ'st *n.* Lack of rest; restlessness, disturbance, agitation. [ME, f. UN-² 2 + REST²]
ŭnrĕ'stful, ŭnrĕ'stĭng, ŭnrėstôr'ed (-ôr'd), **ŭnrėstrai'ned** (-nd), **ŭnrėstrĭ'ctėd, ŭnrėtûr'ned** (-nd), **ŭnrėvea'led** (-ld), **ŭnrėvêr'sed** (-st), **ŭnrėvī'sed** (-zd), **ŭnrėvō'ked** (-kt), **ŭnrėwar'dėd** (-ôr'-), **ŭnrhėtŏ'rĭcal** (-rĭt-), **ŭnrhȳ'med** (-rī'md), **ŭnrhȳ'thmĭcal** (-rĭ'th- *or* -rĭ'dh-), **ŭnrī'dable, ŭnrĭ'dden,** *adjs.* See UN-² 1.
ŭnrĭ'ddle *v.t.* Solve, explain, (mystery etc.). [f. UN-¹ 1 + RIDDLE¹]
ŭnrĭ'g *v.t.* (-gg-). Remove rigging from (ship); undress. [f. UN-¹ 2 + RIG¹]
ŭnrī'ght (-ī't) *n.* (arch.) Injustice, wrong. [OE *unriht* (as UN-² 2, RIGHT³)]
ŭnrī'ghteous (-ī'ch*u*s) *a.* Not righteous, unjust, wicked, dishonest; hence ~LY² *adv.*, ~NESS *n.* [OE *unrihtwīs* (as UN-² 1, RIGHTEOUS)]
ŭnrĭ'p *v.t.* (-pp-). Open by ripping. [f. UN-¹ 1 + RIP²]
ŭnrī'pe, ŭnrĭ'sen (-z-), *adjs.* See UN-² 1.
ŭnrī'valled, *-aled, (-*a*ld) *a.* Having no equal, peerless. [f. UN-² 1; see RIVAL]
ŭnrĭ'vėt *v.t.* See UN-¹ 1.
ŭnrō'be *v.t.* & *i.* Disrobe; undress. [f. UN-¹ 2 + ROBE]
ŭnrō'll *v.t.* & *i.* Open out from rolled-up state; display or be displayed thus. [ME, f. UN-¹ 1 + ROLL²]
ŭnromă'ntĭc *a.* See UN-² 1.
ŭnro͞o'f *v.t.* Remove roof of. [f. UN-¹ 2 + ROOF]
ŭnro͞o'fed (-ft) *a.*, see UN-² 1; **ŭnro͞o'st** *v.t.*, UN-¹ 3.
ŭnro͞o't *v.t.* Uproot; (fig.) eradicate. [ME, f. UN-¹ + ROOT²]
ŭnrō'pe *v.t.* & *i.*, see UN-¹ 3; **ŭnroy'al, ŭnrŭ'ffled** (-feld), **ŭnru'led** (-o͞o'ld), *adjs.*, UN-² 1.
ŭnru'l|ȳ (-o͞o'-) *a.* Not easily controlled or disciplined, disorderly; *unruly* MEMBER; hence ~**ĭ**NESS *n.* [ME, f. UN-² 1 + *ruly* (RULE, -Y²)]
UNRWA (ŭ'nrah) *abbr.* United Nations Relief and Works Agency.
ŭnsā'fe, ŭnsai'd (-ĕ'd), **ŭnsă'larĭed** (-ĭd), **ŭnsā'leable** (-l*a*-), **ŭnsa'ltėd** (-aw'- *or* -ŏ'-), **ŭnsă'nctĭfīed** (-īd), **ŭnsă'nctioned** (-nd), **ŭnsă'nĭtarȳ, ŭnsătĭsfă'ctorȳ, ŭnsă'tĭsfīed** (-īd), **ŭnsă'tĭsfȳĭng,** *adjs.* See UN-² 1.
ŭnsă'tūrātėd (*or* -ch*er*-) *a.* Not saturated; (Chem.) able to combine with another substance, esp. hydrogen, to form a third by addition of molecules with elimination of double or triple bonds. [f. UN-² 1; see SATURATE]
ŭnsā'vour|ȳ (-*er*ĭ), ***-or|ȳ,** *a.* Disagreeable to taste, smell, or feelings, disgusting; distasteful; morally offensive; hence ~**ĭ**LY² *adv.*, ~**ĭ**NESS *n.* [ME, f. UN-² 1 + SAVOURY]
ŭnsay' *v.t.* (for forms see SAY²). Retract (statement). [ME, f. UN-¹ 1 + SAY²]
ŭnsay'able, ŭnscā'lable, *adjs.*, see UN-² 1; **ŭnscā'le** *v.t.*, UN-¹ 2; **ŭnscâr'red** (-âr'd) *a.*, UN-² 1.
ŭnscā'thed (-dhd) *a.* Without suffering any injury. [ME, f. UN-² 1; see SCATHE]
ŭnscĕ'ntėd, ŭnschĕ'dūled (-shĕ'dūld), **ŭnschŏ'larlȳ** (-sk-), **ŭnscho͞o'led** (-sko͞o'ld), *adjs.* See UN-² 1.
ŭnscientĭ'f|ĭc *a.* Not familiar with science; not in accordance with scientific principles; hence ~ICALLY *adv.* [f. UN-² 1 + SCIENTIFIC]
ŭnscră'mble *v.t.* Restore from scrambled state, esp. interpret (scrambled conversation etc.). [f. UN-¹ 1 + SCRAMBLE]
ŭnscree'ned (-nd) *a.* Not provided with a screen; not shown on a screen; not passed through a screen (lit. or fig.). [f. UN-² 1; see SCREEN]
ŭnscrew' (-o͞o') *v.t.* Unfasten by turning or removing screw(s); loosen (screw). [f. UN-¹ 1 + SCREW]
ŭnscrĭ'ptėd *a.* (Of speech etc.) delivered without a prepared script. [f. UN-² 1 + SCRIPT + -ED²]
ŭnscrĭ'ptural (-choor-) *a.* Not in accordance with Scripture; hence ~LY² *adv.* [f. UN-² 1 + SCRIPTURAL]
ŭnscru'pūlous (-o͞o'-) *a.* Not having scruples, shameless, unprincipled; hence ~LY² *adv.*, ~NESS *n.* [f. UN-² 1 + SCRUPULOUS]
ŭnsea'l *v.t.* Break seal of, open, (letter etc.). [ME, f. UN-¹ 1 + SEAL²]
ŭnsea'led (-ld) *a.* See UN-² 1.
ŭnsea'm *v.t.* Unfasten seams of (garment). [f. UN-¹ 1 + SEAM]
ŭnsear'chable (-êr'-), **ŭnsear'ched** (-êr'cht), **ŭnsea'sonable** (-z*o*-), **ŭnsea'soned** (-z*o*nd), *adjs.* See UN-² 1.
ŭnsea't *v.t.* Remove from (esp. parliamentary) seat; dislodge from horseback. [f. UN-¹ 3 + SEAT]
ŭnsea'worthȳ (-êrdhĭ), **ŭnsĕ'condėd, ŭnsėcūr'ed** (-ūr'd), *adjs.* See UN-² 1.
ŭnsee'dėd *a.* (Of tennis-player etc.) not seeded. [f. UN-² 1; see SEED]

For other words in *un-* see UN-, UN-¹, UN-².

ŭnsee′ĭng *a.* Blind; unobservant; hence ~LY[2] *adv.* [f. UN-[2] 1; see SEE[1]]

ŭnsee′mlȳ *a.* See UN-[2] 1.

ŭnsee′n *a.* & *n.* **1.** *a.* Not seen; (of translation) done without previous preparation. **2.** *n.* ‖Unseen translation. [ME, f. UN-[2] 1 + SEEN]

ŭnsĕ′grėgātėd, ŭnsėlĕ′ct, ŭnsĕlfcŏ′nscious (-sh*u*s), **ŭnsĕ′lfĭsh, ŭnsĕnsā′tional, ŭnsĕntĭmĕ′ntal, ŭnsĕ′parātėd, ŭnsẽr′vĭceable** (-s*a*b-), *adjs.* See UN-[2] 1.

ŭnsĕ′ttle *v.* **1.** *v.t.* Disturb settled state or arrangement of; derange. **2.** *v.i.* Become unsettled. [f. UN-[1] + SETTLE[2]]

ŭnsĕ′ttled (-t*e*ld) *a.* Not (yet) settled; liable to or open to change or further discussion; (of bill etc.) unpaid. [f. UN-[2] 1; see SETTLE[2]]

ŭnsĕ′x *v.t.* Deprive of qualities of one's (esp. female) sex. [f. UN-[1] 2 + SEX]

ŭnsĕ′xed (-kst) *a.*, see UN-[2] 1; **ŭnshă′ckle** *v.t.*, UN-[1] 1; **ŭnshā′dėd, ŭnshā′keable** (-k*a*-), **ŭnshā′ken, ŭnshā′pelȳ** (-plĭ), **ŭnshar̃′ed** (-ar̃′d), **ŭnshā′ved** (-vd), **ŭnshā′ven,** *adjs.*, UN-[2] 1; **ŭnshea′the** (-dh) *v.t.*, UN-[1] 1; **ŭnshĕ′d** *a.*, UN-[2] 1; **ŭnshĕ′ll** *v.t.*, UN-[1] 3; **ŭnshĕ′ltered** (-*e*rd) *a.*, UN-[2] 1.

ŭnshĭ′p *v.t.* (**-pp-**). Remove or discharge (cargo, passenger) from ship; (Naut.) remove (mast, oar, etc.) from fixed position. [ME, f. UN-[1] 3, 1 + SHIP[1,2]]

ŭnshŏ′ckable, ŭnshŏ′d, *adjs.*, see UN-[2] 1; **ŭnshoe′** (-o͞o′) *v.t.*, UN-[1] 2; **ŭnshor̃′n, ŭnshrĭ′nkable, ŭnshrĭ′nkĭng,** *adjs.*, UN-[2] 1.

ŭnsī′ghtėd (-ī′t-) *a.* Not sighted or seen; prevented from seeing. [f. UN-[2] 1; see SIGHT[2]]

ŭnsī′ghtl|ȳ (-ī′t-) *a.* Unpleasing to the sight, ugly; hence ~ĬNESS *n.* [ME, f. UN-[2] 1 + SIGHTLY]

ŭnsī′gned (-ī′nd) *a.* See UN-[2] 1.

ŭnsī′zed[1] (-zd) *a.* Not made to a size; not sorted by size. [f. UN-[2] 1; see SIZE[1]]

ŭnsī′zed[2] (-zd) *a.* Not treated with size. [f. UN-[2] 1; see SIZE[2]]

ŭnskĭ′lful *a.* See UN-[2] 1.

ŭnskĭ′lled (-ld) *a.* Not having or needing skill or special training. [f. UN-[2] 1 + SKILLED]

ŭnskĭ′mmed (-md), **ŭnslee′pĭng,** *adjs.*, see UN-[2] 1; **ŭnslĭ′ng** *v.t.*, UN-[1] 1; **ŭnsmī′lĭng, ŭnsmō′ked** (-kt), *adjs.*, UN-[2] 1.

ŭnsnar̃′l *v.t.* Disentangle. [f. UN-[1] 1 + SNARL[2]]

ŭnsō′ciable (-sh*a*-) *a.* See UN-[2] 1.

ŭnsō′cial (-sh*a*l) *a.* Not social; not seeking or suitable for society; antisocial. [f. UN-[2] 1 + SOCIAL]

ŭnsoi′led (-ld), **ŭnsō′ld,** *adjs.*, see UN-[2] 1; **ŭnsŏ′lder** *v.t.*, UN-[1] 1; **ŭnsŏ′ldierlȳ** (-j*e*rlĭ), **ŭnsolĭ′cĭtėd, ŭnsŏ′lvable, ŭnsŏ′lved** (-vd), *adjs.*, UN-[2] 1.

ŭnsophĭ′stĭcātėd *a.* Natural, ingenuous, innocent; not adulterated or artificial; hence ~LY[2] *adv.*, ~NESS *n.* [f. UN-[2] 1; see SOPHISTICATE]

ŭnsor̃′dĭd, ŭnsor̃′tėd, ŭnsou′ght (-aw′t), *adjs.* See UN-[2] 1.

ŭnsou′nd *a.* Not sound; diseased, unhealthy, rotten, wicked, ill-founded, fallacious, unreliable; **of ~ mind,** insane; hence ~LY[2] *adv.*, ~NESS *n.* [ME, f. UN-[2] 1 + SOUND[1]]

ŭnsou′ndėd, ŭnsour′ed (-owr′d), **ŭnsow′n** (-ō′n), *adjs.* See UN-[2] 1.

ŭnspar̃′ĭng *a.* Profuse, lavish; merciless. [f. UN-[2] 1 + SPARING]

ŭnspea′kab|le *a.* That cannot be expressed in words; indescribably bad or objectionable. [ME, f. UN-[2] 1 + SPEAK + -ABLE]

ŭnspĕ′cĭfied (-īd), **ŭnspĕctă′cūlar,** *adjs.*, see UN-[2] 1; **ŭnspĕ′ll** *v.t.*, UN-[1] 3; **ŭnspĕ′nt, ŭnspĭ′lled** (-ld), **ŭnspĭ′lt, ŭnspĭ′rĭtūal, ŭnsplī′ced** (-st), **ŭnsplĭ′nterable, ŭnspoi′led** (-ld), **ŭnspoi′lt, ŭnspō′ken, ŭnspor̃′tĭng, ŭnspor̃′tsmanlīke,** *adjs.*, UN-[2] 1.

ŭnspŏ′ttėd *a.* Not marked with spot(s); (fig.) morally pure; unnoticed. [ME, f. UN-[2] 1; see SPOT[2]]

ŭnsprŭ′ng *a.* See UN-[2] 1.

ŭnstā′b|le *a.* Not stable; changeable; showing tendency to sudden mental or emotional changes; *unstable* EQUILIBRIUM; hence ~LY[2] *adv.* [ME, f. UN-[2] 1 + STABLE[1]]

ŭnstai′ned (-nd), **ŭnstă′mped** (-pt), **ŭnstar̃′ched** (-cht), **ŭnstā′tėd, ŭnstā′tesmanlīke** (-ts-), *adjs.* See UN-[2] 1.

ŭnstă′tūtab|le *a.* Contrary to statute(s); hence ~LY[2] *adv.* [f. UN-[2] 1 + STATUTABLE]

ŭnstea′dfast (-ĕ′-) *a.* See UN-[2] 1.

ŭnstea′d|ȳ (-ĕ′-) *a.* Not steady or firm; changeable, fluctuating, not uniform or regular; hence ~ĬLY[2] *adv.*, ~ĬNESS *n.* [f. UN-[2] 1 + STEADY]

ŭnstĭ′ck *v.t.* (**unstu′ck**). Separate (thing stuck to another); (colloq.) cause (aircraft) to leave ground; **come unstuck,** (colloq.) come to grief, fail. [f. UN-[1] 1 + STICK[1]]

ŭnstĭ′ntėd, ŭnstĭ′ntĭng, ŭnstĩr′red (-ẽr′d), *adjs.*, see UN-[2] 1; **ŭnstĭ′tch** *v.t.*, UN-[1] 1.

ŭnstŏ′p *v.t.* (**-pp-**). Free from obstruction; remove stopper from. [ME, f. UN-[1] 1 + STOP[1]]

ŭnstŏ′ppable *a.*, see UN-[2] 1; **ŭnstŏ′pper** *v.t.*, UN-[1] 2; **ŭnstrai′ned** (-nd), **ŭnstră′tĭfied** (-īd), **ŭnstrea′med** (-md), *adjs.*, UN-[2] 1.

ŭnstrĕ′ssed (-st) *a.* Not subjected to stress; not pronounced with stress. [f. UN-[2] 1; see STRESS]

ŭnstrĭ′ng *v.t.* (**unstru′ng**). Remove or relax string(s) of (bow, harp, etc.); remove from string; (esp. in *p.p.*) unnerve. [f. UN-[1] 2 + STRING]

ŭnstrŭ′ctured (-kch*e*rd) *a.* Not structured; informal. [f. UN-[2] 1; see STRUCTURE]

ŭnstŭ′dĭed (-ĭd) *a.* Easy, natural, spontaneous. [f. UN-[2] 1; see STUDY[2]]

ŭnstŭ′ffed (-ft) *a.* See UN-[2] 1.

ŭnstŭ′ffȳ *a.* Not stuffy; informal, casual. [f. UN-[2] 1 + STUFFY]

ŭnsubdūe′d (-ū′d), **ŭnsŭ′bjugātėd** (-jo͝o-), *adjs.* See UN-[2] 1.

ŭnsubstă′ntial (-sh*a*l) *a.* Having little or no solidity or reality or factual basis; hence ~ITY (-shĭă′l-) *n.*, ~LY[2] *adv.* [ME, f. UN-[2] 1 + SUBSTANTIAL]

ŭnsubstă′ntĭātėd (-shĭ-) *a.*, see UN-[2] 1; **ŭnsuccĕ′ss** (-ks-) *n.*, UN-[2] 2; **ŭnsuccĕ′ssful** (-ks-), **ŭnsu′gared** (-sho͝o′g*e*rd), **ŭnsuggĕ′stĭve** (-s*u*j-), **ŭnsui′table** (-sū′- *or* -so͞o′-), **ŭnsui′tėd** (-sū′- *or* -so͞o′-), **ŭnsŭ′llĭed** (-ĭd), **ŭnsŭ′mmoned** (-nd), *adjs.*, UN-[2] 1.

ŭnsŭ′ng *a.* Not sung; not celebrated in song. [ME, f. UN-[2] 1 + SUNG]

ŭnsŭ′nned (-nd) *a.* Not reached by or affected by or exposed to sunlight. [f. UN-[2] 1; see SUN]

ŭnsupplī′ed (-ī′d), **ŭnsuppor̃′table, ŭnsuppor̃′tėd, ŭnsur′e** (-shoor′), **ŭnsurpa′ssable** (-ah′-), **ŭnsurpa′ssed** (-ah′st), **ŭnsurvey′ed** (-ā′d), **ŭnsuscĕ′ptĭble, ŭnsuspĕ′ctėd, ŭnsuspĕ′ctĭng, ŭnsuspĭ′cious** (-sh*u*s), **ŭnsustai′ned** (-nd), *adjs.*, see UN-[2] 1; **ŭnswā′the** (-dh) *v.t.*, UN-[1] 1; **ŭnsway′ed** (-ā′d) *a.*, UN-[2] 1.

ŭnswear′ (-ar̃′) *v.t.* (**unswor′e; unswor′n**). Retract (thing sworn). [f. UN-[1] 1 + SWEAR]

ŭnswee′tened (-nd), **ŭnswĕ′pt,** *adjs.* See UN-[2] 1.

ŭnswẽr′vĭng *a.* Not turning aside; steady, constant; hence ~LY[2] *adv.* [f. UN-[2] 1; see SWERVE]

ŭnswor̃′n, ŭnsȳmmĕ′trĭcal, ŭnsȳmpathĕ′tĭc, ŭnsȳstemă′tĭc, *adjs.*, see UN-[2] 1; **ŭntă′ck** *v.t.*, UN-[1] 1; **ŭntă′lentėd, ŭntā′meable** (-m*a*-), **ŭntā′med** (-md), *adjs.*, UN-[2] 1; **ŭntă′ngle** (-ngg*e*l) *v.t.*, UN-[1] 1; **ŭntă′nned** (-nd), **ŭntă′pped** (-pt), **ŭntar̃′nĭshed** (-sht), **ŭntā′stėd,** *adjs.*, UN-[2] 1.

ŭntau′ght (-aw′t) *a.* Not taught; not instructed

by teaching, ignorant; not acquired by teaching, natural, spontaneous. [ME, f. UN-^{2} 1 + TAUGHT]
ŭntă'xed (-kst) *a.*, see UN-^{2} 1; **ŭntea'ch** *v.t.*, UN-^{1} 1; **ŭntea'chable, ŭntear'able** (-tār'-), **ŭntĕ'chnĭcal** (-kn-), **ŭntĕ'mpered** (-*erd*), **ŭntĕ'nable, ŭntĕ'nantėd, ŭntĕ'ndėd, ŭntĕ'stėd,** *adjs.*, UN-^{2} 1; **ŭntĕ'ther** (-dh-) *v.t.*, UN-^{1} 3; **ŭntĕ'thered** (-dh*erd*), **ŭnthă'nked** (-kt), **ŭnthă'nkful, ŭnthă'tched** (-cht), *adjs.*, UN-^{2} 1; **ŭnthĭ'nk** *v.t.*, UN-^{1} 1.
ŭnthĭ'nkab|le *a.* That cannot be conceived in thought or grasped by the mind; (colloq.) highly unlikely or undesirable; hence ~LY^2 *adv.* [ME, f. UN-^{2} 1 + THINKABLE]
ŭnthĭ'nkĭng *a.* Thoughtless; unintentional, inadvertent; hence ~LY^2 *adv.* [f. UN-^{2} 1 + THINKING^2]
ŭnthou'ght (-aw't), **ŭnthou'ghtful** (-aw't-), *adjs.* See UN-^{2} 1.
ŭnthrea'd (-rĕ'd) *v.t.* Take thread out of (needle); find one's way out of (maze). [f. UN-^{1} 1 + THREAD^2]
ŭnthrĕ'shed (-sht) *a.*, see UN-^{2} 1; **ŭnthrĭ'ft** *n.*, UN-^{2} 2; **ŭnthrĭ'ftȳ** *a.*, UN-^{2} 1; **ŭnthrō'ne** *v.t.*, UN-^{1} 3; **ŭntī'dȳ** *a.*, UN-^{2} 1.
ŭntie' *v.t.* (*part.* **unty'ing**). Unfasten (knot etc.); unfasten cords etc. of (package etc.); release from bonds or attachment. [OE *untīgan* (as UN-^{1}, TIE^1)]
ŭntie'd (-ī'd) *a.* See UN-^{2} 1.
untĭ'l *prep.* & *conj.* = TILL^2 (used esp. when its clause or phrase stands first: *until you told me, I had no idea of it*, and in formal style: *resided there until his decease*). [orig. north. ME *untill* f. ON (= OE, OS) *und* as far as + TILL^2]
ŭntĭ'llable, ŭntĭ'lled (-ld), *adjs.*, **ŭntī'melȳ** (-mlĭ) *a.* & *adv.*, **ŭntĭ'nged** (-njd), **ŭntīr'ĭng, ŭntī'tled** (-teld), *adjs.* See UN-^{2} 1.
ŭ'nto (-o͞o *or* -o) *prep.* (arch.) = TO^1 (in all uses except as sign of infinitive; *do unto others*; *sick, faithful, unto death*; *a* LAW^1, *take, unto oneself*). [ME; formed f. UNTIL, w. TO^1 repl. north. TILL^2]
ŭntō'ld *a.* Not told; not (able to be) counted (*untold wealth*). [OE *untēald* (as UN-^{2}, TOLD)]
ŭntou'chable (-ŭ'-) *a.* & *n.* **1.** *a.* That cannot or must not be touched. **2.** *n.* Member of hereditary Hindu group held to defile members of higher caste on contact. [f. UN-^{2} 1 + TOUCHABLE]
ŭntou'ched (-ŭ'cht) *a.* See UN-^{2} 1.
ŭntow'ard (-tō'-; *or* -towôr'd) *a.* Perverse, refractory; awkward; unlucky; unseemly; hence ~LY^2 *adv.*, ~NESS *n.* [f. UN-^{2} 1 + TOWARD^1]
ŭntrā'ceable (-s*a*-), **ŭntrā'ced** (-st), **ŭntrai'ned** (-nd), **ŭntră'mmelled** (-ld), **ŭntrănslā'table** (*or* -z-; *or* -trah-), **ŭntrănspôr'table** (*or* -trah-), *adjs.* See UN-^{2} 1.
ŭntră'velled, *-eled, (-*e*ld) *a.* That has not travelled; that has not been travelled over or through. [f. UN-^{2} 1; see TRAVEL]
ŭntrī'ed (-ī'd) *a.* Not tried or tested, inexperienced; not tried by a judge. [f. UN-^{2} 1 + TRIED]
ŭntrŏ'dden *a.* See UN-^{2} 1.
ŭntrou'bled (-rŭ'b*e*ld) *a.* Not troubled; calm, tranquil. [ME, f. UN-^{2} 1; see TROUBLE]
ŭntrue' (-o͞o') *a.* Not true; contrary to what is the fact; not faithful or loyal (*to*); deviating from accepted standard; hence **ŭntru'**LY^2 (-o͞o'-) *adv.* [OE *untrēowe* etc. (as UN-^{2}, TRUE)]
ŭntrŭ'ss *v.t.*, see UN-^{1} 1; **ŭntrŭ'ssed** (-st), **ŭntrŭ'stworthȳ** (-ẽrdhĭ), *adjs.*, UN-^{2} 1.
ŭntru'th (-o͞o'-) *n.* (*pl. pr.* -dhz *or* -ths). Being untrue; false statement (*told me an untruth*). [OE *untrēowth* etc. (as UN-^{2} 2, TRUTH)]
ŭntru'thful (-o͞o'-) *a.*, see UN-^{2} 1; **ŭntŭ'ck** *v.t.*, UN-^{1} 1; **ŭntū'ned** (-nd), **ŭntū'neful** (-nf-), **ŭntûr'ned** (-nd), **ŭntū'tored** (-*erd*), *adjs.*, UN-^{2} 1; **ŭntwī'ne, ŭntwĭ'st,** *vbs. t.* & *i.*, UN-^{1} 1;
ŭnū'sed (-zd *or* -st) *a.*, UN-^{2} 1.
ŭnū'sual (-zho͞o*a*l) *a.* Not usual; exceptional, remarkable; hence ~LY^2 *adv.*, ~NESS *n.* [f. UN-^{2} 1 + USUAL]
ŭnŭ'tterab|le *a.* Inexpressible; beyond description (*unutterable torment, joy, fool*); hence ~LY^2 *adv.* [f. UN-^{2} 1 + UTTER^2 + -ABLE]
ŭnŭ'ttered (-*erd*), **ŭnvă'ccĭnātėd** (-ks-), *adjs.* See UN-^{2} 1.
ŭnvă'lūed (-ūd) *a.* Not regarded as valuable. [f. UN-^{2} 1; see VALUE]
ŭnvâr'ĭed (-ĭd) *a.* See UN-^{2} 1.
ŭnvâr'nĭshed (-sht) *a.* Not varnished; (fig., of statement or person) plain and straightforward. [f. UN-^{2} 1; see VARNISH]
ŭnvâr'ȳĭng *a.* See UN-^{2} 1.
ŭnvei'l (-ā'l) *v.* **1.** *v.t.* Remove veil from; remove concealing drapery from (statue etc.) as part of ceremony of first public display; (fig.) disclose, reveal, make publicly known. **2.** *v.i.* Remove one's veil. [f. UN-^{1} 2 + VEIL]
ŭnvĕ'ntĭlātėd, ŭnvĕ'rĭfīable, ŭnvĕ'rĭfīed (-īd), *adjs.* See UN-^{2} 1.
ŭnvẽr'sed (-st) *a.* Not versed or experienced (*in*). [f. UN-^{2} 1 + VERSED^1]
ŭnvī'olātėd, ŭnvĭ'sĭtėd (-z-), **ŭnvĭ'tĭātėd** (-shĭ-), *adjs.* See UN-^{2} 1.
ŭnvoi'ced (-st) *a.* Not spoken; (Phonet.) not voiced. [f. UN-^{2} 1; see VOICE]
ŭnwa'ntėd (-ŏ'-), **ŭnwar'līke** (-ôr'-), **ŭnwar'med** (-ôr'md), *adjs.* See UN-^{2} 1.
ŭnwa'rrantab|le (-wŏ'-) *a.* Indefensible, unjustifiable; hence **~le**NESS (-b*e*ln-) *n.*, ~LY^2 *adv.* [f. UN-^{2} 1; see WARRANTABLE]
ŭnwa'rrantėd (-wŏ'-) *a.* Unauthorized; unjustified. [f. UN-^{2} 1; see WARRANT^2]
ŭnwâr'ȳ *a.* See UN-^{2} 1.
ŭnwa'shed (-ŏ'sht) *a.* Not washed; not usually washed or clean (**the great ~**, the rabble). [f. UN-^{2} 1; see WASH^1]
ŭnwa'tched (-ŏ'cht), **ŭnwa'tchful** (-ŏ'-), **ŭnwa'tered** (-aw't*erd*), **ŭnwā'verĭng, ŭnwea'ned** (-nd), **ŭnwear'able** (-âr'-), **ŭnwear'ĭed** (-ĭd), **ŭnwear'ȳ, ŭnwear'ȳĭng,** *adjs.*, see UN-^{2} 1; **ŭnwea've** *v.t.*, UN-^{1} 1; **ŭnwĕ'd, ŭnwĕ'ddėd, ŭnwee'dėd, ŭnwei'ghed** (-ā'd), **ŭnwĕ'lcome,** *adjs.*, UN-^{2} 1.
ŭnwĕ'll *a.* Not in good health; (somewhat) ill. [ME, f. UN-^{2} 1 + WELL^3]
ŭnwĕ'pt *a.* Not wept (for). [f. UN-^{2} 1 + WEPT]
ŭnwĕ'ttėd, ŭnwhĭ'pped (-pt), **ŭnwhī'tened** (-nd), **ŭnwhō'lesome** (ŭnhō'ls-), *adjs.* See UN-^{2} 1.
ŭnwie'ld|ȳ *a.* Slow or clumsy of movement, difficult to use or manage, owing to size or weight or shape; hence **~ĭ**LY^2 *adv.*, **~ĭ**NESS *n.* [ME, f. UN-^{2} + (now dial.) *wieldy* active f. WIELD + -Y^2]
ŭnwĭ'llĭng *a.* Not willing or inclined (*to* do, *for* thing, *for* thing *to* be done, *that*, or abs.); hence ~LY^2 *adv.*, ~NESS *n.* [OE *unwillende* (as UN-^{2}, WILLING^2)]
ŭnwī'nd *v.t.* & *i.* (**unwou'nd**). (Cause to) become drawn out at length after having been wound; (colloq.) relax. [ME, f. UN-^{1} 1 + WIND^3]
ŭnwĭ'nkĭng *a.* Not winking; watchful, vigilant; hence ~LY^2 *adv.* [f. UN-^{2} 1; see WINK]
ŭnwĭ'sdom (-z-) *n.* Being unwise; folly; imprudence. [OE *unwīsdōm* (as UN-^{2} 2, WISDOM)]
ŭnwī'se (-z) *a.* Foolish, imprudent; injudicious; hence ~LY^2 (-zlĭ) *adv.* [OE *unwīs* (as UN-^{2}, WISE^1)]
ŭnwĭ'shed (-sht) *a.* Not wished for or *for.* [f. UN-^{2} 1; see WISH]

For other words in *un-* see UN-, UN-^{1}, UN-^{2}.

ŭnwĭ'thered (-dherd), **ŭnwĭ'tnėssed** (-st), *adjs.* See UN-² 1.
ŭnwĭ'ttĭng *a.* Not aware or conscious; unintentional; hence ~LY² *adv.* [OE *unwitende* (as UN-², WIT¹, -ING²)]
ŭnwo'manlў (-wŏŏ'-), **ŭnwō'ntėd, ŭnwŏŏ'dėd, ŭnwŏŏ'ed** (-ŏŏ'd), **ŭnwor'kable** (-ér'-), **ŭnwor'ked** (-ér'kt), **ŭnwor'kmanlike** (-ér'-), *adjs.* See UN-² 1.
ŭnwor'ldl|ў (-ér'-) *a.* Not worldly; spiritually-minded; hence ~**ĭ**NESS *n.* [f. UN-² 1 + WORLDLY]
ŭnwōr'n *a.* That has not been worn or impaired by wear. [f. UN-² 1 + WORN]
ŭnwor'shĭpped (-ér'shĭpt) *a.* See UN-² 1.
ŭnwor'th|ў (-ér'dhĭ) *a.* Not worthy or befitting the character (*of*); discreditable, unseemly; contemptible, base; hence ~**ĭ**LY² *adv.*, ~**ĭ**NESS *n.* [ME, f. UN-² 1 + WORTHY]
ŭnwou'nd, ŭnwou'ndėd (-ŏŏ'-), **ŭnwō'ven,** *adjs.*, see UN-² 1; **ŭnwră'p** (ŭnr-) *v.t.*, UN-¹ 1; **ŭnwrĭ'nkled** (ŭnrĭ'ngkeld), **ŭnwrī'table** (ŭnr-), *adjs.*, UN-² 1.
ŭnwrĭ'tten (ŭnr-) *a.* Not written; (of law etc.) resting originally on custom or judicial decision, not on statute. [ME, f. UN-² 1 + WRITTEN]
ŭnwrou'ght (ŭnraw't), **ŭnwrŭ'ng** (ŭnr-), *adjs.* See UN-² 1.
ŭnyie'ldĭng *a.* Not yielding to pressure etc.; hence ~LY² *adv.*, ~NESS *n.* [f. UN-² 1; see YIELD]
ŭnyō'ke, ŭnzĭ'p, *vbs. t.* See UN-¹ 1.
ŭp *adv., prep., a., n.,* & *v.* (**upp-**). **1.** *adv.* To or in high(er) place, position, degree, amount, value, etc., ||to or in capital or university, to or in place farther north or otherwise regarded as high(er), (*bird flew up to the eaves*; *high up in the air*; *what is he doing up there?*; *lives four floors up*; *a few feet farther up*; *flames mount up, total mounts up*; *tide is coming up*; *water came up to his chin*; *roll your sleeves up*; *lift up your head*; *up in Scotland, up to Scotland from London, up to London* or *town from the country*; *is high up in the school*; *went up three places in class*); to earlier time; towards source of river; inland; (of jockey) in the saddle; (of sword, arch.) in scabbard; (of points etc. in game) registered on score-board, forming total score for the time being, constituting one player's or team's lead over another, (of player etc.) holding such lead; before magistrate etc. (*was had up* or *brought up for speeding*); in position of gain (*£5 up on the transaction*); at or to high(er) price (*meat is up, has gone up, this week*; *prices $3 and up*); (of theatre-curtain) raised etc. to reveal stage; ALL-*-up*. **2.** To the place or time in question or in which the speaker etc. is (*child came up and asked me the time*; *went straight up to the door*; *all the time up till now*; *sure to* TURN¹ *up late*). **3.** To or in erect or vertical or inflated position (lit. or fig.) esp. as favourable to activity, out of bed or from lying or sitting or kneeling posture, in(to) condition of efficiency or activity, (*sprang up from his seat*; *stand up*; *turn your collar up*; *put your umbrella up*; *pump up the tyres*; *was (already) up early this morning*; *was (still) up late last night*; *must be up and doing*; *matter is up for discussion*; *house is up for sale*; *stir up sedition*; *screw up your courage*; *wind up your watch*; *radio takes a long time to warm up*); (as *int.*) get, stand, etc., up (**up with you,** get up; **up with it,** put it up; *up with the revolution!*); instructed (*is well up in mathematics*); advanced (*is up with the leaders*); (of ship's helm) with rudder to leeward; in rebellion (*up in* ARM²*s*); (of hunt etc.) in progress; (of sun etc.) having risen; (of road etc.) with surface broken or removed during repairs; *up and* ABOUT; *his* BLOOD¹ *is up*; **something is up,** something unusual is happening; **what's up?** what is going on? what is the matter? **4.** (Expr. complete or effectual result etc.; *eat, drink, burn, dry, tear, use, up*; *sawn up into logs*); into compact or accumulated state (*pack, bind, store, save, up*); securely (*lock, chain, tie, fasten, fix, nail, seal, up*); *the* GAME¹ *is up*; **time is up,** allowance of time is exhausted; CHEER², CLEAR², FOLLOW, HUNT¹, HURRY², SPEAK, WASH¹, *up*; HARD *up*; **it is all up with him,** his case is hopeless. **5.** See BEAR³ *up*, BRING *up*, COME *up*, GET¹ *up*, GIVE¹ *up*, GO¹ *up*, KEEP¹ *up*, MAKE¹ *up*, PUT¹ *up*, RUN¹ *up*, SEND¹ *up*, SET¹ *up*, TURN¹ *up*. **6. Up against,** close to, in(to) contact with, (colloq.) confronted with (*up against a problem*); *up against it*, in great difficulties; **up and down,** (fig.) to and fro (*marching up and down*), in every direction (*have looked for it up and down*); **up to,** until (*up to the present*), not exceeding in number (*can take up to six guests*), less than or equal to (*sums up to £5*), comparable with (*not up to your usual standard*), incumbent on (*it is up to us to do something*), capable of or fit for (*am not up to walking 20 miles*), *up to* DATE², ||*up to the* KNOCKER, *up to the* MARK¹, *up to the* MINUTE¹, *up to* SNUFF¹, *up to* one's or person's TRICK*s*. **7.** *prep.* Upwards along, through, or into, from bottom to top of, (*climbed up the ladder, up the hill*; *smoke goes up chimney*); towards source of (river); along (*walk up the street*); **up and down,** (fig.) to and fro along; **up hill and down dale,** up and down in every direction, taking the country or (fig.) the situation as it comes; **up stage,** at or to back of theatre stage. **8.** At or in a higher part of (*lives farther up the road*; *somewhere up the river*; *some dust up my nose*; *sitting up a tree*); *up the* POLE¹; *up the* SPOUT. **9.** *a.* Directed upwards; **up beat, draught, grade, platform, -stroke, train** (in senses opposite to those of DOWN⁵); **up-and-coming,** (colloq.) enterprising, alert, and likely to succeed; **up-and-over,** (of door etc.) opened by being raised and turned into horizontal position. **10.** *n.* **On the up-and-up,** (colloq.) (1) steadily improving, (2) on the level, honest(ly); **ups and downs,** rises and falls, undulating ground, alternately good and bad fortune. **11.** *v.i.* (colloq.) Start up, begin abruptly to say or do something (*he ups and says*); ~ **with,** raise, pick up, (*he upped* (or *up*) *with his fist, with his stick*). **12.** *v.t.* (colloq.) Raise, esp. abruptly. [OE *up(p)*, *uppe*, = OS *up(pa)*, ON *upp(i)*, rel. to OHG *ūf*]
ŭp- *pref.* **1.** As *adv.* to *vbs.* & vbl derivs., = prec. 1, 3: **upbear',** (arch.) sustain aloft; **u'pheaped,** accumulated, piled up; **uphea've,** lift forcibly; **uprai'se,** raise to higher level; **upri'se,** rise (to standing position, to higher level etc.). **2.** As *prep.* to *ns.*, forming *adjs.* & *advs.*, = prec. 7, 8; **up-country,** towards the interior, inland; **u'pfield,** in or to a position farther along a football etc. field. **3.** As *a.* to *ns.*, = prec. 9: UPBEAT, UPLAND; **up-stroke** (see UP 9). [OE *up(p)*-, = MDu. *op*-, OS *up*-, OHG *ūf*-, ON *upp*-, = UP]
U.P. *abbr.* (sl.) = UP 4 (*it is all U.P. with him*); Uttar Pradesh (formerly United Provinces), India.
Upă'nĭshăd (ŏŏ-) *n.* Each of a series of philosophical compositions concluding exposition of the Vedas. [Skr. (*upa* near, *ni-shad* sit down)]
ū'pas *n.* ~(**-tree**), (Bot.) Javanese tree yielding milky sap used as arrow-poison, (Myth.) Javanese tree thought to be fatal to whatever came near it, (fig.) pernicious influence, practice, etc.; poisonous sap of upas and other trees. [Malay *ūpas* poison]
ŭ'pbeat *a.* Optimistic, cheerful. [f. UP- 3 + BEAT²]

For other words in *up-* see UP-

ŭpbrai'd *v.t.* Chide, reproach (person etc. *with* or *for* fault etc., or abs.); hence ~ING[1] *n.* [OE UP(*brēdan* = *bregdan* BRAID[2] in obs. sense 'brandish')]

ŭ'pbrĭngĭng *n.* Bringing up (of child), education. [f. obs. *upbring* to rear (UP- 1, BRING) + -ING[1]]

ŭpca'st[1] (-ah'-) *v.t.* (**upca'st**). Cast up. [ME, f. UP- 1 + CAST[1]]

ŭ'pcast[2] (-ah-) *n.* Casting up, upward throw; (Mining) shaft through which air leaves a mine; (Geol.) = UPTHROW. [f. UP- 1 + CAST[2]]

ŭpdā'te *v.t.* Bring up to date. [f. UP- 1 + DATE[3]]

ŭp-ĕ'nd *v.t.* & *i.* Set or rise up on end. [f. UP- 1 + END[2]]

ŭpgrā'de *v.t.* Raise in rank etc. [f. UP- 1 + GRADE]

ŭ'pgrowth (-ōth) *n.* Process or result of growing upwards. [f. UP- 1 + GROWTH]

ŭphea'val (ŭp-h-) *n.* Heaving up; (Geol.) upward displacement of part of earth's crust; (fig.) violent social etc. change. [f. UP*heave* + -AL 2]

ŭphĭll (ŭp-h-) *n.*, *a.*, & *adv.* **1.** *n.* (ŭ'-). Upward slope. **2.** *a.* (ŭ'-). Sloping up, ascending, (fig.) arduous, difficult, (*uphill work*). **3.** *adv.* (-ĭ'l). In ascending direction, on an upward slope. [f. UP- 2 + HILL]

ŭphō'ld (ŭp-h-) *v.t.* (**uphe'ld**). Hold up, keep erect, support; give support or countenance to (person, practice, etc.); maintain, confirm, (decision, verdict). [ME, f. UP- 1 + HOLD[1]]

ŭphō'lder (ŭp-h-) *n.* In vbl senses; (as guild--name) upholsterer. [ME, f. prec. + -ER[1]]

ŭphō'lster (ŭp-h-) *v.t.* Furnish (room etc.) with hangings, carpets, furniture, etc.; provide (chair etc.) with textile covering, padding, springs, etc., cover (chair etc. *with* or *in* tapestry etc.); **well-~ed,** (joc., of person) fat. [back form. f. foll.]

ŭphō'lsterer (ŭp-h-) *n.* One whose trade it is to upholster; **~-bee** (that furnishes its nest with cut leaves etc.); so **ŭphō'lst**ERY (1, 2) (ŭp-h-) *n.* [f. obs. *upholster* n. f. UPHOLD (in obs. sense 'keep in repair') + -STER, + -ER[1]]

ū'phrōe *n.* (Naut.) Long wooden block with holes through which ropes of crowfoot are rove. [f. Du. *juffrouw* young lady, (Naut.) dead-eye (*jong* young, *vrouw* woman)]

ŭ'pkeep *n.* (Cost or means of) maintenance in good condition. [f. UP- 1 + KEEP[1]]

ŭ'plănd *n.* & *a.* (Of) higher or inland parts of a country. [f. UP- 3 + LAND[1]]

ŭplĭ'ft[1] *v.t.* Raise (in rank, moral elevation, etc.; one's voice in praise etc.). [ME, f. UP- 1 + LIFT]

ŭ'plĭft[2] *n.* Being raised; (colloq.) morally or intellectually elevating influence. [f. UP- 1 + LIFT 4]

ŭ'pmōst. See UPPERMOST.

upŏ'n *prep.* (more formal, but usu. idiomatically interchangeable with) ON[1]; idiomatic preferences are *once upon a time*; *upon my word*; *on the whole*; *tier upon tier of seats*; *fell upon him unawares*; *had him on toast*; *came at once on receiving your message*; *take it on trust*; *will go on the chance*; *went on the spree*; *thrown upon his own resources*. [ME, f. UP + ON[1], after ON *upp á*]

ŭ'pper *attrib. a.*, & *n.* **1.** *a.* Higher in place, situated above another part, (*upper lip*, *arm*, *atmosphere*, *circle* in theatre, *Jurassic*, etc.), situated on higher land (*Upper Egypt*); *upper* CASE[2]; **~-cut** *n.*, & *v.t.*, (hit with) blow delivered upwards with arm bent; *have* or *get* or *gain* **the ~ hand,** mastery, control, dominance; *upper* JAW; *upper* PARTIALS; **~ regions,** the sky, heaven; *upper* STOREY; **~ works,** part of ship that is above water when laden for voyage. **2.** Higher in rank, dignity, etc., (*the upper class*, *servants*); **the U~ Bench,** (Hist.) King's BENCH during Commonwealth in England; **the U~ House,** (in legislature, esp.) House of Lords; **the ~ ten (thousand)**, (colloq.) **the ~ crust,** the aristocracy, the highest social group. **3.** *n.* Part of boot or shoe above sole; **on** one's **~s,** in financial difficulties. [ME, f. UP 9 + -ER[3]]

ŭ'ppermōst *a.* & *adv.* **1.** (*or* **ŭ'pmōst**) *a.* Highest in place or rank. **2.** *adv.* On or to the top or front or most prominent position (lit. or fig.). [ME, f. prec. + -MOST]

ŭ'ppĭsh *a.* Self-assertive; putting on airs; hence ~LY[2] *adv.*, ~NESS *n.* [f. UP + -ISH[1]]

ŭ'ppĭty̆ *a.* (colloq.) Arrogant, snobbish. [fanciful f. UP]

ŭ'prīght (-rīt; *or* ŭprī't in pred. use) *a.* & *n.* **1.** *a.* Erect, vertical, (*an upright post*, *posture*; *stood upright*; *set it upright*); (of book, picture, etc.) greater in height than breadth; **~ piano** (with vertical strings). **2.** Righteous, strictly honourable or honest; hence ~LY[2] *adv.*, ~NESS *n.* **3.** *n.* Post or rod fixed upright esp. as support to some structure; upright piano. [OE UP(*riht* RIGHT[1])]

ŭprī'sĭng (-z-) *n.* Insurrection; (arch.) rising from bed. [ME, f. UP- 1 + RISING[1]]

ŭ'proar *n.* Tumult, violent disturbance, clamour; hence **ŭproar'**IOUS *a.* (often of laughter, high spirits, etc.). [f. Du. *oproer* (*op* up, *roer* confusion), assoc. w. ROAR]

ŭproo̅'t *v.t.* Pull from ground etc. together with roots; (fig.) eradicate, destroy. [f. UP- 1 + ROOT[2]]

ŭ'prŭsh *n.* Upward rush, (esp., Psych.) from the subconscious. [f. UP- 1 + RUSH[2] 7]

ups-a-daisy. Var. of UPSY-DAISY.

ŭpsĕ't[1] *v.* (**upse't**). **1.** *v.t.* & *i.* Overturn, be overturned, (*carriage* (*was*) *upset*). **2.** *v.t.* Disturb composure or temper or digestion of (*the news quite upset him*; *ate something that upset him*). **3.** Shorten and thicken (metal, esp. tire) by hammering or pressure. [f. UP- 1 + SET[1]]

ŭ'psĕt[2] *n.* & *a.* **1.** *n.* Upsetting or being upset (*stomach upset*); surprising result in game etc. **2.** *a.* **~ price,** lowest acceptable selling price of property in auction etc., reserve price. [f. UP- 1 + SET[2]]

ŭ'pshŏt *n.* Final issue, conclusion; general effect, the long and the short, (*of* a matter). [f. UP- 1 + SHOT[1]]

ŭpsīde-dow'n *adv.* & *a.* With the upper part under, with top where bottom should be, inverted; in total disorder (*everything was turned upside-down*). [ME, orig. *up so down*, perh. = 'up as if down']

||**ŭpsī'des** (-dz) *adv.* (colloq.) **~ with,** equal with (person) by retaliation etc. [f. *upside* = top part (UP- 3, SIDE[1]) + -S[3]]

ŭpsi'lon *n.* Twentieth Greek letter (Υ, υ) = u. [Gk, = slender U (*psilos* slender), w. ref. to its later coincidence in sound with Gk *oi*]

ŭpstā'ge *a.*, *adv.*, & *v.t.* **1.** *a.* & *adv.* Nearer back of theatre stage; (fig.) snobbish(ly). **2.** *v.t.* Move upstage from (actor) to make him face away from audience, (fig.) divert attention from (person) to oneself, put at a disadvantage, outshine. [f. UP- 2 + STAGE[1]; cf. UP 7]

ŭpstair's *adv.* & *n.*, **ŭ'pstair(s)** *a.*, (-z). Up the stairs; (to, on, of) upper floor of house etc.; KICK[2] person *upstairs*. [f. UP- 2 + STAIR]

ŭpstă'ndĭng *a.* Standing up; well set up; honest, straightforward. [ME, f. UP- 1 + STANDING[2]]

ŭ'pstârt *n.* & *a.* (Person) who has risen suddenly from humble position; (person) who assumes arrogant tone. [f. UP- 1 + START[1]]

***ŭ'pstāte** *a.*, *adv.*, & *n.* (Pertaining to, in) part of state remote from large cities, esp. northern part. [f. UP- 2 + STATE[1]]

ŭ'pstream *a.* & *adv.* In the direction opposite to that in which a stream or river flows. [f. UP- 2 + STREAM]

ŭ'psûrge *n.* Upward surge, rise. [f. UP 1 + SURGE]

ŭ'pswĕpt *a.* (Of hair) combed up and arranged on top of head; curved or sloped upwards. [f. UP- 1 + SWEPT]

ŭ'pswĭng *n.* Upward movement or trend. [f. UP- 1 + SWING]

ŭ'psȳ-daisȳ (-zĭ) *int.* expr. encouragement to child rising after fall or being lifted. [f. earlier *up-a-daisy* f. UP; cf. LACKADAISICAL]

ŭ'ptāke *n.* Lifting; understanding, apprehension, (*quick in* or *on the uptake*). [f. UP- 1 + TAKE²]

ŭ'pthrow (-ō) *n.* Throwing upwards; (Geol.) upward dislocation of strata. [f. UP- 1 + THROW²]

ŭ'pthrŭst *n.* Upward thrust, e.g. of fluid on immersed body; (Geol.) = UPHEAVAL. [f. UP- 1 + THRUST]

ŭptī'ght (-ī't; *or* ŭ'-) *a.* (colloq.) Nervously tense; angry. [f. UP- 1 + TIGHT]

ŭ'ptown *a.* & *n.* (Pertaining to, in) higher or *residential part of town or city. [f. UP- 2 + TOWN]

ŭptûr'n¹ *v.t.* Turn upwards; turn up (ground in ploughing etc.); (in *p.p.*) turned upside-down. [f. UP- 1 + TURN¹]

ŭ'ptûrn² *n.* Upheaval; improvement, upward trend. [f. UP- 1 + TURN²]

U.P.U. *abbr.* Universal Postal Union.

ŭ'pward *a.* & *adv.*, **ŭ'pward|s** (-z) *adv.* **1.** (Moving, extending, pointing, leading) towards what is higher, superior, more important, larger in amount, or earlier; hence ~LY² *adv.* **2.** ~(s) **of,** more than (*found upward(s) of 40 specimens*). [OE *upweard(es)* (as UP, -WARD(s))]

ŭ'pwarp (-ôrp) *n.* (Geol.) Broad surface elevation, anticline. [f. UP- 1 + WARP²]

ŭ'pwĭnd *a.* & *adv.* In the direction opposite to that in which the wind is blowing. [f. UP- 2 + WIND¹]

ur- (oor) *pref.* Primitive, original, earliest. [G]

ūr'acĭl *n.* (Chem.) Crystalline compound formed by hydrolysis of RNA. [f. UREA + ACETIC + -IL]

ūrae'm|ĭa, *-ē'm|ĭa, *n.* (Path.) Morbid condition due to presence in blood of urinary matter normally eliminated by kidneys; hence ~IC *a.* [f. Gk *ouron* urine + *haima* blood; see -AEMIA]

ūrae'us *n.* Serpent (emblem of power) as represented on head-dress of Egyptian divinities and sovereigns. [mod. L, f. Gk *ouraios*, repr. the Egypt. wd for 'cobra']

Ural-Altā'ic (ūr*al*-ăl-) *a.* Of (the people of) the *Ural* and *Altaic* mountain ranges; (Philol.) of a family of Finno-Ugric, Turkic, Mongolian, and other agglutinative languages of N. Europe and Asia.

ūr'anĭsm *n.* Homosexuality, esp. of males. [f. G *uranismus* f. Gk *ouranios* heavenly, taken as 'spiritual'; see -ISM]

ūrā'nĭum *n.* Radioactive grey heavy metallic element, capable of nuclear fission and hence used as a source of nuclear energy; hence **ūră'n**IC, **ūr'an**OUS, *adjs.* [mod. L, f. URANUS + -IUM; cf. *tellurium*]

ūrano-¹ *comb. form.* The heavens, as: **~graphy** (-ŏ'g-), descriptive astronomy; **~metry** (-ŏ'm-), measurement of stellar distances, map showing positions and magnitudes of stars. [f. Gk *ouranos* heaven(s) + -O-]

ūrano-² *comb. form.* Uranium. [f. URANIUM + -O-]

Ur'anus (ūr'-; *or* ūrā'n-) *n.* Planet discovered by Herschel in 1781, outermost of solar system except Neptune and Pluto. [L, f. Gk *Ouranos* heaven, Uranus, in Gk Myth. the son of Gaea (Earth) and father of Kronos (Saturn), the Titans, etc.]

ūr'āte. See URIC.

ūr'ban *a.* Of, living or situated in, a city or town (*urban districts, population*; opp. *rural*); ‖~ **district,** (Hist.) group of urban communities governed by elected council; ~ **guerrilla** (operating in towns by kidnapping etc.); *~ **renewal,** slum clearance; ~ **sprawl,** uncontrolled expansion of urban areas. [f. L *urbanus* (*urbs urbis* city; see -AN)]

ūrbā'ne *a.* Courteous, suave, elegant or refined in manner; hence ~LY² (-nlĭ) *adv.* [f. F *urbain* or f. L *urbanus* (see prec.)]

ūr'ban|ĭsm *n.* Urban character; study of urban life, whence ~IST (3) *n.* [f. URBAN + -ISM]

ūr'banīte *n.* Dweller in city or town. [f. URBAN + -ITE¹]

ūrbă'nĭtȳ *n.* Courtesy, polished manners; urban life. [f. F *urbanité* or f. L *urbanitas* (as URBAN; see -ITY)]

ūr'banīz|e, -īs|e (-īz), *v.t.* Make urban; remove rural character of (district); hence ~A'TION *n.* [f. F *urbaniser* (as URBAN; see -IZE)]

ūr'ceolate *a.* (Bot.) Pitcher-shaped, with large body and small mouth. [f. L *urceolus* dim. of *urceus* pitcher + -ATE²]

ūr'chĭn *n.* **1.** Roguish or mischievous boy; boy, youngster; ~ **cut,** cut-short hair-style for women. **2.** = SEA-*urchin*; (arch.) hedgehog, goblin. [ME *hirchon, urcheon* f. ONF *herichon*, OF *heriçon* f. Rom. **hericio* f. L (*h*)*ericius* hedgehog]

Ur'du (oor'dōō) *n.* Indic language, allied to Hindi but with large admixture of Persian, and usu. written in Persian script, an official language of Pakistan. [f. Hind. (*zabān i*) *urdū* (language of the) camp, f. Pers. *urdū* f. Turki *ordū* (see HORDE)]

-ure *suf.* forming *ns.* w. sense (1) (result of) action or process (*composure, enclosure, failure, figure, scripture, seizure*), (2) function, state, rank, dignity, office, (*judicature, prefecture*), (3) collective body of agents (*legislature*), (4) that by which the action is effected (*closure, ligature*). [f. or after OF *-ure* f. L *-ura*]

ūr'ėa (*or* -ĭ'a) *n.* (Chem.) Soluble colourless crystalline compound contained esp. in urine of mammals. [mod. L, f. F *urée* f. Gk *ouron* urine]

-ūrĕt *suf.* (Chem.) forming names of binary compounds, now for the most part replaced by -IDE. [f. mod. L *-uretum* first applied to F wds in *-ure*]

ūrē'ter *n.* Duct by which urine passes from kidney to bladder or cloaca; hence ~AL, **ūrētĕ'r**IC, *adjs.*, ~I'TIS, **~ŏ'**TOMY, *ns.* [f. F *uretère* or mod. L *ureter* f. Gk *ourētēr* (*oureō* urinate)]

ūrĕ'thāne (*or* ūr'-) *n.* (Chem.) Crystalline amide, ethyl carbamate. [f. F *uréthane* (as UREA, ETHANE)]

ūrē'thr|a *n.* (*pl.* **~ae** *or* **~as**). Duct by which urine is discharged from bladder; hence ~AL *a.*, ~I'TIS, **~ŏ'**TOMY, *ns.* [LL, f. Gk *ourēthra* (as URETER)]

ūrge *v.t.*, & *n.* **1.** *v.t.* Drive forcibly, impel, hasten, cause to proceed with effort, (*urged his horse forward; urged him on; urged our flight northwards*); entreat earnestly or persistently (*urge him to action, to take steps, his going, that he should go*); advocate (measure etc.) pressingly (*on* or *upon* person); ply (person etc.) hard with argument or entreaty; dwell earnestly or emphatically upon, esp. as reason or justification, (*urged his youth, the difficulty of getting supplies; argument was urged in vain*). **2.** *n.* Urging impulse or tendency; yearning. [f. L *urgēre* press, drive]

For other words in *up-* see UP-.

ûr'g|ent *a.* Pressing, calling for immediate action or decision or attention, (*am in urgent need*; *the matter is urgent*; *an urgent demand*); importunate, earnest and persistent in demand; hence ~ENCY *n.*, ~**ent**LY[2] *adv.* [ME f. F (as prec.; see -ENT)]

U.R.I. *abbr.* upper respiratory infection.

-ûr'ĭa *suf.* forming *ns.* denoting that a substance is (excessively) present in the urine (*albuminuria*, *pyuria*). [mod. L, f. Gk *-ouria* (as URINE; see -IA[1])]

ûr'ic *a.* Of urine; ~ **acid** (found in small quantities in healthy urine of man and mammals, chief constituent in that of birds and reptiles); hence **ûr'**ATE[1] (3) *n.* [f. F *urique* (as URINE; see -IC)]

-ûr'ĭent *suf.* forming *adjs.* w. sense 'desiring (to do something)' (*esurient*). [f. L *-urient-* part. st. of desiderative vbs.; see -ENT]

ûr'ĭm *n.* ~ **and thummim,** objects of now unknown nature worn in or on breastplate of Jewish high priest (Exod. 28:30). [Heb. *'ûrîm* pl. of *'ôr* a light, *tummîm* pl. of *tōm* completeness]

ûr'ĭnal (*or* -ī'-) *n.* Vessel or receptacle for use in urination, e.g. by invalid in bed; structure containing such receptacles. [ME f. OF, f. LL *urinal* neut. (as n.) of *urinalis* (as URINE; see -AL)]

ūrĭnă'lȳs|ĭs *n.* (*pl.* ~**es** *pr.* -ēz). Chemical analysis of urine esp. for diagnostic purposes. [f. URINE + ANALYSIS]

ûr'ĭnarȳ *a.* Of or relating to urine (*urinary organs*, *diseases*). [f. med. L **urinarius* (as URINE; see -ARY[1])]

ûr'ĭn|āte *v.i.* Discharge urine; hence ~A'TION *n.* [f. med. L *urinare* (as foll.) + -ATE[3]]

ûr'ĭn|e *n.* Pale-yellow fluid secreted from the blood by the kidneys and (in man and higher animals) stored in bladder and discharged at intervals through urethra; hence ~OUS *a.* [ME f. OF, f. L *urina*]

ûrn *n.*, & *v.t.* **1.** *n.* Vase with foot and usu. with rounded body, esp. as used for storing the ashes of the cremated dead or as vessel or measure; (poet.) anything in which dead body or its remains are preserved, e.g. grave. **2.** Large vessel with tap, in which tea, coffee, etc., is made or kept hot. **3.** ~**-flower,** S. Amer. bulbous plant of genus *Urceolina*, with yellow and green urn-shaped flower. **4.** Hence ~'FUL 2 *n.* **5.** *v.t.* Enclose in urn. [ME, f. L *urna*, rel. to *urceus* pitcher]

ûr'nĭng *n.* Homosexual (usu. male). [G, f. *Urania*; cf. URANISM]

ûr'o-[1] *comb. form.* Urine, as: ~**ge'nĭtal,** pertaining to urinary and genital products or organs; ~**logy** (-ŏ'l-), study of urinary system. [f. Gk *ouron* urine + -O-]

ûr'o-[2] *comb. form.* Tail, as: ~**chord,** notochord of tunicate; ~**dele** [f. Gk *dēlos* evident], amphibian with adult tail, e.g. newt; ~**py'gium,** rump of bird. [f. Gk *oura* tail + -O-]

Ur'sa (ẽr'-) *n.* ~ **Major, Minor,** Great, Little, BEAR[1]. [L, = (she-)bear]

ûr'sīne *a.* Of or like a bear. [f. L *ursinus* (*ursus* bear; see -INE[1])]

Ur'sūlīne (ẽr'-) *a.* & *n.* (Nun) of an order founded by St. Angela in 1537 for nursing the sick and teaching girls. [f. St. *Ursula*, founder's patron saint, + -INE[1]]

ûrtĭcâr'ĭa *n.* (Path.) Nettle-rash. [mod. L, f. L *urtica* nettle (*urere* burn)]

ûr'tĭc|āte *v.t.* Sting like a nettle; so ~A'TION *n.* [f. med. L *urticare* (L *urtica*; see prec.) + -ATE[3]]

ûr'us *n.* = AUROCHS 1. [L, f. Gmc **ūrus*]

us. See WE.

U.S. *abbr.* United States (of America); unserviceable.

U.S.A. *abbr.* *United States Army; United States of America.

usable. See USE[2].

U.S.A.E.C. *abbr.* (Hist.) United States Atomic Energy Commission.

U.S.A.F. *abbr.* United States Air Force.

ū'sage (ū'z-) *n.* Manner of using or treating, treatment, (*met with harsh usage*; *damaged by rough usage*); habitual or customary practice esp. as creating a right or obligation or standard (*sanctified by usage*; *an ancient usage*; *contrary to the usage of the best writers*; *modern English usage*); (Law) habitual but not necessarily immemorial practice. [ME f. OF (*us* USE[1]; see -AGE)]

ū'sance (ū'z-) *n.* Time allowed by commercial usage for payment of foreign bills of exchange. [ME f. OF, f. Rom. **usantia* (**usare*; see USE[2], -ANCE)]

ūse[1] *n.* **1.** Using, employment, application to a purpose, (*should recommend the use of a saw*; *for external use only*; *put it to good use*; *is meant for use not ornament*; *has passed out of use*; *is in daily use*; *becomes easier with use*; *worn and polished with use*); **make ~ of,** employ, apply, benefit from. **2.** Right or power of using (*requested the use of the piano*; *lost the use of his left arm*). **3.** Availability, utility, purpose for which thing can be used, (*a blunt knife is of use, of no use, for this work*; *a torch will be found of* (*great*) *use*; *it is* (*of*) *no use talking* or *to talk*; *what is the use of talking?*; *talking is no use*; *find a use for banana-skins*); **have no ~ for,** be unable to find a use for, (fig.) dislike, be impatient with. **4.** Custom, familiarity, (*long use has reconciled me to it*; *use and* WONT[3]). **5.** Ritual and liturgy of a church, diocese, etc., (SARUM, *Anglican*, *Roman*, *use*). **6.** (Law). Benefit or profit of lands and tenements, esp. in the possession of another who holds them solely for the beneficiary. [ME f. OF *us*, f. L *usus* (as foll.)]

ūse[2] (ūz) *v.* **1.** *v.t.* Cause to act or serve for a purpose, handle as instrument, consume as material, exercise, put into operation, avail oneself of, (*seldom uses a knife*; *should use oil for frying*; *we seem to use a great deal of butter*; *never uses a dictionary*; *learn to use your hands, your wits*; *must use the services of an agent*; *shall use every means*; *must use your opportunities*; *use your discretion*; *should at least use some moderation*); apply (name, title, etc.) to oneself; ~ person's **name,** quote him as authority, reference, etc. **2.** Treat in specified manner (*has used me shamefully*; *how is the world using you?*). **3.** (in *past*, usu. *pr.* ūst, esp. when followed immediately by *to*; neg. **used not, did not use,** (colloq.) **use(d)n't** *pr.* ū'sent, or **didn't use**). Had as one's or its constant or frequent practice or state (*I used to take the bus, be the manager*; *does not come as often as he used* (*to*); *there used to be a law against it*). **4.** ~ **up,** consume the whole of (material etc.), find use for (remaining material etc.), exhaust, wear out e.g. with overwork. **5.** Hence **ū's**ABLE (ū'z-) *a.* [ME, f. OF *user* f. Rom. **usare* frequent. of L *uti us-* use]

ūsed *a.* **1.** (ūzd). In vbl senses; (of clothes, vehicles, etc.) second-hand. **2.** (ūst). ~ **to,** having become familiar with by habit or custom (*am not used to this sort of thing, to being called a liar*; *become used to eating horse-flesh*). [p.p. of prec.]

ū'seful (ū'sf-) *a.* **1.** Of use, serviceable, producing or able to produce good results (*to* person, *for* thing; *gave me some useful hints*); ~ **load** (carried by aircraft etc. in addition to its own weight); **make oneself ~,** perform services. **2.** (sl.) Highly creditable or efficient (*a useful performance*). **3.** Hence ~LY[2] *adv.*, ~NESS *n.* [ME, f. USE[1] + -FUL]

ū'selėss (ū'sl-) *a.* Serving no useful purpose, unavailing, (*useless erudition*; *contents were rendered useless by damp*; *protest is useless*); hence ~LY[2] *adv.*, ~NESS *n.* [f. USE[1] + -LESS]

ū'ser[1] (ū'z-) *n.* In vbl senses; drug addict. [f. USE[2] + -ER[1]]

ū'ser[2] (ū'z-) *n.* (Law). Continued use or enjoyment of a right etc.; **right of ~**, (1) right to use, (2) presumptive right arising from user. [inferred f. NON-USER]

ŭ'sher *n.*, & *v.t.* **1.** *n.* Officer or servant acting as door-keeper of court etc., showing persons to seats in public hall etc., ||or walking before person of rank, as (*gentleman usher of the*) BLACK[1] *Rod*; ||(arch. or joc.) under-teacher, assistant schoolmaster; hence ~ETTE (3) (esp. in cinema), ~SHIP, *ns.* **2.** *v.t.* Act as usher to, precede (person) as usher; announce, show *in* etc. (lit. or fig.). [ME, f, AF *usser*, OF *u(i)ssier*, var. of *huissier* f. med. L *ustiarius* for L *ostiarius* (*ostium* door; see -ARY[1], -ER[2])]

U.S.I.A., U.S.I.S., *abbrs.* United States Information Agency, Service.

U.S.N. *abbr.* United States Navy.

***U.S.O.** *abbr.* United Service Organization.

ŭ'squėbaugh (-aw) *n.* Whisky. [f. Ir. & Sc. Gael. *uisge beatha* water of life; cf. WHISKY[1]]

U.S.S. *abbr.* United States Ship; ||Universities Superannuation Scheme.

U.S.S.R. *abbr.* Union of Soviet Socialist Republics.

ū'sual (ū'zhŏŏal) *a.* Such as commonly occurs or is observed or done, customary, habitual, (*asked the usual questions*; *with his usual disregard of convention*; *the courtesy usual with him*; *it is usual to tip the waiter*; *came earlier than* (*was*) *usual*; *have forgotten something as* (*is*) *usual* or (vulg. or joc.) *as per usual*); **the ~, my ~,** (drink etc.); hence ~LY[2] *adv.*, ~NESS *n.* [ME, f. OF *usual*, *usuel* or f. LL *usualis* (as USE[1]; see -AL)]

ūsūcā'ption, ūsūcā'pĭon, (ūz-) *n.* (Law). Acquisition of title or right to property by uninterrupted and undisputed possession for prescribed term. [f. OF *usucap(t)ion* or f. L *usucap(t)io* f. *usucapere* acquire by prescription (*usu* by USE[1], *capere capt-* take); see -ION]

ū'sūfrŭct (ū'z-) *n.*, & *v.t.* **1.** *n.* Right of enjoying the use and advantages of another's property short of destruction or waste of its substance; so ~**ŪARY**[1] (-ŭ'k-) *a.* & *n.* **2.** *v.t.* Hold in usufruct. [f. med. L *usufructus* f. L *usus* (*et*) *fructus* (*usus* USE[1], *fructus* FRUIT)]

ū'surer (ū'zher-) *n.* One who lends money at exorbitant interest. [ME f. AF; OF *usureor* (*usure* f. L *usura*; see USURY)]

ūsûr'p (ūz-) *v.* **1.** *v.t.* Seize, assume, (throne, office, power, property, etc.) wrongfully. **2.** *v.i.* Encroach (*up*)*on*. **3.** Hence or cogn. ~A'TION (-zer-), ~ER[1], *ns.* [ME, f. OF *usurper* f. L *usurpare* seize for use]

ū'surў (ū'zherĭ) *n.* **1.** Practice of lending money at exorbitant interest, esp. at higher interest than is legal; hence **ūsûr'ĭ**OUS (ūz- *or* ūzh-) *a.* **2.** Such interest; (usu. fig.) interest (*the service was repaid with usury*). [ME, f. AF **usurie* or f. med. L *usuria* f. L *usura* (as USE[1]; see -URE, -Y[1])]

U.T. *abbr.* universal time.

ūtĕ'nsĭl *n.* Instrument, implement, esp. one in working or domestic use (*writing, cooking, utensils*) or in religious use. [ME, f. OF *utensile* f. med. L, neut. (as n.) of L *utensilis* usable (as USE[2]; see -IL)]

ū'terĭne *a.* Of or relating to the uterus; born of same mother but not same father (*brother, sister, uterine*). [ME, f. LL *uterinus* (as foll.; see -INE[1])]

ū'ter|us *n.* (*pl.* ~**i** *pr.* -ī). Womb; hence ~I'TIS *n.* [L]

ū'tĭle *a.* Having utility, useful. [ME f. OF, f. L *utilis* (*uti* use; see -IL)]

ūtĭlĭtār'ĭan *a.* & *n.* Of, consisting in, based on, utility; (holder) of utilitarianism. [f. UTILITY + -ARIAN]

ūtĭlĭtār'ĭanĭsm *n.* Doctrine that actions are right because they are useful; doctrine that greatest happiness of greatest number should be guiding principle of conduct. [f. prec. + -ISM]

ūtĭ'lĭtў *n.* & *a.* **1.** *n.* Usefulness, profitableness; useful thing; = PUBLIC *utility*. **2.** *a.* Made or serving for utility; severely practical and (e.g. in wartime) standardized (*utility clothes, furniture*); ~ **man,** actor of the smallest speaking parts in plays, footballer etc. who can play in various positions, *odd-job man; ~ **room** (containing large fixed domestic appliances, e.g. washing-machine); ~ **vehicle** (serving various functions). [ME, f. OF *utilité* f. L *utilitas -tatis* (as UTILE; see -ITY)]

ū'tĭlĭz|e, -ĭs|e (-īz), *v.t.* Make use of, turn to account, use; hence ~ABLE *a.*, ~A'TION *n.* [f. F *utiliser* f. It. *utilizzare* (as UTILE; see -IZE)]

-ū'tion (*or* -ōō'-) *suf.* forming *ns.* w. senses as -ATION (*solution*). [F, f. L *-u-* of vbs. in *-vere*]

uti possidetis (ūtĭpŏsĭdē'tĭs) *n.* Principle that leaves belligerents in possession of what they have acquired. [L, = as you possess]

ŭ'tmōst (*or* -ost) *a.* & *n.* **1.** *a.* Furthest, extreme, (*the utmost limits*); that is such in the highest degree (*showed the utmost reluctance*). **2.** *n.* Utmost point, degree, etc.; one's ~, all that one can do. [OE *ūt(e)mest* (as OUT, -MOST)]

Utō'pĭa (ū-) *n.* Imaginary place with perfect social and political system; ideally perfect place or state of things. [title of book by More (1516), mod. L, = nowhere, f. Gk *ou* not + *topos* place; see -IA[1]]

Utō'pĭan (ū-), **ū-,** *a.* & *n.* (Inhabitant) of Utopia; (characteristic of an) ardent but unpractical reformer, etc., whence **ūtō'pĭan**ISM (3) *n.* [f. mod. L *Utopianus* (as prec.; see -AN)]

U'trĕcht (ū'trĕkt) *n.* ~ **velvet,** mohair plush for furniture. [~ in Holland]

ū'trĭcle *n.* Small cell or sac of animal or plant, esp. one in the inner ear; hence **ūtrĭ'cūl**AR[1] *a.* [f. F *utricule* or f. L *utriculus* dim. of *uter* leather bag; see -CULE]

ŭ'tter[1] *attrib. a.* Complete, total, unqualified, (*utter misery*; *saw the utter absurdity of it*; *an utter denial*); ||~ **barrister** (junior, addressing court from outside bar within which Q.C. pleads); hence ~LY[2] *adv.*, ~MOST *a.*, ~NESS *n.* [OE *ūter(r)a*, *ūttra*, compar. adj. f. *ūt* OUT; cf. OUTER]

ŭ'tter[2] *v.t.* Emit audibly (cry, groan, sigh, etc.); express in spoken or written words (one's sentiments, a lie, the truth, etc.); put (forged bank notes, base coin, etc.) into circulation. [ME, f. MDu. *ūteren* make known, assim. to prec.]

ŭ'tterance[1] *n.* Uttering, expressing in words, (*gave utterance to his rage*); power of speech (*defective utterance*); spoken words (*his pulpit utterances*); (Ling.) spoken or written words forming complete expression of a thought. [ME, f. prec. + -ANCE]

ŭ'tterance[2] *n.* (literary). *Fight* etc. **to the ~**, to the bitter end. [ME, f. OF *outrance* (*outrer* surpass, f. L ULTRA; see -ANCE)]

U.V. *abbr.* ultraviolet.

ū'vŭl|a *n.* (*pl.* ~**ae**). Pendent fleshy part of soft palate; similar process in bladder or cerebellum; hence ~AR[1] *a.* [ME f. LL, dim. of L *uva* grape]

ŭxŏr'ĭcīd|e *n.* Killing of one's wife; one who kills his wife; hence ~AL *a.* [f. L *uxor* wife; see -CIDE]

ŭxŏr'ĭous *a.* (Excessively) fond of one's wife; (of action etc.) showing such fondness; hence ~LY[2] *adv.*, ~NESS *n.* [f. L *uxoriosus* (*uxor* wife) + -OUS]

U'zbĕk, U'zbĕg, (ŭ'-) *n.* Member or language of a Turkic people in central Asia. [Uzbek]

V

V, v, (vē) *n.* (*pl.* **Vs** *or* **V's**). Twenty-second letter of alphabet; V-shaped thing, e.g. joint; aircraft formation; (as Roman numeral) 5 (**vi** 6, **vii** 7, **viii** 8); **V1, V2,** weapons used by Germany near end of war of 1939–45 [f. G *vergeltungswaffe* reprisal weapon]; **V8,** (vehicle having) engine with eight cylinders in V form; **V sign** (made by hand with fingers clenched except the first and second outspread in V shape, as gesture symbolizing victory, approval, or vulgar derision).

V *abbr.* volt(s).

v. *abbr.* verse; verso; versus; very; *vide*.

V *symb.* vanadium.

V.A. *abbr.* *Veterans' Administration; Vicar Apostolic; Vice-Admiral; ||Order of Victoria and Albert.

Va. *abbr.* Virginia.

||**văc** *n.* (colloq.) Vacation; vacuum cleaner.

vā'cancy̆ *n.* Being vacant or empty or unoccupied; emptiness of mind, idleness, listlessness; unoccupied post or place (*has a vacancy on his staff*; *no vacancies at present in this hotel*). [f. foll. + -ANCY, or f. LL & med. L *vacantia*]

vā'cant *a.* **1.** Empty, not filled or occupied, (*house is still vacant*; *a vacant compartment*; *have no vacant space*; *will amuse your vacant hours*; *applied for a vacant post*); ||~ **possession,** ownership of house etc. without prior occupant. **2.** Not mentally active, not rationally occupied, empty-headed, thoughtless, listless, stupid, (*his mind seems completely vacant*; *received the news with a vacant stare*; *given up to vacant frivolities*); hence ~LY[2] *adv.* [ME f. OF, or f. L *vacare* (as foll.; see -ANT)]

vacā't|e (*or* vā'-) *v.t.* Go away from so as to leave empty or unoccupied, give up occupation or possession of, (military position, place, house, throne, office); (Law) annul (judgement, contract, etc.); hence ~ABLE *a.* [f. L *vacare* be empty + -ATE[3]]

vacā'tion (*or* vā-) *n.*, & *v.i.* **1.** *n.* Vacating (of house, post, etc.); part of year constituting fixed period of cessation from work, esp. in ||lawcourts and universities, (*Christmas*, *Easter*, *Whitsun*, *long* or *summer vacation*); *~**land,** area providing recreations for holiday-makers. **2.** *n.*, & *v.i.* *(Take) holiday; hence ~IST (1) *n.* [ME f. OF, or f. L *vacatio* (as prec.; see -ATION)]

vă'ccin|āte (-ks-) *v.t.* Inoculate with vaccine to procure immunity from smallpox or with vaccine of any disease in order to produce it in mild form and so prevent serious attack; hence ~A'TION, ~**ātor,** *ns.* [f. foll. + -ATE[3]]

vă'ccine (-ks-; *or* -ēn) *a.* & *n.* **1.** *a.* Of cows or cowpox or vaccination. **2.** *n.* Virus of cowpox as used in vaccination; modified micro-organism of any disease similarly used; hence **vă'ccĭn**AL (-ks-) *a.* [f. L *vaccinus* (*vacca* cow; see -INE[1])]

văccĭ'nia (-ks-) *n.* (Med.) Cowpox, esp. inoculated. [mod. L, f. as prec. + -IA[1]]

vă'cĭll|āte *v.i.* Move from side to side, oscillate, waver; fluctuate in opinion or resolution; so ~A'TION *n.* [f. L *vacillare* sway + -ATE[3]]

vă'cū|ōle *n.* (Biol.) Minute cavity in organ or cell, containing air, fluid, etc.; hence ~**ol**AR[1] *a.*, ~**ol**A'TION *n.*, formation of vacuoles. [F, dim. of L *vacuus* empty]

vă'cūous *a.* Empty; evacuated; unintelligent, expressionless, (*vacuous remark*, *stare*); hence or cogn. **vacū'**ITY, ~NESS, *ns.*, ~LY[2] *adv.* [f. L *vacuus* empty (as VACATE) + -OUS]

vă'cūum *n.* (*pl.* **va'cua** *or* **va'cuums**), & *v.* **1.** *n.* Space entirely devoid of matter; space or vessel from which air has been almost or completely removed by pump etc. (TORRICELLIAN *vacuum*); decrease of pressure below normal atmospheric value; (fig.) absence of normal or previous content of a place, environment, etc.; (colloq.) vacuum cleaner. **2.** ~ **brake,** continuous train-brake in which pressure is caused by exhaustion of air; ~**-clean** *v.t.* & *i.*, clean by use of ~ **cleaner,** apparatus for removing dust etc. from carpets etc. by suction; ||~ **flask,** vessel with double wall enclosing vacuum so that liquid in inner receptacle retains its temperature; ~**-gauge** (for testing pressure after production of vacuum); ~**-packed,** sealed after partial removal of air; ~ **pump** (for production of vacuum); ~ **tube,** sealed tube with almost perfect vacuum for free passage of electric current. **3.** *v.t.* & *i.* (colloq.) Use vacuum cleaner (on). [mod. L, neut. (as n.) of L *vacuus* empty]

V.A.D. *abbr.* (Member of) Voluntary Aid Detachment.

vādė-mē'cum (*or* vahdĭmā'-) *n.* Handbook or other thing carried constantly about the person. [F f. mod. L, = go with me]

vă'gabŏnd *a.*, *n.*, & *v.i.* **1.** *a.* Having no fixed habitation, wandering; driven or drifting to and fro, straying. **2.** *n.* Wanderer, vagrant, esp. idle and worthless one; (colloq.) scamp, rascal; hence ~AGE (2), ~ISM (2), *ns.*, ~ISH[1] *a.*, ~IZE (2) *v.i.* **3.** *v.i.* Wander about as vagabond. [ME f. OF, or f. L *vagabundus* (*vagari* wander)]

vā'gal. See VAGUS.

vagar'y̆ (*or* vā'gerĭ) *n.* Whimsical or extravagant notion; caprice; freak; hence **vagar'ĭ**OUS *a.* [f. L *vagari* wander]

vagī'n|a *n.* (*pl.* ~**ae** *or* ~**as**). **1.** Canal between womb and external genital orifice of female mammal; similar canal in insect etc.; hence **văgĭnī**'TIS *n.* **2.** (Bot.) Sheath formed round stem by base of leaf. **3.** Hence ~AL *a.* [L, = sheath, scabbard]

văgĭnĭ'smus (-z-) *n.* Painful spasmodic contraction of vagina. [mod. L (as prec.; see -ISM)]

vā'gr|ant *a.* & *n.* **1.** *a.* Wandering, roving, straggling, itinerant, (*vagrant musician*; *indulging in vagrant speculations*); being a vagrant; hence ~ANCY *n.*, ~**ant**LY[2] *adv.* **2.** *n.* Wanderer, idle rover, vagabond; idle and disorderly person without settled home or regular work. [ME f. AF *vag(a)raunt*, perh. alt. f. AF *wakerant* etc. by assoc. w. L *vagari* wander]

vā'grom *a.* = prec. [illit. alt. of prec.; see Shak. *Much Ado* III. iii. 26]

vāgue (-g) *a.* Indistinct, not clearly expressed or identified, of uncertain or ill-defined meaning or character, (*returned only a vague answer*; *has some vague idea of going to Canada*; *have not the vaguest notion of his reasons*; *heard a vague rumour to that effect*); (of person or mind) imprecise, inexact in thought or expression; hence ~'LY[2] (-glĭ) *adv.*, ~'NESS (-gn-) *n.*, **vā'gu**ISH[1] (-gĭ-) *a.* [F, or f. L *vagus* wandering, uncertain]

vā'g|us *n.* (*pl.* ~**i** *pr.* -gī). (Anat.) Pneumogastric nerve, either of tenth pair of cranial nerves with branches to heart etc.; hence ~AL *a.* [L (see prec.)]

vail^{1} *v.* (arch. or poet.) **1.** *v.t.* Lower or doff (one's plumes, pride, crown, etc.) esp. in token of submission. **2.** *v.i.* Yield, give place, remove hat as sign of respect etc. [ME f. obs. *avale* f. OF *avaler* (*a val* down, f. *val* VALE^{1}) to lower]

vail^{2} *n.* (arch.; usu. in *pl.*). Gratuity, tip; occasional profit from office. [ME, f. obs. *vail* AVAIL^{1}]

vain *a.* **1.** Unsubstantial, empty, trivial, (*vain boasts, triumphs, distinctions*); useless, unavailing, followed by no good result, (*in the vain hope of dissuading him*; *all resistance is vain, to resist is vain, it is vain to resist*); **in ~,** with no result, to no purpose, uselessly, (*we protested in vain, it was in vain that we protested*; TAKE^{1} person's *name in vain*). **2.** Conceited (*of* one's beauty etc.). **3.** Hence ~'LY^{2} *adv.*, ~'NESS (-n-n-) *n.* [ME f. OF, f. L *vanus* empty, without substance]

vainglōr'|ў (-n-g-) *n.* Boastfulness, extreme vanity; so **~ious** *a.* [ME, after OF *vaine gloire*, L *vana gloria*]

vair *n.* **1.** (arch.) Squirrel-fur widely used for medieval linings and trimmings. **2.** (Her.) Fur represented by small shield-shaped or bell--shaped figures usu. alternately azure and argent. [ME f. OF, f. L (as VARIOUS)]

Vai'sya (vī'-) *n.* (Member of) third of four great Hindu castes, comprising the merchants and agriculturalists. [f. Skr. *vaiśya* peasant, labourer]

vă'lanc|e, vă'lenc|e^{1}, *n.* Short curtain round frame or canopy of bedstead, above window, or under shelf; hence ~ED^{2} (-st) *a.* [ME, perh. f. AF **valance* (*valer* = OF *avaler* descend; see VAIL^{1}, -ANCE)]

vāle^{1} *n.* (arch. or poet. exc. in place-names). Valley (*o'er field and vale*; *Vale of the White Horse*); **this ~, the ~ of tears,** etc., the world as scene of life, trouble, etc.; **~ of years,** old age. [ME, f. OF *val* f. L *vallis, valles*]

vā'lė^{2} *int.* & *n.* Farewell. [L, imper. of *valēre* be well or strong]

vălėdĭ'ction *n.* (Words used in) bidding farewell. [f. L VALE^{2}(*dicere dict-* say) bid farewell, after *benediction*]

vălėdĭ'ct|orў *a.* & *n.* **1.** *a.* Serving as valediction. **2.** *n.* *Valedictory oration, esp. as given by (usu. highest-ranking) member of graduating class (the **~ōr'ĭAN** *n.*). [f. prec. + -ORY]

vā'lence^{1}. See VALANCE.

vā'lence^{2} *n.* **1.** (Chem.) Combining or replacing power of an atom as compared with hydrogen atom as standard (*hydrogen, carbon, has a valence of one, four*); *valency; **~ electron** (in outermost shell of atom). **2.** (Biol. etc.) Ability to interact. [f. LL *valentia* power, competence (as VALE^{2}; see -ENCE)]

Vălenciennes (vălahṅsyĕ'n) *n.* Rich kind of lace. [~ in N.E. France, where made in 17th & 18th c.]

||**vā'lencў** *n.* (Chem.) Unit of combining power (*carbon has 4 valencies*); = VALENCE^{2}. [f. as VALENCE^{2}; see -ENCY]

vă'lentīne *n.* **1. St. V~'s day,** 14 Feb., feast of St. Valentine, on which birds were supposed to pair. **2.** Sweetheart chosen on this day; amatory or satirical letter or card or picture sent, often anonymously, to person of opposite sex on this day. [ME, f. OF *Valentin* f. L *Valentinus*, name of two saints]

valēr'ĭan *n.* Herb of genus *Valeriana*, esp. **common ~,** with pink or white flowers and strong smell liked by cats; root of this used as medicinal stimulant. [ME, f. OF *valeriane* f. med. L *valeriana* (*herba*), app. fem. of L *Valerianus* of Valerius; see -IAN]

valĕ'rĭc *a.* (Chem.) Derived from valerian (**~ acid,** fatty acid occurring in valerian root; hence **vă'ler**ATE^{1} (3) *n.*). [f. prec. + -IC]

vă'lėt (*or* -lā) *n.* & *v.* **1.** *n.* Gentleman's personal attendant who looks after clothes etc.; hotel etc. employee with similar duties. **2.** *v.t.* & *i.* Act as valet (to). [F, = OF *valet, vaslet*, VARLET, f. Rom. **vassellittus* dim. of **vassus* (see VASSAL)]

valē'ta. See VELETA.

vălėtūdĭnār'ĭan *a.* & *n.* **1.** *a.* Of infirm health; seeking to recover health; unduly anxious about one's own health. **2.** *n.* Valetudinarian person. **3.** Hence or cogn. ~ISM (2) *n.*, **vălėtū'dĭn**ARY^{1} *a.* & *n.* [f. L *valetudinarius* in ill health (*valetudo -dinis* health f. *valēre* be well; see -TUDE, -ARIAN, -ARY^{1})]

vă'lgus *n.* Deformity involving outward turning of foot. [L, = bandy-legged]

Vălhă'lla *n.* (Norse Myth.) palace in which souls of slain heroes feasted; building used for honouring the illustrious. [mod. L, f. ON *Valhöll* (*valr* the slain, *höll* HALL)]

vă'liant (-ya-) *a.* (Of person or conduct) brave, courageous; hence ~LY^{2} *adv.* [ME, f. AF *valiaunt*, OF *vail(l)ant* f. Rom. **valiens* f. L *valēre* be strong; see -ANT]

vă'lĭd *a.* (Of reason, objection, argument, etc.) sound, defensible, well-grounded; (Law) sound and sufficient, executed with proper formalities, (*valid contract*; *the marriage was held to be valid*); legally acceptable (*valid passport*); hence or cogn. **valĭ'd**ITY *n.*, ~LY^{2} *adv.* [f. F *valide* or f. L *validus* strong (as prec.; see -ID^{1})]

vă'lĭd|āte *v.t.* Make valid, ratify, confirm; hence ~A'TION *n.* [f. med. L *validare* f. L (as prec.) + -ATE^{3}]

vā'line (-ēn) *n.* (Chem.) White crystalline amino-acid forming essential ingredient in human and vertebrate diet. [f. VALERIC + -INE^{5}]

vali'se (-ē's *or* -ē'z) *n.* *Kind of small portmanteau; kitbag. [F, f. It. *valigia* corresp. to med. L *valisia*, of unkn. orig.]

Vă'lkўrie (*or* -kēr'ĭ) *n.* (Norse Myth.) Each of Odin's 12 handmaidens who selected those destined to be slain in battle. [f. ON *Valkyrja* lit. chooser of the slain (*valr* the slain + **kur-*, **kuz-* cogn. w. CHOOSE)]

văllĕ'cūl|a *n.* (*pl.* **~ae**). (Anat. & Bot.) Groove, furrow; hence ~AR^{1}, ~ATE^{2}, *adjs.* [LL, dim. of L *vallis* valley]

vă'lley *n.* **1.** Low area more or less enclosed by hills and usu. with stream flowing through it; any depression compared to this; **~ of the shadow of death,** (period of) close approach to death, extreme affliction (Ps. 23:4, prob. orig. meaning 'valley of deep shadows'). **2.** (Archit.) Internal angle formed by intersecting planes of roof. [ME, f. AF *valey*, OF *valee* f. Rom. **vallata* f. L *vallis, valles*; cf. VALE^{1}, -Y^{4}]

vă'llum *n.* (Rom. Ant.) Rampart and stockade as defence. [L, collect. f. *vallus* stake]

valō'nĭa *n.* Acorn-cups of the Levantine evergreen **~ oak** (*Quercus aegilops*), used in tanning, dyeing, and making ink. [f. It. *vallonia* ult. f. Gk *balanos* acorn]

***vă'lor.** See VALOUR.

vă'lorīz|e, -īs|e (-īz), *v.t.* Raise or fix price of (commodity etc.) by artificial means, esp. by government action; so ~A'TION *n.* [back form. f. *valorization* f. F *valorisation* (as foll.; see -IZE, -ATION)]

vă'lour (-ler), ***vă'lor,** *n.* (poet., formal, or joc.) Personal courage esp. as shown in fighting, prowess; so **vă'lor**OUS *a.* [ME f. OF, f. LL *valor -oris* (*valēre* be strong; see -OR)]

valse (vahls *or* vawls) *n.* Waltz. [F, f. G (as WALTZ)]

vă'lūable *a.* & *n.* **1.** *a.* Of great value or price or worth (*valuable property, land, furniture, information, assistance*). **2.** *n.* (usu. in *pl.*) Valuable thing(s), esp. small article(s) of personal property, (*sent all her valuables to the bank*). [f. VALUE 9 + -ABLE]

vălūā'tion *n.* Estimation (esp. by professional valuer) of a thing's worth, worth so estimated, price set on a thing, (*valuation of land; disposed of at a low valuation; sets too high a valuation on his abilities*). [f. VALUE 9 + -ATION]

vă'lūātor *n.* One who makes valuations, valuer. [f. prec. + -OR]

vă'lūe *n.*, & *v.t.* **1.** *n.* Worth, desirability, utility, qualities on which these depend, (*now learnt the value of fresh water, a friend, quinine, accuracy, regular exercise*). **2.** Worth as estimated, valuation, (*sets a high value on his time*). **3.** Purchasing power, power of a commodity to purchase others, amount of money or (Econ.) other commodities for which thing can be exchanged in open market. **4.** Equivalent of a thing, what represents or is represented by or may be substituted for a thing, (*paid him the value of his lost property*); ability of a thing to serve a purpose or cause an effect (*news value*); (in *pl.*) one's principles or standards, one's judgement of what is valuable or important in life; meaning *of* word etc.; quality *of* a spoken sound; (Mus.) duration of sound signified by note; relative rank or importance of playing-card, chess piece, etc., according to rules of game; (Paint.) relation of one part of picture to others in respect of light and shade, part characterized by a particular tone. **5.** (Math.) Amount or quantity denoted by algebraical term or expression. **6.** (Biol.) Rank in classification. **7.** (Phys. etc.) Numerical measure of a quantity (*value of gravity at the equator*); (Chem. etc.) number giving content etc. of a substance expressed on some conventional scale (*iodine value as measure of unsaturated fats*). **8.** **~-a'dded tax,** tax on amount by which value of an article has been increased at each stage of its production; **~ for money,** something well worth the money spent; **~-judgement,** subjective estimate of quality etc.; **~ received,** money or its equivalent given for bill of exchange. **9.** *v.t.* Estimate the value of, appraise (professionally, whence ||**vă'lū**ER[1] *n.*, or otherwise), (*should value the whole at £2,000*); have high or specified opinion of, attach importance to, prize, esteem, appreciate, pride one*self*, (*value sincerity* (*beyond all things*); *a valued friend; values himself on* or *for his conversational powers*). [ME f. OF, fem. p.p. of *valoir* be worth f. L *valēre*]

vă'lūelėss (-ūl-) *a.* Having no value, worthless; hence **~**NESS *n.* [f. prec. + -LESS]

valū'ta *n.* Value of a currency with respect to another; a currency thus considered. [It., = VALUE]

vălv|e *n.* **1.** Automatic or other device for controlling passage of liquid or gas or the like through pipe etc., usu. to allow movement in one direction only; SAFETY-*valve*; || = THERMIONIC *valve*. **2.** (Anat. & Zool.) Membranous part of organ etc. allowing flow of blood etc. in one direction and not in another (*valves of the heart, of the veins*). **3.** (Conch.) Each of two or more separable pieces of which shell consists, whole shell in one piece. **4.** (Bot.) Each of the segments into which a capsule dehisces; lidlike part of anther. **5.** (Mus.) Device for varying length of tube in brass wind instrument. **6.** (arch.) Leaf of folding door. **7.** Hence or cogn. **~'**ATE[2] (Bot.), (-)**~**ED[2] (-vd), **~'e**LESS (-vl-), *adjs.*, **~'**ULE *n.* [ME, f. L *valva* leaf of folding door]

vă'lvūl|ar *a.* Having (form or function of) valve(s); so **~**I'TIS *n.*, inflammation of valves of heart. [f. mod. L *valvula*, dim. of L *valva* (see prec.) + -AR[1]]

vă'mbrāce *n.* (Hist.) Defensive armour for forearm. [ME, f. AF *vaunt-bras*, OF *avant-bras* (*avant* before, see AVAUNT; *bras* arm)]

***vamoo'se** *v.i.* & *t.* (sl.) Depart hurriedly (from). [f. Sp. *vamos* let us go]

vămp[1] *n.* & *v.* **1.** *n.* Upper front part of boot or shoe; vamped or patched-up article; improvised musical instrument. **2.** *v.t.* Put new vamp to (boot, shoe); repair, furbish usu. *up*; make *up* by patching or from odds and ends. **3.** *v.t.* & *i.* Improvise musical accompaniment (to); improvise (musical accompaniment). **4.** Hence **~'**ER[1] *n.* [ME, f. AF *vaumpé*, OF *avantpié* (*avant* before, see AVAUNT; *pied* foot)]

vămp[2] *n.* & *v.* (colloq.) **1.** *n.* Adventuress, woman who exploits men; unscrupulous flirt. **2.** *v.t.* (Of woman) allure, exploit, (man). **3.** *v.i.* Act as vamp. [abbr. of foll.]

vă'mpīre *n.* **1.** Ghost or reanimated body (usu. of wizard, heretic, criminal, etc.) supposed to leave grave at night and suck blood of sleeping persons; person who preys ruthlessly on others; = prec. **2.** **~** (**bat**), S. Amer. etc. bat actually or supposedly biting horses, cattle, and sleeping persons, and lapping their blood. **3.** (Theatr.) small spring trapdoor used for sudden disappearances. **4.** Hence **vămpĭ'r**IC *a.* [F, or G *vampir*, f. Magyar *vampir* perh. f. Turk. *uber* witch]

vă'mpīrĭsm *n.* Belief in existence of vampires; action of a vampire (lit. or fig.). [f. prec. + -ISM]

vă'mplāte *n.* (Hist.) Iron plate protecting hand when lance was couched. [ME, f. AF *vauntplate* (as VAMBRACE, PLATE[1])]

văn[1] *n.* Testing of ore quality by washing on shovel or by machine; (arch.) winnowing fan; (arch. or poet.) wing. [ME, southern & western var. of FAN[1], perh. partly f. OF *van* or L *vannus*]

văn[2] *n.* Vanguard (lit. or fig.; *in the van of civilization*). [abbr.]

văn[3] *n.* Covered vehicle for conveying furniture or other goods or horses etc. or prisoners; ||railway carriage for luggage (**luggage ~**) or goods or for use of guard (**guard's ~**); ||gipsy caravan. [abbr. of CARAVAN]

||**văn**[4] *n.* (Tennis colloq.) = ADVANTAGE[1] 3. [abbr.]

vanā'dĭum *n.* Hard grey metallic element used in small quantities for strengthening some steels; hence **vă'nad**ATE[1] (3) *n.*, **vană'd**IC, **vă'nad**OUS, *adjs.* (Chem.). [mod. L, f. ON *Vanadís* name of the Scand. goddess Freyja + -IUM]

Văn A'llen (ă'-) *n.* **~** (**radiation**) **belt** or **layer,** one of two regions partly surrounding earth at heights of several thousand kilometres, containing intense radiation and many high-energy charged particles. [f. J. A. ~, Amer. physicist b. 1914]

||**V. & A.** *abbr.* Victoria & Albert Museum.

Vă'ndal *a.* & *n.* **1.** (Member) of a Germanic people that in 4th–5th c. ravaged Gaul, Spain, N. Africa, and Rome, destroying many books and works of art. **2.** (*v~*). Wilful or ignorant destroyer or damager of works of art or other property; hence **~**ISM (2) *n.*, **~**IZE (1) *v.t.* **3.** Hence **~**IC (-ă'l-) *a.* [f. L *Vandalus* f. Gmc **Wandal-* etc.]

văndȳ'ke *n.*, *a.*, & *v.t.* **1.** *n.* Each of a series of large points forming border to lace, cloth, etc.; cape, collar, etc., with these. **2.** *a.* (*V~*). In the style of dress, esp. with pointed borders, common in portraits by Van Dyck; **V~** (neat pointed) **beard; V~ brown,** deep rich brown.

3. *v.t.* Cut (cloth, edge of lawn, etc.) in vandykes. [f. Sir A. *Van Dyck*, Anglicized *Vandyke*, Flem. painter d. 1641]

vāne *n.* Weathercock; similar device exposed to current of water etc.; blade of windmill, turbine, screw propeller, etc.; sight of surveying instruments, sight of quadrant etc.; flat part of bird's feather formed by barbs; hence **vān**ED² (-nd), ~′LESS (-nl-), *adjs.* [ME, southern & western var. of obs. *fane* f. OE *fana* banner, = OS, OHG *fano*, ON *fani*, Goth. *fana* f. Gmc **fanon*]

vaně′ssa *n.* Butterfly of genus *Vanessa*, e.g. red admiral, painted lady. [mod. L]

văng *n.* (Naut.) Each of two guy-ropes running from end of gaff to deck. [earlier *fang* = gripping-device, OE f. ON *fang* grasp f. Gmc **fang-*]

vă′nguard (-n-gard) *n.* Foremost part of army or fleet advancing or ready to do so; (fig.) leaders of movement, of opinion, etc. [earlier *vandgard*, *(a)vantgard*, f. OF *avan(t)garde* (*avant* before, see AVAUNT; *garde* GUARD¹)]

vanĭ′lla *n.* Tropical climbing orchid of genus *Vanilla*, with fragrant flowers; ~(**-pod**), fruit of this; extract obtained from vanilla-pod or synthetically and used for flavouring ice cream, chocolate, etc. [f. Sp. *vainilla* pod dim. of *vaina* sheath, pod, f. L VAGINA]

vanĭ′llĭn *a.* Fragrant principle of vanilla. [f. prec. + -IN]

vă′nĭsh *v.* & *n.* **1.** *v.i.* Disappear suddenly; disappear gradually, fade away; cease to exist; (Math.) become zero; ~**ing-cream,** emollient that leaves no visible trace when rubbed into skin; ~**ing-point,** point at which receding parallel lines viewed in perspective appear to meet, (fig.) state of complete disappearance. **2.** *v.t.* Cause to disappear. **3.** *n.* (Phonet.) Slight sound with which a principal sound ends (e.g. ŏŏ, ĭ, at end of ō, ā). [ME, f. OF *e(s)vaniss-* stem of *e(s)vanir*; see EVANISH]

vă′nĭtorў *n.* Wash-basin surrounded by flat top for use as dressing-table. [P]

vă′nĭtў *n.* **1.** Futility, unsubstantiality, unreality, emptiness, unsubstantial or unreal thing, (*the vanity of worldly wealth, of political distinction, of human achievements; these things are vanity* or *vanities; all is vanity; pomps and vanity of this wicked world*); **V~ Fair,** the world (allegorized in Bunyan's *Pilgrim's Progress*) as scene of vanity. **2.** Empty pride, desire for admiration, based on personal attainments or attractions or qualities; ~ **bag, case,** (carried by woman and containing small mirror, powder-puff, etc.). **3.** Ostentatious display. **4.** *Dressing-table. [ME, f. OF *vanité*, f. L *vanitas -tatis* (as VAIN; see -ITY)]

vă′nquĭsh *v.t.* (literary). Conquer, overcome, (lit. or fig.); hence ~ABLE *a.*, ~ER¹ *n.* [ME *venkus, -quis*, etc., f. OF *vencus* p.p., and *-quis* past tense, of *veintre* f. L *vincere*; assim. to -ISH²]

va′ntage (vah′-) *n.* = ADVANTAGE¹ (esp. in Tennis, cf. VAN⁴; COIGN *of vantage*; ~**-ground,** advantageous position for defence or attack). [ME f. AF, f. OF *avantage* ADVANTAGE¹]

vă′pĭd *a.* Insipid, flat, (*vapid beer, conversation, remark, pleasures, moralizings*); hence **vapĭ′d**ITY, ~NESS, *ns.*, ~LY² *adv.* [f. L *vapidus*; see -ID¹]

***vā′por.** See VAPOUR.

vā′por|ize, -ise (-īz), *v.t.* & *i.* Convert or be converted into vapour; hence or cogn. ~**iz**A′TION, ~**iz**ER¹ (2), *ns.*, ~(**iz**)ABLE *adjs.* [f. foll. + -IZE]

vā′pour (-per), ***vā′por,** *n.*, & *v.i.* **1.** *n.* Moisture or other substance diffused or suspended in air, e.g. mist, smoke; (Phys.) gaseous form of a normally liquid or solid substance (cf. GAS¹), present above it and into which it is entirely converted when heated above boiling-point, whence **vāporĭ′**FIC, **vā′porĭ**FORM, *adjs.*, **vāporĭ′**METER *n.*; medicinal agent to be inhaled; unsubstantial thing, vain imagination; (in *pl.*, arch.) depression, melancholy, hypochondria, hysteria, or similar nervous disorder, whence ~ISH¹ *a.* **2.** ~ **bath,** bath in vapour or steam, apparatus or apartment for this; ~**-burner,** apparatus for vaporizing and burning a hydrocarbon for producing light or heat; ~ **density** (of gas or vapour relative to hydrogen etc.); ~**-engine** (driven by steam or other vapour); ~ **pressure** (of vapour in contact with its liquid or solid form); ~ **trail,** condensation trail. **3.** Hence or cogn. **vā′por**OUS, ~Y², *adjs.* **4.** *v.i.* Rise as vapour; utter idle boasts or empty talk, whence ~ER¹ *n.* (~**er moth,** tussock-moth), ~ING¹ *n.* [ME f. OF, or f. L *vapor* steam, heat]

vaquer′ō (-kār′ō) *n.* (*pl.* ~**s**). (Sp. Amer. etc.) Herdsman. [Sp. (*vaca* cow)]

var. *abbr.* variant; variety.

vară′ctor *n.* Semiconductor diode with capacitance dependent on applied voltage. [f. *varying reactor*]

Vară′ngĭan (-nj-) *n.* Norse rover, esp. one of those who penetrated into Russia in 9th–10th c.; ~ **guard,** bodyguard of Byzantine emperors formed of Varangians. [f. med. L *Varangus* f. med. Gk *varaggos* f. ON *Væringi* lit. confederate (*várar* oaths) + -IAN]

vă′rĕc *n.* Seaweed = KELP 2. [f. F *varec(h)* f. ON **wrek* WRECK]

vār′ĭable *a.* & *n.* **1.** *a.* That can be varied or adapted, (*rod of variable length; the pressure is variable*); (of gear) designed to give varying speeds, e.g. slow advance and quick return; apt to vary, not constant, fickle, unsteady, (*variable mood, temper, fortune*); (of wind, currents) tending to change direction; (Astron., of star) periodically varying in brightness or magnitude; (Math., of quantity) indeterminate, able to assume different numerical values; (Bot. & Zool., of species) including individuals or groups that depart from the type; (Biol., of organism) tending to change in structure or function; hence **vārĭ**ABI′LITY, ~NESS (-beln-), *ns.*, **vār′iab**LY² *adv.* **2.** *n.* Variable thing (esp. quantity or star); (Naut.) shifting wind, (in *pl.*) region between N.E. and S.E. trade winds. [ME f. OF, f. L *variabilis* (as VARY; see -ABLE)]

vār′ĭance *n.* Disagreement, difference of opinion, dispute, lack of harmony, (*on that point we are at variance (among ourselves); at variance with the authorities; have had a slight variance with him; this theory is at variance with all that is known on the subject*); (Law) discrepancy between statements or documents; (Statistics) quantity equal to square of standard deviation; *permission to depart from usual rules. [ME f. OF, f. L *variantia* difference (as VARY; see -ANCE)]

vār′ĭant *a.* & *n.* **1.** *a.* Differing in form or in details from the one named or considered, differing thus among themselves, (*a variant reading in some MSS.; 40 variant types of pigeon*); variable, changing. **2.** *n.* Variant form, spelling, type, reading, etc., (*'enure' is a variant of 'inure'; difficult to choose between these variants*). [ME f. OF (as VARY; see -ANT)]

vār′ĭate *n.* (Statistics). Quantity having a numerical value for each member of a group; variable quantity, esp. one whose values occur according to a frequency distribution. [f. p.p. of L *variare*; see VARY, -ATE¹]

vārĭā′tion *n.* **1.** Varying, departure from a former or normal condition or action or amount or from a standard or type, extent of this, (*prices are subject to variation; repeated variations of temperature; is subject to a variation of several* *degrees*); (Astron.) deviation of heavenly body from mean orbit or motion (**periodic, secular,** ~, compensated in short, in very long, period); (of magnetic needle) declination; (Biol.) structural or functional deviation from type; (Math.) change in a function etc. due to small changes in values of constants etc. (*calculus of variations*). **2.** Thing that varies from a type; (Mus.) tune or theme repeated in a changed or elaborated form; (Ballet) solo dance. **3.** Hence ~AL *a.* [ME f. OF, or f. L *variatio* (as VARY; see -ATION)]

văricĕ'lla *n.* Chicken-pox. [mod. L, irreg. dim. of VARIOLA]

vă'rĭcocēle *n.* Tumour composed of varicose veins of spermatic cord. [f. as VARIX + -O- + -CELE]

vār'ĭcoloured, *-ored, (-kŭlerd) *a.* Variegated in colour; of various or different colours. [f. L *varius* VARIOUS + COLOURED]

vă'rĭc|ōse *a.* Of or affected with varix (*varicose ulcer, vein*); hence ~O'SITY *n.* [f. L *varicosus* (VARIX; see -OSE¹)]

varied. See VARY.

vār'ĭeg|āte (-rĭg-) *v.t.* Diversify in appearance, esp. in colour; mark with irregular patches of different colours; (in *p.p.*, Bot.) having two or more colours of leaves; hence ~A'TION *n.* [f. L *variegare* (*varius* VARIOUS) + -ATE³]

varī'etĭst *n.* One whose habits etc. differ from what is normal. [f. foll. + -IST]

varī'etў *n.* **1.** Being various, diversity, absence of monotony or uniformity, many-sidedness, (*was struck by the variety of his attainments, of his conversation, of the scene*; *London has for me the charm of variety*; *cannot live without variety*). **2.** Quantity or collection of different things (*turned over a variety of silks*; *for a variety of reasons*); ~ (**entertainment** or **show**), series of dances, songs, comedy acts, acrobatic feats, etc.; *~ **meat,** edible offal of animals; *~ **store** (selling many kinds of small items); ~ **theatre** (for variety shows etc.). **3.** (Specimen or member of a) class of things differing in some common qualities from the rest of a larger class to which they belong; different form *of* thing, quality, etc. **4.** (Biol.) Individual or group usually fertile within the species to which it belongs but differing from the species type in some qualities capable of perpetuation; subspecies; cultivar; hence **varī'et**AL *a.* [f. F *variété* or f. L *varietas* (as VARIOUS; see -TY¹)]

vār'ĭfōrm *a.* Having various forms. [f. L (as VARIOUS) + -FORM]

varī'ol|a *n.* Smallpox; hence ~AR¹, **vār'ĭol**OID, ~OUS, *adjs.* [med. L, = pustule, pock (as VARIOUS)]

vār'ĭōle *n.* Shallow pit like smallpox mark; spherule in variolite. [f. med. L (see prec.)]

vār'ĭol|ite *n.* Rock with embedded spherules causing on surface an appearance like smallpox pustules; hence ~ĭ'TIC *a.* [f. as prec. + -ITE¹]

vārĭŏ'mėter *n.* Device for varying the inductance in an electric circuit, or for indicating aircraft's rate of change of altitude. [f. as VARIOUS + -O- + -METER]

vārĭōr'um *a.* & *n.* **1.** *a.* With notes of various editors or commentators (*a variorum* (*edition of*) *Horace*). **2.** *n.* Variorum edition. [L, gen. pl. masc. of *varius* VARIOUS, short for *cum notis variorum*]

vār'ĭous *a.* **1.** Different, diverse, (*the modes of procedure were various*; *types so various as to defy classification*). **2.** Separate, several, more than one, (*came across various people*; *for various reasons*). **3.** Hence ~LY² *adv.*, ~NESS *n.* [f. L *varius* changing, diverse + -OUS]

vār'ĭ|x *n.* (*pl.* ~**ces** *pr.* vă'rĭsēz). (Path.) permanent abnormal dilatation of vein or artery; vein etc. thus dilated; (Conch.) each of the ridges across the whorls of a univalve shell. [ME f. L *varix -icis*]

vār'lėt *n.* (Hist.) knight's attendant; (arch. or joc.) menial, low fellow, rascal; hence ~RY (1) *n.* [ME f. OF, var. of *vaslet*; see VALET]

vār'mĭnt *n.* (dial. or U.S.) Mischievous or discreditable person or animal, esp. fox. [var. of *varmin*, VERMIN]

vār'na *n.* Any of the four great Hindu castes. [Skr., = colour, class]

vār'nĭsh *n.*, & *v.t.* **1.** *n.* Resinous solution in oil or spirit applied to wood, metal, etc., to give hard shiny transparent coating; other preparation for similar purpose, e.g. ‖NAIL¹ varnish. **2.** Artificial or natural glossiness; superficial polish of manner; external appearance or display without underlying reality; ~**-tree** (from which varnish-resin is obtained). **3.** *v.t.* Apply varnish to (wood, picture, etc.; (fig.) character, person, action, account; or abs.); gloss over (fact); ~**ing-day,** day before exhibition of pictures on which exhibitors may retouch and varnish their pictures already hung. [ME, f. OF (*verniss*(*i*)*er* v. f.) *vernis* n. f. med. L *veronix* SANDARAC 2 or med. Gk *berenikē* prob. f. *Berenice* in Cyrenaica]

vār'sĭtў *n.* **1.** ‖(colloq., esp. w. ref. to sports). University. **2.** *University etc. sports team. [abbr.]

vārsoviĕ'nne (-vyĕ'n), **vārsovia'na** (-vyah'-), *n.* (Music for) dance resembling mazurka. [F & It., = (dance) of Warsaw (*Varsovie, Varsovia*) in Poland]

vār'us *n.* Deformity involving inward turning of foot. [L, = knock-kneed]

vārv|e *n.* Annually deposited layers of clay and silt in lake used to determine chronology of glacial sediments; hence ~ED² *a.* [f. Sw. *varv* layer]

vār'ў *v.* **1.** *v.t.* Change, make different, modify, diversify, (*can vary the pressure at will*; *seldom varies the routine*; *varies the treatment according to circumstances*; *style is not sufficiently varied*; *a varied scene*). **2.** *v.i.* Undergo change, be(come) different in degree or quality, be of different kinds, (*he, his mood, varies from day to day*; *temperature varies from 30° to 70°*; *tried with varying success*; *varies from the type*; *opinions vary on this point*). **3.** ~ (**directly**) **as,** ~ **inversely as,** be in direct, inverse, proportion to (*attraction of bodies varies* (*directly*) *as their masses and inversely as the square of their distance*). [ME, f. OF *varier* or f. L *variare* (as VARIOUS)]

văs *n.* (*pl.* ~**a** *pr.* vā'sa). (Anat.) Vessel, duct; ~ **de'ferens,** spermatic duct of testicle; hence **vā'**SAL *a.* [L, = vessel]

vă'scūlar *a.* Of, made up of, containing, vessels or ducts for conveying blood, sap, etc., (*vascular functions, tissue, system*); ~ **plant** (with woody conducting elements); hence ~ITY (-ă'r-) *n.*, ~IZE (3) *v.t.*, ~LY² *adv.* [f. mod. L *vascularis* f. L VASCULUM; see -AR¹]

vă'scūl|um *n.* (*pl.* ~**a**). Botanist's (usu. metal) collecting-case with lengthwise opening. [L, dim. of VAS]

vase (vahz) *n.* Vessel of earthenware, metal, etc., usu. tall and circular, used as ornament or container (*flower-vase*); ~**-painting,** decoration of vases with pigments esp. among ancient Greeks, instance of this; hence ~'FUL 2 (-zf-) *n.* [F, f. L VAS]

vasĕ'ctom|ў *n.* (Surg.) Removal of part of each vas deferens esp. for sterilization of patient; hence ~IZE (1) *v.t.* [f. VAS + -ECTOMY]

vă'selīne (*or* -ēn) *n.*, & *v.t.* (Treat with) type of petroleum jelly used in ointments etc. [**P** as noun f. G *wasser* water + Gk *elaion* oil + -INE⁵]

vā'sĭfŏrm (-z-) *a.* Duct-shaped; vase-shaped. [f. L *vasi-* (VAS; see -I-) + -FORM]

vāsō- *comb. form.* Vessel, esp. blood-vessel, as: **~-a'ctive, ~-mo'tor,** causing constriction or dilatation of blood-vessels; so **~-constri'ctive, ~-dila'ting**; **~pre'ssin,** pituitary hormone acting to reduce diuresis and increase blood pressure. [f. L VAS + -O-]

vă'ssal *n.* (Hist.) holder of land by feudal tenure on conditions of homage and allegiance (**great, rear, ~**, holding directly from king, holding from great vassal); (rhet.) slave, humble dependant; so ~AGE (1, 2) *n.* [ME f. OF, f. med. L *vassallus* retainer, of Celt. orig., the simplex *vassus* corresp. to OBret. *uuas*, W *gwas*, Ir. *foss*; cf. VAVASOUR]

vast (vah-) *a.* & *n.* **1.** *a.* Immense, huge, very great, (*a vast expanse of water*; *vast plains*; *shook his vast frame*; *a vast multitude, scheme*); (colloq.) great (*gave him vast satisfaction*; *makes a vast difference*); hence ~'LY[2] *adv.*, ~'NESS *n.* **2.** *n.* (poet. or rhet.) Vast space (*the vast of ocean, of heaven*). [f. L *vastus* void, immense]

văt *n.*, & *v.t.* (-tt-). **1.** *n.* Large tub, cistern, tank, or other vessel, esp. for holding liquids or holding something in liquid in process of manufacture, as in brewing, tanning, dyeing; dyeing liquor in which textile is soaked to take up colourless soluble dye afterwards coloured by oxidation in air; hence ~'FUL 2 *n.* **2.** *v.t.* Place or treat in vat. [ME, southern & western var. of *fat*, OE *fæt*, = OS, ON *fat*, OHG *faz* f. Gmc **fatam* vessel]

V.A.T. (*or* văt) *abbr.* value-added tax.

vă'tĭc *a.* Prophetic, inspired. [f. L *vates* prophet + -IC]

Vă'tĭcan *n.* Pope's palace and official residence in Rome; (fig.) papal government; ~ **City,** independent papal state in Rome 1929–; ~ **Council,** (1) ecumenical council held 1869–70 and proclaiming infallibility of pope when speaking *ex cathedra*, whence ~ISM (3), ~IST (2), *ns.*, (2) similar council held 1962–65. [F, or f. L *Vaticanus* name of hill in Rome]

vatĭ'cĭn|āte *v.t.* & *i.* Prophesy; so ~A'TION, ~ātOR, *ns.*, ~ātORY *a.* [f. L *vaticinari* (*vates* prophet) + -ATE[3]]

vau'devĭlle (*or* vō'-) *n.* Variety entertainment; satirical or topical song with refrain; light stage-play with interspersed songs. [F, orig. of convivial song esp. any of those composed by O. Basselin, 15th-c. poet born at *Vau de Vire* in Normandy]

Vaudois[1] (vōdwah') *a.* & *n.* (*pl.* same). (Inhabitant or dialect) of Vaud in Switzerland. [F (*Vaud*, *-ois* -ESE)]

Vaudois[2] (vōdwah') *a.* & *n.* (*pl.* same). (Member) of the Waldenses. [F, repr. med. L *Valdensis*; see WALDENSES]

vault[1] (*or* vŏ-) *n.*, & *v.t.* **1.** *n.* (Archit.) Arched roof, continuous arch, set or series of arches whose joints radiate from central point or line. **2.** Vaultlike covering (*the vault of heaven*); arched apartment; arched or other cellar or subterranean chamber as place of storage (*bank vaults*, WINE-*vault*, etc.), of interment beneath church or in cemetery (*family vault*), etc. **3.** (Anat.) Arched roof of a cavity. **4.** *v.t.* (esp. in *p.p.*). Make in form of, furnish with, vault(s). **5.** Hence ~'ING[1] (6) *n.* [ME f. OF (*vouter* v. f.) *voute*, *vaute*, f. Rom. **vol(vi)ta* for *voluta* fem. p.p. of L *volvere* roll]

vault[2] (*or* vŏ-) *v.* & *n.* **1.** *v.i.* Leap, spring, esp. while resting on the hand(s) or with help of pole, (*vault over the gate*, *from the saddle*, *on to a horse*); **~'ing-horse,** gymnast's wooden block for use in vaulting. **2.** *v.t.* Spring over (gate etc.) thus. **3.** Hence ~'ER[1] *n.* **4.** *n.* Leap so performed. [f. OF *vo(u)lter* leap, f. Rom. **vol(u)tare* frequent. of L *volvere* roll, assim. to prec.]

vaunt *v.i.* & *t.*, & *n.* Boast, brag; boast of, extol boastfully, so ~'ER[1] *n.* (arch.). [ME, f. AF *vaunter*, OF *vanter* f. LL *van(i)tare* f. L *vanus* VAIN; partly obs. *avaunt* v. f. OF *avanter* (*a* intensive, *vanter*)]

vau'nt-courĭer (-kŏŏ-) *n.* (arch.) Forerunner. [f. *avant-courier* f. F *avant-courrier* (*avant* before; see AVAUNT, COURIER)]

vă'vasorў *n.* (Hist.) Estate of vavasour. [f. OF *vavasorie* or f. med. L *-oria* (as foll.; see -Y[1])]

vă'vasour (-oor) *n.* (Hist.) Vassal holding from great lord and having other vassals under him. [ME, f. OF *vavas(s)our* f. med. L *vavassor*, perh. f. *vassus vassorum* VASSAL of vassals]

vaw'ard. Var. (arch.) of VANGUARD.

V.C. *abbr.* Vice-Chairman, -Chancellor, -Consul; Victoria Cross.

V.D. *abbr.* venereal disease; Volunteer (Officer's) Decoration.

've *v.* (colloq., chiefly after pronouns). = HAVE[1]. [abbr.]

VE *abbr.* Victory in Europe; ~ **day,** 8 May 1945.

veal *n.* Calf's flesh as food; hence ~'Y[2] *a.*, like veal, (fig.) immature. [ME, f. AF *ve(e)l*, OF *veiaus veel* f. L *vitellus* dim. of *vitulus* calf]

vĕ'ctor *n.*, & *v.t.* **1.** *n.* (Math.) Quantity having both magnitude and direction, esp. as determining position of one point in space relative to another (RADIUS *vector*); course to be taken by aircraft; hence **vĕctŏr'**IAL *a.* **2.** Carrier of disease or infection from one organism to another. **3.** *v.t.* Direct (aircraft in flight) to desired point. [L, = carrier (*vehere vect-* convey; see -OR)]

Vē'da (*or* vā'-) *n.* (in *sing.* or *pl.*) Ancient Hindu scriptures, esp. **Rig, Sāma, Yajur, Atharva,** -~, four collections of hymns etc. [f. Skr. *vēda*, lit. (sacred) knowledge]

Vėdā'nt|a (*or* vādah'-) *n.* **1.** Upanishads. **2.** Monistic Hindu philosophy founded on the Upanishads. **3.** Hence ~IC *a.*, ~IST (3) *n.* [f. Skr. *vēdānta* (as VEDA, *anta* end)]

Vĕ'dda *n.* Aborigine of Sri Lanka. [f. Sinh. *veddā* hunter]

vėdĕ'tte *n.* Mounted sentry placed in advance of an outpost. [F, = scout, f. It. *vedetta*, *veletta* f. Sp. *vela(r)* watch f. L *vigilare*]

Vē'dĭc (*or* vā'-) *a.* & *n.* **1.** *a.* Of Veda(s). **2.** *n.* Language of the Vedas, old form of Sanskrit. [f. F *védique* or G *vedisch*; see VEDA, -IC]

vee *n.* (Thing shaped like) letter V. [name of the letter]

***Veep** *n.* (colloq.) Vice-President. [f. abbr. V.P.]

veer[1] *v.t.* (Naut.) Slacken, let out, (rope, cable, etc.); ~ **and haul,** tighten and slacken (rope etc.) alternately, (fig.) deal with problem by skilful manœuvres. [ME, f. MDu. *vieren*]

veer[2] *v.* & *n.* **1.** *v.i.* Change direction esp. (of wind; cf. BACK[2]) clockwise; (Naut.) = WEAR[3]. **2.** *v.i.* & *t.* (fig.) Change in course or opinion or conduct or language. **3.** *n.* Change of direction, shifting round. [f. F *virer* f. Rom. **virare*, perh. alt. f. L *gyrare* GYRATE[2]]

vĕg (-j) *n.* (colloq.) Vegetable(s). [abbr.]

vē'gan *n.* & *a.* (Person) eating no animals or animal products; strict(ly) vegetarian. [f. VEGETARIAN]

vĕ'gėtable *a.* & *n.* **1.** *a.* Of (the nature of), derived from, concerned with, comprising, plants, esp. opp. *animal* or *mineral* (*vegetable* BUTTER[1], IVORY, *kingdom*, MARROW, OYSTER, PARCHMENT, SPONGE[1], TALLOW, WAX[1]); (of life etc.) like that of vegetable, uneventful, monotonous. **2.** *n.* Plant, esp. herbaceous plant or part of one used for food, e.g. cabbage, potato, turnip, bean, pumpkin, yam; person living vegetable life through injury or lack of ambition. [ME f. OF, or f. LL *vegetabilis* animating (as VEGETATE; see -ABLE)]

vĕ'gėtal *a.* Of (the nature of) plants; vegetative; **the ~ functions** (of growth, circulation, nutrition, etc.). [f. med. L *vegetalis* f. L *vegetare* animate; see -AL]

vĕgėtār'ian *n.* One who abstains from animal food, esp. that obtained by killing animals, and whose diet includes roots, green vegetables, cereals, seeds, fruit, and nuts, with or without eggs and dairy products; hence ~ISM (3) *n.* [irreg. f. VEGETABLE + -ARIAN]

vĕ'gėtāte *v.i.* Grow as plants do, fulfil vegetal functions; (fig.) live an uneventful or monotonous life. [f. L *vegetare* animate (*vegetus* f. *vegēre* be active) + -ATE³]

vĕgėtā'tion *n.* Vegetating (lit. or fig.); plants collectively, plant life, (*luxuriant vegetation*; *no sign of vegetation for miles round*); (Path.) abnormal plantlike growth on surface of body. [f. med. L *vegetatio* growth (as VEGETATE; see -ATION)]

vĕ'gėtātive *a.* Concerned with growth and development, opp. (sexual) reproduction; of vegetation; hence ~LY² (-vlĭ) *adv.*, ~NESS (-vn-) *n.* [ME, f. OF *vegetatif* -*ive* or f. med. L *vegetativus* (as VEGETATE; see -IVE)]

vē'hėm|ent (vē'ĭ-) *a.* Showing or caused by strong feeling, impetuous, ardent, passionate, (*a vehement desire, protest*; *man of vehement character*); (arch.) acting with great force, violent, (*a vehement wind, onset*); hence or cogn. ~ENCE *n.*, **~ent**LY² *adv.* [ME, f. F *véhément* or f. L *vehemens* -*entis*, perh. f. **vemens* deprived of mind, assoc. w. *vehere* carry]

vē'hĭcle (vē'ĭ-) *n.* Carriage or conveyance of any kind used on land or in space; liquid etc. used as medium for suspending pigments, drugs, etc.; thing or person used as medium for thought or feeling or action (*used the pulpit, the press, as a vehicle for his political opinions*; *will not be used as the vehicle of your resentment*); so **vėhĭ'cūl**AR¹ *a.* [f. F *véhicule* or f. L *vehiculum* (*vehere* carry; see -CULE)]

vehm|gericht (fā'mgerĭχt) *n.* German system of secret tribunals prevailing esp. in Westphalia *c.* 1200–1550; such tribunal; so ~IC *a.* [G (*vehm* punishment, *gericht* tribunal)]

veil (vāl) *n.*, & *v.t.* **1.** *n.* Piece of usu. more or less transparent material attached to woman's hat or otherwise forming part of head-dress, esp. one serving to conceal the face or as protection against sun, dust, etc.; piece of linen etc. as part of nun's head-dress, falling over head and shoulders (**take the ~**, become nun); curtain, esp. that separating sanctuary in Jewish Temple, (**beyond the ~**, in the unknown state of life after death); (fig.) disguise, pretext, (*under the veil of religion*); **draw a ~ over,** avoid discussing or calling attention to. **2.** = VELUM; (Photog.) slight fogging. **3.** Slight huskiness of voice, natural or due to a cold etc. **4.** Hence ~'ING¹ (3) *n.*, ~'LESS (-l-l-) *a.* **5.** *v.t.* Cover (one's face, one*self*, or abs.) with veil; (fig.) partly conceal, disguise, mask, (*veiled threat, resentment*). [ME, f. AF *veil*(*e*), OF *voil*(*e*) f. L *vela* pl. of VELUM]

vein (vān) *n.*, & *v.t.* **1.** *n.* Membranous tube forming part of system by which blood is conveyed to heart (cf. ARTERY). **2.** (pop.) Any blood-vessel (*has royal blood in his veins*). **3.** Nervure of insect's wing; slender bundle of tissue forming part of framework of leaf; (Geol. & Mining) fissure in rock filled with deposited material, e.g. ore (**~'stone,** gangue). **4.** Streak or stripe of different colour in wood, marble, cheese, etc. **5.** Distinctive character or tendency, cast of mind or disposition, mood, (*was of an imaginative vein*; *said this in a humorous vein*; *other remarks in the same vein*). **6.** Hence ~'LESS, ~'LIKE, ~'Y², *adjs.*, ~'LET *n.* **7.** *v.t.* (esp. in *p.p.*) Fill or cover (as) with vein(s); hence ~'ING¹ (6) *n.* [ME, f. OF *veine* f. L *vena*]

vē'la. See VELUM.

vėlā'|men *n.* (*pl.* **~mina**). Enveloping membrane esp. of aerial root of orchid. [L (*velare* cover)]

vē'lar *a.* Of a veil or velum; (Phonet., of sound) pronounced with back of tongue near soft palate. [f. L *velaris* (VELUM; see -AR¹)]

vĕld, vĕldt, (vĕld *or* vĕlt *or* fĕlt) *n.* (S. Afr.) Open country neither cultivated nor true forest; **~'schoen** (fĕ'lskōōn), shoe of untanned hide. [Afrik., = FIELD]

velē'ta, valē'ta, *n.* Ballroom dance in triple time. [Sp., = weather-vane]

vĕlĭtā'tion *n.* (arch.) Slight skirmish, controversy. [f. L *velitatio* (*velitari* skirmish f. *veles velitis* light-armed skirmisher; see -ATION)]

vĕllē'ĭtў *n.* Low degree of volition not prompting to action; slight wish or inclination. [f. med. L *velleitas* f. L *velle* to wish; see -ITY]

vĕ'llum *n.* Fine parchment orig. from skin of calf; manuscript written on this; smooth writing-paper imitating vellum. [ME, f. OF *velin* (as VEAL; see -INE¹)]

vėlŏ'cĭpēd|e *n.* **1.** (Hist.) Light vehicle propelled by rider, esp. early form of bicycle; hence ~IST (3) *n.* **2.** *Child's tricycle. [f. F *vélocipède* f. L *velox -ocis* swift + *pes pedis* foot]

vėlŏ'cĭtў *n.* Quickness or rate of motion or action usu. of inanimate things; (Mech.) speed in a given direction; **~ of escape,** = ESCAPE¹ *velocity*; **~ of light,** constant rate (about 300,000 km. per sec.) at which radiation travels in vacuum; so **vėlocĭ'**METER *n.* [f. F *vélocité* or f. L *velocitas* (as prec.; see -ITY)]

velour', velours', (-oor') *n.* Plushlike woven fabric or felt; hat of such felt. [F *velours* velvet f. OF *velour*, *velous* f. L *villosus* hairy (*villus*; see VELVET)]

velou'té (-ōō'tā) *n.* Sauce of white stock mixed with cooked butter and flour. [F, = velvety]

velskoon. Var. of VELD*schoen*.

vē'l|um *n.* (*pl.* **~a**). (Anat., Bot., & Zool.) Membrane or membranous covering, esp. the soft palate. [L, = sail, curtain, covering, veil]

vėlū'tĭnous *a.* (Bot. & Entom.) Velvety. [perh. f. It. *vellutino* (*velluto* VELVET)]

vĕ'lvėt *n.* & *a.* **1.** *n.* Closely woven fabric (orig. of silk) with thick short pile on one side; furry skin covering a growing antler; profit, gain; **on ~**, in an advantageous or prosperous position; hence ~ED², ~Y², *adjs.* **2.** *a.* Of, like, soft as, velvet; **~ bean,** annual bean of southern U.S. used as fodder; **~ glove,** outward gentleness or suavity cloaking inflexibility (*with an iron hand in a velvet glove*). [ME, f. OF *veluotte* (*velu* velvety f. med. L *villutus* f. L *villus* down)]

vĕlvėtee'n *n.* Cotton fabric with pile like velvet; (in *pl.*) trousers etc. made of this. [f. prec.]

Ven. *abbr.* Venerable (as title of archdeacon).

vēna cā'va *n.* (*pl.* **-ae -ae**). Each of usu. two veins conveying blood into heart. [L, = hollow vein]

vē'nal *a.* (Of person) that may be bribed, ready to sell one's influence or services or to sacrifice principles from sordid motives; (of conduct etc.) characteristic of venal person; hence or cogn. **vēnă'l**ITY *n.*, ~LY² *adv.* [f. L *venalis* (*venum* thing for sale; see -AL)]

vėnā'tion *n.* Arrangement of veins in leaf, insect's wing, etc.; hence ~AL *a.* [f. L *vena* vein + -ATION]

vĕnd *v.t.* **1.** (Law). Sell; hence ~EE' *n.* **2.** Offer (small wares) for sale; hence (-)~'ER¹ *n.*;

~'ing-machine (for automatic retail of small articles). **3.** Hence ~'IBLE *a.* [f. F *vendre* or f. L *vendere* sell (as VENAL, *dare* give)]

vĕ'ndāce *n.* Small delicate fish (*Coregonus albula*) found in some British lakes. [f. OF *vendese*, *-oise* f. Gaulish **vindesia* (**vindos* white)]

vĕndĕ'tta *n.* Blood feud in which family of injured or murdered man seeks vengeance on offender or his family; this practice as prevalent in Corsica etc.; prolonged bitter hostility. [It., f. L *vindicta*; see VINDICTIVE]

vendeuse (vahndêr'z) *n.* Saleswoman, esp. in fashionable dress-shop. [F]

vĕ'ndor *n.* **1.** (esp. Law). One who sells. **2.** = VEND*ing-machine*. [AF *vendo(u)r* (as VEND, -OR)]

***vĕndūe'** *n.* Public auction. [f. Du. *vendu(e)* f. F *vendue* sale (*vendre* VEND)]

vėneer' *v.t.*, & *n.* **1.** *v.t.* Cover (wood, furniture, etc.) with thin coating of finer wood; (fig.) disguise (character etc.) under superficial polish of manner etc.; so ~ING¹ (1, 2, 4) *n.* **2.** *n.* Thin outer coating, veneering (lit. or fig.); **~-moth,** moth of subfamily Crambidae, whose colouring suggests veneer. [earlier *fineer* f. G *furni(e)ren* f. OF *fournir* FURNISH]

vĕ'nėpŭncture, vĕ'nĭ-, *n.* (Med.) Puncture of vein esp. with hypodermic needle to withdraw blood or for intravenous injection. [f. L *vena* vein + PUNCTURE]

vĕ'ner|able *a.* Entitled to veneration on account of character, age, associations, etc., (*venerable priest, relics, beard, ruins*; in Ch. of Engl. as title of archdeacon, in R.C. Ch. as title of one who has attained a certain degree of sanctity but is not fully beatified or canonized); hence ~ABI'LITY, **~able**NESS (-beln-), *ns.*, **~ab**LY² *adv.* [ME f. OF, or L *venerabilis* (as foll.; see -ABLE)]

vĕ'nerāt|e *v.t.* Consider worthy of and regard with deep respect or warm approbation; revere; so ~OR *n.* [f. L *venerari* adore, revere + -ATE³]

vĕnerā'tion *n.* Deep respect, reverence; venerating or being venerated. [ME, f. OF, or f. L *veneratio* (as prec.; see -ATION)]

vėnēr'ėal *a.* Of sexual desire or intercourse; relating to ~ **disease** (contracted by sexual intercourse with person already infected); hence ~LY² *adv.* [ME, f. L *venereus* (*venus veneris* sexual love) + -AL]

vėnērėŏ'log|y̆ *n.* Study of venereal diseases; hence **vėnērėolŏ'g**ICAL *a.*, ~IST (3) *n.* [f. as prec. + -O- + -LOGY]

vĕ'nery̆¹ *n.* (arch.) Hunting. [ME, f. OF *venerie* (*vener* to hunt f. Rom. **venare* for L *venari*; see -ERY)]

vĕ'nery̆² *n.* (arch.) Sexual indulgence. [f. med. L *veneria* (as VENEREAL; see -Y¹)]

vĕ'nėsĕction, vĕ'nĭ-, *n.* Phlebotomy. [f. med. L *venae sectio* cutting of VEIN; see SECTION]

Vėnē'tian (-shan) *a.* & *n.* **1.** *a.* Of Venice; **v~ blind,** window blind of horizontal slats that may be adjusted so as to admit or exclude light and air; ~ **carpet** (with worsted warp and usu. with striped pattern); ~ (= FRENCH) **chalk**; ~ **glass,** delicate glassware made at Murano near Venice; ~ **pearl,** imitation pearl of solid glass; ~ **red,** reddish pigment of ferric oxides; ~ **sumac,** a Eur. smoke-tree with large panicles of flowers; ~ **window** (with three separate openings, central one being arched and highest). **2.** *n.* Native or dialect of Venice. **3.** (*v~*). Venetian blind, whence **v~**ED² (-nd) *a.* [ME, f. OF *Venicien*, assim. to med. L *Venetianus* (*Venetia* Venice; see -AN)]

vĕ'ngeance (-njans) *n.* Punishment inflicted or retribution exacted for wrong to oneself or to person etc. whose cause one supports; **with a ~,** in a higher degree than was expected or desired, in the fullest sense of the word(s), and no mistake, (*this is punctuality with a vengeance*). [ME f. OF (*venger* avenge f. L, as VINDICATE; see -ANCE)]

vĕ'ngeful (-njf-) *a.* Disposed to revenge, vindictive; hence ~LY² *adv.*, ~NESS *n.* [f. obs. *venge* avenge (as prec.) + -FUL]

vē'nĭal *a.* (Of sin or fault) pardonable, excusable, not very wrong, (Theol.) not mortal; hence ~ITY (-ă'l-), ~NESS, *ns.*, ~LY² *adv.* [ME f. OF, f. LL *venialis* (*venia* forgiveness; see -AL)]

vĕ'nĭpŭncture, -sĕction. See VENEPUNCTURE etc.

vėnīr'ė *n.* (Law). **1.** ~ (**facias** *pr.* fā'shĭăs), (Hist. or U.S.) writ directing sheriff to summon jury. **2.** *Panel of persons thus summoned; **~man,** member of this. [f. L *venire facias* make or cause to come]

vĕ'nĭson (*or* -z-; *or* -ns- *or* -nz-) *n.* Deer's flesh as food. [ME, f. OF *veneso(u)n* f. L *venatio -onis* hunting (*venari* to hunt; see -ATION, -ISON)]

Vėnī'tė *n.* Canticle consisting of Ps. 95. [ME f. L, = come ye, its first word]

Vĕnn *n.* ~ **diagram,** set of circles etc. representing logical classes which may or may not coincide, intersect, etc. [f. J. ~, Engl. logician d. 1923]

vĕ'nom *n.* Poisonous fluid secreted by serpents, scorpions, etc., and introduced into system of victim by bite or sting; (fig.) malignity, virulence of feeling or language or conduct; hence ~ED² (-md) *a.* [ME, f. OF *venim*, var. of *venin* f. Rom. **venimen* f. L *venenum* poison]

vĕ'nomous *a.* Containing or full of venom; secreting venom, inflicting poisonous wounds by this means; (fig.) virulent like venom, spiteful, malignant; hence ~LY² *adv.*, ~NESS *n.* [ME, f. OF *venimeux* (*venim*; see prec., -OUS)]

vē'nōse *a.* Having many or very marked veins. [f. L *venosus* (*vena* vein; see -OSE¹)]

vē'nous *a.* (Anat., Zool., & Bot.) Of, full of, contained in, veins; hence or cogn. **vēno**'SITY *n.*, ~LY² *adv.* [f. L as prec., or f. L *vena* vein + -OUS]

vĕnt¹ *n.* & *v.* **1.** *n.* ~(**-hole**), hole or opening allowing motion of substance out of or into confined space, e.g. touch-hole of gun, hole in top of barrel to admit air while liquid is being drawn out, finger-hole in musical instrument (also ~'AGE *n.*), flue of chimney, fumarole of volcano. **2.** Anus esp. of lower animal, serving for both excretion and reproduction. **3.** (fig.) Outlet, free passage, free play, (*gave vent to his indignation*; *impatience found a vent*). **4.** Venting of otter etc. **5. ~-peg, ~-plug,** (for stopping vent of barrel etc.). **6.** Hence ~'LESS *a.* **7.** *v.t.* Make vent in (gun, cask, etc.); give vent or free expression to (one's SPLEEN; *vented his disgust in an epigram, with a snort, on the office boy*). **8.** *v.i.* (Of otter or beaver) come to surface for breath. [partly f. F *vent* f. L *ventus* wind, partly f. F *évent* f. *éventer* expose to air f. OF *esventer* f. Rom. *EX¹(*ventare* f. L *ventus* wind)]

vĕnt² *n.* Slit in garment, esp. in back of coat. [ME, var. of *fent* f. OF *fente* slit f. Rom. **findita* fem. p.p. (as n.) f. L *findere* cleave]

vĕ'ntidŭct *n.* (Archit.) Air-passage, esp. for ventilation. [f. L *ventus* wind + -I- + *ductus* DUCT]

vĕ'ntĭfăct *n.* Stone shaped by wind-blown sand. [f. L *ventus* wind + -I- + *factum* neut. p.p. of *facere* make]

vĕ'ntĭl *n.* (Mus.) Valve in wind instrument; shutter for regulating air-flow in organ. [G, f. It. *ventile*, f. med. L *ventile* sluice f. L *ventus* wind]

vĕ'ntĭl|āte *v.t.* Cause air to circulate freely in (room etc.); purify by air, oxygenate, (blood); submit (question, subject, grievance, etc.) to public consideration and discussion; hence or cogn. ~A'TION, **~ā**TOR (esp., appliance or aperture for ventilating room, compartment, mine, etc.), *ns.*, ~**ātive** *a.* [f. L *ventilare* blow, winnow (*ventus* wind) + -ATE[3]]

vĕ'ntral *a.* & *n.* (Anat. & Zool.) Of or on the abdomen (opp. DORSAL); (Bot.) of the front or lower surface; ~ (**fin**), either of the ventrally placed fins; hence ~LY[2] *adv.* [f. *venter* abdomen f. L + -AL]

ventre à terre (vahṅtrahtār') *adv.* At full speed. [F, lit. with belly to ground]

vĕ'ntrĭcle *n.* (Anat.) Cavity in the body, hollow part of organ, esp. one of four in the brain or two in the heart; hence **vĕntrĭ'cūlAR**[1] *a.* [ME, f. L *ventriculus* dim. of *venter* belly; see -CULE]

vĕ'ntrĭcōse *a.* Having a protruding belly; (Bot.) distended, inflated. [irreg. f. prec. + -OSE[1]]

vĕntrĭ'loqu|ĭsm *n.* Act or art of speaking or uttering sounds in such a manner that the voice appears to come from some source other than the speaker; so ~IST (1), ~Y[1], *ns.*, **vĕntrĭlō'quiAL**, ~**ĭ'stIC**, ~OUS, *adjs.*, ~IZE (2) *v.i.* [ult. f. L *ventriloquus* ventriloquist (*venter* belly, *loqui* speak)]

vĕntrĭ'potent *a.* (literary). Large-bellied; gluttonous. [F, f. med. L *ventripotens* (as prec., POTENT)]

vĕ'nture *n.* & *v.* **1.** *n.* Undertaking of a risk, risky undertaking, (*declined the venture*; *ready for any venture*); commercial speculation (*one lucky venture made his fortune*); (arch.) thing at stake, property risked; **at a** ~, at random, without previous consideration; **V~ Scout,** senior Scout. **2.** *v.i.* Dare, not be afraid, (*did not venture to stop him*; *I venture to differ from you*); dare to go etc. (*shall not venture out*); take risks; ~ **(up)on,** dare to engage in, make, etc. **3.** *v.t.* Dare to make or advance or put forward, hazard, (*would not venture an opinion, a guess, a step*); expose to risk, stake, (*men who venture their lives for the cause*; *will venture a small bet on it*; *nothing venture, nothing gain* or *have* or *win*). **4.** Hence **vĕ'nturER**[1] (-cher-) *n.*, (esp. Hist.) one who undertakes or shares in a trading venture, ~SOME[1] (-chers-) *a.* [f. *aventure* = ADVENTURE[1,2]]

vĕntūr'ĭ *n.* Short piece of tube between wider sections for measuring flow-rate or exerting suction. [f. G. B. *Venturi*, It. physicist d. 1822]

vĕ'nūe *n.* **1.** (Law). County etc. within which jury must be gathered and cause tried (orig. neighbourhood of crime etc.); **change the** ~ (to avoid riot, prejudiced jury, etc.). **2.** Appointed place of meeting esp. for match etc., rendezvous. [F, = coming, fem. p.p. (as n.) of *venir* come f. L *venire*]

vĕ'nūle *n.* (Anat.) Small vein adjoining capillaries. [f. L *venula* dim. of *vena* vein; see -ULE]

Vē'nus *n.* **1.** (Rom. Myth.) Goddess of love. **2.** Planet second from sun in solar system; hence **Vĕnū'sIAN** (-z-) *a.* & *n.* **3.** Sexual love, amorous influences or desires. **4.** Beautiful woman. **5.** ~**'s comb,** = SHEPHERD'*s needle*; ~**'s fly-trap,** herb *Dionaea muscipula*, with leaves that close on insects etc.; ~**'s girdle,** ribbon-like ctenophore; ~**'s slipper,** = LADY'*s slipper*. [OE, f. L *Venus Veneris*]

verā'cious (-shus) *a.* Speaking, disposed to speak, the truth; (of statement etc.) true, not (meant to be) false; hence ~LY[2] *adv.*, **veră'cITY** *n.* [f. L *verax veracis* (*verus* true; see -ACIOUS)]

verā'nda, -dah, (-*a*) *n.* Open portico or gallery along side of house with roof supported on pillars. [f. Hindi *varandā* f. Port. *varanda*]

vĕ'ratrĭne (*or* -ēn) *n.* Poisonous compound from sabadilla etc. used esp. as local irritant in treatment of neuralgia and rheumatism. [f. F *vératrine* f. L *veratrum* hellebore; see -INE[5]]

vērb *n.* (Gram.) Part of speech that predicates, word whose function is predication (e.g. italicized words in Time *flies*, Salt *is* good, You *surprise* me). [ME, f. OF *verbe* or f. L *verbum* word, verb]

vēr'bal *a.* & *n.* **1.** *a.* Of or concerned with words (*verbal distinctions*, *subtleties*, *critic(ism)*, *accuracy*, INSPIRATION). **2.** Oral, not written (*a verbal communication*, *contract*; *verbal evidence*). **3.** (Of translation) literal, word for word. **4.** (Gram.) Of (the nature of) a verb (*verbal inflexions*); ~ **noun,** noun derived from verb and partly sharing its constructions (e.g. E nouns in -ING[1]); ~ **senses,** those of a corresponding verb. **5.** Hence ~LY[2] *adv.* **6.** *n.* Verbal noun; verbal statement, esp. one made to police. [ME f. F, or f. LL *verbalis* (as prec.; see -AL)]

vēr'bal|ĭsm *n.* Minute attention to words, verbal criticism; (merely) verbal expression; so ~IST (2) *n.*, ~**ĭ'stIC** *a.* [f. prec. + -ISM]

vēr'balīz|e, -īs|e (-īz), *v.* **1.** *v.t.* Make (noun etc.) into a verb; express in words. **2.** *v.i.* Be verbose. **3.** Hence ~A'TION *n.* [f. F *verbaliser*, or f. VERBAL + -IZE]

verbā'tĭm *adv.* & *a.* In exactly the same words, word for word (*copied it verbatim*; *a verbatim reprint*). [ME f. med. L (adv.), f. L *verbum* word; cf. LITERATIM]

verbē'na *n.* Plant of genus *Verbena*, vervain; **lemon** ~, similar plant (*Lippia citriodora*) with lemon-scented leaves. [L, = sacred bough of olive etc., in med. L vervain]

vēr'bĭage *n.* Needless accumulation of words, verbosity. [F (obs. *verbeier* chatter f. *verbe* word; see VERB, -AGE)]

vēr'bĭcīde *n.* (joc.) Destruction of, or one who destroys, sense or value of a word. [f. as VERB + -I- + -CIDE]

verbō'se *a.* Using or expressed in more words than are wanted, prolix; hence or cogn. ~LY[2] (-slĭ) *adv.*, ~NESS (-sn-), **verbo'sITY**, *ns.* [f. L *verbosus* (*verbum* word; see -OSE[1])]

verboten (ferbō'ten) *a.* Forbidden, esp. by authority. [G]

vērb. să'p. *int.* expr. absence of need for further explicit statement. [abbr. of L *verbum sapienti sat est* a word is enough for the wise person]

vēr'dant *a.* (Of grass etc.) green, fresh-coloured; (of field etc.) covered with green grass etc.; (of person) unsophisticated, raw, green; hence **vēr'dANCY** *n.*, ~LY[2] *adv.* [perh. f. OF *verdeant* part. of *verdoier* be green f. L **viridiare* (*viridis* green)]

vērd-ănti'que (-ē'k) *n.* Ornamental usu. green serpentine; green incrustation on ancient bronze; green porphyry. [obs. F, = antique green]

‖**vēr'derer** *n.* Judicial officer of royal forests. [AF, earlier *verder*, OF *verdier* f. Gallo-Rom. **viridarius* f. L *viridis* green; see -ER[2]]

vēr'dĭct *n.* **1.** Decision of jury on issue of fact in civil or criminal cause (*brought in a verdict of not guilty, a verdict for the plaintiff*); **open** ~ (affirming commission of crime but not specifying criminal, or occurrence of violent death but not specifying cause); **partial** ~ (finding person guilty of part of the charge); **sealed** ~ (written, and delivered to clerk of court when court has adjourned during deliberation of jury); **special** ~ (stating facts as proved but leaving court to draw conclusion from them). **2.** Decision, judgement, (*the verdict of the public was in his favour*; *does not dispute your verdict*). [ME f. AF *verdit*, OF *voirdit* (*voir, veir* true f. L *verus, dit* f. L DICTUM saying)]

vēr'dĭgrĭs (*or* -ēs) *n.* Green crystallized substance formed on copper by action of acetic acid and used in medicine and as pigment etc.; green rust on copper or brass. [ME, f. OF *verte-gres*, *vert de Grece* green of Greece]

vĕr'dĭter *n.* Basic copper carbonate as blue or green pigment. [f. OF *verd de terre* green of earth]

vĕr'dur|e (-dyer) *n.* Greenness of vegetation, green vegetation, whence ~ED² (-dyerd), ~OUS, *adjs.*; (fig.) freshness. [ME f. OF (*verd* green f. L *viridis*; see -URE)]

Verey. Var. of VERY².

vĕrge¹ *n.* **1.** Extreme edge, brink, border, (usu. fig.; *drew near to the very verge of the stream*; *on the verge of 70, destruction, tears, betraying his secret*). **2.** Grass edging of flower-bed, road, etc.; (Archit.) edge of tiles projecting over gable (**~-board,** = BARGE-BOARD). **3.** Wand or rod carried before bishop, dean, etc., as emblem of office. **4.** (Hist.) Area of jurisdiction of Lord High Steward. [ME f. OF, f. L *virga* rod]

vĕrge² *v.i.* Incline downwards or in specified direction (*the now verging sun*; *verge towards old age, to a close*); ~ **on,** border on, approach closely, (*path verges on the edge of a precipice*; *a solemnity verging on the tragic*). [f. L *vergere* bend, incline]

vĕr'ger *n.* Official in a church who shows persons to their seats etc.; ‖officer who bears staff before bishop, (vice-)chancellor of university, etc.; hence ~SHIP *n.* [ME, f. AF **verger* (as VERGE¹; see -ER²)]

ver'glas (vār'glah) *n.* Thin coating of ice or sleet. [F]

vėrĭ'dĭcal *a.* Truthful; (Psych., of visions etc.) coinciding with realities; hence ~LY² *adv.* [f. L *veridicus* (*verus* true, *dicere* say) + -AL]

vĕ'rĭėst. See VERY¹.

vĕ'rĭ|fȳ *v.t.* Establish the truth or correctness of by examination or demonstration (*must verify the statement, his figures*; *always verify your references*); (of event, action, etc.) bear out, make good, fulfil, (prediction, promise); (Law) append affidavit to (pleadings), support (statement) by proofs; hence or cogn. ~FICA'TION, ~fīER¹, *ns.*, ~fīABLE *a.* [ME, f. OF *verifier* f. med. L *verificare* (*verus* true; see -FY)]

vĕ'rĭlȳ *adv.* (arch.) Really, truly, in very truth. [ME, f. VERY¹ + -LY², after OF & AF]

vĕrĭsĭmĭ'lĭtūde *n.* Appearance of being true, semblance of actuality, (*the verisimilitude of the tale*; *verisimilitude is not proof*); statement etc. that seems true; so **vĕrĭsĭ'mĭl**AR¹ *a.* [f. L *verisimilitudo* f. *verisimilis* probable (*veri* gen. of *verus* true, *similis* like); see -TUDE]

vĕr'ĭsm *n.* Realism in literature or art; so **vĕr'**IST (2) *n.* [f. L *verus* or It. *vero* true + -ISM]

vĕrĭ'smō *n.* (*pl.* **~s**). = prec. (esp. of opera). [It. (as prec.)]

vĕ'rĭtab|le *a.* Real, rightly so called, (*a veritable boon*); hence ~LY² *adv.* [OF (as foll.; see -ABLE)]

vĕ'rĭtȳ *n.* Truth (of statement etc.); true statement, esp. one of fundamental import; really existent thing; **of a** ~, (arch.) in truth, really. [ME, f. OF *ver(i)té* f. L *veritas -tatis* (*verus* true; see -ITY)]

vĕr'juice (-ōōs) *n.* Acid liquor got from crab--apples, sour grapes, etc., and formerly used in cooking and medicine; (fig.) bitterness. [ME, f. OF *vertjus* (VERT¹ green, *jus* JUICE)]

verkrampte (ferkrǎ'mpte) *a.* (S. Afr.) Regarded as relatively reactionary or unprogressive, esp. towards Negroes. [Afrik.]

verligte (ferlĭ'χte) *a.* (S. Afr.) Regarded as relatively progressive or enlightened, esp. towards Negroes. [Afrik.]

vĕr'meil (-māl *or* -mĭl) *n.* Silver gilt; orange-red garnet; (poet.) vermilion. [ME f. OF; see VERMILION]

vĕr'mĭ- *comb. form.* Worm, as: **~cide,** drug that kills worms; **~form,** worm-shaped (*vermiform* APPENDIX); **~fuge,** (drug) that expels intestinal worms; **~vorous** (-ĭ'v-), feeding on worms. [f. L *vermis* worm; see -I-]

vĕr'mĭan *a.* Of worms, wormlike. [f. L *vermis* worm + -AN]

vĕrmĭcĕ'llĭ *n.* Pasta made in long slender threads. [It., pl. of *vermicello* dim. of *verme* f. L *vermis* worm]

vermĭ'cūlar *a.* Like a worm in form or movements, vermiform; (Med.) of or caused by intestinal worms; marked with close wavy lines. [f. med. L *vermicularis* f. L *vermiculus* dim. of *vermis* worm; see -AR¹]

vermĭ'cūlate *a.* = prec. (usu. fig.); worm-eaten. [f. L *vermiculatus* p.p. of *vermiculari* be full of worms (as prec.; see -ATE²)]

vermĭcūlā'tion *n.* Being eaten or infested by or converted into worms; vermicular marking; worm-eaten state. [f. L *vermiculatio* (as prec.; see -ATION)]

vermĭ'cūlite *n.* Hydrous silicate mineral usu. resulting from alteration of mica, and expandable into sponge by heating. [f. as VERMICULATE + -ITE² (2)]

vermĭ'lion (-yon) *n.*, *a.*, & *v.t.* **1.** *n.* Cinnabar; brilliant red pigment made by grinding this or artificially. **2.** *n.* & *a.* (Of) this colour. **3.** *v.t.* Colour (as) with vermilion. [ME, f. OF *vermeillon* (*vermeil* f. L *vermiculus* dim. of *vermis* worm; see -OON)]

vĕr'mĭn *n.* (usu. treated as *pl.*) Mammals and birds injurious to game, crops, etc., e.g. foxes, weasels, rats, mice, moles, owls; noxious insects, e.g. fleas, bugs, lice; parasitic worms or insects; (fig.) vile persons; so ~OUS *a.* [ME f. OF *vermin, -ine* f. Rom. **verminum, -ina* collect. f. L *vermis* worm]

vĕr'mĭn|āte *v.i.* Breed vermin; become infested with parasites; so ~A'TION *n.* [f. L *verminare* (*vermis* worm) + -ATE³]

vĕr'mouth (-ōōth *or* -uth) *n.* White wine flavoured with wormwood or other aromatic herbs; **French, Italian,** ~, dry, sweet, kind. [f. F *vermout* f. G *wermut* WORMWOOD]

vernă'cūlar *a.* & *n.* **1.** *a.* (Of language, idiom, word) of one's native country, native, indigenous, not of foreign origin or of learned formation; ~ **architecture** (concerned with ordinary buildings, not cathedrals etc.). **2.** *n.* The language or dialect of the country (*Latin gave place to the vernacular*); language of a particular class or group; homely speech. **3.** Hence ~ISM (4), ~ITY (-ă'r-), *ns.*, ~IZE (3) *v.t.*, ~LY² *adv.* [f. L *vernaculus* domestic, native (*verna* home--born slave) + -AR¹]

vĕr'nal *a.* Of or like, appearing or occurring or done in, appropriate to, spring, (*vernal breezes, flowers*, EQUINOX, *migration, fancies*); ~ **grass,** sweet-scented Eur. grass grown for hay; hence ~LY² *adv.* [f. L *vernalis* (*vernus* f. *ver* spring; see -AL)]

vĕrnalizā'tion *n.* Cooling of seed before planting, in order to accelerate flowering; hence **vĕr'nal**IZE (1) *v.t.* [(transl. of Russ. *yarovizatsiya*) f. prec. + -IZE + -ATION]

vernā'tion *n.* (Bot.) Arrangement of leaves in leaf-bud (cf. AESTIVATION). [f. mod. L *vernatio* f. L *vernare* bloom (as VERNAL; see -ATION)]

Vĕr'ner *n.* **~'s law** (relating to voicing of orig. fricatives in Germanic languages, giving e.g. *sodden* as p.p. of *seethe*). [f. K. A. ~, Da. philologist d. 1896]

vĕr'nĭcle *n.* = VERONICA 2. [ME f. OF, earlier *ver(o)nique* f. med. L VERONICA]

vĕr'nĭer *n.* Small movable graduated scale for obtaining fractional parts of the subdivisions on fixed scale of barometer, sextant, etc.; ~ **engine,** auxiliary engine for slight changes in motion of space rocket etc. [f. P. *Vernier*, Fr. mathematician d. 1637]

vĕ'ronal *n.* Sedative drug, derivative of barbituric acid. [G, f. *Verona* in Italy]

verŏ'nĭca *n.* **1.** Plant of genus *Veronica*, speedwell. **2.** Cloth with representation of Christ's face, esp. one miraculously so impressed after being used by St. Veronica to wipe sweat from Christ's face as he went to Calvary; any similar picture of Christ's face. **3.** Matador's movement of cape away from charging bull. [med. L, f. woman's Christian name *Veronica*]

vĕrru'c|a (-rōō'-) *n.* (*pl.* **~ae** *pr.* -sē). (Path., Zool., & Bot.) Wart, wartlike elevation; so **vĕ'rruc**OSE[1], **vĕ'rruc**OUS, (-rōō-) *adjs.* [L]

vẽr'sant *n.* Extent of land sloping in one direction; general slope of land. [F (*verser* f. L *versare* frequent. of *vertere vers-* turn; see -ANT)]

vẽr'satīle *a.* Turning easily or readily from one subject or occupation to another, capable of dealing with many subjects, (*versatile author, genius, disposition, mind*); (Bot. & Zool.) moving freely about or up and down on a support (*versatile anther, head, antennae*); changeable, inconstant; hence or cogn. ~LY[2] (-l-lĭ) *adv.*, **vẽrsatĭ'l**ITY *n.* [F, or f. L *versatilis* (as prec.; see -IL)]

vers de société (vār de sōsĭātā') *n.* Light witty topical verse. [F]

vẽrse *n.* & *v.* **1.** *n.* Metrical line in accordance with rules of prosody (*quoted some verses of the Iliad*; CAP[2] *verses*); group of definite number of such lines, stanza; metrical composition in general, particular type of this, (*wrote pages of verse*; *expressed in indifferent verse*; *what is not prose is verse*; *a prize for Latin verse*). **2.** Each of the short divisions of chapter in Bible (CHAPTER *and verse*); versicle; solo part of anthem etc. **3.** Hence ~'LET (-sl-) *n.* **4.** *v.t.* Express in verse. **5.** *v.i.* Compose verses. [OE *fers* (OHG, ON *vers*) f. L *versus* (*vertere vers-* turn) turn of plough, furrow, line (of writing); in ME reinforced by OF *vers* f. L *versus*]

vẽrsed[1] (-st) *a.* Experienced, practised, skilled, proficient, (*in* subject, occupation, etc.). [f. F *versé* or f. L *versatus* p.p. of *versari* be engaged in (as VERSANT; see -ED[1])]

vẽrsed[2] (-st) *a.* Reversed (*versed* SINE). [f. mod. L (*sinus*) *versus* turned (sine) f. as VERSE]

vẽr'sėt *n.* (Mus.) Short prelude or interlude for organ. [F, dim. of *vers* VERSE; see -ET[1]]

vẽr'sĭcle *n.* Short sentence, esp. of each series of short sentences in liturgy said or sung alternately by minister or priest and people. [ME, f. OF *versicule* or f. L *versiculus* dim. of *versus* (see VERSE, -CULE)]

vẽr'sĭcoloured (-kŭlerd) *a.* Variegated; changing from one colour to another in different lights. [f. L *versicolor* (*versus* p.p. of *vertere* turn, *color* colour)]

versĭ'cūlar *a.* Of (esp. Biblical) verses or versicles. [f. L (as VERSICLE) + -AR]

vẽr'sĭ|fȳ *v.* **1.** *v.t.* Turn (prose) into verse; express in verse. **2.** *v.i.* Compose verses. **3.** So ~FICA'TION, **~fīer**[1], *ns.* [ME, f. OF *versifier* f. L *versificare* (as VERSE; see -FY)]

vẽr'sīn(e) *n.* = *versed* SINE. [f. VERSED[2] *sine*]

vẽr'sion (-shon) *n.* **1.** Book etc. when translated into another language; AUTHORIZED*d*, REVISE*d* (**Standard*), *Version*. **2.** Piece of translation, esp. into foreign language, as school exercise. **3.** Account of a matter from particular person's point of view (*now let me have your own version of the affair*); special form or variant of a thing. **4.** (Obstet.) Turning of foetus in womb to improve presentation. **5.** Hence ~AL *a.* [F, or f. med. L *versio* f. L *vertere vers-* turn; see -ION]

vers libre (vārlē'br) *n.* Verse composition in which different metres are mingled, or prosodic restrictions disregarded, or variable rhythm substituted for definite metre; hence **vers-li'br**IST (vārlē'-) *n.*, writer of *vers libre*. [F, = free verse]

vẽr'sō *n.* (*pl.* **~s**). Left-hand page of open book; back of leaf (opp. RECTO); reverse of coin. [f. L *verso* (*folio*) = turned (leaf), abl. p.p. as VERSE]

vẽrst *n.* Russian measure of length, about ⅔ mile. [f. Russ. *versta*]

vẽr'sus *prep.* (esp. Law & Sport, abbr. *v.* or *vs.*) Against (*Rex versus Crippen*; *Surrey v. Kent*). [L, = towards, in med. L against]

vẽrt *n.* & *a.* **1.** *n.* (Law, Hist.) All that bears green leaves in forest; right to cut this. **2.** *n.*, & *a.* (usu. placed after *n.*) (Her.) Green. [ME f. OF, f. L *viridis* green]

vẽr'tėbr|a *n.* (*pl.* **~ae**). Each segment of backbone; (in *pl.*) backbone; so **~AL** *a.* [L (*vertere* turn)]

vẽr'tėbrate (*or* -āt) *a.* & *n.* (Animal) having spinal column or notochord, esp. (member) of the (sub)phylum Vertebrata, including mammals, birds, reptiles, amphibians, and fishes. [f. L *vertebratus* jointed (as prec.; see -ATE[2])]

vẽrtėbrā'tion *n.* Division into vertebrae or similar segments; (fig.) firmness. [f. VERTEBRA + -ATION]

vẽr't|ĕx *n.* (*pl.* **~ices** *pr.* -ĭsēz, *or* **~exes**). **1.** Highest point, top, apex; (Anat.) crown of head. **2.** (Geom.) Each angular point of triangle, polygon, etc.; point at which axis meets curve or surface; meeting-point of lines that form an angle. [L, *vertex -ticis* whirlpool, crown of head, vertex (*vertere* turn)]

vẽr'tĭcal *a.* & *n.* **1.** *a.* Of or at the vertex or highest point; at, or passing through, the zenith; perpendicular to plane of horizon; in direction from top to bottom of picture etc.; (Anat.) of the crown of the head; combining all stages in hierarchy (sense 3), or in production of a class of goods (*vertical* INTEGRATION); **~ angles,** each pair of opposite angles made by two intersecting lines; **~ fin** (dorsal, anal, or caudal); **~ plane** (perpendicular to the horizon); **~ take-off** of aircraft (directly upwards); hence ~ITY (-ă'l-) *n.*, ~LY[2] *adv.* **2.** *n.* Vertical line, plane, or circle; **out of the ~**, not vertical. [F, or f. LL *verticalis* (as prec.; see -AL)]

vẽr'tĭcĭl *n.* (Bot. & Zool.) Whorl, set of parts arranged in circle round axis; hence **vertĭ'cĭll**ATE[2] *a.* [f. L *verticillus* whorl of spindle, dim. of VERTEX]

vẽr'tĭgō (*or* vertī'-) *n.* (*pl.* **~s**). Giddiness, dizziness; condition with sensation of whirling and tendency to lose balance; so **vertĭ'gĭn**OUS *a.* [L *vertigo -ginis* whirling (*vertere* turn)]

vertu. See VIRTU.

vẽr'vain *n.* Herbaceous plant of genus *Verbena*, esp. one with small blue, white, or purple flowers, formerly believed to have various virtues and used as amulet etc. [ME, f. OF *verveine* f. L VERBENA]

vẽrve (*or* vārv) *n.* Enthusiasm, energy, vigour, esp. in artistic or literary work. [F, earlier = form of expression, f. L *verba* words]

vẽr'vėt *n.* Small greyish Afr. monkey. [F]

vĕ'rȳ[1] *a.* & *adv.* **1.** *attrib. a.* (arch.) Real, true, genuine, that is such in the truest or fullest sense, (*very God of very God*; *has shown himself a very knave*; *the veriest simpleton knows that*; *in very truth*; *must consent from very shame*). **2. The, this, that, his,** etc., ~ (emphasizing identity, coincidence, significance, or extreme degree; *this is the very spot I found it on*; *the very* SAME; *those were his very words*; *speaking in this very room*; *did it that very day*; *the very fact of his presence is enough*; *you are the very man I am looking for*; *a needle is the very* *thing* (*for our purpose*); *come here this very minute*; *grieves me to the very heart*; *the very stones cry out*; *his very servants bully him*; *drank it to the very dregs*; *at the very edge of the cliff*; *a very little more will do*; *give me only a very little*). **3.** *adv.* (w. superl. *adjs.* or *own*). In the fullest sense (*drink it to the very last drop*; *the very last thing I expected*; *did the very best I could*; *did my very utmost*; *may keep it for your very own*). **4.** (w. *adjs.*, adjectival participles, & *advs.*) In a high degree (*that is very easy*, *very annoying*, *very easily done*; *a very trying time*; *very often fails*; *find very few instances*; *gives very little trouble*; *Very* REVEREND; *very much better*; *very much annoyed*); **not ~**, (1) in a low degree, (2) far from being; *not* so[1] *very*; **~ high frequency** (in range 30 to 300 megahertz); **~ good, ~ well,** (formula of consent or approval). [ME, f. OF *verai* f. Gallo-Rom. **veraius* f. L *verus* true]

Vě'rÿ[2] (*or* vēr'ĭ) *n.* **~ light,** flare projected from **~ pistol** for signalling or temporarily illuminating part of battlefield etc. [f. S. W. ~, inventor (1877)]

vėsī'ca *n.* **1.** (Anat. & Zool.) Bladder, esp. urinary bladder. **2.** **~** (**piscis** or **piscium** = fish's or fishes'), pointed oval used as aureole in medieval sculpture and painting. **3.** Hence **vě'sĭcAL** *a.* [L]

vě'sĭc|āte *v.t.* Raise blisters on; hence **~ANT**, **~ātORY**, *adjs.* & *ns.*, **~A'TION** *n.* [f. LL *vesicare* (as prec.) + -ATE[3]]

vě'sĭcle *n.* (Anat., Zool., Bot., & Geol.) Small bladder, cell, bubble, or hollow structure; (Path.) blister; so **vėsĭ'cūlAR**[1], **vėsĭ'cūlATE**[2], *adjs.*, **vėsĭcūlA'TION** *n.* [f. F *vésicule* or f. L *vesicula* dim. of VESICA; see -ULE]

vě'sper *n.* **1.** (*V~*). Venus as evening star, (poet.) evening. **2.** (Eccl., in *pl.*) (Office of) sixth of the canonical hours of prayer; evensong; **~(-bell)**, bell that calls to vespers. [f. L *vesper* evening (star), or f. OF *vespres* f. eccl. L *vesperas* f. L *vespera* evening]

vě'spertīne *a.* Of or occurring in the evening; (Bot., of flower) opening, (Zool.) flying, in the evening; (Astron.) setting near the time of sunset. [f. L *vespertinus* (VESPER; see -INE[1])]

vě'spĭarÿ *n.* Nest of wasps. [irreg. f. L *vespa* wasp, after *apiary*]

vě'spīne *a.* Of wasps. [f. L *vespa* wasp + -INE[1]]

vě'ssel *n.* **1.** Hollow receptacle esp. for liquid, e.g. cask, cup, pot, bottle, dish. **2.** Ship, boat, esp. large one. **3.** (Anat.) duct, canal, holding or conveying blood or other fluid, esp. BLOOD[1]-*-vessel*; (Bot.) woody duct carrying or containing sap etc. **4.** (Bibl., or allus. esp. joc.). Person viewed as recipient or exponent of a quality; **weak ~**, unreliable person; **weaker ~**, woman (1 Pet. 3:7); *vessels of* WRATH. **5.** Hence **~FUL** 2 *n.* [ME, f. AF *vessel(e)*, OF *vaissel(le)* f. LL *vascellum*, (pl.) *-ella*, dim. of VAS]

věst[1] *n.* **1.** (‖Commerc.) Waistcoat. **2.** Knitted or woven undergarment worn on upper part or whole of trunk. **3.** Piece, usu. V-shaped, on front of body of woman's dress, esp. to fill opening at neck. **4.** (arch.) Clothing, dress. **5.** **~-pocket,** of a size suitable for the (waistcoat-) pocket, very small. [f. F f. It. *veste* f. L *vestis* garment]

věst[2] *v.* **1.** *v.t.* (esp. in *pass.*) Furnish (person *with* authority, powers, property, etc.); ~ (property, power) **in** (person), confer formally on him an immediate fixed right of present or future possession of; **~ed interests, rights,** etc., (possession of which is established in a person by right or by long association and usu. gives rise to expectation of gain). **2.** (poet.) Clothe. **3.** *v.i.* **~ in,** (of property, right, etc.) come into the possession of (person); **~'ing day** (on which this takes place). [ME, orig. p.p. f. OF *vestu* (*vestir* f. L *vestire -it-* clothe, as prec.)]

vě'sta *n.* Short wooden or (**wax ~**) wax match. [f. *Vesta*, Rom. goddess of hearth and household, L = Gk *Hestia*]

vě'stal *a.* & *n.* Of the Roman goddess Vesta or the vestal virgins; **~** (**virgin**), virgin consecrated to Vesta, vowed to chastity, who shared charge of sacred fire perpetually burning on the altar, (fig.) chaste woman, esp. nun. [ME, f. L *vestalis* a. & n. (as prec.; see -AL)]

věstee' *n.* = VEST[1] 3. [f. VEST[1] + -EE]

vě'stĭarÿ *n.* & *a.* **1.** *n.* Vestry, robing-room, or cloakroom. **2.** *a.* Relating to clothes or dress. [ME, f. OF *vestiarie*, *vestiaire*; see VESTRY]

vě'stĭbūle *n.* **1.** Antechamber, hall, lobby, next to outer door of house and from which rooms are reached by door(s); porch of church etc. **2.** *Enclosed entrance to railway-carriage; **~ train** (with corridor). **3.** (Anat.) Chamber or channel communicating with others; part of mouth outside teeth; central cavity of labyrinth of inner ear. **4.** ***~ school** (for training new industrial employees). **5.** Hence **věstĭ'būlAR**[1] *a.* [F, or f. L *vestibulum* entrance-court]

vě'stĭge *n.* Trace, evidence, sign, (*vestiges of an earlier civilization*; *found no vestiges of his presence*); slightest amount, particle, (*without a vestige of clothing*; *has not a vestige of evidence for this assertion*); (Biol.) part or organ now degenerate and of little or no utility but well developed in ancestors; hence **věstĭ'gIAL** *a.* (esp. Biol.). [F, f. L *vestigium* footprint]

vě'stĭture *n.* Investiture; clothing; (Zool.) hair, scales, etc., covering a surface. [ME, f. med. L *vestitura* f. L *vestire* (see VEST[2], -URE)]

vě'stment *n.* Garment, esp. official or state robe; any of the official garments of clergy, choristers, etc., worn during divine service, esp. chasuble. [ME, f. OF *vestiment*, *vestement* f. L *vestimentum* (as VEST[2]; see -MENT)]

vě'strÿ *n.* **1.** Room or building attached to church and in which vestments are kept and put on. **2.** ‖(Hist.) Meeting of parishioners usu. in vestry for parochial business; body of parishioners meeting thus; **~-clerk,** officer chosen by vestry to keep parish accounts etc.; **~man,** member of a vestry; hence **vě'strAL** *a.* [ME, f. AF **vest(e)rie* alt. of OF *vestiarie*, *vestiaire*, f. L *vestiarium* (as VEST[1]; see -ARIUM, -ERY)]

vě'sture *n.*, & *v.t.* (poet. or rhet.) **1.** *n.* Garments, dress, clothes; covering. **2.** *v.t.* Clothe. [ME f. OF, f. med. L *vest(it)ura* (as VEST[2]; see -URE)]

vět[1] *n.*, & *v.t.* (**-tt-**). (colloq.) **1.** Veterinary surgeon. **2.** *v.t.* Examine and pass fit, treat, (animal); (fig.) make careful examination of (scheme, work, candidate, etc.). [abbr.]

***vět**[2] *n.* (colloq.) Veteran. [abbr.]

větch *n.* Plant of pea family esp. of genus *Vicia*, largely used, wild or cultivated, for forage; **common ~**, tare; **kidney-~**, perennial herb (*Anthyllis vulneraria*) with red or yellow flowers; hence **~'Y**[2] *a.* [ME, f. AF & ONF *veche* f. L *vicia*]

vě'tchlĭng *n.* Plant of genus *Lathyrus*, allied to vetch. [f. prec. + -LING[1]]

vě'teran *n.* & *a.* **1.** *n.* Person who has grown old in or had long experience of (esp. military) service or occupation (*a veteran of two world wars*; *a veteran golfer*); *ex-service man (***V~s' Day,** 11 Nov.). **2.** *a.* Of a veteran; composed of veterans; ‖**~ car** (made before 1916, or before 1905). [f. F *vétéran* or f. L *veteranus* a. & n. (*vetus -eris* old; see -AN)]

věterĭnār'ĭan *n.* Veterinary surgeon. [f. L *veterinarius* (as foll.) + -AN]

vĕ'terĭnarў *a.* & *n.* **1.** *a.* Of or for (treatment of) diseases and injuries of farm and domestic animals; ~ **surgeon,** one skilled in such treatment. **2.** *n.* Veterinary surgeon. [f. L *veterinarius* (*veterinae* cattle)]

vĕ'tĭver *n.* = CUSCUS[1]. [f. F *vétiver* f. Tamil *vettivēru* (*vēr* root)]

vē'tō *n.* (*pl.* ~es), & *v.t.* **1.** *n.* Constitutional right of sovereign, president, governor, upper house of legislature, etc., to reject a legislative enactment (*POCKET[1] *veto*; **suspensive** ~, one suspending but not necessarily preventing completion of measure); right of permanent member of U.N. Security Council to reject a resolution; (official message conveying) such rejection; prohibition (*put a* or *his veto on the proposal*). **2.** *v.t.* Exercise veto against (bill etc.); forbid authoritatively. [L, = I forbid, w. ref. to its use by Roman tribunes of the people in opposing Senate's measures]

vĕx *v.t.* Anger by slight or petty annoyance, irritate, (*this would vex a saint*; *how vexing!*); (arch.) grieve, afflict; (poet. or rhet.) put (sea etc.) into state of commotion; **a** ~**ed** (difficult and much discussed) **question.** [ME, f. OF *vexer* f. L *vexare* shake, disturb]

vĕxā'tion *n.* Vexing, being vexed; harassing by means of malicious or trivial litigation; state of irritation or distress; annoying or distressing thing (*subjected to many vexations*). [ME f. OF, or f. L *vexatio -onis* (as prec.; see -ATION)]

vĕxā'tious (-sh*u*s) *a.* Causing or tending to cause vexation; (Law) not having sufficient grounds for action and seeking only to annoy defendant; hence ~LY[2] *adv.*, ~NESS *n.* [f. prec. + -OUS]

vĕxĭllŏ'logў *n.* Study of flags. [f. as foll. + -o- + -LOGY]

vĕxĭ'll|um *n.* (*pl.* ~**a**). (Rom. Ant.) military standard esp. of maniple, body of troops under this; (Bot.) large upper petal of papilionaceous flower; vane of a feather; (Eccl.) flag on or wound round bishop's staff, processional banner or cross. [L (*vehere vect-* carry)]

V.G. *abbr.* very good; Vicar-General.

V.H.F. *abbr.* very high frequency.

***V.I.** *abbr.* Virgin Islands.

vī'a *prep.* By way of, through, (*from Exeter to York via London*; *sent it via his secretary*). [L, abl. of *via* way, road]

vī'able *a.* (Of foetus or new-born child) capable of maintaining life; (of plant, animal, etc.) able to live or exist in particular climate etc.; (of seed) able to germinate; (of plan etc.) feasible, practicable esp. from economic standpoint; so **vīABI'LITY** *n.* [F (*vie* life f. L *vita*; see -ABLE)]

vī'adŭct *n.* Long bridgelike structure, esp. series of arches, for carrying road or railway over valley or dip in ground; such road or railway. [f. L *via* way, after *aqueduct*]

vī'al *n.* Small (usu. cylindrical glass) vessel for holding liquid medicines etc.; **pour out** ~**s of wrath,** take vengeance (Rev. 16:1), (colloq.) give vent to anger; hence ~FUL 2 *n.* [ME, var. of *fiole* etc.; see PHIAL]

via media (vīa mē'dĭa; *or* vēa mĕ'-) *n.* Middle way or course between extremes. [L]

vī'and *n.* (usu. in *pl.*) Article(s) of food, victual(s). [ME, f. OF *viande* food f. Rom. **vi(v)anda* for L *vivenda*, neut. pl. gerundive of *vivere* live]

vīă'tĭc|um *n.* (*pl.* ~**a**). Provisions or official allowance of money for journey; Eucharist as given to person (in danger of) dying. [L, neut. (as n.) of *viaticus* (*via* road; see -ATIC)]

vībes (-bz) *n. pl.* (colloq.) Vibraphone; vibrations. [abbr.]

vībră'cūl|um *n.* (*pl.* ~**a**). Whiplike appendage of bryozoans, serving to bring food within reach by lashing movements; hence ~AR[1] *a.* [mod. L (as VIBRATE; see -CULE)]

vī'brant *a.* Vibrating; thrilling *with* (action etc.); responding readily to emotions etc.; (of sound) resonant. [f. L *vibrare* (see VIBRATE, -ANT)]

vī'braphōn|e *n.* Percussion instrument of metal bars with motor-driven resonators and metal tubes giving vibrato effect; hence ~IST (3) *n.* [f. VIBRATO + -PHONE]

vībrā'te *v.* **1.** *v.i.* & *t.* Move to and fro like pendulum, (cause to) oscillate. **2.** *v.i.* (Of sound) throb (*on* ear, *in* memory, etc.); (Phys.) move unceasingly to and fro, esp. rapidly; thrill, quiver, (*with* passion etc.). **3.** *v.t.* (Of pendulum) measure (seconds etc.) by vibrating. **4.** Hence **vī'bratIVE, vī'bratORY,** *adjs.* [f. L *vibrare* shake, swing + -ATE[3]]

vī'bratile *a.* Capable of vibrating; (of cilia etc.) used in vibratory motion. [f. VIBRATORY (see prec.) after *pulsatile* etc.]

vībrā'tion *n.* Vibrating, oscillation; (Phys.) (rapid) motion to and fro esp. of the parts of a fluid or an elastic solid whose equilibrium has been disturbed or of electromagnetic wave; (in *pl.*) mental (esp. occult) influence; hence ~AL *a.* [f. L *vibratio* (as VIBRATE; see -ATION)]

vibra'tō (vēbrah'-) *n.* (*pl.* ~**s**). (Mus.) Tremulous effect in singing or of playing stringed instrument by rapid slight variation of pitch; cf. TREMOLO. [It., p.p. of *vibrare* VIBRATE]

vībrā'tor *n.* Person or thing, that vibrates; (Mus.) reed in reed-organ; (Med.) electric or other instrument used in massage. [f. VIBRATE + -OR]

vibrĭ'ssae *n. pl.* Stiff coarse hairs near mouth of most mammals (e.g. cat's whiskers) and in human nostril; bristle-like feathers near mouth of insectivorous birds. [L (as VIBRATE)]

vībûr'num *n.* Shrub of genus *Viburnum* w. usu. white flowers, e.g. guelder rose and wayfaring-tree. [L, = wayfaring-tree]

Vic. *abbr.* Victoria.

vĭ'car *n.* **1.** (In Ch. of England) incumbent of parish where tithes formerly belonged to chapter or religious house or layman (cf. RECTOR); Episcopal clergyman deputizing for another. **2.** ~ **of Bray,** systematic turncoat [w. ref. to 18th-c. song]; **lay** ~, cathedral officer singing some parts of service; ||~ **choral,** clerical or lay assistant in some (esp. musical) parts of cathedral service; ~**-general,** Anglican official assisting (arch)bishop in ecclesiastical causes etc., R.C. bishop's assistant in matters of jurisdiction etc.; **cardinal** ~, pope's delegate acting as bishop of diocese of Rome; ~ **apostolic,** R.C. missionary or titular bishop; ~ **forane** (fŏrā'n) [= FOREIGN], dignitary appointed by R.C. bishop to exercise limited local jurisdiction; **V**~ **of (Jesus) Christ,** the pope. **3.** Hence **vĭcar'ĭATE**[1] (1), ~SHIP, *ns.* [ME, f. AF *viker(e)*, OF *vicaire* f. L *vicarius* substitute f. *vicis* (see VICE[4], -ARY[1])]

vĭ'carage *n.* Benefice or residence of vicar. [ME, f. prec. + -AGE]

vĭcār'ial *a.* Of, or serving as, a vicar. [f. VICAR + -IAL]

vĭcār'ious *a.* Deputed, delegated, (*vicarious authority*); acting or done for another (*vicarious work*; ~ **suffering** esp. of Christ in place of sinner); experienced imaginatively through another person (*vicarious pleasure*); hence ~LY[2] *adv.*, ~NESS *n.* [f. L *vicarius* (see VICAR, -IOUS)]

vice[1] *n.* **1.** Evil (esp. grossly immoral) habit or conduct, (particular form of) depravity, serious fault, (*has the vice of gluttony*; *drunkenness is not among his vices*; *vice is duly punished and virtue rewarded in fifth act*); **has no redeeming** ~ (to relieve overpowering rectitude). **2.** Defect, blemish, (*of* character, literary style, etc.); fault(s) or bad habit(s) in horse etc.; ~ **squad,** police department enforcing laws against prostitution etc. **3.** (Hist.) Character in a morality play representing a vice. [ME f. OF, f. L *vitium*]

‖**vīce**², ***vīse,** *n.*, & *v.t.* **1.** *n.* Instrument with two jaws between which thing may be gripped usu. by operation of screw so as to leave the hands free for working upon it, esp. attached to carpenter's or metal-worker's bench; hence ~′LIKE (-sl-) *a.* **2.** *v.t.* Secure (material to be worked upon, or fig.) in vice. [ME, = winding stair, screw, f. OF *vis* f. L *vitis* vine]

vīce³ *n.* (colloq.) = VICE-*president* etc. [abbr.]

vī′cė⁴ *prep.* In the place of, in succession to, (*gazetted as captain vice Captain Jones promoted*). [L, abl. of **vix vicis* change]

vīce- *pref.* forming *ns.* w. sense 'person acting or qualified to act in place of, or next in rank to', and derivs. of these, as: **~-a′dmiral,** ADMIRAL of third grade; **~-a′dmiralty,** office of vice-admiral (‖~-*admiralty courts*, tribunals with admiralty jurisdiction in British colonial possessions); *vice-chair′man(ship)*; ‖**~-cha′mberlain** (esp. deputy of Lord Chamberlain); **~-cha′ncellor,** deputy chancellor (esp. of university, discharging most of the administrative duties); *vice-cha′ncellorship*; *vice-co′mmodore*; *vice-co′nsul (ship)*; *vice-co′nsulate*; *vice-go′vernor*; **~-ki′ng,** = VICEROY; *vice-ma′ster*; *vice-pre′sident-(ship)*, *-pre′sidency*, *-preside′ntial*; *vice-pri′ncipal*; **~-quee′n,** = VICEREINE; *vice-re′gent*; *vice-she′riff*; *vice-war′den*. [f. prec.]

vīcegĕ′r|ent (-sj-; *or* -ēr′-) *a.* & *n.* (Person) exercising delegated power, deputy, (*of* God, king, etc.); hence ~ENCY *n.* [f. med. L *vicegerens* (as VICE⁴ + L *gerere* carry on; see -ENT)]

vīcĕ′nnĭal *a.* Lasting, occurring every, twenty years. [f. LL *vicennium* period of 20 years (*vicies* 20 times f. *viginti* 20, *annus* year) + -AL]

vī′cereine (-srān) *n.* Viceroy's wife; woman viceroy. [F (as VICE-, *reine* queen)]

vī′ceroy (-sr-) *n.* Ruler exercising authority on behalf of sovereign in colony, province, etc.; hence **vīcerē′g**AL, **vīceroy′**AL, *adjs.*, **vīceroy′al**TY¹, ~SHIP, *ns.*, (-sr-). [F (as VICE-, *roy* king)]

vīcĕ′sĭmal *a.* Vigesimal. [f. L *vicesimus* twentieth + -AL]

vīcė vēr′sa *adv.* With the order of terms changed, the other way round: *the man blames his wife and* ~ (she him); *the cat stole the dog's dinner and* ~ (he hers); *calls black white and* ~ (white black). [L, = the position being reversed (as VICE⁴, *versa* abl. fem. p.p. of *vertere* turn)]

Vi′chy (vē′shĭ) *n.* ~ **(water),** effervescent mineral water from Vichy freq. bottled. [~ in central France]

vĭchȳssoi′se (-shĭswah′z) *n.* Creamy soup of leeks and potatoes, served chilled. [f. F *vichyssois -oise* of Vichy (cf. prec.)]

vĭ′cĭnage *n.* Neighbourhood, surrounding district; relation of neighbours. [ME, f. OF *vis(e)nage* f. Gallo-Rom. **vecinatus* (*vecinus* for L *vicinus* neighbour)]

vĭ′cĭnal (*or* -sī′-) *a.* Neighbouring, adjacent; of a neighbourhood, local. [F, or f. L *vicinalis* (*vicinus* neighbour; see -AL)]

vĭcĭ′nĭtȳ *n.* Surrounding district; nearness in place (*to*); close relationship (*to*); **in the** ~ **(of),** near. [f. L *vicinitas* (as prec.; see -ITY)]

vĭ′cious (-shus) *a.* **1.** Of the nature of vice, morally evil or injurious, (*vicious tendencies, habits, life*); addicted to vice (*vicious companions*); (of horse etc.) having vices. **2.** (Of language, document, reasoning, etc.) incorrect, faulty, unsound, corrupt, (*vicious* CIRCLE¹; so ~ **spiral,** continual interaction causing e.g. steady increases of both prices and wages). **3.** Bad-tempered, spiteful, (*vicious dog, mood, remarks*); severe (*vicious weather*). **4.** Hence ~LY² *adv.*, ~NESS *n.* [ME f. OF, or f. L *vitiosus* (as VICE¹; see -OUS)]

vĭcĭ′ssĭ|tūde *n.* Change of circumstances esp. of fortune; (arch. or poet.) regular change, alternation; hence **~tū′dĭn**OUS *a.* [F, or f. L *vicissitudo -dinis* f. *vicissim* by turns (as VICE⁴; see -TUDE)]

vĭ′ctĭm *n.* Living creature sacrificed to a deity or in performance of religious rite; person or thing injured or destroyed in seeking to attain an object, in gratification of a passion etc., or as result of event or circumstance, (*the victims of his relentless ambition*; *fell a victim to his own avarice*; *the victims of disease, of a railway accident, of an earthquake*); prey, dupe, (*the numerous victims of the confidence trick*). [f. L *victima*]

vĭ′ctĭmīz|e, -īs|e (-īz), *v.t.* Make (person etc.) a victim; cheat (person); make (striker etc.) suffer by dismissal or other exceptional treatment; hence ~A′TION *n.* [f. prec. + -IZE]

vĭ′ctor *n.* (rhet.) Conqueror in battle or contest; ~ **ludor′um,** most successful competitor in school etc. sports; so **vĭ′ctr**ESS¹ *n.* [ME, f. AF *victo(u)r* or f. L *victor* (*vincere vict-* conquer; see -OR)]

vĭctōr′ĭa *n.* **1.** Low light four-wheeled carriage with seat for two and raised driver's seat and with collapsible top. **2.** Gigantic S. Amer. water-lily of genus *Victoria*. **3.** Species of crowned pigeon; variety of domestic pigeon. **4.** Large red luscious variety of plum. **5. V~ Cross,** decoration awarded to members of the Commonwealth armed services for conspicuous act of bravery, founded by Queen Victoria in 1856. [f. Queen *Victoria* of England d. 1901]

Vĭctōr′ĭan *a.* & *n.* Of, (person, esp. author) living in, characteristic of, the reign of Queen Victoria (1837–1901); ‖**Royal ~ Chain** (order founded by Edward VII in 1902 and conferred by sovereign on special occasions); ‖**Royal ~ Order** (founded by Queen Victoria in 1896 and conferred usu. for great service rendered to sovereign); so **Vĭctōrĭ**A′NA *n. pl.* [f. as prec. + -AN]

vĭctōr′ĭous *a.* Conquering, triumphant; marked by victory (*victorious day*); hence ~LY² *adv.*, ~NESS *n.* [ME f. AF; OF *victorieux*, f. L *victoriosus* (as foll.; see -OUS)]

vĭ′ctorȳ *n.* Defeating one's enemy in battle or war or one's opponent in contest (lit. or fig.; *battle ended in a decisive victory for him*; *fought hard for victory*; *hero of many victories*; *gained a* or *the victory over his passions*); *Cadmean* or PYRRHIC², MORAL, *victory*. [ME, f. AF *victorie*, OF *victoire*, f. L *victoria* (as VICTOR; see -Y¹)]

vĭ′ctual (vĭ′tal) *n.* & *v.* (‖-ll-). (formal). **1.** *n.* (usu. in *pl.*) Food, provisions, esp. as prepared for use; hence ~LESS (-l-l-) *a.* **2.** *v.t.* Supply with victuals. **3.** *v.i.* Obtain stores; eat victuals. [ME, f. OF (*vitaillier* v. f.) *vitaille* f. LL *victualia*, neut. pl. of L *victualis* (*victus* food, cogn. w. *vivere* live; see -AL)]

vĭ′ctualler, *-aler, (vĭ′tler) *n.* One who furnishes victuals, ‖esp. **licensed** ~, innkeeper licensed to sell alcoholic liquor etc.; ship employed to carry stores for other ships. [ME, f. OF *vitaill(i)er*, *vitaillour* (as prec.; see -ER²)]

vĭcuña (-kōō′nya *or* -kōō′na) *n.* S. Amer. mammal allied to llama, with fine silky wool; (imitation of) cloth made from its wool. [Sp., f. Quechua]

vide (vī′dĭ *or* vĭ′dā *or* vē′dā) *v.t.* (*imper.*, in reference to passage in book etc.). See, consult; QUOD² *vide*. [L, imper. of *vidēre* see]

vidĕ'lĭcĕt *adv.* = VIZ. [ME f. L (*vidēre* see, *licet* it is permissible)]

vĭ'dĕō *n.* (*pl.* ~**s**) & *a.* **1.** *n.* *Television. **2.** *a.* Relating to (recording for) broadcasting of photographic images; ~ **frequency** (in the range used for video signals in television); ~**phone,** telephone transmitting picture of person speaking; ~ **signal** (containing information for producing television signal); ~ **tape** *n.*, & *v.t.*, (make recording of, by use of) magnetic tape suitable for records of television pictures and sound. [L, = I see]

vĭ'dĭmus *n.* Inspection or certified copy of accounts etc. [L, = we have seen (*vidēre* see)]

vie *v.i.* (*part.* **vying** *pr.* vī'ĭ-). Strive for superiority, carry on rivalry, (*with* another *in* quality, *in* doing). [prob. f. ME, as ENVY²]

viĕ'lle *n.* Hurdy-gurdy. [F, f. OF *viel(l)e*; see VIOL]

Viĕ'nna *n. Vienna* SCHNITZEL; ~ **steak,** fried rissole of minced meat; hence **Vienne**'SE *a.* & *n.* [~ in Austria]

Viĕtnamē'se (-z) *a.* & *n.* (*pl.* same). (Native, inhabitant, or language) of Vietnam in S.E. Asia. [f. *Vietnam* + -ESE]

vieux jeu (vyẽr zhẽr') *a.* Old-fashioned, hackneyed. [F, lit. 'old game']

view (vū) *n.* & *v.* **1.** *n.* Inspection by eye or mind, survey, (*of* surroundings, subject, etc.); (Law) inspection by jury of place, property, etc., concerned in a case, or of dead body; PRIVATE *view.* **2.** Power of seeing, range of vision, (*came into view*; *passed from our view*; *house has a view of the sea*); what is seen, scene, prospect, (*a superb view*); picture etc. representing this. **3.** Manner of considering a subject, opinion, mental attitude, (*takes a different view*; *his view is that we are the aggressors*; *takes a* DIM OR POOR, *a favourable, view of her conduct*; *holds extreme views* (*in politics* etc.)); *take the* LONG¹ *view.* **4.** (arch.) Intention, design, (*will this meet your views?*). **5. In** ~ **of,** able to see, or to be seen by or from, (*came in view of the church*; *stood in full view of the audience*), having regard to, considering, (*in view of recent developments we do not think this step advisable*), in anticipation of; **on** ~, being shown (for inspection); **with a** ~ **to, with the** or **a** ~ **of,** for the purpose of, as a step towards; **with a** ~ **to,** with the aim of attaining; **to the** ~, openly, in public. **6. Have in** ~, have as one's object, bear (circumstance) in mind in forming judgement etc.; POINT¹ *of view*; ~'**finder,** part of camera showing extent of picture; ~ **halloo'**, huntsman's shout on seeing fox break cover; ~'**point,** point of view, standpoint. **7.** *v.t.* Survey with the eyes; survey mentally, form mental impression or judgement of, (*subject may be viewed in different ways*; *does not view the matter in the same light*); inspect (house etc.); see (fox) break cover. **8.** *v.i.* Watch television. **9.** Hence ~'ABLE *a.* [ME f. AF *v(i)ewe*, OF *vēue* fem. p.p. (as n.) f. *vēoir* see f. L *vidēre*]

view'er (vū'-) *n.* In vbl senses; television-watcher; device for looking at film transparencies etc. [f. prec. + -ER¹]

view'lėss (vū'-) *a.* Having no opinions; (poet. or rhet.) invisible. [f. VIEW + -LESS]

view'ÿ (vū'ĭ) *a.* (colloq.) Holding odd or fanciful opinions. [f. VIEW + -Y²]

vĭgĕ'sĭmal *a.* Of twentieths or twenty; reckoning or reckoned by twenties; hence ~LY² *adv.* [f. L *vigesimus* (*viginti* twenty) + -AL]

vĭ'gĭl *n.* Keeping awake during the time usually given to sleep, watchfulness, (*keep vigil*); (usu. in *pl.*) nocturnal devotions; eve of a festival, esp. eve that is a fast. [ME, f. OF *vigile* f. L *vigilia* (*vigil* awake)]

vĭ'gĭl|ance *n.* Watchfulness, caution, circumspection; *~**ance committee,** self-appointed body for maintenance of order etc. in imperfectly organized community; so ~ANT *a.* [F, or f. L *vigilantia* (*vigilare* keep awake f. as prec.; see -ANCE)]

vĭgĭlă'ntė *n.* Member of a vigilance committee or similar body. [Sp., = vigilant]

vĭ'gneron (vē'nyerawṅ) *n.* Vine-grower. [F (*vigne* VINE)]

vignĕ'tt|e (vēnyĕ't) *n.*, & *v.t.* **1.** *n.* Ornament round capital letter etc. or in blank space; illustration, esp. on title-page of book, not enclosed in definite border; photograph or portrait showing only head and shoulders with background gradually shaded off; (fig.) character sketch, short description. **2.** *v.t.* Make portrait of (person) in vignette style, shade off (photograph or portrait); hence ~ER¹, ~ING¹, ~IST (3), *ns.* [F, dim. of *vigne* VINE; see -ETTE]

vĭ'gorous *a.* Strong and active, robust; (of plant) growing strongly; full of vigour, showing or requiring physical strength or activity; forceful, acting or done with vigour; hence ~LY² *adv.*, ~NESS *n.* [ME f. OF, f. med. L *vigorosus* f. L *vigor* (see foll., -OUS)]

vĭ'gour (-*ger*), ***vĭ'gor,** *n.* Active physical strength or energy; flourishing physical condition; healthy growth, vitality, vital force; mental strength or activity as shown in thought or speech or literary style, forcibleness, trenchancy, animation; hence ~LESS *a.* [ME f. OF *vigour* f. L *vigor -oris* (*vigēre* be lively; see -OR)]

vĭhâr'a *n.* Buddhist temple or monastery. [Skr.]

Vī'kĭng *n.* Scandinavian trader and pirate of 8th–10th c. [f. ON *víkingr*, perh. f. OE *wīcing* (*wīc* camp; see -ING³)]

vĭla'yĕt (-ah'-) *n.* Province of Turkey. [Turk., f. Arab. *wilāya* district]

vīle *a.* Morally base, depraved, shameful, abject, disgusting; (arch.) worthless; (colloq.) abominably bad (*vile weather*); hence ~'LY² (-l-lĭ) *adv.*, ~NESS (-ln-) *n.* [ME, f. OF *vil vile*, f. L *vilis* cheap, base]

vĭ'lĭ|fȳ *v.t.* Defame, traduce, speak evil of; hence ~FICA'TION, ~fīER¹, *ns.* [ME in sense 'lower in value', f. LL *vilificare* (as prec.; see -FY)]

vĭ'lĭpĕnd *v.t.* (arch.) Treat contemptuously, disparage. [ME, f. OF *vilipender* or f. L *vilipendere* (as VILE, *pendere* consider)]

vĭ'lla *n.* **1.** Country residence; ‖detached or semi-detached house in suburban or residential district, whence ~DOM *n.*, Suburbia; house for holiday-makers at seaside etc. **2.** (Rom. etc. Hist.) Country estate. [It. & L]

vĭ'llag|e *n.* Group of houses etc., larger than hamlet and smaller than town; *small municipality with limited corporate powers; inhabitants of a village; hence ~ER¹ (4) (-ĭj-) *n.* [ME f. OF, f. L *villa*; see -AGE]

vĭ'llain (-*an*) *n.* Person guilty or capable of great wickedness, scoundrel; character in play whose evil actions or motives are important in the plot; (colloq., playfully) rascal (without serious imputation of badness); (arch.) rustic, boor; hence ~ESS¹ *n.* [ME f. OF *vilein, vilain* f. Rom. **villanus* f. L *villa*; see -AN]

vĭ'llainous (-*lan*-) *a.* **1.** Worthy of a villain, vile, wicked; so **vĭ'llain**Y¹ (-*lanĭ*) *n.* **2.** (colloq.) Abominably bad (*villainous weather*). **3.** Hence ~LY² *adv.*, ~NESS *n.* [ME, f. prec. + -OUS]

vĭllanĕ'lle *n.* Form of poem of 19 lines on two rhymes with some lines repeated. [F, f. It. *villanella* fem. of *villanello* rural, dim. of *villano* (as VILLAIN)]

-vĭlle *suf.* (colloq.) forming names of fictitious places w. ref. to particular quality etc. (*they must* *come from Squaresville*). [f. F *ville* town, as in many U.S. town-names]

villeggiatura (vĭlĕjatoor'a) *n.* Stay or retirement in the country. [It. (*villeggiare* live at VILLA or in the country)]

vĭ'llein (-ĭn) *n.* (Hist.) Feudal serf, tenant entirely subject to lord or attached to manor; so ~AGE *n.*, tenure or status of villein. [ME, var. of VILLAIN]

vĭ'll|us *n.* (*pl.* ~**i** *pr.* -ī). (Anat.) each of the short hairlike processes on some membranes, esp. on mucous membrane of small intestine; (Bot., in *pl.*) long soft hair covering fruit, flowers, etc.; hence or cogn. ~IFORM, ~OSE[1], ~OUS, *adjs.*, ~O'SITY *n.* [L, = shaggy hair]

vĭm *n.* (colloq.) Vigour. [perh. f. L, acc. of *vis* energy]

vĭmĭ'nėous *a.* (Bot.) Of or producing twigs or shoots. [f. L *vimineus* (*vimen viminis* osier; see -EOUS)]

vī'na (vē'-) *n.* Indian four-stringed musical instrument with fretted finger-board and a gourd at each end. [f. Skr. & Hindi *vīṇā*]

vīnā'ceous (-sh*u*s) *a.* Wine-red. [f. L *vinaceus* (*vinum* wine; see -ACEOUS)]

vĭnaigrĕ'tte (-nĭg-) *n.* Small ornamental bottle for holding aromatic salts etc., smelling-bottle; ~ (**sauce**), salad dressing of oil and wine vinegar. [F, dim. of *vinaigre* VINEGAR; see -ETTE]

vĭ'ncible *a.* That can be overcome or conquered; ~ **ignorance** (that can be overcome by the ignorant person himself). [f. L *vincibilis* (*vincere* overcome; see -IBLE)]

vĭ'ncŭl|um *n.* (*pl.* ~**a**). (Alg.) line drawn over several terms to show that they have a common relation to what follows or precedes (e.g. $\overline{a+b}\times c=ac+bc$, but $a+b\times c=a+bc$; $a-\overline{b+c}=a-b-c$); (Anat.) ligament, fraenum. [L, = bond (*vincire* bind)]

vĭ'ndĭc|āte *v.t.* Justify (person, religion, etc.) by evidence or argument; clear of suspicion etc.; establish the existence or merits or justice of (one's veracity, courage, conduct, character, assertion); hence or cogn. ~A'TION, ~**ātor**, *ns.*, ~ABLE, ~ATIVE, *adjs.* [f. L *vindicare* claim, avenge (*vindex -dicis* claimant, avenger) + -ATE[3]]

vĭ'ndicātorў *a.* Tending to vindicate; (of laws) punitive. [f. prec. + -ORY]

vĭndĭ'ctive *a.* Revengeful, tending to seek revenge; ~ **damages** (exceeding simple compensation and awarded as punishment of defendant); hence ~LY[2] (-vlĭ) *adv.*, ~NESS (-vn-) *n.* [f. L *vindicta* vengeance (as VINDICATE) + -IVE]

vīne *n.* Climbing or trailing woody-stemmed plant of genus *Vitis*, whose fruit is the grape; (*any plant with) slender stem that trails or climbs; ~**-borer,** beetle or moth whose larva destroys vines; ~**-dresser,** one who prunes, trains, and cultivates vines; hence **vī'ny**[2] *a.* [ME f. OF *vi(g)ne* f. L *vinea* vineyard (*vinum* wine)]

vĭ'nėgar *n.* Sour liquid got from wine, cider, etc., by fermentation and used as condiment or for pickling; (fig.) sour behaviour or character; **aromatic** ~ (containing camphor etc. in solution); MOTHER[3] *of vinegar*; RASPBERRY *vinegar*; **V~ Bible,** 1717 ed. with *parable of the vinegar* (for *vineyard*) in heading above Luke 20; hence ~ISH[1], ~Y[2], *adjs.* [ME, f. OF *vyn egre* f. Rom. **vinum acrum* sour wine f. L *vinum* wine + *acer acre* sour]

vī'nerў *n.* Vine greenhouse. [f. VINE + -ERY]

vĭ'neyard (-ny-) *n.* Plantation of grape-vines, esp. for wine-making; (fig.) sphere of action or labour. [ME, f. VINE + YARD[2]]

vingt(-et)-un (vănt(ā)ẽr'n̆) *n.* Card-game in which the object is to reach as nearly as possible the number of 21 pips on one's cards without exceeding it; hand of 21 pips in this. [F, = 21]

vī'nĭ- *comb. form.* Wine, as: ~**culture,** cultivation of vines; ~**fica'tion,** conversion of grape-juice etc. into wine. [f. L *vinum* wine + -I-]

vin ordinaire (văn ŏ̄rdĭnār') *n.* Cheap (usu. red) wine as drunk in France mixed with water. [F, = ordinary wine]

vī'nous *a.* Of, like, due to, addicted to, wine, (*vinous flavour, fermentation, eloquence*); hence **vīno**'SITY *n.* [f. L *vinum* wine + -OUS]

vin rosé (văn rōzā') *n.* = ROSÉ. [F]

vīnt[1] *v.t.* Make (wine). [back form. f. VINTAGE]

vĭnt[2] *n.* Russian card-game like auction bridge. [Russ., = screw]

vĭ'ntage *n.* & *a.* **1.** *n.* (Season of) gathering grapes for wine-making; (wine made from) season's produce of grapes, (fig.) (thing made etc. in) a particular year etc.; (poet. or rhet.) wine; wine of high quality kept separate from others. **2.** *a.* Of high quality esp. from the past; of a past season; ‖~ **car** (made 1917–1930). [alt. (after *vintner*) f. ME *vendage, vindage* f. OF *vendange* f. L *vindemia* (*vinum* wine, *demere* remove)]

vĭ'ntager *n.* Grape-gatherer. [f. prec. + -ER[1]]

vĭ'ntner *n.* Wine-merchant. [ME, f. AL *vintenarius, vinetarius* f. AF *vineter*, OF *vinetier*, f. med. L *vinetarius* f. L *vinetum* vineyard (*vinum* wine; see -ER[2])]

vī'nў. See VINE.

vī'nўl *n.* Plastic made by polymerizing a compound containing the ~ **group,** CH_2CH; (esp.) POLYvinyl chloride. [f. L *vinum* wine + -YL]

vī'ol *n.* Medieval (usu. 6-)stringed musical instrument, similar to violin etc. but held vertically; BASS[3] *viol*. [ME *viel* etc. f. OF *viel(l)e*, alt. f. *viole* (whence mod. E sp.) f. Prov. *viola*, *viula*, prob. f. Rom. **vitula* f. L *vitulari* be joyful; cf. FIDDLE]

vĭō'la[1] *n.* **1.** Kind of large violin, alto or tenor violin; its player. **2.** Viol; ~ **da bra'ccio** (brah'chō), viol corresponding to modern viola; ~ **da ga'mba,** viol held between player's legs, esp. corresponding to modern violoncello; ~ **d'amor'e** (dămŏ̄r'ā), sweet-toned tenor viol. [It. & Sp., prob. f. Prov. (see prec.)]

vī'ola[2] *n.* Plant of genus *Viola*, e.g. pansy and violet; (esp.) cultivated hybrid of this genus. [L, = violet]

violā'ceous (-sh*u*s) *a.* Of violet colour; (Bot.) of violet family Violaceae. [f. L *violaceus* (as prec.; see -ACEOUS)]

vī'ol|āte *v.t.* Disregard, fail to comply with, act against the dictates or requirements of, (oath, treaty, law, terms, conscience); treat profanely or with disrespect (sanctuary etc.); break in upon, disturb, (person's privacy etc.); rape; so ~ABLE *a.*, ~A'TION, ~**ātor**, *ns.* [ME, f. L *violare* treat violently + -ATE[3]]

vī'olence *n.* Quality of being violent; violent conduct or treatment, outrage, injury, (**do** ~ **to,** act contrary to, outrage); (Law) unlawful exercise of physical force, intimidation by exhibition of this. [ME f. OF, f. L *violentia* (as foll.; see -ENCE)]

vī'olent *a.* **1.** Involving great physical force (*a violent storm; came into violent collision*); ~ **death** (resulting from external force or from poison; cf. NATURAL). **2.** Involving unlawful exercise of force (*laid violent hands on him*). **3.** Intense, vehement, passionate, furious, impetuous, vivid, (*violent pain, abuse, controversy, discrepancy, revulsion, contrast, dislike, shock, colours; is of* or *was in a violent temper*). **4.** Hence ~LY[2] *adv.* [ME f. OF, f. L *violentus*; see -LENT]

vī'olet *n.* & *a.* **1.** *n.* Plant of genus *Viola* etc. with blue, purple, white, or other flowers, esp. **sweet**(-scented) ~; DOG[1]-*violet*; **shrinking ~**, shy person. **2.** *n.* & *a.* (Of) the colour seen at end of spectrum opposite red, produced by slight admixture of red with blue. **3.** *n.* Violet pigment; violet clothes or material. [ME, f. OF *violet(te)* dims. of *viole* f. L VIOLA[2]]

violi′n *n.* Musical instrument with 4 strings of treble pitch played with bow; violinist (FIRST, SECOND, *violin*); hence ~IST *n.*, player of violin. [f. It. *violino* dim. of VIOLA[1]]

vī′olist[1] *n.* Player of viol. [f. VIOL + -IST]

viō′list[2] *n.* Player of viola. [f. VIOLA[1] + -IST]

violoncĕ′ll|ō (-chĕ′-; *or* vē-) *n.* (*pl.* **~os**). Bass instrument like large violin, 4-stringed and held upright on floor by seated player; hence ~IST (3) *n.* [It., dim. of *violone* large viol (VIOLA[1]; see -OON)]

V.I.P. *abbr.* very important person.

vī′per *n.* Venomous snake of family Viperidae, esp. **common ~** or adder, the only poisonous snake in Gt. Britain; (fig.) malignant or treacherous person (**~ in** one's **bosom,** person who betrays those who have helped him); **~'s bugloss,** stiff bristly blue-flowered plant (*Echium vulgare*); **~'s grass,** scorzonera; hence or cogn. ~ĬFORM, ~INE[1], ~ISH[1] (fig.), ~-LIKE, ~OUS (fig.), *adjs.* [f. F *vipère* or f. L *vipera* (**vivipera* f. *vivus* alive + *parere* bring forth)]

virā′gō (*or* -ah′-) *n.* (*pl.* **~s**). Turbulent woman, termagant; (arch.) woman of masculine strength or spirit. [OE, f. L, = female warrior (*vir* man)]

vīr′al. See VIRUS.

vī′rėlay *n.* Short (esp. old French) lyric poem with two rhymes to a stanza variously arranged. [ME, f. OF *virelai*]

vīr′ement (vīr′m-; *or* vĕr′mahṅ) *n.* Power to transfer items from one financial account to another. [F (*virer* turn; see VEER[2], -MENT)]

vī′rėō *n.* (*pl.* **~s**). Small greenish Amer. song-bird of family Vireonidae. [L, perh. = greenfinch]

virĕ′sc|ence *n.* Greenness; (Bot.) abnormal greenness in petals etc. normally of some bright colour; so ~ENT *a.* [f. L *virescere*, incept. of *virēre* be green; see -ESCENCE]

vīr′gate[1] *a.* (Bot. & Zool.) Slim, straight, and erect. [f. L *virgatus* (*virga* rod; see -ATE[2])]

vīr′gate[2] *n.* (Hist.) Varying measure of land, esp. 30 acres. [f. med. L *virgata* (rendering OE *gierd-land* yard-land) f. L *virga* rod + -ATE[1]]

Vīrgĭ′lĭan *a.* Of, or in the style of, the Roman poet Virgil (d. 19 B.C.). [f. L *Vergilianus* (P. *Vergilius* Maro, Virgil; see -AN)]

vīr′gĭn *n.* & *a.* **1.** *n.* Person (esp. woman) who has had no sexual intercourse; **~'s bower,** clematis; hence or cogn. ~HOOD, **vīrgĭ′n**ITY, *ns.* **2.** Member of any order of women under a vow to remain virgins. **3. The (Blessed) V~ (Mary)**, mother of Christ. **4.** Picture or statue of the Virgin. **5.** Female insect producing eggs without impregnation. **6.** (*V~*). *The* zodiacal sign Virgo. **7.** *a.* That is a virgin; of or befitting a virgin (*virgin modesty*); undefiled, spotless; not yet used or penetrated or tried (*virgin soil*); (of clay) not fired; (of metal) made from ore by smelting; (of wool) not yet, or only once, spun or woven; (of insect) producing eggs without impregnation. **8. ~ birth,** (1) doctrine of Christ's birth without human father, (2) parthenogenesis; **~ comb** (that has been used only once for honey and never for brood); **~ forest** (in its untouched natural state); **~ honey** (taken from virgin comb, or drained from comb without heat or pressure); **~ queen,** unfertilized queen bee; **the V~ Queen,** Queen Elizabeth I of England. [ME, f. AF & OF *virgine* f. L *virgo -ginis*]

vīr′gĭnal *a.* & *n.* **1.** *a.* That is or befits or belongs to a virgin; hence ~LY[2] *adv.* **2.** *n.* ~, **(pair of) ~s,** legless early form of spinet in box, used in 16th–17th c. [ME f. OF, or L *virginalis* (as prec.; see -AL); n. perh. because intended for use by young women]

Vīrgĭ′nĭ|a *n.* Tobacco from Virginia; **~a creeper,** N. Amer. vine cultivated for ornament; ***~a reel,** a country dance; **~a stock,** branching plant with white or pink flowers; so ~AN *n.* & *a.* [f. ~ in U.S.A., orig. the first English settlement (1607), f. VIRGIN *Queen* + -IA[1]]

Vīr′gō *n.* **1.** Sign of the ZODIAC, the Virgin. **2. v~ inta′cta,** virgin with hymen intact. [OE, f. L, = virgin]

vīr′gūle *n.* Slanting line to mark division of words or lines; = SOLIDUS 2. [F, = comma, f. L *virgula* dim. of *virga* rod; see -ULE]

virĭdĕ′sc|ent *a.* Greenish, tending to become green; hence ~ENCE *n.* [f. LL *viridescere* f. L *viridis* (see foll., -ESCENT)]

virĭ′dĭan *a.* & *n.* (Chromium oxide pigment of) bluish-green (colour). [f. L *viridis* green (*virēre* be green)]

virĭ′dĭtȳ *n.* Greenness, verdancy. [ME, f. OF *viridité* or f. L *viriditas* (*viridis* green; see prec., -ITY)]

vĭ′rīle *a.* **1.** Of man as opp. to woman or child; **~ member,** (arch.) penis. **2.** Of or having procreative power. **3.** (Of mind, character, literary style, etc.) having masculine vigour or strength. **4.** So **virĭ′l**ITY *n.* [ME, f. F *viril* or f. L *virilis* (*vir* man; see -IL)]

vĭ′rilism *n.* (Path.) Development of secondary male characteristics in female or precociously in male. [f. prec. + -ISM]

virŏ′log|ȳ *n.* Scientific study of viruses; hence **virolŏ′g**ICAL *a.*, ~IST (3) *n.* [f. VIRUS + -O- + -LOGY]

vīrtu′, vĕrtu′, (-ōō′) *n.* **1.** Love of fine arts; **article** or **object of ~** (interesting from workmanship, antiquity, rarity, etc.). **2.** Virtuosity. [f. It. *virtù* VIRTUE, virtu]

vīr′tūal *a.* **1.** That is such for practical purposes though not in name or according to strict definition, (*is the virtual manager of the business*; *take this as a virtual promise*; *constitutes a virtual exculpation*). **2.** (Opt.) Relating to points at which rays would meet if produced backwards (*virtual focus, image*). **3.** (Mech.) Relating to infinitesimal displacement of point in system. **4.** Hence ~ITY (-ă′l-) *n.*, ~LY[2] *adv.* [ME, f. med. L *virtualis* f. L *virtus* after LL *virtuosus*; see -AL]

vīr′tūe *n.* **1.** Moral excellence, uprightness, goodness, (*virtue is its own reward*; *make a virtue of* NECESSITY); particular moral excellence (*patience is a virtue*); **the (seven) cardinal ~s (natural ~s,** justice, prudence, temperance, fortitude; **theological ~s,** faith, hope, charity). **2.** Chastity esp. of woman (EASY *virtue*); good quality (*has the virtue of being adjustable, of resisting heat*); inherent power, efficacy, (*no virtue in such drugs*); one of seventh ORDER[1] of ninefold celestial hierarchy; **by** or **in ~ of,** on the strength of, on the ground of, (*claims it in virtue of his long service*; *is entitled to it by virtue of his prerogative*). **3.** Hence ~LESS (-ūl-) *a.* [ME, f. OF *vertu* f. L *virtus -tutis* (*vir* man)]

vīrtūō′s|ō *n.* (*pl.* **~i** *pr.* -ē, *or* **~os**). Person with special knowledge of or taste for works of art or virtu; person skilled in the technique of a fine art, esp. performance of music; hence ~IC *a.*, **vīrtūo′**SITY, ~ŌSHIP, *ns.* [It., = learned, skilful, f. LL (as foll.)]

vīr′tūous *a.* Possessing or showing moral rectitude; chaste; hence ~LY[2] *adv.*, ~NESS *n.* [ME, f. OF *vertuous* f. LL *virtuosus* (*virtus* VIRTUE; see -OUS)]

vĭ'rŭl|ent (*or* -rōō-) *a.* Poisonous; (of disease) malignant or violent; (fig.) malignant, bitter, (*virulent animosity, tone, abuse*); hence ~ENCE *n.*, ~**ent**LY² *adv.* [ME, orig. of poisoned wound, f. L *virulentus* (as foll.; see -ULENT)]

vīr'|us *n.* Any of numerous kinds of very simple organisms smaller than bacteria, mainly of nucleic acid in protein coat, multiplying only in living cells and able to cause diseases; (arch. or fig.) poison, source of disease; hence ~AL *a.* [L, = slimy liquid, poison]

vis (vĭs) *n.* (Mech.) ~ ***inertiae*** (ĭnĕr'shĭē), inertia; ~ ***viva*** (vī'va), 'living force' (= mass × square of velocity) of moving body, twice its kinetic energy. [L, = strength, force]

Vis. *abbr.* Viscount.

vi'sa (vē'za) *n.*, & *v.t.* (~**ed** *or* ~**'d,** *pr.* -ad). **1.** *n.* Endorsement on passport etc. showing that it has been found correct, esp. as allowing holder to enter or leave a country. **2.** *v.t.* Mark with visa. [F, f. L *visa* neut. pl. p.p. of *vidēre* see]

vĭ'sag|e (-z-) *n.* (literary). Face, countenance; hence (-)~ED² (-zĭjd) *a.* [ME f. OF, f. L *visus* sight (as prec.); see -AGE]

vis-à-vis (vēzahvē') *adv.* & *n.* (*pl.* same). **1.** *adv.* In a position facing one another; opposite to; in relation to. **2.** *n.* Person or thing facing another, esp. in some dances; person occupying corresponding position in another group; *social partner. [F, = face to face (*vis* face f. L, as prec.)]

Visc. *abbr.* Viscount.

vĭscă'cha *n.* S. Amer. burrowing rodent with valuable fur. [Sp., f. Quechua (*h*)*uiscacha*]

vĭ'scera *n. pl.* The interior organs in the great cavities of the body (e.g. brain, heart, liver), esp. in the abdomen (e.g. the intestines). [L, pl. of VISCUS]

vĭ'sceral *a.* Of the viscera; relating to inward feelings; ~ (= SYMPATHETIC) **nerve.** [f. prec. + -AL]

vĭscerotŏ'nĭc *a.* Like endomorph in temperament, with predominantly social interests. [f. VISCERA + -O- + TONIC]

vĭ'scĭd *a.* Sticky, glutinous; semifluid; hence ~ITY (-ĭ'd-) *n.* [f. LL *viscidus* f. L *viscum* birdlime; see -ID¹]

vĭ'scōse *n.* (In the manufacture of rayon etc.) cellulose in highly viscous state (suitable for drawing into yarn) formed by treatment with sodium hydroxide solution and carbon disulphide. [f. LL *viscosus* (as VISCOUS; see -OSE¹)]

vĭscŏ'sĭtў *n.* **1.** Quality or degree of being viscous. **2.** (Phys., of fluid) internal friction, power of resisting a change in the arrangement of the molecules; quantity expressing this (**dynamic** ~, measuring the force needed to overcome internal friction; **kinematic** ~, measuring the force per unit density); hence **vĭscŏ'**METER, **vĭscosĭ'**METER, *ns.* [ME, f. OF *viscosité* or f. med. L *viscositas* (as VISCOUS; see -ITY)]

vĭ'scount (vī'k-) *n.* British nobleman ranking between earl and baron; hence ~CY, ~SHIP, ~Y⁴, *ns.* [ME, f. AF *viscounte*, OF *vi(s)conte* f. med. L *vicecomes -mitis* (as VICE-, COUNT³)]

vĭ'scountėss (vī'k-) *n.* Viscount's wife or widow; woman holding rank of viscount in her own right. [ME, f. prec. + -ESS¹]

vĭ'scous *a.* Sticky, glutinous; (Phys.) having high viscosity; semifluid; hence ~NESS *n.* [ME f. AF, or f. LL *viscosus* (as VISCID; see -OUS)]

vĭ'scus *n.* (Anat.) Any of soft internal organs of body (usu. in *pl.* VISCERA). [L]

***vise.** See VICE².

visé (vē'zā) *n.*, & *v.t.* (~**d** *or* ~**'d,** *pr.* -ād). (arch.) = VISA. [F, p.p. of *viser* scrutinize f. Rom. **visare* f. L *vidēre vis-* see]

Vĭ'shnu (-ōō) *n.* Hindu god regarded by his worshippers as supreme deity and saviour, by others as second member of triad including Brahma and Siva; hence ~ISM (3) *n.*, ~ITE¹ (1) *n.* & *a.* [f. Skr. *Vishṇu*]

vĭsĭbĭ'lĭtў (-z-) *n.* Being visible; (Meteorol. etc.) possibility of seeing, range of vision, as determined by conditions of light and atmosphere. [f. F *visibilité* or f. LL *visibilitas* f. L *visibilis* (see foll., -ITY)]

vĭ'sĭble (-z-) *a.* **1.** That can be seen by the eye; (of light) within the range of wavelengths to which the eye is sensitive; that can be perceived or ascertained, apparent, open, (*has no visible means of support*; *spoke with visible impatience*); prepared to receive callers; (of exports etc.) consisting of actual goods (cf. INVISIBLE). **2. The Church ~,** whole body of professed Christian believers; *visible* HORIZON; **~ speech,** system of alphabetical characters designed to represent position of vocal organs in all possible articulate utterances. **3.** Hence ~NESS (-beln-) *n.*, **vĭ'sĭb**LY² (-z-) *adv.* [ME f. OF, or f. L *visibilis* (*vidēre vis-* see; see -IBLE)]

Vĭ'sĭgŏth (-z-) *n.* West Goth, member of branch of Goths who settled in France and Spain in 5th–8th c. [f. LL *Visigothus*]

vĭ'sion (-zhon) *n.*, & *v.t.* **1.** *n.* Act or faculty of seeing, sight, (*has impaired his vision*); **field of ~,** all that comes into view when the eyes are turned in some direction. **2.** Thing or person seen in dream or trance (SEE¹ *visions*); supernatural or prophetic apparition, phantom; thing seen vividly in the imagination (*the romantic visions of youth*; *had visions of roast beef and plum pudding*); person etc. of unusual beauty; hence ~AL *a.*, ~IST (3) *n.* **3.** Imaginative insight; statesmanlike foresight, sagacity in planning. **4.** What is seen on television screen. **5.** *v.t.* See, present, (as) in a vision. [ME f. OF, f. L *visio -onis* (as prec.; see -ION)]

vĭ'sionar|ў (-zho-) *a.* & *n.* **1.** *a.* Given to seeing visions or to indulging in fanciful theories; existing only in a vision or in the imagination; imaginary, fanciful, unpractical; hence ~**ĭ**NESS *n.* **2.** *n.* Visionary person. [f. prec. + -ARY¹]

vĭ'sĭt (-z-) *v.* & *n.* **1.** *v.t.* Go or come to see (person, place, etc., or abs.) as act of friendship or ceremony, on business or for a purpose, or from interest; go or come to see for purpose of official inspection or supervision or consultation or correction; hence ~ABLE *a.* **2.** (Of disease, calamity, etc.) come upon, attack, (*be visited by* or *with the plague*); (Bibl.) punish (person, sin), inflict punishment for (his sins etc.) *upon* person, (arch.) comfort, bless, (person *with* salvation etc.). **3.** *v.i.* Be visitor; *~ **with,** visit, converse with; **~ing professor** (spending some time at another university). **4.** *n.* Act of visiting, call on a person or at a place, temporary residence with person or at place, (*was on a visit to some friends*; *paid him a long visit*; *during his second visit to the East*); *chat; occasion of going *to* doctor, dentist, etc.; formal or official call for purpose of inspection etc.; DOMICILIARY *visit*; *right of visit* (see VISITATION). [ME, f. OF *visiter* or f. L *visitare* go to see, frequent. of *visare* view f. *vidēre vis-* see; n. f. v., or perh. f. F *visite*]

vĭ'sĭtant (-z-) *a.* & *n.* **1.** *a.* (arch. or poet.) Visiting. **2.** *n.* Migratory bird temporarily in a particular locality; visitor, esp. supposedly supernatural one. [F, or f. L *visitare* (as prec.; see -ANT)]

vĭsĭtā'tion (-z-) *n.* **1.** Official visit of inspection or the like, esp. bishop's examination of the churches of his diocese; (colloq.) unduly protracted visit or social call; boarding of vessel belonging to another State to learn her character and purpose (**right of ~** or **visit,** right to do this, not including right of search). **2.** Divine dispensation of punishment or reward, notable experience compared to this; (Eccl.) festival on 2 July in honour of visit of the Virgin Mary to Elizabeth (Luke 1:39); **Nuns of the V~,** R.C. order founded 1610, now concerned esp. with education. **3.** (Zool.) Unusual and large migration of animals. [ME f. OF, or f. LL *visitatio* (as VISIT; see -ATION)]

visitatorial. See VISITOR.

vĭ'sĭtĭng (-z-) *n.* Paying visits, making calls; **have a ~ acquaintance with, be on ~ terms with,** know well enough to visit; **~-book** (for names of persons calling or to be called upon); *visiting*-CARD². [ME, f. VISIT + -ING¹]

vĭ'sĭtor (-z-) *n.* One who visits a person or place; migratory bird (cf. VISITANT); ||(in college etc.) official with right or duty of occasionally inspecting and reporting, whence or cogn. **visĭt(at)ŏr'**IAL (-z-) *adjs.*; **~s' book** (in which visitors to church, embassy, etc., write their names and addresses and occas. remarks). [ME, f. AF *visitour*, OF *visiteur* (as VISIT; see -OR)]

vi'sor (-z-), **vī'zor,** *n.* **1.** (Hist.) Movable part of helmet covering face. **2.** Projecting front part of cap; (Hist.) mask. **3.** Shield (fixed or movable) at top of vehicle windscreen to protect eyes from bright sunshine etc. **4.** Hence ~ED² (-zerd), ~LESS, *adjs.* [ME f. AF *viser*, OF *visiere* (*vis* face f. L *visus*; see VISAGE)]

vĭ'sta *n.* Long narrow view as between rows of trees; long succession of remembered or anticipated events etc., mental prospect or retrospect, (*opened up new vistas* or *a new vista to his ambition*); hence ~ED² (-*a*d) *a.* [It., = view]

vĭ'sual (-zhyoo- *or* -zyoo-) *a.* Of, concerned with, or used in, seeing (*visual nerve, organ*); **~ aid,** diagram etc. as aid to learning; **~ angle** (formed at the eye by rays from the extremities of an object viewed); **~ field** (of vision); **~ point,** effective position of eye in optical analysis; **~ purple,** light-sensitive pigment in retina; **~ ray,** line from object to eye; hence ~ITY (-ă'l-) *n.*, ~LY² *adv.* [ME, f. LL *visualis* (*visus* sight f. *vidēre* see; see -AL)]

vĭ'sualīz|e (-zhyoo- *or* -zyoo-), **-īs|e** (-īz), *v.t.* Make visible esp. to the mind (thing not visible to the eye); make visible to the eye; hence ~A'TION *n.* [f. prec. + -IZE]

vī'tal *a.* & *n.* **1.** *a.* Of or concerned with or essential to organic life (*vital energies, functions; wounded in a vital part*); **~ power** (to sustain life). **2.** Essential to existence of a thing or to the matter in hand (*a vital question; question of vital importance; secrecy is vital to the success of the scheme*). **3.** Affecting life; fatal to life or to success etc., (*a vital wound, error*); full of life or activity. **4. ~ capacity,** volume of air that can be expelled from lungs after taking deepest possible breath; **~ force,** *élan vital*; **~ statistics,** number of births, marriages, deaths, etc., (colloq.) measurements of woman's bust, waist, and hips. **5.** Hence ~LY² *adv.* **6.** *n.* (in *pl.*) Vital parts, e.g. lungs, heart, brain. [ME f. OF, f. L *vitalis* (*vita* life; see -AL)]

vī'tal|ism *n.* (Biol.) Doctrine that life originates in a vital principle distinct from chemical and other physical forces; hence ~IST (2) *n.*, **~ĭ'st**IC *a.* [f. F *vitalisme*, or f. prec. + -ISM]

vītă'lĭtў *n.* Vital power, ability to sustain life; animation, liveliness; (fig., of institution, language, etc.) ability to endure and to perform its functions. [f. L *vitalitas* (as VITAL; see -ITY)]

vī'talīz|e, -īs|e (-īz), *v.t.* Endow with life; infuse with vigour; hence ~A'TION *n.* [f. VITAL + -IZE]

vĭ'tamĭn *n.* Any of a number of accessory food factors present in many foodstuffs and essential to normal growth and nutrition of man and other animals; **~ A** (found in fish-liver oils etc.); **~ B_1, B_2, B_{12}, H,** members of group found in yeast etc.; **~ C** (found in fruit and vegetables, and preventing scurvy); **~ D,** group of several vitamins (D_1, D_2, etc.) found in fish-liver oils and egg-yolk, and preventing rickets; **~ E** (found in wheat-germ and green leaves, and preventing sterility); **~ H** (see above); **~ K** (found in green leaves etc., and assisting blood--clotting); hence ~IZE (1) *v.t.* [orig. *vitamine* f. G *vitamin* f. L *vita* life + G *amin* AMINE, because orig. thought to contain an amino-acid]

vītĕ'llĭn *n.* (Chem.) Chief protein constituent of yolk of egg. [f. foll. + -IN]

vītĕ'll|us *n.* (*pl.* ~*i pr.* -ī). Yolk of egg; protoplasmic contents of ovum; hence ~ARY¹, ~INE¹, *adjs.* (**~ine membrane,** yolk-sac). [L, = yolk]

vĭ'tĭ- *comb. form.* Vine, as: **~culture,** grape--growing. [f. L *vitis* vine]

vĭ'tĭāt|e (-shĭ-) *v.t.* Impair the quality or efficiency of, corrupt, debase, contaminate, (*person's constitution vitiated by intemperance; vitiated air, blood, mind, judgement*); make invalid or ineffectual (*a single word may vitiate a contract*); so **vĭtĭ**A'TION (-shĭ-), ~OR, *ns.* [f. L *vitiare* (*vitium* VICE¹) + -ATE³]

vĭ'trėous *a.* Of (the nature of) glass; like glass in hardness, brittleness, transparency, structure, etc. (*vitreous enamel*); **~ body** or **humour,** (Anat.) transparent jelly-like tissue filling eyeball; hence or cogn. ~NESS, **vĭtre'**SCENCE, *ns.*, **vĭtr**E'SCENT, **vĭ'trĭ**FORM, *adjs.* [f. L *vitreus* (*vitrum* glass) + -OUS]

vĭ'trĭ|fȳ *v.t.* & *i.* Convert or be converted into glass or glasslike substance esp. by heat; hence or cogn. ~FA'CTION, ~FICA'TION, *ns.*, **~fīable** *a.* [f. F *vitrifier* or f. med. L **vitrificare* (as prec.; see -FY)]

vĭ'trĭol *n.* Sulphuric acid or a sulphate, orig. one of glassy appearance; (fig.) caustic speech, criticism, feeling, etc.; **blue** or **copper ~,** copper sulphate; **green ~,** iron sulphate; **white ~,** zinc sulphate; **oil of ~,** concentrated sulphuric acid; **~-throwing,** throwing oil of vitriol in person's face as act of vengeance etc.; hence **vĭtrĭŏ'l**IC *a.*, ~IZE (1) *v.t.* [ME f. OF, or f. med. L *vitriolum* f. L *vitrum* glass]

Vĭtru'vĭan (-oo'-) *a.* **~ scroll,** convoluted scroll pattern in frieze decorations etc. [f. M. *Vitruvius* Pollio, Roman architect of 1st c. B.C. + -AN]

vĭ'tt|a *n.* (*pl.* ~**ae**). (Bot.) oil-tube in fruit of some plants; (Zool.) stripe of colour; so ~ATE² *a.* [L, = band, chaplet]

vĭtū'per|āte *v.t.* Revile, abuse; hence or cogn. ~A'TION, **~ātor,** *ns.*, ~ATIVE *a.* [f. L *vituperare* (*vitium* VICE¹) + -ATE³]

viva¹ (vē'va) *int.* & *n.* (The cry) 'long live' as salute etc. [It., 3 sing. pres. subj. of *vivere* live f. L]

||**vī'va**² *n.*, & *v.t.* (~**ed** *or* **~'d,** *pr.* -*a*d). (colloq.) = VIVA VOCE 2, 3. [abbr.]

vivace (vēvah'chā) *adv.* (Mus.) In a lively brisk manner. [It., f. L (as foll.)]

vĭvā'cious (-sh*u*s) *a.* Lively, sprightly, animated; hence or cogn. ~LY² *adv.*, **vĭvă'**CITY *n.* [f. L *vivax -acis* (*vivere* live; see -ACIOUS)]

vivandière (vĭvahṅdyār') *n.* (Hist.) Woman attached to continental esp. French regiment and selling provisions and liquor. [F]

vĭvār'ĭ|um *n.* (*pl.* ~**a**). Place artificially prepared for keeping animals in (nearly) their natural state. [L, = warren, fishpond (*vivus* living f. *vivere* live; see -ARIUM)]

vī'văt (*or* vē'-) *int.* & *n.* = VIVA¹. [L, 3 sing. pres. subj. of *vivere* live]

vīva vō'cė (*or* vō'chĭ) *adv.*, *a.*, *n.*, & *v.t.* **1.** *adv.* & *a.* Oral(ly). **2.** *n.* Oral examination. **3.** *v.t.* (w. hyphen). Examine viva voce. [med. L, = with the living voice]

vī'văx *n.* Malaria parasite (*Plasmodium vivax*) causing tertian fever. [mod. L, f. L (see VIVACIOUS)]

vīvĕ'rrīne *a.* Of the civet family or subfamily. [f. mod. L *viverrinus* f. L *viverra* ferret; see -INE[1]]

vī'vers (-z) *n. pl.* (Sc.) Food, victuals. [f. F *vivres* (*vivre* live f. L *vivere*)]

vĭ'vĭd *a.* (Of light or colour) strong, intense, glaring, (*a vivid flash of lightning*; *of a vivid green*); (of person) lively, vigorous; (of mental faculty or impression) clear, vigorous, strongly marked, (*has a vivid imagination*; *gave a vivid description*; *have a vivid recollection of the scene*); hence ~LY[2] *adv.*, ~NESS *n.* [f. L *vividus* (*vivere* live; see -ID[1])]

vĭ'vĭ|fȳ *v.t.* (esp. fig.) Give life to, enliven, animate; so ~FICA'TION *n.* [f. F *vivifier* f. LL *vivificare* f. L *vivus* living (*vivere* live; see -FY)]

vīvĭ'parous *a.* (Zool.) bringing forth young alive, not hatching by means of egg, (cf. OVI[1]*parous*); (Bot.) producing bulbs or seeds that germinate while still attached to parent plant; hence **vĭvĭpă'r**ITY, ~NESS, *ns.*, ~LY[2] *adv.* [f. L *viviparus* (*vivus*, see prec., -PAROUS)]

vĭ'vĭsĕct *v.t.* Perform vivisection on. [back form. f. foll.]

vĭvĭsĕ'ction *n.* Dissection or other painful treatment of living animals for purposes of scientific research; (fig.) unduly detailed or ruthless criticism; hence ~AL *a.*, ~IST (2, 3), **vĭ'vĭsĕct**OR, *ns.* [f. L *vivus* living (see VIVIFY), after *dissection*]

vĭ'xen *n.* She-fox; quarrelsome woman, termagant; hence ~ISH[1], ~LY[1], *adjs.* [ME *fixen* f. OE **fyxen* (= MHG *vühsinne*) fem. of FOX; see -EN[3]]

viz. (*or* nā'mlĭ) *adv.* That is to say, in other words, namely, (usu. following words that promise or more or less clearly require explanation etc., as: *under the following conditions, viz. that* etc.; *a permanent board of three, viz.* etc.). [abbr. of VIDELICET, *z* being med. L symbol for abbr. of *-et*]

vĭ'zard *n.* (arch.) = VISOR 2. [f. VISOR + -ARD]

vizcacha. Var. of VISCACHA.

vĭzier' (*or* vĭ'zĭer) *n.* High official, esp. State minister, in some Muslim countries; **grand** ~, prime minister in former Turkish empire and other Muslim countries; hence ~ATE[1] (1), ~SHIP, *ns.*, ~IAL (-ēr'-) *a.* [ult. f. Arab. *wazir* caliph's chief counsellor]

vĭ'zor. See VISOR.

vĭ'zsla (-zhl*a*) *n.* Hungarian hunting-dog with deep-red coat. [f. *V*~ in Hungary]

VJ *abbr.* Victory over Japan; ~ **day,** ||15 August 1945, *2 September 1945.

v.l. *abbr.* variant reading. [f. L *varia lectio*]

Vlăch (-k) *a.* & *n.* (Member) of a Romanian-speaking people in S.E. Europe. [Bulg., f. OSlav. *Vlachŭ* Romanian etc. f. Gmc **Walh* foreigner]

vlei (flā) *n.* (S. Afr.) Hollow in which water collects during rainy season. [Du. dial., f. Du. *vallei* valley]

||**V.O.** *abbr.* Royal Victorian Order.

vō'cable *n.* Word, esp. w. ref. to form rather than meaning. [F, or f. L *vocabulum* (*vocare* call)]

vocă'būlarȳ *n.* (List, arranged alphabetically with definitions or translations, of) the (principal) words used in a language or usu. in a particular book or branch of science etc., or by a particular author, (*a Livy with notes and vocabulary*; *a word not found in the Chaucerian vocabulary*; *the ever-increasing scientific vocabulary*); person's range of language (*his vocabulary is limited*); set of artistic or stylistic forms or techniques, esp. range of set movements in ballet etc. [f. med. L *vocabularius, -um* (as prec.; see -ARY[1])]

vō'cal *a.* & *n.* **1.** *a.* Of, concerned with, uttered by, the voice, (*a vocal communication*); ~ **cords,** folds of lining membrane of larynx about the opening of the glottis, with edges vibrating in air-stream to produce voice; ~ **music** (written for or produced by the voice with or without accompaniment); ~ **score,** musical score showing voice parts in full. **2.** Expressing one's feelings freely in speech (*was very vocal about his rights*); (poet., of trees, water, etc.) endowed (as) with a voice; (Phonet.) voiced, sonant. **3.** Hence or cogn. **vocă'l**ITY *n.*, ~LY[2] *adv.* **4.** *n.* Musical performance with singing; (R.C. Ch.) person entitled to vote in certain elections. [ME, f. L *vocalis* (as VOICE; see -AL)]

vocă'lĭc *a.* Of or consisting of vowel(s). [f. prec. + -IC]

vō'calism *n.* Use of voice in speaking or singing; vowel sound or system. [f. VOCAL + -ISM]

vō'calĭst *n.* Singer (opp. to *instrumentalist*). [f. VOCAL + -IST]

vō'caliz|e, -īs|e (-īz), *v.* **1.** *v.t.* Form (sound), utter (word), with the voice, esp. make sonant, (f *is vocalized into* v); write (Hebrew etc.) with vowel points. **2.** *v.i.* (joc.) Speak, sing, hum, shout, etc. **3.** (Mus.) Sing florid passage to vowel(s). **4.** Hence ~A'TION *n.* [f. VOCAL + -IZE]

vocā'tion *n.* **1.** Divine call to, or sense of fitness for, a career or occupation, (*felt no vocation* (*for the ministry*); *has never had the sense of vocation*; *little or no vocation to literature*). **2.** Employment, trade, profession, (*all vocations are overcrowded*). **3.** Hence ~AL *a.* [ME f. OF, or f. L *vocatio* (*vocare* call; see -ATION)]

vŏ'catĭve *a.* & *n.* (Gram.) ~ **(case),** case of nouns etc. in inflected languages, used in addressing or invoking person or thing. [ME, f. OF *vocatif -ive* or f. L *vocativus* (*vocare* call; see -ATIVE)]

vocĭ'fer|āte *v.t.* Utter (words etc., or abs.) noisily; shout, bawl; hence or cogn. ~ANCE, ~A'TION, **~ātor**, *ns.*, ~ANT *a.* & *n.* [f. L *vociferari* (*vox* voice, *ferre* bear)]

vocĭ'ferous *a.* (Of person, his speech, etc.) noisy, clamorous; insistently and forcibly expressing one's views; hence ~LY[2] *adv.*, ~NESS *n.* [f. as prec. + -OUS]

vŏ'dka *n.* Alcoholic spirit made esp. in Russia by distillation of rye etc. [Russ., dim. of *voda* water]

vōe *n.* Small bay, creek, in Orkney and Shetland. [f. Norw. *vaag*, ON *vágr*]

vōgue (vōg) *n.* *The* prevailing fashion (*the vogue for large hats*; *large hats are the vogue*); popular use or reception (*has had a great vogue*); **in** ~, in fashion, generally current; **~-word,** word currently fashionable; hence **vō'gu**ISH[1] (-gĭ-) *a.* [F, f. It. *voga* rowing, fashion (*vogare* row, go well)]

voice *n.*, & *v.t.* **1.** *n.* Sound formed in larynx etc. and uttered by mouth, esp. human utterance in speaking, shouting, singing, etc., (*heard a voice*; *spoke in a low voice*; *did not recognize her voice*; *the voice of the cuckoo*; *cried out in a loud voice*); ability to produce this (*has laryngitis and has lost her voice*); **in (good)** ~, in proper vocal condition for singing or speaking; *at the* TOP[1] *of* one's *voice*; hence **-voic**ED[2] (-st) *a.* **2.** Use of the voice, utterance esp. in spoken or (fig.) written words, opinion so expressed, right to express opinion, (*gave voice to his indignation in a pamphlet*; *dog gave voice to his joy*; *I have no voice in the matter*); agency by which opinion is expressed; **the ~ of God,** expression of God's will, wrath, etc.; **with one** ~, unanimously. **3.** (Phonet.) Sound uttered with resonance of vocal cords, not with mere breath. **4.** (Gram.) Set of forms of a verb showing relation of the subject to the action (ACTIVE, PASSIVE, MIDDLE[1], *voice*); verb in this form. **5.** (Mus.) Vocal part in composition; constituent part of fugue. **6. ~-box,** larynx; **~-over,**

narration in film not accompanied by picture of speaker; **~-print,** visual record of speech, analysed with respect to frequency, duration, and amplitude; ***~ vote** (taken by noting relative strength of calls of *ay* and *no*). **7.** *v.t.* Give utterance to, express, (*believe I am voicing the general sentiment when I say*; *letter voices our opinion*); (Mus.) regulate tone-quality of (organ-pipes), whence **voi'**CER[1] *n.*; (Phonet., esp. in *p.p.*) utter with voice, make sonant. [ME, f. AF *voiz*, OF *vois* f. L *vox vocis*]

voi'ceful (-sf-) *a.* (poet. or rhet.) Vocal; sonorous. [f. prec. + -FUL]

voi'celėss (-sl-) *a.* Speechless, dumb, mute; (Phonet.) surd, not voiced; hence ~NESS *n.* [f. VOICE + -LESS]

void *a.*, *n.*, & *v.t.* **1.** *a.* Empty, vacant; (of office) vacant (*bishopric fell void*); (of hand) having no cards *in* a suit. **2.** (esp. Law, of deed, promise, contract, etc.) invalid, not binding, (*null and void*); (poet. or rhet.) ineffectual, useless. **3. ~ of,** lacking, free from, (*a proposal wholly void of sense*; *his style is void of affectation*). **4.** Hence ~'NESS *n.* **5.** *n.* Empty space (*vanished into the void*; (fig.) *cannot fill the void made by death*); unfilled space in wall or building; (Bridge etc.) absence of cards *in* a particular suit. **6.** *v.t.* Render invalid; evacuate (excrement etc., or abs.); hence ~'ABLE *a.* [ME, f. OF dial. *voide*, OF *vuide*, *vuit* f. Rom. **vocitus* cogn. w. L *vacare* VACATE; v. partly f. AVOID, partly f. OF *voider* f. Rom. **vocitare* (**vocitus*)]

voi'dance *n.* Vacancy in benefice; voiding. [ME f. OF (as prec.; see -ANCE)]

voi'dėd *a.* In vbl senses; (Her., of bearing) having the central area cut away so as to show the field. [p.p. of VOID]

voile *n.* Thin semitransparent cotton, woollen, or silken dress-material. [F, = VEIL]

voir dire (vwar̂dėr') *n.* (Law). Oath to give true answers to questions affecting one's competence as juror etc. [OF (*voir* truth, *dire* say)]

vol. *abbr.* volume.

vō'lant *a.* (Zool.) flying, able to fly; (Her.) represented as flying; (literary) nimble, rapid. [F (*voler* f. L *volare* fly; see -ANT)]

vō'lar *a.* (Anat.) Of the palm or sole. [f. L *vola* hollow of hand or foot + -AR[1]]

vŏ'latīle *a.* & *n.* **1.** *a.* Evaporating rapidly (*volatile salts*); ~ (= ESSENTIAL) **oil. 2.** (fig.) Lively, gay, changeable, (*volatile wit, writer, disposition*); transient. **3.** Hence or cogn. ~NESS (-ln-), **vŏlatĭ'l**ITY, *ns.* **4.** *n.* Volatile substance. [f. OF *volatil* or f. L *volatilis* (*volare -at-* fly; see -IL)]

volă'tĭlīz|e, -īs|e (-īz), *v.t.* & *i.* (Cause to) evaporate; hence ~ABLE *a.*, ~A'TION *n.* [f. prec. + -IZE]

vŏl-au-ve'nt (-ō-vah'ṅ; *or* vŏ'-) *n.* Small pie of puff pastry filled with meat, fish, etc., and sauce. [F, lit. 'flight in the wind']

vŏlcă'n|ic *a.* Of, like, produced by, a volcano; **~ic bomb,** mass of ejected lava usually rounded and sometimes hollow; **~ic glass,** obsidian; hence ~ICALLY *adv.*, **vŏlcanĭ'**CITY *n.* [f. F *volcanique* (*volcan* volcano f. as foll.; see -IC)]

vŏlcā'nō *n.* (*pl.* ~es). Mountain or hill having opening(s) in earth's crust through which lava, cinders, steam, gases, etc., are or have been expelled continuously or at intervals (*active, dormant, extinct, volcano*); (fig.) violent esp. suppressed feeling, state of things likely to cause violent outburst. [It., f. L *Volcanus* Vulcan, Rom. god of fire]

vŏlcanŏ'logy̆. Var. of VULCANOLOGY.

vōle[1] *n.* (arch.) Winning of all tricks at cards. [F (*voler* fly f. L *volare*)]

vōle[2] *n.* Small ratlike or mouselike herbivorous rodent of family Cricetidae. [orig. *vole-mouse* f. Norw. **vollmus* (*voll* field, *mus* mouse)]

vŏ'let (-lā) *n.* Panel or wing of triptych. [F (*voler* fly f. L *volare*)]

vŏ'lĭtant *a.* (Zool.) = VOLANT. [f. L *volitare* frequent. of *volare* fly; see -ANT]

volĭ'tion *n.* Exercise of the will; power of willing (**of** or **by** one's **own ~**, voluntarily); hence ~AL, **vŏ'lĭt**IVE, *adjs.* [F, or f. med. L *volitio* (*volo* I wish; see -ITION)]

völkerwanderung (fėr'lkervahnderōōng) *n.* Migration of peoples, esp. of Germanic and Slavic peoples into Europe in 2nd–11th c. [G]

vŏ'lley *n.* & *v.* **1.** *n.* Simultaneous discharge of missiles, missiles so discharged; (fig.) noisy emission (*of* oaths etc.) in quick succession; (Lawn Tennis etc.) return of ball in play before it touches ground; (Football) kicking of ball in play before it touches ground; (Cricket) pitching of ball, ball pitched, right up to batsman or stumps without bouncing; **half-~,** (Lawn Tennis) return of ball as soon as it touches ground, (Cricket) ball so pitched that batsman may hit it as it bounces, hit so made; **~-ball,** game for two teams of six volleying large ball by hand over net. **2.** *v.t.* Return or send (ball, or abs.) by volley, whence ~ER[1] *n.*; discharge (missiles, abuse, etc., or abs.) in volley. **3.** *v.i.* (Of missiles) fly in a volley; (of guns etc.) sound together; make sound like volley of artillery. [f. F *volée* f. Rom. **volata* fem. p.p. (as n.) of L *volare* fly; see -Y[4]]

vŏ'lplāne *n.*, & *v.i.* (Aeron.) Glide. [f. F *vol plané* (*vol* flight, *plané* p.p. of *planer* hover); see PLANE[3]]

vols. *abbr.* volumes.

vŏlt[1] *v.i.*, & *n.* **1.** *v.i.* Make a volte. **2.** *n.* Var. of VOLTE. [f. F *volter* (VOLTE)]

vōlt[2] *n.* Unit of electromotive force, the difference of potential that would carry one ampere of current against one ohm resistance. [f. as VOLTAIC]

vō'ltage *n.* Electromotive force expressed in volts. [f. prec. + -AGE]

vŏltā'ĭc *a.* (arch.) Of electricity from a primary battery, galvanic, (*voltaic battery*, PILE[2]). [f. A. *Volta*, It. physicist d. 1827 + -IC]

Vŏltair'ėan, -ĭan, *adjs.* & *ns.* (Follower) of Voltaire; critical(ly) sceptic(al); hence ~ISM (3) *n.* [f. de *Voltaire*, later surname of F. M. Arouet, Fr. author d. 1778 + -EAN, -IAN]

vŏltă'mėter *n.* Instrument for measuring electric currents by their electrolytic effects. [f. as VOLTAIC + -METER]

vŏlte *n.* (Fenc.) quick movement to escape thrust; sideways circular movement of horse. [F, f. It. *volta* turn, fem. p.p. (as n.) of *volgere* turn f. L *volvere* roll]

vŏlte-fa'ce (-tfah's) *n.* Turning round, esp. (fig.) complete change of front in argument, politics, etc. [F, f. It. *voltafaccia* (*voltare* turn f. Rom. **volvitare* frequent. of L *volvere* roll; as FACE[1])]

vō'ltmēter *n.* Instrument for measuring electric potential in volts. [f. VOLT[2] + -METER]

vŏ'lūb|le *a.* **1.** (Of speech or speaker) fluent, glib; hence or cogn. **vŏl**UBI'LITY, **~le**NESS (-beln-), *ns.*, ~LY[2] *adv.* **2.** (arch.) Revolving, rotating. **3.** (Bot.) Twisting round a support, twining. [F, or f. L *volubilis* (*volvere* roll; see -UBLE)]

vŏ'lūme *n.* **1.** Set of (written or usu. printed) sheets of paper bound together and forming part or the whole of a work or comprising several works (*issued in 3 volumes*; *an odd volume of 'Punch'*; *library of 12,000 volumes*; SPEAK *volumes*); (Hist.) scroll of papyrus etc., ancient form of book. **2.** (usu. in *pl.*) Wreath, coil, rounded mass, *of* smoke etc. **3.** Solid content, bulk; amount or quantity *of* (business etc.). **4.** (Mus. etc.) Quantity or power of sound; fullness of tone. **5.** Hence (-)**vŏ'lūme**ED² (-md) *a.* [ME f. OF *volum(e)*, f. L *volumen -minis* roll (*volvere* to roll)]

vŏlūmĕ'tr|ic *a.* Of or pertaining to measurement by volume; hence ~ICALLY *adv.* [f. prec. + METRIC]

volū'min|ous (*or* -lōō'-) *a.* Consisting of many volumes; (of writer) producing many books etc.; of great volume, bulky, (of drapery etc.) loose and ample; hence ~O'SITY, ~OUSNESS, *ns.*, **~ously²** *adv.* [f. LL *voluminosus* (as VOLUME; see -OUS)]

vŏ'luntar|ism *n.* **1.** Doctrine of independence of Church etc. (see foll. 5). **2.** (Philos.) Doctrine that the will is a fundamental or dominant factor. **3.** Principle of relying on voluntary action rather than compulsion. **4.** So ~IST (2) *n.* [irreg. f. foll. + -ISM]

vŏ'luntar|ў *a.* & *n.* **1.** *a.* Done, acting, able to act, of one's own free will, not constrained or compulsory, intentional, (*a voluntary gift*; *there was no voluntary misstatement*; *was a voluntary agent in the matter*; *voluntary service, army*); **~y confession** (of criminal, not prompted by promise or threat); (Law) **~y conveyance** or **disposition** (made without compensation in money or other consideration). **2.** Brought about, produced, etc., by voluntary action; (of institution) supported by voluntary contributions; ||**V~y Aid Detachment,** group of organized voluntary first-aid and nursing workers. **3.** (Of limb, muscle, movement) controlled by the will. **4.** Hence **~ĭly²** *adv.*, ~ĬNESS *n.* **5.** *n.* Organ solo played before, during, or after church service; music for this; (arch.) extempore performance esp. as prelude to other music; (arch.) one who holds that the Church or the schools should be independent of the State and supported by voluntary contributions; (in competitions) special performance left to performer's choice. [ME, f. OF *volontaire* or f. L *voluntarius* (*voluntas* will; see -ARY¹)]

vŏ'luntarў|ism *n.* = VOLUNTARISM 1, 3; so ~IST (2) *n.* [f. prec. + -ISM]

vŏlunteer' *n.* & *v.* **1.** *n.* Person who spontaneously undertakes task etc.; person who voluntarily enters military or other service, esp. member of any of corps of voluntary soldiers formerly organized in U.K. and provided with instructors, arms, etc., by the State; (*attrib.*, of vegetation) growing spontaneously. **2.** *v.t.* Undertake, offer, (one's services, remark, explanation, etc.; *to* do) voluntarily. **3.** *v.i.* Make voluntary offer of one's services (*for* campaign, purpose); be a volunteer. [f. F *volontaire* (as VOLUNTARY), assim. to -EER]

volŭ'ptūarў *a.* & *n.* Concerned with, (person) given up to, luxury and sensual pleasure. [f. L *volupt(u)arius* (as foll.; see -ARY¹)]

volŭ'ptūous *a.* Of, tending to, occupied with, derived from, sensuous or sensual pleasure; hence ~LY² *adv.*, ~NESS *n.* [ME, f. OF *voluptueux* or f. L *voluptuosus* (*voluptas* pleasure; see -OUS)]

volū't|e *n.* & *a.* **1.** *n.* Spiral scroll characteristic of Ionic, Corinthian, and Composite capitals; hence ~ED² *a.* **2.** (Spiral shell of) gastropod of genus *Voluta*. **3.** *a.* (Bot. etc.) Rolled up. [F, or f. L *voluta* fem. p.p. (as n.) of *volvere* roll]

volū'tion (*or* -lōō'-) *n.* Rolling motion; spiral turn; whorl(s) of spiral shell; (Anat.) convolution. [f. as prec., after *revolution* etc.]

vŏ'lva *n.* (Bot.) Membranous covering enclosing immature fungus. [L (*volvere* wrap)]

vō'mer *n.* (Anat.) Small thin bone separating nostrils in man and most vertebrates. [L, = ploughshare]

vŏ'mit *v.t.*, & *n.* **1.** *v.t.* Eject (matter, or abs.) from stomach through mouth; (fig., of volcano, chimney, etc.) eject violently, belch forth. **2.** *n.* Matter vomited from stomach; (arch.) emetic; **black ~,** (black substance vomited in) yellow fever. [ME, f. (OF *vomite* n. or L *vomitus* f.) L *vomere -it-*, or f. frequent. L *vomitare*]

vŏmĭtŏr'ĭ|um *n.* (*pl.* **~a**). = foll. 2. [L; see foll.]

vŏ'mitorў *a.* & *n.* **1.** *a.* Emetic. **2.** *n.* (Rom. Ant.) Each of a series of passages for entrance and exit in (amphi)theatre. [f. L *vomitorius* a., *-um* n., (as VOMIT; see -ORY)]

vōō'dōō *n.*, & *v.t.* **1.** *n.* Use of, belief in, religious witchcraft as prevalent among W. Ind. etc. Negroes; person skilled in this; voodoo spell; hence ~ISM (3), ~IST (2, 3), *ns.* **2.** *v.t.* Affect by voodoo, bewitch. [f. Dahomey *vodu*]

-vora. See -VOROUS.

vorā'cious (-sh*u*s) *a.* Greedy in eating, ravenous, (lit. or fig.; *voracious schoolboy, readers*); hence or cogn. ~LY² *adv.*, ~NESS, **voră'**CITY, *ns.* [f. L *vorax* (*vorare* devour; see -ACIOUS)]

-vōre. See foll.

-vorous *suf.* forming *adjs.* (usu. w. intermediate -I-) w. sense 'feeding on' (*carnivorous*); so **-vora,** forming names of groups of animals classified by their food (*Insectivora*), **-vore** (vōr), forming name of individual of such group (*herbivore*). [f. L *-vorus* (*vorare* devour) + -OUS]

vŏr't|ĕx *n.* (*pl.* **~ices** *pr.* -ĭsēz, *or* **~exes**). Mass of whirling fluid, esp. whirlpool or whirlwind; (Phys.) portion of fluid whose particles have rotatory motion; any whirling motion or mass, esp. (fig.) system, occupation, pursuit, etc., viewed as swallowing up or engrossing those who approach it (*the vortex of society*); **~ex-ring,** vortex whose axis is a closed curve, e.g. smoke-ring puffed from smoker's lips or pipe; hence ~ĬCAL, ~ĬCOSE¹, ~Ĭ'CŪLAR¹, *adjs.*, ~Ĭ'CITY *n.* [L *vortex -icis* eddy, var. of VERTEX]

vŏrtĭcĕ'lla *n.* Bell-shaped animalcule of family Vorticellidae found in stagnant water etc. [f. mod. L *vorticella*, dim. of prec.]

vŏr'tĭc|ist *n.* **1.** (Metaphys.) Person regarding the universe, with Descartes, as a plenum in which motion propagates itself in circles. **2.** (Art). Painter etc. of futurist school using 'vortices' of modern civilization as basis. **3.** So ~ISM (3) *n.* [f. as VORTEX + -IST]

vŏrtĭ'ginous *a.* (arch.) Whirling, vortical. [f. L *vortigo -ginis*, var. of VERTIGO, + -OUS]

vō'tar|ў *n.* Person vowed to the service *of* (God etc.); ardent follower, devoted adherent or advocate, (*of* person, system, occupation, etc.); hence ~ESS¹, ~IST (1), *ns.* [f. L *vot-* (see foll.) + -ARY¹]

vōte *n.* & *v.* **1.** *n.* Formal expression of will or opinion in regard to election of officer etc., sanctioning law, passing resolution, expressing thanks, etc., signified by ballot, show of hands, voice, or otherwise, (*shall give my vote to* or *for the Labour candidate*; *was put to the vote and passed without a dissentient vote*; *let us take a vote on it*). **2.** Opinion expressed, ||money granted, by majority of votes (*Government received a vote of confidence*; *the army vote*); *the* collective votes (that may be) given by a party etc. (*will lose the Labour, Conservative, vote*); *the* right to vote (*Swiss women now have the vote*); ticket etc. used for recording vote; hence ~'LESS (-tl-) *a.* **3.** *v.i.* Give a vote (*for* or *against* person or measure, *to* do). **4.** *v.t.* Enact, resolve, (*that*), grant (sum), by majority of votes; (colloq.) pronounce, declare, by general consent (*was voted a failure*); (colloq.) announce one's proposal (*that*); **~ down,** defeat (proposal etc.) by votes; **~ in,** elect by votes. **5.** Hence **vō'**TABLE *a.*, **vō'**TER¹ *n.* [ME, (n. f. L *votum*) f. p.p. st. *vot-* of L *vovēre* vow]

vō'tĭng *n.* In vbl senses; **~-machine** (for automatic registering of votes); **~-paper** (used in voting by ballot in election of M.P. etc.); **~ stock** (entitling holder to a vote). [f. prec. + -ING[1]]

vō'tĭve *a.* Offered or consecrated in fulfilment of a vow, (*votive offering, tablet, picture*). [f. L *votivus* (as VOTE; see -IVE)]

vouch *v.* **1.** *v.t.* (arch.) Confirm, uphold, (statement) by evidence or assertion; cite as authority. **2.** *v.i.* Answer *for*, be surety *for*, (*will vouch for the truth of this, for him* or *his honesty*). [ME, f. OF *vo(u)cher* summon etc., ult. f. L *vocare* call]

vou'cher *n.* In vbl senses; document, receipt, etc., establishing the payment of money or the truth of accounts; document which can be exchanged for goods or services as token of payment made or promised by holder or another (||LUNCHEON *voucher*). [AF (as prec.; see -ER[4]), or f. prec. + -ER[1]]

vouchsā'fe *v.t.* Condescend to give or grant (*vouchsafed me no answer*); condescend (*to* do). [ME, f. VOUCH in sense 'warrant' + SAFE[2]]

vou'ssoir (vōō'swar) *n.* Each of the wedge-shaped or tapered stones forming an arch [f. OF *vossoir* etc., f. pop. L *volsorium*, ult. f. L *volvere* roll]

vow *n.*, & *v.t.* **1.** *n.* Solemn promise or engagement esp. in the form of an oath to God or other deity or to saint; **baptismal ~s** (given at baptism by baptized person or by sponsors); **monastic ~s** (by which monk binds himself or nun herself to poverty, chastity, and obedience); **lovers'** or **marriage ~s** (promises of fidelity); **under a ~**, having made a vow. **2.** *v.t.* Promise solemnly (thing, conduct; *vowed a temple to Apollo*; *vow obedience, vengeance against oppressor*). **3.** (arch.) Declare, esp. solemnly, (*that*, or abs.). [ME, f. AF *v(o)u*, OF *vo(u)*, f. L (as VOTE); v. f. OF *vouer*, in sense 3 partly f. AVOW]

vow'el *n.* Each of the more open sounds uttered in speaking, sound capable of forming a syllable, made with vibration of vocal cords but without audible friction, (opp. to, but not sharply divided from, CONSONANT); letter(s) representing this, as *a, e, i, o, u, aw, ah*; **neutral** or **obscure ~** (heard in second syllable of *cousin, reason, haddock*; cf. SCHWA); **~ gradation,** = ABLAUT; **~ mutation,** = UMLAUT; **~-point,** each of a set of marks indicating vowels in Hebrew etc.; hence (-)~**LED**[2] (-ld), ~LESS (-l-l-), ~**LY**[2], *adjs.* [ME, f. OF *vouel, voiel* f. L *vocalis* (*littera*) VOCAL (letter)]

vow'elize, -ise (-īz), *v.t.* Insert the vowels in (Hebrew etc., shorthand). [f. prec. + -IZE]

vox (vŏks) *n.* **~ *angelica,*** organ-stop with soft tremulous tone; **~ *humana*** (hūmah'na), organ-stop with tone supposed to resemble human voice; **~ *populi*** (pŏ'pūlī), the people's voice (i.e. public opinion, the general verdict, popular belief, or rumour). [L, = voice]

voy'ag|e *n.* & *v.* **1.** *n.* Journey, esp. long one by sea or water or air or in space; account of this. **2.** *v.i.* & *t.* Travel or traverse by water or air, or fig.; hence ~**EABLE** (-ĭja-) *a.*, ~ER[1] *n.* [ME, f. AF & OF *veiage, voiage* f. L *viaticum*; see -AGE; V. f. F *voyager*, or f. n.]

voyageur (vwahyahzhėr') *n.* Man employed in transportation of goods and passengers between trading posts; Canadian boatman. [F, = VOYAGER]

voyeur' (vwahyėr') *n.* One who obtains sexual gratification from looking at others' sexual actions or organs; hence ~ISM (2) *n.* [F (*voir* see)]

V.P. *abbr.* Vice-President.

V.R. *abbr.* Queen Victoria [f. L *Victoria Regina*]; variant reading.

||**vraic** *n.* Seaweed found in Channel Islands, used for fuel and manure. [F dial.; cf. VAREC]

||**V.R.D.** *abbr.* Volunteer Reserve Decoration.

V.R.I. *abbr.* Victoria, Queen and Empress. [f. L *Victoria Regina Imperatrix*]

vs. *abbr.* versus.

V.S. *abbr.* Veterinary Surgeon.

||**V.S.O.** *abbr.* Voluntary Service Overseas.

V.S.O.P. *abbr.* Very Special Old Pale (brandy).

Vt. *abbr.* Vermont.

V.T.O.(L). *abbr.* vertical take-off (and landing).

vŭlcă'nĭc etc. Var. of VOLCANIC etc.

Vŭ'lcanĭst *n.* (Geol.) Holder of PLUTONIC theory. [f. F *vulcaniste, volcaniste* (as VOLCANO; see -IST)]

vŭ'lcanite *n.* Hard black vulcanized rubber, ebonite. [f. as foll. + -ITE[1]]

vŭ'lcaniz|e, -is|e (-īz), *v.t.* Treat (rubber or rubberlike material) with sulphur etc. esp. at high temperature to increase elasticity and strength; hence ~ABLE *a.*, ~A'TION, ~ER[1] (1, 2), *ns.* [f. *Vulcan*, Rom. god of fire and metal-working + -IZE]

vŭlcanŏ'log|y̆ *n.* Scientific study of volcanoes; hence **vŭlcanolŏ'g**ICAL *a.*, ~IST (3) *n.* [f. as prec. + -O- + -LOGY; see VOLCANO]

vŭ'lgar *a.* **1.** Of or characteristic of the common people, plebeian, coarse in manners, low, (*vulgar expressions, mind, tastes, finery*). **2.** In common use, generally prevalent, (*vulgar errors*); **the ~ (**Christian**) era; ~ fraction** (expressed by numerator and denominator, not decimally); *vulgar* LATIN; **the ~** (national, vernacular, esp. formerly as opp. to Latin) **tongue. 3.** Hence or cogn. ~ISM (4, 2), ~ITY (-ă'r-), *ns.*, ~LY[2] *adv.* [ME, f. L *vulgaris* (*vulgus* common people; see -AR[1])]

vŭlgār'ian *n.* Vulgar (esp. rich) person. [f. prec. + -IAN]

vŭ'lgariz|e, -is|e (-īz), *v.t.* Make (person, manners, etc.) vulgar, infect with vulgarity; spoil (scene, sentiment, etc.) by making too common or frequented or well known; popularize; hence ~A'TION *n.* [f. VULGAR + -IZE]

Vŭ'lgate (*or* -āt) *n.* Latin version of the Bible prepared mainly by St. Jerome in late 4th c.; official R.C. text as revised 1592; (*v~*) traditionally accepted text of any author. [f. L *vulgata* (*editio* edition), fem. p.p. of *vulgare* make public (*vulgus*; see VULGAR)]

vŭ'lner|able *a.* That may be wounded (lit. or fig.); susceptible of injury, exposed *to* damage by weapon, criticism, etc.; (Contract Bridge) having won one game towards rubber and therefore being liable to higher penalties; hence ~ABI'LITY, ~**able**NESS (-beln-), *ns.*, ~**ab**LY[2] *adv.* [f. LL *vulnerabilis* f. L *vulnerare* to wound (*vulnus -eris* wound); see -ABLE]

vŭ'lnerary̆ *a.* & *n.* (Drug, unguent, etc.) useful or used for healing of wounds. [f. L *vulnerarius* (*vulnus*; see prec. and -ARY[1])]

vŭ'lpīne *a.* Of (the nature of) a fox; crafty, cunning. [f. L *vulpinus* (*vulpes* fox; see -INE[1])]

vŭ'ltur|e *n.* Large bird of prey of order Raptores with head and neck more or less bare of feathers, feeding chiefly on carrion and reputed to gather in anticipation of a death; (fig.) rapacious person; CULTURE *vulture*; hence or cogn. ~INE[1], ~ISH[1], ~OUS, (-cher-) *adjs.* [ME, f. AF *vultur*, OF *voltour* etc., f. L *vulturius*]

vŭ'lv|a *n.* (Anat.) External female genitals, esp. external orifice of vagina; hence ~AR[1] *a.*, ~I'TIS *n.* [L, = womb]

vv. *abbr.* verses; volumes.

vȳ'ĭng. See VIE.

W

W, w, (dŭ'b*e*lyōō) *n.* (*pl.* **Ws** *or* **W's**). Twenty-third letter of alphabet.

W. *abbr.* watt(s); Welsh; west(ern); women's (size).

w. *abbr.* wicket; wide; wife; with.

W *symb.* tungsten. [f. mod. L *wolframium*]

W.A. *abbr.* Western Australia.

Waac (wăk) *n.* Member of Women's Army Auxiliary Corps (‖1914–18 or *1942–48). [f. initials *W.A.A.C.*]

‖**Waaf** (wăf) *n.* Member of Women's Auxiliary Air Force (1939–48). [f. initials *W.A.A.F.*]

wabble. See WOBBLE.

***W.A.C.** *abbr.* Women's Army Corps.

wă'cke (-k*e*) *n.* Greyish-green or brownish rock resulting from decomposition of basaltic rock. [G, f. MHG *wacke* large stone, OHG *wacko* pebble]

wă'cky̆ *a.* & *n.* (sl.) Crazy (person). [orig. dial., = left-handed, f. WHACK + -Y[2]]

wad (wŏd) *n.*, & *v.t.* (**-dd-**). **1.** *n.* Lump or bundle of soft material used esp. to keep things apart or in place or to stuff up opening, esp. disc of felt etc. keeping powder or shot in place in gun; *roll of notes, money; (in *sing.* or *pl.*) large quantity esp. of money; ‖(sl.) bun, sandwich, etc. **2.** *v.t.* Press (cotton etc.) into wad or wadding; line or stuff (garment, coverlet), protect (person, walls, etc.), with wadding; stop up (aperture, gun-barrel), keep (powder etc.) in place, with wad. [perh. rel. to Du. *watten*, F *ouate* padding, cotton-wool]

wa'ddĭng (wŏ'd-) *n.* Soft pliable material usu. of cotton or wool used to line or stuff garments, quilts, etc., or to pack fragile articles in, cotton wool; material from which gun-wads are made. [f. prec. + -ING[1]]

wa'ddle (wŏ'-) *v.i.*, & *n.* **1.** *v.i.* Walk with the rocking motion natural to stout short-legged person or to bird with short legs set far apart as duck or goose. **2.** *n.* Waddling gait. [perh. frequent. of WADE; see -LE 3]

wa'ddy̆ (wŏ'-) *n.* Australian aboriginal's war-club. [Aboriginal wd, perh. f. WOOD]

wāde *v.* & *n.* **1.** *v.i.* Walk through water or other impeding medium e.g. snow, mud, sand; make one's way with difficulty or by force; (fig.) ~ **in,** (colloq.) intervene, make vigorous attack on one's opponent; ~ **into,** (colloq.) attack (person, task) vigorously; ~ **through,** read (book etc.) in spite of its dullness etc. **2.** *v.t.* Ford (stream) on foot; hence **wā'd**ABLE *a.* **3. Wading bird,** long-legged water-bird that wades (opp. short-legged web-footed swimmers). **4.** *n.* Spell of wading. [OE *wadan*, = OHG *watan*, ON *vatha* f. Gmc **wadhan* go (through) f. IE **wadh-*]

wā'der *n.* In vbl senses; wading bird; (in *pl.*) high waterproof boots, or waterproof garment for body and legs, worn in fishing etc. [f. prec. +-ER[1]]

wa'dĭ (wah- *or* wŏ'-) *n.* Rocky watercourse dry except in rainy season (in N. Africa etc.). [f. Arab. *wādī*]

***W.A.F.** *abbr.* Women in the Air Force.

w.a.f. *abbr.* with all faults.

wā'fer *n.*, & *v.t.* **1.** *n.* Very thin sweet crisp biscuit now chiefly eaten with ice cream; thin disc of unleavened bread used in Eucharist; small disc of dried paste formerly used for fastening letters, holding papers together, etc.; disc of red paper stuck on legal document instead of seal; **~-thin,** very thin. **2.** *v.t.* Attach or seal with wafer. [ME f. AF *wafre*, ONF *waufre*, OF *gaufre* (cf. GOFFER) f. MLG *wāfel* waffle; cf. foll.]

wa'ffle[1] (wŏ'-) *n.* Small crisp batter cake baked in **~-iron** usu. of two shallow metal pans hinged together. [f. Du. *wafel, waefel* f. MLG *wāfel*; cf. prec.]

‖**wa'ffle**[2] (wŏ'-) *v.i.*, & *n.* (Indulge in) verbose but aimless or ignorant talk or writing. [orig. dial., frequent. of *waff* = yelp, yap; imit.]

waft (wah- *or* wŏ-) *v.* & *n.* **1.** *v.t.* & *i.* Convey or travel easily (as) through air or over water; sweep smoothly and lightly along. **2.** *n.* Whiff of odour; transient sensation of peace, joy, etc. **3.** (Naut.) Distress signal, e.g. ensign rolled or knotted or garment flown in rigging. [orig. 'convoy (ship etc.)', back form. f. obs. *waughter, wafter* armed convoy-ship, f. Du. or LG *wachter* (*wachten* to guard)]

wăg[1] *v.* (**-gg-**) & *n.* **1.** *v.t.* & *i.* Shake to and fro, oscillate; *dog* **~s tail,** shows pleasure thus; **tail ~s dog,** less or least important member of society or section of party or part of structure has control; *wag* one's FINGER *at*; ~ one's **head** (in derision or amusement); **beards, chins, jaws, tongues, are ~ging,** talk is going on. **2.** *v.i.* (arch., of the world, times, etc.) Go along with varied fortune or characteristics. **3. ~'tail,** small bird of genus *Motacilla* (*grey, pied, yellow,* etc., *wagtail*) with long tail in frequent motion. **4.** *n.* Single wagging motion (*with a wag of his tail, head,* etc.). [ME *waggen* f. root of OE *wagian* sway, = OHG *wagōn*, ON *vaga*]

wăg[2] *n.* Facetious person, one given to jesting or practical jokes; ‖(sl.) truant (esp. *play wag* or *the wag*); hence, **~'**GERY (4) *n.*, **~'**GISH[1] *a.*, (-g-). [prob. f. obs. *waghalter* one likely to be hanged (as prec., HALTER)]

wāge[1] *n.* (in *sing.* or *pl.*) Amount paid at regular intervals esp. by the day or week or month, for time during which workman or servant is at employer's disposal (*gets good wages*; *brings his wages home*; *at a wage* or *at wages of £40 a week*; **living ~,** wages that allow earner and family to live without fear of privation; SUBSISTENCE *wage*); (fig.) requital (*the wages of sin is death*); (Econ., in *pl.*) part of total production that rewards labour rather than remunerating capital; (in *attrib.* use, usu. in *sing.*:) ~(s) **council,** board of workers' and employers' representatives determining wages where there is not collective bargaining; *wage* FREEZE; ~ **slave,** person dependent on income from labour in conditions like slavery; ~ **stop,** limitation of supplementary benefit at level of normal wage. [ME f. AF & ONF; OF *g(u)age* f. Gmc **wadhjam* (cf. GAGE[1], WED)]

wāge[2] *v.t.* Carry on (war, conflict). [ME 'pledge, gage', f. AF *wager*, ONF *wagier*, OF *guagier* (*guage*; see prec.)]

wā'ger *n.*, & *v.t.* **1.** = BET. **2.** *n.* (Hist.) ~ **of battle,** ancient form of trial by personal combat between the parties or their champions; ~ **of law,** trial by evidence of witnesses on oath. [ME, f. AF *wageure* (*wager*; see prec.)]

wă'ggle *v.i.* & *t.*, & *n.* (colloq.) = WAG^1; (Golf) swing (of) club-head to and fro over ball before playing shot; hence **wă'ggl**Y^2 *a.*, unsteady. [f. WAG^1 + -LE 3]

Wagnē'rĭan (vah-) *a.* & *n.* (Admirer) of the music of Wagner; like Wagner's grandly-planned dramatic operas. [f. R. *Wagner*, Ger. composer d. 1883 + -IAN]

wă'gon, ||wă'ggon, *n.* Four-wheeled vehicle for drawing heavy loads, often with removable semicylindrical tilt or cover, usu. drawn by two or more horses, (**hitch** one's ~ **to a star,** utilize powers higher than one's own); trolley for conveying tea etc.; ||open railway vehicle or railway van for goods; *small vehicle or cart, van, motor car; (**water-**)~, vehicle for carrying water, whence *on the* (*water-*)~, (sl.) teetotal; *wagon* TRAIN 11; **~-roof, -vault,** (shaped like wagon-tilt). [earlier *wagan*, *wag*(*h*)*en*, f. Du. *wag*(*h*)*en*, cogn. w. OE *wægn* WAIN]

wă'g(g)oner *n.* Driver of wagon. [f. Du. *wagenaar* (as prec., -ER^1)]

wăg(g)onĕ'tte *n.* Four-wheeled horse-drawn pleasure vehicle (open or with removable cover) with facing side-seats. [f. WAGON + -ETTE]

wagon-lit (văgawnlē') *n.* Sleeping-car on continental railway. [F]

Waha'bĭ, Wahha'bĭ, (wahah'-) *n.* One of a sect of Muslim puritans following strictly the original words of the Koran. [f. Abd-el-*Wahhab*, founder in 18th c. + -I]

wahi'nė (wah-hē'nĭ) *n.* (N.Z.) Woman, wife. [Maori]

waif *n.* **1.** Ownerless object or animal, thing cast up by or drifting in sea or brought by unknown agency. **2.** Homeless and helpless person, esp. unowned or abandoned child. **3. ~s and strays,** odds and ends, homeless or neglected children. [ME, f. AF *waif*, *weif*, ONF *gaif*, prob. of Scand. orig.]

wail *v.* & *n.* **1.** *v.i.* Lament with wail or with words suggesting wail; (of wind etc.) make sound like person wailing; **W~ing Wall,** high wall in Jerusalem said to stand on site of Solomon's temple, where Jews traditionally pray and lament on Fridays. **2.** *v.t.* (poet. or rhet.) Bewail, wail over. **3.** *n.* Prolonged plaintive inarticulate loud high-pitched cry; sound like or suggestive of this; hence ~'FUL *a.* (poet.). [ME, f. ON **veila* (*vei* int. = WOE)]

wain *n.* (poet. or dial.) Wagon; = CHARLES's WAIN; **~'wright,** wagon-builder. [OE *wæg*(*e*)*n*, *wǣn*, = OHG *wagan*, ON *vagn*, f. Gmc **wagnaz*, **wegnaz* f. IE **wogh-*, **wegh-* carry; cf. WAY, WEIGH]

wai'nscot *n.*, & *v.t.* **1.** *n.* Wooden panelling or boarding on lower part of room-wall; ||(Hist.) imported oak of fine quality. **2.** *v.t.* Line with wainscot; hence ~ING^1 (3) *n.* [ME, f. MLG *wagenschot*, app. f. *wagen* WAGON + *schot* of uncert. meaning]

waist *n.* **1.** Part of human body below ribs and above hips, usu. of smaller circumference than these. **2.** Narrower middle part of normal human figure; similar narrow part in middle of long object, e.g. violin or hour-glass or wasp. **3.** Middle part of ship, between forecastle and quarterdeck. **4.** Part of garment encircling or covering waist; narrow middle part of woman's dress etc.; part of garment between neck and waist; *blouse or bodice. **5. ~'band, ~-belt,** (worn round waist); **~-cloth,** = LOIN-*cloth*; **~-dee'p, -hi'gh,** *adjs.* & *advs.*, up to waist; **~'line,** outline of size of person's waist, e.g. as indicator of fatness. **6.** Hence (-)~'ED^2 *a.* [ME *wast*, perh. repr. OE **wæst*, **weahst* (= Goth. *wahstus* growth), f. root of WAX^2]

||wai'stcoat (*or* -sk-) *n.* Man's garment for upper part of body, usu. buttoned and sleeveless, normally worn under jacket but partly visible in front; woman's similar garment. [f. prec. + COAT]

wait^1 *v.* **1.** *v.i.* Defer action or departure for specified time or until some expected event occurs, be expectant or on the watch, (*for*, *till*; *wait a minute*; *waited* (*for*) *an hour*; *shall not wait here any longer*; *kept me waiting* or *made me wait*; *have a month to wait yet*; *will do it for you while you wait*; *wait till I come*, *for high water* or *a fine day*; *waited to see what would happen*); **~ and see,** await progress of events; **~ for it!,** (colloq.) do not begin before the proper moment; **~ for me!,** do not go so fast that I am left behind; **cannot ~,** is impatient; *that* **can ~,** need not be dealt with at present, since it is unimportant; **you ~!** (as threat of retribution). **2.** *v.t.* Await, bide, (*is waiting his opportunity*; *you must wait your turn*, *my convenience*); defer (meal etc.) till another's arrival. **3.** *v.i.* ~ (**at** or ***on table**), act as waiter or as servant with similar functions; act as attendant. **4. ~-a-bit,** plant with hooked thorns etc. that catch the clothing; **~ (up)on,** await convenience of, serve as attendant to, pay respectful visit to; **~ up,** not go to bed but wait (*for* someone to arrive). [ME, f. ONF *waitier* = OF *guaitier*, f. Gmc **wahtan* (**wak-* WAKE^1)]

wait^2 *n.* **1.** ||(in *pl.*) Street singers of Christmas carols; (Hist.) official bands of musicians maintained by a city or town. **2.** Act or time of waiting (*had a long wait for the train*); watching for enemy, ambush, (*lie in* or *lay wait*, usu. *for*). [ME, partly f. ONF **wait*, *wet* (*waitier*; see prec.), partly f. prec.]

wai'ter *n.* In vbl senses; man who takes orders, brings food, changes plates, etc., at hotel or restaurant tables, whence **wai'tr**ESS^1 *n.*; tray, salver; DUMB *waiter*; TIDE^1-*waiter*. [f. WAIT^1 + -ER^1]

wai'tĭng *n.* In vbl senses; stopping of motor vehicle at side of road even without leaving it (*no waiting*); (period of) official attendance at court (LADY, LORD, etc., *-in-waiting*); **~ game,** abstention from early action in contest etc. so as to act more effectively later; **~-list** (of persons waiting for vacancy, next chance to obtain thing, etc.); **~-room** (provided for persons to wait in, esp. by doctor, dentist, etc., or at railway or bus station). [ME, f. WAIT^1 + -ING^1]

waive *v.t.* Refrain from insisting on or using, tacitly or implicitly relinquish or forgo, (right, claim, opportunity, legitimate plea, etc.); hence **wai'v**ER^4 *n.* (Law). [ME, f. AF *weyver*, OF *gaiver* allow to become a '**WAIF**', abandon]

wāke^1 *v.* (*past* **woke** *pr.* wōk, *or* **~d;** *p.p.* **~d, wo'ken,** *or* **woke**). **1.** *v.i.* & *t.* ~ (**up**), cease to sleep, cause to cease sleeping, (lit., or fig.: *spring wakes all nature*; *nature wakes*; *shouting woke the echoes*; *woke up to the fact that he meant it*). **2.** *v.i.* Be awake (arch. exc. in part. or gerund: *in his waking hours*; *waking or sleeping*; *waking* DREAM^1). **3.** *v.i.* & *t.* ~ (**up**), cease or rouse from sloth, torpidity, inactivity, or inattention (*needs something to wake him up*); rise or raise from the dead. **4.** *v.t.* Disturb (silence, place) with noise, make re-echo. **5. ~-robin,** ||arum, esp. cuckoo-pint, *plant of genus *Trillium*. [goes back to two OE forms: (a) strong v. **wacan wōc *wacen*, (b) weak v. *wacian* (cf. OS *wakon*, OHG *wahhēn*, *-ōn*), f. Gmc **wak-*; cf. WATCH^2]

wāke^2 *n.* **1.** (Hist.) Vigil commemorating church dedication, merry-making or fair on the occasion. **2.** (usu. in *pl.*) Annual holiday in (industrial) northern England. **3.** (Ir.) Watch by corpse before burial, lamentations and merry-making in connection with it. [partly f. OE

**wacu* (= OHG *wahha*, ON *vaka*), rel. to prec.; in ME partly f. prec.; sense 'vigil' perh. f. ON]

wāke[3] *n.* Strip of smooth-looking water left behind moving ship (**in the ~ of,** behind, following, as result of, after the example of); turbulent air left behind moving aircraft etc. [prob. f. MLG, f. ON **vaku, vök* hole or opening in ice]

wā'keful (-kf-) *a.* Unable to sleep, (of night etc.) passed with little or no sleep; vigilant; hence ~LY[2] *adv.*, ~NESS *n.* [f. WAKE[1] + -FUL]

wā'ken *v.t.* & *i.* Cause to be, become, awake (lit. or fig.). [f. ON *vakna*, = OE *wæcnan*, Goth. *-waknan* f. Gmc **wak-* WAKE[1]; cf. -EN[6]]

Wa'lach (wŏ'lak) *n.* = VLACH; hence ~IAN (-lā'k-) *a.* & *n.* [f. as VLACH]

Waldĕ'ns|ēs (wŏ-; -z) *n. pl.* Puritan religious sect orig. in S. France, now chiefly in Italy and America, founded *c.* 1170 and much persecuted; hence ~IAN *a.* & *n.* [f. Peter *Waldo* of Lyons, founder]

wāle *n.*, & *v.t.* **1.** *n.* = WEAL[2]; ridge on woven fabric, e.g. corduroy; specially woven strong band round woven basket; (Naut.) broad thick timber along ship's side; **wale-knot** or **wall-knot** (made at end of rope by intertwining strands to prevent unravelling or act as stopper). **2.** *v.t.* Provide or mark with wales. [OE *walu* stripe, ridge, = LG *wāle*, ON *vala* knuckle]

Wā'ler *n.* Horse imported (esp. Hist. for Indian army) from New South Wales. [f. *Wales* + -ER[1]]

walk[1] (wawk) *v.* **1.** *v.i.* (Of person or other biped) progress by advancing each foot alternately; never having both feet off ground at once; go *backwards, sideways*, etc., with similar movements; go with gait usual except when speed is desired; (of quadruped) go with slowest gait, always having at least two feet on ground at once; *be released from suspicion or charge; (Baseball) reach first base on BALL[1]*s*. **2.** Travel or go on foot (*walk into shop, down hill*, etc.); take exercise thus (*walks for two hours each day*); (of GHOST) be visible. **3.** (arch.) Live with or in specified principle or manner, conduct oneself, (*walk in love, humbly, with God*, etc.). **4.** *v.t.* Perambulate, traverse on foot at walking speed, tread floor or surface of; **~ the boards,** be actor or actress; **~ the hospitals** or **wards,** be medical student; *walk the* PLANK[1]; **~ the streets,** (1) traverse streets esp. in search of work etc., (2) be prostitute; hence ~'ABLE *a.* **5.** Cause to walk with one; accompany in walking; ride or lead (horse, dog, etc.) at walking pace; take charge of (hound-puppy at walk); (Baseball) allow to reach first base on BALL[1]*s*; ~ person **off his feet** or **legs,** exhaust him with walking. **6. ~ about,** stroll; **~'about** *n.*, Austral. Aboriginal's period of wandering in bush, informal stroll among crowd by royal person etc.; **~ away from,** easily outdistance; **~ away with,** = *walk off with*; **~ in,** enter; **~ into,** (colloq.) encounter through unwariness (*walked into the trap*), (sl.) attack forcefully, eat (meal etc.) heartily; **~ it,** (1) perform journey on foot, not ride, (2) have easy victory; **~ off,** depart (esp. abruptly); **~ off with,** (colloq.) steal, win easily; **~-on,** = WALKING[1]*-on part* or its player; **~ on air,** be transported with joy; **~ out,** ||go for walks (*with*) in courtship, depart suddenly and angrily, whence *~-out* n. (esp. as protest or strike); **~ out on,** desert, leave in the lurch; **~ over,** (1) treat contemptuously, (2) traverse (racecourse, or abs.) at walk if one wishes or with little effort, owing to absence or inferiority of competitors, whence *~-over* n., easy victory or achievement; **~ tall,** be proud; **~ up!** (showman's invitation to circus etc.); **~ up to,** come near to (person); ***~-up** *n.* & *a.*, (building) with access to upper floors only by stairs. [OE *wealcan* roll, toss, wander, corresp. to MDu. & MLG *walken* to full, cudgel, ON *valka* drag about f. Gmc **walk-*]

walk[2] (wawk) *n.* **1.** Walking gait or pace, person's action in walking, (*go at, never gets beyond, a walk; know him by his walk; win* etc. **in a ~,** without effort). **2.** Traversing of distance by walking (*is only ten minutes' walk from here*); excursion on foot, stroll, constitutional, (*go for, take, take person for, a walk; to the castle and back is a good walk*); journey on foot completed to earn money promised for charity etc.; SPACE[1] *walk*. **3.** Person's favourite walking-ground; round of hawker, postman, etc.; place or track or route intended or suitable for strollers or foot-passengers, promenade, colonnade, footpath; place where hound-puppy is sent to accustom it to various surroundings; place where gamecock is kept (COCK[1] *of the walk*); part of forest under one keeper; ROPE-*walk*; ||SHEEP-*walk*; **~ of life,** calling, profession, occupation. **4. ~'way,** passage for walking along (esp. one connecting different sections of a building), wide path in garden etc. [ME, f. prec.]

wa'lker (waw'k-) *n.* In vbl senses; wheeled framework for person (e.g. baby or cripple) unable to walk unaided; bird of kind that walks instead of hopping or swimming. [ME, f. WALK[1] + -ER[1]]

wa'lkĭe-talkĭe (waw'kĭtawkĭ; *or* -taw'-) *n.* Radio transmitting- and receiving-set carried on the person to provide two-way communication as one walks about. [f. WALK[1] + TALK + -IE]

wa'lkĭng[1] (waw'k-) *n.* In vbl senses; **heel-and-toe ~** (in which both heel and toe are used, as required in walking-races); **~-o'n part** (in which actor or actress appears on stage but does not speak); **~ papers,** (colloq.) dismissal; **~-stick,** (1) stick carried when walking, esp. as added support, (2) *STICK[2]-insect; **~-tour,** pleasure-journey of some days on foot. [ME, f. WALK[1] + -ING[1]]

wa'lkĭng[2] (waw'k-) *a.* In vbl senses; **~ delegate,** trade-union official who visits members and their employers for discussions; **~ dictionary** or **encyclopaedia,** person able to provide much miscellaneous information; **~ fern,** Amer. evergreen fern of genus *Camptosorus*, whose fronds take root at their ends; **~ gentleman** or **lady,** theatrical performer without speaking part, needed for appearance only; **~ leaf,** (1) = *walking fern*, (2) = leaf-insect; **~ wounded** (able to walk despite injuries). [ME, f. WALK[1] + -ING[2]]

wall (wawl) *n.*, & *v.t.* **1.** *n.* Continuous and usu. vertical and solid structure of stones, bricks, concrete, timber, etc., narrow in proportion to length and height, serving to enclose (partly) or protect or divide off town, house, room, field, etc.; surface of inner side(s) of room, esp. as place for display of pictures etc.; *with* one's BACK[1] *to the wall*; **blank ~** (without door or gate or window, or without decoration); **bang** or **run** one's **head against a** (**brick**) **~,** attempt the impossible; **see through a brick ~,** have miraculous insight; **~s have ears,** eavesdroppers are or may be present; PARTY[1]-*wall*; RETAIN*ing wall*; (*drive* or *send* person) **up the ~,** (colloq.) crazy or furious; WRITING *on the wall*. **2.** Thing resembling wall in appearance or effect; steep side of mountain; protection or obstacle consisting of weapons etc.; vertical outermost part of hollow structure; (Anat., Zool., & Bot.) outermost layer of organ, cell, etc.; (Mining) rock enclosing lode or seam. **3.** (arch.) (Position next to) wall as opp. gutter side of street footpath (**give** person **the ~,** allow him cleaner and safer part in passing; **take the ~ of,** refuse this courtesy to). **4.** Side as opp. centre of road (*the weakest* **goes to the ~,** is pushed aside, gets the worst in competition). **5.** **~-barley,** wild barley as weed; **~-board** (made from wood-pulp etc. and used to cover walls); **~-cress,** plant of genus *Arabis* growing in stony places; **~-fern,** common polypody; **~'flower,** yellow-flowered plant of genus *Cheiranthus* growing wild on old walls, fragrant spring garden-plant (*C. cheiri*) with usu. orange or brown or yellow clustered flowers, (colloq.) woman sitting out dances for lack of partners; **~-fruit** (of trees fastened against wall for protection and warmth); ||~ **game,** Eton form of football played beside a wall; **~-painting** (on wall usu. of room, esp. fresco); **~'paper** (for pasting over room-walls, freq. with decorative printed patterns); **~-pepper,** pungent kind of stonecrop; **~-plate,** timber laid in or on wall to distribute pressure of girder etc.; **~-rue,** small fern with leaves like rue, growing on walls and rocks; **~-to-~,** (of carpet) covering whole floor of room. **6.** Hence ~-LESS *a.* **7.** *v.t.* (esp. in *p.p.*) Provide or protect with wall; hence ~'ING[1] (2) *n.* **8.** Block *up* (aperture etc.) with wall; shut *up* (person) within wall. [OE, =OS *wal*, f. L *vallum* rampart (*vallus* stake)]

wa'llabў (wŏ'-) *n.* **1.** Small species of kangaroo; **on the ~ (track),** (Austral.) vagrant, unemployed. **2.** (in *pl.*, colloq.) Australians, esp. Australian international Rugby Union team. [f. Aboriginal *wolabā*]

Wallach. Var. of WALACH.

wallah (wŏ'la) *n.* (orig. Anglo-Ind., now sl.) Person employed about or concerned with something, -man; BOX[2]-*wallah*; **competition-~,** Indian civil servant appointed by competitive examination. [f. Hindi -*wālā* suf. = -ER[1] (3)]

wallarōō' (wŏ-) *n.* Large brownish-black kangaroo (*Macropus robustus*). [f. Aboriginal *wolarū*]

wa'llĕt (wŏ'-) *n.* **1.** (arch.) Bag for carrying personal necessaries, food, etc., on journey, esp. as used by pilgrim or beggar. **2.** Flat case for holding banknotes etc. [ME *walet*, prob. f. AF **walet*, perh. f. Gmc **wall-* roll]

wa'll-eye (waw'lī) *n.* Eye with iris showing whitish opacity or streaking, or turned outwards in squint; Amer. pike with large prominent eyes. [back form. f. foll.]

wa'll-eyed (waw'līd) *a.* Having wall-eye; *(of fish) having large prominent eyes. [ME, f. ON *vagleygr* (**vagl*, cf. Icel. *vagl* film over eye; *auga* EYE[1])]

wa'll-knŏt (waw'ln-) *n.* See WALE. [perh. rel. to Norw. & Sw. *valknut* double or secure knot]

Wallōō'n *n.* & *a.* **1.** *n.* Member or language (a French dialect) of a Gaulish people in S. Belgium and neighbouring parts of France. **2.** *a.* Of the Walloons or in their language. [f. F *Wallon* f. med. L *Wallo -onis* f. Gmc **walhaz* foreign; cf. WELSH[1]]

wa'llop (wŏ'-) *v.t.*, & *n.* (sl.) **1.** *v.t.* Thrash, beat; hit hard; (in *part.*) big, strapping, thumping; hence ~ING[1] (1) *n.* **2.** *n.* Heavy resounding blow; beer or other drink. [earlier senses 'gallop', 'boil', f. ONF (*walop* n. f.) *waloper*, OF *galoper* f. Frank. **wala hlaupan* (**wala* well, **hlaupan* run, LEAP[1]; cf. GALLOP)]

wa'llow (wŏ'lō) *v.i.*, & *n.* **1.** *v.i.* Roll about in mud, sand, water, etc.; take gross or unrestrained delight *in* sensuality etc. **2.** *n.* Act of wallowing; place to which buffaloes etc. resort to wallow, resulting depression in ground. [OE *walwian* roll f. WG **walwōjan* f. Gmc **walw-*, **welw-* roll f. IE **wolw-*, **welw-*]

Wa'll Street (waw'l-) *n.* American financial interests or money-market. [street in New York City]

wa'lnut (waw'l-) *n.* (Tree of genus *Juglans* yielding) nut containing delicate-flavoured kernel in pair of boat-shaped shells; timber of walnut-tree used in cabinet-making. [OE *walh-hnutu* f. Gmc **walhaz* foreign + **hnut-* NUT]

Walpur'gĭs nīght (vahlpoor'gĭs-nīt) *n.* Eve of 1 May, when (acc. to G legend) witches meet on the Brocken or elsewhere and hold revels with the Devil. [f. G *Walpurgisnacht* (*Walpurgis* gen. of *Walpurga* 8th-c. Engl. woman saint, *nacht* NIGHT)]

wa'lrus (waw'l- *or* wŏ'l-) *n.* Large amphibious carnivorous arctic long-tusked mammal (*Odobenus rosmarus*) related to seal and sea-lion; **~ moustache** (long, thick, and hanging down at sides). [prob. f. Du. *walrus*, *-ros*, perh. by metath. after *walvisch* 'whale-fish' f. wd repr. by OE *horschwæl* 'horse-whale']

waltz (wawlts *or* wawls *or* wŏ-) *n.* & *v.* **1.** *n.* (Music for) dance in triple time with graceful flowing melody, performed by couples who progress and rotate simultaneously. **2.** *v.i.* Dance waltz; dance *in*, *out*, *round*, etc., in joy etc.; move easily or casually. **3.** *v.t.* Move (person) in or as in waltz; *waltz* MATILDA. **4.** Hence ~'ER[1] *n.*; **~'ing mouse** (of breed unable to walk straight). [f. G *walzer* (*walzen* revolve)]

wa'mpum (wŏ'-) *n.* Beads made from shells and strung for money or decoration or as mnemonic patterns by N. Amer. Indians. [f. Algonquin *wampumpeag* (*wap* white, *umpe* string, *-ag* pl. suf.)]

wan (wŏn) *a.* (Of person or his complexion or look) pale, looking worn or exhausted; (of heavenly body or its light) faint, partly obscured; (arch., of night, water, etc.) dark, black; hence ~'LY[2] *adv.*, ~'NESS (-n-n-) *n.* [OE *wann* dark, black, of unkn. orig.]

wand (wŏ-) *n.* Slender rod for carrying in hand or setting in ground as temporary mark; magician's or music-conductor's baton; staff symbolizing some officials' authority. [ME, f. ON **vandur*, *vöndr*, = Goth. *wandus*, prob. f. Gmc **wanduz* (**wend-*, **wand-*; cf. WEND[1], WIND[3])]

wa'nder (wŏ'-) *v.* & *n.* **1.** *v.i.* Go from country to country or from place to place without settled route or destination; go aimlessly *in*, *off*, etc.; (of river or road) wind, meander; **~ing Jew,** (1) legendary person supposed to be still living from when Christ said 'Thou shalt wander on the earth till I return' as punishment for an insult, (2) person who never settles down, (3) climbing plant of genus *Tradescantia* etc.; **~ing sailor,** moneywort; **~-plug** (to be fitted into any of various sockets in electrical device); hence ~ER[1] *n.* **2.** Stray, diverge from the right way (lit. or fig.), get lost, depart from home. **3.** Talk or think irrelevantly or disconnectedly or incoherently, stray from subject in hand, be inattentive or delirious, (*his mind wandered*; *wanders in his talk*). **4.** *v.t.* Traverse in wandering (*you may wander the world* (*through*) *and not find such another*). **5.** Hence ~ING[1] (1) *n.* (esp. in *pl.*). **6.** *n.* Act of wandering. [OE *wandrian*, = MLG, MDu. *wanderen* f. WG **wandrōjan* (as WEND[1]; see -ER[5])]

wa'nderlŭst (wŏ-; *or* vah'nderlo͝ost) *n.* Eager desire or fondness for travelling or wandering. [G]

wanderōō' (wŏ-) *n.* Langur or macaque of Sri Lanka. [f. Sinh. *wanderu* monkey]

wa'ndōō (wŏ'-) *n.* W. Austral. eucalyptus with white bark and durable brown wood. [Aboriginal]

wāne *v.i.*, & *n.* **1.** *v.i.* Decrease in brilliance, size, or splendour; (of moon) decrease in apparent size after the full (cf. WAX²); lose power or vigour or importance or repute, decline. **2.** *n.* Process of waning; **on the ~**, waning, declining. **3.** Defect of plank etc. that lacks square corners; hence **wā'ney**² *a.* [OE *wanian* lessen, = OS *wanon*, OHG *wanōn*, *wanēn*, ON *vana*, Goth. **wanan* f. Gmc **wanōjan* (**wana-* lacking f. IE **wa-*)]

wă'ngle (-nggel) *v.t.*, & *n.* (sl.) **1.** *v.t.* Secure (favour, desired result) by scheming or contrivance; show in the desired light, fake, (report etc.). **2.** *n.* Act of wangling. [19th-c. printers' sl.; orig. unkn.]

wa'nion (wŏ'nyon) *n.* (arch.) **With a ~** (*to*), with a curse (on), with a vengeance. [var. of *waniand* part. of WANE (waning moon = unlucky hour)]

Wă'nkel (*or* v-) *n.* **~ engine,** rotary internal combustion engine with continuously rotated and eccentrically pivoted nearly triangular shaft. [f. F. ~, Ger. engineer b. 1902]

want¹ (wŏ-) *n.* **1.** Lack, absence, deficiency, *of* (*ship rotting for want of paint*; *took this for want of anything better*; *shows great want of thought, care, sense, judgement*). **2.** Need *of*, need of sustenance, poverty, (*is in want of money, a gardener*, etc.; *living in great want*). **3.** Desire for thing held necessary to life or happiness or success or completion, thing so desired, (*a man of few wants*; *meets a long-felt want*; *can supply your wants*); ***~ ad,** newspaper advertisement by person seeking to obtain employee or thing. [ME, f. ON *vant* neut. of *vanr* lacking = OE *wana*, f. as WANE]

want² (wŏ-) *v.* **1.** *v.t.* Be without or deficiently supplied with; fall short by (specified amount) *of* specified limit. **2.** *v.i.* Be in want (*for*; *let him want for nothing*; *must not be allowed to want*). **3.** *v.t.* Require, need, (thing, doi*ng*, *to be* done, *to* do). **4.** Desire, wish for possession or presence of, (*to* do, thing, person; *I want some sugar, it done, you to try*; *call me if I am wanted*); **do not ~ to,** (1) am unwilling to, (2) ought not to (*you don't want to overdo it*); **~ed (by the police)**, suspected to be criminal etc. **5.** *v.i.* (U.S. & Sc. colloq.) Desire to come or go or get (*want out*). [ME, f. ON *vanta* (as prec.)]

wa'ntĭng (wŏ'-) *a.* Lacking in quality or quantity; unequal to requirements; absent; deficient (*is wanting in judgement*); **be found ~**, not meet requirements. [ME, f. prec. + -ING²]

wa'nton (wŏ'-) *a.*, *n.*, & *v.i.* **1.** *a.* Sportive, gambolling, playful, irresponsible, capricious, (*wanton child, kid, wind, mood*); luxuriant, unrestrained, wild, (*wanton growth, ringlets, profusion*). **2.** Licentious, unchaste, lewd, (*a wanton woman*; *wanton thoughts*). **3.** Motiveless, serving no purpose, random, arbitrary, (*wanton mischief, destruction*). **4.** Hence **~LY**² *adv.*, **~NESS** (-n-n-) *n.* **5.** *n.* Licentious person. **6.** *v.i.* Sport, gambol, move capriciously; behave licentiously (*with*). [ME *wantowen* (*wan-* UN-², *towen* f. OE *togen* p.p. of *tēon* discipline, cogn. w. TEAM)]

||**wă'pentāke** (*or* wŏ'-) *n.* (Hist.) Hundred or division of shire (in areas of England that had large Danish population). [OE *wǣpen(ge)tæc* f. ON *vápnatak* (*vápn* weapon, *tak* taking f. *taka* TAKE¹); perh. w. ref. to voting in assembly by show of weapons]

wa'pĭtĭ (wŏ'-) *n.* N. Amer. elk, resembling red deer but larger. [f. Cree *wapitik* white deer]

war¹ (wŏr) *n.* **1.** Strife usu. between nations conducted by force; state of open hostility and suspension of ordinary international law prevalent during such strife, military or naval or air attack or series of attacks; period of such strife (TROJAN *War*; *Wars of the* ROSE¹*s*; **the War,** one in progress or recently ended); (fig.) hostility or contention between persons, efforts to combat crime, disease, poverty, etc., natural conflict compared to war (**~ of the elements,** storms and catastrophes in nature). **2. Art of ~**, strategy and tactics; **at ~**, engaged in hostilities (*with* enemy); **carry the ~ into the enemy's camp** or **country,** (fig.) make counter-accusations etc., not confine oneself to defence; CIVIL *war*; **cold ~**, unfriendly relations between nations (esp. U.S.S.R. and West after Second World War), with hostile propaganda but not fighting; COUNCIL *of war*; **declare ~**, announce imposition of hostilities (*on* nation or fig. institution, practice, etc.); **dogs of ~**, (poet.) havoc accompanying war; **gang ~**, fighting between members of rival gangs of criminals etc.; **go to ~**, begin hostile operations; **go to the ~s,** (arch.) serve as soldier; **a good ~**, (colloq.) an enjoyable time during a war; **holy ~** (waged in support of a religious cause); HOT¹ *war*; **have been in the ~s,** (colloq.) show signs of injury or rough usage; **laws of ~**, limitations on belligerents' action recognized by civilized nations; MAN¹-*of-war*; **private ~**, feud between persons or families disregarding law of murder etc., or hostilities against members of another State without sanction of one's own government; **rights of ~** (permitting belligerents certain acts illegitimate in peace); SHOOTING *war*; TOTAL *war*; **trade of ~**, soldier's profession; TUG *of war*; *war of* ATTRITION; **~ to the knife,** relentless struggle to the bitter end esp. between persons; **~ of nerves,** attempt to wear down opponent by gradual destruction of morale; WORLD *war*. **3. ~ baby,** (esp. illegitimate) child born in wartime; **~ bride,** woman who marries soldier etc. met as result of war; **~ chest,** funds for war or other campaign; **~-cloud,** state of international affairs that threatens war; **~ correspondent** (employed to send reports from scene of war); **~ crime, criminal,** (perpetrator of) action violating laws of war; **~-cry,** phrase or name shouted in charging or rallying to attack, party catchword; **~ damage** (caused by events resulting from war); **~-dance** (performed by primitive peoples before war or after victory); **~ department,** State office in charge of army; **~-game,** kriegspiel, or similar exercise testing tactical knowledge; **~-gaming,** conduct of battles with toy soldiers; **~-god,** one worshipped as giving victory in war, esp. the Greek Ares or Roman Mars; **~ grave** (of person killed in fighting); **~'head,** explosive head of missile, torpedo, or similar weapon; **~-horse,** knight's or trooper's powerful horse, (fig.) veteran soldier or politician; ||**~ loan,** stock issued by Government to raise funds in wartime; **~-lord,** military commander(-in-chief); **~ memorial,** monument etc. commemorating those killed in a war; **~'monger,** one who seeks to bring about war; ||**War Office,** (Hist.) State department in charge of army; **~-paint,** paint put on body esp. by N. Amer. Indians before battle, (colloq.) ceremonial costume, full fig, cosmetics; **~-path,** (route of) warlike expedition of N. Amer. Indians (*be, go, on the ~-path*, (fig.) be engaged in, enter upon, any conflict, have taken, take, hostile attitude); **~-plane,** military aircraft; **~ poet** (writing on topics relating to wars, esp. the two world wars); **~'ship** (for use in war); **~-song** (inciting to war, or celebrating martial deeds); **~'time,** period when war is being waged; **~-weary,** dejected by prolonged war; **~-whoop,** yell esp. of N. Amer. Indians in charging; **~-widow,** woman whose husband has been killed in war; **~-work,** work done on account of a war; **~-worn,** experienced in or damaged or exhausted by war. [ME *werre* f. AF, ONF, var. of OF *guerre* f. WG **werra* (cf. OHG *werra* confusion, strife, OS, OHG *werran* embroil), f. Gmc **werz-*, **wers-* (cf. WORSE)]

war² (wôr) *v.* (**-rr-**). **1.** *v.i.* (arch.) Make war. **2.** *v.t.* Bring or beat *down* by war. **3.** (in *part.*) Rival, competing, inconsistent, (*warring creeds, factions, principles*). [ME, f. prec.]

War. *abbr.* Warwickshire.

wa'ratah (wŏ'-) *n.* Austral. crimson-flowered shrub of genus *Telopea.* [Aboriginal]

war'ble¹ (wôr'-) *v.* & *n.* **1.** *v.i.* & *t.* (Esp. of bird, also fig. of person or sound) sing in gentle continuous trilling manner. **2.** *v.t.* Speak or utter in manner suggestive of warbling bird's song; express in song or verse. **3.** *n.* Warbled song or utterance. [ME, f. ONF *werble(r)* f. Frank. *hwirbilōn* whirl, trill]

war'ble² (wôr'-) *n.* Hard lump on horse's back from galling of saddle; (tumour on cattle etc. produced by) larva of ~ **fly** beneath skin. [16th c.; orig. uncert.]

war'bler (wôr'-) *n.* In vbl senses; small bird of family Sylviidae or *Parulidae, e.g. blackcap, whitethroat, and chiff-chaff, sometimes not remarkable for song. [f. WARBLE¹ + -ER¹]

ward¹ (wôrd) *n.* **1.** (arch.) Act of guarding or defending place etc. (cf. WATCH¹ 2); bailey of castle. **2.** (arch.) Confinement, custody, guardian's control. **3.** Minor under care of guardian; ~ **(of court)**, minor, insane person, etc., under protection of court such as Court of Chancery. **4.** Administrative division of city or town esp. for elections. **5.** Separate room or division in prison (*condemned* etc. *ward*) or hospital (ISOLATION etc. *ward*; WALK¹ *the wards*) ||or (Hist.) workhouse (CASUAL etc. *ward*). **6.** (in *pl.*) Notches and projections in key and lock designed to prevent opening of lock by wrong key. **7.** **Ward*-HEEL²*er*; **~-maid,** woman employed to clean etc. in hospital ward; ||**~-mote,** (Hist.) meeting of citizens or liverymen of ward [f. as MOOT]; **~'room** (in warship, for commissioned officers). [OE *weard,* = OHG *warta* watch, ON *vartha* cairn f. Gmc **wardho* (**wardh-* extended form of **war-* WARE²,³; cf. GUARD¹)]

ward² (wôrd) *v.t.* **1.** ~ **(off)**, parry (blow), avert (danger, poverty, etc.). **2.** (arch.) Guard, protect. [OE *weardian,* = OS *wardon,* OHG *wartēn,* ON *vartha* f. Gmc **wardhōjan* (as prec.)]

-ward *suf.* forming *adjs.* w. sense 'having specified direction or tendency' (*backward, downward, eastward, homeward, onward, toward*), also used as *advs.* (= -WARDS) and *ns.* (*to the eastward*); **to usward,** (arch.) towards us. [f. or after OE *-weard* f. Gmc **-wardha* (**wardh-* var. of **werth-* turn)]

war'den¹ (wôr'-) *n.* **1.** President or governor (*of* some colleges, schools, hospitals, *prisons, youth hostels, etc.). **2.** Official appointed to perform supervisory duties (CHURCH¹*warden,* GAME¹-*-warden,* ||TRAFFIC *warden*), esp. **(air-raid)** ~ (helping civilian population in air raids). **3.** Hence ~SHIP *n.* [ME, f. AF & ONF *wardein,* var. of OF *g(u)arden* GUARDIAN]

war'den² (wôr'-) *n.* Kind of cooking pear. [ME, of unkn. orig.]

war'der (wôr'-) *n.* **1.** ||Gaoler, whence **war'dr**ESS¹ (wôr'-) *n.* **2.** (Hist.) Staff of authority carried by commander and used to give signals. **3.** (arch.) Sentinel, watchman. [ME, f. AF *wardere, -our* f. ONF *warder,* OF *garder* (see GUARD¹, -ER²); sense 2 partly f. *warderer* perh. f. obs. *wardererе* look out behind!]

War'dour Street (wôr'der-) *n.* Antique and imitation-antique furniture trade (~ **English,** affectedly archaic); cinema film trade. [name of street in London]

war'drōbe (wôr'-) *n.* Place where clothes are kept, esp. large cabinet or movable cupboard with pegs, shelves, etc.; person's or persons' stock of clothes; department of royal household in charge of garments; ~ **bed,** bed that can be folded up into wardrobe; ~ **dealer,** dealer in second-hand clothes; ~ **master,** ~ **mistress,** one who has charge of professional wardrobe of an actor, actress, or theatrical company; ~ **trunk** (fitted with separate drawers, coat-hangers, etc., and designed to stand on end, serving as wardrobe). [ME, f. ONF *warderobe,* OF *garderobe* (as GUARD², ROBE)]

-wards (-z) *suf.* forming *advs.* (and *adjs.*) w. sense 'to or in the direction of' (*backwards, downwards, eastwards, homewards, onwards, towards*). [f. as -WARD + -S³]

war'dshĭp (wôr'-) *n.* Tutelage, guardian's care, (*under wardship; has the wardship of*). [ME, f. WARD¹ + -SHIP]

wāre¹ *n.* **1.** Things manufactured for sale, esp. pottery of any kind, or in comb. (*hardware, ironware,* ||*smallwares*). **2.** (usu. in *pl.*) Articles that person etc. has for sale (usu. *his* etc. *wares*). **3.** (With distinctive epithet) kind of manufactured material, esp. pottery (*Wedgwood, Delft, biscuit,* etc., *ware*), named from inventor, place of manufacture, or some characteristic. **4.** **~'house** *n.*, building in which goods are stored, repository, wholesale or large retail store; **~'house** (*or* -z) *v.t.*, store (esp. furniture or bonded goods) temporarily in repository; **~'houseman,** worker in or owner of repository; cf. ITALIAN. [OE *waru,* = MDu., MLG *ware,* ON *vara* f. Gmc **warō,* perh. orig. = 'object of care', cogn. w. foll.]

wāre² *pred. a.* (poet.) Aware. [OE *wær,* = OS *war,* OHG *giwar,* Goth. **wars* f. Gmc **war-*; cf. WARD¹]

wāre³, 'wāre, (*or* wôr) *v.t.* (esp. in *imper.*) Look out for, be cautious about, avoid, (*ware hounds, wire, traps!,* esp. in hunting-field). [OE *warian,* = OS *waron,* OHG *-warōn,* ON *vara* f. Gmc **war-* (as prec.), & f. ONF *warer* f. Gmc]

war'fāre (wôr'-) *n.* State of war, campaigning, being engaged in war, (*after long warfare; bacteriological, chemical, warfare; his warfare is over*). [ME, f. WAR¹ + FARE¹]

war'like (wôr'-) *a.* Martial, fond of or skilful in war; military, of or for war, (*warlike preparations*); bellicose, threatening war. [ME, f. WAR¹ + -LIKE]

war'lŏck (wôr'-) *n.* (arch.) Sorcerer, wizard. [OE *wǣr-loga* traitor (= OS *wār-lǫgo*) f. *wǣr* covenant + **log* cogn. w. LIE²]

warm¹ (wôrm) *a.* & *n.* **1.** *a.* Of or at fairly high temperature (*hot, warm, tepid, cool, cold; warm water, weather, countries*); (of blood) remaining at temperature well above that of the surroundings as in mammals and birds; (of person etc.) (1) at natural temperature, not cold, (2) having temperature of skin raised by exercise or excitement or external heat; **keep a place** ~, occupy it temporarily on behalf of another. **2.** (Of clothes etc.) serving to keep one warm; (of exertion etc.) making one warm. **3.** (Of friendly relations or actions or agents) enthusiastic, hearty, zealous, (*a warm partisan, friend,* WELCOME, RECEPTION; *warm thanks*). **4.** Animated, heated, exciting or excited, in or resulting from sanguine or offended or indignant or unreserved mood, (*when warm with wine; the dispute* or *disputants grew warm*). **5.** (Of position etc.) difficult or dangerous to maintain or meet (*warm* RECEPTION or WELCOME; **make it** or **things** ~ **for** person, create strong feeling against him). **6.** (Of feelings etc.) sympathetic, cordial, affectionate, susceptible, (*has a warm heart, smile*); (of temperament) amorous, prone to sexual desire; (of description etc.) intended to appeal to erotic feelings. **7.** (Of colour) suggestive of warmth, esp. containing rich reds or yellows. **8.** (Of scent in hunting) fresh and strong, indicating recent passage of quarry; (of seeker in children's hiding games etc.) near the object sought, on verge of finding. **9.** ||(colloq.) (Of person) comfortably off, rich. **10. ~-blooded,** having warm blood, (fig.) ardent, passionate; **~ front** (of advancing mass of warm air); **~-hearted,** affectionate, cordial; **~ work,** keen or dangerous conflict (and cf. sense 2). **11.** Hence ~'ISH[1] 2 *a.*, ~'LY[2] *adv.*, ~'TH[1] *n.* **12.** *n.* Warmth of atmosphere; warm thing, esp. BRITISH *warm.* [OE *wearm,* = OS, OHG *warm,* ON *varmr* f. Gmc **warmaz,* prob. f. IE **ghworm-* etc.]

warm[2] (wôrm) *v.* & *n.* **1.** *v.t.* Make warm, excite, (*fire warms room, person,* etc.; *wine to warm the heart; warm oneself at fire* etc.). **2.** *v.i.* Warm oneself at fire etc.; **~ (up)**, become warm or animated or sympathetic (*room is warming up; he warmed up as he got into his subject, warmed to his subject; my heart warms to him*). **3. ~ up,** (of radio, engine, etc.) reach temperature of efficient working; (of athlete etc.) prepare for contest by exercise or practice; hence *~-up* n.; **~ed-up** or ***-over,** (of food, lit. or fig.) reheated, stale. **4. ~'ing-pan,** flat closed long-handled usu. brass vessel for holding live coals formerly used for warming inside of bed before it was occupied, (fig.) person holding office temporarily to keep it for another not yet ready. **5.** Hence (-)~'ER[1] (2) *n.* **6.** *n.* Warming or being warmed (*must have, give it, another warm first*). [OE *werman* v.t. (= OS *wermian,* OHG *wermen,* ON *verma,* Goth. *warmjan,* f. Gmc **warmjan*), & OE *wearmian* v.i. (= OHG *war(a)mēn*) f. Gmc **warmǣjan;* cf. prec.]

warn (wôrn) *v.t.* Give notice to, put on guard, admonish, (person, or abs.; *of* danger or consequences or future or unknown present circumstance, *against* person or thing or do*ing, that* something impends or must be reckoned with, *that* he is neglecting or has neglected to do something, *to* (= that he must) do); **~ off,** tell person to keep away (from), (Racing) prohibit from attending races (at); **~'ing coloration,** (Biol.) conspicuous colouring that warns an enemy against attacking. [OE *war(e)nian, wearnian,* = OHG *warnōn, warnēn,* f. WG **warnōjan, -ǣjan* f. Gmc **war-;* cf. WARE[2]]

war'nĭng (wôr'-) *n.* In vbl senses (**take ~,** change one's course of action when warned of its danger); thing that serves to warn (*palpitation is a warning of heart trouble; let this be a warning to you*); **give ~,** (arch.) give notice, announce that employment, tenancy, etc., is to terminate in specified (e.g. a month's) time. [OE *war(e)nung* etc. (as prec., -ING[1])]

warp[1] (wôrp) *v.t.* & *i.* **1.** Make or become crooked or perverted, change from straight or right or natural state, bias, (*sun had warped the boards; seasoned timber does not warp; hardship warped his disposition; judgement warped by self-interest; has a somewhat warped sense of humour*). **2.** (Naut.) Haul (ship) in some direction by rope attached to fixed point; progress thus. **3.** *v.t.* Fertilize by inundating with warp; choke *up* (channel) with alluvial deposit. [OE *weorpan* throw, = OS *werpan,* OHG *werfan,* ON *verpa,* Goth. *wairpan,* f. Gmc **werp-,* **warp-*]

warp[2] (wôrp) *n.* **1.** Threads stretched lengthwise in loom to be crossed by weft. **2.** Rope used in towing or warping, or attached to trawl-net. **3.** Crooked state produced in timber etc. by uneven shrinkage or expansion; (fig.) perversion or perverse inclination in mind. **4.** Sediment or alluvial deposit, esp. that left by turbid water kept standing on poor land. [OE *wearp,* = OHG *warf,* ON *varp,* f. Gmc **warp-* (cf. prec.), or f. prec.]

warragal. Var. of WARRIGAL.

wa'rrant[1] (wŏ'-) *n.* **1.** Thing or person that authorizes (person in) action (*have no warrant for this action; his promise* or *order, our strength, is our warrant; I will be your warrant; with the warrant of a good conscience*). **2.** Voucher, written authorization to receive money (*dividend warrant*), obtain or supply goods or services (*travel warrant;* ROYAL *warrant*), carry out arrest or search (DISTRESS[1]-, SEARCH-, *warrant*), represent principal in lawsuit (*warrant of attorney*), etc. **3.** Certificate of service rank held by **~-officer** (between commissioned officers and N.C.O.s). [ME f. ONF *warant, -and,* var. of OF *guarant, -and,* f. Frank. *werēnd* (*giwerēn* be surety for)]

wa'rrant[2] (wŏ'-) *v.t.* **1.** Serve as warrant for, justify, (*nothing can warrant such insolence*); hence ~ABLE *a.*, that can be warranted, (of stag) old enough to be hunted (5 or 6 years). **2.** = GUARANTEE 2, (esp.) answer for genuineness etc. of; **I** or **I'll ~ (you)**, (usu. parenth.) I am certain, no DOUBT[1]; hence ~ER[1], ~OR, ~EE' (one to whom warranty is given), *ns.* [ME, f. OF *warantir, -dir,* vars. of *g(u)arantir, -dir,* (as prec.)]

wa'rrantў (wŏ'-) *n.* Authority or justification (usu. *for* doing or saying or supposing); (Law) express or implied undertaking on vendor's part that thing sold is vendor's and is fit for use or fulfils specified conditions, often accepting responsibility for necessary repairs over a specified period; undertaking by insured person of truth of statement or fulfilment of condition. [ME, f. AF *warantie,* var. of *garantie* (as WARRANT[1]; see -Y[1])]

wa'rren (wŏ'-) *n.* Piece of ground in which rabbits abound or are preserved or (Hist.) game is preserved; (fig.) densely populated district, region with many narrow winding streets etc.; so ~ER[2] *n.*, person in charge of rabbit-warren or game-warren. [ME, f. AF & ONF *warenne,* OF *garenne* game-park f. Gaulish **varrenna* fenced-off area (**varros* post)]

wa'rrĭgăl (wŏ'-) *n.* & *a.* (Austral.) **1.** *n.* Dingo dog; untamed horse; wild Aboriginal. **2.** *a.* Wild, untamed. [Aboriginal]

wa'rrĭor (wŏ'-) *n.* Fighting man; (rhet. or poet.) distinguished or veteran soldier; member of any of the fighting services (UNKNOWN *Warrior*); COLD[1] *warrior;* (*attrib.*, of nation etc.) martial; **~ ant** (that makes slaves of other species). [ME, f. ONF *werreior* etc., OF *guerreior* etc. (*werreier, guerreier,* make WAR[1]; see -ER[2], -OR)]

wart (wôrt) *n.* **1.** Small hardish roundish excrescence on skin caused by virus-induced abnormal growth of papillae and thickening of epidermis (**~s and all,** without concealment of blemishes or unattractive parts). **2.** Similar lump on stem etc. of plant; (colloq.) objectionable person. **3. ~-grass, -weed, -wort,** kind of spurge with juice thought to cure warts; **~-hog,** large-headed Afr. wild pig of genus *Phacochoerus,* with warty lumps on face and large curved tusks. **4.** Hence ~'Y[2] *a.* [OE *wearte,* = OS *warta,* OHG *warza,* ON *varta* f. Gmc **wartōn*]

wār'|ў *a.* Given to caution, habitually on the look-out, circumspect; cautious *of* person, thing, or do*ing;* showing, or done with, caution; hence ~ĬLY[2] *adv.*, ~ĬNESS *n.* [f. WARE[2] + -Y[2]]

was. See BE.

wash[1] (wŏ-) *v.* **1.** *v.t.* Cleanse with liquid esp. water (*wash* one's *face* etc., *oneself,* or any object); ~ thing **out,** clean its inside by washing; *wash* one's *dirty* LINEN; ~ one's **hands,** (fig.) decline responsibility usu. *of*, (euphem.) go to lavatory. **2.** (fig.) Purify (*wash me throughly from mine iniquity*). **3.** Take (stain, dirt, etc.) *out* or *off* or *away* by washing. **4.** ~ **up,** *wash one's face and hands, ||wash (table utensils etc.; usu. abs.) after use. **5.** *v.i.* Wash oneself or esp. one's (face and) hands (*must wash before dinner*); wash clothes. **6.** (Of coloured material or dye) bear washing without loss of colour; (of stain etc.) be taken *off* or *out* by washing; **won't** ~, (colloq., of argument etc.) will not stand examination; **~ed out,** faded by washing, (fig.) enfeebled, limp, demoralized; hence ~'ING² *a.* (*washing prints*). **7.** *v.t.* Moisten (*roses washed with dew*); (of river, sea, etc.) touch (coast, bank, country) with its waters. **8.** (Of moving liquid) carry along in specified direction (*a wave washed him overboard*; *was washed up* (*by the sea*); *beef washed down with ale*); erode, denude, (*sea-washed cliffs*); scoop out (*water had washed a channel*); ~ **out,** cause wash-out of (road etc.); **~ed up,** (sl.) defeated, having failed. **9.** *v.i.* Go splashing or sweeping *over, along, out, in,* or *into*. **10.** *v.t.* Sift (ore) by action of water. **11.** Brush thin coating of watery colour over (paper in water-colour or sepia painting, wall), coat (inferior metal) thinly *with* gold etc.; ~ **out,** (colloq.) cancel. **12.** **~-and-wear** *a.*, (of garment) easily washed, quickly dried, and needing no ironing; **~-basin** (for washing one's hands etc.); **~-boiler,** clothes-washing cauldron, copper; **~-bottle,** apparatus for purifying gases etc. by passage through liquid; **~-bowl,** = *wash-basin*; **~-cloth,** = ||DISH¹*cloth*, * = FACE¹-*cloth* (1); ||**~-hand** *a.*, for use in washing one's hands (*wash-hand basin*; *~-hand stand*, piece of furniture to hold basin, jug, soap, etc.); **~-house,** (esp. out)building where clothes are washed; **~-leather,** chamois or similar leather; **~-out,** breach in railway or road track caused by flood, heavy rainfall, etc., (sl.) complete failure, fiasco, (sl.) useless or inefficient person; **~-pot,** (arch. w. ref. to Ps. 60:8) vessel for washing one's hands; ***~-rag,** = FACE¹-*cloth* (1); ***~-room,** lavatory; **~-stand,** = *wash-hand stand*; **~-tub,** tub for washing clothes; ***~-woman,** washerwoman. **13.** Hence ~'ABLE *a.* [OE *wæscan* etc., = OS, OHG *wascan*, ON *vaska* f. Gmc **wa(t)skan* (**wat*- WATER¹)]

wash² (wŏ-) *n.* **1.** Washing or being washed (*give it a good wash*; *must get* or *have a wash*); **the** ~, treatment at laundry (*send the clothes to the wash*; **come out in the** ~, (fig.) eventually reach satisfactory state); quantity of clothes just (to be, being) washed. **2.** Visible or audible motion of agitated water, esp. waves caused by passage of vessel; turbulent air behind moving aircraft. **3.** Soil swept off by water, alluvium; sandbank exposed only at low tide. **4.** Kitchen slops and scraps given to pigs. **5.** Malt etc. fermenting before distillation; thin or weak or inferior liquid food (*this soup, tea, claret, is mere wash*); liquid food for animals; (fig.) twaddle, wish-wash. **6.** Liquid for spreading over surface to cleanse or heal or disinfect or colour; lotion, cosmetic (EYE¹*wash*); thin coating of water-colour, wall-colouring, or metal. **7.** **~'board,** board of ribbed wood or sheet or corrugated zinc for use when scrubbing clothes in washing, (fig.) road surface worn to similar shape; **~-day** (on which clothes are washed); **~-drawing** (made with washes of esp. black or grey water-colour). [ME, f. prec.]

Wash. *abbr.* Washington.

wa'sher (wŏ'-) *n.* In vbl senses (DISH¹*washer*); flat ring or perforated piece of leather, rubber, metal, etc., used to give tightness to joint, nut, fastening, etc.; **~woman,** laundress. [ME, f. WASH¹ + -ER¹]

wa'sherў (wŏ'-) *n.* Place where coal etc. is washed. [f. WASH¹ + -ERY]

wa'shĭng (wŏ'-) *n.* In vbl senses (BOND¹-*washing*; BRAIN*washing*); clothes etc. sent to the wash; **get on with the** ~, (sl.) stop wasting time; **~-day,** = WASH²-*day*; **~-machine** (for the washing of clothes etc.); **~-powder** (of soap or detergent for washing clothes etc.); **~-soda,** sodium carbonate, used dissolved in water for washing and cleaning; ||**~-u'p,** washing of table utensils after use (*~-up machine*, = DISH¹*washer* (2)). [ME, f. WASH¹ + -ING¹]

Washĭngtō'nĭa (wŏ-) *n.* Californian fan palm of genus *Washingtonia*. [f. G. *Washington*, Amer. statesman d. 1799 + -IA¹]

wa'sh|ў (wŏ'-) *a.* (Of liquid food etc.) too watery, weak, thin, insipid; (of colour) faded-looking, thin; (of style, sentiment, etc.) diffuse, feeble, lacking vigour or compression; hence ~ĭLY² *adv.*, ~ĭNESS *n.* [f. WASH¹,² + -Y²]

wasn't. See BE.

wasp (wŏ-) *n.* Hymenopterous social or solitary often carnivorous insect of superfamily Vespoidea, esp. common kind (of genus *Vespa*) with black and yellow transverse stripes, very slender waist, liking for fruit and sweets, and formidable sting; **~-bee, -beetle, -fly,** kinds having some resemblance to wasps; **~-waist,** (esp. woman's) very slender waist. [OE *wæfs, wæps, wæsp* = OS *wepsia* etc., OHG *wafsa, wefsa*, f. WG **wabhis*-, **waps*- f. IE **wobhes*-, **wops*-, perh. cogn. w. WEAVE (from weblike form of nest)]

W.A.S.P. (wŏsp) *abbr.* (usu. derog.) White Anglo-Saxon Protestant.

wa'spĭsh (wŏ'-) *a.* Irritable, petulant, ill-tempered, sharp in retort; hence ~LY² *adv.*, ~NESS *n.* [f. WASP + -ISH¹]

wa'ssail (wŏ'-; *or* -sal) *n.*, & *v.i.* (arch.) **1.** *n.* Festive occasion, drinking-bout; kind of liquor drunk on such occasion; **~-bowl** etc. (from which healths were drunk, esp. on Twelfth Night and Christmas Eve). **2.** *v.i.* Make merry, hold carousing festivities. [ME *wæs hæil* etc., f. ON *ves heill*, corresp. to OE *wes hāl* 'be in good health', form of salutation (cf. HALE¹)]

Wa'ssermann (vah'-) *n.* ~ (**test**), test for syphilis using reaction of patient's blood serum. [f. A. von ~, Ger. pathologist d. 1925]

wast. See BE.

wā'stage *n.* Amount wasted or that runs to waste, loss by use, wear, decay, leakage, etc.; loss of employees other than by dismissal. [f. WASTE² + -AGE]

wāste¹ *a.* **1.** (Of district etc.) desolate, desert, uninhabited, uncultivated, as result of natural barrenness etc. or of ravages or catastrophe; **lay** ~, ravage; **lie** ~, be uncultivated; ~ **land** (not used for cultivation or building). **2.** (fig.) Monotonous, presenting no features of interest, (*the waste periods of history*). **3.** Superfluous, refuse, no longer serving a purpose, left over after use; ~ **paper,** paper regarded as spoiled or valueless; **~-paper basket,** basket for temporary storage of waste paper; ~ **products,** useless by-products of manufacture or of physiological process. [ME, f. ONF *wast*, var. of OF *g(u)ast* f. Rom. **wasto* f. L *vastus*]

wāste² *v.* **1.** *v.t.* Lay waste, ravage; treat (documents etc.) as waste paper. **2.** Expend or employ to no purpose or for inadequate result, use extravagantly or ineffectually, squander (*waste money, time, food*, etc., or abs.: *waste not, want not*); give (advice etc.) without effect (*on* person); ~ **breath** or **words,** talk uselessly. **3.** *v.t.* & *i.* Wear gradually away, wither, (cause to) lose substance, make or become weak, (*his resources were wasted, were rapidly wasting; a wasting asset; a wasted arm, a wasting disease; is wasting away for lack of food*). **4.** *v.i.* Run to waste (*that water is wasting*). **5.** Hence **wā'st**ABLE *a.* [ME, f. ONF *waster*, var. of OF *g(u)aster* f. Rom. **wastare* for L *vastare* (*vastus* = prec.)]

wāste[3] *n.* **1.** Desert, waste region, dreary scene, (**a ~ of waters,** unbroken expanse of sea or floods). **2.** Being used up, diminution by wear and tear; hence ~'LESS (-tl-) *a.* **3.** Waste material or food, useless remains, refuse, scraps, shreds; = COTTON[1] *waste.* **4.** Act of wasting, throwing away or extravagant or ineffectual use of money, time, food, etc.; **go to ~, run to ~,** (of liquid or fig. of affection etc.), be wasted. **5.** (Law). Injury to estate caused by act or neglect esp. by a life-tenant. **6. ~-basket,** = (esp.) WASTE[1]-*paper basket*; ~(**-pipe**) (to carry off waste material, esp. from washing etc.). [ME, f. ONF *wast(e)*, var. of OF *g(u)ast(e)* f. L *vastum* neut. of *vastus* WASTE[1]; partly f. ONF *waster* (see prec.)]

wā'steful (-tf-) *a.* Extravagant; causing or exhibiting waste; hence ~LY[2] *adv.*, ~NESS *n.* [ME, f. prec. + -FUL]

wā'ster *n.* In vbl senses; article spoilt or flawed in manufacture; (sl.) good-for-nothing person. [ME, f. AF *wastere* (as WASTE[2], -ER[2]), & f. WASTE[2] + -ER[1]]

wā'strel *n.* Thing spoilt in making; neglected child, waif; good-for-nothing person; wasteful person. [f. WASTE[2] + -REL]

watch[1] (wŏ-) *n.* **1.** Period of wakefulness at night; ancient division of night-time; **in the ~es of the night,** while one lies awake, in the night-time; **pass as a ~ in the night,** be soon forgotten. **2.** Alert state, being on the look-out, vigilance, constant observation or attention, (*keep watch* or *a watch, good* or *a good watch*); **~ and ward,** (orig.) guard by night and day (now merely emphatic for *watch*); **on the ~,** waiting usu. for expected or desired or feared occurrence; SET[1] *a watch.* **3.** (Hist.) Man or body of men charged with patrolling streets at night, guard. **4.** (Hist.) irregular Highland troops in 18th c.; BLACK[1] *Watch.* **5.** Four-hour spell of duty on board ship (DOG[1]-*watch*; SET[1] *the watch*); one of the halves (**starboard** and **port ~** from position of men's bunks) into which ship's crew is divided to take alternate duty; **~ and ~,** such arrangement; **~ below,** time when one is off duty. **6.** Small portable spring-driven timepiece usu. worn on wrist or carried in pocket; STOP[1]-*-watch.* **7. ~-case,** outer metal case enclosing works of watch; **~-chain,** metal watch-guard; ||**W~ Committee,** (Hist.) committee of a county borough council dealing with policing etc.; ***~ crystal,** = *watch-glass* (1); **~-dog,** dog kept to guard property etc., (fig.) guardian against infringement etc.; **~-fire** (at night in camps etc.); **~-glass,** (1) glass disc covering dial of watch, (2) similar piece of glass used as receptacle for experimental material; **~-guard,** chain etc. for securing watch when worn on the person; **~-key** (for winding up works of watch); **~'man,** man employed to look after empty building etc. at night, (arch. or Hist.) sentinel or member of night-watch; **~-night,** last night of year, religious service then celebrated; **~ oil,** thin kind for lubricating works of watches and clocks; **~-pocket** (in garment esp. waistcoat, or separate for attachment to bed etc., holding watch); **~-spring,** mainspring of watch; **~-strap** (for fastening watch on wrist); **~-tower,** post for observation of approaching danger; **~'word,** phrase expressing briefly the principles of a party etc. (e.g. *Equal pay for equal work*), (Hist.) military password. [OE *wæcce* (**wæccan*; see foll.)]

watch[2] (wŏ-) *v.* **1.** *v.i.* (arch.) Remain awake for devotions etc. **2.** Be on the watch, keep watch, be vigilant, take heed, look out *for* opportunity etc., exercise protecting care *over*; **~'ing brief** (of barrister who follows case for client not directly concerned, or fig.); **~ out,** be on one's guard. **3.** *v.t.* Keep eyes fixed on, keep under observation, follow observantly, (*had him watched by detectives; was watching the television; boy was paid to watch sheep; shall watch your career with interest; am having to watch my weight; watch him do it* or *doing it*); *watch the* CLOCK[1]; **~** one's **step,** (colloq.) **~ it** or one**self,** take care or precautions; **~ed pot never boils,** strained waiting makes time seem long. **4.** Look out for, await, (opportunity; **~** one's **chance,** wait for right moment). **5.** Hence ~'ER[1] *n.* [OE **wæccan*, doublet of *wacian* (WAKE[1]), repr. WG **wakæjan*]

wa'tchful (wŏ'-) *a.* Accustomed to or engaged in watching, vigilant, (*about, against, for, of, over, to* do); showing vigilance; (arch.) wakeful; hence ~LY[2] *adv.*, ~NESS *n.* [f. WATCH[1] + -FUL]

wa'ter[1] (waw'-) *n.* **1.** Colourless transparent tasteless odourless compound of oxygen and hydrogen in liquid state convertible by heat into steam and by cold into ice, liquid consisting chiefly of this (in seas, lakes, streams, springs, rain, tears, sweat, saliva due to appetite, urine, serum, amniotic fluid (usu. in *pl.*), morbid accumulation of fluid, etc.), body of this as sea or lake or river (*across* or *over the water*), (HOT[1] and *cold, salt* and *fresh* or *sweet,* SMOOTH[1] or *still* and *rough* or *troubled,* HARD and SOFT, *aerated, saline, chalybeate, thermal,* BLUE[1], HEAVY, HOLY, MINERAL, RUNNING[2], TABLE-, etc., *water; the upper waters of the Thames*); water as supplied (esp. through pipes) for domestic use; (in *pl.*) part of sea etc. (*in Icelandic waters; cross the waters*), mineral water at spa etc. (*take* or *drink the waters*); STRONG *waters.* **2.** BACK[2] *water*; BACK[1]*water*; *between* WIND[1] *and water*; **by ~,** using ship, barge, etc., for travel or transport; **cast** one's **bread upon the ~s,** do good without expecting gratitude or immediate or definite reward; **in deep ~(s),** floundering, in great difficulties, in affliction; *still waters run* DEEP[3]; FIRE[1] *and water*; FISH[1] *out of water*; FISH[2] *in troubled waters*; *keep* one's HEAD[1] *above water*; HOLD[1] *water*; *spend money, shed blood,* etc., **like ~,** lavishly or recklessly; **make ~,** (1) urinate, (2, of ship) leak; *pour* OIL[1] *on the waters*; **on the ~,** (fig.) in boat or ship; **pass ~,** urinate; **pour** or **throw cold ~ on,** disparage or discourage (scheme etc.); TREAD *water*; UNDER *water*; UNDERWATER; **~s of forgetfulness,** Lethe, oblivion, death; **~ of life,** spiritual enlightenment; **~ under the bridge** or **over the dam,** irrevocable past; **writ(ten) in ~,** (of achievements etc.) transient. **3.** State of tide (HIGH, LOW[1], *water*). **4.** Solution of specified substance in water, e.g. LAVENDER-, ROSE[1]-, etc., *water,* SODA-*water,* DILL-*water.* **5.** Transparency and brilliance of gem esp. diamond; **of the first ~,** of finest quality or extreme degree (*diamond, genius, blunder, of the first water*). **6.** (Finance). Amount of nominal capital added by WATER[2]ing. **7.** *attrib.* (in compounds, of which those especially that distinguish varieties of plants and animals are too numerous to be given separately). Found in or near, growing in, used or employed on, etc., the water; of, for, worked or effected by, made with, containing, using, yielding, etc., water. **8.** ||**~-bailiff,** (1, Hist.) custom-house officer at port, (2) official enforcing laws on shipping or on fishing; **~-bath,** bain-marie, (Chem.) vessel containing heated water for evaporation etc. of substances; **~-bear,** = TARDIGRADE 2; **~-bed,** rubber mattress filled with water (esp. for invalid to avoid bedsores); **~-biscuit,** unsweetened biscuit made from flour and water; **~-blister** (containing colourless fluid, not blood or pus); *water*-BLOOM[1]; **~-boatman,** aquatic bug of genus *Notonecta*, swimming upside-down on water; **~-borne,** (of goods) conveyed by water, (of disease) communicated or propagated by use of contaminated drinking-water; **~-bottle** (for drinking-water, esp. of glass for dining-table, bedroom, etc., or of metal etc. in soldier's kit); **~-brain,** = STURDY[2]; **~brash,** pyrosis; *water*-BREAKER[2]; **~-buck,** S. Afr. antelope of genus *Kobus*, frequenting river-banks; **~-buffalo,** the common domestic Indian buffalo; **~ bus,** river or lake boat carrying passengers on regular run; **~-butt,** barrel used to catch rain-water; **~-cannon,** device for shooting powerful jet of water to disperse crowd etc.; **~-carriage,** conveyance of goods etc. by water; **W~-carrier,** *the* zodiacal sign Aquarius; **~-cart,** (esp.) cart carrying water for sale or for sprinkling roads; **~-clock** (measuring time by flow of water); **~-closet,** (room etc. containing) lavatory with arrangement for flushing bowl with water; **~-colour,** artists' paint made of pigment diluted with water and not oil, picture painted with such colours, art of painting such pictures; *water* COMPRESS[1]; **~-cooled** (by circulating water); **~-cooler,** tank of cooled drinking-water; **~course,** (1) brook, stream, artificial channel for flow of water, (2) its bed; **~-craft,** (1) skill in sailing etc., (2) vessel(s) travelling on water; *water*-CRANE[1] 2; **~cress,** hardy perennial cress growing in springs etc., with pungent leaves used as salad; **~-cure,** hydropathy; **~-diviner,** dowser (see DOWSE[2]); **~-dog** (trained to retrieve waterfowl, etc.); **~-drinker,** (esp.) total abstainer from alcohol; **~fall,** stream falling over precipice or down steep hillside; **~-finder,** dowser (see DOWSE[2]); **~-flea,** small aquatic crustacean hopping like flea; **~fowl** (usu. collect. as *pl.*), birds frequenting water, esp. swimming game-birds; **~front,** part of town adjoining river, lake, etc.; **~-gas** (got by decomposing steam with red-hot coke, mainly hydrogen and carbon monoxide); **~-gate,** (1) flood-gate, (2) gate giving access to river etc.; **~-gauge,** (1) glass tube etc. indicating height of water inside reservoir, boiler, etc., (2) pressure expressed in terms of head of water; **~-glass,** (1) tube with glass bottom enabling objects under water to be observed, (2) solution of sodium or potassium silicate used as a vehicle for fresco-painting, for hardening artificial stone, or for preserving eggs; **~-hammer,** percussion made by water in pipe when tap is turned off, or by water in steam-pipe when live steam is admitted; **~-heater,** device for heating (esp. domestic) water; **~-hemlock,** poisonous herb of genus *Cicuta*, found in marshes etc.; **~-hen,** bird of family Rallidae, esp. a gallinule (*Gallinula chloropus*); **~-hole,** shallow depression or cavity in which water collects (esp. in the bed of a river otherwise dry); **~-hog,** capybara; **~ hyacinth,** tropical river-weed (*Eichhornia crassipes*); **~-ice,** confection of flavoured and frozen water and sugar; **~-jacket,** case filled with water and enclosing part of machine that is to be heated or (esp.) kept cool; **~-jump,** place where horse in steeplechase etc. must jump over water; **~-laid,** (of rope) = CABLE[1]-*laid*; **~-lens,** magnifying lens made of transparent cell filled with water; **~-level,** (1) (height of) surface of water in reservoir etc., (2) plane below which ground is saturated with water, (3) level using water to determine horizontal; **~-lily,** aquatic plant of family Nymphaeaceae, with broad flat floating leaves and white or blue or yellow or red flowers; **~-line,** (1) line along which surface of water touches ship's side (marked on ship for certain specified conditions of loading; cf. LOAD[1] *line*), (2) linear watermark; **~logged,** (of wood) so saturated, (of vessel) so filled, with water as barely to be able to float, (of ground) made useless by saturation with water; **~-main,** main pipe in water-supply system; **~man,** (1) boatman plying for hire, (2) oarsman, *good, bad*, etc., at keeping boat truly balanced etc.; **~mark,** (*n.*) faint design visible in some paper when viewed by transmitted light, indicating name of maker etc., (*v.t.*) impress such mark on (paper) in making; **~-meadow** (kept fertile by being flooded periodically by stream); **~-melon,** (plant bearing) elliptical melon with smooth green skin, red pulp, and watery juice; **~-meter,** apparatus registering amount of water supplied to house etc.; **~-mill** (worked by water-wheel); **~-mole,** (Austral.) platypus; **~-monkey,** jar with long narrow neck for water, used in hot countries; **~-moth,** caddis-fly; **~-nymph** (inhabiting or presiding over water); *water* OUZEL; ***~-parting,** = WATERSHED 1; **~-pepper,** acrid plant found in wet places; **~-pheasant,** jacana, pintail, or goosander; **~-pipe,** (1) pipe for conveying water, (2) hookah; **~-pistol,** toy pistol shooting jet of water etc.; **~-plane** (passing through ship's water-line); **~-plantain,** ditch-plant of genus *Alisma*, with plantain-like leaves; **~-platter,** = VICTORIA 2; **~ polo,** game played by swimmers with ball like football; **~-power,** (1) mechanical force got from weight or motion of water, (2) fall in stream capable of being utilized as force; **~proof,** (*a.*) impervious to water; (*n.*) waterproof garment or material, (*v.t.*) make waterproof; **~-rail,** bird of genus *Rallus*; **~-ram,** hydraulic ram; **~-rat,** = *water-vole*; **~-rate,** charge made for use of public water-supply; **~-repellent,** not easily penetrated by water; **~-sail** (below lower studding-sail close over water); **~-scorpion,** aquatic bug of family Nepidae; **~-seal,** body of water used in bent pipe etc. to prevent passage or escape of gas; **~-shoot,** pipe or trough for overflow of water; **~side,** margin of sea, lake, or river; **~-skater,** insect moving on surface of water; **~-ski** (on pair of which a person towed by a motor boat can travel skimming surface of water; so as *v.i.*); **~-skin,** skin bag for carrying water; **~-softener,** apparatus for softening hard water; **~-soldier,** aquatic plant with plumelike flowers above surface; **~-soluble,** soluble in water; **~ souchy** (sōō′shĭ), fish boiled and served in its own liquor; **~-spaniel,** large spaniel of variety used for retrieving waterfowl; **~-splash,** part of road submerged by stream or pool; **~spout,** (1) gyrating column of water and spray formed by whirlwind between sea and cloud, (2) sudden violent fall of rain; **~-supply,** providing and storing of water, or amount of water stored, for use of town, house, etc.; **~-table,** (1) string-course arranged to throw water off building, (2) = *water-level* (2); **~-tiger,** larva of water-beetle *Dytiscus*; **~tight,** (of joint, shoes, cask, compartment in ship, etc.) tightly enough fastened or fitted to prevent ingress or egress of water, (fig., of argument etc.) unassailable; *~tight compartment*, part of ship separated by watertight partitions for safety, (fig.) place for subject etc. kept entirely separate; **~ torture** (by exposing victim to incessant sound of dripping water); **~-tower** (supporting elevated tank to secure pressure for distributing water-supply, or for delivering water at great height in fire-fighting); **~-vole,** vole frequenting water, esp. *Arvicola amphibius*; *water*-WAGON; **~ wagtail,** common pied wagtail; **~-wave,** wave in the hair produced by the use of water; **~way,** (1) route for travel by water, navigable channel, (2) thick plank at outer edge of deck along which channel is hollowed for water to run off by; **~-weed,** aquatic plant without special use or beauty; **~-wheel,** wheel driven by water to work machinery, or used to raise water; **~-wings,** inflated floats fixed behind shoulders of person learning to swim; ***~-witch,** (1) dowser (see DOWSE^2), (2) quick-diving water-bird; **~works,** establishment for managing water-supply, (sl.) shedding of tears, (sl.) urinary system. **9.** Hence ~LESS *a.* [OE *wæter*, = OS *watar*, OHG *wazzar*, f. WG **watar* f. Gmc **wat-*, f. IE **wod-*, cogn. w. WET]

wa'ter² (waw'-) *v.* **1.** *v.t.* Sprinkle (road, plants, etc.), adulterate (milk, beer, etc.), (of river etc.) supply (place), with water. **2.** Give drink of water to (horse etc.). **3.** *v.i.* (Of animal) go to pool etc. to drink; (of ship, engine, etc., or person in charge of it) take in supply of water. **4.** (Of smarting eyes) secrete tears; (of mouth when food is seen or food or pleasure eagerly anticipated) run with saliva (**makes** one's **mouth ~**, excites desire or envy, whence *mou'th-*~ING^2 *a.* **5.** (esp. in *p.p.*) Produce irregular wavy damask-like markings on (material) by moistening and pressing in manufacture (*watered silk*). **6.** (Finance). Increase (company's debt, or nominal capital) by issue of new shares without corresponding addition to assets. **7. ~ down,** dilute, make (story, doctrine, etc.) less vivid or forceful or horrifying. [OE *wæterian* (as prec.)]

Wa'terford (waw'-) *n.* **~ glass,** clear colourless flint glass. [~ in Ireland]

wa'terĭng (waw'-) *n.* In vbl senses; **~-can, ~-pot,** portable vessel for watering plants, with long tubular spout often ending in perforated sprinkler; **~-cart,** = WATER^1-*cart*; **~-place,** (1) pool etc. at which animals water, (2) place where water is obtained, (3) spa or seaside resort. [OE *wæterung* (as WATER^2, -ING^1)]

Waterlōō' (waw-) *n.* Crushing blow, decisive contest, (*meet* one's *Waterloo*). [~ in Belgium, where Napoleon was finally defeated in 1815]

wa'tershĕd (waw'-) *n.* **1.** Line of separation between waters flowing to different rivers or basins or seas. **2.** (fig.) Turning-point e.g. in history. **3.** (pop.) Catchment area. [f. WATER^1 + *shed* ridge of high ground (cogn. w. SHED^1), after G *wasserscheide*]

wa'ter|ў (waw'-) *a.* (Consisting) of water (**~y grave,** place where person lies drowned); containing too much water, over-moist, sodden, (esp. of cooked vegetables or fish); (of eyes or lips) suffused or running with water; (of liquid) too thin, actually or apparently diluted, resembling water; (fig., of expression, talk, style, etc.) vapid, insipid, uninteresting, feeble, (of colour) pale, washed out; suggestive of rain (*a watery moon, sky*); hence ~ĭNESS *n.* [f. OE *wæterig* (as WATER^1, -Y^2)]

Wa'tson (wŏ'-) *n.* Stolid person acting as foil to genius. [f. Dr. ~, character in SHERLOCK Holmes stories]

watsō'nĭa (wŏ-) *n.* S. Afr. plant of genus *Watsonia*, resembling gladiolus. [f. W. *Watson*, Engl. botanist d. 1787, + -IA^1]

watt (wŏt) *n.* Unit of power, rate of working of one joule per second, corresponding to electric circuit where electromotive force is one volt and current one ampere; **~-hour,** energy used when one watt is applied for one hour; hence ~'AGE *n.*, amount of electrical power expressed in watts; ~'METER *n.* [f. J. *Watt*, Sc. engineer d. 1819]

Wa'tteau (wŏ'tō) *n.* **~ back** (of woman's dress with broad pleat from neck to hem without girdle); **~ bodice** (with square neck-opening and short ruffled sleeves); **~ hat** (shallow, with wide brim, and flowers as decoration). [f. A. ~, Fr. painter d. 1721]

wa'ttle¹ (wŏ'-) *n.*, & *v.t.* **1.** *n.* Interlaced rods and twigs as material of fences, walls, or roofs, (**~ and daub,** this plastered with mud or clay to make huts etc.); (in *sing.* or *pl.*) rods and twigs for such use. **2.** Austral. acacia with long pliant branches supplying such twigs, having bark used in tanning, and bearing golden flowers adopted as national emblem; (dial.) wicker hurdle. **3.** *v.t.* Construct of wattle; interlace (twigs etc.); enclose or fill up with wattles. [OE *watul*, of unkn. orig.]

wa'ttl|e² (wŏ'-) *n.* Fleshy appendage on head or throat of turkey and other birds; BARB^1 of fish; hence ~ED^2 (-teld) *a.* [16th c.; orig. unkn.]

waul *v.i.* Give loud harsh cry like cat. [imit.]

wāve¹ *v.* **1.** *v.i.* Vibrate or be stirred with sinuous or sweeping motions like those of flag or tree or field of corn in wind, flutter, undulate. **2.** *v.t.* Impart waving motion to; brandish (sword) as encouragement to followers etc.; ~ one's **hand** (*to* person), move hand to and fro in greeting or as signal. **3.** *v.i.* Wave hand or thing held in it (*to* person); give direction thus to person *to* do. **4.** *v.t.* Tell (person) thus to go *away, on*, etc.; direct (person) thus *to* do; express *farewell* etc. thus; **~ aside,** dismiss as intrusive or irrelevant; **~ down,** wave as signal to (vehicle or its driver) to stop. **5.** Give undulating surface or course or appearance to (hair of head, lines in drawing, etc.), make wavy. **6.** *v.i.* (Of hair, line, etc.) have such appearance, be wavy. [OE *wafian*, = MHG *waben*, f. Gmc **wabh-* move to and fro; cf. WAVER]

wāve² *n.* **1.** Ridge of water between two depressions; long body of water curling into arched form and breaking on shore, breaker; **the ~(s)**, (poet. or rhet.) the sea, water. **2.** Body of attackers, immigrants, etc., coming in one of successive groups advancing like sea-waves. **3.** (Phys.) Disturbance of particles of a fluid medium into a ridge-and-trough oscillation by which motion is propagated or heat, light, sound, electricity, etc., conveyed in some direction without corresponding advance or without any advance of the particles in that direction; single curve in the course of such motion. **4.** Temporary heightening of some influence or condition or feeling (*a wave of enthusiasm, prosperity, depression*; **heat, cold, ~**, spell of hot, cold, weather, rise or fall of temperature travelling over large area). **5.** Undulating line or outline or surface, waviness. **6.** Gesture of waving; waving of hair (COLD^1 *wave*; PERMANENT *wave*). **7. ~'band,** range of wavelengths between specified limits; **~ equation,** differential equation expressing properties of motion in waves; **~-form,** curve showing shape of wave at given time; **~-front,** surface containing points affected in same way by a wave at given time; **~ function** (satisfying wave equation and describing properties of wave); **~'guide,** metal tube etc. confining and conveying electromagnetic waves; **~'length,** distance from one crest of wave to the next, corresponding distance between points in sound wave or electromagnetic wave, this as distinctive feature of radio waves from a particular transmitter or (fig.) of an individual's line of thought; **~ mechanics,** method of analysis of behaviour esp. of atomic phenomena with particles represented by wave equations; ~ **number,** number of waves in unit distance; ~ **theory,** undulatory theory of light etc.; ~ **train,** sequence of similar waves. **8.** Hence ~'LESS (-vl-) *a.*, ~'LET (-vl-) *n.* [alt. f. ME *wawe, wage* cogn. w. WAG[1], after prec., or f. prec.]

wā'ver *v.i.* Falter, become unsteady, begin to give way; be irresolute or undecided *between* different courses or opinions, be shaken in resolution or belief; (of light etc.) flicker; hence ~ER[1] *n.* [ME, f. ON *vafra* flicker, = MHG *waberen*, f. Gmc **wabh-*; see WAVE[1]]

wā'vey. See WAVY[2].

wā'v|ÿ[1] *a.* Undulating, (of line or surface) consisting of or showing alternate contrary curves, (*wavy hair*); ||**W~y Navy,** (colloq., Hist.) R.N.V.R. (from wavy gold stripes or rings on sleeve); hence ~ĭLY[2] *adv.*, ~ĭNESS *n.* [f. WAVE[1,2] + -Y[2]]

wā'vÿ[2]**, wā'vey,** *n.* The snow-goose. [f. *wawa* f. Cree *wehweh*, Ojibwa *wĕwe* goose]

wa'-wa (wah'wah) *n.* Sound of trumpet etc. with mute moved in and out of bell. [imit.]

wawl. Var. of WAUL.

wăx[1] *n.*, & *v.t.* **1.** *n.* Sticky plastic yellowish substance secreted by bees as material of honeycomb cells, beeswax; white translucent odourless tasteless material got from this by bleaching and purifying and used for candles, in modelling, as basis of polishes, and for other purposes; **be ~ in** person's **hands,** be entirely subservient to him; **lost ~,** *cire perdue*; **mould** person **like ~,** form his character on desired lines or induce him to act just as desired. **2.** Substance resembling wax in some respect, e.g. secretion of some other insects (esp. scale-insect), EAR[1]-wax, fossil resin (**mineral ~**) esp. ozocerite, bee-bread, PARAFFIN wax, **vegetable ~** (exudation of certain plants such as sumac), SEAL[2]*ing-wax*, COBBLER'*s wax*. **3.** (colloq.) (Material for manufacture of) gramophone record. **4.** *attrib.* Made of wax. **5. ~'berry,** (fruit of) candleberry-myrtle; **~'bill,** small weaver-bird with translucent bill; **~-chandler,** maker or seller of wax candles; **~'cloth,** oilcloth; ~ **doll** (with face etc. of wax); **~-insect** (that secretes wax); **~-light,** taper or candle of wax; **~-myrtle,** candleberry-myrtle; **~-painting,** encaustic; **~-palm,** (1) S. Amer. palm with stem coated in mixture of resin and wax, (2) carnauba; **~-paper** (waterproofed with layer of wax); **~-pocket,** bee's abdominal sac to store wax; **~-pod,** yellow-podded bean; **~-tree** (yielding vegetable or insect wax); *wax* VESTA; **~'wing,** bird of genus *Bombycilla* with small tips like red sealing-wax to some wing-feathers; **~'work,** (making of) objects modelled in wax, esp. dummies of persons with face and hands of coloured wax clothed to look as in life and be exhibited, (in *pl.*) such exhibition. **6.** *v.t.* Smear, polish, encrust, treat surface of, with wax; (colloq.) record for the gramophone. [OE *wæx, weax,* = OS, OHG *wahs*, ON *vax* f. Gmc **wahsam*]

wăx[2] *v.i.* **1.** (Of moon between new and full) have progressively larger part of visible surface illuminated (cf. WANE); **~ and wane,** (fig., of influence etc.) undergo alternations of increase and decrease. **2.** (arch. or poet.) Grow, increase; (w. adj. compl.) pass into specified condition or esp. mood or tone (*wax fat, old, merry, facetious, indignant, pathetic, wroth, angry*). [OE *weaxan,* = OS, OHG *wahsan*, ON *vaxa*, Goth. *wahsjan* f. Gmc **wahs-* f. IE **woks-*, **auks-*]

wăx[3] *n.* (sl.) Fit of anger (*is in, got into, put him in, a wax*). [19th c., of uncert. orig.; perh. f. WAX[2] *wroth* etc.]

wă'xen *a.* (arch.) Made of wax; having smooth pale translucent surface as of wax; able to receive impressions like wax, plastic. [f. WAX[1] + -EN[5]]

wă'x|ÿ *a.* Resembling wax in some way, esp. easily moulded or having smooth pale translucent surface; (of tissue) degenerated to consistency resembling wax; (sl.) angry, quick-tempered; hence ~ĭLY[2] *adv.*, ~ĭNESS *n.* [f. WAX[1,3] + -Y[2]]

way *n.* & *adv.* **1.** *n.* Road, track, path, (lit. or fig.) provided for passing along; place of passage through door etc.; (in *pl.*) structure of timber etc. down which new ship is slid when launched, parallel rails etc. as track for movement of machine; (as name of road or street, ancient: *Appian Way, Icknield Way,* or modern); *the house* **across** or **over the ~,** opposite; MILKY *Way*; PARTING *of the ways*; PAVE *the way for*; ||PERMANENT *way*; **go the ~ of all the earth, of all flesh, of nature,** die (see also FLESH[1]); **go the ~ of all good things,** be inevitably lost; **the Way of the Cross,** series of paintings of stations of the Cross in church or along road. **2.** Best route, or route taken or contemplated, between two places or *to* place, method or plan for attaining object, person's desired or chosen course of action, (*ask the* or one's *way*; *there is a right way and a wrong way of using the tool*; *that is not the way to do it*; *do it this way, my way*; *don't like the way she smiles*; *the way the* COOKIE *crumbles*; *where there's a* WILL[2] *there's a way*); BOTH *ways*; **by ~ of,** through, by means of, (see also sense 12); ||EACH *way*; FEEL one's *way*; **find a ~,** (fig.) discover means of attaining object; **find its** or one's or **the ~,** reach destination, arrive at specified point; **get** or **have** one's (**own**) **~, have it** one's (**own**) **~,** get what one wants, see one's orders carried out or one's desires gratified; **go** one's ~ or (now dial.) **~s,** depart; **go** one's **own ~,** act independently esp. against others' advice; **go** person's ~, (colloq.) accompany him, (of things) be favourable to him; **lead the ~,** act as guide or leader, show how to do something; **lose** one's or **the ~,** go astray; ***no ~,** it is impossible; **not, nothing, out of the ~,** common or unremarkable (thing); **one ~ and another,** taking various aspects of the matter jointly; **one ~ or another,** by some means; **out of the ~,** remote, inaccessible, (see also sense 4); **out of** one's **~,** not on one's intended route; **go out of the** or one's **~,** make special effort, act gratuitously or without compulsion (*to be rude, to be helpful*); **put** oneself **out of the ~,** inconvenience oneself to serve another; *out of* HARM'*s way*; SEE[1] one's *way to*; **take its** or one's **~,** go usu. *to* or *towards*; **the Way,** the Christian religion; **~s and means,** methods of achieving something, esp. (Parl.) means of providing money. **3.** (in *sing.* or *colloq. in *pl.*) Travelling-distance, length of road etc. (to be) traversed, (*India is a long way away* or *off*; *went a little, a good, a long, some, way with* or *to meet him,* lit. or fig.; ||ONCE *in a way*; *is still a long way off perfection, from being perfect*); **all the ~,** the whole distance, completely; HALF-*way*. **4.** Unimpeded opportunity of advance, space free of obstacles, region or ground over which advance is desired or would naturally take place; **clear the ~,** remove obstacles, stand aside; **give ~,** fail to resist, be dislodged or broken under load, make concessions, allow precedence (*to*), abandon oneself (*to* grief etc.), (see also sense 9); *give ~ to*, be superseded by; **in** one's or **the ~,** forming obstacle or impediment; LION *in the way*; **make ~,** allow room (*for* others) to proceed, (see also sense 9); **out of** one's or **the ~,** no longer an obstacle or impediment, disposed of, settled, (of person) imprisoned or killed, (see also sense 2); **put** person **in the ~,** give him opportunity *of*; RIGHT³ *of way*. **5.** Being engaged, or time spent, in movement from place to place (lit. or fig.; *with songs to cheer the way*; *met him on the way out* or *back* or *home*); **by the ~,** during journey, (fig.) incidentally, as a more or less irrelevant comment; **in a fair ~,** likely *to*; **on the** or one's **~,** travelling, approaching, having progressed (*is well on the* or *its way to completion*), (colloq., of child) conceived but unborn; **on the ~ out,** (colloq.) about to disappear, fail, or perish; **(be) on your ~!,** begone!. **6.** Specified direction (usu. in adv. phr. without prep.; *which way is he looking, going?*; STEP¹ *this way*; *will call next time I'm your way*; (colloq.) *lives somewhere Brighton way*); *(in *pl.*) parts into which thing is divided (*split it three ways*); **come** one's **~,** (fig.) fall to one's lot, become available; **look the other ~,** avoid looking at person who is looking at one, deliberately ignore something one should notice; **the other ~ about** or **round,** reversed, inverted. **7.** Custom, manner of behaving, habit, personal peculiarity, (*is not my way to deceive people*; *has a way of leaving his bills unpaid*; *these bright ideas have a way of turning out badly*); *the* normal course of events (*that is always the way*); ability to attain one's object (*has a way with him*; *the way of a man with a maid*); specific manner of life or procedure (*I soon got into his ways, into the way of it* or *things*); **in its ~,** if regarded from a particular standpoint appropriate to it; **only his, pretty Fanny's,** etc., **~,** unseemly or unpleasing behaviour having no special significance; **~ of life,** principle(s) or habit(s) governing all one's actions etc.; (to one's) **~ of thinking,** (according to one's) customary opinion of matters; **~ of the world,** conduct no worse than is customary. **8.** Scope, sphere, range, line of occupation, branch of business, (*hunting is not, does not lie* or *come* or *fall in my way*; *is in the grocery way*; *want a few things in the stationery way*). **9.** Advance in some direction, impetus, progress, (*fight, push*, etc. one's *way to* or *through* place); movement of ship etc. (*gather, lose, way*; *have way on*; **under ~,** not anchored or fast, (usu.) in motion, (fig.) in progress); **give ~,** (of oarsmen) row hard, (see also sense 4); **make ~,** advance (lit. or fig.) (see also sense 4); **make** one's **~,** go (*home* etc.); **make** one's **(own) ~ (in the world),** progress, prosper; **make** or **pay its ~,** be profitable; **pay** one's **~,** not get into debt. **10.** Respect (*not a bad fellow in some ways*; *is satisfactory in one* or *a way*); **in a ~,** to a limited extent, not altogether, (see also sense 12); **in more ~s than one** (calling attention to multiple meaning etc.); **in no ~,** not at all. **11.** Ordinary course (*did it in the way of business*). **12.** Condition, state, degree, (*things are in a bad way*; *we are all in the same way*); **any ~,** = ANYWAY; **by ~ of,** as substitute for or form of, with intention of, (*carries a stick by way of weapon*; *did it by way of apology, of discovering the truth*), imagining or representing oneself as do*ing* (*is by way of making a great effort, of being a humorist*), habitually do*ing*, (see also sense 2); **either ~,** in either case or event; ‖**in a (great) ~,** (colloq.) agitated; *in a* BIG *way*; *in a* or *the* FAMILY *way*; **in a small ~,** unambitiously, on a small scale. **13. ~-bent,** wall-barley; **~-bill,** list of passengers or parcels on vehicle; **~'farer, ~'faring,** traveller, travelling, esp. on foot; **~'faring-tree,** white-flowered Eur. & Asian shrub (*Viburnum lantana*) common along roadsides, with berries turning from green through red to black; **~lay',** lie in wait for, wait for or stop to rob or interview; **~-leave,** right of way rented to mine-owner, electricity company, etc.; **~'mark,** natural or artificial object as guide to traveller; **~'side,** (land at) side of road (esp. *attrib.*: *wayside flowers, inn*); ***~ station,** minor station on railway; ***~ train** (stopping at way stations); **~-worn,** tired with travel. **14.** *adv.* (colloq.) To a considerable extent, far, (*way off the target*); **~ back,** long ago; **~-out,** unusual, eccentric, avant-garde, progressive, excellent. [OE *weg*, = OS, OHG *weg*, ON *vegr*, Goth. *wigs* f. Gmc **wegaz* (**weg-* move, carry, cf. WAIN, WEIGH); in sense 14 f. AWAY]

-way *suf.* = foll. [f. prec.]

-ways (-z) *suf.* forming *adjs.* & *advs.* indicating direction or manner (*crossways, lengthways, sideways*); cf. -WISE. [f. WAY + -'s 1]

way'ward *a.* Childishly self-willed or perverse, capricious, unaccountable, freakish; hence **~**LY² *adv.*, **~**NESS *n.* [ME, f. obs. *awayward* turned away (AWAY, -WARD); cf. FROWARD]

way'zgōōse *n.* Printing-house's annual festivity. [earlier *waygoose*, 17th c., of unkn. orig.]

Wb *abbr.* weber(s).

W.C. *abbr.* water-closet; West Central.

W.C.C. *abbr.* World Council of Churches.

W/Cdr. *abbr.* Wing Commander.

W.D. *abbr.* ‖War Department; Works Department.

wē (*or* wĭ) *pron.* (*obj.* **us** *pr.* us *or, when stressed*, ŭs; also 's; *refl.* OURSELF, OURSELVES, arch. **us;** *poss.* OUR, OURS). Pl. of I² (used also for *I* by royal person in proclamations etc. and by writer of editorial article in newspaper etc.); I and other person(s), = ONE 7; I and you; (colloq.) I (*give us a chance*); (colloq.) you (*how are we feeling today?*); **~ and they, us and them,** the group including, and the group regarded as opposed to, our social class etc. [OE, = OS *wi, wē*, OHG *wir*, ON *vér, vær* f. Gmc **wiz*; *us* f. OE *ūs*, = OS *ūs*, OHG *uns*, ON *oss* f. Gmc **uns* f. IE **n̥s*, **nes*]

‖**W.E.A.** *abbr.* Workers' Educational Association.

weak *a.* **1.** Deficient in strength or power or number, fragile, easily broken or bent or defeated, (*weak barrier, rope*; *candidate weak in algebra*; *weak resistance, team*); (of crew) short-handed; (of syllable etc.) unstressed; **~'er brethren,** less able members of a group; **~ ending,** unstressed syllable in normally stressed place at end of verse-line; **~ hand** (deficient in high cards); **~ knees,** (usu. fig.) inability to stand firm, lack of resolution, so **~**-*kneed* a.; **the ~er sex,** women; **~ sister,** ineffective person; *weak* VESSEL; *weaker* VESSEL. **2.** Deficient in vigour, not acting strongly, sickly, feeble, (*weak health, imagination, intellect*; *weak demand for goods, market is weak*); **~ constitution,** lack of power to resist disease etc.; **~ eyes** or **sight** (easily tired, or not seeing well); **~ heart** (acting feebly); **~ interaction,** (Phys.) weakest form of interaction between elementary particles (cf. STRONG *interaction*); **~ mind** or **head** (below average in intelligence, verging on idiocy); **~-mi'nded,** (1) having weak mind, (2) lacking resoluteness; **~ nerves,** nervousness; **~ stomach** (easily upset); **~ voice** (easily tired or not reaching far). **3.** Deficient in resolution or power of resisting temptation, easily led, (*weak character, man*; person's *weak side* or *point*); (of action) indicating lack of resolution (*a weak surrender, compliance*); **in a ~ moment,** at a time when one is unusually compliant or temptable. **4.** Unconvincing, logically deficient, (*weak logic, evidence*; *a weak case, argument*). **5.** (Of mixed liquid or solution) watery, thin, dilute, (*weak tea, brandy-and-water, brine*). **6.** (Of style etc.) not vigorous or well-knit, diffuse, slipshod. **7.** (Gmc Gram.) (Of verb) forming inflexions by addition of suffix to, not by vowel-change in, stem, (of noun or adjective declension) corresponding to original stems in *-n*, (opp. STRONG 4); **~ grade,** unstressed ablaut-form. **8.** Hence ~'EN[6] *v.t.* & *i.*, ~'ISH[1] 2 *a.* [ME, f. ON *veikr*, = OE *wāc* pliant, insignificant, OS *wēk*, OHG *weih* f. Gmc **waikaz* (**waik-* yield)]

***wea'kfĭsh** *n.* (*pl.* usu. same). Marine food-fish of genus *Cynoscion.* [f. obs. Du. *weekvisch* (*week* soft f. as prec.; *visch* FISH[1])]

wea'klĭng *n.* Feeble person etc. [f. WEAK + -LING[1]]

wea'klȳ[1] *adv.* In adj. senses. [ME, f. WEAK + -LY[2]]

wea'klȳ[2] *a.* Sickly, not robust, ailing. [f. WEAK + -LY[1]]

wea'knėss *n.* In adj. senses; weak point, defect; inability to resist a particular temptation; self-indulgent liking or inclination *for.* [ME, f. WEAK + -NESS]

weal[1] *n.* (literary). Welfare, prosperity, good fortune, (esp. *weal and* WOE, *weal or woe*, *for the public* or *general weal*). [OE *wela*, = OS *welo* f. WG **welon* (as WELL[3])]

weal[2] *n.*, & *v.t.* (Mark with) ridge raised on flesh by stroke of rod or whip. [var. of WALE, infl. by obs. *wheal* suppurate]

‖**weald** *n.* **The** ~, formerly wooded district including parts of Kent, Surrey, Hampshire, and East Sussex; **~-clay,** beds of clay, sandstone, limestone, and ironstone, forming top of wealden strata, with abundant fossil remains. [OE, = *wald* WOLD]

‖**wea'lden** *a.* & *n.* **1.** *a.* Of the weald; resembling the weald geologically. **2.** *n.* Series of lower-Cretaceous freshwater deposits above oolite and below chalk, best exemplified in the weald. [f. prec. + -EN[5]]

wealth (wĕl-) *n.* Riches, large possessions, opulence; being rich; abundance, *a* profusion or great quantity or display, *of* (*a wealth of illustration, wit, fruit; wealth of words is not eloquence*); (arch.) welfare, prosperity; ~ **tax** (on personal capital); hence ~'Y[2] *a.* [ME *welthe*, f. WELL[3] or WEAL[1] + -TH[1], after *health*]

wean[1] *v.t.* Accustom (infant or other young mammal) to food other than milk; (fig.) disengage or cure (*away*) *from* habit, specified company, etc., by enforced abstinence or counter-attractions; hence ~'ER[1] *n.*, young animal recently weaned. [OE *wenian* accustom, = OS *wennian*, OHG *-wennen*, ON *venja*, f. Gmc **wanjan* (**wanaz* accustomed; cf. WONT[1])]

wean[2] *n.* (Sc.) Child. [contr. of *wee ane* little one]

wea'nlĭng *n.* Newly-weaned child etc. [f. WEAN[1] + -LING[1]]

wea'pon (wĕ'p-) *n.* Thing designed or used or usable as instrument for inflicting bodily harm, e.g. gun, bomb, rifle, sword, spear, stick, hammer, poker, horn, claw; action or procedure or means used to get the better in a conflict (*irony is a double-edged weapon*; *use the weapon of a general strike*; *tears, the woman's weapon*); hence ~LESS *a.*, ~RY (1) *n.* [OE *wǣp(e)n*, = OS *wāpan*, OHG *waf(f)an*, ON *vápn*, Goth. **wēpn* f. Gmc **wǣpnam*, of unkn. orig.]

wear[1] (wār) *v.* (**wore; worn**). **1.** *v.t.* Be dressed habitually or on some occasion in (*wears green, serge, shorts*, etc., as usual colour etc.; *is wearing* or *wore* or *intends to wear diamonds*, on this occasion); **~'ing apparel,** clothes; **worn clothes** (that have been put on at least once; see also sense 5); ~ **the crown, sword, gown, willow, breeches** or **trousers,** be a monarch or martyr, soldier, lawyer, desolate lover, husband-ruling wife. **2.** Have on, or as part of, one's person (*wear a beard, glasses, perfume; wear* one's *hair long, short*, etc.; *wear a joyful face, sour look*, etc.); *wear* one's HEART *on* one's *sleeve*; ~ **in** one's **heart,** be devoted to (person or principle); ~ one's **years well,** remain young-looking. **3.** (Of ship) fly (flag); (colloq., usu. w. neg.) accept, tolerate. **4.** Hence ~'ABLE *a.*, ~'ER[1] *n.* **5.** *v.t.* & *i.* Injure surface of, partly consume or obliterate, damage, attenuate, or alter, by rubbing or stress or use, suffer such injury or consumption or change, come or bring into specified state by use, rub or be rubbed or (fig.) pass *off* or *out* or *away* or *down*, (*step worn with pilgrims' knees; inscription has been worn*, or *has worn, away; wear the freshness, the nap, off; impression, novelty, soon wears off; wear* one's *trousers, trousers have been worn, into holes* or *bagginess; seams wear threadbare; care-worn, toil-worn; is worn to a shadow with care; stick wears down to a stump*); (**well-**)**worn,** (of joke etc.) stale, (of clothes) damaged by use; ~ **out,** use or be used till usable no longer (see also sense 6); ~ **thin,** (fig., of patience etc.) be over-used. **6.** Exhaust, tire or be tired *out*, put *down* by persistence, (*worn with travel; a wearing occupation, companion*, etc.; *wear out* one's WELCOME; *his patience wore*, or *was worn, out at last; succeeded in wearing down the opposition*). **7.** *v.i.* Endure continued use *well, badly*, etc., remain for specified time in working order or presentable state, last long; person **~s well,** retains youthful strength or esp. look. **8.** *v.i.* & *t.* (Of time) go slowly or tediously, (of time) pass, pass (time) gradually away, (*winter, time, day, wears on* or *away*; *wear away* or *out* one's *life* or *time* or *youth in trifles*); ~ **through the day,** survive it somehow. **9.** *v.t.* (Of water etc.) make (hole, groove, channel) by rubbing or attrition (usu. of incidental or undesigned action). [OE *werian*, = OHG *werien*, ON *verja*, Goth. *wasjan* clothe, f. Gmc **wazjan* (**was-* clothing)]

wear[2] (wār) *n.* **1.** Wearing or being worn on person, use as clothes, (*the best materials for Sunday, working, spring, seaside*, etc., *wear*); **in general** ~, fashionable; **in** ~, being regularly worn by person. **2.** Thing to wear, fashionable or suitable apparel (*sportswear*), (collect.) things to wear in or on specified part or place (*footwear, underwear, beach wear*). **3.** ~ (**and tear**), damage sustained as result of ordinary use; **the worse for** ~, damaged by use, (fig.) injured. **4.** Capacity for resisting wear and tear (*there is a great deal of, no, wear* (*left*) *in it*). [ME, f. prec.]

wear[3] (wār) *v.t.* & *i.* (**wore**). Bring (ship), (of ship) come, about by turning head away from wind (cf. TACK[1] 9). [17th c., of unkn. orig.]

wear'|**ȳ** *a.* & *v.* **1.** *a.* Unequal to or disinclined for further exertion or endurance; **~y Willie,** (sl.) habitually weary person, tramp. **2.** Disgusted at the continuing *of*; impatient *of.* **3.** Tiring, tedious, irksome. **4.** Hence ~ĭLY[2] *adv.*, ~ĭNESS *n.* **5.** *v.t.* Make weary (esp. *of* or *with* importunity or monotony); hence ~ĭSOME[1] *a.* **6.** *v.i.* Grow weary (*of* importunity or importunate person); hence ~ĭLESS *a.* **7.** (chiefly Sc.) Long *to* do or *for.* [OE (*wēr(i)gian* v. f.) *wērig*, *wǣrig*, = OS *-wōrig*, OHG *wuarag* drunk, f. WG **wōriga*, **wōraga*]

wea'sand (-z-) *n.* (arch. or dial.) Windpipe, gullet, throat. [OE *wāsend*, = OS *wāsend(i)*, OHG *weisant*, perh. orig. part.]

wea'sel (-z-) *n.*, & *v.i.* **1.** *n.* Small nimble reddish-brown white-bellied slender-bodied ferocious carnivorous quadruped (*Mustela nivalis*) allied to stoat and ferret; stoat; tracked vehicle for use in snow, bog, etc.; **~-faced,** with thin sharp features; ***~ word** (used to remove any real force from expression containing it). **2.** **v.i.* Equivocate, quibble; default *on*, get *out* of obligation. [OE *wes(u)le*, = OHG *wisula* f. WG **wisulōn*, of unkn. orig.]

wea'ther[1] (wĕ'dh-) *n.* & *a.* **1.** *n.* Atmospheric conditions prevailing at a place and time, combination produced by heat or cold, clearness or cloudiness, dryness or moisture, wind or calm, high or low pressure, and electrical state, of local air and sky, (*favourable*, *seasonable*, *good*, FAIR², FINE², *bad*, FOUL, *cold*, *dull*, *rainy*, *windy*, etc., *weather*; *goes out in all weathers*); **under stress of ~**, owing to storms etc.; CLERK *of the weather*; **make good** or **bad ~ of it,** (Naut., of ship) behave well or badly in storm; **make heavy ~ of,** (fig.) find trying or needlessly difficult; **above the ~**, (Aeron.) in calm region above clouds; **under the ~**, (colloq.) indisposed, out of sorts. **2. ~-beaten,** seasoned by or bearing the marks of exposure to storms; **~-board,** (*n.*) sloping board attached at bottom of door to keep out rain, (*v.t.*) supply with **~-boarding** or **-boards,** horizontal boards of which each overlaps the next below to throw off rain as protective casing to wall etc.; **~-bound,** unable to proceed owing to bad weather; **~-box,** indicator with figures of man and woman, one issuing to foretell rain, the other fine weather; **~-chart,** diagram showing state of weather over wide area; **~cock,** revolving pointer often in shape of cock mounted in high place esp. on church spire to show whence wind blows, (fig.) inconstant person; **~-contact** or **-cross,** leakage from one telegraph wire to another due to wet weather; **~ forecast,** prediction of weather for next few hours or longer period; **~-glass,** barometer; **~-house,** = *weather-box*; **~man,** (1) meteorologist, esp. one who broadcasts a weather forecast, (2) *member of violent revolutionary group; **~-map,** = *weather-chart*; **~-moulding,** dripstone; *weather*PROOF²; **~-prophet,** person who foretells weather; **~-service, -ship, -station,** organization, ship, post, for meteorological observations; **~-strip,** piece of material used to make door or window proof against rain or wind; **~-tiles** (arranged to overlap like weather-boarding); **~-vane,** = *weathercock*; **~-wise,** able to forecast weather; **~-worn,** damaged by storms etc. **3.** *a.* (Naut.) Windward (*on the weather side*, *quarter*, *beam*, *bow*, etc.); *weather gage* or GAUGE¹; **keep a** or one's **~ eye open,** (fig.), be watchful; *weather* HELM²; hence ~MOST *a.* [OE *weder*, = OS *wedar*, OHG *wetar*, ON *vethr* f. Gmc **wedhram*, prob. f. root **we-* to blow (WIND¹)]

wea'ther² (wĕ'dh-) *v.* **1.** *v.t.* Expose to atmospheric changes, esp. deliberately to dry, season, etc.; (usu. in *pass.*) discolour or partly disintegrate (rock, stones) by exposure to air. **2.** *v.i.* Be discoloured or worn thus. **3.** *v.t.* (Of ship or its crew) get to windward of (cape etc.); come safely through (storm, lit. or fig.). **4.** Make (boards, tiles) overlap downwards; hence ~ING¹ (2) *n.* [ME, f. prec.]

wea'therl|ȳ (wĕ'dh-) *a.* (Naut.) (Of ship) making little leeway, capable of keeping close to wind; hence ~ĭNESS *n.* [f. WEATHER¹ + -LY¹]

weave¹ *v.* (**wove** *pr.* wōv; **wo'ven** *or* WOVE¹) & *n.* **1.** *v.t.* Form (thread etc.) into fabric, (fabric) out of thread etc., by interlacing long threads running in two directions. **2.** *v.i.* Make fabric thus, work at loom. **3.** *v.t.* Make (basket, wreath, etc.) by interlacing rods, flowers, etc.; work up (facts etc.), introduce (details), *into* story or connected whole, fashion (poem, tale, etc.); contrive (plot). **4.** *n.* Style of weaving. [OE *wefan*, = OHG *weban*, ON *vefa* f. Gmc **webhan* f. IE **webh-*]

weav|e² *v.i.* Move repeatedly from side to side; take devious course esp. to avoid obstructions; (R.A.F. sl.) manœuvre aircraft thus, take evasive action; **get ~ing,** (sl.) hurry, begin action. [prob. f. ME *weve*, var. of *waive* f. ON *veifa* WAVE¹]

wea'ver *n.* In vbl senses; one whose occupation is weaving; **~(-bird)**, tropical bird of family Ploceidae remarkable for elaborate or dextrously made woven nests; **~'s knot,** SHEET³-*-bend* used in weaving. [ME, f. WEAVE¹ + -ER¹]

wea'zen. See WIZENED.

wĕb *n.* & *v.* (**-bb-**). **1.** *n.* Woven fabric, amount woven in one piece, (lit., or fig.: *a web of lies*); **(spider's) ~**, cobweb; similar product of any spinning creature, gossamer, etc. **2.** Membrane filling spaces between toes esp. of swimming bird or animal; connective tissue; vane of feather. **3.** (Large roll of paper used esp. in newspaper-printing, made on) endless wire-mesh on rollers. **4.** Thin flat part connecting more solid parts in machinery etc., e.g. part of railway-carriage wheel between hub and rim. **5. ~-fingered, ~-toed,** having **~-fingers** or **-toes** (abnormally or normally connected with web); **~-foot** (with web-toes), whence **~-footed; ~-offset,** offset printing on web of paper; **~-wheel** (with plate or web instead of spokes, or with rim, spokes, and centre, in one piece as in watch-wheels); ***~-worm,** gregarious caterpillar spinning large web in which to sleep or to feed on enclosed foliage. **6.** Hence ~BED² (-bd) *a.* **7.** *v.t.* & *i.* Weave web (on). [OE *web(b)*, = OS *webbi*, OHG *weppi*, *wappi*, ON *vefr*, f. Gmc **wabhjam* (**wabh-* var. of **webh-* WEAVE)]

wĕ'bbĭng *n.* Strong narrow closely-woven fabric such as is used to support upholstery, for belts, etc. [f. prec. + -ING¹]

we'ber (vā'-) *n.* Unit of magnetic flux, causing electromotive force of one volt in circuit of one turn when generated or removed in one second. [f. W. E. *Weber*, Ger. physicist d. 1891]

wĕd *v.t.* & *i.* (**-dd-**; *p.p.* occas. **wed**). **1.** (rhet.) (Of party to marriage, priest, or parent etc.) = MARRY¹; unite (qualities often separated; *wed efficiency to economy*). **2.** (in *p.p.*) Married (*wedded pair*, WIFE; **newly-~s,** newly wedded pair); of marriage (*wedded life*, *bliss*); so devoted *to* opinion, occupation, etc., as to be unable to abandon it. [OE *weddian* to pledge, = OHG *wettōn*, ON *vethja*, Goth. *gawadjōn* f. Gmc **wadhjōjan* (**wadhjam* a pledge; cf. GAGE¹)]

Wed. *abbr.* Wednesday.

wĕ'ddĭng *n.* Marriage ceremony (and festivities); anniversary of this (DIAMOND, GOLDEN, RUBY, SILVER¹, *wedding*); **~ breakfast,** meal etc. usual between wedding ceremony and departure for honeymoon; **~-cake,** rich decorated cake of which portions are distributed to guests at wedding and sent to absent friends; **~-card** (with names of bride and bridegroom sent to friends as announcement of wedding); **~-day,** day or anniversary of wedding; **~-favour,** (arch.) white rosette or knot of ribbons worn in honour of wedding; **~ garment,** (fig.) qualification for participating in feast of some kind (ref. to Matt. 22:11); **~ march,** march (esp. by Mendelssohn) played at wedding; **~-ring** (put on bride's finger at wedding-ceremony and usu. worn there constantly as distinctive mark of married woman, or similarly worn by married man). [OE *weddung* (as WED, -ING¹)]

wĕdge *n.*, & *v.t.* **1.** *n.* Piece of wood, metal, etc., one end of which is an acute-angled edge formed by two converging planes used to split wood or rock or widen opening or tighten structure or exert force in various ways, a form of inclined plane; **thin end of the ~**, change, measure, action, etc., that will open the way to further changes or developments and is therefore of more importance than it seems. **2.** Thing resembling wedge in being chiefly outlined by two planes or lines converging at acute angle (*a wedge of cake* etc.; *the seats are arranged in wedges*); (shoe with) wedge-shaped heel; golf-club with wedge-shaped head used for approach shots. **3. ~-shaped,** (1) shaped like solid wedge, (2) V-shaped; **~-tailed,** (of bird) having middle tail-feathers longest. **4.** Hence ~'WISE (-jw-) *adv.* **5.** *v.t.* Tighten or fasten by use of wedge; thrust or pack (*in*) tightly like a wedge between other things or persons, or *together*; push *off* or *away* like a wedge. [OE *wecg*, = OS *weggi*, OHG *weggi*, *wecki*, ON *veggr* f. Gmc **wagjaz*]

Wĕ'dgwŏŏd (-jw-) *n.* Kind of fine pottery esp. with white cameo design, made by Wedgwood and his successors; blue colour characteristic of this. [f. J. ~, Engl. potter d. 1795]

wĕ'dlŏck *n.* The married state; **born in, out of, ~** (legitimately, illegitimately). [OE *wedlāc* (*wed* pledge, cogn. w. WED, *-lāc* suf. denoting action) marriage vow]

Wĕ'dnesday (wĕ'nz-; *or* -dĭ) *n.* & *adv.* **1.** *n.* Day of week, following Tuesday; ASH[2] *Wednesday.* **2.** *adv.* (cf. FRIDAY 2). [f. ME *wednesdei*, OE *wōdnesdæg* day of (the god) Odin, transl. of LL *Mercurii dies* day of planet Mercury]

wee[1] *a.* (**weer** *pr.* wē'*er*; **weest** *pr.* wē'ĭst). **1.** (esp. childish or Sc.) Little, very small. **2.** (colloq.) Extremely small, tiny, (*a wee bit*). **3. Wee Frees,** (nickname for) minority of Free Church of Scotland that refused inclusion in the United Free Church in 1900. [orig. Sc. n., f. north. ME *wei* (small) quantity f. Anglian *wēg*(*e*) = West Saxon *wǣg*(*e*); cf. WEY]

wee[2]. Var. of WEE-WEE.

weed *n.* & *v.* **1.** *n.* Wild herb growing where it is not wanted; **the (Indian, soothing,** etc.) **~,** (arch.) tobacco; (**the**) **~,** (sl.) marijuana. **2.** Lanky and weakly horse or person. **3. ~-grown,** overgrown with weeds; **~-killer,** substance used to destroy weeds or other plants. **4.** Hence ~'LESS, ~'Y[2], *adjs.* **5.** *v.t.* Clear (ground etc.) of weeds (lit. or fig.); sort *out* (inferior parts or members of a quantity or company) for removal, rid (quantity or company) of inferior members etc. **6.** *v.i.* Cut off or uproot weeds. **7.** Hence ~'ER[1] (1, 2) *n.* [OE (*wēodian* v. f.) *wēod*, = OS *wiod*, of unkn. orig.]

weeds (-z) *n. pl.* **(Widow's) ~,** deep mourning worn by widow. [OE *wǣd*(*e*) garment, = OS *wād*(*i*), OHG *wāt*, *giwāti*, ON *váth* f. Gmc **wǣdhiz*, **gawǣdhjam*]

week *n.* **1.** Period of seven days reckoned usu. from and to midnight on Saturday–Sunday (**what day of the ~ is it?,** is it Sunday, Monday, Tuesday, Wednesday, Thursday, Friday, or Saturday?); **~ of Sundays, ~ of ~s,** seven weeks; **feast of ~s,** = PENTECOST 1; KNOCK[1] *into the middle of next week.* **2.** Period of seven successive days reckoned from any point (*can you come to us for a week?*; *have not seen you for weeks*; *did it weeks ago*); **a ~ (from) today,** or **today, this day, Monday,** etc., **~,** 7 days before or esp. after today etc.; *week* IN[2], *week out.* **3.** The six days between Sundays, or the five days between Sunday and Saturday (*never go there in the week*); period of work done during these (*42-hour week*). **4. ~'day,** any day other than Sunday; **~-end,** (*n.*) Sunday and (part of) Saturday (occas. longer period) as time for holiday or visit, (*v.i.*) make week-end visit etc.; **~-long** *a.* & *adv.*, (lasting) for whole week; **~-night,** evening or night of weekday. [OE *wice*, = OS *-wika*, OHG *wehha*, *wohha*, ON *vika*, Goth. *wikō* f. Gmc **wikōn*, prob. orig. = sequence]

wee'klȳ *a.*, *adv.*, & *n.* **1.** *a.* & *adv.* (Produced or occurring) once every week; of or for or lasting a week. **2.** *n.* Weekly newspaper or periodical. [f. prec. + -LY[1,2]]

ween *v.t.* (arch. or poet.) **1.** Be of opinion; **I ~** (*that*, or abs.), I think or suppose. **2.** Expect *to* get etc. [OE *wēnan*, = OS *wānian*, OHG *wan*(*n*)*ēn*, ON *vǣna*, Goth. *wēnjan* f. Gmc **wǣnjan* (**wǣniz* hope)]

wee'nȳ *a.* (childish or colloq.) Tiny; **~-bopper,** girl like teeny-bopper but younger. [f. WEE[1] after *tiny*, *teeny*]

weep *v.* (**wept**) & *n.* **1.** *v.i.* Shed tears (*for* or *over* person or thing; *at* event etc.; *for* or *with* pain, joy, etc.). **2.** *v.t.* Shed (tears); shed tears for, lament over, bewail; **~ out,** utter with tears; **~** one's **eyes** or **heart out,** weep excessively or for a long time. **3.** *v.i.* & *t.* Send forth or be covered with drops; come or send forth in drops, exude, drip; **~ing eczema** (with exudation); **W~ing Cross,** (Hist.) wayside cross for penitents to pray at (*come home by W~ing Cross*, be made to repent one's conduct etc.). **4.** *v.i.* (Of tree) have drooping branches (chiefly in *part.* as distinctive epithet of variety or species: *weeping birch, willow*, etc.). **5.** *n.* Fit or spell of weeping. [OE *wēpan*, = OS *wōpian*, OHG *wuofan*, ON *ǽpa*, Goth. *wōpjan* f. Gmc **wōp-*, prob. imit.]

wee'per *n.* In vbl senses; hired mourner at funeral; small image on monument, representing mourner; (in *pl.*, Hist.) crape hatband worn by men at funerals, widow's black crape veil or white cuffs; capuchin monkey. [ME, f. prec. + -ER[1]]

wee'pĭe *n.* (colloq.) Sentimental or mournful film, play, etc. [f. WEEP + -IE]

wee'pȳ *a.* & *n.* (colloq.) **1.** *a.* Inclined to weep, tearful. **2.** *n.* = prec. [f. WEEP + -Y[2,3]]

wee'ver *n.* Sea-fish of genus *Trachinus*, with sharp venomous dorsal spines. [perh. f. OF *wivre*, *guivre*, serpent, dragon, f. L *vipera* VIPER]

wee'vil *n.* Beetle of family Curculionidae, with head extended into a proboscis, feeding on grain, nuts, fruit, and bark; any insect damaging stored grain; hence ~Y[2] *a.* [ME, f. MLG *wevel* = OE *wifel* beetle, OS *-wivil*, OHG *wibil*, ON **vifill* f. Gmc **webhilaz* (**webh-* move about briskly; cf. WAVE[1], WEAVE[1])]

wee-wee *n.*, & *v.i.* (sl.) **1.** *n.* Urination; urine. **2.** *v.i.* Urinate. [20th c.; orig. unkn.]

w.e.f. *abbr.* with effect from.

wĕft[1] *n.* Transverse threads woven into warp to make web; yarn for these; something woven (lit. or fig.); filling-strips in basket-weaving. [OE *weft*(*a*), = ON *veptr*, *vipta*, MHG *wift* fine thread, f. Gmc **weft-* (**webh-* WEAVE[1])]

wĕft[2]. Var. of WAFT 3.

Wehr'macht (vār'mahχt) *n.* (Hist.) German armed forces. [G, = defensive force]

weigh (wā) *v.* & *n.* **1.** *v.t.* Find weight of with scales or other machine; balance in hands (as if) to guess weight of (*meditatively weighed his stick in his hand*); **~ out,** take a definite weight of, take specified weight from larger quantity, distribute in definite quantities by aid of scales, (*weigh out butter, portions* or *3 lb. of butter*). **2.** *v.i.* & *t.* **~ out, in,** (of jockey before, after, race); **~ in** (of boxer etc. before contest); **~ in with** *argument* etc., (colloq.) introduce with some confidence. **3.** *v.t.* Estimate relative value or importance of, compare (*with* or *against*, or abs.) consider with a view to choice or rejection or preference, (*weigh the consequences, pros and cons, argument with* or *against* another; *weigh claims* or *merits of candidates*); **~ up,** (colloq.) appraise, form estimate of; **~** one's **words,** select such as express neither more nor less than one means. **4.** *v.t.* & *i.* Be equal to (specified weight), balance in the scales, (fig.) have specified importance, exercise pressure or influence, have weight or importance, be heavy or burdensome, (*weighs a* TON¹, *very little, light, heavy, heavily*); ~ (**heavy** etc.) (**up**)**on,** be burdensome or depressing to; ~ **with,** be regarded as important by (*the point that weighs with me*). **5.** *v.t.* Bring *down* by weight lit. or fig., (of counterweight) force *up*, (*fruit weighs down branch; branches weighed down by fruit; weighed down with cares*). **6.** Raise from below water (*weigh* ANCHOR¹). **7.** **~-beam,** portable steelyard suspended in frame; **~'bridge,** weighing-machine with plate set in road on to which vehicles etc. can be driven to be weighed; **~-house,** building in which goods can be weighed officially; **~'ing-machine** (usu. for greater weights or of more complicated mechanism than simple balance); **~-lock,** canal lock with provision for weighing barges; **~'man,** man employed to weigh goods, esp. mined coal at colliery. **8.** Hence ~'ABLE *a.* **9.** *n.* Process or occasion of weighing; **under** ~, = *under* WAY 9. [OE *wegan*, = OS, OHG *wegan*, ON *vega* lift, weigh, Goth. **wigan* shake, f. Gmc **wegan* (**weg-*, **wag-*, **wǣg-*, f. IE **wegh-* etc.; cf. WAG¹, WAIN, WAY)]

weight¹ (wāt) *n.* **1.** Force with which body tends to centre of attraction, esp. (of terrestrial things) degree of downward tendency in body produced as resultant of earth's gravitation and centrifugal force (*the weight of a body varies with latitude and altitude but its mass does not*). **2.** Relative mass or quantity of matter contained and giving rise to downward force, heaviness, regarded as a property of bodies (*superior both in size and in weight; he is twice your weight; kept in position by its weight*); surface density of cloth etc. as measure of its suitability for particular season, garment, etc.; ATOMIC *weight*; DEAD *weight*; ~ **of metal,** total amount that can be thrown by ship's gun(s) at one discharge; **throw** one's ~ **about,** (colloq.) act with (unpleasant) self-assertiveness. **3.** Body's mass numerically expressed in some recognized scale (*what is your weight?; goods sold by weight not quantity*); scale or notation for expressing weights (TROY, AVOIRDUPOIS, *weight*); BOX⁵*ing-weights*; PULL¹ one's *weight*. **4.** Heavy body (*keep papers down with a weight; clock is worked by weights; must not lift weights*); piece of metal etc. of known mass used in scales for weighing articles (*where is the ounce weight?*); heavy object thrown or PUT¹ by athletes, e.g. SHOT¹. **5.** Load to be supported (*the pillars have a great weight to bear*); force to which LEVER is applied; heavy burden *of* care, responsibility, etc. **6.** Importance, convincing effect, influence, preponderance, (*considerations without weight; men of weight; has great weight with me; the weight of evidence is against him*); relative value assigned to an observation etc.; **carry** ~, be influential or important. **7.** **~-cloth,** lead-weighted saddle-cloth to make up difference between weight horse is to carry and weight of jockey; **~-lifter,** one who engages in **~-lifting,** athletic sport or exercise of lifting heavy objects; **~-watcher,** one who takes care not to become unduly fat. **8.** Hence ~'LESS *a.* (esp. in free-falling space-craft etc.). [OE (*ge*)*wiht*, = ON *vétt*, *vætt* f. Gmc -*wehtiz* (**weg-*; cf. prec.)]

weight² (wāt) *v.t.* Attach a weight to, hold down with a weight or weights; impede or burden with load (lit. or fig.); assign handicap weight to (horse); treat (fabric) with mineral etc. to make it seem stouter; (Statistics) multiply components of (average) by factors to take account of their importance; hence ~'ING¹ *n.*, (esp.) extra pay or allowances given in special cases, e.g. to allow for higher cost of living in London. [f. prec.]

wei'ght|ў (wā'tĭ) *a.* Weighing much, heavy; momentous, important; well-weighed, giving evidence of earnest thought, deserving of consideration; influential, authoritative; hence ~ĭLY² *adv.*, ~ĭNESS *n.* [ME, f. WEIGHT¹ + -Y²]

Weimara'ner (wī- *or* vī-; -ah'-) *n.* (Usu. grey) variety of pointer used as gun dog. [G, f. *Weimar* in Germany (where developed)]

weir (wēr) *n.* Dam across river to raise level of water upstream or regulate flow; enclosure of stakes etc. set in stream as trap for fish. [OE *wer* (= OS *werr*) f. *werian* dam up]

weird¹ (wērd) *n.* (esp. Sc.) Fate, destiny; DREE one's *weird*. [OE *wyrd* destiny, = OS *wurd*, OHG *wurt*, ON *urthr* f. Gmc **werth-*, **warth-*, **wurth-* become; cf. WORTH²]

weird² (wērd) *a.* Connected with fate (**the ~ sisters,** (1) the Fates, (2) witches); supernatural, uncanny, unearthly; (colloq.) queer, odd, old-fashioned, strange, incomprehensible; hence ~'IE, ~'O, ~'Y³, *ns.*, (colloq.) eccentric person; ~'LY² *adv.*, ~'NESS *n.* [ME, attrib. use of prec., in *weird sister*(*s*)]

Wei'smannism (vī'-) *n.* Theory of heredity assuming continuity of germ-plasm and non-transmission of acquired characteristics. [f. A. *Weismann*, Ger. biologist d. 1914 + -ISM]

Wĕlch¹. Var. of WELSH¹ (now only in *Royal Welch Fusiliers*).

wĕlch²(er). See WELSH².

wĕ'lcome *int.*, *n.*, *v.t.*, & *a.* **1.** *int.* of greeting = know that your coming here gives pleasure (often w. *adv.*: *welcome home*, *to England!*). **2.** *n.* Saying 'welcome' to person; kind or glad reception or entertainment of person or acceptance of offer, gift, etc.; **bid** person ~, assure him he is welcome; **wear out** or **outstay** one's ~, go too often or stay too long as visitor etc.; **give warm** ~, (1) show great joy at person's arrival, (2) make vigorous resistance. **3.** *v.t.* Say 'welcome' to, greet on arrival (*home* etc.), receive (guest, arrival, news, opportunity, event) with pleasure or signs of it; greet or receive *with* (embrace, gunfire, etc.). **4.** *a.* Gladly received (*a welcome guest, interruption, gift, rest, denial, sight*, etc.); **make** person ~, let him feel so; hence ~NESS (-mn-) *n.* **5.** *pred. a.* Ungrudgingly permitted *to* do or given right *to* thing, absolved of thanking or recompensing, (*you are welcome to take it, you may have it and welcome; any one is welcome to my share, to any service I can do*); **you are** ~, no thanks are required. [orig. OE *wilcuma* (*wil-* desire, pleasure, *cuma* comer) one whose coming is pleasing, w. later change to *wel-* = WELL³ after OF *bien venu* (or ON *velkominn*)]

wĕld¹ *n.* (Plant, *Reseda luteola*, yielding) yellow dye formerly used. [ME, f. OE **w*(*e*)*alde*, = MDu. *woude*, MLG *walde*]

wĕld² *v.* & *n.* **1.** *v.t.* Unite (pieces of metal, esp. iron) into homogeneous mass by hammering or pressure (usu. when iron is softened by heat but not melted), or by fusion with electric arc etc.; make by welding; (fig.) unite closely, bring (recruits, parts, arguments, etc.) into or *into* homogeneous whole. **2.** *v.i.* (Of iron etc.) admit of being welded *easily* etc. **3.** Hence ~'ABLE *a.*, ~'ER¹ *n.* **4.** *n.* Joint made by welding. [alt. f. WELL² in obs. sense melt or weld (heated metal), prob. infl. by p.p.]

wĕ'lfāre *n.* Satisfactory state, health and prosperity, well-being, (usu. *of* person, society, etc.); maintenance of members of community in such condition, esp. by statutory procedure or social effort; money etc. thus received by those in need; **W~ State,** country seeking to ensure welfare of all citizens by means of government-operated social services; ~ **work,** organized efforts to improve conditions of living for the poor, the disabled, etc. [ME, f. WELL³ + FARE²]

wĕ'lkĭn *n.* (poet. or literary). Sky, upper air. [OE *wolcen* cloud, sky, = OS, OHG *wolkan*]

wĕll[1] *n.* **1.** (poet. or arch.) Spring or fountain, (fig.) source; ~ **of English undefiled,** Chaucer. **2.** Mineral spring; (in *pl.*) spa. **3.** Shaft sunk in ground and lined with stone or other protection for obtaining subterranean water, oil, etc., (ARTESIAN *well*). **4.** Enclosed space more or less resembling well-shaft; space in middle of building from basement to roof containing stairs or lift or surrounded by stairs or open for light and ventilation; ||railed space for solicitors etc. in lawcourt; (Phys.) region of minimum potential etc.; = INK-*well*; depression for gravy etc. in dish or tray. **5.** **~-deck,** space on main deck of ship, enclosed by bulwarks and higher decks; **~-head,** (1) source, fountain-head, (2) top of well; **~-spring,** = *well-head* (1). [OE *wella*, = OHG *wella* wave, ON *vella* boiling heat f. Gmc **wall-*; cf. foll.]

wĕll[2] *v.i.* (literary). Spring (as) from fountain (*up, out, forth*). [OE *wællan, wellan* boil, melt, causative of *weallan*, = OS, OHG *wallan* boil, gush forth, f. WG **wallan*]

wĕll[3] *adv.* & *a.* (BETTER[1], BEST[1]). **1.** *adv.* In good manner or style, satisfactorily, rightly, (*the work is well done*; *that is well said*; *a well situated house*; *you did well to come*; *is eating well now*; *well begun is half done*); ~ **done!, run!,** etc., (cry of commendation); ~ **met!** (arch. greeting to person one has been wanting to meet); **come off** ~, have good luck, distinguish oneself; DO[1] one*self well*; DO[1] *well for* one*self*; DO[1] *well* (*out of*); LIVE[2] *well*; ~ **out of it,** ~ **rid of them,** disengaged without disaster etc. **2.** Thoroughly, with care or completeness, sufficiently, to a considerable distance or extent, with margin enough to justify description, quite, (*look well to it*; *judge well and truly*; *thrash him, polish it, well*; *is well up in the list, well on in life, well over retiring age, well past forty, well among the leaders of thought, well in the lead*; PRETTY *well*); ~ **away,** having started or made considerable progress; ~ **and truly,** decisively (beaten etc.). **3.** Heartily, kindly, laudatorily, approvingly, on good terms, (*love* or *like* person *well*; *treat* person *well*; *think* or *speak well of*); SPEAK *well for*; **stand** ~ **with** person, be approved by him; **wish** person ~, hope that he prospers. **4.** Probably, not incredibly, easily, with reason, wisely, advisably, (*it may well be that you are right*; *cannot very well refuse the offer*; *you may well ask*; *we might well make the experiment*). **5.** **As** ~, (1) in addition, to an equal extent, not less truly, (2) with equal reason, preferably, without worse consequences, (*that* **is just as** ~, need not be regretted), (3) advisable (*it would be as well to inquire*); **as** ~ **as,** in addition to (*gave me clothes as well as food*; *you were there as well as I*; *as well as help me she continued her own work*). **6.** *pred. a.* In good health (*is she well or ill?*; *will soon be better*; *is best in the winter*; *quite well thank you*; *am perfectly well*); in satisfactory state or position, satisfactory, advisable, (*am very well where I am*; *all's well*; *it would be well to inquire*); ALL *very well*; **let** or **leave** ~ (**enough**) **alone,** not meddle needlessly; ~ **enough,** tolerably good or attractive; ~ **and good** (formula of dispassionate acceptance of decision; *if you choose to take my advice, well and good*); ~ **off,** fortunately situated, fairly rich; **~-to-do,** fairly rich; VERY[1] *well*. **7.** *attrib. a.* In good health (*a well man should not be dawdling in bed*; *the well are impatient of the sick*). [OE *wel*(*l*), = OS *wel*(*a*), OHG *wela, wola*, ON *vel*, Goth. *waila*, prob. f. same st. as WILL[1]]

wĕll[4] *int.* expr. great astonishment (*well, who would have thought it?*; *well, I* NEVER*!*), relief (*well, here we are at last*), concession (*well, come if you like*; *well, perhaps you are right*; *well then, say no more about it*), resumption or continuation of talk (*well, who was it?*; *well, he says he must see you*; *well, that's a difficult question*); qualified recognition of point (*well, but what about Jones?*), expectation (*well then?*), resignation (*oh well, it can't be helped*), etc.; **ah** ~, (expr. resignation); ~, ~! (expr. surprise). [ellipt. uses of prec. adv.]

wĕll(-) *pref.* = WELL[3] *adv.* **1.** To *ns.* & *adjs.*: **~-being,** welfare; **~-doer,** virtuous person; **-doing,** virtuous conduct; **~'nigh,** (rhet.) almost; **~-wisher,** person who wishes well to another. **2.** To participles in -ED[1], -ING[2], etc., and to *adjs.* in -ED[2], (usu. w. hyphen except in pred. use of past participles in -ED[1] etc. not having restricted force: *my watch is well regulated*; *I do not think his action was well-advised*; cf. *he is not well advised by his friends*): **~-advi'sed,** (of person or action) prudent, wise; **~-affected,** favourably disposed *to*(*wards*), loyal; **~-appointed,** having all necessary equipment; **~-balanced,** sane, sensible, equally matched; **~-behaved,** having good manners or conduct; **~-beloved** *a.* & *n.*, dearly loved (person); **~-born,** of noble family; **~-bred,** having good breeding or manners, (of horse etc.) of good or pure stock; ~ **chosen** (esp. of words or phrases); **~-condi'tioned,** in good physical or moral condition; **~-conducted,** characterized by good conduct or organization; **~-connected,** connected by blood etc. with good families; **~-defined,** clearly indicated or determined; **~-disposed,** having good disposition or friendly feeling (*towards*); ~ **done,** (of meat) cooked thoroughly; ~ **earned,** fully deserved; **~-favoured,** good-looking; **~-found,** = *well-appointed*; ~ **founded,** (of suspicion or other belief or sentiment) having foundation in fact or reason; **~-groomed,** (of person) having carefully tended hair, skin, clothes, etc.; ~ **grounded,** (1) = *well founded*, (2) well trained in rudiments; **~-heeled,** (colloq.) wealthy; **~-informed,** having well-stored mind or access to reliable information; **~-intentioned,** having or showing good intentions; **~-judged,** (of action) showing good judgement or tact or good aim; **~-knit,** (esp. of person) compact, not loose-jointed or sprawling; **~-liking,** (arch.) with well-fed prosperous look (*fat and well-liking*); **~-looking,** of attractive appearance; ~ **made,** (of person or animal) having good build, (of thing) skilfully manufactured; **~-mannered,** having good manners; ~ **marked,** distinct, easy to detect; *well* MATCH[2]*ed*; **~-meaning,** ~ **meant,** = *well-intentioned* (but ineffective or unwise); ~ **oiled,** (fig., of expression) complimentary, (sl.) drunk; ~ **ordered,** arranged in orderly manner; ~ **paid,** liberally rewarded for work, service, etc.; ~ **preserved** (esp. of old person not showing signs of age); **~-read,** having read much [cf. -ED[1] (2)], with mind well stored by reading; **~-rounded,** complete and symmetrical, (of sentence) complete and well expressed; **~-seen,** (arch.) accomplished *in*; ~ **set,** skilfully placed or adjusted, (of batsman) accustomed to the bowling and unlikely to be out; ~ **set up,** (of person) compact, firmly knit; ~ **spent** (esp. of money, time, or effort); **~-spo'ken,** ready or refined in speech; **~-thought-out,** carefully devised; ~ **thumbed,** bearing marks of frequent handling; ~ **timed,** opportune, timely; **~-tried,** often tested with good result; **~-trodden,** (of path etc.) frequented; ~ **turned,** (of compliment, phrase, verse) neatly expressed; *well*-UPHOLSTER*ed*; **~-worn,** (esp.) trite, stale.

wĕ'lladay, wĕ'llaway (-*a*-wā), *ints.* (arch. or joc.) of grief. [OE *wei lā wei* alt. f. *wā lā wā* (woe, lo! woe) after OScand. *_wei_; _welladay_ 16th c. alt. after _lackaday_ (see LACKADAISICAL)]

wĕ'llies (-ĭz) _n._ (colloq.) Wellingtons. [abbr.; see -IE]

wĕ'llington _n._ High boot covering knee in front; rubber waterproof boot usu. reaching knee. [f. 1st Duke of _Wellington_, Brit. general and statesman d. 1852]

wĕllĭngtō'nĭa _n._ = SEQUOIA. [f. as prec. + -IA[1]]

Wĕ'llsĭan (-z-) _a._ Characteristic of Wells's writings, esp. in predicting conditions of the future. [f. H. G. _Wells_, Engl. writer d. 1946 + -IAN]

wĕls _n._ Sheat-fish. [G]

Wĕlsh[1] _a._ & _n._ (Celtic language, (as _pl._) people) of Wales; _Welsh_ CORGI; ~ **dresser** (with open shelves above cupboard); ~ **harp** (with three rows of strings); ~**'man,** ~**'woman,** native of Wales; ~ **lamb** or **mutton** (from small Welsh mountain sheep); ~ **onion,** species (_Allium fistulosum_) forming clusters of bulbs; ~ **rabbit** or by pop. etym. **rarebit,** dish of melted or toasted cheese on toast. [OE _Welisc_, _Wælisc_, etc., = OHG _wal(a)hisc_, _walesc_ Roman, Italian, French, ON _valskr_ Gaulish f. Gmc *_walhaz_ foreign f. L _Volcae_, name of a Celtic people]

wĕlsh[2], **wĕlch**[2], _v.i._ & _t._ (Of loser of bet, esp. bookmaker) decamp without paying; hence ~'ER[1] _n._ [19th c.; orig. unkn.]

wĕlt _n._, & _v.t._ **1.** _n._ Strip of leather sewn round edge of boot or shoe upper to serve as attachment to sole; WEAL[2]; heavy blow; ribbed etc. border or edging of garment etc., trimming. **2.** _v.t._ Provide with welt; raise weals on, beat, flog. [ME _welte_, _walt_, of unkn. orig.]

Weltanschauung (vĕltahnshow'ōōng) _n._ Philosophy of life; conception of the world. [G (_welt_ world, _anschauung_ perception)]

wĕ'lter[1] _v.i._, & _n._ **1.** _v.i._ Roll, wallow, be washed about, lie prostrate or be soaked or steeped _in_ blood etc. **2.** _n._ General confusion, disorderly mixture or aimless conflict _of_ creeds, policies, errors, etc. [ME, f. MDu., MLG _welteren_]

wĕ'lter[2] _n._ **1.** Heavy rider or boxer; ~ (**race** etc.), race etc. for heavyweight riders; ~**-weight,** (1) heavyweight rider, (2) weight carried in addition to weight assigned according to age, (3) see BOX[5]_ing-weights_. **2.** (colloq.) Heavy blow; big person or thing. [19th c.; orig. unkn.]

Weltpolitik (vĕltpŏlĭtē'k) _n._ Participation (esp. in leading role) in international politics. [G (_welt_ world, _politik_ politics)]

Weltschmerz (vĕ'ltshmārts) _n._ Apathetic or vaguely yearning outlook on life. [G (_welt_ world, _schmerz_ pain)]

wĕn[1] _n._ More or less permanent benign sebaceous tumour on skin esp. of scalp; (arch.) goitre; (fig.) abnormally large or congested city (**the great** ~, London). [OE _wen(n)_, _wæn(n)_, of unkn. orig.; cf. Du. _wen_, MLG _wene_, LG _wehne_ tumour, wart]

wĕn[2] _n._ Runic letter in OE & ME, later replaced by _w_. [OE, var. of _wyn_ joy (see WINSOME), used as beginning with this letter; cf. THORN]

wĕnch _n._, & _v.i._ **1.** _n._ (dial. or joc.) Girl or young woman. **2.** (arch.) Prostitute. **3.** _v.i._ (arch.) (Of man) consort with prostitutes; hence ~'ER[1] _n._ [ME _wenche(l)_ f. OE _wencel_ child; cf. OE _wancol_ weak, tottering]

wĕnd[1] _v._ (literary). **1.** _v.t._ ~ one's **way,** go. **2.** _v.i._ (arch.) Go. [OE _wendan_, = OS _wendian_, OHG _wentan_, ON _venda_, Goth. _wandjan_, causative of Gmc *_windan_ WIND[3]]

Wĕnd[2] _n._ One of a Slavic people formerly spread over N. Germany, and now inhabiting E. Saxony; hence ~'IC, ~'ISH[1], _adjs._ [f. G _Wende_ f. OHG _Winida_, of unkn. orig.]

Wĕ'nsleydāle (-zlĭ-) _n._ Variety of white or blue cheese; breed of long-woolled sheep. [~ in North Yorkshire]

wĕnt. See GO[1].

wĕ'ntletrăp (-telt-) _n._ Shellfish of genus _Scalaria_ with spiral shell of many whorls. [f. Du. _wentletrap_ winding stair, spiral shell]

wĕpt. See WEEP.

were(n't). See BE.

wer'ewol|f, wer'wol|f, (wēr'wōolf; _or_ wēr'-) _n._ (_pl._ ~**ves** _pr._ -vz). (Myth.) Human being able to be turned at times into wolf. [OE _werewulf_, = MDu. _weerwolf_, MHG _werwolf_; first element perh. f. OE _wer_ man = L _vir_]

wert. See BE.

Werthēr'|ĭan (vertēr'-) _a._ Morbidly sentimental; so ~ISM (3) _n._ [f. _Werther_, hero of Goethe's 'Sorrows of Werther' (1774) + -IAN]

Wĕsleyan (wĕ'zlĭan, wĕ's-, _or_ arch. wĕzlē'an) _a._ & _n._ (Hist.) (Member) of the Protestant denomination founded by Wesley; hence ~ISM (3) _n._ (cf. METHODISM). [f. J. _Wesley_, Engl. evangelist d. 1791 + -AN]

wĕst _adv._, _n._, & _a._ **1.** (Towards, at, near) point of horizon where sun sets at the equinoxes (cardinal point 90° to left of North); (**to the**) ~ (**of**), in a westward direction (from); EAST _and west_; ~ **wind,** wind blowing from the west; **go** ~, (sl.) be killed, lost, wrecked, etc. **2.** _n._ (usu. _W_~). Part of world or country or town lying to the west (***the W**~, part of U.S. lying west of originally settled areas or of the Mississippi; ***Far W**~, region beyond Great Plains; ***Middle W**~, region adjoining the northern Mississippi; WILD _West_); western part of late-Roman world; European in contrast to Oriental civilization; non-Communist States of Europe and America; card-player occupying position designated 'west'. **3.** ~**'about,** westwards; ~**'bound,** travelling westwards; _west_ BY[1] _north_ or _south_; **W**~ **Country,** south-western counties of England; ||**W**~ **End,** fashionable part of London incl. Mayfair and Piccadilly; _West_ INDIAN; _West_ INDIES; ~**-north-**~, compass point midway between west and north-west (so ~**-south-**~); ***W**~ **Side,** western part of Manhattan. **4.** Hence ~'WARD _a._ & _n._, ~'WARD(s) _adv._ [OE, = OS, OHG _west_, ON _vestr_ f. Gmc *_westaz_ f. IE *_wes-_]

wĕ'sterĭng _a._ (Esp. of sun) tending towards the west. [f. _wester_ v. ME f. prec. + -ER[5]]

wĕ'sterlў _a._, _adv._, & _n._ In a western position or direction; (wind) blowing (nearly) from the west. [f. _wester_ a. f. OE _westra_ (WEST) + -LY[1]]

wĕ'stern _a._ & _n._ **1.** _a._ Of or (dwelling) in the west; lying or directed towards the west; **W**~ **Church,** part of Christian Church that continued to acknowledge popes after schism, Latin Church; **W**~ **Empire** (cf. ROMAN[2] _Empire_); _Western_ HEMISPHERE; **W**~ **roll,** high-jumper's technique of turning body over bar; hence ~ER[1] (4) _n._, ~IZE (3) _v.t._, make (Oriental person etc.) more like the West in ideas, institutions, etc., ~MOST _a._ **2.** _n._ Film or novel dealing with cowboys etc. in western N. America. [OE _westerne_ (as WEST, -ERN)]

wĕ'stĭng _n._ (Naut. etc.) Distance travelled or measured westward; westerly direction. [f. WEST + -ING[1]]

||**Wĕ'stmĭnster** _n._ (Houses of) Parliament in London; past or present member of Westminster School. [~ in London, where Houses of Parliament (_Palace of_ ~) are]

wĕt _a._, _v.t._ (**-tt-; wet** _or_ **we'tted**), & _n._ **1.** _a._ Soaked, covered, splashed, moistened, or supplied, with or _with_ water or other liquid (_wet sponge_, _land_, _road_, _table_, _clothes_, _feet_; ~ **behind the ears,** immature, inexperienced; ~ **to**

the skin, ~ through, with clothes soaked through); used with or using water; (of day, weather, etc.) rainy; comprising or supplying, or allowing the sale of, alcoholic liquor; (of paint, ink, etc.) recently applied and not yet dry; (sl.) mistaken, stupid, inept. **2.** ***~'back,** (colloq.) illegal immigrant from Mexico to U.S.; **~ bargain** (closed with drink); *wet* BLANKET[1]; ‖*wet*-BOB[5]; **~ bulb** (of thermometer, covered with wet muslin etc. to give measure of air humidity by its lower temperature due to evaporation of water from it into the air); **~ dock** (in which ship can float); **~ dream,** erotic dream with involuntary emission of semen; **~ fly,** artificial fly used under water by angler; **~'lands,** swamps and other damp areas of land; **~ look,** shiny surface of fabric; **~-nurse,** (*n.*) woman employed to suckle another's child, (*v.t.*) act as wet-nurse to (child), (fig.) treat as if helpless; **~ pack,** therapeutic wrapping of body in wet cloths etc.; **~ plate,** (Photog.) sensitized collodion plate exposed while wet; *wet* STEAM[1]; **~ suit,** porous garment worn by skin-diver etc. **3.** Hence ~'NESS *n.*, **~'TISH**[1] 2 *a.* **4.** *v.t.* Make wet (**~ bargain,** close it with drink; **~ one's whistle,** (colloq.) drink); urinate in or on; **~'ting agent,** substance that helps water etc. to spread or penetrate; hence **~t'**ABLE *a.*, **~'t**ING[1] (1) *n.* **5.** *n.* Moisture, liquid that wets something, rainy weather or season; (sl.) a drink; *one who favours sale of alcoholic liquor; (sl.) stupid or inept person. [OE (*wǣtan* v. f.) *wǣt* a. & n., = ON *vátr*, superseded in ME by p.p. of the v.; cogn. w. WATER[1]]

wĕ'ta *n.* (N.Z.) Large wingless horned grasshopper whose grubs bore in wood. [Maori]

wĕ'ther (-dh-) *n.* Castrated ram. [OE, = OS *withar*, OHG *widar*, ON *vethr*, Goth. *withrus* f. Gmc **wethruz*]

W.E.U. *abbr.* Western European Union.

wey (wā) *n.* Former unit of weight or volume varying with different kinds of goods, e.g. 3 cwt. of cheese. [f. OE *wǣg(e)*, balance, weight, OS, OHG *wāga*, ON *vág* f. Gmc **wǣg-* WEIGH]

w.f. *abbr.* (Print.) wrong fount.

W.F.T.U. *abbr.* World Federation of Trade Unions.

Wg. Cdr. *abbr.* Wing Commander.

whăck *v.t.*, & *n.* **1.** *v.t.* (colloq.) Strike heavily with stick etc., thwack, whence ~'ING[1] (1) *n.*; ‖(in *p.p.*) tired out; bring *up* etc. by vigorous action. **2.** *n.* (colloq.) Heavy resounding blow esp. with stick; attempt *at*. **3.** *v.t.*, & *n.* (sl.) Share; ***out of ~,** out of order. [imit., or alt. f. THWACK]

whă'cker *n.* (sl.) Thing (esp. a lie) or person big of its kind. [f. prec. + -ER[1]; cf. *whopper* etc.]

whă'ckĭng *a.* & *adv.* (sl.) **1.** *a.* Big of its kind. **2.** *adv.* Very (*big* etc.). [f. as prec. + -ING[2]; cf. *whopping* etc.]

‖**whă'ckō** *int.* (sl.) expr. joy. [f. WHACK + -O]

whă'ckȳ. Var. of WACKY.

whāle *n.* (*pl.* **~s** *or* ~) & *v.* **1.** *n.* Fishlike marine mammal of order Cetacea, esp. large one hunted for oil, spermaceti, whalebone, ambergris, etc., (**right ~,** kind yielding best whalebone); **very like a ~** (ironical assent to absurd statement; see Shak. *Hamlet* III. ii. 399). **2. A ~ of a,** (colloq.) an exceedingly (great); **a ~ at, for, on,** very good at or keen on; **~-back,** structure shaped like whale's back; **~-boat,** double-bowed boat (like those) used in whaling; **~'bone,** elastic horny substance growing in thin parallel plates in upper jaw of some whales, used as stiffening etc.; **~-head,** Afr. bird allied to herons and storks; **~-oil,** train-oil or sperm oil got from whales; **~-shark,** huge tropical shark. **3.** *v.i.* Be engaged in whale-fishing; **wha'ling-gun** (for firing harpoon etc. at whales); **wha'ling-master,** captain of a whaler. **4.** *v.t.* & *i.* *(colloq.) Beat, thrash. [OE *hwæl*, = OHG *wal*, ON *hvalr*]

whā'ler *n.* Whaling ship or man; whale-boat; Austral. shark of genus *Carcharhinus*. [f. prec. + -ER[1]]

***whā'lĭng** *a.* (sl.) = WHACKING. [f. WHALE + -ING[2]]

whăm *int.*, *n.*, & *v.* (**-mm-**). **1.** *int.* expr. sound of forcible impact. **2.** *n.*, & *v.i.* & *t.* (Make, strike with) such sound. [imit.]

***whă'mmȳ** *n.* (Thing with) supernatural power, esp. one bringing bad luck. [20th c., of unkn. orig.]

whăng *v.* & *n.* (colloq.) **1.** *v.t.* Strike heavily and loudly, whack. **2.** *v.i.* (Of drum etc.) sound (as) under blow. **3.** *n.* Whanging sound or blow. [imit.]

whăngee' (-nggē') *n.* (Cane made from) Chinese or Japanese bamboo of genus *Phyllostachys*. [f. Chin. *huang* old bamboo-sprouts]

wha'rė (wŏ'-) *n.* Maori hut or house. [Maori]

whar|f (-ōrf) *n.* (*pl.* **~fs,** *or* **~ves** *pr.* -vz), & *v.t.* **1.** *n.* Wooden or stone platform beside which ship may be moored for (un)loading etc.; hence **~'f**AGE (1, 4) *n.* **2.** *v.t.* Moor (ship) at, store (goods) on, wharf. [OE *hwearf*, = MLG *warf*, *werf* mole, dam, wharf]

whar'fĭnger (-ōr'fĭnj-) *n.* Wharf-owner. [app. f. earlier **wharfager*, f. WHARFAGE + -ER[1]; cf. *messenger*]

what (-ŏt) *a.*, *pron.*, & *adv.* **1.** *interrog. a.* (asking for selection from indefinite or (colloq.) definite number: *what books have you read?; don't know what plan he will try*; (colloq.) *what book have you chosen?*; or asking for statement of amount or number or kind: *what men, money, abilities, has he?; what news?; what kind of man is he?; I know what time to start, what difficulties there are*); **~ matter?,** what does it matter?; **~ good** or **use is it?,** what purpose will it serve?; ‖*what* PRICE*?*. **2.** *excl. a.* How great or strange or otherwise remarkable (*what a fool you are!; what impudence!; what luck!; what a swindle!; what an idea!; what genius he has!*); (before *a.* & *n.*) how (*what partial judges we are!*). **3.** *rel. a.* The . . . that, any . . . that, as much or many . . . as, (*dispose of what difficulties there are; lend me what money* or *men you can; will give you what help is possible*); *what* TIME[1]. **4.** *interrog. pron.* What thing(s)? (*what is your name?; how I wonder what you are; cannot guess what he meant; don't know what she said; what followed is unknown*); (in rhet. questions equiv. to neg. statement: *what is the use of trying?*); (asking for repetition or confirmation of something not properly heard or understood, or for agreement: *what?; you did what?; what, do you really mean it?; what, are you stepping westward?*; ‖(colloq.) *nice day, what?*); **~ about,** what is the news concerning, how do you dispose of the question of, what do you think of, I suggest (*what about a game of chess?*); **~-d'you**(or **d'ye**)**-call-it** etc., **~'s-its**(or **his**)**-name, ~ is it, ~ you may call it,** (substitutes for name that cannot be recalled); **~ for?,** for what reason or purpose? (GIVE[1] person *what for*); **~ have you,** anything else (similar) that there may be or that one can think of; **~ ho!** (excl. of greeting or hailing); ~ (would result) **if; ~ is he,** what is his occupation, character, social status, etc.?; **~ is it** etc. **like** (asking for description etc.); **~ next?,** (fig.) what more absurd or impudent thing is possible?; **~ not,** many other similar things; **~'not,** (1) indefinite or trivial thing, (2) 19th-c. stand with shelves for small objects; **~ of,** what is the news concerning; **~ o'f it?,** = *so* WHAT*?* (1); **~ do you say, *~ say,** (colloq.) I suggest that (*what do you say we have a rest*); ~ **will people say?,** is it a respectable thing to do?; **I'll tell you** ~, my assertion or proposal is this; ~ **then?,** what would happen next or be the consequence?; *what* THOUGH; *I* or *you* KNOW[1] *what* (*he* or *it is*); KNOW[1] *what's what*; **or** ~ (indefinite alternative following question: *are you trying to kill me, or what?*); **so** ~**?,** (1) that fact has no immediate relevance or interest, (2) there is no obvious solution or procedure. **5.** *excl. pron.* What thing(s)!, how much!, etc., (*what he must have suffered!*). **6.** *rel. pron.* That or those which, the thing(s) that, anything that, a thing that, (*what followed was unpleasant*; *this is what I mean*; *did what he was attempting*; *what I have written I have written*; *what I don't know isn't knowledge*; *give me what you can*; *what is called 'the general reader'*; COME *what may*; *tell me what you remember of it*; *but, what even you must condemn, he was lying*; *will do what I can for you*; *use no arguments but what you yourself believe in*); (vulg.) who, which, (*it's the poor what gets the blame*); BUT[1] *what*; NOT *but what*; ~ **is more,** and as an additional point, moreover. **7.** *adv.* To what extent or degree (*what do we care?*; *what does it matter?*); ~ **with,** on account of (usu. more than one thing). [OE *hwæt* = OS *hwat*, OHG (*h*)*waz*, ON *hvat*, Goth. *hwa* f. Gmc **hwat* f. IE **q*^{w}*od* neut. of **q*^{w}*os* WHO]

whatĕ'ver (-ŏt-), **whate'er'** (poet.; -ŏtār'), *a.* & *pron.* **1.** = prec. 3, 6 (with addition of or emphasis on indefinite sense: *whatever I have is yours*; *whatever measures are considered necessary*; *do whatever you like*). **2.** (In indef. concessive clause) though any(thing) (*whatever results follow, whatever happens, whatever friends we may offend, we shall have done our duty*). **3.** (w. neg. or interrog.) At all, whatever it, he, etc., may be, (*there is no doubt whatever*; *is there any chance whatever?*; *no one whatever would accept*; *cannot see any one whatever*); **or whatever,** or anything similar. **4.** (colloq.) = *what* EVER. [ME, f. prec. + EVER]

wha'tsō (-ŏ't-) *a.* & *pron.* (arch.) = prec. 1, 2. [ME, = WHAT + SO[1], f. OE *swā hwæt swā*]

whatsōĕ'ver (-ŏt-), **whatsōe'er'** (poet.; -ŏtsōār'), *a.* & *pron.* = WHATEVER 1, 2, 3. [ME, f. prec. + EVER]

whaup *n.* (Sc. & N. Engl.) Curlew. [imit. of cry]

wheal. Var. of WEAL[2].

wheat *n.* (Highly nutritious seeds of) cereal plant of genus *Triticum* bearing dense four-sided spike of grain, an important source of flour for bread; *separate wheat from* CHAFF; ~**-belt,** region where wheat is chief agricultural product; ~**-grass,** couch-grass; ‖~**-meal,** (esp. wholemeal) wheat-flour; hence ~'EN[5] *a.* [OE *hwæte*, = OS *hwēti*, OHG *wei*(*z*)*zi*, ON *hveiti*, Goth. *hwaiteis* f. Gmc **hwaitjaz* (**hwit*- WHITE[1])]

whea'tear *n.* Small bird of genus *Oenanthe*, esp. species with white belly and rump. [app. f. *wheatears*, **whiteeres* (as WHITE[1], ARSE[1])]

Whea'tstōne *n.* ~ **bridge,** apparatus for measuring electrical resistances by equalizing potential at two points of circuit. [f. C. *Wheatstone*, Engl. physicist d. 1875]

whee *int.* expr. joy or excitement. [imit.]

whee'dl|e *v.t.* Coax *into* doing or *into* good temper etc., persuade by flattery or endearments, cajole; get (thing) *out of* person by wheedling; cheat (person) *out of* thing by wheedling; hence ~ER[1] *n.*, ~ING[2] *a.* [perh. f. G *wedeln* fawn, cringe (*wedel* tail)]

wheel[1] *n.* **1.** Circular frame or disc arranged to revolve on axle and used to facilitate motion of vehicle or for various mechanical purposes; machine etc. of which a wheel is an essential part; object resembling a wheel (CATHERINE *wheel*); = POTTER[1]'*s*, SPINNING-, STEER[1]*ing-*, *wheel* (**at the** ~, driving a vehicle or directing a ship, (fig.) in control of affairs); *bicycle; set of short lines concluding stanza; *BIG *wheel*; **break on the** ~, maim (and kill) on medieval instrument of torture that revolved with victim bound to it and beaten; *break* BUTTERFLY *on wheel*; FLY[1] *on wheel*;. (**Fortune's**) ~, wheel which Fortune is depicted as turning, (symbol of) vicissitudes; *go* **on** (**oiled**) ~**s,** smoothly; OIL[2] *the wheels*; SHOULDER *to the wheel*; *put a* SPOKE[1] *in* person's *wheel*; ~ **and axle,** machine using leverage given by difference in circumference between wheel and its axle; ~ **of life,** (1) zoetrope, (2) endless sequence of individual's lives in Buddhism; ~**s of life,** vital processes etc.; ~**s within** ~**s,** intricate machinery, (fig.) indirect or secret motives or agencies. **2.** Motion as of wheel, circular motion, motion of line as on pivoted end esp. as military movement (**right, left,** etc., ~, words of command to company etc. in line to swing round on right, left, flank as pivot). **3.** ~**-animal**(**cule**), rotifer; ~**-back,** chair with back shaped like, or containing design of, wheel; *wheel*BARROW[2]; ~**'base,** distance between front and rear axles of vehicle; ~**'chair,** invalid's chair on wheels; ~**-horse,** wheeler, *(fig.) steady worker; ~**-house,** steersman's shelter; ~**-lock,** (gun with) antiquated lock having steel wheel to rub against flint etc.; ~**'man,** cyclist, *steersman; ~**-race,** part of mill-race where mill-wheel is placed; *~**'sman** (-z-), steersman; ~**-spin,** rotation of vehicle wheels without traction; ~**-tree,** Austral. tree with circular flower-clusters; ~ **window** (circular with spokelike tracery); ~**'wright,** maker or repairer of (esp. wooden) wheels. **4.** Hence (-)~ED[2] (-ld), ~'LESS (-l-l-), *adjs.* [OE *hwēo*(*go*)*l*, = MDu. *wiel*, MLG *wēl*, ON *hjól*, *hvél* f. Gmc **hwe*(*g*)*ula* f. IE **q*^{w}*eq*^{w}*lo*- (**q*^{w}*elo*- move around)]

wheel[2] *v.* **1.** *v.t.* & *i.* Turn on axis or pivot, swing round in line on one flank as pivot; ~ (**about** or **round**), (cause to) change direction (lit. or fig.) or face another way. **2.** *v.t.* Push or pull (wheeled thing esp. wheelbarrow or pram or wheelchair or bicycle or its load or occupant, or furniture on castors) in some direction. **3.** *v.i.* Go in circles or curves; travel in wheeled vehicle; ride on bicycle; *~ **and deal,** engage in political or commercial scheming. [ME, f. prec.]

whee'ler *n.* In vbl senses; horse harnessed next to wheels and behind another (cf. LEADER); wheelwright; *~**-dealer,** one who wheels and deals. [ME, f. WHEEL[1,2] + -ER[1]]

wheez|e *v.* & *n.* **1.** *v.i.* Breathe with audible whistling sound. **2.** *v.t.* ~**e out,** utter with wheezing. **3.** *n.* Sound of wheezing; hence ~'Y[2] *a.* **4.** (sl.) Joke, anecdote, etc., interpolated by actor during performance; catch-phrase; clever expedient; scheme, plan. [prob. f. ON *hvæsa* to hiss]

whĕlk[1] *n.* Marine spiral-shelled gastropod mollusc of genus *Buccinum* etc., esp. species used as food. [OE *wioloc*, *weoloc*, of unkn. orig.; perh. infl. by foll.]

whĕlk[2] *n.* Pimple. [f. OE *hwylca* (*hwelian* suppurate)]

whĕlm *v.t.* (poet. or rhet.) Engulf, submerge, overwhelm. [OE **hwelman* = *hwylfan* overturn, whence dial. *whelve*]

whĕlp *n.* & *v.* **1.** *n.* Young dog, pup; (arch.) cub, young lion, tiger, bear, wolf, etc.; disagreeable or ill-bred child or youth; (Naut., esp. in *pl.*) projection on barrel of capstan or windlass. **2.** *v.i.* Produce whelp(s) or (derog.) child. **3.** *v.t.* Give birth to (esp. derog. of human mother); originate (evil scheme etc.). [OE *hwelp*, = OS *hwelp*, OHG (*h*)*welf*, ON *hvelpr*]

whĕn *adv., conj., pron., & n.* **1.** *interrog. adv.* At what time?, on what occasion?, how soon?, how long ago?, (*when did, shall, you see him?*; *don't know when it was*); (in rhet. question equiv. to neg. statement: *when shall we see his like again?*); **say ~** (process is to begin or stop, esp. when enough drink has been poured). **2.** *rel. adv.* (W. ref. to time) at which (*the time when such things could happen is past*; *there are occasions when one must yield*; *have seen the day when that would not have been allowed*). **3.** *conj.* At the or any time that, on the or any occasion that, at whatever time, as soon as, (*he exclaimed when he saw me*; *when it rains he stays at home*; *shall have it when you ask politely*; (ellipt.) *he looked in when passing, when found make a note of, myself when young*); (introducing excl. clause without main clause: *when I think what I have done for that man!*). **4.** Although, considering that, (*walks when he might ride*; *how could you, when you knew it might kill him?*; *how convince him when he will not listen?*). **5.** After or upon which, but just then, and then, (*the conflict began, when it soon appeared which was stronger*; *we were just coming to the point when the bell interrupted us*). **6.** *pron.* What time?, which time, (*till when can you stay?*; *from when does it date?*; *since when things have been better*). **7.** *n.* Time, date, occasion, (*told me the when and the how of it*; *and have they fixed the where and when?*). [OE *hwanne, hwenne*, etc., = OS *hwan(na)*, OHG *wanne, wenne*, Goth. *hwan*, f. interrog. st. **hwa-* (WHO, WHAT); cf. THEN f. **tha-*]

whĕnce *adv., conj., pron., & n.* (arch. or literary). **1.** *interrog. adv.* From what place or source? from where? (*no one knows whence she comes*). **2.** *conj.* (W. ref. to place) from which (*the source whence these evils spring*); to the place from which (*return whence you came*); = *and thence*; **~soe'ver** (-s-s-), from whatever place or source. **3.** *pron.* What place?, which place, (*from whence does it come?*; *the source from whence it springs*). **4.** *n.* Source (*we know neither our whence nor our whither*). [ME *whannes, whennes*, (*whanne, whenne* f. OE *hwanon(e)* whence, f. as prec., + -s[3]; cf. THENCE)]

whĕnĕ'ver, whĕne'er' (poet.; -ār'), *conj.* & *adv.* **1.** At whatever time, on whatever occasion; (Sc. & Ir.) as soon as; every time that; **or whenever,** or at any similar time. **2.** (colloq.) = *when* EVER. [ME, f. WHEN + EVER]

whĕnsōĕ'ver, whĕnsōe'er' (poet.; -ār'), *conj.* & *adv.* = WHENEVER 1. [ME, f. *whenso* f. OE **swā hwanne swā*; cf. WHATSOEVER]

where (-ār) *adv., conj., pron., & n.* **1.** *interrog. adv.* In or to what place or position (lit. or fig.)?, in what direction?, in what respect?, (*where is Dorothy?*; *where are you going?*; *showed me where they were*; *where does it concern us?*; *where are you looking?*; cf. COME *in*); in what book etc.? (*where did you read that?*); in what situation or condition? (*where will you be if that happens?*); (in rhet. question equiv. to neg. statement: *where is the sense of it?*). **2.** *rel. adv., & conj.* (W. ref. to place) in which or to which (*places where they sing*; (ellipt.) *where he is weakest is in his facts*); in or to the or any place, in the direction or part or respect, in which (*where your treasure is*; *go where you like*; *is, send him, where he will be taken care of*; *that is where you are wrong*; *where the ancients knew nothing we know a little*; (ellipt.) *delete where inapplicable*); and there (*reached Crewe, where the car broke down*). **3.** *pron.* What place? (*where do you come from, are you going to?*); (vulg.) which place (*the town where he comes from*). **4.** *n.* Place, scene of something, (cf. WHEN 7; ANYWHERE, EVERY*where*, NOWHERE, SOMEWHERE). **5.** **~abou'ts** *adv.*, where? (within considerable limits or vaguely; *whereabouts is he?*; *don't know even whereabouts to look*); **~'abouts** *n.* (as *sing.* or *pl.*), person's or thing's location roughly defined; **~a'fter,** (formal) after which; **~a's** *conj.*, taking into consideration or having as premiss the fact that (esp. in legal preambles), in contrast or comparison with the fact that, but (in contrast with what has been said); **~a't,** (arch.) at which place, for which reason; **~by',** by what means? by which means, in consequence of which; **~'fore,** (*adv.*) for what reason?, why?, for which reason, (*n.*) reason (*the whys and wherefores*); **~fro'm,** (arch.) from which; **~i'n,** (formal) in what place or respect? in which place or respect; **~i'nto,** (arch.) into which; **~o'f,** (formal) of what? of which; **~o'n,** (arch.) on what? on which; **~ou't,** (arch.) out of which; **~throu'gh,** (arch.) through which; **~to',** (formal) to what? to which; **~u'nder,** (arch.) under which; **~u'nto,** (arch.) to what? to which; **~upo'n** (*or* wār'-), immediately after which, in consequence of which, (arch.) upon which; **~wi'th,** (arch.) with what? with which; **~'withal** *n.*, (colloq.) money etc. needed for a purpose (*has not the wherewithal to do it*). [OE *hwǣr, hwār* = OS *hwār*, OHG *(h)wār, wā*, ON *hvar*, Goth. *hwar* f. st. **hwa-* (see WHEN); cf. HERE, THERE]

wheresōĕ'ver (-ārs-), **wheresōe'er'** (poet.; -ārsōār'), *conj.* & *adv.* = foll. 1. [ME, f. *whereso* f. OE **swā hwǣr swā*; cf. WHATSOEVER]

whereĕ'ver (-ār-), **where'er'** (poet.; -ārār'), *conj.* & *adv.* **1.** In or to whatever place; in every place that; **or wherever,** or in any similar place. **2.** (colloq.) = *where* EVER. [ME, f. prec. + EVER]

whĕ'rrȳ *n.* Light shallow rowing-boat usu. for carrying passengers; ‖large light barge; ‖**~man** (employed on wherry). [ME, of unkn. orig.]

whĕt *v.t.* (-tt-), & *n.* **1.** *v.t.* Sharpen by rubbing on or with stone etc.; stimulate (appetite, interest, desire); **~'stone,** shaped stone for tool-sharpening, (fig.) thing that sharpens the wits. **2.** *n.* Sharpening; small quantity taken to create or creating appetite for more; dram of liquor. [OE *hwettan*, = OHG *wezzan*, ON *hvetja* f. Gmc **hwatjan* (**hwattaz* sharp)]

whĕ'ther[1] (-dh-) *a.*, & *interrog.* & *rel. pron.* (arch.) Which of the two. [OE *hwæther, hwether*, = OS *hwethar*, OHG *(h)wedar*, ON *hvatharr*, Goth. *hwathar* f. Gmc **hwa-*, **hwe-*; cf. WHEN, WHO, EITHER, OTHER]

whĕ'ther[2] (-dh-) *conj.* **1.** (Introducing indirect question expr. doubt or choice between alternatives: *don't know whether he will be here* (*or not*), *don't know whether he is here or* (*whether he is*) *in London*; *am doubtful, must decide, the question is, whether to go* (*or not*); DOUBT[2] *whether*; *whether or* NO[2]). **2.** (With following *or* or *or whether*, introducing alternative conditions in conditional sentence, = *if . . . and likewise if . . .*: *the result will be bad whether we stay or whether we go, whether we stay or go, whether we stay or not, whether or* NO[2]). [OE, = prec.]

whew (hwū, *or* a whistle) *int.* expr. surprise, consternation, or relief. [imit.]

whey (-ā) *n.* Watery part of milk that remains liquid when the rest forms curds; **~-faced,** (arch.) pale esp. with fear. [OE *hwæg, hweg*, = MDu. *wey*, f. LG **hwaja-*]

whĭch *a.* & *pron.* (*poss.* in sense 4 **of which,** *or* **whose**). **1.** *interrog. a.* (asking for selection from alternatives conceived as limited in number or known: *which Jones do you mean?*; *which way shall we go?*; *say which chapter you prefer*). **2.** *rel. a.* And, now, although, since, etc., this or these (usu. w. n. serving to sum up details of compound or vague antecedent: *a smile and a shilling, which equipment is within most people's reach, will suffice*; *for ten years, during which time he spoke to nobody*;

which things are an allegory). **3.** *interrog. pron.* Which person(s) or thing(s)? (*which of you am I to thank for this?*; *say which* (*of these books*) *you would like best*); **~ is ~?**, which of two etc. given persons etc. corresponds to one of given descriptions etc., and which to another?; T'OTHER *from which.* **4.** *rel. pron.* (cf. THAT¹ 4, WHO; used to convert what would in the simplest grammar be an independent sentence into a subordinate clause by taking the place of a noun expressed in that sentence and expressed or implied in another sentence; used of things and (arch.) of persons; used esp. to introduce a clause not essential for identification: *the meeting, which was held in the Park, was a failure*; *Our Father, which art in Heaven*; *he said he saw me there, which* (statement) *was a lie*; occas. in clause preceding antecedent: *moreover, which you will hardly credit, he was not there himself*); **the ~**, (arch.) = *which* rel. (a. or pron.). [OE *hwilc*, = OS (*h*)*wilik*, OHG (*h*)*welih*, ON *hvílikr*, Goth. *hwileiks* f. Gmc **hwa-*, **hwe-*, **hwi-* + **likam* body, form; cf. LIKE¹, -LY¹, SUCH]

whĭchĕ'ver *a.* & *pron.* **1.** Any (of a definite set of persons or things) which; that or those which. **2.** (colloq.) = *which* EVER. [ME, f. prec. + EVER]

whĭchsōĕ'ver *a.* & *pron.* (arch.) = prec. 1. [ME; cf. WHATSOEVER]

whĭ'dah (-d*a*) *n.* Small Afr. weaver-bird of genus *Vidua*, the male having mainly black plumage and tail-feathers of great length. [orig. WIDOW-*bird*, altered f. assoc. w. *Whidah* (now Ouidah) in Dahomey]

whiff *n.* & *v.* **1.** *n.* Puff of air, smoke, odour, (fig.) scandal, etc. (*want a whiff of fresh air*); minor discharge *of grape-shot* etc.; small cigar; ‖light narrow outrigged sculling-boat. **2.** *v.t.* & *i.* Blow or puff lightly. **3.** *v.i.* Smell (unpleasant). [imit.]

whĭ'ffl|e *v.* & *n.* **1.** *v.i.* & *t.* (Of wind) blow lightly, shift about. **2.** *v.i.* Be variable or evasive, whence ~ER¹ *n.*; (of flame, leaves) flicker, flutter; make the sound of a light wind in breathing etc. **3.** *n.* Slight movement of air. [f. WHIFF + -LE 3]

***whĭ'ffletree** (-felt-) *n.* = SWINGLE*tree*. [var. of WHIPPLETREE]

Whĭg *n.* & *a.* (Hist.) **1.** 17th-c. Scottish Presbyterian. **2.** ‖(Member) of political party that, after the Revolution of 1688, aimed at subordinating the power of the Crown to that of Parliament and the upper classes, passed the Reform Bill of 1832, and in the mid-19th c. was succeeded by the Liberals (opp. TORY). **3.** *Supporter of American Revolution; (member) of political party 1834–56, succeeded by the Republicans. **4.** Hence **~'g**ERY (4), **~'g**ISM (3), *ns.*, **~'g**ISH¹ *a.*, (-g-). [prob. abbr. of *whiggamer*, *-more*, Scottish rebel of 1648, f. *whig* to drive + MARE²]

whīle¹ *n.*, & *v.t.* **1.** *n.* Space of time, time occupied by or spent in some action etc., (*have been waiting all this while*; *happened a* (*long*) *while ago* or *back*; *go away for a while*); **in a little ~**, soon; **once in a ~**, occasionally, at long intervals; **(for) a ~**, for some time; *have not seen him* **for a long ~**, for a long time past; **a good** or **great ~**, a considerable time; **between ~s**, in the intervals between other actions; **worth ~** or one's **~**, repaying the time spent in doing it etc.; **the ~**, during some other process, (poet.) during the time that; **all the ~**, during the whole time (that). **2.** *v.t.* Pass (time, hour, etc.) *away* in leisurely or interesting manner. [OE *hwīl* = OS, OHG *hwīla*, ON *hvíla*, Goth. *hweila* f. Gmc **hwīlō* f. IE **qwi-*]

whīle² *conj.* **1.** During the time that, for as long as, at the same time as, (*please write while I dictate*; *Jones got 98 runs while Smith at the other end was making 15*; *while there is life there is hope*; (w. ellipsis of pron. subj. and BE) *while reading I fell asleep*; *we are safe while in his care*; *he retained the consciousness of it while asleep*). **2.** In more or less marked contrast with the fact that simultaneously, although, whereas, (*Nero fiddling while Rome burns*; *while I have no money to spend, you have nothing to spend money on*; *while I admit his good points I can see his bad*; *while convinced it is true, I cannot prove it*). [abbr. of OE *thā hwīle the*, ME *the* WHILE¹ *that*]

whīles (-lz) *conj.* (arch.) = prec. [f. WHILE¹ + -S³, orig. in *somewhiles*, *otherwhiles*, advs.]

whī'lom *adv.* & *a.* (arch.) **1.** *adv.* Once, formerly. **2.** *a.* Former (*his whilom friend*). [OE *hwīlum*, dat. pl. of *hwīl* WHILE¹]

‖**whīlst** *conj.* = WHILE². [ME, f. WHILES; cf. AGAINST]

whĭm *n.* **1.** Sudden fancy, caprice, freakish idea. **2.** Kind of windlass for raising ore or water from mine. [17th c.; orig. unkn.]

whĭ'mbrel *n.* Small curlew, esp. *Numenius phaeopus*. [f. foll. (imit.); cf. *dotterel*]

whĭ'mper *v.* & *n.* **1.** *v.i.* Make feeble querulous or frightened sounds, cry and whine softly. **2.** *v.t.* Utter whimperingly. **3.** Hence ~ER¹ *n.* **4.** *n.* Sound of whimpering. [imit., f. dial. *whimp* + -ER⁵]

whĭ'msĭcal (-z-) *a.* Capricious; odd-looking, fanciful; hence ~ITY (-ă'l-) *n.*, ~LY² *adv.* [f. foll. + -ICAL]

whĭ'msy̆, whĭ'msey, (-zĭ) *n.* = WHIM 1. [rel. to foll.; cf. *flimsy*]

whĭ'm-whăm *n.* (arch.) Plaything, toy; = WHIM 1. [redupl., of uncert. orig.]

whĭn¹ *n.* (in *sing.* or *pl.*) Gorse, furze; **~'chat,** small brownish sweet-singing bird (*Saxicola rubetra*). [prob. Scand.; cf. Norw. *hvine*, Sw. *hven*]

whĭn², whĭ'nsĭll, whĭ'nstōne, *n.* (Piece of) hard dark (esp. basaltic) rock or stone. [ME, of unkn. orig.; see SILL, STONE]

whīn|e *v.i.* & *t.*, & *n.* (Make) long-drawn complaining cry (as) of child or dog; (make) shrill prolonged sound like this; (utter) querulous talk or petty complaint; utter in whining tone; hence ~'ER¹ *n.*, ~'Y² *a.* [OE *hwīnan*, = ON *hvína* whiz]

whĭ'nnȳ *v.i.*, & *n.* (Give) gentle or joyful neigh. [imit.; cf. prec.]

whĭp¹ *v.* (-pp-). **1.** *v.t.* & *i.* (w. *adv.* or *prep.*) Move with sudden or unexpected or rapid motion, snatch, dart, (*whip behind the door*; *whipped up her toy terrier*; *whip out sword, knife*; *whip off* one's *coat*); **~-graft,** graft with tongue of scion in slit in stock and vice versa; ‖**-round,** appeal for contributions from a group to charitable cause. **2.** *v.t.* Bind (cord, stick) with close covering of twine, overcast (hem etc.). **3.** Flog, lash, (horse, body, etc.); use whip to bring hounds *in*, *off*, *together*; strike or reprove vigorously; fish (stream) with whipping motion; urge *on* with whip; bring (fault, etc.) *out of* person by flogging; beat (cream or eggs) into froth; spin (top) with whip; (sl.) excel, defeat; **~ up,** summon (attendance), generate (attack, feeling), by vigorous action. **4.** Hence **~'p**ING¹ (1, 4) *n.*; **~ping-boy,** (Hist.) boy educated with and chastised instead of young prince, (fig.) scapegoat; **~ping-post** (to which persons were tied to be whipped, usu. in public); **~ping-top** (kept spinning by blows of lash). [ME (*h*)*wippen*, prob. f. MLG & MDu. *wippen* swing, leap, dance, f. Gmc **wip-* move quickly]

whĭp² *n.* **1.** Instrument for urging on or punishing with lash attached to short or long stick (*fair* CRACK[1] *of the whip*); coachman (*good, poor, etc., whip*). **2.** Hunt official subordinate to huntsman and charged with management of hounds; ||(Parl. etc.) (1) official appointed to maintain discipline among, secure attendance of, and give necessary information to, members of his party, (2) written notice (variously underlined with number of lines representing degrees of urgency, as **three-line** ~) requesting attendance on particular occasion, (3) party discipline and instructions (*ask for, take, the Liberal whip*). **3.** Rope-and-pulley hoisting apparatus. **4.** Food made with whipped cream etc. **5.** **~-bird,** Austral. bird with cry like crack of whip; **~'-cord,** tightly twisted cord such as is used for making whiplashes, close-woven worsted fabric; **~-crane,** light derrick with tackle for hoisting; **~-fish** (with dorsal fin elongated into filament like whiplash); **~-gin,** = sense 3; **~ hand,** hand that holds whip; *have the* ~ *hand* (*of* or *over*), be in position to control; **~'lash,** lash of whip, flagellum; *~lash injury* (to neck, caused by sudden jerk of head in collision of vehicle etc.); **~-ray,** sting-ray; **~-saw,** (*n.*) narrow saw-blade with ends held by frame, *(*v.t.* & *i.*) cheat, be cheated, by joint action on or by two others; **~-scorpion,** arachnid with long slender abdomen; **~-snake** (slender); **~-stitch** (made by whipping); **~'stock,** handle of whip. [ME, partly f. prec., partly f. MLG *wip(pe)* quick movement]

whĭ'pper *n.* In vbl senses; **~-in,** (Hunting) = WHIP[2] 2; **~-snapper,** small child, young and insignificant but presumptuous or intrusive person [perh. for *whipsnapper*, implying noise and unimportance]. [f. WHIP[1] + -ER[1]]

whĭ'ppĕt *n.* Cross-bred dog of modified greyhound type used for racing. [prob. f. obs. *whippet* move briskly, f. *whip it*]

whĭ'ppletree (-pelt-) *n.* = SWINGLE*tree*. [app. f. WHIP[1] + TREE]

whĭ'ppoorwĭll *n.* Amer. nightjar (*Caprimulgus vociferus*). [imit. of cry]

whĭ'pp|ȳ *a.* Flexible, springy; hence ~ĭNESS *n.* [f. WHIP[2] + -Y[2]]

whĭ'pster *n.* = WHIPPER-*snapper*. [app. f. WHIP[1] + -STER]

whîr. See WHIRR.

whîrl *v.* & *n.* **1.** *v.t.* & *i.* Swing round and round, revolve rapidly (*whirling* DERVISH). **2.** Send (missile etc.), (of moving body) travel, swiftly in orbit or curve; convey or go rapidly *away* etc. in wheeled conveyance. **3.** *v.i.* (Of brain, senses, etc.) be giddy, seem to spin round, (of thoughts etc.) follow each other in bewildering succession. **4.** *n.* Whirling movement (lit. or fig.; *my thoughts are in a whirl*); bustling activity (*the social whirl*); *(sl.) attempt (*give it a whirl*). **5.** **~'pool,** circular eddy in sea, river, etc., often causing suction to its centre; **~'wind,** mass of air whirling rapidly round and round in cylindrical or funnel shape (*sow the wind and reap the ~wind,* suffer worse results of bad action), (fig.) confused tumultuous process, (*attrib.*) very rapid (*whirlwind courtship, tour*); **~'ybird,** (sl.) helicopter. [ME; v. f. ON *hvirfla*, n. f. MLG & MDu. *wervel* spindle & ON *hvirfill* circle f. Gmc **hwerbhilaz* (**hwerbh-* turn)]

whîr'lĭgĭg (-g-) *n.* Spinning or whirling toy; (fig.) revolving motion (~ **of time,** changes of fortune); merry-go-round; water-beetle of family Gyrinidae that circles about on surface. [ME, f. prec. + obs. *gig* whipping-top]

whîrr, whîr, *v.i.* (**-rr-**), & *n.* (Make) continuous buzzing or softly clicking sound as of bird's wings quickly flapping or cog-wheels in rapid action. [ME, prob. Scand.; cf. Da. *hvirre*, Norw. *kvirra*, perh. rel. to WHIRL]

whĭsht. (Ir.) Var. of WHIST[1].

whĭsk *n.* & *v.* **1.** *n.* Bunch of grass, hair, twigs, etc., to flap dust off, flies away, etc., with; instrument for beating up eggs or cream; quick movement (as) of whisk or of animal's tail. **2.** *v.t.* Flap (dust, fly, etc.) *away* or *off*; beat (eggs etc.) into a froth; take *away* or *off* with sudden motion (*waiter whisked my plate away*). **3.** *v.t.* & *i.* Convey or go lightly and quickly esp. out of sight (*was whisked away in a helicopter; mouse whisks into its hole*). **4.** *v.t.* Brandish lightly or flip or wave about (*went whisking a cane, her tail*). [ME *wisk*, prob. Scand. cf. ON *visk* wisp, Sw. *viska* to whisk (off)]

whĭ'sker *n.* **1.** (usu. in *pl.*) Hair of man's face, esp. cheek (cf. MOUSTACHE, BEARD[1]); SIDE[1]-*-whiskers*. **2.** Bristle growing from upper lip of cat etc., set of such bristles on one side; CAT[1]*'s whiskers*. **3.** (colloq.) Small distance (*within a whisker of*). **4.** Strong hairlike crystal of metal. **5.** Hence (-)~ED[2] (*-erd*) *a.* [f. prec. + -ER[1]]

whĭ'skey *n.* Var. of foll. (esp. U.S. and of Irish whisky).

whĭ'sk|ȳ[1] *n.* Spirit distilled from malted barley, other grains, or potatoes etc.; drink of this; **~ified,** (joc.) affected by whisky-drinking; **~y-jack,** Canadian jay. [abbr. of obs. *whiskybae*, var. of USQUEBAUGH]

whĭ'skȳ[2] *n.* (Hist.) Kind of light gig or chaise. [f. WHISK, w. ref. to lightness of motion]

whĭ'sper *v.* & *n.* **1.** *v.i.* Speak without vibration of vocal chords; talk with intention of being audible only close at hand or *to* confidant; converse privately, indulge in slander or plotting; (of leaves, stream, etc.) rustle; **~ing--gallery,** gallery, dome, etc., in which some acoustic peculiarity causes least sound made at a particular point to be audible at another far off. **2.** *v.t.* Convey (statement etc. *to* person), inform or order (person *that* or *to* do), by whispering; covertly make known (tale, *that*). **3.** Hence ~ER[1], ~ING[1] (1), *ns.* **4.** *n.* Whispering speech (*always talks in a whisper* or *in whispers*); whispered remark (STAGE[1] *whisper*); rumour of unknown origin, insinuation, mysterious hint; rustling sound. [OE *hwisprian*, early Flem. *wisperen*, f. Gmc **hwis-* (imit.)]

||**whĭst**[1] (arch. or dial.) *int.* enjoining silence. [ME, imit.; cf. HIST, HUSH[2]]

||**whĭst**[2] *a.* (arch.) Silent. [ME, f. prec.]

whĭst[3] *n.* Card-game of mingled skill and chance for four or exceptionally three or two persons; **long, short,** ~, with ten, five, points to game; RUBBER[3] *of whist*; ~ **drive,** PROGRESSIVE whist party usu. with prizes. [f. earlier *whisk*, perh. f. WHISK; infl. by WHIST[1] (w. ref. to the silence usual in the game)]

whĭ'stle (-sel) *v.* & *n.* **1.** *v.i.* Make—with the lips or with instrument for the purpose, or (of bird etc.) with the voice, or (of missile, wind, etc.) by rapid motion—clear shrill sound (as) of breath forced through small orifice formed with lips; make such sound as signal (*to* person, *for* thing; *becalmed superstitious sailors* ~ **for a wind,** whence ~ **for,** (colloq.) seek in vain; **let** person **go** ~, disregard his wishes) or expr. surprise, derision, etc.; ~ **in the dark** (lit. or fig.; to overcome one's fears). **2.** *v.t.* Give (tune) etc. by whistling; ~ (**up**), summon or give signal to (dog, attendant) by whistling; ~ **down the wind,** turn (hawk) loose, (fig.) let go, abandon. **3.** *n.* Whistling sound or note. **4.** Instrument for producing such sound; **penny** or **tin** ~, tin pipe with six holes giving different notes; **steam** ~, whistle sounded by jet of steam; **pay for** one's ~, pay high for a caprice [w. ref. to story of B. Franklin]; **as clean, clear, dry, as a** ~ (prov. similes);

*~-**stop,** small unimportant town on railway, politician's brief pause for electioneering speech on tour, rapid superficial visit. **5.** (colloq.) Throat (WET one's *whistle*). [OE *(h)wistlian* v., *(h)wistle* n., of imit. orig.; cf. ON *hvísla* whisper, MSw. *hvisla* whistle]

whĭ'stler (-sl-) *n.* In vbl senses; kind of marmot; bird that whistles. [OE *hwistlere* (as prec., -ER[1])]

whĭ'stlĭng (-sl-) *a.* In vbl senses; (of bird or animal) characterized by uttering clear shrill sound; ~-**buoy** (fitted with whistle sounded by movement of waves); ~ **kettle** (fitted with whistle sounded by steam when contents are boiling). [f. WHISTLE + -ING[2]]

whĭt[1] *n.* (arch. or literary). Particle, least possible amount, (**every** ~, the whole, wholly; **no** ~, **not** or **never a** ~, not at all). [earlier *w(h)yt*, app. alt. f. WIGHT in phr. *no wight* etc.]

Whĭt[2] *a.* ~ **Sunday,** seventh Sunday after Easter, commemorating descent of Holy Spirit at Pentecost (Acts 2); ~ **Monday, Tuesday,** those following, ~ **week(-end)**, that containing, Whit Sunday. [OE *Hwīta Sunnandæg*, lit. white Sunday, prob. f. white robes of newly-baptized at Pentecost]

whīte[1] *a.*, & *v.t.* **1.** *a.* Resembling a surface reflecting sunlight without absorbing any of the visible rays, of the colour of milk or fresh snow or common salt or the common swan's plumage; approaching such colour, pale esp. in face (*white as a sheet*; *white with rage*; so *in a white rage*); that is an albino (*white mouse*); less dark than other things of the same kind; (of hair) having lost its colour esp. in old age; **bleed** ~, (fig.) drain of wealth etc. [w. ref. to hanging of killed calf to whiten veal]. **2.** Characterized by presence of some white (in many -ED[2] compounds used esp. in describing animals etc., as *white-bellied*, *-crowned*, *-eyed*, *-faced*, *-headed*, *-rumped*, *-tailed*, *-throated*, *-winged*); (of plant) having white flowers, light-coloured bark, etc. **3.** (Of water, air, glass) transparent, colourless; (fig.) innocent, unstained, of harmless kind. **4.** Of (the class of) or reserved for white men (see *white man* below; *white culture*, *civilization*, *woman*, etc.; *the White Australia policy*). **5.** (Polit.) Of royalist or counter-revolutionary or reactionary tendency (opp. *red*). **6.** *White* ADMIRAL; ~ **ant,** termite; ~'**bait,** small silvery-white fish prob. the young of herring, sprat, etc., eaten fried in quantities, (N.Z.) young inanga; ~'**beam,** tree (*Sorbus aria*) with silvery downy under-side of leaf, and red berries; ~ **bear,** polar bear, *grizzly bear; **W~boy,** member of 19th-c. illegal agrarian association in Ireland wearing white shirts at nightly meetings and outrages; ~ **bread** (made from fine bolted flour); ~ **bronze** (containing much tin); ~-**caps,** breakers far out at sea; ~ **cell,** leucocyte; ~ **coal,** = WATER[1]-*-power* (1) [F *houille blanche*]; ~ **Christmas** (with snow); ||~ **coffee** (with milk or cream); ~-**collar,** (of worker) not engaged in manual labour; **W~ Continent,** Antarctica; ~ **corpuscle,** leucocyte; *white* CROW[1]; *white* CURRANT; ~ **dwarf,** (Astron.) small very dense faint star; *white* ELEPHANT; ||*white* ENSIGN; ~-**-eye,** bird with white ring round eye; ~**face,** white make-up of actor etc.; *white* FEATHER[1]; ~ **fish,** (1) light-coloured esp. silver fish, e.g. cod, haddock, (2) lake-fish of genus *Coregonus* etc.; *white* FLAG[4]; ~ **fly,** small insect of family Aleyrodidae attacking shrubs etc.; *White* FRIAR; *white* FROST; ||~ **gloves** (Hist., presented to assize judge finding no criminal cases to try); ~ **gold,** pale alloy of gold with nickel etc.; *~ **goods,** white household fabrics or equipment (refrigerators etc.); ~ **grouse,** ptarmigan; ~-**haired** or ~-**headed boy,** highly favoured person; ~ **hands,** (fig.) innocence or integrity; ~-**heart cherry** (orig. ~ **heart-cherry**), pale cultivated heart-shaped kind; ~ **heat,** temperature at which metal emits white light, (fig.) state of intense passion or activity; ~ **hope,** person who is expected to attain renown; ~ **horses,** (fig.) white-crested waves at sea; ~-**hot,** at white heat; **W~ House,** official residence of U.S. president in Washington; ||~ **land** (restricted to agricultural use); *white* LEAD[1]; ~ **leather,** = WHITLEATHER; ~ **leg,** MILK[1]-*leg*; *white* LIE[1]; ~ **light** (colourless, e.g. ordinary daylight); ~-**lipped** (esp. with fear); ~-**livered,** cowardly, dastardly; *white* MAGIC; ~ **man,** member of one of the human groups with relatively pale complexion, chiefly inhabiting or having inhabited Europe, and characterized by a certain type of civilization (*the ~ man's burden*, supposed task of leading the coloured peoples forward), (colloq.) person of honourable character, good breeding, etc.; ~ **matter,** fibrous part of brain and spinal cord; ~ **meat,** poultry, veal, rabbit, pork; ~ **metal,** white or silvery alloy; ~ **monk,** Cistercian; ~ (sleepless) **night** [F *nuit blanche*]; ~ **noise** (containing many frequencies with about equal energies); ~-**out,** atmospheric condition, esp. in polar regions, marked by dense snow-cloud and total obscuration of physical features [after BLACK[3]-*out*]; ||**W~ Paper,** report issued by Government to give information; *white* PEPPER[1]; *~ **ribbon,** badge of temperance; ~ **rose,** emblem of Yorkshire, or of House of York in Wars of the Roses; **W~ Russian,** Belorussian; ~ **sale** (of household linen); *white* SAUCE; ~ **sheet,** penitent's garb (usu. *stand in a ~ sheet*, confess sin etc.); ~ **slave,** woman entrapped (and sent abroad) into prostitution (*the ~-slave traffic*, ~ *slavery*); ~'**smith,** (1) worker in tin, (2) polisher or finisher of metal goods; ~ **spirit,** light petroleum fraction used as solvent etc.; *white* SQUALL; ~ **stock,** STOCK (sense 4) made from veal, chicken, etc., and uncoloured; ~ **sugar** (purified); ~ **supremacy,** doctrine based on supposed inherent inferiority of Negroes and other non-white races; *White* TERROR; ~'**thorn,** hawthorn (cf. BLACK[1]*thorn*); ~-**throat,** species of warbler or Amer. sparrow with white patch on throat; ~ **tie,** man's white bow-tie worn as part of full evening dress; **white* TRASH; *white* VITRIOL; ~ **war,** war without bloodshed, economic warfare; ~ **water,** shallow or foamy water; ~ **whale,** northern cetacean, white when adult; ~ **wine** (of amber or golden or pale yellow colour, opp. *red wine*); ~ **witch** (using power for beneficent purposes only); ~'**wood,** light-coloured wood esp. prepared for staining etc. **7.** Hence ~'LY[2] (-tlĭ) *adv.*, ~'NESS (-tn-) *n.*, **whī'tish**[1] 2 *a.* **8.** *v.t.* (arch.) Make white (*whited* SEPULCHRE). [OE *hwīt*, = OS *hwīt*, OHG *(h)wīz*, ON *hvítr*, Goth. *hweits* f. Gmc **hwītaz* f. IE **kwitnos*]

whīte[2] *n.* **1.** White or nearly white colour; white pigment (CHINESE etc. *white*); white clothes or material (*dressed in white*); blank space in printing. **2.** Albuminous part round yolk of egg; visible part of eyeball round iris; white person (*mean* or *POOR *white*); white butterfly; (colloq., in *pl.*) leucorrhoea; white ball in billiards etc.; (player of) white men in chess etc. [OE; f. prec.]

Whī'techăpel (-t-ch-) *n.* **1.** ~ **(cart)**, light two-wheeled sprung cart used by shopkeepers etc. **2.** (Cards). Lead of singleton with a view to subsequent trumping. **3.** (Bill.) Pocketing of opponent's ball. [~ in London]

||**Whī'tehall** (-t-hawl) *n.* British Government;

its offices or policy. [street in London where there are many Government offices]

whi'ten *v.i.* & *t.* Make or become white(r) (lit. or fig.). [ME, f. WHITE[1] + -EN[6]]

whi'tening (-tn-) *n.* In vbl senses; = WHITING[1]. [f. prec. + -ING[1]]

whi'tewash (-twŏ-) *n.*, & *v.t.* **1.** *n.* Solution of quicklime or of whiting and size for brushing over walls, ceilings, etc., to give clean appearance, (fig.) means employed to conceal faults etc. in order to clear person or institution of imputations. **2.** *v.t.* Cover with whitewash, (fig.) attempt by concealment to clear reputation of, (in *pass.*, of insolvent) get fresh start by passage through bankruptcy court; *defeat (opponent) without allowing any opposing score. [n. f. v., f. WHITE[1] + WASH[1]]

Whī'tey *n.* (usu. derog.) White person; white persons collectively. [f. WHITE[1] + -Y[3]]

whi'ther (-dh-) *adv.*, *conj.*, & *n.* (arch. or rhet.) **1.** *interrog. adv.* To what place or position (lit. or fig.); what is the future of (*Whither Democracy?*). **2.** *rel. adv.*, & *conj.* (W. ref. to place) to which; to the, or (also **~soe'ver**) any, place to which; = *and thither*. **3.** Hence ~WARD(s) *adv.* **4.** *n.* Destination (cf. WHENCE 4). [OE *hwider* f. Gmc **hwi-*; cf. WHICH, HITHER, THITHER]

whī'ting[1] *n.* Chalk prepared by drying, grinding, etc., for use in whitewashing, plate-cleaning, etc. [ME, f. WHITE[1] + -ING[1]]

whī'ting[2] *n.* Small white-fleshed food-fish (*Merlangus merlangus*). [ME, f. MDu. *wijting*, app. f. as WHITE[1] + -ING[3]]

whi'tleather (-lĕdh-) *n.* Tawed leather. [ME, f. WHITE[1] + LEATHER]

||**Whi'tley** *n.* ~ **Council** (of representatives of employers and workers for discussion and settlement of industrial or civil-service relations and conditions); hence ~ISM (-ĭĭ-) *n.*, use of such methods for dealing with industrial problems. [f. J. H. ~, chairman of committee (1916) that recommended creation of such councils]

whi'tlow (-ō) *n.* Inflammatory sore on finger esp. near the nail, usu. with suppuration. [ME *whitflaw*, *-flow*, app. = WHITE[1] + FLAW[1] in sense 'crack', but perh. of LG orig.; cf. Du. *fijt*, LG *fīt* whitlow]

Whi'tsun *n.* **~day,** (1) = WHIT[2] *Sunday*, (2, Sc.) 15 May, a quarter-day; ~**(tide)**, Whit Sunday and following days; ~ **week,** Whit week. [ME, f. *Whitsun Day* = WHIT[2] *Sunday*]

whi'ttle[1] *n.* (arch. or dial.) Long knife, esp. such as is used by butchers. [var. of ME *thwitel* f. OE *thwītan* to cut off + -LE 1]

whi'ttle[2] *v.t.* Trim, carve, slice off pieces from, (wood, or abs.: *whittle at*) with knife; ~ **(down, away)**, reduce amount or effect of by repeated subtraction. [f. prec.]

Whi'tworth *n.* ~ **thread,** standard screw-thread for metal. [f. Sir J. ~, Engl. engineer d. 1887]

whī'tȳ *a.* Inclining to white (usu. in comb. with other colour-name, esp. *whity-brown*); cf. WHITEY. [f. WHITE[1] + -Y[2]]

whiz, whizz, *v.i.* (-zz-), & *n.* (Make) sound given by friction of body moving at great speed through air; move quickly; **~-bang,** (sl.) high-velocity shell from a small-calibre gun, whose passage is heard before the gun's report; **~-kid,** (colloq.) exceptionally brilliant or successful young person. [imit.]

who (ho͞o *or, when unstressed,* ho͝o) *pron.* (*obj.* **whom** *pr.* ho͞om, colloq. **who;** *poss.* **whose** *pr.* ho͞oz). **1.** *interrog.* What person(s)?, which person(s)?, what sort of person(s) in regard to position or authority?, (*who said so?*; *whom*, colloq. *who, do you mean?*; *told him who they were*, *whom* or colloq. *who to look out for*; *whose son is he?*); (in rhet. questions equiv. to neg. statement: *who would have thought it?*; *it was Jones, of course—who else?*; *who am I that I should object?*); (asking for repetition of person's name not properly heard; *you saw whom?*, colloq. *who?*, *it was Mr. who?*); *know* **~'s ~**, who or what each person is; *a* **~'s ~**, list with facts relating to notable persons; **~-does-what dispute** or **strike,** one about which of the trade unions is to do a particular job; ~ **goes there?** (see GO[1] 6); ~ **is it** (substitute for name that cannot be recalled). **2.** *rel.* (Person or persons) WHICH or THAT[1] (*the man whom*, colloq. *who, you saw*; *those for whose benefit it was done*; *anyone who chooses can apply*; *there is no one who we can believe is, whom we can believe to be, competent*). **3.** (arch.) The or any person(s) that (*who steals my purse, steals trash*; *whom the gods love die young*); **as ~ should say,** like a person who said, as though one said. **4.** = and, but, though, since, if, etc., he or him or they, etc. (*sent it to Jones, who passed it on to Smith*; *is flirting with Dick, whom she actually detests*). [OE *hwā*, = OS *hwē*, OHG (*h*)*wer*, Goth. *hwas* f. Gmc **hwas*, **hwes* f. IE **q*ʷ*os*, **q*ʷ*es*; *whom* f. OE dat. *hwām*, *hwǣm*; *whose* f. gen. *hwæs*]

W.H.O. *abbr.* World Health Organization.

whoa *int.* (to horse etc.) expr. command to stop or stand still. [var. of HO]

whodŭ'(n)nĭt (ho͞o-) *n.* (colloq.) Detective or mystery story, play, etc. [= *who done* (illiterate for *did*) *it?*]

whoĕ'ver (ho͞o-), **whoe'er'** (poet.; ho͞oār'), *pron.* (*obj.* **whomever, whome'er,** colloq. **whoever;** *poss.* **whosever;** *pr.* as at WHO). **1.** The or any person(s) that (*whoever comes will be welcome*). **2.** (In indef. concessive clause) though anyone (*whoever else objects, I do not*; *whosever it is, I mean to have it*). **3.** (colloq.) = *who* EVER. [ME, f. WHO + EVER]

whōle (hōl) *a.* & *n.* **1.** *a.* (arch.) In good health, well, (*thy faith hath made thee whole*). **2.** In sound condition, uninjured, not broken, intact, (*hope you will come back whole*; *got off with a whole skin*; *there is not a plate left whole*; *has swallowed a plum whole*). **3.** Integral, consisting of one or more units, without fractions; ~ **number** (that can be got from zero by adding or subtracting units). **4.** Undiminished, without removal of part (*whole milk*; *whole blood*; *was talking the whole time*); *bread made of* ~ **meal** (not deprived of some constituents by bolting). **5.** Not less than (*spent whole years of misery*; *went up a whole foot*; *lasted three whole days*; *whole regiments were cut down*; *talked a whole lot of nonsense*); all that there is of (*the whole truth, world, duty of man*; *do* thing **with** one's ~ **heart,** heartily, with concentrated effort, etc., without doubts etc.); all members etc. of (*the whole priesthood*). **6.** ~ **cloth** (of full size as manufactured; **out of ~ cloth*, entirely fabricated and false); **~-coloured,** all of one colour; **~-hearted,** (of person) completely devoted, (of action) done with one's whole heart (see sense 5); **~-ho'gger,** one who goes the *whole* HOG[1]; ~ **holiday,** day taken entirely as holiday (opp. *half holiday*); **~-hoofed,** with undivided hoofs; **~-length,** (of portrait) representing person from head to foot; ~ **life insurance** (for which premiums are payable throughout life of insured person); **~'meal** (see sense 4); ***~ note,** semibreve; ~ **number** (cf. sense 3); ~ **plate,** photographic plate or film 16·5 × 21·6 cm; **~-souled,** = *whole-hearted*; ***~ step,** = *whole tone*; **~-time,** full time; ~ **tone,** (Mus.) interval of one TONE[1]; **~-tone** *a.*, (Mus.) using intervals composed of whole tones without semitones; ~ **wheat** (not separated into parts by bolting; cf. sense 4). **7.** Hence ~'NESS (-ln-) *n.* **8.** *n.* Thing complete in itself; all that there is of or *of* something (*the golden rule contains the whole of morality*); all members etc. *of* (*the whole of London knows it*); **as a ~**, (considered etc.) as a unity, not as separate parts; **on the ~**, taking into consideration everything that bears on the question, after weighing pros and cons etc. **9.** Organic unity, complete system, total made up of parts, (*nature is a whole*; *the whole and the parts*). [OE *hāl*, = OS *hēl*, OHG *heil*, ON *heill*, Goth. *hails* f. Gmc **hailaz*]

whō′lesāl|e (hō′ls-) *n.*, *a.*, *adv.*, & *v.t.* **1.** *n.* Selling of articles in large quantities to be retailed by others. **2.** *a.* & *adv.* By or relating to wholesale, at wholesale price (*I can get it for you wholesale*), (transf.) on a large scale (*a wholesale slaughter took place*; *sends out Christmas cards wholesale*). **3.** *v.t.* Sell wholesale; hence ~ER[1] *n.* [ME, orig. *by whole sale*]

whō′lesome (hō′ls-) *a.* Promoting physical or moral health, salubrious, prudent, not morbid, (*wholesome food, air, exercise, advice, respect, excitement*); hence ~LY[2] (-mlĭ) *adv.*, ~NESS (-mn-) *n.* [ME, f. OE **hālsum* (as WHOLE, -SOME[1])]

whō′llȳ (hō′l-lĭ) *adv.* Entirely, without limitation or diminution, (*I am wholly at a loss*); exclusively, without admixture, (*a wholly bad example*). [ME, f. OE **hāllīce* (as WHOLE, -LY[2])]

whom, whomever, etc. See WHO, WHOEVER, etc.

whōōp (*or* hōōp) *v.i.*, & *n.* (Utter) loud cry (as) of excitement etc.; **~′ing cough,** infectious bacterial disease, esp. of children, with short violent cough followed by long sonorous inspiration; **~′ing crane, swan,** (species that make whooping or whistling sound); **~ it up,** engage in revelry, *make a stir; **~s!** (colloq. apology for obvious mistake). [ME; imit.]

whōō′pee (*or* -ē′) *int.* & *n.* **1.** *int.* expr. exuberant joy. **2.** *n.* (colloq.) **Make ~**, rejoice noisily or hilariously. [f. prec.]

whōō′per (*or* h-) *n.* In vbl senses; whooping swan. [f. WHOOP + -ER[1]]

whŏp *v.t.* (**-pp-**). (sl.) Thrash, (fig.) defeat, overcome; (in *part.*) very large or remarkable of its kind (esp. *a whopping lie*), whence **~′PER**[1] *n.* [ME, var. of (dial.) *wap*, of unkn. orig.]

whōre (hōr) *n.*, & *v.i.* **1.** *n.* Prostitute; **~-house,** brothel; **~-master, -monger,** fornicator; **~′son,** (arch.) disliked person. **2.** *v.i.* (arch.) (Of man) commit fornication; (fig.) commit idolatry or iniquity (esp. *go a-whoring after strange gods* etc.). [OE *hōre*, = OHG *huora*, ON *hóra*, f. Gmc **hōrōn* f. IE **qār-*]

whōrl *n.* Ring of leaves or other organs round stem etc. of plant; complete circle in fingerprint; one turn of a spiral; small wheel on spindle steadying its motion; hence ~ED[2] (-ld) *a.* [ME *wharwyl*, *whorwil*, app. var. of WHIRL, infl. by *wharve* n. = whorl of spindle]

whor′tleberrȳ (wēr′telb-) *n.* = BILBERRY. [16th c., S.W. Engl. dial. form of *hurtleberry*, ME, of unkn. orig.]

whose. See WHO and WHICH.

whosever, whoseso(ever). See WHOEVER, WHOSO(EVER).

who′sō (hōō′-) *pron.* (*obj.* **whomso,** *poss.* **whoseso;** *pr.* as at WHO). (arch.) = WHOEVER 1, 2. [ME, = WHO + SO[1], f. OE *swā hwā swā*]

whosōĕ′ver (hōō-), **whosōe′er′** (poet.; hōōsōār′), *pron.* (*obj.* **whomso-,** *poss.* **whoseso-;** *pr.* as at WHO). = WHOEVER 1, 2. [ME, f. prec. + EVER]

whȳ[1] *adv.* & *n.* (*pl.* **~s**). **1.** *interrog. adv.* On what ground?, for what reason?, with what purpose?, (*why did you do it?*; *cannot think why you came*; (often ellipt.) *You are late*; *why?*); **~ so?** (demand for grounds of statement or view). **2.** *rel. adv.* On account of which (*the reasons why he did it are obscure*). **3.** *n.* Reason, explanation, (cf. WHERE*fore*). [OE *hwī*, *hwȳ* instr. of *hwæt* WHAT, f. Gmc **hwī*, IE **qʷei*, locative of **qʷo-* WHO]

whȳ[2] *int.* expr. surprised discovery or recognition (*why, it is surely Jones!*; *why, what a bruise you have got!*; *why, of course, that was it*), protest at simplicity of question etc. (‘*What is twice two?*’ ‘*Why, four.*’; *why, a child could answer that*), pause for reflection (‘*Is it true?*’ ‘*Why, yes, I think so*’), objection (*why, what is the harm?*), introduction of apodosis (*if silver will not do, why, we must try gold*), etc. [ellipt. uses of prec. 1]

whydah. Var. of WHIDAH.

W.I. *abbr.* West Indies; ||Women's Institute.

wĭch-. See WYCH-.

wĭck[1] *n.* (Piece of) fibrous or spongy material by which lamp or candle flame is kept supplied with melted grease or oil; (Surg.) gauze strip inserted in wound to drain it; **get on** person's ~, (sl.) annoy him. [OE *wēoce*, *-wēoc*, = MDu. *wiecke*, MLG *wēke*, OHG *wiohha*, of unkn. orig.]

wĭck[2] *n.* Town, hamlet, district, (now dial. exc. in compounds e.g. *bailiwick*, and in place-names e.g. *Hampton Wick*, *Warwick*); (dial.) dairy farm. [OE *wīc*, = OS *wīc*, OHG *wīh*, Goth. *weihs*, prob. f. L *vicus* street, village]

wĭ′ckėd *a.* (**~er, ~est**). **1.** Sinful, iniquitous, vicious, given to or involving immorality (**~ Bible,** edition of 1632 with *not* omitted in seventh commandment), offending intentionally against what is right; **the ~**, (abs.) wicked persons. **2.** Spiteful, ill-tempered, intending or intended to give pain; playfully mischievous, roguish; (colloq.) very bad or formidable. **3.** Hence ~LY[2] *adv.*, ~NESS *n.* [ME, f. obs. *wick* in same senses (perh. adj. use of OE *wicca* wizard) + -ED[1] as in *wretched*]

wĭ′cker *n.* Plaited twigs or osiers as material of baskets, chairs, mats, protective covers, etc.; **~work,** (things made of) wicker. [ME, f. E. Scand.; cf. Sw. *viker* willow cogn. w. *vika* bend]

wĭ′ckėt *n.* **1.** ~(**-door, -gate**), small door or gate, esp. one beside or within larger one and used when latter is not open. **2.** *Aperture in door or wall usu. closed with sliding panel; *croquet hoop. **3.** (Cricket). Set of three stumps and two bails defended by batsman (**keep ~**, be **~-keeper,** fieldsman stationed close behind batsman's wicket; **at the ~**, batting; *catch* **at the ~**, by wicket-keeper); batsman's avoidance of being out (**~ is down** or **lost** or **taken, ~ falls,** batsman is out (in any manner); **third ~**, period between second and third dismissals of batsmen in side's innings; **win by two ~s,** score necessary runs with three batsmen not out); = PITCH[3] 4 (*went down the wicket to drive*); state of pitch (**on a good,** STICKY, **~**, (fig.) in advantageous, unfavourable, position). [ME, f. AF & ONF *wiket*, OF *guichet*, of uncert. orig.]

wĭ′ckĭup *n.* Amer. Indian hut of frame covered with grass etc. [f. Fox *wikiyap*]

widdershins. See WITHERSHINS.

wīde *a.*, *adv.*, & *n.* **1.** *a.* Measuring much or more than other things of same kind across or from side to side, broad, not narrow, (*wide door, road, river, brim, sleeve, margin, cloth, angle, interval*); **~ margin,** (fig.) a good deal more allowed than is (likely to be) needed; **~ screen,** cinema screen much greater in width than in height. **2.** (Appended to measurement) in width (*a strip 3 ft. wide*); (as *suf.*) extending over the whole of (*nation-wide*). **3.** Extending far, embracing much, of great extent, (*has a wide range*; *a wide domain*; *has wide experience*; *reached a wide public*; *a man of wide reading*; *there is a wide difference between*); **of ~ distribution,** occurring in many places; **of ~ fame,** known to many;

~ **generalization** (covering many particulars); **the ~ world,** all the world great as it is; hence ~'LY² (-dlĭ) *adv.* **4.** Not tight or close or restricted, loose, free, liberal, unprejudiced, not specialized, general, (*wide trousers*; *takes wide views*); ~ **guess,** one allowing margin for errors of detail; **give ~ berth to,** not go too near, keep clear of, avoid. **5.** Open to full extent (*staring with wide eyes*). **6.** At considerable distance from a point or mark, not within reasonable distance *of*; ~ **ball,** (Cricket) ball judged by umpire to pass wicket beyond batsman's reach and counting one to his side; ~ **of the mark,** (fig.) quite incorrect. **7.** ‖(sl.) Shrewd, skilled in sharp practice (*wide boy*). **8.** Hence **wī'**DEN⁶ *v.t.* & *i.*, **wī'**DISH¹ 2 *a.* **9.** *adv.* Widely (*ranges* FAR¹ *and wide*); to full extent (*open your mouth wide*; *wide awake*); far from target etc. (*is shooting wide*; *arrow fell wide of target*); ~ **open,** (fig.) exposed (*to* attack etc.), *(of town etc.) lenient in enforcing regulations. **10.** *n.* Wide ball; **the ~,** the wide world; *broke* etc. **to the ~,** completely; **dead to the ~,** unconscious. **11. ~-angle,** (of lens) having short focal length and field covering wide angle; ~ **awake,** (colloq., fig.) wary, knowing; **~'awake,** soft wide-brimmed low-crowned felt hat; **~-eyed,** surprised or naïve; **~-ranging,** covering an extensive range; **~'spread,** widely disseminated or distributed. [OE *wīd* a., *wīde* adv., = OS *wīd*, OHG *wīt*, ON *víthr* f. Gmc **wīdaz*]

wĭ'(d)geon (wĭ'jon) *n.* Wild duck, esp. *Anas penelope* or **Anas americana*. [perh. f. imit. **wi-*, after *pigeon*]

wĭ'dgėt *n.* (colloq.) Gadget, (unspecified) device. [perh. alt. of GADGET]

wĭ'dow (-ō) *n.*, & *v.t.* **1.** *n.* Woman who has lost her husband by death and not married again (GRASS *widow*; **golf** etc. ~, woman whose husband often leaves her and plays golf etc.); **~'s cruse,** supply that looks small, but seems or is inexhaustible (see 1 Kgs. 17:10–16); **~'s mite,** small money contribution (see Mark 12:42); **~'s peak,** V-shaped growth of hair towards centre of forehead; *widow's* WEEDS. **2.** Extra cards dealt separately and taken by highest bidder; (Print.) break-line at top of page or column; BLACK¹ *widow*; **the ~,** (sl.) champagne [f. the Veuve (F = widow) Cliquot brand]. **3. ~-bird,** whidah. **4.** Hence ~HOOD *n.* **5.** *v.t.* (usu. in *p.p.*) Kill husband or mate of, deprive of husband or wife or mate, make into widow or widower, (fig.) deprive *of*. [OE *widewe* etc., = OS *widowa*, OHG *wituwa*, Goth. *widuwō*, f. IE **widhewo* a.]

wĭ'dower (-ōer) *n.* Man who has lost his wife by death and not married again; GRASS *widower*. [ME, f. prec. + -ER¹]

wĭdth *n.* Measurement from side to side; large extent; comprehensiveness or liberality *of* mind, views, etc.; piece of material of full width as woven (*shall want three widths of it*); hence ~'WAYS, ~'WISE, *advs.* [17th c. (WIDE, -TH¹), repl. *wideness*]

wield *v.t.* Control, command, hold and use, manage with the hands or otherwise, (*wield power*, *the sceptre*, *a kingdom* etc. chiefly poet., *weapon* lit. or fig.). [OE *wealdan*, *wieldan* = OS, Goth. *waldan*, OHG *waltan*, ON *valda* f. Gmc **waldh-*]

wie'ner (vē'-) *n.* *Frankfurter; *Wiener* SCHNITZEL. [G, = Viennese]

wife *n.* (*pl.* **wives** *pr.* -vz). **1.** Old and rustic or uneducated woman (esp. in **old wives' tale,** foolish or superstitious tradition); (in *comb.*) woman engaged in selling etc. (FISH¹*wife*, HOUSEWIFE, MIDWIFE). **2.** Married woman esp. in relation to her husband (*his wife*; *the wife of the President*; *will make a good wife*); **wedded, lawful, ~,** (emphatic phrs. in contrast w. *mistress*, *concubine*, etc.); THE *wife*; *all the* WORLD *and his wife*; *have*, *take*, **to ~,** (arch.) as wife; **~-swapping,** (colloq.) sexual activity of various men with one another's wives. **3.** Hence ~'HOOD (-fh-), **wī'f**IE, *ns.*, ~'LESS, ~'LIKE, ~'LY¹, (-fl-) *adjs.* [OE *wīf* woman, = OS *wīf*, OHG *wīp*, ON *víf*; ult. orig. unkn.]

wĭg¹ *n.* Artificial head of hair worn to conceal baldness or to change or disguise appearance, or as part of official dress esp. of judge or lawyer or of servant's livery, or (Hist.) as part of fashionable costume; **~s on the green,** (arch.) a free fight; hence (-)~GED² (-gd), ~'LESS, *adjs.* [abbr. of PERIWIG; cf. WINKLE]

wĭg² *v.t.* (**-gg-**). Rebuke sharply, rate; hence (esp.) **~'g**ING¹ (1) (-g-) *n.* [app. f. prec. in sl. or colloq. sense 'rebuke' (19th c.)]

wigeon. See WIDGEON.

wĭ'ggle *v.* & *n.* (colloq. or dial.) **1.** *v.t.* Cause (thing) to move repeatedly from side to side. **2.** *v.i.* Move from side to side; ~ **out of,** extricate oneself from by wiggling. **3.** *n.* Act of wiggling; **get a ~ on,** *(sl.) make haste; hence **wĭ'ggl**Y² *a.*, showing wiggles, having small irregular undulations. [ME, f. MLG & MDu. *wiggelen*, frequent. of **wig-*; cf. WAG¹, WAGGLE, -LE 3]

wĭ'ggle-wăggle *v.* & *n.* (colloq.) = prec. (with emphasis on alternation of movement). [redupl. f. prec. + WAGGLE]

wīght (wīt) *n.* (arch. or joc. or dial.) Person (esp. *luckless*, *wretched*, etc., *wight*). [OE *wiht*, = OS, OHG *wiht*, ON *vættr* fem., Goth. *waihts* fem.; orig. unkn.]

wĭ'gwăg *v.i.* (**-gg-**). (colloq.) Move lightly to and fro; wave flags thus in signalling. [redupl. f. WAG¹]

wĭ'gwăm (*or* -ŏm) *n.* N. Amer. Indian's tent or hut of skins or mats or bark on poles; similar structure for children etc.; *headquarters of political organization. [f. Ojibwa *wigwaum*, Algonquin *wikiwam* their house]

wĭ'lcō *int.* expr. compliance or agreement. [abbr. of *will comply*]

wīld *a.*, *adv.*, & *n.* **1.** *a.* (Of animal or plant) not domesticated or cultivated (esp. of species or varieties allied to others that are not wild; *wild beast*, *plant*; *wild ass*, *duck*, *rose*, *vine*); not civilized, barbarous; (of scenery etc.) having conspicuously desolate appearance; ~ **and woolly,** lacking refinement(s), barbarous. **2.** (Of horse, game-bird, etc.) shy, given to shying, easily startled, hard to get near. **3.** Unrestrained, wayward, disorderly, irregular, out of control, unconventional, (*a wild fellow*; *settled down after a wild youth*; *hair hanging in wild locks*; *living in wild times*; *room is in wild disorder*); (of playing-card) having any rank chosen by player holding it; **run ~,** grow unchecked or undisciplined or untrained. **4.** Tempestuous, violent, (*a wild wind*, *night*, etc.). **5.** Intensely eager, excited, frantic, passionate, distracted, mad, (*is wild with excitement*, *to try it*; *wild delight*, *excitement*, *enthusiasm*, *grief*, *rage*); (of looks, appearance, etc.) indicating distraction; (colloq.) angry, infuriated; ~ **about,** enthusiastically devoted to (person or subject); **drive ~,** madden. **6.** Haphazard, rash, ill-considered, ill-aimed, disturbed by excitement, (*a wild guess*, *shot*, *blow*, *venture*; *wild opinions*, *bowling*). **7.** ~ **boar,** tusked wild pig (*Sus scrofa*) from which domestic pigs are descended; ~ **cat,** medium-sized wild feline, esp. European species (*Felis sylvestris*); **~'cat,** (fig.) hot-tempered or violent person; **~'cat** *a.*, reckless, financially unsound, (of strike) sudden and UNOFFICIAL, (of well) drilled for oil etc. where there is only a possibility of success; **~'fire**

= *Greek* FIRE[1], will-o'-the-wisp, (fig.) thing that spreads rapidly; **~'fowl,** game-bird(s); **~-goo'se chase,** foolish or hopeless or fruitless quest; **~ horse,** horse not domesticated or broken in (*~ horses would not drag* etc. *it from me,* I refuse to disclose the secret); *wild* HYACINTH; **~'life,** wild animals collectively; **~ man,** (1) savage, (2) political extremist; **~** *man of the woods*, orang-utan; *wild* OATS; **~ rice,** tall grass of genus *Zizania* yielding edible grains; **~ silk,** silk from wild silkworms, or imitation of this from short silk fibres; *wild* THYME; **W~ West,** western U.S. in time of lawlessness; **~'wood,** (poet.) uncultivated or unfrequented woodland. **8.** Hence ~'ISH[1] 2 *a.*, ~'LY[2] *adv.*, ~'NESS *n.* **9.** *adv.* In wild manner (*shooting wild*). **10.** *n.* Desert, wild tract; **(out) in the ~s,** (colloq.) far from towns etc. [OE *wilde* = OS, OHG *wildi*, ON *villr*, Goth. *wiltheis*, f. Gmc **wilthijaz*]

wi'ldèbeest (*or* v-) *n.* Gnu. [Afrik. (as prec., BEAST)]

wi'lder *v.t.* (arch. or poet.) Lead astray; bewilder. [perh. based on foll.]

wi'lderness *n.* **1.** Desert, uncultivated and uninhabited tract; **voice (crying) in the ~** etc., unregarded advocate of some reform, w. ref. to Matt. 3:3 etc.; **in the ~,** (of political party) out of office, w. ref. to Num. 14:33 etc. **2.** Part of garden left with uncultivated appearance. **3.** Confused assemblage *of.* [f. OE *wild(d)ēornes*, f. *wil(d)dēor* wild deer; see -NESS]

wi'lding *n.* Plant sown by natural agency, esp. wild crab-apple; fruit of such plant. [f. WILD + -ING[3]]

wile *n.*, & *v.t.* **1.** *n.* (usu. in *pl.*) Trick, cunning procedure, artifice. **2.** *v.t.* Lure or entice *away*, *into*, etc.; = WHILE[1] 2. [ME *wil*, perh. f. Scand. (ON *vél* craft)]

wi'lful, *wi'llful, *a.* (Of action or state) for which compulsion or ignorance or accident cannot be pleaded as excuse, intentional, deliberate, due to perversity or self-will, (*wilful murder, waste, ignorance, disobedience*); obstinate, self-willed, headstrong, refractory; hence ~LY[2] *adv.*, ~NESS *n.* [ME, f. WILL[2] + -FUL]

wi'lga *n.* (Austral.) Small white-flowered drought-resistant tree of genus *Geijera*. [Aboriginal]

wi'liness. See WILY.

will[1] *v.t.* & *aux.* (*pres.* **will,** *or* **'ll** (after pers. pron., or colloq.), exc. 2 *sing.* (arch.) **wilt** *or* **'lt,** *neg.* **will not, 'll not,** (colloq.) **won't** *pr.* wōnt; *past* **would** *pr.* wŏŏd *or* wud, *or* **'d** (after pers. pron., or colloq.), exc. 2 *sing.* (arch.) **wouldst** *pr.* wŏŏdst, *or* **wouldest** *pr.* wŏŏ'dĭst, *or* **'dst,** *neg.* **would not, 'd not,** (colloq.) **wouldn't** *pr.* wŏŏ'dent; no other parts used). **1.** *v.t.* (In all persons, with more or less of orig. sense of volition). Desire (thing; arch.; *what wilt thou?*; *what would they?*); want or desire or choose to (*the haven where I would be*; *come when you will*; *I will* or *would have you know that I am the one who gives the orders here*; **would-be** *a.* & *adv.*, as (unachieved) aspiration or intention: *a would-be gentleman, smart saying*); wish that or *that* (esp. (*I*) *would* expr. unfulfilled wish: *it shall be as you will*; *said it should be as we would*; *would* or *I would I were a bird!*; *would it were otherwise!*; **would God** *that I had died!*, if only God had wished, or perh. ellipt. for 'I would to God'; *I would to heaven I was dead*); consent or be persuaded to (*will* or *would not go any farther*; *wound would not heal*; *this window won't open*; *would you pass the salt?*; *would not do it for £100*); have habitual or inevitable tendency to (*boys will be boys*; *accidents will happen*; *you will have your way*; *you* would *do that!*; *he will* or *would get in my light*); be accustomed or observed from time to time to (*will sit there for hours*; *now and then a blackbird would call*; *will succeed once in ten times*); be likely to turn out to (*this will be Reading, I suppose*; *I don't know who it would be*). **2.** *v. aux.* In 2nd and 3rd person (1st having *shall, should,* exc. colloq.) forming simple future or conditional statement or order or question (*you,* colloq. *I, will hear soon enough*; *the battalion will attack at dawn*; *would have been killed if they had let go*; *will* or *would you, they, be able to hear at such a distance?*, but cf. SHALL 6). **3.** In 1st person (others having *shall, should*) forming future or conditional statement expressing speaker's will or intention (*I will not be caught again*; **~ do,** (colloq.) I will do that; *we would have come if you had given us longer notice*). **4.** (Less often than *shall, should*) in sentences of type 2 changed in reporting to 1st from other person (*you say I will, said I would, never manage it,* reporting *you will never*). **5.** Replacing *shall* or *should* in sentences of type 2 changed in reporting from 1st to other person (*he said he would never manage it,* reporting *I shall never*). **6.** In reporting 1st pers. sentences of type 3 (*you promised you would not be caught again*). **7.** (colloq.) = SHALL 8 (*I would like to disagree*; **I wouldn't know,** (as is to be expected) I do not know). [OE **willan*, *wyllan* = OS *willian*, ON *vilja*, Goth. *wiljan* f. Gmc **wel(l)jan* f. IE **wel-*, **wol-*]

will[2] *n.* **1.** Faculty by which person decides or conceives himself as deciding upon and initiating action (*mind consists of the understanding and the will*); **freedom of the ~, free ~,** power of determining one's choice of action independently of causation or fate; **a ~ of** one's **own,** (euphem.) obstinacy, wilfulness of character. **2.** **~(-power)**, control exercised by deliberate purpose over impulse, self-control, (*has a strong, weak,* etc., *will*; *overcame her shyness by will-power*). **3.** Deliberate or fixed desire or intention (*the patient's will to live is the surgeon's best ally*; *did it against my will*); **free ~,** inclination to act without suggestion from others (*did it of my own free will*); **where there's a ~ there's a way,** determination will overcome any obstacle. **4.** Energy of intention, power of effecting one's intentions or dominating other persons; *do* thing **with a ~,** energetically or resolutely. **5.** (arch.) Contents of the will, what is desired or ordained by person, (*thy will be done*); **what is your ~?,** what do you wish done?; **have** one's **~,** get thing desired. **6.** Arbitrary discretion; **at ~,** whenever one pleases; *tenant* **at ~,** who can be turned out without notice. **7.** Disposition towards others, wishing of good or ill, (GOOD or ILL *will*; cf. GOODWILL); **with the best ~ in the world,** however good one's intentions. **8.** Directions (usu. written) in legal form for disposition to be made of person's property after his death (often *last will and testament*; *make* one's *will*). **9.** Hence (-)~ED[2] (-ld), ~-LESS, *adjs.* [OE *willa,* = OS *willio*, OHG *will(i)o*, ON *vili*, Goth. *wilja* f. Gmc **wiljon*, **weljon* (**wel-* be pleasing; cf. prec.)]

will[3] *v.t.* **1.** Have as object of one's will, intend unconditionally, (*God wills, willeth, willed, that man should be happy*; *can we will what we are told to will?*; *he who wills success is half-way to it*). **2.** (abs.) Exercise will-power (*has no power to will*; *willing and wishing are not the same*). **3.** Instigate or impel or compel by exercise of will-power (*you can will yourself into contentment*; *willed the genie into his presence*). **4.** Bequeath by will (*shall will my money to a hospital*). [OE *willian* (as prec.)]

wi'llèt *n.* (*pl.* same). Large N. Amer. shore-bird like snipe. [f. *pill-will-willet*, imit. of its cry]

***wi'llful.** See WILFUL.

wĭ'llies (-iz) *n. pl.* (sl.) Nervous feeling of discomfort or fear (*gives me the willies*). [19th c.; orig. unkn.]

wĭ'lling¹ *n.* In vbl senses; cheerful intention (*show willing*). [f. WILL¹,³ + -ING¹]

wĭ'lling² *a.* Disposed to consent or undertake (*to* do, or abs.; *do not spur a willing horse*; *am willing to admit he is right*); of, given etc. by, willing person (*willing hands, help*, etc.); hence **~LY**² *adv.*, **~NESS** *n.* [ME, f. OE **willende* (as WILL¹, -ING²)]

will-o'-the-wĭ'sp (-dh-) *n.* **1.** Phosphorescent light on marshy ground perh. due to combustion of methane. **2.** Person of uncertain whereabouts or appearances. **3.** Delusive hope or plan. [orig. *Will with the wisp*; *wisp* = handful of (lighted) hay etc.]

wĭ'llow (-ō) *n.* **1.** Tree or shrub of genus *Salix*, with pliant branches, growing usu. near water in temperate climates, many kinds of which yield osiers or timber used for cricket bats and other purposes; WEAR¹ *the willow*; **~-pattern,** conventional design of Chinese type done in blue on white china etc., introduced in England 1780. **2.** Cricket-bat. **3.** **~-herb,** plant of genus *Epilobium* etc., esp. one with leaves like willow and pale purple flowers; **~-warbler,** bird of genus *Phylloscopus*. [OE *welig*, = OS *wilgia*, MLG *wilge*]

wĭ'llowy̆ (-ōĭ) *a.* Abounding in willows; bordered by willows; lithe and slender. [f. prec. + -Y²]

willy̆-nĭ'lly̆ *adv.* & *a.* (Existing or occurring) whether one likes it or not. [= *will I, nill I* (WILL¹, NILL)]

wĭ'lly̆-willy̆ *n.* (Austral.) Cyclone or dust-storm. [Aboriginal]

wilt¹. See WILL¹.

wilt² *v.* & *n.* **1.** *v.i.* (Of plant, leaf, flower) wither; lose vigour, droop. **2.** *v.t.* Cause to wilt. **3.** *n.* Disease of plants that causes wilting. [orig. dial., perh. alt. f. *wilk, welk*, of LDu. orig.]

Wĭ'lton *n.* Kind of carpet like Brussels, with loops cut into thick pile, first made at Wilton. [~ in Wiltshire]

Wilts. *abbr.* Wiltshire.

wī'l|y̆ *a.* Full of wiles, crafty, cunning; hence **~ĭLY**² *adv.*, **~ĭNESS** *n.* [ME, f. WILE + -Y²]

wĭ'mple *n.* & *v.* **1.** *n.* Covering of linen or silk worn by nuns and formerly by other women, arranged in folds about head, cheeks, chin, and neck. **2.** *v.t.* Put wimple on, veil; arrange in folds. **3.** *v.i.* Fall in folds. [OE *wimpel*, = OS *wimpal*, OHG *winfila*, ON *vimpill*]

Wĭ'mpy̆ *n.* (colloq.) Hamburger served in plain bun. [P]

Wĭ'mshûrst (-z-h-) *n.* **~ machine,** device for generating electric charge by turning glass discs in opposite directions. [f. J.~, Engl. engineer d. 1903]

wĭn *v.* (**-nn-; won** *pr.* wŭn) & *n.* **1.** *v.t.* Secure as result of fighting, competition, betting etc., or effort, (*win victory, fortress, prize, honour, fame, fortune, wife*, person's *confidence*; *won £5 from me at cards*); get (ore etc.) from mine; (sl.) steal; **~** one's **spurs,** be knighted, (fig.) get recognition as expert at something; **~** one's **way,** progress by struggle etc. **2.** Be victorious in (*win battle, game, bet, race*); **~ the day** or (arch.) **field,** be victorious in battle (lit. or fig.); *win the* TOSS. **3.** *v.i.* Win race, contest, money, etc., (*win by a* HEAD¹, *in a* CANTER, HAND¹*s down, by two* etc. *lengths, easily*, etc.; *usually wins at cards*; *let those laugh who win*); **you can't ~ (them all),** (colloq.) there is no way of achieving (universal) success. **4.** *v.t.* (arch.) Make one's way to (*win the shore, summit*, etc.). **5.** *v.i.* Make one's way, or (w. compl.) become by successful effort, (*win home*; *win through*, (colloq.) *out, through all difficulties*; *win free, clear*, etc.). **6.** *v.t.* Persuade, induce *to* do, gain *over* (*soon won his audience over*). **7.** *v.i.* (arch.) Exercise increasing attraction *upon* (*a theory that wins upon one by degrees*). **8.** *n.* A success or victory in a game (*has had three wins and no defeats*). [OE *winnan*, = OS, OHG, Goth. *winnan*, ON *vinna*]

wince¹ *v.i.*, & *n.* **1.** *v.i.* Show bodily or mental pain or distress by slight start or loss of composure, flinch, (*under* or *at*). **2.** *n.* Act of wincing. [ME, f. AF **wencir* = OF *guenchir* turn aside, f. WG **wenkjan*; cf. WINCH, WINK]

‖**wĭ'nce**² *n.* Roller for moving textile fabric through dyeing-vat. [var. of WINCH]

wĭ'ncey *n.* Strong material of wool and cotton or wool and linen used for shirts etc.; hence ‖**~E'TTE** (2) (-ĭĕ'-)*n.*, lightweight napped flannelette formerly used for night-clothes etc. [orig. Sc.; app. f. *woolsey* in LINSEY-WOOLSEY]

winch *n.*, & *v.t.* **1.** *n.* Crank of wheel or axle; ‖reel of fishing-rod; hoisting-machine, windlass; = WINCE². **2.** *v.t.* Lift with winch. [OE *wince* f. Gmc **winkjōn* (**wenk*; cf. WINCE¹)]

Wĭ'nchėster *n.* **~ (quart),** (bottle holding) standard quart as orig. deposited at Winchester, about half a gallon. [~ in Hampshire]

wind¹ (poet. also wī-) *n.* **1.** Air in more or less rapid natural motion, breeze or gale, (*hot, cold, whistling, variable*, etc., *wind*); **north** etc. **~,** wind blowing from the north etc.; **fair ~** (helping ship's course); CONTRARY *wind*; ILL *wind*; **before the ~,** helped by its force; **between ~ and water,** at a vulnerable point; **close to the ~,** (sailing) as nearly against it as is consistent with using its force, (fig.) close to indecency or dishonesty; **down the ~,** in the direction in which it is blowing (WHISTLE *down the wind*; DOWNWIND); **how the ~ blows** or **lies,** (fig.) what developments are likely, what is the state of opinion; **in the ~,** (fig.) happening or about to happen; **like the ~,** swiftly; **near the ~,** = *close to the wind*; **off the ~,** (Naut.) with the wind on the quarter; **on a ~,** (Naut.) against a wind on either bow; **on the ~,** (of sound or scent) carried by the wind; RAISE *the wind*; **to the (four) ~s,** in all directions, into state of abandonment or neglect; *in the teeth of the wind* (see TOOTH); UPWIND; WHIRL*wind*; **~ and weather,** exposure to influence of wind, rain, etc.; **~(s) of change,** force or tendency for reform; **in the ~'s eye,** directly against it; **~ is in that quarter,** (fig.) things are in that (particular) state; **take the ~ out of** person's **sails,** frustrate him by anticipating his arguments, etc. **2.** Windward position or *weather* GAUGE¹ (*take* or *get the wind of*). **3.** Mere empty words, meaningless rhetoric. **4.** Artificially produced air-current (esp. for sounding an organ or other wind instrument), air stored for use or used as current, (collect.) part of orchestra or band consisting of wind instruments, (*organ fails when the wind is exhausted*; *was knocked down by the wind of the missile*; *the strings were drowned by the wind, and the* WOOD*-wind by the brass*). **5.** Smell carried by the wind, indication of thing's whereabouts or existence, commencing publicity; **get ~ of,** smell out, begin to suspect, hear rumour of; **take** or **get ~,** be rumoured, become known. **6.** Gas generated in bowels etc. by indigestion, flatulence; **break ~,** release it by anus; **get** or **have the ~ up,** (sl.) become or be frightened; **put the ~ up,** (sl.) frighten. **7.** Breath as needed in exertion or speech, power of breathing without difficulty while running or making similar continuous effort, spot below centre of chest where blow temporarily paralyses breathing, (*have lost, let me recover* or *get, my wind; has a good, bad,* LONG[1], SHORT, *wind*); **broken ~,** condition of being BROKEN-winded; **second ~,** recovery of wind in course of exercise after initial breathlessness, (fig.) renewed energy for effort; **sound in ~ and limb,** in full physical health; **have** one's **~ taken,** be paralysed by blow in the wind. **8. ~'bag,** wordy orator; **~ band,** wind instruments as band or part of orchestra; **~'bound,** unable to sail because of contrary winds; **~-break,** row of trees, fence, shrubs, etc., or temporary wall, serving to break force of wind; ***~'breaker,** ||**~-cheater,** jacket for protecting person from cold wind; **~-chest,** (Mus.) box for compressed air supplied to pipes or reeds in organ; **~-cone,** = *wind-sock*; **~-egg,** soft-shelled unfertilized or imperfect egg incapable of producing chicken; **~'fall,** fruit blown down, (fig.) unexpected good fortune, esp. legacy; **~-flower,** anemone; **~-force** (esp. stated on Beaufort etc. scale); **~-gall,** (1) soft tumour on horse's fetlock-joint, (2) coloured sun-halo; **~-gauge,** (1) anemometer, (2, Mus.) instrument showing amount of wind in organ, (3) apparatus attached to sights enabling allowance to be made for wind in shooting; ||**~'hover,** kestrel; **~ instrument,** musical instrument in which sound is produced by current of air, e.g. organ, & esp. by breath, e.g. flute, trumpet; **~-jammer,** merchant sailing-ship; **~ machine** (Theatr., for producing blast of air or sound of wind); **~'pipe,** breathing-tube from throat to lungs, trachea; **~-rose,** diagram of relative frequency of wind directions at a place; **~-row,** line of raked hay, corn-sheaves, peats, etc., made to allow drying by wind; **~-sail,** canvas funnel conveying air to lower parts of ship; ||**~'screen,** ***~'shield,** (of glass in front of motor-vehicle driver); **~-sleeve, ~-sock,** canvas cylinder or cone flying from mast-head to show direction of wind at airfield etc.; **~-sucker, -sucking,** (horse with) bad habit of noisily drawing in and swallowing breath; **~-swept,** exposed to (high) winds; **~-tunnel,** tunnel-like apparatus for producing air-stream of known velocity past model of aircraft etc. to investigate flow or effect of wind pressure on structure. **9.** Hence **~'**LESS *a.* [OE, = OS *wind*, OHG *wint*, ON *vindr*, Goth. *winds* f. Gmc **windaz* f. IE **went-* part.]

wīnd[2] (in sense 1 wī-) *v.t.* (in sense 1 also **wound**). **1.** Sound (horn, bugle, blast, call) by blowing. **2.** Detect presence of by scent (*hounds, deer, wind the fox, stalkers*). **3.** Make breathe quick and deep by exercise, exhaust wind of by exertion or blow, renew wind of by rest, (*give horse a gallop to wind him; am quite winded by the climb; rested to wind the horses*). [ME, f. prec.]

wind[3] *v.* (**wound**) & *n.* **1.** *v.i.* Go in circular, spiral, curved, or crooked course, meander, (*path, river, winds; herd wind slowly o'er the lea; creeper winds round pole*); **~ing staircase** (spiral). **2.** *v.t.* Make one's or its *way* etc. circuitously, insinuate one*self into*, (*brook winds its way; wound himself* or *his way into my affections*). **3.** *v.t.* & *i.* Coil, wrap closely, (*wind cotton on reel, wool into ball,* etc.); provide (reel etc.) with coiled cotton etc.; coil (wool) into ball from skein; **~ off** (*adv.* or *prep.*), unwind; *wind round* one's FINGER. **4.** *v.t.* Surround (as) with coil, embrace, (*wound the blanket round him, her arms round the child, the child in her arms*); coil string round (TOP[3]). **5.** Hoist or draw by use of windlass etc. (*wind ship out of harbour, men* or *ore up from mine, window of vehicle down*); wind up (clock etc.). **6. ~ down,** unwind (lit. or fig.); **~ up,** coil the whole of (*wind up piece of string*), tighten coiling or coiled spring or fig. tension or intensity or efficiency of (*wind up* (*spring* or *weights of*) *clock* etc.; *is winding himself up for an effort to do it; person is wound up to fury; expectation was wound up to a high pitch*), bring to a conclusion, conclude, (*wound up his speech,* or *wound up, by declaring; shot his wife and child and wound up by stabbing himself*), arrange affairs of and dissolve (company), (of company) cease business and go into liquidation, (colloq.) arrive finally (*he'll wind up in prison*); **~-up** *n.*, conclusion, finish. **7.** Hence **~'**ER[1] (1, 2) *n.* **8.** *n.* Bend or turn in course; single turn in winding clock, string, etc. [OE *windan,* = OS *windan*, OHG *wintan*, ON *vinda*, Goth. *-windan* f. Gmc **windan* rel. to WANDER, WEND[1]]

wĭ'ndage *n.* Difference between projectile's and gun-bore's diameter allowing escape of gas; (allowance for) influence of wind in deflecting missile; friction of air against moving part of machine. [f. WIND[1] + -AGE]

wī'ndĭng *n.* In vbl senses; (Electr.) coils of wire round armature etc.; **~-engine** (for hoisting); **~-sheet** (in which corpse is wrapped for burial). [OE *windung* (as WIND[3], -ING[1])]

wĭ'ndlass *n.*, & *v.t.* **1.** *n.* Machine for hauling or hoisting on wheel-and-axle principle, with horizontal axle. **2.** *v.t.* Hoist or haul with windlass. [alt. (perh. by assoc. w. dial. *windle* to wind) f. obs. *windas* f. AF, = OF *guindas* f. ON *vindáss* (*vinda* WIND[3], *áss* pole)]

||**wĭ'ndlestraw** (-dels-) *n.* Old dry stalk of grass. [OE *windelstrēaw* grass for plaiting (*windel* basket f. as WIND[3], -LE 1; *strēaw* STRAW[1])]

wĭ'ndmĭll (*or* -nm-) *n.* Mill worked by action of wind on sails (**fight** or **tilt at ~s,** battle with imaginary enemy or grievance, w. ref. to Don Quixote; **throw** one's **cap over the ~,** act recklessly or unconventionally); toy of stick with revolving light card etc. [ME, f. WIND[1] + MILL[1]]

wĭ'ndow (-ō) *n.* **1.** Opening in wall or roof of building, ship, vehicle, etc., usu. filled with glass in fixed or sliding or hinged frames to admit light and often air to room etc. and allow occupants to look out or objects within to be seen; (fig.) opportunity to observe; space for display behind window of shop etc. (**have all** one's **goods in the** (**front** or **shop-**)**~,** be superficial); aperture in wall for issue of tickets etc.; **blank, blind, false, ~,** moulding or recess as for window but without aperture; FRENCH *window*; **out of the ~,** (colloq.) no longer taken into account. **2.** Opening or transparent part in envelope to show address written on letter; range of electromagnetic spectrum for which a medium is transparent; interval during which positions of planets etc. allow specified journey by spacecraft; ||strips of metal foil in air to obstruct radar detection. **3. ~-box,** box on outside window-sill in which flowers are grown; **~-dressing,** art of arranging goods attractively in shop-window, (fig.) adroit presentation of statistics etc.; **~ envelope** (with opening or transparent part allowing address to show); **~-ledge,** sill of window; **~-seat,** usu. upholstered seat against window in room; **~-shopping,** looking (for pleasure or for comparison of prices etc.) at the goods displayed in the shop-windows without buying; ||**~-tax,** (Hist.) tax on any windows or window-like openings (1695–1851). **4.** Hence (-)**~**ED[2] (-ōd), **~**LESS, *adjs.* [ME, f. ON *vindauga* (as WIND[1], EYE[1])]

Wĭ'ndsor (-nz-) *n.* **House of ~,** name of British Royal Family since 1917; **~ chair** (all of wood with curved frame and upright rods as support for back); **~ soap** (brown or white scented kind); ||**~ uniform,** blue coat with red collar and cuffs sometimes worn at Windsor by the royal household and guests having royal permission. [~ in Berkshire, site of royal residence at ~ Castle]

wi'ndward *a.* & *n.* (Region) lying in the direction from which the wind blows, exposed to the wind, (*look to windward*; *the windward side*); **anchor to ~**, safety precaution; **get to ~ of,** avoid smell of, (fig.) gain advantage over. [f. WIND¹ + -WARD]

wi'nd|y̆ *a.* Wind-swept (*windy hill-top, plain, situation*); in which wind is high (*windy night, weather, crossing*); wordy, verbose, empty, (*windy eloquence, logic, speaker*); generating or characterized by flatulence; (arch.) windward (**on the ~y side of,** safely away from); (sl.) nervous, frightened; hence **~ILY²** *adv.*, **~INESS** *n.* [OE *windig* (as WIND¹, -Y²)]

wine *n.* & *v.* **1.** *n.* Fermented grape-juice as alcoholic drink (DRY¹ and *sweet*, STILL¹ and *sparkling*, WHITE¹ and RED, *wine*); SPIRIT¹(*s*) *of wine*; *good wine needs no* BUSH¹; **new ~ in old bottles,** new principle too powerful to be restrained by ancient forms; **take ~ with,** pledge and be pledged by at table; **in ~,** exhilarated or drunk with wine. **2.** Fermented drink resembling wine made from specified fruit etc. (*cowslip, currant, ginger, palm, wine*). **3.** Dark red colour of red wine. **4. ~-apple,** large red apple with winy flavour; **~'berry,** = MAKO²; **~'bibber,** tippler, drunkard, [f. *bib* to tipple]; **~-biscuit** (served with or flavoured with wine); **~'bottle,** glass bottle for wine; *wine*-CELLAR; **~-coloured,** having colour of wine (see sense 3); **~-cooler,** vessel in which winebottles are cooled with ice; **~'fat,** (arch.) = *winepress*; **~'glass,** any glass for drinking wine from; **~'glass(ful),** this as measure of liquid, esp. of size used for sherry, = four tablespoons; **~-grower,** cultivator of grapes for wine; so **~-growing** *n.*; **~-palm,** kind from which palm wine is made, e.g. coquito; **~'press** (in which grapes are squeezed); **~'sap,** large red American winter apple; **~'skin,** whole skin of goat etc. sewn up and used to hold wine; **~-stone,** = TARTAR¹ 1; **~-tasting,** judging quality of wine by tasting it; **~-vault,** (1) cellar in which wine is kept, (2) bar etc. where wine is retailed. **5.** Hence **~'LESS** (-nl-), **wi'ny²**, *adjs.* **6.** *v.i.* Drink wine. **7.** *v.t.* Entertain to wine; **~ and dine,** entertain to dinner with wine. [OE *wīn*, = OS, OHG *wīn*, ON *vín*, Goth. *wein* f. Gmc **wīnam* f. L *vinum*]

wi'nery̆ *n.* Establishment for making wine. [f. prec. + -ERY]

wĭng *n.* & *v.* **1.** *n.* One of the limbs or organs by which the flight of a bird, bat, insect, angel, etc., is effected; part in non-flying bird or insect corresponding to this; winglike supporting part of aircraft; **clip** person's **~s,** limit his movements or ambitions or expenditure; *come* **on the ~s of the wind,** swiftly; **lend ~s to,** accelerate; **on the ~,** flying; SINGE one's *wings*; **spread** or **stretch** one's **~s,** (fig.) develop one's full powers; **take under** one's **~,** treat as protégé; **his ~s are sprouting** etc., his virtues are too great for a being below the degree of an angel; **take ~,** fly away; *money* **takes to itself ~s,** disappears. **2.** More or less separate projecting part of something, esp. of building or battle array (*north wing was added in 17th century*; *cavalry were massed on left wing*); (in *pl.*) sides of theatre stage, pieces of side scenery (**waiting in the ~s,** (fig.) holding oneself in readiness); ||mudguard of motor vehicle; extreme section of political party. **3.** (Footb., Hockey, etc.) Forward etc. whose place is at either end of the line; side part of playing-area. **4.** Air-force unit of several ||squadrons or *groups. **5.** (in *pl.*) Pilot's badge in R.A.F. etc. **6.** (Anat. & Bot.) Lateral part or projection of organ or structure. **7. ~-beat,** one complete set of motions with wing in flying; **~-case,** horny cover, a modified fore-wing, protecting some insects' flying wing; **~-chair** (with side-pieces projecting forwards at top of high back); **~-collar,** man's high stiff collar with upper corners turned down; ||**~ commander,** officer of Royal Air Force commanding wing (sense 4); *wing*-COVERT²; **~-footed,** (poet.) swift; ||**~-game,** game-birds; **~-nut** (with projections for thumb and fingers to turn it on screw); **~-span, ~-spread,** measurement across wings when extended, or between tips of aircraft's wings; **~-stroke,** = *wing-beat*; **~-tip,** outer end of wing of bird, aircraft, etc. **8.** Hence **-~ED²** (-ngd), **~'LESS,** *adjs.*, **~'LET** *n.* **9.** *v.t.* Equip with wings, enable to fly or mount, send in flight, lend speed to, (*wing arrow with eagle's feathers*, or *at the mark*; *vengeance winged the shaft*; *ambition wings his spirit*; *fear winged his steps*); **~ed god,** Mercury; **~ed horse,** Pegasus, poetry; **W~ed Victory,** statue of Greek goddess of victory with wings; **~ed words** (going swiftly like arrows to mark, significant). **10.** Wound (bird) in wing or (person) in arm. **11.** *v.i.* & *t.* Travel or traverse on wings (*bird wings its way, wings to its mate, wings the air*). [ME pl. *wenge, -en, -es* f. ON *vængir*, pl. of *vængr*]

***wi'ngding** *n.* (sl.) Wild party; drug addict's real or feigned seizure. [20th c.; orig. unkn,]

wi'nger *n.* Wing forward etc. (see WING 3); LEFT¹, RIGHT¹, *-winger*. [f. WING + -ER¹]

wink *v.* & *n.* **1.** *v.i.* Close and open eye(s), blink, (of eye) close and open; **as easy as ~'ing,** very easy; **like ~'ing,** (sl.) very quickly or vigorously. **2.** Momentarily close one eye to awaken attention of or convey private intimation to (or *at*) person. **3.** (Of light, star, etc.) twinkle, shine intermittently. **4. ~ at,** (fig.) shut one's eyes to, purposely avoid seeing, pretend not to notice, connive at, (abuse, transgression, etc.). **5.** *v.t.* Close and open (eye or eyes); give (signal etc.) by flashing lights. **6.** *n.* Act of winking, esp. as signal etc. (TIP² person *the wink*; **in a ~,** very quickly); short sleep (**not a ~,** no sleep at all; FORTY *winks*). [OE *wincian*, = OS *wincon*, OHG *winchan* stagger, nod, f. Gmc **wink-* etc.; cf. WINCE¹, WINCH]

wi'nker *n.* In vbl senses; (usu. in *pl.*) horse's blinker; motor vehicle's flashing light to indicate intended change of direction of travel. [f. prec. + -ER¹]

wi'nkle *n.*, & *v.t.* **1.** *n.* Edible gastropod of genus *Littorina*, periwinkle; **~-picker,** (sl.) long pointed shoe. **2.** *v.t.* **~ out,** extract or eject (as a winkle from its shell with a pin). [abbr. of PERIWINKLE²; cf. WIG¹]

wi'nner *n.* In vbl senses; successful thing (*her new book is a winner*). [ME, f. WIN + -ER¹]

wi'nnĭng¹ *n.* In vbl senses; (in *pl.*) money won in betting etc.; **~-post** (marking end of race). [ME, f. WIN + -ING¹]

wi'nnĭng² *a.* In vbl senses; persuasive, attractive, (*a winning smile*); that brings victory or advantage (*winning hit*, HAZARD, *card*, etc.); hence **~LY²** *adv.* [f. WIN + -ING²]

wi'nnow (-ō) *v.t.* Blow (grain) free of chaff etc. in wind or air-current, blow (chaff etc.) *away* or *out* or *from*; sift, separate, clear of refuse or inferior specimens or falsehood, clear (refuse etc.) *out* or *away*, examine, sort, weed out; (poet.) fan (air with wings), flap (wings), stir (hair etc.); hence **~ER¹** (1, 2) *n.* [OE *windwian* (as WIND¹)]

wi'nō *n.* (*pl.* **~s**). (sl.) Alcoholic. [f. WINE + -O]

wi'nsome *a.* (Of person or his or her appearance,

manner, smile, etc.) charming, attractive, bright; hence ~LY² (-mlĭ) *adv.*, ~NESS (-mn-) *n.* [OE *wynsum* (*wyn* joy; see -SOME¹)]

wĭ'nter *n.*, *a.*, & *v.* **1.** Coldest season of the year, in N. hemisphere Dec.–Feb. (Astron., from winter solstice to vernal equinox). **2.** (poet. or rhet., usu. in *pl.* with number etc.) Year of life or age (*a man of fifty winters*). **3.** *a.* Characteristic of or used etc. in or lasting for the winter; (of fruit) ripening late or keeping until or during winter; (of wheat or other crop) sown in autumn and reaped in spring; *winter* ACONITE; ~ **cress,** cress of genus *Barbarea* formerly cultivated for winter salad; **~-fallow,** (land) lying fallow during winter; ~ **garden,** garden or conservatory of plants flourishing in winter; **~-green,** plant (esp. of genus *Pyrola* or *Gaultheria*) remaining green through winter; *winter* JASMINE; *Winter* OLYMPICS; ~ **quarters** (esp. to which troops retire for winter); ~ **sleep,** hibernation; *winter* SOLSTICE; ~ **sports,** open-air sports on snow or ice esp. in winter (e.g. skiing); **~-tide** (poet.), **~-time,** season of winter; **~-weight,** (of clothes) suitable in weight for use in winter. **4.** Hence ~LESS, ~LY¹, *adjs.* **5.** *v.i.* Pass the winter (*at* or *in* place). **6.** *v.t.* Keep or feed (plants, cattle) during winter. [OE, = OS, OHG *wintar*, ON *vetr*, Goth. *wintrus* f. Gmc **wentrus*, prob. rel. to WET]

wĭ'nteriz|e, -is|e (-iz), *v.t.* Adapt for operation, or for use, in cold weather. [f. prec. + -IZE]

wĭ'ntr|ȳ *a.* Having the temperature, storminess, or appearance appropriate to winter, cold, windy, cheerless, (*wintry weather, day, sun, scene*); (of smile, greeting, etc.) lacking warmth or interest or vivacity; hence ~ĬNESS *n.* [OE *wintrig*, or f. WINTER + -Y²]

wī'nȳ. See WINE.

wipe *v.t.*, & *n.* **1.** *v.t.* Clean or dry surface of by rubbing with cloth, paper, hand, etc., (*wipe table, dish, face, hands*, etc.); ~ one's **eyes,** dry tears, cease weeping; ~ person's **eye,** (sl.) get advantage by anticipating him; ~ **the floor with,** (sl.) inflict humiliating defeat on; ~ **out** (bath or other hollow utensil); *wipe the* SLATE¹ *clean.* **2.** Get rid of, clear *away* or *off* (*the* MAP¹) or *up*, take *up*, wash *out*, by wiping (*wipe your tears* (*away*)); ~ **off,** annul (debt etc.); ~ **out,** remove (disgrace) by atonement, (insult etc.) esp. by vengeance, utterly destroy, annihilate, (*the whole army was wiped out*); *~-out* n., (1) obliteration of one radio signal by another, (2) fall from surf-board. **3.** Spread (substance) over surface in thin layer. **4.** *n.* Act of wiping (*give this plate a wipe*); (sl.) sweeping blow; (sl.) handkerchief. [OE *wīpian*; cf. OHG *wīfan* wind round, Goth. *weipan* crown; rel. to WHIP]

wī'per *n.* In vbl senses; cam or tappet; (Electr.) moving contact; rubber strip mechanically moved to and fro across windscreen to remove rain etc. [f. prec. + -ER¹]

W.I.P.O. *abbr.* World Intellectual Property Organization.

wire *n.* & *v.* **1.** *n.* (Piece of) metal drawn out into form of thread or slender flexible rod; quantity of this as barrier, framework, etc.; **pull (the) ~s,** operate puppets etc., (fig.) exert hidden influence. **2.** Piece of wire used to carry electric current esp. of telegraph or telephone; **by ~,** by telegraph; **private ~** (reserved for person's exclusive use); **get** one's **~s crossed,** (fig.) become confused and misunderstand. **3.** (colloq.) Telegram or cablegram (*sent me a wire*). **4.** **~-bird,** St. Helena plover living on wire-grass; **~-brush** (for cleaning rusty metal, or making hissing sound with cymbal etc.); **~-cloth** (woven from wire); **~-cutter,** tool for cutting wire; **~'draw,** draw (metal) out into wire, elongate, protract unduly, (fig., esp. in *p.p.*) refine or apply or press (argument, point, etc.) with idle or excessive subtlety; **~-edge,** turned-back edge formed when blade is badly sharpened; ~ **gauge,** (1) gauge for measuring diameter of wire etc., (2) standard series of sizes in which wire etc. is made; **~gauze** (woven from wire); **~-grass** (with wiry stems); **~-gun** (made by coiling flat wire round tube); **~-haired,** (esp. of dog) with stiff or wiry hair; **~'man,** installer or repairer of electric wires; ~ **mattress,** wires stretched in frame as support for canvas etc. mattress; ~ **netting** (of wire twisted into meshes); **~'puller,** politician etc. who pulls wires; ~ **rope** (made by twisting wires together as strands); **~'scape,** obtrusive electric wires spoiling natural scenery; **~-tapping,** eavesdropping on telephone conversations by taking current from wires; **~-walker,** acrobat performing feats on wire rope; ~ **wheel,** vehicle-wheel with spokes of wire; ~ **wool,** mass of fine wire used esp. for cleaning kitchen utensils; **~-worm,** destructive larva of click beetle; **~-wove,** (of paper) = WOVE. **5.** *v.t.* Provide, fasten, strengthen, etc., with wire(s); snare (bird, rabbit, etc.) with wire; (Electr.) install circuits for lighting in (a house etc.); (Croquet, usu. in *pass.*) obstruct (ball, shot, player) by hoop. **6.** *v.t.* & *i.* (colloq.) Telegraph (*wire me the result*; *wired to him*; *was wired for*). [OE *wīr*, = MLG *wīre*, ON **vírr*, prob. cogn. w. WITHE]

wīr'eless (wīr'l-) *a.*, *n.*, & *v.* **1.** *a.* Without wire(s) (~ **telegraphy,** radio, transmission of signals by electromagnetic waves); ||of or pertaining to radio (~ **set,** radio receiver). **2.** *n.* Wireless telegraphy or telegram; ||radio receiving set or broadcast or programme. **3.** *v.i.* Send radio message. **4.** *v.t.* Send (message), inform (person), by radio. [f. prec. + -LESS]

wīr'ing *n.* In vbl senses; electrical circuit(s) esp. in a building. [f. WIRE + -ING¹]

wīr'|ȳ *a.* Made of wire; tough and flexible as wire, (of person) sinewy, untiring, whence ~ĬLY² *adv.*, ~ĬNESS *n.* [f. WIRE + -Y²]

wis *v.i. pres.* (pseudo-arch., parenth.) *I, you*, etc., know well. [orig. *I wis* = obs. *iwis* 'certainly' f. OE *gewis* (Y-, WIT¹), erron. taken as 'I know' and as pres. tense of *wist* (WIT¹)]

Wis. *abbr.* Wisconsin.

Wisd. *abbr.* Wisdom of Solomon (Apocrypha).

wĭ'sdom (-z-) *n.* Being wise; (possession of) experience and knowledge together with the power of applying them critically or practically; sagacity, prudence, common sense; wise sayings (**W~ of Solomon, W~ of Jesus the Son of Sirach** = Ecclesiasticus, books of Apocrypha); **W~ literature,** (1) books of philosophical reflections on life written in ancient Babylonia or Egypt, (2) biblical books of Job, Proverbs, Ecclesiastes, Wisdom of Solomon, Ecclesiasticus, Epistle of James; ~ **tooth,** hindmost molar usu. cut at about 20 years of age (*cut* one's ~ *teeth*, gain discretion). [OE *wīsdōm* = OS *wīsdōm*, OHG *wīstuom*, ON *vísdómr* (as WISE¹; see -DOM)]

wise¹ (-z) *a.* & *v.* **1.** *a.* (Of person) having, (of action, course of action, speech, opinion, etc.) dictated by or in harmony with or showing, experience and knowledge judiciously applied; sagacious, prudent, sensible, discreet; having knowledge; ~ **after the event,** (of person) who explains but has failed to foresee; *came away* **none the** or **not much** or **no ~r** or **as ~ as he went,** knowing no more than before; **without anyone's being the ~r,** undetected. **2.** (arch.) Having occult power or knowledge of mysterious things; ~ **man,** wizard, esp. one of the Magi;

||~ **woman,** (1) witch, fortune-teller, (2) midwife. **3.** Suggestive of wisdom, oracular, (*with a wise shake of the head*); **~'crack** *n.*, & *v.i.*, (colloq.) (make) smart pithy remark or witticism; **~ guy,** (colloq.) know-all; **~ saw,** proverbial saying. **4.** *(sl.) **Be** or **get ~ to,** be or become aware of; **put** person **~ (to)**, inform him (of), enlighten him (concerning). **5.** Hence ~'LY² (-zlĭ) *adv.* **6.** *v.t.* & *i.* ***~ up,** (sl.) = *put* or *get wise*. [OE *wis*, = OS, OHG *wis(i)*, ON *víss*, Goth. *-weis* f. Gmc **wisaz* (**wittos* f. IE **weid-*, cogn. w. WIT¹)]

wise² (-z) *n.* (arch.) Way, manner, guise, (*in solemn* etc. *wise*; esp. *in some, no, any, wise*; *on this wise*). [OE *wise* = OS, OHG *wisa*, ON *vísa* f. Gmc **wisōn*, **wisō* f. **wit-* WIT¹]

-wise (-z) *suf.* forming *adjs.* & *advs.* of manner (*clockwise, crosswise, lengthwise, nowise*) or respect (*moneywise*); cf. -WAYS. [f. as prec.]

wī'seăcre (-zāker) *n.* One who pretends to, or affects an air of, wisdom. [f. MDu. *wijsseggher* soothsayer, prob. f. OHG *wissago, wizago*, w. assim. to WISE¹, SAY²*er*, ACRE]

wi'sent (wē'z-) *n.* European bison (*Bison bonasus*). [G; cf. BISON]

wĭsh *v.* & *n.* **1.** *v.t.* Have as a desire or aspiration (*that*-clause with *that* usu. omitted, or obj. and compl.: *wish* (*to God that*) *I had never been born, were* or *was a bird, may live to see it*; *wish you would be quiet*; *could not wish it better*; *wish* one*self dead, home*, etc.; *wish* person *happy, miles away*, etc.); *it is* **to be ~ed** *that*, desirable; ***I ~* it may not** *prove true*, fear it will. **2.** Want with the kind of desire that tends to affect result (*to* do, person or thing *to* do, person or thing and p.p., or w. simple obj. esp. pron.: *I wish to go, you to do it, it finished* or *to be finished*; *what do you wish?*; *they say they wish peace, an interview*). **3.** Have desire that succeeding *well* or *ill* may befall or happen *to* (*wishes me well, well to all men, nobody ill*), whence (-)~'ER¹ *n.* **4.** Say one hopes for (joy, luck, pleasant journey, sorrow, etc.) to happen to person (*I wish you joy, wish success to each and all*); ~ person **'good day'** etc., greet him thus; ~ person **joy of,** (iron.) hope he will enjoy. **5.** (colloq.) Foist (*up*)*on* person. **6.** *v.i.* Have desire or aspiration; ~ **for,** desire to have, express wish that one may have. **7. ~'bone,** forked bone between neck and breast of bird (longer part of it from cooked bird when it is broken between two persons being said to entitle holder to magic fulfilment of any wish), object of similar shape. **8.** *n.* (Expression of) desire or aspiration, request, implied command, (**the ~ is father to the thought,** we believe thing because we wish it true; *if wishes were horses beggars would ride*; *has a great wish to go to sea*; *cannot grant your wish*; *has disregarded my wishes in the matter*), whence ~'FUL *a.*, desiring (*to* do; **~ful thinking,** belief founded on wishes rather than facts); **best** or **good ~es,** hopes felt or expressed for another's happiness etc.; **~-fulfilment,** tendency of subconscious desire to be satisfied in fantasy etc. **9.** Thing desired (*have got my wish*). [OE *wȳscan*, OHG *wunsken*, = ON *æskja* f. Gmc **wunskjan*, ult. cogn. w. WEEN, WONT¹]

wĭ'sh-wash (-ŏsh) *n.* Washy drink or talk or writing. [redupl. of WASH²]

wĭ'shy̆-washy̆ (-wŏ-) *a.* (Of tea, soup, etc.) weak, sloppy; feeble or poor in quality or character. [redupl. of WASHY]

wĭsp *n.* **1.** Small bundle or twist of straw etc.; small separate quantity *of* smoke, hair, etc.; small thin person etc.; hence ~'Y² *a.* **2.** Flock (of snipe). [ME, of uncert. orig.; cf. WFris. *wisp*, and WHISK]

wĭst. See WIT¹.

wĭstăr'ĭa, wĭstēr'ĭa, *n.* Climbing plant of genus *Wistaria*, with pendulous racemes of blue, purple, or white flowers. [f. C. *Wistar* (or *Wister*), Amer. anatomist d. 1818 + -IA¹]

wĭ'stful *a.* (Of person or looks etc.) affected with or betraying vague yearnings or mournfulness or unsatisfied desire to understand; hence ~LY² *adv.*, ~NESS *n.* [app. assim. of obs. *wistly* adv. intently (cf. WHIST¹,²) to *wishful*, w. corresp. change of sense]

wĭt¹ *v.* (*sing. pres.* 1, 3 **wot,** 2 **wo'ttest;** *past* & *p.p.* **wist;** *inf.* **wit;** *part.* WITTING; no other parts used). **1.** (arch.) Know (*of*); **God wot** (knows); **I wot** (know well). **2. To ~,** that is to say, namely. [OE *witan*, = OS *witan*, OHG *wizzan*, ON *vita*, Goth. *witan*, f. Gmc **wait-*, **wit-*, f. IE **woid-* etc.]

wĭt² *n.* **1.** (in *sing.* or *pl.*) Intelligence, understanding, (*has not the wit, the wits, wit enough, to see*; *remedy is past the wit of man to devise*; *has quick, slow*, etc., *wits, a nimble wit*, whence **(-)~'TED²** *a.*); **out of** one's **~s,** mad, distracted; **have** or **keep** one's **~s about** one, be alert or observant or of lively intelligence; **at** one's **~'s** or **wits' end,** utterly at a loss; **live by** one's **~s** (by ingenious or crafty expedients, without settled occupation); SET¹ one's *wits to*; **the five ~s,** (arch.) the senses or the mind. **2.** (Power of giving sudden intellectual pleasure by) unexpected combining or contrasting of previously unconnected ideas or expressions (*possessed of both wit and humour*; *pages sparkling with wit*). [OE *wit(t)*, *gewit(t)*, = OS *wit*, OHG *wizzi*, ON *vit*, Goth. *-witi* f. as prec.]

wĭt³ *n.* **1.** (arch.) Wise man. **2.** Witty person; person who talks wittily; hence ~'LING¹ 2 *n.* [f. prec.]

wĭtch *n.*, & *v.t.* **1.** *n.* Woman practising sorcery (WHITE *witch*; *witches'* SABBATH); (fig.) fascinating or bewitching woman; ugly old woman, hag; flat-fish resembling the lemon sole. **2. ~ ball,** coloured glass ball as formerly hung to repel witches; **~'craft,** sorcery, use of magic; **~-doctor,** tribal magician of primitive people; **~es' broom,** tufted gall caused by mites on birch etc.; **~-hunt,** search for witch(es), (fig.) search for suspected Communists or other persons with unorthodox views; **~-meal,** pollen of club-moss. **3.** *v.t.* Bewitch (**the ~ing time of night** [Shak. *Hamlet* III. ii. 406], time when witches are active, midnight); (fig.) fascinate, charm, whence ~'ERY (4, 5) *n.*, ~'ING² *a.* [OE *wicca* masc., *wicce* fem. (*wiccian* v., of unkn. orig.)]

wĭtch-. See WYCH-.

wĭ'tchetty̆, -ety̆, *n.* (Austral.) Large white larva of beetle or moth, eaten as food by Aborigines. [Aboriginal]

wĭtenagĕmō't (-g-) *n.* (Hist.) Anglo-Saxon national council or parliament. [OE, f. *witena* gen. pl. of *wita* wise man (as WIT¹) + *gemōt* meeting (cf. MOOT)]

wĭth (-dh) *prep.* **1.** In antagonism to, against, (*fight, quarrel, struggle, dispute, argue, compete, vie, with*). **2.** In or into company of or relation to, among, beside, (*come, go, walk, eat, live, spend the day* or *night with*; *king is expected with* or *together with queen and court*; *numbered with the transgressors*; *(un)connected with*; *associate oneself with*; COMPARE¹ *with*; *have a* WORD¹, WORD¹*s*, (*nothing*) *to* DO¹, *with*; DEAL² *with*; SLEEP² *with*); employed by (*he is with Shell*); ~ **God,** dead and in heaven; **have ~ you,** (arch.) I accept your offer or challenge; **~ it,** (colloq.) up to date, progressive, following latest fashions; **not ~ you,** (colloq.) unable to follow your meaning. **3.** Agreeably or in harmonious relations to (*I feel, think, sympathize, with you*; *am with you on that point*; w. neg. wds in opp. sense: *I disagree with you*; *he that is not with me is against me*; *vote with the Liberals*; *blue* *does not* GO[1] *with green*); **one ~,** part of same whole as. **4.** Having, carrying, possessed of, characterized by, (*vase with handles*; *man with sinister expression*; *walking with a gun*; *went out with no hat on*); **~ child** or **young,** pregnant. **5.** In the care or charge or possession of (*have no money with me*; *leave child, parcel, with nurse, porter*; *it rests with you to decide*; *the deal, decanter, next move, is with you*). **6.** By use of as instrument or means (*cut it with a knife*; *have no pen to write with*; *walks with a crutch*; *damn with faint praise*). **7.** By addition or supply or acquisition or possession of as material (*fill it, overflowing, with water*; *crawling with vermin*; *laden with baggage*; *threaten with dismissal*; *blessed with beauty*; *adorn with frescoes*). **8.** In same way or direction or degree or at the same time as (*changes with the seasons*; *quantity varies directly* or *inversely, increases, with another*; *rise with the sun*; *with his death the barony becomes extinct*); **~ that,** thereupon, simultaneously, saying or having just said that; BEGIN *with.* **9.** Because or by operation of, owing to, (*trembles with fear*; *is down with measles*; STIFF *with cold*). **10.** Displaying or so as to display, under favourable or unfavourable circumstances of, (*heard it with calmness*; *fought with courage*; *handle with care*; *won with ease, difficulty, a good deal to spare*; *shot well with a good, wretched, light*); under accompanying conditions of (*sleep with the window open*; *speak with* one's *mouth full*; *holiday with all expenses paid*; *with a song in my heart*). **11.** In regard to, concerning, in the sphere of, in the mind or view of, (*be patient with him*; *with God all things are possible*; *it is holiday time with us*; *has great influence with the President*; *my dealings with the plaintiff*; *what do you want with me?*; *can be dispensed with*); **away, down,** OFF, **on, up, to the devil,** etc., **~ him** or **it,** take or send or put him or it, he may go, away etc. **12.** Despite, notwithstanding, the presence of (*with all his learning, he is the simplest of men*; *with many admirable qualities, the best of intentions, he failed completely*). [OE, = OS *with*, prob. shortened f. Gmc prep. corresp. to OE *wither*, OHG *widar* against]

wĭtha'l (-dhaw'l) *adv.* & *prep.* (arch.) **1.** *adv.* With it, in addition, moreover, as well, at the same time. **2.** *prep.* (esp. at end of rel. clause or question) With (*what shall he fill his belly withal?*). [ME, f. prec. + ALL]

wĭthdraw' (-dh-) *v.* (**withdrew'**; **~n**). **1.** *v.t.* Pull aside or back (*withdraw curtain*, one's *hand*); take away, remove, (child from school, coins from circulation, money from bank, horse from race, troops from position, favour etc. from person); retract (offer, statement, promise, or abs.; in *imper.*, as demand that a speaker shall retract something as unparliamentary etc.); (in *p.p.*) mentally detached, unsociable. **2.** *v.i.* Retire from presence or place, go aside or apart; adopt detached mental attitude; **~ing-room,** (arch.) drawing-room. [ME, f. *with-* away (as WITH) + DRAW[1]]

wĭthdraw'al (-dh-) *n.* Act of withdrawing; process of ceasing to take addictive drugs, often with unpleasant physical reaction (*withdrawal symptoms*). [f. prec. + -AL 2]

wĭthe (*or* -dh *or* widh), **wĭ'thȳ** (-dhĭ), *n.* Tough flexible branch esp. of willow or osier used for binding bundles etc. [OE *withthe, withig,* = OHG *wit(hi)* etc., ON *vith(ja)* f. Gmc **withōn*, cogn. w. WIRE]

wĭ'ther (-dh-) *v.t.* & *i.* Make or become dry and shrivelled (*up*), deprive of or lose vigour or vitality or freshness or importance (*away*), decline, languish, decay, (*has a withered arm*; *flowers and beauty wither*; *age cannot wither her*); blight with scorn etc., put out of action with gun-fire etc., whence **~**ING[2] *a.* [ME, app. var. of WEATHER[2], different. for certain senses]

wĭ'thers (-dh*erz*) *n. pl.* Ridge between horse's shoulder-blades (**my ~ are unwrung,** imputation etc. does not affect me, f. Shak. *Hamlet* III. ii. 252). [app. reduced f. (16th c.) *widersome* or *-sone*, f. *wider-*, *wither-* against (cf. WITH), as the part that resists strain of collar; second element obscure]

wĭ'thershĭns (-dh-; -z), **wĭ'dder-,** *adv.* (esp. Sc.) In a direction contrary to apparent course of sun (considered as unlucky), anticlockwise. [f. MLG *weddersins* f. MHG *widersinnes* (*wider* against, *sin* direction)]

wĭthhō'ld (-dh-h-) *v.t.* (**withhe'ld**). Refrain from putting into action, refuse to grant, (*withhold* one's *consent, support*); hold back, restrain, (*from*); ***~ing tax** (deducted from income at source). [ME, f. *with-* away (as WITH) + HOLD[1]]

wĭthĭ'n (-dh-) *adv.* & *prep.* **1.** *adv.* (arch. or literary). Inside, to or at or on the inside, in(to) house or room, internally, (*clean within and without*; *as seen from within*; *beauty without and foulness within*); in spirit (*make me pure within*); *Bishopsgate* **~**, inside the walls. **2.** *prep.* To or on or in the inside of, enclosed by, (**~ doors,** in or into house; WHEEL[1]*s within wheels*). **3.** Not beyond, not too far for, not transgressing, so as not to pass or exceed, subject to, (*live* or *keep within* one's *income*; *acting within* one's *rights*; *keep it within bounds*; *a task well within his powers*); **~ the meaning of the Act** etc., covered by it; **~ the law,** not illegal; **~ oneself,** not putting forth whole power; *within* REASON[1]. **4.** Not too far for, near enough to affect or be affected by, not farther off than (*of* w. sense 'from', or abs.; *is within three miles of a station*; *was within an ace of destruction*); **~ reach,** SIGHT[1], **call,** near enough to reach or be reached etc. (*within sight of port*). **5.** In a time no longer than, before expiration or since beginning of, (*of* w. sense 'from', or abs.; *shall have it within an hour*; *within a year of his death, within the* or *a year, all was changed*; *have seen him within these last three days*). [OE *withinnan* on the inside (as WITH, *innan* adv. & prep. within, f. as IN[2])]

wĭthou't (-dh-) *adv., prep.,* & *conj.* **1.** *adv.* (arch. or literary). Outside, to or at or on the outside, out of or outside house or room, externally, (*white within and without*; *as seen from without*; *stands disconsolate without*; *listening to the wind without*); in outward appearance (*a prince without but a beggar within*); *Bishopsgate* **~**, outside the walls. **2.** *prep.* (arch.) On the outside of, outside, (*met us without the gates*; *is without the pale of civilization*); **things ~ us,** all that is not ourselves. **3.** Not having, not with, with no, devoid of, lacking, in want of, free from, with freedom from, not feeling or showing, in or with absence of, (*came without a hat*; *a rose without a thorn*; *am without friends* or *money*; *did it without difficulty* or *being discovered*; *act without hesitation*; *cannot live without her, go away without thanking you*; *is absolutely without fear, anxiety*; *times without* NUMBER[1]; *train left without us*; *one cannot make an* OMELETTE *without breaking eggs*; *without health happiness is impossible*); DO[1] or GO[1] *without* (thing expressed or implied); *without (a)* DOUBT[1]; **~ end,** infinite, eternal; *without* FAIL[1], PREJUDICE, RESERVE[2]; *go without* SAYING. **4.** *conj.* (arch. or vulg.) Unless. [OE *withūtan* (as WITH, *ūtan* from outside f. as OUT)]

wĭthstă'nd (-dh-) *v.* (**withstoo'd**). **1.** *v.t.* Resist, oppose, (person, force, hardship, wear, etc.). **2.** *v.i.* Make opposition, offer resistance. [OE *withstandan* (*with-* against, cf. WITH; STAND[1])]

withy. See WITHE.

wĭ'tlėss *a.* Foolish; crazy; stupid; lacking wit; hence ~LY² *adv.*, ~NESS *n.* [OE *witlēas* (as WIT², -LESS)]
wĭ'tlĭng. See WIT³.
wĭ'tloof (-ōf) *n.* Chicory plant; its salad leaves. [Du., = white leaf]
wĭ'tnėss *n.* & *v.* **1.** *n.* Testimony, evidence, (**bear ~ to** or **of,** state one's belief in, state or be fact(s) tending to establish); confirmation (*stands there in witness of the event*; **call to ~,** appeal to for confirmation); thing or person whose existence, position, state, etc., serves as testimony *to* or proof *of* (*is a living witness to my clemency*). **2.** = EYE¹*witness*; person present at event. **3.** Person giving sworn testimony in lawcourt or for legal purpose; person attesting genuineness of signature to document by adding his own signature; ||**~-box, *~ stand,** enclosure in lawcourt from which witnesses give evidence. **4.** *v.t.* (arch.) State in evidence (thing, *that,* etc.); indicate, serve as evidence of, (*a deathly pallor witnessed his agitation*). **5.** See, be spectator of; act as witness of (document, signature, etc.). **6.** *v.i.* Give evidence (*against, for*); serve as evidence (*agqinst, for, to*); (**as**) **~ my poverty,** of which let my poverty be proof. [OE *witnes* (as WIT², -NESS)]
wĭ'ttĭcĭsm *n.* (usu. derog.) Witty remark, jest. [coined by Dryden (1677) f. WITTY, after *criticism*]
wĭ'ttĭng *a.* Aware, intentional; hence ~LY² *adv.* [ME, f. WIT¹ + -ING²]
wĭ'ttol *n.* (arch.) Acquiescent cuckold. [ME *wetewold,* app. formed by substitution of *wete* WIT¹ for first syllable of *cokewold* CUCKOLD]
wĭ'tt|ȳ *a.* Full of WIT² (sense 2); capable of or fond of saying things that are brilliantly or sparklingly amusing; hence **~ĭLY²** *adv.*, **~ĭNESS** *n.* [OE *wit(t)ig* (as WIT², -Y²)]
wive *v.t.* & *i.* (arch.) Provide with, take, wife. [OE *wīfian* (as WIFE)]
wī'vern. Var. of WYVERN.
wives. See WIFE.
wiz *n.* & *a.* (sl.) Wizard. [abbr.]
wĭ'zard *n.* & *a.* **1.** *n.* Magician, sorcerer; person who effects seeming impossibilities; conjurer; hence ~RY (4, 5) *n.* **2.** *a.* (sl.) Wonderful, excellent. [ME, f. WISE¹ + -ARD)]
wĭ'zened (-nd), **wĭ'zen, wea'zen,** *a.* Of shrivelled or dried-up appearance (chiefly of person or his face or look). [p.p. of *wizen* shrivel f. OE *wisnian,* = OHG *wesanēn,* ON *visna* f. Gmc **wis-*]
wk. *abbr.* weak; week; work.
Wm. *abbr.* William.
W.M.O. *abbr.* World Meteorological Organization.
W.N.W. *abbr.* west-north-west.
wō *int.* = WHOA. [var. of *who* int., HO]
W.O. *abbr.* Warrant Officer.
w.o. *abbr.* walk-over.
woad *n.*, & *v.t.* **1.** *n.* (Plant, *Isatis tinctoria,* yielding) kind of blue dye now superseded by indigo. **2.** *v.t.* Dye with woad. [OE *wād,* = OHG *weit* f. Gmc **waida-*, **waisda-*]
wŏ'bbėgŏng *n.* (Austral.) = CARPET-*shark.* [Aboriginal]
wŏ'bbl|e, wa'bbl|e (wŏ'-), *v.i.*, & *n.* **1.** *v.i.* (Of top or revolving body) revolve with changing inclinations, rock; (of person, missile, etc.) go unsteadily, vibrate from side to side, swerve, stagger; (fig.) vacillate, waver, act inconsistently, be inconstant; (of voice or sound) quaver, pulsate; hence ~ER¹ *n.*, ~Y² *a.* **2.** *n.* Wobbling movement, change of direction or policy, swerve, piece of vacillation. [corresp. to LG *wabbeln,* ON *vafla* waver f. Gmc **wabh-*; cf. WAVE¹, WAVER, -LE 3]
||**wŏdge** *n.* (colloq.) Chunk, lump. [alt. f. WEDGE]
wōe *n.* (arch., literary, or joc.) Affliction, bitter grief, distress, (*tale of woe*; **weal and ~,** prosperity and adversity; **~ is me,** alas; **~ be (un)to,** a curse upon; *woe* WORTH² *the day*); (in *pl.*) calamities, troubles; **~'begone,** dismal-looking [*begone* p.p. of *bego* f. OE BE(*gān* GO¹) surround]. [OE *wā, wǣ,* = OS, OHG *wē,* ON *vei, væ,* Goth. *wai,* f. Gmc **wai,* natural excl. of lament]
wō'eful (wō'f-) *a.* Afflicted with distress; bad, unpleasant, wretched; hence ~LY² *adv.* [ME, f. prec. + -FUL]
wŏg *n.* (sl., derog.) Native of Middle East; foreigner. [20th c.; orig. unkn.]
wŏ'ggle *n.* Loop of leather round Scout's neckerchief. [20th c.; orig. unkn.]
woke(n). See WAKE¹.
wōld *n.* Piece of open uncultivated esp. elevated country, downland or moorland. [OE *wald,* = OS, OHG *wald* forest, ON *völlr* field f. Gmc **walthus,* perh. rel. to WILD; cf. WEALD]
wolf (wŏŏ-) *n.* (*pl.* **wolves** *pr.* -vz), & *v.t.* **1.** *n.* Erect-eared straight-tailed coarse-furred tawny-grey fierce usu. gregarious carnivorous doglike mammal of genus *Canis,* esp. *Canis lupus,* preying on sheep etc. or combining in packs to hunt larger animals; **cry ~ (too often),** raise false alarms (till genuine one is disregarded); **have** or **hold a ~ by the ears,** be in a precarious situation; **keep the ~ from the door,** avert hunger or starvation; **lone ~,** person who prefers to act alone; **~ in sheep's clothing,** malicious person who pretends friendship; **throw to the wolves,** sacrifice without compunction. **2.** Rapacious or greedy person; (sl.) man who aggressively seeks women for sexual purposes. **3.** (Mus.) Jarring sound from some notes in bowed instrument; out-of-tune effect when playing certain chords on old organs (before present 'equal temperament' was in use). **4. ~-cub,** (1) young wolf, (2) ||(former name for) Cub Scout; **~-dog,** (1) dog kept to guard sheep from or hunt wolves, (2) dog-and-wolf hybrid; **~-fish,** large voracious blenny of genus *Anarhichas*; **~'hound,** borzoi or other dog used (orig.) to hunt wolves; **~-pack,** attacking-group of submarines or aircraft; **~'sbane,** aconite; **~'s-claw, ~'s-foot,** club-moss; **~'-skin,** (mat, cloak, etc., made of) wolf's skin; **~'s-milk,** spurge; **~ spider** (of family Lycosidae, chasing instead of netting prey); **~-tooth,** supernumerary premolar in horse; **~-whistle,** whistle of a man admiring sexually, and trying to attract the attention of, a woman. **5.** Hence ~'ISH¹ *a.* **6.** *v.t.* Devour or swallow greedily (*down*). [OE *wulf,* = OS *wulf,* OHG *wolf,* ON *ulfr,* Goth. *wulfs* f. Gmc **wulfaz* f. IE **wlq^{w}os*]
wo'lfram (wŏŏ'-) *n.* **1.** ~(ite), ore yielding tungsten, native tungstate of iron and manganese. **2.** Tungsten. [G, perh. f. *wolf* WOLF + *rahm* cream, or MHG *rām* dirt, soot]
wo'lverine (wŏŏ-; -ēn), **-ēne,** *n.* Amer. GLUTTON 2; ***W~ State,** Michigan. [16th c. *wolvering,* somehow derived f. *wolv-*, st. of WOLF]
wolves. See WOLF.
wo'man (wŏŏ'-) *n.* (*pl.* **women** *pr.* wĭ'mĭn), & *v.t.* **1.** *n.* Adult human female; *make an* HONEST *woman of*; INNER *woman*; LITTLE *woman*; OLD *woman*; **the other ~** (who attracts married man so that he deserts or neglects his wife); OUTER *woman*; **play the ~,** weep or show fear; *woman with a* PAST¹; SCARLET *woman*; **~ of the streets,** prostitute; *woman of the* WORLD 6; ||**Women's Institute,** organization of women in rural areas to meet regularly and engage in crafts etc.; **Women's Lib(eration),** movement urging liberation of women from domestic duties and

subservient status; **~'s** or **women's rights,** position of legal and social equality with men. **2.** The average or typical woman, the female sex, any woman, (*how does woman differ from man?*); (in *pl.*) women as partners in illicit sexual activity; **man born of ~,** mortal man; **~'s wit,** instinctive insight or resource. **3.** (colloq.) Charwoman; (arch.) queen's or great lady's female attendant, lady-in-waiting; ||**~ of the bedchamber** (ranking below LADY *of the bedchamber*). **4.** Man with feminine characteristics (*is a woman in tenderness*); OLD *woman*. **5.** *The* feminine emotions (*all the woman in her rose in rebellion*; *stirred the woman in him*). **6.** *attrib.* Female (*woman driver, doctor, friend*; *women doctors*); *woman* SUFFRAGE. **7.** *suf.* (chiefly in terms correl. to compounds in *-man*). Woman concerned or dealing or skilful with or describable as (*countrywoman*, HORSE[1]*woman*, NEEDLE*woman*, GENTLEWOMAN). **8.** **~-hater,** misogynist; **~-kind, wo'menkind,** women in general (one's *~kind*, the women of one's family); **wo'menfolk,** women, one's womankind. **9.** Hence **~**HOOD *n.* (= female maturity, womanly instinct, womankind), **~**LESS, **~**LIKE, *adjs.* **10.** *v.t.* (arch.) Make behave like a woman, cause to weep etc. **11.** Equip with staff of women; address or speak of as 'woman' (not 'lady'). [OE *wīfmon(n)*, *-man(n)* (as WIFE, MAN[1]), a formation peculiar to English, the ancient wd being WIFE]

wo'manĭsh (wŏŏ'-) *a.* (Of man or his feelings, conduct, looks, etc.) like women or their ways etc. (usu. derog.), effeminate; hence **~**LY[2] *adv.*, **~**NESS *n.* [ME, f. prec. + -ISH[1]]

wo'manize (wŏŏ'-), **-ise** (-īz), *v.* **1.** *v.t.* Make womanish. **2.** *v.i.* (Of man) philander, consort illicitly with women. [f. WOMAN + -IZE]

wo'manl|ÿ (wŏŏ'-) *a.* (Of woman or her feelings, conduct, etc.) having or showing the qualities befitting a woman, not masculine or girlish, (*womanly modesty, compassion, tact,* etc.); hence **~**ĭNESS *n.* [ME, f. WOMAN + -LY[1]]

womb (wōōm) *n.* Organ in woman and other female mammals in which child or young is conceived and nourished till birth, uterus, (**fruit of the ~,** child(ren)); (fig.) place of conception and development (*future events in the womb of time*). [OE *wamb, womb,* = OHG *wamba*, ON *vömb*, Goth. *wamba*]

wŏ'mbăt *n.* Australian herbivorous marsupial mammal esp. of genus *Phascolomis*, like small bear. [Aboriginal]

women. See WOMAN.

won. See WIN.

wo'nder[1] (wŭ'-) *n.* **1.** Miracle, prodigy, strange or remarkable thing or specimen or performance or event, (**do** or **work ~s,** do miracles, succeed remarkably; **~s will never cease,** (iron.) this is indeed surprising); marvellously successful thing, precocious child, etc.; NINE *days' wonder*; **the seven ~s of the world,** seven remarkable structures so called in antiquity; **the ~ is,** what is surprising is; **for a ~,** (esp.) by way of welcome exception (*you are punctual for a wonder*); **what ~, small ~, it is no ~, no ~,** (**that**), naturally, inevitably, of course, one cannot be surprised or might have guessed that. **2.** Emotion excited by what surpasses expectation or experience or seems inexplicable, surprise mingled with admiration or curiosity or bewilderment, (*were filled with wonder*; *looked at him in silent* or *open-mouthed wonder*). **3.** **~land,** fairyland, land full of surprises or marvels; **~-stricken, -struck,** filled with or made dumb by wonder; **~-worker,** one who performs miracles. [OE *wundor*, = OS *wundar*, OHG *wuntar*, ON *undr*, of unkn. orig.]

wo'nder[2] (wŭ'-) *v.* **1.** *v.i.* Be filled with wonder, feel surprise, (*at, to see* etc., or abs.); **I shouldn't ~ if,** (colloq.) I think it likely that; hence **~**ING[2] *a.*, **~**MENT *n.* **2.** *v.t.* Be surprised to find (*that*). **3.** Feel curiosity about, desire to know (*wonder what the time is, how to proceed,* etc.); express tentative inquiry (*I wonder whether I might open the window*); **I ~,** (as excl.) I very much doubt it. [OE *wundrian* (as prec.)]

wo'nderful (wŭ'-) *a.* Marvellous, surprising, exceeding (esp. better than) what was expected, remarkable, admirable; hence **~**LY[2] *adv.* [OE *wunderfull* (as WONDER[1], -FUL)]

wo'ndrous (wŭ'-) *a.* & *adv.* (poet. or rhet.) **1.** *a.* Wonderful; hence **~**LY[2] *adv.*, **~**NESS *n.* **2.** *adv.* (qualifying *adjs.* only). Wonderfully (*wondrous kind* etc.). [alt. f. obs. *wonders* a. & adv. (gen. of WONDER[1]; cf. -S[3]), after *marvellous*]

wŏ'nga(-wŏnga) *n.* Large Austral. pigeon. [Aboriginal]

||**wŏ'nkÿ** *a.* (sl.) Shaky, groggy; unreliable. [fanciful formation]

wōnt[1] *pred. a.* (arch.) Accustomed *to* do (*as he was wont to say*). [OE *gewunod* p.p. of *gewunian* (*wunian* dwell)]

wōnt[2] *v.* (3 *sing. pres. ind.* **~s** *or* **~**; *past* **~** *or* **~'ed**). (arch.) **1.** *v.t.* Accustom *to.* **2.** *v.i.* Be accustomed. [ME, f. prec. or as back form. f. WONTED]

wōnt[3] *n.* (arch.) What is customary in general or habitual to a person (*according to his wont*; *it is my wont to*; **use and ~,** established custom). [16th c., of doubtful orig., perh. f. obs. *wone* habit and WONT[1]]

wōn't. See WILL[1].

wō'ntėd *attrib. a.* Habitual to person, accustomed, usual, (*heard me with his wonted courtesy*; *met with the wonted obstacles*). [either f. WONT[3] + -ED[2], or an extension of WONT[1] with -ED[1]]

wōō *v.t.* (literary). **1.** Ask in marriage, court, (woman, or abs.); hence **~'**ER[1] *n.* **2.** Pursue, seek to win, (fame, fortune, etc.); coax, importune, try to persuade, (person usu. *to*, do or *to* compliance etc.). [OE *wōgian* v.i., *āwōgian* v.t., of unkn. orig.]

wŏŏd *n.* **1.** (in *sing.* or *pl.*) Growing trees occupying fairly densely a considerable tract of ground; one **cannot see the ~ for the trees,** details impede general view; **out of the ||~** or ***~s,** out of danger etc.; **don't halloo till you are out of the ||~** or ***~s,** do not assume too soon that difficulties are over; hence (-)**~'**ED[2] *a.* **2.** Hard compact fibrous substance between pith and bark of trunks and branches of tree, whether growing or cut for timber or fuel or use in arts and crafts; timber, fuel, etc., of this; **touch ~, *knock (on) ~,** put hand etc. against something wooden (as superstition to avert ill luck, or to avoid capture in children's game). **3.** *The* cask or unbottled storage of wine etc. (*in, from, the wood*). **4.** (Bowls) = BOWL[2] 1; (Golf) wooden-headed club. **5.** **~ alcohol,** methyl alcohol; **~ anemone,** wild spring-flowering anemone; **~'bine** or **~'bind,** wild honeysuckle, *Virginia creeper; **~-block** (from which woodcuts are taken); **~'cock,** game-bird related to snipe; **~'craft,** (1) knowledge of forest conditions esp. as applied in hunting etc., (2) skill in woodwork; **~'cut,** (print, usu. as illustration in book, taken from) engraving made on wood; **~'cutter,** (1) man who cuts wood, (2) maker of woodcuts; **~-engraver,** (1) maker of woodcuts, (2) beetle that bores in wood; **~-fibre,** fibre got from wood esp. as material for paper; **~-gas** (from distillation of wood, used for lighting etc.); ||**~ grouse,** capercaillie; *wood* HYACINTH; **~ ibis,** Amer. wading bird frequenting wooded swamps; **~'land,** wooded country, woods, (often attrib.: *woodland scenery*); **~'lark,**

lark (*Lullula arborea*) perching on trees; **~-leopard,** spotted moth whose larva bores into trees; **~-louse,** small isopod land crustacean of genus *Oniscus* etc. found in old wood, often able to roll itself into a ball; **~'man,** forester, wood-cutter; **~-notes,** spontaneous bird-song or poetry; **~-nymph,** (1) dryad or hamadryad, (2) species of humming-bird and moth; **~ paper** (made of wood-pulp); **~'pecker,** bird of family Picidae that clings to tree-trunks and taps them to discover insects: **~'pie,** greater spotted wood-pecker; **~-pigeon,** ring-dove; **~'pile,** stack of wood esp. for fuel (NIGGER *in the woodpile*); **~-pulp,** wood-fibre reduced chemically or mechanically to pulp as material for paper; **~'ruff,** white-flowered plant of genus *Asperula*, esp. *sweet ~ruff* grown esp. for fragrance of its whorled leaves when dried or crushed; *wood*-SCREW; **~-shed** (where wood is stored esp. for fuel); **~'sman** (-z-), dweller in or frequenter of woods, person skilled in woodcraft; **~-smoke** (from burning of wood); **~ sorrel,** plant of genus *Oxalis* with trifoliate leaves and white or pink flowers; **~ spirit,** crude methyl alcohol got from wood; **~-spurge,** species of spurge with greenish-yellow flower-clusters; **~ tar** (got from wood); **~-warbler,** bird *Phylloscopus sibilatrix*, *warbler; **~-wasp,** wasp that hangs nests in tree or burrows in rotten wood; **~'waxen,** dyer's broom [OE *weaxe* (as WAX²)]; **~-wind,** orchestral wind instruments made (orig.) of wood; **~-wool,** fine pine etc. shavings used as surgical dressing or for packing; **~'work,** (1) work done in wood, (2) things made of wood, esp. the wooden part of a house etc.; **~'worm,** wood-boring larva of furniture beetle; **~-yard** (where wood is used or stored). **6.** Hence ~'LESS *a.* [OE *wudu, wi(o)du,* = OHG *witu*, ON *vithr* f. Gmc **widuz*]

Wŏŏ'dbury̆ty̆pe *n.* (Process of making) print from metal plate to which gelatine film from photographic negative is transferred. [f. W. B. *Woodbury*, Engl. inventor d. 1885, + TYPE¹]

wŏŏ'dchŭck *n.* Reddish-brown and grey N. Amer. marmot. [f. Amer. Ind. name; cf. Cree *wuchak, otchock*]

wŏŏ'den *a.* **1.** Made of wood (*wooden stool, leg*); **~ horse** (by use of which Troy was taken; cf. TROJAN); *wooden* SPOON¹; **~ walls,** ships as defence. **2.** Like wood, stiff, clumsy, without animation or flexibility, inexpressive, (*wooden movements, manners, stare, face,* etc.); **~head(ed),** stupid (person); hence ~LY² *adv.*, ~NESS (-n-n-) *n.* [f. WOOD + -EN⁵]

***wŏŏ'dsy̆** (-zĭ) *a.* Silvan. [irreg. f. WOODS + -Y²]

wŏŏ'd|y̆ *a.* (Of region) abounding in woods, well-wooded; of the nature, consisting, of wood (*the woody parts of a plant; woody stem, tissue*); (of plant) forming stem and branches of wood (*woody* NIGHTSHADE); hence ~ĬNESS *n.* [ME, f. WOOD + -Y²]

wŏŏ'er. See WOO.

wŏŏf¹ *n.* = WEFT¹. [OE *ōwef*, alt. f. *ōwebb* (after *wefan* WEAVE¹) f. as A- 1, WEB; *w-* f. assoc. w. *warp*]

wŏŏf² *n.*, & *v.i.* (Give) gruff bark of dog; hence ~'ER¹ *n.*, loudspeaker for accurately reproducing low-frequency signals (cf. TWEET*er*). [imit.]

wŏŏl *n.* **1.** Kind of hair distinguished by fineness, softness, wavy structure, and scaly surface, forming fleece of sheep, goat, alpaca, etc., and occurring mixed with ordinary hair in coat of some other animals; DYE²*d in the wool*; **much cry and little ~,** much talk or effort but disappointing result, fiasco; **go for ~ and come home shorn,** have tables turned on one; **pull the ~ over** person's **eyes,** deceive him; hence **(-)~(l)**ED² (-ld) *a.* **2.** Woollen yarn, worsted, (*spent an hour matching wools*); woollen garments or cloth (*safest to wear wool*). **3.** Soft short under-fur or down. **4.** Negro's short curly hair, (joc.) any person's hair; **lose** one's **~,** (sl.) show anger. **5.** Kinds of wool-like substance (COTTON¹, GLASS, LEAD¹, STEEL, WIRE, WOOD-, *wool*); **mineral ~** (made from molten slag subjected to strong blast, and used for packing walls etc.). **6.** **~-carding, -combing,** processes by which short, long, wool is prepared for spinning; **~-dyed,** DYE²d in the wool; **~-fat,** lanolin; ||**~-fell,** skin of sheep etc. with fleece still on; **~-gathering,** absent-minded(ness), dreamy or inattentive (mood); ||**~-grower,** one who breeds sheep for wool; **~-oil,** suint; **~-pack,** fleecy cumulus cloud, (Hist.) bale of wool; ||**~'sack,** large wool-stuffed cushion on which Lord Chancellor sits in House of Lords (*reach* etc. *the ~sack*, become Lord Chancellor; *take seat on the ~sack*, open proceedings in House of Lords); **~-skin,** = *wool-fell*; **~-sorters' disease,** anthrax; **~-stapler,** one who grades producer's wool and sells to manufacturer; **~-work,** embroidery with wools on canvas etc. [OE *wull*, = OHG *wolla*, ON *ull*, Goth. *wulla* f. Gmc **wullō* f. IE **wḷna*]

wŏŏ'llen, *wŏŏ'len, *a.* & *n.* **1.** *a.* Made (partly) of wool, esp. from short fibres. **2.** *n.* Woollen fabric, as blanket, flannel, cloth; (in *pl.*) woollen garments; **~-draper,** (Hist.) retailer of woollens. [OE *wullen* (as prec., -EN⁵)]

wŏŏ'lly̆ *a.* & *n.* **1.** *a.* Bearing or naturally covered with wool or wool-like hair; (Bot.) downy; **~-bear,** large hairy caterpillar esp. of tiger-moth. **2.** Resembling or suggesting wool (*woolly hair, clouds*). **3.** (Of sound) indistinct; (Paint.) lacking in definition or luminosity or incisiveness; (of mind or thought) confused and hazy; WILD *and woolly*. **4.** Hence **wŏŏ'llĭ**NESS *n.* **5.** *n.* Woollen garment, ||esp. knitted one or *undergarment. [f. WOOL + -Y²]

wŏŏ'mera *n.* (Austral.) Aboriginal throwing-stick for dart or spear, or club used as missile. [Aboriginal]

***wŏŏ'z|y̆** *a.* (colloq.) Dizzy, unsteady; dazed or slightly drunk; vague; hence ~ĬLY² *adv.*, ~ĬNESS *n.* [19th c., of unkn. orig.]

wŏp¹. Var. of WHOP.

***Wŏp²** *n.* (sl., derog.) Italian or other S. European, esp. as immigrant in U.S. [20th c.; orig. unkn.]

Worcester (wŏŏ'ster) *n.* **~(shire) sauce,** pungent sauce first made in Worcester. [~ in England]

Worcs. *abbr.* Worcestershire (former county in England).

word¹ (wêrd) *n.* **1.** Any sound or combination of sounds (or its written or printed symbol, customarily shown with a space on either side of it but none within it) forming meaningful element of speech, conveying an idea or alternative ideas, and capable of serving as a member of, the whole of, or a substitute for, a sentence; basic unit of expression of data and instructions in computer; **at a ~,** as soon as requested; **have no ~s for,** be unable to express; **in a** or **one ~,** briefly, to sum up; **in other ~s,** expressing the same thing differently; **not a ~ of it,** no part whatever (of story etc.); *is* **not the ~ for it,** not an adequate description; **put into ~s,** express in speech or writing as well as in thought; **~ for ~,** (repeat etc.) in exactly the same words, (translate) literally; **a ~ to the wise,** = VERB. SAP. **2.** Speech (*honest in word and deed; bold in word only*); **by ~ of mouth,** in speech (only). **3.** (in *sing.* or *pl.*) Thing said saying, remark, conversation; (in *pl.*) text of song, actor's part, etc.; **(hard, high,** etc.) **~s,**

angry talk (*have* ~*s*, quarrel *with*); thing (merely) said (and not done); BIG *words*; EAT one's *words*; **of few ~s,** taciturn; GOOD *word*; **have a ~ to say,** know something worth hearing; **have a ~,** converse briefly (*with*); HOUSEHOLD *word*; LAST³ *word*; **of many ~s,** talkative; (**not**) **in so many ~s,** (not) explicitly or bluntly; **say the ~,** give the order etc.; **say a few ~s,** make a short speech; **suit the action to the ~,** do at once what has been threatened etc.; **take** person **at his ~,** act on assumption that he means what he says; **too** *funny* etc. **for ~s** (inexpressibly); WASTE² *words*; **~ of command,** word or phrase giving instruction (esp. in drill etc.); **~s fail me,** I am too surprised to express my thoughts; **W~ (of God),** (1) Bible or part of it, (2) title of Christ, = LOGOS; *a word in* SEASON; **not have a ~ to throw at a dog,** be unsociably or superciliously taciturn. **4.** News, intelligence, a message, (*send* or *leave word that* or *of*; *word came that* or *of*; *the word got round that*; *the word is, word has it, that*); **send ~,** have message taken (*that, to* do, etc.). **5.** One's promise, assurance, or responsible statement; **give** person, **give, pledge,** one's ~, make promise; **keep, break,** one's ~, do, fail to do, what one has promised; **I give you my ~ for it,** promise it shall be or state that it is so; **take** person's **~ for it,** accept his statement that it is so; **upon my ~** (form of asseveration); (**upon**) **my ~** (excl. at something that shocks or surprises); **~ of honour,** promise or statement made upon one's HONOUR¹; **a man of his ~,** one who keeps his promises; **be as good as, better than,** one's ~, fulfil, exceed, what one has promised; **his ~ is (as good as) his bond** (may be relied on). **6.** Command, order, password, motto, (*his word is law*; *give the word to* do or *for*; *act promptly at the word*; *must give the word before you can pass*); SHARP¹'*s the word*. **7. ~-blind, -deaf,** incapacitated by kinds of brain defect from attaching meaning to words seen or heard; **~'book,** book with list(s) of words, vocabulary; **~-game** (in which words are thought of, guessed, etc.); **~ order,** arrangement of words in sentence etc.; **~-painter, -painting,** vivid descriptive writer, writing; **~-per'fect,** knowing part, lesson, etc., by heart; **~-picture,** piece of word-painting; **~-play,** joke using features of words, pun, etc.; **~'smith,** skilled user or maker of words; **~-square,** set of words of equal length so chosen that when they are written under each other the letters read downward in columns give the same words, e.g. *too old ode*. **8.** Hence **~'**AGE (1) *n.*, **~'**LESS *a.* [OE, = OS *word*, OHG *wort*, ON *orth*, Goth. *waurd* f. Gmc **wordam*]

word² (wẽrd) *v.t.* Put into words, phrase, select words to express; hence **~'**ING¹ (1, 2, 6) *n.* [ME, f. prec.]

wor'd|ȳ (wẽr'-) *a.* Tending to use, expressed in, (too) many words; in, consisting of, words (*wordy warfare*); hence **~ĭLY²** *adv.*, **~ĭNESS** *n.* [OE *wordig* (as WORD¹, -Y²)]

wōre. See WEAR¹,³.

work¹ (wẽrk) *n.* **1.** Expenditure of energy, striving, application of effort or exertion to a purpose, (*all work and no play*; *never does a stroke of work*; *never liked, will do no, work*); **at ~,** engaged in work, operating; **set to ~,** (cause to) begin operations; **~-to-rule,** act of WORK²-ing to rule. **2.** (Phys.) Exertion of force overcoming resistance or producing molecular change (*convert heat into work*); **internal ~** (exerted on molecules of a body). **3.** Task (to be) undertaken, materials (to be) used in task, (*the work of converting the heathen*); **have** one's **~ cut out** (**for** one), have a hard task, have as much as one can do; *all in the* DAY'*s work*; **the ~ of** *a moment* etc., a task occupying (only) a specified time. **4.** Thing done by work, result of action, achievement, thing made; book or piece of literary or musical composition, (in *pl.*) all such compositions by author, composer, etc.; literary or other product *of*; (Theol., usu. in *pl.*) meritorious act as opposed to faith or grace; **a good day's ~,** much accomplished; GOOD *works*; PIECE *of work*; **a ~ of art,** fine picture, building, poem, etc.; **~s of mercy,** charitable actions; *works of* SUPEREROGATION. **5.** Doings or experiences of specified kind (*sharp, bloody, wild, work*; *thirsty, dry, work*); DIRTY, NICE, *work*; *make* SHORT *work of*. **6.** Employment, esp. the opportunity of earning money by labour, laborious occupation, (*is out of, is in regular, wants, is looking for, work*; *many hands make light work*). **7.** (usu. in *pl.* or in *comb.*) Piece of fortification, structure for defence, (*the works are impregnable*; *advanced, detached, defensive, work(s)*; EARTH¹*work*). **8.** (in *pl.*) Operations in building etc. (CLERK *of* (*the*) *works*; **public ~s,** such operations done by or for the State). **9.** (in *pl.*) Acting or operative part of machine (*of* clock etc.; *something must be wrong with the works*); (sl.) all that is available (**give** person **the ~s,** give him or tell him everything, (esp.) kill him). **10.** (in *pl.*, often treated as *sing.*) Place where manufacture etc. is carried on (*ironworks, gasworks*; *the works is* or *are closed next week*); **~s council,** group of employees representing those employed in a works etc. in discussions with employer. **11.** (Articles having) ornamentation of specified kind, things or parts made of specified material or with specified tools etc., (*covered with elaborate work*; *rustic, embossed, beaten, frosted,* etc., *work*; WOOD*work*, IRON¹*work*, STONE*work*; FANCY¹*-work*, NEEDLE*work*, POKER¹*-work*); needlework, knitting, etc.; (Naut.) UPPER *works*. **12. ~'aday,** fit for or used or seen on workdays, ordinary, everyday, practical, (*this workaday world*); **~-bag, -basket, -box,** (holding materials and implements for work, esp. for needlework); **~-bench** (for mechanical work, esp. carpentry); **~-camp** (for work esp. by volunteers helping a community); **~'day,** day on which work is usu. done; **~-force,** (number of) workers engaged or available in an industry etc.; **~-horse,** horse (or fig. person or machine etc.) that performs arduous labour; **~'house,** ‖(Hist.) public institution for reception of paupers in parish or union of parishes, *house of correction for petty offenders; **~-load,** amount of work to be done by particular employee etc.; **~'man,** man hired to do manual labour, person *good, bad, skilled,* etc., at his job (*a bad workman blames, quarrels with, his tools*); **~'manlike,** characteristic of a good workman; **~'manship,** person's relative skill in doing task, relative finish or execution seen in manufactured article or work of art, thing made (*the world is God's workmanship*); **~'mate,** one engaged in same work as another; **~'people,** people employed in labour for wages; **~'piece,** thing worked on with tool or machine; **~-room** (in which work is done); **~'sheet,** paper for recording work done, calculations in progress, etc.; **~'shop,** (1) room or building in which manufacture is carried on, (2) meeting of several persons for intensive discussion etc.; **~-shy,** disinclined to work; **~ study,** system of examining performance of jobs so that they can produce the best results for employees and employers; **~-table** (with drawers for sewing-materials etc.); **~'woman,** female worker or operative. **13.** Hence **~'**LESS *a.* [OE *weorc* etc., = OS *werk*, OHG *werc*, ON *verk* f. Gmc **werkam* f. IE **wergon*]

work[2] (wě̄rk) *v.* (**~ed;** *or* **wrought** *pr.* rawt, arch. exc. in formal use in senses 1, 4, 5, and 8). **1.** *v.i.* Engage in bodily or mental work, carry on operations (*at* or *on* thing), make efforts (*for* or *against* cause), be craftsman *in* some material (*worked* or *wrought in brass* etc.); ~ **away** or **on,** continue to work; *work double* TIDE[1]*s*; ~ **to rule,** follow rules of one's occupation pedantically to reduce efficiency, usu. as protest; ~ **with,** work jointly with (person), be workmate of. **2.** (Of machine, plan, etc.) operate, act, do its appointed work, (*charm, drug, pump, scheme, works* or *will not work*); (of part of machine) run, revolve, go through regular motions, (*wheel works on axle, works freely, stiffly*, etc.). **3.** *v.t.* (Of person) put or keep (machine etc.) in operation, keep (person, horse, machine, etc.) going or at work, exact toil from, (*work ship, typewriter, lift,* ||*the* ORACLE; *works his men too hard, that idea to death*; *work* one's *fingers to the* BONE[1]); carry on, manage, control, (*work mine, scheme*; *my partner works the Liverpool district*; *is worked by wires, electricity*, etc.). **4.** *v.i.* Have influence or effect, exercise influence (*up*)*on*, (*work upon* person, *his mind*, etc.; *all these things have worked together for good*; *the appeal wrought powerfully upon him*; OVERWROUGHT). **5.** *v.t.* Bring about, effect, accomplish, produce as result, (*work wonders, cures, mischief, a change*); ~ one's **will,** accomplish one's purpose (*upon* person or thing); *will* ~ **it** *if I can*, (sl.) bring it about, achieve desired result. **6.** *v.i.* Be in motion, be agitated, cause agitation, ferment (lit. or fig.), (*face, features, worked violently*; *waves work to and fro*; *thoughts, conscience, working within him*; *yeast began to work*). **7.** *v.i.* & *t.* Make way or make (way etc.) or cause to make way slowly or with difficulty or by shifting motions (usu. w. *adv.* or *prep.*), gradually become (loose, free, tight, etc.) by motion, (*socks work down, shirt works up*; *needle worked out eventually from her arm*; *ferrule has worked off, loose*; *work your knife through the card*; *was trying to work round to that question*; *angler working upstream*; *grub works its way into* or *out of*; *wind has worked round*); (Naut.) sail against wind (*ship is working eastwards*). **8.** *v.t.* Knead, hammer, fashion, into shape or desired consistency (*work dough, clay*, etc.; *work flour and butter into a paste*; *butter should be thoroughly worked*); **wrought iron** (forged or rolled, not cast). **9.** Artificially and gradually excite *into* (*worked his audience into enthusiasm, himself into a rage*). **10.** *v.i.* & *t.* Do, make by, needlework or the like (*reads to them while they work*; *work pattern, initials*, etc., *on linen*, etc.; *is working a shawl*). **11.** *v.t.* Solve (sum) by mathematical processes. **12.** Purchase (one's PASSAGE[1] etc.) with labour instead of money (lit. or fig.); obtain by labour the money for (one's way through university etc.). **13.** ~ **in,** find place for (illustration, subject, etc.; *will work it in somewhere*); ~*-in* n., take-over by workers etc. of factory threatened with closure; ~ **off,** get rid of, get over, find customers etc. for, by work or activity; ~ **out,** find (amount etc.) or solve (sum) by calculation, (of amount etc.) be calculated *at* (*works out at £6·50*), (of sum) give definite result (*will not work out*), exhaust with work (person, *a mine*, etc., *is quite worked out*), accomplish or attain with difficulty (*work out* one's *salvation*), have result (*plan did not work out well*), provide for or plan all details of (*has worked out a scheme of invasion*); ~*-out* n., (esp. in Boxing etc.) a practice or test; ~ **over,** examine thoroughly, (colloq.) treat with violence; ~ **up,** bring gradually into efficient state, elaborate in description, advance gradually *to* (climax), excite (person, expectations, etc.) by degrees, mingle (materials) into whole, acquire familiarity with (subject) by study. [OE *wyrcan* (Gmc **wurkjan*), *wircan* (Gmc **werkjan*), & *we*(*o*)*rcan* (f. *we*(*o*)*rc* n.); see prec.]

wor'kab|le (wě̄r'-) *a.* That can be worked, that will work, that is worth working, practicable, feasible; hence **~**ABI'LITY, **~able**NESS (-beln-), *ns.*, **~ab**LY[2] *adv.* [f. prec. + -ABLE]

wor'ker (wě̄r'-) *n.* In vbl senses; employee esp. in manual or industrial work; neuter or undeveloped female of various social insects (bee, ant, etc.); ~ **priest,** French R.C. priest who engages in non-religious (esp. industrial) work for part of his time. [ME, f. WORK[2] + -ER[1]]

wor'kĭng[1] (wě̄r'-) *n.* In vbl senses; way thing works or result of its working; mine, quarry, etc., or part of it in which work is being or has been done (*was found in a disused working*); ~ **capital** (used in actual carrying on of business); ~ **day,** (1) = WORK[1]*day*, (2) portion of the day devoted to work; ~ **drawing** (to scale, serving as guide for building or construction); ~ **hours,** those normally devoted to work; ~ **hypothesis** (used as basis for action); ~ **knowledge** (adequate to work with); ~ **lunch** etc., meal at which business, policy, etc., are discussed; ~ **order,** condition in which machine etc. works (satisfactorily); **~-out,** calculation of results, elaboration of details. [ME, f. WORK[2] + -ING[1]]

wor'kĭng[2] (wě̄r'-) *a.* In vbl senses; engaged in manual or industrial labour (*working man*; *the working class*); ~ **model** (of machine etc., able to operate though on reduced scale); ~ **party,** (esp.) ||committee etc. appointed to advise on improving efficiency in an industry etc. or to investigate and report on some question. [ME, f. WORK[2] + -ING[2]]

world (wě̄r-) *n.* **1.** Time or state or scene of human existence; **the** or **this** ~, mortal life; **out of this** ~, (colloq.) incredibly good etc., indescribable; **the other** or **next** ~, **the** ~ **to come,** life after death; *the* LOWER[3] *world*; **Prince of this** ~, *the* Devil; **bring into the** ~, (1) possess at one's birth, (2) deliver (child) at birth, (3) beget or bear (child); **come into the** ~, be born; **get** etc. **the best of both ~s,** benefit from both secular and spiritual (or other partly conflicting) interests; **the end of the** ~, cessation of all mortal life by destruction of universe or otherwise; ~ **without end,** for ever. **2.** Secular interests and occupations (**the** ~, **the flesh, and the devil,** kinds of temptation). **3.** The universe, all creation, everything, (*the best of all possible worlds*); **in the** ~, at all, that exists, etc., (*who, how, what, in the world was it?*; *nothing in the world*); **for all the** ~ **like,** precisely like; **carry the** ~ **before** one, have rapid and complete success. **4.** Everything that exists outside oneself (**the external** ~, all phenomena; DEAD *to the world*; **the** ~ **of dreams,** things as they seem in dreams); anything however valuable (*would not do it for the, to gain the whole, world*; *she is all the world to me*; *think the world of her*; *would give the world to know*). **5.** The earth, heavenly body supposed to resemble it, its countries and their inhabitants, all people, the earth as known or in some respect limited, (*go round the world*; *a universe of worlds*; *are there other worlds than ours?*; *all the world's a stage*; *make a* NOISE *in the world*; **all the** ~ **knows,** it is generally known; (**all**) **the** ~ **over,** throughout the world; **the ~'s end,** farthest attainable point of travel; **the wise old** ~, general experience and custom; **give to the** ~, publish; *on* TOP[1] *of the world*; **the Old W~,** Europe, Asia, and Africa, part known by ancients to exist (OLD-*world*); **the New W~,** America; **the Roman** etc. ~, as much of the world as concerned Rome etc.; *the* THIRD *World*); (*attrib.*) affecting many nations (*world politics, tendency*), of all nations (*world champion, record*). **6.** Human affairs, their course and conditions, active life, (*so wags the world; how goes the world with you?*); **know, see, the ~,** have, acquire, experience; **man** or **woman of the ~,** practical tolerant person experienced in life or society; **all's right with the ~** (expression of optimism); **take the ~ as it is, as one finds it,** be adaptable. **7.** Average or respectable or fashionable society or people or their customs or opinions; **the great ~,** fashionable society; **all the ~ and his wife,** (1) all with pretensions to fashion, (2) any miscellaneous large assembly; **what will the ~ say?,** dare we defy public opinion?. **8.** All that concerns or all who belong to specified department or class, sphere, domain, (*the literary, scientific, sporting, animal, ancient, world; the world of letters, art, sport*). **9.** A vast or infinite number or amount or extent (*a world of meaning, trouble, faults; will do him a* or *the world of good*); **a ~** or **~s** *too wide* etc., by far. **10. W~ Bank,** (colloq.) International Bank for Reconstruction and Development; **~-beater,** person or thing surpassing all others; **W~ Cup,** quadrennial competition between association football teams representing various countries; **~-famous,** known throughout the world; **~ language,** (1) artificial language for universal use, (2) language spoken in many countries; **~-line,** (Phys.) curve in space-time joining positions of a particle throughout its existence; **~ power,** nation having influence in world politics; **W~ Series,** U.S. championship for baseball teams; **~-shaking,** important enough to affect the whole world; **~-view,** *Weltanschauung*; **~ war,** war involving many important nations (*First, Second, W~ War*, of 1914–18, 1939–45); **~-weary,** weary of (the life of) the world; **~-wide,** covering, occurring in, known in, all parts of the world. [OE *w(e)orold, world,* = OS *werold,* OHG *weralt,* ON *veröld* f. Gmc **weraz* man + **aldh-* age (see OLD)]

wor'ldling (wẽr'-) *n.* Worldly person. [f. prec. + -LING¹]

wor'ldl|y̆ (wẽr'-) *a.* Temporal, earthly, (**~y goods,** property); exclusively or mainly concerned with or devoted to the affairs of this life, esp. to pursuit of wealth or pleasure (**~y wisdom,** esp. prudence in advancing one's own interests); **~y-minded,** intent on worldly things; **~y-wise,** having worldly wisdom; hence **~ĭNESS** *n.* [OE *woruldlic* (as WORLD, -LY¹)]

worm¹ (wẽrm) *n.* **1.** Invertebrate limbless or apparently limbless slender burrowing or creeping animal, esp. segmented in rings or parasitic in intestines or tissues; wormlike larva of insect, esp. one feeding on fruit, timber, etc.; SHIP¹-*worm*; blind-worm or SLOW-WORM; maggot supposed to eat dead bodies in the grave (**food for ~s,** dead person); (fig.) inward torment; (in *pl.*) internal (esp. intestinal) parasites; **(even) a ~ will turn,** the meekest will resist or retaliate if pushed too far. **2.** Abject or insignificant or contemptible person. **3.** Spiral part of screw; spiral pipe of still in which vapour is cooled and condensed. **4.** Ligament under dog's tongue. **5. ~-cast,** convoluted tubular mass of earth voided by earthworm on surface of ground; **~'eaten,** eaten into by worms, full of worm-holes, (fig.) antiquated; **~-fishing** (with worm for bait); **~-gear,** arrangement of toothed wheel worked by revolving spiral; **~-hole** (left in wood, fruit, etc., by passage of worm); **~-seed,** (plant e.g. santonica bearing) seed used to expel intestinal worms; **~'s-eye view,** (joc.) view as seen from below or from humble position (opp. *bird's-eye view*); **~-wheel,** wheel of worm-gear. **6.** Hence **~'Y²** *a.* [OE *wyrm,* = OS, OHG *wurm,* ON *ormr* serpent, Goth. *waurms* f. Gmc **wurmiz, *wurmaz*]

worm² (wẽrm) *v.* **1.** *v. refl.* & *i.* Insinuate one*self* or oneself *into* (favour, person's confidence, etc.). **2.** *v.t.* & *i.* Convey one*self*, progress, make one's way, with crawling motion (*wormed himself* or *his way* or *wormed through the bushes*). **3.** *v.t.* Draw (secret etc.) by crafty persistence *out* (*of* person) or *from* (person). **4.** Cut worm of (dog's tongue). **5.** Rid (plant, dog, etc.) of worms. [f. prec.]

wor'mwood (wẽr'-) *n.* Perennial herb of genus *Artemisia* with bitter, tonic, and stimulating qualities used in preparation of vermouth and absinth and in medicine; bitter mortification or its cause. [ME, alt. f. obs. *wormod* f. OE *wormōd, wermōd,* (OS *wer(i)moda,* OHG *wer(i)muota,* of unkn. orig.), after *worm, wood*; cf. VERMOUTH]

worn. See WEAR¹.

wo'rrit (wŭ'-) *v.* & *n.* (colloq.) = foll. [orig. vulg. alt. f. foll.]

wo'rrỹ (wŭ'-) *v.* & *n.* **1.** *v.t.* (Of dog) bite or seize esp. at throat (rat, sheep, dog) repeatedly, shake or pull about with the teeth; attack repeatedly; **~ out,** obtain (solution to problem etc.) by dogged effort. **2.** Tease, harass, importune, be continuously or intermittently troublesome to, allow no rest or peace of mind to (**~ oneself,** take needless trouble); (in *p.p.*) uneasy (**much** or **very worried,** full of uneasiness; **wears a worried look,** looks anxious or troubled). **3.** *v.i.* Give way to anxiety, let the mind dwell on troubles, fret; **I should ~,** (colloq.) it doesn't trouble or concern me at all; **not to ~,** (colloq.) do not worry, there is no need to worry; **~ along** or **through,** manage to advance by persistence in spite of obstacles. **4.** Hence **wo'rrĭMENT** *n.*, **wo'rrĭSOME¹** *a.*, (wŭ'-). **5.** *n.* Dog's worrying of quarry; (usu. in *pl.*) care(s), thing(s) that worry person; cares, worried state, over-anxiety; **~ beads,** string of beads for fiddling with to occupy one's hands or calm oneself; **~-guts, ~-wart,** (colloq.) person who habitually worries unduly. [OE *wyrgan* kill, = OHG *wurgan* f. WG **wurgjan*]

worse (wẽrs) *a., adv.,* & *n.* **1.** *a.* & *adv.* More bad or badly or evil or ill; (as *pred. a.*) in or into less good health (*is worse today; is getting worse*), in less good condition or circumstances (*is none the worse for it; the worse for* LIQUOR, *for* WEAR²); *for* BETTER¹ (*or*) *for worse*; **~ luck!,** excl. of disappointment at unlucky event; *worse* OFF; **~ and ~,** increasingly worse; hence **wor'SEN⁶** (wẽr'-) *v.t.* & *i.* **2.** *n.* Worse thing(s) (*have worse to tell; but worse followed; you might do worse than* (*to*) *accept*); **from bad to ~,** into even worse state; **or ~,** or as an even worse alternative; **the ~,** defeat in contest, worse condition (*a change for the worse*); **if worse comes to* WORST. [OE *wyrsa, wiersa,* = OS *wirsa,* OHG *wirsiro,* ON *verri,* Goth. *wairsiza* f. Gmc **wersizon* (**wers-*; cf. WAR¹)]

wor'ship (wẽr'-) *n.* & *v.* (‖**-pp-**). **1.** (arch.) Worthiness, merit, recognition given or due to these, honour and respect, (**men of ~,** persons of repute). **2. Your, His, W~** (title used to or of certain magistrates, or to show respect for person of higher station or ironical pretence of this). **3.** Reverence paid to God or god, esp. in church service (*public worship; do worship*; **freedom of ~,** = *freedom of* RELIGION; **place of ~,** church); adoration or devotion comparable to this felt or shown towards person or principle (*an object of worship; regarding her with worship in his eyes; the worship of wealth, intellect, athletics*). **4.** *v.t.* Adore as divine, pay religious homage to; idolize, regard with adoration, (*worships the ground she walks on*). **5.** *v.i.* Take part in (public) worship;

be full of adoration. **6.** Hence ~(**p**)ER[1] *n.* [OE *weorthscipe* (as WORTH[1], -SHIP)]

wor'shĭpful (wěr′-) *a.* **1.** (arch.) Entitled to honour and respect. **2.** ||(Title given to justices of the peace, recorders, London City companies and Freemasons' lodges and their masters). **3.** Imbued with spirit of veneration. **4.** Hence ~LY[2] *adv.*, ~NESS *n.* [ME, f. prec. + -FUL]

worst (wěr-) *a.*, *adv.*, *n.*, & *v.t.* **1.** *a.* & *adv.* Most bad or badly or evil or ill. **2.** *n.* Worst part, feature, state, possible assumption, event, possible issue, or action (*the worst of the storm is over*; *that is the worst of being clever*; *saw him at his worst*; *if the worst happens*; *prepare for the worst*; *when things are at the* or *their worst*); **at (the)** ~, in the worst possible case; **get** or **have the ~ of it,** be worsted; ||**if the ~ comes to the ~, *if worse comes to ~,** if the worst happens; **do your, let him** etc. **do his** etc., ~, (expression of defiance). **3.** *v.t.* Get the better of, defeat, outdo. [OE *wierresta, wyrresta* a., *wyr(re)st* adv., = OS *wirsista*, OHG *wirsisto*, ON *verst(r)* f. Gmc **wersistaz* (**wers-* WORSE; see -EST[1])]

wor'stĕd (wŏŏ′s-) *n.* Fine smooth yarn spun from combed long-staple wool; fabric woven from this. [f. *Worste(a)d* in Norfolk]

wort (wěrt) *n.* **1.** Plant, herb, (arch. exc. in names of plants: *St. John's wort*; *woundwort*; *liverwort*). **2.** Infusion of malt before it is fermented into beer. [sense 1 f. OE *wyrt*, = OS *wurt*, OHG *wurz*, ON *urt*, Goth. *waurts*; sense 2 f. OE *wyrt*, = OS *wurtja* spicery, MHG *würze*; both cogn. w. ROOT[1]]

worth[1] (wěrth) *pred. a.* (governing *n.* like *prep.*) & *n.* **1.** *a.* Of value equivalent to (*is worth much, little, nothing, about £1*; BIRD *in the hand is worth two in the bush*; *what is the house worth?*; *the rarer it is the more it is worth*). **2.** Deserving, worthy of, bringing compensation for, (*worth doing, hearing, notice, the trouble*, (one's) WHILE[1], one's SALT, *an effort*); **~ it,** (colloq.) worth while; **well ~,** certainly worth (doing etc.); *I give you, you must take, this* **for what it is ~,** without guarantee of its truth, wisdom, etc. **3.** Possessed of, having property amounting to, (*is, died, worth a million pounds*; *spent all he was worth on it*); **for all** one **is ~,** (colloq.) with one's utmost efforts, without reserve. **4. ~'while,** that is worth WHILE[1] (*a worthwhile undertaking*). **5.** *n.* What a person or thing is worth, value, merit, high merit or excellence, (*of great, little, no, worth*; *persons of worth*; *true worth often goes unrecognized*); hence ~'LESS *a.* **6.** Equivalent of money etc. in commodity (*give me a pound's worth of stamps*); MONEY'*s-worth*; PENNY*worth*; SHILLING*sworth*. [OE *w(e)orth* etc. a. & n., = OS *werth*, OHG *werd*, ON *verth(r)*, Goth. *wairth(s)*]

worth[2] (wěrth) *v.t.* 3 *sing. pres. subj.* (arch.) **Woe ~,** cursed be (*the day* etc.). [OE *weorthan* become, = OS *werthan*, OHG *werdan*, ON *vertha*, Goth. *wairthan* f. Gmc **werthan* f. IE **wert-*]

wor'th|ў (wěr′dhĭ) *a.* & *n.* **1.** *a.* Estimable, having some moral worth, of a fair degree of merit, respectable, (*a grave and worthy man*; *has lived a worthy life*); (with patronizing effect, cf. HONEST) no more than moderately estimable (*I asked the worthy rustic whether*). **2.** Deserving *of* or *to* be or do, (arch.) deserving of, (*is worthy of* or *worthy remembrance* or *being remembered*; *is worthy to be remembered, to take the lead*). **3.** Corresponding to the worth *of* or (arch.) of, adequate, appropriate, of sufficient worth or merit, (*in words worthy of* or *worthy the occasion*; *he is not worthy of her*; *a foeman worthy of your steel*; *has found a worthy opponent*; *received a worthy reward*). **4.** Hence **~ĭLY**[2] *adv.*, **~ĭNESS** *n.* **5.** *n.* Worthy person; person of some distinction in his country, time, etc.; (joc.) person. [ME *wurthi* etc., f. WORTH[1] 5 + -Y[2]]

-worthў (wěrdhĭ) *suf.* forming *adjs.*, w. sense 'deserving of' (*blameworthy*, *noteworthy*, *praiseworthy*), 'suitable or fit for' (*newsworthy*, *roadworthy*, *seaworthy*). [f. prec.]

wŏt('tĕst). See WIT[1].

would, would-be, wouldn't, would(e)st. See WILL[1].

Woulfe, Woulff, (wŏŏlf) *n.* **~ bottle,** (Chem.) jar with more than one neck, used for passing gas through liquid etc. [f. P. *Woulfe*, Engl. chemist d. 1803]

wound[1] (wōō-) *n.*, & *v.t.* **1.** *n.* Injury done by (deliberate) cut or stab or blow or tear to animal or vegetable tissues including and usu. going beyond the cutting or piercing or breaking or tearing of the skin or bark or other integument, (fig.) injury done to person's reputation etc. or pain inflicted on his feelings, (poet.) pangs of love, (*receive, inflict, make, heal, a wound*; *open, incurable, festering, mortal, wound*); **~'wort,** plant formerly supposed to have healing properties, esp. kidney-VETCH or plant of genus *Stachys*; hence ~'LESS *a.* **2.** *v.t.* Inflict wound on (lit. or fig.; *wounded soldiers, feelings*). [(v. f. OE *wundian*) f. OE *wund*, = OS *wunda*, OHG *wunta*, ON *und*]

wound[2]. See WIND[2,3].

wou'nd|ў *a.* & *adv.* (arch.) **1.** *a.* Very great, extreme; hence **~ĭLY**[2] *adv.* **2.** *adv.* Extremely, excessively. [f. *wounds* int. of asseveration (cf. ZOUNDS) + -Y[2]]

wōve[1] *a.* (Of paper) made on wire-gauze frame and so having uniform unlined surface. [var. of *woven*, p.p. of WEAVE[1]]

wōve[2], **wō'ven.** See WEAVE[1].

wow[1] *int.*, *n.*, & *v.t.* **1.** *int.* expr. astonishment or admiration. **2.** *n.* (sl.) A sensational success. **3.** *v.t.* (sl.) Impress or excite greatly. [orig. Sc.; imit.]

wow[2] *n.* Slow pitch-fluctuation in sound-reproduction, perceptible in long notes. [imit.]

wow'ser (-z-) *n.* (Austral.) Puritanical fanatic; spoil-sport; teetotaller. [20th c.; orig. unkn.]

W.P. *abbr.* weather permitting.

w.p.b. *abbr.* waste-paper basket.

||**W.P.C.** *abbr.* woman police CONSTABLE.

w.p.m. *abbr.* words per minute.

W.R. *abbr.* West RIDING[2].

||**W.R.A.C.** *abbr.* Women's Royal Army Corps.

wrăck *n.* Wreck(age); = RACK[1,7]; seaweed cast up, or growing below high-water mark, and used for manure etc. [ME f. MDu. *wrak* or MLG *wra(c)k*, a parallel form. to OE *wræc*, rel. to *wrecan* WREAK; cf. WRECK, RACK[1]]

||**W.R.A.F.** *abbr.* Women's Royal Air Force.

wraith *n.* Person's double or apparition supposedly seen shortly before or after his death; ghost, apparition. [16th c., orig. Sc., of unkn. orig.]

wră'ngle (ră′nggel) *v.i.*, & *n.* Brawl, (engage in) loud or angry argument or altercation or quarrel; *herd (cattle). [ME, prob. f. LDu.; cf. LG *wrangelen*, frequent. of *wrangen* to struggle, cogn. w. WRING]

wră'ngler (-ngg-) *n.* In vbl senses; *cowboy; (Camb. Univ.) person placed in first class of mathematical tripos (**senior ~,** first in the class when it was arranged in order of merit), whence ~SHIP *n.* [f. prec. + -ER[1]]

wrăp *v.* (**-pp-**) & *n.* **1.** *v.t.* **~ (up),** enfold, enclose or pack or conceal in folded or soft encircling material, (*wrap it in paper, cotton wool*; *wrap up parcel*; *mountain, affair, is wrapped in mist, mystery*; *wraps up his meaning in tortuous sentences, in allegory*); **~ up,** finish off, settle, (dealings etc.);

~**ped up,** engrossed or involved (*mother, country's prosperity, is wrapped up in her child, its shipping*). **2.** *v.i.* ~ **over,** (of garment) overlap itself when worn; ~ **up,** put on wraps (*mind you wrap up well if you go out*), (in *imper.*, sl.) be quiet; ~**'around** *a.* & *n.*, (object) that extends round a thing. **3.** *v.t.* Arrange or draw (flexible covering) *round* or *about* person or thing (*wrapped her shawl closer about her*); hence ~**'PING**[1] (3) *n.* **4.** *n.* (usu. in *pl.*) Shawl(s), rug(s), coat(s), cloak(s), neckerchief(s), etc., as addition to ordinary indoor clothes; **take the ~s off,** disclose; **under ~s,** in concealment or secrecy. [ME, of unkn. orig.]

wră'ppage *n.* Wrapping(s). [f. prec. + -AGE]

wră'pper *n.* In vbl senses; (loose indoor garment resembling) dressing-gown; paper enclosing newspaper or similar packet for posting; paper enclosing sweet, chocolate, etc.; (freq. detachable) paper cover of book; tobacco-leaf of superior quality enclosing cigar. [ME, f. WRAP + -ER[1]]

wrăsse *n.* Thick-lipped strong-toothed bright-coloured rock-haunting sea-fish of family Labridae. [f. Corn. *wrach*, mutated f. *gwrach*, = W *gwrach*, lit. 'old woman']

wrath (rŏ- *or* raw-) *n.* (poet., rhet., or joc.) Anger, indignation; **vessels** or **children of** ~, persons destined to undergo divine chastisement; VIALS *of wrath*; **slow to** ~, not irascible; hence ~'FUL, *~'Y[2], *adjs.* [OE *wrǣththu* (*wrāth* WROTH + *-*ithō* -TH[1])]

wreak *v.t.* **1.** (arch.) Avenge (wrong, wronged person). **2.** Give play or satisfaction to, put in operation, (*vengeance*, *rage*, etc., usu. (*up*)*on* enemy etc.; *effort* etc.); cause (damage etc.). [OE *wrecan* drive, avenge, etc., = OS *wrekan*, OHG *rehhan*, ON *reka*, Goth. *wrikan* persecute, f. Gmc **wrekan* (**wrek-*, cf. WRACK, WRECK, WRETCH, f. IE **wreg-*)]

wreath *n.* (*pl. pr.* -dhz *or* -ths). Flowers or leaves strung or woven or wound together into ring for wearing on head or for decorating statue, building, etc., or placing as mark of respect on coffin etc.; carved imitation of this; similar ring of soft twisted material such as silk, (Her.) representation of this below crest; curl *of* smoke, circular or curved band of cloud, light drifting mass of snow etc. [OE *writha* f. weak grade of *wrīthan* WRITHE]

wreathe (-dh) *v.* **1.** *v.t.* Encircle as or (as) with wreath (*face wreathed in smiles*); form (flowers, silk, etc.) into wreath; wind (one's arms etc. or (of snake etc.) it*self*) *round* person etc.; make (garland). **2.** *v.i.* (Of smoke etc.) move in shape of wreaths. [partly back form. f. *wrethen* (see foll.); partly f. prec.]

wrea'then (-dh-) *a.* (arch.) Wreathed, intertwined. [ME *wrethan*, *writhen*, p.p. of WRITHE]

wrĕck *n.* & *v.* **1.** *n.* Ruin, destruction, disablement, esp. of ship (cf. SHIP[1]*wreck*; *save ship*, one's *fortunes*, *from wreck*; *gale caused many wrecks*; *the wreck of the Hesperus*, *of his happiness*). **2.** Ship that has suffered wreck, greatly damaged or disabled building or vehicle or person, disorganized remains or wretched remnant *of*, (*shores are strewn with wrecks*; *person is a physical* or *mental wreck*; *is but a* or *the wreck of his former self*). **3.** (Law). Goods etc. cast up by the sea (*wreck of the sea belongs to the Crown*). **4.** ~**-master,** officer appointed to take charge of goods etc. cast up from wrecked ship. **5.** *v.t.* Cause wreck of (ship, train, hopes, undertaking, person or his fortunes); (in *p.p.*) involved in shipwreck (*wrecked sailors, goods*). **6.** *v.i.* Suffer wreck; *deal with wrecked vehicle(s) etc. [ME, f. AF *wrec* etc. (cf. VAREC), f. ON **wrek* f. Gmc **wrekan* to drive; cf. WREAK]

wrĕ'ckage *n.* Wrecked material, remnants, fragments; action or process of wrecking. [f. prec. + -AGE]

wrĕ'cker *n.* In vbl senses; one who tries from shore to bring about shipwreck with view to profiting by wreckage, or who steals such wreckage; person employed in demolition, or in recovering wrecked ship or its contents; *person who repairs damaged vehicles; *vehicle or train used in recovering damaged one. [f. WRECK + -ER[1]]

wrĕn[1] *n.* Small usu. brown short-winged song-bird of family Troglodytidae, esp. European species with erect tail. [OE *wrenna*, rel. to OHG *wrendo*, *wrendilo*, Icel. *rindill*]

||**Wrĕn**[2] *n.* Member of the Women's Royal Naval Service; hence ~**'NERY** (3) *n.* (joc.). [orig. in pl., f. abbr. W.R.N.S.]

wrĕnch *n.*, & *v.t.* **1.** *n.* Violent twist or oblique pull or tearing off, (fig.) pain caused by parting, (*gave a wrench to his ankle*, *at the door-handle*; *leaving home was a great wrench*). **2.** Implement like spanner (usu. adjustable) made to grip and turn nuts, bolts, etc. **3.** (Phys.) Combination of couple with force along its axis. **4.** *v.t.* Twist or pull (thing, or abs.) violently round or sideways, injure or pull *off* or *away* by twisting, (*wrenched the door open*, *at the handle*, *his horse's head round*, *his ankle*, *fowl's head off*, *opponent's sword from him*); pervert, distort, (facts etc.). [n. f. v., f. OE *wrencan* twist, = OHG *renchen*, of unkn. orig.]

wrĕst *v.t.*, & *n.* **1.** *v.t.* Twist, deflect, distort, pervert, (*wrests the law to suit himself*; *wrest the facts*, *sense* or *words of a passage*, etc.); obtain by effort or with difficulty; force or wrench away from person's grasp (*wrested his sword from him*). **2.** *n.* (arch.) Key for tuning harp, piano, etc.; ~**-block** or **-plank,** part of piano holding ~**-pins,** to which strings are attached. [OE *wrǣstan*, = ON **wreista* f. Gmc **wraistjan*, rel. to WRIST]

wrĕ'stl|e (-sel) *v.* & *n.* **1.** *v.i.* Grapple with and try to throw adversary esp. in sporting contest under code or rules (*with*, or abs.); contend, grapple, do one's utmost to deal, *with* evil, temptation, duty, task, problem, etc.; ~**e with God** or **in prayer,** pray fervently; hence ~ER[1], ~ING[1], (rĕ'sl-) *ns.* **2.** *v.t.* Have wrestling-match with; move with efforts as if wrestling. **3.** *n.* Wrestling-match; hard struggle. [OE **wrǣstlian*; cf. MLG *wrostelen*, OE *wraxlian*]

wrĕtch *n.* Very unfortunate or miserable person; despicable person, person without conscience or shame (often as term of playful depreciation). [OE *wrecca*, = OS *wrekkio*, OHG *reccho* exile, adventurer, f. WG **wrakjo* f. Gmc **wrak-* (cf. WREAK)]

wrĕ'tchėd *a.* Miserable, unhappy, afflicted; inferior, of bad quality or no merit, contemptible, unsatisfactory, causing discontent or discomfort or nuisance, confounded, (*wretched weather*, *health*, *horse*, *inn*, *accommodation*, *poetry*, *poet*, etc.); **feel** ~, be much embarrassed or very unwell; hence ~LY[2] *adv.*, ~NESS *n.* [ME, irreg. f. prec. + -ED[1]; cf. WICKED]

wrĭck. See RICK[2].

wrĭ'ggle *v.* & *n.* **1.** *v.i.* (Of worm etc.) move body with short twistings, (of animal or person) make wormlike motions, (fig.) be slippery, practise evasion; make way *along*, *through*, *out*, *in*, etc., by wriggling (lit. or fig.; *wriggle out of a garment*, *a difficulty*). **2.** *v.t.* Move oneself, one's *body*, *tail*, *hand*, etc., with wriggling motion; make one's *way* by wriggling. **3.** *n.* Wriggling movement. [ME, f. MLG *wriggelen* frequent. of *wriggen*; see -LE 3]

wright (rīt) *n.* Craftsman, maker, (arch. exc. in comb., as *shipwright*, *wheelwright*, *playwright*).

[OE *wryhta*, *wyrhta*, = OS *wurhtio*, OHG *wurhto* f. WG **wurhtjo* (**wurk*-; cf. WORK[2])]

wrĭng *v.t.* (**wrung**), & *n.* **1.** *v.t.* Squeeze, squeeze and twist esp. to remove liquid (*out*), twist forcibly, break by twisting; distress, torture; ~ person's **hand,** press it with emotion; ~ one's **hands,** squeeze them together in sign of great distress; **~ing wet,** (colloq.) **~ing,** so wet that moisture can be removed by wringing; ~ **neck of,** kill chicken etc. by twisting its head round. **2.** Extract by squeezing, get *out* by pressure or importunity, extort, (*wring water, groan, consent, money, from* or *out of* or *out*). **3.** Hence (-)~'ER[1] (2) *n.* (esp. device for squeezing wet clothes etc. between rollers). **4.** *n.* Squeeze (*gave my hand, give those clothes, a wring*). [OE *wringan*, = OS *-wringan*, OHG *ringan*, rel. to WRONG]

wrĭ'nkle *n.* & *v.* **1.** *n.* Furrow-like crease or depression or ridge in the skin (esp. of the kind produced by age) or other flexible surface; hence **wrĭ'nkl**Y[2] *a.* **2.** (colloq.) Piece of serviceable information not generally known, tip, dodge, (*is full of wrinkles*; *gave me, put me up to, a wrinkle or two*). **3.** *v.t.* Produce wrinkles in (*he wrinkled his forehead*; *wrinkled with age*). **4.** *v.i.* Form wrinkles; become marked with wrinkles. [orig. repr. OE *gewrinclod* sinuous]

wrĭst *n.* Joint connecting hand with forearm; corresponding part in animal; part of garment covering wrist; (effect got in fencing, ball-games, sleight-of-hand, etc., by) ~(**-work**), working of the hand from the wrist alone; ~(**-pin**), (Mech.) stud projecting from crank etc. as attachment for connecting-rod; **~'band,** band forming or concealing end of shirt-sleeve, cuff; **~-drop,** inability to extend hand through paralysis of forearm muscles; **~-watch** (worn on strap etc. round wrist). [OE, = MHG *rist*, ON *rist* instep f. Gmc **wristiz*, prob. f. **wridh-*, weak grade of base of WRITHE]

wrĭ'stlėt *n.* Band or ring worn on wrist to strengthen or guard it or as ornament, bracelet, handcuff, etc.; ||~ **watch,** = WRIST-*watch*. [f. prec. + -LET]

wrĭt[1] *n.* **1.** Form of written command in name of sovereign, State, court, etc., issued to official or other person and directing him to act or abstain from acting in some way (*writ of attachment, habeas corpus, subpoena*, etc.); **serve ~ on** person, deliver it to him; ~ **runs** *in district* etc., is theoretically valid or is actually respected. **2.** Crown document summoning peer to Parliament or ordering election of member(s) of Parliament. **3.** HOLY or *Sacred Writ*. [OE, = OHG *riz* written stroke, ON *rit*, Goth. *writs* f. as WRITE]

wrĭt[2]. See foll.

wrīte *v.* (**wrote** *pr.* rōt, arch. **writ**; **wrĭ'tten,** usu. arch. **writ**). **1.** *v.i.* Form or mark symbols representing word(s) esp. with pen or pencil or typewriter on paper or parchment or other surface (*write legibly, in ink*; *cannot* or *does not read or write*). **2.** *v.t.* Form or mark (such symbols), form or mark the symbols that represent or constitute (word, special script, etc.), (*writes a good* etc. HAND[1] 7; *write* one's *name*; *writes his name with a final 'e'*; *notice is written on wall*; *can write his alphabet, the Greek letters, Greek, shorthand*); enter (data) in computer store, esp. on magnetic tape. **3.** (fig., esp. in *p.p.*) Indicate (quality or condition) by appearance *on* etc. person's face etc. (*has honesty written in his face*; *guilt was written all over her*); cause to be recorded (*name written in* BOOK[1] *of life*; *writ(ten) in* WATER[1]); **writ large,** on a large scale, in a magnified or emphasized form. **4.** Fill, draw up or fill in, with writing (*has written three sheets*; *paper written all over*; *write cheque, certificate, application*, etc.); underwrite (insurance policy). **5.** *v.t.* & *i.* Compose for written or printed reproduction or publication, put into literary etc. form and set down in writing, be engaged temporarily or permanently in such composition, compose books etc. *well* etc., (*is writing a book, an article, his life, poetry, a novel, report, letter, play, symphony, opera*, etc.; *New Testament was written in Greek*; *writes a little, in* or *for the papers, for a living*, etc.); bring (character, episode) *into* or *out of* story by suitable changes of text. **6.** Write and send letter (*to* person, or abs.), (U.S., Commerc., or colloq.) write and send letter to (person), (*writes home once a week*; *nothing to write* HOME[1] *about*; *have written to him*; *we wrote you last week*; *will write (off) for a fresh supply*). **7.** *v.t.* Send or convey (*to* person news, *that, how*, etc.) by letter (*write me all the news, the result, how you got home*; *wrote to his mother that he was bullied*). **8.** State in writing or print (*Herodotus writes, it is written, that*). **9.** (arch.) Describe in writing as (*writes himself esquire*). **10.** ~ **down,** (1) record or take note of in writing, (2) write as if for those considered inferior, (3) disparage in writing, (4) reduce nominal value of (stock, goods, etc.); ~ **in,** (1) send letter to firm etc., (2) *add (extra name) on list of candidates when voting (so *~-in* n.); ~ **off,** write and send letter, compose with facility, cancel, recognize in writing the non-existence or annulment of, (bad debts, sums absorbed by depreciation, lost or destroyed goods, etc.; so *~-off* n., esp. vehicle etc. so badly damaged as to be not worth repairing); ~ **out,** write the whole of, exhaust one*self* by writing (*has written himself out*, has no ideas etc. left); ~ **up,** (1) praise in writing, (2) write full account of (incident etc.; so *~-up* n.), (3) make entries to bring (diary etc.) up to date. **11.** Hence **wrī't**ABLE *a.* [OE *wrītan* scratch, score, write, = OS *wrītan* cut, write, OHG *rīzan* tear, draw, ON *rita* score, write, f. Gmc **wrītan*; orig. of symbols inscribed with sharp tools on stone or wood]

wrī'ter *n.* In vbl senses; clerk, esp. in Navy or in government offices; scribe; author; **the (present)** ~, myself; **W~ to the Signet,** Scottish solicitor conducting cases before Court of SESSION; **~'s cramp,** muscular spasm due to excessive writing. [OE *wrītere* (as prec.; see -ER[1])]

wrīthe (rīdh) *v.* & *n.* **1.** *v.i.* Twist or roll oneself about (as) in acute pain, squirm; shrink mentally, be stung or bitterly annoyed, (*under, at*, insult etc.; *with* shame etc.). **2.** *v.t.* Twist (one's body etc.) about. **3.** *n.* Act of writhing. [OE *wrīthan*, = OHG *rīdan*, ON *rítha*, rel. to WREATHE]

wrĭ'then (-dh-) *a.* (arch.) Writhing, twisting, intertwined. [ME, p.p. of prec.]

wrī'tĭng *n.* In vbl senses; handwriting; written document; piece of literary work done, book, article, etc., (*the writings of Plato*; **W~s,** Hagiographa); **at this (present)** ~, at the time when this is being written; **put** thing **in** ~, write it down; **~-case** (holding writing-materials); **~-desk,** desk for writing at, esp. with compartments for papers etc.; **~-ink** (opp. *printing-ink*); **the ~ on the wall,** ominously significant event etc. (Dan. 5:5, 25:28); *writing*-PAD[3]; **~-paper,** paper for writing on, esp. cut to size usual for letters; **~-table,** table for writing at, usu. with drawers etc. [ME, f. WRITE + -ING[1]]

wrĭ'tten. See WRITE.

||**W.R.N.S.** *abbr.* Women's Royal Naval Service.

wrŏng *a.*, *n.*, *adv.*, & *v.t.* **1.** *a.* Out of order, in(to) bad or abnormal condition, (*something is wrong with him, with the engine*; *my watch has gone wrong*); **what's ~ with . . .?,** (colloq.) surely no alternative or substitute for . . . is wanted. **2.** Contrary to law or morality, wicked, (*knows the right from the wrong*; *lying is wrong*). **3.** Other than the right or suitable or the more or most desirable (*always does the wrong thing*; *backed the wrong horse*; *took the wrong road*; *the wrong answer, move*); **in the ~ box,** unsuitably or awkwardly placed, in a difficulty, at a disadvantage; **get hold of the ~ end of the stick,** (fig.) be quite mistaken in attempt to understand; **~ fount,** (of printed letter etc.) size, shape, etc., other than what is wanted; **~ side,** side (of fabric etc.) not meant to be exposed or used (*~ side out*, inside out), less good or undesired side (of door, the BLANKET¹, specified age, etc.; *out of* BED¹ *on the wrong side*; cf. LAUGH 1, TRACK¹ 1, 5); *get wrong* SOW² *by ear*; BARK⁵ *up wrong tree*; **~ 'un,** (colloq.) person of bad character, (Cricket) googly; **go down the ~ way,** (of food) enter windpipe instead of gullet; **(the) ~ way round,** in opposite of proper or usual orientation. **4.** Mistaken, in error, (*a wrong opinion, guess, decision, hypothesis*; *clock is wrong by ten minutes*; *I think you are, can prove you, wrong*); **~-headed,** perverse and obstinate. **5.** Hence ~'LY² *adv.*, ~'NESS *n.* **6.** *n.* What is morally wrong, wrong action, (*the difference between right and wrong*; *can two wrongs make a right?*); **do ~,** sin, offend, transgress. **7.** Injustice, unjust action or treatment, (*do wrong to*; *suffer wrong*; *has done me a great wrong*); **do** person **~,** malign or mistreat him. **8. In the ~,** in position of or responsibility for having caused quarrel, made the mistake, been the offender, etc., (*you were, they are both, in the wrong*); **put** person **in the ~,** show or make it appear that he was the offender. **9.** *adv.* (usu. placed last). In wrong direction or manner, with incorrect result, (*aim, guess, answer, do sum, sort things, wrong*; *you told, led, me wrong*); **get** person **~,** misunderstand him; *(colloq.) **get in ~ with** person, incur his dislike, **get** person **in ~,** bring him into disfavour; **go ~,** take wrong path, (fig.) depart from virtuous behaviour. **10.** *v.t.* Treat unjustly, do wrong to, (*his deeply wronged wife*); mistakenly attribute bad motives etc. to (*I assure you you wrong me*). [OE *wrang* f. ON **wrangr, rangr* awry, unjust, rel. to WRING]

wrŏ'ngdo|er (-dōō-) *n.* Person who violates law or morality; so ~ING¹ *n.* [f. prec. 6 + DOER]

wrŏ'ngful *a.* Characterized by unfairness or injustice; contrary to law; (of person) not entitled to position etc. occupied; hence ~LY² *adv.*, ~NESS *n.* [ME, f. WRONG + -FUL]

wrŏ'ngous *a.* **1.** (arch.) Wrongful. **2.** (Sc. Law). Illegal, unjust. **3.** Hence ~LY² *adv.* [alt. f. ME *wrangwis* (*wrang* wrong + *-wīs*, after *rihtwīs* RIGHTEOUS)]

wrōte. See WRITE.

wrōth *pred. a.* (rhet., poet., or joc.) Angry. [OE *wrāth*, = OS *wrēth*, OHG *reid*, ON *reithr* f. Gmc **wraith-*, **writh-*; cf. WRITHE]

wrought. See WORK².

wrŭng. See WRING.

‖**W.R.V.S.** *abbr.* Women's Royal Voluntary Service.

wrȳ *a.* (**~'er** *or* **wri'er, ~'est** *or* **wri'est,** *pr.* rī'-). Distorted, turned to one side, skew, (**~ face, mouth, smile,** grimace expressing disgust or disappointment or mockery); **~'bill,** N.Z. plover with sharply deflected bill; **~'mouth,** blenny of genus *Cryptacanthodes*; **~'neck,** (1) torticollis, (2) bird of genus *Jynx* allied to woodpeckers able to turn head over shoulder; hence ~'LY² *adv.*, ~'NESS *n.* [f. *wry* v. f. OE *wrīgian* tend, incline, in ME deviate, swerve, contort; cf. OFris. *wrīgia* bend]

W.S. *abbr.* Writer to the Signet.

W.S.W. *abbr.* west-south-west.

wt. *abbr.* weight.

Wu (wōō) *n.* Chinese dialect of Yangtze valley. [Chin.]

wu'nderkĭnd (vōō'nderkĭnt) *n.* Person who achieves great success while relatively young. [G (*wunder* wonder, *kind* child)]

W.Va. *abbr.* West Virginia.

***WW** *abbr.* World War (I, II, etc.).

WX. *abbr.* women's extra large size.

wȳ'andŏtte *n.* American breed of fowl, usu. black and white. [name of Amer. Ind. tribe]

wȳch-, wĭch-, wĭtch-, *pref.* in names of trees with pliant branches: **~-alder,** Amer. plant akin to witch-hazel, with alder-like leaves; **~-elm,** species of elm (*Ulmus glabra*); **~-hazel,** (1) Amer. shrub of genus *Hamamelis* whose bark yields astringent lotion, (2) = *wych-elm*. [OE *wic(e)* app. f. Gmc **wik-* bend, cogn. w. WEAK]

Wȳ'kehamĭst (-kam-) *a.* & *n.* (Past or present member) of Winchester College. [f. mod. L *Wykehamista* f. William of *Wykeham*, bishop of Winchester & founder (d. 1404) + -IST]

wȳn. Var. of WEN².

wȳnd *n.* (Sc.) Narrow street, alley. [ME, app. f. st. of WIND³]

Wyo. *abbr.* Wyoming.

wȳ'vern *n.* (Her.) Winged two-legged dragon with barbed tail. [f. ME *wyver*, f. OF *wivre*, *guivre*, f. L *vipera*; for *-n* cf. BITTERN]

X

X, x, (ĕks) *n.* (*pl.* **Xs** *or* **X's,** *pr.* ĕ'ksĭz). Twenty-fourth letter of alphabet; (Alg., usu. *x*) first unknown quantity; (Geom.) first co-ordinate; unknown or unspecified person etc.; (as Roman numeral) 10 (**xi** 11, **xv** 15, **xx** 20, **xl** 40, **xc** 90); cross-shaped symbol esp. used to indicate position (*X marks the spot*) or incorrectness or to symbolize a kiss or vote, or as signature by person unable to write his name.

-x (-z) *suf.* equiv. to -s¹, retained in *pl.* of many *ns.* in *-u* taken from French (*beaux, jeux d'esprit, tableaux*). [F]

‖**X** *symb.* (Of films) not suitable for persons under 18.

xă'nth|ĭc (z-) *a.* Yellowish; **~ic acid,** colourless unstable acid; hence ~ATE¹ (3) *n.*, yellow salt of xanthic acid. [f. Gk *xanthos* yellow + -IC]

Xănt(h)ĭ'ppė (zăntĭ'-) *n.* Shrewish woman or wife. [name of Socrates' wife]

xănthō'ma (z-) *n.* (*pl.* **~s** *or* **~ta**). (Path.) Skin disease with irregular yellow patches on neck etc. [f. as XANTHIC + -OMA]

xă'nthophȳll (z-) *n.* Dark brown compound associated with chlorophyll and causing yellow colour of leaves in autumn. [f. as XANTHIC + -O- + Gk *phullon* leaf]

X-chrōmosōme (ĕ'kskr-) *n.* Chromosome of which number in cells of one sex (in humans, the female) is twice that in cells of the other sex. [f. *X* as arbitrary label + CHROMOSOME]

x.d. *abbr.* EX² dividend.

Xe *symb.* xenon.

xē′běc (z-) *n.* Small three-masted Mediterranean vessel with lateen and usu. some square sails. [alt. (after Sp. *xabeque*) f. F *chebec* f. It. *sciabecco* f. Arab. *šabāk*]

xě′no- (z-) *comb. form.* Foreign(er), other, as: **~gamy** (-ŏ′g-), cross-fertilization; **~lith,** (Geol.) stone or rock occurring in a system to which it does not belong; **~phobe, ~pho′bia,** (person with) morbid dislike of foreigners. [f. Gk *xenos* strange(r), foreign + -o-]

xě′nŏn (z-) *n.* (Chem.) Heavy inert gaseous element. [Gk, neut. of *xenos* strange]

xērā′nthėmum (z-) *n.* Annual herb of genus *Xeranthemum*, with everlasting composite flowers. [mod. L, f. Gk *xēros* dry + *anthemon* flower]

xēr′o- (z-; *or* zē′ro) *comb. form.* Dry, as: **~graphy** (-ŏ′g-), dry copying process in which black or coloured powder adheres to parts of surface remaining electrically charged when it is exposed to light from bright parts of image of what is to be copied; **~philous** (-ŏ′f-), (of plant) adapted to extremely dry conditions; **~phile, ~phyte,** plant able to grow in very dry conditions, e.g. in desert. [f. Gk *xēros* dry + -o-]

Xēr′ŏx (z-; *or* zē′r-) *n.*, & *v.t.* (Reproduce by) a certain process of xerography. [P as noun]

Xhō′sa (kō′-; *or* kaw′-) *a.* & *n.* (Member or language) of a Bantu people of Cape Province, S. Africa. [native name]

xi (*or* gzī *or* zī) *n.* Fourteenth Greek letter (Ξ, ξ) = x. [Gk]

x.i. *abbr.* EX² interest.

-xion (-kshon) *suf.* forming *ns.* (see -ION) from L *p.p.* stems in *-x-* (*fluxion, inflexion*).

xi′phoid (z-) *a.* Sword-shaped; **~ process** (at lower end of sternum). [f. Gk *xiphoeidēs* (*xiphos* sword; see -OID)]

Xmas (krĭ′smas) *n.* = CHRISTMAS. [abbr., with X for initial chi of Gk *Khristos* Christ]

xō′an|ŏn (z-) *n.* (*pl.* **~a**). (Gk Ant.) Primitive usu. wooden image of deity supposed to have fallen from heaven. [Gk (*xeō* carve)]

X-ray (ě′ks-) *n.*, & *v.t.* **1.** *n.* (in *pl.*) Electromagnetic radiation of short wavelength, able to pass through opaque bodies. **2.** Picture made by effect of X-rays on photographic plate, esp. showing position of bones etc. by their greater absorption of the rays. **3.** *v.t.* Photograph, examine, or treat with X-rays. [transl. of G *x-strahlen* pl., so called by their discoverer (see ROENTGEN) from their then unknown nature]

Xt(ian) *abbrs.* Christ(ian). [cf. XMAS]

xȳ′lěm (z-) *n.* (Bot.) Woody tissue (opp. PHLOEM). [f. Gk *xulon* wood]

xȳ′lēne (z-) *n.* (Chem.) One of three isomeric hydrocarbons formed from benzene by substitution of two methyl groups, obtained from wood etc. [f. as prec. + -ENE]

xȳ′lo- (z-) *comb. form.* Wood, as: **~carp(ous),** (having) hard woody fruit; **~graph,** (esp. early) wood-engraving; **~graphy** (-ŏ′g-), (esp. early or primitive) engraving on wood, use of wood blocks in printing; **~phagous** (-ŏ′f-), (of insect) eating, or boring into, wood. [f. Gk *xulon* wood + -o-]

xȳ′lonīte (z-) *n.* Celluloid. [irreg. f. *xyloidin* (as prec., -OID, -IN) + -ITE¹]

xȳ′lophōn|e (z-) *n.* Musical instrument of flat wooden bars graduated in length and struck with small wooden hammer(s); hence **~IST** (3) *n.* [f. Gk *xulon* wood + -o- + -PHONE]

xȳ′st|us (z-) *n.* (*pl.* **~i** *pr.* -ī). Covered portico used by ancient-Greek athletes for exercise; (Rom. Ant.) garden walk or terrace. [L, f. Gk *xustos* smooth (*xuō* scrape)]

Y

Y, y, (wī) *n.* (*pl.* **Ys** *or* **Y's**). Twenty-fifth letter of alphabet; (Alg., usu. *y*) second unknown quantity; (Geom.) second co-ordinate; Y-shaped arrangement of lines, piping, roads, etc., forked clamp or support; **Y-cross,** Y-shaped cross esp. on chasuble, suggesting figure of crucified Christ; **Y-moth** (of genus *Plusia*, with mark like Y on wings).

y̆- *pref.* (arch.) of *p.p.*, collective *ns.*, etc., (*yclept*); cf. AMONG, ENOUGH, HANDIWORK. [OE *ge-* f. Gmc *ga-]

-y̆¹ *suf.* forming *ns.* denoting (1) state, condition, or quality, (*courtesy, fury, glory, synchrony*); (2) action or its result (*colloquy, remedy, subsidy*); (3) object formed (*company, library*); (4) name of country etc. (*Italy*). [f. or after F *-ie* f. Rom. f. L *-ia*, Gk *-(e)ia*, or L *-ium*; cf. -ACY, -ERY, -GRAPHY, etc.]

-y̆² *suf.* forming *adjs.* f. *ns.* & *adjs.*, w. sense 'full of', 'having the quality of', 'addicted to', (*gluey, horsy, icy, messy, slangy, thorny*), & f. *vbs.* w. sense 'inclined to', 'apt to', (*preachy, runny, sticky*). [f. or after OE *-ig* f. Gmc **-iga*, **-aga*]

-y̆³ *suf.* forming dim. *ns.*, pet names, etc., (*granny, jenny, Sally*). [ME; orig. Sc. (cf. -IE)]

-y̆⁴ *suf.* forming *ns.*, & *adjs.* (esp. Her.), (*army, county, easy, paly*). [f. AF & OF *-e(e)* f. L *-atu-*, *-ata-*; cf. -ATE¹·²]

Y. *abbr.* yen; Yeomanry; * = Y.M.C.A. or Y.W.C.A.

y. *abbr.* year(s).

Y *symb.* yttrium.

yă′bbȳ, yă′bbĭe, *n.* (Austral.) Small freshwater crayfish often used as bait. [Aboriginal]

yacht (yŏt) *n.*, & *v.i.* **1.** *n.* Light sailing-vessel kept, and usu. specially built and rigged, for racing; vessel propelled by sails, steam, electricity, or motive power other than oars, and used for private pleasure excursions, cruising, travel, etc.; similar vessel for travel on sand or ice; **~-club** (esp. for yacht-racing); **~′sman,** person who yachts. **2.** *v.i.* Race or cruise in yacht; hence **~′ING¹** (1) *n.* [f. early mod. Du. *jaghte* = *jaghtschip* fast pirate-ship f. *jag(h)t* chase (*jagen* to hunt) + *schip* SHIP¹]

yăck (**etȳ-yă′ck**) *n.*, & *v.i.* (sl., derog.) (Engage in) trivial or unduly persistent conversation. [imit.]

yă′ffle *n.* (dial.) Green woodpecker. [imit. of its laughing cry]

yager. Var. of JAEGER¹.

yah *int.* expr. derision or defiance. [imit.]

yahōō′ (ya-h-) *n.* Brute in human shape; coarse person of bestial passions and habits. [name of imaginary race of brutish men in Swift's *Gulliver's Travels*]

Yah′veh, Yah′weh, Yah′vĭst, etc. See JEHOVAH, JEHOVIST.

yăk *n.* Long-haired humped grunting wild or domesticated ox of Tibet. [f. Tibetan *gyag*]

Yāle *n.* **~ lock,** type of lock for doors etc., with

revolving barrel. [f. L. ~, Amer. inventor d. 1868; **P**]

yăm *n.* (Edible starchy tuber of) tropical or subtropical climbing plant of genus *Dioscorea*; *sweet POTATO. [f. Port. *inhame* or Sp. *iñame*, of unkn. orig.]

yă'mmer *v.i.*, & *n.* (colloq. or dial.) Lament, wail, grumble; (utter) voluble talk. [OE *geōmrian* (*geōmor* sorrowful)]

yăng *n.* (Chin. Philos.) Active male principle of universe (opp. *yin*). [Chin.]

yănk^{1} *v.t.*, & *n.* (colloq.) **1.** *v.t.* Pull (lever etc., or abs.) with a jerk. **2.** *n.* Sudden hard pull. [19th c.; orig. unkn.]

Yănk^{2} *n.* (colloq.) = foll. [abbr.]

Yă'nkee (-kĭ) *n.* *Inhabitant of New England; *inhabitant of northern States, Federal soldier in Civil War; ||inhabitant of U.S., American; type of bet on four or more horses to win (or be placed) in different races; (*attrib.*) of or as of the Yankees; ~ **Doodle,** (1) American tune and song regarded as a national air, (2) = *Yankee*; hence ~DOM, ~ISM (2, 4), *ns.*, ~FY *v.t.* [perh. f. Du. *Janke* dim. of *Jan* John used derisively (1683), or pe[illegible]. orig. pl. f. *Jengees*, Amer. Ind. pronunc. of [illegible]*ish*]

[illegible]. See YOGHURT.

yap *v.i.* (**-pp-**), & *n.* **1.** *v.i.* Bark shrilly or fussily; (colloq.) talk noisily or foolishly or complainingly. **2.** *n.* Sound of yapping. [imit.]

yă'pŏck *n.* S. Amer. water-opossum, with webbed hind feet. [f. *Oyapok*, *Oiapoque*, N. Brazilian river]

||**yăpp** *n.* Kind of bookbinding with limp leather cover projecting to fold over edges of leaves. [name of London bookseller *c.* 1860, for whom first made]

yar'borough (-r*o*) *n.* Whist or bridge hand with no card above a 9. [f. Earl of *Yarborough* (d. 1897), said to have betted against its occurrence]

yard^{1} *n.* **1.** Unit of linear measure, = 3 feet or 0·9144 metre; = SQUARE^{2} or CUBIC yard (*of* sand etc.); yard-length of material (*a yard and a half of cloth*); **by the ~,** (fig.) at great length; ||~ **of ale,** (contents of) deep slender glass for liquor; ||~ **of clay,** long clay pipe; ||~ **of tin,** coachman's horn. **2.** Cylindrical spar tapering to each end slung horizontally (*square yard*) or slantwise (*lateen yard*) across mast to support sail (*lower topsail, topgallant, royal, yard,* according to sail supported); **man the ~s,** place men, stand, along yards as form of salute. **3. ~-arm,** either end of yard (sense 2); ~ **measure,** rod, tape, etc., a yard long and usu. divided into feet, inches, and quarters or fifths; **~'stick,** rigid yard-measure, (fig.) standard of comparison. [OE *gerd*, **gierd*, *gyrd*, = OS *gerdia* twig, OHG *gart(e)a*, *gerta* f. WG **gazdjō*; cf. GADFLY]

yard^{2} *n.*, & *v.t.* **1.** *n.* Piece of enclosed ground, especially one surrounded by or attached to building(s) or used for some manufacturing or other purpose (BRICK^{1}, CHURCH^{1}, COURT^{1}, DOCK^{4}, FARM^{1}, GRAVE^{1}, SHIP^{1}, STOCK, *-yard*, VINEYARD); *garden of house; ||**the Y~,** (colloq.) SCOTLAND YARD; **~-man,** man working in railway-yard or timber-yard, *gardener or one who does various outdoor jobs; **~-master,** manager of railway-yard. **2.** *v.t.* Put (cattle) into stockyard. [OE *geard* enclosure, region, = OS *gardo*, OHG *gart(o)*, ON *garthr* (cf. GARTH), Goth. *gards* house, *garda* enclosure, f. Gmc **gardaz*; cf. GARDEN]

yar'dage *n.* Total number of yards; (payment for) use of a stockyard etc. [f. YARD^{1,2} + -AGE]

yar'mulka *n.* Skull-cap worn by Jewish men. [Yiddish]

yarn *n.*, & *v.i.* **1.** *n.* Any spun thread esp. of kinds prepared for weaving, knitting, or rope-making. **2.** (colloq.) Story, traveller's tale anecdote, rambling discourse, (SPIN^{1} *a yarn*). **3.** *v.i.* (colloq.) Tell yarns. [OE *gearn*, = OHG, ON *garn*]

yă'rrow (-ō) *n.* Perennial herb of genus *Achillea*, esp. milfoil. [OE *gearwe*, = OHG *gar(a)wa*, of unkn. orig.]

yă'shmăk *n.* Veil worn in public by Muslim women of some countries, concealing whole of face except eyes. [f. Arab. *yašmak*, Turk. *yaşmak*]

yă'taghăn (-găn) *n.* Sword without guard and often with double-curved blade, used in Muslim countries. [f. Turk. *yātāğan*]

yaw *v.i.*, & *n.* (Naut. & Aeron.) **1.** *v.i.* (Of ship, aircraft, spacecraft, etc.) fail to hold straight course, fall off, go unsteadily (esp. turning from side to side). **2.** *n.* Yawing of ship etc. from course. [16th c., of unkn. orig.]

yawl *n.* Ship's jolly-boat with four or six oars; two-masted fore-and-aft sailing-boat with mizen-mast stepped far aft; small kind of fishing-boat. [f. MLG *jolle* or Du. *jol*, of unkn. orig.; cf. JOLLY^{2}*-boat*]

yawn *v.* & *n.* **1.** *v.i.* (Of chasm etc.) gape, be wide open, (*a yawning gulf, rent,* etc.). **2.** (Of person or animal) open the mouth wide and inhale as effect of drowsiness, boredom, etc. **3.** *v.t.* Utter or say with a yawn. **4.** *n.* Act of yawning; (sl.) something boring. [OE *ginian*, *geonian*, = OHG *ginōn*]

***yawp** *v.i.*, & *n.* (Utter) harsh or hoarse cry, or foolish talk. [ME; imit.]

yaws (-z) *n. pl.* (usu. treated as *sing.*) Contagious bacterial skin-disease of tropical countries, with raspberry-like excrescences. [17th c.; orig. unkn.]

Yb *symb.* ytterbium.

Y-chrōmosōme (wī'kr-) *n.* Chromosome occurring in cells of only one sex (in humans, the male), whose presence or absence in zygote determines sex of new individual formed in reproduction. [f. *Y* as arbitrary label + CHROMOSOME]

ўclĕ'pt *a.* (arch. or joc.) Called (by the name of). [OE *gecleopod* p.p. of *cleopian* call f. Gmc **klipōjan*]

yd(s). *abbr.* yard(s).

yē^{1} (*or* yĭ) *pron.* (*obj.* YOU, occas. **ye,** *refl.* YOURSELVES *or* **you** *or* **ye,** *poss.* YOUR, YOURS). (poet., arch., religious, dial., or joc.) Pl. of THOU^{1} (*blessed are ye; ye zephyrs gay; how d'ye do?*); **ye gods (and little fishes)!** (joc. int. of astonishment). [OE *ge*, = OS *gi*, *ge*, OHG *ir*, ON *ér*, forms assim. to *we* etc. ult. f. Gmc **juz* (cf. YOU)]

yē^{2} (*or as* THE) *a.* (pseudo-arch.) = THE (*ye olde tea-shoppe*). [var. sp. due to use of *y*-shaped letter THORN in 14th c.]

yea (yā) *adv.* & *n.* (arch.) **1.** *adv.* Yes (*let your communication be* ~, ~, **nay, nay,** yes and no without oaths); indeed, nay, (*ready, yea eager*). **2.** *n.* The word 'yea'; **~s and nays,** ayes and noes, affirmative and negative votes; ~ **and nay,** shilly-shally. [OE *gea*, *ge*, = OS, OHG *jā*, ON *já*, Goth. *ja*, *jai* f. Gmc **ja*, **je*]

yeah (yĕ*a*) *adv.* (colloq.) Yes; (**oh**) **~?** (expr. incredulity). [casual pronunc. of YES]

yean *v.t.* & *i.* (arch.) Bring forth (lamb or kid). [perh. f. OE **geēanian* (as Y-, *ēanian* to lamb)]

yea'nling *n.* (arch.) Young lamb or kid. [f. prec. + -LING^{1}]

year (*or* yēr) *n.* **1.** Time occupied by the earth in one revolution round the sun (**astronomical, equinoctial, natural, solar, tropical,** ~, 365d. 5h. 48m. 46s. in length) or (**sidereal** ~, longer by 20m. 23s. because of precession) by the sun in returning to the same position in relation to the fixed stars; **great** or

Platonic ~, period (estimated by ancient astronomers at about 26,000 years) occupied by the celestial bodies in returning to same relative positions. **2.** (**Calendar** or **civil**) **~,** period of days (esp. **common ~** of 365 or LEAP² ~ of 366 reckoned from 1 Jan.) used for time-reckoning in ordinary affairs, commencing on a certain day and corresponding more or less exactly in length to the astronomical year; **lunar ~** (of 12 lunar months); LUNISOLAR *year*; *year of* GRACE, *of Our* LORD; ||**in the ~ dot** or **one,** (colloq.) very long ago; FROM *year to year*, *year* BY¹ *year*; *year* IN² *year out*; **of the ~,** chosen as outstanding in a particular year (*award to Sportsman of the Year*). **3.** Period of same length as civil year commencing at any day; group of students entering college etc. in same academic year; **Christian, Church, ecclesiastical, ~,** round of sacred seasons reckoned from and to Advent; **financial** or **fiscal** or **tax ~** (reckoned from ||1 or 6 Apr. or *1 Jan. or July for taxing and accounting purposes); SABBATICAL *year*; **academic** or **school ~** (usu. reckoned from beginning of autumn term); **a ~ and a day,** period specified in some legal matters to ensure completion of a full year; **a ~ (from) today** etc., 12 months before or esp. after today etc. **4.** (in *pl.*) Age, time of life; **young for his ~s,** not showing much sign of his age; (**getting on**) **in ~s,** old. **5.** (in *sing.* or *pl.*) Very long time. **6. ~-book,** annual publication bringing information on some subject up to date; **~-long,** lasting a year, lasting the whole year; **~-round,** existing etc. throughout the year. [OE *gē(a)r*, = OS, OHG *jār*, ON *ár*, Goth. *jēr* f. Gmc **jǣram* f. IE **jēr-*, **jōr-*]

year'lĭng (*or* yēr'-) *n.* & *a.* **1.** *n.* Animal more than one and less than two years old; racehorse in calendar year after year of foaling. **2.** *a.* A year old, having existed or been such for a year, (*yearling heifer, bride*); intended to terminate after one year (*yearling bonds*). [f. prec. + -LING¹]

year'lȳ (*or* yēr'-) *a.* & *adv.* (Produced or occurring) once every year, annual(ly); of or for or lasting a year. [OE *gēarlic, -lice* (as YEAR, -LY¹,²)]

yearn (yẽrn) *v.i.* Be filled with longing or compassion or tenderness (*for* or *after* rest, home, affection, etc.; *to* do; *towards* or *to* person etc.); hence **~'ING¹** *n.*, **~'ING²** *a.* [OE *giernan*, = OS *girnean*, ON *girna*, Goth. *gairnjan* f. Gmc **gernjan* (**gernaz* eager)]

yeast *n.* Yellowish frothy viscous substance consisting of fungous cells developed by germination in contact with saccharine liquids and producing alcoholic fermentation, used in brewing beer, making wine, distilling spirit, and raising bread etc.; dried form of this used in baking. [OE **g(i)est, gist*, = MDu. *ghist*, MHG *jist*, ON *jöstr*]

yea'st|ȳ *a.* Frothy like yeast; in a ferment, working like yeast; wordy, superficial; hence **~ĭLY²** *adv.*, **~ĭNESS** *n.* [f. prec. + -Y²]

***yĕgg** *n.* (sl.) **~('man),** travelling burglar or safe-breaker. [said to be a surname]

yĕll *v.* & *n.* **1.** (Make, utter with) sharp loud cry of pain or anger or fright or delight or derision (*yelled with pain, fury, laughter; yelled curses, my name, a refusal, defiance; with yells of horror* etc.). **2.** *n.* *Organized cry used by students e.g. in encouraging their representatives in athletic contests. [OE *g(i)ellan*, = OHG *gellan*, ON *gjalla* f. Gmc **gel-*, **gal-*; cf. NIGHTINGALE]

yĕ'llow (-ō) *a.*, *n.*, & *v.* **1.** *a.* Of the colour between green and orange in the spectrum, coloured like buttercup or primrose or lemon or egg-yolk or gold, (as distinguishing epithet of plants, animals, etc.: *yellow* RATTLE², ROCKET¹, *wagtail, ochre*; often also in comb. with parts of body etc.: *yellow-bill, -legs, -root, -rump, -seed, -shank, -tail, -throat, -top, -wood*, forming animal and plant names); of the colour of faded leaves, ripe wheat, etc.; having yellow skin or complexion. **2. ~back,** cheap novel etc. in yellow cover; **~-belly,** (1) a coward, (2) fish with yellow under-parts; **~ cedar,** evergreen ornamental tree from N.W. America (*Chamaecyparis nootkatensis*); ***~ dog,** mongrel; ***~-dog** *a.*, antagonistic to trade unions; **~ fever,** tropical virus disease with fever and jaundice; *yellow* FLAG⁴; **~hammer,** bunting of which the male has yellow head, neck, and breast [*-hammer* of uncert. orig.]; **~ Jack,** = *yellow fever* or *flag*; *the* SEAR¹, *the yellow leaf*; **~ metal,** brass of 60 parts copper and 40 parts zinc; **~ pages,** section of telephone directory on yellow paper and listing business subscribers according to goods or ser[vices] they offer; **the ~ peril,** the supposed dang[er that th]e yellow races may overwhelm the whit[e or] overrun the world; **the ~ press,** unscrupulously sensational newspapers; **~ soap,** common household soap; **~ spo[t],** point of acutest vision in retina; **~ streak,** trai[t] of cowardice. **3.** (fig.) (Of looks, mood, feelings, etc.) jealous, envious, suspicious; (colloq.) cowardly. **4.** Hence **~ISH¹** 2, **~Y²**, *adjs.*, **~LY²** *adv.*, **~NESS** *n.* **5.** *n.* Yellow colour; yellow pigment; yellow clothes or material (*dressed in yellow*); yellow ball in snooker etc.; (colloq.) cowardice; yellow moth or butterfly; **the ~s,** jaundice of horses etc., *a peach-disease with yellowed leaves. **6.** *v.t.* & *i.* Make or become yellow (*paper yellowed with age; the yellowing leaves*). [OE *geolu, geolo*, = OS, OHG *gelo* f. WG **gelwa* f. IE **ghelwo-*, rel. to GOLD]

yĕlp *v.i.*, & *n.* (Utter) sharp shrill cry (as) of dog in pain or excitement; hence **~'ER¹** *n.* [OE *gielp(an)* boast, imit.; cf. YAWP]

yĕn¹ *n.* (*pl.* same). Japanese monetary unit. [Jap., f. Chin. *yüan* round, dollar]

***yĕn²** *n.*, & *v.i.* (**-nn-**). (sl.) **1.** *n.* Longing, yearning. **2.** *v.i.* Yearn. [Chin.]

yeo'man (yō'-) *n.* (*pl.* **yeo'men**). **1.** Man holding and cultivating small landed estate; (Hist.) person qualified by possessing free land of annual value 40 shillings to serve on juries, vote for knight of shire, etc.; (Hist.) servant in royal or noble household. **2.** ||Member of the yeomanry force; ||**~ (of signals),** petty officer in Navy, concerned with visual signalling; *petty officer performing clerical duties on board ship. **3. ~('s) service,** efficient or useful help in need; ||**Y~ of the Guard,** = BEEF*eater*; ||**Y~ Usher,** deputy of Black Rod. **4.** Hence **~LY¹** *a.* [ME *yoman, yeman*, etc. prob. f. YOUNG + MAN¹]

yeo'manrȳ (yō'-) *n.* Body of yeomen; ||(Hist.) volunteer cavalry force raised chiefly from yeoman class (1794–1908). [ME, f. prec. + -RY]

***yĕp.** Var. (colloq.) of YES.

-yer *suf.* var. of -IER, esp. after *w* (*bowyer, lawyer, sawyer*).

yẽr'ba *n.* **~ maté,** = MATÉ. [Sp., = herb]

yĕs *adv.* and *n.* **1.** The answer to your question is affirmative, it is as you say or as I have said, your request or command will be complied with, the statement made or course intended is correct or satisfactory, the negative statement etc. made is not correct ('*It isn't ready*'—'*Yes, it is*'); **~ and, ~ or,** (forms for introducing stronger phr.: *I could endure, yes, and enjoy it; he would beat me, yes, and you too*); **~?,** indeed?, is that so?, what do you want?; **~, ~** (emphat.). **2.** (In answer to summons or address) I am here,

I hear or am attending to you. **3.** *n.* The word or answer *yes* (**say ~,** grant request, accept proposal, confirm statement); **~-man,** (colloq.) characterless, obedient, weakly acquiescent person. [OE *gēse, gise,* prob. f. **gia* YEA + *sīe* 3 sing. pres. subj. of *bēon* BE]

yĕster- *comb. form.* (poet. or arch.) Of yesterday, that is last past, (*yester-eve, yestermorn, yesternight*); **~-year,** last year. [OE *geostran,* = OHG *gestaron*]

yĕ'sterday (*or* -dĭ) *n.* & *adv.* (On) the day before today (*arrived yesterday; yesterday was her birthday*); (in) the recent past (*is but of yesterday; not* BORN *yesterday*); **~ morning, afternoon,** etc., (*ns.* & *advs.*) (*in*) the morning etc. of yesterday. [OE *giestran dæg* (as prec., DAY)]

yĕt *adv.* & *conj.* **1.** *adv.* As late as now or then, with continuance to this or to that time, still, (*there is yet time; is he yet living?; there is life in the old dog yet; much yet remains to be done; his greatest achievement yet; his yet unfinished task; I seem to see him yet; while it was yet morning*); AS¹ *yet.* **2.** (w. neg. or interrog.) So soon as now or then, by this or by that time, so far, in the immediate future, (*it is not time yet; is he dead yet?; they have not yet heard; I have never yet lied; need you go* (*just*) *yet?; it will not happen just yet; these things are not yet*). **3.** Again, in addition, (*yet once more; another and another and yet another; yet again; more and yet more*); **nor ~,** and also not (*won't listen to me nor yet to her*). **4.** Before the matter is done with, before all is over, in the time that still remains (though not hitherto), (*he will win, I will be even with you, yet*). **5.** (w. compar.) Even (*a yet more difficult, easier, task*). **6.** Nevertheless, and in spite of that, but for all that, (*it is strange, and yet it is true; strange and yet true; the logic seems sound, but* or *and yet it does not convince me*). **7.** *conj.* But at the same time, but nevertheless, (*the work is done, yet what is the use of it all?; faint yet pursuing*). [OE *giet*(*a*), = OFris. *iēta,* of unkn. orig.]

yĕ'tĭ *n.* Native (Sherpa) name for the ABOMINABLE Snowman. [Tibetan]

yew *n.* **~(-tree),** slow-growing dark-leaved evergreen coniferous tree of genus *Taxus* often planted in churchyards; its wood, used formerly as material for bows and still in cabinet-making. [OE *īw, ēow,* = OS *īh,* OHG *iwa,* ON *ýr* bow f. Gmc **īhw-,* **igw-*]

Y'ggdrasĭl (ĭ'-) *n.* (Scand. Myth.) Ash-tree whose roots and branches join heaven and earth and hell. [f. ON *yg*(*g*)*drasill* (*Yggr* Odin, *drasill* horse)]

||**Y.H.A.** *abbr.* Youth Hostels Association.

Yĭd *n.* (sl., derog.) Jew. [back form. f. foll.]

Yĭ'ddĭsh *a.* & *n.* (Of) language used by Jews in or from central and eastern Europe, orig. a Middle Rhine dialect, with words from Hebrew and several modern languages; hence **~ER¹** *a.* & *n.,* (person) speaking Yiddish. [f. G *jüdisch* Jewish]

yield *v.* & *n.* **1.** *v.t.* Give or return or bring as fruit or result (*earth yields her increase; land yields good crops; investment yields 15%; betting tax yields a large revenue*); (abs., of land etc.) repay cultivation etc. *well, poorly,* etc. **2.** Give up, deliver over, surrender, resign, comply with demand for, concede, (*yield fortress* etc.; *yield oneself prisoner; yield possession,* one's *pride of place; yield precedence to; yield the* PALM¹; *yield up the* GHOST; **~ the point,** concede it in argument). **3.** *v.i.* Surrender, make submission *to,* give consent or change one's course of action in deference *to,* comply with demand, respond as desired *to,* be inferior or confess inferiority *to,* (*town yielded without awaiting assault; yield to superior force, persuasion, treatment, seducer; courage never to submit or yield; I yield to none in appreciation of his merits*); give right of way (*to* other traffic); *allow another the right to speak in debate etc. **4.** *n.* Amount yielded or produced, output, return; **~ point,** (Phys.) stress beyond which material becomes plastic. [OE *g*(*i*)*eldan,* = OS *geldan,* OHG *geltan,* ON *gjalda,* Goth. *-gildan* f. Gmc **geldhan* pay]

yĭn *n.* (Chin. Philos.) Passive female principle of universe (opp. *yang*). [Chin.]

***yĭp** *v.i.* (-pp-), & *n.* = YELP. [imit.]

yĭ'ppee *int.* expr. delight or excitement. [cf. HIP⁵]

yĭ'ppĭe, yĭ'ppy̆, *n.* Politically active Amer. hippie. [f. *Y*outh *I*nternational *P*arty, after HIPPIE]

-y̆l *suf.* (Chem.) forming *ns.* denoting a radical (*amyl, ethyl, phenyl*). [f. F *-yle* f. Gk *hulē* wood, substance]

y'lăng-ylăng (ē'l-; -ēl-) *n.* Malayan tree (*Cananga odorata*) from the fragrant yellow flowers of which a perfume is distilled; the perfume itself. [f. Tagalog *álang-ilang*]

Y.M.C.A. *abbr.* Young Men's Christian Association.

-y̅ne *suf.* (Chem.) forming names of unsaturated compounds containing a triple bond (*ethyne* = acetylene). [alt. f. -INE⁵]

yŏb('bō) *n.* (*pl.* **~s**). (sl.) Lout, hooligan. [back sl. for BOY; see -o]

yŏd *n.* Tenth and smallest letter of Hebrew alphabet; the sound (y). [f. Heb. *yōḏ* (*yaḏ* hand)]

yō'del *v.* (||-ll-) & *n.* **1.** *v.t.* & *i.* Sing with melodious inarticulate sounds and frequent changes between falsetto and normal voice in the manner of Swiss and Tyrolean mountain-dwellers. **2.** *n.* Yodelling cry. [f. G *jodeln*]

yō'g|a *n.* Hindu system of philosophic meditation and asceticism designed to effect reunion with the universal spirit; = HATHA YOGA; hence **~IC** (-g-) *a.* [Hind. f. Skr., = union]

yŏgh (-χ *or* -k) *n.* Middle-English letter used for certain values of *g* and *y.* [ME]

yŏ'ghurt (-gert), **yŏ'gurt, yaourt** (yah'oort), *n.* Semi-solid sourish junket-like or curd-like food prepared from milk fermented by added bacteria. [f. Turk. *yoğurt*]

yō'g|ĭ (-gĭ) *n.* Devotee of yoga; hence **~ISM** (3) *n.* [Hind. (YOGA)]

yō'-heave-hō *int.* & *n.* = HEAVE¹ *ho.*

yō-(hō-)hō' *int.* used to attract attention, or = prec. [cf. prec. & HO]

yoicks *int.* Fox-hunter's halloo. [orig. unkn.; cf. *hyke* call to hounds, HEY¹]

yōke *n.* & *v.* **1.** *n.* Wooden cross-piece fastened over necks of two oxen etc. and attached to the plough or wagon that they are to (help to) draw; (Rom. Hist.) uplifted yoke or arch of three spears symbolizing it under which defeated enemy was made to march (*army passed under the yoke*); (fig.) sway or dominion or servitude (*submitted to his yoke; had never endured the yoke*); (fig.) bond of union, esp. the marriage tie. **2.** Pair *of* oxen etc. (*pl.* often same after numeral); (arch.) amount of land that one yoke of oxen can plough in a day. **3.** Piece of timber shaped to fit person's shoulders and support pail etc. at each end. **4.** Separately made shoulder-piece of shirt or coat or blouse, or fitted to top part of skirt, from which the rest hangs. **5.** Object shaped like yoke; crossbar on which bell swings; crossbar of rudder to whose ends ropes are fastened; bar of soft iron between poles of electromagnet. **6.** **~-bone,** cheek-bone connecting bones of head and face; **~'fellow, ~'mate,** partner in marriage, work, etc. **7.** *v.t.* Put yoke on; couple or unite (esp. pair) in marriage or otherwise, link (one *to* another). **8.** *v.i.* Match or work together. [OE *geoc*, = OS *juc*, OHG *joh*, Goth. *juk*, ON *ok* f. Gmc **jukam* f. IE **jugom*]

yō'kel *n.* Rustic, country bumpkin. [perh. f. dial. *yokel* green woodpecker]

yōlk[1] (yōk) *n.* Yellow internal part of egg, nourishing the young before hatching; (Biol.) corresponding part of any animal ovum; **~-bag, -sac,** membrane enclosing yolk of egg; hence (-)~ED[2] (-kt), ~'Y[2], *adjs.* [OE *geol(o)ca* (*geolu* YELLOW)]

yōlk[2] (yōk) *n.* = SUINT. [OE **eowoca*]

Yŏm Kĭ'ppur *n.* = *Day of* ATONEMENT. [Heb.]

yŏn *a.*, *adv.*, & *pron.* (arch. or poet. or dial.) **1.** *a.* & *adv.* Yonder; HITHER *and yon.* **2.** *pron.* Yonder person or thing. [OE *geon*, = OHG *jenēr*, ON *enn*, Goth. *jains* that]

yŏ'nder *a.* & *adv.* (literary). (Situated) over there, at some distance in the direction towards which I am looking or pointing, within or conceived as within view but distant. [ME; cf. OS *gendra*, Goth. *jaindrē*]

yō'nĭ *n.* Symbol of female genitals venerated by Hindus etc. [Skr.]

yōō'-hōō *int.* expr. desire to attract person's attention. [spontaneous utterance]

yôre *n.* **Of** ~, formerly, in or of old days. [OE *geāra*, *geāre*, etc., adv. forms of uncert. orig.]

Yôrk[1] *n.* **~ and Lancaster,** rival parties in the Wars of the Roses (*~-and-Lancaster rose*, red and white particoloured kind); **House of ~,** English kings from Edward IV to Richard III. [f. 1st Duke of ~ (cf. YORKIST), f. ~ in England f. OE *Eoforwīc* f. L *Eboracum* + *wīc* dwelling]

yôrk[2] *v.t.* (Cricket). Bowl with yorker. [backform. f. foll.]

yôr'ker *n.* (Cricket). Ball so bowled as to pitch immediately in front of batsman's block. [prob. f. YORK[1], as introduced by Yorkshire players, + -ER[1]]

Yôr'kĭst *a.* & *n.* (Adherent) of family descended from 1st Duke of York (d. 1402, 5th son of Edward III) or of the White Rose party supporting it in the Wars of the Roses. [f. YORK[1] + -IST]

Yorks. *abbr.* Yorkshire.

Yôr'kshire (*-er or* -ēr) *n.* **~man, ~woman,** (born or living in Yorkshire); **~ pudding,** batter baked and eaten with or before roast meat, esp. beef; **~ terrier,** small shaggy blue and tan toy kind; *Yorkshire* TYKE. [~, former county in England]

Yŏ'ruba *n.* Member or language of a Negro people on W. Afr. coast, esp. in Nigeria. [native name]

you (ū *or* yŏŏ) *pron.* (*obj.* **you;** *refl.* YOURSELF, YOURSELVES, arch. **you;** *poss.* YOUR, YOURS). **1.** Sing. (w. pl. vb.) and pl. pron. of 2nd pers. (for phrs. see HE[1]); the person(s) or thing(s) addressed; (as *voc.* w. n. in excl. statement: *you fool(s)!*; *you darling!*; *you idiot, you!*); ***~-all,** (colloq.) you; **~'re another** (colloq. phr. retorting accusation on person who makes it); **~-know-what** or **-who,** something or someone unspecified but understood; *you and* YOURS; *not quite you* (cf. HER[1] 2). **2.** (In general statements) one, any one, all concerned, every one, a person, (*you never can tell*; *what are you to do with a child like this?*; *it is bad at first, but you soon get used to it*; *there's a shot for you!*). [OE *ēow* acc. & dat. of *gē* YE[1], = OS *ju*, OHG *iu(h)* f. WG **iwwi(z)*; supplanting *ye* f. more frequent use of obj. case, and *thou* and *thee* as more courteous form]

young (yŭ-) *a.* (**~'er, ~'est,** *pr.* -ngg-) & *n.* **1.** *a.* Not far advanced in life or growth or development or existence, of recent birth or origin or formation, not yet old, still vigorous, immature, youthful, inexperienced, (*a young child, man, animal, plant, wine, nation, institution*; *young for his* YEARS); (of night, year, century, etc.) still near its beginning; (w. surname etc.) son as dist. f. father (*young Jones*; *the Young* PRETENDER), (in compar.) person as dist. f. older one of same name (*the younger Pitt*; *Teniers the younger*); felt in or characteristic of youth (*young love, ambition*, etc.); **the ~,** young people; **~ and old,** everyone. **2.** *Young* BLOOD[1]; one's **~ day(s)** (when one was young); **Y~** *England, Liberals*, etc., political group claiming to speak for younger members of the population; **~ family** (of young children); *young* FUSTIC; **~ girl,** unmarried adolescent girl or young woman; **~er hand,** (Cards) second player of two; *young* HOPEFUL; *young* IDEA; **~ lady** or **man** (sweetheart, girl- or boy-friend; or lit., esp. as *voc.*); *young* MARRIEDs; **~ person** (arch., esp. as viewed by the respectable elderly; ||in Law, usu. between 14 and 17 years old); **you ~ rascal** etc. (usu. playfully to child); *old head on young* SHOULDERS; **~ thing** (arch., indulgent description of young person); **Y~ Turk,** (1) member of revolutionary party in Turkey 1908, (2) member of rebellious group in political party; **~ turk,** violent child or youth; **~ 'un,** (colloq., usu. as *voc.*) youngster; **~ woman** (sweetheart or girl-friend; or lit., esp. as *voc.*). **3.** Hence ~'ISH[1] 2 *a.*, ~'LING[1] *n.* (arch.) **4.** *n.* (collect.) Offspring esp. of animals before or soon after birth (**with ~,** pregnant). [OE *g(e)ong*, = OS *jung*, OHG *junc*, ON *ungr*, Goth. *juggs* f. Gmc **ju(wu)ngaz* f. IE **juwnkos*]

you'ngster (yŭ'-) *n.* Child, esp. active or lively boy; young person. [f. prec. + -STER, after foll.]

you'nker (yŭ'-) *n.* (arch.) = prec. [f. MDu. *jonckher* (*jonc* YOUNG, *hēre* lord); cf. JUNKER]

your (ūr *or* yôr *or, when unstressed*, yer) *poss. pron. attrib.* **1.** Of you(rself or -selves) (for phrs. see HER[2], OUR). **2.** (colloq., usu. derog.) Much talked of, well known, familiar, (*no one so fallible as your expert in handwriting*; *your facetious bore is the worst of all*). [OE *ēower* gen. of *gē* YE[1], = OS *iuwar*, OHG *iuwēr*, & OE *ēower* poss. adj., = OHG *iuwar*]

yours (ūrz *or* yôrz) *poss. pron.* & *pred. a.* **1.** *pron.* The one(s) belonging to or of you (for phrs. see HERS); your letter; **you and ~,** you together with your family, property, etc. **2.** *a.* Belonging to you, at your service, (*it is yours if you will accept it*); ~, or ~ EVER, FAITHFULLY, *obediently*, SINCERE*ly*, *truly*, *to* COMMAND[1], or EVER etc. ~, (formulae preceding signature of letter); **~ truly,** (joc.) I (the speaker or writer); **what's ~?,** (colloq.) what would you like to drink?. [ME, f. prec. + -S[3]]

yoursĕ'lf (ūr- etc., as YOUR) *pron.* Emphat. & refl. form corresp. to YOU sing. (for uses cf. HERSELF); **how's ~?,** (sl.) how are you? (esp. after answering similar inquiry). [ME, f. YOUR + SELF]

yoursĕ'lves (ūr- etc. as YOUR; -vz). *pron.* Emphat. & refl. form corresp. to YOU pl. (for uses cf. HERSELF). [f. prec. + -S[1]]

youth (ūth) *n.* (*pl. pr.* ūdhz). **1.** Being young, adolescence, (the vigour or enthusiasm or weakness or inexperience or other characteristic of) the period between childhood and full manhood or womanhood, (*has all the appearance of extreme youth*; *in my hot, raw, vigorous*, etc., *youth*; *from youth onwards*; *youth's a stuff will not endure*; *the secret of perpetual, of keeping* one's, *youth*); early stage of development etc. **2.** Young man (*as a youth of 16*). **3.** (as *pl.*) Young people collectively (*the youth of the country*; *loves to be surrounded by youth*); **~ centre** or **club,** place or organization provided for leisure-time activities of young people; **~ hostel,** place where hikers

etc. (~ *hostellers*) can put up for the night. [OE *geoguth*, = OS *juguth*, OHG *jugund* f. WG *jugunth-, juwunth- f. Gmc *juwung- (see YOUNG)]
you'thful (ū'-) *a.* (Still) young; characteristic of the young (*youthful impatience*); having the freshness or vigour of youth (*youthful complexion*); hence ~LY² *adv.*, ~NESS *n.* [f. prec. + -FUL]
yowl *n.*, & *v.i.* (Utter) loud wailing cry (as) of cat or dog in distress, pain, etc. [imit.]
yō'-yō *n.* (*pl.* ~**s**). Toy consisting of pair of discs with deep groove between them in which string is attached and wound, and which can be made to fall and rise by its weight and momentum. [20th c., of unkn. orig.]
yr. *abbr.* year(s); younger; your.
yrs. *abbr.* years; yours.
ўttēr'bĭum *n.* (Chem.) Metallic element of lanthanide series. [mod. L, f. *Ytterby* in Sweden + -IUM]
ў'ttrĭum *n.* (Chem.) Trivalent metallic element, resembling those of lanthanide series. [f. as prec.]
yüa'n (yōōah'n) *n.* (*pl.* same). Monetary unit of China. [Chin.; see YEN¹]
yŭ'cca *n.* American white-flowered plant of genus *Yucca*, with swordlike leaves. [Carib]
Yu'goslav, Ju'goslav, (ū'goslahv) *a.* & *n.* (Native or inhabitant) of Yugoslavia; hence ~IAN (-ah'-) *a.* & *n.* [Austrian G *Jugoslav* f. Serb. *jugo-* (*jug* south) + SLAV]
yule (ūl) *n.* ~(**-tide**), (arch.) the Christmas festival; ~**-log** (large, burnt in hearth on Christmas Eve). [OE *gēol(a)*; cf. ON *jól*; ult. orig. unkn.]
yŭ'mmў *a.* (colloq.) Tasty, delicious. [f. foll. + -Y²]
yŭm-yŭ'm *int.* expr. pleasure from (prospect of) eating. [imit.]
***yŭp.** Var. of YEP.
yurt (yoort) *n.* Mongolian nomads' circular skin- or felt-covered tent, with collapsible frame. [f. Russ. *yurta*]
Y.W.C.A. *abbr.* Young Women's Christian Association.

Z

Z, z, (zĕd) *n.* (*pl.* **Zs** *or* **Z's**). Twenty-sixth letter of alphabet; (Alg., usu. *z*) third unknown quantity; (Geom.) third co-ordinate; *from A to Z* (see A).
zabagliō'ne (zahbahlyō'nā) *n.* Italian sweet of whipped and heated egg yolks, sugar, and (esp. Marsala) wine. [It.]
ză'ffre (*-er*), ***ză'ffer,** *n.* Impure cobalt oxide used as blue pigment. [f. It. *zaffera* or f. F *safre*]
zăg *n.* Sharp change of direction in zigzag course. [f. ZIGZAG]
ză'mbō *n.* (*pl.* ~**s**). = SAMBO 1. [Sp.; see SAMBO]
zamĭ'ndār. See ZEMINDAR.
Z.A.N.U. (zah'nōō) *abbr.* Zimbabwe African National Union.
zā'nў *n.* & *a.* **1.** *n.* (Hist.) Attendant clown awkwardly mimicking chief clown in shows, merry andrew. **2.** Person given to buffoonery, foolish jester. **3.** *a.* Characteristic of a zany; comically idiotic, crazily ridiculous. [f. F *zani*, or f. It. *zan(n)i*, Venetian form of *Gianni*, *Giovanni* John]
zăp *v.t.* (**-pp-**). (sl.) Hit, attack, knock out, kill. [imit.]
zapatėa'dō (zah-; -ah'-) *n.* (*pl.* ~**s**). (Sp. dance with) rhythmic stamping of feet. [Sp. (*zapato* shoe)]
Z.A.P.U. (zah'pōō) *abbr.* Zimbabwe African People's Union.
zarape. See SERAPE.
Zarathustrian. See ZOROASTRIAN.
zari'ba (-rē'-), **zarē'ba,** *n.* Hedged or palisaded enclosure for protection of camp or village in the Sudan etc. [f. Arab. *zarība* cattle-pen]
zăx. See SAX¹.
zeal *n.* Earnestness or fervour in advancing a cause or rendering service; hearty and persistent endeavour; so ~'OUS (zĕ'l-) *a.* [ME *zele* f. eccl. L f. Gk *zēlos*]
zea'lot (zĕ'l-) *n.* Zealous person; uncompromising or extreme partisan, fanatic; (*Z*~) one of a Jewish sect aiming at world Jewish theocracy and resisting the Romans until A.D. 70; hence ~RY (4) *n.* [f. eccl. L f. Gk *zēlōtēs* (as prec.; see -OT²)]
zĕ'bĕc(k). Var. of XEBEC.
zĕ'bra *n.* **1.** Striped Afr. quadruped of genus *Equus* allied to ass and horse. **2.** *attrib.* Striped like zebra (*zebra finch*); ||~ (**crossing**), striped street-crossing where pedestrians have precedence over vehicles; ~ **wolf,** = TASMANIAN *wolf*. **3.** Hence **zĕ'brINE**¹ *a.* [It. or Port., f. Congolese]
zē'bū *n.* Humped ox (*Bos indicus*) of India, E. Asia, and Africa. [f. F *zébu*, of unkn. orig.]
Zech. *abbr.* Zechariah (O.T.).
||**zĕd** *n.* Letter Z. [f. F *zède* f. LL f. Gk *zēta*; cf. ZETA]
zĕ'dōarў *n.* Aromatic ginger-like substance made from rootstock of E. Ind. plants of genus *Curcuma* and used in medicine, perfumery, and dyeing. [ME, f. med. L *zedoarium* f. Pers. *zidwār*]
***zee** *n.* Letter Z. [17th c., var. of ZED]
Zee'man (zā'-) *n.* ~ **effect,** (Phys.) splitting of spectrum line into several components by magnetic field. [f. P. ~, Du. physicist d. 1943]
zē'ĭn *n.* Principal protein of maize. [f. *Zea* generic name of maize + -IN]
Zeitgeist (tsī'tgīst) *n.* Spirit of the times; trend of thought and feeling in a period. [G (*zeit* time, *geist* spirit)]
zėmĭ'ndār, zamĭ'ndār, *n.* (Ind. Hist.) District governor and revenue-farmer under Mogul empire; Indian landed proprietor paying land-tax to British Government. [Hind., f. Pers. *zamīndār* (*zamīn* earth, *dār* holder)]
Zĕn *n.* Form of Buddhism emphasizing value of meditation and intuition; hence ~'(**n**)IST (3) *n.* [Jap., = meditation]
zėna'na (-ah'-) *n.* That part of house in which women of high-caste families are secluded in India and Iran; ~ **mission** (Hist., of women visiting zenanas to spread medical and other reform among inmates). [f. Hind. *zenāna* f. Pers. *zanāna* (*zan* woman)]
Zĕnd *n.* Interpretation of the Avesta, each Zend being part of the ~**-Avesta,** Zoroastrian scriptures of Avesta or text and Zend or commentary. [f. Pers. *zand* interpretation]
Zē'ner *n.* ~ **cards,** set of 25 cards with 5 different symbols, used in E.S.P. research. [f. K. E. ~, Amer. psychologist b. 1903]
zĕ'nĭth *n.* **1.** Point of heavens directly above

observer (opp. NADIR); ~**-distance,** arc intercepted between celestial body and zenith, complement of body's altitude. **2.** Highest point, time or place of greatest power or prosperity or happiness, (*is at his, its, the, zenith*). **3.** Hence ~AL *a.*; ~**al projection** (of part of globe on plane tangent at centre of the part, showing correct directions of all points from centre). [ME, f. OF or med. L *cenit* ult. f. Arab. *samt* (*ar-ra's*) path (over the head)]

zē'olīte *n.* One of a number of minerals consisting mainly of hydrous silicates of calcium, sodium, and aluminium, able to act as CATION exchangers. [f. Sw. & G *zeolit* f. Gk *zeō* boil + -LITE (from their characteristic swelling and fusing under the blowpipe)]

Zeph. *abbr.* Zephaniah (O.T.).

zĕ'phyr *n.* **1.** Soft mild gentle wind or breeze. **2.** Athlete's thin gauzy jersey for running, rowing, boxing, etc. in; light dress-material. [f. F *zéphyr* or f. L f. Gk *zephuros* (god of the) west wind]

Zĕ'ppelĭn *n.* Large dirigible airship of type built, orig. for military use in Germany, in early 20th c. [f. Count F. von ~, Ger. airman d. 1917, first constructor]

zēr'ō *n.* (*pl.* ~**s**) & *v.* **1.** *n.* Figure 0, nought, cipher; no quantity or number, nil; starting-point of scale from which positive or negative quantity is reckoned; temperature of freezing-point of water or other point selected to graduate thermometer-scale from (**absolute** ~, temperature at which the particles whose motion constitutes heat would be at rest, −273·15°C.); GROUND¹ *zero.* **2.** ~ (**hour**), (orig. & esp. Mil.) hour at which timed programme is to begin. **3.** Lowest point, nullity, nonentity. **4.** Hence ~TH² *a.*, coming next before what is regarded as 'first' in series. **5.** *v.t.* Adjust (instrument etc.) to zero point. **6.** *v.i.* Set gun-sights for firing; ~ **in on,** take aim at (target etc.), focus attention on. [f. F. *zéro* or f. It. f. OSp. *zero* f. Arab. *ṣifr* (CIPHER¹)]

zĕst *n.* Piquancy, stimulating flavour, (esp. fig.; *adds a zest to*); keen enjoyment or interest, relish (*for*), gusto, (*entered into it with zest*); piece of orange or lemon peel as flavouring; hence ~'FUL, ~'Y², *adjs.* [f. F *zeste* orange or lemon peel, of unkn. orig.]

zē'ta *n.* Sixth Greek letter (Z, ζ) = z. [f. Gk *zēta*]

zētĕ'tĭc *a.* Proceeding by inquiry. [f. Gk *zētētikos* (*zēteō* seek; see -IC)]

zeu'gma *n.* Figure of speech using a verb or adjective with two nouns, to one of which it is strictly applicable while the word appropriate to the other is not used (e.g. *kill the boys and* [sc. *destroy*] *the luggage, with weeping eyes and* [sc. *grieving*] *hearts*); cf. SYLLEPSIS; hence **zeugmă'tic** *a.* [L, f. Gk *zeugma -atos* (*zeugnumi* to yoke, *zugon* yoke)]

Zeus *n.* (Gk Myth.) Supreme god of Olympus; **by** ~!, = *by* JOVE. [Gk]

zhō. Var. of DZHO.

zĭ'bėt, *zĭ'bėth (-t), *n.* Asian or Indian civet (*Viverra zibetha*); its perfume. [f. med. L *zibethum* (see CIVET)]

zĭ'ggurăt *n.* Pyramidal tower in ancient Mesopotamia, surmounted by temple. [f. Assyr. *ziqquratu* pinnacle]

zĭ'gzăg *a., adv., n.,* & *v.i.* (**-gg-**). **1.** *a.* & *adv.* With abrupt alternate right and left turns, with alternating salient and re-entrant angles, with motion as of tacking ship, (*a zigzag line, course, road, fence, trench, flash of lightning*). **2.** *n.* Zigzag line or (esp. for ascending steep hill) road or (in sieges) set of trenches. **3.** *v.i.* Move in zigzag course. [F, f. G *zickzack*, symbolic form.]

zĭ'llah (-*a*) *n.* Administrative district in India, containing several pergunnahs. [f. Hind. *ḍilah* division]

***zĭ'llion** (-lyon) *n.* Indefinite large number. [f. z (perh. = unknown quantity) + MILLION]

zĭnc *n.,* & *v.t.* (**-c-** *or* **-k-** *or* **-ck-**, *pr.* -k-). **1.** White metallic element used as component of brass and German silver, as roofing material, as coating for sheet iron (cf. GALVANIZE), in electric batteries, and in printing-plates; (*zinc*) BLENDE; **flowers of** ~ or ~ **oxide,** powder used as white pigment and in ~ **ointment;** hence ~'IC *a.*, ~'ĬFY *v.t.*, ~'Y² *a.* (*or* **-k-** *or* **-ck-**; *pr.* -k-). **2.** *v.t.* Coat or treat with zinc. [f. G *zink*, of unkn. orig.]

zĭ'ncō *n.* (*pl.* ~**s**) & *v.* = foll. [abbr.]

zĭ'nco|graph (-ahf) *n.* & *v.* **1.** *n.* Zinc plate with design etched in relief on it for printing from; print taken from this. **2.** *v.t.* & *i.* Etch on zinc; reproduce (design) thus. **3.** So ~GRAPHY (-ŏ'g-) *n.*, ~TYPE¹ *n.* = *zincograph.* [f. ZINC + -O- + -GRAPH]

zĭng *n.,* & *v.i.* (colloq.) **1.** *n.* Vigour, energy; hence ~'Y² *a.* **2.** *v.i.* Move swiftly or shrilly. [imit.]

Zĭ'ngar|ō (-ngg-) *n.* (*pl.* ~**i**). Gipsy. [It.]

zĭnk-. See ZINC.

zĭ'nnĭa *n.* Composite plant of genus *Zinnia*, with showy rayed flowers of deep red and other colours. [f. J. G. *Zinn*, Ger. physician and botanist d. 1759 + -IA¹]

Zī'on *n.* (Holy hill of) ancient Jerusalem; the Jewish religion; the Christian Church; the Heavenly Jerusalem or kingdom of heaven; ‖nonconformist chapel. [OE, f. eccl. L *Sion* f. Heb. *ṣiyôn*]

Zī'on|ĭsm *n.* Movement founded 1897 that has sought and achieved the re-establishment of a Jewish nation in Palestine; so ~IST (2) *n.* [f. prec. + -ISM]

zĭp *n.* & *v.* (**-pp-**). **1.** *n.* Light sharp sound, as of bullet passing through air, the sudden tearing of cloth, etc. **2.** (fig.) Energy, vigour; hence ~'PY² *a.* **3.** ~(**-fastener**), fastening device consisting of two flexible strips with interlocking projections closed or opened by sliding clip pulled along them; ~**-bag** etc. (equipped with zip-fastener for closing). **4.** ***Zip code,** system of five-figure numbers used to identify postal delivery areas [f. *z*one *i*mprovement *p*lan]. **5.** *v.t.* & *i.* Fasten (*up*) with zip-fastener; hence ~'PER¹ *n.*, zip-fastener. **6.** *v.i.* Move with zip or at high speed. [imit.]

zīr'con *n.* Zirconium silicate of which some translucent varieties (HYACINTH, JARGON²) are cut into gems. [f. G *zirkon*; cf. JARGON²]

zīrcō'nĭum *n.* Grey metallic element found chiefly in zircon and used in various industrial applications. [f. prec. + -IUM]

zĭ'ther (-dh-) *n.* Simple flat many-stringed instrument placed horizontally and played partly with fingers of left hand and partly with plectrum on right thumb and with fingers of right hand; hence ~IST (1) *n.* [G (as CITHERN)]

zlŏ'tȳ *n.* (*pl.* ~**s** *or* same). Monetary unit of Poland. [Pol., lit. 'golden']

Zn *symb.* zinc.

zō'dĭăc *n.* Belt of the heavens limited by lines about 8° from the ecliptic on each side, including all apparent positions of the sun, moon, and planets as known to the ancients, and divided into 12 equal parts called **signs of the** ~ (Aries, Taurus, Gemini, Cancer, Leo, Virgo, Libra, Scorpio, Sagittarius, Capricorn(us), Aquarius, Pisces), each formerly containing the similarly named constellation but now by precession of equinoxes coinciding with the constellation that bears the name of the preceding sign; diagram of these signs; (fig.) complete cycle, circuit, or compass. [ME, f. OF *zodiaque* f. L *zodiacus* f. Gk *zōidiakos* (*zōidion* sculptured animal-figure, dim. of *zōion* animal); see -AC]

zodī'acal *a.* Of or in the zodiac; ~ **light,** luminous area of sky shaped like tall triangle occas. seen in east before sunrise or in west after sunset, esp. in tropics. [F (as prec.; see -AL)]

zō'ĕtrōpe *n.* Optical toy in form of cylinder with series of pictures on inner surface which give impression of continuous motion when viewed through slits with cylinder rotating. [irreg. f. Gk *zōē* life + *-tropos* turning]

zō'ĭc *a.* Of animals; (Geol., of rock etc.) containing fossils, with traces of animal or plant life. [prob. back form. f. AZOIC]

Zö'llner (tsẽr'-) *n.* **~'s lines,** parallel lines made to appear not parallel by short oblique intersecting lines. [f. J. K. F. ~, Ger. physicist d. 1882]

zollverein (tsŏ'lferīn) *n.* Customs union, esp. of German states in 19th c. [G]

zŏ'mbĭe, *zŏ'mbĭ, *n.* Corpse said to be revived by witchcraft; (colloq.) person resembling this, dull or apathetic person. [W. Afr.]

zŏ'nda *n.* Hot dusty N. wind in Argentina. [Amer. Sp.]

zōne *n.*, & *v.t.* **1.** *n.* (arch.) Belt or girdle worn round the body. **2.** Encircling band or stripe distinguishable in colour or texture or character from rest of object encircled. **3.** (Geog.) Any of five divisions of the earth bounded by circles parallel to the equator; **frigid ~s** (N. of Arctic, S. of Antarctic, Circle); **torrid ~** (between the tropics of Cancer and Capricorn); **temperate ~s** (between frigid and torrid zones). **4.** Area enclosed between two exact or approximate concentric circles; part of surface of sphere enclosed between two parallel planes, or of cone, cylinder, etc., between such planes cutting it perpendicularly to axis. **5.** Any well-defined region of more or less beltlike form; **(time) ~,** range of longitudes where a common standard time is used; (Geol. etc.) region between specified limits of depth. **6.** Area having particular features, properties, purpose, or use, (*danger, demilitarized, erogenous, smokeless, zone*). **7.** Hence **zō'n**AL, **zō'n**ARY[1], **zō'n**ATE[2] (Bot. & Zool.), *adjs.* **8.** *v.t.* Encircle as or with zone; arrange or distribute by zones; assign as or to zone (sense 6), whence **zō'n**ING[1] *n.* [F, or f. L f. Gk *zōnē* girdle]

zōō *n.* (colloq.) Zoological garden. [abbr.]

zō'o- *comb. form.* Of animals, of animal life, as: **~geo'graphy,** zoology dealing with local distribution of animals; **~graphy** (-ŏ'g-), descriptive zoology; **~latry** (-ŏ'l-), worship of animals; **~mancy,** divination from appearances or behaviour of animals; **~mor'phic,** (1) dealing with or represented in animal forms, (2) having gods of animal form; so **~mor'phism; ~phyte,** plantlike animal, esp. coral, jellyfish, sea anemone, or sponge; so **~phy'tic** (-fĭ'-) *a.*; **~pla'nkton,** plankton consisting of animals; **~spore,** spore capable of motion; **~tomy** (-ŏ't-), dissection or anatomy of animals. [f. Gk *zōio-* (*zōion* animal; see -o-)]

zō'oid *n.* Organic body or cell resembling but not being animal or plant; more or less independent organism given by gemmation or fission; member of compound organism; hence **zōoi'd**AL *a.* [f. as prec. + -OID]

zōŏ'log|ў *n.* Science of animal structure, physiology, classification, habits, and distribution; hence or cogn. **zōolŏ'g**ICAL *a.* (**~ical garden**(s), public garden or park with collection of animals for exhibition and study), ~IST (3) *n.* [f. mod. L *zoologia* (as ZOO-, -LOGY)]

zōōm *v.i.*, & *n.* **1.** *v.i.* Force aeroplane to mount at high speed and steep angle; move quickly, esp. with buzzing sound; (of camera) change (esp. quickly) from long shot to close-up. **2.** *n.* Aeroplane's steep climb; ~ **lens,** (Photog. etc.) lens which by variation of focal length allows (esp. quick) transition from long shot to close-up. [imit.]

zōōt *a.* ~ **suit,** (colloq.) man's suit with long loose jacket and high-waisted tapering trousers. [rhyming on SUIT]

zŏ'rĭ *n.* Japanese straw sandal. [Jap.]

zŏ'rĭl *n.* Carnivorous Afr. quadruped allied to skunk and weasel. [f. F *sorille* f. Sp. *zorrilla* dim. of *zorro* fox]

Zŏrōă'strĭan, Zărathu'strĭan (-thŏŏ'-), *a.* & *n.* (Follower) of Zoroaster or Zarathustra, (adherent) of the dualistic religious system taught by him and his followers in the Zend-Avesta based on the conflict between Ormuzd or (Ahura) Mazda god of light and good and Ahriman spirit of darkness and evil (the religion of the magi and ancient Persia still followed by Parsees); hence ~ISM (3) *n.* [f. (L f. Gk *Zōroastrēs* f.) Avestan *Zarathustra*, Persian founder of the religion 6th c. B.C. + -IAN]

zou'ave (zōō'ahv *or* zwahv) *n.* Member of French light-infantry corps orig. formed of Algerians and retaining their Oriental uniform. [F, f. *Zouaoua*, name of tribe]

||**zounds** (-z) *int.* (arch.) expr. indignation. [= (God)'*s wounds* (i.e. those of Christ on the Cross)]

Z.P.G. *abbr.* zero population growth.

Zr *symb.* zirconium.

zucchĕ'ttō (tsŏŏk-) *n.* (*pl.* ~s). R.C. ecclesiastic's skull-cap, black for priest, purple for bishop, red for cardinal, and white for pope. [f. It. *zucchetta* dim. of *zucca* gourd, head]

zucchi'nĭ (zŏŏkē'-) *n.* (*pl.* same *or* ~s). Courgette. [It., pl. of *zucchino* dim. of *zucca* gourd]

zu'gzwang (tsŏŏ'ktsvahng) *n.* (Chess). Obligation to move in one's turn even when this must be disadvantageous. [G (*zug* move, *zwang* compulsion)]

Zu'lu (zōō'lōō) *n.* & *a.* (Member or language) of a S. Afr. Bantu people. [native name]

zwie'băck (*or* tsvē'bahk) *n.* Kind of biscuit rusk or sweet cake toasted in slices. [G, = twice baked]

Zwĭ'nglĭan (-ngg-; *or* tsv-) *a.* & *n.* (Follower) of Zwingli. [f. U. *Zwingli*, Swiss religious reformer d. 1531 + -IAN]

zwĭ'ttĕrĭon (*or* tsv-) *n.* Molecule or ion having separate positively and negatively charged groups. [G (*zwitter* a hybrid); see ION]

zȳ'gal *a.* H-shaped (esp. of brain-fissures). [f. as foll. + -AL]

zȳ'go- *comb. form.* Joining, pairing, as: **~da'ctyl** *a.* & *n.*, **~da'ctylous** *a.*, (bird) with two toes pointing forward and two backward; **~mor'phic, ~mor'phous,** (of flower) divisible into similar halves only by one plane; **~spore,** spore formed by conjugation of two similar gametes. [f. Gk *zugo-* (*zugon* yoke; see -o-)]

zȳgō'ma *n.* (*pl.* ~ta). Bony arch of cheek, yoke-bone; hence **zȳgomă't**IC *a.* [f. Gk *zugōma* -*atos* (*zugon* yoke; see -OMA)]

zȳgō's|ĭs *n.* (*pl.* **~es** *pr.* -ēz). (Biol.) Conjugation. [mod. L, f. Gk *zugōsis* joining (*zugoō* to yoke f. *zugon* yoke; see -OSIS)]

zȳ'gōte *n.* (Biol.) Cell formed by union of two gametes. [f. Gk *zugōtos* yoked (*zugoō*; see prec.)]

zȳ'māse *n.* Enzyme of group orig. found in yeast, causing breakdown of glucose. [F, f. Gk *zumē* leaven; see -ASE]

zȳmō's|ĭs *n.* (*pl.* **~es** *pr.* -ēz). Fermentation;

zymotic disease. [mod. L, f. Gk *zumōsis* f. as prec.; see -OSIS]

zȳmŏ'tĭc *a.* Of fermentation; **~ disease,** epidemic, endemic, contagious, infectious, or sporadic disease regarded as caused by multiplication of germs introduced from outside. [f. Gk *zumōtikos* (as prec.; see -OTIC)]

zȳ'murgȳ *n.* Branch of applied chemistry dealing with use of fermentation in brewing etc. [f. Gk *zumē* leaven, after *metallurgy*]

ADDENDA

‖**A.C.A.S.** (ā'kăs) *abbr.* Advisory, Conciliation, and Arbitration Service.

air[1]**. 6. ~ traffic controller,** person employed at airport to give radio instructions to pilots seeking to take off or land.

a.s.a.p. *abbr.* as soon as possible.

banana. ‖**go ~s,** (sl.) become crazy or angry.

batter[1]**. 1. ~ed wife** (subjected to repeated violence by her husband).

bīŏ'nĭc *a.* Relating to bionics; having mechanical body-parts, or superhuman powers resulting from these. [f. BIONICS; see -IC]

bouncer. (Also, Cricket) = BUMPER.

bridge[2]**. bridging loan,** loan made to cover short interval between buying a house etc. and selling another.

Bundestag (bŏŏ'ndeztahg) *n.* Lower House of Parliament in Federal Republic of Germany. [G (*bund* federation, *tagen* confer)]

cagou'le (kagōō'l) *n.* Hooded thin windproof garment worn in mountaineering etc. [F]

capital[2]**. 7.** ‖**~ transfer tax** (levied on transfer of capital by gift, bequest, etc.).

cash[1]**. 2. ~ flow,** movement of money as affecting liquidity of firm etc., or as measure of profitability.

chair. 6. ~'person, chairman or chairwoman.

child. 3. ‖**~ benefit,** State benefit replacing family allowance.

day. 10. ~ care, supervision of young children during day, esp. while mothers are out at work.

dēcrĭ'mĭnalīz|e, -is|e (-īz), *v.t.* Treat (action etc.) as no longer illegal; hence **~A'TION** *n.* [f. DE- + CRIMINAL + -IZE]

dėsêrtĭfĭcā'tion (-z-) *n.* Making or becoming a desert; so **dĕsertīzā'tion** (-z-) *n.* [f. DESERT[2] + -I- + -FICATION]

devolution. 2. Esp. of delegation to regional administrations in Scotland and Wales; hence **~IST** (2) *n.*

dial. 3. ~ling code, sequence of numbers dialled to connect telephone to another exchange appropriate for the telephone being called.

emir. ~ate also pr. (ĕ'mĭrat).

Euro-. ~communism, form of Communism in European countries, seeking to be independent of the Soviet Communist Party.

extend. 2. ~ed family (including relatives living near).

first. 5. ~ past the post, (of election-candidate) winning because having the most votes though perhaps not having absolute majority; ‖**~ school** (for children from 5 to 9 years old).

flash[1]**. 2.** (Also, sl.) briefly display oneself indecently.

flĕ'x(ĭ)time *n.* (System of) working-hours with set total but with times partly as chosen by employee. [f. FLEXIBLE + TIME[1]]

gay. (Also, *n.*, sl.) homosexual.

genetic. 2. ~ engineering, deliberate modification of hereditary features by treatment of DNA to transfer certain genes.

go[1]**. 35. go-go,** (also, of dancer, music, etc.) full of verve, movement, and excitement.

goal. 3. ~ difference, difference between numbers of goals as in *goal average*, now used similarly to decide league-rank of teams having equal numbers of points from wins and draws.

granny. 2. ~ flat, part of house, made into self-contained accommodation for a relative.

green[1]**. 10. ~ pound,** currency exchange unit for payments to agricultural producers in E.E.C.

gŭnge (-nj) *n.* = GUNK. [imit.]

hard. 12. ~ core, (also, *attrib.* w. hyphen) blatant, uncompromising, (*hard-core pornography*).

hatch[1]**. ~'back,** (vehicle with) large sloping rear door hinged at top.

hī'ya *int.* (colloq.) of greeting. [corrupt. of *how are you?*]

holocaust. (Esp., *H~*) w. ref. to mass murder of Jews by Nazis 1939–45.

home[1]**. 10. ~land,** (also) = BANTUSTAN.

index. 3. ~-linked, calculated in accordance with index number. **11.** (Also) relate (wages etc.) to value of price index; hence **~A'TION** *n.*

inner. 1. ~ city, central area of city, usu. with overcrowding and poverty.

Irish. 1. ~ coffee, = GAELIC *coffee.*

job[1]**. 5.** ‖**~'centre,** employment exchange displaying information about available jobs.

jump[1]**. 6. ~-leads,** device for conveying current from one battery to recharge another.

keg. ~ beer (supplied from metal container).

kĕ'ndō *n.* Japanese sport of fencing with two-handed bamboo swords. [Jap., = sword-way]

kerb. ~-crawling, driving slowly along and seeking to persuade some person on the pavement to get into the vehicle.

knacker. 2. *v.t.* (sl.) Kill; (fig., esp. in *p.p.*) exhaust, wear out.

knee[1]**. 4. ~-capping,** shooting in the legs as punishment; **~s-up,** lively party.

Kru'gerrand (-ōō'-; -ahnt) *n.* S. Afr. gold coin depicting President Kruger. [f. S. J. P. *Kruger*, S. Afr. statesman d. 1904, + RAND[2]]

Lă'ssa *n.* **~ fever,** acute febrile virus disease of tropical Africa. [~ in Nigeria]

Lib. ~-Lab, Liberal and Labour (Parties).

lĭ'mbō[2] *n.* (*pl.* **~s**). W. Ind. dance in which dancer bends back and passes repeatedly under horizontal bar gradually lowered to just above ground. [Caribbean name]

liquid. 1. ~ crystal, turbid liquid in intermediate state between crystalline solid and ordinary liquid.

litre, *liter. Hence **~AGE** (1) (lē'terĭj) *n.*

look. 7. *~-alike, person or thing closely resembling another.

male. 1. ~ chauvinist, man showing excessive loyalty to other men and prejudice against women.

martial. 2. ~ arts, fighting sports such as judo and karate.

metre[2]**, *meter**[3]**.** Hence **~AGE** (1) (mē'terĭj) *n.*

middle[1]**. ~ school,** (1) middle forms of independent or grammar school, (2) school for children from about 9 to 13 years old.

minimum. ~ lending rate, = BANK[3] *Rate.*

M.L.R. *abbr.* minimum lending rate.

mock[3]. **3. put the ~ers on,** (sl.) bring bad luck to.

mō'dĕm *n.* Combined device for modulation and demodulation, e.g. between computer and telephone line. [portmanteau wd]

mountain. 2. (Also) large surplus stock esp. of a commodity.

music. 4. ~ centre, equipment combining radio, record-player, and tape-recorder.

Mū'zăk *n.* System of music transmission by wire or cable for playing in public place; recorded light music as background. [**P**]

năn, nă'nna, *n.* (colloq.) Grandmother. [childish pronunc.]

national. 2. N~ Front, U.K. organization with extreme reactionary views on immigration etc.

N.E.B. *abbr.* || (also) National Enterprise Board.

neutron. ~ bomb (type using neutrons to do harm to life rather than buildings etc.).

||**N.F.** *abbr.* National Front.

no[1]. **4. no-go',** impossible to achieve; impossible to enter (because of barricade, prohibition, etc.). [*no* GO[2]]

no[2]. **no can do,** (colloq.) I am unable to do it.

non-. ~-ne't, (of book) not subject to minimum selling-price.

nŭ'tter *n.* (sl.) Crazy person. [f. NUT + -ER[1]]

ŏ'cker *n.* (Austral. sl.) Boorish or aggressively Australian person. [20th c.; orig. uncert.]

ŏncŏ'logy̆ *n.* Study of tumours. [f. ONCO- + -LOGY]

one. 8. ~-night stand, (also) sexual liaison lasting only from one day to the next; **~-two,** (also) passing of football from one player to another and immediately back to the first.

Ostpolitik (ŏstpŏlĭtē'k) *n.* Politics of a European country with reference to Communist countries of E. Europe. [G (*ost* east)]

paedo-, *pedo-. ~phile, person displaying paedophilia.

***păstra'mĭ** (-ah'-) *n.* Seasoned smoked beef. [Yiddish]

plea. ~ bargaining, practice of agreeing to drop charge(s), or sentence leniently, if accused pleads guilty to other charge(s).

P.L.O. *abbr.* Palestine Liberation Organization.

plough[1], **plow**[1]. **5. ~man's lunch,** meal of bread and cheese etc.

pole[1]. **1. ~ position,** most favourable position at start of motor race [orig. next to inside boundary-fence].

poly-. 1. ~unsa'turated, (of chem. compound) containing several double or triple bonds, and therefore reactive.

porridge. (Also, sl.) imprisonment.

poverty. ~ trap, situation in which increase of pay leads to no greater total income, because of loss of benefits.

preventive. 1. ~ medicine (seeking to prevent disease rather than cure it).

punk[2]. **3. ~ rock,** style of simple rock music played with great vigour but lacking polish.

quad. (Also) quadraphonic (see foll.).

quadraphŏ'n|ic (-ŏd-) *a.* (Of sound-reproduction) using four transmission channels; hence ~ICALLY *adv.*, ~Y[1] (-ă'fonĭ) *n.* [f. QUADRI- + STEREOPHONIC]

Quă'ngō (-nggō) *n.* (*pl.* **~s**). Semi-public body with financial support from and senior appointments made by Government. [abbr. of *quasi-non-governmental organization*]

rabbit[1]. **2. ~ on,** (sl.) talk pointlessly, waffle.

Răstafār'ĭan *a.* & *n.* (Member) of a Jamaican sect regarding Blacks as a chosen people. [f. *Ras Tafari*, title of Emperor Haile Selassie of Ethiopia d. 1975, venerated by the sect as a god, + -AN]

roustabout. 1. (Also) labourer on oil rig.

scă'ndĭum *n.* (Chem.) Trivalent metallic element, resembling those of lanthanide series. [mod. L, f. *Scandia* Scandinavia + -IUM]

self-. 4. ~-ca'tering, occupying rented accommodation on holiday etc. but providing one's own food.

sex. 1. Hence ~'ISM *n.*, prejudice or discrimination against people (esp. women) because of their sex; ~'IST (2) *n.*

shuttle. 1. ~ diplomacy, negotiations conducted by mediator who travels to several countries at brief intervals.

sight[1]. **6. lower** one's **~s,** become less ambitious.

skate[2]. **1. ~'board,** (*n.*) short narrow board like large roller-skate on which person stands with both feet, (*v.i.*) travel on this.

S.L.A.D.E. *abbr.* Society of Lithographic Artists, Designers, Engravers, and Process Workers.

snake. 1. the ~, system of interconnected exchange rates for currencies of E.E.C. countries.

spoiler. (Also) similar device on vehicle to prevent it from being lifted off the road at speed.

tail[1]. **5. ~'back,** queue of traffic unable to proceed freely; **~-gate,** (4) hatchback door of estate car.

tă'ndoor *n.* (Ind.) Clay oven; **~ĭ** *n.*, food cooked over charcoal in tandoor. [Hind.]

Tă'nnoy *n.* Type of public-address loudspeaker system. [**P**]

Te *symb.* tellurium.

tool[1]. **~-pusher,** worker directing drilling on oil rig.

tră'nny̆ *n.* (sl.) Transistor radio. [abbr.; see -Y[3]]

tree. 2. ~-house, structure in tree for children to play in.

Trŏt[2] *n.* (sl.) Trotskyist. [abbr.]

wănk *n.*, & *v.i.* (vulg.) (Engage in) masturbation; hence ~'ER[1] *n.* (also, contemptible person). [20th c.; orig. unkn.]

welsh[2], **welch**[2]. (Also) evade an obligation; **~ on,** fail to carry out one's promise to (person), fail to honour (obligation).

Wĕ'ndy̆ *n.* **~ house,** children's small houselike structure for playing in. [character in Barrie's *Peter Pan*]

yellow. 2. ||**~ lines** (painted on road beside pavement to indicate restriction on parking of vehicles).

APPENDIX I

WEIGHTS AND MEASURES

Note. The conversion factors are not exact unless so marked. They are given only to the accuracy likely to be needed in everyday calculations.

1. BRITISH AND AMERICAN, WITH METRIC EQUIVALENTS

Linear Measure

1 inch	= 25·4 millimetres exactly
1 foot = 12 inches	= 0·3048 metre exactly
1 yard = 3 feet	= 0·9144 metre exactly
1 (statute) mile = 1,760 yards	= 1·609 kilometres

Square Measure

1 square inch	= 6·45 sq. centimetres
1 square foot = 144 sq. in.	= 9·29 sq. decimetres
1 square yard = 9 sq. ft.	= 0·836 sq. metre
1 acre = 4,840 sq. yd.	= 0·405 hectare
1 square mile = 640 acres	= 259 hectares

Cubic Measure

1 cubic inch	= 16·4 cu. centimetres
1 cubic foot = 1,728 cu. in.	= 0·0283 cu. metre
1 cubic yard = 27 cu. ft.	= 0·765 cu. metre

Capacity Measure

British

1 pint = 20 fluid oz.	= 0·568 litre
= 34·68 cu. in.	
1 quart = 2 pints	= 1·136 litres
1 gallon = 4 quarts	= 4·546 litres
1 peck = 2 gallons	= 9·092 litres
1 bushel = 4 pecks	= 36·4 litres
1 quarter = 8 bushels	= 2·91 hectolitres

American dry

1 pint = 33·60 cu. in.	= 0·550 litre
1 quart = 2 pints	= 1·101 litres
1 peck = 8 quarts	= 8·81 litres
1 bushel = 4 pecks	= 35·3 litres

American liquid

1 pint = 16 fluid oz.	= 0·473 litre
= 28·88 cu. in.	
1 quart = 2 pints	= 0·946 litre
1 gallon = 4 quarts	= 3·785 litres

Avoirdupois Weight

1 grain	= 0·065 gram
1 dram	= 1·772 grams
1 ounce = 16 drams	= 28·35 grams
1 pound = 16 ounces	= 0·4536 kilogram
= 7,000 grains	(0·45359237 exactly)
1 stone = 14 pounds	= 6·35 kilograms
1 quarter = 2 stones	= 12·70 kilograms
1 hundredweight = 4 quarters	= 50·80 kilograms
1 (long) ton = 20 hundredweight	= 1·016 tonnes
1 short ton = 2,000 pounds	= 0·907 tonne

See also APOTHECARY and TROY in the Dictionary.

2. METRIC, WITH BRITISH EQUIVALENTS

Linear Measure

1 millimetre	= 0·039 inch
1 centimetre = 10 mm	= 0·394 inch
1 decimetre = 10 cm	= 3·94 inches
1 metre = 10 dm	= 1·094 yards
1 decametre = 10 m	= 10·94 yards
1 hectometre = 100 m	= 109·4 yards
1 kilometre = 1,000 m	= 0·6214 mile

Square Measure

1 square centimetre	= 0·155 sq. inch
1 square metre	= 1·196 sq. yards
1 are = 100 sq. metres	= 119·6 sq. yards
1 hectare = 100 ares	= 2·471 acres
1 square kilometre	= 0·386 sq. mile

Cubic Measure

1 cubic centimetre	= 0·061 cu. inch
1 cubic metre	= 1·308 cu. yards

Capacity Measure

1 millilitre	= 0·002 pint (British)
1 centilitre = 10 ml	= 0·018 pint
1 decilitre = 10 cl	= 0·176 pint
1 litre = 10 dl	= 1·76 pints
1 decalitre = 10 l	= 2·20 gallons
1 hectolitre = 100 l	= 2·75 bushels
1 kilolitre = 1,000 l	= 3·44 quarters

Weight

1 milligram	= 0·015 grain
1 centigram = 10 mg	= 0·154 grain
1 decigram = 10 cg	= 1·543 grain
1 gram = 10 dg	= 15·43 grain
1 decagram = 10 g	= 5·64 drams
1 hectogram = 100 g	= 3·527 ounces
1 kilogram = 1,000 g	= 2·205 pounds
1 tonne (metric ton) = 1,000 kg	= 0·984 (long) ton

3. TEMPERATURE

Fahrenheit: Water boils (under standard conditions) at 212° and freezes at 32°.
Celsius or Centigrade: Water boils at 100° and freezes at 0°.
Kelvin: Water boils at 373·15° and freezes at 273·15°.

$F = 9C/5 + 32$ or $F + 40 = 9(C + 40)/5$

$C = 5(F - 32)/9$ or $C + 40 = 5(F + 40)/9$

$K = C + 273{\cdot}15$

4. THE POWER NOTATION

This expresses concisely any power of ten (any number that is composed of factors 10), and is sometimes used in the dictionary. 10^2 or ten squared $= 10 \times 10 = 100$; 10^3 or ten cubed $= 10 \times 10 \times 10 = 1{,}000$. Similarly, $10^4 = 10{,}000$, and $10^{10} = 1$ followed by ten noughts $= 10{,}000{,}000{,}000$. Proceeding in the opposite direction, dividing by ten and subtracting one from the index, we have $10^2 = 100$, $10^1 = 10$, $10^0 = 1$, $10^{-1} = \frac{1}{10}$, $10^{-2} = \frac{1}{100}$, and so on; $10^{-10} = 1/10^{10} = 1/10{,}000{,}000{,}000$. See also POWER 9 in the Dictionary.

5. THE METRIC PREFIXES

	Abbreviations	*Factors*
deca	da	10
hecto	h	10^2
kilo	k	10^3
mega	M	10^6
giga	G	10^9
tera	T	10^{12}
deci	d	10^{-1}
centi	c	10^{-2}
milli	m	10^{-3}
micro	μ	10^{-6}
nano	n	10^{-9}
pico	p	10^{-12}
femto	f	10^{-15}
atto	a	10^{-18}

Pronunciations and derivations of these are given at their alphabetical places in the dictionary. They may be applied to any units of the metric system: hectogram (abbr. hg) = 100 grams; kilowatt (abbr. kW) = 1,000 watts; megahertz (MHz) = 1 million hertz; centimetre (cm) $= \frac{1}{100}$ metre; microvolt (μV) = one millionth of a volt; picofarad (pF) $= 10^{-12}$ farad.

6. CHEMICAL NOTATION

The symbol for a molecule (such as H_2O, CH_4, H_2SO_4) shows the symbols for the elements contained in it (C = carbon, H = hydrogen, etc.), followed by a subscript numeral denoting the number of atoms of each element in the molecule where this number is more than one. For example, the water molecule (H_2O) contains two atoms of hydrogen and one of oxygen.

APPENDIX II
THE GREEK ALPHABET

Capital	*Lower-case*	*Name**	*English transliteration in this dictionary*
Α	α	alpha	a
Β	β	beta	b
Γ	γ	gamma	g
Δ	δ	delta	d
Ε	ε	epsilon	e
Ζ	ζ	zeta	z
Η	η	eta	ē
Θ	θ	theta	th
Ι	ι	iota	i
Κ	κ	kappa	k
Λ	λ	lambda	l
Μ	μ	mu	m
Ν	ν	nu	n
Ξ	ξ	xi	x
Ο	ο	omicron	o
Π	π	pi	p
Ρ	ρ	rho	r
Σ	σ, (at end of word)ς	sigma	s
Τ	τ	tau	t
Υ	υ	upsilon	u
Φ	φ	phi	ph
Χ	χ	chi	kh
Ψ	ψ	psi	ps
Ω	ω	omega	ō

ʽ (rough breathing) over vowel = prefixed h (ἁ = ha)
over rho = suffixed h (ῥ = rh)

ʼ (smooth breathing) over vowel: not transliterated

ͺ (iota subscript) under vowel = suffixed i (ᾳ = ai)

*Pronunciations are given in the dictionary entries for these words.

THE RUSSIAN ALPHABET

Capital	Lower-case	Approx. Pronunciation of Name	English transliteration in this dictionary
А	а	(ah)	a
Б	б	(bě)	b
В	в	(vě)	v
Г	г	(gě)	g
Д	д	(dě)	d
Е	е	(yě)	e
Ё	ё	(yǒ)	ë
Ж	ж	(zhě)	zh
З	з	(zě)	z
И	и	(ē)	i
Й	й	(ēkră′tkŏyě)	ĭ
К	к	(kah)	k
Л	л	(ěl)	l
М	м	(ěm)	m
Н	н	(ěn)	n
О	о	(ŏ)	o
П	п	(pě)	p
Р	р	(ěr)	r
С	с	(ěs)	s
Т	т	(tě)	t
У	у	(o͞o)	u
Ф	ф	(ěf)	f
Х	х	(χah)	kh
Ц	ц	(tsě)	ts
Ч	ч	(chě)	ch
Ш	ш	(shah)	sh
Щ	щ	(shchah)	shch
Ъ	ъ	(tvyo͡r′dĭznahk)	" ('hard sign')
Ы	ы	(ĭ)	y
Ь	ь	(myah′k-kĭznahk)	' ('soft sign')
Э	э	(ěŏb*er*ŏ′tnŏyě)	é
Ю	ю	(ū)	yu
Я	я	(yah)	ya

APPENDIX III

PRINCIPAL MONETARY UNITS OF THE WORLD

Afghanistan	1 afghani	= 100 puls
Albania	1 lek	= 100 qintar
Algeria	1 dinar	= 100 centimes
Argentina	1 peso	= 100 centavos
Australia	1 dollar	= 100 cents
Austria	1 schilling	= 100 groschen
Bangladesh	1 taka	= 100 paise
Belgium	1 franc	= 100 centimes
Bolivia	1 peso	= 100 centavos
Brazil	1 cruzeiro	= 100 centavos
Bulgaria	1 lev	= 100 stotinki
Burma	1 kyat	= 100 pyas
Canada	1 dollar	= 100 cents
Chile	1 peso	= 1,000 escudos
China	1 yuan	= 100 fen
Colombia	1 peso	= 100 centavos
Costa Rica	1 colón	= 100 céntimos
Cuba	1 peso	= 100 centavos
Cyprus	1 pound	= 1,000 mils
Czechoslovakia	1 koruna	= 100 heller
Denmark	1 krone	= 100 öre
Dominican Republic	1 peso	= 100 centavos
Ecuador	1 sucre	= 100 centavos
Egypt	1 pound	= 100 piastres
Ethiopia	1 dollar	= 100 cents
Finland	1 markka	= 100 penniä
France	1 franc	= 100 centimes
The Gambia	1 dalasi	= 100 bututs
Germany (East & West)	1 mark	= 100 pfennig
Ghana	1 cedi	= 100 pesewa
Greece	1 drachma	= 100 lepta
Guatemala	1 quetzal	= 100 centavos
Haiti	1 gourde	= 100 centimes
Honduras	1 lempira	= 100 centavos
Hong Kong	1 dollar	= 100 cents
Hungary	1 forint	= 100 fillér
Iceland	1 króna	= 100 aurar
India	1 rupee	= 100 paise
Indonesia	1 rupiah	= 100 sen
Iran	1 rial	= 100 dinars
Iraq	1 dinar	= 1,000 fils
Ireland (Republic of)	1 pound	= 100 pence
Israel	1 pound	= 100 agorot
Italy	lira	—

Jamaica	1 dollar	= 100 cents
Japan	yen	—
Jordan	1 dinar	= 1,000 fils
Kenya	1 shilling	= 100 cents
Khmer Republic	1 riel	= 100 sen
Korea (North & South)	1 won	= 100 jeon
Kuwait	1 dinar	= 1,000 fils
Laos	1 kip	= 100 ats
Lebanon	1 pound	= 100 piastres
Liberia	1 dollar	= 100 cents
Libya	1 dinar	= 1,000 dirhams
Luxemburg	1 franc	= 100 centimes
Malagasy Republic	franc malgache	—
Malawi	1 kwacha	= 100 tambala
Malaysia	1 dollar	= 100 cents
Malta	1 pound	= 100 cents
Mauritius	1 rupee	= 100 cents
Mexico	1 peso	= 100 centavos
Mongolia	1 tugrik	= 100 mongo
Morocco	1 dirham	= 100 centimes
Nepal	1 rupee	= 100 paisa
Netherlands	1 gulden	= 100 cents
New Zealand	1 dollar	= 100 cents
Nicaragua	1 córdoba	= 100 centavos
Nigeria	1 naira	= 100 kobo
Norway	1 krone	= 100 öre
Pakistan	1 rupee	= 100 paisa
Panama	1 balboa	= 100 cents
Paraguay	1 guarani	= 100 céntimos
Peru	1 sol	= 100 centavos
Philippines	1 peso	= 100 centavos
Poland	1 zloty	= 100 groszy
Portugal	1 escudo	= 100 centavos
Rhodesia	1 dollar	= 100 cents
Romania	1 leu	= 100 bani
El Salvador	1 colón	= 100 centavos
Saudi Arabia	1 riyal	= 100 halalas
Seychelles	1 rupee	= 100 cents
Sierra Leone	1 leone	= 100 cents
Singapore	1 dollar	= 100 cents
South Africa	1 rand	= 100 cents
Spain	1 peseta	= 100 céntimos
Sri Lanka	1 rupee	= 100 cents
Sudan	1 pound	= 100 piastres
Sweden	1 krona	= 100 öre
Switzerland	1 franc	= 100 centimes
Syria	1 pound	= 100 piastres
Taiwan	1 dollar	= 100 cents
Tanzania	1 shilling	= 100 cents
Thailand	1 baht	= 100 satangs

Tunisia	1 dinar	= 1,000 millimes
Turkey	1 lira	= 100 kuruş
Uganda	1 shilling	= 100 cents
United Kingdom	1 pound	= 100 pence
United States	1 dollar	= 100 cents
Uruguay	1 peso	= 100 centésimos
U.S.S.R.	1 rouble	= 100 copecks
Venezuela	bolívar	—
Vietnam (North)	1 dong	= 100 xu
Vietnam (South)	1 dong	= 100 cents
Yugoslavia	1 dinar	= 100 paras
Zaire	1 zaire	= 100 makuta
Zambia	1 kwacha	= 100 ngwee

Many of these words are further described in their places in the Dictionary.

NOTES

NOTES

NOTES

NOTES

NOTES

NOTES

NOTES

NOTES

NOTES

NOTES

NOTES

NOTES

NOTES

NOTES